THE SYNONYM FINDER

The Synonym Finder

J. I. RODALE
Editor-in-Chief

Edward J. Fluck, Ph.D.
Associate Editor

Collaborators

Gordon Marshall Pitts, Ph.D.
Assistant Professor of English
West Virginia University

Marguerite Wheaton Pitts, M.A.
Formerly of University of Pennsylvania

E. D. Gross, M.A.
of Russell Sage College

Rodale Books, Inc.
Emmaus, Pennsylvania

INTRODUCTION

There have been many synonym books and thesauri. I have worked with and used most of them, but I have also found that they either do not provide enough up-to-date synonyms per key-word, or are arranged in a manner that makes them difficult to use, and necessitates an exasperating amount of page-turning in searching out a confusing number of cross-references. In this book we have tried to remedy both failings. We have compiled many more synonyms than contained in any other book, and have placed them in the one place where they belong—under the word that is being looked up.

In order to augment the number of words in each group we have taken the license of including many words that may not be exact synonyms but are very close in meaning to the key-word under which they are listed. This entailed the use of a kind of magnifying focus to attract quantities of near-synonyms and words related by either extension of meaning or subdivision of connotation (secondary, implied meanings) to the specific key-word to which you would most naturally refer. Thus, for example, where other existing dictionaries of synonyms would cross-reference *boat* by directing you to leaf out over a vexatious number of pages for an examination of the material under *ship* (or refer you from the word *man* to other related words contained under *mankind, servant,* etc.), we have in both cases and under all similar circumstances gathered all this related matter under the first key-word to which you would be most likely to direct your first attention.

Within the contents listed under each individual key-word, the subdivision (if any) into sub-classes according to various classifications of meaning (*e.g.,* 1, 2, 3, etc.) follows the method of procedure of the excellent *American College Dictionary* (Random House) in putting the commonest, most literal and most modern meanings first, in category 1, and all other meanings (figurative, transferred, specialized, rare, and obsolete or archaic) under subsequent numerical groupings (2, 3, 4, etc.). Thus, though the words given preferred billing by being placed in early categories merit this priority because they have been selected on the basis of frequency and currency of usage, we caution you to remember that one word may have a variety of different meanings and that other words may be its synonyms in one sense but not in another. You should, therefore, examine carefully all the various subdivisional meanings of a word; do not merely take the first one. You must carefully sift out all the meanings in order to find the one that will fit best into the context you have in mind.

J. I. RODALE
Edward Fluck, Ph.D.

List of Abbreviations Used in The Synonym Finder

abbr.—*abbreviation*
adj.—*adjective*
adv.—*adverb*
Afr.—*Africa*
Anat.—*anatomy*
Anthrop.—*anthropology*
Antiq.—*antiquities*
Arab.—*Arabic*
arch.—*archaic*
Archaeol.—*archaeology*
Archit.—*architecture*
Arith.—*arithmetic*
Astron.—*astronomy*
Auto.—*automobile*
Aviat.—*aviation*
Bacteriol.—*bacteriology*
Bibl.—*Biblical*
Bibliog.—*bibliography*
Biol.—*biology*
Bot.—*botany*
Br., Brit.—*British*
Budd.—*Buddhist*
Can.—*Canada*
cap.—*capitalized*
Carp.—*carpentry*
Cent.—*century*
Ch.—*church*
Chem.—*chemistry*
civ.—*civil*
Class.—*classical*
coll., colloq.—*colloquial*
Com., Comm.—*commerce*
comb.—*combining*
conj.—*conjunction*
contempt.—*contemptuous*
crim.—*criminal*
Cryst.—*crystallography*
Dent.—*dentistry*
derog.—*derogatory*
dial.—*dialect*
dim., dimin.—*diminutive*
Dram.—*dramatic*
eccl.—*ecclesiastical*
Ecol.—*ecology*
Econ.—*economics*
Elect.—*electricity*
Eliz.—*Elizabethan*
Embryol.—*embryology*
Entomol.—*entomology*
erron.—*erroneous*
esp.—*especially*
euphem.—*euphemistic*
Falc.—*falconry*
fem.—*feminine*
fig.—*figurative*

fol., foll.—*followed*
Fort.—*fortification*
Fr.—*French*
Geog.—*geography*
Geol.—*geology*
Geom.—*geometry*
Ger.—*German*
Gov., Govt.—*government*
Gk., Gr.—*Greek*
Gr., Br.—*Great Britain*
Gram.—*grammar*
Hebr.—*Hebrew*
Her.—*heraldry*
Hind.—*Hindu*
Hist.—*historical*
hum., humor.—*humorous*
Hort.—*horticulture*
I.—*Island*
imit.—*imitative*
Ind.—*India*
interj.—*interjection*
Ir.—*Irish*
It., Ital.—*Italian*
Jap.—*Japanese*
Jew.—*Jewish*
joc.—*jocose*
Jour.—*journalism*
L., Lat.—*Latin*
La.—*Louisiana*
Lang.—*language*
l. c.—*lower case*
leg.—*legal*
lit.—*literal*
Lit.—*literature*
Log.—*logic*
Mach.—*machinery*
masc.—*masculine*
Math.—*mathematics*
Mech.—*mechanics*
Med.—*medicine*
Metall.—*metallurgy*
metaph.—*metaphorical*
Metaphy.—*metaphysics*
Meteorol.—*meteorology*
Mex.—*Mexican*
Mil.—*military*
Min.—*mineralogy*
mod.—*modern*
Moham(m).—*Mohammedan*
Mus.—*music*
n.—*noun*
Naut.—*nautical*
Nav.—*naval*
Navig.—*navigation*
nr.—*near*

occas.—*occasionally*
Ordn.—*ordnance*
Ornith.—*ornithology*
Paleontol.—*paleontology*
Parl. Proc.—*Parliamentary Procedure*
Pathol.—*pathology*
Penol.—*penology*
pert.—*pertaining*
Petrog.—*petrography*
Pharm.—*pharmacy*
Philol.—*philology*
Philos.—*philosophy*
Phonet.—*phonetics*
Photog.—*photography*
Phys.—*physics*
pl., plur.—*plural*
Poet.—*poetical*
Pol.—*politics*
Port.—*Portuguese*
prec.—*preceded*
prep.—*preposition*
Print.—*printing*
pron.—*pronoun*
Pros.—*prosody*
prov.—*provincial*
Psychol.—*psychology*
q. v.—*which see*
R. C.—*Roman Catholic*
ref.—*reference*
reflex.—*reflexive*
Relig.—*religion*
restr.—*restricted*
Rhet.—*rhetoric*
Rom.—*Roman*
Rus.—*Russian*
S.—*south*
Scand.—*Scandinavian*
Sci.—*science*
Scot.—*Scottish*
sing.—*singular*
sl.—*slang*
Sp.—*Spanish*
spec.—*specifically*
Surg.—*surgery*
Teleg.—*telegraphy*
Teut.—*Teutonic*
Theat.—*theater*
Theol.—*theology*
Turk.—*Turkish*
v.—*verb*
Veter.—*veterinary*
vulg.—*vulgar*
Zool.—*zoology*

ABACK

ABACK, *adv.* Behind, back, backward, to the rear, rearward, hindward, retrogressively, regressively, retrogradingly.

ABAFT, *adv.* Sternward, astern, behind, back, aft, rearward, in the rear.

ABANDON, *v.* 1. Relinquish, give up, discard, discontinue, cease, forsake, quit, desert, leave, depart from, have done with, leave behind, let alone, evacuate, drop, abjure, repudiate, reject, retract, fall away from, stop, forbear, forswear, give over, cast off, ostracize, neglect, throw away, retire from, withdraw from.
2. Lay aside, abdicate, surrender, throw off, resign, renounce, forego, waive, give up, vacate, let go, part with, lay down, demit, deliver up, yield, cede, concede, secede from, emigrate from, apostasize, lose hope of, despair of.

ABANDON, *n.* 1. Wantonness, intemperance, immoderation, incontinence, unrestraint, lawlessness, profligacy, surrender.
2. Ease, freedom, élan, spontaneity, animation, impetuosity, ardor, dash, spirit, enthusiasm, verve.

ABANDONED, *adj.* 1. Neglected, relinquished, alone, solitary, lonely, forlorn, lorn, deserted, discarded, outcast, adrift, left, forsaken, rejected, cast away, cast aside, cast off, thrown overboard, given up, given over, demitted, shunned, scorned, destitute, desperate, helpless, hopeless, wretched, mournful, unfortunate, friendless.
2. Accursed, depraved, dissipated, lewd, low, vicious, corrupt, dissolute, sinful, wicked, lost, profligate, flagitious, immoral, impure, unchaste, unprincipled, hardened, incorrigible, shameless, irreformable, unrepentant, graceless, vitiated, irreclaimable, obdurate, impenitent, disreputable, dead to honor, lost to shame, demoralized, bad, blackhearted, infamous, degraded, despised, worthless, odious, reprobate, detestable, unrestrained.

ABANDONMENT, *n.* 1. Desertion, dereliction, forsaking, decampment, relinquishment, defection.
2. Abnegation, renunciation, disavowal, denial, disowning, resignation, abjuration, dismissal, rejection, demission, surrender, cession.

ABASE, *v.* 1. Level, throw down, cast down, let down, reduce, lower, depress, detrude, sink, drop, let fall.
2. Demean, discredit, mortify, disgrace, mock, humiliate, dishonor, degrade, humble, bring low, take down, bring down a peg, debase, depose, belittle, devaluate, expose, shame, denigrate, vilify, calumniate, vitiate, slander, vituperate, defame.

ABASEMENT, *n.* 1. Fall, reduction, prostration, descent, lowering, downfall, depravation, vitiation, deterioration, degradation, debasement, degeneration, perversion, depression, detrusion.
2. Disgrace, obloquy, ignominy, turpitude, infamy, baseness, abjectness, vileness, meanness, degeneracy, despicableness, disrepute, dishonor, contemptibleness, ingloriousness, shame.
3. Servility, submission, condescension, self-abasement, mortification, resignation, meekness, humiliation, humbleness, humility, lowliness.

ABASH, *v.* Daunt, discomfit, intimidate, shame, embarrass, bewilder, discountenance, put out of countenance, mortify, confuse, disconcert, make ashamed, put to shame, overawe, cow, confound, discompose, put down, humble, humiliate, snub, take down, set down, browbeat, chagrin, dismay, nonplus, dumfound, overwhelm, dishearten, cast down.

ABASHED, *adj.* Confused, embarrassed, awestruck, mortified, ashamed, disconcerted, shy, humiliated, chagrined, overawed, daunted, self-conscious, humiliated, bashful, subdued, dumfounded, nonplused.

ABASHMENT, *n.* Awe, discomfiture, shyness, embarrassment, shame, bashfulness, confusion, mortification, chagrin, self-consciousness.

ABATE, *v.* 1. Ease, alleviate, allay, relax, dull, quiet, mollify, appease, mitigate, assuage, pacify, tranquilize, moderate, temper, compose, soften, attemper, soothe, quell, qualify, cool, palliate, slake, blunt, calm, relieve.
2. Abolish, destroy, flatten out, batter down, quash, liquidate, raze, beat down, demolish, lay low, bring down, restrain, curtail, reduce, remove.
3. Restrict, restrain, hold in, lower, relax, damp, reduce.
4. Rebate, subtract, bate, remit, allow, deduct, abridge.
5. (*Legal*) Annul, void, remove, suspend, put an end to, defalcate, terminate, suppress. Be frustrated, fail, be defeated, be overthrown.
6. Fall, lessen, decline, fade away, fall off, fall away, wane, ebb, intermit, slacken, fade, subside, decrease, diminish, sink.

ABATEMENT, *n.* 1. Qualification, moderation, extenuation, remission, alleviation, assuasion, mitigation, diminution, lessening, decrease, decrement.
2. Let-up, wane, evanescence, evanishment, fading, lowering, ebb, sinking, subsidence, settling, decline, relief.
3. Reduction, discount, deduction, allowance, drawback, rebate, annulment, mitigation, redress, remission, depreciation, suspension.

ABATTOIR, *n.* Slaughterhouse, slaughter-pen, shambles, butchery.

ABBE, *n.* Abbot, priest, ecclesiastic, minister, divine, clergyman, monk, padre, curate, prior, pastor, friar, Jacobin, Dominican.

ABBEY, *n.* Hermitage, priory, cloister, friary, monastery, convent, nunnery.

ABBREVIATE, *v.* Lessen, shorten, condense, reduce, compress, contract, curtail, cut down, cut short, abridge, abstract, summarize, epitomize, synopsize.

ABBREVIATION, *n.* 1. Lessening, shortening, condensation, compression, contraction, curtailment, reduction.
2. Brief, compendium, abstract, abridgment, epitome, synopsis, outline, summary, syllabus, digest, sketch, précis, résumé, conspectus.

ABDICATE, *v.* Relinquish office, vacate the throne, surrender a right, resign from an office, quit possession of, give up claim to, renounce claim to, tender resignation, cede, forego, lay down, abandon, give up, part with, quit.

ABDICATION, *n.* Renouncement, retirement, abandonment, renunciation, relinquishment, resignation, vacation, surrender.

ABDOMEN, *n.* Venter, epigastrium, visceral cavity, ventral region, stomach, belly, paunch.

ABDOMINAL, *adj.* Stomachic, visceral, hemal, celiac, ventral.

ABDOMINOUS, *adj.* Big-bellied, large-bellied, pot-bellied, paunchy, gor-bellied, great-bellied, tun-bellied, obese, round-bellied.

ABDUCT, *v.* Rape, take forcibly, run off with, take by stealth, kidnap, carry off, shanghai, run away with, spirit away, drag away, transport, convey away, make off with, impress, hold for ransom.

ABDUCTION, *n.* Rape, man-stealing, kidnapping.

ABECEDARIAN, *adj.* Alphabetical, beginning, rudimentary, primary, elementary.

ABECEDARY, *n.* Beginner, tyro. Abecedarium, primer.

ABERRANT, *adj.* 1. Variable, divergent, out of the right way, erratic, erroneous, errant, devious, wandering, rambling.
2. Anomalistic, erratic, eccentric, irregular, abnormal, uncommon, unusual, unconformable, unnatural, strange, singular, peculiar, exceptional, disconnected, preternatural, inconsequent, idiotic, monstrous.

ABERRATION, *n.* 1. Aberrancy, abnormality, anomaly, irregularity, lapse, rambling, wandering, divergence, departure, deviation.
2. Idiosyncrasy, eccentricity, monstrosity, abnormity, strangeness, singularity, peculiarity, unconformity.
3. Vagary, unsoundness, mistaken idea, lapsus mentis, illusion, hallucination, monomania, self-deception, delusion, alienation, derangement, dementia, madness, insanity, lunacy, frenzy, delirium.

ABET, *v.* 1. Advance, prompt, sustain, endorse, maintain, befriend, back, cooperate with, uphold, support, subsidize, take part with, succor, second, help, aid, assist, embolden, instigate, incite, urge, spur, animate, goad, stimulate, arouse, fire, egg on, foment, be accessory to.
2. Inspire, promote, further, patronize, stick up for, countenance, be subsidiary to, excite, advocate, connive at, sanction, favor, encourage.

ABETTOR, *n.* 1. Aide, assistant, adjutant, ally, helper, attendant, coadjutor, colleague, retainer, cooperator, henchman, auxiliary, follower, participator, comrade, associate, consociate, partner, adherent, companion.
2. Agent, promoter, encourager, instigator, adviser, inciter, advocate.
3. Confederate, accomplice, accessory.

ABEYANCE, *n.* 1. Suspension, inactivity, rest, remission, suppression, inaction, sublation, pause, intermission, reservation, dormancy, quiescence, latency, interim, status quo.
2. *(Legal)* Expectancy, prospect, anticipation, waiting, contemplation, calculation.

ABEYANT, *adj.* Inert, inactive, static, dormant, latent, resting, suspended, undeveloped, pausing, inoperative, potential, stationary, unexerted, expectant, waiting, quiescent, undetermined.

ABHOR, *v.* 1. Despise, dislike, hate, execrate, loathe, detest, abominate, recoil at, not be able to stomach, feel aversion toward, be nauseated by, shrink from, view with horror, shudder at, revolt against.
2. Avoid, eschew, shun, reject, disdain, scorn, object to, deprecate.

ABHORRENCE, *n.* Repugnance, detestation, aversion, contempt, antipathy, dislike, disgust, animosity, revulsion, loathing, distaste, hatred, odium, execration, abomination, deprecation, horror, noisomeness.

ABHORRENT, *adj.* Detestable, repulsive, foul,

abominable, loathsome, repellent, nauseating, horrible, nauseous, hateful, disgusting, obnoxious, odious, revolting, heinous, repugnant, hideous, noisome, offensive, fulsome, horrifying, shocking, ignominious, infamous, forbidding, opprobrious, unpleasant, distasteful, disagreeable, opposed to, displeasing, remote from.

ABIDE, *v.* 1. Bide, lodge, house, stay, tarry, stop, take up quarters, quarter, sojourn, pitch tent, rest, sit, lie, keep.
2. Settle, anchor, get foothold, inhabit, dwell, subsist, reside, plant oneself, live, maintain.
3. Persist, exist, remain, persevere, continue, be constant, go on, be steadfast, keep on.
4. Survive, be enduring, last, adhere, outlive, be immovable, be immutable, endure, inhere, be indestructible, be permanent.
5. Expect, wait for, attend, await expectantly, be in readiness for, stand in hand, be in store for.
6. Submit to, tolerate, stomach, endure, put up with, stand, suffer, sustain, brook, bear with, conform to, stick to.

ABIDE BY, *v.* Observe, conform to, fulfil, act up to, discharge a promise, comply with, adhere to, persist in, hold to, keep, obey, acknowledge, stand by.

ABIDING, *adj.* Eternal, enduring, everlasting, steadfast, permanent, immutable, durable, stable, continuing, immortal, unending, lasting, constant, indestructible, unchangeable, changeless, inherent, indissoluble.

ABILITY, *n.* 1. Adeptness, efficacy, aptitude, talent, proficiency, skill, skillfulness, mastery, dexterity, adequacy, energy, strength, cleverness, knack, adroitness, aptness, address, readiness, facility, quickness, ingenuity, expertness, power, strength, vigor, efficiency, might, force, potency, ableness.
2. Endowment, competency, acumen, wisdom, sufficiency, capacity, knowledge, qualification, intelligence, eligibility, gumption, understanding, attributes, accomplishments, attainments.
3. Gift, powers, bent, flair, forte, caliber, turn, reach, parts, capability, genius, capableness, faculty.

ABJECT, *adj.* 1. Mean-spirited, degraded, base, base-minded, contemptible, debased, low, abased, vile, reptilian, despicable, low-minded, squalid, sorry, beggarly, groveling, dirty, pitiful, prostrate, obsequious, paltry, inferior, servile, slavish, poor, sordid, earth-born, worthless, ignoble, cringing, undignified, menial, earth-bred, sneaking, shabby, oppressed, brought-low, wretched, destitute, miserable, depressed, scurvy, mean.
2. Stark, sheer, blank, utter, irremediable, downright, hopeless, disheartening, humiliating, desperate.

ABJECTION, *n.* 1. Humbling, humiliation, servility.
2. Abasement, baseness, meanness, vileness, debasement, degradation, degeneracy.

ABJECTNESS, *n.* Degradation, contemptibleness, servility, shabbiness, vileness, worthlessness, sordidness, baseness, obsequiousness, meanness, despicableness, wretchedness, destitution.

ABJURATION, *n.* 1. Rejection, renouncement, repudiation, renunciation, discarding, surrender, abandonment, disowning, abnegation, relinquishment.
2. Revocation, disclaiming, repeal, retraction, denial, disclamation, disaffirmation, disavowal, recantation, recall, reversal, rejection, negation, refutation.

ABJURE, v. 1. Abrogate, forswear, relinquish, forsake, resign, abandon, apostasize, repudiate, depart from, give up, reject, renounce, disown, discard, desert, forego.

2. Renege, take back, disavow, deny, disclaim, dismiss, recall, retract, go back on, disown, recant, resign, revoke, withdraw.

ABLAZE adj. 1. Flaming, burning, illuminated, blazing, aflame, lighted, alight, gleaming, fiery, glowing, luminous.

2. Excited, desirous, eager, fervent, vehement, fervid, ardent, impassioned, intense, perfervid.

3. Angry, irate, wrathful, wroth, incensed, heated.

ABLE, adj. 1. Proficient, practiced, ingenious, skilful, experienced, expert, learned, inventive, dexterous, facile, accomplished, adept, versed, apt, efficient, quick, adroit, finished, talented, au fait, clever, practical, good.

2. Competent, equal to, adequate, qualified, fitted, sagacious, intelligent, dynamic, profound, fit.

3. Talented, highly endowed, gifted, capable, able-bodied, strong, robust, mighty, stalwart, powerful, athletic, muscular, sinewy, physically qualified, brawny, potent, sturdy, vigorous:

4. Telling, effective, masterly, fresh.

ABLE-BODIED, adj. Lusty, stalwart, muscular, sound, robust, powerful, athletic, stout, vigorous, herculean, potent, strong, brawny, able, sturdy, strapping.

ABLUTION, n. Washing (ritualistic), bathing, laving, cleansing, purification, baptism, lavation, bath, wash, cleaning.

ABNEGATE, v. Deny, refuse, reject, renounce, abjure, retract, recall, gainsay, disown, disavow, forbear.

ABNEGATION, n. Disavowal, denial, negation, disclaimer, renunciation, rejection, abjuration, abandonment, renouncement, surrender, refusal, disallowance.

ABNORMAL, adj. 1. Preternatural, unheard of, freakish, unnatural, monstrous, irregular, queer, amorphous, peculiar, heteroclite, unconformable, outlandish, anomalous, erratic, aberrant, bizarre, unconventional, exceptional, odd, unusual, rare, eccentric, divergent, strange, curious, grotesque, nondescript, teratogenic.

2. Beside oneself, morbid, crazy, unhinged, crackbrained, disordered, frenzied, moonstruck, frenetic.

ABNORMALITY, n. Malformation, aberration, oddity, peculiarity, singularity, exception, freak, variation, eccentricity, monstrosity, deformity, irregularity, perversion, idiosyncrasy, anomaly, unconformity.

ABOARD, adv. On board, on deck, in the vessel, on ship, within, inside.

ABODE, n. 1. Domicile, address, hearthstone, quarters, lodging, dwelling-house, habitation, house, mansion, home, headquarters, place, seat, residence, tenement, country, hearth, fireside, vine and figtree, lares and penates, homestead, berth, chimney corner, ingleside.

ABOLISH, v. 1. Repeal, do away with, revoke, supersede, rescind, reverse, quash, disestablish, abrogate, deprive of force, cancel, vitiate, nullify, annul, inhibit, invalidate, make void, dispense with, set aside, vacate, repudiate, declare null and void, disannul, supplant, nol-pros.

2. Terminate, put an end to, extinguish, make an end of, demolish, destroy, ravage, subvert, remove, overthrow, eradicate, annihilate, cut out, extirpate, obliterate, stamp out, suppress, crush out, batter down, raze, squelch, not leave one stone upon another.

ABOLITION, n. 1. Disendowment, rescinding, annulment, repudiation, nullification, defeasance, countermand, revocation, recantation, rescission, abrogation, cancellation, dissolution, repeal.

2. Removal, extinction, extirpation, overthrow, abolishment, destruction, subversion, eradication, obliteration, annihilation, disestablishment, extinguishment, suppression.

ABOMINABLE, adj. 1. Heinous, ignominious, odious, hateful, execrable, reprehensible, horrid, nefarious, flagitious, villainous, damnable, hellish, horrible, detestable, accursed, criminal, obscene, cursed, frightful, atrocious, infamous, malicious.

2. Abhorrent, obnoxious, disagreeable, fetid, loathsome, offensive, repellent, disgusting, foul, nauseous, repugnant, nauseating, revolting, stinking, sickening, hideous, shocking, repulsive.

3. Vile, base, unclean, shabby, sorry, squalid, wretched, extremely bad, scurvy.

ABOMINATE, v. 1. Execrate, deprecate, loathe, despise, hate, abhor, recoil from, shrink from, shudder at, revolt at, nauseate, detest, hold in aversion, regard with horror.

ABOMINATION, n. 1. Antipathy, abhorrence, execration, hatred, detestation, disgust, loathing, extreme aversion, repugnance.

2. Loathsomeness, depravity, corruption, taint, foulness, uncleanness, defilement, contamination, impurity, pollution, corruptness, odiousness.

3. Villainy, evil, iniquity, hateful thing, curse, crime, offense, wickedness, shame.

4. Annoyance, nuisance, torment, infliction, plague, bête noire.

ABORIGINAL, adj. Original, indigenous, prime, autochthonous, primeval, native, primitive, first, pristine, old, primordial, underived, primary, earliest, autochthonic.

ABORIGINES, n. First residents, aboriginals, indigenes, original inhabitants, natives, primitive inhabiters, autochthones, indigenous people.

ABORT, v. Deliver prematurely, miscarry, fail, develop incompletely, force, frustrate, check.

ABORTION, n. 1. Premature birth, premature labor, miscarriage, untimely birth, forced birth, premature delivery, unnatural birth, arrested development.

2. Frustration, failure, vain attempt, defeat, lack of success, fiasco, disappointment, blunder, circumvention, bringing to nought.

ABORTIVE, adj. 1. Untimely, not viable, failing, imperfectly developed, immature, rudimental, miscarrying, incomplete, rudimentary, stunted.

2. Fruitless, unproductive, sterile, profitless, of no account, unavailing, idle, worthless, nugatory, unsuccessful, vain, unprofitable, ineffective, inept, futile, useless, bootless, inoperative, ineffectual.

ABOUND, v. 1. Be filled, overflow, teem, be rich in, superabound, be plentiful, be prolific, be extremely prevalent, swarm, multiply, increase, be numerous, stream, swell, rain, flow, shower down.

2. Flourish, luxuriate, be well furnished, be well supplied, exuberate, wanton, revel.

ABOUNDING, adj. Rife, replete, rich, lavish, bountiful, unstinted, sufficient, exuberant, full, teeming, affluent, copious, prolific, plentiful, fertile, ample, abundant, plenteous, flush.

ABOUT, *adv.* 1. In the reverse direction, half round, hind part before, around.

2. Nearby, on every side, in every direction.

3. To and fro, here and there, hither and thither, from one place to another, in various places, far and wide, helter-skelter.

4. More or less, approximately, nearly, not far from, virtually, some, towards, well-nigh, almost, near.

5. On the move, ready, on the eve, on the point.

ABOUT, *prep.* 1. Around, on every side of, surrounding, encircling, round, circuitously.

2. Close to, near to, in, near, not far from, near at hand, nigh, hereabouts.

3. Regarding, in regard to, with regard to, in relation to, respecting, with respect to, anent, with reference to, referring to, relative to, of, relating to, connected with, concerning, touching, concerned with.

4. Here and there in, in all parts of, all over, over, through.

ABOVE, *adv.* 1. In a higher place, aloft, into the firmament, overhead, on high, in the celestial heights, in excelsis, toward the sky.

2. Previously, before in order, in a former part, aforesaid.

3. Higher in rank or power, surpassing, superior to.

ABOVE, *prep.* 1. In a higher place than, atop of, on top of, aloft of.

2. More in quantity or number than, greater than, exceeding, over and above, in excess of, beyond.

3. Superior to, beyond.

4. Too great in integrity for, too high for, too magnanimous for, too proud for.

ABOVE ALL, *adv.* Chiefly, in the first place, first and foremost, as the chief end, as the main object, before all other considerations.

ABOVE-BOARD, *adv.* Guilelessly, ingenuously, unequivocally, fairly, undisguisedly, sincerely, candidly, honestly, frankly, openly, equitably, in plain sight, without artifice, in full view.

ABRACADABRA, *n.* 1. Incantation, invocation, spell, charm, magic, apotropaion, fetish, hocus pocus, conjuration, open sesame.

2. Jargon, bosh, gibberish, nonsense, empty sound, mere words.

ABRADE, *v.* 1. Rub particles from, wear down, wear off, wear away, grind away, erode, scrape, file, scour, sand, smooth, clean, polish, erase.

2. Exhaust, irritate, rasp, grate, make sore, fret, chafe, fray.

ABRASION, *n.* 1. Friction, filing, wearing down, wearing off, wearing away, scraping, rubbing down, rubbing off, rasping, scouring.

2. Erosion, detrition, attrition, disintegration, granulation, pulverization, comminution, trituration, excoriation.

ABRASIVE, *n.* Grater, rasp, file, grinder, quern, grindstone, millstone, sander, sharpening stone, whetstone, brush.

ABREAST, *adv.* 1. Abeam of, by the side of, over against, opposite, on a line with, alongside, beside, side by side, aligned, in alignment, in one line, bow to bow, stem to stem, against, off.

2. Equally advanced, up to the same plane, parallel, matched, even, tied, equal, alike.

ABRI, *n.* Shelter, dugout, shed, cave, thatch, trench, foxhole.

ABRIDGE, *v.* 1. Summarize, shorten, make an abstract of, abstract, epitomize, contract, digest, condense, compress, brief, synopsize.

2. Cut down, truncate, curtail, shrink, lessen, abbreviate, reduce, decrease, diminish, retrench, slash, trim, pare down, prune, dock, clip, lop, blue-pencil.

3. Debar from, deprive of, divest of, cut off, restrict, dispossess of, amputate, restrain, abate.

ABRIDGMENT, *n.* 1. Abbreviation, conspectus, abstract, compend, compendium, analysis, digest, epitome, outline, summary, précis, résumé, brief, aperçu, review, breviary, syllabus, recapitulation, sketch, bird's-eye-view, substance, notes.

2. Lessening, retrenchment, condensation, shortening, contraction, reduction, compression, curtailment, diminution, compacting.

3. Dispossession, divestiture, deprivation, limitation, restriction, abatement.

ABROACH (to set), *v.* 1. Tap, leave running, draw from.

2. Give rise to, spread abroad, give vent to, diffuse, give utterance to, publish, disseminate, start, propagate.

ABROAD, *adv.* 1. Far and wide, ubiquitously, in all directions, omnipresently, widely, broadly, expansively, extensively, unrestrainedly.

2. Away, out of the house, out, in the open air, elsewhere, yonder, forth, not at home, not present, absent, gone out.

3. In foreign parts, out of the country, far away, overseas, on the continent, beyond seas, wandering, adrift, on one's travels, distant, afar off.

4. At large, astir, in circulation, before the public, publicly.

5. Wide of the truth, puzzled, bewildered, at the end of one's wits, confused, dazed, off the scent, quite confounded, on the wrong track, aside of the mark, off the course, without the least clew, abstracted, preoccupied, perplexed.

ABROGATE, *v.* Nullify, disestablish, disannul, annul, retract, rescind, repudiate, repeal, recant, renounce, revoke, countermand, cancel, overrule, abolish, override, quash, dissolve, set aside, make void, destroy, void, recall, vacate, withdraw, do away, invalidate, undo, reverse, abjure, nol-pros, throw overboard.

ABROGATION, *n.* Cancellation, retractation, voidance, recantation, repeal, recall, abolition, countermand, rescinding, rescission, counterorder, annulment, repudiation, revocation, dissolution, setting aside, defeasance, invalidation, reversal, nullification, undoing, overruling, overriding, vacatur *(law)*, nolle prosequi.

ABRUPT, *adj.* 1. Sharp, craggy, uneven, rough, rugged, irregular, zigzag, jagged, broken, cragged.

2. Precipitous, declivitous, shelving, acclivitous, steep, sheer.

3. Sudden, instantaneous, hasty, subitaneous, precipitate, headlong, swift, hurried, unexpected, unforeseen, unlooked for, unannounced, rapid, unanticipated, rash, out-of-hand, unseasonable, ill-timed.

4. Blunt, gruff, curt, short, bluff, rude, rough, brusque, impetuous, violent, bold, discourteous, ungracious, unceremonious, uncomplaisant, uncivil, impolite, premature, broken off.

5. Jerky, broken, cramped, angular, inelegant *(as style),* disconnected, harsh, transient, stiff.

ABSCESS, *n.* Ulcer, carbuncle, boil, gall, sore, canker, pustule, fester, gathering, purulent tumor.

ABSCOND, *v.* 1. Depart in haste, flee, leave, decamp, make off, sneak off, take to one's heels, retreat, escape, take oneself off, slink away, run away, steal off, slip away, bolt, run off, disappear, fly, pack off, evade, give the slip, quit the scene, withdraw, take French leave, take flight, make off with oneself, give leg bail, elude, bundle off, elope, vamoose, vanish, skedaddle.
2. Conceal oneself, secrete oneself, hide away, hole up.

ABSENCE, *n.* 1. Inexistence, non-attendance, non-residence, non-appearance.
2. Absorption, preoccupation, daydreaming, withdrawal, abstraction, revery, woolgathering, inattention, musing, brown study, heedlessness, absence of mind, distraction.
3. Unavailability, lack, need, want, deficiency, requirement, default, scarcity, defect.
4. Privation, emptiness, negation, destitution, void, vacuum, vacuity, vacancy.

ABSENT, *adj.* 1. Nonattendant, away, abroad, nonresident, gone, not at home, not present, lost, elsewhere, otherwhere, wanting, astray, flown, missing, out, A. W. O. L., omitted.
2. Unthinking, inattentive, thoughtless, blank, absent-minded, oblivious, abstracted, heedless, preoccupied, absorbed, musing, dreamy, vacuous, distracted, lost, unconsidering, napping, listless, unconscious, unaware, woolgathering, faraway, removed.

ABSENT, *v.* Decamp, abscond, stay away from, retire from, remove oneself, keep oneself away, refuse to attend, withdraw oneself, play truant, fail to appear, not show up, shirk, evade, vacate, slip away, hold aloof, cut, ignore.

ABSENTEE, *n.* Deserter, truant, malingerer, shirker, slacker, skulker, quitter, fugitive, exile, backslider, renegade, runaway.

ABSENTEEISM, *n.* Truancy, failure in duty, malingering, shirking, French leave, avoidance, evasion, abstention, inaction, desertion, neglect, delinquency, dereliction, slow-down, sneaking out.

ABSENT-MINDED, *adj.* Abstracted, unmindful, preoccupied, absent, musing, distrait, inattentive, dreamy, unheeding, rapt, forgetful, engrossed, unconscious, unaware, oblivious, withdrawn, lost, remote, thoughtless, heedless, listless, napping, inadvertent, distracted, woolgathering, removed, faraway, in a brown study.

ABSOLUTE, *adj.* 1. Unqualified, unrestricted, unrestrained, unlimited, unconditional, complete, total, perfect, independent, unconditioned, free, unbounded, self-existent, self-determined, utter, unmixed, pure, ideal, out-and-out, supreme, full, *causa sui*, fixed, settled, self-sufficing, inalienable, infinite, unalloyed.
2. Autocratic, self-willed, domineering, lordly, imperative, imperious, dogmatic, authoritative, official, commanding, despotic, overbearing, tyrannous, tyrannical, controlling, peremptory, exacting, arbitrary, arrogant, haughty, dictatorial, irresponsible, irrepressible, compelling, stark.
3. Positive, conclusive, decisive, true, actual, essential, real, demonstrable, demonstrated, undoubted, indubitable, unquestionable, veritable, decided, accurate, confirmed, unreserved, plenary, determinate, categorical, plain, downright, sure

terminative, infallible, axiomatic, unalterable, definite, genuine, reliable, confident, unequivocal, certain, consummate, simple.

ABSOLUTELY, *adv.* 1. Wholly, purely, verily, utterly, completely, unconditionally, definitely, perforce, without limitation.
2. Incontestably, infallibly, undoubtedly, truly, unquestionably, indubitably, positively, really, beyond peradventure, in reality, actually, indeed, in truth, in fact, unequivocally, decidedly.

ABSOLUTENESS, *n.* 1. Independence, ideality, unlimitedness, unrestrained power, arbitrariness, despotism, supremeness, perfection.
2. Positiveness, actuality, substantiality, reality.

ABSOLUTION, *n.* Pardon, forgiveness, quittance, dispensation, remission, exoneration, exculpation, acquittal, deliverance, dismissal, vindication, release, discharge, condonation, intercession, shriving, liberation, extenuation, forgetfulness, clearance, amnesty, overlooking, justification, oblivion, sanctification, indemnity, indulgence.

ABSOLUTISM, *n.* Sovereignty, arbitrariness, absoluteness, imperialism, iron rule, dictatorship, tyranny, domination, despotism, autocracy, Caesarism, czarism, kaiserism, monarchism, personal government, man-on-horsebackism.

ABSOLVE, *v.* Adjudge innocent, remit, quit, exonerate, acquit, exculpate, reprieve, exempt, clear, release from imputation, set free, liberate, declare removed, discharge, loose, vindicate, justify, deliver, overlook, forgive, condone, pardon, excuse, shrive.

ABSONANT, *adj.* 1. Discordant, out of tune, dissonant, unharmonious, cacophonous, grating, harsh, jarring, jangling, untuneful, unmusical.
2. Unreasonable, disagreeing, incongruous, contrary, inconsistent, contradictory, dissident, incompatible, discrepant, conflictory, opposite, repugnant, at variance, dissentient.

ABSORB, *v.* 1. Suck in, take in, receive in, imbibe, ingest, ingurgitate, take up, suck up, appropriate, drink in, incorporate, embody, use up, assimilate, sponge up, intercept.
2. Swallow up, engorge, engulf, consume, merge, devour, exhaust, destroy, overwhelm.
3. Occupy wholly, engross completely, enwrap, immerse, engage, fix, arrest, rivet, monopolize, fascinate.

ABSORBED, *adj.* Thoughtful, occupied, intent, engrossed, preoccupied, engaged, rapt, plunged, buried, sunken in, deep in, lost in, concentrated, fascinated, incorporated, swallowed up.

ABSORBENT, *adj.* Pervious, imbibing, spongy, permeable, penetrable, absorptive, receptive, sorbefacient, retentive, porous, spongiose, thirsty.

ABSORBING, *adj.* Engrossing, prepossessing, occupying, captivating, winning, fascinating, interesting, soul-stirring, exciting, thrilling, inspiring.

ABSORPTION, *n.* 1. Imbibition, imbibing, swallowing up, taking in, reception, digestion, engulfment, inosculation, ingurgitation, merging, appropriation, incorporation, assimilation, union, engorgement, consumption, fusion, blending.
2. Preoccupation, prepossession, immersion, concentration, engrossment, monopolization, engagement, fascination, occupation, interest, reverie, musing, brown study, close application.

ABSTAIN, *v.* Keep one's hands off, forbear, stay one's hand, refrain voluntarily from, withhold oneself from, deny oneself, restrain oneself, cease, desist, avoid, let alone, turn aside from, refuse, decline, fast, eschew, teetotal, look not upon the wine when it is red, get on the water wagon, take the pledge.

ABSTAINER, *n.* Teetotaler, temperance advocate, Rechabite, prohibitionist, nephalist, puritan, dry *(colloquial),* blue-ribbonist, water-drinker, hydropot.

ABSTEMIOUS, *adj.* Habitually abstinent, teetotal, temperate, non-indulgent, moderate, sober, frugal, austere, sparing, self-denying, ascetic, continent, self-controlled, non-alcoholic.

ABSTEMIOUSNESS, *n.* Habitual abstinence, teetotalism, temperance, non-indulgence, sobriety, frugality, moderation, austerity, self-denial, self-control, asceticism, blue-ribbonism, nephalism, Volsteadism, puritanism.

ABSTENTION, *n.* Abstaining, forbearance, holding off, refraining, avoidance, self-restraint, non-indulgence, non-participation, inaction.

ABSTERGE, *v.* Wash, cleanse, make clean, wipe, purge, purify, elutriate, scour, scrub, rinse.

ABSTERGENT, *n.* Cleansing agent, detergent, purifier, purgative, cathartic.

ABSTINENCE, *n.* 1. Abstention, abstaining, forbearance, avoidance, withholding, refraining, abnegation, keeping aloof.
2. Frugality, abstemiousness, sobriety, self-restraint, self-control, self-denial, asceticism, non-indulgence, continence, moderation, fasting, temperance, soberness, teetotalism, nephalism, blue-ribbonism, Rechabitism, austerity, Puritanism.

ABSTINENT, *adj.* Moderate, abstemious, sparing, frugal, sober, self-restraining, self-denying, self-controlling, non-indulgent, ascetic, continent, temperate, teetotal, austere, puritanical.

ABSTRACT, *adj.* 1. Theoretic, immaterial, pure *(as mathematics),* conceptual, notional, refined, non-particular, general, indefinite, abstracted, metaphysical, subtle, attenuated, rarefied.
2. Difficult, abstruse, recondite, occult, vague, hidden, obscure, dark, enigmatical, mysterious, profound, remote, undetermined, ill-defined.
3. Ideal, transcendental, imaginary, visionary, spiritual, intellectual, not concrete, generalized, non-representational *(as art).*

ABSTRACT, *v.* 1. Detach, separate, dissociate, disunite, isolate, disengage, disjoin, consider by itself, take out of context, remove from its proper whole, distinguish, discriminate, consider as a generality, view partially, regard one-sidedly, draw off, distract, divert, remove, eliminate, deduct, analyze, draw from, withdraw.
2. Appropriate, take away, seize, steal, purloin, remove by stealth, embezzle, plagiarize.
3. Synopsize, abbreviate, summarize, shorten, condense, epitomize, contract, compress, reduce, compact, abridge, prune, cut down, make an abstract of, curtail, outline.

ABSTRACT, *n.* 1. Epitome, compendium, draft, compend, condensation, epitomization, synopsis, abridgment, résumé, brief, abbreviature, outline, abbreviation, breviary, summary, précis, review, aperçu, digest, conspectus, analysis, contraction, recapitulation, syllabus, reduction, compression, sum, substance, note, drift, prospectus, concise statement, gist, general contents, sketch, head note, docket, bulletin, minute.
2. Essence, quintessence, extracts, excerpts,

fragments, cuttings, analects, citations, clippings, symposium, compilation.
3. Generality, universality, main, common run, average.

ABSTRACTED, *adj.* 1. Separated from matter, apart, subtle, refined, ideal, esoteric, withdrawn, disconnected, removed, abstruse, difficult, aerial, profound, unsubstantial, theoretical, volatile, transcendental.
2. Absorbed, indifferent, inattentive, heedless, oblivious, preoccupied, engrossed, lost in thought, thoughtful, dreaming, distrait, musing, listless, remote, absent-minded, thoughtless, negligent, in a reverie, unobservant, in a brown study.

ABSTRACTION, *n.* 1. Generality, concept, idea, visionary notion, theory, vague representation.
2. Disconnection, isolation, disjunction, partial consideration, taking from context, separation, non-consideration of the whole.
3. Engrossment, preoccupation, remoteness, inattention, self-communing, reverie, detachment, musing, aloofness, absent-mindedness, brown study, distraction.
4. Drawing off, seizure, deduction, removal, taking, appropriation, subtraction, withdrawal, stealing, embezzlement, pilfering, purloining, theft.

ABSTRUSE, *adj.* Remote from apprehension, difficult to understand, incomprehensible, occult, profound, transcendental, recondite, acroamatic, esoteric, mysterious, remote, hidden, secret, deep, dark, obscure, enigmatical, mystic, ambiguous, vague, far-fetched, metaphysical, unfathomable, indefinite, abstract, complex, attenuated, subtle, rarefied, cabalistic, unintelligible, impenetrable, refined, nebulous.

ABSTRUSENESS, *n.* Obscurity, reconditeness, incomprehensibility, profundity, unintelligibility, impenetrability, unfathomableness, insolubility, inscrutability, ambiguousness, enigmaticalness, vagueness, intricacy, inexplicableness.

ABSURD, *adj.* 1. Contrary to reason or common sense, unreasonable, senseless, ill-advised, daft, ill-considered, irrational, nonsensical, crazy, mad, meaningless, amphigoric, unwise, impractical, ill-judged.
2. Obviously false or foolish, illusive, fabulous, fallacious, sophistic, incorrect, preposterous, erroneous, chimerical, impossible.
3. Logically contradictory, self-contradictory, paradoxical, illogical, anomalous, inconsistent, incongruous, inept, self-annulling.
4. Ridiculous, asinine, fatuous, inane, stupid, silly, wild, farcical, laughable, funny, childish, ludicrous, derisible, egregious, extravagant.

ABSURDITY, *n.* 1. Unreasonableness, delusion, irrationality, error, fallacy.
2. Idiocy, imbecility, *bêtise,* fatuity, nugacity, drivel, inanity, asininity, foolishness, silliness, folly, nonsensicality, comicality, stupidity.
3. Illogicality, hysteron proteron, paralogism, logical contradiction, paradox, inconsistency, sophistry, incongruity.
4. Balderdash, fiction, farcical fantasy, fable, bosh, myth, romance, chimaera, canard, mare's nest, moonshine, twaddle, gibberish, jargon, old wives' tale, fiddle-faddle, cock-and-bull story, amphigory.
5. Burlesque, travesty, farce, extravagance, caricature, farrago, buffoonery, mummery, parody.

ABUNDANCE, *n.* 1. Overflowing quantity, great supply, amplitude, full measure, copiousness, fullness, profusion, fertility, bounty, exuberance, multiplicity, great sufficiency, luxuriance, flood, heap, plenteousness, store, richness, enough, fund, mine, bonanza, cornucopia, horn of plenty, fat of the land, wherewithal.

2. Surfeit, satiety, repletion, superfluity, glut, excess, supersaturation, redundance, oversupply, surplus, plethora, drug on the market.

3. Wealth, affluence, resources, means, riches, prosperity, opulence, comfort, fortune, treasure, *embarras de richesses*.

ABUNDANT, *adj.* Profuse, copious, overflowing, rife, brimming, abounding, superabundant, rich, plenteous, generous, plentiful, bounteous, lavish, affluent, exuberant, in large measure, luxuriant, fertile, replete, fully sufficient, big, large, great, ample, thick, liberal, chock-full, well-provided, bountiful, teeming, swarming, prolific, prodigal, productive, unstinted, unmeasured, superfluous, inexhaustible, redundant.

ABUSE, *v.* 1. Use wrongly or improperly, put to bad use, misuse, mishandle, pervert, profane, misemploy, defile, prostitute, debase, desecrate, pollute, dishonor, misapply, degrade.

2. Do wrong to, maltreat, injure, victimize, act injuriously toward, wrong, harm, ill-treat, ruin, persecute, oppress, overwork, overburden, overtax, overstrain, impose upon, ill-use.

3. Reproach coarsely, revile, inveigh against, execrate, vituperate, vilify, blacken, denigrate, malign, berate, censure, defame, disparage, speak ill of, traduce, objurgate, scold, asperse, slander, calumniate, upbraid, carp at, denounce, libel, run down, decry, slur, backbite, lampoon, rail at, pasquinade, satirize, pour contumely on, lash, stigmatize, insult, blaspheme, curse, scorn, sneer at, bullyrag, blackguard, belittle, criticize, pull to pieces, anathematize.

4. Molest, ravish, violate, deflower, outrage, rape, debauch.

ABUSE, *n.* 1. Wrong or improper use, pollution, misuse, mishandling, misemployment, defilement, misappropriation, misapplication, profanation, desecration, debasement, perversion, degradation, prostitution.

2. Ill-use, ill-treatment, maltreatment, outrage, victimization, injury, persecution, bad treatment.

3. Insulting language, calumniation, censure, vituperation, derogation, vilification, execration, revilement, denigration, disparagement, slander, condemnation, defamation, aspersion, contumely, tongue-lashing, railing, objurgation, upbraiding, stigmatization, berating, invective, denunciation, stricture, tirade, diatribe, obloquy, malediction, philippic, detraction, opprobrium, libel, vicious scolding, red-hot salvo, ribaldry, scurrility, vile reproof, billingsgate, blasphemy, blackguardism, insult.

4. Offense, crime, malversation, malfeasance, corrupt practice, fault.

5. Ravishment, violation, rape, molestation, defilement, indecent assault.

ABUSIVE, *adj.* 1. Harsh, disparaging, libelous, reproachful, derogatory, condemnatory, offensive, denunciatory, depreciatory, defamatory, carping, slanderous, censorious, calumniatory, indecent, contumelious, vilificatory, vituperative, insulting, scurrilous, thersitical, opprobrious, licentious, Fescennine, obscene, ribald, foul-mouthed, vile, railing, reviling, invective, insolent, sarcastic, injurious, hurtful, outrageous, scurvy, satirical, blackguard, biting, acrimonious, loud-mouthed, cynical, low, mean, gross, rude.

2. Wrongly used, corrupt, missapplied, undue, improper, inappropriate, unjustified, unwarranted, perverted.

ABUT, *v.* Meet end to end, border on, adjoin, lean against, be contiguous, join, butt, approach, be adjacent to, be juxtaposed, be conterminous, touch, reach, project, approximate, impinge, extend.

ABUTMENT, *n.* 1. Junction, contiguity, contact, joint, juxtaposition, adjacency, conterminousness, conjunction, adhesion, attachment, appendage, union, appurtenance.

2. Buttress, retaining wall, supporting wall, end-pier, support, anchorage, thrust wall, shore, adjoinment, stay, brace, prop.

ABUTTAL, *n.* 1. Adjacency, touching, nearness, meeting, conjunction, contiguity, juxtaposition, union, convergence, confluence.

2. Border, boundary, bourn, terminus, bound, confine, limit, mete, termination.

ABYSMAL, *adj.* Down-reaching, unfathomable, profound, fathomless, boundless, deep, endless, bottomless, dark, infinite, vast, immeasurable, enormous.

ABYSS, *n.* 1. Cleft, fissure, gorge, void, depth, deep pit, deep, chasm, crevasse, gulf, gap, abysm, couloir, profound, great immensity, infinitude, hiatus, hollow, yawning cavity, womb of earth, primal chaos.

2. Infernal regions, inferno, netherworld, the bottomless pit, lower world, underworld, the pit, the nadir, limbo, purgatory, hell, Sheol, Tophet, Gehenna, Erebus, Hades, Tartarus, Avernus, Naraka (*Hindu and Buddhist*), Malebolge (*Dante*), Nastrond (*Norse*), Niflheim (*Norse*), Amenti (*Egyptian*), Aralu (*Babylonian*).

ACADEMIC, *adj.* 1. Of an academy, of a college or university, scholastic, lettered, erudite, liberal, scholarly, learned, classical, collegiate.

2. Theoretical, not practical, ivory-towered, general, speculative, pedantic, formal, accepted, cut-and-dried, conventional, traditional, remote, bookish, stiff, ivy-walled.

ACADEMIC, *n.* Member of an academy, holder of degree, academician, collegian, schoolman, professor, instructor, don (*English*), doctor, man of letters, fellow, gownsman, learned person, philosopher, scholar.

ACADEMICALS, *n.* Cap-and-gown, robe, gown, vestments, hood, mortarboard (*colloquial*), dress prescribed in an institution of learning, colors, stripes, insignia.

ACADEMY, *n.* 1. Private intermediate school, secondary school, preparatory school, day school, boarding school, seminary, institute, gymnasium, high school, lyceum, grammar school, Latin school.

2. Learned institution, college, university, school for instruction in a particular science or art (*Military Academy, Academy of Fine Arts*), phrontisterion (*facetious or disparaging*), educational establishment, conservatory (*Academy of Music*).

3. Association of artists or scientists, body of experienced persons in any group (*Academy of Political Science,* etc.), scientific body, association of literary men.

ACCEDE, v. 1. Concur, assent, accord, approve, agree, acquiesce, grant, consent, acknowledge, concede, admit, permit, close with, echo.

2. Comply, conform, yield, submit, accept, obey, subscribe to, defer to, abide by.

3. Enter upon (an office), attain (a dignity), succeed to (as heir), assume, come to inherit, arrive at, reach, come to.

4. Become a party to, associate oneself with, unite oneself, give one's adherence to, be joined, be added.

ACCELERATE, v. Express, forward, precipitate, urge forward, press forward, expedite, advance, hasten, further, dispatch, hurry, step up, speed up, facilitate, hustle, quicken, spur, promote, drive on, urge on, push on, move forward in time, antedate.

ACCELERATION, n. Speeding up, hastening, increase of speed or velocity, stepping up, dispatch, expedition, advanced transportation, advanced production, advanced time, mounting intensity.

ACCENT, v. Stress, emphasize, accentuate, utter or mark with accent, put the ictus on, render emphatic, bring out distinctly, articulate forcibly, give prominence to, intensify.

ACCENT, n. 1. Syllable stress, attack, prominent pulsation, rhythmical emphasis, articulative emphasis, force of utterance, stress accent, mark, sign.

2. Tone, inflection, pronunciation, intonation, vocalization, modulation, pitch, quality of sound, significant tone, cadence, twang, articulation, enunciation, utterance, distinguishing character, distinctive mode of expression, significance, mood.

ACCENTUATE, v. 1. Pronounce or write with accent, mark with accent, stress a syllable, lay stress upon.

2. Bring into prominence, give emphasis to, emphasize, call attention to, underline, feature, underscore, punctuate, give point to, intensify, deepen, heighten, strengthen, make clear.

ACCEPT, v. 1. Take willingly, receive something offered, receive with favor or approval, endure, gain, acquire, get, obtain, secure, come by.

2. Admit as satisfactory or sufficient, acquiesce in, consent, accede to, allow, resign oneself to, comply, agree to, confirm, assent to, sign, accord recognition to, embrace, approve, adopt, avow, believe, acknowledge.

3. Receive into the mind, consider as true, estimate, assume, credit, regard, esteem, value, understand, construe, interpret, put a sense upon.

ACCEPTABLE, adj. 1. Pleasing to the receiver, attractive, inviting, welcome, pleasant, likable, agreeable, felicitous, prepossessing, becoming, popular, delightful, desirable, comfortable, gratifying, pleasurable, refreshing, admirable.

2. Capable of being accepted, timely, passable, opportune, seasonable, allowable, satisfactory, convenient, expedient.

3. Worthy of being accepted, meritorious, deserving, fit, suitable, meet, due, proper, seemly, decorous, advisable, worthwhile, commendable, creditable, reputable, estimable, wise, exemplary.

ACCEPTANCE, n. 1. Accepting, taking, receipt, reception.

2. Suitableness, favorable reception, approval, favor, approbation, affirmation, recognition,

acknowledgment, ratification, confirmation, sanction, satisfaction, gratification.

3. Assent to, belief in, compliance with, submission to, acquiescence in, resignation to.

4. Trade acceptance (commercial), signature, accepted bill (of exchange), signed contract, indorsement, guarantee, agreement, order, draft, certification.

ACCEPTATION, n. 1. Favorable regard, cordial reception, approval, adoption, admission, assent, currency, vogue.

2. Accepted meaning, sense, interpretation, import, signification, explanation, significance, construction, understanding, implication, purport, denotation, connotation, drift, force.

ACCEPTED, adj. Favorably received, approved, chosen, acceptable, popular, current, in vogue, conventional, standard, orthodox, stereotyped, formally admitted, acknowledged, recognized, accredited, established, sanctioned, unopposed, settled, allowed, preferred, authorized, authentic, time-honored, fashionable, confirmed.

ACCESS, n. 1. Act or privilege of coming to, accessibility, approachability, advent, entrance, admittance, admission, introduction, reception, interview, audience.

2. Way or means of approach, entrance, adit, entrance-way, passageway, path, course, inlet, route, communication, road, highroad.

3. Paroxysm, fit, seizure, attack, onset, throe, outburst, recurrence, raptus, spasm, convulsion.

4. Increase, accession, addition, enlargement, increment, gain, aggrandizement, augmentation, extension, expansion, accretion.

ACCESSIBILITY, n. Convenience, affability, ease of approach, approachability, attainability, procurability, susceptibility, openness, weakness, impressibility, vulnerability, receptiveness, geniality, sociability.

ACCESSIBLE, adj. 1. Approachable, get-at-able, free of entrance, come-at-able, affable, civil, easy, companionable, complaisant, sociable, obliging, conversable, unconstrained, courteous, friendly, familiar.

2. Possible, procurable, reachable, available, attainable, obtainable, achievable, compassable.

3. Open to the influence of, vulnerable, weak, easily influenced, assailable.

ACCESSION, n. 1. Act of coming near or on, approach, arrival, advent, admittance, access, influx.

2. Coming into office or power (as a new dynasty), taking over, induction, inauguration, elevation, installation, investment, attainment.

3. Something added, addition, augmentation, increment, annexation, enlargement, accretion, aggrandizement, increase, extension, reinforcement.

4. Coming on of disease or passion, raptus, seizure, onset, paroxysm, attack, outburst, spasm.

5. Agreement, consent, acquiescence, assent, acceptance, adherence.

ACCESSORY, adj. Contributory, appurtenant, subsidiary, secondary, auxiliary, adscititious, subservient, ancillary, additional, complementary, supplementary, collateral, subordinate, adjunct, helpful, abetting, assisting, of minor importance, giving aid, privy, allied, adventitious, incidental, unessential, extra.

ACCESSORY, n. 1. Something added for effect or adornment, adjunct, appurtenance, appendage, attachment, accompaniment, auxiliary, minutia, minor particular, subordinate part, subsidiary, concomitant, complement, belongings, gear, appropriate detail, fashionable accent.

2. Abettor, accomplice, helper, assistant, ally, coadjutor, confederate, henchman, participant, retainer, associate, colleague, companion, partner, consociate, adherent, co-partner, attendant, follower, figurant.

ACCIDENT, *n.* 1. Unforeseen occurrence, event, occasion, adventure, happening, circumstance, incident, befalling.

2. Fortuity, chance, hap, hazard, luck, crisis, fortune, possibility, contingency, modification, alteration, change.

3. Adversity, affliction, casualty, catastrophe, calamity, disaster, mishap, misfortune, blunder, mischance, fluke, oversight, contretemps, crash, miscarriage, misadventure, mischief, hurt, ruin, wreck, smash-up, collision, undoing, downfall, blow, collapse.

ACCIDENTAL, *adj.* 1. Unintentional, unusual, undesigned, unpremeditated, not planned, stray, unexpected, unpurposeful, unintended, random, adventitious, fortuitous, unforeseen, haphazard, casual, chance.

2. Dependent, incidental, subsidiary, accessory, subordinate, contingent, conditional, secondary, non-essential, dispensable, not requisite, extrinsic, collateral, extraneous, adscititious, external, not pertinent, irrelevant, beside the point.

ACCIDENTALLY, *adv.* Unwittingly, casually, unintentionally, inadvertently, undesignedly, not purposely, unexpectedly, involuntarily, incidentally, fortuitously, randomly, haphazardly.

ACCLAIM, *v.* Salute with voice or sound, crown with acclamation, applaud, praise, cheer, shout, hail, greet, pay homage to, extol, laud, magnify, glorify, exalt, sing praises of, celebrate, idolize, pay tribute to, eulogize, congratulate, felicitate, compliment, encore, prize, honor, approve, cry up, call out loudly, noise abroad, rejoice in, declare.

ACCLAMATION, *n.* Acclaim, shout of applause, plaudit, paean, loud homage, hosanna, hurrah, huzza, cheer, outcry, jubilation, gratulation, exultation, adulation, salutation, approbation, laudation, commendation, éclat, magnification, glorification, eulogization, praise, tribute, ovation, triumph, rejoicing.

ACCLIMATE, *v.* Inure to a climate, acclimatize, habituate to an environment, accustom to, season, naturalize, adapt to, become habituated to, 'get used to.

ACCLIMATION, *n.* Acclimatement, acclimature, acclimatation, acclimatization, getting used to, inurement to climate, adaptation, adjustment, seasoning, hardening.

ACCLIVITY, *n.* Grade, gradient, ascent, slope, rise, pitch, cant, glacis, incline, inclination, bank, slant, upgrade, elevation, eminence, uphill-way, steep, hillside, height, hillock.

ACCLIVOUS, *adj.* Sloping upward, uphill, rising, ascending, upward, inclining, mounting, climbing, heaving up, looming up, springing up, gradient, towering up.

ACCOMMODATE, *v.* 1. Aid, assist, oblige, do a favor for, favor, convenience, serve, do a service for, save trouble to, help, meet the wants of, furnish, provide, supply, attend to the convenience of, make comfortable, tender to.

2. Have capacity for, be capable of holding, contain, furnish room for, have as contents, lodge, receive, supply accommodations for, entertain comfortably, comprise, include.

3. Adjust, adapt, fit, make suitable, make correspond, make conform, bring into consistency.

4. Make agree, bring into harmony, reconcile, make accord, settle amicably, harmonize, adjust, compose, bring to terms.

ACCOMMODATING, *adj.* Obliging, helpful, considerate, benevolent, amiable, gracious, kind, complaisant, friendly, neighborly, attentive, kindly, polite, unselfish, warm-hearted, cordial, well-disposed, benignant, favorable, easy to deal with, conciliatory, pliable, yielding.

ACCOMMODATION, *n.* 1. Favor, advantage, interest, service, convenience, assistance, aid, help, provision of wants, supply of conveniences.

2. Lodging, space, arrangements, quarters, room, maintenance.

3. Adjustment, adaptation, agreement, fitness, conformity, congruence, suitableness, uniformity, correspondence.

4. Adjustment of differences, accordance, settlement, harmonization, reconciliation, concord, compromise, restoration of harmony, abatement of differences, pacification, harmony.

5. Act of accommodation, favor, helping hand, assistance, lift, good turn, kindness, obligingness, help, generosity, loan of money.

ACCOMPANIMENT, *n.* 1. Association, escort, partnership, company, convoy, suite, retinue, train, entourage, cortege.

2. Concomitant, appanage, appurtenance, accessory, adjunct, appendage, attachment, circumstance, attendant, complement, context, attribute, coexistence.

3. Attendant music, obligato, minor harmony, subsidiary part, supplementary part.

ACCOMPANY, *v.* 1. Conduct, escort, squire, go with, usher, attend, keep company with, wait upon, associate with, convoy, chaperon, guard, tend, join in action, follow, consort with, go along with, companion, couple with, go side by side with.

2. Coexist, occur with, occur in association with, be connected with, append, characterize, add.

3. Play or sing an accompaniment to.

ACCOMPANYING, *adj.* Concomitant, attendant, accessory, coexistent, incidental, associated with, coupled with, fellow, joint.

ACCOMPLICE, *n.* Partner in wrongdoing, ally, associate in guilt, accessory, right-hand man, confederate, assistant, abettor, stool-pigeon, aider, companion, colleague, helpmate, confrere, mate, follower, attendant, henchman, retainer, recruit, consociate, copartner, co-operator, collaborator, co-worker, comrade, helper, coadjutor, auxiliary, supporter, *particeps criminis, socius criminis.*

ACCOMPLISH, *v.* 1. Carry into effect, bring to pass, work out, execute fully, consummate, carry through, perfect, negotiate, perform, achieve, put over, effect, work out, dispatch, complete, carry out, discharge, compass, win, engineer, bring about, do, produce, turn out, realize, attain, fulfil, effectuate, expedite, manage, contrive, operate, get, act.

2. Bring to an end, put an end to, finish, close, conclude, wind up, terminate.

3. Make complete, equip thoroughly, furnish completely, polish.

ACCOMPLISHED, *adj.* 1. Expert, practiced, up to the mark, dexterous, deft, adroit, skilful, apt, proficient, gifted, talented, masterly, trained, experienced, finished, resourceful, neat-handed, nimble-fingered, able, *au fait,* ripe, perfected, consummate, clever.

2. Well-grounded, educated, learned, lettered, instructed, cultivated, versed, qualified, scholarly, well-informed, well-read, well-educated, erudite, intellectual.

3. Cultured, refined, fashionable, well-bred, urbane, polished, genteel, fine, polite, elegant, graceful, artistic, thoroughbred.

4. Completed, effected, established, consummated.

ACCOMPLISHMENT, *n.* 1. Complete performance, completion, transaction, execution, fulfilment, achievement, realization, dispatch, consummation, culmination, perfection.

2. Deed, feat, act, exploit.

3. Acquired art or grace, polite attainment, acquirement, adornment, embellishment, finish, ornament, graceful acquisition, finesse, forte, talent, gift, savoir-faire, mental resources.

4. Proficiency, skill, address, qualification, dexterity, adroitness, expertness, deftness, competence, capability.

ACCORD, *v.* 1. Be in accordance, be in unison, be as one, be harmonious, attune, be in tune with, harmonize, chime in with, comport with, correspond, concur, agree, assent, acquiesce, tally, conform, adjust, square, adapt, quadrate.

2. Vouchsafe, deign, bestow, award.

3. Concede, accede, grant, admit, allow, accept, yield, give, permit, tolerate.

ACCORD, *n.* 1. Harmonious union, harmony, unison, concert, correspondence, accordance, consonance, concord, concordance, unanimity, consensus, consentience, comport, keeping with, conjunction, rapport, sympathy, conformation, congruity, conformity, uniformity, communion, coincidence.

2. Act of reconciliation, compliance, assent, acquiescence, accession, concurrence, agreement, concession, obedience, submission, consent.

3. Spontaneous impulse, voluntary choice, volition, will, free will, free agency, discretion, determination.

ACCORDANT, *adj.* In accord with, conformable, adapted, consonant, fit, congruous, agreeing, complementary, responsive, answering, consistent, compatible, correspondent, acquiescent, willing, compliable, consenting, fitting, agreeable, suitable, harmonious, symphonious.

ACCORDINGLY, *adv.* 1. In a conformable manner, compliantly, conformably, agreeably, correspondingly, consistently, compatibly.

2. In accordance therewith, wherefore, thus, therefore, consequently, hence, thence, whence, then, thereafter, whereupon, in due course, so, and so, in which case.

ACCORDING TO 1. After the manner of, in accordance with, in conformity with, in the light of, conformably to, agreeably to.

2. Proportionately, in proportion with.

3. On the authority of, as stated by, as believed by.

ACCOST, *v.* Address, salute, hail, appeal to, call to, speak first to, converse with, halloo, greet, make up to, invoke, apostrophize, solicit, draw near, confront, approach, assail, waylay.

ACCOUCHEMENT, *n.* (Fr.) Confinement, labor, travail, giving birth to, bearing, child-bearing, childbirth, childbed, bringing forth, nativity, birth, delivery, parturition, gestation, lying-in, prolification, eutocia *(easy),* dystocia *(difficult),* bringing into life.

ACCOUNT, *v.* 1. Hold to be, consider, believe, look upon, value, deem, judge, view, regard, rate, think, take for, esteem, estimate, count, compute, calculate, reckon, appraise, set a value on.

2. Give an explanation of, refer to some cause, exhibit the reason, show the grounds, ascertain the cause, attribute, expound, elucidate, clear up, accredit, credit, impute.

3. State the terms of, render an account, put to the credit of, furnish an accounting, give a reckoning, answer for, assign to.

ACCOUNT, *n.* 1. Record of debits and credits, statement of pecuniary transactions, methodical calculation, computation, enumeration, reckoning, tally, count, score, valuation, invoice, bill, charge, tick, balance sheet, entry.

2. Recitation, recital, chronicle, record, word, rehearsal, relation, explanation, statement, sketch, description, version, recountal, delineation, tale, story, history, narrative, portrayal, memoir, representation, report, detail, commentary, tidings, declamation.

3. Statement of reasons, reference to grounds, investigation into causes, clearing up, unfolding, explanation, exposition, detailment.

4. Concern, sake, interest, ground, cause, reason, score, consideration, motive, regard.

5. Esteem, importance, value, worth, merit, honor, consequence, estimation, reputation, note, distinction, rank, dignity, repute.

6. Gain, profit, utility, expediency, service, advantage, good, benefit, avail, advancement, weal, use.

ACCOUNTABILITY, *n.* Responsibility, bounden duty, responsibleness, accountableness, liability, trustworthiness, obligation, answerableness, amenability.

ACCOUNTABLE, *adj.* Answerable, liable, subject, responsible, amenable, open to, obligated, in duty bound, beholden.

ACCOUNTANT, *n.* Bookkeeper, auditor, actuary, controller, teller, cashier, clerk, inspector of accounts, expert in accounts, calculator, reckoner, examiner of business accounts, analyst, certified accountant, CPA, chartered accountant *(Eng.),* computer, comptroller, sirkar *(Anglo-Ind.).*

ACCOUNT OF, ON Because of, by reason of, for the sake of, on behalf of, in the interest of.

ACCOUTER, *v.* Array in mail, harness, rig out, caparison, fit out, equip, garb, dress, attire, trap, apparel, invest, clothe, adorn, deck, habit, arm, supply, provide, equip for the field.

ACCOUTERMENTS, *n.* Trappings, caparison, array, appurtenances, gear, appointments, dress, equipage, equipment, paraphernalia, ornaments, housings, arms, outfit, livery, apparel, garb, attire, raiment, habiliment, vesture, rigging, investiture, clothing, harness.

ACCREDIT, *v.* 1. (Followed by *with.*) Ascribe to one's credit, attribute to, give credit for, assign to.

2. Receive as credible, believe, credit, put trust in, acknowledge.

3. Furnish with credentials, invest with credit, bring into authority, vouch for officially, certify

as standard, sanction, authorize, empower, credit as an envoy, depute, commission, deputize, assign to an embassy.

ACCREDITED, *adj.* Publicly authorized, officially sanctioned, provided with credentials, empowered, authorized, commissioned, deputed, confirmed, endorsed, sanctioned, approved, acknowledged, accepted as valid, guaranteed as standard, vouched for.

ACCRETION, *n.* 1. Organic growth, formation by external additions, increase by inclusion, extraneous addition, augmentation by adhesion, accession of parts, natural growth, coherence of particles, accumulation, matter added, fusion, increment, enlargement, extension, expansion, amplification.

2. *(Pathol.)* Growing together of parts into a whole, adhesion of parts normally distinct, piling up of substance, conglomeration.

3. *(Law)* Increase by deposit of alluvium, extension of boundaries, gradual accumulation of soil, increase of property by surrender of a coheir.

ACCRUAL, *n.* Increase, maturing, accruement, accretion, accumulation, gain, yield, acquirement, outcome, advantage, right.

ACCRUE, *v.* 1. Come as a natural result or addition, follow by increase or advantage, issue as a result, arise in due course, proceed, fall from, emanate from, flow from, result, redound, ensue, come in, be added by growth, accumulate, be derived, be gained, yield, bring in, mature, fall due, fall to one's share.

2. *(Law)* Vest as a right, come into existence as an enforceable right or claim.

ACCUMULATE, *v.* 1. Heap up, mass, pile up, gather into a mass, amass, muster, stack up, aggregate, agglomerate, scrape together, collect a bulk of, heap together, assemble, bring together, rake up, lump together, load up.

2. Hoard, store up, harvest, garner, save up, husband, bank, deposit, treasure up, set by, stow up, garner up, lay by, lay up, lay in, stock up, preserve, reserve, conserve.

3. Increase in quantity, swell, augment, wax, mount, grow, rise, enlarge, deepen, heighten, expand, extend, congregate, agglomerate, be heaped up, multiply, accrue, cumulate.

ACCUMULATION, *n.* Collecting together, bulk, amassing, gathering, hoarding, growth by addition, pile, compilation, collection, accretion, aggregation, conglomeration, agglomeration, stock, mass, heap, assemblage, amassment, store, drift, fund, accruement, concentration, acervation, coacervation, centralization.

ACCURACY, *n.* Freedom from error, conformity to truth, accurateness, exactitude, exactness, nicety, precision, correctness, justness, fidelity, faithfulness, regularity, carefulness, strictness, minuteness, severity, closeness, accordance, perfection, truthfulness, veracity, verity, truth, probity, soundness, equity, integrity, validity, rectitude, propriety, faultlessness.

ACCURATE, *adj.* Careful, executed with care, defect-free, errorless, faultless, exact, punctilious, precise, true, veracious, truthful, correct, close, minute, scrupulous, conscientious, severe, strict, rigorous, perfect, right, unerring, blameless, particular, nice, faithful, just, proper, definite, mathematical, absolute, conclusive, sure, certain, authoritative, scientific, thorough, regular,

unmistaken, trustworthy, dependable, reliable, sterling, conformable to standard, clean-cut, meticulous.

ACCURSE, *v.* Devote to destruction or evil, curse, anathematize, revile, invoke misery upon, damn, imprecate, maledict, denounce, execrate, doom, bedevil, proscribe, curse by bell, book and candle.

ACCURSED, *adj.* 1. Subject to a curse, doomed to evil, curse-laden, anathematized, execrated, unsanctified, condemned, unholy, blighted, banned, ruined, bedeviled, stricken, undone, unhappy, miserable, unfortunate, ill-fated, woeful, abandoned, unblest, hopeless.

2. Worthy of curses, dire, diabolic, devilish, infernal, hellish, execrable, abominable, base, vile, odious, wicked, hateful, detestable, horrid, abhorrent, horrible, malign, sinister, damnable, atrocious, revolting, loathsome, repugnant, foul, nauseous, offensive, repulsive, baleful, corrupt, villainous, pernicious, pestilential, noxious, deadly.

ACCUSATION, *n.* 1. Charge, imputation of wrongdoing, plaint *(law)*, indictment, challenge, arraignment, inculpation, crimination, true bill, incrimination, impeachment, allegation, taxing, complaint, attack, denunciation, delation, libel, citation, information.

2. Taking to task, calling to account, censure, reproach, blame, vituperation, slur, invective, recrimination.

ACCUSE, *v.* 1. Lodge a complaint, charge with, denounce, impeach, criminate, incriminate, tax with, arraign, indict, inculpate, implicate, impute, recriminate, inform against, challenge, cite, sue, prosecute, hail to court, appeal to law, litigate, bring to trial, prefer or file a charge, serve with a summons, delate, libel, bring a charge against.

2. Upbraid, blame, take to task, reproach, call to account, reprehend, attack, inveigh, declaim against, asperse, censure, stigmatize, slur, impugn, brand, revile, decry, vilify, malign, execrate.

ACCUSER, *n.* Libelant, judicial party, suitor, petitioner, litigant, prosecutor, plaintiff, delator, complainant, adversary, opposer, opponent, informer, informant.

ACCUSTOM, *v.* Make familiar by use, make wonted or used, break in, habituate, train, drill, familiarize, discipline, ingrain, harden, toughen, inure, season, acclimate, acclimatize, naturalize, addict, apply habitually, expose to, give one the hang of, make routine.

ACCUSTOMED, *adj.* 1. Habituated, wonted, used to, addicted to, given to, in the habit of, wedded to, acclimated, seasoned, hardened, toughened, inured, confirmed, broken in, trained, familiar through use, familiarized, disciplined, ingrained, acclimatized.

2. Habitual, routine, usual, established, set, customary, regular, normal, ordinary, general, prevailing, prevalent, common, frequent, fixed, everyday, household, well-known, rooted, well-trodden, commonplace, stock, prescriptive, conventional.

ACE, *n.* 1. Single mark on card, single spot on die, single pip, one-spot, a card so marked, winning card, head of suit.

2. Very small quantity or degree, unit, one, minute particle, atom, molecule, ion, corpuscle, granule, mote, grain, mite, scrap, snip, nip, bit,

speck, trifle, iota, jot, whit, tittle, scintilla, fig, rap.

3. Highly skilled person, adept, expert, winner, specialist, crack, master-hand, skilled hand, seasoned fighter pilot.

ACERBATE, *v.* 1. Render sour or bitter, make crabbed or harsh, sour, aggravate, worsen, heighten, increase, exaggerate.

2. Exasperate, provoke, inflame, excite, vex, infuriate, enrage, envenom, embitter, anger, gall, nettle, chafe, incense, annoy, fret, ruffle, irritate.

ACERBITY, *n.* 1. Bitterness, sourness, roughness of taste, unsavoriness, mordancy, acidity, tartness, causticity, acridness, acridity, sharpness, acidness, astringency, pungency, acidulousness.

2. Irritability, irascibility, acrimoniousness, asperity, captiousness, acrimony, harshness, rudeness, sternness, testiness, churlishness, severity, choler, rancor, venomousness, pique, snappishness, crabbedness, sullenness, moroseness, ill nature, ill temper, dudgeon, ill feeling, virulence, gruffness, austerity, surliness, brusqueness.

ACETOUS, *adj.* 1. Sour, vinegary, bitter, acid, tart, acrid, acidulated, biting, acidulous, sharp, caustic, pungent, stinging, piquant.

2. Acerb, acrimonious, mordant, cutting, harsh, austere, severe, morose, sullen, virulent, unkind, churlish, crabbed, crusty, gruff, moody, splenetic, sulky, surly.

ACHE, *v.* 1. Be in continued pain, feel or suffer pain, be distressed, be disquieted, be anguished, sorrow, grieve, suffer, mourn.

2. Inflict suffering upon, be painful, give pain, torment, torture, wound, distress, disquiet, be sore, trouble, afflict, hurt, twinge, shoot, smart, gnaw, pierce, gripe, pinch, throb.

3. Be eager, yearn, long, wish ardently, fret, be discontented, pine for, crave, hanker for, desire earnestly.

ACHE, *n.* 1. Protracted aching, dull pain, local pain, continued pain, agony, suffering, throe, twitch, smarting, pang, torture, twinge, hurt, torment, paroxysm, gripe, pinch, shooting, stab, soreness, throb, lancination, spasm.

2. Misery, affliction, woe, heartache, dolor, desolation, grief, sorrow, anguish, loneliness, distress, uneasiness, longing, craving, yearning, hankering after, pining for.

ACHIEVABLE, *adj.* Attainable, obtainable, possible, feasible, practicable, manageable.

ACHIEVE, *v.* 1. Effect, carry out, execute, bring to pass, accomplish, effectuate, contrive, bring about, work out, consummate, do, perform, compass, realize, fulfil, actualize, encompass, carry through, dispatch.

2. Complete, perfect, finish, end, terminate, bring to a successful end, bring to a conclusion, conclude, transact.

3. Acquire by effort, wrest, gain, win, get, procure, obtain, attain, succeed in gaining, earn.

ACHIEVEMENT, *n.* 1. Realization, accomplishment, attainment, performance, fulfilment, completion, consummation, execution, dispatch, effectuation, contrivance, encompassment, actualization.

2. Act, heroic deed, brilliant accomplishment, bravura, exploit, feat, meritorious work, feather in the cap.

3. *(Her.)* Escutcheon, shield, shield armorial, hatchment, funeral shield.

ACHROMATIC, *adj.* Free from color, colorless, hueless, uncolored, untinged, pale, gray, color-free, neutral, perfectly transparent, transmitting light, refracting light, free from iridescence, lighter in color than normal, resisting dyes, without coloring matter.

ACHROMATISM, *n.* Absence of color, freedom from chromatic aberration, achromaticity, want of color, freedom from color, transparency, colorlessness, paleness, dye-resistance, grayness, freedom from iridescence.

ACHROMATIZE, *v.* Render achromatic, make non-iridescent, render completely transparent, deprive of color, render translucent.

ACHROMATOPSY, *n.* Total color-blindness, acritochromacy, monochromatism, deuteranopia, protanopia, tritanopia, dichromatism.

ACID, *adj.* 1. Sour, vinegarish, bitter, tart, harsh, sharp, caustic, stinging, astringent, pricking, keen, pungent, acetous, acidulated, cutting, biting, burning, scalding, corrosive.

2. Acerb, acidulous, acrid, acrimonious, rough, crabbed, ill-tempered, severe, mordant, sarcastic, satirical, ironical.

ACIDIFY, *v.* Convert into acid, turn, ferment, acidulate, sour, embitter.

ACIDITY, *n.* 1. Sourness, vinegariness, bitterness, tartness, harshness, sharpness, causticity, astringency, keenness, pungency, acidulousness.

2. Acerbity, asperity, roughness, crabbedness, ill-humoredness, acridity, acrimony, severity, ill-temperedness, sarcasm, mordancy, ironicalness.

ACIDULOUS, *adj.* 1. Sourish, sub-acid, bitter, somewhat acid, sharp, tart, caustic, stinging, cutting, biting, burning, scalding, corrosive.

2. Sour-tempered, severe, sarcastic, satirical, virulent, scathing, mordant, sardonic, ironical, mocking.

ACKNOWLEDGE, *v.* 1. Admit to be real or true, declare belief in, recognize authority of, own the validity of, admit, grant, allow, accept, indorse, avow, profess, subscribe to, agree to, vouch for, certify, ratify, accede, concur, approve, concede, yield, assent, acquiesce, consent.

2. Recognize existence of, take cognizance of, notice, be aware of, respect, hold in remembrance.

3. Show appreciation of, express gratitude for, recompense, requite, thank, respond, answer, reply, reward, compensate, remunerate, settle, pay, give thanks for.

ACKNOWLEDGED, *adj.* Admitted, confessed, unquestioned, recognized, accepted, accredited.

ACKNOWLEDGMENT, *n.* 1. Recognizance, recognition, greeting, salutation, salute, address.

2. Avowal, profession, affirmation, admission, declaration, allowance, acceptance, indorsement, ratification, confession, concession, acquiescence, assent.

3. Voucher, certification, receipt, acquittance, deed, discharge, quittance, clearance, release.

4. Expression of gratitude, thanks, response, answer, return, reply, replication.

ACME, *n.* 1. Top, crest, summit, crown, peak, pinnacle, topmost point, apogee, utmost height, apex, zenith, culmination, vertex, extreme limit, *ne plus ultra*, turning point, culminating point, meridian, crisis.

2. Perfection, highest attainment, consummate achievement.

3. Full maturity of life, heyday, flush, prime, bloom, flower.

ACOLYTE, *n.* 1. Follower, retainer, henchman, satellite, assistant, attendant, helper, coadjutor, aide, auxiliary, adherent.

2. Altar boy, candle-lighter, candle-bearer, ministerial assistant, underclergyman, novice.

ACQUAINT, *v.* 1. Cause to have acquaintance with, introduce to, familiarize, make conversant with, make familiar.

2. Furnish with knowledge, cause to know, make known to, advise, let know, apprise, notify, make cognizant, disclose, discover to, announce, inform, enlighten, reveal, make aware, signify to, admonish, give notice, mention to, tell, divulge, report, send word to, impart, communicate to, advertise of, give intelligence of, intimate, hint, counsel concerning, suggest.

ACQUAINTANCE, *n.* 1. Personal knowledge, state of being acquainted, experience, familiarity, cognizance, awareness, close insight.

2. Reciprocal knowledge, social relations, intimacy, companionship, association, fellowship, friendliness, friendship.

3. Person known, group known, visiting circle, round of social relations, familiar, intimate, associate, companion, friend, colleague.

ACQUAINTED WITH 1. More or less familiar with, having personal knowledge of, informed of, apprised of, aware of, enlightened concerning, instructed in, conscious of, privy to, let into, alive to, conversant with, versed in, *au courant, au fait.*

2. Friendly with, at home with, in social relation with, sociable with, on a friendly basis with, companionable with, on amicable terms with, on visiting terms, on speaking terms, knowing personally.

ACQUIESCE, *v.* Assent tacitly, consent to, bow to, agree, accept passively, comply quietly, admit, submit, concede, yield, accede, concur, accord, conform, subscribe to, fall in with, join in the chorus, go with the stream, acknowledge, agree to, recognize, grant, remain without active opposition, allow, resign oneself, be reconciled to, rest, rest satisfied.

ACQUIESCENCE, *n.* Passive consent, tacit assent, concurrence, accordance, agreement, compliance, yielding, quiet submission, semi-approval, resignation, acknowledgment, willingness, sufferance.

ACQUIESCENT, *adj.* Accordant, agreeing, assenting, consenting, complying, yielding, willing, submitting, nothing loath, amenable, obedient.

ACQUIRE, *v.* 1. Come into possession of, fall into, attain, arrive at, compass, achieve, make, come to have, gain for oneself, obtain, inherit, secure, procure, realize, get as one's own, win, earn, reap, glean, pick up, get possession of, get one's hands on, receive, come by, adopt.

2. Cultivate, master, affect, pick up knowledge of, lay hold of, learn thoroughly, become adept in, make oneself master of.

ACQUIREMENT, *n.* Attainment, endowment, accomplishment, mental embellishment, turn, forte, gift, faculty, parts, stock of knowledge, mental resources, attributes, ability, talents, qualifications.

ACQUISITION, *n.* Acquirement, obtainment, attainment, procurement, purchase, inheritance, benefaction, gift, donation, gain, possession, take, conquest, prize, winnings, pickings, perquisite, proceeds, godsend, windfall.

ACQUISITIVE, *adj.* Fond of acquiring, eager for gain, greedy, avid, possessive, grasping, covetous, craving, rapacious, predacious, extortionate, grabbing, avaricious, appetitive, exacting, sordid, prehensile, hoarding, saving, with an itching palm.

ACQUISITIVENESS, *n.* Love of acquiring, greed, eagerness for gain, avidity, possessiveness, craving, graspingness, covetousness, rapacity, cupidity, predaciousness, avariciousness, avarice, appetitiveness, propensity to get property.

ACQUIT, *v.* 1. Release from obligation, remit, exempt, let off, pay off, deliver, liberate, excuse, absolve, relieve of burden, quit, settle a claim.

2. Pronounce not guilty, declare innocent, discharge from accusation, exonerate, exculpate, pardon, forgive, set free, clear, vindicate, justify.

ACQUIT ONESELF, *v.* Act, behave, conduct oneself, deport oneself, comport oneself, demean oneself.

ACQUITTAL, *n.* 1. Discharge, liberation, release, remission, exemption, letting off, deliverance, absolution, relief from, quittance, amnesty, pardon.

2. Exoneration, exculpation, acquittance, judicial vindication, clearance, justification, forgiveness, quietus, reprieve, respite.

ACQUITTANCE, *n.* 1. Payment of indebtedness, satisfaction of obligation, receipt, voucher, quittance, acknowledgment.

2. Discharge from responsibility, clearance, release, deliverance, quietus.

3. Vindication, acquittal.

ACRID, *adj.* 1. Stinging, biting, pricking, sharp, burning, irritating, caustic, astringent, corrosive, pungent, acid, keen, bitter, tart, piquant, hot, mordant.

2. Acrimonious, acerbic, harsh, severe, rough, vitriolic, sarcastic, virulent, mordacious, violent, sour-tempered, acidulous, trenchant.

ACRIDITY, *n.* 1. Acridness, causticity, acidity, astringency, corrosiveness, pungency, piquancy, poignancy, tartness, bitterness, sharpness, sourness, acetosity.

2. Acrimony of speech or temper, asperity, sarcasm, severity, sharpness, crabbedness, irritability, harshness, acerbity, virulence, hardness, roughness.

ACRIMONIOUS, *adj.* 1. Caustic, stinging, bitter, acrid, corrosive, sharp, tart, biting, sour, cutting, harsh.

2. Sarcastic, mordacious, vitriolic, virulent, rancorous, envenomed, galling, spiteful, testy, splenetic, peevish, petulant, snappish, waspish, cross-tempered, ill-natured, gruff, rude, rough, censorious, captious, severe, blistering, snarling, pettish, snapping, crabbed, malignant, scathing, resentful, inimical, irascible, choleric, irritable, huffy, touchy.

ACRIMONY, *n.* 1. Sourness, tartness, pungency, astringency, bitterness, sharpness, corrosiveness, causticity, acridity.

2. Acerbity, asperity, harshness, severity, virulence, animosity, crabbedness, sarcasm, moroseness, rudeness, churlishness, roughness, unkindness, abusiveness, ill temper, irascibility, rancor, venom, anger, spitefulness, choler, bile, dudgeon, malevolence, malignity, resentment, malice, grudge, pique, gall, spleen.

ACROBAT, *n.* Tightrope-walker, rope-dancer, flying trapezist, funambulist, bar-swinger, circus athlete, somersaulter, aerosaltant, tumbler, aerial gymnast, contortionist, high-vaulter, stunt-man, aerial athlete, equilibrist, balancer.

ACROBATICS, *n.* Acrobatic feats, gymnastics, agonistics, athletics, calisthenics, trapeze displays, tightrope displays.

ACROPOLIS, *n.* Fortified height, citadel, high point of city, stronghold, fort, fortress, fastness, keep, bulwark, earthwork, castle, rampart.

ACROSS, *prep. and adv.* From side to side of, from one side to another, athwart, thwart, in a crossing position, transversely, contrariwise, crosswise.

On the other side of, over, beyond, opposite, fronting.

ACT, *n.* 1. Single exertion of power, deed, feat, exploit, achievement.

2. Process of doing, action, performance, procedure, doing, course, step, turn, exercise, accomplishment, execution, consummation, conduct, operation, transaction, working.

3. Measure, enactment, edict, motion, law, statute, ordinance, judgment, decree, resolution, bill.

4. Main division of a play or opera, unit of dramatic action. individual part of a variety show, scene.

ACT, *v.* 1. Execute, carry into effect, be in process, be in action, move, go about, carry on, persevere, work, be active, keep going, put forth energy.

2. Exert power, produce an effect, operate, perform actions, have influence, be effective, have effect, function, be operative.

3. Behave as befits, comport oneself, conduct oneself, deport oneself, demean oneself, acquit oneself.

4. Feign, counterfeit, simulate, dissemble, dissimulate, pretend, make believe.

5. Represent a character, play a part, play dramatically, impersonate, personate, play the role of, enact, mimic, mime, take the part of.

6. Make, do, perform, perpetrate, execute, achieve, carry into execution, commit, produce.

7. Have the essential character of, function as, do the duties of, show the qualities of, realize, actualize, be.

ACT FOR, *v.* Do the work of, serve as, take the place of, pinch-hit, represent, substitute, be agent for.

ACTING, *n.* Histrionic art, dramaturgy, stage-playing, representation, personation, playing, impersonation, simulation, performance, dramatic action, stagecraft, rendition, theatricals, mimicry.

ACTION, *n.* 1. Exertion of power or force, energetic activity, energy, instrumentality, agency, mechanism, workmanship, operation, process, measure, influence, working, activity, exercise of activity, motion, movement.

2. Work, labor, task, execution, perpetration, business, occupation, employment, pursuit.

3. Something done, act, deed, feat, exploit, achievement, performance, transaction, doings, enterprise, accomplishment, dealings, procedure.

4. Battle, fray, engagement, affray, combat, encounter, brush, skirmish, contest, fight, affair, conflict, hostile meeting, rencontre, collision, struggle.

5. Deportment of an actor, gesticulation, gestures, expression, performing, enacting, air, representation, playing, performance, acting,

posture, attitude, histrionics, putting on the boards.

6. Series of events in a play or novel, main subject, story, plot, fable, disentangling of intricacies, unfolding, denouement.

7. *(Law)* Judicial proceeding, lawsuit, suit, case, process, prosecution, suit in law, cause, judicial contest, litigation, assumpsit, replevin, arraignment, accusation, presentment, true bill, indictment, libel, trespass.

ACTIONS, *n.* Habitual or usual acts, conduct, behavior, deportment, demeanor, comportment, address, bearing, mien, air, port, carriage, ways, manners, mannerisms, line of action, career, manner of life, *modus vivendi,* practice, policy, dealings, doings, mode of action, customary course, procedure.

ACTIVATE, *v.* 1. Make active, excite to action, energize, give energy to, work upon, set going, animate, give force to, actuate, drive, stimulate, enliven, impel, stir, prompt, start development, place in an active status.

2. *(Physics)* Render radioactive, ionize.

3. *(Chem.)* Make more active, render capable of adsorption, hasten reactions, aerate.

ACTIVE, *adj.* 1. In a state of action, in actual progress, operative, functioning, in process, working, acting, in effect, serviceable, effectual, efficacious, efficient, effective, at work, in force, exertive, in play.

2. Full of activity, constantly engaged in action, busy, painstaking, diligent, industrious, indefatigable, unremitting, watchful, vigilant, wakeful, laborious, assiduous, sedulous, restless, bustling, persevering, occupied, plodding, hardworking, busily employed, intent, strenuous, earnest, vigorous, fervent, ebullient, ardent, astir.

3. Causing change, capable of exerting influence, enterprising, influential, zealous, up-and-coming, go-ahead, wide-awake, pushing, up-in-arms, officious, aggressive, resolute, forward, energetic, ambitious, mettlesome, forceful, self-assertive, progressive.

4. Having power of quick motion, nimble, spry, mobile, agile, brisk, quick, expeditious, animated, alert, sharp, smart, spirited, vivacious, alive, sprightly, keen, lively, instant, mercurial, prompt, hustling, stirring, light, chipper, supple, ready, kinetic, volant.

5. *(Med.)* Acting quickly, drastic, potent, producing immediate effects, strong, powerful.

ACTIVITY, *n.* 1. Quality of acting promptly, quickness, alacrity, alertness, vivacity, briskness, dispatch, expedition, sprightliness, celerity, dash, agility, nimbleness, liveliness, go, animation, promptitude, rapidity, speed, fleetness, hustle, stir.

2. Exercise of energy or force, exertion, vim, spirit, snap, intensity, vigor, strength, power, forcefulness, stress, pressure, zeal, eagerness, efficacy.

3. Specific deed or action, enterprise, essay, endeavor, transaction, doing, act, undertaking, venture.

ACTOR, *n.* 1. Stage-player, Thespian, histrio, photoplayer, performer, dramatic artist, player, histrionic performer, personator, impersonator, theatrical performer, mime, mummer, masker, pantomimist; comedian, tragedian; star, headliner, principal, protagonist, deuteragonist, understudy, tritagonist, leading man *(or woman),* juvenile, villain, heavy lead, character man, ingénue, soubrette, extra, mute, supernumerary, *dramatis persona;* hamfatter, variety performer, farceur, vaudevillist, barnstormer; caricaturist, comique, buffoon, burlesquer; monologist, repertory player; gallery-player, scene-stealer, clown, pantaloon, harlequin, columbine, pierrot, pierrette, Punch, Judy, punchinello.

2. Doer, perpetrator, operator, executor, agent, representative, deputy, practitioner, emissary, participant, mover, promoter, factor.

3. One who behaves as if acting a part, simulator, poseur, dissembler, pretender, cheat, hypocrite, impostor, deceiver, humbug, quack, charlatan, mountebank, counterfeiter.

ACTUAL, *adj.* 1. Existing in act or fact, real, factual, genuine, authentic, true, absolute, not imaginary, positive, veritable, demonstrable, unimagined, truthful, veracious, legitimate, valid, rightful, well-founded, well-grounded, objective, categorical, developed, determinate, certain, decided, very, reliable, unquestionable, sure, unimpeachable, undisguised, unvarnished, gospel-true, incontestable, irrefragable, irrefutable, not fictitious, indubitable, confirmed, certified, in fact, accurate, *bona fide,* unsupposed, *de facto, de jure.*

2. Now existing, existent, present, extant, current, prevalent, tangible, palpable, sensible, perceptible, material, substantial, embodied, now in being, solid, corporeal, concrete, in hard fact, essential, realistic, un-ideal, in act, at this moment, in process, here and now, this present.

ACTUALITY, *n.* 1. State of being real or actual, absoluteness, true being, essentiality, actual existence, corporeality, substantiality, tangibility, palpability, perceptibility, sensibility, materiality.

2. That which is actual, reality, fact, realness, phenomenal reality, verity, truth, certainty, matter of fact, entity.

3. Realism (*as in art*), truth to nature, fidelity, graphicalness, naturalness, naturalism.

ACTUALIZE, *v.* Make actual, make real or realistic, realize in action or fact, externalize, exteriorize, objectify, transform from ideality to reality, substantiate, embody, put into substance, incorporate, bring to existence, carry into being, bring about, bring to pass, work out, effectuate.

ACTUALLY, *adv.* In fact, in act, indeed, in reality, in truth, truly, veritably, positively, really, absolutely, decidedly, certainly, categorically, assuredly, as a matter of fact, *de facto,* in effect, to all intents and purposes, literally, genuinely, *bona fide.*

ACTUARY, *n.* Overseer, superintendent, agent, supervisor, clerk, notary, registrar, executive agent, computing manager, keeper of accounts, accountant, statistician, one skilled in calculation, adviser of an insurance company, calculator of insurance risks and premiums, compiler of statistical tables of mortality.

ACTUATE, *v.* Incite to action, quicken, stimulate, animate, rouse, arouse, instigate, work upon, urge, sway, influence, persuade, induce, prevail upon, move, stir, excite, inspire, dispose, incline, draw, lead, drive, force, compel, impel, promote, prompt, act upon, activate.

ACT UPON, *v.* 1. Act in accordance with, regulate one's conduct according to.

2. Affect, influence, have influence upon, exert influence on.

ACT UP TO, *v.* Come up to in practice, carry out in practice, adhere to, be faithful to, practice, live up to, fulfil, conform to, abide by.

ACUMEN, *n.* Quickness of perception, sagacity, perspicacity, percipience, perspicuity, mental acuteness, keenness, discernment, insight, smartness, shrewdness, mother-wit, *esprit,* sharpness, cleverness, ingenuity, quick sense, quick intelligence, astuteness, long-headedness, penetration, intuition, comprehension, judgment, foresightedness, wisdom, subtlety.

ACUTE, *adj.* 1. Sharp at the end, ending in a point, pointed, acute-angled, acuminate, cuspated, cuspidate, peaked, prickly, spinous, needle-shaped, aciculate, apiculate, acanthaceous, echinate, pectinated.

2. Sharp in effect, severe, cutting, trenchant, intense, fierce, piercing, excruciating, poignant, distressing, piquant, pungent, exquisite.

3. Sharply sensitive, discerning, subtle, astute, sagacious, penetrating, perspicacious, knowing, keen-sighted, clear-witted, longheaded, sapient, shrewd, quick, cunning, sharp, keen, ingenious, smart, discriminating, bright, intelligent, sage, perceptive, lively, up-to-snuff, brainy, intuitive, quick-witted, prompt, apt.

4. High in pitch, shrill, piping, treble, high-toned, strident, thin-toned.

5. (*Med.*) Not chronic, sudden, brief, limited, temporary, violent, critical, crucial.

ACUTELY, *adv.* Intensely, severely, sharply, deeply, keenly, poignantly, exquisitely, painfully, profoundly, extremely.

ACUTENESS, *n.* 1. Spinosity, cuspidation, acuity, sharpness, acumination, pointedness, peakedness, mucronation.

2. Severity, trenchancy, incisiveness, intensity, fierceness, poignancy, pungency.

3. Sensitivity, discernment, subtlety, sagacity, astuteness, penetration, perspicacity, perspicuity, acumen, keen-sightedness, clear-wittedness, quick-wittedness, longheadedness, sapiency, smartness, shrewdness, sharpness, keenness, ingenuity, brightness, intelligence, mother-wit, *esprit,* quick parts, cleverness.

4. Shrillness, stridency, thinness, highness.

ADAGE, *n.* Wise antique observation, proverb, axiom, aphorism, apothegm, sententia, maxim, precept, dictum, saying, saw, byword, truism, self-evident truth, motto, epigram, formulary, rule, principle, theorem, postulate, cliché, commonplace, moral.

ADAMANT, *n.* An impenetrably hard mineral or metal, diamond, crystallized carbon, infrangible rock, indestructible stone, stone of impenetrable hardness, unbreakable obstacle.

ADAMANT, *adj.* Hard-hearted, inexorable, immovable, inflexible, unyielding, stubborn, firm, unfeeling, unbending, uncompassionate, merciless, obdurate, intractable.

ADAMANTINE, *adj.* 1. Made of adamant, very hard, unbreakable, infrangible, impenetrable, imperishable, indestructible, enduring, everlasting.

2. Solid, massive, rigid, stony, flinty.

ADAPT, *v.* 1. Adjust, temper, qualify, conform, accommodate, fit, suit, naturalize, assimilate, coordinate, level to, transmute, comply, reconcile, harmonize, attune to, attemper, square to, regulate, arrange, proportion.

2. Make suitable to requirements, modify fittingly, change, remodel, alter, transform, compose, prepare, fashion, match, shape, frame, make conformable, convert, apply to.

ADAPTABILITY, *n.* Pliability, flexibility, conformability, pliancy, tractability, plasticity, ductility, accommodativeness, applicability, malleability, docility, manageability, governableness, compliancy, amenability, changeability, variability, versatility, many-sidedness, usability.

ADAPTABLE, *adj.* Pliable, flexible, pliant, usable, tractable, tractile, plastic, ductile, accommodative, conformable, adaptive, applicable, malleable, docile, manageable, governable, compliant, amenable, open to, teachable, submissive, changeable, modifiable, utilizable, serviceable.

ADAPTATION, *n.* 1. Process of making fit, suiting, preparation, adjustment, accommodation, conformation, acclimatization.

2. Alteration, modification, qualification, modulation, variation, change.

3. Suitableness, accordance, appropriateness, fitness, adaptability, applicability, appositeness, conformability, consonancy, reconcilement, concord, harmony, unison.

ADAPTED, *adj.* Fit, suitable, fitted, acclimated, conformable, compliant, appropriate, apposite, apt, proper, meet, right, correct, fitting, befitting, becoming, accordant, consonant, pertinent, seemly, adequate, qualified.

ADD, *v.* 1. Put with, attach, annex, affix, join, adjoin, subjoin, append, tack on, superpose, superadd, tag, connect, unite, combine, adject, suffix, postfix, interpolate.

2. Find the sum of, put together mentally, add together, aggregate, sum up, compute, cast up, enumerate, number, calculate, reckon, foot up, figure up, count up, total, cipher.

3. Increase, amplify, enlarge, augment, join on, magnify, extend, raise, lengthen, supplement, fill up.

4. Say or write further, go on to say.

ADDENDUM, *n.* Addition, additament, affix, appendage, appurtenance, annex, attachment, adjunct, subscript, postscript, appendix, pendant, tailpiece, codicil, supplement, complement, increment, concomitant, acquisition, extension, improvement.

ADDER, *n.* Viper, horned viper, puff adder, death adder, spreading adder, milk adder, banded adder, krait, poisonous snake, serpent.

ADDICT, *v.* Habituate, give over to, give up to, accustom, inure, wont, apply habitually, incline, familiarize, cause to incline, dedicate, devote, indulge in, surrender to.

ADDICT, *n.* One addicted, victim, prey, dopefiend, practitioner, alcoholic, fetishist.

ADDICTED, *adj.* Given up to, given, given over, devoted, dedicated to, prone to, disposed toward, wedded to, habituated, accustomed, attached to, inclined toward, predisposed, wont, used to, surrendered to, indulgent in.

ADDICTION, *n.* Indulged inclination, habituation, leaning, bent, predilection, proclivity, tendency, propensity, addictedness, absorption, devotion, surrender, indulgence, enslavement, enthrallment, subjugation, yielding, immersion.

ADDITION, *n.* 1. Joining, adjoining, subjoining, adding, tacking on, appending, attaching, annexing, uniting, combining.

2. Summing up, summation, adding together, computation, enumeration, calculation, reckoning, counting up, totaling.

3. Increase, increment, accession, accretion, augmentation, superaddition, enlargement, annexation, extension, subjunction, interpolation, continuation, prolongation, reinforcement.

4. Appendage, additament, appendix, adjunct, appurtenance, affix, prefix, suffix, subscript, postscript, addendum, tailpiece, pendant, sequel, rider, attachment, codicil, supplement, extension, annex, wing, ell.

ADDITIONAL, *adj.* Added, supplementary, extra, supplemental, adscititious, super-added, further, adventitious, advenient, supervenient, appended, spare, more, else, fresh, new, other.

ADDITIONALLY, *adv.* Besides, plus, over, to boot, furthermore, too, more, likewise, also, again, over and above, moreover, into the bargain, not only so, as well as, together with, along with, conjointly, in conjunction with, *au reste.*

ADDITIVE, *adj.* To be added, accessory, tending to increase, auxiliary, contributory, addititious.

ADDLE, *v.* 1. Make or become spoiled or rotten *(as eggs)*, corrupt, render barren, abort, make unfruitful, rot, render putrid.

2. Make or become muddled or confused, make inefficient, render worthless.

ADDLED, *adj.* 1. Spoiled *(as eggs)*, worthless, incapable of producing, empty, fruitless, barren, unfruitful, unproductive, unfertile, unprolific, infecund, sterile, abortive, putrid, rotten, corrupt.

2. Mentally confused, muddled, unsound, idle, good-for-nothing, weak.

ADDLE-HEADED, *adj.* Mentally confused, dull, muddled, stupid, brainless, witless, destitute of reason, irrational, obtuse, foolish, absurd, oafish, doltish, blockish, idiotic, block-headed, noodle-headed, shallow-pated, cloddish, lack-witted, fat-headed, wooden-headed, dunder-headed, soft-brained, sottish, weak-minded, half-witted, dull-witted, shallow-brained, feeble-minded, thick-skulled, short-witted, muddle-headed, addlepated, crack-brained, half-baked, weak in the upper story.

ADDRESS, *n.* 1. Appeal, application, petition, entreaty, invocation, prayer, imploration, request, suit, supplication, solicitation, orison, importunity, adjuration.

2. Formal communication, speech, lecture, talk, discourse, sermon, oration, harangue, parley, declamation, palaver, salutation, apostrophe, eulogy, valedictory.

3. Manner of a person in speaking, delivery, bearing, deportment, demeanor, mien, manners, port, politeness, courtesy, ceremonious behavior, air.

4. Skilful management, skill, dexterity, ability, cleverness, readiness, adroitness, expertness, art, facility, faculty, aptness, knack, ingenuity, tact, management, discretion.

5. Superscription, direction for receiving correspondence, place by post or mail, home, post office, residence, habitation, dwelling, abode, domicile, locality, house, lodging, place of business, quarters, housing, berth.

ADDRESS, *v.* 1. Apply to, invoke, appeal to, entreat, implore, request, supplicate, importune, solicit, appeal to, memorialize, apostrophize, call upon.

2. Direct words to, speak to, salute, accost, hail, call to, greet, approach, declaim, hold forth, harangue, orate, rant, spout, lecture, sermonize, discourse, expatiate.

3. Pay court to, make suit to, court, woo, make up to, pay addresses to, make love to, serenade.

4. Direct a letter to, superscribe, consign, destine.

ADDRESSES, *n.* Courtship, suit, love suit, love-making, attentions, blandishments, wooing, serenading.

ADD TO, *v.* Increase, augment, enlarge, widen, broaden, lengthen, expand, magnify, amplify, greaten, make greater, aggrandize, make larger, heighten, advance, raise, reinforce, extend, fill out, prolong, continue, dilate.

ADDUCE, *v.* Bring forward, present, offer, aver, introduce, produce, advance, give, proffer, evidence, allege, claim, cite, quote, instance, refer to, assign, name, mention, allude, assert, declare, affirm, propound.

ADEPT, *adj.* Well-skilled, skilful, adroit, apt, deft, dexterous, handy, clever, able, proficient, good at, expert, experienced, trained, versed, gifted, practiced, talented, finished, accomplished, ingenious, sharp, smart, capable, crack (*colloq.*), at home with, conversant with, master of, *au fait*, qualified.

ADEPT, *n.* Master hand, skilled hand, master, connoisseur, expert, genius, artist, virtuoso, proficient, veteran, past master, old hand, old stager, authority, specialist, savant, capital hand, good hand, practiced hand, nice hand, crackajack (*colloq.*), top sawyer, prizeman, picked man, master mind.

ADEQUACY, *n.* Sufficiency, sufficientness, adequateness, enough, satisfaction, wherewithal, competency, competence, completeness, adequate resources, plenty, fitness, contentment.

ADEQUATE, *adj.* 1. Equal to requirement or occasion, fully sufficient, enough, ample, full, proportionate, commensurate, correspondent, due, equivalent, plenty, plentiful, plenteous, well-provided, satisfactory, equal to, adapted, merited, qualified.

2. Suitable, capable, fit, fitted, fitting, effectual, competent, able, effective, up to the mark.

ADHERE, *v.* 1. Stick fast, hold firmly, stick, cleave, cling, take hold, be firmly fixed, hold fast, fasten, unite, coalesce, cohere, attach, join, glue, agglutinate.

2. Belong, be appendant to, be connected with, pertain, appertain, constitute a part of, be appurtenant, have relation to, be intimately related.

3. Be attached, be faithful, be devoted, be true, stand by, remain fixed, give support, be loyal, be constant, keep to, comply with, abide by, observe, fulfil.

ADHERENCE, *n.* 1. Adhesion, cohesion, sticking together, cohesiveness, cementation, concretion, accretion, tenacity, glutinousness, viscosity, stickiness, tenaciousness.

2. Steady attachment, continued observance, devotion, constancy, faithfulness, fidelity, fealty, loyalty, allegiance, inseparability.

ADHERENT, *adj.* Sticking, clinging, adhering, tenacious, viscous, sticky, glutinous, viscid, sizy, cohesive, gummy, gluey, mucilaginous, tacky.

ADHERENT, *n.* Upholder, supporter, advocate, partisan, sectary, votary, devotee, follower, disciple, pupil, assistant, dependent, hanger-on, parasite, sycophant, henchman, vassal, retainer, attendant, acolyte, satellite, backer, seconder, ally,

helper, aider, abettor, champion, patron, partner, confederate, confidant, accomplice, companion, approver, accessory.

ADHESION, *n.* 1. Clinginess, stickiness, tendency to adhere, glutinousness, mucilaginousness, viscosity, viscidity, tenacity, ropiness.

2. Steady attachment, strong connection, union, affinity, alliance, association, junction, devotion, fidelity, close identification, intimate relationship.

3. Assent, concurrence, consent, agreement, acquiescence, approbation.

ADHESIVE, *adj.* Sticky, clinging, tenacious, sticking fast, tending to adhere, gummed, viscid, glutinous, viscous, gummy, mucilaginous, ropy, emplastic, smeary, stringy, dauby, clammy.

ADHESIVE, *n.* 1. Adhesive plaster, sticking plaster, court plaster, gummed tape, sticker, label, stamp.

2. Glue, sealing wax, cement, paste, sizing, mortar, solder.

ADIEU, *interj.* Good-by, farewell, fare-you-well, God-bless-you, Godspeed, best wishes, to God (*lit.*), addio! (*It.*), adiós! (*Sp.*), adeus! (*Portug.*), vale! (*Lat.*), vive valeque! (*Lat.*), sayonara! (*Jap.*), au revoir! (*Fr.*), a rivederci! (*It.*), so long (*slang*), auf Wiedersehen! (*Ger.*), lebewohl! (*Ger.*), bon voyage! (*Fr.*), glückliche Reise! (*Ger.*), bye-bye (*colloq.*).

ADIEU, *n.* Leave-taking, act of taking leave, parting salutation, valediction, valedictory, *congé*, separation, setting out, departure, leave, good-by, farewell.

ADIPOSE, *adj.* 1. Fat, fatty, oleaginous, oily, greasy, unctuous, sebaceous, pinguid.

2. Corpulent, obese, plethoric, fleshy, stout, plump, chubby, pursy, pudgy, thick-set, rotund, abdominous, paunchy, potbellied, bulky, burly, gross, portly, brawny, unwieldy, hulking, puffy, cumbrous, ponderous, lumpish, heavy, swollen, bloated.

ADIPOSITY, *n.* Tendency to fatness, state of being fat, corpulence, obesity, embonpoint, bulk, avoirdupois, heaviness, expanse, pinguidity, weight, plumpness, obeseness, polysarcia (*med.*), stoutness, fleshiness, chubbiness, pursiness, pudginess, rotundity, paunchiness, burliness, grossness, portliness, brawniness, unwieldiness, cumbrousness, ponderosity, lumpishness.

ADJACENCY, *n.* Contiguity, conterminousness, contact, touching, meeting, tangency, junction, juxtaposition, abuttal, abutment, propinquity, proximity, nearness, closeness, neighborhood, vicinity, vicinage, adjoinment, attingency.

ADJACENT, *adj.* Contiguous, conterminous, touching, meeting, abutting, bordering, adjoining, neighboring, lying near to, attached, beside, close to, near, next, nigh, juxtaposed, in contact, in proximity, proximate, approximate, approaching, in juxtaposition, attingent, vicinal.

ADJECTIVE, *n.* Qualifying word, descriptive term, attributive name, modifier, attribute, adjunct, limiting word, qualifying term, adnoun, accessory, addition, dependent.

ADJOIN, *v.* 1. Touch, abut upon, border upon, march upon or with, lie near to, lie next, lie close to, be in connection with, be in contact with, be contiguous to, be juxtaposed to, open into, be adjacent to.

2. Join to, attach, append, unite, add to, affix, annex, join on, subjoin, conjoin, connect.

ADJOINING, *adj.* Contiguous, conterminous, attingent, bordering on, connected, adjacent, abutting, touching, neighboring, close, vicinal, next, near, proximate, nigh.

ADJOURN, *v.* 1. Suspend the meeting of, break off, break up, prorogue, recess, interrupt, end for the time, terminate, close, dissolve, intermit, stop, discontinue.
    2. Put off, defer, delay, lay over, stave off, remand, table, shelve, reserve, protract, retard, procrastinate, postpone, continue, temporize, stay.

ADJOURNMENT, *n.* 1. Suspension, prorogation, breaking off, recess, interruption, end, close, termination, dissolution, discontinuation.
    2. Putting off, deferment, delay, postponement, respite, procrastination, continuation.

ADJUDGE, *v.* 1. Pronounce formally, ordain, order, rule, decree authoritatively, decide, settle, determine, arbitrate, adjudicate, confirm, doom, try, sentence, condemn.
    2. Award judicially, allot, apportion, assign, bestow, grant, dispense, mete out, deal, destine, distribute.
    3. Deem, consider, appraise, judge, estimate, regard, hold, rate, assess.

ADJUDGMENT, *n.* Award, allotment, bestowal, grant, dispensation, judgment, decision, finding, verdict, sentence, decree, arbitration, appraisal, estimate, valuation, assessment.

ADJUDICATE, *v.* 1. Determine, decide, umpire, arbitrate, referee, sit in judgment, judge, settle, adjudge, decree, ordain, award, assign.
    2. Try, hear, pass sentence on, pass judgment on, give judgment, reach an official decision, doom, condemn, rule, pronounce.
    3. Reckon, consider, regard, deem, esteem.

ADJUDICATION, *n.* 1. Deciding, arbitrament, adjudgment, settlement, ordainment.
    2. Hearing, sentence, decision, determination, decree, judgment, verdict, award, resolution, ruling, opinion, finding.

ADJUDICATOR, *n.* Arbiter, arbitrator, umpire, referee, judge, censor, inspector, assessor, ruler, moderator, master, determiner, controller, justice, justiciar, bencher.

ADJUNCT, *n.* 1. Something added, additament, addition, addendum, appendage, affix, annex, attachment, appurtenance, accessory, dependency, acquisition, reenforcement, supplement, support, complement, modifier, attribute, subordinate part, auxiliary, ancillary, minor detail, incident, aid, accompaniment, appanage, advantage, help.
    2. Assistant, colleague, associate, confrere, coadjutor, collaborator, co-aid, partner.

ADJURATION, *n.* Vehement appeal, swearing, solemn charging, act of adjuring, conjuration, solemn entreaty, importunity, obtestation, plea, imprecation, supplication, imploration, oath.

ADJURE, *v.* 1. Appeal to, supplicate, implore, beseech, pray, obtest, entreat, beg, invoke, bid, conjure, ask, request, solicit, importune, plead.
    2. Charge, bind, command, enjoin solemnly, order, require, urge, direct, prescribe to.
    3. Invoke upon oath, take oath upon, attest, swear by, witness to.

ADJUST, *v.* 1. Arrange in order, classify, sort, size, grade, methodize, systematize, rectify, trim, match, straighten, set right, put in order, set to rights, attune, tune up, put in tune, put in proper trim, order, organize.
    2. Regulate, put in working order, set, bring to a proper state, true, bring into line, collimate, focus, square, right, time, gauge, balance, make exact.
    3. Bring into agreement, settle, make up, free from differences, reconcile, compose, bring to a satisfactory state, harmonize, pacify, justify, even, counterpoise, negotiate, amend, redress.
    4. Bring into proper relations, proportion, fit, make correspondent, adapt, suit, measure, make conformable, accommodate, coordinate, fashion, alter, modify, orient, frame, shape.

ADJUSTABLE, *adj.* Adaptable, conformable, tractable, compliant, adaptive, applicable, flexible, movable, utilizable, disposable.

ADJUSTMENT, *n.* 1. Arrangement, setting right, classification, rectification, putting in order, putting in proper trim, organization, adjusting, disposal, disposition.
    2. Regulation, putting in working order, setting, making exact, good order, accurate arrangement, method, system.
    3. Bringing into agreement, settlement, making up, reconciliation, mutual understanding, freeing from differences, pacification, harmonization, negotiation, accordance, compromise.
    4. Adaptation, fitting, suiting, accommodation, making conformable, conformity, coordination, correspondence, proportionment, modification.

ADJUTANT, *n.* 1. Assistant, coadjutor, adjuvant, cooperator, helper, aider, auxiliary, subaltern, subordinate, underling.
    2. *(Mil.)* Subordinate through whom orders are issued, assistant staff officer, executive officer, order-aide.

ADMINISTER, *v.* 1. Provide with, dispense, mete out, measure out, serve out, give out, deal out, supply, furnish, tender, offer, proffer, apply, contribute, distribute, make application of, disburse, impose.
    2. Have executive charge of, preside over, perform officially, superintend, govern, direct, control, regulate, conduct, manage, rule, lead.
    3. Contribute assistance, conduce, tend toward, be helpful to, bring aid, minister, succor, relieve.
    4. Perform duties of an administrator, settle, execute, enforce, take charge of, discharge, deal with.

ADMINISTRATION, *n.* 1. Dispensation, giving, ministration, distribution, tendering, application, contribution, meting out, supplying, furnishment.
    2. Executive charge, performance of executive duties, superintendence, presidency, direction, control, regulation, conduct, management, rule, leadership, headship, oversight, jurisdiction, dominion, regime.
    3. Executive department, executive officers, the Government, ministry, cabinet, council, body of ministers, governmental organization, official tenure, President and advisers, commonwealth, period of service.
    4. Management of a legal estate, settlement, execution, disposal.

ADMINISTRATIVE, *adj.* Executive, directorial, skilful in administration, authoritative, directive, gubernatorial, magisterial, official, jurisdictional, legislative, bureaucratic, departmental.

ADMINISTRATOR, *n.* Manager, director, head of affairs, executive, administrative head, head, organizer, superintendent, overseer, supervisor, conductor, leader, curator, guardian, custodian, intendant, head of government, president, regent, commander, commandant, chief, governor, ruler.

ADMIRABLE, *adj.* Awaking admiration, striking, wonderful, marvelous, excellent, fine, estimable, astonishingly good, glorious, great, high, perfect, superior, masterly, desirable, praiseworthy, rare, commendable, meritorious, laudable, valuable, worthy, exciting approval, superb, capital, of the first water, choice, transcendent, sterling, prime, first-rate, first-class, first-grade, of the highest order.

ADMIRATION, *n.* 1. Fond approbation, liking, fondness, love, high regard, high opinion, honor, appreciation, approval, veneration, reverence, esteem, pleasurable contemplation, adoration, respect, praise.
2. That which is admired, object of wonder or approbation, pride and joy, delight, sensation, marvel, prodigy, wonder, astonishment, surprise, amazement.

ADMIRE, *v.* 1. Regard with approbation, revere, venerate, have a high opinion of, esteem high, think wonderful, wonder at, think highly of, rate high, prize, value highly, regard as fine, consider brilliant, contemplate pleasurably, extol, approve, applaud, praise, honor, respect.
2. Like much, love, adore, idolize, be taken with, be extravagantly fond of, delight in, have a yen for, carry a torch for, have affection for, be in love with, be enamored of, be captivated by, be pleased with, appreciate, enjoy.

ADMIRER, *n.* 1. Reverer, venerator, esteemer, one with high esteem for, champion, enthusiast, one who values greatly, adherent, follower, partisan, votary, supporter, disciple, devotee, zealot.
2. Lover, wooer, adorer, suitor, swain, beau, truelove, sweetheart, gallant, cavalier, paramour, inamorato.

ADMISSIBLE, *adj.* Allowable, permissible, legal, legitimate, lawful, passable, approvable, proper, equitable, meet, just, fair, reasonable, justifiable, warrantable, considerable, concedable, possible, likely, not unlikely, probable, tolerable, worthy, fit, suitable, right, unprohibited, not impossible, free.

ADMISSION, *n.* 1. Entrance, entry, access, power of entrance, ingress, entrée, introduction, grant of entry, admittance, initiation, privilege of admission, reception, approach, permission, inclusion, accession.
2. Price of entrance, charge, cost, fee, receipt, tariff, cover charge.
3. Recognition, acknowledgment, exposure, avowal, assent, acquiescence, concurrence, acceptance, allowance, concession, profession, confession, disclosure, divulgence, revelation, expression, utterance, declaration.

ADMIT, *v.* 1. Give access to, allow to enter, let in, yield passage to, afford means of entrance to, give right of entry to, open the door to, take in, receive, accept, welcome, include.
2. Induct, install, initiate, inaugurate, invest, vest, institute.
3. Concede as true, grant in argument, avow, acknowledge, recognize, profess, declare, own, agree to, confess, tell, assent to, acquiesce in, accede to, concur.
4. Allow, permit, grant opportunity, admit of, be compatible with, bear, have capacity for, let, tolerate, stand, suffer.

ADMITTANCE, *n.* 1. Means of approach, adit, ingress, portal, access, approach, introduction, passage, entrance, initiation, induction.
2. Right of entrance, liberty of approach, permission to enter, admission, *admittatur,* entry, entrée, acceptance, inclusion, reception, welcome, lodgment.

ADMITTEDLY, *adv.* By acknowledgment, truly, avowedly, confessedly, acceptedly, concededly, authoritatively, authentically, genuinely, really, certainly, surely, assuredly, veritably, actually, validly, legally, legitimately, unquestionably.

ADMIX, *v.* Mix with, commix, mingle with, add to something else, commingle, interlard, unite with, combine, blend, compound, intermingle, sprinkle with, tinge with, flavor with, season with, adulterate, modify, temper, alloy, amalgamate, incorporate, interfuse.

ADMIXTURE, *n.* 1. State of being mixed, blend, mixture, mingling, commixture, intermixture, intermingling, combination, compound, mélange, composition, medley, hash, hodgepodge, olio, farrago, salmagundi, mingle mangle, gallimaufry, mishmash, potpourri, olla-podrida, ragout, jumble.
2. Added ingredient, spice, sauce, seasoning, relish, condiment, flavoring, leaven, taste, savor, dash, sprinkling, smack, twang, touch, tinge, tincture, cast, infusion, trace, suggestion, streak, soupçon, suspicion, hint, bit, particle.

ADMONISH, *v.* 1. Counsel against, caution, advise against, dissuade, enjoin, warn, forewarn, put on one's guard.
2. Reprove mildly, notify of a fault, censure, chide, blame, reproach, rebuke, objurgate, scold, reprehend, reprimand, remonstrate, expostulate, take to task, upbraid, rate, berate, disapprove.
3. Give notice of, apprise, inform, enlighten, acquaint, make aware, recall to duty, remind, exhort, incite, urge.

ADMONISHER, *n.* Monitor, warner, cautioner, adviser, counselor, mentor, tutor, instructor, guide, director, prompter, reminder.

ADMONITION, *n.* 1. Reminder of a fault, act of discipline, friendly reproof, censure, rebuke, reproach, remonstrance, expostulation, reproval, reprehension, reprimand, rap on the knuckles.
2. Caution, warning, forewarning, monition, commonition, injunction, counsel, advice, notice, instruction, prediction.

ADMONITORY, *adj.* Monitory, precautionary, premonitory, cautionary, warning, forewarning, admonitive, counseling, mentorial, threatening, reproving, ominous, minatory.

ADO, *n.* 1. A doing, work, troublesome business, trouble, travail, toil, pains, labor, difficulty, care, bother, worry.
2. Unnecessary activity, bustle, fluster, flutter, flurry, hurry, stir, fanfare, hubbub, excitement, noise, din, bluster, to-do, turmoil, confusion, ferment, rout, tumult, hurly-burly, fuss, pother, excessive ceremony, fuss and feathers, agitation, perturbation, botherment, commotion.

ADOLESCENCE, *n.* Youth, youthfulness, teens, juvenescence, pubescence, puerility, juvenility, boyishness, boyhood, juniority, wardship, tender age, minority, pupilage, nonage, growing up, growing time, springtide of life, flower of youth, dayspring of life, bloom of life, flower of life, prime of youth, seedtime of life, golden season of life, heyday of youth, rising generation.

ADOLESCENT, *adj.* Youthful, juvenescent, green, growing to manhood, pubescent, juvenile, under age, in the teens, young, unripe, tender, callow, immature, fresh, blooming, budding, beardless, smooth-cheeked, downy-cheeked, new-fledged, unfledged.

ADOLESCENT, *n.* 1. The youth of tomorrow, youth, lad, boy, youngster, teen-ager, juvenile, schoolboy, junior, minor, cadet, cub, youngling, young hopeful, stripling, fledgling, scion, sapling, seedling, slip, sprig, sprite, pixy, leprechaun, whipster, whelp, lambkin, whippersnapper, cherub.

2. Girl, schoolgirl, lass, lassie, mademoiselle, damsel, maiden, maid, virgin, nymph, tomboy, hoyden.

ADOPT, *v.* 1. Choose for oneself, appropriate, arrogate, make one's own, take to oneself, select as one's own, choose, assume, affect, acclimatize.

2. Vote to accept, approve, avow, receive, espouse, attach oneself to, maintain, support, embrace, affiliate with, elect, take up, take over, welcome, follow, conform to.

3. Take as one's own child, naturalize, foster, affiliate, father, mother.

ADOPTION, *n.* 1. Choosing, appropriation, arrogation, selection, assumption, affectation.

2. Acceptance, approval, avowal, reception, espousal, attachment to, maintenance, affiliation with, election of, support, acknowledgment.

3. Taking as one's own child, naturalization, fosterage, guardianship, affiliation, fathering, mothering.

ADORABLE, *adj.* 1. Deserving divine honors, deserving of worship, worthy of adoration, holy, divine, sacred, celestial, angelic, worthy of the highest love, venerable, worthy of honor, godlike, sacred.

2. Dear, lovable, sweet, lovely, admirable, winsome, charming, attractive, engaging, dearly beloved, enchanting, bewitching, captivating, fascinating, beloved, darling, precious, prized, pet, cherished, treasured, idolized.

ADORATION, *n.* 1. Worship, deification, honor, apotheosis, magnification, glorification, homage, exaltation, laudation, reverence, veneration, idolization, incense, praise, deference, kneeling, genuflection, divine service, invocation, orison, supplication, prayer.

2. Excessive fondness, love, devotion, hero worship, admiration, infatuation, tender passion, enchantment.

ADORE, *v.* 1. Worship, do service to, venerate, revere, reverence, glorify, extol, magnify, exalt, idolize, deify, apotheosize, pay homage to, honor, hallow, praise, burn candles to, burn incense before, bow down before, prostrate before, bless, genuflect before, kneel before, kiss the feet of, lift up the heart to, invoke, supplicate.

2. Hold dear, dote on, admire, love, cherish, fancy, set the affections on, be enamored of, put on a pedestal, carry the torch for, wear one's heart on the sleeve for.

ADORER, *n.* 1. Worshiper, idolater, celebrant, communicant, congregation (*collective*), reverer, iconolater, venerator, votary, devotee.

2. Great admirer, sweetheart, swain, suitor, lover, wooer, truelove, gallant, cavalier, beau, inamorato.

ADORN, *v.* Make pleasing, make more attractive, decorate, embellish, beautify, lend beauty to,

dignify, set off to advantage, enrich, ornament, add to the splendor of, emblazon, blazon, stud, bestud, render pleasing, deck, bedeck, set, gild, beset, add luster to, varnish, enamel, prink out, trim, garnish, furbish, polish, array, attire, invest, dress up, trap out, accouter, crown, glorify, grace, trick out, bedizen, paint, spangle, bead, bespangle, embroider, elaborate, figure, illustrate, illuminate, miniate (*as a manuscript*), rubricate.

ADORNED, *adj.* Ornamented, decorated, trim, bedecked, beautified, spruce, trig, appareled, caparisoned, accoutered, glorious, rich-wrought, fancy, new-spangled, gilt, gilded, begilt, inlaid, inwrought, filigreed, fretted, festooned, ornate, magnificent, florid, figured, rich, rococo, garish, baroque, grandiose, flamboyant, resplendent, refulgent, glittering, brilliant, dazzling, flashy, gorgeous, showy, gaudy, tawdry, meretricious.

ADORNMENT, *n.* Ornament, ornamentation, decoration, embellishment, beautification, display, enrichment, emblazonment, bedizenment, luster, floridness, flourish, splendor, magnificence, show, ostentation, ornateness, flamboyance, garnish, baroqueness, veneer, gloss, glitter, spangle, tinsel, embroidery, finery, frippery, trimming, array, trappings, attire, dress, gear, trim.

ADRIFT, *adj., adv.* 1. Cut loose from moorings, in a drifting state, floating unanchored, drifting unmoored, at the mercy of wind and current, borne by the tide, moving aimlessly, afloat, derelict, bobbing with flotsam and jetsam.

2. Lost, confused, perplexed, at sea, astray, without destination, purposeless, random, stray, wavering, inconstant, uncertain, irresolute, in an abandoned state, insecure, unstable, unsettled, swayed by chance impulse, guideless, away from the point.

ADROIT, *adj.* 1. Deft, dexterous, skilful, handy, clever, able, ready, nimble, quick, apt, expert, masterly, talented, gifted, smart, versatile, facile, proficient, slick, practiced, ingenious.

2. Ready-witted, cunning, crafty, artful, sly, sharp, shrewd, subtle, tricky, wily.

ADROITNESS, *n.* 1. Deftness, dexterity, skill, handiness, cleverness, ability, address, faculty, facility, readiness, quickness, art, knack, talent, ingenuity, expertness, aptitude, masterliness, versatility, proficiency, practice.

2. Ready-wittedness, cunning, slyness, subtlety, craftiness, artfulness, sharpness, shrewdness, trickiness, wiliness.

ADSCITITIOUS, *adj.* Added, additional, extra, derived from without, superadded, adventitious, advenient, supervenient, spare, further, fresh, accessory, not essential, superfluous, redundant, extraneous, extrinsic, supplemental, new, alien, other, artificial, supplementary.

ADULATE, *v.* Flatter servilely, fawn upon, pay court to, compliment excessively, make much of, praise inordinately, show pretended devotion to, curry favor with, truckle to, toady to, bootlick, kiss the feet of, lickspittle, pander to, ingratiate oneself with, wheedle, pet, blandish, cajole, jolly, humor, coddle, blarney, soft-soap, butter (*colloq.*).

ADULATION, *n.* Hypocritical flattery, abject adoration, servile laudation, fulsome praise, inordinate compliment, blandishment, cajolery, wheedling, fawning, flummery, honeyed words, obsequiousness, vernility, sycophancy, servility, parasitism, flunkeyism, toadyism, incense, soft soap, homage, buncombe, blarney, palaver, jollying, tufthunting, butter, apple sauce (*colloq.*).

ADULATOR, *n.* Fulsome eulogist, excessive laudator, servile flatterer, fawner, cringing parasite, sycophant, hanger-on, toady, cringer, truckler, bootlicker, lickspittle, tufthunter, flunkey, spaniel, timeserver, wheedler.

ADULATORY, *adj.* Flattering, servile, cajoling, rich in compliments, obsequious, sycophantic, wheedling, truckling, blandishing, fulsome, oily, fawning, cringing, honeyed, candied, smooth, smooth-tongued, unctuous, mealy-mouthed, buttery, specious.

ADULT, *adj.* Having attained full size, grown to full strength, full-grown, fully developed, ripe, ripened, mature, of age, grown up, of mature age, of legal majority.

ADULT, *n.* Mature person, grown-up person, person of age, full-grown man, fully developed person, one who has attained legal majority, one who has attained 21 years *(common law)*, a male of 14 *(civil law)*, a female of 12 *(civil law)*.

ADULTERATE, *v.* Make lower in quality, make impure, alloy, mingle with, mix with, blend, water down, thin out, infuse, debase, defile, contaminate, taint, pollute, denature, vitiate, impair, corrupt, degrade, deteriorate, change, weaken, lower, depreciate, render counterfeit, render spurious.

ADULTERATED, *adj.* Fraudulent, vitiated, not genuine, spurious, mixed, impure, corrupted, debased, contaminated, deteriorated, factitious, falsified, alloyed.

ADULTERATION, *n.* Corruption by admixture, admixture, watering down, thinning out, lowering in quality, impairment, debasement, deterioration, vitiation, contamination, pollution, corruption, defilement, alloyage.

ADULTERER, *n.* Nest fouler, married reprobate, rake, libertine, man of pleasure, illicit sensualist, debauchee, violator of marriage vows, pollutor of the marriage bed, free liver, roué, voluptuary.

ADULTERESS, *n.* Mistress, paramour, demirep, concubine, kept woman, jade, illicit lover, doxy, demimondaine, call girl.

ADULTEROUS, *adj.* Committing adultery, impure, unchaste, illicit, unlawful, concupiscent, illegal, corrupt, immoral, dissolute, licentious, lascivious, prurient, incontinent, libidinous, rakish, lecherous, salacious.

ADULTERY, *n.* Illicit intercourse, violation of the marriage vows, sexual unfaithfulness of a married person, fouling the nest, pollution of the marriage bed, marital infidelity, cuckoldry, extramarital relations, criminal unchastity, unlawful carnality, criminal conversation, amour, unhallowed liaison, libertinism, extramarital promiscuity, intrigue.

ADUMBRATE, *v.* 1. Represent the shadow of, indicate by partial disclosure, give a faint resemblance of, shadow forth, outline, sketch slightly, represent approximately, trace dimly, delineate vaguely, hint at, approximate, suggest, indicate.

2. Represent beforehand by emblem, denote, symbolize, foreshadow vaguely, prefigure, stand for, allegorize, show in outline, be a parable of, typify, image.

3. Partially conceal, darken, obscure, hide, shade, overshadow, overcast, obfuscate, bedim, enshadow, becloud, place in penumbral light, put into partial eclipse, cloud over, make dark, make dim.

ADUMBRATION, *n.* 1. Imperfect portrayal, dim representation, vague outline, faint sketch, vague approximation, blurry image, suggestion, hint, indication, sketchy delineation, shadowing forth, faint resemblance.

2. Vague foreshadowing, symbol, prototype, symbolic representation, type, presage, shadow, prefiguration, image, premonition, sign, omen, portent, dark prophecy.

3. Overshadowing, shade, obscuration, eclipse, obfuscation, shadow, enshadowment.

ADVANCE, *v.* 1. Put farther to the front, move forward, bring toward the front, push forward, send onward, set forward, shove, propel.

2. Bring to notice, call attention to, bring to view, present, bring forward, offer, proffer, lay down, allege, adduce, propound, assign.

3. Bring forward in time, accelerate, hasten, help forward, further, forward, promote, amend, make better, improve, assist, strengthen, foster, benefit, aid the progress of, facilitate, speed up, quicken, expedite, help on, abet, boost, conduce to.

4. Cause to move higher, raise in rank, lift to a higher place, promote, exalt, lift to preferment, elevate, aggrandize, ennoble, dignify.

5. Raise in rate, make higher, make greater, increase *(as price)*, augment, heighten, enhance.

6. Supply in advance, pay before due, supply beforehand, pay beforehand, furnish on credit, pay in expectation of reimbursement, lend, loan, accommodate.

7. Go forward, progress, proceed, forge ahead, move forward, make way, edge forward, gain ground, march forward, get along, step forward, go on, get on, rise, come on, inch along, get ahead, push forward, take the lead, lead the van, make headway.

8. Make progress, make improvement, thrive, prosper, flourish, increase, develop, improve, grow.

ADVANCE, *n.* 1. Moving forward, progress in space, movement to the front, forwarding, forward movement, forward march, progression, procedure, headway, way.

2. Improvement, step forward, advancement, promotion, preferment, enhancement, progress, growth, elevation, furtherance.

3. Act of personal approach, proposal, tender, overture, offer, proffer, proposition, addresses.

4. Giving beforehand, payment beforehand, anticipated payment, loan.

5. Addition to price, increase of price, rise in price.

ADVANCED, *adj.* 1. Ranged at the front, placed in advance, set in the van, ahead.

2. At a forward stage *(for its years)*, early, precocious, premature.

3. At a late stage, far on in time or course, well along, far on in time, beyond the elementary.

4. Far on in progress, before others in ideas, progressive, ultra.

ADVANCE GUARD, *n.* 1. Front rank, first line, fore rank, vanguard, van, way-clearer, outrider.

2. Forerunner, precursor, harbinger, herald, van-courier, avant-courier, pioneer, leader.

ADVANCEMENT, *n.* 1. Act of moving forward, progression, forward movement, forward march, progress.

2. Promotion in rank, elevation in standing, preferment, exaltation, furtherance, uplift,

aggrandizement.

3. Improvement, growth, advance, proficiency, enlightenment, edification.

ADVANTAGE, *n.* 1. Favoring circumstance, edge, odds, favorable opportunity, superior situation, best estate, vantage ground, play, leverage, best plight, purchase, hold, dominating position, upper hand, whip hand.

2. Precedence, ascendancy, prevalence, power, preeminence, supremacy, prestige, superiority, authority, mastery.

3. Profit, benefit, gain, help, avail, vantage, expediency, improvement, return, utility, success, emolument, weal, boon, blessing, service, good, compensation, prize, windfall.

4. Concern, behalf, regard, behoof, account, support, interest, defense.

5. Prerogative, right, favor, privilege, comfort, supply of wants, accommodation, convenience, easement.

ADVANTAGE, *v.* Give superiority to, help, be of service to, favor, serve, prove beneficial to, advance, be of advantage to, avail, yield gain to, profit, further, benefit, promote.

ADVANTAGEOUS, *adj.* Conferring advantage, to one's interest, to one's good, valuable, useful, beneficial, helpful, serviceable, gainful, well, convenient, good, favorable, salutary, profitable, lucrative, remunerative, expedient, fortunate, auspicious, opportune, propitious, encouraging.

ADVENT, *n.* 1. Coming into view or being, reaching, approach, arrival, appearing, accession, appearance, visitation.

2. *(Cap.)* Coming of Christ, Incarnation, appearance of the Lord, season preceding Christmas.

ADVENTITIOUS, *adj.* Coming from without, not inherent, foreign, alien, superadded, added extrinsically, not essential, extraneous, advenient, supervenient, casually acquired, accidental, fortuitous, incidental, accessory, supplemental, casual.

ADVENTURE, *n.* 1. Risk, hazard, venture, trial, fortuity, jeopardy, chance, fortune, contingency, experiment, stake.

2. Perilous enterprise, venturesome exploit, bold undertaking, daring feat, gallant deed.

3. Exciting experience, striking event, affair, stirring incident, episode, happening, occurrence, accident, transaction, circumstance, passage, engagement, crisis, contingency.

4. Commercial speculation, hazardous trading, taking a "flyer," venture.

ADVENTURE, *v.* 1. Risk, jeopardize, put in risk, hazard, put to hazard, endanger, put in danger, imperil, expose to peril, venture, jeopard, sail near the wind.

2. Take the chance of, run the risk involved, dare, try the chance, take the risk, run the hazard, wager, chance, stake, suggest venturesomely, venture to utter.

ADVENTURER, *n.* 1. Wanderer, voyager, rover, traveler, wayfarer, roamer, itinerant, vagabond, gadabout, explorer.

2. Soldier of fortune, mercenary, daredevil, fire-eater, madcap, swashbuckler, free shooter, free lance.

3. Undertaker of commercial risk, speculator, gambler, gamester.

4. Seeker of fortune by underhand means, desperado, sharper, trickster, knave, swindler, rogue, impostor, pretender, deceiver, charlatan.

ADVENTUROUS, *adj.* 1. Willing to incur hazard, daring, courageous, brave, audacious, gallant, bold, doughty, valiant, chivalrous, venturesome, fearless, enterprising, intrepid, undaunted, valorous.

2. Rash, temerarious, foolhardy, presumptive, reckless, headlong, precipitate, incautious, hasty, errant.

3. Attended with risk, dangerous, perilous, hazardous, requiring courage, full of peril, fraught with hazard, uncertain, risky.

ADVERSARY, *n.* Opponent, antagonist, enemy, foe, foeman, adverse party, contestant, emulant, competitor, rival, opposer, disputant, assailant, counterlitigant, the Devil, Satan.

ADVERSE, *adj.* 1. Being or acting in a contrary direction, opposing, against, conflicting, head *(as winds)*, counteracting, diametrically opposite.

2. Antagonistic, having opposing interests, hostile, unfriendly, inimical, belligerent, bellicose, acting against, oppugnant, opposed, injurious, detrimental, hurtful, harmful, pernicious.

3. Opposing one's interests or desire, untoward, unprosperous, unpropitious, unlucky, calamitous, unfavorable, unfortunate, afflictive, disastrous, catastrophic, cataclysmic, ruinous.

4. Averse, disinclined, reluctant, loath.

ADVERSITY, *n.* Adverse fortune, misfortune, mishap, mischance, disaster, calamity, hardship, catastrophe, affliction, trial, trouble, distress, misery, bereavement, ill luck, ill fate, bad luck, reverses, buffeting, storm and stress, suffering, woe, tribulation, misadventure, disappointment, failure, crash, wreck, undoing, setback, ruin, downfall, suffering, destitution, broken fortunes, hard times, evil day, frowns of fortune, ills of life, unlucky fate, stroke of ill fortune, a sea of troubles, rainy day, ill wind, hard luck.

ADVERTENCE, *n.* Notice, attention, observation, heed, regard, consideration, awareness, mindfulness, observance, heedfulness, attentiveness, advertency.

ADVERTISE, *v.* 1. Make known by printed public notice, make public announcement of, give information to the public concerning, announce publicly, publish abroad, call public attention to, lay before the public, give public notice of, placard, circulate, circularize, post, blazon, promulgate, divulgate, noise abroad, blaze abroad, bruit abroad, propagate, diffuse, disseminate, spread abroad, trumpet, proclaim, make known, make proclamation of, give out, press agent.

2. Praise the good qualities of, commend to the public, vaunt, cry up, make conspicuous, describe.

3. Offer for sale, bill, exhibit, push.

4. Give advice to, advise, give notice to, apprise, inform, notify, report, acquaint, warn.

ADVERTISEMENT, *n.* 1. Printed public notice, paid announcement, poster, placard, bill, circular, handbill, flyer, broadside, leaflet.

2. A giving notice, notification, announcement, report, proclamation, divulgation, promulgation, publication, trumpeting, noising abroad, rumor, news.

ADVERTISER, *n.* 1. Hawker, huckster, trader, merchant, tradesman, monger, peddler, vendor, retailer, shopkeeper, mercantile agent, dealer, proprietor, owner.

2. Informant, notifier, adviser, newsmonger, relator.

ADVERT TO, *v.* 1. Turn the attention to, regard, notice, observe, take notice of, view, mark, pay attention to, remark, give heed to, take heed, attend to, consider, look to, mind, see to, glance at, have an eye to, look after, give a thought to.

2. Call attention to, make a remark about, refer to, touch upon, relate, mention, hint about, allude to, suggest, insinuate, intimate, indicate, imply.

ADVICE, *n.* 1. Opinion recommended, counsel, recommendation regarding a course of action, advisement, suggestion, instruction, injunction, charge, admonition, monition, caution, warning, dissuasion, persuasion, encouragement, word to the wise, exhortation.

2. Communication containing information, tidings, news, word, report, announcement, notice given, notification, account, information, intelligence, knowledge.

ADVISABILITY, *n.* Recommendability, fitness, suitability, seemliness, propriety, desirability, judiciousness, wisdom, advisableness, prudence, expediency, sensibleness, appropriateness, aptness, justness, profitability, advantageousness, usefulness.

ADVISABLE, *adj.* Recommendable, suitable, commendable, meet, seemly, proper to be done, fitting, desirable, judicious, wise, discreet, fit to be advised, advantageous, prudent, expedient, politic, befitting.

ADVISE, *v.* 1. Offer an opinion to, counsel, give counsel to, give advice to, recommend to, give suggestions to, admonish, caution, dissuade, warn, exhort, encourage, enjoin, charge, guide, teach, instruct, persuade.

2. Give information to, inform, apprise, direct, acquaint, notify, give notice to, send word to, make known to, communicate to, tell, enlighten, impart.

3. Take counsel with, confer with, consult with, hold a conference, deliberate, consider.

ADVISED, *adj.* 1. Thought out, done with forethought, considered, intended, deliberate, prudent.

2. Informed, counseled, instructed, aware, conscious, wary.

ADVISEDLY, *adv.* 1. After due consideration, with forethought, deliberately, by design, with due consideration, purposely, intentionally, knowingly, designedly, consciously, thoughtfully.

2. Carefully, heedfully, circumspectly, warily, discreetly, cautiously, prudently.

ADVISEMENT, *n.* Process of observing by thought, careful deliberation, consideration, contemplation, consultation.

ADVISER, *n.* Counselor, director, instructor, teacher, tutor, prompter, preceptor, admonitor, coach, consultant, mentor, monitor, Nestor, Solon, referee, backseat driver, guide.

ADVISORY, *adj.* 1. Having power to advise, giving advice, consultative, consultatory, acting under advice, prudential.

2. Given as advice, not mandatory.

ADVOCACY, *n.* Support, countenance, assistance, favor, championship, backing, patronage, active espousal, endorsement, subscription, sanction, recommendation, seconding, act of pleading for, defense, vindication, justification, intercession.

ADVOCATE, *v.* Recommend publicly, speak in favor of, plead for, counsel, back, second, press for, propose, suggest, champion, urge, espouse, endorse, subscribe to, prescribe, promote, take

the side of, propagate, speak for, defend by argument, uphold, favor, abet, argue for, justify, maintain, stand up for, vindicate, support, cry up, countenance, applaud.

ADVOCATE, *n.* 1. Backer, espouser, patron, seconder, sustainer, spokesman, propagator, promoter, supporter, upholder, vindicator, pleader, defender, apologist, propagandist, proponent, maintainer, countenancer, friend, abettor, favorer.

2. Lawyer, attorney, attorney-at-law, legal adviser, counselor, counsel-at-law, barrister, limb of the law, solicitor, jurisconsult.

3. Intercessor, go-between, mediator, comforter, arbitrator, paraclete.

AEGIS, *n.* 1. Shield of Zeus and Athena, buckler, defensive armor, breastplate, breast protection.

2. Protecting influence, defense, safeguard, protection, surety, guaranty, guard, sponsorship, shelter, championship, patronage, favor, support, aid, auspices.

AERATE, *v.* 1. Expose to air, impregnate with air, aerify, infuse air into, pass air through, permeate with air, air, fill with air, ventilate, oxygenate.

2. Charge with carbon dioxide, treat with gas, make effervescent.

3. Etherealize, make ethereal, make delicate, spiritualize, elevate.

AERIAL, *adj.* 1. Atmospheric, aural, vaporous, aeriform, airy, gaseous, volatile.

2. Rising high in the air, reaching far into the air, high, lofty, towering, elevated, high-reaching, soaring, distant, remote, faraway, aloft, celestial, empyreal, empyrean, supernal.

3. Light, invisible, attenuated, tenuous, thin, rarefied, indistinct, fugitive, elusive, ethereal, flimsy.

4. Imaginary, unsubstantial, incorporeal, ideal, spiritual, visionary, unreal, dreamy, fairylike, theoretic.

AERIE, *n.* 1. Nest of a predatory bird, eyrie, eagle's nest, crag-perched nidus.

2. Brood in the nest, the young of a bird of prey.

3. Elevated habitation, secure retreat, house situated on a height, high situation.

AERIFORM, *adj.* 1. Having the form of air, airy, aerial, with the nature of air, air-like, vaporous, gaseous, gassy, volatile.

2. Unsubstantial, unreal, incorporeal, rare, ethereal, intangible, tenuous, rarefied.

AERONAUT, *n.* Pilot of lighter-than-air craft, balloonist, aerial navigator, aviator, airman, pilot, aeroplanist, flyer, birdman.

AERONAUTICS, *n.* Aerial navigation, aviation, ballooning, aerostatics, flying, flight, volitation, aerodonetics, science of flight in aircraft, art of navigating in the air, volation, aerodynamics, airmanship, aerography, aeromechanics.

AESTHETE, *n.* 1. Cultivator of the sense of the beautiful, one very sensitive to the beauties of art, votary of art, man of good taste, connoisseur, critic, *cognoscente* (*It.*), *arbiter elegantiae* (*Lat.*).

2. One who affects a great love of art and indifference to practical matters, pretender to taste, dilettante, amateur, sensitive soul, wearer of the green carnation.

AESTHETIC, *adj.* 1. Founded on the idea of beauty, pertaining to the sense of the beautiful, artistic, beautiful, tasteful, gratifying to the taste, graceful, dainty, attractive, in good taste, to one's taste, exquisite, lovely, charming, comely, delicate.

2. Having a sense of the beautiful, loving the beautiful, characterized by a love of beauty, cultured, cultivated, refined, polished, elegant, discriminative, manifesting taste, fastidious.

3. Sensitive, easily affected, impressionable, responsive, susceptible, alive to, tender, weak, thin-skinned, finical, squeamish, precious.

AESTHETICS, *n.* Science of the principles of art, science of the beautiful, theory of the fine arts, doctrines of taste, philosophy of taste.

AFAR, *adv.* Far away, at a distance, a long way off, far off, far afield, afar off, far and wide, wide apart, away, beyond range, out of range, a great way off, remote, distant, beyond, yonder, over the hills and far away.

AFFABILITY, *n.* 1. Ease of approach, readiness to converse, approachability, neighborliness, accessibility, conversableness, friendliness, candor, amiability, sociability, sociableness, cordiality, companionableness, unreservedness, openness, frankness.

2. Ease of manner, courteousness, courtesy, politeness, graciousness, civility, complaisance, obligingness, benignness, gentleness, kindliness, good manners, mannerliness, good breeding, gentlemanliness, condescension, soft-spokenness, blandness, fluency, ease of manner, courtliness, suavity, urbanity, comity, amenity.

AFFABLE, *adj.* 1. Easy to approach, accessible, approachable, open, neighborly, amiable, easy, friendly, sociable, familiar, accostable, free and easy, companionable, unreserved, easy-going, easy to talk to, communicative, conversable, amicable, cordial.

2. Expressing affability, courteous, respectful, polite, deferential, gracious, civil, complaisant, obliging, benign, gentle, mild, kindly, mannerly, condescending, well-mannered, fair-spoken, suave, soft-spoken, well-bred, bland, fluent, urbane, courtly, debonair.

AFFAIR, *n.* 1. Private concern, personal business, function, office, duty, matter, interest, question, thing, circumstance, case, subject, topic, calling, job, employment, occupation, profession, pursuit, avocation.

2. Occurrence, undertaking, operation, action, proceeding, performance, transaction, incident, event, happening, fact, adventure.

3. Love affair, *affaire d'amour, affaire de coeur,* amour, amourette, amorous intrigue, illicit love affair, unlawful love connection, liaison, love making.

4. Affair of honor, *affaire d'honneur,* duel, fight, engagement, conflict, contest, encounter, skirmish, brush, collision, passage, fight, combat.

AFFAIRS, *n.* Practical concerns, matters of action, personal business, financial activities, finances, estate, property, pecuniary ventures.

AFFECT, *v.* 1. Concern, be of interest to, regard, be in relation with, refer to, relate to, pertain to, be of importance to.

2. Produce an effect upon, effect, influence, act on, impress, work upon, produce a change in, change, alter, transform, modify.

3. Lay hold of, act upon contagiously, attack, seize, take hold, grip, infect, nip, taint.

4. Move, soften, touch, stir, melt, trouble, hurt, grieve, perturb, agitate, chasten, overcome, subdue, smite, pierce, thrill.

5. Have a liking for, be fond of, love, like, be attracted by, be drawn toward, be given to, take pleasure in, show tendency toward, aim at, aspire to, yearn for, desire.

6. Do for effect, put on, make a show of, profess ostentatiously, put on a pretense of, take on, pretend to, assume, adopt, feign, counterfeit, simulate, pose, make believe.

AFFECTATION, *n.* Airs, mannerisms, pretense, pretension, artificiality of manner or conduct, unnaturalness, affectedness, studied attempt, shallow display, outside show, simulation, sham, feigning, pretext, make-believe, acting, finical airs, foppery, frills, dandyism, coxcombry, mincingness.

AFFECTED, *adj.* 1. Acted upon, influenced, impressed, worked upon, moved, touched, melted, concerned, reached, grieved, compassionate, sympathetic, tender, sorry, troubled, distressed, overwrought.

2. Influenced injuriously, attacked, laid hold of, seized, afflicted, diseased, impaired, tainted.

3. Assumed artificially, not natural, pretended, feigned, simulated, artificial, unnatural, stilted, mannered, in outward semblance only, insincere, canting, pedantic, hypocritical, self-conscious, overdone, overacted, stagey, theatrical.

4. Given to false show, swaggering, conceited, pretentious, ostentatious, self-important, upstage, high-hat, vainglorious, egotistic, pompous, vain, foppish, coxcombical, modish, mincing, finical, simpering, namby-pamby, missish, prim, priggish, prudish.

AFFECTING, *adj.* Having power to move the feelings, tending to stir the affections, moving the emotions, exciting sympathy, moving, touching, pathetic, sad, piteous, heart-rending, melting, tender, poignant, soul-stirring, impressive, overpowering, stirring, piercing, nerve-wracking, agitating, powerful, thrilling, striking.

AFFECTION, *n.* 1. Feeling, emotion, natural impulse, inclination, disposition, predisposition, proneness, propensity, tendency, proclivity, bent, penchant, leaning, bias, frame of mind.

2. Zealous attachment, love, passion, fondness, regard, devotion, liking, ardor, desire, heart, tenderness, endearment, partiality, predilection, good will, solicitude, kindness, friendliness.

3. Attribute, characteristic, quality, character, property, mark, note, peculiarity.

4. Disorder, ailment, sickness, disease, illness, malady, morbid state, complaint.

AFFECTIONATE, *adj.* Loving, warm-hearted, tender, devoted, tender-hearted, fond, fervent, ardent, amorous, amatory, erotic, passionate, enamored, lovesick, doting, caring, attached, warm, cordial, earnest, friendly, amiable, kind, sympathetic, solicitous.

AFFIANCE, *v.* 1. Betroth, plight faith, pledge faith for marriage, engage, contract to marry, agree to marry, promise to wed, bind by promise of marriage, espouse.

2. Promise solemnly, assure by pledge, pledge, covenant.

AFFIANCE, *n.* 1. Marriage contract, pledging of faith, marital covenant, plighted faith, betrothal, engagement, espousal, promise to marry.

2. Trust, faith, confidence, reliance, belief in.

AFFIDAVIT, *n.* Written testimony sworn to before a magistrate, written declaration upon oath, sworn statement, voluntary attestation under oath, deposition, evidence, voucher, proof, witness, affirmation.

AFFILIATE, *v.* 1. Adopt, receive into the family as a child, take as one's own child, fix the paternity of, filiate.

2. Attach on terms of fellowship, place on friendly terms, come into intimate relations, associate, connect, join with, unite, bring into close relationship, league, make belong, relate closely, incorporate, ally, band together, graft upon, annex, be friendly, consort, fraternize.

AFFILIATION, *n.* 1. Adoption, acknowledgment of a child, treating as a child, filiation.

2. Friendly association, relationship, intimate connection, alliance, league, fraternity, union with, incorporation, annexation, fraternization, membership, consortium.

AFFINITY, *n.* 1. Natural liking for, attraction to, inclination, drawing toward, proclivity, sympathy, propensity, friendliness.

2. Soul mate, other half, alter ego, second self, inseparable friend, flame, sweetheart, mistress, inamorata, ladylove, beau, lover, suitor, spark, truelove.

3. Relationship by marriage, kinship, kindred, connection, interconnection, alliance, propinquity, union, attachment, bond, association.

4. Inherent likeness, resemblance, similarity, similitude, correspondence, close agreement, parallelism, analogy, correlation, conformity, parity, homogeneity, homology.

AFFIRM, *v.* 1. State positively, declare to be fact, assert absolutely, tell with confidence, aver, maintain as true, avouch, vouch, attest, testify, depose, witness, bear witness to, asseverate, hold, contend, allege, propound, make known, claim, proclaim, pronounce, enunciate, promulgate, say, announce, profess, predicate, acknowledge, protest.

2. Make firm, confirm, corroborate, establish, sustain, support, vouch for, ratify, guarantee, indorse, certify, warrant, approve.

3. Declare solemnly, give solemn declaration, pledge one's word, make attestation, make averment, give deposition, make asseveration.

AFFIRMATION, *n.* 1. Positive statement, factual declaration, absolute assertion, word, testimony, vouchment, averment, profession, avouchment, allegation, asseveration, protestation, avowal, acknowledgment, announcement, pronouncement, saying, predication, deposition.

2. Confirmation, corroboration, establishment, approval, ratification, indorsement, certification, warranty.

3. Solemn declaration, legal pledge, attestation, solemn avowal, averment.

AFFIRMATIVE, *adj.* 1. Giving affirmation, answering "yes," assenting, affirmatory, assertory, declaratory, declarative, positive, not negative, asseverative, dogmatic, emphatic, absolute, insistent, categorical, predicative, assertive.

2. Confirmative, corroborative, establishing, ratifying, indorsing, approving, acknowledging, affirming, acquiescent, concurring.

AFFIX, *v.* Fix, fasten, join, subjoin, conjoin, put with, attach, add, connect with, append, annex, set to, adjoin, unite with, tack on, tag, stick to, impress *(as a seal or stamp).*

AFFIX, *n.* That which is appended, appendage, postfix, suffix, prefix, adjunct, annexation, tab, attachment, addendum, appendix, pendant, tag, subscript.

AFFLATUS, *n.* Inspiration, impelling inward mental force, elevating natural impulse, supreme insight, awakening creative impulse, inspired state, fire, genius, spiritual exaltation, beatific vision, rhapsody, ecstasy, supernatural influence, divine communication, revelation, theopneusty, divine impartation.

AFFLICT, *v.* Distress physically or mentally, trouble grievously, oppress with suffering, plague, torment, wound, lacerate, stab, hurt, agonize, pain, sting, strike, scourge, rack, grieve, smite, grind, gall, fret, gnaw, grate, chafe, exercise, harass, persecute, try, beset, vex, disquiet, cut up, punish, chasten, burden, make sorrowful.

AFFLICTED, *adj.* Suffering affliction, distressed in body or mind, filled with woe, grieved, sad, desolate, bereaved, mortified, pitiable, oppressed, troubled, unfortunate, grievously depressed, mentally impaired, diseased, disabled, burdened.

AFFLICTION, *n.* 1. Distress of body or mind, tribulation, hardship, trial, scourge, plague, misery, wretchedness, pain, bereavement, agony, suffering, torture, torment, anguish, sore worry, desolation, sorrow, grief, dolor, woe, grievous trouble, care, anxiety, burden, load, heartache, unhappiness, heartbreak, heavy heart, desolation, bitterness.

2. That which causes distress, adversity, blow, setback, reverse, calamity, catastrophe, bad luck, misfortune, mishap, misadventure, mischance, oppression, visitation, disaster, reverse of fortune, persecution, stroke, ill, shock, ordeal, buffeting, curse, undoing, evil, destruction, ruin, disease, blight, sickness, disability.

AFFLICTIVE, *adj.* Tormenting, grievous, sore, hard to bear, painful, trying, troublous, baleful, harrowing, dire, disastrous, calamitous, unlucky, catastrophic, unfortunate, stricken, harassing, distressing, hard, heavy, woeful, severe, piteous, vexatious, sorrowful, miserable, mournful, sad, unhappy, wretched, deplorable.

AFFLUENCE, *n.* 1. Abundant supply, plenitude, fulness, plenty, richness, exuberance, profusion, luxuriance, no lack, amplitude, ample store, copiousness, plethora, abundance.

2. Abundance of material goods, opulence, wealth, riches, fortune, gold, capital, mint of money, ample means, mine of wealth, resources, substance, independence, easy circumstances, prosperity, money.

AFFLUENT, *adj.* 1. Abundant, ample, exuberant, full, luxuriant, plenteous, bounteous, bountiful, abounding, teeming, rife, plentiful, copious, lavish, superabundant, plethoric, profuse.

2. Abounding in riches, wealthy, rich, opulent, moneyed, well off, well-to-do, flush, in the chips, in easy circumstances, on easy street, well-heeled, in the dough, capitalistic.

AFFLUENT, *n.* Tributary stream, branch, feeder, confluent, ramification of a river.

AFFORD, *v.* 1. Be financially able, have the means, have sufficient means for, well afford, bear the expense of, incur without detriment to financial condition, be able to meet the expense of, spare the price of, command money, endure with advantage, stand, support, sustain, bear.

2. Yield, give forth, produce, furnish, supply, provide, contribute, generate, beget, engender, bring forth.

3. Confer upon, accord, award, grant, bestow, give, offer, accommodate with, favor with, lend, dispense, assign, communicate, impart.

AFFRAY, *n.* Public brawl, noisy quarrel, breach of the peace, disturbance of the peace, strife, row, scuffle, tussle, fracas, melee, conflict, fray, contest, scrimmage, skirmish, tumultuous assault, tumult, fisticuffs, fight, encounter, collision, broil, set-to, rumpus, outbreak, uproar, brush, feud, vendetta, duel, riot, *émeute (Fr.),* rencontre, mill, dispute, wrangle, dissension, contention, affair, commotion, battle, squabble, altercation.

AFFRIGHT, *v.* Impress with sudden fear, strike terror, terrify, scare, frighten, alarm, appal, put in fear, startle, overawe, intimidate, browbeat, cow, shock, astonish, astound, daunt, dismay, dishearten, dispirit, confound, confuse.

AFFRONT, *v.* 1. Treat with incivility, insult, injure with insolence, illtreat, abuse, outrage, wrong, defy.

2. Aggravate, exasperate, displease, offend, put to the blush, put out of countenance, confuse, confound, put to shame, give offense to, annoy, provoke, irritate, vex, pique, wound, anger, gall, nettle, make angry, chafe, fret, miff, disoblige, tease, molest, mock.

3. Meet in hostile manner, face in defiance, confront, accost, encounter face to face, strike upon, cross, oppose, clash with.

AFFRONT, *n.* 1. Intentional slight, contemptuous wrong, rude treatment, offensive act, marked disrespect, purposed indignity, discourtesy, rudeness, indignity, insult, outrage, dishonor, injury, ill-treatment, abuse, contumely, insolence.

2. Offense to one's dignity, provocation, irritation, vexation, annoyance, impertinence.

3. Shame, degradation, disgrace, ignominy, humiliation, sense of shame, abasement, chagrin, mortification.

AFOOT, *adv., adj.* 1. Pedestrially, walking, on foot.

2. Astir, in motion, up, abroad, in full swing, in action.

3. In progress, in process of accomplishment, in course of preparation, on the tapis, on the carpet, on the anvil, forthcoming.

AFORESAID, *adj.* Mentioned previously, said in a preceding part, said before, said, named, aforementioned, forementioned, beforementioned, aforenamed, aforestated, forenamed, preceding, aforecited, aforegiven, aforegoing, antecedent, above-mentioned, above-named, former, anterior, foregoing, previous, specified.

AFORETHOUGHT, *adj.* Previously in mind, thought of beforehand, premeditated, prepense, intended beforehand, deliberate, well-considered, with forethought, planned beforehand, contrived in advance, devised beforehand, reflective, designed, purposed, collected.

AFORETIME, *adv.* In a former time, in time past, at a previous time, in past ages, heretofore, of eld, of yore, formerly, bypast, in days gone by, in days of old, long ago, of old, bygone, formerly, anciently, in times of old.

A FORTIORI *(Lat.)* For a still stronger reason, by a stronger reason, with the greater force, all the more, by so much the more, even more certain, still more surely.

AFRAID, *adj.* Frightened, terrified, alarmed, fearful, affrighted, scared, haunted by fear, apprehensive, shrinking, timorous, timid, uneasy, nervous, solicitous, anxious, distrustful, diffident, terror-stricken, aghast, panic-stricken, panicky, faint-hearted, dreading, tremulous, shaky, white-livered, craven, cowardly, pusillanimous, cautious.

AFRESH, *adv.* Once more, after rest or interval, anew, again, newly, over again, *de novo.*

AFT, *adv.* *(Naut.)* Toward the stern of a ship, near the stern, astern, abaft, back, behind, in the rear, backward, rearward.

AFTER, *prep.* 1. Later in time than, following the expiration of, subsequent to, at the close of, following successively, in succession to, because of, in consequence of.

2. Following behind, behind in place, in the rear of, in the wake of, in back of.

3. Below in rank, next to in order, back of, below.

4. Moving toward from behind, following the course of, in pursuit of, in search of, in desire for, with desire for.

5. About, concerning, in relation to, for.

6. In proportion to, in accordance with, in conformity to, according to, in agreement with.

7. In the manner of, in obedience to, in the pattern of, in imitation of the style of, on the model of, from, for.

8. For the sake of, by the name of, with the name of, for.

AFTER, *adj.* 1. Succeeding, later in time, next, following later, subsequent, second, successive, sequential, attendant, ensuing, consequent, latter.

2. *(Naut.)* Farther aft, situated in the rear, posterior, rearward, back, hind, hinder, astern.

AFTER, *adv.* 1. Later in time, afterward, at a succeeding time, afterwards, subsequently, following in time.

2. Behind, in the rear.

AFTER ALL On the whole, all things having been considered, when all is said and done, at last, finally, eventually, in the end, ultimately, in spite of every consideration to the contrary, notwithstanding.

AFTERLIFE, *n.* 1. Later life, subsequent life, ensuing years.

2. Life after death, life beyond the grave, future state, the hereafter, immortality, eternity, perpetuity, deathlessness, eternal continuance, heaven, abodes of bliss, the eternal rest, the New Jerusalem, Abraham's bosom, Paradise, Zion, Elysium, Elysian fields, happy hunting grounds, Isles of the Blessed, Valhalla, Nirvana.

AFTERMATH, *n.* 1. Consequences, results, issue, outcome, upshot, effect, outgrowth, offshoot, afterclap, turnout, end, sequel, event, penalty, development, fruit, reward.

2. Second stand of grass in the same season, second mowing, second growth, aftergrass, fog, aftercrop, aftergrowth, lattermath, eddish, arrish, rowen.

AFTERMOST, *adj.* 1. *(Naut.)* Aftmost, nearest the stern, farthest aft, sternmost.

2. Hindmost, hindermost, rearward, last, last in time or order.

AFTERNOON, *n.* 1. 'Twixt noon and sundown, before sunset, *post meridiem (Lat.),* p.m.

2. The latter part, middle age, maturity, the closing part, decline, ebb, wane.

AFTERTHOUGHT, *n.* Reflection after an act, subsequent meditation, afterwit, second thought, later expedient, reconsideration, later thought, reexamination, review, deliberation, wisdom out of time, retrospection.

AFTERWARD, *adv.* In subsequent time, after, subsequently, in aftertime, thereafter, latterly, later, posteriorly, ensuingly, at a later time, in the sequel, thereupon, then, thereon, another time, ultimately.

AGAIN, *adv.* 1. Once more, another time, over, anew, afresh, newly, freshly, a second time, bis, encore, repeatedly, *de novo (Lat.), da capo (It.),* reiteratively, recurrently, anon, ditto.
2. In the next place, moreover, furthermore, in an additional instance, besides, further.
3. In reply, in return, in answer, in restitution, back, as a result, in consequence.
4. On the contrary, contrariwise, on the other hand.
5. In the opposite direction, to the same place, over the same course, back again.

AGAIN AND AGAIN Often, repeatedly, over and over, recurrently, reiteratively, frequently, in quick succession, on and on, at short intervals, with frequent repetitions, oftentimes, many a time and oft, ever and anon, incessantly, monotonously, unremittingly, pertinaciously, harpingly, ceaselessly, continuously, insistently, persistently, perseveringly, doggedly.

AGAINST, *prep.* 1. Facing, over against, close up to, fronting, opposite to, abreast of, toward, off.
2. From an opposite direction, in contact with, upon.
3. In the face of, directly into.
4. On the other side of, counter to, opposed to, contrary to, in contrariety to, in opposition to, adverse to, versus, antagonistic to, in violation of, resistant to, obstructive of, unfavorable to, counteracting.
5. In preparation for, in provision for, in anticipation of, in expectation of, for.
6. For protecting from, in resistance against, in compensation for, to counterpoise, to match, to countervail, to counterbalance, in requital for, in equalization of, in contrast with.

AGAINST THE GRAIN 1. Oblique to the fiber of wood, against the fiber of wood.
2. Counter to the natural bent, against the natural disposition, against one's inclination, in violation of one's preference, contrary to one's feelings, *au rebours (Fr.),* irritating, the wrong way.

AGAPE, *adv.* 1. Yawning, open-mouthed, with mouth wide open, wide asunder.
2. In an attitude of wonder, wonderstruck, staring with open mouth, spellbound, astonished, surprised, amazed, breathless, dumfounded, dazed, blank, stupefied, awestruck, thunderstruck, struck all of a heap, confounded.
3. Gazing eagerly, eagerly attentive, expectant, in an attitude of eagerness, waiting.

AGE, *n.* 1. Length of life, duration of existence, period of life, time of life, lifetime, stage of life, generation.
2. Maturity, mature years, majority, years of discretion, seniority, full age, adulthood, period of life at which one becomes qualified for anything.
3. The latter part of life, advanced age, old age, advanced period of life, agedness, decline of life, declining years, vale of years, senescence, senectitude, senility, anility, caducity, grand climacteric, dotage, second childhood, ripe old age, superannuation, decrepitude, gray hairs, "sear and yellow leaf," longevity.

4. Period of time or history, date, era, epoch, time, cycle.
5. A great length of time, decade, century, millennium, chiliad, eon, years.

AGED, *adj.* 1. Advanced in life, stricken in years, old, senile, senescent, past one's prime, elderly, waning, hoary, grayheaded, time-honored, old as Methuselah, venerable, veteran, ancient, decrepit, patriarchal, superannuated, time-worn, declining, antiquated, mellow, old as the hills, with one foot in the grave.
2. At the age of, of the age of, having lived for, old.

AGENCY, *n.* 1. State of being in action, state of exerting power, instrumentality, active power, means, action, activity, influence, appliance, means of producing effects, efficiency, force, operation, procurement, intermediation, medium, mediation, intervention, causation.
2. Public service bureau, commercial bureau, agent's place of business, the office of agent, direction, supervision, superintendence, charge, management, maintenance.

AGENDA, *n.* Things to be done, matters to be attended to, order of the day, items of business, program of business, docket, memoranda, record of details, schedule of affairs, register.

AGENT, *n.* 1. Active cause, moving force, object used for obtaining specific results, effective principle, acting element, modifying force, power, reagent.
2. Doer, perpetrator, actor, mover, operator, practitioner, performer, worker, executor, artisan, mechanic, promoter, artificer.
3. Deputy, intermediary, mediary, procurator, representative, go-between, middleman, attorney, commissioner, broker, minister, factor, actuary, viceregent, principal, emissary, envoy, canvasser, solicitor, proctor, negotiator, advocate, coagent, functionary, negotiant, ambassador, comprador, chargé d'affaires, steward, factotum, substitute, servant, proxy, delegate, commissary, traveling salesman, syndic, consignee.

AGGLOMERATE, *v.* Gather into a mass, roll into a ball, bring together into a cluster, cluster, crowd densely, condense in a mass, collect, mass together, wind together, gather together, lump together, accumulate, heap up, pile up, conglomerate, join together.

AGGLOMERATION, *n.* Orderless mass, pile of things clustered together, indiscriminate heap, random assemblage, aggregation, conglomeration, lump, accumulation, collection, crowd, cluster, congeries, compages.

AGGLUTINATE, *v.* Cause to adhere, unite by adhesion, glue, cement, stick together, attach, join, fasten together, fix together, fuse, blend, amalgamate, commingle, conglutinate, combine, weld, merge, cluster.

AGGLUTINATION, *n.* 1. Process of uniting by tenacious substance, gluing together, cementing together, clumping, combining, sticking together, fastening together, fusing, amalgamating, welding.
2. Adhesion, cohesion, union, combination, coalescence, conjunction, fusion.

AGGRANDIZE, *v.* 1. Enlarge, extend, magnify, add to, augment, increase, widen in scope, lengthen, spread, enhance, enrich, intensify, strengthen.
2. Promote, advance, exalt, give grandeur to,

dignify, raise to preferment, make great, elevate, honor, ennoble, extend the power of.

AGGRANDIZEMENT, *n.* 1. Increase in size, enlargement, augmentation, accession, extension, expansion, spread, growth, increment, accretion.

2. Increase in honor, promotion, elevation, exaltation, advancement, preferment, enrichment, magnification, ennoblement, glorification.

AGGRAVATE, *v.* 1. Render worse, make more severe, worsen, make more serious, heighten in evil, intensify, increase, render less tolerable, increase inflammation in, inflame, excite fever, sharpen disorder.

2. Exaggerate, overestimate, overstate, color, enhance, magnify.

3. *(Colloq.)* Exasperate, exacerbate, irritate, provoke, enrage, vex, annoy, nettle, anger, fret, ruffle, roil, rile, embitter, sour, envenom, offend, infuriate, mock, insult, tease, affront.

AGGRAVATION, *n.* 1. Irritation, inflammation, heightening of something evil, intensification, sharpening, worsening.

2. Exaggerated representation, exaggeration, overestimation, overstatement, stretching, high coloring, hyperbole.

3. *(Colloq.)* Annoyance, vexation, provocation, exasperation, exacerbation, embitterment.

AGGREGATE, *v.* Collect into a mass, amass, mass, unite into a sum, bring together, heap up, pile up, gather up, get together, assemble, scrape together, accumulate, sum up, cumulate, make as a sum, amount to the number of.

AGGREGATE, *adj.* Collected in a mass, formed by collection of individuals into a sum, total, gathered into a whole, combined, compound, united, agglomerate, clustered together, complete, all, entire, composite, collective.

AGGREGATE, *n.* Entire quantity of something, complete whole, totality, entirety, total, sum of particulars, gross amount, sum total, summation, congeries, assemblage, aggregation, collection, combination, composite, compound, heap, mass, body, amount.

AGGREGATION, *n.* Combined whole, aggregate of particulars, union into a mass, accumulation into a sum, collection, composite, gathering, agglomeration, group, assembly, congregation, multitude, throng, force, body, mass, pile, heap.

AGGRESS, *v.* Commit the first act of hostility, attack first, make an attack, seize the initiative, be the aggressor, begin a quarrel, attack, set upon, encroach, infringe, trespass, transgress, intrude, make inroad, commit an offense, offend.

AGGRESSION, *n.* Unprovoked attack, offensive action, first assault, provocation, act of hostility, practice of encroachment, first act leading to a war, violation of another's rights, transgression, trespass, inroad, infringement, injury, offense, onset, onslaught, incursion, irruption, intrusion, illapse, foray, thrust for conquest, sally, sortie, forced entrance, outbreak, surprisal, storming, raid, beleaguerment, besiegement.

AGGRESSIVE, *adj.* 1. Combative, pugnacious, belligerent, bellicose, disposed to attack, invasive, offensive, assailant, prone to encroach, provoking, incursive, transgressive, trespassing, contentious.

2. Self-assertive, pushing, inclined to take the initiative, bumptious, obtrusive, vigorous, active, alert, enterprising, energetic, vigilant, watchful, wide-awake, ready, up and coming, live-wire, go-ahead, zealous, resolute, assiduous.

AGGRESSOR, *n.* One who begins hostilities, provocator, assailant, attacker, assaulter, assailer, invader, first offender, antagonist, prime mover, beginner, initiative seizer.

AGGRIEVE, *v.* Wrong grievously, grieve, cause sorrow to, injure by injustice, give pain to, wound the feelings of, trouble, distress, wrong, inflict hardship upon, give cause for just complaint, oppress, bear heavily upon, abuse, maltreat, ill-treat, ill-use, persecute, impose upon.

AGHAST, *adj.* 1. Horrified, alarmed, dismayed, frightened, terrified, appalled, panic-stricken, scared, horror-struck, petrified, afraid.

2. Flabbergasted, astounded, confounded, startled, amazed, astonished, dumbstruck, taken aback, dumfounded, thunderstruck, overcome with consternation, thrown off one's balance, surprised, stunned, stupefied.

AGILE, *adj.* Light in movement, nimble, spry, lithe, supple, brisk, sprightly, deft, dexterous, easy-moving, fleet, swift, rapid, fast, prompt, ready, winged, active, tripping, swift-footed, alive, light-footed, mentally quick, smart, alert, lively, bustling, expeditious, dapper.

AGILITY, *n.* Nimbleness, spryness, litheness, suppleness, briskness, sprightliness, deftness, dexterity, fleetness, swiftness, rapidity, activity, promptness, readiness, promptitude, expedition, dispatch, liveliness, smartness, alertness, celerity, quickness, alacrity.

AGITATE, *v.* 1. Move with violent action, shake, toss, set in motion, keep in motion, move briskly, move to and fro, rock, jar, convulse, upheave, heave, stir, quake, displace, vibrate, oscillate, churn, jostle, undulate, tumble, fan, brandish, wave.

2. Disturb, disquiet, distract, trouble, perturb, discompose, work up, stir up, disconcert, rouse, ferment, ruffle, unsettle, alarm, excite, upset, flutter, fluster, confuse, flurry, hurry.

3. Call attention to by speech or writing, excite discussion over, discuss excitedly, engage in discussion, keep discussion going, debate, dispute, controvert, argue.

4. Revolve in the mind, consider on all sides, meditate on, excogitate, deliberate, investigate, ventilate, contrive busily, devise, plot.

5. Arouse public interest in, keep alive interest in, keep constantly before the public, excite public action, ferment, instigate, kindle, revive.

AGITATED, *adj.* 1. Shaking, tremulous, jerky, convulsive, spasmodic, twitching, quavering, saltant, quivering, vibrating.

2. Ripply, rough, choppy, tempestuous, wild, turbulent, boiling, stormy, violent, tumultuous, boisterous, vehement.

3. Excited, wrought up, distraught, frantic, hysterical, disturbed, shaken, uneasy, unquiet, restless, atwitter, disquieted, ruffled, ebullient, impatient, flurried, aflutter.

AGITATION, *n.* 1. Shake, concussion, succussion, quake, stir, tremor, shake, ripple, jog, jolt, jar, hitch, jerk, quiver, shock, quaver, pulsation, undulation, backwash, commotion, fury, tossing, upheaval, jactation, throb, paroxysm, ripple.

2. Perturbation, excitement, trepidation, fret, turmoil, tumult, turbulence, ebullition, fever, commotion, disturbance of mind, emotion, hurry, disconcertion, discomposure, disquiet, distraction, unrest, uneasiness, restlessness, unquiet, flurry, fluster, flutter, hurry-skurry, ruffle, fume.

3. Keeping a matter before the public, open debate, persistent public urging, disputation, active discussion, demagogy, canvassing, inquiry, controversy, ventilation, consideration, argument, investigation, examination.

AGITATOR, *n.* 1. Zealous advocate, reformer, active partisan, ardent champion, exciter of public debate, active supporter.
2. Popular ringleader, demagogue, firebrand, incendiary, rabble rouser, stirrer up of strife, soapbox orator, troublemaker, stormy petrel, labor baiter, radical, leftist.

AGNOSTIC, *n.* Skeptic, nullifidian, unbeliever, doubter, doubting Thomas, Pyrrhonist, atheist, phenomenalist, empiricist, disbeliever in God, deist, freethinker, infidel, heretic, heathen.

AGNOSTIC, *adj.* Skeptical, doubting, incredulous, unbelieving, indisposed to believe, disbelieving, godless, distrustful, phenomenalistic, questioning.

AGNOSTICISM, *n.* Skepticism, nullifidianism, Pyrrhonism, empiricism, disbelief, incredulity, unbelief, phenomenalism, freethinking, atheism, heresy.

AGO, *adj.* Gone, gone by, past, bygone, over, passed away, elapsed, extinct, former, earlier, previous, antecedent, sometime, pristine, late, quondam, prior.

AGO, *adv.* In the past, in past time, in time gone by, agone *(poetical),* formerly, of old, of yore, erstwhile, time was, aforetime, heretofore, once, one day, ere now, since.

AGOG, *adj.* In a state of eager curiosity, curious, looking forward to, impatient, expectant, astir, on tiptoe, worked up, wrought up, highly excited, in eager desire, alert, more than ready, vigilant, watchful, wakeful, open-eyed, open-mouthed, breathless, anxious, anticipatory, desirous.

AGONIZE, *v.* 1. Subject to extreme agony, rack, torture, torment, cause to suffer greatly, distress with pain, excruciate, wring, put in great pain, pain severely, convulse, harrow, harass.
2. Be in agony, suffer violent anguish, writhe with extreme pain, be tormented, be distorted with pain, wince, bleed, struggle with sorrow, grieve.
3. Make great effort, exert oneself, strive earnestly, strain desperately, struggle, wrestle, labor, toil, endeavor, flounder in distress.

AGONIZING, *adj.* Woeful, painful, torturous, tormenting, aching, severe, extreme, poignant, intense, grave, acute, sharp, sore, excruciating, cruel, corroding, cutting, excoriating, grievous, crushing, harrowing, rending, insupportable, insufferable, unbearable, intolerable.

AGONY, *n.* 1. Extreme pain, intense suffering, anguish, torment, torture, distress, misery, rack, throe, pang, paroxysm, convulsion, spasm, woe, excruciating ache, affliction, sorrow.
2. Violent contest, earnest striving, arduous effort, vital struggle.

AGRARIAN, *adj.* Agricultural, agronomical, geoponic, georgic, praedial, rural, campestral, rustic, agrestic, bucolic, pastoral.

AGREE, *v.* 1. Yield assent, consent, fall in with, think alike, be of one mind, concede, grant, accept, admit, approve, consent, acquiesce, side with, accede, comply, subscribe, acknowledge, go along with, come to the same conclusion.
2. Concur, harmonize, accord, gee with, jibe with, be in unison, coincide, stand with, chime in with, fit, suit, match, correspond, conform, tally, dovetail, parallel, match, equal, square, cohere, comport, resemble, be appropriate.
3. Promise, undertake, bargain, covenant, contract, make an agreement, bind oneself, stipulate, pledge one's word, engage, guarantee, give assurance, take upon oneself.
4. Arrive at a settlement, compromise, come to an arrangement, come to an understanding, compound, come to one mind, reconcile, see eye to eye.

AGREEABLE, *adj.* 1. Pleasant, attractive, tasty, delightful, gratifying, pleasing, pleasurable, to one's fancy, welcome, inviting, comely, elegant, handsome, graceful, nice, enjoyable, acceptable, goodly, charming, to one's mind, likable, to one's taste, luscious, palatable, delectable, delicious, sweet, dulcet.
2. Genial, amiable, congenial, good-natured, amenable, gracious, suave, winning, neighborly, polite, complaisant, friendly, cordial, courteous, well-disposed, sociable, favorably disposed, gentle, willing.
3. Suitable, appropriate, apropos, fitting, meet, becoming, befitting, fit, proper, adapted, apt, expedient, apposite, conformable, congruous, correspondent, accordant, compatible, consonant, concordant, harmonious, consistent.

AGREEMENT, *n.* 1. Mutual understanding, accord, accordance, concord, consensus, amity, concordance, concurrence, conformity, harmony, unison, unanimity, consonancy, communion, sympathy, rapport.
2. Compact, contract, pact, promise, treaty, word, proposal, bargain, covenant, transaction, concordat, deal, stipulation, acknowledgment, obligation, guaranty, guarantee, arrangement, cartel, convention, warranty.
3. Similitude, resemblance, affinity, harmony, similarity, correspondence, congruence, analogy, coherence, symmetry, uniformity, coincidence, consistency, compatibility, adjustment, approval, acquiescence, compliance, propriety, acceptance, accommodation, affirmation, corroboration, collusion.

AGREE WITH, *v.* 1. Prove suitable, be good for, be accommodated, be adapted, conduce to one's health, have a beneficial effect, suit, be wholesome for, be healthful for, promote one's health.
2. Tally with, be in rapport with, chime in with, comport with, fall in with.
3. Make a bargain with, covenant, stipulate, compact, strike hands with.

AGRICULTURE, *n.* Farming, market-gardening, husbandry, geoponics, agronomy, agronomics, cultivation, tillage, gardening, kitchen gardening, fruit raising, crop raising, stock raising, dairying, terraculture, horticulture, viticulture, forestry, floriculture, arboriculture.

AGRICULTURIST, *n.* Farmer, husbandman, tiller of the ground, cultivator of the soil, agronomist, granger, yeoman, gardener, producer, truck gardener, horticulturist, livestock raiser, terraculturist, floriculturist, arboriculturist, dairyman, viticulturist.

AGROUND, *adj., adv.* 1. Stranded, foundered, shipwrecked, wrecked, swamped, grounded, on the ground, touching on the shore, resting on the bottom, on a rock, stuck in the mud, stuck fast, beached, ashore, not afloat, cast away.
2. At a standstill, brought to a stop, high and

dry, exhausted in resources, at a loss, run out, hard up, helpless, in a pass, in straits, in a fix, put to it, straitened, graveled, foundering.

AGUE, *n.* 1. Chills and fever, malarial fever, intermittent fever, chills, sweating fits.

2. Chill, rigor, chilliness, cold, fit of shivering, shakes, quaking.

AHEAD, *adv.* In front, to the front, in the front, before one's path, in the direct line of one's course, in advance, on, onward, forward without pausing, toward a position in advance, farther forward than another, at the head of, forward, before, toward something in front, toward an earlier point of time.

AHEAD OF More advanced than, quicker than, having the advantage of, surpassing, outstripping, gone beyond, outdistancing, beating, getting on, overreaching, securing the lead, winning out, progressing, outwitting, in the lead, outranking, superior to.

AID, *v.* 1. Lend assistance, assist, give support to, help, stand by, support, sustain, abet, back, second, cooperate with, befriend, encourage, strengthen, foster, uphold, bolster, minister to, boost, supply, accommodate, defend, take part with, relieve, alleviate, bestead, prosper, serve, subserve, favor, patronize, speed, stimulate, take turn with, intercede for, shield, protect, subsidize, contribute.

2. Give a helping hand, succor, give alms to, relieve, supply the necessities of, do kindness to, put on their feet.

3. Further, forward, seek to push forward, advance, help on, promote, improve, facilitate, make easy, render less difficult.

AID, *n.* 1. Help, helping hand, assistance, lift, support, cooperation, encouragement, promotion, furtherance, service, good offices, maintenance, accommodation, ministry, protection, interest, favor, defense, championship, alleviation, rescue, mitigation, ministration, deliverance, comfort.

2. Succor, bounty, charity, patronage, dole, subsidy, subvention, relief, alms, donation, gift, contribution, subscription, allowance, remedy, supplies, stores, means, manna in the wilderness.

3. Aider, helper, assistant, associate, friend, ally, abettor, subsidiary, adjutant, subordinate, auxiliary, adherent, adjunct, coadjutor, supporter, colleague, promoter, friend, sympathizer, patron, partisan, champion, friend in need, helpmeet, helpmate, advocate, comforter, cooperator, ally, confrere, collaborator, co-worker, contributor, seconder, backer, upholder, Man Friday, stooge, right-hand man, accessory, accomplice, follower, satellite, acolyte, henchman, retainer, stool, tool, decoy.

AIDE-DE-CAMP, *n.* Assistant military or naval officer, subordinate officer, camp assistant, deputy, confidential assistant to a superior officer, staff officer, attaché, appointed agent, right-hand man.

AIL, *v.* 1. Affect with pain, trouble bodily or mentally, be the matter with. afflict, distress, make ill, sicken, disturb, cause disease in, cause uneasiness in, disorder.

2. Be somewhat ill, be unwell, be affected with pain, feel uneasiness, suffer, be in pain, decline, be indisposed, peak, weaken, pine, languish, dwindle, droop, flag, waste away, lose strength, lie abed.

AILING, *adj.* Indisposed, unsound, unhealthy, unwell, sickly, poorly, ill, diseased, poisoned, sick, palsied, paralytic, consumptive, tubercular, phthisic, cancerous, lame, halt, crippled, infirm, maladive, delicate, weakly, faint, feeble, morbid, languishing, pathologic, invalided, valetudinarian, disordered, in a bad way, miserable, complaining, down, aching, sore, suffering, out of sorts, under the weather, not up to snuff, on the sick list, laid up, confined, bedridden, on the shelf, done for.

AILMENT, *n.* Morbid physical affection, illness, indisposition, disorder, malady, disease, sickness, complaint, infection, derangement, invalidism, infirmity, weakness, affliction, valetudinarianism, neurosis, mental uneasiness, morbidity.

AIM, *v.* 1. Direct, train, point, level, sight, peg, prepare to fire.

2. Direct the purpose, have in mind, plan, fully intend, purpose, design, tend toward, mean, be at.

3. Direct efforts toward, steer for, aspire to, strive toward, struggle toward, work toward, labor for, drive at, head for, try for, endeavor, essay, propose to oneself, have in view, have an eye to, attempt to reach, be after, aspire after, look after, seek, long for, yearn for, affect, want, wish, desire, crave.

AIM, *n.* 1. Pointing of a weapon, line of sighting, marksmanship.

2. Inclination, proclivity, drift, bent, bearing, tendency, course, direction, drive.

3. Objective, target, goal, mark, point, desire, destination, desideratum, wish, aspiration, object, ambition, intention, end, purpose, intent, view, design, determination, reason, scheme, attempt, undertaking, effort, endeavor.

AIMLESS, *adj.* 1. Undirected, blind, purposeless, objectless, without aim or end, random, chance, haphazard, fortuitous, accidental, stray, drifting, rudderless, erratic, wandering, desultory, to no purpose, pointless.

2. Capricious, fitful, wayward, unreasoning, wanton, indecisive, irresolute, variable, mutable, inconstant, fickle, frivolous, volatile, flighty.

AIR, *v.* 1. Aerate, aerify, expose to air, ventilate, change the air of, fan, winnow, freshen, refresh, revivify, cool, purify, oxygenate.

2. Expose for public notice, exhibit, parade, display ostentatiously, flaunt, show forth, make ostentation of, utter abroad, rumor, make public, publish, give expression to, publicize, broadcast, noise abroad, bruit abroad, divulgate, diffuse, vent, disseminate.

AIR, *n.* 1. Atmosphere, aerosphere, troposphere, stratosphere, blue sky, the open, open air, sky, heaven, welkin, al fresco.

2. Ether, ozone, oxygen, gaseous matter, something volatile.

3. Breeze, light wind, breath of air, zephyr, draft, air in motion, current of air, ventilation.

4. Weather, climate, clime, circumambience, environment, surrounding influence, pervading condition.

5. Utterance abroad, publicity, outlet, vent, currency, exposure, publication, dissemination, divulgation, diffusion.

6. Outer appearance, aspect, semblance, look, personal quality, apparent character, mien, style, manner, cast, bearing, demeanor, carriage, gait, conduct, attitude, gesture, deportment, behavior, peculiar action, personal address, presence.

7. Unceremonious dismissal, removal from

office, discharge, firing, ejection, displacement, expulsion.

8. Tune, aria, melody, song, ditty, canzonetta, ballad, carol, strain, lay, descant, theme, ariette.

AIRINESS, *n.* 1. Lightness, nimbleness, agility, light-footedness, buoyancy, volatility, litheness, gracefulness, grace, lissomness, flexibility, pliancy.

2. Delicacy, tenuousness, thinness, gauziness, gossameriness, flimsiness, diaphaneity, sheerness, limpidness, translucency, etherealness, featheriness, transparency, pellucidness, weightlessness.

3. Frivolity, gayety, insouciance, breeziness, levity, flippancy, jauntiness, sprightliness, vivacity, jocundity, liveliness, gladsomeness, blitheness, joviality, lightheartedness, cheeriness.

AIRING, *n.* 1. Promenade, jaunt, walk, ramble, stroll, saunter, outing, hike, outdoor exercise, tramp, turn, constitutional, circuit, excursion, tour, peregrination, trek, perambulation, drive, wayfaring, motoring, ride.

2. Aeration, exposure to air, ventilation, aerification, admission of air, fanning.

3. Exposure to public notice, divulgation, promulgation, dissemination, ostentatious display, diffusion, exhibition, flaunting, parading.

AIR PIPE, *n.* Vent, blowhole, air hole, air tube, breathing hole, spiracle, bung, bunghole, flue, air shaft, air trunk, chimney, ventilator, louver, funnel, air passage, nostril, nozzle.

AIRS, *n.* Artificial manner, posing, parade of vanity, pretense, pretension, affected manner, arrogance, superciliousness, swank, pomposity, affectedness, show of style, haughtiness, swagger, frills, mannerisms, assumed manner.

AIR-TIGHT, *adj.* 1. Not allowing air to enter, hermetically sealed, impermeable to air, closed, shut tight, impenetrable to air, impervious to air.

2. Having no weak points, incontrovertible, unassailable, invincible, irrefragable, undeniable, inexpugnable, indisputable, incontestable, irrefutable, impregnable.

AIRY, *adj.* 1. Out of doors, in the open, windy, breezy, exposed, al fresco, *à la belle étoile,* open, ventilated, fluttering, breezy.

2. Aerial, ethereal, immaterial, unsubstantial, aeriform, tenuous, thin, rare, graceful, delicate, light, subtle, empyreal, pliant.

3. Frivolous, gay, insouciant, flippant, jaunty, sprightly, vivacious, jocund, lively, gladsome, jovial, blithe, lighthearted, cheery, buoyant, volatile, jolly, merry, animated, brisk, perky, sportive, cheerful, frolicsome, easy.

4. Superficial, gaudy, garish, showy, pranked out, pretentious, ostentatious, putting on airs, flashy, flaunting, swaggering, pompous.

AISLE, *n.* Passageway, walk, passage, gangway, alley, lane, path, way, ingress, egress.

AJAR, *adv.* 1. Neither quite open or shut, agape, gaping, yawning, dehiscent, on the turn, unclosed, unlatched.

2. Out of harmony, in a state of discord, discordant, inharmonious, harsh, jarring, rough, grating, clashing, jangling, cacophonous.

AKIMBO, *adv.* Hand-on-hip, with elbow bent outward, angular, at an angle, tilted, raised, crooked, bent, oblique.

AKIN, *adj.* 1. Related by blood, consanguineous, cognate, agnate, german, kindred, kin, of the same stock, of one's blood, affiliated, connected, sib.

2. Allied by nature, similar in nature, alike,

analogous, resembling, like, parallel, **germane,** corresponding, correlative, associated, collateral, of a piece, in the same category, of the same kind, homogeneous, homologous, partaking of the same qualities.

ALACK, *interj.* Alas! woe is me! alas the day! lackaday! alackaday! welladay! ah me! too bad! heigh-ho! *O tempora, O mores* (Lat.).

ALACRITY, *n.* 1. Cheerful readiness, briskness, willingness, promptitude, swiftness, expedition, speed, haste, promptness, zeal, eagerness, avidity, enthusiasm, alertness, activity, quickness, celerity, facility.

2. Animation, vivacity, liveliness, cheerfulness, sprightliness, hilarity, gayety, high spirits.

A LA MODE *(Fr.)* In fashion, fashionable, in style, stylish, in vogue, modish, chic, smart, according to fashion.

ALARM, *v.* 1. Rouse to vigilance, call to arms, give notice of approaching danger, put on the alert, summon to arms, alert, arouse, sound an alarm, warn, signal, ring the tocsin.

2. Throw into excitement, panic, intimidate, unnerve, dismay, excite with sudden fear, daunt, frighten, terrify, startle, scare, consternate, affright, throw into fear, appall, disturb, agitate, surprise with apprehension of danger, fill with anxiety, shock.

ALARM, *n.* 1. Tocsin, alarum, warning sound, summons to arms, call to arms, sound for notifying of danger, sound of trumpet, beat of drum, notice of danger, alarm bell, alarm gun, war cry, hue and cry, signal of distress, SOS, siren, danger signal, red light.

2. Fear of danger, trepidation, apprehension, fear, terror, consternation, dismay, fright, scare, panic, affright, funk, dread, timidity, disquiet, perturbation, misgiving, solicitude.

ALARMED, *adj.* Apprehensive, fearful, uneasy, solicitous, concerned, aroused to vigilance, excited by fear, agitated, disturbed, anxious, afraid, terrified, distrustful, suspicious, troubled, timorous, faint-hearted, frightened, nervous, haunted with fear.

ALARMING, *adj.* Awful, portentous, ominous, ill-boding, inauspicious, unpropitious, startling, premonitory, terrifying, frightful, threatening, fearful, dreadful, imminent, terrible, formidable, precarious, hazardous, perilous, dangerous, disturbing.

ALARMIST, *n.* Calamity-howler, scaremonger, pessimist, terrorist, decrier, croaker, panicmonger, Cassandra.

ALBEIT, *conj.* Even though, even if, although, notwithstanding that, admitting.

ALBUM, *n.* Scrapbook, portfolio, register for names, depository for photographs, blank book for autographs, visitor's register, memory book, printed compilation, commonplace book, memorandum book, notebook.

ALCHEMY, *n.* Preternatural transmutation, black art, magic, thaumaturgy, magical power, sorcery, witchcraft, occult art, wonder-working, pseudo art, pseudo science.

ALCOHOL, *n.* Intoxicating principle, spirits of wine, pure spirit, fermented liquor, *spiritus frumenti (Lat.),* John Barleycorn, Demon Rum, blue ruin, booze, grog, intoxicant, stimulant, moonshine, hooch, firewater, home-brew.

ALCOHOLIC, *adj.* Intoxicating, inebriating, hard, spirituous, ardent, strong, distilled, fermented.

ALCOHOLIC, *n.* Dipsomaniac, toper, drunkard, tippler, winebibber, hard drinker, addict, boozer, inebriate, sot, carouser, reveler, bacchanalian.

ALCOHOLISM, *n.* Dipsomania, intemperance, drunkenness, inebriety, insobriety, inebriation, intoxication, winebibbing, delirium tremens, D.T.'s.

ALCOVE, *n.* Recess, booth, retreat, bay, niche, nook, corner, hollow, place of retirement, bower, compartment, cubicle, cubbyhole, secluded spot, garden-house, summerhouse, grotto, pergola, arbor, kiosk.

ALEMBIC, *n.* Ancient retort, still, beaked vessel, heater, distillation apparatus, crucible, converter, condensation-causer, transformer, purifier, refiner.

ALERT, *adj.* 1. Vigilant, Argus-eyed, lynx-eyed, keen-eyed, watchful, wide-awake, open-eyed, attentive, circumspect, guarded, wary, chary, precautious, careful, heedful, regardful, cautious, on guard, on the lookout, observant, on the watch, on the *qui vive*, on the alert, thoughtful, discreet, mindful, prudent, roused, awake.
2. Brisk, spry, supple, agile, nimble, moving with celerity, ready to act, active, prepared, bustling, instant, spirited, alive, frisky, sprightly, smart, lively, astir, enterprising, vivacious, quick, prompt, expeditious, assiduous, sedulous, swift, speedy, rapid, fleet, animated, fast, on one's toes.

ALERTNESS, *n.* 1. Vigilance, watch and ward, watchfulness, wakefulness, attention, surveillance, lookout, circumspection, heedfulness, caution, wariness, guardedness, precaution, prudence, discretion, care, solicitude.
2. Dispatch, expedition, alacrity, celerity, quickness, promptness, liveliness, sprightliness, nimbleness, agility, briskness, haste, promptitude, speed, activity, action, spryness, animation, snap, smartness, vivacity, spirit, dash.

ALIAS, *adv.* Otherwise, *alias dictus (Lat.),* at another time, otherwise called, previously, heretofore, in another place, elsewhere, in other circumstances.

ALIAS, *n.* Another name, assumed name, false name, pseudonym, fictitious name, pen name, nom de plume.

ALIBI, *n.* Plea of being in another place, defense of being elsewhere, way out, plausible excuse, any excuse *(colloq.).*

ALIEN, *n.* Foreigner, stranger, emigrant, one of another race, immigrant, outlander, outsider, newcomer, resident foreigner, one excluded from some body or privilege.

ALIEN, *adj.* 1. Of foreign origin, unnaturalized, foreign, not native, introduced from abroad, adventitious, exotic, extrinsic, outlandish, distant, barbarian, tramontane, remote, strange.
2. Wholly different in nature, dissimilar, unlike, conflicting, contradictory, inappropriate, contrary, contrasted, differing, irrelevant, not assimilated, impertinent, incongruous, unallied, unharmonized, inconsistent with, unconnected, separated, unrelated, inapplicable.
3. Hostile, opposed, adverse, unsympathetic, repugnant, inimical, antagonistic.

ALIENATE, *v.* 1. Transfer title to another, make over, part voluntarily with ownership of, consign, deliver over, lease, surrender, devolve, convey, assign, surrender, dispose of, forfeit.

2. Make indifferent or averse, make inimical, turn away, estrange, disunite, disaffect, separate, withdraw the affections of, wean away, make unfriendly, set against, come between, divide.

ALIENATION, *n.* 1. Transfer of title to another, demise, abalienation, transference, drawing off, conveyance, consignment, delivery, surrender, assignment, disposal.
2. Withdrawal, estrangement, coolness, breach, disaffection, rupture, separation, weaning away, division, variance, diverting, deflection.
3. Mental or psychiatric illness, derangement, insanity, lunacy, madness, mania, aberration, delirium, dementia, hallucination, unsoundness of mind, craziness, frenzy, delusion, obsession.

ALIGHT, *v.* 1. Stop after flight, drop down on, come to rest upon some support, descend and settle, stay after descending, lodge, perch, fall upon, strike, reach, light on, pitch upon, come down on, ground oneself, locate on.
2. Get down from, dismount, spring down, descend, land, detrain, disembark.
3. Chance upon, come upon unexpectedly, hit upon, encounter accidentally, come across, light upon.

ALIGN, *v.* 1. Adjust to a line, lay out by line, regulate by line, arrange in line, place in line, range, line up, collimate, make parallel, make even, dress, straighten.
2. Array on the side of, join with others in a cause.
3. Come into line, fall into line, form in line, get in line, be in line.

ALIKE, *adj.* Having similarity, similar, having resemblance, resemblant, exhibiting no difference from, indistinguishable, akin, selfsame, identical, like, twin, duplicate, copied, facsimile, parallel, corresponding, same, uniform, mated, matched, fellow-paired, even, equivalent, equal, cognate, tantamount, interchangeable, consubstantial, homogeneous, synonymous, homologous, allied, analogous, correlative, kindred, of a piece, one and the same, ditto.

ALIKE, *adv.* In the same manner, to the same degree, of the same form, akin, together, in common, equally, both.

ALIMENT, *n.* Food, nutriment, nurture, victuals, diet, comestibles, eatables, edibles, provision, fare, board, keep, commissariat, regimen, viands, meal, repast, rations, cheer, meat, flesh, bread, staff of life, meat and drink, cuisine, foodstuff, means of support, sustenance, the necessaries of life, subsistence, pabulum, feed, provender, corn, fodder, pasture, pasturage, forage, nourishment.

ALIMENTARY, *adj.* Nourishing, wholesome, nutritive, digestible, nutritious, dietetic, nutrient, comestible, strengthening, alimental, eutrophic, sustentative, eupeptic, salutary, invigorating, succulent, supplying sustenance, providing maintenance, esculent.

ALIMENTATION, *n.* Nourishment, nutrition, sustentation, sustenance, support, mode of being nourished, process of affording nutriment, maintenance.

ALIMONY, *n.* 1. Separation money, divorce settlement, maintenance-allowance, heart balm, court order.
2. Sustenance, means of living, maintenance, support, nourishment, aliment.

ALIVE, *adj.* 1. In a living state, in existence, existent, existing, live, viable, having life, alive and kicking, breathing, subsisting, extant, vivified, animate, quick, not dead, above ground.

2. Open to impressions, impressionable, easily impressed, sensitive to, aware of, responsive to, susceptible, having susceptibility, with keen perceptions, attentive to, awake, vigilant, alert to, conscious of, cognizant of, aware.

3. In a state of action, in motion, in force, in operation, in existence, active, operative, in full vigor, unextinguished, unexpired, unquenched, glowing.

4. Full of life, lively, spirited, sprightly, in an animated state, joyous, cheerful, sportive, brisk, vivacious, spry, agile, vigorous, energetic, eager, restless, bustling, busy.

5. Filled with living things, thronged, replete, swarming, teeming, rife, fraught, overflowing, full, abounding.

ALL, *adj.* 1. The whole number of, the entire extent of, every one of, each, each and every, any, any and every, every part of, any whatever, total, complete, the sum of, every member of, undivided, perfect, integral, universal, full, only, alone, nothing except, nothing but.

2. The greatest possible, the utmost possible, as much as possible.

ALL, *n.* Total, whole, aggregate, sum, entirety, totality, everything, completeness, *tout ensemble (Fr.),* collectiveness, complexus, undividedness, integrality, allness, omnitude, universality, sum total, intactness, organic unity, integer, length and breadth of, everybody, gross amount.

ALL, *adv.* In complete or highest degree, totally, altogether, completely, wholly, entirely, quite, utmost, exclusively, only, solely, alone, very, exceedingly, apiece, each, to a man, just, even, at the exact time or place.

ALLAY, *v.* 1. Put at rest, quiet, cause to subside, cause to be still, still, silence, quell, calm, lay, compose, subdue, hush, lull, smooth, restrain, tranquilize, appease, pacify, check, repress, suppress.

2. Mitigate, relieve, alleviate, assuage, soothe, moderate, temper, soften, mollify, lighten, ease, qualify, palliate, blunt, dull, slake, quench, lessen, slacken, reduce, diminish.

ALLEGATION, *n.* 1. Positive declaration, formal averment, affirmation, claim, asseveration, charge, avouchment, assertion without proof, predication, avowal, profession, statement, deposition, thesis, accusation, argument.

2. Justification, plea, excuse, pretext.

ALLEGE, *v.* 1. Declare with positiveness, affirm to be true, claim, asseverate, aver, avouch, assert without proof, predicate, maintain, avow, state, profess, say, protest, depose, testify, bear witness to, vouch.

2. Urge as a reason, bring forward as a ground, produce, introduce, present, offer, lay down, propose, adduce, advance, impute, assign, ascribe, attribute, plead in support of, cite, name, quote.

ALLEGIANCE, *n.* Fidelity, fealty, loyalty, duty owed, faithfulness, constancy, devotion, homage, obligation, troth, observance of obligation, deference, subjection, submission, compliance, subservience, adherence.

ALLEGORICAL, *adj.* Figurative, not literal, representative, significative, typical, metaphorical, tropical, symbolic, emblematical.

ALLEGORIZE, *v.* 1. Use allegory, turn into allegory, narrate in allegory, figure, shadow forth, adumbrate, typify, symbolize, represent, make a parable of, prefigure, image forth, illustrate.

2. Understand figuratively, treat as allegorical, interpret allegorically.

ALLEGORY, *n.* 1. Figurative treatment of one subject under the guise of another, figurative representation, symbolical narration, fiction, tale, veiled presentation, fable, parable, apologue, myth, story.

2. Suggestive resemblance, comparison, figure, metaphor, simile, analogy, trope, illustration.

3. Type, image, emblem, symbol, token.

ALLEVIATE, *v.* Assuage, mitigate, palliate, diminish, lessen, slacken, reduce, remit, succor, relieve, temper, attemper, qualify, smooth, calm, remedy, lighten, allay, moderate, mollify, soften, soothe, still, quiet, quell, appease, abate, lull, ease, compose, dull, blunt, tranquilize, hush, deaden, smother, weaken, check, tame, curb, restrain, subdue, solace, console.

ALLEVIATION, *n.* Lessening, abatement, relief, diminution, moderation, assuagement, mitigation, palliation, reduction, easement, amelioration, softening, sedation, slackening, remittance, allayment, mollification, appeasement.

ALLEY, *n.* 1. Back street, byway, narrow street, lane, mall, back-passage, slum, footway, dead end, cul-de-sac, crow-way.

2. Garden path, enclosed walk, bordered way, covered way, passageway, way, passage, aisle, pathway, thoroughfare.

ALLIANCE, *n.* 1. Union, junction, combination, fusion, coalition, league, association, confederacy, federation, confederation, trust, combine, society, partnership, copartnership, company, syndicate, joining of interests, convention, amalgamation.

2. Formal agreement, treaty, compact, pact, covenant, concordat, contract, bargain, *entente cordiale (Fr.).*

3. Marriage, intermarriage, affinity, kinship, relation, nuptial tie, wedlock.

4. Relationship in qualities, connection, similarity, affiliation, concurrence, sympathy.

ALLIED, *adj.* 1. Joined by treaty, confederated, leagued, federate, corporate, incorporated, amalgamated, connected, united, associated, bound, joined, cooperating, in cooperation.

2. Analogous, similar, alike, like, resembling, cognate, corresponding, kindred, akin, related, germane, congeneric.

ALL-INCLUSIVE, *adj.* Comprehensive, extensive, all-embracing, complete, without omissions, full, compendious, capacious, synoptic, comprising, encircling.

ALLOT, *v.* 1. Distribute by lot, partition, divide, apportion, share, mete out, deal out, parcel out, portion out, dole out, measure, give out, quarter, dispense.

2. Appropriate to a special purpose, earmark, allocate, detail, destine, prescribe, assign, specify, appoint, fix, set apart, select, destinate, design, intend, ordain, designate, apply, determine, adjudge, administer.

3. Hand over, grant, give, bestow on, present, render.

ALLOTMENT, *n.* 1. Distribution by lot, award, apportionment, assignment by share, partition, division, deal, dispensation, consignment, grant, appointment, dole, gift, appropriation, allocation, administration, designation.

2. Share, portion, dividend, part, lot, ration, quota, measure, allowance, meed, pittance, stint, grant for support, stated maintenance.

ALL-OUT, *adj.* 1. Using all resources, complete, total, full, entire, thoroughgoing.

2. Aggressive, offensive, vigorous, determined, full pelt, pulling no punches, no holds barred, energetic, powerful, forcible, mighty, resolute.

ALLOW, *v.* 1. Interpose no obstacle in the way of, permit, suffer to occur, let, indulge, authorize, empower, give permission to, favor, oblige, grant leave to, privilege, vouchsafe, license, warrant, enfranchise.

2. Admit, own, acknowledge, confess, concede, recognize, grant, take for granted.

3. Suffer, bear, endure, tolerate, bear with, put up with, take patiently, submit to, yield to, brook, abide, stand.

4. Let have, assign as one's right, grant, allot, give, afford, spare, accord, yield, relinquish.

5. Approve of, give consent to, sanction, justify, accept.

6. Take into account, set apart, deduct, abate, make allowance for, remit.

ALLOWABLE, *adj.* Permissible, warrantable, justifiable, admissible, proper, not improper, not objectionable, unprohibited, lawful, unforbidden, licit, legitimate, legal, legalized, chartered, sanctioned, conventional, tolerated, suffered, tolerable, excusable, acceptable, venial, pardonable.

ALLOWANCE, *n.* 1. Allotment, grant for support, stated maintenance, settled rate, stipend, salary, remittance, fee, pay, recompense, hire, wages, quarterage, viaticum, commission, stint, pittance, gift, contribution, pension, aid, annuity, alimony, subvention, subsidy, dole, hand out, largesse, bounty, pin money, pocket money.

2. Limited amount, portion, share, ration, stated quantity, quota, dosage, mess, diet.

3. Permission, sufferance, leave, assent, license, sanction, authorization, approval, approbation, tolerance, connivance, authority, permit.

4. Acceptance, admission, acknowledgment, recognition, concession, acquiescence.

5. Discount, abatement, deduction, reduction, rebate, margin for deviation from standard, qualification, modification, extenuation.

ALLOY, *n.* 1. Metallic compound, combination of metals, amalgam, alloyage, admixture, fusion, combine, synthesis.

2. Less costly metal mixed with a more valuable one, pinchbeck, deleterious ingredient, baser element, adulteration, deterioration, depreciation, impairment, debasement.

3. Standard, quality, fineness.

ALLOY, *v.* 1. Admix a metal with a baser one, mix metals, modify by admixture, intermix, fuse, interfuse, compound, amalgamate, blend, form into an alloy, adulterate, combine by mixing.

2. Reduce the purity of, reduce in value, debase, impair, degrade, depreciate, lower, abate, deteriorate, allay, temper, moderate.

ALL RIGHT 1. Safe and sound, well, healthy, unimpaired, uninjured, hale, perfect, complete, whole.

2. Yes, okay.

3. Quite correct, satisfactory, true.

4. Without fail, beyond doubt, certainly, assuredly.

ALLUDE, *v.* Make indirect reference to, refer casually, suggest, hint, imply, indicate, advert,

relate, insinuate, intimate, mention, point, touch upon, signify, cite, quote, convey.

ALLURE, *v.* Tempt, lure, attract, draw, lead on, invite, decoy, bait, troll, ensnare, entrap, charm, entice, seduce, lead astray, beguile, captivate, bewitch, fascinate, exercise attraction, intrigue, engage, engross, enchant, cast a spell, tantalize, whet the appetite, induce, persuade, prevail on, win over, coax, cajole, inveigle, toll.

ALLUREMENT, *n.* Enticement, attraction, bait, magnetism, fascination, charm, enchantment, bewitchery, temptation, seduction, witchery, decoy, ensnarement, beguilement, captivation.

ALLURING, *adj.* Tempting, enticing, seductive, fascinating, charming, bewitching, enchanting, captivating, enrapturing, ravishing, irresistible, prepossessing, winsome, tantalizing, appealing, inviting, winning, attractive, beauteous, sensuous, stirring, exciting, voluptuous.

ALLUSION, *n.* Incidental mention, insinuation, casual reference, implied indication, intimation, hint, inference, innuendo, indirect implication, suggestion, quotation, citation.

ALLUSIVE, *adj.* Having reference to something not fully expressed, suggestive, referential, hinting.

ALLUVIUM, *n.* Earthy material deposited by floods, sediment, detritus, silt, deposit, gravel, drift, wash, sand.

ALLY, *v.* Join by alliance, connect by formal agreement, unite, confederate, league, combine, bind together, connect by marriage, bring into affinity, make similar, band together, bring into close relationship.

ALLY, *n.* Assistant, helper, helpmate, helping hand, coworker, cooperator, collaborator, aider, colleague, confrere, associate, coadjutor, partner, mate, friend, auxiliary, supporter, upholder, backer, seconder, advocate, adherent, companion, accessory, confederate, abettor, accomplice.

ALMANAC, *n.* Calendar, astronomical table, ephemeris, year book, register of the year, registry, farmer's almanac, nautical almanac, statistical almanac, world almanac, *fasti (Lat.).*

ALMIGHTY, *n.* The Omnipotent, King of Kings, the Most High, the First Cause, the Infinite, the Divine Being, the Eternal, the Deity, the Supreme Being, Jehovah, God Almighty, Divine Father, Sovereign of the Universe, the Creator, Providence, the Absolute, the All-Father, Author of all things, the Lord of Lords, the All-wise, the All-Powerful, the Omniscient, the Triune God, the All-knowing, God the Father, the King of Glory, the Maker, the Light of the World, the All-sufficient.

ALMONER, *n.* Alms-dispenser, distributor of alms, dispenser of charity, distributor of bounty, steward, functionary, treasurer, alms-giver, church official.

ALMOST, *adv.* Nearly, well-nigh, all but, for the most part, in large part, within a little, towards, a little short of, not quite, very nearly, *circa (Lat.),* approaching, approximately, bordering on, virtually, partially, in part, thereabouts, about that, adjoining, not far from, nigh, about, close to, roughly, touching, hard by, next door to, in sight of, on the verge of, at the point of, within an inch of.

ALMS, *n.* Dole, bounty, gratuity, baksheesh, cumshaw *(China),* douceur, gift for the relief of the poor, benefaction, beneficence, work of mercy, charity, charitable donation, offerings, eleemosynary aid, maundy-coins, contribution, public subscription, subsidy, present, assistance, pittance, largess, sportula, hand out, Christmas box.

ALMSGIVING, *n.* Benefaction, munificence, benevolence, beneficence, subvention, charity, philanthropy, liberality, generosity, altruism, humanitarianism, large-heartedness, public spiritedness.

ALMSHOUSE, *n.* Poorhouse, house for paupers, eleemosynary institution, asylum, refuge, shelter, workhouse *(Brit.)*.

ALOFT, *adv.* 1. In a higher place, on high, in the air, high above the ground, skyward, in the sky, heavenward, in heaven, in the clouds, high up, above, overhead, up, above, heaven-high.
2. *(Naut.)* At the masthead, in the top, in the upper rigging.

ALONE, *adj.* 1. Without any company, sharing with no other, single, solitary, apart from others, lonely, lonesome, isolated, separate, unattended, unaccompanied, without company, forlorn, *solus,* companionless, forsaken, deserted, abandoned, desolate.
2. To the exclusion of all others, only, sole, all by oneself, lone, of one's self, on one's own power, unaided, unassisted, without any aid, without help.
3. Without any equal, with no competitor, unparalleled, matchless, unique, incomparable, unmatched, peerless.

ALONE, *adv.* Singly, solely, by oneself, solitarily, without help, single-handedly, separately, *per se,* merely, only, simply.

ALONG, *prep.* From one end to the other of, through the length of, throughout, through, in the course of, alongst, by the side of, on the border of, on the line of, in the direction of.

ALONG, *adv.* 1. Lengthwise, by the length, in a line with the length, longitudinally, parallel to the length.
2. With a progressive motion, onward, in a line, forward.
3. In company, as a companion with one, together, by the side, side by side, beside, at the same time, simultaneously.

ALONGSIDE, *adv.* By the side of, close to the side, along the side, at the side, beside, abreast.

ALOOF, *adv.* At a distance, withdrawn, apart, separately, away, afar, off, by oneself, not wishing to associate with others, not in sympathy with others.

ALOOF, *adj.* Distant, remote, standoffish, formal, removed in distance or interest, reserved, cool, cold, frigid, offish, unapproachable, unsociable, unsympathetic, unneighborly, uncommunicative, unresponsive, disinterested, indifferent, haughty, high-hat.

ALOUD, *adv.* 1. With the speaking voice, with ordinary vocal strength, with the natural tone of the voice, not whisperingly, in a clear voice, distinctly, audibly, plainly, clearly.
2. With a loud voice, vociferously, at the top of one's lungs, obstreperously, loudly, noisily, sonorously, clamorously, lustily, in full cry, blatantly, thunderingly, deafeningly, uproariously, ear-splittingly, stentoriously, clangorously.

ALPHABET, *n.* 1. The letters of a language,

symbols, characters, signs, hieroglyphs, graphic representation, pictograph, ideograph, syllabary, rune, consonants and vowels, system of characters.
2. First rudiments, elements of a subject, the A B C, beginnings, first steps, first principles.

ALPHABETIZE, *v.* Furnish with an alphabet, arrange alphabetically, express by alphabetical symbols.

ALPINE, *adj.* Very high, high-reaching, elevated, mountainous, lofty, towering, rangy, soaring, aerial, heaven-kissing, cloud-capped, ice-peaked, snow-clad.

ALREADY, *adv.* 1. By the time mentioned, by this time, even now, but now, just now, by now.
2. Prior to some specified time, before that time, previously, beforehand, formerly, before now.

ALSO, *adv.* In addition, besides, likewise, withal, additionally, moreover, further, furthermore, in like manner, to boot, over and above, including, in conjunction with, conjointly, more than that, along with, together with, as well as, ditto, therewithal, thereto, yet, *au reste (Fr.).*

ALTAR, *n.* 1. Sacrificial structure, raised place, place of sacrifice, elevation for offerings.
2. Place devoted to prayer, shrine, place of worship, sanctuary, holy place, Holy of Holies, *sanctum sanctorum, penetralia,* inner shrine, high altar, adytum.
3. Communion-table, Lord's table, holy table, God's board.

ALTER, *v.* 1. Make different, make some change in, modify, qualify, transform, transmute, shift, transfigure, commute, vary, change, adjust, turn, convert, metamorphose, exchange, emend, invert, shuffle, reconstruct, remodel, transpose, recast, diversify, remold, reverse.
2. Geld, castrate, spay, emasculate, deprive of the ovaries.
3. Become different, reform, moderate, amend, become better, mend.

ALTERATION, *n.* Change, mutation, exchange, permutation, transmutation, transfiguration, modification, qualification, adjustment, shifting, conversion, metamorphosis, variation, deviation, vicissitude, variance, transposition, transition, turn, change-over, innovation, reduction, revolution, inversion, transference, reversal.

ALTERCATE, *v.* Argue with heat, differ, clash, spar, spat, brawl, tiff, have words, be at variance, quarrel, wrangle, disagree, expostulate, dispute, jangle, squabble, contend in words, fall out, remonstrate, bicker.

ALTERCATION, *n.* 1. Angry dispute, heated debate, controversy, wrangle, war of words, wordy contest, logomachy, disagreement, strife, jangling, jarring, contention, quarrel, bickering, sparring, disputation, divergence, dissension, discord, difficulty, difference, variance, argument.
2. Affray, broil, fracas, scene, scuffle, scrap, row, brawl, spat, rumpus, melee, feud, contest, tumult, riot, disturbance.

ALTERNATE, *adj.* 1. One after another, being by turns, following each the other, reciprocal, first one and then the other, reciprocative, changing back and forth by turns, consecutive, successive, succeeding regularly, following in a series.
2. Every other, every second, separated by

one, interrupted by one, following an interval of one, the next but one.

3. On each side alternately, on different sides successively, not opposite, opposite to the intervals between.

ALTERNATE, *v.* 1. Reciprocate, rotate, change about by turns, follow one another reciprocally, act interchangeably, vary, interchange, take turns, reverse direction periodically, pass back and forth between, vacillate, crossruff.

2. Perform by turns, perform responsively, interchange successively, cause to succeed by turns, interchange regularly, cause to alternate, change by alternation, intermit.

ALTERNATE, *n.* Substitute, second, person authorized to take the place of another, deputy, proxy, representative, *locum tenens (Lat.),* vicar, understudy, pinch hitter.

ALTERNATION, *n.* Interchange, reciprocation, rotation, alternate succession, occurrence by turns, change by turns, appearance by turns, recurrence, periodicity, taking of turns, passage from one place to another, interpolation, substitution, variation, oscillation, vacillation.

ALTERNATIVE, *n.* Choice between two things, option, preference, remaining course, other choice, horn *(of a dilemma),* selection, election, recourse, pick, shift, substitute, *embarras de choix (Fr.).*

ALTHOUGH, *conj.* Admitting that, granting that, supposing that, even though, though, be it that, for all that, in spite of the fact that, even if, even supposing, notwithstanding that, albeit that, despite the fact that.

ALTITUDE, *n.* 1. Vertical elevation, height above sea level, perpendicular distance, extent upward, distance upward, loftiness, tallness, pitch, stature, extreme limit, celsitude.

2. Exalted position, sublimity, culmination, grandeur, eminence, dignity, apex, ascendancy, zenith, vertex.

ALTOGETHER, *adv.* 1. In complete degree, wholly, with no exception, completely, totally, entirely, quite, utterly, throughout, *in extenso (Lat.),* thoroughly, out and out, on the whole, to the full, in the main, *in toto (Lat.),* perfectly, fully, in general, outright, wholesale, finally, permanently.

2. Collectively, as a whole, in the aggregate, in sum total, bodily, in a body, in a mass, all, all in all, conjointly, *en masse (Fr.), en bloc (Fr.), tout ensemble (Fr.).*

ALTRUISM, *n.* Regard for the interests of others, devotion to others, universal good will, love of others, public spirit, unselfishness, benevolence, humanitarianism, generosity, liberality, action in behalf of others, large-heartedness, magnanimity, disinterestedness, beneficence.

ALTRUISTIC, *adj.* Devoted to others, friendly to man, humanitarian, public-spirited, attached to the common weal, large-hearted, humane, benevolent, considerate, thoughtfully kind, disinterested, magnanimous, beneficent, liberal, generous, bountiful, charitable, philanthropic, unselfish.

ALUMNUS, *n.* 1. A foster son, a male ward or pupil, disciple.

2. Male graduate of an institution of learning, scholar with degree, former student.

ALWAYS, *adv.* 1. Perpetually, eternally, forever, ever, evermore, for aye, to the end of time, throughout all time, continually, through all

ages, sempiternally, everlastingly, unceasingly, coeternally, endlessly, round-the-clock, through thick and thin, unremittingly, incessantly, all the time.

2. At all times, invariably, uniformly, on every occasion, constantly, regularly at stated intervals, whenever opportunity offers, uninterruptedly, on every contingency, consistently, at all times, infallibly.

AMAIN, *adv.* 1. With full force, forcibly, with might and main, violently, vehemently, headlong, furiously.

2. At full speed, quickly, without delay, in great haste, hastily.

3. Suddenly, all at once.

4. Exceedingly, greatly, to a high degree.

AMALGAM, *n.* 1. Alloy of mercury with another metal, mercurial compound, mixture of other metals with quicksilver, alloy of silver and mercury.

2. Mixture, commixture, combination, union, compound, composite.

AMALGAMATE, *v.* 1. Combine with mercury, blend with another metal, alloy.

2. Mix so as to make a combination, combine into a whole, commix, commingle, merge in a single body, unite, consolidate, incorporate, blend, compound, unify.

AMALGAMATION, *n.* 1. Combination with mercury, alloy.

2. Mixture, commixture, intermingling, union, commingling, blending, coalescence, coalition, consolidation, combination, compound, fusion, interfusion, junction, conjunction, alliance, merger, intermixture.

3. Intermarriage of different racial stocks, miscegenation, biological fusion of diverse races.

AMANUENSIS, *n.* Secretary, scrivener, scribe, copyist, transcriber, recorder, registrar, writer, stenographer, clerk, quill-driver.

AMARANTHINE, *adj.* 1. Of or like the amaranth.

2. Unfading, everlasting, immortal, imperishable, indestructible, incorruptible, undecaying, fadeless, abiding, enduring, undying, deathless, everfresh, ever-blooming, ever-vernal, perennial.

3. Purplish red, bluish red, amethystine, purpureal.

4. Sweet-scented, nectared, luscious, fragrant, redolent, odorous, ambrosial, elysian, perfumed, balmy, rosy.

AMASS, *v.* Gather for oneself, collect as one's own, accumulate, pile up, heap up, store up, hoard, scrape together, bring together, rake up, gather into a pile, aggregate, assemble, cumulate, build up, muster, concenter, reserve, treasure, save.

AMATEUR, *n.* 1. Nonprofessional cultivator of an art, one with a taste for, devotee, admirer, dilettante, connoisseur, critic.

2. Superficial worker, unskilled practitioner, neophyte, tyro, novice, dabbler, dabster, beginner, greenhorn, Corinthian, volunteer, one who toils for joy.

AMATORY, *adj.* Erotic, amorous, passionate, impassioned, fervent, lovesome, tender, devoted, Anacreontic, fond, rapturous, lovesick, doting, languishing, sentimental, romantic.

AMAZE, *v.* Astonish greatly, overwhelm with surprise, stagger, dumfound, daze, stupefy, stun, flabbergast, astound, startle, petrify with wonder, strike with wonder, perplex, confound, bewilder, confuse, dazzle, electrify, take away one's breath, strike dumb.

AMAZEMENT, *n* Overwhelming surprise, awe, stupefaction, bewilderment, perplexity, confusion, astonishment, marvel, wonder, wonderment, amazedness.

AMAZING, *adj.* Causing great surprise, fabulous, marvellous, miraculous, prodigious, wondrous, wonderful, portentous, preternatural, striking, highly extraordinary, surprising, stupendous, strange, incredible, unexpected, inconceivable, remarkable, unprecedented, singular, astounding, astonishing, bewildering, confounding, perplexing, confusing.

AMAZON, *n.* Female warrior, aggressive female, formidable woman, virago, termagant, Tartar, Xanthippe, Penthesilea, spitfire, fury, brawler, shrew, scold, vixen.

AMBAGES, *n. pl.* 1. Sinuosities, winding paths, turnings, circuits, anfractuosities, serpentine courses.
2. Indirections of speech, circumlocution, periphrasis, verbiage, largiloquence, volubility, wordiness, diffuseness, redundancy, pleonasm, verbosity.
3. Ambiguities, evasions, tortuous courses, roundabout ways, quibbles, quirks, subterfuges.

AMBAGIOUS, *adj.* 1. Circuitous, serpentine, roundabout, tortuous, devious, sinuous, winding, anfractuous, meandering.
2. Indirect, ambiguous, amphibolous, evasive, full of subterfuge.
3. Circumlocutory, periphrastic, pleonastic, diffuse, redundant, voluble, wordy, largiloquent.

AMBASSADOR, *n.* 1. Resident representative of a foreign state, minister of the highest rank, minister of state, official diplomatic agent, envoy, plenipotentiary, legate, deputy, dignitary, nuncio, commissioner, emissary.
2. Authorized messenger, herald, proclaimer, publisher, announcer, harbinger, courier, agent, intermediary.

AMBIENT, *adj.* 1. Completely surrounding, lying round about, encompassing on all sides, enclosing, investing, enfolding, circumambient, enveloping, embosoming, environing, encircling, circumjacent.
2. Circulating, moving round about, moving in a circle.

AMBIGUITY, *n.* 1. Uncertainty of meaning, equivocalness, doubtfulness, vagueness, duplexity, obscurity, indefiniteness, incertitude, dubiousness, unintelligibility, reconditeness, amphibology, abstruseness.
2. Double meaning, *double-entendre (Fr.),* ambiguous expression, play upon words, pun, paradox.

AMBIGUOUS, *adj.* 1. Having a double meaning, capable of being understood in more than one sense, open to various interpretations, doubtful, amphibolous, susceptible of more than one meaning, problematical, dubious, paradoxical, doubtful, ambagious, equivocal, enigmatical, uncertain, quibbling.
2. Of uncertain nature, puzzling, mystifying, difficult to comprehend, perplexing, apocryphal, unintelligible, cryptic, oracular, mysterious, delphic, occult, recondite, abstruse, misleading.
3. Lacking clearness, not clear, indefinite, indeterminate, not plain, vague, indistinct,

obscure, unsettled, inconclusive, questionable, disputable, mistakable, confused.

AMBITION, *n.* 1. Desire for superiority, love of glory, eagerness for distinction, appetite for fame, aspiration, emulation, yearning.
2. Object sought after, objective, goal, dream, desideratum, hope, purpose, design, intent, resolve, aim, destination.
3. Desire for work or activity, energy, zeal, drive, striving, spirit, vigor, animation, activity, intensity, mettle, impetus, verve, vim, dash.

AMBITIOUS, *adj.* 1. Eager for superiority, emulous of fame, high-reaching, aspiring, anxious for power, vaulting, highflying, soaring, ardent, longing, Icarian, bold.
2. Inordinately eager, greedy, desirous, avid, intent, appetitive, covetous, wishful, worldly, discontented, dissatisfied, grasping, avaricious, envious.
3. Showing ambition, enterprising, energetic, daring in undertaking, wide-awake, aggressive, pushing, zealous, active, forcible, mettlesome, strenuous, alert, in earnest.
4. Ostentatious, showy, aiming at effect, pretentious, conspicuous, assuming.

AMBLE, *v.* 1. Move to an easy pace, go at a gentle gait, pace, jiggle, jog trot, dogtrot, lope, canter.
2. Walk affectedly, dawdle, saunter, meander, jaunt, ramble, stroll, traipse *(colloq.),* toddle, mince, paddle, bowl along, jog on, prance.

AMBROSIA, *n.* Immortality-giving food, food of the gods, heavenly food, food fit for the gods, savory fare, delectable sustenance.

AMBROSIAL, *adj.* 1. Especially delicious to taste, luscious, dainty, delectable, palatable, savory, honeyed, sweet, sugary, toothsome, mouth-watering.
2. Sweet-smelling, odoriferous, fragrant, spicy, scented, aromatic, balmy, odorous, redolent, perfumed, amaranthine.
3. Worthy of the gods, heavenly, celestial, divine, ethereal, glorious, golden, everlasting, beatific.

AMBULATE, *v.* Walk about, move about, go on foot, go from place to place, course, rove, roam, range, traverse, perambulate, stroll, saunter, foot it, jaunt, ramble, promenade, wend one's way.

AMBULATORY, *adj.* Capable of walking, not stationary, adapted to walking, walking, moving, shifting about, mobile, movable, changeable, itinerant, peripatetic, not confined to bed *(Med.).*

AMBUSCADE, *n.* 1. Act of hiding to surprise adversaries, lying in wait, lurking, concealment.
2. Place of hiding, ambush, secret-place, trap, retreat, lurking-place, hiding-place, means of concealment, cover, snare, pitfall, screen, blind, lure.

AMBUSH, *v.* Wait in an ambuscade, lie in wait for, lie concealed, lurk, skulk, keep out of sight, set a trap for, ensnare, entrap, attack from a concealed position, waylay, bait the hook, spread the toils, decoy, hook-in, benet.

AMELIORATE, *v.* 1. Make better, better, mend, meliorate, improve, amend, correct, reform, rectify, advance, promote, raise, elevate.
2. Allay, soften, relieve from pain, ease, help, mitigate, mollify.

AMELIORATION, *n.* 1. Betterment, melioration, improvement, amendment, reformation, revision, correction, rectification, advancement, promotion, elevation.

2. Easement, mitigation, relief, mollification, assuagement, alleviation, palliation.

AMEN, *interj.* It is so, so it is, be it so, so be it, so shall it be, let it be so, would that it were so.

AMEN, *adv.* Verily, truly, assuredly.

AMENABILITY, *n.* 1. Liability, accountability, answerableness, responsibility, responsibleness to authority, amenableness.

2. Openness to suggestions, docility, pliancy, compliancy, willingness, readiness, obedience, yieldingness, acquiescence, inclination, agreeableness, submissiveness, tractability, responsiveness, adaptability.

AMENABLE, *adj.* 1. Liable, accountable, subject to authority, answerable, responsible, obligated.

2. Open to suggestions, docile, able to be influenced by, within the reach of, tractable, responsive, compliant, manageable, yielding, pliant, obedient, submissive, willing, acquiescent, agreeable, persuadable, reasonable.

AMEND, *v.* 1. Alter by due formal procedure, revise, emend, add to.

2. Change for the better, adjust, better, heal, remodel, ameliorate, reclaim, reorganize, restore, repair, reconstruct, mend, redeem, purify, cleanse, compensate, recompense, relieve, remedy, mitigate, advance.

3. Remove faults in, correct, rectify, free from faults, put right, set right, edit, doctor, touch up, polish.

4. Grow better by reforming oneself, become better, improve, mend.

AMENDMENT, *n.* 1. Change for the better, improvement, amelioration, betterment, revision, reformation, alteration, correction, emendation, reorganization, melioration.

2. Modification of a law, motion, legislative addition, bill.

AMENDS, *n.* Recompense, compensation for loss, reparation, restoration, restitution, indemnity, requital, redress, indemnification, quittance, sop, payment, reward, guerdon, peace offering, *quid pro quo,* consideration, return, acknowledgment, salvage, propitiation, retribution, douceur, hush-money, atonement, satisfaction, expiation, apology.

AMENITY, *n.* 1. Pleasantness, agreeableness, niceness, gentleness, mildness, delightfulness, softness, delectableness.

2. Polish, gallantry, suavity, chivalry, comity, politeness, urbanity, good breeding, amiability, good behavior, good manners, obliging manner, complaisance, affability, geniality, refinement, gentility, blandness, pink of politeness, courtesy, graciousness, civility.

AMERCE, *v.* Punish by a pecuniary penalty, fine, mulct, impose a fine upon, penalize, sconce, estreat, forfeit, deprive of, confiscate, strip of, escheat, sequestrate.

AMERCEMENT, *n.* Pecuniary penalty, sconce, mulct, escheat, estreat, forfeiture, deprivation, fine, confiscation, sequestration.

AMIABILITY, *n.* Agreeableness, pleasantness, attractiveness, winsomeness, charm, sweetness, lovableness, kindliness, graciousness, politeness, suavity, blandness, cordiality, urbanity, amenity, complaisance, friendliness, amicableness, good humoredness, affability, benignity, sweet temper, sweetness of disposition, kindheartedness, obligingness.

AMIABLE, *adj.* Agreeable, pleasing, attractive, charming, winning, engaging, winsome, sweet, lovable, kindly, gracious, pleasant, polite, suave, bland, cordial, urbane, complaisant, obliging, friendly, amicable, affable, benign, gentle, nice, sweet-tempered, good-humored, kind-hearted, good-natured, well-disposed, benignant, lovely, worthy of love.

AMICABLE, *adj.* Showing good will, friendly, sociable, neighborly, fraternal, companionable, familiar, obliging, benevolent, hearty, cordial, well-disposed, kind, warm-hearted, sympathetic, kindly, agreeable, advantageous, kindhearted, propitious, favorable, harmonious, peaceable, concordant, pacific, affectionate.

AMICABLENESS, *n.* Friendliness, sociability, amity, neighborliness, cordiality, friendly feeling, good will, friendship, kindliness, benevolence, kindheartedness, warm-heartedness, concordance, agreeableness, harmoniousness, peaceableness.

AMIDST, *prep.* Amid, mid, midst, among, in the middle of, amongst, encompassed by, with, surrounded by, between, betwixt, mingled with.

AMISS, *adj.* Done out of suitable order, beside the mark, untimely, inopportune, misdirected, improper, erroneous, fallacious, wrong, faulty, inaccurate, incorrect, inexact, false, untrue, ill, mistaken, abortive, awry, untoward, unpropitious, disadvantageous, inappropriate, perverse, unwise, unfavorable, injudicious, unsuitable, unworthy, bad.

AMISS, *adv.* Out of the proper course, astray, beside the mark, out of order, wrong, improperly, wrongly, in a faulty manner, faultily, incorrectly, inaccurately, inexactly, falsely, erroneously, ill, mistakenly, badly, unfittingly, untowardly.

AMITY, *n.* Friendliness, amicableness, friendship, fraternity, brotherhood, good understanding, mutual good feeling, peaceful relations, accord, agreement, sympathy, good will, fellowship, affection, cordiality, unity, harmony, unanimity, peace, concord, tranquility.

AMMUNITION, *n.* 1. Materials of combat, store of arms, military stores, munitions, matériel, sinews of war, supplies of projectiles, provisions, armament, firearms, means of attack.

2. Explosives, powder and shot, gunpowder, charge, cartridges, rockets, missiles, bullets, ball, slug, shells, propellants, shrapnel, torpedoes, bombs, grenades, mines, pyrotechnics, chemicals.

AMNESIA, *n.* Loss of memory, impairment of memory, obliteration of the past, obliviousness, morbid forgetfulness, oblivion, inability to recall, gap in one's memory, lapse of memory, *lapsus memoriae (Lat.),* Lethe, waters of oblivion.

AMNESTY, *n.* General pardon, absolution from penalty, universal forgiveness of past offenses, immunity, acquittal, non-remembrance, peace, protection against punishment, overlooking, truce, reconciliation, reprieve.

AMONG, *prep.* 1. Amid, amongst, amidst, in the midst of, in the middle of, mingled with, in intercourse with, in association with, surrounded by, in connection with, encompassed by, betwixt, between, in dispersion through.

2. To each of, for distribution to.

3. In the number of, in the group of, in the class of, in the company of, in the country or time of, according to the customs of.

4. With all, by all, by the whole of, by joint action of, by the reciprocal action of, affecting all of, shared by the generality of.

5. Each with the other, mutually.

AMOROUS, *adj.* 1. Influenced by sexual appetite, erotic, full of sexual passion, having a propensity for sexual activity, prone to sexuality, lustful, carnal, lecherous, libidinous, lascivious, sensual, voluptuous, lewd, licentious, prurient, salacious, concupiscent, lickerish, unchaste, passionate, wanton.

2. In love, enamored, fond, loving, ardent, longing, tender, affectionate, devoted, sweet upon, lovesick, smitten, over head and ears in love, doting, infatuated.

3. Amatory, impassioned, Anacreontic.

AMOROUSNESS, *n.* 1. Sexual appetite, venery, passion, sensuality, lust, concupiscence, sexuality, lecherousness, libidinousness, voluptuousness, carnality, lasciviousness, lewdness, wantonness, licentiousness, pruriency, salaciousness, dalliance.

2. Ardency, fondness, tenderness, devotion, lovesickness, infatuation, affection.

AMORPHOUS, *adj.* 1. Having no specific shape, shapeless, lacking definite form, formless, unshapely, irregular, unshapen, unsymmetrical.

2. Of no particular kind or character, vague, characterless, indeterminate, unorganized, clumsy, anomalous, heterogeneous, nondescript, confused, disorganized, chaotic, anarchic, misshapen.

3. *(Geol.)* Structureless, non-crystalline, without stratification, uncrystallized, occurring in a mass.

AMOUNT, *n.* 1. Aggregate, totality, sum total, sum, net quantity, whole, lot, pack, deal, mass, footing up.

2. Full effect, total substance, purport, value, import, significance, sum and substance, result, harvest.

AMOUNT TO, *v.* 1. Reach in the aggregate, be equal in quantity to, aggregate, be in the whole, be in all, total up to, sum up to, foot up to, rise by accumulation to, come to, mount to, extend to.

2. Be equivalent to, be substantially, average, be in effect, approximate, approach, come near.

AMOUR, *n.* Love affair, amourette, romance, affair, *affaire de coeur (Fr.),* affair of gallantry, *affaire d'amour (Fr.),* love intrigue, illicit relation, liaison, clandestine intimacy.

AMPLE, *adj.* 1. Of great size, large, big, great, commodious, capacious, extensive, expansive, bulky, wide, spacious, vast, outspread, roomy, extended, immense, broad, considerable, huge, voluminous, boundless.

2. In full measure, abundant, affluent, full, unstinted, unrestricted, plentiful, abounding, plenteous, copious, rich, profuse, lavish, liberal, bountiful, complete, overflowing, exuberant, luxurious, handsome, generous, munificent.

3. Enough and to spare, fully sufficient for the purpose, adequate to the needs, plenty, satisfactory, commensurate.

AMPLIFICATION, *n.* 1. Enlargement, expansion, extension, broadening, greatening, development, dilation, heightening, increasing, augmentation, swelling.

2. Expatiation, copious discourse, extended remark, full detail, diffuse narrative, elaboration, fulness, prolixity, descant, comment on a subject, verbosity, minute detail.

AMPLIFY, *v.* 1. Make larger, enlarge, extend, magnify, expand, greaten, widen, heighten, add to, lengthen, increase in scope, augment, dilate, raise, swell, spread out.

2. Make copious, expand in stating, go into detail, add something to what has been said, discourse at length, expatiate on, treat more fully, dilate on, speak with fulness of illustration, make more explicit, present in all aspects, fill out the details, develop, unfold, supplement, continue, branch out.

3. Exaggerate, overstress, overstate, overcharge, render more important, strain, stretch, overdo, overcolor, hyperbolize, overdraw, draw a long bow, romance, embroider, enhance.

AMPLITUDE, *n.* 1. Extension in space, size, greatness of extent, bigness, greatness, fulness, largeness, capaciousness, spaciousness, width, breadth, extent, volume, bulk, dimensions, mass, bulkiness, roominess, vastness, latitude, capacity, magnitude, measure.

2. Large or full measure, abundance, plenty, copiousness, exuberance, profusion, richness, fulness, plenitude, sufficiency, completeness, luxuriance, affluence, repletion, plethora.

3. Range, sweep, compass, scope, extent, reach, expanse, swing, field.

AMPUTATE, *v.* Remove by cutting, cut off, cut away, sever, clip, separate, prune, lop, curtail, excise, dismember, mutilate, dislimb, disjoint.

AMUCK, *adv.* In a murderous frenzy, crazedly, berserk, maniacally, ferociously, violently, in indiscriminate attack, with frenzied fury, blood-thirstily.

AMULET, *n.* Protecting charm, rabbit's foot, phylactery, talisman, preservative, safeguard, anything with occult protective power, abraxas, apotropaion, periapt, telesm, tefillin, swastika, scarab, triskelion, gammadion, merrythought, wishbone, furcula, horseshoe.

AMUSE, *v.* 1. Hold the attention agreeably, stir with pleasing emotions, please, entertain, divert, beguile, interest, occupy, engross, absorb, cheer, charm, gladden, relax, recreate, enliven, solace, disport, gratify, cause time to pass agreeably, dally, regale, exhilarate, rejoice, take one's fancy, do one's heart good.

2. Excite mirth in, cause to be merry, raise a smile, titillate, convulse with laughter, tickle to death.

AMUSEMENT, *n.* 1. Gratification, entertainment, diversion, pleasure, fun, recreation, relaxation, enjoyment, cheer, delight, merriment, joviality, merrymaking, pleasantry, jocoseness, distraction, jollity, drollery, tomfoolery, mummery, gaiety, dalliance, pastime, jollification, revelry.

2. That which amuses, spectacle, game, sport, play, festivity, fete, festival, carnival, junket, gambol, romp, prank, practical joke, antic, lark, skylarking, spree, escapade.

AMUSING, *adj.* 1. Pleasantly entertaining, light, pleasing, diverting, distracting, delighting the fancy, pleasurable, interesting, absorbing, lively, engrossing, recreative, beguiling, sportive.

2. Exciting mirth, ludicrous, ridiculous, risible, laughable, comical, funny, facetious, farcical, droll, witty, jocose, jovial, hilarious, jolly, joyful, sidesplitting, humorous, witty, salty, waggish, jocular.

ANACHRONISM, *n.* Chronological error, error in assigning a date, misdate, occurrence out of its proper time, misplacement in time, incongruity in point of time, antedate, prolepsis, prochronism (*before the real date*), postdate, metachronism (*after the real date*).

ANACREONTIC, *adj.* 1. Convivial, symposiac, wine-bibbing, festive, festal, jovial, gay.
2. Amatory, amorous, passionate, impassioned, ardent, erotic, fervent.

ANACREONTIC, *n.* Erotic song, amatory poem, madrigal, drinking song.

ANALECTS, *n. pl.* Selected passages, selections, extracts, selected pieces, quotations, citations, excerpts, collection of literary fragments, literary gleanings, collectanea, analecta, compilation, sayings, fugitive pieces, anthology, florilegium, cuttings.

ANALEPTIC, *adj.* Giving strength after disease, roborant, tonic, restorative, strengthening, invigorating, comforting.

ANALEPTIC, *n.* Analeptic medicine, restorative, strengthening medicine, roborant, tonic.

ANALGESIA, *n.* Insensibility to pain, absence of sense of pain, painlessness.

ANALOGOUS, *adj.* Resembling in some particular, related, associated, similar in relations, same, like, akin, kindred, cognate, comparable, parallel, equivalent, correspondent, correlative, identical, homogeneous, homologous, allied, of a piece.

ANALOGY, *n.* Resemblance, agreement, partial similarity, likeness, similitude, comparison, parity, affinity, coincidence, correspondence, proportion, parallelism, relation, semblance, correlation, connection.

ANALYSIS, *n.* 1. Resolution of a compound into its parts, determination of the elements of a compound, decomposition, dissection, partition, dissociation, subdivision, anatomy, reduction, disintegration, breakup, breakdown, separation of a whole into its constituents.
2. Brief presentation of essential features, outline, summary, synopsis, syllabus, résumé, abstract, précis, epitome, digest, condensation, brief, aperçu, conspectus, abridgment, review, compendium, abbreviation.
3. Examination, investigation, study, inquiry, consideration, sifting, test of elements, search, induction.
4. Psychoanalysis, psychiatry, psychotherapy.

ANALYST, *n.* 1. A person skilled in making analyses, fact-sifter, investigator, inquisitor, examiner, catechist, assayer.
2. Psychiatrist, alienist, neuropsychiatrist, psychoanalyst.

ANALYTICAL, *adj.* Resolving into first principles, resolvent, treating of analysis, separative, solvent.

ANALYZE, *v.* 1. Subject to analysis, decompose into constituent parts, resolve into elements, determine the essential features of, anatomize, dissect, separate, disintegrate, examine minutely.
2. Examine critically, investigate, compare critically, collate, discriminate, inquire into, review, study, question, catechize.

ANARCHICAL, *adj.* Lawless, ungoverned, riotous, disordered, turbulent, tumultuous, disobedient, unruly, ungovernable, rebellious, seditious, Red, subversive, tending to overthrow, mutinous, insurgent, revolutionary, nihilistic, Bolshevik, anarchistic.

ANARCHIST, *n.* Revolutionist, subverter, Red, nihilist, terrorist, insurgent, mutineer, Jacobin, disorder-promoter, revolt-exciter, rabble-rouser, demagogue, extreme radical, malcontent, renegade.

ANARCHY, *n.* Absence of government, political disorder, lawlessness, social upheaval, terrorism, avowed hostility to government, nihilism, reign of violence, misrule, sedition, tumult, turmoil, revolution, rebellion, riot, chaos, disorganization, confusion, insubordination, derangement, mutiny, insurgence, uprising, insurrection.

ANATHEMA, *n.* 1. Ecclesiastical curse, malison, imprecation of divine punishment, malediction, commination, fulmination, proscription, ban, denunciation, abomination, condemnation, execration, excommunication.
2. A person or thing consigned to damnation.

ANATHEMATIZE, *v.* Pronounce an anathema against, denounce, execrate, maledict, call down curses on the head of, fulminate against, damn, imprecate, proscribe, ban, excommunicate, revile, condemn, comminate, accurse, curse with bell, book and candle.

ANATOMIZE, *v.* 1. Cut asunder for examination, dissect, vivisect, hominisect, anatomatize, display the anatomy of.
2. Examine minutely, analyze, pull to pieces, scrutinize, lay open, probe, sift, discriminate carefully.

ANATOMY, *n.* 1. Dismemberment, vivisection, dissection for study of structure, hominisection, zootomy, phytotomy.
2. Structure, framework, constructional plan, structural form.
3. Skeleton, bony structure, anatomical model, body (*humorously*).

ANCESTOR, *n.* Progenitor, primogenitor, genitor, forefather, forebear, forerunner, predecessor, precursor, author, begetter, procreator, patriarch, originator.

ANCESTRAL, *adj.* Lineal, hereditary, inherited, patrimonial, racial, patriarchal.

ANCESTRY, *n.* 1. Lineage, race, house, family, series of ancestors, line, caste, ancestral descent, pedigree, stock, birth, genealogy, heredity, root, extraction, parentage, progeniture, stem, trunk, stirps, family tree, breed.
2. Honorable descent, high birth, nobility, hereditary rank, noble blood.

ANCHOR, *n.* 1. Mooring, ground tackle, kedge, grapnel, killick, grappling iron, sheet anchor, drag anchor, drift anchor, floating anchor, screw anchor, mushroom anchor, bow anchor, waist anchor, sea anchor.
2. Safeguard, mainstay, sure protection, hold, security, support, stay, defense, a reliance in danger, means of stability.

ANCHOR, *v.* 1. Secure by anchor, affix firmly, fix securely, fasten, fix in a stable condition, moor.
2. Drop anchor, cast anchor, ride at anchor, hold fast, take firm hold, rest, tarry, stop, abide, settle.

ANCHORAGE, *n.* Place for anchoring, harbor, roadstead, port, resting-place, harborage, refuge, berth, security, mooring, secure connections.

ANCHORITE, *n.* Recluse, hermit, mortifier of the flesh, cenobite, eremite, anchoret, solitary, *solitaire (Fr.)*, ascetic, troglodyte, monk, nun, pillar saint.

ANCIENT, *adj.* 1. In time long past, dating in a

remote period, pristine, olden, old, primitive, of eld, primordial, immemorial, primeval, of old time, prehistoric, belonging to times long past.

2. Aged, of great age, of long duration, very old, superannuated, veteran, venerable, hoary, patriarchal, gray, senior, decrepit, time-honored, timeworn.

3. Obsolete, obsolescent, antiquated, antique, out-of-date, old-fashioned, archaic, former, past, out-of-fashion, bygone, outworn, outmoded, passé.

ANCIENTLY, adv. In olden times, in days of yore, in ancient times, a long while ago, in days long gone by, of old.

ANCILLARY, adj. 1. Serving as an aid or adjunct, accessory, auxiliary, contributory, instrumental, helpful.

2. Subordinate, subsidiary, secondary, inferior, subservient, dependent, minor.

ANDIRON, n. One of a pair of metal hearth supports for firewood, firedog, fireplace lift, dog.

ANDROGYNOUS, adj. Uniting the characters of both sexes, bi-sexed, bisexual, hermaphroditic, being both male and female.

ANECDOTE, n. Short narrative of a particular incident, brief account of an interesting event, story of private life, biographical account, short story, sketch, legend, myth, story, tale, relation, reminiscence, history, memoir, yarn, instance, illustration.

ANECDOTIST, n. Storyteller, raconteur, relator, narrator, romancer, chronicler, yarn-spinner, describer.

ANEMIA, n. 1. Deficiency of hemoglobin, lack of blood, reduction of red blood cells, poverty of blood, bloodlessness.

2. Pallor, weakness, breathlessness, wanness.

ANEMIC, adj. 1. Thin-blooded, deficient in blood, lacking red blood cells, deficient in hemoglobin.

2. Pallid, wan, pale, bluish-white, breathless, weak.

ANESTHESIA, n. Local insensibility to pain and other sensations, loss of sense of feeling, stupor, insentience, unconsciousness of pain, suspended consciousness, numbness, suspended sensibility, coma, analgesia, narcosis.

ANESTHETIC, n. Pain-suppressing agent, drug, gas, dope, sedative, opiate, soporific, novocaine, agent inducing insensibility, ether, chloroform, cocaine, chloral, nitrous oxide, morphine.

ANEW, adv. As a new act, newly, in a new or different manner, over again in a different way, afresh, once more, again, de novo (Lat.).

ANFRACTUOUS, adj. Crooked, twisted, bent, sinuous, serpentine, turning, winding, devious, circuitous, meandering, tortuous, ambagious, intricate, mazy, labyrinthine, spiraling, circling, flexuous.

ANGEL, n. 1. Glorified spirit, supernatural being, winged being, seraph, cherub, ministering spirit, celestial spirit, attendant of God, heavenly spirit, archangel, invisible helper, guardian spirit, messenger of God.

2. A person resembling an angel in character or beauty, saint.

3. Financial backer, patron, Maecenas, friend in need, fairy godmother, tutelary angel, special providence.

ANGELIC, adj. 1. Heavenly, ethereal, spiritual, divine, celestial, saintly, seraphic, cherubic, archangelic.

2. Pure, good, righteous, ideal, beautiful, adorable, entrancing, transporting, rapturous, lovely, enrapturing.

ANGER, n. Emotion of displeasure, revengeful passion, feeling of antagonism, fury, ire, ill temper, hot temper, hot blood, rage, wrath, irascibility, animosity, flare-up, exasperation, gall, exacerbation, frenzy, choler, dander, spleen, huff, pique, umbrage, indignation, bile, resentment, annoyance, tiff, vexation, disapprobation, hatred, irritation, provocation, enmity, tantrum, vials of wrath, impatience, petulance, fretfulness, chagrin, acrimony, distemper, sharpness, dudgeon, violence.

ANGER, v. Annoy, provoke, exasperate, ruffle, exacerbate, irritate, vex, gall, nettle, chafe, rile, incense, fret, affront, offend, embitter, arouse, displease, rouse, enrage, madden, infuriate, inflame, excite to wrath, keep at the boiling point, arouse the ire, make bad blood, stir up a hornet's nest.

ANGLE, n. 1. (Geom.) Space within two planes diverging from a common line, difference of direction of two lines, point where two lines meet, divergence, obliquity, flare.

2. Angular projection, projecting corner, bend, elbow, crook, knee, fork, crotch, edge, notch, shoulder, cusp, Y, branch.

3. Nook, corner, cantle, recess, niche, coign, out-of-the-way place.

4. Point of view, standpoint, viewpoint, attitude of mind.

5. Aspect, side, phase, guise, stage.

6. Hook, fishhook.

ANGLE, v. Fish with hook and line, bob, bait.

ANGLE FOR, v. Try by artful means to get, plot for, scheme for, maneuver for, try to attain by artifice, hint for, intrigue for, strive for.

ANGLER, n. Fisherman, piscator, fisher, baiter.

ANGLICISM, n. English idiom, characteristic English quality, Briticism.

ANGLICIZE, v. Give an English form to, make English in character, introduce into English.

ANGRY, adj. Annoyed, provoked, exasperated, exacerbated, displeased, vexed, irritated, chafed, galled, riled, incensed, nettled, piqued, indignant, resentful, offended, affronted, wroth, enraged, sullen, splenetic, choleric, irate, furious, huffy, irascible, hostile, rabid, infuriated, infuriate, raging, storming, mad, impassioned, in high dudgeon, out of temper, in a pet, in the tantrums, in a passion, out of humor, fuming, fiery, fierce, ferocious, steamed up, flown off the handle, inflamed (as a sore), at the boiling point, purple in the face, with one's back up.

ANGUISH, n. Agony of mind or body, pang, acute suffering, severe distress, intense pain, excruciating torment, agonizing torture, throe, rack, paroxysm, affliction, wound, aching, misery, excessive grief, anxiety, woe, dolor, sorrow, heartache, remorse.

ANGUISH, v. Distress with grief or pain, affect with anguish, torture, torment, rack, put in great pain, wring, excruciate, trouble, harry, make miserable, disturb, worry, agonize.

ANGULAR, adj. 1. Pointed, with corners, sharp-cornered, crooked, bent, forked, bifurcate, jagged, divaricate, crotched, V-shaped, Y-shaped, scraggy.

2. Bony, rawboned, gaunt, spare, lean, lank, lanky, scrawny.

3. Acting or moving awkwardly, ungraceful, uncouth, ungainly, gauche, maladroit.

4. Stiff in manner, unbending, abrupt, edged, sharp, crabbed.

ANILE, *adj.* Like a weak old woman, aged, doting, old-womanish, superannuated, infirm, childish, feeble-minded, foolish, simple, imbecile.

ANILITY, *n.* Old-womanishness, decrepitude, caducity, weakness, imbecility, superannuation, dotage.

ANIMADVERSION, *n.* Critical remark, censure, censorious comment, reproof, rebuke, reproach, adverse criticism, check, disapproval, stricture, reflection, blame, aspersion, reprehension, fault-finding, condemnation, reprobation, chiding.

ANIMADVERT UPON, *v.* Remark by way of censure, comment critically, pass criticism, make censorious remarks, censure, reprove, disapprove, find fault with, protest against, remonstrate, expostulate, object to, take exception to, criticize severely.

ANIMAL, *n.* 1. Sentient being, creature, living being, created being.

2. Any animal other than man, dumb creature, dumb animal, irrational creature, beast, zoon (*zool.*), vertebrate, invertebrate, mammal, beast of the field, quadruped, denizen of the deep, fowl of the air.

3. Inhuman person, brutish person, brute, monster, fiend, sensualist.

ANIMAL, *adj.* 1. Sentient, living, sensate, existing, animate.

2. Derived from animals, composed of flesh, meaty.

3. Physical, fleshly, natural, unspiritual, bodily, carnal, sensual, brutish, beastlike, gross, beastly, coarse, low, vulgar, impure, obscene.

ANIMAL SPIRITS, *n.* 1. Vital principle, *élan vital (Fr.)*, nervous force, life, nervous fluid, creative force.

2. Vigor, energy, spirit, animation, élan, spiritedness, impulsiveness, light-heartedness, impetuosity, exuberance, buoyancy of spirit, good humor.

ANIMATE, *v.* 1. Impart life to, quicken, inform, vitalize, make alive, vivify, arouse, give life to, endue with life, furnish with vital principle.

2. Energize, invigorate, give energy to, make lively, strengthen, fortify, keep alive.

3. Actuate, move to action, impel, instigate, stimulate, incite, rouse, arouse, activate, waken, stir, kindle, goad, urge, work up, provoke, whet, prompt, warm, fire, heat, excite, enkindle, set on, enliven, spur on, imbue, move.

4. Inspire, embolden, hearten, encourage, elate, inspirit, enhearten, flush, elevate, erect, cheer, gladden, exhilarate, delight.

ANIMATED, *adj.* Spirited, hearty, fervent, ardent, alive, glowing, buoyant, airy, sprightly, vivacious, brisk, full of action, lively, full of life, full of spirit, elated, blithe, gay, jocund, sportive, passionate, quick, hot, bright, vivid, active, vigorous, sanguine, breezy, glad, zealous, alert, mettlesome, earnest.

ANIMATING, *adj.* Vivifying, elevating, inspiriting, spirit-stirring, life-giving, rousing, exhilarating, enlivening, exciting, cheering, encouraging, stimulating, heart-stirring, inspiring.

ANIMATION, *n.* 1. Vitalization, inbreathing of life, vivification, stimulation, act of making alive.

2. Vitality, vital power, breath of life, vital spark, life.

3. Activity, alacrity, liveliness, briskness, vigor, buoyancy, promptitude, enthusiasm, alertness, vivacity, spiritedness, sprightliness, airiness, fire, elasticity, force, energy, strength, courage, ardor, warmth, fervency, verve, spirit, edge, glow, dash, élan, eagerness, mettle, brightness, gaiety, cheer, exhilaration, animal spirits, good spirits, high spirits.

ANIMOSITY, *n.* Feeling of antagonism, malice, malevolence, malignity, hatred, enmity, hostility, vehement opposition, antipathy, dislike, anger, detestation, abhorrence, rancor, spite, resentment, spleen, hate, ill will, unfriendliness, pique, gall, umbrage, grudge, animus, acerbity, acrimony, bitterness, virulence, rankling aversion, loathing, feud, contention, invidiousness.

ANIMUS, *n.* 1. Hostile spirit, feeling of hatred, malice, animosity, partisan feeling.

2. Purpose, mind, will, intention, inclination, general tone, temper, disposition, spirit, animating nature.

ANNALIST, *n.* Historian, chronicler of yearly events, recorder, historiographer, writer of annals, memorialist, biographer.

ANNALS, *n.* History in the order of years, relation of events in chronological order, narrative of events in their order of time, yearly history, chronicles, records, historical rolls, registers, historical memoirs, archives, journal, state-papers, documents, diary.

ANNEAL, *v.* Subject to high heat, smelt, heat to remove internal stress, heat in order to fix laid-on colors, reduce brittleness, bake, temper by slow cooling, harden, toughen, make enduring.

ANNEX, *v.* 1. Join, adjoin, subjoin, affix, append, attach, add to, superadd, tack to, tag, suffix, add at the end, postfix.

2. Make an integral part of something larger, incorporate, consolidate, unite, connect, combine, blend, merge.

3. Appropriate, expropriate, seize, take to oneself.

ANNEXATION, *n.* 1. Attachment, annexment, joining, adjoining, affixing, appending, accession, suffixment, additament, augmentation, addition.

2. Incorporation, consolidation, connection, union, conjunction, combination, junction, merger.

3. Appropriation, expropriation, seizure.

ANNIHILATE, *v.* 1. Put to death, slay, kill, cut down, mow down, massacre, slaughter, decimate, murder, execute, do to death.

2. Put an end to, put out of existence, destroy utterly, exterminate, eradicate, extirpate, crush, raze, demolish, ruin, blast, wreck, ravage, root out, dismantle, dissolve, quench, extinguish, blot out from being, overthrow, obliterate, consume, end, devour, expunge, efface, reduce to nothing, cause to cease to exist, bring to naught, unmake, undo, do away with.

3. Cancel the effect of, annul, nullify, make void, invalidate, render of no effect, destroy the force of, vitiate, revoke.

ANNIHILATION, *n.* 1. Slaying, killing, cutting down, mowing down, massacre, assassination, decimation, slaughter, murder, finishing stroke, execution, deathblow.

2. Utter destruction, extermination, ruination,

eradication, extirpation, demolition, wreckage, ravagement, dissolution, extinction, obliteration, expungement, effacement, end, undoing, wiping out, unmaking, abolition, disestablishment, nullification.

3. Cessation of being, nonexistence, oblivion, non-being, nothingness, nullity, nihility, eternal blank, vacuum, *non-esse (Lat.), tabula rasa (Lat.).*

ANNIVERSARY, *adj.* Returning each year, yearly, recurring yearly, happening at a fixed time annually, commemorated at the same date each year, performed each year, annual.

ANNIVERSARY, *n.* Yearly recurrence of the date of a past event, commemoration of a past event, yearly observance of an event, memorable date, celebration of a date, day of annual celebration, annual festival, feast-day, fete, red-letter day, holiday, birthday, natal day, saint's day, annual meeting, centenary, biennial, triennial, octennial, quadrennial, quinquennial, sextennial, septennial, novennial, decennial, silver anniversary, golden anniversary, diamond jubilee, sesquicentennial, bicentenary, tercentenary, etc.

ANNOTATE, *v.* 1. Furnish with explanatory notes, remark upon in notes, supply with notes, equip with critical notes, gloss, gloze, interlineate, marginalize.

2. Commentate, elucidate, interpret, expound, explain, illustrate, clear up, shed light upon, account for.

ANNOTATION, *n.* 1. Marginal notes, marginalia, footnotes, gloss, scholium, postil, critical notes, glossary.

2. Critical explanation, exegesis, exposition, interpretation, elucidation, illustration, remark, observation, commentary.

3. Act of annotating, supplying with notes, making of notes, commenting.

ANNOTATOR, *n.* Writer of annotations, scholiast, commentator, glossarist, interpreter, expounder, expositor, explainer.

ANNOUNCE, *v.* 1. Make known publicly, publish, broadcast, advise, proclaim, tell, inform, notify, enunciate, declare roundly, assert, affirm, state, acquaint, report, reveal, propound, set forth, apprise, call out, disseminate, give out, signal, sound abroad, bruit, blazon, promulgate, bill, circulate, cry out, bulletin, post, placard, trumpet, advertise, noise abroad, communicate, spread abroad, lay before the public, herald abroad, give notice of, bring before the notice of the public, make proclamation of.

2. State the approach or presence of, usher in, give notice of the arrival of, herald the coming of, harbinger, foretell.

3. Predict, forecast, prognosticate, prophesy, presage, augur, bode, forebode, foretoken, give intimation of, shadow forth, betoken, portend, signify, make known to the mind, make manifest.

ANNOUNCEMENT, *n.* 1. Public advertisement, formal notice, notification, promulgation, decree, divulgation, disclosure, communication, rescript, annunciation, declaration, enunciation, mention, proclamation, recital, statement, affirmation, publication, publicity, broadcast.

2. Message, bulletin, news, tidings, report, pronunciamento, communiqué, manifesto, edict, banns, prospectus, advices, information, word, letter, telegram, wire, cable, handbill, bill, post, placard, affiche, circular, poster, broadside, form letter, encyclical, leaflet, pamphlet, brochure, letter-card, missive, flier.

3. Prediction, prognostication, presagement, forecast, prophecy, augury, signification, manifestation.

ANNOY, *v.* Injure by repeated acts, harm, **pain,** wound, do harm to, molest, torment, **plague,** tantalize, bother, pester, tease, hector, **heckle,** badger, harry, harass, worry, irritate, ruffle, **irk,** chafe, fret, vex, roil, nettle, pique, **persecute,** trouble, discommode, inconvenience, **incommode,** disturb, displease, disquiet, provoke, **embarrass,** offend, affront, gall, distress, discompose, **hamper,** distract, nag, pinprick, raise the hackles.

ANNOYANCE, *n.* 1. State of being annoyed, vexation, worry, uneasiness, solicitude, malaise, discomfort, molestation, disturbance, trouble, stew, mortification, chagrin, discomposure, hurt, inconvenience, harassment, distress, displeasure, disquiet, botheration, pique, abomination, care, dissatisfaction, resentment, umbrage, distress, torment, irritation, infliction, misery, unhappiness, despair, torture, grief, sorrow, heartache, anxiety.

2. That which annoys, affliction, scourge, bane, thorn, plague, trial, ordeal, tribulation, burden, load, fret, bore, canker, nuisance, pest, bother, bitter pill, gall and wormwood, thorn in the flesh, affront.

ANNOYING, *adj.* Irritating, aggravating, tedious, galling, bothersome, tiresome, troublesome, harassing, thorny, painful, irksome, provoking, vexatious, unpleasant, disagreeable, distasteful, unwelcome, obnoxious, odious, execrable, taxing, distressing, afflictive, mischievous, inconvenient, burdensome, onerous, oppressive, disheartening, plaguing, pestering, enough to provoke a saint.

ANNUAL, *adj.* Yearly, recurring once a year, occurring every year, anniversary, reckoned by the term of a year, valid for use during one year, performed in a year, lasting a year, living only one growing season, expiring each year.

ANNUAL, *n.* 1. Yearbook, literary production published annually, illustrated yearly gift book, yearly report, yearly record, annals of science or letters, yearly transactions.

2. *(Bot.)* Plant living only one year or season.

ANNUALLY, *adv.* Yearly, by the year, once a year, *per annum (Lat.),* year after year, every year.

ANNUITY, *n.* Specified income payable for life, amount of money payable yearly, money coming in, annual allowance, income, pension, yearly sum granted in fee, return from an investment of capital, revenue.

ANNUL, *v.* 1. Render null and void, make of no effect, nullify, disannul, invalidate, quash, cancel, revoke, retract, recall, rescind, recant, overrule, override, set aside, vacate, countermand, reverse, counteract, withdraw, repeal, abrogate, abolish, dissolve, supersede, avoid, nol-pros *(Leg.),* break off, contravene, repudiate, disclaim, disestablish, suspend, discharge, counter-order, contradict.

2. Reduce to nothing, annihilate, destroy, do away with, extinguish, obliterate, blot out, undo, efface, put an end to, stop.

ANNULAR, *adj.* Ring-shaped, ringlike, having the form of a ring, forming a ring, ringed, banded or marked with rings, circular, rounded, orbed, annulated, orbicular, spherical, globular, discoid, globose, cylindrical, rotundate.

ANNULET, *n.* 1. Little ring, annulus, circlet, hoop, loop, eyelet, grommet, orb, disc, band, coil.

2. (*Arch.*) Fillet, encircling band, cincture, list, tenia, listel, molding.

ANNULMENT, *n.* Nullification, abrogation, recall, rescission, retractation, repeal, recantation, repudiation, revocation, invalidation, cancellation, vacatur (*Leg.*), annulling, disestablishment, nolle prosequi (*Leg.*), reversal, countermand, avoidance, counterorder, dissolution, quashing, discharge, defeasance, undoing, abolition.

ANODYNE, *n.* Pain-killer, analgesic, agent to diminish sensibility, medicine to remove pain, sedative, calmative, distress-easer, mitigative, stupefacient, assuasive, palliative, lenitive, opiate, demulcent, hypnotic, narcotic, nepenthe, poppy, opium, laudanum, mandragora, morphine, salve, mandrake, soothing syrup, ointment, balm in Gilead, febrifuge.

ANOINT, *v.* 1. Put oil on, rub over with unctuous matter, smear with oily liquid, pour oil on, apply an unguent to, oil, salve, grease, lubricate, lard, chrism, balsam, moisten, spread over, anele.

2. Consecrate by unction, hallow, sanctify, inunct, render reverend, dedicate, devote, set apart as sacred.

ANOMALOUS, *adj.* Deviating from the common rule or type, not conforming to the usual, queer, unusual, aberrant, abnormal, irregular, erratic, unconformable, eccentric, anomalistic, peculiar, exceptional, unnatural, preternatural, monstrous, odd, strange, singular, unaccountable, out of the way, out of keeping, uncommon, amorphous, disordered, heteroclite, rare, unique.

ANOMALY, *n.* Deviation from the common rule, abnormality, abnormity, irregularity, something out of keeping, aberration, departure, exception, unconformity, eccentricity, monstrosity, peculiarity, singularity.

ANON, *adv.* 1. In a little while, in a short time, soon, early, quickly, shortly, presently, ere long, before long, eftsoons, betimes.

2. Immediately, at once, straightway, directly, forthwith, on the instant, instanter, without delay, apace.

3. At another time, then, again, afterward.

4. In the same direction, straight ahead.

ANONYM, *n.* Assumed name, false name, alias, pseudonym, fictitious name, sobriquet, pen name, nom de plume, nom de guerre, stage name, nom de théâtre.

ANONYMOUS, *adj.* Nameless, unnamed, bearing no name, innominate, without a name, having no acknowledged name, not disclosing a name, of unknown authorship, pseudonymous, without the name of the author, pseudo.

ANOTHER, *adj.* 1. A different, a distinct, some other, a separate, of a different kind, divergent, heterogeneous, variant, unidentical, unlike, not the same, dissimilar, contrastive, any other.

2. A second, a further, an additional, one more, a later.

ANSWER, *v.* 1. Give back words in return, reply, give answer, retort, rejoin, say in reply, make answer, respond, return, retaliate, act in response to, acknowledge, echo, comply, react, replicate.

2. Be responsible, undertake responsibility, be liable, be surety, be accountable, be security.

3. Have similarity, correspond, conform, be similar, be like, be counterpart, be correlated.

4. Meet requirements, meet a want, serve the purpose, be sufficient, be adequate, be enough, pass muster, do, pass, suit, be satisfactory, do

well enough, be of use, be an equivalent.

5. Suffer in consequence of, pay for, atone for, make amends for, expiate, redeem, make reparation for, settle, satisfy a demand.

6. Speak in defense against, refute, meet by argument, controvert, defend, rebut, account for, counterclaim, recriminate, surrejoin, surrebut, plead, countercharge, counterblast.

7. Give a solution to, solve, satisfy, set at rest, determine, elucidate, explain, interpret, discover, hunt out, inquire.

ANSWER, *n.* 1. Rejoinder, response, replication, reply, retort, repartee, respondence, return, echo, acknowledgment, reverberation, antiphon.

2. Reply to a charge, plea, counterstatement, defense, countercharge, counterclaim, refutation, recrimination, counterblast, rebuttal, confutation, surrejoinder, surrebuttal, retaliation.

3. Solution to a problem, explanation, clue, satisfaction, disclosure, discovery, elucidation, interpretation, key.

ANSWERABLE, *adj.* 1. Liable to be asked to give account, accountable, responsible, obligated to answer, subject, amenable.

2. Capable of being answered, refutable.

3. Correspondent, accordant, corresponding, conformable, correlative, proportionate, adapted, commensurate, agreeable, harmonious, suitable, fit, suited.

ANT, *n.* Emmet, pismire, formicid, formican, termite, carpenter ant, foraging ant, harvesting ant, leaf-cutting ant, mason ant, soldier ant, white ant, black ant.

ANTAGONISM, *n.* Hostility, animosity, antipathy, opposition, aversion, contrariety, repugnance, abhorrence, detestation, loathing, dislike, distaste, hatred, enmity, feud, conflict, discord, repulsion, repellence, adversity, rivalry, emulation, relation of contending parties, competition, activity of conflicting forces, opposing force or tendency, resistance, counterplot, collision, contradiction, clashing, incongruity, incompatibility, dissonance, discordance, inconsistency, disharmony, cacophony.

ANTAGONIST, *n.* Opponent, oppositionist, foe, adversary, disputant, rival, contestant, competitor, assailant, enemy, foeman, opposer, adverse party, sworn enemy, passive resister, objector, die-hard, malcontent, bitter-ender.

ANTAGONISTIC, *adj.* Acting in opposition, at loggerheads, opposing, opposed, counteractive, hostile, inimical, belligerent, adverse, combating, conflicting, unfriendly, irreconcilable, repugnant, uncongenial, loath, contrary, renitent, up in arms, recalcitrant, contradictory, incompatible, on bad terms, incongruous, inconsistent, inharmonious, discordant, dissonant, at variance, at daggers drawn.

ANTAGONIZE, *v.* 1. Make hostile, repel, offend, make an antagonist of, alienate, estrange, make unfriendly, render inimical, disaffect, incur the hostility of, produce antagonism, embitter, turn against, set against.

2. Struggle against, contend with, oppose, act in opposition to, conflict with, counteract, check, be hostile to, work against, compete with, hinder, dispute the mastery with, rival, be at feud with, act in antagonism.

ANTECEDE, *v.* 1. Precede, go before in time or place, preexist, forecome, forerun.

2. Surpass, have precedence, outrank, outstrip,

lead, head, forestall, be beforehand, have the start, anticipate.

3. Usher in, presage, herald, announce, present, introduce.

ANTECEDENCE, *n.* Act of going before, state of being before, anteriority, precedence, priority, preexistence, seniority, superiority, preeminence, preference.

ANTECEDENT, *adj.* Going before, precursory, anterior, forerunning, preceding, preexistent, first, precedent, previous, former, prior, introductory, earlier, preparatory, preliminary, precedaneous, prefatory, prevenient, foregoing, aforementioned, aforesaid.

ANTECEDENT, *n.* 1. Precursor, avant-courier, forerunner, predecessor, harbinger, foreloper, herald, pioneer, outrider, ancestor.

2. (*Pl.*) Family, ancestry, family tree, stock, lineage, genealogy, house, extraction, pedigree, line, progeniture.

3. (*Pl.*) Earlier events of one's life, previous history of an individual, incidents of one's past life, one's past history, record, previous course, preceding circumstances.

4. (*Gram.*) Preceding noun to which a subsequent pronoun refers.

5. (*Logic*) First proposition in an enthymeme, premise, cause.

ANTEDATE, *v.* 1. Be of older date than, occur earlier than, precede in time, forego, go before, be anterior to, antecede, forerun, come first.

2. Date before the true date, predate, misdate, assign to an earlier date, mistime, overdate, date earlier than the fact, date back, anachronize, transfer to an earlier date, accelerate, cause to happen sooner.

3. Take in advance, take before the true time, anticipate, experience beforehand, foretaste, forestall.

ANTEDILUVIAN, *adj.* 1. Before the Flood, before the Deluge, antediluvial.

2. Antique, ancient, old, aboriginal, primitive, troglodytic, primeval, primordial, prehistoric, archaic, immemorial, obsolete, antiquated, old as the hills, timeworn, crumbling, old-fogyish, old as history.

ANTERIOR, *adj.* 1. Previous in time, antecedent, going before in time, earlier, former, foregoing, prior, preceding, going before, introductory, precedent, precursory, preliminary, prevenient, aforesaid.

2. Situated more to the front, placed before, fore, front, forward, in front.

ANTERIORITY, *n.* 1. Antecedence, precedence, priority in time, precedency, preexistence.

2. Position in advance, location at the head, situation in the forefront.

ANTEROOM, *n.* Antechamber, small room with access to a chief apartment, vestibule, lobby, hall, outer room, waiting room, outer office, reception room, fore court.

ANTHEM, *n.* Hymn of devotion, sacred choral composition, sacred song, solemn song, paean, plainsong, chant, motet, antiphon, response, song of praise, offertory, responsory, psalm, song of patriotism.

ANTHOLOGY, *n.* Selections from authors, choice extracts, collection of flowers of literature, *excerpta (Lat.),* literary digest, thesaurus, treasury, compilation, compendium, collection of epigrams, florilegium, literary garland, fugitive pieces,

spicilegium, miscellany, collectanea, analects, pastiche.

ANTHROPOLOGY, *n.* Anthropography, science of the origin of man, anthroposophy, ethnology, science of the natural history of man, science of the varieties of mankind, study of man's cultural development, history of man's divergence from other animals, science of man and his works, archaeology.

ANTHROPOPHAGI, *n., pl.* Cannibals, eaters of human flesh, man-eaters, bloodsuckers.

ANTIC, *adj.* Bizarre, fantastic, grotesque, wild, fanciful, whimsical, extravagant, outlandish, odd, singular, incongruous, ludicrous, preposterous, strange, ridiculous.

ANTIC, *n.* 1. Fantastic action, ludicrous behavior, prank, frolic, romp, caper, gambol, monkeyshine, trick, freak, vagary, sport, dido, rig, lark, spree, skylarking, escapade, tomfoolery, practical joke, mummery, grotesque gesture, ludicrous posture.

2. One who practices odd gesticulations, clown, harlequin, zany, jester, buffoon, merry-andrew, scaramouch, fool, wearer of cap and bells, mime, mountebank, pickle-herring, jack-pudding, punch, farceur, wearer of the motley, pantaloon, witling, caricaturist, madcap.

ANTICIPATE, *v.* 1. Perform an action before another has had time to act, act sooner than, be quicker than, be before another in doing something, get the start on, forestall, preclude, obviate, prevent, intercept, beat to the draw.

2. Accelerate, precipitate, cause to happen earlier.

3. Mention before the proper time, take up beforehand, do beforehand, consider in advance, discharge an obligation before it is due, pay in advance.

4. Look forward to, look toward, expect, count upon, pin hope on, long for, await, look for, hope for, reckon upon, prepare oneself for, calculate upon.

5. Have a previous view of, foretaste, forefeel, experience beforehand, preconceive, precognize, presume, surmise, apprehend, intuit, forecast, predict, foresee.

ANTICIPATION, *n.* 1. Confident expectation, expectancy, prospect, outlook, hope, trust, looking forward, contemplation, preoccupation.

2. Previous notion, slight previous impression, hasty generalization, prematurity of opinion, ill-grounded notion.

3. A prior knowledge, realization in advance, instinctive prevision, presentiment, foreseeing, prescience, foresight, forethought, forefeeling, foretaste, antepast, preassurance, apprehension, prevision, intuition, foreboding, forecast, prior realization, preconception, experience beforehand.

4. Action beforehand, forestalling, obviation, prevenience, prevention, preclusion.

ANTICIPATIVE, *adj.* Presentient, precognoscent, foreseeing, apprehensive, intuitive, foreboding, expectant, sanguine, looking forward, hopeful, precocious, premature, prevenient, proleptic.

ANTICLIMAX, *n.* Falling off in importance, come-down, let-down, bathos, ludicrous descent from the lofty to the less impressive, inglorious conclusion, drop.

ANTIDOTE, *n.* 1. Counterpoison, anti-poison, mithridate, alexipharmic, counteragent, theriac, counteractant, countervenom, antiphlogistic, emetic, preventive.

2. Remedy, corrective, cure, restorative, tonic, specific.

ANTINOMY, *n.* Opposition between laws and principles, mutual contradiction of two principles, irreconcilability between principles, unconformity, self-contradiction, paradox.

ANTIPATHETIC, *adj.* 1 Naturally repugnant, constitutionally opposed, averse, antagonistic, abhorrent, loath, disinclined, reluctant, unwilling.

2. Having a natural contrariety, contrary, counter, antipodean, diametrically opposite, negatory.

ANTIPATHY, *n.* 1. Constitutional aversion, settled dislike, instinctive antagonism, natural repugnance, abhorrence, detestation, reluctance, disgust, distaste, disrelish, disinclination, disfavor, disapprobation, repulsion, nausea, uncongeniality, incompatibility, unfriendliness, ill will, animosity, loathing, hatred, horror, hostility, unwillingness.

2. Instinctive contrariety, opposition in feeling, disagreement, clashing, opposition.

ANTIQUARY, *n.* One versed in the knowledge of ancient things, collector of antiquities, dealer in antiquities, custodian of antiquities, curator of antiquities, paleologist, archaeologist, student of antiquity, antiquarian, archaist.

ANTIQUATE, *v.* 1. Make old and useless by a new and better substitute, render obsolete, cause to have seen its day, make void as out of date, outdate, unmodernize, age.

2. Make antique, give an antique character or appearance to, bring into conformity with the antique.

ANTIQUATED, *adj.* 1. Antique, archaic, bygone, grown very old, aged, ancient, superannuated, of the old school, of other times, antediluvian, gone by, primitive, old-world, timeworn, quaint.

2. Adapted to a former time rather than to the present, ill adapted to present use, disused, outworn, passé, fallen into desuetude, out-of-use, out-of-date, old-fashioned, obsolete, obsolescent, out-of-fashion, unfashionable.

ANTIQUE, *adj.* 1. Belonging to former times, dating from an early period, come down from ancient times, ancient, archaic, bygone, old, aged, superannuated, pristine, timeworn.

2. Old-fashioned, antiquated, outmoded, passé, obsolete, out-of-date, superseded.

ANTIQUE, *n.* 1. Ancient artifact, object of art of a former period, ancient rarity, monument, relic.

2. The antique style, style of ancient art.

ANTIQUITY, *n.* 1. Remote times, former ages, ancient times, early times, the olden time, days of yore, days of eld, hoary eld, early ages, the time before the Middle Ages.

2. State of being ancient, ancientness, great age, oldness.

3. People of ancient times, aboriginals, the ancients.

4. *(Pl.)* Monuments of the past, early remains, relics of ancient times, ancient artifacts.

ANTISEPTIC, *n.* Germicide, disinfectant, agent to destroy microorganisms that produce sepsis, putrefaction-preventive, prophylactic.

ANTITHESIS, *n.* 1. Setting of one clause against another *(rhet.),* balanced contrast, opposition, contraposition, contrariety, dualism.

2. The direct opposite, strong contrast, reverse,

contrary, inverse, converse, antipode, setoff, foil, other extreme, counterpart, pole.

ANTITHETICAL, *adj.* Placed in contrast, directly contrasted, strongly opposed, made up of two opposing qualities, opposite, antipodean, reverse, converse, inverse, diametrical, counter, polar, oppositive.

ANTITOXIN, *n.* Toxin-neutralizer, neutralizing agent, antibody formed by the introduction of a toxin, defensive proteid, preventive, antipoison, antiserum, antiseptic.

ANXIETY, *n.* 1. Mental distress, uneasiness of mind, disquietude, inquietude, solicitude, worry, concern, care, trouble, vexation, disturbance of mind, fretfulness, disquiet, mental anguish, pain, grief, perplexity, suspense, apprehension, dread, misgiving, foreboding, fear, psychic tension.

2. Solicitous desire, eagerness, intentness, wariness, watchfulness.

ANXIOUS, *adj.* 1. Greatly troubled, solicitous, uneasy, disquieted, unquiet, restless, distressed, thoughtful, worried, apprehensive, disturbed, perplexed, fretful, concerned, subject to disturbing suspense, fraught with anxiety, fearful, afraid, exercised, ill at ease, vexed, watchful, vigilant.

2. Earnestly desirous, having the desire intently fixed, intent, eager, earnest, fond, fervent, keen, zealous, sedulous, ardent, avid, impatient.

ANY, *adj.* 1. Whatever or whichever it may be, any one, one, a, an, a single one.

2. Some, in whatever quantity.

3. Every.

4. *(With a negative)* None at all.

ANY, *adv.* Somewhat, to any extent, at all, in any degree, in the least.

ANYHOW, *adv.* 1. In any manner, in any way, whatever, anywise, by any means.

2. In any case, at all events, however that may be, notwithstanding, at any rate, in any event, nevertheless.

3. In a careless manner, indifferently, without arrangement, haphazard, unorderly.

ANYTIME, *adv.* No matter when, any time when, whenever, at any moment, at your convenience, when you will.

ANYWAY, *adv.* 1. In any way or manner at all, anywise.

2. At all events, anyhow, nevertheless, after all.

3. In any case, no matter what happens, in any event, whether wanted or not, regardless, in spite of.

4. Carelessly, haphazard.

APACE, *adv.* At a quick pace, quickly, rapidly, swiftly, speedily, posthaste, hastily, with dispatch, at a great rate, full speed, in full sail, under press of sail, in double quick time, with rapid strides, expeditiously, whip and spur, at top speed, in high gear.

APACHE, *n.* Parisian gangster, desperado, bandit, terrorist, gunman, racketeer, ruffian, bludgeon man, hooligan, ugly customer, criminal, tough.

APART, *adv.* 1. Separately, one from another, singly, severally, individually, independently, privately.

2. To one side, at one side, by oneself, by itself, in isolation, aloof, alone, aside, away, afar, distant, lonely.

3. In two or more parts, part from part, to pieces, asunder, in pieces, disjointly.

APARTMENT, *n.* 1. Set of rooms, suite, flat, story, lodging, tenement.

2. Single room in a building, chamber, hall, compartment, cell, stall, nook, cabin.

APATHETIC, *adj.* 1. Void of feeling, exhibiting no emotion, unemotional, unfeeling, insensible, unimpressible, unsusceptible, cold-blooded, cold, thick-skinned, frigid, stolid, unmoved, impassible, impassive, passionless, stoical, Laodicean, stony, soulless, listless, lethargic, spiritless, torpid, inert, supine, sluggish, unaffected, unanimated, obtuse, dull, phlegmatic, callous, dead, insentient.

2. Indifferent, careless, unconcerned, heedless, pococurante, lukewarm, insouciant, nonchalant, uninterested, lackadaisical, half-hearted, languid, inattentive.

APATHY, *n.* 1. Lack of feeling, unconsciousness of emotion, absence of emotion, dispassion, want of passion, immobility, impassivity, phlegm, inertness, lethargy, sluggishness, hebetude, want of feeling, dulness, lassitude, torpor, coldness, frigidity, torpidity, stolidity, supineness, languor, passiveness, insensibility, unfeelingness, stoicism, impassibility, Laodiceanism, adiaphorism, sang-froid, calmness, composure.

2. Lack of interest, indifference, nonchalance, pococurantism, insouciance, inattention, coolness, heedlessness, listlessness, lukewarmness, unconcern, carelessness.

APE, *n.* 1. Monkey *(tailless)*, simian, anthropoid, quadrumane, gorilla, orang-utan, chimpanzee, baboon, gibbon, pongo.

2. Slavish imitator, copier, mimic, copyist, parrot, echo.

APE, *v.* 1. Mimic *(in good sense)*, personate, imitate, impersonate, simulate, mirror, reflect, take the appearance of, echo, parallel, emulate, reproduce, do like, follow suit, model after.

2. Mimic *(in bad sense)*, copy slavishly, affect, imitate absurdly, sham, parrot, parody, take-off, caricature, travesty, burlesque, counterfeit, mock, represent grotesquely, forge.

APERIENT, *n.* Mild laxative, gentle purgative, cathartic, deobstruent.

APERTURE, *n.* Opening, outlet, inlet, mouth, embouchure, orifice, entrance, vomitory, postern, gate, wicket, hatch, door, trap door, portal, oriel, window, dormer, lattice, spiracle, open passage, foramen, open space, hiation, dehiscence, rent, patefaction, pandiculation, gap, cleft, slit, slot, crack, cranny, chink, rime, crevice, rift, scissure, gash, chasm, gulf, fissure, perforation, puncture, hole, dent, indentation, breach, bore, interstice, caliber, vent, pore, eye, break, eyelet, eyehole, pinhole, porthole, peephole, mousehole, keyhole, pigeonhole, loophole.

APEX, *n.* 1. Top, brow, summit, highest point, utmost height, crest, pinnacle, tip, crown, cusp, crowning point, culminating point, vertex, cap, peak, nib, pointed end, extreme point, capstone, head, maximum, extreme, angle, meridian, *ne plus ultra.*

2. Acme, climax, crisis, zenith, apogee.

APHORISM, *n.* Terse statement of a general truth, axiom, maxim, proverb, adage, dictum, apothegm, saw, saying, sententious precept, moral, self-evident truth, truism, byword, motto, epigram, gnome, pithy statement, elementary principle, brocard, mot, commonplace, cliché, stereotyped saying.

APHRODISIAC, *n.* 1. Inordinate sexual desire, sensual desire, venery, lechery, lust, carnality, libidinousness, violent sexual passion, salacity, concupiscence, pruriency, lubricity, lewdness, whoredom, rut, nymphomania, lasciviousness, satyriasis, sensuality.

2. Sexual coition, coitus, copulation, relations, commerce, fornication, intercourse, seduction, defloration, defilement, violation, rape, wenching, stupration, ravishment. debauchery.

APHRODISIAC, *adj.* 1. Arousing sexual desire, stimulating sexual appetite, inducing lust, titillating, inflammatory, seductive, enticing, alluring.

2. Fond of sensual pleasures, lustful, carnal, lascivious, voluptuous, wanton, incontinent, lewd, prurient, lecherous, salacious, lickerish, obscene, libidinous, concupiscent, dissolute, adulterous, erotic.

APIARIST, *n.* Beekeeper, breeder of bees, beemaster, bee student, keeper of an apiary, apiarian.

APIARY, *n.* Collection of beehives, bee-house, beehive-frame, bee-shed, bee-stand, floating apiary, house-apiary, railway-apiary, out-apiary.

APIECE, *adv.* For each one, for each, to each one, one by one, individually, separately, for each several article, severally, respectively, in detail, distributively, seriatim, each.

APLOMB, *n.* Imperturbable self-possession, self-command, self-reliance, poise, collectedness, self-confidence, self-assurance, self-balance, grit, confidence, calmness, stability, balance, coolness of mind, level-headedness, equilibrium, boldness, composure, sang-froid, resolution, intrepidity, backbone.

2. *(Lit.)* Upright posture, perpendicularity, erect carriage, erectness.

APOCALYPSE, *n.* 1. Prophecy of St. John the Divine, divine communication of truth, divine unveiling.

2. Revelation, disclosure, showing forth of things secret, discovery, manifestation, afflatus, inspiration.

APOCALYPTIC, *adj.* 1. In or from the book of *Revelation.*

2. Affording a revelation, prophetic, fatidical, predictive, prognosticative, vaticinal, haruspical, oracular, given to interpreting prophecy, inspired, revelatory of mysteries, mystical, theopneustic, precious.

APOCRYPHAL, *adj.* Of doubtful authenticity, unauthentic, questionable, unauthenticated, false, unauthorized, unsustained, unverified, of doubtful sanction, of doubtful authorship, legendary, mythical, fabulous, fictitious, uncanonical, ungenuine, spurious, dubious, problematic, enigmatic, equivocal, ambiguous, uncertain, doubtful. discredited, disputed, incredible.

APOGEE, *n.* Highest point, most distant point, farthest point, apex, summit, top, vertex, zenith, pinnacle, acme, culmination, meridian, climax, culminating point, crowning point, crest.

APOLOGETIC, *adj.* 1. Defending by discourse, defensive, vindicatory, refuting allegations, exonerative, exculpatory, excusatory, palliatory, extenuatory, mitigatory, justificatory.

2. Expresing regret for fault or failure, sorry, regretfully acknowledging, regretful, penitential, self-condemnatory, self-reproachful, remorseful, contrite, compunctious, propitiatory, expiatory, rueful.

APOLOGIST, *n.* Arguer in defense, defender, vindicator, advocate, supporter, pleader, friend, justifier, patron, favorer, upholder.

APOLOGIZE, *v.* Express regret, make apology, ask pardon, acknowledge delinquency, offer an excuse, give satisfaction, make amends, atone for, shrive, do penance, appease, expiate, redeem, propitiate, absolve, palliate, plead in defense.

APOLOGUE, *n.* Moral fable, didactic narrative, parable, homily, sermon, allegory, tale, story, fiction.

APOLOGY, *n.* 1. Expression of regret, disclaimer of intentional offense, acknowledgment of error, confession, admission, self-reproach.
2. Reparation, satisfaction, amends, expiation, *amende honorable (Fr.),* peace offering, redress, recompense, compensation, indemnification, atonement, propitiation.
3. Assignment of reasons in defense, formal defense, explanation, justification, vindication, exculpation, extenuation, palliation.
4. Makeshift, temporary expedient, stopgap, shift, pinch hitter, poor specimen, poor excuse, meager substitute, flimsy pretext, *pis aller (Fr.).*

APOSTASY, *n.* 1. Total departure from one's faith, abandonment of religion, renunciation of religious obligations.
2. Desertion of principles in general, defection, perfidious backsliding, traitorous abjuration, going back on, disloyalty, recreancy, heresy, relapse, lapse, dereliction, recidivism, forsaking, fall, secession, perversion, tergiversation, reversal, revocation, recantation, retraction, disavowal, withdrawal, recession.

APOSTATE, *n.* One who forsakes his party or cause, deserter, backslider, recreant, renegade, traitor, turncoat, pervert, retractor, recanter, recidivist, abjurer, tergiversator, seceder, dissenter, straddler.

APOSTATE, *adj.* Guilty of apostasy, perfidious, disloyal, unfaithful to moral allegiance, faithless, recreant, renegade, untrue, false, traitorous, treacherous, backsliding, tergiversating, recusant, recidivous, schismatic, heretical, apostatic.

APOSTATIZE, *v.* Forswear one's faith, change one's mind, shift one's ground, be a traitor, commit apostasy, forsake one's principles, abjure, recant, retract, revoke, renounce, repudiate, relinquish, backslide, tergiversate, recidivate, secede, relapse, veer round, change sides, go over to, desert, depart from, lapse, abandon, disavow, disclaim, discard, disown.

APOSTLE, *n.* 1. One of the Twelve Disciples, one deputed by our Lord, Apostolic father.
2. One sent forth on foreign missions, zealot, evangelist, proselyte, messenger, missionary, propagandist, devoted proclaimer, pioneer of any great moral reform, zealous preacher, reformer, revivalist, advocate, disciple, witness.

APOSTOLIC, *adj.* Founded by the Apostles, authorized by the Twelve, evangelical, orthodox, ecclesiastical, catholic, according to the spirit and customs of the primitive church, conferred by the Pope, papal.

APOSTROPHE, *n.* 1. Personal address to someone not present, direct address, abrupt interjectional speech, alloquy, allocution, appeal, interpellation, invocation, salutation, obtestation, supplication, imploration, solicitation, entreaty, imprecation, soliloquy, digressive address.
2. Sign of contraction, sign of omission, sign of the possessive case, sign of certain plurals.

APOTHECARY, *n.* Druggist, pharmacopolist, pharmacist, pharmaceutist, chemist, prescription-filler.

APOTHEGM, *n.* Instructive dictum, maxim, mot, axiom, gnome, adage, proverb, aphorism, saw, sententious precept, truism, pithy saying, word, byword, cliché, epigram, moral, phylactery, motto.

APOTHEOSIS, *n.* 1. Deification, exaltation to the rank of a god, enrollment among the gods, conferment of immortality, canonization, homage with divine honors, glorification, enthronement, enshrinement, dignification, elevation, celebration, consecration, idolatry, hero worship.
2. Glorified ideal, glorified personification, perfect incarnation.

APOTHEOSIZE, *v.* Deify, place among the gods, worship, idolize, put on a pedestal, bow down to, prostrate oneself before, burn incense to, make sacrifice to, enshrine, enthrone, enroll among the gods, translate to heaven, immortalize, sing praises to, canonize, consecrate, glorify, exalt to the skies, elevate, honor greatly, signalize.

APPALL, *v.* 1. Fill with consternation, overcome with fear, fill with horror, horrify, terrify, alarm, affright, frighten, impress with fear, dismay, cow, dishearten, daunt, abash, deter, discourage with fear, consternate, scare, startle, shock, awe, astound, overawe, strike with terror, petrify with fear, unman, palsy with dread, paralyze with fright, harrow, unnerve, intimidate.
2. Disgust, offend, sicken, revolt, nauseate, repel, be detestable, be abhorrent.

APPALLING, *adj.* Fearful, terrible, frightful, dismaying, horrifying, dreadful, dire, alarming, awful, shocking, horrible, awe-inspiring, lurid, unearthly, terrific, tremendous, formidable, grim, ghastly, horrid, hideous, loathsome, intolerable, grisly, insufferable, distressing, revolting.

APPARATUS, *n.* Set of implements, materials for a particular use, assemblage of machinery, mechanism, equipment, machine, appliance, gear, outfit, tools, instruments, complex device, tackle, contrivances, means, matériel, paraphernalia, fixtures, plant, rigging, utensils.

APPAREL, *n.* Clothing, clothes, attire, dress, garb, garments, vestments, vesture, garmenture, array, raiment, robes, habiliments, habit, toilet, toilette, costume, trousseau, wardrobe, drapery, suit, palliament, finery, ensemble, turnout, livery, trappings, gear, rig, outfit, adornment, covering, togs, duds *(colloq.),* accouterment, caparison, guise, equipment.

APPAREL, *v.* Put clothes upon, clothe, dress, dress up, attire, tire, invest with raiment, array, robe, vest, enrobe, habit, fit out, rig out, deck out, trick out, rig, accouter, enclothe, dight, drape, garb, habilitate, encase, sheathe, don, slip on, equip.

APPARENT, *adj.* 1. Exposed to the sight, open to view, capable of being seen, visible to the eye, discernible, perceptible, clearly perceivable, easily seen, in full view, appearing, in full sight, able to be seen, in focus, distinct.
2. Manifest to the understanding, patent, clear, evident, obvious, understandable, palpable, easily understood, tangible, certain, definite, plain, open, overt, conspicuous, notorious, clear as day, indubitable, unmistakable, self-evident,

express, well-defined, salient, unambiguous, transparent.

3. Seeming, likely, specious, presumable, not real, ostensible, pretended, semblable, avowed, assigned, shown, declared, exhibited, professed, external, superficial, not actual, probable, unreal, quasi, as it were.

APPARENTLY, *adv.* 1. Plainly evident to the senses, obviously, patently, evidently, clearly, openly, manifestly, plainly, palpably, tangibly, overtly, conspicuously, indubitably, expressly, transparently, perceptibly, at a glance, to the eye, at first view, in plain sight, unmistakably, at first sight.

2. Judged by appearances, on the face of it, seemingly, ostensibly, in semblance, in show, speciously, presumably, avowedly, externally, superficially, probably, quasi, as far as can be told.

APPARITION, *n.* 1. Act of becoming visible, appearing, materialization, appearance, epiphany, manifestation, coming to view, presence.

2. Visible object, form, shape, being, thing appearing, phenomenon, image, vision, sight, spectacle.

3. Preternatural appearance, phantom, specter, ghostly appearance, ghost, phantasm, double-ganger, *Doppelgänger* (*Ger.*), spirit, shadow, shade, revenant, visual hallucination, illusion, sprite, bogy, hobgoblin, wraith, banshee, spook, immaterial appearance, illusory appearance, eidolon, chimera, will-o'-the-wisp, *ignis fatuus* (*Lat.*), fairy, fay, fetch.

APPEAL, *v.* 1. (*Law*) Seek reference of a case from one court to another, remove from a lower to a higher court for review, apply for review of a case to a higher tribunal, transfer by appeal from one court to another.

2. Call upon, apply to, turn to, sue to, make earnest entreaty, plead with, call for aid, petition, supplicate, address, entreat sympathy, beseech, invoke, implore, solicit, make application to, refer to, resort for settlement.

3. Offer a peculiar interest, awaken response, attract, invite, entice, allure, tempt, fascinate, engage.

APPEAL, *n.* 1. Petition, plea, call for aid, prayer, entreaty, supplication, solicitation, suit, address, imploration, application, invocation, earnest request, adjuration.

2. Recourse to some higher power, resort to superior authority, reference to some authority for corroboration, application for review by a higher tribunal, request for decision.

3. Power to attract, capacity for moving the feelings, interest, engagingness.

APPEAR, *v.* 1. Be within view, be in sight, become visible, come into sight, loom up, come into view, present itself, show itself, turn up, issue, arrive, arise, crop up, enter the picture, cut a figure, come to light, heave in sight, show up, show one's face, come forth, burst forth, dawn, peep forth, break forth.

2. Come into public notice, come before the public, see the light, be placed before the public, come upon the stage, present oneself on the stage, present oneself as an author, come out in published form.

3. (*Law*) Come formally before a tribunal, stand in judgment, present oneself, be present to answer, come into court, enter an appearance.

4. Come to mental apprehension, be patent,

become clear to the mind's apprehension, be manifest, be plain, be obvious, be certain, be clear, be open, be known, be made clear by evidence, declare itself, be self-evident.

5. Have an appearance, seem, seem likely, have a certain semblance, look, show, present the appearance, wear the aspect, have the expression, strike one as being.

APPEARANCE, *n.* 1. Act of appearing in sight, arrival into view, coming, advent, apparition, manifestation, emergence, rise, publication, introduction, debut, exhibition.

2. A thing seen, form, being, shape, image, sight, phenomenon, eidolon, phantasm, vision.

3. (*Law*) Coming into court of a party to a suit, being present in court.

4. Outward look, external aspect, air, mien, look, demeanor, cast, complexion, figure, port, expression, manner, carriage, personal presence, deportment, visage, features, hue, view.

5. Outward show, external seeming, semblance, likeness, show, exterior, face, guise, fashion, phase, color, pretense, pretext, presentment, likelihood, probability, plausibility.

6. (*Pl.*) Circumstances, indications.

APPEASE, *v.* 1. Bring to a state of quiet, reduce to a state of peace, pacify, quiet, calm, placate, tranquilize, compose, still, silence, lull, hush, temper, attemper, moderate, qualify.

2. Soothe, allay, assuage, alleviate, mollify, mitigate, slake, quench, abate, ease, dull, quell, blunt, lessen, humor, make favorable, satisfy.

3. Accede to belligerent demands by a sacrifice of justice, conciliate, propitiate, reconcile, satisfy demands.

APPEASEMENT, *n.* Pacification, mollification, propitiation, conciliation, reconciliation, amends, satisfaction, assuagement, submission, assuasion, accommodation, adjustment, settlement, peace-offering, restoration of harmony, reparation.

APPELLATION, *n.* 1. Name, proper name, style, appellative, designation, denomination, cognomen, agnomen, praenomen, surname, patronymic, title, descriptive name, epithet, by-name, handle, alias, moniker, nickname, sobriquet, assumed-name, pseudonym, *nom-de-guerre,* pen name, *nom-de-plume,* stage name, *nom-de-théâtre.*

2. Act of calling by name, naming, nomination, nuncupation, nomenclature.

APPEND, *v.* 1. Attach as a pendant, hang, make to depend, suspend, swing, sling, make dangle, fasten.

2. Add as an accessory, join, subjoin, affix, suffix, prefix, annex, superadd, tack on, tag, subscribe, supplement.

APPENDAGE, *n.* 1. Subsidiary superaddition, subordinate attached part, accessory, adjunct, attachment, appurtenance, addition, addendum, additum, appendant, appendix, accompaniment, attendant, appliance, tailpiece, concomitant, tag, supplement, extension, auxiliary, codicil, pendant, arm, leg, feeler, tentacle, limb, projecting part, member, extremity.

2. Person in constant attendance upon another, hanger-on, sidekick (*colloq.*), shadow, parasite, leech, sponge, sycophant, trencher-friend, flunky, lackey, toady, stooge.

APPENDANT, *adj.* Adjunct, attached as an appendage, annexed, hanging to, dependent, attendant, concomitant, belonging as a right, pendent, hanging, suspended, swinging, subjoined, added, additional, appurtenant, supplementary, suffixed, associated as a consequence.

APPENDIX, *n.* 1. Appendage, appendant, rider, adjunct, appurtenance, addition, addendum, codicil, postscript, additum, accompaniment, sequel.

2. Supplementary matter, supplement, tabular matter, explanatory matter, statistical material, excursus, bibliographic matter.

APPERTAIN TO, *v.* 1. Belong as a part or attribute, be part of, be characteristic of, be incident to, inhere in, adhere to, be proper to, pertain to, belong to, be the property of.

2. Have relation to, concern, relate to, refer to, regard, touch, affect, bear upon, answer to, behoove.

APPETENCE, *n.* 1. Natural craving, intense desire, fixed longing, appetite, passion, libido, lust, hunger.

2. Instinctive inclination, natural tendency, instinct, leaning, propensity, predilection, bent, proclivity, partiality, penchant, liking, affection, fondness, love, taste for.

3. Material affinity, chemical attraction.

APPETITE, *n.* 1. Desire for food or drink, longing to supply a bodily want, physical craving, hunger, thirst, innate demand for.

2. Voracity, ravenousness, voraciousness, gluttony, insatiability, omnivorousness, edacity, belly-worship, gormandizing, rapacity, gulosity, crapulence.

3. Relish, zest, gusto, liking, taste, fondness, enjoyment, palate, pleasure, stomach, keenness, edge of appetite, sweet tooth, mouth watering, chop licking.

APPETIZER, *n.* Appetite-stimulant, aperitif, hors d'oeuvres, antipasto, canape, spread, tidbit, dainty, delicacy, *bonne bouche (Fr.),* relish, condiment, sauce.

APPETIZING, *adj.* Stimulating the appetite, whetting the appetite, mouth-watering, savory, succulent, tasteful, tasty, delicious, delectable, luscious, ambrosial, nectareous, toothsome, palatable, flavorous, gustable, spicy, piquant, tempting, tantalizing, inviting.

APPLAUD, *v.* 1. Clap the hands, cheer, hail, huzza, root, encore, stomp, chirrup, recall, shout admiration, whistle, make the rafters ring.

2. Express approval of, give vent to loud approbation, acclaim, laud, extol, exalt, sing the praises of, cry up, congratulate, eulogize, praise, compliment, commend, magnify, glorify.

APPLAUSE, *n.* Hand clapping, cheering, cheers, plaudits, acclaim, acclamation, huzza, hurrah, shout of approbation, burst of approbation, open approval, paean, demonstration of approval, marked commendation, ovation, triumph, fanfare, loud praise, encomium, eulogy, panegyric, noisy admiration, exultation, hosanna, homage, bravo-calling, encoring.

APPLIANCE, *n.* 1. Application, applying, putting to use, carrying into operation, use, practice, exercise.

2. Piece of apparatus, tool, machine, device, instrument for a particular use, mechanism, gear, contrivance, attachment, arrangement, equipment, furnishing, appointment, appurtenance.

3. Agency, means, instrumentality, measure, resource, step, expedient, ways and means.

APPLICABLE, *adj.* 1. Capable of being applied,

able to be fitted to, able to be put on, adjustable, adaptable.

2. Suitable, fit, befitting, meet, seemly, apt, fitting, appropriate, convenient, opportune, due, timely, proper, right, apposite, apropos, relevant, relative, pertinent, germane, compatible, useful, adapted, to the point, to the purpose, bearing on, pat.

APPLICANT, *n.* One who applies, office seeker, place hunter, job seeker, want ad answerer, interviewee, aspirant, candidate, competitor, inquirer, petitioner, suppliant, solicitor, asker, suitor, claimant, postulant.

APPLICATION, *n.* 1. Act of applying, laying on, touching, bringing into contact, putting to, juxtaposing.

2. That which is laid on, thing applied to the body as a remedial device, lotion, wash, balm, ointment, poultice, stimulant, rubefacient, salve, emollient, plaster, unguent, pomade, pomatum, nard, cataplasm, fomentation.

3. Putting to special use, employment as a means, appliance, exercise, practice, use, resort, recourse.

4. Meaning, significance, signification, point, inference, bearing, import, purport, sense, gist, drift, tenor, intention, interpretation.

5. Act of requesting, solicitation, petition, request, appeal, entreaty, suit, requisition, demand.

6. Quality of being usable for a particular purpose, reference to practice, use in detail, utilization, usableness, relevance, pertinence, appositeness, germaneness, suitability, fittingness, appropriateness, opportuneness, compatibility.

7. Close attention to, persistent effort, sedulity, assiduity, sedulousness, diligence, perseverance, industry, constancy, persistency, intense study, intentness, addiction, devotion to.

APPLY, *v.* 1. Lay on, bring into physical contact, touch to, put to, lay over, rub into, massage into.

2. Put to use, employ, use, exercise, convert to use, ply, administer, adapt, adjust, utilize, resort to, put the hand to, direct.

3. Put into practical operation, execute, bring into effect, carry out, practice, put in practice, bring to bear.

4. Devote to some specific purpose, assign, appropriate, allot.

5. Attend closely, devote oneself, dedicate, turn attentively, bend with diligence, address, addict, direct, engage diligently, concentrate, study, persevere, persist, be assiduous, give wholly to, be sedulous, be industrious, buckle down to.

6. Have reference, refer, be pertinent, have some connection with, pertain, be in relationship with, have bearing upon, bear upon, relate to, fit the case, hit the case, hold good, be in point, hold true, come into play, suit, fit, be adapted to, be suitable to, be applicable to, allude.

7. Make application, make formal request, make suit, become a candidate, solicit, petition, request, call upon, have recourse to, appeal to, address, ask, seek, entreat, canvas.

APPOINT, *v.* 1. Nominate, assign to a position, place in an office, designate to a post, depute, delegate, set apart, single out, detail, select, elect, empower, deputize, commission, name to fill an appointment.

2. Institute, ordain, fix by decree, enjoin, command, decree, order, direct, bid, **require,**

authorize, dictate, predetermine, impose.

3. Determine by agreement, fix by decision, settle, set, fix the time and place of, prescribe, establish, decide upon, arrange, mark out, allot, apportion.

4. Provide with what is requisite, equip, fit out, supply, furnish, prepare.

APPOINTEE, *n.* Person appointed, nominee, delegate, deputy, incumbent, representative, agent, commissioner, surrogate, legate, emissary, envoy, vice-regent, factor.

APPOINTMENT, *n.* 1. Act of appointing, placing in office, nomination, designation to office, assignment to position, commissioning, deputation, delegation.

2. That to which one is appointed, situation, position, post, station of authority, office, sphere of occupation, place of employment.

3. Agreement as to time and place of meeting, assignation, engagement, date *(colloq.)*, meeting, rendezvous, interview, arrangement for meeting, tryst.

4. Bidding, order, decree, command, edict, enactment, law, ordinance, ordination, mandate, ordainment, dispensation, prescription, precept, requirement, establishment, direction.

5. *(Pl.)* Equipment, furnishings, equipage, accouterments, outfit, furniture, paraphernalia, gear.

APPORTION, *v.* Distribute proportionally, assign in just proportion, divide according to some rule, make an apportionment of, portion out equitably, allocate, allot, measure out, dispense, award, grant, detail, cast, deal out, parcel out, mete out, dole, partition, part, administer, adjust, appoint, appropriate, share, subdivide, admeasure.

APPORTIONMENT, *n.* 1. Act of apportioning, distribution, allotment, equitable assignment, just division, fair deal, consignment, appropriation, allocation, partition, division, issuance, allowance, administration, dispensation.

2. That which is apportioned, share, lot, dose, measure, ration, portion, dividend, dole, part, meed, pittance, certain quality, quantum, quota, parcel, contingent.

APPOSITE, *adj.* Relevant, pertinent, to the purpose, well adapted to the point, apropos, fit, relative, appropriate, timely, seasonable, germane, fitting, befitting, seemly, proper, suitable, meet, well-applied, pat, well put, applicable, congenial.

APPOSITION, *n.* Act of adding to, application, placing side by side, placing together, placing in contact, state of juxtaposition, unanimity one with the other.

APPRAISAL, *n.* Estimated value, appraisement, evaluation, judgment, assessment, setting of price, estimate, valuation, estimation, price survey, appreciation.

APPRECIABLE, *adj.* Material enough to be recognized, large enough to be estimated, definite, noticeable, perceptible, discernible, estimable, ascertainable, visible, apparent, distinguishable, cognizable, perceivable, sensible, detectable, evident.

APPRECIATE, *v.* 1. Place a sufficiently high estimate on, estimate justly, hold in high regard, rate high, value rightly, esteem to the full the worth of, fully appraise, put a just value on, realize the worth of, formulate a correct estimate of, prize, cherish.

2. Be fully conscious of, be aware of, be alive to, be sensitive to, be fully sensible of, recognize, be cognizant of, feel, detect, see the full import of, adequately perceive, note, realize, understand, comprehend, feel for, sympathize.

3. Be grateful for, applaud, acclaim, respect, honor, admire, savor, relish.

4. Raise in value, increase the market price of, raise the value of, enhance the degree of, make of greater value, advance, improve, boost.

APPRECIATION, *n.* 1. Just estimate, just sense of worth, correct valuation, full recognition of worth, high estimation, full appraisal, esteem, sympathetic recognition of excellence, complete appraisement.

2. Clear perception, recognition through the senses, sensitive awareness, sensitiveness to, keen apprehension, delicate distinctions.

3. Expression of gratification, regard, relish, admiration, honor, praise, gratitude, thankfulness.

4. Critical notice, critique, review, commentary, critical examination, critical remarks.

5. Increase in value, added monetary worth, rise in value, increased price, advance in worth.

APPRECIATIVE, *adj.* Understanding, sensible of, aware of, cognizant of, conscious of, alive to, sensitive to, acquainted with, *au fait (Fr.)*, capable of appreciating, no stranger to, sympathetic, critical, manifesting appreciation, thankful, under obligation, grateful, obliged, indebted, beholden.

APPREHEND, *v.* 1. Seize by legal warrant, take into custody, detain by criminal process, arrest with authority, catch, capture, make a prisoner of, take prisoner, imprison, incarcerate, place in confinement, jail, put in duress, put in durance.

2. Comprehend with the mind, lay hold of with the mind, grasp the meaning of, understand, hold opinions concerning, cognize, know, conceive, have a mental impression of, imagine, appreciate.

3. Perceive through the senses, discover by observation, view, look at, note, regard, discern, see, recognize, become aware of through the senses, sense emotionally, intuit, feel, take in, realize.

4. Think, suppose, fancy, opine, surmise, ween, conjecture, presume, formulate opinions about.

5. Entertain suspicion of, mistrust, dread, fear, have a presentiment of, be in fear of, forebode, anticipate with apprehension, expect with unease, forecast, be prescient of, have foreknowledge of, have premonition of.

APPREHENSION, *n.* 1. Fear of coming evil, foreboding, presentiment, presage, premonition, anticipation of adversity, solicitude, anxiety, care, uneasiness, misgiving, concern, dread, suspicion, alarm, distrust, apprehensiveness, dismay.

2. Faculty of apprehending, grasping with the intellect, understanding, intellection, cognition, comprehension, grasp.

3. Mind, intellect, intelligence, reason, nous *(Gk. philos.)*, insight, memory, imagination, sense.

4. Notice, observation, taking in, cognizance, discernment, perception, recognition.

5. Result of apprehending mentally, idea on any subject, sentiment, view, opinion, impression, belief, fancy, supposition, conjecture, judgment, notion, thought, conception, conclusion.

6. Act of arresting, seizure, arrest, capture, detention, holding in custody.

APPREHENSIVE, *adj.* 1. Uneasy, suspicious, distrustful, disquieted, afraid, fearful, anxious, worried, solicitous, alarmed, mistrustful, nervous, tremulous, terror-stricken, panic-stricken, scary, quavering, anticipative of evil, expectant, fidgety, hesitant, timid, cowardly, pusillanimous, haunted by fears, terrified.

2. Quick to learn, quick to understand, seizing quickly with the mind, capable of apprehending, discerning, awake to, aware, perceptive.

APPRENTICE, *n.* Learner of a trade, indentured assistant, articled probationer, student, pupil, novice, neophyte, beginner, bound journeyman, tyro.

APPRENTICE, *v.* Set at work as an apprentice, indenture to an employer, bind for instruction, article.

APPRISE, *v.* Give notice to, notify, inform, tell, advise, acquaint, make acquainted, communicate, advertise, publish, disclose to, make known to, bring to the ears of, enlighten, let know, make aware, point out, announce, report, send word, tip off, make cognizant of, give to understand, instruct, impart knowledge of, divulge, reveal, admonish, counsel, warn.

APPROACH, *v.* 1. Come nearer to, draw nigh to, advance nearer, go near, move towards, edge close to, gain upon, overtake, hail, salute, accost, confront, address, greet, speak to, near.

2. Broach a subject to, make advances to, make a proposal to, address confidentially, make overtures to.

3. Bring near to, push forward, advance, carry toward, tend toward, converge, abut.

4. Come near in quality or condition, resemble closely, be much like, nearly equal, approximate.

5. Begin work on, take preliminary steps toward, set about.

APPROACH, *n.* 1. Act of drawing near, coming nearer, advent, advance.

2. Advances made to a person, wily addresses, confidential overtures, tenders, proposal, offer, proposition, proffer.

3. Nearness, close approximation, tendency, gradual convergence.

4. Steps taken in setting about a task, method followed. preliminaries, procedure.

5. Access, admittance, admission, liberty to approach, audience, interview, entrance, *entrée (Fr.)*, permission to enter, reception, acceptance.

6. Means of access, passage, passageway, way, entrance, path, adit, avenue, portal, doorway, gate, hallway, lobby, vestibule, door.

APPROACHABLE, *adj.* Accessible, open, affable, easy to approach. get-at-able *(colloq.)*, attainable, come-at-able *(colloq.)*, friendly, gracious, sociable, companionable, familiar, democratic, congenial.

APPROBATION, *n.* 1. Acceptance, approval, favorable opinion, esteem, favor, regard, liking, admiration, laudation, good word, commendation, praise, congratulation, compliment, encomium, eulogy, applause, acclamation, recommendation, encouragement.

2. Official sanction, authoritative support, formal assent, consent, endorsement, concurrence, ratification, confirmation, attestation, advocacy, corroboration, adoption.

APPROPRIATE, *v.* 1. Take possession of, take for oneself, take as one's own, take to oneself in exclusion of others, apply to one's own uses, claim by preeminent right, avail oneself of, annex, treat as one's own, usurp, expropriate, abstract, assume.

2. Misappropriate, steal, borrow, embezzle, rob, defalcate, arrogate.

3. Assign to a particular use, set apart for a specific purpose, allot, allocate, apportion, devote, appoint, allow for, disburse.

APPROPRIATE, *adj.* Belonging peculiarly, fit, special, specially suitable, well-suited, congruous, conformable, applicable, adapted, pertinent, apt, relevant, apposite, apropos, germane, agreeable, felicitous, harmonious, concinnous, condign, due, befitting, fitting, meet, seemly, to the purpose, to the point, proper, convenable, likely, timely, congenial, expedient, convenient, seasonable, becoming, rightful, opportune.

APPROPRIATENESS, *n.* Suitability, suitableness, fitness, aptness, applicability, felicity, congruity, becomingness, concinnity, congruence, decorum, harmoniousness, propriety, expediency, relevancy, appositeness, pertinence.

APPROPRIATION, *n.* 1. Act of appropriating, taking to oneself, annexing, arrogation, capture, usurpation, ascription, expropriation, seizure, theft, larceny, confiscation, misappropriation, embezzlement, defalcation.

2. Application to a particular purpose, assignment, devotion, adoption, conversion.

3. That which is appropriated, sum set apart for a special purpose, money earmarked for a specific use, allotment, allocation, allowance.

APPROVAL, *n.* 1. Act of approving, approbation, reception with favor, acceptance, concurrence, consent, good opinion, confirmation, permission, agreement, compliance, acquiescence, patronage, support, favor, liking, countenance, advocacy, blessing, hearty accord, eulogy, respect, regard, honor, applause, acclamation, acclaim, praise, commendation, encouragement, leave, backing.

2. Official permission, license, imprimatur, sanction, ratification, endorsement.

3. On approval, on appro. *(abbr.)*, primarily for examination, subject to a purchaser's decision to accept, without obligation to buy.

APPROVE, *v.* 1. Have a very good opinion of, consider good, pronounce worthy, commend, think highly of, judge favorably, think favorably of, express a favorable opinion of, regard as worthy of acceptance, be pleased with, speak well of, look upon with favorable attention, form a favorable judgment concerning, recommend, praise, appreciate, prize, value, admire, receive with favor, respect, believe in, cherish, esteem, eulogize, extol, like.

2. Confirm officially, pronounce legal, ratify, sanction, authorize, endorse, second, subscribe to, homologate, rubber stamp, make valid, affirm, sustain, support, uphold, assent to, consent to, concur in, accede to, corroborate, acquiesce in, advocate, maintain, vote for, establish, allow, go along with.

APPROXIMATE, *adj.* 1. Near, close together, close to, drawn very near, situated very close together, coming near, approaching, proximate, adjacent, bordering.

2. Nearly equal, nearly correct, nearly true, nearly perfect, nearly accurate, almost exact, near to correctness, not perfectly accurate, rough, inexact, relative, comparative.

3. Very similar, nearly resembling, quasi.

APPROXIMATE, *v.* Approach in amount, come near in position or character, come close to, approach closely to, advance near to, draw near to, border on, lean toward, nearly equal, almost come up to, closely resemble, nearly rival, look like, savor of, hint at, adumbrate, suggest.

APPROXIMATELY, *adv.* Very nearly but not absolutely, about, circa, ca. *(abbr.),* not far from, in the vicinity of, in the neighborhood of, close to, generally, roughly, comparatively, near to, incompletely, relatively, almost, around.

APPROXIMATION, *n.* 1. Approach, being near, drawing near, gradual convergence, moving nigh, advancing near, nearness, neighborhood, vicinity, proximity, propinquity, vicinage, contiguity.
2. Enumeration, summing up, reckoning, tally, estimate, computation, calculation, account, score, rough measure.
3. Likeness, similarity, resemblance, similitude, semblance, correspondence, parallel, affinity, rough equivalent.

APPURTENANCE, *n.* 1. Minor thing attached to a principal one, appurtenant, dependency, annex, accessory, addendum, additament, attachment, adjunct, appendage, appendency, supplement, incidental.
2. *(Pl.)* Apparatus, mechanism, paraphernalia, gear, accessories, props, belongings, property.

APPURTENANT, *adj.* 1. Belonging to something else more important, appertaining legally, suited, pertaining, pertinent, appropriate, incident.
2. Appended, attached, annexed, accessory, subsidiary, auxiliary, ancillary.

A PRIORI 1. Proceeding from antecedent to consequent, from cause to effect, from a general law to a particular instance, deductive, inferential.
2. Theoretical, presumptive, in accordance with one's previous notions, from assumed principles, previous to examination, according to prepossessions, before trial, prior to experience.
3. Valid independently of observation, from the nature of the case, furnishing the basis of experience, independent of all experience, from pure reason, innate, absolute, constitutional, necessary, apodictic, aboriginal, primordial.

APROPOS, *adj.* Suited to the time or occasion, timely, opportune, seasonable, just the thing, suitable, apt, fit, pat, to the point, pertinent, relevant, apposite, appropriate, applicable, to the purpose, well put, fitting, befitting, germane.

APROPOS, *adv.* 1. With regard to, with respect to, with reference to, as suggested by, while the matter's up, in that connection, which reminds me, speaking of which, by the way, by the bye, incidentally.
2. To the purpose, at the proper time, in the proper way, pertinently, appropriately, suitably, opportunely, seasonably, timely.

APT, *adj.* 1. Having a natural tendency to, likely, habitually tending, inclined, given to, subject to, prone, disposed to, liable.
2. Quick to learn, unusually intelligent, good at, bright, gifted, accomplished, clever, skilful, deft, adroit, proficient, master of, competent, at home in, able, qualified, prepared, ready, prompt, handy, sharp, expert, dexterous, smart, *au fait (Fr.).*
3. Suited to the purpose or occasion, adapted to its purpose, fitted, appropriate, apropos, to the point, apposite, germane, applicable, fitting, admissible, meet, befitting, suitable, fit, suited, felicitous, neat, pat, *ad rem (Lat.),* to the purpose, related to, important to, pertaining to the matter in hand, pertinent, relevant, consonant, proper, harmonious, concordant, expedient, congruous,

becoming, opportune, seasonable, timely.

APTITUDE, *n.* 1. Quickness of understanding, readiness in learning, intelligence, innate ability, natural capacity, talent, aptness, cleverness, gift, endowment, faculty, genius, knack, capability, deftness, adroitness, adeptness, address, happy faculty, dexterity, sharpness, tact, skill, facility, expertness, finish, proficiency, resourcefulness, competence, inventiveness, ingenuity, mastery, forte, efficiency, felicity, qualification, smartness, brightness, sharpness.
2. Natural tendency, predisposition, acquired inclination, turn, leaning, propensity, proclivity, penchant, proneness, bent, bias, predilection, mind set.

APTNESS, *n.* Quality of being apt, special fitness, suitability, suitableness, applicability, pointedness, appropriateness, relevancy, felicity, pertinency, appositeness, propriety, felicitousness, point, adaptation, admissibility, seasonability, seemliness, timeliness, opportuneness, expediency, germaneness, congruousness, harmoniousness, concordance, consonance.

AQUARIUM, *n.* Fish tank, pond, globe, display of fish in a vivarium, aquatic establishment, fishery, fish pond.

AQUATIC, *adj.* 1. Pertaining to water, nautical, maritime, marine, naval, littoral, lacustrine, oceanic, pelagic, fluvial.
2. Living in water, growing in water, native to water, frequenting the margin of water, amphibian.
3. Practiced on water, carried on in water, engaged in on water, occurring in water, natatory, seafaring.

AQUEDUCT, *n.* Artificial water channel, channel for the passage of water, water conduit, structure for conveying a canal over a hollow, water duct, water conductor, watercourse.

AQUEOUS, *adj.* 1. Of water, containing water, like water, of the nature of water, made from water, watery, waterish, moist, damp, humid, wet, dewy, dripping, lymphatic, serous.
2. Diluted, thinned with water, adulterated, insipid, vapid, weak, tame, feeble, spiritless, flat, tasteless, wishy-washy.

AQUILINE, *adj.* Eagle-like, resembling an eagle, beaked, hooked like an eagle's beak, curved, bent, curving, prominent, Roman-nosed.

ARAB, *n.* 1. Bedouin, Hadji, Arabian, Moor, Saracen, Sabaean, Minaean, Semite.
2. Vagrant, nomad, itinerant, wanderer in the street, wanderer, roamer, peripatetic, homeless outcast, street Arab, hoodlum, gamin.

ARABESQUE, *n.* Floral ornamentation, fanciful pattern, intricate design of interlaced lines, Moorish decoration, Arabian fret, anthemion.

ARABLE, *adj.* Fit for plowing, suitable for cultivation, cultivable, capable of producing crops by means of tillage, plowable, tillable, fertile, that may be plowed, cultivatable, fruitful, fruit-bearing, productive, prolific, exuberant, fecund.

ARBITER, *n.* 1. One authorized to decide points at issue, referee, umpire, linesman.
2. One qualified to give an opinion, judge, adjudicator, arbitrator, moderator, mediator, negotiator, intermediary, referendary, intercessor.
3. One with absolute power, controller, ruler, authority, lord, sovereign, governor, determiner, master.

ARBITRAMENT, *n.* 1. Arbitration, right of deciding, power of absolute decision, settlement, judgment, umpirage, determination, trial, test.

2. Sentence pronounced by an arbiter, verdict, decree, finding, opinion, decision of an arbitrator, dictum.

3. *(Law)* Award of an arbitrator, adjudication, determination.

ARBITRARINESS, *n.* 1. Absolutism, despotism, autocracy, tyranny, imperiousness, summariness, absoluteness.

2. Self-will, wilfulness, capriciousness, want of principle, unreasonableness, opinionativeness, obstinacy, noncompliance, indocility, contumacy, intractability, intransigence, obduracy, perversity, unyieldingness, mulishness, stubbornness.

ARBITRARY, *adj.* 1. Bound by no law, absolute in power, using unlimited power, unrestrained by law, uncontrolled, autocratic, despotic, tyrannous, tyrannical, dictatorial, unlimited, high-handed, harsh, imperious, summary, domineering, stern, peremptory, overbearing, inexorable, magisterial, stiff-necked, stringent, hidebound, unyielding, obdurate, uncompromising, oppressive, dogmatic, unbending, strait-laced.

2. Subject to individual will, capricious, wilful, fanciful, whimsical, depending on the will alone, determined by no principle, discretionary, erratic, voluntary, optional, uncertain, done at pleasure, without adequate determining principle, toplofty, unreasonable, non-rational, self-willed, wayward, unaccountable, crotchety, inconsistent, bumptious, irresponsible, opinionated, supercilious, self-assertive.

ARBITRATE, *v.* 1. Decide as arbiter, adjudicate, judge, adjudge, determine a point at issue, pass judgment, pronounce judgment, umpire, referee, settle, try a case, sit in judgment, fix, decree, sentence, give a verdict.

2. Act as arbiter, decide between opposing parties, mediate, intervene, intercede, interpose, conciliate, step in, negotiate, reconcile, pour oil on troubled waters, come between, parley, bring to terms, placate, interfere.

3. Submit to arbitration, settle by arbitration,

ARBITRATION, *n.* 1. Hearing a dispute between parties, determining of a controversy, judgment, adjudication, adjudgment, arbitrament, decision, determination, trial, test, umpirage, settlement.

2. Intermediation, interference, intercession, mediation, intervention, interposition, negotiation, peacemaking, conciliation, reconciliation, parley, compromise.

ARBITRATOR, *n.* 1. Person chosen to decide a contest, umpire, referee, judge, arbiter, mediator, adjudicator, intercessor, go-between, reconciler, peacemaker, negotiator, intermediary, interagent, moderator.

2. One with absolute power to ordain, master, controller, ruler, sovereign, governor, director, lord, determiner, autocrat, potentate, dictator, monarch, king, prince, liege.

ARBOR, *n.* 1. Latticework bower, trellis, pergola, summerhouse, gardenhouse, pavilion. pleasance, kiosk, pandal *(S. India)*, shaded retreat, grotto, shaded walk, recess.

2. *(Mach.)* Axle, spindle, mandrel, shaft, bar, beam, axis.

ARBOREAL, *adj.* 1. Of the nature of trees, arborescent, arboreous, pertaining to trees, in the form of a tree, treelike, dendral, dendriform, arboriform.

2. Inhabiting trees, sylvan, frequenting woods, living among trees, wood-dwelling, bosky, copsy, situated among trees, woodsy.

ARBORESCENCE, *n.* Treelike form, branching, arborization, ramification, ramosity, divarication, forking, radiation.

ARBORESCENT, *adj.* Having the nature of a tree, arboreal, arboreous, treelike in size and form, dendroid, dendriform, resembling a tree in size and appearance, dendritic, branching like a tree, arboriform, ramose, ramifying, ramous, having crystallizations disposed like the branches of a tree.

ARC, *n.* Curvation, curvature, incurvity, bend, conflexure, part of a circle, curved line, bow-shaped object, meniscus, arcuation, crescent, half moon, lunule, thing in the shape of an arch, curve, bow, parabola, luminous bridge *(Elect.)*, voltaic arc.

ARCADE, *n.* Series of supported arches, range of arches with supporting columns, vaulted roof, roofed-in gallery, covered passageway, peristyle, cloister, portico, colonnade, loggia, piazza.

ARCANUM, *n.* 1. Something hidden from the mass of men, inner secret, esoteric mystery, sealed book.

2. Secret and powerful remedy, extract of the vital nature of something, potent natural agent, elixir, nostrum, panacea.

ARCH, *adj.* 1. First, principal, most important, most eminent, consummate, first-class, first-rate, chief, greatest, extreme, highest.

2. Inoffensively saucy, sportively mischievous, characterized by clever artlessness, frolicsome, roguish, playful, waggish, merry, mirthful, jocose, tricksy, lively, wily, sly, cunning, subtle, shrewd, designing, intriguing.

ARCH, *n.* 1. Curvature, bow-like curve, arc, bend, convexity, camber.

2. Curved structure, fornix, cove, span, dome, cupola, vault, ogive, catenary arch, cinquefoil arch, cycloidal arch, elliptical arch, horseshoe arch, multifoil arch, semicircular arch, triangular arch, trefoil arch.

ARCH, *v.* 1. Make into the shape of an arch, bend into the form of an arch, form into an arch, curve, embow, camber, deflect.

2. Span with an arch, provide with an arch, span, vault, cover with an arch, arch over.

ARCHAEOLOGIST, *n.* Specialist in archaeology, archaeologian, paleologist, paleontologist, antiquarian.

ARCHAEOLOGY, *n.* Study of antiquity from relics and remains, scientific study of prehistoric culture, investigation of man's relics, study of material remains of past human life, branch of anthropology, paleology, paleontology, science of antiquities, antiquarianism.

ARCHAIC, *adj.* Marked by the characteristics of an earlier period, primitive, ancient, antiquated, old, antique, obsolete, obsolescent, antediluvian, prehistoric, patriarchal, bygone, gone out of use, passé, out of date, out of fashion, old-fashioned, whilom, extinct, of other times, after-age, behind the times, old as the hills.

ARCHAISM, *n.* Borrowing from older usage, use of what is archaic, relic of the past, affectation of archaic language, obsolete diction, archaic word or expression, archaic style, antiquated term. old-fashioned word, obsolete idiom.

ARCHBISHOP, *n.* Highest-ranking bishop, chief bishop, titular bishop, primate, prelate, diocesan, metropolitan, church dignitary, divine, suffragan, hierophant, ecclesiarch, eminence, reverence, grace, churchman, hierarch.

ARCHED, *adj.* 1. Spanned with an arch, covered over with an arch, furnished with an arch, cambered.

2. Having the form of an arch, forniciform, curved, enarched, vaulted, camerated, fornicated, concave, bowed, embowed, domed, curviform, falciform, hemispherical.

ARCHER, *n.* User of bow and arrow, devotee of archery, arrow-shooter, bowman, toxophilite, sagittary, longbowman, crossbowman, arbalester.

ARCHETYPE, *n.* Original pattern, first form, primitive model, protoplast, prototype, original, primal form, primitive form, original ancestor, exemplar, example, paragon, paradigm, realized ideal, Absolute Idea *(Philos.),* the Self-existent, the Absolute.

ARCHITECT, *n.* 1. Designer of buildings, builder, planner of structures, director of construction, director of building, master builder, constructor, person skilled in the art of architectonics.

2. Creator, maker, author, deviser, planner, contriver, originator, former, inventor, founder, prime mover.

ARCHITECTURE, *n.* 1. Science of building, art of construction, architectonics, art of designing buildings, decorative building art, ecclesiology, science of constructing edifices, production of structural forms, construction, building technology.

2. Style of building, system of building, character of building.

3. Workmanship, structure, fabric, framework, frame, execution, craftsmanship.

ARCHIVES, *n.* 1. Building for public records, depository of historic public documents, place where historical documents are kept.

2. Documents, annals, muniments, chronicles, statistics, records, registers, rolls, registry, lists, reports, entries, public papers, memoirs, ledgers, memorabilia, testimonials, *procès-verbaux (Fr.),* depositions, certificates, memoranda, memorials.

ARCHWAY, *n.* Arch over a passage, passage under an arch, arched passage, arched opening, vaulted entrance, arcade.

ARCTIC, *adj.* 1. Near the North Pole, under the northern constellation, under the Bear, lying under the Great and the Little Bear *(Astron.),* boreal, septentrional, hyperborean, far northern, polar.

2. Cold, wintry, icy, frigid, brumal, hibernal, gelid, bleak, glacial, algid, raw, freezing, frozen, snowy, niveous, frost-bound, icebound.

ARDENT, *adj.* 1. Causing a sensation of burning, hot, burning, warm, baking, calid, fiery, red, shining, flashing, inflammable, incandescent, glowing.

2. Amorous, amatory, erotic, loving, lovesick, passionate, affectionate, fond, devoted, rapturous, voluptuous, sensual, carnal, salacious, lascivious, concupiscent, licentious, libidinous, lecherous, lustful, wanton.

3. Intense in desire, vehement in emotion, fervent, fervid, perfervid, impassioned, earnest, impetuous, fierce, zealous, enthusiastic, excitable, enterprising, sharp, eager, keen, excited, spirited, heated, assiduous, animated, feverish, sedulous,

ambitious, aspiring, impatient, high-spirited, active, intense, violent.

ARDOR, *n.* 1. Burning heat, intense light, glow, warmth, ardency, hotness, flame, incandescence, fire, blaze, inflammableness.

2. Amorousness, eroticism, passion, affection, fondness, lovesickness, devotion, rapture, lust, voluptuousness, sensuality, carnality, salacity, concupiscence, lasciviousness, licentiousness, lechery, wantonness, libidinousness.

3. Warmth of feeling, intense desire, fervency, fervor, perfervor, excitement, feverishness, spirit, sharpness, intensity, vehemence, fierceness, soul, impetuosity, keenness, animation, verve, mettle, élan, vigor, zeal, enthusiasm, empressement, eagerness, earnestness, heartiness, cordiality, good will.

ARDUOUS, *adj.* 1. Difficult of ascent, hard to climb, steep, high, uphill, acclivous, lofty.

2. Requiring great exertion, toilsome, difficult, hard, operose, laborious, onerous, troublesome, involving great labor, Herculean, formidable, offering difficulties, not easy, severe, wearisome, beset with difficulties, fraught with difficulties, full of hardships, tiresome, fatiguing, exhausting, trying, hard to endure, heavy, burdensome, tough, intricate.

AREA, *n.* 1. Portion of the earth's surface, extent of surface, field, range, tract, stretch, expanse, scope, arena, sphere, domain, territory, realm, region, district, circuit, compass, province, zone, ground, room, terrain, locality, precinct.

2. Enclosed ground around a building, close, enclosure, plot, yard surrounding a house, sunken court adjoining a basement, kitchen-yard, areaway.

3. Open space, piece of unoccupied ground, clear level surface outside a building, clearing, esplanade, square.

4. *(Geom.)* Surface, amount of surface, plane surface, two-dimensional extent, superficies, contents, measurement, superficial contents.

ARENA, *n.* 1. Enclosed oval space in Roman amphitheatres, Colosseum, hippodrome, circus, stadium, bowl, field, stage, platform, gymnasium, course, lists, cockpit.

2. Sphere of action, scene of contest, field of conflict, theater of endeavor, scene of conflict, area of combat, place of contest, playing field, battlefield, battle ground, Aceldama.

ARGENT, *adj.* Silvery, argentine, silvery-white, snowy, frosted, snow-white, niveous, canescent, albescent, fair, radiant, bright, resplendent, radiant, refulgent, effulgent, beaming, shining, brilliant.

ARGOSY, *n.* 1. Large merchant ship, brigantine, merchantman, cargo ship, trader, large ship of commerce, carack, galleon, schooner, topsail.

2. Fleet of vessels, flotilla, armada, escadrille.

ARGOT, *n.* Language peculiar to special groups *(thieves, hoboes, etc.),* class jargon, idiom, lingo, dialect, secret language, cant, code, cipher, patois, brogue, slang in general.

ARGUE, *v.* 1. Present reasons for or against, reason, offer reasons, use arguments, justify, explain, support, logicize, labor a point, reason about.

2. Contend in argument, dispute with, cross verbal swords, remonstrate, expostulate, disagree, wrangle, battle verbally, controvert, carry on an argument, bandy words, chop logic, ratiocinate,

try conclusions, debate, discuss, sift, question, moot, reason upon, maintain in reasoning, influence by argument, contest, persuade by reasoning, quibble.

3. Furnish proof of, exhibit by inference, render capable of inference, manifest, evince, betoken, indicate, denote, mean, imply, show, establish, demonstrate.

ARGUER, *n.* Logomachist, eristic, logic-chopper, controversialist, disputant, debater, reasoner, logician, dialectician, casuist, polemic.

ARGUMENT, *n.* 1. Statement tending to prove a point, address intended to convince others of the truth of something, discourse designed to convince, expression of opinion for or against, statement offered in proof, reason for or against, proof, evidence, ground, chain of reasoning, ratiocination, course of reasoning, demonstration, data, argumentation, discussion, disputation, logomachy, polemics.

2. Disagreement between persons, contention, controversy, oral contention, dispute, contest in reasoning, expression of contrary opinions, war of words, quarrel, feud, altercation, difference, verbal contest, conflict, wrangle, squabble, row, clash, discord, imbroglio, embroilment, variance, dissension, bickering, strife, spat, tiff, schism.

3. Subject-matter, gist, matter in hand, subject, thesis, theme, topic, matter, question, proposition, case.

4. Outline, general contents, abstract, epitome, summary, précis, conspectus, compendium, brief, abridgment, synopsis, digest, syllabus, sum and substance.

ARGUMENTATION, *n.* Setting forth of reasons and conclusions drawn from them, pattern of reasoning, chain of reasoning, ratiocination, logic, course of reasoning, polemics, dialectics.

ARGUMENTATIVE, *adj.* 1. Disputatious, given to controversy, addicted to arguing, bickering, quarrelsome, dissentient, contentious, combative, discordant, wranglesome, cantankerous, petulant, exceptious, peevish, deaf to reason.

2. Characterized by argument, controversial, polemical, logomachous, containing a process of reasoning, moot, debatable, doubtful.

3. Concerned with argument, logical, making inferential statement of facts, presumptive, indicative, dialectical, apologetic, ratiocinative, forensic.

ARGUS-EYED, *adj.* Vigilant, alert, wakeful, on the alert, watchful, prudent, all-observant, wary, circumspect, discerning, perspicacious, keen-eyed, quick-sighted, sharp-sighted, hawk-eyed, eagle-eyed, lynx-eyed, all-seeing, on the *qui vive,* on one's guard, broad-awake, wide-awake, on the watch for, on the lookout.

ARIA, *n.* Elaborate operatic solo, melody sung by a single voice, air, tune, song, arietta, ariette, canzonet, air buffa, aria cantabile, aria da capo, aria da chiesa, aria di bravura, aria d'imitazione, aria parlante.

ARID, *adj.* 1. Dry, without moisture, anhydrous, waterless, sear, rainless, dried up, parched with heat, burning, desert, desiccated, dehydrated, drought-scourged, bare, unfertile, unfruitful, infecund, barren, unproductive, uncultivable, sterile, torrid, thirsty, having insufficient rainfall to support agriculture without irrigation.

2. Wanting in interest, devoid of feeling, dull, lacking in life, lifeless in spirit, uninteresting,

dreary, dry as dust, jejune, pithless, pointless, without profit, unimaginative, unsuggestive, bald, stupid, flat, monotonous, tedious, soporiferous, humdrum, prosy.

ARIDITY, *n.* 1. Intense dryness, desiccation, parchedness, siccity, dehydration, aridness, want of moisture, arefaction, drought, barrenness, rainlessness, infertility, sterility, infecundity, unproductiveness, unfruitfulness.

2. Want of interest, dryness, dulness, flatness, tediousness, jejuneness, pithlessness, dreariness, pointlessness, unprofitableness, monotonousness, unsuggestiveness, prosaicness, baldness, torpidity, insensibility.

ARIGHT, *adv.* In a right way or form, correctly, properly, rightly, not amiss, without error, fitly, appropriately, suitably, exactly, without mistake, aptly, worthily, quite, satisfactorily, well, truly.

ARISE, *v.* 1. Move upward, come up from a lower to a higher position, ascend, move to a higher place, climb, mount, go up, scale, top, soar, tower, escalade, clamber up.

2. Get up from sitting or lying, get up from sleep or repose, rise from sleep, get out of bed, leave one's bed, rise, get up, stand up, start up, turn out.

3. Come into being or action, commence, originate, begin, begin existence, enter upon life, come into existence, come up, spring forth, crop up, spring up, open, start, take birth, take rise, set in, dawn, transpire, come to pass, become operative.

4. Appear above the horizon, become visible, appear, rise, emerge, come into notice, come in sight, become noticeable, come into view, show itself, present itself, reveal itself, discover itself, come to light, make its appearance, befall, occur, betide, happen.

5. Be excited, be stirred up, rise up in anger, revolt, mutiny, rebel, rise in sedition, rise in violence, rise threateningly.

6. Revive from death, rise from the dead, come up from the grave, leave the tomb, rise again, resurrect.

7. Grow out of, result, accrue, issue, flow, emanate, proceed, ensue, follow, be derived, originate, eventuate.

ARISTOCRACY, *n.* 1. Rule by the best, state characterized by the rule of a nobility, rule of the upper classes, government by a privileged class.

2. Class of hereditary nobility, patriciate, body of nobles, body of persons holding exceptional privileges, peerage, noblesse, gentry, privileged class, the quality, persons of rank, patricians, optimates, high society, élite, *haut monde, beau monde (Fr.),* upper classes, upper ten, *pur sang (Fr.),* gentility, upper ten thousand, fashionable world, high life, four-hundred, upper crust, F.F.V.'s *(First Families of Virginia).*

ARISTOCRAT, *n.* 1. Believer in government by the higher classes, advocate of rule by the privileged, advocate of privilege, oligarch.

2. Member of the ruling classes, patrician, optimate, hereditary noble, nobleman, peer, lord, chevalier, grandee, don, hidalgo, magnifico, polished gentleman, swell *(colloq.),* man of fashion, silk-stocking, blue-blood.

3. One with the manners of a superior group, person of supercilious feeling, snob, haughty fellow, overbearing person.

ARISTOCRATIC, *adj.* 1. Vesting power in the

upper classes, favoring the aristocracy, oligarchic, pertaining to the aristocracy, of the privileged.

2. Patrician, lordly, titled, noble, highbred, of gentle blood, blue-blooded, high born, of high rank, gentlemanly, senatorial *(Rom.)*, princely, courtly, basilic, royal, wellborn, *bon ton,* silk-stocking, refined, dignified.

3. Socially exclusive, snobbish, supercilious, arrogant, lordly, disdainful, cavalier, imperious, proud, haughty, domineering, overweening, overbearing, tyrannical, despotic, insolent, consequential, high-toned, undemocratic.

ARK, *n.* 1. Noachian vessel during the Flood, clumsy flat-bottomed boat, floating abode, refuge, retreat, last resort, asylum, haven, screen, abode, protection, safeguard, a large uncomfortable building *(colloq.)*.

2. Ark of the Covenant, chest of great sanctity, holy box, most sacred object of the Tabernacle, portable sanctuary.

ARM, *n.* 1. Upper limb of the human body, anterior limb, fore limb, thoracic limb, anterior member, brachium, antebrachium, humerus, forearm.

2. Some part of an organism likened to an arm, any armlike part, appendage, projecting part, projection, limb, branch, scion, bough, offshoot, ramification.

3. End of a yard *(Naut.)*, axle spindle, branch of an angle iron, hammer handle, windmill-sail spar, gearwheel spoke, projecting member of an anchor, crosspiece on a telegraph pole.

4. Inlet of the sea, fiord, firth, frith, estuary, ostiary, mouth, gulf, cove, bay, bight, lagoon, indraught, strait, sound, kyle.

5. Arm of the law, power, potency, might, puissance, strength, authority, warrant, sway, command, support, protection, defense.

6. Combat branch of the military service, organized branch of national defense.

7. *(Usually pl.)* Weapon of offense or defense, instrument of warfare, offensive or defensive implement for use in war.

ARM, *v.* 1. Equip with arms, accouter, furnish with weapons, array, gird, outfit, fit out, supply with instruments of warfare, provide with arms.

2. Prepare for resistance or attack, forearm, man, prime, gird up one's loins, get into harness, buckle on one's armor, prime and load, shoulder arms, take up arms, draw the sword, unsheathe the sword, fit out for action, make ready, ready arms, keep one's powder dry, hold oneself in readiness.

3. Fortify, put in a state of defense, furnish with a means of defense, prepare for resistance, make sure against, add security, add force, strengthen, clothe protectively, guard, protect, add superior power to, cover with whatever will add strength.

4. Enter into a state of hostility, ready for war, make warlike preparations, collect munitions of war, gather an army, muster one's forces, be fitted with arms.

ARMADA, *n.* Fleet, squadron of warships, navy, flotilla of armed ships, escadrille, argosy, wooden walls.

ARMAMENT, *n.* 1. Process of equipping or arming for war, accouterment, array, outfitting.

2. Equipment of war, armamenture, combined number and weight of guns, explosives, guns, cannon, arms, firearms, small arms, munitions of war, ammunition, weapons, mortars, howitzers,

field guns, artillery, automatic pistols, machine guns, ordnance, panoply, muskets, rifles, pistols, revolvers, grenades, shells, bombs, torpedoes, shrapnel, rockets, land mines, mine throwers, fortifications, transport.

3. Land, sea or air force equipped for war, nation's military strength, military personnel, manhood power of nation, army, military forces engaged in an expedition, land or naval force, equipment for hostile action, raw materials for war, war industries, accumulation of war products.

ARMISTICE, *n.* Suspension of hostilities by agreement, cease-fire, temporary truce, cessation of arms by convention, temporary peace, interval in fighting, respite from war, stoppage of gunfire, halt in hostilities, remission of war, interruption of warfare, discontinuance of belligerence, break in conflict, intermission from fighting, battle recess, breathing space in combat, lull in warfare.

ARMOR, *n.* 1. Protective covering against weapons of offense, defensive clothing, chain mail armor, defensive equipment, coat of mail, defensive arms for the body, shield, aegis, buckler, cuirass, leg armor, panoply, hauberk, habergeon, breast plate, corselet, lorica, plastron, brigandine, jambeaux, greaves, helm, helmet, steel helmet, trench helmet, casquetel, casque, head piece, siege-cap, vizor, morion, basinet, sallet, heaume, armet, targe, gauntlet, bulletproof vest.

2. Plate armor, armor plate, splint armor, decorative armor, armature, metallic sheathing, metal plates, outer metallic wrapping.

3. Protection, defense, safeguard, security, shelter, safety, guard, preservation.

ARMORY, *n.* 1. Storage place for war equipment, place for the safekeeping of guns, arsenal, depot of arms, depository of weapons, magazine of arms, military storehouse, repository of arms, ammunition dump.

2. Drill center of a National Guard unit.

ARMS, *n.* 1. Instruments of war, weapons, mean[?] of offense and defense, muniments, armamen[?] deadly weapons, armor, accouterments, harnes[?] panoply, martial array, mail, guns, small arn[?] firearms, lethal weapons, weapons of sm[?] caliber operated by hand, rifles, pistols, ordnan[?] submachine guns, machine guns, artillery.

2. Military service, profession of war, d[?] of valor, deeds of arms, feats of war, mil[?] exploits, war, warfare, heroic acts.

3. Heraldic bearings, heraldic devices, he[?] emblems, armorial ensigns, armorial bea[?] blazonry, emblazonry, blazonment, coat of emblazonment, escutcheon, scutcheon, device, crest, official insignia.

ARMY, *n.* 1. Military forces of a nation, [?] armament, military machine, men-of-w[?] forces of a nation, regular army, standi[?] soldiery, soldiers, body of troops tra[?] armed for war, militia, troops, arme[?] legion, phalanx, cohort, battalion, d[?] brigade, regiment, platoon, division, corps, squadron, squad, section, col[?] detail, garrison, battery, guard, pic[?] cavalry, infantry, artillery, air forc[?]

2. Vast multitude, host, great nur[?] array, vast assemblage, crowd, press aggregation, swarm, concourse, coll[?] congregation, herd, jam *(colloq.[?]* gang, crew, band, bevy, knot.

AROMA, *n.* 1. Agreeable odor,

redolence, perfume, fragrance, spicy smell, sweet scent, delicate savor, bouquet, odoriferousness, exhalation, trail, trace, emanation, aura.

2. Characteristic subtle quality, subtle essence, delicate characteristic, ethereal spirit, supreme quality, fine flavor.

AROMATIC, *adj.* Having an agreeable scent, odoriferous, aromatous, redolent, exhaling a rich odor, fragrant, sweet-smelling, sweet-scented, scented, spicy, pungent, savory, piquant, olent, strong-scented, balmy, ambrosial, perfumed, flavored, incense-laden.

AROMATIZE, *v.* Perfume, make aromatic, scent, imbue with fragrance, spice, season, flavor, give a spicy scent to.

AROUND, *adv.* 1. Round, about, round about, in a course making a circle, along a circuit, in a sphere, in a circle, in circumference, on all sides, circuitously, on every side, all about, right and left, out in all directions from a point, in various directions, on various sides, entirely about.

2. In the reverse direction, to the rear, in rotation, backwards.

3. Here and there indefinitely, from place to place.

4. Somewhere near, in the neighborhood, somewhere in the vicinity, neighboring, nigh, thereabouts, close about.

AROUND, *prep.* 1. So as to make the circuit of, along the whole outer boundary of, past all sides of successively, about the circuit of, on all sides, around, about, on all sides of at the same time, encompassing, encircling, enclosing, surrounding, on every side of, ambient, circumambient.

2. In all directions outward from, from one part to another of, random through, on another side of, on various sides of.

3. Here and there in the vicinity of, near in time or amount, approximately, about the time of, circa, ca. *(abbr.),* near to, in the region of, nigh to, bordering on, neighboring to.

AROUSE, *v.* Awaken, rouse, wake-up, waken, revive from sleep, summon up, cause to exert force, excite into action, infuse life into, give new life to, quicken, sharpen, stimulate, stir, incite, animate, warm, kindle, fire, spur, inspirit, stir up, goad, fillip, urge, instigate, foment, fan, foster, heat, provoke, put in motion, put in exertion, call forth, hurry on, set on, electrify, move, touch to the quick, rivet the attention, impress, strike, penetrate, disturb, alarm, startle, whet.

ARRAIGN, *v.* 1. Call before a court to answer an accusation, bring before a court to answer to a charge, cite, summon, bring to trial, prosecute.

2. Accuse in general, charge, indict, call to account, inculpate, incriminate, implicate, take to task, impeach, denounce, censure, tax, impute.

ARRAIGNMENT, *n.* 1. Act of arraigning, true bill, bringing to trial, summons, presentment, prosecution, legal action, indictment.

2. A calling in question for faults, calling to account, taking to task, censure, crimination, denunciation, impeachment, citation, accusation, inculpation, charge.

ARRANGE, *v.* 1. Place in proper order, class properly, classify, sort, assort, file, group, range, array, dispose in convenient order, marshal, rank, distribute in desired order, set in order, set out, parcel, systematize, organize, regulate, bring into

order, reduce to order, methodize, assign places to, pose, prearrange, allocate.

2. Come to an understanding concerning, settle, agree as to the terms of, determine the details of, fix upon, adjust, come to an agreement.

3. Settle details in advance, settle plans, plan, get ready beforehand, prepare, project, concoct, make preparations, construct, devise, lay out, contrive, mature, shape, premeditate, ordain, design.

4. *(Music)* Score, orchestrate, harmonize, adapt a composition for a particular mode of rendering.

ARRANGEMENT, *n.* 1. Putting in an orderly condition, disposition in suitable form, disposal, organization, classification, systematization, distribution, allocation, collocation, arraying, grouping, reducing to order, methodization, assortment, assignment, categorization, ordination.

2. Manner in which things are arranged, mode of arranging, make-up, style in which something is arranged, form, structure, system of parts according to some scheme.

3. Something made by arranging parts or things together, combination, amalgamation.

4. *(Usually pl.)* Measure taken in advance, settlement of details in advance, preparation, preparatory measure, provision.

5. Final settlement, adjustment by agreement, compromise, contract, covenant, compact, terms, accommodation.

6. Management, procedure, regulation, system, codification, ordinance, direction, economy.

7. *(Music)* Adaptation of a composition to voices or instruments, instrumentation, orchestration.

ARRANT, *adj.* 1. Utter, downright, through and through, thorough, thoroughgoing, overt, patent, glaring, stark-staring, consummate, rank, gross, out and out, undisguised, barefaced, brazen, bold, confirmed, pronounced, perfect, unmitigated.

2. Infamous, scandalous, vile, wicked, foul, base, low, ignominious, blackguard, notorious, atrocious, monstrous, preeminently bad, flagrant, egregious, flagitious, nefarious, outrageous, shocking, disgraceful, shameful, disreputable, shameless, rascally, heinous, unscrupulous.

ARRAY, *n.* 1. Regular order, state of special preparation, imposing disposition, order of battle, regular arrangement, collocation, marshalling, battle array, line of battle.

2. Marshalled force, body of persons placed in order, militia force, army, troops, battalions, soldiery, hosts.

3. Impressive group of things on exhibition, imposing series of things, display, show, parade, impressive collection, ostentation, pageantry, sight.

4. Ornamental clothing, attire, fine clothes, beautiful apparel, rich raiment, vestments, finery, elegant garments.

5. *(Law)* Body of jurors, panel.

ARRAY, *v.* 1. Range in desired positions, rank, place in proper order, arrange, set in order, dispose, marshal, draw up, set in line, draw out in line of battle, deploy, group.

2. Clothe with ornamental garments, attire, accouter, adorn with dress, wrap, invest, enrobe, robe, vest, dress, habit, envelop, don, put on, bedeck, deck, betrap, embellish, betrim, garnish, ornament, bedizen, prank, decorate, set off, fit out, trick out, outfit, equip.

ARREARS, *n.* That which is behind in payment, something overdue and unpaid, debt unpaid though due, outstanding debt, liability, obligation, outstandings, debit, claim, arrearage, deficiency, deficit, unpaid bills, balance remaining due, remainder after part of a debt has been paid.

ARREST, *v.* 1. Stop suddenly, stop the course of, bring to a standstill, end, stay, check the motion of, hinder the action of, block, inhibit, restrain from further motion, keep back, bring to a state of inactivity, obstruct, delay, interrupt, suspend, withhold, prevent, suppress, quiet, stunt, dwarf, nip in the bud.
2. Seize by legal warrant, take by authority, take into custody, take prisoner, imprison, jail, incarcerate, apprehend, capture, catch, detain, hold, secure, collar.
3. Catch and fix, attract and hold, seize on, hold the attention of, engross, engage, occupy, rivet, absorb, electrify, galvanize.

ARREST, *n.* 1. Act of stopping, stoppage, delay, cessation, interruption, hindrance, obstruction, prevention, suspension, suppression, restraining, check, stay.
2. Police detention, seizure, apprehension, capture, taking by force, taking into custody, imprisonment, incarceration, legal restraint, duress, durance, constraint.

ARRIVAL, *n.* 1. Act of arriving, advent, coming, access, reaching a place from a distance, return, reaching one's destination, meeting, approach, appearance, accession, alighting, dismounting, landing, debarkation, disembarkation, reception, welcome.
2. Person that has arrived, comer, visitant, visitor, passenger, incomer, newcomer, transient.

ARRIVE *v.* 1. Come to certain point in the course of travel, reach one's destination, reach a stopping place, come to the end of a journey, get to, gain, join, put in, come in contact, overtake, appear, drop in, visit, meet, enter, return, land, alight, light, dismount, disembark, detrain.
2. Reach in any course or process, attain, come to, touch, consummate, compass as an object, attain by effort, be successful, prosper, flourish, reach that toward which one has progressed.
3. Come at length, occur, happen, present itself, come into view, befall, take place, come to pass, eventuate, supervene, betide, chance, turn up.

ARROGANCE, *n.* Offensive exhibition of assumed superiority, overweening assurance, overbearing pride, overbearance, insolence, haughtiness, airs, exorbitant estimation of worth, lordliness, vanity, loftiness, self-assurance, self-conceit, ostentation, egotism, hauteur, swagger, bluster, toploftiness, conceit, self-assumption, superciliousness, disdain, pretension, vainglory, presumption, excessive assumption of superiority, presumptuousness, imperiousness, self-assertion, effrontery, audacity, bumptiousness, disrespect, contempt, contumely, uppishness, despotism, tyranny, self-importance, braggadocio.

ARROGANT, *adj.* Making unwarrantable claims to superior importance, overbearingly assuming, making exorbitant claims of rank, giving oneself an undue degree of importance, self-important, imperious, domineering, overweening, arbitrary, dictatorial, despotic, authoritative, vainglorious, presumptuous, high and mighty, toplofty, full of

mighty airs and graces, dogmatic, magisterial, supercilious, insolently proud, cavalier, pompous, self-conceited, self-assertive, self-assuming, lordly, egotistic, self-assured, haughty, swaggering, blustering, bumptious, contemptuous, disdainful, insulting, contumelious, rude, scornful, stuck-up (*colloq.*), offensive, audacious, impertinent, on one's high horse, impudent, high-handed, uppish.

ARROGATE, *v.* 1. Claim unwarrantably, make undue claims to, assume without right, appropriate to oneself unduly, take without grounds, help oneself to, commandeer, make free with, possess oneself of, usurp, expropriate, seize, take, demand presumptuously, make unjust pretensions to, adopt to oneself.
2. Assign to another without just reason, attribute unjustly, impute unrightfully, ascribe falsely.

ARROW, *n.* 1. Sagitta, dart, feathered shaft, bolt, pointed missile weapon, missile, barbed reed, bobtailed arrow, barreled arrow, bearing arrow, chested arrow, whistling arrow, spirally feathered crossbow-bolt, vire, quarrel (*for crossbow*), flight (*volley*), arbalester, matras (*Celtic*), cloth-yard shaft (*for early English longbow*), quiver (*pl.*), sumpit (*Malayan poisoned dart*).
2. Indicator, pointer, marker, director, figure used in maps etc. to indicate direction.

ARROW-HEADED, *adj.* Sagittate, triangular, barbed, wedge-shaped, cuneiform.

ARROWY, *adj.* 1. Like an arrow in shape, slim, reedlike, straight, pointed, feathered, slender, gracile, graceful, light, delicate, slight, narrow.
2. Flexible, supple, limber, lithe, lissome, svelte, sinuous, pliant, easily bent.
3. Swift, fleet, rapid, flying, rushing, darting, fast, speedy, quick.
4. Sharp, cutting, piercing, penetrating, biting, pricking, sarcastic, mordant, acrimonious, stinging.

ARSENAL, *n.* 1. Magazine of arms, depository of military stores, repository of military matériel, storehouse of arms, depot of ammunition, cache of weapons, armory, military warehouse, store of military equipment, entrepot (*Fr.*), ammunition dump.
2. Building for the training of troops, armory, drill center, headquarters of a National Guard unit.
3. Public establishment for the manufacture of arms, armorer's shop.

ARSON, *n.* Incendiarism, pyromania, deliberate burning of property, criminal setting of fires, set conflagration, malicious burning of other's property, firing, wilful burning of one's own property when insured.

ARSONIST, *n.* Incendiary, pyromaniac, firebug, pétroleur (*Fr.*), one who sets fires illegally.

ART, *n.* 1. Exercise of skill, mastery, address, dexterity, facility, expertness, adroitness, skill, aptitude, cleverness, ingenuity, knack, readiness, sagacity, aptness, virtuosity, genius.
2. Department of skilled performance, system of rules to facilitate performance, aesthetics, general principles of a craft.
3. Skilled workmanship, production of what is beautiful, creation of beauty, embodied beauty, that which is produced by the application of skill and taste, cultural achievement, illustration, depiction.
4. Branch of learning or university study, a

science, field of learning, learning, liberal arts.

5. Execution, agency, profession, business, trade, calling.

6. Immoral shrewdness, craft, cunning, slyness, craftiness, trickery, duplicity, subtlety, finesse, trickiness, wiliness, foxiness, astuteness, artifice, wile, strategy, insidiousness, deception, deceit, guile, artfulness, artful device, contrivance, skilful plan.

7. Studied action, artificiality of behavior, affectation, mannerism, affectedness, assumed manners, unnaturalness, affected manner, airs, pretense.

ARTERY, *n.* 1. Blood vessel, vessel, aorta, vein.

2. Main channel of communication, path of transportation, way, road, roadway, passage, avenue, thoroughfare, turnpike, boulevard, lane, highway, trunkline, supply route, course, pathway, corridor, conduit, duct, canal.

ARTFUL, *adj.* 1. Shrewd, astute, sharp, subtle, scheming, designing, insidious, contriving, wily, machinating, cunning, sly, intriguing, strategic, Machiavellian, Jesuitical, diplomatic, politic, maneuvering, crafty, tricky, trickish, deceitful, underhand, double-faced, shifty, crooked, foxy, stealthy, cautelous, subdolous, versute, pawky, disingenuous, canny, snaky, vulpine, feline.

2. Skilful in adapting means to ends, adroit, dexterous, deft, adept, ready, quick, clever, able, ingenious, apt, knowing, masterly, proficient, smart, gifted, resourceful, inventive, talented, facile, nimble-fingered, neat-handed.

3. Done with skill, characterized by art, artistic.

ARTHRITIS, *n.* Arthropathy, collagen disease, inflammation of a joint, gout, rheumatism.

ARTICLE, *n.* 1. Definite division, individual piece, item, particular, distinct detail, division, member, branch, part, portion, paragraph, head, heading, point, count.

2. Independent literary composition on a specific subject, essay, commentary, brief paper, feuilleton, sketch, review, study, critique, item, write-up, skit, contribution, appreciation, notice, feature, editorial, dissertation, treatise, thesis, theme, tract, written discourse, disquisition, descant, discussion.

3. Particular object, material thing, substance, matter, commodity, object, something, subject.

4. Clause in a contract, condition, stipulation, proviso, provision, distinct proposition, covenant, term, *sine qua non (Lat.).*

5. Item of religious belief, point of doctrine, tenet, dogma, creed, canon, catechism, summary of belief, credo.

6. *(Gram.)* Particle of logical quantity, limiting adjective, quantifying adjective.

ARTICLE, *v.* 1. Bind by articles of covenant or stipulation, indenture, apprentice, bind to service.

2. Specify, formulate in distinct particulars, set forth in articles, make specific charges, charge, accuse specifically, object in writing to the credibility of depositions *(Law).*

ARTICULATE, *adj.* 1. Clearly enunciated, not speechless, spoken so as to be intelligible, audible in distinct syllables, distinctly uttered, divided into consecutive syllables, capable of speech, characterized by division into syllables, distinct, clear, manifest, united to form speech.

2. Composed of segments, expressed in clearly distinguished parts, jointed, having joints, formed with joints, articulated.

ARTICULATE, *v.* 1. Sound in distinct syllables, utter distinct syllables, enunciate, enounce, give utterance to, set forth in speech, express, articulate a speech sound *(Phonet.).*

2. Connect by articulation, unite articularly, form a joint, put together with joints, unite by joints, fasten together, connect, join, fit into a systematically interrelated whole.

ARTICULATION, *n.* 1. Distinct utterance, speech sound, enunciation, syllabic differentiation, division into syllables, pronunciation, elocution, diction, process of articulating speech *(Phonet.),* adjustment of speech organs involved in pronouncing a particular sound.

2. Segmented composition, jointed formation, joint, juncture, connection, hinge, mode of union, point of junction.

ARTIFICE, *n.* 1. Invention, contrivance, design, art, measure, expedient, effort, step, course, procedure, bright idea, clever stroke, ingenuity.

2. Stratagem, crafty device, clever trick, artful contrivance, ruse, cabal, plot, subterfuge, wile, feint, coup, maneuver, finesse, hoax, blind, trap, sleight, shift, evasion, dodge, fetch, fraud, circumvention.

3. Strategy, machination, intrigue, trickery, craft, guile, deceit, deception, artfulness, slyness, wiliness, cunning, imposture, duplicity, subtlety, imposition, diplomacy, shuffle, double-dealing, cheatery, doubling, crookedness, falsehood, cozenage, Machiavellism, hocus-pocus, delusion.

ARTIFICER, *n.* 1. Craftsman, handicraftsman, skilful worker, artistic workman, artisan, hand, mechanic, machinist, operative, artist in handicraft.

2. Inventor, one skilful in devising ways of making things, deviser, contriver, machinator, framer, skilful designer, artist, maker, wright, architect, manufacturer, builder, mason, smith.

ARTIFICIAL, *adj.* 1. Made by human labor, made by art, not natural, factitious, contrived by art, manufactured, modified by human skill, unnatural, made-up, constructed, cultivated.

2. Made in imitation of, made as a substitute, ersatz *(Ger.),* not genuine, mock, synthetic, sham, counterfeit, spurious, specious, pseudo, simulated, imitated, false, unreal, forged, adulterate, base, alloyed, hollow, make-believe, bogus, bastard, fraudulent, catchpenny, meretricious, illegitimate, brummagem.

3. So-called, feigned, fictitious, assumed, pretended, imaginary, fabulous, supposititious, trumped up.

4. Full of affectation, affected, forced, labored, unnatural, strained, stilted, stagy, theatrical, canting, insincere, *maniéré (Fr.),* mannered, overdone, overacted, self-conscious.

ARTILLERY, *n.* 1. Ordnance, mounted guns, cannon, missile engines of war, enginery, great guns, group-served firearms, battery, mortars, howitzers, flying artillery, heavy artillery, light artillery, field artillery, foot artillery, seacoast artillery, siege artillery, engines for discharging heavy missiles, catapults, ballistae, fieldpieces, culverins, carronades, falconets, jingals, swivel guns, mitrailleuses *(Fr.),* machine guns.

2. Branch of the army concerned with the service of the guns.

3. Science treating of the use of such guns, gunnery, theory of ordnance, art of handling artillery, cannonry.

ARTILLERYMAN, *n.* Gunner, artillerist, matross,

cannoneer, mitrailleur, machine gunner, fusilier, bombardier.

ARTISAN, *n.* One skilled in an industrial art, one engaged in a manual enterprise, mechanic, one trained to dexterity in some mechanic trade, handicraftsman, craftsman, artificer, laborer, operative, mechanician, machinist, hand, worker.

ARTIST, *n.* 1. Proficient practitioner of a fine art, consummate performer, virtuoso, masterhand, master, one who exhibits art in his work, one who makes an art of his employment, adept, artificer, skilled hand, finished practitioner in any occupation requiring skill, skilled workman, handicraftsman.

2. Designer, projector, contriver, architect, perpetrator, author, builder, promoter, agent.

3. Painter, colorist, limner, delineator, watercolorist, drawer, cartoonist, caricaturist, cubist, illuminator, pastellist, landscapist, draughtsman, depictor, portraitist, miniaturist, enamelist, impressionist, futurist, sketcher.

4. Sculptor, modeler, lapidary, statuary, carver, figuriste, engraver, graver, molder, chaser, etcher.

5. Member of one of the histrionic professions, actor, singer, musician, dancer, artiste *(Fr.)*.

6. A trickster, a schemer, an artful person, rogue, knave, sharper, swindler, impostor, cheat, deceiver, peculator, embezzler, counterfeiter, forger.

ARTISTIC, *adj.* 1. Conformable to the standards of art, aesthetically excellent, appealing to the aesthetic nature, admirable, beautiful, attractive, lovely, pretty, handsome, shapely, well-made, well-proportioned, symmetrical, harmonious, graceful, exquisite, delicate, elegant, enchanting, pleasing, ornamental, magnificent, classical, chic, becoming, stylish, exhibiting skill in applying the principles of beauty, tasteful, in good taste.

2. Befitting an artist, skilful, accomplished, talented, aesthetic, cultured, refined, polished, discriminative, proficient, expert, masterly.

3. Bohemian, unconventional, unconformable, eccentric, *sui generis (Lat.),* original, bizarre, *outré (Fr.),* impractical, visionary.

ARTISTRY, *n.* 1. Artistic workmanship, artistic effect *or* performance *or* quality *or* ability *or* virtuosity *or* touch *or* style.

2. Pursuit of art, artistic pursuits.

ARTLESS, *adj.* 1. Sincere, candid, plain-spoken, frank, truthful, straightforward, aboveboard, open-hearted, true, fair, honest, straight-out, free, simple-minded, free from deceit or cunning, not crafty, guileless, unsophisticated, naive, innocent, childlike, ingenuous, simple, simple-hearted, pure, unselfconscious, unaffected, natural, undesigning, single-minded, trustful, confiding, unsuspicious, plain, devoid of stratagem.

2. Not artificial, inartificial, natural, without marks of art, plain, simple, classic, unadorned, chaste, homespun.

3. Without artistic skill or taste, wanting in skill, lacking knowledge or art, ignorant, rude, unskilful, inartistic, uncultured, unlearned, crude, untalented, untaught, devoid of artistic quality, awkward, clumsy, untutored, gauche, bungling, blundering, uncouth.

ARTLESSNESS, *n.* 1. Guilelessness, sincerity, candor, simplicity, naivete, ingenuousness, purity, unsophistication, innocence, frankness, honesty, truthfulness, openness, rough diamond, plainness, unself-consciousness, single-mindedness, pureness, naturalness.

2. Unskilfulness, awkwardness, clumsiness, crudeness, gaucherie, uncouthness, ignorance, benightedness, rusticity.

AS, *adv.* and *conj.* 1. To the extent in which, to the degree that, in the same proportion that, in proportion to which, to the same extent, in equal degree, equally, no less than, to whatever extent, to such a degree or extent.

2. By way of example, for example, *exempli gratia (Lat.),* e.g. *(abbr.),* to wit, namely, *videlicet (Lat.),* viz. *(abbr.),* for instance, thus, in the same manner with, of the same kind with, in a manner like that of, after the manner of.

3. In the idea or character of, under the name of, considered in the state of, viewed like, taken in the character of.

4. At the time when, while, when, during the time that, at the same time that.

5. Because, inasmuch as, forasmuch as, for the reason that, as, since, by reason of, it being the case that, on account of, in consideration of, on the score that.

6. However, though.

7. *(Relative pronoun)* That, who, which, being of the kind which, being of the class who.

ASCEND, *v.* 1. Move upward upon, climb, scale, clamber, go up, get up along, work one's way up, scramble, shin *(colloq.),* mount, surmount, escalade, top, overtop, scrabble.

2. Rise, uprise, arise, tower, soar, fly aloft, rise to a higher point or degree, proceed from an inferior to a superior level, advance, shoot up, slope upward, heave up, spring up, wing up, swerve up, run up, creep up, float, levitate.

3. Go backward in time, go toward the source or beginning.

4. *(Music)* Rise in pitch, pass from any tone to a higher one.

ASCENDANCY, *n.* 1. Controlling authority, edge, governing influence, paramount power, dominion, domination, dominance, mastery, sway, control, rule, reign, supremacy, sovereignty, command, masterdom, superiority, government, prevalence, preponderance, pull, predominance, advantage over, upper hand, whip hand, hegemony, victory, preeminence, majority, triumph, conquest, state of being in the ascendant.

2. Ancestry, progenitors.

ASCENDANT, *n.* 1. Position of dominance, place of supreme power, superior influence, supremacy, preeminence, predominance, domination, control, lordship, chiefdom, seigniority, suzerainty, hold, hegemony, leadership, mastership, grasp, iron sway, rod of empire, command, rule, controlling influence, weight, pressure.

2. Ancestor, antecedent, progenitor, forebear, forefather, sire.

3. Horoscope, sign of the zodiac rising above the eastern horizon.

ASCENDANT, *adj.* 1. Rising above the horizon, moving up in space, climbing, towering, raised, mounting, scandent, elevated, uplifted, upturned, curved upward.

2. Superior in power or rank, dominant, ruling, supreme, predominant, preeminent, prevailing, surpassing, prevalent, rampant, over-swaying, controlling.

ASCENSION, *n.* Act of ascending, ascendance, rising, ascent, rise, mounting, moving upward, upward flight, uphill climb, voyage up, scaling, act of traveling up.

ASCENT, *n.* 1. Rising from a lower to a higher state or grade, advancement in status, promotion.

2. Procedure toward a source or beginning.

3. Hill, acclivity, rising ground, ascending path, upward slope, rise, upgrade, grade, gradient, that by which one ascends, climb, incline, ramp, eminence, elevation, height, inclination.

ASCERTAIN, *v.* 1. Verify, determine, establish, adjudge, settle, decide, certify, make sure, make certain, estimate.

2. Find out by trial, discover, investigate, espy, ferret out, unearth, descry, make out, detect, spy out, try out, prove, learn for a certainty, get at with precision, come to know.

ASCETIC, *adj.* 1. Abstemious, puritanic, austere, self-denying, over-abstinent, rigorous, practicing rigid abstinence, stern, severe, harsh, given to severe self-denial, strict, temperate.

2. Unduly strict in religious exercises, self-mortifying, flagellant, flagellatory.

ASCETIC, *n.* Practitioner of religious austerities, holy man, religious devotee, monk, anchorite, nun, anchoress, anchoret, penitent, flagellant, fakir *(Moham.),* yogi *(Hindu),* sannyasi *(Hindu),* dervish *(Moham.),* calender *(Persian),* puritan, mortifier of the flesh, stylite, pillar saint, eremite, solitary, *solitaire,* recluse, hermit, one who leads an abstemious life, self-tormentor, self-denier.

ASCETICISM, *n.* Monasticism, self-abnegation, abstemiousness, austerity, rigorous self-discipline, over-abstinence, self-denial, total abstinence, self-renunciation, self-mortification, puritanism, penance, sackcloth and ashes, fasting, scourging, flagellation, flagellantism, hair shirt.

ASCRIBABLE, *adj.* Imputable, referable, due to, assignable, attributable, chargeable, traceable, owing to, accountable, explicable.

ASCRIBE, *v.* Assign, impute, refer, attribute, charge to, lay to, father upon, trace to, saddle with, account for, derive from, blame on, allege to belong, accredit to, credit with, appropriate, owe to, arrogate.

ASCRIPTION, *n.* 1. Act of ascribing, attribution, assignment, reference to, charging, imputation, setting down, laying, alleging, accounting for, derivation, appropriation, arrogation.

2. Text ascribing praise to the Almighty, praises to the Deity, exaltation, magnification, adoration, extolling, homage, allelujah, hosannah, glorification, Magnificats, Glorias, *Te Deums.*

AS FAR AS To the extent that, insofar as, to the degree that.

AS GOOD AS Of equal goodness with, up to the measure of, the same as, equal to, tantamount to, equivalent to being, practically.

ASHAMED, *adj.* 1. Embarrassed, abashed by guilt, conscience-stricken, chagrined, mortified, affected by consciousness of impropriety, bashful, humiliated, disconcerted, hangdog, put to shame, out of countenance, chapfallen, crestfallen, confused, bewildered, perplexed, confounded, diffident, shamefaced.

2. Fearing to perform some action because of the shame connected with it, verecund, pudent, prudish, squeamish, deterred by anticipation of shame, reluctant, restrained, unwilling through fear of shame.

ASHEN, *adj.* 1. Consisting of ashes, made of ash, cinereous, favillous.

2. Resembling ashes in color, ashen-gray, wan, ashy, pale, pallid, blanched, hueless, colorless, gray, ash-colored, pale-faced, ghastly.

ASHES, *n.* 1. Favillae, lapilli, scoriae, cinders, slag, embers, remains of what is burned, ruins from destruction by fire.

2. Any ruined or blasted thing, dust, bitterness, disappointment, symbol of grief.

3. Mortal remains, corpse, dead body, dust and ashes, reliquiae, relics, clay.

ASHORE, *adv.* 1. On shore, on land, not at sea, not afloat, not on board a vessel, on dry land, on terra firma.

2. To shore, to the land, to the beach, to the breakers, with the intide.

3. Aground, stranded, run out, at a loss, come to grief, hard up, in difficulties.

ASHY, *adj.* 1. Consisting of ashes, cineraceous, favillous, composed of ashes, covered or strewn with ashes, sprinkled with ashes, cinereous.

2. Whitish, gray, ash-colored, pale as ashes, light-gray, pale with rage, angry.

ASIDE, *adv.* 1. To the side, to one side, beside, laterally, sidewise, sideways, alongside, abreast, abeam, at a short distance, apart so as to deviate, away from some position, by.

2. Away from one's thoughts or considerations, out of mind, out of thought, out of consideration, out of character, off the line, wide of the mark, out of relation, out of connection, off, away from further use.

3. In a state of exclusion, apart from, except for, excluding, separately, put by, in private, set to one side, astray, away, aloof, secretly, so as not to be overheard.

ASIDE, *n.* 1. Something said so as not to be overheard, whisper, under-breath, soliloquy, side-remark, monologue, apostrophe, by-play.

2. Anything apart from the main thing, side issue, incidental consideration.

AS IF As though, as it were, as it would be if, as if it were, the same that it would be if, as might be, supposing, so to speak, quasi.

ASININE, *adj.* Ass-like, assish, doltish, loutish, witless, stupid, silly, senseless, blockish, foolish, brainless, fatuous, dullard, duncish, half-witted, obtuse, dunderheaded, feeble-minded, obstinate, idiotic, nonsensical, irrational, ridiculous, absurd, thick-headed, thick-skulled, muddle-brained.

ASININITY, *n.* Act of folly, inanity, foolishness, stupidity, assishness, fatuity, idiocy, imbecility, doltishness, loutishness, brainlessness, obtuseness, duncishness, nonsensicality, absurdity, nugacity.

AS IT WERE So to say, so to speak, so to express oneself, in a manner, in some sort, as it would seem, as it seems.

ASK, *v.* 1. Question, query, interrogate, inquire of, put questions to, quiz, catechize, interpellate, sound out, pump, cross-examine, put through the third degree, grill.

2. Seek to be informed about, make inquiry concerning, seek information about, inquire into, investigate.

3. Request the presence of, invite, summon, bid.

4. Seek by words to obtain, express a desire for, solicit from, request of, desire, crave, beg, petition, beseech, plead, supplicate, implore, sue, importune, seek, canvass, entreat, pray for, beg a boon, adjure, conjure, clamor for, beg leave, earwig, appeal to, make petition for, make suit, make application for, invoke.

5. Expect as a right, require, demand, claim, call for, exact, dun, order, requisition, press, urge.

ASKANCE, *adv.* 1. At an angle, obliquely, awry, slantwise, askant, sideways, aslant, with a side glance, asquint, askew, out of the corner of one's eye, with an indirect glance, crooked, edgewise.

2. Disdainfully, with envy, with distrust, with suspicion, with disapproval, distrustfully, meaningfully, significantly.

ASKER, *n.* Inquirer, inquisitor, querist, quizzer, questioner, catechist, examiner, investigator, petitioner, seeker, solicitor, suitor, solicitant, suppliant, postulant, applicant, supplicant, beggar.

ASKEW, *adv.* With a wry look, awry, in a twisted position, atwist, crookedly, distortedly, aslant, askance, askant, skewed, obliquely, sidewise, aside, sidelong, crosswise, turned to one side, asquint, out of proper position, out of line, asymmetrically.

ASLANT, *adv.* At a slant, slantingly, in a slanting position, slantwise, aslope, athwart, across, at an angle, askance, sidewise, edgewise, obliquely.

ASLANT, *adj.* Inclined, slanting, sloping, oblique, uphill, rising, ascending, acclivous, downhill, falling, descending, declivitous, tilted, skew, slant, bias, indirect, diagonal, transverse.

ASLEEP, *adj.* 1. In a state of sleep, in a sound sleep, sleeping, fast asleep, dead asleep, sound asleep, slumbering, somnolent, soporous, heavy with sleep, napping, dozing, comatose, drowsy, reposing, resting, in the arms of Morpheus, taking a siesta, dormant, anaesthetized, dreaming.

2. Inactive, quiescent, in abeyance, quiet, inert, motionless, torpid, sluggish, leaden, lethargic, supine, passive, stagnant, lifeless, inanimate, dull, languid.

3. Numb *(of the foot)*, tingling, benumbed, prickling.

4. In the sleep of death, dead, at rest, in the last sleep, defunct, extinct, departed, deceased, late.

ASP, *n.* Venomous snake, hooded serpent, adder, horned viper, Egyptian cobra, uraeus *(Archaeol.),* Naje haje.

ASPECT, *n.* 1. Appearance to the eye, look, mien, air, figure, peculiar feature, facial expression, salient characteristic, countenance, visage, face, physiognomy, complexion, lineaments, manner, cast, bearing, deportment, carriage, posture.

2. Appearance to the mind, way in which a thing may be regarded, light, condition, attitude, state, phase, side, viewpoint, angle, conception, respect, selected view of a subject.

3. Position with regard to direction or outlook, situation, outlook, prospect, relative position, direction, exposure, view commanded, side facing a given direction, landscape, scene, view.

ASPERITY, *n.* 1. Roughness of surface, rugosity, ruggedness, corrugation, spinosity, unevenness.

2. Harshness of taste, tartness, corrosiveness, sourness, acridness, bitterness, sharpness, acidity, acidulousness, causticity, pungency, piquancy, poignancy.

3. Harshness of sound, grating, hoarseness, huskiness, raucity.

4. Sharpness of temper, crabbedness, acerbity, churlishness, ill temper, acrimony, sullenness, moroseness, petulance, ill humor, irritability, irascibility, crossness, spleen, bile, gall, procacity,

resentment, huff, virulence, discourtesy, surliness, captiousness, choler, sternness, severity.

5. Hardship, difficulty, bleakness, inclemency, rigor.

ASPERSE, *v.* 1. Assail with damaging charges, slander, circulate injurious reports about, cast aspersions, calumniate, defame, decry, disparage, discredit, censure harshly, vilify, traduce, impugn, slur, libel, denigrate, revile, sneer at, vilipend, avile, malign, abuse, run down, detract from, pull to pieces, pick a hole in one's coat, derogate, depreciate, besmirch, blacken, defile, brand, fling dirt, befoul, blemish, give a dog a bad name, speak ill of, vituperate, cast obloquy upon, gibe at, sully, cast reproach upon, tarnish, accuse falsely, dishonor, reflect upon, animadvert upon, cast reflections on, reproach, bring scandal upon, assail, attack, lampoon, backbite, rate, berate.

2. Sprinkle, besprinkle, bespatter.

ASPERSION, *n.* 1. Damaging imputation, libel, derogatory criticism, slanderous charge, censure, defamation, detraction, obtrectation, reflection, evil-speaking, vituperation, obloquy, lampoon, squib, pasquinade, *chronique scandaleuse,* abuse, envenomed tongue, backbiting, traducement, reviling, calumny, vilification, depreciation, fling, reproach, animadversion, disparagement, railing, brickbats.

2. Shower, spray, sprinkle, diffusion, lustration, dissemination.

ASPHYXIATE, *v.* Suffocate, stifle, strangulate, garrote, choke, throttle, smother, stop the breath, produce asphyxia in.

ASPHYXIATION, *n.* Suffocation, strangulation, throttling, garrote, stifling, choking, smothering, suspended respiration, death by intake of noxious gases.

ASPIRANT, *n.* 1. Ambitious person, aspirer, one who seeks honor or advancement.

2. Candidate, seeker, petitioner, supplicant, postulant, solicitant, claimant, solicitor, suitor, competitor, rival, would-be, applicant.

ASPIRATION, *n.* 1. Inhalation, inspiration, sigh, drawing in of air in breathing, respiration, breath, pronunciation with the rough breathing *(Phonet.).*

2. Lofty desire, sanguine expectation, earnest longing, ardent wish for what is above one's reach, airy hopes, fond hope, yearning, upward looking, spiritual elevation, eager desire to gain, craving after excellence, presumption, endeavor, expectancy, design, end, goal, mark, intention, object, purpose, ambition, aim, objective, wish, daydream, golden dream, castles in the air, dream of Alnaschar.

ASPIRE, *v.* Be eagerly desirous, have an earnest longing for something high and good, presume to, live in hope of, hold out for, bid for, desire ardently, yearn for, long for, thirst after, hanker after, wish for, pant after, covet, seek, endeavor to attain, aim at, indulge an ambition for, venture to make suit for, entertain hopes of, venture to seek ambitiously, hope against hope for, purpose, project.

ASPIRING, *adj.* Eager for advancement, winged, ambitious, resolved to obtain preferment, high-reaching, of lofty purpose, enterprising, hopeful, hard-working, sanguine, expectant, optimistic, enthusiastic, vaulting, emulous, striving after excellence, high-flying.

ASQUINT, *adv.* With an oblique glance, awry,

obliquely, sidelong, to one side, askance, with averted glance, so as to see distortedly.

ASS, *n.* 1. Small long-eared equine, *equus asinus* (*Lat.*), jackass, donkey, onager, kiang, burrico, burro, jenny (*fem.*), jack (*male*), moke (*Eng.*), neddy (*slang*), cuddy (*slang*), Jerusalem pony, beast of burden.

2. Person with asinine qualities, booby, lout, noodle, dolt, blockhead, numskull, nincompoop, ninny, witling, simpleton, fool, tomfool, dunce, halfwit, bonehead, lunkhead, clod, Simple Simon, oaf, idiot.

ASSAIL, *v.* 1. Attack physically, set upon with violence, assault belligerently, oppugn, strike at, thrust at, deal a blow at, fly at, fall upon, bear down upon, pounce upon, make aggression on, beset, waylay, kick against, lunge at, charge at, invade, accost, encounter, molest, maltreat. (see ATTACK.)

2. Attack by non-physical means, importune with arguments or entreaties, bombard, besiege, storm, ply, harry, pepper, pitch into. (see IMPORTUNE.)

3. Asperse, malign, impugn, defame, snipe at, calumniate, vituperate, slander, vilify, hoot at, censure, abuse. (see ASPERSE.)

4. Undertake with the purpose of mastering, approach in order to overcome, bend to one's task.

ASSAILABLE, *adj.* Vulnerable, open to attack, impugnable, not impregnable, censurable, weak, sensitive, exposed, liable to injury, defenseless, accessible.

ASSAILANT, *n.* Assaulter, attacker, aggressor, assailer, adversary, foe, enemy, antagonist, opponent, challenger, accoster, accuser, plaintiff.

ASSASSIN, *n.* 1. Murderer by surprise, slayer by secret assault, killer, cutthroat, assassinator, manslayer, butcher, Cain, hatchet man, garroter, strangler, throttler, mugger, dagger man, gunman, Apache, executioner, sicarian, slaughterer, thug, destroyer, desperado, hired murderer of a public person, bravo (*professional assassin*).

2. One of a sect of Oriental fanatics practicing assassination.

ASSASSINATE, *v.* 1. Kill by secret assault, slay, murder by premeditated attack, morganize, shed blood, despatch treacherously, remove by killing, burke, butcher, massacre, destroy treacherously, murderously assail, exterminate, put to death, do to death, run through, put to the sword, put an end to, slaughter, garrote, choke, strangle, suffocate, smother, asphyxiate, knife, shoot, bump off (*slang*), mug, throttle, take for a ride, knock on the head.

2. Stab (*one's reputation*), destroy, blight. (see ASPERSE and DEFAME.)

ASSASSINATION, *n.* Murder by premeditated assault, killing by treachery, homicide, slaying, manslaughter, dispatch, bloodshed, death blow, finishing stroke, suffocation, mugging, choking, strangulation, knifing, shooting, violent death.

ASSAULT, *n.* 1. Violent attack, aggressive action, onset with force, onslaught, lunge, pass, thrust, aggression, charge, invasion, incursion, irruption, illapse, sally, sortie, raid, foray, push, drive, assailing with blows, buffet, shock, brunt, offense, holdup.

2. Storming, boarding, escalade, investment, siege, bombardment, fusillade, broadside, air raid, cannonade.

3. Rape, debauchery, fornication, defloration, defilement, sexual abuse, molestation, outrage, violation, stupration.

ASSAULT, *v.* 1. Attack, affront hostilely, assail, fall upon with hostile intention, fly at, lunge at, bear down upon, make aggression on, assail with blows, batter upon, pitch into, batter down, set upon, accost bellicosely, oppugn, descend upon, invade, charge.

2. Storm, board, besiege, invest, bombard.

3. Rape, debauch, defile, violate, stuprate, abuse sexually, molest, attack, deflower, outrage.

ASSAY, *n.* 1. Determination of the amount of metal in an ore, chemical analysis of an alloy to ascertain its ingredients and their proportions, trial to determine the quality of metals.

2. Test, examination, experiment, touchstone, proof, endeavor, attempt, effort.

ASSAY, *v.* 1. Analyze metallic substances, subject to analysis, submit to test, examine by trial, put to trial, try in combat, test, make an assay of, prove by touchstone, make trial of, try, judge the quality of, evaluate.

2. Attempt, endeavor, essay, undertake.

ASSEMBLAGE, *n.* 1. Collection, accumulation, amassment, cumulation, conglomeration, store, aggregation, stock, congestion, conflux, cluster, aggregate, group, number, bunch, body, mass, congeries, clump, pack. crew, flock, herd, drove, roundup, bevy, swarm, shoal, flood, circle, pile, gang, knot, troupe, batch, heap, lump, litter, medley, jumble.

2. Assembly, levee, reunion, convention, convocation, conclave, conference, confluence, congregation, crowd, rout, concourse, throng, meeting, gathering, mustering, forgathering, convergence, mobilization, big concentration.

3. Combination, conjunction, association, act of fitting together parts of a machine, union, union of parts, unification.

ASSEMBLE, *v.* 1. Collect, round up, muster, marshal, convene, convoke, concentrate, gather into one place, congregate, call together, bring together, summon, levy, amass, accumulate, compile, lump together, mass, rake up, heap, pile up, join together, unite.

2. Collect and put together the parts of, fit parts together, manufacture, fabricate.

3. Meet together, flock, herd, swarm, stream, surge, crowd, throng, huddle, bunch, cogather, draw together, rally, hold a meeting, come together, get together, resort.

ASSEMBLY, *n.* 1. Concourse, throng, press, rout, crush, galaxy, group, muster, confluence, mass, multitude, audience, community, flock, crowd, group, host, horde, assemblage, congregation, bloc.

2. Lower house of a legislature, chamber of deputies, states-general, congress, parliament, legislative body, diet, convocation, conclave, council, synod, conventicle, caucus, consistory, federal council, directory, comitia, camarilla, camera, conference, junta.

3. Ball, salon, dance, dancing party, soiree, reception.

ASSENT, *v.* Give assent, agree by expressing acquiescence, express concurrence, concur, yield, acquiesce, accede, conform to, comply, consent, subscribe to, coincide, accept, accord, approve, permit, admit, endorse, visé, seal, corroborate, validate, verify, testify, accredit, ratify, confirm, substantiate, sustain, uphold, recognize, concede, acknowledge, own, allow, avow, confess, grant, homologate, countersign, clinch *(colloq.)*, chime in, fall in with, defer to, go with the stream, be in the fashion, join in the chorus, echo, go with the current, reciprocate.

ASSENT, *n.* Agreement, consent, compliance, concession, concurrence, acquiescence, admission, allowance, approbation, affirmation, recognition, nod, acknowledgment, avowal, accord, unison, acceptance, approval, unanimity, acclamation, consensus, chorus, consentience, ratification, visé, confirmation, corroboration, endorsement, belief, verification, sanction, assentience, accordance, confession, accession, understanding.

ASSERT, *v.* 1. Declare the truth of, state as true, affirm, asseverate, aver, avow, predicate, avouch, protest, profess, propound, enunciate, pronounce, express, state, say, tell, set forth, lay down, broach, propose, utter, announce, put forward.
2. Maintain by words or force, allege, swear, testify, warrant, attest, certify, depose, guarantee, contend, justify, vindicate, defend, accentuate, maintain, claim, enforce, advance, stress, uphold, lay down the law, insist upon, make felt, emphasize, press, sustain.

ASSERTION, *n.* 1. Positive statement, averment, unsupported declaration, allegation, profession, avowal, predication, protestation, asseveration, affirmation, acknowledgment, position, assurance, word, observation, expression, utterance, saying, statement, communication, dictum, manifesto, sentence, representation.
2. Vindication, defense, insistence on a right or claim, maintenance, support, emphasis, stress, force of utterance.

ASSERTIVE, *adj.* Positive, decided, dogmatic, confident in statement, emphatic, certain, wilful, absolute, categorical, insistent, unconditional, peremptory, forceful, offensively self-assertive, aggressive, bumptious, outspoken, domineering, pushing, arbitrary.

ASSERTORY, *adj.* Declarative in the affirmative or negative, declaratory, assertorial, maintaining, affirming, supporting, assertive, no longer problematic.

ASSESS, *v.* 1. Estimate officially the value of as a basis for taxation, fix the amount of a tax, charge with one's share, impose one's share on, levy, exact, demand, require, ask, impose a charge on, lay upon.
2. Appraise, set a price, compute, value, rate, estimate, account, appreciate, calculate, size up *(colloq.)*, determine the amount of, measure, price.

ASSESSMENT, *n.* 1. Official valuation of taxable property, taxation, exactment, exaction, appraisal.
2. Tax, levy, fee, impost, charge, rate, toll, amount assessed as payable, subsidy.
3. Price, worth, value, appraisement, face value.

ASSETS, *n.* Personal resources, property, real property, securities, notes, inventories, admitted assets, cash, goods, chattel, effects, possessions, estate, capital, wealth, bonds, money, credit, net assets, frozen assets, assets by descent, assets in hand, equitable assets, intangible assets, liquid assets, personal assets, real assets.

ASSEVERATE, *v.* Assert emphatically, declare solemnly, aver earnestly, affirm positively, allege,

assure, avow, avouch, maintain, protest, depose, guarantee, testify, predicate, state, say. (See ASSERT.)

ASSEVERATION, *n.* Solemn averment, emphatic assertion, protestation, assurance, certification, positive affirmation, declaration, vow, oath. (See ASSERTION.)

ASSIDUITY, *n.* 1. Constant industry, sedulity, diligence, painstaking, assiduousness, constancy, sedulousness, indefatigation, continuous effort, activity, exertion, intentness, perseverance, labor, persistence, endurance, patience, devotedness, care, pains, carefulness, close application, zeal, constant attention.
2. *(Pl.)* Devoted attentions, faithful personal attention, vigilance, watchfulness.

ASSIDUOUS, *adj.* 1. Diligent, untiring, tireless, indefatigable, never-tiring, untiring, unremitting, unwearied, unintermitting, sedulous, industrious, busy, active, persistent, persevering, painstaking, patient, constant, careful, laborious, studious, zealous, intent, unsleeping, plodding, occupied, hard-working, bustling, busy as a bee, engrossed, close, earnest, determined, alert, brisk, vigorous.
2. Obsequiously attentive to a person, devoted, attached.

ASSIGN, *v.* 1. Give in distribution, apportion, allocate, allot, set apart for a particular use, appropriate, administer, mete out, cast, distribute, dispense, share, portion out, partition, assign to, grant, award, consign, hand over.
2. Point out with precision, fix, particularize, specify, determine, set, designate, detail, depute, prescribe, delegate, commission, appoint to a post of duty, nominate, name, intrust, charge, enroll, authorize, empower, accredit, put in commission, invest, ordain, dedicate, induct, install.
3. Account for with reasons, ascribe, attribute, refer, bring forward, adduce, point out, allege, show, state, advance.
4. *(Law)* Transfer ownership of in writing, make over to another, convey, deliver, hand over, surrender to another, award, adjudge.

ASSIGNATION, *n.* Appointment of time and place for a meeting, guilty appointment, appointment for criminal converse, illicit love meeting, clandestine meeting, tryst, rendezvous, date *(colloq.)*.

ASSIGNEE, *n.* 1. One to whom some right is transferred either for himself or in trust, trustee, transferee, executor, appointer, recipient.
2. One empowered to act for another, assignee in bankruptcy, assignee in insolvency.
3. Assigned servant.

ASSIGNMENT, *n.* 1. Apportionment, allocation, allotment, distribution, allowance, share, award, part.
2. Specification, attribution, ascription, office, determination, arrangement, designation, agency, nomination, ordination, delegation, commission, mandate, embassy.
3. Allegement, adducing, showing, offering, presentation, giving, imputation, referral.
4. Something assigned, task, duty, stint, part, emplacement, charge, lesson, errand.
5. *(Law)* Conveyance, transfer of property or right.

ASSIMILATE, *v.* 1. Turn to one's own substance, transform into a homogeneous part of something, digest, take into the organism, absorb into the system, incorporate as one's own, make part of oneself, completely appropriate, convert food into the substance of the body, homogenize, resolve into.

2. Cause to become more accordant with, cause to resemble, make alike, harmonize, render conformable, bring into resemblance, adapt.

3. Compare, liken, represent as like.

ASSIMILATION, *n.* 1. Conversion of absorbed food into the substance of the body, digestion, total process of nutrition, homogenization, transformation, resolution, reduction, anabolism, transmutation, incorporation, absorption, constructive metabolism.

2. Adjustment, accommodation to, accordance, harmonization, adaptation.

3. Comparison, resemblance, likeness.

ASSIST, *v.* 1. Act as assistant to, be associated with as a helper, be of service, aid, help, abet, render help, serve, cooperate with, give support to, take part with, minister to, work for, befriend, lend a hand, support, reinforce, uphold, back up, sustain, patronize, accommodate, oblige, favor, subserve, subsidize, second, promote, advance, speed, further, be auxiliary to, adjuvate, tend, attend, wait on, take in tow, espouse the cause of, stand by, stick by, side with, prop, coadjuvate, collaborate, have a finger in the pie.

2. Give support to in distress, succor, give alms to, tide over, relieve, set on one's legs, benefit, supply.

3. Act interchangeably, alternate with, spell out.

ASSISTANCE, *n.* 1. Aid, help, furtherance, lift, reinforcement, backing, cooperation, patronage, collaboration, support, helping hand, protection, good offices, championship, favor, countenance, accommodation, encouragement, subservience, defense, service, adjuvancy, helpfulness.

2. Alms, sustenance, succor, relief, sympathy, maintenance, subsidy, subvention, manna in the wilderness, charity, bounty, contribution, comfort.

ASSISTANT, *n.* 1. Aider, helper, abettor, mate, helpmate, helping hand, right-hand man, co-aid, adjutant, coadjutor, cooperator, collaborator, accessory, ally, confederate, adjuvant, confrere, accomplice, copartner, co-worker, companion, partner, supporter, follower, adherent, colleague, friend, ancillary, friend in need, auxiliary.

2. One who assists a superior, subordinate, aide, clerk, underworker, subaltern, underling, agent, henchman, retainer, satellite, stooge, tool, puppet, parasite, dependent, hanger-on, attendant, man-Friday, candleholder, servant, apprentice, domestic, menial, second.

ASSOCIATE, *v.* 1. Bring into association, make a partner, join as a companion, conjoin, unite, connect by some relation, affiliate, combine with, link together, couple, yoke, bind together, bring into close relation, correlate, ally, pair, marry, league, confederate.

2. Enter into a league, join in action, unite for a common purpose, fraternize, consort, be in intimate intercourse, mingle, mix, club, federate, amalgamate, unionize, band together, coalesce, accompany, be in company, be in contiguity, herd together, blend, come together, jostle elbows, hobnob.

ASSOCIATE, *n.* 1. One who is habitually in the company of another, familiar, crony, chum, pal, buddy, companion, mate, yokefellow, bedfellow, fellow, comrade, consort, consociate, compeer, follower, adherent, peer, helpmate, friend, ally,

confederate, accomplice, brother, bosom friend, messmate, colleague, condisciple, shipmate, alter ego, intimate, confidant, house mate, clansman, entourage, other self, side kick.

2. Partner in interest, copartner, cooperator, co-worker, collaborator, confrere, abettor.

3. Anything closely connected with another, accompaniment, concomitant, accessory fact, attending circumstance.

4. One admitted to a subordinate degree of membership in an association, fellow.

ASSOCIATION, *n.* 1. Union, conjunction, bond, combination, connection, federation, consortium, consociation, coadjuvancy, affiliation, mingling, relationship, resemblance, affinity, homogeneity, tie, cluster, similarity, analogy.

2. Companionship, intercourse, fraternization, intimacy, fellowship, familiarity, friendliness, friendship, camaraderie, membership, participation, cooperation, acquaintance.

3. Organization of people with a common purpose, assemblage, society, alliance, sodality, community, fraternity, coterie, clique, combine, club, lodge, league, confederacy, joint concern, confederation, cartel, trust, firm, corporation, federation, partnership, house, guild, body, band, company, group, institute, craft, trade, camorra, chapter, troop, brigade, brotherhood, sisterhood, friary, coalition, party, syndicate, denomination, circle, clan, bloc.

4. Mental connection, connection of ideas in thought, idea suggested by a subject of thought, memory, train of thought.

ASSORT, *v.* 1. Class, classify, grade, graduate, range, rank, group, arrange in lots, distribute according to kind, separate, sort, dispose, set in order, sift, file, list, register, catalogue, tabulate, index.

2. Make up a variety, furnish with a variety, make varied, variegate.

3. Make of the same sort, adapt, coordinate, match, make harmonize.

4. Agree in kind, fall into a class or group, be matched, be suited, harmonize, associate, consort.

ASSORTED, *adj.* 1. Consisting of selected kinds, selected, matched, arranged in sorts, classified, suited, grouped, separated.

2. Of various sorts, consisting of various kinds, varied, diverse, various, miscellaneous, arranged in varieties, variegated, mixed, heterogeneous.

ASSORTMENT, *n.* 1. Act of assorting, arranging, classification, arrangement, distribution, grouping, allotment, disposition.

2. Class into which things are assorted, group, batch, lot, set, category, division, head, collection, denomination, grade.

3. Stock of various things whether of the same or different kinds, package, pack, store, selection, quantity.

4. Variety of sorts, many kinds, salmagundi, mixture, miscellany, medley, olio, hodgepodge, farrago, gallimaufry, melange.

ASSUAGE, *v.* 1. Make milder, make less severe, cause to be less harsh, mollify, mitigate, relieve, alleviate, palliate, moderate, lenify, soften, allay, addulce, soothe, deaden, smother, lay, take the edge off, temper, abate, lessen, attemper, still, quiet, quell, tranquilize, lull, compose, qualify, dull, obtund, blunt, subdue, check, curb, chasten, ease, comfort, solace, remedy, heal, extenuate, diminish, hush.

2. Appease, satisfy, slake, quench, fulfill, sate, gratify, indulge, satiate.

3. Pacify, calm, calm down, sober, tone down, smooth down, pour balm into, salve up.

ASSUAGEMENT, *n.* 1. Act of assuaging, letup, mitigation, palliation, easement, tranquilization, remission, abatement, softening, soothing, relief, alleviation, deliverance, pacification, comfort, appeasement.

2. That which assuages, sedative, alleviative, palliative, lenitive, demulcent, balm, calmative, anodyne.

3. Gratification, fulfilment, satiation, refection, refreshment, regalement, indulgence, satisfaction.

ASSUASIVE, *adj.* Alleviative, palliative, gentle, mild, mildening, bland, lenitive, healing, stilling, demulcent, emollient, soothing, sedative, balmy, mitigative, balsamic, relieving, anodyne, lulling, softening, lenient, allaying, laying, tranquilizing, abating, quelling, tempering, easing, moderative, mollifying, quieting, pacifying, that soothes and persuades at once, composing.

ASSUME, *v.* 1. Take for granted, take without proof, treat as conceded, suppose as a fact, infer, understand, presuppose, presume, imply, suspect, consider as true, postulate, hypothesize, theorize, predicate, speculate, posit *(Logic),* premise, draw the inference, gather, judge at random, imagine, conjecture, surmise, guess, fancy, divine, consider, believe, think, deduce.

2. Claim unduly, usurp, appropriate, arrogate, make free with, make unjust pretensions to, help oneself to, possess oneself of, commandeer, take as one's own, adopt, accroach, intercept, seize, dispossess, expropriate.

3. Enter upon, begin, resume, take on oneself, put on oneself, attempt, set about, pursue, take care of, undertake, be willing to bear, become responsible for, attend to, shoulder, contract for, venture, accept.

4. Take the semblance of, feign, affect, put on deceitfully, counterfeit, outwardly seem, ape, simulate, make believe, profess, pretend to, sham, dissemble, don, pose, attitudinize, take the part of, dissimulate, personate, play the part.

ASSUMED, *adj.* 1. Fictitious, make-believe, false, adopted, hypocritical, pretended, sham, feigned, counterfeit, pseudo, spurious, so-called, bogus, pseudonymic.

2. Given, granted, stated, taken as known, postulated, presupposed, supposed, suppositional, hypothetical.

ASSUMING, *adj.* 1. Disposed to arrogate to oneself more than is proper, presumptuous, bold, nervy, forward, unabashed, audacious, cheeky *(colloq.),* self-assertive, shameless, unblushing, blustering, brazen, swaggering, brazen-faced, immodest, pretentious, assumptive.

2. Imperious, arrogant, haughty, supercilious, high and mighty, magisterial, overbearing, uppish, toplofty, high-handed, overweening, bumptious, dictatorial, commanding, domineering, arbitrary, superior, conceited, self-conceited, snobbish, vainglorious, egotistical, consequential, self-sufficient.

ASSUMPTION, *n.* 1. Act of taking for granted, supposing, something taken for granted, premise, presumption, presupposition, supposition, axiom, guesswork, conjecture, hypothesis, postulation, postulate, theory, thesis, guess, surmise, inference, deduction, condition.

2. Act of taking upon oneself, undertaking, becoming responsible for, adoption.

⁻3. Taking to oneself, arrogation, usurpation, appropriation, seizure, dispossession, imposition, expropriation, encroachment, infringement, exaction.

4. Disposition to assume too much, effrontery, forwardness, boldness, audaciousness, audacity, nerve, cheek *(colloq.),* bumptiousness, assurance, impertinence, impudence, brazenness, shamelessness.

5. Arrogance, haughtiness, toploftiness, airs, superciliousness, superiority, lordliness, boasting, swaggering, self-conceit, conceitedness, conceit, self-importance, gasconade, putting-on, pretense, bluffing, rodomontade, braggadocio, affectation, pretension, bluster, vaporing, vaingloriousness, overbearance, insolence, hauteur, pride, big talk.

ASSURANCE, *n.* 1. Positive declaration intended to give confidence, earnest declaration, solemn assertion, protestation, averment, profession, asseveration, affirmation.

2. Promise, warranty, engagement, proof, oath, pledge, earnest, word of honor, guaranty, surety, security, reassurance, troth, vow, guarantee, seal, contract, certification.

3. Mental state of being assured, assuredness, full confidence, reliance, sureness, reassurance, certainty, certitude, freedom from doubt, belief, conviction, persuasion, ground of confidence, credence.

4. Freedom from timidity, courage, aplomb, intrepidity, self-reliance, self-confidence, coolness, self-possession, self-assurance, collectedness, self-poise.

5. Presumptuous boldness, nerve, effrontery, cheek *(colloq.),* brass *(colloq.),* bumptiousness, cocksureness, audacity, self-assertion, insolence, rudeness, impudence, impertinence, front, face, arrogance.

6. *(Law)* Insurance.

ASSURE, *v.* 1. Inform positively, tell confidently, declare earnestly, assert absolutely, endeavor to impart conviction to, offer assurances to, affirm, asseverate, solemnly promise, vow to, vouch to, avouch, avow, attest, aver to, pledge, warrant, guarantee, answer for, underwrite, subscribe to, certify, make assurance double sure.

2. Cause to feel certain, free from doubt, make one sure, deliver from uncertainty, convince, persuade, reassure.

3. Make a future event sure, ensure, render certain, clinch, secure, confirm, render safe, make stable, corroborate.

4. Embolden, enhearten, encourage, hearten, make confident, confirm in conviction.

5. *(Law)* Insure, secure against loss, contract to indemnify for loss.

ASSURED, *adj.* 1. Made sure, sure, undoubted, certain, indubitable, settled, fixed, guaranteed, unquestionable, positive, indisputable, infallible, official, reliable, unerring, trustworthy, secure, dependable, authoritative.

2. Not afraid, bold, confident, self-confident, self-possessed, sanguine, unquestioning, hardy, unhesitating, unwavering, self-reliant.

3. Bold to excess, overconfident, self-assertive, bumptious, impudent, presumptuous, autocratic, opinionated, bigoted, domineering, peremptory, imperious.

ASSUREDLY, *adv.* 1. Truly, in very truth, very true, surely, certainly, certes, doubtless, no doubt, undoubtedly, indubitably, unquestionably, even so, positively, actually, just so, to be sure, of course, exactly, precisely, indeed.

2. With assurance, with confidence, with firmness, unwaveringly, unhesitatingly.

ASTERN, *adv.* 1. (*Naut.*) In the direction opposite to a ship's course, to the rear of, in a backward direction, rearward, back, behind.

2. In the rear, in a position behind, aft, abaft, at any point behind.

ASTHENIA, *n.* Depression of vital power, atony, atonicity, cachexia, adynamia, marasmus, loss of power, general debility, debilitation, exhaustion, lack of strength, weakness, feebleness, languor, prostration, enervation.

ASTHENIC, *adj.* Debilitated, debile, infirm, on its last legs, strengthless, adynamic, cachectic, weak, prostrated, exhausted, faint, feeble, powerless, wasting away, marasmic, wasted, spent, weak as water.

ASTIR, *adj.* and *adv.* 1. Out of bed, up and about, moving about, afoot, on foot.

2. On the move, in full activity, in motion, brisk, active, moving, alert, stirring, roused, up in arms, excited, in full swing, agog.

ASTONISH, *v.* Amaze, startle, shock, take by surprise, surprise greatly, stagger, electrify, stupefy, dazzle, stun, daze, strike dumb, strike with overpowering wonder, dumbfounder, perplex, flabbergast *(colloq.)*, astound, overwhelm with surprise, petrify with wonder, confound, confuse, bewilder, astound, take aback, dismay, impress, disconcert, take one's breath away, make one's hair stand on end, galvanize.

ASTONISHMENT, *n.* 1. Overpowering wonder, great surprise, amazement, mental excitement, wonderment, bewilderment, confusion, dismay, consternation, perplexity, stupefaction.

2. Object or cause of amazement, wonderwork, marvel, prodigy, miracle, portent, phenomenon, *rara avis (Lat.),* rarity, curiosity.

ASTRADDLE, *adv.* With one leg on each side, in a straddling position, astride, bestriding, athwart, pickaback.

ASTRAL, *adj.* 1. Pertaining to the stars, starry, starlike, sidereal, stellar, star-shaped.

2. Susceptible to influence from the stars, supersensible, spiritual, immaterial, unearthly, extramundane.

ASTRAY, *adj.* and *adv.* Off the track, away from the right path, out of one's bearing, out of the right way, adrift, abroad, at sea, not at home, away, wandering, straying, lost, afield, distant, off, on the wrong scent, at a loss, at fault, dazed, at the end of one's wits, quite confounded, off the course, without the least clew, confused, aside of the mark, in a dilemma, in a maze, into error, misguided, misled, mistaken.

ASTRINGENT, *adj.* 1. Constrictive, contractive, binding, constipative, styptic, astrictive, costive, constringent, stegnotic.

2. Sour, bitter, tart, puckery, rough, acrid, raw, acid.

3. Austere, harsh in disposition, severe, stern.

ASTROLOGER, *n.* Interpreter of the influence of heavenly bodies on human affairs, Chaldean, astromancer, astroalchemist, seer, soothsayer, reader of the stars, horoscopist, star diviner.

ASTRONOMER, *n.* One versed in the science of the stars, observer of celestial bodies, stargazer, astrochemist, astrophysicist, astrographer, cosmo-

grapher, astrognostic, astrophotographer, uranographer, uranologist, cosmologist, cosmogonist.

ASTUTE, *adj.* Quick of apprehension, of keen perception, sharply discerning, penetrating, keen, perspicacious, cunning, shrewd, knowing, acute, calculating, designing, sharp, bright, smart, clever, quick-witted, intelligent, clear-headed, sagacious, long-headed, discriminating, wise, ingenious, deep, wide-awake, sharp-sighted, keen-sighted, quicksighted, clear-sighted, far-sighted, eagle-eyed, lynx-eyed, hard-headed, hawk-eyed, diplomatic, politic, Machiavelian, subtle, subdolous, wily, foxy, artful, crafty, sly.

ASTUTENESS, *n.* Sagacity, mother wit, brains, parts, genius, good judgment, quick parts, guile, acumen, acuteness, keenness, smartness, cunning, brightness, apperception, intelligence, ability to fathom wiles, understanding, discernment, slyness, shrewdness, penetration, perspicacity, sharpness, hard-headedness, quick-wittedness, depth, wiliness, keen-sightedness, subtlety, artfulness, ingenuity.

ASUNDER, *adj.* and *adv.* 1. Into separate parts, in pieces, into pieces, piecemeal, in two, sundered, dissected, disjoined, rent, carved, dismembered, *disiecta membra (Lat.),* torn apart, dissevered, broken apart.

2. In a different place or direction, widely separated, apart, far apart, divided, distinct, isolated, divergent, discordant.

ASYLUM, *n.* 1. Inviolable refuge, secure retreat, place of refuge, sanctum, adytum, *sanctum sanctorum (Lat.),* sanctuary, place of immunity, haven, harbor, *dernier ressort (Fr.),* covert, abri, hiding place, shelter, home, protection, defense, ark, rock, fastness, stronghold.

2. Charitable institution, shelter for the afflicted, poorhouse, almshouse, eleemosynary institution, hospital, sanatorium, sanitarium, *maison de santé (Fr.), hôtel-Dieu (Fr.),* nursing home, state hospital, insane asylum, madhouse, bedlam, lazaretto.

ASYMMETRY, *n.* Lack of symmetry, want of coordination, want of proportion, irregularity, formlessness, amorphism, anamorphosis, contortion, misproportion, deformity, malformation, distortion.

AT, *prep.* 1. Occupying the precise position of.

2. In contact with, on, upon.

3. In the vicinity of, in the region of, in proximity to, near, about.

4. Within the limits of, within, in, present in.

5. In the direction of, in reference to, upon the thought of, in pursuit of, applying to, toward, after.

6. By way of, through, from.

7. During the lapse of, in, by.

8. On the stroke of, upon the point of, upon the coming of.

9. On the happening of, on the occasion of, on the utterance of, in response to, because of, by means of, with, through the agency of.

10. Up to, amounting to, to the extent of, corresponding to.

11. Engaged in, occupied with, connected with, dependent on, in a state of, in a condition of.

AT ALL 1. In any degree, to any extent, in the least degree, in the least.

2. For any reason, in any event, under any circumstances, whatever, ever, in any case.

3. In any way, in any manner, in any respect.

AT ALL EVENTS Whatever happens, in any case, in the worst case, at any rate, no matter what else may be, anyhow, in any event, happen what may, whatever be the case, come what may, be as it will, at least.

AT A LOSS 1. In a state of bewilderment, in a dilemma, in a quandary, not knowing what to do, perplexed, posed, nonplused, in confusion, puzzled, at one's wits' end, unable to determine, uncertain, staggered, in a state of uncertainty, beyond one's depth, in difficulty, put to it, put to one's trumps, hard-pressed, out, hard up, in a state of embarrassment for lack of something, stranded, cornered, at a stand, in doubt.

2. At so low a price as to result in a loss.

AT A STAND 1. Interrupted, stopped, halted, in abeyance, at a standstill, at a stop.

2. In a state of perplexity, perplexed, in a perplexing situation, embarrassed.

ATAVISM, *n.* *(Biol.)* Recurrence to an ancestral type, intermittent heredity, reappearance in an individual of characteristics of a remote ancestor that have been absent in intervening generations, reversion to an earlier type, hereditary resurgence, throwback.

AT EASE 1. In a state free from bodily discomfort, free from pain, comfortable, relaxed, drawing a long breath, at rest.

2. In a state free from mental concern, untroubled, cheerful, carefree, worriless, without anxiety.

3. *(Mil.)* Position of rest in which soldiers may relax but not fall out of rank or talk.

ATELIER, *n.* Workshop of an artist, studio, loft, workroom, attic, shop, boutique.

AT FAULT 1. Off the scent, on the wrong track, wide of the mark, all astray, unable to proceed, in trouble or embarrassment, misguided, lost, abroad, adrift, at sea, thrown off the track, in trouble, wrong.

2. Puzzled, perplexed, on the horns of a dilemma, in a quandary, in a maze, in the dark, uncertain, confused, dubious, at a loss, at a nonplus.

3. Open to censure, censurable, blamable, in the wrong, blameworthy, reprehensible, guilty.

AT FIRST 1. In the beginning, at the outset, at the commencement, at the start, first off, in the first place.

2. At first sight, at first blush, at the first view, on first consideration, on first presentation, at first thought.

AT HAND 1. Within reach, near, near by, close by, fast by, hard by, within range, nigh, within a stone's throw, next door to, but a step, not far from.

2. Near in time, drawing near, imminent, approaching, impending, almost come, at the point of, close at hand, on the verge of, on the brink of, one of these days, on the eve of, soon, about to.

3. Ready for use, at one's finger's end, under one's nose, at the service of, handy, convenient, at the disposal of, available.

AT HEART 1. In inmost disposition, in one's feelings, in one's heart, in one's character, inwardly, in reality, really, in principle, at the center, essentially, at the core, substantially, at bottom, in the grain, bred in the bone, ingrained, inborn, deep-rooted.

2. Held dear, from the bottom of one's heart, *ab imo pectore (Lat.), con amore (Sp.),* heart and soul, in true regard, in esteem.

ATHEISM, *n.* Denial of God, disbelief in God, skepticism, agnosticism, deism, heresy, disregard of God, godlessness in life and conduct, unbelief, nullifidianism, irreligion, irreverence, infidelity, antichristianism, materialism, positivism, free-thinking, Pyrrhonism, dogmatic atheism, negative atheism, critical atheism, skeptical atheism, nihilism, rationalism, iconoclasm.

ATHEIST, *n.* Denier of the existence of God, disbeliever in God, agnostic, skeptic, heretic, deist, pagan, heathen, giaour *(Turk.),* zendik *(Arab.),* godless person, nullifidian, infidel, irreligionist, rationalist, materialist, positivist, Pyrrhonist, unbeliever, nonbeliever, freethinker, *esprit fort (Fr.),* doubter, iconoclast.

ATHEISTIC, *adj.* Given to atheism, godless, agnostic, heretical, irreligious, irreverent, profane, Pyrrhonean, materialistic, rationalistic, doubting, nullifidian, antichristian, skeptical, freethinking, positivistic, disbelieving, unbelieving, impious, blasphemous, iconoclastic.

ATHIRST, *adj.* 1. Thirsty, wanting water, dry, parched with thirst, droughty.

2. Keenly desirous, eager for, with fierce desire, longing, orectic, craving, covetous, avid, burning, fervent, ardent, all agog, fain, bent on, dying for, devoured by desire.

ATHLETE, *n.* Gymnast, one trained to exercises of physical agility and strength, agonist, acrobat, contestant in physical games, Olympian, contender for victory, pancratiast, strong-man, combatant, champion, competitor in physical exercises, pole-vaulter, trained contestant, muscular expert, boxer, wrestler, ball player, swimmer, rower, trackman, jumper, discus-thrower, weight-lifter, pugilist, prize fighter, runner.

ATHLETIC, *adj.* 1. Gymnastic, acrobatic, pertaining to athletics, indulging in athletics, agonistic, palaestral, pancratic.

2. Physically strong, muscular, brawny, burly, sinewy, strapping, made of iron, iron-muscled, robust, lusty, stout, sturdy, stalwart, mighty, powerful, vigorous, able-bodied, Herculean, wiry, husky, hardy, strong as a lion, manly, virile.

ATHLETICS, *n.* 1. Gymnastics, sports, games of strength, games depending on feats of physical strength, muscular contests, agonistics, outdoor exercises, field events, calisthenics, acrobatics, Olympics.

2. Track events, running, rowing, boxing, pugilism, prize fighting, boxing, wrestling, polo, swimming, baseball, football, soccer, cricket, golf, lacrosse, basketball, handball, tennis, high-jump, pole-vaulting, discus-throwing.

3. Practice of athletic exercises, principles of athletic training.

ATHWART, *adv.* 1. From side to side, across, transversely, crosswise, sidewise, obliquely, awry, askant.

2. So as to thwart, perversely, contrariwise, counter to, in conflict with, at cross purposes, against the grain, against, versus.

3. *(Naut.)* At right angles to a ship's keel.

ATHWART, *prep.* 1. From side to side of, in the direction of the breadth of, over, across.

2. In opposition to, contrary to, against, versus, counter to.

3. *(Naut.)* Across the line or course of.

AT LAST 1. Finally, ultimately, in the end, in conclusion, in the upshot.

2. At length, after a great while, at the end of

a certain period, after delay, after a long time, at long last, after much has intervened, *en fin (Fr.)*.

AT LENGTH 1. In full extent, at full length, without omission, without contraction, without abbreviation, in full detail, with fulness, in full, *in extenso (Lat.)*.

2. After a long period, after a great while, at the end of a long time, at last, at the conclusion.

3. (With *stretch* or *lie*) Out, in one's whole stature, in entire dimensions.

ATMOSPHERE, *n.* 1. Gaseous fluid surrounding the earth, gaseous envelope surrounding heavenly bodies, air, element, troposphere *(inner layer of atmosphere)*, stratosphere *(layer outside the troposphere)*, tropopause *(boundary layer between the foregoing)*, ionosphere *(ionized layers of earth's atmosphere beyond the stratosphere)*, Heaviside layer *(lower regions of ionosphere, about 60 miles up)*, Kennelly-Heaviside layer, ozone *(outer portion of stratosphere, about 20 miles up)*.

2. Climatic condition, climate, weather, clime.

3. Environing influence, environment, general effect, pervading tone, quality producing a predominant impression, mood, flavor, tone.

ATMOSPHERIC, *adj.* 1. Aerial, airy, pneumatic, meteorological, pneumatic, climatic.

2. Moody, impressionistic, vivid, real.

AT ODDS Quarrelsome, disputatious, factious, litigious, bickering, at strife, disagreeing, in disagreement, dissentient, in dissension, on bad terms, discordant, embroiled, torn, disunited, at variance, at loggerheads, at daggers drawn, at issue, at cross purposes, at sixes and sevens, at feud, with bad blood between, dissonant, at words.

ATOM, *n.* 1. Smallest unitary constituent of a chemical element, monad, ultimate particle, indivisible particle, molecule, aggregate of protons, neutrons and electrons, particle of matter so minute as to admit of no division.

2. Minute quantity, mite, mote, speck, grain, smithereen, iota, jot, tittle, scrap, bit, particle, corpuscle, whit, dot, crumb, shred, point, ace, scintilla, morsel.

ATOMIC, *adj.* 1. Molecular, corpuscular, nuclear, fissionable.

2. Infinitesimal, minute, tiny, extremely small, inappreciable, divided into minute particles, wee, microscopic, minikin.

3. Propelled or driven by atomic energy.

AT ONCE 1. Straightway, without delaying, forthwith, directly, immediately, instantaneously, in no time, in less than no time, *presto, subito, instanter,* instantly, in a trice, in a moment, at a stroke, like a shot, like greased lightning, in the twinkling of an eye, at a leap, *per saltum (Lat.),* in one's tracks, all at once, at one fell swoop, plump, on the spot, before you could count ten, before you could say Jack Robinson, no sooner said than done, touch and go, on the spur of the moment, suddenly, at short notice, extempore.

2. At exactly the same time, at the same instant, in the same breath, together, in one body, simultaneously, at one and the same time, at the same point of time.

ATONE, *v.* 1. Make amends for, make expiation, expiate, propitiate, do penance for, appease, redeem, ransom, make reparation for, render satisfaction for, pay for, answer for, countervail,

make up for, absolve, purge, shrive, pay the penalty, remunerate, recompense, acknowledge, apologize, *faire l'amende honorable (Fr.),* serve as a set-off.

2. Harmonize, make harmonious, bring into unity, be at one, agree.

ATONEMENT, *n.* 1. Satisfaction for a wrong or injury, expiation, propitiation, amends, *amende honorable (Fr.),* redemption, reclamation, peace offering, reparation, redress, recompense, ransom, indemnification, compensation, requital, apology, remuneration.

2. Penitential act, penance, sackcloth and ashes, self-mortification, flagellation, fasting, purgation, shrift.

ATONIC, *adj.* 1. *(Pathol.)* Asthenic, marked by agony, languid, exhausted, muscularly weak, lacking in tone or energy, wanting vigor, without nervous energy.

2. *(Phonet.)* Aspirate, merely breathed, surd, aspirated, unaccented, without accentual mark, without vocal sound, non-sonant, voiceless.

ATRABILIOUS, *adj.* Melancholic, saturnine, hypochondriacal, moody, hipped, dispirited, glum, doleful, dejected, depressed, gloomy, long-faced, desponding, lugubrious, sorrowful, downcast, sad, low-spirited, blue, downhearted, heavy-hearted, chapfallen, down in the mouth, singing the blues, calamity-howling, in the dumps, woebegone, lachrymose, mumpish, dumpish, rueful, mopish, cheerless, joyless, unhappy, dismal, somber, dark, gloomy, triste, funereal, Acherontic.

AT RANDOM 1. Without definite aim or purpose, in a haphazard way, unmethodical, aimlessly, at haphazard, by chance, without selection, just as it happens, casually, as may chance, without choice, without direction, irregularly, without rule.

2. Without restraint, at liberty, neglected, without attention.

AT REST 1. In a quiescent state, in repose, resting, inactive, motionless.

2. Free from disquietude, at ease, free from pain, comfortable, untroubled.

3. Dead, in the last sleep, in the bosom of God, passed away, departed, late.

ATROCIOUS, *adj.* 1. Extremely cruel, fiendish, shockingly wicked, savage, barbarous, outrageous, villainous, heinous, nefarious, facinorous, arrant, scelerous, flagitious, felonious, criminal, flagrant, infamous, enormous, grievous, diabolical, hellish, inhuman, monstrous, black, infernal, horrible, dark, pitiless, vile, iniquitous, vicious, violent, bad, ignominious, opprobrious, brutal.

2. Shockingly bad, lacking in taste, execrable, uncouth, inelegant, unpolished, in poor taste, gaudy, garish, meretricious, overdecorated, flashy, gimcrack, brummagem, ostentatious.

ATROCITY, *n.* 1. Great cruelty, brutality, villainy, depravity, barbarity, barbarism, ferocity, blackness, heinousness, flagrancy, flagitiousness, nefariousness, atrociousness, recklessness, ruffianism, savagery, wickedness, fiendishness, ruthlessness, inhumanity, mercilessness, truculence, enormity.

2. Atrocious deed, crime, iniquity, flagitious villainy, deed of savagery, enormity, horror, ferocious act, outrage, monstrosity, felony, gross offense, wrong, delinquency.

ATROPHY, *n.* Marasmus, consumption, wasting away, emaciation from lack of nourishment, decline, withering, degeneration, stoppage of growth, lack of development, lack of use.

AT STAKE In danger, endangered, at hazard, hazarded, pledged, risked, involved, implicated, on the anvil, on the tapis, in question, concerned, put to proof, at risk, in jeopardy, at the caprice of fortune.

ATTACH, *v.* 1. Join, connect, fasten to, make fast to, tie, unite, add, fix, affix, conjoin, subjoin, append, pin, stick, tack, hitch, set to, annex, engraft, cement, yoke, chain, combine, secure, bind, wed.

2. Attribute, assign, ascribe, associate, put in relation.

3. Bind by ties of affection, lay hold on by affection, attract, enamor, captivate, unite to oneself by love, endear, win, charm, gain over, engage, fascinate.

4. *(Law)* Take property by legal authority, distrain, seize, arrest for contempt of court.

5. Adhere, pertain, belong as a proper adjunct, be incident, apply.

ATTACHMENT, *n.* 1. Act of attaching, binding, affixture, confixation, annexation, insertion, union, subjunction, cohesion.

2. That which attaches, nexus, bond, copula, tie, fastening, connection, link, junction.

3. Anything attached as an adjunct, annex, supplementary device, appurtenance, appendage, addendum, additum, appendix, fixture.

4. Affection binding one person to another, love, esteem, liking, regard, fondness, estimation, friendship, predilection, devotion, adhesion, heed, fidelity, adherence, endearment, penchant, respect, tenderness, affinity, inclination, partiality.

5. *(Law)* Seizure of property by legal authority, distrainer, annexation, writ of arrest for contempt of court, judicial proceeding for taking property into custody of court to await ulterior proceedings.

ATTACK, *v.* 1. Set upon with force, attempt violence to, begin hostilities against, assail, beset, assault, invade, storm, charge, make an onset against, tackle, engage, oppugn, fall upon, have at, run at, fly at, rush upon, bear down upon, ride full tilt against, spring upon, have a cut at, make aggression on, push, beleaguer, besiege, bombard, combat, strike, sally forth, trespass against, waylay, pitch into, pelt, stone, torpedo, fire upon, shoot at, snipe at, draw a bead on, open fire, pepper, shell, fusillade, enfilade, rake, close with, cut and thrust, stab, bayonet, saber, take the offensive, strike the first blow, go over the top.

2. Direct unfavorable criticism against, blame, abuse violently, censure, lampoon, impugn, reflect upon, criticize, calumniate, denigrate, slander, traduce, blacken.

3. Abuse sexually, rape, assault, stuprate, defile, debauch, violate, deflower, outrage, molest.

4. Begin action upon, make a beginning upon, undertake, take up, go to work on a thing forcefully, set about a task vigorously.

5. *(Med.)* Begin to affect injuriously, cause to waste or decompose, seize.

ATTACK, *n.* 1. Offensive military operation, jab, assault, onslaught, onset, aggression, intrusion, encroachment, incursion, inroad, illapse, invasion, irruption, outbreak, sally, sortie, raid, skirmish, foray, assailment, storming, zero hour, cannonade, bombardment, air raid, *coup de main (Fr.),* thrust, charge, encounter, offense, surprisal, firing,

fusillade, shooting, volley, burst, barrage, siege, broadside, sharpshooting, enfilade, curtain of fire, cross fire, *rafale (Fr.),* boarding, escalade, lunge, investment, blockade, beleaguerment, trespass.

2. Slanderous criticism, vilification, censure, impugnment, calumniation, denigration, slander, aspersion, defamation, vituperation, lampoon, libel, pasquinade, disparagement, beratement.

3. Rape, stupration, defilement, debauchment, violation, outrage, molestation.

4. First movements toward an undertaking, decisive and spirited commencement, beginning of action.

5. *(Med.)* Seizure by disease, raptus, spell, fit, stroke, paroxysm, visitation, access of disease, affection.

ATTACKER, *n.* Assailant, assailer, aggressor, assaulter, invader, antagonist, enemy, foe.

ATTAIN, *v.* 1. Procure by effort, gain by exertion, achieve by continued effort, acquire, obtain, win, earn, grasp, master, bring off successfully, fulfill, compass, secure, accomplish, score a success, effect, execute, realize, reap, carry by storm.

2. Succeed in reaching, reach, get to, arrive at in due course, approach, come to, make, attain to.

ATTAINABLE, *adj.* Capable of being attained, achievable, obtainable, practicable, compassable, workable, feasible, possible, *in posse (Lat.),* on the cards, accessible, reachable, available, within the bounds of possibility, surmountable, within reach, within measurable distance, on the dice.

ATTAINMENT, *n.* 1. Act of attaining, getting, consummation, completion, fulfilment, mastery, achievement, realization, securement, acquisition, accomplishment, gaining, winning.

2. Something attained, personal acquirement, accomplishment, enlightenment, learning, higher education, scholarship, erudition, lore, wisdom, information, store of knowledge, culture, grace, mental resources, attributes, parts, qualification, talents, capability, competence, cleverness, skill, proficiency, technique, finish, finesse, ability, craft.

ATTEMPER, *v.* 1. Temper, moderate, modify, qualify, reduce, regulate, keep within bounds, attune.

2. Make suitable, accommodate, adapt, bring into harmony, fit, proportion.

3. Soothe, appease, mollify, mitigate, alleviate, allay, lenify, blunt, dull, take off the edge, soften, tone down, smooth down, tranquilize, assuage, lull, quell, hush, still, smother, deaden, rebate, abate.

ATTEMPT, *v.* 1. Endeavor to effect, strive, try, essay, make an effort at, aim, make an attempt, venture, seek, make trial of, make essay, drive at, experiment, incur the hazard, do all that in one lies, work at, strain every nerve, do one's best, leave no stone unturned, put forth an effort, undertake, set out to, go about, take in hand, take upon oneself, tackle, take a whack at, take a crack at, whack away at, make a go at, aspire to.

2. Make an effort against, try to overcome, attack, assault, assail.

ATTEMPT, *n.* 1. Trial, effort, endeavor, essay, try *(colloq.),* experiment, test, venture, emprise, exertion, struggle, aim, undertaking, enterprise, speculation.

2. Effort to effect a purpose by violence, onset, assault, attack, onslaught.

ATTEND, *v.* 1. Be present at, visit, frequent, go to, resort to, haunt.

2. Accompany, conduct, escort, usher, keep company with, chaperon, go hand-in-hand with, squire, convoy, watch over, guard, protect, tend, see to, look after, superintend, supervise, oversee, overlook, provide for, care for, have in keeping, have charge of, take care of, wait within hearing, stand by.

3. Follow as a result, go with as a concomitant, be associated with, be connected with, go along with, be consequent on.

4. Wait upon, serve, devote one's services to, minister to, be attendant on, dance attendance on, accompany as a servant.

5. Listen, heed, hearken, give ear, hear, give heed to, pay attention, pay regard, notice, mind, observe, be attentive to, take notice of, give a thought to, be mindful of, mark, note, remark.

ATTENDANCE, *n.* 1. Act of attending, presence, visitation, sojournment, being there, going to.

2. Persons collectively that attend any service or entertainment, persons attending, persons present, number present.

3. Attendants collectively, retinue, entourage, persons ministering, body of attendants, suite, train, staff, followers, cortege, escort, bodyguard, convoy, honor guard.

4. Act of being in waiting, ministration, duty, service, waiting on, tendance, labor for another, business, employment, office.

ATTENDANT, *adj.* 1. Concomitant, consequent, accompanying in causal connection, attending, following, concurrent.

2. Ministrant, ministrative, being present, being in attendance.

ATTENDANT, *n.* 1. One who is present, person present at a meeting, attender, frequenter.

2. One who attends another for company, adherent, follower, companion, associate, fellow, attender, escort, bodyguard, shadow, hanger-on, suitor, satellite, chaperon.

3. One who attends another for service, lackey, servant, domestic, liveried manservant, footman, flunky, valet, squire, page, steward, butler, usher, waiter, cupbearer, Ganymede, footboy, orderly, servitor, vassal, retainer, henchman, dependant, underling, acolyte, helper, menial, aide, outrider, understrapper, equerry, groom, hostler, courtier, train-bearer, liegeman, employee, attaché, gillie, caddie, bus boy, seneschal, chamberlain, herald, major-domo, subaltern, secretary, keeper, nurse, pursuivant, forerunner, precursor, harbinger, handmaid, *femme de chambre (Fr.)*, servant of all work, factotum, guide, cicerone.

4. Something that accompanies, concomitant, natural consequence, accompaniment, consequent, attendant circumstance, accessory, appendage.

ATTENTION, *n.* 1. Observant care, watchful observation, advertence, heed, heedfulness, note, notice, observance, mindfulness, regard, wariness, consideration, circumspection, alertness, vigilance, intentness.

2. Mental concentration upon an object, vigorous direction of mental powers to a specific object, maximal integration of the higher mental processes, scrutiny, investigation, reflection, study, deliberation, thought, thoughtfulness, voluntary attention, close attending, contemplation, special consideration, reflex attention, non-voluntary attention.

3. Courtesy, politeness, civility, deference, respect, homage, service.

4. Acts indicating regard as in courtship, act of gallantry, amorous service, court, devotion, suit, addresses, wooing, devoirs.

5. *(Mil.)* Command to take an erect position, order to assume a posture of readiness.

ATTENTIVE, *adj.* 1. Applying the mind to, alert, giving attention, observant, regardful, mindful, heedful, considerate, thoughtful, listening, alive to, careful, awake to, intent, on the alert, on the lookout, wide awake, watchful, conscious, aware, wary, sharp, discreet, circumspect, vigilant.

2. Occupied with, absorbed in, rapt, enrapt, taken up with, engrossed in, wrapped up in, studious, assiduous, diligent, sedulous, zealous, painstaking, persevering.

3. Polite, courteous, gallant, accommodating, deferential, respectful, chivalrous, complaisant, courtly, gracious, obliging, debonair, persistent in attentions, devoted, lover-like, wooing.

ATTENUATE, *v.* Make thin, make small, make fine, thin out, rarefy, make rare, make slender, make slim, reduce in size, render threadlike, spin out, draw out, subtilize, decrease, lessen, impair, enfeeble, enervate, pulverize, triturate, dilute, adulterate, water down, weaken in force, reduce in intensity, reduce in strength, diminish in effect, lessen in value, narrow down in quantity.

ATTENUATE, *adj.* Slight, slender, slim, sheer, lean, thin, fine-spun, fine-drawn, drawn-out, airy, gossamer, transparent, air-spun, thread-like, weak, delicate, frail, enfeebled, starveling, emaciated, infirm, shriveled, gaunt, lank, scraggy, scanty, flimsy, meager, diluted, contracted.

ATTENUATION, *n.* 1. Process of attenuating, thinning out, rarefaction, making slender, making thread-like, fine-drawing, diminution, weakening, watering down.

2. Tenuity, thinness, exiguity, gossameriness, slenderness, fineness, slimness, flimsiness, delicacy, lightness, rareness, etherealness, airiness, leanness, gauntness, emaciation.

ATTEST, *v.* 1. Witness, bear witness to, testify to, certify as true, declare to be true, confirm as correct, corroborate, vouch for as genuine, bear out, declare the truth of, affirm in an official capacity, endorse, ratify, authenticate, support, seal, set one's hand and seal to, depose, warrant, guarantee, subscribe.

2. Evince, manifest, give evidence of, prove, demonstrate, verify, give proof of, show, exhibit, betoken, display, confess, tell of, declare, make clear, assert, assure, affirm.

ATTESTATION, *n.* Authenticated confirmation, proof, corroboration, ratification, certification, deposition, statement made in attesting, attesting declaration, witness, testimony, evidence, seal, voucher, warrant record, averment, affirmation, demonstration.

ATTIC, *adj.* 1. Of Athens, Athenian, of Attica.

2. *(l.c.)* Chaste, classic, classical, pure, correct, refined, elegant, polished, in good taste, simple, delicate.

3. *(l.c.)* Pointed, incisive, witty, intelligent, cultured, subtle, penetrating.

ATTIC, *n.* Garret, mansard, loft, clerestory, head *(humorous)*, cockloft, "sky parlor," "upper story" *(humorous)*.

ATTICISM, *n.* 1. Attic peculiarity of style, Attic idiom, Attic elegance of diction.

2. Elegant expression, felicitous phrase, happy phrase, well-turned expression, concise expression.

ATTIRE, *v.* Clothe, dress, apparel, deck, adorn, drape, garb, robe, enrobe, gown, costume, invest, enclothe, rig out, array, trick out, fit out, equip, accouter, dight, harness, caparison, encase, don, swathe, sheathe, wrap, muffle, put on, wear, slip on.

ATTIRE, *n.* Rich dress, splendid garments, garb, ornamental clothing, habiliments, clothes, array, raiment, vestment, vesture, wardrobe, wearing apparel, toilette, finery, outfit, trousseau, gear, habits, costume, suit, uniform, livery, harness, rigging, trappings, accouterments, equipment, turn-out, caparison, things *(colloq.)*, togs, duds *(colloq.)*, glad rags *(colloq.)*

ATTITUDE, *n.* 1. Physical position, stance, stand, position of the body appropriate to an action or emotion, composition of a figure, mode of being placed, arrangement of body, posture, pose *(in ballet)*, set *(colloq.)*, twist, figure, gesticulation, turn.
2. Disposition of mind, state of feeling, mind set, manner with regard to, settled behavior or conduct indicative of opinion, habitual mode of regarding anything, frame of mind, condition of mind, mood, air, demeanor.

ATTITUDINIZE, *v.* Assume attitudes, pose for effect, pose affectedly, strike a pose, put on, strike attitudes.

ATTORNEY, *n.* 1. Public attorney, attorney at law, lawyer, legal adviser, counselor, counselor at law, counsel, solicitor, barrister, member of the bar, advocate, proctor, limb of the law, pettifogger, shyster.
2. Private attorney, one duly empowered by another to transact business for him, attorney in fact, agent, deputy, factor, proxy, one designated by another to act in his stead, substitute.

ATTRACT, *v.* 1. Draw by physical influence, pull, drag, cause to adhere, magnetize, cause to approach, bring into proximity, exert a force that tends to draw towards.
2. Affect favorably, lure, allure, interest, invite, tempt, entice, win, engage, fascinate, captivate, inveigle, charm, enamor, seduce, endear, enchant, ensorcel, decoy, bait, take the fancy, feed the eye, catch the eye.

ATTRACTION, *n.* 1. Drawing power, magnetism, gravity, affinity, inclination, tendency, gravitation, pull, traction.
2. Attractiveness, charm, appeal, glamor, lure, allure, fascination, enchantment, inveiglement, enticement, witchery, inducement, temptation, seduction.
3. That which allures, pleasing object, graces, attractive qualities, charms.

ATTRACTIVE, *adj.* Appealing, to one's liking, having the power of attracting, drawing forth interest, enticing, winsome, charming, engaging, winning, prepossessing, taking, agreeable, comely, interesting, inviting, alluring, seductive, tempting, enchanting, fascinating, captivating, bewitching, fetching, sightly, becoming, likable, delightful, tasteful, elegant, shapely, fair, beautiful, pretty, handsome, lovely, sweet, pleasing, dainty, artistic, pleasant, picturesque, aesthetic.

ATTRIBUTABLE, *adj.* Assignable, accountable, ascribable, imputable, traceable, chargeable, due to, referable, explicable, owing to, to be imputed to, to be attributed to, to be ascribed to, to be charged to, to be laid at the door of, to be fathered upon.

ATTRIBUTE, *v.* Ascribe to, impute, assign to, refer to, consider as belonging, regard as owing to, charge to, father upon, lay to, trace to, blame on, saddle with, set down to, point to, bring home to, lay at the door of, account for, derive from, invest with, attach to, accredit with, associate, connect with.

ATTRIBUTE, *n.* 1. Quality, feature, property, something attributed as belonging, faculty, mark, characteristic, character, peculiarity, specialty, endowment, note, virtue, gift, predicate, grace, acquirement, attainment, ability, accomplishment.
2. *(Fine Arts)* Distinctive mark, characteristic token, emblem, symbol, adjunct, belonging, concomitant sign.

ATTRITION, *n.* Abrasion, confrication, friction, affriction, rubbing, wearing down, grinding, rubbing away, scraping, erasure, disintegration, arrosion, detrition.

ATTUNE, *v.* 1. Adjust to harmony, tune, put in tune, harmonize, modulate, accord, tune up, syntonize.
2. Make accordant, bring into agreement, fit for a purpose, adapt to sympathetic relationship, attemper, prepare, accommodate, acclimatize, adjust.

AUBURN, *adj.* Chestnut-colored, nut-brown, reddish-brown, golden-brown, citron-colored, carrot-colored, copper-colored, rust-colored, russet, titian, henna, cinnamon, tawny.

AU COURANT *(Fr.)* With the stream *(lit.)*, up to date, up with the times, well informed on current matters, fully acquainted with.

AUCTION, *n.* Public sale at which goods are sold to the highest bidder, vendue, public sale, roup *(Scottish)*, auction sale, cant *(Irish)*.

AUDACIOUS, *adj.* 1. Courageous, valiant, bold, dauntless, daring, undaunted, fearless, stalwart, lion-hearted, venturesome, stout-hearted, plucky, doughty, intrepid, valorous, mettlesome, hardy, enterprising, adventurous, spirited, self-reliant, strong-willed, unflinching, unshrinking, ambitious, cool, manly, virile.
2. Foolhardy, rash, temerarious, indiscreet, imprudent, injudicious, heedless, overconfident, madcap, devil-may-care, reckless, death-defying, hot-headed, breakneck, harebrained, headlong, desperate, wild, daredevil, harum-scarum.
3. Forward, impudent, presumptuous, defiant of decorum, assuming, glaring, brazen-faced, rude, cheeky, shameless, insolent, impertinent, self-assertive, bumptious, malapert, unabashed, saucy, fresh *(colloq.)*, barefaced, overbearing, pert, full of effrontery.

AUDACITY, *n.* 1. Confidence in one's powers, courage, hardihood, boldness, self-reliance, dash, fearlessness, intrepidity, resoluteness, derring-do, venturesomeness, spirit, bravery, valor, backbone, grit, nerve, spunk *(colloq.)*, assurance, enterprise.
2. Overconfidence, rashness, temerity, leap in dark, foolhardiness, imprudence, indiscretion, injudiciousness, desperation, hot-headedness, recklessness.
3. Impudence, gall, bumptiousness, effrontery, presumptuousness, insolence, presumption, front, shamelessness, cheek, face, brass, impertinence, lip *(colloq.)*, freshness, malapertness, brazenness, sauciness, rudeness, forwardness, self-assertiveness.
4. Departure from precedent, bold originality, disregard of conventionality.

AUDIBILITY, *n.* Audible capacity, distinctness of sound, carrying quality, sonority, sonorousness, sound, acoustics, tone, resonance, reverberation, clearness.

AUDIBLE, *adj.* Perceptible by the ear, actually heard, loud enough to be heard, capable of being heard, distinct, hearable, aloud, resounding, clear.

AUDIENCE, *n.* 1. Gathering of persons to listen, hearers, assembly of hearers, assemblage, gallery of spectators, auditory, congregation, assembly, house, gallery gods, persons attending, listeners.
2. Persons reached by a book or broadcast, public, reading public, readers of a book.
3. Formal interview, formal reception, hearing, opportunity to be heard, liberty of speaking to a person, admittance to a hearing, access, court, ear, levee, consultation, discussion, tête-à-tête, conference, parley, interlocution, communion, converse, colloquy, reception, *conversazione (It.),* intercourse, powwow, palaver, pourparler.

AUDIT, *v.* 1. Examine accounts officially, verify an account by reference to vouchers, make audit of, keep accounts, take stock, balance accounts, make accounts square, bring to book, check, scrutinize, investigate.
2. Attend classes as an auditor, listen in on without actual participation.

AUDIT, *n.* 1. Official verification of financial records, rendering and settling of accounts, official examination of accounts.
2. Final statement of accounts, balance sheet, accompts, commercial arithmetic, money matters, statistics, budget, books, ledger, bookkeeping.

AUDITION, *n.* 1. Power of hearing, sense of hearing, act of hearing, ability to hear.
2. Something heard, what is heard, a mere sound.
3. Hearing given to a musician or actor to test performance, hearing to try out a performer, test performance, audience, test hearing, trial hearing.

AUDITOR, *n.* 1. Member of an audience, hearer, listener, one who listens critically, eavesdropper.
2. Examiner of accounts, accountant, expert accountant, certified public accountant, C.P.A. *(abbr.),* chartered accountant, verifier of balance sheets, actuary, bookkeeper, comptroller.

AUDITORIUM, *n.* Hall of audience, building for public gatherings, auditory, assembly hall, lecture hall, concert hall, theatre, stalls, parquet, boxes, orchestra, pit, cockpit, parterre, balcony, gallery, front of the house, dress circle, house, coliseum, congregation, peanut heaven, durbar, pump room, public meeting place, casino.

AU FAIT *(Fr.)* To the fact *(lit.),* familiar with the facts of, having practical knowledge of, good at, experienced, skilled, versed, proficient, skilful, expert, at home in, in one's element, a good hand at, well-instructed, trained, crack, accomplished, master of, up to.

AU FOND *(Fr.)* At bottom, to the bottom, in the main, thoroughly, in reality, fundamentally.

AUGMENT, *v.* 1. Enlarge in size or extent, swell, increase, magnify, amplify, add to, expand, make larger, distend, make bigger, extend, double, deepen, heighten, lengthen, raise, boost, inflate, spread, stretch out, strengthen, thicken, heap up, reinforce, redouble, accrue.
2. Grow larger, wax, multiply, mount, sprout, ascend, spring up, branch out, grow, burgeon, rise.

AUGMENTATION, *n.* 1. Enlargement, increase, expansion, extension, amplification, development, accession, dilation, dilatation, spread, annexation, growth, inflation, intensification, multiplication, aggrandizement, enhancement, reinforcement.
2. That by which anything is augmented, addition, annex, accretion, addendum, additum, appendage, increment, supplement, adjunct.

AUGUR, *n.* Ancient Roman official charged with interpreting omens, haruspex, observer of signs, foreteller of future events, seer, prophet, diviner, soothsayer, oracle, fortuneteller, prognosticator, geomancer, monitor, vaticinator.

AUGUR, *v.* 1. Prophesy, predict, prognosticate, soothsay, forecast, vaticinate, divine, augurate, presage, foretell, signify, ominate, premonish.
2. Afford an omen of, portend, foreshow, be an omen, foreshadow, bode, forebode, threaten, presignify, forewarn, foretoken, hold out hope, bid fair, promise, lead one to expect, excite expectation.
3. Conjecture from signs, guess, take an augury.

AUGURY, *n.* 1. Art of an augur, divination, prognosis, foretelling, forecast, prognostication, mantology, vaticination, hariolation, omination, soothsaying, prophecy, prediction, clairvoyance, sortilege, premonstration, prefigurement, auspices, foreboding, second sight.
2. Indication of the future, omen, prognostic, auspice, portent, sign, presage, token, foretoken, bodement, promise, harbinger, forerunner, herald, precursor, sign of the times, bird of omen, gathering clouds, warning.

AUGUST, *adj.* Inspiring admiration, imposing, glorious, awe-inspiring, majestic, sublime, grand, stately, dignified, exalted, lofty, illustrious, royal, distinguished, supreme, worshipful, of supreme dignity, of venerably majestic grandeur, solemn, inspiring reverence, impressive, pompous, superb, magnificent, imperial, royal, venerable, eminent, of high birth, of high rank, regal, princely, noble, kingly.

AURA, *n.* 1. Subtle essence, emanation, effluence, exhalation, expiration, effluvium, aroma, odor, vaporous spirit, atmosphere, distinctive air, distinctive character, pervasive influence.
2. Gentle breeze, zephyr, wind, breath, stream, puff, current, draught.

AUREATE, *adj.* 1. Gold-colored, golden, gilded, gilt, flavous, fulvous, xanthous, citrine, tawny, yellow, saffron-colored.
2. Like gold in resplendence, brilliant, ornate, splendid.

AUREOLE, *n.* Halo, aureola, nimbus, radiance surrounding head or figure of a sacred personage, encircling ring of light, circle of glory, glory, blaze of glory, effulgence, irradiation, luminous cloud, luminosity, light, radiance, crown of light, phosphorescence, luminescence, transplendency, corona, luster, resistant, fulguration.

AU REVOIR *(Fr.)* Till we meet again, to the seeing again, good-by for the present, fare you well, Godspeed you, bon voyage, *a rivederci (It.),* *auf Wiedersehen (Ger.),* hasta la vista *(Sp.),* so long!

AURORA, *n.* 1. *(Mythol.)* Goddess of the Dawn, herald of the day, personification of Morning, Eos *(Greek.)*
2. Roseate glow of early morning, sunrise, daybreak, dawn, matins, sunup, peep of day,

cockcrow, break of day, rising light, light of day, first blush of morning.

3. Rise of something, first period, beginning.

4. Electrical atmospheric phenomenon, polar lights, aurora borealis, northern lights, aurora polaris, southern lights, aurora australis, southern streamers.

AUSPICE, *n.* 1. Haruspication, prognostication, divination from birds.

2. Omen, bodement, forecast, augury, portent, prognostic, presage, sign, indication of the future, prefigurement, sign of the times.

3. Circumstance indicating the promise for the future, propitious circumstance.

AUSPICES, *n.* Favoring influence, benign favor, patronage, support, protection, aegis, palladium, championship, safeguard, wardenship, tutelage, guidance, support, care, countenance, advocacy, control, charge, superintendence, guardianship, authority, leadership.

AUSPICIOUS, *adj.* 1. Presaging to good fortune, of good omen, propitious, favorable, promising, encouraging, reassuring, golden, bright, roseate, rosy, fair, betokening success, felicitous, timely, opportune, seasonable, smiling, sunny, hopeful.

2. Favored by fortune, fortunate, thriving, flourishing, successful, prosperous, providential, well off, palmy, halcyon, red-letter, favonian, lucky, expedient, happy.

AUSTERE, *adj.* 1. Harsh in manner, forbidding, stern in appearance, dour, grim, grave, serious, sober, uncompromising, relentless, unrelenting, unyielding, acrimonious, sharp, acerbic, sarcastic, caustic, morose, difficult, peremptory, pitiless, hard.

2. Severe in disciplining oneself, morally strict, Catonian, ascetic, stringently moral, abstemious, strait-laced, puritanic, prudish, flagellatory, rigid, rigorous, stiff, formal in conduct.

3. Severely simple, without ornament, plain, unadorned, unembellished.

4. Rough to the taste, harsh in flavor, bitter, acetous, sour, astringent.

AUSTERITY, *n.* 1. Harshness, sternness, asperity, grimness, sobriety, seriousness, gravity, hardness, relentlessness, peremptoriness, acrimoniousness, acerbity, sharpness, dourness, failure to show leniency, severity, rigor, strictness, inflexibility, stiffness, formality.

2. Severe discipline, self-restraint, asceticism, abstemiousness, chasteness, puritanism, scourging, self-mortification, sackcloth and ashes, penance, fasting, flagellation, hardship, self-discipline, hair shirt.

3. Severe simplicity, lack of luxury, plainness.

AUTHENTIC, *adj.* 1. Entitled to acceptance and belief, trustworthy, dependable, reliable, official, authoritative, standard, accepted, received, valid, canonical, orthodox, accredited, accurate, from competent sources, accordant with the facts, of approved authority, worthy of belief, bona fide, from the original data, not garbled, credible, well-founded, unquestionable, attested, factual.

2. Genuine in origin, of the origin reputed, really coming from the alleged source, real, sure, true, veritable, legitimate, pure, unadulterated, actual, not spurious, not false, not fictitious, not apocryphal, what it purports to be, uncorrupted, literal, faithful.

AUTHENTICATE, *v.* 1. Make authoritative, seal, verify, certify, avouch, attest, give validity to,

countersign, guarantee, vouch, warrant, assure, insure, underwrite, endorse, give legal force to, validate.

2. Establish as genuine, show to be authentic, confirm, prove, demonstrate the genuineness of.

AUTHENTICATION, *n.* Verification, attestation, confirmation, establishment, guaranty, warranty, assurance, insurance, voucher, guarantee.

AUTHOR, *n.* 1. Originator, prime mover, former, beginner, first cause, founder, planner, creator, maker, father, projector, organizer, contriver, inventor, begetter, producer, parent, framer.

2. Person who writes or composes, composer, writer, litterateur, scribe, penman, playwright, dramatist, historian, novelist, fictioneer, essayist, pamphleteer, romancer, poet, librettist, journalist, newspaperman, reporter, correspondent, publicist, contributor, columnist, editorial writer, reviewer, critic, annotator, commentator, compiler, hack, lexicographer, encyclopedist, epistolographer, short story writer, free lance, quill-driver, pot-boiler.

3. Literary productions of a writer, author's writings collectively.

AUTHORITATIVE, *adj.* 1. Official, having due authority, having the weight of authority, ruling, ex cathedra, executive, administrative, sovereign, gubernatorial, bureaucratic, regnant, supreme, in the ascendant, entitled to obedience, worthy of acceptance, sound, weighty, decisive, imposing, impressive, duly sanctioned, valid, standard, orthodox, canonical.

2. Having an air of authority, peremptory, positive, dictatorial, imperious, magisterial, exercising authority, commanding, imperative, dogmatic, despotic, autocratic, lordly, arrogant, masterful.

AUTHORITY, *n.* 1. Right to command, right to control, sovereignty, jurisdiction, administration, right to adjudicate, right to determine, right to settle issues, government, empire, reign, dynasty, prerogative, divine right, rule by rank, control, ascendancy by office, sway, supremacy, mastery, power to direct others, domination, dominion, predominance, hegemony, regency, lordship, force.

2. Person in whom command is vested, official, magistrate, ruler, person in office, in (colloq.), powers that be, the government, governor, head, regent, president, director, commander, emperor, sovereign, potentate, king, lord, czar.

3. Person of commanding knowledge, leading expert, standard author, connoisseur, specialist, adept, proficient, master, mastermind, crackajack, accepted source of information, person cited as voucher, commanding scholar, leading man of science, authoritative textbook, final court of appeal.

4. Judicial decision establishing a rule, ruling, statute, court rule, precedent, decision, judgment, dictum, citation, command, warranty, permit, license, precept, sanction, liberty, carte blanche, order.

5. Weight of evidence, warrant for action, justification, commanding attestation, credibility, authorization, right, testimony, witness.

6. Title to respect, respectability, weight of character, dignity, commanding influence, credit, importance, prestige, esteem, respect, competency, trustworthiness.

AUTHORIZE, *v.* 1. Give authority to, empower,

license, commission, permit, give permission to, allow, give leave to, enable, invest, depute.

2. Give authority for, formally sanction, give warrant for, legalize, support by authority, sustain by authority, vouch for, entitle, approve, confirm, certify, accredit, establish.

3. Afford a ground for, warrant, justify.

4. Establish by usage, sanction the use of.

AUTOBIOGRAPHY, *n.* Self-written account of one's personal life, personal history, memoirs, own story, personal narrative, journal, letters, confession, life, fortunes, experiences, adventures.

AUTOCHTHONOUS, *adj.* Sprung from the soil, domestic, native, indigenous, developed at the place where found, enchorial, original, aboriginal, primeval, primitive, pristine, primary, first.

AUTOCRACY, *n.* 1. Unlimited authority over others invested in a single person, dictatorship, despotism, tyranny, absolute monarchy, arbitrary power, absolutism, czarism, kaiserism, monarchy, Caesarism, monocracy, absolute supremacy, iron rule.

2. Self-derived power, independent power, self-sustained power, uncontrolled action, autonomy.

AUTOCRAT, *n.* Person invested with absolute authority, absolute ruler, supreme ruler, monarch by inherent right, ruler not subject to restrictions, unlimited monarch, absolute emperor, dictator, despot, Caesar, czar, Kaiser, tyrant, overlord.

AUTOCRATIC, *adj.* 1. Absolute, irresponsible, holding independent powers of government, unlimited, arbitrary, royalistic, monarchical, monocratic.

2. Tyrannous, despotic, tyrannical, oppressive, magisterial, overbearing, severe, high-handed, iron-handed, coercive, peremptory, imperious.

AUTOGRAPH, *n.* 1. One's own signature, John Hancock, author's original signature, name-writing, moniker.

2. A person's own handwriting, hand, seal, chirography, countersign.

3. A manuscript in the author's handwriting, holograph, that which is written with one's own hand.

AUTOMATIC, *adj.* 1. Having the power of self-motion, self-moving, self-regulating, self-acting, self-propelling, mechanical, robotian, robotesque, push-button, under its own power, under its own steam, having inherent power of action.

2. Occurring independently of volition, reflex, involuntary, not controlled by volition, instinctive, spontaneous, unbidden, not under the control of the will.

3. Done unconsciously, done from force of habit, acting mechanically, blind, acting from inherent forces.

AUTOMATON, *n.* 1. Robot, mechanical figure that acts as if spontaneously, automatic puppet, marionette, fantoccino, self-moving machine, power-generating mechanism.

2. Person who acts without active intelligence, one who acts in routine manner, living being with involuntary actions, person who acts in a mechanical manner, pawn.

3. Something capable of acting without external impulse, anything capable of spontaneous movement.

AUTONOMOUS, *adj.* 1. Self-governing, self-directing, self-ruling, free, independent, subject to its own laws only, sovereign, autonomic,

existing as independent entity, allodial, absolute, freeholding, uncoerced, unrestricted.

2. Not under conscious control, spontaneous.

AUTONOMY, *n.* 1. Self-government, political independence, home rule, self-legislation, self-determination, freedom, autocracy, self-derived power, liberalism, non-interference.

2. Self-governing community, free land, freehold, allodium.

3. *(Philos.)* Ethical self-determination of the will, power of self-control.

AUTOPSY, *n.* 1. Post-mortem examination, post-mortem, necropsy, dissection of a body after death, examination of a cadaver by dissection, critical dissection.

2. Personal observation, ocular evidence, act of seeing with one's own eyes, personal inspection.

AUTUMN, *n.* 1. Fall, harvest-time, fall of the leaf, third season of the year, autumnal equinox, Indian summer, St. Luke's summer *(English Indian summer in October),* St. Martin's summer *(English Indian summer in November).*

2. Period of maturity passing into decline, period of ripeness, period of incipient decay, time of decline, caducity, decadence, falling off, climacteric, eventide.

AUXILIARY, *adj.* 1. Giving support, assisting, helping, aiding, helpful, adjuvant, cooperative, abetting.

2. Subordinate, subsidiary, supplementary, ministrant, ancillary, accessory, subservient, additional.

3. Used as a reserve.

AUXILIARY, *n.* 1. Giver of aid, helper, helpmate, helping hand, assistant, adjuvant, cooperator, coadjutor, collaborator, copartner, co-worker, accessory, right-hand man, companion, comrade, mate, buddy, sidekick, shadow, ally, accomplice, abettor, confederate, associate, colleague, puppet, confrere, partner, subordinate, cat's-paw, stooge, tool, satellite, hanger-on, parasite, dependent.

2. *(Pl.)* Foreign troops allied with a nation at war, mercenary soldiers, mercenaries.

AVAIL, *v.* 1. Help, be of value to, be of profit to, do good to, advantage, assist in accomplishing a purpose, aid, succor, stand one in good stead, promote, boot, conduce.

2. Have force, have efficacy, be of use, be of advantage, serve, bestead, work well, succeed, bear fruit, turn out well, answer the purpose, meet the demand, suffice.

AVAIL, *n.* Efficacy for a purpose, use toward success, usefulness, advantage to an end, good, serviceableness, advantage, benefit, profit, help, aid, service, utility, importance, consequence, significance, moment, weight, value, worth, productiveness.

AVAILABLE, *adj.* 1. Suitable for use, likely to answer an end, suitable for the accomplishment of a purpose, having sufficient efficacy, having enough power, sufficient in power for producing a desired result, effectual, valid, able to be turned to account, of use, of service, profitable, advantageous, capable of being employed with advantage, usable, beneficial.

2. Ready for use, at hand, convenient, handy, at one's command, at one's disposal, at one's elbow, accessible, obtainable.

AVAIL ONESELF OF Give oneself the advantage of, utilize, make use of, turn to account, employ, use, take advantage of, put to use, apply, set in motion, call into play, resort to, profit by, have recourse to, lay one's hands on, try, press into service, requisition, fall back upon, put to task.

AVALANCHE, *n.* 1. Large mass of falling snow, sliding of an ice mass down a mountain slope, snowslide, snowslip, landslide, landslip, overwhelming descent of anything.
2. Anything like an avalanche in sudden destructiveness, catastrophe, cataclysm, disaster, inundation, deluge, flood, debacle.

AVANT-GARDE, *n.* Van, vanguard, outrider, avant-coureur, leader, precursor, forerunner, pioneer, herald, harbinger, advance-guard.

AVARICE, *n.* Insatiable greed for riches, passion for getting riches, cupidity, graspingness, avidity, covetousness, rapacity, sordid desire to possess wealth, miserliness, tenacity, desire to hoard wealth, inordinate desire of gain, greediness, parsimony, penuriousness, stinginess, worship of the golden calf, niggardliness, lust for money, *auri sacra fames* (Lat.).

AVARICIOUS, *adj.* Immoderately desirous of accumulating wealth, covetous, eager to hoard, greedy of wealth, grasping, extortionate, sordid, rapacious, mercenary, venal, usurious, close-fisted, tight-fisted, tight, close, hard-fisted, strait-handed, penny-wise, miserly, stingy, penurious, tenacious of money, parsimonious, mean, niggardly.

AVATAR, *n.* 1. Descent of the soul into cosmic life, descent of a deity to earth in some manifest shape.
2. Concrete manifestation, visible material display, embodiment, incarnation, epiphany, worldly appearance.
3. Exaltation into an object of worship, graven image, fetishism.

AVAUNT, *adv.* Begone, be off, along with you, hence, away, away with, get you gone, go along, go away, go your way, off with you, go about your business, depart, get out, beat it, disappear.

AVENGE, *v.* Take vengeance for, repay, requite, exact satisfaction for, award just punishment for, punish, wreak punishment upon, inflict injury in return for, wreak vengeance, bring retributive justice to bear, visit punishment upon, retaliate, revenge, vindicate by punishment.

AVENUE, *n.* 1. Broad road bordered by trees, wide street, principal thoroughfare, boulevard, parkway, roadway, footway, highroad, highway, walk, alley.
2. Opening for entrance, perron, adit, passage, entry, main way of approach, access, doorway, passageway, gate.
3. Channel, artery, pass, course, passage, way, route, means of access, means of attainment.

AVER, *v.* Affirm with confidence, maintain, state, assert peremptorily, asseverate, depose, contend, declare in a positive manner, allege as a fact, pronounce, represent, predicate, avouch, avow, take one's stand upon, profess, protest, insist, emphasize roundly, lay stress upon, assure, verify, certify, guarantee, put in an affidavit, swear by bell, book and candle.

AVERAGE, *n.* 1. Quotient of a sum divided by the number of its terms, arithmetical mean, mean amount, mean quantity, mean proportion, medial estimate, medium, intermediate quantity.
2. Mean standard, norm, standard, run, rule, golden mean, mediocrity, medium grade, normal, ordinary amount, common run, normal rate, typical kind, general type.

AVERAGE, *adj.* 1. Mean, intervening, estimated by average, medium, middle, forming an average, intermediate, medial, median, typical in amount, normal, standard.
2. Usual, ordinary, middling, mediocre, so-so, indifferent, passable, tolerable, fair, moderate, decent, pretty well, well enough, rank and file, milk-and-water, betwixt and between, not bad, run-of-the-mill, not amiss.

AVERAGE, *v.* 1. Calculate arithmetical means of, reduce to a mean, find an average value for, reduce to an average, equate, split the difference, strike a balance.
2. Result in an arithmetical mean, amount to a mean quantity, show an average, occur as a mean rate.
3. *(Com.)* Apportion on the average, divide, distribute proportionally, proportion, equalize, balance.

AVERMENT, *n.* Positive statement, affirmation, affirmance, declaration, predication, profession, protestation, asseveration, assertment, remark, word, avowal, avouchment, adjuration, assurance, deposition, allegation, attestation, establishment by evidence, verification, proof.

AVERSE, *adj.* Turned away in mind or feeling, disinclined, reluctant, renitent, recalcitrant, loath, counter, contrary, backward, slow, laggard, shy of, unwilling, indisposed, moved by dislike, hostile, conflicting, adverse, inimical, opposed, restive, unfavorable.

AVERSION, *n.* 1. Rooted dislike, averted state of mind, fixed opposition, strong disinclination, unreasoning desire to avoid, distaste, disrelish, unwillingness, reluctance, backwardness, disfavor, repugnance, disapprobation, displeasure, prejudice.
2. Hatred, dyspathy, antipathy, antagonism, repulsion, abhorrence, abomination, detestation, horror, loathing, nausea, disgust, dislike, rancor, animosity, hostility, odium, grudge, umbrage, ill will, enmity.

AVERT, *v.* 1. Turn away, turn aside, sidetrack, move from the main course, turn off, divagate.
2. Make possible the avoidance of, prevent, preclude, obviate, debar in advance, ward off, keep off, parry, divert, forestall, hinder, inhibit, arrest, draw off, shield from, forefend, avoid, stave off, remove, nip in the bud.

AVIARY, *n.* Spacious enclosure in which birds are kept, large cage, bird-cage, bird-house, bird sanctuary, vivarium, pigeon-house, dovecote.

AVIATION, *n.* Aeronautics, aerial navigation, science of flying by mechanical means, art of flying with heavier-than-air craft, aerodynamics, aerostatics, aeromechanics, flight, wind, volation, volitation, aeroplaning, airmanship, flying.

AVIATOR, *n.* Aeronaut, aeroplanist, pilot of an airplane, operator of a flying machine, airman, flyer, aerial navigator, birdman, eagle, ace, scout, aviatrix, birdwoman, observer, bomber, spotter, fighter pilot, jet pilot, hydroplanist.

AVID, *adj.* 1. Keenly desirous, eager, covetous, acquisitive, grasping, extortionate, concupiscent, greedy, craving, rapacious, prurient.
2. Keen with hunger, appetitive, famished, ravenous, ravening, voracious, omnivorous, insatiable, unsated, sharp-set, edacious, esurient, hungry.

AVIDITY, *n.* 1. Intense desire, longing, craving, hankering, yearning, covetousness, concupiscence, eagerness, ardor, appetency, cupidity, prurience, lust, itching palm, greediness, grasping, rapacity.

2. Strong appetite, eager relish, ravenousness, voracity, voraciousness, sharp-set hunger, canine appetite, edge of appetite, torment of Tantalus, stomach, sweet tooth, edacity, esurience, empty stomach, famishment, omnivorousness, mouth-watering.

AVOCATION, *n.* 1. *(Colloq.)* Regular occupation, vocation, pursuit, line, calling, business, concern, job, duty, craft, work, task, trade, employment, profession, office, function.

2. Minor occupation, occasional business, side interest, hobby, distraction, diversion, by-concern, by-business.

AVOID, *v.* 1. Keep at a distance from, steer clear of, go wide of, keep away from, keep out of the way of, keep clear of, hold aloof from, fight shy of, dodge, evade, shirk, elude, eschew, malinger, shun, escape, avert, balk at, hold back, desert, abandon, forsake, have nothing to do with, flit, decamp, retreat, vamoose, depart from, make off, part company, make oneself scarce, abscond, cut and run, bolt, play truant, flee from, fend off, parry, beware of, abhor, blink at, boycott, not do, abstain from, forbear, refrain from, cannot help, decline.

2. *(Law)* Make of no effect, void, invalidate, annul, make inoperative, vacate, refute, defeat.

AVOIDANCE, *n.* 1. Keeping away from, go-by, evasion, parrying, escape, shunning, eschewment, forbearance, elusion, abstention, abstinence, flight.

2. *(Law)* Annulment, vacatur, making void, dismissal, invalidation, voidance.

AVOIRDUPOIS, *n.* 1. System of weights used for ordinary purposes of trade, weight.

2. *(Colloq.)* Heaviness, gravity, ponderosity, ballast, embonpoint, corpulence, plumpness, obesity.

AVOUCH, *v.* 1. Make frank acknowledgment of, make open affirmation of, allege on one's word, declare with positiveness, assert positively, avow, proclaim, asseverate, aver, say, maintain, state, protest, affirm, profess, confirm, authenticate, certify, depose.

2. Assume responsibility for, guarantee, vouch for, give assurance, assure, insure, be answerable for, pledge one's word, warrant.

3. Admit, confess, acknowledge.

AVOW, *v.* Declare openly, admit frankly, allow, aver, avouch, profess, acknowledge, own, confess, make a clean breast, unburden one's mind, lay bare, unbosom oneself, come out with, blurt out, let out, divulge, disclose, advertise.

AVOWAL, *n.* Open statement of affirmation, frank admission, confession, acknowledgment, profession, public declaration, allegation, word, assertion, affirmation, averment, protestation, assurance, manifesto, exposure, exposé.

AVOWEDLY, *adv.* Confessedly, openly, candidly, frankly, affirmatively, manifestly, to one's face, as freely acknowledged, cards on the table, in the open, in broad daylight, without reserve, on oath, in plain words, unfeignedly, bona fide, by my troth, to be sure, certes, eyes are opened, the murder is out.

AWAIT, *v.* 1. Wait for, look for, keep in view, have in prospect, stay for, abide, expect, look forward to, anticipate, contemplate, watch for, be in readiness for.

2. Be ready for, be prepared for, attend, tarry, be in waiting for, bide, sit up for, hang fire, be reserved for, be contingent upon.

3. Approach, impend, hang over, near, come on, threaten.

AWAKE, *adj.* 1. Waking, not sleeping, not asleep.

2. Attentive, vigilant, watchful, wide-awake, circumspect, open-eyed, observant, heedful, alert, mindful, conscious, aware, alive to, on the qui vive, on the alert, keen, astute, acute, intent on, bright, sharp.

AWAKEN, *v.* 1. Wake up, waken, awake, wake, rouse from sleep.

2. Bring to a realization of the truth, rouse to action or attention, arouse, kindle, excite, fire, animate, spur, work upon, incite, stimulate, work up, quicken, provoke, fan the fire, stir up, give new life to, infuse life into, prod, call forth, whet, summon up, vivify, revive, move, impress.

AWAKENING, *n.* 1. Waking up, awaking, rising from sleep.

2. Arousal, excitation of feeling, quickening of interest, revival of interest, kindling, suscitation, renascence, stimulation, stirring, galvanization, animation, agitation.

AWARD, *v.* Adjudge to be due, allot, apportion, decree to be merited, assign, grant, bestow by judicial decree, appoint by deliberate judgment, determine, judge, adjudicate, decide, consign, grant the enjoyment of, allow.

AWARD, *n.* 1. Assignment, allotment, present, gift, bestowal, trophy, meed, prize, honorarium, honor, guerdon, reward, premium, decoration, medal, cup, laurels, palm, blue ribbon, *cordon bleu (Fr.),* citation, bays, chaplet, wreath, crown.

2. *(Law)* Judicial sentence, decree, decision of arbitrators on points submitted to them, decision after consideration, determination, arbitrament, dictum, adjudication.

AWARE, *adj.* Possessing knowledge of, informed through the senses, familiar with, cognizant of, apprised, certified, observant, mindful, conscious of, percipient, sentient, sensible of, awake, sure, certain, assured, persuaded, convinced, knowing, enlightened, acquainted with, conversant, alive to, wide-awake.

AWAY, *adv.* 1. From this place, off, absent, gone, from home, not at home, not present.

2. Far apart, aloof, at a distance, remote.

3. Aside, from contact, in another direction.

4. Out of possession, out of notice, out of use, out of existence, to an end, into extinction, into termination.

5. Continuously, on, without break.

6. Without hesitation, without delay.

7. Away with, take away, begone, avaunt, get you gone.

AWE, *n.* 1. Reverence, reverential fear, solemn exaltation, veneration, adoring wonder, admiring solemnity, respect, amazement, abashment.

2. Dread mingled with veneration, fearfulness, fear, horror, shock, panic, apprehension, alarm, fright, affright, dismay, consternation, quaking, disquietude, trepidation, perturbation, quivering, trembling.

AWE, *v.* 1. Inspire with awe, solemnize, make reverent, influence by profound respect, fill with reverence.

2. Overawe, restrain by awe, constrain by fear, terrify, intimidate, affright, daunt, cow, appall, fill with consternation, dismay, abash, astonish, amaze, alarm.

AWE-INSPIRING, *adj.* Formidable, portentous, imposing, impressive, terrible, ghastly, awesome, appalling, weird, redoubtable, fearsome, dreadful, shocking, tremendous, horrific, horrendous, eerie, overwhelming.

AWE-STRUCK, *adj.* 1. Filled with awe, solemn, reverent, reverential, filled with grave exaltation, inspired with awe, awed.

2. Held in check through awe, horror-struck, abashed, dismayed, daunted, cowed, frightened, appalled, horrified, overwhelmed, intimidated, terrified.

AWFUL, *adj.* 1. Inspiring reverential awe, dread, solemnly impressive, awesome, awe-inspiring, reverend, solemn, sublime, majestic, imposing, grand, august, venerable, stately, noble.

2. Inspiring fear, horrific, horrendous, fearful, dreadful, terrific, shocking, horrible, horrifying, alarming, terrible, dire, appalling, formidable, frightful, tremendous, overwhelming, portentous, monstrous, heinous, calamitous, redoubtable, stupendous, gruesome, hideous, distressing.

3. Full of awe, reverential, feeling awe.

4. *(Colloq.)* Extremely bad, unpleasant, ugly, grotesque.

AWHILE, *adv.* For a short time, for a brief respite, for a brief period, for some time, some time, for a while.

AWKWARD, *adj.* 1. Lacking dexterity, without skill, unskilful, bungling, inexpert, maladroit, inapt, inefficient, clumsy, without expedition, inept.

2. Ill-adapted for use, unwieldy, inconvenient, unhandy, difficult to handle, bulky, lumbering, unmanageable, unfit, ill-proportioned, ponderous, cumbersome.

3. Gauche, ungraceful, ungainly, unpolished, uncouth, rude, coarse, rough, unrefined, wooden, uncourtly, inelegant, untoward, stiff, slouching, gawky, loutish, rustic, boorish, lubberly, uneasy, constrained, shuffling, indelicate, crude, homely, grotesque, backward, dowdy.

4. Requiring caution, somewhat hazardous, dangerous to deal with.

5. Embarrassing, trying, not easily dealt with, unpleasant, uneasy.

AWNING, *n.* Shelter of canvas, roof-like covering, canopy, tilt, baldachin, canvas roof, sunshade, shade. protection from the sun.

AWRY, *adv.* 1. Out of the proper direction, with a twist to one side, askew, turned toward one side, athwart, obliquely, asquint, askant, out of the right course, crosswise, distortedly, crookedly.

2. Away from the truth, away from reason, unreasonably, perversely.

3. Amiss, wrong, erroneously.

AX, *n.* Adz, dolabra, mattock, hatchet, cleaver, celt, securis, broadax, battle-ax, poleax, pickax, ax-hammer, chopping-ax, chipping-ax, dock-ax, listing-ax, felling-ax, fire-ax, grubbing-ax, ice-ax, holing-ax, logging-ax, lopping-ax, bullhead-ax, peeling-ax, flesh-ax, granite-ax, head-ax, slate-ax, double-ax, two-bladed ax, labrys, grooved-ax.

AXIOM, *n.* 1. Postulate, established rule, truism, universally accepted principle, settled principle not necessarily true, assumed truth, recognized truth, commonly received proposition, law drawn from experience, self-evident proposition, self-evident truth, intuitive truth, necessary truth.

2. Aphorism, motto, precept, proverb, saying, maxim, saw, dictum, adage, apothegm, byword, gnome.

AXIOMATIC, *adj.* 1. Self-evident, apodictic, a priori, manifest, certain, absolute, necessary, positive, gnomic, unquestionable.

2. Aphoristic, apothegmatic, preceptive, based upon axioms, proverbial, abounding in axioms, characterized by axioms.

AXIS, *n.* 1. Shaft, arbor, spindle, axle, cob, stem.

2. Line about which a rotating body turns, line around which something is symmetrically arranged, central line of any symmetrical body, line of revolution, line of rotation, geometric line round which a turning body revolves, line of symmetry, verticle.

3. *(Fig.)* Pivotal point, that on which any matter hinges.

4. Alliance of two or more states, entente, coalition, compact.

AYE, *adv.* Always, ever, eternally, at all times, forever, continually, evermore, unchangingly, ceaselessly, incessantly, unendingly, immutably, changelessly.

AYE, *n.* Affirmative vote, expression of assent, yea, yes.

AZURE, *adj.* 1. Blue, cerulean, sky-blue, cobalt blue, sky-colored, ultramarine, smalt.

2. Like the clear sky, cloudless, spotless.

AZURE, *n.* 1. Clear blue, sky-color, cerulean, blue of unclouded sky.

2. The clear sky, empyrean, cerulean vault, blue expanse, arch of heaven, heaven, welkin, depths of space, blue vault of heaven.

B

BAA, *v.* Bleat, cry, call.

BABBLE, *v.* Patter, twattle, talk incoherently *or* foolishly *or* nonsensically, sputter, blather, gibber, prattle, drivel, chatter, tattle, gab, blab, twaddle, gabble, rattle on, gush, prate, cackle, palaver, clack, clatter, maunder, blabber. (see also PRATE, *v.*)

BABBLE, *n.* 1. Chitchat, childish *or* foolish talk, stuff and nonsense, rubbish, simple-minded talk, blather, twaddle, patter, cackle, clack, clatter, drivel, blabber, gab. (see also BALDERDASH, *n.*)

2. Garrulity, loquaciousness, multiloquence, loquacity, talkativeness, volubility, flippantness, volubleness, glibness, flippancy, effusion.

BABBLER, *n.* Talker, tattler, prattler, blabber, prater, blab, magpie, gabbler, chatterer, driveler, maunderer, jay, parrot, poll, windbag. (see also BABBLE, *n.*)

BABBLING, *adj.* Blathering, garrulous, talkative, loquacious, voluble, glib, multiloquous, flippant, effusive. (see also BABBLE, *n.*)

BABE, *n.* 1. Infant, child, etc. (see BABY, *n.*)

2. Innocent, beginner, neophyte, novice, tyro, abecedarian, tenderfoot, greenhorn, catechumen, alphabetarian, recruit, inceptor, apprentice, novitiate.

BABY, *adj.* 1. Childish, babyish, etc. (see BABYISH, *adj.*)

2. Small, infinitesimal, diminutive, tiny, little, wee, teeny, petite, weeny, minute, miniature, Lilliputian, minikin, exiguous, pygmy, pygmaean, dwarfish, midget, pocket, pocket-size, undersized, runty, stunted, bantam, microscopic *(loosely)*.

BABY, *v.* Coddle, pet, fondle, humor, indulge, nurse, pamper, caress, treat with fondness, make much of, dandle, cocker, cosset, cuddle, spoil, mollycoddle.

BABYHOOD, *n.* Babehood, childhood, infancy, diaper days, early childhood, suckling days, nursery days, cradle days.

BABYISH, *adj.* 1. Childish, juvenile, infantine, baby, babylike, infantile, childlike, juvenile, puerile.

2. Simple, soft, green, foolish, etc. (see FOOLISH, *adj.*)

BACCALAUREATE, *n.* (See BACHELOR, *n.,* 2)

BACCHANAL, *n.* (*Often* BACCHANALS.) 1. Drunken bout, orgy, revelry, revels, carousal, debaucherie, frolic, potation, compotation, spree, wassail, Saturnalia, drunken feasts, merrymaking, conviviality, carousing, jollification, feast, festival, libation, Dionysia, festivity, junket, carnival, symposium. (see also BAT, *n.* 6)

2. Reveler, carouser, wassailer, merrymaker, bacchant, bacchante, convivialist, frolicker, maenad.

BACCHANAL, *adj.* Riotous, reveling, wild, gay, festive, orgiastic, bacchant, bacchantic, bacchic, bacchanalian, Dionysiac, Dionysian, entertaining, jovial, merry, jocund, frolicsome, hilarious, sportive. (see also GAY, *adj.*)

BACHELOR, *n.* 1. Unmarried man, celibate, single man, misogamist, misogynist.

2. B.A., college graduate, baccalaureate.

BACHELORHOOD, *n.* Bachelorship, celibacy, unmarried state, single life, singleness, single blessedness.

BACK, *adj.* 1. Remote, secluded, rural, etc. (see BACKWOODS, *adj.*)

2. Hindmost, dorsal, posterior, rear, hinder, hind, after, caudal, tergal, spinal.

3. Former, tardy, forgotten, late, in arrears, belated, behind, dilatory, delayed, past, bygone, gone, elapsed, expired, obsolete, forgotten, past.

BACK, *adv.* 1. Ago, formerly, of old, of yore, since, hitherto, heretofore, once.

2. Aback, backward, etc. (see BACKWARDS, *adv.*)

BACK, *n.* 1. Rear, end, hinder part, buttocks (of a ship), hind part, posterior, tail end, breech (of a gun), reverse, reverse side, occiput (of the skull), nape *and* scruff (of the neck), behind, wake, stern, afterpart, heel.

2. Spine, dorsum, etc. (see BACKBONE, *n.,* 1)

3. Rump, backside, fundament, buttocks, loins, hindquarters, croup (of animals).

BACK, *v.* 1. Help, endorse, vouch for, back up, maintain, stand up for, aid, encourage, second, assist, plead for, advocate, recommend, praise, protect, guard, promote, succor, sanction, abet, corroborate, patronize, cooperate with, sponsor, subsidize, approve, uphold, support, countenance, bolster, reinforce, strengthen, sustain, favor, hold up, take side with, attest, bear witness, validate, testify for, affirm, certify, verify, substantiate, confirm, make out a case for, warrant, ensure, guarantee.

2. Retrogress, back up, decline, retreat, recede, retract, withdraw, retire, abduce, pull back, move backward, resile, ebb, recoil, rebound, spring back, reverse, return, back down, revert, regrade, turn round, turn tail, beat a retreat, relapse, draw *or* fall back.

BACKBITE, *v.* Run down, belittle, traduce, stab, revile, smirch, blemish, decry, speak ill of, pick *or* pull to pieces, depreciate, denounce, throw mud at, scandalize, abuse, vilipend, malign, libel,

defame, slander, gossip, blame, asperse, vilify, disparage, calumniate, stigmatize, vituperate, blacken, denigrate, belie, derogate, bespatter, injure, damage, hurt, attack, assail, steal one's reputation, censure, condemn, bear false witness against, dispraise, discommend, reprobate, detract, recriminate.

BACKBITING, *n.* Vituperation, invective, hurt, traduction, scandal, vilification, scurrility, abuse, traducing, obloquy, reviling, blackening, abusing, denigration, belittling, contumely, vilipending, calumny, smirching, decrying, assailing, slander, gossip, attack, damage, aspersion, defamation, detraction, maliciousness.

BACKBONE, *n.* 1. Spine, spinal column, chine, vertebrae, spina, rachis, dorsum, breech, ridge, vertebral column.

2. Mettle, ardor, fortitude, firmness, quality, grit, endurance, valor, stamina, courage, bravery, steadfastness, dauntlessness, manhood, hardihood, manliness, spirit, pluck, daring, resolve, tenacity, inflexibility, resoluteness, indefatigability, bulldog courage, gallantry, intrepidity, soundness, stiffness.

BACKER, *n.* Second, partner, adherent, patron, supporter, friend at court, guardian angel, aider, champion, upholder, partisan, well-wisher, sharer, favorer, confrere, cooperator, right hand, helper, reliever, subsidizer, sponsor, assistant, colleague, crony, accessory, accomplice, follower, Maecenas, ally, adjuvant, adjunct, mate, fautor, coadjutor, conspirator, collaborator, coadjutrix, satellite, disciple, votary, worshipper, confidante, ensurer, guarantee, guarantor, warrantor, sympathizer, endorser, promoter, abettor.

BACKFIRE, *v.* 1. Discharge, explode, detonate, burst, flash back, flow back, reverberate.

2. Boomerang, bounce, bounce back, recoil, turn the tables, rebound, spring back, fly back, resile, ricochet.

BACKGROUND, *n.* 1. Distance, rear, backdrop, mise-en-scène *(Fr.),* skyline, foil, scene, seascape, landscape, décor, offing, setting, stage.

2. Groundwork, antecedents, milieu, scheme, local color, underlying factors, environment, fabric, circumstances, framework.

3. Upbringing, rearing, training, experience, environment, education, breeding, knowledge, preparation, foundation, grounding, credentials, qualification.

4. (*Preceded by* in the) In obscurity, in the shadows, out of the limelight, in the rear, in the dusk, in the shade, unnoticed, inconspicuous, in the back seat, out of sight, unseen, behind the scenes.

BACKHANDED, *adj.* 1. (*Of handwriting*) Inclining *or* sloping *or* slanting to the left.

2. Awkward, insincere, clumsy, left-handed, indirect, hollow, mendacious, false, sly, cunning, unfavorable, backhand, unveracious, Janus-faced, unfair, underhanded, crafty, dishonorable, artful, insidious, tartuffish, hypocritical, double-tongued, sneaking, inappropriate, ill-contrived, unsuitable, unnecessary, gauche, tactless, heavy-handed, maladroit, inconsiderate, unapt, dirty, uncalled for, two-faced, untoward, ungracious, unkind.

3. Biting, bitter, sarcastic, scathing, mordant, mordacious, incisive, caustic, trenchant, cutting, mean, cruel, scurrilous, spiteful, harsh, galling, taunting, acrimonious, keen-edged, splenetic, sharp, insulting.

BACKHOUSE, *n.* Latrine, necessary, outhouse, privy, outdoor toilet, water closet, cloaca.

BACKING, *n.* Help, assistance, seconding, relief, support, cooperation, subsidy, approval, succor, advocacy, commendation, encouragement, grant, maintenance, championing, sustenance, aid, lift, furtherance, helping hand, propping, bracing, bolstering, strengthening, comfort, defense, favor, protection, abetting, endorsement, collaboration, warranty, guarantee, security, surety, adherence, sponsorship, collateral, assurance, partisanship, sympathy, promotion.

BACKLASH, *n.* 1. *(Of machinery)* Rebound, jar, recoil, snag, obstruction, stoppage, hitch, kick, dislocation.
2. Snarl, catch, knot, tangle, entanglement, snag, ravel.

BACKSET, *n.* 1. Turn of the tide, setback, rebuff, discouragement, repulse, check, misfortune, curb, reverse, reversal, upset, miscarriage, throwing back, damper, restraint, relapse.
2. Eddy, countercurrent, backflow, ebb, reflux, back-surge, regurgitation, backwash, backwater, return, deflection, reflection.

BACKSLIDE, *v.* Desert, fall, regress, relapse, fail, break faith, lapse, renege, apostatize, fall away, weaken, retrogress, retrograde, revert, deteriorate, tergiversate, degenerate, decline, droop, return, secede, recant, retract, abandon *or* adjure *or* forswear *or* relinquish *or* disavow *or* unsay *or* renounce *or* forsake *or* discard *or* cast off *or* reject *or* repudiate one's principles or beliefs.

BACKSLIDER, *n.* Turncoat, renegade, pervert, tergiversator, defectionist, traitor, nonconformist, deserter, recidivist, forsaker, abandoner, heretic, apostate, dissenter, schismatic. (see also BACKSLIDE, *v.*)

BACKWARD, *adj.* 1. Remiss, laggard, slack, slow, averse, renitent, recalcitrant, opposed, hesitant, antipathetical, stubborn, wavering, unconsenting, uncomplying, noncompliant, restive *(of horses),* wayward, balky, protesting, unwilling, obdurate, mulish, pigheaded, loath, perverse, reluctant, pervicacious, disinclined, refractory, unyielding, contumacious, withstanding, unruly, unamenable.
2. Reluctant, shy, coy, etc. (see BASHFUL, *adj.*)
3. Retarded, dull, inapt, inept, undeveloped, stupid, stolid, unprogressive, slack, slow-witted, thick-skulled, moronic, idiotic, imbecile, feeble, feeble-minded, witless, unintelligent, wanting, rattle-brained, soft, slow, insulse, doltish, asinine, childlike, simple, fatuous, simple-minded, weak-, addle-, blunder-, muddled-, gross-headed, vacant, blockish, unteachable, Boeotian, foolish, silly, senseless, irrational.
4. Late, overdue, laggard, detained, retarded, slow, belated, unpunctual, slack, leisurely, tardy, sluggish, hindered, impeded, snail-like, lingering, behindhand, slow-paced, in arrears, loitering, lagging, tardigrade, dawdling.
5. Receding, refluent, reversionary, ebbing, regressive, retrogressive, returning, relapsing, retrospective, retrograde, recessive, recidivous, reflex, lapsing, counterclockwise.

BACKWARDS, *adv.* also **BACKWARD.** Aback, towards the back *or* rear, at the back, behind, aft *(Naut.),* abaft *(Naut.),* astern, after, in the rear, backward, rearward.

BACKWASH, *n.* 1. Wake *(of a vessel),* backwater, churning, wash, train, rear, track, path.
(see also BACKSET, *n.,* 2)
2. Agitation, result, repercussion, concussion, effect, reverberation, sequela, disturbance, storm,

succussion, succussation, commotion, convulsion, ferment, tumult, turmoil, perturbation, tremor, trepidation, vibration, discomposure, fervor, disquietude, excitement, rebound, recoil, upshot, consequence, outcome, aftermath, outgrowth, issue.

BACKWATER, *adj.* 1. Reflux, eddy, etc. (see BACKSET, *n.* 2)
2. Rural, rustic, etc. (see BACKWOODS, *adj.*)

BACKWOODS, *adj.* Frontier, backwater, hick, out-of-the-way, sequestered, jerkwater, rustic, remote, distant, secluded, lonely, inaccessible, removed, provincial, country, outdoor, pioneer, backwoodsy, countrified, isolated, pastoral, Arcadian, agrestic, geoponic, bucolic, Georgic.

BACKWOODS, *n.* Timberlands, forests, woods, woodlands, hinterland, country, outdoors, bush, greenwood, jungle, undergrowth, sticks.

BACTERIA, *n.* Germ, bacillus, microbe, virus, microorganism, infusoria, pathogen.

BACTERICIDE, *n.* Germicide, antiseptic, phage, disinfectant, antitoxin, prophylactic, serum, bacteriophage.

BAD, *adj.* 1. Evil, wicked, nefarious, heinous, vicious, baneful, baleful, pernicious, malicious, malignant, malevolent, offensive, dangerous, poisonous, noisome, mischievous, noxious, mean, hurtful, naughty, wrong, spiteful, bestial, crooked, injurious, unwholesome, corrupt, unprincipled, iniquitous, demoralized, dissolute, profligate, libertine, accursed, hardened, incorrigible, base, felonious, rotten, infamous, unrighteous, sinister, unscrupulous, miscreant, unlawful, reprobate, disreputable, knavish, vile, arrant, shameful, immoral, villainous, degenerate, dishonorable, depraved, criminal, disreputable, ' scandalous, blackhearted, opprobrious, scoundrelly, brutish, foul, reprehensible, treacherous, false, faithless, gross, flagrant, turpitudinous, scurvy, soulless, insidious, sinful, untrustworthy, Machiavellian, blackguard, uncommendable, facinorous, hellish, blameworthy, inexpiable, evil-minded, infernal, evil-disposed, Satanic, fiendish, demoniacal, guilty, diabolic, devilish, scampish, disgraceful, stygian, atrocious, Mephistophelian, irreclaimable, culpable, obdurate, peccable, censurable, illaudable, virtueless, obliquitous, peccant, flagitious.
2. Defective, below standard, worthless, faulty, lacking, poor, unfit, second-rate, inferior, thin, deficient, imperfect, sparing, scrimp, inadequate, meager, paltry, stinted, skimpy, weak, unsound, mutilated, below par, inefficacious, inefficient, inept, ineffectual, valueless, useless, unavailing, inutile, incompetent, incapable, unendowed, wretched.
3. Erroneous, untrue, unsound, fallacious, false, questionable, untrustworthy, unreliable, incorrect, sham, falsified, impure, adulterated, illicit, contraband, illegitimate, bastard, bogus, artificial, factitious, fraudulent, scamped, feigned, pretended, counterfeit, faked, spurious, wrong, inaccurate, inexact, illogical, unreal, ungrounded, groundless.
4. Rotten, decayed, spoiled, turned, foul, fetid, noisome, stinking, malodorous, rank, rancid, sour, fusty, musty, putrefied, decomposed, corrupted, vitiated, contaminated, defiled, poisonous, carious, poisoned, polluted, tainted, infected, putrescent, rotted, diseased, festered, gangrenous, mouldering, septic, blighted, mouldy, mildewed, cankered,

envenomed, putrefacient, putrid, reeking, maggoty, flyblown, mucid, purulent.

5. Unfavorable, ill, threatening, unpleasant, unwelcome, inauspicious, unpropitious, adverse, sad, distressing, discouraging, oppressive, gloomy, frightening, depressing, untoward, disappointing, disadvantageous, troublesome, troubling, trying, disturbing, afflicting, tormenting, melancholy, dark, dull, woeful, painful, mournful, somber, grave, disheartening, joyless, unhappy, upsetting, forlorn, comfortless, desolate, doleful, solemn, grim, unnerving, heavy, hopeless, desperate, unpromising, ill-omened, lowering, ill-boding, sinister, menacing, minatory, hard, grievous, harsh, dismal, deplorable, moving, touching, pathetic, rueful, dreary, disquieting, unbearable, unendurable, shocking, appalling, crushing, dire, dreadful, heartbreaking, harrowing, disastrous, calamitous, tragic, desolating, baleful, withering, unfortunate, ill-starred, regrettable, sorrowful, lamentable, sickening, burdensome, agonizing, onerous, vexatious.

6. Harmful, injurious, hurtful, etc. (see BALEFUL, adj., 1)

7. Disagreeable, unpleasant, nasty, filthy, sour, distasteful, upsetting, unpalatable, displeasing, uninviting, unsatisfactory, annoying, irritating, unsavory, bitter, acrimonious, offensive, foul, vile, disgusting, repulsive, revolting, ill-favored, harsh, rough, acrid, obnoxious, repugnant, nauseous, objectionable, sickening, loathsome, detestable, fulsome, unappetizing, inedible, uneatable, odious, undesirable, abhorrent, insufferable, horrid, execrable.

8. Ill, sick, distressed, sorry, upset, diseased, infirm, ailing, sickly, feeble, indisposed, off color (colloq.), unwell, nauseated, not well, poorly, in bad health, unhealthy, qualmish, queasy, under the weather (colloq.), unsound, weakly, sickish, drooping, flagging, suffering, failing, wretched, valetudinary, affected, languishing, miserable.

9. Severe, distressing, painful, aching, piercing, keen, sharp, hurtful, afflicting, acute, sore, harsh, agonizing, horrible, grating, grinding, searing, racking, excruciating, consuming, cutting, cruel, caustic, gripping, galling, grave, hard, stinging, stabbing, pricking, gnawing, torturing, punishing, convulsive, telling, smarting, serious, grievous, dangerous, dreadful, disastrous, aggravating, heavy, harrowing.

10. False, counterfeit, bogus, forged, unsound, phony (slang), pretended, deceptive, unreliable, fraudulent, misrepresented, untrustworthy, not genuine, supposititious, scamped, illegal, simulated, imitation, misstated, falsified, fabricated, sham, feigned, fictitious, tampered with.

11. Disastrous, catastrophic, ruinous, serious, damaging, unfortunate, unlucky, fatal, terrible, crushing, frightful, calamitous, tragic, desolating, hopeless, incurable, irreparable, irretrievable, immedicable, immitigable, irremediable, irrevocable.

BADGE, n. 1. Shield, device, ensign, star, token of office, official star, insignia, seal, marker, phylactery, cordon, brassard, brand, chevron, motto, decoration, medallion, medal, escutcheon, cockade, feather, emblem, rosette, button, ribbon, crest, weeper, cuff band, epaulet, aglet, aiguillette, sigil, signet, laticlave and angusticlave (Rom. Antiq.)

2. Sign, mark, token, stamp, brand, stigma, indication, token, criterion, label, tab, symptom, trademark, note, earmark, trait, characteristic,

diagnostic, livery, uniform.

BADGER, v. Bait, tease, annoy, provoke, bother, pester, nag, persecute, vex, heckle, irritate, bully, try one's patience, victimize, hector, nettle, sting, trouble, goad, hound, chevy, ride, torment, irk, gripe, disquiet, perturb, haunt, disturb, worry, inconvenience, discommode, harry, gall, rile, ruffle, roil, plague, tweak, fret, oppress, harass, dragoon (Mil.), rag, pother, beset, infest, chafe, afflict.

BADINAGE, n. Raillery, chaff, persiflage, etc. (see BANTER, n.)

BAFFLE, v. 1. Foil, balk, thwart, check, etc. (see BALK, v., and BAR, v., 2)

2. Delude, confuse, cheat, outwit, nonplus, puzzle, disconcert, perplex, bewilder, confound, distract, mystify, elude, evade, foil, trick, hoax, perplex, stagger, daze, befog, bemuddle, amaze, surprise, astonish, astound, dumfound, spoof, flabbergast, hoodwink, blind, pull the wool over one's eyes, bluff, throw off the scent, frustrate, make a fool of.

3. Cheat, defraud, do, jockey, gyp, diddle, swindle, hoax, cozen, chouse, bilk, pluck, gull, victimize, circumvent, inveigle, trick, bamboozle, overreach, beguile, decoy, waylay, humbug, lime, illaqueate, befool, fleece, bite, play or foist upon, hook, entoil, practice upon, trepan, snare, use wiles, gammon, mulct, peculate, fuddle, outwit, befuddle.

BAG, n. 1. Sack, pouch, pack, portmanteau, case, suitcase, reticule, wallet, valise, bundle, sachet, receptacle, satchel, knapsack, poke, pocketbook, packet, ditty bag, purse, handbag, gunny sack, sabretache (Mil.), sporran (Scot.), quiver, vanity bag, haversack, rucksack, feedbag, holster, grip, kitbag, saddlebag, carpetbag, Gladstone, briefcase, container.

2. (Anat.) Sac, vesicle, saccule, utricle, cyst, capsule, bladder, theca, crop, craw.

BAG, v. 1. Bulge, swell, belly, project, protrude, pout, hang over, beetle, bunch, bouge, sag, hang, swell out, dangle, droop.

2. Take, seize, capture, catch, entrap, trap, snare, ensnare, get, gain, win, obtain, procure, gather, annex, cull, nab, cop, collect, acquire, snatch, pocket, hook, shoot, shanghai, spirit away, grab, carry off, bear away or off, abduct, steal, filch, lift, pilfer, kidnap, abstract, crimp, appropriate, apprehend, pluck up, clasp, grip, grapple, fasten upon, lay by the heels, help oneself, collar, snip up, whip up, commandeer.

BAGATELLE, n. (see BAUBLE, n.)

BAGGAGE, n. 1. Luggage, encumbrances, pack, impedimenta, things, truck, viaticals, viaticum, trunk, valise, suitcase, effects, movables, gear, paraphernalia, accouterments, equipment.

2. Jade, hussy, wench, flapper, trollop, vixen, harridan, minx, hoyden.

BAGGY, adj. Swelling, swelled, swollen, puffed, flabby, flaccid, full, unshapely, loose, slack, limp, plump, soft, lumpy, bunchy, bulbous.

BAGNIO, n. 1. Bath, bathing house, etc. (see BATH, n.)

2. Stew, brothel, etc. (see BAWDY HOUSE, n.)

3. Confine, prison, etc. (see PRISON, n.)

BAIL, n. 1. Security, warranty, plight, pledge, tie, sponsorship, mainprise, hostage, collateral, bond, vadium, guarantee, deposit, surety.

2. Handle (of a pail, etc.), hoop, ring.

3. Hoop, ring, support, crinoline, bustle.

4. Pail, scoop, ladle, bucket, dipper, baler.

5. Bar, pole, partition, stake, palisade, pale, paling, fence, guard.

BAIL, *v.* 1. Post a bond for, post bail, warrant, underwrite, assure, insure, give security *or* surety, go bail, deliver, release, guarantee.

2. Dip, ladle, scoop, spoon, lade, dish, empty.

BAILIFF, *n.* 1. Proxy, deputy, catchpoll, officer, tipstaff, deputy-sheriff, deputy-marshal, deputy-constable, constable.

2. Usher, overseer, steward, agent, seneschal, major-domo, oeconomus *(L.),* policeman, factor, manciple, manager, supervisor, wapentake. (see also BEADLE, *n.*)

BAILIWICK, *n.* Domain, province, field, territory, jurisdiction, sphere, orbit, sway, authority, realm, dominion, empery, estate, lands, region, ground, department, ward, beat, pale, diocese, parish, constituency, circuit, tithing, kingdom.

BAIRN, *n.* (see BABY, *n.*)

BAIT, *n.* 1. Snare, trap, decoy, noose, gin, lure, pitfall, plug, springe, springle, ground bait.

2. Allurement, enticement, temptation, bribe, inducement, attraction, distraction, seduction.

BAIT, *v.* 1. Put bait upon (see BAIT, *n.,* 1).

2. Worry, harry, hound, etc. (see BADGER, *v.*)

3. Mislead, attract, seduce, entice, allure, whet one's appetite, titillate, appetize, tantalize, induce, draw on, beckon, stimulate, magnetize, persuade, captivate, fascinate, intrigue, charm, bewitch, coax, lure, inveigle, suborn, tempt.

BAKE, *v.* 1. Chafe, indurate, scorch, sear, sun, incinerate, decrepitate, calcine, warm, burn, heat, torrefy, dry, fire, anneal, parch, harden by heat.

2. Roast, grill, braise, broil, barbecue, toast, fry, frizzle, pan, cook.

BALANCE, *n.* 1. Weighing scale, weighing machine, steelyard, weighing scales, beam, weigh scale, measure, spring balance, scalebeam, pair of scales, weigh beam, weigh bridge, balances, lever.

2. Sanity, evenness, poise, equanimity, ballast, composure, self-possession, sobriety, assurance, sagacity, wiseness, sapience, reason, aplomb, level-headedness, dispassion, coolness, presence of mind, self-command, self-restraint, steadiness, perspective, self-control, good temper, carriage, rationality, judgment, discernment, discretion, stability, common sense, acumen, consistency, long-headedness, discrimination, perspicacity, consistency, prudence.

3. Equipoise, counterpoise, equivalence, poise, equiponderance, equality of weight, par, symmetry, parity, equalization, equipollence, equipollency.

4. Estimate, judgment, opinion, esteem, appraisal, estimation, comparison, weighing, assessment, consideration, valuation.

5. *(Colloq.)* Residuum, rest, remnant, excess, superfluity, remainder, residue, leavings, surplus, extra, relics.

6. Weight, compensation, compensating force, counterpoise, countercheck, ballast, equalizer, stabilizer, equilibrant, plumb, plummet.

BALANCE, *v.* 1. Compensate, poise, make equal, make level, make steady, tie, co-ordinate, adjust, readjust, square, equate, trim, nullify, match, level off, pair off, parallel, restore, neutralize, countervail, correspond, accord, harmonize,

cancel, tune, stabilize, attune, steady.

2. Test, judge, try, collate, contrast, ponder, deliberate, consider, reflect, cogitate, consider, compare, estimate, weigh.

3. *(Comm.)* Settle, equate, square, reckon, tot up, audit, tell, count, tally, total, overhaul, take stock, compute, calculate, enumerate, sum up.

4. Sway, waver, oscillate, fluctuate, rock, shake, vibrate, pendulate, undulate, hesitate, vacillate, falter, librate, debate, dillydally, hover, wobble, shilly-shally, boggle, demur, alternate, straddle, blow hot and cold.

BALANCER, *n.* Equilibrist, acrobat, tumbler, contortionist, rope-dancer, juggler, funambulist, high-vaulter, flying-trapezist, tightrope walker.

BALANCE SHEET, *n.* Account, annual report, tally, score, sum total, budget, bill, reckoning, report, statement, journal, ledger, list, running account, account-current, cashbook, liability and asset sheet, expenses, expenditures.

BALCONY, *n.* 1. Loggia, terrace, veranda, stoop, porch, piazza, portico.

2. Loges, boxes, amphitheater, foyer, upper-circle.

BALD, *adj.* 1. Glabrous, hairless, tonsured, polled, shaven, destitute of hair, depilated, without hair.

2. Barren, treeless, without vegetation, bare, verdureless, uncovered, plain, austere, coverless, uninteresting, unsheltered, monotonous, naked.

3. Unadorned, inelegant, simple, severe, plain, unornamented, colorless, uncolored, undecorated, unembellished.

4. Literal, laconic, evident, open, bare, simple, unvarnished, straightforward, mere, vapid, tame, meager, dull, prosaic, blunt.

5. Unsupported, mere, uncorroborated, sheer, unqualified, undisguised, glaring, open, flagrant, evident, obvious, signal, outright, out-and-out, unmitigated, arrant.

BALDACHIN, *n.* Canopy, cover, tilt, tent, marquee, awning.

BALDERDASH, *n.* Claptrap, rant, gibble-gabble, prattle, gibberish, gabble, drivel, jargon, babble, jibberish, jabber, fudge, buncombe, bunk, idle discourse, froth, prating, prate, nonsense, bosh, moonshine, rigmarole, flummery, abracadabra, platitude, fustian, inanity, absurdity, tomfoolery, stuff, verbiage, palaver, piffle, flapdoodle, bunk, twaddle, bombast, chatter, hocus-pocus, trash, tommyrot.

BALDNESS, *n.* 1. Alopecia, hairlessness, lack of hair.

2. Plainness, bareness, barrenness, meagerness.

3. Inelegance, simplicity, straightforwardness, severity, austerity, unembellishment, plainness.

BALE, *n.* (see also BAIL) 1. Pack, case, fardel, parcel, package, packet, bunch, bundle, lading, load, truss.

2. Woe, misery, anguish, sorrow, despair, pain, grief, distress, dolor, pang, affliction, gloom, chagrin, unhappiness, tribulation, wretchedness, heartache.

BALEFUL, *adj.* Malignant, despiteful, evil, hurtful, malicious, dispiteous, morbific, deadly, pestilential, afflictive, ruinous, noxious, fatal, disastrous, baneful, malefic, malevolent, dire, destructive, envenomed, nocuous, calamitous, pernicious, prejudicial, injurious, venomous, virulent, deleterious, poisonous, mephitic, spiteful.

BALK, *n.* 1. Hindrance, let, impediment, check,

obstruction, bar, obstacle, defeat, disappointment, block, impedition, stoppage, oppilation, restraint, restriction.

2. Beam, support, cross beam, tie beam, rafter, timber, joist, brace, lath. (see BEAM)

3. Blunder, slip, error, mistake, miss, failure, bloomer, botchery, lapse, fault, miscarriage, boner.

BALK, *v.* 1. Disappoint, check, block, hinder, prevent, thwart, frustrate, impede, circumvent, baffle, foil, estop, defeat, obstruct, bar, impedite, retard, restrict, restrain, dissatisfy.

2. Shirk, refuse, avoid, refuse to go on, shy away from, shun, eschew, evade, elude, have nothing to do with, steer clear of, fight shy of, shrink from, draw back, recoil from, dodge, blench, flinch.

BALKY, *adj.* Perverse, rebellious, defiant, obstinate, recalcitrant, restive, stubborn, contrary, disinclined, pigheaded, wayward, refractory, ungovernable, unmanageable, disobedient, unruly, intractable, bullheaded, stiff-necked, mulish, pertinacious, dogged, froward.

BALL, *n.* 1. Globe, clew, pellet, sphere, marble, knot, globule, round body, conglobation, drop, glomeration, pommel, pill, orb.

2. Missile, shot, grape, shell, bullet, projectile, ammunition, slug.

3. Dance, masquerade, prom, assembly, levee, evening party, dance festival, soirée, hop.

4. Game of ball, ball game, baseball, football.

BALLAD, *n.* Folk song, ditty, carol, light poem, barcarole, narrative poem, lay, song, doggerel poem, broadside, fable, fabliau, fado.

BALLADMONGER, *n.* 1. Minstrel, gleeman, troubadour, minnesinger, seller of ballads, scald, ballad-crier, street singer, scop, jongleur.

2. Poetaster, rhymer, rhymist, hack, doggerel poet, versifier, grubstreet poet.

BALLAST, *n.* 1. Counterpoise, counteraction, compensation, counterbalance, weight, packing, equiponderance, equalization, ballasting, filling, countercheck.

2. Counterpoise, sense, judgment, discernment, discretion, balance, acumen, self-control, long-headedness, equipoise, sagacity, perspicacity, stability, steadiness, foresight, consistency.

BALLAST, *v.* Stabilize, steady, equalize, poise, countercheck, balance, trim, weight, weight down, counterbalance, counterpoise, offset.

BALLET, *n.* Choreography, pantomime, the dance.

BALLET DANCER, *n.* Coryphée, figurante, danseuse, ballerina, ballet girl.

BALLISTICS, *n.* Science of projectiles, gunnery, science of propulsion.

BALLOON, *n.* Non-dirigible aerostat, blimp, mongolfier, aerostat, dirigible, airship, free balloon, captive balloon, kite balloon, zeppelin, observation balloon.

BALLOON, *v.* Inflate, swell up, distend, fill out, increase, expand, amplify, magnify, puff out, bloat, enlarge, dilate.

BALLOT, *n.* 1. Voting-ticket, slate, voting-ball, ticket.

2. Vote, suffrage, franchise, voice, placet, poll, election, *vox populi (L.),* plebiscite, referendum, cumulative vote, plumper.

BALLOT, *v.* Vote, exercise the franchise, poll,

elect, coopt, decide, select, cast votes, take a ballot.

BALM, *n.* 1. Salve, ointment, unguent, lotion, emollient, demulcent, aromatic oil, cerate, liniment, embrocation.

2. Mitigant, lenitive, cataplasm, sinapism, assuager, vulnerary, healing fluid, anodyne, nepenthe, collyrium, poultice, physic, ptisan, medicament, cordial, theriac, lozenge, potion, elixir, plaster, electuary, drug, linctus, panacea, catholicon, sedative.

3. Balsam, balm of Gilead, balsam of Peru, balsam of Tolu, resin.

BALMINESS, *n.* Fragrancy, scent, perfume, aroma, sweet smell, sweet odor, redolence, ambrosia, freshness.

BALMY, *adj.* 1. Calm, soothing, calmative, mild, sedative, helpful, lenitive, mitigating, healing, bland, easing, vulnerary, refreshing, gentle.

2. Fragrant, spicy, aromatous, aromatic, fresh, perfumed, ambrosial, sweet-smelling, odorous, thuriferous, odoriferous, redolent.

3. Fair, gentle, temperate, clement, soft, mild, lenient, pleasant, refreshing, fine, calm.

4. Balsamic, resinous.

BALUSTER, *n.* 1. Post, support, banister, upright, stanchion.

2. Bolster, pilaster, column, pillar, post.

BALUSTRADE, *n.* Railing, banisters, support, handrail, barrier.

BAMBOOZLE, *v.* 1. Befool, outwit, fleece, abuse, swindle, pluck, deceive, victimize, lure, cheat, delude, rook, dupe, gammon, mulct, beguile, hoodwink, impose on, fraud, inveigle, humbug, trick, gull, do, cozen, overreach, diddle, chouse, circumvent, gyp, defraud, play upon, hoax, foist upon, practise upon, take in.

2. Perplex, mystify, baffle, puzzle, tease, spoof, bluff, mislead, throw dust in the eyes.

BAMBOOZLER, *n.* Cheat, deceiver, beguiler, fraud, inveigler, trickster, adventurer, humbug, pretender, impostor, swindler, charlatan, rogue, mountebank, empiric, knave, quack, plagiarist, shark.

BAN, *n.* 1. Decree, bull, decretal, breve *(leg.),* pronouncement, edict, ordination, writ, notice, announcement, proclamation.

2. Malison, fulmination, anathema, execration, objurgation, curse, denunciation, oath, censure, imprecation, malediction, excommunication, reprobation, reprehension.

3. Interdict, interdiction, forbiddance, taboo, prohibition, condemnation, outlawry, exclusion, proscription, embargo, ostracism, preclusion, omission, rejection, exception.

BAN, *v.* Prohibit, preclude, ostracize, forbid, interdict, exclude, taboo, debar, disallow, inhibit, outlaw, reject, banish, bar, forfend.

BANAL, *adj.* Humdrum, unimaginative, stock, matter of fact, wanting originality, conventional, dull, ordinary, bromidic, fatuous, simple, insipid, vapid, inane, jejune, wishy-washy, stereotyped, flat, platitudinous, stale, trite, commonplace, common, hackneyed.

BANALITY, *n.* Platitude, truism, triteness, cliché, commonplace, inanity, bromide, hackneyed phrase, jejuneness, jejunity, vapidity, vapidness, conventionalism.

BAND, *n.* 1. Vinculum, bond, copula, nexus, tie, joint, joining, affection, link, connection.

2. Fillet, baldric, stripe, strip, frontlet, cestus,

ribbon, collar, sash, surcingle, maniple, girdle, withe, ferrule, strap, streak, belt, binding, brace, cincture, hoop, thong, zone, braid, cordon, ring, hatband, waistband, wristband, cummerbund.

3. Crowd, mob, group, troupe, company, club, party, coterie, clique, set, circle, horde, tribe, swarm, force, order, association, society, sodality, gang, crew, junto, fellowship, cabal, league, pack, squad, confederacy, throng, bunch, gathering, assembly, multitude, rout, rabble, mob, crush.

4. Orchestra.

BAND, *v.* Unite, confederate, join, fuse, ally, combine, affiliate, federate, coalesce, consolidate, merge, incorporate, gather together, associate, muster, join together.

BANDAGE, *n.* Fillet, ligature, deligation, truss, fasciation, compress, band, dressing, binding, pledget, cincture, spica, fascia *(med.),* tourniquet.

BANDAGE, *v.* Bind, tie, swathe, deligate, dress, fillet, truss.

BANDEROLE, *n.* Banner, flag, ensign, colors, streamer, standard, pennant, insignia, banneret, bannerol, labarum, oriflamme, pennon, pendant, burgee, gonfalon, ancient, jack, bunting.

BANDIT, *n.* Desperado, knight of the road, thief, outlaw, road agent, vandal, looter, despoiler, marauder, hoodlum, ladrone, highwayman, thug, buccaneer, robber, filibuster, rustler, brigand, spoiler, ruffian, burglar, cracksman, cutthroat, gunman, bravo, blackleg, sandbagger, freebooter, plug-ugly, footpad, crook, poacher, plunderer, racketeer, depredator, pickpocket, pirate, apache, larrikin, scoundrel, bunco steerer, highbinder, nihilist, terrorist, public enemy, strongarm-man, housebreaker, pilferer, rifler, pillager, pickeerer, dacoit, corsair, privateer, rapparee, picaroon, viking, wrecker.

BANDY, *v.* 1. Toss, interchange, exchange, swap, shuffle, toss about, agitate, change hands, trade, commute, permute, transpose, reciprocate.

2. Swap, barter, trade, pass, shuffle.

BANDY, *adj.* Crooked, bent, bowlegged, bow-kneed.

BANE, *n.* 1. Virus, toxicant, poison, pollution, toxin, venom, contamination.

2. Plague, nuisance, pest, detriment, trouble, infection, bale, scourge, mischief, calamity, pain, curse, misery, ruin, mishap, evil, destruction, harm, disaster, injury, tragedy, torment, wrong, hurt. (see also BALE)

BANEFUL, *adj.* Hurtful, bad, destructive, evil, poisonous, venomous, toxic, noisome, noxious, baleful, ruinous, unwholesome, deadly, harmful, deleterious, lethal, pestilential, pernicious, fatal, injurious, morbific, hurtful, sinister, threatening.

BANG, *n.* 1. Boom, sound, whang, crepitation, smack, clap, report, burst, explosion, clangor, jangle, discharge, clang, shot, salvo, rap, slam, knock, tap, snap, click, clash, crash, plump, pop, thump, whack.

2. Whack, stroke, lash, stripe, cuff, pommel, blow, beating, thump, box, wallop, tap, whop, hit, smack, buffet, slap, thwack, lick, knock, rap. (see also BAT *n.,* 5.)

3. Fringe (of hair).

BANG, *v.* 1. Whack, beat, clap, rap, jab, hit, slap, strike, pound, knock, pat, cuff, buffet, lash, sock, smite, poke, clip, punch, bump, pommel, thrash, slug, swipe, belabor, cudgel, thwack, beat, dab, tap, bat, thump, box, wallop. (see BAT *v.)*

2. Slam, plump, crack, rap, snap, tap, knock,

click, pop, clap, thump, clash, resound, jangle, ring, clang, boom, sound, crepitate, fulminate, crackle, thunder, peal, beat, re-echo.

BANGLE, *n.* Anklet, bracelet, ornament, trinket, armlet.

BANISH, *v.* 1. Exile, ostracize, deport, isolate, outlaw, relegate, expatriate, transport, extradite, send to Coventry, excommunicate, expel, dismiss, cast out.

2. Abandon, blacklist, proscribe, drop, reject, ban, damn, dismiss, shut out, eject, evict, exclude, oust, exterminate, eradicate, eliminate, cast out, cast away, dislodge, repudiate, discharge, discard, send off, send away, bar, prohibit, shake off, dispel, remove, drive out, eliminate, get rid of, do away with.

BANISHMENT, *n.* Exile, isolation, exclusion, deportation, proscription, expulsion, outlawry, relegation, ostracism, elimination, extradition, expatriation, dismissal, excommunication.

BANISTER, *n.* Baluster, balustrade, railing, handrail. (see BALUSTER)

BANK, *n.* 1. Mound, barrow, terreplein, terrace, embankment, dune, knoll, heap, acclivity, ramp, ascent, pile, rise, ridge, tumulus, dike, gradient, grade, shock, cock, mole, parapet.

2. Shore, ripa, edge, coast, rim, foreshore, littoral, alluvion, bound, border, beach, marge, margin, strand, brink, brim.

3. Shoal, reef, scar, syrtis, coral reef, sunken rocks, sand bank, snags, bar, shallows, shelf, flat.

4. Seat, thwart, bench, beam, tier (of oars), rowing-beam.

5. String, succession, row, tier, chain, train, series, course, progression, file, rank, line, range, concatenation, catenation.

6. Moneylender's banking house, exchequer, finance company.

7. Depository, treasury, almonry, fisc, purser's, vault, coffer, strongbox, safe.

8. Reserve, store, accumulation, pile, savings, stock-pile, fund, thesaurus.

BANK, *v.* 1. Border, surround, surround with a bank, embank, dike.

2. Keep an account, save, salt away, deposit, lay up.

3. Heap up, pile up, stack, shock, cock, mass.

4. Rely on, stake, depend, trust, count on, pin one's faith on, take for granted, lean on, build on, credit, swear by, confide in.

BANKRUPT, *adj.* Broken, ruined, wiped out, broke, insolvent, impoverished, aground, on the rocks, depleted, dead beat, beggared, gazetted, stripped, unmoneyed, impecunious, pauperized, destitute, indigent, strapped, bereft, necessitous, penniless, poverty-stricken.

BANKRUPT, *n.* Insolvent debtor, pauper, beggar.

BANKRUPT, *v.* Drain, impoverish, exhaust, ruin, deplete, cripple financially, reduce to beggary.

BANKRUPTCY, *n.* Failure, financial ruin, insolvency, liquidation, financial disaster, penury, destituteness, straitened circumstances, distress, economic death, destitution, indigence, pauperism, privation, beggary, impecuniosity.

BANNER, *n.* Standard, pennant, gonfalon, flag, vexillum, banderole, streamer, oriflamme, colors, labarum, ensign, pendent, burgee, ancient, jack, pennon, eagle. (see also BANDEROLE)

BANQUET, *n.* Feast, public dinner, carousal, meal, repast, spread, picnic, entertainment, treat, refection, regalement, symposium, jollification, wassail.

BANQUET, *v.* Feast, dine, be regaled with food, picnic, junket, eat one's fill, revel, carouse, make merry.

BANSHEE, *n.* Fay, spirit, vision, ghost, shee, fairy, faery, sprite, gnome, pixie, evil spirit, elf, goblin, brownie, puck, nix, nixie, leprechaun, wraith, fiend, imp, demon, washer of the ford, ghoul, apparition, spectre, phantom, djin, troll, genie, clurichaune, bogy, spook.

BANTAM, *adj.* Miniature, small, diminutive, tiny, little, minute, stunted, atrophied, dwarfish, runted, microscopic, puny, petty, pocketsized, exiguous, scanty, spare, Lilliputian, weeny, wee, petite, teeny, minikin.

BANTAM, *n.* Skipjack, jackanapes, upstart, fop, whippersnapper, braggart, popinjay, swaggerer, puppy, coxcomb, dandy, gascon, cockalorum, self-important person, bluff.

BANTER, *n.* Joking, jesting, chaff, quizzing, teasing, raillery, fun, kidding, asteism, badinage, persiflage, derision, ragging, ribbing, joshing, pleasantry, mockery, drollery, jocularity, ridicule, facetiousness, waggery, repartee, quiddity, wordplay.

BANTER, *v.* Jeer, rally, fleer, quip, josh, rag, taunt, kid, make fun of, make a butt of, mock, jig, jest, deride, laugh at, twit, chaff, quiz.

BANTLING, *n.* Brat, urchin, kid, bratling, elf, cub, unlicked cub, whippersnapper, hobbledehoy, chit.

BAPTISM, *n.* Ablution, pedobaptism, ritual, rite, parabaptism, immersion, lustration, aspersion, baptismal regeneration, dedication, sacrament.

BAPTIZE, *v.* 1. Dip, immerse, sprinkle, asperse, administer baptism to.
2. Christen, name, chrism, dedicate.

BAR, *n.* 1. Stake, stick, tool, jimmy, handspike, betty, casting, batten, crosspiece, crosshead, rod, grating, crossbar, crowbar, pole, lever, boom, fid, rib, sprag, sprit *(naut.)*, spar.
2. Ingot, block, stick, nugget.
3. Block, stumbling-block, prevention, check, impediment, estoppel *(leg.)*, stop, barricade, ban, barrier, difficulty, curb, preclusion, prohibition, limitation, disallowance, dam, snag, impedition, catch, stoppage, obstruction, oppilation, restraint, restriction, repression, obstacle, foreclosure *(leg.)*, barrage, forbiddance, retardment, embarrassment, hindrance, retardation, cohibition, trammel, balk, bridle, proscription, embargo, injunction, stopper, constraint, enjoining.
4. Pale, paling, gunwale, balustrade, palisade, rail, railing, fence, guard, stile.
5. Tribunal, judicatory, bench, court, board, *curia (L.)*, inquisition, court of justice, court of law, court of arbitration, forum, assize, sessions, Areopagus, divan, court-martial.
6. Legal profession, gentlemen of the long robe, legal fraternity, body of lawyers, solicitors, attorneys, legists, advocates, counselors, jurists.
7. Shelf, shoal, reef, ridge, sand bar, flat, spit, bank, sand bank, delta, shallow, tongue, rocks, snags, gravel bank.
8. Saloon, counter, taproom, tavern, cocktail lounge, barroom, alehouse, public house, hotel, hostel, inn, canteen, restaurant, cafeteria, grill room, lunchroom, luncheonette, café, rotisserie, caravansary, diner, *estaminet (Fr.)*, speakeasy.

9. Stripe, strip, band, stroke, pale *(her.)*, line, streak, mark, slice, blaze, stria.

BAR, *prep.* Without, less, omitting, lacking, but, excluding, barring, with the exception of, save, except, deducting, minus, bating.

BAR, *v.* 1. Bar up, fasten with a bar, block up, close up, embar, bolt, lock, barricade, padlock, secure, fasten.
2. Barricade, block, curb, preclude, embarrass, forbid, taboo, hinder, limit, dam up, oppilate, repress, avert, obviate, obstruct, stop, stay, ban, impede, restrict, circumscribe, draw the line, prevent, shut off, choke off, prohibit, interdict, embar, restrain, frustrate, thwart, foreclose, plug up, estop, debar, disallow, occlude, trammel, bridle, retard, cohibit.
3. Banish, oust, ostracize, debar, eliminate, proscribe, cast aside, cast out, lock out, reject, refuse, omit, relegate, exclude, thrust out, leave out, spurn, blackball, boycott, excommunicate, exile, outlaw, isolate.

BARB, *n.* 1. Beard, wattle, barbel, whiskers, tuft, appendage, bristles, barblet.
2. Point, prickle, guard *(of a hook)*, arrow, spine, jag, spike, spur, snag, spicule, bristle, tip, acumination, nib, prong, tine, cusp, barbule.

BARB, *v.* Tip, sharpen, spiculate, acuminate, fit with barbs, bard, point.

BARBARIAN, *n.* 1. Foreigner, stranger, outsider, alien, tramontane, outlander.
2. Savage, vandal, Goth, Hun, brute, Yahoo, cannibal, troglodyte.
3. Hooligan, lout, ruffian, tough, rowdy, ugly customer, bully, hoodlum, roughneck, larrikin.
4. Philistine, opponent of culture, obscurantist, anti-intellectual, plebeian, bourgeois, proletarian, peasant, obscurant.

BARBARIAN, *adj.* 1. Barbarous, barbaric, rude, uncivilized, ill-mannered, savage, crude, Gothic, unpolished, outlandish, unlettered, mean, vulgar, low, churlish, boorish, loutish, rough, ill-bred, uncivil, untamed, uncultivated, uncultured, wild, heathenish, ignorant, untutored, troglodytic.
2. Inhuman, unkind, hard-hearted, heartless, vicious, marble-hearted, relentless, savage, fierce, merciless, bloody, untamed, truculent, homicidal, fell, ruthless, unrelenting, remorseless, ferocious, brute, brutal, brutish, bloodthirsty, sanguinary, unfeeling, cruel, feral, ferine, atrocious, pitiless, devilish, demoniacal, diabolic, slaughterous, hellish.

BARBARIC, *adj.* 1. Savage, rude, unpolished, etc. (see BARBARIAN, *adj.* 1.)
2. Uncouth, gaudy, boisterous, showy, florid, ostentatious, ornate, coarse, outlandish, flamboyant, vulgar, unrefined, wild, garish, crude, flashy, meretricious, unregulated, coarsely luxuriant, loud, unrestrained, unsubdued, grotesque, unbeseeming, tawdry, crass, unseemly, unpresentable, inelegant, bedizened, incorrect, bizarre.

BARBARISM, *n.* 1. Vulgarism, impropriety, slip, misusage, misuse, solecism, impurity of style, catachresis, malapropism, error, anachronism, slang, faulty grammar, infelicity, bull, cacophony.
2. Cruelty, act of violence, atrocity, ferocity, fell deed, ill usage, wrong, outrage, brutality.
3. Barbarity, Gothicism, savagism, savagery, outlandishness, churlishness, loutishness, lack of culture, boorishness, depravity, ill-manners, rudeness, roughness, crudeness, vulgarity, crudity, ignorance, crassness.

4. Vandalism, destruction, aggression, ferity, ruthlessness, destructiveness, harshness, ferocity, savageness, brutality, brutishness, ferociousness, cruelty, unkindness, truculence, savagery, atrocity, inhumanity, hard-heartedness.

BARBARITY, *n.* 1. Cruelty, savageness, etc. (see BARBARISM, *n.*, 2 and 4)
2. Crudeness, roughness, etc. (see BARBARISM, *n.*, 3)

BARBAROUS, *adj.* 1. Uncivilized, rough, etc. (see BARBARIAN, *adj.*, 1)
2. Cruel, inhuman, etc. (see BARBARIAN, *adj.* 2)
3. Improper, infelicitous, incorrect, unseemly, uncouth, harsh, awkward, vulgar, contrary to good usage, impure, solecistic, cacophonous, wrong.
4. Foreign, tramontane, strange, outlandish, alien.

BARBECUE, *n.* 1. Grill, roast.
2. Picnic, feast, roast, junket.

BARBECUE, *v.* Cook, roast, broil, grill, toast, bake, torrefy.

BARBED, *adj.* 1. Wattled, bearded, whiskered.
2. Thorny, aculeate, prickly, pointed, tipped, acuminate, spicular, nibbed, pronged, spined, sharp, barbellate.
3. Armored (said of horses), mailed, barded, accoutered, protected.

BARBER, *n.* Haircutter, hairdresser, tonsor.

BARBER, *v.* Trim, dress, arrange, shave, shear, cut, tonsure, raze.

BARBETTE, *n.* (see BATTLEMENT)

BARCAROLE, *n.* Melody, tune, song, air, strain, refrain, serenade.

BARD, *n.* (see also BALLAD-MONGER) Poet, poetaster, versifier, rhymster, rhymer, sonneteer, maker, writer, author, poetess, composer of poetry, writer of poems, poetizer, singer, harper, minstrel, scop, minnesinger, troubadour, jongleur, gleeman, scald, trouvère.

BARE, *adj.* 1. Naked, nude, unrobed, disrobed, divested, exposed, denudate, stripped, undressed, unclad, unappareled, stark naked, unclothed, peeled, uncovered, denuded, unveiled, undraped, callow (of a bird.)
2. Threadbare, napless, depilous, worn.
3. Unveiled, revealed, unconcealed, uncovered, exposed, displayed, shown, exhibited, disclosed.
4. Unembellished, uncolored, destitute, gaunt, unadorned, unvarnished, bald, stark, jejune, raw, unfinished, blank, scanty, bleak, desolate, barren, unsheltered, unshielded, destitute, uninteresting, inelegant, plain, austere, meager, unornamented, colorless, unprotected; verdureless, monotonous, treeless, without vegetation.
5. Mere, utter, unvarnished, open, pure, poor, meager, simple, devoid, straightforward, laconic, sheer, tame, dull, brief, prosaic, literal, naked, bald, stark, short, stinted. (see also BALD, *adj.* 4.)

BARE, *v.* 1. Strip, unrobe, undress, unsheathe, discase, make bare, denude, denudate, unmask, expose, reveal, undrape, depilate, divest, uncloak, dismantle, undisguise, divulge, disclose, dismask, unveil, unseal, unfold, bring to light, evince, exhibit, display.
2. Abrade, rub off, fret, erode, peel, shave, skin, strip, bark. (see also BARK, *v.*, 2)

BAREFACED, *adj.* Saucy, bold-faced, immodest, impertinent, bold, unabashed, daring, audacious, unreserved, impudent, presumptuous, shameless, frank, plain-spoken, brazen, insolent, flippant, indecent, forward, fresh, malapert, precocious, pert, brash, unblushing, cheeky, indecorous, outspoken, bluff, plain, candid, unseemly.

BARELY, *adv.* 1. Nakedly, etc. (see BARE, *adj.*, 1)
2. Without concealment, etc. (see BARE, *adj.*, 3)
3. Not quite, just, only, hardly, scarcely, by the skin of one's teeth, with difficulty.
4. Faintly, imperceptibly, imperfectly, feebly, sparingly, slightly, meagerly, scantily, weakly, insufficiently, not wholly.

BARENESS, *n.* 1. Nakedness, nudeness, nudity, undress, disrobement, divestment, divestiture.
2. Unadornment, baldness, unembellishment, uncoloredness, plainness, gauntness, jejuneness, blankness, scantiness, rawness, unornamentation, bleakness, desolateness, desolation, inelegance, barrenness, austerity, meagerness, colorlessness.
3. Poorness, emptiness, straightforwardness, brevity, laconism, meagerness, purity, simplicity, openness, tameness, dullness, prosaism, literality, nakedness, sheerness.

BARGAIN, *v.* 1. Sell, transfer goods, exchange, trade, chaffer, dicker, haggle, higgle, vend, swop, traffic, truck, buy and sell, transact, deal, barter. (see BARTER, *v.*)
2. Contract, agree, pledge, stipulate, covenant, make a bargain, make a pact, engage, promise, plight, transact, deal, settle, negotiate, come to terms, make terms.

BARGAIN, *n.* 1. Pledge, compact, promise, pact, agreement, transaction, contraction, indenture, deal, stipulation, negotiation, treaty, settlement, understanding, convention, covenant, cartel, mise, bond, contract, entente *(Fr.)*, concordat *(Eccl.)*.
2. Purchase, cheap purchase, discount, good buy, reduction, marked down price.

BARGAIN FOR Expect, anticipate, calculate on, look for, contemplate, foresee, prepare for, count upon, think likely, surmise.

BARGAINING, *n.* Dickering, negotiating, traffic, commerce, trade, nundination, etc. (see BARTER, *n.*, 1)

BARGE, *n.* 1. Houseboat, state barge, vessel of state, pleasure-boat, bucentaur.
2. Canal-boat, transport, flat-bottomed boat, boat of burden, hoy.
3. *(Naut.)* Powerboat, launch, pinnace, flag officer's boat, motorboat.

BARK, *v.* 1. Roar, bellow, bay, howl, cry, yelp, ululate, bell.
2. Shout at, etc. (see BARK AT)
3. Hull, peel, skin, decorticate, flay, scrape, strip, girdle, abrade, rub off, fret, shave, skin, desquamate, denudate, uncover, depilate, husk, shell, pare, scalp, excoriate, exfoliate, denude, bare.
4. Tan, infuse with bark.

BARK, *n.* 1. Cry, yelp, yap, ululation, latration, bay, bellow, howling, croak, roar, howl, belling.
2. Vessel, argosy, galleon, carrack, barkentine, cutter, sloop, clipper, schooner, ship, yawl, brig, dandy, brigantine, ketch, smack, windjammer, outrigger, sailing-ship.
3. Husk, rind, cortex, shell, case, sheathing, crust, cuticle, integument, pellicle, hide, coat, periderm, skin, rind, peel.

BARK AT Vociferate, threaten, menace, snarl, growl, bully, intimidate, thunder, bellow, screech, holler at, bluster, shout at, snap at, abuse, scold, scream, shriek, censure. (see ASPERSE, v.)

BARK UP THE WRONG TREE Be deceived, be misled, be under a false impression, blunder, misconceive, misapprehend, misunderstand, err, miscomprehend, muddle, mistake, miscalculate, misreckon, miscount, misjudge, get the wrong sow by the ear, misestimate, be on the wrong scent, bungle, botch, muff, fumble, stumble, be on the wrong track, flounder.

BARN, n. Stable, shed, cow shed, agricultural housing.

BARNSTORMER, n. Actor, player, performer, strolling-player, Thespian, Roscius.

BARON, n. 1. Nobleman, peer, baronet, knight, lord, aristocrat.
2. Tycoon, king.

BAROQUE, adj. Rococo, florid, ornate, garish, gaudy, bizarre, showy, ostentatious, flashy, odd, rocaille (Fr.), extravagant, outré (Fr.), fantastic, outlandish, strange, grotesque.

BARRACKS, n. Quarters, military enclosure, camp, encampment, shelter, garrison, casern, fort, cantonment, bullpen.

BARRAGE, n. 1. Barrier, canopy of fire, curtain of fire, deluge of steel, artillery fire, drumfire, protective fire, covering fire, cannonade, assault, bombardment, cross fire, battery, shelling, salvo, broadside, volley, concentration, box barrage, creeping barrage, emergency barrage, standing barrage.
2. Barrier, block, etc. (see BARRIER, n., 1)
3. Blast, burst, salvo, shout, outcry, clamor, vociferation, roar, volley, blare, verbal assault.

BARREL, n. 1. Tub, container, tun, rundlet, keg, cask, hogshead, puncheon, butt, tierce, vessel, vat, firkin, kilderkin.
2. Tube (of a gun), bore.

BARREN, adj. 1. Unproductive, sterile, effete, unprocreant, impotent, agenetic, incapable of bearing young, farrow (of cows), childless, infecund.
2. Unfructuous, sterile, acarpous, infecund, effete, unproductive, infructiferous, unfertile, arid.
3. Poor, bare, dry, arid, bald, waste, desolate, dead, naked, miserable, uncultivable, exhausted, uncultivatable, meager, scanty, worn out, empty, lean, forlorn, impoverished, depleted, austere, severe. (see also BARE, adj., 4)
4. Devoid, idle, tame, prosaic, stupid, jejune, dull, ineffectual, uninteresting, uninstructive, otiose, uninspiring, unprofitable, unsuggestive, fruitless, useless, leading to nothing, infecund, unproductive, inefficacious, futile, inutile, stale, flat, inept, impotent, unendowed, worthless.

BARRENNESS, n. 1. Sterility, unproductiveness, infertility, unprolificness, childessness, agenesis, infecundity, effeteness, impotence, unfructuosity, unfertileness, unfertility.
2. Dryness, baldness, poverty, desolation, aridity, etc. (see BARENESS, n., 2).

BARRICADE, n. Bar, barrier, barricado, fence, blockade, impediment, bulwark, rampart, etc. (see BARRIER, n.)

BARRICADE, v. Block up, close up, embar, bar, padlock, lock, bolt, fence in, picket, fortify, defend, fence round, obstruct, barricado.

BARRIER, n. 1. Moat, ditch, barricade, cordon, stop, check, wall, hedge, boom, fence, railing, dam, breastwork, rampart, balustrade, bulwark, bank, blockade, block, roadblock, stockade, bar, parapet, fortification, safeguard, dike, parados, earthwork, mole, contravallation, glacis, abatis, circumvallation. (see also BATTLEMENT, n.)
2. Obstruction, hurdle, difficulty, restriction, prohibition, partition, boundary, impediment, stumbling block, obstacle. (see also BAR, n., 3)

BARRING, prep. Excepting, precluding, etc.

BARRISTER, n. Advocate, jurisconsult, legist, publicist, civilian, jurist, legal advisor, officer of court, solicitor, attorney, counsel, member of the bar, counselor, attorney at law, limb of the law.

BARROOM, n. Saloon, taproom, public house, inn, tavern, speakeasy, grill, cocktail lounge, bar, canteen, alehouse. (see also BAR, n., 8)

BARROW, n. 1. Pushcart, carriage, wheelbarrow, dumpcart, handtruck, handbarrow, ricksha, gocart.
2. Burial mound, hillock, tumulus, monticle, heap, sepulchral mound, grave, funeral pile, cairn, burial place.

BARTER, n. 1. Business, commutation, truckage, selling, sale, commerce, exchange, traffic, dealing, negotiation, interchange, transaction, bargaining, auction, higgling, chaffering, nundination, truck, speculation, intercourse, peddling, dickering, vending, haggling.
2. Merchandise, goods, bargain, commodity, wares, stock, produce, stock in trade, effects.

BARTER, v. Sell, buy and sell, trade, dicker, deal, truck, vend, interchange, peddle, auction, traffic, bargain, higgle, chaffer, haggle, bandy, huckster, beat down, swop, commute, exchange.

BASAL, adj. 1. Fundamental, elementary, basic, underlying, substratal, substrative, radical, vital, sustentative, supporting, basilar, indispensable, essential, constant, intrinsic, inherent, primary, infixed, necessary.
2. Least, lowest, bottom, minimum, smallest.

BASE, adj. 1. Adulterated, debased, counterfeit, inferior, impure, alloyed, forged, sham, pseudo-, fake, ungenuine, cheap, worthless, meretricious, spurious, artificial, bogus, scamped, simulated, bastard, false, unsound, rotten, trashy, paltry, gimcrack, putrid.
2. Degraded, venal, miserable, mean, menial, wretched, sneaking, unmanly, despicable, dirty, low, mealy-mouthed, sycophantic, ignominious, unworthy, hangdog, mean-spirited, degenerate, cowardly, abject, low-minded, recreant, dastardly, contemptible, ungenerous, parasitical, groveling, sorry, ignoble, pitiful, ungentlemanly, worthless, petty, vulgar, pettifogging, inglorious, cringing, fawning, sniveling, slavish, servile, scurvy, sordid, prostrate, scabby, scrubby, craven, obsequious, beggarly, abased, common, shabby, discreditable, pusillanimous, subservient, churlish, paltry.
3. Treacherous, vicious, reprehensible, beastly, shameful, sinister, scoundrelly, felonious, wrong, brutish, corrupt, reprobate, foul, disreputable, bad, disgraceful, discreditable, false, faithless, black-hearted, wicked, villainous, nefarious, vile, opprobrious, infamous, scandalous, soulless, scurvy, turpitudinous, miscreant, dishonorable, dirty, disloyal, flagrant, incorrigible, profligate, gross, iniquitous, demoralized, depraved, steeped in iniquity, uncommendable, facinorous, sinful, blameworthy, dissolute, inexpiable, evil-minded,

evil-disposed, unprincipled, lawless, unworthy, culpable, objectionable, illaudable, rancorous, invidious, malicious, maleficent.

BASE, *n.* 1. Stand, support, basis, foundation, fundus, pedestal, bed, ground, groundwork, bottom, foot, dado, plinth, wainscot, baseboard, substructure, substratum, prop, caudex *(Bot.),* footing, socle.

2. Principal, component, rudiments, essence, root, origin, source, essentials, elements, stem, foundation, core, heart, radical, ground, vital principle, groundwork.

3. Starting point, camp, site, station, seat, post, anchorage, settlement, mooring, home.

BASEBORN, *adj.* 1. Vulgar, ignoble, plebeian, lowborn, common, peasant, untitled, proletarian, lowly, humble, obscure, of low birth, of obscure birth, beggarly, of low parentage, earthborn, of low extraction, lowbred, parvenu.

2. Vile, mean, etc. (see BASE, *adj.,* 2)

BASELESS, *adj.* 1. Bottomless, foundationless, groundless, etc. (See BASE, *n.,* 1)

2. Ungrounded, groundless, unfounded, unreal, unsupported, illogical, erroneous, unsubstantial, without reason, unjustifiable, without cause, gratuitous, uncaused, unsound, unreasonable, unsubstantiated, uncorroborated.

BASEMENT, *n.* Cellar, underground story, wine cellar, storage room, cellarage, underground chamber, hold *(Naut.).*

BASE-MINDED, *adj.* Mean, low, vile, groveling, etc. (see BASE, *adj.,* 2)

BASENESS, *n.* 1. Beggary, meanness, servility, slavishness, slavery, sordidness, unworthiness, unmanliness, cowardice, ignominy, ignobility, fawning, inferiority, abjection, pusillanimity, humiliation, debasement, contemptibleness, disgrace, dishonor, abasement, despicableness, worthlessness, low-mindedness, obsequiousness, groveling, abjectness, venality, wretchedness, degradation, degeneracy, recreancy, cringing, sniveling, shabbiness, paltriness, pettifogging, vulgarity, ungentlemanliness, pettiness, scurviness, cravenness, scabbiness, prostration, subserviency, poltroonery.

2. (See BASE, *adj.,* 3)

BASE ON Settle-, found-, place-, stablish-, fix-, fasten-, stand-, institute-, form-, organize-, hinge-, depend on *or* upon.

BASHFUL, *adj.* Shy, modest, over-modest, coy, shamefaced, reserved, retiring, shrinking, demure, sheepish, diffident, unobtrusive, constrained, blushing, unconfident, timorous, timid, skittish, seemly, unassuming, unostentatious, verecund.

BASHFULNESS, *n.* Shyness, modesty, reserve, sheepishness, demureness, diffidence, humility, timidity, hesitation, unobtrusiveness, constraint, coyness, timorousness, skittishness.

BASIC, *adj.* Elementary, fundamental, essential, etc. (see BASAL, *adj.,* 1)

BASICALLY, *adv.* Intrinsically, fundamentally, essentially, vitally, primarily, radically, inherently, originally.

BASILIC, *adj.* Kingly, royal, regal, majestic, noble, imperial, princely, sovereign, monarchial.

BASILICA, *n.* 1. Public assembly hall, forum, judgment hall, assembly hall.

2. Church, temple, shrine, sanctuary (see also CHURCH, *n.*)

BASIN, *n.* 1. Pan, bowl, sink, punch bowl, dish, porringer, boat.

2. *(Geog.)* Bottom, reservoir, hollow, valley, depression, cup, crater, indentation, vale, dell, dingle, strath.

BASIS, *n.* (see BASE, *n.*)

BASK, *v.* 1. Lie in the sunshine, sunbathe, toast oneself, sun oneself, chafe oneself, warm, lie warming, luxuriate.

2. Delight in, rejoice, indulge in, feel *or* experience *or* receive pleasure, enjoy, relish, prosper, revel in, wallow in, thrive on, flourish, luxuriate.

BASKET, *n.* Hamper, scuttle, creel, bassinet, pannier, punnet, dosser.

BASS, *adj.* Low, deep, grave, sonorous.

BASTARD, *n.* Natural child, love-child, whoreson, illegitimate child.

BASTARD, *adj.* 1. Adulterine, illegitimate, born out of wedlock *or* of illicit union, unfathered, misborn, baseborn, misbegotten, unlawfully begotten, natural.

2. Spurious, untrue, mock, faked, pseudo-, fraudulent, adulterine, adulterate, adulterated, inferior, supposititious, simulated, imitation, so-called, make-believe, artificial, bogus, factitious, counterfeit, ungenuine, sham, substandard.

BASTARDIZE, *v.* Make a bastard of, misbeget, illegitimatize.

BASTARDY, *n.* 1. Illegitimacy.

2. Misbegetting, illicit procreation.

BASTE, *v.* 1. Thrash, buffet, batter, lash, rap, pommel, belabor, pound, cuff, drub, thump, punch, cudgel, cane, wallop, whip, smite, trounce, flog, flagellate, fustigate, beat. (see also BEAT, *v.*)

2. Moisten with fat, pour fat on, drip grease on, prepare with fat *or* grease.

3. Sew, sew loosely, tack, secure, pin, stitch loosely, fasten temporarily.

BASTILLE, *n.* 1. Tower, fortification, fort, fortress, citadel, castle, stronghold, bulwark, rampart, château.

2. Prison, confine, donjon, dungeon, keep, oubliette, panopticon, limbo, house of detention.

BASTINADO, *n.* 1. Bastinade, blow, whipping, flagellation, fustigation, flogging, beating. (see BEATING, *n.*)

2. Stick, cudgel, etc. (see BAT, *n.,* 1)

BASTINADO, *v.* Lash, thrash, trounce, drub, beat, wallop, pound, pommel, leather, belabor, flog, baste, cudgel, flagellate, fustigate. (see also BEAT, *v.*)

BASTION, *n.* Bulwark, fort, stronghold, citadel, fortress. (see BASTILLE, n., 1 and BATTLEMENT, n.)

BAT, *v.* Buffet, strike, tap, hit, smack, smite, bang, thump, thwack, rap, slap, cuff, knock, box, punch, slug, swipe, lick, slam, wallop, pat, dab, bump, beat, whack, tamp, cudgel, belabor, jab, pound, whip, lash, sock, poke, clip, batter.

BAT, *n.* 1. Stick, racket, mallet, club.

2. Cudgel, bludgeon, club, stick, truncheon, cane, life preserver, staff.

3. Blow, stroke, tap, hit, smack, strike, buffet, thump, thwack, rap, slap, cuff, box, knock, sock, punch, poke, slug, swipe, lick, bang, slam, pat, wallop, impact, dab, fillip, carom, jab, hit.

BATCH, *n.* Quantity, allotment, mass, measure,

quota, amount, lot, bunch, crowd, collection, stock, sum, aggregate, number, volume.

BATE, v. Abate, retrench, moderate, repress, subside, wane, ebb, suppress, dwindle, remit, lessen, cut down, diminish, decline, decrease, lapse, rebate, slump, drop, fall.

BATH, n. 1. Washing, irrigation, ablution, dip, infiltration, dilution, immersion, bathing, plunge, lavement, cleansing.
2. Bagnio, thermae, sudatorium, lavatory, tub, bathroom, shower, washroom, toilet.
3. Tank, pool, bowl, basin, sink.

BATHE, v. 1. Wash, dip, foment, cleanse, wet, shower, immerse, soak, douse, lave, irrigate.
2. Suffuse, immerse, cover, swaddle, envelop, enwrap, surround, infold.

BATHOS, n. Sentimentalism, anticlimax, slush, insincere pathos, mawkishness, maudlinness, false sublimity, emotional silliness, soppiness, mushiness, poignancy, slushiness.

BATON, n. Rod, stick, staff of office, fasces, eod, sceptre, crosier, crook, bar, wand, truncheon, shaft, staff, caduceus (med.)

BATTALION, n. Army, forces, division, body, legion, companies, host, force, body of troops, horde, multitude, platoons, groups, squadrons, units, corps, wing, column, detachment, garrison, brigade, batteries, sections, squads, phalanx, contingent, regiment, military force.

BATTEN, v. 1. Fasten down, fasten with battens, screw down, board up, secure, make fast, clamp down.
2. Fatten, feed, thrive, grow fertile, grow fat, grow rank, wax, prosper, flourish, fructify, make plump, enrich, increase.
3. Feed gluttonously, gormandize, devour, guzzle, gorge, glut, cram, stuff, gulp, raven, bolt, gobble, overeat, satiate, sate, surfeit, surcharge, cloy, saturate.

BATTER, v. 1. Beat, smite, assault, thump, ram, pommel, attack by battery, pound, wallop, smash against, strike repeatedly.
2. Break, break up, crush, destroy, demolish, overwhelm, mangle, smash, crumble, shake to pieces, shiver, mutilate, shatter, maim, bruise, cripple, devastate, quell, squash, lay in ruins, level, deal destruction, lay waste, ravage, gut, raze, pulverize.
3. Deteriorate, disfigure, mar, eat away, wear away, deface, deform, abrade, dilapidate, indent, undermine, truncate, impair, defeature, disfeature, disintegrate, crumble.
4. (Masonry) Incline, slant, slope, slope back, retreat, fall back, recede.

BATTER, n. 1. Mixture, paste, liquid paste.
2. Batsman, hitter, player, striker, man in.
3. (Masonry) Slope, inclination, recession.

BATTERY, n. 1. Assault, offense, attack, onset, onslaught, charge, offensive, offensive action, aggression, surprisal, raid, storming, incursion, drive, invasion, inroad, sally, foray, boarding, escalade, siege, bombardment, cannonade, volley.
2. Troop, artillery, guns, cannon, armament, musketry, group of guns, field pieces, ordnance, howitzers, mortars.

BATTLE, v. 1. Contend, skirmish, cope with, combat, come to blows, contest, beat, fight, pommel, resist, engage, conflict with, encounter, war, make war, war against, go to war, storm,

attack, struggle, strive, pitch into, ride against, assault, meet, joust, tilt, quarrel, tussle, take the field, broil, row, brawl, resist, tourney, feud, duel.
2. Dispute, litigate, debate, altercate, argue, agitate, wrangle, dissent, be at variance with, be at loggerheads, bicker.

BATTLE, n. 1. Encounter, affair, combat, bout, tournament, strife, contention, collision, war, rencounter, warfare, struggle, fight, contest, fray, skirmish, conflict, action, distraction, storm, showdown, Armageddon, attack, melee, gehenna, hostile meeting, engagement, quarrel, brush, duel, fracas, feud, clash of arms, tussle, scuffle, brawl, affray, joust, tourney, assault, hostility, campaign, crusade, bloodshed, broil, row, resistance, tilt, carnage, massacre.
2. Dispute, controversy, quarrel, war of words, paper war, litigation, debate, polemics, round, altercation, logomachy, argument, agitation, wrangle, disputation, dissension, discord, variance.

BATTLE CRY, n. 1. War cry, whoop, gathering cry, war whoop.
2. Slogan, catchword, motto, shibboleth, party cry, watchword.

BATTLEFIELD, n. 1. Theater of war, scene of battle, scene of action, arena, lists, no man's land, field of war, seat of battle, place of contest, battle ground.
2. Arena, circus, ring, cockpit, court, field, gridiron, diamond, rink, amphitheater, campus, coliseum.

BATTLEMENT, n. Wall, parapet, outworks, embrasure, breastwork, fortification, bulwark, rampart, barbette, bastion, stronghold, fortress, fort, citadel, crenelated wall, defense, fastness, redoubt, embankment, mound, bank, abutment, fence, paling, banquette, palisade, stockade, barrier, barricade, boom, ravelin, redan, buttress, demilune.

BATTLESHIP, n. Floating fortress, armed vessel, man of war, dreadnought, battle wagon, battle cruiser, cruiser, destroyer, corvette, warship, ironclad, line of battle ship, ship of the line, war vessel, superdreadnought, torpedo boat, sloop of war, gunboat, monitor, frigate, flagship, submarine, submarine chaser, submersible, U-boat, flattop, carrier.

BAUBLE, n. Ornament, bagatelle, bric-a-brac, tinsel, plaything, gimcrack, gaud, kickshaw, triviality, knack, tawdry thing, picayunish thing, junk, rubbish, trash, clinquant, finery, frippery, trifle, spangle, toy, pinch-beck, gewgaw, trinket, brummagem.

BAWD, n. Procurer, procuress, pander, purveyor, whoremaster, securer, pimp.

BAWDRY, n. Obscenity, concupiscence, rudeness, pornography, scatology, salaciousness, impurity, libidinousness, wantonness, smut, indecency, lewd talk, impropriety, indecorum, indecorousness, indelicacy, coarseness, ribaldry, vulgarity, lasciviousness, nastiness, dirt.

BAWDY, adj. Dissolute, immoral, licentious, carnal, voluptuous, lickerish, prurient, ruttish, obscene, Paphian, shameless, risqué, immodest, double entendre, pornographic, impure, dirty, scatological, lustful, salacious, libidinous, gross, crude, wanton, off-color, lewd, improper, rude, smutty, indecorous, indelicate, unchaste, coarse, ribald, filthy, vulgar, bestial, lascivious.

BAWDY-HOUSE, n. Stew, whorehouse, house of

ill-fame, house of ill-repute, house of lewdness, bagnio, brothel, bordel, lupanar, kip.

BAWL, *v.* 1. Call, call out, cry, sing out, exclaim, squall, give cry, rend the air, make the welkin ring, shout at the top of one's voice, bring down the roof, yelp, proclaim, hoot, bellow, mewl, hollo, shout, howl, roar, screech, yell, caterwaul, squeel.
2. Wail, weep, cry, sob, blubber, keen, snivel, whimper, whine.

BAWL, *n.* Vociferation, outcry, clamor, yell, howl, roar, shout, hoot, cry, squalling, calling out, bellowing, boohooing, hollering, screech, proclaiming, ejaculation, yelping, caterwauling, wail, squeel, hubbub, hullabaloo, bleating.

BAY, *adj.* Reddish-brown, rust, tan, dun, bronze, terra cotta, russet, foxy, copper, maroon, roan, fawn, sorrel, chestnut, henna, auburn, hazel, ginger, brick.

BAY, *v.* 1. Bark, yelp, cry. (see BAY, *n.*, 4)
2. Pursue, chase, put to flight, follow, track down, flush, start, take after, trail.

BAY, *n.* 1. Cove, gulf, loch, frith, firth, fiord, estuary, bayou, arm of the sea, mouth, inlet, lagoon, creek, bight, natural harbor, sound, strait, narrows, roads.
2. Recess, aperture, embrasure, cavity, nook, depression, channel, compartment, alcove, niche, cubicle, carrell, carol.
3. Bay-tree, magnolia, sweet laurel, laurel tree, European laurel.
4. Bark, cry, bellowing, calling, yelping, roar, howling, yapping, clamor, hooting, hue and cry.
5. Hopelessness, desperation, last stand, lost cause, despair, fight to the death, last resort.
6. Standstill, restriction, debarring, hindrance, constraint, check, thwart, curbing, prohibiting, boxing up, hemming in.
7. Bay window, bow window, embrasure, oriel, lattice, casement, dormer.

BAYONET, *v.* Stab, kill, impale, cut and thrust, transfix, spear, transpierce, pink, jab, stick, lance, spike, spit, run through, point.

BAYONET, *n.* Blade, cold steel, naked steel, side arms.

BAYS, *n.* 1. Laurel crown, chaplet, palm, prize, wreath, citation, decoration, reward, ribbon, garland, laurel, distinction, medal, trophy, cup.
2. Repute, celebrity, éclat, acclaim, distinction, recognition, renown, eulogy, applause, praise, fame, approval, honors, glory, kudos.

BAZAAR, *n.* 1. Emporium, arcade, dime store, exchange, market, mart.
2. Fair, fancy fair, charity fair.

BE, *v.* 1. Exist, have being, live, have life, be alive, subsist, inhere in, consist in, lie in, be comprised in, be extant, seem, appear, have reality, have substance, coexist, breathe, inhabit, vegetate.
2. Remain, abide, endure, last, continue, stay, persist.
3. Occur, happen, take place, prevail, come to pass, develop, chance, befall, betide.

BEACH, *n.* Water's edge, edge, shore, strand, ground, coast, sands, land, seacoast, margin, rim, seashore, bank, shingle, seaside, seaboard, dry land, ripa, foreshore, littoral.

BEACH, *v.* Run ashore, run aground, strand, be stranded, put aground.

BEACHCOMBER, *n.* 1. Wave, ripple, comber,

white horses, surge, rollers, swell, billow, ground swell, breaker, surf.
2. Vagrant, poor white, tramp, hobo, riffraff, derelict, human wreck, vagabond, renegade, rover, loafer, wanderer, bum, stiff, swagman, roamer, sundowner, meanderer, panhandler, ragamuffin, tatterdemalion, pariah.

BEACHED, *adj.* 1. Stranded, high and dry, stuck, aground, castaway, marooned.
2. Abandoned, deserted, left, discarded, cast off.

BEACON, *n.* 1. Balefire, signal-fire, bonfire, smoke signal, watch fire, beacon fire, torch, pilot light, fiery cross, smudge pots.
2. Mark, signal, guide, warning, sign, buoy, searchlight, rocket, flare, brand, firebrand, sign board, pointer, arrow, indicator, guide post, sign post, landmark, sea mark, weathercock, milepost, weathervane, very light *(Mil.)*, watchtower, lighthouse, pharos, balize.

BEACON, *v.* Sign, warn, signal, illuminate, kindle, enlighten, brighten, flash, glow.

BEAD, *n.* 1. Globule, little ball, spherule, pellet, vesicle, pea, shot.
2. Drop, particle, speck, dot, iota, dab, pill, blob, droplet.
3. Moulding, trimming, openwork, skirting, fringe work, border, ornature, decoration, edging, ornament, embellishment, astragal.

BEAD, *v.* 1. Decorate, embellish, ornament, trim, mould, edge.
2. Deck with beads, thread, string.

BEADLE, *n.* 1. Mace-bearer, summoner, usher, law-officer, proclaimer, messenger, herald, bum bailiff, apparitor, servitor, steward, court crier, catchpoll, tipstaff, lictor.
2. Church servitor, sexton, verger, custodian, caretaker, churchwarden, sacristan, acolyte.

BEADROLL, *n.* List, catalog, roster, series, roll of honor, register, scroll, screed, muster roll, slate, panel, docket, inventory, gazette, archive, calendar, schedule, directory, file, annals, terrier, chronicles, genealogy, cartulary, table, gazetteer.

BEADS, *n.* Necklace, pendant, pearls, string of jewels, rosary, peag, wampum, chaplet, necklet, passementerie.

BEADSMAN, BEADSWOMAN, *n.* 1. Retainer, liegeman, servitor, intercessor, pleader, adjuror, suppliant, supplicant.
2. Mendicant, beggar, pauper, starveling, almsman, mumper.

BEAK, *n.* 1. Bill, proboscis, snout, mandible, nozzle, snozzle, pincers, chela, neb, nib, nose, rostrum.
2. Prow, bowsprit, projecting lip, spout, bow, stem.

BEAKED, *adj.* Pointed, aquiline, sharp, hook-shaped, crook-shaped, nibbed, arched.

BEAKER, *n.* Glass, goblet, cup, tumbler, bowl, chalice, tankard, mug, flagon, pot, wineglass, toby, stoup, tass, noggin, rummer, pannikin, horn, hogshead, stein.

BEAM, *n.* 1. Support, prop, trestle, brace, lintel, girder, joist, rafter, spar, timber, pole, boom, lath, furring strip, stud, scantling, pile, balk, transverse.
2. Ray, glimmer, flicker, shimmer, glitter, glare, streak, twinkle, glint, glow, stream of light, chink, pencil, gleam. (see GLIMMER)
3. Width, breadth, thickness, expanse, widest

point, caliber, bore, radius, latitude, amplitude, extent, expanse, compass.

BEAM, *v.* Radiate, shine, emit light, gleam, glare, glisten, glitter, beacon, glance, glimmer, glow, scintillate, shed luster, shine upon, phosphoresce, coruscate.

BEAMY, *adj.* 1. Bright, vivid, lambent, glowing, illuminated, illumined, enlightened, radiant, beaming, lightened, gleaming, flashing, flaming, glistening, sparkling, shining, brilliant, luminous, lustrous, effulgent, refulgent.
2. Brilliant, bright, scintillating, joyous, radiant, gladsome, glowing, shining, sparkling.
3. Beam-like, massive, gigantic, enormous, large, bulky, huge, ponderous, big, great, massy, sturdy, thick, hulky, elephantine, pachydermous, unwieldy.

BEAR, *v.* 1. Hold up, support, sustain, uphold, shoulder, lift, bolster up, shore up, upbear, prop, underprop, underpin, underset, brace, lend support, cradle, pillow.
2. Transmit, tote, carry, shift, transfer, convoy, conduct, transplant, convey, haul, fetch, displace, portage, bring, take, move, remove, transport.
3. Contain, possess, have, be equipped with, be furnished with, hold, be marked with.
4. Abide, suffer, tolerate, feel, withstand, put up with, persist, endure, thole, aby, undergo, submit to, bear with, stand, take, brook, go through, weather, stomach, brave, bide.
5. Warrant, signify, permit, admit, allow, be capable of.
6. Maintain, uphold, keep up, sustain, carry on, support, assume responsibility.
7. Heed, keep in mind, entertain, cherish, regard, take cognizance of, harbor.
8. Create, generate, produce, render, yield, give, cause, engender, fructify, turn out, form, develop, germinate.
9. Reproduce, give birth, breed, carry, deliver, germinate, procreate, propagate, bring forth, be parturient, be pregnant, spawn, cast, hatch, lay, bring into being, gestate, drop *(of animals).*
10. Exhibit, wear, put on, assume, be marked with, don, show, display.
11. Press, force, bear down, drive, compel, coerce, enforce, constrain, influence, affect, cause, push, be oppressive.
12. Act, assume a duty, operate, work, take office, assume a responsibility, succeed, take effect.
13. Appertain, belong, pertain, touch upon, affect, concern, regard, be pertinent, have to do with, refer, have respect to, have bearing on, relate, tend.
14. Bend, turn, deviate, curve, be directed at, be aimed at, be pointed at, be aligned with, diverge.

BEAR, *n.* 1. Bruin, Ursus, musquaw.
2. Grouch, crosspatch, churl, boor, snarler, growler, crab, frump, "sourpuss."
3. Underseller, speculator, depreciator of the market.

BEARABLE, *adj.* Sufferable, endurable, passable, admissible, supportable, tolerable.

BEAR A HAND 1. *(Naut.)* Shake a leg, shake a timber, pull an oar, make haste, be quick, hurry, hurry up, scurry, scuttle, scramble, hustle, make short work of, bestir one's self, get a move on, scud, hie.
2. *(Colloq.)* Buckle to, ply the oar, put one's shoulder to the wheel, cooperate, contribute,

lend assistance, give *or* stretch a hand, give a lift *or* turn, help, aid, assist, afford help, subscribe to, support, back up, second, abet.

BEARD, *n.* Whiskers, Vandyke, burnsides, tuft, awn, goatee, mutton chops, imperial, brush, shag, mane, bristles. (see BARB)

BEARD, *v.* 1. Pluck by the beard, take the bull by the horns, bell the cat, march up to the cannon's mouth.
2. Defy, brave, oppose, stand up against, snap the fingers at, affront, show scorn for, look in the face, dare, face.

BEARDED, *adj.* 1. Hairy, barbate, bewhiskered, bristly, bushy, shaggy, maned, unshaven, hirsute, whiskered.
2. Barbed, spined, sharp, prickly, pointed, tufted.
3. *(Bot.)* Awned, bristly, bristled, tufted, aristate.

BEARDLESS, *adj.* 1. Smooth-faced, clean-shaven, shaven, glabrous-cheeked, hairless.
2. Youthful, immature, unfledged, young, callow, green, raw, puerile, boyish, juvenile, naive, adolescent.

BEAR DOWN UPON 1. Attack, assail, draw near, converge on, rush upon, gain upon, set upon, overtake, come to close quarters, charge, close in on, march against, approach, press on, move upon, advance upon, run down, have at, overhaul.
2. *(Naut.)* Set in towards, veer towards, sail towards, draw near, approach, put at, put into.

BEARER, *n.* Carrier, porter, transporter, owner, possessor, messenger, conductor, sustainer, holder, conveyor, supporter.

BEARING, *n.* 1. Comportment, port, attitude, manner, air, behavior, mien, look, gait, guise, deportment, demeanor, acquittal, carriage, front, conduct, observance, presence.
2. Pertinence, relation, relevancy, belonging, appertaining, application, reference, connection, appositeness, concern, dependency, cognation, interconnection, relationship, applicability, correlation, applicableness, association.
3. Abiding, endurance, enduring, putting up with, standing, taking, submitting to, swallowing, going through, patience, toleration, weathering, fortitude, brooking, withstanding, sufferance.
4. Position, drift, tendency, dip, divergence, fluctuation, direction, course, aim, reading, set, aspect, trend, compass reading.
5. Significance, signification, sense, purport, tenor, drift, import, connotation, effect, essence, scope, spirit, sum and substance, tendency, gist, compass, core, meaning, scope.
6. Giving birth, pregnancy, delivering, bringing forth, germination, procreation, producing, casting, propagation, yielding fruit, breeding, spawning, reproduction, hatching, gestation, dropping *(of animals),* laying, conception, parturience.
7. Joint, journal, gudgeon, pivot, fulcrum, socket, pin, hinge, receptacle, ball bearing, ball and socket.
8. *(Her.)* Device, charge, supporters, armorial bearing, escutcheon, field, blazon, coat of arms, depiction, chief, base, dexter, sinister, fess, heart, navel, nombril, livery, badge, crest, brassard, hatchment, shield.

BEARISH, *adj.* Cross, unfriendly, surly, churlish, quick-tempered, thin-skinned, grouchy, impolite, ungentlemanly, rough, mean, rude, unkind, fierce, coarse, boorish, discourteous, angry, uncivil, mad, out-of-sorts, peevish, saturnine, ill-willed, sullen, loutish, unbred, harsh, blunt, unaffable, snappy, savage, irascible, morose, crabbed, crusty, sour, moody, frumpish, splenetic, sharp, tart, short, choleric, testy, peppery, touchy, fractious, huffy, waspish.

BEAR ONE'S SELF Behave, be mannerly, put up a front, look, acquit—, conduct—, deport—, demean—, comport—, quit one's self, act.

BEAR OUT Ratify, warrant, make absolute, authenticate, sustain, endorse, maintain, sanction, confirm, authorize, defend, substantiate, uphold, verify, justify, make good, circumstantiate, corroborate, establish, vindicate.

BEAR THE BELL Excel, transcend, challenge comparison, stand proof, carry all before, possess the field, win hands down, be the leader, have the best of it, vanquish all comers, be supreme, surpass, play first fiddle, carry the day, prevail, preponderate, predominate, take precedence, take the cake, rank foremost, bear the palm.

BEAR THE CROSS Quaff the bitter cup, drain the cup of misery, labor under afflictions, endure trials, endure hardship, fall on evil days.

BEAR UP 1. Support, etc. (See BEAR, *v.* 1)
2. Endure, etc. (See BEAR, *v.* 4)

BEAR UPON (See BEAR, *v.* 13)

BEAR WITH (See BEAR, *v.* 4)

BEAR WITNESS Give evidence, vouch for, aver, certify, attest to, depone, testify, asseverate, state, depose, give an affidavit, affirm, verify, declare, substantiate, confirm, swear, corroborate, avow, give deposition.

BEAST, *n.* 1. Creature, dumb animal, brute, wild animal, quadruped, four-footed creature.
2. Brute, monster, swine, savage, sensualist, voluptuary, glutton, pig, hog, satyr, lecher, goat, seducer, libertine, whoremonger, monstrosity, fornicator, adulterer, Bluebeard. (see also BARBARIAN, *n.* 2)

BEASTLIKE, *adj.* 1. Theriomorphic, theroid, animal-like, animal-shaped, bestial, having brute *or* animal form.
2. Fierce, savage, mean, etc. (see BARBARIC, *adj.,* 2 and BEARISH, *adj.*)

BEASTLY, *adj.* Gross, vulgar, nasty, loathsome, savage, vile, unclean, piggish, boarish, swinish, hoggish, base, carnal, abominable, irrational, prurient, degraded, inhuman, repulsive, obscene, gluttonous, greedy, coarse, sensual, bestial, brutal, brutish. (see also BARBAROUS, *adj.* 2 and BAWDY, *adj.*)

BEAT, *v.* 1. Strike, smack, tap, rap, slap, cuff, box, wallop, pat, dab, bump, knock, hit, larrup *(colloq.),* curry, fillip, buffet, lace, spank, tamp, jab, smite, switch, flog, whip, persecute, punish, club, lambaste, cane, cudgel, punch, trounce, bat, batter, flail, lash, ram, welt *(colloq.),* chastise, pound, bastinade, whack *(colloq.),* bang, thwack, thrash, maltreat, scourge, castigate, flagellate, swinge, whale *(colloq.),* baste, swat, fustigate, hammer, leather, chasten, horsewhip, strap, birch, trim, pommel, thump, bethump, belabor, slug, clout, drub, maul.
2. Hammer, forge, malleate, beetle, pound.
3. Pound, bruise, pulverize, etc. (See BATTER, *v.,* 1 & 2)
4. Conquer, destroy, knock down, overwhelm, crush, quell, squash, master, smash, discomfit, rout, reduce, humble, subject, nonplus, overcome, subdue, worst, triumph over, vanquish, subjugate,

checkmate, defeat, overpower, whip, drub, lick, put down, get the better of, prevail over, be victorious over, get the upper hand of, get the whip hand of, surmount, have on the hip, best.
5. Eclipse, outstrip, surpass, excel, outdo, bear the palm, carry all before, outflank, bear the bell, be the leader, rank foremost, transcend, challenge comparison, stand proof, possess the field, win hands down, carry by storm, have the best of it, vanquish all comers, be supreme, play first fiddle, preponderate, predominate, prevail, take the cake, take precedence, overmatch.
6. Agitate, churn, mill, thresh, stir, whip, mix, shake, mash.
7. Conduct, lead, wield the baton, beat time, direct.
8. Cheat, defraud, swindle, etc. (see BAFFLE, *v.* 3)
9. Palpitate, pulse, pulsate, throb, flap, flutter, flap, fluctuate, quake, quiver, quaver, shake, go pitapat, vellicate, pitch, pound, vibrate, librate, oscillate, wobble, waggle, flicker, wriggle, roll, wiggle, bounce, totter, flop, bandy, brandish, flourish, tremble, shiver, dither, twitch, writhe, bob, buffet, sway, agitate, reel, jerk, pendulate, jounce, toss.
10. *(With back)* Throw back, repel, dispel, put to flight, drive back, scatter, rebuff, repulse, hold at bay, resist, oppose, chase, send away, reject, make run.

BEAT, *n.* 1. Stroke, blow, etc, (see BEAT, *v.,* 1)
2. *(Music, poetry, etc.)* Rhythm, accent, sound, cadence, time, measure, pace, pulse, throb, lilt, thrumming, swing, periodicity, rise and fall, scansion, emphasis.
3. Lap, way, sphere, walk, routine, rounds, road, ambit, compass, tour, trek, circumference, bounds, zone, area, orbit, path, tack, perimeter, traversal, course.

BEATEN, *adj.* 1. Well-trodden, threadbare, much used, smooth, napless, much traveled.
2. Exhausted, jaded, enervated, tired, drained, expended, emptied, impoverished, used up, worn out, weakened, depleted, fatigued, done in *(colloq.),* debilitated, weary, fagged, oppressed, weighed down, emasculated, drooping, haggard, footsore, wayworn, toilworn, effete, faint, spent, ready to drop, played out, enfeebled, sickly, unsteady, groggy. (see also BEAT, *v.*)
3. Hackneyed, trite, commonplace, etc. (see BANAL, *adj.*)
4. Defeated, conquered, vanquished, etc. (see BEAT, *v.,* 4)

BEATIFIC, *adj.* Wonderful, glorious, enchanting, pleasure-giving, pleasurable, enrapturing, happy, delightful, glad, blissful, heavenly, rapt, divine, transporting, ecstatic, Elysian, Arcadian, sacred, Olympian, celestial, paradisaic, angelic, supernal, enravishing, rapturous.

BEATIFICATE, *v.* (see BEATIFY, *v.*)

BEATIFICATION, *n.* (see BEATITUDE, *n.*)

BEATIFY, *v.* 1. Pronounce in bliss *(by the Pope),* beatificate, canonize, bless, hallow, revere, sanctify, consecrate, laud, macarize, enshrine, venerate.
2. Enrapture, delight, enchant, make joyful, transport, charm, enthral, enravish, felicitate, gladden, entrance, make happy, give blessedness. (see BEATITUDE, *n.* 2)

BEATING, *n.* (see BEAT, *n.* and *v.*)

BEATITUDE, *n.* 1. Encomium of virtue, blessing,

declaration, pronouncement of blessing (*in the Sermon on the Mount*).

2. Delight, joy, exaltation, bliss, felicity, holy joy, blessedness, enchantment, ecstasy, serenity, blissfulness, elation, happiness, heavenly peace, divine rapture, fruition, enjoyment, pleasure.

BEAU, *n.* 1. Fop, dandy, cavalier, man about town, coxcomb, playboy, ladies' man, popinjay, carpet knight, fine gentleman, jack-a-dandy, prig, young blood, puppy, jackanapes, exquisite, swell, dude, blade, spark, Dundreary, *élégant (Fr.)*, Sir Fopling Flutter *(the prototype)*, silk-stocking.

2. Lover, admirer, swain, fiancé, pursuer, love, follower, cavalier, inamorato, paramour, flame, adorer, suitor, true love, sweetheart, betrothed, cicisbeo *(It.)*, young man *(colloq.)*, boy friend *(colloq.)*, beloved, amorist, wooer, dear, darling, Romeo, Lothario, Casanova, lion among ladies.

BEAU IDEAL *(Fr.)*, *n.* Ideal, pattern, standard, model, example, mirror, paradigm, exemplar, criterion, prototype, archetype, design, mould, precedent, paragon, ne plus ultra *(L.)*, module, acme, nonpareil.

BEAUTEOUS, *adj.* (see BEAUTIFUL, *adj.*)

BEAUTIFUL, *adj.* Fair, pretty, magnificent, fine, attractive, bonny, personable, seemly, sightly, charming, blooming, exquisite, artistic, handsome, captivating, alluring, fascinating, winning, elegant, bewitching, graceful, charming, enticing, superb, enchanting, good-looking, comely, stately, noble, becoming, gracious, shapely, lovely, choice, nitid, delicate, dainty, gorgeous, resplendent, dazzling, radiant, shining, lustrous, beauteous, glamorous, divine, seductive, winsome, engaging, effulgent, ravishing, matchless, pulchritudinous.

BEAUTIFY, *v.* Adorn, paint, enrich, elaborate, make beautiful, prettify, set, grace, primp, array, arrange, sweeten, garnish, bedeck, enhance, deck, heighten, prink, prank, preen, prune, ornament, emblazon, embellish, set off, polish, burnish, gild, adonize, smarten, furbish, dress up, titivate, fret, spangle, bespangle, embroider, emboss, illuminate.

BEAUTY, *n.* 1. Pulchritude, grace, loveliness, charm. (see BEAUTIFUL, *adj.*)

2. Belle, fascinator, enchantress, goddess, Venus, charmer *(colloq.)*.

BECALM, *v.* 1. Mollify, allay, appease, pacify, calm, soothe, still, compose, tranquilize, stay, lull, hush, quell, quiet, moderate, soften, sober, repose, make quiescent, quench, propitiate.

2. Make motionless, stand still, stop, halt.

BECAUSE, *conj.* or **BECAUSE OF** For, since, on account of, inasmuch as, whereas, forasmuch as, due to the fact, as, by virtue of, due to, through, owing to, by reason of, therefore, as a result, consequently.

BECHANCE, *v.* Fall, happen, befall, occur, come about, betide, chance, hap, turn out, take place, come to pass, become, prove, eventuate, result, ensue, take effect, crop up, arise, start, intervene, supervene, transpire *(colloq. in this sense)*, arrive, emanate from, issue, overtake (one).

BECHARM, *v.* Bewitch, seduce, entice, allure, captivate, fascinate, put *or* cast a spell on, take, enchant, attract, delight, rejoice, please, endear, gratify, engage, hypnotize, enamor, transport, turn one's head, enrapture, bedevil, witch, lure, magnetize, inveigle, tempt, ravish, enravish, mesmerize.

BECK, *n.* 1. Nod, gesture, gesticulation, sign, call, signal, bow, glance, wink, shrug, touch, nudge.

2. Bidding, call, desire, whim, fancy, wish, want, command, summons, order, word, request, behest, ruling, dictation, charge, instructions, beck and call.

BECKON, *v.* 1. Nod, gesture, gesticulate, crook the finger at, give a sign, motion, call, wave, signal to come.

2. Summon, call, invite, draw towards, draw, attract, allure, lure, coax, bid, call upon, claim, send for, lead, cite, pull.

BECLOUD, *v.* Shade, envelop, shadow, gloom, dim, cloud over, lower, fade, pale, grow dim, overcast, befog, bedim, overshadow, obscure, darken, adumbrate, tone down, eclipse, throw *or* spread gloom over, obfuscate, cover, screen, hide, shroud, veil, cloak, bemask.

BECOME, *v.* 1. Happen, befall, occur, etc. (see BECHANCE, *v.*)

2. Turn into, change into, appear as, pass into, be transformed, grow into, grow, mature, alter, mellow, wax, ripen into, develop into, convert, be transmuted, be transfigured, be remodeled, be metamorphosed, be reorganized, be reduced to, reform oneself, be translated, vary, come to be, get, lapse, shift, assume the form *or* shape *or* state of, melt into, settle into, resolve oneself, be reformed, be converted into.

3. Suit, enhance, fit, be appropriate, behoove, befit, harmonize with, accord with, beseem, be proper to, grace, embellish, be consistent with, match, enrich, adorn, garnish, heighten, belong to, ornament, go with.

BECOMING, *adj.* Seemly, proper, comely, decent, fit, apt, relevant, worthy, fitting, consistent with, conformable, decorous, congruous, appropriate, gainly, shapely, graceful, attractive, ornamental, decorous, harmonious, stylish, chic *(colloq.)*, suitable, tasteful, meet, accordant, concordant, congenial, in keeping with, consistent, befitting, proportionate, compatible, cute *(colloq.)*.

BED, *n.* 1. Cot, couch, crib, cradle, resting place, pallet, paillasse, bunk, mattress, bedstead, litter, hammock, four-poster, berth, mat, bassinet, land of nod, truckle bed.

2. Matrix, bottom, foundation, support, base, grounding, fundus, plinth, socle, substructure, substratum. (see BASE, *n.*, 1)

3. Layer, underlayer, stratum, band, course, zone, belt, tier, seam, deposit, vein, floor, lode, accumulation.

4. Plot, bank, plat, lot, patch.

BED, *v.* 1. Couch, recline, rest, lie, repose, sleep, slumber, nod, drowse, turn in, retire, nap, lodge, snooze, hibernate, bed down, put up, lay, quarter, billet, camp, encamp, bivouac, roost, house.

2. Bottom *(with* on *or* upon*)*, ground, found, base, embed, set, enclose, intern, insert, implant, immerse, immerge, bury, fix in, be buried in.

BEDAUB, *v.* 1. Smudge, stain, blacken, smear, spot, smutch, blur, smirch, salve, grease, dab, besmear, soil, blot, begrime, splash, blemish, bespatter, deface, mar, blotch.

2. Coat, overspread, veneer, varnish, tar, gild, stucco, plate, lacquer, japan, enamel, whitewash, parget, plaster.

3. Smear, vilify, disparage, etc. (see BACKBITE, *v.*)

4. Ornament, adorn, embellish, etc. (see ARRAY, *v.*)

BEDCLOTHES, *n.* Blanket, sheets, coverlets, comforter, counterpane, quilt, spread, bedspread, duvet.

BEDDING, *n.* Mattress, litter, pillows, bolsters, bedclothes. (see also BEDCLOTHES, *n.* and BED, *n.*, 1)

BEDECK, *v.* (see BEAUTIFY, *v.*)

BEDEVIL, *v.* 1. Bewitch, hypnotize, etc. (see BECHARM, *v.*)
2. Tease, worry, etc. (see BADGER, *v.*)
3. Confuse, muddle, etc. (see BAFFLE, *v.*, 2)
4. Adulterate, corrupt, ruin, spoil, debase, rot, warp, taint, pollute, defile, contaminate, deprave, debauch, pervert, degrade, abase, wreck, ruin, infect, demoralize, poison, envenom, corrode, canker, blight, vitiate, undermine, subvert, change for the worse, mar, despoil, blemish, wither.

BEDEW, *v.* Soak, saturate, moisten, wet, damp, sprinkle, humidify, dampen, drench, sodden, sop, make dank *or* muggy, water, besprinkle, imbue, humect, make roscid, bathe.

BEDIM, *v.* (see BECLOUD, *v.*)

BEDIZEN, *v.* (see BEAUTIFY, *v.*)

BEDLAM, *n.* 1. Insane asylum, retreat, sanctuary, sanatorium, madhouse, hospital for the insane, institution.
2. Uproar, pandemonium, turmoil, etc. (see BABEL, *n.*)

BEDLAMITE, *n.* Madman, lunatic, energumen, dement, insane person, crazy person, phrenetic, deranged person, raver, paranoiac, demoniac, maniac. (see also MAD, *adj.*)

BEDRAGGLE, *v.* (see BEDRAGGLED, *adj.*)

BEDRAGGLED, *adj.* Wet, soiled, sodden, dirty, draggled, untidy, mussed, soggy, sloppy, dripping, soaking, muddied, slovenly, messy, draggletailed, unkempt, unclean, filthy, grimy, splashed, stained, wringing wet, drenched, drenched to the skin.

BEDRID or BEDRIDDEN, *adj.* Decrepit, laid on one's back, crippled, paralyzed, incapacitated, confined to bed, disabled, helpless, bedfast.

BEEFY, *adj.* Fat, plump, fleshy, brawny, stolid, pudgy, dumpy, thickset, corpulent, stout, bulky, portly, obese, burly, muscular, podgy, chubby, hulky, lumpish, puffy, swollen, bloated, rotund, squab, well-fed, stalwart, large, big, ample, full, massy, massive, bouncing, buxom, elephantine, chunky, ponderous.

BEEHIVE, *n.* Bee-house, apiary.

BEELINE, *n.* Direct route, direct line, direction as the crow flies, shortest distance, straight *or* most direct line *or* route, short cut, straight shot.

BEELZEBUB, *n.* Evil one, Satan, Lucifer, Belial, Mephistopheles, Samael, the prince of darkness, Apollyon, Abaddon, Mammon, the wicked one, the tempter, the author of evil, Ahriman, Old Nick (*colloq.*).

BEER, *n.* Lager, ale, stout, porter, bock, malt liquor.

BEETLE, *v.* 1. Overhang, stick out, lean over, protrude, pout, bunch, belly, overtop, extend, be pendent, be prominent, poke out, shoot out, jut out, impend, sag, bouge, bulge, bristle, swell over, hang over, jut over, project.
2. Hammer, forge, etc. (see BEAT, *v.*, 2)

BEETLEHEAD, *n.* (see DUNCE, *n.*)

BEFALL, *v.* (see BECHANCE, *v.*)

BEFIT, *v.* (see BECOME, *v.*, 3)

BEFITTING, *adj.* (see BECOMING, *adj.*)

BEFOG, *v.* 1. Shadow, dim, cloud over, etc. (see BECLOUD, *v.*)

2. Confuse, mystify, perplex, etc. (see BAFFLE, *v.*, 2)

BEFOOL, *v.* (see BAMBOOZLE, *v.*, 1 and 2)

BEFORE, *adv.* 1. In front, out front, ahead, in advance, in the van, foremost, headmost, in the lead, in the foreground, in preference, forward, first, pre—, ante—.
2. In time past, previously, prematurely, early, beforetime, beforehand, prior, formerly, betimes, afore, yet, aforetime, pre—, ante—, sooner, in anticipation, in advance, first.

BEFORE, *prep.* 1. In front of, ahead of, by, in the face of, in advance of, outside, under the eyes *or* nose of, face to face with, pre-, ante-, in the foreground of, in the presence of, in the vicinity of, near.
2. Ahead of, previous to, earlier than, sooner than, on the eve of, in anticipation of, prior to, previous to, pre-, ante-.

BEFOREHAND, *adv.* (see BEFORE, *adv.*)

BEFRIEND, *v.* Make friends with, help, assist, aid, succor, stand by, relieve, rescue, lend a hand, support, take in tow, set on one's legs, promote, further, forward, favor, patronize, advance, tend, minister to, take care of, stick by, work for, take up the cause of, smile upon, side with, foster, cherish, protect, encourage, look after, benefit, countenance, contribute to, subscribe to, uphold, prop, bolster, serve, smile upon, conduce to, incline towards, be favorably disposed to, keep an eye on, get acquainted with, keep company with, have dealings with, sympathize with, regale, fraternize, embrace, receive with open arms, hold out a hand to, associate with, consort with, entertain, welcome, sustain. (see also BACK, *v.*, 1)

BEFUDDLE, *v.* Intoxicate, muddle, bemuddle, confuse, inebriate, exhilarate with liquor, make drunk, make tipsy *or* tight, fuddle (*colloq.*), stupefy, make mellow, make groggy (*colloq.*), fuzzle. (see also BEFUDDLED, *adj.*)

BEFUDDLED, *adj.* Drunk, intoxicated, tight, tipsy, inebriate, inebriated, fuddled (*colloq.*), bemuddled, muddled, overcome, boozy (*colloq.*), groggy (*colloq.*), unsteady on the legs, stupefied, in one's cups, temulent, merry, elevated (*colloq.*), flustered, plastered (*slang*), obfuscated, crapulous.

BEG, *v.* 1. Beseech, entreat, implore, supplicate, importune, appeal to, ask, crave, sue for, urge, plead, petition, request, pray, obtest, conjure, press, adjure, solicit, apply to, apostrophize, requisition, call to, canvass.
2. Seek alms, mendicate, cadge, panhandle, bum (*slang*), sponge, go from door to door, live from hand to mouth, live on charity, want, lack, starve, be on one's uppers.

BEGET, *v.* 1. Procreate, generate, father, sire, engender, get, breed, propagate, reproduce, spawn, produce, originate, fecundate, impregnate, fertilize, pollinate, progenerate.
2. Effect, bring about, etc. (see CAUSE, *v.*)

BEGGAR, *n.* Pauper, mendicant, almsman, hobo, mumper, starveling, vagrant, tramp, panhandler, derelict, meanderer, vagabond, tatterdemalion, beadsman, canter, schnorrer, fakir, beachcomber, dervish, cadger. (see also BEACHCOMBER, *n.*, 2)

BEGGAR, *v.* 1. Impoverish, pauperize, etc. (see BANKRUPT, *v.*)
2. Baffle, surpass, exceed, eclipse, outstrip,

excel, outdo, transcend, challenge, preponderate, vanquish, predominate, prevail over, overmatch, go beyond, belittle, surmount, overwhelm, quell, master, humble, make inadequate.

BEGGARLY, *adj.* Mean, vile, contemptible, etc. (see BASE, *adj.*, 2)

BEGGARY, *n.* Pauperism, privation, indigence, distress, misery, squalor, penury, want, poverty, destitution, mendicancy, mendicity, straits, need, bankruptcy, lack, pennilessness, necessity, ruin, neediness, impecuniosity, insolvency, starvation, begging, poorness, scarcity, dearth, the wolf at the door, straitened circumstances, paucity, bare subsistence, scantiness, exigency.

BEGIN, *v.* 1. Start, commence, take the first step, initiate, inaugurate, originate, spring, arise, enter, derive, rise, dawn, set in, open, embark, set out, break ground, make a start, incept, undertake, usher in, precede, come into existence, take birth, introduce, inchoate, launch, broach, handsel, make a debut, come into existence, burst forth, break out, spring up, crop up, break the ice, cross the Rubicon.
2. Found, establish, institute, organize, admit, introduce, enter, originate, set in motion, initiate, inaugurate, open, launch, inchoate, germinate, handsel, conceive, auspicate, head, kindle, lay the foundations, sow the seeds of, produce, lay the first stone, create, induce, provoke, promote, get up (*colloq.*).

BEGINNER, *n.* 1. Originator, creator, author, inceptor, starter, initiator, inaugurator, founder, organizer, begetter, producer, sponsor, prime mover. (see also BEGIN, *v.*)
2. Student, recruit, catechumen, abecedarian, alphabetarian, tyro, novice, learner, neophyte, novitiate, amateur, babe, freshman, understudy, pupil, apprentice, probationer, rooky (*slang*), greenhorn (*colloq.*), tenderfoot (*slang*).

BEGINNING, *n.* Origin, source, fountain, spring, starting point, outbreak of, infancy, conception, birth, onset, emergence, commencement, outset, start, inception, incipience, initiation, nascency, inauguration, fountainhead, zero hour, exordium, preface, forward, embryo stage.
(see also BEGIN, *v.*)

BEGIRD, *v.* 1. Bind, wrap, bandage, swaddle, gird, belt, pinion, buckle, truss, couple, swathe, tie.
2. Circumscribe, surround, confine, limit, hem in, enclose, envelop, embrace, case, encompass, incase, encircle, contain, ring, hedge, corral, pen, box in, shut in, bound, rail in, fence round, skirt, picket, circle, circumvent, environ, enshrine, enfold, enclasp.

BEGONE, *interj.* Go away!, get out!, out!, be off!, depart!, avaunt!, scram! (*slang*), scat (*slang*), vamoose! (*slang*). (see also GO, *v.*)

BEGRIME, *v.* Bedaub, smudge, stain, blacken, smear, spot, sully, smirch, grease, besmear, tar, soil, dirty, tarnish, blur, draggle, spatter, mess, befoul, defile, bemire, muddy, beslime, maculate, blotch, smutch, contaminate, drabble, muss.

BEGRUDGE, *v.* Grudge, envy, loathe to give, give *or* allow reluctantly, repine at another's prosperity, covet, be discontented at, be mean *or* niggardly towards, be unwilling to give, crave, withhold, lust after, be jealous of.

BEGUILE, *v.* 1. Delude, cheat, deceive, dupe, etc. (see BAMBOOZLE, *v.*, 1)
2. Divert, charm, etc. (see BECHARM, *v.*)

3. Entertain, amuse, cheer, while away, solace, delight, occupy, enliven, please, interest, treat, recreate, titillate, make merry, sport, disport, revel, junket, carouse, romp, caper, game.
(see also AMUSE, *v.*)

BEHALF, *n.* In prepositional phrases as in *or* on behalf of.
Side, support, advantage, interest, benefit, use, defense, behoof, account, place, representation, sake, profit, service, stead. *Phrases*: by proxy for, for, acting for, deputizing for, in the name of, under authority of, under orders from, by order of, in aid of, in favor of, in the name of, on the part of, for the sake of, in furtherance of.

BEHAVE, *v.* 1. Act, conduct, comport, acquit, quit, deport, demean, carry oneself, manage oneself, bear oneself, govern oneself, regulate oneself, proceed, discharge one's duties.
2. React, act, do, operate, function, work, execute oneself *or* itself, perform, take effect, counteract, respond, meet, readjust to, cope with, fit oneself, adapt, fall in with, conform to, be regulated *or* governed by, comply with, adjust to, accommodate oneself to.

BEHAVIOR, *n.* 1. Carriage, manners, conduct, deportment, demeanor, breeding, attitude, mien, manner, actions, act, ethics, deed, comportment, air, port, morals, code, address, guise, bearing, presence, rôle, ways, habits, practice, course, dealings, observance.
2. Reaction, act, deed, response, performance, function, operation, work, execution, adaptation, adjustment, conformance, compliance, counteraction.

BEHEAD, *v.* Decapitate, execute, guillotine, send to the ax, decollate, bring to the block, bring to the scaffold, chop off the head of, ax, give to the headsman.

BEHEST, *n.* Command, mandate, injunction, request, wish, bidding, dictate, order, precept, solicitation, will, word, charge, decree, imposition, direction, instruction, beck, nod, call, rule, ruling, fiat, sanction, demand, exaction, writ, ordination, edict, summons, authority, compulsion, pleasure, commission, authorization, regulation, requisition, ultimatum, appointment, fixture, desire, choice, want, requirement.

BEHIND, *adv.* 1. Back in the rear, behindhand, rearward, toward the back, astern, aback, aft (*Naut.*), abaft (*Naut.*), backward, at the heels of, in the background, sternmost, rearward, in the wake of.
2. After, later, subsequently, afterwards, next, since, close upon, thereafter, following.
3. Backward in progress, etc. (see BACKWARD, *adj.*, 3)
4. Slow, late, etc. (see BACKWARD, *adj.*, 4)

BEHIND, *prep.* (see BEHIND, *adv.*)

BEHINDHAND, *adj.* (see BACKWARD, *adj.*, 4)

BEHOLD, *v.* Look, look at, examine, inspect, pay attention to, heed, glance at, observe, see, espy, notice, remark, note, discern, contemplate, descry, regard, sight, witness, look upon, watch, gaze at, scan, be a spectator to, view, survey, consider, take cognizance of, eye, mark, perceive, discover, glimpse, stare, scrutinize.

BEHOLDEN, *adj.* 1. Indebted, owing, under obligation, thankful, grateful, appreciative, bound, obliged, obligated, in one's debt.
2. Answerable, liable. responsible, accountable, amenable.

BEHOLDER, *n.* Watcher, spectator, onlooker, bystander, witness, eyewitness, looker-on, viewer, kibitzer *(colloq.),* inspector, passer-by, sightseer, observer.
(See also BEHOLD, *v.)*

BEHOOF, *n.* (see BEHALF, *n.)*

BEHOOVE, *v. (Usually impersonal)* Be necessary, be incumbent upon, be proper for, befit, suit, be apt, become, be appropriate, be one's duty *or* obligation, beseem, devolve on, be required *or* expected, be bound, be needful, be right, be correct, be requisite.

BEING, *n.* 1. Existence, life, reality, occurrence, living, existing, subsistence, coexistence, ubiquity, omnipresence, presence, actuality, *esse* (Lat.), abiding, *ens* (Lat.), inherence in, preexistence, residing in, consisting in.
2. Nature, personality, individuality, essence, character, disposition, temperament, complexion, temper, psyche, soul, spirit, mind, intellect, vital principle, inner reality, root, core, center, heart, true being, quiddity, truth, veracity, hypostasis, prime constituent, substance, essential being, life, lifeblood.
3. Entity, body, creature, fellow creature, soul, earthling, person, personality, sentient, individual, living thing, character, specimen, bion, morphon, organism, somebody, someone, one, inhabitant, man.
(Pl. only) Folk, people.

BELABOR, *v.* (See BEAT, *v.,* 1)

BELATED, *adj.* Delayed, retarded, late, tardy, slow, dilatory, behindhand, backward, overdue, unpunctual, deferred, procrastinated, obstructed, tabled, impeded, prevented, barred, restrained, slack, laggard, tardigrade, behind time, long delayed.

BELCH, *v.* 1. Eruct, hiccup, hiccough, eructate, burp.
2. Emit, spew forth, eject, vomit, gush, erupt, void, cough up, expel, evacuate, discharge, issue forth, outpour, send forth, vent, blow, squirt, spurt, disgorge, emanate, disembogue, spit out *or* forth, extravasate, expectorate, puke, blast forth.

BELDAM or **BELDAME,** *n.* 1. Hag, crone, old woman, dotard, harridan, witch *(loosely),* granny *(colloq.),* hellhag.
2. Vixen, fury, virago, termagant, shrew, scold, Xanthippe, spitfire, dragon, tartar, amazon, tigress, demon, wildcat.

BELEAGUER, *v.* Blockade, surround, encompass, beset, besiege, siege, invest, compass, enclose, close, hem in, encircle, loop, girdle, hedge, pen in, confine, embrace, engird, skirt, circumscribe, ensphere, corral, begird, picket, fence in, bound.

BELFRY, *n.* Turret, cupola, bell tower, steeple, clocher, campanile, spire, dome, minaret, apse.

BELIE, *v.* 1. Calumniate, slander, abuse, asperse, scandalize, backbite, disparage, traduce, malign, defame, revile, libel, blacken, run down, belittle, cry down, blemish, decry, depreciate, vilipend, stigmatize, vituperate, derogate, condemn, tell lies about, gossip about, speak maliciously of, vilify, pull to pieces, bear false witness against, detract, bespatter, denigrate.
2. Misrepresent, falsify, fake, pervert, distort, disguise, garble, gloss over, color, varnish, put a false construction on, exaggerate, magnify, lie about, amplify, overstate, understate, minimize, stretch, wrest the meaning *or* sense of, belittle,

misinform about, deceive, mislead *or* misguide *or* misdirect *or* misinstruct concerning.
3. Be false, be unfaithful, contradict, oppose, go against, contravene, violate, defy, backslide, apostatize, renege, desert, fail, leave in the lurch, deny, gainsay, repudiate, set aside, ignore, give the lie to, negate, negative, counteract, neutralize, run counter to, be at cross purposes with, go back on *(colloq.),* forsake, abandon. (See also BACKSLIDE, *v.)*

BELIEF, *n.* 1. Understanding, faith, confidence, trust, hope, conviction, feeling, intuition, credit, expectation, knowledge, persuasion, assurance, credence, assent, reliance, certainty, conception, opinion, view, surmise, conclusion, judgment, impression, fancy, apprehension, presumption, supposition, presupposition, assumption, axiom, acceptance, suspicion, convincement, plerophory, mind, thinking, hypothesis, postulation, theory, thesis, theorem, conjecture, guess, divination, deduction, inference, notion.
2. *(Often in plural)* Religion, persuasion, sect, creed, principles, doctrine, dogma, canon, faith, convictions, tenet, affiliation, confession, symbol, catechism, leaning, profession, cult, communion, denomination, teaching, maxim, article (of faith), rules, way of thinking, declaration.

BELIEVE, *v.* 1. Maintain, trust, assert, credit, hope, think, suppose, guess, acknowledge, deem, consider, presume, judge, regard, fancy, imagine, know, feel, realize, surmise, opine, hold, perceive, understand, apprehend, conceive, be convinced, be certain, accept, postulate, theorize, conjecture, divine, infer, deduce, dare say, take it, be assured, be persuaded, be satisfied.
2. *(With* in *or* on) Trust, confide, put faith in, rely on, depend on, lean upon, cling to, count on, rest assured in, be confident of, calculate on, pin one's faith on, build on, be sure of, swear by, anchor on, **repose in.**

BELITTLE, *v.* 1. Dwarf, make small, decrease, diminish, reduce, lessen, shrink, abridge, shorten, contract, subtract from, compress, retrench, boil down, curtail, attenuate, extenuate, overshadow, narrow, condense, deflate, bedwarf, obtruncate, elide, truncate, shrivel, wither, bate, beggar.
2. Mitigate, make light of, minimize, neglect, underestimate, underrate, undervalue, misprize, underpraise, underreckon, think nothing of, set no store by, ignore, fail to count on.
3. Decry, depreciate, disparage, derogate from, detract from, satirize, lampoon, poke fun at, deride, scorn, disdain, pour scorn upon, jeer at, mock, scoff at, ridicule, discredit, contemn, slight, spurn, laugh at, sneer at, pooh-pooh, humiliate, cheapen, lower, mortify, shame, disgrace, vilify, slur, jibe at, malign, traduce, defame, asperse, misprize, criticize, pull to pieces, brand, slander, libel, calumniate, dispraise, anathematize, carp at, cavil at, caricature.
(See also BACKBITE, *v.)*

BELL, *v.* (See BAY, *v.)*

BELL, *n.* 1. Tocsin, angelus, curfew, carillon, gong, campana, tintinnabulum, chime, buzzer.
2. Alarm, ding-dong, tolling, curfew, chimes, angelus, tocsin, tintinnabulation, siren, carillon, signal, hooter, gong, whistle, ringing, pealing, campana.

BELLE, *n.* (See BEAUTY, *n.,* 4)

BELLICOSE, *adj.* Warlike, pugnacious, litigious, belligerent, quarrelsome, contentious, aggressive, martial, militant, warmongering, hostile, warring, unpeaceful, pugilistic, gladiatorial, unfriendly, antagonistic, inimical, petulant, factious, fighting, battling, contending, disputatious, dissentious, perverse, wrangling, combative, opposed, peppery, irascible, irritable, bad *or* ill tempered, captious, fiery, cantankerous, exceptious, fractious, touchy, inaffable, splenetic, testy, angry.

BELLIGERENT, *adj.* 1. Unfriendly, warlike, hostile, etc. (See BELLICOSE, *adj.*)

2. Participating, wrestling, striving, opposed, engaging, active, wrangling, fighting, contending, rival, enemy, combatant, combating, struggling, disputant, polemic, competing.

BELLOW, *v.* (See BAWL, *v.*, 1)

BELL-TOWER, *n.* (See BELFRY, *n.*)

BELLY, *n.* 1. Abdomen, stomach, paunch, craw, intestines, venter, front, corporation (*colloq.*), epigastrium, vitals, entrails, ingluvies (*Zool.*), gizzard (*of birds*), crop (*of birds*), maw, guts (*now coarse*), chitterlings (*of animals*), underpart.

2. Appetite, desire, hunger, etc. (See APPETITE, *n.*)

3. Depths, bowels, interior, recesses, abysses, deepest parts, inmost parts, interior, innermost recesses, cavities.

BELLY, *v.* (See BAG, *v.*, 1)

BELONG, *v.* (*Usually followed by* to) 1. Be an attribute *or* adjunct of, appertain, relate, bear upon, form part of, merge with, be a component of, be part of, inhere in, be a constituent of, interpenetrate, permeate, be pertinent to, apply to, correlate with, tend to, concern, have to do with, affect, have respect to, touch upon, have relationship to, have applicability to, regard, be associated with, be affiliated with, be allied to, refer to, be linked *or* joined to, be appurtenant to, be appendant to, attach to, adhere to, go with.

2. Be the property of, be in the possession of, be owned by, be in the hands of, be at the disposal of, be the right of, be vested in, be occupied by, be held by, be enjoyed by.
(See also BELONGINGS, *n.*)

3. Be a member of, be allied to, be linked with, be akin to, be related to, be the same family as, be included in, range with, be bound to, be contained in, owe allegiance *or* support to, be classified *or* counted among.

BELONGINGS, *n.* Property, goods, accessories, things, possessions, chattels, appendages, effects, movables, appurtenances, paraphernalia, gear, equipment, holdings, assets, accoutrements, stuff, personalty (*Leg.*).

BELOVED, *adj.* Favorite, loved, dear, precious, popular, darling, pet, hallowed, respected, doted on, admired, worshipped, idolized, treasured, revered, cherished, prized, highly valued, well liked, endeared, esteemed, highly regarded, cared for, favored, nearest to one's heart, dearest, fondled, caressed, cosseted.

BELOVED, *n.* (See BEAU, *n.*, 2)

BELOW, *adv.* and *prep.* 1. Lower than, beneath, down, downwards, under, underneath, subjacent to, downstairs, belowstairs, sub- (*Comb. form*).

2. On earth, in this world, under the sun, here below, in this vale of tears, in this life, in one's mortal flesh *or* mortal coil.

3. In Hell, in Hades, etc. (See Hell, *n.*)

4. (*Prep. only*) Lower than, inferior to, less, than, secondary to, subordinate to, subservient to, under, beneath, subject to.

5. Unworthy of, unbecoming of, discreditable to, unbefitting, degrading to, debasing to, not becoming *or* behooving (see BEHOOVE, *v.*), shameful to.

BELT, *n.* 1. Girdle, sash, cummerbund, etc. (See BAND, *n.*, 2)

2. Zone, area, tract, region, strip, layer, band, circle, tropic, circuit, zonule, zonula (*L.*), circlet, circumference, perimeter, meridian, cingulum (Zool.), zodiac, sphere, latitude, cordon, areola.

BELT, *v.* 1. Begird, encircle, girdle, etc. (See BEGIRD, *v.*)

2. Thrash, flay, pelt, etc. (See BEAT, *v.*, 1)

BEMIRE, *v.* (See BEGRIME, *v.*)

BEMOAN, *v.* Wail, moan, groan, lament, fret over, bewail, rend the air, mourn, sorrow, regret, deplore, grieve, cry about, wring one's hands, sob about, tear one's hair, complain, beat one's breast, languish over, pine about, yearn over, repine, whimper about, shriek *or* yell *or* howl *or* squawk *or* squall *or* yelp *or* screech about, shed tears for, sigh *or* suspire for, express pity for.

BEMUSE, *v.* Confuse, muddle, stupefy, etc. (See BEFUDDLE, *v.*, 2)

BENCH, *n.* 1. Seat, pew, stool, settee, settle, long seat, form, ottoman, box, bank, dickey, stall.

2. Counter, board, table, trestle, workbench.

3. Tribunal, court, etc. (See BAR, *n.*, 5)

BEND, *v.* 1. Turn, twist, loop, deflect, worm (*Naut.*), reel, wind, curve, warp, crimp, crinkle, arch, inflect, crook, camber, pervert, contort, flex, circle, wheel, coil, curl, incline, buckle, swerve, serpentine, detour, meander, incurvate, sinuate, veer, round, put about, slue, fork, spiral, bifurcate, diverge, divaricate, ramify, branch, zigzag.

2. Stoop, bow, genuflect, lean, give way to, salaam, curtsy, scrape, kowtow (*Chin.*), bend the knee to, prostrate, kneel, show obeisance *or* reverence, cower, crouch, level oneself, incline the head, uncover, pay homage to, grovel, fawn, toady, lick the feet of, crawl to, truckle to.

3. Yield, submit, succumb, defer to, accede, give, give in, relax, relent, soften, mellow, falter, capitulate, surrender, comply, do one's bidding, unbend, resign.

4. Subjugate, conquer, overcome, force one's will upon, persuade, sway, compel, shape, dispose, rule, dominate, domineer, master, gain the upper hand *or* better of, prevail over, override, coerce, predominate, control, govern, overpower, make a puppet of, boss, lead by the nose, twist around one's little finger, mould, influence, incline, direct, actuate, bias, overbear.

5. Apply oneself to, buckle to, attend to, look after, pay attention, strain at, occupy oneself with, turn to, heed, mind, be engaged in, become absorbed in, give one's mind to, devote oneself to, buckle down, set one's shoulder to the wheel, set one's mind on, lean to, advert to, give oneself to, throw oneself into, put one's heart into, exert oneself, strive, wade through, work, toil, labor, fag, drudge, sweat at, slave, moil, bestir oneself, busy oneself with, peg away, plod, slog at, persist, persevere, stick at, tackle vigorously *or* diligently, be strongly disposed *or* inclined to.

BENEATH, *prep.* (See BELOW, *prep.* and *adv.*)

BENEDICTION, *n.* Closing prayer, prayer, blessing, invocation, grace, dedication, benison. (See also PRAYER, *n.*)

BENEFACTION, *n.* Gift, present, gratuity, alms,

bounty, donation, liberality, offering, charity, endowment, bequest, benefit, oblation, bestowal, boon, presentation, conferment, dispensation, almsgiving, generosity, philanthropy, subsidy, aid, benevolence, contribution, help, succor, relief, sportula, largess, favor, subvention, devise, legacy, award, beneficence, subscription.
(See also BENEVOLENCE, *n.*)

BENEFICE, *n.* Rectory, vicarage, curacy, diocese, pastorate, see, bishopric, archbishopric, prebend, preferment, provostship, sinecure, primacy, parish, episcopate, deanery, chaplaincy, abbacy.

BENEFICENCE, *n.* (See BENEVOLENCE, *n.*)

BENEFICIAL, *adj.* Healthful, desirable, salutary, propitious, wholesome, favorable, benign, helpful, advantageous, beneficent, profitable, serviceable, curative, valuable, useful, improving, fortunate, pleasant, pleasing, suitable, good, agreeable, fit, congenial, edifying, compatible, gainful, availing, invaluable, commodious, convenient, conducive, contributive, efficacious, lucrative, remunerative, proficuous, salubrious, bracing, tonic, healing, invigorating, sanative, salutiferous, balsamic, anodyne, restorative, remedial, nutritious, paying, auspicious, productive.
(See also SOOTHING, *adj.*)

BENEFICIARY, *n.* Receiver, recipient, legatee, heir, donee, grantee, possessor, inheritor, assignee (*Leg.*), feoffee (*Leg.*), dower, accipient, devisee, stipendiary, releasee, almsman, pensioner.

BENEFIT, *n.* 1. Gift, gratuity, alms, etc. (See BENEFACTION, *n.*)
2. Profit, advantage, welfare, betterment, gain, help, aid, promotion, good, interest, behoof, favor, improvement, behalf, emolument, enjoyment, use, well-being, convenience, consumption, service, utilization, harvest, good fortune, blessing, value, edification, reward, remuneration, return, prize, recompense, guerdon.

BENEVOLENCE, *n.* 1. Bountifulness, love, good, will, mercy, generosity, humanism, cordiality, munificence, liberality, kindliness, beneficence, assistance, charity, humaneness, sympathy, good nature, compassion, clemency, goodness, favor, Samaritanism, consideration, amiability, succor, helpfulness, friendship, kindness, support, kind treatment, benignity, patronage, benignancy, good works, graciousness, obligingness, philanthropy, altruism, tolerance, charitableness, almsgiving, unselfishness, tenderness, humanity, good deeds.
2. Contribution, gift, alms, donation, etc.
(See BENEFACTION, *n.*)

BENIGN, *adj.* (See BENEVOLENT, *adj.*)

BENIGNANCY, *n.* (See BENEVOLENCE, *n.*)

BENT, *adj.* (See BEND, *v.*)

BENT, *n.* Aptness, aptitude, trend, susceptibility, flection, disposition, inclination, ability, liability, tendency, direction, affection, mind, genius, flair, gift, ply, conatus, conation, attraction, turn, set, appetency, proneness, twist, temperament, liking, fondness, feeling, facility, skill, adroitness, bias, proficiency, competence, partiality, predilection, knack, capacity, predisposition, proclivity, leaning, faculty, propensity, capability, prepossession, penchant, endowment, prejudice.

BENUMB, *v.* Drug, dull, stun, numb, anesthetize, hypnotize, obtund, stupefy, petrify, paralyze, deaden, freeze, blunt, chill, narcotize, hebetate, mesmerize, make stupid, daze, obfuscate, stagger, lethargize, electrify, make torpid, reel, magnetize.

BEQUEATH, *v.* 1. Leave, endow, settle upon, will, devise, demise.
2. Give, donate, bestow, accord, grant, award, confer, apportion, allot, assign, present, impart, dispense, deliver to, transfer, transmit, turn over, consign, cede, render, communicate, commit, entrust.
(See also BESTOW, *v.* 2)

BEQUEST, *n.* Legacy, will, dot, dowery, dower, devise, heritage, devisal, fideicommissum, gift, dotation, endowing, endowment, voluntary settlement, appanage, settlement.
(See also BEQUEATH, *v.*)

BERATE, *v.* Chide, reprove, censure, upbraid, scold, reprimand, blame, condemn, denounce, reprobate, rebuke, reproach, reprove, tongue lash, admonish, execrate, objurgate, vituperate, rate, browbeat, fulminate against, dispraise, disparage, depreciate, deprecate, animadvert on, chastise, castigate, stigmatize, defame, bawl out (*colloq.*), express disapprobation of.
(See also ASPERSE, *v.*)

BEREAVE, *v.* Deprive, dispossess, steal, make destitute of, wrench from, wrest from, take away from, afflict with a loss, despoil, strip.
(See also BEREAVEMENT, *n.*)

BEREAVEMENT, *n.* Deprivation, loss, mourning, privation, sorrow, grief, affliction, adversity, blow, distress, anguish, hardship, tragedy, tribulation, misfortune, trouble.

BERTH, *n.* 1. (*Naut.*) Anchorage, dock, harbor, wharf, pier, landing stage, port, quay, dry dock, floating dock, haven, graving dock, jetty, mole, resting place.
2. Bed, bunk, etc. (See BED, *n.* 1)
3. Billet, job, situation, employ, engagement, living, office, incumbency, place, position, post, appointment, capacity.
4. Lodgings, quarters, billet, apartment, seat, domicile, habitation, abode, dwelling, residence, nest, housing, house, home, diggings (*colloq.*), address, lair, den, cell, retreat, tent, barrack, camp, shelter, encampment, bivouac, cantonment.

BESEECH, *v.* (See ADJURE, *v.* and BEG, *v.*, 1)

BESEEM, *v.* (See BEHOOVE, *v.*)

BESET, *v.* 1. Besiege, encompass, surround, begird, etc. (See BELEAGUER, *v.*, 1 and 2)
2. Harass, perplex, worry, etc. (See BADGER, *v.*)
3. Fix, deck, beautify, enrich, dress up, set, trim, bestud, array, bedeck, bedizen, bestick, stud, prink, gild, spangle, bespangle, smarten, bead, embroider, furbish, emboss, fret, embellish, ornament, garnish, decorate, emblazon, blazon, illuminate.

BESIDE, *prep.* 1. Near by, close at hand, close to, by, with, alongside, adjacent to, next to, close upon, abreast, next door to, cheek by jowl, side by side, but a step from, on the verge *or* brink of, at the door of, at one's elbow, in juxtaposition with, bordering upon.
2. Over and above. (See BESIDES, *adv.*)

BESIDES, *adv. & prep.* Moreover, over and above, beyond that, into the bargain, aside from, in addition to, as well as, other than, not counting, also, furthermore, additionally, likewise, further, to boot, too, else, in conjunction with, together with, along with, conjointly.

BESIEGE, *v.* (See BELEAGUER, *v.*)

BESMEAR, *v.*
(See BEDAUB, *v.*, 1 & BEGRIME, *v.*)

BESMIRCH, *v.* (See BEGRIME, *v.*)

BESOT, *v.* (See BEFUDDLE, *v.*, 2)

BESPATTER, *v.* 1. Soil, sully, etc. (See BEDAUB, *v.*, 1)

2. Slander, abuse, defame, etc. (See ASPERSE, *v.*)

BESPEAK, *v.* 1. Foretell, predict, prophesy, portend, augur, presage, forecast, prognosticate, foresee, read, forewarn, signify, point to, divine, auspicate, declare, intimate, hint at, proclaim, herald, announce, advise, bode, foreknow, be the precursor, forebode, foreshow, foretoken, have a presentiment of, soothsay, prefigure, foreshadow.

2. Betoken, indicate, imply, proclaim, declare, evince, show, signify, mean, express, purport, import, point to, denote, suggest, symbolize, reflect, connote, intimate, manifest, tell of, affirm, breathe, testify, bear witness to, attest to, reveal, give a token *or* sign of, disclose, exhibit, display, represent, demonstrate, betray, savor of.

3. Stipulate for, solicit, speak for, request, ask for, reserve, requisition, bid for, secure, sue for, engage, order, pre-engage, arrange for, procure, assure, obtain.

BESPRINKLE, *v.* (See BEDEW, *v.*)

BEST, *adj.* (superl. of GOOD. See GOOD, *adj.*)

BEST, *v.* Conquer, overcome, surpass, etc. (See BEAT, *v.* 5 and 6)

BESTIAL, *adj.* (See BEASTLY, *adj.*)

BESTIR, *v.* Stir up, stir, move, rouse, vivify, awaken, rouse to action, speed, hasten, bustle, fuss, hustle, hurry, scurry, scuttle, scramble, quicken, accelerate, spur, urge, press, drive, hie, goad, prod, agitate, be busy, be lively, exert oneself, disturb, stimulate, jostle, shake, animate, inspire, strive, excite, prick, incite, speed, prompt, arouse, push, push forward, poke, jolt, set going, start.

BESTOW, *v.* 1. Use, apply, spend, utilize, put to task, occupy, turn to account, consume, expend, put to advantage *or* profit, direct, devote, employ, adopt, administer, dispose of, adhibit.

2. Give, give away, grant, impart, confer, present, endow, afford, vouchsafe, award, thrust upon, pour upon, favor, deliver, hand, pass, turn over to, dole, mete, donate, assign, yield, cede, concede, consign, bequeath, shower (down) upon, divide, dispense, distribute, subscribe, settle upon, lavish, deal out, apportion, allot, render to, commit, entrust.

BESTRADDLE, *v.* (See BESTRIDE, *v.*)

BESTREW, *v.* Scatter, disseminate, broadcast, sow, radiate, propagate, diffuse, spread, shed, strew, cast, sprinkle, spatter, distribute, ted, overspread, circulate, dispense, disperse, cast forth, circumfuse.

BESTRIDE, *v.* 1. Bestraddle, arch over, straddle, cross, ride *or* sit *or* stand astride of, ride, perch, mount.

2. Stride, mount, cross, traverse, pace-, tread-, walk-, step-, stump-, march-, plod-, stalk-, trudge-, *or* jump over.

BET, *n.* Gamble, blind bargain, plunge, risk, chance, pledge, toss up *(colloq.)*, speculation, venture, sweepstake, random shot, lottery, wager, ante, blind, stake, flier *(slang)*, hazard, betting, fall of the dice, pitch and toss, luck, fortune, lot, game of chance, pig in a poke, uncertainty, shot in the dark, raffle, odds, long shot, chance-medley.

BET, *v.* Gamble, punt, lay, wager, make a bet, stake, speculate, risk, chance, toss up *(colloq.)*, venture, hazard, trust, tempt fortune, game, play for, put up *(colloq.)*, put money down, cover *(with money)*, dice.
(See also BET, *n.*)

BETIDE, *v.* (See BECHANCE, *v.*)

BETOKEN, *v.* 1. Signify, denote, indicate, etc. (See BESPEAK, *v.*, 2)

2. Foreshadow, foretell, presage, etc. (See BESPEAK, *v.*, 1)

BETRAY, *v.* 1. Mislead, delude, deceive, trap, ensnare, etc. (See BAMBOOZLE, *v.*, 1)

2. Reveal, disclose, give away, show, lay bare, discover, let the cat out of the bag *(colloq.)*, blab *(colloq.)*, inform against, expose, divulge, let slip, bare, bring to light, blurt out, vent, whisper about, unmask, uncover, reveal the secrets of, tell, violate a confidence, double cross *(slang)*.

3. Deliver into the hands of the enemy, let down, sell, sell out *(colloq.)*, play Judas, deliver up, play false, trick, knife *or* stab in the back, break faith with, give the Judas kiss to, break one's promise, be false-hearted to, go over to the enemy.

4. Seduce, dishonor, jilt, abandon, beguile, lure, deceive, undo, delude, inveigle, play one false, disgrace, lead astray, entice, lure with cajolery *or* blandishments, use honeyed words, violate, ruin, debauch, defile, abase, deflower, corrupt.

BETRAYAL, *n.* Bad faith, breach of faith, revolt, treachery, treason, double-crossing *(colloq.)*, perfidy, faithlessness, disloyalty, sedition, mutiny, rebellion, insurrection, subversion, revolution, revolt, double-dealing, duplicity, intrigue, Judas kiss, falseness, Iscariotism, chicanery.

BETRAYER, *n.* Traitor, false friend, renegade, Judas, recreant, archtraitor, plotter, complotter, conspirator, Catilinarian.
(See also BETRAY, *v.*)

BETROTH, *v.* Engage, promise, contract, plight, affiance, bind, espouse, pledge, plight faith, pledge (in marriage), tie *or* commit oneself to, undertake to marry, give one's hand, bestow one's hand upon, publish the banns, affy.

BETROTHAL, *n.* Contract, engagement, bond, promise, espousal, sponsalia, betrothing, vow, plighting, alliance, covenant, handfast, obligation, subarrhation, marriage compact, betrothment, match.
(See also BETROTH, *v.*)

BETTER, *adj.* (comparative of GOOD, *adj.*) Superior, excelling, surpassing, preferable, more acceptable. (See GOOD, *adj.*)

BETTER, *v.* 1. Ameliorate, promote, meliorate, help, correct, remedy, rectify, redress, enhance, improve, heighten, exalt, aggrandize, relieve, mend, repair, advance, restore, enrich, mellow, refine, develop, cultivate, strengthen, revivify, refresh, recreate, invigorate, freshen, forward, further, emend, polish, reform, remodel, uplift, reconstruct, refashion, ennoble, raise, regenerate, make over, touch up, brush up, brighten up, cure, redact, heal, rebuild, reorganize, renew, revive, recondition, temper, mitigate, palliate, increase.

2. Excel, surpass, exceed, etc. (See BEAT, *v.*, 6)

BETTER, *n.* Wagerer, gambler, speculator, sport, hazarder, gamester, bookmaker, bookie *(colloq.)*, punter, dicer, venturer, layer, backer, adventurer, manipulator. (See also BET, v.)

BETWEEN, *prep.* Amidst, among, betwixt, in between, amid, in the thick of, at intervals, in the midst of, midway, halfway, interjacent to, 'mid, sandwich-wise to.

BEVEL, *n.* Angle, slant, inclination, incline, list, slope, skew, obliquity, leaning, bezel, ramp, tilt, bias, cant, declination, bend, chamfer.

BEVERAGE, *n.* Potables, liquor, drink, draft, broth, soup, swill, nip, dram.

BEVY, *n.* 1. Flock, shoal, swarm, covey, pack, drove, herd, flight, school, kennel, array, cluster, pack, hive, litter, brood, farrow, nest, cloud. (See also below, 2)
(Of women)
2. Assemblage, collection, company, group, squad, crowd, knot, gathering, gaggle, throng, multitude, rush, deluge, mob, press, horde, body, tribe, crew, gang, band, party, galaxy, troop, host, force, army, legion, sea.

BEWAIL, *v.* (See BEMOAN, *v.*)

BEWARE, *v.* *(Usually followed by* lest, of, how, that)
Take heed, watch, be on one's guard, be careful, look out, mind, avoid, shun, be cautious, take warning, be wary, take precautions, be prepared, be forewarned *or* prewarned, be on the alert, think twice, look before one leaps, count the cost, keep at a respectful distance, keep out of harm's way, be on the safe side, be guarded, be wary, be stealthy *or* chary, shy off, be circumspect *or* prudent.

BEWILDER, *v.* (See BAFFLE, *v.* 2)

BEWITCH, *v.*
(See BECHARM, *v.* and BEDEVIL, *v.*)

BEYOND, *adv & prep.* Far, farther, yonder, at a distance, abroad, far off, far away, away, beyond range, out of range, far and wide, farthest, aloof from, ultimate, extreme, remotest, wide of, clear of, distant from, a good *or* great *or* long way off, out of the way *or* reach of, further, over the border of, out of touch with, out of the sphere of, wide of the mark, outside, apart, asunder, at arm's length.

BIAS, *n.* 1. Angle, slope, inclination, etc. (See BEVEL, *n.*)
2. Bent, disposition, propensity, prejudice, tendency, misjudgment, misconstruction, hasty conclusion, miscalculation, misconception, fixed idea, preconception, predilection, preconceived idea, obsession, partiality, one-sidedness, favor, warp, twist, fad, aversion, leaning, proneness, prenotion, whim, craze, quirk, crotchet, blind eye, whimsey, perverse fancy, blind side, narrow view, narrow mind, obstinacy, intolerance, dogmatism, bigotry, opinionativeness.
3. Turn, ability, aptitude, facility, skill, etc. (See BENT, *n.*)

BIB, *n.* Apron, pinafore, napkin, chemisette, tucker, dickey.

BIBLE, *n.* 1. *(Used with the prefixed)*
Holy Scripture, the Good Book, the Book of books, Holy Writ, the Gospel, the Word of God, the Scriptures, Good Tidings, Glad Tidings, the Old and New Testaments, inspired writings.
2. Handbook, manual, text, authority, primer, guidebook, vade mecum, treatise, text, textbook, enchiridion.

BIBLIOGRAPHY, *n.* List, catalog, compilation,

compendium, history *or* account of books, booklore.

BIBLIOPHILE, *n.* Book-lover, book-worm, bibliomaniac, bibliolater, bibliognost, bibliopole, antiquary, bibliomanian, bibliosoph, bibliotaph.

BIBULOUS, *adj.* 1. Drunken, drinking, sottish, bibacious, given *or* addicted to drink, intemperate, tippling, carousing, soaking, cup-loving, guzzling, bacchanalian, revelling, wassailing, bacchant, convivial, frolicking, merrymaking, alcoholic, dipsomaniacal.
2. Assimilating, imbibing, soaking, absorbent, sorbefacient *(Med.)*, receptive, absorbefacient, porous, absorptive, spongy, permeable, pervious.

BICKER, *v.* 1. Contend, wrangle, dispute, argue, litigate, altercate, agitate, dissent, be at variance, be at loggerheads, quarrel, squabble, spat, tiff, spar, jangle, brawl, conflict, clash, jar, disagree, differ, controvert, row *(colloq.)*, nag, fall out, have words, bandy words, fence, tilt, scrap, fight, battle. (See also BATTLE, *v.*, 1)
2. Flutter, shake, quiver, agitate, flicker, quaver, shudder, quake, tremble, vibrate, shiver, oscillate, convulse, flap, wag, waggle, flitter, flit, totter, teeter, shimmy, didder, vacillate, waver, fluctuate, reel, undulate, wave, librate, twitter, dodder, potter, stagger, sway, wiggle.

BICYCLE, *n.* Velocipede, cycle, tandem, bike *(colloq.).*

BID, *v.* 1. Promise, propose, suggest, advance, submit, extend, bestow, proffer, offer, volunteer, tender, pay, be willing to pay.
2. Instruct, charge, dictate, adjure, conjure, admonish, command, direct, enjoin, decree, enact, ordain, prescribe, set, give orders, require, exact, demand, summon, call, appoint, tax, task, insist upon, cite, beckon, rule.

BIDDING, *n.* Bid, command, invitation, request, summons, mandate, behest, desire, dictate, order, charge, commandment, instruction, injunction, direction, summoning, call, citation, convening, convoking, evoking, eliciting, educing, enjoining, word, requisition, appointment, ordinance, beck, regulation, nod, precept, claim, demand, exaction.

BIER, *n.* Coffin, litter, feretory, catafalque, pyre, hearse, funeral pile, casket, sarcophagus, pall.

BIG, *adj.* 1. Corpulent, fat, fleshy, etc. (See BEEFY, *adj.*)
2. Bulky, massive, huge, large, grand, great, immense, tall, ample, spacious, extensive, gross, mighty, stout, massy, strapping, bumper, sizable, considerable, substantial, voluminous, capacious, towering, enormous, gigantic, Titanic, monstrous, vast, stupendous, elephantine, mammoth, giant, colossal, Brobdingnagian, Gargantuan, abundant, prodigious, Cyclopean, comprehensive, monster, imposing, grandiose, majestic, august, whacking, overgrown, thumping.
3. Important, chief, top, main, leading, high, eminent, elevated, exalted, foremost, momentous, grand, supreme, head, distinguished, significant, consequential, weighty, notable, esteemed, vital, famous, well-known, illustrious, renowned, prime, noteworthy, influential, powerful, outstanding, dignified, prominent, material, considerable, marked, salient, paramount, essential, principal, radical, primary, capital.
4. Magnanimous, great, noble, honorable, just, magnificent, glorious, majestic, splendid, superb, generous, high-minded, unselfish, benevolent, gracious, kind, forgiving, humane, altruistic,

liberal, self-denying, fair, impartial, unbiased, unprejudiced, princely, chivalrous, heroic, lofty, sublime, exalted, handsome.
(See also BENEVOLENCE, *n.*)

BIGHT, *n.* Bay, inlet, creek, etc. (See BAY, *n.,* 1)

BIGOT, *n.* Enthusiast, partisan, zealot, devotee, dogmatist, formalist, adherent, Pharisee, fanatic, sectary, puritan, ranter, precisian, stickler, know-all, die-hard, monomaniac.

BIGOTED, *adj.* Prejudiced, intolerant, etc. (See BIAS, *n.,* 2)

BILK, *v.* Cheat, defraud, swindle, etc. (See BAMBOOZLE, *v.,* 1)

BILL, *n.* Beak, nib, rostrum, etc. (See BEAK, *n.*)

BILL, *n.* 1. Account, tally, reckoning, amount, check, charges, statement, list, expenditures, note, expenses, score, record, draft, accounts payable, invoice, cost, figure, demand, dues, manifest, bill of lading, budget, fee.
2. Placard, poster, handbill, billboard, leaflet, hoarding, advertistment, broadside, affiche *(Fr.),* circular, notice, announcement, dodger, folder, broadsheet, encyclical, program, bulletin, brochure.
3. Bank note, treasury note, currency, paper money, greenback, silver certificate.
4. I.O.U., promissory note, bond, debenture, evidence of debt, draft, pledge, tie, chit.
5. Measure, act, protocol, legislation, law, statute, regulation, decree, rule, enactment, fiat, charter, canon, institution, ordinance, instrument, proclamation, decision, precept, mandate, bylaw.
6. Schedule, program, list, prospectus, agenda, card, panel, poll, muster, roster, register, outline, sketch, calendar, docket, scheme, cadre, catalog, inventory, enumeration, syllabus, ticket, contents, synopsis, table, index.

BILL, *v.* 1. Make a bill, etc. (See BILL, *n.*)
2. Kiss, fondle, embrace, hug, caress, smile upon, pet, make love to, cuddle, clasp, snuggle, court, trifle, dally, woo, nestle, nuzzle, cosset, osculate.

BILLET, *n.* Quarters, lodgings, etc. (See BERTH, *n.,* 4)

BILLFOLD, *n.* Wallet, purse, pocketbook, pocket, handbag, card case.

BILLOW, *n.* Wave, breaker, etc. (See BEACHCOMBER, *n.,* 1)

BILLOWY, *adj.* Waving, rolling, surging, rising, undulating, heaving, tossing, rippling, undulant, swelling, rising and falling, ebbing and flowing, swirling.

BIMONTHLY, *adj.* Appearing every two months, bimestrial, bimensal.

BIN, *n.* Box, crib, frame, enclosure, receptacle, hutch, hold, container, caddy, casket, hamper, rack, canister, can.

BIND, *v.* 1. Pinion, chain, enchain, fetter, gyve, enfetter, shackle, constrict, astrict, trammel, tie, hamper, manacle, muzzle, tether, hitch, fasten, secure, pin, fix, tape, attach, join, connect, strap, tighten, lash, lace, buckle, truss, splice, bracket, moor, hook, yoke, couple, interlock, interlace, weave, entwine, plait, string, leash, bridle, hobble, hopple, pin *or* peg down, handcuff.
2. Restrain, obligate, restrict, limit, constrain, hold, hamper, hinder, force, impel, press, enforce, inhibit, encumber, handicap, burden, cramp, clog, cumber, confine, bound, stint.

3. Impose a duty *or* responsibility *or* obligation, require, necessitate, stipulate, prescribe, assign, oblige, condition, insist upon, tie up, have strings attached *(coll.),* have provision.
4. Bandage, swathe, wrap, etc. (See BANDAGE, *v.*)
5. Stick, solidify, cohere, set, gel, agglutinate, stick together, hold fast, adhere, cake, congeal, clot, coagulate, glue, cement, paste, consolidate, gum, thicken, curdle, inspissate, harden, stiffen, conglutinate, lute, compact, constipate, gelatinize, jellify, fuse, coalesce, merge, blend, combine, connect, unite, agglomerate.
6. Edge, rim, border, fringe, hem, marginate, margin, trim, garnish, line, purfle, purl.
7. Incase, cover, put a jacket on, sew into boards.

BIOGRAPHY, *n.* Life story, personal narrative, life, personal account, diary, journal, personal record, life history, memoir *or* memoirs, experiences, adventures, confessions, fortunes, autobiography *(of oneself).*

BIOLOGY, *n.* Science of life, natural history, nature study, natural science, life lore.

BIRD, *n.* Fledgling, warbler, songster, feathered tribe *(pl.),* fowl, avifauna *(pl.),* cageling *(spec. one confined in a cage).*

BIRTH, *n.* 1. Origin, source, start, etc. (See BEGINNING, *n.,* 2)
2. Genesis, nativity, parturition, confinement, delivery, childbirth. (See BEARING, *n.,* 6)
3. Background, parentage, ancestry, pedigree, extraction, stock, house, line, blood, stirps, race, family, derivation, descent, blood line, genealogy, strain, affiliation, origin, lineage.
(See also GENEALOGY, *n.*)

BIRTHDAY, *n.* Anniversary, natal day, birthday celebration.

BIRTHMARK, *n.* Nevus *(Med.),* blemish, blot, disfigurement, mole, patch, freckle, macule *or* macula, cicatrice *(from a scar),* maculation, lentigo.

BIRTHRIGHT, *n.* Right, inheritance, heritage, legacy,[t] prerogative, patrimony, primogeniture, privilege, due, droit *(Leg.).*

BISCUIT, *n.* Cracker, bun, cookie, pretzel, rusk, cracknel, muffin, scone, zwieback.

BISECT, *v.* Divide, halve, cut in two, separate equally, split, cleave, dimidiate, dichotomize, hemisect.

BISEXUAL, *adj.* Hermaphrodite, hermaphroditic, epicene, androgynous, gynandrous, monoclinous *(Bot.).*

BISHOP, *n.* Prelate, divine, pontiff, archbishop, primate, coadjutor, exarch *(Eastern Ch.),* angel, diocesan, suffragan, metropolitan.

BISHOPRIC, *n.* See, diocese, primacy, prelacy, archbishopric, episcopate, episcopature, prelature, episcopacy, archiepiscopacy, pontificate, prelate-ship, bishopdom.

BIT, *n.* 1. Piece, slice, portion, part, fragment, trace, fraction, segment, item, lump, chip, chunk, scrap, sample, cantle, moiety, installment, cut, sector, subdivision, division, share, dose, morsel, particular, collop, taste, mouthful, shard, detail, snatch, paring, shaving, drop, rasher, snip, scale, shred, splinter, gob *(coll.),* remnant, hunk *(coll.),* stub, stump, butt. (See also below 2)
2. Mote, mite, trifle, speck, snippet, particle, molecule, jot, iota, smitch, smidgen, whit, tittle,

grain, ace, crumb, modicum, minimum, atom, corpuscle, point, dot, dab, tinge, pinch, scintilla, sliver, scrap, fleck, touch, minutia (*chiefly pl.* minutiae), drop, droplet, sip, spice, tincture, tag, driblet, splinter, shive, shadow, spark, gleam, suspicion, granule, sup, sprinkling, sop, pittance, seed, fritter, hair.

BITCH, *n.* Slut, female dog, gyp, lewd woman. (See WHORE.)

BITE, *v.* 1. Chew, masticate, gnaw, nibble, eat, crunch, munch, snap, nip, champ, ruminate, mumble.
    2. Smart, sting, pain, burn, nettle, prick, cut, nip, gripe, gall, fret, grate, chafe, agonize, eat into, corrode, stab, grind, convulse, rub, tweak, pinch, lancinate, excruciate, rack, torture.
    3. Corrode, eat away, burn, sear, erode, rust, dissolve, deteriorate, decay, wear away, oxidize, consume, gnaw, rot.
    4. Pierce, puncture, etc. (See STAB, *v.*)
    5. Defraud, cheat, swindle, etc. (See BAMBOOZLE, *v.*, 1)

BITING, *adj.* Caustic, cutting, sarcastic, etc. (See BITTER, *adj.*, 4)

BITTER, *adj.* 1. Acrid, astringent, sour, unsweet, acid, acidulous, constringent, unpalatable, nasty, disagreeable, unsavory, distasteful, acrimonious, tasting like gall *or* vinegar, subacid, acerb, harsh, vinegarish, unpleasant, unlikable, unappetizing.
    2. Cross, mean, unkind, etc. (See BEARISH, *adj.*)
    3. Painful, sad, poignant, tragic, tearful, grim, mournful, sorrowful, grievous, dejecting, onerous, distressing, lamentable, burdensome, calamitous, afflicting, unhappy, dreadful, ruinous, disastrous, desolate, oppressive. (See *also* SAD, *adj.*)
    4. Sarcastic, keen, cutting, biting, severe, acid, virulent, scathing, unkind, caustic, acrimonious, burning, corrosive, mordant, crusty, tart, sour, crabbed, sharp, trenchant, venomous, splenetic, contumelious, scornful, hurtful, brutal, smarting, stern, harsh, austere, stinging, painful, pricking, pungent, pointed, violent, malicious, rancorous, unamiable, uncharitable, spiteful, malevolent, maleficent, despiteful, envenomed, invidious, grinding, galling.

BIVOUAC, *n.* Quarters, lodging, etc. (See BERTH, *n.* 4)

BIWEEKLY, *adj.* Fortnightly, semiweekly, twice monthly.

BIZARRE, *adj.* Outlandish, strange, odd, etc. (See BAROQUE, *adj.*, 2)

BLAB, *v.* Chatter, gab, gush, etc. (See BABBLE, *v.*, 1)

BLACK, *adj.* 1. Dark, jet, raven, sable (*Poet.*), ebony, coal-black, sooty, swarthy, inky, murky, livid, somber, atramentous, ink-like, nigrescent, swart, pitchy, of the deepest dye *or* color, dusky, dingy, pitchy, nigrous, nigritudinous, nigrine, blackish.
    2. Evil, wicked, nefarious, etc. (See BAD, *adj.*, 2)
    3. Threatening, oppressive, unpropitious, etc. (See BAD, *adj.*, 4)
    4. Dark, smoky, cloudy, Stygian, sooty, dirty, sunless, gloomy, overcast, overclouded, grimy, murky, dusky, sullen, Cimmerian, shadowy, dim, lowering, leaden, obscure, dingy, lightless, shady, tenebrous, unilluminated, rayless, somber, lurid, umbrageous, caliginous, tenebrose, unlighted, moonless, starless, nubilous. (See also OPAQUE, *adj.*)

BLACKBALL, *v.* Ostracize, cast out, debar, etc. (See BAN, *v.*)

BLACKEN, *v.* 1. Calumniate, slander, backbite, etc. (See ASPERSE, *v.*)
    2. Stain, sully, tarnish, etc. (See BEGRIME, *v.*)

BLACKGUARD, *n.* Scoundrel, knave, rascal, etc. (See BEGGAR, *n.*, 2)

BLACKGUARD, *v.* (See ASPERSE, *v.*)

BLACKMAIL, *n.* 1. Extortion, squeezing, shakedown (*slang*).
    2. Tribute, ransom, hush money, protection, bribe.

BLACKNESS, *n.* (See BLACK, *adj.*)

BLACK SHEEP, *n.* Scapegrace, outcast, pariah, n'er do well, reprobate, prodigal, recreant, roué, good-for-nothing, debauchee, wastrel, locust, rake.

BLADDER, *n.* Sac, vesicle, blister, saccule, bag, utricle, cyst, capsule, theca, pocket, sacculus, bleb, vesica (*L.*), sound (*of a fish*), bursa, pericarp, udder.

BLADE, *n.* 1. Frond, lamina, phyllome, needle, bract, petal, leaf, flag, bractlet, sepal, peduncle, leaflet, foliole, sprig, switch, stem, stalk, spray, petiole.
    2. Sword, sabre, cutlass, etc. (See SWORD, *n.*)
    3. Cutting edge, knife, edge tool, razor, lancet, scalpel, bistoury, chisel, cutter, cutlery (*pl.*), penknife, jackknife.

BLAIN, *n.* Sore, boil, pimple, pustule, swelling, blister, ulcer, abscess, gall, fester, eruption, wen, gathering, canker, rash, pock, corn, carbuncle, bunion, wart, papule (*Med.*), wheal, impostume, whitlow, breaking out, excrescence, inflammation, gumboil, whelk, tumor, tumefaction, tumescence, noma, stomatitis (*of the mouth*), ulceration, sarcoma, hive, brash, exanthema.

BLAMABLE, *adj.* Blameworthy, culpable, guilty, faulty, reprehensible, censurable, delinquent, at fault, answerable, uncommendable, reprovable, peccable, illaudable, chargeable, impeachable, accusable, imputable, in the wrong, wrong.

BLAME, *n.* Accusation, reproof, disapprobation, admonition, rebuke, reproach, animadversion, censure, denunciation, stricture, condemnation, criticism, reprehension, castigation, objurgation, chiding, reprobation, frowning upon, attribution, imputation, reflection, disparagement, complaint, expostulation, remonstrance, charge, implication, inculpation, exprobation, incrimination, obloquy, indictment, impeachment, arraignment, diatribe, slur, recrimination, tirade, jeremiad, Philippic.

BLAMELESS, *adj.* Innocent, guiltless, unerring, sinless, clear, unbribed, incorruptible, stainless, uncorrupted, undefiled, childlike, virtuous, good, inculpable, irreproachable, irreprovable, taintless, irreprehensible, unobjectionable, unimpeachable, above suspicion, unspotted, unsoiled, unsullied, unblemished, without sin *or* fault, unoffending, virtuous, moral, upright, incensurable, faultless, sterling, saintly, saint-like, peerless, uniniquitous, matchless, admirable, estimable, unblamable, noble.
    (See also various meanings of GOOD, *adj.*)

BLAMEWORTHY, *adj.* (See BLAMABLE, *adj.*)

BLANCH, *v.* Decolor, decolorize, achromatize, discolor, etiolate, whiten, pale, make white *or* light, bleach, albify, achromatize, silver, besnow, frost, fade, wash out.

BLAND, *adj.* 1. Smooth, soothing, gentle, kindly, soft, quiet, courteous, polite, urbane, civil, even, well-spoken, soft-spoken, mannerly, reverential, cordial, amiable, gracious, obliging, deferential, winsome, winning, tactful, graceful, respectful, benign, benignant, tender, quiet, complaisant, mild, moderate, modulate, equable, untroubled, calm, unruffled, tranquil, peaceful, peaceable.

2. Moderative, soft, balmy, lenitive, calmative, non-irritating, soothing, assuaging, demulcent, smooth, gentle, mollifying, mitigating. (See also BALM, *n.,* 1 & 2)

BLANDISH, *v.* 1. Flatter, wheedle, coax, cajole, compliment, humor, coquet, butter *(coll.),* fawn on, ingratiate, adulate, praise, puff, overpraise, truckle to, pet, beslaver, praise to the skies, curry favor, soft-soap *(coll.).*

2. Tempt, allure, entice, etc. (See BEWITCH, *v.*)

BLANK, *adj.* 1. Plain, desolate, bleak, etc. (See BARE, *adj.,* 4)

2. Pale, white, colorless, unmarked, untouched, clean, unsullied, empty, vacant, clear, unfilled, void, snowy. (See also WHITE, *adj.*)

3. Dazed, nonplused, confounded, etc. (See AMAZED, *adj.*)

4. Staring, gaping, bovine, expressionless, dull, vacuous, vacant, hollow, void, inexpressive, silly, thoughtless, inane, asinine, foolish, incogitant, incogitative, unoccupied, empty.

5. Futile, useless, unrewarding, unproductive, wasted, empty, unavailing, leading nowhere, vain, bootless, fruitless, ill-spent, worthless, valueless, idle, unprofitable, profitless, gainless, nugatory, ineffectual, nugacious, inconsequential, insignificant, uneventful.

BLANK, *n.* 1. Emptiness, vacancy, hollowness, void, vacuum, tabula rasa *(L.),* nullity, nothing, nothingness, nil, zero.

2. Space, gap, break, hiatus, interruption, gulf, interval, caesura, lacuna, separation.

BLANKET, *n.* 1. Cover, comforter, etc. (See BEDDING, *n.*)

2. Cover, wrapper, layer, wrapping, envelope, casing, coating, carpet, muffler, wadding, lining, padding, coverage, coverture, mantle, coat, cloak, overlayer, spread, veneer, film, investment, bed, integument, stratum.

BLARE, *v.* Trumpet, blast, honk, hoot, flourish, toot, sound, scream, wail, whine, roar, bellow, screech, shriek, trill, boom, buzz, clamor, peal, make a fanfare, be blatant, swell, thunder, hum, resound, rend the air, clang.

BLARNEY, *n.* Flattery, cajolery, blandishment, coaxing, wheedling, soft soap *(coll.),* adulation, fawning, sycophancy, flummery, blandiloquence, captation, flunkyism, obseqiousness, overpraise, guile, palaver, coquetry, suaviloquence, incense, honeyed words, soft phrases, mealy-mouthedness, sawder *(coll.),* buncombe *(coll.),* beslavering, empty encomium, hollow commendation.

BLASE, *adj.* Surfeited, glutted, satisfied, gorged, overfed, replete, full, insensible to pleasure, sick of, saturated, palled, bored, weary, spoiled, indifferent, tired, cloyed, apathetic, phlegmatic, jaded, unconcerned, uninterested, unastonished, insouciant, nonchalant, pococurante, unattracted by, careless, mindless of, listless, unamazed, flagging, spiritless, life-weary. (See also INDIFFERENT, *adj.*)

BLASPHEME, *v.* 1. Revile, calumniate, abuse, etc. (See ASPERSE, *v.*)

2. Swear, curse, be impious *or* profane *or* irreverent *or* sacrilegious *or* irreligious, profane, desecrate, execrate, utter an oath *or* profanity, damn, scoff, commit sacrilege.

BLASPHEMOUS, *adj.* Irreligious, unregenerate, impious, irreverent, ungodly, profane, hardened, ribald, sacrilegious, unhallowed, unsanctified, perverted, reprobate, godless, undevout. (See also BLASPHEME, *v.,* 2)

BLAST, *n.* 1. Storm, hurricane, tempest, tornado, breeze, gale, zephyr, gust, flurry, whirlwind, high wind, squall, blow, breeze, blizzard, northwester, thundersquall, cyclone, twister, southeaster, stiff wind, southwester, flaw, typhoon. (See also WIND, *n.*)

2. Blare, clang, noise, sound, peal, whistle, shriek, screech, toot, boom, wail, whine, scream, trumpet-sound, fanfare, alarm, swell, roar, bang.

3. Detonation, explosion, volley, concussion, crash, roar, discharge, blowup, burst, flash, bang, boom, report, fulguration, eruption, crack, shot, salvo, percussion, repercussion, rumble, thunder, roll, fulmination.

4. Hardship, curse, trouble, blight, affliction, trial, scourge, bad fortune, ill luck, visitation, adversity, woe, plague, pestilence, infestation, stroke, blow, cut, shock, aggravation, grievance, pest, vexation, oppression, tribulation, infliction, injury, hurt, wound.

BLATANT, *adj.* 1. Noisy, loud, piercing, bawling, boisterous, vociferous, obstreperous, clamorous, harsh, screaming, shrieking, blaring, booming, whining, roaring, uproarious, deafening, shrill, ear-splitting, stentorian, clamant, turbulent, deep, sonorous, full, powerful, multisonous, rending the air, rackety, blustering, tonant, reverberating, clattering, clarion-voiced.

2. Crying, bleating, bawling, lowing, ululant, latrant, mugient, bellowing, reboant, reboantic, rebellowing, braying, whinnying, caterwauling, neighing, baying, mewling. (See also BAY, *v.,* 1)

3. Obtrusive, coarse, vulgar, rude, common, crude, cheap, uncouth, unpolished, ill-mannered, ill-bred, uncivil, indecorous, unseemly, offensive, undignified, ungracious, uncultured, in bad taste, rowdy, gross, ribald, loutish, crass, loud, rough, flaunting, scurrilous, raffish, vulgarian, unrefined, indelicate, improper, unpresentable, ungenteel, ungentlemanly, ill-behaved.

BLAZE, *n.* 1. Flame, fire, conflagration, bonfire, ingle, flaring, scintillation, combustion, ignition, sheet of fire, sea of flames.

2. Coruscation, flash, flicker, fulguration, glow, gleam, glint, glimmer, streak, radiance, shimmer, glare, glitter, streak, beam, ray, twinkle.

3. Outburst, flaring up, outbreak, eruption, burst, rush, torrent, explosion, blast, flash.

BLEACH, *v.* (See BLANCH, *v.*)

BLEACHERS, *n.* Grandstand, stadium, benches, tiers, stands.

BLEAK, *adj.* 1. Lonely, desolate, barren, gloomy, cheerless, comfortless, uninviting, depressing, joyless, dismal, comfortless, dreary, melancholy, disheartening, distressing, somber, drear, weary, sad, mournful, monotonous, dull, flat.

2. Exposed, raw, windy, wind-swept, bitter, biting, cold, frosty, freezing, chilly, chilled, icy, stormy, cutting, nipping, rigorous, severe, wintry, unsheltered, bare, piercing, algid, inclement, keen, shivery, pinching, hiemal, boreal, arctic, brumal.

3. Destitute, bare, plain, waste, etc. (See BARE, *adj.,* 4 & BARREN, *adj.,* 3)

4. Dark, gloomy, murky. (See BLACK, *adj.*, 2)

BLEAR, *v.* Fog, befog, render dim, obfuscate, obscure, mist, bemist, enmist, shadow, overcast, shade, overshadow, darken, cloud over, nubilate, adumbrate, make smoky, make watery, bedarken, gloom, eclipse, make murky, bedim. (See also BEDIM, *v.*)

BLEAT, *v.* (See BAA, *v.*)

BLEED, *v.* 1. Shed blood, discharge blood *or* gore, emit blood *or* gore, flow (*as a wound*), be gory *or* bloody, ooze (*as a wound*).
   2. Let blood, cup (*Med.*), open a vein, take blood, withdraw blood, venesect, phlebotomize.

BLEMISH, *n.* Spot, stain, maculation, macule, freckle, lentigo, mole, nevus, birthmark, blotch, discoloration, blot, smudge, speckle, bruise, pock, disfigurement, disfiguration, defacement, tarnish, patch, smirch, smutch, blain, wart, pimple, knob, lump, node, nodule, tubercle, taint, flaw, blur, scar, cicatrice. (See also BLAIN, *n.*)

BLENCH, *v.* Wince, flinch, shrink, recoil, weaken, quail, start aside *or* back, hesitate, falter, quiver, shudder, quake, flutter, shiver, shake, tremble, shy, fly, cower, skulk, crouch, evade, elude, shun, eschew, avoid, hang back, retire, turn tail, blink, dodge, give way, give place, stand aghast, jib, funk (*coll.*), swerve, sheer off, take to one's heels.

BLEND, *v.* Merge, harmonize, mix, combine, associate, unite, intermingle, incorporate, shade, compound, fuse, amalgamate, commingle, alloy, embody, interfuse, assimilate, interlard, coalesce, impregnate, intertwine, interweave, melt together, inosculate, anastomose, centralize, synchronize, syncretize, agglutinate, contemper, bemingle, scramble, levigate, unify.

BLESS, *v.* 1. Consecrate, hallow, glorify, sanctify, dedicate, beatify, ordain, justify, absolve, edify, exalt, honor, enshrine, anoint, baptize, canonize, make *or* pronounce holy, give benediction, make the sign of the cross over.
   2. Sanction, approve, support, help, aid, allow, succor, permit, smile upon, endorse, assent, say amen to, consent, ratify, subscribe to, enable, countenance, be in favor of, approbate.

BLESSED, *adj.* 1. Holy, sanctified, consecrated, revered, glorified, exalted, sacrosanct, reverenced, divine, sacred, hallowed.
   2. Sainted, baptized, canonized, etc. (See BEATIFY, *v.*, 1)
   3. Happy, joyous, glad, etc. (See BLITHE, *adj.*)

BLESSING, *n.* 1. Grace, invocation, benison, etc. (See BENEDICTION, *n.*)
   2. Profit, advantage, gain, etc. (See BENEFIT, *n.*, 2)
   3. Bounty, kindness, liberality, gift, etc. (See BENEFACTION. *n.*)

BLIGHT, *n.* Mildew, canker, mould, impairment, decay, rot, corruption, pollution, contamination, pest, fungus, pestilence, affliction, infliction, dry rot, plague, scourge, worm, locust, cankerworm, mucor, must, adulteration. (See also BLAST, *n.*, 4)

BLIND, *adj.* 1. Purblind, eyeless, visionless, unseeing, sightless, amaurotic (*Med.*).
   2. Dim-sighted, dull-sighted, weak-eyed, snow-blind, feeble-eyed, bleary-eyed, hemeralopic, filmy-eyed, nyctalopic.
   3. Unperceiving, unseeing, unobserving, slow

of comprehension, obtuse, inattentive, mindless, unobservant, unmindful, thoughtless, inadvertent, unreflecting, undiscerning, respectless, negligent, disregardful, heedless, neglectful, cursory, stupid, indiscriminating, uncomprehending, dull-witted, senseless, dense, non-understanding, incognizant, bovine, insulse, unenlightened, ignorant, unaware, unknowing, unacquainted, unapprised, unversed, uninformed, nescient, unconversant, insensible, insensitive, insusceptible, unconcerned, mindless, uninterested, insouciant, unimpressible, unfeeling, unconscious, unemotional, dispassionate, indifferent.
   4. Concealed, obscure, hidden, closed, sealed, impassable, obstructed, blocked, dead, dead-end, without exit, shut-off, barricaded, barred, shut, stopped-up, blockaded. (See also BARRIER, *n.*)

BLIND, *n.* 1. Screen, cover, blinder, shutter, veil, shield, shade, blinker, mantle, mask, curtain, protection, drapery.
   2. Subterfuge, trick, decoy, device, dodge, net, shift, feint, catch, fraud, fake, snare, trap, cloak, disguise, camouflage, masquerade, pretext, wile, pretense, swindle, delusion, falsification, artifice, stratagem, contrivance, maneuver, chicanery, guile, duplicity, finesse, evasion, smoke screen, ruse. (See also TRICK, *n.*)
   3. Ambush, pitfall, trap, etc. (See AMBUSH, *n.*)
   4. Cul-de-sac, one way, dead end, blind alley, impasse, standstill. (See also BLIND, *adj.*, 4)

BLIND, *v.* 1. Make sightless, put out one's eyes, blindfold, render blind. (See also BLIND, *adj.*)
   2. Hoodwink, cheat, defraud, etc. (See BAMBOOZLE, *v.*)

BLINDFOLD, *v.* Cover the eyes of, bandage eyes of. (See also BLIND, *v.*)

BLINK, *v.* 1. Recoil, shirk, wince, etc. (See BLENCH, *v.*)
   2. Wink, nictate, nictitate, squint, screw up the eyes, look askance, flick the eyelids.
   3. Glance peer, glimpse, squint, perceive, spy, descry, spot, espy, see with half an eye. (See also GLIMPSE, *v.*)
   4. Sparkle, glister, flash, coruscate, shimmer, dance, waver, flutter, flicker, scintillate, shine, beam, glitter, glimmer, twinkle, glow, flare, blaze, phosphoresce, fulgurate, radiate, shoot out beams, reflect light, be lustrous, bedazzle.

BLISS, *n.* Delight, happiness, enchantment, glee, felicity, ecstasy, paradise, joy, blessedness, cheer, gladness, elation, rapture, pleasure, jubilation, delectation, beatitude, exaltation, transport, Eden, heaven, elysium, luxury, halcyon days, sunshine, ravishment, glory, oblectation, joyance, Arcadia, Utopia, seventh heaven, gratification, enjoyment, relish, exhilaration.

BLISTER, *n.* (See BLAIN, *n.*)

BLITHE, *adj.* Happy, cheerful, glad, jocund, jolly, gladsome, mirthful, pleased, sprightly, joyous, jovial, merry, joyful, cheery, light-hearted, elated, genial, animated, sunny, contented, ecstatic, airy, smiling, optimistic, winsome, in good spirits, free and easy, debonair, buoyant, flippant, spry (*coll.*), jaunty, convivial, gleeful, hilarious, frolicsome, spirited, jocular, jocose, exultant, jubilant, frisky, sparkling, bubbling, effervescent, rejoicing, riant, playful, sportive, skittish, flushed, brisk, waggish, gamesome, rollicking, blithesome, enthusiastic, carefree.

BLIZZARD, *n.* Gale, tempest, storm, blow, snow, windstorm, blast, snowstorm, hurricane, cyclone, whirlwind, typhoon, snowfall, hailstorm, driven snow, snow blast, flurry, tornado, snow squall. (See also BLAST, *n.*, 1)

BLOAT, *v.* Swell, distend, puff up, dilate, expand, enlarge, grow, wax, increase, fill out, inflate, pad, balloon, amplify, stretch, sufflate, pump up, pack, stuff, cram, magnify, aerate, incrassate, make turgid *or* swollen *or* puffy *or* lumpy, intumesce.

BLOB, *n.* Globule, drop, etc. (See BEAD, *n.*, 1 & 2)

BLOC, *n.* Union, combination, cabal, faction, coalition, entente, ring, combine, junto, coterie, clique, circle, camarilla, group. (See also BODY, *n.*, 4)

BLOCK, *n.* 1. Piece, lump, chunk, cake, wedge, brick, cube, bar, square, loaf, ingot, stick, mass, nugget, slice, wad, clod, briquette.
2. Scaffold, gallows, guillotine, ax *(in this sense)*.
3. Bar, obstacle, hindrance, etc. (See BARRIER, *n.*, 1 and BAR, *n.*, 3)
4. Fool, dolt, dunce, idiot, blockhead, booby, simpleton, chump, dullard, dullhead, dunderpate, beetlehead, bullhead, blunderhead, clod, oaf, lout, lubber, gawk, shallowbrain, imbecile, moron, nitwit *(sl.)*, Boeotian, scatterbrain, rattlebrain, rattlehead, harebrain, addlebrain, featherbrain, ignoramus, tomfool, sap *(sl.)*, nincompoop *(coll.)*, witling, halfwit, goose *(coll.)*, ass *(coll.)*, donkey *(coll.)*, mooncalf, dummy, duffer, greenhorn, bonehead *(sl.)*, numskull *(coll.)*, dimwit *(sl.)*, natural-born fool, lackwit, yokel, clodhopper, rube *(sl.)*, clodpate, clodpoll, thickhead *(coll.)*, cabbagehead *(coll.)*, jackass, ninny, noodle, owl, ninnyhammer, Simple Simon, driveler, fathead, wiseacre, blunderbuss.

BLOCK, *v.* (See BAR, *v.*)

BLOCKADE, *n.* (See BARRIER, *n.*)

BLOCKHEAD, *n.* (See BLOCK, *n.* 4)

BLOND, BLONDE, *adj.* Fair-haired, fair, light, fair-skinned, towheaded, whitish, high in tone, ivory, pearly, gray-white, platinum, creamy, pale, snowy, blanched, bleached, milky, niveous, albino.

BLOOD, *n.* 1. Gore, cruor *(Med.)*, vital fluid, ichor *(Mythol.)*, grume, life-fluid, sap *(of plants)*, juice *(of insects)*, plasma *(Med.)*
2. Consanguinity, extraction, lineage, etc, (See BIRTH, *n.*, 2)

BLOODLESS, *adj.* Wan, pallid, pale, blanched, colorless, hueless, pasty, anemic, faint, haggard, cadaverous, sallow, tallow-faced, jaundiced, sickly.

BLOODSHED, *n.* Slaughter, killing, homicide, murder, slaying, manslaughter, carnage, butchery, pogrom, massacre, internecion, trucidation. (See also BATTLE, *n.*)

BLOODSHOT, *adj.* Bloody, inflamed, suffused with blood, sanguine, blood-red, blood-stained, red, gory. (See also RED, *adj.*)

BLOODTHIRSTY, *adj.* (See BARBAROUS, *adj.*, 2)

BLOODY, *adj.* (See BLOODSHOT, *adj.*)

BLOOM, *n.* 1. Flower, blossom, inflorescence, bud, burgeon, flowerage, florification, anthesis, floweret, floret.
2. Flush, glow, florescence, flowering, health, blossoming, efflorescence, strength, vigor, luster, soundness, brilliance, radiance, prime, heyday. (See also BEAUTY, *n.*)

BLOOM, *v.* Flower, flourish, grow, prosper, bud, fructify, wax, thrive, be in health, batten, blow, succeed, luxuriate, sprout, burgeon, fare well, bear fruit, germinate, pullulate.

BLOSSOM, *n.* (See BLOOM, *n.*, 1)

BLOT, *n.* 1. Spot, blotch, stain, blur, blemish, mark, smudge, splotch, speck, macule, smear, daub, smirch, speckle, taint.
2. Disfigurement, impairment, etc. (See BLEMISH, *n.*)

BLOT, *v.* 1. Smear, stain, sully, etc. (See BESMIRCH, *v.*, 1)
2. Cancel, erase, destroy, obliterate, expunge, efface, delete, scratch out, annihilate, rub out, expurgate, wash out, deface, dele, render illegible, strike out, extinguish, exterminate, extirpate, abolish.

BLOTCH, *n.* (See BLOT, *n.* and BLEMISH, *n.*)

BLOTTER, *n.* Book, record, etc. (See BOOK, *n.*)

BLOW, *n.* 1. Storm, gale, blizzard, etc. (See BLAST, *n.*, 1 and BLIZZARD, *n.*)
2. Thump, knock, smack, etc. (See BAT, *n.*, 5)
3. Blossom, bloom, bud, etc. (See BLOOM, *n.*, 1)

BLOW, *v.* 1. Bloom, blossom, etc. (See BLOOM, *v.*)
2. Puff, pant, breathe hard, gasp, respire, huff, exhale, suspire, sigh. wheeze, bluster.
3. *(With up)* Distend, inflate, balloon, etc. (See BLOAT, *v.*)

BLOWZY, *adj.* 1. Coarse, bloated, turgid, puffy, plethoric, pursy, chubby, red, red-faced, ruddy, swollen, sanguine, florid, rubicund, flamboyant, tumid.
2. Slovenly, untidy, uncombed, bedraggled, tousled, slipshod, frowzy, frumpish, unkempt, sloppy, dowdy. messed, uncouth, slatternly, mussy. (See also BEDRAGGLED, *adj.*)

BLUBBER, *v.* Cry, wail, whimper, etc. (See BAWL, *v.*, 2)

BLUDGEON, *n.* Cudgle, staff, club, etc. (See BAT, *n.*, 1)

BLUE, *adj.* Azure, navy, aquamarine, cerulean, bluish, indigo, sapphire, cerulescent, turquoise, cyanic, cyaneous, amethystine, marine, cobalt, Prussian blue.

BLUFF, *adj.* 1. Steep, perpendicular, precipitous, abrupt, vertical, sheer, sudden, rising, ascending, acclivous, bold, towering, plumb.
2. Frank, open, blunt, unceremonious, abrupt, outspoken, curt, rude, downright, plain-spoken, candid, straightforward, uncivil, brazen, insolent, bold, barefaced, impudent, plain, brusque, direct, ungracious, short, impolite, insulting, ungallant, unflattering, discourteous, unmannerly, trenchant, disrespectful, brash, gruff, drastic, harsh, brutal, cruel, biting, sharp, cutting, piercing, stinging, inconsiderate, blustering, headlong.

BLUFF, *n.* 1. Cliff, bank, slope, height, peak, escarpment, headland, foreland, promontory, ridge, knoll, precipice, crag, steep, wall, scarp, palisade.
2. Pretense, fake, sham, etc. (See BLUFF, *v.*)

BLUFF, *v.* 1. Deceive, mislead, fake, sham, hoax, pretend, delude, lie, counterfeit, blind, humbug, throw dust in the eyes, practice deception. (See also BAMBOOZLE, *v.*, 1)
2. Brag, bluster, etc. (See BOAST, *v.*)

BLUNDER, *n.* Oversight, fault, flaw, mistake,

impropriety, error, fumble, gaucherie, bloomer *(sl.)*, boner *(sl.)*, misconception, inadvertence, misunderstanding, omission, slip-up, slip, howler *(sl.)*, inaccuracy, solecism, bull, malapropism, spoonerism, indiscretion, foolish procedure, folly, stupidity, imprudence, botchery, bad job, default, deficiency. (See also BLUNDER, *v.*)

BLUNDER, *v.* Flounder, stumble, bungle, slip, be at fault, botch, miscalculate, misjudge, mistake, err, be deceived, misreckon, miscount, fail, miss, fall short, miss the mark, miscarry, falter, spoil, boggle, fumble, mess up, hash up, muff, foozle *(coll.)*, put one's foot into it *(coll.)*, misfire.

BLUNDERBUSS, *n.* 1. Shotgun, musket, large-bore rifle, musketoon.
2. Dolt, blunderhead, blunderer, etc. (See BLOCK, *n.*, 4)

BLUNT, *adj.* 1. Dull, obtuse, insensitive, etc. (See BLIND, *adj.*, 3)
2. Abrupt, tactless, curt, etc. (See BLUFF, *adj.*, 2)
3. Dulled, unpointed, edgeless, unsharpened, thick, not sharp.

BLUR, *v.* 1. Darken, obscure, becloud, etc. (See BEDIM, *v.*)
2. Smudge, smear, smutch, etc. (See BEDAUB, *v.*, 1)

BLURT, *v.* Utter impulsively, gush, blab, etc. (See BABBLE, *v.*)

BLUSH, *v.* Redden, flush, color, grow red, glow, mantle, crimson, turn red *or* scarlet.

BLUSTER, *v.* 1. Puff, pant, huff, etc. (See BLOW, *v.*, 2)
2. Brag, boast, swagger, etc. (See BOAST, *v.*)

BOARD, *n.* 1. Council, tribunal, etc. (See BAR, *n.* 5)
2. Clapboard, wallboard, plank, siding, lath, shingle, panel, strip of wood, piece of timber, slab.
3. Table, stand, counter, tablet, slab, support.
4. Spread, repast, food, etc. (See MEAL, *n.*)
5. Edge, rim, skirt, etc. (See BORDER, *n.*)

BOARD, *v.* 1. Close with, come to quarters with, attack, land on, grapple with, bring to bay, take, commandeer, beset, assault, assail, press down upon, bear down upon, storm, take by storm. (See also ATTACK, *v.*)
2. Feed, lodge, quarter, take care of, cater to, house, billet, harbor, room, bed, put up *(coll.)*.

BOAST, *v.* Swagger, bluster, brag, crow, swash, vapor, vaunt, blow, flaunt, gasconade, puff, show off, flourish, strut, blow one's own trumpet *(coll.)*, draw the long bow, give oneself airs, pat oneself on the back, roister, exult, bluff, parade.

BOASTFUL, *adj.* Bragging, blustering, crowing, vaunting, blowing, bombastic, inflated, swollen, proud, pretentious, fanfaronading, thrasonical, vainglorious, conceited, puffed up, vain, cocky, pert, egotistic, overproud, overweening, priggish, overbearing, swell-headed, arrogant, haughty, pompous, grandiloquent, magniloquent, bravado, rodomontade, braggadocio.

BOAT, *n.* Ship, vessel, bark, craft, shell, skiff, dinghy, liner, steamer, pinnace, yacht, rowboat, dory, cutter, freighter, packet, galley, tug, canoe, transport, dugout, scow, ferry, sailboat, tender, hulk, merchantman, ark, punt.
(See also BARK, *n.*,2 and BATTLESHIP, *n.*)

BOB, *v.* 1. Nod, jerk, weave, oscillate, vibrate,

quiver, quaver, shake, flicker, waggle, palpitate, vellicate, wobble, tremble, twitch, jounce, duck, dither, buffet, librate. (See also BEAT, *v.*, 10)
2. Tap, slap, dab, tamp, jab, bump, knock, rap, thump, hit, strike. (See also BEAT, *v.*, 1)
3. Cut, trim, shorten, clip, shear, prune, crop, dock, lop, mow, skive, shingle, pare, bobtail, curtail.

BODE, *v.* Foretell, prophesy, predict, presage, augur, etc. (See BESPEAK, *v.*, 1)

BODILESS, *adj.* Without substance, immaterial, disembodied, incorporeal, discarnate, incorporal, unsubstantial, intangible, impalpable, unfleshly, unembodied, spiritual, extramundane, animistic, unreal, superphysical, spectral, ghostly, phantom, wraithlike, supernatural, chimerical, visionary, ethereal, airy, imponderable, illusory, shadowy, fanciful, figmental, vapory.

BODILY, *adj.* Real, actual, fleshly, physical, true, earthly, material, substantial, solid, corporeal, tangible, unspiritual, somatic, carnal, palpable, hylic, parenchymatous *(Anat.)*, existent, factual, concrete.

BODILY, *adv.* 1. Corporeally, physically, actually, etc. (See BODILY, *adj.*)
2. Wholly, collectively, *in toto (L.)*, *en masse (Fr.)*, entirely, altogether, totally, fully, all, as a whole, as a body, completely, in the mass *or* main or aggregate, substantially, *en bloc (Fr.)*, all put together, one and all, intact, to the limit, in full measure.

BODY, *n.* 1. Corpse, carcass, cadaver, remains, dust, ashes, clay, relics, bones, skeleton, mummy.
2. Person, figure, being, torso, trunk, form, shape, individual, creature, presence, frame, cast, physique, appearance, embodiment, incarnation, build.
3. Substance, flesh, reality, matter, corporality, physical condition, flesh and blood, materiality, stuff, bodily nature, substance, condition, etc. (See BODILY, *adj.*)
4. Community, group, gathering, gang, party, collection, side, troop, band, squad, order, school, denomination, class, sect, faction, interest, bloc, division, union, combination, cabal, coalition, entente, ring, combine, junto, clique, coterie, set, circle, camarilla, fellowship, knot, club, crowd, bunch, sodality, brotherhood, fraternity, league, society, federation, confederation, institute, tribe, congress, session, caucus, seance, levee, throng, corps, force, multitude, horde, host, legion, mob, array, bevy, galaxy, rabble, herd, drove, cluster, lot, accumulation, agglomeration, conglomeration, batch. (See also BATTALION, *n.*)
5. Heart, core, essential part, etc. (See BASE, *n.*, 2)

BOG, *n.* Mire, slough, swamp, quagmire, morass, fen, pocosin *(South. U.S.)*, peat bog, quicksand, marsh, swampland, wash, salt marsh, sump.

BOGEY, *n.* Spirit, specter, ghost, etc. (See BANSHEE, *n.*)

BOGGLE, *v.* 1. Blunder, flounder, bungle, botch, etc. (See BLUNDER, *v.*)
2. Shy, hesitate, avoid, etc. (See BLENCH, *v.*)
3. Hide, cover up, etc. (See CONCEAL, *v.*)

BOGUS, *adj.* Sham, spurious, false, etc. (See BASTARD, *adj.*, 2)

BOHEMIAN, *adj.* Unconventional, careless, loose, carefree, nonconformist, informal, grotesque, strange, fanciful, bizarre, freakish, disorganized, rococo, free and easy, irregular, heteroclite, aberrant, wanton, abnormal, unorthodox, odd, uncustomary, unusual, curious, peculiar, *outré* (*Fr.*), exotic. (See also BIZARRE, *adj.*)

BOIL, *n.* Sore, pimple, etc. (See BLAIN, *n.*)

BOIL, *v.* 1. Seethe, cook, stew, poach, scald, steam, simmer, parboil, ebullate, decoct, brew, heat, bring to the boil.

2. Bubble, well up, effervesce, simmer, gurgle, fizzle, fizz, guggle, burble (*coll.*), froth, mantle, foam, ferment.

3. Be angry, be indignant, rage, rave, storm, fume, foam, rampage, roar, ferment, fulminate, rant, burn (*coll.*), stew (*coll.*), run wild, run riot, run amuck, run berserk, flare up, explode, lose one's temper, quiver, chafe, fret, sizzle (*coll.*), smolder, bristle, seethe. (See also ANGRY, *adj.*)

BOISTEROUS, *adj.* Noisy, unrestrained, out of hand, turbulent, tumultuous, vehement, roaring, clamorous, rollicking, tempestuous, rough, raging, furious, stormy, hilarious, blatant, blustering, loud, rampageous, rambunctious (*sl.*), riotous, uproarious, unquiet, disturbed, troublous, wild, frenzied, rampant, vociferous, blustery, violent, tumultuary, disorderly, obstreperous, brawling, strident.

BOLD, *adj.* 1. Impudent, insolent, rude, etc. (See BAREFACED, *adj.*)

2. Brave, fearless, impavid, unfearful, manly, reckless, unapprehensive, unafraid, dauntless, dashing, daring, enterprising, stout-hearted, lion-hearted, undismayed, stalwart, adventurous, venturous, venturesome, stout, defiant, plucky, unflinching, confident, sturdy, gritty (*coll.*), audacious, unshrinking, heroic, resolute, valiant, ironhearted, courageous, aweless, intrepid, fiery, valorous, unalarmed, spirited, unblenching, assured, mettlesome, indomitable, temerarious, doughty, foolhardy, rash, daredevil, dreadless.

BOLSTER, *v.* Support, underbrace, mainstay, lend support, pillow, cradle, brace, buttress, underset, upkeep, maintain, underpin, underprop, uphold, sustain, shoulder, lift, hold up, shore up, bear up.

BOLT, *n.* 1. Arrow, quarrel (*Hist.*), shaft, vire, missile, reed, dart, flight, volley, projectile, trajectile.

2. Charge, assault, etc. (See ATTACK, *n.*)

3. Lock, latch, pin, padlock, catch, fastener, spike, tie, clinch, holdfast, clamp, pawl, dog, click, detent, stop, bar. (See also BAR, *n.*, 1)

4. Thunderbolt, flash, fulguration, stroke of lightning, brand, ball of lightning, sheet of lightning.

5. Screw, nut, rivet, pin, spike, staple, brad, nail, peg, skewer, dowel.

BOLT, *v.* 1. Swallow, gulp, gobble, gorge, etc. (See BATTEN, *v.*, 3)

2. Blurt, utter, etc. (See BLAB, *v.*)

3. Fasten down, secure, etc. (See BATTEN, *v.*, 1)

4. Dislodge, drive forth, etc. (See DISCHARGE, *v.*)

5. Run, rush, escape, take off (*coll.*), dash, retreat, turn tail, fly, flee, abscond, make a run for it, sprint, scoot, flit, tear off, start, start forth, speed, hurry, hasten, post, spank, scud, spurt.

BOMB, *n.* Grenade, fireball, torpedo, missile, high explosive, petard, shell, blockbuster, carcass (*Mil.*), mine, land mine, explosive.

BOMBARD, *v.* Fire upon, cannonade, barrage,

pepper, shoot, shoot at, open fire on, strafe, shell, blitz, fusillade, torpedo, bomb, rain explosives upon. (See also ATTACK, *v.*, and BATTER, *v.*, 2)

BOMBARDMENT, *n.* (See BARRAGE, *n.*, 1 & 3)

BOMBAST, *n.* Grandiosity, tumidity, turgidity, flatulence, pomposity, magniloquence, fustian, tympany, extravagance, rodomontade, bravado, rant, gasconade, highflown language, turgescence, lexiphanicism, grandiloquence, sesquipedality, altiloquence. (See also BALDERDASH, *n.*, and BOMBASTIC, *adj.*)

BOMBASTIC, *adj.* Inflated, swollen, flatulent, turgid, pompous, magniloquent, ranting, bloated, highflown, impressive, pretentious, lexiphanic, altiloquent, grandiose, mouthy, orotund, lofty, flaunting, swelling, sonorous, grandisonant, florid, sesquipedalian, stilted, declamatory, sententious, showy, flowery, euphuistic, fustian, affected, ornamental, ornate, flamboyant, flashy, over-loaded, plethoric, Johnsonian.

BONBON, *n.* Candy, sugarplum, chocolate, taffy, confection, caramel, fondant, lollipop, sweetmeat, toffee, nougat, mint, peppermint.

BOND, *n.* 1. Tie, link, connection, etc. (See BAND, *n.*, 1)

2. Covenant, contract, agreement, pledge, guarantee, compact, engagement, understanding, pact, promise, obligation, bargain, deal (*coll.*), indenture (*Leg.*), stipulation, transaction, nego-tiation.

3. Security, share, stock, scrip, scrip dividend, certificate, deed, debenture.

4. Promissory note, I.O.U., note, etc. (See BILL, *n.*, 4)

BOND, *v.* (See BIND, *v.*, 1)

BONDAGE, *n.* Serfdom, slavery, servitude, yoke, subjugation, enslavement, durance, vassalage, duress, thraldom, helotry, restraint, constraint, villenage (*Hist.*), subordination, bonds, manacles, trammels, reins, shackles, fetters, chains.

BONE, *n.* 1. Marrow, marrowbone, cartilage, gristle, rib.

2. (*In plural*) Skeleton, carcass, etc. (See BODY, *n.*, 1)

BONUS, *n.* Dividend, reward, tip, gratuity, share, interest, benefit, premium, bounty, subsidy, prize, commission, compensation, largess, sportula, gift, handsel.

BOOK, *n.* Volume, tome, work, edition, writing, publication, lucubration, monograph, treatise, manual, album, portfolio, brochure, pamphlet, text, libretto, tractate, tract, dissertation, thesis, textbook, magazine, periodical, octavo, quarto, folio, copy, opus (*L.*), enchiridion, opuscule, vade mecum (*L.*), codex, incunabula, opuscle, (See also HANDBOOK, EDITION, NOVEL, MAGAZINE)

BOOK, *v.* 1. Reserve, engage, bespeak, request, pre-engage, arrange for, procure, order, assure, make reservations.

2. Schedule, line up (*coll.*), list, program, slate, calendar, bill.

3. Enter, write down, record, list, put down, register, catalog, tally, enroll, inscribe, tabulate, post, docket, index, file, chronicle, calendar, jot down, mark down, insert, note, report.

BOOKISH, *adj.* 1. Pedantic, scholarly, academic, formal, stiff, starched, precise, highbrow, erudite, learned, scholastic, pedagogical. (See also BOMBASTIC, *adj.*)

2. Learned, well-read, studious, well-posted, given to studying *or* reading, scholarly, informed, educated, well-instructed, bibliophilic, sedulous, intellectual, diligent, assiduous, industrious, able, lettered, well-grounded, accomplished, erudite.

BOOKKEEPER, *n.* Clerk, accountant, auditor, public accountant, chartered accountant, actuary, reckoner, examiner, registrar, recorder.

BOOKWORM, *n.* Scholar, student, bibliophile, pedant, great reader, academician, litterateur, scholiast, bookman. (See also BIBLIOPHILE, *n.*)

BOOM, *n.* 1. Retort, roar, loud noise, etc. (See BANG, *n.,* 1)

2. Pole, shaft, lever, etc. (See BAR, *n.,* 1)

3. Growth, expansion, progress, upsurge, push, prosperity, sudden development, boost, thrust, impetus, impulse, momentum, increase, sudden advance *or* appreciation, flood, spread, sudden improvement, gain.

BOON, *n.* (See BENEFIT, *n.,* 2)

BOOR, *n.* Lout, churl, rustic, peasant, clown, yokel, bear, bumpkin, lubber, oaf, hayseed *(coll.),* clodpole, rube *(coll.),* plowman, hobnail, countryman, hick *(sl.),* lumpkin, chuff, looby, gaffer, vulgarian. (See also BLOCK, *n.,* 4 and BARBARIAN, *n.,* 3 & 4)

BOOT, *n.* Shoe, footwear, oxford, wellington, clog, brogue, bootee, bootikin.

BOOTH, *n.* 1. Shed, stall, hut, hutch, manger, box, compartment, cubbyhole, pen, coop, cote.

2. Stall, tent, counter, table.

BOOTLESS, *adj.* Nugatory, useless, vain, fatuous, unsuccessful, idle, profitless, inefficacious, inane, gainless, unprofitable, unremunerative, ineffectual, empty, unproductive, futile, worthless, abortive, lame, without result *or* effect, effete, sterile, void, fruitless, barren, unyielding.

BOOTY, *n.* Spoil, plunder, loot, prize, pillage, gains *(of war),* pickings, swag *(sl.),* seizure, prey, takings.

BORDER, *n.* 1. Edge, periphery, margin, fringe, circumference, brink, brim, precinct, extremity, terminal, confine, verge, curb, skirt, outskirt, rim, frame, side, hem, brow, bound, perimeter, pale, bourn, boundary, purlieus, termination, compass, ambit, limit.

2. Frontier, line, boundary, march, limit.

BORDER, *v.* 1. Fringe, befringe, skirt, rim, bind, hem, marginate, margin, line, dado, trim, purfle, purl, bound, verge, edge.

2. Be contiguous, touch, meet, join, adjoin, connect with, append, neighbor, conjoin, abut, verge upon, flank, skirt. (See also BORDER, *n.,* 1)

BORE, *v.* 1. Drill, mine, tap, pierce, penetrate, perforate, puncture, stick, prick, pink, stab, sink, punch, auger, trepan, riddle, tunnel, ream, gouge out, lower, burrow, broach.

2. Weary, annoy, tire, jade, exhaust, wear out, irk, harp at, harass, pester, buttonhole, bore stiff, fag, burden, oppress, tax one's patience.

BORROW, *v.* 1. Ask *or* take a loan, go into debt, get temporary use of, run up a score. (See also CHARGE, *v.* and HIRE, *v.*)

2. Take, get, acquire, imitate, pocket, grab, appropriate, use, steal, usurp, arrogate, purloin, help oneself, take possession of, commandeer, pirate, plagiarize, snatch, copy, filch, abstract, pilfer. (See also STEAL, *v.*)

BOSOM *n,.* 1. Breast, heart, bust, chest, mamma, mammary, thorax, papilla, nipple, teat, dug *(of animals),* udder *(of cows).*

2. Center, heart, essence, innermost being, inmost nature, soul, core, heart's core, spirit, pith, nucleus, heartblood. (See also BASE, *n.* 2)

BOSOM, *adj.* Dear, cherished, close, etc. (See BELOVED, *adj.*)

BOSS, *n.* *(Coll.)* Chief, foreman, superintendent, manager, director, leader, executive, supervisor, head, governor, master, overseer, overlooker, overman, intendant, organizer, employer.

BOTCH, *v.* Muff, blunder, bungle, fumble, trip, flounder, stumble, mar, spoil, mismanage, make a mess *or* hash of, butcher, bosh, err, fail, fall down, execute clumsily, do unskillfully, misjudge, be mistaken, misreckon, miscalculate, misapply, misestimate, miscompute, misconstrue, put one's foot in it *(coll.),* misconjecture.

BOTH, *adj.* The two, both together, both the one and the other.

BOTHER, *n.* 1. Trouble, turmoil, turbulence, disturbance, commotion, hubbub, tumult, bluster, convulsion, stir, perturbation, ado, fuss, pother, racket, fracas, melee, scramble, riot, confusion, rumpus *(coll.),* pandemonium, Babel, distraction, scurry, bewilderment, flurry, muddle, bustle, stew *(coll.),* disconcertion, befuddlement, ferment.

2. Trouble, nuisance, inconvenience, burden, annoyance, aggravation, fret, vexation, irritation, worry, problem, load, care, anxiety, tribulation, stress, drag, onus, hindrance, cumbrance, trial, tax, affliction, impediment, strain, responsibility, hardship, oppression, pest, encumbrance, care, molestation, gall, mortification.

3. Perplexity, confusion, bewilderment, puzzle, muddle, befuddlement, quandary, confoundment, embarrassment, puzzlement, bafflement, dilemma, nonplusation, botheration, *(coll.),* mystification.

BOTTLE, *n.* Flask, jar, decanter, phial, canteen, vial, carafe, demijohn, cruse, ewer, flasket, stoup, carboy.

BOTTOM, *n.* 1. Bed, floor, benthos *(of the sea),* depths, lowest part, deepest part.

2. Socle, support, dado, wainscot, baseboard, base, basis, foundation, fundus, plinth, ground, groundwork, foot, pedestal, bed, lowest part, substructure, substratum, prop, caudex *(Bot.),* footing, sole, nadir, flooring.

3. Underneath, belly, undermost part, under part, nether parts, underside.

4. Essence, root, origin, source, stem, radical, foundation, core, heart, ground, groundwork, vital principle, principal component, principle, substance, center, inmost nature, cause, quiddity, bosom, gist, pith, backbone, nub *(coll.),* matter, quintessence, intrinsic truth, sum and substance, mainspring, fountainhead, spring, base, inception, wellspring, rudiments, derivation, beginning, prime mover, primordium.

BOTTOMLESS, *adj.* Deep, soundless, baseless, unfathomable, fathomless, plumbless, abysmal, unfathomed, abyssal.

BOUDOIR, *n.* Private room, bedroom, chamber, apartment, private chamber, sanctum, dressing room.

BOUGH, *n.* Shoot, limb, twig, branch, member, bush, sprig, switch, spray, runner, stem, sprout, sarmentum, offshoot, ramage *(pl.)*, stalk, bine, tendril. (See also BLADE, *n.*, 1)

BOULDER, *n.* Stone, rock, sarsen.

BOULEVARD, *n.* Avenue, thoroughfare, street, roadway, highway, drive, driveway, main road, parkway, road, highroad, terrace, row.

BOUNCE, *v.* 1. Rebound, jump, leap, spring, bob, recoil, bound, flounce, buck, jounce, bump, jerk up and down, ricochet, resile, spring back, hop, skip, boomerang.
2. Bump, thump, bang, etc. (See BANG, *v.*)

BOUND, *n.* 1. Boundary, limit, confine, border, edge, enclosure, frontier, landmark, line, margin, termination, verge, march, end, rim, brim, curb, skirt, fringe, hem, side, periphery, frame, purlieus, extremity, compass, line of demarcation, pale.
2. Borderland, domain, territory, province, orb, region, bailiwick, area, quarter, part, department, section, district, realm, demesne, precinct, pale, compass, orbit, range, circle, ambit, field.
3. Spring, rebound, jump, leap, hop, saltation, skip, vault, upspring, gambol, caper, antic, frisk, start, prance, bob, flounce, curvet, buck, dance, demivolt *(of horses)*, gambado, bounce.

BOUND, *v.* 1. Limit, confine, border, edge, end, enclose, mark, surround, circumscribe, encircle, encompass, restrict, restrain, demarcate, delimit, hem in, wall in, pen in, shut in, hedge in, rail in, engird, ensphere, begird, embrace, skirt, hedge, define, determine, fix, surround.
2. Border, adjoin, be near, be next to, be adjacent to, be contiguous to, join, neighbor, abut, verge upon, conjoin, touch, stand by, connect, fringe, edge.
3. Bounce, rebound, resile, spring, saltate, hop, jump, upspring, start, bob, buck, leap, gambol, caper, flounce, prance, frisk, curvet, dance, skip, romp.

BOUNDARY, *n.* Limit, confine, border, frontier, landmark, line, termination, margin, verge, pale, march, periphery, extremity, compass, purlieus, line of demarcation, frame, side, hem, fringe, skirt, brim, rim, end, fence.

BOUNDLESS, *adj.* Immense, vast, unbounded, limitless, inexhaustible, illimitable, measureless, infinite, unlimited, unrestricted, immeasurable, interminable, endless, undefined, interminate, innumerable, termless, incalculable, unceasing, indeterminate, perpetual, constant, uninterrupted, without end, uncircumscribed, unending.

BOUNTEOUS, *adj.* 1. Liberal, generous, giving, munificent, philanthropic, benevolent, charitable, unsparing, kind, beneficent, unselfish, altruistic, free, princely, unsparing, unstinting, openhanded, bountiful, eleemosynary, big-hearted, large-hearted, magnanimous.
2. Plentiful, ample, large, overflowing, full, plenteous, rich, abundant, unstinted, abounding, prolific, copious, lavish, superabundant, profuse, generous, teeming, prolix, prodigal, exuberant, extravagant.

BOUNTIFUL, *adj.* (See BOUNTEOUS, *adj.*)

BOUNTY, *n.* 1. Benevolence, philanthropy, help, munificence, unselfishness, free-handedness, aid, altruism, big-heartedness, almsgiving, goodness, giving, hospitality, grace, assistance, relief, succor, donating, liberality, open-handedness, generosity, kindness, indulgence, self-sacrifice.
2. Subsidy, recompense, subvention, bestowal, benefaction, gift, donation, presentation, grant, endowment, tribute, gratuity, concession, largess,

contribution, offering, bonus, handsel, present, honorarium, remuneration, solatium, guerdon, meed.

BOUQUET, *n.* 1. Aroma, odor, scent, etc. (See AROMA, *n.*)
2. Boutonniere, posy, nosegay, garland, spray, bunch (of flowers), wreath, chaplet, festoon, boughpot.

BOURGEOIS, *adj.* Common, middle-class, hoi polloi *(Gr.)*, ordinary, uncultivated, proletarian, plebeian, *roturier (Fr.)*, peasant, obscurantist, Philistine, working-class, sans-culotte.

BOURN, *n.* 1. Stream, brook, riverlet, etc. (See BROOK, *n.*)
2. Limit, boundary, etc. (See BORDER, *n.*, 1)

BOUT, *n.* 1. Conflict, trial, contest, round, set-to, fray, affray, match, affair, encounter, engagement, battle, combat, fight, brush, tilt, skirmish, action, collision, clash, scuffle, struggle, embroilment, melee, duel, scrimmage, quarrel, tournament, scrap *(sl.)*, meeting, passage of arms, altercation, contention.
2. Cycle, course, revolution, turning, circuit, returning, turn, series, twist, rotation, curvature, curve, rota, flexure.

BOUTONNIERE, *n.* (See BOUQUET, *n.*)

BOVINE, *adj.* Dull, stupid, cowlike, sluggish, inane, empty, oxlike, obtuse, hebetate, Boeotian, sottish, blockish, dumb, doltish, insulse, oafish, dense, blunt, thick, stolid, uncomprehending. (See also BLIND, *adj.*, 3)

BOW, *v.* 1. Stoop, salaam, prostrate oneself, etc. (See BEND, *v.*, 2)
2. Subdue, sway, master, etc. (See BEND, *v.*, 4)

BOW, *n.* 1. Bend, curve, arch, twist, loop, turn, warp, crimp, crook, circle, wheel, spiral, coil, curl, arc, crescent, curvature, incurvation, hook, flexure, aduncity, arcade, meniscus, half moon, semicircle, horseshoe, lune *(Geom.)*, parabola, hyperbola, vault, sweep, inflection, arcuation, concameration, sinus, catenary, caustic *(Optics)*.
2. Catapult, slingshot, longbow, crossbow, sling, arbalest.
3. *(Naut.)* Prow, bowsprit, front, etc. (See BEAK, *n.*, 2)

BOWELS, *n.* 1. Vitals, vital organs, insides, guts *(vulg.)*, intestines, viscera, entrails, chitterlings *(of animals)*, colon, rectum, anus. (See also BELLY, *n.*, 1)
2. Depths, recesses, penetralia, midst, heart, core, center, interior, interior parts, inside, womb, bosom, vault, hollows, abysses, cavities, bottom.

BOWER, *n.* Arbor, retreat, nook, summerhouse, grotto, refuge, cell, shady retreat *or* den *or* lair, seclusion.

BOWL, *n.* 1. Goblet, cup, chalice, etc. (See BEAKER, *n.*)
2. Dish, basin, porringer, boat, vessel, pan, tureen, receptacle, container. (See also BASIN, *n.*, 1)
3. Depression, hollow, cavity, valley, etc. (See BASIN, *n.*, 2)

BOWL, *v.* Move, roll, travel, spin, gyrate, trundle, troll, rotate, revolve, whirl, turbinate, pirouette, reel, wheel, twirl, swivel, gurge. (See also RUN, *v.*)

BOWLEG, BOWLEGGED, *adj.* (See BANDY, *adj.*)

BOX, *n.* Canister, carton, case, chest, coffer, bin,

BOX 111 BRAVE

caddy, hutch, crib, caisson, pyxis, casket, crate, bandoleer, trunk, skippet, vasculum, monstrance *(Eccl.)*, file, shrine, bunker.

BOX, *v.* 1. Hit, cuff, strike, etc. (See BAT, *v.*)

2. Engage, encounter, spar, fight, grapple with, play at fisticuffs, contend, contest, combat, battle, struggle, scramble, tussle, strive, skirmish, broil, scuffle, pitch into, brawl, come to blows with. (See also BATTLE, *v.*, 1)

3. Coop up, pen up, shut up, hem in, wall in, bolt *or* bar in, incarcerate, entomb, impound, immure, cage, confine, imprison, lock up, case in, cork up, bottle up, cloister, seal up *or* in.

BOY, *n.* Youth, youngster, lad, stripling, cadet, whippersnapper *(coll.)*, puppy *(coll.)*, schoolboy, cub *(coll.)*, male child, little gentleman, little guy *(coll.)*, small fry *(coll.)*, junior.

BOYCOTT, *v.* Exclude, cut off, shut out, banish, ostracize, oust, debar, eliminate, proscribe, cast aside, reject, refuse, pass over, omit, ban, bar, blackball, thrust out, spurn, leave out, relegate, excommunicate, isolate, outlaw, lock out, picket, black-list.

BOYCOTT, *n.* Exclusion, ostracism, debarring, ousting, elimination, rejection, refusing, omission, banning, ban, barring, blackballing, spurning, isolation, black-listing, boycottage, embargo, cutting, excommunication.

BOYISH, *adj.* Puerile, boylike, youthful, green, raw, callow, unfledged, newfledged, immature, inexperienced, childish, childlike, sappy, unripe, infantile, juvenile, juvenescent, tender, underage, budding, beardless, kiddish *(coll.)*.

BRACE, *v.* 1. Tie, join, fasten, etc. (See BIND, *v.*, 1)

2. Support, reinforce, hold up, etc. (See BEAR, *v.*, 1)

BRACE, *n.* 1. Support, stanchion, band, strut, reinforcement, rib, shore, buttress, stay, bracket, strengthener, prop, bearing, upholder, block, peg, stirrup, arm, mainstay, sustainer, stave, bracer, raker *(Arch.)*, guy, shroud *(Naut.)*, splint, skid.

2. Buckle, clasp, tie, chain, joint, coupling, clamp, clinch, holdfast, hasp, clip, fastener, band, staple, bonder, bandage, fillet, withy.

3. Two, duet, pair, etc. (See COUPLE, *n.*)

BRACELET, *n.* (See BANGLE, *n.*)

BRACING, *adj.* Stimulating, invigorating, tonic, refreshing, roborant, strengthening, restorative, corroborant, recuperative, revivatory, reviviscent, remedial, brisk, crisp. (See also BENEFICIAL, *adj.*, 1.)

BRACKET, *v.* Couple together, unite, yoke, pair, couple, tie, join, combine, connect, merge, weld, amalgamate, attach, truss, link, harness, associate, hitch, conduplicate, hook up, pinion, affix, clip together, mate, span.

BRACKET, *n.* (See BRACE, *n.*, 1)

BRACKISH, *adj.* Salty, saline, briny, saltish, salted.

BRAG, *v.* Boast, vaunt, extol oneself, gasconade, talk big *(coll.)*, be windy, inflate oneself, brave, bluster, swagger, bluff, puff oneself up, flourish, give oneself airs, exaggerate, crow, vapor, strut, be vainglorious, blow one's own trumpet *or* horn, glorify oneself, crack *(coll.)*, hug oneself, roister, pat oneself on the back, be swell-headed.

BRAGGART, *n.* Fanfaron, trumpeter, blowhard, windbag, Braggadocio, Rodomont, Thraso, Sir

Oracle, Gascon, strutter, swaggerer, peacock, swashbuckler, blatherskite.

(See also BOAST, *v.*, and BOASTFUL, *adj.*)

BRAID, *v.* Weave, twist, entwine, interlace, knot, interweave, ravel, interthread, inosculate, raddle, mat, interleave, anastomose, intertie, intertwist, interdigitate, knit, wreathe, twine, plat, pleat, plait, twill, entangle, interlock, bind together, mortise, splice, intort, convolve, let in, dovetail, work together.

BRAIN, *n.* *(Often in plural)* Mentality, mind, intellect, psyche, soul, intelligence, wit, capacity, wits, understanding, reason, rationality, wisdom, intellectual faculties, senses, consciousness, head, percipience, capability, genius, judgment, ability, intuition, conception, gray matter *(coll.)*, sapience, perception, apperception, discernment, faculties, powers, discrimination, thinking ability *or* power, nous, sensorium, cogitative faculties, comprehension, sagacity, grasp, acuteness, depth, common sense, acumen, penetration, perspicacity, profundity, aptitude, foresight, mental poise, observation, insight, cognition.

BRAMBLE, *n.* Thorn, brier, prickly shrub, burr, nettle, thistle, cleaver, catchweed, thistle sage, goose grass.

BRANCH, *n.* 1. Shoot, limb, spray, etc. (See BOUGH, *n.*)

2. Office, division, subdivision, section, bureau, chapter, member, offshoot, department, category, part.

3. Offshoot, ramification, arm, spur, limb, leg, scion, wing, fork, bifurcation, divergence, prong, separation, forking, divarication, tributary, feeder, channel, filiation.

BRANCH, *v.* Bifurcate, divide, ramify, shoot off, divaricate, diverge, fork, dichotomize, aberrate, separate, radiate, go off at a tangent, furcate.

BRAND, *n.* 1. Disgrace, stigma, mark, spot, blot, slur, taint, stain, smirch, smutch, imputation. (See also BLEMISH, *n.*)

2. Sign, mark, token, emblem, etc. (See BADGE, *n.*, 2)

3. Torch, light, flambeau, firebrand.

4. Make, type, kind, class, label, trademark, quality, sort, stamp.

BRAND, *v.* 1. Burn, scorch, sear, mark with a branding iron, singe, burn in, cauterize.

2. Mark, stigmatize, etc. (See BRAND, *n.*, 1)

BRANDISH, *v.* Wield, swing, shake, flourish, flaunt, wave, flap, whisk, jerk, switch, swing, wag, waggle, bandy, vibrate, hold before the eyes, display, exhibit, show off *(coll.)*.

BRASH, *adj.* 1. Hard, brittle, etc. (See BRITTLE, *adj.*)

2. *(Colloq.)* Saucy, impudent, etc. (See BAREFACED, *adj.*, 2)

BRASSY, *adj.* Impudent, brazen, saucy, etc, (See BAREFACED, *adj.*, 2)

BRAT, *n.* Chit, bantling, cub, urchin, kid *(sl.)*, whelp, imp, rascal, whippersnapper, sprig, slip, bratling, puppy, ill-mannered child, annoying child, minx *(of girls)*, whipster, hoyden *(of girls)*.

BRAVADO, *n.* Braggadocio, vaunting, boasting, puffing, gasconade, rodomontade, blowing, rant, storming, bullying, swaggering, raging, fuming, crowing, railing, bluff, fanfaronade, pomposity, self-glorification, grandiosity, bombast, hot air *(coll.)*, braggartry, swelling. (See also BRAG, *v.*)

BRAVE, *adj.* Unflinching, bold, courageous,

doughty, undaunted, fearless, intrepid, herolike, unshrinking, stout-hearted, valiant, mettlesome, hardy, heroic, stalwart, daring, audacious, plucky, lion-hearted, manful, dauntless, unafraid, stout, undismayed, iron-hearted, unappalled, dreadless, unblenching, gallant, spirited, gritty *(coll.)*, game, awless.

BRAVE, *n.* Hero, warrior, soldier, fighting man, paladin, champion, chevalier, Hercules, fighter.

BRAVE, *v.* 1. Face, defy, dare, outbrazen, beard, oppose, stand up to, withstand, confront boldly, refuse to be cowed by, breast, buffet, look in the face *or* eye, bell the cat, take the bull by the horns, stand up against.

2. Endure, bear, suffer, put up with, tolerate, sustain, abide, aby, carry on, stand, brook, take bravely, undergo, swallow, weather, bide, persist, stomach.

BRAVO, *n.* (See BANDIT, *n.*)

BRAWL, *n.* Fracas, fight, broil, fray, scrimmage, scrap *(sl.)*, uproar, quarrel, wrangle, encounter, scuffle, affair, embroilment, commotion, turmoil, brangle, altercation, scramble, dispute, squabble, bickering, disturbance, imbroglio, spat *(coll.)*, dissension, disruption, tiff, outbreak, huff, strife, contention, rumpus, clash, litigation.

BRAWN, *n.* Muscles, robustness, strength, power, sturdiness, physical ability, vigor, lustiness, sinew, stalwartness, brawniness, muscular development, might. (See also BRAWNY, *adj.*)

BRAWNY, *adj.* Burly, muscular, mighty, robust, powerful, stout, sound, husky, hale, rugged, able, Herculean, sinewy, Atlantean, broad-shouldered, lusty, strapping, hardy, vigorous, athletic, tough, stalwart, well-developed, strong, thewy, forcible, healthy, sturdy, solid, Cyclopean.

BRAY, *v.* 1. Call, cry, bleat, blat, blare, ululate. (See also BLARE, *v.*)

2. Crush, grind, pulverize, rub, beat, pound, triturate, spread thin, powder, comminute, mash, crumble, disintegrate, granulate, rub down, grate, abrade, crunch, craunch, bruise.

BRAZEN, *adj.* 1. Of brass, made of brass, of brassy quality, brass-like.

2. Loud, harsh, strong, strident, penetrating, ear-splitting, grating, jarring, piercing, raucous, stertorous, cacophonous, jangling, inharmonious, dissonant, screeching, shrill, stentorian, deafening, clanging, trumpet-voiced *or* trumpet-tongued, discordant.

3. Saucy, open, presumptuous, shameless, immodest, daring, indecorous, outspoken, bluff, plain, frank, candid, barefaced, unseemly, bold, unabashed, unreserved, plain-spoken, insolent, flippant, indecent, bold-faced, impertinent, fresh *(coll.)*, forward, malapert, pert, precocious, rude, brash, cheeky, brazen-faced, arrogant, obtrusive, familiar, procacious, disrespectful, unmannerly, petulant, impudent, unblushing, audacious.

BREACH, *n.* 1. Difference, rupture, schism, gap, discord, dissension, chasm, rent, rift, variance, incompatibility, misunderstanding, disruption, jar, faction, disunion, clash, division, split, disparity, cleft, disagreement, break, friction, antagonism, enmity, conflict, bitterness, rancor, alienation, estrangement, irreconciliation, animosity, bad blood, antipathy, hostility, resentment.

2. Violation, oversight, infraction, inattention, transgression, infringement, fault, flaw, defect, trespass, nonobservance, diregard, laxity, neglect, disobedience, omission, misfeasance, dereliction,

misdemeanor, indiscretion, failure, delinquency, contravention, noncompliance, thoughtlessness, defiance.

3. Fissure, opening, split, cleft, fracture, crack, crevice, cranny, rift, rent, hole, scission, fission, cut, chink, gap, incision, gash, break, rupture, slit, puncture, hiatus. (See also BREAK, *v.*, 1)

BREADTH, *n.* Width, broadness, latitude, span, expanse, spread, spaciousness, gauge, roominess, extensiveness, diameter, caliber, bore, thickness, radius, expansion, stretch, extent, dimensions, coverage, compass, area, reach, measure, scope, tread.

BREAK, *n.* 1. Rupture, split, schism, breach, rift, disruption, variance, difference, dissension, tiff, dispute, altercation, falling out, disagreement, division, breaking off, disparity, dissent, quarrel, misunderstanding, contention.

2. Split, crack, fracture, cleft, crevice, fissure, gap, flaw, breach, rent, gash, scissure, chasm, chink, hole, cavity, leak.

3. Gap, interval, omission, flaw, intermission, division, hiatus, caesura, lacuna, lapse, pause, interlude, breach, cessation, space.

BREAK, *v.* 1. Shatter, splinter, crush, crumble, crack, destroy, mangle, grind, fragmentize, wreck, ruin, batter, demolish, pulverize, crumple, pound, chop, chip, crash, mutilate, shiver, snap, burst, mash, beat, powder, disintegrate, granulate, tear, mince, hash, lacerate, pull to pieces, fracture, hack up, wrench, scramble, damage.

2. Destroy, annihilate, ruin, raze, etc. (See BATTER, *v.*, 2)

3. Bankrupt, impoverish, cripple, deplete, etc. (See BANKRUPT, *v.*)

4. Separate, cleave, part, divide, burst, sunder, split, disjoint, disarrange, fracture, disband, rive, disconnect, sever, rend, dismember, take to pieces.

5. Subdue, tame, override, etc. (See BEND, *v.*, 4)

6. Violate, transgress, disregard, neglect, fail, disobey, omit, defy, infringe, slight, take no note of, set aside, ignore, overlook, forget, shirk, let slip *or* slide, be guilty of infraction, oversight, etc. (See also BREACH, *n.*, 2)

7. Demote, cashier, degrade, humiliate, unseat, dismiss, discharge, displace, fire, depose, remove from office, oust, unsaddle, unfrock *(Eccl.)*, dethrone, unthrone, disbar, uncrown.

8. Lessen, mitigate, diminish the force of, etc. (See ASSUAGE, *v.*)

9. Disclose, divulge, reveal, give away, etc. (See BETRAY, *v.*, 2)

10. Interrupt, discontinue, stop, halt, arrest, stem, suspend, intermit, check, shut down, pause, stay, cease, intervene, interpose, intrude, interfere, restrain, choke off, hinder, impede, retard, inhibit. (See also BAR, *v.*, 2)

11. *(With* DOWN*)* Anatomize, dissect, resolve, etc. (See ANALYZE, *v.*)

BREAKABLE, *adj.* Fragile, brittle, delicate, weak, frangible, frail, splintery, friable, crisp, crumbly, easily broken, flimsy, shattery, unstable, dainty, gossamery, jerry-built *(coll.)*, unsteady, shaky, tottering, wobbly, teetering, decrepit, slight.

BREAKDOWN, *n.* Upset, overthrow, ruination, crash, wreck, debacle, demolition, devastation, collapse, breakup, shipwreck *(fig.)*, crackup *(coll.)*, failure, downfall, cave-in *(coll.)*, smash, undoing. (See also ILLNESS, *n.*)

BREAKER, *n.* (See BEACHCOMBER, *n.*, 1)

BREAKWATER, *n.* Sea wall, mole, jetty, pier, embankment, groin, jutty, wharf.

BREAST, *n.* 1. Bosom, chest, bust, mammary, mamma, thorax, papilla, nipple, teat, dug *(of animals).*
2. Heart, core, center, depths, deepest part, inmost parts, bowels, interior, inside, innermost recesses, penetralia, kernel, middle, pitch, gist, marrow.

BREATH, *n.* 1. Respiration, breathing, wind, inhalation, exhalation.
2. Life, life force, vital spark, vital principle, breath of life, divine spark, vital spirit, pneuma, soul, existence, essence of existence, lifeblood, anima, animation, spirit, vitalization.
3. Breath of air, etc. (See BREEZE, *n.*)

BREATHE, *v.* Respire, inhale, exhale, draw in, draw breath, inspire, snuff in, expire, suspire *(Poet.).*

BREATHLESS, *adj.* 1. Lifeless, inanimate, etc. (See DEAD, *adj.*)
2. Panting, gasping, choking, wheezing, out of breath, exhausted, short-winded, windless, blown, winded, puffing and blowing, dyspneal, asthmatic, anhelous, breathy.
3. Surprised, amazed, etc. (See ASTONISHED, *adj.*)

BREECH, *n.* 1. Posterior, haunches, dorsal *or* lumbar region, seat, hind part, hind quarters, rump, fundament, podex *(Zool.),* buttocks, croup *(of quadrupeds),* crupper *(of horses),* nates.
2. Rear part *(of a firearm),* loading place.

BREECHES, *n.* Trousers, pantaloons, corduroys, pants *(coll.),* knickerbockers, jeans, smallclothes, slacks, drawers, culottes.

BREED, *n.* Race, stock, kind, species, type, sort, blood, stamp, brand, genus, strain, family, nature, order, feather, tribe, caste, variety, subspecies, subgroup, suborder.

BREED, *v.* 1. Bring forth, produce, engender, beget, etc. (See BEAR, *v.,* 10)
2. Raise, foster, bring up, nurture, cultivate, cross, develop.

BREEDING, *n.* 1. Reproduction, propagation, generation, begetting, gemination, parturition, hatching, spawning, bearing, progeneration, birth, multiplication, laying, producing, bringing forth, yielding, dropping *(of animals),* procreation.
2. Extraction, parentage, kin, family, blood, strain, lineage, ancestry, posterity, race, house, clan, stock, descent, line, bloodline, genealogy, stirps, pedigree, heredity.
3. Manners, courtesy, politeness, behavior, cultivation, civility, gentility, upbringing, rearing, training, background, conduct, bearing.

BREEZE, *n.* Breath of air, zephyr, draft, gust, gentle wind, current of air, puff of wind, stir of air, whiffet, whiff of air.

BREEZY, *adj.* 1. Windy, gusty, squally, blustery, airy, blowy, blasty, flawy.
2. Light, airy, pert, fresh, vivacious, peppy, animated, energetic, chipper *(coll.),* cheerful, spirited, frisky, brisk, sprightly, dynamic, vivid, spry, jaunty, debonair, buoyant, mirthful, jovial, jocular, blithesome, joyous, resilient, sportive, elated, jubilant, in high spirits, in high humor, free and easy, carefree, gay, sunny, merry, zippy *(coll.),* gleeful, happy.

BREVIARY, *n. (Eccl.)* Prayer book, service book,

church book, canon, rubric, missal, lectionary, ordinal, farse, litany, euchology.

BREVITY, *n.* 1. Shortness, briefness, quickness, succinctness, curtness, compactness, compression, terseness, pointedness, laconism, conciseness, compendiousness, crispness.
2. Transience, impermanence, ephemerality, volatility, evanescence, fugacity, perishableness, caducity, preterience, perishability, mortality.

BREW, *v.* 1. Cook, cook up, decoct, concoct, make, prepare, mix, seethe, levigate, knead, stir up *or* hash up, commix. (See also BOIL, *v.,* 1)
2. Hatch, concoct, arrange, think up, foment, contrive, originate, plot, project, devise, produce, plan, formulate, germinate, scheme, conspire, complot, arrange, initiate, inchoate, concert. (See also PLAN, *v.,* and BEGIN, *v.*)

BRIBE, *n.* Reward, gift, hush money, sop, lure, corrupt money, remuneration, compensation, gratuity, price, graft. (See also BOOTY, *n.*)

BRIBE, *v.* Lure, tempt, entice, corrupt, influence, coax, suborn, buy, grease the palm *(coll.),* square *or* seduce with money, give a bribe *or* sop *or* price to, etc. (See also BRIBE, *n.*)

BRIC-A-BRAC, *n.* (See BAUBLE, *n.*)

BRIDAL, *adj.* Conjugal, hymeneal, wedding, matrimonial, marital, spousal, nubile, connubial, nuptial, wedded.

BRIDE, *n.* Newly married woman, spouse, mate, partner.

BRIDGE, *n.* 1. Pontoon, viaduct, plank, catwalk, drawbridge, gantry, span, overpass, ford.
2. Bond, tie, link, association, etc. (See BAND, *n.* 1)

BRIDGE, *v.* Cross, go over, connect, span, travel over, link, unite, unify, consolidate, bind, conjoin, league, band, couple, bracket, yoke, traverse.

BRIDLE, *v.* Restrain, hinder, obstruct, etc. (See BAR, *v.,* 2)

BRIDLE, *n.* Hindrance, oppilation, check, etc. (See BAR, *n.,* 3)

BRIEF, *adj.* 1. Short, abrupt, cursory, concise, epitomized, shortened, reduced, abridged, curt, contracted, curtailed, summarized, laconic, neat, limited, condensed, compact, abbreviated, pithy, thumbnail, pointed, compendious, crisp, precise, aphoristic, terse, epigrammatic, exact, bare, compressed, sententious, elliptical.
2. Transitory, fugacious, vanishing, transient, impermanent, temporary, sudden, quick, fugitive, flying, fleeting, swift, evanescent, passing, elusive, brisk, hasty, hurried, momentary, short-lived, ephemeral.

BRIEF, *n.* Digest, epitome, outline, compendium, draft, conspectus, prospectus, abstract, summary, abridgment, condensation, pandect, synopsis, syllabus, analysis, sum and substance, extract, minutes.

BRIGADE, *n.* Unit, body of troops, detachment, corps, column, force, legion, host, group, wing, squadrons, garrison, batteries, sections, squads, cohorts, contingent, regiment, companies, phalanx.

BRIGAND, *n.* Outlaw, thug, spoiler, looter, thief, bandit, robber, desperado, vandal, despoiler, hoodlum, buccaneer, pirate, rustler, highwayman, ruffian, burglar, smuggler, gunman, cutthroat, bravo, crook, racketeer, depredator, pickpocket, Apache, larrikin, strongarm-man, pilferer, rifler, pillager, freebooter, dacoit, corsair, privateer, viking, rapparee, picaroon, terrorist, filibuster.

BRIGHT, *adj.* 1. Glowing, shining, beaming, beamy, luminous, illumined, argent, incandescent, silvery, resplendent, white, golden, polished, vivid, effulgent, refulgent, lustrous, nitid, glossy, brilliant, gleaming, scintillating, burnished, light, orient, fulgent, fulgid, luciferous, lambent, sheeny, sparkling, glowing, splendid, glittering, glistening, twinkling, irradiant, coruscating, shimmering, dazzling, beautiful, relucent.

2. Joyous, happy, gladsome, auspicious, fair, palmy, inspiring, exhilarating, favorable, lenient, mild, pleasant, promising, cheerful, cheering, clement, opportune, lucky, providential, halcyon, fortunate, felicitous, rosy, inspiriting, assuring, roseate, rose-colored.

3. Gay, debonair, happy, glad, etc. (See BLITHE, *adj.*)

4. Apt, brilliant, clever, intelligent, able, gifted, talented, adroit, expert, dextrous, handy, brainy *(coll.),* proficient, accomplished, quick, masterful, deft, competent, efficient, capable, ingenious, inventive, resourceful, shrewd, sharp, precocious, witty, teachable, knowing, keen, alive, profound, alert, wide-awake, clear-headed, discerning, wise, sage, calculating, argute, intellectual, sagacious, acute, astute, quick-witted, aware, observant, apperceptive, perceptive, percipient, far-sighted.

BRIGHTEN, *v.* 1. Polish, shine, furbish, rub up, touch up, scour, gild, lighten, illuminate, illumine, burnish, buff, varnish, wax, gloss, glaze, luster, mercerize. (See also BRIGHT, *adj.,* 1)

2. Light, illuminate, enlighten, cast light upon, illumine, illume, lighten, irradiate, beam upon, shed luster.

3. Cheer, comfort, make happy, glad, etc. (See BLITHE, *adj.*)

BRILLIANT, *adj.* 1. Shining, glowing, gleaming, etc. (See BRIGHT, *adj.,* 1)

2. Clever, intelligent, acute, etc. (See BRIGHT, *adj.,* 4)

BRIM, *n.* 1. Edge, verge, margin, etc. (See BORDER, *n.,* 1)

2. Shore, beach, etc. (See BANK, *n.,* 2)

BRINDLED, *adj.* Streaked, dappled, mottled, freckled, blotched, banded, spotted, variegated, speckled, flecked, pied, piebald, marbled, pepper and salt, bespotted, besprinkled.

BRINE, *n.* Salty water, salt water, sea water, salt solution.

BRING, *v.* 1. Carry, transport, convey, fetch, etc. (See BEAR, *v.,* 2)

2. *(With* ABOUT) Engender, originate, etc. (See BEGIN, *v.,* 1)

3. *(With* FORTH) Procreate, reproduce, propagate, etc. (See BEAR, *v.,* 10)

BRINK, *n.* 1. Edge, verge, margin, etc. (See BORDER, *n.,* 1)

2. Shore, beach, bank, etc. (See BANK, *n.,* 2)

BRISK, *adj.* 1. Lively, animated, energetic, spry, dynamic, sprightly, busy, pert, snappy *(coll.),* peppy *(coll.),* ready, sharp, alert, agile, spirited, prompt, quick, active, swift, smart, breezy *(coll.),* vivacious, chipper *(coll.),* frisky *(coll.),* speedy, bustling.

2. Invigorating, refreshing, stirring, etc. (See BRACING, *adj.*)

BRISTLE, *n.* Barb, point, prickle, spine, thorn, jag, spike, spur, snag, spicule, tip, quill, barbule, acumination, nib, prong, tine, cusp, wattle, tuft, appendage, barblet.

BRISTLE, *v.* Prickle, stick *or* stand *or* start up, be hairy, rough, setose, etc. (See BRISTLY, *adj.*)

BRISTLY, *adj.* Wattled, thorny, prickly, pointed, tipped, barbed, whiskered, acuminate, nibbed, pronged, spined, barbellate, spicular, sharp, hairy, hirsute, setaceous, setose, hispid, strigose *(Bot.),* shaggy, trichomic, horrent, quilled.

BRITTLE, *adj.* Fragile, breakable, crisp, friable, crumbly, crushable, splintery, shivery, delicate, shattery, frail, lacerable, frangible, pulverizable, pulverable, brash *(of timber).*

BROACH, *v.* 1. Tap, pierce, perforate, etc. (See BORE, *v.,* 1)

2. Open, mention, express, utter, break, begin, suggest, take the plunge, propound, start, open up, propose, institute, bring about, launch, touch off, set off, introduce, set going.
(See also BEGIN, *v.*)

BROAD, *adj.* 1. Wide, extended, extensive, large, spacious, ample, immense, roomy, capacious, expansive, outspread, outstretched, thick, beamy *(Naut.).*

2. Liberal, catholic, broad-minded, charitable, tolerant, receptive, unbigoted, democratic, lenient, impartial, unprejudiced, magnanimous, indulgent, open-minded, unbiased, undogmatic, responsive, latitudinarian, unprovincial, unswayed, amenable, accessible.

3. Sweeping, far-reaching, extensive, inclusive, comprehensive, ecumenical, general, universal, world-wide, wholesale, all-embracing, prevalent. (See also COMMON, *adj.,* 1)

BROADCAST, *v.* 1. Publish, proclaim, report, trumpet, spread abroad, sow, speak, air, publish abroad, propagate, circulate, spread, make known, declare, voice, announce, advertise, divulge, tell, write in the sky *(fig.),* scatter, disseminate, bruit, blazon, evulgate, utter, diffuse, herald, make public, noise abroad.

2. Send out, cable, telecast, televise, telegraph, transmit, relay, radio, put on the air, telephone, radiograph, radiogram.

BROADEN, *v.* Widen, extend, amplify, make larger, expand, spread, stretch, thicken, increase, dilate, distend, enlarge, augment, develop, swell, aggrandize, make more roomy *or* capacious, etc. (See BROAD, *adj.,* 1)

BROAD-MINDED, *adj.* (See BROAD, *adj.,* 2)

BROADSIDE, *n.* 1. Bill, poster, placard, etc. (See BILL, *n.,* 2)

2. Cannonade, volley, salvo, etc. (See BARRAGE, *n.,* 1)

BROCHURE, *n.* Booklet, leaflet, folder, circular, pamphlet, chapbook, monograph, tractate.

BROIL, *n.* 1. Boiling, stewing, simmering, frying, seething, steaming, heating, grilling, roasting, baking, toasting, cooking, warming.

2. Fracas, brawl, fray, litigation, clash, strife, rumpus, contention, scrimmage, scrap *(coll.),* uproar, quarrel, wrangle, scuffle, encounter, affair, embroilment, huff, outbreak, tiff, disruption, dissension, commotion, turmoil, brangle, dispute, altercation, scramble, squabble, bickering, spat *(coll.),* disturbance, imbroglio.

BROIL, *v.* 1. Heat, warm, chafe, boil, simmer, cook, bake, seethe, stew, fricassee, steam, sear, baste, roast, grill, fry, griddle, toast, parboil.

2. Burn, torrefy, scorify, parch, heat, warm, blister, scorch, singe, bake, sear, roast, toast, fry, grill.

BROKEN, *adj.* 1. Ruptured, fractured, rent, split, gashed, cracked, shattered, destroyed, pulverized, smashed, crushed, mangled, mutilated, lacerated, bruised, damaged, injured, crumbled.

2. Interrupted, spasmodic, irregular, discrete, discontinuous, unsuccessive, intermittent, uneven, disconnected, disjunct, desultory, fitful, unequal, inconstant, variable, unsteady.

3. Defeated, beaten, discomfited, overthrown, vanquished, conquered, overpowered, overridden, outdone, outmatched, fallen, subdued, quelled, suppressed, crushed, reduced, ruined, undone, licked *(coll.)*, worsted, trimmed *(coll.)*, hard-hit, knocked down, checkmated.

BROKEN-HEARTED, *adj.* Sad, miserable, wan, melancholy, mournful, wretched, sorrowful, heartbroken, crushed, gloomy, disconsolate, comfortless, poor, infelicitous, inconsolable, woeful, cheerless, woebegone, stricken, unhappy, heavy-laden, despairing, in despair, hopeless, forlorn, overcome, dashed, bowed-down, doleful, dejected, despondent, crestfallen, spiritless, glum, lamenting, depressed, long-faced, prostrated, rueful, careworn.

BROKER, *n.* Stockbroker, dealer, agent, factor, insurer, underwriter, exchange broker, insurance broker, money changer, money broker, mortgage broker, cambist, cotton broker, bill broker.

BRONZE, *adj.* Bronzy, brown, copper, mahogany, reddish-brown, rust, russet, tan, henna, chestnut, terra-cotta, auburn, liver-colored, titian, sorrel, foxy, roan, brick, fawn, bay.

BROOCH, *n.* Pin, clasp, decoration, trinket, piece of jewelry, broach, jewel, lavaliere, chatelaine, buckle.

BROOD, *n.* 1. Litter, nest, fry, farrow, offspring, family, progeny, issue, spawn, young, spat.

2. Species, kind, sort, type, description, order, genus, family, strain, tribe, breed, subspecies, subgroup, suborder, extraction.

BROOD, *v.* 1. Hatch, incubate, sit upon, cover.

2. Meditate, think, contemplate, mull over, reflect, ruminate, speculate, ponder, daydream, dream, mope, muse, deliberate, consider, fret over, sulk, dwell upon, worry, be in a brown study.

BROOK, *n.* Stream, streamlet, rivulet, creek, rill, branch, fresh, runnel, runlet, bourn.

BROOK, *v.* Endure, abide, suffer, etc. (See BEAR, *v.,* 4)

BROOM, *n.* Brush, whisk, mop, sweeper, whisp, feather duster, swab.

BROTH, *n.* Soup, bouillon, chowder, consommé.

BROTHEL, *n.* Stew, bordel, bagnio, house of ill-repute, bawdy-house, whorehouse, house of harlotry, house of prostitution, house of lewdness.

BROTHER, *n.* 1. Kinsman, twin, blood brother, brother-german.

2. Double, mate, twin, match, correlative, analogue, correspondent, equivalent, counterpart, complement, fellow, image, congener, parallel, sister *(in this sense).*

3. Priest, father, friar, monk, monastic, cleric, Carmelite, Dominican, Augustinian, Fransciscan, Jesuit, Loyolite, Trappist, Cistercian, Benedictine, Carthusian, preaching friar, White Friar, Black Friar, Gray Friar.

BROTHERHOOD, *n.* 1. Kinship, consanguinity, relationship, blood relationship, filiation, family connection, affiliation.

2. Fellowship, body, group, fraternity, order, confraternity, fraternal order. (See also ALLIANCE, *n.,* and BLOCK, *n.*)

3. Friendship, amity, friendliness, fraternity, cordiality, comradeship, intimacy, harmony, good will, affection, concord, neighborliness, sympathy, benevolence, amiability, helpfulness, consideration. (See also BENEVOLENCE, *n.*)

BROW, *n.* 1. Eyebrow, forehead, front, temple, countenance, features, visage. See also FACE, *n.,* 1)

2. Top, summit, apex, crown, peak, highest point, pinnacle, zenith, cap, culmination, acme, tip, vertex.

3. Edge, brim, brink, etc. (See BORDER, *n.,* 1)

BROWBEAT, *v.* Bully, cower, hector, bulldoze *(coll.),* cow, overbear, abash, subdue, beat down, intimidate, terrorize, badger, threaten, discourage, daunt, frighten, petrify, scare, harass, dragoon, domineer.

(See also BLUSTER, *v.,* 2)

BROWN, *adj.* Dun, maroon, fawn, hazel, russet, tan, drab, khaki, bay, snuff-colored, beige, ecru, bronze, chocolate, cinnamon, liver-colored, dust, tawny, brownish, puce, fuscous, musteline, coffee, cocoa, umber, mahogany, rust, terra-cotta, foxy, copper, roan, sorrel, chestnut, henna, auburn, ginger, brick.

BROWSE, *v.* 1. Graze, crop, pasture, feed, bite, munch, nibble, ruminate, champ, batten upon, peck, masticate, chew, mumble.

2. Wander here and there, read here and there, scan, glance at, go through carelessly *or* in a desultory manner, peruse, check over, look over, examine cursorily, run over *or* through, skim, dip into, flip through, survey, glance through, inspect loosely, pass the eye over, look through, skip.

BRUISE, *n.* Discoloration, mark, blemish, black mark, scratch, gash, scuff, laceration, abrasion, mutilation, contusion.

BRUISE, *v.* 1. Grind, pulverize, powder, etc. (See BRAY, *v.,* 2)

2. Hit, strike, etc. (See BEAT, *v.,* 1)

3. Mar, disfigure, blemish, deface, bloodstain, mangle, injure, contuse, maul, mark, abuse, buffet, blacken, suggilate, damage, harm, mutilate, scratch, lacerate.

BRUNET, *adj.* Dark, dark-haired, brown-haired, melanic, melanous, olive-skinned. (See also BROWN, *adj.*)

BRUNT, *n.* Shock, full force, force, percussion, impact, stress, violence, strain, bump, charge, concussion.

BRUSH, *n.* 1. Encounter, engagement, fracas, etc. (See BATTLE, *n.,* 1)

2. Forest, greenwoods, undergrowth, etc. (See BACKWOODS, *n.*)

3. Bush, brushwood, shrubbery, deadwood, thicket, underwood, undergrowth, boscage, copse, fern, bracken, gorse, sedge, scrub, whin.

4. Broom, whisk, duster, besom, mop, wisp.

BRUSH, *v.* 1. Clean, sweep, groom, rub down, whisk, flick, cleanse.

2. Touch, graze, glance off, kiss, stroke, touch lightly, feel, caress, flick, lick, sweep.

BRUSHWOOD, *n.* (See BRUSH, *n.,* 3)

BRUSQUE, *adj.* Blunt, abrupt, frank, bluff, rude,

unreserved, gruff, forward, plain-spoken, drastic, outspoken, downright, unvarnished, brash, curt, harsh, sharp, keen, trenchant, stern, austere, tart, acrimonious, caustic, virulent, brutal, stringent, cruel, bearish, churlish, discourteous, impolite, inaffable, unceremonious, ill-bred, uncivil, hasty, ungracious, ungentle, unmannerly.

BRUTAL, *adj.* Inhuman, vicious, unkind, brutish, hard-hearted, cruel, bloody, fell, fierce, mean, ruthless, unfeeling, ferocious, hellish, demoniacal, diabolic, heartless, merciless, unrelenting, pitiless, remorseless, inexorable, bloodthirsty, untamed, homicidal, sanguinary, murderous, feral, ferine, atrocious, savage, wild, barbaric, barbarous.

BRUTE, *n.* 1. Animal, beast, creature, quadruped, wild animal, dumb creature, beast of the field, irrational animal.

2. Monster, swine, savage, monstrosity, vandal, hog, satyr, lecher, fornicator, adulterer, seducer, goat, tiger, hyena, barbarian, wild beast, beast, fiend, demon, devil.

BUBBLE, *v.* Burble, effervesce, boil, blob, foam, gurgle, fizzle, spume, froth, guggle, percolate.

BUBBLE, *n.* 1. Globule, blister, bleb, etc. (See BLOB, *n.*)

2. Trifle, bagatelle, etc. (See BAUBLE, *n.*)

BUCCANEER, *n.* Pirate, freebooter, privateer, corsair, robber, bandit, bravo, outlaw, spoiler, cutthroat, viking, desperado, despoiler, smuggler, thief, pilferer, rifler, pillager, filibuster.

BUCK, *n.* 1. Male deer, stag.

2. Blade, fop, dandy, dude *(coll.)*, coxcomb, beau, exquisite, popinjay, swell, spark, cavalier, playboy, man about town, fine gentleman, blood, gallant, Dundreary, élégant *(Fr.)*, carpet knight, macaroni, jackanapes, jack-a-dandy, silk-stocking, young puppy.

BUCK, *v.* Spring, jump, leap, bound, hop, vault, skip, prance, caper, bob, bounce, gambol, frisk, leapfrog, buckjump.

BUCKET, *n.* Pail, scuttle, growler *(sl.)*.

BUCKLE, *n.* 1. Button, clip, clasp, hasp, hook and eye, catch, fastening, fastener.

2. Bend, knot, warp, twist, curl, coil, distortion, contortion, twisting, screw, whirl, kink, curlicue, twirl, whorl, loop, crimp, curve, crinkle, crook, flexion.

BUCKLE, *v.* 1. Warp, crinkle, crimp, distort, curl, contort, twist, gnarl, double up, crook, bend. (See also BEND, *v.*, 1)

2. Tie, join, yoke, fasten, etc. (See BIND, *v.*, 1)

BUD, *v.* Germinate, sprout, shoot up, blossom, grow, burgeon, put forth, open, burst forth, put forth shoots, develop, pullulate, vegetate, bloom, flower, begin to grow.

BUD, *n.* Shoot, stem, floweret, floscule, burgeon, sprout, spray, twig, blade, praefoliation.

BUDGE, *v.* Move, move slightly, go, stir, remove, dislodge, pass, roll, slide, flit, move over, shift, change position, give way, advance, progress, set in motion, propel, render movable, inch, proceed, push. (See also MOVE, *v.*)

BUDGET, *n.* 1. Bag, sack, pack, etc. (See BAG, *n.*)

2. Financial statement, financial plan, cost of operation, etc. (See BILL, *n.*, 1)

3. Resources, salary, treasure, purse, principal, purchasing power, pocket, means, stock, assets,

substance, finances, exchequer, moneys, funds, supplies, reserves, income.

BUFF, *adj.* Yellow, yellowish-red, gold, canary, citron, lemon, sulphur, sallow, luteous, sandy, saffron, tawny, fulvous, apricot, peach, straw, flaxen, ocherous, xanthous, aureate.

BUFF, *v.* (See BRIGHTEN, *v.*, 1)

BUFFER, *n.* Shock-absorber, bumper, fender, pad, protector, cowcatcher, guard, shield, screen.

BUFFET, *v.* Push, thrust, bump, clip, beat, box, pound, knock, slap, thwack, strike, poke, jab, pat, dab, wallop, butt, cuff, hit, bang, rap, ram, thump, bunt, impel, jostle.

BUFFET, *n.* 1. Snack bar, lunch counter, lunch stand, cafeteria, automat.

2. Sideboard, cupboard, cabinet, closet, shelf, bureau.

BUFFOON, *n.* Fool, clown, comedian, harlequin, jester, mimic, antic, zany, pantaloon, funnyman, stooge, comic, merryandrew, mummer, mime, Punch, Scaramouch, acrobat, contortioner, wag, juggler, mountebank, pickle-herring, wit, droll, punchinello, Pierrot, goliard, gracioso.

BUGBEAR, *n.* 1. Specter, bugaboo, goblin, etc. (See BANSHEE, *n.*)

2. Bête noire *(Fr.)*, anathema, hate, bugaboo, fetish, bogy, hydra, abomination, nightmare, specter, scarecrow, terror, horror, phantom, ogre, Gorgon, monster, fear, curse, dread, dismay, consternation, anxiety. (See also BANE, *n.*, 2)

BUGLE, *n.* Cornet, trumpet, horn, tooter, tromba, clarion.

BUILD, *v.* 1. Form, shape, make, set up, rear, elevate, construct, fabricate, compose, fashion, erect, create, evolve, manufacture, edify, produce, put together, bring about, frame, devise, put up, weave, carve, chisel, compile, hew, model, mould, cast, block out, figure, hammer out, sculpture, forge.

2. Establish, found, originate, etc. (See BEGIN, *v.*)

BUILDING, *n.* Construction, house, structure, compages, erection, fabric, edifice, pile, frame, framework, superstructure.

BULB, *n.* 1. Bud, tuber, corm, root, bulblet, bulbil.

2. Blob, swelling, protuberance, etc. (See BLAIN, *n.*, and BULGE, *n.*)

BULGE, *v.* Bag, belly, project, protrude, hang over, beetle, sag, bunch, bouge, swell out, dangle, droop, dilate, pout, excurvate, bilge, puff out, be rounded *or* swollen, stand out, stick out.

BULGE, *n.* Swelling, protuberance, intumescence, bulb, convexity, protrusion, tumefaction, dilation, nodule, nodulation, excrescence, prominence, tuberosity, salience, sagging, bagginess, bunching, projection, outgrowth, growth, appendage, excess, exuberance, superfluity.

BULK, *n.* 1. Quantity, size, measure, capacity, matter, weight, extent, dimensions, substance, magnitude, massiveness, largeness, capaciousness, bigness, amplitude, corpulency, bulkiness, fatness, greatness, proportions, hugeness, immensity, enormity, volume, mass.

2. Major part, lion's share, majority, main part, most, body, gross, heft *(coll.)*, principal part, staple, greater part, nearly all, best, best part, more than half, plurality, preponderance, predominant part.

BULKY, *adj.* 1. Big, large, massive, great, ample,

sizable, considerable, substantial, voluminous, capacious, goodly, huge, gigantic, enormous, mammoth, titanic, elephantine, mighty, colossal, monstrous, prodigious, immense, vast.

2. Fat, plump, lumpish, obese, stout, beefy, brawny, puffy, swollen, inflated, stalwart, pudgy, corpulent, rotund, tubby (coll.), portly, paunchy, big-bellied, thick-bodied.

3. Ponderous, clumsy, awkward, lumpish, unwieldy, hulky, cumbersome, lubberly, unmanageable, cumbrous, ungainly, ungraceful, lumbering.

BULLET, n. Projectile, missile, shot, cartridge, shell, ball, bolt, slug, piece of ammunition, trajectile, dumdum.

BULLETIN, n. 1. News report, announcement, message, news, statement, information, dispatch, news sheet, communication, communiqué, note, telegram, notification, aviso, intelligence, tidings, word.

2. Placard, poster, etc. (See BILL, n., 2)

BULLY, n. Hector, roisterer, tyrant, intimidator, bulldozer, coercer, tough, ruffian, blusterer, fury, rowdy, browbeater, vaporer, swaggerer, ranter, raver, oppressor, despot, hard master, inquisitor, hellcat, terror.

BULLY, v. Domineer, tyrannize, browbeat, cow, frighten, intimidate, scare, coerce, overbear, rage, overawe, ride over, bulldoze, hector, terrorize, harass, dragoon, bluster, threaten, lord it over, trample, tread on, dictate, exact, lay down the law to, thunder, storm, swagger, rant, rave, bluff, petrify, dismay, put fear into, daunt, disconcert, make one tremble.

BULWARK, n. 1. Bastion, rampart, battlement, citadel, fort, fortress, stronghold, redoubt, mound, abutment, barrier, barricade, breastwork, fastness, fortification, bank, fence, embrasure, parapet, barbette, defense, paling, palisade, stockade, wall, boom, ravelin, redan, demilune, outworks, mole, crenelation, bulkhead, buffer, portcullis, buttress, dam, weir, earthwork, fieldwork.

2. Security, protection, defense, safeguard, shelter, sconce, shield, tower of strength, screen, preservation, caution, support, surety, palladium, rock, sheet anchor.

BUMP, n. 1. Blow, knock, buffet, jolt, impact, crack, smack, tap, crash, rap, clap, slam, stroke, cuff, hit, pummel, box, whop, whack, thwack, lick, thud, clump, clunk, plump, pat, appulse, smash, encounter, collision, slap, punch, slug, swipe, wallop (sl.), poke, sock, jab.

2. Prominence, lump, protuberance, swelling, nodule, bulge, excrescence, convexity, rising, bulb, hump, hunch, knob, gnarl, knot, clump, swell, salient, intumescence, tumescence, bulbil (Anat.), bulblet, node, bunch.

BUMP, v. 1. Strike, beat, bat, tap, hit, smack, bang, thump, thwack, rap, slap, cuff, box, knock, punch, slug, swipe, lick, slam, wallop (sl.), pat, dab, whack, tamp, jab, pound, whip, lash, sock, smite, poke, clip.

2. Collide, encounter, crash into, smash into, meet, run into, butt, jostle, jolt, jar, jounce, buffet, crash, clash.

BUMPER, n. Cupful, glassful, flowing bowl or glass, beakerful, brimming cup or goblet, mugful, bowlful, tumblerful, tankardful.

BUMPKIN, n. Yokel, chawbacon (sl.), yahoo, clown, churl, plowman, swain, lubber, lout, gawk, hobnail, hind, rustic, boor, lumpkin, lummox, peasant, clodpoll, rube (coll.), hick (sl.), looby, farm hand, joskin (sl.).

BUMPTIOUS, adj. Conceited, fanfaronading, self-assertive, obtrusive, pompous, presumptuous, forward, pushing, aggressive, insolent, egotistic, vain, opinionated, boastful, braggart, vainglorious, vaunting, thrasonic, pushing, haughty, arrogant, proud, high-handed, contumelious, supercilious, overbearing, overweening, self-esteeming, smug, self-loving, priggish, complacent, gasconading, strutting, bragging, swaggering, precocious. (See also BOMBASTIC, adj.)

BUNCH, n. 1. Hunch, lump, protuberance, bulge, prominence, nodule, swelling, node, tumescence, bulblet, bulbil (Anat.), intumescence, excrescence, convexity, rising, swell, hump, knob, gnarl, knot, clump, bulb, salient.

2. Cluster, group, knot, gathering, glomerule (Bot.), clump, tuft, batch, galaxy, host, bundle, shock, stack, sheaf, wisp, lock, tussock, thicket, fascicle, inflorescence (Bot.), pompon.

3. Group, assembly, aggregate, cluster, stack, batch, number, host, lot, quantity, amount, mass, assortment, collection, crowd, multitude, array, bevy, flock, sum, gathering, company, band, gang, tribe, crew, squad, string, team, troop, force, covey, pack, set.

BUNCH, v. Gather, group, cluster, crowd, herd, crowd together, collect, huddle, muster, amass, mass, agglomerate, accumulate, assemble, flock together, draw together, unite, round up, heap, cram together, compile, lump together, mobilize, truss, tie, bind, fasten.

BUNDLE, n. 1. Packet, parcel, package, hamper, bag, bale, sheaf, fagot, wisp, budget, roll, pack, tuft, stack, truss, bunch, tussock. (See also BUNCH, n., 2)

2. Cluster, clump, batch, gathering, collection, group, lot, fascicle, concentration, muster, heap, congregation, pile, mass, assemblage, assortment, quantity, crowd, multitude, array, bevy, flock, sum, stack.

BUNDLE, v. 1. Assemble, tie together, bunch, package, parcel, pack, gather together, round up, concentrate, collect, cram, lump together, amass, compile, accumulate, agglomerate, muster, truss, heap up, gather, congregate, batch together, cluster, flock, crowd together, huddle.

2. Hurry, hustle, speed, move quickly, sprint, make haste, post, scud, spank, scuttle, scoot, step along or lively, race, go all out, accelerate, make a spurt, spur, hasten, quicken, rush, scamper, be in haste, press forward, bestir oneself, lose no time.

BUNGLE, v. Blunder, spoil, muff, fumble, mar, mismanage, butcher, execute clumsily, stumble, misreckon, trip, miscalculate, misdirect, misapply, botch, make a mess or hash of, foozle (coll.), flounder, bosh, do unskillfully, misjudge, err, fail, misestimate, put one's foot in it (coll.), fall down, miscompute, misconstrue, misconjecture, be mistaken.

BUNGLER, n. Botcher, blunderer, duffer, muffer, mismanager, clumsy oaf, flounderer, rattlehead, blunderhead, block, fumbler, butterfingers (coll.), marplot, donkey, gawk, lubber, looby, ignoramus, dunce, greenhorn, bonehead (sl.), featherbrain, numskull, scatterbrain, harebrain, giddyhead, addlebrain, addlehead.

BUNGLING, adj. Inexpert, ungainly, maladroit, clumsy, blundering, lubberly, stupid, incompetent, gauche, unskillful, awkward, botching, graceless, muffing, floundering, stumbling, unaccomplished, gawky, ill-qualified, unfit, inept, inapt, unhandy, unteachable, blockish, ungraceful, unskilled, oafish, slovenly, untrained.

BUNK, *n.* Bed, berth, couch, doss *(sl.)*, cot, pallet, hammock.

BUNKER, *n.* Crib, bin, box, case, canister, chest, coffer, casket, crate, caddie, rack.

BUOY, *n.* Marker, guide, beacon, float, life buoy.

BUOYANCY, *n.* 1. Buoyance, lightness, levity, imponderability, weightlessness, floatability, floatiness.

2. Sprightliness, gaiety, light-heartedness, glee, cheerfulness, happiness, gladness, alacrity, mirth, vivacity, animation, airiness, briskness, levity, good spirits, merriment, hilarity, jollity, joviality, jocularity, blithesomeness, joy, joyousness, cheer, sunniness, hopefulness, good humor, optimism, playfulness, enthusiasm, aspiration, geniality, exhilaration, animal spirits, breeziness, jocundity, jauntiness, brightness.

BUOYANT, *adj.* 1. Floatable, light, weightless, floating, feathery, imponderable, ethereal, corky, floaty.

2. Sprightly, gay, light-hearted, cheerful, glad, happy, vivacious, lively, animated, airy, brisk, mirthful, gleeful, merry, jolly, jovial, blithesome, jocular, joyous, optimistic, sunny, hopeful, genial, breezy, jaunty, bright, elastic, resilient, sportive, elated, jubilant, in high spirits, in high humor, volatile, full of life, debonair, carefree, free and easy.

BURDEN, *n.* **BURTHEN** 1. Load, care, anxiety, encumbrance, responsibility, oppression, hardship, handicap, strain, impediment, grievance, trial, gravamen, affliction, sorrow, tax, cumbrance, trouble, hindrance, onus, cross, nuisance, hamper, vexation, millstone around one's neck, lumber, drag, pressure, stress, tribulation, clog, incubus.

2. Weight, capacity, load, lading, cargo, bale, shipload, carload, wagonload, freight.

BURDEN, *v.* Strain, load, oppress, encumber, handicap, afflict, tax, cumber, trouble, hinder, vex, drag, overload, surcharge, try, overcharge, obligate, press down, weigh down, hamper, load with, saddle with, overlay, overwhelm, pile, lade, overtask, task with.

BURDENSOME, *adj.* 1. Bulky, weighty, onerous, ponderous, cumbersome, oppressive, massive, heavy, unwieldy, hefty *(coll.)*, cumbrous.

2. Oppressive, exacting, taxing, strenuous, fatiguing, exhausting, tiring, arduous, difficult, hard, trying, onerous, irksome, troublesome, wearisome, tiresome, afflictive, crushing, severe, bothering, harassing, worrying, vexatious, painful, toilsome, laborious.

3. Painful, aching, grave, melancholy, rueful, mournful, deplorable, dismal, distressing, pitiable, lamentable, sad, cheerless, unpleasant, agonizing, displeasing, hard, harsh, acute, severe, cruel, sore, dolorous, dreary, insufferable, heartbreaking, intolerable, unendurable, harrowing, grievous, grim, rending, heart-rending, disagreeable, bitter, piteous.

BUREAU, *n.* 1. Chest of drawers, dresser, locker, wardrobe, chiffonier, commode, chifforobe, sideboard, repository, depository, cabinet.

2. Office, agency, department, secretariat, division, portfolio, branch.

BURGESS, *n.* Burgher, townsman, householder, freeman, villager, citizen, oppidan.

BURGLAR, *n.* Robber, thief, felon, cracksman, safecracker, housebreaker, larcener, safeblower,

crook *(coll.)*, yegg *or* yeggman *(sl.)*, marauder, spoiler, pillager, second-story man, prowler, rifler, filcher, pilferer.

BURGLARY, *n.* Robbery, theft, forcible entry, larceny, felony, housebreaking, stealing, looting, appropriation, pilfering, plundering, safecracking, raiding, safebreaking, safeblowing, thievery, filching.

BURIAL, *n.* Funeral, burying, exequies, funeral rites *or* ceremonies, obsequies, entombment, interment, sepulture, inhumation.

BURIAL GROUND, *n.* Graveyard, necropolis, golgotha, potter's field, cemetery, memorial park, polyandrium *(Gr. Antiq.)*, boneyard *(sl.)*, God's acre, charnel house.

BURLESQUE, *adj.* Farcical, ludicrous, grotesque, mock, parodying, droll, ridiculous, caricatural, comic, macaronic, Hudibrastic, travestying, apish, ridiculing, exaggerated, satirical, mock-heroic, sarcastic, derisive, quizzical, bantering, ironical, mimic.

BURLESQUE, *n.* Farce, mockery, parody, satire, caricature, travesty, mock-heroic, take-off, mock tragedy, burletta, paratragoedia, slapstick, macaronic, cartoon.

BURLESQUE, *v.* Imitate, mock, mimic, take-off, satirize, travesty, parody, ridicule, laugh at, ape, laugh to scorn, exaggerate, caricature, buffoon, make ludicrous, make foolish, stultify, render absurd.

BURLY, *adj.* Fat, plump, corpulent, beefy, portly, chubby, stout, hefty, bulky, obese, fleshy, well-fed, sizable, big, large, substantial, hulking, full, ponderous, lumpish, lubberly, unwieldy, bloated, swollen, overgrown, puffy, rotund, tubby *(coll.)*, bouncing, strapping, stalwart, paunchy, thickset, chunky *(coll.)*, pudgy, dumpy.

BURN, *v.* 1. Incinerate, set on fire, consume with flames, ignite, kindle, rekindle, enkindle, fire, cremate, reduce to ashes, increate, conflagrate.

2. Scorch, char, sear, singe, roast, scald, brand, bake, calcine, oxidize, wither, shrivel, torrefy, parch, kiln, toast, heat, cauterize.

3. Blaze, flame, incandesce, smolder, be in flames, be ablaze, smoke, be on fire, flicker, glow, flare, flash.

4. Tan, suntan, embrown, brown, sunburn, bronze.

5. Prickle, be feverish, be hot, be flushed, tingle, sting, swelter.

BURNING, *adj.* 1. Smoldering, roasting, fiery, smoking, ignited, flaming, aflame, incandescent, raging, blazing, heated, afire, alight, reeking, sizzling, ustorious, comburent, glowing, fervid.

2. Passionate, enthusiastic, ardent, eager, alive with, zealous, vehement, fevered, excited, raging, agitated, glowing, earnest, frenzied, fanatic, hot, frantic, unquenched, unextinguished, devout, fiery, aglow, impetuous, fervent, intense, impassioned, devoured by, fervid, resolute, forward, heated, boiling, red-hot, sincere.

3. Caustic, sharp, cutting, painful, stinging, smarting, prickling, biting, irritating, corroding, acrid, excruciating, racking, tormenting, strong, agonizing, pungent, poignant, searing, piercing, acute, incisive, trenchant, astringent.

BURNING, *n.* Incineration, flaming, igniting, kindling, firing, cremation, incremation, boiling, conflagration, combustion, oxidation, roasting, torrefaction, scorification, parching, singeing, scorching, scalding, cauterizing, baking, searing.

BURNISH, v. Smooth, glaze, plane, buff, rub up, planish, beautify, wax, varnish, polish, brighten, make glossy, scour, furbish, sandpaper, pumice, make lustrous.

BURROW, n. Hole, excavation, hollow, furrow, concavity, groove, rut, den, lair, nook, dugout, refuge, retreat, shelter, lodge, cavity.

BURROW, v. Dig, delve, root out, tunnel, scoop out, render concave, excavate, penetrate, gouge out, furrow, deepen, hollow out.

BURSAR, n. Cashier, cashkeeper, depositary, purser, treasurer.

BURST, v. 1. Explode, break into pieces, rupture, part, pop, open, break open, disintegrate, split open, be torn asunder, crack, split, detonate, fulminate, blast, divide, shatter, discharge, go off, crash, deflagrate (Chem.), blow up, blow out.
2. Issue, emerge, rush, run, break into, spring forth, flow in, inpour, inrush, pop in, barge in (coll.), press or thrust or push in, enter suddenly, fly in or out, surge or gush forth, jet, spout.

BURY, v. 1. Submerge, sink, merge, enclose, infold, incase, submerse, engulf, immerge, hide, conceal, cover, cover up, embosom, shroud, cache.
2. Inearth, entomb, tumulate, enshrine, inhume, inter, deposit in the earth, lay in the grave, inurn, ensepulcher, sepulture, hearse, consign to the tomb or grave.

BUSH, n. 1. Clump, shrub, sapling, scrub, vine, creeper.
2. Brush, underbrush, boscage, etc. (See BRUSH, n., 3)

BUSINESS, n. 1. Job, line, avocation, profession, following, calling, activity, station, career, place, vocation, occupation, pursuit, employment, living, livelihood, means of support, work, bread and butter (coll.), office, duty, function, province.
2. Industry, enterprise, commerce, affairs, trade, barter, trading, traffic, dealings, ventures, intercourse, merchantry, mercantile business, truck, transaction, negotiation, bargaining, selling, merchandizing, exchange.
3. Affair, subject, matter, topic, concern, text, transaction, thing, theme, motif, material, point, problem, proposition, gist, thesis, point at issue, question, case, facts, proceeding, consequence, pith.
4. Enterprise, undertaking, trading, concern, shop, store, company, corporation, firm, house, establishment, partnership, venture.

BUSINESSLIKE, adj. Practical, efficient, well-ordered, thorough, industrious, methodical, orderly, regular, correct, systematic, diligent, sedulous, careful, painstaking, assiduous, prompt.

BUST, n. Figure, model, statue, representation, carving, head, statuette, figurehead, sculpture, image, effigy, portrait sculpture.

BUSTLE, v. Move quickly, hurry, stir, bestir, fluster, scurry, be active, flutter, hustle (coll.), scramble, make the most of one's time, lose no time, not let the grass grow under one's feet, make haste, scamper, rush, scuttle, work against time, be quick, be swift, dash, press on, spur oneself, urge oneself, prod or drive oneself.

BUSY, adj. 1. Working, engaged, engrossed, hard at work, occupied, on duty, in harness, absorbed, intent, toiling, striving, slaving, laboring, plying the oar, travailing, grinding, drudging, plodding.
2. Strenuous, active, engaged, diligent, full, sedulous, notable, energetic, untiring, unwearied,

studious, never idle, indefatigable, unflagging, assiduous, bustling.
3. Busybody, meddling, interfering, officious, meddlesome, intrusive, pushing, prying, nosy (coll.), inquisitive, snooping, forward, obtrusive, interposing, tampering, interloping, encroaching.

BUSY, v. Work, engross, occupy, employ, toil, strive, labor, travail, plod, grind, drudge, ply, exercise, concern, spend time, practice, pursue, toil, hammer away, plug away (coll.).

BUSYBODY, n. Snoop, pry, meddler, gossip, pragmatic, newsmonger, quidnunc, talebearer, scandalmonger, telltale, blabber, chatterer, Paul Pry, chatterbox, muckraker, intruder, slanderer, backbiter, libeler, defamer, intriguer, eavesdropper.

BUT, conj. However, yet, further, on the other hand, nevertheless, still, notwithstanding, on the contrary, even so, be that as it may, for all that, as a matter of fact, actually, in actuality, in fact, in reality, in truth.

BUT, prep. Omitting, without, not including, less, excepting, deducting, save, with the exception of, barring, except, bating.

BUT, adv. Merely, simply, barely, just, only, no more than, singly, solely, purely.

BUTCHER, n. 1. Meat seller, meat-merchant.
2. Slaughterer, killer, slayer, murderer, manslayer, bloodshedder, cutthroat, executioner, assassin.

BUTCHER, v. Kill, slaughter, slay, destroy, put to death, massacre, annihilate, exterminate, put to the sword, murder, execute, finish, dispatch, decimate, sacrifice, immolate, assassinate, cut to pieces, shed the blood of, cut down, do to death.

BUTCHERY, n. Carnage, massacre, slaughter, extermination, cutting down, internecion, pogrom, bloodshed, bloodletting, homicide, manslaughter, assassination, noyade, trucidation, dispatching, killing, slaying, annihilation, immolating, sacrifice, decimation.

BUTT, n. 1. Keg, barrel, tank, cask, firkin, tun, puncheon, kilderkin, rundlet.
2. Laughingstock, victim, dupe, target, game, jestingstock, gazingstock, gull, sucker (sl.), fool, mark, hoaxee, goat, byword.
3. End, extremity, tip, extreme, tag, stub, tail, bottom, shaft, hilt, haft, shank.
4. Target, aim, mark, bull's-eye, objective, point, destination.
5. Impulse, thrust, push, impetus, shove, bunt, jostle, ramming, blow, thump, knock, buffet, rap, smack, hit, wallop, poke, jab, cuff, dab, pat.

BUTT, v. Push, thrust, impel, shove, bunt, jostle, poke, ram, thump, knock, rap, buffet, smack, hit, cuff, wallop, poke, jab, dab, strike, thwack, slap, box, knock, swipe, lick, bump, clip.

BUTTOCK, BUTTOCKS, n. Posterior, seat, hind quarters, rump, fundament, nates, crupper (of horses), croup (of quadrupeds), podex (Zool.), dorsal or lumbar region, haunches, hind part.

BUTTON, n. Stud, link, clip, clasp, hook and eye, hook, buckle.

BUTTRESS, n. 1. Support, prop, stanchion, band, strut, reinforcement, rib, shore, stay, bracket, strengthener, upholder, sustainer, maintainer, mainstay, shoulder.
2. Rampart, fortification, bastion, etc. (See BULWARK, n., 1)

BUXOM, adj. Robust, healthy, strapping, bonny,

chubby, hearty, plump, winsome, rosy, jolly, comely, vigorous, ruddy, well-fed, bouncing, fresh, blooming, florid, rosy-cheeked, lusty.

BUY, *v.* 1. Acquire, pay for, get, obtain, invest in, shop, market, procure, gain, purchase, put money into, make a buy.

2. Corrupt, bribe, buy off, tickle the palm of, square, tip, subsidize, throw a sop to, suborn, influence, grease the palm, seduce with money. (See also BRIBE, *v.*)

3. Redeem, repurchase, ransom, reclaim, set free, recover, retrieve, rescue, deliver, liberate, emancipate, save, render free.

BUZZ, *v.* 1. Gossip, chatter, murmur, talk, chat, whisper, tattle, prate, gabble, clatter, babble, blab, rumor, noise, breathe, jabber, gibber, gab.

2. Bombilate, whizz, thrum, drone, boom, bombinate, whir, purr, sibilate, hiss, wheeze, saw, fizzle, sizzle, burr, snort.

BY, *adv.* 1. Near, at, in, on, alongside of, at hand, in close proximity to, beside, abreast, neck and neck, by the side of, next to, opposite, parallel to.

2. Aside, apart, on the side, away, out of the way, on one side.

3. Past, beyond, near by, over, through, by way of, via.

BY, *prep.* 1. Toward, near, at, in, on, in close proximity to, beside, abreast of, next to, by the side of, opposite, parallel to, along with.

2. Through the medium of, by means of, with, by virtue of, by the help of, by dint of, by the agency of, by the aid of, through, with the assistance of, helped by.

BYGONE, *adj.* Belonging to the past, past, gone by, old, antiquated, ancient, historical, former, departed, obsolete, passed away, elapsed, extinct, forgotten, outdated, expired, bypast, of yore, olden *(Poet.)*, archaic, pristine, primeval, dead, primitive, old-fashioned, outworn, outmoded, lost, unremembered, unrecollected.

BY-NAME, *n.* Nickname, cognomen, epithet, stage name, sobriquet, appellation, pen name, nom de plume, pseudonym, *nom de guerre* (Fr.), byword.

BY-PASS, *n.* Detour, short cut, temporary route, side road, byroad, circuit, indirect road, bypath, roundabout road, roundabout.

BY-PATH, *n.* Private road, side road, byroad, by-pass, indirect road, lane, path, trail, alley, pass, footpath, backway, byway, unfrequented road, third class road.

BYSTANDER, *n.* Onlooker, spectator, witness, observer, beholder, eyewitness, viewer, passer-by, gazer, looker-on, attender, gaper.

BYWORD, *n.* 1. Reflection, gnome, epigram, law, saying, axiom, conclusion, adage, rule, saw, moral, precept, aphorism, motto, principle, truth, maxim, dictum, apothegm, pet expression.

2. Laughingstock, victim, dupe, target, goat, game, jestingstock, gazingstock, butt, gull, sucker *(sl.)*, fool, mark, hoaxee.

3. Byname, nickname, *nom de guerre* (Fr.), stage name, pseudonym, nom de plume, pen name, appellation, sobriquet, epithet, cognomen.

C

CAB, *n.* Conveyance, cabriolet, car, vehicle, fly, taxicab, closed carriage, brougham, hansom, hack, hackney, four-wheeler, *fiacre (Fr.), droshky* (Rus.), driver's compartment, covered part of a locomotive.

CABAL, *n.* 1. Clique for some sinister purpose, secret group, coterie, band, party, set, crew, gang, ring, camarilla, junto, push, faction, union, coalition, combination, league, confederacy, council, conclave.

2. Intrigue, plot, plan, scheme, complot, design, conspiracy, machination, connivance, racket.

CABAL, *v.* Intrigue, plot, complot, connive, form an alliance, conspire, machinate, unite secretly.

CABALA, *n.* Mysticism, mystic art, occultism, esoteric science, theosophy, secret doctrine, secret science, mystery.

CABALISTIC, *adj.* Occult, secret, mysterious, mystic, mystical, obscure, concealed, hidden, covert, dark, cryptic.

CABARET, *n.* Tavern, wineshop, grogshop, beer garden, public house, house of entertainment, restaurant furnishing entertainment, night club, casino, *café* (Fr.), *Hofbrau* (Ger.), rathskeller.

CABIN, *n.* Small house, log building, cottage, cot, humble dwelling, shack, shanty, hut, hovel, hideout, wigwam, lodge, vacation retreat, room in a ship, enclosed part of an airplane.

CABINET, *n.* 1. Case, chest, breakfront, whatnot, cupboard, china closet, set of drawers, box, file, commode, safe, repository, receptacle.

2. Advisory council, ministry, body of advisers, administrators, governing body, board, assembly, group of counselors, the official family of the President.

3. Private room, private apartment, boudoir, side room, byroom, closet.

CABLE, *n.* 1. Rope, wire rope, wire line, line, cordage, strand, chain, fastening, bundle of wires, stranded conductor of electricity, mooring, hawser.

2. Cablegram, telegram from abroad, news, submarine telegram, submarine telegraph, message.

CABOOSE, *n.* 1. End car of freight train, kitchen of train, work-car, workmen's car on train, cabin car.

2. Cookroom of ship, galley, deckroom for cooking, deckhouse.

CACHE, *n.* 1. Hiding place, hide-out, storage place, hole, secret storehouse, crypt, hidden repository, secret arsenal.

2. Hoard, loot, hidden treasure, hidden goods, store of provisions, concealed implements, hidden weapons.

CACHE, *v.* Deposit secretly, put away, bury, store, hoard, save, hide, conceal, secrete.

CACHINNATION, *n.* Immoderate laughter, loud laugh, guffaw, horselaugh, hysterical laughter, hilariousness, roar, haw-haw.

CACKLE, *n.* 1. Chatter, clack, cluck, quack, gabble, babble, gibberish, broken laughter.

2. Prattle, idle talk, small talk, empty loquacity.

CACKLE, *v.* 1. Make a noise like a hen or goose, cluck, clack, chuckle, giggle, titter, snicker, laugh brokenly, snigger, chortle.

2. Chatter, prattle, babble, jabber, talk idly, talk nonsense.

CACOPHONOUS, *adj.* Discordant, harsh, grating, strident, scraping, screechy, screaky, raucous, jarring, ill-sounding, dissonant, inharmonious, hoarse, unmelodious.

CACOPHONY, *n.* Discord, harsh sound, jarring, dissonance, jangle, grating, croaking, rasping, hoarseness.

CAD, *n.* Ungentlemanly person, vulgarian, boor, bounder, bear, churl, lout, galoot, ragamuffin, scrub, low-bred person, dastard, caitiff, mean fellow.

CADAVER, *n.* Corpse, dead body, remains, stiff, subject for dissection, carcass.

CADAVEROUS, *adj.* 1. Corpselike, deathlike, ghastly, gaunt, haggard, grim, hideous, horrible, revolting, sickening.
2. Pale, pallid, wan, ashen, chalky, blanched, sallow.

CADDISH, *adj.* Ungentlemanly, unmannerly, ill-mannered, vulgar, lowbred, underbred, illbred, common, low, inferior, unrefined, barbarous, ignoble, base, uncouth, rude, crude, uncivil, raw, impolite, crass, mean, obnoxious, contemptible, despicable, obtrusive, presumptuous, presuming.

CADENCE, *n.* 1. Measure, meter, beat, rhythm, accent, accentuation, rate of stepping in marching.
2. Rise and fall of sound, modulation of the voice, intonation, inflection, characteristic accent.
3. Musical run, musical embellishment, flow, trill, concluding strain.

CADENZA, *n.* Flourish, brilliant solo, ornamental flight, bravura.

CADRE, *n.* Nucleus, skeleton, framework.

CADUCITY, *n.* 1. Infirmity of old age, senility, decline, dotage, decadence, degeneracy, decay, deterioration, weakness.
2. Transience, transitoriness, passing away, perishableness, deciduousness, impermanence, frailty.

CADUCOUS, *adj.* 1. Tending to fall, dropping off, deciduous, non-persistent, subject to shedding.
2. Transient, transitory, passing away, temporary, fleeting, ephemeral, evanescent.

CAFÉ (Fr.), *n.* Restaurant, coffee-house, eating house, public dining room, cafeteria, barroom, rathskeller.

CAGE, *n.* 1. Enclosure, receptacle, pen, coop, aviary, mew, crib, corral, crawl, box, prison, cell.
2. Enclosed elevator platform, car of an elevator, framework, skeleton of a building.
3. Baseball backstop, catcher's mask, hockey goal.

CAGE, *v.* Imprison, confine, lock up, shut in, coop up, mew up, trap, encage, hem in, rail in, immure, impound, incarcerate, intern, jail, pen, inclose, incase, cloister, restrict, restrain, corral.

CAITIFF, *n.* Despicable person, good-for-nothing, villain, wretch, knave, rascal, recreant, coward, sneak, miscreant, scoundrel, mean fellow, thug, blackguard, scapegrace, varlet, vagabond, scamp, rogue, ruffian, reprobate, scalawag, apostate, renegade, dastard, evildoer, cad, tough, rowdy, cur, reptile, skunk.

CAJOLE, *v.* Coax, wheedle, flatter, blandish, ply with smooth words, persuade by promises, charm, beguile, entice with false words, influence by artful arguments, inveigle, importune, jolly, softsoap.

CAKE, *v.* Harden, solidify, become firm, bake, coagulate, congeal, consolidate, agglomerate, thicken, form a compact mass, condense, indurate.

CAKE, *n.* 1. Sweetened bread, cookie, wafer, pancake, griddlecake, layer cake, loaf cake, sweet bun, fritter, *éclair* (Fr.), charlotte russe, cupcake.
2. Floe, mass, block, crust.

CALAMITOUS, *adj.* Disastrous, ruinous, adverse, unfortunate, untoward, ill-fated, ill-starred, fatal, distressful, deplorable, grievous, baleful, afflictive.

CALAMITY, *n.* Disaster, misfortune, catastrophe, mishap, mischance, ill fortune, stroke of ill luck, reverse, blow, trouble, affliction, infliction, evil, distress, misery, ill, casualty, fatality, hardship, tragedy, sea of troubles, woe, undoing, downfall, ruin, misadventure, scourge, ill wind, fiasco, bale, cataclysm, failure, adversity.

CALCINE, *v.* Burn, reduce to ashes, powder, pulverize, oxidize, roast, convert to calx, frit.

CALCULABLE, *adj.* 1. Computable, measurable, reckonable, discoverable, ascertainable, countable.
2. Reliable, dependable, to be counted on, trustworthy.

CALCULATE, *v.* 1. Compute, determine, work out, ascertain mathematically, count, figure, cast, measure, forecast, estimate, weigh, gauge, sum up, reckon, enumerate, figure up, take into account, predict.
2. Make suitable, adjust, adapt, fit, intend, plan, design, prepare one's self for.

CALCULATING, *adj.* 1. Scheming, designing, crafty, contriving.
2. Shrewd, wary, careful, sharp, far-sighted, circumspect, discreet, prudent, politic, judicious.

CALCULATION, *n.* 1. Computation, reckoning, count, estimation, estimate.
2. Expectation, expectancy, anticipation, forecast, prospect, prediction.
3. Forethought, foresight, wariness, caution, circumspection, care, deliberation, discretion, cautiousness, prudence.

CALCULUS, *n.* 1. Method of calculation, system of algebraic notation, computation, branch of mathematics, process of reasoning by the use of symbols.
2. *(Med.)* Morbid concretion, stone, gravel, calcified mass.

CALDRON, CAULDRON, *n.* Boiler, large kettle, vessel, pot, vat, container, utensil, receptacle.

CALENDAR, *n.* 1. System of reckoning time, record of yearly periods, tabular register of the year, almanac, ephemeris, menology, chronology.
2. List, table, schedule, register, docket, agenda.

CALIBER, CALIBRE, *n.* 1. Size of an internal cylindrical cavity, diameter, bore, dimension.
2. Capacity, scope, talent, ability, capability, faculty, endowment, parts, gifts, compass of mind, quality, importance, power, excellence, merit.

CALISTHENICS, CALLISTHENICS, *n.* Bodily exercise, promotion of grace and strength, drills, physical exercise, physical training, gymnastics.

CALL, *v.* 1. Cry out, utter a characteristic cry, attract attention vocally, speak in a loud voice, utter loudly, shout, clamor, vociferate, exclaim, roar, bellow, bawl, scream, yell, halloo, hollo, signal by whistling, telephone to, hail.
2. Name, designate, term, denominate, title, entitle, style, dub, christen.
3. Call together, summon, invite, ask to come, assemble by summons, muster, convoke, convene, collect.
4. Reckon, consider, estimate, judge.
5. Appeal to, invoke, pray to, supplicate, ask for, petition, entreat, demand, request, command, conjure.
6. Visit, make a visit, pay a visit, stop on business.

CALL, *n.* 1. Cry, outcry, shout, cooee, animal note, signal.

2. Summons, bidding, invitation, appeal, notice, request.

3. Demand, claim.

CALLING, *n.* Occupation, business, profession, pursuit, trade, craft, employment, work, job, vocation, office, mission, forte, specialization, speciality, *metier (Fr.),* line.

CALLOUS, *adj.* 1. Hard, hardened, indurate, inured, tough, stubborn, horny, pachydermatous, stiff, thick-skinned.

2. Unfeeling, insensible, insensitive, insentient, insensate, impenitent, unsympathetic, obdurate, hard-hearted, unsusceptible, apathetic, indifferent, unaffected by, uncaring.

CALLOW, *adj.* 1. Featherless, unfledged, naked, bare, bald.

2. Immature, undeveloped, unformed, unripe, green, inexperienced, shallow, puerile, young, unsophisticated, sophomoric, juvenile, childish, infantile, awkward.

CALM, *adj.* 1. Motionless, still, quiet, windless, waveless, stormless, smooth, unruffled, restful, undisturbed.

2. Serene, passionless, impassive, unperturbed, peaceful, placid, unagitated, reposeful, composed, collected, cool, cool-headed, unexcited, staid, tranquil, halcyon, self-possessed, untroubled, sedate.

CALM, *v.* Still, compose, tranquilize, smooth, quiet, pacify, soothe, lull, hush, allay, settle, cool off, becalm, subside.

CALMNESS, *n.* Repose, quietness, tranquillity, composure, self-possession, coolness, serenity, peace, peacefulness, dispassion, placidity, stillness, equanimity, steadiness, *sang-froid* (Fr.), doldrums.

CALUMET, *n.* Peace pipe.

CALUMNIATE, *v.* Slander, malign, traduce, sully, defame, vilify, revile, abuse, libel, blacken, accuse falsely, speak evil of, depreciate, asperse, belie, disparage, besmirch, denigrate.

CALUMNY, *n.* Slander, defamation, aspersion, malicious falsehood, scandal, scandal-mongering, imputation, detraction, false accusation, obloquy, backbiting, revilement, disparagement, abuse, libel, denigration.

CAMARADERIE, *n.* Comradeship, good will, close friendship, close association, friendliness, good-fellowship, companionship, companionableness.

CAMARILLA, *n.* 1. Cabal, clique, group, coterie, council, set, assembly, private advisers, secret advisers, irresponsible advisers.

2. Room, small chamber, meeting-place.

CAMEL, *n.* Ship of the desert.

CAMOUFLAGE, *n.* Disguise, deceptive covering, mask, screen, cloak, blind, concealment, false appearance, false pretense, deception.

CAMP, *n.* Place of temporary lodgment, bivouac, encampment, collection of tents, cantonment, hut, army establishment, rustic resort, strongly entrenched position, homogeneous group, lodging, quarters.

CAMP, *v.* Lodge temporarily, encamp, pitch a tent, pitch a camp, tent, bivouac, take a position stubbornly.

CAMPAIGN, n. Battle, plan of offensive, series of military operations, operation.

CAMPAIGN, *v.* Conduct a military operation, war, crusade, canvass, electioneer, solicit votes, compete politically for office, lobby, beat the drums, take to the stump, open a push, stump the countryside, barnstorm.

CAMPANILE, *n.* Bell tower, belfry, separate structure to house a bell.

CAMPUS, *n.* Roman military or sports field, college grounds, school grounds, academic world.

CAN, *n.* Container, receptacle, vessel for holding liquids, jar, tin, drinking cup, tankard.

CAN, *v.* 1. Be able to, be possible to, have power to, have permission to.

2. Preserve, keep, put up, process.

3. *(Slang)* Dismiss, fire, discharge.

CANAILLE, *n.* The populace, the rabble, the mob, the multitude, the million, the vulgar, the crowd, the common mass, the vulgar herd, lowest class of people, dregs of society, plebeians, riffraff, proletarians, ragtag and bobtail, tagrag, trash, *ignobile vulgus (Lat.),* hoi polloi *(Gr.).*

CANAL, *n.* 1. Artificial waterway, narrow arm of the sea, conduit, aqueduct.

2. Duct, pipe, tubular passage, channel.

CANARD, *n.* False story, falsehood, report intended to delude, hoax, malicious rumor, cock-and-bull story, fabrication.

CANCEL, *v.* 1. Obliterate, efface, erase, expunge, blot out, rub out, scratch out, cross out, strike out, wipe out, render invalid, mark off, stamp across, delete, omit, dele, write off.

2. Annul, rescind, revoke, abrogate, repeal, recall, abolish, nullify, repudiate, make void, invalidate, quash, set aside, countermand, recant, retract, vacate.

3. Neutralize, counterbalance, compensate for.

CANCER, *n.* 1. Malignant growth, carcinoma, sarcoma, tumor, cancerous tissue, malignant tumor.

2. Malignant evil, ruthless killer, spreading corruption.

CANDELABRUM, *n.* Chandelier, candleholder, branched candlestick, ornamental candlestick, lampstand, luster, girandole, sconce, *torchère (Fr.).*

CANDID, *adj.* 1. Frank, open, free, ingenuous, artless, plain, downright, outright, direct, blunt, open-hearted, aboveboard, unreserved, outspoken, straightforward, plainspoken, straight from the shoulder, unvarnished.

2. Honest, impartial, fair, truthful, sincere, unbiased, unprejudiced, just.

CANDIDACY, *n.* Candidature, running for office, candidateship.

CANDIDATE, *n.* 1. Political contestant, aspirant, office-seeker, applicant, nominee.

2. Postulant, confirmand, probationer.

CANDIED, *adj.* 1. Preserved with sugar, sugared, impregnated with sugar, incrusted with sugar, converted to sugar, crystallized, granulated.

2. Flattering, honeyed, sweet, over-sweet.

CANDLE, *n.* Taper, tallow light, rush light, dip, bougie, *cierge (Fr.),* paschal.

CANDLESTICK, *n.* Candleholder, support for a candle, sconce, standard, candelabrum, luster, dicerion, tricerion, paschal, chandelier, girandole, *torchère (Fr.).*

CANDOR, *n.* 1. Frankness, openness, simplicity, ingenuousness, artlessness, straightforwardness, outspokenness.

2. Fairness, impartiality, truthfulness, honesty, sincerity, freedom from prejudice, freedom from bias.

CANDY, *n.* Confectionery, confection, sweetmeat, sweet.

Specifically, bonbon, comfit, fondant, toffee, sugarplum, taffy, hard candy, nougat, cream, fudge, peanut brittle, caramel, praline, lollipop, kiss, chocolate.

CANE, *n.* 1. Hollow stem, stalk, sugar cane.
2. Walking stick, stick, staff, rod, alpenstock.

CANE, *v.* Beat, strike, drub, switch, baste, flog, belabor, smite, hit, whip, rap, whack, trounce, tan, wallop, thrash.

CANKER, *n.* 1. Disease, mouth sore, gangrenous sore, ulcer, tree bark lesion.
2. Corrosion, corruption, infection, irritation, that which destroys, blight.

CANKER, *v.* 1. Corrode, eat away, destroy slowly.
2. Infect, corrupt, blight.

CANNIBAL, *n.* Eater of one's own kind, ogress, man-eater, anthropophagus, anthropophagite, ogre.

CANNIBALISTIC, *adj.* Man-eating, Thyestian, anthropophagic, anthropophagical, anthropophagous.

CANNONADE, *n.* Discharge of cannon, barrage, bombardment, broadside, battering, firing upon, shelling, pounding, continuous firing.

CANNONADE, *v.* Discharge cannon, attack with cannon, cannon, attack with heavy artillery, bombard, bomb, batter, shell.

CANNY, *adj.* 1. Careful, prudent, cautious, wary, watchful, vigilant, alert, open-eyed, circumspect, politic.
2. Knowing, sagacious, shrewd, astute, clever, intelligent, wise, sharp-witted, cunning, skilful, artful, perspicacious.
3. Skilled, expert, dexterous.
4. Comfortable, cozy, snug, quiet.
5. Thrifty, frugal, saving.

CANOE, *n.* Light narrow boat, canvas-covered boat, pleasure boat, birch bark boat, outrigger, kayak, pirogue, pitpan, dugout.

CANON, *n.* 1. Critical standard, criterion, decree, test, law, rule, fundamental principle, established principle.
2. *(Ecclesiastical)* Law, principle, regulation, standard, order, decree, decretal, code, rule of doctrine, constitution, rule of religious conduct.
3. Clergyman, prebendary, church dignitary.
4. List, catalog, catalog of saints, genuine books of Holy Scripture.

CANONICAL, *adj.* Authorized, according to the canon, established by a canon, recognized, accepted, lawful, approved, orthodox, standard, Biblical.

CANONIZE, *v.* Declare a saint, enroll in the canon, glorify, dignify, make canonical.

CANOPY, *n.* 1. Awning, tilt, tester, baldachin, cope, overhanging projection, cover, covering, shelter, roof, hood, shade, pavilion.
2. Sky, vault, heaven, dome.

CANT, *n.* 1. Whining talk, singsong speech, pious prating, sanctimonious phrases, pharisaism, rant.
2. Hypocrisy, affected piety, sham holiness, affectation in speech, insincere statements, pretense.
3. Peculiar form of speech, slang, professional

parlance, partisan vocabulary, shibboleths of sect, conventional talk, jargon, special idioms, thieves' vocabulary, argot, lingo.
4. Salient angle, turn, tip, tilt, slant, slanting surface, bias, slope, pitch, change of direction, toss, change of position.

CANT, *v.* Whine, beg, snivel, affect piety.

CANTANKEROUS, *adj.* Contentious, fractious, quarrelsome, disagreeable, cranky, disputatious, sullen, difficult, peevish, waspish, perverse, sharp, irritable, grouchy, splenetic, choleric, irascible, crabbed, morose, testy, huffy, short, ill-natured, contrary, ill-tempered, churlish, crusty, snappish, argumentative, grumpy, sulky, forward, iracund, touchy, quick-tempered, peppery, bearish, boorish.

CANTEEN, *n.* 1. Club, bar, Post Exchange, sutlery.
2. Flask, pocket flask, bottle, flasket.

CANTER, *n.* 1. Whiner, crier, beggar, mendicant, pauper, beadsman, vagrant, tramp, panhandler, hobo, derelict, wanderer.
2. Lope, trot, dogtrot, scamper, amble, jog trot, easy gallop, gentle gallop, leisurely gait.

CANTER, *v.* Lope, trot, dog trot, scamper, gallop gently, amble, go at a leisurely gait, bound *or* leap gently along.

CANTING, *adj.* Whining, insincere, hypocritical, tartufian, two-faced, pharisaic, unctuous, double-tongued, sanctimonious, dissembling, sniveling, mealy-mouthed, Janus-faced, smooth-tongued, bland.

CANVAS, *n.* Cloth, coarse cloth, sailcloth, fabric, woven fabric, material, drill, tarpaulin, artists' cloth, embroidery cloth.

CANVASS, *v.* 1. Survey, scrutinize, examine, scan, peruse, investigate, go over, look into, overhaul, explore, inspect, analyze, sift, break down, take stock of, search, consider, contemplate.
2. Discuss, debate, argue, consider, discourse, contemplate, air, treat, descant, comment upon, dissertate, ventilate, dispute, logomachize, discept, reason.
3. Solicit, bespeak, request, poll, invite, apply, electioneer, ballot, entreat, press, urge, endeavor to obtain, petition, sue for, appeal for.

CANYON, *n.* Ravine, divide, gorge, gulch, notch, gap, cut, water gap, chasm.

CAP, *n.* 1. Headdress, hat, bonnet, headgear, lid *(sl.),* fez, mitre, turban, hood, wimple, snood, beaver, castor, toque, beret, shako, biggin, calpac, biretta *(Church),* barret, zucchetto *(R. C. Church),* tarboosh, calotte, montero.
2. Lid, top, plug, cork, stopper, coverce, bung, stopple, ferrule, capsule.
3. Crown, tip, acme, vertex, zenith, peak, crest, culmination, point, pinnacle, height, apex, top, summit.

CAP, *v.* 1. Cover, tip, top, crown, bung, stopple, cork up, put a lid on.
2. Match, meet, rival, give and take, retort in kind, complement, requite, pattern, return the like, reciprocate, give *or* repay in kind, parallel.
3. Outplay, surpass, exceed, take the lead, transcend, outrank, beat, defeat, overtop, outdo, predominate, win over, overmatch, overpass, be superior to, override, throw into the shade, bear the palm, prevail, outpoint, outstrip, bear the bell, outdistance, eclipse, have the better of, take precedence, have the ascendancy, excel.

CAPABILITY, *n.* 1. Capacity, ableness, adequacy, qualification, possibility, efficacy, faculty, power, proficiency, efficiency, sufficiency, competence, capableness, potency, potentiality.

2. Cleverness, ability, adroitness, competency, power, dexterity, skill, facility, craft, ingenuity, mastery, calibre, efficiency, knowledge, capacity, scope, aptitude, knack, genius for, talent for, gift for, proficiency, attainment in.

CAPABLE, *adj.* 1. Able, efficient, sufficient, equal, adequate, competent, adapted, suited, effective, effectual, fitted, qualified, proficient, efficacious, suitable, open to, admitting of, susceptible to, receptive.

2. Able, skillful, deft, fitted, competent, adept, expert, intelligent, proficient, clever, masterly, dexterous, versatile, efficient, ingenious, adroit, accomplished, gifted, qualified.

CAPACIOUS, *adj.* Vast, vasty, widespread, big, great, spacious, comprehensive, immense, ample, large, extended, expanded, full, broad, massive, wide, voluminous, roomy, huge, commodious.

CAPACIOUSNESS, *n.* Expanse, vastness, width, comprehensiveness, expansiveness, extensiveness, greatness, amplitude, immensity, voluminousness, largeness, breadth, extent, roominess, openness.

CAPACITATE, *v.* Equip, make suitable, qualify, render capable, empower, enable, endue, endow, fit.

CAPACITY, *n.* 1. Volume, size, holding ability, dimensions, compass, scope, extent, reach, size, sweep, range, mass, amplitude, magnitude, bulk, containing power, largeness, content, burden, measure, room, power, proportions, quantity, sufficiency.

2. Intelligence, wit, grasp, discernment, reason, wisdom, intuition, sense, power, faculty, calibre, subtlety, aptness, mind, brain, acumen, sagacity, endowment, talent, gift, forte, ability, reasoning, penetration, perspicacity, quality, head, intellect, judgment.

CAPARISON, *n.* Outfit, equipment, adornment, trappings, dress, clothing, coverings, harness *(of horses),* accouterment, wardrobe, livery, things, apparel, wear, garments, drapery, impedimenta, costume, array, gear, rigging.

CAPE, *n.* 1. Point, peninsula, promontory, naze, foreland, headland, point of land, head, tongue, neck of land, chersonese, ness.

2. Wrap, cloak, mantle, fichu, cope *(Eccl.),* overdress, pelisse, manta, pelerine, mantelletta *(R. C. Church),* shawl, gaberdine, tabard, paletot.

CAPER, *n.* 1. Jump, leap, hop, skip, spring, trip, bound, romp, gambol, frisk, prance, dance, buck, cavort, curvet, gambado.

2. Antic, jape, trick, dido, escapade, frolic, revel, lark, prank, adventure, spree, practical joke, monkey trick.

CAPER, *v.* Leap, hop, skip, jump, bound, bounce, romp, prance, trip, frolic, frisk, dance, gambol, cavort, bob, flounce, caracole, buck.

CAPILLARY, *adj.* Slender, hair-like, flagelliform, filiform, finespun, attenuate, wiredrawn, fibriform, filamentar, fibrilliform, filamentary, filamentous, thread-like, thin, delicate.

CAPITAL, *adj.* 1. Main, chief, principal, central, foremost, primary, first, leading, supreme, prime, dominant, outstanding, highest, uppermost, vital, paramount, crowning, pre-eminent, predominant, top, greatest, ruling, key, head, master, major, important.

2. Punishable with death, carrying the death sentence.

3. Fine, excellent, supreme, first-class, tiptop, choice, select, best, peerless, matchless, superior, unapproached, champion *(coll.),* superexcellent, unparalleled, superlative, incomparable, of the first water, unmatched, unsurpassed, inimitable, unrivaled, unequaled, beyond compare, superfine, consummate, perfect, superb.

CAPITAL, *n.* 1. Majuscule, capital letter, large letter, upper case letter, initial letter.

2. Chief city, metropolis, seat of government, first city, center of government.

3. Stock, supply in hand, funds, wealth, nest egg, working assets, reserve, savings, resources, supply, cash, principal, investments, available means, moneys, finances, treasure, pecuniary resources, riches.

CAPITALISM, *n.* Free enterprise, competitive enterprise system, private ownership.

CAPITALIST, *n.* Financier, investor, plutocrat, business tycoon, banker, broker, stockbroker, moneyed man, millionaire, billionaire, wealthy man.

CAPITALIZE, *v.* Make money, gain, invest, turn to profit, thrive, prosper, profit, make capital out of, succeed in business, realize, clear, harvest, treasure up, accumulate wealth, obtain a return.

CAPITOL, *n.* Statehouse, legislative building, government house.

CAPITULATE, *v.* Surrender, give up, succumb, sue for peace, hoist the white flag, submit, yield, cede, acknowledge defeat, lay down *or* give up one's arms, come to terms, give ground, cry quits, comply, acquiesce, bend the neck, bow to, defer to, accede.

CAPITULATION, *n.* 1. Surrender, submission, yielding, cession, submittal, resignation, coming to terms, compliance, acquiescence, nonresistance.

2. Heading, enumeration, numeration, subject heading, numbering, summation.

CAPRICE, *n.* Whim, notion, fad, fit, idiocrasy, vagary, humor, crotchet, quirk, crank, erraticism, turn, maggot, craze, fancy, idiosyncrasy, oddity, peculiarity, twist, whimsy.

CAPRICIOUS, *adj.* Fitful, fickle, irresponsible, wayward, unsteady, erratic, whimsical, uncertain, inconstant, flighty, volatile, variable, impulsive, mercurial, changeable, fanciful, irregular, moody, deviative, wanton, lawless, heteroclite, spasmodic, stray, uneven, crotchety, skittish, faddish, infirm of purpose, changeful, unstable, wavering, shilly-shallying, irresolute, indecisive, undecided, vacillating.

CAPSIZE, *v.* Turn turtle, overturn, turn over, upset, keel over, tip over, be reversed, overset.

CAPSULE, *n. (Bot.)* Sac, blister, vasculum, boll, bladder, pericarp, follicle, silique, bleb, pocket, cyst, case, vesicle, utricle, saccule, bursa, legume, calyx, cell.

CAPTAIN, *n.* 1. Head, chief, leader, commander, skipper, foreman, boss, chieftain, commandant, master, overlord, headman, principal, governor, chief officer.

2. Master of a vessel, skipper, commander, sailing master, chief officer, old man *(Naut. sl.).*

CAPTION, *n.* 1. Heading, title, overline, banner, headline, scarehead, screamer, imprint, head.

2. Seizure, capture, apprehension, abduction, arrest, taking, appropriating, trapping, catching, commandeering, prehension *(chiefly zool.).*

CAPTIOUS, *adj.* 1. Insidious, entangling, subtle,

ensnaring, crafty, artful, vulpine, astute, subtile, arch, shrewd, tricky, Machiavellian, scheming, deep-laid, stealthy, sly, cunning, deceptive, conniving, perfidious, treacherous, collusive, guileful, elusive, delusive.

2. Carping, faultfinding, cutting, reproachful, nagging, caviling, critical, censorious, impugning, hypercritical, biting, disapprobatory, deprecating, disapproving, condemnatory, denunciatory, objurgatory, chiding, reprehensive, disapproving, picking, animadverting, scoffing, discommending.

CAPTIVATE, *v.* Fascinate, attract, enrapture, seduce, bewitch, enravish, enchain, enamor, lure, ravish, dazzle, enslave, transport, charm, enchant, infatuate, bedevil, becharm, vamp, mesmerize, hypnotize, delight, titillate, inflame, carry away, tantalize, take the fancy, turn one's head, enthrall.

CAPTIVE, *n.* Bondman, prisoner, slave, hostage, convict, cageling.

CAPTIVITY, *n.* Imprisonment, bondage, limbo, constraint, restraint, servitude, enslavement, subjection, slavery, duress, confinement, custody, incarceration, impoundment, committal, durance, detention, internment.

CAPTURE, *n.* 1. Seizure, arrest, caption, taking, apprehension, appropriating, trapping, abduction, commandeering, catching, prehension *(chiefly zool.),* snaring, snatching, grabbing, laying hold of, taking prisoner, rape, ensnaring, grasping, clutching, gripping.

2. Trophy, plunder, booty, gain, spoils, loot, pickings, prey, stealings, filchings, pillage, seizure, take, haul, swag *(sl.),* prize.

CAPTURE, *v.* Take captive, seize, wrest, catch, trap, ensnare, lay hold of, grab, clasp, arrest, apprehend, bag, ravish, rape, take by assault, clutch, fasten onto, nab *(sl.),* snag, snare, take prisoner, lay by the heels, kidnap, abduct, collar *(coll.),* take into custody, carry off.

CAR, *n.* 1. Carriage, vehicle, cart, van, wagon, coach, conveyance, chariot, phaeton, buggy, trap, break, landau, runabout, hackney, hack, cabriolet, hansom.

2. Automobile, motor car, auto, machine, auto car, roadster, limousine, sedan, tourer, coupé, convertible.

3. Railway car, coach, carriage, parlor car, Pullman, sleeper, diner, freight car, box car, baggage car, caboose, smoker, compartment.

CARAFE, *n.* Bottle, flask, flagon, decanter, phial, flasket, carboy, canteen, caster, cruse, demijohn, cruet.

CARAVAN, *n.* 1. Procession, company, group of travelers, cavalcade, column, parade, train, band, team, wagon train, coffle.

2. Wagon, van, covered wagon, Conestoga wagon, cart, prairie schooner.

CARAVANSARY, *n.* Inn, hotel, hostel, public house, lodging place, khan *(Near East),* resting place, tavern.

CARCASS, *n.* 1. Body, stiff, cadaver, dead body, corpse, remains, bones, carrion, skeleton.

2. *(Contemptuous)* Body, mold, torso, build, physique, person, anatomy, figure, form, shape.

3. Hulk, shell, remains, frame, framework, structure, ruin, relic, skeleton, debris, derelict.

CARD, *n.* 1. Ticket, pasteboard, cardboard, postcard, visiting card.

2. Slate, bill, line-up, schedule, program, order of the day, agenda, list, calendar, docket.

CARDINAL, *adj.* Main, basic, chief, foremost, principal, primary, central, first, leading, ruling, supreme, dominant, predominant, outstanding, highest, uppermost, paramount, capital, prime, crowning, pre-eminent, top, greatest, vital, key, head, master, essential, most important, intrinsic, underlying, elementary, necessary, indispensable, basal, necessary, constant, infixed.

CARDINAL, *n.* Prelate, ecclesiastical dignitary, ecclesiastical prince, hierarch, pontiff, Eminence, cardinal bishop, primate, prince of the church.

CARE, *n.* 1. Grief, sorrow, affliction, oppression, hardship, trouble, misfortune, misery, anguish, wretchedness, desolation, heartache, unhappiness, sadness, despair.

2. Concern, solicitude, anxiety, worry, trouble, vexation, stress, pressure, responsibility, incubus, encumbrance, load, handicap, strain, impediment, onus, hindrance, gravamen, tax, cross, nuisance, annoyance, tribulation, charge.

3. Attention, heed, caution, carefulness, pains, thought, heedfulness, consideration, application, diligence, concern, regard, exactness, precaution, meticulousness, conscientiousness, particularity, scrupulousness, fastidiousness, discrimination, nicety.

CARE, *v.* 1. Be cautious, heed, take care, attend, be careful, consider, regard, mind, think, take pains, bother.

2. *(With* for*)* Love, be fond of, have affection for, have regard for, like, prize, cherish, treasure, revere, adore, idolize.

3. *(With* for*)* Want, desire, wish for, have a longing for, fancy, hope for, yearn for, hunger *or* thirst after, aspire after, long for, prefer, be pleased with, incline towards.

CAREEN, *v.* Tilt, lean, incline, list, sway, slope, keel, sag, slant, lurch, be at an angle, tip, veer, sheer.

CAREER, *n.* 1. Profession, job, line, vocation, following, calling, activity, lifework, occupation, pursuit, livelihood, work, employment, walk of life, metier.

2. Flow, course, passage, set, flux, direction, onrush, road, route, run, track, march, tack, line, beat, way, lap, circuit, trek, ambit, round.

CAREER, *v.* Run, move, scurry, hustle *(coll.),* scramble, make haste, scamper, rush, scuttle, bustle, bowl, be swift, dash, speed, sprint, spank, scoot, bolt, dart, fly, race, shoot, tear, sweep, bundle along, go.

CAREFREE, *adj.* Happy, gay, light-hearted, glad, cheerful, without worry, sprightly, buoyant, airy, mirthful, unworried, gleeful, jolly, jovial, jocular, free and easy, jubilant, debonair, elated, sportive, breezy, jaunty, optimistic, sunny, joyous, brisk, bright, in high spirits, elastic, resilient, laughing, riant, smiling, nonchalant, careless, easygoing, happy-go-lucky.

CAREFUL, *adj.* 1. Cautious, wary, heedful, alert, prudent, discreet, chary, on guard, observant, circumspect, judicious, mindful, apprehensive, thoughful, attentive, regardful, politic, guarded, stealthy, vigilant, watchful, solicitous, concerned.

2. Fine, nice, diligent, exact, scrupulous, fussy, fastidious, particular, meticulous, conscientious, attentive, accurate, painstaking, precise, faithful, correct, punctilious.

CARELESS, *adj.* 1. Untroubled, happy, gay, free from care, light-hearted, without worry, buoyant, sprightly, airy, mirthful, unworried, optimistic, gleeful, jolly, jovial, jocular, free and easy, elated, jubilant, debonair, sportive, breezy, jaunty, brisk, sunny, joyous, bright, in high spirits, in high humor, riant, elastic, resilient, laughing, smiling, nonchalant, happy-go-lucky, easygoing.

2. Neglectful, heedless, imprudent, indiscreet, injudicious, thoughtless, unthinking, disregardful, inconsiderate, forgetful, reckless, rash, incautious, temerarious, inattentive, insouciant, indifferent, lax, unmindful, loose, remiss, unconcerned, unwary, slack, nonobservant, unheeding, inadvertent, unguarded, absent-minded, uncircumspect.

3. Sloppy, untidy, messy, slovenly, slapdash, casual, slipshod, sluttish, slack, lax, remiss, loose, inexact, inaccurate, incorrect, offhand, indifferent, nonchalant, untrustworthy, disorderly, apathetic, perfunctory, lackadaisical, forgetful, slatternly, listless.

CARESS, *n.* Kiss, embrace, gentle touch, smack, fondling, osculation, brush, grazing, hug, stroking, blandishment.

CARESS, *v.* Touch, fondle, rub, handle, stroke, pat, massage, brush, graze, lick, embrace, sweep, kiss, pass the fingers over, cuddle, hug, clasp, nuzzle, nestle, cosset, coddle, snuggle, pet, toy with, pamper.

CARETAKER, *n.* Janitor, sexton, custodian, keeper, watchman, overseer, warden, curator, steward.

CAREWORN, *adj.* Tired, weary, haggard, spent, exhausted, effete, wasted, woebegone, oppressed, worn, heavy-laden, oppressed, crushed, beaten, fatigued, drooping, enfeebled, fagged, tuckered *(coll.),* faint, toilworn, footsore, overwearied, weakened, flagging, dispirited, life-weary, sorry, stricken.

CARGO, *n.* Load, lading, weight, capacity, bale, shipload, carload, wagonload, freight, contents, burden, shipment, goods, haul, charge.

CARICATURE, *n.* Take-off, cartoon, burlesque, parody, travesty, satire, mockery, burletta, farce, macaronic, slapstick, grotesque rendition *or* portrayal, lampoon.

CARICATURE, *v.* Satirize, take-off, mimic, ape, portray grotesquely, imitate, mock, exaggerate, parody, ridicule, stultify, render absurd, buffoon, make ludicrous, burlesque, make foolish, laugh at, laugh to scorn, lampoon.

CARILLON, *n.* Set of bells, peal of bells, tocsin, angelus, chimes, tintinnabulum, campana, gong, dingdong.

CARNAGE, *n.* Massacre, bloodshed, destruction, wholesale killing, butchery, mass-murder, mass homicide, pogrom, slaughter, slaying, trucidation, internecion, havoc, effusion of blood, saturnalia of blood.

CARNAL, *adj.* 1. Sensual, worldly, profane, secular, mundane, earthly, unspiritual, physical, terrestrial, corporeal, fleshly, bodily.

2. Sexual, fleshly, physical, bodily, animalistic, voluptuous, theroid, lustful, lickerish, libidinous, erotic, lascivious, lewd, lecherous, brutish, crude, bestial, concupiscent, prurient, salacious, wanton, unchaste, indecent, impure, ruttish, venereal, gross.

CARNALITY, *n.* 1. Worldliness, unspirituality, sensuality, profaneness, earthliness, fleshliness, carnal nature, secularity, physical nature, earthly nature.

2. Desire, sexuality, concupiscence, passion, lust, lewdness, satyrism, venery, lasciviousness,

lechery, libidinousness, bestiality, salaciousness, pruriency, wantonness, crudeness, bodily appetite, grossness, impurity, ruttishness.

CARNIVAL, *n.* 1. Festival, celebration, revelry, jollification, feasting, spree, fete, masquerade, Mardi gras, merrymaking, carousing, Saturnalia, frolic, junket, bacchanal, gala, jamboree *(sl.),* heyday, holiday, carousal, jubilee, conviviality.

2. Sideshow, merry-go-round, circus, peep show, puppet show, freak show, Punch-and-Judy show, raree show, carousal.

CARNIVOROUS, *adj.* Carnivoral, flesh-eating, predaceous, predatory, zoophagous, omophagous, ichthyophagous *(of fish eaters).*

CAROL, *n.* Hymn, song, song of praise, canticle, chant, noel, Christmas song, anthem, doxology, paean, glorification, spiritual, madrigal, glee.

CAROL, *v.* Sing, chant, pipe, vocalize, warble, descant, intone, chirp, chirrup, lilt, sing a paean, sing jubilantly, sing with joy, praise in song, trill, yodel, troll.

CAROUSAL, *n.* Carouse, jollification, bacchanal, spree, revelry, banquet, festivity, merrymaking, fete, frolic, junket, Saturnalia, potation, wassail, conviviality, orgy, drunken bout, debaucherie, compotation, libation, carnival, gala affair, bout, romp, frisk, caper, heyday.

CAROUSE, *v.* Drink, tipple, quaff, make merry, revel, junket, frolic, wassail, paint the town red *(sl.),* guzzle, imbibe, drown one's sorrows, sup, banquet, be convivial, feast.

CARP, *v.* Complain, cavil, find fault, nag, pick, depreciate, censure, reprehend, faultfind, quibble, animadvert, wrangle, peck at, blame, reproach, pull to pieces, disparage, disapprove, cast a slur on, deprecate, belittle, decry, jibe at, sneer at, slight, discredit, deride.

CARPENTER, *n.* Woodworker, cabinetmaker, joiner, builder *(in wood),* chips *(sl.),* journeyman.

CARPET, *n.* Rug, floor covering, matting, mat, flooring, scatter rug, mohair rug, Oriental rug, Persian rug, Turkish rug, Indian rug, Chinese rug.

CARPET, *v.* Floor, overlay, cover, pave, conceal *(the floor with),* lay down a covering, superpose, superimpose, overspread.

CARPING, *adj.* Caviling, faultfinding, nagging, cutting, bitter, critical, biting, disapprobatory, reproachful, hypercritical, censorious, scoffing, disapproving, condemnatory, animadverting, denunciatory, objurgatory, chiding, deprecating, reprehensive, picking, impugning, discommending.

CARRIAGE, *n.* 1. Comportment, attitude, front, deportment, demeanor, quital, acquital, bearing, behavior, manner, gait, look, cast, presence, mien, guise, observance, air, port, build, physique, pose, posture, aspect, poise.

2. Vehicle, conveyance, wagon, van, four-wheeler, coach, stage-coach, hansom, cabriolet, phaeton, chariot, brougham, trap, surrey, dogcart, gig, buggy, sulky, dearborn, curricle, rockaway, runabout, chaise, hackney, two-wheeler, tilbury, landau, victoria, Tally-ho, barouche, dos-à-dos, calash, tumbrel, coupé.

3. Transportation, transference, conveyance, freight, carrying, portage, postage, asportation, cartage, truckage, freightage, shipment, haulage, trans-shipment, convection, conduction, porterage, waftage, carry, ferriage.

CARRIER, *n.* Porter, transporter, messenger, coolie, tranter, conductor, conveyor, sustainer, supporter, holder, bearer.

CARRION, *n.* Putrefying meat *or* flesh, remains, corpse, bones, dead body, offal, cadaver.

CARRY, *v.* 1. Transport, tote, transmit, displace, bear, waft, move, take, bring, portage, convey, fetch, haul, transplant, conduct, convoy, transfer, shift, cart, lug.

2. Uphold, prop, pillow, cradle, lend support, underset, brace, underpin, underprop, shore up, bear, shoulder, lift, sustain, support, hold up, maintain, buttress, mainstay.

3. Urge, impel, drive, actuate, induce, thrust, persuade, bring round, bring over, move, turn the scale, influence, determine, motivate, prompt, push, goad, poke, prod, instigate, incite, whip, spur, stimulate, press, propel.

4. (With *off*) Take captive, seize, catch, grab, clasp, bag, ravish, rape, abduct, take by assault, clutch, fasten upon, nab *(sl.),* capture, kidnap, take prisoner, collar *(coll.).*

CART, *n.* Wagon, two-wheeler, tumbrel, dray, gig, dogcart, curricle, dumpcart, tipcart, trap, handcart, tilbury, handbarrow, pushcart, gocart, barrow.

CART, *v.* Transport, haul, lug, carry, tote, bear, transmit, move, take, bring, portage, convey, fetch, convoy, conduct, transplant, transfer, transmit.

CARTE BLANCHE, *n.* Unconditional power, free license, open sanction, free authority, full right, unconditional permit.

CARTON, *n.* Cardboard box, packing case, case, cardboard container, pasteboard box, strawboard box, box, paper box.

CARTOON, *n.* 1. Sketch, design, image, tracing, outline, pencil sketch, drawing, charcoal drawing, picture, representation, depiction, portraiture, delineation, caricature, portrayal, pastiche, likeness.

2. Satire, burlesque, take-off, travesty, parody, pastiche, extravaganza, caricature.

CARTOONIST, *n.* Artist, sketcher, caricaturist, drawer, portrayer, designer, draftsman, depicter.

CARTRIDGE, *n.* Shell case, explosive capsule, casing, cylinder, cap, ball cartridge, cartouche, charge.

CARVE, *v.* 1. Cut, hew, shape, sculpture, chisel, mold, model, form, fashion, insculp, roughhew, pattern, trim, roughcast, block out, tool, engrave, incise, etch, stipple, enchase, grave, scrape.

2. Cut, slice, hack, sunder, quarter, decimate, cleave, saw, chop, split, hew, slash, whittle, rend, dissever, divide, gash, trench, mince, abscind, rive, dissect.

3. Serve, apportion, divide, allot, partition, portion, quarter.

CASCADE, *n.* Waterfall, chute, rapids, niagara, cataract, fall, series of small waterfalls.

CASE, *n.* 1. Container, carton, box, receptacle, coffer, casket, crib, caisson, bin, chest, caddie, pyxis, crate, canister, cartouche, cabinet, holder, tray.

2. Sheath, sheathing, wrapper, envelope, cover, covering, jacket, capsule, protection, housing, shelter, shroud, overlay, coverage, integument, casement.

3. *(Bot.)* Sac, cell, bursa, calyx, legume, pocket, saccule, utricle, vesicle, cyst, follicle, silique, boll, bleb, pericarp, bladder, vasculum, blister.

4. Example, sample, illustration, instance, case in point, representation, exemplification.

5. Circumstance, situation, condition, clause, provision, stipulation, specification, arrangement, requisite, reservation, prerequisite, exemption, exception.

6. Proposition, premise, argument, assumption, position, postulation, supposal, presupposition, thesis, hypothesis, theorem, subject.

7. Patient, invalid, victim, sickling, sufferer, valetudinarian, sick person.

8. Inflection, declension, grammatical ending, conjugation, grammatical suffix, grammatical prefix.

9. Suit, appeal, lawsuit, plea, trial, litigation, proceedings, cause, action, hearing, indictment, inquiry, dispute, arraignment, impeachment.

10. Event, happening, occurrence, emergency, circumstance, incident, episode, matter, business, transaction, contingency, affair, concern, advent, occasion, proceeding, eventuality, supervention, situation, experience, adventure.

11. Dispute, controversy, quarrel, altercation, litigation, argument, agitation, wrangle, discord, disputation, debate, dissension.

CASEHARDENED, *adj.* Unrelenting, relentless, stony-hearted, ruthless, thick-skinned, inflexible, callous, hard-hearted, unaffected, uninfluenced, insensible, hard-boiled *(coll.),* unfeeling, tough, hardened, remorseless, insensitive, unsusceptible, inured, heartless, impassive, coldhearted, coldblooded, unconcerned, indifferent.

CASEMENT, *n.* Sash, lattice, wicket, bay window, bow window, dormer, oriel, window frame.

CASH, *n.* 1. Legal tender, coin, coinage, mintage, coin of the realm, lucre *(coll.),* dough *(sl.),* bill, specie, hard money, bank note, change, currency.

2. Stock, supply in hand, capital, funds, riches, wealth, working assets, reserve, savings, supply, resources, pecuniary resources, treasure, finances, moneys, available means, investments, principal, wherewithal.

CASH, *v.* 1. Turn into money, change, exchange, realize in cash, liquidate assets.

2. Pay, remit, pay cash, reimburse, discharge, refund, settle, square accounts, clear, pay in full, defray, honor a bill, pay on the line, put down *or* lay down money, pay the costs, redeem.

CASHIER, *n.* Teller, cashkeeper, bursar, receiver, accountant, cambist, treasurer, purser, banker, depositary.

CASHIER, *v.* Dismiss, displace, break, remove, discharge, disbar, deprive of office, drum out, cast out, depose, divest of office, unfrock, oust, unseat, disestablish, fire *(coll.),* bust *(sl.),* let go.

CASINO, *n.* Clubhouse, gambling establishment, dance hall, betting house, roadhouse, gambling den, Domdaniel, honky-tonk, poolroom.

CASK, *n.* Vat, butt, rundlet, barrel, keg, tun, tub, firkin, kilderkin, hogshead, puncheon, vessel, tierce, pipe.

CASKET, *n.* 1. Container, box, case, receptacle, coffer, crib, caisson, bin, chest, caddie, pyxis, crate, canister, cabinet, holder, tray, reliquary, shrine.

2. Coffin, box, pall, sarcophagus, catafalque.

CASSEROLE, *n.* Saucepan, skillet, baking dish, frying pan, tureen, terrine, covered dish.

CAST, *n.* 1. Throw, toss, pitch, heave, expulsion, hurling, shy, fling, sling, propulsion, launching, ejection, shooting, projection.

2. Glance, glimpse, sight, view, regard, aspect, spying, eyeshot, cursory look, flicker, twinkle, peep.

3. Humor, mood, disposition, aspect, tendency, temperament, spirit, tone, streak, stripe, temper, vein, quality, nature, constitution, propensity, proclivity, predilection, predisposition, proneness, grain, inclination, leaning, twist, bent, bias, warp, course.

4. Shape, form, mold, set, pattern, type, turn, stamp, impression, duplicate, model, replica, counterpart, casting, reproduction.

5. Manner, appearance, complexion, seeming, look, expression, mien, tone, color, air, carriage, semblance, guise, bearing, attitude, deportment, observance, front, behavior, demeanor, acquittal, quittal, pose.

6. Players, actors, dramatis personae, persons in the play, company, troupe, performers, list of characters.

CAST, *v.* 1. Throw, toss, hurl, dash, heave, dart, shy, sling, chuck, pitch, discharge, jerk, propel, project, ejaculate, expel, shoot, catapult, let fly, precipitate, send, launch.

2. Scatter, disseminate, sprinkle, spread, strew, diffuse, radiate, distribute, bestrew, broadcast, disperse, spatter, bespread, ted, circulate, shed, sow, broadcast.

3. Mold, set, shape, model, sculpture, form by molding, fix, stamp, mint, roughcast, knead, work into shape.

4. Pick (actors), apportion, allot, choose, give parts, appoint, detail, allocate.

5. (*With* AWAY) Reject, throw out, refuse, repulse, eject, expel, oust, discard, fling away, forswear, disclaim, decline, put aside.

6. (*With* OUT) Exclude, bar, ban, prohibit, reject, banish, ostracize, taboo, debar, disallow, outlaw, preclude, forfend, interdict, eliminate, relegate, remove, repudiate, excommunicate, shut out, exile, disbar (*Leg.*).

7. (*With* UP) Throw up, expel, eject, spew, vomit, disgorge, belch forth, extrude, emit, send forth, gush, pour out, spurt, squirt, jet, issue forth, vent, discharge, void, evacuate, expectorate, spit forth.

CASTAWAY, *adj.* Shipwrecked, abandoned, lost, marooned, derelict, deserted, stranded, aground, adrift, grounded, wrecked, stuck, forsaken.

CASTAWAY, *n.* 1. Shipwrecked person, derelict, marooned person.

2. Castoff, outcast, pariah, leper, waif, stray, foundling, vagrant, vagabond, flotsam and jetsam, jettison, beachcomber, renegade, outlaw, rover, wanderer, man without a country, meanderer.

CASTE, *n.* Class, rank, order, race, grade, social order, position, standing, condition, station, place, status, sphere, degree, lineage, descent, ancestry, blood, family, clan, group.

CASTIGATE, *v.* 1. Flog, beat, whip, lash, spank, chastise, scourge, lace, strike, flagellate, trounce, bastinado, flail, thrash, drub, cane, birch, cudgel, fustigate, horsewhip, baste, cuff, box, pummel, smite, thump, swinge, strap.

2. Punish, chasten, chastise, upbraid, rebuke, reprimand, correct, chide, bring to retribution, admonish, reproach, objurgate, scold, berate, take to task, penalize, reprove, put on the carpet (*coll.*), discipline, dress down, haul over the coals (*coll.*), censure.

CASTLE, *n.* 1. Fortification, fortress, stronghold, keep, chateau, tower, donjon, fort, citadel, hold,

acropolis, fasthold, safehold, fastness.

2. Hall, stately dwelling, chateau, mansion, manor house, palace, chalet, messuage, grange, tower.

CASTRATE, *v.* 1. Capon, eunuchize, geld, alter (*coll.*), unman, effeminize, emasculate, deprive of virility *or* manhood, spay (*of female animals*).

2. Weaken, reduce, debilitate, impair, exhaust, sap, impoverish, extenuate, incapacitate, enfeeble, devitalize, attenuate, enervate, unstrengthen, emasculate.

CASTRATION, *n.* Effeminization, emasculation, gelding, orchotomy, unmanning, altering, spaying (*of female animals*).

CASUAL, *adj.* 1. Unintentional, unpremeditated, accidental, fortuitous, adventitious, unlooked-for, contingent, incidental, unexpected, involuntary, random, undesigned, unpurposed, undirected, unplanned, haphazard, unforeseen, chance.

2. Random, indefinite, careless, thoughtless, desultory, haphazard, offhand, unsystematic, irregular, occasional, vague, disorderly, aimless, unmethodical, undirected, indiscriminate, unsure, disorganized, orderless, unarranged, straggling, equivocal, ambiguous, dubious, questionable, uncertain, unsettled, unfixed.

3. Blasé, unconcerned, nonchalant, indifferent, inconstant, uninterested, insouciant, pococurante, careless, lackadaisical, inattentive, apathetic, listless.

CASUALTY, *n.* 1. Event, chance, occurrence, accident, happening, incident, adventure, episode, contingency, experience, occasion, fortuity, hazard.

2. Misfortune, disaster, catastrophe, mischief, tragedy, emergency, mishap, accident, adversity, unfortunate occurrence, misadventure, calamity, mischance, stroke, blow, grief, reverse, visitation, setback, infliction, sorrow, scourge, contretemps, cataclysm.

3. Wounded man, injured man, fatality.

CASUISTRY, *n.* Sophistry, sophism, chicanery, equivocal reasoning, philosophism, speciousness, philosophastry.

CAT, *n.* Feline, mouser, pussy, tomcat, house cat, tabby, Angora, grimalkin, Maltese cat, Persian cat, gib, tortoise-shell, kitten (*dim.*), catling.

CATACLYSM, *n.* 1. Flood, deluge, earthquake, disaster, upheaval, avalanche, inundation, debacle, washout, eruption, convulsion, alluvion.

2. Disaster, tragedy, catastrophe, mishap, blow, calamity, stroke, debacle, mischief, emergency, visitation, scourge, infliction, contretemps, reverse.

CATACOMB, *n.* (*often plural*) Vault, sepulcher, subterranean cemetery, crypt, burial chambers, tomb, underground ossuary.

CATALOGUE, *n.* Index, enumeration, list, brief record, register, file, table, syllabus, schedule, calendar, panel, beadroll, prospectus, draft, roll bulletin, inventory, screed, directory, cartulary, classification, docket, terrier, gazetteer, archive, slate, muster roll, gazette.

CATALOGUE, *v.* Arrange, list, classify, register, record, file, group, tabulate, alphabetize, codify, rank, docket (*Leg.*), ticket, graduate, segregate, digest, calendar, enroll, chronicle, summarize.

CATAPULT, *n.* Sling, slingshot, arbalest, mortar, trebuchet, ballista.

CATAPULT, *v.* Hurl, fling, eject, throw, shoot

fire, let fly, heave, pitch, cast, expel, precipitate, send, discharge, toss, propel, sling, shy, chuck.

CATARACT, *n.* 1. Waterfall, fall, cascade, race, torrent, niagara, rapids, sault, debacle.

2. Deluge, flood, inundation, washout, debacle, downpour, alluvion.

CATASTROPHE, *n.* Cataclysm, disaster, tragedy, misfortune, mishap, calamity, hardship, casualty, misery, visitation, blow, upheaval, debacle, ruin, stroke, emergency, reverse, scourge, infliction, contretemps, eruption, convulsion, misadventure, alluvion, avalanche, affliction, desolation, havoc, devastation, ravage, fatality, wreck, grief, crash, accident, mischance.

CATCALL, *n.* 1. Whistle, hoot, shout, rude cry, hiss, boo, jeer, gibe, heckling, raspberry *(sl.).*

2. Hooter, rattle, whistle, noisemaker, clacker, clapper, tick-tock.

CATCH, *v.* 1. Grasp, snatch, nab, seize, clutch, snap, swoop on, take, grab, pick, pounce on, grip, snare, pluck, claw, clench, hook, fasten upon, snag.

2. Apprehend, seize, nab, capture, take, snare, arrest, ensnare, intercept, stop, cop, noose, collar *(coll.),* net, lasso, corral, corner, pit, take captive, lay hold of, bag, kidnap, take into custody.

3. Contract, get, come down with, break out with, receive, incur.

4. Surprise, detect, espy, discover, come upon, discern, spot *(coll.),* find out, descry, uncover, unearth, take off guard, startle, disclose, reveal, show up, bring to light, unmask, bare.

5. Fascinate, attract, enthrall, enrapture, trap, transport, enravish, enchain, bewitch, mesmerize, seduce, enamor, ravish, allure, dazzle, enslave, charm, enchant, infatuate, captivate, hypnotize, bedevil, becharm, vamp, turn one's head, take the fancy, carry away, tantalize, inflame, titillate, delight.

CATCH, *n.* 1. Clasp, hasp, lock, clip, fastening, fastener, buckle, crotch, detent, union, coupling, latch, click, latchet, holdfast, clinch, clamp, cog, snap, dog, pawl, hook.

2. Troll, round, song, rondo, madrigal, canon.

3. Bag, take, haul, capture, catchment, seizure, find, pickings, swag *(sl.),* prey, pillage, plunder, loot, spoils, gain, trophy, booty, prize.

CATCHING, *adj.* 1. Communicable, pestilential, inoculable, infectious, pestiferous, contagious, miasmatic, taking, epidemic, epizootic, pandemic.

2. Appealing, charming, desirable, fascinating, alluring, seductive, engrossing, ravishing, taking, glamorous, engaging, enchanting, bewitching, entrancing, absorbing, tempting, inviting, elegant, tantalizing, attractive, enthralling, transporting, dazzling, delightful, captivating, winning, lovely, intriguing, fetching, provocative, enticing, fair, handsome, pretty, magnificent, graceful, bonny, beauteous, seemly, sightly, blooming, exquisite, superb, good-looking, comely, magnetic, radiant, gorgeous, resplendent, lustrous, effulgent.

CATCHING, *n.* Seizure, arrest, caption, trapping, apprehension, taking, appropriating, abduction, commandeering, prehension *(chiefly zool.),* snaring, snatching, grabbing, clutching, taking prisoner, laying hold of, rape, ensnaring, grasping, gripping.

CATCHUP, *n.* Sauce, catsup, ketchup, condiment, relish, seasoning, tomato sauce.

CATCHWORD, *n.* 1. Signal, cue, cue word.

2. Clew-word, tag, signature, marginal clew.

3. Slogan, watchword, motto, battle cry, party cry, war cry, password, shibboleth.

CATECHIZE, *v.* 1. Coach, instruct, teach, tutor, inform, edify, inspire, familiarize, ground, school, enlighten, acquaint, impart, show, indoctrinate, implant, imbue, inculcate, indue, instill, educate, nurture, discipline, drill, train, initiate, rudiment, preach, descant, discourse.

2. Pump, query, quiz, inquisite, inquire, grill *(coll.),* cross-examine, interpellate, investigate, cross-question, interrogate, examine, question, put through the third degree *(coll.).*

CATECHUMEN, *n.* Tyro, beginner, abecedarian, novice, proselyte, recruit, learner, alphabetarian, novitiate, amateur, pupil, freshman, apprentice, probationer, newcomer, tenderfoot, initiate, neophyte, convert.

CATEGORICAL, *adj.* Absolute, implicit, positive, pronounced, direct, exact, unconditional, concise, actual, detailed, unequivocal, marked, emphatic, unmistakable, express, flat, certain, unqualified, downright, peremptory, dogmatic, unreserved, explicit.

CATEGORY, *n.* Classification, class, status, type, compilation, distribution, heading, subdivision, province, sphere, family, genus, sort, designation, kind, variety, denomination, species, arrangement, division, head, department, assortment, section, order, rank, enumeration, coördination, grouping.

CATER, *v.* 1. Purvey, forage, supply, provender, mess, provide, victual, furnish, procure.

2. *(With TO)* Gratify, satisfy, please, humor, spoil, indulge, pamper, pander to, favor, curry favor.

CATERWAUL, *v.* Howl, wail, cry, miaul, bawl, clamor, vociferate, screech, whimper, proclaim, whine, yelp, give cry, rend the air, sing out, hoot, boohoo, mewl, bellow, squall, shout, roar, bray, shriek, squawk, scream, squeal, stridulate, mew.

CATHARSIS, *n.* Purification, purgation, ablution, release, abstersion, purging, depuration, epuration.

CATHARTIC, *adj.* Cleansing, purifying, purging, aperient, detergent, emetic, purificative, purgative, abstergent, expurgatory, abstersive, ablutionary, lustral, lapactic, laxative, eccritic, deobstruent, depurative, carminative, vomitive.

CATHEDRAL, *n.* 1. Bishop's seat, bishop's chair, bishop's throne, cathedra, episcopal see, chief church *(of a diocese).*

2. Cathedral church, sanctuary, temple.

CATHOLIC, *adj.* 1. Ecumenical, predominant, infinite, prevailing, absolute, preponderant, widespread, rampant, universal, general, world-wide, common, comprehensive, all-inclusive, catholical, all-embracing.

2. Liberal, latitudinarian, unbiased, unbigoted, broad-minded, unsectarian, unprejudiced, broad, impartial, lenient, indulgent, dispassionate, wideminded, uninfluenced, unwarped, unjaundiced, unswayed, undogmatic, open-minded, unfanatical, amenable, responsive, persuadable, freethinking, unopinionated, disinterested.

CATHOLIC, *n.* Roman Catholic, ultramontane, Romanist, papist *(derog.).*

CATTLE, *n.* Livestock, bovine animals, domestic animals, dairy cattle, beef cattle, shorthorns, longhorns, heifers, yearlings, oxen, steers, Jerseys, Holsteins, Guernseys, Galloways, Lancashires, Redpolls, Anguses, Aberdeens.

CAUCUS, *n.* Assembly, gathering, policy-fixing

meeting, meeting (of political leaders), conclave, convention, session, assemblage, council, synod, conventicle, political confluence, conference.

CAUSALITY, n. Causation, cause, prime mover, determining factor, first-cause, influence, reason, occasion, origination.

CAUSATION, n. Causality, origination, invention, causativeness, causativity, determinant.

CAUSE, n. 1. Root, occasion, source, inspiration, prime mover, spring, origin, incentive, excitation, stimulation, motive, inducement, fountainhead, actuation, fomentation, incitation, instigation, reason, provocation, incitement, author, agent, mainspring, derivation, genesis, beginning, primary cause, ultimate cause, primordium, generator, producer.
2. Question, matter, bone of contention, point, subject of dispute, ground, question at issue, problem, topic, theme, point at issue, point in question.
3. Principle, object, purpose, belief, tenet, end, conviction, side, persuasion.
4. Suit, appeal, lawsuit, plea, trial, proceedings, litigation, case, action, hearing, inquiry, dispute, arraignment, indictment, impeachment.

CAUSE, v. Bring about, effect, be the cause of, produce, raise, create, institute, found, neologize, originate, begin, give rise to, make, generate, set up, bring to pass, set afloat, give occasion, induce, lead to.

CAUSEWAY, n. Raised road, bridge, corduroy road, road, viaduct.

CAUSTIC, adj. 1. Mordant, burning, sharp, keen, erosive, escharotic, cutting, biting, penetrating, stringent, corrosive, astringent, piercing, pungent, corroding, consuming.
2. Sharp, keen, painful, agonizing, stinging, biting, burning, piercing, trenchant, penetrating, severe, excruciating, tormenting, torturous, poignant, hurtful.
3. Cruel, unkind, hurtful, sarcastic, ungracious, biting, sharp, keen, cutting, stinging, acrimonious, mean, brutal, brusque, harsh, blunt, abrupt, rude, gruff, brash, curt, drastic, short, austere, stern, tart, virulent, bearish, churlish, discourteous, impolite, inaffable, unceremonious, unmannerly, ill-bred, uncivil, ungentle, scathing, bitter, mocking, satirical, malevolent, venomous, crusty, crabbed, mordacious, derisive, derisory, insulting, excoriating, lashing, malignant, unbenevolent, ill-natured, malicious, maleficent, spiteful, galling, rancorous, envenomed, uncharitable, invidious, unamiable, uncordial.

CAUTERIZE, v. Sear, burn, disinfect by burning.

CAUTION, n. 1. Prudence, care, attention, heed, concern, carefulness, thought, heedfulness, regard, diligence, application, precaution, watchfulness, circumspection, vigilance, sleeplessness, alertness, guardedness, surveillance, mindfulness, wariness, attentiveness, solicitude, deliberation, calculation.
2. Warning, caveat, admonition, dehortation, forewarning, alarm, prewarning, omen.

CAUTION, v. Warn, forewarn, admonish, alarm, notify of danger, advise, put on one's guard, prewarn, premonish, prenotify, precaution, bode, forebode, portend, presage, prognosticate, augur, auspicate, foreshadow, foretoken, preindicate, betoken, presignify.

CAUTIOUS, adj. Circumspect, deliberate, careful, prudent, attentive, heedful, guarded, concerned, regardful, watchful, mindful, vigilant, wary, alert,

aware, judicious, stealthy, thoughtful, sagacious, shrewd, chary, discreet, advised, scrupulous, precautionary, sleepless, wakeful.

CAVALCADE, n. Parade, procession, train, team, retinue, cortege, company, caravan, excursionists, group of travelers, column, safari.

CAVALIER, n. 1. Mounted soldier, knight, rider, horse soldier, cavalryman, cuirassier, dragoon, trooper, lancer, hussar, horseman.
2. Blade, fop, dandy, beau, coxcomb, gallant, exquisite, silk-stocking, popinjay, swell, spark, buck, dapperling, dude, jackanapes, carpet knight, macaroni, élégant (Fr.), Dundreary, blood, fine gentleman, man about town, playboy.

CAVALRY, n. Mounted troops, dragoons, lancers, hussars, horse soldiers, mounted men, squadrons, horse, mounted rifles, mounted soldiers.

CAVE, n. Den, dugout, hollow, cavern, grotto, cavity, subterrane, underground chamber, tunnel, cellar, subway.

CAVEAT, n. Warning, alarm, prewarning, omen, caution, forewarning, dehortation, admonition.

CAVERN, n. Cave, hollow, grotto, subterrane, cavity, underground chamber, tunnel, cellar, den, subway, dugout.

CAVERNOUS, adj. Hollow, sunken, cave-like, yawning, abysmal, pitted, crannied, furrowed, honeycombed, concave, depressed, hollowed out, rimose, indented, retreating, faveolate, alveolate.

CAVIL, v. Complain, quibble, carp, find fault, sneer at, deride, discredit, slight, jibe at, decry, pull to pieces, belittle, criticize, deprecate, cast a slur on, disapprove, disparage, reproach, nag, censure, reprehend, pick, faultfind, animadvert, wrangle, peck at, blame, find flaws in, haggle, censure captiously or frivolously.

CAVITY, n. Cave, cavern, pit, shaft, abyss, deep, chasm, excavation, hollow, impression, crater, crevasse, indentation, concavity, dent, cup, cell, chamber, mine, den, scoop, burrow, cistern, hole, niche, orifice, opening, fissure, crack, slit, breach, aperture, cleft, chink, notch, gap, perforation, rent, bore, tunnel, dell, crypt (Anat.), hiatus, sinus (Anat.), pore, alveolus (Anat. and Zool.), lacuna (Biol.), fossa (Anat.), atrium (Anat.), druse.

CAVORT, v. (Coll. U.S.) Prance, caper, bounce, leap, hop, skip, jump, romp, bound, trip, frolic, frisk, dance, gambol, bob, caracole, buck, flounce.

CEASE, v. Pause, desist, leave off, stop, halt, end, quit, withdraw from, withhold, conclude, bring to an end, give over, finish, drop, forbear, abstain from, break off, intermit, discontinue, refrain, dispatch, consummate, complete, suspend, terminate, die away, pass, rest, lull, repose, stay, surcease, pull up, come to a standstill, abate, check, quell, silence, stanch, suppress.

CEASELESS, adj. Perpetual, incessant, endless, eternal, everlasting, never-ending, interminable, never-failing, perennial, unwearied, undiminished, unimpeded, unfaltering, invariable, unceasing, constant, uninterrupted, stable, steady, Sisyphean, fixed, untiring, unremitting, lasting, unwavering, unintermitting, unending, permanent, continual, continuous, protracted, relentless.

CEDE, v. 1. Yield, grant, deliver, concede, give, bequeath, hand over, donate, tender, relinquish, transfer, abandon, surrender, release, renounce, assign, resign, part with, deliver up, sacrifice, vouchsafe.

2. Acquiesce, bend, capitulate, kneel, comply, quiesce, desist, remise, succumb, surrender, give in, stoop, truckle, defer to, accede, obey.

CEILING, *n.* Top-side, covering, covert, roof, dome.

CELEBRATE, *v.* 1. Solemnize, consecrate, keep, hallow, dedicate, commemorate, memorialize, observe, signalize, ritualize, ceremonialize.

2. Glorify, extol, praise, honor, laud, magnify, exalt, bless, reverence, venerate, revere, belaud, pay homage, commend, acclaim, eulogize, cheer, compliment.

CELEBRATED, *adj.* Renowned, famous, famed, distinguished, prominent, extolled, worshipped, honored, popular, noted, notable, illustrious, eminent, lionized, glorified, prized, respected, toasted, venerable, revered, treasured, important, outstanding, acclaimed, preeminent, far-famed, well-known.

CELEBRATION, *n.* 1. Commemoration, ritual, ceremonial, ceremony, dedication, solemnization, solemnity, observance, keeping, memorialization, remembrance.

2. Festival, festivity, fete, gala, carnival, spree, jubilee, ovation, jollification, Bacchanal, revelry, carousal, frolic, potation, compotation, wassail, Saturnalia, conviviality, feast, libation, holiday, junket.

CELEBRITY, *n.* Dignitary, notable, lion, hero, star, magnate, notability, name, figure, man of note, famous person, personage, worthy, bigwig, somebody, luminary.

CELERITY, *n.* Rapidity, speed, haste, dispatch, promptness, fleetness, hurry, quickness, swiftness, acceleration, expedition, velocity, precipitance, alacrity, legerity.

CELESTIAL, *adj.* 1. Heavenly, empyreal, uranic, astronomical, starry, stellar, astrological, nebular, solar, asteroidal, heliacal, lunular, sphery, astral, planetary, sidereal, supernal.

2. Heavenly, sublime, divine, angelic, seraphic, hallowed, sacred, ethereal, supernal, Olympian, holy, paradisiacal, beatific, god-like, cherubic, Elysian, unearthly, Edenic, Arcadian.

CELIBACY, *n.* Chastity, virginity, singleness, bachelorhood, spinsterhood, continence, pucelage.

CELIBATE, *adj.* Chaste, pure, virtuous, virginal, immaculate, single, unmarried, unwed, continent, spouseless.

CELL, *n.* 1. Chamber, compartment, nook, den, burrow, crib, stall, small room, antechamber, closet, recess, alcove, retreat, booth, cloister, crypt, manger.

2. Cage, lockup, prison, vault, guardhouse *(Mil.),* closure, dungeon, hole, coop, black hole, pound, pen *(sl.).*

3. Sac, calyx, legume, bursa, saccule, vesicle, case, utricle, pocket, capsule, cyst, bleb, boll, silique, follicle, pericarp, bladder, blister, theca, vasculum, vacuole, loculus.

4. Organism, egg, ectoplasm, embryo, germ, ameba, corpuscle.

CELLAR, *n.* Basement, vault, wine cellar, buttery, subterranean room, subbasement, underground room.

CEMENT, *v.* 1. Paste, weld, seal, congeal, glue, agglutinate, crystallize, fix, braze, cleave, harden, coalesce, conglutinate, concrete, coagulate, bind, cohere, adhere, solidify, indurate, amalgamate, set.

2. Plaster, overlay with cement, stucco, parget, roughcast, mortar, concrete.

CEMETERY, *n.* Necropolis, graveyard, sepulcher, charnel house, Golgotha, catacomb, tomb, vault, ossuary, crypt, resting place, God's Acre, burial ground, memorial park, churchyard, potter's field.

CENSOR, *n.* 1. Reader, overseer, expurgator, critic, reviewer, examiner, inspector.

2. Faultfinder, depreciator, knocker *(coll.),* muckraker, calumniator, traducer, vituperator, reprimander, reviler, defamer, slanderer, vilifier, maligner, abuser, chider, libeler, censurer, scold, detractor, caviler, carper, criticaster, castigator.

CENSOR, *v.* Inspect, examine, oversee, abridge, expurgate, cut, read, review, criticize.

CENSORIOUS, *adj.* Complaining, animadverting, disapprobatory, hairsplitting, damnatory, cutting, vituperative, critical, hypercritical, faultfinding, detracting, derogatory, captious, biting, withering, condemnatory, severe, querulous, disparaging, vitriolic, crabbed, reproachful, petulant, scolding, uncharitable, nagging, denunciatory, objurgatory, abusive, fretful, peevish.

CENSURABLE, *adj.* Worthy of blame, at fault, reprehensible, unprovoked, answerable, culpable, chargeable, accusable, reprovable, objectionable, blamable, blameworthy, indefensible, accountable, impeachable, faulty, unjustifiable, guilty.

CENSURE, *n.* Aspersion, obloquy, reprobation, criticism, scolding, diatribe, objurgation, blame, upbraiding, accusation, complaint, remonstrance, objection, calumny, stricture, animadversion, carping, imputation, disapprobation, censorship, charge, disapproval, reproof, crimination, rebuke, inculpation, reproach, philippic, reprehension, reprimand, incrimination, castigation, tirade, vituperation.

CENSURE, *v.* Reprobate, blame, carp at, charge, contemn, asperse, declaim against, remonstrate, attack, denounce, condemn, animadvert, berate, fulminate against, arraign, chide, reproach, decry, inveigh against, admonish, reprimand, reprehend, scold, proscribe, disapprove, disparage, reprove, deprecate, inculpate, incriminate.

CENSUS, *n.* Enumeration, tally, statistics, poll, tabulation, figures, statement, demography, count, census returns, listing, evaluation, nose count.

CENTENARY, *n.* Centennial, centennial celebration, hundredth anniversary.

CENTER, *n.* Core, heart, focus, focal point, hub, middle, midst, middle point, pivot, nucleus, gist, focalization, navel, marrow, omphalos, centriole *(Biol.),* axis, radiant, cynosure, centrality, point of convergence, point of concentration, kernel.

CENTER, *v.* Converge upon, centralize, collect, concenter, concentrate, unify, focus, join, unite, meet, gather, focalize, bring to a focus, close on, concentralize.

CENTRAL, *adj.* 1. Middle, pivotal, centric, focal, median, inner, inmost, intermediate, middlemost, interior, midmost, mesial, centroidal, axial, mean, nuclear, midway, equidistant.

2. Chief, dominant, master, major, important, key, head, vital, ruling, greatest, main, foremost, principal, primary, first, capital, basic, supreme, dominant, outstanding, highest, uppermost, prime, paramount, crowning, preeminent, predominant, top, intrinsic, inherent, infixed, indispensable, supporting, underlying, fundamental, necessary, basal, essential, radical.

CENTRALIZATION, *n.* 1. Confluence, centrality, centralism, concentration, centralness, convergence, focalization.

2. Combination, union, alliance, aggregation, nationalization, unification, coalescence, fusion, joining, coadunation, embodiment, incorporation, absorption, blending, coalition, amalgamation, synthesis.

CENTRALIZE, *v.* 1. Concentrate, join, focalize, meet, unite, bring to a focus, collect, converge, gather, close on, unify, focus, concenter, center.

2. Combine, unify, ally, incorporate, absorb, amalgamate, blend, aggregate, join, coadunate, fuse, coalesce.

CENTRIFUGAL, *adj.* Eccentric, radiating, radial, outward, efferent *(Physiol.),* diverging, diffusive, deviating from the center.

CENTURY, *n.* Centenary, hundred years, period, era, age, time, aeon.

CERAMICS, *n.* Plastic arts, pottery, sculpture, tile work, porcelain work, china work, delft work, working in clay, crockery making.

CEREAL, *n.* Grain, wheat, oats, rice, rye, maize, breakfast food, bran, corn, cornstarch, farina, meal, grout, grit, hominy, porridge, buckwheat, mush.

CEREMENT, *n.* Shroud, cerecloth, winding sheet, graveclothes, garment of the dead, pall.

CEREMONIAL, *n.* Formality, solemnity, service, function, duty, ceremony, ritual, ordinance, rite, invocation, celebration, ceremonialism, practice, sacrament, incantation, observance, formulary, cult, rituality, custom.

CEREMONIAL, *adj.* Ceremonious, liturgic, lofty, august, Pharisaic, dignified, sacramental, solemn, ritual, commemorative, functional, triumphal, stately, formal, imposing, impressive, majestic, ritualistic.

CEREMONIOUS, *adj.* 1. Ceremonial, impressive, majestic, imposing, lofty, formal, stately, solemn, ritual, commemorative, functional, sacramental, triumphal, dignified, Pharisaic, august, liturgic.

2. Fastidious, squeamish, exact, disciplinary, strict, solemn, fussy, particular, finicky, formal, meticulous, punctilious, rigorous, affected, stiff, correct, precise, starched, rigid, scrupulous, methodical.

CEREMONY, *n.* 1. Rituality, custom, practice, cult, formulary, observance, incantation, service, sacrament, ceremonial, ceremonialism, function, rite, celebration, invocation, ordinance, ritual, duty, solemnity, formality.

2. Conformity, etiquette, formality, politeness, decorum, propriety, preciseness, strictness, nicety, formalism, punctilio, minuteness, scrupulosity, finicality, fastidiousness, squeamishness, custom, conventionality, observance, usage, prescription.

CERTAIN, *adj.* 1. Definite, genuine, indubitable, authoritative, true, infallible, unambiguous, sure, unequivocal, unmistakable, unquestionable, plain, unqualified, indisputable, undeniable, undisputed, incontrovertible, incontestable, unerring, cogent, irrefragable, irrefutable, unquestioned, reliable, inappealable, unanswerable, absolute, unconfuted, trustworthy, sound, inescapable, evident, positive, conclusive, past dispute.

2. Undoubting, believing, sure, undoubtful, confident, questionless, assured, satisfied, secure, cocksure *(coll.).*

3. Dependable, steadfast, reliable, unfailing, steady, changeless, stable, settled, unchanging,

infallible, sure, constant, unerring, unshaken, unwavering, staid, firm, unfaltering, fixed, sound, unaltering, unshakable, well-grounded, inviolate, valid, unchangeable, invariable, indefeasible, undeviating, unalterable, inexorable.

4. Special, specific, particular, some, express, precise, singular, individual, especial.

CERTAINTY, *n.* 1. Truth, fact, reality, actuality, factuality.

2. Infallibility, inevitability, unimpeachability, reliability, irrefragability, irrefutability, unqualification, unquestionability, incontrovertibility, undeniability, indisputability, incontestability, ineluctability, conclusiveness, authoritativeness, inescapability.

3. Trust, confidence, reliance, assurance, certitude, surety, conviction, faith, knowledge, positiveness, prescience, confident expectation, sure assumption *or* presumption.

CERTIFICATE, *n.* 1. Certification, document, script, coupon, voucher, attestation, credential, testimonial, covenant, indorsement, affidavit, authentication, frank, pass, instrument, testament, ticket, warranty, warrant, guarantee, indenture, docket, license.

2. Diploma, authority, authorization, brevet, exequatur, commission, sheepskin *(coll.).*

CERTIFY, *v.* Endorse, confirm, validate, verify, substantiate, support, attest, guarantee, ratify, authenticate, warrant, witness, depose, declare, testify to, avouch, assure, aver, corroborate, acknowledge, authorize, swear, give one's word, sanction, underwrite, evidence, manifest, certificate.

CESSATION, *n.* Rest, pause, stop, intermission, leaving off, interruption, recess, stay, lull, end, close, suspension, desisting, quitting, restraint, respite, discontinuation, desistance, abeyance, discontinuance, halt, repose, stoppage, desinence, termination, completion, finish, conclusion, standstill.

CESSION, *n.* Granting, giving, delivery, submittal, acquiescence, capitulation, resignation, submission, conceding, compliance, yielding, surrender, renunciation, concession, abandonment.

CHAFE, *v.* 1. Inflame, kindle, warm, warm by rubbing, frictionize, heat by friction.

2. Rub, affricate, abrase, abrade, fret, scrape, file, scratch, rasp, grind, grate, gall, fray, scrub, excoriate.

3. Inconvenience, infuriate, irritate, torment, aggravate, badger, heckle, bait, tease, tantalize, molest, bullyrag, bother, gall, fret, infest, beset, chevy, discommode, irk, chagrin, provoke, pester, displease, pique, worry, trouble, madden, roil, ruffle, offend, nettle, rankle, harass, incense, harry, plague, try one's patience, weary, enrage, exasperate, anger, goad, hector, ride, tweak, vex.

4. Rage, fume, bemoan, fret, grieve, groan, brood, despond, languish, mope, pine, sorrow, worry, seethe, burn, simmer, fuss, fidget, sizzle, smoke, burst with anger, foam, boil.

CHAFF, *n.* 1. Husks, gleanings, cuttings, casings, hulls, glumes, shells, pods.

2. Trash, rubbish, litter, slag, leavings, refuse, weeds, lumber, sweepings, rubble, scourings, shoddy, stubble, draff, grounds, dregs, tares, junk, waste, discard, offscouring, stuff, debris, dross.

3. Joking, jesting, teasing, fun, kidding, ragging, ribbing, joshing, pleasantry, drollery, jocularity, facetiousness, waggery, repartee, raillery, wordplay, quizzing, banter, humor, badinage, mockery,

persiflage, ridicule, jeering, buffoonery, sally, witticism, high-jinks, jocosity, jocundity, asteism, clowning.

CHAFF, *v.* Jolly, twit, ridicule, gibe, gird, rally, kid, rag, scoff, deride, snigger, snicker at, poke fun at, stultify, clown, roast *(sl.)*, haze, fleer, josh, bandy, banter, jest, quip, illude.

CHAFFER, *v.* 1. Negotiate, bargain, barter, bid, higgle, haggle, transact, drive a bargain, argue over terms, dicker, truck, exchange, stickle, beat down, cheapen, underbid, outbid.
2. Chatter, talk, babble, clack, gab, patter, trifle, prattle, prate, rattle, palaver, drivel, tattle, fiddle-faddle, gibber, smatter, twaddle.

CHAGRIN, *n.* Humiliation, mortification, shame, chafing, vexation, rankling, smarting, grief, despair, frustration, resentment, perturbation, abasement, dismay, annoyance, aggravation, fret, bitterness, desolation, prostration, unhappiness, irritation, botherment, worry, disconcertion, care, sadness, sorrow, dejection, embarrassment, gloom, discomposure, discomfiture, despondency, disquiet.

CHAGRIN, *v. (Chiefly passive)* Humble, vex, disappoint, chafe, mortify, shame, rankle, smart, fret, wince, grieve, despair, thwart, frustrate, humiliate, sadden, disgrace, ruffle, nettle, bother, disconcert, resent, perturb, crush, suppress, abase, repress, droop, repine, dismay, embarrass, abash, displease.

CHAIN, *n.* 1. Cable, catena, fob, steel *or* metal links.
2. Vinculum, bond, tie, link, connection, nexus, joining, copula, ligature, interconnection, couple, yoke, leader, rope, painter, line, cable, hawser, funicle, leash, thong, strap, funiculus, wire, string.
3. Train, string, series, succession, links, row, column, procession, cavalcade, caravan, course, progression, file, line, catena, queue, range, set, cycle, sequence, suit, suite.
4. *(Usually plural.)* Shackles, fetters, bondage, bonds, torque, yoke, servitude, slavery, serfdom, subjugation, enslavement, durance, duress, reins, thralldom, bilboes, gyves, trammels, manacles, subordination, villenage *(Hist.)*, constraint, limbo, restraint, confinement, captivity, detention, imprisonment, incarceration, helotry, entombment, internment, impoundment.

CHAIN, *v.* 1. Tie, secure, fasten, manacle, bind, pinion, string, lash, leash, truss, tether, moor, belay, cord, gird, lace, rope, strap, hitch, cable, enchain, girt.
2. Shackle, fetter, bind, enchain, tie up, make fast, astrict, entrammel, put in irons, manacle, handcuff, gyve.
3. Confine, restrict, limit, hamper, hinder, pen, encumber, coop, entomb, cage, imprison, bind, incarcerate, impound, immure, restrain.

CHAIR, *n.* 1. Seat, bench, stool, armchair, camp-stool, rocker, rocking chair, box, easy chair, Morris chair, taboret, fauteuil *(Fr.)*, elbow chair, chaise longue, form, musnud *(Oriental)*.
2. Seat, throne, office, bench, seat of state, dais, cathedra, gaddi *(India)*, woolsack *(Brit.)*.
3. Professorship, instructorship, readership, fellowship, professorate, tutorage, tutorship.
4. Director, chairman, speaker, supervisor, administrator, executive, governor, manager, toastmaster, moderator, master of ceremonies, leader.
5. Electric chair, execution, electrocution, hot seat *(sl.)*, death chair.

CHAIRMAN, *n.* Director, chair, speaker, manager, supervisor, administrator, executive, master of ceremonies, governor, toastmaster, moderator, leader.

CHALICE, *n.* 1. Goblet, bowl, cup, vessel, font, beaker, glass, tumbler, hogshead, horn, rummer, pannikin, tankard, mug, flagon, pot, wineglass, toby, stoup, tass, noggin, schooner, drinking cup, stein, jorum *(coll.)*.
2. Flower cup, vase, pot, urn, flowerpot, jardiniere.

CHALK, *n.* Crayon, pencil, marking chalk, pastel, coloring pencil, lead.

CHALK, *v.* 1. Blanch, bleach, whiten, make pale, etiolate, albify, whitewash, white, calcimine.
2. Draw, sketch, mark, limn, color, design, pencil, scratch.

CHALKY, *adj.* 1. Pulverulent, comminute, dusty, triturate, cretaceous, powdery, crumbly, flaky, pulverous, chalk-like.
2. White, pale, pasty, blanched, bleached, wan, snowy, pallid, waxen, cretaceous, milky, blond, milk-white, ashen, colorless, ghastly, hoar, sallow, niveous, marmoreal, albescent.

CHALLENGE, *n.* 1. Protest, objection, dispute, expostulation, remonstrance, rejection, difference, denunciation, reproach, attack, charge, retort, slur, imputation, complaint, countercharge, denouncement, allegation, dissension, quibble, contradiction, cavil.
2. Defiance, daring, threat, cartel, gage, glove, gauntlet, menace, commination, summons, daunt.

CHALLENGE, *v.* 1. Dare, defy, brave, accost, encounter, affront, stand up against, beard, snap the fingers at, oppose, bid defiance to, menace, threaten, fulminate, daunt, breast, confront, cheek, scorn, hurl defiance at, fling down the gauntlet.
2. Question, dispute, bring to question, object, protest, differ, slur, attack, charge, impute, retort, denounce, remonstrate, disagree, dissent, take exception, demur, quibble, wrangle, contradict, cavil.
3. Claim, lay claim to, demand one's rights, claim as one's due, require, impose, exact, assert, make a point of, take a stand, insist upon, vindicate.

CHAMBER, *n.* 1. Room, apartment, parlor, hall, sitting room, bedroom, living room, drawing room, reception room, boudoir, dormitory, salon, sanctum, den, cubicle, roomlet, library, study, camera, anteroom, antechamber, hallway, adytum.
2. Closet, cubicle, cell, recess, stall, cabinet, box, booth, alcove, nook, den, crib, retreat.
3. Court, council, congress, diet, assembly, constituency, committee, cabinet, staff, bench, tribunal, judicature, board, forum, house, divan *(Oriental)*, camera *(ital.)*, quorum, caucus, plenum.

CHAMP, *v.* Bite, chew, munch, nibble, gnaw, ruminate, crunch, craunch, masticate, manducate.

CHAMPAIGN, *n.* Plain, table land, downs, heath, prairie, common, moor, moorland, expanse, flat, plateau, meadow, field, savannah, greensward, steppe *(Russian)*, tundra *(Russian)*, links, lawn, veld *(S. Africa)*, pampas *(S. Amer.)*, clearing, park, green, turf, flats, stretch, reaches, wold, vega *(Spanish)*, open country.

CHAMPION, *n.* 1. Defender, protector, upholder, supporter, advocate, votary, fautor, abettor, aider, backer, helper, patron, guardian, paladin.

2. Winner, victor, conqueror, master, hero, subjugator, medalist, leader, laureate, prodigy, prizeman, foremost person, vanquisher, subduer.

3. Campaigner, veteran, soldier, fighter, battler, combatant, scrapper, contestant, contender, gladiator, paladin, belligerent, disputant, warrior.

CHAMPION, *v.* Uphold, support, sustain, defend, maintain, espouse, stand up for, contend for, aid, speak for, advocate, protect, back, help, guard, justify, vindicate, battle for, assist.

CHANCE, *adj.* Casual, unlooked-for, unplanned, undirected, unpurposed, involuntary, random, undesigned, unexpected, unintentional, accidental, fortuitous, adventitious, contingent, unforeseen, incidental, unpremeditated, blind, haphazard, aimless.

CHANCE, *n.* 1. Fortune, hap, luck, hazard, lot, accident, adventure, happening, random, destiny, contingency, fate, kismet, fortuity, casualty.

2. Gamble, risk, odds, liability, possibility, probability, contingency, likelihood, speculation, jeopardy, uncertainty.

3. Opportunity, possibility, opening, occasion, place, advantage, time, means, moment.

CHANCE, *v.* 1. Befall, happen, come about, fall to one's lot, bechance, hap, turn up, come, betide, fall, light, occur, arrive, eventuate, supervene, result.

2. Risk, gamble, take a chance, hazard, dare, venture, jeopard, jeopardize, speculate, stake, adventure, rely on fortune, bet, wager.

CHANDELIER, *n.* Luster, electrolier, gaselier, corona lucis, girandole, candelabrum, sconce.

CHANGE, *n.* 1. Alteration, variation, fluctuation, wavering, modulation, alternating, modification, metamorphosis, metamorphism, veering, shifting, transformation, transfiguration, transmutation, conversion, warping, transshaping, revolution, remodeling, regeneration, transubstantiation, shift, tempering, commutation, qualification, turning, substitution, shuffling, reconstruction, exchange, restyling, reorganization, reformation, disguising, vacillating, switch, permutation, interchange, trade, move, difference, inflection, deviation, diversion, resolution, metastasis, metathesis, transposition, innovation, novelty, vicissitude, variety, swerving, aberration, evolution.

2. Small change, silver, pocket money, coins, small coins, petty cash, pin money.

CHANGE, *v.* 1. Alter, vary, mutate, merge into, modulate, alternate, diversify, modify, fluctuate, metamorphose, veer, shift, transform, transfigure, transmute, convert into, swerve, warp, resolve into, transmogrify *(humor.)*, transshape, remodel, revolutionize, regenerate, render different, turn, transubstantiate, temper, commute, qualify, inflect, substitute, turn, shuffle, diverge, evolve, deflect, translate, reduce, recast, reconstruct, restyle, reorganize, reform, denature, disguise, vacillate, transpose.

2. Exchange, move, budge, shift, interchange, reverse, alter, substitute, shuffle, switch, trade, swap *(coll.)*, permute, give and take.

3. Barter, exchange, trade, buy and sell, deal, dicker, chaffer, transact, haggle, higgle, vend, interchange, peddle, auction, bandy, truck, huckster, bargain, negotiate.

CHANGEABLE, *adj.* 1. Alterable, uncertain, mutable, unstable, unsteady, reversible, revocable, transformable, permutable, modifiable, checkered,

many-sided, transitional, mobile, changeful, inconstant, unreliable, fluctuating, alternating, vacillating, vicissitudinary, irregular, convertible, commutative, substitutive, protean.

2. Fitful, fickle, volatile, mercurial, uncertain, unstable, unsteady, changeful, inconstant, uneasy, unreliable, fluctuating, irregular, uneasy, restless, wavering, unsettled, unquiet, fidgety, spasmodic, desultory, vagrant, wayward, wanton, undecided, shilly-shallying, indecisive, irresolute, faddish, skittish, crotchety, uneven, capricious, fanciful, impulsive, flighty, deviative, undependable, erratic.

CHANGELESS, *adj.* Unchanging, unchangeable, constant, steady, fixed, certain, settled, fast, firm, unalterable, unaltering, abiding, permanent, invariable, eternal, reliable, unwavering, even, enduring, lasting, persisting, unvarying, unfailing, unfading, steadfast, incommutable, undeviating, immutable, undying, indissoluble, imperishable, insusceptible of change, inflexible.

CHANNEL, *n.* 1. Bed, floor, bottom, depths, lowest part, deepest part, benthos, basin.

2. Conduit, coulee *(Western U.S.)*, duct, way, watercourse, waterway, trench, moat, aqueduct, canal, dike, gully, culvert, chasm, ravine, gulch, water gap, flume, riffle, gutter, trough, fosse, sluice.

3. Strait, straits, narrows, inlet, neck, lagoon, creek, roads, sound, estuary, fiord, gulf, bight, bay, cove.

4. Way, path, course, career, lane, artery, approach, pass, passage, passageway, avenue, aisle, corridor, route, run, road, trail, runway, track, fairway, cut, chase.

CHANNEL, *v* Groove, flute, burrow, plow, gash, champfer, streak, hollow out, trench, carve, cut, cut a channel *or* groove *or* furrow, chase, scratch.

CHANT, *n.* 1. Song, carol, madrigal, glee, lay, spiritual, lied, ditty, ballad, ballade, catch, rondo, round, troll, melody, descant, canticle, chantey, aria, arietta, berceuse *(Fr.)*, serenade, cantata, lilt, dirge, canzone *(It.)*, canzonet, cavatina, lullaby, duet, incantation, monody.

2. Hymn, paean, psalm, chorale, recitative, oratorio, benediction, vespers, thanksgiving, exaltation, evensong, matins, glorification, motet, antiphony, response, grace, hallelujah, doxology, *Gloria in Excelsis Deo, Gloria Patri,* Gregorian chant, introit, Magnificat, requiem, laud, Miserere, hosanna.

CHANT, *v.* Sing, warble, serenade, harmonize, chime, trill, quaver, lilt, croon, chirp, descant, hum, intone, carol, yodel, vocalize, cantillate, chirrup, pipe, sol-fa, solmizate.

CHAOS, *n.* Furor, commotion, tumult, rumpus, fracas, disunion, riot, bedlam, turmoil, discord, confusion, upset, pandemonium, babel, uproar, hubbub, turbulence, unrest, stir, stampede, fuss, pother, panic, perturbation, imbroglio, bustle, hurry-scurry, huddle, fray, flurry, ferment, row, excitement, discomposure, agitation, convulsion, ado, muddle, mess, disarray, upheaval, racket, tempest, disquiet, storm, jumble, tumble, bluster, scramble, derangement, disarrangement.

CHAOTIC, *adj.* 1. Haphazard, disordered, wild, disorganized, orderless, topsy-turvy, pell-mell, unsystematic, jumbled, untidy, littered, scattered, askew, awry, ramshackle, desultory, casual, careless, unmethodical, aimless, straggling, random, undirected, shapeless, purposeless, formless, deranged, disarranged, discomposed, slipshod, sloppy (coll.), slovenly, unkempt, muddled, hugger-mugger, mussed (coll.).

2. Disorderly, lawless, orderless, tumultuous, wild, tempestuous, agitated, riotous, turbulent, unquiet, uncontrolled, uproarious, seething, anarchal, unrestrained, unruly, stormy, bustling, fermenting, perturbed, stirred-up, discordant, restless, raging, frenzied, furious, rampageous, mad, frantic, boisterous, tumultuary, harum-scarum (coll.).

CHAP, v. Split, crack, slit, chafe, roughen (as skin), break, make raw, cleave, score, cut, chisel, gash, incise.

CHAP, n. Cleft, slit, chink, crack, break, scratch, gash, cut, cranny, fissure, cavity, indentation, pit, rent, scission, rift.

CHAPBOOK, n. Treasury, anthology, thesaurus, florilegium, collection, corpus, chrestomathy, booklet, garland, gathering, miscellany, posy, spicilege, compilation, album.

CHAPEL, n. Place of worship, church, temple, tabernacle, synagogue, sanctuary, house of God, house of worship, meeting house, minster, shrine, basilica.

CHAPERON, n. Protector, guardian, companion, attendant, duenna, escort, convoy, protectress, custodian, governess, nurse, matron.

CHAPERON, v. Guard, watch, care for, conduct, accompany, convoy, attend, protect, shepherd, safeguard, tend, keep an eye on, matronize, escort.

CHAPFALLEN, adj. Dejected, downcast, gloomy, humiliated, depressed, disheartened, chagrined, low-spirited, cheerless, unhappy, dismal, glum, dismayed, abject, doleful, sorrowful, careworn, melancholy, sad, despondent, crestfallen, shamed, discouraged, mortified, vexed, desolate, out of humor, disconcerted, discomposed, disappointed, drooping, thwarted, frustrated, brought low, out of countenance, subdued, downhearted, heavy-hearted, woeful, woebegone, in the doldrums, spiritless, ashamed, abashed, dashed, bowed-down.

CHAPLAIN, n. Priest, clergyman, minister, padre, father, pastor, churchman, cleric, parson, curate, preacher, ecclesiastic, sky pilot (sl.), curé, rector, vicar, presbyter, rabbi, dominie.

CHAPLET, n. 1. Garland, wreath, crown of flowers, spray, coronal, bays, laurel.

2. Rosary, peag, beads, necklace, string of jewels, pearls, pendant, wampum, passementerie.

CHAPTER, n. 1. Part, section, division, portion, subdivision, clause, article, passage.

2. Council, convocation, synod, consistory, conference, session, presbytery, classis, body, group, directory.

CHAR, v. Burn, scorch, singe, cauterize, corrode, oxidate, oxidize, carbonize, torrefy, cremate, fire, incinerate, scorify, parch, sear, calcine, reduce to charcoal.

CHARACTER, n. 1. Mark, brand, stamp, sign, token, badge, emblem, figure, cipher, digit, rune, number, integer, initial, majuscule, minuscule, ideogram, ideograph, device, marker, label, notation, insignia, symbol.

2. Attribute, quality, property, trait, nature, feature, point, mark, specialty, peculiarity, idiosyncrasy, individuality, personality, cast, turn, bent, temperament, mood, complexion, aspect, style, characteristic, frame, streak, stripe, tone,

particularity, singularity, mannerism, earmark, badge, trademark, diagnostic, symptom, essential, disposition, idiocrasis.

3. Reputation, esteem, honor, name, respect, regard, respectability, repute, personality, glory, notability, note, report, popular favor, credit, prestige, account, éclat, standing, position, station, status, order.

4. Person, individual, being, man, woman, personality, mortal, soul, somebody, specimen, someone, human being.

5. Actor, actress, role, dramatis personae (pl.), piece, portrayal, characterization, personation, part, impersonation, representation.

CHARACTERISTIC, n. Peculiarity, singularity, property, attribute, trait, nature, feature, point, mark, specialty, idiosyncrasy, individuality, essential, personality, cast, turn, bent, mood, style, temperament, complexion, character, aspect, tone, frame, streak, stripe, particularity, mannerism, earmark, badge, trademark, idiocrasy, symptom, diagnostic, disposition, idiocrasis, tendency, bias, propensity, proclivity, penchant, leaning, warp, predisposition, drift, proneness, predilection, animus.

CHARACTERISTIC, adj. Typical, distinctive, particular, pointed, marked, peculiar, special, specific, differentiative, diagnostic, distinguishing, discriminative, unique, representative, emblematic, symptomatic, idiosyncratic, indicative, symbolic, individualistic, individual, diacritical.

CHARACTERIZE, v. 1. Distinguish, signalize, designate, denominate, indicate, define, describe, specify, label, tag, style, name, show to be, identify, stamp, brand, ticket.

2. Delineate, describe, draw, depict, represent, analyze, paint, picture, portray, sketch.

CHARGE, n. 1. Cargo, lading, bale, shipload, freight, contents, burden, shipment, carload, goods, wagonload, freightage.

2. Burden, anxiety, care, load, encumbrance, responsibility, oppression, handicap, incubus, clog, tribulation, stress, pressure, drag, lumber, hamper, millstone, vexation, cumbrance, trouble, tax, sorrow, affliction, gravamen, trial, grievance, impediment, hardship, strain.

3. Care, superintendence, custody, keeping, management, guardianship, guidance, tutelage, auspices, surveillance, safekeeping, patronage, supervision, ward, command, control, protection, jurisdiction, administration, chaperonage, concern.

4. Command, order, behest, bidding, mandate, word, will, direction, injunction, commandment, summons, call, ordinance, exaction, demand, instruction, requisition, regulation, enjoining, summoning, dictate.

5. Accusation, allegation, condemnation, slur, arraignment, blame, complaint, crimination, impeachment, recrimination, objurgation, chiding, incrimination, indictment, imputation, reproof, exprobration, inculpation, denunciation, stricture, disapprobation, rebuke, reproach, animadversion, censure, reprehension, castigation, tirade, diatribe, jeremiad, Philippic, expostulation, attribution.

6. Cost, expense, pecuniary burden, price, amount, figure, assessment, fee, rent, tax, poll, tollage, rate, value, quotation, dues, commission, freightage, truckage, wharfage, brokerage, duty, towage, capitation, custom, obligation, payment, outlay, expenditure, toll.

7. Instruction, direction, precept, injunction, prescript, rule of conduct, exhortation, charging.

8. Attack, onslaught, onset, assault, offense, offensive, invasion, storming, raid, push *(sl.)*, inroad, incursion, dragonnade, aggression, sortie, attempt, sally, expenditure, surprisal, besetment, thrust.

CHARGE, *v.* 1. Load, strain, encumber, press down, weigh down, lade, try, task with, overtask, pile, overwhelm, overlay, saddle with, hamper, obligate, overcharge, burden, surcharge, oppress, overload, drag, vex, hinder, trouble, cumber, tax, afflict, handicap.
2. Pack, load, burden, stuff, fill, lade, freight, weight, pad, pile, implete, stow, lumber, wad, heap, stack.
3. Command, order, bid, direct, demand, urge, instruct, enjoin, dictate, exhort, require, exact, summon, adjure, decree, enact, ordain, prescribe, call upon.
4. Accuse, indict, arraign, blame, tax, attack, incriminate, impeach, challenge, inculpate, twit, condemn, denounce, bring accusation, lay at one's door, lay responsibility upon, criminate, taunt, denunciate, countercharge, lodge a complaint against, fix responsibility, prefer charges, slur, reproach, stigmatize.
5. Impute, ascribe, assign, lay at one's door, fix responsibility on, attribute, saddle upon, set down to, father upon, name as the cause, indicate *(as cause)*.
6. Bear down upon, rush, attack, make a thrust, make a sally, make an onslaught, invade, storm, raid, make an inroad, make an incursion, beset, assail, strike, have at, fall upon, march upon, go for *(coll.)*, ride against, make a dash at, close upon, make an offensive, launch against, tilt at, come at, assault.
7. Consign, intrust, commission, deputize, empower, invest, appoint, nominate, engage, give power to, ordain, delegate, assign, induct, install, name, instate.
8. Ask, require, fix a charge, fix a price, price, exact, levy, assess, put a value on, impose, tax, fine.
9. Take credit, take on account, receive credit, put on the bill, put on one's account, run up an account, incur a debt, debit.

CHARGEABLE, *adj.* Responsible, blameworthy, liable, blamable, indictable, reprovable, censurable, imputable, reprehensible, culpable, answerable, impeachable, reproachable, accusable.

CHARGER, *n.* Steed, war horse, cavalry horse, mount, courser *(Poet.)*, trooper.

CHARILY, *adv.* Carefully, cautiously, gingerly, warily, guardedly, circumspectly, discreetly, alertly, stealthily, wakefully, on the alert, in a chary manner, on the safe side, with care, with caution, heedfully, judiciously, observantly, with both eyes open.

CHARINESS, *n.* Caution, care, circumspection, carefulness, vigilance, concern, apprehension, watchfulness, forethought, providence, wariness, foresight, guardedness, deliberation, solicitude, alertness, prudence, discretion.

CHARITABLE, *adj.* 1. Liberal, open-handed, bountiful, princely, kind, giving, unstinted, ample, generous, benignant, eleemosynary, philanthropic, benevolent, munificent, unselfish, bounteous, free-handed, altruistic, almsgiving, big-hearted, free, magnanimous, unsparing, ungrudging, handsome, great-hearted.
2. Kind, good, amiable, cordial, warm-hearted, tender, considerate, altruistic, well-disposed, well-

meaning, loving, friendly, sympathizing, gracious, soft-hearted, kindhearted, complaisant, obliging, benevolent, benign, hospitable, tolerant, humane, indulgent, clement, compassionate, lenient, mild, good-natured, magnanimous, munificent.

CHARITY, *n.* 1. Liberality, open-handedness, bounty, generosity, benevolence, philanthropy, munificence, unselfishness, free-handedness, help, altruism, almsgiving, big-heartedness, assistance, grace, goodness, hospitality, giving, donating, aid, succor, relief.
2. Kindness, amiability, goodness, tenderness, consideration, warm-heartedness, altruism, love, friendliness, sympathy, soft-heartedness, benignity, kindheartedness, graciousness, benevolence, help, hospitality, tolerance, indulgence, clemency, love of mankind, humanity, compassion, magnanimity, munificence, assistance, humanitarianism, good will, self-sacrifice, unselfishness.
3. Benefaction, gift, donation, help, assistance, relief, succor, bestowal, presentation, concession, endowment, present, grant, tribute, subscription, contribution, gratuity, offering, largess, sportula *(Rom. Antiq.)*, bonus, alms, oblation, handsel.

CHARLATAN, *n.* Deceiver, swindler, cheat, fake, fraud, hypocrite, mountebank, quack, adventurer, humbug, chiseler, trickster, decoy, allurer, rascal, confidence man, enticer, beguiler, twister, hoaxer, impostor, pretender, empiric, fourflusher *(sl.)*, cozener, medicaster, quacksalver.

CHARM, *n.* 1. Exorcism, incantation, conjuration, magic formula, abracadabra, hocus-pocus, spell, mumbo jumbo, sorcery, black magic, witchcraft, necromancy, demonifuge, countercharm.
2. Specific, amulet, lucky piece, periapt, fetish, talisman, phylactery, voodoo, rabbit foot, philter.
3. Enticement, allurement, fascination, draw, attractiveness, irresistible power, inducement, attraction, pull, seduction, bewitchment, lure, blandishment, cajolery, magnetism, temptation, tantalization.

CHARM, *v.* 1. Fascinate, subdue, engross, seduce, captivate, entrance, enrapture, enravish, enchain, transport, enamor, lure, decoy, influence, cajole, intrigue, magnetize, attract, bewitch, allure, invite, electrify, entice, tempt, tantalize, carry away, lead on, ensnare, entangle, enmesh, inveigle, titillate, mesmerize, becharm, inflame, endear, infatuate.
2. Delight, please, amuse, entertain, fascinate, interest, entrance, enrapture, enravish, transport, enamor, give pleasure, satisfy, regale, enthrall, gratify, make happy, thrill, divert, treat.
3. Exorcise, conjure, work magic, cast a spell, practice sorcery *or* black magic, spellbind, hex, bewitch, witch, bedevil, sorcer, practice voodoo *or* juju, hypnotize, mesmerize, command spirits, becharm, demonize.

CHARMER, *n.* Magician, wizard, witch, seducer, temptress, siren, enchantress, conjurer, warlock, necromancer, sorcerer, sorceress, miracle worker, enchanter, bewitcher, thaumaturge, incantator, exorcist, voodooist, theurgist.

CHARMING, *adj.* Graceful, lovely, thrilling, fair, entrancing, attractive, fascinating, prepossessing, seductive, winning, winsome, sweet, transporting, fetching, enchanting, exquisite, beautiful, elegant, agreeable, bewitching, delightful, accomplished, engaging, irresistible, tempting, pleasing, enticing, enrapturing, rapturous, handsome, magnetizing, absorbing, engrossing, enamoring, electrifying, intriguing, tantalizing, titillating, enthralling,

CHART 137 **CHATTY**

gratifying, diverting, provocative, likable, taking, inducing, delectable, catching, alluring.

CHART, *n.* Plan, map, outline, sketch, tabulation, guide, table, graph, blueprint, design, drawing, draft, tracing, scheme, diagram, representation, copy, guidebook, handbook, manual, gazetteer, picture.

CHART, *v.* Plan, map, outline, draw, tabulate, design, diagram, copy, chart a course, steer, pilot, direct, guide, shape a plan, draft, draw up, map out, chalk out, delineate, picture.

CHARTER, *n.* Permit, instrument, imprimatur, sanction, license, agreement, contract, compact, immunity, covenant, concession, lease, franchise, commonage, deed, document, authority.

CHARTER, *v.* 1. Grant, commission, entitle, fix, sanction, allot, delegate, grant by charter, grant a charter to, assign, license, authorize, legalize, prescribe, establish, settle, ordain, constitute, enact.
2. Rent, hire, lease, let, engage, employ, take by the hour, day, month, etc.

CHARY, *adj.* 1. Guarded, discreet, shrewd, astute, cautious, suspicious, vigilant, careful, unwilling, circumspect, prudent, choosy, fastidious, politic, watchful, alert, noncommittal, leery *(sl.),* averse, stealthy, overcareful, overcautious, on guard, on the safe side, disinclined, reluctant, loath, restive, indisposed, squeamish, punctilious, meticulous, renitent, queasy, querulous, exacting, difficult, over particular, precise.
2. Careful, thrifty, frugal, sparing, provident, parsimonious, unwasteful, husbandly, niggardly, saving, stingy, miserly, grudging, penny-wise, penurious, close-fisted, tight-fisted, stinting, pinching.

CHASE, *v.* 1. Fly after, give chase, pursue, dog, follow, bedog, run after, tag, tag after, try to overtake, move behind, trail, tail *(coll.),* make after, go in pursuit, shadow, hound.
2. Hunt, stalk, drive, course, hound, track, trail, pursue.
3. Repel, dispel, repulse, scatter, beat back, oppose, send away, hold off, ward off, thrust back, retrude, oust, cast out, drive out, evict, send packing *(coll.).*

CHASE, *n.* 1. Pursuit, following, pursuing, hunt, shooting, battue, coursing, hunting, field sport, shoot, sport, sporting, hawking.
2. Game, prey, quarry.

CHASM, *n.* Ravine, divide, gorge, gap, canyon, notch, gulf, abyss, gulch, cavity, pit, deep, shaft, crater, crevasse, crevice, concavity, cave, cavern, hollow, fissure, crack, hole, tunnel, breach, gash, aperture, cleft, opening, mine, scoop, scissure, split, rift.

CHASSIS, *n.* Undercarriage, frame, framework, skeleton.

CHASTE, *adj.* 1. Virtuous, pure, innocent, clean, undefiled, continent, immaculate, spotless, vestal, virgin, unsullied, uncorrupted, stainless, unsoiled, untarnished, unstained, unblemished, virginal, snowy.
2. Single, celibate, unmarried, husbandless, unwed, continent, spouseless, abstemious, wifeless.
3. Modest, pure, innocent, decent, decorous, clean, clean-minded, wholesome, moral, delicate, righteous, noble, right-minded, faultless, sinless, virtuous, stainless, untainted, unblemished, nice, unsoiled, unsullied, immaculate, snowy, saintly, exemplary, angelic, upright, meritorious, vestal,

reputable, honorable, creditable, maidenly, prudish.
4. Simple, pure, restrained, reserved, inornate, unaffected, plain, unadorned, severe, unenriched, unornamented, unembellished, strict, ungarnished, unpretentious, classic, Attic, subdued, tasteful, seemly, proper, becoming, sedate, undecked, formal, precise.

CHASTEN, *v.* 1. Punish, castigate, discipline, correct, penalize, afflict, chastise, scourge, scold, humble, inflict punishment, upbraid, reproach, admonish, call down *(coll.),* rebuke, reprimand, exprobrate, objurgate, reprove, chide, reprehend, fulminate against, tongue lash, haul over the coals *(coll.),* roast *(coll.),* have on the carpet *(coll.),* rap on the knuckles, berate, take to task.
2. Clean, purge, absterge, refine, expurgate, purify, depurate, cleanse, deterge, decrassify, soften, epurate.

CHASTISE, *v.* Scourge, lash, whip, beat, inflict punishment, strike, smite, castigate, flog, spank, lace, flagellate, bastinado, strap, swinge, thump, pommel, cudgel, box, cuff, birch, fustigate, flail, trounce, thrash, drub, cane, horsewhip, baste.

CHASTITY, *n.* Virginity, singleness, continence, bachelorhood, spinsterhood, pucelage, celibacy, unmarried state, abstemiousness, immaculateness, virtue, spotlessness.

CHAT, *n.* Conversation, prattle, palaver, informal talk, discourse, parleying, chewing the rag *(sl.),* chatter, chitchat, confabulation, clack, causerie, rattle, gossip, buzzing, prating, babble, tittle-tattle, babblement.

CHAT, *v.* Converse, prate, prattle, palaver, clack, discourse, bandy words, parley, chin *(sl.),* chew the rag *(sl),* chatter, chitchat, confabulate, talk informally, rattle, babble, gossip, tittle-tattle, buzz.

CHATEAU, *n.* 1. Fortification, fortress, fasthold, stronghold, keep, castle, tower, donjon, safe-hold, fort, citadel, acropolis, hold, fastness.
2. Hall, tower, grange, mansion, castle, stately dwelling, messuage, manor house, palace, chalet, palatial dwelling.

CHATTEL, *n. (Usually plur.)* Goods, belongings, effects, personal effects, things, property, assets, possessions, trappings, traps *(coll.),* personalty *(Leg.),* paraphernalia, accouterments, holdings, gear, appointments, appurtenances.

CHATTER, *n.* Prattle, palaver, babble, chitchat, confabulation, clack, gossip, rattle, babblement, prating, gabble, jabber, patter, tattle, maundering, drivel, raving, blather, twattle, twaddle, gushing, blab, blabber, idle talk, chitter-chatter, trifling, blatherskite *(coll.),* buzzing.

CHATTER, *v.* Prattle, gossip, babble, chitchat, confabulate, clack, palaver, rattle, buzz, prate, gabble, jabber, patter, tattle, drivel, rave, blather, maunder, twattle, twaddle, gush, blab, chitter-chatter, gibble-gabble, ramble, talk aimlessly *or* idly, gas *(sl.),* chaffer, trifle, fiddle-faddle, smatter.

CHATTERER, *n.* Chatterbox, blatherskite *(coll.),* magpie, jay, parrot, windbag *(sl.),* windjammer *(sl.),* prattler, talker, jabberer, gabbler, babbler, maunderer, twattler, twaddler, gusher, cackler, gossip, patterer.

CHATTY, *adj.* Effusive, talkative, loquacious, garrulous, windy *(sl.),* gassy *(sl.),* noisy, prattling, clacking, babbling, buzzing, prating, gabbling, jabbering, pattering, tattling, tongue-wagging, driveling, blathering, maundering, multiloquent, rambling, gossiping, voluble, glib, profuse, wordy, verbose, gushing, eloquent, polyloquent.

CHAUVINISM, *n.* Spread-eagleism, jingoism, exaggerated patriotism, vainglorious patriotism, patriolatry, over patriotism.

CHEAP, *adj.* 1. Reasonable, inexpensive, reduced, low-priced, economical, moderate, depreciated, of small *or* little cost, of small price, worth the money, slashed (in price), lowered, marked down.

2. Worthless, trashy, tawdry, gaudy, inferior, gimcrack, paltry, meretricious, beggarly, mean, poor, base, second-rate, commonplace, indifferent, trivial, shoddy, vulgar, shabby, sorry, scrubby, contemptible, meager, mere, measly *(sl.).*

3. Embarrassed, disconcerted, abashed, abased, discomfited, shamed, chagrined, crushed, subdued, humiliated, mortified, degraded, low, chapfallen, uncomfortable, ashamed, dismayed, crestfallen, dashed.

CHEAPEN, *v.* 1. Bargain, negotiate, transact, dicker, barter, drive a bargain, beat down, underbid, higgle, haggle, stickle, chaffer.

2. Lower, depreciate, make worthless, make less, drop in value *or* worth, reduce, mark down, slash, trim the price, decline, slump, fall *or* come down in price.

3. Calumniate, sneer at, slander, libel, brand, pull to pieces, defame, traduce, asperse, misprize, malign, jibe at, decry, depreciate, disparage, slur, derogate, detract from, minimize, belittle, satirize, lampoon, poke fun at, deride, mock, scoff at, ridicule, discredit, vilify, disgrace, pooh-pooh, humiliate, mortify, lower, shame, underestimate, make light of, laugh at, spurn, slight, contemn, scorn, pour scorn on.

CHEAT, *n.* Deceiver, fraud, inveigler, impostor, trickster, swindler, pretender, humbug, blackleg, bilk, adventurer, charlatan, mountebank, rogue, knave, crook, quack, shark, diddler, hypocrite, cozener, dissembler, jockey, fourflusher *(sl.),* fake, scaramouche, chiseler, confidence man, decoy, allurer, enticer, rascal, beguiler, twister, empiric, medicaster, quacksalver, masquerader, bluff, wolf in sheep's clothing, pettifogger, dodger, sharper, picaroon.

CHEAT, *v.* 1. Deceive, swindle, hoax, beguile, dupe, fraud, befool, abuse, inveigle, gull, trick, overreach, circumvent, defraud, practice upon, outwit, victimize, delude, gammon, hoodwink, impose upon, humbug, do, cozen, diddle, fleece, gyp, play upon, foist upon, lure, rook, mulct, bamboozle, ensnare, entrap, entice, bilk, mislead, cajole, jockey, play false, cog, wheedle, baffle, take *(coll.),* gouge *(coll.),* chouse *(coll.),* flam, betray, palm upon, pluck *(sl.),* bunko.

2. Foil, frustrate, thwart, balk, defeat, cross, checkmate, circumvent, baffle, check, deprive of, rob of, bilk, disappoint.

CHECK, *n.* 1. Restriction, restraint, repression, obstacle, block, stumbling block, prevention, bar, estoppel *(Leg.),* barrier, impediment, stop, ban, difficulty, curb, obstruction, barricade, preclusion, prohibition, limitation, trammel, bridle, embargo, proscription, injunction, balk, constraint, stopper, enjoining, disallowance, catch, snag, impedition, oppilation, forbiddance, retardment, retardation, cohibition, dam, stoppage, hindrance, hitch, stay.

2. Repulse, rebuff, setback, reverse, drawback, opposition, rejection, throwing back, reversal,

upset, recession, balk, bafflement, foil, checkmate, disappointment, stalemate, deadlock.

3. Break, breach, gap, interval, division, space, hiatus, falling off, cessation, lacuna, lapse, pause, intermission, interlude, disruption, rift, stopping, discontinuance, arresting, standstill, suspension, respite, abeyance.

4. Control, restraint, tab, restriction, discipline, regulation, curb, supervision, restraining measure, limitation.

5. Standard, criterion, rule, yardstick, pattern, type, scale, test, canon, model, gauge, measure.

6. Checkup, examination, inspection, scrutiny, exploration, search, survey, perusal, indagation, investigation, test, probe.

7. Certificate, stub, ticket, identification, chit, voucher, pass, certification, credential, coupon, docket, paper, scrip, token, tessera.

8. Note, voucher, draft.

9. Plaid, patchwork, checkwork, checkerboard, tessellation, tartan.

CHECK, *v.* 1. Stop, halt, arrest, stay, stall, bring to a standstill, put a stop to.

2. Hold back, restrain, curb, impede, hinder, repress, prevent, bar, balk, constrain, handicap, retard, bridle, obstruct, choke, circumscribe, gag, cohibit, forbid, embarrass, trammel, circumvent, impedite, estop, debar, block, brake, withhold, rein, control, harness, muzzle, inhibit, suppress, limit, hold, smother, frustrate, thwart.

3. Test, examine, explore, inspect, scrutinize, search, survey, peruse, indagate, investigate, look over, probe, take stock of, overhaul, review, study, scan, contemplate, consider.

4. Correspond, tally, agree, conform, accord, fit, harmonize, chime in with, fall in with, be uniform.

CHECKERED, *adj.* Varied, variegated, variable, diversified, versatile, changeful, mutable, uneven, many-sided, changeable, deviative, undependable, spasmodic, fluctuating, inconstant, unsteady, fitful, irregular, unsettled, uncertain, vacillating, alternating, alterable.

CHECKMATE, *v.* Overwhelm, beat, overthrow, defeat, conquer, knock-down, overcome, subdue, vanquish, overpower, subjugate, rout, discomfit, worst, triumph over, whip, drub, get the better of, put down, prevail over, crush, quell, squash, get the upper hand, master, smash, reduce, humble, be victorious over, have on the hip, surmount, lick, floor, overturn, outdo, outwit, outmaneuver, gain the ascendancy, have the whip hand.

CHEEK, *n.* 1. Gill, jowl.

2. *(Coll.)* Nerve, audacity, daring, brazenness, shamelessness, boldness, insolence, impertinence, forwardness, procacity, brashness, malapertness, arrogance, familiarity, rudeness, petulancy, brass, unmannerliness, disrespect, immodesty, sauciness, contumely, impudence, flippancy, gall *(coll.),* effrontery, sauce.

CHEEP, *v.* Peep, chirp, chirrup, tweet, twitter, pipe, chip, twit, carol, chatter, whistle, chitter, lilt, sing.

CHEER, *n.* 1. Animation, merriment, vivacity, jollity, mirth, gaiety, gladness, delight, glee, fun, festivity, frolic, pleasure, joy, joyance, sunshine, delectation, bliss, felicity, transport, ravishment, enchantment, ecstasy, blitheness, geniality, high spirits, animal spirits, liveliness, merrymaking, joviality, revelry, conviviality, rejoicing, jubilee, jubilation, exultation.

2. Huzza, hurray, shout, yell, hurrah.

3. Hope, trust, assurance, confidence, reliance, optimism, good spirit, conviction, reassurance, faith, affiance, hopefulness, buoyancy.

CHEER, v. 1. Gladden, brighten, enliven, make rejoice, regale, exhilarate, inspire, elate, refresh, encourage, animate, inspirit, stimulate, enhearten, invigorate, hearten, buoy up, reassure, quicken, fortify, restore, strengthen, warm, revitalize, revivify, revive, uplift, comfort.

2. Applaud, urge, encourage, clap, root for (sl.), encore, hail, call 'bravo.'

3. Cry, shout, yell, huzza, hurray, hurrah.

CHEERFUL, adj. Happy, gay, debonair, blithe, gladsome, cheery, light-hearted, winsome, jolly, jovial, genial, merry, mirthful, buoyant, joyous, joyful, animated, elated, sprightly, lively, jocund, pleasant, vivacious, airy, sportive, brisk, gleeful, sunny, hopeful, optimistic, resilient, free and easy, volatile, jubilant, carefree, in high humor, in high spirits, bright, breezy, jaunty, chipper (coll.), frisky, pert.

CHEERFULNESS, n. Exultation, merrymaking, jubilation, rejoicing, conviviality, revelry, gaiety, joviality, high spirits, high humor, liveliness, mirth, animal spirits, geniality, blitheness, ecstasy, joy, joyance, festivity, fun, glee, delight, gladness, vivacity, jollity, merriment, animation, cheeriness, jocundity, exhilaration, sprightliness, breeziness, levity, jubilance, sunshine, resilience, briskness, hopefulness, airiness.

CHEERING, adj. Heartening, elating, restoring, encouraging, enlivening, exhilarating, animating, refreshing, inspiriting, stimulating, revitalizing, reassuring, fortifying, revivifying, quickening, inspiring, cheering, promising, propitious, auspicious.

CHEERLESS, adj. 1. Gloomy, dejected, forlorn, sad, downcast, melancholy, depressed, unhappy, miserable, woebegone, glum, sullen, dispirited, downhearted, heavy-hearted, doleful, lugubrious, dolorous, dreary, rueful, joyless, sorrow-stricken, spiritless, disconsolate, desolate, funereal, woeful, heartbroken, hopeless, despondent, lamenting, grieving, sorrowful, mournful, plaintive, tearful, solemn, grim, saturnine, sorrow-burdened, sick at heart, sorrow-worn, sorrow-laden, down in the mouth (coll.), comfortless, lachrymose, morose.

2. Bleak, desolate, deserted, lonely, gloomy, cold, comfortless, bitter, uninviting, depressing, joyless, dismal, barren, austere, somber, dreary, melancholy, grim, sunless, lightless, murky, dingy, lurid, frowning.

CHEERY, adj. Light-hearted, cheerful, gladsome, blithe, debonair, gay, happy, joyous, pleasant, sunny, carefree, bright, breezy, jaunty, chipper (coll.), frisky, pert, in high spirits, in high humor, free and easy, jubilant, volatile, resilient, jocund, optimistic, hopeful, vivacious, airy, gleeful, brisk, sportive, lively, sprightly, elated, animated, jolly, joyful, buoyant, mirthful, merry, genial, jovial.

CHEF, n. Professional cook, food preparer, cook, chef de cuisine (Fr.).

CHERISH, v. 1. Nurse, cradle, foster, nourish, nurture, shelter, succor, guard, defend, comfort, support, sustain, care for, preserve, cultivate, feed, harbor, hold, cling to, prize, value, esteem, revere, take care of, hug.

2. Love, treasure, adore, idolize, prize, revere, hold dear, caress, pet, fondle, value, esteem, idolatrize, dote on, fancy, like dearly, cuddle, clasp, cosset, coddle, embrace.

CHERUB, n. 1. Cherubim, cherubin, celestial being, angel, seraph, winged child.

2. Darling, innocent, beautiful child or baby, curled darling (coll.), babe, infant.

CHEST, n. 1. Bosom, bust, breast, thorax.

2. Container, box, case, carton, receptacle, crib, casket, coffer, bin, shrine, reliquary, cabinet, crate, canister, pyxis, caddie, bunker, strongbox, locker.

CHEW, v. Masticate, ruminate, gnaw, munch, grind, rend, manducate, champ, nibble, crunch, mumble, craunch, scrunch (coll.).

CHICANERY, n. Chicane, knavery, deceit, wiles, trickery, sophistry, intrigue, subterfuge, cheating, rascality, cunning, fraud, tergiversation, betrayal, deception, swindling, bamboozling, fraudulence, cozenage, delusion, duplicity, cajolery, dodgery, humbuggery, dishonesty, pettifoggery, treachery, befooling, beguiling, hoodwinking, luring, duping, fleecing, playing false, inveigling, gulling, hoaxing, guile.

CHIDE, v. Reprove, rebuke, scold, admonish, censure, take to task, upbraid, reproach, berate, reprimand, reprehend, reprobate, disapprove, call to account, exprobrate, lecture, remonstrate, rate, trounce, overhaul, condemn, blame, denounce.

CHIEF, adj. Main, foremost, master, important, major, key, head, vital, ruling, greatest, capital, top, predominant, pre-eminent, prime, crowning, paramount, uppermost, highest, outstanding, dominant, supreme, leading, first, central, front, primary, principal, superior, headmost, ascendant, preponderant, prepotent, prepollent, hegemonic, governing, ruling, commanding, controlling, prevailing, presiding, cardinal.

CHIEF, n. 1. Overlord, lord, chieftain, suzerain, emperor, king, sovereign, monarch, majesty, lord paramount, ruler, paramount, potentate, prince, duke.

2. Head, commander, governor, master, boss (coll.), director, chairman, captain, commandant, general, president, leader, dictator, director, manager, administrator, superintendent, overseer, supervisor, overman, overlooker, ringleader, controller, foreman, proprietor.

CHIEFLY, adv. Usually, generally, principally, mainly, particularly, eminently, predominantly, pre-eminently, especially, expressly, in the main, above all, peculiarly.

CHIEFTAIN, n. Lord, overlord, potentate, king, paramount, lord paramount, headman, sovereign, ruler, majesty, monarch, emperor, suzerain, chief, duke, prince.

CHILD, n. 1. Youngster, youth, stripling, boy, girl, minor, youngling, juvenile, whippersnapper, urchin (contempt.), kid (sl.), shaver (coll.), cub, mite, pickaninny, cherub, innocent, chickabiddy, young fry or small fry (coll.), pubescent, tad, tot, chit, chick.

(For contemptuous terms see BRAT, n.)

2. Offspring, young descendant, scion, heir, son, daughter, chip of the old block (coll.).

CHILDBIRTH, n. Childbed, labor, childbearing, pregnancy, giving birth, propagation, parturition, reproduction, parturience, delivery, confinement, lying-in, accouchement, procreation, delivering, travail, nativity.

CHILDHOOD, n. Boyhood, girlhood, minority, school days, puberty, adolescence, adolescency, juvenility, immaturity, nonage, infancy, youth, pupilage, juniority, incunabula, nursery days, babyhood, "salad days."

CHILDISH, *adj.* 1. Childlike. childly, infantile, juvenile, puerile, immature, youthful, infantine, callow, unfledged, tender, budding, unfeathered, boyish, girlish, kiddish *(coll.)*, youthlike, babyish, beardless, adolescent.

2. Puerile, silly, foolish, senseless, foolheaded, stupid, asinine, unwise, simple, green, naïve, soft, imbecile, inane, inept, inapt, absurd, nonsensical, injudicious, ill-advised, unreasonable, indiscreet, undiscriminating, ill-judged, tactless.

CHILDLIKE, *adj.* 1. Childly, childish, infantile, juvenile, puerile, immature, youthful, infantine, callow, unfledged, tender, budding, boyish, girlish, kiddish *(coll.)*, youthlike, beardless, unfeathered, babyish, adolescent.

2. Naïve, simple, unknowing, overconfident, trustful, innocent, ingenuous, credulous, artless, unsuspecting, overtrustful, gullible, untutored, without suspicion, simple-minded, confiding, unsophisticated.

CHILL, *adj.* 1. Chilling, brisk, bleak, penetrating, cold, clammy, biting, nippy, stinging, inclement, frosty, wintry, cutting, snappy, sleety, fresh, keen, icicled, boreal, arctic, polar, snowy, bone-chilling, frost-riven, teeth-chattering, hyperboreal, hoary, freezing, shivery, hoarfrosted, severe, hibernal, crisp, numbing, sharp, frigid, frost-beaded, cool, bitter, ice-like, ice-cold, gelid, algid, blasting, brumal, icy, glacial, zippy, Siberian, pinching, piercing, hyperborean, draughty, sunless, heatless, lukewarm, tepid.

2. Heatless, cold, shivering, numbed, cooled, frosted, frigid, chilly, coolish, shuddering, gelid, quivering, shaking, chilled to the marrow, algid, chattering, frost-nipped, goose-fleshed, congealed, pinched, frostbitten, frozen stiff, unheated, icy, unthawed, unmelted, glaciated, *frappé (Fr.)*.

3. Callous, cruel, hard, aloof, cold, indifferent, unemotional, unanimated, indurated, impervious, inured, uncaring, untouched, pococurante, obtuse, lethargic, insentient, unmoved, incurious, supine, unstirred, hardened, unfeeling, soulless, languid, insensitive, thick-skinned, stony, inert, undesirous, unexcitable, adamantine, comatose, half-hearted, condescending, flinty, uncommunicative, remote, impassive, harsh, listless, unmindful, passionless, formal, unresponsive, without heart, phlegmatic, stoical, unsusceptible, unconcerned, frigid, stiff, cold-blooded, neutral, insouciant, hostile, icy, uninterested, undemonstrative, unapproachable, unfriendly, spiritless, haughty, unimpassioned, inaccessible, forbidding.

CHILL, *n.* 1. Chilliness, algidity, sharpness, cold, bitterness, iciness, crispness, frigidity, coolness, tepidity, algor, gelidity, draught, want of heat, absence of warmth, bleakness, lukewarmness, glaciation, frostiness.

2. Cold in the head, cold, catarrh, pertussis, bronchitis, flu *(coll.)*, influenza, grippe, rhinitis *(Med.)*, coryza, cough, ague, rheum.

CHILL, *v.* Freeze, make cold, refrigerate, numb, glaciate, benumb, cool, frigorify, infrigidate, ice, congeal, petrify, pinch, cut, bite, nip, air, pierce, ventilate, make one's teeth chatter, make shudder, make shiver, chill to the marrow, chill to the bone.

CHIME, *n.* Peal of bells, set of bells, carillon, tocsin, angelus, tintinnabulum, campana, gong, dingdong.

CHIME, *v.* 1. Ring, sound, toll, peal, jingle, gong,

tinkle, tintinnabulate, knell, clangor, dingdong, ding, tink, ting.

2. Correspond, tally, agree, conform, fit, check, accord, harmonize, be uniform, fall in with, be accordant, be consistent with, jibe *(coll.)*, blend, concur, be harmonious, symphonize, consonate.

3. Descant, trill, chant, cantillate, pipe, sol-fa, solmizate, croon, intone, carol, vocalize, recite, call over, rehearse, yodel, quaver, lilt.

CHIMERA, *n.* 1. Humor, figment, maggot, whim, specter, imagery, daydream, caprice, fancy, ghost, shadow, misapprehension, whimsey, bubble, vapor, misconception, illusion, monster, dream, phantom, imagining, phantasmagoria, vagary, fantasque, mental aberration, derangement, myth, fiction, crotchet, delusion, vision, apparition, deception, hallucination, castle in the air, idle fancy, phantasm, absurdity, fantasy, *bête noire*, bugbear, bugaboo, goblin, hobgoblin, bogey.

2. Imaginary monster, monstrosity, Gorgon, Minotaur, Hydra, Python, salamander, unicorn, lamia, echidna, wivern *(Her.)*, basilisk, dragon, cockatrice, hippocampus, hippogriff, kraken, gyascutus, Centaur, sphinx, androsphinx, dipsas, hippocentaur, hippocerf, manticore, Sagittary, whangdoodle *(humor.)*, roc, griffin, bucentaur, lycanthrope, werewolf, uturuncu.

CHIMERICAL, *adj.* Fanciful, delusive, fantastic, imaginary, notional, whimsical, illusory, unreal, visionary, wild, gossamery, fancied, groundless, mythological, shadowy, utopian, quixotic, vague, feigned, fictitious, figmental, romantic, fabulous, phantasmagorial, imagined, concocted, vaporous, unsubstantial, airy, dreamy, dream-like, spectral, fantasque, legendary, air-built, castle-built.

CHINA, *n.* Earthenware, porcelain, terra cotta, crouch ware, crackle, pottery, crockery, ceramics, chinaware, gombroon, household dishes, salt glazed ware, majolica, eggshell porcelain, basalt, lusterware, porcelain figurine, whiteware, biscuit, blackware, glazed ware, bisque, stoneware, white pottery, ironstone ware, enamelware, clayware, tableware, faience, intaglio ceramics, cottage china, cloisonné, champlevé.

CHINK, *n.* 1. Opening, crack, crevice, rift, cleft, fissure, notch, chasm, chap, hole, breach, leak, aperture, cranny, gap, orifice, ravine, gulch, cut, gully, furrow, scission, gash, rent, fault, rupture, break, rime, split, incision, slit, slot, interval, nick, blaze *(trail marking)*, stria, rut, sulcus, score, crena, flaw, fracture, scissure, trough, trench, scratch, scotch, nock *(archery)*, narrow, interstice.

2. Clink, jingle, tinkle, tink, ting, clank, ring, rattle, ding, dingle, jangle, twang, click, clack.

CHINK, *v.* Jingle, clink, jangle, twang, ding, ting, clank, tinkle, ring, dingle, rattle, click, tink, clack.

CHIP, *n.* Fragment, bit, small piece, sliver, cut, cutting, chunk, scrap, flint, flinder, part, paring, counter, discard, whittling, slice, morsel, splint, particle, speck, tag, shred, piece, flake, splinter, remnant, snick, crumb, lamina, snicking, snip, snippet, chipping, shaving, patch, clipping, bone, gobbet, modicum, cantle, cantlet, snatch, collop, rasher, snack, check, scantling, leaf, wafer, dib, scrip, shive, peel, scale, disk, plate, slug.

CHIP, *v.* 1. Hew, whittle, chisel, cut fragments from, crack off, chop, hack, break, shape bit by bit, gash, haggle, hackle, snip, whack *(coll.)*, incise, sliver, slash, shive, gobbet, nick, crumble, splinter, shiver, fragment, notch, snick.

2. Bird's sound, cheep, chirp, peep, tweet, twitter, chirrup, crick.

3. *(Coll.,with* in) Contribute, participate, pool resources, go shares, share in, pull an oar, join in, take part in, help, pay one's share, do one's share, lend aid, subscribe to, go halves, go Dutch treat *(coll.)*, pull one's weight, defray jointly.

CHIPPER, *adj. (Coll.)* Cheerful, sprightly, well, hearty, active, gay, happy, blithe, spry, lively, of good cheer, jolly, sunny, in fine fettle, in good health, pert, talkative, airy, peppy, spirited, in good spirits, sportive, frisky, elated, gleeful, gay as a lark, playful, debonair, in high spirits, bright, vigorous, buoyant, light-hearted, sparkling, merry, animated, lissom, carefree, waggish, full of life, breezy, laughing, alert, riant, brisk, jovial, joyful, joyous, saucy, dapper, roguish, impish, winsome, lightsome, perky, soaring, nimble, agile, in high feather, volant, bonny, jaunty, jocund, jocular, mirthful, jocose.

CHIROGRAPHY, *n.* Art of writing, penmanship, handwriting, engrossing, calligraphy, hand, script, autography, pencraft, manuscript, graphology, inscribing, scrivening, scrivenery, penscript, runes, inscription, longhand, cerography, stylography, uncial writing, lexigraphy, hieroglyphics, cuneiform, macrography, micrography.

CHIROMANCER, *n.* Fortuneteller (by the hand), chiromancist, reader, interpreter, diviner, palmist, adviser.

CHIROMANCY, *n.* Fortunetelling (by the palm), palmistry, divination, reading, symbology.

CHIRP, *v.* 1. Cheep, chirrup, twit, pipe, carol, crick, tweet, peep, twitter, chatter, whistle, lilt, chitter, sing.

2. Rejoice, carol, exult, crow, joy, frisk, skip for joy, chirrup, sing a paean of triumph, be ecstatic, be merry, lilt, sing, rollic, delight, be gay.

CHISEL, *v.* Cut, sculpture, shape, gouge out, frame, figure, carve, form, engrave, hew out, hammer out, model, forge, cast, furrow, groove, pattern, rough-hew, mold, channel, flute, grave, chip, insculpture, character, tool, chase, fashion, enchase, scratch, score, emboss, incise, contrive, chamfer, hatch, crosshatch, fabricate, stipple.

CHIT, *n.* Child, forward girl, pert young woman, mite *(coll.)*, shaver, tot, elf, cherub, imp, scrap of a child, lass, lassie, bantling, hoyden, tomboy, miss, romp, chickabiddy, dwarf, urchin, midget, dwarfling, manikin, pygmy, Lilliputian, Missy.

CHITCHAT, *n.* Prattle, chat, familiar talk, small talk, trifling talk, gossip, causerie, idle talk, table talk, tattle, powwow, easy conversation, tittle-tattle, scandalmongering, buzz, common talk, babble, grapevine, cackle, tête-à-tête, coze, tea talk, gabble, confabulation, soiree, sociability, confab *(coll.)*, prittle-prattle, town talk, gabfest *(coll.)*, babblement.

CHIVALROUS, *adj.* 1. Gallant, valiant, bold, knightly, valorous, daring, heroic, adventurous, brave, fearless, unflinching, undaunted, hardy, warlike, spartan, doughty, spirited, mettlesome, stout, dauntless, defiant, resolute, venturesome, lion-hearted, plucky, gritty *(coll.)*, venturous, soldierly, undismayed, courageous, unshrinking, intrepid, chivalric, leonine, stone-hearted.

2. High-minded, magnanimous, knightly, loyal, liberal, gentle, upright, generous, courteous, manful, manly, resolute, sterling, unselfish, noble, stout-hearted, jealous of honor, steadfast, constant, gently bred, forbearing, gracious, long-suffering,

exalted, mannerly, self-sacrificing, morally pure, untainted, courtly, charitable, ruthful, clement, illustrious, pitying, compassionate, benign, kind, kindly, merciful, princely, lofty, chivalric, gallant, honorable, unsullied, unstained, complaisant, virtuous, contemptuous of danger, trustworthy, incorruptible, inviolate.

CHIVALRY, *n.* 1. Knighthood, knightly skill, knight-errantry, adventure.

2. Valor, gallantry, courage, prowess, loyalty, heroism, faith, honor, bravery, nobility, defiance of danger, gentleness, courtesy, civility, constancy, morality, fidelity, fortitude, dexterity in arms, loftiness of mind, magnanimity, liberality, mercy, noble resolution, clemency, charity, ruth, pity, compassion, virtue, contempt of danger, mettle, intrepidity, spirit, manliness, complaisancy, probity, integrity, rectitude, courtliness, fealty, uprightness, self-abnegation, forbearance, gentle breeding, humanity, devotion to human welfare, courtly behavior, elevation of spirit *or* purpose, graciousness, amenity, comity, gentility, veracity, good faith, trustworthiness, reliability, hardihood, resoluteness, resolution, generosity, kindness, protectiveness.

CHOCK-FULL, *adj.* Filled to capacity, brimming, crammed, filled to the top, running over, laden, brimful, choked, glutted, topfull, abundant, filled to overflowing, stuffed, overcharged, loaded, overloaded, surcharged, turgid, overflowing, full, chuck-full, replete, bursting, full-charged, ready to burst, choke-full, cram-full, chock *(coll.)*, full to suffocation, excessive, sodden, flushed, sated, saturated, plethorous, surfeited, crowded, heavy-laden, inflated, copious, packed, satiated, compact, closely packed, chuck *(coll.)*, flush, packed like sardines, fraught, full-fraught, solid, dense, close, plethoric, smothered, overfull, gorged, teeming, swarming, enough and to spare, as full as a tick.

CHOICE, *adj.* Select, prime, singled out, rare, exquisite, precious, picked, fine, unique, hand-picked, superfine, dainty, valuable, uncommon, superior, elective, elite, priceless, excellent, best, champion, peculiar, particular, special, preferred, unusual, tiptop, scarce, preferential, preferable, chosen, cream, sterling, prize, ideal, superlative, consummate, paramount, first-rate, first-class, extraordinary, exclusive, singular, restricted, exceptional.

CHOICE, *n.* 1. Election, opinion, volition, vote, pleasure, selection, voice, will, decision, right, conclusion, privilege, free selection, choosing, voluntary decision, discretion, discrimination, selectivity, co-option, co-optation, taste, adoption, determination, judgment, acceptance, espousal, eclecticism, novation *(Law)*, embracement, differentiation, perception of differences, hair-splitting, discernment.

2. Preference, elect, pick, option, propensity, bias, pleasure, considered decision, wish, desire, inclination, excerpt, excerption, predilection, the best part, prepossession, extract, extraction, the most excellent, prejudice, partiality, gem, jewel, pearl, tidbit, cream, prime, treasure, the elect, the select, elite, prize, best, rarest, paragon, prince among men, trump, flower, champion, prodigy, one in a thousand, nonesuch, nonpareil *(Fr.)*, predisposition.

3. Selection, abundance, array, display, supply, surplus, alternatives, large quantity, profusion, variety, host, fund, accumulation, store, stock, *embarras de choix (Fr.)*, embarrassment of riches, multitude, assemblage.

CHOKE, v. 1. Suffocate, smother, throttle, gag, asphyxiate, burke, kill, strangle, stifle, overpower, grab by the throat, stop the breath, gibbet, cut one's air supply, kill by suffocation, wring the neck, strangulate, bowstring, noose, garrote.

2. Overload, overburden, engulf, saturate, glut, satiate, cloy, gorge, fill to overflowing, overlade, surcharge, smother, muffle, envelop, inundate, flood, stifle, constrict, deaden, damp down, gag, deluge, muzzle, repress.

3. Obstruct, block, bar, hinder, clog, blockade, trap, intercede, congest, interfere, interrupt, dam up, impede, check, blight, stop, close, counteract, bridle, tie hand and foot, arrest, tether, put in irons, tie one's hands, hobble, constrict, occlude, shut, plug, stanch, seal up, inhibit, cramp, seal, trammel, hamper, embarrass, cork, stop up, clog the wheels, staunch, restrict, entrammel, brake, deadlock, slacken, debar, shackle, prohibit, bring to a stop, foreclose, preclude, retard, restrain, curb, enmesh, lock in, keep within bounds, hold in leash, surround, hem in, rein in, barricade, constrain.

4. Be choked, suffocate, gasp, smother, burn out, die out, die by asphyxiation, gag, strangle, stick, throttle, be overpowered by strong feeling, become extinguished, be obstructed.

5. (With OFF) Occlude, seal, seal off, make impassable, render mute, interrupt, cut off, gag, muzzle, throttle, stifle, smother, still, hush, cut one short, silence, strike dumb, muffle, quell.

CHOLERIC, adj. Bilious, of fiery nature, hot-tempered, irascible, testy, prone to anger, on edge, quickly aroused to rage, fractious, vengeful, ignitible, excitable, revengeful, rancorous, quick to take offense, acrimonoius, resentful, ready to flare up, irritable, petulant, peevish, touchy, thin-skinned, unruly, undisciplined, uncontrolled, crusty, fitful, cross, spleenful, splenetic, churlish, ill-humored, cross-grained, lacking self-control, atrabilious, sour, bitter, acerbic, jaundiced, huffy, shrewish, peppery, ill-tempered, bad-tempered, emotionally unstable, crabbed, snappish, volcanic, fiery, vixenish, discourteous, rough, rude, sullen, brusque, saturnine, unkind, grouchy, mean, gruff, impolite, ill-willed, loutish, blunt, inaffable, short, morose, short-tempered, sour, sharp, waspish.

CHOOSE, v. Select, prefer, pick, single out, make choice of, adopt, decide on, sort, list, like, draw, judge, will, call for, fancy, take, assign, determine upon, fix upon, opt, appoint, pick out, accept, embrace, cull, co-opt, co-optate, elect, balance, weigh, discriminate between, espouse, take up, exercise discretion, exercise option, discriminate, excerpt, extract, settle on, segregate, set apart, glean, winnow, separate the wheat from the tares, separate, divide the sheep from the goats, make a decision, cast in one's lot, favor, make up one's mind, do of one's own accord, resolve, throw away the scabbard, burn one's bridges, determine, decide, exercise volition, incline toward, prefer, commit oneself.

CHOP, n. 1. Slice, cut, crack, cutlet, piece cut off, cleft, chip, clip, côtelette (Fr.).

2. Act of chopping, hack, whack (coll.), snap, stroke, dint, sharp blow, short abrupt motion (of waves), cutting stroke.

CHOP, v. 1. Cut with a quick blow, fell, hew, sever, sunder, cut down, mark, truncate, cleave, rive, dissever, rend, split, gash, trim, lop, hack, retrench, prune, shear, reap, mow, dismember, strike repeatedly, dislimb, slash, notch, nick, disjoint, clip, crop.

2. Mince, chip, hash, cut into small pieces, dice, cube, crack, hackle, haggle, partition, crush, divide, subdivide, splinter, shiver, reduce to fragments, crumble, grind, break up, disintegrate, pulverize, reduce, granulate, comminute, fritter, triturate, segment, chew, cut up, decimate.

3. Shift, change suddenly, veer, turn with the wind, mutate, turn, jibe, tack, deviate, swerve, warp, vacillate, dodge, shuffle, turn aside, alter, tergiversate, vary, leap, swirl, jib.

4. Cut in, interpose, interrupt, dart, move suddenly, pounce, push in, intervene, break in.

CHOPPY, adj. 1. Full of cracks, rough, full of chaps, unpolished, uneven, furrowed, irregular, coarse, rugged, wrinkled, crinkled, craggy, flaky, homespun, rough-grained, rough-hewn, scaly, rough-cast, cross-grained, coarse-textured, rugose, rugous, corrugated.

2. Rough, stormy, squally, turbulent, with ruffled surface, with short tumbling waves, pecky (coll.), wind-whipped, tempestuous, boisterous, swirling, leaping, wind-lashed.

3. Repeatedly veering about, changeable, variable, mutable, unstable, blown with every wind, shifting, deviating, vacillating, swerving.

CHOPS, n. Chaps, jaws, mouth cavity, fauces (Anat.), mouth of a cannon, opening to a valley, entrance to a channel.

CHORAL, adj. Choric, in unison, in chorus, concert, concerted, operatic, concordant, group, attuned, assonant, psalmodic, accordant, odic, symphonic, psalmic, harmonic, Pindaric, epodic, modal, polyphonic, symphonious, euphonious, harmonious, strophic, antistrophic, contrapuntal, song, consonant.

CHORAL, CHORALE, n. Psalm-tune, sacred song, anthem, paean, response, antiphon, carol, hymn-tune, canticle, offertory, responsory, motet, Passion music, doxology, hymn, psalm, concentus.

CHORD, n. 1. String of a musical instrument, a particular emotion (fig.).

2. Simultaneous harmonizing tones, triad, seventh, ninth.

3. Right line uniting the extremities of an arc (Geom.), secant (Geom.), filament (Anat.), cord (Anat.), horizontal brace (Engineering), tendon (Anat.), filament (Anat.).

CHORE, n. Small job, duty, work, turn, task, job, stint, errand, light task, routine, daily light duty, care, exercise, minor domestic work.

CHORTLE, v. Laugh gleefully, snort, gloat, relish, chuckle, snigger, crow, exult, snicker, chant, sing exultantly, triumph, gloat over, crow over, cackle.

CHORUS, n. 1. Song, refrain, burden, repetend, polyphony, antiphon, antiphony, response, choral ballad, recurring words, choral composition, prologue (Gk. and Eliz. drama), epilogue (Gk. and Eliz. drama), chant, anthem, part song, chorale, Gregorian, harmonized vocal music, part singing, bob, repetition, ritornel, strophe, part music, antistrophe, undersong, ode, epode, outcry, ritornello (Ital.), clamor, baying (of dogs), descant, counterpoint, carol, lusty chirruping (of many insects combined).

2. Choir, glee club, choristers, choral society, Kapelle (Ger.), Liederkranz (Ger.), symphony of voices, carolers, waits, street singers, Liedertafel (Ger.), festival chorus, group of singers, line of dancers, commentator (Eliz. drama).

3. Unity, harmony, consonance, concord, one voice, unison, assonance, concert, unanimity, concordance, consensus, concurrence, accord.

CHRISTEN, *v.* 1. Baptize, sprinkle, confirm, dip, lay hands on, anoint, immerse, consecrate, impose, asperge, dedicate, asperse.

2. Name, denominate, term, call, entitle, open ceremonially, dedicate, designate, dub, title, style, intitle, launch *(of a ship)*, send down the ways *(of a ship)*.

CHRONIC, *adj.* Inveterate, persistent, enduring, continuous, deep-seated, recurring, long-lived, of long duration, constant, abiding, ingrained, lingering, permanent, longevous, lasting, deep-rooted, unyielding, long-established, ineradicable, rooted, virulent, long-continuing, perennial, long-standing, fixed, inborn, inbred, settled, habitual, incessant, unabating, seated, protracted, continual, sustained, intermittent, lifelong, prolonged, long-drawn, hardened, periodic, unmitigated, returning at intervals, persisting, ceaseless, recurrent, unshifting, confirmed.

CHRONICLE, *n.* 1. Register of events, journal, log, calendar, minutes, docket, proceedings, document, diary, transactions, annals, registry, archive, record, public record, Congressional Records, almanac, scroll.

2. Record, history, chronology, story, legend, events in sequence, memoir, archives, account, recital, saga, annals, narrative, memorandum, memorabilia, biography, epic, autobiography, life, narration, memorial(s), document, scroll, relation, factum, journal, fortunes, adventures.

CHRONICLE, *v.* Record, set down, document, chronologize, put on record, register, narrate, report, relate, recite, enter, list, enroll, calendar, take minutes, docket, mark, recount, set forth in order, write an historic account of.

CHRONICLER, *n.* Chronographer, chronologer, annalist, documenter, writer, narrator, reporter, record-maker, recorder, chronologist, registrar, scribe, historiographer, biographist, memorialist, antiquary, antiquarian, autobiographer, historian, autobiographist, clerk, biographer.

CHRONOLOGICAL, *adj.* In sequence, in order of time, chronometric, temporal, horologic, archival, horological, chronographic, measured in time, chronoscopic, chronometrical, properly dated, sequential, sequent, progressive in time, following time order, consecutive, horometrical.

CHUBBY, *adj.* Rotund, plump, pudgy, stubby, stocky, round, squabby, squat, fat, stout, squab, stubbed, thickset, squattish, squabbish, squatty, stumpy *(coll.)*, substantial, dumpy, chunky *(coll.)*, tubby *(coll.)*, rotundate, filled out, full, fleshy, corpulent, gibbous, gibbose, bouncing, lusty, strapping, podgy, ample, well-fed, round-faced, chopping, moonfaced, punchy *(coll.)*, rounded out, stodgy, chumpy *(coll.)*.

CHUCK, *n.* 1. Tap, pat, caress, slight blow, loving poke.

2. Throw, thrust, fling, fillip, heave, chunk, flirt, shy, push, toss, sling, cast, propulsion, peg *(coll.)*, shove, pitch, hurl.

CHUCK, *v.* 1. Tap, pet, caress, poke lovingly, fondle, pat, tickle.

2. Throw, thrust, fling, jerk, pitch, push, toss, shy, cast, pelt, peg *(coll.)*, heave, dart, hurl, let fly, sling, cant, fillip, bat, bowl, chunk, shoot, flirt, shove, tilt, lance, put *(a shot)*, project, drive, propel, force.

CHUCKLE, *v.* Laugh quietly and inwardly, relish, chirrup, chirp, exult, laugh gleefully, chortle good-humoredly, grin complacently, heave with mirth, smile playfully, grin jovially, laugh with contentment, purr, convulse quietly, laugh softly with amusement, rejoice, laugh to oneself, grin like a Cheshire cat.

CHUCKLE, *n.* Suppressed laughter, playful smile, jovial grin, jollity, complacent grin, expression of content, quiet laughter, inward pleasure, silent heaving with mirth, merriment, good-humored chortle, quiet convulsion, Cheshire grin, jocundity.

CHUM, *n.* *(Coll.)* Partner, intimate, friend, habitual companion, playmate, companion, close associate, buddy *(coll.)*, bosom friend, fellow, side kick *(slang)*, familiar friend, playfellow, boon companion, comrade, boonfellow, confidant, intimate companion, fast friend, devoted friend, inseparable, other self, alter ego *(Lat.)*, friend in need, confidential friend, faithful friend, well-wisher, trusted friend, trusty friend, pal *(slang)*, crony *(slang)*, roommate, confident, confidante, mate, devoted friend.

CHUMMY, *adj.* *(Coll.)* Friendly, intimate, genial, affable, sociable, cordial, congenial, fraternal, neighborly, true, steadfast, faithful, familiar, constant, fond, hearty, endearing, confiding, at home with, affectionate, accessible, brotherly, warm-hearted, amicable, sisterly, stanch, tried and true, harmonious, friendlike, sympathetic, close, on familiar terms, near, hand and glove, hand in hand, thick *(coll.)*, devoted, ardent, fast, firm, inseparable.

CHUNK, *n.* *(Coll.)* Piece, lump, wad, batch, loaf, bulk, block, mass, thick slice, squab, stump, hunk *(coll.)*, butt, thick fragment, hunch, gobbet, fair quantity *(fig.)*, thick cut, clod, nugget, gob *(slang)*, mouthful, square, swad *(slang)*, bite-size piece, part, snack, whack *(slang)*.

CHUNKY, *adj.* *(Coll.)* Thick, stocky, bulky, solid, bulging, heavy, thickset, lumpy, stout, stubby, stunted, gross, dwarfish, plump, lumpish, stodgy, stubbed, rotund, rough-ground, tumid, swollen, knobby, bulbous, bellied, pudgy, stumpy *(coll.)*, distended, round, squat, squab, squatty, firm, dumpy, squabby, fat, squabbish, muscular, full, gibbous, corpulent, fleshy, gibbose, bouncing, lusty, hulking, portly, chumpy *(coll.)*, chopping, podgy, strapping, punchy *(coll.)*, ample, brawny, tubby *(coll.)*, bunched, squattish, beefy.

CHURCH, *n.* 1. Temple, meeting house, Lord's house, house of worship, chapel, cathedral, see, sanctuary, synagogue, minster, house of God, tabernacle, shrine, conventicle, oratory, place of worship, basilica, auditorium, sacellum, chantry, bethel, house of prayer, pantheon, mosque.

2. Body of Christians, believers, the elect, congregation, communion, disciples, body, fold, followers, synod, ecclesiastical body, community, members of Christ, fellowship, presbytery, vestry, adherents, conclave, classis, conventicle, imitators of Christ, consistory, congress, ecclesiastical council, Holy Church, convocation, convention, the Bride of the Lamb, Church invisible.

3. Sect, religious order, religion, affiliation, creed, cult, denomination, persuasion, ism, faith, religious society, belief, doctrine, faction, order, sectarism, schism.

4. Divine worship, chapel service, devotions, vespers, morning worship, evening worship, prayer meeting, ceremony, rite, camp meeting, office, duty, ritual, service, exercises, revival meeting, congregational worship, fellowship.

5. Ecclesiastical authority, Christendom, pale, churchdom, Church visible, orthodoxy, the

Vatican, ecclesiastical hierarchy, Popedom, ecclesiastical council, ecumenical council, World Federation of Churches.

6. Parish, pastorate, curacy, classis, living, benefice, prelacy, diocese, see, vicarage, rectory, field.

CHURL, *n.* 1. Rustic, clodhopper, hobnail, hind, peasant, yokel, farmer, countryman, lout, hick *(slang),* greenhorn, swain, Tony Lumpkin, boor, country bumpkin, clown, plowman, drone, son of the soil, lubber, hayseed *(slang),* hodge *(coll.),* son of Martha, chuff, kern *(rare),* galoot *(slang),* clod, joskin *(slang),* jake *(coll.),* rube *(coll.)* lumpkin, looby, tiller of the soil, gaffer, bumpkin.

2. Ill-bred man, curmudgeon, boor, dolt, bear, surly fellow, tyke, codger, cad, bounder *(coll.),* vixen, shrew, chit, screw, numskull, dunce, blockhead, dastard, blackguard, ignoramus, beast, dullard, barbarian, duffer, scoundrel, ribald, cur, oaf, clown, vulgar fellow, groveler, wasp, ne'er-do-well, loafer.

3. Niggard, miser, screw, tightwad *(slang),* moneygrubber, pinchfist, curmudgeon, skinflint, skin *(slang),* Euclio, Daniel Dancer, save-all *(dial.),* codger *(slang),* lickpenny, harpy, hunks, Harpagon, mean fellow, Silas Marner, scrimp *(coll.),* muckworm, pinchpenny *(rare).*

CHURLISH, *adj.* 1. Rude, brusque, surly, sullen, crabbed, petulant, acetous, choleric, acrimonious, bearish, insulting, abrupt, ill-mannered, uncouth, tart, ill-bred, unmannerly, insolent, brazen, gross, obnoxious, acerbic, irascible, sharp, thorny, bluff, grouchy *(coll.),* gruff, bristling, grouty *(coll.),* sarcastic, growling, harsh, uncivil, rough, impolite, brutish, snarling, waspish, peppery, snappish, sour, quarrelsome, splenetic, crusty, sulky, unamiable, unhandsome, coarse, boorish, ungainly, rustic, blunt, glum, swinish, bestial, gloomy, reptilian, beastly, vulgar, grim, perverse, ugly, ungallant, doggish, stubborn, morose, ill-tempered, spiteful, fractious, mean, sordid, base, dastardly, recreant, discourteous, testy, lowbred, callous, crude, crass, resentful, caviling, iracund, of shabby behavior, unwholesome, pusillanimous, offensive, cloddish, loutish, brash, acrid, mordant, curt, currish, short, ungraceful, lubberly, cankered, captious, moody, cynical, clownish, vengeful, irritable, thin-skinned, touchy, jaundiced, saturnine, mordacious, bitter, impudent, bold, umbrageous, arrogant, audacious, presumptuous, contemptible, rancorous, peevish, bilious, cross-grained, shrewish.

2. Niggardly, stinting, stingy, miserly, close, penurious, mean, narrow, illiberal, sordid, close-fisted, penny-wise, gripping, chary, usurious, near, shabby, close-handed, tight-fisted, parsimonious, beggarly, venal, greedy, grasping, avaricious, mercenary, scrimping, extortionate, covetous, rapacious, grudging, pinching, meager, cheeseparing *(coll.),* tight *(coll.).*

3. Wanting pliancy, intractable, ungovernable, obstinate, rebellious, incorrigible, contumacious, unruly, self-willed, stubborn, resistant, fractious, refractory, unmanageable, dogmatic, unbending, stiff-necked, bigoted, prejudiced, insubordinate, hidebound, headstrong, untoward, hard-set, balky, inflexible, defiant, obdurate, arbitrary, perverse, pertinacious, hard-bitten, unyielding, pigheaded, mulish.

CHURLISHNESS, *n.* 1. Rudeness, boorishness, roughness, sulkiness, crustiness, incivility, spleen, bluffness, bluntness, coarseness, petulance, choler, quarrelsomeness, cynicism, sourness, brutishness,

inurbanity, vulgarity, irascibility, acid, disdain, brusqueness, gruffness, sarcasm, lack of breeding, abruptness, sharpness, unmannerliness, insolence, bearishness, mordacity, amarity *(rare),* bestiality, beastliness, causticity, cavil, brazenness, spinosity, arrogance, protervity, hot blood, gall, procacity, temper, crabbedness, sullenness, acrimony, bile, moroseness, tartness, acerbity, harshness, spite, ill temper, bitterness, perverseness, grouchiness *(coll.),* rusticity, grossness, ugliness, perversity, doggishness, mordancy, gloominess, fractiousness, testiness, moodiness, offensiveness, crudeness, baseness, crassness, bad blood, glumness, canker, discourtesy, meanness, pusillanimity, loutishness, curtness, iracundity, ill humor, irritability, rancor, touchiness, peevishness, resentfulness, shortness, brashness, impudence, effrontery, irreverence, ill will, shameless boldness, aspersion, dudgeon, black dog, contemptuousness, unsociability, scowling, umbrage, animosity, melancholy, scornfulness, indignity, contempt, disrespect, presumptuousness, audacity, asperity, insult.

2. Miserliness, niggardliness, parsimony, stint, closeness, chariness, close-fistedness, illiberality, beggarliness, avarice, avidity, greediness, venality, narrowness, penuriousness, sordidness, meanness, shabbiness, tight-fistedness, meagerness, stinginess, scrimping, covetousness, extortion, cupidity, cheeseparing, grudging, rapacity, close-handedness.

3. Inflexibility, obstinacy, bigotry, stiffness, contumacy, incorrigibility, rebelliousness, pigheadedness, unruliness, arbitrariness, prejudice, resistance, insubordination, mulishness, balkiness, pertinaciousness, intractability, refractoriness, perversity, obduracy, stubbornness, unmanageability.

CHURN, *v.* 1. Whisk, shake up, palpitate, shake to the center, toss, whip, beat, agitate, jounce, vibrate, stir up, mash, disturb, cause to foam.

2. Heave, revolve, turn violently, vibrate, foam, shake, palpitate, pulsate, convulse, roll, eddy, swirl, surge, gurge.

CHUTE, *n.* 1. Slide, shoot, sluice, tube, spout, passage, flume, duct, course, drain, canal, trench, pipe, conduit, sloping channel, hopper, sink, shaft, cut, inclined plane, receptacle, way, aqueduct, adit *(Mining),* sewer, scupper, gutter, ditch, moat, culvert, dike, cloaca, funnel, hose, drainpipe, kennel, waterspout, race, raceway, main, trough, drainspout, channel, gargoyle, run, stulm *(Mining).*

2. *(Of water, a river)* Fall, gorge, rapid, chasm, cataract, gully, gulch, steep channel, ravine, quick descent, canyon, watercourse, arroyo, couloir *(Fr.),* waterway, coulee *(West. U.S.).*

3. *(Metal founding)* Gate, runner, tedge, sprue, ingate.

CIMMERIAN, *adj.* Gloomy, dark, shrouded, lightless, umbrageous, somber, pitch-black, ebony, darksome, unilluminated, nigrous, sunless, murky, fuliginous, raven, lurid, dreary, lowering, Nubian, pitchy, night-clad, funereal, Stygian, lackluster, sooty, leaden, dun, night-enshrouded, crepuscular, coal-black, hopeless, pitch-dark, nigrine, shadowy, caliginous, dingy, night-cloaked, inky, clouded, night-filled, obscure, shady, night-hid, tenebrous, depressing, nocturnal, swart, jet-black, night-mantled, tenebrific, dismal, night-veiled, sable, rayless, in eclipse, overcast, swarthy, moonless, atramentous, nubilous, turbid, opaque, starless, lugubrious, cloudy, obfuscated, black.

CINCH, *n.* Girth, girdle, saddle band, belly band, surcingle, belt, girt, latigo.

CINCTURE, *n.* 1. Belt, girdle, ring, sash, crown, band, halo, snood, baldric, cestus, tie, cordon, stripe, ribbon, girth, strip, collar, thong, circlet, cord, zone, lasso, chaplet, coronet, garland, strap, cummerbund, girt, hoop, bracelet, bandage, fillet, armlet, noose, vinculum, wreath, annulet, corona, aureole, necklace, rope, cingulum, fascia, zonule.

2. Enclosure, zone, coop, yard, pen, closure, encompassment, encincture, confine, fold, stall, hen cote, pigpen, sty, sheepfold, pound, paddock, barnyard, farmyard, cage, cell, enclave, premises, precinct, compartment, circuit, bounds, stockade, pinfold, pale, patch plot, booth, piggery, penfold, cattlefold, pasture, stockyard, camp, compound, quadrangle, courtyard, curtilage, square, court, circumvallation, corral.

3. Surrounding, encompassment, encincture, encircling, girdling, circumjacence, hemming in, circumambience, circumcincture, enclosing, siege, skirting, circumvention, restriction, swaddling, circumscription, circumvallation, trussing, walling in, constriction, blockading, hedging, binding, circumfluence, environment, circumflexion, fencing in, confinement, restraint, astriction, swathing, limitation, circumposition.

CINCTURED, *adj.* 1. Surrounded, girdled, belted, encompassed, encircled, roped, girded, engirt, bound, ringed, ensphered, girt, begirt.

2. Circumscribed, confined, imprisoned, zoned, walled, bound, hemmed in, delimited, railed, encompassed, picketed, limited, bounded, pent up, enclosed, fenced in, hedged around, cooped up, corraled, encircled, defined, demarcated, marked off, restricted, walled in, surrounded.

CINDER, *n.* 1. Ash, ember, hot coal, burned-out coal, remnant, scale, clinker, sinter.

2. *(Usually plural)* Ashes, clinkers, embers, sinters, hot coals, carbon, soot, coke, culm, smut, burned-out coals, scale, residue, slag, dross, waste, recrement, coom, scoria, refuse, dràff, slaggy lava, sprue, charcoal, remnants.

CINEMA, *n.* Moving picture, film, motion picture, movie *or* movies *(sl.)*, sound motion picture, talking motion picture, photoplay, talkie *(coll.)*, picture show.

CIPHER, *n.* 1. Zero, naught, nothing, nil, aught, goose egg *or* duck's egg *(sl.)*.

2. Number, numeral, digit, integer, character, figure, symbol, numero, no. *(abbr.)*.

3. Steganogram, cryptogram, cryptograph, code, secret writing, prearranged signal, anagram, device, monogram, acrostic, logogriph.

4. Nonentity, nothing, naught, nobody, nullity, obscurity, person of no account *or* influence.

CIPHER, *v.* 1. Practice arithmetic, write, figure, compute, count up, use figures, codify, analyze, numerate, calculate, score, estimate, count, sum up, enumerate, number, add, total, reckon.

2. Write in code *or* cipher, use secret writing, code, decipher, decode.

CIRCLE, *n.* 1. Round, round plane figure, coin, roundlet, disk, wheel, rondure, hub, nave, roulette, trolley.

2. Circumference, ring, halo, orbit, zone, belt, perimeter, meridian, corona, periphery, hoop, horizon, equator, parallel of latitude, circuit, full turn, twirl, circus, bowl, stadium, zodiac, colure, tropic *(of Cancer, Capricorn)*, aureole, ecliptic, equinoctial, hippodrome, amphitheater, crescent, tier of seats, tire, felly, wheel, vortex, cirque.

3. Orb, globe, ball, pellet, sphere, spherule, drop, vesicle, star, marble, pea, cannon ball,

celestial sphere, apple, globule, planet, orange, billiard ball, knob, bulb, geoid, armillary sphere, spherulite *(Petrog.)*.

4. Cycle, returning series, circuit, revolution, rondure, spiral, gyration, twirl, curl, helix, whorl, corkscrew, round, rondel, involution, tendril, repeated set, rondeau, coil, screw, volute, curlicue, full turn, volution, rondo *(Mus.)*.

5. Enclosure, province, region, compass, zone, area, radius, section, range, part, vicinage, vicinity, purlieus, quarter, district, neighborhood, pale, county, precinct, diocese, township, riding, ward, hundred, commune, parish, shire, canton, field, bailiwick, state, cincture, settlement, colony.

6. Group with mutual interest or status, company, coterie, set, clique, knot, cabal, club, gang, faction, interest, society, fraternity, party, class, association, bunch *(coll.)*, crowd *(coll.)*, outfit *(coll.)*, ring, group, camarilla, junto, walk of life.

7. Sphere *(of activity, influence)*, province, range, region, area, circuit, compass, bounds, field, section, dominion, ambit, premises, hub, tour, lap, turn, nave, bailiwick, precinct, division, stage, scene, theater, niche, sweep, swing, scope, reach, arena, walk, daily round, capacity, notch, expanse, extent, spread, latitude, course, orbit, domain, quarter, department, demesne, realm, stretch, orb *(rare)*, gyration.

8. Ring, belt, discus, hoop, crown, girdle, cincture, cingulum, girt, roundlet, cordon, girth, coronet, wreath, zone, diadem, circlet, ringlet, annulet, cestus, bracelet, eye, loop, band, fascia, baldric, chaplet, garland, cummerbund, eyelet, armlet, fillet, necklace, neckband, aureole, areola, grommet, collar, sash.

CIRCLE, *v.* 1. Encircle, revolve around, ring, wind about, circumscribe, compass, environ, loop, girdle, ensphere, round, double, encompass, gird, enclose, surround, hedge in, curve around, circuit, circumvent, circumflex, curl, ring round, lie around, envelop, belt, twine round, beset, circumnavigate, circumambulate, embrace, coil, cincture, compass about, be circumjacent, spiral, crook, hem in, invest, endue.

2. Revolve, move around, rotate, pivot, turn, wheel, curve, spin, roll, whirl, eddy, circumrotate, involute, twirl, coil, gyrate, incurve, circulate, swivel, reel, pirouette, gurge, circumnavigate, circumambulate, curl, turbinate, volutate, furl, circumvolve, trundle.

CIRCUIT, *n.* 1. Limit, confine, border, edge, enclosure, frontier, pale, line of demarcation, compass, extremity, circumference, purlieus, frame, periphery, side, hem, fringe, skirt, curb, brim, rim, end, march, verge, termination, line, margin, boundary, girdle, perimeter.

2. Area, bounds, pale, compass, section, field, extent, orbit, sphere, beat, province, space, region, jurisdiction, tract, ambit, district, domain, part, territory, bailiwick, quarter, realm, demesne, orb, precinct, orbit, range, premises, zone.

3. Beat, lap, way, sphere, walk, work, routine, road, ambit, compass, tour, trek, circumference, bounds, zone, area, orbit, path, track, perimeter, traversal.

4. Course, journey, travel, tour, perambulation, excursion, trek, peregrination, expedition, trip, outing, airing, jaunt, voyage, run, pilgrimage, wanderings, meanderings, itinerary, route.

5. Path, multiple series, closed circuit, live circuit, loop, leg, series, multiple, parallel, live wire.

CIRCUITOUS, *adj.* Meandering, tortuous, indirect, roundabout, sinuous, flexuous, winding, turning, twisting, serpentine, devious, crooked, ambagious, anfractuous, helical, rambling, zigzag, mazy, labyrinthine.

CIRCULAR, *adj.* 1. Round, ring-shaped, curved, spherical, rotund, discoid, annular, globular, rounded, fasciate, cycloid, orbicular, curviform, perimetric, curvilinear, epicycloid, bent, convex, conical, arched, cupped, spheroidal, peripheral, circumferential, orbiculate, calathiform, gibbous, cylindrical, concave, bowed, globate, globeshaped, hooped, bulbous, circumflex, clockwise, cyclical, columnar, sphincteral.

2. Rotary, swiveling, gyrating, twirling, turning, pivoting, rotating, revolving, curling, coiling, vertiginous, volute, trochilic, involute, spiraling, gyratory, vortical, rolling, helical, helicoid, cochleate, doubling, whirligig.

3. Cyclic, periodic, in repeating series, serial, perennial, returning, regular, rhythmic, remittent, continuous, alternate, recurrent, seasonal, epochal, isochronal.

4. Meandering, roundabout, crooked, mazy, anfractuous, zigzag, rambling, ambagious, devious, twisting, turning, helical, flexuous, serpentine, winding, sinuous, indirect, tortuous.

5. Encyclical, propagatory, annunciatory, declaratory, publicized, distributed, circulated, enunciatory, proclamatory, promulgatory, cyclic, disseminated, form, advertising, common, general, public.

CIRCULAR, *n.* Handbill, duplicated communication, advertisement, encyclical, form letter, propaganda, bill, placard, proclamation, bulletin, follow-up, flier, notice, poster, announcement, official summary, ad *(coll.),* statement.

CIRCULATE, *v.* 1. Spread, disseminate, spread abroad, propagate, report, notify, advertise, run, proclaim, circumfuse, rumor about, make known, whisper about, divulge *(rare),* rumor, issue, bruit abroad, distribute, repeat, give currency to, promulgate, diffuse, scatter, bestrew, intersperse, placard, disperse, publish, publish abroad, vent, blow, noise abroad, put about, hawk about, air, ventilate, broadcast, spray, sprinkle, irrigate, sow, strew, give to the world, bring into the open, give out, put forth, emit, trumpet, put forward, lay before the public, utter, declare, enunciate, proclaim from the housetops, herald, blaze, proclaim at the crossroads, blazon, give voice to, raise a report, publicize, mint, monetize, coin, reissue, set news afloat, remonetize, put into circulation, blaze abroad, tell, announce, bruit, bandy about, evulgate, make public, divulgate.

2. Move round, rotate, revolve, whirl, twist, describe a circle, pivot, spin, curl, roll, curve, trundle, circle, gyre, furl, convolve, wheel, turn, gyrate, round, convolute, move in a circle, circumrotate. coil, incurve, reel, gurge, pirouette, circumvolve, circumvolute, swivel, involute.

3. Spread, have currency, pass, get abroad, flow, be diffused, disperse, emanate, be published, come out, circuit, perform a circuit, go around, compass, go the rounds, meander, encompass, issue, circuiteer, permeate, become public, find vent, acquire currency, pass current, go the length and breadth of the land, spread like wildfire, stream, drift, flit, shift about, pass around, change hands, course, get afloat, travel. get out, go forth, blow about, pass from mouth to mouth.

CIRCULATION, *n.* 1. Motion in a circle, rotation,

circuit, trundle, revolution, circumvolution, gyration, turning, circling, curling, spinning, compassing, curving, rolling, pivoting, whirling, circumgyration, turbination, volutation, circumrotation, circumflexion, involution, incurvation, reeling, gurging, circumambulation, convolution, circumvention, flowing, passing, encompassing, rounding, convolution, circumnavigation, coiling, pirouetting, swiveling.

2. Diffusion, spreading, transmission, currency, flow, dissemination, propagation, becoming public, issuing, issuance, repetition, reporting, notification, bruiting, printing, acquiring currency, distribution, advertisement, circumfusion, ventilation, broadcast, divulgation, rounding, circuity, compassing, excursion, announcement, publicity, flagrancy, general notice, manifesto, publishing, irrigation, proclamation, evulgation, circuiting, traveling, meandering, circuiteering, publication, emanation. dispersion.

3. Currency, circulating medium, medium of exchange, coinage, coin of the realm, specie, paper money, legal tender, mintage, fractional currency, money, sterling *(Eng.).*

4. Extent of subscription, number of takers, number of books lent, number of people reached, area covered, number of copies distributed, number of copies disposed of.

CIRCUMAMBIENT, *adj.* Surrounding, encircling, ambient, encompassing, enveloping, radiating, effulgent, radiant, embracing, containing, going around, enclosing, inclusive, compassing, circling, circumjacent, enfolding, roundabout, around, circumfluent, circumferential, comprehending, comprising, embodying, immersing, supporting, emanating, aural *(from aura).*

CIRCUMFERENCE, *n.* Periphery, perimeter, outline, bound, compass, limit, girdle, border, contour, circuit, felly, confine, line of enclosure, edge, girth, zone, coast line, pale, delineation, lineaments, profile, extent, orbit, silhouette, fringe, horizon, extremities, frame, purlieus, boundary, margin, skirt, rim, tire, hem, gable *(Fr. Art),* ambit, tournure *(Fr.),* circumscription.

CIRCUMJACENT, *adj.* Surrounding, encircling, circumambient, enfolding, lying around, girdling, contiguous, embracing, circumscribing, all around, circumfluent, circumferential, bounding, circumscriptive, binding, hemming in, compassing about, suburban, roundabout, bordering on every side, skirting, engirding, encincturing, enclosing, neighboring, environing, ambient, encompassing, fringing, outlining, outlinear, peripheral, vicinal, adjoining, proximate, juxtapositional, proximal, juxtapositive, neighbor, adjacent, intimate, coastal, perimetric, marginal.

CIRCUMLOCUTION, *n.* 1. Periphrasis, tautology, periphrase, indirect expression, roundabout mode of speech, diffuseness, verbiage, circuit of words, involved expression, wordiness, pleonasm, indirection, tediousness, redundancy, nimiety, battology, tautologism, ambagiousness, rambling, circumbendibus, surplusage, meandering, needless amplification, maundering, redundance, effusive speech, profuseness, superfluity of speech, longwindedness, macrology, perissology *(rare),* ambages *(rare),* digression, garrulity, padding, looseness, excursus, episode, ambiguity, smokescreen of words *(fig.),* vagueness, volubility, repetition, loquacity, discursiveness, prolixity, exuberance, extravagance, cloud of words, longiloquence, frivolous talk, complexity, Jesuitism, verbosity, roundabout phrases, repetitiousness.

2. Quibble, evasion, quiddity, prevarication, subtlety, ambiguity, shifting, dodging, quirk, cavil, carping, begging of the question, tergiversation, shuffling, subterfuge, equivocation, mystification, sophistry, vagueness, indirection.

CIRCUMLOCUTORY, *adj.* 1. Periphrastical, roundabout, involved, prolix, wordy, pleonastic, diffuse, indirect, periphrastic, voluble, effusive, tedious, superfluous, ambiguous, tautological, verbose, redundant, exuberant, garrulous, repetitious, ambagitory, profuse, battological, episodic, circuitous, digressional, loose, loquacious, long-winded, padded, vague, discursive, digressive, ambagious, perissological *(rare)*, needlessly complex, copious, protracted, rambling, devious, extravagant, maundering, lengthy, desultory.
2. Equivocal, quibbling, caviling, carping, evasive, sophistical, shifting, dodging, ambiguous, shuffling, prevaricating, tergiversatory, subtle.

CIRCUMSCRIBE, *v.* 1. Bound, surround, encircle, encompass, environ, shut in, fix bounds of, outline, encincture, enclose, fence in, delineate, picket, ensphere, invest, circumpose *(rare)*, gird, infold, encase, border, enwrap, enclasp, enchase, envelop, belt, girdle, endue, embrace, beleaguer, corral, embay, involve, wrap, round, circuit, lie around, clothe, pack, incase, lie circumjacent to, double, embosom, hem in.
2. Confine, limit, proscribe, bind, define, restrain, restrict, keep within bounds, curb, leash, trammel, incarcerate, cloister, intern, shackle, hold in check, determine, hem in, shut in, pen in, picket, encyst, beset, beleaguer, blockade, collar, interdict, withhold, imprison, hinder, specify, embargo, stay, trim down to size *(coll.)*, impede, condition, qualify, constrain, retain, repress, cage, bridle, hobble, fix, veto, deny, preclude, debar, disallow, forbid, inhibit, prohibit, harass, immure, circumvent, impound, fetter, besiege, check, ban, shorten, bar, taboo, bound, mark off, demarcate, delimit, delimitate, tie one's hands.

CIRCUMSPECT, *adj.* Cautious, careful, heedful, judicious, attentive, prudent, alert, wise, wary, watchful, considerate, vigilant, discreet, chary, observant, wide-awake, mindful, advertent, astute, perceptive, discerning, sapient, discriminative, savant *(Fr.)*, percipient, sage, regardful, politic, discriminating, well-advised, expedient, gingerly, precautious, on one's guard, shy of, on the safe side, close-mouthed, precautionary, sure-footed, noncommittal, open-eyed, stealthy, reserved, contemplative, premeditative, reticent, guarded, deliberative, scrupulous, deliberate, particular, thoughtful, sagacious, economical, provident, calculating, perspicacious, Argus-eyed.

CIRCUMSPECTION, *n.* Caution, watchfulness, care, attention, discretion, propriety, deliberation, scrupulousness, precaution, forethought, caution, cautiousness, solicitude, alertness, judgment, heed, forecast, prudence, vigilance, thoughtfulness, wariness, heedfulness, judiciousness, wisdom, economy, guardedness, regard, astuteness, policy, mindfulness, sagacity, chariness, observation, consideration, perspicacity, percipience, sapience, providence, contemplation, premeditation, sure-footedness, stealthiness, expedience, perception, discrimination, discernment, reserve, observant care, diligent attention, advertency, advisement, examination, concern, husbandry, advertence, scrutiny, reticence.

CIRCUMSTANCE, *n.* Event, incident, condition, occurrence, fact, matter, influencing factor, affair, particular, crisis, feature, accompaniment, point, obligation, contingency, item, case, situation, predicament, casualty, incidental factor, essential condition, casual detail, juncture, provision, plight, exigency, mishap, adjunct, pass, attendant facts, primary qualification, subsidiary factor, concern, stipulation, proviso, eventuality, article, happening, accident, supervention, happenstance *(coll.)*, phenomenon, arrangement, specification, term, place, instance, turn of events, incidence, chance, complement, accessory, cause, fortuity, coincidence, episode, time, clause, concurrent event.

CIRCUMSTANCES, *n.* 1. Situation, position, state of affairs, controlling factors, qualifying factors, how the land lies, current regime, phase, modifying features, accompanying events, the lay of the land, governing agents, case, premise, condition, surroundings, attendant conditions, surrounding facts, motives, promptings, the times, life, course of events, ups and downs, change, fluctuation, vicissitudes, order of the day, bearings, occasion, environment, a tide in the affairs of men, basis, grounds, terms imposed, milieu, setting, scene, background.
2. Pecuniary standing, degree of wealth, financial status, position, terms, rank, degree, way of life, property, monetary condition, financial responsibility, means, footing, standing, assets, vicissitudes of fortune, income, what one is worth, substance, capital, class, notch *(coll.)*, place on the ladder, precedence, sphere, stock in trade, command, resources, estate, prestige, lot, material welfare.

CIRCUMSTANTIAL, *adj.* 1. Indirect, presumptive, founded on circumstances, contingent, limitative, conditional, given, inferential, provisional, subject to, hearsay, tentative, evidential, constructive, deduced, verisimilar, likely, debatable, disputable, controvertible, conjectural, probable, indecisive, inconclusive, presumable, dependent, interpretive.
2. Nonessential, relating to, adventitious, from without, not inherent, acquired, extrinsic, casual, incidental, adscititious, additional, accessory, providential, extraneous, supervenient, ascititious, accidental, fortuitous, contingent, modal, exterior, subsidiary.
3. Particular, detailed, express, exact, minute, clear, containing particulars, particularized, full, declarative, comprehensive, expository, definite, explanatory, unreserved, precise, explicit.

CIRCUMVENT, *v.* 1. Abuse, inveigle, gull, trick, overreach, cheat, befool, fraud, beguile, dupe, hoax, swindle, deceive, defraud, victimize, outwit, practice upon, delude, gammon, humbug, impose upon, hoodwink, do, cozen, diddle, gyp, play upon, foist upon, fleece, lure, rook, mulct, entrap, bamboozle, ensnare, entice, bilk, mislead, cajole, jockey, play false, cog, wheedle, take *(coll.)*, gouge *(coll.)*, baffle, chouse *(coll.)*, flam, betray, palm upon, bunko, pluck *(sl.)*.
2. Disappoint, cheat, foil, frustrate, thwart, defeat, cross, checkmate, baffle, check, rob of, bilk.
3. Avoid, elude, evade, circumnavigate, circle, escape, shun, keep away from, fight shy of, circumambulate, make a detour, go around, circuit.

CIRCUS, *n.* 1. Hippodrome, circular area, arena, stadium, bowl, race course, oval area for special performances, open space surrounded by seats for spectators, big top, coliseum, field, scene of action, turf, gymnasium, bear garden, bull ring, palaestra, amphitheater, campus *(Rom. Antiq.)*, cirque *(Geol.)*, natural amphitheater, enclosed area.

2. Elaborate spectacle, The Big Top, carnival, animal performance, side show, rodeo, feats of skill and daring done for entertainment, exhibitions by trained performers.

CISTERN, *n.* Reservoir, well, tank, natural basin to catch water, wide well to catch rain water, water barrel, receptacle for rain water, rain barrel.

CITADEL, *n.* Castle, bulwark, fortress, fort, fortification, tower, stronghold, chateau, stockade, bastion, safehold, rampart, battlement, buttress, donjon, redoubt, palisade, fasthold, keep, fastness, acropolis, hold.

CITATION, *n.* 1. Summons, official call or notice, bidding, charge, writ of summons, subpoena, habeas corpus, arraignment, venire facias *(Law)*, writ of habeas corpus, implication, command to appear.

2. Enumeration, quotation, allusion, reference, mention, instance, extract, evidence, proof, excerpt, witness, adduction, substantiation, saying, illustration, authority, bringing forward, quoting.

3. Formal eulogy, honor conferred, official recognition, public recognition, award, mark of honor.

CITE, *v.* 1. Summon, enjoin, send for, subpoena, serve with a writ, bid appear, involve, implicate, arraign, call for, direct to appear, attach *(Law)*, distrain *(Law)*, invite forcibly, charge to appear.

2. Quote, adduce, excerpt, allude to, instance, refer to, give as example, indicate, repeat, extract, exemplify, illustrate by.

3. Enumerate, present, call to witness, plead, exemplify, produce as witness, evidence with, attest, manifest, put a case, advance, appeal to, prove, document, call, give as example, denote, indicate, display, assemble, specify, mention, name, allege, bring forward, assign, make clear, make evident, refer to, say.

CITIZEN, *n.* Inhabitant, dweller, civilian, burgher, taxpayer, commoner, townsman, resident, burgess, denizen, freeman, cit *(derog.)*, oppidan, villager, householder, voter, the common man, the man on the street, member of the body politic, John Q. Public.

CITY, *n.* Incorporated town, metropolitan area, urban place, metropolis, municipality, township, burg *(coll.)*, large town.

CIVIC, *adj.* Civil, political, metropolitan, urban, social, public, burghal, communal, municipal, oppidan, community, neighborhood, town.

CIVIL, *adj.* 1. Secular, profane, lay, temporal, worldly, mundane, everyday, laical, unspiritual, nonecclesiastical, outside church jurisdiction.

2. Municipal, civic, public, lawful, political, social, communal, metropolitan, oppidan, urban, burghal, non-military.

3. Intestine, domestic, of the estate *or* nation, internal.

4. Courteous, urbane, suave, affable, gracious, well-behaved, well-mannered, cultivated, cordial, amiable, diplomatic, gentle, mild, fair-spoken, gentlemanly, genteel, mannerly, well-bred, bland, complaisant, obliging, neighborly, conciliatory, politic, respectful, decorous, gallant, refined, polished, deferential, gentlemanlike, chivalrous, polite, genial, civilized.

CIVILIAN, *n.* Non-military person, citizen, private citizen, private person, lay person.

CIVILITY, *n.* Courtesy, civil conduct, manners, good behavior, urbanity, good breeding, suavity, amiability, amity, politeness, courteousness, affability, elegance of manners, social grace, considerateness, cultivation, mildness, moderation, observance of the proprieties, *bienséance (Fr.)*, good will, regard for others, decency, refinement, deference, respect, gentility, comity, cordiality, pleasantness, polish, civilization, tact, presence, good temper, gentle breeding, chivalry, kindliness, finesse, savoir-faire *(Fr.)*, agreeableness, amenity, *prévenance (Fr.)*, gallantry, mansuetude, good manners, graciousness, complaisance, attentiveness to others' needs, neighborliness, friendliness.

CIVILIZATION, *n.* Race *or* national culture, degree of cultivation, state of refinement, level of education, progress, advancement, civility, enlightenment, illumination, material well-being, advancement of knowledge, elevation, social well-being, acculturation *(Anthrop.)*, edification, Kultur *(Ger.)*.

CIVILIZE, *v.* Refine, educate, reclaim from barbarism, elevate, instruct, uplift, help forward, advance, better materially, edify, inform of civilized ways, acquaint with culture, tame, make gentle, rub off the corners *(coll.)*, polish, develop, foster, promote, render civil, humanize, improve, cultivate, enlighten, indoctrinate, acculturize *(Anthrop.)*.

CLABBER, *n.* Sour milk, bonnyclabber, curdled milk, curd(s), coagulated milk, flummery, pap, lopper *(dial.)*, junket, casein, Devonshire cream, clotted cream.

CLACK, *n.* 1. Click, clink, rattle, clatter, clitterclatter, racket, jingle, chink, clutter, chattering, chuck, clamor, rattling, noise, beat, tick, cluck, rattley-bang, crackle, clank.

2. Prate, babble, cackle, gabble, idle talk, gossip, blather, inanity, gibberish, racket, clamor, prattle, babbling, palaver, small talk, empty chatter, bosh *(coll.)*, nonsensical talk, foolish speech, voluble nonsense, unmeaning words, tommyrot, balderdash, senseless jargon, hocus-pocus, humbug, rubbish, claptrap, fiddle-faddle *(coll.)*, gammon *(coll.)*, poppycock *(coll.)*, stuff and nonsense, truck, hogwash *(coll.)*, rot *(slang)*, drivel, patter, gab, hot air *(slang)*, gabbling, jabbering, twaddle, blatherskite, fudge, flummery, buncombe *(coll.)*, bunkum *(coll.)*, gobbledygook *(slang)*.

3. Noisemaker, clapper, clacker, rattle, whizzer, razzle-dazzle, bullroarer, snapper, ticktack, cracker bonbon, cracker, rattlebox.

CLACK, *v.* 1. Click, clatter, clap, chink, snap, rattle, clink, chuck, crackle, smack, clutter, rap, crepitate, chatter, cluck, clank, jingle, jangle, clitterclatter.

2. Prate, chatter, clatter, gossip, tattle, blab, gabble, prattle, clamor, rant, gibber, patter, palaver, utter drivel, blather, talk nonsense, talk idly, pour forth, talk glibly, twaddle, rattle, let the tongue run, jabber, babble.

CLAIM, *n.* 1. Demand, requisition, exaction, plea, requirement, profession, application, entreaty, command, suit, petition, ultimatum, call, request, postulation, reclamation, declaration *(Law)*.

2. Right, title, privilege, power, desert, debt, interest, pretension, ownership, prerogative, due, estate, holding, access, demand, leasehold, need,

license, share, tenure, postulate, assumption, grant, droit (*Law*).

3. Grant, lease, expectancy, tract, legacy, heritage, stake, share, birthright, droit (*Law*), bill (*Law*), freehold, allodium.

CLAIM, *v.* Require, demand, call for, seek as due, apply for, pray, sue, petition, vindicate a right, be entitled to, seek to obtain, appropriate, usurp, exact, take, hold, assert as one's right, lay claim to, challenge, charge, command, insist on, assume, expropriate, qualify for, deserve, be worthy of, postulate, compel, arrogate, have title to, maintain to be one's property, appeal for, request, ask, stand on one's rights.

CLAIMANT, *n.* Owner, applicant, complainant, supplicant, petitioner, suitor, claimer, asserter, asker, plaintiff, pleader, suppliant, prosecutor, candidate, accuser, pretender, inheritor, appellant, heir, postulant.

CLAIRVOYANCE, *n.* 1. Sight beyond physical limits, clear sight, second sight, intuition, seeing in a mesmeric state, mysterious knowledge, clairsentience, crystal vision, sixth sense, insight, subconscious perception, psychometry, sensitive knowledge, clairaudience, inexplicable knowledge, trance-vision.

2. Penetration, insight, divination, perceptivity, intuition, sagacity, immediate cognition, innate knowledge, ready association, subtle sense, depth of understanding, acumen, sapience, sharpness, clearsightedness, mental acuity, discrimination, keen mental vision, perspicacity, discernment, direct perception, quick apprehension, clarity of mind, percipience, apperception.

CLAIRVOYANT, *adj.* 1. Able to see beyond the physical, seeing in trance, clairaudient, psychic, psychometric, clairsentient, second-sighted, seeing by mesmeric influence.

2. Penetrating, divining, perceptive, intuitive, keen, sagacious, discerning, perspicacious, astute, apperceptive, sharp, sapient, discriminating, quick of apprehension, mentally acute, of keen mental vision, clearsighted, percipient, subtle, piercing, apperceptient.

CLAMBER, *v.* Climb with difficulty, tumble over, crawl upwards, scramble up, shin up (*coll.*), scale in disorder, swarm up, scrabble up.

CLAMMY, *adj.* Damp, slimy, sweaty, dough-like, viscous, dauby, ropy, mucid, gelatinous, smeary, wet, adhesive, pasty, fishy, vaporous, glutinous, misty, rainy, gummy, musty, viscid, sticky.

CLAMOR, *n.* Tumult, disturbance, uproar, broil, din, hubbub, hue and cry, agitation, outcry, bray, noise, vociferation, pandemonium, brawl, fracas, commotion, rumpus, Babel, catcalls, importunity, war cry, caterwauling, hissing, shouting, bellow, blast, loud protest, jangle, wild chorus, hell let loose, embroilment, hullabaloo, contention, rout, babble, insistence, racket, Bedlam, Dutch concert (*coll.*), cat's concert (*coll.*), clangor, disruption, storm, complaining.

CLAMOR, *v.* Vociferate, cry out, make uproar, yell, shout, protest loudly, agitate, babble, storm, bawl, chorus wildly, bellow, make the welkin ring, rend the air, make outcries, insist, demand continually, cry importunately, entreat eagerly, fuss, whoop, wrangle, din, be outspoken, raise voice.

CLAMOROUS, *adj.* Vociferous, boisterous, noisy, vehement, blustering, turbulent, protesting, loud, ululant, ear-splitting, howling, bawling, bellowing, hysterical, obstreperous, blatant, deafening, ear-rending, loudmouthed, clattering, clamant, crying, clangorous, tonant, loud-voiced, ear-piercing, stentorian, shrewish, braying, urgent, uproarious, importunate, rampant, insistent, exigent, pressing, rackety, wailing.

CLAMP, *v.* Clutch, hook, fasten, clinch, bracket, clip, press, clasp, vise, gripe, clench, hug, fasten upon, embrace, clap hands on, have an iron grip on, make fast, secure, bind, screw fast, grapple, seize, hold, bolt, wedge, brace, grip.

CLAN, *n.* 1. Race, family, kindred, people, house, nation, tribe, strain, line, lineage, stirps, phylum (*Biol.*), extraction, root, stem, blood relations, ethnic group, sept, gens (*Rom. Hist.*), stock, breed, pedigree.

2. Clique, set, brotherhood, fraternity, class, side, coterie, gang, sodality, association, society, guild, party, faction, knot, ring, cabal, lodge, sect, order, club, junto, circle, company, fellowship, crowd (*coll.*), alliance, federation, union, league, affiliation, outfit (*coll.*), camarilla.

CLANDESTINE, *adj.* Hidden, secret, underhand, concealed for an evil purpose, private, stealthy, surreptitious, furtive, crafty, undercover, elusive, obreptitious, cloaked, dissembled, unrevealed, unseen, skulking, feline, cunning, confidential, underground, disguised, collusive, taciturn, dark, reserved, shrouded, obscure, undisclosed, veiled, screened, masked, with secret design, covert, sly, sneaking, hugger-mugger, ensconced, conspiring, underhanded, privy, arcane, evasive, secretive, secluded, close, feigned.

CLANG, *n.* 1. Clangor, clank, peal, blare, timbre, metallic ringing, crash (*of cymbals*), clash, bong, clashing, reverberation, knell, chime, tolling, din, ringing percussion, jangle, raucity, loud ringing sound, jarring sound, ding-dong, gong, vibration, blast, harsh resonance, sonorousness.

2. Resonant cry (*of birds*), honk (*of geese*), cronk, screech, shrill, strident call (*of birds*).

3. (*Music*) Timbre, Klang (*Ger.*), resonance, tonality, clang color, clang tint, tone color, Klangfarbe (*Ger.*).

CLANG, *v.* Clank, jangle, blare, resound, gong, honk, bray, clash, reverberate, bugle, ring loudly, peal, toll, knell, jar, wind (*a horn*), blast, clangor, trumpet, din, cronk, ding-dong, bong, echo, blow sharply (*a horn*).

CLANGOR, *n.* Clang, racket, blare, noise, clank, ringing, discord, clamor, cacophony, dissonance, stridor, diaphony, harshness, jangle, crashing, jarring, harsh resonance, wild pealing, clash, din, raucity, heavy vibration, gong, percussion, blast, reverberation.

CLANK, *n.* Dull clang, clink, jingle, tinkle, jangle, chink, metallic rattle, tink, ting.

CLANK, *v.* Clang dully, clink, rattle metallically, jingle, chink, jangle, tink, ting.

CLANNISH, *adj.* 1. Akin, close, family, tribal, cognate, associative, brotherly, intimate, related, confederate, racial, of a feather (*prov.*), loyal, unified, fraternal, familial, lineal, root, septal.

2. Narrow, sectarian, unmixing, bigoted, aloof, distant, exclusive, cold, lofty, unreceptive, sortal, superior, snobbish, partisan, denominative, thick (*coll.*), leagued, confined, contemptuous, allied, provincial, restricted, intolerant, illiberal, insular, parochial, supercilious, haughty, holding one at arm's length, family, racial, tribal, selfish, class-conscious.

CLAP, *n.* 1. Blow, slap, rap, smack, slam, bang, poke, knock, tap, fillip, bump, thrust, bat, thump, cuff, clip *(coll.),* sharp impact, hit, whack.

2. Explosion, peal, bang, clack, sharp noise, report, handclap, applause, clapping, clatter, percussion, discharge, concussion, sharp impact, detonation, shot, snap, fulmination, crack, slam, burst.

CLAP, *v.* 1. Pat vigorously, slap, rap, whack, jab, bump, poke, bat, flap *(wings),* clatter, fulminate, detonate, percuss, fillip, clip *(coll.),* thump, cuff, punch, hit, smack, discharge, snap, swat, buffet, smite, thwack, strike together, applaud, come together sharply, bang, slam.

2. Fling, toss, place effectually, set suddenly, force, slam, set forcibly, cast, push, shoot, rush, hurl, pitch, dash, impose, sling, thrust, propel unceremoniously.

3. *(With* up) Imprison, confine, shackle, shut in, jail, lock up, intern, incarcerate, impound, immure, restrain, fetter, handcuff, manacle, shut up, lay under hatches, pen in, cage, box up, coop up, throw in chains, throw in prison, captivate, enthrall, put in irons, clap under hatches.

4. *(With* on) Add hastily, slap on, affix, put on hurriedly, apply vigorously, place emphatically.

CLAPPER, *n.* 1. Tongue of a bell, rattle, clacker, noisemaker, clap, clack, tongue *(coll.),* stick *or* bone used by Negro minstrel.

2. Claquer, paid applauder, claqueur *(Fr.),* hired rooter *(slang).*

CLAP-TRAP, *adj.* Spectacular, sham, histrionic, ostentatious, theatrical, showy but cheap, seeking applause, boastful, inflated, calculated for effect, glittering, burlesque, nonsensical, fanfaron, cant, bombastic, deceptive, devised, posed, swaggering, untruthful, fabricated, quack, tawdry, pretending, gaudy, affected, specious, insincere, pretentious, blustering, fictitious, pretexed, artificial, hollow, twaddling, factitious, casuistic, misleading, empty, foolish, gabbling, flattering, prating, moonshine, babbling, driveling, sophistic, charlatan, feigned, fraudulent, Jesuistic, captious, prattling, fustian, hypocritical, rodomontade, parading, veneered, supposititious, sensational, *ad captandum (Lat.),* mock, glossed, trumped-up.

CLAPTRAP, *n.* Trick for effect, trumpery, sham, jargon, fustian, bosh, mockery, tour de force, stage trick, ostentation, fabrication, rodomontade, deception, flattery, sensationalism, cant, bombast, bluster, swaggering, peacockery, pose, attitude, play for the grandstand, casuistry, buncombe, nonsense, stage effect, *étalage (Fr.),* device to gain applause, untruth, specious argument, gaudiness, feigned appearance, fraud, sophism, empty words, elench, frippery, palaver, hoax, prate, imposture, tawdry behavior, pseudosyllogism, blather, drivel, prattle, gibberish, babble, false show, pretention, display, parade, veneer, airs, cliché, front *(coll.),* inflation, tear jerking, charlatanry, gabble, glitter, hypocrisy, hogwash, moonshine, quackery, gloss, posture, trumped-up story, pretentious language, insincere sentiment, affectation, sophistry, pious phraseology, pretense, Jesuitism, fanfaronade, quibble, sophism.

CLARIFICATION, *n.* 1. Purification, filtration, purgation, clearing, drainage, expurgation, lavage, elutriation, defecation, refinement, edulcoration, ventilation, irrigation, separation, despumation, percolation, lavation, elution *(Chem.),* epuration.

2. Interpretation, elucidation, simplification, exposition, exegesis, light, commentary, solution, resolution, explication, enucleation, illumination, definition, explanation.

CLARIFY, *v.* 1. Purify, make clear, purge, filter, expurgate, separate, winnow, sift, settle, decant, rack, elute, edulcorate, ventilate, drain, chasten, irrigate, skim, percolate, defecate, refine, strain, achromatize, clear, elutriate, despumate, epurate, sieve, screen.

2. Elucidate, make clear, explain, interpret, lay open, render intelligible, expose, bring to light, define, hold up the mirror to, bare, make explicit, resolve, solve, comment upon, make plain, make manifest, disentangle, exhibit, show, demonstrate, expound, enucleate, exposit, manifest, illuminate, make visible, unfold, decipher, unmask, unveil, uncover, simplify, clear up, demonstrate, shed light on.

CLARION, *adj.* Deafening, clear, loud as a trumpet-call, distinct, compelling, imperative, shrill, constraining, trumpet-voiced, sonorous, blatant, emphatic, swelling, plain, rallying, resounding, tonant, resonant, sweetmouthed (of hounds), high-pitched, acute, high-toned, brazen, ringing, declamatory, golden-throated, silver-toned, sharp, piercing, full, clangorous, orotund, blaring, high-sounding, reverberant, commanding.

CLARITY, *n.* 1. Brightness, luster, transparency, purity, distinctness, splendor, clearness, brilliance, translucence, transpicuity, glassiness, limpidity, crystallinity, vitreosity, resplendence, effulgence, cleanness, spotlessness, radiance, immaculateness, lucidity, luminosity, homogeneity, hyalescence, pellucidity, dazzle, whiteness, refulgence, lucence.

2. Purity of line, simplicity, classic simplicity, cleanness of design, absence of ornament, lack of embellishment, lucidity, plainness, chasteness, Atticism, unadornment, severity, restraint.

3. Intelligibility, penetrability, unmistakability, explicability, clearness, distinctness, perceptibility, obviousness, evidence, comprehensibility, lucidity, cognizability, limpidity, legibility, plain speech, simplicity, openness, prominence, manifestness, directness, perspicuity, accuracy, decipherability, precision, transpicuity, transparency, palpability, overtness, evincement, salience, conspicuousness, explicitness, exactness, luminosity.

CLASH, *n.* 1. Collision, encounter, impact, fight, contest, affair, scrimmage, skirmish, fracas, tussle, smash *(coll.),* jar, smashup, impingement, crash, concussion, shock, bump, cannon, blow, meeting, brush, joust, scuffle, engagement, appulse, ruction, percussion, conflict, affray, combat, tilt, dogfight, battle, debate, free-for-all *(coll.),* passage of *or* at arms, argument, fisticuffs, mêlée *(Fr.),* struggle, run-in *(slang),* scrap *(slang),* fray, row, bout, set-to *(coll.),* jolt, imbroglio, striking together.

2. Clang, clangor, crash, rattle, din, diaphony, percussion, clank, cacophony, discord, clashing, stridor, jangle, jumble of sound, tumult, uproar, clutter, dissonance, confused noise, concussion, racket, clatter.

3. Opposition, interference, jarring, resistance, disagreement, conflict, quarrel, antagonism, feud, discord, friction, contravention, cross fire, strife, oppugnancy, disceptation, wrangling, logomachy, impugnation, altercation, litigation, open rupture, passage of words, working at cross-purposes, tiff, dispute, dissent, contention, odds, enmity, faction, squabble, hostility, contradiction, clashing, war of words, jar, contrariety, dissidence, dissension, controversy, antipathy.

CLASH, *v.* 1. Collide, come into collision, strike,

hit, knock, contend, encounter, joust, scuffle, tilt, fight, tussle, engage in battle, jostle, exchange blows, cannon, percuss, impinge, conflict, combat, crap (slang), battle, whack, reluct, close with, grapple with, cross swords, join issue, fall foul of, meet with a shock, crash together, meet, jar, strike against each other, hurtle, brush, bump, smash (coll.).

2. Clank, crash, clatter, jangle, hurtle, percuss, din, make a racket, crack, clang, rattle, clangor.

3. Disagree, interfere, be mutually opposed, rival, contradict, jar, conflict, contravene, dissent, oppugn, controvert, work at cross-purposes, tiff, litigate, impugn, wrangle, lock horns, disceptate, argue, strive, dispute, collide, differ violently, be at variance, altercate, pick a bone with, have words with, take issue, broil, pull different ways, fall foul of, squabble, resist, feud, oppose, act in contrary direction, contend, quarrel, discord.

CLASHING, n. 1. Clang, clangor, crash, clash, clank, din, tumult, cacophony, jumble of sound, confusion of noise, concussion, uproar, discord, rattling, stridor, clutter, jangling, clatter, racket, diaphony, dissonance.

2. Opposition, interference, jarring, dissension, disagreement, contradiction, hostility, misalliance, discord, disunity, discongruity, disharmony, clash, incongruity, dissonance, enmity, irreconciliation, bitterness, contrast, antagonism, antipathy, strife, contrariety, collision, conflict, violent difference, unfriendliness, ill will, animosity, vindictiveness, rancor, alienation, estrangement, hatred, feuding, antithesis, repugnance, quarreling, friction, open rupture, resistance, oppugnancy, disceptation, wrangling, altercation, litigation, impugnation, squabbling, dissidence, faction, controversy, dissent.

CLASP, n. 1. Hook, catch, snap, hasp, grip, bolt, fastener, clamp, holdfast, buckle, lock, bar, brace, coupler, bond, latch, brooch, fastening, copula, link, clinch.

2. Embrace, hold, squeeze, accolade, cincture, hug, clinging, cleaving, zone, circuit, girth, close hold, cordon, encircling, twining, adherence, grappling, baldric, coherence.

3. Grasp, grip, holdfast, clutch, handshake, gripe, iron grip.

CLASP, v. 1. Fasten with a clasp, unite, shut, pin, bind, catch, clamp, clinch, clip, buckle, bracket, bolt, hook, lock, link, adhere, fetter, hold tightly, cohere, latch, snap, hasp, bar, couple, secure.

2. Embrace, fold, squeeze, press, encircle, hug, enclose, entwine, cleave to, hold close, enfold, cling to, cherish, grasp, take to one's arms, fold to the heart, circuit, encincture, hold tightly, fold in one's arms, enwrap, grapple with.

3. Grasp, clutch, put the fingers around, fasten upon, shake (hands), gripe, hold, wrest, seize, take hold of, lay hold of, grapple, grip.

CLASS, n. 1. Category, division, group, set, kind, classification, head, order, section, department, province, domain, heat, collection, character, sort, source, origin, variety, feather, color, grain, suit, make, cast, mold, sect, nature, distinction, breed, denomination, designation, stamp, brand, kidney, type, stripe, the like (coll.), sphere, status, range, grade, selection, species, brood, genus, property, genre, constitution, crasis, temper, aspect, spirit, disposition, vein, tone, streak, persuasion, name, humor, mood, frame, habit, temperament, form, quality, school, subdivision, lot (coll.).

2. Scientific division, kind, designation, name,

branch, distinction, description, sort, group, type, breed.

3. Social rank, title, hierarchy, clan, standing, caste, station, breed, place, degree, sept, position, state, status, stock, lineage, connection, condition, set, coterie, circle, sphere, precedence, high rank, genealogy, stirps, power, pedigree, clique, strain, company, society, derivation, descent, ancestry, extraction, origin, birth, club, nobility, quality, influence, source, prestige, gens (Rom. Antiq.), estate, tribe, family.

4. Set of pupils, grade, seminar, section, lesson, period, assembly, quiz section, meeting for study, course, recitation, form, room, division, session, course of study, group, graduating group.

CLASS, v. Arrange, range, classify, dispose, type, distribute, group, divide, place, put in order, file, assort, rate, label, tag, brand, form into classes, rank, size, grade, bracket, graduate, name, allot, match up, distinguish, divide, segregate, tabulate, list, catalogue, index, codify, ticket, digest, docket, allocate, organize, alphabetize, pigeonhole, place in a category, number.

CLASSIC, CLASSICAL, adj. 1. Of the first class, standard, master, authoritative, first-rate, correct, canonical, absolute, model, of established form, principled, ideal, epic, prototypal, paradigmatic, consummate, humanistic, archetypal, by Greek or Roman rules, neoclassic, masterly, Hellenistic, Augustan, Attic, excellent, aesthetically pure, of proven merit, Ciceronian, prescriptive, appealing to cultivated taste, ancient, instructive, preceptive, non-romantic, heroic, exemplary, enduring, ageless.

2. Elegant, refined, chaste, lucid, simple, clear, formal, polished, pure, Attic, Hellenistic, sober, in good taste, clear-cut, finished, reposeful, of exact proportions, principled, eloquent, patterned, stately, Augustan, symmetrical, dignified, severe, concinnate, balanced, harmonious, Ciceronian, grand, majestic, eurhythmic, inornate, restrained, cultivated, rational, tasteful, artistic, regular.

CLASSIC, n. First-quality work, standard work, masterpiece, enduring work of art, transcendent work, work of ageless power, exemplar, type, original, archetype, paradigm, paragon, criterion, prototype, ideal form, standard, precept, pattern, Greek or Latin work, Greek or Latin author, chef d'oeuvre, model art work, highest achievement, art work of proven merit, author or artist of a classic.

CLASSICISM, n. Reverence for the ancients, pure taste, classicalism, observance of classic principles, formal style, classical taste, proportion, elegance, conventional formality, restraint, lucidity, dignity, nobility, the grand style, propriety, stateliness, refinement, polish, finish, clarity, simplicity, symmetry, balance, concinnity, majesty, rhythm, grandeur, rationalism, Atticism, Ciceronianism, excellence, sobriety, severity, sublimity, high art, established forms, well-turned periods, Hellenism, authority of the ancients, eurhythmy, conformity to classical style, neoclassicism, eloquence, purity.

CLASSIFICATION, n. 1. Arrangement, analysis, grouping, codification, division, systematization, allocation, distribution, methodizing, assignment, reducing to order, categorizing, apportionment, organization, digestion, gradation, regulation by a system, designation, consignment, tabulation, collocation, taxonomy, orderly arrangement, categorization, biotaxy (Biol.), co-ordination, graduation, assortment, disposal, disposition.

2. Arrangement, group, order, system, index, category, rank, disposition, code, analysis, head, method, department, section, family, assortment, species, grade, kind, sort, type, domain, province, denomination, sect, array, designation, directory, status, dictionary, encyclopedia, concordance, lot, grouping, division, distribution, sphere, range, genus, genre *(Fr.)*.

CLASSIFY, *v*. Class, range, distribute, categorize, form into classes, organize, pigeonhole, place in a category, catalogue, segregate, divide, docket, allocate, arrange, reduce to order, label, number, dispose, rank, size, grade, rate, assort, methodize, file, systematize, distinguish, list, tabulate, brand, alphabetize, codify, collocate, ticket, coordinate, digest, name, allot, group, tag, type, put in order, analyze, index.

CLATTER, *n*. Rattling, clattering, racket, noise, commotion, din, raucity, jangle, chatter, clamor, uproar, clank, crash, bang, confused noise, hell broke loose, clutter, brabble, clack, hullabaloo, tumult, crashing, disturbance, sharp noise, sharp echo, pandemonium, concussion, hollow sound, hollow resonance, charivari, crepitation, cracking, crackling, bedlam.

CLATTER, *v*. 1. Rattle, clash, crackle, crepitate, crack, clangor, hurtle, clutter, snap, smack, echo sharply, din, bang, crash, resound, clump along, tramp noisily, be heavy-heeled, racket, jangle, clang, clank, clack.

2. Prate, prattle, clack, gabble, chatter, jabber, talk loudly, tattle, talk idly, gossip, run on, wag the tongue, babble, rattle away.

CLAUSE, *n*. 1. Subordinate unit of a sentence, period, member of a grammatical whole, part of a sentence, simple sentence, passage, paragraph, section, sentential term.

2. Article, provision, condition, stipulation, bond, contract, affix, additament, addendum, addition, adjunct, paragraph, codical, passage, exception, particle, term, specification, appendage, proviso, exemption, usual covenant, reservation, qualification, rider, covenant, proposition.

CLAVIER, *n*. Keyboard, clavichord, manichord, piano, manual, claviature, clavicymbal, virginal, seraphine, spinet, melodeon, organ, choralcelo, pianoforte, clavicembalo, cembalo, vocalion, reed organ, monochord, dummy keyboard, pipe organ, clavial, practice piano, clavicytherium, lyrichord, pair of virginals, piano-violin, symphonion, melodica, Klavier *(Ger.)*, harpsichord, melopiano, harmonium, harmonichord, piano quatuor.

CLAW, *n*. Talon, hook, spur, fang, pincers, paw, griff, nail, clapperclaw, retractile, nipper, pounce, fingernail, tentacle, grapnel, anchor, cant hook, crook, fluke, barb, grappling iron *or* hook, forked end, ungula, chela, unguis, tack-claw, nail-claw, kedge *(Naut.)*, clutching hand.

CLAW, *v*. Tear, scratch, clutch, gouge, prick, dig, spur, goad, scrape, seize, grapple, mangle, rend, snag, lacerate, lancinate, pounce, snatch, laniate, grope, jab, slash, gash, clinch, grip, hook, stab, pierce, fasten upon, puncture, gripe, nip, maul, scrape, clench, grasp, cut.

CLAY, *n*. 1. Argillaceous earth, argil, marl, slip, ground, pottery, kaolin, cloam, bole, potter's clay, pug, mire, mud, soil, sod, terra cotta, fire clay, clayware, loam, green pottery, green brick, glebe *(Poetic)*, china clay, pugged clay, porcelain clay, raw brick, earth, cledge, adobe.

2. Flesh of man, mortal part, mortal body, earthly substance, human flesh, earth, ashes, dust, earthly part, perishable substance, mortal coil.

CLAYEY, *adj*. Earthy, argillous, waxy, cold and damp, fictile, dense, gummy, luteous, responsive, loamy, argilliferous *(Petrog.)*, cledgy, moldable, plastic, impressible, susceptible, tractable, moist, muggy, dank, humid, tenacious, figuline, pliant, pasty, manageable, passive, malleable, formable, impressionable, argillaceous *(Petrog.)*, heavy.

CLEAN, *adj*. 1. Fresh, spruce, newly cleaned, snowy, unstained, tidy, cleaned, orderly, trim, sweet, trig, well-groomed, clean-cut, well-kept, neat, spotless, unsoiled, unspotted, immaculate, bright, speckless, washed, white, dapper, shining, unblemished.

2. Free of impurities, faultless, flawless, clear, expurgate, unadulterated, undefiled, uninfected, whole, complete, perfect, untainted, unpolluted, uncontaminated, purified, unmixed, clarified.

3. Well-made, well-formed, delicate, shapely, well-balanced, graceful, fair, becoming, even, symmetrical, well-molded, well-set, trim, neat, clean-cut.

4. Virtuous, stainless, untainted, unblemished, healthy, healthy-minded, wholesome, immaculate, chaste, decent, decorous, innocent, pure, modest, righteous, moral, clean-minded, unsoiled, snowy, unsullied, exemplary, nice, saintly, meritorious, angelic, upright, reputable, honorable, creditable, prudish, maidenly, vestal.

5. Clever, expert, proficient, adroit, skillful, deft, handy, adept, dexterous, quick, masterful.

6. Polished, swept, dusted, rubbed up, flushed, expunged, vacuumed, neatified, wiped, leached, arranged, mopped, sponged, raked, put in order, combed, whisked, brushed, ordered, scrubbed, carded, scraped, rasped, bathed, scoured, washed.

CLEAN, *adv*. Cleanly, to the utmost, throughout, fore and aft, inside and out, from cover to cover, entirely, out and out, unqualifiedly, absolutely, fully, thoroughly, to the full, to the limit, wholly, altogether, quite, all over, totally, from beginning to end, through and through, perfectly, utterly, completely.

CLEAN, *v*. 1. Cleanse, purify, purge, wash, lave, bathe, launder, deterge, epurate, decrassify, swab, scour, rinse, depurate, defecate, elutriate, hatchel, expurgate, edulcorate, absterge, refine, expunge, polish, flush, lixiviate, sponge, sweep, wipe, soap, put in order, hackle, dust, mop, shampoo, rub up, card, sweep out, leach, whisk, comb, rake, heckle, flush, scrape, rasp, blot, erase, vacuum *(coll.)*, neatify, neaten, tidy, clarify.

2. *(Often with* OUT*)* Defecate, void, sweep out, empty, exhaust, evacuate, drain, deplete, purge, clear.

3. Sanitize, ascepticize, asceptify, antisepticize, Tyndallize, cauterize, pasteurize, sanitate, cleanse, sterilize, disinfect, Listerize, deodorize, fumigate, ventilate, whitewash.

CLEANLY, *adj*. 1. Washing, edulcorating, balneal, decrassifying, clarifying, lavational, expurgative, abluting, lavatory, cleansing, cleaning, purgative, depurative, abstergent, purifying, cathartic, detergent.

2. Fresh, spruce, neat, tidy, dapper, speckless, white, bright, immaculate, sweet, unblemished, spotless, unsoiled, well-kept, clean-cut, orderly, well-groomed, trig, cleaned, snowy.

CLEANSE, *v*. 1. Clean, purify, wash, lave, bathe, launder, deterge, epurate, decrassify, clarify, scour, swab, rinse, depurate, defecate, elutriate, expurgate, edulcorate, absterge, refine, expunge, polish, flush, sponge, sweep, wipe, soap, hackle, dust, mop, shampoo, rub up, hatchel, sweep out, leach, whisk, comb, rake, lixiviate, scrape, rasp, blot, erase, whiten, bleach, vacuum (coll.), tidy, neatify, neaten.

2. Sanitize, asepticize, aseptify, antisepticize, cauterize, pasteurize, sanitate, sterilize, disinfect, Tyndallize, Listerize, deodorize, whitewash, fumigate, ventilate.

CLEANSER, n. Solvent, detergent, disinfectant, purgative, antiseptic, deodorant, cathartic, soap, purifier, fumigant, cleaning powder, cleaner, soap flakes, abstergent, soap powder, lather, abrasive, polish, suds, cleaning agent.

CLEAR, adj. 1. Radiant, beaming, beamy, vivid, gleaming, shining, lambent, glowing, illuminated, enlightened, illumined, flashing, glistening, light, sparkling, flaming, brilliant, luminous, lustrous, effulgent, refulgent, bright, resplendent, twinkling, scintillating, coruscating, blazing, dazzling, nitid, irradiant, luminiferous, luciferous, sheeny, glossy, burnished, sunny, orient, fulgid, incandescent, transparent, lucid, limpid, crystalline, translucent.

2. Faultless, flawless, free of impurities, whole, homogeneous, expurgate, unadulterated, perfect, undefiled, clean, complete, untainted, purified, uncontaminated, unpolluted, uninfected, unmixed, clarified.

3. Definite, true, genuine, authoritative, sure, indubitable, infallible, unambiguous, unequivocal, certain, unmistakable, unquestionable, unqualified, undeniable, incontrovertible, incontestable, sound, unerring, irrefragable, irrefutable, unquestioned, undisputed, reliable, inescapable, unconfuted, past dispute, evident, positive, plain, conclusive, cogent.

4. Unbridled, unrestrained, unobstructed, free, unencumbered, open, unhampered, unhindered, untrammeled, unfettered, unembarrassed, unimpeded, unburdened, unreined, unmuzzled, uncurbed, unprevented, unconstrained, unchained, unbound, unchecked, unshackled.

5. Fine, bright, warm, mild, estival, summery, sunshiny, nice, pleasant, cloudless, genial, serene, calm, undimmed, unobscured, shining, unclouded, fair, halcyon.

6. Free, gratis, for nothing, immune, with no strings attached, excepted, unaccountable, rent free, unsubject, unliable, net, untaxed, costless, expenseless, complimentary, gratuitous, untaxable.

7. Empty, void, dry, drained, forsaken, blank, abandoned, vacuous, barren, desolate, deserted, vacant.

8. Self-evident, comprehensible, graphic, plain, straightforward, express, understandable, decided, well-marked, apparent, unquestionable, manifest, distinct, undisguised, vivid, downright, decisive, articulate, positive, certain, perspicuous, clear-cut, salient, prominent, pronounced, patent, palpable, visible, unmistakable, intelligible, unhidden, disclosed, revealed, unconcealed, uncloaked.

9. Shrewd, prompt, quick, sagacious, astute, penetrating, sage, cognitive, judicious, keen, sharp, discerning, perspicacious, level-headed, argute, quick-witted, alert, wide-awake.

10. Blameless, above suspicion, innocent, unimpeachable, uncensurable, guiltless, sinless, irreprehensible, inculpable, spotless, unblemished, unsoiled, unsullied, upright, irreprovable, stainless.

11. Tuneful, dulcet, sweet, mellisonant, silvery, melodious, mellifluent, dulcifluous, melodic, resonant, euphonious, sonorous, musical, clarion.

12. Audible, distinct, definite, loud enough to be heard, hearable, recognizable, plain, distinguishable, articulate.

13. Released, pardoned, excused, loose, free, freed, at liberty, liberated, acquitted, exempt, exonerated, absolved, quit, scot-free.

CLEAR, v. 1. (Chiefly of weather) Clear off, become fine, break, become fair, become free from clouds, brighten, lighten, illuminate, enlighten, irradiate.

2. Settle, square accounts, liquidate, pay off, cancel debts, wipe off, pay in full, discharge obligations, balance accounts, settle balances, satisfy, meet payment.

3. Cleanse, clean, purify, refine, purge, wash, deterge, epurate, decrassify, clarify, depurate, defecate, elutriate, expurgate, absterge, expunge, flush, strain, drain, lixiviate, filter.

4. Free, unmuzzle, unshackle, untie, untruss, unhandcuff, unleash, untether, unbandage, uncage, unharness, disenthrall, emancipate, liberate, release, unbind, unfasten, unchain, unyoke, manumit, affranchise, unmanacle, unpinion.

5. Disentangle, disengage, free, open, unravel, extricate, disburden, unknot, facilitate, unclog, open, loosen, disembarrass, untie, unstop, unseal, deobstruct.

6. Pardon, amnesty, exculpate, excuse, acquit, reprieve, vindicate, absolve, let go free, exonerate, discharge, forgive, justify.

7. Vault, leap over, hop over, bound over, skip over, pass over, avoid, jump, bounce over, make (coll.).

8. Gain, earn, make, profit, realize a profit, bag, reap, glean, gather, net, come out ahead.

9. (Often with UP) Elucidate, explain, make clear, render intelligible, lay open, define, bring to light, expose, interpret, hold up the mirror to, bare, make explicit, resolve, disentangle, make plain, comment upon, solve, manifest, enucleate, expound, demonstrate, show, exhibit, exposit, make visible, unfold, decipher, unmask, unveil, uncover, simplify, clear up, illuminate, shed light on.

10. (With AWAY) Clean up, deforest, make a clearing, remove underbrush, clear of rubbish, empty, free from encumbrances.

CLEARANCE, n. 1. Clearage, clearing, freeing from obstruction, discharge, disengagement, loosing, extrication, removing encumbrances, disburdening, unraveling, relegation, removal, evacuation, withdrawal, elimination, banishment, eradication, quittance, liquidation, voidance, eviction, disposal, dislodgment, depopulation, dispossession.

2. Discharge, release, acquittal, dismissal, excuse, permission to leave port (Naut. and Com.), vindication, deliverance, exculpation, quietus, liberation, emancipation, payment of debts, reckoning, manumission, disenthrallment, pardon, satisfaction for debts, absolution, exoneration, settlement, liquidation, enfranchisement, disengagement, compurgation (Law), quitclaim (Law), quittance.

3. Space, free passage, altitude, height, free scope, distance between objects, allowance for expansion, room to pass, elbowroom, leeway, room to spare, headway, berth (Naut.), margin.

CLEAR-CUT, adj. Sharply outlined, exact, direct, precise, distinct, well-defined, definite, classic, graphic, to the point, clear, articulate, apparent, specific, particular, unmistakable, positive, open, pronounced, striking, salient, in bold relief, fixed, unclouded, undisguised, evident, patent, vivid, determinate, intelligible, clearly discernible, well-formed, naked, overt, bare, lucid, pellucid, point-blank, concise, sharply defined, perspicuous, prominent, pointed, palpable, express, obvious, understandable, unequivocal, accurate, in the foreground, conspicuous, manifest, detailed, plain, clean-cut, unerring, marked, categorical (Log.), explicit, unambiguous, bald, luminous, in strong focus, translucent, transpicuous, transparent.

CLEAR-EYED, adj. Bright, healthy, open-eyed, far-seeing, straightforward, honest, sagacious, discriminating, critical, keen, acute, shrewd, wide-awake, discretional, prudent, sharp-sighted, farsighted, forehanded, bright-eyed, astute, argute, penetrating, alive, alert, aware, piercing, subtle, quick, undeceived, provident, quick-witted, lynx-eyed, clear-headed, gimlet-eyed, discerning, sage, perceptive, sapient, imaginative, level-headed, cool-headed, ferret-eyed, clear-witted, nobody's fool (slang), Argus-eyed, eagle-eyed, rational, perspicacious, sober-minded, judicious, quick of apprehension, keen-sighted, smart, sharp-eyed, well, wise, sensible, comprehending.

CLEAR-HEADED, adj. Lucid, clear-thinking, sane, free from confused thought, untroubled, steady, discerning, clear-sighted, keen-sighted, cognitive, clear-eyed, of clear understanding, unperturbed, calm, collected, unruffled, composed, unshaken, unexcited, level-headed, unnervous, self-possessed, tranquil, serene, poised, placid, self-restrained, reasonable, comprehending, thinking, resourceful, fully conscious, reliable, dependable, penetrating, right-minded, long-headed, acute, perspicacious, of sound mind, sagacious, shrewd, luminous, prepared, of sound judgment, strong-minded, knowing, oracular, sage, in possession of one's faculties, astute, sharp, sensible, self-controlled, undisturbed, accurate, discriminating, undeceived, prudent, subtle, argute, perceptive, cool-headed, clear-witted, rational.

CLEARING, n. 1. Clearance, clearage, freeing from obstruction, breaking, release, extrication, becoming fair, brightening, discharge, acquittal, loosing, removing encumbrances, disburdening, unraveling, elimination, eradication, quittance, voidance, liquidation, dismissal, disengagement, vindication, exculpation, pardon, exoneration, settlement, freeing, liberation, emancipation, facilitation, cleaning, purification, refinement, flushing, clarification.

2. Open space, cleared land, open field, claim, tract, cultivated land, tilled field, felled forest, field, patch of land, glade, opening in woodland.

CLEARLY, adj. Distinctly, before one's eyes, noticeably, in full view, decidedly, admittedly, unequivocally, beyond question, incontestably, transparently, palpably, patently, starkly, beyond doubt, irrefutably, to all appearances, on the face of it, at the first blush, prominently, undeniably, pronouncedly, undoubtedly, unquestionably, at first sight, uncontrovertibly, to the eye, prima facie (Lat.), visibly, assuredly, certainly, overtly, positively, discernibly, openly, plainly, markedly, definitely, recognizably, irrefragably, manifestly, autoptically, evidently, obviously, unmistakably, surely, perceptibly, observably, in plain sight, indubitably, apparently, seemingly, conspicuously.

CLEAR-SIGHTED, adj. Open-eyed, far-seeing, discriminating, critical, keen, acute, wide-awake, shrewd, discretional, sharp-sighted, far-sighted, astute, penetrating, aware, piercing, subtle, argute,

undeceived, quick-witted, clear-headed, discerning, gimlet-eyed, lynx-eyed, perceptive, percipient, ferret-eyed, sapient, imaginative, clear-witted, quick of apprehension, sharp-eyed, perspicacious, comprehending, judicious, sagacious, prudent, eagle-eyed, Argus-eyed, forehanded, prepared, provident.

CLEAT, n. 1. Belaying pin, wedge, timber, kevel (Naut.), bollard.

2. Strip, rib, ridge, stay, girder, crossbeam, toggle, support, brace, reinforcement, holdfast, crosspiece, crossbrace, bowstring beam, bearing block (Civ. Eng.), truss, plate, check, bearing plate (Civ. Eng.), bonder (Masonry), binder (Masonry), header (Masonry), chock (Naut.), crossbridging (Arch.), purlin (Arch.).

CLEAT, v. Strip, wedge, ridge, support, belay, tie, check, stay, make fast, underbrace, underpin, reinforce, bind, rib, truss, brace, toggle, secure, anchor.

CLEAVAGE, n. Division, separation, cleaving, sunderance, severance, splitting, segmentation, detachment, dismemberment, disengagement, slit, partition, bifidity, dichotomy, halving, discerption, abscission, dilaceration, rending asunder, split, slashing, chopping, incision, rift, fissure, break, abruption, section, rent, rupture, cutting, fission, scission, disconnectedness, disjointure, biforking, ramification, branching, forking, divergence, crotch, fork, divorce, disunion, mitosis (Biol.), cell division (Biol.), line of division, laceration, tearing, abstriction (Bot.), bifurcation, fracture, breach, disruption, avulsion, dissection, divulsion, diremption, dimidiation, dissociation, disjunction, disconnection, bisection, furculum (Anat. and Zool.), divarication, bipartition.

CLEAVE, v. 1. Shear off, cut off, break off, tear, divide, furrow, split, rend, sever, lacerate, carve, rupture, sunder, hew, quarter, dissever, incise, slit, hack, slice, rend in twain, dismember, part, partition, disjoin, disconnect, disunite, separate, divorce, detach, open, bisect, dimidiate, branch, diverge, ramify, lance, furcate, crack, fork, cut a passage, lay open, halve, isolate, rive, gash, plow, flake, laminate, cut, chop, slash, cut in two, disengage, dissociate, dispart, section, dichotomize, bifurcate, abscind, hemisect, divaricate.

2. Adhere, stick, cling, be attached, be true, be devoted, hold close, be faithful, stick together, grow together, remain constant, cohere, be united, be joined, clasp, hold fast, embrace, believe in, cherish, uphold, sustain, coalesce, have faith in, stand by, grasp, grip, hug, hold, stay close, fuse, upbear, hold together.

CLEAVER, n. Butcher's instrument, heavy cutting tool, ax, hatchet, machete, blade, tomahawk, sword, short broad knife, celt (Archaeol.), adz.

CLEFT, adj. Cut, riven, parted, divided, rent, crannied, fractured, dissociated, cloven, halved, bisected, sundered, slashed, crotched, divergent, furcate, disparted, detached, divaricate, bifurcate, branched, pronged, bicuspid, gaping, furrowed, ruptured, slotted, bifid, asunder, rimose, incised, gashed, notched, digitate, disjoined, split, slit, forked, separated, fissured, cracked, dichotomous, hewn, dimidiate, bipartite (Bot.), dismembered, sliced, partitioned, divorced.

CLEFT, n. Crevice, chink, fissure, split, incision, gash, breach, gap, cranny, crack, break, chasm, rift, fracture, flume, flaw, aperture, scissure, crevasse, rent, cleavage, clough, defile, notch, rime, slit, gully, gulch, slot, trench, nick, ditch, fosse, chap, orifice, ravine, bifurcation, trough, divergence, division, separation, couloir (Fr.), interstice, chimney (Mountaineering), cut, gorge, canyon, pass, hiatus, rupture, fork, furrow, crotch.

CLEMENCY, n. 1. Lenity, leniency, mildness, mercy, tenderness, compassion, indulgence, pity, forbearance, readiness to spare, grace, charity, forgivingness, gentleness, toleration, humanity, disposition to mercy, freedom from vindictiveness, favor, chivalry, exorability, soft-heartedness, milk of human kindness, benevolence, yearning, ruth, magnanimity, liberality, longanimity, good will, consideration, patience, propitiousness, moderation, placability, mercifulness, fellow feeling, long-suffering, mitigation, quarter, kindness, sympathy.

2. (Of weather) Softness, mildness, leniency, temperance, moderation, abatement, tranquillity, peace, calm, stillness, diminution of severity, mitigation.

CLEMENT, adj. Lenient, merciful, mild, kind, indulgent, tender, forgiving, gentle, kindhearted, liberal, tolerant, benevolent, moderate, soft, charitable, forbearing, free from vindictiveness, sympathetic, pitiful, ready to spare, placable, ruthful, exorable, yearning, propitiatory, still, peaceful, pacific, pardoning, stormless, halcyon, undisturbed, reasonable, pitying, considerate, temperate, magnanimous, longanimous, patient, peaceable, compassionate, mitigating, tender-hearted, chivalric, soft-hearted, propitious, tranquil.

CLENCH, v. 1. Fix, clinch, secure, fasten, attach, bolt, rivet, lash, truss, latch, belay, hook, couple, clasp, fuse, fetter, cement, clamp, lock, bind, make fast, pinion, tie.

2. Set, set firmly, interlock, stiffen, grit (the teeth), steel (the nerves), strengthen, gird, fortify, buttress, brace (the nerves), set closely, clasp firmly, double up tightly.

3. Grasp firmly, seize and hold, close upon, fasten on, clutch, wrest, lay hold of, grapple, hook, grip, snag, hold fast, have an iron grip on, snatch, collar (coll.), gripe, clinch, clasp, hold firmly.

4. Complete, confirm, establish, fix, endorse, strengthen, make short work of, dispose of, finish off, dismiss, decide, settle, drive home, secure, bind, conclude, dismiss all doubt, convince, set at rest, answer conclusively, confute, make sure, verify, find out, round out, culminate, cinch (slang), crown, cap, wind up.

CLERGY, n. Ministers, clergymen, priesthood, body of ecclesiastics, clericals, ministry, pastorate, holy orders, cassock, priestly office, clerical office, preachers, the Fathers, the pulpit, prelacy, hierarchy, church, episcopacy, clerical order, the cloth, presbytery.

CLERGYMAN, n. Minister, divine, priest, pastor, churchman, rector, preacher, vicar, chaplain, curate, cleric, theologian, clerical, minister of the Gospel, pulpiteer, servant of God, canonist, father, confessor, spiritual director, dignitary, evangelist, penitentiary, missionary, shepherd, parson, bishop, ecclesiastic, dean, padre, curé, parish, priest, presbyter, deacon, dominie (coll.), clerk, sky pilot (slang), Holy Joe (Naut. slang), blackcoat (coll.), reverend (coll.), sermoner, sermonizer, hierophant, cassock.

CLERICAL, adj. 1. Ecclesiastical, ministerial, churchly, cleric, pastoral, priestly, prelatic, papal,

episcopal, canonical, pontifical, apostolic, monkish, monastic, sacerdotal, hierarchic, theocratical.

2. Clerkly, secretarial, stenographic, scribal, sales, bookkeeping, accounting, typing, recorded, written.

CLERK, n. 1. Recorder, registrar, scribe, office worker, secretary, corresponder, bookkeeper, actuary, amanuensis, accountant, stenographer, shorthand writer, notary, notary public, copyist, typist, quill-driver (contempt.), prothonotary, tachygrapher, brachygrapher, calculator, reckoner, logographer.

2. Shop assistant, salesman, saleswoman, sales clerk, salesperson, employee, counterjumper (coll.).

CLEVER, adj. 1. Dexterous, apt, ingenious, ready, quick, expert, adroit, neat, sleight, efficient, cute (coll.), shrewd, capable, handy, masterly, sharp, proficient, deft, facile, keen, knowing, versatile, adept, urbane, piquant, droll, witty, sprightly, humorous, pungent, felicitous, cunning, acute, masterful, Daedalian, resourceful, nimble, smart, sparkling, scintillating, epigrammatic, competent.

2. Able, gifted, talented, wise, subtle, witty, intellectual, intelligent, quick, adroit, expert, alert, argute, alive, fertile, precocious, capable, bright, competent, keen, sharp, sagacious, endowed, fit, skilled, conversant, cunning, qualified, brilliant, accomplished, artistic, astute, quick-witted, apt, crafty, artful, canny, inventive, wily, discerning, perspicacious, well-versed, proficient, clear-headed, wide-awake, perceptive, percipient.

CLEVERNESS, n. Dexterity, adroitness, skill, wit, ingenuity, talent, mastery, address, subtlety, finesse, callidity, keenness, versatility, adeptness, discernment, inventiveness, capacity, sharpness, sagacity, efficiency, deftness, acumen, insight, humor, drollery, piquancy, urbanity, brilliance, intellect, artistry, alertness, faculty, parts, gift, knack, precocity, sleight, resourcefulness, forte, wizardry, aptitude, cunning, ingeniousness, craft, aptness, readiness, quickness, guile, penetration, facility, power, panurgy, ability, felicity, pungency, perspicacity, perception, endowment, sprightliness, competence, smartness, proficiency, expertness, gumption (coll.), clear-headedness.

CLEW, n. 1. Ball of twine, skein of yarn, spool of thread, sphere, twist, hank, coil, winding, loop, ball of yarn, spool, spindle.

2. Guiding thread, direction, hint, indicator, pointer, symptom, token, cue, solution, key, guide, clavis, intimation, implication, light, note, inkling, glimmer, finding, suspicion, insinuation, symbol, sign, suggestion, indication, inference, clue.

CLEW, v. 1. Coil into a ball, roll, wind, loop, form into a skein, twist.

2. Direct or point out by a clue, discover, find, disclose, give a lead, indicate, steer, pilot, set on the trail of, intimate, give a key to, guide, hint, insinuate, shed light, signify, give the cue, give a sign, inform, enlighten, give token of, evidence, evince, show, suggest, manifest, imply.

CLICHE, n. Stereotyped saying, trite phrase, old repeated maxim, hackneyed expression, banality, commonplace, threadbare phrase, banal sentiment, vapid expression, drug-store philosophy (coll.), bromide, platitude, fadaise (Fr.), chestnut (coll.), truism, réchauffé (Fr.), rehashed story, warmed-over tale, warmed-over cabbage (coll.), familiar tune, prosaism, old song (coll.), unthinking repetition.

CLICK, *n.* 1. Slight sharp noise, tick, clack, tink, rattle, jingle, chink, snap, tap, beat, clink, clap.

2. *(Mach.)* Pawl, detent, ratchet, dog, tooth, sliding bolt, catch, pivoted tongue.

CLICK, *v.* Emit a short sharp sound, snap, tick, clack, chink, rattle, tink, clap, tap, beat, clink, vibrate with a click, jingle.

CLIENT, *n.* 1. One under protection *or* patronage, one whose interests are cared for, dependent, ward, pensioner, charge, one under guardianship, one in custody, protégé *(Fr.)*.

2. Employer of professional services, advisee, person represented *(Law)*.

3. Customer, patron, purchaser, buyer, vendee, shopper, marketer, patronizer *(coll.)*, emptor *(Law)*.

CLIENTELE, *n.* Clients, body of customers, trade, people one serves, purchasers of goods *or* services, following, cortege, attendance, buyers, shoppers, custom, clientage, attendants, patronage *(coll.)*, customers, patrons *(coll.)*, cases.

CLIFF, *n.* Precipice, crag, bluff, steep, rocky eminence, steep face of rock, wall, scarp, incline, point, ledge, shelf, peak, scar, escarpment, crest, palisade, rocky headland, overhanging rock, tor, pinnacle, promontory, summit, height, ascent, steep climb, sharp rise, acclivity, mountain, chine, spine, ridge, peña *(S. West U. S.)*, headland, precipitous rock.

CLIMACTERIC, *n.* Crisis, critical period, turning point, change of life, menopause, turn of the tide, critical age, crucial moment, juncture, zero hour, emergency, decisive moment, exigency, conjuncture, climax, culminating point, moment of crisis, crowning circumstance, extremity, crux, pinch, trial, crest, psychological moment.

CLIMATE, *n.* Meteorological character *or* habit, usual weather, prevailing atmospheric conditions, zone, region, quarter, latitude, characteristic weather, meridian, meteorologic conditions.

CLIMAX, *n.* 1. *(Rhet.)* Successive increase of effect, gradual culmination, accumulated power, ascendancy, intensification, enlargement of meaning, rising force.

2. Point of greatest intensity, highest point, acme, culmination, summit, crown, crisis, limit, top, turn, height, zenith, meridian, turning-point, supreme moment, consummation, extreme limit, extremity, utmost, apex, maximum, utmost extent, highest degree, moment of revelation *(Drama)*, catastrophe *(Drama)*, point of highest development, pitch, final turn of events, peak, capsheaf, spire, pinnacle, crowning point, crest, cap, vertex, turn of the tide, supremacy, critical point, ne plus ultra *(Lat.)*, uttermost.

CLIMAX, *v.* Reach *or* bring to a climax, crown, bring to a head, cap, top, crest, culminate, tip, consummate, increase, intensify, ascend, tower, transcend, overtop, surmount, head, result, end, conclude, terminate.

CLIMB, *v.* 1. Ascend gradually, struggle up, mount, ascend, progress upwards, work one's way up, clamber, rise, scale, scramble, surmount, go up, lift, rise hand over hand, shin, escalade, swarm up.

2. Aspire and achieve, improve one's position, work successfully toward a goal, be promoted, work one's way up, ascend gradually, advance, progress, make headway, make strides, get ahead, succeed step by step, rise in the ranks, rise.

3. Grow on a trellis, creep upwards, clamber, trail, run, vine, hold on by tendrils, ramp, curl upwards, twine, wind upwards.

CLINCH, *v.* 1. Lay hold of, seize and hold, wrestle with, wrest, close upon, grab hold of, gripe, clutch, grapple, grasp, fasten on, hold firmly, grip, collar *(coll.)*, clasp.

2. Attach, secure, fasten, rivet, drive in, make fast, couple, fetter, fix, clamp, clasp, set, bolt, tie, belay, bind, lock, pinion.

3. Bring to a conclusion, complete, decide, strengthen, make sure, verify, cinch *(sl.)*, cap, wind up, establish, dispose of, dismiss, settle, secure, conclude, round out, confirm, finish off, drive home, bind, dismiss all doubt, culminate, crown, fix.

CLING, *v.* 1. Adhere, stick to, be attached, hold, hold fast, be united, clasp, coalesce, grasp, grip, hang onto, grow together, stick together, be joined, cohere, fuse, hold together, stay close.

2. Be unwilling to give up, cleave to, embrace, cherish, love, hold onto, refuse to give up, upbear, maintain, remain constant to, hug, hold fast to, believe in, be faithful to, be attached to.

CLINIC, *n.* 1. Study of patients, study of diseases, study of cases before medical students, assemblage of doctors for diagnosis and study of cases.

2. Hospital, infirmary, policlinic, medical center, polyclinic, outpatients' ward.

CLINK, *n.* Click, clack, twang, jangle, dingle, ding, ring, rattle, clank, ting, tinkle, jingle.

CLINK, *v.* Rattle, dingle, ding, ring, click, clack, tinkle, clank, ting, tink, ding, twang, jangle, jingle.

CLINKER, *n.* Ashes, cinders, embers, sinters, hot coals, carbon, soot, coke, culm, smut, burned-out coals, scale, residue, slag, dross, recrement, waste, coom, acoria, refuse, draff, slaggy lava, sprue, charcoal, remnants.

CLIP, *n.* 1. Act of clipping, shearing, cutting, trimming, pruning, cropping, lopping, fleecing, bobbing, snipping, nipping, stunting, curtailment, retrenchment, checking, condensation, reduction, compression, abstraction, docking, abridgment, abbreviation, epitome, paring, constriction, subtraction, deduction, diminishing, withdrawal, removal, cramping, contraction, truncation, shaving, snubbing.

2. Quantity of wool sheared, season's shearing, clipping, piece, snip, snippet, snatch, chip. sliver, paring, cut, cutting, collop, splinter, pollard, tag, shred, gleaning, scrap, sample, remnant, lock *(of hair)*, slip, shaving, flinder.

3. Spring clasp, device for gripping and holding tightly, spring holder, metal clasp, hasp, letter-holder, fastener, hook, holdfast, buckle, coupler, copula, vise, grip, clinch.

CLIP, *v.* 1. Cut off, bob, crop, cut short, shear, trim, pare, prune, truncate, shave, snip, poll, lop, fleece, mow, shorten, stunt, check the growth of, nip, dock, retrench, pollard.

2. Fasten together, clamp, hasp, clinch, buckle, couple, grip, vise, press, hold, fasten, hook.

3. Curtail, cut short, reduce, shorten, cut, take in, abridge, condense, epitomize, retrench, check the growth, abstract, boil down, stunt, compress, contract, compact. dock, deduct, diminish, cramp, subtract, remove, withdraw, constrict.

4. Cut out articles *or* pictures, make clippings, remove to keep, take excerpts, glean *(fig.)*.

CLIPPER, *n.* 1. Fast horse, fast-moving animal *or* person, fast-sailing vessel, low fast sled, cutter, runner, frigate, corsair, speeder, sleigh, bobsled, flier, goer, hustler *(coll.)*, speed demon *(coll.)*, racer, toboggan, stepper.

2. *(In plural)* Shears, pruning tools, cutters, hair-trimmer.

CLIPPING, *n.* Printed matter from paper or book, piece of a growing plant for propagation, sample of fabric, remnant from cutting, excerpt, snip, piece, cutting, snippet, lock of hair, literary gleaning.

CLIQUE, *n.* Coterie, club, brotherhood, knot, set, interest, side, clan, cabal, class, party, gang, ring, circle, private *or* exclusive association, plot, faction, combination, group, cell, caucus, junto, camarilla, lodge, order, alliance, league, outfit *(coll.)*, crowd *(coll.)*, conclave, fraternity, body of partisans, division, coalition, caste, machine, union, federation, Bund *(Ger.)*, sect, sodality, association.

CLOAK, *n.* 1. Mantle, outer coat, wrap, cape, shroud, pall, robe, great coat, poncho, pelisse, capote, domino, dolman, manta, jubbah, pelerine, paletot, blouse, frock, shawl, veil, cope, tunic, burnoose, sagum, smock, cardinal, talma, tabard, gaberdine, mantelet.

2. Mask, veil, pretext, disguise, blind, front, screen, cover, evasion, mantle, appearance, film, concealment, dodge, incognito, vizard, excuse, semblance, feint, subterfuge, misrepresentation, curtain, covert, artifice, veneer, coverage, false colors, camouflage, dust thrown in the eye, gloss, varnish, color, claim, occulter, dissembling, fraud, simulation, deceit, pretense, white lie, haze, side-step, deception, duplicity, bluff, trickery, shroud, guise, borrowed plumes, masquerade, profession, dissimulation, plea, occulting screen, put off, allegation, sham, cloud, ostensible motive, alleged ground.

CLOAK, *v.* Mask, hide, conceal, disguise, evade, shield, coat, mantle, veneer, face, cover, secrete, hoodwink, protect, screen, pretend, dodge, haze, sidestep, dissemble, counterfeit, obscure, blind, shroud, cloud, befog, robe, profess, pretext, allege, tell a white lie, color, varnish, whitewash, slur, feint, throw dust in the eyes, put a good face upon, enamel, gild, gloss, throw into the shade, occult, trick, bluff, deceive, camouflage, veil, guard.

CLOCK, *n.* 1. Timekeeper, horologe, dial, timer, chronometer, timepiece, watch, chronoscope, chronograph, taximeter *(coll.)*, speedometer *(coll.)*, journeyman.

2. Vertical embroidery on stockings, broidery, embroidered figure, ornamentation on hosiery.

CLOCKWORK, *n.* 1. Precision machinery, perfectly timed operation, accurate operation, synchrony, synchronous motions, mechanical movements, wheelworks, epicycle train, wheels within wheels.

2. *(With like)* Precision, regularity, mechanical nature, perfect timing, methodical patience, on schedule, according to plan, synchronization, accuracy, synchronous motion.

CLOD, *n.* 1. Lump of earth, mass of clay, wad, chunk, nugget, clump, fragment of soil, hunk *(coll.)*, gob *(slang)*.

2. Ground, earth, sod, soil, glebe *(Poetic)*, turf, loam, humus, mold, leaf mold, marl *(Poetic)*, subsoil, sward, green, lawn, greensward, gumbo.

3. Clay, flesh of man, base substance, human flesh, dust, ashes, earthly part, mortal coil, earth, mortal part, earthly substance, temporal body, the earthbound, the mundane, terrestrial being,

perishable substance.

4. Stupid person, blockhead, dolt, clown, oaf, clodpoll, dunce, ill-bred man, boor, ignoramus, dullard, tyke, numskull, ne'er-do-well, clodpate, loafer, barbarian, countryman.

CLODHOPPER, *n.* 1. Rustic, swain, bumpkin, churl, yokel, farmer, peasant, boor, hind, clown, countryman, ploughman, lout, hobnail, son of the soil, hick *(slang)*, Tony Lumpkin, drone, lubber, hayseed *(slang)*, country bumpkin, hodge *(coll.)*, chuff, kern, joskin *(slang)*, gaffer, tiller of the soil, rube *(coll.)*, galoot *(slang)*, jake *(coll.)*, son of Martha, looby, lumpkin, greenhorn, clodbreaker.

2. *(Plural)* Heavy shoes, boots, brogan, brogue, clumsy footgear, dog *(slang)*, kick *(slang)*.

CLOG, *n.* 1. Impediment, encumbrance, obstacle, check, drawback, drag, brake, skid, obstruction, barrier, hamper, curb, hitch, remora, determent, delay, dead weight, snag, interruption, stoppage, counteraction, embarrassment, restraint, damper, restriction, holdback, difficulty, stay, checkmate, deadlock, blockage, hurdle, prevention, kill-joy, wet blanket, incubus, dog in the manger, catch, spoke, knot, onus, burden, millstone round one's neck, stumbling block, load, pack, lumber, stop, preclusion, inhibition, preventive, detention, interception, retardation, hindrance, handicap.

2. Trammel, fetter, drag-weight, heavy block, brake, shackle, dead weight, tether, hopple, check, restraint, curb, anchor, drag, hobble.

3. Sabot, wooden shoe, chopine, babouche, patten.

CLOG, *v.* 1. Encumber, hinder, impede, shackle, retard, fetter, put a clog on, act as a drag, saddle, incommode, load, burden, trammel, embarrass, restrain, cumber, hamper, handicap, hobble, balk, check, put a stop to, cramp, interfere, hopple, bar, brake, cross, prevent, interpose, counteract, stop, countercheck, intercept, filibuster, block, delay, debar, barricade, bolt, lock, stay, arrest, restrict, interrupt, slacken, deadlock, checkmate, detain, scotch.

2. Fill with foreign matter, choke, obstruct, close, staunch, fill up, dam up, check, shut off, stop up, block, prevent passage, choke up, retard flow.

CLOISTER, *n.* 1. Arcade, colonnade, piazza, abbey-walk, convent-walk, walk, passage, arched ambulatory, colonnaded court, portico, gallery, peristyle, covered way, corridor.

2. Convent, monastery, nunnery, abbey, place of religious seclusion, priory, hermitage, friary, retreat from the world, cell.

3. Place of quiet seclusion, sanctum, retreat, ivory tower, cell, study, library, private quarters, sanctuary, mew, arbor, bower, resort, haunt, den, asylum, closet, refuge for contemplation, haven, hermitage, hideaway, adytum, covert, shelter, cubicle, sanctum sanctorum.

CLOISTERED, *adj.* Retired from the world, sole, recluse, concealed, isolated, sheltered, monastic, cloistral, monachal, conventual, claustral, hidden, solitary, secreted, secluded, sequestered, closeted, alone, withdrawn, apart, renouncing, dissociated, aloof, separate, confined, remote, close, private.

CLOSE, *adj.* 1. Tight, closed, shut fast, shut in, confining, enclosed, without opening, airtight, watertight, impermeable, impenetrable, imporous, unventilated, fixed, fast, secure, firm, stanch, set, sound, impervious, hermetically sealed.

2. Hidden, secret, guarded, narrowly confined, obscure, covert, enclosed, dark, recondite, privy,

abstruse, clouded, under prohibition, carefully watched, undisclosed, not open to the public, undercover, closed, private, screened, shrouded, eclipsed, inviolate, unrevealable, arcane, retired, mysterious, auricular, underground, clandestine, huggermugger, surreptitious, inviolable, exclusive, withdrawn, concealed, cloistered, secluded, pent up.

3. Close-mouthed, taciturn, reserved, reticent, curt, uncommunicative, disinclined to speak, not loquacious, sparing of words, silent as the grave, speechless, mute, sententious, secretive, indisposed to talk, word-bound, silent, tongue-tied, evasive, laconic, unsociable, mum, retiring, silent as a post, dumb, brief, concise, pauciloquent, wary, obmutescent, cautious.

4. Musty, stagnant, stale-smelling, oppressive, moldy, heavy, stifling, motionless, uncomfortable, fusty, confined, suffocating, stuffy, unventilated.

5. Sultry, muggy, heavy, sweltering, oppressive, uncomfortable, humid, stifling, suffocating, warm, stuffy.

6. Crowded, compressed, compact, dense, solid, cramped, serried, firm, thick, condensed, packed, crushed, wedged, teeming, populous, squeezed, jammed, stuffed, pressed, congested, packed like sardines, clotted, coherent, cohesive, swarming, as thick as hops, as thick as flies, crowded to suffocation.

7. Near in space, time *or* relation, adjoining, imminent, approximate, neighboring, immediate, adjacent, almost, within a little, hard upon, nearby, nigh, on the heels of, within an ace of, near together, within an inch of, resembling, similar, much the same, forthcoming, impending, instant, approaching, tangent, contiguous, bordering, at hand, near the mark, on the brink of, all but, conterminous, juxtapositional, handy, proximate, propinquant, something like, knocking at the door, approaching nearly, near, quasi *(Lat.)*, pseudo, on a level with, vicinal, peer, virtual, on a par with, hairbreadth.

8. Intimate, strongly attached, confidential, based upon strong uniting feeling of love *or* honor, dear, devoted, familiar, bosom, federate, inseparable, indissoluble, firm, hand and glove, hand-in-hand, indivisible, united, indiscerptible, confederate, stanch, loyal, cheek-by-jowl, allied, inseverable, thick *(coll.)*, thick as thieves *(coll.)*, tried and true, fast.

9. Nearly balanced, sharply contested, hard fought, nearly even *or* equal, drawn, tied, almost lost, fifty-fifty, well-matched, nip and tuck, with narrow margin, of comparable strengths, nose to nose, photo finish *(Racing)*, hot *(coll.)*, on even terms, of uncertain outcome, suspenseful, just escaped, unresolved, anybody's *(coll.)*, hairbreadth.

10. Intense, earnest, fixed, assiduous, searching, strict, minute, attentive, trenchant, incisive, sharp, acute, not deviating, scrutinizing, vigilant, vivid, watchful, dogged, unsleeping, lively, keen, cutting, constant, intent, unremitting, regardful.

11. Not deviating from original *or* model, as like as two peas, faithful, accurate, particular, logical, literal, very like, conscientious, lifelike, cast in the same mold, sound, true, speaking, stringent, exact, precise, express, nice, coherent, rigorous, exacting, strictly logical, servile, strict.

12. Parsimonious, penurious, niggardly, tight *(coll.)*, miserly, save-all, close-fisted, mean, near, illiberal, narrow, avaricious, sordid, ungenerous, close-handed, stingy, churlish, stinting, beggarly,

penny-wise, shabby, tight-fisted, venal, grasping, cheese-paring *(coll.)*, mercenary, scrimping, grudging, meager, pinching, greedy.

13. Tightly fitting, snug, slim, slender, tight, glued, scant, hampering, skin-tight, like the paper on the wall, skimpy, constricting, restricting, choking, confining, binding, plastered, narrow, incapacious, limiting, coarctate *(Biol.)*, hugging.

CLOSE, *n.* 1. End, conclusion, completion, finish, termination, expiration, fall of the curtain, term, omega, apodosis, consummation, discontinuance, shutdown, finale, cessation, finis, stoppage, payoff *(slang)*, nightfall, evening, decline, culmination, closure, cloture *(U.S. Parl. Proc.)*, peroration, windup, sundown, dénoument *(Fr.)*.

2. Cathedral *or* abbey precinct, enclosure about *or* beside a building, grounds, courtyard, piazza, churchyard, cloister, square, plaza, arcade, court.

3. Enclosure, yard, grounds, precinct, environ, square, court, back yard, garden, plot, private land, plat, cincture, quadrangle, compound, tract, kitchen garden, courtyard, curtilage *(Law)*.

4. Junction, union, joining, meeting, coupling, accouplement, connection, conjunction, ligation, binding, compagination, copulation, conjugation, conjuncture, concurrence, tie-up.

5. Grapple, hand-to-hand fight, clash, meeting, collision, contiguous battle, grasp, clasp, bump, iron grip, appulse, impact, brunt, firm hold, fast hold, strangle hold, seizure, joining, shock, grip, gripe, close encounter.

CLOSE, *v.* 1. Shut, lock, cover in, encompass, enclose, envelop, fasten, intern, pen, bottle up, box, wall in, wrap, cover, sheathe, secure, bar, trap, button, buckle, immure, impound, imprison, snap, rail, environ, clap, surround, cloister, coop up, cage, confine, besiege, bolt, seal, incase, mew, cork, shut up, plumb, gather around, rope in.

2. Stop, obstruct, clog, block, calk, occlude, stuff, dam, plug, stanch, choke off, hold back, fill in, blockade, bung, staunch, hinder, interrupt, hamper, impede, cram, seal, ram, throttle, curb, cut off, choke, fill, check, prevent passage, retard flow, fill with foreign matter.

3. Unite, coalesce, blend, converge, conjugate, join, merge, incorporate, meet, link, couple, unify, reduce distance between, contract, compact, draw in, group, bunch, narrow, concentrate, compress, fuse, consolidate, connect, come together, become one, be brought together, shrink, articulate, line up together.

4. Terminate, end, cease, put an end to, stay, perfect, halt, leave off, have done with, finish, conclude, drop, run out, dismiss, wind up *(coll.)*, surcease, consummate, dispatch, culminate, quit, perorate, achieve, adjourn, eventuate, suspend operation, be concluded, expire, stop, discontinue, break off, accomplish.

5. *(With* with) Grapple, come to close quarters, clench, confront, embrace, encounter, contend with, strive with, tussle with, join issue, engage with, struggle with, fight hand-to-hand, bring to bay, gripe, grip, lay hold of, wrest, seize, collide, clash, clinch, wrestle, lock horns, tangle with *(slang)*, meet head-on, join combat, fasten upon, fall foul of, measure swords with, cross swords with, clutch, face, stand up against, square off *(coll.)*, come to blows, exchange blows, set to, pitch into *(coll.)*, enter the lists.

6. *(With* with *or* on) Agree, come to terms, clench, clinch, complete, fix by agreement, land, secure, accept *(an offer)*, arrange, adjust, set at rest, straighten out, conclude, decide, settle.

CLOSE-FISTED, *adj.* Niggardly, miserly, mean, penurious, tight-fisted, close-handed, ungenerous, stingy, churlish, stinting, parsimonious, narrow, grudging, meager, scrimping, beggarly, illiberal, pinching, tight *(coll.).*

CLOSE-FITTING, *adj.* Tightly fitting, skin-tight, restricting, choking, limiting, narrow, hugging, confining, skimpy, snug, slender, tight, glued, plastered, hampering, scant, slim, constricting, like paper on the wall, binding, incapacious, coarctate *(Biol.).*

CLOSE-MOUTHED, *adj.* Close, reticent, evasive, uncommunicative, reserved, curt, cautious, brief, taciturn, sparing of words, laconic, unsociable, retiring, silent as a post, disinclined to speak, silent as the grave, mute, secretive, tongue-tied, concise, pauciloquent, obmutescent, speechless, not loquacious, sententious, word-bound, mum, dumb, wary, silent.

CLOSET, *n.* 1. Cabinet, cupboard, small room, enclosed recess, depository, buttery, locker, attic room, cubicle, pantry, larder, coffer, repository, cellaret, cache, compartment, vault, strong room, alcove, ambry, scullery, storeroom, wardrobe, press, clothespress, clothesroom, abditory, safe, safe-deposit box, crypt, cuddy, dressing room.
2. Private room, retiring room, place of quiet seclusion, sanctum, sanctum sanctorum, cloister, ivory tower, cell, study, bower, mew, sanctuary, resort, asylum, library, refuge for contemplation, covert, adytum, shelter, den, hideaway, haven, hermitage, cubicle, retreat, private quarters, camera.

CLOSET, *v.* Admit to intimate interview, talk privately with, sequester, seclude, cloister, put into concealment, confer with in camera, talk with tête-à-tête.

CLOSURE, *n.* 1. Act of closing *or* shutting, occlusion, stoppage, obstruction, clogging, sealing, calking, blockage, plugging, locking, damming, blocking, covering, enveloping, bottling up, cooping up, bolting, corking, stanching.
2. Bringing to an end, conclusion, culmination, decline, curtain, stoppage, cessation, finishing, completion, expiration, termination, peroration, cloture *(U.S. Parl. Proc.),* discontinuance, windup, ending, concluding, payoff *(slang),* consummation, method of ending a debate, *dénouement (Fr.).*
3. State of being shut, blockade, embolism, occlusion, imperforation, imperviousness, infarct, impermeability, cul-de-sac, stoppage.
4. That which closes or shuts, joint, holdback, articulation, connection, stitch, seam, seal, cap, lid, top, stopper, interceptor, barrier, spigot, dam, embolus, commissure, operculum, obstruction, curb, impediment, coupler, juncture, suture, plug, raphe *(Anat. and Bot.),* interrupter, tourniquet, mortise, hitch.

CLOT, *n.* Coagulum, precipitate, lump, mass, gob, coagulation, concretion, thrombus, curd, grume, thickness, coalescence, acid casein, clabber, gout, coagulated protein, conglutination, crassamentum.

CLOT, *v.* Coagulate, curdle, thicken, inspissate, coalesce, form into clots, cause to coagulate, congeal, curd, set, conglomerate, precipitate, fix, condense, solidify, incrassate, cake, conglutinate, concrete.

CLOTH, *n.* 1. Woven fabric, textile, goods, dry goods, texture, felt, rag, material, stuff, tissue.
2. Piece of fabric, table covering, dusting rag, spread, towel, pall, robe, napkin, dishcloth, bib, drapery, curtain, tapestry, cover, cerecloth, doily, backdrop, hanging, serviette, handkerchief, face cloth, sudarium, cerement, altar cloth *or* carpet, cleaning rag, back scene.
3. Clergy, ministers, body of ecclesiastics, ministry, prelacy, clerical office, cassock, holy orders, pastorate, clergymen, priesthood, clericals, preachers, the pulpit, church, hierarchy, prelacy, episcopacy, presbytery.

CLOTHE, *v.* 1. Dress, attire, array, put garments on, garb, habilitate, costume, drape, bedeck, coat, bedizen, trick out, cloak, jacket, muffle up, gown, accouter, caparison, rig out, breech, deck out, bundle up, dizen, don, mantle, gird, disguise, apparel, robe, deck.
2. Provide garments for, accouter, supply with clothes, appoint, equip, outfit, uniform, furnish raiment, fit out, gear, dress, array, buy garments for, garb, costume, frock, fit up, deck, supply with garments.
3. Invest, cover, endow, envelop, wrap, shroud, sheathe, encase, vest, case, swaddle, muffle, coif, enwrap, endue, cloak, bedeck, accouter, costume, veil, enamel, gild, gloss, cloud, screen, veneer, face, disguise, coat.

CLOTHES, *n.* 1. Garments, raiment, attire, dress, clothing, habiliments, garb, costume, vestments, apparel, caparisons, wear, wearables, finery, gear, ensemble, array, toggery *(coll.),* wardrobe, livery, frippery, trousseau, togs *(coll.),* bedizenment, regimentals, toilet, linen, habits, wearing apparel, vesture, guise, regalia, duds *(coll.),* costumery, rags, robes, drapery, trim, rigging, tatters.
2. Bedclothes, linens, covers, bedding, sheets, bedcovers, blankets.

CLOUD, *n.* 1. Visible suspended water *or* ice particles, haze, mist, fog, nebulosity, film, steam, vapor, nebule, frost smoke, smog, drisk, pea soup *(coll.).*
2. Dense mass as of smoke *or* dust, pall, smog, mist, mantle, soot, dust, cloak, screen, veil, smoke screen, dust storm, puff, cover, shade, shadow, shroud.
3. Throng, crowd, multitude, dense mass, host, swarm, flight, shower, flock, volley, congregation, legion, storm, galaxy, vast assemblage, horde, army, vast number.
4. Blur, dark spot, blotch, blemish, shade, spot, stain, smudge, smirch, soil, brand, defect, stigma, flaw, blurred spot, imperfection, taint, smutch, daub, smear, macule, grime, tarnish, patch, speck, maculation, nebula *(Med.).*
5. Darkness, obscurity, despondency, despair, night, fogginess, obscuration, eclipse, occultation, gloom, sorrow, extremity, blighted hope, futility, hopelessness, dark future, grief, woe, evil day, benighted state, confusion, oppression, dimness, depression, bewilderment, trouble of mind, ill fortune, prostration, desolation, perplexity, pall, dilemma, tragedy, wretchedness, hope deferred, catastrophe, reverse, disaster, gloomy outlook, rainy day, trouble of soul, dejection.
6. Anything that obscures, darkens, *or* causes gloom, trouble, suspicion, disgrace, shadow, blot, blight, ill omen, gathering clouds, warning, chill, apprehension, visitation, scourge, shroud, pall, ill wind, premonition, evil, bane, curse, specter, blot in the scutcheon, badge of infamy, affliction, evil dispensation, weight, cancer, ill fortune, woe, thorn in the flesh, canker worm, plague, skeleton in the closet, pestilence, breakers ahead, evil star,

handwriting on the wall, storm brewing, damp, ghost, doubt, scandal, bar sinister, incubus.

CLOUD, v. 1. Overspread, cover with clouds, grow cloudy, overcast, overshadow, darken, fog, mist, haze, nubilate, shade, dim, promise rain, dusk, gloom, adumbrate, murk, darkle, befog, smoke, obfuscate, eclipse, lower, hide, becloud, pale.

2. Darken, obscure, overshadow, eclipse, hide, shroud, shadow, dull, blacken, bedim, blur, shade, begloom, encompass with shadow, obtenebrate, somber, murk, occult, blind, curtain, benight, veil, conceal, cover, cloak, screen, blear, smoke, adumbrate, fog, nubilate, make gloomy, frost, dim.

3. Place under suspicion or disgrace, put to shame, humiliate, mortify, indict, suspect, doubt, mistrust, question, discredit, call in question, set a mark on, challenge, give the lie to, taint, sully, defile, censure, blacken, denounce, gibbet, brand, maledict, blackball, expose, malign, stigmatize, vilipend, tarnish, stain, detract, defame, bespatter, give a bad name, slur, anathematize, derogate from, degrade, vilify.

CLOUDBURST, n. Torrential shower, downpour, sudden heavy rainfall, flash flood, the heavens opened, inundation, deluge, waterspout, cataract, driving rain, flood, drenching rain, pouring rain, cats and dogs (coll.).

CLOUDLESS, adj. 1. Clear, sunny, unclouded, fair, luminous, serene, fine, genial, undimmed, unobscured, transparent, irradiate, light, lucent, pellucid, starlight, moonlight, bright, starlit.

2. Unalloyed, happy, carefree, joyous, blissful, painless, buoyant, flawless, optimistic, guileless, blithe, light-hearted, untainted, faultless, beatific, untarnished, cheerful, beatified, sans souci (Fr.), joyful.

CLOUDY, adj. 1. Clouded, lowering, overcast, darkened, misty, foggy, hazy, nebulous, moonless, overclouded, cloudlike, somber, starless, sunless, gray, moist, damp, wet, madid, humid, muggy, gloomy, leaden, dull, eclipsed, dreary, vaporous, umbrageous, pea-soup (coll.), soupy (slang), lurid, murky, smoky, steamy, fumy, caliginous, volatile, dingy, drizzly, drippy, overshadowed, nubilous.

2. Obscure, dim, confused, indistinct, blurred, befuddled, indefinite, baffling, bleary, occult, pale, unsettled, incomprehensible, dark, faint, vague, unresolved, unclear, ill-defined, veiled, nubilous, obfuscated, hazy, shadowed forth, nebulous, out of focus, baffled, bewildered, mysterious, undefined.

3. Gloomy, dismal, depressing, somber, under a pall, lackluster, sorrowful, oppressive, lowering, oppressed, sullen, dun, dreary, flat, leaden, dusky, heavy, glowering, breeding despair, gray, without a ray of hope, funereal, saturnine, lugubrious, black, umbrageous, dull.

4. Varied with dark spots, mottled, having cloudlike markings, variegated, maculate, shaded, opalescent, blotched, milky, spotted, opaque.

5. Blurred, dimmed, lusterless, muddy, murky, nacreous, dense, viscous, sooty, smoky, fuliginous, foggy, tarnished, unclear, troubled, turbid, thick, unsettled, viscid, nubilous, dirty, unquiet, frosty, stirred-up, agitated, smirched, smeared, opaque, in suspension, emulsified, non-transparent.

6. Under suspicion or disgrace, under a cloud, black, in question, defiled, dubious, suspect, open to challenge, doubtful, in disrepute, mistrusted, defamed, discredited, stigmatized, tainted, sullied,

branded, stained, distrusted, maligned, tarnished, slurred, bespattered, denounced, open to doubt, anathematized, out of countenance.

CLOVEN, adj. Cleaved, cleft, bisected, cut, rent, sundered, halved, dissociated, fractured, crannied, divided, parted, riven, slashed, crotched, furcate, divergent, disparted, detached, divaricate, gaping, bifurcate, branched, pronged, bicuspid, furrowed, ruptured, slotted, bifid, asunder, rimose, digitate, notched, gashed, incised, slit, forked, separated, disjoined, split, cracked, hewn, dichotomous, bipartite (Bot.), sliced, dismembered, partitioned, divorced.

CLOWN, n. 1. Buffoon, jester, comic, joker, wit, fool, droll, funnyman, harlequin, humorist, zany, madcap, scaramouch, Punch, mime, farceur (Fr.), card (coll.), grimacier, merry-andrew, Pantaloon, witling (derog.), wag, pickle-herring, wearer of the motley, jack-a-dandy.

2. Blockhead, stupid person, dolt, clod, dunce, clodpoll, dunderhead, boor, ignoramus, dullard, tyke, oaf, numskull, ne'er-do-well, loafer, jackass, countryman, clodpate, barbarian, blunderhead, thickskull, ninny, wiseacre (sl.), woodenhead, loon, lunkhead (coll.), pighead, pigsconce.

3. Bumpkin, lout, greenhorn, hick (sl.), swain, countryman, rustic, clodhopper, hobnail, yokel, hind, peasant, churl, boor, plowman, drone, son of the soil, lubber, hayseed (sl.), hodge (coll.), chuff, kern, galoot (sl.), clod, joskin (sl.), jake (coll.), rube (coll.), lumpkin, looby, gaffer, tiller of the soil.

CLOWN, v. Make fun, jest, joke, cut up, act the fool, play tricks or pranks, go zany, burlesque, mimic, fool, banter, chaff, wisecrack (slang).

CLOY, v. Satiate, surfeit, pall, glut, sate, fill to excess, suffice, jade, satisfy, overfeed, weary by excess of food, sweetness, pleasure, etc., gorge, choke, fatigue, exhaust, sicken, obtund, deaden the appetite, saturate, spoil, render callous, bore, stupefy, desensitize, overdo, exceed desire, blunt the senses, benumb, nauseate, tire, overload, dull the feelings, cause to feel surfeited or satiated, wear, deaden, numb.

CLUB, n. 1. Bludgeon, cudgel, stick, billy, bat, warclub, mace, shillelagh, blackjack, hammer, mallet, mall, flail, ball-hitting stick (for golf, hockey, etc.), sandbag, truncheon, staff.

2. Association, society, set, fraternity, coterie, sorority, clique, circle, confederacy, union, class, knot, junto, cabal, camarilla, familistery, league, following, confraternity, guild, alliance, house, order, lodge, squad, team, social group, combine, affiliation, federation, organization, brotherhood, trust, pool, bunch (coll.), crowd (coll.), group, ring, company, sodality, membership, community.

3. Building occupied by a group, headquarters, meeting place, haunt, gathering place, hangout (slang), house, resort, center, rendezvous, retreat, rallying point.

CLUB, v. 1. Strike a crushing blow, beat with a club, cudgel, pommel, maul, blackjack, bludgeon, thump, bat, sandbag, hammer, flail, fustigate, lay on, bash, buffet, flog, butt, belabor, batter, bang, swinge, strike.

2. Gather or form into a clublike mass, bunch, clump, aggregate, fagot, agglutinate, mass, conglomerate.

3. Combine, unite, add together, join together, league, aggregate, organize, form a club, unite into a group, federate, cooperate, act in concert, ally, pool interests, form an alliance, associate,

confederate, band together, fraternize, unionize, amalgamate, consolidate, bunch, gang, team with, join forces, cement a union.

4. *(Often foll. by* up *or* together) Contribute, lump, defray by shares, average, unite to share expenses, make a common purse, contribute to a common fund, combine for financial advantage, participate, go shares, apportion costs, split the difference, share and share alike, pay by turns, divide with, pool resources.

CLUCK, *v.* Make the sound of a brooding hen, emit a small throaty sound, call quietly, cry out softly, cackle gently, click, chirk, chirp, chuckle, chirrup, chuck, summon *(as a hen her chicks)*, coo, utter sympathetically, clack.

CLUE, *n.* 1. Guiding thread, direction, indicator, hint, pointer, symptom, token, cue, solution, key, guide, clavis, intimation, implication, light, note, inkling, glimmer, finding, suspicion, suggestion, symbol, sign, indication, insinuation, inference.

2. Ball of twine, skein of yarn, spool of thread, sphere, twist, hank, coil, winding, loop, ball of yarn, spool, spindle, clew.

CLUMP, *n.* 1. Cluster, bunch, group, thicket, grove, sheaf, bundle, aggregate, shock, spinney, pack, stack, lump, agglutination, mass, colony *(Bacteriol.)*, assemblage, collection, packet, copse.

2. Protuberance, projection, nodule, convexity, mass, lump, bulge, node, bump, hunch, knob, gnarl, knot, bulb, knurl, hump, knur.

3. Clumping tread, stamping sound, tramp, bump, clunk, thud, plunk, stumping *(coll.)*, stomping, clumsy gait, lumbering, plodding, plump.

CLUMP, *v.* 1. Step heavily, tramp, stomp, walk clumsily, lumber, plod, bump, plump, clunk, go steadily, thud, stamp, plunk, stump *(coll.)*.

2. Gather into *or* form a clump, aggregate, mass, cluster, bunch, stack, bundle, shock, pack, colonize, group, grow in a bunch, form a thicket, agglutinate, congregate.

CLUMSY, *adj.* 1. Awkward, unhandy, unskillful, inapt, maladroit, bungling, blundering, graceless, unpolished, uncourtly, inelegant, uncouth, rough, without dexterity, ungraceful, clownish, slovenly, without skill, like a bull in a china shop, stiff, gauche *(Fr.)*, left-handed, dull, dense, bovine, thick *(coll.)*, doltish, dumb *(coll.)*, insensitive, all thumbs *(coll.)*, untoward, insulse, slatternly, stolid, obtuse, heavy-handed, inexpert, oafish, butterfingered *(coll.)*.

2. Unwieldy, awkwardly done, ill-contrived, ungraceful, lumbering, heavy, ponderous, rough, ill-made, wooden, lumpish, hulking, crude, ugly, stodgy, heavy-handed, knocked together, stupid, makeshift, lubberly, ill-shaped, cumbersome, dull, boorish, ungainly, crass, thoughtless, amorphous, bulky, hulky, inconsiderate, tactless, inelegant, coarse, gross, obtuse, uncouth, stolid, inept.

CLUSTER, *n.* Clump, bunch, group, confluence, swarm, crowd, assemblage, collection, bevy, set, throng, tuft, thicket, herd, grove, sheaf, bale, lot, covey, galaxy, company, constellation, aggregate, band, truss, wisp, batch, fagot, accumulation, concentration, drift, congeries, raceme *(Bot.)*, panicle *(Bot.)*, fascicle, shoal, cloud, school, flock, pack, drove, conglomeration, congregation, knot, shock, hive, swathe, seroon, caboodle *(coll.)*, pile, convergence, agglomeration, heap.

CLUSTER, *v.* Grow in bunches, collect together, throng, flock, grow in clusters, crowd together, conglomerate, bundle, mingle, converge, colligate, concentrate, mass, truss, drift, accumulate, pile,

amass, group, gather, congregate, assemble, heap, agglomerate, surge, swarm, stream, muster, herd, bunch, aggregate.

CLUTCH, *n.* 1. Grasping hand, claw, talon, chela, pounce, tentacle, prehensile organ, hook, pincers, nippers, manus, unguis, nails.

2. *(Chiefly plural)* Power of disposal, control, grasp, mercy, mastery, hands, retention, talons, grip, dominion, fangs, gripe, hold, whip hand, confinement, detention, custody, dominance, nod, keep, captivity.

3. Grasp, gripe, clasp, clench, seizure, capture, possession, taking, iron grip, tenacity, retainment, tight hold, viselike grip, leech, bulldog grip, grip, adhesion, embrace, apprehension, coherence, snatch, retention, adherence.

4. Forceps, clamp, nippers, pincers, vise, grip, clinch, clasp, holdfast, tongs, tweezers, wrench, clip, grapnel, pliers.

5. Coupling apparatus for engaging parts *(Mach.)*, gear shift.

6. Hatch of eggs, setting, brood, nest, number of eggs produced *or* incubated at one time.

CLUTCH, *v.* 1. Grasp, gripe, clasp, clench, seize, snatch, clinch, claw, wrest, pounce on, spring upon, nip, control, capture, hang on to, take, swoop down on, ensnare, grab, lay hold of, hug, fasten upon, grapple, cleave, cling, hook, snag, cohere, retain fiercely, hold in one's power, grip, embrace, catch at, adhere, nab *(coll.)*, hold to, catch.

2. *(With* at) Grope for, try to grasp, catch at, grapple for, make a grab at, reach desperately for, snatch at.

3. Hatch *(chickens)*, incubate, brood, cover, sit.

CLUTTER, *n.* 1. Confused mass, disorder, odds and ends, confusion, disarray, litter, jumble, mess, motley collection, disorderly heap *or* assemblage, hodgepodge, trash, minglement, hash, mix-up, confused medley, muddle, tangle, patchwork, chaos, farrago, tumble, untidy mass, disheveled state, lumber, rummage, mishmash, scattered parts, olla-podrida, huddle, gallimaufry, topsyturvy.

2. Bustle, clatter, racket, confused noise, din, clack, hubbub, clangor, discord, Bedlam, hell let loose, tumult, clamor, pandemonium, chatter, babel, clattering, rattling.

CLUTTER, *v.* 1. Disarrange, throw into disorder, muddle, tumble, fill full of confused materials, litter, jumble, confuse, strew about, encumber with useless articles, discompose, upset, agitate, derange, disorganize, muss up *(coll.)*, dishevel, huddle, scatter, shuffle, lumber, turn topsy-turvy.

2. Run in disorder, move with bustle and confusion, make unintelligible, confuse, perplex, chatter, clangor, bustle, clamor, clack, rattle, make a clatter, speak rapidly and indistinctly, clatter.

COACH, *n.* 1. Large closed four-wheeled carriage, stagecoach, landau, barouche, brougham, drag, diligence, four-in-hand, tallyho, hackney coach, enclosed automobile, berlin, four-wheeler, fiacre, chariot, railway car, dearborn, phaeton, railroad passenger car, public passenger bus, stage, sedan, omnibus, limousine, clarence, Gladstone, equipage, motorbus.

2. Tutor, trainer of athletes, coacher, private teacher, preceptor, mentor, director of sports, crammer *(coll.)*, *Privatdozent (Ger.)*, private instructor.

COACH, v. 1. Train, teach, give instruction *or* advice, tutor, instruct, direct individually, drill, prime, give extra exercises to, aid in practice, cram *(coll.)*, guide in studies, prepare for examinations.

2. Study with a coach, be instructed by a coach, drill, exercise, practice, train, cram *(coll.)*.

COACHMAN, n. Driver, postilion, charioteer, reinsman, chauffeur, cabman, bus driver, coachy *(coll.)*, jehu *(slang)*.

COACTION, n. Force, compulsion, prohibition, restraint, coercion, pressure, obligation, impetus, propulsion, drive, duress, high-pressure methods, denial, impulse, conscription, impressment, curb, shackle, counteraction, constraint, constriction, draft, projection, shove, stricture, sword's point, absence of choice, check, limitation, hindrance, bondage, restriction, curb, no alternative, push, Hobson's choice, inhibition, trajection, the big stick, enforcement, control.

COADJUTOR, n. Assistant, associate, co-worker, helper, aid, adjunct, auxiliary, companion, coaid, collaborator, helpmate, cohelper, confederate, colleague, aider, copartner, consociate, attendant, coadjuvant, teammate, confrere, adjuvant, ally, cooperator, adjutant, man Friday, succeeding bishop.

COAGULATE, v. Curdle, change from liquid to thickened mass, gel, thicken, clot, curd, congeal, firm, mass, solidify, jelly, condense, inspissate, densify, jellify, agglomerate, consolidate, lopper *(dial.)*, conglomerate, gelatinize, incrassate, jell *(coll.)*, caseate *(Pathol.)*, concrete, set, precipitate.

COAGULATION, n. Precipitation, condensation, curdling, clotting, curding, thickening, concretion, setting, congelation, gelatination, inspissation, consolidation, conglomeration, solidification, jellification, agglomeration, incrassation, caseation *(Pathol.)*.

COAL, n. 1. Combustible mineral substance used as fuel, lignite, black diamonds, anthracite, hard coal, bituminous, soft coal, brown coal, slack, coke, culm, cobbles, blind coal, cob coal, cannel coal, briquette, glance coal, jet.

2. Glowing *or* charred wood, charcoal, clinker, ember, slag, scoria, cinder, live coal, carbon, lava, fire *(pl.)*.

COALESCE, v. 1. Grow together *or* into one body, unite, combine, amalgamate, mix, mingle, fuse, blend, come together, become consolidated, adhere, merge, consolidate, inosculate, compound, alloy, incorporate, converge, coincide, become one, absorb, melt into one, agglutinate, interfuse, intermingle, commix, integrate, consubstantiate, contemper, assimilate.

2. Unite to form one mass *or* community, *etc.*, concur, fraternize, accord, harmonize, come to an agreement, conglomerate, meet, league, ally, coadunate, integrate, federate, club, confederate, combine, herd, throng, crowd, surge, gather, join forces, cluster, team with, form an alliance, band together, swarm, moderate for harmony, convene, consolidate, convocate, concentrate, flock, adapt, embody, coincide, concert, associate, centralize, join, unite, merge, incorporate, amalgamate, syncretize.

COALITION, n. 1. Union into one body *or* mass, compound, combination, fusion, amalgamation, junction, consolidation, alloy, bond, adherence, conglomeration, integration, grafting, absorption, accouplement, concurrence, conjuncture, melting, blending, coadunation, synthesis, agglutination,

coalescence, assimilation, merging, commixture, mingling, conjugation, confluence, inosculation, convergence, connection, agglomeration.

2. Combination of persons, alliance of states, accord, union of factions, bond, confederacy, confederation, affiliation, conjunction, integration, party, consolidation, incorporation, concurrence, embodiment, league, copartnership, fusion of interests, syndicate, amalgamation, cabal, plot, conspiracy, concord, agreement, treaty, sodality, convention, connection, concourse, federation, collaboration, partnership, co-operation, compact, unanimity, harmony, association, cartel, society, community, consubstantiation, coalescence.

COARSE, adj. 1. Lacking fineness *or* delicacy of texture, heavy, rugged, knotty, knobbed, nubbly, scaly, reedy, spiked, homespun, bristling, prickly, barbate, shaggy, bristly, thick, rugose, wrinkled, ridged, hirsute, nodose, nodular, large-meshed, harsh, rough, uneven, rough-grained, encrusted, barbed, coarse-grained, cross-grained, setaceous, hispid *(Bot., Zool.)*, strigose, whiskered, tufted, setose, rough as sandpaper, rough as a nutmeg grater, scratchy, gnarled, bearded, linsey-woolsey.

2. Of large parts *or* particles, large-meshed, lumpy, jagged, broken, rough-hewn, craggy, gross, uneven, roughcast, lacking fineness *or* delicacy of structure, rugged, heavy, unbolted, of large size, clumsy, lumbering, hulky, bulky, unwieldy, roughcut, awkward, unmilled, unground, heavy-grained, rocky.

3. Crude, rough, unpurified, impure, unrefined, rank, rude, in the rough, homespun, unpolished, raw, earthy, formless, shapeless, unsorted, uncut, irregular, rough-hewn, roughcast, unprocessed, unfashioned, unlabored, natural, unfractionated, imperfect, unleavened, rudimentary, unwrought, undistilled *(of water)*, untanned *(of hides)*, not spun *or* twisted *(of fibers)*, not mixed or diluted *(of spirits)*, not tried *(of tallow)*, unbolted *(of grains)*, unformed, unfinished.

4. Of inferior *or* faulty quality, base, gross, low, vulgar, sorry, trashy, vile, foul, odious, low-minded, unworthy, mediocre, lowbred, common, brutal, tawdry, beastly, pitiful, cheap, of inferior breed, not pure *or* choice, homely, ignominious, ordinary, ignoble, worthless, fulsome, swinish, obnoxious, plain, fourth-rate, commonplace, vernacular, unlovely, comtemptible, abject, petty, shabby, paltry, little, shameful, scurvy, prosaic, broad, crude, despicable, uncultivated, plebeian, peccable, peccant, disreputable, discreditable, mean, uncouth, infamous, disgraceful, scrubby, dishonorable, rank, deplorable, beggarly, raffish, unseemly, meretricious, execrable.

5. Lacking delicacy of feeling *or* manner, rude, uncivil, unpolished, not refined, ill-mannered, ill-bred, rough, unhandsome, churlish, clownish, loutish, gruff, impolite, bearish, ungentlemanly, barbaric, rustic, harsh, offensive, cloddish, crude, boorish, sordid, crass, lubberly, improper, bold, ungraceful, indecent, brazen, shameless, vulgar, unblushing, bestial, indelicate, broad, mean, vile, unceremonious, ignorant, plebeian, smutty, gross, licentious, fulsome, ignoble, inelegant, odious, degraded, abandoned, dirty, lewd, obscene, rank, indecorous, prurient, bawdy, lascivious, insensitive, solecistic, defiled, repulsive, loathsome, noisome, blackguardly, abusive, pornographic, unbecoming, scurrilous, brutish, barbarous, unwomanly, brash, unclean, beastly, filthy, foul, ribald, bluff, lacking taste, disgusting, revolting, foul-spoken.

COARSEN, *v.* 1. Roughen, thicken, become heavy, become gross, densify, wrinkle, callous, hornify, ossify, become sclerotic, become stringy, stiffen, enlarge, sclerify *(Bot.)*, cornify.

2. Render insensitive, harden, toughen, blunt, numb, brutify, callous, indurate, obtund, deaden, dull, sensualize, hebetate.

COARSENESS, *n.* Vulgarity, indecency, obscenity, indelicacy, unrefinement, inelegance, incivility, bad taste, loud behavior, misconduct, lewdness, ungentlemanliness, rowdyism, brutishness, low-mindedness, lowness, callousness, cheapness, ruffianism, infamy, crudeness, unseemliness, ignobleness, rudeness, prurience, brashness, brazenness, foulness, vileness, inferior breeding, gaudiness, parvenuism, gaucherie *(Fr.)*, harshness, hardness, baseness, commonness, tawdriness, impropriety, foul speech, ribaldry, Gothicism, rusticity, inurbanity, filthiness, smuttiness, ill breeding, barbarism, unladylikeness, unloveliness, blackguardism, roughness, churlishness, offensiveness, scurrilousness.

COAST, *n.* Land next to the sea, shore, strand, seaside, margin of the sea, brink, brim, bank, seashore, beach, seaboard, seacoast, edge of land, waterside, reclamation, derelict, inning, made land, loom of the land, foreshore, littoral, rim bordering the sea, region bordering on the Pacific Ocean *(Cap., U. S.)*.

COAST, *v.* 1. Glide, move by gravity alone, slide downhill on a sled, continue in motion through momentum, sled, toboggan, bobsled, ski, skim, skate, sweep, glissade, stay in motion, slip, drift, float, waft, move effortlessly, bellywhop *(coll.)*, bellyflop *(coll.)*, volplane.

2. Sail along the coast, border, skirt, ply the coast, lie along the shore, hug shore *or* land, range the coast, make free with the land *(Naut. sl.)*, keep hold of the land *(cant)*.

COASTAL, *adj.* Of *or* at a coast, bordering, shore, marginal, riparian, coastwise, waterside, littoral, beachfront, seaboard, seashore, seaside.

COAT, *n.* 1. Outer garment, jacket, overcoat, ulster, slicker, cloak, smock, talma, great coat, frock coat, mantle, cape, Mackinaw, surcoat, blazer, wrap, cardinal, redingote, pelerine, coatee, mantilla, paletot, fearnought, dreadnought, temiak *(Eskimo)*, spencer, haik *(Arab.)*, toga *(Rom. Antiq.)*, sagum *(Rom. Antiq.)*, raincoat, mackintosh, caftan *(Nr. East)*.

2. Natural integument *or* covering, coating, skin, envelope, capsule, cortex, protective covering, fur, hide, fleece, bark, peel, film, chaff, bran, membrane, pellicle, husk, shell, hull, crust, scale, flake, foil, cyst, sac, vesicle, sheet, lamella, leaf, involucre, lamina, outer layer, hair, wool, exterior, outside, rind, palea, pelt, cuticle, lorica *(Zool.)*, leather, jacket, fell, epidermis, scarfskin, pericarp, epicarp, cover, ectoderm, investment, pod, shuck.

3. Anything that covers *or* conceals, layer, film, glaze, veneer, crust, covering layer, plate, plaster, overlay, pavement, weatherboard, whitewash, varnish, enamel, shingle, clapboard, facing, priming, calcimine, sheathing, shellac, lacquer, roughcast.

COAT, *v.* Cover, spread a covering over, plate, overlay, stratify, laminate, apply, clothe, glaze, plaster, prime, wash, incrust, smear, electroplate, silver-plate, lacquer, gown, encase, envelop, invest, wrap, jacket, whitewash, pave, shingle, sheathe, enamel, shellac, veneer, cloak, mantle,

loricate, gild, gloss, parget, weatherboard, paint, garb, daub, smear over, undercoat, superimpose, calcimine, paper, clapboard, face, robe, put on.

COATING, *n.* 1. Covering, coat, crust, clothing, incrustation, plaster, gilding, cement, plate, rind, lamella, paint, skin, capsule, cortex, membrane, chaff, pellicle, shell, husk, bran, fur, hide, fleece, film, peel, envelope, bark, epicarp, layer, veneer, pavement, shellac, lacquer, shuck, hull, scale, foil, sac, vesicle, leaf, outside, palea, cuticle, jacket, leather, flake, cyst, sheet, involucre, overlay, shingle, priming, sheathing, roughcast, calcimine, varnish, rind, pelt, lorica *(Zool.)*, pericarp, ectoderm, pod, investment, fell, outer layer, weatherboard, wool, exterior, epidermis, hair, scarfskin, plaster, whitewash, clapboard, facing, enamel.

2. Material for coats, suiting, tweed, fleece, worsted.

COAT OF MAIL, *n.* Defensive garment of interlinked metal rings, coat of overlapping metal plates, suit of armor, hauberk, habergeon, lorica, corselet, brigandine, panoply, armature, cuirass, mail, suit of mail, armor, thorax *(Antiq.)*.

COAX, *v.* Wheedle, influence by gentle persuasion, cajole, prevail upon by flattery, move, inveigle, importune, lure, invite, appeal to, manipulate, induce, tease, win over, charm, blandish, beguile, gain one's ends by playful strategy, soft-soap, coquet, soothe, adulate, vamp, entice, wile, cog, sawder *(coll.)*, persuade by fondling, caress, urge, ask affectionately, humor, honey up *(coll.)*, pet, butter *(coll.)*, fawn upon, flatter, get by flattery, tempt, attract, seduce.

COAXING, *adj.* Persuasive, winning, wheedling, bland, flattering, unctuous, cajoling, inducive, adulatory, tempting, seducing, attractive, teasing, appealing, humoring, fawning, charming, urgent, enticing, soft soap, soothing, coquettish, gentle, blandishing, oily, affectionate, beguiling, urging, importunate.

COAXING, *n.* Cajolery, blandishment, adulation, persuasion, teasing, inducement, beguilement, importunity, appeal, humoring, fawning, soft soap, coquetry, effort to influence, attempt to gain one's ends, enticement, seduction, temptation, urging, flattery, wheedling.

COBBLE, *n.* Cobblestone, cobstone, stone used in paving, naturally rounded stone, water-worn stone, round stone larger than a pebble, glacial stone.

COBBLE, *v.* 1. Pave with cobblestones.

2. Do cobbler's work, mend shoes, refurbish shoes, repair shoes, patch, sole, heel, fix shoes, restore leather goods.

3. Be a bungler, botch, put together roughly *or* clumsily, bungle, do bungling work, make roughly, be all thumbs *(coll.)*, tinker, make sad work of, work like a carpenter *(cant)*, fumble, muff, do carelessly, make a mess of *(coll.)*, spoil, mar, blemish, hash *(coll.)*, bosh *(coll.)*.

COBBLER, *n.* 1. Mender of shoes, shoemaker, bootmaker, shoe repairman, Crispin.

2. Clumsy workman, bungler, tinker, fumbler, dunce, ignoramus, blunderer, boggler, botcher, sloven, blunderbuss, butterfingers *(coll.)*, muffer *(coll.)*, bosher *(coll.)*, carpenter *(cant)*, duffer *(coll.)*, careless artisan.

COBWEB, *n.* 1. Spider's web, single thread of a web, filament, cilium, fiber, filamentule, web, capillary, veinule.

2. Network of plot *or* intrigue, entanglement, snare, toils, insidious snare, net, web, perplexity, involution, meander, labyrinth, maze, dilemma, conspiracy, confoundment, machination, paradox, quandary, disconcertion, bafflement, puzzle, nonplus, intricate plot, meshes, bewilderment, tangled skein, complex trap, vexed question.

3. Anything finespun, flimsy *or* unsubstantial, fragile fabric, flimsy *or* frail thing, froth, foam, gossamer, feather, gauze, ephemera, flue, bubble, fluff, straw, thistledown, dust, down, piece of flimsiness, spray, suds, mockery, dream, fantasy, spun glass, spume, fizz, vapor, spindrift, mesh, organdy, tissue, lace, sheer, mosquito netting, ignis fatuus *(Lat.),* voile, cheesecloth, organza, illusion, phantom, shadow, thin air, chaff.

COCK, *n.* 1. Rooster, chanticleer, cockerel, fowl, cockalorum *(dimin.),* barnyard fowl.

2. Cockcrow, crowing, rooster's call, cock-crowing.

3. Tap, valve, spigot, faucet, turn valve, stopcock.

4. Weathercock, vane, wind vane, weather vane, wind indicator.

5. Bend, curve, roll, cast, swing, pivoting, bending, perking, toss, turn.

6. Stack, pile, bank, mass, shock, gathering, rick, sheaf, haycock, hayrick, mow.

COCK, *v.* 1. Strut, swagger, bounce, roister, crow, bluff, be vainglorious, give oneself airs, flourish, glorify oneself, swashbuckle, vaunt, gasconade, vapor, rollick, inflate oneself, puff oneself up, be perky.

2. *(Of the eye)* Squint, look asquint, goggle, screw up *(the eye),* cast *(the eye),* look askance.

3. Stack, sheaf, pile, bank, heap, gather, rick, assemble, shock, collect.

4. Stick up, stand up, be vertical, stand on end, perk up, stand upright, be perpendicular, project, bristle up.

5. Set, ready, make ready for firing, set the hammer *or* cock of, prepare for firing, adjust.

COCKADE. *n.* Rosette, button, ribbon, symbol, emblem, crest, decoration, marker, insignia, device, knot, mark, badge, official shield *or* star.

COCK-A-HOOP, *adj.* Swollen, bombastic, proud, puffed up, arrogant, elated, self-esteeming, vainglorious, thrasonical, gassy *(coll.),* blown, overweening, exulting, bouncing, blustering, egotistic, vaporing, ostentatious, lexiphanic, strutting, vaunting, vain, bragging, boasting, pert, boastful, cocky, gasconading, windy, pompous.

COCKLE, *n.* Crinkle, wrinkle, pucker, fluting, corrugation, pleat, crease, rumple, fold.

COCKLE, *v.* Crinkle, fold, crumple, rumple, ripple, ruck, ruffle, flute, wrinkle, pucker, pleat, crease, corrugate, make into folds.

COCKSURE, *adj.* Presumptuous, opinionated, presumingly certain, dogmatic, confident, dead sure, positive, assured, convinced, satisfied.

COCOON, *n.* Protective envelope, chrysalis, pupa, aurelia *(esp. of lepidopterous insect).*

CODDLE, *v.* 1. Cook slowly, parboil, stew, brew, simmer, seethe.

2. Baby, caress, cocker, fondle, pamper, spoil, indulge, pet, cosset, cuddle, nurse, mollycoddle, dandle, humor, treat with fondness, make much of, dote on, pat. '

CODE, *n.* 1. Digest, body of laws, collection of laws, precepts, principles, constitution, statute, pandect. institute, ordinance, prescript, formulary,

capitulary, canon, charter.

2. Standard, principles, moral principles, propriety, decorum, ethics, morals, morality, moral code.

3. Steganogram, cryptogram, secret writing, cipher, cryptograph, prearranged signal.

CODICIL, *n.* Added provision, appendix, rider, subscript, postscript, suffix, continuation, added clause, supplement, added item, adjunct, additament, addendum, appurtenance, extension.

CODIFY, *v.* Segregate, ticket, arrange, classify, catalogue, digest, graduate, docket *(Leg.),* rank, alphabetize, tabulate, file, register, record, list, systematize, systemize, organize, methodize, co-ordinate.

COEQUAL, *adj.* Of like rank, equipollent, on the same footing, level, even, corresponding, equal, equipotential, equiponderant, parallel, uniform.

COEQUAL, *n.* Fellow, match, peer, compeer, equivalent, parallel, equipollent, confrere, mate, colleague.

COERCE, *v.* 1. Restrict, curb, restrain, constrain, control, hold back, repress, suppress, inhibit, cohibit, check, deter, discourage, disincline, stop, prevent, retard, disallow, interdict, bar, preclude, prohibit, ban, block.

2. Force, enforce, compel, intimidate, oblige, make, bear down upon, drive, press, necessitate, bully, require, dragoon, constrain, cause, induce, prevail upon, insist upon, bind, pin down, drag into, commandeer, draft, conscript, impel, apply pressure, impress.

COERCION, *n.* Pressure, obligation, compulsion, constraint, duress, enforcement, force, driving, inducement, prevailing, insistence, conscription, impelling, impressing, oppression, necessitation.

COEVAL, *adj.* Coetaneous, contemporary, of the same age *or* duration, coexistent, simultaneous, coincident, synchronous, synchronal, coexisting, contemporaneous, concomitant, coextensive.

COEXIST, *v.* Exist together, be contemporary *or* contemporaneous, be concomitant, contemporize, concur, accompany, be synchronous, go hand in hand.

COEXISTENCE, *n.* Coevality, contemporariness, coexistency, coetaneity, contemporaneousness, coincidence, synchronousness, simultaneousness, simultaneity, concomitance, concomitancy, coextension.

COEXISTENT, *adj.* Contemporary, concurrent, coinstantaneous, contemporaneous, synchronal, coeval, coetaneous, coincident, synchronous, simultaneous, concomitant, coextensive.

COFFER, *n.* Container, box, case, receptacle, bin, crib, casket, caisson, chest, shrine, holder, crate, reliquary, cabinet, canister, pyxis, caddie.

COFFIN, *n.* Casket, box, sarcophagus, catafalque, pall.

COG, *n.* Sprocket, tooth, ratchet, projection, jag, catch, saw tooth, tenon.

COG, *v.* Wheedle, cheat, befool, abuse, swindle, outwit, fleece, pluck, deceive, victimize, lure, gyp, delude, rook, dupe, gammon, mulct, hoodwink, beguile, hoax, practice upon, foist upon, defraud, overreach, cozen, chouse, trick, do, bamboozle, inveigle, humbug, fraud, entrap, ensnare.

COGENT, *adj.* Persuasive, telling, convincing, forceful, conclusive, undeniable, unquestionable, incontestable, irrefutable, past dispute, plain, sure, positive, evident, inescapable, sound, trustworthy, unanswerable, irrefragable, certain, unequivocal, infallible, authoritative, definite, incontrovertible, inducive, suasory, suasive, efficacious, weighty, influential, effective, effectual, proving, puissant, valid, demonstrating, forcible, potent, powerful.

COGITATE, *v.* 1. Speculate, contemplate, think, mull over, deliberate, ruminate, meditate, ponder, consider, weigh, muse, concentrate upon, think over, reflect, turn over mentally, con over, dream, trouble one's head about, bethink, apply oneself *(mentally),* be absorbed, ransack the brains, put on one's thinking cap, cudgel the brains, revolve, commune, be engrossed in thought, excogitate, cerebrate, mentalize, intellectualize, philosophize, envision, conceive, imagine.
2. Plan, scheme, plot, hatch a plot, conspire, complot, machinate, design, contrive, concoct a plot, devise, intrigue, cabal, frame a plan, concert.

COGITATION, *n.* 1. Thought, thinking, musing, contemplation, deliberation, meditation, reverie, pondering, weighing, concentration, deliberating, reflection, reflecting, meditating, contemplating, bethinking, absorption, communion, mentalizing, communing, cerebrating, intellectualizing, brown study, revolving, philosophizing, excogitation, rumination, excogitating, application, engrossment.
2. Impression, idea, notion, thought, inkling, reflection, supposition, suspicion, consideration, perception.

COGNATE, *adj.* 1. Allied, related, affiliated, akin, associated, germane, apposite, connatural, alike, paronymous, equiparant, co-ordinate, congeneric, kindred, similar, common, generic, correlative, corresponding, correspondent, affined, collateral.
2. Uterine, consanguine, consanguineous, akin, related, kindred, agnate, german, germane, enatic, relative, fraternal, sororal.

COGNITION, *n.* Knowledge, knowing, wisdom, comprehension, perception, notion, grasp, insight, awareness, cognizance, familiarity, apprehension, acquaintance, apperception, enlightenment, ken, discernment, penetration, intelligence, sensibility, understanding, conversance, conversancy.

COGNIZANCE, *n.* 1. Awareness, consciousness, sensibility, conversance, conversancy, perception, understanding, intelligence, wisdom, penetration, apprehension, notion, grasp, familiarity, cognition, apperception, insight, discernment, enlightenment.
2. Heed, notice, attention, observation, regard, note, scrutiny, study, concentration, inspection, consideration, attentiveness, perusal, examination, investigation.
3. Sign, mark, stamp, brand, token, label, base, livery, uniform, device, crest, heraldic bearing, charge, arms, armorial bearing, escutcheon, field, blazon, coat of arms, depiction, chief, sinister, dexter, fess, heart, nombril, brassard, hatchment, navel, shield, supporters.

COGNIZANT, *adj.* Informed, aware, alive, awake, sensible, conscious, versed, conversant, apprised, acquainted, knowing, perceptive, familiar, wise, discerning, enlightened, intelligent, apperceptive, understanding, cognitive, no stranger to, posted, instructed, well-grounded, knowledgeable, well-conned.

COGNIZE, *v.* Know, take knowledge of, realize, comprehend (the point *or* meaning), understand, have knowledge of, recognize, heed, attend, seize, regard, consider, study, discern, be cognizant of, have cognizance of, fathom, conceive, apprehend, grasp, perceive, be aware of, take notice, observe,

be conscious of, scrutinize, take in, ken, make out, con, gain insight into, gain an impression of, become familiar with, be informed, be sensible of, be conversant with, penetrate, see.

COGNOMEN, *n.* Name, nomination, alias, title, pet name, epithet, cognomination, pseudonym, designation, appellative, appellation, patronymic, denomination, sobriquet, nickname, surname, family name, handle *(sl.),* moniker *(sl.),* by-name, compellation, signature, diminutive name, last name, assumed name. autograph.

COHABIT, *v.* Live together, abide together, dwell together, lodge together, reside together, stay together, room together.

COHERE, *v.* 1. Adhere, set, coagulate, condense, stick together, hold fast, cleave, be attached, hold to, hold together, consolidate, be connected, join, clasp, coalesce, solidify, cement, cake, congeal, stick fast, cling, stick to, agglutinate, be joined, remain constant, concrete, be spliced, be clinched, jelly, gel, gelatinate, consolidate, be bound, be tacked together, be fastened, be glued, be made fast, densify, clabber, be pasted, be cemented, inspissate, curdle, clot, thicken, fuse, fasten, seal, attach, fix, bind, unite, conjoin, affix, combine, unify, connect, weld, compress, squeeze, braze, solder, paste, glue, crystallize, harden, indurate, conglutinate, amalgamate.
2. *(With* WITH) Suit, agree, fit, accord, tally, coincide, square, converge, reconcile, comport, conform, concur, harmonize, correspond, jibe *(coll.),* quadrate.
3. Be consistent, hold good, be common sense, be logically consistent, be rationally connected, be accordant, make sense, be convergent, possess firmness, be congruous, possess solidity, accord with, correspond, agree with, harmonize, tally with, be logically evident, hold water, have basic similarity, make accordant, assent, hold up, hold together, assimilate, be vitally connected, appeal to reason, be related, be associated, be adaptable to, stand to reason, conform to, square with, be reasonable, withstand assault, stand unrefuted, defy criticism.

COHERENCE, *n.* 1. Cohesion, adherence, fusion, agglutination, coagulation, consolidation, sticking, concretion, cementation, congelation, union, set, conglomeration, firm hold, connection, junction, agglomeration, solidification, dependence, clutch, accretion, aggregation, soldering, conglutination, sticking together, conjunction, adhesion, concert, firmness, coherency, amalgamation, homogeneity, tenaciousness, viscosity, inseparability, iron grip, fusion, conglomerate, perseverance, agglomerate, viscidity, indivisibility, condensation, stickiness, glutinousness, retention, tenacity, grasp, embrace, glutinosity, toughness, prehension, interrelation, coadunation, compression, prehensility, blending, interlinking, coalescence, confluence, maintaining, interlocking, stability, maintenance, consistency, fixity, unity, attachment.
2. Consistency, concurrence, correspondence, connection, congruity, accord, intelligibleness, accordance, comprehensibleness, harmony, unity, concord, cognizability, agreement, concordance, conformity, explicability, rationality, concinnity, rapport *(Fr.),* decipherability, comprehensibility, intelligibility, consonance, congruence, legibility, intelligible meaning, conformance, assimilation, correspondency, coincidence, understandability, penetrability, adaptation, apprehensibility.

COHERENT, *adj.* 1. Connected, consolidated,

coagulative, united, concretive, coagulated, firm, adherent, cemented, agglutinative, conglutinative, sticking together, congealed, agglutinate, sticky, cleaving together, cohering, tough, viscid, unified, convergent, compact, converging, cohesive, fixed, grasping, accreted, prehensile, conjoined, joined, compressed, retentive, concerted, amalgamative, confluent, indivisible, adhering, stable, clutching, inseparable, adhesive, conglutinative, interlinked, viscous, interlocked, glutinous, soldered, gripping, interrelated, persevering, accretive, coadunate, tenacious, solid, agglomerative, agglomerate, solidified, conglomerate, conglomeratic, blended, combined, set, homogeneous, aggregate, holding firmly, condensed, fused, coalesced, coalescent.

2. Consistent, meaningful, concurrent, logical, congruous, correspondent, consonant, accordant, corresponding, intelligible, harmonious, unified, concordant, in agreement, in rapport, congruent, in conformity, rational, in keeping, coincident, distinguishable, logically appealing, assimilated, connected, comprehensible, cognizable, legible, comprehendible, understandable, decipherable, apprehensible, explicable, conceivable, penetrable.

COHESION, *n.* 1. Coherence, consistency, union, adherence, agglutination, attachment, coagulation, consolidation, fusion, concretion, cementation, sticking, congelation, conglomeration, firm hold, set, connection, agglomeration, solidification, dependence, junction, accretion, conglutination, aggregation, soldering, sticking together, concert, conjunction, adhesion, firmness, amalgamation, coherency, homogeneity, tenaciousness, viscosity, inseparability, clutch, iron grip, indivisibility, conglomerate, perseverance, viscidity, stickiness, condensation, glutinousness, retention, tenacity, agglomerate, glutinosity, toughness, prehension, grasp, interrelation, coadunation, compression, prehensility, interlinking, coalescence, confluence, maintaining, interlocking, blending, maintenance, stability, fixity, embrace, unity.

2. Cohesive force, compression, conglutination, cohesive attraction, coalescence, conglomeration, accretion, viscosity, blending, adhesion, viscidity, aggregation, toughness, solidification, fusion, agglutination, conglomerate, agglomeration, glutinosity, amalgamation, glutinousness, condensation, agglomerate, homogeneity.

COHORT, *n.* Band, company, swarm, contingent, horde, legion, throng, host, force, squadron, body, battery, troop, regiment, phalanx, platoons, army, groups, multitude of troops *or* soldiers, brigade, column, detachment, wing, division, corps, units, garrison, sections.

COIFFURE, *n.* Hairdo, permanent wave, bun, permanent, pompadour, upsweep, bangs, pigtail, braid, plait, curls, chignon, hair-arrangement, tress.

COIL, *n.* Spiral, rings, circles, windings, whorl, corkscrew, convolution, tendril *(Bot.)*, twirl, roll, helix, volute, worm, scallop, kink, contortion, crook, helicoid, screw, curlicue.

COIL, *v.* Spiral, wind, convolve, twirl, twist, turn, serpentine, screw, curl, plait, braid, plat, raddle, intort, worm, reel, incurvate, entwine, sinuate, wreath, wheel, intervolve.

COIN, *n.* 1. Quoin, wedge, corner, cornerstone, keystone, voussoir, bight, angle.

2. *(Often indicates plural)* Specie, change, hard money, silver, piece, silver *or* gold pieces, copper, hard cash, coinage, rouleau *(roll of coins)*, jingler

(sl.), chinker *(sl.)*, button *(sl.)*, chicken feed *(sl.)*, mintage.

COIN, *v.* 1. Coin, mint, monetize, circulate, issue, put into circulation, stamp coins.

2. Produce, invent, bring about, evolve, hatch, originate, contrive, fabricate, create, devise, make up, concoct, frame, innovate, neologize, dream up, neoterize.

COINAGE, *n.* 1. Specie, change, silver, silver *or* gold pieces, piece, copper, hard cash, hard money, coins, chinker *(sl.)*, jingler *(sl.)*, buttons *(sl.)*, chicken feed *(sl.)*, rouleau *(roll of coins)*.

2. Creation, device, contrivance, fabrication, neologism, neoteric, concoction, innovation, invention, introduction.

3. Making of coins, coining, minting, stamping, circulating, monetizing, monetization.

COINCIDE, *v.* 1. Agree, comport, cohere, accord, suit, match, equal, concur, correspond, quadrate, square, tally, be equivalent, be equal, harmonize, be synonymous, reciprocate, jibe *(coll.)*, fall into agreement.

2. Exist together, be concomitant, accompany, be synonymous, reciprocate, jibe *(coll.)*, fall into, be contemporaneous, be coeval, be simultaneous, be coincident, be contiguous, be concurrent, go with.

COINCIDENCE, *n.* 1. Agreement, concurrence, concurring, connaturalness, equality, synonymity, concord, coherence, conformance, identicalness, accord, consistency, Homoousia, congruency, uniformity, accordance, harmony, concinnity, congruity, consonance, consonancy, parallelism, affinity, apposition, concomitance, correlation, concomitancy.

2. Concomitancy, concomitance, coextension, simultaneity, simultaneousness, synchronousness, contemporaneousness, coexistence, coadunation, contemporariness, coevality, congruity, conflux, coexistency, coetaneity, contingence, confluence, contiguousness.

COINCIDENT, *adj.* 1. Coinciding, synonymous, equivalent, alike, comparable, similar, consilient, corresponding, coordinate, confluent, concurring, concurrent, coadunate, joint, conjoint, conjunct, copulate, united, combined, linked, unified.

2. Contemporary, coinstantaneous, coextensive, concomitant, contemporaneous, simultaneous, synchronal, coexistent, coetaneous, concurrent, coeval, collateral.

COINCIDENTAL, *adj* . Simultaneous, synchronal, coinstantaneous, synchronous, synchronic, synchronical.

COINER, *n.* 1. Neologist *(of words)*, fabricator, maker, neoterist, innovator, inventor, concocter, deviser, framer, creator.

2. Coin maker, coin stamper, mint master, moneyer.

COITUS, *n.* Coition, sexual intercourse, congress, union, copulation, fornication, sexual conjunction.

COLD, *adj.* 1. Devoid of warmth, heatless, cool, cooled, frosted, frigid, chill, chilly, coolish, icy, chilled, frozen, unwarmed, unheated, gelid, algid, unthawed, unmelted, refrigerated, extinguished, lukewarm, tepid, burned out, ice-cold, draughty, sunless, barren, frosty, breezy, dead *(hearth)*, damped, choked, quenched, annihilated, snuffed, windy, airy, unkindled, congealed, invigorated, glaciated, frappé *(Fr.)*, regelated, chilled through, frozen stiff, frostbitten, numbed, goose-fleshed, frost-nipped, chilled to the marrow, chilled to the bone, pinched, mortally chilled, quaking, shaking, quivering, trembling, shuddering, shivering, fireless, aguish.

2. Bleak, brisk, penetrating, frozen, nipping, biting, nippy, sleety, cutting, snappy, frosty, rimy, piercing, chill, pinching, chilly, icicled, boreal, arctic, polar, keen, inclement, snowy, icy, wintry, rigorous, blasting, brumal, algid, gelid, ice-like, ice-cold, cool, bitter, frigid, sharp, frosted, severe, frost-beaded, numbing, frost-chequered, hibernal, hoary, hoarfrosted, shivery, freezing, hyperboreal, hyperborean, chilling, glacial, Siberian, intense, zippy, frost-fettered, teeth-chattering, frost-riven, rime-frosted, bone-chilling, frost-rent, marrow-chilling, stern, harsh, intemperate, slushy, crisp, stinging.

3. Apathetic, heartless, unemotional, reserved, unsympathetic, unresponsive, distant, phlegmatic, stoical, cruel, unfeeling, aloof, hard, passionless, unsusceptible, unimpressible, without heart, icy, frigid, freezing, unconcerned, indifferent, torpid, cold-blooded, dead, sluggish, lukewarm, neutral, impartial, untroubled, unruffled, stolid, averse, insouciant, antipathetic, adverse, serene, poised, calm, antagonistic, hostile, composed, collected, unhurried, bristling, inimical, unperturbed, stiff, unembarrassed, supercilious, reticent, unkindled, hateful, disdainful, disinterested, uninterested, undemonstrative, spiritless, scathing, withering, unfriendly, contemptuous, haughty, chill, formal, unapproachable, inaccessible, forbidding, remote, unimpressionable, unimpassioned, condescending, nonchalant, unmindful, harsh, listless, insensible, half-hearted, impassive, uncommunicative, stony, flinty, steely, irreligious, Laodicean, unambitious, calculous, comatose, adamantine, numb, supine, repellant, unexcitable, languid, undesirous, inert, unsolicitous, callous, obdurate, thick-skinned, unfeeling, soulless, insensitive, hardened, obtuse, sharp, lethargic, bitter, insentient, pococurante, unmoved, incurious, unstirred, untouched, inured, impervious, uncaring, indurated, unanimated, inanimate, cold-hearted.

4. Unaffecting, uninspired, uninteresting, flat, insipid, vapid, spiritless, dull, dead, poor, lifeless, uninspiring, wanting in spirit, lacking in fervor, commonplace, unconvincing, tame, weak, without savor, unanimated, meager, passable, mediocre, ordinary, inconsiderable, unimportant, bloodless, insignificant, drab, uncompelling, indifferent, fair, lackluster, immaterial, inconsequential, trifling, unfruitful, unrewarding, undesirable, unalluring, average, middling, unprepossessing, unattractive, paltry, small, petty, slight, inferior, inappreciable, pallid, colorless, etiolated.

5. Untouched by desire, frigid, unimpassioned, indifferent, without passion, undemonstrative, coldly chaste, unnatural, platonic, reserved, incapable of emotion, wanting ardor, repelled, unresponsive, without natural feeling, passive.

COLD, *n.* 1. Absence of warmth, chill, chilliness, want of heat, tepidity, algor, gelidity, coolness, lukewarmness, refrigeration, shivering, frostbite, goose flesh, horripilation, numbness, congelation, frostiness, mortal chill, iciness, shivers, glaciation, draught, regelation.

2. Coldness, freshness, briskness, chilliness, chill, algidity, gelidity, frost, iciness, bleakness, rawness, sharpness, bite, cut, bitterness, teeth *(of the wind),* Boreas, crispness, severity, frigidity, hoar, rime, coolness, rigor, cold snap, Jack Frost, freezing weather, inclemency.

3. Catarrh, rheum, ague, cough, coryza, cold in the head, ptyalism, rhinitis *(Med.),* hay fever,

rose fever, rose cold, asthma, grippe, influenza, flu *(coll.),* common cold, laryngitis, bronchitis, whooping cough, pertussis.

COLD-BLOODED, *adj.* 1. Apathetic, heartless, unemotional, unsympathetic, unresponsive, cruel, reserved, distant, phlegmatic, stoical, unfeeling, aloof, hard, unsusceptible, unimpressible, without heart, frigid, freezing, passionless, unconcerned, indifferent, impartial, untroubled, disinterested, unruffled, averse, insouciant, cold, dead, torpid, sluggish, lukewarm, neutral, antipathetic, formal, adverse, antagonistic, hostile, composed, listless, collected, bristling, inimical, unperturbed, hateful, unembarrassed, supercilious, reticent, unkindled, disdainful, uninterested, undemonstrative, remote, spiritless, scathing, withering, unfriendly, harsh, contemptuous, haughty, chill, unapproachable, icy, inaccessible, stiff, forbidding, unimpassioned, unimpressionable, nonchalant, unmindful, flinty, insensible, half-hearted, impassive, condescending, uncommunicative, steely, irreligious, Laodicean, repellant, languid, supine, undesirous, calculous, inert, unsolicitous, callous, comatose, adamantine, numb, unexcitable, unambitious, obdurate, stony, thick-skinned, unfeeling, soulless, pococurante, insensitive, hardened, obtuse, sharp, lethargic, bitter, insentient, unmoved, incurious, unstirred, untouched, impervious, uncaring, cold-hearted, inured, indurated, unanimated, inanimate.

2. Deliberate, brutal, cruel, cold, calculating, cool, calculated, heartless, cruel-hearted, bestial, unrelenting, relentless, of evil intent, remorseless, inhuman, unfeeling, ruthless, incompassionate, cold-hearted, pitiless, brutish, savage, inhumane, diabolic, diabolical, demoniac, nefarious, fiendish, Stygian, insidious, fiendlike, devilish, unmerciful, brute, virulent, satanic, unpitying, predetermined, merciless, splenetic, barbarous, unsympathetic, revengeful, inclement, inexorable, treacherous, invidious, unsympathizing, malign, ill-intentioned, malignant, malicious, malevolent, uncharitable, truculent, punitive, vengeful, unkind, despiteful, spiteful, uncordial, insensitive, venomous, hard, unnatural, bloodless, hard-hearted, stony-hearted, flint-hearted, punitory, implacable, bloodthirsty, villainous, flagitious, sanguinary, premeditated, callous, retaliative, immitigable, retaliatory, prepense, envenomed, maledictory, maledictive, despotic, tyrranical, imprecatory, Procrustean, tyrannic.

COLISEUM, *n.* Arena, amphitheater, hippodrome, circus, statium, campus *(Rom. Antiq.),* theater, bowl, field *(for public displays),* Colosseum.

COLLABORATE, *v.* Co-operate, work together, coadjute, coact, work side by side, pull together, concur, labor jointly, conspire, affiliate with, team up.

COLLABORATOR, *n.* Associate, assistant, ally, helper, helpmate, co-helper, co-worker, copartner, adjunct, confederate, colleague, consociate, aid, attendant, confrere, teammate, aider, adjuvant, adjutant, co-operator.

COLLAPSE, *n.* 1. Breakdown, downfall, fiasco, debacle, tumble, smash, prostration, fall, utter failure, dead failure, defeat, destruction, abortion, calamity, cataclysm, catastrophe, flop, slump, cave-in, crackup, break, washout *(sl.),* surrender, deluge, demolition, bankruptcy, overthrow, havoc, discomfiture, desolation, devastation, insolvency, disaster, rout, crash, ruin, checkmate, dissolution, sudden contraction, failure, explosion, smash-up, falling in pieces, falling together, falling apart, nonfulfillment, vain attempt, abortive attempt, comedown (coll.), letdown (coll.), ill success, unfulfillment, unsuccessfulness.

2. Prostration, debility, exhaustion, lipothymy (Med.), extreme depression, sudden illness, fall, nervous breakdown, stroke, weakness, attack, seizure, sudden helplessness, swoon, relapse, coma, syncope (Med.).

COLLAPSE, v. 1. Fall down, fall together, cave in a crash, give way, fall inward or outward, fall to pieces, close together, crumple, crumple up, break apart, tumble, fall into ruin, fold at will (for storage or transportation), contract suddenly, fall through lack of support, be demolished, be pulled down, be cut down, be blown down, be torn down, be felled.

2. Break down, fail, come to nothing, misfire, miscarry, backfire, flounder, fail utterly, go up in smoke, go out in smoke, vanish in thin air, fold up, fail abruptly, not succeed, flop (sl.), fall through, peter out (sl.), fall flat, crash, explode, blow up, be in vain, miss the mark, abort, go amiss, go astray, go to wrack and ruin, dash one's hopes, fall short, miss fire, run aground, come to grief, sink, flunk, flunk out, strike out, have the ground cut out from under one, not have a leg to stand on, acknowledge defeat, surrender, have the wind taken out of one's sails, lick the dust, bite the dust, fall prey, fall victim, be impotent, not make the grade (sl.), cave in, suffer defeat, be disarmed, be undermined, be hamstrung, be checkmated, be incapacitated, be overthrown, bog down, slump, contract suddenly, kick the beam, fizzle out (coll.), smash up, crack up, go broke (coll.), go bankrupt, be gazetted, go up (coll.), go to the dogs (coll.), go to pot (coll.), go on the rocks, go to the wall, become bankrupt, be ruined, become insolvent, fold.

3. Suffer physical breakdown, suffer mental breakdown, fall prostrate, faint, swoon, fall in a swoon, drop, succumb, suffer a relapse, keel over (coll.), be exhausted, give way, fall through lack of support, suffer nervous breakdown, become suddenly helpless, buckle (coll.), suffer a stroke, take sick, become ill, suffer acutely, be stricken, crumple.

COLLAR, n. Neckband, neckpiece, boa, ruff (mainly Hist.), rabato (Hist.), collaret, ruche, gorget, bertha, carcanet.

COLLAR, v. Seize, capture, lay by the heels, take into custody, catch, trap, ensnare, lay hold of, grab, clasp, arrest, apprehend, bag, ravish, rape, take by assault, clutch, fasten upon, nab (sl.), snag, snare, take prisoner, kidnap, abduct.

COLLATE, v. Compare (texts, etc.), edit, revise, prepare, redact, match, analogize, compare notes, put alongside of or set alongside of or set over against (of texts), compare critically, compile.

COLLATERAL, adj. 1. Secondary, supporting, subordinate, incidental, lateral, side by side, relative, accessory, accidental, ancillary, adjuvant, subsidiary, connected, contributory, associated, contributing, dependent, affiliated, auxiliary.

2. Supportive, ratificatory, corroboratory, supporting, verificative, sustaining, warranting, certifying, validating, endorsing, confirmatory, upholding, bearing out, affirming.

3. Concomitant, contemporaneous, coinciding, synchronal, simultaneous, coetaneous, coincident, coeval, coexistent, concurrent, accompanying.

4. Corroborated, established, authenticated, endorsed, ratified, verified, sustained, supported,

confirmed, secured, pignorate, avouched for, guaranteed, warranted, bonded, underwritten, insured, attested to, vouched for.

COLLATERAL, n. Insurance, security, guarantee, pledge, warrant, warranty, pignus (Leg.), plight, endorsement, gage, pignoration.

COLLATION, n. 1. Description, examination, determining (a text), editing, preparing (a text), comparative estimate, revision, compilation, redaction.

2. Light meal, light repast, refreshment, lunch, simple meal, refection, snack, bite (coll.), frugal meal, déjeuner (Fr.).

COLLEAGUE, n. Companion, accessory, fellow-worker, associate, mate, compeer, confederate, accomplice, helpmate, coadjutor, copartner, ally, adjunct, coadjutor, consociate, attendant, fellow, confrere, co-operator, collaborator, teammate, aid, aider, assistant, colaborer, adjuvant, consort, coadjutant, accompanier, coadjutrix, comrade, coadjutress, partner.

COLLECT, v. 1. Assemble, call together, gather, convene, summon, muster, congregate, convoke, bring together, rally, come together, group, hire, flock together, round up (coll.), round in (sl.), cluster, join, unite, meet, gang up (coll.), crowd, foregather, swarm, bunch up, concentrate, surge, center round, throng, herd, associate, huddle, go into a huddle, rendezvous, get together, rejoin, reunite, reassemble.

2. Accumulate, assemble, amass, gather, heap up, glean, garner, aggregate, compile, acquire, raise (funds, contributions), scrape together, get, congregate, conglomerate, draw together, obtain, pack together, hoard, scrape up, bring together, get together, lump together, harvest, get in, whip in, gather in, pile up, rake up, reap, levy, batch together, bunch together, pile, mass, bunch, cull, provide, pick up, agglomerate, demand and obtain payment, heap, pack, group, unite, store, store up, store away, lay in, dig up, husband, file away, stash (sl.), cache, stow away, treasure up, save up, stock, deposit, purchase, recover, reposit.

3. Infer, deduce, gather, draw an inference, consider probable, derive, reckon (coll.), suppose, calculate (coll.), presume, surmise, imagine, fancy.

4. (Of oneself) Regain command of (oneself, one's powers), pick up the pieces (coll.), muster one's strength, gather one's wits, pull oneself together (coll.), recover one's poise, rally one's forces, prepare to begin again, screw up one's courage (coll.), renew one's courage, face the world again (coll.), compose oneself.

COLLECTANEA, n. Excerpts, collection, garland, anthology, compilation, ana, collectarium (Eccl.), thesaurus, florilegium, treasury, miscellany, posy, gathering, chrestomathy, corpus, spicilege, album, analects, delectus.

COLLECTED, adj. Composed, calm, quiet, cool, restrained, nonchalant, serene, placid, quiescent, imperturbable, tranquil, inexcitable, inirritable, unruffled, level-headed, self-controlled, balanced, sane, self-possessed, poised, self-assured, even-tempered, undisturbed, untroubled, cool-headed, steady, recollected, dispassionate, unemotional, peaceful, dégagé (Fr.), at ease, unstirred, temperate, undemonstrative.

COLLECTION, n. 1. Assembly, group, heap, mass, pack, confluence, aggregation, massing, drove, concentration, number, conflux, body, raft, throng, concourse, collocation, colligation, lot, crowd, medley, hodgepodge, swarm, garnering, hoard, set, store, assortment, jumble, array, bevy, clutter, variety, batch, bunch, miscellany, flock, compilation, pile, clump, cluster, concentration, muster, congregation, multitude, stack, gleaning, cumulation, series, gathering, accumulation.

2. Anthology, compilation, ana, collectanea, collectarium (Eccl.), miscellany, delectus, posy, treasury, florilegium, thesaursus, corpus, album, chrestomathy, garland, gathering, spicilege, analects.

3. Composure, calm, quiet, restraint, serenity, placidity, imperturbation, quiescence, quietness, tranquillity, coolness, quietism, quietude, balance, inexcitability, inirritability, level-headedness, self-control, equanimity, self-possession, presence of mind, self-command, poise, aplomb, even temper, self-assurance, constraint, nonchalance.

4. Offertory, donations, oblation, gift.

COLLECTIVE, adj. Collected, comprehensive, gathered, aggregate, composite, as one, unified, accumulated, accumulative, cumulative, majority, cooperative, concerted, representative, in a body, integrated, sum total, mutual, integrative, joint, congregational, congregative, conglobate, of one mind, concurrent, congregate, consonant, of the same mind, cooperative, coadjutant, coactive, coadjuvant, coadunate, coadunative, corporate, like-minded, correal (Civ. Law), leagued, federal, enleagued, compiled (of literary works), of plural origin, of group origin, considered together, seeking harmony and mutual benefit (as with bargaining, farm), federate, federative, compound, confederate, corporative.

COLLECTIVISM, n. Socialism, communion, community of possessions, common ownership, nationalism, social democracy, communalism, communism, Marxism, Bolshevism, Sovietism, communization, communalization.

COLLEGE, n. 1. Company, group, body, guild, association, establishment, league, union, society, corporation, corporate body, community, trust, assemblage, committee, council.

2. University, seminary, academy, school, hall, institute (of learning, technology, etc.), lyceum, polytechnic, conservatory, atheneum, palaestra, gymnasium, varsity (coll.), phrontistery (often derog.), Alma Mater.

COLLIDE, v. Clash, meet, meet head on, run into, crack up, come together, bump into, dash, encounter, smash, impinge, strike against, come into collision, jostle, hit, beat against, hurtle against, knock into, run or fall foul of, buffet, jounce, jolt, jar, butt.

COLLIER, n. 1. Coal miner, coal digger, digger, excavator, miner, ground hog, strip miner.

2. Coal dealer, coal merchant, dealer in coals, coal salesman, coal retailer, coal wholesaler.

3. Coal transport, coaler, coaling vessel, coal barge, coal lighter, coal hoy, coal freighter.

COLLIERY, n. Coal mine, mine, shaft, pit, coal-pit, strip pit, strip mine, excavation.

COLLIGATE, v. 1. Bind, unite, tie, collocate, fasten together, combine, fagot, strap, chain, bundle, bale, gather, assemble, lash, collect, set in order, package, parcel, clump, cluster, group, bunch, shock, aggregate, imbricate, arrange, lump together, join, bind up together, reduce to order, compose, align, sheaf.

2. Gather for logical study, accumulate, unify, derive (a principal), amass, assemble, compile, collocate, generalize from particulars, induce, form into a logical whole, combine, unite, bring

into unity, systematize, methodize, harmonize, co-ordinate, organize, regulate, reduce to order, join, incorporate, arrange, consolidate, classify, codify.

COLLISION, n. 1. Clash, crash, bump, smash, automobile accident, blow, violent encounter, shock, smash-up, jarring, running into, running afoul of, falling afoul of, striking together, fray, appulse, impact, sudden contact, concussion, duel, affray, brush, sharp contest, encounter, tilt, joust, impingement, passage at arms, dogfight, clash of arms, tourney, tournament, tussle, scuffle, riot, contest, combat, disturbance, battle, conflict, action, engagement, skirmish, fight, strife, open rupture, struggle, disruption, brawl, squabble, quarrel, repulse, repulsion, melee, fisticuffs, reencounter, fracas, litigation, scrap (coll.), affair, wrangle, spat (coll.), interruption, interception, check, arrest, jostling.

2. (Of sounds) Percussion, clash, clashing, crashing, dissonance, cacophony, stridor, discord, harshness, atonalism, stridence, raucousness, raucity, stridency, sourness, Babel, bedlam, din, pandemonium, racket, clang, clangor, roar, hell let loose, vociferation, caterwauling, diaphony, confusion worse confounded, atonality, concordia discors (Lat.).

3. Interference, clashing, opposition, conflict, contention, clash, clashing, opposure, strong disagreement, impugnment, contradiction, cross fire, contravention, oppugnance, oppugnancy, impugnation, wrangle, cross current, running counter, counteraction, violent encounter, contest, contention, altercation, strife, struggle, argument, controversy, working at cross purposes, crossing up, jostling, litigation, dispute, disputation, check, interruption, interception, arrest, words.

COLLOCATE, v. Place, assemble, gather, collect, colligate, set, dispose, marshal, array, lay, allot, arrange, install, collate, regulate, put, methodize, organize, co-ordinate, settle, file, systematize, list, codify, digest, set in order, catalogue, tabulate, put in array, sort, allocate, group, line up, rank, align, apportion, grade, graduate, distribute, post, classify, locate, station, situate, deposit, reposit, establish, fix, lodge, assign to a place, consign to a place, quarter, billet.

COLLOCATION, n. Arrangement, placement, disposal, disposition, situation, disposure, placing, grouping, emplacement, distribution, organizing, lodgment, allocation, fixation, sorting, assortment, allotment, deposition, reposition, establishment, apportionment, organization, graduation, division, classification, table, taxonomy (Biol.), biotaxy (Biol.), systematizing, series, order, array, medley, sequence, succession, progression, consecution, collation, codification, categorization, congruence, analysis, assemblage, correspondence, miscellany, correspondency, colligation, congruity, collection, pyramid, pile.

COLLOQUIAL, adj. (Of speech) Conversational, informal, non-literary, familiar, unstudied, local, ordinary, common, unguided, unguarded, of the folk, spontaneous, casual, popular, unwitting, unthinking, vulgar, vernacular, everyday, jargony, unliterary, chatty, undignified, slangy, dialectical, jargonal, dialectal, dialectic, simple, unadorned, plain, homespun, unaffected, unfeigning, homely, unassuming, inartificial, unpretending, workday, plebeian, household, Philistine, natural, native, provincial, undistinguished, modest, artless, naïve, unsophisticated, untutored, unrefined, uncultured, ingenuous, confabulatory, uneducated, shoptalk.

COLLOQUIALISM, *n.* Common speech, dialect, slang, jargon, the vernacular, informality, lingo, familiarity, shop talk, chattiness, ordinariness, commonness, naturalness, spontaneity, simplicity, inartificiality, lack of sophistication, Philistinism, plainness, homeliness, modesty, ingenuousness, lack of pretense, lack of presumption, artlessness, naïveté, native speech, lack of affectation, provincialism, localism, non-literary speech, confabulation.

COLLOQUY, *n.* Dialogue, collocution, converse, conversation, talk, interlocution, debate, speech, conference, disquisition, consultation, discourse, caucus, junta, mutual discourse, interchange of views, verbal intercourse, reasoning together, convention, interview, duologue, trialogue, trial, congress, exchange of views, discussion, talking over, parlance, counsel, parley, negotiation, joint study, session, palaver, consideration, committee meeting, conclave, board meeting, dialogism, council.

COLLUDE, *v.* 1. Participate in fraud, conspire, connive, be partners in crime, confederate, work together surreptitiously, conspire fraudulently, go hand in glove, plot, scheme, cabal, intrigue, play into each other's hands, machinate, concur with evil design, co-operate toward a fraud, act in secret concert.
2. Abet, incite, tolerate, ignore, disregard, be wilfully negligent, overlook, wink at, acquiesce, foment, blink at, shut one's eyes, regard with indulgence, incite by neglect.

COLLUSION, *n.* Colluding, connivance, intrigue, conspiracy, secret understanding for fraud, cabal, conspiring, deceit, fraud, guilty association, plot, confederation, machination, trickery, combination for fraud, participation in fraud, co-operation for fraud, scheme, collusiveness, knavery, pact, legal tricks, concurrence, subreption, slippery dealing, chicanery, pettifoggery, pettifogging, chicane, sharp practice, secret association, guile.

COLLUSIVE, *adj.* Deceitful, conniving, deceptive, fraudulent, conspiratorial, conspirative, dishonest, conspiratorial, trickish, tricky, deceptious, shifty, deceptitious, deceiving, covinous *(Law),* delusory, delusive, flam, cajoling, done in collusion, artful, planned in collusion, insidious, guileful, illusive, illusory, rascally, intriguing, vulpine, designing, crafty, perfidious, slippery, underhand, spurious, treacherous, double-dealing, confidential, furtive, unscrupulous, subreptitious, obreptitious, illicitly covert, untrustworthy, clandestine, underhanded, sly, undercover, hollow-hearted.

COLONIAL, *adj.* Daughter, provincial, Pilgrim, early American, immigrant, emigrant, pioneering, pioneer, imperial, oversea, outland, Anglo-Indian, Puritan, dependent, territorial, dominion, frontier, protectoral, mandated, pre-Revolutionary.

COLONIAL, *n.* Colonist, colonizer, homesteader, founder, Patriot, squatter, nester *(West. U.S.),* Anglo-Indian, habitant *(Can. and La.),* Pilgrim, metic *(Gr. antiq.),* Puritan, redemptioner, settler, planter, pioneer, immigrant, emigrant, emigree, émigré *(Fr.),* outlander, frontiersman.

COLONIST, *n.* Colonial, colonizer, redemptioner, Pilgrim, settler, outlander, pioneer, Anglo-Indian, immigrant, emigrant, planter, Puritan, squatter, emigree, émigré *(Fr.),* Patriot, founder, habitant *(Can. and La.),* nester *(West. U.S.),* homesteader, frontiersman, metic *(Gr. antiq.).*

COLONIZATION, *n.* Settlement, settling, group migration, establishment, establishing, plantation, clearing, founding, peopling, striking roots, expanding, expansion, forging a new home.

COLONNADE, *n.* *(Arch.)* Columns, pillars, row (of trees, posts, etc.), portico, gallery, arcade, peristyle, cloisters, peripteros, columniation, piazza, corridor, columnar building, covered way, series, veranda *(U.S. and Can.),* ambulatory.

COLONY, *n.* Province, clearing, group migration, daughter country, new land, settlement, mandate, dependency, possession, dominion, community, territory, plantation, protectorate, hive, cluster, group, satellite state *or* province, home in the wilderness, swarm, political possession.

COLOR, *n.* 1. Hue, tone, tint, value, intensity, tinge, shade, cast, coloration, coloring, tincture, tinct, chroma, chromaticity, colorimetric quality, undertone, iridescence, chromism, chromatism, polychromasia, luminosity.
2. Pigment, dye, paint, coloring matter, stain, colorant, crayon, coloring, tinction, chromogen, dyestuff, tincture, medium, vehicle, pigmentation, tempera, distemper, nuance.
3. Redness, blush, flush, rosiness, rubescence, bloom, ruddiness, freshness of complexion, glow, rubicundity, erubescence, sanguinity, complexion, floridity, warm complexion, suffusion, race, caste, red complexion, hue of skin.
4. Plea, guise, disguise, pretext, excuse, front, appearance, semblance, false show, justification, outward show, pretense, makeshift, complexion, external appearance, air, turn, cast, ostent, image, prejudice, extenuation, aspect, carriage, bearing, effect, evasion, lip homage, slant, bias, varnish, mein, ostensible ground, ruse, apparent character, allegation, alleged motive, dissimulation, seeming, feint, white lie, cloak, mask, cover, subterfuge, profession, palliation, empty words, gloss, sour grapes, obliquity, blind, assumption.
5. Vividness, emphasis, reality, suggestiveness, lifelikeness, strength, force, picturesqueness, tone, concreteness, imagination, animation, intonation, life, intensity, piquancy, zest, vibrancy, vivacity, timbre, variety, graphicness, dynamic resonance, vigor, word painting, nuance, effectiveness, brilliance, brightness, richness.
6. Aspect, stripe, vein, mold, grain, feather, breed, kidney, cast, strain, brand, kin, the like, stamp.
7. Meaning, essence, significance, sense, gist, purport, import, bearing, implication, hint, drift, suggestion, connotation, denotation, intimation, cast, vein, tenor, disposition, stress, probability, inkling, spirit, glimmer, innuendo, cue, intention, scent, force, effect, inclination, insinuation, intent.

COLOR, *v.* 1. Tinge, tint, stain, dye, paint, infuse, chalk, illuminate, heighten, suffuse, variegate, gild, enamel, gloze, wash, imbue, grain, blazon, daub, emblazon, pigment, crayon, gloss, japan, lacquer, stipple, distemper, fresco, ingrain.
2. Blush, redden, flush, become red, color up, show color, change hue, crimson, glow, mantle, burn, flame, warm, suffuse, become sanguine, become florid, show modesty, show anger.
3. Disguise, distort, pervert, varnish, misstate, counterfeit, twist, garble, gloss over, slur, slant, misrepresent, make plausible, palliate, misquote, exaggerate, falsify, belie, dress up, torture the meaning, present obliquely, put false construction upon, warp, invent, invert, allege, fabricate, bias, tamper with, doctor up *(coll.),* embroider, wrest

the meaning, wrench the sense, stretch, strain, misinterpret, misrender, misconstrue, incline, see through rose-colored glasses, sophisticate, understate, overstate.

COLORABLE, *adj.* 1. Tingible, receptive to color, absorbent.

2. Plausible, apparent, persuasive, impressive, ostensible, specious, credible, believable, tenable, conceivable, feasible, convincing, cogent, telling, seemingly sound, counterfeit, deceptive, feigned, pretended, apparently fair, apparently just, bogus, seemingly valid, outwardly pleasing, exaggerated, palliated, fraudulent, trumped-up, factitious, fake (*coll.*), tricky, false, sham, covinous (*Law*), shady, satisfying, shoddy, so-called, fictitious, simulated.

COLOR BLINDNESS, *n.* Achromatopsy, green blindness, nonrecognition of color, Daltonism, chroma-blindness, achromatopsia, dichromatism, chromatic aberration, chromatism, dichromism, deuteranopia, protanopia, tritanopia, xanthopsia, monochromatism, blue-yellow blindness, red-green blindness, red blindness.

COLORFUL, *adj.* Vivid, realistic, imaginative, animated, forceful, pithy, suggestive, chromatic, picturesque, lifelike, concrete, zestful, full-toned, intense, strong, piquant, vibrant, vivacious, rich, dynamic, emphatic, resonant, varied, spicy, tangy, effective, bright, vigorous, graphic, brilliant, gay, variegated, showy, loud (*coll.*), daedal, lustrous, offensively colored, high-colored, individualistic, multicolor, prismatic, pavonian, pavonine, well-drawn, nacreous, opalescent, kaleidoscopic, parti-colored, versicolor, many-colored, multicolored, polychrome, distinctive, compelling, inspirited, savory, fervent, spirited, inspiring, illustrative, affecting, interesting, depictive, chameleonic, chatoyant, descriptive, delineative.

COLORLESS, *adj.* 1. Uncolored, achromatic, neutral, etiolated, dull-hued, pale, leaden, faint, hueless, whitened, dingy, natural, undyed, faded, unstained, untinged, decolorate, dreary, somber, drab, washed-out, bleached, blanched, watery, pallid, livid, ashen, sallow, decolorized, white, mouse-colored, lacklustrous, glassy, lurid, wan, dun, grayed, dim, lackluster, weak.

2. Pale, ashen, pasty, dun, pallid, pale-faced, white, blanched, wan, anemic, sallow, hueless, bloodless, livid, ghastly, cinereous, ashy, ghostly, cadaverous, lackluster, leucocytic (*Med.*), lurid, tallow-faced, sickly, washed-out (*coll.*), glassy, haggard.

3. Dull, without distinction, prosaic, languid, monotonous, wishy-washy, characterless, sluggish, indifferent, inexpressive, blank, effete, apathetic, stolid, slack, flaccid, neutral, faint, cold, dreary, pale, expressionless, somber, torpid, dead, mousy, lukewarm, nerveless, sinewless, unprepossessing, undistinctive, uninspired, weak, ineffective, tepid, unmoving, spiritless, ineffectual, inconsiderable, unaffecting, powerless, listless, unexciting, vapid, unspirited, unanimated, uninteresting, bloodless, sapless, insignificant, strengthless, insipid, meager, ordinary, flat, mediocre, unconvincing, unvaried, lifeless, commonplace, tame, lacking in fervor, marrowless, dilute, thin, impotent, vague, sickly, drab, watery, jejune, inconsequential, unfruitful, lurid, anemic, petty, paltry, average, unrewarding, slight, inferior, pallid, pale, unattractive, pithless, etiolated.

COLORS, *n.* Badge, device, rosette, ribbon, flag, ensign, cause, arms, dress, cognizance, jockey's cap and jacket, standard, regiment, coat of arms, rallying focus, hostile standard, salute, banner,

escutcheon, pennon, gonfalon, insignia, pennant, livery.

COLOSSAL, *adj.* Gigantic, tremendous, imposing, titanic, herculean, huge, monstrous, elephantine, extreme, terrible (*coll.*), tall, immense, enormous, grand, colossus-size, of great power, prodigious, overwhelming, extraordinarily large, stupendous, vast, mammoth, gross, towering, staggering, great, massive, Brobdingnagian, awe-inspiring, excessive, overpowering, Cyclopean, commanding, massy, sky-scraping, lofty, Gargantuan, bulky, Antaean, Atlantean, mighty, dinotherium, strapping (*coll.*), dinosaurian, jumbo, megatherine, magnitudinous, leviathan, extravagant, spectacular, monumental, giant, exceeding, wonderful, gigantean, inordinate, exorbitant, incredible, ponderous.

COLOSSUS, *n.* Gigantic statue, strong man, giant, Titan, tower of strength, muscle man (*coll.*), Goliath, Hercules, Samson, pillar of strength, man mountain (*coll.*), Atlas, Antaeus, Cyclops, Tarzan, Superman, athlete, gymnast, Polyphemus, palaestrian, wrestler, pancratiast, pancratist, pile, giantess, Titaness, giant refreshed, monster, Gog and Magog, whale, behemoth, hippopotamus, elephant, jumbo, dinosaur, mammoth, mountain, megalosaur, Megatherium, Dinotherium, tower, monument, Megalosaurus, Ceratosaurus, obelisk, skyscraper, troll, leviathan, Gargantua, prodigy.

COLT, *n.* 1. Young of horse and related animals, foal, filly (*fem.*), yearling, weaner (*West. U.S.*).

2. Youngster, novice, beginner, tenderfoot, lad, greenhorn, boy, youth, gosling, lively child, chap, laddie, fellow, master, sonny, cub, initiate, young professional (*Sports*), muchacho (*Sp.*), schoolboy, young hopeful, scion, tyro, imp, devilkin, young nick, whipster, rascal, hobbledehoy, sprig, whelp, whippersnapper, pup, puppy, slip, fledgling, kid (*coll.*), bumpkin, cherub, elf, brat, cadet, child, stripling, shaver, chicken, shaveling, bairn (*Scot.*), chick, urchin, bantling.

COLTISH, *adj.* Frisky, playful, sportive, jaunty, playsome, saucy, rampant, frolicsome, gamesome, gay, waggish, rollicking, roguish, prankish, jolly, lighthearted, pranky, rompish, rollicksome, sunny, tricksy, sparkling, jocular, debonair, jocose, brisk, gamboling, lively, mischievous, dancing, capering, larking, prancing, feeling one's oats (*coll.*), joyful, breezy, spirited, animated, active, skittish, blithe, jubilant, blithesome, elated, ebullient, sprightly, sportful, carefree, perky, happy-go-lucky, lissom, arch, effervescent, joyous, mirthful, mercurial, cheerful, buoyant, bonny, frivolous, nimble, agile, chipper, volant.

COLUMN, *n.* 1. Round pillar, post, shaft, tower, pillar, support, obelisk, monument, peristyle, pier, columella, columna, totem, martello, funiculus (*Anat.*), fasciculus (*Anat.*), memorial, campanile, pilaster, pestal, steeple, minaret, stupe, stalagmite, pagoda, spine, mast, monolith, cylinder, caryatid, atlas, telamon, standard, upright, cylindrical body, pylon, fractionating tube *or* tower (*Chem.*).

2. File, row, procession, string, train, funeral, line, vertical row of figures (*Math.*), cavalcade, parade, caravan, safari, queue, wagon train, line of infantry (*Mil.*), formation (*Mil.*), phalanx (*Mil.*).

3. Editorial, regular feature, signed article, newspaper department.

COLUMNIST, *n.* Journalist, newspaperman, war correspondent, newsman, gentleman of the press, gentleman of the Fourth Estate, editorialist, correspondent, foreign correspondent, interviewer, reporter, publicist, news analyst, editorial writer, press man, columner.

COMA, *n.* 1. (*Med.*) Lethargy, unconsciousness, unnatural sleep, profound slumber, anesthesia, sopor, hypnosis, narcosis, narcotization, stupor, lack of consciousness, insensibleness, insentience, insensibility, trance, swoon, catalepsy, somnolism, cataplexy, absence of consciousness, somnipathy, unimpressibility, estivation, deep sleep, mesmeric sleep, hypnotic somnolence, torpor, hibernation, lipothymy, syncope, morbid drowsiness, oblivion, encephalitis lethargica, lentitude, narcolepsy.

2. (*Astron.*) Envelope, nebulous sheath, halo, aura, aureola, halation, luminescence, radiation, hairy envelope, nebulous mass, chromosphere, nimbus, parhelion (*of the sun*), paraselena (*of the moon*), diffused light.

3. (*Bot.*) Tuft, clump, glomerule, group, crest, fascicle, cluster, bunch, plumule, inflorescence, fascicule, fasciculus, plume, feather, topknot, knot, panache.

COMATOSE, *adj.* Lethargic, stuporous, comatous, stupefied, heavy, inert, lazy, sleepy, unconscious, torpid, drowsy, dormant, stupor-like, somnolent, sluggish, hypnotic, soporiferous, soporose, soporific, languid, listless, phlegmatic, passive, impassible, unresponsive, lipothymial, slow of response, dull, supine, insensible, anesthetic, impassive, frozen, languorous, immobile, numb, lipothymic, obtuse, oblivious, enervated, insentient, insensate, blunt, stolid, apathetic, unfeeling, benumbed, insensitive, impercipient, deadened, thick-skinned, narcotic, narcoleptic, numbed, cataleptic, callous, pachydermatous, imperceptive, slumberous, sleep-drunk, lymphatic, oscitant, otiose, lentitudinous, leaden, lumpish, somnific, indolent, torporific, exanimate, dronish, torpescent, somnolescent, drony.

COMB, *n.* 1. Toilet comb, dressing comb, harrow, fine-tooth comb, serration, serrated edge, rake, toothed edge, card (*for wool, etc.*), crenelation, bur, currycomb.

2. Cockscomb, tuft, caruncle, topknot, beard, panache, head-tuft, top, ridge (*of a helmet*), spine, crest (*of a wave*).

3. Honeycomb, sieve, strainer, cell mass, filter, screen, colander, sifter, cribble, cribbiformity, riddle, porosity, porousness.

COMB, *v.* 1. Dress (*with a comb*), curry, groom, order, smooth, arrange, disentangle, clean, adjust, harrow, sift, untangle, unravel, winnow, riddle, thrash, rake, weed, screen.

2. Curl, break in foam, form whitecaps, crest, roll over.

3. (*Fig., with* OUT) Eliminate, screen, search over systematically, rid, sort, discard.

COMBAT, *v.* 1. Fight, war, battle, strive, contend, struggle, tourney, tilt, joust, contest, jostle, clash, fall foul of, close with, join issue, run foul of, collide, break lance with, bandy blows with, box, skirmish, scuffle, enter the lists, cross swords with, come to blows, fence, thrust and parry, wrestle, give satisfaction, duel, spar, exchange fisticuffs, measure swords with, tussle, make warfare, defy, engage in hostilities, take the field, storm, reluct, bombard, reluctate, go to battle, wage war, take the law into one's own hands, take up the sword, impinge, meet a challenge, take up the cudgels, beset, take up arms, contend against, war against, encounter, attack, engage, join battle with, face, disagree, struggle with, cope with, assault, assail, do battle with, grapple with, lift hand against, march against, take one's stand, confront, stand

one's ground, make a stand against, charge, draw sword against, battle with, repel, repulse, act in opposition to, counteract, keep at bay, brush.

2. Oppose, defy, contradict, disagree, thwart, resist, withstand, restrain, hamper, obstruct, constrain, interfere, curb, barricade, bar, block, preclude, blockade, debar, prohibit, foil, cross, confound, traverse, frustrate, act in opposition to, counteract, recalcitrate, repulse, repel, hinder, militate against, contravene, protest, embarrass, oppugn, restrict, impede, call in question, reluct, stultify, proscribe, veto, embargo, play at cross purposes, be contrary to, interdict, antagonize, reluctate, take the law into one's own hands, inhibit.

COMBAT, *n.* 1. Battle, conflict, contest, skirmish, passage, war, strife, struggle, affray, set-to, fray, tournament, contention, warfare, duel, bout, tilt, joust, affair, brush, encounter, fight, engagement, rencounter, action, concussion, percussion, clash, tourney, scuffle, hostilities, siege, altercation, the sword, fracas, militancy, bombardment, collision, tussle, belligerence, jostle, fisticuffs, opposition, resistance, assault, charge, impingement, dispute, controversy, confrontation, counteraction, match, contrary action, impact, embroilment, bloodshed, feud, onslaught, scrimmage, arms, melee, brush, military operations, vendetta, game.

2. Opposition, resistance, constraint, blockade, barricade, antagonism, defiance, obstruction, interference, contradiction, prohibition, inhibition, restraint, disagreement, preclusion, frustration, debarment, restriction, cross purposes, contrary action, discord, argument, repulsion, protest, counteraction, hindrance, oppugnation, impediment, contravention.

COMBATANT, *n.* Contestant, fighter, foe, battler, antagonist, disputant, participant in fight, athlete, champion, fighting man, wrangler, player, litigant, belligerent, opponent, rival, adversary, assailant, the opposition, obstructionist, gladiator, jouster, tussler, struggler, scuffler, contender, competitor, emulator, duelist, attacker, militarist, soldier, man-at-arms, brave, warrior, serviceman, enemy, militant, pugilist, paladin, assailer, assaulter, controversialist, opposer, aggressor, swordsman, polemic, candidate.

COMBINATION, *n.* 1. Union, aggregate, joining, conjunction, association, aggregation, connection, congregation, junction, medley, miscellany, stew, entanglement, multiformity, mélange (*Fr.*), olio, convergence, varied assortment, polymorphism, anastomosis, inosculation, synizesis (*Pros.*), odds and ends, synaeresis (*Pros.*), variegation, variety, omnium-gatherum, gallimaufry, potpourri, motley array, salmagundi, mosaic, diversity, patchwork, heterogeneity, hodgepodge, ollapodrida, synartesis.

2. Alliance, consolidation, association, coterie, coalition, plot, clique, assemblage, cabal, complot, conspiracy, party, faction, league, confederacy, junto, aggregation, congregation, junta, syndicate, cartel, union, trust, cabinet, merger, pool, ring, company, federation, set, coalescence, aggregate, intrigue, cartelization, gang, racket, triumvirate, camorra, incorporation.

3. Mixture, fusion, blend, composite, alloy, compound, synthesis, admixion, commixture, formation, composition, tissue, amalgam, infusion, impregnation, admixture, multiformity, crasis, interfusion, intermixture, preparation, pervasion,

minglement, amalgamation, levigation, suffusion, permeation, adulteration, miscellany, transfusion, diffusion, penetration, imbuement.

COMBINE, v. 1. Coalesce, unite, mingle, pool, amalgamate, embody, associate, become united, blend, mix, form, lump together, variegate, inlay, dapple, stipple, mottle, striate, polychromize, diversify, commix, inosculate, weave, impregnate, instill, commingle, scramble, alloy, levigate, fuse, throw together, infuse, hybridize, suffuse, connect, transfuse, anastomose, compound, join, converge, put together, couple, tie together, chain, band, link, fasten, coadunate, merge, coordinate, synergize, cooperate.
2. Unite, join, league, associate, incorporate, federate, merge, club together, ally, cooperate, pool effort, form a union, unify, meet, hold together, amalgamate, consolidate, agglomerate, confederate, fraternize, coordinate, synergize, get together, conglomerate.

COMBUSTIBLE, adj. 1. Inflammable, burnable, conflagrant, inflammatory, consumable, tindery, conflagratory, comburent, igneous, ignitible, fiery, combustive, incendiary, accendible, conflagrative, explosive, crematory, candent, calefactory.
2. Irascible, inflammatory, touchy, testy, hot-tempered, fiery, easily excited, irritable, peppery, volcanic, emotional, volatile, excitable, explosive, passionate, caustic, at the boiling point, choleric, ignitible, incendiary, seditious.

COMBUSTION, n. 1. Burning, oxidation, fire, flame, blaze, conflagration, consuming, kindling, cineration, inflammation, cremation, incineration, ingle, ignition, scorification, cautery, coruscation, torrefaction, calefaction, consumption, fritting, cupellation, carbonization, cauterization, calcination.
2. Violent agitation, tumult, ebullition, turmoil, excitement, devouring, uproar, turbulence, riot, ferment, convulsion, hubbub, boiling over, disquiet, confusion, effervescence, agitation, fomentation, pandemonium, commotion.

COME, v. 1. Move toward, approach, bear down upon, advance, near, draw near, converge, gain upon, go toward, impend, make for, accede to, move into view, appear, be in store for, gain upon, lay for (Naut.), be imminent, approximate, come to close quarters, tend hither, draw on, await, hover, lower, menace, threaten, brew, loom, be in the wind, stare one in the face.
2. Get here or there, arrive, reach, gain, reach the destination, attain, appear, drop in, make one's appearance, show up, enter, make, advene, turn up.
3. Move into view, show, be visible, appear, become visible, spring forth, be disclosed, issue, arise, stand out, strike the eye, present oneself or itself, heave in sight, be revealed, come to view, stand forth, emerge, rear its head, loom, rise, materialize, pop up, become manifest.
4. Extend, reach, stretch to, come down or up to, reach as far as, range, parallel, be level with, spread to, touch, go to, attain.
5. Betide, happen, come about, occur, hap, fall, transpire (often regarded as erroneous), bechance, result, ensue, follow, supervene, light, chance, befall, pass, come to pass, take effect, eventuate, take place, arise.
6. (Often with FROM) Be derived, spring from, issue, turn on, descend from, be a product of, result from, follow from, hinge on, accrue from, originate in, emanate, depend on, arise

from, flow from, bud from, be produced by, germinate from.
7. (With ACROSS) Meet, discover, run into, find, turn up, encounter, light upon, stumble upon, dig up, find out, bump into, come into contact with, rencounter, hit, hit upon, root out, burst upon, unearth, fall upon, uncover, expose, bring to light.
8. (With AT) Attack, make a thrust, make a sally, make an onslaught, invade, storm, raid, assault, tilt at, launch against, make an offensive, close upon, make a dash at, ride against, go for (coll.), march upon, fall upon, have at, strike, assail, beset, make an incursion, make an inroad, charge.
9. (With BACK) Return, turn back, react, retire, reverse, ricochet, regrade, regress, retrace one's steps, withdraw, rebound, regurgitate, put back (chiefly nautical), ebb, recoil, recede, resile, retrovert.
10. (With BY) Obtain, get, acquire, earn, win, crop, pick up, reap, rake up, dig up, procure, secure, gather, harvest, take possession of, net, bag, collect, glean, get hold of, lay hands on.
11. (With DOWN) Descend, fall, flop, lapse, gravitate, sag, decline, droop, slide down, plunge, subside, founder.
12. (With DOWN) Misfire, run aground, sink, drown, fizzle out (sl.), end, explode, crash, go to seed, collapse, come to grief, peter out (sl.), take an ugly turn, fail, fall through, flop, turn out ill, backslide.
13. (with FORWARD) Be a candidate, offer one's services, volunteer, present oneself, step forward, stand, offer oneself.
14. (With IN) Enter, inflow, infiltrate, push in, slip in, press in, break in, burst in, set foot in, thrust in, find a way into, penetrate, ingress, interpenetrate, inpour, inrush, go in, come on (stage).
15. (With INTO) Inherit, come in for, come by, succeed to, fall heir to, receive as inheritance or from a will, be left, have handed down to one, have descend to one.
16. (With ON) Make progress, develop, pick up, improve, gain, become or get better, forge ahead, ameliorate, fructify, advance, make steps, make headway, ripen, rally, proceed, make strides, mend, amend, progress, take a favorable turn, make one's way, move forward, edge along.
17. (With OUT) Be published, appear, appear in print, be issued, go to press, be brought out.
18. (With ROUND) Admit, relent, change one's mind, be converted, consent, concede, be induced, submit, accede, tergiversate (implies frequency), yield, concur, acquiesce, mellow, defer to, capitulate, grant, come over, allow, bend, soften, comply, surrender.
19. (With THROUGH) Do as hoped or expected, come off well, prove oneself, fare well, succeed, accomplish, make the grade, follow to a conclusion, achieve, win, be successful, achieve one's purpose, triumph, be victorious, gain one's ends, be triumphant, win through, get through, carry through, see it through.
20. (With TO) Awake, recover consciousness, regain consciousness, recover, revive, wake up, come to life, recuperate, rally, stir, come round, rouse oneself, arouse oneself.
21. (With TO) Total, add up to, equal, match, aggregate, correspond to, number, be tantamount, be equivalent, amount to, mount up to.
22. (With UP) Arise, happen, present itself,

result, occur, ensue, eventuate, follow, chance, take effect, supervene, come about, betide, fall, light, hap, befall, bechance, pass, take place, come to pass.

COMEDIAN, *n.* 1. Comic actor, performer in comedy, clown, jester, impersonator, mimic, thespian, player, comic, writer of comedy, farcist, funnyman, comedienne *(fem.),* wearer of the cap and bells, end man, Columbine, mummer, mime, harlequin, Punch, Punchinello, buffoon, motley fool, grimacer, pantaloon, pickleherring, zany, fool, Scaramouch, jokesmith *(humorous),* skit, merry-andrew.

2. Amusing person, humorist, joker, buffoon, wag, droll, clown, mimic, impersonator, zany, madcap, life of the party, wagwit, wit, witling, puck, cut-up *(coll.),* prankster, funnyman, spark, banterer, reparteeist, caricaturist, burlesquer, parodist, punster, epigrammatist, *bon diable (Fr.),* *bel-esprit (Fr.), drôle de corps (Fr.).*

COMEDY, *n.* 1. Play that ends happily, droll piece, light movie, comic opera, literature of comic theme *or* tone, melodrama, farce, travesty, burlesque, musical, harlequinade, broad humor, *comédie rosse (Fr.),* sock, motley, cap and bells, *comédie bouffe (Fr.),* slapstick, exode *(Rom. Antiq.).*

2. Comic element, wit, drollery, fun, joking, salt, caricature, pleasantry, humorous exchange, banter, Attic salt, badinage, horseplay, chaff, repartee, Attic wit, humor, wittiness, mimicry, waggery, buffoonery, wordplay, foolery, playful raillery, persiflage, jesting.

COMELINESS, *n.* 1. Propriety, fitness, decorum, seemliness, taste, fittingness, refinement, tact, appropriateness, correctness, charm, restraint, polish, simplicity, suitableness, decency, purity, chasteness, harmony, concinnity, becomingness, naturalness.

2. Pleasing appearance, grace, beauty, fairness, prettiness, litheness, sightliness, goodliness, glow, loveliness, pulchritude, gracefulness, elegance, handsomeness, attractiveness, agreeableness, the pink of, shapeliness, wholesomeness, blossom, radiance, appeal, bloom, winsomeness, the flower of, beauty unadorned, symmetry.

COMELY, *adj.* 1. Becoming, seemly, proper, fitting, suitable, decorous, tasteful, refined, fit, correct, appropriate, polished, befitting, decent, nice, charming, tactful, harmonious, natural, concinnate, pure, simple, unaffected, restrained, chaste.

2. Pleasing in appearance, fair, personable, sightly, graceful, pretty, handsome, beautiful, goodly, attractive, good-looking, lovely, elegant, well-proportioned, prepossessing, bonny, shapely, agreeable, buxom, promising, blooming, radiant, lissome, wholesome, appealing, lithe, winsome, winning, rosy-cheeked, glowing, blossoming, well-favored, symmetrical, bright-eyed, engaging.

COMESTIBLE, *n.* 1. Eatable, edible, victual, foodstuff, delicacy, article of food, esculent, gustable, nutriment, aliment.

2. *(Plural)* Food, sustenance, creature comforts, feed, ingesta, fare, aliment, nutriment, refection, nourishment, provisions, refreshment, pabulum, bread *(fig.),* meat *(fig.),* grub *(slang),* chow *(slang),* eats *(coll.),* belly cheer *(slang),* scoff *(slang),* peck *(slang).*

COMFIT, *n.* Dry sweetmeat, confection, candy, sweet, bonbon, candied fruit, comfiture. lozenge, glacé, confect, sugarplum.

COMFORT, *n.* 1. Solace, consolation, relief in affliction, refreshment, respite, serenity, calm, mitigation, composure, lightening, easement, rest, rescue, peace, alleviation, prayer, tranquillity, quiet after the storm, freedom from pain *and* anxiety, lifting of a burden, soothing, lenitive, reassurance, deliverance, amelioration, balm in Gilead, palliation, assuagement, allayment, aid in distress, restorative, help in trouble *or* need, quietism, encouragement, softening of hardship.

2. Ease, enjoyment, gratification, satisfaction of bodily wants, well-being, opulence, sufficiency, creature comforts, bed of roses, complacency, warmth, snugness, luxury, abundance, plenty, cheer, amusement, quiet, pleasure, contentment, paradise, happiness, restfulness, peacefulness, coziness, nepenthe.

3. Comforter, bedcover, quilt, puff, coverlet, eiderdown, down quilt, comfortable.

COMFORT, *v.* Solace, console, cheer, soothe when in grief, make physically comfortable, encourage, gladden, restore, allay, lighten one's burden, quiet one's fears, help one in need, grant respite, calm, sustain, delight, hearten, support, nourish, relieve, reanimate, revivify, revive, aid, palliate, assuage, compose, regale, assist, alleviate, provide easement, ameliorate, satisfy, speak peace, divert, gratify, warm, bolster up, bear up, pamper, put at ease, soften, disburden, enhearten, inspirit, refresh, invigorate, rejuvenate, mitigate, reassure, salve.

COMFORTABLE, *adj.* 1. Giving comfort, quiet, consoling, relieving, solacing, soothing, calming, restoring, assuaging, reassuring, supporting, ameliorative, lenitive, giving ease, restorative, assuring, peace-giving, tranquil, serene, helpful.

2. Agreeable, pleasant, gratifying, acceptable, welcome, congenial, cordial, palatable, sweet, cheering, agreeable, inspiriting, pleasing, easeful, adapted for comfort, convenient, commodious, roomy, satisfactory, luxurious, protected, quiet, easy, cozy, habitable, enjoyable, gladsome, genial, regaling, homelike, peaceful, savory, refreshing, congruous, suitable, grateful, pleasurable, to one's mind *or* taste, homey *(coll.),* amiable, likable, snug, sheltered, loose-fitting, adaptable, restful, pleasure-giving, tranquil, wind-proof, water-tight, fit for a king.

3. At ease, free from pain, well, undisturbed, contented, cared-for, untroubled, cheerful, well-off, flourishing, well-to-do, warm, thriving, in full feather, in good case, in a fair way, in one's element, snug, cozy, peaceful, at rest, at home, content, successful, on a bed of roses, relaxed, prosperous, easy, in clover, unafflicted, without care, placid, tranquil, complacent, unvexed, unplagued, unmolested, serene.

4. Adequate, satisfactory, sufficient, ample, usable, equal to, agreeable, admissible, desirable, acceptable, unexceptionable, unobjectionable, applicable, adaptable, commensurate, satisfying.

COMFORTER, *n.* 1. One who *or* that which comforts, consoler, friend, pacifier, well-wisher, restorer, upholder, balm, deliverer, reliever, advocate, sympathizer, reassurance, support, restorative, palliative, poultice, mollifier, helper, bearer of one's burdens.

2. *(Cap.)* The Holy Spirit, Spirit of Truth, The Holy Ghost, Paraclete, the Spirit of God, the Consoler, the Dove, the Spirit, the Intercessor.

3. Comfort, bedcover, quilt, puff, stuffed coverlet, down quilt, comfortable, eiderdown.

COMFORTLESS, *adj.* 1. Forlorn, cheerless, cold,

distressing, distressful, desolate, miserable, dreary, bleak, joyless, afflicting, grievous, depressing, grim, deserted, wearisome, inhospitable, dismal, uncomfortable, melancholy, drear, wretched, deplorable, lowering, lugubrious, disheartening, funereal, saturnine.

2. Disconsolate, inconsolable, grief-stricken, forlorn, woebegone, broken-hearted, desolate, miserable, distressed, pitiable, destitute, cheerless, unhappy, mournful, woeful, rueful, affecting, touching, sad, pathetic, despondent, doleful, sorrowful, forsaken, unmanned, prostrated, sick at heart, deserted, stricken, crushed, hopeless, desperate, lamenting, lost, despairing, heartbroken, wretched, melancholy, joyless, heartsick, piteous, plaintive, without heart.

COMIC, *adj.* 1. Provoking laughter, droll, funny, comical, risible, witty, prankish, humorous, rich, sportive, diverting, absurd, ridiculous, facetious, mirthful, waggish, merry, jocose, amusing, entertaining, fantastic, laughable, ludicrous, whimsical, doggerel, nonsensical, roguish, playful, quizzical, nimble-witted, farcical, slapstick, burlesque.

2. Humorous, ending happily, light, droll, farcical, burlesque, mimic, slapstick, melodramatic.

COMICAL, *adj.* Comic, droll, funny, amusing, humorous, diverting, ludicrous, laughable, witty, sportive, farcical, provoking laughter, playful, roguish, prankish, burlesque, slapstick, doggerel, ridiculous, nonsensical, rich, risible, whimsical, quizzical, absurd, entertaining, fantastic, jocose, merry, waggish, mirthful, facetious, nimble-witted.

COMING, *adj.* 1. Future, to come, prospective, anticipated, eventual, imminent, progressing, advancing, approaching, hereafter, ulterior, in the wind, due, in store, in prospect, subsequent, in view, immediate, instant, close, hoped for, looked for, fated, written, predestined, nearing, in the womb of time, at hand, about to happen, on the horizon, deserving, preparing, forthcoming, to be, impending, expected, pending, certain, en route (*Fr.*), near, close at hand, foreseen, ordained.

2. On the way to fame *or* success, climbing, ongoing, advancing, arriving, making strides, aspiring, promising, ambitious, better off, shooting ahead, improving one's place, carving one's way, progressing.

COMING, *n.* Approach, advent, appearance, birth, landing, gaining, proximity, nearing, afflux, visit, convergence, propinquity, accession, attaining, reaching, closeness, arrival.

COMITY, *n.* Courtesy, civility, amenity, mildness of manner, suavity, friendliness, amity, affability, graciousness, camaraderie, good-fellowship, good will, amiability, considerateness, deference, peace, mutual respect, cordiality, warm pleasantness, mansuetude, complaisance, disposition to please, neighborliness, fellow feeling, rapport, harmony, concord, accord, congeniality, graceful behavior, compatibility, gentility, urbanity, soft tongue, polish, refinement, presence, cultivation, courtly politeness, easy temper, gentle breeding.

COMMAND, *n.* 1. Order, direction, injunction, charge, behest, instruction, exaction, precept, law, ordinance, dictation, commandment, ultimatum, requisition, bidding, dictum, summons, citation, notification, decree, dictate, imperative, prescript, fiat, caveat, beck, nod, demand, dispensation, hest, requirement, word of command, edict, rule, writ, regulation, warrant, mittimus (*Law*), mandamus

(*Law*), proclamation, pronunciamento, bull, will, request, mandate, say-so (*coll.*), call, act, claim, imposition.

2. Act of commanding *or* ordering, rule, sway, power, authority, control, ascendancy, supremacy, dominion, domination, empire, lead, supervision, government, charge, eminence, directorship, hold, presidency, possession *or* exercise of controlling authority, predominance, compulsion, prepotency, grasp, disposal, mastery, coercion, lordship, grip, primacy, imperiality, royalty, regality, seigniory, protectorate, premiership, dictatorship, prestige, kingship, superintendence, headship, prevalence, prepollency, hegemony, weight, pressure, upper hand, influence, reins, rule, oversight, captaincy, governorship, jurisdiction, suzerainty, prefecture, stewardship, chieftaincy, leadership, magistracy, helm, range, rudder.

3. (*Military*) Division, company, battalion, administrative and tactical unit, area *or* station under a commander, post, regiment, arm, corps, garrison, battery, brigade, group, fort, platoon, camp.

4. Extent of view *or* outlook, dominance of a region by reason of location, advantage, reach, scope, sweep, range, compass, span, visibility, favorable position, vantage ground, high ground, prominence, height, altitude, eminence, eyesight, eyeshot, horizon, field of observation, prospect, control *or* mastery of the field, vista, eyereach, ken, expanse, elevation.

COMMAND, *v.* 1. Order with authority, direct, charge, bid, dictate, call upon, compel, prescribe, appoint, enjoin, require, adjure, instruct, summon, state authoritatively, ordain, make a requisition, enact, decree, task, inflict, authorize, warrant, grant, subpoena, call for, cite.

2. Rule, govern, control, be master of, have the upper *or* whip hand, have at one's bidding *or* disposal, call the signals, have the ascendancy, exercise power over, domineer, conduct, reign, supervise, have authority over, lead, preside over, take possession of, have charge of, override, overbear, hold in hand, keep under, oppress, compel, coerce, predominate, have superiority over, prevail, head, hold office, officiate, occupy a post, manage, direct, sway, guide, superintend, wield the scepter, dominate, have sway, tyrannize, wear the crown, occupy the chair, administer, boss (*coll.*), possess the throne, preponderate.

3. Claim, challenge, compel, exact, demand, ask, call forth a response, require with authority, force, call on, deserve and get, levy, impose, lay under contribution, take one's stand, request, elicit, appropriate, be rewarded, stand upon one's rights, get one's deserts, make a point of, make out a case, incite, kindle, motivate, inspire, reap the fruits of, insist, tax, assess, suscitate, provoke, stimulate, induce, effect, draw down, evoke, wring *or* wrest from, prompt, extort, extract, bring on, charge.

4. Have under vision *or* range, overlook, rise above, dominate, overshadow, tower above, top, surmount, occupy a dominating position, have in sight, control, overlie, overhang, overtop, look down upon, exceed in height.

COMMANDEER, *v.* 1. Conscript, draft, order *or* force into active military service, activate, press, impress, constrain, compel to serve.

2. Seize for military *or* public use, usurp, take presumptuously, appropriate summarily, deprive of, dispossess, expropriate, take by force, put one out, take away from, deprive, distrain, divest,

wrest, confiscate, dislodge, turn out of house and home, eject, oust, evict, accroach, take possession of, assume, arrogate, rout one out (coll.).

COMMANDER, n. Chief, commanding officer, person in authority, commandant, officer, master, controller, captain, leader, head, superior, dean, chief commissioned officer, overlord, paramount, overman, impresario, conductor, principal, senior, supervisor, speaker, chairman, manager, governor, ruler, sovereign, lord, potentate, protector, king, sheriff, official, magistrate, general, administrator, admiral, superintendent, functionary, proprietor, skipper, suzerain, seignior, chieftain, regent, top, comptroller, director, commodore, executive, president, dictator, boss (slang), kingpin (coll.).

COMMANDING, adj. 1. Important, considerable, unforgettable, material, to the point, significant, salient, signal, momentous, noteworthy, eminent, remarkable, substantial, great, big, noble, august, outstanding, imposing, extraordinary, convincing, cogent, valid, exceptional, conspicuous, worthy of notice, distinguished, overshadowing, not to be overlooked, consequential, prominent.
2. Compelling, gripping, powerful, dynamic, vigorous, strong, forceful, potent, impressive, pointed, stirring, striking, puissant, spirited, bold, elevated, slashing, crushing, grand, sublime, vivid, incisive, keen, trenchant, convincing, mordant, cogent, graphic, pungent, pithy, biting.
3. Mandatory, obligatory, imperative, jussive, decisive, decretive, prescriptive, unequivocal, not to be contradicted, compulsory, coactive, binding, compelling, peremptory, forcible, not to be trifled with, inexorable, severe, rigorous, exigent, stern, exacting, absolute, official, authoritative, without appeal, irrevocable, conclusive, strict, preceptive, austere, instructive, decretal, final, arbitrary, coercive, uncompromising.

COMMEASURABLE, adj. Commensurate, having the same measure, equal, coextensive with, level, equally divisible, regular, equidistant, collateral, coexistent, coeval, identical, concentric, aligned, synchronous, in exact agreement, symmetrical, coinstantaneous, coetaneous, equivalent, parallel, synchronal, contemporaneous, coinciding, coincident, coequal.

COMMEASURE, v. Be equal in measure, match, be coextensive with, parallel, correspond, be in relation with, balance, accord with, be relative to, correlate with, be comparable, be proportionate, agree with, be identical, coexist, have the same measure, be equated, border, touch, reach, fellow with, be on a level with, coextend, amount to, even off.

COMMEMORATE, v. 1. Celebrate, solemnize, immortalize, preserve, observe, fix in memory, mark, perpetuate, memorialize, salute, hallow, recall, keep, honor, be mindful of, do homage to, rejoice in, laud, hold jubilee, sing the praises of, recognize the anniversary of, acknowledge the dignity of, signalize.
2. Serve as a memento of, recall, remind one of, prompt reminiscence, renew, keep memory alive or green, bring to mind, revive, conjure up, carry one's thoughts back, perpetuate, summon up the past.
3. Make public notice of, make honorable mention of, grant a testimonial to, commend, praise, glorify, bestow honor upon, aggrandize, ennoble, confer dignity upon, speak highly of, signalize, extol, lionize, elevate, exalt, acclaim,

acknowledge the merits of, compliment, laud, pay tribute, distinguish.

COMMEMORATION, n. 1. Celebration, jubilee, observing, hallowing, recognition, remembrance, keeping, recalling, memorialization, reminiscence, perpetuation, mindfulness, memento, exaltation, revivification, public notice, honorable mention, tribute, acclaim, commendation, aggrandizement, glorification, homage, triumph, toast, summoning up from the past, preservation, testimonial, rejoicing, laud, praise, reanimating the spirit of, saluting the memory of, honoring, reminder, acknowledgment, solemnization, commemorative.
2. Commemorative service, memorial service, celebration, observance, solemnization, holiday, rite, holy day, feast day, festival, fast day, fete, revelry, merrymaking, jubilee, ritual, saint's day, wake, funeral, anniversary, birthday, fiesta (Sp.).
3. Memorial, monument, commemorative slab, statue, pillar, obelisk, tablet, token, gravestone, remembrance, shrine, trophy, medal, tombstone, souvenir, column, monolith, marker, headstone, memento, cairn, testimonial, icon, image, cross, representation, wax figure, cenotaph, escutcheon, shaft, footstone, pyramid, reliquary, hatchment, record, memoria (Eccl.), dolmen (Archaeol.), cromlech (Archaeol.), portrait.

COMMEMORATIVE, adj. Memorial, serving to commemorate, keeping in remembrance, jubilant, celebrating, perpetual, perpetuating, solemn, in honor of, in memory of, kept in remembrance, in commemoration of, ritual, commendatory, in memoriam (Lat.), festive, holiday, fast, observing, feast, preservative, conservatory, recognizing, signalizing, reminiscent, reminding, recalling to mind, ceremonial, hallowing.

COMMENCE, v. Begin, start, institute, originate, open, inaugurate, engage upon, undertake, set in operation, initiate, set about, enter upon, make a beginning, take the first step, take rise, have source in, derive from, embark on, get to, turn to, inchoate, go ahead, lay the first stone, install, pioneer, make off, put one's hand to the plow, put the ball in motion, get going (coll.), take off (coll.), pitch in (coll.), introduce, incept, hit the trail, set forth, be off, venture on, take up, turn one's hand to, plunge into, put one's shoulder to the wheel, put in execution, open fire, set up, launch, usher in, broach, break ground, break the ice, set on foot, fall to, handsel, buckle down (coll.), ring in (coll.), set forward.

COMMENCEMENT, n. 1. Beginning, start, inception, outset, opening, birth, genesis, threshold, initiation, origination, dawn, head, inauguration, first cause, incipience, source, spring, base, rudiments, foundation, rise, onset, inchoation, first beginning, incubation, first move, prelude, preface, preliminary, proem, overture, morning, first attempt, outbreak, raising of the curtain, first stage, unveiling (coll.), debut, installation, coming out (coll.), take-off (coll.), send-off (coll.), kick-off (coll.), derivation, the first step, infancy, embryo, embarkation.
2. (In universities and colleges, etc.) Ceremony of granting diplomas, graduation day, graduation, day of conferring degrees, promotion, completion of a school's curriculum.

COMMEND, v. 1. Mention as worthy of confidence, notice kindness, etc., recommend, guarantee, bespeak regard for, sanction, endorse, approve, back, advocate, speak highly of, acclaim, support, laud, cite, accredit, give credit, stand by, stand back of (coll.), pay tribute to, express esteem for, underwrite, put in a good word for, ratify, certify, assure the merits of, present confidently, warrant, make out a case for, O.K. (coll.).

2. Commit, entrust, yield, consign, surrender, give in charge, deliver with confidence, resign to, transmit, convey, make over, confer, pass over, endow, leave in the hands of, grant, give, submit, relegate, bequeath, vest in, settle on, hand over, transfer.

COMMENDABLE, *adj.* Laudable, praiseworthy, to be commended, worthy, meritorious, desirable, estimable, creditable, deserving, excellent, good, fine, reputable, worthy of estimation, advisable, in favor, unimpeachable, honorable, respectable, above par (coll.), exemplary, admirable.

COMMENDATION, *n.* 1. Act of commending, recommendation, praise, support, approval, good opinion, approbation, respect, endorsement, good word, certification, tribute, backing, acclamation, regard, advocacy, sanction, esteem, ratification, citation, laudation.

2. Something that commends, honor bestowed, title, recognition, trophy, recommendation, laurel, tribute, honorable mention, citation, guarantee, award, decoration, ribbon, medal, certificate, badge.

COMMENDATORY, *adj.* Commending, serving to commend, laudatory, approbative, respectful, recommendatory, advisory, praising, favorable, complimentary, approbatory, in favor of, well-disposed, acclamatory, approving, assenting.

COMMENSURABLE, *adj.* 1. Having a common measure *or* divisor, commeasurable, measurable by a common unit, commensurate, comparable, equally divisible, of equal length *or* volume, of a size, equivalent, identical in size, coextensive with, aligned, concentric, equiparant, the same length, twin, similar, uniform, collateral, accordant, even, consistent, equal, regular, agreeing, coordinate, in unison with, level, coequal, equidistant.

2. Suitable in measure, proportionate, relative, comparable, balanced, regular, corresponding, accordant, proportional, coordinate, consistent, parallel, agreeing, well-proportioned, symmetrical, well-set, even.

COMMENSURATE, *adj.* 1. Commeasurable, in exact agreement, commensurable, having the same measure, equally divisible, regular, of equal extent *or* duration, level, synchronous, symmetrical, concentric, coexistent, coincident, parallel, even, synchronal, coetaneous, equivalent, equidistant, identical, coinstantaneous, concurrent, collateral, contemporary, coeval.

2. Corresponding in amount, magnitude, *or* degree, equal, coextensive, conterminous, identical, balanced, regular, even, symmetrical, coordinate, relative, parallel, fellow, of equal rank, in exact agreement, coinciding, coincident, comparable, proportionate, accordant, equiparant, of similar rank, coequal, level, of relative importance, of a size, regular, consistent, synchronous, equivalent.

3. Adequate, proportionate, proportioned, due, on a proper scale, appropriate, corresponding, sufficient, suitable, equivalent, meet, competent, sufficing, enough, satisfactory, equal to, bearable, passable, ample, admissible, agreeable, acceptable, fit.

4. Having a common measure, contemporary, commensurable, comparable, relative, balanced, corresponding, proportionate, coordinate, similar

in size *or* volume, accordant, consistent, agreeing, coextensive, collateral, concurrent, coincident.

COMMENT, *n.* 1. Explanatory *or* critical matter added to a text, annotation, note, explanation, explanatory note, elucidation, illustration, gloss, commentary, marginal annotation, clarification, exemplification, explication, judgment, exegesis, light, review, definition, expansion, exposition, criticism, interpretation, discourse, illumination, explanatory footnote, scholium.

2. Remark, observation, statement, word, talk, saying, gossip, reflection, interjection, criticism, expression, assertion, allegation, animadversion, affirmation, declaration, postulate, utterance, dictum, whisper, reproof, position, mention, pronouncement.

COMMENT, *v.* 1. Write explanatory *or* critical notes upon a text, annotate, make notes, make comments *or* remarks upon, clarify, clear, review, illuminate, discourse, dilate upon, touch upon, interpret, explain, criticize, elucidate, shed light, render intelligible, exemplify, exposit, expand on, render judgment, gloss, postil, illustrate, descant, interpose, expound, define, discuss, treat.

2. Make remarks, observe, disclose, enucleate, bring out, notice, interpose, touch upon, remark, reprove, reflect, criticize, interject, state, express, utter, say, allege, pronounce, mention, postulate, affirm, posit, assert, opine (humorous), gossip, whisper.

COMMENTARY, *n.* 1. Dissertation, explanatory essay *or* treatise, running comments, notes, thesis, discourse, discussion, monograph, elucidation, explanation, homily, paper, critique, notice, gloss, report, expansion on a text, tractate, explication, critical discussion, essay, handbook, exposition, criticism, exegesis, interpretive study, scholium, review, disquisition, series of comments *or* annotations.

2. Anything serving to illustrate a point, note, comment, annotation, explanation, illumination, footnote, observation, elucidation, illustration, gloss, exemplification, explication, clarification, light, definition, exposition, expansion, reflection, interpretation, criticism.

3. (Usually plural) Record of facts *or* events, familiar narrative, memoirs, personal history, history, graphic account, relation, memorabilia, narration, recapitulation, representation, recital, annals, experiences, adventures, autobiography, biography, journal, memorials, commonplace book, adversaria, chronicle, circumstantial account.

COMMENTATOR, *n.* Annotator, leader writer, expositor, expounder, interpreter, monographer, exponent, explicator, definer, reviewer, exegete, critic, writer of comments, explainer, editorialist, essayist, pamphleteer, publicist, dissertator, news analyst, descanter, discourser, newscaster (Radio), commenter, scholiast, columnist, glossarist.

COMMERCE, *n.* 1. Dealing, trade, interchange of goods *or* commodities, business, reciprocity, exchange, traffic, merchandising, custom, barter, buying and selling, mercantilism, transfer, lease and release, bargain and sale, mercantile relations, system of exchanges.

2. Social relations, intercourse, communication, correspondence, federation, alliance, association, conversance, interlocution, collocation, meeting, joining, communion, conversation, consociation, familiarity, fraternization, conference, converse, companionship, connection, cooperation, union,

joint effort, concurrence, intimacy, consortship, concourse, colloquy, sociability.

3. Illicit sexual intercourse, criminal intimacy, criminal converse, criminal conversation, social evil, prostitution, whoredom, meretricious traffic, concubinage, harlotry, streetwalking, adultery, free love, bordel, cuckoldry, Mrs. Warren's profession, whoremongering.

4. Intellectual interchange, mental *or* spiritual intercourse, conference, passage of words, debate, discussion, tongue-fence, self-council, collocution, interlocution, paper war, verbal contest, thought, logomachy, disputation, conversation, meditation, self-communing, self-consultation, contemplation, cogitation, reflection, secret thoughts, argument, reverie, inmost mind, colloquy, stimulating talk, exchange of ideas, war of words, *guerre de plume (Fr.),* dialogue.

COMMERCIAL, *adj.* 1. Of, or of the nature of, commerce, mercantile, having to do with business, relating to traffic, arising from traffic, of organized trade, trade, retail, wholesale, market, of buying and selling.

2. Engaged in commerce, business, mercantile, skilled in trade, trading, engaged in business.

3. Prepared for sale, mass-produced, saleable, manufactured for sale, vendible, merchantable, staple, trade, marketable.

COMMINATION, *n.* Threat of punishment, ban, denunciation, menace, curse, malediction, tirade, threatening, anathema, malison, condemnation, execration, proscription, aspersion, objurgation, vituperation, denouncing as evil, imprecation, damaging imputation, philippic, intimidation, invective, diatribe, obloquy, censure, challenge, excommunication.

COMMINGLE, *v.* Blend, mingle together, unite, mix, commix, intermingle, amalgamate, combine, intermix, interlace, alloy, hybridize, interweave, fuse, miscegenate, interbreed, intermarry, immix, crossbreed, immingle, commingle, run together, interlink, mingle.

COMMINUTE, *v.* Pulverize, triturate, levigate, bray, powder, grind, break to pieces, granulate, atomize, harrow, mince, crumble, crush, grate, pound, mill, fritter, crumb, contriturate, thresh, disintegrate, chip, reduce to fragments, shiver, crunch, calcine, shatter, turn to dust, file, abrade, erode, scrape, corrode, hash, beat to pieces, make small, bruise, break *or* separate into fine particles, reduce to powder, divide into small bits, break to smithereens *(coll.).*

COMMINUTION, *n.* Pulverization, trituration, levigation, grinding, breaking up, disintegration, braying, bruising, powdering, crushing, hashing, reduction to powder, separation into fine particles, granulation, detrition, atomization, attrition, mincing, frittering, harrowing, crumbling, grating, pounding, milling, crumbling, contrituration, threshing, shattering, shivering, chipping, filing, scraping, corrosion, abrasion, erosion, crunching, tripsis *(Med.),* beating to pieces, calcination, friction.

COMMISERATE, *v.* Feel *or* express sorrow *or* sympathy for, condole, sympathize with, solace, compassionate, pity, feel for, show pity, express fellow feeling, feel sorry for, soothe, grieve with, enter into the feelings of, console, have one's heart bleed for, send one's condolences, share one's sorrow, lament with, comfort, disburden one, relieve one's sorrow, have pity *or* compassion for.

COMMISERATION, *n.* Compassion, sympathy, pity, condolence, comfort, humanity, consolation, tenderness, kindness, relief, solace, lamentation with, soothing, shared grief, charity, fellow-feeling.

COMMISSARY, *n.* 1. Store of equipment and provisions, supply of foods for organized body, ship's store *(Nav.),* quartermaster, feeder, purser, officer of camp store *or* commissariat *(Mil.),* provider, victualer, supplier, steward, maniple, outlet store of a commissariat, military, mining, *or* lumber camp grocery store.

2. One charged with duty by a superior power, deputy, ambassador, consul, agent, legate, proxy, lieutenant, secondary, delegated spiritual officer of remote regions *(Eccles.),* broker, instrument, steward, parliamentary, surrogate, intelligencer, substitute bishop *(Eccles.),* parliamentary agent, delegate, representative, minister, commissioner, negotiator, emissary, attorney, attorney general, solicitor general, envoy, diplomat, plenipotentiary, messenger, vicar, regent, spokesman, mouthpiece.

COMMISSION, *n.* 1. Act of committing *or* giving in charge, entrusting, commitment, consignment, committal, handing over, assignment, confiding, reference, commending, relegating, risk, venture, crediting, placement, making over, passing over, deliverance, loan, putting, investing.

2. Charge, authority granted, direction, trust, authoritative order, office, bidding, full powers, mandate, rank, power of attorney, brevet, place, assignment, appointment, authorization, legation, post, service, chargeship, incumbency, delegation, procuration, consignment, warrant, deputation, position, station, granting of powers, proxy.

3. Warrant of authority, appointment papers, written order, brevet, authorization, assignment, diploma, document granting authority, certificate, official charge, charter, procuration, exequatur, proxy, authorizing order, government order conferring rank *or* office, document giving powers, official communication.

4. Delegation, body of commissioners, board, committee, deputation, legation, council, agency, legislature, representatives, overseers, embassy, cabinet, chamber, congress, mission.

5. Operation, working order, running, shape *(coll.),* condition of anything regarding active service *or* use, state, form, fettle, trim, repair, whack *(sl.),* kilter *(coll.).*

6. Trust, charge, office, duty, task, ward, orb, errand, business, occupation, matter in hand, concern, employment, bidding, assignment, work, place, mission, exercise, stint, agendum, thing to do, function, chargeship, part, province, sphere, capacity, role, scope, compass, berth, post, field, realm, agency, legation, embassy, mandate.

7. Carrying out of evil intent, perpetration, committing *(of crime, error, etc.),* performance of misdeed, criminality, exercise of wrongdoing, violation of law, offense, infringement, trespass, lawbreaking, malfeasance, evildoing, infraction, misconduct, malpractice, disobedience, transgression.

8. That which is committed, deed, crime, evil, felony, sin, error, wrong, misdeed, malefaction, malfeasance, wrongdoing, misdemeanor, breach, infraction, peccancy, fault, offense, infringement, violation, committal, commitment.

9. Sum allowed an agent, compensation, fee, portion, part, share of profits, brokerage, cut *(sl.),* piece, allowance, allotment, dividend, percentage, contingent, rake-off *(sl.),* pay.

COMMISSION, *v.* 1. Authorize, empower, hire, engage, employ, refer matters to, entrust, charge, invest with powers, grant prerogative, nominate, enjoin upon, give a commission to, detail, ordain, accredit, set *or* place over, appoint, station, name, assign, enable, enfranchise, charter, allot, patent, facultate, bid, trust, warrant, entitle, give power of attorney to, relegate power to, license.

2. Depute, delegate, send on a commission, empower to act for another, accredit, dispatch, authorize to represent, consign, assign, relegate, appoint, charge with an errand, entrust with a mission, deputize, commit.

3. Put (*a ship, etc.*) in commission, activate, repair, put in order, furnish, rig up *or* out, adapt, refurbish, prepare for use, take out of mothballs (*coll.*), equip for service, fit out, supply, man, arm, gear, accouter, outfit, provision, munition, put in trim, appoint, provide.

4. Give a commission *or* order for, requisition, command to be supplied, request creation of, require, demand, sponsor, engage, contract for, covenant, indent, agree for, direct to be made.

COMMISSIONER, *n.* Member of a commission, ambassador, emissary, agent, delegate, protector, representative, officer, deputy, factor, commissary, negotiator, viceroy, envoy, messenger, solicitor, attorney, diplomat, consul, spokesman, minister, intelligencer, plenipotentiary, broker, lieutenant, parliamentary agent, regent, vicar, functionary, government official, magistrate, public servant, executive officer, middleman, proxy, surrogate.

COMMISSURE, *n.* Seam, joint, suture, juncture, closure, stitch, joining, connection, articulation, conjunction, hinge, pivot, weld, splice, vinculum, node (*Bot.*), nexus, ligation, miter, mortise, link, intersection, bond, tie, interconnection, ligature, intermedium, raphe (*Anat.* and *Bot.*), dovetail, osculation.

COMMIT, *v.* 1. Entrust, consign, give in trust *or* charge, empower, confide, charge with, assign, relegate to, send, dispatch, commission, depute, delegate, grant authority to, engage, employ, set over, invest with power, authorize, convey, vest in, charge, deputize.

2. Consign (*for safe keeping or preservation*), resign, give over, place, lay, put, deliver, submit, deposit, entrust, put in the hands of, render, pass over, make over, bestow, transfer, discharge, lay away, commend, invest, surrender, store, yield, confide, dispose of, vest in, stow away, salt down (*coll.*), reposit, throw at the feet of, cache, bank, prostrate before, remit, bequeath.

3. Perpetrate, enact, do, perform, effect, act, execute, pursue, carry on, transact, inflict, be a party to, practice, participate in, trespass, violate the law, transgress, infringe the law, have a hand in, disregard the law, disobey the law, be an accomplice, pull (*slang*), pull off (*coll.*).

4. Imprison, send to prison, put in custody, arrest, impound, immure, enthrall, jail, consign, place in confinement, confine, incarcerate, clap up, intern.

5. Engage, pledge, implicate, swear to, bind by pledge *or* assurance, involve, exact, compel, make liable, constrain, oblige, promise, plight, certify, undertake, contract an obligation, become bound to, answer for, guarantee, warrant, require, bear witness, enjoin, vouch, vow, give one's word, assure, attest, consent, mortgage, pawn, covenant, hypothecate, bottomry, impignorate, impose responsibility.

6. (*Parl. Proc.*) Place *or* put in charge of a committee, refer matters to, charge with, leave to, deliver to, give for consideration, hand over to, transfer to, transmit, convey, assign, forward, turn over to, pass over to, enjoin.

7. (*To memory*) Memorize, con, fix in memory, impress on the mind, acquire, learn, get, take in, master, get into one's head, get by rote, learn by heart, learn word for word.

8. (*Oneself*) Take a decisive step, make up one's mind, enter upon a course, make a decision, resolve, conclude, fix upon, seal, settle, take one's stand, give oneself up to, choose, undertake, cast in one's lot with, decide, throw away the scabbard, kick down the ladder, pass *or* cross the Rubicon, determine, take for better or worse, burn one's bridges.

COMMITMENT, *n.* 1. Act of committing, giving over, entrusting, delivering, placing in charge, consignment, transfer, resignation, delivery, committal, entrustment, consignation, handing over, confiding, commending, investment, risk, assignment, venture, reference, relegating, giving in trust, placement, crediting, putting in the hands of, sending, dispatching, submitting, depositing, rendering, bestowal, surrendering, discharge to, yielding, vesting, repositing.

2. State of being committed, resignation, bondage, commission, submission, trust, resting with one, surrender, implication, involvement, convenant, being in one's hands, consignment, obligation, liability, decision, choice, confidence, determination, repository, settlement, resolution, responsibility, deliverance, deposit, investment, bequest.

3. (*Parl. Proc.*) Reference to a committee for consideration, entrusting for decision, committal, placing in charge, leaving, delivery, handing over, turning over, transmission, conveyance, forwarding, assignment, transferring, passing over.

4. Consignment (*to prison or an institution*), committal, imprisonment, restraint, constraint, confinement, internment, impoundment, duress, detention, thrall, putting in custody, placing in confinement, durance, immuring, incarceration, cohibition, inhibition, restriction, constriction.

5. Written court order directing confinement, mittimus, warrant, decree, writ, edict.

6. Commission (*as of crime*), perpetration, committal, performance of misdeed, exercise of wrongdoing, lawbreaking, evildoing, infraction, malpractice, transgression, disobedience, trespass, misconduct, malfeasance, offense, violation of law, infringement, criminality.

7. Act of committing, pledging, *or* engaging oneself, giving in adhesion, pledge, warrant, engagement, unreserved adherence, committal, commendation, submission, resignation, trust, surrender, yielding, obligation, liability, decision, choosing, taking one's stand, determination, resolution, responsibility, undertaking, vouching, vowing, giving one's word, covenanting, taking a decisive step, plighting, making up one's mind, entering upon a course, conclusion, settlement, burning one's bridges, taking for better or worse, passing *or* crossing the Rubicon, casting in one's lot with.

COMMITTEE, *n.* Person *or* group designated to investigate, report, *or* act, person *or* group committed, appointed group, deliberative *or* advisory group, council, board, jury, convocation, subcommittee, court, chamber, cabinet, comitia (*Rom. Hist.*), assignee, trustee.

COMMIX, *v.* Blend, mingle, combine, unite, mix, compound, incorporate, merge, melt into one, coalesce, alloy, absorb, fuse, stir together, immix, immingle, impregnate, embody, consubstantiate, interweave, intermix, amalgamate, commingle, mix together, intermingle.

COMMIXTURE, *n.* 1. Intermingling, blending, commingling, combination, union, compounding, mixing, intermixture, amalgamation, fusing, stirring together, absorption, incorporation, merging, melting into one, coalescence, mixing together, embodiment, impregnation, imbuement, saturation, diffusion, infusion, pervasion, uniting, adulteration, penetration, suffusion, infiltration, permeation, interlarding, interfusion, levigation *(Chem.),* mingling, admixture, consubstantiation, immixture, injection, mixture.
2. Intermixture, blend, tincture, homogeneous mass, infusion, alloy, combination, interfusion, tinge, amalgam, compound, amalgamation, one body *or* substance, composition, mixture, unity, admixture, intertexture, immixture, fusion.

COMMODE, *n.* Chest of drawers, dressing table, night stand, small bureau, night stool, closestool, cupboard, cabinet, lowboy, cellaret, clothespress, dresser, press, washstand, sideboard, end *or* side table with drawers, vitrine, Canterburies.

COMMODIOUS, *adj.* Convenient, roomy, useful, spacious, comfortable, suitable, advantageous, fit, proper, satisfactory for the purpose, usable, applicable, restful, easeful, cozy, snug, valuable, helpful, luxurious, agreeable, capacious, handy, accommodating, appropriate, apt, ready, large, expedient, serviceable, profitable, conducive, to one's liking, acceptable, gratifying, grateful, amiable, pleasant, pleasurable, favorable, ample, contributive, competent, adequate, sufficient, easy, adaptable, unobjectionable, equal to.

COMMODITY, *n.* 1. Article of merchandise, ware, article of trade *or* commerce, vendible, good, staple, effect, necessity, product.
(In pl.) Merchandise, produce, stock, lading, supplies, cargo, capital stock, stores, stock in trade, goods, capital, freight.
2. Belonging, chattel, holding, possession, effect, provision, property, asset, appointment, movable, convenience, appurtenance, seizin *(Law).*
(In pl.) Goods, estate, paraphernalia, luggage, resources, impedimenta, equipage, baggage, means, personalty *(Law).*

COMMON, *adj.* 1. Belonging to all, public, shared by two *or* more, joint, united, for the use of all, pertaining to the whole community, popular, proletarian, plebeian, rife, bourgeois, national, state, civic, civil, international, reciprocal, social, societal, communal, widespread, general, native, universal, world-wide, commutual, collective, generic, extensive, sweeping, comprehensive, used by all, encyclopedic, all-embracing, ecumenical, catholic, proverbial, observed by all.
2. Usual, of frequent occurrence, familiar, habitual, prevailing, current, abundant, popular, plentiful, customary, everyday, often met with, prevalent, average, conventional, wonted, daily, accustomed, normal, domestic, plain, native, natural, sound, unexceptional, homespun, middle-class, pat *(coll.),* known, expected, numerous, garden-variety, stock, household, vernacular, commonplace, indiscriminate, well-trodden, in the beaten path, regular, routine, ritual, repeated, established, consuetudinary, standard, recurrent,

orthodox, according to use *or* custom, according to Hoyle *(coll.),* acknowledged, received, cut and dried, approved, understood, traditional, simple, dime-a-dozen, periodic, betwixt-and-between, matter-of-fact, workday, Philistine, unassuming, informal, salt-of-the-earth, rife, set, settled, in a rut *(coll.),* promiscuous, conformable to rule.
3. Well-known, notorious, ascertained, known by every schoolboy, generally *or* publicly known, recognized, acknowledged, received, widely-known, well-kenned, household, noted, pat *(coll.),* familiar, established.
(Of speech, spoken expression, etc.)
4. Trite, commonplace, stale, prosaic, stock, threadbare, colloquial, worn out, hackneyed, tedious, monotonous, harping, humdrum, trivial, unvaried, platitudinous, everyday, familiar, banal, moth-eaten, tautological, wearisome, stereotyped, warmed-over, indiscriminate, bromidic *(coll.),* conversational, mediocre, homely, worn thin, oft-repeated, singsong, ordinary, non-literary, casual, uneducated, unguided, spontaneous, unthinking, popular, of the folk, vernacular, vulgar, slangy, jargonal, jargony, plain, workday, plebeian, Philistine, unassuming, artless, unsophisticated, untutored, uncultured, unrefined, provincial, confabulatory, undistinguished.
5. Of mediocre *or* inferior quality, ordinary, low, mean, coarse, indifferent, vulgar, inferior, unrefined, vile, cheap, base, illiterate, lewd, poor, depraved, deficient, insipid, wishy-washy, paltry, pitiful, contemptible, inane, middling, tolerable, niggardly, beggarly, wretched, niggling, piddling, of no value, worthless, uncivil, ignoble, trivial, undiscriminating, inadequate, ungentle, trifling, beneath contempt, pedestrian, indelicate, gross, trashy, odious, low-minded, low-bred, ill-bred, tawdry, brutal, beastly, of inferior breed, swinish, ignominious, obnoxious, unlovely, shabby, abject, shameful, scurvy, broad, crude, despicable, rank, peccable, disreputable, discreditable, uncouth, infamous, disgraceful, dishonorable, scrubby, deplorable, unseemly, meretricious, execrable, raffish, rude, unpolished, ill-mannered, churlish, loutish, barbaric, harsh, offensive, cloddish, boorish, crass, indecent, shameless, brazen, unblushing, bestial, smutty, degraded, obscene, indecorous, bawdy, defiled, foul-spoken, brash, ribald, lacking taste, unwomanly, unmanly, foul, abandoned, unbecoming, solecistic, callous, scurrilous.
6. Having no rank, lesser, insignificant, minor, obscure, plebeian, bourgeois, undistinguished by high birth, without attainments, characterless, mediocre, unheard of, subordinate, unnoticed, nameless, inglorious, renownless, inferior, base, unexalted, average, garden-variety, of little *or* no account, no great shakes *(coll.),* immaterial, humble, unessential, expendable, not vital, slight, irrelevant, inappreciable, inconsiderable, puny, nugatory, picayune, petty, idle, ineffectual, base, worthless, unworthy of notice, unworthy of serious consideration, small-fry, dime-a-dozen, unimportant, G. I. *(coll.),* ignoble, lowly, of the street.

COMMON, *n.* Tract of land owned *or* used in common, park, square, public grounds, commons, pleasance, green, campus, village green, mall, quadrangle, greensward, grassplot, open space in town.

COMMONALTY, *n.* The common people *(below the orders of nobility),* the lower classes, the commons, commoners, rabble, multitude, crowd.

proletariat, populace, rank and file, bourgeoisie, people, varletry, ruck, yeomen, rout, canaille, commonage, common run (coll.), salt of the earth, low life, the herd, the million, horde, peasantry, general public, community, society, citizenry, commonwealth, state, world at large, folks, public, the many, democracy, dregs, body politic, riffraff, members of an incorporated body, population, nation, stockholders, shareholders, commonality, participants, underlings, roughscuff (coll.), membership, mob, humbler classes or orders, great unwashed, great unnumbered, hoi polloi.

COMMONER, n. One of the commons or common people, untitled person, common man, plebeian, one of the people, nobody, democrat, republican, underling, citizen, peasant, inhabitant, one of the crowd, John Doe, John Smith, proletarian, man of the street, pleb, roturier (Fr.), one with joint rights in land, yeoman, G. I. (coll.), civilian, burgher, townsman, householder, John Q. Public.

COMMONLY, adv. 1. In a common manner, without distinction, vulgarly, negligently, with bad grace, showing ill breeding, lacking spirit, indifferently, wretchedly, humbly, ignobly, idly, ineffectually, coarsely, lewdly, vilely, basely, by the letter of the law, cheaply, meanly, without originality, superficially, uncivilly, unworthily, without inspiration, sullenly, insolently, tolerably, impudently, perfunctorily, negatively, popularly, contemptibly, indiscriminately, any old way (coll.).

2. Familiarly, ordinarily, popularly, generally, normally, by and large, as a matter of course, on an average, in most instances, day by day, as a rule, again and again, frequently, usually, most often, according to custom, universally, in the natural order of things, repeatedly, constantly, generally speaking, daily, by force of habit, from habit, currently, regularly, conventionally, for the most part, in general.

COMMONPLACE, adj. Trite, stale, hackneyed, mediocre, unimpressive, common, threadbare, worn-out, prosaic, ordinary, familiar, tame, usual, dull, everyday, trivial, banal, monotonous, prosy, pedestrian, matter-of-fact, vulgar, general, not new, stock, tedious, humdrum, platitudinous, stereotyped, homely, oft-repeated, unvaried, dry, undiscriminating, slow, unimaginative, sober, uninteresting.

COMMONPLACE, n. 1. Well-known, customary, or obvious remark, axiom, platitude, truism, twaddle, banality, triviality, trite or uninteresting saying, trite remark, stale saying, cliché, prosaism, old maxim, hackneyed expression, fadaise (Fr.), familiar tune, common sentiment.

2. One of a miscellany, excerpt, passage important for reference, gleaning, memorable selection, memorabile, quotable passage, memory book entry, noteworthy quotation, adversaria entry, memorandum, analects (pl. only), commonplace book item.

COMMONS, n. pl. 1. Commonalty, the common people, commoners, populace, the people, the lower classes, untitled class, rabble, proletariat, crowd, bourgeoisie, varletry, commonage, the million, the horde, general public, citizenry, mob, humble classes, hoi polloi, multitude, rank and file, peasantry, community, common run (coll.).

2. (Cap., usually with The) Lower house of Parliament, House of Commons, elective house of certain governments, lower chamber, the

people's representation, Legislative Assembly.

3. Large dining room at a university, students' dining hall, refectory, mess hall, eating quarters, table shared by a group or organization, eating club.

COMMON-SENSE, adj. Practical, sober, sensible, matter-of-fact, sagacious, free from vagaries, unbiased, intelligent, rational, understandable, sane, sound, logical, well-founded, reasonable, plausible, well-grounded, just, prudent, credible, clear-headed, judicious, solid, expedient, politic, believable, shrewd, astute, hard-headed, keeping to facts, free from fanciful views, experienced, open-minded, uninfatuated, dispassionate, unprejudiced, unjaundiced.

COMMON SENSE, n. Natural sagacity, good sense, good judgment, normal intelligence, native reason, intuition, practical discernment, sound sense or understanding, mental poise, prudence, presence of mind, judiciousness, resourcefulness, shrewdness, reasonableness, ballast, untutored reasoning power, balanced judgment, sobriety, level-headedness, experienced view, rational faculty, worldly wisdom, composure, wisdom arising from experience, unbiased impulse, plain sense, unemotional consideration, unreflective opinion of an ordinary man (Philos.), conceptions natural to one untrained in dialectic (Philos.), calmness, sang-froid (Fr.), sound perception, mother wit, horse sense (coll.), gumption (coll.).

COMMONWEALTH, n. 1. Body of people of a nation or state, the public, commonalty, empire, population, polity, realm, state, nation, body politic, the people, society, community, general public, inhabitants, civil community, populace, citizenry.

2. State in which the supreme power is held by the people, republic, democracy, federation, representative government, constitutional government.

COMMOTION, n. 1. Violent or tumultuous motion, agitation, disturbance, explosion, storm, collision, fulmination, convulsion, perturbation, effervescence, fomentation, tempest, excitement, cataclysm, outbreak, quake, earthquake, burst, upheaval, eruption, outburst, tumult, clash, crash, washout, debacle, revolution, disruption, ado, stir, hubbub, squall, turmoil, turbulence, violence, fury, furor, bustle, ferment, fuming, ebullition, heaving.

2. Turmoil, tumult, disorder, upheaval, pother, ado, to-do (coll.), altercation, ruckus, affray, violence, bustle, furor, uproar, racket, fuss, stir, outbreak, row, clatter, hubbub, riot, quarrel, flurry, hullabaloo, turbulence, fight, encounter, affair, contest, skirmish, fracas, conflict, tussle, concussion, clash, brush, scuffle, appulse, tilt, ruction, combat, bout, fray, set-to (coll.), noisy strife, imbroglio, struggle, pasage of or at arms, fisticuffs, scrap (slang), jolt, mêlée (Fr.), dogfight, embroilment.

3. Political or social disturbance, revolt, riot, revolution, insurgence, rebellion, mutiny, upset, sedition, convulsion, overthrow, outbreak, rising, insubordination, coup d'état (Fr.), insurrection.

COMMUNAL, adj. Pertaining to a commune or community, public, of or belonging to the people of a community, general, common, cosmopolitan, mutual, state, in common, social, national, civil, provincial, commutual, civic, united, joint, used by all, societal, widespread, collective, popular, proletarian, bourgeois, plebeian.

COMMUNE, *n.* 1. Zone, division, community, local corporate body, ward, town, village, city, neighborhood, district, parish, bailiwick, township.

2. Interchange of ideas *or* sentiments, friendly conversation, converse, communication, parley, intercourse, friendly discourse, exchange of ideas, confidence, confabulation, palaver, personal dialogue, chat, interlocution, colloquy, coze, sharing of feelings, consultation, tête-à-tête.

COMMUNE, *v.* 1. Converse, talk together, share feeling, discourse, communicate, talk freely, interchange thoughts *or* feelings, confabulate, chat, be closeted with, have a word with, talk with tête-à-tête, coze, commerce with, chew the rag *(sl.),* chin *(sl.),* bandy words, hold intimate conversation, parley, palaver, dialogue, talk in private, transfer ideas, reach one another's mind, consider together, meditate together, have close fellowship, hold intercourse, bare one's inmost thoughts to, confide mutually, share an aesthetic experience, enjoy a meeting of minds.

2. *(Eccles.)* Receive the communion, partake of the Lord's Supper, partake of the Eucharist, take communion, celebrate the Lord's Supper.

3. *(With oneself or God)* Meditate, pray, take counsel, consider, contemplate, bethink oneself, muse, ruminate, revolve, ponder, reflect, cogitate, repent, sleep on a question, petition, supplicate, think over, search one's soul, think quietly, spend a time apart *or* in solitude.

COMMUNICABLE, *adj.* Capable of being communicated, transferable, contagious, catching, transmittable, infectious, taking, inoculable, epidemic, transmissible, pestilential.

COMMUNICANT, *n.* 1. Worshiper, celebrant, partaker of the Eucharist, member of a church, communionist, participator in divine service, one who shares in the communion.

2. One who communicates, informant, tipper, reporter, spokesman, mouthpiece, messenger, enlightener, correspondent, adviser, notifier, witness, appriser, intelligencer, communicator, teller, annunciator.

COMMUNICATE, *v.* 1. Give to another as partaker, impart, give, convey, share, pass on, infect, contribute, afflict with, confer, donate, grant, allow, accord, vouchsafe, disseminate, offer, render, infuse, instill, infix, deliver, present, contaminate, pervade, tender, teach, inculcate, proffer, propose, put forward, overture, submit, set forth, expound, instruct, preach, exposit, put one in possession of, acquaint with.

2. Impart knowledge of, divulge, reveal, hint, announce, declare, make known, uncover, bring word, articulate, represent, set forth, put forth, pronounce, enunciate, give voice to, pour out, convey, relate, recite, aver, assert, allege, speak out, comment, remark, publish, observe, let fall, blurt out, come out with, narrate, describe, state, point out, tip, signify, emit, utter, breathe, break *(news),* dictate, shout, unbosom, proclaim, advise, inform, express, cable, tell, state, telephone, acquaint with, insinuate, drop *(a hint),* mention, say, write, deliver, apprise of, notify, present, lay before, disclose, promulgate, call attention to, herald forth, enlighten, wigwag, instruct, give one to understand, inculcate, submit, elucidate, demonstrate, impress upon the mind, inform, put into one's head, infuse, instill.

3. Have interchange of thoughts, commune, hold intercourse *or* converse, converse, deal with,

confer, talk, correspond, speak together, discourse together, colloquize, confabulate, chat, convey thoughts, write to, send a letter *or* communication to, reply, answer, transfer ideas, reach another's mind, commerce with, let one know by mail *or* post, epistolize, drop a line to *(coll.).*

4. Have *or* form a connecting passage, connect, afford access, lead into, carry into, be connected, unite, cause to meet, link, bridge, span, abut on, neighbor, border, conjoin, touch, adjoin, come in contact, be contiguous, trench on, encroach, be adjoining, join.

COMMUNICATION, *n.* 1. Imparting, giving, act *or* fact of communicating, transmission, infection, transmittal, conveyance, presentation, delivery, accordance, consignment, conferment, bestowal, sharing, dissemination, infliction, contagion, tendering, dispensation, donation, contamination, rendering, contribution.

2. Imparting *or* interchange of thoughts, opinions, *or* information, intercourse, telling, conversation, speaking, saying, presentation, disclosure, mention, conference, converse, offer, interchange, transmission, expression, narration, description, correspondence, notification, delivery, consultation, utterance, pronouncement, relation, assertion, conveyance, announcement, proposal, declaration, promulgation, advice, overture, instruction, teaching, exposition, submitting, proffer, elucidation, demonstrating, inculcation, informing, acquaintance, publication, writing, observation, remarking, commerce, articulation, enunciation, allegation.

3. That which is communicated *or* imparted, message, dispatch, information, statement, news, account, doctrine, teaching, instruction, word, publicity, declaration, intelligence, talk, tale, report, hint, cognizance, knowledge, light, notice, proclamation, embassage, revelation, secret.

4. Means of imparting views *or* information, letter, document, paper, message, bulletin, communiqué, directive, wire, cable, telegram, epistle, missive, cablegram, dispatch, speech, note, broadcast, billet-doux, the printed page, the written word, telephone call, notice.

5. Opportunity of passage, connection, means of passage, access, continuity, junction, link, contact, union, encroachment, bridge, joint, span, annexation, interconnection, confluence, opening, door, mail service, passage between places, intercourse, abutment, contiguity, coalescence, anastomosis *(Physiol.),* inosculation, concourse, symphysis *(Anat., Zool., and Bot.).*

COMMUNICATIVE, *adj.* Inclined to communicate *or* impart, free, open, unreserved, informative, informational, social, affable, conversable, ready, talkative, sociable, frank, expressive, confiding, candid, ingenuous, intelligential, outspoken, fluent, aboveboard, accessible, receptive, friendly, chatty, voluble, confidential, neighborly, loquacious, forthright, instructive, disclosive, divulgatory, revelatory, straightforward, free-spoken, liberal in manner.

COMMUNION, *n.* 1. Act of sharing, holding in common, participation, concord, association, fellowship, alliance, harmony, partnership, accord, joint possession, friendship, union, bond, relationship, communism, co-operation, gavelkind *(Law),* agreement, accordance, partaking together, sympathy, community of possession *or* goods, copartnership, brotherhood.

2. Interchange of thoughts *or* interests, oral communication, interlocution, intimate talk,

conversation, commerce, confession, sharing confidences, fellowship, dialogue, correspondence, converse, intercourse, concord, sympathy, verbal intercourse, agreement, harmony, disclosure, mutual imparting, conference, transmission, consultation.

3. *(Eccles.)* Group with common faith, order, denomination, fellowship, church, sect, school of thought, faction, persuasion, affiliation, faith, cult, belief, ism.

4. Eucharist, Sacrament, Lord's Supper, the elements, reception of the Eucharist, celebration of the Lord's Supper, transubstantiation, altar, Holy Communion, consubstantiation.

5. *(With oneself)* Meditation, soul-searching, self-communing, prayer, contemplation, musing, consideration, rumination, pondering, revolving, reflection, cogitation, quiet thought, solitary thought, a time apart.

COMMUNIQUE, *n.* Official communication, bulletin, dispatch, official summary, statement for the press, announcement, correspondence from news reporter, message relating an event, report to the public, news item for the press.

COMMUNISM, *n.* Social organization based on communal ownership of property, communalism, community of possessions *or* goods, collectivism, socialism, communalization, state ownership, social democracy, nationalism, phalansterianism, Fourierism, Communist Party, Marxism, Saint-Simonianism, Bolshevism, Sovietism, radical socialism.

COMMUNIST, *adj.* Pertaining to communists *or* communism, communal, collective, socialist, Bolshevist, Marxian, Soviet, Red, Saint-Simonian, Fourierist.

COMMUNIST, *n.* Advocate *or* adherent of communism, communalist, communitarian, Red, socialist, collectivist, revolutionary, Bolshevist, Marxist, Saint-Simonian, Fourierist, fellow-traveler.

COMMUNITY, *n.* 1. *(Often with* the*)* Social group of a locality with common heritage and government, people, public, society, commonalty, commonwealth, nation, social state, body politic, habitancy, colony, settlement, inhabitancy, folk, population, confederacy, neighborhood, populace, citizenry.

2. Common *or* joint possession, enjoyment, liability, *etc.,* partnership, equal responsibility, common ownership, co-operation, concurrence, participation, sharing, cotenancy, collectivism, jointure, partaking, communion, communization, communism, communalism, community of possession *or* goods.

3. *(Eccles.)* Association, brotherhood, society, order, commune, company, phalanstery, faction, fellowship, communion, denomination, sodality, affiliation, faction, persuasion, cult, sect, fraternal order, preceptory, college, corporation, assembly, neighborhood, group, *familistère (Fr.)*.

4. *(Ecol.)* Colony, cluster, group of organisms living together in ecological relation, aggregation, clump, swarm, group of animals *or* plants living in interrelation and interdependence, inhabitants of a region, denizens, growth, occupation.

5. Similar character, identity, agreement, amity, sameness, similarity, likeness, sharing, harmony, sympathy, correspondence, response, congeniality, accord, affinity, membership, solidarity, union, comparability, unanimity, consentaneity, analogy, concurrence, resemblance, homogeneity, like-

mindedness, approximation, compatibility, parity comradeship, rapport, equivalence, concord, good understanding, cordiality, unison, assent, meeting of minds, parallelism, participancy.

COMMUTATION, *n.* 1. Substituting one thing for another, replacement, exchange, substitution, compensation, barter, interchange, reciprocation, counterchange, supplanting, supersession, mutual concession, compounding, atonement, recompense, compromise, indemnification, supersedure, swap *(coll.),* regulation *(of currencies),* subrogation *(Law),* trade, surrogation, indemnity.

2. Replacement of a greater punishment by a less severe *(Law),* respite, exchange of penalties, easement, modification of sentence, mitigation, allayment, relief, softening, remission, palliation, shortening of term, substitution, abridgment, extenuation, mollification, relaxation of severity, diminution of severity, assuagement, deliverance, reduction of penalty.

COMMUTE, *v.* 1. Exchange for another *or* something else, change, substitute, compound, compensate, barter, give and take reciprocally, alter, interchange, traffic, surrogate, reciprocate, counterchange, retaliate, adjust, compromise, recompense, indemnify, supplant, supersede, settle differences, requite, take the place of, succeed, suffect, change for, permute, transpose, switch, shuffle, regulate *(currencies),* concede differences, subrogate, replace, repay, supply, put in place of, atone, trade, swap *(coll.).*

2. Replace a greater punishment with a less severe, reduce, mitigate, abridge, exchange penalties, give easement, grant respite, redeem, remit, modify sentence, alleviate, assuage, relieve, allay, mollify, extenuate, palliate, shorten, relax severity, diminish, deliver, soften.

COMPACT, *adj.* 1. Joined *or* packed together, closely and firmly united, close, dense, solid, compressed, pressed together, of firm texture, concentrated, consolidated, tight, thick, hard, strong, economical of space, conjacent, snug, tidy, trim, thickset, arranged within a relatively small space, impermeable, imporous, impenetrable, massive, serried, crowded, portable, heavy, all of a heap *(coll.),* substantial, teeming, full, crowded to suffocation, stanch, stubby, squat, stocky, in narrow compass, knit, grumous, clustered, united, conjunct, inseparable, shipshape, clotted, stuffed, coherent, conjoined, viscid, corporate, as one, stout, closely put together, firm, solidified, stiff, populous, bunched tightly, gross, orderly.

2. Expressed concisely, pithy, terse, concise, brief, succinct, pointed, compendious, laconic, not diffuse, elliptical, curt, decurtate, summary, full of meaning, abridged, concentrated, crisp, neat, trenchant, compressed, synoptic, pregnant, to the point, epigrammatic, condensed, not verbose, sententious, short, abbreviatory, close.

3. *(With* of*)* Composed of, made of, formed with, fabricated from, including, constructed from, constituted of, comprising, embodying, built of, involving, incorporating, encompassing, comprehending, formulated from.

COMPACT, *n.* Agreement between parties, treaty, contract, covenant, mutual promise, bargain, understanding, stipulation, concordat, convention, pact, alliance, arrangement, *entente cordiale (Fr.),* engagement, warranty, cartel, paction, assurance, guarantee, solemn declaration, pledge, parole, oath, vow, plight, word of honor, undertaking, union, concord, troth, confederacy, coalition, bond, security, combination, word, deal (coll.), gentlemen's agreement, indenture.

COMPACT, v. 1. Join or pack closely together, press together, condense, compress, consolidate, densify, contract, shrink, pucker, crumple, reduce, squeeze, collapse, shrivel, wither, purse, thicken, ram down, tamp down, cram, cockle, wrinkle, crowd, coagulate, clot, cramp, concentrate, draw in or together, narrow, constrict, constringe, interlace, intertwine, coalesce, melt into one, felt, fuse, agglutinate, cause to cohere, join or knit firmly, constrain, coarctate.

2. (Often with of) Make firm or stable, unite, constitute, bind, knit together, join firmly, connect, form or make by close union or conjunction, fuse, make up, embody, compose, strengthen, solidify, unify, cause to adhere, constrain, attach securely, form an alliance, club together, consociate, confederate, clasp, render one, blend, inosculate, federalize, cement a union, go in partnership, amalgamate, incorporate, link, combine, clinch, fabricate, ally, affix, secure, alloy, merge, coalesce, join forces, splice, compile, reinforce, syndicate, team up, consolidate, fix together, syncretize, melt into one.

COMPANION, n. 1. One who accompanies or associates with another, comrade, mate, fellow, associate, compeer, pal, consort, confrere, boon companion, adviser, escort, attendant, aid, friend, colleague, teammate, adjunct, accompanier, peer, buddy, brother, follower, intimate, confidant, chaperon, helper, accompanist, shadow, partner, participant, sharer, chum (coll.), fellow worker, workfellow, shipmate, playmate, yokefellow, classmate, schoolfellow, accessory, assistant, ally, auxiliary, copartner, partaker, abettor, adherent, confederate, participator, accomplice, consociate, coadjutor, concomitant, crony, benchfellow, roommate, messmate.

2. Mate, match, double, second of a pair, twin, analogue, complement, correlative, parallel, congener, equivalent, correspondent, counterpart.

COMPANIONABLE, adj. Fitted to be a companion, sociable, gregarious, affable, social, convivial, accessible, clubbish, conversable, jolly, amicable, friendly, jovial, well-affected, familiar, intimate, well-disposed, warm-hearted, gracious, genial, lovable, cordial, brotherly, neighborly, communicative, warm, ingratiating, affectionate, hearty, harmonious, cosmopolitan, chummy (coll.).

COMPANIONATE, adj. Of, by or like companions, by mutual consent, shared, partaking, collaborative, hand in glove, cooperative, agreed, participatory, participative, amicable, coactive, joint, friendly, leagued, companionable.

COMPANIONSHIP, n. Fellowship, association as companions, partnership, friendship, company, society, mutual confidence, intimacy, sociability, consociation, camaraderie, familiarity, mutual trust, agreeableness, cooperation, acquaintance, cordial understanding, party spirit, esprit de corps (Fr.), comradeship, brotherliness, friendly relations, rapport, colleagueship, community of interests, social intercourse, amity, collaboration, fraternization, close acquaintance.

COMPANY, n. 1. Assemblage, assembly, band, party, attendance, meeting, gathering, assembled body, group, circle, gang, crew, troop, concourse, convention, throng, congregation, audience, mob, community, convocation, multitude, cavalcade, host, lot, number, entourage, congregation, levy,

confluence, conflux, muster, tribe, congress, posse, watch, bunch (coll.), caravan, cohort, drove, covey, brood, mess, conclave.

2. Assemblage for social purposes, party, club, festivity, fete, meeting of friends, social meeting, entertainment, reception, reunion, soiree, levee, at home, get-together (coll.), housewarming, fraternity, sorority, gathering of people.

3. Visitor or visitors, guest or guests, those entertained at home, gathering in one's home, friends assembled, friends calling on one.

4. Fellowship, companionship, society, alliance, association, affiliation, league, conjunction, team, incorporation, combination, federation, close acquaintance, friendship, consociation, social intercourse, fraternization, collaboration, amity, colleagueship, community of interests, friendly relations, comradeship, camaraderie, familiarity.

5. Number of people united or incorporated for joint action especially business, corporation, firm, joint concern, copartnership, association, union, establishment, committee, combination, class, troupe, alliance, confederacy, faction, concern, council, house, guild, outfit (coll.), merger, institute, federation, squad, institution, Bund (Ger.), coalition, league, combine (coll.), partnership, Verein (Ger.).

6. (Mil. and Naval) Subdivision of regiment or battalion, ship's crew, small group of soldiers, platoon, squadron, force, cohort, section, unit, outfit (coll.).

COMPARABLE, adj. 1. Capable of being compared, proportionate, alike, commensurate, like, corresponding in some respect, approximate, analogous, similar, relative, parallel, correlative, quasi, resembling, allied to, akin, matching, near, close, approaching, assonant, rhyming, cognate, alliterative, homologous, kindred, roughly the same, synonymous, congeneric, proportional, affinitive, consonant, connatural, paronymous (of words).

2. Worthy of comparison, equal to, on a par with, as good as, a match for, on a level with, coequal, peer with, in a class with, the equivalent of, tantamount, on a footing with, coordinate, on even terms.

COMPARATIVE, adj. 1. Estimated or judged by comparison, relative, contrastive, metaphorical, approximate, allusive, comparable, not positive or absolute, conditional, modified, contingent, restricted, limited, undefined, inconclusive, with reservation, allegorical, provisional, figurative, tropical, qualified, tralatitious.

2. Proceeding by or founded in comparison, general, noting similar and varying characteristics, taking into account related phenomena.

COMPARE, v. 1. Note the similarities and differences of, collate, bring into comparison, estimate relatively, contrast, measure, weigh, divide, segregate, balance against, set side by side, place in juxtaposition, separate, confront, oppose, set over against, differentiate, relate, estimate, correlate, discriminate between, juxtapose, distinguish between, exercise critical judgment.

2. (Followed by to) Show to be similar or analogous, liken, declare similar, equate, parallel, similize, analogize, allegorize, associate, express by metaphor, show correspondence, identify with, bring into meaningful relation with, correlate, match, represent as resembling, draw a parallel between.

3. Bear comparison, present a resemblance,

admit of comparison, be held equal, simulate, resemble, vie with, hold a candle to, be worthy of comparison, match with, approximate, be equivalent, be as good as, be similar, have the earmarks of, approach, correspond, parallel, agree, be a match for, be in a class with, be on equal footing, be on a par with, be comparable, put one in mind of *(coll.)*, favor *(coll.)*, take after, savor *or* smack of.

COMPARISON, *n.* 1. Act of comparing, collation, association, relating, identification, testing by, exemplification, opposition, close scrutiny, testing by a criterion, observation, likening, balancing, confrontation, dividing, distinguishing between, separation, juxtaposing, correlation, segregation, discrimination, measuring, weighing, comparative relation, relative estimation, bringing together.

2. Comparative estimate *or* statement, simile, metaphor, parable, contrast, relative judgment, similarity, correlation, parallel, discrimination, distinction, illustration, likening, analogy, estimate of likeness and difference, identification, critical judgment, example, connection, measurement, ratio, association, equation.

3. State of being compared, relation, ratio, contrast, assent, consistency, assonance, accord, agreement, relationship, respect, connection, correlation, synonymy, equivalence, significant relation, cognation, identity, juxtaposition, relative position, coincidence, consonance, proportion, unison, balance.

4. Capability of being compared *or* likened, analogy, likeness, ratio, identity, proportion, accord, compare, consistency, comparability, equality in some respect, connection, alliance, comparativeness, concurrence, filiation, kinship, correlation, equipollence, equivalence, contrast, parallelism, relationship, identification, reference, relation, affinity, approximation, resemblance, homology, parity, semblance, commensurability, propinquity, closeness, nearness, proximity, homogeneity, symmetry, apposition, unison, coincidence, similarity.

COMPARTMENT, *n.* Part *or* space marked *or* partitioned off, division, section, department, apartment, locker, stall, room, separation, cell, till, drawer, box, tray, well, cage, booth, pew, kennel, pigeonhole, niche, alcove, recess, pane, cubbyhole, province, bay, stateroom, coffer, partition, corner, vault, manger, ciborium, panel, crib, bunker, pen, nook, hold, crypt, quarter, cabin, closet, enclosure, chest, rack, caddy, bin, case, press, cabinet, district, casket.

COMPASS, *n.* 1. Space within limits, stretch, reach, extent, scope, range, area, spread, span, sweep, amplitude, limits, measure, caliber, swing, expanse, margin, leeway, acreage, circuit, ambit, orbit, demesne, premises, realm, section, quarter, territory, region, zone, play, vicinage, interval, interstice, neighborhood, interspace, orb, part, confines, mileage, distance, width, breadth, length, division, field, sphere, latitude, room, bound, boundary, volume *(Music or speaking voice)*, diapason *(Music)*, gamut *(Music)*.

2. Enclosing line *or* limits of an area, measurement round, circumscription, circumference, rim, curve, enclosure, circular course, circuit, ambit, fringes, ring, perimeter, belt, zone, orbit, meridian, corona, horizon.

3. Instrument for determining directions by the magnetic poles, mariner's *or* surveyor's compass, ship's compass, needle, card compass, earth inductor, induction compass, sun compass, guide,

cardinal points, earth induction compass, card magnetic compass.

4. Due *or* proper limits, moderate bounds, circle, jurisdiction, precinct, purview, capacity, range, scope, limit, limitation, orbit, circuit, orb, vicinage, purlieu, department, district, quarter, function, allowance, restraint, circumscription, latitude, field, zone, scale, territory, stint, height, reach, sphere, area, role, round, temperance, restriction, moderation.

5. A passing round, circuit, detour, excursion, circumscription, peregrination, itinerary, tour, perambulation, cycle, revolution, volution, round, trip along the outskirts, rounding, circumvention.

COMPASS, *v.* 1. Go *or* move around, make the circuit of, environ, encompass, encircle, surround, engird, embrace, stretch round, envelop, bound, circumscribe, border, span, range, spread, sweep, compass about, measure, enclose, ring, revolve around, girdle, ensphere, round, gird, loop, curve around, circumvent, ring round, circumnavigate, circumambulate, cincture, outline.

2. Extend *or* stretch around, encircle, hem in, invest, besiege, hedge in, circumscribe, beleaguer, beset, blockade, wall in, lay siege to, bound, surround, encompass, environ, engird, embrace, envelop, span, ring, girdle, ensphere, include, comprehend, shut in, fix bounds of, encincture, fence in, delineate, circumpose, gird, encase, enwrap, infold, belt, take in, round, incase, confine, embosom, proscribe, define, restrain, cloister, intern, constrain, retain, circumvent, impound, immure, delimit, contain, incorporate, take into account *or* consideration, reckon among, cover.

3. Attain, obtain, achieve, accomplish, get, procure, effect, perform, consummate, carry, realize, execute, gain, grasp, earn, perfect, ripen, succeed, bring to pass, effectuate, render complete, enact, work out, bring through, hammer out, contrive, dispose of, dispatch, manage, make good, carry out, follow to a conclusion, fulfill, discharge, finish, culminate, wind up *(coll.)*, mature, bring about, complete, get through, conclude, reach an end.

4. Contrive, scheme, meditate, plot, purpose, devise, intend, manage, arrange, conspire, think out, invent, motivate, form, coin, concoct, frame, fabricate, finesse, concert, project, hatch, cabal, complot, intrigue, maneuver, machinate, shape, outline, map out, delineate, use strategem, sketch, cast.

5. Grasp with the mind, perceive, comprehend, realize, follow, be cognizant of, know, discern, be master of, know by heart *or* rote, fathom, understand, cognize, have knowledge of, catch, penetrate, conceive, seize, embrace, apprehend, take in *(coll.)*.

COMPASSION, *n.* Pity, commiseration, clemency, fellow feeling, mercy, grace, charity, kindness, consideration, sympathy, lenity, condolence, gentleness, favor, mildness, indulgence, quarter, soft-heartedness, exorability, long-suffering, sorrow for another's sufferings *or* misfortunes, kindliness, forbearance, tenderness, heart, tenderheartedness, bowels of compassion, melting mood, lenience, benevolence, ruth, readiness to spare, toleration, forgivingness, placability, liberality, yearning, magnanimity, chivalry, humanity.

COMPASSIONATE, *adj.* Tender, sympathetic, pitying, merciful, gracious, clement, inclined to pity, full of compassion, soft, gentle, kindhearted, humane, lenient, benignant, mild, indulgent, pardoning, forgiving, placable, benevolent, free from vindictiveness, moderate, ready to spare, ruthful, yearning, magnanimous, benign, touched, chivalric, exorable, liberal, tolerant, charitable, kind, forbearing.

COMPASSIONATE, *v.* Pity, commiserate, be moved with sympathy for, show pity, feel pity for, feel for, sympathize, melt toward, weep for, forbear, relent, condole, enter into the feelings of, give quarter, spare, show kindness, tolerate, share one's sorrows, lament with, console.

COMPATIBILITY, *n.* Unanimity, congeniality, harmony, suitability, concurrence, symphony, adaptability, concord, concert, concinnity, unity, consonance, assonance, conformance, congruity, rapport, response, accommodation, apposition, coincidence, keeping, coherence, consistence, line, congruence, affinity, correspondence, amity, compossibility, good understanding, conjunction, like-mindedness, pertinence, commensurability, coordination, cooperation, propriety, consentience, conformation, consentaneousness, sync *(motion picture and television)*, synchronization, accord, agreement, toleration, unison.

COMPATIBLE, *adj.* Capable of existing together in harmony, congruous, consistent, consonant, suitable, in keeping, in harmony, harmonious, conformable, admissible, apposite, fitting, possible, congenial, reconcilable, agreeable, such as to agree, suiting, agreeing, in accordance, in unison, in accord, concordant, correspondent, of a piece, commensurate, at one, of one mind, appropriate, like-minded, synchronized, of the same mind, cooperative, apt, adaptable, accommodative, compossible, concurrent, in sync *(motion picture and television)*, consentient, becoming, applicable, unanimous, even, meet, fitting, seemly, pertinent, consentaneous, coordinate, tolerable, in rapport, in step, accordant, proportionate.

COMPATRIOT, *n.* Fellow countryman, fellow citizen, countryman.

COMPEER, *n.* Companion, associate, comrade, equal, mate, colleague, coequal, confidant, partner, confrere, equivalent, equipollent, comate, consociate, consort, brother, buddy *(coll.)*, fellow, peer.

COMPEL, *v.* 1. Force, drive secure by force, bring about by force, extort, wring, bring pressure to bear on, require, insist, command, press, move, enforce, exact, control, distrain, necessitate, make, coerce, oblige, constrain, bear upon, elicit, draw forth, draft, conscript, impress, drag into, put the screws on, strong-arm *(coll.)*, employ force, commandeer, impel, squeeze, seize, wrest, cram down the throat, dragoon.
2. Force to submit, subdue, overpower, restrain, circumscribe, bend low, subject, bind, put under, chastise, reduce, harass, inflict, impose, bully, dragoon, grind, oppress, tyrannize, override, curb, control, repress, suppress, smother, check, wreak, intimidate, terrorize, browbeat, cow, bulldoze *(coll.)*, domineer, keep under, pin down, lord it over, inhibit, prohibit, keep within bounds, give no quarter, put under restraint, rule with a rod of iron, ride roughshod over, crush under an iron hand, trample *or* tread upon, put on the screw.

COMPENDIOUS, *adj.* Containing the substance in brief form, concise, abridged, summary, terse, succinct, comprehensive, laconic, compact, brief, short, synoptic, shortened, curt, elliptical, pithy, decurtate, inclusive, neat, sententious, contracted, pointed, epigrammatic, compressed, condensed.

COMPENDIUM, *n.* Comprehensive summary of a subject, concise treatment, epitome, abstract, abbreviation, contraction, synopsis, digest, brief, minute, note, conspectus, sketch, review, pattern, recapitulation, draft, *aperçu (Fr.)*, condensation, compression, syllabus, essence, pandect, outline, diagram, delineation, bulletin, scenario, docket, *abrégé (Fr.)*, précis, analysis, extract, multum in parvo *(Lat.)*, résumé.

COMPENSATE, *v.* 1. Counterbalance, make up for, offset, be *or* furnish an equivalent, produce equilibrium *(Mech.)*, handicap, trim *(of sails or cargo)*, accommodate, strike a balance, equalize, balance, square, equate, counteract, frustrate, nullify, neutralize, dress *(of troops)*, give a headstart, give points, oppose, fit, poise.
2. Make up for something to, recompense, remunerate, atone, reward, reimburse, repay, redeem, make amends, redress, make good, make restitution, annul, settle, compromise, fee, square with, balance, restore, cover, indemnify, make compensation, remit, recoup, replace, repair, pay in kind, refund, return, undo, cancel, guerdon *(Poetic)*, requite, adjust, satisfy, acknowledge.

COMPENSATION, *n.* 1. Return for services, debt, or loss, recompense, reward, payment, earnings, wages, commission, stipend, emolument, profit, reimbursement, remittance, salary, hire, deserts, pay, benefit, honorarium, counterclaim, damages, perquisite, brokerage, defrayal, satisfaction, tip, coverage, settlement, return, consideration, meed, remittal, gratuity, quittance, reckoning, premium, repayment, allowance, equivalent, scot *(Hist.)*, gain, remuneration, fee, price, bonus, guerdon *(Poetic)*, recoupment, indemnity, indemnification.
2. Return for wrong *or* suffering, satisfaction, requital, atonement, reparation, justice, redress, recoupment, measure for measure, commutation, expiation, return, gratification, acknowledgment, redemption, retaliation, reciprocation, settlement, restoration, remission, repair, recompense, price, restitution, amends, adjustment, neutralization, rectification, nullification, counteraction, penalty, reckoning, composition, solatium, equalization, guerdon *(Poetic)*, wergild *(Law)*, bloodwite *(Law)*, quid pro quo *(Lat.)*, making right.
3. Counterpoise, equalization, balance, offset, equivalence, ballast, makeweight, counterweight, adjustment, equation, handicap, accommodation, nullification, reciprocation, recovery, symmetry, reaction, polarity, frustration, counteraction, opposition, squaring, trimming *(sails or cargo)*, counterbalance, countervailing, producing equilibrium *(Mech.)*.

COMPETE, *v.* Contend for prize, profit, *etc.*, strive, engage in a contest, race with, struggle, cope, enter the lists, vie with, be rivals, oppose, try conclusions, emulate, seek the same prize, wrestle, tussle, stem, breast, employ stratagem, combat, joust, tilt, battle, spar, fence, bid, face, bandy with, encounter, clash, attempt to better, attempt to outdo, pit against, lock horns, fight, break a lance with, collide, attempt to outsell, contest, match wits *or* strength with, litigate, grapple, play.

COMPETENCE, *n.* 1. Quality of being competent, ability, capacity, qualification, capability, address, endowment, training, competency, proficiency, skill, fitness, faculty, power, authority, practice, effectiveness, efficacy, conversance, responsibility, mastery, dexterity, quickness, readiness, relation, familiarity with, usefulness, commensurability, adaptability, validity, appropriateness, adequacy, convenience, suitableness, applicability, execution, expertness, craft, experience, eligibility, incidence, pertinence, belonging, implication, connection, relevance, technique, what it takes (*sl.*), the goods (*sl.*), the stuff (*sl.*).

2. A sufficient quantity, sufficiency, satisfaction, enough, plenty, fill, good measure, saturation, impletion, abundance, competency, full supply, satisfactory amount.

3. Income sufficient for necessities without luxuries, sufficient fortune, adequate income, independent support, comfortable means, support, provision, means of independence, enough to live on, plenty, moderate wealth, abundance, living, livelihood, fortune, wherewithal, maintenance, sustenance, subsistence, balanced budget, competency, sufficiency.

COMPETENT, *adj.* 1. Able, capable, qualified, good for the purpose, equal to, skillful, fitted, trained, proficient, efficient, endowed, up to, effectual, applicable, practiced, expert, versed, efficacious, usable, ready, quick, dexterous, well up in, master of, conversant, au fait (*Fr.*), gifted, at home in, a good hand at.

2. Answerable to all requirements, adequate, fit, sufficient, adapted, suitable, appropriate, up to the mark (*coll.*), eligible, commensurate, up to snuff (*sl.*), adaptable, standard, experienced, satisfactory, responsible, commodious, apposite, well-grounded, prepared, seasoned, convenient, proficient, effective, qualified, valid.

3. (*With* to) Rightfully or properly belonging, incident, pertinent, relating, connected, in point, appertaining, implicated, applying, bearing upon, allied, associated with, involved, the right of, relevant, in the scope of, apposite, admissible, connate, characteristic of, affinitive, connatural, germane, in the province of, implying, belonging.

COMPETITION, *n.* Act of competing, rivalry, emulation, contest for prize *or* advantage, strife, contention, handicap, opposition, trial, struggle, race, pitting of strengths *or* wits, athletic event, engagement, clash, encounter, counteraction, litigation, attempt at betterment, joust, attempt to outsell, digladiation, debate, match, scramble, game, conflict, rivalry for patronage, combat, bout, fight, tilt, tournament, antagonism.

COMPETITIVE, *adj.* Competing, rival, based on competition, prompted by emulation, contested, combative, counteractive, litigious, competitory, striving, opposing, conflicting, antagonistic, of *or* pertaining to competition, involving *or* decided by competition, emulous, cutthroat.

COMPETITOR, *n.* One who competes, aspirant, rival, antagonist, emulator, adversary, entrant, racer, enemy, foe, opponent, contestant, corrival, player, bidder, disputant, battler, jouster, fighter, suitor, contender, controversialist, athlete, litigant, sportsman, debator, rival candidate.

COMPILATION, *n.* 1. Act of compiling, joining, compiling, gathering, gleaning, co-ordinating, mustering, colligating, marshalling, accumulating, unifying, incorporating, combining, forgathering, collecting, selecting, garnering, consolidating, arranging, assembling, collocating, aggregating, organizing, codifying, drawing together, ordering, methodizing, systematizing.

2. Collection, gathering, colligation, succession, series, garnering, gleaning, assembly, assemblage, collocation, accumulation, aggregation, selection, combination, assortment, congeries.

3. Anthology, compilation, ana, collectanea, collectarium (*Eccl.*), miscellany, delectus, corpus, treasury, thesaurus, florilegium, chrestomathy, garland, gathering, spicilege, album, analects.

COMPILE, *v.* Accumulate, assemble, congregate, glean, heap up, get together, garner, cull, collect, group together, anthologize, unite, draw together, put together, bring together, accumulate, amass, muster, collocate, colligate, compose.

COMPLACENCE, *n.* **COMPLACENCY** 1. Ease, gratification, contentedness, quietism, peace of mind, tranquillity, imperturbation, contentment, serenity, composure, placidity, content, pleasure, self-satisfaction, satisfaction.

2. Good manners, consideration, mansuetude, congeniality, chivalry, benevolence, bienséance (*Fr.*), cultivation, prévenance (*Fr.*), camaraderie, suavity, comity, pleasantness, agreeableness, graciousness, courtesy, amenity, cordiality, amity, urbanity, friendliness, deference, neighborliness, amiability, kindliness, civil conduct, conviviality, respect, politeness, civility, affability, affableness, good humor.

3. Comfort, solace, mitigation, amelioration, easement, alleviation, lenitive, reassurance, balm, refreshment, aid, restorative, respite, deliverance, assuagement, allayment, consolation, palliation, relief, nepenthe.

COMPLACENT, *adj.* 1. Self-satisfied, composed, serene, placid, tranquil, content, at ease, pleased, easy, glad, delighted, imperturbable, contented, peaceful of mind, smug, gratified.

2. Complaisant, bland, civilized, gentlemanlike, well-mannered, cheerful, pleasant, civil, affable, gracious, compliant, tactful, decorous, diplomatic, chivalrous, courtly, gallant, urbane, conciliatory, cultivated, genteel, well-bred, polite, agreeable, suave, well-behaved, winsome, good-humored, genial, polished, deferential, politic, mannerly, respectful, cordial, amiable, obliging, gentle, mild.

COMPLAIN, *v.* 1. Grumble, growl, grouse (*sl.*), bewail, lament, fret, grouch (*coll.*), fume, pick, clamor, murmur, whine, nag, moan, disapprove, groan, deplore, faultfind, wrangle, criticize, kick (*sl.*), deprecate, animadvert, cavil, carp.

2. State a grievance (*in court*), file a claim, make an accusation, bring suit, bring to litigation, take action, bring action, seek redress, prosecute at law.

COMPLAINANT, *n.* Claimant, petitioner, suitor, prosecutor, libelant, appellant, accusant, accuser, accusatrix (*fem.*), plaintiff.

COMPLAINT, *n.* 1. Expression of grief, pain, *or* resentment, wail, murmur, lament, lamentation, moan, bewailing, grouch (*coll.*), faultfinding, objection, caviling, carping, charge, crimination, blame, animadversion, jeremiad, disapprobation, reproof, reproach, condemnation, remonstrance, censure, disapproval, calumny, diatribe, obloquy, upbraiding, inculpation, objurgation, reprobation, aspersion, stricture, scolding, accusation, tirade, castigation, vituperation.

2. Sickness, malady, illness, disease, condition, chronic condition, infirmity, debility, disturbance, delicate health, affection, impairment, infection, morbidity, ailment, valetudinarianism, disability, disorder, distemper, indisposition, invalidism.

3. Pleading (*of a civil action*), preferment of charges, incrimination, allegation, charge, suit, accusation, prosecution, imputation, gravamen, indictment, inculpation.

COMPLAISANCE, *n.* Good manners, politeness, civility, respect, conviviality, civil conduct, amity, kindliness, friendliness, deference, graciousness, amiability, neighborliness, urbanity, cordiality, courtesy, amenity, benevolence, *prévenance (Fr.)*, cultivation, *bienséance (Fr.)*, consideration, good-humor, mansuetude, congeniality, pleasantness, chivalry, camaraderie, suavity, agreeableness, affability, affableness, comity.

COMPLAISANT, *adj.* Well-mannered, civilized, civil, bland, complacent, gentlemanlike, cheerful, pleasant, gracious, tactful, compliant, decorous, diplomatic, chivalrous, courtly, gallant, urbane, cultivated, genteel, well-bred, polite, agreeable, affable, suave, well-behaved, winsome, polished, good-humored, genial, deferential, politic, cordial, mannerly, respectful, amiable, obliging, gentle, mild, conciliatory.

COMPLEMENT, *n.* Supplement, double, match, mate, counterpart, other half, parallel, brother, sister, twin, fellow, companion, correspondent, equivalent, correlative, pendant, second *or* other part.
2. That which completes, impletion, balance, remainder, rest, supplement, makeweight, filler.
3. Complete allowance, full amount, totality, full number, whole, total, fullness, completeness, wholeness, ensemble, entirety, gross, aggregate, integrity.

COMPLEMENT, *v.* Make complete, whole, *or* entire, perfect, consummate, implete, supplement, fill up, fill out, render complete, supply a lack, make up, make good, bring to fullness, round out, realize, crown, cap, fulfill, bring to maturity, bring to completion, complete.

COMPLEMENTARY, *adj.* **COMPLEMENTAL** 1. Forming a complement, equivalent, correlative, corresponding, mutual, correspondent, reciprocal, interconnected, interdependent, parallel, integral, interrelated, commutual, completing.
2. Paired, mated, doubled, matched, brother, twin, corresponding, sister, fellow, companion.

COMPLETE, *adj.* 1. Whole, entire, intact, perfect, full, absolute, solid, undivided, unbroken, uncut, unabridged, all in one, unshortened, unreduced, undiminished, plenary, self-contained, exhaustive, thorough, gross.
2. Brought to a conclusion, concluded, mature, finished, accomplished, ripe, ended, done, grown, perfected, consummate, terminated, achieved, fully realized, wrought, settled, effected, closed, wrapped up *(coll.)*, performed, discharged, brought through, carried through, dispatched, executed, brought about, clinched, polished off *(coll.)*, made an end of, effectuated, disposed of, set at rest.
3. Free from imperfection, faultless, unhurt, unblemished, unmarred, unimpaired, unspoiled, undamaged, undefective, indefectible, indeficient, unscathed, uninjured, undeformed, unharmed, sound, undefaced, perfect, untainted.

COMPLETE, *v.* 1. Make complete, perfect, fill out whole *or* entire, bring to maturity, implete, consummate, supplement, mature, round out, cap, bring to fullness, realize, crown, fulfill, bring to completion, complement.
2. Render complete, end, finish, conclude, set at rest, close, consummate, make an end of, get through, terminate, polish off *(coll.)*, dispatch, hammer out, clinch, clench, accomplish, execute, effect, effectuate, wrap up *(coll.)*, settle, perform, achieve, discharge, bring through, bring about, dispose of, prosecute to a conclusion.

COMPLETION, *n.* Fulfillment, conclusion, end, finish, finale, finis, achievement, effectuation, effecting, termination, close, ending, execution, dispatch, consummation, attainment, realization, terminus, expiration, windup, settlement, capping, accomplishment, discharge, perfection, crowning.

COMPLEX, *adj.* 1. Composed of interconnected parts, compound, composite, mingled, manifold, composed of several elements, conglomerate, aggregated, compact, acervate, motley, multiple, mosaic, fasciculate, multiform, miscellaneous, multiplex, multifarious, heterogeneous, medley, variegated, compounded, mixed.
2. Characterized by an involved combination of parts, complicated, entangled, intricate, mazy, involved, complected, interwoven, labyrinthine, tangled, inscrutable, unfathomable, impenetrable, undecipherable, enigmatic, obscure, convoluted, difficult, tortuous, confused, puzzling, circuitous, sinuous, tortile, winding, irreducible, meandering, knotted, snarled, perplexed, hidden, anfractuous, ambagious, flexuous, roundabout, imperspicuous, devious, discursive, rambling, Daedalian, twisted, Gordian, disordered, complicate, crabbed, cryptic, inextricable, paradoxical, bewildering, excursive.

COMPLEX, *n.* Complex whole *or* system, skein, complexus, network, conglomerate, complicated assemblage of particulars, aggregate of parts, aggregation, congeries, involution, interrelated elements, integrality, entanglement, intricate web, webwork, compages, complication, functioning organization, totality, ensemble.

COMPLEXION, *n.* 1. Color, tinge, hue, tint, cast, general coloring *(of skin, hair, eyes, etc.)*, tone, degree and kind of pigmentation, skin texture, flush, glow, coloration, relative clarity of skin's condition, natural color and appearance of the skin.
2. Appearance, aspect, character, stamp, look, feature, apparent state, tone, tenor, turn, mood, temper, light, disposition, nature, color, outline, manifestation, ostent, guise, favor, mien, sight, lines, lineaments, figure, shape, countenance, air, contour, outward show, front, semblance, image, seeming, expression, presence, demeanor, bearing, port, carriage, phase, likeness, posture, attitude, quality, crasis, visage, angle, spirit, impression, effect.

COMPLEXITY, *n.* Intricacy, complication, state *or* quality of being complex, entanglement, coil, involved character, tortuosity, ambagiousness, flexuosity, ambages, circuity, inscrutability, kink, obscurity, incomprehensibility, sinuosity, network, complexness, implication, involution, perplexity, wilderness, jungle, webwork, involvement, wheels within wheels, complexus, Hyrcanian wood, knot, ramification, tangled skein, clockworks, arcanum, complicacy, difficulty, predicament, plight, sleave, Gordian knot, raveling, gnarl, twist, labyrinth, enigma, unintelligibility, puzzle, maze, meander, riddle, imbroglio, stew *(coll.)*, bafflement, riddle of the Sphinx, vexed question, dilemma, knotty point, imperspicuity, compositeness, quandary, paradox, confusion, disorder.

COMPLIABLE, *adj.* **COMPLIANT** 1. Willing to yield, acquiescent, resigned, obedient, malleable, submissive, inclined, accommodating, conforming, subdued, adapting, adaptable, tractable, bowing, deferential, deferring, relenting, pliant, ductile, capitulating, willing, manageable, disposed, meek, dutiful, passive, nonresisting, unassertive, yielding, biddable, respectful, assenting, docile, conformable.

2. Subservient, servile, obsequious, truckling, bowing, scraping, self-effacing, self-surrendering, self-abasing, fawning, cowering, cringing, slavish, crawling, toadying, obeisant, ingratiating, abased, bootlicking *(sl.),* prostrate, subdued.

COMPLIANCE, *n.* Yielding, acquiescence, assent, willingness to comply, respect, conformability, resignation, obedience, docility, bowing, pliancy, submission, adaptability, tractability, deference, tractableness, passiveness, meekness, capitulation, passivity, biddableness, homage, nonresistance, dutifulness, complaisance, malleability, malleableness.

2. Subservience, servility, obeisance, toadying, subjection, slavishness, cringing, fawning, bowing, cowering, abasement, bootlicking *(sl.),* truckling, scraping, bending, ingratiation, obsequiousness, submission, subjection, prostration, self-subdual, self-renunciation, self-surrender, self-effacement.

COMPLICATE, *v.* Involve, entangle, embarrass, make intricate, make complex, vex, perplex, clog, obscure, snarl, encumber, confound, muddle, mix up, confuse, tangle, bedevil, render unintelligible, implicate, hinder, hobble, handicap, impede, spike one's guns, hamper, jumble, embroil, darken, conceal.

COMPLICATED, *adj.* Of many inseparable parts, difficult to analyze, understand, *or* explain, deep, irreducible, imperspicuous, obscure, troublesome, complex, complexed, intricate, involved, operose, perplexed, enigmatic, indistinct, raveled, tangled, laborious, formidable, labyrinthine, problematic, flexuous, thorny, hidden, unintelligible, exacting, incomprehensible, beset with difficulties, profound, abstruse, recondite, unclear, ambiguous, puzzling, paradoxical, embarrassing, bewildering, toilsome.

COMPLICATION, *n.* 1. Complicated *or* involved state *or* condition, complexity, entanglement, confusion, difficulty, puzzle, snarl, intrigue, ado, intricacy, perplexity, sinuosity, complexness, coil, implication, incomprehensibility, embarrassment, tortuosity, flexuosity, ambages, obscurity, circuity, inscrutability, involution, hornet's nest, confusion, sea of troubles, tangle, ambagiousness, wheels within wheels, involvement, tangled skein, sleave, complicacy, predicament, Gordian knot, riddle, imbroglio, labyrinth, dilemma, bafflement, quandary, paradox.

2. Mixture, combination, complexus, jumble, confusion, quandary, dilemma, complex, network, conglomerate, congeries, involution, compages, entanglement, webwork, ensemble, skein, intricate web, complex combination of elements *or* things.

3. Complicating element, aggravation, barrier, unforeseen circumstance, irritating addition, clog, fortuitous factor, stumbling block, hindrance, hitch, snag, objection, disadvantage, impediment, obstruction, difficulty, obstacle, handicap, insult added to injury, drawback, one thing too many, drag.

COMPLICITY, *n.* Sharing of crime, conspiracy, criminal participation, guilt, connivance, complot, collusion, association, partnership in wrongdoing, state of being an accomplice, abetment, alliance, collaboration, concurrence, confederacy, cabal, machination, intrigue, collusiveness, combination.

2. Complexity, intricacy, entanglement, maze, tortuosity, ambages, circuity, obscurity, sinuosity, implication, perplexity, confusion, disorder, knot, imperspicuity, bafflement, riddle, meander, coil, imbroglio, enigma, labyrinth, complicacy, tangled skein, difficulty, predicament, network, arcanum,

complexus, complication, flexuosity, complexness, ambagiousness, inscrutability, involution, puzzle, incomprehensibility, unintelligibility, wilderness, jungle.

COMPLIMENT, *n.* 1. An expression of praise, commendation, *or* admiration, commendation, praise, encomium, laudation, good word, ovation, congratulation, panegyric, regards, appreciation, sentiment, posy, bouquet, respects, veneration, tribute, acclamation, homage, honor, celebration, eulogy, blurb, blessing, notice.

2. Formal act *or* expression of civility, regard, *or* respect, commendation, felicitation, welcome, salute, salutation, commemoration, toast, pledge, dedication, laureation, eulogy, recognition, good wishes, greeting.

3. Polite praise *or* commendation, insincere praise, hollow commendation, formal praise, soft phrases, empty encomium, flattery, sycophancy, blarney, flummery, adulation, honeyed words, puff, salve *(coll.),* taffy *(coll.),* soft soap *(coll.),* pretty lies, agreeable humbug, butter *(coll.),* conventional expression of flattery, ceremonious phrase.

4. Present, gift, sentiment, boon, favor, grace, handsel, kindness, largess, gracious gesture, gratuity.

COMPLIMENT, *v.* 1. Pay a compliment to, praise, commend, flatter by expressions of civility, gratify, appreciate, greet, pay tribute to, acclaim, laud, endorse, applaud, favor, eulogize, honor, adulate, extol, glorify, puff, lionize, magnify, venerate, pledge, soft-soap *(coll.),* exalt, cheer, cry up, court, butter *(coll.),* ingratiate oneself with, sing the praises of, speak highly of, make much of, panegyrize, give a bouquet *(coll.),* welcome, salute, celebrate, toast, hail.

2. Show kindness *or* regard by a gift *or* favor, do honor to, make a present, give a gift, be benevolent, do a good turn, render a benefit, bestow largess, pay regard to, indulge with.

3. Congratulate, felicitate, wish joy to, rejoice with, wish one well.

COMPLIMENTARY, *adj.* 1. Of the nature of, conveying *or* addressing a compliment, lost in admiration, commendatory, laudatory, flattering, courteous, encomiastic, eulogistic, praising, showing regard, appreciative, celebrating, finespoken, honoring, plauditory, praiseful, honeyed, fair-spoken, politely flattering, buttery *(coll.),* bland, unctuous, saluting, welcoming, well-wishing, congratulatory, sycophantic, fawning, courtierly, lavish of praise, respectful, panegyric, adulatory, acclamatory.

2. Free, gratis, free as air, for nothing, for love, costless, expenseless, without charge, scot-free, gratuitous, honorary, donated, contributory, given, no strings attached *(coll.),* voluntary.

COMPLOT, *n.* Conspiracy, plot, machination, scheme, plan, intrigue, cabal, frame-up, design, counterplot, collusion.

COMPLOT, *v.* Plot, scheme, plan, conspire, contrive, concoct a scheme, frame, cabal, collude, hatch a plot, counterplot, intrigue.

COMPLY, *v.* *(With* with) Observe, perform, be faithful to, discharge, satisfy, carry into effect, adhere to, complete, attend to orders, chime *or* fall in with, be guided *or* regulated by, accord with, be subject to, adapt, adjust, suit, fit, tally with, correspond, accommodate, truckle to, do one's bidding, knuckle under, compose differences, reconcile oneself to, yield to, consent to, follow the lead of, answer the helm, carry out, abide by, acknowledge, carry into execution, respect, be willing, fall in with, give in, grant, concur, defer to, give way, relent, stoop, succumb, resign to, submit to, obey, meet, fulfill, assent to, agree to, acquiesce in, surrender, bend, bow, accede to, conform to, give consent to, accept, harmonize with.

COMPONENT, *adj.* Composing, constituent, constituting, integral, elemental, integrant, basic, inherent, intrinsic, original, essential, forming, fundamental, primary, radical, indigenous, inbred, congenital, connate, implanted, ingrained, native, innate, inborn, infixed, underlying, elementary, inwrought, fragmentary, sectional, constitutional, inseparable, inalienable, indivisible, fractional, complementary, partial, subsistent, indwelling, immanent.

COMPONENT, *n.* Constituent part, element, ingredient, component part, member, principle, material, unit of composition, integral part, factor, portion, fragment, piece, organ, fraction, segment, feature, one of the contents, part and parcel, division, item, detail, particular, share, allotment, subdivision, detachment, fundamental, radical *(Math.)*, complement, integrant, parcel *(Law).*

COMPORT, *v.* 1. *(Of oneself)* Behave, act, quit, conduct, demean, deport, bear, acquit, carry.
2. *(Followed by* with) Agree, accord, suit, harmonize, fit, become, be suitable to, befit, be accordant, tally, square, fall in, chime in, match, conform, respond, meet, dovetail, fit together, consort, coincide, concur, adapt to, correspond, jibe *(coll.).*

COMPOSE, *v.* 1. Make, form, create, produce, put together, frame, chisel, hammer out, evolve, manufacture, construct, erect, build, carve, coin, fashion, fabricate, weave, contrive, formulate, devise, do, set up, compound, concoct, forge.
2. Be part of, appertain to, combine in, make up, constitute, unite in, go into, belong to, go into the making of, be a portion of, be an appurtenance, be an adjunct, be an element of, be an integral part, be an ingredient, be a constituent, be a component, form, comprise.
3. Put in form *or* order, arrange, classify, allocate, digest, grade, align, divide, group, rank, clarify, reduce to order, codify, array, co-ordinate, line up, segregate, fix, settle, index, organize, systematize, dispose, methodize, place, collocate, range, graduate, catalogue, tabulate, list.
4. Bring to a position of repose, settle, calm, alleviate, dulcify, becalm, placate, mollify, soothe, bring *or* make peace, smooth, make tranquil, pour oil on troubled waters, quell, still, allay, lenify, modulate, mitigate, milden, hush, quiet, palliate, tame, assuage, lull, resolve (differences), soften, tranquilize, pacify, adjust, mend, appease, conciliate, reconcile, propitiate, harmonize.
5. Write, indite, create, make, shape, form, draw up, fashion, originate, prepare, draft, rime, poetize, poeticize.

COMPOSED, *adj.* Calm, quiet, undisturbed, serene, placid, imperturbable, restrained, at ease, nonchalant, collected, cool, quiescent, temperate, unstirred, *dégagé (Fr.)*, peaceful, unemotional, dispassionate, recollected, steady, cool-headed, even-tempered, inexcitable, inirritable, unruffled, level-headed, self-assured, undisturbed, tranquil, untroubled, poised, self-possessed, sane, balanced, controlled, undemonstrative, staid, sedate, serious.

COMPOSER, *n.* 1. Musician, arranger, melodist, symphonist, tone poet.
2. Poet, maker, creator, bard, author, writer, rimer, verse maker, playwright, versifier, elegist, rhapsodist, poetizer, dramatist, librettist, lyrist, epopoeist, bucoliast, satirist, laureate, poetaster *(derog.),* tragedian, sonneteer, idylist, scribbler.

COMPOSITE, *adj.* Compound, complex, mixed, amalgamate, made up of various parts *or* elements, combined, varied, motley, variegated, heterogeneous, medley, mongrel, compounded, mingled, conglomerate, mosaic, manifold, fused, multiple, multiplex, fascicled, fasciculate, multiform, aggregated, compact, miscellaneous, acervate, blended, synthesized, amalgamated.

COMPOSITION, *n.* 1. Act of combining parts *or* elements to form a whole, combination, union, conjunction, arrangement, synthesis, construction, organization, compilation, concoction, designing, establishment, preparation, building, coinage, fabrication, grouping, conformation, formation, efformation, constituting, manufacture, erection, ordination, disposition, ordering, making, fusing, conflation *(Bibliog.),* treatment, technique, balance, sculpturing, chiseling, modeling, printing, typesetting, typography, presswork, consolidation, assemblage, aggregation, congregation, mingling, incorporation, blending, compounding, creation, amalgamation, impregnation, interfusion, framing, fashioning, contriving, formulation, devising, classification, allocation, innovation.
2. Act of composing, invention, production of an art work, creation, synthesis, origination, adherence to the rules of grammar and rhetoric, fabrication, authorship, producing, inditement, instrumentation, hymnody, hymnology, technique, treatment, designing, writing, pencraft, portrayal, representation, making, drafting, fashioning, forming, shaping, innovation, depiction.
3. Artistic production, literary work, design, invention, essay, instrumentation, painting, study, theme, poem, treatise, publication, masterpiece, melody, literary *or* musical effort, manuscript, aria, opus, handwork, copy, work, creation, book, arrangement, booklet, statue, brain child, draft, inscription, production, ana, lucubrations, piece of sculpture, opuscule, disquisition, brochure, virtu, representation, depiction, art object, objet d'art *(Fr.),* coinage, masterwork, canvas, air, medley, written matter, piece.
4. Constitution, make-up, structure, character, embodiment, comprisal, contents, layout, nature, incorporation, compaction, combination, form, organization, arrangement, comprehension, array, conformation, lay, plan, sketch, filling, draft, foundation, setup, getup *(coll.),* crasis, effect, inclusion, outline, synthesis, make, framework, texture, formation.
5. Compound, mixture, composite substance, admixture, fusion, combination, melange, varied assortment, blend, mass, commixture, mosaic, amalgam, salmagundi, aggregate, organism, alloy, compilation, potpourri, miscellany, concoction, medley, gallimaufry, compound, intermixture, interfusion, tinge, immixture, collection, accumulation.
6. Settlement by mutual agreement, sum agreed upon for settlement, compromise, agreement, compounding, mutual *or* reciprocal concession, commutation, adjustment, mean, compensation, mid course, regulation, reciprocal abatement, golden mean, happy medium, moderation, middle ground.

COMPOST, *n.* 1. Manure, fertilizer, composite of soil builders, muck, guano, stercoration, dung, ordure, organic soil, dressing, fertilizing mixture.

2. Compound, composition, blend, commixture, composite substance, combination, fusion, mass, admixture, mixture, amalgam, organism, tinge, aggregate, immixture, concoction, compilation, medley, potpourri, alloy, gallimaufry, interfusion.

COMPOSURE, *n.* Serene state of mind, quiet, tranquillity, calmness, repose, serenity, poise, aplomb, equability, stillness, placidity, self-restraint, coolness, sedateness, moderation, peace, indisturbance, dignity, stability, balance, calm, content, self-command, level-headedness, peace of mind, self-possession, equilibrium, command of temper, imperturbability, ease, evenness, gravity, complacence, assurance, staidness, dispassion, patience, tolerance, stoicism, inirritability, self-control, sobriety, philosophy, quietude, rest, sang-froid *(Fr.)*, nonchalance, equanimity, unruffled calm, inexcitability, quiescence, debauch.

COMPOTATION, *n.* Drinking together, pot companionship, carousal, revelry, wassailing, frolicking, jollity, merrymaking, festivity, spree, bacchanals, orgy, drinking bout, carouse, cups, reveling, saturnalia, bacchanalianism, symposium *(Gr. Antiq.)*, conviviality, jollification, libation *(humorous)*, carnival, shindy *(sl.)*, tippling in company, carousing, debauch.

COMPOUND, *adj.* Complex, composite elements, composed of two or more parts or ingredients, compounded, heterogeneous, involving two or more actions, functions, *etc.*, amalgamated, mixed, combined, synthesized, acervate, medley, compacted, manifold, multiple, multiplex, fused, conglomerate, mingled, variegated, blended, fascicled, miscellaneous.

COMPOUND, *n.* 1. Something formed by compounding or combining parts, elements, *etc.*, mixture, combination, composition, commixture, alloy, concoction, intermixture, medley, jumble, miscellany, conglomeration, concretion, blend, synthetic, amalgam, hodgepodge, salmagundi, olio, hotchpotch, union, farrago, mess, composite, potpourri, miscellany, gallimaufry, admixture, fusion, melange, varied assortment, mass, mosaic, aggregate, compilation, tinge, tincture, infusion, intertexture, hash, chow-chow, constitution.

2. Yard around a building, enclosure, court, close, curtilage *(Law)*, kampong *(Malay)*, plot, grounds, precinct, plat, cincture, quadrangle, courtyard, grounds, environ, village, workers' colony *(S. Africa)*.

COMPOUND, *v.* 1. Put together into a whole, make or form by combining elements, construct, combine, commingle, concoct, mingle, blend, unite, make-up, constitute, comprise, amalgamate, intermix, intermingle, create, prepare, form, make, construct, formulate, devise, fabricate, fashion, coalesce, embody, impregnate, instill, fuse, hybridize, join, merge, coordinate, evolve, coadunate, alloy, frame, manufacture, organize, originate, incorporate, conjoin, consolidate, synthesize, mix.

2. Make a bargain, settle by agreement, come to terms, compromise, agree, compose, arrange, make an arrangement, make mutual concessions, commute, take the mean, arbitrate, strike a balance, settle amicably, settle for less than originally stipulated, come to an agreement, adjust.

COMPREHEND, *v.* 1. Grasp mentally, conceive,

understand the meaning or nature of, know, apprehend, cognize, recognize, make out, see, perceive, discern, imagine, enter into the idea of, penetrate, appreciate, see into, fathom, get to the bottom of, realize, read into, get the hang of *(coll.)*, master, command, assimilate, absorb, digest, savvy *(sl.)*, get *(coll.)*, catch the idea of, seize, gain insight into, be cognizant of, gripe.

2. Comprise, include, embrace, embody, span, compass, enclose, compose, involve, reckon among, constitute, possess, engross, own, hold, enumerate or number among, cover, take in, encircle, incorporate, sum up, contain, admit, subsume, receive, encompass, encincture, infold, take into account or consideration, extend or stretch around, encircle, surround, envelop, circumscribe.

COMPREHENSIBLE, *adj.* Capable of being comprehended, understandable, intelligible, plain, explicit, clear, obvious, graphic, exoteric, vivid, recognizable, perceptible, discoverable, knowable, cognoscible, cognizable, ascertainable, discernible, distinguishable, demonstrable, self-evident, lucid, explicable, conceivable, decipherable, legible, pellucid, easily understood, limpid, unveiled, accountable, apprehensible, perspicuous, simple, articulate, unobscure, unclouded, translucent, distinct, unconfused, unambiguous, clear-cut, luminous, transparent, transpicuous, unhidden, evident, defined, manifest, palpable, express, open, revealed, disclosed, overt, unequivocal, unmistakable, penetrable, patent, perceivable, unconcealed.

COMPREHENSION, *n.* 1. Act or fact of comprehending, inclusion, comprising, comprisal, incorporation, composition, compassing, embracing, embodying, admission, constitution, enclosure, encompassing, embodiment, spanning, engrossing, containing, subsuming, encircling, compaction, surrounding, circumscription, subsumption, envelopment, reception, encompassment, comprehensiveness.

2. That which is comprehended, inclusion, scope, compass, embrace, range, reach, limits, sphere, province, field, latitude, composition, breadth, constitution, precinct, tour, bailiwick, arena, capacity, expanse, extent, walk, premises, dominion, bounds, ambit, zone, measure, region, circuit, realm, course, demesne, sweep, domain, span, orbit, stretch, area, swing.

3. *(Logic)* Sum of attributes which make up a conception, intension, connotation, totality of concept, force, complete conception, range of objects to which a term may be applied, total implication, depth of a notion.

4. Capacity to understand, power to grasp ideas, intelligence, mental capacity, capability, understanding, insight, mind, reason, mental grasp, ability to know, cognition, conception, discernment, realization, assimilation, command of thought, apprehension, perception, awareness, recognition, knowledge, liberality, mastery of thought, penetration, enlightenment, awareness of, apperception, conversance with, perspicacity, familiarity with, cognizance, imagination, sense, intuition, conception, wisdom, intellect.

COMPREHENSIVE, *adj.* Extensive, inclusive, comprehending, thoroughgoing, sweeping, wide-embracing, far-reaching, of great scope, general, expansive, discursive, encyclopedic, of extensive application, capacious, broad, large, wide, fully realized, exhaustive, compendious, inclusory, unexclusive, radical, thorough, sizable, liberal, ample, composite, synthetic, substantial, extended, voluminous, ecumenical, world-wide, widespread, far-going, far-spread, wholesale, full, copious, all-inclusive, overall, catholic, universal.

COMPRESS, v. Press together *or* into, squeeze together *or* into smaller compass, condense, make brief, consolidate, abbreviate, pack, truss up, force into smaller space, ram, cram, crowd, concentrate, compact, tighten, cramp, reduce, shorten, contract, abridge, make terse *or* pithy, shrivel, dehydrate, shrink, restrict in area, bind tightly, constringe, constrict, narrow, coarctate, curtail, reduce volume by pressure, wrap closely, boil down, epitomize, stuff, wedge, desiccate, coagulate, incrassate, inspissate, constipate, abstract.

COMPRESSION, n. 1. Act of compressing, condensation, squeezing, pinching, confining, ramming, cramming, crushing, decrease of size, constringing, pressing together, shortening, abbreviation, densification, thickening, narrowing, consolidation, abstraction, ellipsis, abridgment, epitomization, stricture, hapology *(Philol.),* syncope, synaeresis *(Pros.),* shrinking, atrophy, diminution, astringing, astriction *(Med.),* elision, crowding, reduction, compaction, constraint, constriction, concentration, contraction.
2. Compressed state, brevity, terseness, force, condensation, abridgment, density, solidity, concentration, shortness, briefness, consistence, epitome, constringency, astringency, concretion, compendium, abstract, compactness, closeness, impermeability, *abrégé (Fr.),* succinctness, pithiness, conciseness, denseness, economy *(of speech),* laconism, ellipsis, syncope, consolidation, atrophy.

COMPRISE, v. 1. Comprehend, include, contain, compose, admit, subsume, enclose, embrace, encircle, incorporate, cover, infold, span, take into account *or* consideration, compass, involve, reckon among, number among, take in, embody, encompass, encincture, hold, engross.
2. Consist of, be composed of, be compounded of, amount to, be made of, be formed of, be constituted of, be resolvable into.

COMPROMISE, n. 1. Adjustment of conflicting claims *or* principles by mutual yielding, mutual concession, settlement of differences, agreement, composition, abatement of differences, peacemaking, arbitration, compensation, pacification, reconciliation, reconcilement, conciliation, accord, concession, terms, moderation, establishment of cordial relations, propitiation, appeasement, commutation, reparation, accommodation, placation, rapprochement *(Fr.),* arrangement.
2. Anything resulting from compromise, truce, settlement, agreement, mean, armistice, compact, convention, reparation, satisfaction, conciliation, harmony, accord, abatement of differences, adjustment, happy medium, golden mean, middle state, composition, mediocrity, half measures, balance, amends, *juste-milieu (Fr.),* aurea mediocritas *(Lat.),* pacification, peace, conclusion.
3. Something intermediate between different things, mid-course, middle state, golden mean, happy medium, middle ground, *juste-milieu (Fr.),* mean, fence *(coll.),* middle term *(Logic),* aurea mediocritas *(Lat.).*

COMPROMISE, v. 1. Settle by compromise, make a compromise, adjust, compose, compound, agree, harmonize, commit, arrange, concede, conciliate, commute, take the mean, come to an agreement, come to terms, meet halfway, strike

a mean, come to an understanding, make a deal, make the best of, accommodate, give and take, split the difference, arbitrate, fix by agreement, set at rest, bridge over, make a virtue of necessity, strike *or* preserve a balance, keep the golden mean, go fifty-fifty *(coll.),* conclude.
2. Take an equivocal position, steer a middle course, maintain a middle position, serve two masters, be noncommittal, straddle *(coll.),* sit on the fence *(coll.),* avoid both Scylla and Charybdis.
3. Make liable to danger, suspicion, scandal, etc., imperil, expose the repute of, endanger the reputation of, implicate, hazard, place in a dubious position, involve unfavorably, make vulnerable, discredit, risk, commit, embarrass, jeopardize the name of, bring into danger, put at hazard, put in jeopardy.

COMPTROLLER, n. Controller, registrar, one employed to check expenditures, treasurer, bursar, purser, trustee, accountant, depositary, steward, cash keeper, manager, banker, almoner, cashier.

COMPULSION, n. Act of compelling, state of being compelled, coercion, constraint, application *or* employment of force, pressure, enforcement, coaction, urgency, duress, press, necessity, impressment, demand, restriction, limitation, constriction, the big stick, the sword, high-pressure methods, stress, eminent domain *(Law),* martial law, lynch law, mob law, ultima ratio *(Lat.),* requirement, what must be, inevitability, imposition, choicelessness, unavoidableness, dint, Hobson's choice, arbitrary power, absolutism, domination, check, control, inhibition, vigor, incumbency, cohibition, curb, despotism, pinch, oppression, exigency, controlling force, violence, the strong arm *(coll.),* obligation, requiring force, restraint.

COMPULSORY, adj. 1. Using compulsion, high-pressure, compelling, constraining, binding, forcing, coercive, restrictive, forcible, coactive, compulsatory, compulsive, coercitive, imperious, constrictive, limitary, cohibitive, requisite, urgent, peremptory, importunate, imperative, severe, strong-arm *(coll.),* commanding, demanding, repressive, pressing, oppressive, restraining.
2. Compelled, obligatory, forced, binding, not to be evaded, necessary, enforced, restrictive, rigorous, imperative, required, inevitable, harsh, exacting, inescapable, ineluctable, indefeasible, irresistible, irrevocable, unpreventable, needful, inexorable, prescriptive, jussory, jussive, final, conclusive, decretory, mandatory, demanded, behooving, incumbent on *or* upon, chargeable to, stringent, unavoidable, against one's will, severe, peremptory, inevasible, authoritative, imperious, exigent, urgent, commanded, prescriptory, decretive.

COMPUNCTION, n. Remorse, contrition, regret, penitence, sorrow, repentance, uneasiness of conscience *or* feelings, regret for wrongdoing, sorrow for having pained another, self-reproach, reluctance, misgiving, qualm, sting of conscience, resipiscence, contriteness, shame, attrition *(Theol.),* self-humiliation, sackcloth and ashes, pangs of conscience, bitter regret, reproach of conscience, prick of conscience, self-reproof, self-accusation, self-condemnation, self-conviction, twinge of remorse.

COMPUNCTIOUS, adj. 1. Repentant, contrite, remorseful, conscience-stung, penitential, sorry, touched, regretting, regretful, self-reproaching, self-accusing, conscience-smitten, self-reproving, repining, apologetic, rueful, melted, affected, sorrowful, penitent, self-condemning, softened, self-humiliating, self-convicting.

2. Causing compunction, causing misgiving, conscience-stinging, compunctive, reproaching, accusing, smiting, condemning, convicting, reproving, chiding, reprehending.

COMPUTABLE, *adj.* Calculable, measurable, estimable, numerable, appreciable, countable, reckonable, commensurable, determinable, mensurable, gaugeable, assessable, fathomable, appraisable, commensurate.

COMPUTATION, *n.* 1. Calculation, act, process *or* method of computing, estimation, reckoning, accounting, ciphering, counting, figuring, adding, enumeration, footing, numeration, summation, casting, totaling, compute, deduction, recension, mensuration, appreciation, survey, appraisement, dead reckoning, measurement, accountancy, assessment, evaluation, calibration, bookkeeping, admeasurement, audit, calculus.

2. Result of computing, amount computed, estimate, account, reckoning, footing, sum, cast, total, count, audit, metage, measurement, figures, survey, valuation, statistics, appraisal, assessment.

COMPUTE, *v.* Determine by calculation, reckon, calculate, estimate, add, add up, foot up, total, figure, tally, appraise, sum up, score up, count, number, rate, cast, cast up, take an account of, keep accounts, mensurate, quantify, enumerate, balance accounts *or* books, gauge, survey, meter, mete, fathom, sound, probe, plumb, appreciate, valuate, cipher, approximate, assess, figure up, measure, value, size up (*coll.*), figure out, tell.

COMRADE, *n.* Companion, associate, mate, ally, friend, colleague, consociate, confrere, partner, teammate, copartner, fellow, consort, playmate, shipmate, workfellow, benchfellow, pal (*sl.*), chum (*coll.*), confederate, assistant, helpmate, helper, cohelper, co-worker, co-operator, adjutant, collaborator, aid, aider, adjuvant, compeer, boon companion, playfellow, abettor, coadjutor, peer, accomplice, buddy (*coll.*), adherent, accompanier, faithful friend, devoted friend, bosom friend, other self, intimate, confidant, attendant, crony, close companion, fellow member, accompanist, adjunct.

CON, *adv.* Against, contrary to, opposed to, adversely, contrarily, conversely, oppositionally, inversely, negatively, reversely, contrariwise, contrastedly, versus.

CON, *v.* 1. Learn by heart, learn word for word, learn by rote, commit to memory, learn, study, get, acquire, acquaint oneself with, cram (*coll.*), peruse, examine, scan, master, pore over, grind (*sl.*), memorize, stamp on the memory, hammer *or* drive into one's head, get up, impress on the memory, work up, engrave on the memory.

2. Speculate, contemplate, think, mull over, deliberate, revolve, philosophize, intellectualize, mentalize, cerebrate, put on one's thinking cap, be engrossed in thought, cogitate, be absorbed, ransack the brains, cudgel the brains, commune, bethink, apply oneself (*mentally*), trouble one's head about, dream, turn over mentally, reflect, think over, concentrate upon, weigh, ruminate, muse, meditate, ponder, consider.

CONCATENATE, *adj.* Concatenated, conjoined, linked together (*as a chain*), articulated, related, united, joined, integrated, cumulative, connected, accumulative, associated, consecutive, successive,

merging, interlinking, additive, linked, sequent, serial, interlocked.

CONCATENATE, *v.* Unite in series *or* chain, catenate, unite, link, connect, relate, associate, form a series, join, conjoin, hang together, unify, band, league, fuse, string together, hook up, add together, combine, articulate, integrate, coalesce, blend, merge.

CONCATENATION, *n.* Adding together, union, stringing together, coupling, connection, junction, conjunction, accouplement, uniting, combination, linking, linkage, continuity, conjugation, integration, hookup, interlocking, interlinking, continuousness, consecutiveness, banding, fusion, articulation.

2. Series of interdependent *or* interconnected things *or* events, chain, sequence, train, set, rank, range, thread, string, succession, progression, line, column, file, cavalcade, caravan, tier, catenation, queue, procession, cycle, row, catena, course.

CONCAVE, *adj.* Curving inward, rounded inward, hollow, hollowed out, indented, sunken, dented, cupped, incurved, incurving, incurvate, troughlike, calathiform, cyathiform, poculiform.

CONCAVE, *v.* Render concave, hollow, furrow, dish, dent, dint, indent, depress, scoop out, gouge out, dig out, excavate, groove, channel.

CONCAVITY, *n.* Concave, depression, hollow, indentation, dip, hollowness, pocket, trough, dint, dimple, sink, antrum (*Anat.*), sinus, furrow, cup, ditch, bowl, impression, crater, pit, cutting.

CONCEAL, *v.* 1. Withdraw from observation, hide, dissemble, secrete, cache, disguise, shelter, camouflage, cover, bury, screen, cloak, obscure, mask, ensconce, keep in the background, veil, curtain, becloud, cloud, blind, befog, keep in the shade, render invisible, latentize, keep out of sight, make inconspicuous *or* indiscernible *or* unperceptible *or* unapparent, hugger-mugger.

2. Keep secret, keep clandestine, secrete, hide, dissemble, veil, cover, obscure, mask, camouflage, cloak.

CONCEALED, *adj.* Hidden, secreted, unrevealed, secret, covered, inconspicuous, screened, masked, unperceived, dissembled, obscured, imperceptible, sheltered, buried, unseen, unexposed, delitescent, disguised, camouflaged, indiscernible, unapparent, invisible, clandestine, hugger-mugger.

CONCEALMENT, *n.* 1. Act of concealing, hiding, dissembling, obscuring, camouflaging, disguising, covering, burying, screening, ensconcing, veiling, secretion, masking, sheltering.

2. State of being concealed, dormancy, latency, secretion, quiescence, privacy, obscurity, burial, nonappearance, delitescence, inconspicuousness, imperceptibility, camouflage, disguise, invisibility.

3. Hiding place, ambush, cover, shelter, cache, shield, blind, camouflage, retreat, ambuscade, secret place, covert, coverture, refuge, hideaway, mew.

CONCEDE, *v.* 1. Admit (*to be true, just, etc.*), allow, yield, agree, accede, recognize, acquiesce, own, assent, permit, acknowledge, accept, defer to, abide by, come round to (*a way of thinking*), be persuaded, come over, confess, vouchsafe.

2. Yield, grant, deliver, transfer, give, assign, accede, cede, bequeath, hand over, donate, waive, tender, release, surrender, renounce, relinquish, abandon, vouchsafe, acquiesce, resign, deliver up, give up.

CONCEIT, *n.* 1. Self-love, self-esteem, bragging,

self-estimation, vanity, conceitedness, self-praise, self-importance, boastfulness, overweening pride, arrogance, fanfaronade, braggadocio, vainglory, self-commendation, self-laudation, overbearance, swelled-headedness, self-glorification, haughtiness, complacency, egotism, egoism, self-exultation, self-adulation, self-approbation, self-admiration, swagger, strutting, disdain, self-worship, hauteur, jactation, gasconade, self-inflation, self-applause, vaingloriousness, superciliousness, amour-propre *(Fr.)*.

2. Good *or* favorable opinion, esteem, favor, respect, regard, admiration, honor, estimation, approbation, approval, compliment, appreciation, sanction, praise, commendation, acclamation, laudation, applause.

3. Faculty of conceiving, understanding, grasp, apprehension, capacity, comprehension, faculty, perception, grasp of intellect, cognizance, power, acumen, discernment, perspicacity, recognition, judgment, cognition.

4. Concept, idea, thought, notion, impression, conception, belief, opinion, apprehension, theory, consideration, conviction, persuasion, reflection, sentiment, perception, supposition, presumption, presupposition, surmise, judgment.

5. Fantastic notion, fancy, whim, vagary, fad, idiosyncrasy, idiocrasy, eccentricity, mental twist, peculiarity, freak of the brain, erraticism, crank, quirk, fit, kink, humor, crotchet, caprice, dream, maggot, illusion, fantasy, whimsy.

6. Elaborate image *(in poetry, etc.)*, gongorism, affected expression, elaborate figure of speech, strained metaphor, novel expression, far-fetched simile, verbal ornamentation, ornamentation *(in poetry, etc.)*, metaphysical verbalism, marinism, stylistic extravagance.

CONCEIT, *v.* Adulate, flatter, wheedle, cajole, soft-soap *(coll.)*, puff, lionize, magnify, butter *(coll.)*, fawn, slaver, commend lavishly, praise to the skies, sawder *(coll.)*, blarney, honey.

CONCEITED, *adj.* Self-important, opinionated, egotistical, peacockish, haughty, contemptuous, proud, pompous, self-esteeming, blown, boasting, swell-headed, supercilious, bragging, disdainful, gasconading, snobbish, swollen, stuck-up *(coll.)*, puffed up, overbearing, inflated, strutting, lofty, overproud, fanfaronading, ostentatious, exulting, overweening, cock-a-hoop, lordly, cocky, pert, vain, vainglorious.

CONCEIVABLE, *adj.* Imaginable, apprehensible, thinkable, fanciable, believable, credible, tenable, picturable, supposable, knowable, understandable, cognizable, ponderable, comprehensible, intelligible, perceivable, appreciable.

CONCEIVE, *v.* 1. Form a notion, imagine, think, fancy, excogitate, mull over, realize, deliberate, envision, cogitate, envisage, consider, concentrate upon, ransack the brains, ruminate, philosophize, apply oneself *(mentally)*, meditate, dream, muse, commune, ponder, cerebrate, speculate, bethink, con over, weigh, consider, revolve.

2. Comprehend, understand, grasp mentally, apprehend, recognize, perceive, discern, enter into the idea of, appreciate, fathom, realize, get the hang of *(coll.)*, command, absorb, savvy *(sl.)*, catch the idea of, gain insight into, gripe, seize, be cognizant of, get *(coll.)*, digest, assimilate, master, read into, get to the bottom of, see into, penetrate, imagine, see, make out, cognize, know, understand the meaning *or* nature of.

3. Think, believe, maintain, assume, presume, dare say, be assured, be satisfied, be convinced, accept, embrace an opinion, suppose, apprehend, opine *(humor.)*, deem, be of an opinion, realize, hold, guess, perceive as true, know, look upon, estimate, credit, entertain *(a view, opinion, etc.)*, have it, nurture *or* cherish a belief, trust, adopt *(a belief, opinion, etc.)*.

4. Form an idea, originate, think of, develop, hatch, form, fabricate, coin, fashion, frame, plan, contrive, draft, prepare, make, create, dream up, bring about, launch, sow the seeds of, invent, produce, evolve, build, weave, concoct, innovate, neologize, neoterize, initiate, inchoate, generate, begin, start, give birth to, occasion.

5. Express *(in words)*, say, phrase, voice, put in words, accent, utter, assert, publish, remark, observe, pronounce, emit, vocalize, deliver, word, allege, make known, couch in terms, articulate, enunciate, state, aver, speak, mouth, mention, give tongue to, proclaim, declare.

6. Be pregnant, carry young, come with child, gestate, be fertilized, be impregnated, carry, be fecundated.

CONCENT, *n.* Harmony in singing, etc., accord, concentus, euphony, concord, concinnity, unison, harmony, concert, chime, homophony, symphony, symphonia, attunement, consonance, unisonance.

CONCENTRATE, *v.* 1. Converge to a center, bring into a small compass, bring toward a central point, focus, intensify, gather, embody, localize, strengthen, amass, center, corradiate, accumulate, bring to bear on one point, direct toward one object, converge, constrict, pack, constringe, fix, bring *or* draw to a common center *or* point of union, draw together, contract, assemble, muster, congregate, cluster, bunch, flock together, cramp, compact, agglomerate, aggregate, compress, heap up, swarm, forgather, conglomerate, concenter, narrow, treasure up, stow away, pour in, meet, unite, close in upon, store, salt down *or* away *(coll.)*, hoard, garner, centralize, collect, resort, congest, focalize, cause to come close together.

2. *(With on)* Think intensely, give attention to, meditate upon, ponder, apply the mind to, focus attention on, direct attention to one object, muse over, weigh, consider closely, scrutinize, attend minutely, regard carefully, revolve, contemplate, ruminate, study deeply, analyze, peruse carefully, examine closely, brood over, con over, put one's mind to, be engrossed in, bring thought to bear on one point, think about with absorption, give exclusive attention to, occupy the mind *or* thoughts with.

3. Boil down, reduce by evaporation, rectify, distill, extract, vaporize, purify by removing the foreign and nonessential, strengthen, squeeze *or* press out, refine, evaporate, crystallize, condense, coagulate, thicken, volatize, finestill, volatilize, draw out the essence, clot, precipitate, free from extraneous matter, reduce to extreme purity and strength.

CONCENTRATION, *n.* 1. Concentrated state, condensation, compression into a small compass, assemblage, accumulation, convergence, conflux, centralization, consolidation, collection upon a single point, conglomerate, agglomerate, cluster, aggregate, aggregation, conglobation, congeries, heap, mass, store, lump, hoard, congestion, focus, drift, collection, concentralization, horde, gathering, focalization, congress, conglomeration, concourse, confluence, corradiation, centrality, agglomeration, amassment, multitude, swarm, press, throng.

2. Reduction by evaporation, boiling down, condensation, distillation, purification, thickening, extraction, freeing from extraneous matter, strengthening, volatilization, rectifying, clotting, coagulation, precipitation, crystallization, constriction, contraction, compression.

3. Exclusive attention to one object, close mental application, deep thought, close attention, intense thought, heed, absorption, fixed regard, close application, diligence, intentness, devotion, intensive study, rumination, close perusal, pains, attentive regard, scrutiny, diligent attention, deliberation, minute attention, profound thought, special consideration, speculation, meditation, reflection, engrossment, cogitation, examination.

CONCEPT, *n.* Notion, thought, opinion, image, idea, conception, belief, apprehension, conviction, persuasion, presumption, supposition, judgment, theory, surmise, consideration, abstract idea, formative notion, principle, postulate, conjecture, view, hypothesis, inference, conclusion.

CONCEPTION, *n.* 1. Forming a mental image, act of conceiving, formation of a notion, musing, imagining, philosophizing, meditation, realizing, meditating, deliberating, concentrating, fancying, speculating, speculation, realization, envisioning, cogitating, envisaging, consideration, considering, communing, weighing, excogitating, dreaming, bethinking.

2. Act of conceiving, fashioning, originating, developing, hatching, devising, forming, coining, formation, fabricating, fabrication, contriving, drafting, planning, inventing, producing, evolving, building, inchoating, beginning, bringing forth, generating, occasioning, concocting, innovating, weaving, initiating, launching, creating.

3. Fertilization, fecundation, inception of pregnancy, fertilizing.

4. Concept, thought, idea, belief, conviction, presumption, judgment, surmise, consideration, formative notion, principle, conjecture, inference, conclusion, hypothesis, postulate, view, opinion, abstract idea, supposition, persuasion, image, notion, apprehension.

5. Beginning, origin, outset, inception, source, emergence, genesis, commencement, prime, start, introduction, rise, inauguration, initiation, onset, inchoation, incipience, birth, nativity, nascence, dawn, opening, budding.

6. Draft, design, plan, scheme, arrangement, proposal, outline, planning, method, projection, system, project, motion, delineation, proposition, resolution.

CONCERN, *n.* 1. Thing of moment, matter of interest, business, affair, care, matter, lookout *(coll.)*, matter in hand, exercise, job, mission, chore, transaction, topic, agendum *or* agenda *(plur.)*, duty, concernment, task in hand, charge, thing, point at issue, proceeding, case.

2. Trouble, care, anxiety, worry, solicitude, regard, vexation, stress, pressure, responsibility, annoyance, tribulation, incubus, onus, hindrance, gravamen, tax, cross, nuisance, impediment, load, strain, handicap, encumbrance.

3. Care, caution, carefulness, thought, regard, attention, heed, consideration, application, pains, exactness, heedfulness, diligence, meticulousness, conscientiousness, discrimination, fastidiousness, precaution, nicety, scrupulousness, particularity.

4. Trading concern, undertaking, partnership, house, establishment, business, firm, corporation, company, shop, store, enterprise.

5. Relation, relationship, correlation, bearing,

applicability, applicableness, alliance, association, cognation, dependence, interconnection, rapport, appositeness, connection, reference, application, belonging, appertaining, relevancy, pertinence, tie-in *(coll.)*, affinity, concernment.

CONCERN, *v.* 1. Be related, be connected, affect, be of interest *or* importance, touch upon, relate to, appertain to, bear upon, pertain to, belong to, be allied with, be implicated with, be germane to, regard, be affiliated, connect, apply, have to do with, refer to, have bearing on, be relevant, interest.

2. *(Reflexive, as concern oneself)* Be interested, be involved, be engaged, busy oneself, engage in, make it one's business, be doing, be busy with, carry on, have one's hand *or* fingers in, devote one's time to, have to do with, be about, occupy oneself, be occupied with, employ oneself in.

CONCERNMENT, *n.* 1. Moment, interest, note, mark, significance, weight, importance, emphasis, urgency, press, consequence, eminence, import, consideration, salience, solemnity, prominence, notability, materialness, seriousness, distinction, stress, standing, gravity.

2. Relation, bearing, association, correlation, applicability, applicableness, cognation, alliance, dependence, interconnection, appositeness, tie-in *(coll.)*, connection, reference, relevancy, affinity, application, belonging, appertaining, pertinence, rapport, concern.

3. Solicitude, worry, anxiety, concern, trouble, vexation, care, stress, pressure, responsibility, encumbrance, load, handicap, strain, impediment, onus, hindrance, gravamen, tax, cross, nuisance, annoyance, tribulation, incubus.

4. Thing of moment, matter of interest, affair, business, concern, care, matter, lookout *(coll.)*, matter in hand, exercise, job, chore, transaction, topic, agendum *or* agenda *(plur.)*, duty, mission, task in hand, charge, thing, point at issue, case, proceeding.

CONCERT, *n.* 1. Agreement in a design *or* plan, harmony, accord, combined action, joint concern, concurrence, consonance, accordance, coherence, unity, unison, co-operation, congeniality, assent, concord, concurrency, coaction, correspondence, coworking, synergy, unanimity, hook-up *(coll.)*, fusion of interests, mutual assistance, coincidence, compatibility, coalition, tie-in *(coll.)*, conjunction, alliance, coadunation, collaboration, complicity, collusion, acquiescence, concomitance, synergism, combined action *or* agency, consentience, trust, coadjuvancy, association, conspiracy, corporation, participation, joint operation, coagency, consent, consentaneity, coefficiency, partnership, rapport, coadjument, confederation, consolidation, union, sympathy, merger, pool, teamwork, connivance, syndicate, combination.

2. Public musical performance, philharmonic, musical entertainment, recital, musicale, serenade, symphony, cantata, oratorio, choral performance, popular concert, chamber concert, aubade *(Fr.)*.

CONCERT, *v.* Plan together, contrive, arrange by agreement, act in conjunction, conspire, plot, cooperate, concoct, design, devise, accord, link forces, combine strengths, merge, federate, hatch, associate, cowork, coact, collaborate, collude, concur, project, lay down a plan, shape *or* mark out a course, predetermine, participate, organize, contribute, chip in *(coll.)*, league, work together, stand shoulder to shoulder, make common cause with, line up with *(coll.)*, pull together, frame, pool interests, confederate, play ball *(coll.)*, operate jointly, band together, unite efforts, hunt in couples, be concordant, draw up jointly, lay heads together, outline cooperatively, coadjuvate.

CONCERTED, *adj.* Contrived *or* arranged by agreement, prearranged, planned, devised, united, intended, purposed, willed jointly, predetermined, forehand, consentient, concurrent, concomitant, accordant, agreed, cooperative, concordant, by assent, associate, conjoined, consonant, contrived, concocted, well-weighed, well-laid, premeditated, consentant, consentaneous, assenting.

CONCESSION, *n.* 1. Act of conceding, yielding, consent, compromise, admission, recognition, toleration, relinquishment, allowance, modifying, consideration, assent, cession, adjustment, giving, qualification, tempering, giving in, accession, rebate, discount, reduction, bestowal, donation, acknowledgment, apology, conferment, granting, presentation, consignment, abatement, deduction, dispensation, extenuation, compliance, mitigation. 2. Thing conceded, point yielded, grant, boon, privilege, authorization, exemption, favor, grace, indulgence, brevet, charter, accession, authority, sanction, license, leave, warrant, permit, benefit, permission, allowance, vouchsafement, sufferance, immunity, gratification, prerogative, aid, subsidy, gift, service, alimony, franchise, qualification, condition, exception, reservation, dispensation, provision, limitation.

CONCILIATE, *v.* Overcome distrust *or* hostility, allay anger, pacify, placate, compose, alleviate, arbitrate, satisfy, assuage, reconcile, propitiate, soothe, set straight, win, gain, engage, secure, win over, restore harmony, persuade, bring round, prevail with, render compatible, bring to reason, bring to one's senses, make to be at peace, calm, restore to friendship, speak one fair, settle, adjust, accommodate, make peace between, ingratiate, settle differences, reunite, heal the breach, meet halfway, intervene, gratify, beguile, apologize, intercede, harmonize, mediate, mollify, put in tune, show the white flag, make a peace offering, patch up, pour balm into, make up a quarrel, beg pardon, mend, hold out the olive branch, disarm, pour oil on troubled waters, bring to agreement, bridge over, bring to terms, appease, square, make friendly.

CONCILIATORY, *adj.* Conciliative, tending to conciliate, reconciling, pacific, pacifying, friendly, propitiatory, peacemaking, accommodative, civil, placatory, mediatory, remissive, forbearing, soft, propitiating, reconciliatory, pacificatory, placable, concordant, agreeable, accordant, unrevengeful, congenial, compatible, harmonious, forgiving, unresentful, long-suffering, reconcilable, cordial, atoning, expiatory, merciful, generous, clement, compassionate, winning, persuasive, courteous, bland, polite, urbane, decorous, deferential, on one's knees, prostrate, soothing, obeisant, tactful, soft-spoken, amiable, gracious, affable, mannerly, disarming, respectful, complaisant, magnanimous, obliging, gentle, placative, sacrificial, piacular.

CONCISE, *adj.* Expressing much in few words, brief, succinct, terse, comprehensive, trenchant, compendious, short, laconic, summary, compact, close, neat, crisp, epigrammatic, condensed, curt, compressed, pointed, pithy, curtate, curtailed, to the point, sparing of words, reticent, word-bound, indisposed to talk, uncommunicative, contracted, taciturn, unconversable, abridged, synoptic, sharp, abbreviated, decisive, direct, emphatic, forceful,

straightforward, gnomic, vigorous, pauciloquent, pregnant, sententious, elliptical.

CONCLAVE, *n.* Private meeting, secret council, private assembly, party gathering, convocation, board, council, parley, consistory, conventicle, conference, session, sitting, séance, synod, cabal, convention, camarilla.

CONCLUDE, *v.* 1. End, finish, bring to an end, terminate, close, expire, be all over, run its course, become void, run out, stop, desist, cease, perfect, windup *(coll.)*, leave off, quit, halt, stay, hold, discontinue, drop, break off, attain the goal, stop short, culminate, reach completion, come to a stand *or* standstill, make short work of, fulfill, perform, crown, dispose of, dispatch, discharge, withdraw from, pass away, table, throw up, die, ripen, mature, lapse, surcease, abandon, come to a conclusion *or* close, ring down the curtain, shut up shop, call it a day *(coll.)*, consummate, give over, draw to a close, come to an end, say in conclusion, come to a full stop, knock off *(coll.)*, have done with. 2. Determine by reasoning, reach as an end of reasoning, infer as from premises, deduce, judge, gather as a consequence, draw inferences, imagine, arrive at, deem, make deductions, guess, reason, presume, syllogize, take it *(coll.)*, think, suppose, assume, consider, surmise, distinguish, interpret, reckon, esteem, regard, come to believe, close by inferring *(as an argument)*, take for granted, dare say, fancy, form an opinion, find, determine, perceive, derive, discern, understand, discover, theorize, hypothesize, calculate *(coll.)*, opine *(humorous)*, be inclined to think, realize, conceive, apprehend, estimate, suspect, see, glean, think likely. 3. Determine, decide, resolve, arrive at an opinion *or* judgment concerning, make a final determination *or* judgment, come to a decision *or* conclusion, make up one's mind regarding, judge, ascertain, adjudge, satisfy oneself, dismiss all doubt, assure oneself, make sure of, decree, fix, commit oneself, seal, confirm, set at rest, will, dijudicate, verify, judicate, find, adjudicate. 4. Bring to a decision *or* settlement, settle *or* arrange finally, bring about as a result, bring to pass, do, effect, accomplish, achieve, bring to a successful issue, settle, arrange, complete, adjust, compound, compromise, close with, clinch, make, strike a bargain, consummate, hammer out, reach an understanding, stamp, make good, come to an agreement, commute, attain, set at rest, straighten out, execute, realize, fulfill, round out, perfect, dispose of, perform, discharge, enact, produce, carry out, dispatch, carry through, render, work out, pull *(coll.)*, fix by agreement, compass, cap, come to terms, close, work, contrive. 5. *(Law, generally in passive)* Stop, estop, bar, hinder, cut off, restrain, limit, preclude, forbid, determine, deny, prohibit, interdict, check, curb, stay, disallow, circumscribe, shut off, proscribe, restrict.

CONCLUSION, *n.* 1. Deduction, inference, belief, derivation, proposition inferred from premises *(Logic)*, surmise, assumption, finding, observation, illation, apprehension, notion, concept, reflection, consequence, reason, thought, consideration, idea, hypothesis, theory, connotation, view, corollary, image, presumption, impression, derived principle, self-persuasion, self-conviction, assurance, mind, persuasion, plerophory, conception. 2. Determination, decision, judgment, verdict, outcome, end, opinion, arbitrament, resolution, upshot, finding, ultimatum, declaration, sentence, adjudication, conviction, view, choice, decree, report, award, moral, issue, result.

3. End, close, termination, completion, upshot, finish, summing up, final part, last main division of a discourse, postscript, sequel, windup, crown, cap, ultimate, period, peroration, catastrophe, resolution, denouement, consummation, postlude, fulfillment, event, finale, issue, epilogue, codicil, outgrowth, fruition, expiration, finis, outcome, expiry, fall of the curtain, stoppage, apodosis, term, terminal, final touch, omega, limit, goal, cessation, climax, dissolution, disbanding, izzard *(coll.)*, fait accompli *(Fr.)*, discontinuance, halt, conclude, terminus, desistance, death, surcease, stopping, arrest, check, abandonment, standstill, checkmate, quietus, desinence *(Gram. and Pros.)*, deadlock, culmination, abolition, knockout blow, abolishment, breakup, overthrow, extermination, downfall, extinction, full stop, stand, elimination, extinguishment, annihilation, eradication, decease, effectuation, accomplishment, achievement, coup de grace *(Fr.)*, crowning of the edifice, keystone, arrival, realization, attainment, perfection, coping stone, execution, performance, discharge, last curtain call *(coll.)*, dispatch, last muster *(coll.)*, last roundup *(coll.)*.

4. Settlement *(as of a treaty, bargain, etc.)*, arrangement, establishment, bargain, pact, close, covenant, outcome of discussion *or* arbitration, adjustment, arrival at a plan, agreement, contract, understanding, compact, protocol, convention, compaction, enactment, discharge, working out, rendering, treaty, end of pleading *or* conveyance *(Law)*, compromise, entente, consequence, bond, composition, commutation, effectuation, mutual *or* reciprocal concession, abatement of differences, successful issue, compounding, realization, sequel, fulfillment, decision, concordat, charter, league, summary, pay-off *(coll.)*, fait accompli *(Fr.)*, execution, completion, resolution, alliance.

5. Estoppal, bar to changing position taken, impediment, obstruction, hindrance, prevention, stoppage, preclusion, check, detention, constraint, restraint, inhibition, determent, counteraction, safeguard of consistent action.

CONCLUSIVE, *adj.* Decisive, convincing, telling, serving to settle *or* decide a question, irrefutable, clinching, clenching, undeniable, cogent, strong, definitive, indisputable, demonstrable, powerful, valid, unanswerable, unquestionable, completing, reliable, obvious, accurate, determinative, clear, inappealable, incontrovertible, unimpeachable, crowning, decided, evidential, answering, perfect, testatory, verifiable, confirming, authenticating, authoritative, supportive, weighty, significant, ratificatory, corroborative, authenticated, patent, verificative, overwhelming, first-hand, indubitable, indicative, incontestable, apparent, commanding, manifest, undoubted, documentary, perspicuous, damning, testimonial, testificatory, confirmed, satisfactory, irresistible, categorical, compelling, apodictic, affording proof, evincive, implicative, probative, demonstrative, plain, palpable, defined, certain, suggestive, self-evident, unavoidable, irrevocable, obligatory, infallible, inescapable, conspicuous, substantial, irrefragable.

2. Belonging to close *or* termination, forming an end *or* termination, ending, terminal, settled, terminative, conclusory, eventual, farthest, last, vergent, approaching an end, drawing to a close, extreme, finished, over, final, putting an end to debate *or* question, involving a conclusion *or* decision, completing, crowning, ultimate, closing, absolute, concluding.

3. Final, ultimate, without appeal, imperative, official, absolute, incontestable, authoritative, settled, indisputable, decretive, unavoidable, mandatory, irrevocable, obligatory, inescapable.

CONCOCT, *v.* Make by combining ingredients, contrive, plan, devise, project, brew, frame, mix, prepare, hatch, invent, design, compound, form, fabricate, scheme, formulate, create, originate, imagine, produce, make up, prepare with art, get up, construct, trump up, think up, cook up *(coll.)*, spin, build, coin, forge, cast, shape, innovate, perfect, refine, elaborate, arrange, develop, plot, evolve, compose, fashion, mature.

CONCOCTION, *n.* Compound, mixture, creation, preparation, brew, dose, make-up, fiction, plot, fabrication, invention, contrivance, scheme, plan, manufacture, hatching, production, embroidery, conglomeration, exaggeration, prevarication, lie, falsification, composition, synthesis, fable, yarn, myth, colored tale, far-fetched story, trumped-up story, false statement, forgery, artifice, nostrum, story *(coll.)*.

CONCOMITANT, *adj.* Accompanying, attending, concurrent, conjoined, simultaneous, collateral, coincident, coexistent, synchronous, coterminous, contemporaneous, connected, belonging, agreeing, attendant, accompanimental, associated with, in time, twin, fellow, synchronal, coefficient, joint, coupled with, coinstantaneous, coetaneous, in step, coeval, isochronal, coactive, co-ordinate, concordant, synergetic, synergistic, consilient, in tempo, isochronous, appendant, conjoined with, accessory, contemporary, in sync *(cant)*.

CONCOMITANT, *n.* Concomitant quality, circumstance, *or* thing, attendant, attending *or* accompanying circumstance, accessory, accessary *(chiefly Law)*, companion, attribute, additament, complement, side issue, episode, augmentation, corollary, appanage, addition, appurtenance, obbligato *(Music)*, accessary fact, simultaneous event, adjunct, appendage, affix, coefficient, co-existent factor.

CONCORD, *n.* 1. Agreement between persons, unanimity, concordance, concurrence in opinions *or* sentiments, etc., accord, amity, peace, assent, friendship, harmony, unity, good understanding, love, sympathy, communion, fraternity, response, consensus, congeniality, neighborliness, cordiality, brotherliness, fellowship, brotherhood, oneness, cordial relations, compliance, consentaneity, good will, consentaneousness, rapport *(Fr.)*, conformity, concert, conformance, compatibility, accordance, understanding, like-mindedness, accommodation, cooperation, joint assent, acclamation, one voice, affinity, mutual regard, rapprochement *(Fr.)*, acquiescence, comradeship, union, amicability, reconciliation, pacification, adaptability.

2. Agreement between things, mutual fitness, harmony, accord, unison, coherence, congruence, compatibility, affinity, consonance, coincidence, agreement, adaptation, accordance, fusion, line, concordance, conformity, proportion, symmetry, keeping, consistence, correspondence, assonance, conformance, concinnity, concurrence, organic totality, synthesis, coalescence, amalgamation, integrality, aptitude, relevancy, synchronization, pertinence, applicability, propriety, conjunction, similarity, parallelism, apposition, congeniality, uniformity, congruity, adaptability, conformation, correlation, homoousia, synonymity, equality, connaturalness.

3. Peace, peacefulness, freedom from war, harmony, truce, public tranquillity, pacifism, amity, good will, benevolence, cordial relations, exemption from hostilities, armistice, serenity, composure, calm, placidity, repose, pipe of peace, quietude, equanimity, entente, friendliness, quiet, rest, pacification, mutual understanding, quiescence.

4. *(Music)* Agreeable combination of tones simultaneously heard, harmony, accord, chorus, tunefulness, symphony, euphony, combination of tones not requiring resolution, consonance, attunement, concentus, symphoniousness, chime, consonant chord, concinnity.

5. Agreement by stipulation, compact, treaty, covenant, peace, mutual agreement, contract, understanding, bargain, engagement, promise, assurance, guarantee, pact, bond, convention, consent, warrant, avowal, solemn declaration *or* word, modus vivendi *(Lat.)*, deal *(coll.)*, entente cordiale *(Fr.)*.

CONCORDANT, *adj.* Agreeing, harmonious, symphonious, suiting, agreeable, unanimous, at one, congenial, peaceful, placative, amicable, in accord, accordant, conformable, consistent, even, commensurate, consentaneous, synchronized, in rapport, assenting, concurrent, like-minded, allied, consilient, acquiescent, tranquil, untroubled, in unison with, coincident, united, cooperative, at peace, confluent, conjoined, pacific, conciliated, friendly, fraternal, pacified, cemented, attuned, assonant, symmetrical, proportionate, halcyon, consonant, reciprocal, mutual, euphonious, well-disposed, brotherly, neighborly, sympathetic, cordial, benevolent, propitiating, accommodative, consentient, correspondent, compatible.

CONCORDAT, *n.* Compact, agreement, covenant, convention, bargain, treaty, charter, contract, league, alliance, protocol, stipulation, entente cordiale *(Fr.)*, understanding, pragmatic sanction, Magna Carta, Zollverein *(Ger.)*, customs union.

CONCOURSE, *n.* 1. Assemblage, throng, crowd, gathering, collection, assembly, meeting, rout, multitude, company, congregation, conference, aggregation, large number, attendance, horde, host, legion, rabble, deluge, flood, body of people, festivity, reception, conflux, meet, levee, force, forgathering, soiree, aggregation, cluster, session, convergence, convocation, rally, congress, muster, get-together *(coll.)*, plenum, quorum, caucus, synod, crush, press, reunion, conclave, resort, congeries, swarm, group, roundup, association, mob, convention.

2. Open public place, driveway in a park, turf, promenade, mall, passage, open space in a railroad station, grounds for racing or athletic sports, boardwalk, public walk, track, path, lane, avenue, thoroughfare, causeway, boulevard, underpass, tunnel, esplanade, corridor, communication, course.

3. Coming together, confluence, conflux, mass, flocking together, concentration, focalization, accumulation, amassment, junction, convergence, joining, conjunction, concurrence, conjuncture, conjugation, congestion, drift, heap, aggregation, store, stock, aggregate, conglomeration, running together.

CONCRETE, *adj.* 1. Concerning a single thing *or* instance, specific, special, individual, singular, exact, particular, precise, express, fixed, single, well-defined, restrictive, determinate, limiting, present, instant, direct, faithful, reliable, minute,

pointed, isolated, explicit, separate, peculiar, distinct, plain, vivid, graphic, true, verifiable, strict, literal, clear-cut, factual, unequivocal, valid, definite, authentic, determinative, individualized, corporeal.

2. Constituting an actual thing *or* instance, non-abstract, pertaining to realities, concerning actual instances, specific, tangible, definite, finite, palpable, material, corporeal, based on existing phenomena, sensible, perceptible to the mind, perceivable, drawn from life *or* experience, free from abstraction, realistic, actual, factual, literal.

3. Formed by coalescence of separate particles into a mass, united in a coagulated *(or condensed or solid)* state, made of concrete, firm, solid, solidified, compact, consolidated, hard, cement, substantial, petrified, stone-like, rock-like, lithoid, petrific, lapidified, compressed, indurate, dense, coalesced, unyielding, impervious, calcified, impermeable, coalescent, coherent, cohesive, callous, conglutinative, complex, concreted, formed by admixture, conglomerated, compound, agglomerated, impenetrable.

CONCRETE, *n.* 1. Concrete idea *or* term, title, concrete object *or* thing, specific, instance, item, identity, individual, actuality, reality, entity, being, integer, phenomenon, nomination, detail, appellation, particular, specification, minutia, example, image, representation, style, name, matter, point, fact, notion, concept, quality, denomination, substantiality.

2. Mass formed by coalescence *or* concretion of particles of matter, concretion, mixture, compound, agglomerate, coagulum, congelation, solid, crystal, calcification, admixture. block, cake, condensation, stone, rock, lump, adamant mass, solid body, conglomeration, conglomerate, callous, petrified object, firm combination, cohesion, clot, agglomeration, fossil.

3. Artificial stone-like building *or* paving material, cemented stones and gravel, pavement, paving, macadam, asphalt, mortar, lute.

CONCRETE, *v.* 1. Form into a mass coalescence of particles, solidify, harden, become firm *or* solid, coagulate, congeal, clot, coalesce, cement, unite solidly, block, thicken, indurate, petrify, solder, regelate, conglutinate, weld, fuse, curdle, be consolidated, condense, densify, set, lapidify, granulate. crystallize, braze, fix, callous, cake, ferruminate, precipitate, calcify, render solid, lithify *(Geol.)*, firm, fossilize.

2. Treat *or* lay with concrete, pave, surface, use *or* apply concrete, cement.

CONCRETION, *n.* 1. State of being concreted, act *or* process of concreting, solidification, fusion, crystallization, coagulation, cohering, adhesion, coherence, adherence, cementation, accretion, consolidation, agglomeration, conglomeration, soldering, lithification, densification, curdling, lapidification, petrification, fixation, precipitation, calcification, induration, regelation, cementing, aggregation, brazing, congelation, hardening, setting, firming, conglutination, agglutination.

2. Clot, knot, nodule, lump, solid body, cake, solid mass formed by coalescence *or* cohesion, concrete, abnormal solid *or* calcified mass *(Pathol.)*, gob *(sl.)*, firm combination, compound, stone, rock, coagulum, conglomeration, calculus *(Med.)*, conglomerate, concreted mass.

CONCUBINE, *n.* Mistress, paramour, odalisque, prostitute, jade, courtesan, kept woman. common law wife, doxy *(sl.)*.

CONCUPISCENCE, *n.* Sensual appetite, eager *or* illicit desire, inordinate desire, sensuality, flesh, lubricity, aphrodisia, carnality, animalism, lust, crudeness, grossness, ruttishness, lewdness, Adam, pruriency, animal appetite, bestiality, lechery, libidinousness, lasciviousness, impurity, salacity, venery, satyrism, the beast, the Old Adam, sinful craving, extravagant passion, depraved appetite, morbid longing, salaciousness, wantonness, bodily appetite, animal *or* carnal nature, sexuality, coveting.

CONCUPISCENT, *adj.* Full of ill-regulated passion, inordinately desirous, animalistic, ruttish, lubricious, sensual, lustful, libidinous, salacious, prurient, carnal, physical, gross, crude, unchaste, bodily, Paphian, lewd, wanton, bestial, licentious, voluptuous, shameless, lickerish, lecherous, erotic, lascivious, goatish, satyric, theroid, earthy, fleshly, morbidly passionate, depraved in appetite *or* cravings, brutish, covetous, amorous.

CONCUR, *v.* 1. Accord in opinion, coincide, agree, acquiesce, grant, concede, harmonize, endorse, approve, assent, comport, go along with, cohere, correspond, quadrate, suit, square, meet, respond, chime, reciprocate, conform with, hold with, be uniform, accommodate, comply, gee *(sl.),* lend oneself to, be accordant, go with, receive, consent, dovetail, hitch *(coll.),* adapt to, homologize, hit it off with *(coll.),* give one's voice for, consort, sympathize with, ratify, homologate, uphold, subscribe to, fit, befit, do, accredit, countenance, sanction, approbate, allow, yield, come to an agreement *or* understanding, come to terms, get together *(coll.),* shake on it *(coll.),* admit, tally, jibe *(coll.),* accede, fall in with, acknowledge, accept, cotton *(coll.).*

2. Come together, meet, unite, focus, center, converge, concentrate, focalize, be conjoined, be combined, corradiate, fall in with, close in upon, concenter, concentralize.

3. Co-operate, combine, contribute jointly, work together, conjoin, confederate, help, be associated, conspire, coadjute, collude, coact, aid, coadjuvate, synergize, pull together, unite efforts, fraternize, league *or* band together, collaborate, concert, work *or* operate jointly, coadunate, team, conduce to, consort, join forces, pool interests, play ball *(coll.).*

4. Coincide in time, exist together, be coeval, be synchronous, be concomitant, contemporize, be contemporary, be coincident, be simultaneous, accompany, go with, be contemporaneous, keep in step, synchronize, be contiguous, be concurrent, go hand in hand, keep pace with.

CONCURRENCE, *n.* 1. Act of concurring, a meeting *or* coming together, union, conjunction, coincidence, junction, joining, meeting, joinder, accouplement, concurrency, concourse, conflux, connection, congress, concentration, focalization, concentralization, hookup, conjugation, tie-up *(coll.),* assemblage, confluence, gathering, commissure, coalescence, coadunation, contingence, contiguity, contiguousness, correlation, corradiation.

2. Accordance in opinion, agreement, alliance, consent, acceptance, accord, concord, harmony, concordance, acquiesence, joint approval *or* approbation, concert, concinnity, assonance, congruency, congruity, fitness, suitability, rapport *(Fr.),* sympathy, congruence, conformation, sanction, union, assent, consonance, meeting of minds, coincidence, conformity, consistence, unison, congeniality, affinity, compatibility,

correspondence, consistency, acknowledgment, conformance, compliance, yielding, concession, confirmation, approval, concurrency, accession, affirmation, consensus, unanimity, approbation, consentaneity, understanding, homoousia, chorus, consentience, consilience, consonancy, acclamation, like-mindedness.

3. Simultaneous occurrence, correspondence in time, coincidence, concurrency, coexistency, coetaneity, conjuncture, contemporaneity, timeliness, coevality, synchronism, coexistence, contemporaneousness, simultaneousness, juncture, synchronousness, simultaneity, synchronization, accord, consonance, concomitancy, coextension, concomitance.

4. Co-operation, working together, coagency, concurrency, coworking, coadunation, synergy, association, conjunction, conjugation, alliance, concert, complicity, participation, unified action, joint operation, union, combination, collective action, coadjuvancy, partnership, collaboration, mutual assistance, concomitance, incorporation, consolidation, coadministration, coordination, conspiracy, incorporation, consolidation, coaction, synergism, confederacy, tie-in *(coll.),* coadjument, collusion, concerted effort, coefficiency, hookup *(coll.).*

CONCURRENT, *adj.* 1. Occurring *or* existing together *or* side by side, concurring, collateral, coextensive, alongside, coexistent, united, even, accompanying, coinciding, contingent, contiguous, cognate, congenerous, congeneric, correspondent, adjacent, conterminous, tangent, juxtaposed, running, correlative, adjunctive, commissural, aligned, abreast, equidistant, concentric, parallel, in juxtaposition.

2. Acting in conjunction, co-operating, united, concurring, coactive, conjoined, associate, hand in glove with, attendant, concomitant, coincident, coadunate, synergetic, coadunative, conjoint, in alliance with, conjunctive, corporate, coadjutant, coadjutive, synergistic, co-ordinate, participating, collaborative, banded together, allied, leagued, co-operative, concerted, confederated, helping, incorporated, amalgamated, in league, unified, associated, joint, coefficient, coadjuvant, conjunct, coalitional, in cahoots *(sl.).*

3. Occurring at the same time, synchronous, coincident, conterminous, isochronal, coexisting, contemporary, coeval, coexistent, collateral, concomitant, coinstantaneous, coetaneous, in time, simultaneous, isochronous, isochrone, in tempo, attendant, coterminous, contemporaneous, synchronal, concreate, conjunctive, coeternal, in step, in sync *(cant).*

4. Having equal jurisdiction, joint and equal, co-operative, of equal authority, collateral, on a par, parallel, correspondent, sharing, coequal, collaborative, co-ordinate, co-administrative, in alliance with, equiparant, conjoint, fellow, united, equiponderant, conjunctive, combined, associate, in partnership, equivalent, equipollent, on a footing with, equipotent.

5. Accordant, agreeing, harmonizing, concerted, in agreement, in accordance with, acquiescent, concinnous, sympathetic, unanimous, coincident, consentaneous, consilient, of one mind, of the same mind, at one with, reconcilable, compatible, correspondent, congenial, consistent, harmonious, consonant, concordant, becoming, congruent, congruous, of one accord, approbative, allied, approving, consentient, concentual, like-minded, conformable, commensurate, consensual *(Law),*

answerable, confirmative, affirmative, affinitive, compliant, concessional, concessionary, suitable, assenting, fit, assonant, in harmony with, in unison with, in rapport, in accord, in step.

6. Tending to *or* intersecting at the same point, joining, conjoined, coming together, meeting, coinciding, focused, concentralized, corradiate, gathered in, centralized, centrical, centripetal, confluxible, confluent, pivotal, centrolineal, homocentric, confocal *(Math.)*, convergent, focal, asymptotic *(Math.)*, connivent *(Biol.)*. converging.

CONCUSSION, *n.* Shock occasioned by a blow *or* collision, violent meeting, clash, crash, collision, percussion, encounter, jolt, blow, brunt, jar, jerk, smash, quake, onset, crackup, attack, smash-up, impact, bump, shaking, agitation, jostle.

CONDEMN, *v.* 1. Express strong disapproval of, pronounce adverse judgment on, reprove, blame, censure, pass censure on, upbraid, disapprove, reprehend, rebuke, reproach, inveigh against, heap denunciation upon, cry out against, scold at, rail at, decry, run down, vituperate, vilipend.

2. Execrate, curse, anathematize, proscribe, damn, excommunicate, interdict, prohibit, veto, ban, outlaw, blackball, discountenance.

3. Pronounce to be guilty, find guilty, sentence to punishment, convict, adjudge, doom, pass sentence on, utter judicial sentence against.

4. Judge to be unfit for service, decide to be unfit for use.

5. Pronounce to be taken for public use, confiscate, sequester, sequestrate, declare to be forfeited, impound, commandeer, expropriate, acquire ownership of for a public purpose by right of eminent domain.

CONDEMNATION, *n.* 1. Strong censure, reproof, disapprobation, reprobation, disapproval, reproach, reprehension, invective, denunciation, vituperation.

2. Proscription, banning, execration, anathema, damnation, excommunication, veto, stricture, ban.

3. Cause for condemning, guilt, wrong, sin, grounds of condemnation, shame, error.

4. Sentence of punishment, penalty, doom, conviction, judgment, sentence, death warrant, death penalty, capital punishment.

5. Seizure of property for public use, forfeit, confiscation, sequestration, expropriation.

CONDEMNATORY, *adj.* 1. Denunciatory, utterly disapproving, censorious, reproachful, blaming, reprehensive, opprobrious, vituperative, minatory, damnatory, threatening, minacious.

2. Expressing condemnation, pronouncing sentence, dooming.

CONDENSATION, *n.* 1. Reduction of a gas to a liquid form, act of reducing a vapor to a solid form, compression, solidification, distillation, liquefaction, precipitation, coagulation, cohesion, concretion, congelation, consolidation, thickening, inspissation, incrassation, crystallization, concentration.

2. Condensed state or form, abridgment, reduction, contraction, abbreviation, synopsis, epitomization, epitome, retrenchment, abstraction, curtailment.

CONDENSE, *v.* 1. Make more dense, render more compact, reduce the volume of, compress, concentrate, consolidate, render close, squeeze, fix.

2. Abbreviate, abstract, abridge, contract, epitomize, summarize, shorten, diminish, take in, curtail, retrench, narrow, shrivel, shrink, lessen,

scrimp, truncate, cut, trim, pare down, clip, **lop,** dock, prune, crop, shear, boil down.

3. Become denser, compact, congeal, thicken, coagulate, harden, solidify, inspissate, incrassate, clot, curd, curdle, crystallize, deposit, precipitate.

4. Become liquid as a gas or vapor, liquefy, deliquesce.

CONDENSED, *adj.* 1. Shortened, summarized, concise, terse, brief, abbreviated, compendious, abstracted, compact, summary, curtate, laconic, succinct, epitomized.

2. Dense, concentrated, compressed, solidified, solid, cohesive, thick, close, concrete, coagulated, hard, clotted.

CONDESCEND, *v.* Waive ceremony voluntarily to assume equality with an inferior, behave as if one is conscious of descending from a superior position, humble oneself, descend, lower oneself, so forget oneself, degrade oneself, come down off one's high horse, come down a peg, submit with good grace, accommodate oneself to an inferior, lower one's tone, sing small, yield the palm, assume a patronizing air, patronize, deign, graciously stoop, vouchsafe.

CONDESCENSION, *n.* Gracious descent from dignity, patronizing complaisance, graciousness, gracious favor, courtesy, deference, patronage, civility, compliance, grace, self-abasement, self-effacement, humbleness, lowliness, modesty, affability toward inferiors.

CONDIGN, *adj.* (Said only of punishment) Just, well-deserved, meet, due, merited, fit, appropriate, proper, adequate, suitable, fitting, *selon les règles (Fr.)*, richly deserved, worthy.

CONDIMENT, *n.* Something used to give flavor and relish to food, seasoning, flavoring, dressing, relish, sauce, appetizer, spice, tang, curry, pickle, chutney, salt, pepper, mustard, catsup, allspice, horse radish, herbs.

CONDITION, *n.* 1. Particular mode of being of a person or thing, existing state, state of affairs, case, circumstances, aspect, phase, attitude, look, mien, situation with respect to circumstances.

2. State of being fit, physical fitness, state of health, form, trim, fettle, kilter, state, shape.

3. Plight, predicament, pass, quandary, scrape, dilemma, impasse, fix, corner, pickle, pinch.

4. Social position, birth, standing, rank of life, precedence, grade, estate, order of society, class, *pas (Fr.),* station, place, status, position, degree, caste, regard, footing.

5. Limiting circumstance, consideration, term, modifying circumstance, restricting circumstance, rule of proceeding, arrangement, saving clause, article of agreement, something demanded as an essential part of an agreement, proviso, provision, limitation, allowance, restriction, qualification, modification, requirement, exception.

6. Circumstance indispensable to some result, premise, requisite state, prerequisite, necessary antecedent, necessity, sine qua non, assumption, postulate, hypothesis, contingency, presumption, supposition, presupposition, theory.

CONDITION, *v.* 1. Form or be a condition of, determine as a condition, subject to something as a condition, restrict, limit, assign terms to, assign conditions to, make contingent, put as dependent, provide, insist upon, make a point of, stipulate, make conditional, bind to, tie to, bargain for, contract, qualify, determine terms, subject to particular circumstances, fence in, hem in, hedge in, cognize under limits.

2. Put in fit or proper state, tone up, put in good shape, prepare, capacitate, qualify, enable, equip, adapt, make competent, entitle, empower, fit.

CONDITIONAL, *adj.* 1. Imposing a condition, dependent on conditions, contingent, modified by conditions, subject to, not absolute, conditioned, limited, restricted, granted on certain terms, guarded, hedged in, fenced in.

2. Provisional, provisory, provisionary, limitative, stipulative, hypothetic, prerequisite.

CONDITIONS, *n.* *(pl.)* Provisions, stipulations, terms, postulates, articles, propositions, articles of agreement, clauses, premises, arrangements, sine qua non, circumstances, eventualities, requisites, prerequisites, obligations, covenant, memoranda.

CONDOLE, *v.* Express sympathy for, sympathize, commiserate, feel sorrow in common with, share mutual grief, lament with, compassionate, solace, pity, grieve with, feel for, console, comfort, afford consolation, soothe, express pity.

CONDOLENCE, *n.* Expression of sympathy with a person in affliction, sympathy, condolement, commiseration, pity, compassion, comfort, solace, fellow feeling, utterance of common sorrow.

CONDONATION, *n.* Overlooking of an offense, implied forgiveness, pardon, grace, dispensation, amnesty, reprieve, remission, absolution, excusal, acquittal, exculpation, exoneration, quittance, extenuation, justification, apology, oblivion, release.

CONDONE, *v.* Overlook an offense, forgive, let pass, pardon, excuse, let off, remit, wink at, pass over, acquit, exculpate, exonerate, absolve, clear, release, reprieve, justify, extenuate, let bygones be bygones, bury the hatchet, wipe the slate clean, blot out an offense, pocket the affront, bear with, make allowances for.

CONDUCE, *v.* Contribute towards, tend to, lead to as a result, be subsidiary to, incline to, have a tendency to, make for, trend to, predispose to, bring about, effect, be directed to, influence, bid fair to, dispose, verge, redound to, aid, adjuvate, assist, help in, serve, subserve, forward, promote, advance, cooperate, conspire to.

CONDUCIVE, *adj.* Tending, working towards, in a fair way to, likely to, apt to, liable to, disposed to, calculated to, predisposed to, instrumental in, contributory, ancillary, productive of, favorable to, promoting, contributive, helpful, subservient, useful, accessory.

CONDUCT, *n.* 1. Personal behavior, deportment as a matter of habit, way of acting, comportment, address, carriage, demeanor, bearing, manner, course of conduct, line of action, presence, role, manner of life, career, mode of action, actions, ways, doings, gestures, morals.

2. Process, practice, proceeding, procedure, treating, method, transaction, business.

3. Direction, leadership, management, regime, administration, execution, regimen, supervision, policy, tactics, strategy, generalship, government, statesmanship, stewardship, housekeeping, game, economy, organization, husbandry, campaign, menage, plan.

4. Act of conducting, guidance, escort, convoy, guardianship, attendance.

CONDUCT, *v.* 1. Behave oneself, bear oneself, act, demean oneself, comport oneself, adopt a course, acquit oneself, carry oneself, shape one's course, play one's part.

2. Direct in action, carry on, regulate, manage, look after, supervise, superintend, administer, transact, run affairs, execute, operate, work, rule, govern, control, perform, do, carry out, dispatch, proceed with, discharge, work out, go through, enact, negotiate, deal.

3. Lead, take the lead in, act as conductor, preside over, command, usher, pilot, convoy, escort, steer, accompany, attend, guide, convey, transmit, transport.

CONDUCTOR, *n.* 1. Leader, guide, escort, usher, conveyer, marshal, guard, cicerone, steersman, adviser, precentor, pilot, helmsman, drum major, fugleman, bellwether, coryphaeus, choir master, maestro *(Music),* baton wielder.

2. Official in charge, presiding officer, director, manager, supervisor, superintendent, functionary, overseer, surveyor, administrator, dean, captain, executive, headman, chief, president, bureaucrat, chairman.

3. Carrier, transporter, transferrer, messenger, bearer, porter, courier.

4. Expressman, teamster, wagoner, chauffeur, motorman, truck driver.

5. *(Physics)* Transmitter, propagator, conveyor, lightning rod.

CONDUIT, *n.* Pipe for conveying water, spout, gutter, main, drain, trough, alveus, channel, duct, canal, tube, scupper, flume, pantile, gully, sewer, culvert, cloaca, natural passage, adit, aqueduct, watercourse, race.

CONFABULATE, *v.* Talk together, converse, put in a word, chat, confab, parley, palaver, join in a conversation, bandy words, discourse with, hold converse, confer with, talk it over, be closeted with, talk in tête-à-tête, commune with, consult, have a free and easy talk, gossip, pass the time of day with, prattle, prate, chatter, babble.

CONFECTION, *n.* 1. Sweet preparation, candy, sweetmeat, comfit, confect, sweet, bonbon, toffee, fondant, caramel, butterscotch, sugarplum, conserve, preserve, confetti, *confiture (Fr.),* dainty.

2. Manufacture, preparing, making, process of compounding, preparation, composition.

CONFECTIONARY, *n.* Place where confections are kept, candy store, confectioner's shop, ice cream parlor.

CONFEDERACY, *n.* 1. Body of confederated states, confederation of independent states, union of confederate parties, league, federacy, alliance, federation, coalition.

2. Association, society, guild, club, pool, trust, combine, cartel, ring, band, push, machine, gang, clique, set, coterie, circle, junto, compact, band, syndicate.

3. Combination for unlawful purposes, cabal, conspiracy, plot, complot.

CONFEDERATE, *adj.* Allied in a league, joined, leagued in an alliance, united in federal compact, confederated, federated, federate, incorporated, combined, corporate, federal, amalgamated, organized, syndicated, unionized.

CONFEDERATE, *n.* Associate, accomplice, tool, accessory, ally, coworker, coadjutor, collaborator, cooperator, copartner, assistant, colleague, mate, auxiliary, consort, helper, helpmate, helping hand, right-hand man, abettor, supporter, promoter, confidant, comrade, companion, henchman, cat's-paw, confrere, upholder, advocate, partisan, puppet, creature, adherent, fellow-conspirator.

CONFEDERATE, *v.* League in an alliance, unite in a league, combine, ally, join with, unite, club, associate with, amalgamate, band together, herd, fraternize, unionize, join in a mutual contract, consolidate, incorporate, federate, federalize, centralize, merge, blend.

CONFER, *v.* 1. Bestow as a gift, give as a favor, grant as an honor, vouchsafe, award, present, accord, donate, adjudge, yield, cede, concede, deliver.
2. Compare, collate, balance one against the other, parallel, estimate relatively.
3. Consult together, carry on a deliberation, advise together, deliberate, interchange views, counsel together, compare opinions, discuss, talk together, hold a conference, discourse, converse, parley, palaver, powwow, colloquize, confabulate, collogue.

CONFERENCE, *n.* 1. Act of conferring, parley, consultation on an important matter, discussion, tête-à-tête, *pourparler (Fr.),* talk, interlocution, colloquy, palaver, conversation, communion, powwow, *conversazione (It.).*
2. Meeting for consultation, assembly, muster, convocation, convention, gathering, assemblage, concourse, congress, council, congregation, synod, conclave, conventicle.
3. Interview, audience, sitting, panel, seance, symposium, round table, salon, hearing, caucus, session.

CONFESS, *v.* 1. Acknowledge as a crime, avow as a fault, admit as a sin, own, make a clean breast, plead guilty, spill, come clean, unbosom oneself, disclose, divulge, reveal, lay bare, expose, bring to light, let into the secret, breathe, confide to, utter, vent, speak out, communicate, blurt out, make known, profess, declare.
2. Make confession, go to the confessional, shrive oneself, cry *peccavi,* cry *mea culpa,* beg pardon, humble oneself, rue, repent, be sorry for, declare one's sins to a priest for the obtaining of absolution.
3. *(Poetical)* Reveal by circumstances, attest, show, prove, manifest, evince, exhibit, declare adherence to, acknowledge belief in.

CONFESSION, *n.* 1. Acknowledgment of guilt, admission of fault, avowal of error, declaration, disclosure, revelation, divulgence, utterance, vent, publication, exposure, exposé.
2. Disclosing of sins to a priest to obtain forgiveness, confessional, apology, self-reproach, penance, lustration, shrift, sackcloth and ashes, remission of sins, self-accusation, compunction, repentance, contrition, remorse, penitence, regret, *mea culpa (Lat.), peccavi (Lat.),* penitential act, qualms of conscience.
3. *(Pl.)* Memoirs, biography, autobiography, personalia, journals, letters, memorabilia, life, experiences.

CONFESSIONAL, *n.* Shriving pew, confession booth, confessionary, confession chair, place set apart for the hearing of confessions by a priest.

CONFESSOR, *n.* 1. Shriver, spiritual adviser, priest authorized to hear confessions, penitentiary.
2. Persecuted saint, martyr, faithful believer, one who confesses and adheres to his religion despite persecution and torture, undeviating witness.

CONFIDANT, *n.* Confidante *(fem.),* bosom-friend, trusty friend, intimate, *alter ego (Lat.),* other self, boon companion, dear friend, shadow, side-kick, crony, fidus Achates, sympathizer, partisan, one to whom secrets are confided, adviser, adherent.

CONFIDE, *v.* 1. Confide in, tell in assurance of secrecy, show trust by imparting secrets, rely upon, believe in, put one's trust in, place reliance on, have confidence in, trust, depend upon, put faith in, repose confidence in, swear by.
2. Divulge, disclose, lay bare, bare, reveal, let into the secret, inform, tip off, apprise, blab, let slip, breathe, utter, vent, blurt out, whisper about, break the news, make known, communicate, own, acknowledge, avow, confess, make a clean breast, come clean, unbosom oneself, let one's hair down.
3. Confide to, entrust, commit to the charge or good faith of another, consign, delegate, commission, authorize, depute, empower, accredit.

CONFIDENCE, *n.* 1. Belief in the trustworthiness and reliability of a person, full trust, credence, faith, reliance, dependence, credit.
2. Ground of trust, trustworthiness, mainstay, sheet anchor.
3. Secret, private matter not to be divulged to others, confidential communication, confidential relations, intimacy.
4. Assured expectation, sanguineness, certitude, hope, certainty, conviction, persuasion, credulity.
5. Sureness of oneself, self-reliance, courage, boldness, self-assurance, firmness, fearlessness, resoluteness, manliness, hardihood, intrepidity, faith in oneself, daring, dash, élan, nerve, mettle, grit, sand, pluck, spirit, heart, backbone, spunk, fortitude, tenacity, resolution.
6. Arrogant self-conceit, presumption, over-confidence, cocksureness, plerophoria, audacity.

CONFIDENT, *adj.* 1. Having strong belief, with full assurance, certain, positive, assured, careless, fully convinced, secure, easy in mind, carefree, untroubled, undisturbed, unconcerned, sure, light-hearted.
2. Hopeful, expectant, optimistic, sanguine, in hopes, anticipatory, buoyant, enthusiastic, elated.
3. Sure of oneself, bold, cocksure, self-assured, fearless, dauntless, undaunted, self-sufficient, self-confident, indomitable, forward, courageous.
4. Overbold, presumptuous, impudent, fresh.

CONFIDENTIAL, *adj.* 1. Spoken in confidence, private, secret, privy, *in petto (It.),* not to be spoken of, not to be communicated, not to be disclosed, close, inviolate, irrevealable, esoteric, unmentionable, betokening intimacy.
2. Enjoying another's confidence, entrusted with private affairs, trusty, trustworthy, faithful, familiar, close, bosom, thick, intimate.

CONFIDENTIALLY, *adv.* Privately, secretly, in secret, in strict confidence, in one's sleeve, behind closed doors, *ianuis clausis (Lat.), à huis clos (Fr.), in petto (It.),* under the seal of secrecy, intimately, between ourselves, just between you and me, *entre nous (Fr.), inter nos (Lat.),* sub rosa, under the rose, aside, on the sly, sotto voce, *à la dérobée (Fr.), en tapinois (Fr.),* hush-hush, hugger-mugger, in a whisper, *à la sourdine (Fr.),* it must go no further, "tell it not in Gath," nobody else the wiser.

CONFIGURATION, *n.* Relative disposition of the parts of a thing, structure, external form, shape, figuration, formation, conformation, figure, cast, outline, contour, design, frame, construction, set, build, trim, type, fashion, mold.

CONFINE, *n.* Border, boundary, boundary line, line of demarcation, line of circumvallation, pale, term, bourn, terminus, termination, margin, rim, enclave, frontier, limit, edge, verge, brink, skirt, precinct, zone, *ne plus ultra* (*Lat.*).

CONFINE, *v.* 1. Shut in, restrain, shut up, keep in, trammel, bind, tie, hedge in, fence round, rail in, hedge round, fence in, hem in, box up, bottle up, seal up, wall in, bolt in, cage, impound, coop, corral, picket, pen in.

2. Hold in custody, imprison, incarcerate, jail, immure, detain, lock up, put in irons, clap under hatches, cast into prison, shut up within walls.

3. Enclose within bounds, bound, circumscribe, mark off, limit, demarcate, delimit, delimitate, encircle, encompass, cramp, straiten.

CONFINEMENT, *n.* 1. State of being confined, restraint, limitation, constraint, restriction, check, detention, circumscription, control, curb, keeping, coercion, custody, safekeeping.

2. Imprisonment, incarceration, durance vile, protective custody, captivity, bondage, servitude, thralldom, duress, slavery, limbo.

3. Childbirth, childbed, lying-in, parturition, travail, delivery, labor, accouchement, eutocia (*easy*), dystocia (*difficult*).

CONFINES, *n.* 1. Borders, bounds, boundaries, limits, marches, frontiers, precincts, premises, remote regions, outbounds, outskirts, suburbs, purlieus, banlieus.

2. Place of confinement, pen, yard, fold, coop, corral, kennel, mew, croft, sty, paddock, pound, kraal, compound, cage, aviary, apiary, hive, pit, box, area, court, quadrangle, bridewell, square, cloister, prison, jail, bastille, lockup.

CONFIRM, *v.* 1. Verify, corroborate, guarantee, authenticate, substantiate, validate, uphold, sustain, clinch, bear out, vindicate, prove, make good, warrant, circumstantiate, make out a case, establish, witness to, testify, acknowledge, make certain, make sure.

2. Make valid or binding by some formal act, sanction, ratify, endorse, seal, sign, countersign, visé, accredit, authorize.

3. Approve, assent, acquiesce, agree, comply, accede, concur, consent, subscribe, recognize, accord.

4. Establish firmly, assure, make firm, settle, fix, plant, fasten, rivet, tie, attach, secure.

5. Strengthen, add strength to, make firmer, reinforce, brace, fortify, buttress, gird, steel.

6. (*Eccles.*) Administer the rite of confirmation to, invest with full membership in the Church, admit to the Communion.

CONFIRMATION, *n.* 1. Settlement, attachment, establishment, securement.

2. Corroborative statement, acknowledgment, corroboration, substantiation, sanction, approval, ratification, support, endorsement, visé, evidence, acceptance, proof, authentication, acquiescence, attestation, witness, testimony, assent, admission, agreement, affirmation, consent, recognition, nod, accord, avowal, consensus, verification.

3. (*Eccles.*) Full investiture with the privileges of the Church, sacrament, laying on of hands, imposition of hands, rite administered to baptized persons as a sacrament for confirming and strengthening the recipient in the faith, admission to the Holy Communion.

CONFIRMATORY, *adj.* Assenting, confirmative, serving to confirm, corroborative, corroborating, affirmative, acquiescent, assentive, consentient, agreeing, concurrent.

CONFIRMED, *adj.* 1. Made firm, settled, valid, approved, accepted, ratified, fiducial, established,

admissible, decisive, conclusive, absolute, definite, authentic.

2. Firmly established in a habit or condition, habitual, habituated, in the habit of, habitué, rooted, chronic, inveterate, inured, wont, used to, ingrained, dyed-in-the-wool, given to, addicted to.

CONFISCATE, *v.* Appropriate to public use by way of penalty, seize as forfeited to the public treasury, condemn to public use, cause to be forfeited, seize by authority, take summarily, lay under contribution, commandeer, impound, fine, sequester, sequestrate, accroach, usurp, distrain, dispossess, deprive of, levy, mulct, adeem (*Law*), disseize (*Law*), intercept, help oneself to, make free with.

CONFLAGRATION, *n.* Large and destructive fire, roaring furnace, sheet of fire, lambent flame, general fire, four-alarm fire, blaze, holocaust, bonfire, suttee.

CONFLICT, *v.* 1. Come into collision, collide, be at variance, clash, be inconsistent, be opposed, be in opposition, be inharmonious, be contrary, jar, be contradictory to, come between, interfere, disagree, contradict, diverge, oppose, antagonize, discommode, dispute.

2. Contend, contest, wrangle, quarrel, grapple, do battle, struggle, scramble, wrestle.

CONFLICT, *n.* 1. Discord of action, opposition, clashing, inconsistency, disagreement, dissidence, interference, inharmony, disunion, antagonism, dissent, division, dissension, variance, contention, misunderstanding.

2. Controversy, quarrel, litigation, altercation, dispute, wrangling, bickering, vendetta, turmoil, feud, jangle.

3. Clash of arms, encounter, fight, battle, fray, combat, armed strife, contest, rencounter, affair, prolonged struggle, brush, hostility, engagement, affray, skirmish, passage at arms, warfare.

4. Bout, tussle, scuffle, scrimmage, set-to, broil, fracas, melee.

CONFLUENCE, *n.* 1. Flowing together, conflux, corrivation, junction, union, meeting, appulse, convergence, concentration, concurrence.

2. Coming together of people, forgathering, assemblage, assembly, concourse, congress, host, gathering, ingathering, meeting, collection, army, multitude, throng, congregation, crowd, swarm, horde, mob, press, crush, shoal, covey, galaxy, herd, flock, bevy, drove, bunch, array.

CONFLUENT, *adj.* Flowing together, mingling, running together, blending into one, concurrent, commingling, meeting, joining, growing together, coalescent.

CONFORM, *v.* 1. Make conformable, bring into correspondence, make similar in form, adjust, make harmonize, adapt, accommodate.

2. Become similar in character, agree with, tally, harmonize, correspond, comport, square, become like, fit, suit.

3. Conventionalize, be regular, fall in with, be guided by, obey rules, comply, adapt to, adjust to, reconcile with, run with the pack, swim with the stream, follow the crowd, follow the fashion, travel in a rut, do at Rome as the Romans do, acquiesce, submit.

CONFORMABLE, *adj.* 1. Corresponding in form or character, like, resembling, similar, uniform.

2. Exhibiting agreement or harmony, suitable, agreeable, consistent with, befitting, congruous, congruent, meet, proper, harmonious, appropriate, fit, consonant.

3. Conventional, orthodox, standard, common, customary, usual, habitual, traditional, ordinary, cut-and-dried, formal, strict, stiff, rigid, regular, uncompromising, canonical, Procrustean, well-regulated, according to rule.

4. Obedient, compliant, obsequious, adaptable, submissive, acquiescent, manageable, compatible, tractable, docile, agreeable, congenial.

5. Typical, illustrative, representative, model, exemplary, ideal.

CONFORMATION, *n.* 1. Agreement, compliance, conformity, accordance, obedience, adaptation, acquiescence.

2. Symmetrical arrangement of parts, fashion, structure, symmetry, shape, figure, configuration, form, figuration, manner of formation, make.

CONFORMITY, *n.* 1. Correspondence in form or character, agreement, accord, likeness, similarity, resemblance, accordance, harmony, congruity, affinity, similitude, uniformity.

2. Observance, compliance, obedience, assent, submission, concession, consent, acquiescence, conventionality.

CONFOUND, *v.* 1. Mingle so that the elements cannot be distinguished or separated, entangle, confuse, mingle confusedly, jumble, mix, blend, intermingle, crowd together in disorder.

2. Confuse with each other, regard erroneously as identical, mistake one for another, associate by mistake, mistake between, mix up.

3. Throw into confusion, render uncertain, perplex, nonplus, baffle, muddle, bewilder, pose, rattle, bother, embarrass, mystify, puzzle, throw off the scent.

4. Perplex with sudden surprise, dumfounder, surprise, astound, astonish, startle, amaze, stun, stupefy, daze, strike dumb, petrify, strike with wonder, take by surprise, paralyze, disconcert, dismay, unsettle.

5. Defeat, subvert, destroy, overwhelm, ruin, overthrow, bring to naught, annihilate, demolish, cast down, rout, scatter.

6. Put to shame, abash, shame, mortify, abase, discompose.

7. Damn, imprecate mildly.

CONFOUNDED, *adj.* 1. *(Colloq.)* Abominable, odious, hateful, detestable, accursed, diabolical, cursed, damnable, execrable, infernal, dreadful, wretched.

2. Abashed, ashamed, disconcerted, astounded, blank, nonplused, confused, disordered, chaotic.

3. Extreme, great, excessive, exceeding, huge, monstrous, enormous.

4. Damned *(a euphemism)*.

CONFRONT, *v.* 1. Stand facing, stand in front of, stand over against, face, front.

2. Face in defiance, defy, brave, oppose, stem, resist, withstand, stand opposed, oppugn, stand athwart the path of, challenge, cross, thwart, threaten, rise in hostility before, encounter, cope with, face up to, repel.

3. Set face to face, bring into the presence of, bring face to face, accost, pit against, set opposite, bring together for comparison, contrast.

CONFUSE, *v.* 1. Fail to distiguish between, mix, associate by mistake, commingle, intermingle, confound, blend, tangle, entangle, mistake.

2. Combine without order or clearness, render indistinct, disorganize, disarrange, disorder, litter, disturb, derange, throw into disorder, embroil, jumble, involve, snarl, clutter up, muddle.

3. Perplex, bewilder, render uncertain, befog,

obscure, obfuscate, mystify, nonplus, embarrass, disconcert, baffle, discompose, fluster, befuddle, flutter, pose, rattle, fuss up, perturb, upset, puzzle, unhinge, pother.

4. Shame, abash, mortify, discomfit, chagrin, addle, distract, demoralize.

CONFUSION, *n.* 1. Disorder, confusedness, chaos, lack of clearness or distinctness, disarrangement, disarray, derangement, jumble, dislocation, mess, anarchy, disorganization, complication, mixture, congestion, entanglement, medley, clutter, snarl, muddle, intricacy, maze, muss, litter, untidiness, tangle, hodgepodge, complexity, network, jungle, labyrinth, wilderness, coil, tangled skein, knot, irregularity

2. Turmoil, tumult, pandemonium, turbulence, commotion, stir, ferment, imbroglio, convulsion, bustle, trouble, row, riot, uproar, fracas, melee, rumpus, agitation, to-do, hurly-burly, disturbance, hubbub, Donnybrook, Babel, Bedlam.

3. Perplexity, bewilderment, distraction, daze, embarrassment, astonishment, surprise, fog, haze, stupefaction, demoralization, discomposure, discomfiture, uncertainty, perturbation, mystification, consternation.

4. Abashment, shame, mortification, chagrin.

5. *(Psychiatry)* A disturbed mental state, a clouding of consciousness, disorientation, unhingement.

CONFUTATION, *n.* Refutation, refutal, exposé, disproval, disproof, redargution, invalidation, conviction, *reductio ad absurdum,* knock-down, exposure, answer, retort, rebuttal, clincher, *tu quoque* argument, complete answer.

CONFUTE, *v.* 1. Prove to be wrong, overthrow by argument, overturn, overcome in debate, set aside, convict of error by proof, rebut, defeat, vanquish, demolish, upset, subvert, oppugn, get the better of, put to silence, squelch, silence, put down, quash, contradict, explode, invalidate, give one a set down, clinch an argument, stop the mouth, shut up, confound, not leave a leg to stand on, cut the ground from under one's feet.

2. Parry, negative, disprove, prove to be false, prove to be defective, refute, expose, show up, show the fallacy of, belie, scatter to the winds, bring to naught, confound.

CONGE, *n.* 1. Farewell, leave, valediction, adieu, valedictory, good-by, departure, embarkation, take-off, exit, exodus, hegira, parting.

2. Leave to depart, permission, leave-taking, leave, discharge, demission.

3. Bow, obeisance, genuflection, prostration, curtsy, obeisance, kneeling, salaam, kowtow.

CONGEAL, *v.* 1. Change from a fluid to a solid state, freeze, convert to ice, glaciate, refrigerate, infrigidate, ice.

2. Change from a soft to a rigid state, harden, stiffen, thicken, condense, coagulate.

3. Become frozen, freeze, turn into ice, set, solidify, become fixed.

CONGENIAL, *adj.* 1. Suited in spirit, adapted in feeling, kindred, sympathetic, similar, agreeable, akin, related, cognate, homogeneous, harmonious, after one's taste, concordant, agreeing, accordant, correspondent, consonant, suitable, appropriate, proper, natural, apposite, relevant, conformable, consistent, congruous, compatible, pertinent, fitting.

2. Favorable, genial, pleasing, gracious, jolly, companionable, delightful, pleasant, felicitous, kindly, happy.

CONGENITAL, *adj.* Innate, inborn, connate, in the grain, coeval with birth, inherent, intrinsic, inbred, ingrained, bred in the bone, existing from birth, connatural, natural, native, deep-rooted, inveterate, pathoscopic, connascent, predisposed, imbued with.

CONGERIES, *n.* Collection of several particles or bodies in one mass, aggregate, aggregation, accumulation, amassment, agglomeration, heap, compages, conglomeration, compage, assemblage, pile, cluster, crowd, mass, group, crowded series, sorus, lot, batch, assortment, pack, bunch.

CONGEST, *v.* Fill to excess, surcharge, crowd, supersaturate, overcrowd, pack, cram, drench, jam, gorge, glut, overcharge, overstock, overdose, overfeed, overload, overburden, choke, pile up, mass, cloy, inundate, flood, deluge, drug the market.

CONGESTION, *n.* Redundance, repletion, load, plethora, too much, superfluity, supersaturation, exuberance, nimiety, profusion, surfeit, overflow, more than enough, *satis superque (Lat.)*, excess, engorgement, overplus, overdose, overcrowding, massing, jam, snarl, obstruction, bottleneck, pile-up.

CONGLOMERATE, *adj.* Gathered into a rounded mass, clustered, composite, complex, glomerate, heterogeneous, mixed, agglomerate.

CONGRATULATE, *v.* Express sympathetic joy on a happy occasion, compliment with expressions of sympathetic pleasure, felicitate, gratulate, wish one joy, rejoice with, tender one's congratulations, salute, hail with pride, wish many happy returns of the day.

CONGRATULATION, *n.* Gratulation, felicitation, congratulatory expression, best wishes, happy greeting, good wishes, well-wishing, salute, many happy returns of the day.

CONGRATULATORY, *adj.* Congratulant, genial, complimentary, gratulatory, fair-spoken, exultant, honey-tongued, addressful, rejoicing, jubilant.

CONGREGATE, *v.* 1. Call together, round up, convene, bring together in a crowd, convoke in large numbers, gather together, collect, muster.
2. Meet in large numbers, meet in a body, assemble, throng, crowd together, meet together, come together, get together, cluster, flock, troop, swarm, surge, rush, stream, herd, huddle, mass, associate, resort, forgather, rally, ingather.

CONGREGATION, *n.* 1. Act of congregating, ingathering, mobilization, concourse, levy, levee, conflux, concentration, muster, collection, caucus, convocation, aggregation, assemblage, convention, association, reunion, congress.
2. Congregated body, crowd, multitude, host, throng, assembly, meeting, gathering, horde, mob, crush, press, troupe, gang, corps, band, council, force, shoal, covey, swarm, fold, flock, herd, roundup, bevy, drove, bunch, array, galaxy, clan, tribe, group.
3. Local church society, parish, assembly of persons met for common religious worship, laity, brethren.

CONGRESS, *n.* 1. Convention, muster, gathering, conference, assembly, meeting, concourse, seance, council, sitting, session, hearing, durbar, caucus, powwow, convocation, synod.
2. National legislature of the U.S.A., Senate, House of Representatives, parliament, chamber of deputies, upper house, lower house, House of Lords, House of Commons, states general, general council, federal council, diet, cortes, duma, soviet.
3. Social relations, intercourse, communion, converse.

CONGRUITY, *n.* Suitableness, accord, harmony, keeping, congruence, fitness, agreement, concord, conformity, consistency, concordance, unanimity, consonance, unison, unity, concert, uniformity, consort, homogeneity, correspondence, coherence, appropriateness, compatibility, aptness, relevancy, appositeness, pertinence, applicability, admissibility.

CONGRUOUS, *adj.* 1. Agreeing in character, compatible, accordant, consonant, harmonious, correspondent, consistent, suitable, conformable, in keeping with, homogeneous, congenial.
2. Proper, fitting, fit, befitting, appropriate, apt, apposite, pertinent, relevant, seemly, meet, germane, *ad rem (Lat.)*, applicable, admissible, in point, becoming, apropos, expedient.

CONICAL, *adj.* Having the form of a cone, cone-shaped, coniform, pyramid-shaped, tapering, conic, pyramidal, pointed.

CONJECTURAL, *adj.* Speculatory, suppositional, involving conjecture, speculative, presumptive, problematic, theoretical, hypothetical, academic, suppositive, supposititious, suppository, reputed, surmised, assumed, supposed, putative, allusive, imagined, referential, uncertain, undetermined, doubtful.

CONJECTURE, *v.* Conclude uncertainly, assume, suppose from evidence insufficient to ensure reliability, presume, surmise, predicate, theorize, hypothesize, posit *(Logic)*, doctrinize, speculate, form conjectures, infer, presuppose, suspect, hint, guess, fancy, take it, understand, take for granted, dare say, hazard the conjecture, suggest, intimate, allude to, postulate, judge, think, deem, imagine, believe, regard, consider, view, divine, wonder, forecast.

CONJECTURE, *n.* Expression of an opinion without sufficient evidence for proof, supposition, hypothesis, theory, guess, surmise, presupposition, inference, divination, speculation, association of ideas, guesswork, shot, forecast, fancy, hazard, suspicion, inkling, hint, suggestion, presumption, postulation, augury, notion, opinion, belief, view, assumption.

CONJOIN, *v.* Join together, combine, associate, unite, connect, concatenate, interlace, entwine, hitch, bind, compound, consolidate, band, league, blend, merge, coalesce, mingle, mix, incorporate, embody, yoke, annex, attach, tie together.

CONJOINT, *adj.* 1. Joined together, associated, connected, united, combined, attached, bound together.
2. Formed by two or more in combination, joint, pooled, corporate, conjunct, hand-in-hand, indissoluble, inseparable, indivisible.

CONJUGAL, *adj.* Matrimonial, marital, nuptial, wedded, connubial, hymeneal, bridal, spousal, married, one bone and one flesh, mated, paired, united, coupled, matched, conjugate, yoked.

CONJUNCTION, *n.* Association, union, junction, combination, hook-up, conjugation, network, concatenation, confluence, connection, juncture, meeting, communication, coherence, attachment, embodiment, coincidence, league, assemblage, reunion, concourse, consolidation, alliance, combine, coalition.

CONJUNCTURE, *n.* 1. Concurrence of affairs, combination of circumstances, particular state of affairs, coincidence, association, interchange, union, vicissitude.

2. Critical state of affairs, crisis, emergency, juncture, exigency, contingency, turning-point, predicament, pass, quandary, strait, extremity, pinch, case, pickle, stew, fix.

CONJURATION, *n.* 1. Invoking by a sacred name, adjuration, solemn imploration, sacred summons, solemn entreaty.

2. Supernatural accomplishment by spell, incantation, enchantment, sorcery, magic, occult art, black magic, black art, magic spell, charm, spell, runes, weird, cabala, exsufflation, wand, thaumaturgy, demonology, divination, sortilege, exorcism, witchcraft, hoodoo, voodoo, *diablerie (Fr.),* Shamanism, possession, hocus-pocus, open sesame, abracadabra, mumbo-jumbo, divining rod, necromancy, Aladdin's lamp, magic carpet, caduceus, magic ring, scarab, fetish, talisman, amulet, phylactery, wishing cap.

3. Practice of legerdemain, sleight of hand, prestidigitation.

CONJURE, *v.* 1. Command by invocation, call upon by spell, affect by magic arts, enchant, practice sorcery, call up spirits, charm, fascinate, bewitch, ensorcel, raise ghosts, lay ghosts, taboo, command genii, exorcise, bedevil, wave a wand, rub a ring, rub the lamp, cast a spell, bring into existence by magic, produce by magic.

2. Juggle, practice legerdemain, practice prestidigitation, play tricks, prestidigitate.

3. Appeal to solemnly, supplicate, entreat, beg, beseech, pray, adjure, enjoin earnestly, implore, urge, obtest, solicit.

CONJURER, *n.* 1. One who conjures spirits, sorcerer, necromancer, diviner, enchanter, seer, charmer, exorcist, wizard, witch, wonder-worker, thaumaturgist, fairy, hag, lamia, warlock, voodoo, magus, medicine man, witch doctor, Shaman, Merlin, Katerfelto, Cagliostro, Comus, Hecate, Circe, Lilith, siren, Weird Sisters.

2. One who practices legerdemain, sleight-of-hand artist, prestidigitator, juggler.

3. Solemn entreater, adjurer, supplicator.

CONJURE UP, *v.* 1. Bring into existence by magic, raise up by magic, summon by sorcery, bid to appear, summon, invoke, exorcise.

2. Bring forward by pretense, produce by artificial method, raise by supernatural effort.

3. Bring to mind, recall, recur to the mind, flash across the memory, call up, bethink oneself, recollect, look back to, retrace, review, think back upon, call to mind.

CONNATE, *adj.* 1. Existing from birth, present at birth, innate, inborn, coeval with birth, original, congenital, connascent, connatural.

2. Agreeing in nature, allied, cognate, akin, alike.

CONNECT, *v.* 1. Fasten together, link together, string together, conjoin, join, combine, subjoin, unite, couple, hyphenate, bind, affiliate, attach, clinch, tie, knit, buckle, button, hitch, pinion, lace, sew, splice, truss, gird, lash, chain, tether, moor, yoke, hook, fetter, bracket, nail, pin, bolt, hasp, screw, rivet, cement, solder, fuse, graft, ingraft, clasp, lock, clamp, span, bridge over, adjoin, append, annex, interknit, interweave, plait, intertwine, consolidate, amalgamate, weave together.

2. Establish communication between, put in communication, bring into relation with, cohere, associate, correlate, articulate, be joined, coalesce,

merge, mingle, blend, interlace, interlock, have relation, entwine, interlink, communicate, become connected, lead into each other.

CONNECTED, *adj.* 1. United, combined, joined together, coupled, associated, affiliated, linked, spliced, knit, conjunct, conjoint, corporate, allied, collateral, coherent, compact, consolidated, *en rapport* (Fr.), amalgamated, leagued, federate, hand-in-hand, confederate, inseparable, undivided, unseparated.

2. Related, kindred, consanguineous, cognate, akin, agnate, sib, germane, affinal, affined, to the point, paronymous, affinitive, conjugate, relevant, correlative, homogenous, pertinent, appurtenant, apropos, apposite, congenial.

3. Leading into one another, communicating, consecutive, appended, adjoining, contiguous, continous.

CONNECTION, *n.* 1. Union, alliance, junction, combination, conjunction, association, coalition, relationship, dependence, interrelation, rapport, attachment, reciprocal dependence, propinquity, coherence, liaison, concatenation, league.

2. Anything that connects, bond, link, tie, knot, coupling, nexus, coupler, copula, vinculum, ring, yoke, ligature, cord, catena, leader, clip, clamp, fastening, holdfast, rivet, clasp, catch, buckle, staple, shackle, hook, hook and eye.

3. Intercommunication, intercourse, commerce, meeting of means of conveyance for transfer of passengers without delay, communication.

4. Sexual commerce, intercourse, copulation, coition, sexual conjunction, venery, seduction, coitus, erotic commerce.

5. Contextual relation, sequence of words or ideas, context, bearing, reference, concernment.

6. Consistency, congruity, coherence, harmony, adherence, congruence, conformity, correlation, relevancy, pertinence, applicability, appositeness, affinity.

7. Kinship, consanguinity, relationship, folks, relations, flesh and blood, kith and kin, relatives, kin, kinsfolk, family, in-law, cognate, agnate, sib, affine.

8. Circle of friends or associates, coterie, set, clique, body of persons, cluster, gang, society, affiliation, denomination, fraternity, sodality, sorority.

CONNIVANCE, *n.* Implied assent, tacit consent, tacit encouragement (without participation) to wrongdoing by another, secret approval, indirect abettal, remote participation, collusion, jobbery, underhanded complicity, gentleman's agreement, logrolling, guiltiness, guilt, conspiracy, intrigue, confederacy, corridor intrigue.

2. Blinking the fact, winking at, forbearance of disapproval, voluntary blindness to an act of wrongdoing, voluntary oversight, allowance, pretended ignorance, sufferance, tolerance, secret condonation, toleration.

CONNIVE, *v.* 1. Participate surreptitiously, be in collusion with, cooperate with secretly, allow by inaction, be knowing, privately consent, have a finger in the pie, be a party to, lend oneself to, stand shoulder to shoulder with, join forces, pool, conspire, concert, be secretly accessory, collude.

2. Avoid noticing that which one should oppose but secretly approves, give aid to wrongdoing by forbearance, purposely overlook, take no notice of, forbear to censure, shut one's eyes to, pretend not to notice, blink the fact, wink at, feign ignorance, disregard, make light of, pass

over, gloss over, let pass, pay no regard to, *laisser passer (Fr.)*.

CONNOISSEUR, *n.* Person competent to pass critical judgment in one of the fine arts, one aesthetically versed in any subject, aesthete, cognoscente, aesthetician, critic, critical judge in matters of taste, expert, adept, savant, man of good taste, *arbiter elegantiae (Lat.)*, proficient, specialist, virtuoso, crack, sharp.

CONNOTATION, *n.* Secondary implied meaning, suggestive significance of a word, range of objects to which a term may be applied, set of attributes constituting the meaning of a term, implication, sum of attributes expressed or implied, intention, intent, comprehension, signification, meaning, sense, force, depth, import, purport, drift, tenor, essence, bearing, coloring, spirit, latency, allusion, insinuation, innuendo, adumbration.

CONNOTATIVE, *adj.* Comprising as attributes, implying, expressing, allusive, meaning, implied, expressive, suggestive, significative, latent, in the background, tacit, indirect, inferential, implicit, understood.

CONNOTE, *v.* 1. Signify in addition to the primary meaning, denote secondarily, imply, convey, indicate, signify, designate, mean, infer, suggest, betoken, bespeak, bear a sense, allude to, touch on, involve, have an inference, import, purport.

2. Comprise among its attributes, involve as a condition, imply as attributes, include in its meaning, express as attributes, involve as an accompaniment.

CONNUBIAL, *adj.* Pertaining to marriage, of wedlock, matrimonial, marital, conjugal, wedded; bridal, spousal, nuptial, hymeneal, married, one bone and one flesh.

CONQUER, *v.* 1. Win in war, acquire by force of arms, win by victory, gain by effort, make conquests.

2. Defeat, vanquish, overcome by force, beat, overthrow, subjugate, subdue, overpower, rout, master, thrash, tame, floor, worst, beat hollow, trim, drub, lick, get the better of, put down, quell, silence, discomfit, checkmate, humble, subject, crush, reduce, suppress, drive to the wall, get the upper hand of, down, get the whip hand of, prevail over.

3. Surmount, outwit, outmaneuver, outdo, outgeneral, circumvent, triumph over, whip.

4. Prevail, succeed, triumph, be triumphant, win, overcome, win success.

CONQUEROR, *n.* 1. Vanquisher, subjugator, defeater, bringer under the yoke, subduer, Caesar, humbler, Alexander.

2. Successful contestant, champion, winner, master, superior, victor, victress, victrix.

CONQUEST, *n.* 1. Vanquishment, subjugation, overthrow, subjection, subversion, discomfiture, rout, defeat, reduction, mastery, checkmate, domination.

2. Victory, triumph, ovation, palm, advantage, ascendancy, walkover, upper hand, whip hand, sway, dominion, acquisition, master stroke, coup, feat, hit, killing.

3. Territory acquired by conquering, empire, province.

4. Captivation of favor or affections, person whose favor has been won.

CONSANGUINITY, *n.* 1. Relationship by blood, kinship, ties of blood, blood-relationship, alliance,

cognation, agnation, affinity, affiliation, filiation, connection, propinquity.

2. Parentage, paternity, family, lineage, line, house, household, brotherhood, sisterhood, clan, tribe, stock, race, strain, breed, stirps.

3. Kinsman, kin, kindred, blood-kindred, sib, kinswoman, relation, relative, next of kin, kith and kinsfolk.

CONSCIENCE, *n.* 1. Internal recognition of what is right and wrong as regards one's actions and motives, faculty that enjoins one to conformity with the moral law, faculty which decides upon the moral quality of one's actions and motives, the still small voice, inward monitor, moral faculty, moral sense, ethical judgment, decalogue, sense of duty, moral obligation, call of duty, moral consciousness, scruples, compunction.

2. Clean hands, probity, rectitude, integrity, uprightness, honor, honesty, conscientiousness, faith.

3. In all conscience, in all reason and fairness, in truth, most certainly, assuredly, upon oath, in faith, marry, upon my honor, by my troth, egad, in sober earnest, truly, of a truth, be assured.

CONSCIENCE-STRICKEN, *adj.* Contrite, not hardened, remorseful, penitent, repentant, self-accusing, penitential, conscience-smitten, self-convicted, chastened, reclaimed, unhardened.

CONSCIENTIOUS, *adj.* 1. Done according to conscience, controlled by conscience, fair, moral, high-principled, high-minded, incorruptible, just, virtuous, religious, upright, honest, honorable, faithful, trusty, ethical, equitable, candid, sincere, right-minded, truthful, frank, veracious, dutiful, true, reputable, trustworthy.

2. Painstaking, particular, careful, scrupulous, exact, strict, precise, minute, punctilious, nice, meticulous, accurate, correct, meritorious, regardful, heedful.

CONSCIOUS, *adj.* 1. Inwardly sensible, awake to one's own cognitions, sentient, knowing, present to consciousness, endowed with consciousness, percipient, intelligent, apperceptive, discerning, awakened to an inner realization of.

2. Having the mental faculties awake, thinking, intellectual, rational, reflecting, reasoning, aware of one's own personality, self-conscious, mentally active.

3. Aware of what one is doing, cognizant, apprised, alive to, informed of, *au fait (Fr.)*, sure, certain, assured.

4. Known to oneself, inwardly known, clearly felt, self-admitted.

CONSCIOUSNESS, *n.* Inward sensibility of something, knowledge of one's own cognitions, cognitive faculty, upper level of mental life, intellection, activity of mental faculties, senses, percipience, apperception, cognizance, cognition, understanding, mentality, psyche, *penetralia mentis (Lat.)*, rationality, awareness, intuition, mind, comprehension, apprehension, recognition.

CONSCRIPT, *v.* Compel to serve, draft, enlist, impress, conscribe, enroll, levy, recruit, dragoon, coerce, constrain, enforce, oblige, take by force, commandeer, require, put in force, tax.

CONSCRIPT, *n.* Recruit in the armed forces, rookie, cadet, raw levy, rank and file, regular, tenderfoot, troop, soldier, commando, private, P.F.C., doughboy, cannon fodder, noncom, infantryman, foot-soldier.

CONSCRIPTION, *n.* 1. Compulsory enrollment of men for service in war, impressment for military or naval service, registry of men, draft, enlistment, registration, enforcement.

2. Forced contribution imposed by a government in time of war, compulsory monetary payment exacted by a government, exaction.

CONSECRATE, *v.* 1. Make an object of veneration, hallow, sanctify, make reverend, glorify, enshrine, enthrone, celebrate, exalt to the skies, immortalize, deify, apotheosize, canonize, beatify, anoint, bless, light candles to, burn incense before.

2. Dedicate to the service of the Deity, ordain in holy orders, set apart to sacred uses, induct.

CONSECRATION, *n.* 1. Sanctification, hallowing, beatification, enthronement, enshrinement, celebration, deification, apotheosis, immortalization, exaltation, canonization, glorification.

2. Piety, religiousness, devoutness, veneration, reverence, godliness, religiosity, holiness, sanctity, sanctitude, spirituality, grace, worship, saintliness.

3. Dedication to the service and worship of God, ordination to a sacred office, devotion to holy orders.

CONSECUTIVE, *adj.* 1. Following one another in uninterrupted succession, successive, following in a series, uninterrupted in course, continuous, following seriatim, seriatim, in turn, serial, gradual, progressive.

2. Marked by logical sequences, sequential, sequent, consequent.

CONSENSUS, *n.* General agreement, common consent, unanimity, unison, concord, consenting judgment, concordance, affirmance, affirmation, accord, harmony, concurrence, public opinion, acclamation, chorus.

CONSENT, *n.* 1. Approval, permission, permit, nod of willingness, acquiescence, concurrence, promise, concession, acceptance, compliance, assent, settlement, ratification, confirmation, approbation, endorsement.

2. Agreement in sentiment, consensus, unison, unanimity, unity, harmony, accord, concord, cooperation, coherence.

CONSENT, *v.* 1. Nod willingness, give consent, give approval, indicate willingness, approve, permit, assent, yield assent, concur, acquiesce, allow, concede, deign, vouchsafe, admit, affirm, ratify, confirm, endorse, come to terms.

2. Comply, yield, accede, submit, accept, fall in with, subscribe to, concur, acknowledge, conform.

CONSEQUENCE, *n.* 1. Result, effect, outcome, upshot, sequel, issue, end, event, proceeding, aftermath, afterclap, development, outgrowth, eventuality, aftergrowth, harvest, fruit, crop, termination, denouement, catastrophe.

2. Following as a result of something antecedent, chain of cause and effect, consecution, concatenation, connection, sequence.

3. Conclusion of an argument or inference, inference, deduction.

4. Importance, value, materialness, moment, weight, momentousness, concern, interest, import, significance, consideration, magnitude, gravity, ponderosity, account, avail, emphasis, usefulness, substance, gravamen, seriousness, press, stress, note.

5. Importance in rank or position, distinction, standing, prominence, mark, caliber, figure, notability, influence, self-importance, pomposity, self-consequence.

CONSEQUENT, *adj.* 1. Following as an effect or result, resultant, sequential, consequential, owing to, attendant, subsequent, eventual, due to, caused by, resulting from, derivable from, ascribable to, attributable to, evolved from, derived from, indirect, derivative, secondary.

2. Following as a logical conclusion, logical, logically consistent, deducible, reasonable, inferable.

CONSEQUENTIAL, *adj.* 1. Of consequence, important, weighty, momentous, eventful, full of incident, memorable, notable, striking, signal, salient, considerable, material, influential.

2. Vainglorious, pompous, self-important, overweening, assuming, presumptuous, conceited, big, toplofty, bumptious, uppish, high and mighty, puffed up, inflated, supercilious, haughty, proud, egotistical, lordly, magisterial.

CONSERVATION, *n.* 1. Preservation, keeping in a safe state, maintenance, protection, storage, safekeeping, upkeep, support, sustentation.

2. Official supervision of rivers and forests.

CONSERVATISM, *n.* Disposition to preserve what is established, preservation of the status quo, opposition to innovation, resistance to change, reaction, die-hardedness, law of the Medes and Persians, stability, *vis conservatrix (Lat.)*, right wing, *laissez-faire*, Fabian policy, Fabianism, inaction.

CONSERVATIVE, *adj.* Disposed to preserve existing conditions, opposed to change, moderate, unprogressive, Tory, reactionary, not speculative, cautious, stable, within safe bounds, unchanging, believed to involve little risk, sober.

CONSERVATIVE, *n.* Champion of the status quo, one disposed to preserve the existing order, Tory, opponent of change, resister of innovation, one lacking in vision, reactionary, die-hard, Whig, Federalist, Silk-Stocking *(U. S. History)*, stand-

CONSERVATOR, *n.* Guardian, protector, keeper of a building, preserver, custodian, warden, curator, concierge, janitor.

CONSERVATORY, *n.* 1. Glass-covered house for growing and displaying plants, greenhouse, glasshouse, hothouse, nursery, vinery, viridarium, arboretum, bower, arbor, summerhouse.

2. Storehouse, repository, place for the safekeeping of things, storeroom, storecloset, depository, depot, cache, safe deposit, entrepôt, vault, magazine, warehouse, crib, granary, silo, bunker, larder, buttery, pantry.

3. Place of instruction in music and theatrical arts, school of music, conservatoire, institute, academy, studio.

CONSERVE, *v.* 1. Keep in a safe state, maintain in a sound condition, protect from injury, save, preserve, keep unimpaired, lay by, gather in, uphold, sustain, guard, shield, secure.

2. Prepare with sugar for the purpose of preservation.

CONSERVE, *n.* Mixture of several fruits cooked to jamlike consistency with nuts and raisins, compote, preserve, confection, sweetmeat, jam, comfit, *confiture (Fr.)*, jelly, marmalade, julep, sugarplum, bonbon.

CONSIDER, *v.* 1. Contemplate mentally, weigh, meditate on, examine, ponder, brood upon, study, reflect upon, give a thought to, investigate, pore over, be attentive to, heed, mind, mark, revolve in the mind, gauge, estimate, appraise, give one's patter.

attention to, think about, envisage, envision, keep in view, take into consideration, scan, rate, digest, pass on, review, notice, look into, adjudge, mull over, turn over in one's mind.

2. Pay attention to, regard, respect, care for, regard with respect, value, honor, esteem.

3. Opine, deem, hold, judge, reflect, deliberate, ruminate, cogitate, muse, take thought, think, reason, speculate, cast about.

4. Think about with a view to action, tinker with a notion, flirt with an idea.

CONSIDERABLE, *adj.* 1. Respectable, important, worthy of consideration, notable, noteworthy, estimable, great, extraordinary, intense, valuable, meritorious, influential, remarkable.

2. Rather large in extent, fairly great, sizable, moderately large, goodly, not little, not small, much, a good deal of, substantial, tidy, decent, tolerable, reasonable, big.

CONSIDERATE, *adj.* 1. Thoughtful, reflective, marked by consideration, circumspect, heedful, regardful of consequences, careful, judicious, discreet, prudent, provident, attentive, mindful, deliberate, conscientious, sober, serious, staid, cautious, wary, regardful.

2. Showing regard for another, observant of the rights and feelings of another, thoughtfully kind, kindly, kind-hearted, solicitous, charitable, obliging, unselfish, indulgent, concerned, anxious, patient, forbearing, friendly, neighborly.

CONSIDERATION, *n.* 1. Attention, observation, advisement, notice, advertency, heed, observance, examination, estimation, review, remark, viewing, sight.

2. Deliberation, cogitation, meditation, serious thought, rumination, forethought, premeditation, study, speculation, contemplation, reflection, ponderance, musing, thinking, judgment, counsel, adjudgment, reckoning.

3. Thoughtful regard, sympathetic respect, thoughtfulness of others. kindliness, friendliness, solicitude, esteem, account, estimation, deference, honor.

4. Consideration for service rendered, gratuity, tip, fee, *pourboire (Fr.)*, *Trinkgeld (Ger.)*, sop, perquisite, compensation, recompense, emolument, reward, *quid pro quo (Lat.)*, pay.

5. Importance, significance, value, moment, consequence, weight, import, concern, interest.

6. Reason, inducement, ground, motive, score, cause, sake, account, incentive.

7. Rank, standing, influence, reputation, fame, note, notability, prominence.

CONSIGN, *v.* 1. Convey, remand, remit, send, ship, freight, dispatch, post, mail, express, address, transmit, transfer.

2. Transfer to another's charge, entrust, refer, commit to another's trust, give in trust, assign, delegate, relegate, hand over, deliver formally, resign, bequeath, leave to, commend to, confide to, deposit with, commission, authorize.

3. Set apart to a purpose or use, dedicate, devote.

CONSIGNEE, *n.* Party to whom merchandise is consigned, receiver of goods shipped, factor, agent, transferee, proctor, underwriter.

CONSIGNER, *n.* Merchant, vender, seller, sender, transmitter, shipper, freighter.

CONSIGNMENT, *n.* 1. Shipment, conveyance, shipping, sending, freight, transmission, mailing, transportation, dispatchment, expressage, posting.

2. Goods shipped, merchandise sent, amount freighted.

3. Allotment, apportionment, assignment, deal, appropriation, allocation, distribution.

4. Errand, task, office, commission, warrant, charge, mandate, instruction, mission, agency, trust.

CONSISTENCE, *n.* 1. Material coherence with retention of form, consistency, solidity, body, firmness, degree of density, degree of viscosity, texture, nature, compactness, cohesion, mass, uniformity, stiffness, thickness.

2. Structure, composition, constitution, make, formation, organization, construction, make up, combination.

3. Durability, lastingness, endurance, permanence.

CONSISTENCY, *n.* 1. Degree of density (See CONSISTENCE).

2. Constant adherence to the same course or principles, agreement, congruity, correspondence, compatibility, conformableness, consonance, self-consistency, harmony, coherence, persistency, substantiality, accordance, conformity, compliance.

CONSISTENT, *adj.* 1. Constantly adhering to the same course or principles, not self-opposed, not self-contradictory, true to type, undeviating, logical, steady, persistent, selfsame, identical, regular, uniform, coherent, homogeneous, equable.

2. Agreeing, accordant, concordant, consonant, harmonious, congruous, compatible, suitable, correspondent, conformable, meet, decorous, proper.

CONSIST IN, *v.* Be contained in, be constituted by, be comprised in, inhere in, lie in.

CONSIST OF, *v.* Comprise, include, contain, hold, embrace, embody, incorporate, involve, be made up of, be constituted of, be made of, be formed of, be composed of.

CONSIST WITH, *v.* Agree, accord, agree with, be in accordance with, be compatible with, jibe, be consistent with, conform, be harmonious with, harmonize, suit, befit, accommodate, become.

CONSOLATION, *n.* 1. Sympathy, condolence, commiseration, solace, compassion, comfort, pity.

2. Assuagement, alleviation, relief, soothing, encouragement, mitigation, palliation, easement, amelioration, diversion, relaxation, rest, respite, ease, cheer, support, help, succor, contentment.

CONSOLATORY, *adj.* 1. Sympathetic, pitying, commiserative, compassionate, grieving with, sorrowing for.

2. Soothing, relieving, palliative, ameliorative, assuasive, balmy, lenitive, comforting.

CONSOLE, *v.* 1. Condole with, sympathize, share another's misery, commiserate, express pity, feel for, afford consolation, lament with, comfort, solace, compassionate, express sympathy for, pity, grieve with, express one's sorrow, cheer, raise the spirits of, encourage, sustain, support, hearten, compose, inspirit, freshen, strengthen.

2. Soothe, relieve, alleviate, assuage, calm, ease, hush, quell, mitigate.

CONSOLE, *n.* 1. (*Arch.*) Ornamental bracket-like member for support, bracket, corbel, ancone.

2. Table, cabinet, the desk from which an organ is played.

CONSOLIDATE, *v.* 1. Unite into one, merge, combine, conjoin, bring together in one connected whole, connect, link, couple, federate, embody, incorporate, amalgamate, associate, attach, knit together, fasten together, organize and strengthen.

2. Compress, condense, mass, compact, make solid, solidify, make firm, harden, coalesce, settle firmly, thicken, concentrate, concrete.

CONSOLIDATION, *n.* 1. Union, combination, junction, aggregation, merger, mixture, fusion, unification, incorporation, synthesis, embodiment, amalgamation, association, coadunation, federation, centralization, conjuncture, confederation.

2. Compression, condensation, solidification, compactness, coalescence, concentration, concretion.

CONSONANCE, *n.* 1. Harmony of sounds, chord, tunefulness, euphony, concert, symphony, chime, melody, pleasing combination of tones, resonance.

2. Agreement, accordance, accord, concord, concordance, concurrence, correspondence, unity, conformity, congruence, congruity, adaptation, consistency, unison, unanimity, union, uniformity, coincidence, suitableness.

CONSONANT, *adj.* 1. Agreeable in sound, in tune, harmonious, tuneful, euphonious, musical, symphonic, melodious, resonant, symphonious, pleasant-sounding, in chime.

2. Agreeing, accordant, concordant, suitable, correspondent, conformable, compatible, fit, apt, congruous, congruent, consistent, in agreement, concurrent, uniform, unanimous.

CONSONANT, *n.* 1. (*Phonetics*) One of a class of speech sounds, a sound subordinated to another sound that has greater sonority, a sound made with more or less obstruction of the breath stream in its passage outward, sonorant (*slight obstruction as in "l"*), fricative (*great obstruction as in "s"*), stop (*complete obstruction as in "t"*), sibilant, liquid, sonant, surd, non-vowel.

2. A letter representing a consonant sound.

CONSORT, *v.* 1. Keep company with, go around with, associate with, couple with, pair off with, walk hand in hand with, club together, bear one company, pal around together, fraternize, herd with, accompany, mingle with, mix with, haunt, frequent, attend.

2. Agree, harmonize, jibe, tally.

CONSORT, *n.* Marital companion, wife, husband, spouse, marriage partner, helpmeet, helpmate, mate, yokemate, rib, better half, other half, good wife, gray mare, *femme couverte (Fr.)*, affinity, soul mate, squaw.

CONSPECTUS, *n.* Summary, résumé, précis, outline, synopsis, digest, abstract, syllabus, brief, breviary, epitome, abridgment, compend, survey, compendium, general sketch, abbreviated version, comprehensive view.

CONSPICUOUS, *adj.* 1. Easy to be seen, clear, apparent, noticeable, plain, in plain sight, in broad daylight, visible, perceptible, discernible, evident, patent, manifest.

2. Obvious, marked, salient, glaring, flagrant, striking, tending to attract attention, readily attracting the attention, eye-filling, outstanding, egregious, notorious, signal, arrant.

3. Eminent, prominent, preeminent, renowned, distinguished, famed, famous, notable, celebrated, noted, illustrious, remarkable, brilliant, great, glorious, well-known, memorable, splendid.

CONSPIRACY, *n.* 1. Combination of men for an evil or unlawful purpose, agreement by two or more persons to commit a crime, plot, complot, intrigue, cabal, collusion, machination, compact,

confederacy, wire-pulling, connivance, treasonable alliance, racket.

2. Combination in bringing about a given result, concurrence in action, coalition, harmonious action.

CONSPIRATOR, *n.* Colluder, schemer, abettor, confederate, strategist, machinator, cabalist, Guy Fawkes, traitor, betrayer, archtraitor, stool pigeon, Judas, Catiline, *intrigant (Fr.)*.

CONSPIRE, *v.* 1. Combine for an evil design, confederate for an unlawful purpose, complot, plot, scheme, cabal, intrigue, collude, agree together secretly to do something illegal, hatch, machinate, counterplot, concoct, contrive, something evil, devise treachery, project treason.

2. Contribute jointly to a result, concur in action, act in harmony, form a coalition, act in combination, combine, concert, contribute toward, conduce, cooperate, unite.

CONSTANCY, *n.* 1. Steadiness, steadfastness, resolution, inflexibility, firmness, resoluteness, decision, determination, tenacity of purpose, fortitude, perseverance, application, adherence, persistence, industry, backbone, diligence, grit, sand, mettle.

2. Faithfulness to a person or cause, fidelity, attachment, fealty, devotion, trustiness, faith, truthfulness, loyality, reliability, allegiance, honesty, devotedness, ardor, eagerness, zeal, earnestness, integrity, honor, principle.

3. Freedom from change, invariableness, uniformity, regularity, sameness, immutability, unchangeableness, permanence, continuousness, stability.

CONSTANT, *adj.* 1. Invariable, fixed, abiding, stable, unalterable, immutable, unchanging, unvaried, invariant, permanent, perpetual, abiding.

2. Standing firm in mind, steadfast, steady, firm, resolute, dogged, determined, unwavering, unshaken, unmoved, unswerving, undeviating, pertinacious, unflagging, tried, resolved, unyielding, unwearied, unremitting, sedulous, persistent, through fire and water, through thick and thin, persevering, assiduous, diligent, tenacious, industrious.

⋅ 3. Regular, uniform, even, same, systematic, methodic, identical.

4. Faithful, loyal, stanch, tried and true, trusty, trustworthy, devoted, true-hearted.

5. Continuing without interruption, incessant, unbroken, continual, ceaseless, uninterrupted, always present, regularly recurrent, sustained, interminable, eternal, unintermitted, endless, everlasting.

CONSTELLATION, *n.* 1. Group of stars to which a definite name has been given, zodiac, configuration of stars, sign of the zodiac, Ursa Major, Great Bear, Little Bear, Ursa Minor, Southern Cross, Orion's Belt, Cassiopeia's Chair, Bootes, Cancer, Pleiades, Taurus, Charles's Wain, Big Dipper, Little Dipper, Andromeda, Aquila, Auriga, Camelopardus, Cepheus, Canes Venatici, Coma Berenices, Corona Borealis, Cygnus, Delphinus, Draco, Equuleus, Lacerta, Hercules, Leo Minor, Lynx, Lyra, Ophiuchus, Pegasus, Perseus, Sagitta, Scutum, Serpens, Triangulum, Vulpecula, Aries, Gemini, Virgo, Libra, Scorpio, Sagittarius, Capricornus, Pisces, Aquarius, Antlia, Apus, Ara, Argo, Caelum, Canis Major, Canis Minor, Carina, Centaurus, Cetus, Chamaeleon, Circinus, Columba, Crux,

Corona Australis, Corvus, Crater, Eridanus, Fornax, Grus, Horologium, Hydra, Hydrus, Indus, Lepus, Lupus, Malus, Mensa, Musca, Microscopium, Monocerus, Norma, Octans, Pavo, Phoenix, Pictor, Piscis Australis, Tucana, Reticulum, Sculptor, Sextans, Telescopium, Vela, Piscis Volans, Dorado.

2. Any brilliant assemblage, collection, galaxy, cluster, pattern.

CONSTERNATION, n. Amazement and dread tending to confound the faculties, paralyzing dismay, alarm, fright, affright, panic, sudden fear, horror, terror, dread, apprehension, scare, distraction, astonishment, pavor, trepidation, bewilderment.

CONSTIPATED, adj. Costive, bound, needing a purge, stegnotic, having the bowels obstructed.

CONSTIPATION, n. Bowel condition marked by defective or difficult evacuation, costiveness, stegnosis, obstipation.

CONSTITUENT, adj. 1. Serving to make up a thing, constituting, composing, forming, basic, component, intrinsic, elementary, elemental, material, integral, creative.

2. Having power to frame or alter a political constitution or fundamental law, overruling, electoral, elective, appointing, official, influential.

CONSTITUENT, n. 1. Constituent element, component, ingredient, component part, radicle, principal, integral part, member, subdivision, rudiment.

2. Resident in a district represented by an elective officer, elector, voter.

CONSTITUTE, v. 1. Establish, found, set up, bring about, produce, create, develop, set on foot, determine, institute, fix.

2. Appoint to an office, depute to a function, elect, empower, delegate, ordain, install, induct, inaugurate, invest, authorize, commission, name, confide to, entrust, appoint, nominate.

3. Give legal form to, enact, draft.

4. Compose, make up, form, make, enter into the composition of, frame, compound, aggregate.

CONSTITUTION, n. 1. Way in which anything is constituted, make-up, construction, structure, composition, formation, compounding, texture, make, conformation, figuration, configuration.

2. Condition of mind, disposition, character, characteristic, spirit, nature, quality, condition, humor, temperament, temper, peculiarity, state, essence, quiddity, hypostasis, diathesis, aspect, tenor, mood, grain, idiosyncrasy, individuality, vein.

3. Physical character of the body as to health and strength, mettle, physique, stamina, virility, lustihood, nerve, sinew, muscle, vitality.

4. Corpus juris, fundamental law, charter, code, organic law, pandect, rule, act, canon, enactment, institution, regulation, ordinance, statute, rescript, decree, edict, plebiscite, system of fundamental principles according to which a nation or group is governed.

CONSTITUTIONAL, adj. 1. Inborn, incarnate, innate, inbred, ingenerate, congenital, connate, organic, chronic, in the grain, running in the blood, bred in the bone, temperamental, native, natural, essential, implanted, instinctive, inner, ingrained, indwelling, immanent, fundamental, inherent, intrinsic, indigenous, internal, rooted, radical.

2. In accordance with the constitution of a state, lawful, legal, legitimate, consistent with

the constitution, politic, licit, legalized, vested, chartered, statutory, existing by virtue of a fundamental organic law.

3. For the benefit of one's health, designed to benefit the bodily constitution, salubrious, salutary.

CONSTITUTIONAL, n. Exercise taken for the benefit of the health, walk, stroll, promenade, hike, saunter, turn, peregrination, tramp, outing, perambulation, jogtrot, setting-up exercises, airing.

CONSTRAIN, v. 1. Bring about by compulsion, compel, coerce, oblige, necessitate, drive, force, make, enforce, dragoon, press, pin down, bind, insist on, require, tax.

2. Put under restraint, restrain, harness, pull in, curb, check, restrict, muzzle, bridle, hold in leash, keep under, keep down, repress, prevent, oppress, straiten, constrict, compress, clasp tightly.

3. Confine forcibly, restrain by bonds, enthrall, confine, bind, chain, fasten, enchain, incarcerate, shackle, pinion, fetter, trammel, handcuff, lock up, manacle, hobble, hold in custody, detain, imprison, immure, coop up, impound, clap under hatches.

4. Impel, draw urgently, impel irresistibly, urge, incite, instigate.

CONSTRAINT, n. 1. Compulsion, enforcement, coercion, force, obligation, necessity, pressure, force majeure (Fr.), necessitation, brute force, ultima ratio (Lat.), stress.

2. Repression of natural feelings, suppression of impulses, unnaturalness, unnatural restraint in manner, diffidence, modesty, verecundity, timidity, retiring disposition, unobtrusiveness, bashfulness, mauvaise honte (Fr.), demureness, reserve, blushing, stiffness of manner.

3. Confinement, incarceration, imprisonment, durance, duress, durance vile, detention, chains, bondage, thralldom, servitude, captivity, bonds, enthrallment, restriction, slavery.

CONSTRICT, v. Draw together tightly, tighten, cause to contract, contract, bind, squeeze, crush, pinch, strangle, strangulate, straiten, astringe, cramp, compress, constringe, narrow, condense.

CONSTRICTION, n. 1. Contraction, decrease, compression, coarctation, narrowing, lessening, angustation, reduction, diminution, constraint, shrinking, coalescence, condensation.

2. Tightness, astringency, stricture, choking, contracture, strangulation, strangling, squeezing, binding.

CONSTRUCT, v. 1. Form by putting together parts, put together, fabricate, erect, build, set up, raise, rear, produce.

2. Make, frame, shape, fashion, forge, create, compose, design, formulate, institute, organize, arrange, invent, devise, found.

CONSTRUCTION, n. 1. Act of constructing, erection, fabrication, creation, organization, building, manufacture, production, constitution, establishment, causation, architecture, tectonics, composition.

2. Way in which a thing is constructed, cut, structure, build, formation, conformation, turn, figuration, configuration, figure, form, shape, make, style, format, galbe (Fr.), getup, contour, outline, frame, fabric, framework, type, mold, cast.

3. Explanation, interpretation, éclaircissement (Fr.), elucidation, explication, exegesis, version,

rendering, translation, rendition, reading, syntax, reddition, analysis.

CONSTRUCTIVE, *adj.* Structural, architectural, pertaining to the nature of construction, tectonic.

2. Deduced by interpretation, inferential, implied, implicit, latent, allusive, indirect, virtual.

3. Tending to construct, productive, useful, helpful toward further development.

CONSTRUE, *v.* 1. Show the meaning of, define, explain, interpret, expound, translate, elucidate, put a particular interpretation on, transfuse the sense of.

2. Deduce by interpretation, infer, find out the meaning of, read, spell out, figure out, find the key to, make out, decode, decipher, unravel, puzzle out, resolve, read between the lines, understand, comprehend, accept in a particular sense, put a construction on.

3. Analyze grammatically, parse, explain the syntax of.

CONSUETUDE, *n.* Usage, custom, practice, use, habit, habitude, assuetude, assuefaction, wont, way, run, prescription, tradition, observance, prevalence, conventionality, order of the day, cry.

CONSUETUDINARY, *adj.* Habitual, customary, usual, common, wonted, accustomed, ordinary, conventional, prescriptive, traditional, general, everyday, well-known, set, established, officinal, stereotyped, current, acknowledged.

CONSUL, *n.* Agent appointed by an independent state to reside in a foreign one and discharge certain administrative duties, diplomatic agent, government official, minister, delegate, emissary, envoy, commissioner, commissionaire, legate, diplomatist, *corps diplomatique (Fr.), attaché,* representative, *chargé d'affaires (Fr.).*

CONSULATE, *n.* 1. Residence of the consul, premises occupied by a consul, embassy, legation.

2. Consular term, consulship, archonship, consular office.

CONSULT, *v.°* 1. Refer to for information, seek counsel from, ask advice of, seek the opinion of, seek information from, inquire of.

2. Have regard for a person's interest in making plans, care for, take into account, have an eye to, regard, consider.

3. Talk over a situation with someone to decide points in doubt, take counsel together, deliberate together, confer, discuss together, confabulate, debate about, commune with, lay heads together, collogue with, conspire with, powwow, advise with, counsel with, be closeted with, compare notes about, interchange views in order to throw light on a subject under consideration.

CONSULTATION, *n.* Conference, deliberation, colloquy, collogue, interview, parley, powwow, *pourparler (Fr.),* council, convocation, seance, meeting, session, hearing, palaver.

CONSUME, *v.* 1. Expend by use, use up, drain, spend, exhaust, deplete, empty.

2. Spend wastefully, lavish, squander, waste, prodigalize, dissipate, disperse, spill, misspend, fritter away, throw away.

3. Eat up, devour, drink up, swallow up, absorb, guzzle.

4. Destroy, eradicate, demolish, annihilate,

ravage, burn up, lay waste, devastate, desolate, sack, despoil.

5. Waste away, be consumed, be exhausted, decay, perish, vanish out of being, evanesce, dissolve, fade away, run out, fail, dwindle, run to waste, leak, ebb, melt away, evaporate, disappear.

CONSUMER, *n.* One who uses up a commodity or service, user, buyer, customer, general public, John Q. Public, purchaser, vendee, patron, client, clientele.

CONSUMMATE, *v.* 1. Bring to completion, do, complete, bring to perfection, perfect, perform, finish, accomplish, fulfill, compass, effect, cap, execute, achieve, carry out, work out, realize, bring about, crown, bring to a happy issue, do thoroughly, not do by halves.

2. Complete a marriage by sexual intercourse.

CONSUMMATE, *adj.* 1. Perfect, consummated, finished, complete, exhaustive, thorough, mature.

2. Sheer, unmitigated, regular, unqualified, unconditional, utter.

3. Excellent, best, matchless, transcendent, crowning, glorious, superlative, of the highest quality, uttermost, profound, distinguished, extraordinary, remarkable, eminent, notable, noteworthy, conspicuous, signal.

CONSUMMATION, *n.* Completion, crowning touch, final touch, finishing stroke, last stroke, final polish, last finish, perfection, fulfillment, accomplishment, achievement, realization, close, termination, culmination, attainment, compass, encompassment, execution, issue, end, upshot, conclusion.

CONSUMPTION, *n.* 1. Destruction, extinction, annihilation, dissipation, exhaustion, waste, use, expenditure, dispersion, loss, diminution, ruin, decrement, wear and tear, misuse, devastation, desolation, ravage, damage, detriment, havoc.

2. Squandering, wastefulness, extravagance, prodigality, ineconomy, lavishness.

3. Tuberculosis, T.B., phthisis, tabes, atrophy, wasting disease, gradual wasting, white plague, decline, progressive emaciation, marasmus, cachexia.

CONSUMPTIVE, *adj.* 1. Tending to consume, destructive, wasteful.

2. Tuberculous, phthisic, tabid, marasmic, marantic.

CONTACT, *n.* 1. Touching of bodies, tangency, taction, union, meeting, juncture, conjunction, touch, adhesion, cohesion, impact, connection, collision.

2. Adjacency, contiguousness, juxtaposition, contiguity, close union, immediate proximity, association, communication, appulse, apposition, abutment, abuttal, propinquity, nearness.

CONTAGION, *n.* 1. Contagious matter, disease germs, contagium, virus, poison, taint, infection, pollution, contamination, corruption, pestilence, sepsis, plague, epidemic, endemic.

2. Transmission, communication, transmittal, transference.

CONTAGIOUS, *adj.* 1. Infectious, inoculable, catching, communicable, transmittable, tending to spread from one to another, epidemic, taking, pandemic, endemic, zymotic, epizootic.

2. Causing contagion, pestiferous, noxious, pestilential, deadly, poisonous, virulent, septic, miasmatic, morbiferous, pernicious, toxiferous,

noisome, toxic, nitrogenous, azotic.

CONTAIN, *v*. 1. Have within itself, hold within fixed limits, accommodate, hold, be capable of holding, have capacity for.
2. Have as constituent parts, have as contents, comprise, comprehend, include, enclose, admit, embrace, embody, involve, subsume, implicate, incorporate.
3. Keep within proper bounds, keep in check, restrain, repress, curb, check, hold in leash.

CONTAMINATE, *v*. Render impure by contact or mixture, taint, corrupt, pollute, foul, befoul, defile, poison, infect, vitiate, spoil, soil, sully, tarnish, stain, besmirch, debauch, debase, rot, degrade, putrefy, desecrate, adulterate, canker, envenom, blight, deprave.

CONTAMINATION, *n*. 1. Pollution, defilement, impurity, vitiation, degradation, depravation, debauchment, debasement, desecration, ravage, inroad, havoc, canker, corruption, adulteration.
2. Taint, infection, foulness, stain, cariosity, uncleanness, abomination, filth, decay, mildew, putrefaction, decomposition, rot, putridity, putrescence, mold, blight, must, rust, dry rot.

CONTEMN, *v*. Treat disdainfully, view with contempt, look down upon, hold in contempt, disdain, despise, spurn, scorn, flout, disparage, scout, slight, snap one's fingers at, turn up one's nose at, point the finger of scorn at, laugh to scorn, turn a cold shoulder upon, mock, set at naught, decry, scoff at, vilify, sneer at, ridicule.

CONTEMPLATE, *v*. 1. View with continued attention, look at fixedly, observe thoughtfully, gaze at, look on, view attentively, survey, eye, observe, notice, witness, take in with the eyes, see at a glance, rivet the eyes upon, pore over, regard, eye up and down, behold, scan, inspect, examine, reconnoiter, stare, peer, pry.
2. Have as a purpose, intend, design, think of, purpose, aspire to, aim at, pursue, propose, premeditate, project, calculate, plan, have in view, envisage, envision, have in contemplation, look forward to, bid for, labor for, dream of, talk of.
3. Think studiously, meditate, ponder, study, consider deliberately, reflect upon, revolve in the mind, muse, deliberate, reason about, mull over, cogitate, ruminate, speculate, brood over.

CONTEMPLATION, *n*. 1. View, inspection, regard, survey, observation, ocular inspection, glimpse, glance, look, *coup d'oeil (Fr.)*, sight.
2. Purpose, intention, proposal, fixed purpose, intent, plan, design, project, ambition, envisionment, envisagement.
3. Meditation, cogitation, rumination, study, consideration, pondering, reflection, absorption, musing, deliberation, speculation, engrossment, thought, brown study, reverie, self-communing, lucubration, cerebration.

CONTEMPLATIVE, *adj*. Thoughtful, engrossed, given to contemplation, meditative, cogitative, pensive, reflective, deliberative, museful, intent, studious, introspective, wistful, speculative, rapt, absorbed in thought, lost in thought.

CONTEMPORARY, *adj*. 1. Belonging to the same time, occurring at the same time, of the same age, living at the same time, of the same date, contemporaneous, coeval, simultaneous, coetaneous, coexistent, concomitant, coincident, synchronous.

2. Present-day, current, living, modern-day, of the here and now.

CONTEMPT, *n*. 1. Despisal, disdain, disregard, mean opinion, scorn, derision, mockery, slight, contumely, despite, revulsion, odium, disgust, abhorrence, detestation, feeling with which one regards anything considered mean or worthless.
2. Slight, sneer, insult, slur, spurn, derision, cold shoulder, curled lip, ridicule.
3. Shame, disgrace, humiliation, disesteem, disfavor, disrepute.
4. *(Law)* Open disrespect of the rules of a court, disobedience.

CONTEMPTIBLE, *adj*. 1. Held in contempt, despised, despicable, low, base, mean, wretched, vile, abject, scurvy, sorry, ignominious, shabby, trashy, worthless, trivial, paltry, cheap, pitiable, petty, insignificant, unworthy, miserable, sordid, lamentable, inferior, pitiful.
2. Corrupt, dishonest, infamous, egregious, debased, depraved, degenerate.

CONTEMPTUOUS, *adj*. Manifesting contempt, expressing disdain, scornful, disdainful, insolent, withering, contumelious, arrogant, impertinent, haughty, supercilious, sneering, flouting, lordly, insulting, scurrilous, derisive, cynical, pompous, bumptious, cavalier, toplofty, high and mighty, upstage, with nose in air.

CONTEND, *v*. 1. Assert earnestly, maintain, affirm, claim, hold, allege, put forward, broach, set forth, propound, enunciate, vouch for, aver, insist, propose, avouch, avow, asseverate.
2. Struggle in opposition, strive, fight, clash, combat, contest, battle, war against, tussle, join issue, jostle, wage battle, grapple, spar, wrestle, exchange blows, skirmish, measure swords, enter the lists.
3. Strive in rivalry, rival, compete, vie.
4. Dispute earnestly, strive in debate, argue, debate, wrangle, quarrel, expostulate, altercate, chop logic, ratiocinate.

CONTENT, *n*. 1. Contentedness, contentment, satisfaction, gratification, delight, complacency, felicity, comfort, ease, peace, gladness, peace of mind, quietude, serenity, happiness, pleasure, cheerfulness.
2. Long-suffering, resignation, reconciliation, patience, endurance, perseverance, submission, constancy, moderation, fortitude.
3. Sum of the attributes composing a given conception, matter of cognition, significant part, meaning, real meaning, substance, essence, gist, subject matter, intent, significance, implication, purport, connotation, signification.
4. Power of containing, holding power, size, volume, capacity, quantity, burden, extent, area, space, contents.

CONTENT, *adj*. 1. Contented, satisfied, having the desire limited to what one has, well pleased, happy, glad, cheerful, snug, comfortable, not particular, easygoing, complacent.
2. Easy in mind, serene, quiescent, tranquil, carefree, untroubled, unconcerned, unworried, at ease, at rest.
3. Not disposed to repine or grumble, willing, assenting, favorable, fain, resigned, agreeing, philosophical, conciliatory.
4. Satisfactory, sufficient, ample, adequate, equal, proportionate, commensurate, satisfying, full, gratifying.

CONTENT, *v*. Make content, gratify, satisfy, make contented, suffice, gladden, cheer, please, beguile, comfort, quiet, set at ease, make easy, rest, appease, reconcile, conciliate, propitiate, requite, recompense, remunerate, reward, win over, convince, disarm.

CONTENTED, *adj.* Satisfied with what one has, content, thankful, grateful, well pleased, happy, cheerful, at ease, at peace, easy in mind, gay, comfortable, fortunate, beatific, cheerful, joyful, joyous, light-hearted, merry, delighted, pleased, gratified, charmed, gladdened, blissful.

CONTENTION, *n.* 1. Struggling together in opposition, conflict, contest, combat, encounter, strife, fight, battle, war, fray, affray, skirmish, broil, brush, collision, fracas, affair, scrimmage, melee, clash of arms, dog fight, bout, warfare, tussle, scuffle, pitched battle, hostile meeting, duel, affair of honor, passage of arms.
2. Fisticuffs, pugilism, boxing, sparring, mill, set-to, prize fighting, cauliflower industry, the ring, wrestling, grappling, jujitsu, sumo, the mat, Greco-Roman, catch-as-catch-can.
3. Striving in rivalry, competition, emulation, rivalry, trial, match, game, handicap, athletics, race, games of skill.
4. Quarrel, falling out, rupture, disagreement, variance, difficulty, dissension, discord, dispute, opposition, controversy, altercation, litigation, squabble, wrangling, bickering, feud, polemics, hard feelings, animosity, high words, paper war, logomachy, debate, war of words, strife of words.

CONTENTIOUS, *adj.* 1. Quarrelsome, warlike, pugnacious, belligerent, stormy, hostile, cross, inimical, brawling, wrangling, litigious, peevish, polemical, dissentious, controversial, perverse, petulant, waspish, snappish, combative, bellicose.
2. Disputatious, caviling, captious, dogged, querulous, obstinate, cantankerous, refractory, stubborn, contumacious, obdurate, headstrong, recalcitrant.

CONTENTMENT, *n.* Content, ease, happiness, satisfaction, complacency, gratification, comfort, contentedness, quietude, pleasure, gladness, peace. (See CONTENT.)

CONTENTS, *n.* 1. All that is contained, filling, lading, stuffing, packing, insides, constituents, furnishing, furniture, ingredients.
2. Cargo, shipment, freight, bale, load, pack.
3. Solid dimensions, volume, capacity, solid contents.
4. Text, matters treated, subjects considered, topics, themes, table of contents.

CONTERMINOUS, *adj.* 1. Having the same boundaries, of identical boundaries, identical in limits, coextensive, commensurate, coincident, having the same ending.
2. Meeting at their ends, coterminous, having a common boundary, conterminal, contiguous, adjacent, adjoining, bordering, vicinal, close upon, attiguous.

CONTEST, *n.* 1. Battle, fight, conflict, combat, struggle, fray, affray, melee, fracas, scrimmage, scuffle, tussle, bout, slugging match, slugfest, encounter, rencounter, scramble, skirmish, broil, set-to, scrap, rough-and-tumble, brush, warfare, brawl, engagement, belligerency, pugnacity, feud.
2. Strife in argument, debate, contention, war of words, quarrel, altercation, dispute, wrangle, controversy, high words, polemics, argument, dissension, difference.

3. Conflict between competitors, competition, rivalry, tourney, tournament, joust, match, race, game, emulation.

CONTEST, *v.* 1. Fight for in battle, struggle to defend, grapple, wrestle, scuffle, tackle, strive to hold.
2. Dispute, argue against, controvert, litigate, oppose, challenge, call in question, object, carp, cavil, stickle, disagree, altercate, debate.
3. Contend for in rivalry, vie for, bid for, compete for, strive to carry, make the object of rivalry.

CONTESTANT, *n.* One who takes part in a contest, competitor, rival, contender, combatant, disputant, opponent, antagonist, adversary.

CONTEXT, *n.* Connected thoughts, connection, adjoining matter, words directly preceding or following, parts of a discourse directly connected with a given passage, subject matter, text, gist, sum and substance.

CONTEXTURE, *n.* Weaving together of parts, disposition and union of the constituent parts of anything, structure, texture, composition, framework, constitution, mode of formation, fabric, structural character, textile, context.

CONTIGUITY, *n.* 1. Adjacency, contact, union, conjunction, meeting, touching, contiguousness, abuttal, abutment, juxtaposition, propinquity, nearness, proximity, vicinage, closeness, appulse.
2. Series of things in continuous connection, unbroken extent, expanse, continuous mass, continuous stretch, continuity.

CONTIGUOUS, *adj.* 1. Adjacent, conterminous, contactual, adjoining, touching, attiguous, in contact, meeting, abutting.
2. Near, neighboring, proximate, next, nigh, in close proximity without actually touching, vicinal, close, hard by.

CONTINENCE, *n.* 1. Chastity, purity, virtue, restraint of sexual passion, continency, pudicity, virginity.
2. Vestal virgin, Hippolytus, Diana, Joseph.
3. Temperance, moderation, self-command, self-restraint, forbearance, sobriety.

CONTINENT, *adj.* 1. Free from lust, virtuous, moderate in sexual appetite, characterized by self-restraint in regard to sexual passion, chaste, pure, virginal, undefiled, *virginibus puerisque (Lat.).*
2. Temperate, moderate, self-controlled, self-commanding, restrained, abstemious, ascetic, austere, exercising restraint in relation to the desires in general.

CONTINENT, *n.* One of the six main land masses of the globe (Europe, Asia, Australia, Africa, North America, South America), great tract of land, mainland, continuous extent of land.

CONTINGENCY, *n.* 1. Dependence on chance, fortuitousness, accidentalness, fortuity, fortune, possibility, lot, luck, hap, chance-medley, run of luck, odds, likelihood, tossup, hazard.
2. Contingent event, unforeseen occurrence, a chance conditional on something uncertain, accident, casualty, incident, event, situation, predicament, exigency, conjuncture, juncture, case.

CONTINGENT, *adj.* 1. Accidental, incidental, happening without known cause, adventitious, casual, fortuitous, haphazard, nonessential, random, unforeseen, unexpected.

2. Liable to happen or not, dependent for occurrence on something not yet certain, subject, uncertain, possible, provisional, conditional, provisory, dependent on circumstances.

CONTINGENT, *n.* 1. Proportion that falls to one as a share to be contributed, quota, share, proportional part, dividend, portion, allotment, lot, allocation, measure.
2. Quota of troops furnished, reinforcements, supplies, reserves.
3. Any one of the representative groups composing an assemblage.
4. Contingency, fortuity.

CONTINUAL, *adj.* 1. Uninterrupted, unbroken, proceeding without interruption or cessation, unceasing, incessant, ceaseless, dusk-to-dawn, unremitting, continous, unintermitted.
2. Never ending, endless, eternal, perpetual, unending, interminable, everlasting, permanent, sempiternal, illimitable, infinite, boundless, perdurable, perennial.
3. Of regular occurrence, oft-repeated, very frequent, ofttime, thick-coming, not rare, day-in and day-out, constant, constantly recurring, persistent, habitual.

CONTINUANCE, *n.* 1. Endurance, continuation, lasting, abiding, duration, permanence, stay, persistence, perseverance, constancy.
2. Prolongation, extension, adjournment of a step in a proceeding to a future day *(Law)*, protraction.
3. Sequence, connection, succession, repetition, concatenation.

CONTINUATION, *n.* 1. Extension in time or space, carrying on to a further point, sequence, protraction, prolongation, perpetuation, line, continuance, continuity, succession.
2. That by which anything is continued, tail, sequel, addition, supplement, postscript, suffix, installment, postlude, epilogue, queue, train, peroration, appendix, wake, trail.

CONTINUE, *v.* 1. Go forward in any course, go onward in any action, persist, endure, stick to, pursue, carry on, keep up, keep on, go on, hold out, hold on, maintain its course, drag on, be steadfast, be constant, go on with, persist in, persevere.
2. Exist uninterruptedly for an appreciable length of time, exist without break, last, endure, remain in a particular capacity, be permanent, subsist, be durable.
3. Stay, remain, abide, tarry, linger, keep the field.
4. Prolong, protract, maintain, extend from one point to another, perpetuate, preserve.
5. Sustain, support, uphold, bear up, hold up, follow up.
6. Keep pending, postpone, adjourn, carry over.
7. Carry on from the point of suspension or interruption, resume, proceed, advance, further, say in continuation, add.

CONTINUITY, *n.* 1. Intimate connection, close union, cohesion, connected whole.
2. Continuation, continuousness, protraction, prolongation, extension, perpetuity, constancy.
3. Uninterrupted connection, constant flow, unintermitted duration, contiguity, ceaselessness, unbroken extent, continuum.
4. Succession, sequence, round, progression, suite, train, series, catena, chain, course, scale,

gradation, retinue, column, rank, line, file, row, string, queue, tier, range.

CONTINUOUS, *adj.* 1. Consecutive, progressive, serial, gradual, successive, linear, connected, unbroken, unintermitted, entire, having the parts in immediate connection.
2. Uninterrupted in time, without cessation, unceasing, ceaseless, unremitting, everlasting, incessant, constant, eternal, endless, perennial, interminable, perpetual, continual.

CONTORT, *v.* Bend out of shape, deform, knot, distort, misshape, writhe, gnarl, twist, buckle, screw, wrap, wrench, wring, wrest, wrinkle, curl, crisp, make faces, make a moue.

CONTORTION, *n.* 1. Deformation, malformation, misshapement, deformity, distortion, grimace, twist, misproportion, anamorphosis, ugliness, crookedness, wryness, *moue (Fr.),* pout.
2. Knot, buckle, warp, screw, curl, volute, coil, corkscrew, spiral, helix, whorl.

CONTORTIONIST, *n.* Acrobat, tumbler, rope-dancer, juggler, equilibrist, funambulist.

CONTOUR, *n.* Outline of a figure or body, profile, silhouette, face, visage, physiognomy, countenance, lineament, trait, feature, lines, cut of one's jib, *tournure (Fr.),* shape, figure, form.

CONTRABAND, *adj.* Prohibited from export or import, not allowed, taboo, forbidden, bootleg, smuggled, unlicensed, unauthorized, actionable, illicit, unlawful, illegal.

CONTRABAND, *n.* 1. Illegal traffic, smuggling, rum-running, bootlegging, speakeasy, poaching, violation of law.
2. Embargo, taboo, ban, proscription, veto, prevention, restriction, interdiction, injunction, disallowance, forbiddance, prohibition, Volstead Act, 18th Amendment.
3. Anything prohibited by law from being imported or exported, prohibited articles, goods imported or exported illegally, forbidden fruit.

CONTRACT, *v.* 1. Draw into smaller compass, draw the parts of together, shorten by omitting some elements, abridge, epitomize, concentrate, reduce, lessen, diminish, narrow, pinch, crush, compress, constrict, condense, dwarf, squeeze, boil down, curtail, strangle, tighten, cramp.
2. Be reduced in compass, be drawn together, become smaller, shrink, shrivel, wrinkle, knit, decrease, grow less, dwindle, decline, fall off, abate, subside, fall away, waste, wane, ebb.
3. Incur, bring upon, fall into, expose oneself to, catch, take, take in, absorb, acquire, lie under, be liable.
4. Enter into, form, develop, beget, assume, engender.
5. Establish by agreement, settle by covenant, enter into an agreement, agree on, bargain, stipulate, covenant, make a bargain, pledge, engage, undertake, negotiate, make terms, come to terms, dicker, adjust, circumscribe, limit, bound.
6. Betroth, affiance, engage.

CONTRACT, *n.* 1. Compact, covenant, treaty, concordat, convention, stipulation, bargain, pact, agreement, entente, *entente cordiale (Fr.),* deal, arrangement, understanding, bond, indenture, gentlemen's agreement, settlement, commitment, legal document.
2. Formal agreement of marriage, betrothal, espousal, engagement.

CONTRACTION, *n.* 1. Shortening, reduction,

diminution, decrease, lessening, abbreviation, abridgment, compendium, abstract, contracture, epitomization, epitome, résumé, condensation, précis, compactness, compression.

2. Shriveling, shrinking, corrugation, drawing in, drawing together, constriction, attenuation.

CONTRACTOR, *n.* Builder, architect, artificer, constructor, *padrone (It.),* maker.

CONTRADICT, *v.* 1. Assert the contrary or opposite of, deny directly and categorically, controvert, gainsay, impugn, dispute, dissent, differ from, refute, disprove, overthrow, rebut, confute, belie.

2. Oppose, counteract, contravene, traverse, thwart, disallow, negative, negate, abrogate, be contrary to, annul, alter the case, counter, run counter to.

CONTRADICTION, *n.* 1. Categorical denial, assertion of the contrary or opposite, rejoinder, gainsay, controversion, impugnment, dissension, disagreement, dispute, contravention, difference of opinion, dissent, refutation, confutation, rebuttal, negation, disproof, counterevidence.

2. Incongruity, antagonism, antinomy, direct opposition between things compared, clashing, contrariety, inconsistency.

CONTRADICTORY, *adj.* Asserting the contrary or opposite, contradicting each other, negating, conflicting, refutatory, refutative, paradoxical, countervailing, negatory, opposing, repugnant, antagonistic, irreconcilable, dissentient, opposite, inconsistent, contrary, at odds, unreconciled, at variance, discrepant, incongruous.

CONTRADISTINCTION, *n.* Opposition, foil, distinction by opposition or contrast, contrast, antithesis, dissimilarity, unlikeness, setoff.

CONTRARIETY, *n.* 1. Opposition, antagonism, oppositeness, contradictoriness, incongruousness, repugnance, contradiction, contrast, antipathy, inconsistency, disagreement, discrepancy, clashing.

2. The opposite, the reverse, the converse, inversion, subversion, antistrophe, counterterm, antipodes, the other extreme, reversal, antonym, the inverse.

CONTRARY, *adj.* 1. Opposite in direction or position, opposing, opposed, counter, converse, averse, antithetical, antipodean, diametrically opposite, reverse.

2. Opposite in nature or character, repugnant, antagonistic, discordant, inconsistent, incompatible, hostile, warring, filibusterous, at cross purposes, inimical, negatory, at variance, counteracting, contradictory, at issue, conflicting.

3. Untoward, unfavorable, adverse, ill, foul, inclement, inauspicious, unpropitious, prejudicial.

4. Obstinate, stubborn, headstrong, perverse, wilful, unruly, intractable, refractory, wayward, recalcitrant, cross-grained, unaccommodating, froward, self-willed, humorsome.

CONTRAST, *n.* Striking exhibition of unlikeness, exhibition of differences, antithesis, counterpart, complement, setoff, foil, disparity, dissimilitude, dissimilarity, contrariety, difference, juxtaposition of differences, opposition, variance, divergence, variation, heterogeneity, disagreement, inequality, distinction, contradiction, oppositeness, disparity, incongruousness, adverseness.

CONTRAST, *v.* 1. Set in opposition in order to show unlikeness, set off by opposition, exhibit the differences between, compare, differentiate,

discriminate, distinguish between, compare by observing differences.

2. Afford a contrast to, stand out in opposition, show difference, stand out, differ, vary, disagree with, mismatch, diverge from, depart from, form a contrast, deviate from.

CONTRAVENE, *v.* 1. Contradict, belie, oppose, counteract, countervail, run counter to, be in conflict with, clash with, cross, thwart, obstruct, traverse, militate against, conflict with, go against, hinder, defeat, rebut, refute, confute, tell another story, turn the tables, annul, abrogate, nullify, alter the case, turn the scale.

2. Violate, infringe, transgress.

CONTRAVENTION, *n.* Action counter to something, counteraction, obstruction, opposition, oppugnancy, antagonism, contradiction, violation, traversal, transgression.

CONTRETEMPS, *n.* Inopportune occurrence, embarrassing mischance, misadventure, mishap, misfortune, mischance, evil hour, intempestivity, improper time, impasse, hitch, calamity, rub, catastrophe, disaster, casualty, cross, reverse, check, pinch, setback.

CONTRIBUTE, *v.* 1. Give to a common stock, give for a common purpose, give in common with others, grant as a share, subscribe, bestow, furnish a contribution, present, accord, donate, confer, offer, dispense, hand out, endow, settle upon, enrich, subsidize.

2. Furnish to a magazine, supply to a journal, communicate, provide, equip, accommodate with, indulge with.

3. Conduce, advance, forward, influence, tend, subserve, redound to, have a hand in, determine, decide, turn the scale, lead to, bear a part, be helpful, cooperate, concur, minister, conspire.

CONTRIBUTION, *n.* 1. Bestowal, presentation, conferment, dispensation, endowment, donation, bestowment, grant, subscription, offering.

2. Article contributed, gift, present, sportula, offertory, gratuity, largesse, alms, allowance, subsidy, dole, subvention, tribute, shower, boon. benefaction, favor, bounty, honorarium, bonus.

3. Benevolence, charity, almsgiving, liberality, philanthropy, generosity.

CONTRIBUTOR, *n.* 1. Donor, subscriber, giver, presenter, conferrer, bestower, grantor, investor, fairy godmother.

2. Correspondent to a magazine or journal, columnist, reviewer, free lance, paragraphist, hack writer, critic, reporter, journalist, potboiler, magazinist, penny-a-liner.

CONTRITE, *adj.* Repentant, penitent, broken in spirit by a sense of guilt, sorrowful, regretful, conscience-smitten, self-accusing, unhardened, humbled, penitential, chastened, reclaimed.

CONTRITION, *n.* Sorrow for sin with a true purpose of amendment, qualms of conscience, awakened conscience, stings of conscience, self-reproach, compunction, repentance, remorse, regret, sincere penitence, self- condemnation, self-humiliation, penance, *locus paenitentiae (Lat.).*

CONTRIVANCE, *n.* 1. Faculty of contriving, designing power, inventiveness, creativeness, invention, ingenuity.

2. Piece of mechanism, device, apparatus, gear, instrument, machine, contraption, gadget, engine, appliance, convenience, implement, tool, utensil, equipment, matériel, tackle, harness.

3. Plot, plan, artifice, trick, design, scheme,

stratagem, intrigue, cabal, conspiracy, complot, machination, shift, makeshift, measure, stroke, coup.

CONTRIVE, *v.* 1. Plan with ingenuity, bring about by a device, effect by a stratagem, intrigue, maneuver, manage to do something, shape out a course, organize, systematize, map out, chalk out, hit upon, fall upon, cast, frame, brew, hatch, concoct, plot, design, devise, invent, scheme, project, forecast, draft, sketch.

2. Form designs, set one's wits to work, rack one's brains, cudgel one's brains, consider, cast about, strain one's invention.

CONTROL, *n.* 1. Power of controlling, regulation, domination, authority, command, sway, dominion, direction, rule, ascendancy, government, mastery, superintendence, regimentation, disposition, management, charge, influence, jurisdiction.

2. Check, curb, restraint, bridle, block, clog, stop, hindrance, obstacle, obstruction, barrier, bar, stopper, brake, damper, repression, drag, device for regulating and guiding a machine.

3. Something that serves to control, a standard of comparison in scientific experimentation.

4. Person who acts as a check, controller.

CONTROL, *v.* 1. Exercise direction over, wield restraint over, direct, master, dominate, rule, govern, sway, reign over, superintend, supervise, have charge of, command, guide, regulate, have the direction of, manage, conduct, hold in line, have well in hand, have the cards in one's hand, hold in hand, ride the waves, be in the saddle.

2. Check, hinder, repress, restrain, curb, stop, bridle, subdue, block, hinder, obstruct, bar, put the brakes on.

3. Verify a scientific experiment by a parallel experiment or other standard of comparison.

CONTROVERSIAL, *adj.* 1. Of the nature of controversy, polemical, eristic, argumentative, dialectic.

2. Given to controversy, disputatious, at odds, dissentient, quarrelsome, factious, litigious, at issue, pettifogging, at variance.

3. Subject to controversy, debatable, doubtful, controvertible, disputable, open to discussion, questionable.

CONTROVERSIALIST, *n.* 1. Reasoner, casuist, logician, dialectician, polemicist, hairsplitter, rationalist, agonist.

2. Debator, arguer, disputant, disputer, fighter, wrangler, litigant, belligerent, aggressor, assailant.

CONTROVERSY, *n.* 1. Disputation concerning a matter of opinion, dispute, discussion, war of words, argumentation, contention, strife of words, logomachy, polemics, debate, argument, quarrel, disagreement, altercation, wrangle, squabble, political football.

2. Lawsuit, litigation, suit at law, judicial contest, process in law.

CONTROVERT, *v.* 1. Contradict, dispute, deny, contend against in discussion, counter, contravene, gainsay, negate, disaffirm, refute, impugn, rebut, confute, join issue upon, call in question, belie, give the lie to, disprove.

2. Oppose, contest, canvass, debate, argue, discuss.

CONTUMACIOUS, *adj.* Wilful, obstinate, self-willed, stubborn, headstrong, perverse, *entêté (Fr.)*, heady, intractable, recalcitrant, recusant, refractory, obdurate, tenacious, pertinacious, unruly, unmanageable, ungovernable, restive,

unsubmissive, uncomplying, insubordinate, stiff-necked, impatient of control, cross-grained, stubbornly rebellious, wilfully disrespectful, insolently disobedient, dogged.

CONTUMACY, *n.* 1. Stubborn perverseness, perversity, obstinacy, self-will, stubbornness, old school, pervicacity, doggedness, mulishness, blind side, tenacity, pertinacity, obduracy, headiness, dogged resolution, immovability, inflexibility.

2. Obstinate disobedience to authority, revolt, rebelliousness, insubordination, infraction, non-compliance, indocility, disrespect, insolence, mutiny, rebellion, sedition, outbreak.

CONTUMELIOUS, *adj.* Abusive, insulting, rude, insolent, uncivil, ungracious, opprobrious, bitter, contemptuous, humiliating, calumnious, reviling, slanderous, reproachful, disdainful, scornful, venomous, acerbous, acrimonious, snarling, surly, arrogant, overbearing, supercilious, sarcastic, biting, trenchant, caustic, vilipendent, derisive, scurrilous, withering, cynical, vituperative, objurgatory.

CONTUMELY, *n.* Insulting manifestation of contempt, contemptuous treatment, humiliating rudeness, disdain, scorn, insult, discourtesy, indignity, affront, dishonor, conduct unbecoming a gentleman, *grossièreté (Fr.)*, abuse, scurrility, objurgation, disrespect, procacity, superciliousness, arrogance, insolence, obloquy, opprobrium, vilipendency, vituperation, reproach, hard words, personal remarks, unparliamentary language, invective, *brusquerie (Fr.)*.

CONTUSE, *v.* Injure by a blow without breaking the skin, bruise, squeeze, crush, make black and blue.

CONTUSION, *n.* Injury from a blow with a blunt instrument, bruise, black-and-blue spot.

CONUNDRUM, *n.* A riddle the answer to which involves a pun or play on words, enigma, puzzle, problem, oracle, Sphinx, poser, arcanum, charade, rebus, *crux criticorum (Lat.)*, logograph, anagram.

CONVALESCENCE, *n.* Gradual recovery of health and strength after illness, recuperation, improvement, revival, rally, restoration, bloom, rehabilitation, rejuvenescence, rejuvenation, cure, renascence, strength, euphoria, haleness.

CONVALESCENT, *adj.* Improving in health, recovering, recuperating, redivivous, renascent, none the worse, restored, rejuvenated, euphoric.

CONVENE, *v.* 1. Meet, assemble, collect, gather, come together for some public purpose, hold a session, congregate, muster, cluster, swarm, flock together, herd, mass, throng, associate, resort, forgather.

2. Cause to assemble, convoke, call together, bring together, gather together, summon, round up.

CONVENIENCE, *n.* 1. Accommodation, ease, opportunity, leisure, spare time, vacant hour, spare moments, freedom, idleness, otiosity, time convenient for one, opportune state of affairs, suitable opportunity.

2. Source of comfort, cause of satisfaction, advantage from something convenient, satisfaction, commodiousness.

3. Suitableness, suitability, fitness, handiness, serviceableness, accessibility, utility, adaptability, usefulness.

CONVENIENT, *adj.* Agreeable to the needs or purpose, well suited with respect to ease in use, easy for use, handy, adapted, serviceable, useful, advantageous, helpful, comfortable, beneficial, commodious, suitable, adaptable, opportune, at hand, easily accessible.

CONVENT, *n.* Community of persons devoted to a religious life under a society, society of monks, society of friars, monastery, monkery, hermitage, friary, abbey, cloister, priory, cenoby, lamasery, khankah *(Moham.),* vihara *(Buddhist),* society of nuns *(popular usage),* nunnery.

CONVENTION, *n.* 1. Meeting, caucus, council, diet, conference, formal assembly of representatives or delegates for action on particular matters, synod, assemblage, gathering, convocation, congress, conclave.
2. Conventionality, propriety, accepted usage as a standard of procedure, general agreement or consent, conventionalism, custom, formality, protocol, practice or rule established by general usage, conventional arrangement, standing order, hard and fast rule, punctilio, etiquette.

CONVENTIONAL, *adj.* 1. Usual, in established usage, customary, habitual, accustomed, normal, wonted, common, ordinary, everyday, regular, stereotyped.
2. Conforming to accepted standards, stiff, established by general consent, traditional, rigid, orthodox, methodical, precise, tradition-bound, academic, formal, uncompromising, Procrustean, standard, canonical, decorous, punctilious.

CONVERGE, *v.* 1. Tend to meet in a point or line, incline toward each other, tend to the same point, draw gradually together, approach one another, come together, close in upon, meet, unite, center, focalize.
2. Tend to a common result or conclusion, conduce, concur, conspire.

CONVERGENCE, *n.* Confluence, conflux, union, convergency, concurrence, focalization, meeting, concentration, concourse.

CONVERGENT, *adj.* Gradually approaching, converging, concurrent, confluent, centripetal.

CONVERSABLE, *adj.* Affable, communicative, discoursive, interlocutory, confabulatory, free, chatty, conversational, unreserved, sociable, open, informal.

CONVERSANT WITH 1. Familiar with by use or study, acquainted with, versed in, proficient in, *au fait (Fr.),* skilled in, practiced, tutored, learned, well-informed, up on, *au courant (Fr.).*
2. Having regular or frequent conversation on, intimately associating.

CONVERSATION, *n.* 1. Informal interchange of thoughts by spoken words, converse, colloquy, discourse, speech, talk, interlocution, dialogue, chat, parley, palaver, causerie, gossip, chitchat, tattle, conference, interview, familiar discourse, consultation, audience, tête-à-tête, powwow, *conversazione (It.).*
2. Intimate acquaintance, association, social intercourse, commerce, communion, familiarity.

CONVERSATIONAL, *adj.* Chatty, confabulatory, colloquial, discoursive, communicative, ready to to converse, interlocutory, given to conversation, talkative, garrulous, voluble.

CONVERSE, *v.* 1. Talk together, engage in a conversation, hold a conversation, discourse with, colloquize, speak with, confabulate, confer with, talk over, discuss, collogue, palaver, parley, consult with, prate, chatter, chat, gossip, talk informally with another, interchange thought in speech.

2. Hold inward communion, commune with, hold intercourse.

CONVERSE, *n.* 1. Familiar talk, intimate discourse, conversation, colloquy, talk.
2. Inward communion, intercourse, commerce, fellowship.

CONVERSE, *adj.* Turned about, opposite in direction, contrary in action, reverse.

CONVERSION, *n.* 1. Transformation, progress, transmutation, metamorphosis, change, changeover, reduction, resolution, growth, passage, passing, metastasis, transmigration, metabolism, flux.
2. Interchange, transposition, transition, reversal, inversion.
3. Change of heart, change in character, new birth, regeneration, change of religion, spiritual change, change from one religion to another.
4. Fraudulent conversion, embezzlement, peculation, defalcation.

CONVERT, *v.* 1. Transform, change, transmute, metamorphose, alter, vary, resolve, transfigure, translate, metabolize, transmogrify.
2. Interchange, invert, transpose, reverse, turn about, divert, turn to another purpose, exchange for an equivalent.
3. Change the heart of, regenerate, create anew, recreate, cause to adopt a different religion, proselytize, change in character, cause to turn from an evil life to a righteous one.
4. Appropriate wrongfully to one's own use, expropriate, misapply, assume unlawful rights of ownership, embezzle, peculate, defalcate, steal.

CONVERT, *n.* One who has been converted to a religion or opinion, proselyte, neophyte, disciple.

CONVERTIBLE, *adj.* 1. Capable of being converted, transmutable, transformable.
2. Interchangeable, reciprocal, synonymous, mutual, equivalent.
3. *(Auto.)* Having a folding top.

CONVEX, *adj.* Rounding outwardly, bulging and curved, curved like a circle or sphere when viewed from without, protuberant, tumid, bossed, swelling, swollen, gibbous, bulbous, embowed, hemispheric, arched, salient, raised.

CONVEY, *v.* 1. Carry from one place to another, bear, transport, transmit, bring, fetch, waft, move, conduct, lead.
2. *(Law)* Cede, grant, will, abalienate, transfer, demise, devolve, bequeath, devise, deliver over, make over, alienate.
3. Make known, communicate, impart, tell, relate, disclose, reveal, divulge, confide to.

CONVEYANCE, *n.* 1. Transfer, carrying, carriage, transmission, conveying, communication, transvection, transport, movement, transshipment, freightage, ferriage.
2. *(Law)* Transfer of property, disposal, sale, legacy, assignment, demise, alienation, cession, transference, lease, abalienation, deed, devisal, quitclaim, devise, bequest, bequeathal.
3. Wagon, car, carriage, van, lorry, vehicle, *voiture (Fr.),* chariot, equipage, rig, coach, bus, stagecoach, tallyho, diligence, hackney, cab, fly, hack, hansom, buggy, surrey, gig, cart, sulky, jinricksha, wain, truck, dray, auto.

CONVICT, *v.* Declare guilty of an offense, prove guilty after legal trial, find guilty, sentence, doom, condemn, pass sentence on, adjudge.

CONVICT, *n.* 1. Person proved guilty of an offense, malefactor, criminal, culprit, felon, condemned person, transgressor, delinquent, malfeasant, recidivist, gunman, gangster.

2. Convicted person serving a prison sentence, jailbird, prisoner, captive, outlaw, murderer, gallowsbird.

CONVICTION, n. 1. Proof of guilt, penalty, sentence, judgment, death warrant, death penalty, capital punishment.

2. Opinion, view, firm persuasion, fixed belief, settled belief, certainty, impression, judgment, conclusion, certitude.

3. Doctrine, tenet, creed, dogma, principle, faith, teaching, maxim, articles, canons, gospel, confession.

CONVINCE, v. Persuade by argument, cause to believe in the truth of what is alleged, satisfy by proof or evidence, prevail on, make see the light, influence, induce, impel, assure, convert, indoctrinate, bring to reason, win over, bring round.

CONVIVIAL, adj. 1. Fond of feasting and drinking, relishing merry company, symposiac, merrymaking, jolly, jovial, gay, hospitable, social, genial, affable, gregarious, agreeable, friendly, companionable, intimate, familiar, hail-fellow-well-met, eat-drink-and-be-merry, bibulous, winebibbing.

2. Befitting a feast, festive, festal.

CONVIVIALITY, n. Merrymaking, festivity, good fellowship, joviality, jollity, gaiety, hospitality, cheer, festive board, loving cup, sociability.

CONVOCATION, n. 1. Calling together, muster, convoking, convening, summoning, assembling, gathering together, ingathering, mobilization, forgathering, congregation, collection, levy.

2. Assembly, group of persons met in answer to a summons, meeting, congress, council, house, convention, conclave, conference, diet, synod, levee, caucus, convocation, legislature, senate, parliament, committee, union, lodge, club, society, association, company.

CONVOKE, v. Assemble by summons, summon to meet, convene, muster, call together, bring together, collect, gather together, round up, hold a meeting.

CONVOLUTION, n. 1. Rolling together, coiling together, involution, tortuosity, winding, twist, ambages, meandering, undulation, wave, circuit, sinuousness, sinuosity, twirl, contortion, whorl.

2. Coil, curl, fold, volute, roll, spiral, helix, scroll, tendril, worm, corkscrew, kink, scallop, labyrinth, maze, snake, serpent, eel.

CONVOY, v. Accompany for protection, attend, escort, go along with, keep company with, guard, conduct, support, watch, chaperon.

CONVOY, n. Attendance for the purpose of protection, protection afforded by an escort, escorting force, escort, guard at sea, armed warship that escorts, formation of ships accompanied by a protecting escort, escorted train of vehicles, group of military vehicles traveling together under the same orders.

CONVULSE, v. 1. Throw into spasms, cause violent disturbance, agitate, stir, disturb, shake violently, rend, churn, jerk, hitch, joggle, jolt, tumble, toss.

2. Wring, hurt, harrow, agonize, torture, rack, torment, excruciate, stab, irritate, exacerbate, inflame.

3. Cause to laugh violently, throw into gales of laughter, make hold one's sides.

CONVULSION, n. 1. Contortion of the body caused by violent muscular contractions of the extremities (Pathol.), paroxysm, fit, throe, raptus, spasm, cramp, ictus (Med.), access, attack, epitasis (Med.), orgasm, entasia (Med.), erethism.

2. Violent agitation, disturbance, commotion, tumult, excitement.

3. Violent fit of laughter, gales of laughter, side-splitting.

COOK, v. 1. Prepare food for the table by the action of heating, bake, braise, broil, fry, roast, stew, boil, frizzle, seethe, heat, parboil, simmer, scald, curry, steam, devil, griddle, fricassee, pan, grill.

2. (Colloq.) Concoct, cook up, invent falsely, falsify, brew up, alter surreptitiously, fix, dress up, tamper with, garble, color, give a color to.

3. (Colloq.) Ruin, undo, spoil, wreck.

COOL, adj. 1. Neither warm nor very cold, heat-repelling, somewhat cold, a little cold, moderately cold, rather cold, chill, chilly.

2. Self-possessed, not excited, calm, not hasty, deliberate, composed, undisturbed, collected, unruffled, unexcited, sedate, placid, quiet, staid, imperturbable, wary, dispassionate.

3. Deficient in ardor, unenthusiastic, distant, indifferent, lukewarm, unconcerned, nonchalant, easygoing, unresponsive, apathetic.

4. Lacking in cordiality, unfriendly, frosty, wintry, frozen, icy, gelid, chilling, frigid.

5. Calmly audacious, brazen, impudent, cold-blooded, shameless.

6. (Of a number or sum) Without exaggeration, round, unqualified.

COOL, v. 1. Chill, freeze, congeal, harden, ice, refrigerate, infrigidate, make cool, reduce the heat of, impart a sensation of coolness to.

2. Lessen the intensity of, calm, allay, quiet, temper, moderate, attemper, damp, mitigate, abate.

3. Cool off, grow cool, lose heat.

4. Grow lukewarm or indifferent, lose ardor, be less zealous.

COOP, v. Confine narrowly, shut up, fence in, impound, cage, encage, imprison, rail in, pen up, box up.

COOPERATE, v. 1. Work together, work in unison, act jointly, unite in producing a effect, act in concert, take part, participate, be a party to, share in, lend oneself to, partake of, cast in one's lot with, stand shoulder to shoulder, pull together, work side by side with, play along, fraternize, join forces, take sides with, side with, join hands with, go along with, make common cause with, join with, unite with, cast in one's lot with, bear part in, chip in, second, contribute, espouse a cause.

2. Conspire, concur, conduce, coact, unite one's efforts, collaborate, concert.

COOPERATION, n. 1. Activity shared for mutual benefit, give and take, concurrent effort, joint action, teamwork, joint operation, synergy, collaboration, pulling together, coadjuvancy, participation, union, logrolling.

2. Association, company, partnership, alliance, pool, society, gentlemen's agreement, coalition, confederation, fusion, fraternization, fraternity, fellowship, comradeship.

3. Concert, concurrence, coaction, agreement, unanimity, concord, consentaneity, harmony, accordance.

4. *Esprit de corps (Fr.)*, party spirit, clanship, partisanship.

COOPERATOR, *n.* Co-worker, party to, fellow worker, colleague, participator in, collaborator, associate, assistant, aider, helper, ally, abettor, auxiliary, accomplice, joint operator, adjuvant, adjutant, mate, helping hand, partner, confrere, coadjutor, confederate, accessory.

COORDINATE, *adj.* Of the same order or degree, equal in importance, of the same rank, coequal.

COORDINATE, *v.* Organize, adjust, harmonize, regulate, systematize, methodize, arrange, set in order.

COPARTNER, *n.* 1. Associate, partner, sharer, partaker, compeer, confrere, colleague.
2. Shareholder, cotenant, joint-tenant, coheir.

COPARTNERSHIP, *n.* 1. Association, alliance, partnership, fraternity, colleagueship, cartel, ring, joint stock, trust, pool, combine, interlocking directorate.
2. Establishment, house, firm, company, joint concern, concern, joint-stock company, investment trust.

COPE WITH, *v.* 1. Encounter, struggle with, compete with, contend with, strive with, engage with, encounter, face, confront.
2. Contend on fairly even terms, struggle with a degree of success, encounter successfully, hold one's own with, manage, hold at bay, combat on equal terms.

COPIOUS, *adj.* Large in quantity or number, yielding an abundant supply, exhibiting fullness, profuse, full, ample, abundant, plenteous, liberal, plentiful, overflowing, exuberant, bountiful, extensive, unrestricted, lavish, replete, chock-full, well-provided, cornucopian.

COPIOUSNESS, *n.* Plenty, plenitude, abundance, profusion, amplitude, full measure, exuberance, richness, repletion, surfeit, satiety, luxuriance, fill, affluence, cornucopia, horn of plenty.

COPPER, *n.* 1. Copper coin, cent, penny, English halfpenny.
2. *(Pl.)* Small change, copper money, pin money, *Wechselgeld (Ger.)*.
3. Cauldron, large boiler, container made of copper.

COPSE, *n.* Thicket of small bushes, grove of small trees, coppice, boscage, bosk, brushwood, underwood, brake, *bocage (Fr.)*, scrub.

COPULATION, *n.* Sexual union, coition, coitus, sexual congress, venereal act, intercourse, coupling.

COPULATIVE, *adj.* Linking, connecting, joining, uniting.

COPY, *n.* 1. Imitation of an original, facsimile, counterpart, reproduction, duplicate, similitude, replica, effigy, likeness, semblance, tracing, cast, representation, portrait, transcript, counterscript, offprint, reprint, counterfeit, forgery, chip of the old block.
2. Original, model, archetype, pattern, plan, standard, precedent, example, specimen, sample.
3. Written matter intended to be reproduced in print, manuscript, typescript, text.

COPY, *v.* 1. Follow as a model, imitate, pattern after, follow as a pattern, mirror, reflect, repeat, reproduce, duplicate, mimic, ape, personate, impersonate, simulate, do something in imitation of someone else, parody, burlesque, caricature, travesty, paraphrase, mock, counterfeit.

2. Make a transcript of, transcribe, trace, make a copy of, rewrite.

COPYIST, *n.* 1. Imitator, mimic, copier, echo, parrot, cuckoo, catbird, mocking bird, monkey, ape.
2. Transcriber of documents, amanuensis.

COQUET, *v.* 1. Trifle in love, philander, flirt, pay one's addresses to, pay court to, make love, affect to be in love, make a show of love, play at courtship, play the coquette, dally, pet, neck, spark, spoon, make googoo eyes at, bill and coo, look sweet at, set one's cap at, woo, vamp.
2. Act without seriousness or decision, toy with, be irresolute, will and will not, *chasser-balancer (Fr.)*, play fast and loose, blow hot and cold.

COQUETRY, *n.* Arts of a coquette, affection of love, flirtation, dalliance, philandering, flirting, gallantry, petting, spooning, necking, amorous glances, ogle, sheep's eyes, googoo eyes, addresses.

COQUETTE, *n.* 1. Woman who tries to gain the affections of men for mere self-gratification, jilt, flirt, gold digger, vampire, vamp, belle, Sheba.
2. Male flirt, sheik, lounge lizard, wolf, necker, philanderer.

CORD, *n.* 1. String, twine, small rope composed of several strands twisted together, line, braid, flexible insulated cable *(Elect.)*, gimp, lanyard, gut, tape, ribbon, funicle.
2. Ribbed fabric, corduroy.
3. Bond, vinculum, tie, catena, nexus, link, connection, interconnection, copula.
4. Ligature, tendon, sinew, leader, ligament, thew.

CORDIAL, *adj.* 1. Genial, friendly, warm, hearty, warmly friendly, ardent, affectionate, gracious, whole-souled, familiar, amiable, affable, sincere, ingratiating, good-natured, heartfelt, earnest.
2. Invigorating, refreshing, restorative, tonic, pleasant, stimulating.

CORDIAL, *n.* 1. Liqueur, aromatized spirit, strong aromatic alcoholic liquor, anisette, aquavit, benedictine, cacao, cassis, chartreuse, crème de menthe, forbidden fruit, grand marnier, kümmel, kirschwasser, maraschino, slivowitz.
2. Stimulating medicine, exhilarating draft, stomachic, stomachal.

CORDIALITY, *n.* Warmth of feeling, affectionate regard, heartiness, ardor, sincerity, eagerness, fervor, fervency, earnestness, good will, fellow-feeling, fraternization, good understanding.

CORDON, *n.* 1. Braid worn for ornament, cord worn as a fastening.
2. Ribbon worn diagonally across the breast as a badge of a knightly or honorary order, sash, decoration, riband, blue ribbon, cordon bleu.
3. Cordon sanitaire, quarantine.
4. Line of sentinels inclosing a particular area, military posts for guarding, picketline.

CORE, *n.* 1. Nucleus, kernel, heart, marrow, inmost part, inner part.
2. Pith, substance, gist, sum and substance, essence, center, gravamen, essential part.

CORK, *n.* 1. Outer bark of the cork-oak *(Quercus suber)*.
2. Stopper, stopple, bung, plug, stopcock, tap, spill, spike, tampon.

CORMORANT, *n.* Greedy person, rapacious fellow, glutton, greedy-gut, belly-god, hog, Apicius, gormandizer, gastronome, epicure, gourmand, *bon vivant (Fr.)*.

CORMORANT, *adj.* Gluttonous, greedy, all-devouring, omnivorous, edacious, voracious, swinish, hoggish, crapulent, rapacious, ravenous, insatiable.

CORN, *n.* 1. Cereal grain, any edible grain, wheat *(in England)*, oats *(in Scotland)*.
2. Indian corn, maize.

CORN, *v.* 1. Preserve and season with salt in grains, salt moderately, sprinkle with salt, lay down in brine.
2. Make drunk, make tipsy, intoxicate, fuddle, inebriate, muddle.

CORNER, *n.* 1. Meeting place of two converging lines or surfaces, space between two converging lines near their intersection, angle, elbow, bend, crotch, knee, coign, cusp, cantle, projection.
2. Secluded place, nook, niche, recess, retired place, secluded spot, secret place.
3. End, margin, edge, rim.
4. Awkward or embarrassing situation, cul-de-sac, impasse, dead end.
5. Monopoly of the available supply of a commodity, control, impropriation, exclusive possession.

CORNER, *v.* 1. Drive into a corner, place in a corner, choke off.
2. Force into an awkward or difficult position, nonplus, confuse, confound, pose, bewilder, put to a stand, perplex, puzzle, stymie.
3. Form a corner in a stock or commodity, monopolize, impropriate.

COROLLARY, *n.* Immediate or easily drawn consequence, deduction, inference, illation, moral, ergotism, porism, conclusion, natural result, upshot.

CORONATION, *n.* Ceremony of investing a king or queen with a crown, accession, crowning, enthronement, elevation to the purple, installation, investiture, inauguration.

CORONET, *n.* Small crown, insignia for the head worn by members of nobility, crownlike ornament for the head, chaplet, wreath, garland, laurel, bays.

CORPORAL, *adj.* Bodily, corporeal, substantial, physical, somatoscopic, fleshly, incarnate, not spiritual, material, palpable, somatic, tangible.

CORPORATION, *n.* Company, trust, partnership, merger, pool, corporate body, guild, house, firm, combine, holding company, lawful association of individuals having a continuous existence irrespective of that of its members.

CORPS, *n.* 1. Military unit of ground combat forces, organized military body, body of troops, division of any army, *corps d'armée (Fr.)*, squad, division, host, wing, column, escadrille, phalanx, detachment, garrison, regiment, brigade, battery, squadron, battalion, platoon, company, section, cohort.
2. Group of persons acting together, troupe, assemblage, posse, crew, team, party, band, force, gang.

CORPSE, *n.* Dead body of a human being, clay, carcass, relics, skeleton, remains, cadaver, earth, dust, ashes, mummy, tenement of clay, carrion, "this mortal coil" *(Hamlet)*.

CORPULENCE, *n.* Bulkiness of body, obesity, fatness, embonpoint, fleshiness, plumpness, bulk, rotundity, portliness, polysarcia *(Med.)*, stoutness, pinguitude, corporation *(colloq.)*.

CORPULENT, *adj.* Bulky of body, fat, chubby, obese, fleshy, portly, stout, stocky, thick-set, fat as a pig, plump, rotund, pursy, burly, hulking, cumbersome, squab, bouncing, strapping, puffy, well-fed, chopping, lubberly, lumpish, spanking, thumping, whopping, whacking, plump as a partridge, overgrown, amplitudinous, elephantine.

CORPUSCLE, *n.* 1. Minute body forming a constituent of the blood.
2. Elementary particle of matter, atom, monad, electron, proton, molecule, grain, iota, jot, mite, bit, scrap, whit, tittle, scintilla, ace, pinpoint, minute body forming a more or less distinct part of an organism.

CORPUSCULAR, *adj.* Molecular, infinitesimal, atomic, granular, rudimentary, imperceptible, embryonic, intangible, impalpable.

CORRECT, *v.* 1. Remove the errors or faults of, improve, rectify, mend, repair, amend, emend, make right, remedy, reform, redress, reclaim, better, ameliorate, doctor, touch up.
2. Mark the errors in, change the quality of, modify, alter, adjust so as to bring into accord with a standard.
3. Admonish in order to improve, chasten, discipline, punish, reprove, rebuke, lecture, chide, reprimand, castigate, dress down, chastise, take to task, overhaul, berate, reprehend.
4. Set right, undeceive, straighten out, open the eyes of, disabuse.

CORRECT, *adj.* 1. Conforming to fact or truth, accurate, precise, exact, strict, true, factual, right, faultless, perfect, unerring, free from error, not faulty, unmistaken, infallible.
2. In accordance with an accepted standard, proper, conventional, fitting, meet, seemly, fit, *comme il faut (Fr.)*, appropriate, becoming, suitable.

CORRECTION, *n.* 1. Act of correcting, remedy, rectification, improvement, righting, reparation, repair, amendment, emendment, indemnification, redress.
2. Chastisement, chastening, reproof, punition, punishment, discipline, castigation.
3. Change in quality, modification, alteration, variation, qualification, mutation.

CORRECTIVE, *adj.* Rectifying, counteractive, tending to correct, reformative, reformatory, improving, amendatory, emendatory, modifying, alterative, correctory.
2. Remedial, curative, restorative, salutiferous, palliative, assuasive, healing, therapeutic.
3. Punitive, penal, disciplinary, castigatory, punitory, inflictive.

CORRECTNESS, *n.* 1. Exactness, faultlessness, exactitude, precision, accuracy, nicety, rightness, truth, rectitude, punctiliousness, rigor, probity, integrity, honesty, honor, faith, authenticity, real Simon Pure, orthodoxy, veracity, gospel, verity, *nuda veritas (Lat.)*.
2. Propriety, decorum, *bienséance (Fr.)*, good behavior, suitability, respectability, dignity, fitness.
3. Good taste, elegance, felicity, purity, grace, refinement, concinnity, symmetry, proportion.

CORRELATE, *v.* 1. Bring into reciprocal relation, place in mutual relation, establish in orderly connection.
2. Stand in correlation, correspond, have a mutual relation, have a reciprocal relation, interact, alternate, reciprocate, interchange, exchange, interdepend.

CORRELATION, *n.* Reciprocation, reciprocity, correspondence, interdependence, reciprocalness, mutuality, alternation, equivalence, give-and-take, *quid pro quo* (*Lat.*), exchange, transmutation, interchange, barter, commutation, permutation, intermutation, intercourse, commerce.

CORRELATIVE, *adj.* 1. Reciprocal, equivalent, so related that each implies or complements the other, mutual, correspondent, corresponding, analogous, complementary, complemental.
2. Being in correlation, mutually related, interchangeable, alternate.

CORRESPOND, *v.* 1. Be in agreement, agree, be in conformity, conform, comport with, concur, be accordant, accord, harmonize, tally, dovetail, square, fit, suit, match, answer, cohere.
2. Be similar, be analogous, be equivalent, be complemental, belong, stand counter, correlate, reciprocate.
3. Communicate with by exchange of letters, write letters to, send a letter to, epistolize, reply, answer, drop a line to, keep up a correspondence.

CORRESPONDENCE, *n.* 1. Agreement, fitting relation, conformity, accordance, concurrence, congruity, coincidence, reciprocity, uniformity, accord, reciprocal adaptation.
2. Counterposition, relation of similarity, relation of analogy, complemental relation, correlation.
3. Communication by exchange of letters, epistolary intercourse, epistolography.
4. Letters that pass between correspondents, missives, writings, epistles, notes, lines, billets, *billets doux* (*Fr.*), dispatches, bulletins, postals, postcards.

CORRESPONDENT, *adj.* 1. Suited, adapted, fit, fitted, fitting, suiting, suitable, corresponding, conformable, congruous, agreeable, answerable.
2. Answering, agreeing, correlative, belonging, complementary, corresponsive, complemental, reciprocal, counterposed.

CORRIDOR, *n.* 1. Passage connecting parts of a building, passage into which several rooms open, gallery, vestibule, anteroom, antechamber, court, lounge, foyer, loggia, hall, lobby, cloister.
2. Avenue, approach, channel, perron, artery, adit, alley, lane, aisle.
3. Narrow tract of land forming a passage to the sea, narrow way, defile.

CORRIGIBLE, *adj.* 1. Docile, tractable, pliant, amenable, submissive, teachable, easily taught.
2. Improvable, amendable, curable, remedial, correctable, emendatory, reformatory, reparatory.

CORROBORATE, *v.* Make more certain, uphold, strengthen, establish, confirm, support, sustain, bear out, vindicate, verify, substantiate, validate, authenticate, circumstantiate, prove, assure, visa, affirm, vouch for, certify, attest, ratify, endorse, countersign, warrant, make absolute.

CORROBORATIVE, *adj.* Confirmatory, assenting, corroborating, affirmatory, vindicatory, agreeing, evidential, at one with, of the same mind with.

CORRODE, *v.* 1. Eat away gradually as if by gnawing, eat into, erode, gnaw, consume.
2. Become corroded, canker, rust, oxidize, rot, crumble, decay, wear, molder, rankle, go bad.
3. Waste, wear away, impair, deteriorate, prey upon, disintegrate.
4. Envenom, poison, embitter, blight, shrivel, blast, wither, crush.

CORROSION, *n.* 1. Gnawing, erosion, eating away.
2. Wearing away, decay, dilapidation, atrophy, disintegration, decomposition, disrepair, canker, wear and tear, rottenness, dry rot, blight.
3. Product of corrosion, discoloration, patina, rust, oxidization.
4. Embittering, poisoning, envenoming, blighting.

CORROSIVE, *adj.* 1. Eating away, consuming, corroding, eroding, erosive, catheretic, wasting, gnawing, wearing away.
2. Caustic, acrid, virulent, harsh, astringent, stringent, sarcastic, mordant, trenchant, incisive, cutting, biting, sharp, acute, carking, cankerous.
3. Venomous, envenomed, poisonous, deadly, destructive.

CORROSIVENESS, *n.* Causticity, incisiveness, acrimony, acridness, virulence, harshness, edge, severity, mordancy, poignancy.

CORRUGATE, *v.* Bend into alternate furrows and ridges, draw into folds, furrow, pucker, knit, cockle, flute, groove, striate, wrinkle, chamfer, contract into wrinkles, seam, crease, plicate, etch, pleat, plait, cocker, crinkle, rumple, ruffle, seam, engrave.

CORRUGATION, *n.* 1. Wrinkle, furrow, ridge, groove, channel, flute, stria, crinkle, fold, plait, pleat, crease, hollow, seam, crumple, plication, cockle, dog's-ear, pucker, crow's-feet, flexure.
2. Roughness, unevenness, asperity, rugosity.

CORRUPT, *v.* 1. Destroy the integrity of, cause to be dishonest, bribe, entice, suborn.
2. Lower morally, deprave, pervert, brutalize, vitiate, degrade, debase, seduce, demoralize.
3. Alter for the worse, adulterate, alloy, tamper with, doctor, falsify.
4. Contaminate, defile, taint, pollute, envenom, spoil, infect, poison, canker, blight.
5. Make putrescent, putrefy, putresce, render putrid, decompose, rot, molder, decay.

CORRUPT, *adj.* 1. Without integrity, dishonest, dishonorable, open to bribes, mercenary, venal, susceptible to bribery, purchasable, unprincipled, hireling, hired, racket-ridden, crooked, villainous, shady, knavish, sordid, unscrupulous, fraudulent.
2. Debased in character, depraved, perverted, vicious, wicked, evil, sinful, iniquitous, criminal, base, degenerate, recreant, evilminded, shameless, immoral, dissolute, debauched, reprobate, lewd, profligate, abandoned, lecherous, lickerish, lustful, libidinous, licentious, wanton, lascivious.
3. Impure, contaminated, tainted, spoiled, bad, rotten, putrid, putrescent, putrefactive, carious, fetid, reeking, infected, unsound, moldy, musty, rancid, touched.

CORRUPTER, *n.* Debaucher, seducer, fast man, fornicator, rake, roué, debauchee, voluptuary, gay deceiver, sensualist, lecher, satyr, goat, wolf, Don Juan, whoremonger, adulterer, libertine, Lothario.

CORRUPTION, *n.* 1. Bribery, venality, jobbery, mercenariness, dishonest proceedings, abuse of public trusts, dishonesty, perversion of integrity, want of principle, deviation from rectitude, breach of trust, Tammany, Teapot Dome, graft, nepotism, shuffle, shady deal, fishy transaction, sharp practice.
2. Moral perversion, turpitude, vice, baseness, viciousness, degeneracy, depravity, wickedness, wrongdoing, iniquity, sinfulness, laxity, looseness of morals, immorality, profligacy, lust, sink of

iniquity, fleshpots of Babylon, demoralization.

3. Degradation, depravation, contamination, defilement, vitiation, debasement, adulteration, infection.

4. Putrefactive decay, putrefaction, pollution, putrescence, rottenness, foulness, rot, putridity, cariosity, decomposition.

CORSAIR, *n.* Pirate, privateer, freebooter, viking, buccaneer, sea robber, sea rover, picaroon, Paul Jones, brigand, pillager, marauder.

CORSET, *n.* Close-fitting inner garment stiffened with whalebone and capable of being tightened by lacing, corselett, bodice, stays, foundation garment, girdle, stomacher.

CORTEGE, *n.* 1. Train of attendants, retinue, suite, staff, court, entourage.

2. Procession, parade, cavalcade, caravan, file, column.

CORUSCATE, *v.* Emit vivid flashes of light, shoot out beams, flicker, sparkle, flash, fulgurate, glare, beam, shine, glitter, glister, glisten, gleam, blaze, twinkle, scintillate, glint, phosphoresce, shimmer, glow, glimmer.

CORUSCATION, *n.* Flash of light, emication, gleam, sparkle, scintillation, blaze, resplendency, glitter, fulguration, spark, effulgence, luminosity, dazzlement, luminousness, radiation, renitency, radiance, luminescence, phosphorescence.

COSMOPOLITAN, *adj.* 1. Belonging to all parts of the world, not limited to one part of the world.

2. Free from local ideas or attachments, not provincial, at home all over the world, oppidan, international, gregarious, urban, metropolitan.

3. Philanthropic, humanitarian, large-hearted, altruistic, utilitarian, public-spirited.

COSMOPOLITE, *n.* 1. One who is free from provincial or national prejudices, citizen of the world, cosmopolitan, *amicus humani generis (Lat.).*

2. Philanthropist, humanitarian, communist, altruist.

COSMOS, *n.* Creation, world, nature, empyrean, earth, globe, wide world, welkin, heavens, starry host, firmament, vault of heaven, heavenly bodies, nebulae, stars, galaxy, milky way, *via lactea (Lat.),* universe as an embodiment of order and harmony.

COSSET, *v.* Treat as a pet, coddle, pet, fondle, pamper, caress, dandle, pat on the cheek, chuck under the chin, fold in one's arms, cover with kisses, make much of, make a pet of, cuddle, hug, nestle, nuzzle, cherish, coax, wheedle, cocker, kill with kindness.

COST, *n.* 1. Price paid for anything, valuation, expenditure, expense, charge, outlay, value, rate, price-making factor, amount, worth, quotation, appraisement, figure, demand, hire, fare, money's worth, face value, market price, disbursement, par.

2. Splendor, richness, preciousness, costliness, sumptuousness, gorgeousness, magnificence.

3. Loss, sacrifice, penalty, damage, detriment, pain, suffering.

COST, *v.* 1. Require the expenditure of, be of the price of, be acquired in return for, fetch, sell for, bring in, afford, yield, amount to, come to, mount up to, stand one in.

2. Result in a particular loss or penalty, hurt, harm, injure, do disservice to, work evil, scathe, endamage, weigh down, overburden, bear hard upon.

3. Estimate the cost of, appraise, determine the expense of.

COSTLY, *adj.* 1. Costing much, of great cost, of great value, expensive, dear, of great price, at a premium, high-priced, valuable, extravagant, not to be had for love or money, unreasonable, exorbitant, extortionate.

2. Rich, priceless, precious, sumptuous, lavish, gorgeous, splendid, of priceless value, luxurious, magnificent.

COSTUME, *n.* Style of dress peculiar to a nation or period, garb belonging to another period or place, set of garments, dress appropriate to a particular occasion or season, raiment, apparel, clothing, attire, vestment, vesture, habiliments, clothes, array, gown, robe, habit, toilet, toilette.

COT, *n.* 1. Hut, small house, cottage, cabin, log cabin, shanty, crib, shack, châlet, lodge.

2. Light portable bed of canvas stretched on a frame, low bedstead, couch, pallet, stretcher, crib, trundle bed, litter.

COTERIE, *n.* Social circle, company, club, crew, set of persons associating habitually together, circle of acquaintance, clique, association, circle, sodality, brotherhood, crowd, party, faction.

COTTAGE, *n.* Small country residence, detached suburban house, cabin, small humble house, cot, lodge, hermitage, bungalow, châlet, croft, shack, château, casino, *rus in urbe (Lat.),* shanty, hovel, temporary residence at a vacation resort.

COUCH, *n.* 1. Bed, place for rest, place used for repose, cot, pallet, litter.

2. Sofa, lounge, divan, davenport, settee, dais, musnud, ottoman, *causeuse,* love seat, day bed, chaise longue.

3. Lair of a wild beast, den.

COUCH, *v.* 1. Lie at rest, recline, repose, lie flat, sprawl, loll, lie down.

2. Crouch, squat, bend, stoop, bow, bob, duck, dip.

3. Lie in ambush, lurk, secrete, stow away, screen, cloak, veil, shroud.

4. Lay in an attitude of rest, level, put down, lower, bend down, lower to a horizontal position.

5. Give expression to, phrase, word, give it words, put into words, voice, express, utter, set forth, clothe in words, frame, find words to express.

COUGH, *n.* Sudden expulsion of air from the hack, bark *(slang).*

COUNCIL, *n.* 1. Cabinet, privy council, chamber, ministry, board, directorate, kitchen cabinet, diet, brain trust, bench, staff, committee, syndicate, divan *(Oriental),* Sanhedrin, chapter, court, duma, plenum, legislature, parliament, congress, cortes, states-general, national assembly, junta, House of Lords, soviet, upper house, upper chamber, lower house, senate, House of Commons, chamber of deputies, House of Peers, house of representatives, body of persons specially selected to act in an advisory or legislative capacity.

2. Assembly, meeting, convocation, conclave, synod, convention, conventicle, conference, salon, husting, gathering, concourse, sitting, hearing, consultation, seance, session, palaver, durbar, caucus, powwow, clique.

COUNSEL, *n.* 1. Interchange of opinions as to future procedure, deliberation, referment, parley, reference, consultation, conference, *pourparler (Fr.),* palaver, powwow.

2. Providence, prudence, precaution, foresight, forethought.

3. Deliberate purpose, plan, design, intention, scheme, project, resolve, aim.

4. Advice, suggestion, word to the wise, charge, *verbum sapienti (Lat.)*, admonition, instruction, warning, adhortation, submonition, exhortation, recommendation, opinion, advocacy, injunction, guidance, caution.

5. Legal adviser, lawyer, counselor, advocate, jurist, barrister, legist, jurisconsult, counselor at law, solicitor, attorney, pettifogger, shyster, limb of the law, stuff gown, silk gown.

COUNSEL, *v.* Give advice to, advise, urge the doing of, recommend, prompt, suggest, prescribe, enjoin, instruct, charge, advocate, exhort, warn, caution.

COUNSELOR, *n.* 1. Adviser, admonisher, tutor, mentor, monitor, guide, instructor, Nestor.

2. Lawyer, attorney, counsel, barrister, jurist, advocate, jurisconsult.

COUNT, *v.* 1. Check over one by one in order to ascertain the total number, tell off, number, enumerate, score, tally, figure, reckon, compute, call over, divide off, calculate, reckon up.

2. Estimate, appraise, cast up, rate, account, assess, value, rank.

3. Take into account, include in a reckoning, reckon to the credit of another, ascribe, impute, attribute.

4. Count on, depend, rely, pin faith on.

5. Consider, regard, think, look upon, deem, esteem, judge, adjudge, hold.

6. Enter into consideration, tell, add to the number, swell the number, weigh, be effective.

COUNT, *n.* 1. Act of counting, enumeration, calculation, reckoning, computation, numbering, numeration.

2. Total number, tally, tale, roll call, muster, poll, census, statistics, lustrum *(Rom. Hist.)*.

COUNTENANCE, *n.* 1. Expression of the face, look, appearance, mien, aspect, semblance, air, presence, cast, image.

2. Face, physiognomy, visage, features, lines, lineaments, traits, contour, silhouette, profile, pan *(slang)*.

3. Appearance of favor, moral support, succor, interest, advocacy, patronage, championship, aid, encouragement, defense, auspices, help, sanction, assistance, lift, promotion, furtherance, approval, advancement, approbation, coadjuvancy.

COUNTENANCE, *v.* Show favor to, patronize, give countenance to, approve, support, sanction, advocate, encourage, smile upon, favor, befriend, take up the cause of, back up, work for, back, side with, stand by, take the side of, promote, further, forward, advance, endorse, uphold, assist, aid, help, succor, abet, lend a hand.

COUNTER, *n.* 1. One who counts, computer, enumerator, calculator, reckoner.

2. Stand on which goods are laid for display and examination, table on which business is transacted, table on which money is counted.

COUNTER, *adv.* 1. Contrary, in opposition to, against, versus, in conflict with, counter to, at cross purposes, at variance, at issue, at war with.

2. In the wrong way, contrary to the right course, in the reverse direction, contrariwise, against the grain, against the stream, against the current, against the tide, against the wind, with the wind ahead, with a headwind, with the wind in one's teeth.

3. In spite, in despite, in defiance, in the way of, in the teeth of, in the face of, athwart, where the shoe pinches, across, *per contra (Lat.), quand même (Fr.)*.

COUNTERACT, *v.* 1. Act in opposition to, cross, oppose, frustrate by contrary action, act against, traverse, contravene, resist, thwart, defeat, check, hinder, run counter to, clash with, conflict with, work at cross purposes, antagonize, overcome, overpower, stultify, withstand, impede, restrain, jostle, repress, interfere with, militate against.

2. Counterbalance, countervail, counterpoise, destroy the effect of, offset, neutralize, negative, nullify, annul, cancel, undo.

COUNTERACTION, *n.* 1. Opposition, resistance, contrariety, contradiction, antagonism, polarity, clashing, collision, friction, reaction, recoil, check, interference, contravention, frustration, restraint, neutralization, nullification, hindrance, repression.

2. Counterblast, counterattack, counterblow, counterthrust, countermeasure, countermovement, counterstroke, counterstrike, counterpush, countersmash, counterassault.

COUNTERACTIVE, *n.* Corrective, counteractant, antidote, counteragent, remedy, cure, restorative, medicine, preventive, counterpoison, mithridate *(Hist.)*, countervenom, alexipharmic *(Med.)*, alexiteric *(Med.)*, theriac.

COUNTERBALANCE, *v.* 1. Act against with equal force, weigh against with equal weight, counterpoise, balance.

2. Make up for, compensate, offset, set off, countervail.

COUNTERFEIT, *adj.* 1. Made to imitate and pass for something else, not genuine, spurious, fake, forged, supposititious, fraudulent, imitation, bogus, flash, pseudo, brummagem, artificial, factitious, theatrical, meretricious.

2. Feigned, simulated, mock, sham, specious, hypocritical, put on, false, pretended, fictitious, make-believe, glossy, unreal.

COUNTERFEIT, *n.* 1. Imitation designed to pass as an original, forgery, sham, fraudulent copy, fake, pretense, brummagem, make-believe, paste, fabrication, tinsel, scagliola, gloss, speciousness, plagiarism, fraud.

2. Likeness, portrait, simulation, semblance, image, representation, reproduction.

COUNTERFEIT, *v.* 1. Make counterfeit money, forge, coin, circulate bad money, shove the queer.

2. Make a counterfeit of, make a spurious copy of, imitate fraudulently, reproduce, mimic, copy.

3. Feign, sham, simulate, fake, dissemble, put on the appearance of, malinger.

COUNTERFEITER, *n.* 1. Forger, falsifier, *faux-monnayeur (Fr.)*.

2. Impostor, pretender, imitator, mountebank, feigner, copier, malingerer, plagiarist, charlatan, quack, empiric.

COUNTERMAND, *v.* Counterorder, revoke, stop by a contrary order, recall, rescind, abrogate, repeal, retract, reverse, override, set aside, do away with, annul, disannul, nullify, declare null and void, abolish, cancel, make void.

COUNTERMARCH, *v.* Turn about and march back along the same route, reverse the direction of a march, execute a countermarch, do an about-face, revert, retreat, retrograde, withdraw, fall back, veer round, wheel about, turn tail, turn upon one's heel, beat a retreat, retrace one's steps.

COUNTERPANE, *n.* Coverlet for a bed, quilt, coverlid, comforter, eiderdown, bedspread, bed-cover.

COUNTERPART, *n.* 1. Corresponding part, part that answers to another, one of two parts which fit together, complement, correlative, correlate, supplement, reverse (*to obverse*).

2. Copy, duplicate, facsimile, replica, effigy, similitude, model, reproduction, echo, reflection, likeness.

3. Mate, match, fellow, twin, pair, double, tally, brother, the very image, the spitting image, chip of the old block, equal, like, analogue, congener.

COUNTERPOISE, *v.* Balance by an opposing weight, counterbalance, equilibrate, countervail, balance, bring into equilibrium, counteract by an opposing force, compensate, equalize, make up for, offset, square.

COUNTERPOISE, *n.* Counterbalancing weight, equal weight, counterweight, balance, equipoise, equal power, opposing force, counterbalance, makeweight, neutralizing force, equalization, *quid pro quo* (*Lat.*), equivalence, ballast, equilibrium, compensation, offset.

COUNTERSIGN, *n.* 1. Watchword, identification, password given by authorized persons in passing through a guard, shibboleth, *mot d'ordre* (*Fr.*), *mot de passe* (*Fr.*), catchword, *qui vive* (*Fr.*), cue.

2. Sign used in reply to another sign, seal, authentication, signature.

COUNTERVAIL, *v.* 1. Counterbalance, counter-act, act against with equal force, avail against with equal effect, be of equal force in opposition, balance.

2. Furnish an equivalent for, offset, make up for, compensate.

COUNT ON, *v.* Rely on, rely upon, depend on, depend upon, count upon, be sure of, calculate upon, pin one's faith on, lean upon, reckon upon, build upon, rest upon, lay one's account for, make oneself easy about, take for granted, take on trust, repose implicit confidence in, place reliance on, believe in, swear by.

COUNTRIFIED, *adj.* Rustic, agrestic, agrarian, rural, bucolic, georgic, country, provincial, hick, fresh-water, boorish, rude, unpolished, uncouth, uncultivated, Boeotian.

COUNTRY, *n.* 1. Tract of land considered apart from geographical or political limits, region, land, district, territory, terrain.

2. Territory of a nation, geographical entity, state, realm, nationality, commonwealth, political division, territory demarcated by geographical conditions or by a distinctive population.

3. Native land, fatherland, abiding habitation, home, state, power, land of one's birth, *patria* (*Lat.*), homeland, mother country, native soil.

4. Nation, population, people, public, stock, inhabitants, race, community.

5. Countryside, rural parts, hinterland, sticks (*slang*), provinces.

COUNTRY, *adj.* 1. Rural, agrarian, provincial, rustic, agrestic, bucolic, georgic.

2. Rude, unrefined, uncultivated, unpolished, uncouth, rough, hick, fresh-water, Boeotian, boor-ish.

COUNTRYMAN, *n.* 1. Man of one's own country,

compatriot, fellow citizen, fellow countryman, fellow patriot.

2. Man who lives in the country, peasant, clod, farmer, rustic, swain, husbandman, churl, yokel, plowman, yeoman, bumpkin, hayseed, hick, rube, clodhopper, boor, hind, Tony Lumpkin, tiller of the soil, serf, hobnail, bog-trotter, cider-squeezer, chawbacon, groundling, lout, oaf.

COUNTRYSIDE, *n.* 1. Open country, provinces, rural section, hinterland, rural regions.

2. Landscape, scenery, view, prospect, vista, scene, outlook.

COUNTY, *n.* Political unit next below the state in the U.S., shire, diocese, canton, *arrondissement* (*Fr.*), province, parish, township, constituency, borough, commune, division for purposes of local administration, one of the chief administrative divisions of a country or state, bailiwick.

COUP, *n.* 1. Unexpected and successful stroke, blow, unexpected device or stratagem, move, step, measure, maneuver, bout, passage, *coup de main* (*Fr.*), feat, stunt, exploit, *tour de force* (*Fr.*), achievement.

2. Twinkling, flash, trice, jiffy, crack, breath, burst, flash of lightning, stroke of time, minute, instant, moment, second.

COUP-DE-GRACE, *n.* Bullet in the head to ensure an executed person is dead, death-blow, finishing stroke, last finish, decisive blow, quietus, mercy-stroke.

COUP-D'ETAT, *n.* 1. Stroke of statesmanship, sudden and decisive measure in politics, stroke of sudden usurpation, master stroke of forcible policy, trump card, *cheval de bataille* (*Fr.*), great gun, bold move, clever hit, *tour de force* (*Fr.*), bright idea.

2. Forcible and sweeping change, illegal or forceful change of government, revolution, clean sweep, overthrow, debacle, rebellion, subversion, *bouleversement* (*Fr.*), *le droit du plus fort* (*Fr.*).

COUPLE, *v.* 1. Associate together in a pair, link, fasten together in pairs, join together, conjoin, pair, pair off, connect, unite, yoke, brace, span, tie together, bracket, match off, double, chain, shackle.

2. Unite in matrimony, marry, wed, mate.

3. Copulate, embrace sexually, fornicate, have sexual intercourse, engage in coitus.

COUPLE, *n.* 1. Combination of two, two of the same kind, brace, pair, both, twain, deuce, twins, binary, gemini, yoke, span, fellow.

2. Man and wife, married couple, husband and wife.

3. Coupling, leash, tie, bond, link, catena, nexus.

COUPLET, *n.* Two verses that rhyme, distich, pair of rhymes, pair of successive lines of verse.

COUPON, *n.* Separable part of a certificate entitling the holder to something, detachable portion, separate ticket, certificate, section, premium-ensurer.

COURAGE, *n.* Quality of mind that enables one to encounter danger without fear, ability to meet difficulties with firmness, assurance, audacity, audaciousness, fearlessness, intrepidity, manliness, dauntlessness, stout-heartedness, valor, manhood, virility, heroism, daring, derring-do, defiance, dash, élan, bravado, bravery, boldness, fortitude, gallantry, resoluteness, prowess, pot-valiance, enterprise, determination, great-heartedness, lion-heartedness, hardihood, resolution, self-reliance, confidence, firmness, spirit, integrity, animation, high-heartedness, will-power, virtue, tenacity, endurance, bulldog courage, Spartan approach, effrontery, rashness, chivalry, blood, heart, nerve, backbone, mettle, pluck, sand, grit, pluckiness, spunk.

COURAGEOUS, *adj.* With a bold front, bold as a lion, lion-hearted, brave, bold, heroic, dauntless, epic, defiant, daring, fearless, stalwart, stout-hearted, doughty, manly, manful, virile, valiant, valorous, gallant, chivalrous, chivalric, dashing, audacious, adventurous, venturesome, venturous, hazardous, redoubtable, fortitudinous, confident, enterprising, firm, high-spirited, high-hearted, hardy, intrepid, stanch, stout, spirited, Spartan, resolute, self-reliant, mettlesome, masculine, mighty, indomitable, martial, warlike, soldierly, nervy, plucky, game, spunky, unafraid, unfearful, undismayed, undaunted, unflinching, unshrinking.

COURIER, *n.* Messenger sent in haste, express messenger, runner, dispatch-bearer, estafette, state messenger, envoy, emissary, legate, nuncio, pursuivant, herald, harbinger, forerunner, kavass, precursor, attendant, postrider, letter carrier, Iris, postman, mail carrier, Mercury, Hermes, Ariel.

COURSE, *n.* 1. Onward movement, ongoing, advance in a particular direction, onward motion, march, headway, speed, progression.
2. Channel along which anything moves, path, route, passage, track, way, road.
3. Line of progress, direction, bearing, drift, trend, track, tenor, tack.
4. Progress through time, continuous passage through a succession of stages, procession, lapse, sequence, advancement, flight.
5. Duration, season, period, spell, span, stage, space, tide, term, time, lifetime.
6. Round, orbit, ambit, beat, circle, circuit, run, race, career, trajectory, cursus, racecourse, rotation.
7. Regular order of events, regularity, order, turn, succession.
8. Customary manner of procedure, method, mode, routine, particular manner of proceeding, prescribed system, methodical arrangement, systematized series, process, regimen.
9. Mode of conduct, deportment, line of conduct, behavior, comportment, demeanor, carriage, action, manners, ways, actions.
10. Study, subject, curriculum, recitation, lesson, lecture, discourse.
11. Row, line, layer, stratum, bed, couch, ply, floor, story, tier, lap, fold.
12. Part of a meal served at one time, set of dishes.

COURSE, *v.* 1. Run through, run over, pass through, traverse, ply, range, wander over, travel over, cross in traveling.
2. Pursue, chase, hunt, run after, give chase to, follow closely, stalk, hound, trail, track.
3. Direct one's course, follow a course.
4. Move swiftly, race, run, hasten, hie, haste, scud, hurry, scamper, scurry, sprint, scuttle, scorch, bolt, lope, gallop, career, scour, speed, trip, post.

COURSER, *n.* Race horse, swift steed, racer, charger, blood horse, thoroughbred, galloway, Arab, Pegasus, Bucephalus, Rocinante.

COURT, *n.* 1. Palace, castle, hall, stately dwelling, residence of a sovereign, royal household.
2. Princely retinue, a sovereign and his councilors, royal household, staff, retinue, train, entourage, suite.
3. Formal assembly held by a sovereign, levee, audience.
4. Place where justice is administered, judicial tribunal, bar, court of justice, bench, forum, curia, basilica, Areopagus, Chancery, King's Bench, Probate, Aula Regis, judicatory, judgment seat, mercy seat, Star Chamber, assize, inquisition.
5. Open space wholly or partly enclosed by a wall, courtyard, quadrangle, patio, inclosed area, areaway, peristyle, piazza, cloister, plaza, forum, square, *place (Fr.), cortile (It.).*
6. Assiduous attention directed to gain favor or affection, homage, addresses, solicitations, civilities, respects, flattering attention, courtship, wooing, love-making, serenading, endearment, suit, blandishments.

COURT, *v.* 1. Endeavor to win the affections of, seek the favors of, woo, pay suit to, make love to, pay one's addresses to, make up to, set one's cap at, serenade, address, sue, make love, spoon, flirt, bill and coo, spark, go steady with.
2. Endeavor to ingratiate oneself with, curry favor with, fawn upon, pay court to, try to please, praise, cajole, coddle, flatter, pander to, truckle to, wheedle, coquet, honey, softsoap, butter up, humor, pet.
3. Invite, solicit, strive to gain, seek, hold out inducements to, engage, enlist, bring round, win over, carry, persuade, predispose, influence, urge, lobby, prevail on, sway, induce.

COURTEOUS, *adj.* Showing good manners, kind, polite, courtly, deferential, urbane, well-behaved, respectful, mannerly, gallant, chivalrous, well-bred, bland, suave, genteel, gentlemanly, gracious, complaisant, ceremonious, obliging, affable, attentive, soft-spoken, fair-spoken, civil, agreeable, complimentary, debonair, elegant, facile, genial, familiar, gentle, graceful, social, unctuous, of gentle breeding, winning, complacent, refined, conciliatory, condescending, polished, cultivated, ingratiating, good-humored, cordial, amiable, sociable, diplomatic, tactful, honey-tongued.

COURTESAN, *n.* Concubine, harlot, mistress, paramour, prostitute, strumpet, trull, whore, kept woman, jade, wench, punk, wanton, frail sister, bawd, street-walker, night-walker, woman of ill-fame, public woman, demirep, cocotte, grisette, lorette, drab, quean, lewd woman, *fille de joie (Fr.),* member of the demi-monde, procuress, bonaroba, Cyprian, Messalina, Delilah, call girl, tart, hustler, broad, chippy, fallen woman, slut, trollop, baggage, hussy, bitch, rig, minx, doxy, fornicatress, *petite femme (Fr.),* fancy woman.

COURTESY, *n.* 1. Elegance of manners, polished manners, excellence of behavior, politeness, refinement, gentility, suavity of manner, amenity, affability, comity, civility, urbanity, amiability, address, gentle breeding, good breeding, good behavior, good manners, gallantry, courtliness, chivalry, courteousness, complaisance, *prévenance (Fr.),* complacence, respect, reverence, kindly consideration, deference, familiarity, *bienséance (Fr.),* favor, indulgence, pink of courtesy, pink of politeness, cultivation, culture.
2. Greeting, salutation, welcome, reception, *accueil (Fr.),* regards, devoirs, remembrances, respects.
3. Bow, curtsy, salaam, genuflection, kowtow, proskynesis, obeisance, bowing and scraping, nod, handshake.

COURTIER, *n.* 1. One in attendance at the court of a sovereign, attendant, subject, liegeman, retainer, servitor, squire, train-bearer, castellan, cup-bearer, seneschal, major-domo, chamberlain, groom of the chambers, pursuivant.
2. Knight, lord, duke, count, peer, baron, earl, nobleman, grandee, magnifico, hidalgo, marquis, aristocrat, patrician, viscount, thane, esquire, seignior, margrave.
3. One who seeks favor, sycophant, parasite, flatterer, flunky, lackey, yes-man, apple-polisher, hanger-on, stooge, truckler, pickthank, bootlicker.

COURTLINESS, *n.* 1. Gallantry, chivalry, grace, polish, elegance, civility, *ton (Fr.), bon ton (Fr.),* drawing-room manners, breeding, air, savoir-faire, demeanor, gentlemanliness, refinement, decorum, gentility, *bienséance (Fr.),* formality, punctilio, etiquette, politeness.

COURTLY, *adj.* Aristocratic, chivalrous, knightly, ceremonious, chivalric, thoroughbred, polished, blue-blooded, silk-stockinged, *distingué (Fr.),* poised, *dégagé (Fr.),* high-bred, elegant, gallant, mannerly, gentlemanly, dignified, aulic, graceful, polite, refined, royal, stylish, fashionable, genteel, punctilious, decorous.

COURTSHIP, *n.* Love-making, wooing, suit, solicitation of favors, courting, attentions, amour, addresses, serenading, flirtation, coquetry, gallantry.

COURTYARD, *n.* Space enclosed by walls, court, quadrangle, inclosed area, patio, yard, peristyle, *cortile (It.), place (Fr.),* piazza, plaza, cloister.

COUSIN, *n.* 1. Son or daughter of an uncle or aunt, coz, cousin-german, first cousin, cousin once removed, full cousin, consobrinus.
2. Kinsman, kinswoman, kin, congener.

COVE, *n.* 1. Small recess in a shoreline, bay, arm of the sea, bight, inlet, lagoon, estuary, fiord, firth, frith, ostiary, indraught, creek.
2. Hollow in a mountain, cave, cavern, bottom, narrow pass between mountains, defile.
3. Sheltered nook, retreat.

COVENANT, *n.* Pact, treaty, agreement, bargain, compact, contract, arrangement, convention, concordat, deed, stipulation, article, deal *(colloq.),* understanding, settlement, gentlemen's agreement, bond, indenture, alliance, league, entente.

COVENANT, *v.* Stipulate, provide, undertake, promise, engage, consent, agree, treat, negotiate, make terms, dicker, bargain, contract, strike a bargain, come to terms.

COVER, *n.* 1. Covering, envelope, wrapper, case, integument, tegument, capsule, top, lid, binding, jacket, sheath, vesture, wrap, pod, involucrum, peel, bark, rind, shell, husk, hull, cortex, facing, carapace, veneer, varnish, enamel, gloss, stucco, whitewash, plaster, paint, coating, crust, ceiling, roof, dome, cupola, deck, mansard.
2. Coat, clothing, vestment, skin, fleece, fur, leather, pellicle, hide, pelt, derma, cuticle, epidermis, corium.
3. Veil, screen, cloak, mask, disguise, hood, camouflage, masquerade, shroud.
4. Counterpane, bedspread, quilt, comforter, blanket, eiderdown, coverlet.
5. Shelter, shield, covert, concealment, ambush, protection, defense, guard, safeguard, ambuscade, hiding place.
6. Underbrush, undergrowth, underwood, shrubbery, vegetation, thicket, brake, woods.

7. Set of articles laid at table for one person, serviette.
8. Funds to secure against risk of loss, funds to cover liability, insurance, security, assurance.

COVER, *v.* 1. Put something over, overspread, overlay, superimpose.
2. Clothe, envelop, invest, incase, wrap up, enwrap, sheathe, fold up, jacket, case, veneer, face, paper, shingle, clapboard, weatherboard, coat, stain, paint, incrust, varnish, stucco, japan, cement, plaster, whitewash, calcimine, daub, gild, smear, plate, enamel, lacquer.
3. Hide from view, conceal, curtain, secrete, veil, cloak, shroud, screen, disguise, mask, hood, camouflage, ensconce.
4. Serve as a defense to, protect, defend, guard, shield, shelter.
5. Travel over, pass through, traverse, cross in traveling, range, wander over.
6. Include, comprehend, embrace, embody, comprise, contain, take in, provide for, subsume, number among, involve, inclose, receive.
7: Suffice to defray, offset, counterbalance, compensate for, make good for.
8. Act as reporter of, write up, describe, tell of.

COVERCLE, *n.* Lid, small cover, top, cap, door, operculum, curtain, blind, eyelid.

COVERING, *n.* 1. Awning, canopy, baldachin, tilt, *tente d'abri (Fr.),* marquee, pavilion, tent, parasol, umbrella, *parapluie (Fr.),* sunshade, pall, veil.
2. Bandage, wrapping, lint, plaster, dossil.
3. Tarpaulin, linoleum, oilcloth, blanket, rug, carpet, drugget, floor cloth.
4. Roof, ceiling, cupola, dome, thatch, tiling, slates, shingles, straw roof.
5. Tegument, integument, crust, coating, case, overlay, top, capsule, ferrule, sheathing, pod, cod, involucrum, casing, theca, vesicle, envelope, wrapper.

COVERLET, *n.* Outer covering of a bed, quilt, bedcover, bedspread, counterpane, coverlid, eiderdown, comforter.

COVERT, *n.* 1. Thicket, shade, underwood, brake, shrubbery, jungle, boskage, underbrush, coppice, undergrowth, copse, grove.
2. Lair, den, hiding place, cave, hole, nest, snuggery, cache, *sanctum sanctorum (Lat.),* cell, rookery, aerie, perch, roost, retreat, resort, hive, haunt, habitat.
3. Shelter, protection, covering, concealment, disguise, cover, fastness, screen, shield, abri, refuge, harbor, asylum, sanctuary, defense, hiding place, abode.

COVERT, *adj.* Concealed, hidden, latent, unseen, unsuspected, unknown, invisible, dark, secret, untalked of, untold, unbreathed, undisclosed, disguised, unknown, clandestine, underground, *sub silentio (Lat.),* sub rosa, sly, stealthy, occult, cabalistic, cryptic, mystic, steganographic, private, mysterious, delitescent, muffled, covered, out of sight, sheltered, secluded, unseen, behind the scenes, in the background, behind the curtain, *à perte de vue (Fr.),* nonapparent, sneaking, allusive, tacit, insidious.

COVET, *v.* 1. Desire, wish for eagerly, long for, be desirous of, want, wish, aim after, have an eye to, have at heart, set one's heart upon, be bent upon, aspire to, woo, ogle, court, fancy, care for, yearn for, envy, begrudge.

2. Desire inordinately, lust after, crave, be appetitive of, hanker after, have an appetite for, pine for, desire wrongfully, sigh for.

COVETOUS, *adj.* 1. Enviously desirous, grasping, avaricious, greedy, rapacious, with an itching palm, exacting, sordid, mercenary, parsimonious, niggardly, penurious, miserly, narrow, stingy, jealous, aspiring, ambitious, extortionate, selfish.
2. Appetitive, inclined, fain, craving, hungry, ravenous, voracious, omnivorous, insatiable, insatiate, unsatisfied, unsated, ravening, sharp-set, thirsty, athirst.
3. Eager, ardent, burning, fervent, perfervid, avid, agog, breathless, impatient.
4. Lustful, prurient, libidinous, lickerish, lecherous, concupiscent, salacious, lascivious, carnal.

COVETOUSNESS, *n.* 1. Greed of gain, itching palm, cupidity, inordinate eagerness to possess, grasping, greediness, avidity, acquisitiveness, envy, avariciousness, avarice, rapacity, rapaciousness, mercenariness, greed, parsimony, penuriousness, niggardliness, miserliness, frugality.
2. Appetite, hunger, stomach, thirst, craving, appetency, longing, hankering, yearning, itch, ardor, fervor, impatience, zeal.
3. Lust, libido, biological urge, carnal passion, sexual desire, concupiscence, pruriency, animal appetite, carnality, lechery, venery, lewdness, lasciviousness.

COVEY, *n.* 1. Small flock of birds, brood, bevy, flight.
2. Group, company, set, cluster, array, bunch, galaxy, party, series.

COW, *n.* Female of the genus *Bos,* bovine, bossy, milch cow, moo-cow, heifer, Jersey, Alderney, Holstein, kine *(plural),* calf, maverick, shorthorn, redpoll, yearling.

COW, *v.* Intimidate, subdue by fear, abash, daunt, affright, frighten, overawe, dismay, deter, scare, discourage, terrify, appall, dishearten, break, bear down, browbeat, terrorize, bully, threaten.

COWARD, *n.* Craven, poltroon, dastard, caitiff, base fellow, sneak, funk, recreant, milksop, cur, mollycoddle, wheyface, hare, chicken, lily-liver, nithing, shirker, quitter, slacker, malingerer, shirk.

COWARDICE, *n.* Poltroonery, pusillanimity, the white feather, faint-heartedness, cowardliness, dastardliness, dastardy, want of courage, yellow streak, cold feet, funkiness, funk, abject fear, recreancy, diffidence, cravenness, timorousness, timidity, dread, apprehension, baseness, shyness, effeminacy, dungeon-hill bravery.

COWARDLY, *adj.* Lacking courage, weakly fearful in the presence of danger, dastardly, dastard, craven, faint-hearted, showing the white feather, yellow, funky, caitiff, recreant, sneaking, timorous, pusillanimous, unmanly, timid, base, chicken-hearted, white-livered, lily-livered, milk-livered, apprehensive, afraid, anxious, diffident, nervous, tremulous, shaky, spiritless, ignoble, soft, effeminate, unsoldierly, ignominious, despicable, fearful, frightened, mean-spirited, niddering.

COWBOY, *n.* Man employed in the care of cattle on a ranch, cowkeeper, cattle-herder, cowherd, herdsman, herder, oxherd, vaquero, grazier, neatherd, drover, bunco-steerer.

COWER, *v.* 1. Bend with the knees and back, stand in a bent position, squat, stoop.
2. Crouch in fear, be cowardly, cringe, draw back, shrink, flinch, quail, funk, skulk, sneak, mooch, fight shy, run away, show the white feather.
3. Fawn, grovel, truckle, bootlick, crawl, toady.

COXCOMB, *n.* Beau, fop, conceited dandy, dude, dandiprat, jackadandy, exquisite, peacock, swell, popinjay, macaroni, silk-stocking, jackanapes, man-milliner, toff, blade, blood, buck, spark, Johnny, silk-sock Sam, man about town, gilded youth, wearer of the green carnation, man of dress, *petit maître (Fr.),* showy fellow, effeminate dresser, fribble, jemmy, carpet-knight, prinker, male clotheshorse, fashion-plate, cavalier, fine gentleman, Beau Brummell, masher, pink of fashion, glass of fashion.

COXCOMBICAL, *adj.* Foppish, dudish, spruce, dandified, dandyish, dapper, vain as a peacock, mincing, silk-stocking, finical, priggish, affected, simpering, effeminate, namby-pamby.

COY, *adj.* Overly modest, shrinking, retiring, hard-to-get, skittish, timid, shy, reserved, quiet, timorous, sheepish, blushing, shamefaced, chary, bashful, diffident, demure, prudish, distant, virtuous, virginal, constrained.

COZEN, *v.* Delude, beguile, deceive, hoodwink, gull, humbug, hoax, chouse, dupe, fool, do, nab, diddle, gyp, gammon, trick, bait the hook, take in, inveigle, impose upon, spoof, throw dust into the eyes, draw a herring across the trail, mislead, victimize, swindle, pluck, fleece, abuse, cheat, circumvent, doublecross, play one false, bilk, cully, jilt, outwit, outmaneuver, steal a march upon, overreach, jockey, palm off on, have a smooth tongue, wheedle.

COZENAGE, *n.* Deception, deceit, trickery, fraud, fraudulency, double-dealing, artifice, imposture, imposition, gullery, victimization, delusion, guile, duplicity, treachery, knavery, misrepresentation, covin, circumvention, ingannation, *supercherie (Fr.),* jugglery, sleight of hand, prestidigitation, legerdemain, hocus-pocus, hanky-panky, coggery, chicanery, pettifogging, sharp practice, spoof, hoax, humbug, bluff, *blague (Fr.),* wile, ruse, feint, blind, plant, catch, bubble, swindle, trap, artful dodge, machination, snare, gin, pitfall, bait, noose, hook, decoy, toils, meshes.

COZY, *adj.* 1. Comfortable, snug, comfy, snug as a bug in a rug, sheltered, sheltering, homelike, easy.
2. Talkative, chatty, conversable, sociable, free and easy, conversational, companionable, social, clubby, neighborly, gregarious, hail fellow well met.

CRABBED, *adj.* 1. Sour, acrid, bitter, tart, rough.
2. Ill-tempered, ill-humored, ill-natured, cross, testy, petulant, out of sorts, grouchy, sulky, snappish, peevish, captious, irritable, surly, touchy, contumelious, sullen, churlish, growling, cantankerous, snarling, morose, waspish, virulent, caustic, acrimonious, harsh, crusty, sarcastic, splenetic, censorious, perverse, contrary.
3. Difficult, hard to deal with, trying, tough, intractable, unmanageable.
4. Difficult to decipher, illegible, intricate, undecipherable, squeezed.

CRABBEDNESS, *n.* 1. Sourness, tartness, acridity, acridness, roughness.
2. Acerbity, asperity, churlishness, acrimony, sullenness, moodiness, captiousness, virulence, acrimoniousness, ill-nature, ill-humor, moroseness, harshness, ill-temper, spleen, surliness, gruffness

peevishness, grouchiness, perversity, scowl, frown, contumeliousness, black looks, short answer, sulks.

3. Difficulty, perplexity, intractability, toughness.

CRACK, *n.* 1. Crevice, fissure, break, split, rent, rift, chink, fracture, breach, cleft, cranny, flaw, interstice, opening, slit, gash, scratch, score, rut, streak, cavity, chap, gap, orifice, rime, rupture, scissure, defect.

2. Sudden sharp noise, report, clap, pop, burst, explosion, thunder-clap, detonation, salvo, volley, crash, crackle, shot, fulguration, fulmination, flash, snap of a whip.

3. Loud slap, resounding blow, smack, fillip, slam, bang, punch, thrust, jab, swipe, pelt, cuff, thump, whack, thwack, clout.

4. (*Colloq.*) A try, an opportunity or chance, a venture.

5. (*Colloq.*) Facetious utterance, gibe, jest, wisecrack, joke, witticism, smart saying, quip.

6. (*Colloq.*) Moment, instant, second, minute, flash, twinkling, jiffy, trice, *coup (Fr.),* burst, *coup d'oeil (Fr.),* breath, stroke of time, flash of lightning.

7. One who excels in some respect, expert, masterhand, adept, connoisseur, past master, specialist, professional, veteran, nonpareil, nonesuch.

CRACK, *v.* 1. Break partially, fracture, chip, slit, splinter, rip, nip, slash, split, chop, cleave, rend asunder, lacerate, tear, rive.

2. Open in chinks, burst, become fissured, chap.

3. Make a sudden sharp sound, strike with a sharp noise, crackle, crepitate, thunder, explode, fulminate, fulgurate, detonate, clash, **pop, crash,** clap, snap a whip, fire off.

4. Hit, knock, rap, tap, slap, punch, smack, jab, pelt, cuff, clout, thump, whack, thwack.

5. (With *of*) Brag, bluster, vapor, boast, bluff, vaunt, show off, flourish, gasconade, crow, exult, crow over, trumpet, swagger.

6. Utter a joke, gibe, wisecrack.

7. Craze, madden, drive insane, make unsound mentally, derange, unhinge, dement.

8. Break with grief, affect deeply, move, touch, stir.

CRACK, *adj.* 1. Of superior excellence, above par, best, choice, first-rate, tiptop, capital, first-class, excellent, unparalleled, superfine, of the first water, cardinal, inimitable.

2. Experienced, practiced, accomplished, at home in, masterly, master of, a good hand at, *au fait (Fr.),* thoroughbred, up to, good at, proficient, skillful, deft, dexterous, adroit, slick, expert, fitted for, neat-handed, crackajack.

CRACKED, *adj.* 1. Broken without separation of parts, fissured, fractured, chipped, crannied, crackled, split, damaged, leaky, sprung, faulty, mutilated, imperfect, defective, rimose, gaping, chinky, breachy, reft, cloven, dehiscent, rent, agape, foraminous, pervious.

2. Mentally unsound, insane, crazy, mad, lunatical, crazed, demented, deranged, unhinged, *aliéné (Fr.),* *non compos mentis (Lat.),* touched in the head, not all there, not quite right, daft, barmy, loco, bughouse, with a bee in the head.

3. Crack-brained, fanatical, rabid, hipped, warped, *entêté (Fr.),* infatuated, overzealous, one-sided, narrow-minded, prejudiced, bigoted, biased.

CRACKLE, *v.* Make slight sharp noises rapidly repeated, crepitate, decrepitate, break with a crackling noise, crack, pop, crash, clap, slam, click, clash.

CRADLE, *n.* 1. Little bed built on rockers, crib, baby's bed, trundle bed, bassinet, *crèche (Fr.),* cunabula, incunabula, truckle bed, litter, berth, pallet, tester, cot, bunk, nest, nursery.

2. Source, origin, spring, fountain, *fons et origo (Lat.),* fountainhead, springhead, breeding place, birthplace, hotbed, *nidus (Lat.).*

CRADLE, *v.* 1. Rock in a cradle, tuck in, lay down, pillow, install, ensconce, deposit.

2. Nurture during infancy, foster, nourish, nurse, suckle, cherish, tend, take care of, watch over, train.

CRAFT, *n.* 1. Adroitness, dexterity, aptness, readiness, expertness, cleverness, aptitude, talent, deftness, address, ability, skill, skillfulness, knack, competency, proficiency, felicity, capacity, trick, mastery, efficiency, adeptness, featness, facility, technique.

2. Art, handicraft, employment, trade, business, vocation, profession, occupation, calling, line, commerce, industry.

3. Members of a trade or profession, guild, union, joint concern of craftsmen, association, society, fraternity, corporate body, company.

4. Boat, ship, vessel, bark, skiff, canoe, scull, shell, kayak, gondola, rowboat, motorboat, yacht, sailing vessel.

5. Craftiness, subtlety, finesse, artifice, ruse, intrigue, cunning, wile, strategy, maneuvering, artfulness, guile, shrewdness, art applied to bad purposes, trickery, duplicity, deception, deceit, chicanery, sharp practice, knavery, jugglery, tact, jobbery, circumvention, temporization, diplomacy, machiavelianism.

CRAFTSMAN, *n.* One who practices a craft, hand operative, skilled workman, handicraftsman, artisan, artificer, workman, mechanic, maker, tradesman, wright, manufacturer, mechanician, artist, machinist.

CRAFTY, *adj.* Skilled in underhand or evil schemes, cunning, wily, intriguing, scheming, machiavelian, guileful, subdolous, calculating, designing, foxy, shrewd, *rusé (Fr.),* tricky, subtle, sly, insidious, plotting, vulpine, feline, underhand, double-faced, canny, astute, sharp, artful, politic, diplomatic, pussyfooting, crooked, slippery, fraudulent, shifty, deceptive, deceitful, jesuitical.

CRAG, *n.* Rough steep rock, rugged cliff, clough, steeps, bluff, craig, tor, pike, escarpment, scarp, brae, crest, *arête (Fr.),* palisade, peak, *aiguille (Fr.),* sugar-loaf, cone.

CRAGGY, *adj.* Rocky, precipitous, cragged, steep, scraggy, rough, jagged, broken, uneven, rugged, gnarled, abrupt.

CRAM, *v.* 1. Fill by force with more than it can conveniently hold, stuff, gorge, fill to repletion, choke, fill full, crowd, press, compress, jam, ram down, pack, squeeze, overcrowd, force.

2. Fill with an excess of food, eat to satiety, eat greedily, gorge oneself, glut oneself, guzzle, gluttonize, gormandize, devour, satiate, raven, overeat, indulge, eat one's fill, bolt, gobble up, gulp, play a good knife and fork, surfeit.

3. Prepare for examination, grind, coach, study, train, teach, instruct, tutor.

CRAMP, *n.* 1. Sudden involuntary muscular

contraction, spasm, convulsion, crick, stitch, crink, throe, pang.

2. Small metal bar with bent ends for holding together, clamp, staple, clasp, fastening.

3. Obstruction, restriction, hindrance, check, stoppage, preclusion, restraint, damper.

CRAMP, *v.* 1. Affect with spasms, convulse.

2. Incapacitate, cripple, paralyze, invalidate, undermine, unfit, lame, maim, hamstring.

3. Confine narrowly, restrain, hinder, check, obstruct, restrict, hamper, handicap, encumber, cumber, clog, saddle with, tie the hands.

4. Fasten with a cramp, confine with a cramp, hold with a cramp-iron, secure, clamp.

CRAMPED, *adj.* 1. Inelegant, graceless, stiff, dry, ungraceful, unpolished, formal, harsh, abrupt, blunt, crabbed, *guindé (Fr.)*, forced, awkward, labored, artificial, ponderous, mannered.

2. Crowded, close, incommodious, narrow, tight, limited, convulsive, contracted.

3. Hard to decipher or understand, illegible, difficult, knotty.

CRANE, *n.* Device for moving heavy weights, derrick, lifting machine, davit, lift, gin, jenny, boom, hoist, windlass, winch, capstan, dredger, elevator.

CRANIUM, *n.* Skull of a vertebrate, that part of the skull which encloses the brain, brain-pan, pericranium, cerebrum, brain-box, pate, poll, noddle.

CRANK, *n.* 1. Turning handle, device for communicating motion to, winch, windlass, lift, capstan, gear wheel, tool.

2. Eccentric, impractical person, crackpot, nut, monomaniac, fanatic, *fanático (It.)*, *exalté (Fr.)*, dreamer, rhapsodist, seer, enthusiast, zealot, Don Quixote.

3. Ill-tempered person, grouch, crab, cross-patch, scold, sour-puss *(slang)*, frowner, scowler, calamity-howler.

4. Eccentric notion, whim, caprice, quiddity, quip, quirk, crotchet.

CRANK, *adj.* Easy to be overset, unsteady, shaky, unstable, wobbly, crazy, loose, disjointed.

CRANKY, *adj.* 1. Ill-tempered, ill-humored, cross-grained, out of sorts, out of humor, sulky, sullen, cantankerous, contumacious, perverse, captious, irascible, unreasonable, splenetic, disagreeable, peevish.

2. Eccentric, capricious, crotchety, aberrant, queer, erratic, odd.

3. Shaky, rickety, unsteady, in a bad way, out of order, drooping, tottering, tumbledown, the worse for wear.

CRANNY, *n.* Small narrow opening, aperture, orifice, dehiscence, interstice, gap, crevice, crack, chink, rime, cleft, breach, rift, scissure, fissure, cavity, break, creek, lacuna, hole, chasm, chap, slit, slot, fracture, rent, cut, gash, flaw.

CRAPULOUS, *adj.* 1. Given to gross excess in drinking, inebrious, intemperate, sottish, bibulous, bibacious, temulent, drunken, crapulent, drunk, surfeited with drink, inebriated, intoxicated, tipsy, fuddled, befuddled, muddled, dissipated, lush, in one's cups, *inter pocula (Lat.)*, mellow, boozy, red-nosed, plastered, groggy, sozzled, pot-valiant, potulent, tight, screwed, primed, oiled, corned, raddled, half seas over, three sheets in the wind, under the table.

2. Excessive in eating, gluttonous, edacious,

gormandizing, omnivorous, voracious, greedy-gut, swinish, piggish, porcine, hoggish, bestial, self-indulgent.

CRASH, *n.* 1. Sudden loud noise, thunder, din, racket, shattering sound, blast, burst, splintering uproar, rending, explosion, detonation, boom, clatter, fracas, clangor.

2. Violent falling to ruin, shock of collision and breaking, smash, smash-up, crack-up, clash, hit, concussion, percussion, wreckage.

3. Sudden collapse of a financial enterprise, failure, bankruptcy, financial disaster, ruination, ruin, downfall, failure, fall, debacle.

CRASH, *v.* 1. Break in pieces violently and noisily, dash in pieces, splinter, smash, shatter, shiver, batter.

2. Impinge, collide, bump, butt, meet, telescope, hurtle, jostle.

3. Fall to the ground, tumble, totter, topple, fall to pieces, break up, go to wrack and ruin.

4. Make a loud clattering noise, clash, boom, thunder, explode, detonate, fulminate, roar, rend the air.

5. *(Colloq.)* Enter without invitation or ticket, come uninvited to, gain entrance, intrude, horn in, slip in, invade, butt in.

CRASS, *adj.* 1. Thick-headed, stupid, dull-witted, ignorant, inept, obtuse, Boeotian, slow-witted, doltish, sottish, fat-headed.

2. Unrefined, crude, raw, gross.

3. Thick, coarse, solid, dense, compact, fat.

CRATE, *n.* Framework of wooden slats for packing and transportation, slatted box, hamper, cage, pannier, wickerwork basket.

CRATER, *n.* 1. Cup-shaped orifice of a volcano, pit, cavity, opening, hole, hollow, shaft, well, abyss, gulf, chasm, bowels of the earth.

2. Large vessel, bowl, basin, punch-bowl, cup.

CRAVAT, *n.* 1. Necktie, tie, four-in-hand, bow tie, foulard, ascot, stock.

2. Scarf worn around the neck, neckerchief, neckcloth, ruff, dicky, boa, bandana.

CRAVE, *v.* 1. Desire, long for, hunger for, wish for, yearn for, hanker after, pine for, hope for, want, have an eye to, have a fancy for, be bent upon, covet, sigh for, aim at, need greatly, require, thirst for.

2. Ask earnestly for, implore, sue, solicit, pray, supplicate, entreat, petition, beseech, beg for, request, canvass, plead for, adjure, importune, conjure, plead, demand, obtest.

CRAVEN, *adj.* Cowardly, pusillanimous, yellow, dastardly, base, mean-spirited, fearful, recreant, timid, timorous, lily-livered, chicken-hearted, pigeon-hearted, milksop, sneaking, unsoldierly, showing the white feather, having cold feet.

CRAVEN, *n.* Coward, poltroon, caitiff, dastard, recreant, milksop, sneak, shy-cock, white-liver, nidgit, coistril, cur, runagate, quitter, funk, hare, mollycoddle, wheyface, lily-liver.

CRAVING, *n.* Urgent desire, eager longing, yearning, desirous aspiration, hankering, appetite, appetency, hungering, keenness, thirsting, hunger, stomach, thirst, avidity, itch, pruriency, strong passion, ravenousness, greediness, grasping, zeal, rapaciousness, voracity, rapacity, eagerness, ardor.

CRAW, *n.* First stomach of a bird or animal, crop, maw, ingluvies, gizzard, venter.

CRAWL, *v.* 1. Move slowly by dragging the body

across the ground, move like a reptile on all fours, creep.

2. Progress slowly and laboriously, sneak, go stealthily, go at a snail's pace, lag, drag, lumber, trail, worm one's way, inch, inch along, jog on, flag.

3. Fawn, cower, cringe, grovel, crouch, toady, be servile.

CRAYON, n. 1. Pointed stick of colored clay, pencil of colored chalk, blacklead.

2. Crayon drawing, sketch, outline, pastel.

CRAZE, v. 1. Make crazy, madden, make insane, impair the intellect, drive wild, dement, derange, unsettle, unbalance, unhinge, crack.

2. Excite, enrage, inflame, frenzy, cause to run amuck, make berserk.

3. Make small cracks on the surface of, crackle, become minutely cracked.

CRAZE, n. Short-lived popular fashion, fad, mania, furor, rage, fancy, whim, crotchet, quirk, infatuation, passion, the go, the thing.

CRAZY, adj. 1. Out of one's head, mad, insane, demented, deranged, lunatical, crazed, out of one's wits, non compos mentis (Lat.), aliéné (Fr.), touched, bereft of reason, out of one's senses, unhinged, unbalanced, maniacal, delirious, cracked, daft, crackbrained, moonstruck, stark raving mad, disordered, brain-sick.

2. (Colloq.) Too excited, too enthusiastic, fanatical, infatuated, rabid, crackpot, mad as a hatter, nutty, queer, mad as a March hare, frantic, foolish, irrational, hysterical, fatuous.

3. Liable to break, apt to fall in pieces, rickety, shaky, tottering, tumbledown, dilapidated, weak, decrepit, infirm, sleazy, gim-crack.

CREAK, v. Make a sharp grating sound, squeak, rasp, grind, grate, stridulate, grit, screech, screak, shrill, set the teeth on edge, burr, jar, jangle, clank.

CREAM, n. 1. Fatty part of milk, rich milk, crème (Fr.).

2. Best part, choice part, flower, pick, élite, quintessence, crème de la crème (Fr.), A 1, non-pareil, flower of the flock, gem of the first water, salt of the earth.

3. Gist, kernel, pith, substance, gravamen, sum and substance, core, nucleus, heart.

4. Yellowish white, light tint of yellow, buff.

5. Cosmetic, ointment, pomade, emulsion, pomatum, unguent.

6. Soup containing cream sauce, purée.

CREASE, v. Make creases in, wrinkle, fold, pleat, plicate, plait, crinkle, crankle, curl, cockle up, smock, rimple, corrugate, rumple, frounce, rivel, ruffle, crimple, crumple, turn under, pucker.

CREASE, n. Line produced on anything by folding, wrinkle, fold, ridge, furrow, plicature, pleat, plait, ply, tuck, gather, rimple, crinkle, crankle, crumple, rumple, rivel, ruck, ruffle, crow's-feet, pucker, dog's-ear, corrugation, flounce.

CREATE, v. 1. Originate, bring into being, call into existence, cause to exist, produce, make, effect, cause, construct, rear, erect.

2. Procreate, propagate, breed, engender, beget, generate, duplicate, progenerate, proliferate, sire, fecundate, spawn, father.

3. Design, form, fashion, mold, invent, evolve from one's imagination, dream up, imagine, coin, devise, conceive, forge, frame, contrive, scheme, hatch, make up, develop, shape.

4. Appoint, constitute, found, institute, be the cause of, establish, give rise to, be the occasion of, occasion, sow the seeds of.

5. Be the first to represent a part or role, visualize, envisage, interpret.

CREATION, n. 1. Original bringing into existence of the universe by the Deity, cosmogony, concreation.

2. Production, formation, origination, causation, fabrication, construction, erection.

3. Invention, coinage, imagination, conception, evolution, development.

4. Procreation, propagation, engenderment, generation, progeneration, proliferation, siring.

5. Appointment, establishment, designation, nomination, constitution, institution.

6. Cosmos, universe, world, nature, wide world, macrocosm, empyrean, firmament, starry host, vault of heaven, heavenly bodies, galaxy, milky way, via lactea (Lat.).

7. Product of inventive ingenuity, original work of the imaginative faculty.

CREATIVE, adj. 1. Having the power of creating, prolific, genetic, genital, fertile, fecund, pregnant.

2. Cosmoplastic, demiurgic, omnific, creant, generative, procreative, causal, formative, plastic, productive, originative, causative, at the bottom of, constituent.

3. Imaginative, fanciful, original, inventive, ingenious.

CREATOR, n. 1. Maker of the universe, Supreme Artificer, Demiurge, The First Cause, The Supreme Original, God, The Preserver, The All-Father, Author of all things, The Omnipotent.

2. Maker, author, originator, inventor, framer, producer, designer, fashioner, founder, prime mover, architect, builder, artist, introducer, determinant.

3. Father, generator, procreator, sire, begetter.

CREATURE, n. 1. Being (animate or inanimate), created being, thing, living thing, entity, object, article, something, body.

2. Living being, animal, beast, lower animal, dumb animal, dumb creature, brute, zoon, vertebrate, invertebrate, mammal, quadruped, bird, fish, crustacean, shellfish, mollusk, reptile, worm, zoophyte, insect, animalcule.

3. Man, human being, person, mortal, mankind, individual, personage, somebody, body, someone, one, living soul, party, wight.

4. Person subject to the will or influence of another, dependent, minion, puppet, parasite, vassal, hanger-on, retainer, slave, mercenary, hireling, satellite, protege, yeoman, henchman, ward.

5. Base person, wretch, rascal, miscreant, worker of iniquity, evildoer, scoundrel, caitiff, villain, varlet, rogue, knave, dog, cur, hound, mongrel, whelp.

CREDENCE, n. 1. Trust, confidence, faith, credit, reliance, trustworthiness, assurance, dependency, belief.

2. Acceptance, reception, acknowledgment, allowance, recognition, admission, receptivity, open-mindedness.

CREDENTIAL, n. 1. That which gives a title to belief or confidence, certificate, authority, warrant, passport, diploma, voucher, docket, record, muniment, pièce justificative (Fr.), deed, data.

2. Letter attesting the bearer's right to authority

or confidence, letter of recommendation, exequatur, testimonial, introduction, authorization.

CREDIBILITY, *n.* Credibleness, trustworthiness, believableness, believability, likeliness, likelihood, verisimilitude, *vraisemblance (Fr.),* presumption, probability, plausibility, appearance, prospect, chance, veracity.

CREDIBLE, *adj.* 1. Worthy of belief, believable, to be believed, reliable, trustworthy, veracious, honest, true, upright, straightforward, dependable, uncorrupt.

2. Conceivable, possible, thinkable, imaginable, cogitable, compatible.

3. Probable, likely, presumptive, presumable, apparent, verisimilar, in a fair way, reasonable, well-founded, *ben trovato (It.),* plausible, ostensible, specious.

CREDIT, *n.* 1. Belief, faith, trust, credence, confidence, reliance, trustworthiness, credibility.

2. Influence of a good name, authority resulting from the confidence of others, prestige, status in the estimation of a community, standing, rank.

3. Good name, good repute, good reputation, reputableness, regard, esteem, high character, honor, merit, proof of desert, commendation, high regard, favorable opinion.

4. Ascription of something as due to a person, acknowledgment of merit, source of honor.

5. Trust in future payment, reputation of solvency and probity, confidence in a purchaser's ability and intention to pay, loan, account.

6. Power to buy on trust, tick, cuff *(colloq.),* charge account, strap, paper credit.

7. Evidence of debt on the part of others, lien, mortgage, debentures, bank balance, stocks, bonds, securities.

8. Letter of credit, traveler's check, circular note, draft.

CREDIT, *v.* 1. Put confidence in, trust, have faith in, believe, doubt not, make no doubt of, put faith in, give faith to, rely upon, take upon credit, confide in, put trust in.

2. Assent to, accept, swallow *(colloq.),* receive.

3. Place to one's credit, place to one's account, place to the credit of, carry to the credit of one's account, enter upon the credit side of an account, give credit for, accredit to.

4. Trust for future payment, loan on trust, give out on security, give credit, take credit.

5. Reflect credit upon, do credit to, give reputation to, do honor to, redound to the praise of, deserve praise, recommend itself, pass muster, win golden opinions, stand well in the opinion of.

6. Ascribe to, make ascription of to, impute to, attribute to.

CREDITABLE, *adj.* Estimable, reputable, meritorious, honorable, respectable, laudable, deserving of commendation, worthy, seemly, fitting, up to the mark.

CREDITOR, *n.* One who gives credit in business transactions, one to whom money is due, lender, mortgagee, lessor *(Law),* usurer.

CREDULITY, *n.* Ease in believing, readiness to believe on slight evidence, disposition to believe too readily, credulousness, gullibility, gullibleness, belieffulness, belief, self-delusion, infatuation, self-deception, bigotry, fanaticism, overzealous faith, *Aberglaube (Ger.).*

CREDULOUS, *adj.* Disposed to believe on weak evidence, too ready to believe, prone to be satisfied with insufficient evidence, lax in seeking

evidence, easily convinced, easily duped, gullible, overtrustful, believing, unsuspecting, deceivable, unsuspicious, easily deceived, green, simple, soft, confiding, easy mark, childish, unsophisticated, superstitious, fanatical, infatuated.

CREED, *n.* 1. Authoritative formulated statement of religious belief, formula, doctrine, dogma, faith, belief, tenet, summary of belief, gospel, teaching, canons, articles, profession of faith, credo, confession.

2. Persuasion, conviction, opinion, view, rule, maxim, principle, theory, avowal, position.

CREEK, *n.* 1. Small river, rivulet, stream, run, branch of a river, runnel, streamlet, brook, race, runlet, rill, burn, freshet.

2. Narrow recess in the shore of the sea, small bay, cove, inlet, bight, loch, fiord, firth, frith, estuary.

CREEP, *v.* 1. Move with the body close to the ground, crawl, worm one's way, formicate, swarm, wriggle, writhe, squirm, vermiculate.

2. Steal, glide stealthily, come imperceptibly, come unnoticed, loiter, dawdle, move secretly.

3. Grovel, fawn, behave servilely, play the sycophant, cringe, bootlick.

4. Have a sensation of something creeping over the skin, have goose-flesh, feel pins and needles.

CREEPING, *adj.* 1. Crawling, wriggling, reptant, reptilian, formicant, vermicular, writhing, worming, squirming, serpentine.

2. Slow-gaited, tardy, slow, leisurely, slow-paced, dilatory, lazy, gradual, lagging.

3. Sycophantic, truckling, fawning, obsequious, servile, cringing, groveling.

4. *(Bot.)* Growing on the ground, repent, trailing, growing on supports, running.

CREMATE, *v.* 1. Burn, consume by fire, incinerate, incremate, decrepitate, carbonize, char, calcine.

2. Reduce a corpse to ashes, inurn.

CREMATION, *n.* Reduction to ashes, consumption by fire, burning, incineration, incremation, suttee, carbonization, calcination, sutteeism.

CREMATORIUM, *n.* Establishment for cremating, crematory, burning place, incinerator, pyre.

CRENATE, *adj.* Having the margin notched so as to form rounded teeth, crenated, notched, scalloped, indented, denticulate, dentated, dentate, denticulated, toothed, serrated, palmated.

CREPITATE, *v.* Make a crackling sound, snap, decrepitate, crackle, explode, crack, discharge, smack, burst, detonate, backfire, pop, snap, rattle.

CRESCENT, *n.* 1. Moon in her first or last quarter, new moon, convexo-concave figure of the moon resembling a bow terminating in points, figure of the new moon, lunule, lune, half-moon, demilune, bow, lunette, meniscus.

2. (With *The*) Emblem of the Turkish Empire, Turkish power, Ottoman Empire, Sublime Porte.

3. Islam, Mohammedanism, Islamism, Moslemism.

CRESCENT, *adj.* 1. Crescent-shaped, luniform, lunate, moon-shaped, falciform, lunular, falcate, sickle-shaped, bicorned, crescine, meniscoid, curved, bow-shaped, horned, arcuate, arciform, incurvate, crescentiform, sigmoid, convexo-concave.

2. Waxing, increasing, growing, enlarging, incressant.

CREST, *n.* 1. Plume, tuft, comb, topknot, mane

cockscomb, copplecrown, plumule, panache, headpiece, crown.

2. Armorial bearings, device, seal, coat of arms, arms, hatchment, escutcheon, scutcheon, badge.

3. Ridge, ledge, spine, chine, *arête (Fr.)*, saddle, hogback, spur, peak, summit, apex, horn, highest part, top, head, tip, height, pinnacle.

4. Climax, culmination, zenith, acme, crowning point, heyday, prime, flower, floruit.

CRESTFALLEN, *adj.* Downhearted, discouraged, sad, dispirited, disheartened, cast down, downcast, melancholy, despondent, low-spirited, chapfallen, dejected, woebegone, depressed, gloomy, in the dumps, blue, spiritless, oppressed, down in the mouth, heavy-hearted, in the doldrums, mopish, glum, morose, saturnine, moody, dull, out of heart, a cup too low, weary.

CREVASSE, *n.* Deep cleft in the ice of a glacier, chimney, precipice, abyss, chasm, fissure, breach, *Schrund (Ger.).*

CREVICE, *n.* Crack forming an opening, fissure, interstice, rift, cleft, cranny, chink, scissure, rent, breach, hole, seam, opening, gap, break, hiatus, lacuna, rime, creek, chap, slit, slot, fracture.

CREW, *n.* 1. Ship's complement, company of sailors, company of men who man a boat, common sailors of a ship's company, bluejackets, tars, mariners, seafarers, sea-dogs, *matelots (Fr.),* shellbacks, Jacks, lime-juicers, gobs, able seamen, hands.

2. Gang, squad, company, throng, mob, band, pack, horde, herd, assemblage, party, set, crowd, host, multitude, troupe, posse, corps, team, force.

3. Rabble, *canaille (Fr.),* vulgus, *profanum vulgus (Lat.),* hoi polloi, proletariat, riff-raff, scum of society, commonalty, dregs of the people, the masses, trash, vulgar herd.

CRIB, *n.* 1. Hovel, hut, cabin, shanty, shack, log cabin.

2. Manger, bin, rack, bunker, stall, pen, feeding-place for cattle.

3. Child's bed with enclosed sides, bassinet, truckle bed, trundle bed, cradle, litter.

4. Translation, key, trot, pony *(colloq.),* gloss.

5. Plagiarism, steal *(colloq.),* forgery, fraud, pilfering, purloinment, petty theft, piece of plunder, literary piracy, misappropriation.

CRIB, *v.* 1. Enclose in a crib, shut in, confine, cage, encage, imprison, box up.

2. Plagiarize, pirate, purloin, pilfer, steal, misappropriate, palm off as one's own, lift, filch.

CRICK, *n.* Sharp painful spasm of the muscles, convulsion, cramp, pain, twinge, twitch, ache, kink, stitch.

CRIER, *n.* Town official who makes public announcements, town crier, herald, proclaimer, trumpeter, bellman, pursuivant, apparitor, muezzin *(Moham.),* harbinger.

CRIME, *n.* 1. Act injurious to the public welfare, serious violation of human law, felony, offense of grave character, aggravated misdemeanor, gross offense against law, outrage, enormity, atrocity, capital crime, murder, robbery, rape, homicide, arson, embezzlement, peculation, malfeasance, lawbreaking, treason, foul play, burglary, perjury, manslaughter, misdeed, immorality, fornication, sodomy, assault, battery, recidivism, tort.

2. Transgression, wrongdoing, blameworthy action, evil behavior, delinquency, iniquity, sin, wickedness, unrighteousness, wrong, dereliction,

evil, trespass, malefaction, vice, depravity, guilt, abomination, villainy, corruption, misconduct.

CRIMINAL, *adj.* 1. Illegal, flagrantly contrary to law, illicit, felonious, lawless, murderous, lawbreaking, homicidal, incendiary, burglarious, arsonist, malfeasant.

2. Guilty, culpable, condemnable, censurable, reprehensible, delinquent, blameworthy, flagitious, red-handed, iniquitous, wicked, foul, vile, black, gross, infamous, nefarious, villainous, heinous, flagrant, monstrous, atrocious, opprobrious, evil-minded, steeped in iniquity, sinful, immoral, degenerate, corrupt, depraved, recreant, vicious, disorderly, unrighteous, evil, wrong, bad, errant, derelict, crooked, abominable, outrageous.

CRIMINAL, *n.* 1. Malefactor, felon, offender, culprit, transgressor, trespasser, delinquent, lawbreaker, convict, wrongdoer, evildoer, worker of iniquity, sinner, malfeasant, recidivist, jailbird, outlaw, ruffian, terrorist, rowdy, thug, gunman, gangster, roughneck, apache, hoodlum, hooligan, gallowsbird, knave, rogue, miscreant, reprobate.

2. Murderer, assassin, killer, rapist, kidnapper, arsonist, sodomite, sexual pervert, degenerate, burglar, thief, robber, footpad, highwayman, shoplifter, embezzler, peculator, swindler, defaulter, perjurer, traitor.

CRIMINALITY, *n.* 1. Culpability, guilt, guiltiness, blameworthiness, censurability, reprehensibility.

2. Misconduct, wrongdoing, misbehavior, sinfulness, malpractice, misdoing, turpitude, vice, depravity, badness, corruption, wickedness, villainy, knavery.

CRIMINATE, *v.* 1. Allege to be guilty, charge with a crime, arraign, incriminate, inculpate, impeach, accuse, indict, inform against, denounce, bring an action against, prosecute.

2. Involve in crime, implicate in guilt.

CRIMINATION, *n.* Arraignment, accusation, charge, impeachment, incrimination, inculpation, indictment.

CRIMP, *v.* 1. Press into small regular folds, plait, form into ridges, crease, flute, twist, wrinkle, buckle, coil, roll, crape, scallop.

2. Curl, friz, frizzle, crisp, wave, undulate, meander.

CRIMSON, *adj.* Deep purplish red, ruby, purple, carmine, magenta, blood-red, sanguinary, wine-color, erubescent, cramoisy, damask, cardinal, scarlet, vermilion, *sang-de-boeuf (Fr.),* roseate, coral, cerise, maroon, cherry, carnation, rubric, rufous, vinaceous, claret, flame-colored, rubicund, ruddy.

CRINGE, *v.* 1. Flinch, wince, shrink, quail, recoil, funk, start, blench, dodge, shy, parry, crouch, stoop, duck.

2. Crouch from servility, cower, truckle, fawn, flatter, grovel, crawl, sneak, be servile, toady.

CRINGING, *adj.* Abject, fawning, truckling, obsequious, servile, crouching, sneaking, yellow, prostrate, subservient, submissive, parasitical, slavish, yielding, sycophantic, groveling, mealy-mouthed, morigerous, timeserving, adulatory, sniveling.

CRINKLE, *v.* 1. Curl, wrinkle, corrugate, ripple, crimple, twist, pucker, wave, undulate, twine, turn and twist, wind, twirl, meander, inosculate, entwine, coil, roll, crisp, twill, crimp, scallop.

2. Make slight sharp sounds, rustle, swish.

CRINKLY, *adj.* Wavy, undulatory, kinky, curly,

ripply, convoluted, serpentine, sinuous, flexuous, anfractuous, mazy, frizzly, buckled, crapy.

CRINOLINE, *n.* Petticoat of haircloth worn under a full dress skirt, hoopskirt, farthingale.

CRIPPLE, *v.* 1. Lame, make lame, hamstring, hock, maim, injure, truncate, mutilate, mangle, detruncate, surbate, scathe, harm, hurt, damage, labefy, prostrate, paralyze, geld, castrate, spay, alter, amputate, scotch.

2. Disable, incapacitate, weaken, impair, unfit, unman, enfeeble, cramp, render impotent, put hors de combat, put out of gear, enervate, emasculate, deprive of strength.

CRIPPLE, *n.* Lame man or woman, invalid, paralytic, convalescent, valetudinary, physical wreck, *magni nominis umbra (Lat.),* the halt, the lame and the blind, amputee, wheel-chair patient.

CRISIS, *n.* 1. Turning point, critical juncture, climax, climacteric, decisive turn, acme, height, vitally important stage in the course of anything, critical occasion, hinge, contingency.

2. Emergency, exigency, conjuncture, strait, pass, pinch, rub, push, extremity, crux, trial, entanglement, pickle, uncertainty, muddle, mess, perplexity, kettle of fish, hot water, stew, deadlock, quandary, dilemma, predicament, scrape, imbroglio, fix, plight, hole, corner, impasse, difficulty.

CRISP, *adj.* 1. Hard but easily breakable, friable, brittle, crumbly, short.

2. Frizzled, curled, crinkled, rippled, wrinkled, wavy, curly.

3. Brisk, decided, sharp, blunt, candid, concise, straightforward.

4. Lively, sparkling, pithy, vivacious, energetic, forcible.

5. Bracing, invigorating, cold, nipping, chilly, fresh.

CRITERION, *n.* Standard of judgment or criticism, established principle for testing, test, trial, rule, measure, norm, canon, model, law, scale, gauge for measuring, point of comparison, prototype, original, precedent, pattern, archetype, exemplar, paradigm, example.

CRITIC, *n.* 1. Judge of artistic merit, connoisseur, man of taste, person skilled in judging merits, adept, expert, cognoscente, aesthetician, purist, dilettante, *arbiter elegantiae (Lat.),* virtuoso, amateur, arbiter.

2. Reviewer, commentator, publicist, editor, essayist, verbalist, verbarian, leader writer.

3. Fault-finder, censor, censurer, captious judge, carper, caviler, knocker *(colloq.),* detractor, derogator, defamer, backbiter, slanderer, Zoilist, cynic, diatribist, satirist, lampooner, calumniator, vilifier, libeler, traducer, reviler, vituperator.

CRITICAL, *adj.* 1. Inclined to judge with severity, disparaging, faultfinding, captious, censorious, caviling, carping, exacting, trenchant, derogatory, disapproving, hypercritical, disapprobatory, severe, calumniatory, sarcastic, satirical, cynical, cutting, withering, Zoilean.

2. Of nice discernment, involving skillful judgment as to merit, discriminating, fastidious, analytical, nice, judicious, accurate, exact, acute, discerning, perspicacious, diagnostic, perceptive, fine, keen, diacritical, astute, delicate, exquisite, particular, squeamish, nasute, scrupulous.

3. Decisive, determining, turning, important, of decisive importance, vital, climacteric, eventful, essential, opportune.

4. Urgent, crucial, momentous, pressing, grave, exigent, imperative, serious.

5. Involving risk or peril, precarious, dubious, hazardous, dangerous, ticklish, imminent.

CRITICISM, *n.* 1. Judgment passed as to merits, evaluation, appreciation, appraisal, estimate, discernment, discrimination, keenness, discretion, perspicacity, astuteness, acumen, tact, taste, long-headedness, dissection.

2. Critique, critical remarks, review, strictures, commentary, annotation, comment.

3. Faultfinding, censure, reflection, reproof, animadversion, diatribe, sarcasm, exception, objection, detraction, condemnation, derogation, disparagement, denunciation, ostracism, black ball, black list, boycott.

CRITICIZE, *v.* 1. Examine and estimate as works of art or literature, remark upon the merits or defects of, pass judgment upon, evaluate, make judgments as to merits and faults, judge, adjudge, appraise, discuss, review, treat, dissect, scan, analyze, comment upon, investigate, survey.

2. Censure, pick holes in, find fault with, reprove, cavil, carp, descant, castigate, blame, disapprove, remonstrate, animadvert on, attack, flay, nag, take exception to, view with disfavor, set one's face against, frown upon, reproach, impeach, impugn, accuse, lampoon, denounce, brand, satirize.

CRITIQUE, *n.* Critical remarks, critical essay, critical commentary, critical notice, critical examination, review, appreciation, discussion, article, editorial.

CROAK, *v.* 1. Utter a low hoarse cry, speak with a low hollow voice, make a raucous sound, talk hoarsely, make hoarse sounds, crow, screech, caw, speak thick, utter rough sounds.

2. Talk despondingly, forebode evil, take a gloomy view of things, cry things down, be depreciatory, complain, mutter, murmur, grunt, grumble, maunder, deprecate, lament, grouse, talk dolefully.

3. *(Slang)* Die, perish, kick the bucket.

CROAKER, *n.* One that takes a gloomy view, pessimist, hypochondriac, seek-sorrow, alarmist, complainer, faultfinder, murmurer, malcontent, bitter-ender, decrier, grumbler, depreciator, mope, growler, *laudator temporis acti (Lat.),* gloomy Gus, foreboder, self-tormentor, mopus, *malade imaginaire (Fr.), heautontimorumenos (Greek).*

CROCK, *n.* Piece of crockery, earthen jar, pot, vessel of terracotta, pitcher, flagon, amphora, ewer.

CROCKERY, *n.* Crocks collectively, pottery, ceramics, porcelain, terracotta, earthenware, china.

CRONE, *n.* Old woman *(contemptuous),* hag, grandam, gaffer, gammer, beldam, virago, vixen.

CRONY, *n.* Intimate friend, fast friend, bosom friend, intimate companion, associate, comrade, chum, mate, other half, alter ego, shadow, buddy, sidekick, bedfellow, bunkie, roommate, man after one's own heart, fidus Achates, playfellow, bed-buddy.

CROOK, *n.* 1. Bend, flexion, flexure, turn, curve, curvature, curvity, incurvity, incurvation, arc, conflexure, inflexion, bending, hook, tortuosity, bow.

2. Bent staff, curved appendage, shepherd's crook, staff, bishop's crook, crosier.

3. *(Colloq.)* Dishonest person, sharper, thief,

robber, bandit, filcher, harpy, sharp, pickpurse, rook, blackleg, swindler, defaulter, welsher, embezzler, peculator, forger, malefactor, cheat, evildoer, knave, wrongdoer.

CROOK, *v.* 1. Make a crook in, render curved, bend, bow, turn, round, arcuate, inflect, deflect, incurvate, curve, arch, loop the loop, curl, coil, concamerate.

2. Become crooked, wind, deviate, trend, heel, swerve, bear off, shift, switch, warp, tack, twist, meander, veer, sheer, wheel, turn aside.

CROOKED, *adj.* 1. Not straight, bent, curved, angular, winding, devious, bowed, sinuous, spiral, flexuous, zigzag, tortuous, ambagious, twisted, meandering, incurvated, hooked, serpentine, arcuate.

2. Twisted, askew, awry, wry, aslant, distorted, disfigured, misshapen, deformed, warped, out of shape, irregular, gnarled, asymmetric.

3. Dishonest, unscrupulous, unprincipled, not straightforward, dishonorable, fraudulent, unfair, deceptive, deceitful, underhand, cunning, crafty, knavish, insidious, intriguing, wily, sly, *rusé (Fr.)*, foxy, time-serving, criminal, lawbreaking, shifty, sneaking, double-faced, diplomatic, Machiavelian.

CROON, *v.* Sing low with exaggerated feeling, sing softly, utter a low murmuring sound, hum, vocalize, murmur, whisper, moan.

CROP, *v.* 1. Cut off the head of, remove the top of, lop, clip, cut off a part of, cut short.

2. Pluck, cull, pick, gather, glean, reap.

3. Nibble, browse, graze, feed upon, pasture.

CROP, *n.* 1. Cultivated produce of the ground, return in food obtained from land at the end of a season of growth, yield of produce for a particular season, harvest, amount produced at one cutting, yield, reaping, gathering, gleaning, vintage, ingathering, fruit.

2. Handle of a whip, stock, short riding whip with a loop instead of a lash.

3. First stomach of a bird, digestive organ, pouchlike enlargement of the gullet of many birds, craw, maw, ingluvies.

CROSIER, *n.* Pastoral staff of a bishop or abbot, crook.

CROSS, *n.* 1. Gibbet made of pieces of wood placed transversely, structure upon which persons were formerly put to death, rood, crucifix, crux, crosslet.

2. (With *The*) Christianity, Christendom, Gospel, Holy Writ.

3. Affliction, suffering, infliction, trouble, trial, ordeal, misfortune, vexation, blow, stroke, load, burden, curse, mortification, bitter cup, crown of thorns.

4. Intermixture of species, crossbreeding, hybridization, mixing of breeds, interbreeding.

CROSS, *v.* 1. Carry across, transport, put across, put athwart.

2. Intersect, lie across, intertwine, intertwist, interweave, interlink, crisscross, lace, entwine, weave, wattle, twist, plait, braid, pleat, entangle.

3. Traverse, pass across, pass over, ford, cut across, overpass, go across, ply, travel over.

4. Mark with a line across, cross out, cancel, delete, erase, obliterate, remove, strike out.

5. Obstruct, hinder, interfere with, thwart, baffle, foil, frustrate, oppose, contravene, run counter, contradict, antagonize, face, impede, retard.

6. Mix, intermix, blend, crossbreed, interbreed,

intercross, hybridize, cross-fertilize, cross-pollinate.

CROSS, *adj.* 1. Lying crosswise, lying athwart, transverse, passing across each other, oblique, intersecting, thwart.

2. Involving interchange, reciprocal, mutual.

3. Adverse, unfavorable, mutually opposed, contrary, opposite.

4. Crossbred, hybrid, mixed, mongrel.

5. Ill-tempered, ill-humored, ill-natured, in a bad mood, irritable, crabbed, morose, fretful, petulant, peevish, pettish, querulous, choleric, irascible, cantankerous, fractious, captious, sullen, out of humor, sour, grouchy, splenetic, surly, churlish, touchy, gruff, testy, sulky, waspish, crusty, snappish, snarling, unamiable, intractable, angry, cynical, vexatious, acrimonious, perverse, contrary, exceptious.

CROSS-EXAMINE, *v.* Examine by questions intended to check a previous examination, cross-question, examine for the purpose of disproving testimony, examine minutely, catechize, grill, interrogate, investigate closely, interpellate, challenge, pump.

CROSS-GRAINED, *adj.* Headstrong, obdurate, stubborn, mulish, dogged, willful, intractable, perverse, refractory, recalcitrant, wayward, sulky, contumacious, *entêté (Fr.)*, pig-headed, resistant, restive, stiff-necked, humorsome, froward, deaf to reason, unaccommodating, exceptious, crusty, cantankerous, crabbed, quarrelsome, contrary.

CROSSING, *n.* 1. Intersection, crossroad, grade crossing, interchange, underpass, overpass, traffic circle, cloverleaf, exchange, crossway, crosswalk.

2. Opposing, opposition, thwarting, frustration, obstruction, contradiction, cancellation, interference.

3. Interbreeding, hybridization, cross-fertilization, cross-pollination.

CROSSWISE, *adv.* 1. Transversely, crossways, athwart, thwart, across, over, thwartly, cross, contrariwise, sideways, crisscross, crosswise, awry, askew.

2. Contrarily, perversely, unfavorably, at cross-purposes, at issue, at variance, at daggers drawn.

CROTCH, *n.* Groin, angle, fork, corner, crutch, bifurcation.

CROTCHET, *n.* 1. Small hook, hooklike device, curved instrument with a sharp hook.

2. Odd fancy, whimsical notion, whim, humor, whimsy, whim-wham, vagary, quirk, caprice, *capriccio (It.)*, wrinkle, kink, freak, maggot, fad, hobby, prank, fit, flimflam, bias, warp, twist, partiality, blind side, infatuation, one-sided notion, narrow mind, bigotry, mote in the eye.

CROTCHETY, *adj.* Humorsome, capricious, whimsical, given to odd fancies, full of crotchets, eccentric, fitful, maggoty, erratic, freakish, queer, vagarious, notional, fanciful, odd, fantastic, fussy, wayward, cracked, changeable, fickle, skittish, wanton, unreasonable, warped, *entêté (Fr.)*, one-sided, fanatical.

CROUCH, *v.* 1. Lie close to the ground, lie flat, squat, stoop low, bend low, droop, incline.

2. Cringe, cower, grovel, truckle, fawn, crawl, flatter, bow servilely, sneak, toady, bootlick.

CROUP, *n.* Rump *(of a horse)*, buttocks, crupper, posterior, behind, hind quarters, backside.

CROW, *n.* Oscine bird, corvus, bird with lustrous black plumage and a characteristic harsh cry of "caw," carrion crow, raven, chough, Cornish crow, pied crow, rook, blackneb, scaldcrow, grayback, jackdaw, daw, jay.

CROW, *v.* 1. Utter the characteristic cry of a cock, cock-a-doodle-doo, cackle.

2. Exult loudly, boast, jubilate, gloat, rejoice, triumph, vaunt, brag, bluster, talk big, puff, swagger, bluff, vapor, gasconade, show off, strut, trumpet.

CROWD, *v.* 1. Flock together, huddle, herd, swarm, gather in large numbers, come thick, be numerous, congregate, collect, muster, assemble, surge, cluster, mass, stream, throng, forgather, concentrate, resort, populate.

2. Press forward, elbow one's way, make one's way, advance by pushing, jostle one's way, shove, shoulder one's way.

3. Force into a confined space, press closely together, pack as tight as sardines, congest, press, compress, cram, jam, squeeze, cramp, lump together, bunch, bundle.

4. Fill to excess, fill by pressing into, choke, gag.

5. Press by solicitation, urge, importune, dun, annoy by urging, press upon, solicit, beset, ply, entreat.

CROWD, *n.* 1. Multitude, array, concourse, jam, throng, press, crush, host, bevy, galaxy, swarm, horde, gang, troop, troupe, party, force, flood, rush, shoal, deluge, assemblage, meet, gathering, forgathering, muster, cluster, congregation, flock, batch, conflux, company, confluence, assembly, posse, crew, drove, congeries, collection, set.

2. Rabble, lower classes, the masses, vulgar herd, proletariat, lower orders, commonalty, common people, commoners, populace, mob, *canaille (Fr.), profanum vulgus (Lat.), hoi polloi (Greek),* chaff, scum, riffraff, dregs of society, trash, ragtag and bobtail, rank and file, great unwashed, *faex populi (Lat.), ignobile vulgus (Lat.),* bourgeoisie.

CROWDED, *adj.* 1. Filled to excess, filled with a crowd, packed, populous, thronged, occupied, congested, overflowing, serried, teeming, full, swarming.

2. Uncomfortably close together, cramped, pressed together, squeezed, jammed, dense, solid, compressed, compact, tight, thick, thickset.

CROWN, *n.* 1. Head covering worn as a symbol of sovereignty, diadem, coronet, tiara.

2. Ornamental wreath for the head, decorative fillet, coronal, chaplet, garland, wreath, laurel, bays, circlet.

3. Royal dominion, sovereignty, kingly power, royalty.

4. Honorary distinction, palm, honor, reward, dignity, recompense, prize, trophy, medal, blue ribbon, citation, cup, memento.

5. Highest point, summit, top, crest, acme, vertex, apex, peak, brow, cap, tiptop, pinnacle, zenith, culmen, climax, *ne plus ultra (Lat.).*

6. Head, pate, sinciput, noodle *(slang),* brow.

CROWN, *v.* 1. Invest with a crown, put a crown upon, place a crown upon the head of, install, inaugurate, coronate.

2. Dignify, adorn, honor, decorate, festoon.

3. Reward, recompense, requite, compliment.

4. Put the finishing touch to, perfect, fulfill, bring to perfection, complete worthily, finish, consummate, achieve, bring to a happy issue, round out, bring to an effective conclusion, terminate, compass.

5. Surmount, top, cap, crest, head, overtop, culminate.

CRUCIAL, *adj.* 1. Involving a final and supreme decision, decisive, critical, determinating, final, supreme, searching, pivotal.

2. Severe, grave, trying, acute, climacteric, momentous, exigent, categorical, imperative, at the crossroads, instant, pressing, urgent.

3. Intersecting, transverse, of the form of a cross, cross-shaped, cruciform, secant, mullioned, reticulated, cancellated, latticed, barred, grated, streaked, interfretted.

CRUCIBLE, *n.* 1. Vessel of metal or refractory material employed for heating substances to high temperatures, retort, melting pot, alembic, mortar, caldron, matrix.

2. Severe and searching test, trial, ordeal, assay, proof, touchstone, probation, scrutiny, experiment.

CRUCIFIX, *n.* Cross with the figure of Jesus crucified upon it, holy rood, rosary, reliquary, beads.

CRUCIFY, *v.* 1. Put to death upon the cross, kill, impale, empale, execute.

2. Immolate, sacrifice, exterminate, annihilate.

3. Treat with severity, torment, torture, rack, persecute, wring, harrow, put to the rack, plant a thorn in one's side, agonize, trouble, excruciate.

4. Subdue the passions by Christian principles, mortify, overcome, repress.

CRUDE, *adj.* 1. In a raw state, raw, uncooked, undressed, in an unprepared state.

2. Unripe, green, callow, immature, harsh.

3. Unrefined, coarse, crass, undeveloped, unwrought, lacking finish, unpolished, lacking completeness, incomplete, imperfect, sketchy, unfinished, rough.

4. Uncouth, awkward, clumsy, rude, vulgar, primitive, gross, tasteless, inartistic, lacking refinement.

5. Blunt, churlish, bare, undisguised, abrupt, uncivil, tactless, brusque, gruff, harsh.

CRUEL, *adj.* 1. Disposed to inflict suffering, fell, taking pleasure in the pain of another, sadistic, vicious, indifferent to suffering, fiendish, brutal, inhuman, merciless, unmerciful, unfeeling, ferine, feral, ruthless, pitiless, ferocious, atrocious, dire, savage, sanguinary, bloodthirsty, barbarous, grim, truculent, inexorable, cold-blooded, hard-hearted, uncompassionate, unrelenting, relentless, unkind, implacable, diabolical, devilish, demoniac, hellish, infernal, maleficent, malevolent, remorseless, brutish, heartless.

2. Bitter, cold, inclement, sharp, painful, acute, stinging, biting, excruciating, raw, sore, agonizing, torturous, poignant.

CRUELTY, *n.* Brutality, ferocity, atrocity, ferity, savagery, barbarity, outrage, inhumanity, torture, ruthlessness, fiendishness, truculence, immanity, brutishness, bloodthirstiness, savageness, tyranny, harshness, persecution, torment, ill-usage, hardheartedness, inquisition, severity, implacability, pitilessness, sharpness, austerity, mercilessness, sternness, oppression, deviltry, ruffianism.

CRUET, *n.* Glass bottle for holding vinegar or oil for the table, vial, phial, cruse, caster, vessel, carafe, ewer, decanter, noggin, ampulla, stoup.

CRUISE, *v.* Rove over the sea, sail about, sail to and fro for pleasure, navigate, range, sail over, drift, course, coast, traverse, move hither and thither, circumnavigate.

CRUISE, *n.* Roving voyage, circumnavigation, sail, passage, *periplus (Greek),* marine journey, boat trip.

CRUISER, *n.* Armored cruiser, light cruiser, man-of-war, battle cruiser, capital ship, dreadnought, battleship, corvette, battle wagon, warship of medium tonnage designed for high speed and long cruising radius.

CRUMB, *n.* Small particle that breaks or falls off, minute portion, bit, morsel, scrap, shred, sliver, snip, splinter, slip, snatch, nip, pinch, dot, dash, speck, dab, minim, *soupçon (Fr.),* trifle, fragment, seed, grain, mite, atom, molecule.

CRUMBLE, *v.* 1. Break to pieces, reduce to bits, fragmentate, disintegrate, crush, comminute, part into small fragments, splinter, crack, pulverize, shiver, grate, powder, fritter, rumple.
2. Fall to pieces, become disintegrated, decay, molder, decompose, fall off, waste, vanish, give way, disappear piecemeal, break up, tumble, fade away, come to dust, degenerate, retrograde, fall into decay, decline, go to wrack and ruin, perish.

CRUMBLY, *adj.* Apt to crumble, friable, brittle, breakable, frangible, fragile, frail, shivery, soft, fissile, moldery, rotten.

CRUMPLE, *v.* 1. Draw into irregular folds, ruffle, crinkle, crisp, corrugate, pucker, crimple, twill, rivel, rumple, frizzle, crease, rimple, crush together, wrinkle.
2. Smash to smithereens, squelch, shatter, squash.
3. Collapse, give way, fall, perish, topple, go all to pieces, tumble, break up, go to shivers, fall to pieces, go to smash.
4. Contract into wrinkles, shrivel, shrink.

CRUNCH, *v.* Crush with the teeth, chew with a crushing noise, grind noisily, munch, bite, gnaw, champ, scranch, craunch, cranch, masticate loudly.

CRUSADE, *n.* 1. Holy war carried on under papal sanction, war of liberation, military pilgrimage, military expedition undertaken for the recovery of the Holy Land from the Mohammedans (11th, 12th and 13th centuries), tented field, appeal to the sword, hostilities, warfare, warpath.
2. Campaign, vigorous aggressive movement for the advancement of a cause.

CRUSADER, *n.* 1. Military pilgrim to the Holy Land, palmer, happy warrior, paladin, champion, armigerent, belligerent, fighting man, gladiator.
2. Campaigner, reformer, reformist, disputant, progressive, radical, controversialist, aggressor, fighter, assailant.

CRUSH, *v.* 1. Press and bruise between two hard bodies, mash, squash, squeeze, contuse, compress, squeeze out of normal condition, tread upon, crumple, rumple, trample.
2. Constrict, pinch, strangle, cramp, tighten.
3. Break into small pieces, crumble, shatter, bray, comminute, pulverize, granulate, triturate, levigate, reduce to powder, abrade, scrape, grate, grind, pound, rasp.
4. Break down, destroy, demolish, dilapidate, raze, shatter, shiver, splinter.
5. Vanquish, overcome, overpower, obliterate, overwhelm, conquer, put down, quell, suppress, subdue completely, quash, squelch, blot out.
6. Oppress grievously, persecute, browbeat, put to the blush, shame, degrade, disconcert, disgrace, mortify, abase, abash, humiliate.

CRUST, *n.* 1. Hard outer portion, incrustation, external covering, hard outer shell, hard coating, exterior portion, casing, hull, shell, rind, coat, husk, bark, cortex, involucrum, encrustment, cake.
2. Scab, eschar *(Med.),* scale, slough.

CRUSTY, *adj.* Crabbed, petulant, peevish, surly, ill-tempered, cross, fretful, touchy, acrimonious, unamiable, sullen, morose, woody, glum, cynical, rude, waspish, snappish, churlish, pettish, testy, acetous, sour, harsh, froward, snarling, tart, curt, sharp, short, trenchant, sarcastic, biting, bitter, caustic, virulent, contumelious, venomous.

CRY, *v.* 1. Weep, shed tears, wail, bewail, utter sounds of lamentation, whimper, snivel, blubber, squall, mewl, pule, lament, groan, moan, keen, sob, boo-hoo, mourn, drop large pear-shaped tears, ululate.
2. Cry out, call, make an outcry, exclaim, call out, clamor, give cry, raise the voice, lift the voice, ejaculate, pronounce loudly, sing out, voice, utter.
3. Shout at the top of one's voice, rend the air, make the welkin ring, vociferate, bellow, roar, shriek, shrill, squall, squeak, yell, bawl, hoot, squawk, screech, scream, howl, yowl, whoop, yo-ho, halloo, halloa, yoick, huzza, hurrah, cheer.
4. Bark, bray, neigh, whinny, yelp, whine, caw, squeal, purr, miaow, gabble, peep, quack, cluck, coo, caterwaul, cackle, twitter, chirp, bleat, moo.
5. Announce orally in public, proclaim, make public, publish, make proclamation of, blazon, blaze abroad, bruit, blare, call out, sell by outcry, hawk.
6. Implore, beg for, importune, sue, petition, plead, appeal, solicit.

CRY, *n.* 1. Weeping, crying, wailing, sobbing, sob, plaint, lament, ululation, lamentation, whimper, tears, mewl, squall, whimpering, sniveling, boo-hooing, blubbering, groaning, moaning, keening.
2. Exclamation, outcry, clamor, ejaculation, vociferation, loud utterance, calling, acclamation, call.
3. Shout, scream, screech, shriek, roar, yell, howl, bawl, whoop, hoot, squawk, squeak, bellow, skirl, yowl, hubbub, hullabaloo, chorus, hue and cry, yoicks, halloo, tallyho.
4. Characteristic call of an animal, bark, yelp, bray, neigh, whinny, whine, purr, miaow, caw, caterwaul, peep, cheep, twitter, chirp, cackle, coo, cluck, quack, squeal, moo, bleat, growl.
5. Entreaty, appeal, solicitation, supplication, request, plea, prayer, orison.
6. Oral announcement, proclamation, public report, publication, bruit, blazonment, hawking, call of wares for sale by a street vendor.
7. Political or party slogan, battle cry, signal, shibboleth, password, keynote.

CRYPT, *n.* Catacomb, vault, tomb, sepulcher, pit, recess, chapel, cave, cavity, grave, mausoleum, subterranean chamber used as a burial place.

CRYPTIC, *adj.* Occult, recondite, enigmatical, cabalistic, obscure, oracular, mysterious, mystic, veiled, secret, hidden, dark, ambiguous, vague, equivocal, perplexing, apocryphal, questionable, puzzling, latent.

CUB, *n.* 1. Young of certain animals, young beast, whelp, pup, puppy.
2. Young boy, awkward youth, hobbledehoy, unpolished child, chit, stripling, sprig, slip, brat, whippersnapper.

CUBE, *n.* Regular hexahedron, solid bounded by six equal squares, die, six-sided body.

CUDDLE, *v.* 1. Draw close, move close together, lie snug, lie close, huddle, nestle, squat, snuggle, curl up in going to sleep.

2. Fondle, embrace, caress, hold tight in an affectionate manner, fold warmly up, cling to, hug tenderly, clasp, strain in one's arms, neck, nuzzle, kiss, bill and coo, spoon, dally, make love.

CUDGEL, *v.* Beat with a cudgel, drub, lambaste, cane, baste, buffet, belabor, bludgeon, pommel, curry, flagellate, bat, bang, maul, strike, birch, bastinado, thrash.

CUDGEL, *n.* Short thick stick used as a weapon, bludgeon, club, shillelagh, billy, truncheon, bastinado, staff, mace, baton, quarterstaff, blackjack, ferule, rubber hose.

CUE, *n.* 1. Signal for an actor to speak or enter, catchword, guiding suggestion, hint, intimation, nod, wink, innuendo, insinuation, inkling, word to the wise, *verbum sapienti (Lat.)*, whisper, watchword, sign.

2. Part one is to play, action made necessary by circumstances, prescribed course of action, allotted share in some doing, business, office, role, function.

3. Humor, state of mind, disposition, temper, temperament, mood, vein, frame of mind.

4. Twist of hair, queue, braid, pigtail, plait.

5. File, line, row, queue, rank, series, string, tier, range.

6. Long tapering rod tipped with a soft leather pad, billiard rod, pool stick.

CUFF, *v.* Strike with the open hand, buffet, slap, fillip, beat, box, pommel, punch, smite, knock, rap, blow, clap, tap, lovetap.

CUFF, *n.* 1. Blow with the open hand, slap, box, buffet, stroke, fillip, punch, rap, tap, clap, lovetap.

2. Handcuff, manacle, hand-fetter, bracelets, pinion, gyve, trammel, shackle.

3. Fold at the bottom of a sleeve or a trouser's leg, manchette.

CUIRASS, *n.* Defensive armor for the body, aegis, breastplate, body-jacket, thorax, coat-of-mail, backpiece.

CUISINE, *n.* 1. Kitchen, culinary department.

2. Cookery, style of cooking.

3. Table, bill of fare, menu.

CUL-DE-SAC, *n.* Lane closed at one end, blind alley, impasse, pocket, no-thoroughfare, blind, trap, bag.

CULL, *v.* 1. Pick, select, single out, choose, pick out, elect, fix upon, pitch upon, make choice of, excerpt.

2. Reap, crop, pluck, gather, pick up, collect, winnow, sift, sort out, separate the chaff from the wheat, glean.

CULMINATE, *v.* 1. Reach the highest point, cap, crown, top, surmount.

2. Come to a head, ripen, come to a crisis, climax, reach final effect, end, come to an end, run its course, reach the goal.

CULMINATION, *n.* 1. Topmost point, highest point, utmost height, summit, vertex, acme, zenith, apogee, top, peak, apex, pinnacle, acropolis, maximum, meridian, ascendant.

2. Crisis, head, finish, conclusion, completion, consummation, close, terminus, finale, wind-up, issue, denouement, catastrophe, result, upshot, last stroke, crowning touch, crowning of the edifice, attainment, keystone, *ne plus ultra (Lat.)*, *fait accompli (Fr.)*, work done.

CULPABILITY, *n.* Guilt, blame, censurableness, blameworthiness, censurability, culpableness, blot, criminality, sinfulness, peccability, deviation from rectitude, remissness, faultiness, fault, guiltiness, delinquency, dereliction.

CULPABLE, *adj.* Deserving blame, blameworthy, meriting censure, to blame, censurable, in fault, blamable, reprehensible, peccable, faulty, sinful, transgressive, objectionable, reprovable, guilty, reproachable, weighed in the balance and found wanting, uncommendable, illaudable.

CULPRIT, *n.* Person arraigned for an offense, guilty party, one guilty of an offense, offender, malefactor, felon, criminal, delinquent, convict, miscreant, sinner, evil-doer, lawbreaker, rascal, wrongdoer, transgressor, reprobate.

CULT, *n.* 1. Worship, homage, veneration, hero-worship, reverence.

2. System of religious worship, ceremony, rite, mode of worship, ceremonial, ritual.

3. Sect, denomination, faction, schism, school, persuasion, belief, doctrine.

CULTIVATE, *v.* 1. Bestow labor upon land in raising crops, produce by culture, work the soil, raise crops from, prepare for crops, till, improve by husbandry, farm, garden, grow, till the soil, plow, sow, plant, dress the ground, manure, dig, compost, spade, delve, hoe, harrow, rake, seed, weed.

2. Educate, civilize, refine, discipline, train, develop, improve, elevate, make better, meliorate, liberalize, humanize, enrich, enhance, mellow.

3. Search into, investigate, devote oneself to, study, pursue.

4. Seek the acquaintance or friendship of, woo, pay one's addresses to, make up to, endeavor to curry favor with, court, ingratiate oneself with.

5. Advance, forward, promote, further, foster, patronize, sponsor, cherish, encourage, assist, aid, help.

CULTIVATION, *n.* 1. Agriculture, agronomy, agronomics, geoponics, husbandry, farming, tilth, gardening, culture, tillage.

2. Mental development, menticulture, march of intellect, refinement, improvement, elevation, culture, civilization, polish, amelioration, *Kultur (Ger.)*, advancement, betterment, enrichment.

3. Investigation, study, pursuit, devotion.

4. Promotion, patronage, fosterment, care, nourishing, cherishing.

CULTURE, *n.* 1. Tillage, agriculture, agronomy, agronomics, geoponics.

2. Breeding, refinement, cultivation, urbanity, polish, suavity, elegance, gentility, gallantry, good taste, chivalry, civility, courtliness, manners, grace.

3. Development by education or training, menticulture, enrichment, betterment, elevation, improvement, advancement.

4. Civilization, education, learning, erudition, higher education, liberal education, attainments, enlightenment, acquirements, accomplishments, scholarship, humanism, knowledge, letters.

CULTURED, *adj.* 1. Elegant, well-bred, urbane, mannerly, courteous, gently bred, genteel, polite, polished, refined, chivalrous, gallant, high-class.

2. Well-educated, erudite, intellectual, lettered, learned, well-informed, well-read, bluestocking, literary, high-brow, enlightened, accomplished, savant.

CULVERT, *n.* Channel crossing under a road,

drain, water-way, sewer, conduit, cloaca, ditch, gully, duct, watercourse, canal, gutter, trough, sough.

CUMBER, v. 1. Hamper, hinder, obstruct, choke, cramp, encumber, handicap, trammel, shackle.

2. Overload, burden, weigh down, saddle with, oppress.

3. Embarrass, inconvenience, harass, trouble, put to inconvenience, discommode, plague, worry, distract, torment.

CUMBROUS, adj. 1. Ponderous, unwieldy, hefty, clumsy, unmanageable, awkward, inconvenient, heavy, massive, incommodious, hulking.

2. Onerous, burdensome, oppressive, irksome, cumbersome, vexatious, troublesome, tiresome, worrisome, embarrassing.

CUMULATIVE, adj. Growing by successive additions, continually increasing, successively waxing in force, augmentative, accumulative, superadded, increscent, waxing, crescent, swelling, enlarging, intensitive.

CUNNING, adj. 1. Deceitful, deceptive, crooked, foxy, shifty, underhand, double-faced, insidious, tricky, rusé (Fr.), intriguing, scheming, shrewd, designing, artful, canny, wily, sly, sharp, crafty, sharp-witted, slippery, guileful, arch, diplomatic, astute, knowing, acute, subtle, deep-laid, feline, profound, strategic, politic, Machiavelian, vulpine, Jesuitical, sophisticated, sagacious, timeserving, trickish, stealthy.

2. Skilfully wrought, exhibiting ingenuity, ingenious, curious.

3. Dexterous, skilful, adept, adroit, masterly, deft.

4. (Of children and animals) Pleasing, lovable, interesting, attractive, pretty, cute, dainty, quaint, darling, sweet, petite.

CUNNING, n. 1. Artifice, craft, subtlety, intrigue, craftiness, circumvention, maneuvering, strategy, temporization, guile, deception, deceit, chicane, chicanery, duplicity, sharp practice, concealment, knavery, jugglery, foul play, trickery, wiliness, artfulness, shrewdness, finesse.

2. Diplomacy, address, savoir-faire, know-how, profound knowledge, mother-wit.

3. Ability, dexterity, adroitness, deftness, skill, expertness, genius, talent, parts, aptitude, forte, turn, knack, cleverness.

CUP, n. 1. Small open container to drink from, goblet, chalice, mug, beaker, bowl, glass, tumbler, cylix, patella, pan, basin, cannikin, stein, tazza (It.), tasse (Fr.), rhyton, cyathus, bumper, tankard, jorum.

2. Cupful, unit of capacity (8 fluid ounces; 16 tablespoons), quantity contained in a cup, potion, draught.

3. Hollow, excavation, crater, concavity, pit, hole, furrow, trough, shaft.

4. Ornamental cup of precious metal offered as a prize for a contest, loving cup, reward, trophy.

CUPBOARD, n. Closet with shelves for dishes, buffet, china closet, cabinet, ambry, storeroom, pantry, locker, press, cuddy, bureau, chiffonier, commode, sideboard.

CUPID, n. Roman god of love, son of Venus, Eros (Greek), Amor, Hymen, amoretto (pl. amoretti), amorino.

CUPIDITY, n. 1. Strong desire, lust, prurience, concupiscence, cacoëthes, irresistible urge, mania, eager longing to possess, coveting, yearning,

itching, appetency, appetite, hunger, ardor, zeal, eagerness, hankering, vaulting ambition, aspiration.

2. Inordinate desire for wealth, venality, greed, avarice, avariciousness, covetousness, illiberality, itching palm, rapacity, extortion, avidity, tenacity, auri sacra fames (Lat.), stinginess, miserliness, parsimoniousness, acquisitiveness.

CUPOLA, n. Rounded vault built upon a roof, dome constituting a roof, tholus, beehive, arch, mansard, tower, turret, belfry, lantern, lookout, pyramid, pagoda, campanile, steeple, obelisk, pylon, small towerlike structure on a roof.

CUR, n. 1. Snarling outcast dog, mutt, whelp, hound, mongrel, bitch.

2. Coward, poltroon, dastard, caitiff, nidget, recreant, shy cock, craven, sneak.

3. Low despicable person, scoundrel, miscreant, blackguard, rascal, villain, black sheep, varlet, wretch, reptile, viper, serpent.

CURABLE, adj. That may be cured, healable, remediable, restorable, reparative, reparatory, corrigible, retrievable, recoverable, improvable, mendable, sanable.

CURATE, n. Clergyman employed as assistant or deputy of a rector, perpetual curate, chaplain, residentiary, curate in charge, incumbent, rector, vicar, divine, clergyman, ecclesiastic, churchman, priest, presbyter, clerk in holy orders, parson, minister, pastor, shepherd, padre, abbé, curé, patriarch, reverend, black coat, sky pilot.

CURATIVE, adj. Restorative, remedial, healing, therapeutic, medical, medicinal, serving to cure, sanative, sanatory, recuperatory, recuperative, reparative, reparatory, corrective, prophylactic, beneficial, palliative, salutiferous, alexipharmic, salutary, dietetic.

CURATOR, n. Person in charge of a collection or museum, keeper, custodian, overseer, proctor, superintendent, guardian, procurator, librarian, supervisor, intendant, manager, director, warden.

CURB, n. 1. Repression, restraint, check, bridle, control, hindrance, constraint, rein, yoke, halter, harness, muzzle, collar, gag, bit, leading string, tether, brake, drag, snaffle, picket, chain, guy, bar, bolt, lock, padlock, wall, rail, fence, palisade, barricade, barrier, stay, damper, wet blanket, dissuasion.

2. Brim, edge, margin, brow, brink, confine, verge, border, skirt, frame, side, flange, ledge, rim.

3. Line of joined stones or concrete at the edge of a street, kerb (Br.), curb-stone, edge-stone, retaining-wall, breast-wall.

4. Curb market, mart, bourse, stock exchange.

CURB, v. 1. Restrain, put under restraint, bridle, muzzle, rein in, yoke, harness, collar, gag, put in leading strings, tether, picket, check, restrict, hinder, coerce, constrain, control, hold in check, keep under, repress, compel, govern, hold in leash, pull in, inhibit, suppress, prohibit, limit, trammel.

2. Retard, slacken, hold back, moderate, relax, slow down, decelerate, delay, slow up.

CURD, n. Casein substance obtained from milk by coagulation, coagulated milk, casein, grume, coagulum, clabber, pulp, paste, sponge, dough, pap, jam, pudding, mush.

CURDLE, v. 1. Convert into curds, coagulate, condense, fix, clot, cake, precipitate, deposit, crystallize.

2. Coagulate, cohere, thicken, stiffen, congeal, chill, become solid, solidify, consolidate, set, concrete, take a set.

3. Curdle the blood, terrify, horrify, daunt, make fearful, affright.

CURE, *v.* 1. Eradicate sickness, restore to health, make well, rid of an illness, heal, remedy, treat, sanitate, palliate, doctor, minister to, nurse, drug, attend, medicate, dose, physic, bring round, set on one's legs, effect a cure, make whole, restore, relieve of something detrimental.

2. Preserve from putrefaction, preserve, smoke, prepare for preservation, dry, salt, pickle, kipper, marinate.

CURE, *n.* 1. Course of remedial treatment, faith healing, therapy, method of treatment, medical treatment, therapeutics, healing art, pathology, nosology, etiology, diagnosis, vocational therapy, prognosis, symptomatology, chiropractic, materia medica, pharmaceutics, pharmacology, allopathy, homoeopathy, surgery, osteopathy, psychiatry, dietetics.

2. Means of healing or curing, remedy, drug, corrective, antidote, medicine, specific, reparative, balm, salve, potion, physic, pill, dose, medicament, prescription, nostrum, sovereign remedy, lenitive, panacea, cure-all, antifebrile, counteractive, tonic, antipoison, antitoxin, antibody, antiserum, emetic, germicide, antiseptic, prophylactic, disinfectant, restorative, stimulant, elixir, ointment, liniment, lotion.

3. Restoration to health, successful remedial treatment, healing, convalescence, recuperation, recovery.

CURFEW, *n.* 1. Ringing of the bell at a fixed hour in the evening as a signal for covering or extinguishing fires, evening bell.

2. Night fall, close of day, evening, eventide, dusk, twilight, sundown, cockshut, gloaming, bedtime.

CURIOSITY, *n.* 1. Inquisitiveness, inquiringness, desire to know about something, inquiring mind, thirst for knowledge, mental acquisitiveness, interest, research, questioning, interrogation.

2. Intrusiveness, officiousness, meddlesomeness, prying, meddling, obtrusiveness.

3. Curious thing, rare object, *rara avis (Lat.)*, curio, novelty, novel thing, rarity, phenomenon, marvel, spectacle, sight, wonder, freak, prodigy, oddity, singular thing.

CURIOUS, *adj.* 1. Meddlesome, inquisitive, prying, desirous of learning or knowing what is not properly one's concern, taking undue interest in other's affairs, intrusive, scrutinizing, meddling, peering, inquiring, burning with curiosity, agape, mousing, overcurious, inquisitorial, expectant, questioning, snooping, rubbernecking, long-nosed.

2. Exciting interest because of strangeness, out of the way, unusual, singular, rare, surprising, unique, strange, extraordinary, odd, queer, novel, phenomenal, prodigious, baffling.

3. Elegant, finely wrought, cunning, finished, made with skill and art, skilful, neat, complicated, elaborate.

4. *(Of books)* Pornographic, obscene, indecent, indelicate, smutty, sexy, erotic, risqué, suggestive.

CURL, *v.* Form into a spiral or curved shape, coil, twist, wave, wind, writhe, ripple, spiral, friz, frizzle, wreathe, buckle, turn, undulate, convolve, twine, loop, entwine, twirl, lap, meander, fold, zigzag, roll, wrinkle, scallop, indent, Phrygianize,

contort, wring, crimp, crisp, form into ringlets, crinkle.

CURL, *n.* 1. Tress of hair, ringlet, lovelock, lock, curlicue.

2. Undulation, sinuosity, wave, winding, twirl, flexure, convolution, circuit, contortion, labyrinth, tortuosity, meandering, involution, twist, maze.

3. Roll, coil, spiral, volute, scallop, corkscrew, helix, scroll, worm, tendril, kink.

CURLY, *adj.* Curly-haired, curly-headed, frizzy, kinky, wavy, undulating.

CURMUDGEON, *n.* Irascible churlish fellow, sordid wretch, codger, churl, mean person, miser, niggard, skinflint, lickpenny, hunks, pinchpenny, screw, tightwad, money-grubber, pinchfist, harpy. Harpagon, scrimp, extortioner, usurer.

CURRENCY, *n.* 1. Money, circulating medium, cash, specie, coin, bills, banknotes, medium of exchange, money in actual use, legal tender, greenbacks, hard cash, dollar sterling, long green, paper money, dough, spondulix, jack, wampum, bucks, shekels, velvet, ten spot, five spot, cart wheel, two bits.

2. Publicity, spotlight, notoriety, hue and cry, limelight, *réclame (Fr.)*, flagrancy, report, bruit, *vox populi (Lat.).*

3. General acceptance, general reception, wide acceptance, prevalence, fashion, vogue, success, universality, wide extension, predominance, preponderance, superiority.

4. Transmission from hand to hand, passage, circulation, passing on from person to person, course, transference, communication, diffusion, conveyance, transmittance, dissemination, spread, propagation.

CURRENT, *adj.* 1. Generally accepted, in vogue, common, generally received, general, popular, in every one's mouth, rife, widespread, customary, comprehensive, ordinary, usual, habitual, wonted, regular, accustomed, prevalent, conventional, circulated, rumored, noised abroad.

2. Present, instant, existing, now passing, of the moment, contemporary, prevailing, belonging to the time actually passing, actual, existent, latest, immediate, occurring, contemporaneous, synchronous, simultaneous, concomitant, coeval, coincident, present-day, up-to-date.

CURRENT, *n.* 1. Progression, forward movement, course, progress, onward flow.

2. That which flows, stream, running water, tide, large body moving in a certain direction, race, undertow, torrent, rapids, flood.

3. Air circulation, draft, wind, air, flatus, puff, breath, whiff, whiffet, zephyr, breeze, emanation.

4. Main course, general tendency, gravitation, bearing, drift, set, inclination, direction, turn, aim.

CURRY, *v.* 1. Comb, currycomb, rub and clean with a comb, groom.

2. Thrash, beat, cudgel, bastinado, drub, buffet, lambaste, belabor, bludgeon, pommel, birch.

CURSE, *v.* 1. Wish calamity on, imprecate evil upon, execrate, invoke harm on, maledict, call down evil on, blast, bring a curse upon, doom, destroy, blight, damn, denounce, excommunicate, fulminate, blaspheme, vituperate, anathematize, proscribe, thunder against, devote to destruction, utter curses, swear.

2. Afflict with great evil, torment, scourge, torture, plague, annoy, vex, injure, harass.

CURSE, *n.* 1. Malediction, expression of a wish

that evil befall another, malison, imprecation, execration, fulmination, denunciation, thunders of the Vatican, commination, excommunication, proscription, abomination.

2. Blasphemy, sacrilege, expletive, irreverence, profane oath, swearing, foul invective, profanity.

3. Evil that has been invoked upon one, bane, plague, trouble, annoyance, affliction, bitter pill, torment, scourge, vexation, thorn in the side, crown of thorns, misfortune, harm, fatal mischief.

CURSED, *adj.* 1. Under a curse, damned, undone, accursed, curse-laden, *sacré (Fr.)*, blighted, cast out, devoted to destruction, excommunicated, unhappy, doomed, confounded.

2. Detestable, abominable, hateful, execrable, damnable, odious, diabolic, infernal, hellish.

3. Baneful, troublesome, vexatious, injurious, dire, pernicious, deleterious, destructive, deadly, venomous, virulent, malignant, vexatious, plaguing, scourging, tormenting.

CURSORY, *adj.* Going rapidly over something without noticing details, desultory, immethodical, superficial, careless, slapdash, slight, transient, hasty, brief, passing, perfunctory, rapid, listless, hurried, summary, loose, inattentive, unreflecting, flighty, giddy, scatterbrained.

CURT, *adj.* 1. Concise, brief, short, succinct, to the point, terse, laconic, pithy, crisp, summary, condensed, compact, compendious.

2. Abrupt, brusque, blunt, rude, snappish, tart, uncivil, petulant, harsh, sullen, crusty, short and rude, snappy, taciturn, unceremonious, impolite, bluff, ungracious.

CURTAIL, *v.* Cut off a part of, cut short, prune, shorten, lop, dock, clip, trim, pare down, shear, crop, dwarf, cramp, diminish, lessen, decrease, reduce, retrench, cut, abbreviate, abridge, take in, scrimp, condense, summarize, epitomize, contract, abstract, compress, truncate, amputate.

CURTAILMENT, *n.* Shortening, epitomization, reduction, abridgment, abbreviation, contraction, retrenchment, condensation, cutting down, cutting off.

CURTAIN, *n.* 1. Hanging piece of fabric, arras, drapery, hanging, lambrequin, portiere, valance, purdah, ridel, backdrop, shutter, Venetian blind, shade.

2. Screen, blind, veil, cover, cloak, ambush, shroud, camouflage, ambuscade.

CURTSY, *n.* Bow by women in recognition or respect, bending of the knees and lowering of the body, genuflection, kowtow, obeisance, salaam, bob, bowing and scraping.

CURVATURE, *n.* Incurvation, incurvative, bend, arcuation, curvation, bending, flexure, curvity, camber, curve, crook, hook, deflexion, aduncity, sinuosity, curl, sweep, winding, cyrtosis *(Pathol.)*.

CURVE, *n.* Continuously bending line without angles, arc, bow, loop, arcade, arch, crescent, lunule, meniscus, half moon, festoon, vault, turn, horseshoe, incurve, fold, bend, parabola, oxbow, epicycloid, ellipse, extrados, wave, circle, lune.

CURVE, *v.* Bend in a curve, turn, crook, wind, coil, hook, bow, round, arch, curl, incurve, twist, inflect, deflect, camber, embow, spiral, encircle, wreathe.

CURVET, *n.* 1. Leap, spring, hop, jump, bounce, vault, saltation, capriole, caracole, demivolt, buck, bound, skip, prance.

2. Caper, gambol, dance, prank, gambade, frolic.

CURVET, *v.* 1. Jump about, bound, leap, vault, jump up, hop, spring, trip, skip, caracole, bob, foot it, bounce, start, flounce.

2. Frisk, caper, cut capers, frolic, gambol, romp, dance, have one's fling.

CUSHION, *n.* Case filled with resilient material for support of the body, pillow, bolster, woolsack, pad, hassock, mat, wad, pillion, seat, rest, buffer.

CUSP, *n.* Pointed end, point, horn, angle, peak, corner, cuspis, apex, bend, incisor, tooth, nib, tusk.

CUSPIDATE, *adj.* Ending in a sharp stiff point, cuspidated, acuminated, acuminate, sharp, acute, pointed, spear-like, cusped, salient, spiky, peaked, spiked.

CUSTODIAN, *n.* Curator, guardian, conservator, superintendent, keeper, warden, custos, janitress, janitor, curatrix, concierge, claviger, watchman, warder, preserver, watchdog, protector, duenna, chaperon, guardian angel.

CUSTODY, *n.* 1. Protection, care, charge, watch, keeping, safekeeping, guardianship, trusteeship, safeguard, ward.

2. Charge of officers of the law, possession, holding, detention, arrest.

3. Confinement, prison, imprisonment, duress, durance vile, bondage, restraint, incarceration, fetter.

CUSTOM, *n.* 1. Usual way of acting in given circumstances, habitual practice, group pattern of habitual activity transmitted from one generation to another, habit of a majority, consuetude, rule, usage, practice, ordered procedure, wont, fashion, more or less permanent continuance of a social usage, established way of doing things, routine, convention, precedent, standing order, red tape, rut, groove, habitude, addiction.

2. Formality, form, observance, prescription, conventionalism, conventionality, second nature, etiquette, matter of course, beaten path.

3. Patronage, trade, clientele, clientelage, body of clients.

4. Tax, toll, duty, impost, tribute.

CUSTOMARY, *adj.* Habitual, common, wonted, usual, defined by long continued practice, regular, accustomed, ordinary, general, normal, popular, systematic, prescriptive, conventional, continued, daily, acknowledged, favorite, natural, everyday, consuetudinary, nomic, frequent, traditional.

CUSTOMER, *n.* Purchaser of goods from another, patron, buyer, client, *emptor (Lat.)*, clientele *(collect.)*.

CUT, *v.* 1. Divide by an edged tool, sever, make an incision in, incise, slit, cleave, wound with a cutting instrument, slice, lance, chop, gash, slash, penetrate with a sharp-edged instrument, sunder, separate from the main body, lop off, hack, trim, lacerate, prune, shear, clip, pare, dock, mutilate, mangle, truncate, whittle, shave, split, saw, snip, nip, rend, rive, rip, crack, chip, splinter, tear, break, snap, hack, carve, quarter, anatomize, dissect.

2. Sculpt, sculpture, chisel, carve, shape, form, sketch, block out, fashion, figure.

3. Reap, mow, harvest, gather.

4. Abridge, curtail, shorten by omitting a part, crop, retrench, abbreviate, reduce, diminish, pare down, contract, abstract, epitomize, condense, summarize.

5. Intersect, cross, bisect, interrupt, decussate, divide.

6. Severely wound the feelings of, hurt, move, touch, pierce, affect, grieve, distress, pain, afflict, discomfort.

7. Slight by not recognizing, ignore, refuse to recognize socially, snub, cold shoulder, turn one's back upon, keep at arm's length, freeze, turn on the ice.

8. Dilute, water, adulterate, make less thick, doctor, vitiate, make impure.

9. Excavate, dig, delve, hollow out, scoop out, burrow.

CUT, *n.* 1. Incision, groove, gash, slit, nick, slash, wound, cleft, division, opening, indentation.

2. Excision, deletion, omission, abbreviation, reduction.

3. Slice, quantity cut, piece, chop.

4. Course straight across, channel, passage, furrow, trench.

5. Sarcasm, taunt, dig, cutting remark, fling.

6. Refusal to recognize socially, snub, cold shoulder, slight.

7. Style, fashion, shape, form, manner, ilk, kind.

8. *(Colloq.)* Graft, share, kickback, unjust acquisition, illegal gain.

9. Engraving, etching, woodcut, blockprint, illustration, picture.

CUT CAPERS, *v.* Be merry, frolic, cut up, be frolicsome, play pranks, gambol, cut didos.

CUTICLE, *n.* Dermis, epidermis, scarfskin, skin, superficial integument, pellicle.

CUTPURSE, *n.* Pickpocket, robber, thief, bandit, lightfingers, pickpurse, light-fingered gentry, crook, blackleg.

CUT SHORT, *v.* 1. Shorten by cutting off the end, bring to a sudden close, terminate abruptly.

2. Hinder from proceeding, interrupt, check suddenly, intercept.

3. Diminish, abridge, abbreviate, retrench.

CUTTHROAT, *n.* Assassin, murderer, killer, thug, ruffian, bandit, bravo, slayer.

CUTTING, *adj.* 1. Sharp, keen, keen-edged, sharpened, incisive, dividing by a cut, edged, knife-edged, keen as a razor, penetrating, slashing, secant, intersecting, cleaving, lancinating.

2. Caustic, sarcastic, mordant, mordacious, satirical, tart, wounding the feelings severely, acetous, trenchant, acrimonious, cynical, stern, severe, harsh, pointed, sardonic, withering, disparaging, derogatory, depreciatory.

3. Cold, bitter, nipping, raw, stinging, biting, bleak, piercing, algid, frigid, fresh, keen.

CYCLE, *n.* 1. Recurring period of time in which certain events repeat themselves in the same order, round of years, circle of time, period, epoch, era, revolution of time, eon, age, succession of years.

2. Bicycle, velocipede, bike, tricycle, tandem, hydrocycle, quadricycle, wheel *(colloq.)*, motorcycle.

CYCLONE, *n.* Atmospheric pressure system with low pressure at its center and with counterclockwise wind motion in the northern hemisphere (clockwise in the southern), tropical hurricane, tempest, tornado, windstorm, whirlwind, samiel, typhoon, monsoon.

CYCLOPEAN, *adj.* Colossal, gigantic, enormous, huge, immense, vast, monstrous, elephantine, giant-like, Brobdingnagian, Herculean, Titantic, Gargantuan, hulking, whopping, massive, lusty, towering, strapping.

CYNIC, *n.* 1. Adherent of Antisthenes, follower of Diogenes, Timonist.

2. Misanthrope, man-hater, one who denies the goodness of human motives, sneering faultfinder, scoffer, one who holds a low opinion of mankind, pessimist, sneerer, growler, snarler, satirist, critic, misanthropist, egotist, egoist, detractor, reprover, censurer, carper, caviler, calumniator, reviler, traducer, castigator, vituperator, nullifidian, skeptic.

CYNICAL, *adj.* Bitterly unbelieving, misanthropic, distrusting the motives of others, pessimistic, skeptical, holding a low opinion of mankind, disbelieving in the sincerity or goodness of human motives, sardonic, disdainful, sneering, satirical, censorious, contemptuous, scornful, derisive, sarcastic, carping, morose, sour, crabbed, ill-natured, ill-tempered, faultfinding, caviling, scurrilous, peevish, pettish, waspish, snappish, snarling, churlish, testy, surly, petulant, touchy, fretful, mocking, scoffing, cross-grained, withering, crusty, grouchy, cutting, cross, supercilious.

CYNICISM, *n.* Disbelief in the goodness and sincerity of human motives, misanthropy, hatred of mankind, misanthropism, cynicalism, tartness, sullenness, moroseness, churlishness, virulence, captiousness, acrimony, asperity, hypercriticalness, acerbity, cynicalness.

CYNOSURE, *n.* 1. Lesser Bear, Ursa Minor.

2. Guiding star, polestar, lodestar, loadstar, North Star, point of attraction, something that strongly attracts attention by its brilliance, object of attention, center of attraction, something serving for guidance or direction, paragon.

CYST, *n.* Closed bladderlike sac containing fluid morbid matter, pouch, bladder, vesicle, utricle, bag.

CZAR, *n.* Tsar, autocratic ruler, tyrant, king, absolute monarch, despot, emperor, dictator, sovereign, potentate, overlord, Caesar, kaiser.

D

DAB, *v.* 1. Pat with something soft, rub with a dabber, apply by light strokes, plaster, coat, tar, paint, varnish, besmear, bedaub.

2. Tap gently, strike lightly, tamp, slap, poke at, hit, swat, rap, bat, flap, thump, dash, whack, swap, peck.

DAB, *n.* 1. Light blow, gentle stroke, pat, gentle slap, dint, knock, swipe, whack, tap, rap, quick sharp stroke, fillip, thrust, peck, cut, lunge, poke, smack.

2. Small moist lump, lumpy mass, pat.

3. Small quantity, spot, dole, mite, bit, nip, modicum, pinch, drop, dash, tinge, sprinkling, crumb, drop in the bucket.

4. *(Colloq.)* Skilful person, experienced hand, adept, expert, master hand, practiced eye, nice hand, connoisseur, proficient, good shot, good hand, capital hand, cracksman, genius, past master, top-sawyer, old stager, old hand.

DABBLE, *v.* 1. Wet slightly, besprinkle, spatter, sprinkle, splash, asperge, moisten, dip slightly and often, damp, water, lave, bathe, soak, steep, drench, macerate, douse, souse, baptize, duck, immerse, submerge.

2. Play in water, paddle, slosh, splash about, puddle.

3. Do something in a light manner, make

slight efforts, work superficially, potter, putter, smatter, concern oneself with anything slightly, meddle, tamper, trifle, loaf, idle away time, fool away time.

DABBLER, *n.* One who approaches his activities in a superficial manner *(usually applied to the arts and hobbies),* sciolist, half scholar, one with superficial knowledge, trifler, potterer, novice, smatterer, amateur, dilettante, dabster, greenhorn, tyro, charlatan, quack.

DAEDALIAN, *adj.* 1. Ingenious, skilful, gifted, inventive, talented, cunning, clever, technical, neat-handed, fine-fingered, workmanlike, artistic, felicitous.
2. Showing cunning, crafty, artful, deceitful, sly, arch, subtle.
3. Intricate, complicated, circuitous, involved, anfractuous, flexuous, maze-like, mazy, tortuous, sinuous, daedal, marked with intricate windings, labyrinthine, convoluted, twisted, undulating, serpentine, variegated, diversified, curiously made.

DAFT, *adj.* 1. Insane, crazy, demented, lunatic, bereft of reason, unsettled in one's mind, *non compos mentis (Lat.),* unhinged, deranged, not quite right, possessed, moonstruck, *aliéné (Fr.),* out of one's head, cracked, touched, bug-house, rabid, mad, not all there, shatter-pated, mad as a March hare, maniacal, of unsound mind, not right in one's upper story, irrational, vacant.
2. Simple, foolish, absurd, stupid, doltish, silly, imbecilic, idiotic, moronic, weak-minded, insulse, asinine, brainless, not bright, witless, fatuous, addle-headed, dull-witted, senseless, unwitted, nonsensical, blockish, Boeotian.
3. *(Scot.)* Frolicsome, wanton, sportive, giddy, playful, merry, mirthful, gay.

DAGGER, *n.* 1. Short-edged pointed weapon, dirk, poniard, stiletto, misericord, skean, barong, bowie knife, blade, stylet, knife, falchion, creese, anlace, yataghan, machete, bolo, kukri, bodkin, rapier, point, foil, cold steel, naked steel.
2. *(Printing)* Reference mark, obelisk.

DAGGLE, *v.* Drag through mud, trail in the wet, draggle, spatter, besmear, dirty, soil, bemire, befoul, spot, smear, daub, smudge, smirch, sully, beslime, begrime, splash, stain, maculate, defile, pollute.

DAILY, *adj.* 1. Occuring every day, issued every-day, diurnal, quotidian, recurring day after day, periodic, cyclic.
2. Ordinary, usual, current, customary, day-to-day, common, habitual, constant, repeated, wonted, regular, steady, punctual, regular as clockwork, everyday, frequent, continual.

DAINTY, *adj.* 1. Of delicate beauty *or* charm, exquisite, beautiful, pretty, lovely, comely, well-made, attractive, charming, pleasing, graceful, elegant, choice, tasteful, neat, petite, trim, trig, fine, natty, stylish, chic.
2. Pleasing to the palate, delicious, savory, appetizing, tasty, delectable, palatable, luscious, toothsome, tender, nectareous, piquant, ambrosial, epicurean.
3. Refined in taste, fastidious, particular, nice, discriminating, scrupulous, meticulous, exacting, hard to please, difficult.
4. Too particular, fussy, squeamish, finical, pernickety *(colloq.),* overnice, overrefined, dandified, precious, effeminate.

DAINTY, *n.* Something delicious to the taste, luscious morsel, choice morsel, delicacy, tidbit, nice bit, *bonne bouche (Fr.),* sweetmeat, comfit, sugarplum, kickshaw, confection, bonbon, treat, ambrosia, nectar.

DALE, *n.* Small open river valley partly enclosed by low hills, vale, dell, glen, dingle, bottom, gap, ravine, clough, basin, defile, combe, gorge, canyon, hollow, slade, strath, glade, grove.

DALLIANCE, *n.* 1. Amorous toying, wanton familiarity, endearments, blandishments, petting, spooning, caressing, necking, fondling, billing and cooing, erotic play, passionate embrace, kissing, osculation, love-making, sparking, coquetry, flirtation, sensual titillation.
2. Procrastinating behavior, dilatoriness, delay, dillydallying, postponement, dawdling, pottering, otiosity, trifling away of time, idling, loitering, lingering, lagging, protraction, prolongation, do-nothingness, faineancy, *dolce far niente (It.).*

DALLY, *v.* 1. Interchange caresses, fondle, toy, sport amorously, play erotically, philander, flirt, coquet, wanton, gallivant, bill and coo, make love, neck, spark, cuddle, hug, nuzzle, kiss, pet.
2. Dawdle, drawl, idle away time, waste time, loiter, fritter away time, loaf, lounge, slouch, loll, vegetate, laze, putter, linger, dillydally, fiddle, shillyshally, tarry, lose time, lag, hang back, delay sportively, take a great deal of time, potter, work in a half-hearted way, dabble, spin out, draw out, procrastinate, retard, put off, prolong, protract, defer, delay.

DAMAGE, *n.* 1. Injury that impairs value, hurt, detriment, impairment, scathe, harm, mischief, loss, blemish, spoil, defacement, spoliation, havoc, debasement, inroad, outrage, ravage, vitiation, deterioration, erosion, corrosion, moth and rust, dry rot, blight, atrophy, degeneration, decay, dilapidation, disintegration, wear and tear, blow, disrepair, discoloration, depravation, pollution, contamination, adulteration, corruption, canker, decadence, depreciation, wound, misfortune, evil, wrong, disadvantage, casualty, mishap, ruin, foul play, buffet, scratch, stroke, bruise, tear, rent, laceration, mutilation, gash, accident, disaster.
2. *(Colloq.)* Cost, expense, price, charge, bill, figure, toll, impost, levy, tax, tariff, excise, par value, assessment, exactment, valuation, market price, price current, quotation.

DAMAGE, *v.* Cause damage to, hurt, injure, mar, harm, impair the value of, diminish the soundness of, deface, disfigure, mutilate, lacerate, despoil, mangle, blemish, spoil, ravage, scathe, wrong, maltreat, wound, incapacitate, abuse, vitiate, debase, tamper with, pervert, defile, corrupt, infect, taint, blight, rot, contaminate, pollute, stain, wreak havoc on, gnaw, erode, eat, rust, disintegrate, crumple, molder, corrode, oxidize, mildew, wear away, warp, destroy, dismantle, sap, undermine, gnaw at the root of, deal a blow to, have an adverse effect upon, stab, pierce, scotch, maim, cripple, lame, hamstring, hock, break, split, crack, rend, tear.

DAMAGES, *n.* *(Law)* Indemnity, reparation, estimated money equivalent for injury sustained, satisfaction, forfeiture, fine, mulct, amercement, penalty, retribution, compensation, escheat, cost, expenses, confiscation, the devil to pay.

DAME, *n.* 1. Woman of rank or authority, lady, woman of high social position, wife of a knight or baronet *(Gr. Br.),* baroness, noblewoman, blueblood, optimate, aristocrat, peeress.

2. Mistress of a household, married woman, Mrs., matron, madam, dowager, gammer, squaw, wife, mem-sahib, *madame, signora, señora, Frau, donna, madonna,* good woman.

3. *(Slang)* A woman, petticoat, skirt, bit of fluff, female, moll, doll, nymph, broad, wench.

DAMN, *v.* 1. *(Theol.)* Condemn to hell, condemn to eternal punishment, doom to perdition, curse with hell, condemn to punishment in a future state, torment, anathematize, excommunicate, condemn with bell, book and candle.

2. Swear at, curse, execrate, imprecate evil upon, accurse, call down curses upon, devote to destruction, curse up hill and down dale, rap out an oath, cuss, swear like a trooper, fulminate, thunder against.

3. Ruin by adverse criticism, condemn as a failure, bring condemnation upon, cause to be slighted and rejected, kill *(metaphorically),* not speak well of, censure, brand, proscribe, dispraise, stigmatize, run down, hiss off the stage, hoot, slate, frown upon, criticize, look askance at, hold up to reprobation, discommend, impeach, cry shame upon, raise a hue and cry against, rail at, inveigh against, denounce, declare to be bad.

4. Judge to be guilty, condemn, convict, find guilty, sentence, pass sentence on, sign the death warrant.

DAMNABLE, *adj.* Worthy of damnation, cursed, meriting reprobation, execrable, abominable, vile, atrocious, accursed, very bad, arrant, foul, base, rotten, odious, heinous, nefarious, flagitious, outrageous, villainous, evil, depraved, hateful, confounded, detestable, pernicious, noxious, dark, malign, infamous, hellish, infernal, diabolical, wretched, horrible.

DAMNATION, *n.* 1. Condemnation to punishment in the hereafter, consignment to everlasting perdition, anathema, excommunication, thunders of the Vatican, ecclesiastical fulmination, bell, book and candle, comminations, proscription, ban.

2. Denunciation, execration, malediction, curse, malison, imprecation, reprobation, devotion to destruction, oath expressing anger.

3. Ruination by adverse criticism, destruction of the favorable prospects of an artistic production.

DAMNATORY, *adj.* Conveying condemnation, tending to convict, inculpatory, compromising, denunciatory, objurgatory, vituperative, critical, defamatory, censorious, captious, carping, abusive, disapproving, disparaging, reproachful, ruinous, opprobrious, condemnatory.

DAMP, *adj.* Moderately wet, moist, humid, dank, wettish, muggy, vaporous, watery, foggy, misty, clammy, cold, dewy, rainy, swampy, marshy, boggy, fenny, paludous, muddy, miry, soaked, sodden, soggy, soft, squashy, spongy, sopping, sloppy, dripping, aqueous.

DAMP, *n.* 1. Moderate degree of moisture, moist air, humidity, mugginess, clamminess, dankness, wateriness, fog, mist, vapor, dew, dampness, madefaction, exudation, wet, softness, sogginess, squashiness, soddenness.

2. *(Mining)* Noxious exhalation, firedamp, chokedamp, blackdamp, poisonous gas, foul air, stifling vapor.

3. Dejection, depression of spirits, chill, gloom, drooping spirits, heaviness, melancholy, sadness, despondency, hypochondria, disconsolateness, dumps, blues.

4. Check, curb, hindrance, discouragement, damper, wet blanket, kill-joy, restraint, inhibition.

DAMP, *v.* 1. Make damp, moisten, dampen, wet, bedew, humidify, madefy, sodden, soak, saturate, sop, drench.

2. Check the energy of, slacken, retard the action of, repress, deter, restrain, moderate, lessen the intensity of, allay, temper, abate, check the vibration of, make dull, make faint, muffle, mute, silence, deaden, dull.

3. Dispirit, cast down, depress, discourage, deject, dishearten, darken, chill, cool.

4. Stifle, suffocate, extinguish, quench, bank, choke, smother.

DAMPER, *n.* 1. Check, barrier, obstacle, load, stumbling block, impediment, hindrance, knot, difficulty, disadvantage, objection, snag, hitch, drag, stay, stop, lion in the way, muffler, soft pedal, silencer, mute, *sordino (It.).*

2. Depressing influence, wet blanket, kill-joy, crape-hanger, cold water, rebuff, discouragement, setback.

DAMSEL, *n.* Young unmarried woman, maiden, maid, lassie, lass, girl, young lady, nymph, miss, demoiselle, mademoiselle, damozel, colleen, schoolgirl, virgin.

DANCE, *n.* 1. Successive group of rhythmical steps to music, measured movement, figured motion, "poetry of motion," Terpsichorean art, choreography, eurhythmics, Russian ballet, toe-dancing, interpretive dancing.

2. Dance music, a tune to dance to.

3. Party, social gathering for dancing, ball, hop, assembly, cotillion, promenade, prom, *thé dansant (Fr.),* tea dance, bal masque, fancy dress ball, masquerade, social.

4. Quadrille, square dance, caledonian, jig, coquette, lancers, minuet, Saratoga, march, star, Parisian varieties, Prince Imperial, sociable, standard.

5. Contra dances, Virginia reel, money musk, Sicilian circle.

6. Round dance, Bohemian, Cracovienne, hop, *deux-temps,* esmeralda, polka, galop, mazurka, two-step, schottische, varsovienne, waltz.

7. One-step, fox trot, gavotte, polonaise, morris dance, folk dance, pavane, rigadoon, saraband, bolero, fandango, rumba, samba, tango, maxixe, tarantella, nautch dance, sword dance, hornpipe, reel, Highland fling, pigeonwing, cakewalk, belly dance, shimmy, *danse du ventre,* cancan, black bottom, turkey trot, ragtime, jazz, jitterbug, tap dance, Charleston, Jersey bounce, Lambeth walk.

DANCE, *v.* 1. Move the feet to music, perform the steps of, step rhythmically, execute the figures of, shuffle the feet, cut, tread, trip the light fantastic toe, chassé, glissade, waltz, bob, pirouette, caracole, jeté, turn, glide, prance, flutter, wriggle, wiggle, bounce, shimmy, fox trot, one-step, tango, rumba, samba, jitterbug, shake a mean foot, leap, jump, skip, spring, vault, foot it, curvet, bound, reel, sway, cavort, frisk, caper, hop about, romp, frolic, gambol, move nimbly up and down.

2. Quiver from excitement, sparkle with emotion, flash, vibrate.

3. Toss up and down, bounce on the knee, bob up and down, dandle.

4. Dance attendance, attend solicitously, wait on constantly, pay attentions to, court, spark.

DANDER, *n. (Colloq.)* Anger, ire, choler, wrath,

rage, temper, resentment, indignation, dudgeon, sulks, animosity, hackles, pique, umbrage, huff, miff, tiff, pet, passion, fit, fire and fury, hot blood, vials of wrath, angry mood, *acharnement (Fr.)*, pucker, fume, bile, spleen, gall, acerbity, acrimony.

DANDLE, *v.* 1. Dance on the lap, toss up and down, move about in the arms caressingly, manipulate conveniently.

2. Treat like an infant, pet, pamper, nurse, fondle, caress, play with, cosset, coddle, cherish, hug, cuddle, nestle, nuzzle, cajole, wheedle, look sweet upon, ogle.

DANDY, *n.* 1. Fine gentleman, fastidious dresser, mirror of fashion, pink of fashion, man of fashion, glass of fashion, clotheshorse, fashion plate, man about town, leader of fashion, blade, drawing-room Johnnie, bandbox aesthete, blood, spark, buck, swell, toff, fop, dude, coxcomb, silk-stocking, gallant, beau, exquisite, prettyboy, mannequin, gay dresser, zoot-suiter, sharp dresser, silk-sock Sam, popinjay, jack-a-dandy, fribble, jemmy, dandyling, dandiprat, macaroni, ladies' man, carpet-knight, cicisbeo, cavalier, masher, male coquet, *petit maître (Fr.)*, man milliner, jackanapes.

2. Particularly fine specimen, something first-rate, something very fine, jim-dandy, "daisy," "beauty," "beaut."

DANGER, *n.* Chance of evil, endangerment, risk, exposure to harm, liability to injury, unsafety, insecurity, imperilment, precariousness, jeopardy, instability, hazard, peril, venture, vulnerability, vulnerable point, Achilles' heel, menace, threat, imminence, breakers ahead, clouds on the horizon, storm brewing, gathering clouds.

DANGEROUS, *adj.* Causing danger, full of risk, hazardous, perilous, parlous, risky, in question, chancy, uncertain, insecure, unsafe, ticklish, in a critical position, precarious, serious, shaky, at stake, slippery, unsteady, dubious, dark, lowering, problematical, under fire, vulnerable, exposed, unsheltered, unshielded, nodding to its fall, black, between two fires, between the frying pan and the fire, between the devil and the deep blue sea, between Scylla and Charybdis, trembling in the balance, on the horns of a dilemma, formidable, treacherous, herculean, top-heavy, malignant, nasty, alarming, menacing, minatory, ominous, threatening, impending, imminent.

DANGLE, *v.* 1. Swing loosely as if suspended, hang loosely with a swaying motion, oscillate, librate, hang pendulous, wave pendulously, sway, swing with a shaking motion, pendulate, jiggle, vacillate, wobble.

2. Be suspended, droop, be pendent, depend.

3. Induce by enticement, bait, lure, allure, inveigle, persuade by deceptive arts, lead astray by hoodwinking, wheedle, entice.

4. Follow a person as if seeking favor, hang about, fawn, be obsequious, follow importunately, be a suitor.

DANK, *adj.* 1. Unpleasantly moist, humid, wet, muggy, clammy, dewy, damp, watery, saturated with cold moisture, chilly.

2. Thick, luxuriant, rank, lush, succulent, juicy.

DAPPER, *adj.* 1. Pretty in appearance, smartly dressed, chic, *bien soigné (Fr.)*, well-groomed, stylish, modish, spruce, smart, elegant, spiffy, dandified, finical, natty, trig, trim, fastidious, neat, dainty, jaunty, goodly, well-proportioned.

2. Small and active, brisk, agile, spry, nimble, lively, pert, quick, ready, alert.

DAPPLE, *v.* Make spotted, mark with spots, fleck, mottle, spot, checker, variegate, diversify.

DARE, *v.* 1. Have the necessary boldness for, make bold, presume, be bold enough to undertake, be not afraid.

2. Have the necessary courage for, brave, face, confront, meet, adventure, attempt, nerve oneself, pluck up courage, take heart, stand to one's guns, present a bold front, show fight, face the music, fly in the face of, run the gauntlet, risk, hazard, stake, put at hazard, wager, do something involving risk.

3. Challenge, provoke to action, defy, meet defiantly, oppose, twist the lion's tail, beard, assume a fighting attitude, square off, threaten, hurl defiance at, taunt, stump, fling down the gauntlet.

4. Dare say, assume as probable, have no doubt, think likely.

DAREDEVIL, *adj.* Recklessly daring, incautious, rash, temerarious, imprudent, inconsiderate, uncalculating, heedless, careless, madcap, foolhardy, venturesome, devil-may-care, wanton, wild, desperate, headlong, breakneck, full of sound and fury, harebrained, precipitate, heels over head, adventurous, Quixotic, impetuous, vehement, impulsive, fire-eating, thrasonic, vaporing, audacious, blustering.

DAREDEVIL, *n.* Recklessly daring person, rash adventurer, desperado, madcap, desperate fellow, rashling, Hotspur, fire-eater, *enfant perdu (Fr.)*, brazen-face, swashbuckler, fanfaron, lion, ace *(aviation)*, man of courage, knight-errant, Icarus, gambler, gamester, dynamitard.

DARING, *adj.* 1. That dares, bold, fearless, game, dauntless, undaunted, intrepid, brave, valiant, adventurous, venturesome, valorous, chivalrous, gallant, courageous, enterprising, doughty, lion-hearted, spirited, heart of oak, manly, manful, virile, stalwart, plucky, unflinching, resolute, unabashed, mettlesome, stout-hearted, hardy, self-reliant, spartan, soldierly, bold as brass, heroic.

2. Audacious, devil-may-care, reckless, rash, presuming, presumptuous, impudent, flagrant, arrant, glaring, unreserved, barefaced, brazen, shameless, flaunting, loud.

DARING, *n.* Adventurous courage, boldness, intrepidity, prowess, contempt of danger, pluck, bravery, heroism, mettle, nerve, grit, sand, spunk, backbone, manliness, hardihood, fortitude, élan, firmness, derring-do, dash, gallantry, chivalry, self-reliance, fearlessness, resolution, spirit, valor, heart, audacity, defiance, rashness.

DARK, *adj.* 1. Without light, unilluminated, dull, dim, darkling, shadowy, caliginous, tenebrous, atramentous, fuliginous, ill-lighted, darksome, sunless, cloudy, overcast, murky, lurid, shady, inky, pitchy, Cimmerian, umbrageous, fuscous, opaque, crepuscular, Stygian, grimy, sooty, coaly, dirty, dun, dingy, foggy, cloudy, misty, vesperal, nocturnal, twilit.

2. Not pale, brunet, dark-complexioned, not fair, swarthy, swart, ebon, dusky, black, sable, nigrescent.

3. Hard to understand, obscure, cryptic, faint, enigmatical, recondite, abstruse, deep, occult, mysterious, cabalistic, mystic, supernatural, secret, unknown, transcendental, not easily perceived, indistinct, esoteric, concealed, hidden, ambiguous,

incomprehensible, unintelligible, uncertain, inscrutable.

4. Forbidding, frowning, ominous, somber, sullen, lowering, threatening, sinister.

5. Gloomy, disheartening, without cheer, blue, cheerless, dismal, dreary, hopeless, discouraging, funereal, depressing, sad, melancholy, joyless, sorrowful, doleful, heavy, dolorous, sober, hypochondriac.

6. Destitute of knowledge, uncultured, blind, untaught, unenlightened, unlettered, unrefined, ignorant, benighted, rude, unseeing.

7. Evil, wicked, black-hearted, atrocious, foul, dastardly, infamous, insidious, Machiavellian, nefarious, flagitious, vile, infernal, villainous, damnable, horrible, shameful, deadly, lethal, slippery.

8. Unknown, little known, unheralded, not recognized by the public, ignored, not expected to win.

DARK, *n.* 1. Night, nightfall, nighttime, dead of night, midnight, witching hour, eventide, evening, crepuscule, vespers, twilight, darkness that can be felt.

2. Absence of light, darkness, obscurity, shade, murkiness, duskiness, blackness, opacity, dimness, dullness, penumbra, umbra, obtenebration, black shadows, fulginosity, tenebrosity, gloominess, caliginosity, inkiness, pitchiness, umbrageousness, dinginess, shadow, chiaroscuro, Cimmerian darkness, Stygian darkness.

3. Abstruseness, want of clearness, mystery, unintelligibleness, obscurity, reconditeness, profundity, esotericism.

4. Privacy, concealment, secrecy, stealth, clandestineness, furtiveness, sub rosa, keeping secret, surreptitiousness, hugger-mugger, covering up, indirection, seclusion.

5. Iniquity, wickedness, sinfulness, depravity, moral blindness, turpitude, crime, misdeed.

6. Gloom, despondency, cheerlessness, blues, joylessness, depression, dejection, melancholia, hypochondria.

7. Ignorance, want of knowledge, lack of enlightenment, benightedness, mental obscurity of vision, blindness, sightlessness.

DARKEN, *v.* 1. Exclude light from, overcast, dim, obscure, eclipse, cloud, becloud, bedim, make dim, make dark, shadow, shade, tone down, lower, blur, blacken, overshadow, blind, screen, mask, hide, conceal.

2. Extinguish, put out, blow out, snuff out, smother, douse, stifle.

3. Fill with gloom, sadden, chill, depress, deject, damp, make gloomy, dishearten, dispirit, make despondent, discourage, make blue.

4. Hinder the mental development of, benight, make ignorant, stupefy, stultify, deprive of sight, make obtuse, make crass.

5. Make unintelligible, make intricate, perplex, obfuscate, confuse, obscure, render unmeaningful, mystify, make less clear.

6. Make less white in color, make less fair, render of darker hue, make less pellucid, stain, dim, tarnish, sully, dull, soil, smear, deface, spot, smudge, discolor, blemish, blotch, splotch, tint, smirch, denigrate, maculate, dye, tinge, color, hue, shade.

DARKLING, *adj.* 1. Being in the dark, hidden, concealed, screened, masked, obscure, mystical, mysterious.

2. Unable to see, blinded, groping.

3. Producing obscurity and gloom.

DARLING, *n.* One who is tenderly beloved, object of one's affection, person very dear to another, person dearly loved, person in great favor, dear, minion, truelove, beloved, charmer, favorite, precious, sweet, idol, pet, love, dear one, jewel, sweetheart, apple of one's eye, duck, honey, inamorata, carissima, ladylove, sweetie *(colloq.),* angel, goddess, flame.

DARLING, *adj.* Regarded with especial tenderness, tenderly beloved, dearly beloved, very dear, lovable, adorable, precious, sweet, charming, engaging, alluring, enchanting, captivating, lovely, bewitching, angelic, winsome.

DART, *v.* 1. Throw suddenly, thrust rapidly, hurl, let fly, jaculate, launch, direct with a sudden thrust, propel, push, drive forward, pitch, toss, fling, cast, project, heave, tilt, lance, sling, let off, pelt, discharge, fire off, expel, eject, emit, send off, shoot out, fire off.

2. Move swiftly, spring suddenly, leap, start, bound, fly swiftly, rush, scoot, start quickly, dartle, scud, spurt, scuttle, skedaddle *(colloq.),* flit, whisk, dash, run, swoop, pounce, speed, hie, trip, hasten, sprint, whiz, post, shoot, tear, race, skim, sweep, run like mad, accelerate, hurry, wing one's way, outstrip the wind.

DASH, *v.* 1. Adulterate, mix, imbue, blend, alloy, mingle, throw something into so as to produce a mixture, produce a mixture, pour a small quantity of something into, commingle, infuse, instill. impregnate, lace *(a beverage),* season, flavor, tinge, tincture, suffuse, color, overspread.

2. Splash violently, splotch, bespatter, sprinkle, besprinkle, besplash, slosh, spatter.

3. Hurl forcibly, throw with might, knock against, fling, slam, cast, beat, throw suddenly, thrust.

4. Strike violently so as to break to pieces, smash, shatter, break, crush, destroy, shiver, crack, split, snap, splinter, fracture, crash, rive, rend.

5. Cast down, depress, dispirit, deject, unman, dishearten, discourage, sadden, throw a damper on, prostrate.

6. Disappoint, thwart, frustrate, check, balk, defeat, foil, baffle, bring to naught, overthrow, ruin, blight, scatter, abash, confound, spoil.

7. Compose hastily, write rapidly, push work rapidly, execute carelessly, sketch quickly, make impromptu, dash off.

8. Rush violently, spring, move with violence, bolt, dart, fly swiftly, run impetuously, sprint, hasten, sally, bound, speed.

DASH, *n.* 1. Slight admixture, tinge, tincture, bit, small addition of some other ingredient, infusion, pinch, sprinkling, small quantity, smack, grain, trace, little, touch, hint, suspicion, flavor, *soupçon (Fr.),* intimation, taste, spice, tang, vein, shade, spot.

2. Throwing of water against, sprinkling, splashing, clashing, collision.

3. Rapid blow, violent stroke, vigorous impact, shock, concussion, crash.

4. Sudden forward advance, rush, rapid onset, impetuous movement, sally.

5. Short race decided in one attempt, trotting race, sprint, short swift trial of speed.

6. Spirited action, spirit, impetus, impetuosity, vigor, energy, élan, verve, brio, mettle, vivacity, zeal, animation, quickness, fearlessness, daring, resolution, gallantry, intrepidity, boldness in execution.

7. Vain display, flourish, ostentation, parade, show, splash, figure.

8. Setback, frustration, check, discouragement, disarrangement, sudden defeat, discomfiture.

9. Hasty stroke of a pen, mark, score, streak, imprint, scratch, notch, nick, line.

10. Horizontal line to mark an abrupt break, signal of longer duration than a dot (*Teleg.*).

DASHING, *adj.* 1. Characterized by energy of action, spirited, impetuous, lively, mettlesome, energetic, bold-spirited, brave, gallant, audacious, game, plucky, daring, fearless, venturous, rushing, headlong, precipitate.

2. Inclined to make a display, showy, jaunty, brilliant, ostentatious, pretentious, gay, colorful, swashbuckling, with colors flying, with flourish of trumpet.

3. Stylish, fashionable, in Sunday best, in best bib and tucker, *endimaché (Fr.), en grande tenue (Fr.),* full dress, white-tie-and-tails, fresh from the bandbox, modish, in the latest style, à la mode, toney (*colloq.*).

DASTARD, *n.* Sneaking coward, mean poltroon, craven, recreant, sneak, milksop, shy-cock, cur, white-liver, midget, shirker, runagate.

DASTARDLY, *adj.* Fearful, cowardly, sneaking, lacking courage to face danger, mean, poltroon, base, unsoldierlike, pusillanimous, craven, timid, recreant, dastard, cowering, timorous, unmanly, mean-spirited, skittish, faint-hearted, lily-livered, white-livered, abject, spiritless, smock-faced, in heart a deer, yellow.

DATA, *n.* 1. Known facts, available figures, raw materials, information, memoranda, matters of direct observation, notabilia, notes, documents, papers, dossier, abstracts, evidence.

2. Assumed propositions, things conceded as the basis of an argument, premises, assumptions, given conditions, starting point, grounds for a conclusion.

DATE, *n.* 1. Particular point of time, epoch, age, era, eon, cycle, period of time, chronology, year, month, quarter, semester, lustrum, generation, day.

2. Time during which anything lasts, duration, assigned length of time.

3. (*Colloq.*) Appointment, engagement, assignation, rendezvous.

DATE, *v.* 1. Fix the date of, affix a date to, mark with a date, furnish with a date, note the time of, register, chronicle, mark the time of, ascertain the time of, assign a time to.

2. Reckon from some point in time, use some event as a basis in noting time, measure time.

3. Belong to a particular period, begin, have its origin, have existed from a given date, be dated, be reckoned, bear a date, have a date.

4. (*Colloq.*) Make an appointment with, keep an engagement with, date up, keep company with, go steady with, squire, escort.

DAUB, *v.* 1. Coat with soft adhesive matter, cover with something sticky, smear, spread over something, besmear, bedaub, plaster, dab.

2. Begrime, soil, dirty, spot, smudge, smirch, sully, defile, deface, draggle, bemire, beslime, muddy, befoul, stain, pollute, tarnish, spatter.

3. Splash paint, paint unskilfully, paint without taste, portray badly.

4. Deck tastelessly, adorn gaudily, bedizen, bepaint.

5. Cover with a deceitful exterior, whitewash,

conceal beneath a specious surface, gild, varnish, counterfeit, misrepresent.

DAUB, *n.* 1. Smeary mass, viscous application, sticky patch, smirch, smear.

2. Material of an inferior kind for daubing, inferior mortar, mud-plastering, clay, mud.

3. Coarse painting, crude painting, inartistic painting.

DAUBY, *adj.* 1. Sticky, smeary, viscous, gummy, adhesive, glutinous, mucilaginous.

2. Unskilful, coarsely executed, crude, rough, inartistic, unfinished.

DAUNT, *v.* 1. Overcome with fear, put into a state of fear, intimidate, frighten, cow, alarm, overawe, appall, check by alarm, frighten off, abash, bulldoze, strike terror, unman, petrify, scare, browbeat, threaten, terrorize, affright, bully.

2. Lessen the courage of, dishearten, dispirit, discourage, dismay, thwart, deter from one's purpose, check, bring low, reduce, shake the courage of, tame, subdue, crush, shake.

DAUNTLESS, *adj.* Not to be daunted, undaunted, not to be dismayed, unaffrighted, unafraid, bold, unflinching, unshrinking, unappalled, courageous, indomitable, fearless, intrepid, unconquerable, confident, self-reliant, Spartan, daring, audacious, stout-hearted, lion-hearted, brave, high-spirited, valorous, valiant, manly, doughty, venturesome, stalwart, plucky, mettlesome, hardy, chivalrous, resolute, game, heroic, gallant.

DAWDLE, *v.* Waste time, potter, fiddle, quiddle, piddle, fiddle-faddle, dillydally, dally, idle away time, kill time, fritter away time, fool away time, do nothing, let the grass grow under one's feet, vegetate, trifle, loiter, take one's time, poke, loll, drawl, slouch, loaf, lounge, move lazily, saunter, act in a protracted indecisive way, linger over, shilly-shally, diddle, lag behind, hang about, go at a snail's pace.

DAWDLER, *n.* Laggard, drone, lie-abed, lounger, poke (*colloq.*), sluggard, idler, trifler, droil, snail, mopus, slow-back, fainéant, do-little, lubbard, loafer, *lazzarone (It.),* slow-coach, afternoon farmer, lotus-eater, inefficient person, slow poke, dormouse, tortoise.

DAWN, *v.* 1. Begin to grow light in the morning, grow light with the light of the rising sun, break, begin to shine, grow light, gleam.

2. Begin to open, begin to develop, begin to expand, begin to give promise, appear, open, set in, rise, commence, originate, enter upon, take its rise, inaugurate, initiate, come into existence.

3. Occur, flash on the mind, begin to make an impression, begin to be perceived, begin to be seen, begin to be understood, come to one's knowledge, break suddenly.

DAWN, *n.* 1. First appearance of daylight in the morning, aurora, show of approaching sunrise, daybreak, sunrise, cockcrow, daypeep, peep of day, dayspring, prime of day, dawning, first blush of the morning, rosy fingers of the morning.

2. Rise of anything, advent, first appearance, beginning, birth, first opening, unfolding, first expansion, first awakening.

DAY, *n.* 1. Time between sunrise and sunset, interval of light between two successive nights, period from dawn to dark, daytime, period during which the earth makes one revolution on its axis (*Astron.*), period of 24 hours, mean solar day.

2. Broadly diffused light, sunlight, sunshine,

daylight, broad day, light of day.

3. Period of life, lifetime, generation, time, epoch, age.

4. Portion of a day alloted to labor, period of time occupied by some course of operations, specified period, period of activity.

5. Day of contest, contest.

6. Day assigned to a particular observance, anniversary, jubilee, holiday, feast day, red-letter day, fête.

7. Period of power, period of influence, term of ascendancy, hegemony, heyday.

8. Distance that can be traveled in a day, a day's journey, unit of distance.

9. Appointed time, promised time, set time, day on which something is to occur, particular time, date, day as a point of time.

DAYBREAK, *n.* First appearance of light in the morning, early dawn, dawning, cockcrow, peep of day, break of day, dayspring, first blush of the morning, sunrise, aurora, matins.

DAYDREAM, *n.* Visionary fancy indulged in while awake, idle fancy, dream, vision, phantasm, fantasy, conceit, idle exercise of the imagination, reverie, musing, flight of fancy, pipe dream, myth, woolgathering, visionary scheme, air castle, "such stuff as dreams are made on," castles in Spain, *châteaux en Espagne (Fr.),* illusory vision, poetic creation, fiction, idealized creation, golden dream, figment, romance, extravaganza, illusion, mirage, dream of Alnaschar, Utopia, Atlantis.

DAYLIGHT, *n.* 1. Diffused and reflected light of the sun, sunlight, light of day, sunshine, sunbeam, light of heaven, luminosity.

2. Daytime, beginning of the day, morning, dawn, daybreak.

3. Full knowledge, understanding, light of full understanding, intelligibility, clearness, lucidity, clarity, perspicuity, openness, publicity.

DAZE, *v.* 1. Stun with a blow, overpower by shock, dazzle, bedazzle, blind, benumb, petrify, electrify.

2. Stupefy, bewilder, confound, confuse, strike dumb, perplex, astonish, surprise, amaze, startle, astound, flabbergast, dumfound, stagger.

DAZE, *n.* 1. Stupor, torpor, coma, anesthesia, trance, catalepsy, lethargy, physical insensibility, paralysis, twilight sleep, hypnosis, narcosis.

2. Bewilderment, wonderment, astonishment, dazzlement, confusion, stupefaction, amazedness, surprise.

DAZZLE, *v.* 1. Overpower by intense light, daze, blind by excess of light, dim the vision, bedazzle, confuse the vision of, blaze, glitter, glisten, blur, glance, glimmer, flicker, glare, flare, shimmer, sparkle, scintillate, coruscate, flash.

2. Be overpowered by light, be overwhelmed by light, have the vision confused, be dizzied.

3. Excite admiration by brilliancy, charm with brilliant appearance, "shine," impress, astonish, overpower with display, confound by splendor, bewilder by brilliancy, overawe, surprise, stupefy.

DAZZLE, *n.* 1. Bewildering brightness, splendor, brilliancy, effulgence, dazzling light, luminosity, shimmer, radiance, iridescence, flash, gleam, glint, sparkle, glitter, glare, blaze, flare, coruscation, scintillation, flame, glance.

2. Display, meretricious brilliancy, bravura, surface show, false splendor, ornateness.

DEAD, *adj.* 1. No longer living, lifeless, deprived of life, breathless, not endowed with life, devoid

of life, inanimate, not possessing life, deceased, exanimate, defunct, destitute of life, departed, gone, no more, gone to one's last rest, gathered to one's fathers, at rest with God, perished, still, asleep, clay-cold, inorganic.

2. Insensible, bereft of sensation, frigid, numb, benumbed, unconscious, unimpressible, wanting in vitality, impassive, spiritless, apathetic, callous, indifferent, lukewarm, unfeeling, obtuse, torpid, dull.

3. Still, motionless, inert, inoperative, marked by a stoppage of action, inactive.

4. Ineffectual, not productively employed, sear, unemployed, useless, unprofitable, unproductive, barren, incapable, slow, stagnant, infertile.

5. Unexciting, lacking animation, monotonous, tedious, vapid, flat, unvaried, without variation, tame, quiet, insipid, tasteless, subdued, uniform, without tang or taste, stale, without freshness.

6. Extinct, no longer in existence, obsolete, no longer in use, expired, past, lapsed, disused, fallen into desuetude.

7. Total, entire, complete, absolute, thorough, utter, sheer, unqualified.

8. *(Colloq.)* Utterly exhausted, without vigor, very tired, spent, tired out, dished, played out.

9. Dull in appearance, unburnished, not glossy, not bright, not brilliant, lusterless, lackluster.

10. Without resonance, unresounding, without resilience, without bounce, without elasticity, heavy.

11. Closed at one end, impassable, incapable of being opened, false, blind, giving no light.

12. Sure, certain, crack, unerring, unfailing, direct, straight, exact.

13. *(Law)* Deprived of civil rights, deprived of the rights of property.

14. *(Sports)* Out of play, not to be counted, stopping on striking the ground.

DEAD, *adv.* 1. Wholly, absolutely, to the last degree, utterly, entirely, completely.

2. With abrupt and complete stoppage of motion.

3. Directly, exactly, diametrically.

DEAD, *n.* Depth, midst, dark, still, period of greatest darkness, point of greatest lifelessness, most quiet time, most lifeless period, period of profoundest inertness, gloomiest period.

DEADEN, *v.* 1. Weaken, soothe, assuage, make less forcible, mitigate, moderate, subdue, abate, diminish the vigor of, destroy the force of, make dull, restrain, retard, lessen the velocity of.

2. Impair, incapacitate, devitalize, enfeeble, unfit.

3. Make less sensitive, benumb, numb, blunt, paralyze, make insensible, obtund, hebetate, dope, drug, anesthetize.

4. Muffle, mute, smother, dampen, repress, damp, choke.

5. Make impervious to sound, deafen, render non-conductive of sound.

6. Make flat, make vapid, deprive of gloss, deprive of brilliancy, obscure.

DEADLOCK, *n.* State of neutralization, state in which progress is impossible, counteraction of things producing total stoppage, state of inaction, complete standstill, insoluble difference, blocking of business, stalemate, checkmate, dead stand, dead stop, stoppage, impasse, stay, arrest, block, check, halt, cessation.

DEADLY, *adj.* 1. Tending to cause death, fatal, attended with death, death-dealing, slaughterous, lethal, lethiferous, murderous, deathly, injurious, sanguinary, bloodthirsty, homicidal, deleterious, noxious, destructive, pestiferous, baneful, virulent, pestilential, pernicious, venomous, poisonous, malignant, noisome.

2. Aiming to kill or destroy, implacable, fell, relentless, desperately hostile, rancorous, mortal, unappeasable, internecine, unrelenting, baleful, inexorable.

3. Like death, pallid, ashen, wan, cadaverous, emaciated.

4. (Theol.) Involving spiritual death, not venial.

5. (Colloq.) Excessive, inordinate, very great, terrible.

DEAF, adj. 1. Without hearing, dull of hearing, hard of hearing, lacking the sense of hearing, unable to hear, unable to distinguish sound, earless, stone-deaf.

2. Determined not to be persuaded, unmoved, unconvinced, unwilling to hear, disregardful, regardless, inattentive, refusing to listen, heedless.

3. Muffled, stifled, deadened.

DEAFEN, v. 1. Deprive of the power of hearing, make deaf.

2. Stun with noise, split the ears, confuse with tumult, din.

3. Render a sound inaudible by a louder one, drown out, cause not to be heard, make sound-proof.

DEAL, n. 1. Uncertain amount, degree, extent, indefinite quantity, lot.

2. Cut and shuffle, apportionment, distribution of cards in a game, single round, act of dealing.

3. (Colloq.) Business transaction, bargaining, trade, traffic, arrangement for mutual advantage, agreement, truck, negotiation, barter, marketing, commerce, mercantile business, merchantry, secret understanding.

DEAL, v. 1. Give to one as his share, distribute, apportion, allot, allocate, dispense, bestow, share, assign, divide, parcel, deal out, mete out, dole out, deliver, administer, inflict.

2. Occupy oneself with, treat of, have to do with, be engaged in, practice, have concern, concern.

3. Take action with respect to, attend to, see to.

4. Carry on negotiations, make arrangements, act in mutual relations, have business relations, trade, do business, traffic, have commerce, buy and sell, negotiate, exchange, market, barter, act, conduct oneself toward others, behave.

DEALER, n. 1. Merchant, vendor, tradesman, retailer, jobber, buyer and seller, trader, monger, trafficker, middleman, chandler, salesman, sutler, chapman, huckster, peddler, smouser, colporteur (Fr.), hawker, cadger, costermonger, shopkeeper.

2. Distributor of cards in a game, shuffler, dispenser, divider.

DEALINGS, n. 1. Method of business, behavior, action, doings, proceeding, policy, management, practice, manner of conduct in relation to others, treatment.

2. Buying and selling, commercial enterprise, commerce, commercial intercourse, negotiation, mercature, trade, business, traffic, barter, business transaction, stockjobbing, agiotage, jobbing, job, bargain, exchange.

DEAR, adj. 1. Held in affection, precious in one's regard, darling, beloved, much loved, close to the heart, favorite, cherished, highly esteemed, estimable, valued, prized, regarded fondly.

2. Entailing great expense, high-priced, of great price, expensive, costly, sumptuous, rich, above price, valuable.

3. Difficult to get, rare, choice, at a premium, priceless, beyond price.

DEAR, n. One who is much beloved, pet, darling, beloved, sweetheart, truelove, idol, angel, flame, goddess, inamorata, ladylove, sugarplum, honey, dear one.

DEARTH, n. 1. Insufficiency, inadequacy, stint, deficiency, short supply, rareness, paucity, none to spare, scantiness, emptiness, poorness, ebb tide, depletion, inanition, low water.

2. Lack of a present necessity, exigency, need, indigence, poverty, want, privation, barrenness, famine, starvation, half rations, drought, short commons.

DEATH, n. 1. End of life, cessation of vital functions, debt of nature, loss of life, decease, demise, dissolution, departure, release, exit, end, "crossing the bar," the great adventure, eternal rest, rest, expiration, last rest, passing, quietus, extinction, finis, decay, annihilation, destruction.

2. Grim reaper, destroyer of life, angel of death, personification of mortality, Azrael, man with the scythe, skeleton, skull and crossbones, death's head, river of death, Jordan, Stygian shore.

3. Bloodshed, murder, carnage, slaughter.

4. Pestilence, plague, epidemic.

DEATHLESS, adj. 1. Not subject to death, not liable to die, immortal, imperishable, undying, never-dying, ever-living.

2. Everlasting, endless, eternal, incorruptible, unceasing, perpetual, coeternal, unending, aere perennius (Lat.), unfading, evergreen.

DEATHLIKE, adj. Resembling death, skeletal, corpse-like, ghost-like, cadaverous, pale, ghastly, wan, livid, grisly, gaunt, emaciated, gruesome, deathly, deadly, shocking.

DEBACLE, n. 1. Break up of ice in a river, violent flood, inundation, cataract, cataclysm, deluge.

2. Complete breakdown, downfall, dissolution, collapse, disruption, avalanche, bouleversement, délabrement (Fr.), sudden overthrow, subversion, demolishment, havoc, ruination, crash, ravage, wreck, smash, devastation.

3. Sudden breaking loose, disorganization, wild flight, stampede, rout, violent rush, tumultuous dispersion.

DEBAR, v. 1. Cut off from entrance, bar out, exclude from, shut out, eliminate.

2. Prevent by authority, forbid, prohibit, bar, disallow, hinder, obstruct, restrain, check, deny, withhold, proscribe, interdict, circumscribe, ban, preclude, foreclose, taboo, refuse, restrict, inhibit, suspend.

DEBARK, v. Go ashore, set foot upon shore from a ship, land, disembark, leave ship, cast anchor, come to land, make the land.

DEBASE, v. 1. Lower in value, depreciate, reduce in quality, deteriorate, impair in worth, bring low, abase, depress, adulterate, weaken.

2. Degrade morally, pervert, deprave, corrupt, prostitute, pollute, vitiate, defile, injure, dishonor, take down, shame, disgrace, soil, foul, befoul, contaminate, taint, render unclean, desecrate, stain, debauch.

DEBASED, adj. 1. Vitiated, adulterated, impure, mixed, deteriorated, doctored.

2. Depraved, degraded, degenerate, groveling, base, vile, mean, vicious, fallen, contemptible, ignoble, low.

DEBASEMENT, *n.* 1. Depreciation, impairment, deterioration, decadence, adulteration, reduction.

2. Corruption, perversion, prostitution, lapse, depravation, pollution, defilement, contamination, degradation, abasement, degeneracy, descent, fall, ignominy, abjection, disgrace, baseness, turpitude.

DEBATABLE, *adj.* Capable of being debated, in question, open to question, subject to contention, disputable, arguable, contestable, controvertible, questionable, unsettled, undecided, indeterminate, dubious, problematical, doubtful, uncertain, open, mooted, in dispute, controversial.

DEBATE, *n.* 1. Disputation of any subject, war of words, argumentation for and against, strife in argument, discussion of a public question in assembly, controversy, contest, logomachy, strife of words, paper warfare, *guerre de plume (Fr.),* contention, palaver, dispute, oral slugging match.

2. Deliberation, advisement, meditation, parley, consideration, cogitation, reflection, consultation.

DEBATE, *v.* 1. Argue the pro and con of, dispute argumentatively, engage in oral controversy, cross verbal swords, contend about with argument, engage in discussion, discuss, contend in words, contest by argumentation, engage in logomachy, canvass, moot, bandy, wrangle.

2. Deliberate, consider, meditate upon, think, ratiocinate, reflect, examine a question.

DEBAUCH, *v.* 1. Lead into unchastity, seduce, corrupt by sensuality, treat to lewdness, despoil of virginity, deflower, stuprate, molest, ill-use, abuse, attack, make an assault on, outrage, rape, ravish, violate, prostitute, force, dishonor, subject to carnal appetite.

2. Corrupt in principles, vitiate, pervert, stain, contaminate, demoralize, infect, debase, deprave, pollute, degrade, defile, brutalize, inquinate, lead into vicious practices, lead astray morally, taint, mislead.

3. Indulge in sensual pleasures, plunge into dissipation, rake, live hard, run riot, sow one's wild oats, engage in riotous living, dissipate, carouse, burn the candle at both ends.

DEBAUCHEE, *n.* 1. Lecher, sensualist, libertine, voluptuary, rake, roué, satyr, whoremonger, goat, fornicator, adulterer, rapist, *paillard (Fr.),* loose fish, rip, rakehell, silk-stockinged seducer, Don Juan, Lothario.

2. Habitual profligate, Sybarite, wanton, fast man, man of pleasure, dissipated person, indulger in sensual pleasures, carouser, drunkard.

DEBAUCHERY, *n.* 1. Seduction, carnality, rape, stupration, ravishment, sexual violation, venery, prostitution, wenching, lasciviousness, impudicity, obscenity, lust, salacity, lewdness, lechery, flesh pots of Babylon, harlotry, whoring, fornication, licentiousness.

2. Excess in eating or drinking, gluttony, wine-bibbing, intemperance, dissipation, dissoluteness, grossness, bestiality, incontinence, libertinism, excessive self-indulgence, revelry, orgies, wassail, saturnalia, bacchanalia, carousal, drinking bout, drunken spree.

DEBILITATE, *v.* Deprive of strength, weaken, make feeble, enfeeble, impair the strength of, enervate, unman, prostrate, exhaust, emasculate, incapacitate, make languid, render weak, shake, unbrace, undermine, cripple, reduce.

DEBILITY, *n.* Failure of strength, invalidation, atony, asthenia, adynamia, cachexia, lack of vigor, exhaustion, weakness, infirmity, languor, frailty, impotence, feebleness, prostration, emasculation, enervation, decrepitude, flaccidity, enfeeblement, unmanning, lassitude, faintness, impuissance, weariness, condition of the body in which the vital functions are feebly discharged *(Pathol.),* delicacy.

DEBONAIR, *adj.* 1. Jaunty, airy, blithe, breezy, light-hearted, buoyant, sparkling, vivacious, free and easy, sunny, merry, sprightly, lightsome, sportive, jocund, smiling, cheery, gay as a lark, *allegro (It.),* in high feather, spry, lithe, elegant, graceful, dapper.

2. Of pleasant manners, having gentle bearing, mannerly, courteous, polite, gentlemanly, urbane, chivalrous, suave, affable, gallant, obliging, civil, complaisant, refined, gracious, well-bred, genteel.

DEBOUCH, *v.* March out from narrow confines into open country, fan out, deploy, march out, sally forth, spread out, emerge, issue, open into a wider space, pass out, flow from a small place to a larger one, emanate, pour out of.

DEBRIS, *n.* Remains of anything broken down or destroyed, wreckage, rubbish, ruins, limature, accumulated fragments, trash, junk, rubble, waste, refuse, dottle, drast, dross, dregs, filings, scobs, litter, odds and ends, sweepings, scourings.

DEBT, *n.* 1. Pecuniary due, that which is owed, duty, liability, obligation, arrears, debit, score, claim, account, indebtedness, arrearage, deferred payment, outstandings, deficit, incumbrance, debt of honor, ancestral debt, contingent debt, debt of nature, floating debt, funded debt, future debt, national debt.

2. *(Theol.)* Offense requiring reparation, error, trespass, sin, transgression, fault, neglect of duty, misdoing, shortcoming, demerit, misdemeanor, misdeed, delinquency, dereliction, imperfection, failing, frailty, infirmity, infringement, infraction.

DEBUT, *n.* 1. First public appearance on the stage, entrance upon a career, embarkation on a career, beginning of a professional career, first step, first attempt, *coup d'essai (Fr.).*

2. Formal introduction into society, coming-out, presentation.

DECADENCE, *n.* Deterioration, process of falling into an inferior condition, decline in excellency, declension, degeneration, debasement, decay, fall, retrogression, wane, ebb, recession, degradation, retrogradation, caducity, perversion.

DECADENT, *adj.* 1. Declining, falling off, falling into ruin, deteriorating, degenerating, decaying, retrogressive, caducous, retrograde, on the wane, withering, spoiling, rotten, cankered, tainted, tabid.

2. Abnormal, artificial, neurotic, hypercivilized, effete, morbid, eccentric, perverted, sensuous, depraved.

DECAMP, *v.* 1. Leave a camping-ground, break up camp, depart from camp, strike tents, march off, march away, move off.

2. Depart suddenly, leave unexpectedly, flee unceremoniously, abscond, desert, abandon, bolt, hasten away, go away secretly, pack off, make off quickly, run away, fly, steal away, escape, sneak off, take flight, take off, take to one's heels, quit, vacate, evacuate, make tracks, cut and run, vamoose, skedaddle, slip away, give leg bail, show a light pair of heels, make oneself scarce, take French leave, take congé.

DECANT, *v.* 1. Pour off gently, lade, dip, ladle, bale, draft off.

2. Pour from one container into another, transfuse, remove from a sediment by pouring.

3. Emit, transfer, unload.

DECAPITATE, *v.* 1. Chop off the head, behead, kill by beheading, decollate, bring to the block, bring to the scaffold, guillotine, bring under the headsman's ax, truncate, detruncate, send under the executioner's ax.

2. (*Colloq.*) Dismiss from office, give the sack to, discharge, dismiss, fire, turn out.

DECAPITATION, *n.* Beheading, decollation, sending to the block, truncation, detruncation, sending under the executioner's ax.

DECAY, *v.* 1. Fall away toward dissolution, fail, deteriorate, decline, be impaired, disintegrate, go bad, crumble, fall to pieces, fall into decay, fall off, molder, waste, wither, break up, wear away, perish, waste away, atrophy, degenerate, fade away, ebb, wane, dwindle, sicken, die.

2. Decompose, putresce, putrefy, rot, spoil, be spoiled.

3. Cause to decay, affect by decay, corrode, reduce to component elements.

DECAY, *n.* 1. Progressive decline, disintegration, gradual falling into an inferior condition, falling off, impairment, dilapidation, decrepitude, ruin, decadence, deterioration, caducity, degeneration, dissolution, gradual crumbling, disrepair, wasting away, wear and tear, retrogradation, labefaction, collapse, downfall, extinction, ruination, failure of body, loss of health, corruption, erosion, dry rot, corrosion, moth and rust consumption, the sear and yellow leaf, senescence.

2. Rotting, putrescence, putridity, putrefaction, decomposition, rottenness, cariosity, caries.

3. Failure of worldly prosperity, indigence, poverty.

DECEASE, *n.* Departure from this life, death, demise, dying, dissolution, expiration, extinction, extinguishment. (see DEATH.)

DECEASE, *v.* Depart from this life, die, perish, expire. (see DIE.)

DECEASED, *adj.* Lately dead, lifeless, defunct, departed from this life, late, recent, lost, gone, passed away, sleeping, asleep. (see DEAD.)

DECEIT, *n.* 1. Act of deceiving, concealment of truth, deception, fraudulence, perversion of truth, cheating, fraud, deceptiveness, deceitfulness, lie, imposition, imposture, falsehood, hypocrisy, dark and crooked ways, guile, finesse, duplicity, craft, wiliness, dissimulation, trickery, subtlety, hocus-pocus, chicanery, cozenage, cunning, trickiness, double-dealing, sophistry, intrigue, tergiversation, treachery, misrepresentation, underhandedness, pretense, hanky-panky, jugglery, circumvention, beguilement, trumpery, mendacity, collusion, knavery, insincerity, indirection, sharp practice.

2. Device intended to deceive, trick, stratagem, ruse. wile, artifice, blind, feint, chicane, juggle, swindle, hoax, fake, sham, contrivance.

DECEITFUL, *adj.* 1. Dissembling, false, guileful, fraudulent, treacherous, perfidious, untrustworthy, double-dealing, two-faced, wily, insincere, lying, hypocritical, disingenuous, faithless, intriguing, designing, insidious, cunning, crafty, artful, snaky, Punic, underhanded, indirect, tricky, dishonest, evasive, dodgy, circumventive, crooked, collusive, prevaricative, Janus-faced.

2. Illusive, illusory, misleading, delusive, mock, deceptive, fallacious, elusive, counterfeit, pseudo, hollow, specious, bogus, sham, make-believe, feigned, pretended.

DECEIVE, *v.* Mislead by false appearance, cog, delude, defraud, cheat, lead into error, fool, trick, bamboozle, take in, impose upon, hoax, humbug, hoodwink, outwit, circumvent, overreach, juggle, flimflam, chouse, swindle, victimize, bilk, decoy, beguile, play a trick on, steal a march on, take advantage of, pull wool over the eyes, make a fool of, dupe, cozen, gull, misinform, misguide, betray, play false, sell out, seduce, entrap, betray, ensnare, sail under false colors, throw dust in the eyes, palm off on.

DECEIVER, *n.* Sharper, swindler, trickster, cheat, knave, rogue, impostor, pretender, mountebank, charlatan, humbug, hoaxster, juggler, quack, liar, prevaricator, dissembler, cozener, circumventor, hypocrite, traitor, Judas, hoodwinker, misleader, fraud, deluder, defrauder, beguiler, bamboozler, duper, dodger, outwitter, shuffler, decoy, serpent, snake in the grass, cockatrice, wolf in sheep's clothing.

DECENCY, *n.* 1. Due regard for decorum, moral fitness, propriety, proper formality, etiquette, decorum, conformity to propriety, seemliness, appropriateness, suitableness, becomingness.

2. Freedom from obscenity, purity, modesty, delicacy of conduct, modest demeanor, virtue, respectability, continence, chastity, fineness, honor, pudicity.

DECENT, *adj.* 1. Characterized by propriety of conduct, decorous, seemly, befitting, proper, fitting, *comme il faut,* appropriate. mannerly, suitable, becoming.

2. Free from obscenity, chaste, pure, modest, virtuous, spotless, immaculate, unblemished, stainless, untarnished, clean, worthy, respectable, honest, upright, trustworthy, delicate.

3. Of seemly appearance, good-looking, fair, comely.

4. (*Colloq.*) Sufficient for a required purpose, fair, fairly good, passable, tolerable, mediocre, indifferent, ordinary, moderate, average, so-so, well-enough, not bad, respectable, competent, reasonably satisfying, considerable.

5. (*British*) Kind, obliging, accommodating, courteous.

DECEPTION, *n.* 1. Misleading by falsehood, act of deceiving, imposture, imposition, treachery, trickery, pretense, falsehood, lying, prevarication, mendacity, untruth, equivocation, double-dealing, dissimulation, dupery, hypocrisy, insincerity, indirection, circumvention, deceitfulness, finesse, guile, trickiness, trumpery, chicanery, cunning, beguilement, craft, deceit, cozenage, duplicity, craftiness, coggery, humbug, flimflam, juggling, defraudation.

2. Something that deceives, artifice, ruse, wile, stratagem, chouse, sham, cheat, subterfuge, hoax, fraud, trick, feint, blind, cog, swindle, fabrication, Trojan horse.

DECEPTIVE, *adj.* 1. Calculated to give a false impression, designed to mislead, deceitful, false, illusory, misleading, delusive, illusive, fallacious, specious, spurious, pseudo, counterfeit, hollow, bogus, make-believe, mock, hallucinatory.

2. Fraudulent, dishonest, lying, prevaricating, untrustworthy, hypocritical, insincere, deceitful, disingenuous, mendacious, slippery, tricky, wily.

DECIDE, *v.* 1. Form a resolution, settle in one's

mind, determine, conclude, establish, pass upon, fix, resolve, adjust, end by a decision, conclude, terminate, regulate, arrange, define, solve, unfold, unravel, disentangle.

2. Give judgment, pronounce, rule, pronounce a judgment, adjudge, adjudicate, hold, stipulate, come to a decision, weigh, arbitrate, umpire, referee, decree, judge, ascertain, make a decision.

3. Choose, fix upon, select, elect, make up one's mind which, prefer, have rather, had lief.

DECIDED, *adj.* 1. Free from ambiguity, beyond a doubt, unquestionable, unmistakable, clear-cut, undeniable, unequivocal, indisputable, certain, unqualified, categorical, emphatic, pronounced, positive, beyond all question, incontrovertible, past dispute, absolute, marked.

2. Exhibiting decision of character, free from hesitation, unhesitating, unwavering, settled, determined, decisive, resolute, firm, strong-willed, assertive, definitive.

DECIPHER, *v.* 1. Decode, bring out from a cipher, translate from secret characters, make out, interpret by the use of a key, disentangle, understand, construe, solve, unravel, reveal, read, expound, resolve, unfold, explain, render.

2. Find out the true meaning of, spell out, discover the meaning of, read between the lines.

DECISION, *n.* 1. Act of deciding, determination, conclusion, settlement, result arrived at after consideration, disposal, adjudication, outcome, arbitration, issue.

2. Recorded expression of a formal judgment, pronouncement by a court, that which is decided, judgment, opinion, finding, award, decree, order, sentence, verdict, ruling, edict.

3. Disposition to prompt action, volition, will, purpose, choice, making up one's mind, pluck, resolution, firmness of character, grit, constancy, steadfastness, hardihood.

DECISIVE, *adj.* 1. Putting an end to controversy, determinative, conclusive, definitive, determinant, final.

2. Characterized by decision, determined, resolute, positive, effectual, absolute, decided, prompt, summary, peremptory.

DECK, *v.* 1. Attire in something ornamental, array in finery, put clothes on, invest, cover, dress, apparel, clothe, robe.

2. Embellish, ornament, adorn, decorate, trick out, beautify, enrich, enhance, bedeck, bedizen, garnish, trim, spruce up, elaborate, emblazon, furbish, prink, prank, bedight, preen, spangle, paint, grace.

3. *(Naut.)* Cover with a deck, roof over, cover in.

DECLAIM, *v.* 1. Make a formal speech, deliver oratorically in public, speak rhetorically, orate, enunciate, perorate, harangue, hold forth, speak for oratorical effect, utter aloud in rhetorical manner, pronounce, proclaim, apostrophize, spellbind, lecture, sermonize, speechify *(colloq.).*

2. Deliver a memorized selection, repeat by heart, speak as an exercise in elocution, make a set speech, soliloquize.

3. Inveigh against, rail, denounce, rant, assail, attack, rebuke, reproach, speak against, decry, criticize, censure, rap out, rant, spout, mouth.

DECLAMATION, *n.* 1. Art of declaiming, rhetoric, oratory, elocution, enunciation, delivery, eloquence, command of words.

2. Reciting of a memorized selection, exercise

in oratory, selection, address, discourse, lecture, allocution, sermon, stump speech, recitation, oration, debate.

3. Bombastic oratory, speaking for mere display, altiloquence, magniloquence, mouthing, grandiloquence, impassioned delivery, haranguing, mouthing, ranting, spouting, tirade.

DECLAMATORY, *adj.* 1. Using a formal style of utterance, oratorical, rhetorical, elocutionary, characterized by declamation.

2. Bombastic, pompous, high-sounding, high-flown, altiloquent, grandiloquent, magniloquent, inflated, swelling, fustian, stilted, pretentious, turgid, grandiose, tumid, stagey, theatrical, formal.

DECLARATION, *n.* 1. Positive statement, formal assertion, explicit utterance, affirmation, avowal, averment, avouchment, asseveration, protestation, allegation, profession, deposition, disclosure, oath, acknowledgment, admission, attestation, word, testimony, enunciation, expression, presentation, remark, saying.

2. Public announcement, notification, report, official proclamation, publication, manifesto, pronunciamento, document, bulletin, notice.

DECLARATORY, *adj.* Serving to declare, making known, expressive, enunciative, affirmative, assertive, enunciatory, declarative, predicative, communicative, communicatory, manifesting, explanatory, expository, exegetical.

DECLARE, *v.* 1. Affirm explicitly, asseverate, assert formally, utter with conviction, enunciate, state emphatically, aver, avow, avouch, protest, profess, maintain, acknowledge, pronounce, make due statement of, propose, propound, depose, enounce, allege, divulge, mention, report, reveal, unfold, swear, predicate, assure, certify, give out, testify, tell.

2. Give evidence of, make known, manifest, reveal, disclose, show, signify.

3. Announce officially, proclaim, promulgate, advertise, blazon, bruit, communicate, publish, herald.

DECLINE, *v.* 1. Cause to slope downward, bend down, incline downward, depress, slope down, slant down, descend, sink down, dip down.

2. Stoop to an unworthy object, condescend, lower oneself, trend downward.

3. Turn aside, deviate, stray, diverge, withdraw.

4. Fail in strength, weaken, flag, sink, fail, languish, droop, pine, become feeble, worsen, lose ground, faint, waste, shrivel, wither, fade, crumble, molder, rot, decay.

5. Fail in value, depreciate, deteriorate, be impaired, degenerate, disintegrate, go bad, abate, retrograde, retrogress, hit the skids, be on the toboggan, go downhill.

6. Draw toward the close, wane, fade, ebb, dwindle, lapse, fall away, diminish, decrease, lessen, recede, age, fall into the sear and yellow leaf, die.

7. Withhold consent to do, express negation, negative, turn away, refuse, reject, avoid, fail to accept, shun, turn down, repudiate, veto, spurn, express courteous refusal, abstain from, forego, balk at, eschew, repel, disallow, disapprove.

DECLINE, *n.* 1. Deterioration, period of decrease, degeneration, decadence, gradual impairment, declination, gradual loss, falling off, diminution, declension, failing, abatement, retrogression, retrogradation, descent, lapse, depreciation.

2. Progress toward a close, ebb, wane, last part, dotage, senility, anility, caducity, oldness, age,

the sear and yellow leaf, superannuation, second childhood, debility, decrepitude.

3. Disease, wasting away, consumption, tabes, progressive emaciation, phthisis, languishment, atrophy, cachexia, marasmus, running down, ailment.

4. Downward tendency, down trend, down swing, tailspin, comedown, fall, plunge, slump, setback, downfall, tumble, debacle.

5. Downward incline, declivity, descent, dip, pitch, drop, downgrade.

DECLIVITY, *n.* 1. Downward slope, descending surface, declination, descent, pitch, dip, drop, incline, downgrade, fall, downhill.

2. Deviation from the horizontal, obliquity, inclination downwards, gradual descent of surface.

DECOMPOSE, *v.* 1. Separate into constituent parts, decompound, analyze, dissolve, disintegrate, resolve, decentralize, break up into its elements, reduce, hydrolyze, electrolyze.

2. Fall into decay, decay, undergo dissolution, rot, putresce, putrefy, spoil, become corrupt, go to pieces, crumble into dust.

DECOMPOSITION, *n.* 1. Catalysis, resolution, analysis of a compound into its original elements, breakdown, disintegration, break up, dissection, dissolution, proteolysis *(Physiol. Chem.)*, electrolysis, hydrolysis.

2. Putrefaction, putrescence, putridity, decay, crumbling, corruption, rotting, cariosity, caries, falling to pieces.

DECORATE, *v.* 1. Set off by ornamental accessories, adorn, ornament, furnish with something ornamental, deck, bedeck, garnish, embellish, beautify, bedizen, trick out, dress out, enrich, embroider, emblazon, beset, bestud, trim, elaborate, grace, chase, tool, prink, furbish, gild, polish, varnish, paint, enamel, bead, spangle.

2. Award a decoration to, confer distinction upon, honor with a medal, dignify.

DECORATION, *n.* 1. Act of decorating, decking, ornamentation, embellishment, beautification, adornment, enrichment, garnishment, bedizenment.

2. Ornament, garniture, trimming, finery, fretwork, tracery, filigree, arabesque, flourish, tooling, inlay, parquetry, figurework, embroidery, tinsel, spangle, gingerbread.

3. Mark of honor, badge of an order, medal, mark of distinction, insignia, regalia, trappings, emblem, laurel, palm, wreath, bays, cordon, ribbon, cross, coronet, star, garter, cockade, service stripe, epaulet, chevron, colors.

DECOROUS, *adj.* 1. Characterized by propriety, conventional, suitable for the occasion, correct, becoming, *comme il faut (Fr.)*, due, proper, fit, befitting, *en règle (Fr.)*, decent, seemly, meet, appropriate, formal, ceremonious.

2. Polite, mannerly, well-behaved, gentlemanly, genteel, respectful, deferential.

3. Calm, sedate, composed, serene, unruffled, quiet, settled, modest, demure, sober, steady, grave, regular.

DECORUM, *n.* 1. Requirement of polite society, etiquette, convention, formality, prescribed code of conduct, dictate of society, punctilio, protocol, act demanded by social custom, standard, code of what is fitting, good form, the thing, the proper thing.

2. That which is proper, fitness, congruity, appropriateness, orderliness, becomingness, duty, appropriate behavior, propriety, suitableness,

decency, seemliness, sedateness, respectability, modesty, conformity.

3. Good manners, mannerliness, breeding, *bienséance (Fr.)*, savoir-faire, politeness, gentility, respectful deportment.

DECOY, *v.* Attract by some deceptive device, lead into danger by artifice, lead by inducement, lure, allure, draw on, entice, inveigle, induce, bait on, entrap, ensnare, entangle, beguile, entrammel, seduce, tempt.

DECOY, *n.* Anything that allures into danger, deceptive stratagem, bait, enticement, allurement, lure, inducement, temptation, attraction, magnet, seduction, snare, trap, pitfall, gin, smokescreen.

DECREASE, *v.* 1. Cause to diminish, reduce, make less, attenuate, lessen, lower, curtail, take away, retrench, contract, abridge, shorten, shrink, abbreviate, defalcate, narrow, compress, scale down, minimize, slice, subtract, weaken, impair, whittle.

2. Diminish gradually, wane, ebb, subside, fall off, become less, lessen, decline, abate, ease, moderate, slacken, taper, dwindle, fall away, grow less, drop, sink, languish, waste, melt, depreciate, drop off, dip, wear, decay, crumble, degenerate, shrivel.

DECREASE, *n.* Gradual diminution, lessening, reduction, contraction, subtraction, shortening, declension, downward march, wane, ebb, loss, subsidence, decline, reflux, abatement, mitigation, cutback, waste, shrinkage, curtailment, sinking, abridgment, retrenchment, decrement, dwindling, depreciation, fall, falling off, deterioration, **decay**.

DECREE, *v.* Enjoin authoritatively, ordain, order, dictate, bid, charge, instruct, prescribe, command, appoint by law, enact, decide by decree, issue a judicial decision, determine, adjudge, abitrate, pronounce, rule, sentence, award, find, direct, authorize, regulate, sanction, set, require, exact, demand, inflict, impose, tax with, give orders, establish.

DECREE, *n.* Authoritative decision, dictum, fiat, mandate, manifesto, ordinance, statute, law, edict, enactment, order, regulation, command, act, direction, dictate, caveat, rescript, prescript, bull *(Eccl.)*, decretal, warrant, rule, ruling, writ, ukase, proclamation, dispensation, ordination, award, pronouncement, pronunciamento, assize, official promulgation, judicial decision, judgment, verdict, injunction, finding, sentence, institution, canon, firman.

DECREPIT, *adj.* Weakened by old age, aged, broken down with age, infirm because of age, superannuated, senile, anile, caducous, feeble, enfeebled by age, weakly, weakened, weak, old, ancient, broken in health, valetudinarian, worn, doddering, wasted, decayed, shattered, battered, faded, wilted, worn out, crippled, disabled, done up, palsied, emasculate, effete, laid on one's back, laid on the shelf, time-worn, weatherbeaten, the worse for wear, on its last legs, nodding to its fall, tumble-down, dilapidated, rickety, withered, tottering, shaken, *hors de combat (Fr.)*.

DECREPITATE, *v.* Make a crackling noise, snap, crackle, crepitate, pop.

DECREPITUDE, *n.* Broken state produced by the infirmities of age, infirmity of age, decrepit condition, decline of life, declining years, hoary age, superannuation, senescence, caducity, grand climacteric, vale of years, sear and yellow leaf, senile weakness, senility, anility, dotage, old age, feebleness, general breaking up, ravages of time, dilapidation, falling off, decadence, debility, retrogression, degeneration, deterioration, palsy, invalidation, disablement, incapacity, paralysis, helplessness, prostration.

DECRY, *v.* Speak disparagingly of, lessen the value of by public condemnation, pull to pieces, asperse, disparage, condemn as worthless, censure as faulty, criticize, depreciate publicly, underrate, discredit, knock *(colloq.),* rap *(colloq.),* defame, belittle, traduce, slander, denounce, cry down, deprecate, damn with faint praise, clamor against, run down, remonstrate against, undervalue, make little of, dispraise, bring into disrepute, degrade, bring discredit on, detract from, derogate, revile, malign, vilify, vilipend, blacken, denigrate, brand, backbite.

DEDICATE, *v.* 1. Devote exclusively to the service of religion, consecrate to a sacred purpose, set apart to a deity, hallow, sanctify, enshrine, deify, immortalize, apotheosize, lay on the altar, bless, signalize.

2. Direct energy toward, devote wholly, apply completely, give earnestly, appropriate devotedly, surrender to, offer.

3. Preface with a dedication to a patron, name by way of compliment, inscribe in testimony of affection, address a literary work to a friend.

DEDICATION, *n.* 1. Rite of dedicating to a deity, solemn appropriation, consecration to a deity, setting apart for sacred uses, religious devotion, ordination, enshrinement, deification, immortalization, apotheosis, glorification, celebration, canonization.

2. Voluntary relinquishment to a cause, close appliance, application, adhibition, resort, setting aside for a particular purpose.

3. Message affixed to a book, address, prefixed apostrophe, prefatory inscription.

DEDUCE, *v.* 1. Derive as a conclusion, draw as an implication, arrive at as the result of reasoning, conclude, infer as a necessary result, ratiocinate, reason, presume, gather, glean, collect, interpret, understand, comprehend, reckon, opine, suppose.

2. Trace the derivation of, track down the course of.

DEDUCIBLE, *adj.* Inferable, derivable, sequent, traceable, consequent, sequential, inferential, following.

DEDUCT, *v.* Take from, subtract, remove, take away, take out, abstract, diminish in sum, curtail, eliminate, shorten, remove from an amount, defalcate, separate from a sum, detract, reduce, decimate, retrench, subduct, abate, rebate, bate, allow, recoup, deprive of, weaken, pare, prune, lop off, file.

DEDUCTION, *n.* 1. Subtraction, diminution, taking away, abstraction, taking out, removal, withdrawal, excision, amputation, curtailment, abbreviation, retrenchment.

2. That which is deducted, abatement, offtake, allowance, discount, reduction, defalcation, tare, rebate, remission, subtrahend, recoupment, reprise.

3. Inference by reasoning from generals to particulars, syllogistic reasoning, conclusion, a priori reasoning, corollary, consequence, proof, induction, implication, derivation, illation, result, ratiocination, presumption, decision, effect, demonstration, development.

DEED, *n.* 1. That which is done, accomplishment,

act, action, gest, exploit, feat, achievement, step, *coup,* stroke, blow, move, maneuver, measure, performance, proceeding, perpetration, doing, dealing, job, transaction, effort, derring-do, turn, stunt, handiwork, workmanship, commission, work.

2. Certain fact, reality, actuality, truth.

3. *(Law)* Document executed under seal to effect a conveyance of real estate, indenture, charter, title deed, record, certificate, security, voucher, agreement, instrument.

DEEM, *v.* 1. Hold as an opinion, hold in belief, think, decide as a conclusion, consider, set down as, regard, suppose, believe, hold, look upon, view, calculate, judge, account, count, imagine, estimate, presume.

2. Form an opinion, be of opinion, fancy, take it, opine, conceive, repute, ween, surmise, be cognizant of, become aware.

DEEP, *adj.* 1. Having depth, extending far downward, down-reaching, profound, abysmal, of great depth, bottomless, fathomless, down far, depthless, extending to a depth, immeasurable, yawning, high, reaching backward, having a specified dimension inward, lying below the surface, underground, submerged, subterranean, inmost, buried, deep-seated, rooted.

2. Hard to comprehend, difficult to understand, not obvious, recondite, abstruse, obscure, esoteric, incomprehensible, inexplicable, occult, secret, hidden, involved, knotty, intricate, mysterious, unfathomable.

3. Having penetrating intellectual powers, intelligent, sagacious, shrewd, astute, discerning, learned, wise, philosophical, artful, subtle, skilled, scheming, designing, insidious, profoundly cunning.

4. Characterized by close occupation, absorbed, rapt, much involved, engrossed, immersed, intent, entangled.

5. *(Of sound)* Low in pitch, of sonorous tone, bass, not high, not sharp, full-toned, grave, heavy, resonant, guttural, full-rumbling.

6. *(Of colors)* Of dark hue, not light, intense, rich, extreme, vivid, intensified, dense, strong, dark.

7. *(Of emotions)* Not superficial, heartfelt, profound, earnest, poignant, sincere, serious, great, extreme, complete, thorough, entire.

8. *(Of sleep)* Sound, fast, undisturbed, dead, strong, heavy.

DEEP, *n.* 1. Briny deep, main, ocean, sea, abyss of waters.

2. A deep space, vast expanse, immeasurable extent, depth, abyss, profundity, deepest part, bottom, recess.

3. Part of greatest intensity, most profound part, stillest part, inmost part, midst, stillness, silence.

4. Acme, zenith, apex, culmination.

5. Something too abstruse to be comprehended, mystery, enigma, profound riddle, conundrum.

DEEPEN, *v.* 1. Make deeper, increase the depth of, burrow, excavate, mine, sap, dig, sink.

2. Make darker, make more intense, darken, intensify, increase, enhance, strengthen, make more vivid, heighten, make more impressive.

3. Reduce to a lower pitch, make graver, lower, depress.

4. Become deeper, grow deeper, become more decided, become intenser.

DEEPLY, *adv.* 1. Profoundly, at a great depth,

deep, far down, far below the surface, with depth, far in.

2. Not superficially, to a great extent, greatly, very much, intensely, acutely, in high degree, passionately, soundly, thoroughly, completely, entirely, profoundly.

3. Far on in time or place.

4. At a low pitch, with a deep tone, sonorously, resonantly.

5. Richly colored, vividly, urgently.

6. Skillfully, artfully, intricately.

7. Gravely, seriously, out of one's depth, over head and ears, beyond one's depth.

DEFACE, v. 1. Mar the appearance of, impair the looks of, disfigure, deform, mutilate, blotch, distort, mangle, blemish, scar, damage, injure, warp, lacerate, spoil, make unsightly, blot, daub, sully, soil, tarnish, stain, spot, mark, bruise, blur, maim, blacken, foul, begrime.

2. Blot out, cancel, obliterate, efface, erase, impair the legibility of.

DEFACEMENT, n. 1. Disfigurement, mutilation, injury to outward appearance, deformation, scar, impairment, distortion, deformity, ravage, soiling, marring, damage, blemish, discoloration, wear and tear, oxidation, vandalism, erosion, eyesore.

2. Obliteration, erasure, cancellation, effacement.

DE FACTO 1. In reality, really, as a matter of fact, in fact, actually.

2. Actually existing, really done, real, actual.

DEFALCATE, v. 1. Take away, deduct, curtail, reduce, abate, retrench, cut off, lop off, prune off.

2. Misappropriate money, embezzle money held in trust, fall short.

DEFALCATION, n. 1. Reduction, deduction, set off, lopping off, diminution, abatement, discount, curtailment, shortening, falling off, decrease.

2. Misappropriation of money, reduction of a claim by deducting a counterclaim, shortage, shortcoming, falling short, delinquency, the sum misappropriated, deficiency, default, deficit, failure, fault, fraudulent shortage, breach of trust, embezzlement, nonpayment.

DEFAMATION, n. Unjustified injury to another's reputation, slander, obloquy, false accusation, calumny, libel, detraction, backbiting, aspersion, insinuation, innuendo, abuse, disparagement, derogation, revilement, scandal, reflection, slur, imputation, tarnish, badge of infamy, traducement, vilification.

DEFAMATORY, adj. Injurious to reputation, slanderous, libelous, calumnious, disparaging, abusive, contumelious, disapprobatory, condemnatory, denunciatory, traducing, detractory, scandalous, discreditable, derogatory, vituperative, depreciatory.

DEFAME, v. Attack the good reputation of, cast aspersions on the good fame of, injure the good name of, slander, malign, call names, denigrate, calumniate, abuse, traduce, run down, vilipend, vilify, revile, execrate, speak ill of, libel, smirch, blemish, blacken, disparage, stigmatize, brand, gibbet, sneer at, blackball, blacklist, ostracize, boycott, tarnish, sully, taint, dishonor, degrade, discredit, backbite, detract from, damn, reproach, vituperate, slur, besmirch, bring disrepute upon, disgrace.

DEFAULT, n. 1. Omission of what is due, lapse, failure to act, neglect, fault, shortcoming,

wrongdoing, transgression, imperfection, oversight.

2. Want, absence, lack, deficiency, defect, destitution.

3. Embezzlement, failure to pay, nonpayment, misappropriation, defalcation.

DEFAULT, v. 1. Fail to pay, defalcate, swindle, embezzle, not pay, welsh (colloq.), stop payment, be in arrears, be in debt, fail in satisfying a claim, fail to meet financial engagements, fail to account properly for money, be guilty of defalcation.

2. Fail to keep one's contract, break one's trust, fail to perform, neglect, pass by, back down, lose by failure to appear, lose by default.

DEFAULTER, n. 1. Defalcator, embezzler, lame duck (Stock Exchange), peculator, swindler, insolvent, bankrupt.

2. One who fails to fulfill an obligation, welsher (colloq.), delinquent, offender, misdoer, reprobate.

DEFEAT, v. 1. Gain a victory over an opponent, conquer, ruin by victory, overthrow, overcome in contest, win over, rout, disperse, upset, best, subjugate, worst, overpower, overwhelm, beat, vanquish, prevail over, quell, crush, thrash, outdo, repulse, outwit, floor, lick (colloq.), drub, trim (colloq.), master, reduce, outplay, drive off, sack, rebuff, gain control over, put down, subdue, outmaneuver, outgeneral, surmount.

2. Prevent the accomplishment of, bring to naught, resist successfully, frustrate, block, check, foil, thwart, confound, baffle, nonplus, balk, disconcert, elude, disappoint, discomfit, drive to the wall, checkmate, nullify, counteract, refute, rebut, silence, subvert, get the better of, squelch, demolish, circumvent, deprive of something expected.

3. (Law) Annul, make void, render null and void, vacate.

DEFEAT, n. 1. Act of overcoming in contest, overthrow, loss of a contest, rout, downfall, ruin, vanquishment, repulse, rebuff, subjugation, conquest, discomfiture, beating, drubbing, overcoming, overpowering, reverse, outwitting, failure to win, perdition, deathblow, fiasco, breakdown, collapse.

2. Bafflement, frustration, checkmate, no go, bringing to naught, undoing, abortion, failure, nonsuccess, loss, disappointment, circumvention, thwarting, miscarriage.

DEFECATE, v. 1. Free from impurities, clear of dregs, clarify, refine, purify, purge of extraneous matter, make void of impurities, strain, cleanse, expurgate, depurate, cast off impurities.

2. Relieve oneself, go to stool, evacuate the bowels, void excrement, excrete.

DEFECATION, n. 1. Separation from impurities, purification, cleansing, purgation, clarification, refining.

2. Evacuation of the bowels, going to stool, fecal discharge, voiding excrement, dejection (Med.), cacation, dysentery.

DEFECT, n. 1. Lack, want, deficiency, absence of something essential to completeness, omission, shortcoming, shortage, destitution, insufficiency, inadequacy, default, incompleteness, falling short, failure.

2. Weakness, error, mistake, infirmity, failing, frailty, vice, foible, demerit, weak point, fault, besetting sin, weak side, blind side.

3. Imperfection, blemish, birthmark, cicatrice,

flaw, injury, deformity, scar, stain, spot, blotch, blot, speck, patch, seam, crack, rift, rough spot, break, eyesore.

4. (Psychol.) Subnormal development of intelligence, subnormality.

DEFECT, v. Abandon allegiance, desert from obedience, break fealty, fall away from duty, revolt, secede, withdraw from, mutiny, disobey, fall off, backslide, apostasize, forsake, leave in the lurch, back out of, go back on one's word, recant, quit, take leave of, vacate, bid a long farewell, throw up the game.

DEFECTION, n. 1. Abandonment of allegiance, breaking of fealty, falling away from duty, forsaking of a cause, relinquishment, desertion, withdrawal, revolt, mutiny, sedition, secession, treason, abandonment.

2. Backsliding, recidivism, apostasy, falling off, dereliction, unfaithfulness, faithlessness, perfidy, renunciation, abrogation, recantation.

3. Failure, lack, failing, loss, deficiency in duty.

DEFECTIVE, adj. 1. Lacking, deficient, failing, insufficient, unfinished, inadequate, falling short, incomplete, below par, scanty, short, attenuated, exiguous, meager, slim, wanting in something essential.

2. Having a defect, imperfect, marred, faulty, flawed, impaired, unsound, infirm, weak, poor, inefficient, bad, inaccurate, improper, incorrect, erroneous, garbled, broken, bruised, blemished, disfigured, injured, distorted, hashed, mutilated, out of order, warped, deformed.

3. (Psychol.) Feeble-minded, imbecilic, idiotic, characterized by subnormal intelligence, moronic, half-witted, unsound.

DEFEND, v. 1. Guard against assault, accouter, repel danger from, ward off attack from, resist invasion, stand on the defensive, show fight, save, stand one's ground, safeguard from attack, secure from danger, protect, fortify, shelter, garrison, screen, cover, watch over, keep safe, keep at bay, preserve, parry, fend, man, arm.

2. Stand up for, make a stand for, uphold, maintain by argument, vindicate, justify, stand by, sustain, apologize for, plead, advocate, rally to, champion, support, second, aid, patronize, endorse, espouse, bolster.

DEFENDER, n. 1. Protector, preserver, warden, savior, champion, guardian, bodyguard, keeper, watchman, convoy, escort, friend.

2. Vindicator, upholder, apologist, advocate, justifier, pleader, seconder, maintainer, patron, asserter.

DEFENSE, n. 1. Protection, security, safeguard, custody, maintenance, preservation, guardianship, guard, care, ward, resistance against attack.

2. Means of warding off attack, bulwark, wall, rampart, shelter, fortification, parapet, earthwork, screen, fosse, moat, ditch, entrenchment, dugout, trench, embankment, levee, mine, redoubt, cover, breastwork, battlement, bastion, palisade, covert, buttress, stockade, barricade, barbed wire, citadel, fastness, stronghold, fortress, blockhouse, armor, pill box, muniment, mail, cuirass, arms, shield, aegis, buckler, palladium, tower of strength.

3. Defending of a cause by argument, speech in vindication, argument, apology, plea, excuse, extenuation, vindication, justification, upholding, support, espousal, advocacy.

DEFENSELESS, adj. Destitute of defense, weak, exposed, vulnerable, unfortified, unshielded, sine

ictu (Lat.), unprotected, unsheltered, uncovered, unguarded, unarmed, weaponless, expugnable, powerless, naked, helpless, vincible, pregnable, impotent, insecure, unsafe, precarious.

DEFENSIBLE, adj. 1. Capable of being defended against assault, unattackable, unassailable, armed at all points, invulnerable, impregnable, ironclad, invincible, founded upon a rock, bullet-proof, shell-proof, bomb-proof, panoplied, accoutered, armored, mailed, steel-plated.

2. Capable of being defended by argument, defendable, supportable, justifiable, maintainable, tenable, excusable, allowable, vindicable, venial, pardonable, permissible.

DEFER, v. 1. Decide to do something later on, postpone, procrastinate, put off to a later time, adjourn, suspend, delay, prorogue, remand, stave off, lay over, table, shelve, refrain from action, temporize, filibuster, protract, prolong, respite, dally, wait, retard.

2. Look up to one more competent, submit in judgment to, yield in opinion to, refer, submit for determination, accord superiority to, give in, obey, capitulate, surrender, cede, accede, comply, acquiesce, yield out of respect, give way, give ground.

3. Pay deference to, pay respect to, venerate, think highly of, respect, value, revere.

DEFERENCE, n. 1. Obedience, submission to the judgment of another, compliance, acquiescence, yielding to another's opinion, acceptance, cession, resignation, surrender, capitulation, complaisance, nonresistance, condescension.

2. Respectful regard, esteem, respect, homage, veneration, reverence, consideration, admiration, honor, regardfulness, obeisance, kowtow, civility, politeness.

DEFERENTIAL, adj. Marked by deference, cap in hand, respectful, reverential, obeisant, polite, ceremonious, gentlemanly, courteous, obsequious, attentive, civil, urbane, suave, obedient, dutiful, subservient, submissive, compliant, complaisant, acquiescent, regardful.

DEFERMENT, n. Delay, postponement, reprieve, procrastination, cunctation, wait, putting off, stay, respite, pause, moratorium, suspension, Fabian policy, adjournment, prorogation, prolongation, remand, retardation, protraction, filibuster.

DEFIANCE, n. 1. Challenge to meet in contest, invitation to combat, dare, defial, provocation, gage, bravado, outdaring, confronting, bearding, facing down, impudence, stump (colloq.), threat, intimidation, declaration of hostilities.

2. Disposition to resist, noncompliance, open disregard, opposition, contumacy, disobedience, recalcitrance, bold resistance to authority, despite, contempt, contemptuous resistance, recusancy, spite, waywardness, insubordination, insurgency, insubmission, mutiny, sedition, rebellion, tumult, revolt, uprising, riot, strike, rebelliousness, war cry, sabotage, stubbornness, willingness to fight, war whoop.

DEFIANT, adj. Characterized by bold opposition, resistant, insubmissive, recalcitrant, disobedient, challenging, audacious, bold, provocative, unruly, insolent, contumacious, headstrong, contumelious, obstinate, stubborn, unyielding, recusant, restive, dissentient, antagonistic, ungovernable, undutiful, refractory, scornful, disregardful, devil-may-care, contemptuous, regardless of consequences, lawless, insubordinate, mutinous, rebellious, threatening.

DEFICIENCY, *n.* 1. Insufficiency, incompleteness, inadequacy, shortage, scantiness, scarcity, deficit, meagerness, dearth, lack, want, default, absence, short supply, falling short, paucity, destitution, penury, poverty, indigence.

2. Failing, defect, frailty, flaw, imperfection, infirmity, shortcoming, faultiness, weakness, weak side, blind spot, foible, error, fault.

3. *(Psychol.)* Feeble-mindedness, subnormality.

DEFICIENT, *adj.* Insufficient, defective, lacking, lacking some element, imperfect, not up to par, not up to normal standard, inadequate, hollow, wanting in some characteristic, incomplete, short, scanty, meager, scarce, attenuated, impaired, bad, destitute, exiguous, sketchy, failing, faulty, weak, inferior, flawed, unfinished, unsatisfactory, minus, needed to make up completeness, in arrear.

DEFICIT, *n.* Amount short of what is required, shortage, deficiency in amount, falling short in amount, impairment of capital, financial shortage, arrears, deferred payment, default, bad debt.

DEFILE, *n.* Narrow passage between mountains, long narrow pass, ravine, gorge, gully, canyon, chasm, crevasse, abysm, hollow, basin, clough, gulf.

DEFILE, *v.* 1. Make unclean, dirty, soil, befoul, render filthy, spot, smear, blot, blur, smudge, smirch, draggle, spatter, begrime, besmear, daub, spoil, maculate, inquinate, stain, tarnish.

2. Corrupt the purity of, pollute, contaminate, infect, poison, make impure, vitiate, debase, taint, deprave, degrade, dishonor, sully, demoralize, asperse, darken, blacken.

3. Violate the chastity of, deprive of virginity, debauch, ravish, abuse sexually, force, mistreat, assault, attack, seduce, deflower, prostitute, rape, stuprate.

4. Make ceremonially unclean, profane, treat sacrilegiously, direct to unholy uses, desecrate.

5. March in single file, file off.

DEFILEMENT, *n.* 1. Contamination, pollution, infection, uncleanness, foulness, filth, maculation, taint, sullying, inquination, smudging, spotting, besmirching, smearing, begriming.

2. Debasement, degradation, depravation, vice, corruption, vitiation, demoralization, turpitude, depravity, wickedness, desecration.

3. Debauchery, seduction, stupration, forced intercourse, defloration, violation, rape, sexual abuse, fornication, prostitution, incest.

DEFINABLE, *adj.* 1. Determinable, appreciable, ascertainable, visible, perceptible, describable.

2. Finite, definite, clear-cut, specific, precise, fixed, exact.

DEFINE, *v.* 1. Mark the limits of, limit, delimit, determine the boundaries of, bound, mark out with exactness, demarcate, bring out clearly the limits of, circumscribe, encompass, compass, set bounds to, fix the limits of.

2. State the meaning of, translate, spell out, set forth the signification of, render, literalize, construe, expound, interpret, explain, throw light upon, popularize.

3. Determine the essential qualities of, explain the nature of, describe the properties of, delineate, depict the essential qualities of, exemplify, style, characterize precisely, illustrate, specify, entitle, denominate, designate, distinguish by name, label.

4. Fix with precision, determine exactly, bring into relief, make clear the outline of, establish by authority, fix, prescribe.

DEFINITE, *adj.* 1. Having fixed limits, limited, circumscribed, determinate, definitive, particular, fixed, strictly defined, bounded with precision, concrete, literal, textual.

2. Unmistakable in meaning, clearly defined, not vague, not general, precise, exact, certain, explicit, express, unequivocal, unqualified, plain, clear-cut, sharp-cut, indisputable, well-grounded, conclusive, decisive, absolute, confirmed, graphic, manifest, positive, obvious, known with exactness, categorical, accurate, well-defined, correct, valid, scientific, meticulous, punctilious, substantial, solid.

DEFINITION, *n.* 1. Determining of the boundary, circumscription, encompassment, delimitation, demarcation.

2. Formal statement of meaning, explanation of meaning, defining, interpretation, elucidation, rendering, explication, exposition, *éclaircissement (Fr.)*, exegesis, exact meaning, translation, illustration, commentary, explanation, diagnosis, analogue, synonym.

3. Clarity of outline, sharp relief, distinctness of detail, fixed shape, discernibleness, apparency, perceptibility, manifestation, clearness, visibility, conspicuousness, sharp demarcation of outlines.

DEFINITIVE, *adj.* 1. Serving to settle finally, having the function of settling, limiting extent, final, conclusive, terminative, decisive, bringing to an end, crowning, ultimate, exhaustive, perfect, complete, thorough, mature, consummate.

2. Clearly defined, positive, explicit, express, decided, determinate, categorical, unconditional, affirmative, exact, absolute, emphatic.

DEFLATE, *v.* 1. Release air from, empty, reduce by removal of air, collapse, exhaust, flatten, blow out, shrink, contract, constrict, squeeze, puncture.

2. Prick the ego, humiliate, humble, chagrin, mortify, take the wind out of the sails, take down a peg, bring down from one's high horse.

3. Reduce currency from an inflated condition, devalue, depreciate.

DEFLECT, *v.* 1. Cause to turn aside, cause to deviate, bend, turn aside, press down, refract, divert from a course, curve, crook, flex, twist, shift, switch.

2. Deviate from a straight line, turn from a true course, diverge, swerve, bear off, alter the course, gybe, yaw *(Naut.)*, go about, sheer, tack *(Naut.)*, sidle, edge, veer, wheel, shy, glance off, sidetrack, divaricate, divagate, waver, fluctuate, fork, heel.

DEFLECTION, *n.* Deviation from a straight line, turning aside, bending, divergence, swing, curve, digression, divagation from a given course, crook, diversion, aberration, variation, declination, sheer, swerve, sweep, drift, warp, ramification, forking, divarication, by-pass.

DEFLOWER, *v.* 1. Despoil of chastity, debauch, ravish, rape, force, assault, attack, abuse sexually, mistreat, seduce, deprive of virginity, corrupt to lewdness, stuprate, violate, dishonor, defile.

2. Strip of flowers, rob of its first bloom, rob of charm, ravage, despoil, spoil, deprive of its freshness, render unattractive.

DEFORM, *v.* 1. Spoil the form of, misproportion, render misshapen, mar the natural form of, knot, disfigure, deface, injure, distort, contort, put out of shape, malform, twist, gnarl, warp, mutilate, cripple, mangle, maim, blemish, damage, bend, hurt, misshape.

2. Metamorphose, transmogrify, change the form of, transform.

DEFORMED, *adj.* 1. Misshapen, bowed, warped, misproportioned, ill-proportioned, curved, awry, distorted, contorted, unnatural in form, twisted, gnarled, malformed, unshapely, askew, grotesque, irregular, crooked, crippled, lame, ill-shaped, ill-made, humpbacked, hunchbacked, splayfooted, kyphotic *(Med.)*, clubfooted, taliped.
2. Hateful, offensive, vile, depraved, hideous, monstrous, gross, loathsome, repulsive, revolting, ugly, unsightly.

DEFORMITY, *n.* 1. Deformation, disfigurement, defacement, distortion, contortion, malformation, misshapenness, crookedness, misproportion, knot, disfiguration, unshapeliness, imperfection, screw, crookedness, twisting, obliquity, asymmetry, lack of beauty, anamorphosis, kyphosis *(Med.)*, warp, twist, irregularity of feature, grimace, ugliness, unsightliness, eyesore, blemish, monstrosity.
2. Deviation from propriety, impropriety, gross departure from standard, irregularity, corruption, aesthetic flaw.
3. Hatefulness, depravity, vileness, grossness.

DEFRAUD, *v.* Take by fraud, trick, bilk, chouse, deprive dishonestly, bamboozle, rook, victimize, fleece, swindle, skin, humbug, hoax, gull, dupe, deceive, cheat, hoodwink, circumvent, overreach, cozen, fool, delude, juggle, beguile, impose upon, outwit, take in, mislead.

DEFRAY, *v.* Make payment for, pay the expenses of, meet with payment, settle, bear the costs of, discharge, liquidate, disburse, foot the bill, clear, adjust, remit, satisfy.

DEFRAYAL, *n.* Payment of expenses, quittance, defrayment, settlement of charges, discharge of costs, clearance, liquidation.

DEFT, *adj.* Neat in action, adroit, dexterous, apt, handy, skillful, slick, clever, able, proficient, dab, ingenious, good at, at home in, a good hand at, *au fait (Fr.)*, neat-handed, fine-fingered, expert, quick, ready, resourceful, light, nimble.

DEFUNCT, *adj.* 1. Gone out of existence, dead, deceased, extinct, departed, exanimate, lifeless, clay-cold. (See DEAD.)
2. Inoperative, inactive, not in force, not in action, idle, not working, inefficacious, annulled, void, abrogated, canceled.

DEFY, *v.* 1. Bid defiance to, dare, brave, outface, confront, face, beard, twist the lion's tail, fling down the gauntlet, gage, square off, assume a fighting attitude, declare hostilities on, stand up against, provoke to action, goad to contest.
2. Act in contempt of, resist openly, oppose, disregard, flout, scorn, slight, set at naught, bite the thumb at, disdain, despise, spurn, contemn, snap the fingers at, fly in the face of, trample on, set at defiance, laugh to scorn, mock, taunt, treat with contempt.
3. Offer effective resistance to, resist attempts at, withstand, stand up under, stand against, resist one's power.

DEGENERACY, *n.* 1. Becoming worse, caducity, deterioration, degeneration, declension, vitiation, decline, disintegration, impairment, depravation, corruption, decadency, retrogression, falling off, retrogradation, degradation, depravity, decrease, demoralization, degenerateness.
2. Abasement, low estate, abjection, poorness, lowness, meanness, inferiority, debasement, baseness.

DEGENERATE, *v.* Sink to a lower condition, become notably worse, worsen, decline from a former state, sink, retrograde, deteriorate, grow worse, become impaired, become depraved, wane, run down, ebb, retrogress, fall off, droop, wither, become enfeebled, run to seed, rot, disintegrate, crumble, putresce, go bad, lapse, fail, become perverted.

DEGENERATE, *adj.* Sunken in character, mean, depraved, degraded, corrupt, decadent, worthless, vicious, vice-ridden, low-down, ignoble, debased, base, fallen, deteriorated, inferior, worse, effete, good-for-nothing.

DEGRADATION, *n.* 1. Reduction in rank, fall from repute, demotion, deposition, deprival of honor, dismissal from office, stripping of caste, dishonor, shame, disgrace, ignominy, humiliation, disrepute, discredit, derogation, removal from standing.
2. Reduced condition, depravity, corruption, vitiation, degeneration, deterioration, decadence, perversion, baseness, turpitude, meanness, abasement.
3. *(Geol.)* Wearing away of rocks, abrasion, erosion.

DEGRADE, *v.* 1. Lower in rank, remove from office, take away position from, strip of rank, deprive of caste, reduce to inferior rank, cashier, dedecorate, bust *(colloq.)*, kick upstairs *(colloq.)*, drum out, expel, mortify, humble, humiliate, uncrown, dethrone, demote, depose, disrate, cast out, break, abase, bring low, discredit, disgrace, dishonor, bring shame upon, bring into disrepute, diminish in esteem, unfrock.
2. Debase the nature of, vitiate, deprave, sink, pervert, injure, lower in character, impair, alloy, corrupt, contaminate, adulterate, pollute, lessen in value, degenerate, deteriorate, depreciate, tone down, make mean.

DEGRADED, *adj.* Depraved, degenerate, scurvy, debased, base, abandoned, mean, shabby, abject, disreputable, déclassé, dishonorable, outcast, vile, rascally, low-down, inferior, sordid, low-minded, corrupt, vicious, worthless, fallen, contemptible, coarse, indelicate, gross, vulgar.

DEGREE, *n.* 1. Step in a series, rung, stair, peg, gradation, point, mark, stage of advancement, point arrived at in a process, grade.
2. Rank of social advancement, station in life, standing, class, caste, order, sphere, estate, sort, quality, standard, post, situation, condition, lot, position, manner.
3. Relative amount, certain proportion, extent, measure, rate, quantity, scale, ratio, quota, pitch, height, plane.
4. Reach, range, scope, caliber, tenor, compass.
5. Division, space, line, interval.
6. Shade, strength, intensity.
7. Literary or collegiate distinction, grade in letters, literary title, stage in Freemasonry, distinction, qualification.
8. *(Genetics)* Remove in the line of descent, distance determining the proximity of blood, relationship between persons in the line of descent.

DEHISCE, *v.* Gape open, open, gape, yawn, bulge, burst open.

DEHISCENCE, *n.* Opening, gaping, patefaction, foramen, aperture, hiation, yawning, oscitancy, pandiculation.

DEHISCENT, *adj.* Opening wide, gaping open, wide open, yawning, agape, oscitant, patent.

DEHYDRATE, *v.* Free from moisture, desiccate, dry completely, exsiccate, deprive of water, parch, anhydrate, drain.

DEIFICATION, *n.* Immortalization, apotheosis, exaltation to divine honors, endowing with divine existence, idolization, canonization, celebration, enshrinement, glorification, consecration.

DEIFY, *v.* 1. Immortalize, apotheosize, exalt to the rank of a deity, make a god of, enroll among deities, place among the gods, raise to godhood, render divine, consecrate, enshrine, enthrone, put on a pedestal, worship, adore, canonize, venerate, burn incense to, make sacrifice to, idolatrize, prostrate oneself before, celebrate.

2. Treat as an object of supreme regard, extol, idolize, cherish idolatrously, revere as if a deity, hymn the praises of, elevate, ennoble, exalt, make godlike.

DEIGN, *v.* Deem in accordance with one's dignity, stoop so far as to grant, condescend, think fit, see fit, allow with condescension, deem worthy of notice, vouchsafe, grant, accord.

DEITY, *n.* 1. Divinity, Godhead, Supreme Being, The Divine Nature, Omnipotence, Omniscience, Providence, The Almighty, The Creator, I Am, The All-Father, The Absolute, The First Cause, The Lord of Lords, The King of Kings, Author of All, The All-Powerful, The All-Knowing, The Infinite, The Eternal.

2. God, demiurge, goddess, divine being, idol, tutelary genius, familiar spirit, genius, lares and penates, avatar, fetish, joss, golden calf, graven image.

DEJECT, *v.* Cast down in spirit, dispirit, depress the spirits of, discourage, dishearten, make sad, sadden, make despondent, damp the spirits, put in the doldrums, put in the dumps, break one's heart, dash one's hopes, prey on the mind, sink, unman, prostrate, dull.

DEJECTED, *adj.* Depressed in spirits, gloomy, low-spirited, downhearted, melancholy, funereal, despondent, hypochondriacal, woebegone, dismal, heavy-hearted, sorrowful, disheartened, spiritless, dispirited, blue, sad, forlorn, cheerless, unhappy, desolate, discouraged, out of heart, cast down, heartsick, crestfallen, mournful, chapfallen, wan, doleful, down in the mouth, lachrymose, in the dumps, disconsolate, hipped, somber, long-faced, grim-visaged, rueful, careworn, broken-hearted, lackadaisical, prostrate, hopeless, wretched, glum, sorry, crushed, defeated, moody, morose, mopish, saturnine.

DEJECTION, *n.* Melancholy, hypochondria, blue devils, pessimism, despondency, hopelessness, depression, despair, dolor, sorrow, sadness, blues, dolefulness, gloom, mopishness, dumps, vapors, doldrums, heaviness, weariness, lowness of spirits, disgust of life, discouragement, low spirits, slough of Despond, brokenheartedness, disconsolateness.

DEJEUNER, *n.* *(Fr.)* 1. First meal of the day, morning meal, breakfast.

2. Luncheon *(in Continental use),* collation, lunch.

DE JURE *(Lat.)* By a lawful title, by right, by right of law, according to law, of right, by law, rightfully, legally.

DELAY, *n.* 1. Postponement, deferment, putting off to a future time, procrastination, adjournment, prorogation, suspension, moratorium, cunctation, remand, respite, reprieve, demurral, Fabian policy.

2. Dalliance, dawdling, dilatoriness, tardiness, lagging, loitering, lingering, tarrying, waiting, stay.

3. Hindrance to progress, retardation, setback, suspension of progress, stoppage, obstacle, knot, obstruction, impediment, snag, hitch, hampering, interruption, detention, prevention, inhibition, determent, restriction.

DELAY, *v.* 1. Put off to a later time, pigeonhole, procrastinate, postpone, adjourn, defer, prorogue, suspend, remand, lay over, stave off, filibuster, table, shelve.

2. Cause to move with undue slowness, check, impede the progress of, hinder, retard, interrupt, detain, arrest temporarily, suspend, deter, stay, put on the brake, interfere, hamper, encumber, hold up, stop, prolong, protract, cause to arrive late, clog, choke, keep back, slacken, obstruct, restrain, confine, prevent, inhibit, restrict.

3. Move slowly, linger, loiter, tarry, stop for a time, lag, take time, dally, dillydally, dawdle, shillyshally, stall, temporize, poke, stay behind, wait.

DELECTABLE, *adj.* Highly pleasing, giving great pleasure, pleasurable, full of enjoyment, delicious, pleasant, gratifying, titillating, enjoyable, thrilling, ravishing, charming, agreeable, delightful to the senses, palatable.

DELECTATION, *n.* Pleasure, delight, enjoyment, pleasurableness, gratification, great pleasure, joy, ravishment, rapture, ecstasy, felicity, refreshment, bliss, gladness, diversion, refection, entertainment.

DELEGATE, *n.* Deputy, representative, minister, one empowered to act for another, commissioner, agent, envoy, legate, regent, viceroy, emissary, consul, ambassador, plenipotentiary, appointee, proxy, substitute, alternate, surrogate.

DELEGATE, *v.* 1. Send as deputy, appoint as representative, deputize, commission, name, send on an embassy, nominate.

2. Entrust to the care of another, authorize, commit powers to another as agent, empower, accredit, invest, charge, assign, consign, depute, entrust, transfer.

DELEGATION, *n.* 1. Appointment of a delegate, nomination, commissioning, commitment, charge, deputization, entrustment, ordination, installation, investiture, authorization, mandate, sending away, trust, investing with authority.

2. Body of delegates, mission, embassy, people delegated, deputation, legation, deputies.

DELETE, *v.* Take out, strike out, rub out, wipe out, blot out, remove, erase, expunge, eradicate, cancel, obliterate, omit, elide, destroy, efface, dele.

DELETERIOUS, *adj.* 1. Destructive, lethal, fatal, deadly, pestilential, pestiferous, ruinous, baleful, malignant, baneful, noxious, poisonous, mortal, toxic, venomous, virulent, morbiferous.

2. Injurious to health, unhealthful, pernicious, detrimental, insalubrious, bad, harmful, hurtful, unwholesome, prejudicial, disadvantageous, foul, nocuous, mephitic, septic, noisome.

DELIBERATE, *adj.* 1. Carefully weighed, wary, characterized by reflection, maturely considered, well-advised, dispassionate, not rash, not sudden, determined, thoughtful, considerate, shrewd, discreet, cool, prudent, attentive, slow in deciding, careful, circumspect, cautious.

2. Planned in advance, purposed, intentional, done on purpose, premeditated, prepense, studied, aforethought, prearranged, wilful, not happening

by chance, voluntary, designed, calculated, cold-blooded, predeterminate, predesigned, resolved, reasoned, pondered, cut-and-dried, done with full realization of what one is doing.

3. Slow-gaited, slow-paced, unhurried, gradual, leisurely, measured, lingering, snail-like, gentle, moderate.

DELIBERATE, *v.* 1. Reflect upon, weigh in the mind, ponder reasons for and against, cerebrate, think carefully, consider attentively, reason out, ratiocinate, cogitate, meditate, ruminate, examine carefully, take counsel with oneself, muse, take into consideration, contemplate, speculate, fancy, brood over, mull over, con over, study, bend the mind.

2. Consult, debate, confer formally, discuss, advise together.

3. Hesitate in deciding, stop and think.

DELIBERATELY, *adv.* 1. Designedly, advisedly, on purpose, purposely, intentionally, with intent, with forethought, by design, wittingly, knowingly, predeterminately, premeditatively, in cold blood, voluntarily, with eyes open, all things considered, studiously, pointedly, with a view to, with an eye to, to the end that.

2. Slowly, leisurely, at one's leisure, casually.

DELIBERATION, *n.* 1. Careful consideration before decision, mature reflection, meditation, ratiocination, cogitation, rumination, prudence, thoughtfulness, contemplation, examination, close attention, cerebration, circumspection, wariness, caution, watchfulness.

2. Forethought, distinct intention, cold blood, conscious purpose, deliberateness, determination prepense.

3. Consultation, conference, discussion, debate, parley, palaver, pourparler.

4. Coolness, leisureliness, slowness, steadiness, care in action, measuredness.

DELICACY, *n.* 1. Quality of affording refined pleasure to the senses, deliciousness, savoriness, relish, delightfulness, flavor, gusto, agreeableness, daintiness, pleasantness.

2. Addiction to sensuous pleasure, indulgence, pleasure, gratification, delight, satisfaction, enjoyment.

3. That which pleases a fine taste, something pleasing to the palate, choice morsel, source of pleasure, tidbit, dainty, bonne bouche, rarebit, bonbon, sweetmeat, kickshaw, appetizer, luxury.

4. Fineness of texture, lightness, smoothness, tenuity, diaphaneity, transparency, gossameriness, cobwebbiness, flimsiness, translucency, elegance, etherealness, exquisiteness, softness, tenderness, subtlety.

5. Small size, slender shapeliness, daintiness, very fine workmanship, sensitiveness, slightness, slenderness.

6. Bodily weakness, susceptibility to injury, liability to sickness, frailty, infirmity, fragility, feebleness, frailness.

7. Refined perception, scrupulousness, nicety, critical niceness, perfection in detail, carefulness, subtlety, fastidiousness, scrupulosity, exactness, accuracy, precision.

8. Fitness of perception, gentle consideration of the feelings of others, nicety of action, fineness of feeling as to what is fitting, tact, refinement, taste, discrimination, finesse, grace, sensibility, culture, gentle consideration of the feelings of others, purity, nice sensibility in conduct.

9. Quality of requiring great care, requiring

cautious treatment, involving great tact, difficulty, criticalness, ticklishness, precariousness, arduousness.

DELICATE, *adj.* 1. Dainty, delightful, pleasing, pleasant, agreeable, delicious, savory, luscious, toothsome, palatable, appetizing, mouth-watering.

2. Fine in texture, diaphanous, transparent, translucent, gossamery, cobwebby, sheer, silken, smooth, soft, dainty in quality, elegant, exquisite, nice, choice, ethereal, tenuous, thin, gauzy, tender.

3. Exquisite in action, fine in execution, exact, precise, accurate.

4. Fragile, easily damaged, frail, slender, thin, weakly, feeble, slight, unwell, ailing, perishable, infirm, sickly, attenuated, small, effeminate.

5. *(Of colors)* Soft, faint, muted, subdued, pastel.

6. Marked by consideration of others, careful, regardful of what is proper, refined in perception, sensitive, discriminating, fastidious, scrupulous, distinguishing subtle differences, tasteful, tactful, refined, discerning, diplomatic.

7. Requiring great caution, critical, dangerous, precarious, ticklish, difficult, arduous, touch-and-go.

DELICIOUS, *adj.* 1. Titillating, delectable, rich, luscious, tasty, palatable, toothsome, nectareous, savory, piquant, appetizing, sweet, ambrosial, highly pleasing to the senses.

2. Pleasing in the highest degree, affording exquisite pleasure, pleasant, agreeable, grateful, delightful to the senses, pleasurable, dainty, nice, charming, exquisite.

DELIGHT, *n.* High degree of enjoyment, elation, joy, joyful satisfaction, delectation, gratification, gladness, jubilation, ecstasy, happiness, transport, ravishment, rapture, exhilaration, paradise, bliss, heaven, elysium, beatitude, enchantment, charm, pleasure, exultation, rejoicing, felicity, zest, thrill, blessedness, content, kick *(colloq.),* entertainment, refreshment, gaiety, titillation.

DELIGHT, *v.* 1. Please highly, give great pleasure to, gratify in an extreme degree, charm, enchant, enrapture, enthrall, captivate, fascinate, ensorcel, bewitch, entrance, put into ecstasy, make happy, transport, ravish, gladden, cheer, excite, thrill, titillate, afford pleasure to, entertain, amuse, suit, divert, refresh.

2. Take delight in, be pleased with, feel a deep interest in, have great pleasure in, admire, relish, savor, revel in, feast on, luxuriate in.

DELIGHTED, *adj.* Highly pleased, enraptured, enchanted, captivated, ravished, transported, in paradise, carried away, elated, jubilant, ecstatic, beatific, entranced, blissful, gladsome, overjoyed, joyous, charmed, gladdened, with sparkling eyes, happy, content.

DELIGHTFUL, *adj.* Affording delight, enjoyable, pleasure-giving, highly pleasing, prepossessing, pleasurable, delectable, agreeable, lovely, golden, delicious, thrilling, heavenly, titillating, cheering, exciting, inviting, engaging, winning, enchanting, fascinating, charming, ravishing, enrapturing, transporting, captivating, alluring, inspiriting, enticing, tempting, gratifying, beatific, felicitous, joyous, blissful, attractive, welcome, exquisite, congenial, amiable, winsome.

DELINEATE, *v.* 1. Trace the outline of, sketch in outline, outline, trace out, represent pictorially, represent by diagram, limn, design, draw, figure, draft, block out, contour, profile, silhouette, define, circumscribe.

2. Portray in words, describe, give a mental picture of, set forth, paint, depict, picture.

DELINEATION, *n.* 1. Drawing, figure, draft, tracing, picture, portrait, sketch, design, diagram, outline, *ébauche*, plan, chart, contour, map, main features.

2. Verbal portraiture, portrayal in words, description, relation, narration, account, report, representation, depiction, rendition, projection, exhibition, exposition.

DELINQUENCY, *n.* Misdeed, misconduct, fault, misbehavior, misdemeanor, shortcoming, offense, transgression, trespass, guilt, failure in duty, slip, neglect of obligation, negligence, lapse, misstep, crime, error, infraction, violation, dereliction, omission, failure, default, wrong, sin, peccadillo, vice, malpractice, misdoing, wrongdoing, felony, malfeasance, violation, culpability, criminality, turpitude, corruption, malefaction, malversation, indiscretion, mortal sin, *flagrante delicto (Lat.).*

DELINQUENT, *adj.* 1. Neglectful of obligation, failing in duty, negligent, remiss, derelict, guilty of misdeed, offending, blamable, culpable, red-handed, censurable, reprehensible, blameworthy.

2. Due, unpaid, in arrears, back.

DELINQUENT, *n.* Neglecter of duty, offender, misdoer, malefactor, miscreant, criminal, culprit, misdemeanant, felon, transgressor, wrongdoer, evildoer, lawbreaker, trespasser, sinner, bad man, worker of iniquity, scamp, scapegrace, recreant, defaulter, blackguard, fallen angel, *âme damnée (Fr.),* reprobate, roué, rake, outlaw, black sheep, jailbird, convict.

DELIQUESCE, *v.* Become liquid by absorbing moisture from air, liquefy, dissolve gradually, melt away, run, thaw.

DELIQUESCENT, *adj.* Liquefying, liquescent, melting away, dissolving, thawing, soluble, colliquative, solvent, vanishing, evanescent.

DELIRIOUS, *adj.* 1. Wandering in mind, insane from fever, demented, mad, deranged, crazed, lunatic, disordered, light-headed, bereft of reason, *non compos mentis (Lat.),* unhinged, crazy, daft, moonstruck, raving, irrational, rambling, off one's head, incoherent.

2. Wild with excitement, carried away, hectic, extremely enthusiastic, frantic, frenzied, flushed, beside oneself, out of this world, fanatical, rabid, giddy, dizzy, vertiginous.

DELIRIUM, *n.* 1. Derangement, madness, raving, mental alienation, insanity, incoherent mental action, unsoundness of mind, incoherence, lunacy, feverish wandering, light-headedness, dementia, aberration, delusion, obsession, hallucination, erratic fancy, illusion.

2. Uncontrollable excitement, fever, frenzy, frenzied rapture, violent ecstasy, monomania, craze, fanaticism, infatuation.

DELIVER, *v.* 1. Free from restraint, liberate, emancipate, manumit, set at liberty, release, set free, extricate.

2. Come to the rescue, save, redeem, ransom, succor, preserve.

3. Give into another's keeping, transfer, place in the possession of, commit, turn over, hand over, make over, pass over, convey, impart, present, entrust, remit, bequeath, consign.

4. Give up, surrender, waive, concede, cede, relinquish, grant, yield, resign.

5. Give forth in words, communicate, utter,

enunciate, speak, pronounce, emit, express, recite, declare, promulgate.

6. Send forth vigorously, throw, project, put forth, discharge, deal, direct, cast, launch, expel, eject, fire, shoot.

DELIVERANCE, *n.* 1. Liberation, setting free, emancipation, manumission, release, riddance, extrication, escape, redemption, relief, absolution, pardon.

2. Rescue, acquittance, salvation, ransom, reprieve, respite, armistice, truce.

3. Formal pronouncement, official declaration, judgment expressed, observation, authoritative remark.

DELIVERY, *n.* 1. Transmission, transferal, commitment, intrusting, handing over, giving over, consignment, rendition, impartment.

2. Giving up, surrender, relinquishment, resignation, conveyance.

3. Distribution of mail-matter, shipment, parcel conveyance.

4. Enunciation of words, utterance, elocution, pronunciation, speech, vocal behavior during the presentation of a speech.

5. Parturition, accouchement, lying-in, labor, confinement, childbirth, travail, birth-throe, midwifery, obstetrics, geniture, bringing forth.

6. Giving forth, casting forward, projection, discharge, propulsive force.

7. Setting free, taking from restraint, release, emancipation, manumission, deliverance, rescue, extrication, freeing, liberation.

DELL, *n.* Small secluded valley between low hills, vale, dale, ravine, dingle, glen, gap, glade, grove, bottom, slade, strath, cove, grotto.

DELUDE, *v.* Persuade to believe error, deceive, mislead the mind of, beguile, fool, dupe, hoax, defraud, swindle, bamboozle, gull, victimize, fleece, cheat, chouse, cozen, hoodwink, humbug, befool, take in, practice upon, impose upon, palm off on, foist off, take advantage, outwit, circumvent, overreach, trick, betray, practice chicanery, juggle, conjure, lead astray, lure, seduce, lead into error, inveigle, gammon, throw dust in the eyes.

DELUGE, *n.* Great overflowing of water, flood, inundation, overflow, cataclysm, flash flood, freshet, spate, downpour, cloudburst, waterspout.

DELUGE, *v.* Flow over, submerge, inundate, flood, drown, overflow, overwhelm with a flood of water, engulf, bury, swallow up, swamp.

DELUSION, *n.* 1. False mental conception, vapor, erroneous belief, misconception, misjudgment, mistaken conviction, misapprehension, fallacy, misunderstanding, misinterpretation, error, false impression, self-deception, fancy, aberration, mockery, misbelief, obsession, misconstruction, fool's paradise.

2. Hallucination, illusion, phantasm, mirage, chimera, apparition, deceptive appearance, false show, vision, myth, ignis fatuus, dream, specter, bubble, will-o'-the-wisp, phantasmagoria.

3. Conjuring, magic, legerdemain, jugglery, prestidigitation, sleight of hand, hocus-pocus.

4. Blind, feint, imposture, imposition, trick, stratagem, fraud, dodge, hoax, artifice, ruse, wile, guile, chouse, snare, fetch, finesse, claptrap.

DELUSIVE, *adj.* False, unreal, fancied, mock, make-believe, imaginary, spurious, sham, vain, specious, pseudo, feigned, counterfeit, pretended, fraudulent, bogus, artificial, factitious, misleading, chimerical, fallacious, deceptive, illusive, empty, deceitful, fancied, visionary, illusory, untrustworthy.

DELVE, v. 1. Dig, work with a spade, excavate, gouge, turn over, mine, sap, burrow, tunnel, undermine, plow, harrow, till.

2. Search laboriously, carry on intensive research, search, look for, make inquiry, probe, ransack, sound, explore, rummage, peer, pry, look behind the scenes, penetrate, ferret out, trace up, unearth, fathom, track, hunt, trail, seek a clue, follow the trail, investigate, fish for, pursue, prosecute an inquiry, look into, go deep into.

3. Work hard, slave, drudge, toil.

4. Slope down, dip suddenly, shelve.

DEMAGOGUE, n. Popular agitator, ringleader of the people, factious leader, rabble rouser, red republican, unscrupulous haranguer, firebrand, soapbox orator, mob swayer, reactionist, brawler, malcontent, extremist, unprincipled politician, anarchist, insurgent, communist.

DEMAGOGUERY, n. Skill in arousing prejudices and passions of the populace, inciting the populace by sensational charges and specious arguments for personal gain, attempt to make capital of social discontent by inciting the populace, demagogism, McCarthyism.

DEMAND, v. 1. Ask for with authority, assert a right to, requisition, lay claim to, claim as a right, exact as due, require, make an authoritative request, ask in a bold way, require of others, dun, insist upon, importune, solicit, press, urge, indent, clamor for, extort, impose, order, make a point of.

2. Have pressing need for, necessitate urgently, call for, lack, stand in need of, be in need of, want.

3. (Law) Summon to court, lay formal legal claim to, make application, sue, enjoin.

4. Ask, make a demand, inquire, question, make inquiry, interrogate, cross-question, catechize.

DEMAND, n. 1. Mandate, order, injunction, command, charge, precept, direction, decree, ultimatum, bidding, behest, requisition, legal claim, draft, exaction, requirement, exigency, imposition.

2. Pressing requirement, want, need, call, call for, request, sale, run, market, desire to obtain, essentiality, necessity, indispensability, earnest seeking.

3. Interrogation, catechism, investigation, inquiry.

DEMARCATION, n. 1. Separation by distinct boundaries, defining of boundaries, marking off of boundaries, delimitation, division, termination, definition, partition, ne plus ultra (Lat.).

2. Frontier, limit, boundary, bound, bourne, line, confine, terminus, precinct, marches.

3. Discrimination, distinction, separation, Jim Crowism, segregation, sequestration, limitation, differentiation.

DEMEANOR, n. Deportment, port, carriage, comportment, conduct, behavior, maintien (Fr.), presence, attitude, address, bearing, manner, air, appearance, cast, mien, guise, expression, look, countenance, lineaments, physiognomy, visage, cast of countenance, observance.

DEMENTED, adj. Out of one's mind, deprived of reason, crazed, insane, crazy, daft, deranged, mad, brainsick, aliéné (Fr.), non compos mentis

(Lat.), lunatic, unhinged, loco (slang), beside oneself, off the beam, touched, cracked, bughouse (slang), possessed, irrational, moonstruck, idiotic, crack-brained, mad as a March hare.

DEMENTIA, n. Insanity, lunacy, state of mental disorder, diseased mind, derangement, madness, disordered reason, impairment of mental powers, unsoundness of mind, craziness, loss of the faculty of coherent thought, mental aberration, paranoia, dementia praecox (Med.), screw loose, bats in the belfry (slang).

DEMERIT, n. 1. Censurable quality, error, sin, punishable misaction, delinquency, dereliction, peccadillo, misconduct, misdeed, failure, fault, flaw, wrongdoing.

2. Mark against a person for misconduct, stigma, black mark, blacklist.

DEMESNE, n. 1. Land attached to a manor house, lands held in one's own power, grounds appertaining to a landed estate, landed property, realty, estate, manor, countryseat, messuage, menage, holdings, possessions.

2. Dominion of a sovereign, domain, empire, seignority, realm.

3. Sphere of influence, region of activity, district.

DEMIMONDAINE, n. Kept woman, mistress, woman of the demimonde, courtesan, demirep, woman of easy virtue, fancy woman, concubine, paramour, doxy, socially déclassé woman, woman of doubtful reputation, cocotte, lorette, grisette, frail sister, hustler, streetwalker, Cyprian, fallen woman, prostitute, tart, chippy, strumpet, broad, harlot, whore, fille de joie (Fr.).

DEMISE, n. 1. (Law) Making over, transference, alienation, conveyance, transfer, abalienation, cession, transmission.

2. Death, decease. (See DEATH.)

DEMISE, v. 1. Transfer for a limited time, let, alienate, abalienate, lease, convey, make over, consign, transmit.

2. Bequeath, bestow, leave by will, will, grant by will, devise.

DEMIURGIC, adj. World-making, creative, formative.

DEMOBILIZE, v. Disband an army, disarm, beat swords into plowshares, disperse an army, smoke the peace pipe, change from uniforms to mufti, break off hostilities and scatter, reduce to a peace footing.

DEMOCRACY, n. 1. Government by the people, self-rule, self-government, popular government, government in which supreme power is vested in the people.

2. State having such a government, republic, commonwealth, representative government, autonomous state.

3. State of society characterized by formal equality of rights, political equality, democratic spirit, social equality, society without class distinctions.

DEMOCRAT, n. 1. Advocate of democracy, one who maintains the social equality of men.

2. (U.S.) Have-not (colloq.), donkey (symbol).

DEMOCRATIC, adj. 1. Advocating democracy, characterized by principles of political equality, representative, republican, proletarian, of the people, Jeffersonian (U.S.), popular, plebeian.

2. Tending to level distinctions in rank, free-and-easy, condescending, broadminded, tolerant, neighborly, accessible, sociable, familiar, genial, gregarious.

DEMOLISH, *v.* 1. Destroy by tearing down, raze, level down to the ground, pull down, dismantle, wreck, overturn, overthrow, throw down, ravage, reduce to ruins, batter, subvert, upset, shatter, break up, fell, dash to pieces, smash to pieces, pulverize, ruin the structure of, separate the fabric of, crush.

2. Put an end to, bring to naught, annihilate, eradicate, devastate, lay waste, ruin utterly, make mincemeat of.

DEMOLITION, *n.* Dismantling, dilapidation, razing, overthrow, subversion, dissolution, ruin, breaking up, disruption, devastation, ruination, destruction, havoc, waste, perdition.

DEMON, *n.* 1. Devil, evil spirit, cacodemon, imp, goblin, troll, lamia, evil jinni, malignant spirit, incubus, succubus, barghest, banshee, ogre, ghoul, vampire, bogy, hobgoblin, changeling, nix, elf, leprechaun, brownie, pixy, dwarf, spook, evil influence, boggart, werewolf, *loup-garou (Fr.),* lycanthrope, bad fairy, evil passion.

2. Atrociously wicked person, fiend, cruel person, devil-incarnate, monster of depravity, hell-hound, hellcat, brute, ruffian, Mohock, hooligan, bludgeon man, Frankenstein's monster.

3. Person of great energy, human dynamo, pusher.

4. Guardian spirit, familiar spirit, tutelary deity, numen, genius, supernatural intelligence, genie.

DEMONIAC, *adj.* 1. Devilish, demoniacal, fiendish, diabolical, satanic, Mephistophelian, infernal, hellish, ghoulish, impious, monstrous, wicked, vicious, atrocious, nefarious, detestable.

2. Possessed by an evil spirit, hoodooed, hexed, bewitched.

3. Excessive, terrible, raging, frantic, hectic, insane.

DEMONSTRABLE, *adj.* Capable of positive proof, capable of being demonstrated, provable, inferable, deductible, irresistible, irrefragable, undeniable, conclusive, decisive, positive, actual, certain, veritable, unquestionable, self-evident.

DEMONSTRATE, *v.* 1. Prove indubitably, prove by experiment, make evident by arguments, substantiate, sustain, teach by examples, describe with the help of specimens, show by example, exemplify, illustrate, show beyond the possibility of doubt, verify, make evident, establish, make good, attest, certify, settle the question.

2. Manifest, exhibit, evince, display, show, point out, show publicly, indicate, make clear.

3. Take part in a demonstration, parade, march past.

DEMONSTRATION, *n.* 1. Argumentation, proof by arguments, verification, attestation, testimony, substantiation, evidence, certification, apodixis, corroboration, absolute establishment, certainty, conclusiveness.

2. Description of a process, explanation by experiment, experimentation, trial, test, description of examples.

3. Exposition, pointing out, manifestation, exhibit, display, spread, layout, exhibition, show.

4. Parade, mass meeting, exhibition of force, procession.

DEMONSTRATIVE, *adj.* 1. Perfectly convincing, seeming to prove the truth of anything, able to prove beyond a doubt, indubitably conclusive, proving, probative, conclusive, absolute, decisive, apodictic, certain, cogent, convincing.

2. Given to open exhibition, free in expression of feeling, prone to emotional display, effusive, gushing, unrestrained, unreserved, emotional, ingenuous, inclined to strong expression of the thoughts, communicative, expressive, explanatory, illustrative.

DEMORALIZATION, *n.* 1. Undermining of morals, corruption of morals, vitiation, want of principle, debasement, perversion, pollution, loss of moral standards, depravity, subversion of morals, wickedness, depravation, vice, immorality.

2. Deprivation of spirit, loss of courage, impairment of morale, lack of self-confidence, destruction of discipline, disablement of courage, panic, rout, trepidation, agitation, confusion, state of disorder, discomfiture.

DEMORALIZE, *v.* 1. Undermine the morals of, deprave, debase, vitiate, pervert, pollute, corrupt, destroy the moral principles of, spoil, debauch, defile, brutalize, contaminate.

2. Strip of spirit, deprive of courage, unnerve, unman, break down the morale of, disable the discipline of, panic, agitate, confuse, trepidate, discomfit, impair the fitness of, undermine the confidence of, make unfit, incapacitate, render powerless, dishearten, render incapable of brave action, enfeeble, paralyze, devitalize, rout.

DEMORALIZED, *adj.* 1. Profligate, depraved, corrupt, reprobate, immoral, bad, sinful, debased, perverted, degenerate, infamous, vicious, vitiated.

2. Disorganized, confused, agitated, panicked, routed, at loose ends.

DEMULCENT, *adj.* Mollifying, soothing, mild, assuaging, emollient, lenitive, bland, sedative, gentle.

DEMUR, *v.* 1. Suspend action because of doubt, hesitate, waver, stop to consider, pause, delay decision, hang fire, hang back, be in doubt, stick at, stickle, stall, hedge, be unwilling, boggle, dislike, recoil, shrink from, shy at, fight shy of, duck, temporize.

2. Object, offer difficulties, find fault, take exception, disapprove, bring up scruples, cavil, protest, wrangle, remonstrate, expostulate, dissent.

DEMUR, *n.* 1. Suspension of action, uncertainty, delay, hesitation, doubt, indecision, qualm, recoil, misgiving, shrinking.

2. Objection to proposed action, exception taken, protest, remonstrance, scruple, rejection, unwillingness, recalcitrance, noncompliance, cavil, issue on matter of law.

DEMURE, *adj.* 1. Unnaturally decorous, prim, affectedly modest, puritanical, priggish, prudish, overmodest, strait-laced, stiff, chaste, virtuous, virginal, prissy, finicky.

2. Shy, timid, timorous, bashful, coy, retiring, shrinking, blushing, sheepish, diffident.

3. Decorous, grave, modest, sedate, sober, serious, discreet, solemn, staid, reserved, quiet, constrained, unpresumptuous, meek, downcast, undemonstrative.

DEN, *n.* 1. Cavern, lair, retired place, rookery, cave, subterranean retreat, hollow, hole, cavity, dugout, grotto, recess haunted by animals, hiding place, eyrie, hive, covert, crypt, niche, nook, nest, perch, roost, nidus.

2. Low haunt, squalid abode, vicious resort, vile place, sink of iniquity, joint *(colloq.),* dive, disorderly house, disreputable place, house of ill-fame, brothel, bordello, bagnio, stew, lupanar, bawdyhouse, nest of thieves, opium den.

3. Cozy sanctum for personal use, snuggery, sanctum sanctorum, private room, study, library, rumpus room, smoking room.

4. Hermitage, retreat, cubicle, cell, cloister, convent, adytum.

DENIAL, *n.* 1. Contradiction of a statement, disaffirmation, contrary assertion, controversion, dissension, negation.

2. Renunciation, abnegation, disclaimer *(Law)*, recantation, repudiation, disavowal, abjuration, disacknowledgment, disownment, disallowance, rejection, rebuff, forswearing, refusal to recognize, recusancy.

3. Disbelief in the reality of a thing, refusal to believe a doctrine.

4. Refusal to grant a request, withholding, forbidding, noncompliance.

DENIZEN, *n.* 1. Habitant, inhabitant, indweller, dweller, resident, occupant, lodger, commorant, inmate, tenant, indigene, sojourner, townsman, settler, burgher, oppidan, burgess.

2. *(Brit.)* Naturalized citizen, alien admitted to residence, compatriot, inhabitant admitted to certain rights of citizenship.

DENOMINATE, *v.* 1. Give a name to, name, call by a specific name, supply with an epithet, designate, specify, style, entitle, christen, baptize, label, call, dub, title, term, phrase, characterize, nickname, define.

2. Show, point out, indicate.

DENOMINATION, *n.* 1. Name, designation, title, epithet, appellation, appellative, compellation, cognomen, style, term, specification, moniker, nomenclature.

2. Variety, genus, species, class, category, kind, sort, grouping, rank, grade, set, brand, stamp, breed, feather, genre, mold, make, cast.

3. Sect, party, faction, school, persuasion, clan, cause, fellowship, society, association, body, side, connection, crew, team, caste, family, fraternity, sodality, brotherhood.

4. One of the degrees in a series of designations of quantity.

DENOTE, *v.* 1. Mean, have in mind, indicate, be an indication of, designate, import, purport, connote, signify, betoken, show, express, imply, convey, suggest, intimate, allude to, particularize, drive at, involve, touch on, tell of, point at, note, mark, typify, individualize, mention.

2. Be a name for, be a designation for, be a mark of, be a sign of.

3. Represent by a symbol, symbolize, stand for, represent by a sign, serve as a sign of.

DENOUEMENT, *n.* 1. Unraveling of a plot, catastrophe of a plot, final disentangling of the intricacies of a plot, disclosure, unveiling, exposé, development.

2. Upshot, outcome, issue, winding up, finale, conclusion, termination, solution, result, end, final happening, consummation, finishing stroke, final touch, last finish.

DENOUNCE, *v.* 1. Publicly accuse, incriminate, condemn openly, assail with censure, upbraid, inveigh against, arraign, impugn, charge with, vilify, revile, brand, gibbet, stigmatize, black-list, hiss, blackball, ostracize, boycott, take to task, reprimand, blame, reproach, rebuke, criminate, inculpate, implicate, prosecute, castigate, dress down, rail at, vituperate, cry down, reprehend.

2. Inform against, accuse, delate, make formal accusation against, make charges against, indict, impeach, lodge a complaint.

3. Declare in a threatening manner, proclaim menacingly, damn, imprecate, swear at, execrate, proscribe, anathematize, excommunicate, thunder against, fulminate, devote to destruction, curse by bell, book and candle.

DE NOVO *(Lat.)* Anew, *de nouveau (Fr.)*, newly, afresh, over again, once more, again, bis, encore, from the beginning, *da capo (It.)*.

DENSE, *adj.* 1. With component parts closely compacted together, compressed, thick, crowded, condensed, close, compact, imporous, thickset, serried, close-set, cohesive, solid, impenetrable, heavy, impermeable.

2. Stupid, crass, obtuse, dull-witted, heavy-witted, thick-headed, ignorant, inept, blind, gross.

3. Transmitting little light, opaque, obscure.

DENSITY, *n.* 1. Closeness of parts, compactness, closely crowded condition, concretion, thickness, solidity, mass, denseness, crowdedness, body, impenetrability, impermeability.

2. Stupidity, crassness, ignorance, obtuseness, thick-headedness, grossness, ineptitude, dullness, dull-wittedness, opacity.

3. *(Physics)* Mass per unit of volume.

DENT, *n.* Hollow in a surface, indentation, dint, depression, dimple, pit, concavity, dip, cavity, nick, trough, notch, hole, furrow, intaglio, sinus, antrum.

DENT, *v.* Indent, dint, make a dent in, perforate, pit, depress, ridge, furrow, scratch, nick, notch.

DENTATE, *adj.* Dentated, denticulated, crenated, dentiform, odontoid, cusped, cuspidated, toothed, notched, serrate, jagged, palmated, lobate, peaked, serrulated, having a toothed margin.

DENUDE, *v.* Make naked, bare, divest, denudate, strip the clothes from, unclothe, undress, disrobe, undrape, lay bare, uncover, uncase, take off, peel off, shed, doff, cast off.

DENUNCIATION, *n.* 1. Vehement condemnation, open denouncing as evil, severe censure, censure, fulmination, invective, imputation, stigmatization, execration, reprobation, diatribe, vituperation, utter disapproval, stricture, abuse.

2. Incrimination, charge, inculpation, true bill, indictment, plaint, libel, citation, arraignment, impeachment, accusation of crime before a public tribunal, challenge.

3. Declaration of a threatening purpose, ban, commination, execration, malediction, anathema, excommunication, proscription, proclamation of ill, imprecation, curse, threat, menace, warning.

4. Informing against, delation, exposure.

DENUNCIATORY, *adj.* Condemnatory, abusive, upbraiding, accusatory, criminatory, threatening, recriminatory, incriminatory, stigmatizing, fulminatory, comminatory.

DENY, *v.* 1. Contradict, gainsay, declare not to be true, assert the negative of, nullify, differ, say "no" to, traverse, controvert, contravene, impugn, disaffirm, dispute, protest, refute, disprove, rebut, confute.

2. Reject as erroneous, repudiate, refuse to acknowledge, refuse to believe, disbelieve, not recognize, disown, disavow, disclaim, discredit, doubt, dissent, disagree, demur, call in question.

3. Renounce, recant, abjure, forswear, rescind, retract, abnegate, cast aside, reject.

4. Refuse to grant, withhold, begrudge, veto, forbid, prohibit, oppose, refuse to permit, rebuff, disallow, grudge, turn one's back on, stand aloof, be deaf to, refuse access to.

DEODORANT, *n.* Agent for destroying odors, killer of bad odors, disinfectant, deodorizer, fumigator.

DEODORIZE, *v.* Destroy the odor of, modify the odor of, deprive of odor, disinfect, fumigate, aerate, ventilate, purify, sweeten.

DEPART, *v.* 1. Go forth, go off, issue forth, set out, be off, start out, sally forth, make an exit, take oneself off, take one's departure, take one's leave, get going, get under way, bid farewell, bid adieu, leave, be gone, withdraw, march out, set forth, debouch, push away.
2. Entrain, embark, put to sea, sail, weigh anchor.
3. Vanish, disappear, go away, evanesce, fade off, abscond, absent oneself, recede, retire, cut one's sticks, retreat, break camp, strike tents, decamp, escape, vacate, evacuate, abandon, give up, desert, forsake.
4. Quit this world, die, perish, decease, expire, pass away.
5. Diverge, deviate, turn aside, digress, vary from, swerve, differ, desist.

DEPARTMENT, *n.* 1. Province, district, sector, section, precinct, tract, shire, circuit, territory, range, quarter, area, beat, canton, diocese, parish, constituency, commune, ward, bailiwick, arena, wapentake, pale, portion, division, subdivision, geographical division.
2. Appointed sphere, sphere of duty, station, function, office, jurisdiction, bureau, incumbency, post, administration, dominion, control, lookout, realm, domain, orb, line, field, walk of life, berth, billet, capacity.

DEPARTURE, *n.* 1. Setting out, starting, going away, leaving, setting forth, congé, exit, parting, separation, removal from a place, withdrawal, retirement, recession, flight, retreat, passage, take off, exodus, hegira, outset, embarkation, sailing.
2. Leave-taking, adieu, farewell, valediction, leave, Godspeed.
3. Forsaking, renunciation, desertion, secession, abandonment.
4. Beginning of a new course, fresh start, change of plan.
5. Deviation, divergence, variation, declination, declension, digression, difference, aberration, change.
6. Removal from life, decease, demise, death, dying, exit from life.

DEPEND, *v.* 1. Hang down, be pendent, dangle, be suspended, be sustained by a fastening to something above, trail, draggle, swing, overhang, flap, droop.
2. Hinge *(fig.)*, be related to something as a condition, be conditioned, be conditional, hang, be contingent upon, be subject to, be connected with, be dependent on, turn, be subordinate to *(Gram.)*, be undetermined, be undecided, be pending.
3. Trust in, rely on, have full confidence in, rest with reliance on, pin one's faith on, swear by, reckon upon, build upon, count upon, bank on, lean on, confide in, support oneself by, rest squarely, be in the hand of, repose in, credit.

DEPENDABLE, *adj.* Worthy of being depended on, reliable, trustworthy, trusted, trusty, faithful, unfailing, infallible, sure, honest, true, accepted, secure, established, received, approved, credible, safe, stable, authoritative.

DEPENDENCE, *n.* 1. Conditioned relation of one thing to another, interconnection, concatenation, connection, interdependence, contingency, natural sequence, conditioned existence, logical sequence.
2. Subordination to the direction of another, inability to act independently, inability to provide for oneself, subjection to control, need of, yoke, servility, subservience.
3. That on which one depends, staff, prop, shore, stay, truss, support, crutch, buttress, pillar, post, abutment, supporter, mainstay, alpenstock, stick, bourdon, cane.
4. Confidence, reliance, trust, credit, assurance, faith, troth, hope, belief, credence, persuasion, sanguine expectation.

DEPENDENCY, *n.* 1. Tributary state, dominion, subject territory, colony, province, mandate, fief, protectorate, principality, seigniory, fee, duchy, dukedom, margraviate, sphere of influence.
2. Something non-essential, appurtenance, ell, adjunct, annex, outbuilding, wing.

DEPENDENT, *adj.* 1. Hanging down, suspended, pendent, dangling, pensile, pendulous, drooping.
2. Under the control of something exterior, subject to, subordinate, subservient, conditioned, ancillary, contingent upon something extraneous, unable to exist without, conditional, accessory to, provisory, at the disposal of, sustained by.
3. Needing outside support, clinging, not able to sustain itself, helpless, weak, poor, indigent, minor, immature, in one's nonage.

DEPENDENT, *n.* 1. One who is sustained by another, one who looks to another for support, minor, ward, protégé.
2. Vassal, thrall, churl, minion, client, slave, hanger-on, parasite, sycophant, satellite, servitor, retainer, henchman, hireling, mercenary, yeoman, puppet, bondsman, serf, liegeman, follower, page, subject, subordinate, creature, servant, attendant, squire, cupbearer, trainbearer, equerry, groom, hostler, manservant, orderly, steward, underling, lackey, flunky, footman, menial.
3. Concomitant, sequela, corollary, attendant circumstance, consequence.

DEPICT, *v.* 1. Delineate, limn, outline, figure, form a colored likeness of, draw, pencil, sketch, portray, paint.
2. Set forth in vivid detail, describe, render vividly, represent in words, picture, characterize, narrate, relate, recite, recount, romance, record, chronicle, detail, reproduce.

DEPLETE, *v.* Deprive of that which fills, reduce the amount of, decrease the fullness of, lessen by exhaustion, use up, spend, drain, unload, empty by use, evacuate, exhaust, bleed, weaken, beggar, impoverish, pauperize, exhaust the strength of, drain of resources, render insufficient.

DEPLETED, *adj.* Used up, spent, exhausted, dry, empty, vacant, bare, drained, bereft of, short of, out of, destitute of, devoid of, sucked out, worn, in want, without resources, slack, denuded of, at low ebb.

DEPLETION, *n.* 1. Great reduction of stored materials, entire exhaustion, consumption, using up, expenditure, draining dry, evacuation, paucity, impoverishment, pauperization, emptiness, stint, deficiency, dearth, destitution, vacuity, lack, want, ebb tide, low water.
2. *(Accounting)* Impairment of capital, decline in value caused by consumption of an asset.

DEPLORABLE, *adj.* Causing grief, regrettable, distressing, woeful, pitiable, lamentable, doleful, sad, pathetic, grievous, wretched, calamitous, mournful, desperate, miserable, disastrous, trying, afflicting, melancholy, unfortunate, unhappy, hopeless.

DEPLORE, *v.* Express deep grief for, grieve for, regret profoundly, show concern for, regard with sorrow, mourn, lament, bewail, bemoan, weep over, condole with, sorrow over, groan, sigh for, shed tears over, cry for, keen *(Irish)*, view with regret, fret over, rue, repent of.

DEPLOY, *v.* *(Mil.)* Spread out troops, extend the front and decrease the depth of, spread out in line of battle, form an extended front, take open order, open, expand, display, unfold, march so as to make an extended line fronting the enemy, fan out.

DEPONENT, *n.* One who testifies under oath, witness who takes oath to a written statement, eyewitness, witness who gives testimony in writing.

DEPOPULATE, *v.* Remove the inhabitants from, unpeople, dispeople, eradicate the population of, deprive of inhabitants, turn out of house and home, evict, oust, relegate, deport, unhouse, exile, expatriate, dislodge.

DEPORTATION, *n.* Expulsion, exile, banishment, expatriation, proscription, outlawry, extradition, transportation, transplantation, rogue's march, ostracism, displacement, removal, dislodgment, relegation, expulsion of undesired aliens, sending back of an undesirable alien to his own country.

DEPORTMENT, *n.* Conduct, comportment, port, behavior, bearing, actions, demeanor, carriage, address, mien, manner, breeding, air, look, guise, appearance, *maintien (Fr.)*, course of conduct, observance, etiquette, manners.

DEPORT ONESELF Act, conduct oneself, bear oneself, manage oneself, behave oneself, carry oneself, demean oneself, comport oneself, play one's part, acquit oneself, steer one's course.

DEPOSE, *v.* 1. Remove from high office, deprive of rank, divest of station, demote, oust from office, turn out, displace, disestablish, discharge, get rid of, dismiss, unseat, dispossess, reduce, degrade, humble, strike off the roll, abase, take power away from, bounce *(slang)*, break *(colloq.)*, fire *(slang)*, sack *(slang)*, give one his walking papers, cashier, dethrone, uncrown, unfrock, disbar.
2. State under oath, give sworn testimony, swear, declare under oath, testify, bear witness to, make an affidavit, make deposition, warrant, give evidence, attest, affirm, certify, asseverate, aver, avow, avouch, allege, assert.

DEPOSIT, *n.* 1. Settled matter, sediment, detritus, settlings, deposition, precipitate, diluvium, drift, precipitation, alluvium, accumulation, grounds, sublimate, silt, lees, dregs, sinter *(Geol.)*, loess *(Geol.)*.
2. Earnest, pledge, security, collateral, surety, stake, pawn, guarantee, retainer, vadium *(Law)*, gage, anything given as security, payment, part payment, installment, money in bank, anything entrusted to another for safekeeping.

DEPOSIT, *v.* 1. Cause to adhere chemically, be formed by deposition, precipitate, drop, settle, accumulate, dump, cast down, throw down, let fall.
2. Place in a receptacle, put down, lay down, lay out, plant, repose, convey, send, hand over, transmit, entrust, consign, transfer, deliver over,

remand, commit, give in trust, commit to custody, put in the bank, put for safekeeping.
3. Give as security, give in part payment, ante up.

DEPOSITARY, *n.* Guardian, trustee, fiduciary, treasurer, bursar, purser, cash-keeper, quaestor, banker, steward, accountant, paymaster, cashier, teller, cambist, money-changer, financier, person entrusted with anything.

DEPOSITION, *n.* 1. *(Law)* Giving of testimony under oath, sworn evidence, testimony in writing and sworn to before a magistrate, asseveration, affidavit, attestation, declaration, *procès-verbal (Fr.)*, affirmation, allegation.
2. Precipitation, sediment, deposit, settlings.
3. Dismissal from office, removal from office, deprivation of authority, discharge, dismission, displacement, degradation, ousting, dethronement, expulsion, deposing, bounce *(colloq.)*, walking papers, sack *(colloq.)*, congé.
4. Burial, interment, entombment, sepulture, inhumation.

DEPOSITORY, *n.* Storehouse for safekeeping, place of deposit, warehouse, repository, magazine, depot, treasury, entrepôt, reservatory, thesaurus, cache, bunker, safe, safe-deposit vault, repertory, bank, pantechnicon.

DEPOT, *n.* 1. Railway station, *Bahnhof (Ger.)*, station house, railway terminus, terminal, haven, *gare (Fr.)*, stopping-place, halting-place, airport, destination, harbor.
2. Place of deposit for goods, supply station, depository, warehouse, magazine, safe-deposit, storehouse, repository, cache.

DEPRAVATION, *n.* 1. Impairment of condition, deterioration, degeneration, debasement, injury, abasement, demoralization, inquination, vitiation, contamination.
2. Corruption, depravity, vice, evil, vileness, taint, wickedness, depravity, turpitude, perversion, prostitution, flagitiousness.

DEPRAVE, *v.* Make bad, make worse, inquinate, corrupt, pervert, debase, vitiate, demoralize, rot, defile, degrade, contaminate, pollute, undermine, taint, infect, stain, poison, blight, corrode, mine, sap, weaken, despoil, spoil, seduce, contribute to the delinquency of, debauch, prostitute, desecrate, lead astray.

DEPRAVED, *adj.* Morally debased, lacking in principle, sunk in wickedness, corrupt, debauched, dissolute, profligate, degenerate, rotten to the core, evil-minded, perverted, immoral, degraded, lewd, gross, obscene, licentious, reprobate, sinful, dissipated, lecherous, vile, vitiated, wicked, base, vicious, shameless, abandoned, iniquitous, *contra bonos mores (Lat.)*, facinorous, felonious, low-minded, infamous, nefarious, heinous, flagrant, incorrigible, demoralized, ignoble, black-hearted, villainous, criminal, brutish, lustful, flagitious, sex-maddened.

DEPRAVITY, *n.* Corruption, degradation, crime, evildoing, corruptness, wickedness, viciousness, moral degeneracy, baseness, iniquity, sinfulness, vitiation, vileness, turpitude, immorality, lechery, debauchery, unchastity, animal nature, sensuality, prurience, lewdness, carnality, obscenity, vice, dissoluteness, profligacy, impurity, licentiousness, perversion, lustfulness, libidinousness, blackness, license, low-mindedness, demoralization, foulness, uncleanness, criminality, atrocity, contamination, pollution.

DEPRECATE, *v.* 1. Express earnest disapproval of, regard with disfavor, view with regret, plead earnestly against, urge reasons against, deplore, regret, remonstrate against, object to, protest against, expostulate, take exception to.

2. Seek to avert by supplication, pray to be delivered from, seek deliverance from, try to avert by prayer, make entreaty against, pray not to happen.

DEPRECIATE, *v.* 1. Represent as of little value, disparage, slander, make slighting reference to, decry, derogate, slight, detract, traduce, asperse, malign, defame, calumniate, denigrate, vilipend, vilify, slur, run down, belittle, revile, ridicule, deride, contemn, cry down, clamor against, scoff at, sneer at, spurn, censure, find fault with, knock *(colloq.)*, rap *(colloq.)*, slam *(colloq.)*, roast *(colloq.)*.

2. Reduce the purchasing value of, diminish the price of, lower the value of, cheapen, make little of, undervalue, underrate, underestimate, minimize, set no store by.

3. Decline in value, fall in price, become of less worth, sink in worth, decline, lose value, fall off, slump, drop, diminish, tumble, readjust downward, pejorate.

DEPRECIATION, *n.* 1. Lowering in estimation, disparagement, pejoration, derogation, detraction, underestimation, inappreciation, censure, malism, belittlement, traducement, maligning, pessimism.

2. Decrease in value, decline in purchasing power, decrease in exchange value of money, fall in price, diminution of value, falling off, reduction, slump, tumble, lessening, depression, drop, lowering, shrinkage, inflation, recession.

DEPRECIATIVE, *adj.* Derogatory, disparaging, depreciatory, pejorative, injurious, inappreciative, detractive, indifferent, uninterested, pessimistic, cynical, malistic.

DEPREDATE, *v.* Prey upon, plunder, despoil, lay waste, desolate, spoil, pillage, rifle, ransack, spoliate, pirate, maraud, steal, thieve, rob, sack, purloin, carry off, rustle, make depredations, loot, poach.

DEPREDATION, *n.* Preying upon, privateering, spoliation, despoilment, ravage, rapine, sacking, laying waste, desolation, pilfering, buccaneering, thievery, robbery, pillage, stealing, filibustering, rapacity, latrociny, direption, brigandage, foray, raid, highway robbery, *razzia (It.)*, plundering expedition, freebooting, burglary, highjacking, stripping, carrying off, cattle-rustling.

DEPREDATOR, *n.* Plunderer, pillager, sacker, looter, destroyer, despoiler, spoliator, marauder, pirate, corsair, buccaneer, viking, privateer, thief, freebooter, bandit, brigand, robber, highwayman, pilferer, rifler, ransacker, footpad, housebreaker, picaroon, rapparee, crook, racketeer, pickpocket, cutpurse, burglar, cracksman.

DEPRESS, *v.* 1. Lower, push down, press down, let drop, let fall, detrude, bring down, cast down, flatten, reduce, bow, sink.

2. Lower in force, weaken, keep down the activity of, enfeeble, diminish, depreciate, make dull, deaden, cheapen the price of.

3. Put into a lower position, degrade, demote, debase, abase, bring low, take down, humble, reduce to subjection, humiliate, crush down, dash, mortify, prostrate, precipitate.

4. Lower in spirits, cast gloom upon, dispirit, dishearten, deject, discourage, sadden, chill, dull, make despondent, dampen, damp, oppress, daunt, appal, dismay, weary, weigh down, throw cold water on, desolate, darken.

DEPRESSED, *adj.* 1. Cast down in spirit, glum, dejected, discouraged, dispirited, disheartened, despairing, disconsolate, despondent, melancholy, downhearted, down-in-the-mouth, downcast, low, drooping, low-spirited, spiritless, doleful, somber, dolorous, lugubrious, gloomy, crestfallen, dismal, saturnine, heartsick, heavy, woeful, woebegone, sad, blue, forlorn, dull, morose, prostrate, heavyhearted, sorrowful, desolate, wretched, dumpish, cheerless.

2. Pressed down, lowered in position, sunken, lower than the general surface, flattened down, deadened, dulled, at low ebb.

DEPRESSING, *adj.* Discouraging, disheartening, dispiriting, gloomy, dismal, dreary, woeful, sorry, doleful, rueful, grievous, damping, black, painful, bad, afflictive, sad, melancholy, dejecting, bitter, saddening, distressing, distasteful, unprepossessing, dolorous, uninviting, unwelcome, heartbreaking, cheerless, joyless.

DEPRESSION, *n.* 1. Sunken part, low place, hollow, cavity, indentation, concavity, dip, dent, dimple, pit, dint, excavation, furrow, trough, bed, bowl, impress.

2. Humbling, abasement, degradation, fall, reduction, humiliation, mortification, debasement, diminution.

3. Economic decline, period in which there is a decline in business, recession, economic malaise, economic paralysis, economic dislocation, hard times, inflation, cruel years, financial storm, business inactivity, economic stagnation.

4. Discouragement, dejection of spirits, grief, heaviness of spirit, cheerlessness, mopishness, lugubriosity, hopelessness, disconsolateness, dolor, dispiritedness, disheartenment, melancholia, blues, hypochondria, downheartedness, despondency, dolefulness, gloom, woefulness, ruefulness, gloominess, dumps, low-spiritedness, vapors, doldrums, oppression, unhappiness, lowness, sorrow, dreariness, distress, dumpishness, despair, desolation, misery, bleakness, sadness, darkness.

DEPRIVATION, *n.* Privation, dispossession, loss, bereavement, spoliation, stripping, removal, deprival, seizure, divestment, divestiture, taking away, despoliation, attachment, appropriation, expropriation, confiscation, deposition, disseizin *(Law)*, ademption *(Law)*, lack, want.

DEPRIVE, *v.* 1. Divest of something possessed, take away from, tear away from, wrest from, wring from, dispossess, strip, denude, rob, attach, despoil, bereave, commandeer, expropriate, confiscate, mulct, disseize *(Law)*, adempt *(Law)*.

2. Keep a person from the enjoyment of, debar, hinder from possessing, shut out.

DEPTH, *n.* 1. Measurement downward, extent down from a given point, downward measure, distance backward, perpendicular measurement from the surface, sounding *(Naut.)*, bathometry.

2. Deepness, profundity, depression, bottom, unfathomable space.

3. Pit, shaft, well, crater, hollow, depression, chasm, abyss, crevasse, deep, bottomless pit, bowels of the earth.

4. Innermost part, central part, midst, middle, midmost part, mid-time, stillness, silence *(of night)*, bosom, womb, base, remotest part, part of greatest intensity *(as of winter)*, underlying region *(as of feeling)*.

5. Abstruseness, reconditeness, esotericism, profoundness, obscurity.

6. Intellectual penetration, acumen, sagacity, discernment, astuteness, perspicacity, shrewdness, artfulness, subtlety, wisdom.

7. Thoughtfulness, gravity, seriousness, weight, sobriety, importance, moment.

8. *(Of color)* Richness, intensity, vividness, darkness, strength, abundance.

9. *(Of sound)* Lowness of pitch, tone color, timbre, alto, baritone, basso.

DEPURATE, *v.* 1. Make free from impurities, make pure, purify, cleanse, clean, mundify, rinse, flush, deterge, absterge, despumate, expurgate, purge, elutriate, lixiviate, disinfect, pasteurize, fumigate, ventilate, deodorize.

2. Clarify, clear, make clear, refine, filter, filtrate, drain, strain.

DEPURATION, *n.* 1. Freeing from impurities, purification, cleansing, mundation, purgation, lustration, abstersion, detersion, epuration, lavation, disinfection, fumigation, ventilation, sterilization, deodorization.

2. Clarification, clearing, filtration.

DEPUTATION, *n.* 1. Appointment to represent another, commission, assignment, nomination, investiture, procuration, delegation to act for another.

2. Body of authorized persons, deputies, body of diplomatists, envoys, commissioners, mission, legation, people deputized, embassy, body of delegates.

DEPUTE, *v.* 1. Send out with authority, appoint as agent, commission to represent one, delegate, deputize, transfer to another, turn over to, give power of attorney to, commit to the hands of, charge with, entrust, empower, authorize, invest, accredit, assign, engage, nominate, name, appoint as agent.

2. Assign a charge to a deputy, enjoin, order, instruct, direct.

DEPUTY, *n.* Person authorized to act for another, representative, agent, commissioner, appointee, emissary, delegate, envoy, ambassador, consul, plenipotentiary, minister, legate, factor, alternate, surrogate, vicar, substitute, proxy, lieutenant, *locum tenens (Lat.),* attorney, regent, viceregent, premier, chancellor, provost, warden.

DERANGE, *v.* 1. Throw into disorder, disorder, bring into a state of confusion, confuse, put out of place, misplace, dislocate, disarrange, litter, unsettle, disorganize, put out of order, throw out of gear, turn topsy-turvy, muddle, jumble, tousle, entangle, dishevel, rumple, disjoint, scatter.

2. Disturb the condition of, trouble, upset, discompose, ruffle, perturb, disconcert, confound, complicate, involve, perplex, embarrass, distract, agitate.

3. Break in upon, interrupt, intrude.

4. Make insane, craze, dement, madden, unsettle the reason of, unbalance, unhinge.

DERANGED, *adj.* 1. Disorganized, disordered, displaced, misplaced, dislocated, disarranged, out of order, topsy-turvy, upside down, jumbled.

2. Unsettled, confused, confounded, distrait, distraught, distracted, frantic, hectic, flighty.

3. Of unsound mind, demented, unbalanced, insane, out of one's mind, cracked, brainsick, lunatic, maniacal, delirious, crazy, mad, raving, dotty *(slang),* daft, weak-minded, witless, feeble-minded, possessed, psychopathic, psychotic.

DERANGEMENT, *n.* 1. Disorder, confusion, disorganization, disarrangement, dislocation, mess, irregularity, muddle, muss, litter, jumble, tangle, dishevelment.

2. Disturbance, perturbation, disconcertion, discomposure, distraction, embarrassment.

3. Mental alienation, mental aberration, mental disorder, dementia, insanity, madness, lunacy, mania, craziness, unbalance, mental unsoundness, delirium, hallucination.

DERELICT, *adj.* 1. *(Law)* Given up by the owner, abandoned, left by the guardian of, relinquished, forsaken, deserted, lost, adrift, drifting.

2. Neglectful of duty, negligent of obligation, delinquent, unfaithful, faithless, remiss, careless.

DERELICT, *n.* 1. Ship abandoned at sea, flotsam and jetsam, ship abandoned for unseaworthiness, shipwrecked vessel, wreckage.

2. Person forsaken by society, human wreck, outcast, tramp, pariah, beachcomber, vagrant.

3. One guilty of neglect of duty, delinquent, slacker, loafer, lounger, idler, *flâneur (Fr.),* dawdler, dallier, time-killer.

DERELICTION, *n.* 1. Utter forsaking, desertion, abandonment, relinquishment, renunciation.

2. Culpable neglect, failure in duty, wilful omission of obligation, remissness, delinquency, faithlessness, negligence, fault, unfaithfulness, wrongdoing, shortcoming, carelessness, evasion, nonobservance, nonperformance, noncooperation, infraction, violation, transgression.

DERIDE, *v.* Laugh at in contempt, ridicule, make the object of scorn, jeer, flout, twit, taunt, scoff at, mock, lampoon, make fun of, gibe, scout, chaff, satirize, make sport of, hold up to ridicule, poke fun at, make a butt of, make game of, laugh to scorn, roast *(colloq.),* guy *(colloq.),* rag, rally, heckle, banter, disdain, curl one's lip, hiss, cry down, hoot at, sneer at, pooh-pooh *(colloq.),* slur.

DERISION, *n.* 1. Contemptuous holding up to ridicule, mockery, contempt shown by laughter, scorn, scoffing, jeering, gibing, banter, slur, disparagement, disdain, disrespect, contumely, insult, affront, taunt, grin, snicker, leer, sneer, flout, mimicry, chaff, raillery, persiflage, quip, squib, sarcasm, irony, satire, burlesque, parody, buffoonery, travesty, farce, caricature.

2. Object of ridicule, laughingstock, butt, goat.

DERISIVE, *adj.* Derisory, jeering, scoffing, sardonic, mocking, taunting, ridiculing, ironical, sarcastic, satirical, disdainful, contumelious, contemptuous, scornful.

DERIVABLE, *adj.* Obtainable, evolvable, due to, resulting from, resultant, caused by, owing to, dependent upon, derivative, heritable, imputable, hereditable, attributable, referable, assignable, traceable, ascribable, deducible, inferable.

DERIVATION, *n.* 1. Acquiring from a source, getting, obtaining, deriving, drawing, deducing, accounting, inferring.

2. Origin, source, origination, foundation, root, spring, cause, beginning, rise, commencement, development, causation, causality, fountainhead, springhead, *fons et origo (Lat.),* imputation, rationale.

3. Genealogy, descent, birth, extraction, stock, genesis, paternity, consanguinity, ancestry, house, stem, trunk, tree, stirps, pedigree, lineage, line, family, tribe, race, clan.

4. Etymology, tracing a word from its original root, word-formation, lexicology, philology.

DERIVATIVE, *adj.* Derivate, derived, caused, acquired from some origin, not original, not primitive, secondary, not fundamental, connate, obtained by transmission, transmitted, educed, inferred, evolved, hereditary.

DERIVE, *v.* 1. Draw by logical sequence, receive from a source, get by transmission, obtain from an origin, gain, secure, glean, extract, procure, acquire, inherit.
2. Obtain by reasoning, account for, trace from a source, draw a conclusion, conclude, infer, gather by inference, theorize, attribute to, lay to, ascribe to, impute to, father upon, refer to, blame with, saddle upon.
3. Come from a source, originate, take origin, arise, proceed, come, be descended, hail from, stem from.
4. Etymologize, philologize.

DEROGATE, *v.* 1. Disparage, brand, stigmatize, malign, detract from, withdraw from, take something from, be derogatory of, lessen the reputation of, underrate, misprize, belittle, run down, diminish the value of, compromise the influence of, be hostile to, vilify, defame, slur, asperse, cry down, decry, traduce, depreciate, slander, discredit, criticize, pull to pieces, denigrate, lampoon, calumniate.
2. Degenerate from, fall away in character, disgrace oneself, fall from high estate, reflect dishonor upon, shame, impute shame to, act beneath one's rank, stoop, grovel, degrade oneself, lose caste, seal one's infamy, be inglorious.

DEROGATION, *n.* 1. Seeking to injure in reputation, detraction, depreciation, decrial, disparagement, vilification, obloquy, defamation, underestimation, scurrility, scandal, aspersion, traducement, slander, calumny, obtrectation, libel, lampoon, pasquinade, criticism, sarcasm.
2. Deterioration, impairment of effect, falling off, limiting in application.

DEROGATORY, *adj.* 1. Detracting from value, lessening in good repute, dishonoring, disparaging, depreciatory, belittling, expressive of low estimation, opprobrious, defamatory, calumnious, slanderous, unfavorable, unflattering, injurious, uncomplimentary, discrediting, faultfinding, disdainful, reproachful.
2. Discreditable, ignoble, inglorious, unworthy, scandalous, unbefitting, ignominious, disreputable, undignified, degrading, unmanly, *infra dignitatem (Lat.)*, ungentlemanly, dedecorous.

DESCANT, *n.* 1. *(Music)* Superimposed counterpoint to a simple melody, accompanying melody, tune with variations, varied melody, ornamental variation, strain of melody, song, air, obbligato.
2. *(In part music)* Highest part in a score, soprano, treble.
3. Variation upon anything, comment on a subject, commentary, remarks, animadversion, series of comments, holding forth on a subject, disputation, discourse, discussion, observations, dissertation, disquisition, excursus, obiter dicta.

DESCANT, *v.* 1. Play a descant, sing, warble.
2. Treat of with variety, comment freely, make comments, hold forth with variety of detail, be diffuse, expatiate, dilate, enlarge upon, discourse at length, treat copiously, animadvert freely, amplify, expand, dissertate, digress, ramble, perorate, rant, branch out, spin a long yarn, harp on, dwell on, insist upon.

DESCEND, *v.* 1. Pass from a higher to a lower place, come down, go down, drop, fall, sink, pitch, slope, move downwards, gravitate, dip, pass downward, tumble, droop, slump, decline, set, settle, plunge, trip, stumble, founder, lurch, topple.
2. Dismount, light, alight, get down, get off, disembark, disentrain, detrain, land.
3. Condescend, stoop, come down in social scale, lower oneself, crouch, stoop, grovel, fall prostrate, sprawl.
4. Come down by transmission, pass down from generation to generation, originate by birth, be sprung, be derived, issue, take rise by extraction, arise, come down lineally, proceed, be transmitted, be handed down, devolve upon.
5. Make an attack, make an assault, make a descent, come in force from above, come down in hostile manner, swoop, pounce, raid, invade, assail.

DESCENDANTS, *n. pl.* Offspring, progeny, issue, posterity, seed *(Biblical)*, breed, spawn, brood, family, offshoots, sons, children, scions, heirs, increase, future generations, after ages, olive branch, succeeding generations, chips off the old block.

DESCENDENT, *adj.* 1. Descending, moving directly downward, going down, coming down, falling, downward, down, deciduous, decursive.
2. Steep, sloping, declivitous, precipitous, beetling, overhanging.

DESCENT, *n.* 1. Change from higher to lower, inclination downward, declension, declination, cadence, droop, plunge, drop, downrush, falling, coming down, sinking, subsidence, settlement, lapse, downcome, stumble, tilt, slip, trip, lurch.
2. Alighting, dismounting, descending, getting off, lighting, journey down, disembarkation, landing, detrainment, disentrainment.
3. That over which one descends, declivity, decline, dip, pitch, descending way, slope, grade, passage leading down, stairway leading down, downgrade, gradient, incline, inclination.
4. Avalanche, landslide, snowslide, glissade.
5. Genealogy, lineage, extraction, derivation, ancestry, family tree, parentage, pedigree, stock, line, blood, paternity, breed, origin, birth, strain, kin, filiation, degree in the scale of genealogy, generation, sonship, succession, heredity.
6. Hostile visitation, sudden incursion, assault, unexpected attack, onslaught, foray, sortie, raid, illapse, invasion.
7. Moral sinking, debasement, degradation, abasement, decline, downfall, comedown, tumble, setback, debacle.

DESCRIBE, *v.* 1. Sketch, delineate, limn, trace, circumscribe, draw, mark out, figure, paint, traverse the outline of.
2. Represent by words, set forth in words, tell, convey a verbal image of, depict, portray, observe vividly, detail, recite, explain, narrate, recount, relate, express, give an account of, give the details of, state the particulars of, picture, particularize, elucidate, illustrate, romance, report, chronicle, record, define, epitomize, characterize, specify the peculiarities of.

DESCRIPTION, *n.* 1. Representation by words, statements that describe, explanation, depiction, portrayal, account, delineation, characterization, recital, rehearsal, report, relation, enumeration of the essential qualities, narration, specification, informal definition, record, brief, summary, monograph.

2. History, annals, memorabilia, memoirs, life, letters, experiences, adventures, personalia, ana, journal, biography, autobiography.

3. Fiction, romance, novel, tale, story, short story, mystery story, whodunit, thriller, detective story, yarn, anecdote, fairy story, legend, myth, parable, allegory, fable, epic.

4. *(Geom.)* Outline, sketch, tracing, delineation.

5. Kind, sort, class, variety, species, manner, genus, nature, character, caliber, brand, feather, category, cast, stamp.

DESCRIPTIVE, *adj.* Delineative, expository, true to life, explanatory, illustrative, graphic, forcible, interpretive, clear, pictorial, picturesque, lifelike, narrative, anecdotic, storied, realistic, depictive, vivid.

DESCRY, *v.* 1. Make out by looking, make out in the distance, catch sight of, discern, sight, espy, distinguish, ken, perceive, behold, look, see, have in sight, catch a glimpse of, scan, survey, witness.

2. Discover by observation, detect, find out, determine, recognize, peer, pry, ferret out, spy out.

3. Divulge, communicate, reveal, impart, make known, disclose.

DESECRATE, *v.* Divest of sacred character, put to an unworthy use, divert from sacred to profane purpose, profane, defile, violate the sanctity of, treat sacrilegiously, commit sacrilege, prostitute, abuse, pollute, pervert to impure uses, unhallow, taint, contaminate, misuse, debase, blaspheme, violate, dishonor, outrage, swear.

DESECRATION, *n.* Sacrilegious treatment, abuse, sacrilege, profanation, perversion to unholy uses, violation, blasphemy, dishonoring, contamination, outrage, misuse, prostitution, pollution, impiety, defilement, profaneness, irreverence, unholiness.

DESERT, *adj.* Like a desert, desolate, infertile, without cultivation, lifeless, arid, infecund, wild, waste, barren, untilled, uncultivated, inarable, unproductive, sterile, empty, void, uninhabitable, forsaken, uninhabited, unoccupied, infrequented, blank.

DESERT, *n.* 1. Area deficient in moisture, wild, wilderness, waste, barren, solitude, arid region, deserted region, uncultivated expanse, Sahara, sand dune.

2. Treeless plain, steppe, tundra, heath, mesa, moor, savanna, bush, veldt.

DESERT, *n.* 1. That which is deserved, reward, due, meed, guerdon, requital, recompense, right, compensation, birthright, justice.

2. Demerit, punishment, condign retribution, penalty, chastening.

3. Merit, fact of deserving well, excellence that entitles to praise, quality entitling to just reward, inherent goodness, good behavior, performance of duty, welldoing, virtue, worth, excellence, credit, value.

DESERT, *v.* 1. Depart from, leave, forsake, quit permanently, run away from, abandon without warning, leave in the lurch, fail one at need, go back on, turn one's back upon, have done with, renounce, forego, make oneself scarce, secede, defect, part company, fly, flee, flit, bolt, vacate, relinquish, abdicate, give up, jilt, disappoint, drop, evade, elude, bid a long farewell, take to one's heels, retreat, withdraw, turn tail, cut and run.

2. Run away from military service, abandon one's post, go A.W.O.L., run away from duty, forsake without leave, take French leave, leave unlawfully, give leg bail, play truant, violate one's oath, make off, sneak off, abscond, decamp.

DESERTED, *adj.* 1. Abandoned, uninhabited, in a backwater, unfrequented, tenantless, secluded, unoccupied, sequestered, retired, isolated, out of the way, lonely, lone, solitary, desolate.

2. Left without support, helpless, unfriended, destitute, forlorn, lorn, alone, forsaken, outcast, excluded, estranged, cast off, given up, adrift, relinquished.

DESERTER, *n.* 1. Runaway, absconder, fugitive, refugee, shirker, slacker, quitter, truant, skulker, ratter, abandoner, seceder.

2. Forsaker of allegiance, backslider, recreant, renegade, runagate, delinquent, traitor, recusant, apostate, revolter, turncoat.

3. Renegade from military service, delinquent soldier, A.W.O.L.

DESERTION, *n.* 1. Dereliction, defection, wilful abandonment, secession, withdrawal, abrogation, relinquishment, recreancy, falling away, evasion, forsaking, renunciation, apostasy, elusion, revolt, avoidance, demission, retirement, going back on.

2. Abandonment of a soldier's post of duty, unlawful departure from military service, absence without leave, A.W.O.L., quitting service without discharge.

3. Desolation, desertedness, loneliness, solitude, Godforsakenness, spiritual melancholy, wildness.

DESERVE, *v.* Merit in return for, be worthy of recompense, be entitled to because of acts, earn as due compensation, be deserving, have right to, richly deserve, lay claim to, demand, requisition, exact, insist on, require.

DESERVED, *adj.* Merited, due, just, rightful, earned, entitled to, condign.

DESERVING, *adj.* Worthy of reward, estimable, meritorious, meedful, worthy of praise, laudable, righteous, good, virtuous, dutiful, commendable, well-intentioned, creditable, praiseworthy, well-doing, excellent, admirable, sterling, exemplary.

DESICCATE, *v.* 1. Remove moisture from, free from moisture, exhaust of moisture, render dry, dry thoroughly, dry up, exsiccate, drain, parch.

2. Preserve by depriving of moisture, powder *(as of milk or soup)*, dehydrate, anhydrate, evaporate.

3. Remove spiritual freshness from, render intellectually dry.

DESIDERATE, *v.* Feel a desire for, feel need for, feel the want of, long for, wish for, desire, crave, hanker after, pine for, not be able to do without, require, stand in need of, lack, want, miss, regard as a desideratum.

DESIDERATUM, *n.* Essential object of desire, generally felt want, thing wanted, that which is lacking, something needed, requirement, height of ambition, consummation devoutly to be wished, aspiration, objective, aim, goal, mark, point to be reached, exigency, *sine qua non (Lat.),* breathless impatience.

DESIGN, *v.* 1. Prepare preliminary sketch for, draw up the plans for, mark out in outline, draft, delineate, trace out, sketch, make a drawing of, describe, outline, limn, block out, paint, portray, fashion according to a plan, color, shape, pencil, stencil, arrange, organize, construct, forge, build, erect.

2. Formulate mentally the idea of, map out in

the mind, plan mentally, project, conceive in the mind, devise, organize a scheme of, plot, scheme, plan, frame, contrive, hatch, invent, machinate, propose, create, construct, concoct, brew, intrigue, maneuver, conspire, cabal.

3. Have in mind to do, purpose, destine for, assign in intention, intend, hold in thought, mean, set up a program before oneself, set apart for a purpose, propose to oneself, devote to a purpose, have in view, aim at, aspire to.

DESIGN, *n.* 1. Preliminary sketch, delineation, rough representation, draft, drawing, depiction, outline, *ébauche (Fr.),* blueprint, layout, chart, diagram, map, study, cartoon, plan, tracery.

2. Contrivance, artifice, device, invention, shift, expedient, stratagem, inventiveness, adaptation of means to ends.

3. Make-up, combination of details, formation, arrangement, construction, organization, text, structure, composition.

4. Pattern, model, archetype, prototype, copy, form, shape, figure.

5. Course of action marked out in the mind, intention, purpose in view, intent, end in view, mental project, fixed purpose, ultimate end, goal, object, objective, drift, set, bent, destination, aim, target, bull's-eye, mark, ambition, determination, proposal, program, scheme, plan, schema, final cause, meaning, purport.

6. Underhanded scheme, hostile plan, plot to injure, crafty intrigue, evil intention, machination, cabal, conspiracy, wirepulling, ruthless personal ambition, deliberate scheming.

DESIGNATE, *v.* 1. Define, circumscribe, describe, mark out, characterize, individualize.

2. Mark out and make known, specify, point out, indicate, show, denote, formulate, stipulate, mention, distinguish, select, particularize, note, pinpoint, earmark, express.

3. Call by a distinctive title, identify by name, name, denominate, term, style, entitle, dub, label, christen, baptize, nickname.

4. Indicate for a purpose, select for a duty, set apart for an office, nominate, appoint, choose, elect, assign, allot.

DESIGNATION, *n.* 1. Pointing out, indication, showing, particularization, specification.

2. Appointment for a purpose, assignment, selection, nomination, election.

3. That which designates, distinguishing title, name, appellative, appellation, compellation, title, denomination, style, cognomen, epithet, surname, patronymic, eponym, moniker, nickname, handle to one's name, sobriquet, alias.

4. Description, kind, character, class, turn, ilk, sort, brand, feather.

5. Signification, meaning, intent, intention.

DESIGNEDLY, *adv.* Intentionally, purposely, by design, on purpose, with aforethought, knowingly, with premeditation, deliberately, advisedly, with eyes open, wilfully, all things considered.

DESIGNER, *n.* 1. Creator, inventor, generator, author, producer, deviser, founder, originator, architect.

2. Schemer, intriguer, machinator, conspirator, plotter, planner.

3. One who devises designs, one who executes decorative patterns, painter, limner, caricaturist, one who creates original works of decoration, cartoonist, draftsman, sketcher, drawer, engraver, delineator, illustrator, modeler, carver, sculptor, chaser.

DESIGNING, *adj.* 1. Exercising foresight, heedful, showing forethought, calculating, foreseeing, provident, thoughtful.

2. Contriving schemes, scheming, treacherous, plotting, intriguing, insidious, cunning, subdolous, guileful, subtle, crafty, feline, vulpine, foxy, wily, stealthy, politic, sly, artful, astute, disingenuous, arch, deceitful, tricky, circumventive, diplomatic, crooked, sharp, Machiavellian, shrewd.

DESIRABLE, *adj.* To be desired, fitted to excite desire, admirable, covetable, enviable, profitable, worth having, advantageous, expedient, gainful, remunerative, beneficial, popular, in demand, fine, eligible, excellent, agreeable, appetizing, goodly, meet, fitting, proper, seemly, decorous, becoming, fair, provocative of longing to possess.

DESIRE, *v.* 1. Wish for the enjoyment of, fancy earnestly, crave, desiderate, covet, lust after, set one's heart upon, hunger after, thirst for, pine for, sigh for, long for, hope for, want, yearn for, hanker after, incline to, be bent upon, have an eye to, aspire after, have a mind to, care for, like, take to, cling to.

2. Express a wish to obtain, ask for, pray for, request, solicit, entreat, beg, urge, press.

DESIRE, *n.* 1. Fondness, longing, ardor, craving, aspiration, ambition, eagerness, solicitude, fancy, inclination, predilection, propensity, liking, itch, proclivity, hankering, avidity, appetency, cupidity, covetousness, yearning, appetite, hunger, stomach, relish, thirst, ravenousness, grasping, attraction, rapaciousness, voracity, ardent impulse, frenzy, mania, craze, monomania, torment of Tantalus, rage.

2. Sexual love, sensual appetite, lust, salacity, carnal passion, libido, concupiscence, pruriency, venery, lecherousness, lubricity, lasciviousness, ithyphallicism, priapism, nymphomania, eroticism, amorousness, biological urge, heat, rut, estrus.

3. Expressed wish, request, petition, prayer, requirement, need, want, exigency.

DESIROUS, *adj.* Governed by desire, yearning, eagerly wishing, wishful, longing, craving, hungry, thirsty, athirst, appetitive, greedy, voracious, fain, omnivorous, inclined, partial to, ready, willing, eager, keen, burning, fervent, ardent, avid, agog, breathless, impatient, anxious, solicitous, minded, ambitious, aspiring, vaulting, eager to obtain, covetous, avaricious, rapacious, grasping.

DESIST, *v.* 1. Cease, stop, forbear, abstain, leave off, refrain from, hold, stay, check, break off, pause, mark time, pull up, stop short, hang fire, interrupt, suspend, intermit, remit, arrest, halt, quit, give over, end, give up, conclude, make an end of, drop, discontinue, have done with, rest, come to a stand.

2. Be at an end, die away, wear away, pass away, lapse, disappear, vanish, evanesce.

DESOLATE, *adj.* 1. Destitute of inhabitants, bare, uninhabited, deserted, depopulated, untenanted, unoccupied, unfrequented, bleak, desert, barren, waste, wild, inhospitable, empty.

2. Left alone, forsaken, lonely, solitary, lorn, lonesome, companionless, abandoned by friends, friendless, forlorn, unfriended, bereft, estranged, excluded, isolated, outcast, derelict, forgotten, homeless.

3. In a ruinous condition, ruined, devastated, destroyed, laid waste, ravaged, desolated, gutted, wrecked, dilapidated, in a state of neglect.

4. Dejected, cheerless, downcast, downhearted, wretched, joyless, spiritless, depressed, overcome,

disconsolate, brokenhearted, melancholy, doleful, hypochondriacal, sorrowful, lachrymose, gloomy, woebegone, bereaved, inconsolable, sad, sick at heart, down in the mouth, despondent, miserable, low-spirited, heavy-hearted, discouraged, dreary, dark, somber, dismal, drear, funereal, mournful, prostrate, cut up, crushed, defeated.

DESOLATE, *v.* 1. Ravage, strip of goods, harry, devastate, ruin, despoil, sack, pillage, plunder, deal destruction, destroy, lay waste, make bare, gut, demolish, depredate, sap, mine, blast, ravage with fire and sword.

2. Deprive of inhabitants, depopulate, leave tenantless.

3. Forsake, abandon, leave alone, deprive of companions, turn one's back upon, shut the door upon, reject, repudiate, expel, relegate, thrust out, disown, evict.

4. Fill with sadness, make disconsolate, make wretched, depress, make joyless, make forlorn, discourage, dishearten, dash one's hopes, unnerve, unman, prostrate, sadden, damp.

DESOLATION, *n.* 1. Devastation, havoc, ravage, destruction, despoliation, stripping, depopulation, ruin, laying waste, blight.

2. Deprivation of companionship, loneliness, forlornness, disconsolateness, solitariness, ejection, destitution, seclusion, sequestration, segregation, isolation, exclusion, expulsion, solitude.

3. Barrenness, wildness, bareness, bleakness, dreariness, gloom.

4. Sadness, melancholy, despondency, misery, unhappiness, depression, dejection, affliction, woe, grief, sorrow, dolefulness, cheerlessness, distress, gloominess, blues, hypochondria, deprivation of joy, dolor, low spirits, pessimism. hopelessness.

DESPAIR, *n.* 1. Passive abandonment of oneself to fate, utter hopelessness, complete loss of hope, desperation, despondency, melancholia, malism, hypochondria, utter discouragement, defeatism, disheartenment, pessimism, miserabilism, dashed hopes, disconsolateness, dolor, bitterness, distress, sorrow, grief, brokenheartedness, misery, anguish, wretchedness, prostration, depth of woe, slough of despond.

2. Tribulation, extremity, care, anxiety, weight on the mind, heartache, burden, ordeal, incubus, trial, nightmare, Ephialtes.

DESPAIR, *v.* Have no hope, lose all hope, have a heavy heart, give up all expectation, despond, lose faith in, lose heart, lose courage, abandon oneself to fate.

DESPAIRING, *adj.* Desperate, plunged in tears, given to hopelessness, despondent, heartbroken, melancholy, disconsolate, downcast, infelicitous, forlorn, sorrowing, chagrined, steeped in misery, griefstricken, miserable, cheerless, inconsolable, crushed, concerned, worried, prostrate, wretched, depressed, heavy-hearted, unhappy.

DESPERADO, *n.* Reckless criminal, malefactor, man of desperate deeds, ruthless lawbreaker, thug, apache, gangster, marauder, tough, highwayman, ruffian, knave, blackguard, miscreant, hellhound, rowdy, terrorist, bully, hooligan, thief, murderer, roughneck, hoodlum, gunman, robber, footpad, bad man, outlaw, brigand, jailbird, *enfant perdu (Fr.)*, felon.

DESPERATE, *adj.* 1. Having no hope, beyond hope, despairing, downcast, forlorn, inconsolable, despondent, broken-hearted, wretched.

2. Regarded as irremediable, remediless, past

cure, hopeless, incurable, irreparable, lamentable, irretrievable, irreclaimable, irredeemable, very bad, irrevocable, irrecoverable, despaired of, lost beyond recovery, deplorable.

3. Resorted to in a last extremity, prompted by despair, heroic, done as a last resort, with back to the wall, without care for safety, ready to run any risk, heedless of danger, critical, very serious, extremely perilous, reckless from despair, very dangerous, death-defying.

4. Frantic, mad, violent, wild, infuriated, rabid, furious, rampant, raging, frenzied, harebrained, phrenetic, turbulent, tumultuous, passionate, wild, daring, bold, rash. precipitate, headlong, madcap, extravagant, incautious, imprudent, indiscreet, injudicious, overhasty, unwary, devil-may-care, breakneck, foolhardy.

5. *(Colloq.)* Excessive, outrageous, impossible, extreme, great, intense, vehement, acute, supreme, prodigious, monstrous.

DESPERATION, *n.* 1. Giving up of hope, lost hopes, hopelessness, disconsolateness, dejection, despondency, melancholy, depression.

2. Recklessness of despair, blind fury, madness, rage, brain storm, defiance of consequences, leap in the dark, reckless fury, frenzy, recklessness, rashness, distraction, blind bargain.

DESPICABLE, *adj.* That is to be despised, vile, contemptible, abject, low, base, mean, wretched, worthless, no-account, beneath contempt, paltry, scrubby, sorry, unworthy of notice, scurvy, poor, cheap, shabby, miserable, disgraceful, degraded, disreputable, infamous, outrageous, ignominious, arrant, corrupt, dishonest, ignoble, mean-spirited, caitiff, nameless, shameful, cowardly, beggarly, yellow, servile.

DESPISE, *v.* Have a low opinion of, look upon as degraded, regard as worthless, contemn, look down upon, spurn, scorn, look upon as beneath one's notice, disdain, disregard, hold in contempt, misprize, scout, treat with indifference, disesteem, slight, pass by, ridicule, laugh at, sneer at, turn a cold shoulder on, undervalue, neglect, dislike, loathe, abhor, detest.

DESPITE, *prep.* In spite of, in despite of, against, in contempt of, in defiance of, in the teeth of, in the face of, notwithstanding.

DESPITE, *n.* 1. Malicious anger, resentment, bad blood, malevolence, malignity, spite, malice, gall, extreme aversion, venom, rancor, rankling, ill-will, virulence.

2. Act of insult, act of malignity, contumacy, contemptuous treatment, defiance, antagonism, highhanded abuse, contemptuous opposition, contempt.

DESPOIL, *v.* 1. Deprive violently, strip, denude, divest wantonly, bereave, confiscate, dispossess.

2. Take spoil from, seize the possessions of, rob, loot, sack, plunder, rifle, pluck, skin, fleece, steal, thieve, filch, lift, spoil, spoliate, forage, help oneself to, pirate, rustle, poach, commandeer, make free with, make off with, carry off, seize, snatch, deprive of by force, ravage, devastate, ravish, overrun, lay waste, ransack, prey upon, wreck, depredate, maraud, tear away, wrench away, wrest from, wring from, pillage.

DESPOILMENT, *n.* Despoliation, depredation, stripping, plunder, pillage, loot, spoliation. havoc, thievery, latrociny, direption, predacity, rapine, brigandage, highway robbery, piracy, devastation, privateering, highjacking, laying waste, ravage, sack, inroad, scathe, desolation.

DESPOND, *v.* Be cast down, be dispirited, sink, become discouraged, be mentally depressed, be disheartened, lose heart, lose spirit, lose hope, lose courage, despair, yield to depression, give way, give up, falter, droop, lay to heart, mourn, lament, grieve, sorrow, mope, brood over, fret, pout, pine away, abandon hope.

DESPONDENCY, *n.* Depression of spirits from loss of hope, dejection, disconsolateness, despair, discouragement, sadness, melancholia, doldrums, hypochondria, dolefulness, mopishness, dumps, blues, vapors, heaviness of heart, blue devils, slough of despond, broken heart, sorrow, grief, hopelessness, weariness, disgust of life, malism, prostration, pessimism, miserabilism, dashed hopes, *Weltschmerz (Ger.)*.

DESPONDENT, *adj.* Dejected, depressed, cast down, low-spirited, spiritless, discouraged, blue, disheartened, dispirited, downhearted, downcast, melancholy, hypochondriacal, mopish, woebegone, glum, moody, sullen, sulky, morose, gloomy, sad, sorrowful, lachrymose, prostrate, crushed, sick at heart, crestfallen, heavy-hearted, down in the mouth, splenetic, out of sorts, dismal, saturnine.

DESPOT, *n.* 1. Irresponsible monarch, absolute sovereign, dictator, autocrat, absolute ruler, ruler without constitutional check.
2. Leader of enslaved people, tyrant, oppressor, hard master, arbitrary ruler.
3. *(Hist.)* Master, lord, emperor.

DESPOTIC, *adj.* 1. Imperious, dictatorial, lordly, autocratic, absolute, unlimited, authoritarian, monarchical, despotical.
2. Tyrannical, tyrannous, oppressive, coercive, high-handed, domineering, grinding, iron-handed, arrogant, self-willed, summary, irresponsible.

DESPOTISM, *n.* 1. Autocracy, dictatorship, iron sway, absolutism, absolute power, Caesarism, power not restricted by constitution, authority unlimited and uncontrolled, exercise of absolute authority, autocratic government, imperialism, despotic monarchy, czarism, kaiserism, arbitrary power.
2. Severe rule, tyranny, oppression, coercion, domination, tyrannical control, iron hand, mailed fist.

DESTINATION, *n.* 1. Predetermined end of a journey, journey's end, place set for a journey's end, terminal point of a course, terminus, point aimed at, bourn, halting place, resting place, landing place, goal, station, harbor, port, haven, anchorage, home base.
2. Purpose for which anything is destined, predetermined object, ultimate design, ultimate end, purpose, intention, goal, ambition, objective, aim, mark, point, butt, target, bull's-eye, quintain, drift, scope.

DESTINE, *v.* 1. Determine the future of, decree beforehand, appoint beforehand, foreordain, fate, preordain, ordain, predetermine, predestine, allot, doom, devote, consecrate, predestinate, compel, necessitate.
2. Set apart for a particular purpose, appoint to a distinct end, determine the future condition of, designate, intend, design, reserve, bespeak, dedicate, settle the future position of, purpose, mean, have in view.
3. Impend, threaten, hover, approach, loom, brew, menace, await, hang over.

DESTINED, *adj.* 1. Assigned to go to a designated place, bound for a certain destination, booked, routed.

2. Engaged, bespoken, designed, reserved, set aside, intended, set apart, in reserve.
3. Fated, ordained, doomed, predetermined, predestined, foreordained, predestineal, on the lap of the gods, compulsory, inevitable, ineluctable, inexorable, written in the book of fate, on the cards, that is to be, that will, in store, to come, unborn, imminent, near, at hand, instant, in the wind, impending, looming, forthcoming, brewing, in prospect, menacing, threatening.

DESTINY, *n.* 1. That which is to happen to a particular person, foreordained condition, doom, unavoidable lot, predetermined plan, star, portion, fatality, fortune, end, astral influence.
2. Inevitable necessity, power which determines the course of events, fate, decrees of fate, course of events, divine decree, wheel of fortune, kismet, will of heaven, Clotho, Lachesis, Atropos, Norns, Three Fates, Sisters Three, Parcae, Moirae, God's will, Ides of March, Hobson's choice.
3. Goal, culminating end, future state, womb of time, foreordained future, future existence, hereafter, next world, world to come, prospect, expectation.

DESTITUTE, *adj.* 1. Out of money, moneyless, indigent, poor, poverty-stricken, needy, badly off, bereft of resources, necessitous, hard up, lacking the means of subsistence, impecunious, in need, penniless, in want, broke, flat, *sans le sou (Fr.)*, pinched, reduced in means, beggared, distressed, straitened, insolvent, short of money, financially embarrassed, without resources, in a condition of extreme want, out of cash, unable to keep the wolf from the door, unable to make both ends meet, out of pocket, down and out, high and dry, out at the elbows, down at the heels, seedy, poor as Job's turkey, barefoot, strapped, down on one's luck, poor as a church mouse.
2. Being completely without, not having, void, lacking, deficient, devoid of, bereft, bereaved of, denuded, helpless, stranded, wanting, scarce, dry, lacking, short, insufficient, inadequate, famished, slack, unprovided, unsupplied, naked, bare, unfed, empty, vacant, drained, at low ebb, ill-provided, starved, emaciated, undernourished.

DESTITUTION, *n.* 1. Want of the means of living, indigence, utter poverty, penury, lack of necessities, privation, impecuniousness, beggary, pauperism, pennilessness, insolvency, necessity, neediness, distress, difficulties, straits, *res angusta domi (Lat.)*, straitened circumstances, broken fortunes, mendicancy, wolf at the door, nightmare of need, bare cupboard, empty purse, slender means, narrow means, empty pocket, light purse, rags and patches, want of the means of subsistence.
2. Deprivation, want, need, lack, absence of, deficiency, dearth, exigency, starvation, famine, drought, depletion, exhaustion, ebb tide.

DESTROY, *v.* 1. Cause the downfall of, raze, demolish, level down to the ground, dismantle, knock to pieces, pull down, overturn, subvert, overthrow, upset, ruin, throw down, break up, bring to ruin, wreck, wrench apart, tear down, sap the foundations of, rend, shatter, blast, gut, waste, ravage, desolate, devastate, devour, spoil, consume, swallow up, lay waste, ravage with fire and sword, despoil, overwhelm, squash, scuttle, break down, crush, smash, crash, batter, topple.
2. Annihilate, exterminate, extinguish, cause to vanish, dissolve, quench, obliterate, efface, put an end to, undo the work of, bring to naught, wipe

out, unbuild, abolish, stifle, snuff out, suppress, do away with, remove, take away, cancel, erase, strike out, expunge, delete, quash, quell, blight, end, finish, put down.

3. Kill, slay, take the life of, give a deathblow to, put an end to the existence of, cause to cease to be, cut off, mow down, blot out, sacrifice, cut down, drown, shipwreck, submerge, murder, set fire to, assassinate, strangle, garrote, shoot, choke off, decapitate, smother, hang, knife, pluck up by the roots, extirpate, eradicate, root out, eliminate.

4. Nullify, counteract, neutralize, invalidate, vitiate, render of no avail, render ineffective, annul, show to be false, disprove.

DESTROYER, *n.* 1. Annihilator, exterminator, dealer of destruction, demolisher, vandal, Goth, wrecker, barbarian, savage, iconoclast, nihilist, Hun, anarchist, plague, pestilence.

2. Killer, slayer, assassin, executioner, gunman, hangman, decapitator, guillotiner, slaughterer, cutthroat, strangler, butcher, murderer, lyncher, Cain, hatchet man, poisoner, cannibal, manslayer, incendiary, arsonist, firebrand.

3. Torpedo-boat, submarine-destroyer, war-vessel.

DESTRUCTION, *n.* 1. Tearing down, demolition, overthrow, subversion, wreckage, rack and ruin, downfall, fall, ruination, havoc, crash, smash, shipwreck, crackup, breakdown, cave-in, wreck, debacle, disestablishment.

2. Ravage, holocaust, cataclysm, devastation, desolation, depredation, spoliation, laying waste, vandalism, pillage, incendiarism, revolution, sabotage.

3. Extermination, eradication, extirpation, end, extinction, annihilation, ruin, perdition, loss, bane, undoing, dissolution, removal, abolition, breaking up, disruption, disorganization, suppression, sacrifice, immolation.

4. Murder, assassination, killing, butchery, carnage, massacre, slaying, slaughter, deathblow, doom, crack of doom.

DESTRUCTIVE, *adj.* 1. Productive of serious evil, ruinous, deleterious, pernicious, fell, baleful, dire, fatal, lethal, deadly, mortal, pestilential, mischievous, pestiferous, noxious, noisome, detrimental, hurtful, harmful, injurious, vicious, disruptive, subversive, evil, murderous, poisonous, toxic, suicidal, incendiary, conflagrative, arsonistic, cataclysmal, demolitionary, extirpative, all-destroying, annihilative, eradicative, devastating, internecine.

2. (*Logic*) Employed for refutation, tending to refute, disproving, taking to pieces.

DESUETUDE, *n.* State of being no longer practiced, disusage, want of habit, want of practice, relinquishment, forbearance, abstinence, neglect, inusitation, disuse, discontinuance of use, nonobservance, cessation of practice.

DESULTORY, *adj.* 1. Passing abruptly from one thing to another, veering about from one thing to another, wandering, shifting, unsteady, inconstant, unsettled, hasty, loose, drifting, spasmodic, by fits and starts, unmethodical, unsystematic, irregular, changeable, capricious, rambling, wandering, roving, discursive, digressive, cursory, skipping about, disconnected, disorderly, unsteady, broken, disjointed, drifting, unsystematized, not connected with what precedes.

2. Random, errant, aimless, erratic, fitful, not pertinent, stray, not connected with the subject, out of course, by the way.

DETACH, *v.* 1. Unfasten and separate, disengage, disconnect, unhitch, disjoin, disunite, loosen, dissociate, sever, dissever, divide, sunder, part, unfix, disentangle, free, uncouple, cut off, isolate, segregate.

2. Assign to a special service, separate for a special object, send away on a special mission, detail, appoint to a particular service, draft, pick.

DETACHMENT, *n.* 1. Disconnection, separation, severing, disseverance, disengagement, loosening, division, disunion, disjoining, parting, unfixing, disjunction, dissociation, segregation.

2. State of aloofness, unconcern, isolation, indifference to opinion, preoccupation, faineancy, absentmindedness, inattention, do-nothingness.

3. Freedom from prejudice, impartiality, objectivity, disinterestedness.

4. Number of troops separated from a main force for some special task, party, detail, force, body, company, division, garrison, squadron, squad, corps, platoon, brigade, regiment, men, battalion.

DETAIL, *n.* 1. Individual part of a whole, item, minute part, particular, feature, aspect, article, particularity, circumstance, respect, point, minor part, accessory.

2. Report of particulars, particularized recital, minute relation, narration, report, account, full treatment, narrative, description.

3. Particular assignment of duty, detachment, telling off, appointment to special service, selection for particular duty, sending off.

4. Squad, detachment, patrol, party, body, group.

DETAIL, *v.* 1. Report in particular, tell fully and distinctly, itemize, narrate minutely, relate, recount, enumerate, designate, mention, specify the particulars of, particularize, enter into details, descend to particulars, specialize, set forth, individualize, describe, delineate, depict, portray, rehearse, catalogue.

2. Select for special service, detach, appoint to special duty, assign, send away, tell off, select.

DETAILED, *adj.* Itemized, particularized, minute, individualized, particular, point by point, full, circumstantial, circumstantially depicted, full of details, complete, all-inclusive, comprehensive, seriatim, one after another, exact, precise, fussy, meticulous.

DETAILS, *n.* Minutiae, minute details, distinct parts, particulars, fine points, niceties, items, counts, minor circumstances, trivialities.

DETAIN, *v.* 1. Hold back, keep from proceeding, restrain, check, arrest, stay, retard, stop, hinder, delay, retain, prevent, impede, inhibit, preclude, bar, buttonhole, keep back, withhold.

2. Keep under restraint, confine, hold in custody, lock up, incarcerate, imprison, impound, pen, coop up, clap under hatches, put behind bars, secure.

DETECT, *v.* 1. Descry, espy, spot, catch in the act, expose, discover, uncover, unearth, dig up, trace out, disinter, unveil, bring out, bring to light, ascertain, find out, lay open, disclose, apprehend, get scent of, ferret out, smell out, get wind of, come upon, come across, light upon, stumble upon.

2. Find out the character of, unmask, expose, see through, reveal.

3. Discover the existence of, learn, discern, perceive, observe.

DETECTION, *n.* Finding out, apprehension, discovery, exposure, laying open of what was hidden, disclosure, unfolding, finding, sighting, getting wind of, espial, perception, ascertainment, learning, unearthing.

DETECTIVE, *n.* Police officer assigned to obtain information and evidence, obtainer of secret information, tracer of crime to its source, sleuth, shadow, constable, bull, F. B. I. man, G-man, patrolman, copper, cop, flatfoot, private eye.

DETENTION, *n.* 1. Retardation, delay, stoppage, staying, holding back, check, keeping back, detainment, hindrance, withholding, Fabian policy, retainment.

2. Keeping in custody, retention, restraint, arrest, confinement, custody, durance vile, duress, imprisonment, incarceration, quarantine.

DETER, *v.* Prevent from action by fear of consequences, restrain from acting through doubt, discourage through fear, dissuade, withhold by fear, hinder, hold back, stop, frighten away from, advise against, warn, dismay, dishearten, dispirit, daunt, abash, impede, turn aside, divert from, damp, cool, chill.

DETERGENT, *adj.* Having cleansing qualities, detersive, abstersive, clearing away foul matter, purging, depuratory, cleaning, purificatory.

DETERIORATE, *v.* 1. Debase in quality, make lower in character, make inferior in value, impair, degrade, corrupt, vitiate, lessen in worth, make worse, injure, damage, hurt, harm, scathe, spoil, mar, taint, contaminate, pollute, infect, blight, defile, deprave.

2. Become lower in quality, be reduced in worth, degenerate, worsen, grow worse, pejorate, become impaired, decline, lapse, droop, run to seed, retrograde, shrivel, fade, discolor, wither, molder, rot, decay, go bad, corrode, rust, fall off, disintegrate, crumble, fall away, ebb, fail, have seen better days, become enfeebled, go sour.

DETERIORATION, *n.* 1. Impairment, damage, loss, detriment, injury, harm, ravages of time.

2. Vitiation, corruption, perversion, depravity, debasement, depravation, degradation, pollution, adulteration, alloy, contamination.

3. Caducity, decline, gradual impairment, dry rot, declination, declension, decadence, decay, degeneration, retrogression, pejoration, wane, ebb, recession, retrogradation, depreciation, wear and tear, disintegration, decomposition, disrepair, moth and rust, erosion, corrosion, rottenness, blight, atrophy, dilapidation, demission, falling off.

DETERMINABLE, *adj.* 1. Fixable, capable of being determined, that may be accurately found out, ascertainable, discoverable, admitting of decision, assayable, judicable, definable.

2. *(Law)* Subject to termination, terminable, liable to be terminated, subject to be put an end to.

DETERMINATE, *adj.* 1. Having definite limits, definite, limited, bounded, fixed.

2. Determined upon, decisive, definitive, final, decided, conclusive, invariable, arbitrary.

3. Known, settled, positive, established, exact, explicit, express, absolute, certain, distinct, not uncertain, specific, special, concrete, weighty, actual.

4. Determined, resolute, resolved. (See DETERMINED.)

DETERMINATION, *n.* 1. Act of deciding, formation of a fixed purpose, determining, fixing, settling and ending a controversy, settlement by authoritative decision, resolving of a question by reasoning, ascertainment, adjudication, decision.

2. That which is determined upon, decision arrived at, authoritative opinion, resolution, judgment, decree, verdict, finding, resolve, result ascertained, solution, declaration, conclusion, upshot, end.

3. Fixed direction, aim, tendency toward some object, leaning, proclivity, propensity, trend, impulsion.

4. Quality of being determined, decision of character, resolve, resolution, resoluteness, fixity of purpose, firmness of purpose, grit, stamina, constancy, persistence, steadfastness, tenacity, fortitude, obstinacy, pluck, manliness, boldness, courage, spunk, mettle, strength of will, iron will, will power, backbone, sand, perseverance, push, insistence.

5. *(Law)* Termination, conclusion, cessation.

6. *(Logic)* Rendering of a notion more definite by the addition of differentiating characters, qualification, adding of determinants, addition of predicates, definition of a concept by citing its constituent elements.

DETERMINATIVE, *adj.* 1. Having power to determine, limiting, shaping, directing, deciding, limitive.

2. Decisive, conclusive, authoritative, final, important.

DETERMINE, *v.* 1. Settle by authoritative decision, decide by judicial sentence, reach a definite purpose concerning, come to a decision concerning, adjust, resolve, conclude, set, end, fix conclusively, bring to an end, ordain.

2. Ascertain after reasoning, insure, fathom, render the knowledge of clear and accurate, solve, understand, certify, verify, make out, find out, get at, detect, discover.

3. Set bounds to, set limits to, delimit, fix the boundaries of, limit in extent, restrict, shut in, limit, bound, define.

4. Give direction to, direct to a certain end, influence, effect, impel, fix the course of, lead, incline, induce, turn, dispose, bend, move.

5. Lead to a decision, decide upon, purpose, set one's purpose on, resolve, make a decision.

6. Decide casually, condition, prearrange, fix the form of beforehand, give definite form to, regulate, direct, shape, pass upon, specify, ordain, designate, necessitate, subject to unyielding conditions, compel.

7. *(Law)* Bring to an end, terminate, put an end to, finish, cause to lose binding force, cause to cease to be, have reached a set limit.

8. *(Logic)* Define by adding a differentia, give predicates, condition, limit by adding differentiating characters, give qualifications, give marks, bound.

DETERMINED, *adj.* 1. Fixed, appointed, set, arbitrary.

2. Having settled purpose, resolute, decided, resolved, firm, strong-willed, unyielding, set on, bent on, obstinate, stubborn, dogged, unflinching, stanch, purposeful, inflexible, unfaltering, iron, unwavering, indomitable, steadfast, game, gritty, plucky, tenacious.

DETERMINING, *adj.* Critical, crucial, pivotal, deciding, important.

DETERRENT, *n.* That which deters, curb, check, restraint, hindrance, warning, discouragement, damper, wet blanket, impediment, obstacle, knot, stricture, cohibition, constraint, snag, hitch, bar, stile, barrier, block, buffer, drawback, lion in the path, objection, stumbling block.

DETEST, *v.* Hate extremely, hold worthy of malediction, abominate, feel abhorrence of, abhor, dislike intensely, loathe, despise, shrink from, execrate, revolt against, recoil from, shudder at, nauseated by, disdain, scorn.

DETESTABLE, *adj.* 1. Deserving to be detested, abominable, abhorrent, execrable, odious, vile, hateful, obnoxious, nameless, cursed, accursed, damnable, infamous, hellish, infernal, heinous, repulsive, offensive, repugnant, revolting, shocking.
2. Loathsome, sickening, unpleasant, foul, disagreeable, nauseating, noisome, noxious.

DETESTATION, *n.* 1. Abhorrence, abomination, execration, hatred, detesting, intense dislike, bitter pill, source of annoyance, aversion, disfavor, odium, *bête noire (Fr.).*
2. Loathing, antipathy, disgust, nausea, horror, repugnance, revulsion.

DETHRONE, *v.* Depose, remove from the throne, drive from the throne, divest of royal authority, strip of regal power, uncrown, drive out of power, discrown, force to abdicate, oust, degrade.

DETONATE, *v.* 1. Detonize, cause to explode by the application of sudden force, set off, discharge.
2. Explode with great violence, fulminate, let off, thunder, displode, blow up, burst on the ear.

DETONATION, *n.* Violent explosion, thunder, fulmination, sharp report, sudden discharge, displosion, burst, blow up, clap, volley, blast, dissilience.

DETOUR, *n.* Circuitous route, roundabout course, indirect way, deviation from a direct course, turning, bypass, circuit, temporary substitute for a main route.

DETRACT, *v.* 1. Take away a part, subtract from, lower, withdraw, divert, draw away, abate, lessen, ·diminish, derogate from, depreciate, deteriorate.
2. Take reputation from, disparage, decry, not do justice to, belittle, asperse, damn with faint praise, abuse, pull to· pieces, run down, vilify, calumniate, vilipend, traduce, cry down, defame, blacken, denigrate, brand, malign, libel, slander, lampoon, backbite, revile, sneer at.

DETRACTION, *n.* Taking away from the good name of another, depreciation, derogation, abuse, slander, aspersion, vilification, obloquy, calumny, traducement, disparagement, defamation, censure, denigration, scandal, evil-speaking, backbiting, decrial, sarcasm, cynicism, criticism, Zoilism, libel, lampoon, squib.

DETRACTOR, *n.* Finder of flaws in the character of another, derogator, depreciator, slanderer, asperser, defamer, calumniator, vituperator, vilifier, censurer, censor, backbiter, lampooner, satirist, traducer, libeler, reviler, critic, caviler, carper, knocker *(colloq.),* cynic, Zoilist.

DETRACTORY, *adj.* Detractive, depreciative, injurious, disparaging, defamatory, derogatory, slanderous, calumnious, libelous, scurrilous, foul-mouthed, abusive, sarcastic, biting, acrimonious, satirical, cynical.

DETRIMENT, *n.* Loss, injury, damage, cost, evil, hurt, harm, ill, impairment, spoliation, blow, delaceration, scratch, bruise, buffet, stroke, gash, wound, mutilation, mortal blow, *immedicabile*

vulnus (Lat.), wear and tear, disaster, accident, casualty, mishap, calamity, catastrophe, tragedy, ruin, adversity, foul play, ill turn, outrage, havoc, inroad, ravage, scath, mischief, disadvantage, deterioration.

DETRIMENTAL, *adj.* Injurious, deleterious, bad, damaging, disadvantageous, harmful, hurtful, pernicious, noisome, destructive, mischievous, inimical, grievous, prejudicial, disastrous, noxious.

DETRITION, *n.* Wearing away by rubbing, rubbing off particles, abrasion, attrition, erosion, disintegration, corrosion, pulverization, multure, comminution, granulation, trituration, limation, levigation.

DETRITUS, *n.* 1. Waterworn particles of rock, broken away particles, loose fragments, loose material resulting from rock disintegration, grit, pulverulence, friability, sandiness, powder, dust, sand, drift, alluvium, moraine.
2. Rubbish, waste, debris, dust.

DE TROP, *(Fr.)* 1. Too much, excessive, too many, superfluous.
2. Not wanted, in the way, out of place, fifth-wheel, *persona non grata (Lat.).*

DETRUDE, *v.* Push down forcibly, depress, sink, force down, lower, thrust into a lower place, push away, push aside, extrude, drop out.

DETRUSION, *n.* Thrusting down, pushing down, driving down, extrusion, trajection, depression, lowering.

DEUCE, *n.* 1. Side of a die with two pips, cast in which two aces turn up, card having two pips, two-spot, two.
2. *(Colloq.)* Bad luck, the mischief, the devil, plague, the dickens, demon.

DEVASTATE, *v.* Render desolate, desolate, harry, despoil, waste, lay waste, destroy, spoil, ravage, blast, strip, sack, pillage, plunder, wreck, ruin, lay in ruins, overwhelm, demolish, rifle, ransack, raze, level, gut, deal destruction, overrun.

DEVASTATION, *n.* Ruination, desolation, sack, spoliation, pillage, rapine, destruction, waste, demolition, ruin, havoc, ravishment, predation, depredation, ravage, wholesale destruction by fire and sword, holocaust, incendiarism, extirpation.

DEVELOP, *v.* 1. Cause to pass from a lower to a higher stage, cause to grow, mature, ripen, bring to maturity, bring to a complete condition, bring to a more advanced state, increase the strength of, enlarge, cause to expand, bring out, advance, further, perfect, complete, dilate, spread, widen, extend, augment, spread out, magnify.
2. Bring to light by degrees, work out in detail, unfold, evolve, lay open, reveal, disclose, make known, uncover, unravel, unfurl, disentangle, explicate, display, unroll, exhibit.
3. Bring into being, generate, breed, hatch, bring up, rear, foster, cultivate, institute, invent, fashion, coin, organize, constitute, establish, erect, build, promote, exploit, propagate, work out.
4. Make progress by stages, expand, advance in successive gradation, be developed, flower, wax, grow, progress, swell, fill out, bud, shoot, sprout, germinate, burgeon, burst forth.
5. Come gradually into existence, disclose itself, appear, dawn, become evident, come out, come to light, become apparent, be disclosed.

DEVELOPMENT, *n.* 1. Bringing to light, display, disclosure, exhibition, revelation, unfoldment, explication, unravelment, disentanglement.

2. Series of changes by which an organism passes from a lower to a higher state, progress toward a more perfect state, ripening, maturation, growth, progress to maturity, gradual evolution, progression in an ascending gradation, increase, advancement, improvement.

3. Expansion, elaboration, evolvement, spread, enlargement, amplification, extension, dilation, augmentation, dilatation, increment, attainment, swell, aggrandizement.

4. Occurrence, happening, circumstance, issue, event.

DEVIATE, v. 1. Digress, deflect, yaw, go about, veer, diverge, slew, wheel, tack, curve, swerve, heel, bear off, wheel about, sheer off, turn, bend, shy, jib, glance off, vary, depart, differ, change, sidle, edge, twist, steer clear of, step aside.

2. Turn aside from a course, take a different course, depart from a course, straggle, ramble, stray, meander, rove, drift, err, wander, miss, go astray, lose one's way, go out of one's way.

3. Cause to turn aside, deflect, bend, cause to deviate, divert, cause to swerve, sidetrack, shunt, switch, shift.

DEVIATION, n. 1. Digression, ramification, divagation, divergence, departure, wandering, declination, swerve, sheer, forking, divarication, deflection, turning aside, aberration, straying, diversion, excursion.

2. Variance, variation, difference, alteration, mutation, change, commutation, permutation.

3. Transgression, obliquity of conduct, sin, error, iniquity, offense, misdeed, misdemeanor, delinquency, fault, aberration, mistake, lapse, moral departure.

DEVICE, n. 1. Appliance, apparatus, contraption, gadget, gear, invention, contrivance, equipment, outfit, matériel, mechanism, implement, utensil, machine, tackle, rigging, harness, instrument, tool, means, agent, medium, wherewithal, resort, resource, expedient.

2. Crafty scheme, stratagem, maneuver, hoax, machination, artifice, design, plan, plot, wile, project, ruse, dodge, shift, trick, finesse, trap, subterfuge, flimflam, snare, fabrication, fraud, evasion.

3. Design, figure, pattern, fanciful conception, emblem, sign, symbol, signum, mark, type, badge, motto, trademark, token, note, hallmark, seal, countermark, insigne, signet, crest, artistic figure used as a heraldic bearing, emblazoned bearing, coat of arms, hatchment, escutcheon.

4. (Pl.) Will, desire, inclination.

DEVIL, n. 1. Chief of the apostate angels, archenemy of God, evil spirit at enmity with God, supreme spirit of evil, prince of darkness, author of evil, the Evil One, the Foul Fiend, the Serpent, the Adversary, the Wicked One, the Tempter, the Old One, the Old Boy, Old Nick, Old Harry, Old Scratch, Old Bogy, the Dickens, the Deuce, the Mischief, prince of sinners, god of this world.

2. Mephistopheles, Satan, Lucifer, Apollyon, Abaddon, Ahriman, Eblis, Belial, Samael, Hades, Asmodeus, Azazel, Beelzebub, Moloch, Diabolus, Mammon.

3. Demon, goblin, bogy, ogre, ghoul, vampire, lamia, evil jinni, genie, barghest, cacodemon, fiend, imp, monster, incubus, succubus, nightmare, malicious spirit, atrociously wicked person, malignant person.

4. Person of great cleverness, one of great dash and daring.

5. Unfortunate fellow, wretched person, rogue.

6. Apprentice in a printing office, printer's devil, printer's errand boy.

DEVIL, v. 1. Be devilish, bedevil, harass, hector, torment, plague, tease, annoy.

2. Prepare with savory seasoning, make burn with spices, spice liberally, make hot with seasoning, make piquant.

DEVILISH, adj. 1. Satanical, satanic, impious, diabolical, demoniac, demoniacal, infernal, hellborn, hellish, accursed, fiendish.

2. Nefarious, flagitious, fell, dire, ruthless, brutal, savage, atrocious, malign, maleficent, malicious, malevolent, wicked, vicious, detestable, rancorous, cruel, barbarous, black, inhuman, heinous.

3. Terrible, excessive, enormous, outrageous.

DEVIL-MAY-CARE, adj. 1. Defiant, reckless, rash, temerarious, careless, wanton, madcap, heedless, irresponsible, impulsive, desperate, headlong, breakneck, foolhardy, free-and-easy.

2. Indifferent, insouciant, nonchalant, listless, unconcerned, pococurante, lackadaisical, easygoing.

3. Cavalier, flippant, pert, saucy, forward, impertinent, fresh, malapert, shameless, brazen, unabashed, barefaced, impudent, audacious, presumptuous, jaunty, roistering, blustering, swaggering, swashbuckling, vaporing, posturing.

DEVILTRY, n. 1. Extreme wickedness, satanic evil, cruelty, fiendishness, diabolic magic, black art, *Hexerei (Ger.).*

2. Devilish mischief, wicked conduct, roguery, wanton rollicking, *diablerie (Fr.),* devilment, devilry.

DEVIOUS, adj. 1. Departing from the direct way, out of the regular track, deflected from a straight road, varying from a straight course, indirect, divergent, aberrant, rambling, swerving, desultory, excursive, discursive.

2. Circuitous, roundabout, winding, tortuous, anfractuous, ambagious, labyrinthine, zigzag, mazy, serpentine, crooked.

3. Going astray, turning aside from the way, erratic, stray, straying, vagrant.

4. Erring out of the path of rectitude, sinful, straying from the way of duty, errant, mistaken, transgressing.

5. Deceitful, misleading, treacherous, sly, confusing, disingenuous.

DEVISE, v. 1. Form in the mind, arrange the plan of, prepare, think out, excogitate, hatch, frame, fabricate, concoct, brew, design, scheme, plan, project, contrive, conceive, invent, trump up, plot, imagine, compass, concert, dream up, make up, originate, create, coin, shape up, spin, formulate, construct, improvise, map out, block out, hit upon, get ready, maneuver, machinate.

2. (Law) Transmit by will, bequeath, will, demise, leave by will, bestow, confer, hand down, give away, dispose of, convey, transfer.

DEVISE, n. 1. Bestowal of real estate by will, legacy, bequest, dowry, dot.

2. Will, clause in a will disposing of property.

3. Property disposed of, gift of lands by a last will and testament.

DEVOID, adj. Not possessing, without, unblest with, lacking, wanting, not in possession, bare, unprovided, empty-handed, bereft of, denuded of, bereaved of, barren, destitute, empty, vacant, out of, short of, void.

DEVOIR, *n.* Respectful notice due to another, expression of honorable regard, act of respect, homage, civility, compliment, regards, service, veneration, *égards (Fr.),* duty, politeness, curtsy, deference, obeisance, reverence, bow, bowing and scraping, mark of recognition, "nods and becks and wreathed smiles."

DEVOLVE, *v.* 1. Cause to pass to another, pass on, delegate upon another, transmit, deliver over to a successor, make over, alienate, transfer to, demise, assign, consign, convey, hand over.

2. Fall on a person as a duty or responsibility, fall to one's lot, be incumbent on, be the duty of, behoove, become, befit, beseem, lie upon one's door, rest with, rest on the shoulders of, lie upon one's head.

3. Descend by inheritance, fall by succession, be transferred, pass to, be handed down to.

DEVOTE, *v.* 1. Dedicate by a solemn act, bless, hallow, consecrate, appropriate by vow, set apart, enshrine, signalize, vow.

2. Direct attention to, give oneself up to, apply oneself to, attach oneself to, addict, resign, give up to a particular pursuit, surrender completely to.

3. Preordain, foreordain, ordain, destine, doom, predestine, foredoom, pronounce a curse on.

DEVOTED, *adj.* 1. Dedicated, consecrated, set apart by vow, devout, hallowed, holy, sacred.

2. Feeling strong attachment, attached, fond, affectionate, loving, tender, amorous, erotic, impassioned, passionate, rapturous, warm, close, uxorious, loyal, faithful, sympathetic, constant, cordial.

3. Eager, ardent, fervent, earnest, assiduous, sedulous, zealous.

DEVOTEE, *n.* 1. One devoted to a cause, bigot, partisan, adherent, votary, zealot, fanatic, very devout person, believer, religionist, pietist.

2. Enthusiast, fan, follower, ardent admirer, *aficionado (Sp.).*

DEVOTION, *n.* 1. Dedication, concentration, sanctification.

2. Ready will to perform what belongs to the service of God, piety, devoutness, reverence, religiousness, godliness, saintliness, sanctity, religiosity, spirituality, holiness, religion.

3. Religious observance, act of religious worship, worship, homage, adoration, prayer, service, cult, laudation, exaltation, benediction, magnification, glorification, thanksgiving, grace, hosanna, hallelujah, alleluia, *Te Deum,* vespers, matins.

4. Earnest attachment to, love, affection, passion, yearning, idolization, fondness, liking, devotedness, regard, inclination, infatuation, fancy, admiration, enchantment, addiction.

5. Faithfulness, allegiance, fidelity, fealty, deference, constancy, loyalty, adherence.

6. Zealous application, ardor, fervor, assiduity, sedulousness, enthusiasm, earnestness, eagerness, zeal.

DEVOTIONAL, *adj.* 1. Devout, pious, religious, characterized by devotion, godly, saintly, solemn, spiritual, reverential, worshipful, prayerful, heavenly-minded, spiritual-minded.

2. Used in devotions, sacred, holy, sanctified.

DEVOUR, *v.* 1. Eat up voraciously, gluttonize,

raven, gormandize, swallow down greedily, gorge, gobble up, gulp down, bolt, wolf, stuff, cram, dispatch, tuck in, banquet, feast, eat in a snatch-and-grab way, play a good knife and fork, eat at a speed that invites indigestion.

2. Make away with violently, expend, scuttle, consume destructively, waste recklessly, spend wantonly, dissipate, destroy rapidly, prey upon, devastate, ravage, gut, eradicate, exterminate.

3. Gaze upon with avidity, read eagerly, peruse intently, look at intently, take in greedily with the senses, make one's own, absorb wholly, engulf, engross.

DEVOUT, *adj.* 1. Devoted to divine worship, religious, heavenly-minded, pious, devotional, reverent, worshipful, prayerful, saintly, godly, holy, Christian, seraphic, pure in heart, moral, pietistic, righteous, solemn.

2. Hearty, sincere, heartfelt, earnest, fervid, fervent, ardent, vehement, intense, serious.

DEXTERITY, *n.* 1. Skill in using the hands, manual efficiency, adroitness, deftness, agility, nimbleness, neat-handedness, facility, featness, adeptness, aptness, proficiency, readiness, sleight, quickness, handiness.

2. Mental sharpness, cleverness, address, turn, mental aptitude, smartness, expertness, ability, capability, knack, tact, diplomacy, ingenuity, gift, felicity, *curiosa felicitas (Lat.),* mastery, finish, technique, finesse, talent, faculty, forte, genius.

DEXTEROUS, *adj.* 1. Skilful in the use of the hands, nimble-fingered, fine-fingered, adroit, deft, neat-handed, handy, proficient, facile, feat, slick, crack, ready, quick, adept.

2. Having mental adroitness, clever, smart, ingenious, gifted, talented, competent, efficient, resourceful, experienced, practiced, accomplished, *au fait (Fr.),* up in, good at, at home in, master of.

3. Done with dexterity, workmanlike, expert, artful, happy, finished, felicitous, neat, artistic, masterly.

DIABOLIC, *adj.* Devilish, fiendish, of devil-like nature, Mephistophelian, satanic, infernal, hellish, hellborn, demoniac, impious, outrageously wicked, atrocious, vicious, nefarious, black-hearted, inhuman, pitiless, accursed, flagitious, felonious, flagrant, heinous, scelerous, monstrous, horrible.

DIADEM, *n.* 1. Symbol of rank worn upon the head, crown, tiara, coronet, mitre.

2. Wreath, garland, chaplet, circlet, fillet.

3. Supreme power, royal dignity, sovereignty, regal authority, empire.

DIAGNOSIS, *n.* 1. Distinction of a disease by its characteristic symptoms, summary of symptoms with conclusion arrived at, determination of the nature of a disease through examination, clinical diagnosis, differential diagnosis, pathological diagnosis, prognosis.

2. Analysis, scientific determination, minute investigation, classificatory description, judgment, critical scrutiny, conclusion.

DIAGNOSTIC, *adj.* Aiding in diagnosis, probatory, distinguishing, characteristic, indicative as symptoms, distinctive as characteristics, characterizing, demonstrative, probative, speculative, analytic.

DIAGRAM, *n.* Tabular sketch, graph, scheme of lines, line drawing, delineation, mechanical plan, outline, chart, map, rough projection, figure drawn to aid in demonstration, representation, draft, ground plan, picture, view, illustration, tracing.

DIAL, *n.* Face upon which time is indicated, disk with figures, device for showing time, sundial, gnomon, horologe, graduated circular plate for indication by a pointer, compass.

DIALECT, *n.* 1. Language of a particular district or class, ruralism, provincialism, colloquialism, vernacular, lingo, patter, argot, jargon, patois, brogue, cant, peculiar speech, idiom, slang, accent, broken English, pidgin English.
2. Special branch of a language, language, mother tongue, tongue, form of speech, diction, parlance, phraseology.

DIALECTIC, *adj.* 1. Idiomatic, vernacular, rural, colloquial, slangy, dialectal, jargonic, neological, provincial, barbarous.
2. Argumentative, rationalistic, controversial, analytic, reasoning, disputatious, polemical, logical.

DIALECTIC, *n.* Discussion of a conception by question and answer, determination of truth and error by analysis, art of distinguishing truth from error, art of logical discussion, logic of debate and refutation, logical argumentation, logic of discursive argument, logic of probable reasoning, metaphysics of ideas, argument for purposes of persuasion, Socratic argumentation, negative procedure, progression by negation, logic of illusion, chain of reasoning, mode of reasoning, ratiocination, induction, deduction, disceptation, generalization, polemics, logomachy, disputation.

DIALECTICIAN, *n.* One skilled in dialectic, one who reasons logically, logician, rationalist, casuist, scientific reasoner.

DIALOGUE, *n.* 1. Formal discussion among several persons, colloquy, collocution, parley, conference, converse, conversation, discourse, oral communication, talk, interlocution, communion, commerce, speech, chat, palaver, confabulation, verbal intercourse, duologue, trialogue, causerie, chitchat, powwow, pourparler, tattle, gossip, small talk, table talk, idle talk.
2. Conversational element in a book or play, literary work in the form of a conversation.

DIAMETER, *n.* Distance through the center, length through the center, bore, caliber, breadth, thickness, broadness, width, central chord.

DIAMETRICAL, *adj.* Pertaining to the ends of a diameter, antipodal, subcontrary, fronting, facing, directly adverse, as remote as possible, utterly different, exactly opposite, extremely opposed.

DIAPHANOUS, *adj.* Showing light through its substance, transparent, transpicuous, translucent, clear, limpid, pellucid, lucid, fine, delicate, thin, sheer, gossamer, gauzy, chiffon, silken, cobwebby.

DIARY, *n.* Daily record, register of daily events, systematic account of daily experiences, journal, chronicle, daybook, log, ephemeris, noctuary, chronogram, memorandum book, biography, annals.

DIATRIBE, *n.* 1. Prolonged discussion, argument, disputation, disquisition, dissertation, descant.
2. Abusive language, stream of abuse, violent denunciation, bitter harangue, verbal onslaught, invective, tirade, philippic, jeremiad, vituperation, reviling, rating, railing, objurgation, exprobration, contumely, stinging words, obloquy, screed, censure, animadversion, criticism, curtain lecture, dressing down, sarcasm, reprehension, increpation, rebuke, castigation, jobation.

DICKER, *v.* Trade by barter, make a petty trade, barter, haggle, higgle, truck, chaffer, huckster, stickle for, bargain, drive a bargain, negotiate, have dealings with, deal, bid for, try to arrange matters by mutual bargaining.

DICTATE, *v.* 1. Issue a command, impose an order, give orders, prescribe positively, charge, enjoin, instruct, declare with directive authority, direct, command, ordain, decree, speak with final authority, demand, require authoritatively, bid, enact, order, exercise authority, lay down the law, call the tune, call the shots.
2. Present forcibly and conclusively, decide by necessity, advise, suggest, counsel, prompt, recommend, urge, move, advocate, exhort, warn, persuade, guide, caution.
3. Communicate directly to an amanuensis, say aloud to be taken down in writing, direct the words of, communicate to another for writing down, compose, draw up, formulate, draft, indite, pronounce, speak.

DICTATE, *n.* 1. Injunction, behest, bidding, fiat, command, instruction, decree, regulation, caveat, mandate, rescript, edict, positive order, demand, imperative direction, commandment, ultimatum, ruling, dictation, dictum, charge, requirement, exaction.
2. Rule, authoritative suggestion, prompting, precept, maxim.
3. Instigation, impulsion, instance, suggestion, advice, counsel, advocacy, exhortation, warning, persuasion, incitement, solicitation, admonition, request, guidance, caution, recommendation.

DICTATION, *n.* 1. Arbitrary direction, positive command, imposition of control, prescription, injunction, charge, instruction.
2. Authoritative utterance, mandate, caveat, decree, fiat, ukase, dictum, order, behest. (See DICTATE.)
3. Advice, counsel, adhortation, word to the wise, suggestion, submonition, recommendation, advocacy, guidance, admonition.
4. Message for reproduction in writing, utterance for copying, dictating to a copyist.

DICTATOR, *n.* Person with absolute control in a government, despot, absolute ruler, autocrat, tyrant, master, leader, Duce, Führer, Caesar, czar, kaiser, taskmaster, lord, commander, chief, overlord, headman, adviser, ringleader, man at the wheel, wirepuller, cock of the walk, boss, lord of the ascendant, disciplinarian, martinet, oppressor, sultan, sheik, sirdar, sachem, grand Turk, caliph, imaum, shah, mogul, khan, lama, tycoon, rajah, emir, negus, bashaw, one appointed to absolute power provisionally in time of emergency *(Hist.).*

DICTATORIAL, *adj.* 1. Absolute, arbitrary, hegemonic, unrestricted, unlimited, clothed with authority, overruling, regnant, dominant, positive, supreme, dogmatic, autocratic, categorical.
2. Given to dictating, inclined to command, imperious, doctrinaire, authoritative, stringent, magisterial, peremptory, overbearing, arrogant, domineering, high-handed, iron-fisted, high and mighty, intolerant, supercilious, contumelious, insolent, haughty, pompous, lordly, obstinate, opinionative, bigoted, wilful.

DICTATORSHIP, *n.* Despotic control, imperious direction, autocracy, tyranny, oppression, iron rule, absolutism, arbitrary power, directorship, supreme authority, tight grasp, strong hand, iron sway, coercion, brute force, reign of terror, rule, domination, hegemony, empire, command.

DICTION, *n.* 1. High level of word usage, style,

wording, turn of expression, phraseology, manner of expression, language, command of language, distinction with which words are used, choice of words, vocabulary, literary power, ready pen, eloquence, verbiage, rhetoric, oratory, fluency, locution.

2. Degree of distinctness of speech sounds, articulation, enunciation, elocution.

DICTIONARY, *n.* Wordbook, lexicon, gloss, thesaurus, vocabulary, *Wörterbuch (Ger.),* gradus *(Prosody),* idioticon, alphabetized vocabulary with definitions, terminology, glossary.

2. Alphabetized reference book, encyclopaedia, cyclopaedia, digest, alphabetical summary of information of a particular subject.

DICTUM, *n.* 1. Authoritative pronouncement, positive oracular announcement, saying uttered dogmatically, affirmation, assertion, authoritative statement, dictate, dogmatic principle, proposition.

2. Maxim, adage, proverb, precept, phylactery, moral, gnome, aphorism, truism, saw, epigram, motto, sentence, mot, apothegm, axiom, byword, *ipse dixit (Lat.).*

3. *(Law)* Judicial assertion, extra-judicial opinion, arbitrament, decision, award, judgment, finding, verdict, decree, sentence.

4. Passing remark, incidental opinion, *obiter dictum (Lat.).*

DIDACTIC, *adj.* 1. Fitted to teach, adapted to teach, intended for instruction, instructive, preceptive, expository, edifying, educational, doctrinal, hortative, pedagogic, tutorial, academic, disciplinal, scholastic.

2. Inclined to lecture others too much, teaching some moral lesson.

DIDACTICS, *n.* Science of teaching, art of educating, paedeutics, pedagogy.

DIDDLE, *v.* 1. Dawdle, waste time, idle away time, trifle. (See DAWDLE.)

2. Move rapidly up and down, totter, move by jerks, jiggle, jog, toddle, mark time with one's feet, dance jerkily.

3. Cheat by trickery, deceive, outwit, kid, overreach, hoax, swindle, undo, ruin, take in, do, gyp, chouse, double-cross, bilk, pluck, fleece, mulct, rook, skin, defraud.

4. Borrow.

DIE, *v.* 1. Expire, demise, pass on, decease, leave this world, cease respiration, emit the last breath, relinquish life, part with life, cease to live, suffer death, pass away, meet death, draw the last breath, give up the ghost, cease to exist, breathe one's last, pay the debt to nature, take one's death throes, go the way of all flesh, lose one's life, go to one's last home, be numbered with the dead, lay down one's life, join the choir invisible, go West, pay the supreme sacrifice, be no more, cross the Stygian ferry, cross the Styx, pay Charon, kill oneself, die a violent death, commit suicide.

2. Perish, wither, decline, fade, fade away, decay, deteriorate, degenerate, fall off, droop, lapse, retrograde, break down, totter to a fall, wear away, disintegrate, go bad, lose active qualities, wane, ebb, wither on the vine, run to seed, crumble, molder, rot, rankle.

3. Pass out of existence, pass out of sight, recede, vanish, evanesce, disappear, come to an end, become lost, be heard of no more, come to nothing, cease, stop, halt, pause, come to a full stop, break off, pass, be gone, leave no trace, melt away, dissolve, be lost to view, die away,

be extinguished, peter out, become fainter and fainter, subside.

4. Lose strength, faint, sink, fall, become vapid, become flat, become spiritless, go stale.

5. Pine with desire, be consumed with desire, long for something ardently, desire greatly, want keenly.

DIE, *n.* 1. Cube for gaming, square block, one of a pair of dice, "bone."

2. Cast, stake, hazard, wager, gamble, chance.

3. *(Arch.)* Dado of a pedestal, cube of a pedestal.

4. Device for cutting material in a press, punch, engraved stamp for impressing a design, hollow device of steel for cutting the threads of bolts.

DIE-HARD, *n.* One who fights to the last, one who resists vigorously to the last, bitter-ender, fanatical partisan, zealot, a conservative in politics, reactionary, passive resister, extremist, irreconcilable, intransigent, Adullamite.

DIET, *n.* 1. Regulated course of food and drink with reference to their quality and effects, particular selection of food for curing a disorder, food considered in relation to its effects on health, dietary, manner of living as regards food, dietetics, system of diet, fixed allowance of food, regular provision of food, rule of diet.

2. Nutrition, nutriment, nurture, nourishment, aliment, sustenance, subsistence, board, regimen, commissariat, fare, rations, commons, provision, pabulum, cheer, victuals, viands, comestibles, edibles, foodstuffs.

3. Legislative assembly, formal assembly for acting upon public affairs, general assembly, convention, convocation, council, legislature, congress, parliament, synod.

DIET, *v.* 1. Prescribe a course of food for, regulate the food of, restrict the food and drink of, dose.

2. Take food according to a regimen, eat sparingly, eat by regulation, nourish oneself, take nourishment, supply with food, feed, eat, nourish, nurture, fare.

DIFFER, *v.* 1. Vary, diverge from, deviate from, depart from, be unlike, be dissimilar, be distinct in nature, be mismatched, contrast.

2. Have a dissimilar opinion, disagree in opinion, dissent, be of a different belief, be of a different opinion, think differently.

3. Quarrel, wrangle, fall out, have a difference, dispute, bicker, be at variance, contend, altercate, squabble, brawl, spat.

4. Modify, change, alter.

DIFFERENCE, *n.* 1. Unlikeness, perceivable variation, lack of identity, state of being different, dissimilarity, lack of resemblance, variety, variance, diversity, dissimilitude, inconformity, inconsistency between things that should agree, disagreement, contrariness, contrast, contrariety, divergence, deviation, departure, opposition, oppositeness, adverseness, antithesis, antithetical-ness, contradiction, inequality, incongruity, heterogeneity, nuance.

2. Disagreement in opinion, contention, dispute, controversy, dissension, altercation, quarrel, contest, disaccord, wrangle, bickering, debate, variance, strife, friction, discord, falling out, clash of temperament, spat, alienation, dissonance, disharmony, misunderstanding, breach, schism, irreconcilability, incompatibility, jarring, rupture, embroilment.

3. Discrimination, act of distinguishing, nice

distinction, perception of dissimilarity, separate treatment.

4. Instance of unlikeness, point of dissimilarity, distinguishing characteristic, peculiarity, idiosyncrasy.

5. Amount by which one quantity is greater or less than another, disparity, remainder, discrepancy.

DIFFERENT, *adj.* 1. Dissimilar, unlike, having unlike qualities, differing in character, contrasted, contrary, disagreeing, divergent, discrepant, varied, variant, distinct, deviating, diverse, various, contradistinct, incompatible, incongruous, marked by a difference, not having like nature, varying, discordant, dissonant, inharmonious, off-beat, modified, altered, changed.

2. Not identical, other, another, separate, not the same, distinct, unmatched, unequal, opposite, contrastive, poles apart, disparate.

3. Several, various, divers, variegated, sundry, manifold, many, diversified, miscellaneous, unclassified.

4. Out of the ordinary, unusual, unique, not ordinary, distinctive, characteristic, distinguishing, foreign, peculiar, discriminative, idiosyncratic.

5. Antagonistic, adverse, hostile, irreconcilable, opposed, intransigent.

DIFFERENTIAL, *n.* Distinguishing feature, differentiating trait, distinguishing morphological characteristic *(Biol.)*, infinitesimal difference between two values of a quantity *(Math.)*, infinitesimal increment of a quantity *(Math.)*.

DIFFERENTIATE, *v.* 1. Mark off by differences, make different, constitute a difference between, make a distinction between, distinguish, contrast, separate, set apart, draw the line.

2. Perceive the difference between, discriminate, indicate the specific differences of, discern between, make a distinction.

3. Make different by modification, institute a difference between, cause to become different, develop variation in, adapt, alter, change, modify.

4. Become unlike, become dissimilar, change in character, acquire a distinct and separate character.

DIFFICULT, *adj.* 1. Laborious, arduous, not easy, hard, strenuous, exacting, attended by obstacles, beset with difficulty, requiring much effort, toilsome, burdensome, wearisome, "tough," Herculean, "stiff," formidable, trying, uphill, exhausting, hard-won, onerous, troublesome, irksome, painful.

2. Hard to explain, puzzling, perplexing, complex, intricate, involved, abstruse, hard to solve, complicated, hard to understand, abstract, obscure, inexplicable, knotty, thorny, ticklish, pathless, trackless, labyrinthine.

3. Hard to manage, adamantine, flinty, stony, intractable, unyielding, stubborn, uncompliant, unaccommodating, obstinate, perverse, refractory, hard to induce, hard to persuade, inflexible, rigid, austere, not easy to approach, unmanageable, trying one's patience, not easily accessible, awkward, *difficile (Fr.)*, disconcerting, unwieldy.

4. Hard to satisfy, hard to please, fastidious, squeamish, delicate, dainty, hard to deal with, embarrassing, hard to get on with, crabbed, critical.

5. Hard-pressed, hard up, pinched, straitened, in difficulty, in a scrape, in a pickle, in hot water, in a fix, on the horns of a dilemma, between the Devil and the deep blue sea, between Scylla and Charybdis, between the frying pan and the fire, at a loss, nonplused, puzzled, reduced to straits, at one's wit's ends, on the rocks, stranded, aground, beached, stuck fast, mired, at a standstill.

DIFFICULTY, *n.* 1. Troublesomeness, uphill work, laboriousness, rough going, arduousness, hard sledding, tight squeeze, tough job, dead weight, impracticability.

2. Impediment, barrier, obstacle, hindrance, bar, thwart, obstruction, stumbling block, clog, check, standstill, dead stand, deadlock, quandary, dilemma, predicament, pickle, fix, pinch, exigency, emergency, crux, entanglement, knot, intricacy, matter, trial, trouble, embarrassment, perplexity, stand, set fast, dead set, hard row to hoe, peck of troubles, hard nut to crack, horns of a dilemma, Gordian knot, labyrinth, maze, coil, puzzle, poser, deep water, knotty point, paradox, bafflement, frustration, hitch, critical situation, crisis, strait, rub, pass, vexed question, scrape, hot water, hornet's nest, stew, snag, muddle, mess, botch, slough, swamp, quagmire, quicksands, financial embarrassment, jam, impasse, cul-de-sac.

3. Show of reluctance, demur, objection, unwillingness, obstacle to belief, cavil, obstructive behavior, protest, scruple, kick, remonstrance, squawk.

4. Argument, controversy, misunderstanding, contentious difference, disagreement, quarrel, embroilment, imbroglio, complication.

DIFFIDENCE, *n.* Extreme modesty, timidity, bashfulness, shyness, sheepishness, reserve, want of self-confidence, humility, distrust of oneself, lack of trust in one's own ability, want of self-reliance, timorousness, faint-heartedness, retiring disposition, apprehension, constraint, reluctance, unobtrusiveness, hesitancy, doubtfulness.

DIFFIDENT, *adj.* Lacking confidence in oneself, distrustful of oneself, timorous, faint-hearted, sheepish, shy, bashful, modest, timid, coy, demure, humble, unassuming, reserved, blushing, constrained, retiring, unobtrusive, apprehensive, shrinking, reluctant, hesitant.

DIFFUSE, *v.* 1. Pour out and spread, scatter widely, disperse, disseminate, strew, dissipate, radiate, extend, send abroad, distribute, effuse, cast forth, dispense, expand, disgregate, separate, disintegrate.

2. Publish, put forward, make known, spread abroad, circulate, propagate, promulgate, bruit about, rumor, evulgate, bring before the public, give out to the world, hawk about, buzz about, blaze about, drag into the open, voice, proclaim, herald, give tongue, noise abroad, proclaim from the housetops, set news afloat, raise a hue and cry about.

DIFFUSE, *adj.* 1. Characterized by great length in speaking, long-winded, wordy, prolix, verbose, long-tongued, voluble, copious, discursive, not concentrated, lacking conciseness, long-spun, protracted, rambling, roundabout, spun out, loose, rhapsodic, full, garrulous, loquacious, episodic, multiloquent, polyloquent, digressive, turgid, maundering, pleonastic, redundant, tautological, circumlocutory, periphrastic, exuberant, profuse, ambagious.

2. Widespread, scattered, dispersed, extended widely, vaguely defined.

DIFFUSION, *n.* 1. Diffuseness, prolixity, want of concentration, copious use of words, verbosity, redundancy, circumlocution, ambages, wordiness, profuseness, amplification, verbiage, flow of words, *flux de paroles (Fr.), copia verborum (Lat.)*, loquacity, periphrasis, indirection, padding, roundaboutness, tautology, rhapsody, garrulity, multiloquence, polylogy, volubility, gift of gab, fluency.

2. Circulation, dissemination, dissipation, dispersion, strewing, scattering, distribution, spread, propagation, expansion, extension.

DIG, *v.* 1. Break up and turn over earth, excavate, hollow out, scoop, grub, burrow, delve, work with a spade, penetrate and loosen ground, make a tunnel by removing earth, channel, quarry, unearth, exhume, bring to the surface, plunge, prod, poke, thrust, hoe, till, cultivate, dibble, plough, rake, harrow.

2. Plunge into, force into, thrust into, insert, push into, poke.

3. Study, work hard, find by effort, discover by search, research, search for and bring out by labor, plod, grind.

DIG, *n.* 1. Thrust, punch, poke, push.

2. Cutting sarcastic remark, verbal thrust, taunt, gibe, hoot, jeer, flout, quip, sneer, fling, slap in the face, twit, slur.

3. Student who studies hard, grind.

DIGEST, *n.* 1. Complete code of laws, systematic abstract of a body of law, pandect.

2. Summary, review, abridgment, compend, compendium, résumé, abstract, précis, epitome, abbreviation, brief, breviary, compilation, sum and substance, syllabus, conspectus, outline, bulletin, aperçu, analysis, condensation, draft, recapitulation, pocket edition, arrangement of literary matter in systematic form.

DIGEST, *v.* 1. Prepare food in the alimentary canal for assimilation into the system, promote the digestion of food, convert into chyme, cause to undergo digestion, separate the nutritive and waste elements of food, dissolve, transform.

2. Arrange in methodical order, reduce to a system, methodize, reduce to order, codify, systematize, analyze, classify, summarize, dispose, edit.

3. Arrange methodically in the mind, reflect upon, ponder, bring into system mentally, revolve in the mind, think out, think over, think on, mull over, study, contemplate, weigh, meditate upon, consider, settle.

4. Assimilate mentally, appropriate wholly in the mind, obtain mental nourishment from, comprehend, understand, make one's own, master, absorb.

5. Bear with patience, endure, tolerate patiently, submit to, brook, suffer, put up with, abide, stand, swallow, stomach, pocket.

6. *(Chem.)* Soften by a gentle heat, steep, macerate, soak.

DIGESTION, *n.* 1. Separation of nutritious from waste elements of food, process by which food is digested, conversion of food into chyme, power of digestion of food, eupepsy.

2. Mental reception and assimilation, reduction to order, methodizing, classification, mental appropriation, meditation, comprehension, understanding.

3. *(Chem.)* Steeping, maceration, soaking, softening under heat.

DIGIT, *n.* 1. Terminal organ of a limb, finger, toe, thumb.

2. Ancient measure of length suggested by the thickness of the finger, finger's breadth, breadth

of a finger used as a unit of linear measure, three-fourths of an inch, about two-thirds of an inch.

3. Numerical symbol in the Arabic notation, any of the Arabic figures 1 to 9.

DIGNIFIED, *adj.* 1. Marked by dignity of manner, majestic, stately, grand, august, magisterial, grave, solemn, sublime, noble, magnificent, imposing, distinguished, eminent, *distingué (Fr.)*, decorous, gravely courteous, honorable, proud, lofty, lordly, imperious, courtly, princely, glorious, haughty, portly.

2. Invested with dignities, promoted in rank, honored, exalted, elevated.

DIGNIFY, *v.* 1. Add dignity to, give distinction to, shed luster on, aggrandize, nobilitate, ennoble, grace, glorify, honor, make illustrious, impart dignity to, make worthy of respect, adorn, render impressive, crown, invest, enthrone, signalize, immortalize, deify, enshrine, blazon, lionize.

2. Give high-sounding title to, invest with honors, promote in rank, advance, confer dignity upon, exalt, elevate, prefer to office, raise to distinction.

DIGNITY, *n.* 1. Nobleness of mind, elevation of mind, worthiness, worth, state of being honorable, fame, repute, éclat, eminence, respectability, reputableness, glory, exaltation, greatness, honor.

2. Nobility of manner, stateliness, lofty bearing, loftiness, elevated deportment, majesty, sublimity, grandeur, solemnity, grace, splendor, luster, dignified behavior, gravity, decorum, reserve, augustness, impressiveness of character, serenity of demeanor.

3. High station, elevated rank, honorable place, degree of excellence, relative standing, preferment of office, title, official distinction, honorable position, honor, station, grade of elevation, place, standing, importance, height.

4. Person in office, dignitary, person holding high title, magistrate, peer, magnate, prelate, canon, officer, bigwig *(colloq.)*.

DIGRESS, *v.* 1. Go out of the path, swerve, diverge, deviate, meander, wander, turn aside, sweep, divagate, stray, ramble, deflect, excurse.

2. Dwell on some incidental matter, be episodic, maunder, beat about the bush, descant, rhapsodize, be diffuse.

DIGRESSION, *n.* 1. Ramification, divarication, deviation, divergence, wandering, rambling, elongation, ecbole, divagation, aberration, variation, alteration, deflection, diversion, declination, swerve.

2. Portion of a discourse deviating from the main topic, departure from the main theme, episode, incidental passage, rhapsody, excursus.

DIGRESSIVE, *adj.* Departing from the main subject, episodic, rhapsodic, excursive, cursory, roundabout, discursive, circumlocutory, desultory, rambling, roving, irregular, unmethodical.

DIKE, *n.* 1. Mole, breakwater, levee, bank, estacade, embankment for restraining waters, dam.

2. Ditch, moat, fosse, channel, bank of earth thrown up in excavation, intrenchment, trench, rampart, parapet, mound, breastwork, earthwork.

3. Causeway, raised path, viaduct, causey, bridge.

4. Obstacle, barrier.

DILAPIDATE, *v.* 1. Bring into a ruinous condition by neglect, ruin, impair by neglect, suffer to go to ruin, destroy, injure, deface, mar, pull down, throw down.

2. Fall into ruin, deteriorate, degenerate, crumble, give way, totter, fall to the ground, tumble, topple, fall to pieces, break up, go to dust, go to smash, go to wrack and ruin.

3. Squander, waste, dissipate.

DILAPIDATED, *adj.* Reduced to ruin, fallen into decay, decayed, ruined, in ruins, run-down, wasted, decadent, worn-out, ramshackle, rickety, tumble-down, falling to pieces, impaired, time-worn, crumbling, deteriorated, disintegrated, battered, weathered, unimproved, in disrepair, gone to wrack and ruin, decrepit, broken-down, down at the heels, moth-eaten, mildewed, moldy, moldering.

DILAPIDATION, *n.* Partial ruin from neglect, decay, disrepair, disintegration, downfall, ravages of time, decomposition, decrepitude, collapse, disorganization, *délabrement (Fr.)*, destruction, havoc, inroads, scathe, impairment, injury, moth and rust, wear and tear, erosion, corrosion, dry rot, *disiecta membra (Lat.)*, deterioration, ricketiness.

DILATE, *v.* 1. Make larger, enlarge, make wider, widen, distend, spread, broaden, swell, stretch, inflate, expand, amplify, intumesce, dome, puff out, increase.

2. Enlarge upon, tell in detail, expatiate, dwell on, descant, be diffuse, be prolix, spin a long yarn, talk about at length, branch out, launch forth, discuss diffusely, rhapsodize.

DILATION, *n.* 1. Dilatation, swelling, distention, expansion, augmentation, extension, fullness, amplification, expatiation, enlargement, bloating, swelling, varix, aneurysm.

2. Diffuseness in speech, prolixity, verbosity, profuseness, periphrasis, circumlocution, padding, indirection, tautology, looseness, redundance, exuberance.

DILATORY, *adj.* Inclined to delay, tardy, slow, sluggish, flagging, laggard, loitering, lingering, not prompt, backward, behindhand, procrastinating, dawdling, inactive, delaying, languid, tardigrade, inert, torpid, supine, passive, indolent, slothful, lackadaisical, otiose, remiss, fiddle-faddle, shilly-shally, pottering.

DILEMMA, *n.* Situation requiring a choice between equally undesirable alternatives, puzzling alternative, quandary, embarrassing situation, difficult choice, *embarras de choix (Fr.)*, awkward predicament, strait, plight, pass, poser, puzzle, nonplus, difficulty, perplexity, Hobson's choice, Morton's fork, impasse, corner, fix, pickle *(colloq.)*, mess, pinch, bewilderment, indecision, uncertainty, horns of the dilemma.

DILETTANTE, *n.* 1. Non-professional, one who pursues an art desultorily, trifling cultivator, amateur, dabbler.

2. Pretender to taste in the fine arts, lover of a fine art, man of taste, connoisseur, cognoscente, *arbiter elegantiae (Lat.)*.

DILIGENCE, *n.* 1. Earnest effort to accomplish what is undertaken, persistent exertion, assiduity in one's pursuits, assiduousness, sedulousness, perseverance, steady application to a pursuit, persistence, energy, enterprise, intentness, vigor, constancy, activity, vim, go *(colloq.)*, dispatch, expedition, industry, earnestness, labor, effort, zeal, pertinaciousness, doggedness, stick-to-itiveness.

2. Heed, attention, caution, care, heedfulness, circumspection, vigilance.

DILIGENT, *adj.* 1. Constant in effort to accomplish, acting with assiduous industry, persistent, pertinacious, occupied, busy as a bee, sedulous, assiduous, persevering, industrious, active, busily intent, hard-working, up-and-stirring, attentive, steady, earnest, laborious, zealous, studious, ardent, deeply engrossed, diligently employed.

2. Prosecuted with careful effort, pursued with persevering attention, pursued diligently, painstaking, plodding, businesslike, untiring.

DILLYDALLY, *v.* 1. Be irresolute, waste time by indecision, hang in suspense, hesitate, pause, hover, wobble, boggle, hem and haw, not know one's own mind, debate, balance, falter, waver, vacillate, blow hot and cold, shuffle.

2. Be inactive, trifle, dawdle, dally, linger, loiter, tarry over, delay, stop for time, lag, peddle, piddle, potter, fritter away time, idle away time, fiddle-faddle, putter, dabble, procrastinate, loll, lounge, loaf, take it easy, shillyshally, do nothing, move slowly, let grass grow under one's feet, take one's time, poke, drawl, hang back, slouch.

DILUTE, *v.* 1. Thin with water, make more fluid, make less concentrated, make more liquid, water down, add water to, make thinner, adulterate.

2. Weaken, thin out, attenuate, make weak, make thin, reduce, rarefy, lessen the strength of by admixture, diminish, *mettre de l'eau dans son vin (Fr.)*, make fainter, diffuse.

DILUTE, *adj.* Diluted, watery, aqueous, weak, attenuated, reduced in strength by admixture, adulterated, weak-tea, milk-and-water, wishy-washy *(colloq.)*, light, tasteless, savorless, *fade (Fr.)*, pale, thin, transparent, colorless, vapid, insipid, flat.

DIM, *adj.* 1. Lacking luminosity, somewhat dark, obscure from lack of light, not bright, darkish, dusky, shadowy, gloomy, cloudy, scarce perceptible, blurry, misty, hazy, opaque, vague, nebulous, tenebrous, atramentous, nocturnal, swart, umbrageous, gray, foggy, filmy, bleary.

2. Darkened, obfuscated, clouded, obscured, not clearly seen, indistinct, ill-defined, mysterious, incomprehensible, pale, faint, confused, muffled.

3. Lurid, dun, leaden, overcast, lowering, murky, muddy, gloomy, threatening, somber, ominous, portentous.

4. Tarnished, dulled, not brilliant, lusterless, sullied, blurred, lackluster, dingy, *sfumato (It.)*, smudgy, smirchy, dirty, mat, unglazed.

5. Slow of understanding, slow to see, not quick at perception, obtuse, dull-witted, inapt, purblind, not seeing clearly, crass, dense, doltish, stupid, slow-witted.

DIM, *v.* 1. Darken, cloud, becloud, shade, shadow, obscure, obfuscate, bedim, eclipse, reduce the luster of, cloud over, make dun.

2. Grow dim, blur, dull, fade, pale, lose luster.

3. Glimmer, flicker, blink, twinkle, flutter, waver.

DIMENSION, *n.* 1. Any measurable extent, expanse, extension, measure in one direction, magnitude measured in a particular direction, caliber, bore.

2. Scope, importance.

DIMENSIONS, *n. (pl.)* 1. Magnitude, size, bulk, bigness, volume, capacity, greatness, quantity, amplitude, massiveness, mass, largeness, weight, tonnage, cordage.

2. Linear dimensions, measurements over all, length, breadth and thickness, 3-D.

DIMINISH, *v.* 1. Lessen, contract, make smaller, decrease, reduce, abate, cut, curtail, pare, cause to taper, retrench, dwarf, shorten, abridge, condense, constrict, cramp, cause to be smaller. 2. Reduce in rank, degrade, abase, put down, weaken, disparage, belittle. 3. Decline, subside, taper off, dwindle, melt, narrow, shrivel, shrink, become smaller, be reduced, grow less, wane, ebb, waste, peter out, let up, fall off, fall away. 4. Alleviate, mitigate, temper, attenuate, moderate.

DIMINUTION, *n.* Reduction, contraction, decrease, retrenchment, constriction, curtailment, lessening, diminishing, decrement, shrinkage, abatement, attenuation, abridgment, decrescendo *(Mus.)*, dwindling, decline, decrescence, subsidence, loss, falling off, defalcation, alleviation, palliation, waste, moderation.

DIMINUTIVE, *adj.* Small, little, not large, below average in size, less than average, slight, stunted, dwarfish, puny, pygmy, tiny, nanoid, elfin, minute, contracted, microscopic, infinitesimal, compact, limited, short, dapper, half-pint *(colloq.)*, dumpy, squat, runty, vest-pocket *(colloq.)*, portable, spare, cramped, animalcular, embryonic, undersized, wee, exiguous, Lilliputian, miniature, minikin, inconsiderable, picayune, petty, insignificant, unimportant, on a small scale, in a small compass, in a nutshell.

DIN, *n.* Loud confused noise, racket, clamor, tumultuous sound, crash, clash, clangor, clang, clattering, rattling, bruit, hubbub, uproar, ado, hullabaloo, tumult, to-do, commotion, stir, babel, babble, turmoil, hurly-burly, pandemonium, roar, bombilation, static, welter of discordant sounds, charivari, blare, blast, fanfare, peal, flourish of trumpets, tintamarre, tintinnabulation, tinnitus *(Med.)*, thunderclap, confusion, riot, brawl, fracas, ruckus, rumpus, ruction.

DIN, *v.* 1. Stun with loud and continued noise, harass with clamor, assail with din, sound with a clamor, ring in the ears, strike with clanging sound, rumble, make a din, rattle, clatter, drone, drum in the ear. 2. Repeat tiresomely, iterate insistently, impress by insistent repetition, utter with persistent repetition, harp on, dwell on, ding-dong, urge, insist, reiterate, press repeatedly.

DINE, *v.* 1. Eat the principal meal of the day, take dinner in an elaborate or formal manner, refresh the inner man, partake of a full meal, feast, banquet, gormandize, gluttonize, fall to, tuck in, play a good knife and fork. 2. Entertain at dinner, provide with the principal meal, treat, regale, feed.

DINGY, *adj.* 1. Of a dark color, dusky, swart, dun, brown, tenebrous, lacking brightness, dull, lackluster, somber. 2. Of dirty aspect, smudgy, smirchy, soiled, sooty, pitchy, grimy, muddy, sullied, tarnished, rusty, faded, colorless, drab, murky, smoky, fuliginous, ashen, leaden, livid, lurid, gloomy.

DINING ROOM, *n.* Dining hall, refectory, festive board, triclinium, *salle à manger (Fr.), sala da pranzo (It.), Speisezimmer (Ger.), comedor (Sp.)*, banquet hall, dinette.

DINNER, *n.* Principal meal of the day, main meal, refection, collation, repast, feast, banquet, formal meal in honor of some person or occasion, *dîner (Fr.), pranzo (It.), comida principal (Sp.), Mittagessen (Ger.)*.

DINT, *n.* 1. (In the phrase *by dint of*) Power, potency, force, efficacy, might, effort, active agency, instrumentality, medium, intermediacy, aid, means, energy, puissance, ability, virtue, qualification, pressure, vehicle. 2. Depression made by a blow, concavity, dent, dip, hollow, indentation, cavity, pit, niche, notch, mark left by a blow, impression, crater, basin, dimple. 3. Blow, stroke, punch, thump, jab, fillip, slam, bang, whack, thwack, clout, cuff, knock, tap, rap, slap, smack, pat.

DIOCESE, *n.* District under the pastoral charge of a bishop, episcopacy, episcopate, bishopric, see, prelacy, benefice, prefecture.

DIP, *v.* 1. Place in a fluid and withdraw again, immerse temporarily, plunge into a liquid, lower and raise quickly, submerge, soak, souse, douse, moisten, wet, bathe, duck, immerge, dunk, splash, swash, lave, wash, slosh, drench, steep, macerate, slop, irrigate. 2. Raise by a dipping action, take out with a ladle, lade, bale, ladle, lift by scooping, draft off, decant, shovel. 3. Baptize by immersion, sparge, sprinkle, inundate. 4. Immerse in a solution to destroy germs. 5. Dye, glaze, plate. 6. Incline downward, tend down, decline, slope, turn down, drop down, subside, droop, settle, gravitate, sink, set, descend, verge. 7. Dive, take a plunge, plump, immerse oneself, pitch, duck. 8. Take part slightly, engage cursorily, engage slightly, take a cursory view of, read here and there in a book, skim, browse, perstringe, touch upon lightly, glance at, run over, cast the eyes over, turn over the leaves, delve into, wade through.

DIPLOMA, *n.* 1. Document conferring some honor or privilege, charter, state document, writing under seal conferring some special privilege, public document, official document, warrant, evidence, credential, voucher, letter patent, brevet. 2. Document given by a school in token of graduation therefrom, official graduation certificate, sheepskin *(colloq.)*.

DIPLOMACY, *n.* 1. Science of statecraft, conduct of negotiations between states, statesmanship, art of negotiating, international business. 2. Politics, Machiavellianism, gerrymander, jobbery, lobbyism, backstairs influence, artful management, craft, strategy, maneuvering, tact, savoir-faire, finesse, subtlety, shrewdness, skill, address, dexterity, indirection. 3. Striped-pants technique, silk-hosed pussy-footing.

DIPLOMAT, *n.* 1. Representative of a state at the capital of another, minister, ambassador, envoy, emissary, legate, consul, attaché, chargé d'affaires, plenipotentiary, resident, agent, expert in international affairs. 2. One who is artful in meeting situations, strategist, tactician, Machiavellian, negotiator, diplomatist, politician.

DIPLOMATIC, *adj.* Smoothly skilful in handling others, able to treat people of different types, capable of handling delicate matters, cautious in dealings, skilful at attaining one's ends, deft, prudent in protecting one's interests, scheming, intriguing, strategic, politic, artful, dexterous, discreet, tactful, adept.

DIPPER, *n.* Container with a handle for dipping liquids, long-handled utensil for ladling, ladler, ladle, baler, beaker, scoop, vessel.

DIPSOMANIA, *n.* A morbid and uncontrollable craving for drink, irresistible and periodic thirst for intoxicating drink, alcoholism, winebibbing, habitual drunkenness, chronic intemperance, inebriety, insobriety, bibacity, temulency, habitual tippling, oinomania, compotation, *cacoethes bibendi (Gr.-Lat.).*

DIPSOMANIAC, *n.* One with an insatiable craving for intoxicants, habitual drinker of hard liquor, alcoholic, drunkard, toper, sot, inebriate, tippler, lush, winebibber, hard drinker, heavy drinker, soak, boozer, swill, toss pot, love pot, devotee to Bacchus.

DIRE, *adj.* 1. Attended with great fear, fearful, dreadful, ill-boding, baleful, grim, appalling, evil, ominous, sinister, unpropitious, ill-omened, awful, inauspicious, ill-fated, ill-starred, portentous, direful, dismal, gloomy, horrible, shocking, horrid, deplorable, terrible, fateful, tremendous, woeful, extreme, ultimate, terrific.
2. Attended with great suffering, rending, sad, harrowing, trying, calamitous, disastrous, fatal, catastrophic, cataclysmic, ruinous, destructive, deadly, lethal, cruel, implacable, inexorable, oppressive, unhappy, unfortunate, overpowering.

DIRECT, *adj.* 1. Proceeding by the shortest course, straight, straightaway, not crooked, not oblique, undeviating, unswerving, shortest, as the crow flies, nearest, straight-line, beeline.
2. Categorical, absolute, exact, unambiguous, not equivocal, positive, express, plain.
3. Sincere, without circumlocution, going straight to the point, frank, outspoken, blunt, open, straightforward, downright, ingenuous, open as day, candid, aboveboard, undesigning, unreserved, point-blank, pointed, artless, forward, matter-of-fact, plain-spoken.
4. Without intervening agent, immediate, from the horse's mouth, personal, first-hand, head-on, face-to-face, vis-à-vis, over-the-counter.

DIRECT, *v.* 1. Guide with advice, regulate the course of, act as a conductor, preside, manage, control, govern, conduct, supervise, oversee, see to, overlook, look after, dispose, superintend, engineer, maneuver, orientate, hold the reins, drive, steer, pilot, be at the helm, boss, handle, manipulate, usher, navigate, head, lead, point out a way, show the way to a place, conduct to, put upon the right track, indicate a course to, act as a guide.
2. Command, order, prescribe to, dictate, bid, decree, ordain to, enjoin, give authoritative instructions to, rule.
3. Tend toward, verge, drift, trend, make a beeline for, gravitate toward.
4. Aim toward a place, cause to move forward, point toward an object, train at, level at.
5. Address to a person, superscribe, mark as sent to a particular person, destine for.

DIRECTION, *n.* 1. Point of compass, region, bearing, quarter, course.
2. Line along which anything moves, route,

alignment, line of march, beeline, track, **road,** path, way, line of action, line of motion.
3. Aim, course of procedure, tendency, bent, inclination, bearing, trend, drift, set, run, tenor, dip, tack.
4. Supervision, surveillance, charge, ministry, management, oversight, superintendence, care, stewardship, leadership, administration, eye of the master, directorate, government, conduct, control, reins of government, guidance, lead, authoritative instruction, steerage, pilotage, statesmanship, statecraft, guiding star, polestar, orientation.
5. Command, order, regulation, instruction, prescription.
6. Name and residence on a letter, address, superscription.

DIRECTLY, *adv.* 1. In a direct line, in a straight line, in a straight course, without deviation from course, virtually at right angles to a surface.
2. Straight as an arrow, in a beeline, as the crow flies, point-blank, full tilt at, exactly, precisely.
3. Immediately, at once, instantly, instanter, promptly, quickly, instantaneously, right away, forthwith, straightaway, next in order, speedily, presently, as soon as possible, soon, now.
4. Personally, face-to-face, vis-à-vis, honestly, straightforwardly, openly, candidly, frankly, without circumlocution, in plain terms, wholly, unambiguously, expressly, absolutely, completely.

DIRECTOR, *n.* 1. Counselor, teacher, instructor, adviser, preceptor, mentor, tutor, monitor, guide, cicerone, pilot, helmsman, steerer, fugleman.
2. Manager, superintendent, administrator, master, boss, supervisor, controller, governor, conductor, leader, overseer, surveyor, inspector, dean, regent, executive, organizer, entrepreneur, impresario, coryphaeus, master mind, commander, ruler, principal, head, headman, chief, president, chairman, speaker, officer, functionary, official, superior, steward, trustee, guardian, curator, proctor, foreman, major-domo, agent, factor, statesman, lawgiver, legislator, politician, despot, dictator.

DIRGE, *n.* Funeral song, death song, elegy, obit, lament, requiem, threnody, coronach, keen *(Irish),* ullalulla *(Irish),* threne, epicedium, nenia, toll, myriologue, trental, trigintal, burial hymn, tune expressing mourning, monody, ululation, passing bell, jeremiad, knell, dead march, mournful sound.

DIRK, *n.* Stabbing weapon, dagger, poniard, cold steel, stiletto, stylet, blade, short sword, kris, kukri, creese, cutlass, Toledo.

DIRT, *n.* 1. Foul matter, filthy substance, muck, ooze, mud, mire, slime, sludge, slush, excrement, grime, filth, dust, smoke, soot, smudge, stain, tarnish, rust, slop, sordidness, squalor.
2. Loose earth, loam, ground, soil, pay dirt.
3. Moral filth, vileness, obscenity, indecency, smut, pornography, unclean language, mind in the gutter, evil-mindedness, ribaldry, bawdiness, coarseness, scurrilous language, profanity.
4. Gossip, rumor, defamatory talk, scandal.
5. Something worthless, trash, rubbish, chaff, offal, refuse, leavings, dross, sweepings, garbage, offscourings, scum, froth, slag, scoria, cinders, ashes.

DIRTY, *adj.* 1. Soiled with dirt, unclean, filthy, foul, unwashed, begrimed, grimy, besmeared, muddied, smudgy, smirchy, bedraggled, sullied, tarnished, dirt-encrusted, defiled, squalid, slovenly, sluttish, slatternly, befouled.

2. Dark-colored, blackened, dingy, bleary, filmy, hazy, dun, dusky, clouded, dull, indistinct, blurred, lackluster, shadowy.

3. Mean, despicable, scurvy, vile, contemptible, groveling, base, low-down, sneaking, nasty, pitiful, beggarly, shabby, paltry.

4. Fraudulent, unscrupulous, dishonest, sordid, morally dishonorable, ignoble, infamous, abject, ignominious, corrupt, villainous, deceitful, unfair, treacherous, perfidious, unprincipled, two-faced, crooked.

5. Morally unclean, off-color, smutty, indecent, obscene, risqué, ribald, pornographic, suggestive, coarse, bawdy, nasty, evil-minded, carnal, lewd, perverted, concupiscent, prurient, lascivious, lecherous, libidinous, licentious, salacious, loose, lustful, lickerish, unchaste, wanton.

6. *(Of the weather)* Cloudy, overcast, misty, rainy, sleety, foggy, hazy, disagreeable, sloppy, gusty, stormy, squally, murky, leaden, gloomy, threatening, lowering.

DIRTY, *v.* Make filthy, defile, foul, befoul, soil, smudge, besmirch, begrime, besmear, spot, smear, smirch, muddy, slop up, stain, sully, pollute, splash, spatter, bemire, draggle, blacken, blur, tarnish.

DISABILITY, *n.* Loss of power, want of ability, lack of competent power, disablement, unfitness, incapacity, inability, impotence, helplessness, powerlessness, weakness, incapability, defect, ineptitude, incompetence, disqualification, impuissance, affliction, handicap, decrepitude, superannuation, senility, infirmity, inanition, paralysis, collapse, exhaustion, atony *(Med.),* legal incapacity.

DISABLE, *v.* 1. Render incapable of effective action, take away the ability of, weaken the capability of, enfeeble, deprive of strength, unfit, disenable, devitalize, debilitate, make unable, incapacitate, cripple, prostrate, paralyze, impair, maim, lame, hamstring, injure to a degree to interfere with normal activities, enervate, spay, unman, unbrace, unhinge, unnerve, emasculate, castrate, geld, mutilate, mangle, wound, disfigure.

2. Render *hors de combat,* draw the teeth, put a spoke in one's wheel, put out of gear, tie the hands, spike the guns, clip the wings, scuttle, scotch.

3. Make legally incapable, disqualify, detract from the value of, invalidate, disenable, impoverish.

DISABUSE, *v.* Clear the minds of, open the eyes of, undeceive, unbeguile, free from error, rid of deception, free from a mistaken belief, liberate the mind from a false idea, disillusion, pull the wool off the eyes, disenchant, set straight, set right, correct.

DISADVANTAGE, *n.* 1. Disadvantageousness, deprivation of advantage, inexpedience, weakness, undesirableness, discommodity, inconvenience, weakness, fault, defect, weak point, fly in the ointment, unfavorable circumstance, stumbling block, impediment, obstacle.

2. Injury to interest, handicap, drawback, hindrance, nuisance, bad turn, disservice, hurt, detriment, harm, prejudice, damage, loss, mischief.

DISADVANTAGEOUS, *adj.* 1. Inconvenient, ill-timed, inexpedient, inopportune, unseasonable, undesirable, inadvisable, objectionable, inapt, unfavorable, discommodious, unprofitable, ill-

starred, unwise, imprudent, ill-fated, inauspicious, unpropitious, embarrassing.

2. Injurious, harmful, hurtful, deleterious, damaging, detrimental, prejudicial, troublesome, disserviceable, pernicious, baneful, noxious, obnoxious, baleful, mischievous, calamitous, perverse, disastrous, destructive, untoward, unlucky.

3. Oppressive, burdensome, onerous, clumsy, cumbersome, cumbrous, awkward, unwieldy.

DISAFFECT, *v.* Alienate the affection of, make ill-affected, estrange, set against, make unfriendly, make hostile, sow dissension between, destroy the affection of, harden the heart, cause a rift between, come between, divide, provoke hatred against, make discontented, make disloyal, set by the ears, make unfaithful, envenom, incense, rile, repel, revolt against, irritate.

DISAFFECTED, *adj.* 1. Alienated in feeling, set against, estranged, inimical, hostile, unfriendly, averse from, at variance, at swords' points, at open war with, up in arms against, seditious, mutinous, rebellious, dissatisfied, discontented, disloyal, false, faithless, traitorous, perfidious, unfaithful.

2. Irreconcilable, implacable, not on terms with, antagonistic, revengeful, vindictive, spiteful, bitter, cool, aloof, withdrawn, invidious.

DISAFFECTION, *n.* Alienation of affection, loss of good will, breach, estrangement, aversion, coolness, disfavor, ill will, unfriendliness, feud, discontent, dissatisfaction, disgust, dislike, bad blood, displeasure, disagreement, disloyalty, mutiny, sedition, rebellion, secession, schism, defection, withdrawal, irritation, resentment, hostility, offense, enmity, antagonism, animosity, umbrage, pique, grudge, dudgeon, spleen, rancor, bitterness, revenge, implacability.

DISAGREE, *v.* 1. Be dissimilar, be unlike, be not accordant, not coincide, present notable points of difference, differ, diverge, vary, be not the same, fail to agree, disaccord.

2. Entertain contradictory views, dissent, contradict, be of different opinion, differ in opinion, think differently, oppose, conflict, lack harmony, refuse to agree.

3. Fall out, quarrel, altercate, bicker, dispute, squabble, wrangle, clash, argue, contest.

4. Be unfavorable in effect, be unsuitable, be unfit, conflict in effect, interfere, jar, discommode, be unsuited, be injurious, offend, sicken, nauseate.

DISAGREEABLE, *adj.* 1. Contrary to one's liking, unpleasant, unwelcome, obnoxious, nasty, distasteful, offensive, unpleasing, displeasing, sour, repugnant, repellent, repulsive, harsh, grating, uninviting, unpalatable, unsavory, disgusting, nauseous, bitter, distressing, uncomfortable.

2. Unpleasant in manner, ill-tempered, ill-natured, irritable, unamiable, churlish, gruff, uncongenial, crabbed, morose, cross, peevish, sullen, bad-tempered, grouchy, petulant, surly, moody, irascible, pettish, captious, testy, fretful, acrimonious, splenetic.

DISAGREEMENT, *n.* 1. Unlikeness, lack of agreement, failure to correspond, dissimilarity, dissimilitude, deviation, divergence, difference, nonconformity, variance, diversity, disparity, inequality, discrepancy, incongruity, disaccord, dissonance.

2. Dissent, dissidence, discord, disunity, feud, disunion, division, opposition, antagonism, breach, friction, misunderstanding, quarrel, altercation,

controversy, dissension, contention, strife, at sixes and sevens, bickering, clashing, jarring, wrangle, dispute, squabble, cross-purposes, contest, vendetta.

3. Unwholesome effect (*as of food*), unsuitableness, inappropriateness, incompatibility, unfitness, ineptitude.

DISALLOW, *v.* 1. Forbid, issue an injunction against, prohibit, put a veto to, refuse to allow, veto, refuse permission to, decline to authorize, ban, interdict, embargo, proscribe, bar, debar, restrain, censor.

2. Reject, set aside, refuse to admit the validity of, withhold sanction, decline to sanction, disapprove.

3. Disclaim, repudiate, disown, refuse to accept, disavow, deny.

DISANNUL, *v.* Annul utterly, declare null and void, nullify, make void, invalidate, quash, do away with, abolish, void, abrogate, set aside, vacate, rescind, cancel, dissolve, revoke, repeal, retract, recall, countermand, overrule, recant, repudiate.

DISAPPEAR, *v.* 1. Pass out of sight, vanish from sight, recede from view, cease to appear, cease to be seen, be lost to view, go, depart, withdraw, be gone, exit, abscond, take flight, escape, take French leave, decamp, take wing, leave, quit, vacate, abandon, avaunt, do the disappearing act, retire, vamoose, retire from sight, go off the stage.

2. Cease to exist, cease to be known, pass away, end gradually, melt away, fade away, pass on, leave no trace, evaporate, dissolve, perish, die out, be no more, evanesce, be swallowed up, dissipate, disperse, wane, ebb, undergo eclipse.

DISAPPEARANCE, *n.* Vanishment, evanescence, ceasing to appear, eclipse, vanishing point, fading, occultation, dissolution, ceasing to exist, exodus, evaporation, wane, ebbing away, dissipation, exit, dispersal, recession from view, departure, escape, withdrawal, retirement, hegira, flight, desertion, French leave, congé.

DISAPPOINT, *v.* 1. Fail to fulfil the expectations of, come to nought, founder, end in smoke, fall through, flash in the pan, come to grief, miscarry, run aground, fizzle out, meet with disaster, come to nothing, abort, fall flat.

2. Defeat the fulfilment of plans, thwart, foil, frustrate, balk, baffle, disconcert, bring to nought, hinder from attaining, blight one's hope, tease, tantalize, torment, leave in the lurch, mislead, dumfounder, dumfound, delude, disillusion, put out, disenchant, dissatisfy, disgruntle, stand up.

DISAPPOINTMENT, *n.* 1. Unfulfilment, foiling, nonsuccess, frustration, thwarted expectation, slip 'twixt cup and lip, bafflement, balk, blighted hope, chagrin, mortification, disillusion, fool's paradise, vain expectation, abortion, miscarriage of plan, adversity, check, setback, much cry and little wool, dissatisfaction, discontent, regret.

2. Something that disappoints, fiasco, labor in vain, no go, inefficacy, fizzle, washout, flash in the pan, shipwreck, miscalculation, failure, defeat, cold comfort.

DISAPPROVAL, *n.* Non-approval, disfavor, boo, disapprobation, condemnation, denunciation, derogation, disparagement, detraction, criticism, censure, stricture, check, blame, reprehension, exception, objection, displeasure, dislike, rebuke, disesteem, odium, reproof, reflection, admonition, animadversion, dissatisfaction, chiding, reproach, reprimand, dressing down, remonstrance, frown,

castigation, black look, scowl, catcall, hiss, tirade, obloquy, sarcasm, satire, stigma, black list, bell, book and candle, blackball, boycott, ostracism.

DISAPPROVE, *v.* 1. Condemn in opinion, regard with blame, view with disfavor, regard as wrong, think reprehensible, think ill of, dislike, censure, criticize, perstringe, deprecate, take exception to, set one's face against, object to, frown upon, look askance, think wrong, impugn, impeach, brand, denounce, stigmatize, rebuke, reprehend, chide, reprimand, admonish, berate, reprove, take to task, dress down, chastise, castigate, run down, decry.

2. Reject as inadmissible, disallow, refuse, veto, negative, decline to sanction, refuse assent to, demur, withhold approval from, cavil, find fault.

DISARM, *v.* 1. Unarm, deprive of weapons, deprive of means of defense, weaken, render powerless, debilitate, disable, incapacitate.

2. Lay down arms, demobilize, reduce the military establishment, reduce forces to a peace footing, reduce the armament, disband troops, beat swords into ploughshares.

3. Divest of suspicion, make friendly, remove suspicion, set at ease, conciliate, win over, touch, beguile, soften, melt the heart, reconcile, quell suspicion, allay mistrust.

DISARMAMENT, *n.* Demobilization, reduction of the armament of, laying aside of arms, limitation of armament, swords into ploughshares, *telum imbelle* (*Lat.*), peace pipe, demilitarization.

DISARRANGE, *v.* Disturb the arrangement of, disorder, put out of order, confuse, scramble, throw into confusion, throw into disorder, upset, disorganize, unsettle, turn upside down, derange, displace, dislocate, discompose, turn topsy-turvy, litter, mix, scatter, muddle, ruffle, clutter, jumble, tumble, rumple, tousle, dishevel.

DISARRAY, *n.* 1. Loss of array, want of regular order, disarrangement, disorder, confusion, upset, jumble, mix-up, scramble, disorganization, litter, unsettlement, derangement, dislocation, discomposition, clutter, dishevelment.

2. Disorder of apparel, disorderly dress, lack of dress, dishabille, undress, negligent dress.

DISASTER, *n.* Great mishap, adverse happening, crushing reverse, unfortunate event, mischance, terrible accident, sudden misfortune, catastrophe, misadventure, adversity, calamity, contretemps, cataclysm, casualty, grief, tragedy, ruination, fell stroke, woe, bale, bane, blow, blight, exigency, extremity, trouble, affliction, harm, ill luck, curse, scourge, undoing, crash, wreck, setback, debacle, comedown, evil day, rainy day, frowns of fortune, gathering clouds, visitation, infliction, downfall, overthrow, fiasco.

DISASTROUS, *adj.* Calamitous, ruinous, hurtful, catastrophic, cataclysmic, causing great injury, destructive, harmful, detrimental, deleterious, pernicious, dire, adverse, tragic, ill-fated, hapless, ill-starred, untoward, unlucky, unfortunate, fell, inauspicious, unprosperous, grievous, portentous, withering, blighting, desolating, ill-boding, grim, woeful, baleful, shocking, appalling, dreadful. crushing, harrowing, disheartening, heartbreaking, frightful, horrendous, perverse, afflictive, wretched, deplorable, distressing.

DISAVOW, *v.* Disclaim knowledge of, disaffirm, deny connection with, deny responsibility for, refuse to acknowledge, disown, disallow, reject, repudiate, renounce, retract, recant, forswear, abjure, contravene, controvert, gainsay.

DISBAND, *v.* 1. Discharge from united service, break up, disperse, dismiss, send home, dissolve by dismissal, disorganize, release, demobilize, let go, release.

2. Retire from service, dissociate from an organization, separate, scatter.

DISBELIEF, *n.* 1. Unbelief, skepticism, doubt, lack of conviction, denial of belief, conviction that a doctrine is untrue, non-conviction, heresy, belief of the contradictory of a doctrine, rejection, freethinking, irreligion, nullifidianism, infidelity, irreverence, agnosticism, atheism, want of faith, Pyrrhonism, mental repudiation, godlessness, the gods have fallen, ungodliness, materialism, nihilism, incredulity.

2. Lack of trust, discredit, distrust, miscreance, want of confidence, dissent, nonconformity, challenge.

DISBELIEVE, *v.* Not believe, refuse to credit, lack faith, give no credence to, discredit, consider not to be true, doubt, question, dispute, deny the truth of, reject, dissent, misbelieve, challenge, protest, take exception, shy at, be skeptical, be agnostic, skepticize, be irreligious.

DISBELIEVER, *n.* Doubter, questioner, denier, challenger, opponent, non-adherent, *esprit fort (Fr.),* freethinker, unbeliever, skeptic, agnostic, atheist, deist, infidel, nullifidian, Pyrrhonist, alien, irreligionist, heretic, heathen, gentile, rationalist, materialist, nihilist, giaour *(Turk.),* zendik *(Arab.).*

DISBURDEN, *v.* Remove a burden from, rid of a burden, unburden, lighten, unload, disburthen, disencumber, disembarrass, disentangle, facilitate, deobstruct, relieve of an annoyance, get rid of as heavy, ease, relieve, free, divest oneself of, part with, dispose of, lay aside, discard, cast off, fling aside, jettison, extricate.

DISBURSE, *v.* Give out in payment, pay out, expend, spend, lay out, make distribution of, run through, dissipate, squander, exhaust, waste, use up, loose the purse strings, shell out, fork out.

DISBURSEMENT, *n.* Paying out, spending, funds paid out, laying out, expenditure, outlay, money going out, money expended, payment.

DISCARD, *v.* 1. Throw away, reject, thrust aside, lay aside, abandon, have done with, relinquish, cast aside, dismiss from use, shelve, turn away as useless, dispense with, forsake, get rid of, drop, shed, put from oneself, abjure, throw overboard, jettison.

2. Discharge, dismiss, turn out, sack, fire, give the gate to, bounce, cashier, break, cast off, send away, expel, give one one's walking papers.

3. Cancel, repudiate, abolish, nullify, declare null and void, rescind, revoke, recall, retract, protest.

DISCERN, *v.* 1. Perceive, behold, observe, notice, descry, espy, make out, see, detect, discover, ken, apprehend clearly, ascertain, become aware of, comprehend, experience, cognize.

2. Discriminate, note the distinctions of, see as distinct from other objects, make distinction, mentally appreciate, distinguish mentally, judge, recognize as distinct, differentiate.

DISCERNIBLE, *adj.* Capable of being discerned, distinguishable, perceivable, discoverable, distinct, perceptible, detectible, apparent, manifest, patent, visible, noticeable, evident, appreciable, palpable, obvious, conspicuous, unhidden, open, revealed, observable, exposed to view, clear, well-defined, well-marked, recognizable.

DISCERNING, *adj.* Showing discernment, having keen insight, discriminative, quick to discern, acute, piercing, sharp, keen-sighted, sharp-sighted, clear-sighted, Argus-eyed, eagle-eyed, hawk-eyed, perspicacious, astute, knowing, shrewd, sapient, penetrating, sagacious, judicious, intelligent, wise, sage, clever, subtle, scrutinous, critical, sensitive.

DISCERNMENT, *n.* 1. Discovery, espial, notice, beholding, descrying, perception, ascertainment, act of discerning, seeing, observance, detection, apprehension, apperception.

2. Discriminative ability, discrimination, skill, faculty of discerning, acuteness of judgment, power of observing differences, mental keenness, sharpness, shrewdness, longheadedness, sagacity, astuteness, mentality, brightness, comprehension, intelligence, perspicacity, insight, intuition, quick parts, divination, clairvoyance, mother wit, depth, subtlety, profundity, judgment, penetration, good sense, acumen, ingenuity, cleverness, knowledge, understanding.

3. Taste, refinement, fastidiousness, discretion, meticulosity, nicety.

DISCHARGE, *v.* 1. Send forth, emit, eject, void, project, excrete, send out, throw off, exude, ooze, give forth, leak, gush, empty, disembogue.

2. Fire off, shoot, deliver a charge, send forth a missile from, explode, burst, detonate, let fly, pour forth, give vent to, deliver, set off.

3. Empty of cargo, unload, put off a burden, disburden, free, relieve of a load, unburden.

4. Oust, dismiss, get rid of, give one one's walking papers, sack, bounce, fire, give the gate to, turn out, send packing, turn away, let the axe fall, relieve of obligation, deprive of office, cashier, discard, remove from office.

5. Exonerate, absolve, exculpate, exempt, send away, allow to go, acquit, release, relieve, clear, pardon, liberate, free, manumit, emancipate, set free, respite, reprieve, remit.

6. Meet the requirements of, relieve oneself of an obligation, fulfil, perform, acquit oneself of, execute, accomplish, observe.

7. Abolish, cancel, destroy, void, remove, put away, banish, expel, clear from, annul, rescind, nullify, make void, invalidate.

8. Pay a debt, settle, liquidate, cash.

9. Disband, demobilize.

DISCHARGE, *n.* 1. Emission, ejection, voidance, projection, evacuation, expulsion, emptying, vent, flowing forth, disemboguement.

2. Drainage, flow, flux, exudation, excretion, rheum, phlegm, suppuration, purulence, lochia, pus, maturation, ooze, ichor, gleet, issue.

3. Firing off, fusillade, salvo, volley, blast, pop, shot, explosion, report, burst, detonation, rafale, crash.

4. Emptying of cargo, unloading, disburdening, relieving of a load.

5. Ouster, dismissal, removal, displacement, bounce, sack, congé, riddance, walking papers, the gate, the axe.

6. Exoneration, exculpation, acquittal, pardon, acquittance, absolution, exemption, release, reprieve, clearance, remittance, liberation, setting free, manumission, emancipation, respite.

7. Fulfilment, performance, execution, meeting the requirements of, accomplishment, observance, achievement.

8. Abolition, voidance, banishment, annulment, destruction, nullification, invalidation.

9. Payment of a debt, liquidation, satisfaction, settlement.

10. Demobilization, disbandment.

DISCIPLE, *n.* 1. One who believes the teaching of another, one who receives instruction from another, student, scholar, learner, pupil, *élève (Fr.).*

2. One who follows some doctrine, alumnus, follower, supporter, adherent, successor, convert, partisan, proselyte, neophyte, votary, evangelist, novice, apostle, sectary, client, satellite, pursuer.

DISCIPLINARIAN, *n.* Enforcer of discipline, one who maintains discipline, advocate of strict discipline, martinet, drill sergeant, hard master, trainer, stickler, formalist, bashaw, tyrant, despot, taskmaster.

DISCIPLINE, *n.* Training, diligent exercise, drill, schooling, preparation, drilling, indoctrination, inculcation, systematization, instruction to act in accordance with rules, development, qualification.

2. System of obedience, orderliness, coercion, good order, subordination to rules of conduct, subjection, control, limitation, regulation, check, compulsion, government, restraint, restriction, curb, reins, system of rules.

3. Set of regulations, rule of practice, method of practice, course of exercise, method, routine, established usage, prescribed practice, customary procedure.

4. Elements of culture, curriculum, teaching, course, branch of knowledge, learning, doctrine, lore, education.

5. Correction, castigation, scourge, retribution, chastisement, infliction, reprimand, punishment for the sake of training, reproof.

DISCIPLINE, *v.* 1. Instruct, train by instruction, teach by exercise, exercise, drill, give lessons in, edify, school in, educate, breed, bring up, form, ground, prepare, rear, prime, coach, direct, show, guide, qualify, tutor, inform, enlighten, inculcate, indoctrinate, inure, habituate, break in, initiate, put through paces, familiarize with, put through systematic exercises.

2. Bring to a state of orderly obedience, curb, govern strictly, train to obedience, control, bring under subjection, regulate, restrain, rein in, check, restrict, coerce, harness, bridle, muzzle, hold in leash, keep under, limit, hold in line, pull in, make toe the line, make walk the chalk line.

3. Subject to punishment, punish, visit upon, chastise, castigate, scourge, inflict penance upon, chasten, visit with penance, strafe, reprimand, criticize, reprove, make an example of, even the score with, get even with, inflict upon, correct.

DISCLAIM, *v.* 1. Repudiate connection with, have nothing to do with, deny any knowledge of, wash one's hands of, disavow, discountenance, not hear of, shake the head, be deaf to, decline, ignore, negate, contravene, gainsay, contradict, disaffirm, refuse, controvert.

2. Renounce a claim to, reject, disown, cast off a right to, disallow, annul, abnegate, rescind, revoke, recant, retract, reject the authority of, abjure, forswear, break off, countermand, set aside, cast behind one.

DISCLAIMER, *n.* 1. Repudiation, contravention, contradiction, disaffirmation, disavowal, negation, denial, refusal, abjuration, disowning, declination.

2. *(Law)* Renunciation of a claim, self-denial, relinquishment of a title, waiver.

DISCLOSE, *v.* 1. Lay open to view, bring to light, bring into view by uncovering, uncover, expose, lay bare, cause to appear, allow to be seen, make known, reveal, manifest, exhibit, discover, open up, unearth, unveil, unseal, unmask, throw off the mask, lift the veil, show in its true color.

2. Publish, tell, inform, make known, reveal to knowledge, show, bare, divulge, communicate, divulgate, evulgate, breathe, utter, betray, confess, declare, impart, free from secrecy, let into the secret, blab, peach, squeal, squeak, blurt out, let slip, vent, break the news, speak out, broadcast.

DISCLOSURE, *n.* 1. Act of disclosing, making known, revealing, divulgence, uncovering, vent, exposure, expression, utterance, unveiling, laying bare, manifestation, publication, enlightenment, exposition, betrayal, mention, divulgation.

2. Anything disclosed, exposé, communication, revelation, showdown, declaration, apocalypse, acknowledgment, admission, confession, avowal.

DISCOLOR, *v.* 1. Spoil the color of, give an unnatural color to, change the color of, deprive of color, decolorize, stain, rust, tarnish, etiolate, tinge, streak, achromatize, bleach, blanch, wash out.

2. Change color, fade, become faded, become stained, weather, soil, lose color, turn pale.

3. Give a false complexion to, characterize wrongly, distort, misrepresent.

DISCOLORATION, *n.* Discolored marking, blot, changed hue, discolored appearance, maculation, changed aspect, macula, stain, blotch, etiolation, spot, blemish, bruise, contusion, decoloration.

DISCOMFIT, *v.* 1. Defeat utterly, rout, make short work of, conquer, overcome, overthrow, overpower, worst, lick, drub, floor, vanquish, beat, put to flight, remain in possession of the field, win the day, disperse in flight, get the upper hand of, subdue, put down, overmaster, checkmate, outflank, outmaneuver, outgeneral, put *hors de combat,* carry by storm, beat hollow.

2. Put to confusion, disconcert, confound, foil, circumvent, baffle, frustrate the plans of, thwart, upset, balk, abash, nonplus, perplex, trump, drive into a corner, embarrass, demoralize, shipwreck, drive to the wall, trip up, elude, confuse, capsize.

DISCOMFITURE, *n.* 1. Defeat in battle, repulse, rout, overthrow, subjugation, ruin, subdual, edge, advantage over, beating, drubbing, expugnation, conquest, upperhand, ascendancy, fall, perdition, deathblow.

2. Frustration of plans, disappointment, labor in vain, nonsuccess, failure, miscarriage, abortion, no go, rebuff.

3. Confusion, disconcertion, embarrassment, abashment.

DISCOMFORT, *n.* 1. Absence of comfort, trial, disturbance of peace, lack of pleasure, uneasiness, disquietude, inquietude, annoyance, trouble, care, vexation, distress, dysphoria, malaise, solicitude, disturbance of comfort, wretchedness, displeasure, sorrow, anxiety, worry, concern, discomposure.

2. Pain, ache, affliction, misery, anguish, pang, twinge, smart, throe, torture, torment, hurt, woe, agony, soreness, suffering, convulsion, palpitation, cramp, throb, pinch, gripe, shooting, laceration, nip.

DISCOMMODE, *v.* Cause inconvenience to, put to trouble, put out, trouble, annoy, disturb, chafe, molest, incommode, disquiet, harass, pester, vex, plague, worry, embarrass, bother, harry, badger, beset, importune, persecute.

DISCOMPOSE, *v.* 1. Bring into disorder, confuse, disarrange, disorder, disorganize, derange, disturb, embroil, misplace, throw into confusion, jumble, muddle, tousle, dishevel, displace, unsettle.

2. Disturb the composure of, disquiet, agitate, ruffle, perturb, harass, displease, plague, worry, annoy, fret, trouble, irritate, nettle, vex, chafe, provoke, put out, anger, rattle, make uneasy.

3. Confound, flurry, disconcert, fluster, daunt, bewilder, perplex, abash, embarrass, unbalance, nonplus, dazzle, muddle, unhinge.

DISCOMPOSURE, *n.* 1. Disturbed condition, derangement, disorder, disorganization, confusion, dislocation, inversion, mess, muss, jumble, chaos, litter, tangle, misplacement.

2. Disquietude, perturbation, embarrassment, chagrin, mortification, annoyance, worry, flurry, uneasiness, inquietude, agitation, irritation, care, vexation, malaise, concern, solicitude, anxiety, trial, ordeal, trouble, discontent, *mauvais quart d'heure (Fr.),* bad time of it.

DISCONCERT, *v.* 1. Balk, frustrate, foil, baffle, thwart, hinder, undermine, cut the ground from under one, undo, defeat, upset, override, spoil, mar, counter, circumvent, contravene, interrupt, clip the wings of, cripple.

2. Disturb the self-possession of, faze, throw into a tizzy, discompose, demoralize, throw off one's balance, unsettle, discomfit, agitate, confuse, puzzle, bewilder, perplex, rattle, confound, put out, embarrass, perturb, ruffle, abash, nonplus, trouble, upset, annoy, worry.

3. Throw into disorder, throw into confusion, disarrange.

DISCONNECT, *v.* Sever the connection of, undo the association, interrupt the connection between, detach, disjoin, disengage, part, separate, cleave, dissociate, disunite, uncouple, sunder, segregate, unlink, dissever, rend, rive, take apart, cut off, loose, unfasten, break, isolate, dissolve.

DISCONNECTION, *n.* 1. Lack of union, parting, disengagement, disjunction, disunion, separation, disassociation, severance, isolation, subdivision, partition, cleavage, divorce, detachment, division.

2. Break, interruption, discontinuity, fracture, crack, flaw, gap, hiatus, opening, broken thread, disruption, cessation, breach, fissure, rift, rent, cleft, slit.

3. Unrelatedness, impertinency, irrelevancy, incoherence, unrelation.

DISCONSOLATE, *adj.* 1. Affected with profound dejection, desolate, destitute of consolation, sad, forlorn, grief-stricken, without solace, miserable, inconsolable, heartbroken, unhappy, sorrowful, broken-hearted, woeful, hopeless, heavy-hearted, comfortless, dispirited, dejected, depressed, blue, woebegone, melancholy, hypochondriacal, in the dumps, distressed, discouraged, wretched, doleful, lachrymose, downcast, despondent, low-spirited, moody, down in the mouth.

2. Causing discomfort, cheerless, gloomy, dark, saddening, blighted, dismal, dreary, depressing, somber, funereal, cloudy.

DISCONTENT, *n.* 1. Lack of contentment, envy, dissatisfaction, disappointment, disquiet, repining, uneasiness, inquietude, restlessness, displeasure, discontentment, disaffection, mortification, regret, rue, querulousness, vexation of spirit, bitterness, faultfinding.

2. Malcontent, grumbler, grouch, faultfinder, croaker, irreconcilable, intransigent, Adullamite.

DISCONTINUANCE, *n.* Lack of union, lack of continued connection, lack of cohesion of parts, interruption, suspension, disjunction, disruption, cessation, discontinuation, stoppage, termination, breaking off, separation, intermission, disunion,

pause, stop, stay, postponement, rest, respite, lull, recess, adjournment, interjacence, interpolation, obtrusion, intervention, interval.

DISCONTINUE, *v.* Cause to cease, put an end to, stay, stop, break off, part, disjoin, separate, disunite, disconnect, dissever, interrupt, terminate, cease, quit, desist from, leave off, give up, defer, abstain, suspend, intervene, interpose, withhold, pause, intermit, abandon, drop.

DISCONTINUOUS, *adj.* Not continuous, wanting continuity, wanting cohesion, broken, interrupted, discrete, disconnected, lacking sequence, gaping, punctuated, disjoined, disjunctive, unconnected, detached, broken off, fitful, irregular, desultory, spasmodic, alternate, intermittent, recurrent, periodic, characterized by frequent breaks.

DISCORD, *n.* 1. Difference of opinions, dispute, dissidence, disagreement, dissension, contention, lack of concord between, quarreling, strife, split, incompatibility, break, falling out, rupture, odds, division, clashing, wrangling, cross-purposes, war, variance, opposition, friction, clash, diversity, conflict, disunity, feud, schism, breach, faction, animosity, at sixes and sevens.

2. Want of harmony, discordance, dissonance, absence of harmony, cacophony, inharmonious combination of musical tones sounded together, harsh medley of sounds, confused mingling of noises, din, jangle, clashing, jarring, noise.

DISCORDANT, *adj.* 1. Dissident, dissentient, at sixes and sevens, irreconcilable, conflicting, being at variance, not coincident, disagreeing, opposed, contradictory, paradoxical, inconsistent, adverse, incongruous, divergent, opposite, heterogeneous, discrepant, repugnant, conflictory, incompatible, dissimilar, contrary, differing, different.

2. Disagreeable to the ear, inharmonious, dissonant, cacophonous, out of tune, tuneless, unmusical, unmelodious, untuneful, being out of musical harmony, strident, shrill, screechy, harsh, sounding harshly, grating, jangling, jarring, rough, clashing.

DISCOUNT, *n.* Amount deducted from a sum owing to be paid, deduction, subtraction, setoff, diminution, reduction, rebate, abatement, rake-off, allowance, drawback, percentage, concession, commission, qualification.

DISCOUNTENANCE, *v.* 1. Show disapproval of, treat with disfavor, discourage, frown upon, put an extinguisher on, disfavor, refuse to look with favor upon, disapprove, show disapprobation of, oppose, check, reject, refuse, stand in the way of, throw cold water on, spoil sport, shake the head, set one's face against, turn one's back upon, not hear of, have nothing to do with, wash one's hands of, stand aloof, resist.

2. Put out of countenance, dishearten, abash, disconcert, put to shame.

DISCOURAGE, *v.* 1. Dishearten, lessen the self-confidence of, damp the courage, unnerve, daunt, deprive of courage, unman, prostrate, depress in spirits, break one's heart, deject, dispirit, appall, dismay.

2. Advise against, dissuade, dehort, bulldoze, deter, frighten so as to prevent some action, keep back, divert from, inspire fear, intimidate, cow, abash, overawe, hold back, restrain, oppose.

3. Express disapproval of, destroy confidence in, attempt to prevent, obstruct by opposition, suggest that a contemplated action will probably fail, hinder, impose difficulties.

4. Disfavor, damp, dash one's hopes, dampen spirits, disenchant, cool, chill, throw cold water upon, throw a wet blanket on, put a damper on, cast a pall, set back hopes, prey on the mind, starve the spirit.

DISCOURAGEMENT, *n.* 1. Hypochondria, state of being discouraged, melancholy, dejection, hope deferred, despair, depression, hopelessness, gloom, morbidity, pessimism, prostration, lack of spirit, loss of confidence, despondency, heaviness of spirit, weariness, low spirits, dismay.

2. Dehortation, deprecation, counterinfluence, intimidation, expostulation, remonstrance, act of discouraging, diversion, disheartening, dissuasion.

3. Something that discourages, deterrent, curb, damper, restraint, constraint, check, control, rein, repression, hindrance, impediment, consternation, obstacle, backset, rebuff, mistrust, qualm, cold feet, hesitation, fearfulness, wet blanket, cold water, embarrassment, solicitude.

DISCOURSE, *v.* 1. Converse, confer, colloquize, talk together, advise, confabulate, talk over, hold a conference, parley, discuss, collogue, hold a conversation, engage in a conversation, commune with, chat, communicate thoughts orally, palaver, tattle, prate, chatter.

2. Treat of a subject formally in speech or writing, expatiate, digress, dilate, hold forth, orate, express oneself connectedly in speech, sermonize, give expression to, speak, lecture, harange, rant, declaim, stump, lucubrate, dissertate, spellbind, dissert, deliver a discourse, speechify, spout, read, recite, render.

3. Reason, make inferences, draw conclusions.

DISCOURSE, *n.* 1. Talk, conversation, converse, continuous interchange of ideas, speech, verbal intercourse, oral communication, colloquy, chat, communication of thought by words, communion, interlocution, verbal commerce, chitchat, babble, tittle-tattle.

2. Formal discussion of a subject in speech or writing, dissertation, disquisition, lecture, homily, sermon, harangue, preachment, address, descant, oration, declamation, speech, peroration, parley, rhetorical presentation, exhortation, travelogue, soliloquy, recitation, appeal, salutation, stump speech.

3. Capacity for proceeding in an orderly and necessary sequence, ratiocination, discursive reasoning.

DISCOURTEOUS, *adj.* Lacking courtesy, sharp, showing discourtesy, uncourteous, unmannerly, impolite, rude, uncivil, disrespectful, ill-mannered, ill-bred, ungentlemanly, unladylike, ill-behaved, inurbane, uncourtly, unaccommodating, brusque, uncomplaisant, indecorous, unceremonious, curt, ungallant, ungracious, unpolished, unrefined, pert, trenchant, sarcastic, captious, snarling, grouchy, surly, sullen, peevish, abrupt, blunt, impertinent, crabbed, boorish, churlish, bearish, short, bluff, crusty, harsh, fresh, saucy, forward, impudent, gruff.

DISCOURTESY, *n.* Breach of courtesy, acerbity, disrespect shown in manners, rude behavior, lack of consideration, unmannerly conduct, incivility, impoliteness, inurbanity, rudeness, *brusquerie*, brusqueness, abruptness, bad manners, gruffness, ill-breeding, ungentlemanliness, thoughtlessness, bluntness, unmannerliness, rusticity, disrespect, impudence, misbehavior, vulgarity, tactlessness, crabbedness, grouchiness, moroseness, surliness, peevishness, churlishness, boorishness, sullenness,

captiousness, sourness, virulence, acrimony, tartness, asperity.

2. Impolite act, snub, affront, insult, rebuff, short answer, sulks, scowl, frown, black looks, hard words, contumelious act, humiliating deed.

DISCOVER, *v.* 1. Bring to the knowledge of the world, reveal, divulge, disclose, display, exhibit, lay open, expose to view, give signs of, tell about, communicate, impart, make known, manifest, lay bare, make manifest, show, betray.

2. Detect, bring to light, uncover, ferret out, unearth, dig up, root out, disinter, trace out, ascertain, gain knowledge of something previously unknown, learn of, find out, hear, elicit.

3. Get sight of, catch a glimpse of, descry, espy, spot, make out, discern, notice, behold, see, identify, fathom, recognize, distinguish, perceive.

4. Invent, originate, contrive, devise, design, come upon, meet with, fall in with, light upon, stumble upon, chance upon.

5. Solve, resolve, determine, unravel, find a clue to, see through, interpret, verify, establish, substantiate, clinch, prove, confirm, make certain of, realize.

DISCREDIT, *v.* 1. Show to be undeserving of credit, destroy confidence in, disprove, undermine belief in, shake one's faith.

2. Bring disgrace upon, shame, dishonor, slur, bring reproach upon, degrade, debase, injure the credit of, bring into disfavor, make disreputable, impair the reputation of, vilify, stigmatize, brand, disparage, decry, asperse, defame, tarnish, stain, smirch, taint, sully.

3. Decline to believe, put no faith in, place no confidence in, disbelieve, misbelieve, give no credit to, refuse credence to, challenge, doubt, question, have one's doubts, dispute, deny, give no ear to, hesitate, waver, raise objections.

DISCREDIT, *n.* 1. Loss of repute, lack of esteem, disesteem, disrepute, disgrace, scandal, ill repute, obloquy, opprobrium, odium, impaired reputation, dishonor, reproach, turpitude, disfavor, baseness, derogation, debasement, degradation, humiliation, shame, infamy, ignominy.

2. Stigma, brand, reflection, imputation, slur, stain, spot, tarnish, taint, attaint, blot, smirch.

3. Loss of credence, scruple, qualm, hesitation, refusal to accept as true, loss of belief, lack of confidence, suspicion, disbelief, distrust, mistrust, unbelief, incredulity, indecision, uncertainty, *onus probandi (Lat.),* doubt, question, skepticism, dubiety.

DISCREDITABLE, *adj.* Hurtful to reputation, such as to bring discredit, blameworthy, culpable, reprehensible, censurable, undutiful, shameful, disgraceful, unworthy, scurvy, flagrant, scandalous, dishonorable, ignominious, infamous, inglorious, derogatory, slanderous, defamatory, libelous, bad, degrading, low, vile, base, mean, ignoble, corrupt, opprobrious, depraved, unprincipled, evil, sinful, vicious, wicked, wrong, recreant, black, felonious, nefarious, flagitious, scelerous, atrocious.

DISCREET, *adj.* Wise in avoiding mistakes, not rash, prudent, judicious, having good discernment, sagacious, careful, wary, circumspect, cautious, heedful, vigilant, precautious, sensible, reserved, diplomatic, politic, noncommital, civil, watchful, polite, observant of decencies, trustworthy as a confidant, strategic, chary, awake, alert, guarded.

DISCREPANCY, *n.* Disagreement, dissimilarity, difference, contrariety, disparity, deviation, cross purposes, variance, divergence, inconsistency, incongruity, discordance, misunderstanding, split, division, rupture, breach, subject of dispute, bone of contention, ground of argument, moot point, disputed point, apple of discord, question at issue, vexed question, subject of controversy, point in dispute, knotty point.

DISCREPANT, *adj.* Inharmoniously different, at variance, differing, discordant, clashing, jarring, conflictory, disagreeing, contrary, contradictory, opposite, paradoxical, incongruous, inconsistent.

DISCRETE, *adj.* 1. Not connected with others, disconnected, separate, disjunct, discontinuous, distinct, detached from others.
2. Consisting of individual parts, disjunctive, discretive.

DISCRETION, *n.* 1. Wordly wisdom, instinctive perception of what is wise, judgment, prudence, thoughtfulness, deliberation, considerateness, tact, judiciousness, sound judgment, good sense, mature judgment, maturity, discrimination, discernment, responsibility, sagacity, forethought.
2. Caution, wariness, circumspection, cautious reserve, carefulness, care, vigilance, safety first, watchfulness, heedfulness, Fabian policy.
3. Freedom of choice, liberty of action, power of choosing, velleity, will, pleasure, preference, volition, option, decision, liberty, voluntariness, election, purpose, intent, intention, inclination, wish, desire, mind, disposition, liking.

DISCRETIONARY, *adj.* Optional, exercisable at discretion, left to individual judgment, subject to one's discretion, left to discretion, uncontrolled except by discretion.

DISCRIMINATE, *v.* 1. Distinguish things by their characteristics, discern differences, mince matters, note differences, judge accurately, have exquisite taste, differentiate between, be discriminating, be fastidious, split hairs, turn up one's nose at, disdain, distinguish between the sheep and the goats.
2. Make a distinction for or against, mark the difference between, separate, differentiate, draw a distinction, set apart as different, tell one from the other, draw the line, sift, estimate, sum up, criticize, weigh carefully, take into consideration.

DISCRIMINATION, *n.* 1. Discernment, sagacity, astuteness, keenness, sharpness, shrewdness, good sense, perspicacity, penetration, acumen, insight, acuteness, judgment, wisdom, prudence, caution, forethought, discretion, longheadedness, vigilance, discriminating judgment, carefulness, circumspection.
2. Fastidiousness, finicalness, nicety, taste, tact, hypercriticism, meticulosity, refinement, culture, good taste, finesse, aestheticism, grace, polish, cultivation.
3. Differentiation, differential treatment, bias, distinction, prejudice, blind alley of segregation.

DISCRIMINATIVE, *adj.* 1. Characteristic, that marks distinction, typical, distinguishing, marking a difference, constituting a difference, distinctive.
2. Observing distinctions, perceptive, critical, diacritical, diagnostic, discriminatory.

DISCURSIVE, *adj.* 1. Wandering away from the point, digressive, desultory, excursive, circuitous, roundabout, indirect, passing rapidly from one subject to another, long-winded, prolix, diffuse.
2. Aberrant, errant, devious, roving, rambling, deviating, taking a wide range, cursory.
3. Argumentative, capable of reasoning, not intuitive, proceeding by reasoning.

DISCUS, *n.* Circular plate for throwing, disk, quoit, squail.

DISCUSS, *v.* 1. Debate, examine by argument, argue for and against, ventilate, canvass, consider, reason about, discourse about, contend, wrangle, chop logic, dispute, handle, plead, talk about, treat of, review, present, confer, speak of, parley, altercate, controvert, ratiocinate, discourse, chew the rag, converse, interchange views, present varied opinions.
2. Investigate, find out about by examination, try, examine, put to the proof, analyze, inquire, scrutinize, inspect, look over, study, dip into, probe, thresh out, winnow, anatomize, dissect, pass in review, sift the considerations for and against.

DISCUSSION, *n.* 1. Debate, controversy, parley, argument, disputation, dispute, quarrel, excursus, altercation, war of words, descant, canvass, pros and cons, review, conference, polemics, critical argumentation, dissertation, symposium, reasons, dialogism, disquisition, argumentation, wrangling, logomachy, pilpulism, contention, arguments, forensics.
2. Consideration, examination, study, inquiry, ventilation, canvassing, investigation, inquisition, scrutiny, prosecution, inspection, analysis, sifting, induction, calculation, consideration, dissection, survey, deliberation.
3. Public excitement, commotion, agitation, hubbub, racket, tumult, fuss, bustle, to-do.

DISDAIN, *v.* 1. Be insolent, give oneself airs, lord it over, arrogate, presume, assume, bluster, deem unworthy of one's character, swagger, recoil from with pride, regard with proud contempt, swashbuckle.
2. Consider beneath oneself, deem unsuitable, deem unbecoming, loathe, abhor, detest, despise, look down upon, think unworthy of notice, pass by, consider unworthy of regard, spurn, scout, contemn, disregard, scorn, snub, slight, high-hat, turn one's back upon, curl up one's lip, carry one's nose in the air, turn up one's nose at, sneer at, ridicule, laugh at, deride, flout, mock, think nothing of, pooh-pooh, care nothing for, set no store by, treat with contempt, brush aside.

DISDAIN, *n.* 1. Proud contempt, pride, hauteur, indignant aversion, feeling of superiority and dislike, haughty indifference, icy aloofness, airs, superciliousness, haughtiness, insolence, haughty contempt, arrogance, contemptuousness, conceit, contumely, scornfulness, overbearance, swagger, toploftiness, bluster, bumptiousness, presumption.
2. Derision, scorn, contempt, detestation, lip, abhorrence, disesteem, mockery, sneer, rudeness, spurn, slight, insult, abuse, incivility, discourtesy, cheek, unmannerliness.

DISDAINFUL, *adj.* Filled with disdain, insolent, contemptuous, arrogant, supercilious, unsociable, proud, haughty, scornful, contumelious, with up-turned nose, unapproachable, cold, distant, aloof, icy, high, reserved, imperious, high and mighty, overbearing, intolerant, overweening, withering, insulting, rude, disrespectful, uncivil, bumptious, unmannerly, discourteous, cynical, toplofty, with nose in air, high-hat, upstage, derisive, mocking.

DISEASE, *n.* Bodily deviation from health, fever, morbid condition of the body resulting from disturbance of physiological functions, abnormal state of the body interfering with the functions of one of its organs or systems, departure from functional integrity of the living organism, taint, failure in normal physiological action, seriously abnormal state of body, physical derangement, ailment, illness, sickness, affection, indisposition, malady, disorder, affliction, complaint, distemper, infirmity, discomfort, idiopathy, cachexia, delicate health, invalidism, ill-health, unhealthiness, virus, unsoundness, dyscrasia, plague, pestilence, decline, epidemic, endemic, infection, contagion, chronic disability, depravity, unwholesome condition.

DISEASED, *adj.* In a condition of bad health, sickly, ailing, sick, out of health, disordered, unhealthy, unwell, unsound, infirm, afflicted, ill, affected, indisposed, distempered, drooping, laid up, flagging, valetudinarian, morbid, symptomatic of morbid structural changes in organs *(Pathol.)*, poisoned, cankered, withered, carious, moribund, contaminated, physically depraved, mentally disordered, tainted.

DISEMBARK, *v.* 1. Put on shore from a ship, unload, send ashore.

2. Go ashore from a ship, land, debark, leave a ship, descend the gangplank, make the land, put into, cast anchor.

DISEMBARRASS, *v.* 1. Ease, set free, relieve, clear, release, liberate, disencumber, disburden, debarrass, free from embarrassment, disengage, rid.

2. Disentangle, extricate, deobstruct, unclog, unravel, untie, cut the knot.

DISEMBODIED, *adj.* 1. Divested of the body, free of the flesh, having no material form, aery, incorporeal, bodiless, asomatous, extramundane, immaterial, unbodied, insubstantial, disincarnate, psychical, spiritual, supersensible, unearthly, ghostly.

2. *(Mil.)* Discharged temporarily as a body, disbanded, demobilized.

DISEMBOGUE, *v.* 1. Empty at the mouth by pouring forth the contents, pour out, emit, eject, cast forth, give vent to, evacuate, gush, spout, extravasate, effuse, debouch, excrete, discharge, secrete.

2. Flow out at the mouth, issue, emerge, pour out of, emanate, be discharged.

3. Pass out of the mouth of a river or bay *(said of a ship).*

DISEMBOWEL, *v.* Eviscerate, remove the entrails from, take out the bowels of, gut, embowel, gib, commit hara-kiri, exenterate, gralloch, paunch, draw, wound so as to cause the bowels to protrude.

DISEMBROIL, *v.* Free from embroilment, free from perplexity, extricate from imbroglio, restore order to, disentangle, disengage.

DISENABLE, *v.* Deprive of ability, make unable, disable, incapacitate, unfit, make incapable, render powerless, invalidate, disqualify, undermine, put a spoke in one's wheel, unman, unnerve, cripple, devitalize, put out of gear, spike the guns, draw the teeth, take the wind out of one's sails, tie the hands, paralyze, hamstring, render *hors de combat,* clip the wings.

DISENCHANT, *v.* Free from enchantment, set free from magic spells, disentrance, disillusion, deliver from illusions, free from glamor, remove the spell from, undeceive, disillusionize, deprive of fascination, disabuse, open the eyes to, show in its true colors, show the daylight to, expose the feet of clay.

DISENCUMBER, *v.* Free from encumbrance, disengage, disentangle, extricate, disembarrass,

discumber, disburden, lighten the labor, unload, ease, liberate, release, set free, free from clog, deobstruct, rid.

DISENGAGE, *v.* 1. Loosen that which has been involved, release from attachment, liberate from connection, free from engagement, unfasten, set free, unloose, unfetter, untie, unbolt, disembarrass, unbar, unbind, unchain, extricate, get out of a complicated position, clear, liberate, emancipate, manumit, disenthrall, disentangle, disencumber, deliver, disembroil.

2. Relieve of obligation, free from pledge or vow.

3. Disunite, detach, disjoin, cut off, sunder, sever, dissever, part, separate, dissociate, divide, disconnect, divorce, segregate, sequestrate, break the connection with.

4. Draw off, abstract, become detached, wean, withdraw, break off action with *(Mil.).*

DISENGAGED, *adj.* 1. Detached, separated, out of gear, unattached, disjoined, disentangled, free, released, liberated, separate, apart, asunder, loose, unconnected.

2. Unengaged, at leisure, unoccupied, at ease, not busy, free from care, unemployed, out of harness, one's own master, at large, at liberty, otiose.

3. Not bound by appointment, not engaged matrimonially, not secured to any party or side, unassociated.

DISENGAGEMENT, *n.* 1. Separation, severance, disunion, dissociation, disjunction, disconnection, discontinuity, detachment, cleavage, segregation, divorce, disruption, break, rupture, sequestration, parting, isolation.

2. Setting at large, liberation, release, freeing, emancipation, manumission, deliverance, liberty, extrication, disentanglement, quittance, freedom, license.

3. Freedom from business, leisure, otiosity, freedom from obligation, freedom from care, freedom from toil, *dolce far niente (It.),* doux faire rien *(Fr.).*

4. Gracefulness, ease, relaxation, unconstraint, naturalness, unembarrassment.

DISENTANGLE, *v.* 1. Free from entanglement, untangle, untwist, card, unravel, unwind, unfold, relieve of internal complication, loosen, separate.

2. Straighten out, set right, systemize, arrange, methodize, **organize.**

3. Disengage, disconnect, unfasten, disembroil, clear, unloose, liberate, extricate, free, set free, detach, disencumber, disembarrass.

4. Decipher, solve, explicate.

DISENTHRALL, *v.* Free from thralldom, rescue from slavery, free from bondage, liberate from oppression, set at liberty, enfranchise, manumit, emancipate, disenslave, set free from that which subjects, disimprison, unchain, unmanacle, unfetter.

DISESTABLISHMENT, *n.* 1. Deprivation of the character of being established, annihilation, revocation, abrogation, rescission, annulment, nullification, cancellation, abolition, subversion, overthrow, destruction, extinction, extirpation.

2. Deprivation of public support, withdrawal of State recognition, stripping of State authority, abolition as a State institution.

DISFAVOR, *n.* 1. Unfavorable regard, disregard, lack of favor, disesteem, little esteem, disrespect, slight displeasure, low regard, dislike, disapproval, discountenance, dissatisfaction.

2. State of low estimation, unacceptableness, disrepute, uninfluential position, state of being regarded unfavorably, discredit, disgrace, odium, ignominy, state of being frowned upon.

3. Act of unkindness, disservice, ill turn, act of ill will, slight, neglect, insult, indignity, affront, discourtesy, outrage, unaccommodating act.

DISFIGURE, v. Change the external surface so as to injure the appearance of, mar the aspect of, spoil the figure of, deface, deform, make ugly, render unsightly, blemish, injure, mutilate, scar, mangle, damage, maim, impair, make defective, ruin, bruise, contuse, maul, disfeature, wrench, twist, blur.

DISFIGUREMENT, n. 1. Act of disfiguring, defacement, marring, injury, spoiling, blemishing, deformation, mayhem, mutilation.

2. That which disfigures, blemish, deformity, imperfection, defect, flaw, eyesore, stain, speckle, blot, spot, blur, freckle, patch, blotch, macula, smudge, birthmark, naevus (Med.), cicatrice, rift, mole, pimple, blister, pustule, crack, fissure.

DISFURNISH, v. Render destitute of belongings, deprive of furnishings, unfurnish, disgarnish, dismantle, divest of furniture, strip.

DISGORGE, v. 1. Throw out from the throat or stomach, spew up, vomit forth, throw up, eject, cast up, discharge, empty.

2. Make restitution of unwillingly, give up unwillingly, yield up, relinquish, surrender, give back, return.

DISGRACE, n. 1. State of being in dishonor, ill-favor, condition of infamy, debasement, discredit, ingloriousness, disrepute, disesteem, disfavor, contempt, abasement, degradation, turpitude, vileness, baseness, exclusion from favor.

2. A cause of shame or reproach, that which dishonors, reproach, derogation, disparagement, infamy, ignominy, obloquy, scandal, odium, blot on the escutcheon, smirch, taint, blemish, spot, stigma, brand, stain, attaint, slur, tarnish, badge of infamy, defilement, skeleton in the closet, stain on honorable reputation, shameful notoriety, ill-repute.

DISGRACE, v. 1. Dismiss with discredit, treat with disfavor, abase, put out of grace, strip of honors, dismiss from favor, cause to lose favor, mortify, humble, humiliate, degrade, defame, debase.

2. Reflect shame upon, bring reproach upon, dishonor, affect dishonorably, disparage, attaint, derogate, stigmatize, pollute, brand, vilify, slur, blot, smirch, taint, drag through the mire, heap dirt upon.

DISGRACEFUL, adj. Bringing disgrace, arrant, shameful, shocking, scandalous, disreputable, notorious, flagrant, nefarious, flagitious, odious, dishonorable, opprobrious, infamous, unseemly, ignominious, discreditable, unbecoming, unworthy, degrading, indecent, outrageous, detestable, vile, horrible, heinous, low, ignoble, mean, villainous, inglorious, base, despicable, worthy of contempt.

DISGRUNTLED, adj. Put into a state of sulky dissatisfaction, dissatisfied, discontented, grumpy, displeased, sulky, vexed, disappointed, malcontent, disillusioned, disenchanted.

DISGUISE, n. 1. That which alters the appearance of, that which renders difficult of recognition, something intended for concealment of identity, camouflage, deceptive covering, concealment, counterfeit dress, veil, mask, cover, incognito, screen.

2. False appearance, make up, veneer, show, masquerade, cloak, blind, pretext, pretense, false colors, artifice, guise, speciousness, borrowed plumes, misrepresentation, color, mummery, seeming, semblance, smoke screen, shade, blinker, ass in the lion's skin.

DISGUISE, v. 1. Change the guise of so as to conceal appearance, alter the appearance of, conceal by outward appearance, muffle, cloak, shroud, mask, veil, dissemble, hide, pretend, feign, dissimulate, camouflage, counterfeit, simulate, transform so as to make recognition difficult.

2. Cover up the real state of by a counterfeit form, misrepresent, falsify, gloss over, garble, give a color to, put a false coloring on, varnish, dress up.

DISGUISED, adj. 1. In disguise, incognito, alias, cloaked, veiled, masked, camouflaged.

2. In ambush, under cover, behind a screen, hidden, concealed, clandestine, sub rosa.

DISGUST, n. 1. Strong distaste, disrelish, nausea, sickness, satiety, repletion, surfeit.

2. Repugnance caused by something offensive, antipathy, aversion, dislike, detestation, hatred, abhorrence, abomination, revulsion, repulsion, resentment, animosity, contempt, displeasure, odium, annoyance, disaffection, antagonism, impatient dissatisfaction, taedium vitae (Lat.).

DISGUST, v. 1. Cause nausea in, sicken, fill with loathing, turn one's stomach, pall, cause aversion, go against one's stomach, nauseate, excite queasiness in.

2. Offend the good taste of, displease, be repellent, repel, excite distaste, revolt, shock, scandalize, offend the moral sense of, be repulsive.

DISGUSTING, adj. 1. Sickening, nauseous, nasty, distasteful, unpalatable, uneatable, loathsome, inedible, noisome.

2. Offensive, repulsive, odious, disagreeable, abhorrent, repugnant, hateful, revolting, repellent, foul, detestable, abominable, reprehensible, vile, shameless, horrid, vulgar, shocking, ignominious, displeasing, obnoxious, execrable, insufferable, unsavory.

3. Aggravating, irritating, galling, annoying, irksome, plaguy.

DISH, n. 1. Open shallow container, receptacle, hollow concave vessel, plate, platter, bowl, paten, saucer, utensil, crock, tureen, porringer, trencher, salver, patera, caraffe, pan, skillet, casserole, bonbonniere, epergne, saucepan, gravy boat.

2. Article of food, that which is served in a dish, particular viand, plat (Fr.).

3. Dishful, as much as a dish will hold.

4. Concavity.

DISH, v. 1. Put into a dish, serve in a dish.

2. Make concave, fashion like a dish.

3. Make ready for acceptable presentation.

4. (Colloq.) Undo, seal the doom of, do for, frustrate, balk, thwart, render helpless, put hors de combat, lay up, shelve, upset, defeat, ruin. use up badly.

DISHABILLE, n. 1. Déshabillé, negligent attire. loose morning dress, undress, disarray.

2. Garment worn in undress, kimono, wrapper, housecoat, dressing gown, peignoir, negligee, robe, tea gown, hostess gown.

DISHEARTEN, v. Depress the spirits of, weaken the resolution of, lower the courage of, dispirit, deject, dash, discourage, daunt, dismay, appall.

damp, dampen, deaden, sadden, put down in the mouth, dull, dissuade, disconcert, weary, frighten, intimidate, abash, cow, crush, deter, unnerve, cut up, unman, check, chill, affright, prostrate, break one's heart, take the heart out of, cast a gloom on, wither one's hopes, throw a shadow on, put a wet blanket on, throw cold water on, lie heavy on one, prey on the mind.

DISHED, *adj.* 1. Concave, dish-faced, discoid, hollow.

2. *(Colloq.)* Defeated, frustrated, disconcerted, thwarted, foiled, balked, cheated, baffled, upset, disappointed, ruined, undone, spoiled.

3. *(Colloq.)* Exhausted, done for, done in, worn out, played out.

DISHEVELED, *adj.* Hanging loosely, disordered, in disorder, tossed about negligently, at loose ends, mussed, disarranged, ruffled, tousled, untidy, upkempt, tumbled, disorderly, rumpled, frowzy, uncombed, slatternly, blowzy, slovenly.

DISHONEST, *adj.* Lacking native integrity, false, destitute of good faith, wanting in probity, unjust, faithless, disingenuous, disposed to cheat, unfair, fraudulent, knavish, thievish, roguish, wrongful, corrupt, crooked, covinous, unconscientious, not honest, unscrupulous, dishonorable, underhand, untrustworthy, deceitful, deceptive, misleading, unrightful, unlawful, sinister, inequitable, double-tongued, slippery, immoral, unprincipled, false-hearted, treacherous, perfidious, hypocritical, unfaithful, collusive, spurious, two-faced.

DISHONESTY, *n.* Deviation from rectitude, bad faith, straying from probity, falsity, indirection, lack of integrity, improbity, lack of honesty, foul play, knavery, roguery, villainy, rascality, deceit, scoundrelism, violation of trust, faithlessness, infidelity, betrayal, treachery, perfidiousness, duplicity, double-dealing, trickery, deceitfulness, unfairness, disposition to lie, fraudulency, fraud, breach of trust, falsehood, unrighteousness, guile, unscrupulousness, disingenuousness, insincerity, corruption, disposition to cheat, malpractice, wrongdoing, stealing, professional misconduct, malfeasance, jobbery, venality, sharp practice, graft.

DISHONOR, *n.* 1. Lack of honor, dishonorable character, dishonorableness, ill-repute, ignominy, disgrace, disrepute, discredit, reproach, obloquy, shame, odium, opprobrium, scandal, degradation, infamy, public disgrace, blot, stain, stigma, low estimation, blemish, disparagement, derogation, abasement, humiliation, disfavor.

2. That which lessens honor, indignity, insult, affront, reproach, slight, discourtesy, outrage.

3. *(Comm.)* Failure to accept, pay or retire a note or bill of exchange.

DISHONOR, *v.* 1. Deprive of honor, stigmatize, bring reproach upon the good character of, bring shame on, discredit, disgrace, abase, humiliate, degrade, defame, stain the character of, asperse, sully, humble, debase, attaint, slur, disparage.

2. Subject to indignities, treat with a lack of courtesy, affront, insult, outrage.

3. Violate the chastity of, seduce, betray, rape, debauch, corrupt, deflower, constuprate, attack, ravish, assault, abuse sexually, take virginity from, molest, pollute.

4. *(Comm.)* Refuse to accept, decline to pay, refuse to honor by payment, decline to redeem.

DISHONORABLE, *adj.* 1. Shameful, disgraceful, infamous, scandalous, disreputable, ignominious, notorious, shady, discreditable, ignoble, vile, base,

mean, low, ribald, low-minded, indecent, arrant, improper, foul, opprobrious, unbecoming, *infra dignitatem (Lat.),* unworthy, unmentionable, outrageous, shocking.

2. Shameless, without honor, unconscientious, without good repute, blackguard, unscrupulous, unprincipled, false-hearted, despicable, traitorous, inglorious, unjust, corrupt, fraudulent, perfidious, crooked, treacherous, perjured, forsworn, roguish, venal, unfair, knavish, rascally, slippery, thievish.

DISILLUSION, *v.* Free from illusion, disenchant, disillusionize, disenthrall, open the eyes, disabuse, undeceive, send one's air castles tumbling, show the feet of clay, embitter, burst the bubble, shatter the illusions of youthful inexperience.

DISINCLINATION, *n.* Absence of inclination, indisposition, unwillingness, averseness, aversion, disrelish, repugnance, reluctance, backwardness, displacency, lack of desire, disaffection, distaste, dislike, abhorrence, antipathy, inclination to the contrary, renitence, hesitation, demur, scruple, qualm, shrinking, recoil.

DISINCLINED, *adj.* Indisposed, averse, not in the mood, reluctant, unwilling, loath, grudging, slow to, renitent, backward, unconsenting, not content, unpersuadable, squeamish, scrupulous, shrinking from, hesitant, disaffected, antipathetic.

DISINFECT, *v.* Destroy disease germs in, purify, sterilize, asepticize, fumigate, sanitate, cauterize, antisepticize, cleanse from infection, deodorize.

DISINGENUOUS, *adj.* Not sincere, insincere, not free from concealment, lacking frankness, artful, wanting in candor, uncandid, double-minded, sly, wanting in openness, double-tongued, dishonest, false-hearted, designing, wily, subtle, crafty, false, subdolous, deceitful, mendacious, unveracious, underhanded, deceptive, fraudulent, hypocritical, *Parthis mendacior (Lat.),* hollow, slippery, foxy, mealy-mouthed, insidious, fishy, tricky.

DISINHERIT, *v.* Exclude from inheritance, cut off from inheritance, exheredate, deprive of the right to inherit, deprive of hereditary succession, dispossess of hereditary right, bereave, disown, disherit, oust, divest, evict, prevent from coming into possession of any property.

DISINTEGRATE, *v.* Break into constituent parts, reduce to particles, destroy the cohesion of, wear away the wholeness of, separate into integrant parts, destroy the unity of, divide the identity of, crumble to fragments, decompose, decay, molder, break to pieces, reduce to fragments, dissolve, rot, disunite, erode, cause to fall to pieces, cause to go to wrack and ruin, disperse, diffuse, disband, decentralize, resolve into its elements, disrupt.

DISINTER, *v.* 1. Dig up out of the earth, take out of the place of interment, exhume, disinhume, exhumate, unbury, disentomb, uncharnel.

2. Bring from obscurity into view, bring to light, unearth, uncover, discover, disclose, expose, root out, resurrect.

DISINTERESTED, *adj.* 1. Not influenced by selfish motives, unselfish, not dictated by private advantage, unbiased by personal interest, free from bias, free from self-interest, unprejudiced, lacking prejudice, dispassionate, impersonal, just, neutral, impartial, open-minded, fair, equitable, candid, honest, generous, magnanimous, liberal, not influenced by regard to personal advantage.

2. *(Colloq.)* Not interested, indifferent, lacking interest, apathetic, uninterested, unconcerned, aloof.

DISJOIN, *v.* Sever the connection of, dissever, undo the junction of, prevent the union of, disunite, separate from something else, divorce, part, sunder, cut off, divide, subdivide, disconnect, disengage, uncouple, dissociate, keep apart, rend, segregate, insulate, isolate, dissolve, disjoint, cut, interrupt, dismember, dissect, anatomize, cleave, partition, rive, rupture, split, break, snap, carve, quarter, detach.

DISJOINT, *v.* 1. Divide at the joints, subdivide, luxate, disarticulate, sunder, rend, split, cleave, break up, dissect, disjunct, disunite, undo, carve, separate the joints of, disconnect the joinings of, take to pieces, quarter, dismember, anatomize, unloose the original divisions, sever, detach from a whole.

2. Disarrange, put out of order, derange, break the sequence of, break the coherence of, throw into confusion.

3. Come apart, be dislocated, be put out of joint, fall to pieces, crumble, break into parts, disintegrate.

DISJOINTED, *adj.* 1. Having the joints separated, disconnected, disarticulated, broken, reft, split, cleft, divided, detached, unconnected, unattached, disjunct, apart, separate, loose, asunder, luxated, out of proper order, out of sequence.

2. Incoherent, desultory, rambling, spasmodic, fitful, irregular.

DISJUNCTION, *n.* Disunion, division, cleavage, disassociation, disconnection, separation, divorce, disengagement, partition, severance, detachment, isolation, fracture, break, interruption, rupture, discontinuity, breach, fissure, rift, split, rent, slit, crack, cleft.

DISJUNCTIVE, *adj.* Distinguishing, helping to disconnect, serving to separate, dividing, tending to disjoin, disjoining, discretive, discontinuous, discrete.

DISK, *n.* 1. Discus, quoit, squail.

2. Circular plate, orb, apparently flat circular surface *(of the sun,* etc.), face, disc, circle, dish, roundel, paten, saucer, plate, flan, sabot *(Mil.).*

3. Phonograph record.

DISLIKE, *n.* Distaste, disrelish, disgust, nausea, loathing, aversion, disinclination, antipathy, spite, repugnance, disapprobation, abomination, ill will, abhorrence, displeasure, detestation, reluctance, unwillingness, backwardness, renitency, revulsion, repulsion, disapproval, mislike, disdain, objection, antagonism, dissatisfaction, prejudice, disfavor, disaffection, hatred, rancor, animosity, hostility, malevolence, enmity, animus, malice, dyspathy, odium.

DISLIKE, *v.* Have no taste for, feel repugnance to, consider obnoxious, hold as disagreeable, not like, regard with displeasure, disrelish, look on with aversion, regard with disfavor, mislike, not be able to stomach, be displeased by, disapprove, resent, loathe, detest, abhor, abominate, execrate, hate, antipathize, despise, contemn, turn up the noise at, disesteem, look askance at, object to, mind, shrink from, recoil from, shudder at, shun, scorn, avoid, eschew, be disinclined.

DISLOCATE, *v.* 1. Put out of proper relative position, displace, derange, throw out of order, disorder, upset, disarrange, disturb, put out of place, disorganize, misplace, loosen, discompose, mislay, scatter, litter, mix.

2. Put out of joint, disarticulate, disconnect, disjoint, luxate, displace at a socket, unhinge, disunite, exarticulate, disengage.

DISLOCATION, *n.* 1. Condition of being out of regular arrangement, derangement, displacement, disorder, disarrangement, disturbance, disruption, disorganization, irregularity, mess, jumble.

2. Disjointing of a bone, displacement of the bone of a joint, luxation.

DISLODGE, *v.* Remove from a place of rest, drive from a place of lodgment, push out of a position occupied, force out, oust, eject, evict, expel, expatriate, deport, exile, banish, unlodge, extrude, displace, dismount, dispel, eliminate, dispossess, discharge, unseat, uproot, dismiss, fire, bounce, sack, depose, disestablish, displant, turn out of doors, disturb, compel to abandon an entrenchment *(Mil.).*

DISLOYAL, *adj.* False to one's obligations, two-faced, faithless to a due allegiance, treasonable, recreant, unfaithful, untrue, undutiful, perfidious, treacherous, disaffected, apostate, false-hearted, renegade, inconstant, untrustworthy, Iscariotic, double-tongued, dead to honor, untrue to one's rightful government, subversive.

DISLOYALTY, *n.* 1. Betrayal of trust, infidelity, deliberate breaking of faith, faithlessness, lack of fidelity, unfaithfulness, undutifulness, recreancy, lack of loyalty, inconstancy, apostasy, treachery, disaffection, dereliction of allegiance, perfidy, bad faith, treason, Iscariotism, double-dealing, breach of trust, subversive activity, performance of overt acts to help one's country's enemies, violation of allegiance to a government, wishing harm to one's country.

2. A disloyal act, Judas kiss.

DISMAL, *adj.* 1. Somber, cheerless, dark, gloomy, dreary, rayless, unilluminated, bleak, murky, dull, black, depressing, tenebrous, atramentous, swart, dusky, dingy, shadowy, umbrageous, overcast, dim, foggy, cloudy, wan.

2. Expressing gloom of feeling, in low spirits, joyless, sad, dolorous, doleful, depressed, morbid, dejected, melancholy, hypochondriacal, unhappy, despondent, mournful, lugubrious, funereal, blue, sorrowful, down in the mouth, in the dumps, downcast, disheartened, dispirited, heavy-hearted, disconsolate, forlorn, desolate, lonesome, woeful, lachrymose, long-faced, rueful, grim-visaged, woebegone.

3. Terrible, dreadful, awful, direful, horrible, relating to adversity, disastrous, horrifying, ill-fated, calamitous, troublous, ill-starred, ominous, ill-omened, foreboding.

DISMANTLE, *v.* 1. Demolish, destroy, unbuild, undo, break down, unrig, deprive of equipment, remove the apparatus of, tear down, pull down, raze, fell, level, ruin, subvert, take to pieces, dismount, take apart, remove the assemblage of.

2. Divest of dress, undress, unclothe, strip of covering, lay bare, denude, disrobe, uncover, bare.

DISMAY, *v.* Utterly break down the courage of, fill with consternation, destroy the self-confidence of, completely dishearten, daunt, intimidate, cow, abash, disconcert, discourage, paralyze with fear, appall, affright, alarm, scare, frighten, horrify, terrify, overawe, bulldoze, unman, unnerve, panic, enervate, petrify.

DISMAY, *n.* Utter disheartenment, complete loss of courage, loss of mental resource, panic, fear, sudden consternation, affright, alarm, misgiving, fright, terror, horror, dread, apprehension, shock, trepidation, chagrin, anxiety, discouragement, confusion of the mental faculties by the prospect of imminent danger, state of embarrassment that incapacitates for action, intimidation, mistrust, awe, qualm, scare, funk, cold feet, perturbation, fear and trembling.

DISMEMBER, *v.* Deprive of members, divide limb from limb, dissect, anatomize, separate part from part, dislimb, disjoint, mutilate, perpetrate mayhem on, cut in pieces, amputate, divide into parts and distribute, sever, dilacerate, pull apart, rend asunder, tear off.

DISMISS, *v.* 1. Direct to disperse, give leave to go, allow to depart, bid to go, permit to go, send away, give permission to depart, send forth, let go, release, free, liberate, disband, dissolve, adjourn.
2. Discharge from office, remove from service, put out of a job, oust, fire, sack, bounce, give one one's walking papers, cashier, turn out, discard, send packing, turn adrift, banish, expel, dislodge, send about one's business, drop, shelve, ship.
3. Put aside from consideration, have done with summarily, put out of mind, lay aside, put away, reject, get rid of, set aside, turn away, disclaim, think no more of, turn thumbs down.

DISMISSAL, *n.* 1. Liberty to depart, permission to go, leave to go forth, adjournment, freedom, dissolution, release, manumission, liberation.
2. Peremptory discharge from employment, removal from office, displacement by authority from an office, deposition, sack, bounce, congé, walking papers, expulsion.

DISMOUNT, *v.* 1. Unhorse, bring down, throw down, set afoot, push off, unmount, unseat.
2. Alight from (*a horse*), light, descend, come down, get down, descend from, drop down, slide off, hop to the ground.
3. Deprive of mountings, dismantle, dislodge, displace, put out of position, dismast, render useless, disable, unrig, remove from its mounting.

DISOBEDIENCE, *n.* Omission to do what is commanded to be done, violation of prohibition, doing of what is forbidden, violation of order, refusal to obey, lack of obedience, neglect to comply with an authoritative injunction, mutiny, infraction of a command, defiance, revolt, strike, insurgence, insubordination, intractableness, riot, indocility, noncompliance, nonobservance, neglect of duty, recusance, recalcitrance, insubmission, disregard, dereliction, infringement, waywardness, transgression, undutifulness, unruliness, sedition, stubbornness, obstinacy, perverseness, contumacy, frowardness, indiscipline, rebellion, insurrection, outbreak, uprising, tumult, sabotage, revolution, secession, high treason.

DISOBEDIENT, *adj.* Noncompliant, refusing to obey, recusant, unsubmissive, fractious, froward, refractory, recalcitrant, undutiful, remiss, wilful, dissentient, stubborn, obstinate, unmanageable, naughty (*in children*), mischievous, ungovernable, wayward, perverse, restive, indocile, headstrong, unyielding, contumacious, intractable, mutinous, derelict, unruly, defiant, riotous, revolutionary, lawless, seditious, insurgent, anarchistic.

DISOBEY, *v.* Ignore the commands of, ignore, disregard the authority of, wilfully fail to comply with, neglect to obey, refuse submission to, break the command of, set at defiance, defy, resist, set at naught, disregard regulations, go counter to, infringe, violate, transgress, break rules, secede, contravene, shirk, slack, strike, revolt, rebel, run riot, mutiny, rise in arms, take the law into one's

own hands, kick over the traces, refuse to support, bolt (*Politics*).

DISOBLIGE, *v.* Act contrary to the desire of, act contrary to the convenience of, give offense to, refuse to oblige, fail to accommodate, act in a manner contrary to the wishes of, displease, affront, offend, discommode, cause inconvenience to, incommode, put out, do an ill office to, plant a thorn in the breast, be unaccommodating, malign.

DISOBLIGING, *adj.* Not disposed to oblige, ill-natured, ungracious, unaccommodating, uncivil, discourteous, unkind, unfriendly, unamiable, ill-disposed, unbenevolent, spiteful, uncharitable, uncomplaisant, churlish, sullen.

DISORDER, *n.* 1. Lack of regular order, lack of system, disorderliness, irregularity, derangement, disarrangement, disorganization, confusion, mess, disarray, litter, jumble, clutter, topsy-turvy, want of order, tumble, muddle, tangle, cart before the horse, hugger-mugger, chaos, hysteron-proteron.
2. Public disturbance, tumult, unrest, uproar, commotion, turbulence, tumultuousness, turmoil, riot, bedlam, fracas, melee, ruckus, misconduct, clamor, bustle, anarchy, pandemonium, misdeed, misdemeanor, breach of order, interruption of peace, disorderly conduct, disturbance of peace, infraction of law, minor uprising.
3. Malady, ailment, sickness, derangement of bodily functions, complaint, malaise, distemper, organic disturbance, illness, indisposition, disease.

DISORDER, *v.* 1. Disarrange, throw out of order, destroy the regular arrangement of, discompose, derange, put in confusion, confuse, upset, perturb, disconcert, confound, disturb, unsettle, dishevel, turn topsy-turvy, disorganize, put out of place, jumble, clutter, muss, tumble, tousle, entangle, tangle, botch, muddle, litter, ravel, rumple, ruffle, agitate.
2. Disturb the natural functions of, impair the health of, produce disease in, render morbid in operation.

DISORDERLY, *adj.* 1. Lacking due arrangement, without method, indiscriminate, out of order, out of place, in bad order, turbid, knotted, tangled, raveled, hugger-mugger, topsy-turvy, disjointed, unmethodical, desultory, confused, unregulated, irregular, chaotic, anomalous, deranged, jumbled, disarranged, disordered, unsystematic, pell-mell, helter-skelter, disorganized.
2. Untidy, disheveled, straggling, slatternly, unkempt, slovenly, messy, frowzy, blowzy, slipshod, dowdy, sloppy, careless, frumpish.
3. Lawless, unquiet, turbulent, unmanageable, tumultuous, agitated, rebellious, ungovernable, riotous, unrestrained, mutinous, undisciplined, wild, rough, rowdyish, boisterous, violent, noisy, obstreperous, not amenable to restraint, violating constituted order, constituting a nuisance.
4. Contrary to public morality, offensive to good morals, counter to public decency, obscene, licentious, disreputable.

DISORGANIZATION, *n.* Destroying of order, disruption of constituent parts, breaking up of system, disunion, dissolution, disarrangement, loss of organic unity, derangement, chaos, confusion, absence of orderly arrangement, demoralization, absence of organization, mess, demobilization, anarchy, disbandment.

DISORGANIZE, *v.* Deprive of organization, put out of order, destroy the organic connection of, abolish the organization of, disarrange, throw into disorder, upset, unsettle, confuse, disorder, break up, disturb, disrupt, dislocate, dissolve, disperse, derange, discompose, demoralize, disconcert, disband, demobilize.

DISOWN, *v.* 1. Disclaim the responsibility for, refuse to acknowledge as pertaining to oneself, deny the ownership of, refuse to recognize, refuse to admit as true, disavow, disallow, repudiate, renounce, forsake, recant, retract, abnegate, cast off, abjure, reject, denounce, pass the buck.
2. Disinherit, cut off without a penny, deprive of the right to inherit, disherit, exheredate,

DISPARAGE, *v.* 1. Speak slightingly of, asperse, traduce, slur, slander, vilify, vilipend, defame, malign, abuse, calumniate, censure, scoff at, call names, ridicule, mock, reflect upon, reproach, speak ill of, scandalize, blacken, denigrate, libel, dishonor, treat with scorn, inveigh against, throw mud at, bring reproach upon.
2. Injure by unjust comparison, belittle, decry, depreciate, debase, undervalue, carp at, detract from, lower the estimation of, run down, degrade in estimation, derogate from, cheapen, underrate, discredit, underpraise, underestimate, regard slightingly.

DISPARAGEMENT, *n.* 1. Something that causes loss of reputation, aspersion, slander, defamation, libel, calumniation, traducement, lampoon, slur, denigration, vilification, squib, pasquinade, gibe, censure, ridicule, mockery, reflection, malediction, scandalmongering, blasphemy, invective, sarcasm, jeer, derision, obloquy, denunciation, insinuation, condemnation, innuendo, vituperation, scurrility, philippic, diatribe, tirade, execration.
2. Something that causes loss of dignity, insult, indignity, affront, slight, snub, dishonor, scowl, frown, black look, rebuff, home thrust, chiding, reprimand, rebuke, reproof, dressing down, hoot, scolding, castigation, reprehension, hissing, cat call, rudeness, discourtesy, incivility, contumely, outrage.
3. Unjust comparison with that which is of less worth, act of undervaluing, condition of low estimation or valuation, underrating, detraction, derogation, belittlement, depreciation, dispraise, debasement, degradation, diminution, impairment, stricture, injury, harm, prejudice.

DISPARITY, *n.* Difference, discrepancy, lack of similarity, deviation, divergence, disproportion, inequality, qualitative dissimilarity, dissimilitude, unlikeness, lack of symmetry, incongruity.

DISPART, *v.* Part asunder, divide into parts, sunder, separate into parts, sever, dissever, open, disunite, part, cleave, rend, split, burst, rive, break apart, divaricate.

DISPASSION, *n.* 1. Freedom from passion, even temper, dispassionateness, unemotional state, self-possession, freedom from agitation, collectedness, coolness, calmness, tranquillity, unruffled state, serenity, inexcitability, imperturbability, placidity, composure, sobriety, equanimity.
2. Indifference, unconcern, apathy, aloofness, *sang-froid (Fr.),* torpor, phlegm, insensibility, dulness, lack of feeling, impassibility, coldness, pococurantism, hebetude, passiveness.

DISPASSIONATE, *adj.* 1. Devoid of bias, sober, unbiased, unprejudiced, impartial, uninfluenced by prejudice, disinterested, candid, fair, judicial, not dictated by prejudice, just, equitable, neutral, impersonal, open-minded.
2. Not warped by passion, unimpassioned, cool as a cucumber, unaffected by emotion, devoid of

personal feeling, unexcited, inexcitable, tranquil, imperturbable, collected, serene, composed, calm, unruffled, unmoved, phlegmatic, undisturbed, moderate, quiet.

DISPATCH, *v.* 1. Execute quickly, transact with promptness, dispose of rapidly, expedite, hasten, make short work of, settle, conclude, finish, wind up, complete, urge forward, press on, speed up, accelerate, quicken, forward, hurry on, discharge speedily, ply diligently.
2. Send away in haste, put under way, send off to some assigned destination, send on one's way, consign to, dismiss.
3. Kill summarily, put to death, slaughter, slay, murder, assassinate, shed blood, put an end to, butcher, finish, take for a ride, do to death, run through, bump off, put to the sword, knock on the head, shoot, massacre, strangle, throttle, execute, asphyxiate, pack off to meet one's maker, post out of this world.
4. Eat up quickly, bolt down, gobble up, ply a good knife and fork, devour.

DISPATCH, *n.* 1. Expeditious performance, zeal, promptitude, speedy transaction, ready carrying on, diligent completion, quick discharge, ready conduct, due diligence, quickness, rapidity, haste, celerity, expedition, speed, quick riddance, swift execution, swiftness, rapidity, speedy completion.
2. Forwarding to some destination, sending off to a destination, dismissal on an errand, mission.
3. Putting to death, killing, disposal, doing to death, death by violence, execution, bloodshed, murder, assassination, effusion of blood, butchery, slaughter, massacre.
4. Written message sent in haste, missive, note, official communication sent by special messenger, letter, report, instruction, news issue, telegram, news account transmitted by a reporter to his newspaper, telegraphic dispatch, message by telegraph.

DISPEL, *v.* Drive away by scattering, drive off in various directions, utterly disperse, scatter, rout, remove, banish, dismiss, diffuse, spread, expel, dissipate, disseminate, dissolve, put an end to.

DISPENSABLE, *adj.* 1. Apportionable, capable of being administered to others, distributable.
2. That may be done without, to be dispensed with, sparable, unnecessary, unessential, needless, superfluous, unimportant, removable, useless, of no avail, futile, unavailing, ineffectual, uncalled for, to spare, in excess, *de trop (Fr.).*
3. Pardonable, not binding, excusable, venial, that may be removed by dispensation.

DISPENSATION, *n.* 1. Dealing out, allotment, apportionment, distribution, allocation, partition, consignment, appropriation, division, conferment, administration, diffusion, bestowal, endowment.
2. Stewardship, management, economy, charge, husbandry, menage, regimen, direction, conduct, regulation, guidance, superintendence, auspices, supervision, control, provision.
3. Specific plan, scheme, system, arrangement, course of conduct, line of action, procedure, order.
4. That which is enjoined, privilege, decree, permission, favor.
5. Exemption, remission, relaxation of a law, release from obligation.

DISPENSE, *v.* 1. Divide in portions, give forth diffusively, allot, distribute, deal out, apportion, assign, mete, allocate, detail, share, parcel out, award, dole.

2. Administer, execute, carry out, undertake, enforce, apply, transact, carry into effect, enact, put into practice, officiate, employ oneself in, concern oneself with, make it one's business, have to do with, ply a task, serve, do duty, be engaged in, direct, manage, superintend, supervise, have charge of, control.

3. Grant a dispensation for, exempt, relieve, absolve, pardon, excuse, release.

4. Put up a prescription, distribute medicine.

DISPENSER, *n.* 1. Donor, giver, bequeather, bestower, grantor, presenter, contributor, patron, fairy godmother.

2. Distributor, divider, allotter, apportioner, dealer.

3. Administrator, executor, steward, manager, superintendent, supervisor, overseer, director.

4. Pharmacist, druggist, chemist *(Brit.).*

DISPENSE WITH, *v.* 1. Do without, forego, not use, let alone, not touch, abstain, forbear, waive, give up, relinquish, spare, throw aside, throw overboard, save the necessity.

2. Let off, absolve, exonerate, set aside, release, exempt, discharge, acquit, pass over, disregard, omit, neglect, excuse, give dispensation, grant exemption from, license.

DISPERSE, *v.* 1. Scatter abroad, drive off in various directions, cast forth, eject, rout, banish, dispel, dissipate, dislodge, dismember, disband, separate, dissolve, dismiss, scatter to the winds, cause to vanish, cause to depart in all directions.

2. Break up, be scattered out of sight, vanish, be dispelled, be dissipated, evanesce, disappear.

3. Propagate, radiate, diffuse, circulate, sow, disseminate, bestrew, sprinkle, spatter, spread, broadcast.

DISPERSION, *n.* Dispersal, scattering, diffusion, dissipation, distribution, propagation, broadcast, dissemination, emission, radiation, disjunction, circulation, divergence, separation, allocation, apportionment, allotment, spread.

DISPIRIT, *v.* Deprive of spirit, deject, sadden, depress the spirits of, dishearten, cast down, deter, discourage, render cheerless, make hopeless, tire, weary, jade, throw cold water on, damp, dash, disincline, knock down, prostrate, unman, wither one's hopes.

DISPIRITED, *adj.* 1. Depressed, dejected, glum, showing depression of spirits, downcast, unhappy, disheartened, discouraged, despondent, cheerless, down-hearted, sad, down in the mouth, mopish, chapfallen, crestfallen, heavy-hearted, heart-sick, in the dumps, in the doldrums, low-spirited, out of spirits, weary, disconsolate, forlorn.

2. Lacking in spirit, tame, spiritless, lukewarm, unspirited, vapid, unenthusiastic.

DISPLACE, *v.* 1. Put out of the usual place, mislay, misplace, change the place of, disarrange, move, dislocate, shift from its place, put out of the proper place, disturb, disorder, unsettle, put in a wrong place, derange, confuse.

2. Dislodge, remove, take out, cart away, draft off, empty, unload, transfer, transpose, set aside, replace, take the place of, succeed to, supplant, crowd out, supersede.

3. Depose, dismiss from office, oust from a position, discharge, unseat, cashier, eject, sack, fire, bounce, expel, disestablish, displant, uproot, evict, banish, export, exile.

DISPLAY, *v.* 1. Open out, unfold, spread out, expand, stretch out, extend, unfurl, deploy.

2. Bring into view, make visible, exhibit, show, evince, reveal, hold up to view, betray, manifest, make manifest, disclose, demonstrate, unmask, expose, array, advertise, make public, bring to the attention of others, put in plain sight.

3. Show off, flaunt, parade, boast, vaunt, show ostentatiously, flourish, air, make conspicuous, make a great show of.

DISPLAY, *n.* 1. Demonstration, manifestation, exhibit, exhibition, exposition, show, disclosure, revelation, array, advertisement, presentation, unfoldment, evincement, divulgence, publication, staging.

2. Ostentation, pomp, flourish, parade, pageant, grandeur, blazon, ceremony, splendor, *étalage (Fr.),* magnificence, pretension, pageantry, state, spectacle, solemnity, front, splash, splurge, gloss, glitter, veneer.

DISPLEASE, *v.* Annoy, provoke to disgust, vex, excite annoyance in, irritate, chafe, pique, fret, affront, chagrin, nettle, anger, tease, pester, miff, worry, disturb, rile, exasperate, exacerbate, repel, incommode, torment, incense, harass, disoblige, inflame, grate, offend, disgust, provoke, dislike, disgruntle, be unpleasant, cause displeasure, incur disapproval.

DISPLEASURE, *n.* Annoyance, vexation, anger, irritation, resentment, disaffection, dissatisfaction, discontent, indignant disapproval, indignation, disapprobation, distaste, dislike, wrath, umbrage, ire, dudgeon, pique, chagrin, exasperation, sulks, exacerbation, animosity, choler, irascibility, huff, tiff, pet, tantrum, fit, hot blood, sore subject.

DISPORT, *n.* Amusement, pastime, *passetemps (Fr.),* entertainment, diversion, playfulness, sport, merriment, play, divertissement, recreation, lark, relaxation, pleasure, frolic, jollity, jocosity, antic, mummery, tomfoolery, pleasantry, skylarking, drollery, gambol, romp, spree, escapade.

DISPORT, *v.* 1. Divert, entertain, amuse, cheer, enliven, beguile, recreate, relax, solace, delight, titillate, rejoice, regale.

2. Make merry, amuse oneself, exercise in a sportive manner, game, play pranks, toy, play wantonly, wanton, sport, frisk, gambol, carouse, romp, frolic, caper, revel, merrymake, sow wild oats, drown care, junket, have a fling, paint the town red.

DISPOSAL, *n.* 1. Distribution, arrangement, plan, ordering, disposition, grouping, order, method, array, assortment, adjustment.

2. Power to dispose of a thing, command, control, direction, regulation, ordering, disposure, management, determination, decision, discretion, administration, government, conduct, mercy.

3. Dispensation, transference, transaction, sale, bestowal, settlement, assignment, transfer.

DISPOSE, *v.* 1. Put in a particular order, range properly, arrange, array, marshal, rank, classify, group, organize, order, appoint, place, collocate, set, distribute.

2. Determine the career of, set right, settle, regulate, adapt, adjust, direct, rule, manage, fix, administer, make conform.

3. Give a tendency to, direct the mind of, lead, induce, predispose, influence, prompt, bias, bend, incline, move, actuate, prepare, give a bent to, tempt, affect.

4. Deal out, give, bestow, make over, alienate, distribute, assign, allot, allocate, apply, employ.

5. Decide matters, settle matters, rule, control, regulate, arrange affairs.

6. Make terms, bargain, contract, compound, compact, have an understanding, come to an agreement, covenant.

DISPOSED, *adj.* 1. Minded favorably, inclined, prone, apt, predisposed, having a bias, liable, subject, ready, tending, given, prompted, moved.

2. Conditioned, having a disposition, molded, cast, formed, framed, constituted.

3. Inborn, congenital, inherent, ingrained, deep-rooted, intrinsic, natural, instinctive, dyed-in-the-wool, blown-in-the-bottle.

4. Distributed, regulated, arranged, assigned, adapted.

DISPOSE OF 1. Put up for sale, sell, vend, sell off, part with by sale, effect a sale, dispense, market, peddle off, turn into money, auction, bring under the hammer, bargain away, put out of one's possession, transfer, make over by gift, alienate, convey.

2. Make final disposition of, finish with, deal with definitely, settle, determine the condition of, arrange for, find a place for, find means to occupy.

3. Put away, dismiss, remove, get rid of, cast forth, dump, unload.

4. Make use of, put to use, use, employ, set to work, apply, adhibit, do with, put in action.

DISPOSITION, *n.* 1. Characteristic mood, vein, temper, mental constitution, temperament, turn of mind, nature, prevailing aspect of one's mind, native character, make-up, essential quality of one's nature, native impulses, turn, humor, spirit, delicate balance of one's emotions, frame of mind, animus, passion, qualities, idiosyncrasy, genius, grain, inner man.

2. Inclination, tendency, habitual bent, mental proneness, predisposition, propensity, bias, bent, proclivity, leaning, penchant, aptitude, appetite, direction, liking, willingness, affection, diathesis, predilection.

3. Arrangement, ordering, plan, distribution, disposal, location, array, collocation, organization, classification.

4. Power to dispose of a thing, adjustment, final settlement of a matter, regulation, control, management, direction, administration, appoint-ment, dispensation.

5. Bestowal, sale, transfer, relinquishment by gift, bestowment, disposing by sale.

DISPOSSESS, *v.* 1. Put out of possession, eject from possession, deprive of occupancy, dislodge, drive out, evict, expel, remove, oust.

2. Divest, strip, bereave, expropriate, depose, commandeer, confiscate, impound, take from, take away from, wrest from, disinherit, levy, distrain, disseize.

DISPOSSESSION, *n.* 1. Deprivation, ademption, disseizin *(Law),* bereavement, sequestration, divestment, expropriation, disinheritance, con-fiscation, attachment, garnishment, usurpation.

2. Eviction, ouster, ejection, dislodgment, removal.

DISPRAISE, *n.* 1. Act of dispraising, reproval, description as undeserving, blame, censure, adverse criticism, detraction, condemnation, disapprobation, depreciation, disparagement, decrial.

2. Expression of unfavorable opinion, shame, reproach, opprobrium, discredit, dishonor, rebuke,

disgrace, obloquy, denunciation, stricture, satire, castigation, reprimand.

DISPROOF, *n.* Proof to be false, refutation, proof to the contrary, confutation, rebuttal, counterevidence, redargution, disproval, clincher *(colloq.),* conviction, invalidation.

DISPROPORTION, *n.* 1. Improper proportion, want of due relation between things, lack of proportion, ill proportions, asymmetry, lack of symmetry, unevenness, irregularity.

2. Unequalness, inequality, inadequacy, want of adequacy to an end, insufficiency, disparity, unsuitableness, incommensurateness.

3. Dissimilarity, dissimilitude, unlikeness, divergence, incongruity.

DISPROPORTIONATE, *adj.* 1. Lacking proper adaptation, ill-proportioned, disproportioned, out of proportion, unsymmetrical, incommensurate, wanting in proportion, unsuitable, poorly adapted.

2. Excessive, inordinate, overmuch, too much, overcharged, superfluous, uncalled for, over and above, *de trop (Fr.).*

DISPROVE, *v.* Prove to be false or wrong, refute, prove to the contrary, confute, rebut, invalidate, controvert, deny, prove to be fraudulent, defeat, overthrow, oppugn, negative, parry, expose, show up, upset, demolish, subvert, get the better of, squelch, silence, clinch an argument.

DISPUTABLE, *adj.* That may be disputed, liable to be called in question, questionable, doubtful, dubious, uncertain, of doubtful certainty, open to discussion, contestable, controvertible, arguable, unsettled, problematical, debatable, undecided, undetermined.

DISPUTANT, *n.* One who enters in an argument, controversialist, contender, logomachist, arguer, debater, agonist, disputer, opponent, adversary, dissenter, pilpulist, wrangler, hair-splitter, litigant, polemicist, antagonist, adverse party, brawler, oppositionist, irreconcilable.

DISPUTATION, *n.* Discussion over a question from opposing sides, verbal controversy, dispute, polemics, debate, argumentation, verbal conquest, altercation, disceptation, dissidence, dissension.

DISPUTATIOUS, *adj.* Characterized by dispute, given to disputation, disposed to controversy, apt to cavil, argumentative, contentious, captious, dissentious, bickering, controversial, disputative, discordant, polemical, quarrelsome, logomachical, exceptious, querulous, cantankerous, fractious, testy, hot-headed.

DISPUTE, *n.* 1. Earnest controversial discussion, verbal contention, contest in words, disputation, debate, controversy, polemic, moot.

2. Clash of contrary opinions, discord, feud, alternate expression of sharp differences of opinion, ill-tempered controversy, altercation, quarrel, bickering, squabble, wrangle, dissension, tiff, spat, war of words, strife, disagreement, difference, argument, disturbance, conflict, open rupture, impugnation, brabble, brawl, broil, row, jangle, litigation, friction, outbreak, imbroglio, fracas, scrimmage, rumpus.

DISPUTE, *v.* 1. Argue in opposition, debate, engage in discussion, contend in argument, have verbal controversy over, litigate, ventilate, reason about, discept, agitate, discuss, moot.

2. Argue vehemently, altercate, wrangle, brawl, bicker, quarrel, squabble, have an altercation, fall out, tiff, jangle, spat, spar, have words, differ, clash, row, nag, cavil, split hairs.

3. Question the truth of, rebut, confute, refute, deny the genuineness of, controvert, challenge, impugn, argue against, object to, contradict, gainsay, disagree, oppose by argument, call in question.

4. Strive against, contest, make resistance on, struggle for, fight about, contend for, compete, resist, struggle against.

DISQUALIFICATION, *n.* 1. Disability, inability, want of qualification, incapacitation, impotence, disablement, incapacity, unfitness, impuissance.

2. Invalidity of title, loss of right, forfeiture, disfranchisement, disbarment, deprivation of rights, pronouncement as unqualified.

3. Unproficiency, incompetency, want of skill, indexterity, clumsiness, ineptitude.

DISQUALIFY, *v.* 1. Render unfit, deprive of fitness, unfit, incapacitate, disable, prostrate, put *hors de combat,* invalidate, render impotent, paralyze.

2. Deprive of the rights necessary for any purpose, disfranchise, debar, disenable, disbar, pronounce unqualified, preclude, disentitle.

DISQUIET, *n.* 1. Turbulence, commotion, fuss, agitation, excitement, turmoil, confusion, hubbub, tumult, bustle, racket, rout.

2. Unsettled condition, want of peace, lack of tranquillity, absence of quiet, disquietude, unrest, inquietude, uneasiness, disturbance, vexation, restlessness, anxiety, trouble, misgiving, worry, concern, annoyance, perturbation, discomposure, disconcertion, discomfort.

DISQUIET, *v.* Make uneasy, agitate, disturb, deprive of tranquillity, perturb, discompose, fret, perturbate, exagitate, trouble, make restless, vex, annoy, excite, plague, harass, worry, pester, molest, bother, incommode, disconcert, alarm.

DISQUISITION, *n.* Treatise based on systematic investigation, study, dissertation, thesis, essay, discourse, theme, formal inquiry, lecture, sermon, formal discussion of a subject, memoir, homily, pandect, tract, excursus, composition, review, commentary, critique, oration, speech, effusion.

DISREGARD, *v.* 1. Pass by as undeserving of notice, neglect, overlook, ignore, leave out of consideration, pay no attention to, pass over, pay no heed to, slight, refuse to regard, brush off, take no notice of, push aside, let pass, turn a deaf ear to, gloss over, cut *(colloq.),* skip, defy, contemn, disobey, override, omit, close the eyes to, let in one ear and out the other, not trouble oneself with, pass up, waive, pretermit, blink, wink at, connive at, transgress, flout.

2. Treat without due respect, slight, snub, disdain, shirk paying sufficient attention to, give only superficial attention to something important, slur over, make little of, minimize, set no store by, fail to see because of carelessness, underrate, belittle, deride, run down, decry, ridicule, set at naught, undervalue, depreciate.

3. Insult, affront, outrage.

DISREGARD, *n.* 1. Deliberate lack of attention, want of notice, wilful oversight, pretermission, heedlessness, remissness, neglect, inattention, omission, preterition, ignoration, carelessness, negligence, indifference, oblivion.

2. Lack of respectful regard, disesteem, slight, disfavor, contempt, underestimation, disdain, snub, undervaluation, depreciation, belittlement, inappreciation.

3. Indignity, dishonor, discourtesy, affront,

insult, outrage, rudeness, scoffing, impoliteness, incivility.

DISRELISH, *n.* 1. Lack of palatableness, bad taste, unsavoriness, nauseousness, insipidity, bitterness, disagreeableness, flatness, acidity, sourness, tartness.

2. Feeling of disgust, dislike, distaste, aversion, repugnance, antipathy, disinclination, reluctance, displacency, abomination, abhorrence, loathing, detestation, queasiness, nausea.

DISRELISH, *v.* Have no taste for, have a distaste for, mislike, dislike, feel somewhat of disgust for, have no relish for, regard as offensive, mind, not care for, object to, have no stomach for, have an aversion to, loathe, abominate, detest, abhor, shrink from, eschew, not be able to bear, turn up one's nose at, shudder at, make a wry face, grimace.

DISREPAIR, *n.* State of being out of repair, rags and tatters, decrepitude, dilapidation, impaired condition, unrepair, irrepair, deterioration, decay, ruination, degeneration, decadency, declination, delaceration, damage, *délabrement (Fr.),* injury, wreckage, havoc, inroad, scath, ravage, wear and tear, mouldiness, moth and rust, dry-rot, atrophy, collapse, destruction, shabbiness, raggedness, run-down heels.

DISREPUTABLE, *adj.* Having a bad reputation, being in ill repute, not reputable, in ill odor, of bad character, base, low, unsavory, under a cloud, shady, abject, despicable, unworthy, disgraced, vile, notorious, ignominious, infamous, wicked, dishonorable, opprobrious, heinous, nefarious, iniquitous, rascally, knavish, villainous, corrupt, sneaking, unscrupulous, unconscientious, crooked, unprincipled, slippery, questionable, shocking, arrant, outrageous, unbecoming, shameful, disgraceful, scandalous.

DISREPUTE, *n.* Loss of reputation, disgrace, dishonor, disfavor, disesteem, discredit, ill-favor, shame, infamy, degradation, odium, obloquy, opprobrium, ignominy, ingloriousness, bad odor, debasement, abasement, derogation, ill-repute, bad name, bad character, unpopularity, badge of infamy, bar sinister, stigma, brand, slur, stain, spot, blot, tarnish, taint, smirch, defilement, pollution.

DISRESPECT, *n.* Lack of respect, disregard, hoot, disparagement, detraction, incivility, rudeness, discourtesy, impoliteness, slight, snub, dishonor, indignity, affront, outrage, disdain, contumely, contumacy, contemptuousness, insubordination, neglect, irreverence, disfavor, disesteem, scoff, contempt, derision, insult, hissing, catcall, sneer, taunt, flout, gibe, fling, jeer, mockery, sarcasm.

DISRESPECTFUL, *adj.* Ill-behaved, wanting in respect, characterized by disrespect, contemptuous, derisive, disparaging, slighting, irreverent, pert, insolent, supercilious, arrogant, opprobrious, insulting, impertinent, saucy, impudent, uncivil, uncourteous, discourteous, impolite, rude, fresh, abusive, scurrilous, disdainful, insubordinate, forward, unmannerly, sarcastic, unaccommodating.

DISROBE, *v.* Remove the garments from, strip of covering, undress, divest, unclothe, uncover, denude, bare, make bare, shed, doff, take off, cast off.

DISRUPTION, *n.* 1. Forcible separation into parts, tearing asunder, scission, disjunction, dissociation, breaking up, severance, cleavage, burst, splitting, parting, division, dissolution, disorganization, destruction, fission, schism.

2. Rupture, fissure, slit, cleft, cut, rent, rift, breach, crack, break, fracture.

3. Downfall, debacle, ruin, perdition, crash, smash, *délabrement (Fr.)*, wreck, crack-up, wrack, shipwreck.

DISSATISFACTION, *n.* 1. Uneasiness of mind resulting from disappointed expectations, state of being not satisfied, nonfulfillment, of one's hopes, disappointment, discontent, inquietude, disquiet, discontentment, regret, chafing, querulousness, repining, chagrin.

2. Unhappiness with one's lot, general feeling of dislike for the conditions of one's life, a wish for other conditions, sense of dislike for one's surroundings, vexation, annoyance, disapproval, disapprobation, distaste, displeasure, resentment, fault-finding, disaffection, umbrage, pique, anger, opposition, irritation, offense, provocation, stew, exasperation, plague, botheration.

DISSATISFIED, *adj.* Displeased from failure of expectation, not pleased, discontented, offended, uneasy from disappointment, ungratified, restless, faultfinding, querulous, rebellious, malcontent, hypercritical, unsatisfied, disgruntled, impatient, repining, regretful, sullen, morose, glum, sulky, in high dudgeon, in a pet, in a fume, in bad humor, sour, soured, grumpy, sore, grouchy, out of temper, ill-humored, irritable.

DISSECT, *v.* 1. Cut apart to examine the structure and relation of parts, divide into separate parts, dismember, separate the parts of, divide into portions, cut up, cut in pieces, anatomize, carve, vivisect, quarter, dissever, hack, slice, perform a post-mortem operation, undertake an autopsy, slash.

2. Examine minutely part by part, analyze, investigate, look into, scrutinize, probe, inspect, explore, look over, lay open, discuss in detail, sift, winnow, thresh out.

DISSECTION, *n.* 1. Operation of cutting a biological specimen in pieces for examination, anatomization, dismemberment, cutting apart of tissues, vivisection, callisection *(with anaesthesia)*, sentisection *(without anaesthesia)*, post-mortem, autopsy.

2. Critical examination, inquiry, scrutiny, investigation, inspection, inquest, research, sifting, analysis, criticism.

DISSEMBLE, *v.* 1. Conceal by false appearance, cloak, screen, veil, mask, shroud, curtain, cover, disguise, camouflage, lay down a smoke screen, give a false semblance to, put on the appearance of, make a show of, give the semblance of something else to.

2. Hide by pretending something different, conceal the real nature of, disguise the reality, conceal the real purpose, disguise the feelings, pretend, dissimulate, counterfeit, simulate, feign, make pretense of, imitate, play, act, act the hypocrite, play possum, hoodwink, blind, color, varnish, pass off for, affect, sham, profess, make believe.

3. Represent untruly, falsify, misrepresent, prevaricate, equivocate, deceive, shuffle, play false, beat about the bush, quibble, cant, snuffle.

4. Let pass unnoticed, ignore, gloss over, hush up, stifle, suppress, withhold, reserve, keep from, repress, restrain.

DISSEMBLER, *n.* Disguiser of one's character, pretender, counterfeiter, hypocrite, bigot, fraud,

Tartuffe, pharisee, sophist, Pecksniff, charlatan, quack, mountebank, imposter, humbug, knave, masquerader, masker, guiser, incognito, domino, wolf in sheep's clothing, ass in the lion's skin, snake in the grass, liar, prevaricator, shuffler, rogue, knave, cheat, deceiver.

DISSEMINATE, *v.* Spread abroad, promulgate, broadcast, diffuse, radiate, circulate, scatter, sow the seeds of, dissipate, disperse, distribute, teach, propagate, propagandize, dispense, make public, publish, rumor, evulgate, give out, give to the world, drag into the open, bandy about, blaze about, bruit, hawk.

DISSEMINATION, *n.* Promulgation, spreading abroad, propagation, dispersal, scattering, sowing the seeds of, radiation, circulation, emission, distribution, dissipation, diffusion, broadcasting, publication, propagandism, indoctrination, proselytism.

DISSENSION, *n.* 1. Violent disagreement, strife, contention, quarrel, friction, clashing, caviling, wrangling, bickering, angry disagreement, tiff, controversy, discord, dispute, altercation, affray, misunderstanding, breach of friendship, feud, spat, squabble.

2. Difference of opinion, disagreement with the majority opinion, dissent, nonagreement, nonconcurrence, nonconsent, conflict of opinion, nonconformity, variance, dissentience, heresy, discordance, sectarianism, heterodoxy, apostasy, schism, disaffection, recusancy, separation from an established group, noncompliance.

3. Refusal of agreement, protest, expostulation, remonstrance, contradiction, rejection, demur, protestation.

DISSENT, *v.* 1. Differ in sentiment or opinion, think in a contrary manner, disagree in opinion, contradict, deny, dispute, cavil, quibble, wrangle, protest, withhold approval, object, demur, take exception, call in question, disapprove, oppose, withhold assent, refuse to admit, decline to agree.

2. Differ in religious opinion, refuse to conform to an established church, reject the authority of an established church, be a nonconformist, refuse adherence to, repudiate, secede, retract, withdraw, recant, retire from, forswear, revoke.

DISSENTER, *n.* 1. One who dissents from what is established, one who separates from the service of an established church, heretic, apostate, schismatic, recusant, protestant, separatist, sectarian, nonconformist, seceder, dissident, Raskolnik *(Russia)*.

2. One who declares his disapproval, disputant, dissentient, controversialist, come-outer *(colloq.)*, objector.

DISSENTIENT, *adj.* Dissenting from the majority opinion, disagreeing, not acquiescent, recusant, schismatic, heterodox, apostatical, sectarian, denominational, unorthodox, dissident, negative, contradictory, unconvinced, unconverted, adverse, noncompliant, unconsenting, deaf to, hostile, factious, iconoclastic, contrary, antagonistic, antipathetic, clashing, jarring, irreconcilable.

DISSERTATION, *n.* Extended and argumentative presentation of a subject, formal discourse, thesis, didactic writing, disquisition, treatise, theme, descant, memoir, study, discussion, homily, essay written by a candidate for the Doctor's degree, sermon, lecture, essay, tract, composition, review, exposition, excursus, commentary, critique, appreciation, criticism.

DISSERVICE, *n.* Ill-service, ill-turn, doing one dirt, foul play, bad turn, disfavor, mischief, hurt, harm, wrong, injury, damage, evil, ill, injustice, disadvantage, buffet, machinations of the devil.

DISSEVER, *v.* Sever from something, cut off, lop off, sunder, divide into parts, subdivide, part, separate, disjoin, disunite, dispart, disengage, detach, dismember, dissociate, disconnect, rend, chop, snip, cleave, rive, split, break, tear apart, hack off, hew, slice, carve, quarter, dissect, set apart, anatomize, segregate, cut adrift, loose, unfasten, wrench free, rupture.

DISSIDENCE, *n.* 1. Difference in opinion, feud, separation in sentiment, nonagreement, variance, nonconcurrence, dissension, dissent, disagreement, disaffection, discordance, dissentience, quarrel, strong dissatisfaction with determined opposition, rupture, secession.
2. Separation from the established religion, heterodoxy, protestantism, apostasy, sectarianism, recusancy, recantation, nonconformity, schism.

DISSIDENT, *n.* One who differs from what is established, one who disagrees, dissenter, seceder, sectarian, nonconformist, separatist, protestant, schismatic, recusant, heretic, apostate.

DISSIMILAR, *adj.* Unlike in any respect, not similar, different, divergent, disparate, various, heterogeneous, various, diversified, diverse, new, distinct, unequal, altered, opposite, contrary, unique, novel, unprecedented, nonpareil, nonesuch, original.

DISSIMILARITY, *n.* Unlikeness, difference, want of similarity, divergence, disparity, variety, heterogeneity, variation, diversification, diversity, dissimilitude, contrast, inequality, variance, discrepancy, contrariety, novelty, originality.

DISSIMULATION, *n.* Concealment, practice of feigning, deceit, dissembling, simulation, false pretense, duplicity, deception, sham, imposition, double-dealing, insincerity, hypocrisy, false show, falsehood, falsification, misrepresentation, guile, misstatement, lying, prevarication, equivocation, mendacity, false coloring, perversion of truth, *suppressio veri (Lat.)*, cant, casuistry, shuffling, evasion, fraud.

DISSIPATE, *v.* 1. Disperse, strew, sprinkle, cast, spatter, bestrew, diffuse, disseminate, dispel, sow, scatter, broadcast, break up and drive off, dissolve.
2. Vanish, evanesce, evaporate, run dry, dry up, become scattered, be dispelled, run to waste, ebb, leak, melt away.
3. Squander, spend lavishly, misspend, expend, consume, use up, burn up, fritter away, waste, lavish, throw away, spill, scatter aimlessly, cast away, devour, empty, absorb, deplete, exhaust, drain.
4. Live dissolutely, pursue pleasures to excess, practice debauchery, wallow in dissipation, be dissolute, burn the candle at both ends, enervate oneself, be dissolute in the pursuit of pleasure.
5. Practice extravagance, prodigalize, be a spendthrift, indulge in extravagance, be an idler, be the prodigal son, live luxuriously, worship the golden calf.

DISSIPATED, *adj.* 1. Squandering, wasteful, thriftless, improvident, self-indulgent, sybaritic, self-gratifying, characterized by excess devotion to pleasure, extravagant, lavish, prodigal, pampered, luxurious, excessive, intemperate, unbridled, inordinate, immoderate.
2. Addicted to vicious indulgence, corrupt, depraved, abandoned, dissolute, immoral, sensual, debauched, voluptuous, gross, carnal, brutish, bestial, animal, lascivious, lewd, licentious, evil, lecherous, libidinous, concupiscent, lustful, salacious, goatish, wanton, fast, loose-moraled, wild, rake-hell, rakish, profligate, lax, drunken, crapulous, sottish, inebrious, crapulent, bibacious, boozy, dipsomaniacal, winebibbing.
3. Scattered, dispersed, disseminated, strewn, diffuse, sparse, sporadic, broadcast, stray, wasted, frittered away, squandered.

DISSIPATION, *n.* 1. Intemperate mode of living, debauchery, dissoluteness, profligacy, excessive indulgence in vicious pleasures, loose living, fast living, free indulgence in vices, corruption, orgy, degradation, rakery, saturnalia, revelry, spree, debauch, carousal, high living, license, sensuality, animalism, carnality, voluptuousness, sybaritism, wild oats, crapulence, winebibbing, alcoholism, dipsomania, drunkenness, sottishness, inebriation, intemperance, immoderation, self-gratification.
2. Wastefulness, extravagance, squandering, lavish expenditure, prodigality, consumption, exhaustion, ineconomy, lavishness, prodigalism, wasting by misuse.
3. Dispersion, diffusion, dissemination, spread, dispersal, broadcast, radiation, distribution, emission, vanishing, dissolution, disintegration.

DISSOCIATE, *v.* 1. Break the association of, sever the connection of, separate, disjoin, divide, subdivide, detach, disunite, disconnect, dissever, sever, sunder, part, cut off, segregate, set apart, divorce, disengage, isolate, insulate.
2. Withdraw from association, part company, disband, disperse, disrupt, take leave, quit, go away.

DISSOCIATION, *n.* State of separation, parting, splitting of a whole into disunited parts, disunion, severance, disjoining, disengagement, dissevering, detachment, disconnection, sundering, dividing, divorce, break, discontinuity, breach, cleavage, rupture, rift, split.

DISSOLUBLE, *adj.* 1. Dissolvable, capable of liquefaction, solvent, colliquative, soluble, capable of being converted into a fluid, liquefiable, liquescent, deliquescent.
2. Separable into parts, separate, liable to be dispersed, capable of being sundered, liable to be terminated, temporary.

DISSOLUTE, *adj.* Characterized by vicious indulgence, indifferent to moral restraints, given over to dissipation, addicted to sensuality, lewd, licentious, debauched, loose in morals, lax in conduct, wanton, lecherous, lascivious, lustful, libidinous, carnal, sensual, degenerate, salacious, voluptuous, gross, animalistic, bestial, reprobate, dissipated, depraved, corrupt, rakish, shameless, wild, fast, profligate, free-living, abandoned, vicious, uncurbed, unrestrained, immoral, sunk in iniquity, libertine, Saturnalian, incontinent, unchaste, drunken, intemperate, alcoholic, sinful, sottish, evil-minded, low-minded.

DISSOLUTION, *n.* 1. Change from a solid to a fluid form, deliquescence, melting, liquefaction, solution, thawing.
2. Resolution into parts or elements, diffusion, disintegration, decomposition, decay, overthrow, putrefaction, destruction, ruin.

3. Separation of soul and body, decease, death, demise, extinction of life, doomsday.

4. Breaking up of an assembly or organization, termination, adjournment, prorogation, recess, dismissal, dispersal.

DISSOLVE, *v.* 1. Change from a solid into a fluid condition, make a solution of in a solvent, liquefy, melt, deliquesce, thaw, macerate, fuse, evaporate, soften, become fluid by diffusion in a liquid.

2. Vanish, evanesce, disappear, melt away, fade, scatter, be dissipated.

3. Break up a connection, undo a tie, resolve into parts, disunite, disorganize, break apart, sever, divide, separate, disconnect, interrupt, loose, lixiviate.

4. Cause to perish, destroy, annihilate, ruin, bring to an end.

5. Crumble, disintegrate, decompose, dwindle, decay, waste away, perish.

6. Terminate, put an end to, break up, recess, disband, disperse, adjourn, prorogue, dismiss.

7. Annul, abrogate, nullify, abolish, rescind, deprive of force, break the control of, destroy the binding power of, set aside.

8. Lose power, lose vigor, weaken, become languid.

DISSONANCE, *n.* 1. Disagreeable mingling of sounds, inharmonious sound, discord, cacophony, harsh sound, discordance, want of harmony, jarring, jangle, stridency, grating.

2. Disagreement, dissension, inconsistency, incongruity, discrepancy, difference, controversy, antagonism.

DISSONANT, *adj.* 1. Disagreeable in sound, out of tune, harshly sounding, painful to the ear, discordant, grating, clashing, jarring, jangling, strident, tuneless, inharmonious, unmelodious, raucous, cacophonous.

2. Widely differing, disagreeing in spirit, at variance, different, incongruous, inconsistent in drift, discrepant, contradictory, irreconcilable, opposite, mutually hostile.

DISSUADE, *v.* 1. Turn aside from a purpose, change the purpose of by counsel, divert by persuasion, persuade not to, render averse, deter, discourage, disincline, alter the plans of by pleading, hold back, restrain, hinder, prevent, stop, obviate, divert by appeal, curb, rein in, harness, hold in leash, hold back, pull in, stop short, repress, suppress, put the kibosh on, damp, squelch, blunt.

2. Cry out against, advise against, urge against, dehort, urge not to, exhort in opposition, warn, remonstrate, expostulate, admonish, deprecate, caution.

DISSUASION, *n.* 1. Contrary advice, counter exhortation, dehortation, dissuasive advice, discouragement, remonstrance, expostulation, deprecation, counsel against, diversion.

2. Curb, check, damper, wet blanket, squelch, kibosh, repression, control, constraint, rein.

DISSUASIVE, *adj.* Tending to dissuade, warning, dehortatory, discouraging, deterring, admonitory, monitorial, monitory, repressive, suppressive, expostulatory, remonstrative, deprecatory.

DISTANCE, *n.* 1. State of being distant in place or time, remoteness, degree of removal, farness, far-offness, far-awayness.

2. Distant quarter, remote region, foreign parts, distant point, ultima Thule, antipodes, *ne plus ultra (Lat.),* outskirt, outpost.

3. Length of space between two points, length of separation in space, extent of space intervening between, interval, interspace, remove, interstice, gap, span, reach, stride, ground, range, circuit.

4. Spatial separation, perspective, background, offing, far cry to, horizon, skyline, abyss, chasm, void, vacuum, elongation, drift, transcendence.

5. Aloofness, reserve, reservation, no undue familiarity, offishness, coldness, stiffness, distant behavior, unresponsiveness, restraint, frigidity, coolness, constraint of manner, haughtiness, exclusiveness, condescension.

DISTANCE, *v.* 1. Outdistance, outrun in a race, leave behind at a distance, outreach, outrange, outstrip, outdo, excel, surpass.

2. Keep at a distance, put at a distance, cause to appear distant.

DISTANT, *adj.* 1. Ultramundane, transatlantic, apart in space or time, not near at hand, far-off, separate, remote, far-away, far, afar, outlying, removed, out-of-the-way, inaccessible, at a distance, away, yon, yonder, ulterior, antipodean, transalpine, separated by a specified interval.

2. Not familiar, formal, reserved, stiff, frigid, cool, cold, icy, uncordial, offish, aloof, reticent, unfriendly, unapproachable, uncommunicative, unresponsive, unsociable, unneighborly, haughty, condescending, high-hat, repellent.

3. Faint, obscure, indistinct, uncertain, not obvious, not plain, slight.

4. Different in kind, not conformable, alien, discrepant, repugnant, foreign.

DISTASTE, *n.* 1. Disrelish for food or drink, lack of relish, disgust, queasiness, turn, nausea, offensiveness.

2. Disinclination, displeasure, dislike, hatred, dissatisfaction, disapproval, aversion, repugnance, alienation, displacency, loathing, abomination, horror, detestation, animosity, shuddering, cold sweat, cold feet, reluctance, backwardness, averseness, antipathy, abhorrence.

DISTASTEFUL, *adj.* 1. Unpleasant to the taste, nauseating, nauseous, unsavory, unpalatable, tart, bitter, sour, rancid, turned, curdled, vinegary, unripe, acetous, acidulated, acrid.

2. Loathsome, disgusting, disagreeable, odious, repugnant, offensive, repulsive, displeasing, hateful, repellent, abhorrent, unsatisfactory, undesirable, antipathetic, uninviting, manifesting aversion, expressive of dislike.

DISTEND, *v.* Expand by stretching, spread apart, enlarge, dilate asunder, open out, swell out, bloat, inflate, blow up, puff out, stretch apart, widen, lengthen out, extend, tumefy, fill out, grow, wax, increase.

DISTENTION, *n.* Enlargement, dilation, spread, dilatation, expansion, amplification, stretching, augmentation, extension, inflation, swelling, tumefaction, turgescence, turgidity, intumescence, puffiness, dropsy, edema, increment, increase.

DISTILL, *v.* 1. Give forth in drops, let fall in drops, emit, evaporate, finestill, sublimate, emit vapor, subject to vaporization and condensation, volatilize, release drop by drop, steam.

2. Extract the volatile components of by heat, separate by evaporation, condense, produce by vaporization and condensation.

3. Extract spirit from, purify by distillation, concentrate, cohobate *(Chem.),* draw out, squeeze out, express, press out, draw forth.

4. Become vaporized and condensed, trickle,

drip, drop, fall in drops, exude, trickle forth, issue in a dripping stream, flow in a small stream.

DISTINCT, *adj.* 1. Distinguished as not being the same, observably different, not identical, separate in nature, clearly standing apart, not the same, unlike others, disjoined, disjunct, discrete, individual, diverse, dissimilar, disunited, disconnected, unconnected, asunder.

2. Clear to the senses or intellect, discernible, definite, clear, well-defined, clear-cut, precise, defined, well-marked, plain, obvious, manifest, evident, unambiguous, unequivocal, unmistakable, unconfused, explicit, pointed, articulate, lucid, intelligible, particular, vivid, graphic, visible, apparent, positive, palpable, recognizable, discriminate, distinctive, determinate, perspicuous, distinguishable.

DISTINCTION, *n.* 1. Marking off as different, discrimination, distinguishment, nice perception, differentiation, notice of difference, discreteness, separation, demarcation, discernment.

2. Perceivable dissimilarity, point of difference, distinguishing characteristic, differentia, disparity, characteristic difference, distinguishing quality, individuality, unlikeness, divergency, antithesis.

3. Notability, repute, prominence, reputation, celebrity, mark, figure, rank, fame, glory, honor, dignity, importance, greatness, report, prestige, renown, eminence, name, account, respectability, credit, marked superiority, signality, éclat, vogue, popularity, *aura popularis (Lat.)*, public esteem, popular favor, mark of special favor, designation of honor.

4. Distinguished appearance, ease, elegance, refinement, polish, finish, beauty, taste, felicity, judgment, good taste.

DISTINCTIVE, *adj.* Differentiating, serving to distinguish, indicating difference, discriminative, peculiar, characteristic, special, particular, unique, diacritical, diagnostic.

DISTINCTNESS, *n.* 1. Difference, disconnection, detachment, dissociation, segregation, isolation, disengagement, insulation, separateness.

2. ·Perspicuity, lucidity, definition of outline, clearness, sharpness, precision, conspicuousness, lucidness, explicitness, manifestness, apparentness, perceptibility, discernibleness.

DISTINGUISH, *v.* 1. Mark off as different, discern, make recognizable by peculiarities, designate by special characteristics, pick out as exhibiting recognizable characteristics, differentiate, single out, apprehend the differences between, recognize as separate, discriminate as distinct, perceive clearly, tell apart, descry, notice, see, judge, ascertain, find, know.

2. Characterize, mark out, make distinctive, specify, define, classify, indicate by a mark.

3. Serve to separate as different, divide into classes, be a distinctive characteristic of, abstract, demarcate, define under different heads, set apart.

4. Decide, determine, note differences, make distinction, exercise discrimination, show the difference.

5. Make famous, confer distinction upon, make celebrated, signalize, make prominent, bring into notice, make eminent, make well known, confer celebrity on.

DISTINGUISHABLE, *adj.* 1. To be recognized as distinct, to be distinguished, evident, clearly perceptible, discernible, perceivable, recognizable, capable of being recognized as distinct.

2. Divisible, separable, that may be divided, partible.

DISTINGUISHED, *adj.* 1. Famous, remarkable, noted for great qualities, notable, illustrious, eminent, prominent, preeminent, imperishable, renowned, celebrated, esteemed, eximious, heroic, revered, venerable, immortal.

2. Having an air of distinction, *distingué (Fr.)*, *dégagé (Fr.)*, aristocratic, genteel, to the manor born, well-bred, bred to the purple, proud, blue-blooded, poised, dignified, lordly, grand, stately, imposing, princely, august.

3. Notably separate and distinct, conspicuous, special, superior, transcendent, signal, marked, foremost, peerless, laureate, extraordinary, noble, nonpareil, nonesuch, matchless, shining, splendid, unequaled, unrivaled, brilliant, glorious, sublime, memorable, majestic, magnificent.

DISTORT, *v.* 1. Twist awry, wrench into an unnatural shape, bend out of shape, misshape, deform, warp, make crooked, make deformed, gnarl, contort, screw, knot, buckle, writhe, wrest, wring, deface, mar, mutilate.

2. Torture the sense of, pervert, misinterpret, interpret falsely, misrepresent, give a strained meaning to, strain the sense of, falsify, garble, color, stretch *(colloq.)*, varnish, doctor, change from a proper state, embroider, misuse, misapply, exaggerate, misrender, misquote, misconstrue, misdirect.

DISTORTION, *n.* 1. Forcing out of shape, knot, deformation, twisting motion, wryness, obliquity, crookedness, misproportion, asymmetry, grimace, anamorphosis, malformation, kyphosis *(Med.)*, deformity, twist, contortion, contortedness, warp, buckle, screw, disfigurement, mutilation.

2. Falsification, misrepresentation, straining of meaning, perversion, garbling, wresting the sense, misinterpretation, misrendering, misconstruction, misreading, misusage, misuse, misapplication, mendacity, exaggeration.

DISTRACT, *v.* 1. Draw away the attention of, turn aside, divert, abstract, beguile, entertain, amuse.

2. Divide the attention between objects, draw in various directions, perplex, bewilder, confound, puzzle, dazzle, confuse, disconcert, discompose, daze, mystify, annoy, harass, embarrass, agitate, complicate, worry, torment, tantalize, befuddle, flurry, fluster, rattle.

3. Disturb greatly in mind, put out of one's head, make frantic, trouble, craze, unsettle the reason of, madden, derange, disorder.

4. Disunite, divide, alienate, estrange, rend by dissension or strife.

DISTRACTED, *adj.* 1. Confused, bemused, lost, perplexed, bewildered, confounded, puzzled, in a brown study, mystified, *désorienté (Fr.)*, bushed.

2. Wrought up, overwrought, distraught, wild, troubled, beside oneself, worked up, frantic, mad, frenzied, phrenetic, delirious, raving, deranged, insane, feverish, crazed, excited, *bouleversé (Fr.)*.

DISTRACTION, *n.* 1. Drawing of the mind in different directions, confusion, puzzle, quandary, perplexity, mystification, abstraction, dazzlement, embarrassment, disconcertion, discomposure, befuddlement, complication, flusterment, preoccupation, consternation, bewilderment.

2. Parrying thrust, counterattraction, strategic move, feint, ruse.

3. Perturbation, disturbance, turmoil, agitation.

tumult, commotion, division due to dissension, disorder, discord.

4. Mental aberration, desperation, alienation, madness, brain storm, raving, hallucination, loss of reason, delirium, mental derangement, lunacy, incoherence, disturbance of mind, madness, rage, craziness, insanity, mania, fury.

5. Amusement, pastime, beguilement, diversion.

DISTRAUGHT, *adj*. In a state of distraction, out of one's wits, perplexed, confused, bewildered, mentally disordered, beset with mental conflict, mentally deranged, deeply agitated, crazed, wild, frantic, distracted, fuming, raging, seething, mad, carried away by passion, raving, beside oneself, amuck, ready to burst, overwrought, wrought up, tempest-tossed.

DISTRESS, *n*. 1. Wretched condition, dangerous condition, disaster, calamity, adversity, hardship, tribulation, misfortune, affliction, misery, worry, anxiety, harassment, wretchedness, perturbation, annoyance, woe.

2. Acute suffering, anguish, pain, agony, thorn, torment, gnawing, griping, torture, disturbance, seizure, discomfort.

3. Poignant sorrow, grief, dolor, unhappiness, heartache, bitterness, sadness, dejection.

4. Poverty, privation, penury, exigency, need, indigence, destitution, want, lack, straits, broken fortunes, necessitude, state of extreme necessity, pennilessness, difficulties, wolf at the door, *res angusta domi* (*Lat.*), low water, impecuniosity, insolvency, pauperism, beggary.

DISTRESS, *v*. 1. Afflict with pain, rack, inflict suffering upon, torment, harrow, wound, hurt sorely, cause to feel acute pain, harry, pain.

2. Make sorrowful, sadden, make unhappy, trouble sorely, persecute, make the heart bleed, wring the heart, cut to the heart, draw tears from the eyes, make miserable, subject to strain, worry, oppress, harass, disturb, vex, perturb, depress, plague, bother, grieve, annoy.

3. Force, compel, provoke, constrain, oblige, subject to pressure, exhaust by strain.

DISTRIBUTE, *v*. 1. Divide and bestow in shares, give out among a number, apportion, dole out, allot, allocate, deal out, prorate, assign, dispense, mete, admeasure, set apart, share, parcel out, partition, issue, portion out, administer, dispose.

2. Disperse over an area, scatter, spread out in an even way, convey into all parts, circulate, disseminate, sow, broadcast, diffuse, propagate, radiate, bestrew, strew, sprinkle.

3. Divide into parts of distinct character, class, classify, divide into classes, arrange, systematize, assort, separate, dispose, catalogue, methodize, tabulate.

DISTRIBUTION, *n*. 1. Division among a number, allotment, allocation, apportionment, assignment, partition, assortment, dispensation, prorating, lot, administration, issuance, dole, share, portion.

2. Grouping, arrangement, disposition, array, disposal, sorting, classification, organization, gradation.

3. Scattering, dispersion, propagation, diffusion, dissemination, dissipation, broadcast, divergence, spread, emission, radiation, circulation.

DISTRICT, *n*. Division of territory specifically defined, region, section, neighborhood, locality, area, quarter, tract, province, department, ward, circuit, domain, sphere, commune, realm, country,

state, precinct, canton, land, zone, county, parish, prefecture, clime, constituency, pale.

DISTRUST, *n*. A feeling that appearances are not reliable, disposition to withhold confidence, want of faith, lack of confidence, lack of trust, doubt, misgiving, mistrust, suspicion, unbelief, hesitation, uncertainty, fear, incredulity, apprehension, care, dubiousness, dubiety, qualm, scruple, solicitude, demur, timidity, fearfulness, anxiety.

DISTRUST, *v*. Feel distrust of, lack confidence in, regard with suspicion, withhold reliance from, doubt, suspect, disbelieve in, mistrust, question, feel absence of trust, have one's doubts, falter, hesitate, demur, scruple, shy at, stick at.

DISTRUSTFUL, *adj*. 1. Full of distrust, fearful, unbelieving, skeptical, entertaining doubt, apt to distrust, dubious about, doubtful, suspicious, not confident, apprehensive, uncertain, mistrustful, afraid.

2. Wanting in self-confidence, diffident, timid, shy, modest, timorous, shrinking.

DISTURB, *v*. 1. Shake, agitate, toss, convulse, stir, jostle, buffet.

2. Rouse from repose, move from rest, pique, interrupt the peace and quiet of, harass, bother, arouse, fluster, roust (*colloq.*), molest, disquiet, annoy, disconcert, discompose, perturb, trouble, incommode, plague, vex, make uneasy, badger, ruffle, fuss up, distress, pester, harry, perplex, cause disquiet in, interfere with, interrupt, hinder, discommode.

3. Throw out of natural condition, disarrange, disorder, unsettle, confuse, throw into confusion, meddle with, put into disorder, muddle, displace, remove, dislocate, confound, tumble, throw into commotion, jumble, mix up.

DISTURBANCE, *n*. 1. Agitation, stir, trepidation, commotion, perturbation, flurry, flutter, disquiet, fluster, restlessness, inquietude, unsettlement, ado, derangement, disorder, bustle, fuss, convulsion, confusion, pother, to-do, turbulence, uneasiness, excitement, discomposure, distraction, annoyance, disconcertion.

2. Interference with a lawful right, prevention, molestation, interruption, hindrance.

3. Uproar, tumult, racket, rout, commotion, storm, fracas, altercation, hubbub, turmoil, row, ruckus, disorder, uprising, *émeute* (*Fr.*), rioting, fray, affray, dissension, discord, dispute, quarrel, brawl, broil, contest, conflict, outbreak, clamor, tumultuousness, unruliness, rumpus, insurrection, breach of public peace.

DISUNION, *n*. 1. Severance of union, separation, disconnection, disjunction, division, interruption, partition, detachment, disruption, disjointure, disjoining.

2. Breach, schism, rupture, feud, spat, discord, tiff, disagreement, split, alienation, cross purposes, dissension, variance, lack of union, dissidence, breach of amity, faction, house divided against itself.

DISUNITE, *v*. 1. Abolish union in, disconnect, separate from another, sever the union of, split, dissever, dispart, dissociate, disjoin, detach, part, sunder, divide, rend, interrupt, disengage, disrupt, dismember, dissolve, disband, rupture, disjoint, divorce, insulate, scatter.

2. Set at variance, put discord between, split wide open, alienate, estrange, widen the breach, embroil, entangle, set at odds, pull different ways, render inharmonious, set together by the ears, pit against, put in issue, stir up dissension.

3. Part company with, part, separate, fall out, be separated, fall asunder, come apart.

DISUSE, *n.* 1. Non-use, failure to use, cessation, discontinuance, non-employment, relinquishment, ceasing to use, abrogation, abolition, discarding, abolishment.

2. Desuetude, want of practice, forbearance, neglect, non-observance, disusage, discontinuance of use, cessation from use, inusitation, abstinence.

DITCH, *n.* Long narrow hollow made in the earth by digging, trench, open passage, channel, dike, drain, moat, fosse, excavation, pit, cloaca, scarp, counterscarp, canal, waterway, main, race, watercourse, sewer, gutter, culvert, conduit, duct, run.

DITTY, *n.* Short and simple song, lay, canticle, strain, arietta, chanson, canzonetta. *Lied (Ger.)*, air, little tune, carol, ballad, lyric.

DIURNAL, *adj.* 1. Happening every day, daily, quotidian.

2. What occupies a day, performed in a day, transient, ephemeral, short-lived.

3. Active by day, not nocturnal.

DIVAGATION, *n.* Erratic wandering, deviation, aimless rambling, straying, roaming, digression, turning aside from a course in hand, diversion, departure from, circumambience.

DIVAN, *n.* Long cushioned seat, sofa, couch, love seat, pillowed place for reclining, settee, musnud, davenport, day bed.

DIVARICATE, *v.* Divide into branches, branch off, radiate, ramify, cause to diverge, fork, part, separate into two, open wide, become bifid.

DIVARICATION, *n.* 1. Ramification, radiation, branching, forking, spreading, stretching apart, separation, divergence, straddling.

2. Disagreement, ambiguity, difference in opinion.

DIVE, *v.* 1. Take a plunge, plunge headfirst, take a header, descend swiftly, submerge, go below the surface of the water, nose-dive, glide, loop the loop, spin, pique, pitch, dip, swoop.

2. Penetrate suddenly, plunge deeply, go deep, explore, fathom, sound, enter deeply into, lose oneself in, become engrossed.

DIVERGE, *v.* 1. Move in different directions from a common point, radiate, tend away from each other, tend in different directions, tend to spread apart, go asunder, divide, separate, part, sever, sunder, fly off, swerve, spread, deflect.

2. Branch off, ramify, fork, divaricate.

3. Differ in opinion, dissent, disagree, vary, deviate.

DIVERGENCE, *n.* 1. Radiation, division, spread, separation, severance, deflection, refraction, swerve.

2. Ramification, branching, forking, furcation, divarication, declination, detachment.

3. Difference in opinion, variance, aberration, dissimilarity, diversity, altercation, discrepancy, incongruity, heterogeneity, disparity, irregularity, disagreement.

DIVERGENT, *adj.* 1. Radial, radiant, centrifugal, ever going farther apart, made more and more distant from a common point.

2. Branching, ramifying, forking, bifurcating, furcate, divaricating, varying more and more, taking different courses, parting, receding farther and farther from each other, tending in different directions.

3. Differing, conflicting, disagreeing, different, dissimilar, diverse, deviating, variant, wandering, aberrant, straying.

DIVERS, *adj.* 1. More than one, several, sundry, various, many, numerous.

2. Of different kinds, differing, heterogeneous, manifold, different, diverse, variegated.

DIVERSE, *adj.* Of a different kind or character, varied, motley, differing in characteristic, unlike, varying, diversiform, multifarious, heterogeneous, multiform, dissimilar, divergent, variant, mixed, of various kinds, miscellaneous, assorted, distinct, diversified, manifold, checkered, variegated.

DIVERSIFY, *v.* 1. Make diverse in form or character, give diversity to, vary, make different, variate, give variety to, change, alter, modify.

2. Variegate, streak, dapple, checker, mottle, spot, stripe.

DIVERSION, *n.* 1. Turning aside from a course, deflection, divergence, digression, deviation, variation.

2. Distraction from business or care, pastime, amusement, entertainment, recreation, relaxation, beguilement, play, divertissement, sport, delight, game, fun, merriment, festivity, solace, interest, exhilaration, refreshment, gratification, pleasure, regalement, disport, enlivenment, cheer.

3. Feint intended to draw off attention from point of main attack, ruse, blind, stratagem.

DIVERSITY, *n.* 1. Unlikeness, diversification, difference, dissimilarity, dissimilitude, divergence, disagreement, disparity, variance, unconformity, variation, imparity, contrariety, nonuniformity, irregularity, inequality, unevenness, disproportion.

2. Variety, manifoldness, medley, assortment, variegation, multiplicity, multiformity, miscellany, multifariousness, heterogeneity.

DIVERT, *v.* 1. Turn aside from a path, deflect, draw away from a course, avert, switch, shift, shunt, sidetrack, diverge, deviate, swerve.

2. Entertain, amuse, delight, gratify, recreate, relax, refresh, distract from serious occupation, turn from serious thoughts, charm, exhilarate, beguile, regale, interest, solace, enliven, raise a smile, excite laughter, cheer, rejoice.

3. Distract, call off, withdraw, abstract, draw off to a different object, draw away, turn to a different use, disturb.

DIVEST, *v.* 1. Strip of clothing, undress, disrobe, lay bare, bare, denude, unclothe, uncover, remove, denudate, dismantle, put off, take off, doff, lay open, expose.

2. Dispossess, deprive, strip, bereave, despoil of anything.

3. *(Law)* Annul or take away, alienate.

DIVIDE, *v.* 1. Separate into parts, sunder, cleave, rive, rend, split, dismember, cut off, part, sever, dissever, disunite, disconnect, detach, disengage, disjoin, subdivide, dispart, quarter, bisect, dissect, intersect, halve, dimidiate, comminute.

2. Set at variance, make hostile, disunite, split wide open, pit against, alienate, estrange, make discordant, disaffect, cause to disagree, separate in opinion.

3. Apportion, allot, allocate, deal out, dole, mete out, dispense, distribute, parcel out, share, assign, portion out.

4. Distinguish the kinds of, classify, tabulate, catalogue, demarcate, compart, partition.

5. Diverge, divaricate, branch, go asunder, be separated, open.

DIVIDEND, *n.* 1. Number to be divided by another number.

2. Profits divided, bonus, pro rata share in an amount to be distributed, sum of money paid to shareholders out of earnings, portion of earnings distributed on a percentage basis to stockholders, cut, split, measure, dole, meed, pittance, quantum, ration, quota.

DIVINATION, *n.* 1. Foretelling of future events, discovering of what is obscure, forecast of future events by supernatural means, augury, prophecy, soothsaying, sortilege, hieromancy, hieroscopy, vaticination, vatidiction, fatidiction, thaumaturgy, mantology, prognostication, prediction, presage, horoscope, fortunetelling, sorcery, haruspicium, incantation, magic, clairvoyance, spell, geomancy, charm, omen, oracle, sign, portent, necromancy, auspice, lithomancy, ornithomancy, bibliomancy, hydromancy, halomancy, hariolation, rhabdomancy, spodomancy, graptomancy, gyromancy, pedomancy, astrology.

2. Intuitive perception, discernment, surmise, conjectural presage, instinctive prevision, exercise of intuition, premonition, foreboding, conjecture, guesswork, supposition, assumption, presumption, forewarning, speculation, shot, presentiment by intuition.

DIVINE, *adj.* 1. Godly, godlike, deiform, deific, superhuman, supernatural, sainted, transcendent, religious, holy, sacred, heavenly, angelic, blessed, spiritual, celestial, seraphic, hallowed, dedicated, blest, supernal, ethereal, sanctified, consecrated, venerable, rapturous, supreme, exalted, beatific, hyperphysical, supramundane.

2. Excellent in the highest degree, admirable, superlative, of surpassing excellence, worthy of great admiration.

3. Religious, pious, devout, righteous, patristic, theological, canonical.

DIVINE, *n.* 1. Theologian, one versed in religious subjects.

2. Clergyman, ecclesiastic, churchman, clerk in holy orders, cleric, minister, parson, pastor, vicar, preacher, priest, father, padre, abbé, curé, canon, curate, rector, presbyter, hierophant, evangelist, hierach, shepherd, chaplain, dominie, sky pilot, confessor, black coat, rabbi.

DIVINE, *v.* 1. Foretell by magical means, declare something future by supernatural means, predict, prophesy, prognosticate, vaticinate, ascertain by divination, presage, discover something obscure, foresee, foreknow, forebode, forecast, forewarn, foretoken, portend, auspicate, augur, annunciate, betoken, shadow forth, signify, point to, play the prophet, practice sorcery, be mantic, hariolate, utter presages.

2. Perceive by intuition, intuit, have insight into, conjecture, guess, surmise, fathom, perceive through, bode, suspect, fancy, suppose, assume, speculate, presume, shoot at, theorize, doctrinize, dream, apprehend.

DIVINER, *n.* 1. One who divines, prophet, seer, mantic, oracle, augur, haruspex, Sibyl, Pythia, soothsayer, prognosticator, clairvoyant, sorcerer, fortuneteller, conjurer, magician, necromancer, Chaldean, astrologer, wizard, geomancer.

2. Conjecturer, guesser, surmiser, speculatist, theorist, hypothesist, notionalist, interpreter.

DIVINITY, *n.* 1. Quality of being divine, deity, Godhead, Godhood, divine nature, divine essence, Omnipotence, Omniscience, Providence, Author of all things, Lord, The Absolute, The Infinite, The Eternal.

2. Divine being, deity, god, goddess, celestial being, numen, angel, seraph.

3. Science of divine things, theology, science of God, theosophy, religion, hierology, hagiology, hagiography.

4. Godlike character, divine attribute, supreme excellence, supernatural virtue.

DIVISIBLE, *adj.* Capable of being divided, able to be separated into parts, partible, severable, separable, dissolvable, commensurable, cleavable, dissoluble, dividual, proportionable, fragmentary, dividuous.

DIVISION, *n.* 1. Marking off of a whole into parts, separation into parts, disjunction, splitting apart, disunion, disconnection, dismemberment, detachment, severance, parting, partitionment, segmentation, dimidiation, scissure.

2. One of the parts into which a thing is divided, separate part, segment, section, branch, compartment, subdivision, department, category, group, class, head, portion, share, apportionment, fragment, parcel, piece, slice, allotment, fraction, sector, bit, cutting, chunk, scrap, swatch, moiety, installment, member, component, constituent, leg, arm, limb, wing, joint.

3. Dividing line, demarcation, terminus, limit.

4. Separation in sentiment, disagreement, split, dissension, separation by difference of opinion, difference, disunion, alienation, discord, divorce, estrangement, variance, breach, rupture, faction, schism, feud, spat.

DIVORCE, *n.* 1. Judicial separation of husband and wife, *separatio a vinculo matrimonii (Lat.),* absolute legal dissolution of the marriage contract, *separatio a mensa et a toro (Lat.),* separation from bed and board, termination of cohabitation, judicial declaration of the nullity of a marriage, annulment, divorcement, judgment dissolving a marriage, separate maintenance, diffarreation *(Rom.),* talak *(Moham.),* Ehescheidung *(Ger.).*

2. Disunion of things closely united, forcible severance of any close relation, disjunction, rupture, breach, repudiation.

DIVORCE, *v.* 1. Release from the relationship of husband and wife, dissolve by legal process the marriage of, unmarry, put out of wedlock, annul.

2. Obtain a divorce from, legally discard a wife, reject from bed and board, put away.

3. Repudiate, sever, dissever, cut off, sunder, disunite, separate, banish, isolate, wrest from an intimate relation, segregate.

DIVULGE, *v.* Disclose something secret, reveal something private, make known, publish, proclaim, communicate something confidential, tell, relate, make public, spread abroad, impart, expose, let fall, declare, betray, uncover, inform, acquaint, confide to, blab, breathe, let leak out, let slip, let into the secret, let drop, break the news, peach, blurt out, squeal, whisper about, tattle, unfold, confess, enlighten, apprise, promulgate, broadcast, divulgate, manifest, unbosom.

DIZZY, *adj.* 1. Feeling about to fall, vertiginous, giddy, light-headed, unsteady, swimming, affected with a sensation of whirling.

2. Bewildered, confused, distracted, distraught, delirious.

3. Foolishly capricious, flibbertigibbety, fickle, lacking rational guidance and control, frivolous, thoughtless, careless, heedless, flighty.

4. Foolish, stupid, crazy *(colloq.),* disordered, deranged.

DO, *v.* 1. Attain a desired purpose through effort, bring about, effect, perform, execute, administer, accomplish, commit, work at, achieve, work out, perpetrate, carry out, carry into effect, realize, act, operate, manage.
2. Bring some action to a conclusion, conclude, complete, consummate, finish, terminate, settle, dispatch, end, fulfil, solve.
3. Exert, observe, practice, carry into practice, discharge, put forth, render, pay, show, employ, play, strive vigorously.
4. Transact, proceed, conduct, carry on, shift, contrive, get along.
5. Be the cause of, produce, make, construct, work out.
6. Translate, depict, compose.
7. Arrange, treat with attention, prepare, cook, preserve.
8. Cheat, deceive, defraud, hoax, overreach, swindle, cozen, chouse, trick.
9. Suffice for, serve, answer, avail, suit, pass, answer the purpose, be enough, be sufficient, be satisfactory, serve the object intended.
10. Visit as a tourist, explore, traverse, travel through, cover.
11. Exhaust, overcome, wear out, fatigue, tire out.
12. Repair, mend, clean, arrange, rearrange, decorate, furbish, put in order.
13. Assume the character of, play the part of, represent, act.
14. Prepare, learn, con, fathom.
15. Act, behave, proceed wisely, be in action, conduct oneself, comport oneself, demean oneself.
16. Fare, prosper, be as regards health.

DOCILE, *adj.* 1. Easily taught, teachable, readily trainable, amenable to training.
2. Easily managed, easily handled, tractable, pliant, pliable, plastic, ductile, malleable, lithe, flexible, limber, yielding, supple, facile, tame, manageable, submissive, gentle, meek, mild, easily led, compliant, obedient, inclined to agreement with another's will, easy going, genial, willing, acquiescent, sequacious.

DOCILITY, *n.* Teachableness, docibleness, readiness to learn, willingness to be taught or trained, tractability, tractableness, pliability, pliableness, obedience, malleability, plasticity, ductility, flexibleness, sequacity, persuasibleness, softness, gentleness, tameness, meekness, pliancy, amenability, submissiveness, acquiescence, compliance, willingness.

DOCK, *v.* 1. Cut short, clip, truncate, obtruncate, cut off the end of, curtail, pare down, prune, bobtail, reduce, snip, lop, crop, abridge, retrench, shorten.
2. Deduct a part from, deduct from the wages of, diminish, lessen, make less, deprive, subject to loss.
3. Guide a ship into dock, lay up in a dock, berth, warp, snub, land, put into dry dock for repairs.

DOCTOR, *n.* 1. Person licensed to practice medicine, medical practitioner, medical man, M. D., physician, surgeon, leech, healer, allopath, homeopath, specialist, consultant, sawbones, pill-peddler, osteopath, chiropractor, chiropodist, oculist, ophthalmologist, aurist, otologist, dentist, laryngologist, neurologist, psychiatrist, urinologist, Roentgenologist, pediatrician, obstetrician, geriatrician, gastrologist, orthodontist, veterinarian, interne.

2. Person holding highest degree conferred by a university, one on whom this academic title has been conferred, man of great learning, savant, sage, learned man, adept.
3. Jack-of-all-trades, tinker, factotum.

DOCTRINAIRE, *n.* One who tries to apply some doctrine without regard to practical considerations, impractical theorist, dogmatizer, ideologist, preacher of abstractions, thinker about unpractical matters, one who arrives at a conclusion by considering a subject from a single standpoint only, one whose views are derived from theories rather than facts, opinionist, bigot, *ipse-dixit (Lat.),* know-it-all, Sir Oracle, stump orator, jack-in-office.

DOCTRINE, *n.* 1. Particular principle advocated, that which is set forth for acceptance, accepted belief, tenet, dogma, principle, precept, opinion, rule, theory, teaching, maxim, article of faith, article of belief, thesis, philosophy, conviction, proposition, postulate, rem, creed, gospel.
2. Body of teachings relating to a particular subject, set of opinions held true by a sect, canons, scientific system of principles involved in a particular subject, articles.

DOCUMENT, *n.* Paper furnishing information, manuscript conveying evidence, official writing, record, instrument, certificate, charta, charter, chronicle, memoir, diploma, writ, testament, deed, brevet.

DODDER, *v.* Tremble from age, shake, totter, potter, falter, dither, quiver, quaver, quake, sway, twitter, twitch, shuffle, stagger, bob, reel, shiver, shamble, flounder, flounce.

DODDERING, *adj.* That dodders, shaking, shaky, trembling, tottering, senile, aged, decrepit, anile, superannuated, feeble, infirm, foolish, silly, characterless.

DODGE, *n.* 1. Spring aside, deviation, swerving, sidestep, starting aside, act of shifting, elusion, avoidance.
2. Ingenious contrivance, trick, artifice, shift, evasion, expedient, device, ruse, machination, subterfuge, chicane, stratagem, maneuver, wile, cavil, quibble, tergiversation, sharp practice, underhandedness, knavery, jugglery.

DODGE, *v.* 1. Avoid by suddenly turning aside, step aside, change position suddenly, move aside, shift place suddenly, steer clear of, duck, swerve, sheer off, alter one's course, heel, bear off, jib.
2. Use evasive methods, evade, shuffle, be evasive, use artifice, parry, elude, hedge, shilly-shally, equivocate, prevaricate, quibble, play fast and loose, fight shy of, tergiversate, palter, shy, malinger, hang back, recoil, wince, escape, make off, sneak off, play truant, decamp, make oneself scarce, flit, bolt, abscond, sidetrack.

DODGER, *n.* 1. One who dodges, a shifty person, one who plays tricks, tricky fellow, trickster, one who plays fast and loose, evader, shirker, slacker, quitter, truant, deserter, skulker, renegade, sly boots, runaway, runagate, backslider, malingerer, fox.
2. Small handbill, circular, flyer, throw-around.

DOER, *n.* One who does something, one who performs, performer, actor, perpetrator, operator, executor, author, maker, agent, composer, deputy, factor, worker, practitioner, artificer, builder.

DOFF, *v.* 1. Remove in salutation, tip, take off,

put off, cast off, lay aside, strip off, shed, bare, uncover, denude.

2. Get rid of, throw off, throw away, thrust aside, rid oneself of.

DOG, *n.* 1. Canine, domesticated carnivore, cur, *Canis familiaris,* pup, puppy, whelp, slut, brachet, bitch, mutt, mastiff, mongrel, retriever, hound, harrier, bulldog, collie, spaniel, Saint Bernard, poodle, lap dog, hunter, terrier, deerhound, pug, buckhound, basset, whippet, tyke, dingo, lurcher, beagle, setter, pointer, dachshund, sledge dog, husky, bloodhound, greyhound, Newfoundland, great Dane, Weimaraner, Pinscher, Scotty, house dog, watchdog, sheepdog, Spitz.

2. A mean worthless fellow, despicable fellow, base contemptible fellow, wretch, rascal, villain, scoundrel, miscreant, caitiff, scamp, scapegrace, ne'er-do-well, blacksheep, blackguard, rogue, knave, varlet, *âme de boue (Fr.).*

3. Ostentatious style, affected dignity, putting on airs, pretentious behavior, false dignity.

DOGGED, *adj.* 1. Having the pertinacity of a dog, determined, persistent, strong-minded, wilful, headstrong, perversely resolute, indomitable, doughty, persevering, obdurate, obstinate, not to be moved, stubborn, inflexible, mulish, unyielding, intractable, immovable, unchangeable, inexorable, stiff-necked, refractory, pig-headed, tenacious, pertinacious.

·2. Surly, churlish, sullen, grumpy, morose, glum, grim.

DOGGISH, *adj.* 1. Currish, growling, snarling, barking, snappish, ill-tempered, churlish, morose, sour, surly, sullen, sulky.

2. Stylish, dapper, dandiprat, pretentious. showy.

DOGMA, *n.* 1. Doctrine authoritatively laid down, established belief, accepted principle, tenet, way of thinking, settled opinion, teaching, maxim, article of faith, creed, credo, conviction, theory, rule.

2. System of principles or tenets, school, *credenda (Lat.),* system of doctrine concerning religious truth, statement of religious faith, catechism, articles, canons, gospel, theology.

DOGMATIC, *adj.* 1. Characterized by positive assertion, authoritative, official, orthodox, formal, categorical, doctrinal, settled, absolute, positive, *ex cathedra (Lat.),* making statements without argument or evidence, canonical, standard, authentic, formally enunciated by adequate authority.

2. Expounding dogma, doctrinaire, parochial, systematic, pragmatic.

3. Opinionated, self-opinionated, asserting a matter as if it were a fact, arbitrary, peremptory, magisterial, dictatorial, oracular, bigoted, biased, imperious, arrogant, overbearing, domineering, narrow-minded, one-sided, fanatical, obdurate, *entêté (Fr.), opiniâtre (Fr.),* immovable, warped, unchangeable, illiberal, intolerant.

DOGMATISM, *n.* Authoritative assertion of opinions, dogmatic character, positiveness of opinion, boldness of spirit concerning what one regards as true, system of philosophy which assumes its principles without previous criticism of them, arrogance of assertion, presumption, habit of asserting views uncompromisingly, bias, presumption, highhandedness, imperiousness, intolerance, bigotry.

DOGMATIZE, *v.* Make dogmatic assertions, treat in a dogmatic manner, deliver as a dogma, assert

positively, express oneself arrogantly, speak with an authoritative air, make positive assertions without supporting them by evidence.

DOINGS, *n.* Things done, events, affairs, deeds, acts, matters, course of conduct, actions, march of things, transactions, proceedings, works, ups and downs of life, accomplishments, creations, performances, ongoings, goings-on, current of things, achievements, chapter of accidents, dealings, measures, vicissitudes, social activity, comportment.

DOLE, *n.* 1. Dealing out, allotment, donation, apportionment, distribution, allocation, meting out.

2. That which is doled out, share, portion, lot, meed, driblet, dividend, that which is given for maintenance.

3. Charitable gift, pittance, mite, alms, charity, gratuity, aid, ration for the needy, payment for unemployment.

4. Grief, affliction, heartache, sorrow, woe, distress, anguish.

DOLEFUL, *adj.* 1. Full of dole, full of grief, sad, melancholy, mournful, hypochondriacal, rueful, despondent, dejected, woebegone, woeful, with a long face, lugubrious, unhappy, depressed, soul-sick, sorrowful, pathetic, pitiful, piteous, blue, plaintive, disconsolate, abject, wretched, joyless, comfortless, uncheerful, unlively, spiritless, in the dumps, downhearted, *au désespoir (Fr.),* down in the mouth, heavy-hearted, moody, pensive, lachrymose, sick at heart, *triste.*

2. Dark, dreary, somber, gloomy, dismal, adust, clouded, murky, lowering, Acherontian, funereal, desolate, forlorn.

DOLE OUT, *v.* Dispense in portions, distribute in charity, give out sparingly, apportion in small quantities, allot, deal out, share, assign, divide, administer, parcel out, mete out, put on short commons, put on allowance, partition, hand over, give away, ration out, cut, split, divvy *(colloq.).*

DO-LITTLE, *n.* One who does little though promising much, indolent fellow, drone, idler, laggard, time-killer, sluggard, droil, loafer, eater of the bread of idleness, lounger, dawdler, do-naught, *fainéant (Fr.),* doodle, trifler, do-nothing, lie-abed, slumberer, dormouse, good-for-nothing, sleeping partner, afternoon farmer, slow-poke, mopus, waiter on Providence, lotus-eater.

DOLL, *n.* 1. Toy puppet representing a child or person, baby doll, toy baby, dolly, poupée, manikin, marionnette, *fantoccini (It.),* effigy, figurine, homunculus.

2. Pretty but unintelligent woman.

3. Sweetheart, mistress.

DOLOR, *n.* 1. Sorrow, grief, distress, anguish, lamentation, mourning, woe, heartache, misery, affliction, unhappiness, infelicity, tribulation, wretchedness.

2. Physical pain, suffering, ache, smart, agony, torment, torture, pang, twinge, throe, malaise.

DOLOROUS, *adj.* 1. Pitiable, piteous, woeful, doleful, melancholy, unhappy, sorrowful, sad, lugubrious, lachrymose, woebegone, despondent, rueful, distressed, morose, depressed, dejected, desolate, disconsolate, downcast, mournful, grievous, wretched, miserable, pathetic, touching, affecting.

2. Gloomy, dark, depressing, somber, dreary, cheerless, funereal, dismal, joyless, lamentable, grave.

DOLT, *n.* Dull stupid fellow, idiot, tomfool, loon, blockhead, dunce, simpleton, nitwit, witling, half-wit, fool, numskull, ignoramus, dullard, jackass, thickhead, thickskull, lout, clod, oaf, nincompoop, donkey, ass, ninny, moron, booby, imbecile, dunderhead, shallow-brain, fathead.

DOLTISH, *adj.* Doltlike, stupid, obtuse, asinine, foolish, idiotic, imbecilic, moronic, half-witted, witless, dull-witted, blockish, simple-minded, thick-skulled, duncical, duncish, buffle-headed, insulse, addle-headed, oafish, unintelligent, weak in the upper story, brainless, blunder-headed, fat-headed, fat-witted, weak-minded, senseless, feeble-minded, lack-brained, fatuous, Boeotian, bovine.

DOMAIN, *n.* 1. Sway, dominion, rule, authority, sovereignty, government, suzerainty.
2. Colony, dominion, province, territory, commonwealth, empire, principality, kingdom, duchy, dukedom, palatinate, archduchy, sultanate, khanate, signory.
3. Department, branch, sphere, field of action, region, realm, hemisphere, quarter, precinct, pale, wapentake, district, commune, bailiwick, scene, orb, circuit, county, shire, canton, area, ground.
4. Ultimate ownership and control over the use of land, eminent domain, estate, landed estate, lands, demesne, landed property.

DOME, *n.* 1. Inverted cup-shaped roof, large hemispherical or spheroidal vault, vaulted roof, rotunda, cupola, tholus, canopy, arch, span, ogive.
2. Majestic building, large or fanciful structure, edifice, mansion, cathedral.

DOMESTIC, *n.* Person living with a family and performing household duties, hired household servant, help, retainer, servitor, lackey, flunky, butler, valet, groom, coachman, chauffeur, maid, footman, attendant, squire, footboy, buttons, waiter, livery servant, boots, maidservant, lady's maid, waitress, chambermaid, cook, kitchenmaid, scullion, upstairs girl, parlor maid, maid of all work, laundress, charwoman, servant girl, slavey.

DOMESTIC, *adj.* 1. Pertaining to the home or household affairs, household, family, home.
2. Fond of home, given to the concerns of home, addicted to family life, domesticated, devoted to home life, having home interests, stay-at-home.
3. Living with man, tame, broken, habituated, docile, housebroken.
4. Home rather than foreign, homemade, not foreign, native, not imported, produced at home, native-grown, homegrown, indigenous, intestine, autochthonous, internal.

DOMESTICATE, *v.* 1. Make an inmate of a home, make domestic, accustom to stay at home, attach to home life, convert to domestic uses, domesticize, cause to feel at ease in domestic surroundings, cause to feel at home, make at home, assimilate, domiciliate, naturalize.
2. Bring under the control of man, tame, break in, bust, train, subdue from a state of nature, yoke, harness, hitch up, bridle, drive, ride, bring up, raise, breed, cage, pen-up, attach to the house, housebreak.
3. *(Of plants)* Reduce to cultivation, cultivate, accustom to the garden, acclimatize.

DOMICILE, *n.* Place where one lives, place of abode, residence, house, home, abode, lodging, habitation, dwelling, permanent legal address, home of rest, quarters, maison, mansion, berth,

diggings, seat, housing, headquarters, homestead, nest, chimney corner, fireside, hearth, hearthstone, habitat, haunt, roof, household, hacienda, villa, cottage, lodge, hermitage, château, palace, castle, manor, country seat, halls, bungalow, apartment, flat, maisonette, duplex, suite, rooms, penthouse, tenement, shack, hut, cot, cabin, cote, shanty, igloo, tepee, wigwam, covert, resort, retreat, roost, perch, croft, chalet, lares and penates, *dulce domum (Lat.).*

DOMINANT, *adj.* 1. Controlling by predominant interest, exercising chief authority, first in rank or order, most influential, regnant, governing, hegemonical, predominating, principal, chief, ascendant, paramount, prevailing, predominant, preponderant, preeminent, commanding, ruling, superior, important, weighty, outweighing, overbalancing, authoritative, recognized.
2. Occupying a commanding position, overshadowing, conspicuously prominent, supereminent.

DOMINATE, *v.* 1. Exercise control over, rule over, control, reign over, govern, sway, bend to one's will, keep under, keep in subjection, keep down, domineer, boss, preside over, direct, lead, lord it over, override, overrule, be at the head of, predominate over, have the whip hand, master, tyrannize, enslave, ride roughshod over, wield the scepter, occupy the throne, wear the crown, rule the roost, have it all one's own way, be master of the situation, take the lead, lay down the law, rule with a rod of iron.
2. Occupy a commanding position, command visually, tower above, overlook, overshadow, overtop, surmount.

DOMINATION, *n.* Control by the exercise of power, hegemony, suzerainty, sovereignty, hold, arbitrary sway, dominion, primacy, ascendancy, command, rule, mastery, supremacy, reign, jurisdiction, administration, government, bidding, dictation, grip, grasp, dictatorship, tyranny, rod of empire, despotism, absolutism, czarism, rule of the sword, Caesarism, kaiserism, imperialism, oppression, iron sway, fangs, clutches, talons, predominance.

DOMINEER, *v.* 1. Rule arbitrarily, rule with an iron hand, govern despotically, tyrannize, play the autocrat, oppress, coerce, lay a heavy hand on, boss, command, dictate, lord it, dominate, sway, have control over, be overbearing, lay down the law, deal hard measure to, keep a tight hand, put on the screws, trample under foot, ride roughshod over.
2. Play the bully, browbeat, bully, intimidate, bluster, hector, bulldoze, terrorize, dragoon, act big, swagger, swell, ride a high horse.
3. Tower over or above, loom above.

DOMINEERING, *adj.* Tyrannical, imperious, insolent, ruling arrogantly, haughty, lordly, iron-handed, overbearing, masterful, arbitrary, high and mighty, despotic, dictatorial, arrogant, bossy, commanding, imperative, magisterial, dogmatic, pompous, overweening, supercilious, bumptious, blustering, swaggering, hectoring, bullying, oppressive, coercive, grinding.

DOMINION, *n.* 1. Power of controlling, right of governing, command, sovereign authority, rule, lordship, sovereignty, suzerainty, supremacy, ascendancy, mastery, domination, control, government, seignority, hegemony, domain, dictation, jurisdiction, influence, kingship, empire, dynasty.

2. Territory, country under a particular government, realm, region, province, sphere of influence, district, tract, domains subject to control.

3. *(Law)* Right of absolute possession and use, ownership, power of disposal.

DON, *v.* Invest oneself with, put on, dress in, slip on, assume, wear, enrobe, rig out, fit out, deck, gown, drape, attire, garb, apparel, endue, dight, enclothe, accouter, array, wrap, swaddle, swathe.

DONATE, *v.* Present as a gift, make a gift of, bestow as a gift, present, give away, dispense, dole out, mete out, contribute, grant, give, make a donation of, subscribe, furnish one's quota, deliver, put into the hands of, turn over, fork over, shell out, render, impart, confer, award, consign, assign, bequeath, devise, furnish, favor with, accommodate, indulge, shower upon, lavish, afford, spare.

DONATION, *n.* Offering, present, donative, gift, offertory, benefaction, bounty, boon, honorarium, sportula, largess, *cadeau (Fr.),* gratuity, dole, grant, subscription, contribution, alms, charity, guerdon, meed, oblation, reward, recompense, award, bonus, allowance, subsidy, subvention, bequest, bestowal, philanthropy, munificence, endowment, legacy, devise, dowry, liberality, generosity, voluntary settlement, presentation, peace-offering, handsel, Maundy money, Peter's pence.

DONE, *adj.* 1. Accomplished, effected, executed, wrought out, achieved, performed, rendered, perpetrated, committed, realized.

2. Concluded, terminated, finished, ended, through, completed, transacted, carried out, settled, fulfilled, past.

3. Tired out, exhausted, worn out, used up, spent, fatigued, weary, drooping, done in, toilworn, faint, prostrate, overtired, forspent, ready to drop, more dead than alive, dog-tired, on one's last legs, walked off one's legs, played out, footsore, wayworn.

4. In conformity with fashion and good taste, *comme il faut.*

5. Cooked sufficiently, ripe, thorough.

DONE FOR, *adj.* Defeated, undone, lost, ruined, broken, bankrupt, used up, put out of action, *hors de combat (Fr.),* shelved, dished, spoiled, damned, destroyed, dead, dead beat, ruined root and branch, *flambé (Fr.),* knocked on the head, dashed, frustrated, thwarted, thrown on one's back, thrown on one's beam ends, unhorsed, hard hit, in a sorry plight, left in the lurch, beaten to a frazzle, overwhelmed, unsuccessful, hoist on one's own petard, stillborn, fruitless, ineffective, grounded, stranded, foundered, wrecked, struck down, shipwrecked, capsized, foiled.

DONKEY, *n.* 1. Ass, jackass, onager, jack, moke, jenny, neddy, cuddy, burro, mule.

2. Stupid person, obstinate person, silly fellow, simpleton, fool, oaf, dunce, blockhead, lout, dolt, half-wit, booby, noodle, idiot, imbecile, moron, nitwit, witling, dizzard, ninny, hoddy-doddy, nincompoop, bonehead, numskull, lunkhead, jughead.

DONOR, *n.* 1. Bestower, benefactor, giver, free giver, grantor, investor, subscriber, contributor, testator, settlor, almoner, fairy godmother, Lady Bountiful, Santa Claus.

2. *(Med.)* Person furnishing blood for transfusion, human blood bank.

DO-NOTHING, *adj.* Inactive, lazy, slothful, idle, otiose, indolent, passive, inert, torpid, supine, sluggish, laggard.

DO-NOTHING, *n.* Useless fellow, lazy good-fornothing person, idler, drone, loafer, sluggard, *fainéant (Fr.),* Fabian.

DOOM, *v.* 1. Pass sentence on, fix as judicial consequence, condemn solemnly, find guilty, convict, decree as a penalty, adjudge, pronounce judgment against, sentence, damn, proscribe.

2. Destine to an adverse fate, consign to destruction, predetermine to an evil destiny, ordain to an evil lot, consign to ruin, destine to calamity, appoint, decree, foreordain, preordain, predestine, consecrate, devote.

DOOM, *n.* 1. Formal fixing of penalty, sentence, verdict, condemnatory judgment, unfavorable decision, judicial decree, penal condemnation.

2. Fixed future evil condition, sad irrevocable destiny, terrible ending brought about by fate, unalterable course of events, predetermined plan of events, irrational power which determines events, portion, lot, fate, kismet, ill-fate, fatalism, future state, hereafter, destruction, ruin, finish.

3. Last Judgment, *dies irae (Lat.),* doomsday, end of the world, death.

DOOR, *n.* 1. Movable frame of boards turning on hinges, opening in a wall to permit ingress or egress, entry, entrance, entranceway, portico, portal, doorway, gate, hatch, wicket, gateway, porte-cochère, postern, trap door.

2. Passageway, means of access, access, means of exit, aperture, orifice, mouth, inlet, outlet, avenue, way, lobby, porch, vestibule, hallway, entrance hall, means of approach, threshold, opening, dehiscence.

3. Barrier, obstacle, barricade, obstruction, stockade, boom.

DOORKEEPER, *n.* One who guards a door, janitor, ostiary, concierge, turnkey, porter, tiler *(Masonry),* janitrix, janitress, gatekeeper, durwan *(Hind.),* warder, guard, sentry, sentinel, Janus, Cerberus, watchdog.

DOPE, *n.* 1. Thick liquid, pasty preparation, paste, lubricant.

2. Preparation of opium used for smoking, narcotic agent used to dull and stupefy, opiate, stimulating drug, narcotic, opium, morphine, heroin, cocaine, hashish, marijuana, bhang, drug, sedative, anaesthetic agent, reefer.

3. User of narcotics, dope addict.

4. *(Slang)* A stupid person, square, drip, creep.

5. Advance or confidential information, data, prediction, tip.

DORMANT, *adj.* 1. In a state of rest, fast asleep, sleeping, soporous, hypnotic, somnolent, at rest, lying as if asleep, comatose, lethargic, torpid, torpescent, quiescent, hibernating, in a state of suspended animation, seemingly lifeless.

2. Inactive, latent, delitescent, abeyant, inert, inoperative, suspended, unexerted, not roused to action, passive, not enforced, resting, smoldering, lurking, unapparent, undisclosed, undeveloped, stagnant, nonvegetative, sluggish, dull, indolent, apathetic, inanimate, fallow.

DORMITORY, *n.* Building containing sleeping apartments *(U. S.),* sleeping apartment containing number of beds *(Brit.),* sleeping room, bedroom, chamber.

DOSE, *n.* 1. Quantity of medicine to be taken at one time, prescribed portion, draught, measure, medicament, drench (*Veter.*), pill, bolus, daily dose, lethal dose, toxic dose.

2. Disagreeable lot, unhappy fate, definite portion, bitter pill.

DOSE, *v.* Deal out in doses, administer a dose to, dispense, give a dosage to, apportion for doses, dole out, treat, medicate, drench (*Veter.*), give anything nauseous or objectionable to.

DOSSIER, *n.* Bundle of papers containing a detailed report, bundle of documents all relating to the same matter, collection of memoranda relating to some matter, brief, record, portfolio.

DOT, *n.* 1. Minute spot on a surface, round mark, period, speck, point, particle, mite, mote, jot, iota, dab, tittle, atom, pinprick, little lump, clot.

2. Dowry, dower, marriage portion, jointure.

DOT, *v.* 1. Mark with dots, sprinkle, besprinkle, spot, bespot, fleck, speckle, bespeckle, stipple, maculate, stud, checker, score.

2. Distribute, scatter, disperse, punctuate, place like dots.

3. Delineate by means of dots, sketch lightly.

DOTAGE, *n.* 1. Feebleness of mind from old age, second childhood, fatuity, driveling, vacancy of mind, senile dementia, imbecility, desipience, irrationality, senility, anility, senescence, caducity, superannuation, climacteric, decrepitude.

2. Foolish affection, excessive fondness, extravagant liking.

DOTARD, *n.* 1. One who is weak-minded from old age, one in second childhood, driveler, old fogey, imbecile.

2. One given to extravagant affection or fancies.

DOTE, *v.* 1. Be in one's second childhood, be in one's dotage, be in feeble mind from old age, lose one's senses, be weak-minded from age, be imbecile, drivel, ramble, wander, rave, be incoherent.

2. Be over-fond, love to distraction, idolize, be foolishly fond, bestow excessive love on, lavish foolish fondness, make much of, feast one's eyes on, make calf-eyes at, hold dear, prize, treasure, adore, look sweet upon, be stuck on.

DOTING, *adj.* 1. Extravagantly fond, foolishly affectionate, over head and ears in love, lovesick, smitten, bitten, struck, taken with, sweet upon, enamored, uxorious.

2. Feeble-minded, weak-minded from old age, senile, old-fogeyish, anile, old-womanish, infirm, driveling, childish, imbecile.

DOUBLE, *n.* 1. Quantity increased by a sum equal to itself, twice as much, two-fold size or amount.

2. Fold, plait, plica, plicature, plication, pleat, doubling, ply, crease, bend, coil, lap, flexure.

3. Turning back on the same course, returning upon one's track, sudden backward bend.

4. Piece of duplicity, stratagem, wile, ruse, artifice, trick, shift, maneuver, dodge.

5. Person closely resembling another, copy, counterpart, duplicate, twin, facsimile, alter ego, two peas in a pod, analogue, like, congener, mate, match, fellow, second self, bird of a feather, apparition, wraith.

6. Substitute, understudy, proxy, alternate, pinch hitter, dummy.

DOUBLE, *adj.* 1. Having two of a sort together, composed of two like parts, coupled, paired, binary, binate, geminate, geminous, in pairs, binal, twin.

2. Twice as much, twice as great, multiplied by two, again as much.

3. Twofold, bifold, duplex, biform, biformed, two-ply, dualistic, bifarious, dual, joining two in one, of twofold aspect, duplicate, bifront, bent over, doubled, folded.

4. Ambiguous, hypocritical, equivocal, false, guileful, deceitful, double-dealing, perfidious, double-tongued, two-faced, insincere, dishonest, hollow, knavish, full of duplicity, twofold in character, Janus-faced.

DOUBLE, *v.* 1. Multiply by two, make as much again, make twice as great, geminate, duplicate, increase by adding an equal amount, magnify, increase twofold, grow, enlarge, be doubled, have twice as much as.

2. Fold with one part upon another, fold the parts of together, make of two thicknesses, plait, tuck, turn, furl, redouble, reduplicate, bend over.

3. Couple, associate, copy, facsimile.

4. Elude, go round, sail round, turn back on a course, return upon the same track, pass round.

5. Cause to stoop by a blow, put out of commission.

6. Do over again, repeat, renew, renovate.

7. Play tricks, act deceitfully.

8. Serve for either of two purposes, serve in two capacities.

9. Go rapidly, march at double time.

DOUBLE-DEALER, *n.* Deceiver, cheat, tricker, trickster, blackguard, knave, rogue, rascal, Judas, villain, renegade, truant, recreant, traitor.

DOUBLE-DEALING, *n.* Duplicity, treacherous dealing, guile, deception, treachery, artifice, deceit, trickery, perfidy, falsehood, dissimulation, dishonesty, fraud, infidelity, faithlessness, cant, breach of trust, hypocrisy, lip-service, mouth-honor, bad faith, mendacity, equivocation, foul play, prodition, disloyalty, knavery, roguery, rascality, betrayal, Judas kiss, Punic faith, improbity, Machiavellism.

DOUBLE-ENTENDRE, *n.* 1. Expression with two meanings, ambiguity, quibble, word play, double meaning, paragram, anagram, quirk, paronomasia, equivocation, *équivoque (Fr.)*, amphiboly, ambiloquy, pun, *calembour (Fr.)*.

2. Impurity, indelicacy, indecency, ribaldry, obscenity, smut, bawdry, pornography.

DOUBLE-FACED, *adj.* Practicing duplicity, two-faced, mendacious, deceitful, false-hearted, sly, treacherous, dishonest, Janus-faced, false, wily, perfidious, knavish, fraudulent, untruthful, tricky, untrustworthy, underhand, subdolous, cunning, insidious, intriguing, foxy, stealthy, shifty, bare-faced, evasive, hypocritical, canting, pharisaical, disingenuous, double-tongued, double-dealing, unveracious, crooked.

DOUBLE-MINDED, *adj.* Unstable, unresolved, unsettled, undecided, vacillating, wavering in mind, changeable, mobile, fickle, infirm of purpose, irresolute, pliant, unsteady, drifting, shilly-shally, unsteadfast, unreliable, capricious, irresponsible, volatile, mercurial, giddy, hot and cold, light-minded, fast and loose.

DOUBLET, *n.* 1. Close-fitting outer body-garment worn by men, jerkin, jacket, waistcoat worn with hose.

2. One of a pair, duplicate.

3. Pair of like things, couple, two.

DOUBLY, *adv.* 1. In double measure or degree, in twofold degree, in a twofold manner, twofold, twice, double, once more, over again, bis.

2. In a manner marked by double-dealing, deceitfully.

DOUBT, *v.* 1. Hesitate to accept as true, hold questionable, question, be skeptical concerning, skepticize, query, have doubts about, disbelieve, lack conviction, lack faith, discredit, dispute, be uncertain in opinion about, scruple, object, stickle, contradict, demur.

2. Suspect, distrust, challenge, deny, smell a rat, harbor suspicions, fear, be apprehensive of, mistrust, lack confidence in, shy at.

3. Feel uncertainty as to something, lose the clue, be undecided in opinion, waver in opinion, hesitate, be doubtful, dubitate, entertain doubts, float in a sea of doubt, be in suspense, be in a state of uncertainty, be inclined to doubt, be fluctuating as to truth, be undetermined, be without judgment, not know what to think, not know which way to turn.

DOUBT, *n.* 1. Indecision in opinion, feeling of uncertainty as to fact, undecidedness, state of suspended judgment through lack of certain knowledge, irresolution, faltering, incertitude, vacillation, dubiety, incredulity, dubiousness, lack of certainty, hesitation, uncertainty, suspense, unbelieving state of mind, unsettled opinion, matter of dubitation, perplexity, lack of conviction, quandary, dilemma, mental vagueness, indefiniteness, confusion, ambiguity, open question.

2. Misgiving, suspicion, mistrust, distrust, state of affairs such as to occasion uncertainty, skepticism, agnosticism, reluctance to believe, disbelief, dissent, apprehension.

3. Something that requires settlement, qualm, objection, problem, difficulty, scruple, demur.

DOUBTER, *n.* Disbeliever, unbeliever, skeptic, agnostic, atheist, freethinker, irreligionist, heretic, rationalist, nullifidian, nihilist, *esprit fort (Fr.).*

DOUBTFUL, *adj.* 1. Disposed to question, in the realm of great doubt, experiencing doubt, dubious, reluctant to be convinced, uncertain, undecided, unsettled in opinion, undetermined, skeptical, incredulous, disbelieving, hesitating, wavering, irresolute, vacillating, in suspense, perplexed, suspicious, distrustful, wondering, indecisive.

2. Indistinct in character or meaning, obscure, admitting of doubt, problematical, enigmatical, equivocal, ambiguous, vague, precarious, muddy, of uncertain issue, puzzling, baffling, oracular, nebulous, shrouded in mystery, occult, cryptic, veiled, indefinite, dark, apocryphal, fabulous, incredible, debatable, conjectural, disputable, questionable, indeterminate, undetermined, controvertible.

DOUBTLESS, *adv.* 1. Withou. doubt, for certain, to a certainty, not a shadow of a doubt, beyond peradventure of a doubt, unquestionably, really, undoubtedly, incontestably, indisputably, surely, irrefutably, certainly, certes, no doubt, to be sure, and no mistake, of course, assuredly, in truth, without fail, positively, truly, actually, there is no question, *cela va sans dire (Fr.).*

2. Probably, presumably, mayhap.

DOUGHTY, *adj.* 1. Courageous, valiant, bold, brave, heroic, mettlesome, valorous, intrepid, dauntless, fearless, manly, gallant, resolute, game, adventurous, audacious, chivalrous, high-spirited, plucky, stout-hearted, lion-hearted, unflinching, daring, unshrinking, confident, self-reliant, enterprising, strong-minded, hardy, dashing, redoubtable, dogged, indomitable, determined, strenuous, mighty, formidable.

2. Boastful of bravery, exhibiting bravado, swashbuckling.

DOUR, *adj.* Sullen, gloomy, morose, sour, stern, severe, unyielding, hard, harsh, strict, rigorous, rigid, austere, uncompromising, obdurate, Spartan, inflexible, unsparing, stringent, ironhanded, inclement.

DOUSE, *v.* 1. Plunge into water, dip suddenly, drench, duck, immerse, submerge, souse, plump under water, drown, soak, steep, sprinkle, sparge, bathe, lave, swash, splash, slosh.

2. *(Slang)* Extinguish, put out.

DOVE, *n.* Pigeon, carrier-pigeon, turtle-dove, symbol of purity and peace, lamb, newborn babe, innocent, peacemaker, gentle person, Holy Spirit *(Eccl.).*

DOVETAIL, *v.* 1. Mortise, tenon, fit together compactly, join harmoniously, fit ingeniously, tail, unite, cog, splice, link, inosculate, let in, graft, ingraft, fix together, intersect, connect skilfully to form a harmonious whole.

2. Agree, tally, correspond, cohere in close unity, accord, harmonize, fall in with, concur, match, coincide, equal, square, conform, parallel, resemble.

DOWAGER, *n.* Widow in possession of dower, endowed widow having a jointure, woman who holds some title from her deceased husband *(Br.),* widow of one of noble rank, dignified elderly lady, matron, dame, madam, lady, woman of dower.

DOWDY, *adj.* 1. Untidy, slovenly in dress, drab, carelessly dressed, frowzy, slatternly, not trim, not smart, not stylish, ill-dressed, draggle-tailed, not neat, vulgar-looking, uncleanly, tacky, frumpy, shabby, sluttish.

2. Ill-fitting, in bad taste, lacking in taste, tasteless, awkward.

DOWER, *n.* 1. *(Law)* Widow's life portion of real estate, legacy, inheritance, property, trust, patrimony, heritage, bequest, demise, alimony, settlement, provision, maintenance, substance, pension, annuity.

2. Sum of one's natural gifts, personal endowment, gift.

3. Dowry, dot, marriage portion, jointure.

DO WITHOUT Get along without, dispense with, not use, forgo, let alone, not touch, forbear, abstain, spare, waive, leave off, disuse, have done with, discard.

DOWN, *prep.* 1. In a descending direction along, from a higher to a lower level, from the top to the bottom of.

2. Along the current of, along the course of, adown.

DOWN, *adv.* 1. In downward course, downward, from higher to lower, in descending direction, into a lower position, netherwards, downstairs, belowstairs.

2. Earthward, to the ground, on the ground, on the floor, underground, underfoot, under, underneath, beneath, below, below the horizon.

3. From an upright to a prostrate position, to a position that is lower than before.

4. To a low point, at a low rate, below par, at a low degree, at a low ebb, at the lowest point, to the very bottom, to the point of exhaustion.

5. From an earlier to a later time, from a former time, onward in time or descent.

6. From a greater to a lesser bulk, from a thinner to a thicker consistence.

7. In due state, into close application, in due position.

8. Upon material for writing, on paper, in a book.

9. In cash, on the counter, into the hand, at once, immediately, forthwith, here rendered.

10. Confined to bed with illness, sick, abed, ailing.

11. In distress, humbled, into disgrace, into disrepute, in a degraded condition, low, into disfavor, in a prostrate condition, in adversity.

12. Into subjection, in dependence, under control.

DOWN, *adj.* 1. Directed toward that which is below, downward, going downward.

2. Downcast, depressed, dejected, in the dumps, blue, dispirited, discouraged, disheartened, forlorn, disconsolate, melancholic, despondent, woebegone.

3. Without friends, down and out, destitute, without money, without prospects, bereft of resources.

4. *(Games)* Behind an opponent by a specified number of points, losing, in the hole, back.

DOWN, *v.* 1. Knock down, throw down, fell, floor, overthrow, conquer, subdue, put down.

2. Drink down, swill, toss off, swallow, gulp, bolt, bottoms up.

3. Go down, sink, fall, drop.

DOWN, *n.* 1. A downward movement, a descent, a drop.

2. Soft hairy growth, soft pubescence, hair, fleece, tomentum, fuzz, fluff, floccus, bloom, woolly plumage, first feathering, feathers, soft under plumage, nap, pile, shag, wool, thatch, fur, beard, awn, whiskers, filament, fimbria, fringe, villus, thistledown, cobweb, gossamer.

3. A reverse of fortune, blow.

4. Grass-grown hilltop, upland, dune.

DOWNCAST, *adj.* 1. Directed downward, turned toward the ground, bowed down, descending, decurrent, descendent.

2. Dejected in spirit, low in spirits, unhappy, downhearted, sad, cast down, down-in-the-mouth, in the dumps, dispirited, discouraged, forlorn, disheartened, disconsolate, despondent, depressed, cheerless, joyless, dismal, gloomy, in the doldrums, doleful, lachrymose, woebegone, desolate, crestfallen, sick at heart, chapfallen, pensive, sorrowful, mopish, mournful, hopeless, blue, saturnine, atrabilious.

DOWNFALL, *n.* 1. Descent to a lower position, drop, subsidence, landslide, avalanche, smashup, breakdown, dilapidation, crack-up, wreck, fall, debacle, shipwreck, subversion, comedown, ruin, downcome, crash, overthrow, collapse, perdition, destruction.

2. Adversity, adverse fortune, undoing, slip, disaster, calamity, cataclysm, catastrophe, doom, misfortune, reverse, casualty, defeat, failure, sudden degradation, total debasement, abasement, humiliation, rout, disgrace, ruination, loss of good fame, loss of high position, losing game, extremity, fate of Icarus, nose-dive, false step, trip, stumble, tumble, *faux pas (Fr.)*, slip, crack of doom.

DOWNGRADE, *n.* Downward slope, declivity, descent, slant, grade, dip, downhill, decline, drop, inclination, fall, devexity, easy descent.

DOWNHEARTED, *adj.* Having the heart cast down, downcast, disheartened, sorrowful, cut up, dejected, depressed, discouraged, heavy-hearted,

desolate, crestfallen, chapfallen, dispirited, blue, gloomy, low-spirited, sad, mournful, forlorn, disconsolate, unhappy, mopish, melancholy, dismal, despondent, atrabilious, heartsick, splenetic, saturnine, woebegone, hypochondriac.

DOWNPOUR, *n.* Heavy continuous fall of water, copious and heavy fall, deluge, torrential rain, flood, cloudburst, shower, flash flood, driving rain, pouring rain, monsoon.

DOWNRIGHT, *adj.* 1. Thorough, out-and-out, utter, complete, absolute, positive, clear, definite, undisguised, manifest, evident, distinct, palpable, conspicuous, unmistakable, self-evident, simple, explicit, plain, decided, unequivocal, categorical, stark, sheer, arrant, unconditional, thoroughgoing, unmitigated, rank, incontestable, unmixed, unqualified, flat.

2. Straightforward, outspoken, straight to the point, plain-spoken, candid, frank, sincere, open, honest, direct, aboveboard, matter-of-fact, blunt, unceremonious, artless, unreserved, ingenuous, bluff, abrupt.

DOWNTRODDEN, *adj.* Trodden under foot, trodden down, trampled upon, downtrod, ground down, oppressed, prostrate, tyrannized over, in subjection to, downfallen, overcome, submissive, servile, resigned, enslaved, subservient, cringing, crouching, on bended knee, weak-kneed, non-resisting, undefended, overwhelmed, beaten to a frazzle, under the lash, under the heel of, the puppet of, like dirt under one's feet, a slave to, at the mercy of, in the power of, at the feet of, at one's beck and call.

DOWNWARD, *adv.* From a higher to a lower place or condition, down from a source, down in a descending course, descending in course from that which is more remote, toward the extremities, lower, down, downwards.

DOWNY, *adj.* 1. Covered with soft hairs, lanate, lanuginous, lanated, woolly, pilous, plumose, soft, fleecy, flocculent, pubescent, fuzzy, light, fluffy, feathery, velvety, silky, tomentose.

2. Soothing, calm, restful.

DOWRY, *n.* 1. Dowery, dower, dot, jointure, marriage offering paid by a wife, marriage money given by a woman to her husband, tocher, marriage goods, marriage portion.

2. Natural gift, endowment, possession, share, livelihood.

DOXOLOGY, *n.* Exultant psalm of praise to God as triune, hymn of praise to God, an ascription, glorification, *Gloria in Excelsis, Gloria Patri, Te Deum, nunc dimittis,* halleluiah, hosanna, paean.

DOXY, *n.* Mistress, paramour, concubine, fancy woman, kept woman, call girl, strumpet, whore, prostitute, harlot, street-walker, wench, loose woman, drab, Cyprian, courtesan, adulteress, advoutress, tart, hustler, chippy, broad, jade, *fille de joie (Fr.),* frail sister, fallen woman, bag, demirep, trollop, trull, baggage, hussy, bitch, woman of easy virtue, wanton, demimondaine, cocotte, grisette, lorette, white slave.

DOZE, *v.* Sleep lightly, sleep fitfully, snooze, nap, yield partially to sleepiness, drowse, slumber, be drowsy, take a nap, be in a half-awake condition, snatch forty winks, fall into a light sleep unintentionally, nod, drop off to sleep, take a siesta, pass time in drowsiness, pass listlessly in a doze, be dull.

DOZE, *n.* Unsound sleep, light sleep, snooze, **nap,**

light slumber, drowse, fitful sleep, siesta, forty winks, sand in the eyes, torpor, somnolence, lethargy.

DRAB, *adj.* 1. Dun, brownish-yellow, dull brown, dull gray, yellowish gray, grayish, brownish, achromatic, leaden, murky, mouse-colored, slate-colored.

2. Dingy, dreary, dismal, humdrum, somber, colorless, commonplace, dull, cheerless, sober, monotonous, lackluster.

DRAB, *n.* 1. Whore, prostitute, trull, strumpet, doxy, Cyprian, jade. (See DOXY.)

2. Draggletail, slattern, slut, dowdy, untidy woman, slovenly woman, dirty woman.

DRAFT, *n.* 1. Drawing, selection, conscription, muster, enrollment, registering, enforcement, induction.

2. Pull, drag, haul, yielding to the force that draws.

3. Depth to which a vessel sinks in water when laden, submergence.

4. Drain, demand made on anything.

5. Amount to be drunk at one time, drink, potation, potion, libation.

6. Current of air, breeze, flatus, wind, puff, breath, zephyr.

7. Rough sketch, outline, delineation, rough copy, preliminary form, delineated figure, chart, diagram, design, map, picture, drawing, skeleton, representation, program, synopsis, conspectus, composition, blueprint.

8. Writing down of propositions as drawn up, formulation, inditement, plot, plan.

9. Money order, bill of exchange, writing directing the payment of money on account of the drawer, written order drawn by one person upon another, debenture.

DRAFT, *v.* 1. Detach, select, mark out for, set apart, reserve.

2. Take by draft for military service, take by force, select and draw off for service, conscript, commandeer, impress, press, levy, conscribe.

3. Make an outline of, make a draft of, outline, draw up, make a rough sketch of, delineate, sketch.

4. Outline in writing, compose the first form of, formulate, draw up, frame, plan in written form, block out, contour, trace, describe, depict, diagram, portray, design, project, indite, dictate.

DRAFTSMAN, *n.* Maker of mechanical drawings, sketcher, delineator, designer, drawer, artist, diagrammer.

DRAG, *v.* 1. Pull along by main force, draw by violence in any direction, draw with effort, pull heavily along, take in tow, tow, trail, tug, haul, draw along wearily, trawl, draggle, hale, lug, dredge, rake, draw a grapnel along the bottom of.

2. Move slowly, crawl, make slow progress, pass tediously, protract, take one's time, trudge, linger, elapse, lag, creep, loiter, plod, inch along, jog on, hobble, shuffle, limp along, shamble, flag, falter.

DRAGGLE, *v.* 1. Soil by dragging over damp or muddy ground, trail on the ground so as to soil, daggle, befoul, drabble, bemire, dirty, smear, spatter, besmear, bespatter, beslime, begrime, muddy.

2. Hang trailing, follow slowly, straggle, trail along in the rear, follow leisurely.

DRAGGLETAIL, *n.* Untidy person, slovenly woman, slattern, slut, sloven, drab, dowdy.

DRAGNET, *n.* Net to be drawn along the bottom of a body of water to catch something, drag, trammel, dredge, anything that serves to catch, police system, activities of detectives, crime-sleuthing.

DRAGON, *n.* 1. Fabulous monster variously represented, huge winged reptile with crested head and terrible claws, fire-spouting monster, winged serpent, huge snake, large winged lizard, dangerous saurian, great marine animal, crocodile, embodiment of the evil principle.

2. Fierce violent person, savage or spiteful woman, shrew, virago, termagant, Xanthippe.

3. Severely watchful woman, chaperon, duenna.

DRAGOON, *n.* Cavalryman, horse-soldier, hussar, equestrian, mounted soldier, trooper, Uhlan, chasseur, cavalier, mounted riflemen, cuirassier.

DRAGOON, *v.* Set dragoons upon, force by rigorous measures, rule despotically by armed force, coerce, harass, oppress, haunt, hunt down, hound, harry, grind, compel, drive, persecute, overcome by threats of violent measures, worry into submission, molest, say it must be done, cram down the throat, turn on the screw, put the screws on, ride roughshod over, trample under foot, ride herd over, crack the whip, terrorize.

DRAIN, *v.* 1. Draw fluid from, withdraw liquid gradually from, remove by degrees, filtrate, discharge, make dry of, cause to run off, tap, sluice, "milk," expel, broach, clear of moisture, pump off.

2. Make heavy demands upon, put under a severe strain, tax, deplete, exhaust by means of gradual withdrawals, empty, impoverish, reduce, wear, stint, beggar, ruin, pauperize, sap, bleed white, strain, expend, consume.

3. Flow off gradually, leak away, exude, seep, ooze, well out, filter, flow out, effuse, trickle out, find vent, percolate.

DRAIN, *n.* 1. That by which anything is drained, pipe, conduit, tube, outlet, channel, sewer, ditch, culvert, trench, watercourse, gutter, hydrant, sink, cloaca.

2. Gradual continuous outflow, continuous withdrawal, expenditure, depletion, exhaustion, reduction, strain.

DRAINAGE, *n.* 1. Gradual flowing off of any liquid.

2. That which is drained off, waste water, seepage, sewerage, bilge.

3. System of drains, device for draining, means of draining collectively, material used to facilitate draining.

DRAM, *n.* 1. Unit of apothecaries' weight, 60 grains, ⅛ ounce.

2. Dose, draft, potion, potation, drink, nip, sip, drop, bracer, eye opener, pick-me-up, stimulant, cordial, liqueur.

3. Small quantity of anything, thimbleful.

DRAMA, *n.* 1. Dramatic composition presenting a story involving conflict or contrast of character, theatrical piece, play, spectacle, masque, dramatic representation, tragedy, comedy, farce, mystery, melodrama, miracle-play, pageant, pantomime, dumb-show, burlesque, travesty, playlet, mime, harlequinade, opera, interlude, comedy of manners.

2. Histrionic art, the stage, showmanship, stage business, acting, impersonation, theatricals, Thespianism, stagecraft, dramaturgy, theatrical entertainment.

3. The theatre, the sock, the buskin, Thespis,

the cothurnus, Melpomene (tragic Muse), Thalia (comic Muse), the boards, the footlights.

DRAMATIC, adj. 1. Theatrical, histrionic, tragic, Thespian, buskined, theatric, scenic, spectacular, stagy, comic, tragi-comic, farcical, operatic.
2. Involving emotional tension, rising to a climax, climactic, sensational, striking, thrilling, impressive, sudden.

DRAMATIS PERSONAE, n. Characters of the play, cast, actors, players, Thespians, performers, personages of the drama, interlocutors in the play.

DRAMATIST, n. Writer of dramas, one who writes plays, playwright, dramaturgist, dramatic author.

DRAMATIZE, v. 1. Set forth in dramatic form, put into dramatic form, make a drama from, make into a drama, compose in form of a drama, convert a plot into a play, represent dramatically, put on the stage, adapt for the stage, produce, set.
2. Express dramatically, emote, orate, relate in a theatrical manner, impart dramatic quality to, spout, rant, overdo, tread the boards, play to the gallery, act a part, star, personate, mimic, enact, perform.

DRAPE, v. Hang with cloth in graceful folds, clothe with hanging cloth, cover with drapery, arrange with decorative folds, adjust hangings in folds, adorn with drapery, invest, enwrap, fold, circumvest, envelop, sheathe, swathe, festoon, dress, trim, prink, prank, preen, trick out, bedeck, bedight.

DRAPERY, n. 1. Coverings arranged in loose graceful folds, materials with which anything is draped, hanging garments, clothing, loosely hanging and classical attire, costume, raiment, toilette, habiliment, vesture, palliament, apparel, array, garniture, finery, trappings.
2. Hangings, tapestry, arras, textile fabrics, frills and furbelows, curtains, trimmings, lambrequin, festoon, tassel.

DRASTIC, adj. Acting with force or violence, vigorously effective, extreme in effect, rigorous, radical, powerful, active, efficacious, energetic, dynamic, forcible, strenuous, forceful, intense, severe, keen, sharp, acute, brisk, vigorous, live, strong, harsh, life-and-death, heroic.

DRAW, v. 1. Cause to come in a particular direction by a pulling force, move by a force, pull, haul, drag, hale, pull along, take in tow, tow, tug, exert force on, yank, lead, transport slowly with sustained effort, exert an attracting force on, cause movement by pulling.
2. Attract, allure, lure, entice, magnetize, bring out, persuade, influence, engage, decoy, charm, move, envoke, bring toward, call forth, elicit, lead others to follow, be attractive, fascinate, enamor, rouse.
3. Delineate, portray, depict, trace out, make a picture of, diagram, sketch, mark out, fabricate, define in lines, practice the art of delineation, picture with pencil or crayon.
4. Compose in words, formulate, write, indite, draw up, prepare, draft, frame, put in proper written form, write out.
5. Obtain by logical process, deduce, infer, get, derive, take, receive, conclude.
6. Take out from a receptacle, extract, pull out, draw out, remove by pulling, unsheathe, take out the entrails of, force out, extort, disembowel, gut, eviscerate.
7. Pull out to full length, elongate, stretch,

lengthen out, protract, extend, prolong, make thin by attenuating.
8. Drain, suck dry, siphon, suck, quaff.
9. Take in by respiration, take into the lungs, breathe in, inhale, inspire.
10. Shrink by contraction, wrinkle, contract, distort.
11. Produce inflammation, blister, vesicate, act as an irritant, have an epispastic effect.
12. Have a free draft, cause motion freely, require the depth of in order to float, sink to the depth of, settle in water up to a certain point, have a draft, move, proceed, come, go.
13. Request payment by draft, make a draft, make a demand, levy, call on for, obtain by making application, obtain means, receive supplies by applying to a source.
14. Discontinue without completion, come to a stalemate.
15. Extract the strength of by steeping, prepare by infusion.
16. Drive out, force out, flush, force an animal to quit.

DRAWBACK, n. 1. Obstacle, impediment, fault, anything that checks progress, hindrance, hitch, disadvantage, imperfection, detriment, deficiency, defect, injury, hurt, harm, damage, difficulty, discouragement, objection, check, snag, mischief, stumbling block, encumbrance, nuisance.
2. Amount paid back from a charge made, refund, discount, allowance, deduction, rebate, abatement, reduction.

DRAWING, n. 1. See various meanings of verb DRAW.
2. Delineation of form without reference to color, representation by lines, art of representing, objects by lines made with a point, design made with pencil or crayon, picture, sketch, outline, plan, diagram, cartoon, draft, study, figure, illustration, tracing, copy, portrait, likeness, depiction, composition, black and white, canvas.

DRAWING ROOM, n. 1. Room for the reception of company, salon, reception hall, parlor, room to which guests withdraw after dinner, atrium, state room, sitting room, living room.
2. Private compartment in a railway car, parlor car.

DRAWL, v. 1. Speak with lingering utterance, speak monotonously from indolence or affectation, pronounce slowly and lazily, protract in utterance, mouth, protract one's words, be long drawn out in speech, prolong syllables, linger over one's words, drag words, elongate in speech, lengthen, extend, spin out.
2. While away, pass indolently, dawdle, do nothing, let the grass grow under one's feet, take one's time, poke, slouch, loll, hang back, lounge, loiter, loaf, take it easy, take time in, go to sleep over, consume time, languish, flag, droil.

DRAWLING, adj. Pronouncing lazily, speaking slowly, singsong, monotonous, longsome, languid, uttering spiritlessly, twanging, lazy, otiose, heavy, droning, lagging, dreamy, leisurely, slowpaced, tardigrade, snail-like.

DRAW UP, v. 1. Put in the required legal form of writing, formulate, indite, compose, write out, frame, draft, redact, prepare, pen, make a report, throw on paper, dash off, write down.
2. Form in order, set in array, array, set in line, marshal, set in battle order, deploy.
3. Come to a halt, stop short, halt, pull up before, rein in.

4. Pull up, lift, raise, elevate, haul up, hoist.

DRAY, *n.* 1. Low cart without fixed sides, wain, conveyance, wagon, van, lorry, strong heavy vehicle for loading heavy articles, baggage truck for carrying heavy loads.

2. Sledge, sled.

DREAD, *n.* 1. Apprehension as to something future, terrifying anticipation, alarm, anxiety, unconquerable fright, shrinking horror, great fear, terror, fearfulness, misgiving, suspicion, hesitation, dismay, consternation, timidity, panic, diffidence, scare, cold feet, funk, trepidation, fear and trembling, perturbation, tremor, bogy, nervousness, disquietude, cowardice, agitation, nightmare, *bête noire (Fr.),* bugaboo, bugbear.

2. Deep awe profound respect, reverence, veneration.

DREAD, *v.* Fear greatly, be apprehensive about, be in shrinking anticipation of, be in great fear, anticipate with shrinking horror, be afraid, funk, distrust, hesitate, falter, cower, flinch, shy, shrink, quail, tremble, quiver, shudder, shake, shiver, have cold feet, quake in one's boots.

DREADFUL, *adj.* 1. Causing great alarm, grim, inspiring dread, portentous, alarming, fearful, shocking, frightful, direful, awesome, awful, fell, formidable, terrible, dire, horrid, terrific, dismal, horrible, appalling, grievous, lurid, redoubtable, distressing, ghastly, calamitous, nefarious, woeful, monstrous, hideous, tragic, insufferable.

2. Awe-inspiring, venerable, august, imposing, impressive, awesome.

3. *(Colloq.)* Extremely bad, unpleasant, ugly, repellent.

DREADNOUGHT, *n.* 1. Type of battleship with battery of heavy-caliber guns in turrets, high-speed battleship of heavy armament, warship, superdreadnought, man-of-war, capital ship.

2. One who fears nothing, daredevil.

3. Outer garment of heavy woolen cloth, surcoat, overcoat.

4. Thick cloth with a long pile, felted cloth.

DREAM, *n.* 1. Succession of images present in the mind during sleep, series of mental images and thoughts experienced while sleeping, incubus, sleeping vision, nightmare, ephialtes, trance.

2. Object seen in a dream, fairy, apparition, wraith, phantom, specter, will-o'-the-wisp, shade, *ignis fatuus (Lat.),* bugbear, chimera, shadow, nothingness, insubstantiality, incorporeity.

3. Flight of fancy, idle fancy, figment, conceit, phantasy, vagary, delusion, reverie, daydream, castle in the air, *château en Espagne (Fr.),* involuntary vision occurring to one awake, vapor, illusion, hallucination, romance, visionary idea, vague notion, wild scheme, nebulous conception, imagery.

4. Something of an unreal beauty or charm, something of exotic beauty ordinarily seen only in dreams.

DREAM, *v.* 1. Experience a succession of mental images and thoughts while sleeping, have dreams, have visions during sleep, be in the dream-like condition of consciousness, see in a vision, have a nightmare, go into a trance, have hallucinations.

2. Indulge in fancies, have notions, fancy, muse, conceive, idealize, imagine, conceive of something in a very remote way, suppose, have a remote idea of, think, have a vague idea through the free exercise of imagination, be pensive, be preoccupied, be abstracted.

3. Give free rein to the imagination, fall into reverie, indulge in daydreams, daydream, pass time in dreaming, build castles in the air, ride a magic carpet, seek the rainbow's end, while away in empty speculations.

DREAMER, *n.* 1. One who dreams in sleep, somnambulist, sleepwalker.

2. One who indulges in waking dreams, one who forms projects but does not act, visionary, idle schemer, castle-builder, enthusiast, idealist, romancer, daydreamer, theorizer, John-a-dreams.

DREAMLAND, *n.* Land of dreams, realm of fancy, region of reverie, cloudland, fairyland, land of imagination, world of fancy, Land of Nod.

DREAMY, *adj.* 1. Full of dreams, visionary, rapt, fanciful, illusory, fabulous, fictitious, cloud-built, aerial, imaginative, poetic, romantic, idealistic, Utopian, quixotic, fantastic, whimsical, notional, figmental, thoughtful, speculative, legendary, mythical, chimerical, imaginary.

2. Pensive, in a reverie, abstracted, wandering, absent-minded, preoccupied, wool-gathering, in a brown study, castle-building.

3. Drowsy, somnolent, lethargic, comatose, listless, lackadaisical, lazy, torpid.

4. Characteristic of dreams, vague, dim, faint, indistinct, shadowy, insubstantial, unreal, spectral, dreamlike, immaterial, apparitional, gossamer, ethereal, vaporous, tenuous, incorporeal, bodiless, intangible, impalpable, superphysical, diaphanous, discarnate, asomatous.

DREARY, *adj.* 1. Manifesting gloom, gloomy, drear, dark, bleak, funereal, mournful, somber, depressing, chilling, lowering, joyless, cheerless, dismal, desolate, melancholy, lonely, lonesome, solitary, forlorn, doleful, overcast, murky.

2. Causing weariness, tedious, uninteresting, wearisome, tiresome, dull, humdrum, monotonous, drab, deadly, lifeless, arid, singsong, unvaried, tame.

DREDGE, *v.* 1. Deepen by means of a dredge, clear out with a dredge, gather with a dredge, drag, net, collect, fish up, remove silt from the bottom of, pull up.

2. Seek laboriously or blindly, grope after.

DREGS, *n.* 1. Lees, sediment, grounds, residuum, residue, bottoms, offscourings, precipitate, slag, settlings, feculence, deposit, the coarse part, offal, draff, heeltap, scoriae, sordes.

2. Scum, refuse, dross, waste, trash, rubbish, debris, filth, recrement.

3. Riffraff, *profanum vulgus (Lat.),* rabble, outcasts.

4. Small remnant, small quantity.

DRENCH, *v.* 1. Wet thoroughly, immerse under water, saturate, wet through and through, soak, souse, douse, steep, drown, inundate, moisten, dampen, wash, dip, slosh, macerate, wet to the skin, splash, spatter, dunk.

2. Administer a draft of medicine to an animal *(Veter.),* administer a potion to, force to swallow a draft.

DRESS, *v.* 1. Invest with clothing, equip with clothing, clothe, array, attire, accouter, apparel, garb, trick out, robe, gown, rig, don, put on, slip on, put formal evening clothes on, put best clothes on, make one's toilet.

2. Adorn richly, array elaborately, drape, doll up, enrich, embellish, beautify, deck, ornament, adorn, decorate, trim, set off, garnish, prink, smarten, spruce up, furbish, gild.

3. Cleanse and cover with antiseptic applications, bandage, treat.

4. Prepare by special treatment, prime, get ready, make suitable, fit, make ready, attend, minister to.

5. Put in order, arrange, dispose, adjust, comb out and do up (hair), curry, cultivate (land).

6. Put in a straight line, align, bring into line, make straight, level, flatten, smooth, even, square, cut down, reduce to proper shape, range.

7. Scold, thrash, reprove, berate, rebuke, chide, reprimand, castigate, blame, censure, take to task, lecture, chastise, trounce, rate, rail at, upbraid, accuse.

DRESS, *n.* 1. Gown, robe, frock, costume, suit, woman's garment consisting of a skirt and waist.

2. Clothing, raiment, clothes, garb, vesture, habiliment, garment, palliament, wearing apparel, toilet, attire, vestment, wardrobe, array, habit, guise, get-up, togs, duds, accouterments, uniform.

3. Elegant attire, evening clothes, dress clothes, fashionable clothing, evening dress, white tie and tails, formal costume, tuxedo, dinner jacket, full dress, *grande tenue (Fr.)*, swallowtail, silk hat, court dress, knee breeches and black silk stockings, fine clothes, bedizenment, bravery, glad rags, rich garments, best bib and tucker, finery, livery, trimmings.

DRESSER, *n.* 1. Bureau, chiffonier, dressing table, vanity table, chest of drawers supporting a swinging mirror.

2. One employed to help dress another, valet, maid, wardrobe mistress.

3. One who dresses elaborately with intent to make a fine appearance, clotheshorse, dude, fop, dandy, coxcomb, popinjay, macaroni, pink of fashion, silk-stocking.

DRESSING, *n.* 1. Act of dressing, wearing of elegant attire, putting on of fashionable raiment, donning evening clothes, making one's toilette.

2. Application for a wound, external remedial application for a diseased part.

3. Scolding, flogging, chastising, castigation, whipping, rap on the knuckles, raking over the coals, berating, reprimand, chiding, upbraiding, exprobration, disapprobation, objurgation, hard words, invective, bitter words, cutting words, diatribe, tirade, lecture, rebuke, reproach.

4. Preparing, putting in order, surface tooling of stone, finishing of wood work.

5. Sauce for food, seasoning, condiment, stuffing for a fowl, forcemeat.

DRESSING GOWN, *n.* Loose gown worn when in dishabille, robe worn while making the toilet, wrapper, robe de chambre, peignoir, negligee, kimono, house coat, hostess gown, morning dress, tea gown.

DRESSMAKER, *n.* One whose occupation is the making of women's clothes, seamstress, designer, modiste, couturier (male), couturière (female), clothier, *costumier (Fr.), sarta da donna (It.),* mantuamaker.

DRIBBLE, *v.* 1. Fall in drops, run bit by bit, drip, trickle, well out, gush, spout, ooze, filter, filtrate, flow in small quantities, plash, squirt, spurt, spurtle, exude, transude, percolate, seep.

2. Act without strength or force.

DRIBLET, *n.* Drop formed as if by dribbling, bit, fragment, small portion, small part, dole, item, instalment, mite, morsel, scrap, particle, pittance, petty sum.

DRIFT, *n.* 1. Course, direction, bearing, tendency, gravitation, inclination, bent, leaning, proclivity, penchant, propensity, bias, trend, current, flow, issue, run, set, tack, dip.

2. Intention, intent, purpose, aim, design, objective, object, mark, scope, proposal.

3. Meaning, signification, significance, tenor, purport, tone, vein, implication, sense, import, force, pith, essence, spirit, gist.

4. Urgent force, controlling influence, drive, impetus, overbearing power, sweeping pressure, movement, motion, driving impulse, rush, sweep.

5. Pyramid of matter driven together, mass, lump, heap, piled up heap, driven mass, heaped pile, drifted pile, dune, bank.

6. (Navig.) Course under the impetus of water currents, speed in knots of an ocean current.

7. (Mining) Horizontal passageway in mining underground, underground passage between shafts, tunnel, gallery, excavation.

8. (Geol.) Deposit, diluvium, detritus, diluvial formation, alluvium.

DRIFT, *v.* 1. Be carried along by the current, be wafted by force of circumstances, float, draw near, converge, gain upon, approach, advance, move towards, gravitate, tend, be borne along aimlessly, wander at random.

2. Be driven into heaps, pile into heaps, heap up, accumulate in masses, sweep along, impel, force, drive.

DRILL, *v.* 1. Bore a hole, make a hole by boring, pierce, transpierce, perforate, tap, penetrate.

2. Exercise in gymnastic tactics, train in martial exercises, instruct in formation marching.

3. Instruct thoroughly, discipline, train, teach, practice, ground, impart knowledge by strict discipline, familiarize with, inure, inculcate, rehearse, accustom, school, practice.

4. Sow with seed, plant.

DRILL, *n.* 1. Machine for drilling driven by a brace, cylindrical borer, boring tool.

2. Training in military exercises, gymnastics, calisthenics, athletic routine.

3. Teaching by repeated exercises, practice, methodical exercise, training, inurement, strict instruction, discipline, thorough indoctrination, rehearsal.

4. Furrow made in the soil to sow seeds in, trench for planting, channel.

DRINK, *v.* 1. Imbibe, lap, quaff, gulp, swallow, ingurgitate, sip, take a liquid into the stomach through the throat, absorb, suck in, take a drink, take in, bolt, soak up, ingest, toss off, whet one's whistle, slake one's thirst, swallow down.

2. Be intemperate in drinking, be a drunkard, tipple, guzzle, swill, swig, tope, be a toper, drink like a fish, carouse, overindulge, revel, bibulate.

3. Salute in drinking, toast, drink in honor of, pledge, caulker, eye opener, wishes for.

DRINK, *n.* 1. Liquid swallowed to quench thirst, beverage, draft, potation, libation, potion.

2. As much as may be taken at one time, sip, bumper, nip, dram, bracer, toast, nightcap, swig, pledge, caulker, eye opener.

3. Alcoholic liquor, intoxicant, stimulant, spirits, booze, moonshine, firewater, Demon Rum, John Barleycorn, blue ruin, flowing bowl, the cup that cheers, Bacchus, Dionysus, wassail.

4. Excessive indulgence in strong drink, toping, alcoholism, dipsomania, drunkenness, inebriety,

intemperance, insobriety, intoxication, tippling, overindulgence, winebibbing.

DRINKABLE, *adj.* Suitable for drinking, that may be drunk, fit to drink, potable, potatory.

DRINKER, *n.* One who drinks spirituous liquors to excess, tippler, sot, drunkard, toper, guzzler, boozer, quaffer, lapper, tosspot, inebriate, soak, dipsomaniac, alcoholic, winebibber, sponge, wet (*slang*), devotee to Bacchus, thirsty soul, carouser, compotator, antiprohibitionist.

DRINKING-BOUT, *n.* Debauch, carousal, spree, revelry, season of drinking, carouse, revel, orgies, jollification, compotation, wassail, bacchanalia, saturnalia, libations, cocktail party.

DRIP, *v.* Shed drops, let fall drops, trickle, distil, dribble, ooze, leak, percolate, well, issue, spurt, purl, gurgle, splash, plash, swash, sprinkle, drizzle.

DRIVE, *v.* 1. Send along by compulsion, push forward, impel, force along, propel, hurl, thrust, aim, shoot, accelerate, plunge, lunge, advance, move, urge onward, give a forward impetus to, chase, flush, beat, hunt out, ferret out, rout, repel.
2. Press forward, incite, actuate, keep going, urge, prosecute, carry forward, carry on, carry through, conduct, set in action, keep in action, make an effort to attain, spur, induce, hurry, hustle, promote, quicken, hasten, instigate, encourage.
3. Compel, oblige, coerce, constrain, force, overwork, overtask.
4. Manage as to direction, guide by reins, convey in a vehicle, go driving, take a drive, travel in a driven vehicle, journey, ride, motor, automobile, take a spin, speed, spin, act as driver, be driven, tour.

DRIVE, *n.* 1. Impulse along in a particular direction, tendency, drift, course, movement, advance, onward course.
2. Impelling force, urgent impulse, violent motion, vigorous pressure, effort, energy, source of motivation (*Psychol.*), vigorous onset, strong offensive, united effort to accomplish some purpose, get-up-and-go (*colloq.*), vim, élan, push, concerted action to attain some specific end, campaign.
3. Trip in a driven vehicle, ride, journey, tour, circuit, airing, outing, jaunt, motoring, excursion, automobiling.
4. Road prepared for driving, carriage-road, driving-course, highway, thoroughfare, boulevard, pike, turnpike.

DRIVE AT, *v.* 1. Strive to accomplish a certain end, aim at, intend, endeavor after, tend to, purpose, be after, design, have in view, have an eye to, contemplate, point at, set before oneself, bid for.
2. Mean, have in mind, imply, indicate, allude to, speak of, signify, hint at, suggest, convey.

DRIVE AWAY, *v.* 1. Scatter, dissipate, disperse, drive off, dispel, expel, rout.
2. Labor diligently, toil persistently, peg away at, grind (*colloq.*).

DRIVEL, *v.* 1. Let saliva drip from the mouth, slaver, drool, slobber.
2. Act foolishly, be silly, be imbecilic, talk foolishly, talk idiotically, talk like a fool, act like a dotard, dote, ramble, babble, twaddle, gabble, utter nonsense.

DRIVEL, *n.* 1. Involuntary flow of spittle from the mouth, drool, slaver, slobber, saliva, sputum, spit, mouth-watering.

2. Senseless talk, nonsense, tosh, balderdash, babble, foolish talk, gabble, twaddle, jargon, gibberish, imbecilic prating, prate, inarticulate talk, childish talk, blatherskike, *baragouin (Fr.)*, jabber, *bavardage (Fr.)*, flapdoodle, poppycock, bosh, moonshine, rubbish, blah, inanity, nugacity.

DRIVELER, *n.* 1. Drooler, slaverer.
2. One who talks in a foolish way, one who acts in a silly manner, simpleton, dotard, fool, imbecile, idiot, twaddler, babbler, senseless gabbler, nitwit, chatterbox, windbag, magpie, jay, parrot, poll, maunderer, dunce, witling.

DRIVER, *n.* 1. One who drives a vehicle, drover, wagoner, motorman, operator of a machine that drives, chauffeur, coachman, charioteer, whip, engineer, cabman, teamster, hackman, "cabby," automobilist, motorist, *vetturino (It.)*, *voiturier (Fr.)*.
2. Overseer of a gang of slaves or convicts, foreman, taskmaster.
3. One who is energetic in business, pusher.

DRIZZLE, *v.* Rain gently in fine drops, mizzle, sprinkle, shower, mist, rain slightly, spray, wet, shed in fine drops, dribble.

DROLL, *n.* 1. Professional jester, clown, buffoon, waggish fellow, funny fellow, wit, quipster, one who makes sport by queer pranks, prankster, harlequin, punchinello, punch, scaramouch, fool, mountebank, merry-andrew, jack-pudding, zany, pickle-herring.
2. Amusing exhibition, farce, comic show, burlesque, mimicry, extravaganza.

DROLL, *adj.* 1. Comic, witty, comical, sportive, sporting, playful, funny, amusing, waggish, zany, ludibrious, ludicrous, ridiculous, laughable, *pour rire (Fr.)*, seriocomic, diverting, entertaining, facetious, humorous, jocular, merry, mirthful.
2. Quaint, bizarre, queer, odd, eccentric, rum, whimsical, grotesque, fantastic, outlandish, strange.

DROLLERY, *n.* Something amusingly queer or funny, action of a buffoon, waggishness, droll quality, buffoonery, comicality, humor, comical ways, pleasantry, facetiousness, fun, waggery, harlequinade, jocosity, esprit, attic wit, atticism, tomfoolery, mummery, jesting, amusing tricks, frolic, jollity, gambol, romp, prank, antic, lark, spree, vagary, monkey trick, caprice, gambade, escapade, *espièglerie (Fr.)*, whimsicality, oddity, zanyism, sportiveness, jocularity, jest, facetious tale, joke.

DRONE, *v.* 1. Make a low humming sound, hum, make a continued monotonous sound, buzz, speak in a monotone, utter monotonously, singsong, use a dull utterance, boom.
2. Waste time trifling, idle, kill time, dawdle, burn daylight, lounge, vegetate, do nothing, take it easy, lead an easy life, live in idleness, loaf, loiter, slouch, poke, droil, sleep at one's post.

DRONE, *n.* 1. Hum, buzz, humming noise, drawl, sibilation, susurration, susurrus, monotone, continuous low tone, singsong.
2. One who lives on the labor of others, idle fellow, do-nothing, *fainéant (Fr.)*, loafer, idler, dawdler, sluggard, lounger, lazy fellow, droil, lubbard, good-for-nothing, ne'er-do-well, do-little, male honey-bee, snail, sleeping partner, afternoon farmer, slow-coach, tortoise.

DROOL, *v.* Drop saliva, slobber, drivel, slaver, mouth-water.

DROOP, *v.* 1. Hang down, depend, bend down

lean downward, sink downward, sag, loll, drop, slouch, bow, lapse, stoop, nutate, nod.

2. Sink to a close, gradually decline, fall into a state of physical weakness, wilt, fade, shrivel, wither, run to seed.

3. Sink from weakness, lose vigor, languish, faint, weaken, grow weak, fail, flag, wane, ebb, be dispirited, despond, pine away, become discouraged, mourn, yearn.

4. Allow to hang listlessly, cause to bend over and hang down, let droop, dangle, let bend down, let sink, make hang.

DROP, *v.* 1. Fall in drops, drip, fall in globules, trickle, dribble, distil, sprinkle, bleed, shed.

2. Fall suddenly, fall vertically, have an abrupt descent, precipitate, descend.

3. Sink to the ground as if inanimate, faint, swoon, subside, become motionless, fall prone, collapse.

4. Bring to an end, cease to carry on, leave off, discontinue, break off, intermit, desist from, remit, lapse, dismiss, lay aside.

5. Have done with, forsake, abandon, desert, quit, relinquish, leave, withdraw, disappear, give up, stop, discard, omit, give over, forswear.

6. Fall lower in degree, slide down, lower, let down, depress, dump, sink, let fall, let go.

7. Go into a place casually, pass without effort into, visit informally.

8. Send a note in a casual manner, hint, utter as if without design, communicate incidentally, let slip, let out.

9. Bring to the ground by a blow *or* shot, fell, floor, cause to fall, kill, bring down.

10. Omit in writing *or* pronunciation, elide, leave out.

11. Cease to employ, dismiss, discharge, fire, sack, bounce, give one his walking papers, let go.

12. Give birth to, litter.

DROP, *n.* 1. Small quantity of liquid produced in a spherical mass, liquid globule, gutta, droplet, bead, blob, dewdrop, pearl, tear.

2. Act of dropping, fall, descent, inclination downward.

3. Steep slope, precipice, abyss, vertical depth.

4. Pendant, earring.

5. Small quantity, driblet, very little, minute quantity, least bit, minimum, minim, moiety, dash, particle, dab, sprinkling, mite, nip, trifle, modicum, scanty supply, spot, trickle, fleck, speckle.

6. Platform gallows, trap door, gibbet.

DROSS, *n.* 1. Waste product taken off molten metal during smelting, impurity in melted metal, scoriae, slag, sprue, sinter, clinker, cinders, ashes, scobs.

2. Foreign matter deposited by a liquid, dregs, draff, grounds, lees, sediment, bottoms, heeltap, recrement, scum, froth, offscourings, feculence.

3. Leavings, residuum, offal, exuviae, sullage, sordes, scales, chaff.

4. Waste matter, refuse, trash, rubbish, debris, litter, sweepings, sawdust, shavings, filings, junk, rags, garbage.

DROUGHT, *n.* 1. Dry weather so long continued as to cause vegetation to wither, lack of rain, aridity, aridness, parchedness, desiccation, drouth, dehydration.

2. Dryness of the throat for want of water, thirst.

3. Scarcity of any necessity, dearth, deficiency, lack, want, insufficiency, inadequacy, need, stint, shortage.

DROVE, *n.* 1. Number of animals driven in a group, flock, herd, pack, bevy, covey, gaggle, flight, brood, hatch, litter, shoal, school, swarm.

2. Large crowd of human beings, collection of people in motion, crowd, press, concourse, band, group, company, multitude, throng, mob.

DROWN, *v.* 1. Suffocate by immersion in water, descend to Davy Jones's locker, smother in water, be asphyxiated by water, sink to the bottom, find a watery grave, perish at sea.

2. Inundate, overflow, deluge, flood, submerge, immerse, swamp, drench.

3. Overwhelm, overpower, overcome, engulf, swallow up, extinguish, quench, deaden *(sound),* mute, muffle, silence.

DROWSE, *v.* 1. Be sleepy, be half-asleep, doze, nap, snooze, slumber, sleep, repose, rest, nod, take a nap, snatch forty winks, drop off, take a siesta, pass time in drowsing, hibernate, go to sleep over, visit the sandman, go to the Land of Nod.

2. Be dull *or* sluggish, be listless, languish, flag, relax, be torpid, be comatose.

DROWSY, *adj.* 1. Inclined to sleep, heavy with sleepiness, half-asleep, sleepy, dozy, slumbrous, nodding, dozing, dreamy, heavy-eyed, somnolent, oscitant.

2. Dull, sluggish, torpid, torpescent, lethargic, comatose, dormant, languid, slow, lackadaisical, stupid, lazy, indolent, otiose.

3. Strongly inclining to slumber, soporiferous, soporific, inducing sleepiness, hypnotic, lulling, mesmeric, balmy.

DRUB, *v.* 1. Beat with a stick, give a dressing down to, thrash, cane, birch, flog, cudgel, lace, lay on, baste, belabor, trounce, larrup, wallop, thwack, thump, pound, deal a blow to, pummel, slap, smack, cuff, buffet, trim, lash, scourge, switch, flagellate, towel, horsewhip, beat hollow, lick, rout, floor, worst, give the stick to, beat black and blue, beat to a jelly, fustigate, dust one's jacket, pitch into, lay about one, whip, curry, punish, defeat decisively.

2. Stamp with the feet, tap with the fingers, rap, drum, thump, knock.

DRUBBING, *n.* Caning, birching, cudgeling, rout, sound thrashing, flogging, beating, switching, walloping, larruping, thwacking, cuffing, blow, pommeling, pounding, flagellation, fustigation, bastinado, malling, thumping, trouncing, decisive defeat, discomfiture.

DRUDGE, *n.* One who works mechanically and without spirit, one who labors at servile tasks, one who works hard and constantly, plodder, fag, grind, hard toiler, hard worker, menial, dig, slave, factotum, scullion, hack, penny-a-liner, scrubwoman, cinderella, one condemned to long hours, hod-carrier.

DRUDGE, *v.* Toil constantly without spirit *or* interest, perform servile *or* distasteful work, work hard at slavish task, do heavy menial service, toil, slave, plod, fag, grind, grub, labor, sweat, toil and moil, exert oneself, dig away at, scrub, hack, plow into.

DRUDGERY, *n.* Hard work in any menial occupation, tedious toil, uninteresting labor, mean labor, ignoble toil, toilsome work, hackwork, grind, moil, service marked by weariness and spiritless routine, exertion, travail, sweat of one's brow, hewing of wood and drawing of water, slavery, degradation, servility, subservience, bondage, subjugation, serfdom, enslavement, vassalage, thralldom.

DRUG, *n.* 1. Chemical substance given to prevent *or* cure disease, agent used as medicine, physic, remedy, prophylactic, sedative, stimulant, specific, palliative, febrifuge.

2. Habit-forming medicinal substance, narcotic, opium, morphine, cocaine, hashish, marijuana, anaesthetic.

3. Unsalable commodity, commodity that is overabundant on the market, something in excess of demand, surfeit, plethora, oversupply, glut, superfluity, load, excess, surplusage.

DRUG, *v.* 1. Dose, medicate, mix with a drug, render narcotic by the addition of drugs.

2. Administer soporific drugs to, deaden with narcotics, render insensible, anaesthetize, dope, stupefy, deaden, blunt, benumb, put under the influence of, narcotize.

3. Poison with a drug, dose to excess, stuff with drugs, surfeit, administer something nauseous to, nauseate.

DRUGGIST, *n.* One who compounds drugs according to medical prescription, dealer in drugs, dispensing chemist, pharmacist, apothecary, pharmacopolist.

DRUM, *v.* 1. Play a drum, beat upon a drum, beat rhythmically, roll, rumble, sound, thrum.

2. Drum out, cashier, depose, degrade, drive out, expel to the accompaniment of a drum beat, dismiss in disgrace, strike off the roll, post, discharge.

3. Summon by beating, call, gather together, round up, solicit, canvass, obtain.

4. Force on the attention by persistent repetition, drive home, reiterate, din, harp on, hammer at, battologize, din in the ear.

DRUM, *n.* Musical instrument struck with the hand *or* sticks, tympanum, tom-tom, tabor, gumby, kettledrum, bass drum, side drum, snare drum, traps, tambour, tambourine, Oriental drum, war drum.

DRUNK, *adj.* Overcome by liquor, drunken, the bottle always won, intoxicated, inebriated, sottish, tipsy, fuddled, full, in one's cups, under the influence of liquor, the worse for liquor, half-seas-over, boozy, intemperate, tight, saturated, pickled, one too many, maudlin, crapulous, temulent, unsteady, muddled, stupefied, soused, elevated, under the weather, lit up, groggy, blind drunk, screwed, primed, dead drunk, drunk as a lord, obfuscated, bleary-eyed, in bed in one's boots.

DRUNKARD, *n.* One with whom drunkenness has become a habit, alcoholic, dipsomaniac, sot, tippler, toper, inebriate, drunk, winebibber, hard drinker, soak, boozer, swiller, wassailer, carouser, bacchanalian, reveler, anti-prohibitionist, wet.

DRY, *adj.* 1. Free from moisture, devoid of humidity, not wet, not moist, dried, evaporated, anhydrous, juiceless, desiccated, sapless, having lost the natural sap, unmoistened, not yielding liquid, nonliquid, exsuccous.

2. Sear, dried up, arid, parched, rainless, not fresh, having little *or* no rain, not green, droughty.

3. Craving drink, thirsty, suffering for water, desiring liquid, waterless.

4. Lacking interest, dry-as-dust, uninteresting, vapid, jejune, dull, insipid, tame, pointless, bare, tedious, tiresome, banal, humdrum, prosy, plain, prosaic, unembellished, bald, unadorned, lifeless,

wearisome, unprofitable, fruitless, sterile, meager.

5. Using a sly form of wit, satirical, quietly jocose, sarcastic, cynical, severe, sharp, keen, sly, humorous in an unemotional way.

6. Indifferent, cold, impersonal, aloof, remote, dry-eyed, tearless.

7. Favoring prohibition, teetotaling, temperate, abstemious.

8. Sunny, fair, pleasant, cloudless.

DRY, *v.* 1. Remove the moisture from, desiccate, exsiccate, dehydrate, draw out by evaporation, parch, free from moisture, exhaust the water of, make dry, stop the flow of, preserve, arefy, cure, torrefy, infumate, toast.

2. Become dry, lose moisture, dry up, become hard, shrivel for lack of moisture, wither, wilt.

3. Wipe away, sponge, swab, drain, blot.

DRYAD, *n.* Goddess who presides over woods, deity dwelling in trees, wood nymph, sylvan goddess, sylph, oread, hamadryad, sprite, treespirit.

DUAL, *adj.* Consisting of two parts, denoting two, relating to two, binary, double, twofold, dualistic, biform, geminate, binomial, composed of two, possessing two forms of existence, paired, duplicate, capable of separate attention, consisting of two natures capable of distinctive qualities, duplex, coupled, matched, conjugate, yoked, mated, united.

DUALISM, *n.* 1. State of consisting of two parts, state of being twofold, duality, twofoldness, doubleness, biformity, duplexity, polarity.

2. *(Theol.)* Doctrine that there are two independent divine beings of opposite nature, doctrine of two supreme principles *(good and evil),* Zoroastrianism, Manicheism, Mazdeism, Parseeism.

3. *(Philos.)* Theory holding that there are only two basic and irreducible principles *(mind and body),* doctrine that mind and matter are the two primal realities, natural realism.

DUB, *v.* 1. Strike lightly with a sword in knighting, designate as a knight, bestow the accolade, confer knighthood upon.

2. Invest with a title, confer a name upon, name, denominate, term, designate, style, entitle, call, christen, baptize, nickname, specify, define, characterize, label.

3. Rub to make smooth, smooth, dress, grease.

4. Thrust, poke, push, make a brisk beating.

DUBIETY, *n.* Doubtfulness, doubt, dubiosity, dubitation, incertitude, hesitation, suspense, fog, perplexity, indecision, vacillation, uncertainty, indetermination, ambiguity, quandary, dilemma, bewilderment, vagueness, haze.

DUBIOUS, *adj.* 1. Inclined to doubt, undecided, irresolute, uncertain, wavering in opinion, in a quandary, doubtful, fluctuating, vacillating, indecisive, puzzled, perplexed, bewildered, dilemma-ridden, hesitant.

2. Being a matter of doubt, unsure, difficult of explanation, equivocal, ambiguous, not clear, not plain, indefinite, vague, enigmatic, precarious, apocryphal, not yet settled, obscure, puzzling, perplexing, mysterious, cryptic, of uncertain outcome, undetermined, contingent, problematic, fallible, debatable, untrustworthy, unreliable, unauthentic.

3. Of doubtful propriety, questionable, loose, objectionable, infamous, scandalous, improper.

DUCK, *v.* 1. Plunge momentarily under water, immerse, dip, souse, throw into water, douse, wet thoroughly, baptize, submerge, drench.

2. Bow with a quick motion, lower suddenly, bob, stoop suddenly, make a jerking stoop, curtsy, kowtow, incline, make obeisance, salaam, cringe, yield.

3. Avoid, parry, dodge, recoil, steer clear of, shun, evade, elude, retreat.

DUCT, *n.* Vessel conveying a fluid, conduit, tube, canal, pipe, channel, main, culvert, alveus, flue, funnel, chimney.

DUCTILE, *adj.* 1. Capable of being drawn out, extensible, tensile, elastic, soft, plastic, tractile, capable of being hammered out thin, malleable.

2. Easily bent, flexible, pliant, pliable, supple, lithe, willowy, lissome, limber.

3. Easily led, capable of being molded *or* shaped, tractable, docile, compliant, facile, easy-going, yielding, susceptible, manageable, willing, acquiescent, disposed, persuadable, amenable.

DUCTILITY, *n.* 1. Property of some solids by which they can be extended by drawing out, extensibility, softness, pliableness, pliability, pliancy, malleability, tractility, plasticity, elasticity.

2. Pliancy of disposition, docility, yielding disposition, tractableness, flexibility, compliancy, facility, manageability, susceptibility, willingness, amenableness, acquiescence.

DUDE, *n.* Man unduly devoted to the niceties of dress, dandy, fop, dapper Dan, coxcomb, beau, exquisite, popinjay, swell, fastidious dresser, jack-a-dandy, macaroni, silk-stocking, silk-sock Sam, fine gentleman, toff, blade, spark, blood, buck, man-about-town, fribble, man milliner, carpet-knight, man of fashion, sharp-dresser, pink of fashion, male coquet, *arbiter elegantiae.*

DUDGEON, *n.* Feeling of offense, resentment, sullen displeasure, anger, indignation, ill will, ire, animosity, malice, umbrage, pique, rage, gall, spleen, churlishness, acerbity, sulks, huff, miff, soreness, virulence, bitterness, acrimony, bile, irascibility, choler, fume, rancor, crow to pluck.

DUDS, *n.* 1. Shabby articles of apparel, work clothes, old clothes, tattered garments, togs, raiment, gear, harness, rigging.

2. Little belongings, effects, traps, things, toggery, trappings, frippery.

DUE, *adj.* 1. Owing, to be paid, owed, unpaid, immediately payable, demandable, outstanding, in arrear, unrequited, that should be rendered, justly claimable, accrued.

2. Morally owed, proper, suitable, appropriate, fit, befitting, fitting, becoming, rightful, expedient, bounden, condign, such as is required by propriety, lawful, meet, merited, deserved, correct, equitable, seemly, beholden, sufficient, adequate, appointed, regular.

3. Owing to, attributable, assignable, ascribable, imputable, chargeable, answerable for.

4. Under engagement as to time, expected to be ready, expected to be present, expected to arrive, unrequited.

DUE, *n.* 1. That which is owed, that which should be paid, obligation, debt, legal charge, what is due, toll, duty, fee, tribute, legal exaction, tax, tariff, impost, levy, assessment.

2. Something which is rightfully required, lawful claim, right, desert, just title, privilege, merit.

DUEL, *n.* Prearranged combat between two persons, deadly contest between two people, affair of honor, *passage d'armes (Fr.),* single combat, struggle between two contending parties, clash of arms, engagement, satisfaction, hostile meeting, passage of arms.

DUENNA, *n.* Older woman serving as protector of a young lady, chaperon, governess, nurse, *ayah, amah,* strict female attendant, warder, guardian, custodian, watchdog, keeper, escort, castellan, third person.

DUGOUT, *n.* 1. Rough excavated shelter, rude dwelling excavated in a hillside and faced with logs, cave dug for shelter in the ground and roofed with logs, intrenchment, ditch, trench, hovel, fortification, shelter, barricade, excavation.

2. Boat made by hollowing out a log, kayak, canoe, dory, galliot.

DULCET, *adj.* 1. Pleasing to the ear, canorous, melodious, musical, harmonious, lyrical, tuneful, euphonious, symphonious, mellifluent, clear as a bell, silver-toned, silvery, soft.

2. Agreeable to the taste, delectable, sugary, sweet, saccharine, honeyed, nectareous, delicious, ambrosial, melliferous, delicately luscious to the taste.

3. Pleasing to the mind, pleasant, attractive, delightful, charming, agreeable, felicitous, lovely, enchanting, winsome, ravishing, sweet, soothing, solacing, tranquil, halcyon, calm, mellow.

DULL, *adj.* 1. Having a blunt edge, pointless, not sharp, blunt, not keen, dulled, obtuse, not acute, flat, not acuminate, unfit for cutting.

2. Slow of understanding, unintelligent, dull-witted, blunt-witted, slow in mental processes, obtuse, blockish, stupid, doltish, inapt, backward, lacking imagination, crass, stolid, brutish, dense, slow-witted, witless, thick-headed, vacuous, not smart, Boeotian, half-witted, undiscerning, purblind.

3. Insensible, unfeeling, apathetic, passionless, listless, spiritless, unimpassioned, callous, numb, phlegmatic, unresponsive, dead, lacking keenness of perception in the feelings.

4. Slow in action, not brisk, inert, inactive, not active, stagnant, heavy, lifeless, inanimate, torpid, languid, sluggish, heavy-footed.

5. Exciting little interest, uninteresting, tedious, uneventful, tiresome, wearisome, humdrum, drab, monotonous, irksome, causing ennui, flat, vapid, tasteless, bald, meager, dry, dry-as-dust, jejune, unimaginative, ordinary, run-of-the-mill, indifferent, commonplace, matter-of-fact, prosaic, prosy, flat-minded, trite, platitudinous.

6. Sad, gloomy, melancholy, overcast, dreary, dismal, somber, cheerless, cloudy, bleak, lowering, gray, leaden, murky, drab, sunless, dark.

7. Having little depth of color, lusterless, dim, lackluster, not bright, obscure, opaque, blurred, tarnished, colorless, matte, unglazed, lacking in intensity of color.

8. Muffled, muted, not clear, not distinct, not well-defined, deadened, softened.

DULL, *v.* 1. Render less keen the edge of, make less sharp, obtund, blunt, make blunt, take off the cutting edge.

2. Render insensible, stupefy, make lethargic, benumb, hebetate, render callous, deaden, besot, paralyze, make sluggish, make heavy, render less active.

3. Make less intense, quiet, allay, slack, soften, diminish the violence of, mollify, alleviate, quell, assuage, moderate, mitigate.

4. Discourage, dishearten, depress, throw cold water on, damp, dampen, deject, dispirit, make

gloomy, make dumpish, lay a wet blanket on, restrain, be indifferent, sag into the doldrums, mope.

5. Obscure, dim, bedim, darken, tarnish, sully, bedull, deaden, cloud, becloud, blur.

DULLARD, *n.* One slow to learn *or* perceive, sot, stupid person, dunce, simpleton, clump, oaf, dull fellow, moron, jolthead, dolt, blockhead, booby, ignoramus, fool, tomfool, coot, loggerhead, lout, numskull, stock, idiot, nitwit, witling, clodpate, hoddy-doddy, dunderhead, mooncalf, dotard.

DULY, *adv.* 1. In a due manner, in accordance with what is right *or* required, fitly, becomingly, befittingly, as is fitting, as is proper, decorously, in a suitable manner, rightly, deservingly.

2. In due season, punctually, regularly, at the proper time, in course.

3. Ex officio, de jure, by right.

DUMB, *adj.* 1. Unable to make articulate sounds, without the power of speech, unable to speak, aphonic, incapable of speech, voiceless, non-vocal, inarticulate, abmutescent.

2. Refraining from speaking, mute, silent, still, little addicted to speaking, reticent, taciturn, not using, words *or* sounds, speechless, done without speech, pantomimic, wordless, noiseless, tongue-tied, soundless, mum.

3. *(Colloq.)* Slow-witted, feather-brained, dull, stupid.

DUMFOUND, *v.* Strike dumb with amazement, dumfounder, take by surprise, confound, confuse, stupefy, astound, take aback, astonish, bewilder, amaze, aghast, stagger, flabbergast, stun, surprise, petrify, startle, dazzle, electrify, pose, embarrass, throw on one's beam ends, make one stare, take away one's breath, make one's hair stand on end.

DUMMY, *n.* 1. Mute, deaf-mute, dumb person, silent person.

2. *(Colloq.)* A stupid person, dolt, blockhead, oaf. (See DULLARD.)

3. Imitation, copy, counterfeit, sham, sample, model, substitute.

4. One put forward to act for others while ostensibly acting for himself, goat, scapegoat, double, alternative representative, agent.

DUMP, *v.* 1. Throw down in a mass, fling down, heap, drop heavily, deposit.

2. Empty out by tilting, unload, tipple.

3. Put on the market in large quantities and at a low price, offer for sale at low price, unload on a foreign market goods for which there is little demand at home, sell below ordinary trade rates, undersell.

DUMPS, *n.* Gloomy state of mind, despondency, low-spiritedness, dejection, sadness, blues, mopes, depression, blue devils, vapors, doldrums, gloom, melancholy, repining, drooping spirits, heaviness of heart, hypochondria, pessimism, prostration of soul, despair, moodiness, disconsolateness, Slough of Despond.

DUN, *adj.* 1. Of a dull dark-brown color, grayish-brown, yellowish-brown, muddy, sallow, swarthy, dirty, drab, dingy.

2. Dark, dim, dull, gloomy, cloudy, misty, muggy, fuliginous, obnubilated, overcast, leaden, crepuscular, lurid, livid, somber.

DUN, *v.* Press for the settlement of a debt, make insistent demands upon for payment of a debt, clamor for, urge, importune, require, trouble one for, ask, tax, sue, petition, solicit, call upon for, beseech, adjure, ply, beset.

DUNCE, *n.* Dull-witted person, stupid fellow, oaf, ignorant person, simpleton, tomfool, lout, dolt, fathead, ignoramus, numskull, blockhead, nitwit, thickhead, bullhead, halfwit, witling, dunderhead, dullard, clodpate, dunderpate, addlehead, moron, jolthead, chucklehead, beetlehead, clodpoll, idiot, clodhopper, shallow-brain, lack-brain, mooncalf, hoddy-doddy, booby, ninny, nincompoop, lackwit, changeling, imbecile, giddyhead, ninnyhammer, noodle, noddy, illiterate, innocent, ass, donkey, jackass, goose, calf, loon, stick, noncompos, silly boy, wooden spoon, bonehead, zany, thickskull, *badaud (Fr.), niais (Fr.),* lummox, gawk, clown, fool.

DUNE, *n.* Hill of loose drifting sand heaped by wind, sand ridge formed by the wind, a down, hog's back, mound, hummock, hillock, barrow, knoll, moor.

DUNG, *n.* Excrement, feces, ordure, *merde (Fr.),* manure, compost, sewage, muck, coprolite, guano.

DUNGEON, *n.* Dark underground chamber for close confinement, subterraneous prison, donjon, keep, strong cell, place of incarceration, bastille, vault, jail, cage, coop, den, "solitary," gaol, stir, confine, tower, oubliette, bridewell, clink, pound, jug, lockup, hold, black hole, pen, fold.

DUPE, *v.* Take advantage of the credulity of a person, make a dupe of, trick, cheat, hoodwink, delude, deceive, fool, befool, humbug, hoax, gull, bamboozle, beguile, outreach, overreach, outwit, take in, cully, cozen, chouse, circumvent, impose upon, make a fall guy of, victimize, mislead, defraud, swindle, play false, betray, steal a march on, put something over on, palm off on, throw dust in the eyes, bait, bilk, diddle, flimflam, best, gudgeon.

DUPE, *n.* A person who is deceived, credulous person, one who is misled through overcredulity, gull, victim of fraud, cully, victim of deception, easy mark, soft mark, sucker, pigeon, greenhorn, fall guy, cat's-paw, puppet, tool, laughingstock, butt, April fool, gudgeon.

DUPLICATE, *adj.* 1. Being exactly like another, corresponding to something else, made exactly in correspondence with a copy, similar, alike, made like an original, exactly like something else.

2. Duplex, bifold, double, twofold, consisting of two corresponding parts, growing in pairs, existing in two corresponding parts.

DUPLICATE, *n.* 1. Object similar in form and appearance to an original, copy exactly like an original, ectype, apograph, counterpart, facsimile, transcript, reproduction, imitation, counterfeit, replica.

2. Anything corresponding in all respects to something else, likeness, match, twin, second, fellow, mate, double.

3. Paper containing the same thing as another and having the force of an original, carbon.

DUPLICITY, *n.* Guile, artifice, chicanery, fraud, deceitfulness in speech *or* conduct, acting in two different ways concerning the same matter with intent to deceive, dishonesty, tricky doubleness in character, hypocrisy, cant, pharisaism, falseness, perfidy, evasion, double-dealing, Machiavelism, falsify, insincerity, equivocation, dissimulation, deception, deceit, casuistry, hollowness, flimflam, lip service, mental reservation, concealment, false coloring, mendacity, trickery, bad faith, Judas kiss.

DURABILITY, *n.* 1. Power of long resistance to

change, imperviousness to decay, lasting quality, durableness, endurance, persistence, preservation, changelessness, immutability, diuturnity, survival, perpetualness, everlastingness, longevity, duration, lastingness, permanence, stability, continuance, perdurability.

2. Age, eon, eternity, years, lifetime, long time, blue moon.

DURABLE, *adj.* Able to continue long in the same state, having the quality of enduring, having power to resist decay, impervious to change, not easily worn out, enduring, persisting, permanent, abiding, lasting, continuing, fixed, firm, chronic, stable, longstanding, constant, settled, long-lived, established, immovable, changeless, immutable, unfading, amaranthine, perdurable, imperishable, lifelong, perennial, perpetual, endless, everlasting, resistant, stout, strong, substantial, sound, holding up well.

DURANCE, *n.* Personal restraint, imprisonment, forced confinement, incarceration, duress, chains, captivity, custody, bondage, fetters, coarctation, bond.

DURATION, *n.* 1. Continuation in time, extent, continuance, perpetuation, everlastingness, lasting period, existence, endurance, permanence, long time, the whole time, blue moon.

2. Period of time during which anything lasts, length of time anything continues, extension in time, time, period, epoch, era, eon, cycle, space, age, course, stretch, term, date, stage, span, spell, season, while.

DURESS, *n.* 1. Constraint of personal action by force, compulsion, coercion, coaction, cohibition, enforcement, discipline, control.

2. Forcible restraint of liberty, durance vile, incarceration, captivity, imprisonment, detention, confinement, coarctation, quarantine, keep, care, custody, restringency, curb, arrest, bondage, lock, fetters, bonds, shackles, irons, handcuffs, pinions, manacles, stocks, straitjacket, gyves, bolts, bars, padlock.

DURING, *prep.* Throughout the continuance of, for the period of, within the time of, for the time of, at some period throughout the course of, pending, continuing, within, while, until, over, through, in the course of, in the time of.

DUSK, *n.* State between light and darkness, even, condition of partial darkness, twilight, crepuscule, approach of darkness, oncoming of night, edge of night, nightfall, gloom, eventide, shadowiness, rushlight, firelight, shade, eveningtide, gloaming, sunset, obscurity, blind man's holiday, *entre chien et loup* (Fr.).

DUSKY, *adj.* 1. Rather dark in coloring, darkish, tending to darkness, somewhat dark, fuscous, swarthy, swart, tawny, sable, black.

2. Deficient in light, feebly lighted, obscure, dim, dim-lighted, murky, gloomy, shadowy, misty, tenebrous, atramentous, shady, cloudy, overcast, veiled, unilluminated, fuliginous, dingy, somber, caliginous, mysterious, opaque.

DUST, *n.* 1. Pulverized earthy matter, earth in fine dry particles, substance reduced to powder, powdery dirt, finely powdered substance, cloud of finely powdered matter, ash, soot, smoke, smudge, culm, smut, grime, filth, soil, dirt, detritus, lint, grittiness, sandiness, arenosity, granulation, sand, grit, sawdust, filing.

2. Elementary substances, ashes, grave, corpse, skeleton, bones, carcass, dry bones, relics, earth,

remains, clay, fossils, dead body, that to which anything is reduced by disintegration.

3. Low and despised condition, anything worthless, rubbish.

4. Confusing cloud of words, turmoil, ruckus, controversy, disturbance, stir.

DUST, *v.* 1. Free from dust, wipe the dust from, brush dust away from, clear from dust, cleanse, sweep out.

2. Sprinkle with powder, dab, strew, speckle, fleck.

3. Soil with dust, dirty, spot, smear, smudge, daub, make dirty, drabble, bemire, besmear, befoul, sully, stain.

4. Reduce to dust, levigate, pulverize, crumble, comminute, granulate, triturate, disintegrate.

DUTIFUL, *adj.* 1. Performing the duties required of one, duteous, conscientious, punctilious, docile, tractable, amenable, compliant, moral, virtuous, ethical, righteous, laudable, observant of the obligations of one's position.

2. Expressive of a sense of duty, deferential, reverent, submissive to one's superiors, respectful, filial, pious.

DUTY, *n.* 1. That which one is bound to do by moral obligation, that which one ought to do, moral obligation, bounden duty, responsibility, devoir.

2. Binding force of that which is morally right, oughtness, right, righteousness, incumbency, integrity.

3. Action required by one's position, function, service, work, office, business, engagement, trust, calling, mission, occupation, commission, charge, assignment, routine, task, part.

4. Conduct due to a superior, deference, act of respect, homage, respect, obedience, expression of respectful consideration, reverence, allegiance, fealty.

5. Levy imposed by law on the import *or* export of goods, tariff, assessment, impost, tax, customs, excise, toll, charge, due, rate.

DWARF, *n.* Human being much below ordinary stature, one checked in growth, unnaturally small person, adult human less than four feet tall, tiny replica of the ordinary species, diminutive being, organism smaller than is common to its species, Lilliputian, pygmy, bantam, manikin, Pigwiggen, homunculus, midget, hop-o'-my-thumb, runt, doll, chit, puppet, Negrillo, Negrito, pigwidgeon, pixy, dapperling, fingerling, cock-sparrow, sprite, Tom Thumb, elf, brownie, leprechaun, troll, gnome, imp, goblin, kobold, nis, nixie, droich.

DWARF, *v.* 1. Prevent the due development of, keep below the natural development, stunt, hinder from growth, make dwarfish, atrophy, bedwarf, cramp, restrain the growth of, reduce, diminish, arrest, make diminutive.

2. Become stunted *or* smaller, be little, grow less, dwindle, contract, shrink, shrivel.

3. Overshadow, render smaller, cause to appear small in size by comparison.

DWARFISH, *adj.* Like a dwarf, of unusually small stature, below the ordinary size, nanoid, stunted, undersized, pollard, scrubby, diminutive, dumpy, squat, minikin, tiny, wee, little, miniature, small, Lilliputian, pygmean, elfin, puny, short, runty, undeveloped, atrophied, deformed, minute.

DWELL, *v.* 1. Take up one's abode, live as a settled resident, inhabit, abide as a permanent resident, have a fixed habitation, reside, live in, domicile, sojourn, stay, room, bunk, lodge, tenant, hang out, tarry, be settled, quarter, put up at, have a habitation, tent, keep house, tabernacle, remain, settle, pitch tent, nestle, roost, burrow, hive, perch, encamp, bivouac, people.

2. Continue for a time, linger over in thought *or* words, emphasize, continue long upon, occupy a long time with, pause, expatiate, descant, tarry over, harp on, insist upon.

3. Be deeply interested, hang upon fondly, be absorbed with, be engrossed in.

DWELLER, *n.* One who has a settled place of abode, permanent resident, residiary, habitant, inhabitant, denizen, indweller, occupier, occupant, inhabiter, citizen, householder, lodger, boarder, roomer, abider, tenant, sojourner.

DWELLING, *n.* 1. House occupied as a residence, building used for human habitation, family abode, dwelling house, residence, edifice, establishment, building, place of abode, place of residence, cot, domicile, lodging, quarters, headquarters, place, mansion, villa, cottage, lodge, hermitage, home, country seat, chateau, chalet, castle, tabernacle, pavilion, hotel, manor house, hall, palace, hovel, hut, dugout, hutch, shanty, cabin, shack, hearth, crib, log house, den, cave, ingleside, chimney corner, homestead, hole, lair, barrack, rookery, court, hiding place, cell, eyrie, hive, covert, nest, perch, roost, nidus, tent, wigwam, tepee, igloo, bower, arbor, tenement, bungalow, maisonette, apartment house, flat, suite, kiosk, ranch house, hacienda, farmstead, grange, plantation.

2. Habitual residence, haunt,' resort, refuge, asylum, continued residence.

DWINDLE, *v.* 1. Become smaller and smaller, become less, diminish, lessen, decrease, grow less, grow little, shrink, peter out, disappear, evanesce, vanish.

2. Fall off in quality, decline, waste away, degenerate, fall away from a normal *or* proper condition, sink, decay, crumble, wear, wane, ebb, subside, shrivel, collapse, wizen, fritter, peak.

3. Make smaller and smaller, cause to shrink, attenuate, make less, draw in, narrow, contract, shrink, curtail, shorten, abbreviate, condense, dwarf, reduce, abridge.

DYE, *v.* Fix a color in the substance by soaking in boiling liquid coloring-matter, treat with a dye, color, stain, tinge, impregnate, imbue, ingrain, wash, tinct, tint, tincture, paint, hue, tone, daub, impart color by means of a dye, color by staining with coloring-matter.

DYE, *n.* Fluid used for dyeing, color, tint, hue, tinge, tincture, stain, pigment, paint, shade, cast, tone, coloration, wash, aniline, ingrain, liquid containing coloring for imparting a particular hue to something.

DYING, *n.* Departure from the present life, life's ebb, extinction of life, decease, death, demise, exit from life, dissolution, end of life, release from life, passing away, debt of Nature, Jordan, extremity, obsolescence, Stygian shore, the great adventure, "crossing the bar," jaws of death, last breath, valley of the shadow, last gasp, swan song, death rattle, death watch, death's door, death throes.

DYING, *adj.* 1. Departing from the present life, approaching death, ceasing to live, expiring, near to death, moribund, at the point of death, failing, at death's door, manifested just before death, associated with death, *in extremis (Lat.)*, with one foot in the grave, commorient, at the last

gasp, in the death throes, in the jaws of death, on one's last legs, on one's death, near one's end, tottering on the brink of the grave, gradually drawing to a close, waning, passing.

2. Destined to death, mortal, perishable.

DYNAMIC, *adj.* 1. Pertaining to motion as the result of force, not static, impelling, propulsive, pertaining to forces not in equilibrium, driving, characterized by mechanical force.

2. Characterized by effective action, forceful, active, producing activity, high-powered, potent, puissant, omnipotent, all-powerful, efficacious, vigorous, effectual, efficient, effective, galvanic, magnetic, electric, energetic, almighty, powerful, capable, potential, motive, peppy, trenchant.

DYNASTY, *n.* 1. Sequence of rulers from the same family *or* stock, race of rulers, ruling house, family of sovereigns, succession of royalty, rule of such a succession, era, time.

2. Government, dominion, sovereignty, empire, suzerainty, lordship, reign, regnancy, seignority, regime, mastery, hegemony, dictation, command, sway, rule, control, authority, influence, power, prerogative, jurisdiction, divine right, dynastic rights, absolutism.

DYSENTERY, *n.* Infectious disease marked by inflammation of the lower part of the bowels, severe inflammation of the mucous membrane of the large intestine, diarrhea, looseness, cacation, flux, defecation, evacuation, dejection *(Med.).*

DYSPEPSIA, *n.* Impaired digestion, indigestion, painful chronic digestion, difficulty of digestion.

DYSPHORIA, *n.* Restlessness characteristic of the sick, state of anxiety, fidgets, *Unruhe (Ger.),* malaise, dissatisfaction.

E

EACH, *pron.* 1. Every one of several considered individually, individual, personal, specific, private, separate, respective, particular.

2. One and the other of two, both, all.

EACH, *adv.* Respectively, apiece, severally, per capita, individually, seriatim, separately, one by one, personally, in detail.

EAGER, *adj.* 1. Ardent in desire, impatiently longing, fervent, fervid, perfervid, sanguine, hot, glowing, impassioned, passionate, warm, cordial, excited, hearty, animated, vehement, importunate, burning, intensely desirous, anxious, intent, keen in feeling, earnest, impetuous, enthusiastic, agog, zealous, avid, fain, yearning, greedy, ravenous, open-mouthed, intense, emulous, solicitous, alive, prone, prurient, hasty, spirited, vaulting.

2. Go-ahead, wide-awake, strenuous, diligent, up-and-coming, enterprising, pushing, aggressive, resolute, sedulous, industrious, ambitious, hard-working, persevering, bustling, studious.

EAGERLY, *adv.* 1. Heartily, cordially, fervently, sincerely, earnestly, fainly, gladly, willingly, *con amore*, with all the heart, with heart and soul, from the bottom of one's heart, keenly, longingly, impatiently.

2. Strenuously, actively, briskly, zealously, in full swing, vigorously, intently, with might and main, with life and spirit, with all one's might, full tilt.

EAGERNESS, *n.* 1. Ardent desire, ardor, fervor, warmth, yearning, longing, intensity, intentness, *empressement (Fr.)*, earnestness, devotion, zeal, devotedness, covetousness, avidity, impetuosity, voracity, greediness, fervency, anxiety, appetite, enthusiasm, heartiness, impatience, vehemence, hastiness, solicitude, keenness, sharpness.

2. Enterprise, exertion, activity, energy, vigor, forwardness, ambition, industry, assiduousness, assiduity, perseverance, diligence, application, go, persistence, promptitude, dispatch, alacrity, vim, liveliness, snap, dash, briskness, life, animation, spirit, agility, expedition, bustle, flurry, quickness, stir.

EAGLE, *n.* 1. Aquila, diurnal bird of prey, bird of Jove, falconoid bird, eaglet, falcon, vulture, hawk, golden eagle, bald eagle, black eagle, ern, harpy eagle, sea eagle, erne, ringtail, sore-eagle, griffin *(Mythol.).*

2. Military standard, ensign.

3. Ten-dollar gold coin.

EAGLE-EYED, *adj.* Sharp-sighted, quick-sighted, keen-sighted, far-seeing, hawk-eyed, Argus-eyed, lynx-eyed, clear-sighted, perspicacious, discerning.

EAR, *n.* 1. Organ of hearing, auditory apparatus, acoustic organ, eardrum, labyrinth, auricle, shell, tympanum, pinna, concha, cannon.

2. Lug, handle, knob, knocker, projection.

3. Musical perception, refined sense of hearing, nice perception of the differences of sound, sense of hearing, sensitiveness to the quality of musical sounds.

4. Earshot, carrying distance, reach, hearing distance, sound, hearing.

5. Favorable attention, audience, observance, audition, heed, regard, alertness, intentness, note, thought, advertency, recognition.

6. The part of a cereal plant which contains the flowers, head, spike of grain.

EARACHE, *n.* Pain in the middle *or* internal ear, otalgia, otalgy.

EARED, *adj.* Having earlike appendages, aurate, auriculate, spiked, spiciferous.

EARLY, *adj.* 1. Among the first in a series, being near the beginning of any stated period of time, occurring in the first part of some division, swift, in season, seasonable, timely, opportune, in good time, timeous, punctual, prompt, speedy, sudden, expeditious, alacritous, instantaneous, immediate, instant.

2. About to happen in the near future, near in the future, soon to occur, imminent, coming, impending, overhanging, threatening, at hand, near.

3. Occurring in advance of the usual time, too much before the time, premature, precocious, forward, needlessly before the time, before the appointed time, untimely, inopportune, previous to the necessary time, advanced, anticipatory, preceding, precipitate, unexpected.

4. Belonging to a period far back in time, ancient, primitive, aboriginal, archaic, obsolete.

5. Before the day has advanced very far, at an early hour in the day, dawning, matutinal, youthful.

EARLY, *adv.* 1. During the first part of some division of time, in good time, near the beginning of a particular period of time, in good season, seasonably, on time, on the dot, punctually.

2. Before long, soon, anon, betimes, ere long, straightway, presently, offhand, directly, by and by, at short notice, on the spur of the moment, extempore, on the spot, on the instant, at sight, at once, speedily, quickly, instantaneously, apace,

forthwith, plump, immediately, promptly, shortly, suddenly.

3. In anticipation, unexpectedly, unawares, in advance of the usual *or* appointed time, hastily, precociously, prematurely, beforehand, too soon, forehandedly, precipitately.

4. Far back in time, previously, heretofore, hitherto, erenow.

5. At dawn, at daybreak, matutinally.

EARMARK, *v.* 1. Mark with an earmark, make an earmark on, mark in a distinctive way, crop, dog's-ear.

2. Set aside for a specific use, mark and hold for a particular purpose, reserve.

EARN, *v.* 1. Gain by labor *or* service, get as one's due, make money by, turn a penny, gather, gain as due return, secure, acquire, coin money, pick up, collect, glean, reap and carry, net, bag, bring home, make the pot boil, bring grist to the mill, draw, harvest, profit, clear, obtain a return, win, receive, attain, achieve, realize, procure.

2. Merit as compensation, deserve, be entitled to.

EARNEST, *adj.* 1. Sincerely zealous, animated, enthusiastic, glowing, ardent, fervent, perfervid, importunate, passionate, impassioned, heartfelt, eager, hearty, warm, cordial, vehement, spirited, intense, anxious, emphatic, deep-felt, profound, whole-hearted, showing depth and sincerity of feeling.

2. Serious in intention, intent in purpose, firm, fixed, stable, steady, constant, strong-willed, staid, self-possessed, sincere, diligent, purposeful, sober, determined, resolute, having a purpose, steadily eager in pursuing a purpose, devoted, assiduous, thoughtful, solemn.

3. Having serious importance, urgent, pressing, demanding serious attention, requiring careful consideration, important, weighty, momentous, critical, crucial, imperative, exigent, strenuous, grave.

EARNEST, *n.* 1. Seriousness of intention *or* purpose, good faith, reality, truth, sincerity, grave and intense attention.

2. Indication of what may be expected in the future, foretaste, pledge, first-fruits, adumbration, promise, token.

3. Portion given in advance as a pledge of the remainder, money given to bind a contract, gage, payment that gives assurance of what is to follow, handsel, earnest-money, surety, security, pawn, guaranty, warranty, installment, deposit, stake.

EARNESTNESS, *n.* 1. Cordiality, fervency, gusto, fervor, unction, vehemence, heartiness, warmth, ardor, intensity, zeal, passion, verve, enthusiasm, *empressement (Fr.)*, sincerity, eagerness, spirit, devotion, intentness, keenness, fidelity, good will.

2. Gravity, solemnity, sobriety, seriousness, urgency, matter of life and death, press, stress.

3. Resolution, determination, firmness, vigor, steadfastness, constancy, perseverance, obstinacy, persistence, tenacity, stamina, backbone, energy, sand, grit, iron-will, strength of mind, stick-to-itiveness.

EARNINGS, *n.* Money earned, wages, winnings, profits, compensation to which one has a claim for services rendered, income, proceeds, innings, clean-up, pickings, perquisite, desert, emolument, reward, salary, revenue, hire, returns of any economic good for an economic service *(Pol. Econ.),* pay.

EARRING, *n.* Pendant, eardrop, girandole, stud, ornamental jewel fastened in the ear with a screw.

EARTH, *n.* 1. The planet we inhabit, the planet third in order from the sun, planet in the solar system, globe on which we dwell, world, sphere, terrestrial ball, terraqueous globe, orb, firmament, terra, terrene, universe, wide world.

2. The solid matter of this planet, solid surface of the globe, dry land, ground, soil, turf, clod, *terra firma*, glebe, loam, sod, humus, dirt, clay, marl, gravel, mold, subsoil, sand, mud, carpet *(aviation term)*.

3. Those who inhabit the globe, inhabitants of this planet, mankind, people, the world at large.

4. Worldly matters, mundane interests, human affairs, temporal pursuits, transient interests, material things, secular affairs, worldly aims.

EARTHBORN, *adj.* 1. Born out of the earth, of earthly origin, sprung from the earth, terrigenous, autochthonous, indigenous, anthropoid, human, worldly.

2. Meanly born, of low birth, mean, abject, base, groveling, earthly, of ignoble extraction, low.

3. Mortal, perishable, ephemeral, unspiritual, of terrestrial birth, transient, merely temporal, passing.

EARTHEN, *adj.* Made of earth, made of burnt clay, made of baked clay, fictile, mud, dirt, clay, stone, rock.

EARTHENWARE, *n.* Earthen pottery, vessels of baked clay, ceramics, ceramic ware, crockery, porcelain, majolica, terra cotta, stoneware, china, Satsuma ware, gombroon, Sèvres, faience, delft, delf, crouch ware, salt-glazed ware, Wedgwood, crown Derby,Spode, Staffordshire, Dresden ware, Leeds ware, Meissen ware, Worcester ware, black ware, Lowestoft ware, Limoges, Allervale, white ware, eggshell porcelain, crackle, ironstone ware, willowware, della Robbia, luster ware, basaltes, biscuit, bisque.

EARTHLY, *adj.* 1. Worldly, terrestrial, terrene, terraqueous, sublunary, telluric, tellurian, earthy, subastral, mundane, alluvial.

2. Worldly-minded, earthly-minded, temporal, not exalted, unspiritual, secular, ungodly, bodily, physical, natural, corporeal, material, devoted to the advantages of this present life, mercenary, venal, moneygrubbing, pleasure-loving, vile, low, in contrast with what is heavenly, fleshly, sensual, carnal, gross, base, earthborn, sordid, groveling, mean.

3. That can be found anywhere on the earth, possible, imaginable, conceivable, in the world.

EARTHQUAKE, *n.* Movement of a part of the earth's surface due to the faulting of rocks, sudden undulation of the earth's crust, volcanic quake, seism, earth tremor, temblor, microseism, earth shock, shaking of the ground, volcanic eruption, upheaval, cataclysm.

EARTHWORK, *n.* Fortification made largely of earth, excavation and embankment of earth, fort, intrenchment, breastwork, muniment, ditch, dike, moat, fosse, dugout, parapet, mound, field-work, contravallation, bastion, rampart, bulwark, redan, redoubt, trench, rifle-pit.

EARTHWORM, *n.* 1. Annelid worm that burrows in soil, burrowing terrestrial megadrilic worm, angleworm, dewworm, wiggling chemist below the soil.

2. A mean sordid person, niggard, churl, miser, curmudgeon, pinchpenny.

EARTHY, *adj.* 1. Of the nature of soil, made of earth, terrene, earthlike, clayey, glebous, cloddy, muddy, sandy, dusty.

2. Unrefined, coarse, roughish, dull, lackluster.

3. Gross, material, carnal, sensual, groveling, low.

EAR TRUMPET, *n.* Instrument to collect and concentrate sound, otophone, sonifer, device for intensifying sounds as an aid in defective hearing, auricle.

EASE, *n.* 1. Relaxed physical condition, tranquil rest, freedom from labor *or* effort, repose, still, tranquility, quiescence, leisure, relaxation, solace, easement, quietude, quietness, restfulness, relief, assuagement, state of being comfortable.

2. Quiet state of mind, peace of mind, peace, freedom from concern, content, serenity, gladness, enjoyment, complacency, satisfaction, happiness, contentment, gratification, calmness, consolation, security.

3. Ability to do something without effort, snap, knack, address, dexterity, skill, flair, expertness, facility, readiness, easiness, fluency, capability, adroitness, quickness, ability, aptness, mere child's play, smooth sailing, cinch.

4. Freedom from affectation, unaffectedness, naturalness, freedom from formality, liberty of action, unembarrassment, unconstraint, lightness, freedom from constraint, flexibility, informality, unconcern, affability.

5. Well-being, prosperity, blessings, hedonism, comfort, luxury, luxuriousness, lap of luxury, bed of roses, purple and fine linen, creature comforts, affluence, opulence, fat of the land, milk and honey, bed of down, silken pillow, velvet, clover.

EASE, *v.* 1. Give rest to, make comfortable, set at ease, give repose to, tranquilize, relax, quiet, free from anxiety, calm, still, pacify, smooth the ruffled brow of care, take off a load of care, set free, disburden.

2. Render less painful, give relief to, alleviate, relieve, lighten, assuage, lessen, allay, palliate, mitigate, mollify, appease, soothe, pour balm into, adulce, soften, diminish, abate, subside, smooth, ameliorate, console, comfort, encourage, cheer.

3. Reduce tension, release from pressure, give more room, loosen, slacken, maneuver gently *or* carefully, adjust by slight gradual movements.

4. Render less difficult, make easy, facilitate, lighten the labor, expedite, favor.

5. Relieve by force, rob, deprive, dispossess.

EASILY, *adv.* 1. In an easy manner, smoothly, with ease, without difficulty, with no effort, hands down, without trouble, facilely, skilfully, readily, dexterously, adroitly, glibly, swimmingly.

2. Beyond question, unquestionably, far and away, undoubtedly, beyond the shadow of a doubt.

EASINESS, *n.* 1. Ease of manner, carelessness, nonchalance, casualness, informality, familiarity, naturalness, facility, affability, freedom from constraint.

2. Simplicity, readiness, lightness, gentleness, grace.

3. Credulity, gullibility, proneness to believe, susceptibility to influence, credulousness.

EAST, *n.* 1. Cardinal point of the compass 90 degrees to the right of North, that point of the compass at which the sun rises at the equinox, rising sun, dawn, aurora, point of the compass which lies at the right hand when one faces the North.

2. Orient, Asia collectively, Near East, Far East, Middle East, Asia Minor, Levant.

3. (U.S. Geog.) Atlantic portion of the United States, the region east of the Mississippi River.

EASTER, *n.* Christian festival commemorating the resurrection of Christ, *Ostern (Ger.), Pâques (Fr.), Pascua florida (Sp.), Pasqua (It.),* paschal festival.

EASTERN, *adj.* Lying toward the east, situated in the east, easterly, eastward, east, Oriental, Levantine, auroral.

EASY, *adj.* 1. That may be accomplished without difficulty, requiring no great effort, presenting few difficulties, not burdensome, light, simple, plain sailing, easily done, slight, effortless.

2. Free from worry *or* care, tranquil, without anxiety, untroubled, relieved, unworried, quiet, satisfied, well-pleased, contented, at ease, secure, comfortable, leisurely, carefree, unconcerned, careless.

3. Not hard to persuade, susceptible, not hard to handle, not difficult to influence, complaisant, yielding without a struggle, tractable, amenable, docile, accommodating, compliant, manageable, acquiescent, submissive, facile, credulous, willing.

4. Free from formality, not formal, informal, unconstrained, free from affectation, unaffected, agreeably natural, graceful, suave, urbane, genial, gracious, cordial, smooth, fluent, unforced, free from embarrassment.

5. Not tight, fitting loosely, flowing, smooth.

6. Not harsh, not strict, gentle, unexacting, moderate, not oppressive, lenient, indulgent, mild, light, temperate, unburdensome, convenient, soft, not forced, not hurried.

7. Well-to-do, in comfortable circumstances, not financially straitened, affluent, possessed of a sufficient competence, free from material cares.

EASYGOING, *adj.* Taking the world easily, calm, taking matters in an easy way, careless, carefree, comfortably unconcerned, phlegmatic, apathetic, unconcerned, nonchalant, insouciant, inexcitable, pococurante, heedless, listless, jog-trot, temperate, patient, uncritical, happy-go-lucky, cheerful, not particular, satisfied, mild-tempered, pacific, cool, placid, tranquil, serene, unruffled.

EAT, *v.* 1. Take in as nourishment, partake of for the purpose of appeasing hunger, masticate, bolt, chew and swallow for nourishment, mandicate, ingest, devour, consume, engorge, gorge, crunch, dispatch, gulp, nibble, gobble up, batten upon, champ, munch, bite, ruminate, digest.

2. Rust, corrode, make a hole by gnawing, gnaw at, consume by devouring, ravage, destroy, devastate, demolish, waste away, bore into, use up, act corrosively.

3. Consume food, fare, take a meal, feed, take sustenance, take food, gratify the appetite, lunch, breakfast, dine, sup, take nourishment, refresh the inner man, break bread, tuck away food, fall to, tuck in, banquet, feast, gormandize.

EATABLE, *adj.* Fit to eat, good to eat, esculent, edible, comestible, ciborious, gustable, dietetic, gastronomically pleasurable, nutritive, alimentary.

EATER, *n.* One who eats, luncher, diner, gorger, gourmet, gourmand, devourer, consumer, glutton, epicure.

EATING HOUSE, *n.* A house where food is

served to be eaten on the premises, restaurant, lunch bar, lunch room, dining hall, café, buffet, public house, diner, chophouse, hashhouse, coffee shop, tavern, hotel, inn, cafeteria, automat, one-arm joint *(slang).*

EAU, *n.* Spirituous waters, cologne, perfume, cordial.

EAVES, *n.* Projecting edge of a roof serving to shed rainwater, overhanging lower edge of a roof, rim, balcony.

EAVESDROP, *v.* Give ear clandestinely, prick up one's ears, listen stealthily, overhear, wiretap, try to overhear private conversation, bend an ear, harken, listen in.

EAVESDROPPER, *n.* Listener, hearer, auditor of private conversation, wiretapper, delator, sleuth, Peeping Tom, Paul Pry, gossip.

EBB, *v.* 1. Flow back toward the ocean, recede, flow away, withdraw, regress, retire, retrocede, subside, fall away, abate, retrace, go back, move back, retreat, fall back.

2. Waste away, decline, wane, sink, decrease, fade away, crumble, decay, shrink, deteriorate, dwindle, languish.

EBB, *n.* 1. Recession of tide-water to the ocean, ebb tide, neap tide, spring tide, low tide, outflow, low water, falling of the tide, reflux, flowback of the tide, retrocession, regression, retrogression, refluence, recession, retreat, reflow, outgo.

2. Point of decline, low state *or* condition, decay, decline, deterioration, caducity, subsidence, degeneration, waning.

3. Diminution, decrease, decrement, abatement.

EBON, *adj.* Like ebony, very black, dark, inky, sable, pitchy, swarthy, atramentous, fuliginous, jetty, jet-black, coal-black, sooty, dusky, swart, Ethiopic.

EBONY, *n.* 1. Durable black wood from various tropical trees, hard wood, heavy durable wood, dark wood.

2. Color of ebony, jet, ink, coal, pitch, soot, charcoal, lampblack.

EBULLIENCE, *n.* 1. Ebulliency, boiling over, bubbling over, ebullition, effervescence.

2. Excitement, agitation, overenthusiasm, rush, impetuosity, ferment, bursting vigor, overflow, bursting forth, outburst.

EBULLIENT, *adj.* Boiling up and over, foaming, effervescent, agitated, in a ferment, gushing, hot, effusive, bubbling with enthusiasm, seething with excitement, irrepressible, excited, sparkling, fiery, overflowing with fervor, enthusiastic, exhilarated, manifesting exhilaration, vivacious, ardent, aglow, glowing, red-hot, wrought up, overdemonstrative, feverish.

EBULLITION, *n.* 1. Boiling up, bubbling over, seething, effervescing, exestuation, fermentation, estuation, elixation, decoction.

2. Rushing forth in a state of agitation, stir, excitability, impetuosity, vehemence, turbulence, agitation, excitement, splutter, bustle, commotion, perturbation, bluster, ferment, disquietude.

3. Seething of passion, overflowing of feeling, outburst, paroxysm, fit, outbreak, throe, spasm, convulsion, passion, rage, storm, anger, explosion.

ECCE, *interj.* Lo, behold, lo and behold.

ECCENTRIC, *adj.* 1. Departing from the usual course, peculiar, singular, strange, extraordinary, abnormal, irregular, anomalous, odd, uncommon, queer, quaint, aberrant, unnatural, preternatural, unwonted, bohemian, unorthodox, bizarre, stray, unusual, unique, *sui generis (Lat.),* outlandish, curious, wayward, erratic, cranky, *tombé des nues (Fr.),* crotchety, whimsical, egregious, original, funny *(coll.),* nutty *(sl.),* out of the common run, out of the beaten track, unconventional, idiosyncratic, fantastic, grotesque, *outré (Fr.),* laughable, droll, freakish, deviating from the recognized *or* usual character, differing conspicuously from one's fellows.

2. Deviating from a circular form, parabolic, elliptic, hyperbolic, displaced with respect to a center, decentered, not in the center, having the axis away from the center, far from the center.

3. Not having the same center, with different centers, deviating, circuitous.

ECCENTRIC, *n.* One who is peculiar, one who differs from conventionality, odd fellow, person of queer habits, queer fellow, crank, crackpot, bohemian, character *(coll.),* original, nonesuch, nondescript, monomaniac, unusual person, freak, oddity, fanatic, crotcheteer.

ECCENTRICITY, *n.* 1. Quality of being strikingly different from one's fellows, characteristic marked by oddity, deviation from customary conduct, peculiarity, oddity of conduct, quirk, mannerism, twist, crotchet, idiosyncrasy, *bizarrerie (Fr.),* singularity, irregularity, anomaly, abnormality, unconventionality, queerness, quaintness, oddness, unconformity, bohemianism, freakishness, waywardness, whimsicality, strangeness, aberration.

2. Deviation from circularity, flattening, kink, oblateness, ellipticity.

ECCLESIA, *n.* 1. Body of Christians organized for worship and religious works, congregation, church.

2. In ancient Greece a popular political assembly of the citizens.

ECCLESIASTIC, *n.* One officially set apart for the service of the church, cleric, clergyman, nun, minister, rector, pastor, parson, preacher, priest, father, padre, abbé, curé, divine, hierarch, canon, churchman, presbyter, hierophant, curate, friar, ecclesiarch, eminence, reverence, primate, vicar, prebendary, chaplain, deacon, prelate, missionary, dean, person in holy orders, "religious," monk, theologian, revivalist, black coat, confessor, sky pilot.

ECCLESIASTICAL, *adj.* Relating to the church *or* clergy, of the church, churchly, clerical, not secular, religious, not lay, ministerial, spiritual, sacerdotal, canonical, apostolic, pastoral, papistic, priestly, hierarchical, episcopal, pontifical.

ECHO, *v.* 1. Emit an echo, resound with an echo, give back a sound, reflect the sound of, ring, be repeated by an echo, reply, reëcho, return the sound of, reverberate.

2. Imitate the words *or* sentiments of another person, repeat, reproduce faithfully, copy, mock, mirror, reflect, iterate, reiterate, duplicate, peal, reduplicate, rehearse, chorus, mimic, ape, match, simulate, take off, personate, do like, follow, take after, parallel.

ECHO, *n.* 1. A sound given back by an opposing surface and returned to its source, reflection of sound, repercussion of sound, iteration, return, reverberation.

2. Close imitation, parrotism, parrotry, reëcho, assenting repetition, reproduction of another's views, copying, mimicking, quotation.

3. Sympathetic response, immediate and hearty reply.

4. One who imitates another, mimic, parrot, imitator, poll, copyist, mocking bird.

ECLAT, *n.* 1. Brilliance of conduct *or* action, showiness of achievement, splendor, luster, show, striking effect, effect, pomp, pageantry, parade, ostentation.

2. Outburst of admiring applause, acclamation, burst of approval.

3. Renown, celebrity, glory, honor, reputation, praise, high repute, distinction, note, notability, fame, vogue, popularity, *aura popularis (Lat.),* *succès d'estime (Fr.),* prestige, talk of the town, toast of the town, illustriousness.

4. Notoriety, public exposure, publicity, scandal.

ECLECTIC, *adj.* 1. Selective, excerptive, picking, selecting, choosing from various sources.

2. Made up of what is selected from diverse sources, not following any one system, composed of selections, anthological.

3. Advocating eclecticism, broad in matters of taste and belief, liberal, catholic, comprehensive.

ECLIPSE, *v.* 1. Darken, cloud, becloud, obscure, dim, bedim, veil, cast a shadow upon, shroud, shade, conceal, hide from view, overcast.

2. Extinguish, annihilate, put out, blot out, douse *(coll.).*

3. Make dim by comparison, surpass, outshine, overshadow, outdo, throw into the shade, excel, transcend, exceed, outstrip, cast into the shadow, dim the brightness of, outrival, outvie, put out of competition.

ECLIPSE, *n.* 1. Interception of light, obscuration of light, penumbra, dimming, occultation, hiding, darkening, veiling, clouding, shrouding, shadow, solar eclipse, lunar eclipse, total eclipse, partial eclipse, annular eclipse, central eclipse, vanishing, concealment.

2. Overshadowment, loss of brilliance, loss of splendor, state of being outshone, change from a reputable to a dishonored state.

3. Extinction, annihilation, destruction, blotting out, extinguishment, obliteration.

ECLOGUE, *n.* Dialogue poem with shepherds as principal speakers, short poem upon rural life and scenes, pastoral poem, bucolic, georgic, idyl, short idyllic poem, lyric.

ECONOMIC, *adj.* 1. Pertaining to the distribution and use of income and wealth, pertaining to money matters *or* wealth, relating to the science of economics, relating to the management of the affairs of a government *or* community, concerning public *or* private economy, concerning political economy, plutonomic, plutological.

2. Practical in application, pertaining to the household and housekeeping, pertaining to the means and methods of living well and wisely, utilitarian, housewifely.

3. Economical, avoiding extravagance, saving, thrifty, economizing, scrimping, sparing, frugal, provident, using resources carefully, careful and provident in management, free from waste *or* lavishness, not wasteful *or* extravagant, penurious, chary, cheap, near, managed with prudence and practical wisdom, niggardly, tight-fisted, illiberal, close-fisted, belt-tightening, parsimonious, close-handed.

ECONOMICS, *n.* 1. Science of the distribution and consumption of goods and services, science of the means and methods of living well, science treating of the development of material resources, method of developing public wealth, science of wealth, plutonomy, plutology, Hooverism, public economy, political economy, economization.

2. Household economy, household management, housewifery, housekeeping.

ECONOMIST, *n.* 1. One versed in economics, specialist in economics, one who is proficient in political economy, plutonomist, plutologist, one who manages material resources, physiocrat, one who is careful and thrifty with resources, one who manages concerns with frugality, chrematist, economic pulse-taker.

2. Economical person, pinchpenny.

ECONOMIZE, *v.* 1. Manage economically, use to the best advantage, husband sparingly, save, use prudently, conserve, expend without waste, be economical, spend sparingly, retrench, skimp, be frugal in management, expend with frugality, cut down expenses, stint, be prudent, husband one's resources, practice economy, avoid waste, pinch, avoid extravagance, be parsimonious, be scant, use sparingly.

2. Make both ends meet, cut costs, cut to the bone, cut corners, tighten one's belt, trim the loss, cut one's coat according to one's cloth, keep one's head above water, save against a rainy day, meet expenses.

ECONOMY, *n.* 1. Thrifty management, prudent use of resources, administration of the resources of a community, political economy, plutonomy, law, management, rule, adjustment, government, organization, system, arrangement, plan, careful administration, regulation of finances.

2. Established order, dispensation, disposition of the parts of an organized whole, practical system in which means are adjusted to ends.

3. Frugality in expenditure of money, ménage, disposition to save *or* spare, carefulness in outlay, thriftiness in consumption of materials, freedom from extravagance, good housekeeping, sparing, husbandry, savingness, good housewifery, thrift, stewardship, regimen, saving, prudence, scanting, providence, prevention of waste, retrenchment, parsimony, skimping, meagerness, cheapness of operation, save-all, cheese parings and candle ends.

ECRU, *adj.* Very light brown, light yellowish brown, brownish, raw silk, unbleached, fuscous, fawn, puce, tawny.

ECSTASY, *n.* 1. Sudden access of intense feeling, afflatus, frenzy of poetic inspiration, paroxysm, trance, rhapsody, madness, obsession by powerful feeling, state of being beside oneself, state of trance supposed to accompany inspiration, violent distraction, overpowering exaltation, spell, reverie, daydream.

2. Overmastering feeling, bliss, supreme joy, rapturous delight, thrill, ravishment, immoderate titillation, rapture, transport, pleasure, delectation, ecstatic delight, gratification, relish, exhilaration, felicity, beatitude, orgasm, enjoyment, happiness, paradise, heaven, elysium, jubilation, exultation, seventh heaven, elation, rejoicing, enthusiasm, gladness, sensation, emotion.

ECSTATIC, *adj.* In a state of ecstasy, rapturous, beside oneself, ravished, transported, enraptured, entranced, enchanted, beatific, excited, overjoyed, elated, enthusiastic, felicitous, glad, rhapsodical, blissful, joyful, happy, radiant, delirious with joy, glorious, rapt, heavenly.

ECZEMA, *n.* Itching inflammatory skin disease with exudation of serous matter, eruption of the skin, redness of the skin, scald-head, salt-rheum, moist tetter, running tetter, milk-crust, psydracia (*Med.*).

EDACIOUS, *adj.* Given to eating, gormandizing, voracious, ravenous, omnivorous, gluttonous, crapulent, swinish, hoggish, consuming, greedy, devouring, destroying.

EDACITY, *n.* Excess in eating, ravenousness, big appetite, omnivorousness, gulosity, crapulence, voracity, gluttony, avidity, greediness, epicurism, overindulgence.

EDDY, *n.* 1. Current at variance with the main current in a stream, counter-current, backward-circling current of water.

2. Whirlpool, maelstrom, vortex, whirl, gurge, surge, swirl, rapids, Charybdis, current with a whirling rotary motion.

EDGE, *n.* 1. Cutting side of a blade, thin sharp side of a cutting instrument, featheredge on a razor, bezel, flange.

2. Boundary line of a surface *or* plane, part adjacent to a line of division, abrupt border, rim, dividing line, margin, bound, brim, brink, verge, side, ledge, lip, mouth, bank, bordure, crest, sill, extremity, strip, frame, confine, skirt, hem, welt, selvage, trimming, fringe, flounce, frill, furbelow, valance, molding, brow, curb, periphery, portal, tip, threshold, groundsel, gate, outstart, inception, limen, beginning *or* end, opening *or* close.

3. Sharpness, acuteness, penetration, keenness, animation, intensity, zest, interest, eagerness.

4. Bitterness, sting, sharpness, acrimony, gall, venom, acridity, poignancy, power to wound.

5. (*Coll.*) Advantage, upper hand, handicap head start.

6. Mild degree of intoxication, jag, skate, bun, glow.

EDGE, *v.* 1. Put an edge on, sharpen, trim the edge of.

2. Provide with a border, put an edging on, fringe, hem, rim, border, skirt, bound, marginate, bevel, coast.

3. Move edgewise, move sidewise, move slyly, sidle, inch, inch along, hitch along, hitch up, move little by little, move with caution, advance slowly, move on the edge, force gradually, verge on.

4. Make eager, incite, goad, instigate, egg.

EDGY, *adj.* 1. Sharp-edged, sharply defined, edge-like, angular, brought out too sharply.

2. On edge, irritable, touchy, excitable, sharp-tempered, irascible, critical, snappish, choleric, waspish, fretful.

EDIBLE, *adj.* Fit to be eaten as food, suitable for eating, eatable, comestible, nutritious, alimentary, esculent, ciborious, dietetic, nutritive, succulent.

EDICT, *n.* Decree issued by an authority, that which is uttered by authority as a rule of action, authoritative command, injunction, proclamation, order, rescript, prescript, statute, regulation, fiat, ordinance, ordination, mandate, caveat, decision, bull, dictum, decretal, ukase, firman, enactment, act, law, manifesto, public notice, appointment, ban, judgment, capitulary, constitution.

EDIFICATION, *n.* Moral improvement, spiritual upbuilding, educational benefit, uplifting, tuition, improvement, education, instruction, inculcation, teaching, advancement, enlightenment, direction, indoctrination, initiation, guidance.

EDIFICE, *n.* Building of imposing appearance, structure of large size, institute, house, mansion, hall, pile, dwelling, temple, fabric, compages, erection.

EDIFY, *v.* Upbuild morally, build up the faith of, increase the morality of, benefit morally, give lessons in, nurture in religion, improve, instruct, teach, school, tutor, prime, coach, guide, direct, show, strengthen morally, educate, inform, uplift, enlighten, evangelize, proselytize, inculcate, open the eyes, indoctrinate, sharpen the wits, produce mental improvement, enlarge the mind, prepare, familiarize with, inure, discipline, drill, train, rear, ground, open the eyes.

EDIT, *v.* 1. Arrange materials for publication, oversee the preparation of for publication, direct the preparation of a writing, compile, compose, select, adapt, prepare for the press, annotate and emend, revise and correct, redact, bring before the public, bring out, issue, rectify, polish, make corrections, amend, modify by excisions, touch up.

2. Conduct a journal, manage, act as editor of, direct the policies of.

EDITION, *n.* 1. Issue of a literary work, number, published form of a literary work, impression, printing, redaction, version, one of a number of printings of the same work issued at different times, whole number of copies printed from one set of type at one time.

2. Format in which a literary work is published.

3. Particular form or reproduction of anything, exemplar, model.

EDITOR, *n.* 1. Redactor, reviser, blue-penciler, emender, compiler, composer, annotator, one who prepares the work of another for publication, one who edits material for publication, one who has charge of a department of a newspaper, supervising director of a publication.

2. Author, publicist, journalist, lexicographer, littérateur, contributor, one who writes editorials, writer.

EDITORIAL, *n.* Article in a periodical published as an official expression of opinion, leader, essay, leading article, article of opinion.

EDUCATE, *v.* Develop the faculties of by instruction, give lessons in, teach, train, instruct, tutor, prime, coach, school, drill, discipline, inure, regulate the mental habits of, indoctrinate, guide, prepare, practice, exercise, initiate, edify, inform, form the mind and character of, bring up, rear, breed, nurture, qualify by training for a particular practice, cultivate, civilize, humanize, ground, sharpen the wits, enlarge the mind, wipe out illiteracy, provide education for, send to school, inculcate, implant, infuse, imbue, instil, lecture, enlighten, preach.

EDUCATED, *adj.* Having undergone education, displaying qualities of culture and learning, well-informed, informed by education, having disciplined mental powers, literate, lettered, scholarly, versed, schooled, cultured, learned, accomplished, intelligent, erudite, trained, instructed, skilled, well-versed, well-grounded, savant, bluestocking, literary, enlightened, high-brow, bookish, deep-read, book-learned.

EDUCATION, *n.* 1. Systematic development and cultivation of the normal powers of intellect so as to render them efficient in some particular form of living, imparting of skill, schooling, discipline, preparation, qualification, training, direction, lore, guidance, initiation, teaching, tuition, tutorship, tutelage, instruction, cultivation of the mental abilities, enlightenment, edification, inculcation, systematic training, indoctrination, development by means of study and learning, nurture, culture, breeding, acquisition of knowledge, erudition, learning, scholarship, study, letters, book learning, general information, bookishness, wisdom, higher education, refinement, civilization, knowledge, broadening of one's horizons.

2. Science of teaching, pedagogics, instruction as a science, pedagogy, didactics.

EDUCATIONAL, *adj.* Tending to educate, instructive, informative, didactic, disciplinary, edifying, propaedeutic, homiletical, doctrinal, scholastic, academic, pedagogical, humanistic, cultural.

EDUCATOR, *n.* One who educates, one versed in educational principles and methods, one able to secure intellectual results in training the mind, teacher, instructor, trainer, pedagogue, tutor, don, coach, master, disciplinarian, schoolman, dominie, abecedarian, professor, lecturer, academician, monitor, proctor, preceptor, expositor, mentor, scholar, philosopher.

EDUCE, *v.* Draw forth, draw out, extract, elicit, bring out, evolve, bring forth, call forth, evoke, deduce from data, derive, infer, develop.

EERIE, *adj.* 1. Inspiring fear, awe-inspiring, unearthly, strange, awful, uncanny, ghostly, alarming, spectral, weird, formidable, ominous, redoubtable, mysterious, lonely, portentous, gloomy, horrendous.

2. Affected by vague uneasiness, affected with superstitious fear, haunted, obsessed, fearful, timid, timorous, frightened, uneasy, tremulous, apprehensive, shaky.

EFFACE, *v.* 1. Destroy the face *or* form of, rub out, remove all sign *or* trace of, scrape out, scratch out, wipe out, cross out, strike out, blot out, obliterate, expunge, erase, cancel, excise, dele *(printing)*, delete, take out completely, cause to disappear, do away with, snuff out, destroy, eradicate, annihilate, raze.

2. Make inconspicuous, make not noticeable, put in the background, play down.

EFFECT, *v.* 1. Be the producer of, produce as an effect, cause, create.

2. Bring to an issue of full success, make happen, accomplish, do, perform, make, carry out, bring about, effectuate, execute, achieve, discharge, complete, consummate, realize, attain, compass, enforce, fulfil, perpetrate, conclude, contrive, procure.

EFFECT, *n.* 1. That which is produced by some agency, product of some efficient cause, result, resultant, consequence, upshot, issue, end, event, conclusion, outcome, fruit, aftermath, outgrowth, denouement, act, catastrophe, aftergrowth, afterclap, development.

2. Power to produce results, efficiency, force, validity, efficacy, weight, influence.

3. State of being operative, execution, active operation, accomplishment.

4. Mental state *or* attitude resulting from external impression, mental impression produced, general impression, impress, *ensemble (Fr.)*.

5. Purport, meaning, intent, significance, drift, import, general intent, tenor, bearing, intended and imparted meaning, substantial purport of a statement, result intended.

6. Fact, reality, actuality, truth.

7. *(Pl.)* Goods, movables, things, personal property, chattels, furniture, personal estate, commodities, merchandise, possessions, wares, stock, trappings, assets, luggage.

EFFECTIVE, *adj.* 1. Serving to effect the purpose, producing the expected result, adapted to produce a proper result, efficient, effectual, competent, availing, capable, sufficient, adequate, fit for a destined purpose, valid, useful, serviceable, practical.

2. Potent, forcible, efficacious, cogent, strong, powerful, energetic, puissant, mighty, dynamic, drastic, influential.

3. Producing a striking impression, striking, impressive, characterized by some striking feature, emphatic, telling, brilliant, pointed.

4. Actually in effect, active, operative, actual, real, prevalent, current.

EFFECTUAL, *adj.* 1. Exercising adequate power to produce a designed effect, capable of producing an intended effect, adequate, effective, of adequate power, efficacious, completely efficient, availing, dynamic, powerful, active, energetic, qualified.

2. Prevailing, binding, operative, valid, legally enforceable, authoritative.

EFFECTUATE, *v.* 1. Bring about, achieve, effect, accomplish, secure, execute, bring to pass, carry out, fulfil, realize, do, perform.

2. Render effectual, implement.

EFFEMINACY, *n.* Unmanliness, invirility, lack of manly character *or* appearance, unmanly delicacy, femininity *(of men)*, womanishness, flabbiness, weakness, softness, tenderness, beardlessness, milksopism.

EFFEMINATE, *adj.* Not virile, unmanly, having womanish traits, soft to an unmanly degree, soft, delicate for a man, feminine *(of men)*, womanish, female, sissyish *(coll.)*, mollyish *(coll.)*, weak, characterized by unmanliness, ladylike, wearing silk stockings, emasculate, unmanned, emolliate, androgynous, hermaphroditic, luxury-loving, silk-stockinged, tender-footed, voluptuous, Lydian, self-indulgent, tender, pusillanimous, milksopish, overdelicate, overemotional, pansyish *(coll.)*.

EFFERVESCE, *v.* 1. Give off bubbles of gas, come away in bubbles, bubble, foam, froth, hiss, ferment, boil, fizz.

2. Manifest irrepressible excitement, exhibit fervor, show excitement, be lively, be gay, be vivacious, exhibit exhilaration, sparkle.

EFFERVESCENCE, *n.* 1. Escape of bubbles of gas from a charged liquid, bubbling up, fizzing, ebullition, exestuation.

2. Vivacity, liveliness, ebullience, commotion, irrepressible fermentation, breathless excitement, lively demonstration of feeling, animation.

EFFERVESCENT, *adj.* 1. Giving off bubbles of gas, effervescing, bubbling, boiling, disappearing and dying out in effervescence, fizzing.

2. Lively, sparkling, gay, vivacious, animated, ebullient, irrepressible, breathless, demonstrative, excited.

EFFETE, *adj.* 1. Unable to produce, unfruitful, unproductive, sterile, unprolific, barren, fruitless, incapable of further production, infecund.

2. That has lost its vigor *or* energy, worn out with age, superannuated, spent, wasted, decayed, exhausted, inefficient through decay, aged, old, decrepit, obsolete, stale.

EFFICACIOUS, *adj.* Showing efficacy, effective as a means, capable of achieving a certain end, able to produce an intended effect, effective, efficient, effectual, of adequate power, powerful, energetic, weighty, strong, dynamic, stringent, potent, productive, forcible, qualified, active, operative, prevailing, valid, binding, prevalent, drastic, sovereign.

EFFICACY, *n.* Capacity for serving to produce effects, power to produce an intended effect as shown in the production of it, effective energy, effectiveness, efficiency, vigor, power, potency, force, competency, strength, weight, virtue, value, productiveness, capability, validity, prevalence,

EFFICIENCY, *n.* Power that accomplishes a designed work, quality that produces the most effective service, state of possessing adequate skill for the performance of a calling, competency in performance, productiveness, productivity, potency, efficacy, power, effectiveness, facility, efficaciousness, proficiency, ability, capableness, capability, capacity, aptitude, suitability, validity, adequacy, fitness, thoroughness, qualification, skill, skillfulness, cleverness, adroitness, address, dexterity, expertness, talent, faculty, finish, knack, technical knowledge, know-how, mastery, felicity, excellence, deftness, adeptness, *curiosa felicitas*, painstaking.

EFFICIENT, *adj.* 1. Adequate in performance, having the requisite skill, competent, capable, able, skillful, having power to act effectually, having adequate energy, energetic, high-powered, workmanlike, ready, clever, up in, qualified, apt, fitted, trained, primed, talented, adroit, expert, deft, artful, slick *(coll.)*, proficient, productive, good at, at home in, familiar with, master of, crack, crackajack, accomplished, *au fait (Fr.)*, trouble-shooting, geared to a stop watch, trained at the assembly-line.

2. Producing an effect, actually productive of results, actively causative, effective, efficacious, effectual, active, operative, operant, potent, valid, powerful, cogent, forceful, vigorous, puissant, dynamic, substantial, fitting, suitable.

EFFIGY, *n.* Figure representing the whole *or* a part of a person, sculptured representation, image, portrait, facsimile, statue, icon, idol, likeness, impersonation, straw man, puppet, doll, figurine, manikin, marionette, fantoccini, statuette, copy, scarecrow, picture, resemblance.

EFFLORESCE, *v.* 1. Blossom out, flower, bloom, break into flower, burst into bloom, become florid, break into floral ornament.

2. *(Chem.)* Change to a powdery substance upon exposure to air, become powdery and lose crystalline structure through loss of water of crystallization on exposure to the air, become incrusted with crystals of salt through evaporation *or* chemical change, grow pulverulent on the surface, crust, become covered with a crust of saline particles left by evaporation, come to dust, be reduced to powder, acquire a down.

EFFLORESCENCE, *n.* 1. Period of flowering, flowering bloom, blossoming, blooming forth, period at which a plant expands its blossoms, anthesis, flowery appearance, floridity.

2. *(Chem.)* Powdery substance, pulverulence, incrustation, crust, friability. (See EFFLORESCE, 2.)

3. *(Pathol.)* Eruption, cutaneous rash, breaking out, individual lesions of a rash.

EFFLORESCENT, *adj.* 1. Efflorescing, opening in flower, floriferous, blooming, blossoming out, flowery, floral.

2. (*Chem.*) Covered with an efflorescence, liable to effloresce, forming into white powder, powdery, pulverulent, granular, flocculent, sandy, gritty, friable. (See EFFLORESCE, 2.)

EFFLUENCE, *n.* 1. Outward flow, egress, flowing out, effusion, emanation, outflow, outpouring, efflux, emersion, disemboguement, defluxion, transudation, discharge, issue, profluence.

2. Something that flows out, stream, course, flux, flow, aura.

EFFLUENT, *adj.* Emanating, issuing forth, flowing out, profluent, diffluent.

EFFLUVIUM, *n.* Invisible exhalation, subtle emanation, slight vapor, noxious aura, reek, fume, flatus, gas, air, steam, smoke, miasma, odor, stench, aroma.

EFFLUX, *n.* 1. Outward flow, effluence, issuance, effluxion, effusion, disemboguement, discharge, outpouring, flowing out, gush, outflow.

2. That which flows out, drainage, emanation, effluvium.

EFFORT, *n.* 1. Voluntary exertion of power, force expended toward a definite end, attempt, expenditure of energy to accomplish some object, strenuous endeavor directed to some definite end, venture, essay, trial, laborious application, strain, trouble, struggle, pains, labor, toil, travail, stress, strife, tug, pull, spurt, stretch, spell, try, work, industry, tension, enterprise, practice, exercise, drill, training, discipline, sweat of one's brow, elbow grease, push, operation, movement, display of consciously directed power, aim.

2. Something done by exertion, achievement, feat, opus.

EFFORTLESS, *adj.* 1. Requiring *or* involving no effort, easy, facile, with ease, offhand, smooth, smooth-sailing.

2. Making no effort, passive, supine, inert, putting forth no effort, otiose.

EFFRONTERY, *n.* Barefaced audacity, shameless impudence, insolent assurance, unblushing boldness, hardihood, shamelessness, cheek, nerve, presumptuousness, bumptiousness, brass, gall, face, front, brazenness, presumption, self-assertion, sauciness, brashness, procacity, pertness, insult, petulance, impertinence, hardened front, incivility, immodesty, insolence, arrogance, haughtiness, rudeness, reckless defiance of propriety.

EFFULGENCE, *n.* Shining forth brilliantly, sheen, beaming brightness, brilliancy, luster, shimmer, splendor, streaming light, luminescence, flash, irradiation, emication, scintillation, coruscation, refulgence, radiance, blaze, fulguration, glare, luminosity, renitency, resplendence, ray, beam, incandescence, gleam, glory, nimbus, fluorescence, halo, aureole, illumination, phosphorescence, transplendency.

EFFULGENT, *adj.* Brilliantly shining, bright with splendor, beaming forth light, transplendent, resplendent, fulgent, refulgent, shining, luculent, radiant, luminous, luminiferous, splendent, nitid, luminescent, glowing, aglow, blazing, ablaze, burning, flaming, dazzling, relucent, fluorescent, rutilant, phosphorescent, incandescent, brilliant, splendid, beamy, lustrous, sheeny, glossy, bright as noonday, burnished, sunny, vivid, lambent, lucent.

EFFUSE, *v.* 1. Pour forth, pour out, dispense, spill, shed, emit, secrete, void, egest, open the sluices, turn on the tap.

2. Issue forth, exude, spread forth, come forth, emanate, spout, spurt, squirt, slop, flow out, well out, seep, filter, extravasate, ooze, disembogue, gush, debouch, find vent, diffuse.

3. Harangue, prattle, gabble, chatter, descant, cackle, rattle, blabber, prate, palaver, jabber, spin a long yarn, maunder, blather, expatiate, gossip, rant, ramble, twaddle, babble.

EFFUSION, *n.* 1. Outpouring, emission, efflux, shedding, gush, effluence, outburst, proruption, extrusion, trajection, outflow, diffusion, stream, dispersion, profusion, egestion, voidance, spilling, disgorgement, emanation, discharge, extrusion, extravasation, transudation, secretion.

2. Gushing and unrestrained utterance, gabble, outpouring of sentiment, unrestrained expression of thought, effusive utterance, disquisition, burst of eloquence, descant, harangue, rhapsody, flow of language, oration, lecture, facundity, *copia verborum* (*Lat.*), *flux de paroles* (*Fr.*), rant, talkativeness, speechifying, peroration, sermon, grandiloquence, multiloquence, largiloquence, chatter, prattle, palaver, soliloquy, declamation.

EFFUSIVE, *adj.* 1. Poured abroad, shed around, diffused, spread widely, wide-spreading, flowing out.

2. Unduly demonstrative, overflowing with sentiment, without reserve, unrestrained, profuse, expansive, ebullient, gushing, exuberant, lavish, freely outpouring, generous, overliberal, wordy, verbose, largiloquent, copious, pleonastic, lengthy, long-winded, diffusive, spun out, maundering, prolix, discursive, rambling, episodic, rhapsodic.

EGEST, *v.* Discharge from the body, eject, void, throw out, excrete, expel, evacuate, emit.

EGG, *n.* Simple cell capable of fertilization, ovum, roundish reproductive body, spawn, nucleus, cell, germ, roe, embryo, genesis, fetus, seed, body that is extruded from the ovary of female animals, hen's egg.

EGG, *v.* 1. Give an impulse, push, urge, set on, instigate, incite, encourage, inspire, rouse to, stimulate, animate, prod, goad, spur, prick, lure, sway, exercise influence over, induce, trigger, hurry on, actuate, persuade, prevail upon, tempt, entice, wheedle, coax, inveigle, exhort.

2. Provoke, harry, harass, hector, badger, press, hound, whip, lash.

EGG-SHAPED, *adj.* Shaped like the longitudinal section of an egg, having elongated rounded form, rounded, oval, oviform, ovate, ovoid, elliptical, ellipsoid, obovate, pear-shaped, bell-shaped.

EGO, *n.* Part of the psychic apparatus which experiences and reacts to the outside world, the self of any person, the "I," conscious individual as distinguished from the "not I," subject of each conscious act *or* state, personality, individuality, enduring and conscious element which knows experience, complete man comprising both body and soul, psyche, pneuma, inner man, soul, spirit, *penetralia mentis* (*Lat.*), me, superego, subject, self-assertive and self-preserving tendency, egotistic nature (*coll.*), id, selfishness.

EGOISM, *n.* 1. (*Ethics*) Solipsism, limitation of consciousness to the self, individualism, doctrine that the individual and his self-interest are the basis of all behavior, self-centration, subjective idealism, giving the "I" undue prominence in thought.

2. Habit of valuing everything only with reference to one's personal interest, self-conceit, pure selfishness, egotism, extravagant love of self, self-regard, self-absorption, self-feeling, self-opinionatedness, self-overestimation, vanity, pride, haughtiness.

EGOIST, *n.* 1. Adherent of the metaphysical principle of the ego *or* self, solipsist, philidox, individualist.

2. Self-centered person, selfish person, self-seeker.

EGOISTIC, *adj.* Pertaining to the ego, self-absorbed, characterized by inordinate regard for self, individualistic, self-regarding, introverted, self-centered.

EGOTISM, *n.* 1. Giving the "I" undue supremacy in speech, preoccupation with one's ego, habit of talking too much about oneself, self-worship, self-importance, self-conceit, self-regard, self-esteem, self-concentration, self-glorification, self-applause, self-importance, self-complacency, self-satisfaction, self-assertiveness, self-admiration, self-commendation, self-assurance, boastfulness, bumptiousness, self-exaltation, self-confidence, self-centeredness, obtrusive reference to oneself, excessive emphasis upon one's own importance, self-love, self-interestedness, self-seeking, self-interest.

2. Vanity, conceit, presumption, insolence, arrogance, ostentation, haughtiness, pertness, pride.

EGOTIST, *n.* One given to extravagant self-mention, conceited and boastful person, braggart, braggadocio, gasconader, boaster, swaggerer, self-applauder, rodomont, self-exalter, self-glorifier, prig, coxcomb, peacock, poseur, philodox.

EGOTISTIC, *adj.* Conceited, puffed up, vain, self-centered, self-admiring, self-loving, self-conceited, self-important, self-asserting, boastful, opinionated, bumptious, inflated, overweening, arrogant, assuming, consequential, haughty, high-flown, affected, proud, pretentious, pompous, self-obtruding, selfish, bombastic, turgid, philodoxical, showy.

EGREGIOUS, *adj.* Conspicuous for bad quality, outrageous, monstrous, flagrant, arrant, gross, shocking, notorious, grievous, crying, insufferable, intolerable, immoderate, greatly exceeding others of the same class, excessive, extreme, enormous, distinguished for badness, tremendous, huge, prodigious, signal, extraordinary, remarkable, great.

EGRESS, *n.* 1. Act of going out, passing out, power to go out, departure, emergence, vent, debouchment, outlet, issuance, issue, discharge, escape, emanation.

2. Means of going out, place of exit, passage out, way out, exit, door, doorway, mouth, gate, opening, aperture, porthole, loophole, window.

EIDOLON, *n.* An unsubstantial image, specter, apparition, ghost, phantom, representation, shade, likeness, *umbra (Lat.).*

EITHER, *adj.* and *pron.* 1. One of two, one or the other of two, any one.

2. The one and the other separately, each of two, both by turns.

EITHER, *conj. (coll.)* At all, in any case, also, too.

EJACULATE, *v.* 1. Speak vehemently and briefly, utter in exclamation, exclaim hurriedly, utter suddenly, cry passionately, blurt out, give voice to, rap out, give utterance, call out suddenly, howl, fulminate, vociferate.

2. Discharge male fluid, jaculate, have an orgasm, eject passionately, emit rhythmically, expel spermatozoa, propel semen.

EJACULATION, *n.* 1. Abrupt and exclamatory utterance, vehemently spoken word *or* phrase, brief and sudden utterance, exclamation, cry, ecphonesis, vociferation, uttering of brief and sudden exclamations.

2. Rhythmic discharge of male fluid, orgasm, expulsion of seminal fluid, emission, ejection, jaculation, propulsion of semen, seed, sperm, spermatozoa.

EJECT, *v.* 1. Drive out, force out, evict, oust, dislodge, dispossess, expel, banish, exile, deport, expatriate, ostracize, turn out, extrude, thrust out, put out, discharge, dismiss, eliminate, remove, excommunicate, exclude, give walking papers, cashier, sack, bounce, fire, throw out, cast out, drive out, sweep out, jettison.

2. Emit, send out, dispatch, discharge, spit, exude, spout, expectorate, spurt, throw forth, disgorge, spew, vomit, puke, throw up, belch, evacuate, void, egest, excrete.

EJECTION, *n.* 1. Casting forth, eviction, ouster, dislodgment, turning out, thrusting out, extrusion, expulsion, dispossession, disseizin, exclusion, removal, discharge, dismissal, banishment, exile, deportation, expatriation, firing, cashiering, sacking.

2. Disgorgement, vomiting, eructation, voiding, belching, spewing, eruption, emission, throwing up, evacuation, excretion.

EKE OUT, *v.* 1. Supply what is lacking, make up the deficiency of, supplement, add to so as to make barely sufficient, barely complete, make out with difficulty, piece out, round out, stretch out, fill in, enlarge, extend, increase.

2. Contrive to make *(a living),* manage to support *(existence),* barely make by various makeshifts, produce with difficulty.

ELABORATE, *v.* 1. Produce by labor, develop in detail, work up, develop by thorough and careful work, work out minutely, bestow labor upon, devise, execute, perfect, consummate, effect, achieve, complete, accomplish, compass, fashion with care.

2. Improve with painstaking, ameliorate, ripen, amend, better, improve upon, prepare thoroughly, put finishing touches to, touch up, polish, adorn, finish, garnish, beautify, bedeck, decorate, enrich, embellish, cultivate, enhance, mellow, mature, refine.

ELABORATE, *adj.* 1. Worked out with great nicety of detail, executed with great minuteness, intricately wrought, developed minutely, done with thoroughness, detailed, minute, complicated, perfected, painstaking, finished, elegant, skillful.

2. Marked by excessive effort, operose, labored, fussy, studied, dressy, ostentatious, laborious, ornamented, ornate, showy.

ELABORATION, *n.* 1. Production with detailed completeness, painstaking development, perfect finish, perfection, labor, carefully wrought work, evolution, manufacture, formation, adaptation, preparation, concoction, incubation, completion, amplification.

2. Working of given material into something better, improvement, betterment, amelioration, amendment, enrichment, elevation, increase, enlargement, cultivation, polish, touching up, repair, ripening, maturing.

ELAN, *n.* Impetuous ardor, dash, spirit, brilliant rush of action, eagerness for action, impetus, impulsion, impact, momentum.

ELAPSE, *v.* Slip by, pass by, slide by, glide by, slip away, pass away, lapse, expire, quietly terminate, be spent, be lost, be past, end, go by, flit, steal by, proceed, advance, intervene, roll along, run, crawl, drag, *tempus fugit (Lat.).*

ELASTIC, *adj.* 1. Having the property of recovering shape after deformation, extensible *or* contractile with facility, readily stretched without essential alteration, spontaneously expansive, tensile, tensible, refluent, plastic, springing back, springy, resilient, rebounding, recoiling, supple, ductile, dilating, flexible.
2. Capable of ready adjustment, easily adapted, adaptable, accommodating, yielding, responsive, complaisant.
3. Readily recovering, recuperative, buoyant, returning to a former state.

ELASTICITY, *n.* 1. Capacity for resisting *or* overcoming depression, springiness, resiliency, rebounding quality, extensibility, tensibility, tensility, ductility, plasticity, backlash, ricochet, flexibility.
2. Tendency to recover, stamina, power to endure strain, vitality, lustihood, grit, virility, recoil, capacity for adjustment, adaptability, rebound, recuperativeness, responsiveness.

ELATE, *v.* Raise the spirits of, put in high spirits, inspirit, inspire, encourage, hearten, animate, cheer, elevate, exhilarate, enliven, stimulate, lift up, excite, overjoy, rejoice, delight, gladden, exalt, please, intoxicate, cause to feel exultant, make proud, puff up, inflate, swell, flush.

ELATED, *adj.* Flushed with success, exhilarated, exultant, exalted, in high spirits, in high feather, on stilts, proud, cock-a-hoop, boastful, crowing, puffed up, swollen, jubilant, triumphant, happy, overjoyed, rejoicing, sanguine, pleased, gleeful, joyful, delighted, blithe, glad, merry, optimistic, animated, excited.

ELATION, *n.* Flush of success, exultant gladness, exaltation of spirit, jubilant state of mind, high spirits, buoyant cheer, buoyancy, elevation, joy, excitement, joyousness, happiness, gladsomeness, cheerfulness, enthusiasm, rapture, ecstasy, bliss, delight, rejoicing, jubilancy, jubilation, crowing, enlivenment, intoxication, gratification, animation, satisfaction, gayety, self-approval, high feather, pride.

ELBOW, *n.* 1. Region at the junction of the upper arm and forearm, bend of the arm, joint of the arm between upperarm and forearm, ancon, ulna, crazy bone.
2. Any sharp angle like that of an elbow, bend, sharp turn, flexure, right angle, knob, projection, kink.

ELBOWROOM, *n.* Room for the free use of the elbows, space for moving the elbows, free scope for activity, ample room for action, spare room, roomage, enough space, sweep, swing, range, room enough, latitude, free play, margin, wide berth, liberty of action, opportunity, freedom, fair field, *Lebensraum (Ger.).*

ELDER, *adj.* 1. Having lived longer, older of two *or* more, senior, earlier born, first-born.
2. Previously commissioned, superior in rank, ranking.
3. Earlier in time, prior, former, more ancient, olden.

ELDER, *n.* 1. Person who is older than oneself, one's senior, superior in age, predecessor, parent, forefather, ancestor, forebear.
2. Old man, aged person, venerable man, old-timer, veteran, grisard, graybeard, oldster, fogy, sexagenarian, octogenarian, nonagenarian, centenarian.
3. Head of a tribe *or* patriarchal family, one of the more influential men of a community, person occupying an office requiring the dignity that age confers, senator, counselor, governing officer, presbyter, church dignitary, ruling elder, patriarch.

ELDERLY, *adj.* Approaching old age, somewhat old, between middle and old age, oldish, veteran, quite advanced in life, in later life, aged, ancient, antique, senile, anile, matronly, ripe, mellow, senescent, past one's prime, gray-haired, decrepit, gray-headed, hoary, venerable, patriarchal, time-worn, superannuated, stricken in years, time-honored.

ELECT, *v.* 1. Designate for office by a majority *or* plurality vote, vote, ballot, pole, hold up one's hand, give a voting sign.
2. Select, choose, pick out, cull, make choice of, single out, appoint, set apart, ordain, call, predestinate, reserve, mark out for.
3. Determine in favor of, decide upon, settle, fix upon, distinguish by special selection, make up one's mind, adopt, take up, embrace, espouse.
4. Prefer, fancy, have rather, be fain, had as lief, had liefer.

ELECT, *adj.* 1. Elected to office but not yet in charge of its functions, appointed to office but not yet installed, selected but not yet inducted.
2. Taken by preference from among two *or* more, preferred, chosen, picked out, selected, conscript.
3. Choice, select, of high character, deserving to be chosen, elite, popular.
4. *(Theol.)* Predestinated to salvation, chosen by God for eternal life, set apart unto eternal life, redeemed, chosen to salvation, anointed, saved.

ELECTION, *n.* 1. Selection of a person for office by vote, choosing by vote, balloting, franchise, suffrage, poll, ticket, vote, direct primary, voice.
2. Public vote upon a proposition submitted, popular vote on a question of public policy, plebiscite, referendum, *vox populi (Lat.).*
3. Choice between alternatives, free choice of means to an end, alternative, *embarras de choix (Fr.),* option, pick, discretion, volition, adoption, preferment, discrimination, decision, cooperation, judgment, selection, preference.
4. Liberty, free-will, freedom, power to choose, call, responsibility, determination.

ELECTIONEER, *v.* Work for the success of a candidate in an election, be active in a canvass for votes, endeavor to influence the result of an election, canvass, campaign, stump for, plump, beat the bushes, speak at every whistle-stop.

ELECTIVE, *adj.* 1. Pertaining to the principle of electing to office, pertaining to the right to choose by vote, electoral, relating to suffrage.

2. Passed by vote, chosen by election, bestowed by ballot, dependent on suffrage, constituent.

3. Open to choice, subject to preference, not required, optional, discretionary, voluntary, not obligatory, at choice, on approval, exerting the privilege of choice, having the privilege to choose, arising from choice, selective.

ELECTOR, *n.* 1. Qualified voter, suffragist, one who elects to office, constituent, balloter, chooser.

2. Ruler of the Holy Roman Empire, prince.

ELECTORATE, *n.* Body of persons entitled to vote in an election, those who elect, the mass of voters, constituency, body-politic, citizens of age.

ELECTRIC, *adj.* 1. Relating to electricity, voltaic, marked by electricity, charged with electricity, faradaic, galvanic, magnetic.

2. Electrifying, thrilling, spirited, full of fire, inspiriting, inspiring, exciting, rapturous, stirring, ecstatic, galvanizing, stimulating, soul-stirring, rousing.

3. Instantaneous, swift, rapid, lightning-like, fulminative.

ELECTRIFY, *v.* 1. Subject to electricity, pass an electric current through, charge with electricity, render electric, galvanize, apply electricity to, equip for the use of electric power, magnetize, energize, dynamize, faradize, give an electric shock to.

2. Arouse to sudden and intense interest, fire, rouse, stimulate, animate, thrill, excite suddenly and violently, touch, impress, strike, ravish, rivet the attention, interest, penetrate, kindle, enchant, charm, captivate, bewitch, fascinate, enrapture, ensorcel.

3. Stun, bewilder, startle greatly, stupefy, take one's breath away, petrify, dazzle, daze, amaze, confound, astonish, surprise, astound, stagger, dumfounder, flabbergast, strike dumb.

ELECTROCUTE, *v.* Inflict a death penalty by means of electricity, execute by electricity, kill by electric shock, send to the hot seat, burn *(coll.),* fry *(coll.).*

ELECTRON, *n.* Unit, extremely small negatively charged particle, electrically charged particle which is one of the basic components of the atom.

ELEEMOSYNARY, *adj.* Pertaining to alms *or* charitable donations, existing for the relief of the poor, charitable, gratuitous, sportulary, tributary, supported by charity, costless, gratis, expenseless, without charge, complimentary, rent-free, free of cost.

ELEGANCE, *n.* 1. Symmetry, proportion, balance, rhythm, clarity, purity, felicity, grace, daintiness, gracefulness, choiceness, exquisiteness, fineness, sumptuousness, luxuriousness, delicate structure, delicacy, pulchritude, grandeur, finery, silks and satins, fastidious taste, comeliness, richness in harmonious simplicity, Atticism, beauty resulting from a combination of fine qualities.

2. Refinement, gentility, politeness, courtliness, polish, culture, distinction, restraint, propriety, correctness, nicety.

ELEGANT, *adj.* 1. Exhibiting delicacy of finish, beautiful, richly ornamental, gorgeous, artistic, aesthetic, handsome, exquisite, well-proportioned, symmetrical, rhythmic, shapely, classical, Attic, choice, chaste, pure, tasteful, pleasingly superior in kind, dainty, delicate, felicitous, happy, neat, inspired, ornate, trim, balanced, pleasing, in good taste, appropriate, rich, recherché, well-chosen, smooth, well-made, fine, finished, nice, lovely, comely, excellent, grand.

2. Correctly fine in dress and person, genteel, refined in tastes, discriminative, polished, courtly, cultivated, well-bred, fine in manners, fastidious, luxurious in dress, wearing silk stockings, dapper, silk-hosed, Chesterfieldian, fashionable, cultured, polite, gracious, sumptuous, accomplished, easy, natural, fluent, urbane, debonair, suave, stylish, good-looking, charming, superior, restrained, select.

ELEGIAC, *adj.* Expressing lamentation, elegiacal, epicedial, threnetic, threnodic, dirgelike, plaintive, sorrowful, mournful, funereal, wailful, querulous, crying, tearful, lachrymose, sad.

ELEGY, *n.* 1. Funeral song, song of lamentation, mournful song, melancholy piece of music, keen, threnody, monody, coronach, threne, requiem, pavane, nenia, death song, plaint, ululation.

2. Lyric poem lamenting the dead, reflective poem with sorrowful theme, melancholy poem, plaintive verse.

ELEMENT, *n.* 1. One of the simple substances regarded as constituting the material universe, earth, water, air, fire, materials of the world, substance, simple body, uncompounded body.

2. Fundamental part, essential part, constituent part of a whole, contents, component, ingredient, integral part, component part, factor, feature, unit which builds up substances, germ, member, subdivision, constituent principle, radicle, nucleus.

3. *(Pl.)* Rudiments, basic ideas, first principles, essential parts, outlines, first steps, foundation, origin, essence.

4. Sphere adapted to any person *or* thing, natural habitat, natural medium. proper sphere, native state, environment, weather.

ELEMENTARY, *adj.* Rudimentary, rudimental, fundamental, primary, basic, component, initial, simple, introductory, coming first, undeveloped, imperfect, easy, understandable, plain, clear, first, inchoate, incipient, elemental, basal, original, uncompounded.

ELEPHANTINE, *adj.* 1. Having vast size, heavy, immense, huge, colossal, gigantic, mighty, bulky, enormous, ponderous, amplitudinous, Cyclopean, Herculean, stupendous, monstrous, towering, massive, stalwart, brawny, whopping.

2. Clumsy, ungainly, ungraceful, thundering, unwieldy, lubberly, hulky, lumpish.

ELEVATE, *v.* 1. Move to a higher place, raise to a higher position, rear, place high, lift up, pry, hoist, raise aloft, direct upward, heighten, erect, tilt up, boost, lever, prize, heave, uplift, upraise, uprear, buoy, mount.

2. Raise in standing, raise to a higher station, promote, advance, exalt, aggrandize, ennoble, dignify, improve, extol, honor, cultivate, enhance, glorify, exalt, greaten, enthrone, esteem, respect.

3. Raise the spirits, put in high spirits, elate, exhilarate, cheer, inspire, revive the feelings of, excite, animate, please, render slightly tipsy.

ELEVATED, *adj.* 1. Raised up, upraised, lofty in situation, high, aerial, towering, alpine, erect, tall, commanding, upturned, rampant, conspicuous, alofty.

2. Exalted, noble, lofty in character, sublime, grand, grandiose, dignified, eminent, high-minded, majestic, superior, princely, glorious, honorable, aristocratic, prominent, ennobled, magnificent, stately.

3. Elated, merry, cheerful, slightly tipsy, in high spirits.

ELEVATION, *n.* 1. Altitude, height, eminence, prominence, lift.

2. Elevated place, hill, mount, rising ground, hillock, acclivity, ascent, mountain, ascendant, rise.

3. Loftiness, grandeur, nobleness, superiority, dignity, refinement, nobility, distinction, majesty, fame, sublimity, cultivation.

4. Exaltation, aggrandizement, improvement, state of being elevated, promotion, advancement.

ELEVATOR, *n.* 1. Moving platform for conveying from one level to another, mechanical device for raising persons *or* things, lift *(Brit.)*, dumbwaiter, hoist, chute, spout, moving stairway, escalator.

2. Building for storing grain, silo.

ELF, *n.* 1. Imaginary being with magical powers given to capricious interference in human affairs, mythological being, fairy, peri, sprite, fay, imp, brownie, banshee, leprechaun, puck, pixie, nixie, pygmy, undine, mermaid, merman, incubus, troll, succubus, kelpie, genie, goblin, gnome, kobold, hobgoblin.

2. Small mischievous person, dwarf, pet name for a lively child, small child.

3. Knave, rogue, mischievous *or* malicious animal *or* creature.

ELFISH, *adj.* Elfin, elf-like, mischievous, tricky, prankish, impish, spiteful, fiendish, small and evil, ghoulish, demoniac.

ELICIT, *v.* Bring forth, draw out, extract, bring out, wrest, wring from, wrench, extort, pump, call forth, fetch, derive, deduce, evoke, develop, educe, succeed in obtaining, exact, cause, bring to light, draw forth.

ELIDE, *v.* 1. Cut off a syllable, strike out a vowel *or* syllable in a word, curtail, delete, syncopate, nullify, omit in pronunciation.

2. Suppress, pass over in silence, omit, ignore.

ELIGIBILITY, *n.* Eligibleness, worthiness, fitness to be chosen, suitableness, endowment, propriety, desirability, advantage, expediency, efficiency, utility, opportunity, legal qualification for election *or* appointment.

ELIGIBLE, *adj.* 1. Worthy of being chosen, fit to be chosen, desirable, suitable, fitting, proper, due, seemly, becoming, befitting, expedient, wise, advisable, acceptable, convenient, proper, worthwhile, meet, opportune, accordant, advantageous, applicable, practical, effective, handy, appropriate, feasible, doable, attainable, achievable, possible, performable, worthy of adoption.

2. *(Coll.)* Desirable to marry, unspoken for, unwed, unaffianced, single.

ELIMINATE, *v.* 1. Put out of doors, exclude, eject, cast out, separate and expel, relegate, exile, banish, deport, expatriate, outlaw, maroon, shut the door upon, drive out, thrust out, reject, get rid of, get clear of, score out, discharge, eradicate, erase, abstract, repudiate, blackball, ostracize, throw out, oust, evict, suspend, extrude, dislodge, weed out, abolish, put aside, set apart, segregate, turn one's back upon, make a clean sweep, fire, stamp out, bounce, sack, exterminate, annihilate, blot out.

2. Omit as irrelevant, suppress as unimportant, ignore, except, drop, neglect, pass over, cancel, bar, leave out of consideration.

3. Expel from an organism, void, excrete, egest.

4. Simplify, clarify, refine, disinvolve, restrain, disentangle, abbreviate, reduce to simplicity, strip of ornament, sift, chasten, winnow, purify.

ELIMINATION, *n.* 1. Casting out, getting rid, removal, expulsion, rejection, extrusion, ejection, relegation, deportation, expatriation, exile, sifting, banishment, proscription, omission, exclusion, separation, abstraction.

2. Excretion, voidance, egestion, purification.

ELITE, *n.* Flower of society, the pick, best part of a class of persons, select body, cream, great folks, crème-de-la-crème, silk-stockinged gentry, "silk-stockings," upper class, aristocracy, swells, choice group, fashionable world, high life, *haut monde (Fr.)*, blue bloods, *pur sang (Fr.)*, A-1, none such, nonpareil, salt of the earth, first water, somebody, paragon, pink, pearl, sterling, upper ten, 14-karat, society, best, nobility, choice and master spirits of the age, notables, personages, men of mark, celebrities, bigwigs, stars, peerage, *noblesse (Fr.)*, grandees, hidalgos.

ELIXIR, *n.* 1. Philosopher's stone, alchemic preparation for transmuting base metals into gold *or* for prolonging life.

2. Aromatic sweetened alcoholic liquid used as a vehicle for medicinal agents, sweetened aromatized alcoholic preparation with small quantity of medicinal substance in solution, balm, compound, tincture, cordial, invigorator, sovereign remedy, panacea, cure-all, catholicon, nostrum, theriac, ptisan.

3. Quintessence, refined spirit, essential principle, absolute embodiment of anything, concentrated essence.

ELL, *n.* 1. Addition attached to one side of the rear of a house, shed at the back, el, extension to a building at right angles, wing, annex.

2. Measure of length, 45 inches *(England)*, 37 inches *(Scotland)*.

ELLIPSE, *n.* Closed conic section, plane curve, oval, ovoid, ovum, oval figure, rounded oblong, flattened circle, ellipsoid, cycloid, epicycle, ring, epicycloid, circlet, annulus, hoop, loop, cycle, orb, disc.

ELLIPTICAL, *adj.* 1. Relating to the ellipse, like an ellipse, belonging to the ellipse.

2. Oblong with rounded ends, oval, ovate, ovoid, discoid, egg-shaped, curved, ringlike, equally rounded at both ends, globular, rotundate, cylindrical, orbed.

3. *(Gram.)* Marked by an omission that may be supplied, containing omissions, shortened, incomplete, defective.

ELOCUTION, *n.* 1. Study and practice of public speaking, declamation, management of voice and gesture, faculty of speech, art of delivery, art of oral expression, art of correct intonation and gesture in public speaking, effective oral delivery, oratory, rhetoric, enunciation, pronunciation, articulation, diction, *usus loquendi (Lat.)*.

2. Manner of speaking, utterance, parlance, oral expression, eloquence, facundity, power of speech.

3. Stilted artificial manner of delivery.

ELONGATE, *v.* 1. Render long, make longer, prolong, produce, draw out to greater length, lengthen, extend, stretch out, lengthen out, protract.

2. Grow longer, increase in length, trail out, be comparatively long.

ELOPE, *v.* 1. Run away clandestinely with a

lover, abscond with a paramour, kidnap, abduct.

2. Run away from one's place of duty, escape, depart clandestinely, withdraw secretly, decamp, slip away, flee, abscond, desert, sneak off, flit, bolt, levant, skedaddle, show a light pair of heels, make a get-away, clear well out of, *échapper belle (Fr.)*, make off, slip the collar, wriggle out of.

ELOQUENCE, *n.* 1. Practice of using language with fluency, art of speaking in language expressing strong feeling, art of speaking well in public, oratory, rhetoric, speech, elocution, declamation, diction, address, enunciation, articulation.

2. Eloquent discourse, fluency, graceful utterance, appropriate expression, right words in right places, moving expression, verbal elegance, grandiloquence, multiloquence, polylogy, gift of the gab, *mot précis (Fr.)*, flow of words, *flux de paroles (Fr.)*, *copia verborum (Lat.)*, volubility, loquacity, facundity, mellifluousness.

3. Command of words, loftiness, elevation of expression, expressiveness, grandeur, impassioned utterance, spellbinding.

ELOQUENT, *adj.* 1. Having the power of forcible speech, forceful, persuasive, expressive, cogent, impressive, effective, trenchant, telling, mordant, incisive, biting, pointed, pithy, marrowy, meaty, graphic, vivid, striking, emphatic, spirited, full of feeling, weighty, vehement, burning, vigorous, impassioned, calculated to stir, powerfully expressive in words of strong feeling.

2. Golden-mouthed, silver-tongued, fluent, mellifluous, facund, grandiloquent, Ciceronian, Demosthenean, Tullian, sublime, lofty, exalted, inspired, poetic, oratorical, altiloquent, graceful, ringing, declamatory, rhetorical.

3. Loquacious, talkative, garrulous, voluble, multiloquent, polyloquent, glib, effusive.

4. Visibly expressive of emotion, significant, meaningful, revealing, representing vividly, movingly expressive *(of looks)*.

ELSE, *adv.* 1. Other than the person *or* thing mentioned, additional to, in addition to, instead, differently, in the place of.

2. Otherwise, if the case were different, if it be not true, if not, moreover, besides, further.

ELSEWHERE, *adv.* In *or* to some other place, somewhere else, anywhere else, another place, not here, away, absent, abroad, hence.

ELUCIDATE, *v.* Make lucid, make clear, make plain, throw light upon, clarify, clear up, bring out more clearly the facts concerning, explain, account for, unfold, point out, define, literalize, spell out, expound, demonstrate, illustrate, quote, illuminate, simplify, popularize, interpret, solve, delineate, describe, resolve, comment upon, gloss, annotate, margin.

ELUCIDATION, *n.* 1. Making plain, making intelligible, clearing up, elucidating, unfolding, illustrating, explaining, *éclaircissement (Fr.)*, explication, exposition, interpretation, definition, diagnosis, rendition, construction, version, solution, exemplification, deduction, inference, animadversion, exegesis.

2. Commentary, comment, note, scholium, gloss, annotation, marginalia.

ELUDE, *v.* 1. Escape by artifice, evade the pursuit of by dexterity, slip through the hands of, give one the slip, give the go-by to, wriggle out of, slip away from, steal away from, slip out of, turn away from, get away from, keep clear of,

dodge, shun, avoid, make a get-away, flee, make one's escape, make off, skedaddle, fight shy.

2. Escape the mind of, remain undiscovered by, thwart, escape notice, disappoint, disconcert, balk, circumvent, frustrate, baffle, foil, parry, mystify, equivocate.

ELUSIVE, *adj.* 1. Evasive, slippery, tending to slip away, tricky, fugitive, runaway, fleeting, shifty, evanescent, transient, vainly pursued, lubricous.

2. Eluding complete mental grasp, eluding clear perception, hard to understand, hard to grasp, hard to express *or* define, intangible, impalpable, imponderable, occult.

3. Shuffling, equivocatory, quibbling, subtle, dexterously evasive, baffling, mysterious, furtive, deceptive, insidious, sophisticated.

ELYSIUM, *n.* Greek paradise, Elysian fields, *Champs Elysées (Fr.)*, abode of the blessed after death, bowers of bliss, place of perfect happiness, Isles of the Blessed, heaven, seventh heaven, place of supreme delight, Eden, Arcadia, happy valley, Olympus, happy hunting ground, Nirvana, Valhalla.

EMACIATE, *v.* Make lean by a gradual wasting away of flesh, make very thin, waste, reduce in flesh, make spare, cause to waste away, fall away, weaken, dwindle, shrink, contract, shrivel, wither, lose flesh, wizen, attenuate.

EMACIATED, *adj.* Gaunt, maculent, weedy, tabid, skinny, tabescent, marasmic, marcid, phthisic, consumptive, atrophied, undernourished, ailing, underfed, starved, famine-stricken, malnourished, famished, pinched, peaked, spindling, spindle-shanked, bare-bone, skeletal, rawboned, lean as a rake, thin as a wafer, lank, wasted, wizened, shriveled, spare, haggard, scraggy, scrawny, worn to a shadow, reduced, attenuated, hatchet-faced, lantern-jawed, like a bag of bones, weak as a scarecrow, infirm.

EMACIATION, *n.* Abnormal thinness caused by lack of nutrition *or* by disease, excessive leanness, tabefaction, tabes, marasmus, atrophy, phthisis, consumption, inanition, malnutrition, starvation, half-rations, undernourishment, attenuation, mere skin and bone, famine, wasting away, lankness, pining away, meagerness, feebleness, falling away, barebones, skeleton, shadow, scrag, bag of bones, anatomy, spindleshanks.

EMANATE, *v.* 1. Flow forth, flow out, well, gush out, effuse, trickle, debouch, disembogue, exude, discharge, ooze, filter, percolate, surge out, stream out, give off, exhale, waft out, send forth, emit, fling out, throw out, deluge, come forth, egress.

2. Proceed from, arise, spring, issue, stem, take rise, appear, originate, result, follow, proceed, go out, radiate.

EMANATION, *n.* 1. Flowing out of some origin, arising, issuing, emerging, springing, welling, issuance, emergence, egress, escape, outflow, effusion, oozing, gush, outpour, effluence.

2. That which proceeds from a source, aura, effluvium, emission, discharge, outburst, drainage, exhalation, mephitis, leakage, efflux, vapor, steam, radiation, percolation.

EMANCIPATE, *v.* Free from restraint, release from oppressive authority, liberate, manumit, set free, disimprison, disenthrall, exempt from bondage, redeem from slavery, set at liberty, deliver from restraint, untie, loosen, unfetter, unbolt, unshackle, unbind, unchain, unbar, acquit, unmanacle, rescue, ransom, enfranchise.

EMANCIPATION, *n.* Liberation, manumission, disenthrallment, disimprisonment, deliverance, setting at large, release, freeing, loosing, salvation, redemption, extrication, rescue, liberty, freedom, right, independence, enfranchisement.

EMANCIPATOR, *n.* Liberator, deliverer, freer, manumitter, rescuer, redeemer, preserver.

EMASCULATE, *v.* 1. Deprive of procreative power, destroy the male functions of, castrate, geld, unman, eunuchize, deprive of virility, caponize, maim, cripple, mutilate.
2. Rob of masculine strength, debilitate, don a skirt and petticoat, weaken, emolliate, soften, enervate, deprive of native vigor, effeminize, render effeminate, put silk stockings on.
3. Impair the vigor of a literary work by cutting out what is regarded as objectionable, expurgate, bowdlerize.

EMASCULATION, *n.* 1. Deprivation of masculine functions, loss of virility, unmanning, castration, eunuchization, caponization, mayhem, mutilation.
2. State of being emasculate, effeminacy, weakness, emolliation, enervation, debilitation.
3. Taking away from a literary product its virile character, expurgation, bowdlerization.

EMBALM, *v.* 1. Preserve from decay by aromatics *or* antiseptics, mummify, impregnate with antiseptics, anoint with preservatives, preserve from putrefaction, prepare for burial, lay out, treat with spices *or* drugs.
2. Preserve from oblivion, keep in memory, enshrine in the memory, cherish, memorialize, keep unimpaired, keep the memory green, mind, commemorate, remember.
3. Impart a balmy fragrance to, make fragrant, aromatize, imbue with aroma, perfume, scent, fill with balm.

EMBANK, *v.* Enclose with a bank, confine with a mound, protect with a dike, bank, defend, guard, secure, protect, fend, shield.

EMBANKMENT, *n.* Dike raised to hold back water, breakwater, mole, pier, jetty, quay, wall, barrier, rampart, earthwork, levee, mound, bank, remblai, terreplein, ditch, intrenchment, trench, bulwark, safeguard, parapet, breastwork, field-work.

EMBARGO, *n.* Authoritative stoppage of any special trade, governmental order of prohibition, prohibitory restriction, legal restraint, interdiction, ban, *verboten (Ger.),* proscription, impediment, hindrance, check, inhibition, barrier, quarantine, deadlock, deadstop, full stop, pause, standstill, lull, forbidden fruit.

EMBARK, *v.* 1. Put on board a ship, go on board a ship, board ship, go on shipboard, go aboard, take ship, set sail, sail, put to sea, hoist the blue peter, weigh anchor, get under way.
2. Engage in an enterprise, enter upon, venture, begin, go into, make a beginning in some occupation, take the first step, launch, plunge into, undertake, take up, tackle, set about, turn one's hand to, assume, broach, institute, start.

EMBARRASS, *v.* 1. Put into a disturbed state of mind, render ill at ease, disturb one's equilibrium, discomfort, make uncomfortable, discompose, discomfit, disconcert, abash, mortify, chagrin, shame, upset, render flustered, agitate, bother, pose, make self-conscious, fluster, distract, derange, confound, perplex, confuse, nonplus.

2. Put obstacles in the way of, impede, hamper, hinder, obstruct, encumber, deprive of freedom of movement, clog, handicap, burden, plague, vex, annoy, distress, involve in difficulties, harass, trouble, frustrate, thwart.
3. Render difficult, complicate, make intricate, beset, enmesh, entangle, involve, tangle, snarl, muddle, entrap, ensnare.
4. Beset with financial difficulties, burden with debt, straiten.

EMBARRASSED, *adj.* 1. Mortified, chagrined, redfaced, ashamed, nonplused.
2. In difficulty, in a strait, in hot water, in a fix, in a scrape, at a loss, puzzled, at one's wits' end, between the devil and the deep blue sea, on the horns of a dilemma.
3. Financially straitened, hard-up, pinched, reduced to straits, impecunious, broke, flat, short of cash, fast, tied up, insolvent, in debt, put to one's shifts, under hatches.

EMBARRASSMENT, *n.* 1. Discomposure, shame, mortification, chagrin, abashment, disconcertion, awkwardness, *faux pas (Fr.),* uneasiness of mind caused by bashfulness, discomfiture, discouragement, vexation.
2. Entanglement, involvement, bewilderment, perturbation, confusion, perplexity, maze, knot, quandary, dilemma, puzzle, poser, knotty point, hard nut to crack, fix, matter, trouble, strait, predicament, intricacy, difficulty, pass, pinch, pickle, rub, critical situation, emergency, crisis, exigency, trial, scrape, hot water, stew, imbroglio, mess, muddle, botch, snag, hitch, hobble, plight, constraint, paradox, pressure.
3. Lack of freedom of action, hindrance, impediment, obstacle, encumbrance, handicap, stumbling block, bafflement, frustration, involvement of one's affairs.

EMBASSY, *n.* 1. Ambassadorial office, errand, delegation, commission, mission, deputation, procuration, embassade.
2. Body of persons entrusted with a mission to a sovereign *or* government, ambassador and his staff, legation, ambassadors, envoys, emissaries, commissionaires, *corps diplomatique.*
3. Official headquarters of an ambassador, consulate, legation, ambassadorial residence.

EMBATTLE, *v.* 1. Form in line of battle, arrange in battle station, array in battle order, marshal, draw up, set in battle array, put in line, prepare for battle, arm, equip for battle, mobilize troops, take the field.
2. Make battlements in, crenellate, fortify, furnish with battlements, fix with battlements.

EMBED, *v.* Fix in a surrounding mass, place within, enclose, put into, inlay, bed, locate, base, insert, set, root, graft, ingraft, plant, implant, impaste, install, establish, fix, pin, deposit, lay as in a bed, tuck in, dovetail, intromit, ram in, thrust in, stick in, stuff in, press in, drive in, pop in, impact.

EMBELLISH, *v.* 1. Make beautiful by adding ornamental features, ornamentalize, beautify by ornamentation, decorate, ornament, deck, bedeck, garnish, adorn, enrich, blazon, emblazon, dress up, trick out, prink, bedizen, array, trim, smarten, spruce up, doll up, set off, set out, elaborate, grace, gild, paint, varnish, enamel, polish, lacquer, spangle, bespangle, bead, chase, tool, illustrate, illuminate, miniate, rubricate.
2. Enhance with fictitious additions, color,

embroider, add imaginary details to, heighten the interest of, exaggerate.

EMBELLISHMENT, *n.* 1. Ornamentation, ornature, beautification, adornment, enrichment, decoration, garniture, ornateness, flamboyancy, trimming, fixings, ornament, illumination, illustration.

2. Embroidery, exaggeration, fictitious addition in a statement.

EMBERS, *n.* Live coals, small unextinguished brands, smoldering remains of a fire, smoking remnants, products of combustion, cinders, dross, slag, clinkers, ash, scoriae.

EMBEZZLE, *v.* Appropriate to one's own use fraudulently, take by fraud, misappropriate, peculate, defalcate, divert to one's own use in breach of trust, pilfer, steal, purloin, filch, rob, thieve, swindle, misapply, plunder, defraud, forge, misuse, dip into the public purse, make off with, cheat, swindle, cozen, pluck, fleece, rook, bilk, default, abstract.

EMBEZZLEMENT, *n.* Fraudulent appropriation to one's own use of money entrusted to one's care, fraud, defrauding, defalcation, peculation, misappropriation, abstraction, depredation, theft, direption, latrociny, malversation, malfeasance, thievery, robbery, larceny, pilfering, swindle, stealing.

EMBEZZLER, *n.* Peculator, defalcator, defaulter, thief, robber, brigand, criminal, reprobate.

EMBITTER, *v.* 1. Impart a bitter taste to, make bitter, make sour, acerbate, sour, acidify, acetify, acidulate.

2. Intensify in angry feeling, make rancorous, anger, exasperate, exacerbate, irritate, envenom, aggravate, poison, rankle, pique, annoy, provoke, vex, nettle, fret, rile, inflame, madden, enrage.

3. Make morose, make moody, make unhappy, make pessimistic.

EMBLAZON, *v.* 1. Portray on a heraldic shield, inscribe with armorial ensigns, emblaze with figures of heraldry, display heraldically, blazon, adorn with ensigns armorial.

2. Set off in resplendent colors, adorn, deck with showy ornamentation, embellish, decorate, bedeck, ornament, beautify, show off, set out.

3. Shine forth in glowing colors, illuminate, become bright.

4. Set forth publicly, publish, delineate in glowing terms, herald, proclaim, celebrate, extol, laud, glorify.

EMBLAZONRY, *n.* 1. Heraldic devices, heraldic ornaments, heraldic decoration, heraldry, blazonry.

2. Brilliant representation, embellishment, high coloring, brilliantly colored representation.

EMBLEM, *n.* 1. Representation of an object symbolizing something, allegorical drawing, figurative representation, symbolical picture, allusive figure, conventionalized figure, image, device, a visible sign for an idea, signum, sign, indicium, badge, token, mark, cognizance, motto, attribute, reminder, memento, effigy, design, metaphor, similitude, character, type, example, model, symbol, hieroglyph.

2. Insigne (*sing.*), insignia (*pl.*), regalia, star, impress, hallmark, countermark, monogram, seal, signet, signum, medal, swastika, asterisk, cross, banner, flag, pennant, ensign, standard, eagle, oriflamme, crest, arms, armorial bearings, escutcheon, cockade, epaulet, chevron, service stripes.

EMBLEMATIC, *adj.* Serving as an emblem, typically representative, typical, figurative, symbolical, metaphorical, indicative, allusive, significatory, suggestive, indicant, denotative, hermetical, hieroglyphic.

EMBODIMENT, *n.* 1. That in which something is embodied, bodily representation, material figuration, personification, incarnation, image, flesh and blood, corporeity, incorporation, substantiality, matter.

2. Concrete expression of, organization in an aggregate, realization, manifestation, formation, actualization, materialization, composition, union, constitution, association, conjunction.

EMBODY, *v.* 1. Clothe with a body, invest with a form, make corporeal, corporealize, incarnate, put into bodily form, form into a body.

2. Give a concrete form to, express in concrete form, represent as having external form, actualize, substantiate, substantialize, externalize, exhibit in visible form, exteriorize, personify, materialize, make visible, manifest, exhibit evidence.

3. Collect into a body, include in a body, fuse, incorporate, organize, integrate, concentrate, join, aggregate into an organized whole, collect in a mass, lump together, compact, combine, unite in a body, consolidate, coalesce, alloy, intermix, interfuse, amalgamate, blend, merge, cement.

4. Include, comprise, subsume, hold, contain, embrace, involve, cover, comprehend, inclose, encircle, receive, reckon among, number, count, enlist.

EMBOLDEN, *v.* Infuse courage in, raise hope, give courage to, encourage, hearten, inspire, cheer, buoy up, assure, reassure, nerve, put upon one's mettle, rally, make bold, inspirit, animate, abet, urge, incite, strengthen, impel, stimulate, press, rouse, instigate, enhearten, invigorate.

EMBOLISM, *n.* 1. Intercalation of a day in a year, interpolation of time for the adjustment of the calendar, time *or* period intercalated.

2. (*Pathol.*) Occlusion of a blood vessel by an embolus *or* blood clot, plugging up of an artery by a clot, thrombosis, closure, blockade, obstruction, stoppage.

EMBONPOINT, *n.* Well-rounded *or* filled-out appearance of the body, moderate degree of corpulence, exaggerated plumpness, fleshiness, fatness, stoutness, obesity, "this all too solid flesh," corporation (*humorous*).

EMBOSOM, *v.* 1. Take into the bosom, hold in the bosom, embrace, cherish, foster, nurse, shelter.

2. Place in the midst of something, enwrap, envelop, enclose, surround, enfold, bury, hide, conceal, secrete, screen from view.

EMBOSS, *v.* 1. Raise the surface of into ornaments in relief, raise surface designs in relief, ornament in relief, raise and design by pressing, adorn with raised work, chase, tool, fret, enchase, adorn with rich ornamentation, represent in relief upon a surface.

2. Cause to bulge out, make protuberant, cover with protuberances, stud with bosses, cause to stand out, decorate prominently.

EMBOSSMENT, *n.* 1. A figure in relief, raised work, embossed ornamentation, group of raised figures, embossed ornament, molding, tracery.

2. Boss-like knob, protuberance, bulging, stud,

projection, bulge, protrusion, excrescence, hump, hunch, lump, node, bump, ridge.

EMBOWEL, v. 1. Enclose deeply in, embed, tuck deep inside, conceal, bury, hide.

2. Remove the viscera of, disembowel, take out the entrails of, free from the bowels, gut, eviscerate.

EMBRACE, v. 1. Take in the arms, clasp in the arms, infold in the arms, hug, caress, fondle, cuddle, press to the bosom, embosom, fold to the heart, snuggle, enfold, cling to, squeeze, clasp, twine, entwine, interlace, wind round, cleave to, cherish, clutch to oneself, grasp.

2. Receive eagerly, welcome, take gladly, lay hold on, accept willingly, espouse, take up, adopt, make one's own, make choice of, avail oneself of.

3. Take in with the eye or mind, survey, comprehend.

4. Contain, comprise, include, subsume, hold, embody, incorporate, cover, admit, implicate, involve, reckon among.

5. Enclose, envelop, environ, confine, encircle, encompass, surround, compass, ensphere, gird, engird, inwrap, swathe, hedge, girdle.

EMBRACE, n. 1. Pressing to the bosom, hug, folding to the heart, embosomment, clasping in the arms.

2. Blandishment, fondling, billing and cooing, dalliance, spooning, petting, necking, love-making, bodily entwinement, kiss, osculation, smack, buss, symplegma.

EMBROIDER, v. 1. Ornament with designs in needlework, decorate with ornamental needle-work, work, braid lace.

2. Embellish rhetorically, hatch, concoct romance, trump up, fabricate, invent, dress up, describe with florid language, adorn with fictitious additions, garble, give a false color to, color, varnish the truth, prevaricate, exaggerate, lie, fib.

EMBROIDERY, n. 1. Needlework consisting of raised and ornamental designs upon any woven fabric, variegated needlework, orphrey, orris, sampler.

2. Elaboration of a story in details, rhetorical embellishment, variegated verbal adornment, variegation of the facts, exaggeration, hyperbole, coloring.

EMBROIL, v. 1. Bring into a state of discord, involve in contention, set at variance, implicate in strife, estrange, disunite, set at odds, pit against, enmesh in hostilities.

2. Throw into confusion, throw into tumult, implicate in confusion, confuse, render confused, throw into disorder, disorder, derange, distract, discompose, trouble, disturb grievously, perplex, mix up, entangle, ensnarl, commingle, jangle, complicate, muddle.

EMBROILMENT, n. 1. Strife, quarrel, imbroglio, embranglement, fracas, breach of the peace, scrimmage, rumpus, squall, riot, disturbance, contention, tumult, commotion, Donnybrook Fair, squabble, odds, brouillerie (Fr.), uproar, dissension, differences of opinion.

2. Confused condition, complication, perplexity, entanglement, confusion, disorder, derangement, distraction, discomposure, trouble, disturbance, entanglement, complication, jangle, muddle, mix-up.

EMBRYO, n. 1. Vitalized germ of an organism, organism in the earlier stages of its development, fetus, egg, nucleus.

2. Rudiment, rudimentary state, beginning, first stage, commencement, origin, incipience.

EMBRYONIC, adj. Being in the state of an embryo, incipient, rudimentary, undeveloped, immature, primary, preparatory, imperfect, unfinished, beginning, inchoate.

EMEND, v. 1. Alter the form of a work with a view to improvement, improve the text of, revise, edit, redact, subject to textual criticism, supply with improved readings.

2. Make corrections in, correct, rectify, change for the better, free from faults, amend by removing errors, rid of defects, make over, meliorate, ameliorate, touch up, improve, better, restore, mend, repair, reform.

EMENDATION, n. 1. Correction of textual errors, alteration in a text, editing, redaction, revision, revisal.

2. Critical alteration, changing for the better, correction, removal of errors, amelioration, mend, melioration, betterment, improvement, labor limae (Lat.), amendment.

EMERALD, n. 1. Rare green variety of beryl, valuable gem, precious stone.

2. Clear deep green, verd antique, verdigris, vert, malachite, viridescence, verdancy.

EMERGE, v. 1. Rise out of a fluid, come up, emerse, debouch, gush, disembogue, issue from, come forth from, emanate, escape, emit, come out, discharge, egress, proceed.

2. Come forth into notice, come out of hiding, appear, become apparent, become visible, arise, rise into view, crop up, outcrop, reappear, become manifest.

EMERGENCE, n. 1. Egress, escape, discharge, issue, outburst, outpour, effluence, emanation, issuance, emersion.

2. Coming forth into view, appearance, rising into view, egression, rise, evolution, apparency, outcrop.

EMERGENCY, n. Unforeseen occurrence, sudden and urgent occasion for action, perplexing combination of circumstances, situation in which quick action and judgment are necessary, fix, juncture demanding immediate action, urgency, extremity, exigency, pressing necessity, crisis, pass, turn of events, strait, plight, hole (coll.), corner, impasse, dilemma, quandary, difficulty, pinch, perplexity, contingency, conjuncture, trouble, predicament, last-minute need, eleventh-hour obligation.

EMERGENT, adj. 1. Emerging, rising, emanant, emanating, efflorescent, coming into view, issuing forth, outbound, outgoing, rising into notice.

2. Arising unexpectedly, resulting casually, sudden, urgent, pressing, calling for immediate action.

EMERITUS, adj. Honorably discharged from active duty because of age but retained on the rolls, honorably relieved from duty, retired, revered, venerable, reverenced, respected, in high esteem, time-honored.

EMERSON, n. Rising up out of or from behind something, emergence, coming forth, issuance, appearance, egress, reappearance of a heavenly body after an occultation or eclipse (Astron.).

EMIGRANT, n. One who emigrates from his native country, expatriate, migrant, immigrant, émigré, migrator, colonist, D. P. (displaced person), refugee, fugitive, wayfarer, itinerant, traveler, foreigner, peregrinator, wanderer, bird of passage, vagrant, Okie.

EMIGRATE, *v.* Depart from one land to reside in another, expatriate, migrate, remove from one country to settle in another, move, immigrate, suffer displacement, leave, quit, abandon, go away from, remove permanently, trek.

EMIGRATION, *n.* 1. Departure from one country to reside in another, expatriation, displacement, migration, moving away, exodus, removal, wayfaring, pererration, trekking.

2. Those who emigrate, body of emigrants, emigrants collectively.

EMINENCE, *n.* 1. Place that projects above the general surface of the surroundings, a high place, rising ground, height of ground, hill, elevation, altitude, high point, elevated ground, rise, dune, prominence, promontory, headland, butte, knoll, mount, mountain, alp, bluff, cliff, peak, ridge, upland, down, highland, hummock, hillock, knob, mound, summit, protuberance, projection.

2. High station *or* repute, elevated rank, high position, important station, standing, importance, exaltation, preëminence, prominence, public esteem, notability, note, name, figure, celebrity, fame, renown, report, repute, reputation, honor, distinction, grandeur, loftiness, greatness, glory, dignity, conspicuousness, nobility, preferment, stateliness, excellence, majesty, supereminence, sublimity.

3. Supreme degree, marked degree, title of honor of a cardinal (*Rom. Cath. Ch.*), brilliancy, transcendence, superiority.

EMINENT, *adj.* 1. High, towering, elevated, lofty.

2. Projecting, protruding, prominent, foremost, standing out clearly, in the front rank, outstanding.

3. Conspicuous, evident, noteworthy, notable, remarkable, noted, extraordinary, memorable.

4. High in station *or* repute, high in esteem, celebrated, esteemed, exalted, supreme, superior, paramount, illustrious, distinguished, well-known, *distingué (Fr.),* far-famed, famous, noted, of note, renowned, eximious, noble, honored, grand, glorious, great, important, majestic, august, sublime, peerless, preëminent, supereminent, dignified, honorable, lordly, princely, imposing, transcendent, heroic, notable, paramount, superlative, excellent, independent of other authority.

EMISSARY, *n.* 1. Agent sent on a mission *or* errand, messenger, envoy, legate, courier, herald, representative, intermediary, go-between, nuncio, middleman, mediator, internuncio, deputy, proxy, delegate, commissioner, *commissionaire (Fr.),* ambassador, plenipotentiary, diplomat, substitute, correspondent, vicar.

2. Secret agent, spy, scout, informer, detective, sleuth, *mouchard (Fr.),* stool pigeon.

EMISSION, *n.* 1. Sending out, putting forth, vent, throwing out, emitting, ejection, projection, ejaculation, expression, effusion, radiation, issue, circulation, issuance, utterance, exhalation, exudation, evacuation, voidance, eructation, eruption, trajection, extrusion, disgorgement, vomition, clearance, excretion, egestion, bent.

2. That which is emitted, discharge, emanation, drainage, ejecta, egesta, orgasm.

EMIT, *v.* 1. Eject, send out, throw out, discharge, pour forth, give forth, cast out, outpour, extrude, dispatch, expel, shed, emanate, squirt, shoot, jet, spurt, spill out, slop, spend, expend, secrete, exude, blow, gush, hurl, issue, perspire, give off,

erupt, eructate, belch forth, vomit, excrete, purge, void, evacuate, egest, cast up, throw up, spew, expectorate, spit, slobber, drool, drivel, transmit, extravasate, ooze, breathe out, exhale, deliver, clear off, turn on the tap, open the sluices, issue for circulation, edit, get out, pour out.

2. Give vent to, utter, effuse, express, voice, give utterance, cry, ejaculate, murmur, whisper, aspirate, articulate, enunciate.

EMOLLIENT, *adj.* Allaying irritation, soothing inflammation, lenitive, assuasive, mitigative, mildening, relieving, palliative, demulcent, bland, healing, remedial, restorative, therapeutic, softening, relaxing, making supple, making pliable, analeptic, balsamic, anodyne, sedative.

EMOLLIENT, *n.* Medicinal substance having the power of relaxing living tissues, application to allay soreness, soothing application, lenitive, oil, salve, ointment, cerate, lotion, liniment, mustard plaster, balm, embrocation, sinapism, cataplasm, poultice, epithem.

EMOLUMENT, *n.* 1. Compensation for services, profit arising from employment, remuneration for occupation, recompense, payment, pay, earnings, wages, salary, fees, revenue, income, perquisite, hire, gain, stipend, indemnification, reparation, pecuniary profit, gross receipts, net profit, bonus, premium, lucre, pelf.

2. General advantage, benefit, reward, return, windfall, clean-up, pickings, proceeds, moneymaking.

EMOTION, *n.* 1. Any strong perturbation of the conscious mind, state of excited feeling, passion, intensified feeling, sentiment, sensation, response, excitement of sensibility, mental agitation, deep sense, inward fermentation, affection, impression, somatic reaction, bodily resonance, excitability.

2. Love, ecstasy, thrill, heartstring, tingling, kick (*coll.*), throb, palpitation, flutter, heaving, fire, warmth, glow, vehemence, fervor, concern, ardor, fulness of the heart, zeal, inspiration, sympathy, tenderness, pathos, mental conflict, trepidation, disturbance, worry, tumult, jealousy, apprehension, fear, hate, agitation, shame, grief, remorse, sorrow, sadness, despondency, despair, hypochondria, pride, elation, anger, rage, greed, ire, resentment, covetousness, cupidity, sensuality, lust, lecherousness, prurience, concupiscence, joy, satisfaction, happiness.

EMOTIONAL, *adj.* 1. Easily affected by emotion, controlled by impulses arising in the emotions, temperamental, demonstrative, susceptible, quick to tears, sensitive, feeling, sentient, sensuous, with feeling, not rational, impressible, fervent, ardent, passionate, sentimental, fiery, warm, breathless, glowing, enthusiastic, zealous, impetuous, mobile, impulsive, deep-feeling, emotive, maudlin, rapt, pathematic, high-strung, excitable, wrought up, overwrought, hysterical, lachrymose, languorous, languishing, lackadaisical, responsive, rapturous, ecstatic.

2. Expressive of emotion, moving the feelings, springing from emotion, dramatic, sensational, thrilling, heartfelt, soul-stirring, electric, swelling, poignant, pathetic, heart-throbbing, heart-expanding.

EMOTIONALISM, *n.* 1. Expression of emotion, emotionality, temperamentalism, sentimentalism, emotional utterance, demonstrativeness, hysteria, sentimentality, tendency to morbid emotion, loss of emotional control, subordination of reason to the superficial emotions, lackadaisicalness, morbid excitement, mawkishness, maudlinness.

2. Emotional appeal, excitation of the feelings, sensationalism, stimulation, impressiveness, tears and laughter, galvanism, provocation, fascination, agitation, perturbation, melodrama, entrancement, enravishment.

EMOTIONALIZE, v. 1. Be excited, work oneself up, thrill, tingle, glow, flush, heave, pant, throb, palpitate, go pitapat, be agitated, be ardent, go into a passion, treat as a matter of emotion.

2. Excite the feelings of, stir, touch a chord, touch the heart, fan the flame, move, touch, play on the feelings, affect, enkindle, inspire, set astir, impassion, play on the heartstrings, rouse, kindle, fire.

EMPEROR, n. Supreme ruler of an empire, rex, sovereign, suzerain, crowned head, monarch, bey, king of kings, potentate, autocrat, despot, tyrant, overlord, liege lord, imperator, Caesar, majesty, czar, kaiser, regent, prince, sultan, khedive, inca, pasha, caliph, shah, grand Turk, imaum, mikado, emir, great mogul, khan, rajah, maharajah, negus, nawab, lama, satrap, doge.

EMPHASIS, n. 1. Force of voice in speaking or reading, stress on certain words, strong accent, intensity of expression, force of utterance, tone degree, accentuation, exclamation, vociferation, special impressiveness added to an utterance, ejaculation, articulation, vigorous enunciation.

2. Stress laid upon anything, moment, energy, significance attached to anything, impressiveness, importance, consequence, saliency, weight, mark, ponderosity, prominence, strength, distinctness, insistence, affirmation, cocksureness, dogmatism, peremptoriness, positiveness, decidedness, gravity, assurance, averment, forcibleness, underscoring, seriousness, solemnity, pressure, urgency, matter of life and death, underlining, italics.

EMPHASIZE, v. Articulate emphatically, feature, give emphasis to, stress, lay stress on, accentuate, accent, heighten, underscore, underline, intensify, put in italics, punctuate, mark, bring out clearly and positively, affirm, protest, make more distinct, make impressive, enforce, bear down on, press home, bring into relief, hammer away, pound away, iterate and reiterate, harp on, dwell on.

EMPHATIC, adj. Uttered with emphasis, strong, strongly expressive, laying especial stress, distinct, conveying emphasis, intensive, pointed, marked, flat, broad, round, affirmative, impressive, grave, imperative, exigent, insistent, prominent, solemn, vigorous, forceful, pregnant, trenchant, serious, assertive, definitive, categorical, weighty, cogent, ponderous, telling, pressing, critical, momentous, crucial, instant, powerful, important, irresistible, peremptory, certain, determined, strongly marked, forcibly significant, striking, vivid, positive, clear, energetic, forcible, pronounced, decided, earnest, conspicuous, express, explicit, absolute, dogmatic, unequivocal.

EMPIRE, n. 1. A group of states united under a single sovereign power, aggregate of peoples ruled over by an emperor, a territory of greater extent than a kingdom ruled over by a single sovereign, autocratic government of vast consolidated territory.

2. Supreme power in governing, imperial rule, sovereignty, suzerainty, supreme dominion, orb, supremacy, imperial power, domain, absolute authority, supreme control, absolute sway, reign, autocratic command, autocracy, monocracy, rod

of empire, kingship, hegemony, mastery, lordship, dictation, royalty, regality, monarchy, imperium, scepter, throne, crown, purple, regalia, sword of state, dynasty, regime, regnancy, protectorate, divine right.

EMPIRICAL, adj. 1. Empiric, experiential, based on evidence of the senses, not using science or theory, derived from experience, generalizing hastily from limited facts, guided by experiment, based on observation, depending on observation alone, guided by observation of facts rather than by accepted principles.

2. Hypothetical, probatory, speculative, feeling its way, probationary, tentative, provisional, awaiting verification.

3. Quackish, charlatanic, unskilled, deceptive, fraudulent.

EMPIRICISM, n. 1. (Philos.) Doctrine that all knowledge is derived from experience alone, experientialism, sensationalism, doctrine of the sole, validity of sense, sensualism.

2. Reliance on the evidence of sense alone, dependence on experience, diagnostic, crucial test, reliance on direct individual observation, rule of thumb, experimentum crucis (Lat.).

3. Charlatanism, mountebankery, imposture, quackery, ignorant and unscientific practice, cheating.

EMPLOY, v. 1. Use the services of a person, give employment to hire, keep in one's service, enlist in one's service, keep at work, hire, retain the services of, furnish occupation for, commission, contract for, engage.

2. Make use of instrumentally, apply, use, put to use, set to work, put to task, wield, operate, handle, manipulate, ply, work, utilize.

3. Devote to a certain occupation, engross, absorb, occupy, exercise, busy, reserve.

EMPLOYEE, n. One who works for wages or salary, person working for a business firm for pay, one who is engaged in the service of another, employe, hireling, clerk, workman, hand, hired hand, helper, assistant, attendant, agent, worker, job-holder, wage-earner, workingman, laborer, servant, domestic, butler, steward, waiter, lackey, footman, flunky, maid, bonne (Fr.), apprentice, cook, scullion, cleaning woman, chambermaid, factotum, errand-boy, understrapper, secretary, stenographer, personnel collectively.

EMPLOYER, n. One who employs for wages, one who engages the services of other persons for pay, boss, owner, proprietor, manager, old man (familiar), director, controller, leader, big shot, master, patron, governor, kingpin (coll.), entrepreneur, contractor.

EMPLOYMENT, n. 1. Work upon which one is engaged, that on which one is employed, business, occupation, position, office, vocation, profession, calling, employ, engagement, work, pursuit, post, incumbency, berth, billet, appointment, mission, enterprise, métier, craft, line, trade, job, situation, undertaking, task, stint, chore, assignment, duty, charge, errand, commission, function, services, agency, station.

2. Use, application, exercise, utilization, wear, appliance, recourse, resort, modus operandi (Lat.), operation, maintenance, usefulness, service, utility.

3. Engrossment, busy state, occupation, brown study, absorption, preoccupation.

EMPORIUM, n. 1. Principal center of trade, fair town or place of important commerce, entrepôt, commercial resort, chief mart of a wide territory, trading center, market-overt, open market, mart, market place, bazaar, forum, staple, large market, warehouse.

2. Large store selling a great variety of articles, department store, shop, establishment, *magasin (Fr.)*.

EMPOWER, *v.* 1. Give power to, confer power on, invest with authoritative power, commission, delegate authority to, authorize formally, license, charter, enfranchise, warrant, privilege, sanction, intrust, legalize, qualify, accredit, appoint, entitle, depute, confirm, approve, ratify, allow, permit, assign.

2. Make able, render competent, enable, invest, strengthen, energize, activate, potentialize, endue, endow, impart physical power to, arm, quicken.

EMPRESS, *n.* Woman who rules an empire as its sovereign, female sovereign, queen, *regina (Lat.)*, *impératrice (Fr.)*, consort of an emperor, begum, dowager-empress, queen-mother, sultana, infanta, czarina, maharani.

EMPTINESS, *n.* 1. State of being destitute of contents, empty space, void, vacuum, interruption, vacuity, vacancy, hiatus, chasm, interim, interval, interlude, want, lack, need, deficiency, scarcity, requirement, depletion, exhaustion, inanition, vacantness.

2. Lack of substantial qualities, want of real value, worthlessness, uselessness, meaninglessness, hollowness, mockery, triviality, unreality, vanity, fruitlessness, sham, insignificance, ineptitude, folly.

3. Lack of sense *or* knowledge, senselessness, inanity, stupidity, flummery, nonsense, frivolity, vacuousness, foolishness.

EMPTY, *adj.* 1. Having nothing within, containing nothing, without contents, void of contents, blank, hollow, clear, bare, deflated, depleted, destitute of contents, vacant, vacuous, devoid, exhausted, wanting, flat, shallow, lacking.

2. Having nothing to carry, unloaded, hungry, unburdened, unfurnished, free, unsupplied, being without supplies, unfilled, unfed.

3. Without force *or* effect, unsatisfactory, vain, unsatisfying, unsubstantial, useless, meaningless, valueless, ineffectual, unreal, delusive, having no fruit, futile, without substance, fruitless, barren, sterile, worthless, weak.

4. Destitute of intelligence, having few ideas, having little sense, brainless, witless, senseless, meaningless, without significance, silly, without knowledge *or* sense, stupid, unwise, frivolous, ignorant, inane, foolish, trivial, empty-headed.

5. Verbose, prolix, long-winded, wordy, diffuse, garrulous, voluble, loquacious, talkative, babbling, blabbing, chattering.

EMPTY, *v.* 1. Remove all the contents from, tap, make vacant, draw out, deplete, exhaust, drain, evacuate, make empty, deprive of contents, clear off, remove all of from that which contains it, broach, deflate, sweep off.

2. Cast forth, eject, expel, discharge, pour out, disembogue, void, purge, unload, unburden.

3. Become empty, flow out, be discharged, ebb out, fall, sink.

EMPYREAL, *adj.* 1. Pertaining to the highest heaven, empyrean, aerial, extraterrene, nebular, sphery, pertaining to the sky, celestial, heavenly, uranic, cosmic, starry, astral, stellar, sidereal, interstellar, intersidereal, lunar, solar.

2. Formed of pure fire *or* light, fiery, light, dazzling, igneous.

3. Most highly refined, sublimated, ethereal, sublime, elevated, airy, volatile, fugitive.

EMPYREAN, *n.* Highest heaven containing the pure elements of fire, seventh heaven, upper sky, celestial spaces, firmament, ether, cosmos, the visible heavens, starry heaven, cosmic space, vault of heaven, welkin, canopy of heaven, abode of God and the angels.

EMULATE, *v.* Imitate with effort to surpass, try to equal, strive to excel, rival with some degree of success, challenge comparison, mimic with intent to outdo, vie with, contend with, compete with, cope with, outrival, race, run a race with, spoil one's trade.

EMULATION, *n.* Desire to excel, ambition to surpass, effort to equal, trial of superiority, race, competition, rivalry, contest, vying, point-to-point race, handicap, agonism, antagonism, controversy, game, match, scrimmage, tussle, scuffle, two of a trade, opposition, tug-of-war, corrivalry, war to the knife.

EMULOUS, *adj.* Striving to excel, eager to equal, inclined to rivalry, competitive, rivaling, desirous of equaling, competitory, aspiring to excel, filled with emulation, ambitious, cutthroat, dog-eat-dog.

ENABLE, *v.* 1. Make able, give means *or* ability to, make competent, render capable, supply with adequate means, endow, arm, strengthen, make possible, capacitate, make practicable, make easy.

2. Give authority, empower, authorize, license, permit, sanction, legalize, warrant, commission, delegate, qualify.

ENACT, *v.* 1. Make into a statute, establish by act of authority, decree, ordain by law, pass into a law, order, give legislative sanction to, legislate, institute by law, dictate, enjoin, bid, impose, issue a command, prescribe, charge, appoint by act, transact, ratify, sanction, approve, proclaim, adjudge.

2. Carry out in action, accomplish, perform, execute, do, effect, commit, achieve, perpetrate.

3. Act the part of, personify, impersonate, play the role of, represent on the stage, take the part of.

ENACTMENT, *n.* 1. Statute, law, fiat, act, edict, decree, dictate, mandate, caveat, rescript, firman, prescript, writ, ordination, ukase, measure, order, command, regulation, ordinance, provision of a law, transaction, prescribed requirement, direction, injunction.

2. Accomplishment, performance, perpetration, appointment, institution, execution, achievement, passage.

3. Personification, impersonation, acting, stage representation, playing.

ENAMEL, *n.* Glossy lacquer, glaze, varnish, gloss, glossy opaque substance applied by fusion as an ornament *or* for protection, vitreous composition, japan, external polish, coating, inlay.

ENAMEL, *v.* Overlay with enamel, decorate in enamel, form an enamel-like surface upon, make a glossy surface upon, variegate with colored enamels, varnish, glaze, japan, lacquer, furbish, paint, adorn with many different hues, cover, superpose, overspread, veneer, coat, embellish, enrich, beautify, smarten.

ENAMOR, *v.* Inspire with ardent love, excite love, make exceedingly fond, inflame with passion, enchant, charm, fascinate, bewitch, win the heart, captivate, ensorcel, enthrall, entrance, infatuate, take the fancy of, turn the head, wind round the heart, endear, send one's pulse spinning, attract, draw to, allure, attach, enrapture, entice, engross, seduce.

ENCAGE, *v.* Confine in a cage, coop up, pen, cage, impound, shut up, rail in, bar in, box in, imprison, immure, incarcerate.

ENCAMP, *v.* Settle in a camp, establish in an encampment, camp down, pitch one's camp, pitch tents, form a camp, lodge in tents, pitch tents for a resting place, take up abode, put up at, billet, bivouac, quarter, settle in temporary habitations, plant oneself.

ENCAMPMENT, *n.* 1. Laying out of a camp, castrametation, pitching tents for occupancy, lodgment in a camp.
2. Quarters occupied in camping, cantonment, bivouac, barrack, camping ground, tents and the grounds occupied by them, casern, caravansary.
3. Body of men occupying a camp, company of travelers.

ENCASE, *v.* Enclose in a case, surround with anything, incase, sheathe, swathe, clothe, stocking, hose.

ENCEINTE, *adj.* Pregnant, gravid, with child, big with, fraught with, teeming with, in a family way, expecting, parturient, puerperal, brought to bed, fertile.

ENCEINTE, *n.* Circumvallation, principal line of fortifications surrounding a place, town wall, wall of a fortified place, cincture, girdle, precinct, plot, arena, enclosure, circuit, circle, walk, ring, fence, march, close, enclave, court, cordon.

ENCHAIN, *v.* 1. Fasten with a chain, hold in chains, fetter, enfetter, shackle, trammel, pinion, entrammel, manacle, put in irons, handcuff, bind, put into bilboes, tie the hands, hobble, bind hand and foot, tie up, forge fetters, truss up, attach firmly, restrain, confine, secure.
2. Hold fast the attention, attract, captivate, rivet, magnetize, hypnotize, mesmerize.

ENCHANT, *v.* 1. Practice sorcery upon, subject to magical influence, spellbind, cast a spell upon, control by enchantment, throw under a spell, bewitch, ensorcel, bind by incantations, charm, call up spirits, witch, hypnotize, mesmerize, hoodoo, hex.
2. Delight in a high degree, fascinate, enamor, captivate, transport, enrapture, ravish, catch, win, attract irresistibly, enchain, lead captive, allure, infatuate, entice, enthrall.

ENCHANTER, *n.* One who enchants, worker with the supernatural, sorcerer, wizard, magician, hex, necromancer, thaumaturgist, charmer, conjurer, witch, exorcist, diviner, seer, voodoo, mage, witch doctor, medicine man, powwow doctor, shaman, mesmerist, hypnotist, astrologer, soothsayer.

ENCHANTING, *adj.* 1. Magical, necromantic, incantatory, witching, talismanic, bewitching, cabalistic, Circean, fetishistic.
2. Captivating, charming, seductive, alluring, enticing, fascinating, entrancing, winning, a sight to see, enravishing, ravishing, delightful, engaging, enrapturing, intriguing, irresistible.

ENCHANTMENT, *n.* 1. Act of influencing by magic arts, use of supernatural agencies, magic, black magic, black art, sorcery, wizardry, occult art, thaumaturgy, conjuration, witchery, hex,

ensorcelment, necromancy, hoodoo, voodoo, jinx, exorcism, demonology, witchcraft, charm, spell, bewitchment, evil eye, *mal occhio (It.),* hocus-pocus, spellbinding, *diablerie (Fr.),* obi, wand, abracadabra, sortilege, invocation, divination, shamanism, obsession, possession, magic ring, open sesame, magic carpet, Aladdin's lamp, divining rod, amulet, talisman, fetish, phylactery, philter, magic potion, incantation.
2. Irresistible allurement, illusive charm, bliss, glamor, fascination, ravishment, rapture, delight, transport, ecstasy, entrancement, seduction, animal magnetism, mesmerism.

ENCHANTRESS, *n.* 1. Woman who practices magic, witch, sorceress, hex, siren, lamia, fairy, weird sister, hag, witch of Endor, Circe, Hecate, Lorelei, succuba.
2. Fascinating woman, *femme fatale (Fr.),* woman of bewitching charms, vampire, vamp, charmer, fair enslaver.

ENCHASE, *v.* 1. Enclose a gem in gold, place gems in an ornamental setting, incase in a setting, stud with gems, encircle, set, form a setting to, infix in an encircling mass.
2. Decorate with embossing, emboss, ornament with engraving, chase, enrich with chased work, grave, engrave, incise, carve, cut, inlay, furrow, crosshatch, flute, groove.

ENCIRCLE, *v.* 1. Form a circle round, gird, hem in, girdle, engird, surround with a girdle, span, compass, encompass, ensphere, surround, enclose, enfold, environ, inclose, loop, belt, ring, enring, beset, wind, twine, hoop, wreathe, hedge, pen, confine, circumscribe, besiege, envelop, embrace.
2. Make a circling movement about, make the circuit of, go round, tour around, circle, close in.

ENCLOSE, *v.* 1. Close in on all sides, shut in, circle, encircle, compass, encompass, embrace, surround, circumscribe, put a barrier around, fence in, enclose, embosom, engird, begird, girdle, hedge in, wall in, picket, corral, bound, pound, palisade, hem in, confine, invest, beset, seclude, imprison, blockade.
2. Insert in the same receptacle, put into a cover, cover, envelop, wrap, infold, seal.

ENCLOSURE, *n.* 1. Thing enclosed, that which is enclosed.
2. That which encloses, envelope, case, girdle, wrapper, stockade, fence, corral, fold, kraal, sty, croft, paddock, pound, yard, compound, palisade, hedge, espalier, pale, paling, circumvallation, pen, enceinte, barrier, ring fence, cage, cloister, prison, barricade, wall.
3. Court, plot, patch, close, enclose, field, arena, precincts, march.
4. Boundary, circumference, compass, circle.

ENCOMIAST, *n.* One who praises extravagantly, deliverer of an encomium, laudator, panegyrist, eulogist, extoller, adulator, euphemist, optimist, booster.

ENCOMIASTIC, *adj.* Bestowing praise, eulogistic, acclamatory, panegyrical, laudatory, lavish of praise, commendatory, complimentary, uncritical, benedictory.

ENCOMIUM, *n.* Formal expression of praise, eulogy, eulogium, éloge, laud, laudation, good word, panegyric, homage, compliment, approval, commendation, approbation, plaudit, applause, meed of praise, tribute of praise, admiration, hero worship, acclaim, acclamation, paean, blurb, hosanna, benediction.

ENCOMPASS, *v.* 1. Form a circle about, circle, encircle, girdle, gird, engird, begird, compass, environ, encompass, envelop, surround, enclose, embrace, inclose, skirt, twine around, belt, hedge in, close in, circumscribe, enfold, contain, include.

2. Surround hostilely, besiege, beleaguer, ring, beset, invest, shut in, hem in, blockade, bound the whole circuit of, lay siege to, wall in.

ENCORE, *v.* Call for an encore from a performer, demand by applause a repetition of, shout the word "encore," call back, call for a repetition of, recall, applaud, clap the hands, cheer, acclaim, hail, acclamate, appreciate, honor.

ENCORE, *interj.* Again, over again, once more, another time, *bis*, bravo, twice, afresh, anew.

ENCOUNTER, *n.* 1. Casual *or* unexpected meeting, coming together, junction, joining, rejoining, interview, approach, experience.

2. Meeting in conflict, hostile contest, battle, rencontre, combat, conflict, fight, onset, charge, invasion, attack, assault, brush, scrimmage, melee, fracas, tussle, scuffle, onslaught, duel, action, engagement, affair, bout, broil, fray, affray, tilt, dispute.

3. Collision, crash, clash, shock, brunt, bump, impact, percussion, concussion, impetus, impulsion, momentum.

ENCOUNTER, *v.* 1. Come upon unexpectedly, meet suddenly, meet with, meet face to face, come across, face, confront, come upon, fall upon, bump into, come in contact, join.

2. Undergo, endure, experience, bear, suffer, go through, pass through, find, taste, receive, fall to the lot of, befall, be one's lot.

3. Engage in conflict with, meet in conflict, fight with, do battle with, contend against opposition, resist, grapple with, exchange blows, attack, assail, combat, struggle with, skirmish, battle, measure swords, enter the lists, join issue, compete with, strive with, cope with, stem, breast, buffet the waves.

ENCOURAGE, *v.* 1. Inspire with confidence, increase the hope of, hold out hope, hearten, enhearten, inspirit, stimulate with courage, rally, embolden, nerve, fortify, strengthen, assure, egg on, reassure, buoy up, cheer, animate, boost, console, comfort, actuate, instigate, incite, excite, exhort, impel, spur, goad, whet, prick, sway, prevail on, induce, influence, dispose, incline, persuade, arouse, urge on, give a shot in the arm, build up, invigorate.

2. Promote, advance, prompt, further, help, abet, aid, back, second, patronize, befriend, favor, foster, support, advocate, countenance, approve, forward, help forward, lobby, assist.

ENCOURAGEMENT, *n.* Hope, shot in the arm *(coll.)*, sanguine expectation, sanguineness, enheartenment, stimulation, stimulus, cheer, lift, urging, confidence, trust, promise, assurance, aid, reassurance, security, buoyancy, incentive, spur, assistance, inspiration, persuasion, exhortation, advice, backing, advance, furtherance, promotion, patronage, favor, advocacy, sanction, approval, approbation, inducement, stimulus, goad, solace, influence, prompting, instigation, urge, instance, countenance, comfort, relief, refreshment, help, consolation, opitulation, succor, support, aegis, subministration, championship, good omen, good auspices, bright prospect, clear sky, optimism, enthusiasm.

ENCROACH, *v.* Advance stealthily beyond proper limits, make gradual inroads, overstep boundaries, break in upon by violation, trench on another's limits, invade insidiously, intrude, make inroad, infringe, trespass, assume possession of others' property, usurp, crowd into the rights of others, spread over, appropriate the possessions of another, transgress established bounds, aggress, impinge, obtrude, establish an imperceptible footing, exact, overrun, seize wrongfully, arrogate, dispossess, pass unlawfully within another's boundaries.

ENCROACHMENT, *n.* Act of encroaching, tort *(Law)*, infringement, trespass, transgression, aggression, invasion, infraction, intrenchment, entrance upon the domain of another, inroad, intrusion without permission, advancement, attack, overrunning, overstepping, transilience, usurpation, injustice, arrogation, exaction, seizure, assumption, dispossession, imposition.

ENCUMBER, *v.* 1. Fill with what is superfluous, cumber, block up, clog, impede with obstacles, obstruct in action, hinder in movement, load, overload, burden, overburden, hamper, check, oppress, handicap, act as a drag, cramp, retard, delay, load down, weigh down, saddle with, fetter, lime, pack, trammel, entrammel, incommode, lumber, discommode.

2. Discompose, corner, tree, nonplus, perplex, embarrass, complicate, entangle, involve, ensnare, frustrate, charge with obligations, mortgage.

ENCUMBRANCE, *n.* 1. Anything that renders action *or* motion laborious, that which encumbers, something superfluous, impediment, impedimenta, hindrance, burden, clog, load, fardel, onus, drag, trammel, dead weight, obstacle, difficulty, pack, drawback, obstruction, barrier, lumber, any useless addition, millstone round one's neck, old man of the sea, incubus, disadvantage, baggage.

2. A dependent person, wife, dependent child.

3. *(Law)* Debt, claim on property, mortgage, registered judgment, liability, lien, charge, right of dower.

ENCYCLICAL, *n.* Circular letter by the Pope to all the bishops of the world, bull, manifesto, propagation, proclamation, papal communication to the Holy See, pronouncement, pronunciamento, promulgation.

ENCYCLICAL, *adj.* Intended for wide circulation, general, encyclic, current, public, in circulation, promulgatory.

ENCYCLOPEDIA, *n.* An alphabetized work treating separately various topics from all branches of knowledge, exhaustive work on arts *or* sciences, a work containing information on all subjects, cyclopedia, thesaurus, lexicon, book of knowledge, dictionary, compilation, concordance, a comprehensive summary of knowledge, one possessed of encyclopedic information.

ENCYCLOPEDIC, *adj.* 1. Relating to all branches of knowledge, embracing the whole circle of learning, comprehensive, all-inclusive, exhaustive, universal, comprehending a wide range of topics, possessing extensive knowledge.

2. Erudite, learned, well-informed, scholastic, savant, bookish, omniscient.

END, *n.* 1. An extremity of anything that is longer than it is broad, furthermost part of anything extended in space, extremity of a body extended longitudinally, extreme point, tip, point, nib, terminal point of any material object that has length, head, top, horn.

2. Anything that bounds an object at one of its

extremities, bound, end, boundary, termination, terminus, limit, close, bourne, terminal, ultimate, pole, utmost, uttermost, extreme.

3. Act of coming to an end, concluding part, cessation, expiration, finish, finis, finale, final event, finality, close, period, stoppage, point in time at which some process ceases, wind-up, outcome, denouement, epilogue, consummation, ending, peroration, conclusion, accomplishment, fulfilment, completion, cessation.

4. Closing period, decline, wane, evening, eventide, sunset, final state, ultimate condition.

5. Close of life, death, death-knell, dissolution, deathblow, *coup de grâce (Fr.)*, termination of existence, doomsday, doom, destiny.

6. Overthrow, knockout, K.O., sleeper, sleep punch, catastrophe, destruction, annihilation, ruination, ruin, extermination.

7. Result, issue, consequence, upshot, outcome, sequel, settlement, fulfilment, effect.

8. Object for which a thing exists, final cause, purpose in view, aim, that for the attainment of which means are to be used, objective, goal, destination, intent, design, object, intention, motive, reason.

9. Fragment, fag end, stub, remnant, scrap, foot, heel, tag, butt.

END, *v.* 1. Bring to a natural conclusion, put an end to, conclude, terminate, drop, discontinue, finish, stop, close, abolish, dissolve, make an end of, wind up, cut short, bring to an end, leave off, desist, relinquish, quit, break off, settle, adjourn, suspend, ring down the curtain, consummate, complete, achieve.

2. Put an end to by force, put to death, kill, annihilate, exterminate, eradicate, extinguish, destroy.

3. Come to a close, cease, come to an end, be finished, reach a close, run out, pass away, expire, die, peter out, vanish.

ENDANGER, *v.* 1. Put in danger, bring into danger, hazard, put to hazard, expose to peril, peril, imperil, jeopard, jeopardize, put in jeopardy, venture, stake, dare, commit, compromise, bring under suspicion, sail too near the wind.

2. Cause danger of, make probable, make imminent.

ENDEAR, *v.* Cause to become an object of affection, make beloved, make esteemed, make dear, bind by ties of affection, attach fondly, cause to be loved, secure the affection of, make an object of affection, prize, treasure, idolize, hold dear, smile upon, lose one's heart to, be enamored of, coddle, make much of, cherish, foster, cuddle, hug, fold to the heart, snuggle, nuzzle, nestle, embrace, kiss, bill and coo, court, make love, spark, spoon, dally, pet, philander, coquet, pay court to, serenade, woo, sue, set one's cap at, warm the cockles of one's heart.

ENDEARMENT, *n.* 1. Attachment, fondness, tender affection, close tie, love.

2. Action manifesting affection, utterance of fondness, affectionate term, baby talk, fondling, blandishment, petting, caress, sweet talk, billing and cooing, embrace, kiss, smack, buss, suit, osculation, love-making, courtship, wooing, court, serenade, amorous glances, calf love, ogling, sheep's eyes, flirting, goo-goo eyes, coquetry, gallantry, necking, spooning, philandering, sheiking, vamping.

ENDEAVOR, *v.* Exert oneself to effect something, attempt strenuously, undertake and strive for,

work at, tackle, struggle, labor, essay, make an effort, take a crack at, take a whack at, make a go at, experiment, aim, test, study, seek to, take on, venture, speculate, take one's chance, tempt fortune, adventure, try one's hand, feel one's way, grope, pick one's way, try hard, make a bold push, do one's best, bestir oneself, trouble oneself over, take pains, aspire, go about.

ENDEAVOR, *n.* Attempt to attain something, earnest exertion for an end, strenuous effort, sustained trial, essay, struggle, striving, conatus, nisus, venture, aim, adventure, speculation, *coup d'essai (Fr.)*, try, crack *(sl.)*, whack *(sl.)*, go *(sl.)*, enterprise, quest, scramble, experiment, undertaking, probation.

ENDLESS, *adj.* 1. Having no end in space, being without bounds, unbounded, boundless, infinite, unlimited, illimitable, unfathomable, without end, having no conclusion, interminable, countless, immeasurable, indeterminable, numberless, untold, unnumbered, innumerable, incalculable, limitless, unmeasured, measureless, termless.

2. Enduring everlastingly, everlasting, without temporal limits, eternal, never-ending, perpetual, sempiternal, perdurable, unending, dateless, evermore.

3. Immortal, imperishable, unfading, undying, deathless, never-dying, everliving, amaranthine, perennial.

4. Continually recurring, incessant, unceasing, ceaseless, continuous, unbroken, continual, constant, uninterrupted.

ENDORSE, *v.* 1. Write upon the back of, put the seal to, countersign, superscribe, designate oneself as payee by signing, sign one's name on, indorse, acknowledge payment by placing one's signature on, inscribe one's signature, seal, autograph.

2. Sanction, give sanction to, confirm, warrant, guarantee, ratify, vouch for, underwrite, assure, insure, justify, clench, subscribe, back up, lend one's name to, stand by, support, sustain, favor, recommend, aid by approval, affirm, visa, give credit, corroborate.

ENDORSEMENT, *n.* 1. Writing of one's name on the back of, docketing, superscription, seal, signature, countersignature, execution, stamp, acknowledgement, sigil, signet, cachet, autograph.

2. Approval, sanction, recommendation, visa, ratification, approbation, assurance, advocacy, commendation, acceptance, confirmation, O.K., corroboration.

ENDOW, *v.* 1. Bestow an income upon for an appointed purpose, provide with a permanent source of income, supply with means, furnish with a fund, settle upon, grant, vest in, invest, dispense, award, donate, accommodate with, equip, provide, insure, bequeath, leave, devise, dower, furnish with a dowry, confer a right of dower upon, give a permanent fund to, subscribe, contribute.

2. Furnish with some gift *or* quality, equip with some faculty, confer something desirable upon, endue, clothe, favor with, enrich, grace.

ENDOWMENT, *n.* 1. That with which one is endowed, bestowal, donation, grant, gift, boon, sportula, insurance, largess, favor, bounty, benefaction, present, offering, bonus, honorarium, fee, dower, consideration, offertory, subsidy, subvention, gratuity.

2. Sum settled for the permanent use of an institution *or* person, bequest, legacy, devise, will,

dot, dower, fund, property, foundation, revenue, investment.

3. Gift of nature, mother wit, attribute, bent, cleverness, ingenuity, aptitude, talent, natural power, genius, gift, parts, turn, forte, aptness, flair, ability, faculty, capability, qualification, capacity, resourcefulness, inventiveness, sharpness, habilitation, *curiosa felicitas (Lat.)*.

ENDURABLE, *adj.* That may be endured, livable, supportable, sustainable, bearable, tolerable, withstandable, sufferable, abidable.

ENDURANCE, *n.* 1. Support, upholding, abiding, maintenance, sustainment, tolerance, sufferance, toleration, bearing, withstanding, perseverance, tribulation.

2. Long-suffering, forbearance, fortitude, grit, patience, capacity to endure, ability to suffer without succumbing, submission, resignation, stamina, backbone, pluck, mettle, "guts," bottom, sand, spunk, game, hardihood, even temper, dispassion, composure, indisturbance, *sang-froid (Fr.)*, equanimity, stoicism.

3. Lasting quality, duration, continuing power, continuance, lastingness, persistence, ability to continue despite destructive forces, permanence, vitality, soundness, solidity, durableness, fixity, durability, immovableness, stability, fixedness, diuturnity, resistance, continuation in time, status quo, changelessness, immutability.

ENDURE, *v.* 1. Bear, go through, undergo, pass through, encounter, experience, meet with, meet, taste, fare.

2. Hold out against, withstand, sustain without yielding, support, bear the test of without giving way, weather, bear painfully, sustain with a sense of distress, bear up under, forbear, keep one's chin up, labor under, brave, prove, go on, not give in, be firm and steadfast in trial, bear up under adversity.

3. Take patiently, tolerate, brook, submit to, bear without resistance, abide, stand, withstand, put up with, permit, swallow, stomach, pocket, allow, afford.

4. Continue to exist, have duration, persist, remain, last, continue, be permanent, stay, tarry, rest, hold, bide, abide, be durable, stand fast, wear, hold one's ground, hold on.

ENEMA, *n.* Liquid injected into the rectum as a medicine *or* purge, rectal injection for therapeutic *or* nutritive purposes, clyster.

ENEMY, *n.* 1. One who cherishes harmful designs against another, one who attempts the injury of another, one hostile to another, one who is unfriendly, opponent, adversary, assailant, backbiter, antagonist, foeman, attacker, asperser, slanderer, calumniator, rival, competitor.

2. One who seeks the overthrow of that to which he is opposed, public enemy, enemy to society, anarchist, Red, terrorist, revolutionary, seditionist, traitor, rebel, opposite party, mortal aversion, wolf-pack, the opposition.

3. Opposing military force, armed foe, a nation at war with another, belligerent state, hostile nation, inimical power, one of a hostile army *or* nation.

ENERGETIC, *adj.* 1. Possessing *or* exhibiting energy, acting with prompt and effective force, forceful, forcible, potent, strong, powerful, brisk, puissant, strenuous, high-powered, dynamic, alive, vigorous, emphatic, robust, determined, peppy, mettlesome, enterprising, earnest, persevering, go-ahead, lively, active, hearty, ambitious, not letting the grass grow underfoot, pushing, untiring, sedulous, assiduous, painstaking, diligent, hardworking, spirited, efficacious, industrious.

2. Powerful in effect, effectual, effective, valid, efficient, cogent, weighty, profound, vivid, intense, intensive, keen, sharp, acute, incisive, trenchant, poignant, virulent, caustic, mordant, harsh, drastic, stringent.

ENERGETICALLY, *adv.* In an energetic manner, actively, briskly, powerfully, potently, strongly, vigorously, with might and main, with vim and vigor, *manibus pedibusque (Lat.)*, with all one's might, with life and spirit, strenuously, full tilt, lustily, hammer and tongs, heart and soul, tooth and nail, to the best of one's abilities, by the sweat of one's brow, *unguibus et rostro (Lat.)*, *suo Marte (Lat.)*.

ENERGIZE, *v.* 1. Give energy to, rouse into activity, give force to, strengthen, invigorate, activate, animate, potentialize, nerve, excite to action, stimulate, galvanize, electrify, make the sparks fly, magnetize, endue with activity, kindle, inflame, quicken, vivify, intensify, sharpen, pep up, enliven, spur, goad, prick.

2. Be in operation, put forth energy, be active, bestir oneself, put forth one's strength, do one's utmost, spare no efforts, strain, struggle, labor, toil, drudge, fag, sweat, buckle to, grind, plod, grub, ply, slave, labor.

ENERGY, *n.* 1. Capacity of vigorous activity, exertion of power, force, *vis viva (Lat.)*, vigor, might, puissance, strength, potency, lustihood, stamina, muscle, brawn, sinews, virility, capacity for performing work, potentiality, activity, ergal *(Physics)*, efficiency, efficacy, conation.

2. Forcefulness of expression, animation, life, spirit, pep, punch, intensity, vivacity, go, dash, impetus, momentum, fervor, fire, tone, verve, élan, drive, vim, snap, zeal, emphasis, mettle, push, fizz, backbone, pluck, manliness, animal spirits, vitality, strenuousness, initiative, high pressure, ambition, briskness, smartness, hustle, alacrity, ferment, stir, enterprise.

ENERVATE, *v.* Destroy the vigor of, deprive of strength, unnerve, deprive of nerve, debilitate, enfeeble, weaken, emasculate, unman, effeminize, effeminate, devitalize, render impotent, soften, relax, unbrace, prostrate, cripple, paralyze, sap, exhaust, attenuate, reduce, injure, impair, disable, incapacitate, unfit, shatter, demoralize, invalidate, render ineffective, defeat, break.

ENERVATION, *n.* Failure of strength, debility, debilitation, lassitude, fatigue, weariness, collapse, weakness, prostration, impotence, infirmity, feebleness, languor, exhaustion, impuissance, inability, atony *(Med.)*, emasculation, asthenia, effeminization, effeminacy, flaccidity, delicacy, adynamy, incapacitation, disablement, powerlessness, helplessness, invalidation.

ENFEEBLE, *v.* Make feeble, weaken, debilitate, deprive of strength, disable, disenable, exhaust, deplete of strength, shake, enervate, emasculate, unman, devitalize, unbrace, unnerve, undermine, sap, paralyze, invalidate, impair, break, reduce, attenuate, minimize, lower, diminish, lessen the vigor of.

ENFILADE, *n.* 1. A situation of troops subjecting them to a sweeping fire from along the length of a battery, a position exposed to a raking fire.

2. A fire that may rake lengthwise a line of troops *or* works, a raking fire.

3. Arrangement in opposite and parallel rows,

straight passage through a suite of apartments with their doors opposite one another, a vista down a hallway *or* lane, a view from such rows, lane, aisle, alley, glade.

ENFOLD, *v.* 1. Infold, envelop, wrap up, roll up in, enwrap, lap, overlap, incase, encase, sheathe, swathe, swaddle, shroud, bury, pack up, enclose, encircle, surround, inclasp, invest, muffle up, implicate, involve, wind, gird in, entwine.

2. Embrace, clasp, hug, embosom, inarm.

ENFORCE, *v.* 1. Put in force, have executed, carry out vigorously, execute, prosecute, charge, dictate, sanction, perform, accomplish, fulfil, complete, consummate, administer, achieve.

2. Impress forcibly, support by force, give force to, drive, set forth strongly, make a point of, insist upon, take no denial, urge forcibly, lay stress on, emphasize, impress on the mind, assail with energy.

3. Obtain by force *or* compulsion, impose a course of action upon a person, compel, require, tax, oblige, constrain, exact, extort, impel, enjoin, cram down the throat, say it must be done, press, dragoon, conscript, coerce, force upon, drag into, necessitate, commandeer, bind, pin down, compel obedience to, subject to pressure, whip, lash, goad.

ENFORCEMENT, *n.* Compulsory execution *or* action, compulsion, necessitation, obligation, impulsion, coercion, pressure, constraint, duress, coaction, *force majeure (Fr.),* forcible urging, prompting, dictate, instance, insistence, urge, press, necessity, draft, conscription, brute force, *ultima ratio (Lat.),* eminent domain, martial law, spur, whip, lash, prick, stimulus, goad, fillip.

ENFRANCHISE, *v.* 1. Liberate from slavery, free, set free, disenthrall, manumit, emancipate, restore to liberty, disimprison, release, unfetter, unshackle.

2. Grant a franchise to, admit to the right of voting, admit to citizenship, affranchise, admit as a free man, naturalize, endow with political privilege, free from political disabilities.

3. Empower, license, authorize, privilege, charter, sanction, warrant, qualify.

ENFRANCHISEMENT, *n.* 1. Emancipation, setting free, manumission, disenthrallment, release, liberation, deliverance, restoration to liberty, disimprisonment.

2. Affranchisement, admission to citizenship, investiture with the privileges of a citizen, political rights.

3. Authorization, warranty, license, permission, concession, leave, admission, accordance, *carte blanche (Fr.),* charter, grant.

ENGAGE, *v.* 1. Occupy the attention of, hold the interest of, employ the time of, engross, busy, attract and hold fast, draw and secure, win, arrest, attach, gain over, allure, charm, please, entertain, absorb, interest.

2. Occupy oneself, become involved, take part, be occupied.

3. Secure for use, hire, employ, induce to serve, enlist, retain, book, reserve, secure, appoint, commission, delegate, choose, select, invite, brief.

4. Bind by contract *or* oath, make liable, put under pledge, obligate, commit, covenant, agree, contract, bargain, stipulate, pledge, promise, assume an obligation, warrant, become bound.

5. Plight faith, betroth, pledge in marriage, affiance, espouse.

6. Bring into conflict, encounter in battle, join battle with, contend, attack, fight with, wage war,

grapple with, cope with, take the field, give battle to, combat, carry on hostilities, enter into conflict with, struggle, cross weapons, war with.

7. Take the first step, take up, undertake, embark on, enlist, take employment, set about, launch into, tackle, go about, enter upon, assume, broach, institute.

8. *(Mech.)* Cause to become interlocked, gear with, interlock, enmesh, mesh, involve, interlace, attach, fasten, cause to stick fast.

ENGAGEMENT, *n.* 1. Agreement, promise, word, pledge, word of honor, parole, vow, oath, bond, assurance, stipulation, covenant, contract, faith, obligation, earnest, guarantee, warranty.

2. Betrothal, troth, affiance, plighted faith, espousal, subarrhation, betrothment, marriage contract.

3. Occupation, employment, pursuit, vocation, calling, business, office, place, position, situation, post, incumbency, billet, berth, job, enterprise, profession, undertaking.

4. Social *or* business appointment, affair of business, rendezvous, date, interview, tryst, assignation.

5. Battle, fight, skirmish, conflict, rencontre, combat, collision, contest, affair, brush, action, encounter, scrimmage, fracas, melee, tussle, broil, scuffle, fray, affray, joust, dog fight, warfare, duel.

ENGAGING, *adj.* Attracting interest *or* affection, attractive, prepossessing, amiable, winning, to one's liking, winsome, fascinating, captivating, interesting, absorbing, enchanting, charming, pleasing, taking, sweet, pleasant, entrancing, enravishing, intriguing, bewitching, delightful, lovable, adorable, angelic, agreeable, welcome.

ENGENDER, *v.* 1. Bring into existence, generate, create, give birth to, bear, beget, fecundate, sire, impregnate, progenerate, father, breed, procreate, propagate, conceive, cause to exist, hatch, spawn, develop, usher into the world.

2. Call into being, cause, give rise to, produce, occasion, incite, call forth, stir up, excite, bring forth, sow the seeds of, plant.

ENGINE, *n.* 1. Mechanism designed to convert energy into mechanical work, machine by which power is applied to the doing of work, turbine, machinery, motor, dynamo, generator, battery.

2. Mechanical contrivance, tool, organ, utensil, weapon, implement, gear, instrument, agent, tackle, apparatus, equipment, device, invention, method, means.

ENGINEER, *v.* 1. Construct, manage skilfully, plan *or* construct as an engineer, lay out, guide the course of, superintend the construction of, assume responsibility of, serve in the capacity of engineer, order, pioneer.

2. Carry through by skilful contrivance, plan strategy, arrange artfully, scheme, machinate, maneuver, work schemes on.

ENGINEER, *n.* 1. One versed in the construction and use of engines, designer *or* constructor of engines, maker, artificer, machinist, mechanic, mechanician, inventor, contriver, electrician, manager, architect, contractor, builder.

2. One who manages a stationary *or* locomotive engine, engine driver, engine runner, engine man, motorman, stoker, fireman, conductor.

3. A member of the division of an army which constructs forts and clears roads, member of the navy especially trained in engineering work.

ENGIRD, *v.* Gird, girdle, engirdle, begird, lap,

surround, encircle, environ, encompass, beset, circle, enclose, compass, cincture, embrace.

ENGORGE, *v.* 1. Devour, ingurgitate, gorge, bolt, swallow up, engulf, swallow greedily, gulp down, ingest, imbibe, gobble, raven, guzzle.

2. Fill to excess, cram, stuff, gormandize, glut, overgorge, eat one's fill, satiate.

3. (Pathol.) Congest with blood, obstruct.

ENGRAVE, *v.* 1. Cut in upon some surface, chase designs on a hard surface, carve, incise, grave, chisel, sculpture, ornament with incised designs, hatch, etch, stipple, enchase, print.

2. Impress deeply, infix indelibly, imprint, inscribe, mark, depict.

ENGRAVER, *n.* One whose occupation is to make engravings, graver, etcher, lithographer, lapidary, sculptor, lapicide.

ENGRAVING, *n.* 1. Art of cutting either incised or relief designs, art of forming designs on a hard surface for the purpose of taking off prints of the design so formed, cutting, chiseling, photo-engraving, carving, incising, anastatic process, chalcography, zincography, gypsography glyphography, heliotypography, heliogravure, stippling.

2. An engraved device, a picture printed from an engraved plate, incised design, wood-engraving, xylograph, etching, aquatint, dry point, cerograph, glyptograph, anaglyptograph, graphotype, plate engraving, chalk engraving, photogravure, steel-plate, rotogravure, lithograph, chromolithograph, copperplate, mezzotint, cut, woodcut, intaglio, half-tone, illustration, picture, illumination, vignette, *cul-de-lampe (Fr.),* tailpiece.

3. Impression, copy, print, pull, proof, positive, negative.

ENGROSS, *v.* 1. Occupy completely, immerse, absorb, busy, employ, engage, abstract, take up, fill the attention, drink in, take in, consume, devour.

2. Acquire the whole of a commodity in order to control the market, monopolize, corner, buy up, curb, regrate, impropriate, have all to oneself, have a firm hold of, get into one's hand, forestall.

3. Transcribe in a formal manner, copy in large legible hand, write out, address, superscribe.

ENGROSSMENT, *n.* 1. The state of being wholly occupied with something, intentness, close study, preoccupation, deep reflection, application, depth of thought, involvement, immersion, abstraction, thoughtfulness, reverie, brown study, musing, absence of mind, detachment, woolgathering, daydream, absorption of mind.

2. Act of getting possession of something exclusively and in large quantities, exclusive possession, monopoly, corner, impropriation, forestalling.

3. Transcription, transcript, writing, dash of the pen, inscription, *coup de plume (Fr.),* engrossed document.

ENGULF, *v.* 1. Swallow up in a gulf, suck in, engorge, gulp, ingulf, submerge, submerse, sink, immerse, douse, send to the bottom, send to Davy Jones' locker, drown, inundate, entomb, bury.

2. Destroy, overwhelm, swamp, overcome, deluge, scuttle, shipwreck.

ENHANCE, *v.* 1. Increase in attractiveness, raise to a higher degree, intensify, magnify, boost, double, deepen, strengthen, reinforce, redouble, advance, heighten, amplify, add to, improve, exalt, extol, elevate, show off to advantage, touch up, polish.

2. Raise the price of, advance in value, swell, augment, enlarge, aggrandize, expand, grow larger.

ENHANCEMENT, *n.* Increase, augmentation, enlargement, aggrandizement, intensification, rise, exaltation, advance, exaggeration, premium, zest, finishing touch.

ENIGMA, *n.* 1. Saying containing a hidden meaning, conundrum, dark saying, oracle, riddle, obscure statement, problem, poser, ambiguous saying, paradox, crossword puzzle, anagram, acrostic, logograph, rebus, charade, parable.

2. Anything inexplicable *or* insolvable, sealed book, secret, arcanum, Asian mystery, labyrinth, maze, Hercynian wood, *terra incognita (Lat.), crux criticorum (Lat.), le dessous des cartes (Fr.),* quodlibet, nut to crack, point to be solved, knotty point.

3. An inscrutable person, Sphinx.

ENIGMATIC, *adj.* Resembling an enigma, occult, enigmatical, of hidden meaning, oracular, dark, recondite, abstruse, ambiguous, obscure, esoteric, incomprehensible, unintelligible, secret, hidden, mysterious, perplexing, puzzling, cabalistic, veiled, apocalyptic *(ironically),* equivocal, acroamatic, cryptic, mystic, mystical, problematic, baffling, conjectural, inexplicable, inscrutable, nebulous, intricate, unknown, unsettled, doubtful, hard to understand, metempiric.

ENJOIN, *v.* 1. Admonish authoritatively, advise with authority, counsel, exhort, urge, recommend, suggest, prompt, prescribe, move, advocate, guide, persuade, impress, adjure, entreat.

2. Order to do something, give orders, bid, direct, decree, dictate, command, charge, enact, ordain, instruct, impose a duty, exact, require, enforce, call upon, request, bind over, saddle with.

3. (Law) Prohibit by injunction, forbid, put an injunction on, restrain, inhibit, disallow, debar, bar, hinder, prevent, obstruct, preclude, restrict, interdict, proscribe, ban.

ENJOY, *v.* 1. Experience with joy, derive pleasure from, take pleasure in, be pleased with, rejoice in, delight in, revel in, relish, love, gloat over, bask in, fancy, like, savor, feast on, take to, go into raptures about, smack the lips over, admire, take satisfaction in, find pleasure for oneself, luxuriate in.

2. Have the use *or* benefit of as a good, have the blessing of, have fruition of, possess, hold, have the advantage of, profit from, be possessed of, control, own, command, inherit.

ENJOYABLE, *adj.* Affording enjoyment, pleasing, delightful, pleasurable, agreeable, gratifying, pleasant, felicitous, lovely, nice, sweet, delicious, delectable, palatable, refreshing, zestful.

ENJOYMENT, *n.* 1. The act of deriving enjoyment and satisfaction from an object, particular form *or* source of pleasure, gratification, delight, delectation, relish, zest, gusto, exhilaration, treat, happiness, cheer, sunshine, amusement, gayety, entertainment, diversion, refreshment, merriment, jollity, felicity, joy, gladness, exaltation, bliss, beatitude, ecstasy, round of pleasure, sport, bed of roses, hilarity, ease, comfort, purple and fine linen, creature comforts.

2. Advantageous possession, beneficent use, fruition, use of anything with satisfaction, hold, pleasurable possession, ownership, proprietorship, occupancy, tenure, retention, inheritance.

3. *(Law)* The exercise of a right, prerogative, privilege.

ENKINDLE, *v.* 1. Set fire to, fire, ignite, inflame, kindle into flame, warm, light, set afire, set on fire, apply the match to, rekindle, relume, add fuel to the flame, fan, poke the fire, blow the coals, stir the embers, heat.

2. Play on the feelings, excite, warm the blood, set astir, waken, awaken, rouse, incite, stir to action, call forth, evoke, summon up, arouse, stimulate, inspirit, quicken, vivify, give new life to.

3. Enrage, envenom, incense, exasperate, rile, exacerbate, aggravate, enchafe, irritate, nettle.

ENLARGE, *v.* 1. Increase in extent, make larger, magnify, expand, amplify, add to, make greater, augment, distend, inflate, dilate, extend, broaden, widen, thicken, greaten, aggrandize, spread, fill out, stretch, spread out, increase the capacity of, make more comprehensive, give wider scope to.

2. *(Photog.)* Print larger than the original negative, blow up, reproduce in larger form.

3. Speak *or* write at large, express oneself at length, speak of diffusively, expatiate, descant, amplify on, branch out.

4. Grow, wax, protuberate, tumefy, swell out, grow larger, expand, overgrow, develop, shoot up.

ENLARGEMENT, *n.* 1. Expansion, extension, growth, amplification, augmentation, increase, spread, dilation, dilatation, development, swell, inflation, tumefaction, aggrandizement, fullness, increment, accession, intensification, addition.

2. *(Photog.)* Print larger than the original negative, blown-up picture.

3. Diffusiveness in discourse, length and fullness of statement, extended remark, descant, expatiation, copious discourse.

4. *(Rare)* Setting at large, liberty, freedom, release, deliverance, manumission, emancipation, disenthrallment, disimprisonment.

ENLIGHTEN, *v.* Give intellectual light to, impart knowledge to, illumine with spiritual light, bring out of the wilderness, cause to see clearly, teach, inform, instruct, inculcate, edify, educate, counsel, indoctrinate, make intelligent, train, make aware, communicate, tell, acquaint, apprise, advise, notify, admonish, civilize, bring culture to.

ENLIGHTENED, *adj.* Instructed, erudite, savant, learned, lettered, informed, educated, brought out of ignorance, intelligent, well-informed, knowing, highbrow, aware, cognizant, made acquainted with, *au fait (Fr.)*, apprised of, sensible of, wise, well-read, versed, insightful, shrewd, scholastic, bookish, profound, book-learned, accomplished, refined, cultured, sagacious, reasonable, rational, fully civilized.

ENLIGHTENMENT, *n.* Culture, civilization, ken, great moral and intellectual advancement, lore, sapience, wisdom, knowledge, erudition, science, education, learning, edification, understanding, instruction, teaching, information, acquaintance, comprehension, appreciation, perception, insight, experience, familiarity, *éclaircissement (Fr.)*, elucidation, intelligence, explication, explanation, cultivation, refinement, freedom of thought, rationalism.

ENLIST, *v.* 1. Recruit, beat up for recruits, levy, enroll, press into service, list, register, conscribe, record, procure, muster, engage for military *or* naval service by enrolling after mutual agreement.

2. Take service in the army *or* navy, enroll

oneself in the armed forces, join up, be in the service, serve one's country, sign up.

3. Gain the interest and assistance of, induce to serve, obtain the aid of, secure for some cause, persuade to enter into a cause.

4. Pledge one's assistance, covenant, contract, engage, embark.

ENLISTMENT, *n.* 1. Voluntary enrollment and muster-in of recruits, conscription, engagement for service, signing up, recruitment, levy.

2. The period of years for which a man engages to serve in the armed forces of his country.

3. The written document binding one enlisted.

ENLIVEN, *v.* 1. Make vigorous and active, pep up, rouse, animate, inspirit, invigorate, stimulate, quicken, reanimate, encourage, inspire, brighten, elate, arouse, give freshness to, stir up, spark, imbue with liveliness, vivify, fire, hearten, excite, refresh, recreate, instigate, comfort, solace.

2. Make gay, render vivacious, make sprightly, cheer up, gladden, exhilarate, rejoice, entertain, delight, beguile.

ENLIVENMENT, *n.* Cheerfulness, geniality, good humor, spirits, happiness, gayety, joy, joyousness, gladness, light-heartedness, buoyancy, optimism, hopefulness, sunniness, liveliness, glee, merriment, vivacity, hilarity, sprightliness, blithesomeness, exhilaration, animation, airiness, merrymaking, jollity, rejoicing, jocularity, joviality, playfulness, sportiveness.

EN MASSE *(Fr.)* In a mass, in a body, bodily, all together, in the aggregate, ensemble, as a group.

ENMESH, *v.* Ensnare in meshes *or* a net, catch in a net, inmesh, immesh, mesh, tangle, snarl, illaqueate, entangle, involve, entrap, trap, betray, mislead, lure, inveigle.

ENMITY, *n.* Hate, hatred, rancor, malevolence, animosity, antagonism, unfriendliness, antipathy, repugnance, hostility, ill will, malice, bitterness, venom, acrimony, malignity, implacability, anger, dislike, aversion, feud, grudge, odium, contention, spite, pique, umbrage, invidiousness, opposition, discord, alienation, ill feeling, estrangement.

ENNOBLE, *v.* 1. Elevate in excellence, uplift in respect, honor, do honor to, exalt, look up to, glorify, dignify, aggrandize, engreaten, promote, advance, raise, heighten, enthrone, immortalize, signalize, lionize.

2. Confer a title of nobility on, accolade, raise to the peerage, promote to nobility.

ENNOBLEMENT, *n.* Exaltation, supereminence, advancement, elevation, promotion, preëminence, aggrandizement, enlargement, eminence, dignity, celebrity, nobility, excellence.

ENNUI, *n.* Feeling of weary discontent arising from satiety, boredom, lack of interest, languor, tedium, *taedium vitae (Lat.)*, listlessness from lack of occupation, defatigation, fatigue, dullness, lassitude, monotony, tediousness, tiresomeness, doldrums, irksomeness, pococurantism, mental weariness produced by satiety, apathy, wearisomeness.

ENORMITY, *n.* 1. Outrageous character, badness, wrongdoing, sinfulness, depravity, turpitude, vice, viciousness, atrociousness, baseness, heinousness, nefariousness, wickedness, iniquity, misconduct, flagitiousness, malignity, flagrancy, transgression, facinorousness.

2. Atrocious crime, atrocity, villainy, outrage,

misdeed, crime, felony, offense, trespass, injury, violation, capital crime, sin.

3. Hugeness, immensity, enormousness, mass, magnitude, exorbitance, greatness, vastness, bulk, largeness, massiveness, amplitude, great size.

ENORMOUS, *adj.* 1. Stupendous, monstrous, vast, greatly exceeding the common size, inordinately large, extreme, tremendous, immense, mammoth, huge, gigantic, colossal, bulky, giant, megatherian, towering, mighty, massive, excessive, prodigious, titanic, elephantine, unconscionable, mountainous, Gargantuan, Herculean, ponderous, Cyclopean, incalculable, astonishing, miraculous, Brobdingnagian, extraordinary.

2. Outrageous, atrocious, abominable, heinous, facinorous, egregious, flagrant, arrant, flagitious, wicked beyond measure, villainous, sheer.

ENOUGH, *n.* An ample supply, adequate quantity, adequacy, sufficiency, *quantum sufficit (Lat.),* as much as desired, plenty, abundance, copiousness, plenteousness, plenitude, amplitude, profusion, repletion, surfeit, satiety, fill, competency, full measure.

ENOUGH, *adj.* Adequate for the demand or need, sufficient for the purpose, ample to satisfy desire, plenty, plenteous, equal, plentiful, satisfactory, abundant, copious, competent, up to the mark, commensurate, full, well-provided, chock-full, replete, lavish.

ENOUGH, *adv.* 1. To the requisite extent, in a degree that answers the purpose, satisfactorily, to one's satisfaction, in a quantity that satisfies a need or desire, sufficiently, in abundance, fully, plentifully, plenteously, adequately, abundantly, competently, with no sparing hand, without stint, to one's heart's content, *ad libitum (Lat.).*

2. Quite, very.

3. In a tolerable degree, tolerably, reasonably, passably, fairly, to an ordinary degree.

ENOUNCE, *v.* 1. Pronounce, articulate, enunciate, vocalize, utter, accentuate, aspirate, emit, deliver, mouth.

2. Give verbal expression to, declare, assert, profess, put forward, advance, allege, proclaim, announce, propose, broach, set forth, speak out.

3. State definitely, affirm, maintain, contend, depone, depose, asseverate, swear, make one's oath, aver, avow, avouch, make an affidavit, vow, vouch, certify.

ENRAGE, *v.* Put into a rage, infuriate, stir to violent anger, provoke a display of wrath, inflame with anger, lash into a fury, madden, exacerbate, craze, incense, anger, irritate, chafe, exasperate, aggravate, enchafe, nettle, envenom, embitter, set by the ears, rile, arouse suddenly to vehement anger, affront, pique, displease, agitate.

EN RAPPORT *(Fr.)* In accord, in agreement, in sympathy with, congenial, in a connection of mutual understanding.

ENRAPT, *adj.* Transported, overjoyed, ecstatic, enraptured, thrown into ecstasy, beside oneself, rapt, overpowered by emotion, out of this world, ravished, charmed, captivated, entranced, blissful, enchanted, fascinated, beatific.

ENRAPTURE, *v.* Move to rapture, delight beyond measure, transport with pleasure, please intensely, entrance, enthrall, enchant, enravish, captivate, ravish, bewitch, beatify, charm, gratify, gladden, excite, thrill, rejoice, send *(coll.),* fascinate, enamor, spellbind, allure, infatuate.

EN REGLE *(Fr.)* According to rule, in due form, in due order.

ENRICH, *v.* 1. Make rich, supply with abundant possessions, make wealthy, give money to burn, fill one's pockets, feather one's nest, millionize, aggrandize, endow.

2. Make finer in quality by supplying desirable elements, beautify, adorn, ornament, deck, prink, embellish, decorate, ornamentalize, bedeck, gild, bedizen, garnish, furbish, polish, enamel, impart a richer quality to.

3. Increase the knowledge of, cultivate the capacities of, develop, improve, mellow, refine, elaborate.

ENRICHMENT, *n.* 1. Endowment, aggrandizement, millionization. *(See the verb.)*

2. Decoration, embellishment, beautification, ornamentation, adornment, ornament.

3. Advancement, advance, promotion, increase, preferment, elevation, improvement, cultivation.

ENROLL, *v.* 1. Write a name on a roll, insert a name in a register, place upon a list, list, enlist, catalogue, register, engross, enter, poll, inscribe, impanel, affix, assign, sign, mark.

2. Put in a record, place on record, record, chronicle, calendar, slate, matriculate, fill in, hand down to posterity, commit to writing.

3. Roll, wrap up, coil, fold, ball.

ENROLLMENT, *n.* 1. Enlistment, matriculation, the act of recording officially, registration, listing, roster, record, register.

2. An enrolled entry, number enrolled.

EN ROUTE *(Fr.)* On the road, on the way, in transit.

ENSCONCE, *v.* 1. Fix securely or comfortably in some place, settle snugly, place, locate, put, set, seat, install, lodge, house, nestle.

2. Make safe, shelter, shield, hide securely, secure, protect, flank, ward, screen, cover, guard, conceal, shroud, muffle, smother, enshield, harbor, fortify, intrench.

ENSEMBLE, *n.* 1. All the parts of a thing taken together so that each part is considered only in relation to the whole, the whole, aggregate, parts viewed as a whole, composite.

2. Total effect, general impression, general effect, general appearance.

3. The entire costume of an individual when all the parts are in harmony, toilette, coordinates.

4. United performance of a full number of musicians.

5. Group of performers, troupe, string quartet, chamber musicians.

ENSEMBLE, *adv.* Simultaneously, together, all at once.

ENSHRINE, *v.* 1. Enclose in a shrine, entemple, place in a fane, inshrine, sanctify, consecrate, beatify, hallow, dedicate, blow the trumpet, deify, crown with laurel.

2. Treasure up in the memory, cherish, keep unimpaired, preserve and keep sacred, embalm in the memory, signalize, immortalize.

ENSHROUD, *v.* Shroud, envelop with a shroud, cover, conceal, enwrap, hide.

ENSIGN, *n.* 1. Banner of a nation, flag, standard, pennon, pennant, pendant, bandrol, oriflamme, banneret, insigne, insignia, streamer, eagle, jack, labarum, gonfalon, tricolor, stars and stripes, Union Jack, burgee, blue peter, cornet, figurehead.

2. Badge of office, insignia of authority, rank

marks, mark of distinction, brassard, sash, stripe, chevron, aiguillette, epaulette, bar, eagle, crown, star, anchor, crest, coat of arms, heraldry, tab, armorial bearings, hatchment, escutcheon, shield, cockade, shoulder strap.

3. Token, sign, symbol, signal, brand, emblem, criterion, type, figure, cipher, device, index, seal, marker, sigil, signet, paraph.

4. Color-sergeant in the British army, standard bearer.

5. *(U.S. Navy)* Lowest commissioned officer ranking next below a lieutenant junior grade, sub-lieutenant, midshipman, cadet, subaltern, shavetail, noncom.

ENSLAVE, *v.* 1. Reduce to slavery, make a slave of, enthrall, hold in bondage, indent, enfetter, enchain, helotize, keep down, yoke, hobble, forge fetters, put in irons, put into bilboes, tie up, lead captive, handcuff, manacle, pinion, bridle, fetter, trammel, shackle, hold in leading strings, repress, drag at one's chariot wheels, trample under foot, hold under, break in, subjugate, subject, bond, overmaster, dominate, overcome, overpower.

2. Addict, bewitch, ensorcel, mesmerize, bring under the domination of some unworthy or injurious influence, hypnotize, captivate.

ENSLAVEMENT, *n.* 1. Involuntary servitude, helotry, thralldom, serfdom, bondage, vassalage, feudality, villenage, subjugation, captivity, collar, slavery, subjection, enthrallment, drudgery, yoke, domination, mastery, enfetterment, enchainment, submission, halter, harness, irons, gyve, shackle.

2. Domination by some pernicious or baleful influence, addiction, bewitchment, ensorcelment, mesmerism, hypnotism, captivation.

ENSNARE, *v.* 1. Involve in a snare, capture, hook in, entoil, entrap, benet, trepan, illaqueate, trap, catch, sniggle.

2. Lay a trap for, set a snare for, bait the hook, forelay, spread the toils, lime, decoy, lure, waylay.

3. Take by craft, beguile, inveigle, seduce, gull, mislead, allure, deceive, cheat, betray, dupe, hoax, bamboozle.

4. Involve in difficulties, embarrass, encumber, entangle, enmesh, snarl, mesh.

ENSUE, *v.* 1. Follow in order, be subsequent to, come next, succeed, attend as consequence, come afterward in immediate succession.

2. Follow as a result, result, arise, proceed, issue, be derived, flow, spring, happen, occur, transpire, eventuate, chance, come to pass, turn out, present itself, befall, betide, turn up, crop up, intervene, supervene, take its course.

ENSURE, *v.* Make sure, make certain, secure, bring surety to, insure, assure, make assurance double sure, dismiss all doubt, set at rest, clinch, warrant, guarantee, make safe from harm, make certain to come.

ENTAIL, *v.* 1. Involve by consequence, bring on by necessity, devolve as a necessary consequence, transmit by necessity, be the cause of, occasion, give origin to, bring on, bring about, produce, inaugurate, induce, open the door to, superinduce, draw down, evoke, elicit, provoke, necessitate, settle, impose.

2. Cause anything to descend to a fixed series of successors, limit the inheritance of an estate to a specified line of heirs, tie up property, settle on inalienably, transfer by inalienable title, make incapable of conveyance.

ENTANGLE, *v.* 1. Make tangled, disorder, twist, intertwist, twine, intertwine, snarl, tangle, ravel, interweave, knot, confuse by crossing, mat, kink, interlace, disarrange, jumble, discompose, ruffle, rumple, muss.

2. Involve in a tangle, enmesh, entrap, insnare, catch, inveigle, illaqueate, decoy, waylay, seduce, lure, allure, ensnare.

3. Involve in difficulties, foul up, complicate, embroil, encumber, beset, implicate, compromise, embarrass, perplex, nonplus, bewilder, puzzle.

ENTANGLEMENT, *n.* 1. Tangled skein, network, knot, snag, hitch, Gordian knot, maze, coil, snare, labyrinth, jungle, wilderness, complexity, tangle, complication, involution, intricacy, disorder, jumble.

2. Imbroglio, involvement, dilemma, obstacle, predicament, fix, quandary, bafflement, confusion, embarrassment, bewilderment, frustration, slough, perplexity, obstruction, quagmire, quicksand.

ENTENTE, *n.* Good understanding, friendship, concord, accord, fraternization, cordiality, union, fellow-feeling, sympathy, camaraderie, compact, rapprochement, reciprocity, combination, unison, contract, harmony, concert, unanimity, consort, conciliation, peacemaking, arbitration, alliance, entente cordiale, treaty, friendly agreement between two governments.

ENTER, *v.* 1. Pass from without to the interior of, make an entrance, go in, go into, pass into, come into, make a way into, set foot on, board, burst in upon, intrude, invade, butt in, horn in, trespass, pass through in going in, penetrate, pass beyond, approach, effect an entrance, come upon the stage, arrive, stand on the threshold, run in, pierce, perforate, filter into, infiltrate.

2. Make a record of, list, register, enroll, tally, index, record, inventory, set down, file, chronicle, schedule, catalogue, calendar, jot down, inscribe, note, take down, docket, post, tabulate, book, bill, slate, poll, invoice, manifest, score.

3. Admit, obtain admission for, cause to be admitted, matriculate, put in, set in, insert.

4. Make a beginning of, begin upon, start, take up the consideration of, commence, embark on, broach, take the first steps in, set out on, launch.

5. Enlist in, join, engage in, become involved in, be initiated into, become a member of, become a party to, form a constituent part of, belong to, be a component of, appertain to, combine with, merge with, unite, participate in, take an interest in, partake of, share, sympathize with, acquiesce, assent, agree.

6. Assume the obligation of, undertake, bind oneself, engage, commit oneself, pledge oneself, take upon oneself, pledge one's word, plight faith.

7. *(Law)* Place a writ in regular form before a court, make an entry in under claim of a right to possession, file an application for public lands, take possession of, occupy.

ENTERPRISE, *n.* 1. That which one attempts to perform, undertaking requiring energy, project of importance, emprise, business, task, work, plan, effort, endeavor, attempt, scheme, venture, move, movement, cause, crusade, affair, occupation, operation, adventure, campaign, essay.

2. Boldness in undertaking, adventurous spirit, willingness to make a venture, courage, spirit, initiative, go, go-ahead, push, dash, élan, energy, snap, vim, vigor, activity, briskness, readiness, animation, life, vivacity, smartness, promptitude, alertness, dispatch, alacrity, expedition.

ENTERPRISING, *adj.* 1. Ready to undertake projects of difficulty, venturesome, adventurous, courageous, bold, audacious, daring, mettlesome, soldierly, heroic, chivalrous, gallant, valiant, high-spirited, valorous, intrepid, dashing, manly, virile, plucky, lion-hearted, stout-hearted, stalwart, self-reliant, dauntless, fearless, venturous.

2. Eager, ambitious, alert, aggressive, energetic, progressive, up and coming, go-ahead, resolute, zealous, ardent, intent, keen, earnest, strenuous, prompt, active, wide-awake, live-wire, audacious, snappy, smart, efficient, brisk, quick, ready, busy, sharp, instant, pushing, indefatigable, persevering, plodding, hard-working, occupied, industrious, sedulous, assiduous, painstaking, diligent.

ENTERTAIN, *v.* 1. Amuse, divert, beguile, hold the attention of agreeably, pleasantly occupy the attention of, please, charm, recreate, exhilarate, enliven, raise a smile, cheer, rejoice, interest, inspirit, engage, relax.

2. Receive as a guest, welcome, regale, treat hospitably, extend hospitality to, fete, treat, give reception to, give a party, keep open house, have the latchstring out, play host to, do the honors, exercise hospitality, kill the fatted calf, provide entertainment for guests.

3. Admit into the mind, heed, mind, take into consideration, admit for deliberation, consider, take cognizance of, recognize, make note of, contemplate, occupy oneself with, attend, advert to, take notice.

4. Hold in the mind, keep in the mind, harbor, nurture, cherish, shelter, imagine, bear in mind.

ENTERTAINER, *n.* 1. Host, hostess, one who extends hospitality.

2. Professional amuser, actor, actress, clown, comedian, comedienne, tragedian, tragedienne, thespian, monologist, reader, lecturer, chanteuse, singer, cantatrice, diva, opera star, strong man, musician, dancer, ballerina, acrobat, master of ceremonies, circus performer, M.C., fortune teller, animal trainer, performer who takes part in public entertainments, palmist.

ENTERTAINMENT, *n.* 1. Agreeable occupation for the mind, amusement, bodily enjoyment, fun, recreation, diversion, divertissement, relaxation, pastime, *passetemps (Fr.),* sport, pleasure, jollity, frolic, jollification, play, merriment, gratification, pleasure, titillation, gusto, relish, cheer, gambol, romp, lark, skylarking, carousal, merrymaking, festivity.

2. Provision for the wants of guests, welcome, hospitality, hospitable treatment, accommodation, quarters, reception.

3. Social gathering, function, party, soirée, bal masque, matinée at home, levee, fête, festival, gala, *ridotto,* carnival, garden party, theatricals, *fête champêtre (Fr.),* ball, dance, prom, concert, hop, play, mummery, exhibition, performance.

4. Festive board, feast, dinner, tea, banquet, repast, collation, refection, regale, treat, cocktails, refreshment, junket, picnic, symposium.

ENTHRALL, *v.* 1. Hold in thralldom, send under the yoke, make a bondsman of, enslave, keep in servitude, put under restraint, subjugate, keep in bondage, subject, vanquish, enchain, overpower, master, subdue, tread down, trample under foot, weigh down, keep under, lead captive, overcome, cast in irons.

2. Captivate, fascinate, enrapture, attract, hold spellbound, spellbind, charm, enchant, ensorcel,

enamor, enravish, ravish, bewitch, transport, take one's fancy, allure, excite, thrill, entrance.

ENTHRALLMENT, *n.* 1. Thralldom, subjugation, bondage, slavery, servitude, yoke, imprisonment, serfdom, captivity, vassalage, reduction, drudgery, enslavement, feudalism, subjection, conquest.

2. Captivation, fascination, attraction, winning ways, enchantment, ensorcelment, entrancement, witchery, allurement, bewitchment, enravishment, seduction.

ENTHRONE, *v.* 1. Place on a throne, seat upon a throne, invest with sovereign power, endue with episcopal authority.

2. Make preëminent, elevate, signalize, exalt, immortalize, raise to preëminence, exalt to the skies, deify, crown with laurel, do homage to, aggrandize, nobilitate.

ENTHUSIASM, *n.* 1. Absorbing possession of the mind by any interest, lively interest, vehemence, mental excitement, heat of imagination, zealous admiration, ardor, zeal, passion, fervor, devotion, *empressement (Fr.),* devotedness, eagerness, keenness, fervency, intentness, earnestness, spirit, fire, glow, warmth, liveliness, vivacity, animation, inspiration, ebullience, exaltation of soul, verve, fanaticism, ecstasy, rapture, elation, transport, force.

2. Optimism, assurance, hopefulness, reliance, buoyancy, aspiration, sanguineness, faith, belief.

ENTHUSIAST, *n.* 1. Person of ardent zeal, bigot, fanatic, zealot, devotee, *fanatico (It.), exalté (Fr.), aficionado (Sp.),* one who is inspired *or* possessed, votary, partisan, crank, eccentric, nut *(sl.).*

2. An ardent and imaginative person, visionary, castle builder, dreamer, knight errant, rhapsodist, Don Quixote.

3. Live wire, human dynamo, hustler, rustler, man of action, go-getter, pusher.

ENTHUSIASTIC, *adj.* 1. Fanatical, possessed of, zealous, rabid, bigoted, partisan.

2. Ardent, fervent, fervid, perfervid, glowing, burning, impassioned, passionate, vehement, alive to, flaming, eager, earnest, excited, fiery, devoted, gushing, spirited, mettlesome, vivacious, lively, ebullient, expressive, excitable, irrepressible, mobile, demonstrative.

3. Visionary, dreamy, romantic, extravagant, high-flown, ecstatic, flighty, rhapsodic, Utopian, quixotic, ideal, unreal, in the clouds, optimistic.

ENTICE, *v.* Persuade with promise held out, lead astray, draw on by exciting desire, lure, allure, induce to evil, charm, draw on, attract, inveigle, bait, decoy, tempt, solicit, seduce, troll, wheedle, cajole, coax, importune, entrammel, entrap, incite, invite, captivate, fascinate, intrigue, bewitch, carry away, magnetize, tantalize, beguile.

ENTICEMENT, *n.* Allurement, attraction, charm, witchery, bewitchment, spellbinding, temptation, seduction, lure, cajolery, blandishment, *agacerie (Fr.),* beguilement, inveiglement, honeyed words, incitement, provocation, solicitation, persuasion, inducement, allectation, magnetism, fascination, glamor, spell, voice of the tempter, song of the Sirens, Lorelei's song, forbidden fruit, golden apple.

ENTIRE, *adj.* 1. Having all the parts *or* elements, perfect, integral, integrate, complete, whole, intact, unbroken, not broken, unimpaired, undiminished, undivided, solid, undividable, indivisible, being wholly of one piece, indissoluble, self-contained, continuous, sound, hale.

2. Total, gross, all, full, plenty, plenary, pure, sheer, unqualified, exhaustive, radical, thorough, universal, sweeping, thoroughgoing, wholesale, comprehensive, all-inclusive, absolute, concrete, unconditional, unreserved, unabridged, aggregate, unalloyed, free from admixture, unmitigated, unmixed, unmingled.

ENTIRELY, *adj.* Wholly, fully, totally, *in toto (Lat.), in extenso (Lat.),* completely, perfectly, in all respects, in every respect, altogether, outright, quite, utterly, thoroughly, positively, unreservedly, all hollow *(coll.),* at all points, from head to foot, at length, throughout, out and out, through and through, from first to last, from top to toe, cap-a-pie, every inch, every whit, 100%, to the backbone, in a body, as a whole, all in all, in the main, *en masse (Fr.),* in the whole, substantially, plenarily, exclusively, solely, purely, arrantly, sheerly, absolutely, lock, stock and barrel.

ENTIRETY, *n.* 1. State of being entire, totality, completeness, intactness, plenitude, integrality, entireness, wholeness, omnitude, allness, ensemble, collectiveness, *tout ensemble (Fr.),* integrity, solidarity, undividedness, indivisibility, length and breath of, universality, Alpha and Omega, be-all.
2. That which is entire, the whole, entire amount, sum total, all, undiminished quantity, integer, organic unity, complexus, aggregate, compages, compaction, assemblage, integral, total, sum, gross amount, everything, everybody.

ENTITLE, *v.* 1. Designate by a title, give a title to, call by a particular name, denominate, name, term, dub, title, style, christen, baptize, nickname, characterize, specify, label, nominate, phrase.
2. Furnish with grounds for laying claim, give a claim to, endow with the right to, authorize, qualify, capacitate, enable, empower, sanction, legalize, warrant, ordain, assign, impute, fit for.

ENTITY, *n.* 1. Something that has a real existence, that which actually exists, a thing, object, article, something, being, creature, person, created being, substance, body, lump of matter, contrivance, monad, individual, *ens, entia (Lat.).*
2. The essential nature of a thing, quiddity, any individuality regarded as complete in itself, quid, essence, vital spark.
3. True being, existence, mere being, all being, subsistence, life, life force, vital principle, vitality, reality, actuality, truth, verity, certainty, fact, matter of fact.

ENTOMB, *v.* 1. Place in a tomb, lay in the grave, lay to rest in a mausoleum, intomb, deposit ashes in an urn, inurn, inter, bury, inhume.
2. Imprison, immure, incarcerate, wall in, seal up, box up, enclose, encage, clap under hatches.
3. Secrete, conceal, hide, cache, screen, veil, cover.

ENTOMBMENT, *n.* 1. Burial in a mausoleum, sepulture, intombment, inurnment, interment, burial.
2. Imprisonment, incarceration, coarctation, immurement, enclosement, durance.

ENTOURAGE, *n.* 1. Attendants of a person of rank, suite, retinue, associates, companions, followers, train, escort, cortege, convoy, following, bodyguard, court, staff.
2. Surroundings, neighborhood, atmosphere, medium, milieu, locale, environment, background, whereabouts, scene, setting.

ENTRAILS, *n.* The internal parts of the trunk of an animal body, viscera, inwards, inner parts, bowels, intestines, colons, guts, insides.

ENTRAIN, *v.* Board a train, go aboard a train, put aboard a train, depart, go away, leave a terminal, ensconce in a railway coach.

ENTRAMMEL, *v.* 1. Trammel, fetter, shackle, enchain, hobble, bind hand and foot, tie up, pinion, truss up.
2. Involve in trammels, embarrass with hindrance or limitations, impede, hamper, entangle, restrain.

ENTRANCE, *n.* 1. Act of entering, introgression, ingress, approach, access, penetration, incoming, infiltration, entrée, influx, intrusion, trespassing, coming in, invasion, inroad, incursion, illapse, irruption.
2. Place of entering, opening for entering, place of ingress, entry, entryway, passage, gate, passageway, gateway, door, portal, doorway, hallway, porch, lobby, foyer, postern, wicket, threshold, stile, turnstile, vestibule, hall, foregate, portico, *porte-cochère (Fr.),* avenue, adit, inlet, aperture, orifice, mouth.
3. Power *or* liberty of entering, admittance, admission, entree, reception, accession.
4. Start, commencement, starting point, outset, beginning, introduction, overture, prelude, onset, outbreak, coming out, debut, initiation, immission, incipience, inception, dawn, birth, opening.

ENTRANCE, *v.* 1. Put into a trance, hypnotize, mesmerize, magnetize, cast a spell on, hoodoo, hex, wave a wand, rub the ring.
2. Fill with delight, enchant, bewitch, charm, enrapture, send into raptures, transport, throw into ecstasy, ravish, enravish, allure, intrigue, enamor, delight, attract, please, take, captivate, fascinate, spellbind, infatuate, carry away with emotion, overpower with bliss.

ENTRANT, *n.* 1. Applicant for admission, suitor, petitioner, solicitor, candidate.
2. New member, novice, neophyte, plebe, tyro, beginner, proselyte, catechumen.
3. Competitor in a contest, rival, opponent, antagonist.

ENTRAP, *v.* 1. Catch in a trap, ensnare, entoil, illaqueate, benet, entrammel, bag, trepan.
2. Bring unawares into danger *or* evil, entice, allure, beguile, inveigle, hook in, mislead, lure, seduce, decoy, waylay, bait the hook, forelay, spread the toils, lime, tangle, deceive, fool.
3. Draw into contradiction *or* damaging admission, pose, catch in difficulties, embarrass, involve in contradictions, implicate, perplex, nonplus, stagger.

ENTRAPMENT, *n.* Snare, ambush, ambuscade, pitfall, gin, trap, springe, noose, hook, net, toils, meshes, *guet-à-pens (Fr.),* ruse, stratagem, trick, decoy, bait, decoy duck, tub to the whale, baited trap.

ENTREAT, *v.* 1. Make supplication to, beseech, supplicate, plead, pray, implore, beg, petition, make earnest petition, importune, solicit, appeal to, obsecrate, impetrate, obtestate, proffer a prayer to, invoke, enjoin, canvass, adjure, crave, conjure.
2. Ask earnestly for, request, urge, press, beg a boon, apply to, call to, cry to, kneel to, clamor for, exhort.

ENTREATY, *n.* Earnest request, supplication, plea, petition, appeal, prayer, beseechment, obsecration, impetration, obtestation, invocation, imploration, adjuration, solicitation, suit, cry, importunity, call, intercession.

ENTREE, *n.* 1. Right of entering, admittance, free and easy access, admission, reception, *carte blanche (Fr.),* privilege of entry.

2. Any food other than a roast served as the main course, *pièce de résistance (Fr.),* principal dish of a meal.

3. Dinner dish served before the main course *or* between the regular courses, side dish, entremets.

ENTRENCH, *v.* 1. Dig trenches for defensive purposes around oneself, fortify, dig in, protect with defensive work, fence round, establish in a strong position.

2. Trench on, encroach, trespass, infringe, overstep, overreach, intrude, invade, intrench on, transgress.

3. Verge on, be near, adjoin, hang about, border upon, approximate.

ENTRENCHMENT, *n.* 1. An entrenched position, trench, defensive work, ditch with parapet, mound, fortification for protection against enemy fire, earthwork, breastwork, fieldwork, gabions, muniment, bulwark, fosse, moat, dugout, embankment, sunk fence, parados, mole, bank, bastion, redan, redoubt, defense, protection.

2. Encroachment, infringement, transilience, trespass, infraction, invasion, intrusion, transgression, extravagation.

ENTRE NOUS *(Fr.)* Between ourselves, between you and me, *inter nos (Lat.),* confidentially, in strict confidence, under the veil of secrecy, secretly, privately, not for public hearing, in one's sleeve, in one's ear, in a whisper, *sotto voce (It.).*

ENTREPRENEUR, *n.* 1. Employer of productive labor, contractor, one who undertakes to carry out any enterprise, one who starts and conducts an enterprise, undertaker.

2. One who originates and manages entertainments, impresario, theatrical director, manager, producer.

ENTRUST, *v.* 1. Invest with a trust, give a responsibility to, charge with a specified duty involving trust, depute, commit with confidence, delegate, put into the hands of, intrust, rely, confide, hand over, make over, deliver, commit in trust to, consign, confide for care *or* use, assign, turn over to, place in charge of.

2. Credit, give credit to, accredit, authorize, keep an account with.

ENTRY, *n.* 1. The act of coming *or* going in, introgression, penetration, access, approach, ingress, admission. (See ENTRANCE, 1.)

2. Place of ingress, passage into, inlet, portal, entrance hall, vestibule, foyer, anteroom, lobby, corridor, avenue. (See ENTRANCE, 2.)

3. Statement recorded in a book, memorandum, memo, memorabilia, note, record, minute, item, jotting, brief, account, reminder, thought, debit, bulletin, posting, booking, deposition, signature, inscription, registration, expenditure, credit.

4. Beginning, starting point, debut, first attempt, essay.

5. One entered in a contest, contestant, rival, competitor, antagonist.

6. *(Theat.)* A coming upon the scene.

ENTWINE, *v.* 1. Twine with *or* together, twine about *or* around, intwine, intertwine, wreathe,

weave, interweave, lace, interlace, splice, link, intertwist, interlink, braid, wattle, plat, plait, crisscross, interlock, entangle, wind around.

2. Surround, encircle, clasp, embrace, hug, compass, encompass, hem in, beset.

ENUMERATE, *v.* Name one by one, specify in a list, mention separately as if in counting, compute, calculate, reckon, estimate, numerate, check, count, tick off, cite, run over, tell off, take an account of, score, cipher, number, sum up, reckon up, total, catalogue, approximate, divide off, mark, tally, take stock, call the roll, muster, poll, take census of, call over, relate in detail, detail, tell over, recapitulate, recount, rehearse, narrate, relate.

ENUMERATION, *n.* Reckoning, numeration, numbering, computation, counting, calculation, tally, itemized list, catalogue, inventory, record, register, scroll, schedule, roster, muster, roll call, poll, census, statistics, detailed mention of things in succession, recapitulation, rehearsal, narration.

ENUNCIATE, *v.* 1. Pronounce in a distinct manner, voice, articulate, modulate, intone, emit, vocalize, accentuate, give out, deliver, express.

2. State formally, make a definite statement of, declare definitely, affirm, assert, asseverate, proclaim, announce, propose, propound, profess, relate, put forward, allege, promulgate, enounce, publish, set forth, broach, maintain, claim, insist, contend, depose, aver, avow, avouch.

ENUNCIATION, *n.* 1. Distinct utterance, tone, articulation, vocalization, intonation, modulation, pronunciation, ecphonesis *(Rhet.),* elocution, *vox (Lat.),* accentuation, delivery, vociferation, stress, emphasis.

2. Announcement, profession, affirmation, assertion, acknowledgment, declaration, avowal, expression, open attestation, asseveration, allegation, averment, protestation, pronouncement, enouncement, confirmation, corroboration, assurance.

ENUNCIATIVE, *adj.* 1. Vocal, phonetic, oral, modulated, voiced, spoken, intonated, distinct, articulate, emphatic, stressed, accentuated.

2. Expressive, enunciatory, corroborative, affirmative, declarative, declaratory, affirmatory, confirmatory, asseverative.

ENURESIS, *n.* Bed-wetting, incontinence of urination, involuntary discharge of urine.

ENVELOP, *v.* 1. Put a covering about, put a wrapper around, enclose in surrounding material, wrap up in a covering, cover closely, encase, sheathe, invest, inclose, inwrap, fold about, case, enfold, pack, shroud, enshroud, clothe, overlay, hood, cloak, shield, screen, protect, shelter, hide, conceal.

2. Surround entirely, environ, encompass, involve, encircle, embrace, embosom.

ENVELOPE, *n.* Wrapper with gummed edges for sealing, wrapping, covering, cover, case, sheathe, casing, vesture, integument, jacket, pod, cod, capsule, wrap, skin, facing, inclosure, garment, shroud, veil, cap, hood, cloak, receptacle, theca, ferrule, ring.

ENVELOPMENT, *n.* *(Mil.)* Encirclement, pincers, simultaneous frontal and flank attack, inclosure, encompassment, forcing into pocket, cutting off, blockade, beleaguerment, besiegement.

ENVENOM, *v.* 1. Impregnate with venom, make poisonous, poison, empoison, taint with venom, infect, contaminate, canker, corrupt, deprave, pollute, vitiate, inquinate, corrode.

2. Taint with spite, render malignant, fill with spleen, embitter, fill with hatred, provoke hate, estrange, alienate.

3. Kindle wrath, enrage, anger, incense, make irate, make furious, stir the blood, inflame, stir up bile, sting, nettle, irritate, rile, ruffle, provoke, madden, enchafe, exacerbate, aggravate, chafe, exasperate, wound, vex, enkindle, add fuel to the flame, fan into flames.

ENVIABLE, *adj.* Worthy to be envied, capable of exciting ardent desire of possession, desirable, of a nature to excite desire, sufficient to attract envy, covetable.

ENVIOUS, *adj.* Disposed to envy, invidious, covetous, desirous, jealous, resentful, yellow-eyed, jaundiced, green with envy, grudging, displeased suspicious, distrustful.

ENVIRON, *v.* 1. Form a circle around, encircle, form a ring around, enclose, gird, girdle, begird, engird, envelop, surround, compass, encompass, involve, enfold, ensphere, embrace, belt, loop, skirt, circumscribe, hem, hedge.

2. Beleaguer, blockade, invest, beset, besiege, hem in, pen in, confine.

ENVIRONMENT, *n.* Aggregate of surrounding things and influences, external conditions, milieu, surroundings, background, setting, surroundings amid which anything is seen, scene, *mise en scène (Fr.),* living conditions, habitat, circumstances, entourage, encompassment.

ENVIRONS, *n.* Surrounding districts of a city, circumjacencies, encompassing regions, vicinage, vicinity, neighborhood, precincts, confines, outskirts, suburbs, faubourgs, purlieus, *alentours (Fr.), banlieue (Fr.).*

ENVISAGE, *v.* 1. Contemplate, consider, view, visualize, realize, idealize, empathize, apprehend directly *or* intuitively, imagine, conceive, fancy, strain one's imagination, dream of, conjure up a vision of, picture to oneself, see before the mind's eye, indulge in reverie.

2. Look in the face of, meet vis-à-vis, meet squarely, confront, present a bold front, face the issue, show fight.

ENVOY, *n.* 1. Diplomat dispatched on a special mission, second-rank diplomatic agent next in dignity after an ambassador, legate, minister, consul, diplomatist, envoy-extraordinary, minister plenipotentiary, plenipotentiary, *chargé d'affaires (Fr.), attaché (Fr.), corps diplomatique (Fr.),* resident.

2. Any accredited messenger *or* representative, anyone entrusted with a mission, emissary, nuncio, internuncio, delegate, deputy, commissioner, *commissionaire (Fr.),* intermediary, courier, runner, herald, agent.

3. Postscript to a book sometimes serving as a dedication, stanza concluding a poem in certain archaic metrical forms, *envoi (Fr.).*

ENVY, *v.* 1. Regard with envy, cast a jaundiced eye at, begrudge, grudge, be envious of, repine at another's well-being, view with jealousy, hate for excellence, feel ill will toward, feel resentful and spiteful for not having what someone else has, be invidious of, be discontented at, be yellow-eyed.

2. Long for what someone else possesses, covet, hanker after, crave, desire emulously, emulate.

ENVY, *n.* 1. Feeling of discontent at seeing another's advantage *or* success, desire for some

advantage possessed by another, jaundiced eye, green-eyed monster, jealousy, heartburn, spite, discontent at another's good fortune, enviousness, invidiousness, grudging, resentment, hate on account of excellence, hatred, ill will, rivalry, mortification, malice, malignity, malevolence, emulation, cupidity, covetousness.

2. Object of envious feeling, person to be envied, cynosure of desire.

ENWREATHE, *v.* Surround with a wreathe, mat, inwreathe, garland, festoon, entwine, interweave, interlace, twine, twist, wreathe, plait, braid, plat.

ENZYME, *n.* Any of various complex organic substances originating from living cells and capable of producing by catalytic action certain chemical changes in organic substances, leaven, unorganized ferment, any ferment formed within the living organism, catalytic agent, barm, yeast.

EON, *n.* Largest division of geologic time comprising two or more eras, cosmic cycle, geologic cycle, an age of the world, indefinitely long period of time, aeon, incalculable period, immeasurable time, an eternity.

EPAULET, *n.* Ornamental badge worn on the shoulders as part of the full-dress uniform of commissioned officers in the army and navy, shoulder ornament, shoulder strap, shoulder-knot, frog, crescent and fringe, *aiguilette (Fr.),* aglet, *épaulette (Fr.),* insigne, ensign, rank marks, insignia of authority, bar, double-bar, pip, stripe, chevron, brassard, *cordon (Fr.),* star, crown, eagle, anchor.

EPHEMERAL, *adj.* Lasting but a day, beginning and ending in a day, monohemerous, enduring only a very short time, short-lived, diurnal, passing, momentary, transitory, transient, fleet, fugacious, fleeting, evanescent, elusive, caducous, impermanent, temporal, temporary, flitting, fugitive, vanishing, deciduous, brief, meteoric, volatile, summary, hurried, cursory, mortal, perishable, mushroom, fungous, provisional, occasional.

EPIC, *adj.* 1. Denoting poetic composition in which a series of heroic achievements is dealt with at length, Homeric, Vergilian, narrative, descriptive, graphic, historic, biographical, expository, anecdotic, storied, mythical, fabulous, traditional, legendary, rhapsodic.

2. Of heroic scale *or* mold, heroic, imposing, of heroic character, elevated, sublime, exalted, superhuman, colossal, stupendous, noble, poetic, dramatic, dignified.

3. Bombastic, wordy, multiloquent, pompous, grandiloquent, fustian, sesquipedalian, stilted, high-sounding, altiloquent, swollen, tumid, long-drawn-out, turgid, inflated, prolix, tedious.

EPIC, *n.* A poem in which heroic actions in related sequence are presented by narration and description, epic poem, epos, saga, rhapsody, narrative poem, historic poem, legend, tradition, story, tale, historiette.

EPICURE, *n.* 1. One who cultivates a refined taste in eating and drinking, one devoted to the fastidious gratification of appetite, one given to the pleasures of the table, gourmet, gourmand, gastronome, gastronomist, gustatory sensualist, palatist, deipnosophist, bon vivant, connoisseur of foods, dainty feeder, aristologist, Apicius, one who displays a nice fastidiousness in his tastes, Brillat-Savarin, high liver.

2. One given up to sensual enjoyment, hog,

voluptuary, sensualist, hedonist, Paphian, Sybarite, man of pleasure, one devoted to the pursuit of pleasure or luxury, libertine, wine bibber, glutton, cormorant, pig from the sty of Epicurus (Horace), belly-god.

EPICUREAN, n. Disciple of Epicurus, adherent to the doctrine that pleasure and freedom from disturbance are the highest good, eudaemonist, hedonist.

EPICUREAN, adj. 1. Given to luxury and refinement, adapted to luxuriousness, bred in the lap of luxury, fastidious, refined, cultivated, cultured, dainty, nice, delicate, finical, meticulous, hard to please, précieuse (Fr.), overrefined, Sybaritic, Paphian, silky, indulged, pampered.

2. Indulgent in sensual pleasures, sensual, voluptuous, licentious, dissolute, rakish, fast, debauched, of intemperate tastes in eating and drinking, full-fed, gluttonous, bibulous, brutish, crapulous, swinish, piggish, porcine, hoggish, bestial, carnal, self-indulgent, orgiastic, lewd, saturnalian, libidinous, lecherous.

EPICUREANISM, n. 1. The doctrine that the external world resulted from a fortuitous concourse of atoms and that the highest good in life is pleasure consisting in freedom from disturbance or pain, Epicurism, eudaemonism, hedonism.

2. Luxurious living, indulgence of dainty appetites, free living, gastronomy, high living, gluttony, crapulence, self-indulgence, Sybaritism, sensuality, luxurious living, edacity, gulosity, overindulgence, pleasure-madness, voluptuousness, silkiness, effeminacy, softness, carnality, worldly-mindedness, dissipation, carousing, revelry, Saturnalia, licentiousness, debauchery, lechery, libidinousness, wine, women and song.

EPIDEMIC, adj. 1. Prevalent, general, pandemic, prevailing, affecting great numbers in a locality and spreading from person to person for a limited period of time, widespread, endemic, epizootic, sporadic.

2. Pestiferous, pestilential, virulent, toxic, venomous, morbiferous, morbific, mephitic, zymotic, contagious, infectious, communicable, catching, taking.

EPIDEMIC, n. A rapidly spreading or widely prevalent attack of disease, temporary prevalence of a disease, disease affecting large numbers of people and spreading over a wide area, infection, visitation, contagion, taint, pollution, septicity, endemic, pandemic, virus, pox, murrain, plague, pestilence, pest, illness, sickness, ailment, malady, morbosity, complaint, disorder, distemper.

EPIDERMIS, n. Outer nonvascular layer of the skin cuticle, dermis, scarfskin, skin, outerskin, pellicle, hide, pelt, integument.

EPIGRAM, n. 1. Witty and pointed saying tersely expressed, witty expression often involving an apparent contradiction, jeu d'esprit (Fr.), play of wit, mot, bon mot, atticism, Attic salt, aphorism, proverb, pithy phrasing, nuggety word-grouping, smart saying, witticism, dictum, gnome, adage, shrewd observation, maxim, apothegm, saw, quip, phylactery, plaisanterie (Fr.), sally of wit, riposte, persiflage, badinage, repartee.

2. A short satirical poem dealing concisely with a single subject and ending with an ingenious turn of thought.

EPIGRAMMATIC, adj. Ingenious in expression, pointed, to the point, full of point, ben trovato (It.), well-turned, neat, compact, succinct, terse,

concise, pithy, trenchant, sharp, piquant, brief, antithetic, pregnant, compendious, condensed, laconic, elliptical, crisp, sententious, pungent, aphoristic, proverbial, phylacteric, gnomic, witty, salty, Attic, jocose, waggish, sparkling, sprightly, merry and wise, spirituel (Fr.), comic, keen, mordacious, acrimonious, acid, bitter, stinging.

EPIGRAMMATIST, n. Humorist, reparteeist, wag, wit, gag-man, bel esprit (Fr.), punster, wit-snapper, jester, quipster, jokesmith, jokester, gaillard (Fr.), banterer, drôle de corps (Fr.), persifleur (Fr.), spark.

EPIGRAPH, n. 1. Inscription carved on a stone building or statue.

2. Apposite quotation at the beginning of a book or chapter, the superscription prefixed to a book, motto, posy.

EPIPHANY, n. 1. Divine appearance, apparition, manifestation of a deity.

2. Christian festival (Jan. 6) commemorating the manifestation of Christ to the Gentiles in the persons of the Magi, Twelfthtide.

EPISCOPACY, n. 1. Church government in which the three distinct orders of ministers consist of bishops, presbyters and deacons, government of the church by bishops, Episcopalianism.

2. The body of bishops collectively, canonry, prebendary, prelacy, bishopric, pontificate, primacy.

EPISCOPAL, adj. 1. Pontifical, prelatical, papal, apostolic, canonical, archiepiscopal, hierarchical, capitular, clerical, sacerdotal, priestly, pastoral.

2. Recognizing a governing order of bishops, having a government vested in bishops.

EPISCOPALIAN, n. A member of the Protestant Episcopal Church, member of the Church of England, Anglican, non-Roman Catholic, an adherent of the episcopal system, believer in prelacy.

EPISCOPATE, n. The incumbency of a bishop, term of bishop's office, office of a bishop, dignity of a bishop, prelacy, pontificate, archiepiscopacy, primacy, archbishopric, bishopric, (see diocese).

EPISODE, n. 1. Incident in the course of a series of events in a person's life or experiences, incidental event, occurrence, happening, affair, circumstance, scene, transaction, proceeding, action, doing, fact, phenomenon, particular case, adventure, experience, outcome, result, issue, consequence, sequel, end.

2. Digression in the course of a story, incidental narrative, excursus.

EPISODIC, adj. Digressive, rhapsodic, rambling, excursive, discursive, roundabout, ambagious, diffusive, spun out, maundering, incidental, spasmodic, sporadic.

EPISTLE, n. 1. Letter of a formal or didactic character, written communication, missive, billet, message, note, line (coll.), favor, dispatch, billet-doux, correspondence, post, bulletin, bull, encyclic, decretal, rescript.

2. One of the apostolic letters in the New Testament, extract from one of the Epistles of the New Testament forming part of the Eucharistic service in certain churches.

EPITAPH, n. 1. Commemorative inscription on a tomb or mortuary monument, elegy, hic jacet, terra tibi sit levis (Lat.).

2. Any brief writing resembling such an inscription.

EPITHALAMIUM, *n.* Marriage poem, nuptial song, hymeneal, poem in honor of a bride and groom, nuptial benediction, epithalamion.

EPITHET, *n.* Word *or* phrase used as an adjective to describe some quality of a person, appellation, by-name, meaningful name, term applied to a person to express an attribute, appellative, designation, denomination, qualifying term, descriptive cognomen, title, ascription, sobriquet, handle to one's name, pet-name, nickname, agnomen, praenomen.

EPITOME, *n.* Condensed account of a literary work, brief and compact treatise, simplified representation, sum and substance, summary, digest, condensation, synopsis, breviary, brief, précis, résumé, aperçu, outline, conspectus, sketch, compendium, syllabus, review, abstract, abbreviation, abridgment, recapitulation, *multum in parvo (Lat.),* draft, minute, contraction, argument.

EPITOMIZE, *v.* 1. Make an epitome of, make an outline of, outline, compress, summarize, make an abstract of, condense, abridge, shorten, contract, curtail, abbreviate, abstract, diminish, lessen, reduce, digest.
2. Contain in small compass, recapitulate, comprise succinctly, review, sum up, restate briefly, skim, run over.

EPOCH, *n.* Particular period of time as marked by distinctive character and events, period in the outward course of history from which succeeding years are counted, point of time distinguished by a particular state of affairs, main division of a geological period representing the time required for making a geological series, beginning of any distinctive period in the history of anything, date, age, era, eon, cycle, series of years, definite period of history, interval of time, time of life, stage, spell, season, year, decade, reign, dynasty, administration, kalpa *(Hindu),* yuga *(Hindu),* Manvantara *(Hindu),* nonce, crisis, time being, day, hour.

EQUABLE, *adj.* 1. Of uniform condition at all times, free from variations, not varying, not changing, invariable, free from extremes, steady, even, level, par, equal, regular, always the same, free from inequalities or irregularities, smooth, consistent, just, equitable.
2. Even-tempered, tranquil, unruffled, not easily disturbed, serene, calm, impartial, dispassionate.

EQUABLENESS, *n.* 1. Evenness, steadiness, uniformity, invariableness, levelness, regularity, parity, sameness, consistency, justness, equitability.
2. Evenness of temper, tranquillity, serenity, inexcitability, calmness, impartiality, dispassionateness.

EQUAL, *adj.* 1. As great as another, neither greater nor less, like in quantity *or* degree, equivalent, tantamount, comparable with, similar, of the same degree *or* rank, identical in value, same, selfsame, one and the same, ditto, twin, duplicate, homologous, of a piece, cognate, synonymous, analogous.
2. Evenly proportioned, proportionate, proportional, commensurate, coordinate, correspondent, balanced, coextensive, symmetrical, coinciding, correlative, matchable.
3. Uniform in operation *or* effect, even, not changeable, level, equable, coequal, regular, unvarying, unfluctuating.
4. Having adequate powers, adequate, up to,

competent, up to the mark, on a par with, on a level with, fit, sufficient, of enough ability, on the same level, neck-and-neck.

EQUAL, *n.* 1. Equivalent, counterpart, duplicate, copy, facsimile, analogue, homologue, parallel, like.
2. A person equal to another, compeer, peer, match, fellow, mate, twin, congener, double, brother, sister, pair, second self, alter ego.

EQUAL, *v.* 1. Be *or* become equal to, rise up to the same level with, match, rival, parallel, keep pace with, run abreast, come up to, tie, run neck and neck with.
2. Make something equal to, equalize, make alike, coordinate, equate, identify with, make identical, level, dress ranks, poise, adjust, trim, balance, handicap, restore equilibrium, readjust, strike a balance.
3. Meet adequately, fulfil the requirements of, be adequate to, be equal to, be sufficient for, do justice to, vindicate, hold the scales even, make equal return, recompense fully, be commensurate with.

EQUALITY, *n.* 1. State of being equal, identical value, parity, similarity, correspondence, poise, symmetry, balance, equipoise, equilibrium, analogy, isonomy.
2. Uniform character, uniformity, plainness, evenness, levelness, monotony.
3. Sameness of rank, equivalence, equipollency, agreement, coequality.
4. Distinction without a difference, equal division, fifty-fifty, quits, two-way split, square deal, fair deal, tie, draw, drawn game, dead heat, neck-and-neck race.
5. Equity, impartiality, justice, justness, fairness, neutrality, fair play, fair treatment, propriety, disinterestedness, dispassion, *suum cuique (Lat.),* scales of justice, fair field and no favor.

EQUALIZE, *v.* 1. Make of equal status, make equal, equate, coordinate, match, make alike, liken, level, even, trim, adjust, handicap, equal, level off, tie.
2. Make uniform, make constant, restore equilibrium, poise, balance.

EQUANIMITY, *n.* Steadiness and calmness amid trying circumstances, evenness of temper, serenity of disposition, composure, poise, self-control, self-possession, placidity, regularity, equability, tranquillity, tranquil mind, peace, coolness, sangfroid, unruffled temper, imperturbability, sobriety, inexcitability, undisturbed feeling, dispassion, staidness, quietude, gravity, self-command, stoicism, philosophy, forbearance, phlegm, presence of mind, long-suffering, submission, resignation, fortitude, acquiescence, sufferance, endurance, patience.

EQUATE, *v.* 1. Make equal to, equalize, regard *or* represent as equivalent, collate, confront, offset, compare, pit against another, place side by side, indicate equality between, contrast, balance, draw a parallel, identify, *parva componere magnis (Lat.).*
2. Make such correction *or* allowance in as will reduce to a common standard of comparison, reduce to an average, average, express an equation, equalize, counterbalance, strike a balance, split the difference.

EQUATOR, *n.* 1. The great circle of the earth equidistant from the North and South Poles, imaginary circle on the earth's surface.
2. That great circle of a sphere which has a

center at each pole and lies equidistant between them, a circle separating a surface into two congruent parts, colure, ecliptic, orbit.

EQUATORIAL, *adj.* Near an equator, like the regions at the earth's equator, resembling conditions at the equator in climate, torrid, warm, sizzling, hot, tropical, estival, stifling, canicular, sultry, suffocating, oppressive, baking, reeking, sweltering, sudorific, humid, steaming, sweaty.

EQUERRY, *n.* 1. Officer of a household of princes *or* nobles charged with the care of horses, officer in the department of the Master of the Horse (*Eng.*), officer who attends on the British sovereign.
2. Groom, hostler, ostler, jockey, stable servant.
3. The stables of a prince *or* noble, livery, manège.

EQUESTRIAN, *n.* 1. One skilled in horsemanship, performer on horseback, horseman, rider, rough rider, jockey, bareback rider, postilion, huntsman.
2. Horse trainer, breaker of horses.
3. Horse soldier, knight, chevalier, cavalier, caballero, mounted rifleman, cavalryman, horse, dragoon, hussar, trooper, chasseur, Cossack, cuirassier.

EQUILIBRATE, *v.* 1. Balance equally, hold in equilibrium, maintain in equipoise, keep in balance, poise, librate, equiponderate, even.
2. Be in equilibrium, counterpoise, counter-balance.

EQUILIBRIST, *n.* One skilled in the practice of balancing, one who practices balancing in unnatural positions and hazardous movements, balancer, ropewalker, funambulist, ropedancer, high-wire artist, acrobat, gymnast, tumbler, contortionist, acrobatic dancer, prestidigitator, juggler.

EQUILIBRIUM, *n.* 1. State of rest due to the action of forces that counteract each other, even balance, poise, equipoise, neutralization of forces, counterpoise, state of balance produced by the counteraction of two *or* more forces, equality of weight, equipollence, equality of pressure, equal balance, symmetrical scales.
2. Mental balance, equanimity, mental poise, mental neutrality.

EQUIP, *v.* 1. Provide with all that is necessary for a successful undertaking, furnish with whatever is needed for service, fit out with essential materials, supply with necessary apparatus, outfit, fit up, harness, caparison, gird, arm, forearm, appoint, rig with, make provision for, train, prepare, store, endow with, man.
2. Array, dress out, accouter, attire, clothe, apparel, garb, costume, invest, swathe, encase, endue, robe, gown, drape.

EQUIPAGE, *n.* 1. Completely equipped carriage with horses and servants. turnout, coach and four, vehicle, phaeton, landau, victoria, barouche, brougham, shay, sulky.
2. Outfit, equipment, appointments, gear, tackle, rigging, matériel, appliances, trappings, harness, fittings, caparison, paraphernalia, bag and baggage, accouterments, impedimenta, effects, baggage, luggage, chattels, furniture, apparatus, habiliments, military apparel.
3. Imposing display, state, parade, flourish, show, ostentation, *étalage (Fr.),* array, pomp, glitter, dash, magnificence, splendor, spectacle, pageantry, exhibition, foppery, frippery.

4. Procession, train, cortège, retinue, suite, attendance, entourage, staff, court, cavalcade.

EQUIPMENT, *n.* 1. Material, supplies, outfit, wherewithal, paraphernalia, apparatus, matériel, gear, rigging, accouterments, tackle, harness, furnishings, trappings, kit, appointments, arms, fixtures, appliances, implements, utensils, tools, contrivances, fittings, chattels, apparel, belongings, armament, armor, machinery.
2. Knowledge and skill necessary for a task, know-how, temperamental resources, mental traits.

EQUIPOISE, *n.* Equal distribution of weight, equilibrium, even balance, equiponderance, equality of force, counterpoise, counter-balancing force, even scales.

EQUITABLE, *adj.* 1. Characterized by equity and just dealing, high-principled, conscientious, lawful, moral, right, proper, due, *en règle (Fr.),* meet, just, fair, right-minded, reasonable, creditable, up to the mark, *selon les règles (Fr.),* legitimate.
2. Of unwarped judgment, impartial, unbigoted, unprejudiced, dispassionate, unbiased, square, unexceptionable, even-handed, upright, veracious, honest, broad-minded, open and aboveboard, as good as one's word, virtuous, honorable, righteous.

EQUITY, *n.* 1. Quality of being equal and fair in any and all circumstances, uprightness, justness, justice, probity, rectitude, fair play, integrity, fairness, reasonableness, righteousness, principle, impartiality, fair field and no favor, court of honor.
2. That which is fair and just, propriety, right, reason, honesty, goodness, honor, good faith, *bona fides (Lat.),* purity, clean hands.
3. (*Law*) Common law, unwritten law, *jus civile (Lat.),* chancery.
4. (*Law*) Application of the dictates of conscience to the settlement of controversies, recourse to the principles of natural justice, theoretically ideal justice, spirit of law, *esprit des lois (Fr.).*
5. (*Law*) Equitable claim, right.

EQUIVALENCE, *n.* Essential equality in value *or* force, parity in significance, parity of value, equipollence, equipollency, equivalency, equality in result, identity, similarity, equivalent meaning, convertible terms, apposition, correspondence, analogy, synonym, homonym, distinction without a difference, amounting to the same thing.

EQUIVALENT, *adj.* 1. Equal in value or effect, tantamount, comparable with, commensurate, equipollent, coordinate, convertible, correlative, correspondent.
2. Of the same meaning, synonymous, of similar import, analogous, consignificant, identical, similar, cognate, complementary, interchangeable, alike, all one, all the same, literal, word for word, homologous.

EQUIVOCAL, *adj.* 1. Doubtful in meaning, of uncertain significance, capable of being taken in a double sense, capable of twofold interpretation, amphibolous, ambiguous, amphibolic, not clear, misleading, sophistical, casuistical, paradoxical, double-tongued, oracular, having different meanings equally possible.
2. Of doubtful nature, undetermined, dubious, indeterminable, uncertain, indeterminate, cryptic, doubtful, questionable, suspicious, enigmatical, problematic, vague, shady, indefinite, obscure,

apocryphal, puzzling, veiled, perplexing, hazy, evasive, mysterious, indistinct, unintelligible.

EQUIVOCATE, *v.* Use ambiguous expressions with a view to mislead, use words of doubtful meaning, mislead by double meanings for the purpose of deception, evade the truth, employ equivocal expressions, dodge, shuffle, quibble, palter, fence, shift, trim, mince the truth, beat about the bush, tergiversate, prevaricate, lie, dissemble, cavil, subtilize, elude, mystify, trifle, weasel, simulate.

EQUIVOCATION, *n.* 1. Use of ambiguous expressions with a view to mislead, ambiguity of speech, amphibology, ambiloquy, sophistry, verbal dissimulation, paralogy, casuistry, Jesuitry, word-fence, chicanery, quiddity, fencing verbally, paltering, quibbling, shuffling, speciousness, false reasoning, subtlety, meshes of sophistry, evasion, tergiversation, prevarication, mental reservation, *suggestio falsi (Lat.),* deceit, pretense, fraud.
2. Quibble, half-truth, *équivoque (Fr.),* double meaning, double-entendre, pun, paragram, *calembour (Fr.),* anagram, word-play, *jeu de mots (Fr.),* a fallacy depending on the double significance of a word *(Logic).*

ERA, *n.* 1. Period of time marked by distinctive character *or* events, period to which anything is to be assigned, extent of time characterized by changed conditions and new undertakings, signal stage of history, an age marked by remarkable events, epoch, time, cycle, aeon, eon, *kalpa (Hindu),* century, decade.
2. System of chronological notation reckoned from a given date, period during which years are numbered from a particular point of time in the past, point of time from which succeeding years are numbered, date forming the beginning of any distinctive period, major division of geological time.
3. Series of years marked by any administration, succession of years, reign, dynasty, interregnum, administration, duration, generation, stage, space, span, spell, season, course.

ERADICATE, *v.* 1. Root up, pull out by the roots, pull up, root out, tear out, extirpate, deracinate, averruncate, aberuncate, outroot, unroot, weed out, pluck up, unearth, pluck out, grub out, rake out, wrench out, extract, extricate, eject, eliminate.
2. Destroy thoroughly, do away with completely, cause to cease summarily, annihilate, exterminate, get rid of, blot out, erase, obliterate, efface, stamp out, wipe out, leave no vestige *or* trace of, remove utterly, demolish, abolish, extinguish, black out, strike out, expunge, delete.

ERADICATION, *n.* Pulling up by the roots, uprooting, rooting out, weeding out, deracination, averruncation, aberuncation, extraction, evulsion, avulsion, elimination, dislodgment, extrication, wrenching out, ejection, extermination, extinction, extirpation, annihilation, complete destruction and removal.

ERASE, *v.* Efface written characters, apply the sponge, rub with a rubber eraser, wipe out, wash out, sponge out, wipe off, wipe away, blot out, scrape out, scratch out, obliterate, delete, rub out, rub off, expunge, strike out, render illegible, cancel, rase, deface, destroy, eliminate, nullify.

ERASURE, *n.* Rubbing out, sponging out, blotting out, scratching out, obliteration, cancellation, expunging, rasure, effacing, deletion, cassation, erasion, attrition, confrication, abrasion, clean

slate, *tabula rasa (Lat.).*

ERE, *prep.* and *conj.* 1. Before in time, aforetime, on the eve of, in anticipation of, erewhile, afore, prior to, earlier than, previously to.
2. Sooner than, rather than, liefer than.

ERECT, *v.* 1. Set in a vertical position, place upright, put in a perpendicular position, render vertical, set up, raise on its legs, rear, hoist, upraise, uprear, uplift, heave, elevate, pitch, mount, straighten, lift, stand up, tilt up, stick up, boost, cock up, pry, lever, prize, perk up, perch up.
2. Construct, build, assemble the parts of and set in place for use, edify, put together, run up, fabricate.
3. Create, form, establish, constitute, institute, organize, found, evolve, compose, plant, design, contrive.
4. Encourage, cheer, rouse, stir, excite mentally, inspirit, animate, exalt.
5. Distend, swell, stiffen, harden, thicken, dilate, inflate, bloat, enlarge, expand.

ERECT, *adj.* 1. Upright in position *or* posture, standing up straight, firmly uplifted, raised, bolt upright, plumb, rampant, not prone, unrecumbent, elevated, directed upward, turned upward, vertical, perpendicular.
2. Hard, stiff, swollen, distended, rigid, thick, enlarged, dilated, inflated, puffed up, tumescent, ithyphallic.
3. Firm of spirit, bold, unabashed, undaunted, unquailing, unterrified, undismayed, shoulders squared, chin up, resolute.

ERECTION, *n.* 1. Construction, fabrication, edification, architecture.
2. Something erected, building, structure, pile, edifice, tower, fabric.
3. *(Physiol.)* Turgid state of an organ, rigid condition of a part containing erectile tissue, ithyphallus, penis erectus, tumescence.

ERELONG, *adv.* Before much time has passed, before long, soon, anon, in a short while, shortly, presently, forthwith, betimes, early, punctually, eftsoons, in good time, in due time, in time, time enough, at once, before one can say "Jack Robinson," straightway, almost immediately, in no long time, apace, at the first opportunity, directly, in a while, by and by.

EREMITE, *n.* A religious solitary, cenobite, anchoret, ascetic, *solitaire (Fr.),* recluse, hermit, sabbatarian, troglodyte, pillar saint, Simon Stylites, castaway, outcast, ruralist, anchorite, Timon of Athens.

EREMITIC, *adj.* Cenobitic, anchoritic, hermitic, ascetic, reclusive, troglodytic, austere, puritanical, *sauvage (Fr.),* living in seclusion, solitary, lonely, isolated, sequestered, retiring, delitescent, in a backwater, out of the world, "the world forgetting by the world forgot," unfriended, unsociable, desolate, forlorn, lorn, outcast, derelict, single, stay-at-home.

ERGO, *adv.* and *conj.* Therefore, wherefore, hence, whence, thence, consequently, accordingly, thus, because, seeing that, since, so, for which reason, inasmuch as.

ERODE, *v.* Eat into by gnawing, destroy by slow consumption, consume, corrode, eat out, wear away, canker, eat away, disintegrate, waste, fret, despoil, rub, ravage, make inroads on, macerate, form a channel by wearing away the earth's surface, wash away.

EROSION, *n.* Process by which the surface of the

earth is worn away by the action of water *or* wind, detrition, attrition, land despoliation, eating away, washout, wearing away, disintegration, corrosion, consumption, denudation, destruction, deterioration, wear and tear, decomposition, dilapidation, ravage, inroad, havoc.

EROSIVE, *adj.* Having the power of gnawing and wearing away, serving to erode, corrosive, eating, caustic, virulent, acrid, catheretic.

EROTIC, *adj.* 1. Pertaining to sexual love and appetite, strongly affected by sexual desire, inflamed with eroticism, passionate, amorous, libidinous, lickerish, prurient, lustful, lecherous, lewd, carnal, bestial, animal, concupiscent, lascivious, wanton, profligate, shameless, risqué, suggestive, smutty, obscene, ithyphallic, impure, pornographic, debauched, dissolute, immodest, unchaste, ribald, ruttish, indecent, aphrodisiac, bawdy, voluptuous, salacious, aroused to venery.
2. Loving, ardent, amatory, fervent, fond, affectionate, tender, sweet upon, lovesick, rapturous, enamored, infatuated.

ERR, *v.* 1. Be in error, be mistaken, be incorrect, be wrong, be at fault, make a mistake, misjudge, slip up, blunder, nod, be deceived, deceive oneself, misapprehend, misunderstand, miscalculate, miss intellectual truth, mistake.
2. Deviate from the right course, go astray, stray, lose oneself, be lost, trip, stumble, wander, ramble, be wide of the mark, rove, misstep.
3. Go astray morally, lapse from virtue, sin, transgress, trespass, do wrong, do amiss, offend, misconduct oneself, misbehave, commit a fault, be vicious, slip into the paths of sin.

ERRAND, *n.* 1. A trip to convey a message or execute a commission, short journey for a specific purpose, the object of a going *or* coming, purpose of any trip.
2. A special business entrusted to a messenger, message, assignment, mandate, mission, embassy, commission, communication, delegation, office, deputation, charge, duty, care, task, trust, matter in hand, undertaking, thing to do, agendum, job, work, chore, transaction, iron in the fire.

ERRANT, *adj.* 1. Traveling as a medieval knight in quest of adventure, roving adventurously, journeying, itinerant, peripatetic, vagrant, stray, wandering, rambling, wayward, free, not confined, foot-loose, committed to the open road, nomadic.
2. Deviating from the proper course, erring, devious, stray, undirected, circuitous, indirect, zigzag, erratic.

ERRATIC, *adj.* 1. Deviating from the usual course in conduct, not conforming to rules *or* standards, eccentric, notional, crotchety, moody, quirked, capricious, queer, peculiar, odd, strange, unnatural, abnormal, fitful, fanciful, wayward, wanton, whimsical, freakish, unconventional, bohemian, bizarre, irregular, anomalous, fantastic, unusual, aberrant, inconsistent, mercurial, fickle, flighty, volatile, giddy, frivolous.
2. Straying, wandering, not fixed, having no certain course, rambling, roving, deviating, uncertain, changeable, spasmodic, variable, mutable, shifting, circuitous, unstable, nomadic, unsettled, vagrant, desultory, unsystematic, zigzag, fluctuating, vacillating, moving hither and yon, planetary.

ERRATICALLY, *adv.* By fits and starts, by fits, intermittently, sporadically, irregularly, off and on, without rime or reason, at one's own sweet will, capriciously, here and there, slapdash, wide of the mark, carelessly, circuitously, desultorily.

ERRATUM, *n.* 1. Error in printing *or* writing, misprint, *lapsus calami (Lat.),* slip of the pen, mistake, blunder, slip, boner, oversight.
2. A note calling attention to an error, correctio, corrigendum, errata *(pl.).*

ERRONEOUS, *adj.* 1. Wrong, false, untrue, incorrect, devoid of truth, fallacious, inaccurate, inexact, faulty, unfounded, ungrounded, unsound, illogical, apocryphal, mistaken, amiss, spurious, counterfeit, fictitious, wide of the mark, out in one's reckoning, blundering.
2. *(Law)* Not in accordance with legal form, irregular, deviating, aberrant, unsustainable.

ERROR, *n.* 1. Fallacy, belief in what is untrue, false belief, deviation from correctness, mistake, inaccuracy, erroneousness, incorrectness, blunder, deviation from the truth, unsoundness, untruth, misconception, misapprehension, misconstruction, misjudgment, miscalculation, misstatement, slip, misprint, erratum, oversight, bungle, bull *(sl.),* solecism, malapropism, Spoonerism, slip of the tongue, *lapsus linguae (Lat.),* slip of the pen, *lapsus calami (Lat.),* flaw, blot, *non sequitur (Lat.),* omission, falsity, misunderstanding, false impression, delusion, illusion, hallucination, mirage.
2. Sin, moral offense, violation of duty, trespass, transgression, misdeed, wrongdoing, iniquity, delinquency, shortcoming, misstep, fault, defect, foible, vice, peccadillo, lapse from virtue.

ERSTWHILE, *adj.* Former, pristine, quondam, whilom, late, heretofore, at a time past, once, erst, past, *ci-devant (Fr.),* bygone, gone, passed away, over with, foregone, prelapsed, elapsed, no more, expired, that has been, blown over, run out, never to return, extinct, irrecoverable, recent, forgotten, preterite, pluperfect, exploded.

ERUCTATION, *n.* Eruction, ructation, belching, burping, bringing up gas, violent emission, vomition, disgorgement, eruption, voidance, ejection, egestion, expulsion, extrusion.

ERUDITE, *adj.* Characterized by erudition, highbrow, learned, well-conned, omniscient, well-read, enlightened, instructed, tutored, scholarly, refined, polished, cultured, well-educated, book-learned, bookish, pedantic, wise, sapient, savant, profound, scholastic, proficient, well-versed, *au fait (Fr.),* accomplished, sage, shrewd, sagacious.

ERUDITION, *n.* Store of knowledge, wealth of information, profound learning, bibliomania, bibliolatry, acquired knowledge gained by study, book learning, bookishness, omniscience, culture, pantology, scholarship, historical lore, reading, letters, higher education, literary learning, wisdom, acquirements, attainments, refinement, accomplishments, enlightenment, appreciation, perception, cognition, ken, familiarity, sagacity, proficiency.

ERUPT, *v.* 1. Give vent to eruptions, be in eruption, burst forth, boil over, break out, go off, explode, displode, thunder, detonate, blow up, eruct, vomit, belch forth, stream with molten lava, emit hail of pumice stones, flash, flare, fulminate, detonize, fulgurate, send forth plumes of fiery smoke.
2. Eject matter, cast forth violently, hurl forth, eject, emit, expel, send out, discharge, pour out, let fly, cast up, spew out, squirt, spill, spurt.

ERUPTION, *n.* 1. Ejection of molten rock from

a volcano, upheaval, earthquake, quake, temblor, cataclysm, explosion, displosion, volley, blast, dissilience, proruption, blow up, detonation, split in a volcanic crater, ebullition, debacle, emission of lava, trajection, discharge, outpour.

2. Violent commotion, issuing forth suddenly and violently, outburst, outbreak, sally, sudden excursion.

3. (Med.) Breaking out, rash, exanthema, eczema, psoriasis, prickly heat, lichen tropicus, hives, nettle rash, herpes, shingles, herpes zoster, scabies, itch, pimple, carbuncle, sore, ulcer, abscess, fester, imposthume, boil, gathering, canker, felon.

ESCALADE, v. Scale by means of ladders in an assault upon a fortified place, enter by means of ladders, scale the walls, mount, climb, clamber, ramp, scramble up, swarm, surmount, scale the heights, attack, assault, assail, charge, storm, beset, besiege, beleaguer, invest, lay siege to.

ESCALATOR, n. Inclined continuous runway used for raising or lowering passengers, moving stairway, mechanical incline, self-propelling stairs.

ESCAPADE, n. 1. Reckless proceeding, wild prank, vagary, mad antic, frolic, roguish trick, espièglerie (Fr.), caper, romp, gambol, lark, spree, skylarking, monkey trick, tomfoolery, drollery, whoopee, gambade, fredaine (Fr.), échappé (Fr.), boutade (Fr.), practical joke, prankish adventure, caprice, whimsy.

2. Impropriety, indiscretion, act of folly, faux pas, indecorum, misstep, mistake, blunder, lapse.

3. Escape from confinement, runaway, flight from restraint.

ESCAPE, v. 1. Slip away from confinement, get away from restraint, break loose, break away, gain one's liberty, make a getaway, fly the coop, break one's bonds, make one's way to freedom, bolt, flit, fly, flee, levant, snake off, make off, skedaddle, run away, decamp, abscond, take French leave, take to flight, take oneself off, depart, cut and run, take to one's heels, beat a retreat, whip off, be among the missing, steal off, slink away, effect one's escape.

2. Avoid capture, slip away from pursuit, get out of reach of by some artifice, keep clear of, get off, make off, give one the slip, get through without harm, get away safely, emerge into safety, keep free of something, succeed in avoiding, get out of the way of, avoid, evade, elude pursuit, wriggle out of, dodge. shun, keep out of the path of, enjoy immunity from, avert.

3. Issue from a confining enclosure, flow out, emanate, stream, gush, spurt, debouch, exit, sally forth, emerge, be emitted, evaporate, leak out.

4. Fail to be noticed or recollected by a person, elude one's memory, be forgotten, be passed over, slip away from inadvertently, slip through the fingers, be omitted, pass unobserved, come in at one ear and go out at the other.

ESCAPE, n. 1. Flight, departure, exodus, hegira, desertion, evasion, elusion, retreat, recoil, French leave, recession, decampment, withdrawal.

2. Release from imminent danger, narrow escape, hairbreadth escape, close call, close shave, extrication, deliverance, liberation, immunity, rescue, freedom, riddance, avoidance, exemption, impunity.

3. Outflow, effluence, efflux, outgush, outpour, outburst, outrush, outlet, leakage, seepage, egress, running out.

4. Mental distraction, oblivion, forgetfulness, avoidance of reality.

ESCAPIST, n. one who seeks mental flight from unpleasant realities, one who avoids reality by absorption of the mind in imaginative activity, non-realist, dreamer, obscurantist, evader, fugitive, ostrich (coll.), runaway, runagate, refugee.

ESCARPMENT, n. 1. Precipitous clifflike ridge of land formed by fracturing of the earth's crust, scarp, abrupt declivity, steep descent, cliff, wall of rock, precipice, steep slope, precipitous face of a ridge, ridge, bluff, butte, crag, peak, tor, clough, brae, headland, promontory, ledge, edge.

2. Ground cut into an escarp about a fortification, fortification, inner slope of the ditch surrounding a rampart.

ESCHEW. v. 1. Abstain from, let alone, shun, avoid, stand off, keep clear of, keep shy of, steer clear of, keep away from, hold aloof, take no part in, have no hand in, keep out of the way of, keep one's distance, flee from, have nothing to do with, turn away from, set one's face against, have done with.

2. Dislike, disrelish, mind, object to, not care for, have rather not, have no stomach for, have an aversion to, recoil from, detest, abhor, shrink from, abominate, shudder at, turn up the nose at, make a wry face, look askance at, make a grimace, loathe.

ESCORT, v. Accompany as an escort, pilot, convoy, patrol, picket, scout, protect, guard, lead the way for, defend, ward, safeguard, watch over, mount guard, attend, conduct, usher, cover, flank, screen, shelter, take precautions, support, wait upon.

ESCORT, n. 1. Person accompanying another for protection or guidance, attendant, companion, conductor, usher, guide, marshal, squire, tutor, cavalier, gallant, protector, defender, custodian, chaperon, duenna, guardian angel, tutelar, nurse, watchman, watchdog, warden, bodyguard, convoy, armed guard, guardian, burkundas (India), bonne (Fr.), governess, ayah (India), amah (Oriental).

2. Protection, safe conduct, safeguard, ward, guardianship, custody, tutelage, accompaniment as protection.

3. Retinue, suite, cortège, attendance, company, entourage

ESCULENT, adj. Suitable for use as food, fit for food, edible, eatable, cibarious, comestible, succulent, nutritive, nutritious, alimentary, dietetic, culinary.

ESCUTCHEON, n. 1. Shield on which armorial bearings are depicted, coat of arms, arms, device, heraldric shield, hatchment, scutcheon, ensign armorial, heraldry, crest.

2. Blot on the escutcheon, stain on one's honor or reputation, stigma, onus, disgrace, skeleton in the closet.

ESOPHAGUS, n. Musculo-membranous tube through which food and drink pass from the pharynx to the stomach, tube connecting the mouth with the stomach, canal extending from the pharnyx to the stomach, gullet, oesophagus.

ESOTERIC, adj. Confined to a select circle, understood by a select few, confidential, private, known only to the initiate, privy, inner, inmost, irrevealable, secret, acroamatic, abstruse, arcane, recondite, cabalistic, mystic, occult, cryptic, not to be spoken of, veiled, dark, close, inviolate, undisclosed, untold, inviolable, confined to a charmed circle, hidden, concealed, behind a screen, *in petto (It.)*, not to be divulged, covert, inscrutable, obscure, deep, profound, mysterious.

ESPECIAL, *adj.* 1. Special, uncommon, unusual, exceptional, singular, unique, exclusive, peculiar, particular, peculiar to a particular one, pertaining chiefly to one thing *or* person, private, respective, individual, personal, essential, specific, proper, not general.

2. Principal, master, outstanding, preëminent, chief, eminent, extraordinary, marked, worthy of note, distinguished, noteworthy.

ESPECIALLY, *adv.* 1. Specially, particularly, in particular, *ad hominem (Lat.)*, chiefly, most of all, mostly, primarily, firstly, truly, definitely, in a definite manner, expressly, specifically, mainly, principally.

2. Extraordinarily, uncommonly, unwontedly, unusually, singularly, exceptionally, markedly.

ESPIAL, *n.* Act of spying, keeping watch, seeing, watching in secret, *espionnage (Fr.)*, discovery, regard, survey, reconnaissance, *coup d'oel (Fr.)*, contemplation, observation, notice, view, glance, look, ken, glimpse, peep, glint.

ESPIONAGE, *n.* 1. Practice of spying on others, undercover work, offensive surveillance, private-eye work, systematic secret observation of the words and conduct of others, prying, subversive activity, reconnoitering, reconnaissance, search made for useful military information, secret watching.

2. Systematic use of spies by a government to discover the military and political secrets of other nations, underground agency. (See SPY.)

ESPLANADE, *n.* Promenade, walk, marina, lane, level open space for promenading, terrace, glacis, estrade, parterre, lawn, slope, grassy plot, green, sward, parade, mall, circus, piazza, quadrangle, court, patio, close, yard, alley, road.

ESPOUSAL, *n.* 1. Adoption of a principle, favor, advocacy of a cause, championship, furtherance, support, aidance, patronage, defense, opitulation, assistance, taking sides, promotion, countenance, succor, auspices, subvention.

2. Betrothment, betrothal, marriage contract, engagement rite, match, spousal, affiance, bridal, wedding, nuptials, assumption of intent, leading to the altar, wedding knot, Hymen, marriage ceremony.

ESPOUSE, *v.* 1. Take up the cause of, champion, assume interest in, adopt, embrace a cause, elect, defend, support, maintain, stand up for, sustain, make one's own, choose, coöpt, uphold, take up the cudgels for, stick up for, back up, second, work for, abet, advocate, lend oneself to, favor, patronize, smile upon, take in hand, side with, enlist under the banners of, lend one's aid, hold out a helping hand, befriend, further, promote, forward.

2. Give a woman in marriage, affiance, plight, betroth, promise in wedlock, publish the banns, give away in marriage.

3. Take in marriage, wive, wed, marry, take to oneself a wife, be spliced, lead to the altar, take for better *or* worse, tie the nuptial knot, give one's hand to.

ESPRIT, *n.* Wit, lively intelligence, sprightliness, Attic salt, smartness, mother wit, shrewdness, gray matter, sagacity, parts, quick parts, intelligence,

grasp of intellect, subtlety, acumen, discernment, sapience, perspicacity, wisdom, brains, rationality.

ESPRIT DE CORPS *(Fr.)* Group interest, group feeling, teamwork, party spirit, mutual interest, morale, unanimity, sense of union, bond of union, cooperation, community, sodality, comradeship, sociality, fellowship, companionship, clubbism, sense of common interests and responsibilities developed among a group of persons associated together, clanship, solidarity, confraternity.

ESPY, *v.* See at a distance, descry, make out, catch sight of, distinguish, discern, spy, perceive, sight, catch a glimpse of, discover, see with one's own eyes, see unexpectedly, recognize, witness, ken, be a spectator, look on, observe closely, behold, detect, inspect, peer at, take a peep, fix the eyes upon, strain the eyes to see.

ESQUIRE, *n.* 1. Man belonging to the order of English gentry ranking next below a knight, sir, English country squire, gentleman, silk-stocking, landed proprietor, patrician, aristocrat.

2. Polite title after a man's last name, title of courtesy.

3. *(Middle Ages)* Attendant upon a knight, aspirant to knighthood, armiger, shield-bearer, armorbearer, squire, escort.

ESSAY, *v.* 1. Make an effort to perform, try, aim, attempt, endeavor, venture, undertake, strive, seek to, strain, adventure, speculate, tempt fortune, feel one's way, throw out a feeler, send up a pilot balloon, fish for, angle for, see how the wind blows, try one's fortune at, take a crack at, take a wack at, make a go at, undertake.

2. Put to the test, try out, test, experiment, make trial of, make an experiment, assay, refine, purify, render.

ESSAY, *n.* 1. Short literary composition on a particular subject, brief discourse, dissertation, monograph, paper, article, disquisition, treatise, thesis, tractate, theme, editorial, commentary, tract.

2. Effort to perform something, attempt to accomplish something, endeavor, trial, struggle, venture, aim, try, experiment.

ESSAYIST, *n.* 1. Writer of essays, litterateur, author, *homme de lettres (Fr.)*, man of letters, scribe, penman.

2. One who essays to do anything, one who makes trials, experimenter.

ESSENCE, *n.* 1. That in which the real character of a thing consists, that by which a thing is what it is, important elements of a thing, essential part, true constitution of, intrinsic nature, quintessence, inmost substance, central nature, vital element, necessary constituent, hypostasis, principle, entity, inwardness, being, actuality, reality, essentialness, main features, quiddity, pith, backbone, heart, kernel, marrow, soul, core, gist, keynote, sum and substance, life, lifeblood, flower, truth, purport, verity, spirit, import, tenor, drift, significance, sense.

2. Substance obtained from a plant *or* drug by distillation and containing its characteristic properties in concentrated form, extract, volatile part, concentrate, elixir, alcoholic solution of an essential oil.

3. Odor, attar, perfume scent *or* the volatile matter of which it consists.

4. Wine made from the pure juice of the ripest grapes.

ESSENTIAL, *adj.* 1. That which is in the natural

composition of a thing, comprised within the nature of a thing, fixed from the beginning as a permanent constituent of a thing, fundamental, constitutional, vital, basic, inherent, indispensable, intrinsic, inward, organic, ingrained, indigenous, immanent, substantial, material, needful, radical, requisite, highly important, characteristic, basal, urgent, imperative, absolute, cardinal, principal, main, leading, capital.

2. Constituting the essence of a thing, having the nature of an essence, highly rectified, volatile, pure, diffusible.

ESSENTIAL, *n.* 1. Indispensable element, main ingredient, chief point, vital part, characteristic, absolute requisite, primary constituent, quality, life, attribute, peculiarity, trait, feature, mark, qualification, virtue.

2. First principle, first step, rudiment, outline, first requirement, fundamental.

ESTABLISH, *v.* 1. Set up on a firm basis, secure, ground, plant, place, root, ensconce.

2. Install in a position, fix securely, stabilize, settle in a business, secure, make stable, make firm, consolidate, sustain, set on its legs, set on its feet, place on a permanent footing, station.

3. Organize, institute, found, create, raise, rear, erect, build, constitute, form, compose, evolve, bring about, frame, contrive, fashion, fabricate, construct, coin.

4. Enact unalterably, ordain for permanence, appoint as a law, decree, rule, seal, authorize, vest, charter, make of a thing a state institution, decide, determine, conclude, clinch, adjudicate, judge, pass upon, hold.

5. Cause to be permanently accepted, confirm, ratify, indorse, sanction, approve, corroborate, sustain, uphold, warrant.

6. Show to be valid *or* well grounded, validate, authenticate, substantiate, make good, make out a case for, verify, prove, circumstantiate.

ESTABLISHMENT, *n.* 1. Act of establishing, upbuilding, erection, installation, confirmation, substantiation, verification, ordainment, founding, authorization, settlement, appointment.

2. Premises occupied by an organization, firm, institution, business, concern, company, combine, house, corporation, trust, syndicate, association, society, plant, emporium, shop, store, building and equipment occupied by a business, mart.

3. Constituted order, system, permanent force *or* organization, recognition of a thing by the state as official.

4. Household, ménage, domestic arrangements, place of residence and everything connected with it, dwelling, home.

5. Settled allowance, fixed income, subsistence, regular means of support, stipend, salary, living.

ESTATE, *n.* 1. Material things which are owned, piece of landed property of large extent, property capable of being handed down to descendants *or* otherwise disposed of in a will, personal estate, possessions, effects, chattels, goods, fortune, real estate, money, valuables, securities, realty, land and buildings, interests, holdings, demesne, grounds, wealth, assets, belongings, means, wares, resources, circumstances, collective assets above *or* against liabilities, commodities, merchandise, stock.

2. Interest in a species of permanent property, ownership, legal status of an owner with respect to his property.

3. Position in society, rank, station, political

group, grade, class, social status, social standing, sphere, order, division, high rank, circumstances with reference to worldly prosperity, dignity.

4. Period of life, condition of life, situation, state, settled form *or* state of being, trait, habit, characteristic, quality, attribute.

ESTEEM, *v.* 1. Regard favorably, approve, like, appreciate highly, admire, value, prize, set great store by, regard as valuable, look up to, honor, pay homage to, venerate, revere, reverence, defer to, respect, worship, glorify, think much of, set a great value on, attach importance to a thing because of its worth, think highly of, commend, praise, recommend, indorse, uphold, stand up for.

2. Consider as of a certain value, calculate, regard, account, deem, look upon as, think, hold, believe, imagine, fancy, suppose.

3. Exercise perception in realizing the worth of something, appraise, estimate, rate, value, set some value on, reckon, repute, judge, adjudge.

ESTEEM, *n.* 1. Good opinion, high regard, honor, approving judgment, favorable repute, reverence, fame, respect, favor, veneration, credit, homage, approbation, commendation, approval, deference combined with admiration and affection, kudos, trust.

2. Judgment of merit *or* demerit, appraisal, valuation, estimate, opinion, account, reckoning, consideration, appreciation.

ESTIMABLE, *adj.* 1. Meriting good opinion, dear, worthy, meritorious, deserving, laudable, worthy of regard, praiseworthy, excellent, unimpeachable, admirable, good, valuable, precious, worshipful, adorable, lovable, venerable, emeritus, deserving of esteem, commendable, time-honored, esteemed, respectable, reputable, valued, respected, creditable.

2. Appreciable, computable, capable of being estimated, calculable, appraisable, reckonable.

ESTIMATE, *v.* 1. Form an approximate judgment of the value of, calculate approximately, reckon, appraise, compute, measure, consider, rate, judge, count, account, value, gage, weigh carefully, set a value on, evaluate, assess, prize, rank, price, set a price on, size up *(coll.)*, form an opinion of, tell off, numerate, enumerate, number, deem, consider, think, ascertain, deliberate.

2. Submit approximate figures of the cost of work to be done, budget.

ESTIMATE, *n.* 1. Approximate judgment of the value of something, estimation, valuation, report, assessment, appraisal, appraisement, appreciation, opinion of the qualities of a person *or* thing, criticism, review, critique, notice.

2. Computation, approximation, approximate statement of the costs for certain work to be done, rough *or* approximate calculation.

ESTIMATION, *n.* 1. Judgment, consideration, point of view, viewpoint, opinion, supposition, surmise, conjecture.

2. Respect, appreciation, admiration, favorable opinion, regard, esteem, honor, reverence, fame, veneration, deference, approval, reputation, standing.

3. Approximate calculation, estimate, account, appraisal, assessment, valuation, appraisement, appreciation, computation, rating.

ESTOP, *v. (Law)* Hinder by estoppel, bar, debar, stop, stay, impede, inhibit, preclude, prevent, put a stop to, foreclose, obstruct, stop the progress of, scotch, contravene, prohibit.

ESTRANGE, v. 1. Disaffect, turn away in feeling *or* affection, make disaffected, abalienate, alienate the affections of, destroy one's affections, turn from attachment to enmity *or* indifference, make unfriendly, make inimical, make indifferent, set against, harden the heart, cause to break with, repel, sow dissension, set by the ears, provoke an aversion to, cause to fall out, come between, sever, sunder, cause to bear malice, cause to take umbrage, embroil, entangle, disunite, set at odds, widen the breach, pit against, envenom, incense, wean away from.

2. Remove to a distance, separate, withdraw, withhold, keep away, keep oneself at a distance, keep aloof, part, part company, leave, take leave, quit, go away, hold at arm's length.

3. Divert from the original use *or* possessor, apply to a foreign purpose, transfer, reassign.

ESTRANGEMENT, n. Alienation of affections, abalienation, disaffection, discord, disagreement, dissidence, dissension, unfriendliness, animosity, antagonism, hostility, antipathy, aversion, dislike, disfavor, house divided against itself, disunion, split, rupture, feud, breach, schism, difference, drawing off, withdrawal, removal.

ESTUARY, n. That part of the mouth of a river in which its current meets the sea's tides, wide lower part of a tidal river, fiord, firth, frith, inlet, arm of the sea, armlet, lough, bay, gulf, bight, ostiary, cove.

ET CETERA (*Lat.*) 1. And others, and the rest, other things unspecified, and so forth, and so on, etc. (*abbr.*).

2. (*Pl.*) Extras, sundries.

ETCH, v. 1. Engrave by corrosion of an acid, corrode with an acid, eat out, bite in, scrape, furrow, carve.

2 Draw with an etching-needle, enchase, chase, incise, crosshatch, engrave, stipple, grave, dry point, outline by scratching lines with a pointed instrument, form a design in furrows which when charged with ink will give an impression on paper, lithograph.

ETERNAL, adj. 1. Lasting throughout eternity, without beginning *or* end, having always existed, superior to time, self-originated, self-active, eterne (*Poetic*), self-existent, absolute, indeterminate, necessary, almighty, inevitable, timeless, infinite, unbegotten.

2. Going on without ceasing, never stopping, never-ending, sempiternal, everlasting, going on continually, ever-enduring, interminable, eonian, unending, of infinite duration, perpetual, forever abiding, illimitable, ceaseless, unceasing, constant, without end, boundless, incessant, unintermittent, persistently recurrent, perennial.

3. Existing outside of all relations of change, not subject to change, unchangeable, immutable, indestructible, imperishable, unfading, immortal, amaranthine, perdurable, ever-living, never-dying, undying, deathless, enduring through all future time, incorruptible.

4. Continued without intermission, continuous, continuously renewing, continual, uninterrupted, persistent, incessant, unbroken, unflagging, never failing.

ETERNALLY, adv. Forever, ever, evermore, aye, for aye, throughout eternity, for everlasting, *in saecula saeculorum* (*Lat.*), throughout all ages, in all ages, forever and ever, world without end, to the end of time, till the crack of doom, till doomsday, endlessly, timelessly, always, forever and a day, constantly, everlastingly, perpetually, ceaselessly, interminably, continually, at all times, incessantly, morning, noon and night, day in and day out, day and night.

ETERNITY, n. 1. Duration without beginning *or* end, endless duration, unceasingness, endlessness, everlastingness, continuity, sempiternity, absence of time, perpetuity, interminableness, timelessness, infinite time, infinite duration, boundlessness, illimitableness, unendingness, eternalness, no time, infinite time, coeternity, perdurability.

2. Immortality, unending existence beyond the present life, hereafter, futurity, time to come, future existence, future state, next world, after life, everlasting life, supramundane being, world to come.

3. Seemingly endless period of time, seeming endlessness, age, ages and ages, drearily unbroken expanse of time.

ETHER, n. 1. The upper regions of space, azure, the atmosphere that fills them, air, the clear sky, welkin, the heavens, hyaline (*Poetic*), empyrean, blue vault above, crystalline spheres, firmament, canopy of heaven, stratosphere.

2. A volatile and colorless highly inflammable liquid obtained by the action of sulfuric acid on alcohol and used as a solvent and anesthetic, anesthetic agent.

ETHEREAL, adj. 1. Volatile, gaseous, vaporous, airy, aerial, heavenly, pertaining to the earth's atmosphere, empyreal, uranic, celestial, supernal.

2. Delicate, light, tenuous, attenuated, slender, thin, rare, sublimated, subtilized, subtle, fragile, intangible, impalpable, insubstantial, flimsy, fine, gossamery, exquisite, fairylike, spiritlike.

ETHEREALIZE, v. Make ethereal, spiritualize, make spiritual, refine, subtilize, rarefy, attenuate.

ETHEREALNESS, n. Unsubstantiality, delicacy, immateriality, incorporeity, tenuity, tenuousness, airiness, fragility, fairy-like flimsiness, sheerness, gossameriness, cobwebbiness, featheriness, "such stuff as dreams are made on," silkiness, buoyancy, vaporousness, transparency, diaphaneity, "baseless fabric of a vision," volatility, ethereality, rarity, subtileness.

ETHICAL, adj. 1. Pertaining to morals, dealing with the principles of morality, pertaining to right and wrong in conduct, deontological, aretological, ethological, pertaining to ethos.

2. Right, conscientious, decorous, decent, just, seemly, correct, proper, fit, dutiful, virtuous, pure, in accordance with the rules for right conduct, conforming to professional standards of conduct, in accordance with the standards of a profession, good, righteous.

ETHICS, n. 1. Principles of morality including both the science of the good and the nature of the right, aretology, deontology, ethology, science of morals, moral philosophy, ethical science, the science of ideal ends of human action, hedonics.

2. Rules of conduct recognized in respect to a particular class of human actions, decalogue, Ten Commandments, moral practice, code of right and wrong.

3. Moral principles of an individual, bounden duty, moral obligation, accountability, liability, onus, responsibility, conscientiousness, conscience, virtue, inward monitor, rectitude, sense of duty, uprightness, good behavior.

ETHNOLOGY, n. Anthropology, anthropometric data, science of races dealing with the mental and physical differences of racial groups of men, science that treats of the distinct subdivisions of mankind.

ETIOLATE, *v.* 1. Render white, cause to whiten by excluding light, bleach, blanch, deprive of color, decolorize, achromatize, wash out, tone down, make pale.

2. Lose color, turn pale, blench, fade, become colorless, pale, be white, whiten through lack of light.

ETIOLATED, *adj.* Whitened, blanched, blenched, bleached, colorless, achromatic, hueless, pallid, pale, light-colored, white, milky-white, snow-white, hoar, blond, chalky.

ETIQUETTE, *n.* Sense of what is becoming for a person of good breeding, conventional forms and usages, conventional ceremonial of polite society, proprieties of conduct, prescribed form of behavior, fashionable ceremony, conventional requirements as to social behavior, forms of good breeding, accepted decorum, ceremonial code, fashion, manners, formality, usage, savoir-faire, punctilio, politeness, gentility, mannerly customs, good form, *bienséance (Fr.),* conventionality, mannerliness, respectable modes, observance of the formal requirements governing behavior in polite society, established conventions of morals and good taste, seemliness, decency, gallantry, protocol.

ETUDE, *n.* Musical composition intended mainly for the practice of some point of technique, piece embodying a specific technical exercise, study piece for practice of some special point, exercise.

ETYMOLOGY, *n.* 1. Science of etymons, study of primitive linguistic roots, study of word roots, study of historical linguistic change as applied to individual words, lexicology, philology.

2. History of a word showing its source and its development in form and meaning, account of the history of a particular word, derivation of a word, etymological meaning of a word.

ETYMON, *n.* Primary linguistic form from which derivatives are formed, primitive *or* root word, radix, radical, stem, stirps, stock, term, vocable, primitive signification of a word.

EUCHARIST, *n.* 1. Sacrifice of the Mass, Holy Communion, sacrament of the Lord's Supper, Christian Sacrament, Communion, consecrated elements of bread and wine, intinction, liturgy, impanation, transubstantiation, elevation of the Host, consecrated wafer, viaticum, real presence, spiritual communion with the One God, oblation.

2. Giving of thanks, thanksgiving, gratefulness.

EUDEMON, *n.* Good demon, eudaemon, tutelar, good spirit, angel, good fairy, fay, peri, genius, good genius, demiurge, familiar spirit, ministering spirit.

EUGENICS, *n.* Euthenics, stirpiculture, process of race improvement, genetics, careful selection of parents, race meliorism, science of improving offspring, science of improving the qualities of the human race.

EULOGIST, *n.* Praiser, lauder, *laudator (Lat.),* panegyrist, encomiast, extoller, booster, courtier, touter, *claqueur (Fr.),* euphemist, adulator, toady, flatterer, whitewasher, sycophant.

EULOGIZE, *v.* Deliver a eulogy about, praise highly, bepraise, laud, extol, cry up, belaud, rate highly, applaud, panegyrize, crack up *(coll.),* boost, tout, speak in strong commendation of, commend, pay tribute to, celebrate, compliment,

glorify, magnify, *prôner (Fr.),* puff *(coll.),* say a good word for, exalt to the skies, speak in high terms of, sing the praises of, cheer, acclaim, gush, acclamate, overesteem, appreciate publicly, approve ringingly, sanction heartily.

EULOGY, *n.* 1. Set oration in honor of a deceased person, *élogy (Fr.),* eulogium, panegyric, formal utterance of praise, encomium, eulogistic speech.

2. High praise, laud, laudation, good word, tribute of praise, commendation, applause, meed of praise, homage, plaudit, acclamation, paean, hosannah, blurb.

EUNUCH, *n.* Castrato, emasculated attendant in a harem, chamberlain, castrated man employed as an officer of state by Oriental rulers.

EUPEPSIA, *n.* Good digestion, sound digestion, good state of health, normal digestion.

EUPHEMISM, *n.* 1. Substitution of mild *or* vague expression for a harsh *or* blunt one, softened expression to avoid offending by indelicacy, mock modesty, substitution of an inoffensive word, verbal extenuation, mild name for something disagreeable, word in verbal good taste.

2. Overdelicacy, affected refinement, restraint, Victorianism, prudishness, unctuousness, propriety.

EUPHEMISTIC, *adj.* Extenuative, metaphorical, given to the use of euphemisms, euphemous, soft, mild, vague, indirect, figurative, tropical.

EUPHONIOUS, *adj.* Agreeable to the ear, clear as a bell, well-sounding, euphonic, mellifluous, silvery, musical, canorous, singing, sweet-toned, pleasing in sound, smooth-sounding, harmonious, sweetly flowing, fluent, melodious, dulcet, mellow, free from harshness, golden-toned, rhythmical, balanced, periodic *(Rhet.).*

EUPHONY, *n.* Agreeable sound in language, smoothness of utterance, homophony, pleasing effect to the ear, sweet sound, melliffluousness, harmonious succession of words having a pleasing sound, dulcet language, melodious speech, well-rounded periods, canorousness, concinnity.

EUPHORIA, *n.* The sense of well-being, feeling of well-being, health, ability to bear pain.

EUPHUISM, *n.* 1. Linguistic purism, fastidious delicacy in language, affected elegance of diction, linguistic cultism, Gongorism, finicalness of style, excessive elegance of language, mannerism in expression, affectation of elegance in writing, Marinism.

2. High-flown periphrastic style, ornate style of expression, pompous language, Alexandrianism, extravagantly ornate diction, linguistic flourish, flowers of rhetoric, inflation, altiloquence, verbal floridness, grandiloquence, magniloquence, rant, fustian, high-sounding words, *sesquipedalia verba (Lat.),* macrology, sesquipedalianism, turgidity, orotundity, purple patches, prose run mad.

EUTHANASIA, *n.* Painless death, mercy killing, easy death, happy release, practice of painlessly putting to death an incurably diseased person.

EVACUANT, *adj.* Producing evacuation, emetic, eliminant, cathartic, purgative, diuretic, ejective, abstergent, cleansing, emptying.

EVACUANT, *n.* Purgative medicine, purgative, evacuant agent, cathartic.

EVACUATE, *v.* 1. Empty, make empty, free from contents, remove, draw out, drain, scour, hollow, exhaust, deplete.

2. Remove inhabitants from a place, quit a

country, leave a town because of threats of attack, withdraw from, vacate, leave empty, abandon, desert, relinquish, retire from, forsake, go away.

3. (*Physiol.*) Discharge waste matter through the excretory passages, eject from the bowels, purge, excrete, eliminate, defecate, void, expel, emit, throw out, clean out.

EVACUATION, *n.* 1. Act of emptying, making empty of contents, exantlation, removal, draining off, depletion, exhaustion.

2. Withdrawal, abandonment, quitting, exodus, clearance by removal of inhabitants *or* troops, removal, departure, hegira, retreat, retirement, flight.

3. (*Physiol.*) Expulsion of waste matter from the bowels, excretion, purgation, catharsis, stool, voidance, defecation, discharge, ejection, egesta, expulsion, excrements, feces, elimination, going to stool, cacation, dysentery, dejection.

EVADE, *v.* 1. Escape by cleverness, escape from by trickery, get away from by artifice, steal away from, steer clear of, shy away from, save oneself from, foil, baffle.

2. Avoid doing *or* fulfilling, get around, dodge, elude, shun, funk, parry, neglect, decline, ignore, violate, shirk, malinger, not do, leave undone, skip, omit, close one's eyes to, hedge, duck, eschew.

3. Dodge by answering indirectly, equivocate, quibble, tergiversate, sophisticate, cavil, subtilize, fence, shuffle, palter, split hairs, shift, beg the question, beat about the bush, sidestep, reason in a circle, carp.

EVALUATE, *v.* Ascertain the amount of, fix the value of, appraise carefully, estimate, rate, assess, sum up, express numerically.

EVANESCE, *v.* Disappear gradually, vanish, be seen no more, be dissipated, dissolve, melt away, pass, go, avaunt, fade away, recede, evaporate, lapse, be transient, flit, fleet, pass away like a summer cloud, be gone, leave no trace, "leave not a rack behind," undergo an eclipse, go off the stage, be lost to view, retire from sight.

EVANESCENCE, *n.* Evanishment, gradual fading from view, gradual disappearance, vanishing, dissipation, tendency to vanish, eclipse, fugacity, occultation, exit, departure, vanishing point, flash in the pan, evaporation, transience, transientness, cursoriness, ephemeralness, impermanence, nine days' wonder, transitoriness, volatility, mortality, deciduousness, caducity, bubble.

EVANESCENT, *adj.* 1. Vanishing, disappearing, passing away, fading, shifting, *spurlos versenkt* (*Ger.*), becoming imperceptible by diminution, scarcely perceptible, lost to view, gone, invisible.

2. Transient, transitory, cursory, short-lived, ephemeral, perishable, mortal, fugitive, fugacious, impermanent, fleeting, flitting, flying, cometary, meteoric, brief, quick, momentary, temporary, unenduring, volatile, caducous, deciduous, flighty, unstable.

EVANGEL, *n.* 1. Gospel, Scripture, word of God, Holy Writ, inspired writings, Christian revelation, glad tidings, good news, message.

2. Doctrine held to be of prime importance, teaching taken as a guide, doctrine regarded as having special sanction.

EVANGELICAL, *adj.* 1. Evangelistic, according to the Gospel, based on the New Testament, in keeping with the Gospel and its teachings, divine,

scriptural, apostolic, canonical, textuary, sacred, orthodox, ecclesiastical, biblical.

2. Designating a sect which emphasizes the authority of the Scriptures in opposition to that of the church itself, adhering to the letter of the Gospel, earnest for the message of the Gospel.

3. Zealous for practical Christian living, deeply pious, fervent, devout, spiritually minded.

4. Emphasizing salvation through atonement of Christ, seeking the conversion of sinners, stressing the importance of personal experience of sin and redemption.

EVANGELIST, *n.* 1. Preacher of the Gospel, field preacher, missionary, propagandist, bringer of the Gospel, revivalist, sky pilot, blackcoat, itinerant pastor, minister, clergyman, converter of sinners, Billy Sunday.

2. Writer of one of the four Gospels, inspired writer, apostle, disciple, saint.

EVANGELIZE, *v.* Act as an evangelist, instruct in the Gospel, preach the Gospel to, convert to Christianity, proselytize, propagandize, spread the faith.

EVAPORATE, *v.* 1. Remove moisture by means of heat, dehydrate, desiccate, make dry, dry up, parch, sear, cause to shrivel, concentrate.

2. Drive off vapor, vaporize, extract in the form of vapor, disperse in vapor, convert into a gaseous state, gasify, dissipate, boil away.

3. Give off moisture, emit vapor, exhale, fume, steam, reek, smoke.

4. Pass off in vapor, volatilize, cohobate (*Chem.*), distill, finestill, fly off in vapor, escape and be dissipated, diffuse.

5. Vanish, evanesce, dissolve, melt away, pass away, fade away, disappear, pass off without effect.

EVAPORATION, *n.* 1. Act of drying *or* concentrating by expelling moisture, change from a liquid *or* solid state into vapor, vaporization, gasification, volatilization, vaporescence, steaming away, distillation, cohobation (*Chem.*), dehydration, boiling away, desiccation, sublimation, finestillation, exhalation of moisture, emanation.

2. Disappearance, evanishment, evanescence (See EVANESCENCE.)

EVASION, *n.* 1. Escape by trickery *or* cleverness, avoidance by subterfuge, elusion, flight, retreat, recoil, recession, departure from, foiling, abstention, dodging, baffling.

2. Means of evading, trick to get around something, excuse to avoid something, shuffling, shift, sophistry, subterfuge, equivocation, deceit, tergiversation, casuistry, quibbling, specious reasoning, prevarication, bluff, artifice, chicanery, Jesuitry, fallaciousness, deception, chicane, hairsplitting, begging of the question, shilly-shally, loophole, sophism, amphiboly, paralogism, ambiguity, pilpulism, subtlety.

EVASIVE, *adj.* 1. Escaping perception, elusive, evanescent, fugitive, fugacious, runaway, shifty, slippery.

2. Avoiding by artifice, characterized by evasion, seeking to evade, shuffling, sophistical, equivocating, deceptive, misleading, elusory, hairsplitting, tricksy, casuistic, Jesuitical, specious, pilpulistic, tergiversatory, fallacious, paralogical, plausible, illusive, hollow, deceitful, paltering.

EVE, *n.* 1. Evening before any date *or* event, night preceding, night before.

2. Period immediately preceding some important event.

3. Evening (*Poetic*).

EVEN, *adj.* 1. Without elevation *or* depression, smooth, plane, level, flat.

2. Without irregularities, having no flaw *or* blemish, uniform, free from variations *or* fluctuations, unvaried, equable, regular, steady, symmetrical, proportionate.

3. In the same plane *or* line, on a level, true, parallel, straight, plumb, on the same level, flush, in line with, abreast, alongside.

4. Having nothing due on either side, fully paid *or* revenged, square, quits, having no advantage on either side.

5. Just, fair, impartial, dispassionate, unbiased, unprejudiced, equitable, straightforward.

6 Even-tempered, calm, placid, not easily excited, not quick to anger, unruffled, not readily disturbed.

7. Exactly expressible in integers, without fractional parts, divisible by 2.

EVEN, *adv.* 1. Exactly, precisely, just, just so, even so, truly, very true, true, yes, yea, aye, granted, well and good, to be sure, surely, that's just it, assuredly, indeed, certainly, certes, of course, to be sure.

2. At the very time, even now, at this moment, but now, just now, on the present occasion.

3. Freely, quite.

4. In like manner, likewise, to a like degree, but also, not only so, regularly, evenly.

EVEN-HANDED, *adj.* Impartial, equitable, fair, just, treating all alike, square, fair and square, fair-dealing, virtuous, honorable, upright, right, honest, straightforward, over and aboveboard, unbiased.

EVENING, *n.* 1. The period from sunset *or* from the evening meal to ordinary bedtime, eve, even, eventide, dusk, gloaming, vespers, evensong, fall of day, nightfall, twilight, close of the day and early part of night, nightfall, decline of day, sundown, sunset, curfew, cockshut (*dial.*).

2. Period of an evening's entertainment, soirée, evening reception.

3. Any concluding *or* declining period, the latter portion, old age, "sear and yellow leaf," vale of years, decay, decrepitude, caducity, years.

EVENING STAR Bright planet seen in the west after sunset, Venus, Vesper, Hesper, Hesperus.

EVENSONG, *n.* 1. Form of worship said *or* sung at evening, evening service, vespers, compline, evening prayer, evening hymn, complin, angelus.

2. The last but one of the seven canonical hours.

EVENT, *n.* 1. Anything that happens *or* comes to pass, incident, occurrence, episode, occasion, happening, accident, circumstance, fact, fortuity, affair, case, proceeding, transaction, hap, casualty, eventuality, contingency, particular, phenomenon, scene, concern, business, matter, fortune, chance.

2. Momentous occurrence, experience, crisis, pass, emergency.

3. Issue, result, consequence, upshot, outcome, conclusion, end, termination, sequel.

EVENTFUL, *adj.* Full of incidents, attended by important *or* noteworthy events, full of events of a striking character, memorable, consequential, remarkable, interesting, notable, epochal, striking, signal, stirring, having important issue *or* results, momentous, weighty, important, critical, salient.

EVENTUAL, *adj.* 1. Pertaining to the event *or* issue, consequent, coming, ultimate, inevitable, final, ulterior, future, prospective, imminent, next, impending, near, close at hand.

2. Depending upon uncertain events, dependent on events, contingent, possible, conditional.

EVENTUALLY, *adv.* In the event *or* outcome, as the final result or outcome, ultimately, finally, in course of time, sooner or later, in the end, at last, impendingly, in store, to come, instant, at hand, imminently, in the wind, in prospect.

EVENTUATE, *v.* 1. Issue, have issue, end, result, ensue, close, terminate, culminate, conclude.

2. Be the issue, be the outcome, come about, take place, come to pass, present itself, befall, betide, bechance, occur, happen, come off, draw on, fall out, turn out, arise, supervene.

EVER, *adv.* 1. At any time, on any occasion, at any period, at any point of time, in any possible case, by any chance, at all.

2. Eternally, always, evermore, for aye, at all times, forever, under all circumstances, endlessly, perpetually, in all ages, to the end of time, till the crack of doom, till doomsday, constantly, incessantly, without end, everlastingly, "to the last syllable of recorded time," continually.

EVER AND ANON Often to be met with, oft, often, frequently, not unfrequently, many a time and oft, in quick succession, at short intervals, every now and then, at one time and at another, repeatedly, continually, commonly, from time to time, *toties quoties (Lat.),* day and night, again and again, morning, noon and night.

EVERLASTING, *adj.* 1. Eternal, unending, lasting *or* enduring forever, endless, ceaseless, unceasing, never-ceasing, incessant, unintermitting, constant, perpetual, continual, never-ending, interminable, infinite in duration, uninterrupted.

2. Undying, immortal, never-dying, deathless, imperishable, ever-living, amaranthine, evergreen, eonian.

3. Wearisome, monotonous, tiresome, tedious from repetition, dragging on over a long period, disgustingly protracted.

4. Wearing indefinitely, durable, perdurable, indestructible.

EVERMORE, *adv.* 1. Always, forever, eternally, ever, for aye, to the end of time, world without end, through all ages, at all times, perpetually, constantly, continually.

2. Ever again, at any future period, in the future.

EVERY, *adj.* 1. Each of several, all taken one by one, collective, universal, world-wide, general, any, generic, individual, either, each and all, everyone.

2. The greatest possible degree of, all possible, very great.

EVERYDAY, *adj.* Pertaining to every day, daily, such as is met with every day, ordinary, common, commonplace, customary, workaday, routine, set, usual, homely, run-of-the-mill, conventional, trite, accustomed, wonted, habitual, habituated, stock, inveterate, frequent, household, familiar, regular, well-trodden, hackneyed, established, stereotyped.

EVERYWHERE, *adv.* In every place, in every quarter, in all places, universally, omnipresently, ubiquitously, far and wide, all over, right and left, throughout the length and breadth of the land, here, there and everywhere, under the sun, from pole to pole, in the wide, wide world, from

China to Peru, from Dan to Beersheba, from Indus to the pole, at all points of the compass, on the face of the earth, to the uttermost parts of the earth, to the four winds, extensively, in all climes, throughout the world.

EVICT, *v.* 1. Turn out of house and home, put out of a house by legal process, unhouse, turn out of doors, dispossess, bundle out, sweep out, eject, eliminate, dislodge, oust, thrust out, kick out, remove, expel, extrude.

2. Recover property by virtue of superior legal title, wrest property from.

EVICTION, *n.* Forcible expulsion from property, driving out, dislodgment, dispossession, removal, ouster, ejectment, extrusion, expulsion, ejection, throwing out, deprivation, recovery of property from another's possession by due course of law.

EVIDENCE, *n.* 1. Body of facts on which belief *or* judgment is based, that which tends to furnish proof, ground for belief, that which tends to prove *or* disprove something, testimony, affidavit, deposition, attestation, voucher, exhibit, premises, document, data, facts, burden of proof, certificate, deed, record, token, substantiation, affirmation, citation, indication, information furnished in a legal investigation to support a contention, surety, argument, admission, averment, declaration, seal, outward sign, exemplification, demonstration, illustration, certainty, confirmation, ratification, corroboration, authentication, credential, warrant, diploma, signature, countersign, quotation, reference.

2. One who gives testimony, eyewitness, one who bears witness, bystander, observer, deponent, earwitness, testifier.

EVIDENCE, *v.* Bear witness, give evidence, tell, depose, witness, swear, avouch, vouch, testify, document, make manifest, make clear, indicate, display, evince, manifest, show clearly, prove, demonstrate, attest, certify, involve, imply, betoken, denote, bespeak, speak for itself, speak volumes, have weight, circumstantiate, exemplify, acknowledge, quote, adduce, cite, instance, refer to, allege, confess, confirm, ratify, corroborate, indorse, bear out, validate, vindicate, establish, authenticate, sustain, uphold, verify, substantiate, warrant, make out a case, make good.

EVIDENT, *adj.* Clear to the sight, plain to the understanding, obvious, open to the vision, bald, conspicuous, apparent, patent, palpable, manifest, distinct, overt, indubitable, unmistakable, lucid, unequivocal, downright, perceptible, standing out clearly, staring one in the face, visible, tangible, perspicuous, notable, discernible, unquestionable, glaring, undeniable, unconcealed, transparent.

EVIDENTIAL, *adj.* Furnishing evidence, evincive, evidentiary, indicative, documentary, supportive, demonstrative, corroborative, confirmatory, first-hand, ratificatory, conclusive, decisive, weighty, determinative, cumulative, significant, veridical, final, veracious, overwhelming.

EVIDENTLY, *adv.* Clearly, patently, plainly, obviously, manifestly, apparently, visibly, openly, perceptibly, in an evident manner, literally, from the context, unquestionably.

EVIL, *adj.* 1. Exhibiting bad moral qualities, base, immoral, iniquitous, wicked, bad, sinful, vicious, violating moral law, vile, corrupt, unprincipled, perverse, nefarious, facinorous, flagitious, wrong, felonious, scelerous, heinous, malign, malicious, malevolent, unregenerate, villainous, recidivistic, profligate.

2. Mischievous, injurious, hurtful, detrimental, harmful, pernicious, villainous, baneful, deleterious, noxious, damaging, malefic, dire, fell, maleficent, having qualities tending to injury and mischief, disadvantageous, prejudicial, sinister.

3. Accompanied by misfortune, unpropitious, calamitous, catastrophic, cataclysmic, disastrous, adverse, woeful, unhappy, unfortunate.

4. Due to bad character *or* conduct, shameful, disreputable, shameless, of ill repute, deserving of condemnation, offensive, repulsive, unrighteous, unholy, infamous, treacherous.

EVIL, *n.* 1. Wrongdoing, iniquity, unregeneracy, sin, wickedness, corruption, viciousness, badness, depravity, moral badness, turpitude, degradation, sinfulness, baseness, malignity, wrong, outrage, enormity, brutality, bestiality, atrocity, foul play, impiety, villainy, knavery, vice, lewdness, crime, licentiousness, wantonness, obscenity, unchastity, lust, abomination.

2. Calamity, adversity, catastrophe, cataclysm, debacle, disaster, accident, casualty, misfortune, mishap, reverse, sorrow, misery, ill, woe, buffet, affliction, blow.

3. Mischief, hurt, injury, harm, curse, bale, bane, damage, blast, loss, canker, disease, pain, suffering, affliction, disadvantage, perniciousness, drawback, detriment.

EVILDOER, *n.* One who works evil, malefactor, evil-worker, worker of iniquity, criminal, sinner, wrongdoer, delinquent, offender, malfeasant, cur, culprit, black sheep, villain, rascal, miscreant, knave, brute, scoundrel, ruffian, desperado, rogue, Apache, recidivist, blackguard, scamp, scapegrace, caitiff, ne'er-do-well, wretch, good-for-nothing, reprobate, monster, fiend, demon, devil incarnate, witch, ghoul, ogre, beast, hellhound, oppressor, vulture, snake, serpent, viper, tyrant, terrorist, incendiary, anarchist, firebrand, nihilist, savage, destroyer, barbarian, vandal, Goth, Hun, jailbird, murderer, convict, felon, outlaw, gangster, bully, gunman, hooligan, hoodlum, roughneck, hijacker, racketeer, tough, cutthroat, thief, robber, footpad, burglar, safecracker, assassin, forger, debauchee, crook, mischief-maker, marplot, libertine, rake, wanton, rapist.

EVIL-MINDED, *adj.* 1. Excessively sex-minded, salacious, lewd, lecherous, pornographic, smutty, obscene, lickerish, licentious, bestial, libidinous, carnal, shameless, mind-in-the-gutter.

2. Wicked, vicious, malignant, depraved, cruel, malicious, malevolent, malign, fiendish, demoniac, devilish, diabolical, Satanic, hellish, cold-blooded, infernal, atrocious, truculent, inhuman, untamed, barbarous, fell, baleful, relentless, brutal, savage, ferocious, feral, spiteful, rancorous, hard of heart, ruthless.

EVIL ONE Satan, Lucifer, Belial, Devil, Samael, Beelzebub, Mephistopheles, Mephisto, Asmodeus, Moloch, Azazel, Abaddon, Eblis, Ahriman, Old Nick, Diabolus, Apollyon, Archfiend, Power of Darkness, Demon, the Evil Spirit, the Tempter, the Old Serpent, the Wicked One, the Prince of Darkness, Prince of the Devils, the Foul Fiend, the Archenemy, Father of Evil, the Author of Evil, Ruler of Darkness, fallen angel, unclean spirit, Old Harry.

EVINCE, *v.* 1. Prove, make manifest, show in a clear manner, manifest, evidence, make evident, establish, demonstrate, certify, bespeak, make clear.

2. Reveal the possession of, indicate, exhibit, present, disclose, reveal, show, display, bring to view, divulge, expose.

EVISCERATE, *v.* 1. Disembowel, take out the bowels of, gut, paunch, exenterate, viscerate, draw.

2. Deprive of vital *or* essential parts, devitalize, deprive of force.

EVOCATION, *n.* Summoning, conjuration, calling up by incantation, invocation, act of calling forth.

EVOKE, *v.* 1. Produce memories *or* feelings, call out, excite, elicit, arouse, rouse, provoke, cause, educe.

2. Summon, call up, call forth, summon forth, cause to appear, evocate, invoke, invite, obtest, adjure, conjure, superinduce, induce.

EVOLUTION, *n.* 1. Growth, process of formation *or* growth, development, evolvement, unfolding, creation, flowering, fruition, production, ripening, elaboration, unrolling.

2. (*Biol.*) Natural history, phylogeny, descent by continuous differentiation, continuous genetic adaptation, ascent from simplicity to complexity, phylogenesis, Darwinism, Lamarckism, theory of preformation, morphology.

3. Manifestation of related events *or* ideas in an orderly succession.

4. Figure in close-order drill, curvet, marching, changing of positions, circuition, convolution, gyration, movement forming one of a series of motions.

EVOLVE, *v.* 1. Develop gradually, expand, unroll, open, unfold, uncoil, emanate, work out, derive, construct, produce, develop by a process of differentiation to a more highly organized condition.

2. Come forth gradually into being, develop, undergo evolution, emerge, result.

EWER, *n.* Wide-mouthed pitcher, pitcher with a wide spout, tall slender vessel with a base, vessel having a spout and a handle, jar to hold water for ablutions, jug, ampulla, cruse, carafe, crock, cruet, urn, decanter, bottle, flagon, demijohn, flask.

EXACERBATE, *v.* 1. Exasperate, enrage, inflame, irritate, provoke, infuriate, excite, madden, add fuel to the flame, envenom, enkindle, suscitate, foment, enchafe, incense.

2. Increase the violence of, aggravate, render worse, embitter, sour, intensify.

EXACERBATION, *n.* Exasperation, irritation, provocation, anger, malignity, paroxysm, increase of violence, resentment, aggravation, increased severity, embitterment, annoyance. (See EXASPERATION, AGGRAVATION.)

EXACT, *adj.* 1. Allowing no departure from the standard, admitting of no deviation, strict, rigid, rigorous, severe, stringent, undeviating, specific.

2. Exercising strict care, careful, scrupulous, meticulous, punctilious, methodical, orderly, systematic, punctual, conscientious.

3. True to the letter, literal, line for line, word for word, verbatim, faithful, true to life, nice, sensitive, fine, critical, delicate, particular, scientific.

4. Strictly accurate, precise, faultless, without any error, true, not merely approximate, express,

explicit, correct, close, clear-cut, right, to the point, apposite, machine-tooled.

EXACT, *v.* 1. Impose, call for, require, ask, requisition, compel, demand, enforce, claim, take, wrest, extract, insist upon, tax with, task, enjoin, charge, bid, levy, draw from.

2. Force the payment of, mulct, extort, elicit, extract, squeeze.

EXACTING, *adj.* 1. Unduly severe in demands *or* requirements, strict, hard, stern, rigorous, exigent, unsparing, critical, exactive, rigid, demanding, imperious, arbitrary, oppressive, burdensome, harsh, peremptory.

2. Requiring close application, demanding close attention, difficult, arduous, trying, operose, involving much labor, calling for continuous exertion.

3. Characterized by exaction, extortionate, grasping, greedy, covetous, rapacious, predacious, predatory, sordid, *alieni appetens* (*Lat.*), insatiable.

EXACTION, *n.* 1. Act of exacting, compulsion to furnish, extortion, demand, oppression, levying by force, requisition, seizure, imposition, lion's share, expropriation.

2. Something exacted, ransom, blackmail, *chantage* (*Fr.*), bribe, hush money (*coll.*), douceur, mulct, toll, tax, dues, duty, levy, impost, excise, tariff, custom, assessment, taxation.

EXACTLY, *adv.* 1. In an exact manner, according to rule *or* measure, accurately, precisely, strictly, to a T, aright, faithfully, plumb, on the dot, explicitly, minutely, absolutely, fully, quite, *ad unguem* (*Lat.*), completely, perfectly, literally, line-for-line, word-for-word, verbatim.

2. That's right, quite so, that's just it, as you say, indeed, truly, certainly, certes, of course, assuredly, unquestionably, just so.

EXACTNESS, *n.* 1. Accuracy, precision, nicety, clockwork, correctness, faultlessness, truthfulness, faithfulness, exactitude, rigor, perfection, fidelity, literality.

2. Strictness, carefulness, scrupulousness, meticulousness, punctiliousness, punctilio, system, scrupulosity, rigidity, method, regularity.

3. Sensitiveness, delicacy, fastidiousness, fineness.

EXAGGERATE, *v.* Magnify beyond the limits of truth, represent disproportionately, enlarge on, delineate extravagantly, overstate, hyperbolize, embroider, color, overcolor, color too highly, romance, depict extravagantly, strain, overstrain, stretch, overcharge, caricature, heighten, draw a long bow, overdraw, overestimate, overshoot the mark, misrepresent, overvalue, overestimate, overdo, enhance, amplify on, pile up, increase immoderately, out-Herod Herod, puff, brag, boast.

EXAGGERATED, *adj.* Hyperbolically stated, overstated, overdone, colored, embroidered, far-fetched, extravagant, greatly magnified, enlarged upon, abnormally large, outsized, unqualified, sweeping, tall, steep, undue, fishy (*coll.*), excessive, hyperbolical, preposterous, egregious, bombastic, magniloquent, heightened.

EXAGGERATION, *n.* Overstatement, hyperbole, stretch of the imagination, extravagant statement, high coloring, embroidery, fringe, unreasonable amplification, misleading enlargement, caricature, yarn, traveler's tale, fish story, old wives' tale, tall story, tall talk, boastful talk, gasconade, rodomontade, *fanfaronnade* (*Fr.*), flourish of trumpet, braggardism, buncombe, vaporing, fine talking, bombast, magniloquence, gas, hot air, much cry and little wool, much ado about nothing, sounding brass and tinkling cymbal, tempest in a teapot, puffery, boasting, rant, Pelion upon Ossa, Baron Munchausen.

EXALT, *v.* 1. Raise on high, raise aloft, raise high, make lofty, lift up, rear, erect, heighten, raise, elevate, promote, advance, uplift, uprear.

2. Praise highly, laud, belaud, bepraise, extol, recommend, boost, make much of, applaud, commend, appreciate.

3. Elate, uplift, inspire, inspirit, stimulate.

4. Honor, ennoble, glorify, dignify, magnify, aggrandize, idealize, deify, apotheosize, canonize, adore, enthrone, worship.

EXALTATION, *n.* 1. Elation of mind *or* feeling, rapture, ecstasy, transport, bliss, inspiration, rhapsody.

2. Elevation, nobility, dignity, grandeur, glory, loftiness, apotheosis, deification, canonization, enthronement.

EXALTED, *adj.* 1. Elevated, raised up *or* aloft, high, upreared, lofty.

2. Magnificent, proud, aristocratic, glorious, noble, dignified, notable, sublime, illustrious, grand, honorable, imperial, transcendent, of high station, imposing, lordly, princely, kingly, regal, royal.

3. Rapturously excited, rapturous, ecstatic, blissful, transported, inspired, rhapsodic.

EXAMINATION, *n.* 1. Act of examining, casual glance over something, observation, inspection, scanning, prying.

2. Careful noting of details, scrutiny, search, investigation, quest, inquiry, survey, exploration, reconnaissance, research, perusal, probing, check up, assay, analysis, rummaging, ventilation, study, sifting, dissection.

3. Trial by questions, interrogation, inquest, inquisition, questioning, probation, prosecution, catechism, third degree, cross-examination, interpellation.

4. Test itself, quiz, list of questions asked, questionnaire.

EXAMINE, *v.* 1. Observe, inspect, scan, review, behold, look over, ponder, pore over, take stock of, audit, animadvert, watch, survey, attend, make note of, contemplate.

2. Look into, investigate, search, probe, explore, inquire into, scrutinize carefully, sift, reconnoitre, inquire about, search into, analyze, winnow, test, study, consider, dip into, canvass, sound, fathom, weigh, thresh out, rummage, ransack, overhaul, put to the proof, subject to inquiry.

3. Subject to legal inquisition, interrogate in order to ascertain truth, put to question in regard to conduct *or* knowledge of facts, question, query, put through the third degree, quiz, grill, roast, cross-examine, pump, interpellate, catechize, try, badger, heckle, cross-question.

EXAMINER, *n.* 1. Questioner, questionist, quizmaster, querist, inquisitor, investigator, catechist, catechizer, inspector, scrutinizer, inquirer, analyst, searcher, reviewer, auditor, observer, censor, critic.

2. *(Law)* A court officer empowered to administer the oath and take testimony.

EXAMPLE, *n.* 1. One of a number of things taken to show the character of the whole, pattern,

original, archetype, prototype, exemplar, sample, specimen, sampler, copy, piece.

2. Instance suitable for imitation, precedent, parallel case.

3. Something to be imitated, ideal, model, standard, criterion, norm, rule, paradigm, pink, paragon, *beau idéal (Fr.)*, phoenix, acme of perfection, *ne plus ultra (Lat.)*, pattern, mirror, trump.

4. Instance serving for illustration, illustration, case in point, exemplification, representative.

5. Warning, caution.

6. Problem, exercise, task.

EXANIMATE, *adj.* 1. Inanimate, lifeless, defunct, dead, departed this life, bereft of life, stonedead, deceased, clay-cold.

2. Spiritless, disheartened, inert, leaden, slack, lumpish, torpid, sluggish, languid, indolent, otiose, lethargic, dormant, comatose, supine, heavy, dull, inactive, motionless, listless, dronish.

EXANTHEMA, *n.* Skin disease accompanied by rash, breaking out of the skin, eruptive disease, eruption, rash, eruptive excrescence, blotch, pox, pustule, measles.

EXASPERATE, *v.* 1. Rouse and roughen the temper of, annoy extremely, irritate to a high degree, chafe, nettle, peeve, huff, provoke, fret, sting, ruffle, vex, offend, pique, rankle, try the patience, enkindle, enchafe, displease, envenom, gall, infuriate, incense, lash into fury, inflame the anger of, anger, affront, make angry, madden, enrage, excite, tantalize, tease, harass, badger.

2. Increase the intensity of, aggravate, make grievous, exacerbate, intensify, embitter, make more violent.

EXASPERATION, *n.* 1. Extreme annoyance, tiff, vexation, resentment, displeasure, indignation, animosity, affront, acerbity, asperity, acrimony, bitterness, virulence, pique, heat, dudgeon, huff, umbrage, pet, tantrum, angry mood, irascibility, sulks, irritation, provocation.

2. Anger, wrath, violent passion, choler, fury, towering rage, ire, vehemence, outburst, spleen, *acharnement (Fr.)*, hot blood, bile, gall, vials of wrath, high words, explosion, paroxysm.

3. Heightening, exacerbation, intensification, aggravation, worsening, increase.

EX CATHEDRA, *adj. (Lat.)* 1. From the seat of authority, authoritative, with authority, from high authority, from the bench, official, by virtue of one's office.

2. Dogmatic, imperious, officious, peremptory, dictatorial, magisterial, despotic, consequential, lordly, domineering.

EXCAVATE, *v.* Make hollow by removing the inner part, make a hole in, form into a hollow, hollow out, remove by digging, scoop out, dig out, lay bare by digging, cut out, burrow, mine, sap, undermine, tunnel, stave in, gouge, delve, unearth.

EXCAVATION, *n.* Hole, hollow, opening, cavity, burrow, trench, trough, furrow, pit, crater, cut, cutting, depression, indentation, dent, dint, cave, cavern, ditch, dugout, quarry, drift, shaft, mine, sap, stope, groove.

EXCEED, *v.* 1. Go beyond the limits of, outride, transgress, overstep, trespass, burst the bounds of, surmount, go by, pass, cap, transcend, overdo, outreach, distance, shoot ahead of, overshoot the mark, outrun, outpace, outdistance, outstrip.

2. Be greater than, excel, surpass, beat, outvie, outrival, outdo, be superior to, preponderate, rise

above, outpeer, outrank, take precedence, come first, out-Herod Herod, throw into the shade, eclipse, outweigh, outplay, predominate.

EXCEEDINGLY, *adv.* Over and above, greatly, especially, surpassingly, supremely, to a great degree, superlatively, eminently, notably, to an unusual degree, vastly, very highly, enormously, amazingly, excessively, astonishingly, extremely, preëminently, by far, beyond measure, too high for, immeasurably, incomparably, transcendently.

EXCEL, *v.* 1. Go beyond, exceed, cap, transcend, overstep, distance, outreach, overtop.

2. Be better than others in achievement, make more successful effort than others, outdo, tower above, surpass, outclass, lead, outstrip, outrival, outbalance, outvie, outweigh, outrank, beat, beat hollow, outplay, be superior to, throw into the shade, eclipse, outshine, take the shine out of, have the advantage, have the upper hand, take precedence, come first, predominate, prevail, rank first, break the record, take the cake, take the prize, win distinction, win eminence, bear the palm, attain superiority.

EXCELLENCE, *n.* 1. Transcendence, distinction, preëminence, superiority, greatness, quintessence, eminence, outstandingness, supereminence, perfection.

2. Excellent feature, great merit, good quality, virtue, integrity, fineness, goodness, worth, value, desert, credit, purity, uprightness, probity, honor, valuable property, strong point, advantage.

EXCELLENT, *adj.* 1. Superior, transcendent, of the highest order, of great worth, sterling, select, first-class, first-rate, fine, choice, prime, tiptop, admirable, of the first grade, of the first water, of the highest quality, topnotch, matchless, perfect, nonpareil, superfine, A-1, superlative, preëminent, capital, classic, sovereign, exemplary.

2. Highly deserving, worthy of great praise, meritorious, estimable, laudable, virtuous, noble.

EXCEPT, *v.* 1. Exclude, bar, shut out, leave out, omit, pretermit, reject, eliminate, remove, pluck out, repudiate, pass over, weed out, strike out.

2. Object, challenge, call in question, impeach, entreat against, deprecate, oppose, cavil, dissent, find fault.

EXCEPT, *prep.* With the exclusion of, excluding, with the exception of, excepting, barring, saving, exclusive of, leaving out, save, omitting, besides, but, other than, more than.

EXCEPT, *v.* 1. Exclude, bar, shut out, leave out, 2. Otherwise than, but, for other reason than.

EXCEPTION, *n.* 1. Leaving out, non-inclusion, exclusion, elimination, debarment, repudiation, rejection, segregation, reservation, limitation, omission, separation, seclusion, isolation.

2. Objection, adverse criticism, opposition of opinion, demurral, dissent, complaint, challenge, affront, disapprobation, stricture, disparagement, denunciation, condemnation, blackball, ostracism, derogation, dispraise, disesteem, detraction, boycott.

3. That which is not covered by a rule, rarity, deviation from the rule, anomaly, unusual case, instance to be excepted, case not conforming to the general rule, irregularity, peculiarity, oddity, unconformity, inconsistency.

EXCEPTIONAL, *adj.* 1. Anomalous, forming an unusual instance, irregular, peculiar, unexampled, abnormal, singular, unnatural, uncommon, queer, unusual, unparalleled, unwonted, aberrant, odd,

extraordinary, out of the way, unheard of, rare, unprecedented, exceptive, phenomenal.

2. Better than average, superior, outstanding, special, remarkable, wonderful, incomparable, marvelous, excellent, inimitable, Simon-pure, unique.

EXCERPT, *v.* Take out from a book *or* literary article, quote, cite, select, pick and choose, pick out, extract, single out, cull, glean, mark out, set apart.

EXCERPT, *n.* Quoted passage, quotation, citation, pericope, selection, extract, selected passage, bar, gleaning, scrap, choosing, portion, clause, verse, paragraph, section, sentence, phrase, measure *(Music),* theme.

EXCESS, *n.* 1. Unwonted abundance, redundance, superabundance, overabundance, surfeit, plethora, undue amount, oversupply, surplusage, glut, too much, supersaturation, repletion, superfluity, too many, fulsomeness, profusion, exuberance, plenty, congestion, inundation, avalanche, lavishness, deluge.

2. Surplus, remainder, waste, residue, overplus, overdose.

3. Overdoing, immoderation, unrestraint, going beyond ordinary limits, prodigality, extravagance, exorbitancy, inordinacy.

4. Immoderate self-indulgence, intemperance, debauchery, drunkenness, spree, orgies, debauch, hot time, revels, saturnalia, carousal, dissipation, dissolute living, overindulgence, free living, high living, dissoluteness, license, licentiousness, flesh pots of Babylon, crapulence, inebriety, sensuality, animalism, venery.

EXCESSIVE, *adj.* 1. Characterized by excess, exceeding what is usual, disproportionate, undue, overmuch, too great, uncalled for, supernumerary, redundant, superabundant, superfluous, needless, unnecessary, *de trop (Fr.),* exuberant, prodigal, replete, profuse, lavish, copious, overflowing, fulsome.

2. Unreasonable, enormous, extravagant, rank, exorbitant, inordinate, outrageous, preposterous, unconscionable, monstrous, crass, gross, extreme, egregious, unbounded, immoderate, intemperate, exaggerated.

EXCESSIVELY, *adv.* Inordinately, immoderately, extravagantly, exorbitantly, acutely, vehemently, over and above, overmuch, too much, extra, to a fault, beyond the mark, unreasonably, out of all proportion, unduly, superabundantly, in a high degree, extremely, monstrously, preposterously, violently.

EXCHANGE, *v.* 1. Give up for something else, part with for something equivalent, part with for a substitute, take something else in place of, swap, substitute, replace by something else, change for another, trade off, barter, traffic, truck, shuffle, buy and sell, market, make a deal.

2. Give and receive reciprocally, interchange, commute, permute, transpose, bandy, reciprocate, counterchange, give and take, requite, give in return, transfer for a recompense, turn the tables.

EXCHANGE, *n.* 1. Act of substituting one thing in the place of another, barter, dealing, truck, swap, traffic, trade, shuffle, substitution, change, bargaining, marketing, commerce, mercantilism, business intercourse, merchantry, commercialism, buying and selling, supply and demand, commerce.

2. Interchange, commutation, reciprocity, give and take, permutation, *quid pro quo (Lat.),* tit

for tat, intermutation, transposal, reprisal, retort, retaliation, requital, cross fire, retribution.

3. Place for buying and selling open only to members, place where business interests of a special character are brought together, exposition, place where things are exchanged, market, mart, fair, staple, bazaar.

4. Stock exchange, bourse, curb market, stock market, financial center, Wall Street .

5. Speculative dealing in securities, agiotage, brokerage, jobbing.

6. Central office, central exchange, telephone switchboard.

7. Conversion of the money of two countries, percentage charged for exchanging currencies, rate of exchange.

EXCHANGEABLE, *adj.* 1. Able to be replaced by something else, interchangeable, transmutable, returnable, convertible, commutable, substitutive.

2. Capable of being reciprocally put in each other's place, reciprocal, mutual, give and take, complementary, interchanging, correspondent, correlative, equivalent.

EXCHEQUER, *n.* 1. Governmental department in charge of public revenues, treasury, national banking account, thesaurus, bank, almonry, fisc, fiscus, bursary, administrative department having the management of the public revenue.

2. *(Coll.)* Pecuniary resources of any person, funds, finances, cash, money, purse, pocketbook, *portemonnaie (Fr.),* purse strings, moneybag, wallet, pecuniary possessions.

EXCISE, *v.* 1. Cut out, cut off, remove, extract, efface, eradicate, pluck out.

2. Expunge, censor, bowdlerize, expurgate.

3. Impose a duty on, tax, impost.

EXCISE, *n.* Tax upon home products, internal revenue tax, impost, internal duty, custom, toll, *octroi (Fr.),* tariff, assessment, taxation, supertax, levy, sales tax, surtax.

EXCISION, *n.* Cutting out, cutting off, removal of a part, surgical removal, abscission, lopping, pruning, eradication, extermination, extirpation, destruction, annihilation, extinction, suppression, erasure, doing away with.

EXCITABLE, *adj.* 1. Unusually susceptible to stimuli, nervously high-strung, easily excited, neurotic, temperamental, moody, sensitive, edgy, impressible, nervous, emotional, galvanic, skittish, mercurial, feverish, hysterical, delirious, fidgety, petulant, vehement.

2. Demonstrative, enthusiastic, mobile, quick, impulsive, impetuous, impatient, uncontrolled, heedless, reckless, ungovernable, irrepressible, hasty, rash.

3. Irritable, irascible, choleric, hot-headed, quick-tempered, passionate, hot-blooded, stormy, volcanic, waspish, peevish, wild, violent, fanatical, fierce, inflammable, rabid, turbulent, fiery.

EXCITE, *v.* 1. Stir up the feelings of, animate, arouse, stimulate, incite, rouse, move, affect, spur, touch, impress, strike, prompt, impel, instigate, provoke, kindle to passionate emotion, enkindle, fire, inflame, goad, quicken, whet, electrify, thrill, go to one's heart, touch to the quick, rivet the attention, possess the soul, galvanize.

2. Bring about, create, elicit, evoke, call forth, summon up, raise, give rise to, bring into activity, put in motion, infuse life into, awaken, energize, actuate, influence.

3. Agitate, perturb, ruffle, fluster, flurry, flutter, disturb, disquiet, upset, make nervous, disconcert, discompose, harass.

4. Irritate, pique, sting, cut, madden, infuriate, anger, enrage, annoy, tease, aggravate.

EXCITED, *adj.* 1. Keyed-up, high-strung, tense, nervous, temperamental, tumultuous, distracted, feverish, wrought up, overwrought, apprehensive, frantic, frenzied, disconcerted, perturbed, beside oneself, wild, seething, delirious, hysterical, edgy, agitated, ruffled, discomposed, uneasy, restless, fidgety.

2. Impassioned, ardent, aroused, eager, elated, hot, red-hot, impatient, ebullient, demonstrative, intoxicated.

3. Angry, furious, fiery, blustering, foaming, fuming, raging, flaming, incensed.

EXCITEMENT, *n.* 1. Agitation, disturbance, ado, activity, bustle, to-do, commotion, ferment, flurry, flutter, fluster, tempest, fuss, turmoil, trepidation, tumult, perturbation, whirl, stir, furor, tension, frenzy.

2. Sensation, stimulation, thrill, kick, passion, emotional appeal, fascination, intoxication, heat, enravishment, entrancement, feeling, eagerness, enthusiasm, elation, ebullition, electrification, fire, ardor, warmth, flush, fever, animation, excitation.

3. Irritation, choler, fury, burst, fit, paroxysm, explosion, outbreak, outburst, scene, violence, melodrama.

EXCITING, *adj.* Producing excitement, thrilling, stimulating, stirring, rousing, provocative, biting, interesting, overpowering, overwhelming, racy, inspiring, soul-stirring, impressive, melodramatic, moving, sensational, impelling, hair-raising, sexy, electrifying, astonishing, piquant, bracing, silken, tantalizing, spicy, risqué titillating, voluptuous, appealing, seductive, glamorous, affecting.

EXCLAIM, *v.* Cry out suddenly, call out, clamor, call aloud, vociferate, give cry, shout, ejaculate, rap out, speak vehemently, say loudly, lift the voice, proclaim, rend the air, make the welkin ring, shout at the top of one's voice, howl.

EXCLAMATION, *n.* 1. Abrupt and clamorous outcry, cry expressing sudden emotion, utterance, sharp utterance expressive of strong feeling, call, vociferation, ejaculation, loud complaint, clamor, protest, shriek, bark, hoot, howl, yell, scream, squawk, screech, squeak, squall, hue and cry, roar, bellow, plaint, yelp, ululation, boohoo, wail, whimper.

2. Ecphonesis, interjection.

EXCLUDE, *v.* 1. Keep out, hinder from entrance, prevent the entrance of, bar, debar, reject, shut the door upon, shut out, ostracize, blackball, boycott, embargo, blockade, regard as not proper to be received.

2. Expel, banish, drive out, throw out, thrust out, eject, eliminate, remove, extrude, weed out, segregate, isolate, repel, cut, send to Coventry, exile, expatriate, relegate, outlaw, drum out, fire, cashier, oust, evict, excommunicate.

3. Shut out from consideration, not include, set aside as unwanted, except, leave out, repudiate, omit.

4. Prevent, preclude, prohibit, hinder, obviate, restrain, forbid, refuse, ban.

EXCLUSION, *n.* Non-admission, lockout, exile, blocking entrance, debarment, ejection, rejection, expulsion, elimination, banishment, expatriation, ostracism, boycott, embargo, blockade, relegation, deportation, excommunication, prohibition, cut, prevention, preclusion, exception, dislodgment, omission, repudiation, separation, segregation, seclusion, isolation, extrusion, eviction, discharge, dismissal.

EXCLUSIVE, *adj.* 1. Select, disposed to resist the admission of outsiders, restrictive, cliquish, aloof, clannish, fastidious in social relations, snobbish, admitting of only a socially restricted patronage, invidiously choice, unneighborly, excluding others from participation in.

2. Aristocratic, luxurious, silk-stocking, stylish, fashionable, chic.

3. In which no others have a share, sole, only, particular, peculiar, special, alone, single, in a place all by itself, individed, limited.

4. Not admitting of something else, excluding from consideration, debarring, desiring to shut out, non-inclusive, prohibitive, preclusive, leaving out of count, inadmissible, not taking into account.

EXCOGITATE, *v.* 1. Think out carefully, devise ingeniously, contrive, invent, imagine, make up, coin, create, hatch, fabricate, frame, forge, brew, concoct.

2. Cogitate, reflect, consider, deliberate, weigh, reason, meditate, ponder, con over, speculate, turn over in the mind, take counsel, commune with oneself, ruminate.

EXCOMMUNICATE, *v.* 1. Unchurch, expel from the church, curse, anathematize, accurse, thunder from the Vatican against, ban with bell, book and candle.

2. Expel in disgrace from any organization, cut off from membership, dismiss, oust, suspend, drum out, cashier, outlaw, proscribe, denounce.

EXCOMMUNICATION, *n.* 1. Exclusion from the church and all its rights and advantages, malison, suspension from the sacraments, anathema, curse, malediction, denunciation, execration, thunders of the Vatican, commination, fulmination, bell, book and candle, ecclesiastical sentence by which a person is excommunicated.

2. Expulsion, banning, dismissal, proscription, cutting off from membership, ouster, suspension, outlawry.

EXCORIATE, *v.* 1. Strip the skin from, remove the hide from, skin, flay, scalp, abrade, score, scar, scarify, gall the skin, scrape the cuticle of, desquamate.

2. Flay verbally, vituperate, denounce, censure, criticize harshly, inveigh against.

3. Strip off bark, decorticate, shell, pare, peel, husk, bark.

EXCREMENT, *n.* Waste matter discharged from the body, excreted matter, feces, dung, *merde (Fr.)*, ordure, stool, excreta, fecal matter, alvine discharges, dejecture, filth, egesta, droppings, diarrhea, frass, fumet, castings.

EXCRESCENCE, *n.* 1. Unnatural and disfiguring growth, swelling, lump, growth, intumescence, morbid protuberance, tumor, wart, fungus, boil, papule, pimple, pustule, blister, carbuncle.

2. Abnormal increase, superfluity, appendage, useless attachment, outshoot.

EXCRETE. *v.* Separate and eliminate from an organic body, expel from the tissues, discharge, throw off waste matter, eject, defecate, evacuate, go to stool, egest, emit, expel, pass, exude, void, perspire, sweat, urinate.

EXCRETION, *n.* 1. Evacuation, elimination, the getting rid of waste matter, voidance, extrusion,

separation and discharge, secernment, secretion, exudation.

2. Substance excreted, excreted matter, urine, excrement, smegma, perspiration, sweat. (See EXCREMENT.)

EXCRUCIATE, *v.* Inflict severe pain upon, rack, agonize, torment, torture, harrow, hurt, wound, lacerate, pierce, stab, cut, lancinate, wring, double up, convulse.

EXCRUCIATING, *adj.* 1. Extremely painful, raw, agonizing, tormenting, torturing, sharp, racking, acute, intense, insufferable, unbearable, poignant, severe, cruel, cutting, unendurable, aching.

2. *(Coll.)* Extremely fastidious, overfinical, prissy, excessively elaborated.

EXCRUCIATION, *n.* Extreme pain, agony, rack, torment, torture, anguish, pang, shooting, cut, laceration, lancination, spasm, seizure, raptus, paroxysm, throe, convulsion.

EXCULPATE, *v.* Clear from a charge of guilt, absolve of fault, vindicate from unjust reproach, set right, acquit, exonerate, clear, pardon, remit, free from blame, justify, relieve from, apologize for, defend, forgive, excuse, exempt, whitewash, set free, reprieve, respite.

EXCULPATION, *n.* Freeing from blame, defense, clearing, exoneration, absolution, pardon, respite, clearance, vindication, remission, justification, acquittal, reprieve, apology, immunity.

EXCULPATORY, *adj.* Exonerative, vindicatory, apologetic, excusatory, tending to clear from alleged guilt, vindicative.

EXCURSION, *n.* 1. Trip primarily for pleasure, short journey for a special purpose, expedition, voyage, pleasure trip, tour, sortie, junket, cruise, globetrotting, sightseeing, peregrination, outing, pilgrimage, wandering, circuit, sally, jaunt, walk, ramble, trek, hike, stroll, tramp, airing, drive, ride.

2. Digression, deviation, wandering from the subject, episode, wandering off, departure from a proper course.

EXCURSIONIST, *n.* One of a party on a pleasure trip, tripper, traveler, voyager, tourist, journeyer, wanderer, migrant, rover, hiker, rambler, nomad, trekker, junketer, gadder, rider, pilgrim, wayfarer.

EXCURSIVE, *adj.* 1. Wandering, roving, giving to making excursions, journeying, ambulatory, roaming, rambling, traveling, peripatetic, gadding, vagrant, migratory, nomadic, wayfaring, itinerant.

2. Desultory, devious, erratic, disconnected, changeful, digressive.

EXCURSUS, *n.* Dissertation added to a work, detailed discussion of some point in a book, disquisition, discussion added by way of appendix, treatise, tract, essay, thesis, discourse, memoir, lecture.

EXCUSABLE, *adj.* Forgivable, venial, allowable, pardonable, defensible, justifiable, permissible, condonable.

EXCUSATORY, *adj.* Justificatory, exonerative, exculpatory, vindicatory, palliative, extenuating, intended to excuse, apologetic.

EXCUSE, *v.* 1. Pronounce innocent of wrong, acquit, clear, exonerate, exculpate, absolve, give up the wish to punish, remit, reprieve.

2. Constitute an apology for, condone, excuse for, extenuate, palliate, mitigate, justify, defend,

apologize for, seek to remove the blame of, vindicate.

3. Judge with indulgence, pardon, forgive, let bygones be bygones, overlook some offense, bear with, treat as venial, regard indulgently, varnish, pass over, wink at, whitewash, gloss over, make allowances for, think no more of.

4. Release from obligation *or* duty, exempt, let off, free, spare, grant exemption to, immunize, dispense with, not exact from.

EXCUSE, *n.* 1. Plea offered in extenuation of a charge *or* fault, explanation for some delinquency, justification, apology, defense, ostensible reason, extenuation, ground for excusing, palliation, argument, claim, mitigation, allowance, allegation.

2. Acquittal, exoneration, exculpation, release, clearance, absolution, vindication, ession *(Law)*, dispensation, remission, pardon, forgiveness, indulgence.

3. False show, subterfuge, pretext, evasion, feint, bluff, pretense, disguise, guise, semblance, color, makeshift, mask, blind, shift, gloss, glaze, varnish, whitewash, loophole.

EXECRABLE, *adj.* 1. Deserving to be execrated, damnable, accursed, cursed, detestable, vile, base, hateful, abhorrent, odious, abominable, heinous, outrageous, villainous, horrifying, diabolical, horrible, nefarious, confounded, infamous, flagitious.

2. Nauseating, nauseous, obnoxious, offensive, sickening, revolting, shocking, disgusting, repulsive, loathesome.

3. *(Coll.)* Very bad, poor, inferior, faulty, wretched, defective, imperfect, unsuitable.

EXECRATE, *v.* 1. Detest utterly, abhor, hate, loathe, shrink from view with horror, revolt against.

2. Curse, revile, accurse, imprecate evil upon, invoke curses on, damn, call down curses on, anathematize, fulminate, swear at, devote to destruction, excommunicate, thunder against, proscribe, scold, denounce, accuse, curse with bell, book and candle.

EXECRATION, *n.* 1. Abhorrence, detestation, abomination, hate, Hymn of Hate, horror, odium, hatred, loathing, repugnance, antipathy, aversion.

2. Thing held in abomination, execrated object, *bête noire (Fr.)*, bugbear, curse, horror.

3. Malediction, anathema, curse, imprecation of evil, malison, fulmination, swearing, ban, profanity, condemnation, denunciation, aspersion, proscription, excommunication, thunders of the Vatican, blasphemy.

EXECUTE, *v.* 1. Put to death according to law, inflict capital punishment on, hang, swing from the gallows, lynch, decapitate, guillotine, behead, decollate, electrocute, send to the electric chair, send to the lethal chamber, gas, impale, crucify, garrote, strangle, dispatch, slay, slaughter, kill, massacre, murder, assassinate, butcher, immolate.

2. Pursue to the end, accomplish, consummate, complete, fulfil, finish, carry out, achieve, carry through, perpetrate, effectuate, effect, perform, do, carry into effect, work out, realize, engineer, discharge, mete out.

3. *(Law)* Make valid, give effect to, give force to, enforce, administer, carry out the terms of, transact, deliver, seal, give validity to.

EXECUTION, *n.* 1. Infliction of capital punishment, hanging, decapitation, beheading, killing, guillotining, electrocution, gassing, lynching, garroting, strangling, shooting, firing squad,

impalement, crucifixion, burning at the stake, martyrdom, slaughter, euthanasia.

2. Carrying into effect, achievement, fulfilment, accomplishment, consummation, completion, administration, transaction, perpetration, effectuation.

3. Stamp, seal, authentication, signature, signing, endorsement.

4. Rendition, mode of performing an artistic work, interpretation, performance, touch, finish, technique, technical skill.

EXECUTIONER, *n.* One who puts to death, killer, hangman, headsman, electrocutioner, garroter, lyncher, strangler, carnifex, official who inflicts capital punishment in pursuance of a legal warrant, Jack Ketch.

EXECUTIVE, *adj.* 1. Suitable for carrying into effect, of the kind requisite for practical direction, skilful in execution, executory, administrative.

2. Charged wth administrative afairs, in charge of execution of laws, responsible for carrying into effect.

EXECUTIVE, *n.* 1. Official, chief magistrate, person charged with administrative work, head of government, head of the nation, leader of affairs, administrative head, person in whom supreme executive power is vested, director, manager, administrator, governor, executor, supervisor, superintendent, overseer, president, chairman, officer, functionary.

2. Executive branch of the government, body charged with administration, administration, administrative body.

EXECUTOR, *n.* 1. One who carries out *or* fulfills, performer, agent, doer, enforcer, perpetrator, operator.

2. Person named by a decedent to carry out the provisions of his will.

EXEGESIS, *n.* Explanation of the language and thought of a literary work, critical explanation, interpretation, exposition, explication, auxesis, elucidation, amplification, explanatory note, comment, gloss, annotation, scholium, hermeneutics.

EXEGETICAL, *adj.* Serving to explain, expository, explanatory, explicative, explicatory, interpretative, hermeneutical, illustrative, elucidative, annotative, scholiastic.

EXEMPLAR, *n.* 1. Model to be copied *or* imitated, pattern, original, archetype, prototype, copy, ideal, standard, paradigm, precedent.

2. Typical instance, example, exemplification, representation, illustration, specimen, sample.

EXEMPLARY, *adj.* 1. Worthy of imitation, praiseworthy, commendable, laudable, estimable, meritorious, deserving of approval, virtuous, righteous, noteworthily good, admirable, sterling, excellent, noble, innocent, correct, ideal, model.

2. Serving for an illustration, illustrative, close, typical, representative, in point, normal, pattern-like, serving for a specimen, closely adherent to the original, faithful, exact, punctilious, rigorous.

3. Serving as a warning, monitory, admonitory, condign, due.

EXEMPLIFICATION, *n.* 1. Illustration by example, practical demonstration, typical instance, case in point, example.

2. *(Law)* Certified and sealed copy of a record, transcript.

EXEMPLIFY, *v.* 1. Show by example, illustrate, instance, cite, quote, elucidate, explain, embody, furnish an example of, define, represent, evidence, demonstrate.

2. *(Law)* Make a certified copy of, transcribe, make an attested copy of under seal.

EXEMPT, *v.* Free from an obligation to which others are subject, confer the privilege of special freedom upon, release from liability, let off, excuse, exonerate of a burden, grant immunity to, relieve, except, pass over, spare, absolve, clear, privilege, exculpate, discharge, remit, acquit, dispense with, pass by, set at liberty.

EXEMPT, *adj.* Not subject to, exempted, not liable, immune, possessed of immunity, released from, at liberty, scot-free, free, clear, liberated, privileged, absolved, excluded, not responsible, void of, unrestrained, unimpeded, unbound, unshackled, untrammeled, unrestricted, untaxed, uncontrolled, unconfined, unchecked, favored.

EXEMPTION, *n.* Freedom from requirements imposed upon others, release from liability, special privilege, immunity, exception, quittance, disengagement, discharge, excuse, exoneration, exculpation, absolution, dispensation granting freedom from duty, franchise, license, impunity, irresponsibility, relief, respite, acquittal, liberty.

EXEQUIES, *n.* Funeral ceremonies, obsequies, burial rite, obit, interment, sepulture, funeral procession, entombment, inhumation, tolling, dead march, passing bell, dirge, muffled drum, funeral cortege.

EXERCISE, *v.* 1. Put through a regimen designed to train, discipline, rear, form, ground, train, prepare, qualify, drill, indoctrinate, school, break in, inculcate, inure, habituate to practice, develop, improve by practice, teach, instruct, tutor, harden, familiarize with, initiate, graduate, accustom, toughen.

2. Discharge a function, perform, execute, practice, pursue, prosecute, carry on, put into action, buckle to.

3. Display in one's actions, exert constantly, make use of, employ, utilize, use, apply, occupy, turn to account, put to use, bring into play, avail oneself of, give employment to.

4. Have as an effect, wield, produce, effect, effectuate, impart, exhibit.

5. Afflict, make uneasy, worry, try, annoy, burden, agitate, trouble, make anxious, perturb, distress, harass, fill with solicitude, tax, vex.

EXERCISE, *n.* 1. Practice to acquire skill, use, exercitation, adhibition, application, appliance, employment, agency, usage, custom, working, performance, operation, plying, play, function.

2. Exertion for the sake of training, effort, energy, work, labor, travail, toil, action, spurt, spell, strain, tug, pull, activity, stress, force, pressure, sweat of one's brow, elbow grease.

3. Drill, sports, field sports, gymnastics, feat, calisthenics, disciplined play, training, schooling, discipline.

4. A set task for a pupil, assignment, lesson, problem, task, praxis, study, test lesson, theme, composition, etude, examination, example for practice.

EXERT, *v.* 1. Exercise ability, put forth power, put in operation, put into action, set in motion, put to work, employ, put to use, use, make use of, utilize, bring into play, wield, practice, bend, administer, strain, strive.

2. Avail oneself of, apply, adhibit, resort to, fall back upon, have recourse to, recur to, take to, lay one's hands on, try.

EXERTION, *n.* 1. Exercise of power *or* faculties, exercitation, application, adhibition, use, resort, utilization, employment, recourse, avail, putting into action, operation, working, drill, practice.

2. Vigorous action, effort, energy, push, strong attempt, endeavor, essay, trial, struggle, stretch, strain, stress, pull, tug, pains, trouble, toil, labor, work, industry, drudgery, travail, sweat of one's brow, elbow grease, grind.

EXERT ONESELF, *v.* Work hard, toil, labor, take pains, put forth one's powers, put forth one's strength, use one's efforts, make great efforts, strain, struggle, endeavor, strive, try, do one's best, bring to bear, buckle to, set one's shoulder to the wheel, fall to work, bestir oneself, do double duty, work with a will, do one's utmost, leave no stone unturned, strain every nerve, spare no effort, ply the oar, grub, toil and moil, plod, grind, drudge, fag, sweat, slave.

EXFOLIATE, *v.* 1. Cast off from the surface in scales, fall off in scales, desquamate, molt, mew, shed, scale off, depilate, flake off, shell off, peel off in thin fragments, husk, pare.

2. Remove the surface of in laminae, separate into sheets.

EXFOLIATION, *n.* 1. Peeling off, desquamation, molting, mewing, depilation, decortication.

2. That which is scaled off, matter molted, integument, pellicle, skin, flake, peel, shell, coat, husk.

EXHALATION, *n.* 1. Breathing, respiration, expiration, emission of vapor, vaporization, evaporation, exsufflation.

2. That which is exhaled, breath, flatus, puff, whiff, zephyr, breeze, gust, squall, blast, flurry.

3. Emanation, aura, effluvium, exudation, fog, fume, vapor, smoke, steam, reek.

EXHALE, *v.* 1. Emit breath, breathe, respire, breathe out, transpire, expire, exsufflate.

2. Puff, blow, pant, gasp, wheeze, sough, sigh, murmur, snuffle, sniffle, whistle, whiffle, whiff, waft.

3. Throw off in effluvia, emit in vapor, smoke, reek, fume, steam, evaporate, emanate, pass off vapor, give out an effluence, rise in vapor.

4. Expel, send out, emit, spout, give off, cast forth, vent, belch, exude, eject, pour out.

EXHAUST, *v.* 1. Empty by drawing out the contents, drain off completely, draw, deplete, clear off, clean out, deflate.

2. Expend the whole of, spend, pour forth like water, waste, consume completely, squander, dissipate, use up, run through, fritter away, lavish, impoverish, spill, overdraw, finish, scrape the bottom of the barrel, reach the end of.

3. Fatigue greatly, drain of strength, deplete of energy, weaken, tire, tire out, fag, sap, weary, debilitate, overtire, deprive of strength, overtask, overwork, wear out, disable, tax, strain, enervate, prostrate, unman, cripple, burn the candle at both ends.

4. Treat thoroughly, study fully, examine all that is essential in a subject, discuss exhaustively, develop completely, go carefully over the full ground of, drive home, not do by halves.

EXHAUST, *n.* 1. Escape of gases from the cylinder of an engine.

2. Parts of an engine through which the exhaust is ejected, vent, valve, opening.

3. Gaseous material exhausted, steam ejected, noxious fumes, reek.

EXHAUSTED, *adj.* 1. Tired out, overfatigued, dog-tired, played out, done in, all in, overtired, ready to drop, weary, worn out, haggard, feeble, toilworn, wayworn, footsore, spent, depleted of strength, flagging, drained of energy, unmanned, prostrated, faint, drowsy.
2. Short of breath, winded, panting, breathless.
3. Used up, consumed, emptied.
4. Deprived of its essential properties, jaded, wasted, depleted of fertility, effete.

EXHAUSTING, *adj.* Fatiguing, wearying, tiring, tiresome, wearisome, weakening, draining, hard, unmanning, toilsome, laborious, arduous, tedious, difficult.

EXHAUSTION, *n.* 1. Deprivation of strength, fatigue, debilitation, enfeeblement, lassitude, weariness, tiredness, languor, faintness, collapse, feebleness, asthenia, prostration, swoon, syncope *(Med.)*, extreme weakness, weakened condition.
2. Depletion, consumption, draining, misuse, dissipation, emptying, vacuation, inanition, ebb, impoverishment, expenditure, dispersion, wastefulness, unthriftiness, prodigality.

EXHAUSTIVE, *adj.* All-inclusive, comprehensive, thorough, thorough-going, radical, sweeping, full, all-embracing, unabridged, complete, plenary, total, entire, all-out.

EXHIBIT, *v.* 1. Present for inspection, expose to view, show, reveal to public notice, place on show, display, unveil, uncover, lay open, bring to light, set forth, evidence, manifest, betray, disclose, point out, divulge, make known, bring forward, produce, bring forth, demonstrate.
2. Be ostentatious, air, parade, flaunt, show off, brandish, dangle, wave, blazon forth, cut a dash, make a splurge, put up a front, swagger.
3. *(Law)* Submit in evidence in a court of law, present for consideration, file charges, present officially, attest.

EXHIBITION, *n.* 1. Presenting to public view, presentation, demonstration, exposition, showing, production, disclosure, revelation, evincement, unveiling, uncovering, divulgence, manifestation, display, array.
2. Performance, representation, rendition, play, spectacle, scene, staging, *étalage (Fr.),* review.
3. Parade, pomp, pageantry, ostentation, gloss, flourish, pomposity, splurge, splash, veneer, front, tinsel, glitter, frippery.

EXHIBITIONIST, *n.* Extrovert, show-off, fop, attitudinarian, swashbuckler, clotheshorse.

EXHILARATE, *v.* Fill with high spirits, make cheerful, cheer, gladden, make joyous, make merry, delight, rejoice, brighten, hearten, elate, invigorate, stimulate, enliven, animate, inspire, inspirit, encourage, refresh, entertain, make happy, gratify, satisfy, comfort, console, solace.

EXHILARATION, *n.* Elevation of spirits, gaiety, geniality, jollity, joviality, joyousness, hilarity, cheerfulness, gleefulness, gladness, happiness, light-heartedness, buoyancy, good humor, high spirits, animal spirits, glee, vivacity, sunniness, levity, animation, stimulation, zest, pleasure, exultation, jubilation, flush, merriment, mirth, enthusiasm, merrymaking, rejoicing, laughter, playfulness, sportiveness, blithesomeness, airiness, liveliness, sprightliness.

EXHORT, *v.* 1. Persuade, encourage to do well, stimulate, inspirit, incite, urge, prompt, put up to, induce, inspire, rouse, prevail upon, animate, instigate, impel, spur, goad, egg, importune, press upon, enjoin, entreat.
2. Admonish urgently, appeal to earnestly, offer advice, counsel, advise, preach, lecture, instruct, charge, suggest, recommend, prescribe, advocate, give exhortation, admonish, warn, caution earnestly.

EXHORTATION, *n.* 1. Persuasion, incitement, encouragement, inducement, instigation, attempt to arouse, urging, injunction, adhortation, charge, entreaty, admonition, advocacy, preachment, caution, word to the wise, advice, counsel, recommendation.
2. Address containing serious advice, sermon, persuasive discourse, homily.

EXHUME, *v.* Dig something buried out of the earth, unearth, disinter, exhumate, disinhume, unbury, disentomb, resurrect.

EXIGENCY, *n.* 1. Circumstance rendering prompt action necessary, critical period, crisis, juncture, emergency, conjuncture, extremity, strait, corner, impasse, difficulty, predicament, quandary, fix, dilemma, plight, pinch, pass, hole, situation demanding remedy.
2. Pressing necessity, requirement, demand, urgency, want, need.

EXIGENT, *adj.* 1. Requiring prompt action, demanding immediate remedy, critical, urgent, pressing, necessary, imperative, arbitrary.
2. Requiring more than is reasonable, taxing, exacting, demanding, severe, distressful, strict, harsh, hard, stern, stiff, austere, rigorous, relentless, stringent, Spartan, unsparing, ironhanded, despotic, tyrannical, extortionate, grinding, oppressive, coercive.

EXIGUITY, *n.* Littleness, smallness, parvitude, inextension, diminutiveness, scantiness, thinness, meagerness, slenderness, exility, fineness, poverty, attenuation, paucity, tininess, slimness, minuteness.

EXIGUOUS, *adj.* Small, little, tiny, wee, petty, diminutive, minute, microscopic, pocket-sized, miniature, minikin, puny, attenuated, slim, fine, meager, slender, scanty.

EXILE, *n.* 1. Expulsion from one's native land, deportation, banishment, proscription, outlawry, ostracism, displacement, relegation, prolonged separation from one's country, expatriation.
2. Banished person, expellee, outlaw, outcast, pariah, Ishmael, vagabond, rank outsider, leper, isolated person, displaced person, D. P., émigré, expatriate, absentee.

EXILE, *v.* Expel from native land, banish, deport, proscribe, ostracize, outlaw, separate from country, expatriate, forbid a return to, cut off from, drive out, thrust out, relegate, eject, exclude, isolate, maroon.

EXIMIOUS, *adj.* Famous, illustrious, far-famed, renowned, distinguished, glorious, eminent, rare, excellent, admirable, estimable, peerless, select, best, choice, elect, prime, recherché, superfine, unparalleled, extraordinary.

EXIST, *v.* 1. Be, have actual being, subsist, vegetate.
2. Live, have animation, have life, be alive, breathe.
3. Continue to be, endure, survive, remain, abide, last, stay.
4. Have being in a specified place, be found under certain conditions, occur, happen, obtain,

take place, prevail, befall, betide, come off, crop up, bechance, ensue.

EXISTENCE, *n.* 1. Possession of animate vital being, existing, being, subsistence, *esse (Lat.),* ens *(Philos.),* actuality, mode of being, reality, presence, fact, living.

2. Matter clothed with form, something that exists, entity, essence, being, thing, creature.

3. Life, vital principle, animation, nature, quid, quiddity.

4. Continuance in being, duration, lastingness.

EXIT, *n.* 1. Way of departure, passage out, outlet, vent, way out, egress, mouth, opening, door, doorway, gate, path, pathway, porthole, loophole, skylight, window.

2. Going away, departure, emergence, exodus, emersion, withdrawal, escape, issue, emanation, evacuation, recession.

3. Death, decease, demise, expiration, end.

EXODUS, *n.* Large migration, departure of many people from a country, emigration, going forth, going out, flight, exit, hegira, exile.

EX OFFICIO, *adj.* By virtue of office *or* official position, officially, authoritatively.

EXONERATE, *v.* 1. Clear of a charge, relieve from accusation, free from blame, exculpate, acquit, absolve, set right, vindicate, justify, gloss over, extenuate, palliate, mitigate, excuse, soften, whitewash, forgive, pardon, give *carte blanche.*

2. Relieve from obligation, discharge, exempt, disburden, except, let off, free, release, remit, spare, pass over, excuse, liberate, dismiss, give dispensation, dispense with.

EXONERATION, *n.* 1. Freeing from accusation, exculpation, clearance, acquittal, vindication, justification, extenuation, palliation, mitigation, remission, absolution, pardon.

2. Apology, excuse, extenuating circumstances, compurgation.

3. Exemption, irresponsibility, release, liberty, discharge, liberation, freedom from, letting off, exception, reprieve, respite, *carte blanche (Fr.),* impunity, immunity, license, dispensation.

EXORABLE, *adj.* Susceptible of being persuaded, able to be moved by entreaty, lenient, yielding to prayer, forbearing, sympathetic, clement, ruthful, merciful, gracious, capable of relenting.

EXORBITANCE, *n.* 1. Gross deviation from normalcy, immoderation, excessiveness, too much, too many, redundance, enormity, excess, overplus, immensity, superfluity, nimiety, going beyond proper limits.

2. Expensiveness, dearness, costliness, high price, extravagance, overcharge, profiteering, extortion.

EXORBITANT, *adj.* 1. Going beyond usual limits, exceeding the bounds of reason, extreme, excessive, inordinate, immoderate, outrageous, preposterous, unconscionable, undue, overmuch, over and above, extortionate, *de trop (Fr.),* unreasonable, uncalled for, *outré (Fr.),* crass, monstrous, enormous, overweening, intemperate, unmerciful, gross, astronomically high, fabulous.

2. Expensive, dear, extravagant, high-priced, costly, priced out of the market, fancily priced.

EXORCISE, *v.* Expel by means of conjuration, deliver from evil spirits, cast out demons, purify from malignant influence, seek to expel an evil spirit by adjuration, disenchant, drive away by incantation, pronounce exorcisms over, conjure spirits, exsufflate.

EXORCISM, *n.* 1. Conjuration of evil spirits, exsufflation, enchantment, hoodoo, voodoo, evil eye, bewitchery, witchcraft, sorcery, black magic.

2. Incantation, spell, formula of exorcism, charm, weird, rune, cabala, abracadabra, mumbo jumbo, hocus-pocus, countercharm.

EXORDIUM, *n.* 1. Beginning of anything, opening, introduction.

2. Introductory part of an oration, preamble, prologue, preface, prelude.

EXOTERIC, *adj.* 1. Not belonging to the inner *or* select circle, unreserved, uninitiated, suitable for the general public, *ad populum (Lat.),* for the masses, common, vulgar, public, open, outer, superficial, external, exterior.

2. Expressing ideas fit for popular understanding, readily comprehensible, intelligible, explicit, simple, commonplace, literal, clear as daylight, palpable, ostensible, overt, patent.

EXOTIC, *adj.* 1. Introduced from a foreign country, belonging to another part of the world, foreign, of foreign origin, alien, extraneous, not native, not indigenous, outlandish, out of the way, derived from abroad, isolated, extrinsic, strange, exceptional, peculiar, unusual.

2. *(Coll.)* Colorful in effect, strikingly unusual in appearance, oriental, almond-eyed, slant-eyed.

EXPAND, *v.* 1. Extend, make to occupy more space, increase in range, enlarge, amplify, augment, magnify, aggrandize, widen, lengthen, broaden, deepen, heighten, elevate.

2. Lay open by extending, spread out, unfold, unfurl, outspread, open, evolve, develop, deploy.

3. Dilate, stretch, swell, intumesce, tumefy, distend, blow up, inflate, puff out, bloat, fatten, fill out, wax, grow, be distended, increase in bulk.

4. Express in fuller form, develop in greater detail, enlarge on, descant.

EXPANSE, *n.* Wide extent of space, uninterrupted space, continuous area, expanded surface, field, margin, scope, stretch, reach, breadth, spread, compass, range, latitude, amplitude, immensity, magnitude, sweep, size, length, measure, amount, sphere, arena, infinity, proportions, distance, spaciousness, expansion, open space, free space, leeway, elbowroom, *Lebensraum (Ger.),* void, abyss, chasm, waste, desert, wilderness.

EXPANSION, *n.* 1. Enlargement, extension, increase, amplification, augmentation, growth, magnification, aggrandizement, development, diffusion.

2. Spreading out, unfolding, unfurling, deploying, expanding, opening, evolution.

3. Swelling, dilation, inflation, dilatation, distension, increment, intumescence, puffiness, tumefaction, diastole.

4. Expanse, extent, stretch, spread, space.

EXPANSIVE, *adj.* 1. Capable of enlarging, tending to expand, dilatable, expanding.

2. Having a wide range, wide-reaching, bulky, extensive, widespread, far-reaching, generous, sizable, voluminous, capacious, spacious, diffusive, swollen, overgrown, bloated, comprehensive, elastic.

3. *(Psychol.)* Characterized by delusions of greatness, grandiose, bombastic, effusive, open, unrestrained, free.

EX PARTE *(Lat.)* Relating to one side only, in the interest of one party, one-sided, partisan, biased, bigoted, prejudiced, partial, unilateral.

EXPATIATE, *v.* 1. Enlarge on in discourse, rant, descant, be copious in discussion, be diffuse, pad, amplify on, maunder, protract, harp upon, dwell on in detail, digress, beat about the bush.

2. Wander about without restraint, range at will, ramble, rove at large, roam.

EXPATRIATE, *v.* 1. Force a person from his own country, banish from native land, exile, expel from one's homeland, deport, relegate, ostracize, outlaw, proscribe, exclude, seclude, isolate, maroon, cast out.

2. Withdraw oneself permanently from residence in one's native country, withdraw from allegiance to, change one's citizenship.

EXPATRIATE, *n.* Exile, banished person, D. P., émigré, outcast, outlaw, pariah, castaway, expellee, displaced person.

EXPECT, *v.* 1. Regard as likely to happen, look for the coming of, anticipate the occurrence of, look to some future event, await, look ahead to, watch for, have in prospect, look forward to, keep in view, contemplate, foresee.

2. Look for with justification, rely upon, hope for, calculate upon, count upon, reckon upon, envisage, promise oneself, consider in duty bound, trust, require.

3. *(Coll.)* Suppose, surmise, conjecture, believe, presume.

EXPECTANT, *adj.* 1. Existing in expectation, looking forward to, awaiting, in suspense, on tenterhooks, open-eyed, vigilant, open-mouthed, agape, gaping, wait-and-see, foreseeing, having in prospect, anticipatory, on tiptoe, with bated breath, apprehensive, provident, ready, eager.

2. Expecting the birth of a child, pregnant, enceinte, gravid, with child.

EXPECTATION, *n.* 1. Anticipation, expectancy, prospect, contingency, contemplation, awaiting, looking forward to.

2. Expectant mental attitude, hope, assurance, trust, reliance, confidence, presumption, promise, dependence, reckoning, calculation, anticipatory desire.

3. Suspense, abeyance, apprehension, torment of Tantalus, tenterhooks, tiptoe.

EXPECTORATE, *v.* Clear the throat, cough up, expel phlegm from the throat, eject from the trachea, spit, salivate, hawk up, slobber, drool, drivel, slabber.

EXPEDIENCY, *n.* 1. Desirableness for a given purpose, suitableness, expedience, opportunism, propriety, advisability, desirability, timeliness, fitness.

2. That which is most practicable, advantage, profit, sense of self-interest, policy, utility.

3. Advantageousness, profitableness, usefulness, judiciousness, efficiency, adaption to end.

EXPEDIENT, *adj.* 1. Fit for the purpose, proper, suitable under the circumstances, desirable for the end proposed, worth-while appropriate, wise, tending to promote some desired aim, acceptable, seemly, politic, judicious, needful, necessary, due, meet, fitting, befitting, becoming, indispensable, convenient, eligible, essential.

2. Conducive to advantage, advantageous, to one's interest, profitable, opportune, practicable, useful, practical, favorable, feasible, performable, doable, attainable, achievable, possible.

EXPEDIENT, *n.* That which furthers a desired end, resource, contrivance, device, resort, dodge, measure, shift, makeshift, stopgap, machination,

creephole, feint, subterfuge, ruse, artifice, trick, stratagem, plan, scheme, design, invention, bold stroke, agency, instrumentality, trump card, means of accomplishing anything.

EXPEDITE, *v.* Speed up the progress of, carry through with dispatch, hasten the movement of, accelerate, push, give a shove to, quicken, hurry, press forward, urge on, precipitate, facilitate, forward, help forward, advance, further, foster, encourage, assist, promote, support, make short work of, railroad *(coll.)*, whip on, hustle, dash off, accomplish promptly, dispatch, make rapid strides.

EXPEDITION, *n.* 1. Excursion made for some specific purpose, voyage for a definite purpose, trip, tour, jaunt, journey, circuit, peregrination, outing, airing, trek, tramp, pilgrimage, wayfaring, exploration, cruise, sail, passage, travel, junket, mission, enterprise.

2. Hostile undertaking, campaign, crusade, march, invasion, raid.

3. Speed in accomplishing something, velocity, celerity, haste, dispatch, promptitude, quickness, alacrity, swiftness, alertness, readiness, rapidity, agility, nimbleness, fastness.

EXPEDITIOUS, *adj.* 1. Speedy, swift, rapid, fast, quick, immediate, prompt, instant, fleet, hasty, light-footed, punctual.

2. Ready, awake, alert, nimble, diligent, active, snappy, up and coming, live-wire, wide-awake, go-ahead, spirited, brisk, agile.

EXPEL, *v.* 1. Cut off from membership, remove by penalty, oust, dismiss, suspend, discharge, fire, sack, bounce, blackball, drum out, cashier.

2. Exile, banish, expatriate, deport, relegate, ostracize, excommunicate, unchurch, proscribe, disown, maroon, outlaw.

3. Eject, drive out, evict, dispossess, extrude, thrust forth, reject, discard, cast out, drive away, put out, repudiate, force away.

4. Eliminate, egest, excrete, void, evacuate.

EXPEND, *v.* 1. Consume, use up, exhaust, drain, devour, absorb, wear out, empty, deplete, waste, scatter, squander, dissipate, prodigalize, disperse, burn up, fritter away, run through.

2. Pay out, disburse, give, donate, spend, lay out, shell out, ante up, fork out, outlay, reward, subsidize, remunerate.

3. Use, exert, wield, employ, exhibit, adhibit. apply.

EXPENDITURE, *n.* 1. Disbursement, cost, price, expense, outlay, charge, overhead, outgo, general costs.

2. Payment, settlement, pay, remuneration, fee, garnish, subsidy, deposit, installment, investment, purchase.

EXPENSE, *n.* 1. Laying out of resources, money expended, source of expenditure, cost, quotation, outlay, charge, price, amount, rate, figure, fare, hire, wages, par, money's worth.

2. Drain on resources, loss due to a detracting cause, costliness, expenditure, disbursement, upkeep.

EXPENSIVE, *adj.* 1. Higher in price than the average person's usual purchases, entailing great expense, costly, dear, high-priced, dear bought, precious, of great price, necessitating great outlay, running into money, in the upper price brackets, sumptuous.

2. Beyond one's means, extravagant, prodigal,

exorbitant, unreasonable, extortionate, wasteful, lavish.

EXPERIENCE, *n.* 1. Acquiring of knowledge by use of one's own faculties of sense, sensibility, actual observation, sensation, sentiment, emotion, response, impression, feeling, actual trial, insight, experiment, contact.

2. Practical wisdom gained from observation, thorough acquaintance with facts, enlightenment, knowledge gained from observation, cognizance, privity, familiarity, comprehension, appreciation, information, ken.

3. Endurance, sufferance, school of hard knocks.

4. Event, adventure, episode, incident, affair, happening, occurrence, transaction, vicissitude, contingency, crisis.

EXPERIENCE, *v.* 1. Feel, sense, apprehend, ken, know, realize, understand, perceive, comprehend, cognize, discern, appreciate, fathom, make out, be aware of, find, discover, have experience of, actually observe, have practical acquaintance with, have before one's own sense, have in one's perception, hear of, prove by trial, test, taste.

2. Undergo, meet with, encounter, fall to the lot of, be one's lot.

3. Endure, suffer, stand, brave, sustain, brook, go through, pass through, support, abide, labor under, be subjected to.

EXPERIENCED, *adj.* Taught by experience, able, having learned through experience, accomplished, trained, tutored, primed, initiated, instructed, practiced, versed, acquainted with, wise in the ways of, skilful, skilled, qualified, capable, expert, efficient, competent, fitted, knowing, veteran, old, old-hand, finished, familiar.

EXPERIMENT, *n.* 1. Prearranged examination, organized observation, investigation, verification, experimentation, research, probation, assay.

2. Tentative procedure, essay, tryout, analysis, test, trial, proof, ordeal, touchstone, criterion.

3. Venture, endeavor, attempt, flyer, random shot, speculation, leap in the dark, feeler, trial balloon, *ballon d'essai (Fr.)*, straw in the wind.

EXPERIMENT, *v.* 1. Operate by trial, make trial of, conduct an experiment, try, essay, test in order to find something out, put to the test, rehearse, verify, prove, break with tradition.

2. Grope for, feel one's way, fumble, throw out a feeler, send up a trial balloon, toy around with, see how the wind blows, feel the pulse, fish for, angle, try one's fortune.

EXPERIMENTAL, *adj.* 1. Founded on fact, tried, ascertained by observation, experiential, verified by experiment, tested, empirical.

2. Actually undergone, personally experienced, really suffered, inwardly felt.

3. On trial, on examination, under probation, on approval, probative, probatory, probational, probationary, tentative, pending verification, trial, speculative, analytic.

EXPERT, *adj.* Trained by practice, possessing special skill, skilful, skilled, practiced, qualified, experienced, learned, accomplished, professional, masterly, *au fait (Fr.)*, adroit, facile, ingenious, dexterous, deft, adept, able, proficient, versatile, wise, clever, prompt, ready, apt, crackajack, crack, sharp.

EXPERT, *n.* One with special knowledge and skill in some particular field, authority, connoisseur, specialist, masterhand, skilled hand, crackajack,

virtuoso, adept, dabster, shark, proficient, prima donna, top sawyer, first fiddle, prizeman, picked man, medalist, crack shot, trouble-shooter, dead shot, veteran, old hand, old stager, genius, mine of information, mastermind, pastmaster, walking encyclopedia, old campaigner, prodigy of learning.

EXPIATE, *v.* Do penance for, atone for, make amends for, make reparation for, redeem, make good, repair, pay the penalty, absolve, propitiate, purge, shrive, stand in a white sheet, repent in sackcloth and ashes, set one's house in order, wipe off old scores, make matters up, compensate, give satisfaction for, requite, appease, blot out, ransom, reclaim.

EXPIATION, *n.* 1. Removal of guilt by suffering punishment, atonement, propitiation, redemption, reparation, compensation, acquittance, apology, quits, indemnification, reclamation, conciliation, amends.

2. Penitential act, peace offering, flagellation, sacrifice, expiatory offering, penance, lustration, fasting, maceration, sackcloth and ashes, hair-shirt, purgation, scapegoat.

EXPIRATION, *n.* 1. Coming to an end, stoppage, termination, conclusion, cessation, running out, completion, close, finish, finis, finale, wind-up, end.

2. Emission of breath, respiration, exhalation, breathing.

3. Outbreathing of life, death, demise, decease, dissolution, release, debt of nature.

EXPIRE, *v.* 1. Come to an end, end, come to a close, terminate, conclude, cease, stop, wind up, close, finish, discontinue, run out, lapse.

2. Emit from the lungs, breathe out, respire, exhale, puff, pant, blow out from the mouth *or* nostrils.

3. Breathe one's last, draw one's last breath, die, decease, give up the ghost, pass away, perish, depart, pay the debt to nature.

EXPLAIN, *v.* 1. Assign a meaning to, make plain, demonstrate, throw light upon, make manifest, cause to be understood, clear of obscurity, clear up, unfold, resolve, explicate, clarify, illustrate, elucidate, interpret, expound, comment on, define, annotate, illuminate, describe, give an account of, teach.

2. Solve, decipher, unriddle, rationalize away, account for, trace to causes, fathom, give the reasons for, justify, warrant.

EXPLAINABLE, *adj.* That may be explained, explicable, solvable, interpretable, accountable, understandable, intelligible.

EXPLANATION, *n.* 1. Statement made to clarify something, explication, exposition, *éclaircissement (Fr.)*, clarification, exegesis, elucidation, making intelligible, definition, unfoldment, description, interpretation, commentary, note, illustration, gloss.

2. Solution, accounting, warrant, signification, answer, key, secret, deduction, reason, meaning, justification, significance.

EXPLANATORY, *adj.* Expository, commentarial, serving to explain, exegetical, accounting for, justificatory, descriptive, elucidative, illustrative, interpretative, expressive.

EXPLETIVE, *n.* 1. Something serving to fill out, addition, expletive word, embellishment.

2. Exclamatory oath, interjectory word, curse, exclamation, emphatic statement, profanity.

EXPLICABLE, *adj.* Capable of explanation, able

to be accounted for, explainable, lending itself to solution, solvable, able to be made intelligible.

EXPLICATE, *v.* Make plain, clarify, make clear, clear from involvement, explain, resolve, solve, untangle, unriddle, unfold, interpret, elucidate, expound, detail, develop.

EXPLICATION, *n.* Detailed description, exegesis, full analytical account, clarification, explanation, unfolding of causes, resolution, *éclaircissement (Fr.)*, solution, definition, annotation, exposition, interpretation, illustration.

EXPLICIT, *adj.* 1. Clearly expressed, categorical, having nothing merely implied, clear, plain, vivid, express, clearly formulated, well-developed, lucid, precise, definite, exact, specific, comprehensible, positive, distinctly stated, unreserved, explanatory, determinate, perspicuous, pointed, unconditional, definitive, obvious, unmistakable, unambiguous, having no disguised meaning, unequivocal.
2. Unreserved in expression, straightforward, outspoken, point-blank, direct, frank, candid, blunt.

EXPLODE, *v.* 1. Make to expand violently, rend, cause to burst in pieces by force, burst, discharge, detonate, displode.
2. Expand with force and noise due to rapid chemical decomposition, burst forth with sudden violence and noise, break in pieces violently, fly into pieces, break up violently with a loud report, burst forth, be discharged, fulminate, pop, erupt, flash noisily with flame, blast, backfire.
3. Cause to be rejected, refute, disprove, scorn, destroy the repute of, expose, cry down, discard, discredit, treat with contempt, scout, contemn, repudiate, reject, spurn, show the fallacy of.

EXPLOIT, *v.* 1. Turn to practical account, put to use, get the value out of, put to service, get the usefulness out of, profit by, utilize for profit, milk *(coll.)*, work.
2. Use selfishly for one's own ends, misapply, misuse.

EXPLOIT, *n.* Striking accomplishment, notable achievement, deed of renown, heroic act, feat, spirited action, ingenious performance, tour de force.

EXPLORATION, *n.* 1. Investigation of unknown regions, geographical research, reconnaissance, survey of the general geographical characteristics of a region.
2. Examination, inquiry, research, inquisition, investigation, scrutiny, probe, questioning, search, election of courses in various fields to determine aptitudes.

EXPLORE, *v.* 1. Range over for the purpose of discovery, traverse an unknown region, examine unknown lands geographically, travel through observingly.
2. March forward into the unknown, see how the land lies.
3. Subject to examination, examine, look over in order to examine, investigate, scrutinize, probe, inquire into closely, search into, penetrate, feel out, pry into, ransack, rummage through, plumb, prospect, fathom, spy out, dissect.

EXPLOSION, *n.* 1. Violent bursting with noise, sudden discharge, fulmination, detonation, shock, displosion, ignition, shattering sound, concussion, clap, blast, report, volley, shot, crack, pop.
2. Outbreak, paroxysm, violent outburst of feeling.

EXPLOSIVE, *n.* Substance capable of causing an explosion by sudden combustion, explosive agent, dynamite, gunpowder, fulgurite, cordite, thorite, trinitrotoluene, T.N.T., nitroglycerine, melinite, tonite, lyddite, ammonal, ammunition, fireworks, pyrotechnics.

EXPLOSIVE, *adj.* Liable to explode, fulminant, fulgurous, violent, expulsive, vehement, abrupt, boisterous, hard, sharp.

EXPONENT, *n.* 1. Symbol, specimen, example, token, sample, type, representative, illustration, indication, index.
2. One who represents the character *or* principles of something, exemplifier.
3. One who explains, explainer, interpreter, expounder, expositor, advocate.

EXPORT, *v.* Send out merchandise from one country to another, dispatch to other lands, ship overseas, market abroad, send commodities out of a country in trade.

EXPORT, *n.* Commodity exported, merchandise sent abroad, shipped wares, article of trade sent from one country to another.

EXPOSE, *v.* 1. Uncover, denude, divest, strip, bare, make bare, air.
2. Put out into an unsheltered place, abandon, deprive of protection, leave to the action of any circumstance, place and leave in probably a fatal position, cast out, turn out.
3. Lay open to harm, jeopardize, imperil, risk, endanger, hazard, put to hazard, venture, put in peril, compromise, make liable, subject to danger.
4. Present to view, offer, submit, display, show, set in view, place so as to be seen, exhibit, put in a conspicuous place, evidence, advertise, vent, publish, make known, set forth, divulge, let out.
5. Deprive of concealment, uncover, disclose, unveil, reveal, descry, bring to light, show up, detect, unearth, evince, manifest, indicate, lay open.
6. Hold up to public reprehension *or* ridicule, denounce, brand, gibbet, stigmatize, abase, show in one's real light, betray, strip of disguise, take the wraps off, show openly, muckrake, smoke out, impugn, impeach, accuse, refute.

EXPOSE, *n.* 1. Deprecatory publication, exposure of something discreditable, denunciation, report, muckraking, disclosure, divulgement, divulgence, complete setting forth of sordid details, whole truth, revelation, telltale.
2. Formal statement, manifesto, asseveration, exposition, exhibit, declaration.

EXPOSITION, *n.* 1. Fair, bazaar, staple, exhibit, exhibition, display, show, World's Fair, market, mart, market place.
2. Bringing to view, exposure, manifestation, laying open, displaying, presentation, disclosure, divulgence, revelation, demonstration.
3. Detailed explanatory statement, annotation, explanation, elucidation, explication, explanatory treatise, *éclaircissement (Fr.)*, note, exegesis, interpretation, commentary, illustration, gloss, key, scholium, rationale, solution, answer, clue.
4. Abandonment, putting out in an unsheltered place, casting out, exposure.
5. Part of a dramatic composition that unfolds the plot, denouement, untangling of the intricacies of a plot, outcome, solution.

EXPOSITOR, *n.* Exponent, expounder, explainer, commentator, interpreter, scholiast, demonstrator, annotator, metaphrast, paraphrast.

EXPOSITORY, *adj.* Serving to set forth clearly,

explanatory, elucidative, descriptive, illustrative, graphic, narrative, realistic, declarative, critical, explicative, explicatory, disquisitional, exegetical, hermeneutic, interpretive, annotative, scholastic.

EX POST FACTO *(Lat.)* By subsequent action, subsequently, retroactively, retrospectively.

EXPOSTULATE, *v.* Reason earnestly against, deprecate, dissuade, remonstrate, disapprove of, exhort against, dehort, enter a protest, complain of, object, rebuke, reproach, contend, altercate, admonish, warn, caution, dishearten.

EXPOSTULATION, *n.* Earnest protest, caution, remonstrance, deprecation, disapprobation, plea against some course of action, protest, dissuasion, dehortation, contention, altercation, admonition, complaint, objection, rebuke, exhortation against, disapproval, reproach.

EXPOSURE, *n.* 1. Disclosure of something private, vent, presentation to view in a public manner, laying open, divulgation, revelation, exposition, exposé, laying bare, muckraking, publication, show-up, betrayal, blazonment, unmasking.
2. Accessibility to anything that may affect adversely, openness to danger, subjection to the influence of, risk, liability, vulnerability, danger, peril, jeopardy, hazard, insecurity.
3. Situation with regard to sunlight *or* wind, position with reference to points of the compass, location, front, frontage, vista, prospect, outlook.

EXPOUND, *v.* 1. State in detail, describe, give a full account of, rehearse, hold forth, discourse at length, teach, instruct, inform, present, descant, develop fully, express.
2. Set forth the significance of, explain, make plain, clear up, elucidate, interpret, comment on, commentate, reveal, unriddle, construe, solve, define.

EXPRESS, *v.* 1. Put into words, word, describe, put, speak, say, utter, declare, enunciate, voice, couch in terms, give vent to, state, assert, emit, vent, air, tell, give voice to, phrase, pronounce, discourse, herald, communicate, clothe in words, style, call, dub.
2. Set forth, manifest, evince, reveal, show, evidence, exhibit, demonstrate, present, embody, make known.
3. Represent by a symbol, symbolize, show by a likeness, betoken, indicate, designate, signify, delineate, depict, mean, denote, intimate, imply, import, suggest, connote, purport.
4. Send by express, hasten, expedite, direct, post, ship, mail.
5. Extract by pressure, press out, squeeze out, extort by force, distill.

EXPRESS, *adj.* 1. Set forth with unmistakable distinctness, clearly indicated, distinctly stated, positive, explicit, unequivocal, plain, clear, direct, unambiguous, definite, categorical, determinate, outspoken, intentional, advised, point-blank, trenchant, emphatic.
2. Exactly resembling an original, accurate, exact, faithful, close, duly formed, precise, true, exactly represented, vivid.
3. Special, specific, particular, specially prepared, intended for a particular purpose.
4. Pertaining to quick conveyance, adapted for high speed, quick, swift, speedy, rapid, with all possible speed, expeditious, fast, posthaste.

EXPRESS, *n.* 1. Special train making limited number of stops, speedy conveyance, system for prompt transportation, swift transmission.
2. Specially sent messenger, special courier.
3. Special communication sent with speed, despatch.

EXPRESSION, *n.* 1. Setting forth in words, vocal embodiment of thought, saying, utterance, remark, communication, emission, voicing, declaration, affirmation, assertion, representation, statement, observation.
2. Particular word, turn of speech, locution, phrase, form of words, idiom, term, metaphor, trope.
3. Wording, phrasing, diction, phraseology, language, style, choice of words, literary power.
4. Facial aspect as indicative of feeling, mien, indication of feeling on the face, look, cast of countenance, aspect, air, play of features, visible and outward attitude, appearance.
5. Manifestation, sign, symbol, signification, token, indication, representation.
6. Style of execution, general tone, pervasive effect.
7. Modulation, intonation, enunciation, accent, articulation, shading nuance, interpretation, touch, stylized execution, performance, virtuosity.

EXPRESSIONLESS, *adj.* Blank, soulless, dull, wooden, vacuous, dead-pan, inscrutable, sphinx-like, poker-faced.

EXPRESSIVE, *adj.* 1. Indicative of power to express, full of expression, meaningful, indicative, significant, significatory, suggestive, pregnant, allusive, informative, eloquent, fraught with meaning.
2. Vivid, forcible, forceful, strong, emphatic, pithy, graphic, felicitous, lively, energetic, terse, demonstrative, weighty, momentous, wise.
3. Finely modulated, executed with feeling, sympathetic, understanding, appropriate, artistic.

EXPRESS ONESELF Set forth one's feelings in words, make known one's opinions, speak one's mind, deliver oneself, air one's opinions, speak one's piece.

EXPROBRATE, *v.* Brand, abuse, stigmatize, slur, gibbet, denounce, reproach, vituperate, censure, upbraid, revile, vilify, rail at, anathematize, call names, speak daggers, objurgate, inveigh against, fulminate against, lash with the tongue, inculpate.

EXPROBRATION, *n.* Abuse contumely, slur, opprobrium, reproach, obloquy, denunciation, vituperation, invective, objurgation, evil-speaking, inculpation, delation.

EXPULSION, *n.* 1. Act of expelling, ejectment, throwing out, elimination, extrusion, ejection, discharge, ousting, eviction, driving out, dislodgment.
2. Exile, banishment, deportation, expatriation, relegation, transportation, proscription, rustication, suspension.
3. Permanent exclusion, separation from membership, debarment, excommunication, ostracism, isolation, segregation, removal.

EXPUNGE, *v.* Wipe out, wash out, sponge out, rub out, blot out, strike out, scrape out, scratch out, erase, eradicate, obliterate, efface, delete, rase, annihilate, destroy, cancel, leave no trace of.

EXPURGATE, *v.* Amend by removing offensive matter, bowdlerize, purge, cleanse, refine, free from objectionable content, castrate, emasculate.

EXQUISITE, *adj.* 1. Satisfying the aesthetic faculties, elegant, dainty, carefully wrought, fine, nice, delicate, ethereal, marked by beautiful workmanship, of rare excellence of execution, high-wrought, rich-wrought.

2. Of high quality, choice, select, precious, excellent, valuable, rare, admirable, splendid, consummate, perfect, matchless, incomparable, superlative, peerless.

3. Of peculiar beauty and charm, beautiful, charming, good-looking, comely, bonny, winsome, handsome, attractive, striking.

4. Discriminating, fastidious, refined, keenly sensitive, finical, meticulous, very careful.

5. Intense, sharp, acute, keen, poignant, thrilling, sensational.

EXQUISITE, *n.* Man overnice in dress, dandy, fop, dude, beau, coxcomb, popinjay, macaroni, buck, spark, toff, fine gentleman, silk-stocking, dandiprat, jack-a-dandy, jackanapes, Beau Brummell, Edwardian, Johnnie, man about town, wearer of the green carnation, vain fellow, man milliner, aesthete, effeminate dresser, clotheshorse, dapper Dan, dapperling, silk-sock Sam, gallant.

EXSICCATE, *v.* Dry, dehydrate, anhydrate, dry up, desiccate, drain, dry out, evaporate, parch, remove moisture from, make dry, sear.

EXTANT, *adj.* Still existing, still to be found, existent, in existence, subsistent, in being, not lost, surviving, undestroyed, living, present, in current use, visible.

EXTEMPORANEOUS, *adj.* 1. Done extempore, without preparation, unprepared, extempore, extemporary, offhand, unpremeditated, on the spur of the moment, spontaneous, at a moment's notice, improvised, impromptu, *ad libitum (Lat.),* informal, unstudied, made for the occasion, occasional, unexpected, sudden.

2. Spoken extempore, given to speaking without prepared material, unmemorized, delivered without preparation, made up as one goes along, spoken without notes.

EXTEMPORE, *adv.* Without preparation, by improvisation, unpremeditatedly, suddenly, offhand, unexpectedly, extemporaneously, without notes, impromptu, *ad libitum (Lat.).*

EXTEMPORIZE, *v.* Speak extempore, deliver without preparation, speak without notes, make an offhand address, improvise, ad-lib, make up as one goes along, cook up, compose, devise for the occasion.

EXTEND, *v.* 1. Draw in a given direction, draw out, stretch out, reach forth, reach out, put forth, run, cause to reach from point to point, carry forward, straighten out.

2. Make larger, lengthen out, elongate, draw out to full length, protract, prolong, increase the length of, place at full length, spin out.

3. Enlarge the scope of, spread out in area, make more comprehensive, enlarge, broaden, widen, lengthen, deepen, heighten, increase, fill out, augment, aggrandize, amplify, magnify, dilate, expand, deploy, project.

4. Hold forth, hold out, stretch forth, offer, proffer, grant, give, bestow, impart, favor, yield.

5. Postpone beyond time originally agreed upon, defer, delay.

6. Sprawl, lie, range, stretch, spread, reach, droop, trail.

EXTENSIBLE, *adj.* Capable of expansion, pliant, elastic, extensile, extendible, tractile, protractile, ductile, plastic, pliable, yielding, dilatable, protrusile, sequacious.

EXTENSION, *n.* 1. Expansion, prolongation,

enlargement, augmentation, amplification, spatial continuance, increase, distension, dilatation, dilation, stretching out, spread, aggrandizement, growth, accretion, diffusion, continuation, projection, lengthening.

2. That by which something is extended, branch, addendum, appendix, annex, wing, ell, appendage, addition, outrigger.

3. Range of extending, degree of extensiveness, extent, expanse, stretch, sweep, spread, play, swing, compass, latitude.

4. Postponement of the time set for a procedure, deferment, delay, prorogation.

EXTENSIVE, *adj.* 1. Of great extent, broad, wide, large, spacious, capacious, great, vast, ample, extended, considerable, big, commodious, bulky, voluminous, gigantic, massive.

2. Far-reaching, world-wide, comprehensive, all-inclusive, long-range, thorough, universal, diffusive, nation-wide, cosmopolitan, far-flung.

EXTENT, *n.* 1. Expanse, expansion, amplitude, spaciousness, spread, capaciousness, wideness.

2. Magnitude, bulk, size, capacity, amount, volume, content, degree, quantity, fullness.

3. The limit to which anything reaches, space to which a thing extends, compass, area, length, proportions, dimensions, measure, reach, span, stretch, distance, limit, limitations, term, circuit, gauge, duration, continuance, period, bounds, borders.

4. Latitude, longitude, scope, range, field, tract, territory.

5. Distance from end to end, height, depth, width, breadth.

EXTENUATE, *v.* 1. Represent as less blameworthy than it might be, make less serious, excuse, absolve, apologize for, remit, condone, palliate, mitigate, varnish, smooth over, clear, exculpate, exonerate, acquit, reprieve, justify, gloss over, qualify, soften, vindicate, forgive, pardon, overlook, make allowance for, gloze, whitewash.

2. Underestimate, underrate, make light of, treat as of small importance, depreciate, derogate.

3. Reduce in size, attenuate, make thin, lessen, weaken, diminish, decrease, lighten, moderate.

EXTENUATION, *n.* 1. Partial excuse, apology, palliation, mitigation, softening, explanation, gloss, varnish, allowance, vindication, acquittal, justification, exoneration, exculpation, pardon, forgiveness, dispensation, whitewashing, reprieve, condonation, remission, absolution, quittance.

2. Underestimation, depreciation, derogation, disparagement.

3. Attenuation, reduction in size, diminution, abatement, lessening, decrease.

EXTERIOR, *adj.* 1. Being on the outer side, outer, outermost, outlying, outward, outside, outdoor, superficial, surface.

2. From without, foreign, extraneous, extrinsic.

3. Noted by the senses, visible, apparent, patent, manifest, evident, palpable, tangible.

EXTERIOR, *n.* 1. Outer surface, superficies, covering, integument, skin, rind, coat, finish, polish, face, façade, outer shell, facet.

2. Outward appearance, external features, outward conduct, observable traits.

EXTERMINATE, *v.* Get rid of by destroying, uproot, eradicate, deracinate, extirpate, root out, averruncate, cut off, destroy totally, annihilate, kill, abolish, put an end to, wipe out, blot out, obliterate, efface, undo, extinguish, quench, raze, quash, ruin, overthrow, ravage, demolish, lay in ruins, devastate, gut, desolate, blast, eliminate.

EXTERNAL, *adj.* 1. Visible from the outside, relating to the surface of a body, without the boundaries of a thing, outward, outermost, outer, exterior, surface, superficial, outside.

2. Outside the mind, belonging to the space world, physical, corporeal, apparent.

3. Coming from without, extraneous, foreign, extrinsic, alien, exoteric.

EXTERNALS, *n.* Outer surface, outside, outward parts, visible forms, things seen, evidence, façade.

EXTINCT, *adj.* 1. Having come to an end, ended, terminated, lapsed, closed, non-existent, no longer existing, dead, gone, deceased, no longer living, passed away, defunct, lifeless, exterminated, lost, without a living representative, without a survivor, obsolete, vanished, departed, superseded.

2. Having ceased burning, quenched, put out, extinguished, doused *(coll.).*

EXTINCTION, *n.* 1. Extermination, destruction, annihilation, slaying, killing, murder, ruination, extirpation, eradication, abolition, overthrow, eclipse, liquidation, excision, suppression, havoc, devastation, waste, laying waste, ravage, crack of doom, obliteration, effacement.

2. Dying out, coming to an end, death, dissolution, breaking up, decease, oblivion.

EXTINGUISH, *v.* 1. Put out the flame of, quench, douse, smother, stifle, suffocate, damp, choke, snuff out, quell, blow out, blot out, darken.

2. Put an end to, bring to an end, wipe out of existence, destroy, eradicate, quash, efface, obliterate, cancel, nullify, erase, dispel, sink, dissipate, swamp, engulf, overwhelm, subdue, put down, subvert, suppress, annul, end, annihilate, extirpate, demolish, ravage.

3. Obscure by superior brilliance, throw into the shade, eclipse.

EXTIRPATE, *v.* 1. Pull up by the roots, uproot, root up, root out, eradicate, deracinate, weed out, averruncate, extract, grub up, unearth.

2. Remove utterly, do away with, destroy totally, exterminate, annihilate, raze, demolish, abolish.

EXTIRPATION, *n.* 1. Uprooting, eradication, deracination, averruncation, extraction, evulsion, avulsion, excision, total removal, cutting out.

2. Extermination, annihilation, suppression, extinction, abolition.

EXTOL, *v.* Praise highly, eulogize, panegyrize, laud, commend highly, glorify, magnify, exalt, celebrate, elevate, compliment, congratulate, sing the praises of, cry up, be laudatory of, approve, admire, honor, adore, flatter, bless, applaud, clap, cheer, acclaim.

EXTORT, *v.* 1. Wring from by violence, exact by force, elicit by threat, blackmail, compel by intimidation, despoil, fleece, milk, wrest from, tear from, deprive of, bereave, wring from by terrorism, constrain by force, put the screws to, squeeze, extract, wrench, require by abuse of authority, demand illicitly.

2. Charge excessively for, overcharge.

EXTORTION, *n.* 1. Taking by undue exercise of power, oppressive exaction, blackmail, skin game, illegal compulsion, shakedown, tribute, bloodsucking, vampirism, squeeze, elicitation, oppression, venality, rapacity, greed, avidity, tenacity, cupidity, heavy hand, usury, blood money.

2. Overcharge, exorbitant charge, exorbitance, excessive price, fancy price, highway robbery, heavy pull upon the purse.

EXTORTIONATE, *adj.* 1. Exacting, oppressive, grasping, sordid, venal, harsh, hard, severe, avid, avaricious, rapacious, voracious, bloodsucking, ravenous, greedy, covetous, insatiable.

2. Grossly excessive, high-priced, dear, above price, exorbitant, unreasonable, extravagant, priced out of the market.

EXTORTIONIST, *n.* Blackmailer, shakedown artist, exacter, wrester, wringer, fleecer, leech, vulture, bloodsucker, vampire, succubus, harpy, oppressor, extortioner.

EXTRA, *adj.* Being over and above what is required, more than usual, additional, accessory, added, supplemental, supplementary, further, spare, new, fresh, other, auxiliary, contributory, redundant, superfluous, supernumerary.

EXTRACT, *v.* 1. Get out by force, draw forth, draw out, pry out, pull out, drag out, take out, exact, wrest, extort, extricate, remove, eliminate, tear out, pluck out, wring from, wrench, root up, eradicate, deracinate, averruncate, extirpate.

2. Evoke, educe, elicit, deduce, evolve, bring forth, derive, pump, obtain.

3. Separate from a mixture by pressure, derive by chemical process, squeeze out, distill, express, press out.

4. Select from a literary work, excerpt, quote, cite, cull, glean.

EXTRACT, *n.* 1. Passage taken from a book, quotation, citation, excerpt, selection, analect, abstract, fugitive piece, clipping, cutting, note, minute.

2. Essence, juice, distillation, quintessence, decoction, tincture, infusion.

EXTRACTION, *n.* 1. Pulling out, elimination, removal, extrication, evulsion, eradication, extirpation, deracination, ejection, drawing out.

2. Ancestry, descent, lineage, genealogy, stock, stirps, parentage, family, race, origin, birth, pedigree, strain, breed.

3. Distillation, essence, quintessence.

4. Derivation, elicitation, evocation, educement.

EXTRADITE, *v.* Send to another state for trial, give up to another authority, surrender the custody of, turn over to, deliver.

EXTRANEOUS, *adj.* 1. Coming from without, extrinsic, external, exterior, foreign, alien, exotic, adventitious.

2. Having no essential relation to a subject, not proper to a thing, not pertinent, irrelevant, unessential, not germane, inappropriate, inadmissible, incidental.

EXTRAORDINARY, *adj.* 1. Out of the regular order, not ordinary, unusual, uncommon, rare, singular, phenomenal, abnormal, out of the way, unwonted, unheard of, exceptional, prodigious, egregious, monstrous, amazing, special, unique, curious, odd, strange, queer, quaint, *sui generis (Lat.),* unfamiliar, preternatural, unconventional, unprecedented, unparalleled, fantastic, fabulous, astonishing, miraculous, portentous, grotesque, peculiar, preposterous, surprising, striking, vast, startling, enormous.

2. Illustrious, famous, glorious, grand, signal, prominent, remarkable, distinguished, important, lofty, renowned, majestic, august, sublime, *tombé*

des nues, noteworthy, noted, notable, eminent, memorable, wondrous.

EXTRAVAGANCE, *n.* 1. Excessive expenditure of money, inordinate outlay, prodigality, luxury buying, wastefulness, economic folly, financial recklessness, lavishness, profligacy, spendthrift ways.

2. Unrestrained excess, immoderation, exorbitance, fantastic enormity, unreasonableness, preposterousness.

3. Irregularity, absurdity, wildness, folly, flightiness, capriciousness.

EXTRAVAGANT, *adj.* 1. Needlessly lavish in outlay, going beyond necessity in expenditure, wasteful, spendthrift, prodigal, thriftless, profuse, squandering, unthrifty, economically imprudent.

2. Extreme, excessive, inordinate, exorbitant, immoderate, extortionate, unreasonable, unconscionable, preposterous, improvident, outrageous.

3. Wild, irregular, foolish, exceeding the bounds of reason, impracticable, romantic, unreal, imaginary, visionary, flighty, quixotic, Utopian, fantastic, fanciful, high-flown, unsubstantial, fabulous, legendary, mythical, chimerical, absurd, irrational.

EXTRAVAGANZA, *n.* Fantastic composition, caricature, divertissement, burletta, harlequinade, spectacular romance, strange story, vagary, rhapsody, fantasy, farce burlesque, *opéra bouffe (Fr.),* wild flight of sentiment.

EXTREME, *adj.* 1. Situated at the farthest limit, farthest removed, most remote, most distant, very far out, outermost, farthest, utmost, uttermost, endmost.

2. Exceeding great, greatest, of the highest degree, highest, supreme, crowning, towering.

3. Terminal, final, last, ultimate, concluding, terminating, ending, finishing, hindermost, rear, lowest.

4. Uncompromising in one's views, radical in one's demands, ultra, exacting, severe, strict, stringent, *outré (Fr.),* advanced, fanatical, rabid, intransigent, froward, insurgent, revolutionary.

5. Exceeding the bounds of moderation, going to the utmost lengths, immoderate, excessive, inordinate, undue, exorbitant, unreasonable, sheer, outrageous egregious, arrant, drastic, intense.

EXTREME, *n.* 1. Extremity, end, terminal point, limit, boundary, term, confine, either of the two ends of anything.

2. Utmost point, utmost, highest degree, acme, apogee, summit, height, climax, pink, apex, verge.

3. Extravagance, exorbitance, undue departure from the mean.

4. Distress, calamity, danger, peril, jeopardy.

EXTREMIST, *n.* Supporter of extreme doctrines, radical, zealot, fanatic, intransigent, malcontent, irreconcilable, die-hard, bitter-ender, demagogue, disputant, oppositionist, obstructive, conscientious objector, wrangler, reactionary, passive resister.

EXTREMITY, *n.* 1. Farthest end, terminal point, termination, terminus, limit, verge, border, edge, extreme, tip, point, nib, tail, stub, fag, top, horn, head, butt, margin.

2. Highest degree, utmost point, last resource, *dernier cri (Fr.),* last cry, extreme measures, undue excess, point of greatest intensity.

3. Limb of the body, appendage, arm, hand, leg, foot, finger, toe.

4. Condition of extreme need, utmost distress, dire circumstances, state of want and misery,

destitution, adversity, greatest difficulty, necessity, need, indigence, hard luck, hardship, losing game, trouble, misfortune, undoing, frowns of fortune, downfall, broken fortunes, disaster, comedown, setback, reverse.

EXTRICATE, *v.* Disentangle, disengage, unfetter, disembarrass, disencumber, disembroil, liberate, unbind, release, relieve, free, deliver, loose, clear, detach, rescue, redeem, ransom.

EXTRINSIC, *adj.* 1. External, pertaining to things outside, outward, extraneous, alien, adventitious, foreign.

2. Being external to the nature of an object, objective, not inherent, nonsubjective, irrelevant, nonessential, unessential, contingent, adscititious, collateral, accidental, incidental, fortuitous, casual, chance.

EXTROVERSION, *n.* Interest directed outside the self, turning of the thoughts to outward things, propensity for finding one's satisfactions in external things.

EXTROVERT, *n.* One whose emotions are moved by external interests, person concerned chiefly with what is objective, exhibitionist, show-off.

EXTRUDE, *v.* Thrust out, detrude, drive away, push out, eject, force out, expel, oust, drive out, dislodge, eliminate.

EXUBERANCE, *n.* Abundance, affluence, wealth, plenitude, fulness, amplitude, galore, lots, satiety, full measure, copiousness, luxuriance, cornucopia, horn of plenty, flood, outpouring, redundancy, abounding variety, superabundance, superfluity, repletion, excess, rankness, overflow, profusion, lavishness, overgrowth.

EXUBERANT, *adj.* Abundant, affluent, marked by great plentifulness, plenty, copious, luxuriant, plenteous, replete, flush, chock-full, liberal, rich, abounding, inexhaustible, prolific, fertile, fruitful, flowing, superabundant, excessive, rank, redundant, lavish, profuse, lush, overflowing, superfluous.

EXUDATION, *n.* Sweating, perspiration, leakage, sweatlike discharge through pores, sweat, issue, transudation, discharge, filtering, efflux, effusion, excretion, secretion, emission, percolation, effluence.

EXUDE, *v.* 1. Send out like sweat, sweat, secrete, perspire, excrete, discharge through the pores, throw out, emit, give off.

2. Come out gradually in drops, ooze through pores, leak, trickle, percolate, filter, infiltrate, find vent, drain, seep, gush, spout, flow out, well out, effuse, escape, issue, transude.

EXULT, *v.* 1. Manifest delight, be in high spirits, rejoice exceedingly for success, triumph, jubilate, be glad, leap for joy, fling up one's cap, be in ecstasy, be in transport, show lively joy, glory, skip, be highly elated, dance, make merry, be jubilant, be exhilarated.

2. Boast, crow, gloat, vaunt, brag, flourish, put on the dog, strut, swagger, bluster, gasconade, blow one's own horn, talk big, give oneself airs, peacock, prance, ride a high horse, plume oneself.

EXULTANT, *adj.* 1. Highly elated, transported, pleased, jubilant, triumphant, joyous, overjoyed, flushed, excited, exhilarated, rejoicing, delighted, satisfied, happy.

2. Boastful, proud of oneself, braggart, windy, vainglorious, bombastic, pompous, toplofty, cock-a-hoop, high-flown, grandiose, vaunting, uppish, puffed up, highfaluting.

EXULTATION, *n.* 1. Triumphant joy, jubilation, elation, transport, delight, triumph, acclamation, exultancy, rejoicing, gladness, flush, glory, praise, reveling, paean, happiness, rapture, enjoyment, ecstasy, plaudit, applause, shouting, reveling.

2. Boasting, vaunting, braggadocio, gasconade, flourish, fanfaronade, swagger, brag, *blague (Fr.)*, bluster, bravado, rodomontade, bombast, swank, pomposity, ostentation, side.

EXUVIAE, *n.* Cast skins, parts shed by animals, slough, castings, shell, morphew, fossil remains of animals, scurf.

EYE, *n.* 1. Visual organ, oculus, organ of sight, orb, optic, "glim," "lamp," "peeper."

2. Visible structure within and surrounding the orbit, retina, pupil, iris, cornea, white, eyeball.

3. Eyesight, perception, power of seeing, view, discernment, sight, look, vision, ken, glint, gaze, glimpse, glance, blink, peep, peek, stare, *coup d'oeil (Fr.)*.

4. Discriminating visual perception, estimate, appreciation, judgment, point of view, viewpoint.

5. Attentive look, close observation, vigilance, surveillance, contemplation, inspection, watchful care, watch, regard, survey, notice, reconnoitre, reconnaissance, look out.

6. Hole, perforation, foramen, aperture, eyelet, loop, peephole, eyelet hole, small loop to receive a hook.

EYE, *v.* 1. Fix the eyes upon, look at fixedly, rivet the eyes upon, view, observe narrowly, peek, watch, scrutinize, survey, look on, have an eye on, glance, peep, peer, pry, squint, leer, scan, lay eyes on, gaze at, keep in view, reconnoitre, espy, catch sight of, see, inspect, stare at, goggle, glare, pore over, notice, behold.

2. Throw amorous glances at, ogle, make eyes at, give the wink to, give the up and down to, undress with a glance.

EYE DOCTOR, *n.* Ophthalmologist, optometrist, oculist.

EYELESS, *adj.* Lacking vision, visionless, blinded, sightless, unseeing, blind, stark-blind, blind as a bat, blind as a mole.

EYELET, *n.* Small opening usually buttonholed, small round hole, eyelet-hole, aperture, foramen, slot, perforation, eye, eyehole, ring, peekhole, peephole, loophole.

EYESIGHT, *n.* 1. Faculty of seeing, vision, sight, optics, power of sight, sense of seeing.

2. Observation, contemplation, regard, survey, inspection, reconnaissance, watch, look, glimpse, espial, ken, glance, peep, view, range of the eye, extent of vision.

EYESORE, *n.* Something unpleasant to look at, something that offends the eye, blemish, offense, deformity, disfigurement, defacement, scarecrow, defect, ugliness, fright, blot on the landscape, sight.

EYEWITNESS, *n.* One who sees an occurrence with his own eyes, witness, beholder, spectator, onlooker, observer, inspector, viewer, looker-on, bystander, passer-by, one who testifies what he has seen, giver of evidence, deponent, testifier.

F

FABIAN, *adj.* 1. Avoiding battle, inactive, chary, purposely delaying, cautiously dilatory, cautious, do-nothing, wary, guarded, *cavendo tutus (Lat.)*, cautelous, shy of, prudent, vigilant, careful, procrastinative.

2. Late, tardy, slow, behindhand, unpunctual, belated, backward.

FABLE, *n.* 1. Short tale to teach a moral, brief story invented to embody a moral, fictitious story, legend, myth, story about supernatural persons and incidents, parable, allegory, apologue, nursery tale, fairy tale, romance, extravaganza, story of supernatural and highly marvelous happenings.

2. Fiction, invention, fabrication, figment, fib, coinage of the imagination, forgery, moonshine, story *(euphemistic)*, lie, prevarication, falsehood, untruth, tall story, whopper *(colloq.)*, fish story, yarn, cock-and-bull story, traveler's tale, canard, bosh, concoction.

FABLE, *v.* 1. Relate fictitious matter, spin a yarn, invent stories, tell tales, write fiction, fabricate stories, compose, romance.

2. Talk about as if true, lie, prevaricate, talk idly, tell untruths, feign, simulate, profess, make believe, affect, sham, counterfeit, misrepresent, speak falsely.

FABRIC, *n.* 1. Woven or knitted material, cloth made by weaving or knitting fibers, tissue, textile, webbing, web, stuff, drill, homespun, twill, tweed, serge, canvas, mat, frieze, linsey-woolsey, fustian, gossamer, silk, acetate, rayon, Nylon, Dacron, Orlon, satin, wool.

2. Texture of the woven material, contexture, intertexture, conformation, grain, workmanship, fiber, nap, make.

3. Structure, superstructure, substructure, pile, stratification, compages, organization, make-up, frame, configuration, construction, substance, build.

4. Building, edifice, erection, architecture.

FABRICATE, *v.* 1. Form into a whole by uniting parts, make by assembling standard parts, frame, assemble, compose, produce, build, construct, manufacture, form, fashion, spin, weave, shape, erect, raise, rear.

2. Make up, invent, devise, create, originate, imagine, concoct, hatch, coin, scheme up, design, formulate, contrive, mint.

3. Devise falsely, forge, fake, feign, embroider, misrepresent, color, varnish, doctor up, dress up, misstate, falsify, counterfeit, pretend, prevaricate, make believe, garble, gloss over, fib, lie, romance, trump up, fable, pass off for, simulate.

FABRICATION, *n.* 1. Construction, assemblage, composition, production, building, manufacture, fashioning, erection, structure.

2. Untruthful statement, falsehood, coinage of the imagination, fiction, invention, concoction, figment, lie, prevarication, fib, mendacity, fable, untruth, forgery, yarn, myth, fairy tale, tall story, whopper *(colloq.)*, fish story, traveler's tale, bosh, cock-and-bull story, moonshine, canard.

FABULOUS, *adj.* 1. Told about in fables, fabled, storied, imaginary, fictitious, legendary, mythical, traditional, mythological, fantastic, fanciful, not true, romancing, apocryphal, invented, fabricated, feigned, coined, marvelous, chimerical, figmental, supposititious, Cinderellaesque, unreal.

2. Incredible, quite unbelievable, astonishing, amazing, extravagant, preposterous, passing the limits of belief, *outré (Fr.)*, excessive, inordinate, extraordinary, wonderful, supernatural.

FAÇADE, *n.* Principal face of an edifice, frontal appearance, front of a building, frontage, front view, forefront, exterior features, face.

FACE, *n.* 1. Front part of the head from the forehead to the chin, combination of the features, physiognomy, visage, features, countenance, mug, lineaments, silhouette, profile, pan *(slang),* phiz *(slang),* half-face.

2. Personal presence, immediate cognizance, sight.

3. Expression on the face, mien, aspect, smirk, air, cast of countenance, demeanor, *moue (Fr.),* grimace, pout, facial contortion.

4. Outward appearance, semblance, superficial showing, outward show, external aspect, disguise, pretense, outward impression.

5. Good name, prestige, dignity, reputation, repute.

6. Boldness, audacity, self-assurance, gameness, confidence, nerve, pluck, mettle, spunk, grit, lip, hardihood, front, effrontery, brass, impudence, sauce, cheek.

7. Surface, superficies, external part, exterior, outside, right side, cover, finished side, facet, side upon which the use of a thing depends.

8. Principal side of anything, most important side, front, front part, forepart, façade, frontage, frontal, obverse *(Numismatics),* forefront, breast, escarpment.

FACE, *v.* 1. Look to, confront, meet face to face, meet in front, turn toward, encounter, envisage, meet, front, breast, front toward, stand opposite to, stand over against, contemplate.

2. Oppose, resist, withstand, brave, buck, dare, beard, defy, challenge, grapple with, stand at bay, make a stand, show a bold front.

3. Put a surface on, smooth the surface of, dress, polish, level.

4. Cover with a different material in front, cover with another kind of material, put a facing on, coat, veneer, incrust, superimpose, line, case, overspread, envelop, encase.

5. Put face upward, turn the face up.

6. Be turned toward, lie with the front toward.

FACET, *n.* 1. One of the small plane polished surfaces of a cut gem, lozenge, surface, templet, shape, cut, small face of some geometric form.

2. One of several sides of anything, aspect, phase.

FACETIOUS, *adj.* 1. Given to pleasantry, jocular, jocose, witty, humorous, comical, joking, waggish, droll, funny, Attic, salty, whimsical, jesting, apt at badinage, full of persiflage, ready at witty sayings, replete with bons mots, full of pleasantries, good at banter, dealing in quips, gifted with a flair for piquant expressions, bright with amusing remarks, master of ready wit, dealing in repartee, inventive of puns and conceits.

2. Trying to be amusing, playful, entertaining, sportive, merry, gay, nimble-witted, lively, keen, sprightly, *spirituel (Fr.),* clever, smart, mirthful, sparkling, epigrammatic, full of point.

FACE TO FACE 1. To one's face, confronting one another, tête-à-tête, vis-à-vis, before one's face.

2. Without anything interposing, in front, in the foreground, in the van, ahead, right ahead, dead ahead, in one's path.

3. At close quarters, cheek by jowl, close, side by side, hard by, in close proximity, within reach, under one's nose.

FACILE, *adj.* 1. Easily done, easy, practicable, proceeding with ease, not difficult to do, readily mastered, easily surmountable, feasible.

2. Working with ease, dexterous, adroit, deft, expert, quick, ready, fluent, skilful, handy, apt, quick, ingenious, artful, proficient, clever.

3. Easy in manner, easygoing, unconstrained, courteous, affable, agreeable, complaisant, mild, cordial, gentle, free, approachable, conversable, accessible, not austere.

4. Easily persuaded, easily influenced, flexible, easily acted upon, yielding, tractable, malleable, pliable, pliant, plastic, ductile, docile, compliant, manageable, submissive.

FACILITATE, *v.* Lessen the labor of, make less difficult, make easier, free from difficulty, lighten, disburden, disencumber, clear, smooth, ease, aid, alleviate, assist the progress of, pave the way, make way for, favor, advance, accelerate, further, open the way for, promote, encourage, expedite, foster, help, push, forward, speed up, bridge over, help forward, clear the ground, clear the way, open the door to.

FACILITY, *n.* 1. Easiness in doing, freedom from difficulty, feasibility, practicability, plain sailing, mere child's play, cinch, snap, ease.

2. Quickness due to practice, readiness because of skill, capability, dexterity, deftness, adroitness, address, expertness, skill, proficiency, cleverness, ability, aptness, knack, forte, turn, bent.

3. Easiness to be persuaded, pliancy, docility, readiness of compliance, tractableness, ductility, malleability, flexibility, pliability.

4. Easy-flowing manner, affability, smoothness, complaisance.

5. *(Usually pl.)* Something that makes possible the easier performance of any action, aid, means, advantages, resources, conveniences, appliances, ways and means, opportunities.

FACING, *n.* Outer layer of different material, a covering in front for any purpose, any material used for facing, cover, lining, veneer, coating, envelope, trimming.

FACSIMILE, *n.* Duplicate, exact copy, replica, transcript, reproduction, reprint, reflex, likeness, counterpart, imitation, apograph, image, forgery, photograph, reflection, resemblance, counterfeit, same, selfsame, ditto.

FACT, *n.* 1. Anything that is done, something that comes to pass, incident, occurrence, event, happening, thing done, transaction, adventure, circumstance, experience, deed, act, proceeding, performance, affair, phenomenon, episode, scene, particular, result achieved.

2. What has really happened, what is the case, anything strictly true, something concrete, reality, real existence, actuality, matter of fact, certainty, *fait accompli (Fr.),* verity, truth, certitude, naked truth, gospel, scripture, the very thing, not an illusion, *nuda veritas (Lat.),* real Simon Pure.

FACTION, *n.* 1. A number of persons combined for a common purpose, combination against, ring, cabal, camarilla, machine, junto, group, gang, clique, set, party, circle, side, denomination, cause, crew, team, knot, push, sect, coterie, party within a party, company, splinter party, smaller group of people within a larger one.

2. Party strife, partisanship, sedition, rebellion, seditiousness, recalcitrancy, insubordination, feud, dissension, discord, disagreement, refractoriness, insurgency, dissidence, difference, disorder, party spirit, variance, tumult, turbulence, division, split, schism, rupture, incompatibility, cross-purposes, contention, clashing, jar, quarreling, clash, break, disruption, breach.

FACTIOUS, *adj.* 1. Addicted to form parties and raise dissensions, unilateral, inclined to act for party purposes, cliquish, cliquy, selfish, thick as thieves, demagogic, extremely partisan.

2. Quarrelsome, dissentious, seditious, polemic, rebellious, recalcitrant, refractory, insubordinate, contentious, turbulent, dissident, discordant, torn, incompatible, at strife, disagreeing, disputatious, heated, inimical, hostile, at loggerheads, at odds, at cross-purposes, at variance, at sixes and sevens, embroiled, disunited, at daggers drawn, up in arms.

FACTITIOUS, *adj.* Artificial, false, mock, sham, not natural, not spontaneous, make-believe, made by art, counterfeit, forged, faked, pseudo, bogus, so-called, fraudulent, bastard, meretricious, made, manufactured, unnatural, simulated, brummagem, spurious, trumped up, feigned, pretended, tinsel, pinchbeck.

FACTOR, *n.* 1. One of the elements contributing to bring about a given result, determining circumstance, instrument, cause, contributing force, constitutive element, constituent, influence, means, aid, measure, agency, medium.

2. *(Brit.)* Agent in commercial transactions, commission merchant, broker, one who transacts business for another, representative, middleman, go-between, negotiator, commissioner, solicitor, consignee, proxy, substitute, attorney, emissary, deputy, delegate, envoy, messenger, manager, bailiff, steward, clerk, secretary, proctor.

FACTORY, *n.* 1. A building with equipment for manufacture of goods, manufacturing plant, manufactory, plant, works, workshop, mill, foundry, hive of industry, manufacturing establishment, shop, laboratory, industrial fabric.

2. An organization of agents in a country other than their own for carrying on business with the inhabitants, trading station.

FACTOTUM, *n.* One who has many diverse activities, do-all, doer of all work, jack-of-all-trades, working bee, laboring oar, worker ant, shaft-horse, general servant, handy man, man of all work, hewer of wood and drawer of water, navvy, hand, man, day laborer, hack, tool, beast of burden, drudge, fag, servitor, menial, lackey, flunky, domestic, butler, valet, groom, footman.

FACTUAL, *adj.* Pertaining to facts, of the nature of fact, real, veritable, genuine, valid, actual, positive, objective, true to the facts, veracious, correct, close, literal, scrupulous, faithful, official, authentic, exact, in fact.

FACULTY, *n.* 1. Ability for a particular kind of action, inherent physical capability, capacity, power, endowment, attribute, qualification, property, virtue, quality, enablement, gift, genius, reason, wits, sense, talent, art.

2. Executive ability to manage, skilfulness, skill, efficiency, dexterity, deftness, adroitness, proficiency, address, aptitude, expertness, ingenuity, cleverness, competency, aptness, native facility, adeptness, mastery, finish, technique, craft, turn, knack, felicity, *curiosa felicitas (Lat.),* sharpness, readiness, quickness, forte, bent.

3. Department of learning in a university, body of a learned profession, teaching staff, body of professors, teaching body, professorate, officers of instruction in a college or university.

4. *(Law)* Privilege conferred, license, power, right, prerogative, dispensation, authority, authorization.

FAD, *n.* Temporary fashion, passing fancy, popular innovation, capricious hobby, irrational pursuit, craze, mania, rage, furor, latest word, *dernier cri (Fr.),* latest thing, the go, prevailing taste, style, vogue, *ton (Fr.),* mode, crotchet, whim, gimcrack, whim-wham, frenzy.

FADE, *v.* 1. Lose color, pale, blanch, blench, bleach, etiolate, achromatize, whiten, grow dim, become colorless, lose brightness, lose luster, cloud, become dull, lose clarity.

2. Lose strength, lose vigor, lose health, decline, wither, droop, languish, faint, flag, wane, fail, ebb, fall off, retrograde, decay, shrivel, molder, rot, crumble.

3. Disappear, vanish, evanesce, dissolve, die gradually, pass away, recede, disperse, dissipate, be seen no more, melt away, depart, be gone, leave no trace, be lost to sight, perish.

FAG, *v.* 1. Tire by labor, weary oneself by working, fatigue, tire out, wear out, tax, task, strain, overwork, overburden, jade, exhaust, knock up, prostrate, tucker out, harass, irk, bore.

2. Drudge, toil, labor, sweat, slave, work hard, exert oneself, tax one's energies, wade through, strive, strain, pull, stretch a long arm, ply the oar, do menial service, be a fag.

3. Grow weary, droop, flag, be tired, become fatigued, sink, drop, swoon, faint, succumb.

4. Make a fag of, require menial service from, compel to drudge, make a slave of.

FAG, *n.* 1. One who does menial service for another, drudge, slave, menial, helot, serf, toiler, hard worker, work horse, shaft horse, bee, worker ant.

2. Drudgery, toil, slavery, hard labor, tiresome work.

3. *(Colloq.)* Cigarette, butt, gasper, cheroot, weed.

FAGGED, *adj.* Wearied, weary, spent, worn out, tired, toilworn, fatigued, dog-tired, played out, exhausted, beat up, knocked up, tuckered, used up, drooping, haggard, done in, footsore, faint, prostrate, ready to drop, more dead than alive, walked off one's legs, *épuisé (Fr.).*

FAGOT, *n.* Bundle of sticks used for fuel, fascine, firewood, log, kindling wood.

FAIL, *v.* 1. Fall short, stop short of, not reach, come short of, be deficient, be insufficient, be wanting, be lacking, prove lacking, disappoint, flunk, not answer expectations, prove inadequate, be defective, prove useless, turn out badly.

2. Not succeed, miss the mark, come to nothing, fall through, fizzle out, miscarry, abort, end in smoke, be unsuccessful, founder, come to grief, go to pot, run aground, be frustrated, flash in the pan, fall to the ground, collapse, succumb, fall stillborn, miss fire, flat out, hang fire, go to wrack and ruin, stick in the mud, shipwreck, go to the wall, falter, meet with disaster, slip up, trip, stumble, blunder, prove of no use to.

3. Omit to perform, neglect to observe, desert, forsake, ignore, slight, evade, give the go-by to, cut, shut one's eyes to, avoid, renounce, forswear, escape, transgress.

4. Waste away, decline, perish gradually, pine away, languish, fade away, disappear, become extinct, cease, pass away, give out, wane, droop, ebb, sink, collapse, sicken, become weaker, flag, lose vigor, dwindle, decay, deteriorate, peak, crumble.

5. Become unable to meet one's business obligations, go out of business, drown in red ink, become bankrupt, become insolvent, go under, go to smash, default on payment, not pay, go up

FAILING, *n.* 1. Wasting away, decline, decay, collapse, languor, debilitation, decrepitude, atony, asthenia, cachexia *(Med.).*

2. Failure, nonsuccess, nonfulfilment, labor in vain, no go, vain attempt, fizzle, fiasco, washout, miscarriage, abortion.

3. Weak side, shortcoming, fault, frailty, foible, flaw, imperfection, defect, blemish, infirmity, weakness, blind side.

4. Delinquency, dereliction, indiscretion, lapse, offense, peccadillo, slight mistake, slip, error, errancy, omission, negligence, inadvertency, recreancy, backsliding, apostasy.

FAILURE, *n.* 1. Lack of success, nonsuccess, nonfulfilment, labor in vain, no go, botch, fizzle, fiasco, washout, muff, flash in the pan, frustration, disappointment, losing game, checkmate, ill success, inefficacy, vain attempt, abortion, miscarriage, breakdown, collapse, wild-goose chase, sleeveless errand, debacle, sinking ship.

2. Omission of something due, nonperformance of something required, dereliction, delinquency, negligence, miss, slip, oversight, neglect, nonobservance, default, pretermission.

3. Running short, insufficiency, shortcoming, deficiency, want, lack.

4. Rebuff, repulse, defeat, overthrow, discomfiture, beating, drubbing.

5. Mishap, slip, trip, stumble, faux pas, blunder, error, scrape, mess, muddle, botch, misfortune, mischance, blow, deathblow, tragedy.

6. Loss of strength, decline, deterioration, decay, declension, failing.

7. Financial disaster, bankruptcy, insolvency, suspension of payment, crash, wreck, ruination, downfall.

FAIN, *adj.* 1. Ready and willing, desirous, nothing loath, minded, disposed, inclined, favorably minded, in the mood, in the humor, avid, keen for, bent upon, set on, appetitive, dying for, partial to, predisposed, propense, eager, anxious, ready, enthusiastic, zealous, earnest.

2. Relatively satisfied, contented, pleased, glad, rejoiced.

3. Constrained, obliged, beholden.

FAINT, *v.* 1. Lose consciousness temporarily, swoon, suffer syncope, black out, faint away, drop, succumb, collapse.

2. Decline, grow weak, languish, droop, sink, flag, fade, fail, lose strength.

3. Lose courage, give way, despond, be dejected, be discouraged, lose heart, be dispirited, fall into dejection, be downhearted.

FAINT, *adj.* 1. Giddy, vertiginous, feeling dizzy, about to swoon, fainting away, light-headed, lipothymial *(Med.).*

2. Overcome with physical exhaustion, feeble, exhausted, lacking strength, weak, worn out, fagged out, drooping, languid, torpid, sluggish, fatigued, wearied.

3. Slight, inconsiderable, little, small, meager, bare, scarce, feeble, thin.

4. Lacking in brightness, wanting in distinctness, dim, indistinct, dull, almost imperceptible, pale, ill-defined, low, stifled, muffled, muted, faltering, irresolute, obscure, faded, soft, gentle, inaudible, muttered, whispered, soft, dulcet.

5. Despondent, dejected, dispirited, depressed, discouraged, disheartened, drooping.

6. Lacking courage, faint-hearted, timorous, timid, pusillanimous, cowardly, dastardly, diffident, fearful, funky, lacking spirit, half-hearted.

FAIR, *adj.* 1. Showing no more favor to one side than another, treating all sides alike, impartial, unbiased, disinterested, unprejudiced, square, even-handed, dispassionate, equitable, just, proper, reasonable, affording no undue advantage.

2. Free from dishonesty, honorable, virtuous, upright, veracious, frank, candid, honest, ingenuous, sincere, truthful, aboveboard, manly.

3. Pretty good, not bad, middling, average, medium, ordinary, moderately satisfactory, not amiss, passable, tolerable, reasonably good, fairish, respectable, decent, reasonable, so-so, above mediocrity, indifferent, milk-and-water, run-of-the-mill.

4. Marked by favoring conditions, promising, propitious, fortunate, lucky, of good omen, auspicious, hopeful.

5. Sunny, cloudless, bright, not stormy, unclouded, pleasant, sunshiny, fine, halcyon.

6. Easy to see, bright, limpid, distinct, clear, plain, evident, legible.

7. Of a light hue, not dark, blond, white, lily-white, pale, creamy, argent.

8. Free from imperfection, spotless, clean, pure, immaculate, unspotted, unblemished, untarnished, stainless, unsullied, impeccable, cleanly, unsoiled, unstained.

9. Handsome, good-looking, beautiful, comely, lovely, bonny, well-favored, winsome, attractive, sweet, personable, graceful, shapely, pretty, seemly, charming.

10. Fair-spoken, courteous, civil, gracious, polite, pleasant, affable, suave.

FAIR, *n.* 1. Competitive exhibition of farm products and live stock, county fair, competitive exhibition of wares, market, mart, staple, marketplace, bazaar, exchange, exposition.

2. Exhibit and sale of fancy articles for some charitable benefit.

FAIRLY, *adv.* 1. Equitably, in a just way, justly, in a fair manner, impartially, without unfair advantage, honestly, reasonably, candidly, rightly, properly, legitimately.

2. Moderately, tolerably, slightly, rather, somewhat, pretty well, fairly well, passably.

3. Actually, completely, positively, absolutely, fully.

4. Clearly, distinctly, openly, evidently, plainly, legibly.

5. Auspiciously, agreeably, favorably, pleasantly, beautifully, handsomely.

6. Courteously, politely, civilly, affably.

FAIRNESS, *n.* 1. Probity, justice, integrity, equity, impartiality, justness, veracity, uprightness, principle, rectitude, honesty, right, faith, honor, good faith, *bona fides (Lat.),* candor, equitable treatment, fair play.

2. Loveliness, sweetness, beauty, handsomeness, winsomeness, charm, exquisiteness, attractiveness, comeliness.

FAIR-SPOKEN, *adj.* 1. Courteous, civil, gracious, polite, complaisant, mannerly, gallant, chivalrous, urbane, suave, soft-spoken, well-bred, gentlemanly, polished, refined, cultured, affable, cordial.

2. Plausible in speech, smooth-tongued, specious, bland, flattering, adulatory, servile, sycophantic, fulsome, blandiloquent, honeyed, honey-mouthed, unctuous, oily.

FAIRY, *n.* 1. Diminutive supernatural being having magical powers, mythical being, sprite, fay, leprechaun, elf, brownie, nix, nixie *(fem.),* pixy, troll, kobold, kelpie, peri, gnome, banshee, hobgoblin, oaf, genie, sylph, nymph, Puck, Oberon, Mab, Titania.

2. Sex deviate, pervert, homosexual, pederast, Sodomite, Lesbian.

FAIRYLAND, *n.* Imaginary realm of the fairies, dreamland, cloudland, happy valley, place of magical charm and delicate beauty, place of enchantment, Arabian nights, dream of Alnaschar.

FAITH, *n.* 1. Trust, belief, assurance, dependence, confidence, reliance, hope, security, sanguine expectation, credence, hopefulness, buoyancy, sheet anchor, mainstay, optimism, aspiration, certitude, certainty.

2. Assent of the mind to Gospel truth without other evidence, open profession of religious truth, belief in God, creed, persuasion, conviction, tenet, doctrine, dogma, religion, teaching, opinion, principle, position, avowal, confession.

3. Faithfulness, trustworthiness, fidelity, constancy, loyalty, truthfulness, honesty, sincerity, veracity, credibility, believability.

4. Verbal pledge, word of honor, obligation, promise, engagement.

FAITHFUL, *adj.* 1. Steady in the performance of duty, loyal, true, devoted, leal, steadfast, tried, stanch, stable, incorruptible, unwavering, unswerving, true-blue, firm in adherence.

2. True to one's word, conscientious, trustworthy, trusty, reliable, dependable, worthy of credit, worthy of confidence.

3. Veracious, truthful, high-principled, honest, upright, virtuous, sincere, scrupulous, religious, sound.

4. True to fact, adhering to an original, exact, accurate, close, strict, nice, punctilious, precise, true to life, lifelike, similar.

FAITHFUL, *n.* Believing members of a church, adherents of a faith, belonging to "the Faith" *(Mohammedan),* body of loyal members of a group.

FAITHLESS, *adj.* 1. Unbelieving, agnostic, nullifidian, skeptical, atheistic, freethinking, incredulous, not believing in religion.

2. Untrustworthy, disloyal, traitorous, treacherous, perfidious, unfaithful, recreant, false, untruthful, deceptive, dishonest, dishonorable, unreliable, unscrupulous, unprincipled, delusive, truthless, lost to shame, dead to honor, Iscariotic, false-hearted, double-tongued, two-faced, fraudulent, deceitful, unstable, inconstant, mercurial, fickle, shifting, variable, vacillating, wavering, mutable, fluctuating, unsteady, untrue, hypocritical.

FAITHLESSNESS, *n.* 1. Agnosticism, nullifidianism, skepticism, atheism, freethinking, incredulity, unbelief, doubt.

2. Perfidy, treachery, traitorousness, treason, untrustworthiness, disloyalty, recreancy, prodition, dishonesty, insidiousness, improbity, fraudulence, lying, unrighteousness, infidelity, double-dealing, Judas kiss, Iscariotism, betrayal, breach of trust, apostasy.

FAKE, *v.* 1. Get up something deceptive, prepare something specious, contrive, fabricate, make up by artificial means, counterfeit, forge, hatch, concoct, foist off.

2. Conceal the defects of, cover up, alter with intent to deceive, garble, gloss over, disguise, color, varnish, furbish up, doctor up.

3. Pretend, simulate, dissemble, dissimulate, lie, sham, swindle, trick, defraud, cheat, gull, hoax,

bamboozle, live by one's wits, juggle, make a show of, malinger.

FAKE, *n.* 1. Something made to appear otherwise than it actually is, counterfeit, forgery, eyewash, window dressing, sham, brummagem, make-believe, tinsel, paste, false jewelry, imitation.

2. Imposition, trick, delusion, imposture, contrivance, humbug, cheat, fraud, deceit, trickery, chicanery, artifice, dodge, cozenage, treachery, subterfuge, finesse, stratagem, ruse, hoax, specious scheme, borrowed plumes.

3. One who fakes, faker, impostor, pretender, charlatan, quack, mountebank, phony, wolf in sheep's clothing, ass in a lion's skin.

FAKIR, *n.* Holy beggar, mendicant monk, religious ascetic, priest living on alms, Hindu yogi, dervish.

FALDERAL, *n.* 1. Meaningless syllables forming the refrain of various old songs.

2. Mere nonsense, foolish talk, twaddle, nonsensical ideas, gibberish, jargon, balderdash, inanity, gibblegabble.

3. Trifling ornament, piece of imitation finery, trifle, gimcrack, gewgaw, bagatelle, trinket, kickshaw, knickknack, whim-wham, frippery, trumpery.

FALL, *v.* 1. Descend from a higher to a lower place through loss of support, drop, descend, be overthrown, be lowered, sink, drop down, slip, slide, tumble, topple, pitch, plunge, gravitate, plop, come down suddenly, collapse, be precipitated, cease to be erect, become prostrate, crumple, faint, swoon, stumble, trip.

2. Hang downward, extend down, droop, slope.

3. Drop down wounded, drop dead, be slain, die, perish, come to destruction.

4. Decrease, become less, abate, ebb, wane, fail, decline, subside, depreciate, be diminished.

5. Succumb to temptation, depart from rectitude, sin, transgress, lapse, err, commit a fault, misconduct oneself, misbehave, go astray, act amiss.

6. Lose dignity, lose high position, lose moral character, degenerate, become depraved in character, come to grief.

7. Be captured, succumb to siege, be destroyed, be taken, pass into enemy hands, surrender, capitulate.

8. Come by lot, befall, happen, come to pass, chance, occur, arrive.

FALL, *n.* 1. Drop from a higher to a lower place, dropping, descent, downfall, tumble, stumble, spill, trip, plunge, slip, plummet, gravitation, prostration.

2. Lowering, becoming less, diminution, sinking to a lower level, slump, decline, decrease, ebb, wane, subsidence, sinking, depreciation, settlement, downcome.

3. *(Usually pl.)* Waterfall, cataract, cascade.

4. Downward slope, declivity, obliquity, incline, dip, downhill, inclination.

5. Succumbing to temptation, loss of innocence, lapse into sin, seduction, spiritual ruin, going astray, deviation from virtue, slip, error, apostasy, backsliding.

6. Humiliation, degradation, depravation, loss of eminence, comedown, setback, shame, debasement, abjection, turpitude, disrepute, discredit, bad name, disgrace, abasement.

7. Destruction, ruin, overthrow, subversion, downfall, surrender, capitulation, capture, collapse, demolition, failure, crash, smash, wreck,

crackup, undoing, breakdown, debacle, perdition, death.

8. Cadence, sinking of the voice, close, setting.

9. Autumn, fall of the leaf, harvest time, autumnal equinox, Indian summer.

FALLACIOUS, *adj.* 1. Erroneous, false, misleading, deceptive, deceiving, disappointing, fraudulent, faulty, mistaken, out in one's reasoning, spurious, delusive, illusory, illusive, untrue, insidious, guileful.

2. Logically unsound, containing a fallacy, paralogistic, sophistical, illogical, unfounded, invalid, unsubstantial, untenable, inconsistent, inexact, ungrounded, groundless.

FALLACY, *n.* 1. False notion, deceptive belief, misleading notion, illusion, delusion, error, mistake, misconception, misapprehension, misjudgment, miscalculation, erroneousness, inexactness, liability to err, deceptiveness, aberration, deceit, deception, false appearance, chimera, fraud, falsehood, absurdity, deviation from truth.

2. Unsound argument, sophistry, erroneous reasoning, sophism, *non sequitur (Lat.),* inconsistency, paralogism, *fallacia consequentis (Lat.),* quibble, worthless argument, casuistry.

FALL AWAY 1. Withdraw allegiance, renounce support of, rebel, defect, revolt, become disaffected, become disloyal, forsake the cause of, fall off, backslide, apostatize.

2. Decline, decay, perish, fade away, evanesce, vanish, disappear gradually.

3. Lose flesh, grow lean, become emaciated, attenuate, pine away, languish.

FALL BACK 1. Retreat, retire, recede, give way, yield, stand at bay.

2. Have recourse to, resort to, make use of, employ, put to use, put in action, call into play, betake oneself to.

FALLIBILITY, *n.* Liability to be misled, frailty, unreliability, untrustworthiness, imperfection, failing, weakness, errancy, liability to error, uncertainty, incertitude, doubtfulness.

FALLIBLE, *adj.* Liable to be erroneous, prone to be inaccurate, liable to mistake, prone to error, unreliable, untrustworthy, questionable, in question, debatable, uncertain, ignorant, weak, frail, imperfect, deceivable.

FALL IN 1. Sink inward, fall to pieces inwardly, cave in, fall into dilapidation, succumb to decay.

2. Take one's proper place in line, queue up, come into line, form ranks.

3. (Followed by WITH) Comply with, assent, agree, consent, concur, acquiesce, swim with the stream, go with the current, favor, conform to, yield to, harmonize with, unite with, join forces with.

FALL OFF 1. Drop, come loose, be detached, drop off, be loosened from support.

2. Separate, withdraw, retire, retreat, step aside.

3. Decline, dip, slump, wane, fail, deteriorate, dwindle, decrease, wither, fade, decay, perish, die off, diminish.

4. Become estranged, withdraw from allegiance, fall away, backslide, apostatize, desert, become disaffected, revolt, defect.

FALL ON 1. Attack, assail, assault, fall upon, rush upon, swoop down on.

2. Light upon, chance upon, descend upon, meet with, discover, bump into.

FALL OUT 1. Leave one's place in rank, drop out of one's place in line.

2. Have differences with, disagree, quarrel, wrangle, feud, bicker, altercate.

3. Occur, happen, chance, come about, befall, come to pass, result, issue, take place, turn out, prove to be.

FALLOW, *adj.* 1. Unplowed, untilled, unsown, unsowed, unseeded, unplanted, uncultivated, unproductive, neglected, unused.

2. Idle, dormant, inactive, inert, sluggish, resting.

3. Light brown, dun, pale brown, sallow, pale yellow, reddish brown.

FALL SHORT Fail to reach a particular amount or standard, be smaller than, not reach, not come up to, disappoint, prove insufficient, be deficient, give out, be wanting.

FALL TO 1. Set about, begin, commence, start, take in hand, take up, tackle, go about, betake oneself to, apply oneself to, put one's hand to, put one's shoulder to the wheel, undertake.

2. Come to blows, do battle, come to grips with, engage, measure swords with, cross swords, draw the trigger, fight, combat.

3. Begin to eat, tuck in, feed, fare, dispatch.

4. Close of itself, drop into place.

FALSE, *adj.* 1. Not correct, incorrect, wrong, erroneous, untrue, mistaken, inaccurate, not well founded, unfounded, improper, unsound, invalid, inexact, faulty, wide of the mark, off key, off pitch, not in tune.

2. Used to deceive, deceptive, deceitful, evasive, delusive, disappointing, misleading, fallacious, artful, tricky, meretricious, apocryphal, fraudulent.

3. Treacherous, traitorous, perfidious, falsehearted, perjured, forsworn, faithless, unfaithful, disingenuous, dishonest, two-faced, dougle-tongued, canting, pharisaical, tartuffish, hypocritical, affected, insincere, inconstant, recreant, disloyal, dishonorable, Machiavellian, double-dealing, cunning, wily, sly, yellow *(colloq.).*

4. Uttering what is untrue, lying, fibbing, mendacious, fabricative, untruthful, contrary to truth, unveracious, unauthentic.

5. Not genuine, spurious, factitious, artificial, sham, theatrical, make-believe, feigned, pretended, flash, hollow, pseudo, supposititious, bogus, bastard, counterfeit, forged, made-up, fictitious, falsified, mythological.

FALSEHOOD, *n.* 1. Lack of conformity to truth, nonconformity to fact, falseness, falsity, inveracity, untruthfulness, inaccuracy, falsification, deceptiveness, dishonesty, error.

2. Act of lying, mendacity, mendaciousness, prevarication, false swearing, perjury, equivocation, mental reservation, deliberate suppression of truth to deceive, concealment, malingering, perversion, misstatement, misrepresentation, evasion, dissimulation, dissembling, deceit, guile, false coloring, exaggeration, distortion.

3. False statement, lie, fib, untruth, fabrication, fiction, canard.

4. Casuistry, Pharisaism, cant, hypocristy, duplicity, lip-service, cajolery, flattery, mealy-mouthedness, insincerity, perfidy, bad faith, double-dealing, two-facedness, Judas kiss, cunning, buncombe.

5. Imposture, forgery, invention, counterfeit, simulation, pretense, sham, hollowness, mere

show, quackery, humbug, charlatanism, flimflam, fraud, artifice.

FALSETTO, *n.* Artificially high-pitched voice, head voice, *voce di testa (It.),* unnatural register, childish treble, squeak.

FALSIFY, *v.* 1. Make false so as to deceive, alter fraudulently, represent falsely, misrepresent, pervert, distort, exaggerate, embroider, doctor, color, varnish, dress up, garble, gloss over, adulterate, fake, disguise, pass off for, counterfeit, coin, forge, trump up, hatch, spin, concoct, invent, sham, malinger, dissimulate, cook up, belie.
2. Lie, fib, prevaricate, tell falsehoods, make false statements, fabricate, misstate, misquote, misinterpret, equivocate, bear false witness, forswear, perjure oneself.
3. Show to be false, disprove, prove unsound, refute, confute, rebut, oppose by contrary proof.

FALTER, *v.* 1. Hesitate in speaking, stammer, stutter, hem and haw, splutter, speak brokenly, pause, halt, lisp.
2. Become unsteady in movement, stagger, dodder, teeter, stumble, hitch, limp, shamble, totter, tremble, fail, flag, hobble, reel, toddle, mince.
3. Waver, hesitate, vacillate, fluctuate, be undecided, blow hot and cold, demur, debate, balance, hover, dilly-dally, shilly-shally, be irresolute, give way, remain neuter, show weakness, be afraid, shuffle, straddle, palter, alternate, shirk, quail, flinch, recoil, hang back, lag, delay, be infirm.

FAME, *n.* 1. Widespread favorable reputation, repute, public esteem, kudos, prestige, celebrity, notability, éclat, vogue, popularity, *aura popularis (Lat.),* illustriousness, glory, renown, mark, name, figure, account, regard, high respect, eminence, prominence, rank, standing, preëminence, honor, luster, greatness, distinction, note, notoriety, estimation, laurels, one's hour in the sun, a walk into the pages of history.
2. Report generally diffused, hearsay, rumor, bruit, gossip, talk of the town.

FAMILIAR, *adj.* 1. Having an intimate knowledge of, well acquainted, well versed, thoroughly conversant, informed of, cognizant of, aware, experienced, *au fait (Fr.),* no stranger to, conscious of, apprised of, at home in, proficient, seasoned, habitué.
2. Closely intimate, close, confidential, thick, near, bosom, hand in hand with, hand and glove, cozy.
3. On a friendly footing, on friendly terms, brotherly, fraternal, neighborly, sociable, amicable, affable, genial, clubby, chatty, accessible, kindly, civil, polite, courteous, conversable, companionable, complaisant, jovial, hospitable, convivial, gracious, suave.
4. Informal, unceremonious, unconventional, free and easy, unconstrained, *dégagé (Fr.),* quite at home, unreserved, careless, slack, Bohemian, at ease, on visiting terms, hail fellow well met.
5. Unduly intimate, taking liberties, too free, forward, lacking in proper reserve, disrespectful, deficient in due respect, impudent, bold, presuming, intrusive.
6. Well-known, generally seen, frequent, common, habitual, accustomed, customary, traditional, every-day, homely, domestic, hackneyed, commonplace, trite, usual, ordinary, wonted, general, household, banal, bromidic, stereotyped, cliché,

conventional, stock, well-trodden, received, accepted, current, vernacular, colloquial.

FAMILIAR, *n.* 1. Intimate friend, bosom friend, boon companion, best friend, close acquaintance, fidus Achates, pal, crony, chum, buddy, bunkie, mate, side-kick, shadow, bedfellow, other self, alter ego, confidant.
2. Familiar spirit, tutelary genius, tutelar, demiurge, demon at call.

FAMILIARITY, *n.* 1. Thorough knowledge, close acquaintance, experience, familiar association, cognition, comprehension, apperception, insight, privity, ken, information.
2. Friendship, amity, fellowship, intimacy, sodality, brotherhood, fraternity, neighborliness, brotherliness, fellow feeling, companionship.
3. Sociableness, sociability, friendliness, affability, conversance, kindliness, good will, benevolence, sociality, intercourse, agreeableness, courtesy.
4. Absence of ceremony, informality, unconstraint, unreserve, ease, naturalness, freedom, liberty, frankness, candor, openness.
5. Undue intimacy, excessive freedom of behavior, undue liberty, overfamiliarity, impropriety, indecorum, unseemliness, impudence, impertinence, presumption, disrespect.

FAMILIARIZE, *v.* 1. Habituate, accustom, season, harden, caseharden, inure, make used to, train, acclimatize, naturalize, initiate.
2. Make conversant, make familiarly acquainted, indoctrinate, teach, inform, instruct, edify, school, tutor, prime, coach, enlighten, inculcate, discipline, educate, nurture.
3. Make well known, bring into common knowledge, give a familiar form to, divest of strangeness.
4. Establish in friendly intimacy, make to feel at ease with.

FAMILY, *n.* 1. Parents and children, household, menage, brood, people *(coll.),* domestic circle.
2. Kinsmen, next to kin, relatives, relation, kinsfolk, kith and kin, group of persons closely related by blood, kindred, folk.
3. Progeny, issue, posterity, offspring, descendants from a common progenitor, generation.
4. Extraction, ancestry, parentage, lineage, forebears, forefathers, paternity, family tree, pedigree, stirps, stem, trunk, genealogy, descent, birth, line, house, dynasty, tribe, race, clan, breed, stock, strain, blood.
5. Major subdivision of an order, class, genus, group of genera, kind, order.

FAMINE, *n.* 1. General scarcity of food, starvation, extreme hunger, famishment, meager diet, half rations, xerophagy.
2. Dearth, insufficiency, want, need, deficiency, lack, shortage, paucity, inanition, stint, meagerness, scantiness, depletion, emptiness, exhaustion, destitution, indigence, poverty, rareness, infrequency, exigency, necessity, short allowance, none to spare, bare subsistence.

FAMISH, *v.* 1. Cause to suffer extreme hunger, starve, destroy with hunger, distress with hunger, exhaust by hunger, deprive of nutriment, pinch, stint, skimp, gripe, dole out, hold back, withhold.
2. Starve to death, perish with hunger, die of hunger, perish for lack of food.
3. Be distressed by hunger, fast, be distressed by hunger pangs, dine with Duke Humphrey, live upon nothing.

FAMOUS, *adj.* 1. Celebrated in public report, renowned, well-known, far-famed, noted, eminent, distinguished, *distingué (Fr.),* illustrious, prominent, notable, eximious, conspicuous, remarkable, immortal, great, historical, fabled, legendary, heroic, brilliant, glorious, memorable, noble, lustrous, grand, notorious, egregious.
2. *(Colloq.)* First-rate, excellent, signal, transcendent, surpassing, splendid.

FAN, *v.* 1. Cause air to blow upon, cool with a fan, ventilate, infrigidate, aerate, use a fan upon, refresh with a fan, stir up a breeze.
2. Agitate, beat gently, move, stir to activity, stimulate, excite, stir up, rouse, fire, enkindle, foment, provoke, encourage.
3. Spread out, fan out, deploy, unfurl, unfold, shake out.

FAN, *n.* 1. Devotee, enthusiast, votary, ardent admirer, lover of, champion, booster, follower, adherent, *aficionado (Sp.),* bobby soxer.
2. Instrument for producing artificial current of air, flabellum, palm leaf, punkah *(India),* blower, thermantidote, colmar.

FANATIC, *n.* Person affected by excessive enthusiasm, unreasoning enthusiast, partisan, zealot, *exalté (Fr.),* devotee, votary, sectarian, bigot, visionary, extremist, radical, die-hard.

FANATICAL, *adj.* Actuated by unreasoning zeal, excessively enthusiastic, hipped *(colloq.),* impassioned, zealous, glowing, ardent, burning, fiery, fervent, rabid, frenzied, raving, mad, wild, feverish, vehement, violent, hot-headed, uncompromising, biased, prejudiced, narrow-minded, dogmatical, partisan, extreme, radical, unreasonable, partial, overzealous, infatuated, ultra, hysterical, intolerant, stubborn, obstinate, extravagant, visionary, superstitious.

FANATICISM, *n.* Unreasoning zeal, excessive enthusiasm, ruling passion, fixed idea, blind side, monomania, bigotry, zealotry, opinionativeness, dogmatism, prejudice, bias, narrow-mindedness, partiality, infatuation, intemperate belief, credulity, intolerance, unfairness, wild and extravagant notions, insanity, frenzy.

FANCIFUL, *adj.* 1. Guided by fancy rather than by reason, imaginative, visionary, quixotic, original, inventive, creative, poetic, romantic, impracticable, extravagant, capricious, whimsical, crotchety, eccentric, flighty, erratic, dreamy, unstable.
2. Exhibiting fancy, imaginary, unreal, chimerical, fantastic, baroque, grotesque, rococo, bizarre, outlandish, odd, quaint, curious, queer, strange, freakish.

FANCY, *n.* 1. Invention of the imaginary and fantastic, imagination exercised in a whimsical mood, capricious creation, fantasy, faculty of creating decorative imagery.
2. Generic image, eidolon, mental image, striking thought, pleasing conceit, bright stroke, happy conception.
3. Opinion with little foundation, hallucination, phantasy, daydream, vision, reverie, illusion, chimera, mirage, apparition.
4. Whim, caprice, megrim, vagary, humor, whimsy, odd fancy, notion, quirk, crotchet, freak, kink, maggot, frolic, escapade, prank, trick.
5. Thought, idea, impression, concept, supposition, surmise, conception, notion, sentiment, observation, apprehension, perception, conjecture.
6. Liking, penchant, inclination, proclivity, propensity, leaning, bent, partiality, fondness, yearning, capricious preference, desire, longing, hankering, predilection, wish, taste, relish, approval, esteem.
7. Hobby, fad, passing fancy, craze, mania, rage.

FANCY, *adj.* 1. Adapted to please the taste, of superfine quality, de luxe, custom, special, unusual, distinctive, of particular excellence, specially selected, superior to the average.
2. Ornamental, elegant, showy, ostentatious, ornate, florid, elaborate, intricately wrought, rococo, baroque, gingerbread.
3. Imaginative, chimerical, quixotic, grotesque, notional, fantastic, cloud-built, visionary, unreal, fictitious, fabulous, mythical.
4. Depending on caprice, capricious, whimsical, crotchety, quaint, freakish, irregular, eccentric.
5. Beyond all real worth, exorbitant, extravagant, high-priced, sumptuous.

FANCY, *v.* 1. Picture to oneself, imagine, conceive, dream, create a conception of.
2. Believe without being sure, ween, suspect, surmise, suppose, think, comprehend, apprehend, presume, be inclined to think, assume, accept, opine, judge, conjecture, deem, take it, hold.
3. Take a liking to, experience love for, take to, be pleased with, have an eye to, like, be bent upon, have a mind to, have a fancy for, covet, crave, hanker after, yearn for, long for, relish, enjoy, **love.**

FANE, *n.* Place of worship, holy place, temple, church, sanctuary, shrine, sacrarium, sanctum, sanctum sanctorum, inner sanctum, altar, Holy of Holies.

FANFARE, *n.* 1. Flourish of trumpets, trumpet blast, tintamarre, blare, blast, peal, alarum.
2. Showy outward display, flourish, ostentatious parade, noisy demonstration, charivari, colors flying, illuminations, fireworks, *feu d'artifice (Fr.).*

FANFARON, *n.* 1. Bully, brawler, roisterer, blusterer, hector, brazen-face, terrorist, roughneck, hooligan, hoodlum, ruffian.
2. Empty boaster, braggadocio, braggart, windbag, blowhard, hot air merchant, swaggerer, vaporer, vain pretender, blatherskite, Gascon, Bombastes Furioso, Thraso, Parolles, fourflusher, *soi-disant (Fr.),* swashbuckler.

FANFARONADE, *n.* 1. Bluster, bravado, rant, swaggering, highfalutin, puffery, bragging, flourish, braggardism, braggadocio, gasconade, hectoring, bullying, swashbuckling.
2. Ostentation, vain pretense, vaporing, bluff, swank, bombast, empty boasting, fanfare, buncombe, fine talking, tall talk, magniloquence, heroics, much cry and little wool.

FANG, *n.* 1. Venom-ejecting tooth, pointed tooth, tusk, canine tooth, poison tooth, stinger.
2. Talon, claw, nail, point.

FANTASIA, *n.* 1. Musical composition in fanciful irregular form, roulade, rhapsody, fantastical air, capriccio.
2. Phantasmagoria, fantasy.

FANTASTIC, *adj.* 1. Capricious, whimsical, grotesque, bizarre, queer, odd, quaint, mad, freakish, eccentric, wild, strange, erratic, giddy, quixotic, fitful, absurd, ridiculous, ludicrous, irrational, antic, crotchety, peculiar, outlandish.
2. Imaginary, visionary, chimerical, not real, romantic, merely ideal, groundless, pie-in-the-sky,

impractical, illusive, illusory, far-fetched, extravagant, unsubstantial, uncommon.

3. Tawdry, ostentatious, showy, rococo, baroque.

FANTASY, *n.* 1. Unrestrained imagination, fiction, forming of grotesque mental images, mental prepossession, visionary idea, supposition based on no solid foundation.

2. Grotesque mental image, hallucination, illusion, chimera, mirage, will-o'-the-wisp, *ignis fatuus (Lat.),* vision, dream, phantasm, apparition, phantom, unreality, daydream, imaginative sequence fulfilling a psychological need.

3. Capricious mood, caprice, whim, vapor, vagary, freak, conceit, notion, humor.

FAR, *adj.* 1. At a great distance, remote, distant, far-away, far-off, not near, way off, yon, yonder, utmost, uttermost.

2. More distant of two, remoter, farther, ulterior.

3. Inaccessible, unapproachable, out of the way, extreme, transatlantic, transalpine, ultramundane, antipodean.

4. Widely different, apart, asunder, separated, alienated, estranged, hostile.

FAR, *adv.* 1. At a great distance, to a remote point, a long way off, remotely, afar, far off, far away, beyond range, wide of, clear of, distantly, widely, abroad, yonder, over the hills and far away, to the ends of the earth, from pole to pole.

2. To a great degree, very much, greatly, transcendently, incomparably, immeasurably.

3. Well-nigh, almost, mostly, in great part.

FARCE, *n.* 1. Light dramatic composition of satirical cast, burlesque, parody, travesty, caricature, mime, pantomime, dumb-show, amphigory, harlequinade, low comedy, after-piece, play light in tone, extravaganza, take off.

2. Buffoonery, tomfoolery, ridiculousness, drollery, *boutade (Fr.),* absurdity, nonsense, *bêtise (Fr.).*

3. Mockery, empty parade, ridiculous pageantry, ridiculous sham, open pretense.

FARCICAL, *adj.* Ridiculous, nonsensical, ludicrous, absurd, droll, laughable, comical, derisible, amusing, funny, risible, facetious, waggish, witty, burlesque, asinine, silly, inane, amphigoric, foolish, senseless, preposterous, grotesque, curious, strange, queer, odd.

FARE, *v.* 1. Be entertained with food and drink, feed, partake of food, eat, devour, swallow, take, fall to, tuck in, gormandize, feast upon, do justice to, banquet.

2. Journey, travel, go forth.

3. Experience good or bad fortune, be situated with respect to what may befall, get on, go through an experience, prosper, turn out, happen, be in any state, be treated, thrive.

FARE, *n.* 1. Price of passage, cost of conveyance, price of a ticket, passage money, charge, expense of transportation, hire.

2. Something that nourishes, food, victuals, comestibles, provisions, commons, food and drink, viands, regimen, diet, board, table, aliment.

3. State of things, condition, outcome, fortune, luck, experience.

FAREWELL, *interj.* May you fare well! Godspeed! good-by! adieu! adios! addio! vale! vive valeque! leb' wohl! au revoir! a rivederci! hasta la vista! auf Wiedersehen! bon voyage! bye-bye! glückliche Reise! sayonara! so long!

FAREWELL, *n.* 1. Parting compliment, valediction, valedictory, expression of good wishes at parting, swan song, dismissal, send-off.

2. Departure, leave-taking, parting, congé, setting out, furlough, last look, embarkation, sailing.

FAR-FETCHED, *adj.* From a remote place, remotely connected, forced, strained, abstruse, recondite, studiously sought, quaint, recherché, catachrestic, strange, fantastic.

FARINA, *n.* Meal made from cereal grains, flour, bran, starch, spore, sporule, powdery substance.

FARINACEOUS, *adj.* Made of flour, consisting of meal, containing starch, starchy, mealy in nature, like meal, granular, floury, branny, furfuraceous, powdery, pulverulent, flocculent.

FARM, *n.* 1. Tract of land devoted to agriculture, land used for cultivation, landed estate, plantation, ranch, farmstead, grange, barton, croft, hacienda, estancia, countryseat.

2. Farmhouse, barn, stable, byre, cow shed.

3. System of collecting revenue by letting out a territory in districts, process of farming out taxes.

FARM, *v.* 1. Cultivate land, till soil, do farmer's work, practice husbandry, engage in agronomy, garden, sow, seed, plant, grow, reap, mow, cut, harvest, manure, dress the ground, produce crops, plow, hoe, harrow, rake, weed.

2. Let out for a fixed sum, contract for the maintenance and care of at a fixed price, take on lease.

FARMER, *n.* 1. Agriculturist, agrarian, tiller of the soil, cultivator of land, guardian of the soil, husbandman, landsman, yeoman, agronomist, farm operator, granger, gardener, horticulturist, hardy son of toil, agricultural laborer, rustic, peasant, countryman, hayseed *(colloq.),* rube *(colloq.).*

2. One who undertakes some service at a fixed price, tax-gatherer, publican, lessee of taxes, collector, one who leases a government monopoly, one who agrees to perform certain duties for a fixed sum.

FARMING, *n.* 1. Business of operating a farm, husbandry, agriculture, geoponics, agronomy, agronomics, soil culture, tillage, cultivation, gardening.

2. Letting out taxes for collection, business of collecting taxes.

FARRAGO, *n.* Confused mixture, mélange, medley, jumble, hodgepodge, gallimaufry, salmagundi, potpourri, ollapodrida, mishmash, miscellany, mulligatawny, goulash, stew.

FARRIER, *n.* 1. Blacksmith who shoes horses, horseshoer, non-commissioned officer of mounted troops responsible for the shoeing of horses.

2. Veterinary surgeon, veterinarian, vet, horse-doctor.

FAR-SIGHTED, *adj.* 1. Seeing to a great distance, seeing objects at a distance more clearly than those near at hand, hypermetropic, presbyopic, long-sighted.

2. Foreseeing future results wisely, of great foresight, foresighted, seeing to remote consequences, far-seeing, of good judgment, provident, prudent, anticipatory, watchful, discreet, judicious, prescient, shrewd, sagacious, thoughtful, sensible, acute.

FARTHER, *adv.* 1. Further, more remotely, to a greater distance, beyond, past, at a greater distance.

2. Furthermore, moreover, besides, in addition, additionally, more completely.

FARTHER, *adj.* 1. More remote, at a greater distance, beyond, more distant, ulterior, further, remoter, more extensive, beyond the present point, extending to a greater distance.

2. Further, additional, more detailed, more complete.

FARTHEST, *adj.* Furthest, most distant, farthermost, most remote, remotest, ultimate, final, utmost, last, most advanced, uttermost, extreme, longest, most extended.

FARTHINGALE, *n.* Framework for expanding a woman's skirt, hoop used to extend a petticoat, crinoline, hoop skirt.

FASCIA, *n.* Band, fillet, sash, belt, sheath, bandage *(Surg.).*

FASCICLE, *n.* 1. Small bundle, bunch, cluster, group, small collection.

2. One of the divisions of a book published in parts, number of printed sheets bound together, part of a printed work, fasciculus.

FASCINATE, *v.* Attract and hold irresistibly by delightful qualities, captivate, ravish, enchant, charm, entrance, enrapture, transport, enamor, enravish, allure, bewitch, delight, grip the attention of, hold spellbound, spellbind, transfix, overpower, infatuate, engross, engage, absorb, win over, rivet, deprive of the power of resistance.

FASCINATION, *n.* Irresistibly charming influence, powerful attraction, attractiveness, pleasurableness, invitingness, winning ways, enchantment, entrancement, captivation, absorption, allurement, bewitchery, enravishment, blandishment, seduction, spell, charm, witchery, glamor, infatuation.

FASCISM, *n.* Strongly centralized government permitting no opposition or criticism, aggressively nationalistic government, totalitarianism, Hitlerism.

FASCIST, *n.* Advocate of fascism, black shirt, silver shirt, Bundist.

FASHION, *n.* 1. Prevailing style of dress, custom as respects dress.

2. Fashionable people *(collectively),* people of fashion, *monde (Fr.),* the *beau monde (Fr.),* good society, high life, élite, smart set, silk-stockinged set, silk-stockings, gentry, upper ten thousand, four hundred, Vanity Fair, Mayfair, Park Avenue, F. F. V.'s, bon ton.

3. Prevailing taste, conventional usage, style, mode, conventionality, general practice, conventionalism, usage.

4. Vogue, fad, the latest thing, the go, taste, the craze, the rage, all the go, *haut ton (Fr.), dernier cri (Fr.),* ton, *haute couture (Fr.).*

5. Etiquette, manners, politeness, gentility, breeding, savoir-faire, decorum, propriety, ceremony, *bienséance (Fr.),* protocol, Mrs. Grundy, Lord Chesterfield, punctilio, formality.

6. Appearance, guise, trim, shape, form, figure, configuration, conformation, pattern, mold, stamp, model, cast, cut.

7. Manner, way, mode of action, behavior, demeanor. attitude, air, wise, tenor.

FASHION, *v.* 1. Give a particular shape to, shape, form. frame, construct, pattern, mold, design, contrive, compose, create, make, give figure to, execute, devise, originate, forge, produce, invent, fabricate, carve, cut out. turn, hew, mint.

2. Accommodate, adapt, adjust, fit. suit.

FASHIONABLE, *adj.* 1. In accordance with prevailing fashion, in vogue, in fashion, à la mode, stylish, smart, chic, modish, all the go, all the rage, elegant.

2. Observant of fashion, conforming to fashion, punctilious, decorous, conventional, *comme il faut (Fr.),* meticulous, proper.

3. Genteel, polished, refined, polite, self-possessed, poised, easy, *dégagé (Fr.),* well-bred, thoroughbred, high-bred, blue-blooded, silkstockinged, courtly, *distingué (Fr.),* aristocratic, gentlemanly, ladylike, urbane, suave, cosmopolitan, continental, international.

4. Customary, prevailing, usual, current, popular, approved, accepted.

FAST, *n.* 1. Abstinence from food, fasting, religious limiting of food, famishment, starvation, meager diet, xerophagy, short commons, Bantingism, hunger strike, diet.

2. Fast day, day of fasting, *jour maigre (Fr.),* period of fasting, banyan day, Lent, quadragesima.

FAST, *v.* 1. Abstain from food, practice abstinence as a religious exercise, abstain from meat, go without food, go hungry, forbear eating, starve, famish.

2. Diet, restrict one's diet by eating sparingly, eat only sparingly.

FAST, *adv.* 1. Tightly, tenaciously, firmly, securely, closely, soundly, fixedly, immovably.

2. Rapidly, quickly, swiftly, speedily, in quick succession, hastily, posthaste, readily, expeditiously.

3. In a dissipated way, dissolutely, profligately, prodigally, extravagantly, loosely, wildly, recklessly.

FAST, *adj.* 1. Characterized by quick motion, taking a comparatively short time, quick, swift, rapid, fleet, speedy, agile, expeditious, express, nimble, light-footed, brisk, nimble-footed, active, flying, winged, hasty, hurried, precipitate, accelerated, spry.

2. Extremely active in pursuing pleasures immoderately, dissipated, wild, dissolute, thriftless, extravagant, reckless, giddy, profligate, immoral, loose, voluptuous, self-indulgent, lax, intemperate, orgiastic, wanton, crapulous, drunken, sottish, gluttonous, rakish, Sybaritical, gross, carnal, salacious, concupiscent, lecherous, lustful, sensual, fleshly, animal, lewd, lascivious, licentious, libidinous.

3. Firmly fixed in place, not easily moved, securely attached, firm, secure, fastened, stationary, adhesive, firmly tied, taut, inseparable, immovable, indissoluble, tenacious, rigid.

4. Firm in adherence, loyal, steadfast, constant, stanch, faithful, reliable, stable, unwavering, unswerving, resolute, permanent, abiding, steady, enduring, lasting, durable, true.

5. Fortified, resistant, impregnable, impervious, inexpugnable, strong, invulnerable, invincible, sure, solid, ineradicable.

6. Not easily disturbed, deep, sound, profound.

7. Deceptive, insincere, inconstant, unreliable.

FASTEN, *v.* 1. Fix firmly in a given position, hold fixed, hold immovable, take a firm grip with, secure, attach, make fast, make secure, tie, tether, bind, restrain, enchain, trammel, manacle, handcuff, hobble, lock, link, gird, clamp, rivet, bolt, chain, pinion, pin, nail, screw, bolt, lace, cleat, strap, hasp, clinch, clasp, hook, moor, affix, sew, stitch, knit, button, buckle, hitch, truss, lash, splice, yoke, couple, bracket, picket, barricade, peg, spike, muzzle, rope, tag, anchor.

2. Associate, put together, unite, hold together, connect, join, solder, cement, weld, fuse, mortise, miter, dovetail, ingraft, dowel, skewer, cotter.

3. Take firm hold, seize, clutch, catch hold, cling, cleave, fix oneself.

FASTENING, *n.* Something that fastens, vinculum, nexus, catch, clasp, bond, chain, latchet, latch, tether, lock, padlock, spring hook, snap hook, snap, clip, tie, clinch, clamp, holdfast, lace, hook and eye, rivet, staple, ring, buckle, bolt, bar, link, shackle, coupler, coupling, copula, yoke, tack, nail, pin, dowel, tholepin, peg, spike, cleat.

FASTIDIOUS, *adj.* 1. Hard to please, difficult, excessively critical, finical, fussy, pernickety, particular, meticulous, precise, finicking, exacting, scrupulous, querulous, squeamish, queasy, disdainful, gingerly, punctilious, proper, priggish, prim, prudish, strait-laced, thin-skinned, hypercritical.

2. Delicate, exquisite, overrefined, dainty, precious, nice, niminy-piminy, prunes-and-prisms, *précieuse (Fr.),* overnice, overdelicate, fine, elegant, effeminate, dandified, silk-stockinged, dapper, dudish.

3. Discerning, discriminative, judicious, astute, keen, sharp, subtle, perspicacious, sagacious.

FASTNESS, *n.* 1. Secure place, fortress, fort, stronghold, fortfied place, castle, capitol, stockade, donjon, tower, barracoon, blockhouse, turret, barbette, redoubt, redan, citadel, refuge, retreat, asylum, ark, acropolis, arx, keep, last resort, sanctuary.

2. State of being fixed, firmness, fixedness, immovability.

3. Quickness, expeditiousness, expedition, celerity, swiftness, rapidity, haste, speed, light-footedness.

4. Quality of being dissipated in behavior, dissoluteness, profligacy, dissipatedness, immorality, wantonness.

FAT, *adj.* 1. Having much flesh other than muscle, corpulent, obese, stout, plump, thickset, stocky, fleshy, portly, chubby, bulky in figure, heavily-built, heavy, pudgy, squab, well-fed, pursy, paunchy, pot-bellied, upholstered in suet, lumpish, beefy, bouncing, amplitudinous, thick-waisted, hulking, elephantine, gigantic, Gargantuan, burly.

2. Containing fat, fatty, oleaginous, sebaceous, adipose, greasy, unctuous, oily, butyraceous, pinguid, lardaceous, soapy, saponaceous, blubbery, tallowy, suety.

3. Gross, sluggish, heavy, dull, slow-witted, obtuse, stupid, thick-headed.

4. Lucrative, remunerative, profitable, rewarding, fortunate, prosperous, rich, opulent, affluent, thriving, palmy, luxuriant, affording good opportunities, productive, fruitful, fertile.

5. Well-stocked, plentiful, plenteous, replete, copious, abundant, chock-full, flush, well-furnished.

FATAL, *adj.* 1. Causing death, deadly, lethal, lethiferous, mortal, tragic, internecine, suicidal, homicidal, murderous.

2. Causing destruction, destructive, involving ruin, ruinous, disastrous, dire, calamitous, catastrophic, cataclysmic, pestilential, pestiferous,

pernicious, baleful, baneful, harmful, injurious, malignant, poisonous.

3. Decisively important, fateful, critical, crucial, ominous.

4. Decreed by fate, inevitable, inescapable, ineluctable.

FATALISM, *n.* 1. Belief that all events are subject to inevitable predetermination, doctrine that all things are subject to fate, determinism, necessarianism, destinism, necessitarianism, predestination, inexorable necessity, dictates of Providence.

2. Submission to fate, acceptance of all events as inevitable, passive resignation, stoicism.

FATALITY, *n.* 1. Disaster resulting in death, casualty, calamity, misfortune, mishap.

2. Quality of causing death, fatal influence, deadliness, mortality.

3. Condition of being destined to disaster, predetermined liability to disaster.

4. Unalterably predetermined course of things, destiny, fate, kismet, foredoom, predestination, preordination, foreordination, inevitable necessity.

FATE, *n.* 1. Predestination, predetermination, destination, inevitable necessity, destiny, prophetic declaration of what must be, fixed sentence by which the order of things is prescribed, that which is inevitably predetermined, kismet, no choice, stacking of the deck.

2. Lot, doom, die, cup, wheel of fortune, portion, predetermined event, weird experience, dispensation, God's will, will of heaven, stars, planets, astral influence, book of fate.

3. Disaster, downfall, debacle, ruin, ruination, destruction, death, knockout, finish, sentence, end, curtain.

4. Ultimate fortune, future, hereafter, future state, next world, world to come, prospect, expectation.

FATED, *adj.* 1. Predetermined by fate, preordained, predestinated, predestined, foredoomed, doomed.

2. Appointed, chosen, set apart, destined, elect, devoted.

FATEFUL, *adj.* 1. Involving momentous consequences, momentous, decisive, decisively important, crucial, critical.

2. Fatal, deadly, disastrous, destructive, ruinous, lethal.

3. Prophetic, ominous, portentous, fatidic.

FATES, *n.* Three goddesses of destiny, Destinies, Three Sisters, Weird Sisters, Parcae, Moerae, Norns, Clotho (spinner of the thread of life), Lachesis (measurer of it), Atropos (cutter of it).

FAT-HEADED, *adj.* Stupid, thick-witted, dull, heavy, obtuse, crass, insulse, blunt, stolid, blockish, bovine, Boeotian, doltish, asinine.

FATHER, *n.* 1. Male parent, pater, paterfamilias, sire, *père (Fr.), Vater (Ger.),* dad, papa, pop *(slang),* old man *(colloq.),* governor *(colloq.),* daddy.

2. Founder of a race or line, male ancestor, progenitor, forefather, patriarch, elder.

3. Maker, begetter, procreator, creator, author, originator, inventor, founder.

4. Supreme Being, Creator, God, the First Person in the Trinity.

5. Priest, abbé, curé, padre, pastor, cleric, shepherd, parson, confessor, dignitary of the church, superior of a monastic house.

6. One who exercises paternal care over another, fatherly provider, patron.

7. Oldest or presiding member of an associated group, leading man of a town or council, one to whom filial respect is due.

FATHER, *v.* 1. Beget, sire, engender, procreate, generate, reproduce, propagate, proliferate.
2. Charge with the begetting of, name the father of, trace the source of.
3. Treat as a father, look after, care for, provide for.
4. Act as a father toward, become a moral father to, adopt, asume as one's own, take the responsibility of.
5. Originate, be the author of, acknowledge.

FATHERHOOD, *n.* Paternity, fathership, progenitorship, parentage, paternal headship.

FATHERLAND, *n.* One's native country, native land, mother country, native soil, natal place, home, country, blighty *(Brit. slang)*.

FATHERLY, *adj.* Like a father, befitting a father, full of natural affection, paternal, parental, kind, kindly, beneficent, tender, benign, affectionate, protective, shielding, sheltering, forbearing, indulgent, obliging, benevolent, well-meaning, sympathetic, proprietary.

FATHOM, *n.* Nautical unit of length equal to six feet, two yards.

FATHOM, *v.* 1. Reach in depth by measurement in fathoms, sound, measure by a sounding-line, take soundings, plumb, measure the depth of by sounding, penetrate to the bottom of, find the extent of, try the depth of.
2. Understand thoroughly, comprehend, divine, penetrate, probe, hunt out, get to the bottom of, bring out, draw out, ferret out, root out, hunt out, fish out, worm out, make sure of.

FATHOMLESS, *adj.* Impossible to fathom, soundless, bottomless, measureless, profound, abysmal, immeasurable, unfathomable, deep as a well, deep-sea, impenetrable, obscure, incomprehensible.

FATIDICAL, *adj.* Prophetic, oracular, Sibylline, Delphic, predictive, vaticinatory, vaticinal, fatidic, prescient, haruspical, extispicious, clairvoyant.

FATIGUE, *n.* 1. Weariness from exertion, tiredness, lassitude, exhaustion, fatigation, debilitation.
2. Ennui, boredom, tedium, enervation, languor, heaviness, yawning, drowsiness.
3. Cause of weariness, labor, exertion, toil, drudgery, hardship, strain, vexation, trouble.

FATIGUE, *v.* Weary with exertion, exhaust the strength of, tire, fag, tucker, jade, prostrate, wear out, suck dry, defatigate, harass, irk.

FATNESS, *n.* 1. Corpulence, obesity, plumpness, stoutness, stockiness, fleshiness, portliness, pudginess, pursiness.
2. Oiliness, greasiness, oleaginousness, sebaceousness.
3. Richness, fertility, productivity, fecundity, prolificness.

FATTEN, *v.* 1. Make fat, expand, distend, cram, bloat, feed for slaughter.
2. Grow fat, batten, grow obese.
3. Make fertile, fertilize, enrich, mellow.

FATTY, *adj.* Containing fat, oleaginous, adipose, oily, greasy, unctuous, tallowy, lardaceous, blubbery, suety.

FATUITY, *n.* 1. Want of intelligence, complacent stupidity, clouded perception, vacancy of mind, feebleness of intellect, lack of understanding, desipience, stupidity, hebetude, foolishness, idiocy, imbecility, nugacity, ineptitude, irrationality.
2. Something foolish, frivolity, folly, utter absurdity, madness, infatuation, trifling, silliness.

FATUOUS, *adj.* 1. Vacant in mind, foolish in a complacently unconscious manner, stupid, brainless, idiotic, witless, dull, asinine, silly, driveling, obtuse, deranged, irrational, imprudent.
2. Ridiculous, nonsensical, absurd, senseless, infatuated, puerile.
3. Illusory, unreal, deceptive as the *ignis fatus*.

FAT-WITTED, *adj.* Stupid, heavy, insulse, dull-witted, brainless, shallow, *borné (Fr.)*, obtuse, not bright, unteachable, blockish, Boeotian, weak-minded, doltish, rattle-brained, addle-pated, thick-skulled, sottish, vacant, asinine, stolid.

FAUBOURG, *n.* Part of a city outside of the walls, suburb, outskirts, purlieu, precinct, *environs (Fr.), banlieue (Fr.)*.

FAUCET, *n.* Device for controlling the flow of liquid from a pipe, spigot, stopcock, cock, tap.

FAULT, *n.* 1. Imperfection, blemish, defect, flaw, spot, taint, stain.
2. Want of principle, weakness, infirmity, weak point, foible, failing, frailty.
3. Moral shortcoming, wrongdoing, evil doing, misdeed, offense, misdemeanor, besetting sin, dereliction, delinquency, wrong, vice, transgression, peccadillo, indiscretion, misconduct.
4. Mistake of judgment, error, negligence, oversight, nonobservance, slip, lapse, cause for blame, culpability, blunder, demerit, omission.

FAULTFINDER, *n.* One who complains, objector, critic, censor, censurer, reprover, detractor, castigator, disapprover, murmurer, repiner, cynic, caviler, carper, word catcher, knocker, lampooner, calumniator, defamer, slanderer, daw plucker, grumbler, snarler, *laudator temporis acti (Lat.)*, Thersites, Zoilus.

FAULTFINDING, *adj.* Disposed to complain, prone to object, hypercritical, disapproving, complaining, grumbling, carping, captious, censorious, critical, discontented, malcontent, murmuring, repining, querulous, caviling, dissatisfied, touchy, contentious, disparaging, derogatory, depreciatory, satirical, sarcastic, sharp, cutting, biting, withering, caustic, trenchant, abusive, calumniatory, reproachful, condemnatory, denunciatory.

FAULTLESS, *adj.* 1. Free from imperfection, in perfect condition, free from defect, perfect, scathless, without blemish, intact, whole, flawless, without fault, ideal, finished, complete in itself.
2. Virtuous, undefiled, innocent, pure, dove-like, lamb-like, sinless, chaste, stainless, immaculate, impeccable, irreproachable, blameless, unimpeachable, guiltless, unblemished, spotless, unspotted, inculpable, above suspicion.

FAULTY, *adj.* 1. Defective, imperfect, unsound, out of order, injured, impaired, warped, awry, amiss, peccable, wrong, incorrect, inaccurate, inexact, untrue, mistaken, false, erroneous, unreliable, unsatisfactory, improper, perverse, bad.
2. Insufficient, deficient, short, partial, scanty, limited, inadequate, unsuitable, below par, second-rate, inferior.
3. Morally blamable, vicious, corrupt, blameworthy, culpable, reprehensible, censurable, obnoxious, transgressive.

FAUN, *n.* Rural god represented as having the ears, horns, tail and hind legs of a goat, woodland deity, sylvan sprite, satyr.

FAUX PAS (*Fr.*) False step, misstep, wrong step, trip, stumble, error, fault, omission, miss, oversight, blunder, bull, boner, indiscretion, mistake in conduct, misconduct, misdeed, peccadillo, offense, transgression, dereliction, slip in manners, breach of etiquette, impropriety, lapsus.

FAVOR, *v.* 1. Regard with favor, approve, commend, be in favor of, esteem, have in one's good books, sanction, go in for, fawn upon.

2. Countenance, encourage, smile upon, befriend, patronize, take up, side with.

3. Have a preference for, treat with partiality, indulge, deal with gently, spare, humor, stretch a point, ease, extenuate, palliate.

4. Resemble in features, take after in aspect, look like, be the image of.

5. Make easier, facilitate, expedite, ease, be propitious to.

6. Support, advocate, show favor to, oblige, help, succor, second, assist, aid, abet, foster.

FAVOR, *n.* 1. Kind approval, friendly disposition, kindly regard, good opinion, appreciation, esteem, good will, friendliness, kindness, propitious aspect, benignity, pleasure, auspices.

2. Kind act, something done out of good will, act of grace, boon, benefaction, good turn, benefit, good deed, dispensation, courtesy, indulgence, accommodation, obligation.

3. Present, gift, good-will token, love-token, grant, honorarium, offering.

4. Patronage, countenance, support, championship, espousal, advocacy, sanction, aid, defense, commendation.

5. Protection, advantage, cover, guidance.

6. Leaning, prejudice, unfair partiality, favoritism, bias, partisanship, nepotism.

7. Permission, leave, good will, pardon, consent to sexual intimacy (*pl.*).

8. Ribbon worn in evidence of loyalty, bunch of ribbons, rosette, badge, knot, decoration.

FAVORABLE, *adj.* 1. Manifesting favor, friendly, amicable, kind, congenial, approving, commendatory, well-disposed, benign, sympathetic.

2. Propitious, auspicious, fair, promising, lucky, opportune, timely, providential, fortunate, happy.

3. Minded, fain, disposed, inclined, in the mood, willing, enthusiastic, eager, predisposed, propense, conducive.

4. Affording aid, beneficial, advantageous, fit, helpful, serviceable, convenient, suitable, adapted.

FAVORITE, *adj.* Regarded with particular preference, welcomed, especially liked, popular, to one's taste, to one's liking, to one's heart, pet, preferred, choice.

FAVORITE, *n.* 1. Pet, idol, minion, cosset, fair-haired boy, white-headed boy, jewel, apple of one's eye, spoiled child, *enfant gâté (Fr.)*, darling, beloved, dear, duck, honey, sweetheart, *persona grata (Lat.)*.

2. Probable winner, front-runner, choice.

FAVORITISM, *n.* 1. Favoring of one over others having equal claims, partiality, partisanship, unilateralism, one-sidedness, prejudice, bias, prepossession, inequity, unfairness, unjustness, injustice, nepotism.

2. Leaning, predilection, penchant, proclivity, weakness for.

FAWN, *v.* 1. Show fondness by crouching before, cringe, stoop, kneel, creep before, bow to, fall on one's knees before, kiss the boots of, bootlick, kiss the feet of, cower before, crawl before, grovel before.

2. Seek favor by servile demeanor, curry favor, toady to, play the sycophant, truckle, flatter, hang to the sleeve of, be servile to, dance attendance on, pander to, blandish, pay court to, court, woo, cajole, wheedle.

FAWNER, *n.* Toady, sycophant, hanger-on, parasite, truckler, cringer, flunky, sponge, courtier, pickthank, timeserver, bootlicker, lickspittle, flatterer.

FAWNING, *adj.* Slavish, servile, cringing, obsequious, subservient, sycophantic, bootlicking, groveling, creeping, timeserving, parasitical, abject, truckling, sniveling, mealy-mouthed, smooth-tongued, flattering, adulatory, honeyed, soapy, oily, unctuous, fulsome, fair-spoken, blandiloquent.

FAWNING, *n.* Servility, sycophancy, slavishness, obsequiousness, subserviency, cringing, flunkyism, abasement, mean flattery, toadying, truckling, adulation, blandishment, wheedling, flummery, incense, honeyed words, buncombe, applesauce, blarney, butter, soft soap, rose water.

FAY, *n.* Fairy, peri, elf, nix, nixie, pixie, sylph, sprite, brownie, gnome, genie, kobold.

FAZE, *v.* (*Colloq.*) Disturb, daunt, intimidate, worry, discomfit, disconcert, upset the composure of, fret.

FEALTY, *n.* 1. Vassal's obligation to be faithful to a lord, loyalty to a feudal lord, homage, allegiance, deference, obedience, compliance, tie, duty, respect.

2. Faithfulness, fidelity, constancy, good faith, loyalty, devotion, honor.

FEAR, *n.* 1. Painful feeling of impending danger, apprehension, dread, fright, alarm, scare, funk, terror, affright, phobia, consternation, dismay, horror, cold feet, panic, gnawing threat.

2. Outward manifestation of fear, trembling, quaking, quivering, tremor, shaking, nervousness, restlessness, disquietude, perturbation, flutter, trepidation, palpitation.

3. Pusillanimity, cowardness, timidity, white feather, timorousness.

4. Worry, anxiety, care, concern, solicitude, misgiving, qualm, diffidence, mistrust, suspicion, hesitation.

5. Bugbear, bugaboo, *bête noire (Fr.)*, bogy, hobgoblin, nightmare, specter, incubus.

6. Reverential awe, reverence, veneration, reverential regard, dread.

FEAR, *v.* 1. Regard with fear, be afraid of, dread, apprehend, be anxious, be concerned about, be solicitous, distrust, hesitate, falter, funk, be cowardly, cower, crouch, skulk, have cold feet, sneak, shy, run away, show the white feather, mistrust.

2. Be afraid, take fright, be alarmed, be scared, be frightened, be in a cold sweat, start, wince, flinch, shrink, quail, shake, tremble, shudder, shiver, quiver, quake, quaver, flutter, blanch, blench, stand aghast, live in terror.

3. Revere, reverence, venerate, have reverential awe of, stand in awe of.

FEARFUL, *adj.* 1. Apprehensive, afraid, solicitous, haunted with fear, frightened, alarmed, anxious, aghast, unmanned, distrustful, uneasy.

2. Diffident, timid, timorous, nervous, easily frightened, superstitious, intimidated, tremulous, panic-stricken, shaky, faint-hearted, unmanly, cowardly, pusillanimous, white-livered, chicken-hearted, showing the white feather, craven.

3. Causing fear, formidable, dreadful, terrible, appalling, alarming, portentous, ominous, dire, frightful, horrible, shocking, perilous, dread, fell, terrific, tremendous, redoubtable, horrid, lurid, gruesome, ghastly, eerie, terrifying, grim, distressing, revolting.

4. Full of awe, awe-inspiring, awful, to be reverenced.

FEARLESS, *adj.* 1. Undaunted, undismayed, dreadless, dauntless, unterrified, unafraid, unappalled, unawed, unabashed, unblenching, unshrinking, unapprehensive, unflinching.

2. Brave, bold, courageous, intrepid, valiant, valorous, daring, gallant, spirited, mettlesome, manly, plucky, game, confident, self-reliant, chivalrous, resolute, upright, spartan, stouthearted, lion-hearted, indomitable, audacious, hardy, heroic, firm, adventurous, foolhardy.

FEASIBILITY, *n.* Practicability, workability, workableness, feasibleness, expediency, desirability, desirableness, fitness, propriety, efficiency, utility, advantageousness, potentiality, potency, possibility.

FEASIBLE, *adj.* 1. Capable of being done, able to be effected, easy to accomplish, workable, doable, performable, achievable, attainable, actable.

2. Suitable, desirable to do, expedient, advisable, wise, acceptable, convenient, worth-while.

3. Likely, probable, possible, practicable, able to happen, potential, within reach, accessible, surmountable, attainable, obtainable.

FEAST, *n.* 1. Sumptuous meal for many guests, large social repast, banquet, refection, collation, symposium, carousal, regale, treat, junket, picnic, festive board, spread, blowout *(colloq.),* feed *(colloq.),* good cheer, fare, barbecue, potluck, festivity, saturnalia, bacchanal.

2. Gala day, red-letter day, saint's day, festival, fête, fiesta, holiday, day of feasting, festal day, joyful anniversary, jubilee, festive celebration, day of rejoicing.

3. Refreshment, animal gratification, bodily enjoyment, delight, round of pleasure, titillation, gusto, entertainment, jollification, merrymaking.

FEAST, *v.* 1. Partake of a feast, eat richly, fare sumptuously, be fed expensively, dine, wine and dine, banquet, refresh the inner man, fare, gormandize, gluttonize, glut, gorge, stuff, cram, overeat, satiate, indulge, eat one's fill, play a good knife and fork, revel, carouse, make merry.

2. Entertain expensively, feed luxuriously, wine and dine.

3. Dwell with delight on, delight in, gladden, gratify, rejoice, make much of, hold dear, be wedded to.

FEAT, *n.* 1. Extraordinary achievement, noteworthy act, heroic accomplishment, bold deed, skilful exploit, masterful stroke, bold stroke, tour de force, striking maneuver, momentous performance, great attainment.

2. Act of dexterity, trick, stunt, sleight-of-hand, legerdemain, jugglery.

FEAT, *adj.* 1. Fit, suitable, appropriate, apt.

2. Dexterous, skilful, nimble, adroit, deft, agile.

3. Neat, elegant, fine.

FEATHER, *n.* 1. Epidermal appendage constituting the plumage of birds, plume, plumule, filoplume, quill, tuft, tussock, pinion, remex, hackle, fledge, rachis, crest, scapular, covert, barb.

2. Something light like a feather, fluff, down, thistledown, cobweb, gossamer, dust, mote.

3. Mark of distinction, panache, aigrette, honor, ornament, decoration, laurel, palm, bays, epaulet, shoulder knot, frog.

4. Kind, character, class, species, nature, sort, lot.

5. Condition of health, bloom, vigor, soundness, state of the spirits.

FEATHERY, *adj.* 1. Clothed with feathers, covered with plumes, feathered, plumigerous, plumed, plumose, plumous, plumate, tufted, downy, fluffy, fledged, pennaceous.

2. Resembling feathers, lightweight, gossamery, light, airy, unsubstantial, imponderous, weightless, ethereal.

FEATURE, *n.* 1. Lines of the face, form of the face, cast of the face, lineament, turn of expression, countenance, look, visage, physiognomy, profile, silhouette, aspect, appearance.

2. Formation, conformation, configuration, cut, shape, figure, build, set, frame, stamp, type, *tournure (Fr.),* fashion, make.

3. Prominent part, highlight, drawing card, main bout, main item.

4. Distinctive trait, outstanding property, conspicuous characteristic, earmark, attribute, quality, peculiarity, mark, hallmark, marked character, idiosyncrasy.

FEBRILE, *adj.* Fever-ridden, feverish, in a fever, in a sweat, sudorific, hectic, flushed, inflamed, in a heat, in a glow, hysterical, delirious.

FECES, *n.* 1. Waste matter discharged from the intestines, excreta, defecated matter, excrement, ordure, dung, alvine dejections, *merde (Fr.),* muck, manure, coprolite, sewage, night soil, stool, guano, compost.

2. Dregs, lees, grounds, settlings, sediment, heeltap, refuse, offal, sordes, dross.

FECULENCE, *n.* Foul matter, refuse, sediment, settlings, dregs, dross, residuum, scum, recrement, sprue, clinker, draff, rubbish.

FECULENT, *adj.* Abounding in foul matter, foul, dreggy, turbid, muddy, unsettled, nasty, filthy, stercoraceus, excrementitious, putrid, offensive, purulent, roily.

FECUND, *adj.* Capable of producing offspring in abundance, fruitful, fructiferous, frugiferous, fertile, prolific, impregnated, teeming, productive, pregnant, uberous, parturient, puerperal, enceinte, big with, fraught with, feracious.

FECUNDATE, *v.* 1. Make prolific, make productive, fructify, make fruitful, enrich.

2. Impregnate, make pregnant, get with young, cover with germinal fluid, cause to germinate, fertilize, spermatize, procreate, generate, beget, progenerate, engender.

FECUNDATION, *n.* 1. Enrichment, making fertile, causing to be prolific.

2. Fertilization, impregnation, germination, generation, epigenesis, genesis, breeding, conception, fructification, flowering, fruition.

FECUNDITY, *n.* Capacity of producing young in great numbers, prolificness, fruitfulness, productiveness, fertility, uberty, richness, feracity, luxuriance, capacity of abundant production.

FEDERAL, *adj.* 1. Pertaining to alliance, relating to treaty.

2. Federated, in league, leagued, united, in partnership, confederate, in alliance, bonded,

banded, linked together, federative, joint, corporate, fraternal.

FEDERATE, v. Organize on a federal basis, unite in a league, band in a federation, confederate, league, unify, combine, enter into partnership with, cartelize, cement a party, keep together, hold together, club together, stand shoulder to shoulder, make common cause, be in league with, join hands with, side with, join with, act in concert, join forces, fraternize, cling to one another, concert.

FEDERATION, n. 1. Formation of a political unity into a central government, union in a league, federation, confederation, formation into a confederacy, leaguing, combination, amalgamation, fusion, coagency, coöperation, concert, participation.

2. Alliance, league, federal union, confederacy, coalition, association, colleagueship, copartnership, federal compact, federacy, union, axis, *Verein (Ger.), Bund (Ger.)*, combine, syndicate, federated body formed by a number of states retaining control of their own internal affairs.

FEE, n. 1. Pay for professional services, salary, perquisite, due, wages, stipend, remuneration, compensation, honorarium, charge, toll, tariff, emolument, recompense, hire, fare.

2. Tip, gratuity, *pourboire (Fr.), Trinkgeld (Ger.)*, douceur, conciliatory gift, handout, sop, palm grease, bribe, graft, bait, commission, allowance.

3. Sum paid for a privilege, reward, meed, guerdon, bounty, bonus, premium.

4. Fief, absolute possession, ownership, unconditional tenure, benefice, fee-simple, feud.

FEE, v. Reward, remunerate, requite, recompense, pay, give a fee to, compensate, reimburse, indemnify, bribe, tip, grease the palm, cross the palm with silver, oil *(colloq.)*.

FEEBLE, adj. 1. Physically weak, not strong, weakly, debilitated, enervated, languid, infirm, emasculated, unmanned, sickly, delicate, fragile, slight, asthenic, anemic, ailing, languishing, frail, doddering, drooping, impotent, powerless, declining, decrepit, puny, unhealthy, forceless, nerveless, senile, impuissant.

2. Faint, dim, hazy, nebulous, misty, indefinite, indistinct, lacking clarity of outline, wanting in vividness, blurred, vague, uncertain.

3. Ineffective, vapid, insipid, flat, meager, spiritless, flimsy, bald, colorless, poor, dry, dull, watery, prosy, tame, prosaic, slight, inexact, lame, lax, loose, slipshod, slovenly, careless, ineffectual, unsatisfactory, meager, paltry, inadequate, wishywashy, passive.

FEEBLE-MINDED, adj. 1. Feeble in intellect, lacking normal mental powers, half-witted, weakminded, addle-headed, stupid, idiotic, imbecilic, moronic, defective, deranged, irresponsible, puerile, childish, senile, fatuous, foolish, senseless.

2. Lacking firmness of mind, irresolute, undecided, half-hearted, rambling, drifting, infirm of purpose, shilly-shallying.

FEEBLENESS, n. Debility, infirmity, weakness, impuissance, impotence, incapacity, asthenia, atony, enervation, bodily attenuation, disability, decrepitude, exhaustion, fatigue, frailty, faintness, languor, inability.

FEED, v. 1. Give food to, supply with nourishment, furnish with edibles, cater, victual, feast, wine and dine, forage.

2. Furnish for consumption, provide for, provision, purvey, supply, contribute to, recruit, equip, outfit, provide with requisite materials for operation.

3. Foster, nurture, cherish, nourish, sustain, strengthen, support, maintain.

4. Satisfy, minister to, gratify, pander to.

5. Take food, take nourishment, eat, fare, devour, fodder, graze, consume, swallow, bolt, dispatch, crunch, gulp, masticate, nibble, peck, gnaw, browse, crop, munch, champ, stuff, ruminate, gorge.

FEED, n. 1. Food for animals, fodder, forage, provender, corn, feed-stuff, mash, pasturage, pasture.

2. Feeding mechanism, automatic stoker, feeder.

FEEL, v. 1. Examine by touch, have perception by touch, perceive by the feel, have feeling.

2. Find by touching, feel of, probe, sound, thumb, finger, grope for, pursue one's way by cautious moves, test, fumble, grabble, search with the hands, handle, touch.

3. Have a sensation of being, receive an impression, have the consciousness of being, perceive, understand, comprehend, know, discern, see, note, remark, respond.

4. Experience the effects of, bear, endure, support, brook, abide, sustain, brave, withstand, stand, suffer, labor under.

5. Be emotionally affected by, be moved, be stirred, be excited, be wrought up, sympathize, have compassion, be perturbed, be agitated, be warmed, have sympathy, glow, blush, flush, crimson, change color, pale, blanch, blench, mantle, tingle, heave, thrill, pant, palpitate, throb, tremble, flutter, quiver, twitter, wince, shake.

FEELER, n. 1. Organ of touch, hand, finger, forefinger, thumb, paw, tentacle, antenna, palpus, palp, tactor, vibrissa, horn, whisker.

2. Pilot balloon, *ballon d'essai (Fr.)*, proposal designed to bring out the opinions of others, straw to show the wind, tentative method, *tâtonnement (Fr.)*, experiment, exploratory hint, tentative remark, inquiry, leading question.

FEELING, adj. 1. Easily affected, accessible to emotion, emotional, susceptible, demonstrative, sentient, sensuous, sensitive, tender, sympathetic, compassionate, merciful.

2. Indicating emotion, pathetic, affecting, touching, moving, melting, telling, striking, impressive, solemn, deep, profound, deep-felt, heartfelt, soul-stirring, electric, thrilling, earnest, warm, passionate, zealous, glowing, ardent, vivid.

FEELING, n. 1. Tactile sense, sense of touch, power of perceiving by touch, tactile physical sensation, sentience, sensation, impression, response.

2. Tingling, thrill, excitement, agitation, shock, kick, quiver, flurry, fluster, blush, flush, tremor, twitter, pulsation, throb, palpitation, panting.

3. Sentiment, sensibility, sensation experienced when one is stirred to emotion, pathos, passion, heart-strings, soul, tenderness, concern, pity, sympathy, compassion, affection, fine feeling, susceptibility, delicate sentiment, love, kindness.

4. Fervor, zeal, spirits, fervency, gusto, vehemence, cordiality, heartiness, eagerness, gush, earnestness, *empressement (Fr.)*, warmth, ardor, verve, ecstasy, enthusiasm.

5. Subjective point of view, personal viewpoint, attitude, opinion, conviction.

FEIGN, v. 1. Devise deceptively, forge, counterfeit, fabricate, invent, concoct, imagine.

2. Put on an appearance of, simulate, dissemble, dissimulate, affect, make believe, assume, imitate deceptively, sham, malinger, profess, create a false appearance, personate, put on, pretend to, make a show of, allege, claim, represent fictitiously.

FEIGNED, adj. Sham, counterfeit, forged, spurious, false, mock, fictive, make-believe, fictitious, mythical, fabulous, imaginary, pretended, simulated, fabricated, fraudulent, illegitimate, faked, pseudo, bogus, unauthentic, not genuine, artificial, factitious, assumed, disguised, untrue, trumped up, so-called, soi disant, self-styled, supposititious, fictitiously invented.

FEINT, n. 1. (Mil.) Appearance of aiming at one point when another is the real object of attack, movement made for the purpose of deceiving an adversary, mock attack, deceptive movement, sham attack.

2. Stratagem, trick, ruse, wile, artifice, pretense, blind, cheat, plant, bubble, fetch, catch, hoax, swindle, hocus-pocus, juggle, chicane, shift, pretext, excuse, subterfuge, color, cloak, disguise, false appearance, mask, make-believe, sham, humbug, camouflage, counterfeit, bait, pitfall, trap, snare, sleight-of-hand, legerdemain, prestidigitation.

FELICITATE, v. 1. Compliment upon a happy event, wish joy to, tender congratulations, congratulate, gratulate, wish many happy returns of the day, rejoice with.

2. (Rare) Make happy, delight, beatify, bless, fill with happiness.

FELICITATION, n. Expression of good wishes, compliments of the season, best wishes, congratulation, gratulation, salute, wish for happiness, well-wishing, beatification.

FELICITOUS, adj. 1. Appropriate, fit, happy, neat, becoming, pertinent, apt, to the point, in point, ad rem (Lat.), apposite, apropos, germane, seasonable, timely, opportune, well-timed, pat, meet, ingenious, skilful, graceful, well-expressed, inspired, well-chosen.

2. Fortunate, lucky, successful, prosperous, propitious, auspicious, full of promise, of good omen, de bon augure (Fr.), roseate, rose-colored, couleur de rose (Fr.).

FELICITY, n. 1. State of being happy in a high degree, bliss, ecstasy, supreme enjoyment, ravishment, blissfulness, beatitude, blessedness, rapture, gladness, heavenly contentment, transport of happiness, beatification, ecstatic joy, enchantment, summum bonum (Lat.), gratification, pleasure, delight.

2. Skilful faculty, aptitude, knack, flair, aptness, appropriateness, grace, fitness, suitableness, readiness, felicitousness, ingenuity.

3. Good fortune, success, good luck, comfort, content, prosperity, well-being.

FELINE, adj. Characteristic of cats, aeluroid, catty, cattish, catlike, subtle, insidious, sly, cunning, crafty, artful, designing, wily, tricky, canny, shifty, treacherous, stealthy, slinking, sneaking, prowling, pussy-footing.

FELL, adj. Fierce, savage, ferocious, bloodthirsty, sanguinary, destructive, deadly, lethal, barbarous, wild, truculent, furious, raging, violent, ruthless, pitiless, remorseless, unmerciful, relentless, implacable, marble-hearted, hard-hearted, inhuman, brutal, merciless, barbaric, vandalic, malignant, malicious, malign, murderous, cruel, dreadful, horrible.

FELL, v. Cause to fall, strike down, cut down, hew down, knock down, hurl down, mow down, lay down, bring to the ground, floor, ground, beat down, prostrate, horizontalize, level, raze, knock prostrate, overthrow, demolish.

FELLOW, n. 1. Man, boy, male, homo, mister, Mr., monsieur, Herr (Ger.), signor (It.), señor (Sp.), hombre, don, hidalgo, caballero, sahib, sir, gentleman, esquire, person, individual, chap, guy, yeoman, gaffer (colloq.), customer (colloq.), cove (Br. slang).

2. Person of small worth, no-account, wight, clown, knave, codger, vauxrien (Fr.), Taugenichts (Ger.), good-for-nothing.

3. Comrade, companion, partner, associate, copartner, co-worker, confrere, colleague, consort, pal, buddy, boon companion, side-kick, chum, shadow, bedfellow, bunkie, playmate, compatriot, hail fellow well met.

4. One belonging to the same class, peer, compeer, equal, brother.

5. One of a pair, twin, double, second self, alter ego, bird of a feather, congener, counterpart, mate, match, duplicate, facsimile, copy.

6. Beau, sweetheart, suitor, boy friend, swain, blade, gallant, cavalier, lover, admirer, escort, wooer, inamorato, true love.

7. Graduate student of a university to whom an allowance is granted for special study, incorporate member of a college entitled to certain privileges, member of a college instructing and sharing its revenues, don, dean, scholar, savant, pundit, member of a learned society.

FELLOW FEELING, n. Feeling of mutual understanding, sense of joint interest, sympathetic feeling, sympathy, compassion, humanity, mercy, forbearance, clemency, goodness of heart, benignity, charity, brotherly love, philanthropy, benevolence, altruism, good will, kindliness, lovingkindness, bonhomie, kind-heartedness, good Samaritanism, pity, commiseration, affection.

FELLOWSHIP, n. 1. Community of interest, friendliness, brotherhood, comradeship, intimacy, familiarity, companionship, friendship, fraternity, sodality, entente cordiale, association of persons having similar interests, club, society, band, company.

2. Joint interest, participation, membership, partnership, corporation, guild.

3. Intercourse, relations, fraternization, converse, communion.

4. Amity, sociability, affability, cordiality, sociableness, kindliness, amicableness, good companionship.

5. Foundation for the maintenance of a scholar, endowment, emolument of a fellow of a university, sum for the maintenance of a fellow in a university.

FELON, n. 1. Malefactor, criminal, misdemeanant, worker of iniquity, wrongdoer, miscreant, culprit, bad man, evildoer, jailbird, convict, outlaw, delinquent, rascal, scoundrel, villain, rough, rowdy, ruffian, hoodlum, hooligan, thug, mugger, blackguard, rogue, recreant, offender, reprobate.

2. Acute inflammation of the deeper tissue of a digit, whitlow.

FELONIOUS, adj. 1. (Law) Done with intent to commit crime, wilfully criminal, showing criminal purpose, with evil intent, with malice prepense, unlawful, illegal, illicit.

2. Wicked, iniquitous, malign, malignant, malicious, vicious, heinous, nefarious, flagitious, base, villainous, infamous, sinister, scurvy, atrocious, foul, gross, vile, black, facinorous, flagrant, fiendish, cruel, sadistic, devilish, hellish, corrupt, depraved, perverse, despicable, pernicious, injurious, virulent, malevolent.

3. *(Rare)* Disloyal, perfidious, traitorous.

FELONY, *n.* Offense of graver character than a misdemeanor, crime punishable by death, misdeed punishable by imprisonment for more than a year, heinous misconduct, gross misbehavior, malefaction, iniquity, trespass, transgression, delinquency, burglary, murder, rape.

FEMALE, *adj.* 1. Belonging to the sex which brings forth young, offspring-bearing, child-bearing, breeding, conceiving, gynecic, fertile.

2. Characteristic of womankind, feminine, delicate, tender, soft, sympathetic, gentle, womanly, weak, ladylike.

3. *(Mech.)* Designating some part into which a corresponding part fits.

FEMININE, *adj.* 1. Like a woman, womanly, delicate, gentle, tender, soft, girlish, maidenly, ladylike.

2. Effeminate, womanish, unmanly, unvirile, lacking in manly qualities, sissyish.

FEMININITY, *n.* 1. Female quality, feminality, womanliness, womanhood, womankind, women collectively.

2. Unmanliness, lack of masculine character, effeminacy, effeminateness, sissiness, weakness, softness.

FEN, *n.* Low land covered wholly or partly by water, bog, boggy land, wet muddy terrain, marsh, swamp, morass, moor, quagmire, moss, sump, wash, slough, marish.

FENCE, *n.* 1. Protective enclosure, circumvallation, wall, weir, hedge, rail, railing, barrier around, paling, post-and-rail framing, wire-guard, stockade, palisade, boarding, barricade, hedgerow.

2. Shield, palladium, protection, defense, guard, bulwark.

3. Swordplay, fencing, art of self-defense, swordsmanship.

4. Cleverness in repartee, defensive argumentation, skill in refutation, skill in debate.

5. Receiver and disposer of stolen goods.

FENCE, *v.* 1. Enclose with a fence, circumscribe by a barrier, secure by an enclosure, surround, encircle, encompass, hedge, corral, pen, box, case, incase, envelop, shut in.

2. Defend, protect, guard, forfend, fend, shield, fortify, screen, arm against danger, fend off danger from, repel, propugn.

3. Practice fencing, use a foil, use the sword, stave.

4. Parry arguments, strive to evade giving direct answers, quibble, shuffle, palter, equivocate, trim, prevaricate, beat about the bush, hedge, mince the truth.

FENCING, *n.* 1. Art of using a foil for defense and attack, manual defense with swords, swordplay, swordsmanship, gladiatorship, art of self-defense, gladiature.

2. Evasion of direct answers, parrying of arguments, skilful debate.

FEND, *v.* Defend, forfend, ward off, keep off,

repel, propugn, avert, parry, avoid, protect, guard.

FENDER, *n.* 1. That which protects or wards off, buffer, apron, guard, screen, shield, fence, bumper, bulwark, safeguard, security, shelter, defense.

2. Pressed and formed sheet metal part mounted over the road wheel of an automobile, mudguard of a horse-drawn vehicle, splashboard.

FENNY, *adj.* Marshy, paludal, swampy, fennish, boggy, quaggy, moorish, plashy, poachy, soft, muddy, squashy, spongy.

FERAL, *adj.* Existing in a state of nature, having escaped from domestication and become wild, ferine, brutish, beastlike, bestial, wild, ruthless, untamed, savage, cruel, dangerous, deadly, bloodthirsty, ferocious, fierce, ravenous, rapacious, predaceous.

FERIAL, *adj.* Pertaining to a holiday, red-letter, commemorative.

FERMENT, *n.* 1. Leaven, yeast, barm, mold, zyme, diastase, pepsin, enzyme.

2. Fermentation, transformation, ebullience, ebullition, effervescence, seething, foaming, bubbling, working, raising.

3. Agitation, state of unrest, restlessness, jactitation, tumult, turbulence, turmoil, commotion, heat, stew, glow, fever, hurly-burly, bustle, fuss, racket, hubbub, rout, confusion, uproar.

FERMENT, *v.* 1. Cause to undergo fermentation, set in fermentation, produce fermentation in, leaven, pepsinate.

2. Undergo fermentation, be fermented, work, foam, boil, bubble up, froth, seethe, raise, turn, effervesce.

3. Agitate, excite, heat, flurry, fluster, stir with emotion, foment, inflame.

FERN, *n.* Pteridophyte, bracken, venus hair, maidenhair, brake, polypody.

FEROCIOUS, *adj.* 1. Untamed like a wild animal, bestial, brutish, ravenous, rapacious, predatory, predaceous, ferine, feral, ravening.

2. Violently cruel, savagely fierce, inhuman in conduct, barbarous, fell, brutal, truculent, violent, malevolent, ruthless, grim, remorseless, relentless, cold-blooded, atrocious, merciless, pitiless, murderous, deadly, bloodthirsty, sanguinary, malignant, maleficent, fiendish, diabolic, demoniac.

FEROCITY, *n.* Savage fierceness, savagery, ferity, ferociousness, rapacity, truculence, violence, bloodthirstiness, brutality, immanity, malignancy, fury, fiendishness, barbarity, atrocious cruelty, inhumanity, outrage, atrocity.

FERRET OUT, *v.* Drive out by means of a ferret, hunt with ferrets, search out, track down, trace up, hunt out, unearth, disinter, bring to light, fish out, dig out, root out, grub up, fathom, pry into, worm out.

FERRY, *v.* 1. Convey over in a boat, transport from shore to shore across a body of water, carry over.

2. Cross by ferry, pass over water in a boat.

FERTILE, *adj.* 1. Producing abundantly, bearing offspring freely, prolific, fecund, puerperal, uberous, proliferous, generative.

2. Pregnant, enceinte, parturient, gravid, heavy, big with, gestant, with child.

3. Productive, fruitful, luxuriant, copious, fructuous, rich, exuberant, plenteous, teeming, plentiful, lush, fat, abundant.

4. Female, fruit-bearing, fertilized, fecundated, fructiferous.

5. Creative, inventive, formative, constructive, imaginative.

FERTILITY, *n.* 1. Ability to produce offspring, power of reproduction, fecundity, uberty, fertileness, propagation, multiplication, fructuousness, feracity.

2. Fruitfulness, productivity, productiveness, plenteousness, abundance, exuberance, luxuriance.

3. Fertile invention, creativeness, imaginativeness.

FERTILIZE, *v.* 1. Supply with semen, spermatize, furnish with pollen, pollinate, fructify, inseminate, impregnate, fecundate, render capable of development by union with the male element.

2. Render productive, make fertile, make fruitful, enrich, develop the latent powers of.

3. Feed the land, dress the soil, manure, compost.

FERTILIZER, *n.* Material for fertilizing land, plant food, soil tonic, manure, compost, guano, dressing, marl, phosphate, lime, dung, chemicals, bone dust.

FERULE, *n.* Flat piece of wood for punishing children, rod, cane, stick, scourge, rattan, birch rod, switch, cudgel, truncheon.

FERVENT, *adj.* 1. Warm in feeling, earnest, zealous, eager, impassioned, passionate, fervid, ardent, vehement, fiery, heated in enthusiasm, animated, intense, fierce, keen, enthusiastic, sincere, affectionate, hearty, spirited, cordial.

2. Burning, seething, boiling, hot, calid, glowing.

FERVOR, *n.* 1. Warmth of feeling, fervency, ardor, zeal, passion, intensity, verve, fire, force, energy, élan, vehemence, earnestness, heartiness, eagerness, *empressement (Fr.),* enthusiasm, animation, gush, gusto, cordiality, keenness, rapture, ecstasy, love, inspiration.

2. Intense heat, warmth, glow.

FESTAL, *adj.* Pertaining to a gala occasion, befitting a feast, convivial, festive, gala, joyous, social.

FESTER, *v.* Generate purulent matter, cause progressive poisoning, generate pus, produce morbid matter, suppurate, cause ulceration, ulcerate, maturate, putrefy, rot, rankle, corrupt, become malignant, grow virulent.

FESTER, *n.* 1. Rankling sore, ulcer, pustule, imposthume, abscess, boil, carbuncle, whitlow.

2. Suppuration, festering, rankling, maturation, decay, putrescence, putrefaction, tainture, fetor, rot, canker.

FESTIVAL, *n.* Time of feasting, anniversary for festive celebration, periodic feast, jubilee, red-letter day, gala day, festive commemoration, carnival, Mardi gras, fête, holiday, day of rejoicing, memorable occasion, banquet, repast, regale, treat, symposium, carousal, merrymaking, fiesta.

FESTIVE, *adj.* Festal, convivial, joyous, merry, gay, jovial, jolly, mirthful, uproarious, gala, sportive, *en fête (Fr.),* social, genial.

FESTIVITY, *n.* 1. Festive celebration, carousal, revelry, rejoicing, joyousness, merrymaking, jollity, merriment, gaiety, joyfulness, enjoyment, pleasure, felicity, mirth, glee, hilarity, amusement, sport, recreation, funmaking, conviviality.

2. Festive proceedings, frolic, whoopee, heyday, lark, spree, festival.

3. Banquet, repast, regale, festive board.

FESTOON, *n.* Garland hanging in a curve between two points, chain of flowers suspended in a curve, wreath, lei, chaplet, string of foliage, looped garland.

FESTOON, *v.* 1. Decorate with looped garlands, hang with festoons, ornament, trim, array, bedeck, deck, bedight.

2. Form into festoons, connect by festoons, string, wreathe, loop up.

FETCH, *v.* 1. Go and bring from a particular place, get and bring back, bring to, go and bring things, get, carry, tote, convey to, conduct to, retrieve, transport.

2. Perform, execute, effect, achieve, bring to accomplishment, make, accomplish, attain by exertion.

3. Sell for, cost, yield, bring in, afford, bring as a price.

4. (*Naut.*) Arrive at, reach, come to, attain, get to.

5. (*Colloq.*) Fascinate, captivate, charm, allure.

FETCH, *n.* 1. Evasion, trick, stratagem, ruse, wile, artifice, dodge, blind, feint, plant, bubble, catch, chicane, sharp practice, juggle, hocus, bite.

2. Apparition of a living person, wraith, delusion.

FETCHING, *adj.* Charming, fascinating, captivating, attractive, pleasing, alluring, provocative, tantalizing, titillating, exciting, stimulating, piquant.

FETE, *v.* Entertain at a fête, feast, treat, regale, wine and dine, honor with an entertainment, give a party for, banquet.

FETE, *n.* 1. Festal day, holiday, anniversary, gala day, field-day.

2. Social gathering, party, gala, *ridotto (It.),* carnival, Mardi gras, bal masque, Saturnalia, *fête champêtre (Fr.),* outdoor festival, garden party.

3. Festive celebration, epulation, entertainment, festival, feast, banquet, treat, regale, symposium, wassail, carousal, junket, jamboree.

FETID, *adj.* Having an offensive odor, malodorous, graveolent, mephitic, noisome, rank, foul, rancid, strong-smelling, stinking, musty, ill-smelling, tainted, rotten, putrid, suffocating, asphyxiative, strong, gamy, moldy.

FETISH, *n.* 1. Inanimate object regarded as being the embodiment of a potent spirit, object of superstitious awe, talisman, charm, phylactery, periapt, amulet, telesm, idol, golden calf, graven image, avatar, joss, wishbone, merry-thought, medicine, scarab, swastika, material object supposed to possess magical powers, object of blind reverence, totem.

2. (*Psychiatry*) Inanimate object used to attain sexual satisfaction (such as: silk stockings, shoes, underwear, furs, gloves, neckpieces, locks of hair).

FETISHISM, *n.* 1. Relief in fetishes, use of fetishes, fetish-worship.

2. (*Psychiatry*) Compulsive use of some inanimate object in attaining sexual gratification, fixation of erotic interest on a part of the body, cross-dressing, transvestitism.

3. Blind devotion, unreasoning attachment, superstitious regard, obsession, possession, *idée fixe (Fr.).*

FETISHIST, *n.* User of fetishes, devotee of inanimate objects, cross-dresser, transvestite, lover of silk stockings.

FETOR, *n.* Strong offensive smell, bad smell, offensive odor, foul smell, malodor, graveolence, mephitis, stench, stink, fume, fumette *(of game)*, foulness, reek, rancidity, fetidness, fustiness, mustiness.

FETTER, *v.* 1. Shackle the feet, put in irons, put into bilboes, enchain, chain, trammel, entrammel, put fetters on, hobble, hamper, clog, pinion, manacle, handcuff, truss up, bind hand and foot, pin down, tie up, tie down.

2. Restrain, shut in, cage, confine, encumber, clap under hatches, impede.

FETTER, *n.* 1. Anything that restrains, shackle for the feet, chain, bond, irons, pinion, gyve, trammel, manacle, handcuff, bracelets, darbies, clog, hamper.

2. Confinement, coarctation, restraint, imprisonment, durance, duress, curb.

FETTLE, *n.* State, condition, situation, status, circumstance, shape, kilter, trim, mode, manner, style, character, way, form, build, tone, tenor.

FETUS, *n.* The young of an animal in the womb, embryo, germ.

FEUD, *n.* 1. Bitter continuous hostility between two families, blood-feud, vendetta, hereditary enmity, family-feud, clan-quarrel, inveterate strife between families.

2. Quarrel, dissension, strife, fray, conflict, affray, contest, controversy, altercation, contention, broil, clashing, fracas, row, rupture, dispute, bickering, falling out, breach, schism, faction, disagreement, wrangle, brawl, jar, clash, discord, dissidence, embroilment, spat, tiff, fuss, argument, division in the camp, animosity, enmity, hard feelings, bitter ill-will, hostility.

FEUDATORY, *n.* 1. One who holds his lands by feudal tenure, feudal vassal, palatine, dependent, subject.

2. Fief, fee.

FEVER, *n.* 1. Morbid bodily condition characterized by undue rise of temperature and pulse, febrile disease, feverishness, pyrexia *(Med.)*, febricity, calenture, inflammation, ague, malaria, typhus, scarlatina, yellow jack.

2. Intense nervous excitement, agitation, ferment, heat, fire, flush, glow, ardor, desire.

FEVERISH, *adj.* 1. Pyrexic, hot, red-hot, pyretic, feverous, febrile, fevered, flushed, fiery, showing increased heat and thirst, parched, inflamed, burning, delirious, rapidly fluctuating from chill to fever, hectic.

2. Restless, excited, wrought up, irritable, nervous, high-strung, angry, frantic, fitful.

3. Impatient, ardent, mercurial, overeager, impassioned, desirous.

FEW, *adj.* Not many, hardly any, scanty, scant, sparse, thin, rare, few and far between, scarce, scarcely any, sporadic, occasional, exiguous, small in number, limited, meager, infrequent, uncommon, unusual, rare, unique.

FEWNESS, *n.* 1. Scantiness, scarcity, sparsity, paucity, sparseness, exiguity, rarity, infrequency, uncommonness, seldomness, drop in the bucket, thimbleful, small quantity, handful, minority, the smaller number, the less, modicum, drop, minimum, sprinkling, dash, dab, spark, tittle, dole, tinge, nip, mite, pinch, bit, snatch, fraction, trifle, scrap.

2. Diminution, reduction, thinning, lessening, weeding, elimination, decimation, eradication.

FEZ, *n.* Conical red felt cap ornamented with a long black tassel, tarboosh, turban, caftan.

FIANCE, *n.* Fiancée *(fem.)*, person engaged to be married, affianced person, intended, betrothed.

FIASCO, *n.* Ignominious failure, fizzle, botch, abortive attempt, *affaire flambée (Fr.)*, nonsuccess, nonfulfilment, abortion, miscarriage, labor in vain, *brutum fulmen (Lat.)*, flash in the pan, no go, frustration, inefficacy, losing game, complete disaster, mess, foozle, breakdown, muddle, blunder.

FIAT, *n.* Positive and peremptory command, authoritative sanction, order, decree, act, dictum, ordinance, hest, proclamation, decretal, manifesto, bull, edict, mandate, precept, bidding, bann, ukase, firman, charge, injunction, prescript, caveat, writ.

FIB, *n.* Trivial falsehood, white lie, bosh, half truth, intentional untruth, fabrication, invention, story, tale, whopper, forgery, fiction, fairy tale, cock and bull story, myth, moonshine, prevarication, mendacity, inveracity, untruthfulness.

FIBER, *n.* 1. Thread, threadlike structure, fine strand, slender filament, tendril, fibril, staple, pile, wire, harl, gossamer, cobweb, hair, cilia, yarn.

2. Essential character, characteristic quality, grain, texture, tissue, nap, grit, tooth, warp and woof, surface.

FIBROUS, *adj.* Threadlike, fibrilose, filamentous, filiform, stringy, filamentary, filar, thready, wiry, ropy, hairlike, capilliform.

FIBULA, *n.* 1. *(Anat.)* The outer of the two bones that form the skeleton of the lower leg.

2. Broach, clasp, pin, safety pin, buckle.

FICHU, *n.* Triangular piece of light material worn about the neck by women, head kerchief, dickey, scarf, collar.

FICKLE, *adj.* Likely to change from caprice, capricious, whimsical, mercurial, volatile, giddy, light-headed, frivolous, feather-brained, wayward, erratic, flighty, feather-headed, unreliable, irresolute, changeful, irresponsible, faithless, inconstant, not fixed or firm, of a changeable mind, fast and loose, fitful, undecided, moonish, skittish, pliant, uncertain, inconsistent, fanciful, crotchety, variable, spasmodic, fluctuating, wavering, unstable, unsteady, mutable, vacillating, unsettled, half-hearted, shifting, veering, like a weather vane.

FICKLENESS, *n.* Caprice, levity, pliancy, capriciousness, indecision, irresolution, inconstancy, instability, changeableness, vacillation, unfaithfulness, fluctuation, tergiversation.

FICTILE, *adj.* 1. Plastic, fashioned by art, full-fashioned, capable of being molded, malleable, ductile, yielding, soft, waxy.

2. Made of molded earth, earthen, made of clay.

FICTION, *n.* 1. Fictitious literature, literary work of imaginative narration, prose work in narrative form, work of fiction, romance, novel, tale, short story, anecdote, yarn, mystery story, thriller, detective story, whodunit *(slang)*, fairy tale, myth, legend, parable, fable, allegory, saga, epic.

2. That which is feigned or imagined, creation of the brain, brain child, mind's eye, invention, fantasy, fancy, imagination, figment, castle-building, rhapsody, extravaganza.

3. Story which is without basis in reality, false statement intended to deceive, made-up story, fabrication, falsehood, forgery, coinage, lie, fib, whopper *(colloq.)*, concoction, canard, yarn, fish story, cock-and-bull story, traveler's tale, moonshine, bosh.

FICTITIOUS, *adj.* 1. Created by the imagination, having no real existence, imaginatively set forth, imaginary, fanciful, invented, feigned, unreal, assumed, untrue, purely ideal, non-real, unfounded, *ben trovato (It.),* imagined, air-built, air-drawn, fabulous, mythical, legendary, romantic, extravagant, in the clouds, *in nubibus (Lat.),* chimerical, visionary, notional, fantastic, far from the truth, theoretical, hypothetical.

2. Artificial, counterfeit, not genuine, spurious, bogus, dummy, false, supposititious, trumped up, fabricated, fictive, sham, unauthentic, fraudulent, forged, simulated.

FIDDLE, *n.* Stringed musical instrument of the viol type, violin, viol, viola d'amore, viola da gamba, viola da braccio, Stradivarius, Guarnerius.

FIDDLE, *v.* 1. Play on a violin, sweep the strings, bow.

2. Make aimless movements with the hands, keep the fingers actively moving, drum with the fingers.

3. Dawdle, idle away time, waste time, poke, droil, lag, lose time, fritter away time, go to sleep over, piddle, potter, putter, fool away time, trifle, dabble, faddle, fribble, dally, dilly-dally.

FIDDLE-DE-DEE, *interj.* Stuff and nonsense! nonsense! pish! pish and tush! rubbish! rot! bosh! moonshine! hogwash! bunk! applesauce! fudge! figs! humbug! bah! tell it to the marines!

FIDDLE-FADDLE, *n. (Colloq.)* Something trivial, stuff and nonsense, trifling talk, twaddle, gibble-gabble, prate, jargon, jabber, mere words, balderdash, rant, fustian, palaver, babble, flummery, *bavardage (Fr.), niaiserie (Fr.),* frivolity, tommyrot, bosh, drivel, rubbish, moonshine, *vox et praeterea nihil (Lat.),* sounding brass and tinkling cymbal, empty sound, flapdoodle.

FIDELITY, *n.* 1. Strict observance of duty, dutiful adherence, keeping of good faith, fealty, loyalty, faithfulness, trustworthiness, dutifulness, good faith, devotion, devotedness, true-heartedness, constancy, stanchness, steadfastness, allegiance, sincerity, earnestness, truthfulness, honor, probity, integrity, honesty.

2. Adherence to fact, accuracy, exactitude, exactness, precision, closeness, faithfulness, reliability, correspondency.

FIDGET, *v.* 1. Move about restlessly, move by fits and starts, move nervously about, hitch, twitch impatiently, stir jerkily, have a tic.

2. Worry, be anxious, be in a stew, chafe, fret, fuss, be restive, be uneasy, toss, be impatient.

FIDGET, *n.* Restlessness manifested by constant changes of position, fidgetiness, fantod, tic, nervousness, agitation, uneasiness, dysphoria, impatience, ruffle, fuss, flurry, fluster, ferment, disquietude.

FIDGETY, *adj.* Restless, unquiet, uneasy, nervous, tremulous, impatient, restive, irritable, apprehensive.

FIDUCIAL, *adj.* 1. Deserving of confidence, trustworthy, trusty, reliable, loyal, dependable.

2. Confident, trustful, undoubting, believing, assured, sure, certain, completely convinced, positive, cocksure.

3. Based on trust, confidential, indicative of faith, held in trust, not to be disclosed, private, secret, not to be communicated.

FIDUCIARY, *n.* Person entrusted with property to hold and manage for another, depositary, trustee, guardian, curator, agent, factor, commis-

sionaire, steward, bailiff, questor, functionary, placeman, treasurer, custodian, caretaker.

FIEF, *n.* Tenure of land subject to feudal obligations, feudal estate, estate in land held by a feudal lord, feud, fee seigniory, territory held in fee, real estate held under feudal tenure and carrying with it a privilege of nobility *(Fr.—Can.).*

FIELD, *n.* 1. Piece of open ground suitable for tillage, tract of land for pasture, cultivated ground, cleared land, clearing, open country, pasture, lea, meadow, mead, glebe, croft, grassland, patch, heath, sward, sod, green, lawn, common, plot, lot.

2. Area of active military operation, scene of conflict, battleground, theater of war, scene of military operation, field of battle, the battle itself.

3. Piece of ground devoted to sports, course, hippodrome, turf, arena, campus, playground, court, diamond, gymnasium, cockpit, ring, lists.

4. Region characterized by a particular feature or product, domain, realm, department, province, bailiwick.

5. Surface, reach, stretch, sweep, play, elbow-room, leeway, margin, area, range, scope, expanse, extent, amplitude, orb, room, opportunity.

FIEND, *n.* 1. Devil, demon, evil spirit, malignant supernatural being, power of darkness, cacodemon, hellhound, infernal spirit, satan, arch fiend.

2. Diabolically wicked person, devil incarnate, monster, incubus, succubus, cruelly malicious being, brute, wolf, barbarian.

3. *(Colloq.)* Hopeless addict, monomaniac, devotee, fan, enthusiast, aficionado.

4. Person very clever at some study, wizard, past master, master hand.

FIENDISH, *adj.* Diabolically wicked, devilish, satanic, hellish, diabolical, demoniac, infernal, tartarean, atrocious, reveling in cruelty, malignant, nefarious, unspeakable, malicious, malign, monstrous, malevolent, inhuman, barbarous, pitiless, implacable, detestable, impious, terrible.

FIERCE, *adj.* 1. Wild in temper, eager to harm or kill, ravenous, truculent, fell, ferocious, savage, feral, bloodthirsty, murderous, tigerish, leonine, bellicose, brutal, barbarous, infuriate, furious, violent, cruel, grim, merciless, voracious, dreadful, raging, enraged.

2. Vehement in action, fervid, fervent, impetuous, intensely eager, passionate, fiery, overpowering, overwhelming, turbulent, unrestrained, untamed, uncurbed, unbridled, tearing, racking.

3. *(Slang)* Extremely bad, unpleasant, bitter, tough.

FIERY, *adj.* 1. Containing fire, igneous.

2. Intensely hot, heated, thermal, calid, torrid, tropical, calorific, burning, inflammable, flaming, glowing, glaring, flashing, blazing, smoldering, ablaze, afire, alight, intensely red, lurid, sweltering.

3. Feverish, febrile, fevered, pyretic *(Med.),* parched, inflamed.

4. Fervent, fervid, ardent, passionate, impassioned, vehement, zealous, impetuous, demonstrative, mettlesome, spirited, temperamental, high-strung, hasty, impulsive, enthusiastic.

5. Easily angered, angry, wrathful, irate, readily provoked, choleric, irascible, hotheaded, irritable, excitable, nervous, agitated.

FIESTA, *n.* Religious celebration, saint's day, religious festival, holiday, feast day, festivity, fête, gala.

FIG, *n.* 1. Tree of the moraceous genus Ficus, turbinate or pear-shaped fruit which is eaten fresh or preserved or dried.

2. Value of a fig, merest trifle, least bit, valueless thing, unimportant article, straw, pin, button, feather, pinch of snuff, jot, rap, continental.

3. Gesture of contempt, fico.

FIGHT, *v.* 1. Contend with in battle, war against, battle, do battle, wage war, take up arms, measure swords, cross swords, draw the sword, combat, go to war, join issue, exchange shots, rise up in arms, take up the cudgels, enter the lists, take up the gauntlet, couch one's lance, appeal to arms, let slip the dogs of war, take the field, engage, strike, set to, fall to, ply one's weapons, measure strength, come to grips with, break a lance with, draw the trigger, come to close quarters with, join battle with, encounter, engage, tilt with, fence.

2. Engage in fisticuffs, fall to blows, come to loggerheads, box, spar, scuffle, buffet, skirmish, exchange blows, grapple, wrestle, tussle.

3. Maintain a quarrel, feud with, pick a bone with, brawl, dispute, wrangle, altercate, clash, broil.

4. Oppose, make resistance, struggle against, act in opposition, resist, repulse, contest, contend, strive with, contend against.

5. Carry through by fighting, gain, win the day, maintain, cope with, sustain.

6. Manage in battle, maneuver, conduct, carry on, wage.

FIGHT, *n.* 1. Armed encounter to settle a dispute, hostile meeting, battle, combat, contest, conflict, skirmish, strife, engagement, rencounter, affray, appeal to arms, melee, fracas, battle royal, clash of arms, passage of arms, collision, affair, brush, armed action, quarrel, tug of war, tussle, scuffle, bout, broil, dogfight, death-grapple, attack, scrimmage, war, Armageddon, pitched battle, death struggle, hand-to-hand struggle for supremacy, duel, fray.

2. Altercation, contention, quarrel, feud, controversy, wrangling, bickering, squabble, brawl, row, broil, disturbance, riot.

3. Inclination to fight, belligerency, bellicosity, pugnacity, pugnaciousness, disposition to struggle, fighting temper, mettle, resistance, spirit, pluck, gameness, sand, grit, combativeness.

4. Pugilism, prizefight, boxing, sparring, fisticuffs, bout, event, set-to, free-for-all, round, the ring, the squared circle, cauliflower industry, modified murder, grappling, wrestling, the mat, jujitsu, sumo.

FIGHTER, *n.* 1. Warrior, combatant, militarist, soldier, belligerent, fighting man, military man, red-coat, janissary, myrmidon, Tommy Atkins, doughboy, *poilu (Fr.),* infantryman, footsoldier, guardsman, artilleryman, gunner, cannoneer, cavalryman, trooper, dragoon, hussar, lancer, cuirassier, private, guerrilla, volunteer, conscript, recruit, rookie, man at arms, champion, adventurer, mercenary, Mameluke, soldier of fortune, free lance, adventurer, swordsman, swashbuckler, gladiator, spearman, archer, bowman, musketeer, knight, franc-tireur, sharpshooter, rifleman, fusileer, grenadier.

2. Pugilist, boxer, prizefighter, bruiser, sparrer, cuffer.

3. Person of spirit or mettle, scrapper, cam-

paigner, veteran, pugnacious individual, brave, vindicator, contestant, contender, assailant.

FIGMENT, *n.* Mere product of the imagination, pure invention, something imagined, feigned story, fiction, fabrication, concoction, fable, falsehood, story, canard.

FIGURATIVE, *adj.* 1. Involving a figure of speech, used in a sense not literal, metaphorical, tropical, catachrestical, hyperbolical, allegorical, parabolic, tralatitious, anagogical, ironic, satirical.

2. Addicted to figurative speech, flowery, ornate, florid, euphuistic, euphemistic, figured, embellished, rich, ornamented, beautified, rhetorical, high-flown, showy, ostentatious, pompous, bombastic, orotund, lexiphanic.

3. Illustrative, typical, symbolic, representative, emblematical, allusive, imitative, graphic, pictorial, descriptive, tropical, imagistic.

FIGURE, *n.* 1. Written character representing a number, numerical symbol, number, digit, numeral, cipher.

2. Value expressed in numbers, price, cost, amount, sum.

3. Figure of speech, metaphorical expression, metaphor, simile, trope, image, imagery, phrase, personification, metonymy, synecdoche, catachresis, antonomasia, enallage, satire, irony, allegory, apologue, parable, fable, illustration.

4. Pictorial likeness, image, effigy, statue, bust, representation, icon.

5. Form determined by outlines, shape, outline, contour, configuration, conformation, body form, frame, cut, cast, build, body.

6. Design, pattern, device, drawing, diagram, schema, plan, type, representative, sign, illustration, cut, symbol, emblem, mold, fashion, cast.

7. Impression made by a person, effect, impression, appearance as regards action, person as presented before the eyes of the world, personage, somebody, character of distinction, presence, one who plays a prominent part.

8. Splendor, magnificence, show, pomp.

9. Dance evolution, pattern in dancing, balletic combination, movement, division of a dance.

FIGURE, *v.* 1. Count, calculate, cipher, compute, numerate, cast, express in figures, work with numerical figures, total, reckon, add up, sum up, find the amount of, appraise, assess.

2. Portray by speech or action, act, personify, impersonate, take the part of, perform, appear.

3. Adorn with figures, ornament, diversify, variegate, mark with a pattern, embellish with a design.

4. Outline, shape, form, image, schematize, sketch, picture, limn, delineate, blazon, depict, portray, draw, make a drawing of.

5. Personify, metaphorize, allegorize, fable, shadow forth, adumbrate, prefigure, allude to, foreshow.

6. Symbolize, typify, be typical of, signify, emblemize, mean, express.

7. Image, conceive, picture, have an idea of, envisage, envision, form a mental image of, represent.

8. Think, opine, judge, suppose, believe, surmise, conjecture.

9. Take a prominent part, be conspicuous, shine, shine forth, cut a figure, make a distinguished appearance, glitter, scintillate, make a splash, flaunt, make a noise in the world, cut a dash, show off, make a great show, attract atten-

tion, strut, swashbuckle, make a display, blow one's horn, enjoy popularity, come to the front.

FIGUREHEAD, *n.* 1. *(Naut.)* Ornamental figure over the cutwater of a ship, image projecting from the prow of a vessel.

2. Nominal but not real chief, assumed head, one with no real authority or responsibility, nonentity, cipher.

FIGURINE, *n.* Small figure, statuette, small-scale sculptural representation, ornamental model, puppet, doll, aglet, manikin, marionette, *fantoccini (It.).*

FILAMENT, *n.* 1. Very fine thread, fiber, strand, cilia, hair, tendril, fibril, cirrus, gossamer, wire, harl, staple, funicle, cobweb.

2. Single element of textile fiber, silk, mechanically produced fiber, rayon, nylon, orlon, dacron, linen, cotton.

3. Thread, yarn, packthread, twist.

4. Strip, shred, slip, band, fillet, lath, shaving, splinter.

FILAMENTOUS, *adj.* Resembling a filament, fibrillous, threadshaped, filamentar, filamentary, filar, fibrous, fibrillose, filiform, threadlike, thready, stringy, ropy, wiry, hairy, hairlike, capilliform.

FILCH, *v.* Steal something of small value, pilfer, purloin, snitch, thieve, rob, lift, bag, prig, nim, crib, shoplift, cabbage, palm, crimp, make off with, carry off, spirit away, abduct, kidnap, shanghai, plagiarize, appropriate, pirate, maraud, swipe, poach, embezzle, swindle, peculate, mulct, defalcate, rook, bilk, pluck, fleece, diddle, skin, pigeon.

FILE, *n.* 1. Device in which things are classified for convenient reference, string on which papers are strung for preservation and reference, cabinet, filing cabinet.

2. Collection of papers so arranged, bundle of papers, dossier, inventory, register, roll, list, rota, row, score, tally.

3. Metal tool with small cutting ridges for smoothing, toothed tool, rasp, emery board, abrasive.

4. Line of persons arranged one behind another, row, queue, rank, series, chain, string, range, tier.

FILE, *v.* 1. Arrange methodically for convenient reference, place on file, pigeonhole, record, classify, list, enter, tabulate, inventory, catalogue, set in order, chronicle, calendar, book, insert, make an entry of, docket, register, enroll, store, preserve, keep, lay in.

2. Smooth with a file, polish, rasp, rub down with a file, scrape, abrade, grind, grate, bray, pound, reduce, attenuate, chip, grind, shear, shave, plane, burnish, pulverize, comminute, granulate, triturate, levigate, glaze, calender.

3. March in a file, walk in line, march in procession, defile, file off, queue up, walk Indian-fashion, follow the leader, line up one after another.

4. Make application, apply for, petition, prefer a claim.

FILIAL, *adj.* Befitting a son or daughter, sonlike, daughterly, bearing the relation of a child to a parent, becoming to a child in relation to his parents, dutiful, affectionate, respectful.

FILIBUSTER, *n.* 1. Attempt to obstruct legislation by dilatory tactics, delay in legislation, obstruction in congressional action.

2. Prevention, preclusion, stoppage, intercep-

tion, hindrance, impedition, obtrusion, interference, opposition.

3. Postponement, cunctation, procrastination, prorogation, retardation, protraction, demurrage, prolongation, Fabian policy.

4. Irregular military adventurer, freebooter, lawless adventurer, buccaneer, pirate, sea-robber, corsair, viking, privateer, rover, ranger, brigand, bandit, marauder, desperado, pillager, depredator.

FILIFORM, *adj.* Filamentous, filaceous, fibrous, fibrillous, threadshaped, thready, threadlike, wiry, stringy, ropy, long and slender.

FILIGREE, *n.* 1. Ornamental work of fine wires, lacy jeweler's work of scrolls and arabesques, jewelry resembling lacework, wirework, ornamental openwork, fretwork, tracery, reticle, grille, grating, plait.

2. Anything too delicate to be durable, fanciful thing.

FILL, *v.* 1. Put as much as can be held into, make full, fill up, inject with, pervade, penetrate, permeate, overspread, run through, charge to repletion, occupy to the full capacity, saturate, load, pack, suffuse, infuse, impregnate, plug, stop up, ram down.

2. Satisfy *(as food),* sate, satiate, cram, stuff, gorge, glut, cloy, pall, content, gluttonize, congest.

3. Provide, lay in, lay by, outfit, provision, supply, store, furnish, replenish, renew, make plentiful throughout, stock, supply deficiencies, make up, eke out, make good.

4. Expand, distend, dilate, dilatate, stretch, spread, widen, extend, diffuse, blow up, puff, fatten, inflate.

5. Occupy and perform the duties of, fulfil, meet requirements satisfactorily, officiate in, serve, act, function, execute, do duty, preside, discharge, carry out.

FILLET, *n.* 1. Thin narrow strip of material, band to encircle the hair, ribbon bound around the hair, diadem, tiara, riband, fascia, wreath, garland, crown, corona, coronet, chaplet, snood, circlet, areola, roundlet, annulus, ringlet.

2. Piece of muscle or lean meat, thick slice of boned fish.

FILLIP, *v.* 1. Strike with a fingernail snapped from the end of the thumb, make a fillip with the fingers, snap with the finger.

2. Strike smartly, tap, bat, rap, slap, dab, flap, pat, whack.

3. Stimulate, spur, urge, goad, prick, egg on, whet, sharpen, hurry on.

FILLIP, *n.* 1. Smart tap, stroke, blow, dint, rap, knock, slap, pat, smack, dab, slam, clout, whack, cuff, swap, jab, swipe.

2. Anything that tends to arouse, stimulus, impulsion, impulse, impetus, incitement, instigation, incentive, spur, goad, whip, provocative, whet.

FILLY, *n.* 1. Female colt, female foal, young mare, jade.

2. Lively young girl, bold girl.

FILM, *n.* 1. Thin layer, coating, thin skin, caul, membrane, pellicle, integument, membranous covering, scale, coat, sheet, peel, veil, scum, overspread, flake, lamina, gauze, nebula, cloud, haze, mist, milkiness, pearliness.

2. Cobweb thread, filament, delicate thread, sheer web, gossamer.

3. Motion picture, movie, cinema, cinematograph, kino, bioscope, biograph, movies, screen.

FILMY, *adj.* 1. Covered with a film, pellicular, scaly, membranous, flaky, squamous.

2. Gauzy, flimsy, gossamery, unsubstantial, thin, fine, delicate, subtile, sheer, finespun, diaphanous, transparent, see-through, silken, silky, cobwebby, chiffon, pellucid.

3. Hazy, cloudy, misty, murky, opaque, obfuscated, opalescent, pearly, milky, frosted, mat.

FILTER, *v.* 1. Pass through a filter, remove by the action of a strainer, strain, filtrate, purify, refine, clarify.

2. Percolate, transcolate, transude, exude, leak, run through, seep, distill, ooze, drain, well out, dribble, trickle, effuse, find vent, escape.

FILTER, *n.* Device through which something is passed to remove impurities, sieve, strainer, screen, porous mass through which fluids are passed to separate them from matter held in suspension, riddle.

FILTH, *n.* 1. Offensive dirt, nastiness, filthiness, uncleanness, impurity, immundity, defilement, contamination, foul matter, ordure, excrement, excreta, dung, feces, sewage, muck, coprolite, night soil, guano, manure, decay, putrescence, slop, squalor, trash, lees, dregs, sediment, putridity, garbage, carrion, offal, spawn, discharge, silt, mire, mud, sludge, slush, slime, grime, smudge, smoke, soot, dust, pig sty, Augean stables, pollution.

2. Moral impurity, foul language, pornography, smut, ribaldry, obscenity, grossness, indelicacy, indecency, impudicity, bawdiness, *double entendre,* suggestiveness, lewdness, dirty-mindedness, vileness, rottenness, nastiness.

FILTHY, *adj.* 1. Disgustingly dirty, foul, unclean, soiled, defiled, besmeared, begrimed, grimy, muddy, sooty, smoky, slimy, mucky, feculent, dusty, dirt-smeared, squalid, bedraggled, uncleanly, slovenly, slatternly, sluttish, unkempt, unscoured, unwashed, unswept, musty, piggish, hoggish, fetid, gone bad, polluted, rotten, tainted, fly-blown, maggoty, putrid, purulent, carious, fecal, stercoraceous, excrementitious.

2. Morally unclean, depraved, corrupt, gross, impure, offensive, objectionable, indelicate, indecent, nasty-minded, coarse, sordid, shameless, vile, vulgar, foul-mouthed, immodest, obscene, bawdy, lewd, smutty, pornographic, ribald, suggestive, risqué, loose, broad, crapulous.

FIN, *n.* Membranous paddlelike process of an aquatic animal, flipper, fish's tail, finlike organ used for propulsion and steering, rudder.

FINAL, *adj.* 1. Coming at the end, concluding, terminal, terminating, ending, hindermost, rear, rearmost, closing, last in time or order, latest, farthest, ultimate, eventual, extreme, last-minute.

2. Conclusive, decisive, determinate, definitive, exhaustive, complete, thorough, finished, decided, irrevocable, unappealable.

FINALE, *n.* Closing part, close, completion, finish, finis, conclusion, denouement, wind-up, catastrophe, epilogue, peroration, last stage, fall of the curtain, termination, end, upshot, issue, result.

FINALITY, *n.* 1. Conclusiveness, completeness, intactness, entirety, totality, integrity, wholeness, perfection, finish, maturity, elaboration, definitiveness, terminality, final character.

2. Final act, final arrangement, final settlement.

FINALLY, *adv.* 1. At the final point, ultimately, lastly, at the last moment, in the end, at length, at the last, at an end, in conclusion, at last, eventually.

2. In a final manner, once and for all, to crown all, conclusively, definitively, determinately, after all, settled, done with.

FINANCE, *n.* 1. Transaction of money matters, monetary theory, banking, art of monetary relations, theory of fiscal relations, money-making, theory of investments, pecuniary management, money-market, bourse, Wall Street, Lombard Street.

2. Money, revenue, accounts, funds, treasure, currency, specie, circulating medium, coin of the realm, hard cash, dollars, sterling, pounds, shillings and pence, guineas, lucre, shekels, roll, jack, dough, spondulics, wads, pile, gold, silver, copper, nickle, bar, ingot, bullion, nugget, wampum, mite, farthing, sou, penny, cent, centime, chicken feed, ducat, sawbucks, eagles, grand, long green, mint, paper money, rupees, greenbacks.

FINANCES, *n.* 1. (*Colloq.*) Resources, income, proceeds, circumstances, personal affairs, money matters, property, breeches pocket, purse, money in hand, ready money, pocket-money, pin-money.

2. Pecuniary resources, revenues, capital, stock, assets, wealth, cash, public funds, fiscus, exchequer, public resources, fiscal resources, treasury, wherewithal, almighty dollar.

FINANCIAL, *adj.* Pertaining to monetary receipts and expenditures, relating to money matters, pecuniary, fiscal, crumenal, numismatical, sterling, sumptuous, bursal.

FINANCIER, *n.* One skilled in money matters, cambist, large-scale investor, money-lender, money-changer, broker, banker, capitalist, man of means, man of substance, rich man, silk-stocking, moneyed man, plutocrat, millionaire.

FIND, *v.* 1. Come upon by chance, encounter, meet with, come across, light upon, fall in with, stumble upon, bump into, come at, chance upon.

2. Discover, unearth, dig up, ferret out, hit upon, uncover, disinter, obtain by search, come by, track down, detect, expose.

3. Espy, descry, catch sight of, discern, spot.

4. Attain by effort, acquire, gain, get, glean, pick up, collect, gather, win, earn, procure, scrape up, succeed in attaining, arrive at, recover, retrieve, get back, repossess.

5. Perceive, observe, apprehend, ken, notice, remark, ascertain, experience, learn, hear of.

6. (*Law*) Determine after judicial inquiry, pronounce as an official act, declare a verdict, decide, settle, adjudge, adjudicate, determine an issue, decree, rule, confirm, sentence, doom, award.

FIND, *n.* Valuable discovery, acquisition, catch, bargain, good buy, bonanza, windfall, godsend, *trouvaille (Fr.),* hit, lucky hit.

FIND FAULT, *v.* Express dissatisfaction, complain, find cause of blame, criticize unfavorably, grumble, disapprove, object to, take exception, view with disfavor, frown upon, shake the head at, disparage, condemn, knock, censure, reproach, impugn, reprehend, chide, admonish, call to account, reprove, rake over the coals, lecture, rebuke, damn with faint praise, scoff at.

FINDING, *n.* Verdict after judicial inquiry, decision, decree, sentence, judgment, award, conclusion arrived at, result of judicial inquest.

FIND OUT 1. Discover in the course of time,

detect by search, bring to light by inquiry, learn, catch, detect, hear of.

2. Make out, decipher, decode, unriddle, solve, get at, ascertain.

FINE, *adj.* 1. Little, small, minute, comminuted, delicate, slender, very thin, svelte, slight, dainty, fragile.

2. Flimsy, gossamery, cobwebby, delicate in texture, tenuous, lightweight, fine in texture, sheer, silken, silky, transparent, diaphanous, delicately fashioned, thin, airy, dainty, ethereal.

3. Consisting of small particles, ground, powdered, pulverized, not coarse, refined.

4. Keen, sharp, precise, accomplished, highly skilled, finished, having special attainments, consummate, perfect, brilliant, acute, subtle, skilful, polished.

5. Clear, bright, pure, refined, unadulterated, pleasant, sunny.

6. Elegant, fastidious, exquisite, discriminating, sensitive, refined, nice, smart, smartly dressed, well-groomed, chic, *bien soignée (Fr.)*, stylish, modish.

7. Handsome, good-looking, beautiful, pretty, comely, bonny, fair, attractive, well-favored.

8. Of the highest grade, of very high quality, free from imperfections, choice, admirable, splendid, rare, excellent, superior, superb, magnificent, very good, dandy, bully, nifty, nobby, tasteful.

FINE, *v.* Subject to a pecuniary penalty, penalize, mulct, amerce, impose a fine upon, punish by a fine, inflict a penalty upon, sequestrate, confiscate, sequester.

FINE, *n.* Pecuniary penalty, forfeiture, mulct, amercement, forfeit, damages, confiscation, assessment, sequestration, sum paid by way of settlement.

FINERY, *n.* Showy dress, elegance, frippery, frills and furbelows, fine things, fine ornaments, excessive decoration, trimmings, paraphernalia, accouterments, gewgaws, tinsel, trappings, trinkets, clinquant, spangles, sequins, pinch-beck, brummagem.

FINESPUN, *adj.* 1. Spun out to a fine thread, attenuated, thin, tapered, slim, gracile, slight, delicate, gossamery, cobwebby, sheer, silken, transparent, diaphanous, unsubstantial.

2. Excessively subtle, hair-splitting, casuistical, Jesuitical, sophistical.

FINESSE, *n.* 1. Delicacy of execution, subtlety of discrimination, tact, knowledge of the world, savoir-faire, worldly wisdom, discretion, taste, refinement, polish, elegance, grace.

2. Artful management, craft, strategy, artifice, stratagem, subterfuge, ruse, wile, shift, evasion, juggle, subtle contrivance, cunning, maneuver, dodge, side-blow, trickery, intrigue, adroitness, artfulness, guile, trick, diplomacy, deception.

FINESSE, *v.* Use finesse, employ stratagem, use artifice, intrigue, maneuver, live by one's wits, gerrymander, practice tricks, contrive, double, temporize, circumvent, steal a march upon, surprise, outdo, cheat.

FINGER, *n.* One of the five terminating members of the hand, organ of touch, forefinger, ring finger, thumb, digit, pointer, index finger, feeler, palpus.

FINGER, *v.* 1. Touch with the fingers, feel, thumb, paw, graze, brush, stroke, pass the fingers over, twiddle, massage, knead, rub, manipulate, palpate, tickle, toy with, caress with the fingers, play with, meddle with, handle.

2. Take with thievish intent, seize, pilfer, filch, steal, purloin.

FINIAL, *n.* (*Arch.*) Ornamental foliated termination of a pinnacle or gable, turned ornament capping another form, vertical termination, terminating detail, terminal, pinnacle, carved peak.

FINICAL, *adj.* 1. Fussily elegant, dapper, foppish, spruce, silk-stockinged, dandyish, affected, coxcombical, dainty, trim, too particular, fussy, affectedly fine, overfastidious, overnice, finicky, squeamish, delicate, *maniéré (Fr.),* dandified, jaunty, mincing, simpering, namby-pamby, prunes-and-prisms, effeminate, pernickety, pranked out, natty, niminy-piminy.

2. Precise, strict, exact, nice, careful, meticulous, scrupulous, exacting, difficult, hard.

FINIS, *n.* End, conclusion, close, windup, denouement, finale, final curtain, ending, last stage, issue, result, upshot, *fait accompli (Fr.),* work done, *coronat opus (Lat.),* that's it, crowning touch, curtain, death, dissolution, deathblow, coup de grâce, K.O.

FINISH, *v.* 1. Arrive at the end of, come to the end, end, conclude, close, terminate, bring to a close, put an end to, bring to an end, discontinue, windup, cease, stop, draw to a close, clinch, seal.

2. Bring to completion, carry out, carry through, consummate, accomplish, fulfill, achieve, get done, do, execute, complete, perform, deliver the goods, make good, fill the bill, bring to a happy issue, effect, crown, cap, round out, get out of the way, dispatch, knock off, dispose of, discharge, realize, compass, settle, do thoroughly, not do by halves.

3. Perfect in detail, put the final touches on, polish, refine, improve, develop, elaborate, make perfect, prepare for entrance into society.

4. Surface, glaze, face, veneer, varnish, lacquer, gild, coat, dress.

5. (*Colloq.*) Overcome completely, defeat, destroy, kill, put out of the way, get rid of.

FINISH, *n.* 1. End, termination, close, expiration, finis, finale, windup, last, stoppage, conclusion, limit, boundary, bottom, last stage, peroration, epilogue, fall of the curtain, ending, curtain, denouement, catastrophe, final event, goal, objective, butt, closing period, evening, eventide, completion.

2. Death, extermination, annihilation, ruin, deathblow, coup de grâce, K.O., destruction, dissolution, knock-out, K.O., sleeper punch, sleeper hold, fate, kismet, doomsday, *dies irae (Lat.).*

3. Polish, smoothness, beauty, shapeliness, symmetry, proportion, balance, harmony, congruity, regularity, evenness, order, form, eurhythmy, elegance, perfection, elaboration, refinement, consummation.

4. Finishing touches, last touch, polishing, surface, veneer, lacquer.

5. Educational or social polish, urbanity, politeness, mannerliness, suavity, social graces, savoir-faire, tact, accomplishments, finesse, felicity, qualification, capability, habilitation, endowment, gift, turn, genius.

FINISHED, *adj.* 1. Concluded, completed, ended, final, complete, perfect, consummated, whole, entire, full.

2. Polished to the highest degree of excellence, perfected in all details, rounded, highly wrought, faultless, ideal, elegant, impeccable, immaculate, shapely, beautiful, well-set, refined, indefectible, flawless, scatheless, choice, prime, classic.

3. Highly accomplished, talented, skilled, gifted, proficient, able, practiced, experienced, qualified, trained, expert, deft, artful, feat, slick, thoroughbred, good at, at home in, master of, masterly, conversant with, crackajack, up in, capable, up to the mark, fitted for, prepared, initiated, primed, neat-handed, fine-fingered, artistic.

FINITE, *adj.* Having definable limits, limited, bounded, terminable, definable, measurable, not infinite or infinitesimal, subject to limitations, contracted, conditioned, restricted, capable of being ended, not everlasting, applied to human life which has an end on this earth, capable of being completely counted *(Math.).*

FIORD, *n.* Long narrow arm of the sea bordered by steep cliffs, armlet, bay, gulf, bight, estuary, inlet, frith, firth, ostiary, mouth, lagoon, indraught, cove.

FIRE, *n.* 1. Combustion, evolution of light and heat, intense heat, caloricity, ignition.

2. Burning mass of material, conflagration, blaze, phlogiston, flame, spark, ingle, coal, flash, bonfire, balefire, beam, wildfire, sheet of fire, lambent flame.

3. Luminous appearance, luminosity, radiance, effulgence, luster, splendor, brilliancy, scintillation, glow, incandescence, redness, flush, suffusion, illumination, flashing light, refulgence.

4. Discharge of firearms, fusillade, volley, firing, broadside, salvo, sharpshooting, sniping.

5. Liveliness of imagination, inspiration, force of sentiment, imaginativeness, genius.

6. Burning passion, ardor, enthusiasm, vivacity, energy, force, power, might, life, vigor, fervor, impetuosity, fervency, animation, intensity, spirit, vehemence, gusto, earnestness, eagerness, *empressement (Fr.),* dash, verve, élan, pep, punch, backbone, mettle, vim, driving power, alacrity, bustle, quickness, unction.

7. Fever, inflammation, flush, febricity, pyrexia *(Med.).*

8. Severe trial, trouble, exposure to fire by way of torture, ordeal, persecution, affliction, holocaust.

FIRE, *v.* 1. Set fire to, kindle, enkindle, light, ignite, set on fire, burn, cause to glow, inflame, set burning.

2. Expose to the action of fire, subject to heat, illuminate, calefy, heat, warm, bake, overheat, make white hot, incandesce, smelt, scorch, torrefy, toast, singe, cauterize, brand, sear, cremate.

3. Inflame with passion, fill with ardor, animate, arouse, stir, stimulate, excite, goad, spur, inspirit, whet, fillip, urge, instigate, incite, rouse, stir up, enliven, infuse life into, foster, foment, electrify, galvanize, inspire, motivate, trigger, vitalize, quicken.

4. Project a missile by discharging from a gun, discharge, fire off, fire a volley, shoot, make go off, detonate, open fire, level at, enfilade, subject to explosion, bombard, shell, draw a bead on, pop at, snipe at, pepper, fusillade, torpedo, draw the trigger, expel, eject, hurl, rake.

5. *(Colloq.)* Dismiss peremptorily from service, eject forcibly, oust, depose, remove from office, sack, bounce, give one his walking papers.

FIREARM, *n.* Small arms, explosive weapon, pistol, rifle, musket, firelock, fowling piece, blunderbuss, matchlock, harquebus, shotgun, breechloader, muzzleloader, carbine, revolver, repeater, fusil, automatic pistol, shooting iron, six-shooter, rod *(slang)*, cannon, saker, ordnance, field piece,

big Bertha, mortar, howitzer, pompom, anti-aircraft gun, aërogun, machine gun, submachine gun.

FIREBRAND, *n.* 1. Brand, torch, fireball, piece of burning wood, live coal, faggot, ember.

2. One who kindles strife, dangerous man, inflamer of passions, mischief-maker, agitator, instigator, incendiary, *agent provocateur (Fr.),* ugly customer, anarchist, communist, terrorist.

FIRE-EATER, *n.* 1. Juggler who pretends to eat fire.

2. One who creates occasion to fight or quarrel, quarrelsome brawler, bully, hector, swashbuckler, domineering fellow, hot spur, tartar, pepperpot, spitfire, berserker, blusterer, vaporer, swaggerer, mock hero, Squire Western (*Tom Jones).*

FIREMAN, *n.* 1. Man employed to tend fires, fire tender, stoker.

2. Man employed to extinguish or prevent fires, fire fighter.

FIREPLACE, *n.* Part of a chimney in which fuel is burned, hearth, grate, firebox, inglenook, hob.

FIREPROOF, *adj.* Proof against fire, relatively incombustible, uninflammable, asbestic, asbestine.

FIRESIDE, *n.* 1. Hearth, place near the fire, ingleside, hearthstone, chimney corner.

2. Home life, home, household gods, Lares and Penates, *dulce domum (Lat.),* paternal domicile, homestead.

FIREWORKS, *n.* 1. Combustible devices, pyrotechnics, *feu d'artifice (Fr.),* fizgig, illuminations, rocket, Roman candle, Catherine wheel, parachute light, Véry light, star shell, bonfire, *feu de joie (Fr.).*

2. Fiery display of temper, tantrum, towering passion, *acharnement (Fr.),* angry mood, fit of rage, paroxysm, fire and fury, rage, hot blood, high words, dander, ferment, explosion.

FIRKIN, *n.* 1. Unit of capacity, the fourth part of a barrel.

2. Small wooden vessel, cask, tub, tun, butt, hogshead, kilderkin, keg, barrel, ampulla.

FIRM, *adj.* 1. Hard, stiff, rigid, solid, dense, not soft, implastic, compact, compressed, not fluid, unbending, unyielding, adamantine, stony, rocky, flinty, steely, brassy, horny, bony.

2. Securely fixed in place, fast, secure, stable, rooted, anchored, moored, settled, established, immovable, unalterable, confirmed, impenetrable, impregnable, close, tight, taut, indissoluble.

3. Unchanging in purpose, steadfast, resolute, determined, resolved, stanch, positive, strong-willed, strong-minded, earnest, serious, dead-set, decided, peremptory, unflinching, unwavering, unshaken, constant, steady, obstinate, inflexible, inexorable, tenacious, obdurate, grim, stern, unfaltering, fearless, invincible.

4. Strong, sturdy, stout, robust, sinewy, hardy, tough, inured, durable, stalwart, vigorous, manly.

FIRM, *n.* Unincorporated association of persons for carrying on a business, company, commercial house, concern, establishment, house, *maison (Fr.),* trust, partnership, copartnership, corporation *(loosely).*

FIRMAMENT, *n.* Heaven, sky, the vault of heaven, the arch of the sky, the welkin, empyrean, azure, blue, ether, celestial spaces, starry host, canopy of heaven.

FIRMNESS, *n.* 1. Hardness, stiffness, rigidity,

inflexibility, solidity, compactness, callosity, durity, petrifaction.

2. Strength, stability, toughness, soundness, immutability, endurance, valor, grit, fortitude, nerve, backbone, manhood.

3. Steadfastness, resoluteness, iron will, strength of mind, resolve, intransigence, obstinacy, tenacity, constancy, steadiness, determination, intrepidity, courage, pertinacity, confidence, assurance, resolution.

FIRST, adj. 1. Chief among others of the same class, foremost, leading, principal, main, prime, capital, highest, head, superior, paramount, preëminent, supreme, preceding all others, fore, essential, vital, cardinal, radical.

2. Original, earliest, eldest, authentic, premier.

3. Elementary, initial, rudimentary, primary, introductory, incipient, initiative, inaugural, embryonic.

4. Pristine, primordial, primeval, primitive, primal, aboriginal, autochthonous.

FIRST, adv. 1. For the first time, in the first place, firstly, imprimis (Lat.).

2. At the outset, initially, in the beginning, before anything else, first and foremost, primarily, originally, in the bud, in embryo, from the beginning, heretofore, formerly.

3. In preference to something else, rather, sooner, liefer, before, by choice, by preference.

FIRST-RATE, adj. Excellent, very good, best, tiptop, crack, choice, select, picked, elect, superfine, prime, superior, of the highest order, of the best quality, of the first class, A-1, first-class, of the highest grade, of the first water, admirable, gilt-edged, capital, cardinal, worth its weight in gold.

FISC, n. Royal treasure, state fiscus, exchequer, thesaurus, bank, bursary, coffer, chest, depository, till, cash box, money box.

FISCAL, adj. Pertaining to the public revenues, pertaining to financial matters, financial, monetary, pecuniary, crumenal, sumptuary, numismatical, sterling.

FISH, v. 1. Angle, cast for, hook, bob, net, cast one's net for, trawl, troll, catch, draw in, grapple.

2. (With FOR) Seek by indirection, aim at, aim after, follow up, set after, woo, hint after, beat the bushes, grope for, fish out, nose out, ferret out, trail, seek a clue, try to get at, look about for, sound, reconnoiter.

FISHERMAN, n. Angler, fisher, piscator, stream sportsman, Izaak Walton, piscatorian.

FISHERY, n. Piscary, aquarium, fish hatchery, fishing establishment.

FISHING, n. Practice of catching fish, angling, hooking, netting, trolling, trawling, piscation, halieutics.

FISHY, adj. 1. (Colloq.) Of questionable character, suspicious, unreliable, dishonest, unscrupulous, slippery, shady.

2. (Colloq.) Exaggerated, hyperbolical, extravagant, embroidered, improbable.

3. Dull, expressionless, vacant, lusterless, lackluster, glassy-eyed.

FISSION, n. Breaking into parts, scission, splitting, cleaving, disjunction, disunion, disengagement, disconnection, dissociation, parting, division, rupture, break, cleavage, severance, disintegration, disruption.

FISSURE, n. Narrow opening made by the part-

ing of any substance, crack, break, breach, cleft, gap, cranny, interstice, split, rift, slit, mesh, slot, chink, chasm, hiatus, lacuna, interspace, interval, crevice, rime, creek, fracture, rent, orifice, aperture, cavity, hole, chap, notch, cut, incision, gash, leak, flaw.

FIST, n. 1. Tightly closed hand with fingers doubled into the palm, clenched hand, duke (slang), nieve (Brit.), mitt (slang), paw.

2. Clutch, firm hold, grasp, grip, gripe, iron grip.

3. Threat, menace, intimidation, defiance.

FISTIC, adj. Pertaining to boxing, pugilistic, palestral, gladiatorial, pugnacious, fighting, combative, bellicose, contentious.

FISTICUFF, n. 1. Blow with the fist, hook, cuff, hard knock, rap, stroke, punch, pummel, thump, buffet, jab, swipe, pelt, hard knock, smack, slap, slam, pat, whack, bang, thwack, clout, thrust, lunge.

2. (Pl.) Combat with the fists, fist fight, pugilism, boxing, spar, mill, set-to, round, scrap, bout, event, prize fighting, the ring, free-for-all, shindy, fracas, scuffle, rumpus, row, tussle, melee, fray, affray, scrimmage, broil, collision, personal encounter, brush, battle royal, hammer and tongs.

FISTULOUS, adj. Hollow, fistular, tubelike, pipeshaped, tubular, fistulose, cannular, pervious, permeable, tubulous, tubulated, piped, foraminous.

FIT, n. 1. Convulsion, paroxysm, spasm, ictus (Med.), throe, spell, sudden acute attack, violent stroke, access, raptus, seizure, epitasis (Med.), outbreak, outburst, agitation, qualm, violent manifestation.

2. Whim, whimsy, notion, fancy, caprice, temporary affection, humor, crotchet, kink, quirk, freak, vagary, passing mood, pet, tantrum, impulsive and irregular action.

FIT, adj. 1. Competent, qualified, capable, capacitated, fit for, fitted, initiated, prepared, primed, adequate, efficient, trained, ready, mature, ripe, eligible.

2. Suitable, well adapted, apt, appropriate, apropos, apposite, adapted, accordant, correspondent, consonant, pertinent, relevant, ad rem (Lat.), in point, applicable, expedient, timely, seasonable, opportune, meet, proper, right, correct, decorous, seemly, fitting, befitting, becoming, good, convenient, felicitous, congruous, coherent, worthy, deserving.

3. In good physical condition, in good health, toned up, in trim, strong, healthy.

FIT, v. 1. Adjust, make suitable, adapt, suit to, graduate, calibrate, rectify, correct, regulate, shape aright, fashion, full-fashion.

2. Agree, accord, harmonize, correspond, tally, be adapted, be suitable for, become, befit, conform, match, equal, dovetail, concur, coincide, be in agreement with, cohere, be of the right size, be of the right shape for.

3. Make qualified, make competent, qualify, prepare, equip, get ready, prime, arrange, capacitate, enable, empower, entitle, arm, forearm, put in a condition of readiness, train.

FITFUL, adj. 1. Coming by spells, irregularly intermittent, sporadic, spasmodic, convulsive, unsteady, unstable, mutable, changeable, fluctuating, unsettled, inconstant, uncertain, uneven, mutable, variable, flickering.

2. Impulsive, fickle, mercurial, whimsical, ca-

pricious, fanciful, maggoty, crotchety, odd, humorsome, erratic, rhapsodical, touch-and-go, desultory, rambling, wayward, vagrant, frivolous, giddy, volatile.

3. Full of vicissitudes, vicissitudinous, checkered, eventful, kaleidoscopic, protean, ever-changing.

FITFULLY, *adv.* In a fitful manner, irregularly, intermittently, off and on, see-saw, by fits and starts, by turns, at intervals, without rhyme or reason, at one's own sweet will.

FITNESS, *n.* 1. Suitableness, applicability, appositeness, aptness, appropriateness, aptitude, pertinence, relevancy, admissibility, compatibility, convenience, expedience, congruity, correspondence.

2. Propriety, decorum, seemliness, becomingness, *bienséance (Fr.),* correctness, the thing, the proper thing.

3. Preparation, qualification, capability, skill, capacity, endowment, ability, competency, efficiency, readiness, eligibility.

FIT OUT, *v.* 1. Dress, habilitate, garb, accouter, apparel, tire, attire, robe, drape, array, vest, invest, clothe, rig.

2. Furnish with requisites, equip, harness, caparison, arm, fit up, fettle, fledge, supply with necessaries.

FIX, *v.* 1. Place permanently, fasten in position securely, secure, attach, make fast, connect, bind, tie, pinion, lock, buckle, hitch, truss, gird, tether, link, fetter, yoke, clinch, stay, couple, nail, screw, bolt, hasp, clamp, clasp, solder, rivet, cement, weld, fuse, pin.

2. Make permanent against change, establish, settle, stabilize, ground, found, institute, organize, install, confirm, plant.

3. Determine definitely, conclude, define, resolve, will, purpose, decide, seal, limit, delimit, appoint.

4. Direct steadily, attract and hold, magnetize.

5. Harden, make rigid, consolidate, solidify, stiffen, congeal, take on a more solid form, become set, become stable in consistence, be reduced from volatility to a more permanent state.

6. Repair, patch up, mend, renovate, put in good condition, adjust.

7. *(Colloq.)* Privately arrange matters with so as to secure favorable action, dishonestly dispose.

8. *(Colloq.)* Put in a position to make no further trouble, fix one's feet, cook one's goose, do for, get even with, get revenge upon, retaliate, take retribution.

FIX, *n. (Colloq.)* Position of embarrassment, position from which it is difficult to escape, predicament, jam, spot, strait, pass, pinch, plight, dilemma, critical situation, pickle, difficulty, quandary, scrape, hot water, stew, imbroglio, mess, muddle, involvement, entanglement, awkward spot, ticklish situation, perplexity.

FIXATION, *n.* Fixed idea, *idée fixe,* obsession, complex, delusion, monomania, *mentis gravissimus error (Lat.),* infatuation, intoxication, prepossession, predilection, crotchet, quirk, fetishistic regard, fool's paradise.

FIXED, *adj.* 1. Firmly implanted, made fast, rendered stable, definitely placed, firm, settled, fastened, set, stationary, motionless, rigid, immovable, stable, rooted.

2. Set upon something, intent on, steadily directed at, persistent, resolute, resolved, obstinate, determined.

3. Definite, not fluctuating, not varying, unwavering, unbending, unpliant, constant, steady.

4. Put in order, repaired, mended.

FIXITY, *n.* Permanence, stability, persistency, endurance, durability, standing, status quo, maintenance, preservation, conservation, tenacity, unchangingness, law of the Medes and Persians.

FIXTURE, *n.* Equipment, apparatus, appointment, equipage, paraphernalia, permanently attached part, appendage, attachment, thing firmly fastened in place, person established in a place.

FIZZ, *n.* Hissing sound, effervescence, fizzle, fermentation, bubbling, froth, fume, spume, spray, swish, sizzle, rustle, buzz, whiz, sparkle, sibilation.

FIZZLE, *v.* 1. Make a sputtering sound that dies out weakly, effervesce, ferment, aerate, foam, froth, spume, sparkle, gurgle, bubble, hiss, fizz.

2. *(Colloq.)* Fail ignominiously, make a failure of, misfire, fizzle out, fall short, break down, collapse, come to nothing, fall through, miss the mark, end in smoke, come to grief, founder, cave in.

FIZZLE, *n. (Colloq.)* Fiasco, botch, abortion, abortive attempt, ignominious failure, nonfulfilment, nonsuccess, miscarriage, labor in vain, no go, flash in the pan, scrape, *brutum fulmen (Lat.),* muddle, foozle, jam, mess.

FLABBERGAST, *v. (Colloq.)* Overcome with surprise and bewilderment, astonish, astound, take aback, strike with wonder, surprise, amaze, dumfound, confound, abash, confuse, disconcert, stagger, startle, stun, nonplus, dazzle, stupefy, bewilder, petrify, throw on one's beam ends, throw off balance, take one's breath, strike dumb, make one's hair stand on end, make one stare.

FLABBINESS, *n.* Limpness, softness, pliableness, laxness, laxity, flaccidity, flexibility, irresilience, pliancy, ductility, inelasticity, clay, wax, dough, pudding.

FLABBY, *adj.* Hanging loosely, drooping limply, soft, tender, yielding, supple, pliant, flexible, mollient, inelastic, weak, limp, flaccid, wanting firmness, feeble, nerveless, baggy, downy, spongy, doughy, soft as butter.

FLACCID, *adj.* Soft and limber, not firm, limp, drooping, pendulous, hanging loose, baggy, inelastic, irresilient, lax, yielding, flabby, weak, nerveless, unstrung, relaxed.

FLACCIDITY, *n.* Limpness, pendulousness, flabbiness, flaccidness, softness, laxity, inelasticity, relaxed condition, inductility, irresilience, inextensibility.

FLAG, *v.* 1. Hang limply, droop loosely, be yielding, be limp.

2. Fall off in vigor, grow spiritless, decline, languish, be weak, give way, faint, fail, sink, pine, succumb, sag, lag, pall, become dejected, crumble, totter, dodder, fade, tire, grow weary, lose interest, become vapid, grow stale.

FLAG, *n.* Banner, standard, pennant, pennon, colors, eagle, ensign, oriflamme, gonfalon, streamer, vexillum, blue peter, jack, union jack, bannerol, tricolor, stars and stripes, stars and bars, Old Glory, bunting, Mr. Bunting.

FLAGELLATE, *v.* Horsewhip, whip, lash, scourge, fustigate, castigate, bastinado, thrash, strap, flog, birch, cane, give the stick, switch, drub, cudgel, beat black and blue, comb, towel.

FLAGELLATION, *n.* Fustigation, castigation,

strappado, *estrapade (Fr.)*, bastinado, *argumentum ad baculum (Lat.)*, flogging, horsewhipping, beating, lashing, thrashing, stick law, mauling, pommeling, cudgeling, scourging, drubbing, gantlet.

FLAGITIOUS, *adj.* Shamefully wicked, guilty of enormous crimes, scandalously vice-ridden, corrupt, profligate, abandoned, flagrant, nefarious, facinorous, felonious, depraved, iniquitous, criminal, heinous, atrocious, outrageous, monstrous, abominable, execrable, shocking, infamous, villainous, notorious, arrant, egregious, reprehensible, ignominious, incarnate, accursed, vile, foul, black, scurvy, base, diabolical, impious, infernal, grievous.

FLAGON, *n.* Large bottle, canteen, jug, crock, carafe, cruse, ewer, jar, decanter, amphora.

FLAGRANCY, *n.* 1. Audacity, immodesty, shamelessness, brazenness, conspicuousness, openness, plainness, prominence, parade, open display.
2. Evildoing, wickedness, wrongdoing, corruption, depravity, atrocity, infamy, brutality, obliquity, knavery, immorality, debauchery, wantonness, grossness, lewdness, lechery, vice, enormity, excess.

FLAGRANT, *adj.* 1. Glaring, obvious, bold, shameless, brazen, daring, loud, red-handed, audacious, immodest, flaunting, barefaced, arrant, sheer, risqué, crying, notorious, flaming into notice, scandalous.
2. Wicked, nefarious, flagitious, facinorous, felonious, heinous, monstrous, enormous, villainous, atrocious, depraved, infamous, iniquitous, violent, profligate, brutal, bestial, immoral, lewd, lecherous, carnal, libidinous, lustful.

FLAGSTONE, *n.* Rock which can be split into slabs for paving, slab, flat paving stone, flag.

FLAIL, *v.* Thresh, thrash, strike, flog, beat, knock, hit, bash, beat, batter, pelt, buffet, belabor.

FLAIR, *n.* 1. Talent, aptitude, keen perception, genius, gift, forte, turn, parts, endowment, faculty, capacity, ingenuity, instinctive discernment, discriminating sense, taste combined with aptitude.
2. Fondness, inclination, bent, propensity, proclivity, predilection, penchant.
3. *(Hunting)* Scent, sense of smell.

FLAK, *n.* Anti-aircraft fire, ack-ack, ground-defense fire.

FLAKE, *n.* Flat thin piece, small detached mass, scale, layer, stratum, lamina, sheet, foil, wafer, coat, peel, pellicle, membrane, leaf, slice, integument, film, lamella, shaving.

FLAKE, *v.* Come off in flakes, peel off, separate into flakes, scale off, desquamate, chip off from, fall in flakes.

FLAMBEAU, *n.* Flaming torch, brand, torch for use at night in illuminations, link, torch of pitch and tow.

FLAMBOYANT, *adj.* 1. Flame-like in form or color, resplendent, flaming, bright, flashing.
2. Florid, ornate, rococo, baroque, showy, rich, pompous, ostentatious.
3. *(Arch.)* Characterized by waving curves and tracery, wavy, sinuous.

FLAME, *v.* 1. Burn with a flame, burst into flames, blaze, flare, flash, glow with flame, shine brilliantly, glare, flicker.
2. Break out in violence of passion, break into open anger, burn with passion, thrill, be fervid.

FLAME, *n.* 1. Burning vapor, portion of ignited gas, light flare, blaze, fire, ingle, conflagration, scintilla, spark, glare, flash, gleam, sparkle, shimmer.
2. *(Pl.)* State of blazing combustion, glow, inflamed condition, brilliant light, scintillation, luster, brightness, effulgence, coruscation, luminosity, refulgency, phosphorescence.
3. Color of flame, bright coloring, streak of color, bright reddish-orange.
4. Ardor, fervency, fervor, burning zeal, passion, affection, enthusiasm, warmth.
5. Excitement, agitation, fume, tumult, violence, turbulence, ebullition.
6. Object of passionate love, sweetheart, lover, ladylove, inamorato, beau.

FLAMING, *adj.* 1. Emitting flames, blazing, fiery, afire, burning, inflammable, igneous, glowing, smoldering, ablaze, alight, incandescent, lambent.
2. Flagrant, glaring, vehement, intense, violent, agitated, passionate, fervent, ardent, fervid, ebullient, stormy.

FLANGE, *n.* Projecting edge on an object for keeping it in place, margin for strengthening an object, collar, ridge, lip, shoulder, rim, rib, brim, skirt, border.

FLANK, *n.* Side of a human being between the ribs and hip, thigh of an animal, pleuron, paries, flitch, loin, hand, haunch, thin slice of flesh from the flank.

FLANK, *v.* 1. Border upon, lie along, lie at the side of, skirt, wing, border, shut in at the side.
2. Protect, cover, ward, screen, shroud, secure, shelter, guard.
3. Attach on the side, pass round the flank of, turn the flank of, approach on the side, outflank, outmaneuver, enfilade.

FLAP, *n.* 1. Hanging piece, lug, leaf, lap, lappet, tab, fly, apron, skirt, tuck, pendant, tail, pocket cover.
2. Pendulous motion, flop, flapping, swinging, flutter, vibration, wave, undulation.
3. Slapping stroke, fillip, slap, flail, blow, dab, knock, tap, smack, rap, jab, pat, swat, poke, buffet, cuff, thwack, whack.

FLAP, *v.* 1. Swing loosely, flutter, vibrate, oscillate, wave about, switch, whisk, beat, shake, swish, tumble.
2. Brandish, agitate, convulse, toss, move to and fro, bat.

FLAPDOODLE, *n.* Nonsense, bosh, fiddle-faddle, rubbish, drivel, rot, moonshine, twaddle, jargon, rant, wish wash, twattle, fudge, trash, balderdash, stuff and nonsense, food for fools, specious talk.

FLAPJACK, *n.* Pancake, griddlecake, johnnycake, turnover.

FLARE, *v.* 1. Burn unsteadily, blaze with a swaying flame, flash, flame, scintillate, coruscate, fulgurate, phosphoresce, glitter, glow, glisten, glister, glimmer, gleam, twinkle, glare, beam, sparkle, flicker.
2. Burst out suddenly, explode, go off, displode, thunder, blow up, erupt, fulminate, start up fiercely.
3. Spread outward gradually, widen out, splay, project beyond the perpendicular.

FLARE, *n.* 1. Swaying flame, flaring light, unsteady glare, brief blaze, spark, scintilla, facula, flash, emication, coruscation, fulguration, sudden burst of flame, phosphorescence, luminescence, radiation, luminosity, renitency, refulgence, shimmer.

2. Torch, taper, rushlight, flambeau, brand, link, Roman candle, star shell, Véry light, parachute light, light used as a signal.

3. Outward curvature, gradual spread outward in form.

FLARE UP, *v.* Lose one's temper, burst out suddenly in anger, get angry, fly into a passion, boil over with rage, be excited, flash up, work oneself up, seethe, foam, simmer, fume, rage, rant, rave, break out, fly off the handle, explode, go off at a tangent, take fire, flame up, go into hysterics, look black as thunder, run mad, run amuck, go berserk, raise Cain.

FLASH, *v.* 1. Send forth fire in sudden flashes, emit a sudden light, sparkle, scintillate, coruscate, fulgurate, gleam, glitter, shimmer, glisten, glance, twinkle, glimmer, flicker, flame, blaze, glare, glow, flash, glint, beam, glister, shine.

2. Communicate instantaneously, telegraph, crackle, snap.

3. Break forth suddenly, rampage, run amuck, rage, roar, riot, blow up, storm, explode, go off.

4. Make ostentatious display of, show suddenly and dramatically, cut a dash.

FLASH, *n.* 1. Transitory outburst of flame, light of transient brilliancy, sudden burst of light, momentary blaze, streak of light, beam, glow, shimmer, glare, gleam, glisten, glitter, glance, glint, spark, scintilla, sparkle, fulguration, coruscation, fulmination, flare, flicker, lightning.

2. Time occupied by a flash, second, minute, trice, moment, instant, twinkling of an eye, jiffy, crack, breath, *coup (Fr.),* lightning flash.

3. Ostentatious display, pomp, parade, fanfare.

FLASHY, *adj.* 1. Sparkling superficially, brilliant for the moment, pretentiously smart, gaudy, flamboyant, garish, loud, ostentatious, showy, pretentious, florid, tawdry, meretricious, sporty, obtrusive, flaunting, pompous, dazzling, glaring, bedizened, tricked out, pranked out, gingerbread, tinsel, theatrical, glittering, coruscant, gay, rowdy, raffish, vulgar, in bad taste.

2. Tasteless, insipid, vapid, stale, flat, savorless, mawkish.

FLASK, *n.* Bottle-shaped container, leather bottle, narrow-necked vessel, cruse, ewer, decanter, canteen, jar, flagon, cruet, flasket, crock, carafe, vial, phial, urn, gourd.

FLAT, *adj.* 1. Level, horizontal, horizontally level, flush, champaign.

2. Without inequalities of surface, smooth, unbroken, plane, even, homaloidal, without prominences, complanate, oblate.

3. Lying at full length, reclining, spread out, prone, recumbent, supine, prostrate, level with the ground, low.

4. Laid low, overthrown, thrown down, fallen, defeated, destroyed, ruined, powerless.

5. Deflated, punctured, blown out, collapsed, depressed, compressed.

6. Without funds, impecunious, indigent, broke, penniless.

7. Having lost its flavor, tasteless, savorless, vapid, insipid, stale, mawkish, dead, unflavored, *fade (Fr.),* unpalatable, unsavory, watery, milk and water.

8. Uninteresting, tedious, boring, monotonous, spiritless, lifeless, heavy, prosy, prosaic, characterless, unanimated, without point, pointless, uni-

form, jejune, frigid, barren, meager, sterile, lean, thin, wishy-washy.

9. Commercially inactive, sluggish, idle, slack, off-season.

10. *(Art)* Lacking contrast or shading, characterized by lack of clearness, free from gloss, mat, dull, unglazed, unglossed.

11. *(Music)* Below the true pitch, off key, minor.

12. Unqualified, peremptory, direct, absolute, positive, plain, thorough, downright, clear, unmistakable, exact.

FLAT, *n.* 1. Flat level ground, stretch, expanse, reach, level land, open country, lowland, champaign, plain, basin, prairie, downs, grassland, wold, heath, moor, pampas, savanna, llano, campo, steppe, tundra, mesa, tableland, plateau.

2. Shallow, shoal, strand, morass, marsh, bar, sand bank.

3. Suite of rooms on one floor, apartment, floor, story *(Brit.),* tenement.

FLAT-FOOTED, *adj.* 1. Having flat feet, splayfoot, with fallen arches.

2. Showing an uncompromising attitude in a matter, intransigent, firm and explicit, unwavering, determined, resolute.

FLATIRON, *n.* Iron with a flat face for smoothing cloth, smoothing iron, sadiron, roller, tailor's goose, steam iron.

FLATTEN, *v.* 1. Make flat, level, smooth, plane, flat, even, lay, dress, compress, deflate, deplanate.

2. Become flat, become savorless, lose fizz, wilt, droop, make insipid, render stale.

3. Deject, depress, discourage, dishearten, dispirit.

4. Throw down, fell, raze, prostrate, squelch, squash, mow down, ground, floor, knock down.

FLATTER, *v.* 1. Seek to please by complimentary speech, eulogize, laud, belaud, panegyrize, compliment, praise insincerely, overpraise, adulate, gratify by praise, puff, represent too favorably, congratulate, extol, exalt to the skies.

2. Play upon the vanity and susceptibilities of, beguile, cajole, blandish, wheedle, gloze, suavify, coax, humor, ingratiate, court, coquet, pet, coddle, jolly, fawn upon, truckle to, pander to, make much of, curry favor with, pamper, honey, blarney, butter up, soft-soap, apple-polish.

3. Inspire with false hope, please oneself with the thought that, deceive, delude.

FLATTERER, *n.* 1. Adulator, eulogist, laudator, panegyrist, encomiast, *prôneur,* puffer, booster, whitewasher, optimist.

2. Sycophant, fawner, cringer, truckler, bootlicker, lick-spittle, flunky, wheedler, parasite, spaniel, toady, toad-eater, pickthank, apple-polisher, tufthunter, hanger-on, blandisher.

FLATTERY, *n.* 1. Excessive compliment, insincere commendation, adulation, eulogy, encomium, panegyric, false praise.

2. Sycophancy, obsequiousness, flunkeyism, toadyism, wheedling, fawning, tufthunting, cajolery, servility, blandishment, blarney, palaver, honeyed words, buncombe, soft sawder, butter, jollying, apple sauce, soft soap, blandiloquence.

FLATULENCE, *n.* 1. Intestinal windiness, gas, eructation, borborygmus *(Med.),* belch.

2. Bombast, empty talk, idle words, mere words, twaddle, babble, fustian, rant, claptrap, hot air, humbug, windbag eloquence, bull, boasting.

FLATULENT, *adj.* 1. Having gas in the alimentary canal, windy, gassy, ventose.

2. Pretentious, bombastic, vain, pompous, inflated, turgid, verbose, wordy, garrulous, prolix, diffuse, long-winded.

FLAUNT, *v.* 1. Parade conspicuously, display oneself boldly, make a show, be ostentatious, cut a dash, show off, put up a front, swagger, make a splurge, strut, swashbuckle, make a showy appearance, disport, exhibit boastfully, exult, boast, vaunt, air.

2. Wave conspicuously in the air, toss, flourish, brandish ostentatiously, dangle, sport, blazon forth, emblazon.

FLAUNTING, *adj.* 1. Gaudy, garish, ostentatious, tawdry, showy, flashy, loud, florid, gay, glittering, dashing, conspicuous, pretentious, ambitious, pompous, vainglorious, swaggering, swashbuckling.

2. Unreserved, barefaced, brazen, bold, shameless, glaring, daring.

FLAVOR, *n.* 1. Characteristic taste, savor, sapidity, relish, *gout (Fr.),* gusto, gust, piquancy, tang.

2. Flavoring, seasoning, lacing, condiment.

3. Smell, aroma, odor, smack, twang, aftertaste, spice, tinge, vein, streak, strain, trace, hint, suggestion, soupçon, dash, shade, thought.

4. Noticeable element in the taste of a thing, essence, extract, subtle quality, spirit, soul, perfume, tincture.

FLAVORLESS, *adj.* Insipid, vapid, tasteless, savorless, stale, unpalatable, jejune, gustless, ingustable, mawkish, milk and water, weak, flat, *fade (Fr.),* wish-washy, mild.

FLAVOROUS, *adj.* Full of flavor, flavorsome, savory, sapid, gustable, tasteful, tasty, palatable, appetizing, toothsome, relishable, gustatory, saporous, delicious, spiced, piquant.

FLAW, *n.* 1. Marring feature, blemish, defect, fault, imperfection, speckle, speck, spot, fleck, injury, deformity, disfigurement, defacement, taint, eyesore, stain, blur, blot, patch, freckle, blotch, macula, smudge, mend, tear, seam, scar, cicatrice.

2. Crack, break, cleft, breach, fissure, crevice, rift, slit, chink, cranny, gap, fracture, hole, puncture, gash, cut.

3. Weak spot, loophole, error, mistake, shortcoming, frailty, foible, failing, vice.

FLAWLESS, *adj.* Sound, perfect, faultless, without blemish, impeccable.

FLAXEN, *adj.* Of a light soft straw color characteristic of flax, of the pale-yellowish color of dressed flax, yellowish, buff, aureate, golden, flavous, fulvous, sandy, xanthous, cream-colored, saffron-colored.

FLAY, *v.* 1. Strip the skin from, skin, excoriate, scalp, strip off the outer covering, decorticate, pare, peel, bark, desquamate.

2. Strip of money or property, fleece, plunder, dispossess.

3. Reprove with scathing severity, censure harshly, criticize, castigate.

FLECK, *v.* Mark with flecks, dapple, speckle, streak, spot, variegate, stripe, checker, bespeckle, besprinkle, stipple, maculate, dot, bespot, brindle, mottle, striate.

FLECK, *n.* 1. Spot, mark on the skin, freckle, patch of color, mole, macula, speck, speckle, dot, blemish.

2. Small bit, iota, dot, drop, jot, tittle.

FLECKED, *adj.* Dappled, spotted, pied, piebald, skewbald, pepper and salt, mottled, powdered, freckled, studded, striated, brindled, streaked, striped, barred, veined, variegated.

FLEE, *v.* 1. Run away from, escape, skedaddle, decamp, levant, abscond, make off, make one's escape, hasten away, cut and run, skip, turn tail, make a get-away, fly the coop, take to one's heels, show a light pair of heels, take flight, scud, forsake, abandon, hasten off, disappear, vanish, fly away, speed off.

2. Wriggle out of, avoid, evade, elude, shun, dodge.

FLEECE, *v.* 1. Deprive of fleece, shear, clip, shave.

2. Overspread with fleece, fleck with fleecelike masses, cover fleecily, shroud softly, cloud softly over.

3. Strip of belongings or money, defraud, plunder, despoil, rob, steal from, pluck, bleed, sponge, rook, bilk, skin, dispossess, diddle, swindle, mulct, rifle, cheat, spoliate, gut, extort, pilfer, purloin, filch, loot, sack, pillage.

4. Overcharge, surcharge, make pay through the nose, pauperize, impoverish, ruin, bring to the poorhouse.

FLEECY, *adj.* Fleece-like, woolly, lanuginous, downy.

FLEER, *v.* Jeer, grin mockingly, laugh coarsely, deride, sneer, gibe, mock, scoff, flout, grimace in a coarse manner, make a wry face in contempt.

FLEET, *n.* Organized unit of naval ships grouped for tactical purposes, organization of warships under the command of a single officer, flotilla, armada, escadrille, navy, squadron, convoy, argosy, naval division, nautical caravan, naval force, vessels carrying armed men, first line of defense, wooden walls *(Hist.).*

FLEET, *adj.* Moving with velocity, fast, swift, quick, rapid, speedy, nimble, light-footed, nimble-footed, fast of foot, swift-footed, winged, eagle-winged, meteoric, cometary, volatile, summary, hasty, hurried, cursory, pressed for time, brisk, ready, prompt, transient, evanescent, brief, sudden, spasmodic, momentary, instantaneous, active, short, not lasting, transitory.

FLEETING, *adj.* Swiftly passing, gliding swiftly away, fugacious, fugitive, evanescent, ephemeral, transient, transitory, passing, caducous, deciduous, short-lived, diurnal, monohemerous, brief, flitting, temporary, temporal, flying, elusive, here today and gone tomorrow, vanishing, perishable, impermanent, mortal, momentary, unenduring, volatile, quick, precarious.

FLEETNESS, *n.* Quickness, velocity, celerity, speed, swiftness, rapidity, expedition, haste, acceleration, nimbleness, swift-footedness, dispatch, promptitude, spurt, sprint, dash, burst, rush, clip, pace, race, swoop, round, scamper, descent, flight, scurry, gallop, scuttle, split second, twinkling, jiffy, trice, flash, greased lightning, wind, hurricane, cyclone, rocket, bullet, cannon ball, arrow, dart, quicksilver, race horse, antelope, gazelle, hare, greyhound, Mercury.

FLESH, *n.* 1. Soft substance of an animal body, muscle and fat, muscular tissue, brawn, meat, game, animal food.

2. Fatness, weight, avoirdupois, embonpoint, corpulence.

3. Body as distinguished from the spirit, soma,

materiality, corporeity, flesh and blood, clay, physique, natural man, animal force, muscular energy, strength, power, vigor.

4. Animal nature, animality, carnality, bodily desire, sensual appetite, sensuality, libido, grossness, voluptuousness, fleshpots, lust, lechery.

5. Living creatures generically, humanity, mankind, human race, mortality, the world, man, people.

6. The color of the skin of the white race, complexion, surface of the body with respect to color, flesh color, pinkish-white, pinkish-cream.

7. Pulp, soft pulpy substance of fruit, part which is fit to be eaten, meat.

FLESHINESS, *n.* Corpulence, corpulency, plumpness, fatness, avoirdupois, embonpoint, obesity, rotundity, pursiness, stoutness.

FLESHLY, *adj.* 1. Human, bodily, corporeal, corporal, of flesh, physical, somatic, incarnate, tangible, palpable, ponderable, mundane, secular, unspiritual, worldly.

2. Sensual, carnal, desirous, lustful, licentious, animal, lickerish, sexual, lewd, hot, libidinous, lecherous, lascivious.

FLESHY, *adj.* Fat, corpulent, plump, obese, stout, meaty, portly, bouncing, upholstered with suet, chubby, thick-set, pursy.

FLEXIBILITY, *n.* 1. Pliableness, pliability, pliancy, softness, suppleness, flexibleness, elasticity, extensibility, litheness, limberness, plasticity, flaccidity, sequacity, sequaciousness.

2. Yielding disposition, tractableness, malleability, compliance, complaisance, tractability, ductility, easy temper, affability, facility.

FLEXIBLE, *adj.* 1. Easily bent, characterized by plasticity, plastic, elastic, flexile, pliant, pliable, soft, supple, lithe, limber, extensible, flexuous, sequacious, mollient, bendable.

2. Willing to yield to the influence of others, adaptable, manageable, tractable, ductile, malleable, tractile, disposed to yield, submissive, pliable, pliant, docile, amiable, genial, mild, easy, easily managed, gentle, compliant, complaisant, responsible to change, affable, readily adjustable, facile, obsequious.

FLEXUOUS, *adj.* Full of curves, convoluted, twisted, winding, tortile, bending, sinuous, tortuous, sinuate, curvaceous *(colloq.),* undulatory, wavy, serpentine, snaky, anguilliform, vermiform, sigmoidal, crooked, circling, labyrinthian, helical, turbinated, coiled, spiral, meandering, mazy, circuitous, anfractuous.

FLEXURE, *n.* 1. Flexion, conflexure, devexity, recurvity, sinuosity, aduncity, incurvation, curving, bending.

2. Part bent, turn, crook, hook, bend, curvature, fold, deflexion, arcuation, deviation, detour, sweep, curve, bow, arc, crescent, meniscus, lunule, horseshoe, crane-neck, loop, festoon, parabola, elbow, joint, bough, curl, twist.

FLIBBERTIGIBBET, *n.* 1. Restless imp, little devil, street angel and house devil, sprite, fiend, demon, malignant spirit.

2. Chattering or flighty person, blatherskite, chatterbox, gossip, butterfly, featherhead.

FLICK, *n.* Sudden light blow, stroke, flip, fillip, whip, tap, jab, dab.

FLICKER, *v.* 1. Shine with a wavering light, burn unsteadily, glitter, glow, glisten, glister, glimmer, flutter, shimmer, glare, flare, scintillate, sparkle, coruscate, blaze, flash, gleam, beam.

2. Wave to and fro, flutter, vibrate, quiver, undulate, oscillate, librate, nutate, dangle, swing, pulsate, throb, wag, waggle, shake, quaver, wriggle, tremble, waver, fluctuate, vacillate, reel, quake, falter, pendulate, sway, rock, wobble.

FLIGHT, *n.* 1. Passing through the air by the use of wings, volitation, flying, aviation, soaring, journey by air, winging.

2. Swift movement, hasty departure, hegira, exodus, leaving, fleeing, rout, stampede, escape, retreat, withdrawal, evasion, French leave, absconding, decamping, desertion, abandonment, removal.

3. Volley *(of arrows),* drove, shower, rain, deluge, rush, flock, storm.

4. Staircase, stairs, steps from one landing to another.

FLIGHTINESS, *n.* Volatility, mercurialness, levity, lightness, giddiness, frivolity, flippancy, lightheadedness, capriciousness, fickleness, inconstancy, humorsomeness, whimsicalness, crotchetiness, eccentricity, variability.

FLIGHTY, *adj.* 1. Given to flights of fancy, fanciful, notional, indulging in flights of imagination, imaginative, quixotic, wayward, wanton, giddy, volatile, mercurial, wild, hare-brained, extravagant, capricious, frivolous, fickle, whimsical, fitful, without ballast, flyaway, scatterbrained, hoity-toity, moonish, light-headed, erratic, reckless, thoughtless, woolgathering, irresponsible, inattentive, inconstant, mutable, changeable, variable, indecisive, irresolute.

2. Deranged, unbalanced, unhinged, slightly delirious, mildly crazy, mad, of disordered mind, cracked.

FLIMFLAM, *n.* Trick, hollowness, mere show, eyewash, window dressing, quackery, charlatanism, gammon, buncombe, trifling, nonsense, humbug, mountebankery, hocus pocus, deception, lie.

FLIMSY, *adj.* 1. Without material solidity, light, slender, tenuous, slight, unsubstantial, thin, of frail texture, immaterial, airy, frail, fragile, delicate, filmy, transparent, diaphanous, ethereal, sheer, silken, gossamer, cobwebby, gauzy, chiffon, silky.

2. Weak, inadequate, feeble, worthless, poor, unreal, foolish, superficial, shallow, puerile, vain, idle, petty, frivolous, paltry, not carefully thought out, trivial, trifling, niggling, piddling, without reason, without plausibility.

3. Ramshackle, two-by-four, cheap, gimcrack, trashy, rubbishy, rickety, tumbledown, scrubby, scurvy, meager, sorry, shabby, wretched, dilapidated, jerry-built, sleazy.

FLINCH, *v.* Shrink under pain, shrink from, withdraw from, wince, draw back from, shy, start, fly, retreat, hold back, swerve, falter, funk, crouch, cower, cringe, skulk, quake, quaver, tremble, quiver, shake, shudder, shiver, flutter, blench, quail, dodge, recoil.

FLINDERS, *n.* Small pieces, little bits, fragments, splinters, shavings, chips, parings.

FLING, *v.* 1. Throw with force, project, hurl, cast, toss, propel, launch, jaculate, emit, pitch, put, dart, heave, dash, drive, jerk, lance, tilt, sling, pelt, send forth, let fly, flirt, precipitate.

2. Throw the body about, jig, flounce, dash.

3. Send forth suddenly and rapidly, dash, move with haste, fly into violent motions, start angrily.

4. Throw aside, throw off, throw to the ground, cast aside.

5. Utter harsh or abusive language, jeer, insult, fleer, gibe, mock, censure, castigate, excoriate, flay.

FLINT, *n.* Rock, hard kind of stone, silica, chip, quartz, pebble, adamant, anything hard and obdurate.

FLINTY, *adj.* 1. Hard as flint, unimpressible, indurate, adamantine, unyielding, impenetrable, stony, rocky, granitic, horny.

2. Unfeeling, stony-hearted, cold-hearted, obdurate, cruel, unmerciful, hard-hearted, stubborn, rigid, stiff, unbending, firm, stark, inflexible, inexorable.

FLIPPANCY, *n.* Pertness, impertinence, sauciness, cheek, malapertness, insolence, rudeness, unmannerliness, incivility, inconsiderate glibness, sauce, lip, impudence, self-assertion, superficial assurance, dicacity, nerve, freshness, front, face, gall, effrontery, unscrupulous smartness, brashness, bumptiousness, procacity, swagger, bounce.

FLIPPANT, *adj.* Pert, malapert, impudent, saucy, fresh, impertinent, insolent, smart in speech, rude, unmannerly, cheeky, disrespectful, characterized by disrespectful levity, lippy, brash, bumptious, forward, free and easy, devil-may-care, insouciant, pococurante, superficial, frivolous, thoughtless, nonchalant.

FLIRT, *v.* 1. Play at love, trifle in love, dally, make a show of love, wanton, play at courtship, pretend to be in love, make love, philander, coquet, cast sheep's eyes at, look sweet at, wink at, wolf-whistle at, ogle, make calf eyes at, undress with a glance, pay court to, display a well-filled pair of silk stockings, play fast and loose, set one's cap at, woo, serenade, court, bill and coo, spoon, pet, neck, spark, *faire les yeux doux (Fr.).*

2. Toy with an idea, trifle, entertain.

3. Move with a jerk, dart about, propel with a toss, throw with a jerk, fling suddenly, flounce, hurl, shy, chuck, pitch, toss, fillip.

4. Give a sudden motion to, wave smartly, flutter, twirl briskly, whisk, whirl.

FLIRT, *n.* 1. Coquette, vampire, vamp, belle, gold digger, Sheba, jilt, hussy, tart, wanton.

2. Philanderer, gallant, fast man, playboy, masher, lady-killer, sheik, tea-hound, lounge-lizard, cake-eater, petter, necker, spooner, wolf.

3. Quick throw, sudden jerk, toss, sudden fling, darting motion, flutter, whisk, whirl, twirl.

FLIRTATION, *n.* 1. Affectation of love, philandering, dalliance, coquetry, gallantry, serenading, sheep's eyes, wink, wolf-whistle, ogle, side-glance, calf love, amorous glances, goo-goo eyes.

2. Love affair which is not serious, romance, amour, intrigue, necking, petting, spooning, billing and cooing.

FLIRTATIOUS, *adj.* Affecting to be in love, coquettish, philandering, flirty, wanton, spoony, fast-and-loose, dallying, wolfish.

FLIT, *v.* Move lightly and swiftly, skim along, move with celerity, take wing, take flight, dart along, fly rapidly, hasten, leave, depart, disappear, abscond, speed, soar, wing, hover, flutter, flicker, scud, remove, migrate, pass, rove, be transient, gallop, vanish.

FLITTING, *adj.* Moving swiftly, passing quickly, fluttering, transitive, transitory, transient, fleeting, fugitive, fugacious, ephemeral, evanescent, shifting, temporary, cursory, short-lived, deciduous,

brief, quick, brisk, meteoric, cometary, itinerant, skimming.

FLOAT, *v.* 1. Rest on the surface of a liquid, be light, be buoyant, be buoyed up, ride, waft, swim, move gently on the surface, drift along, sail, soar, glide, ride the waves, skim over, tide, be held suspended within the body of a fluid.

2. Buoy up, keep afloat, carry on the surface, bear up, give support to, launch, transport, convey, hold up.

3. Shift from one's proper position, be unstable, make frequent changes, drift about free from attachment.

4. Cover with water, flood, irrigate, inundate.

5. Sell on the market, purvey, set going.

FLOAT, *n.* 1. Raft, pontoon, outrigger, floating mass, buoy, inflated bag to sustain a person in water, life preserver, lifesaver.

2. Wheeled platform bearing a display and drawn in a procession, pageant.

FLOATING, *adj.* 1. Buoyed up, natant, drifting, buoyant, borne along, afloat.

2. Not fixed in a definite place, not settled, migratory, away from its proper position, in circulation, shifting, not stationary, variable, movable, wandering, unattached, moving about, fluctuating, temporary.

FLOCCULENT, *adj.* Covered with a soft woolly substance, bearing long soft hairs, downy, velvety, floccose, cottony, flocky, tufted, lanate, lanuginous, tomentous, hairy, filamentous, pilous, shaggy, villous.

FLOCK, *n.* 1. Herd, roundup, drove, pack, kennel, fold, litter, covey, bevy, brood, hatch, flight, gaggle, set, school, swarm, shoal, team, troupe, group, band, aggregation, collection, multitude, company, array, galaxy, assemblage, crowd, concourse, large number, gathering, mob, throng.

2. Congregation, pastorate, parish.

3. Lock of wool or hair, tuft, crest.

4. Shearings of cloth, cotton and woolen refuse, old cloth torn to pieces and used for stuffing.

FLOCK, *v.* Go in a crowd, muster, assemble, congregate, cluster, swarm, herd, rush, surge, stream, gather in large numbers, mass, crowd, throng, huddle, gather together.

FLOE, *n.* Low free mass of floating ice, iceberg, ice floe, berg, field of floating ice formed on the surface of the sea, sheet of ice.

FLOG, *v.* Beat hard with a whip, horsewhip, whip, lash, thrash, thresh, drub, flagellate, castigate, scourge, spank, cane, birch, switch, strap, paddle, fustigate, lay on, beat black and blue, leather, strike, smite, cuff, cowhide, lambaste, lace, pommel, trounce, larrup, lick, buffet, belabor, club, cudgel, maul, baste, wham, thump, thwack, bang, punish, rub down with a wooden towel, make run the gauntlet, whack.

FLOGGING, *n.* Scourging, whipping, lashing, beating, fustigation, flagellation, forty lashes, bastinado, estrapade, strappado, blow, stripe, cuff, buffet, pommel, gauntlet, stick law, castigation, licking, dressing down.

FLOOD, *n.* 1. Great flowing of water over land not usually submerged, deluge, inundation, overflow, flash flood, freshet, downpour, drencher, waterspout, shower, monsoon, rains, tide, high tide, cloudburst, diluvian, cataclysm.

2. Great outpouring, spate, stream, current, race, sluice, mill race, torrent, rapids, whirlpool,

eddy, vortex, maelstrom, cascade, fall, waterfall, cataract, swell, heave, downrush.

3. Any large body of water, the sea, a river, a lake, rivulet, creek, run, bourn, jet, spout, splash, rush, gush.

4. Abundant excess, abundance, superabundance, plenitude, copiousness, amplitude, galore, profusion, lots, full measure, saturation, too much, nimiety, *satis superque (Lat.),* more than enough, plethora, engorgement, outpouring, repletion, redundance, satiety.

FLOOD, *v.* 1. Cover with a flood, overflow in a flood, deluge, inundate, fill to overflowing, drown, submerge, flow over, surge, swirl, splash, plash, swash, discharge itself, disembogue, open into, drain into.

2. Overwhelm with an abundance of something, abound, exuberate, teem, rain down on, stream, pour in, swarm, spill, shower down, irrigate, drench.

FLOODGATE, *n.* Gate designed to regulate the flow of water, water gate, sluice, sluice gate, weir, penstock, outlet, vent, spout, tap, conduit, lock, valve, waterworks, vomitory, out-gate, lower gate of a lock, gate serving to control indiscriminate passage.

FLOOR, *v.* 1. Furnish with a floor, put a floor on, cover with a floor, pave, deck.

2. Bring down to the floor, knock down, fell, ground, prostrate, overthrow, lay level with the floor, finish, make an end of, beat, defeat, conquer, vanquish.

3. Prevail over in argument, silence, quell, quash, take the wind out of an adversary's sails, nonplus, confound, pose, embarrass, stagger, checkmate, upset, trump, trip up, put one's nose out of joint, drive to the wall, discomfit, overpower, beat hollow, rout, lick, worst, drub, put hors de combat.

FLOOR, *n.* 1. Pavement, paving, story, deck, parquet, flag, flooring, baseboard, washboard, plinth, dado, wainscot, sill, beam, rafter, girder, planking.

2. Lower enclosing surface upon which one walks, level supporting surface, foundation, *fond (Fr.),* ground, earth, groundwork, footing.

3. Prepared level area for a particular use, platform, stage, dais, rostrum, stand, bed, keel, scaffold.

4. Flat bottom of a more or less hollow place, flat extent of surface.

5. Minimum charged or paid, base rate, base.

FLOOR COVERING, *n.* Floorcloth, carpet, rug, scatter rug, linoleum, tile, mosaic.

FLOP, *n.* 1. Fall, downfall, jog, jolt, jar, jerk, shock, succussion, sound of flopping, thud.

2. *(Colloq.)* Failure, fiasco, fizzle, no-go, labor in vain, something that falls flat, something that disappoints expectations, flash in the pan, foozle.

FLORA, *n.* Plants of a country listed by species, vegetable life, vegetation, plant kingdom, verdure, botany, plant life.

FLORAL, *adj.* Pertaining to flowers, flowery, verdant, verdurous, herbaceous, botanic, sylvan, arborary, arboreous, arborescent, dendritic, woodsy, grassy, mossy.

FLORESCENCE, *n.* 1. Flowering bloom, efflorescence, anthesis, blossoming, period of blooming, flourishing, floruit.

2. Development, outgrowth, fruit, product, bud, crop, harvest, ear, first fruits.

FLORET, *n.* Little flower, floweret, flowerlet, blossom, bloom, bud, floscule, posy.

FLORICULTURE, *n.* Cultivation of flowering plants and flowers under glass, landscape gardening, arboriculture, horticulture, spade husbandry.

FLORID, *adj.* 1. High-colored, ruddy, rubicund, red-complexioned, ruddy-faced, flushed, red-faced, blowzy, hectic, inflamed, blooming, erubescent.

2. Flowery, excessively ornate, highly embellished, showy, abounding in decorative features, elaborate, ostentatious, flamboyant, rococo, baroque, brilliant, gorgeous, figured, luxuriant, high-flown, euphuistic, rhetorical, figurative.

FLOSSY, *adj.* 1. Resembling floss, silken, silky, filamentous, downy, fluffy.

2. Stylish, chic, modish, dolled-up, fancy, showy in appearance.

FLOTSAM, *n.* Part of the wreckage of a ship and its cargo found floating on the water, floating goods, jetsam.

FLOUNCE, *v.* Go with an impatient fling of the body, throw the body about, fling about, throw oneself with a jerk, flop, twitch, slosh, bob, bounce, leap, jump at, hop, spring, vault, bound, trip, gambol, skip, caper, prance, curvet, shamble, dance.

FLOUNCE, *n.* 1. Flouncing movement, spring, jerk, bound, leap, hop, jump, saltation, vault, caper, curvet, capriole, caracole, demivolt.

2. Furbelow, frill on a gown, fringe, valance, trimming, ruffle, ornament, edging, skirting, hem, selvedge.

FLOUNDER, *v.* 1. Wallow, struggle, stumble, shamble, welter, totter, flop, flounce with stumbling movements, plunge clumsily, toss about, tumble, hobble, limp, stagger, proceed clumsily.

2. Blunder, bungle, muddle, come to grief, lose, meet with disaster, turn out badly, succumb, collapse, go up, end in smoke, fall through, hang fire, flash in the pan, fizzle out.

3. Hesitate, waver, falter, halt, boggle, be uncertain, miss one's way, lose oneself, wander aimlessly, not know which way to turn, float in a sea of uncertainty, beat about.

FLOUR, *n.* Finely ground meal of grain, farina, bran, spore, sporule, bolted wheat, ground wheat, fine soft powder.

FLOUR, *v.* 1. Make into flour, grind and bolt, pulverize, powder, break up into fine globules.

2. Sprinkle, dredge with flour.

FLOURISH, *v.* 1. Grow luxuriantly, thrive, bloom, blossom, flower, vegetate, fructify, bear fruit.

2. Succeed, prosper, be successful, turn out well, light on one's feet, swim with the tide, get ahead, get on, rise in the world, make a place for oneself in the world, have a run of luck, feather one's nest, bask in the sunshine, make one's pile.

3. Attain one's prime, exercise one's full powers, be at the height of one's excellence.

4. Speak in flowery or pretentious language, brag, boast, vapor, vaunt, gasconade, use florid language.

5. Make a show, strut, puff, show off, swagger, swashbuckle, bluster, be ostentatious, blow one's trumpet, talk big, blow hard, draw the long bow, give oneself airs, put on dog, make a flourish, show off, cut a dash, parade, flaunt.

6. Sound a trumpet call, play a fanfare.

7. Make flourishes with a brandished weapon, wave about in the air, swing, brandish, flap,

wield, agitate, shake, convulse, whisk, switch, sweep, swish, twirl.

8. Add embellishments to, embellish with sweeping curves, adorn with decorative designs.

FLOURISH, *n.* 1. Parade, ostentatious display, ostentation, show, dash, *étalage (Fr.)*, splash, glitter, strut, pomp, array, highfaluting, dog, side, swagger, toploftiness, swashbuckling, swank, fuss, grand doings.

2. Parade of fine language, bombast, altiloquence, grandiloquence, fustian, rant, highsounding words, flowery speech, magniloquence, boasting, vaunting, pretensions, braggadocio, puff, bluff, gasconade, rodomontade, hot air, heroics, bravado.

3. Fanfare, trumpet call, tantara, tantivy, blast, fanfaronade, blare, tintamarre, alarum.

4. A showy musical passage, cadenza, bravura.

5. Embellishment in writing, decoration, fanciful strokes of a pen, decorative figure, scroll, volute, coquillage, curlycue.

6. Brandishing, shake, waving, oscillation, vibration, libration, undulation, agitation, quiver, jactitation.

FLOURISHING, *adj.* 1. Vigorous in growth, thriving, booming, fresh, verdant, growing, mushrooming, in full feather.

2. Auspicious, propitious, *couleur de rose (Fr.)*, rose-colored, in the pink, well-off, palmy, halcyon, successful, lucky, fortunate, in a fair way, happy.

3. Prosperous, well-to-do, lucrative, remunerative.

FLOUT, *v.* Jeer, sneer, gibe, fleer, scoff, taunt, deride, ridicule, laugh at, twit, niggle, guy, rag, chaff, mock, snigger, insult, mock, treat with disdain, poke fun at.

FLOUT, *n.* Mocking insult, mockery, sneer, gibe, jeer, scoffing, fling, taunt, gleek, sarcasm, quip, wipe, hiss, hoot, slap in the face.

FLOW, *v.* 1. Move along in a liquid stream, stream, roll along, pour, run, gush, spout, trickle, jet, rush forth copiously, pour out, spurt, leak, exude, discharge, drain, seep, ooze, filter, well out, effuse, dribble, drop, drip, disembogue, purl, gurgle, swirl, deluge, splash, plash, swash, surge.

2. Emanate, proceed from a source, issue, well forth, arise, well up, spring, be derived, result, follow, grow, come, egress, originate, come forth.

3. Liquefy, melt, deliquesce, become fluid.

4. Proceed continuously and smoothly, sweep along, glide, move along smoothly, glissade, circulate, drift, slide, roll, ripple.

5. Overflow, abound, be copious, run, be full.

6. Fall at full length, hang loosely, float, wave, undulate, waver.

FLOW, *n.* 1. That which flows, current, stream, tide, flood, torrent, rapids, mill race, sluice.

2. Gush, flux, spout, spurt, jet, trickle, discharge, leakage, oozing, drainage, outpour, effluence, effusion, efflux, debouchment, outflow, dribble.

3. Drift, course, stir, ebb.

4. Copiousness, abundance, plethora, plenty.

FLOWER, *n.* 1. Blossom of a plant, floweret, floret, floscule, bloom, posy, blow, bud, nosegay, floral glory, perennial, annual.

2. Finest part, best, pick, choicest, best part, essence, élite, cream, *crème de la crème (Fr.)*.

3. State of efflorescence, most flourishing

period, floruit, acme, prime, springtide of life, youth, early vigor.

4. Ornament, adornment, embellishment, ornamentation, decoration.

5. Floral design, rosette, acanthus, floriation.

FLOWER, *v.* 1. Produce flowers, put forth blooms, blossom, be in flower, bloom, effloresce, abound in flowers, come out into full development, develop, vegetate, blow, unfold, bud, burgeon, come to full bloom.

2. Decorate with a floral design, deck with flowers, strew with blossoms.

FLOWERY, *adj.* 1. Covered with blossoms, blossomy, bloomy, blooming, blossoming, flowering, floral, flosculous, florescent, efflorescent, floscular, florulent, full of flowers.

2. Containing highly ornate language, ornate, figurative, rhetorical, florid, tropical.

FLOWING, *adj.* 1. Moving in a stream, running, gushing, gliding, issuing, fluvial, meandering, flexuous, streamy, tidal, fluid, liquid, effluent.

2. Proceeding smoothly and easily, gracefully continuous throughout the length, cursive, fluent, easy, glib, facile, graceful, round, full, harmonious, voluble, abundant, copious.

3. Falling at full length, hanging loosely.

FLUCTUATE, *v.* 1. Move in waves, undulate, oscillate, vacillate, swing, wave, vibrate, sway, deflect, swerve, float backward and forward, shift to and fro, flicker, flutter, pulsate, shuffle, librate, move up and down, toss, pitch.

2. Alternate between one direction and another, rise and fall, roll hither and thither, bob up and down, pass and repass, ebb and flow, come and go, shuttle, vary irregularly, veer, alter, change continuously from one course to another.

3. Be irresolute, be undetermined, waver, hang in suspense, pause, think about twice, hesitate, hover, boggle, wobble, hum and haw, demur, not know one's own mind, debate, be unsettled, balance, blow hot and cold, will and will not, shuffle, falter, palter, dawdle, dillydally, be inconstant.

FLUCTUATION, *n.* 1. Wave-like motion, vacillation, oscillation, rolling, swing, rising and falling, seesaw, vibration, wavering, unsteadiness, nutation, pulsation, alternation, libration.

2. Continual change from one course to another, alternating variation, changeableness, restlessness, unrest, agitation, vicissitude, change, shifting.

3. Rise and fall, ebb and flow, flux and reflux, ups and downs, peaks and valleys, shifting sands, kaleidoscope, pendulum.

4. Inconstancy, hesitation, instability, infirmity of purpose, irresolution, indecision, uncertainty, hesitancy, ambivalence, suspense, changefulness, fickleness, caprice.

FLUE, *n.* 1. Smoke passage in a chimney, smokevent, smokestack, funnel, air pipe, gully, tunnel, main, shaft, blowhole.

2. Heating tube in a boiler, heat-pipe, duct, passage, chimney.

3. Downy matter, fluff, cobweb, gossamer, nap, downy fur, soft down, feather, mote, thistledown.

FLUENCY, *n.* 1. Liquidness, flowing quality, smoothness, cursiveness, circulation.

2. Ready flow of words, mellifluousness, affluence, *copia verborum (Lat.)*, *flux de paroles (Fr.)*, ease of speech, ready utterance, felicity of expression, command of language, eloquence, volubility,

loquaciousness, multiloquence, polylogy, grandiloquence, sonority, gift of gab.

FLUENT, *adj.* 1. Flowing smoothly and easily, fluid, liquid, current, gliding, running.

2. Smooth, graceful, rhythmical, legato *(Music)*, melodious, harmonious, euphonious, suave, bland, silky.

3. Able to speak readily, ready in speech, talkative, glib, voluble, facile, smooth-spoken, silvertongued, mellifluous, smooth-tongued, multiloquent, polyloquent, garrulous, loquacious, effusive, soft-spoken.

FLUFF, *n.* Light downy particles, downy mass, flue, lint, nap, pile, floss, fur, flossy hair, down, plush, velvet, wool.

FLUFFY, *adj.* 1. Soft and light as fluff, downy, nappy, flossy, feathery, fleecy, fuzzy, pilous, wooly, velvety, flocculent, lanate, lanuginous, tomentous.

2. *(Theat.)* Inclined to forget one's lines, of uncertain memory, ruffled easily.

FLUID, *adj.* 1. Fluent, running, liquid, gaseous, flowing.

2. Watery, rheumy, ichorous, serous, sanious *(Med.)*, lymphatic, sappy, juicy, succulent, liquefied, soluble, uncongealed.

3. Changing readily, shifting, floating, not fixed, unstable, not stable, not rigid.

FLUID, *n.* 1. Nonsolid substance capable of flowing, liquid, vapor, gas, solution, decoction.

2. Water, lymph, ukum, latex, juice, sap, chyle, ichor, blood, gore, claret *(slang)*, cruor *(Physiol.)*, grume.

FLUIDITY, *n.* 1. Liquidity, fluidification, liquidness, liquefaction, solubility, fluency.

2. Instability, unstableness, changeableness, changeability, inconstancy, insecurity, fickleness.

3. Easy adaptability, pliability, pliancy, smoothness, facility, versatility.

FLUKE, *n.* 1. Accidental advantage, lucky chance, lucky stroke, stroke of luck, hazard, scratch, score by accident, windfall, potluck, lot, fate, good luck, wheel of fortune, random shot, gamble, flier, leap in the dark, pig in a poke.

2. Flat triangular piece at the end of each arm of an anchor, grappling-flap, anchor-flake, barb, hook, barbed head, cusp, crane, fork, angle, bifurcation.

FLUME, *n.* Narrow defile containing a mountain torrent, gorge with a mountain stream flowing through it, ravine with flowing current, millrace, race, chute, inclined channel for conveying water from a distance.

FLUMMERY, *n.* 1. Nonsense, trash, chaff, froth, fudge, frippery, moonshine, inanity, frivolity, trifle, rubbish, bosh, stuff and nonsense, fiddle-faddle, flapdoodle, balderdash, rigmarole, humbug, *niaiserie (Fr.)*, hocus-pocus.

2. Bombast, jargon, gibberish, palaver, rant, fustian, mere words, jabber, babble, verbiage, rodomontade, *bavardage (Fr.)*, platitude, cliché.

3. Flattery, empty compliment, agreeable humbug, blandishment, blandiloquence, blarney, adulation, gloze, wheedling, fawning, sycophancy, bootlicking, cajolery, unctuousness, incense, honeyed words, apple sauce, soft soap, butter, blancmange, buncombe, placebo, rose water, mouth honor, lip homage, tickletoe.

FLUNKY, *n.* 1. Male servant in livery, man-servant in silk stockings and knee breeches, footman, lackey, livery-servant, valet, valet de chambre,

boots, page, buttons, footboy, servitor, butler, groom.

2. Servile follower, parasite, sycophant, obsequious person, toady, flatterer, wheedler, tuft-hunter, yes-man, lap dog, spaniel, bootlicker, hanger-on, stooge, doer of dirty work, tool.

FLURRY, *n.* 1. Sudden and brief commotion in the weather, squall, sudden gust of wind, flaw, light gusty shower, light snowfall, blast, capful of wind, fresh breeze, half a gale, precipitation, puff.

2. Sudden excitement, nervous hurry, bustle, flutter, fluster, fuss, ferment, whirl, agitation, commotion, confusion, disturbance, turbulence, perturbation, trepidation, ruffle, flush, fever, heat, hurry-skurry, tumult, haste, discomposure, fidgets, restlessness, impatience.

FLURRY, *v.* Put into a flurry, fluster, make nervous, disturb, excite, agitate, hurry, confuse, perturb, disconcert, trouble, rattle, perplex, ruffle, confound, flutter, bewilder, panic, alarm.

FLUSH, *v.* 1. Cleanse by flooding, flood with water, wash out, drench, drain, clean, rinse, mop, sponge, scour, swab, scrub.

2. Flow with a rush, flow and spread suddenly, rush rapidly, start forth.

3. Drive from cover, cause to start up, rouse, cause to fly off.

4. Make flush, make even, level, even off, smooth.

5. Redden, color, mantle, blush, crimson, rouge, cause to glow, incarnadine, rubricate, miniate, empurple.

6. Excite, animate, elate, elevate, make proud, puff up, erect, rouse, thrill.

FLUSH, *adj.* 1. Flushed with color, blushing, of a ruddy color, crimson, purple, florid.

2. Vigorous, fresh, lusty, spirited, full of life and vigor, bright, hardy, stanch, robust.

3. Fertile, fecund, prolific, exuberant, fully supplied, overflowing, well filled, well-equipped, abundant, lavish, prodigal, affluent, replete, enough and to spare, ample, full, plenteous, copious, chock-full, abounding, wealthy, prosperous.

4. Level with a surface, in one plane, even, smooth, flat, plane, on a level with the adjacent surface.

FLUSH, *n.* 1. Tinge of color, tint, tincture, shade, hue, rosy glow, ruddiness, blush, redness, rosiness, bloom, complexion.

2. Heat, glow, fever, febricity, pyrexia.

3. Rush of emotion, thrill, shock, elation, jubilation, exultation, excitement, tingling, kick, quiver, flutter, flurry, fluster, twitter, tremor, panting, palpitation.

4. Overspreading flow of water, deluge, inundation.

FLUSHED, *adj.* 1. Excited, feverish, wrought up, overwrought, in a fever, in a ferment, all of a flutter, all of a dither, hectic, hysterical.

2. Blushing, glowing, warm, rosy, ruddy, florid, blowzy, rubicund.

3. Cheerful, in high spirits, in high feather, gay as a lark, allegro, buoyant, debonair, lighthearted, airy, jaunty, animated, lively, sparkling, vivacious, breezy.

4. Hopeful, elated, sanguine, exultant, enthusiastic, confident, secure, assured, certain.

5. Proud, vain, haughty, lofty, high and mighty, swollen, puffed up, blown, vainglorious, conceited, inflated.

FLUSTER, *v.* 1. Excite, make nervous, disturb, ruffle, flurry, perturb, agitate, flutter, shake, faze, startle, stagger, give one a shock.
2. Confuse, befuddle, muddle, discompose, confound, disconcert, throw off balance, put out, perplex, bewilder, dazzle, daze.

FLUTIST, *n.* Flute-player, flautist, fifer, piper, piccolo Pete *(colloq.)*.

FLUTTER, *v.* 1. Fly with flapping movements, flap the wings quickly, hover, soar, wing.
2. Wave in the air, move rapidly, flit, flirt, flap, flicker, stir, undulate, shift, shuffle, shake, sway, blink, beat fast and irregularly, move in irregular motions, vibrate, agitate, quiver.
3. Beat tremulously, tremble, palpitate, throb, be tremulous, be perturbed, be agitated, twitter, reel, wince, be thrown into a state of nervous excitement.
4. Go with aimless course, be unsteady, waver, vacillate, oscillate, fluctuate.

FLUTTER, *n.* 1. Quick motion, agitation, quiver, vibration, tremor, tremble.
2. Sensation, stir, ripple, shock, tingling, thrill, kick.
3. Nervous excitement, mental agitation, twitter, fluster, flurry, hurry-skurry, hurry, commotion, confusion, perturbation.

FLUX, *n.* 1. Flow, stream, current, run, course, profluence, effluence, defluxion, flood, outflow.
2. Continuous passage, continuous change, transit, transmigration, transition, mutation, shifting, continuous succession of changes.
3. Progress, motion, growth, lapse, process, succession, duration, tide, sweep, step, march.
4. *(Med.)* Lax state of the bowels, diarrhoea, dysentery, looseness, abnormal and morbid discharge.
5. Liquefaction, solution, infusion, decoction, apozem, lixivium.
6. Fusing agent, diluent, alkahest, solvent, fusing mixture, protective nonmetallic salt substance.

FLY, *v.* 1. Take wing, take the air, soar, mount, aviate, take off, hop, zoom, climb in the air, linger in the air, hover, drift, glide, volplane, plane, pilot, loop the loop, roll, bank, sideslip, spiral, dive, nosedive, spin, pancake, open up the throttle, be borne through the air, move through the air on wings, travel through the air.
2. Agitate tremulously, undulate, wave, flutter, float, sail, vibrate, flicker, quiver, quaver, shake, shiver, toss, wag, waggle, flirt, flap.
3. Explode, burst, detonate, fulminate, go off, discharge, blow up, flash, fulgurate, flare.
4. Let fly, shoot, scatter, spread, radiate, disperse, branch off.
5. Move swiftly, move with a rush, pass rapidly, run, rush, hurry, flit, speed, dart, post, sprint, trip, hasten, spurt, hie, scud, whiz, race, swoop, tear, whisk, dash, sweep, skim, bolt, scurry, accelerate, scamper, outstrip the wind, gallop.
6. Flee from, run away, avoid, shun, escape, evade, elude, wriggle out of, skedaddle, break away, make a get-away, vanish, slip away, make off, steal away, pack off, slink away, abscond, decamp, depart, take to one's heels, take to flight, disappear.

FLY, *n.* 1. Housefly, *musca domestica,* one of the family *Muscidae,* winged insect belonging to the order *Diptera,* dipteron, May fly, firefly, gadfly.
2. *(Brit.)* Light public carriage for passengers, cab, hackney-coach, cabriolet, bus, hansom.

3. Apparatus above the stage in a theater, scene-shifting gallery, stage gallery.
4. Strip sewn along one edge of a garment to conceal the fasteners or buttons, flap, lap, zipper.
5. Fishhook dressed with silk so as to resemble an insect.
6. Act of flying, flight, volation, volitation.

FLY AT, *v.* Rush upon, assail by flying, attack suddenly, spring upon, assault, fall upon, swoop down on, pounce upon, pitch into, strike at, thrust at, have a fling at, dash at, have at, let out at.

FLYAWAY, *adj.* 1. Streaming, fluttering, waving, undulating.
2. Frivolous, flighty, giddy, volatile, unrestrained, fly-by-night, irresponsible, unreliable.

FLY-BY-NIGHT, *n.* Person who leaves secretly by night to avoid paying his debts, one who escapes by night from his creditors, insecurely financed speculator, fleecer, flimflam artist.

FLYER, *n.* 1. Something that flies, bird, fowl, insect, bat, volator.
2. That which moves with great speed, express, fast train.
3. Aviator, airman, ace, birdman, aeronaut, eagle, pilot, navigator.
4. Flying jump, leap.
5. Financial venture outside of one's ordinary business, speculation, experiment, random shot, leap in the dark, feeler, pilot balloon.
6. Straight flight of steps, stairs, single step, stairs of straight flights.
7. Advertisement scattered abroad in great numbers, leaflet, small handbill, circular, notice.

FLYING, *adj.* 1. Making flight, passing through the air, volitational, moving freely in the air, volant.
2. Floating, fluttering, waving, extending through the air, streaming.
3. Moving swiftly, hasty, fast, rapid, hurried, brief, speedy, winged, quick, fleeting, swift.
4. Running away, fleeing, taking flight, fugitive, fleeting, evanescent, transitory, transient.

FLYING, *n.* Act of moving through the air on wings, flight, volation, volitation, aerial navigation, avigation *(cant)*, airmanship, aviation, soaring, winging.

FLYING MACHINE, *n.* Contrivance which sustains and propels itself through the air, aeroplane, airplane, *avion (Fr.)*, monoplane, biplane, triplane, quadruplane, multiplane, plane, aircraft, cabin plane, transport plane, cargo plane, passenger plane, seaplane, hydroplane, glider, sailplane, helicopter, aerodrome, autogiro, airship, crate *(slang)*, jenny *(slang)*, jet, flying boxcar, rocket ship, Nike, ornithopter, dirigible, Zeppelin, blimp, Whirlybird *(humorous)*, jet.

FOAL, *n.* The young of the horse, filly, colt, pony, roan, jade, jument, palfrey, mare, gelding, stallion, cob, hobby, mustang, broncho.

FOAM, *n.* 1. Aggregation of minute bubbles formed on the surface of a liquid by agitation or fermentation, spray, spume, lather, suds, froth, head, cream, scum, yeast, bubbles, globules, fizz.
2. Sparkle, effervescence, spumescence, bubbling, ebullience, ebullition, fermentation.

FOAMY, *adj.* Covered with foam, frothy, spumous, spumy, spumescent, scummy, foaming, creamy, yeasty, lathery, effervescent, bubbling, sparkling, heady, fizzy, *mousseux (Fr.)*, up *(colloq.)*.

FOB, *n.* 1. Small pocket just below the waistline in trousers, pouch to hold watch, watch pocket.

2. Short chain worn hanging from the pocket, ribbon with a seal.

FOCUS, *n.* 1. Point at which rays meet after being refracted, point from which diverging rays appear to proceed, point of concentration, central point, converging point, point of convergence, central point of attraction, primary center, focal point, focal distance of a lens, nucleus, core, point of corradiation.

2. Gathering place, rendezvous, rallying point, center of activity, headquarters, haunt, retreat, resort, trysting place, place of meeting, *point de réunion (Fr.).*

FOCUS, *v.* 1. Bring into focus, focalize, center, concenter, bring to a point, converge, concentrate, adjust, nucleate, corradiate.

2. Rally, meet, rendezvous.

FODDER, *n.* Coarse roughage used as feed for livestock, forage, provender, feed, silage, ensilage, stover, provision, ration, pasture, pasturage, subsistence, sustenance.

FOE, *n.* 1. One who entertains enmity against another, enemy, foeman, adversary, antagonist, assailant, opponent, attacker, combatant, contestant, contender, rival, competitor.

2. One who opposes on principle anything prejudicial or injurious, oppositionist, wrangler, disputant, obstructionist, filibusterer, extremist, bitter-ender, die-hard.

3. Ill-wisher, malcontent, irreconcilable, agitator, demagogue, reactionary, anarchist, revolutionary, seditionist, rebel, Red.

4. Backbiter, slanderer, traducer, vilifier, betrayer.

FOG, *n.* 1. Thick mist, darkened state of the atmosphere, haze, smog, brume, vapor, murkiness, soup *(slang),* pea soup *(Brit.),* dirty sky, dampness, cloud, nebula, film, wetness, drizzle, steam.

2. State of mental perplexity, daze, stupor, bewilderment, haze, smog, mental confusion, vagueness, haziness, obscurity, indefiniteness, ambiguity.

FOGGY, *adj.* 1. Thick with fog, hazy, brumous, cloudy, beclouded, overcast, smoky, soupy *(slang),* smoggy, murky, muggy, lowering, dirty, filmy, nebulous, vaporous, steamy, humid, gray, damp, thick, misty.

2. Resembling fog, dim, obscure, confused, vague, dark, shadowy, dusky, indistinct.

FOGY, *n.* 1. Old-fashioned person, excessively conservative person, one behind the times, old fogey, conservative, fogramite, fogrum, fossil, mossback, dotard, square-toes, driveler.

2. Dull person, tomfool, simpleton, oaf, lout, dullard, numskull, beetlehead, lack-wit.

FOIBLE, *n.* Weakness of character, frailty, fault, defect, failing, imperfection, weak side, weak point, besetting sin, blindside, shortcoming, infirmity, deficiency, whimsy, crotchet, quirk, eccentricity.

FOIL, *v.* Render vain, cause to be nugatory, frustrate, thwart, baffle, balk, circumvent, contravene, counter, override, cut the ground from under, clip wings, bring to naught, discomfit, disappoint, disconcert, checkmate, check, defeat, vanquish, prevent, hinder, cripple, overthrow, subdue, spoil.

FOIL, *n.* 1. Metallic substance rolled and hammered into very thin sheets, thin layer of metal,

lamina, flake, lamella, plate, sheet, film, leaf, scale, wafer, membrane, ply.

2. Anything that serves to set off another thing distinctly or to advantage by contrast, contrast, setoff, background, striking difference, contrariety, antithesis.

3. Failure, repulse, defeat, frustration, contravention, circumvention, checkmate.

4. Blunt fencing sword with a button at the point, blunted rapier, glaive, side arms, blade, steel.

FOIST, *v.* Impose unwarrantably, palm off fraudulently, thrust upon surreptitiously, interpolate wrongfully, practice upon, pass off, take in, bait the hook, lure, beguile, trick, trump, slip over on.

FOLD, *n.* 1. Pen for sheep, cote, cot, enclosure for domestic animals, corral, pound, pinfold, shed, sty, stall, paddock, croft, yard, compound, close, stockyard, barnyard, stockade, cattlefold.

2. Flock of sheep, the church *(fig.),* congregation, parish.

3. Part that is folded, plication, plica, plicature, plait, pleat, crease, flexure, folding, doubling, layer, thickness, bend, coil, lap, ply, tuck, gather, crinkle, crumple, corrugation, cockle, furrow, dog's-ear, ruffle, flounce, wrinkle, pucker, crow's-feet.

4. Embrace, hug, embosomment, envelopment, clasp.

FOLD, *v.* 1. Lay one part over another part of, bend over upon itself, lay in folds, double, plicate, pleat, plait, lap, crease, wrinkle, gather, ruffle, pucker, rumple, corrugate, crumple, crinkle, curl, tuck, ruck, hem, dog-ear.

2. Shut by laying parts together, wrap, infold, enclose, wind round, surround, interlace, envelop, inwrap, bring into a compact form by bending, enclose within folds, encircle, furl.

3. Entwine within the arms, embrace, hug, embosom, clasp to the breast, lay close to the body.

FOLIACEOUS, *adj.* 1. *(Min.)* Consisting of leaf-like plates, lamelliform, laminated, lamellate, lamellar, lamellated, laminiferous, schistose, micaceous, flaky, scaly, foliated, filmy, membranous, squamous, stratified.

2. *(Bot.)* Bearing leaves, leafy, foliate, foliated.

FOLIAGE, *n.* Leaves of a plant, frondescence, clusters of leaves, foliation, leafage, vernation, prefoliation, verdure, boskage.

FOLIO, *n.* 1. Sheet of paper folded once to make two leaves (four pages), leaf of a manuscript or book, leaf of a book numbered only on the front side, page number of a book.

2. Volume having pages of the largest size, tome, codex, quarto, octavo.

FOLK, *n.* 1. Group of kindred people, kindred, people in general, mankind, persons, public, society, demos, body politic, masses, commons, people of lower culture in any homogeneous social group, peasantry, tribe, nationality, race, nation, state, realm, community.

2. *(Pl.)* The persons of one's own family, one's relatives, kith and kin, kinfolk, blood relations, family.

FOLKLORE, *n.* The lore of the common people, traditional legends and customs of a people, popular beliefs, superstitions, prescription, traditions, traditional sayings preserved unreflectively among a people, immemorial usage, common law.

FOLLICLE, *n.* 1. *(Anat.)* Small cavity, sac, gland, cyst, cellule, pit, antrum, sinus, alveolus, dint, deep narrow-mouthed depression, small lymph node.

2. (*Bot.*) Dry one-celled seed vessel consisting of a single carpel, fruit, vesicle.

FOLLOW, *v.* 1. Come after, go behind, move behind in the same direction, proceed in the wake of, tread in the rear of, tread on the heels of, walk in the steps of, bring up the rear.

2. Come after in natural sequence, succeed, take the place of, come next, step into the shoes of, replace, supplant.

3. Endeavor to overtake, go in pursuit of, pursue, run after, chase, go after, tag after, track, hunt, stalk, shadow, tail, hound, dog, trail, trace, camp on the trail, hang on the skirts of.

4. Lag, loiter, linger, fall behind, tarry, saunter.

5. Come after as a consequence, ensue, result from, happen after something else, occur as a consequence, be subsequent to, come next as an event, supervene, arise, emanate, issue, flow, spring, be inferable, be deducible.

6. Go along with as a companion, attend, escort, accompany, go along with, dance attendance on, keep company with.

7. Act in accordance with, heed, obey, comply with, yield to, conform to, be guided by, observe, notice, mind, note, regard, watch.

8. Accept as a guide or leader, accept as an authority, yield allegiance to, follow the example of, imitate, echo, copy, pattern after, take after, copy after, take as an example, borrow, adopt, duplicate, ape, mimic.

9. Engage in as a pursuit, be concerned with, attend to, practice, prosecute, press to a conclusion, carry on.

10. Endeavor to attain to, aim at, strive for, strive after, cultivate, emulate, cherish, seek, court, woo.

11. Understand, comprehend, savvy (*colloq.*), grasp, catch on, keep up with.

FOLLOWER, *n.* 1. One who demonstrates allegiance to a person or cause, one who follows another in regard to his beliefs, disciple, adherent, proselyte, sectary, partisan, pupil, admirer, apostle, protégé, advocate, votary, devotee.

2. Copyist, imitator, copy-cat (*colloq.*), emulator, echo, duplicate, successor, heir.

3. Pursuer, chaser, stalker, shadow, tail (*slang*), heeler, hound, hunter.

4. Male admirer, beau, sweetheart, boy friend.

5. Servant, servitor, attendant, dependent, retainer, henchman, stooge, hanger-on, dangler, parasite, sycophant, toady, satellite, accessory, acolyte, associate, tool, partner, companion.

FOLLOWING, *adj.* 1. That comes after in time, that comes next in order, succeeding, next after, ensuing, consecutive, successive, consequent, sequential, sequent, subsequent.

2. That is now to follow, now to be mentioned, below.

FOLLOWING, *n.* Body of followers, clientele, clientage, sequela, adherents, dependents, train, retinue, suite, entourage, attendance.

FOLLY, *n.* 1. Lack of understanding, want of sense, senselessness, fatuity, foolishness, unwisdom, fatuousness, irrationality, idiocy, imbecility, mental dullness, shallowness, doltishness, brainlessness, inanity, ineptitude, insipience, desipience.

2. Foolish action, tomfoolery, absurdity, frivolity, levity, trifling, giddiness, infatuation, eccentricity, extravagance, indiscretion, imprudence, puerility, nonsense.

3. Scandalous crime, sin, wantonness, lewdness.

4. An excessively costly or unprofitable undertaking, ridiculous expenditure.

5. (*Pl.*) Theatrical revue, girly show, burlesque, strip tease.

FOMENT, *v.* 1. Promote the development of, stimulate the growth of, stir up, brew, incite, urge, instigate, excite, galvanize, encourage, foster, sharpen, abet, agitate, quicken, rouse, kindle, suscitate, inflame, exacerbate, irritate, aggravate, raise a storm, make a riot, kick up a fuss, fan the fire, blow the coals, stir the embers, fan into flame.

2. Apply medicated liquid, apply cloths dipped in liquid to the surface of the body, stupe, poultice, bathe with warm lotions, embrocate, wash, heat, warm, chafe, stive, make hot.

FOMENTATION, *n.* 1. Instigation, suscitation, encouragement, excitement, galvanization, stimulation, stirring up, brewing, promoting, abetting, provocation, agitation, perturbation, excitation, incitement, emotional appeal.

2. Application of warm lotion to the body, poultice, embrocation, local bathing with warm liquid.

FOND, *adj.* 1. Liking, loving, affectionate, tender, devoted, ardent, impassioned, amorous, erotic, sentimental, enamored, attached, desirous, passionate, appetitive, prizing highly.

2. Overaffectionate, doting, foolishly loving, weakly indulgent, overfond, uxorious, partial.

3. Credulous to the point of folly, gullible, overly trusting.

FONDLE, *v.* Caress, touch fondly, stroke lovingly, pet, coddle, hug, embrace, blandish, cosset, coddle, clasp to the bosom, fold in one's arms, nestle, nuzzle, spoon, bill and coo, titillate, tickle.

FONDNESS, *n.* 1. Affectionateness, tenderness, strong affection, ardent love, endearment, attachment, amorousness, infatuation, passion, regard, devotion, desire.

2. Partiality, penchant, inclination, propensity, predilection, leaning, preference, whim, animus, bent, instinctive liking, fancy.

3. Appetite, taste, relish, keenness, hunger, stomach, thirst, appetency, gusto.

4. Foolish love, doting affection, uxoriousness, excessive tenderness.

5. Complacent credulity, credulousness, gullibility, delusion.

FONT, *n.* 1. Stone receptacle for baptismal water, receptacle for holy water, stoup, baptistery, baptismal vessel.

2. Complete assortment of type of one style and size.

3. Oil reservoir in a lamp.

FOOD, *n.* 1. What is taken into the body for nourishment, nutrition, nutriment in solid form, aliment, sustenance, victuals, board, provisions, fare, bread, meat, viands, cheer, regimen, diet, rations, subsistence, foodstuffs, manna, belly-timber, pabulum, commons, eatables, edibles, comestibles, refreshments, ambrosia, whatever supplies nourishment to organic bodies, anything serving as material for consumption.

2. Fodder, feed, forage, provender, pasturage, grub, prey, bait.

FOOL, *n.* 1. Stupid person, dunce, dolt, bonehead, blockhead, simpleton, Simple Simon, chump, nitwit, lunkhead, nincompoop, ninny, donkey, ass, noddle, dullard, oaf, clod, rube, clodpate, booby, mooncalf, witling, driveler, lout, lubber, goose, sap, saphead, coot, silly-willy, numskull, ignoramus, dunderhead, beetle-head.

2. Person deficient in judgment, idiot, moron, imbecile, half-wit, defective, tomfool.

3. One who professionally counterfeits folly, professional jester, buffoon, clown, droll, dunce, harlequin, zany, merry-andrew, antic, punch, scaramouch, punchinello, pierrot, wiseacre.

4. One who has been imposed on by others, dupe, gull, butt, toy, tool, stooge, cat's-paw.

FOOL, *v.* 1. Make a fool of, befool, kid, gull, hoax, cozen, delude, deceive, beguile, dupe, flimflam, trick, cheat, hoodwink, bamboozle, humbug, bluff, take in, defraud, victimize, overreach, circumvent, best, do, bilk, diddle.

2. Jest, joke, act the fool, play the monkey, wear the cap and bells, be a zany, cut capers, frolic.

3. Potter aimlessly, waste time, fritter away, spend foolishly, trifle, toy, dally, dawdle, idle, loiter, tarry, spend time in idle pursuit.

4. Make believe, pretend, feign.

FOOLERY, *n.* 1. Nonsense, absurdity, foolishness, folly, insipience, desipience, idiotism, imbecility, moronism.

2. Foolish conduct, buffoonery, zanyism, mummery, tomfoolery, mischievous behavior, prankishness.

FOOLHARDY, *adj.* Daring without judgment, foolishly venturesome, venturous, adventurous, audaciously bold, rash, brash, incautious, imprudent, indiscreet, temerarious, reckless, daredevil, madcap, careless, heedless, regardless, thoughtless, impetuous, impulsive, headlong, precipitate, hare-brained, hot-headed, desperate, hasty, headstrong.

FOOLISH, *adj.* 1. Idiotic, imbecilic, moronic, weak-minded, half-witted, stupid, dull, insensate, irrational, brainless, buffle-headed, shallow, thick-skulled, witless, daft, fatuous, destitute of reason, loony, bone-headed, demented, senseless, simple-minded, inept, inane, apish, doltish, deficient in understanding.

2. Ill-considered, unwise, short-sighted, ill-judged, imprudent, indiscreet, unintelligent, insagacious, incautious, irresponsible, ill-advised, unreasonable.

3. Ridiculous, derisible, laughable, nonsensical, asinine, ludicrous, preposterous, quixotic, hard-brained.

FOOLISHNESS, *n.* 1. Stupidity, imbecility, moronity, idiotism, fatuity, dullness, madness, lunacy, idiocy, fatuousness, doltishness, shallowness.

2. Folly, absurdity, asininity, nonsense, extravagance, indiscretion, imprudence, irrationality, preposterousness, insagacity, ineptitude, childishness, puerility, triviality, wild-goose chase.

FOOT, *n.* 1. Terminal part of the leg, organ of locomotion, *pes (Lat.), pedes (pl.),* lower extremity, heel, toe, sole, trotter, tootsy, understanding, dog, bowwow, kicker, silk-stocking form, pedal, tread, pad, paw, hoof.

2. Ground part, bottom, base, foundation, lower part.

3. Unit of length derived from the length of the human foot, 12 inches, 30.48 centimeters.

4. *(Mil.)* Foot-soldiers, infantry, rank and file, rifles, cannon fodder.

FOOT, *v.* 1. Walk, go on foot, traverse on foot, ambulate, perambulate, step, pace, tramp, march.

2. Move the feet to music, dance, tread the light fantastic toe.

3. Set foot on, walk on, tread.

4. Add up figures, sum up, total, aggregate.

5. Settle a bill, pay, pay on the line, discharge an obligation, stand expense, cough up, pay the piper, come across, shell out, fork over.

FOOTBOY, *n.* Boy in livery employed as a servant, page, squire, usher, buttons, donzel, cup-bearer, train-bearer, lackey, runner.

FOOTFALL, *n.* Footstep, sound of one's step, tramp, tread, step, clip, port, carriage, rate, pace, stride, gait.

FOOTHOLD, *n.* 1. Hold for the feet, place to stand on, *locus standi (Lat.), pou sto (Gk.),* footing, standing, foundation, support, purchase, vantage ground, basis for operation, beachhead, bridgehead, spearhead, grip.

2. Firm footing, secure position, stable position, firm place.

FOOTING, *n.* 1. Establishment, settlement, secure position.

2. Basis on which anything is established, groundwork, foundation.

3. Support for the feet, surface to stand on, foothold, *locus standi (Lat.), pou sto (Gk.),* standing, purchase, basis for operation, beachhead, bridgehead, spearhead, grip.

4. Act of adding up a column of figures, addition, aggregate, total.

5. Position assigned to a person in estimation, rank, status, situation, condition, state, grade, standing, station.

6. Terms of social intercourse, mutual standing, reciprocal relation.

FOOTLIGHTS, *n.* Row of lights in the front of the stage, the stage, the theater as a profession, acting profession, theatricals, buskin, sock, cothurnus, the boards, histrionic art, dramaturgy, Thespis, Melpomene and Thalia.

FOOTMAN, *n.* Liveried servant, man in waiting, lackey, butler, flunky, male servant in silk stockings and knee breeches, menial, valet, valet de chambre, manservant, servitor.

FOOTPAD, *n.* Highwayman who robs on foot, knight of the road, freebooter, bandit, robber, brigand, ladrone, thug, thief, marauder, forager, pillager, plunderer, rifler, pilferer, burglar, pirate, buccaneer, raider, corsair, picaroon, filcher, cutpurse, pickpocket, shoplifter.

FOOTPATH, *n.* Narrow way for pedestrians only, beaten track, beaten path, footway, trail, pathway, bypath, byway, shortcut, bridlepath, carrefour, private road, trot-toir, pavement, sidewalk.

FOOTPRINT, *n.* Impression left by the foot, footmark, track, vestige, mark of the foot, trace, wake, trail, spoor, *piste (Fr.),* soleprint.

FOOT SOLDIER, *n.* Infantryman, footman, private, doughboy, regular, trooper, rookie, legionary, shavetail, standard-bearer, non-com, line troop, rank and file, cannon-fodder, food for powder, sepoy, peltast.

FOOTSTALK, *n.* Leafstalk, pedicle, pedicel, peduncle.

FOOTSTEP, *n.* 1. Sound of one's step, stepping, tread, footfall, step, clamp.

3. Mark left by the foot, footmark, footprint, trace, track, trail, vestige, wake, *piste (Fr.)*.

4. Mark, token, indication, sign.

2. Distance covered by the feet in stepping, pace, stride, degree of progress.

FOOTSTOOL, *n.* Low stool upon which to rest one's feet, ottoman, hassock, faldstool, prie-dieu, tabouret, tripod.

FOOZLE, *v.* Bungle, play clumsily, blunder, slip, make a mess of, botch, not succeed, make vain efforts, bring to naught, labor in vain, fall short of, flunk, flounder, run aground.

FOP, *n.* Man who is excessively concerned about his appearance, dandy, dude, fashion plate, coxcomb, exquisite, buck, blade, dasher, man about town, prettyboy, silk-stocking, popinjay, jack-a-dandy, beau, toff, spark, jackanapes, silk-sock Sam, green-carnation wearer, swell, man milliner, fine gentleman, dandiprat, macaroni, blood, fribble, carpet-knight, masher, Johnnie, Beau Brummel.

FOPPERY, *n.* Showiness of dress, foppishness, dandyism, dudishness, dudism, exquisitism, coxcombry.

FOPPISH, *adj.* Showy in dress, dandified, dandyish, coxcombical, dapper, spruce, natty, exquisite, affected, vain, finical, fop-like.

FOR, *prep.* 1. By reason of, in consequence of, as the effect of, because of, inasmuch as, considering.

2. On account of, in behalf of, for the sake of, in consideration of, in the interest of, with the object or purpose of.

3. Instead of, in the place of, in return for, in exchange as the equivalent of, in requital of, as an offset to.

4. As far as concerns, concerning, with regard to, with respect to, respecting, as regards.

5. In spite of, notwithstanding, despite, for all one's.

6. In favor of, in support of, pro, on the side of, in championship of, favorably inclined toward.

7. Appropriate to, adapted to, beneficial to, conducive to, intended to be used in connection with.

8. During, during the continuance of, during the term of, throughout the extent of, in the space of time of, during the incumbency of.

9. With the purpose of reaching, having as goal or object, in order to obtain, with a view to, in quest of, with inclination toward.

FOR, *conj.* On the account that, since, because, seeing that, for the reason that, on the ground that.

FORAGE, *v.* Take forage, wander in search of forage, hunt, search about, raid, plunder, maraud, rob, strip of supplies, loot, ravage, depredate, despoil.

FORAGE, *n.* Food for horses and cattle, feed, provender, fodder, pasture, pasturage.

FORAMEN, *n.* Opening, hole, perforation, orifice, aperture, fenestra, short passage, hiatus, mouth.

FORAMINATED, *adj.* Provided with an opening, having an orifice, perforated, foraminous, apertured.

FORASMUCH AS, *conj.* In view of the fact that, in consideration that, inasmuch as, seeing that, whereas, because, since.

FORAY, *n.* Hostile invasion, predatory incursion, invasion, irruption, inroad, inimical descent, depredation, sudden attack, raid.

FORBEAR, *v.* 1. Cease, stop, refrain from, pause, desist from, leave off, break off, hold, stay, relinquish, quit.

2. Do without, abstain, hold back, endure the privation of, discontinue, renounce, resign, give up.

3. Keep back, withhold, restrain.

4. Decline, shun, avoid, eschew, omit.

5. Show forbearance, be tolerant, be patient, endure, suffer, tolerate, brook, put up with, treat with indulgence, spare, bear with, submit.

FORBEARANCE, *n.* Forbearing conduct, patient endurance, lenity, patience, indulgence, long-suffering, self-restraint, command of temper, mildness, tolerance, submission, endurance, lenience, clemency, mercy, pardon, pity, meekness, avoidance, abstinence, self-denial, temperance, respite, moderation, longanimity.

FORBID, *v.* Put an interdiction against, interdict, enjoin, prohibit, proscribe, embargo, veto, taboo, ban, disallow, debar, command not to do, render impossible, hinder, prevent, impede, exclude, obstruct, oppose, refuse, preclude, restrain, gainsay, forfend.

FORBIDDANCE, *n.* Edict against a thing, debarment, taboo, ban, embargo, prohibition, boycott, veto, interdiction, proscription, inhibition.

FORBIDDING, *adj.* Causing dislike, disagreeable, offensive, odious, unpleasant, abhorrent, repulsive, repellent, unseemly, horrible, dangerous-looking, ugly, disgusting, grisly, hideous, grim, sinister, threatening, inhospitable, prohibitory.

FORCE, *v.* 1. Necessitate, oblige, compel, constrain, coerce, effect, make by force, impose forcibly upon, overcome the resistance of, overpower, shove down the throat, enforce.

2. Drive against resistance, impel, propel, press, push, urge, stress, strain, obtrude, thrust, elbow.

3. Obtain by force, exact, extort, twist from, shear.

4. Hasten growth artificially, cause to mature at an increased rate by artificial means.

5. Take by violence, capture by assault, storm, overpower, break open, wrest.

6. Rape, ravish, violate, constuprate, assault, attack, deflower.

FORCE, *n.* 1. Energy, vigor, might, power, strength, vim, emphasis, stress, pith, weightiness, virtue, caliber, elan, impetus, nerve, stamina, animation, activity, striking ability, vitality, brunt.

2. Capacity of producing an effect, ability, efficiency, efficacy, validity, potency, puissance, cogency, agency, impact, binding effect, prevalence.

3. Special signification, significance, value, meaning, import.

4. Compulsion, coercion, duress, constraint, enforcement, vehemence, violence.

5. (*Pl.*) Army, soldiery, troops, legion, squadron, host, battalion, phalanx, detachment, regiment, division, patrol, convoy, armament, body of men prepared for action, posse, vigilantes.

FORCED, *adj.* 1. Constrained, obliged, made to, compelled, enforced, involuntary, compulsory, emergency.

2. Strained, labored, far-fetched, recherché, studiously sought, artificial, catachrestic, unnatural, affected.

FORCEFUL, *adj.* Full of power, vigorous, effective, mighty, dynamic, virile, potent, puissant, active, powerful, robust, energetic, emphatic, intensive, cogent, valid, vivid.

FORCIBLE, *adj.* 1. Strong, powerful, potent, puissant, herculean, all-powerful, mighty, sturdy, vigorous, energetic.

2. Weighty, cogent, impressive, irresistible, graphic, pithy, producing a powerful effect, convincing, effective, telling, efficacious, striking, emphatic, urgent.

3. Compulsory, coercive, coerced, obligatory, required, binding, incumbent.

4. Vehement, violent, unrestrained, drastic, intense, impetuous.

FORCIBLY, *adv.* 1. Compulsorily, by force, against one's will, violently, coercively, at gun point, *vi et armis (Lat.),* by coercion, perforce, necessarily, of necessity, *ex necessitate rei (Lat.),* needs must, *nolens volens (Lat.),* willy-nilly, willing or unwilling, *coûte que coûte (Fr.), bon gré mal gré (Fr.),* under protest, against one's will.

2. Vigorously, energetically, with might and main, puissantly, powerfully, effectively, efficaciously.

FORD, *v.* Cross a river by wading, wade across a shallows, wade through, cross by a ford, cross on foot, traverse.

FORD, *n.* Place where a body of water may be crossed by wading, shallows, shallow crossing, wading-place.

FORE, *adj.* 1. Previous, preceding, antecedent, anterior, foregoing, prior, former, first.

2. Situated toward the front, at the front, frontal, headmost, face, front, forward.

3. Leading, foremost, chief, head, most advanced, first.

FOREBEAR, *n.* Forefather, ancestor, genitor, progenitor, procreator, begetter, forerunner, grandsire, grandfather, great-grandfather.

FOREBODE, *v.* 1. Look into the future, have foreknowledge of, foreknow, have prescience of, be prescient of, have a presentiment of, have a premonition of, predict, presage, prognosticate, foresee, foretell, forecast, prophesy, vaticinate, soothsay, divine, have an inward conviction of, surmise.

2. Be an omen of, indicate beforehand, signify, betoken, foreshow, shadow forth, foreshadow, ominate, prefigure, augur, portend, be ominous, warn, forewarn, threaten.

FOREBODING, *n.* 1. Presentiment, premonition, prognostic, augury, omen, portent, apprehension, dread, boding, misgiving, anticipation.

2. Prediction, prognostication, presage, foreknowledge, preapprehension, forecast, prophecy.

FORECAST, *v.* 1. Conjecture beforehand, predict, prognosticate, auspicate, foreknow, presage, prophesy, foretell, make a forecast of, calculate beforehand, foresee, anticipate, expect, divine, surmise, guess, picture to oneself, envision, envisage.

2. Serve as a forecast of, betoken, foreshadow, portend, augur, foretoken, bode, point to, signify, forewarn.

3. Plan beforehand, prearrange, predetermine, contrive, design, devise, project, invent, hatch, scheme, concoct, plan ahead.

FORECAST, *n.* 1. Foresight of consequences and provision against them, conjecture as to something in the future, forethought, foreknowledge, prescience, prevision, precognition, prediction, prophecy, prognostication, vaticination, presage,

premonition, augury, provident regard to the future, anticipation, conjecture, presentiment, prognosis.

2. Foresight in planning, providence, prudence, predetermination, contrivance, circumspection.

FORECLOSE, *v.* 1. Close beforehand, debar, shut out, exclude, bar, keep off, stop, stave off, forfend, estop, antevert, prevent, hinder, preclude, obviate.

2. *(Law)* Deprive of the power of redeeming property, take away the right to redeem a mortgage.

3. Establish an exclusive claim to, hold exclusively.

FOREDOOM, *v.* Doom beforehand, predestine, predestinate, predict as a doom, ordain, preordain, foreordain, devote, have in store for.

FOREFATHER, *n.* Forbear, foregoer, forerunner, father, author, begetter, procreator, genitor, progenitor, primogenitor, originator, ancestor, ancient, patriarch, grandsire, grandfather, graybeard.

FOREGOER, *n.* 1. Forerunner, one who leads, predecessor, precursor, harbinger, herald, avant-courier, advance guard, pioneer.

2. Ancestor, forefather, forbear, progenitor, father.

FOREGOING, *adj.* Going before, preceding, antecedent, anterior, fore, former, previous, prior, forenamed, aforesaid, *ci-devant (Fr.),* last, latter, recent.

FOREGONE, *adj.* 1. Prejudged, predesigned, predetermined, decided beforehand, prepense, premeditated, advised, studied, calculated, aforethought, intended, fixed, set, cut and dried.

2. That has gone before, previous, bygone, former, past, earlier, prior, antecedent.

FOREHANDED, adj. 1. Providing for the future, thrifty, provident, prudent, beforehand, mindful of the future, foresighted, seasonable, timely, done in time.

2. In easy circumstances, comfortable as regards property, well-to-do, well-off.

FOREHEAD, *n.* That part of the face above the eyes, brow, front upper part of the head, temple, sinciput, metopion.

FOREIGN, *adj.* 1. Coming from another land, derived from another country, alien, not native, not domestic, from abroad, tramontane, ultramarine, transatlantic, transpacific, transmarine, exotic, outlandish, barbarous, distant, remote, unfamiliar, strange, peregrine, heathenish, transpontine, unknown.

2. Not belonging where found, extraneous, exterior, extrinsic, external, outward, outside, not organically connected, not naturally related, unnatural, unrelated, not related with the thing under consideration, not pertinent, not congruous, inappropriate, impertinent, inapposite, inapplicable, irrelevant, unessential, inadmissible, beside the point, adventitious.

FOREIGNER, *n.* Person coming from a foreign country, alien, non-native, immigrant, emigrant, newcomer, outsider, *novus homo (Lat.), Ausländer (Ger.), étranger (Fr.), aubain (Fr. Law), straniero (It.), extranjero (Sp.), forastero (Sp.),* stranger, tramontane, outlander, barbarian, heathen, gentile, pagan, tenderfoot, Wop *(slang),* Dago *(slang),* Polack *(slang),* Hunky *(slang),* Frog *(slang),* Kraut *(slang),* Chink *(slang).*

FOREIGNISM, *n.* Alienism, exoticism, foreign idiom or custom, deviation from accepted speech standards that comes from the influence of a foreign language, Gallicism, Briticism, Germanism, foreign quality.

FOREKNOWLEDGE, n. Knowledge of things before they happen, second sight, clairvoyance, prevision, foresight, precognition, prescience, preconception, prenotion, previous knowledge, presentiment, foresightedness, anticipation, presage, prospect, prognostication, premonition, foreboding, portent, forecast.

FORELAND, n. Cape, promontory, headland, butte, bluff, cliff, point of land, tor, rock projecting into the sea, peak, escarpment, dune.

FOREMAN, n. 1. Man in charge of a group of workers, supervisor, superintendent, overlooker, overseer, master workman, chief workman, head, boss, straw boss, inspector, taskmaster.

2. Chairman of a jury, presiding juryman.

FOREMOST, adj. 1. First, initial, prime, primary, primal, inaugural.

2. Forward, fore, front, uppermost.

3. Chief in rank or dignity, head, leading, most advanced, grand, supreme, capital, paramount, preëminent, essential, vital, cardinal.

FORENSIC, adj. 1. Used in courts of law, judicial, juridic, juristic, legal, lawful.

2. Adapted to argumentation, argumentative, polemical, controversial, disputative, rhetorical, oratorical, proper to public debate.

FOREORDAIN, v. Appoint beforehand, doom, foredoom, predestine, predestinate, predetermine, preordain, foreshadow, have in store for.

FORERUN, v. 1. Go before, precede, antecede, go in the van, go in advance, run in front of, precurse, be the precursor of, usher in, introduce as a harbinger, herald, announce, lead the way, head.

2. Anticipate, forestall, be beforehand, be in advance of, steal a march upon, have the start on.

3. Outrun, outstrip, take the lead, get before, get ahead, get in front of, shoot ahead of, gain upon.

FORERUNNER, n. 1. Messenger sent before to give notice of approach of others, one who foreruns, precursor, predecessor, herald, harbinger, announcer, avant-courier, pioneer, outrider, foreloper, foregoer, antecedent, usher, proclaimer, advance guard.

2. Ancestor, progenitor, forefather, forebear.

3. Omen, portent, prognostic, token, foretoken, sign, presage, premonition, augury.

FORESEE, v. 1. Look into the future, presage, augur, divine, forebode, foretell, prophesy, predict, prognosticate, forecast, have prescience of, be prescient, be clairvoyant, have second sight, look into a crystal ball.

2. Look forward to, look ahead, expect, contemplate, envisage, envision, surmise, conjecture.

3. Exercise forethought, be farsighted, be provident, be prudent.

FORESHADOW, v. Indicate beforehand, suggest in advance, shadow forth, adumbrate, signify, presignify, bode, forebode, prefigure, foretoken, presage, ominate, prognosticate, forecast, preshow, betoken, portend, augur, point to, herald, lead one to expect.

FORESIGHT, n. 1. Power of foreseeing, clairvoyance, second sight, foreknowledge, precognition, prevision, prescience, prenotion, preconception.

2. Provision for the future, longsightedness,

farsightedness, sagacity, providence, prudence, provident care, shrewdness, forethought, precaution, discretion, wisdom, premeditation.

3. View into the future, prospect, vista, perception gained by looking forward, vision.

4. Foreboding, presentiment, premonition, portent, presage, forecast, prediction, prognostic, omen, boding, apprehension.

FOREST, n. Dense growth of trees and underbrush, large tract of land covered with trees, extensive wooded area, woods, woodland, wooded tracts, timberland, grove, sylvan thicket, copse, coppice, covert, bosk, bush, jungle, virgin forest, greenwood, wildwood, chaparral, underbrush, brake, canebrake, plantation, chase (Brit.).

FORESTALL, v. 1. Thwart by action in advance, be beforehand with, get ahead of in action, steal a march upon, gain the start on, anticipate, meet in advance of the natural time, deal with a thing in advance, hinder by prior action, frustrate, preclude, prevent, obviate, shut off.

2. Buy up in advance in order to enhance the price, monopolize, regrate, get a corner on, impropriate, have all to oneself, corner, engross, get control of, get exclusive possession of, get into one's hand, have a firm hold of.

FORESTRY, n. Science of planting and taking care of forests, dendrology, silviculture, woodcraft, forestation, afforestation, management of growing timber.

FORETASTE, n. Antepast, pregustation, prelibation, taste beforehand, partial enjoyment in advance, anticipation, first experience of anything, handsel.

FORETELL, v. 1. Tell of beforehand, forecast, prophesy, predict, auspicate, augurate, vaticinate, prognosticate, divine, foresee, soothsay, act the seer, announce in advance, tell before occurrence, cast a horoscope, tell fortunes.

2. (Of things) Portend, forebode, foretoken, augur, bode, foreshadow, foreshow, betoken, presignify, shadow forth, presage, signify, point to, forewarn, lower, threaten.

3. Herald, usher in, announce, proclaim, promulgate, advise, annunciate, cry.

FORETHOUGHT, n. 1. Thinking of something beforehand, premeditation, previous consideration, anticipation, precaution, predeliberation, presurmise, prior thought, prospicience, deliberation, prepensation.

2. Provident care, providence, prudence, foresight, sagacity, longsightedness, farsightedness, shrewdness, wariness, circumspection, carefulness, discrimination, caution, heed.

FORETOKEN, n. Premonitory token, premonition, augury, omen, portent, presage, prognostic, sign, writing on the wall, thunder on the left.

FOREVER, adv. Evermore, ever, always, endlessly, unceasingly, incessantly, aye, for aye, perpetually, everlastingly, eternally, without ever ending, in saecula saeculorum (Lat.), to the end of time, world without end, pour toujours (Fr.), auf immer und ewig (Ger.), per sempre (It.), por siempre jamás (Sp.), till doomsday, till the crack of doom, for a limitless time, at all times, in all ages, for good and all, through endless ages, undyingly, unremittingly, continually, constantly, ceaselessly, interminably.

FOREWARN, v. Give previous warning to, caution in advance, warn beforehand, prewarn, premonish, admonish, give notice, advise, menace, put on one's guard, put on the qui vive, sound the alarm, sound the tocsin.

FOREWORD, *n.* Introductory statement, introduction, preface, prolegomenon, exordium, preamble, proem, prelude, prologue.

FORFEIT, *n.* Penalty, assessment, fine, amercement, forfeiture, damages.

FORFEIT, *v.* 1. Lose because of some offense, alienate by breach of condition, have to pay as a forfeit, become liable to lose in consequence of fault, fail to keep an obligation, default, escheat *(Law),* meet with a loss, experience a loss, miss, let slip, allow to slip through the fingers, squander, be without, waste.

2. Violate, infringe, transgress, break, trample under foot, do violence to.

3. Penalize, make penal.

FORFEITURE, *n.* 1. Amercement, confiscation, sequestration, loss because of some neglect, deprivation, penal retribution, punishment, chastisement, penalization, penance, *peine forte et dure (Fr.),* incurment of damages.

2. (See FORFEIT, *n.*)

FORFEND, *v.* 1. Fend, defend, secure, protect, shield, preserve, secure, save, screen, shroud.

2. Avert, fend off, prevent, forbid, hinder, keep off, ward off, obviate, antevert, stave off, turn aside, draw off, nip in the bud.

FORGATHER, *v.* 1. Gather together, convene, assemble, muster, congregate, hold a session, come together.

2. Encounter, meet by accident, bump into, happen on, confront, face, meet with, come upon.

3. Associate, fraternize, consort, mingle, keep company.

FORGE, *n.* Furnace in which metal is heated before shaping, smithy, ironworks, stithy, shinglingmill, smithery, bloomery.

FORGE, *v.* 1. Beat molten metal into shape, form by heating and hammering, hammer out, fabricate, extund.

2. Make in any way, shape, figure, create, invent, achieve, compose, conceive, coin, frame, devise, contrive, produce, fashion, shape.

3. Imitate fraudulently, fabricate by false imitation, counterfeit, feign, falsify, trump up, commit forgery, circulate bad money, circulate the queer *(slang).*

4. Sign a false signature to a check or money transaction.

FORGER, *n.* 1. Falsifier, coiner, counterfeiter, *faux monnayeur (Fr.).*

2. Signer of false signature.

FORGERY, *n.* 1. Making of a fraudulent imitation of a thing which is put forth as genuine, fabricating falsely, counterfeiting, falsification, misrepresentation, imposture, fraudulence, cheating, imposition, deception, false imitation.

2. Something produced by forgery, counterfeit, fake, sham, brummagem, make-believe, fraud, tinsel, paste, false jewelry, scagliola, ormolu, German silver.

3. Simulated signing of another person's name.

FORGET, *v.* 1. Cease to remember, fail to recollect, be unable to recall, be forgetful, disremember, lose the remembrance of, let slip from the memory, lose the memory of, have a short memory, be unable to recall, obliterate, have escape the memory.

2. Omit unintentionally, overlook, lose sight

of, think no more of, consign to oblivion, write off, let bygones be bygones.

3. Omit to take, leave behind inadvertently.

4. Omit to mention, leave unnoticed, pass over, miss, skip, pass by, let pass, gloss over, let slip.

5. Neglect willfully, cease to care for, slight, disregard, treat with inattention, ignore, take no note of.

FORGETFUL, *adj.* 1. Apt to forget, amnesic, insensible to the past, Lethean.

2. Inattentive, negligent, neglectful, heedless, unmindful, absent-minded, mindless, oblivious, careless, listless.

FORGETFULNESS, *n.* 1. Failure of memory, amnesia, obliteration of the past, oblivescence, obliviousness, shortness of memory, lapse of memory, *lapsus memoriae (Lat.),* aptness to forget, absent-mindedness.

2. Oblivion, forgottenness, waters of oblivion, Lethe, lotus-eating.

3. Carelessness, heedlessness, negligence, neglectfulness, inattention, woolgathering, inadvertence, unobservance, slip, disregard, remissness, thoughtlessness.

FORGET ONESELF, *v.* 1. Be guilty of what is unworthy of one, do something improper, commit an indiscretion, misconduct oneself, misbehave, deviate from virtue, offend, commit a faux pas, trespass, err, do amiss, go astray, sow one's wild oats, lose self-control.

2. Fail to remember, lapse, slip, trip.

3. Neglect oneself, slight oneself, fail to take care of oneself, be entirely unselfish.

4. Become absent-minded, become lost in thought, go into a brown study, woolgather, be lost in reverie, build aircastles.

5. Lose consciousness in sleep, fall asleep, doze off.

FORGIVE, *v.* 1. Grant free pardon for, pardon, remit the penalty of, acquit, absolve, excuse, give absolution, blot out offenses, wipe the slate clean, let bygones be bygones, clear, pass by, reprieve, exonerate, exculpate, overlook, discharge, condone, pass over, release, set free.

2. Cease to feel resentment against, think no more of, bear with, bury the hatchet, allow for, make allowances for, pocket the affront, start afresh.

3. Give up all claim on account of, waive, remit a debt.

FORGIVENESS, *n.* 1. Absolution, pardon, remission, exoneration, exculpation, extenuation, dispensation, condonation, acquittal, reprieve, amnesty, quittance, grace, respite, excuse, release, indulgence, mercy, willingness to forgive, disposition to pardon, justification, apology, essoin *(Law).*

2. Conciliation, reconciliation, appeasement, forbearance, satisfaction, propitiation, pacification.

FORGIVING, *adj.* 1. Absolvatory, absolutory, acquitting, clearing, excusing, exonerative, exculpatory, pardoning, releasing, placable.

2. Compassionate, merciful, clement, magnanimous, generous, conciliatory, lenient, indulgent, charitable, humane, forbearing, sparing, patient, kindhearted, reconcilable.

FORGO, *v.* Abstain from, refrain from, do without, give up, renounce, resign, surrender, waive, yield, forbear, eschew.

FORGOTTEN, *adj.* Past recollection, gone out of

one's head, gone from one's mind, out of mind, gone, out of one's recollection, unremembered, lapsed, lost, bygone, irrecoverable, on the other side of Lethe, sunk in oblivion, buried in the past.

FORK, *n.* 1. Instrument with tines used for piercing and holding, pronged instrument for taking up and pitching, trident.

2. Bifurcation, divarication, branching, dividing into branches, division, angulation.

3. Branch, notch, crutch, angle, bend, elbow, knee, crotch.

4. Choice of two alternatives, dilemma, crisis, crossroads, crux.

FORK, *v.* Divide into branches, bifurcate, divaricate, branch, ramify, branch out, diverge, form a fork, bend, hook.

FORKED, *adj.* Dividing into two or more prongs, bifurcated, bifurcate, bifid, biforked, furcated, furcate, branching, divaricated, forficate, Y-shaped, V-shaped, sharp-cornered, crotched, cleft, angular, zigzag, oblique, staggered.

FORLORN, *adj.* 1. Abandoned, deserted, bereft, forsaken, desolate, lost, lonesome, bereaved, solitary, friendless, helpless, destitute, forgotten, lone.

2. Unhappy, dejected, depressed, broken-hearted, disconsolate, dispirited, abject, woebegone, pathetic, pitiable, wretched, miserable, hopeless, in pitiful plight, lamentable, doleful, comfortless, cheerless, dreary, dismal, desperate, inconsolable.

FORM, *n.* 1. Shape as regards structure, formation, conformation, figuration, configuration, figure, outline, pattern, build, *galbe (Fr.),* contour, mold, cut, turn, cast, tournure, construction, set, frame, get-up, format, particular structural character, make, orderly arrangement of parts, matrix, scheme, structure, style, design, plan.

2. Variety, type, sort, kind, species, genus, genre, class, order, model, stamp, brand, character, denomination, race, color, description.

3. Feature, outward appearance, lineament, phase, aspect, characteristic.

4. Body, figure, person, individual, being, fellow, creature, presence, image, resemblance, likeness, semblance.

5. Good condition with reference to fitness for performing, condition of health and training, fitness, trim, fettle, kilter, state.

6. Regularity, orderliness, disposition, system, systematization, symmetry, shapeliness, harmony, order, arrangement.

7. Fixed and formal way of proceeding, procedure, prescribed method of doing something, established practice, manner, way, formula, formulary, mode, ritual, set order, rite.

8. Conduct regulated by custom, conventional behavior, conventionality, deportment as judged by social standards, conformity to the usages of society, conventional method of acting, propriety, formality, punctilio, etiquette, observance, ceremony, ceremonial, decorum, ordinance.

9. Printed document with blank spaces for insertion of information, questionnaire, questionary.

10. Rank of students, grade in school, class.

11. Long seat without a back, bench, settle, settee.

FORM, *v.* 1. Give shape to, fashion, shape, figure, mold, carve, sculpture, sculpt, model, cut, chisel, hew, roughhew, block out, shape up, cast, stamp, trim, knead, pattern.

2. Make, produce, construct, build, erect, fabricate, frame, put together, create, institute, prepare, effect, manufacture.

3. Invent, conceive, contrive, devise, coin, mint, forge.

4. Serve to make up, compose, constitute, serve for, make up, incorporate, embody.

5. Contract, acquire, develop, beget, breed, engender, generate, incur, grow into.

6. Train, teach, instruct, exercise, drill, develop, discipline, advance, unfold, expand.

7. Place in order, organize, systematize, arrange, dispose, adjust.

FORMAL, *adj.* 1. Being in accordance with conventional requirements, official, authoritative, in due form, observant of form, academic, ceremonial, ritualistic, liturgical, methodic, systematic, orderly, definite, symmetrical, regular.

2. Conventional, ceremonious, punctilious, precise, stiff, starched, prim, exact, rigid, set, fixed, inflexible, uncompromising, Procrustean, strict, strait-laced, prudish, proper, tartuffish, solemn, pompous, decorous, bombastic, stilted, Pharisaic.

3. Being a matter of form only, external, perfunctory, outward, apparent, as mere form.

4. In evening clothes, *en grande tenue,* coattails and top hat, full dress.

5. Essential, vital, constitutional, constituent, organic, inward, innate, primordial, a priori, formative, indispensable.

FORMALITY, *n.* 1. Compliance with formal or conventional rules, accordance with prescribed or customary form, observance of form, red tape.

2. Rigorously methodical character, excessive regularity, stiffness, precision, rigidity.

3. Established mode of proceeding, settled method, custom, rule of procedure, punctilio, etiquette, conventionality, ceremonial, ceremony, ritual, rite, mere form, propriety, manners, decorum.

FORMAT, *n.* 1. Shape and size of a book as determined by the number of times the original sheet has been folded to form the leaves.

2. Size and general style of a publication, make-up, getup, form, general physical appearance of a book, type face, binding, quality of paper, margination.

FORMATION, *n.* 1. Manner in which a thing is formed, formal structure, make-up, make, texture, nature, construction, organization, composition, constitution, arrangement, shape, conformation, synthesis.

2. Production, creation, genesis, development, fabrication, manufacture, generation, establishment.

FORMATIVE, *adj.* 1. Giving form and shape, forming, fashioning, molding, plastic, shaping, creative, formable, fictile, moldable, modeling, determinative.

2. Impressible, sensitive, susceptible, impressionable, pliant, supple.

FORMER, *adj.* 1. Earlier, foregoing, previous, anterior, preexistent, antecedent, prior, preceding, preliminary.

2. Bygone, gone by, gone, over, passed away, past, elapsed, lapsed, foregone, late, *ci-devant (Fr.),* old-time, ancient, quondam, pristine, whilom, expired, extinct, sometime.

3. First mentioned, aforementioned, aforesaid, first named, before-mentioned.

4. Being the first of two, preceding in order.

5. Having held a particular office in the past, ex—.

FORMERLY, *adv.* Aforetime, heretofore, in times past, of yore, of old, in days of yore, in ages past, long ago, anciently, in the olden time, in time gone by, hitherto, previously, erst, erstwhile, whilom, time was, ago, once, one day, long ago, ere now, lately.

FORMIDABLE, *adj.* 1. Exciting fear, causing apprehension, frightful, fearful, menacing, dread, dreadful, appalling, threatening, terrifying, alarming, deterring, shocking, horrible, terrific.
2. Of alarming strength, indomitable, redoubtable, impregnable, invincible, arduous, huge, difficult, tremendous, doughty.
3. Such as to inspire apprehension of defeat or failure, dangerous, serious, risky, ticklish.

FORMLESS, *adj.* Wanting form, inform, without a determinate form, shapeless, unshapely, misshapen, amorphous, indeterminate, unformed, unhewn, unfashioned, unshapen, asymmetric, unsymmetrical, rough, wanting regularity of shape, chaotic.

FORMULA, *n.* Set form for use in any ceremony, fixed conventional method in which anything is to be done, formulary, prescription, rule, recipe, model, principle frequently expressed, formal statement of doctrine, creed, credo, ritual, code.

FORMULARY, *n.* 1. Collection or system of formulas, book of forms.
2. Set form of words, canon, model, formula, rule, creed, precept.
3. Ceremonial, ritual, sacrament.

FORMULATE, *v.* Express in precise form, state systematically, reduce to a formula, indite, frame, institute, shape up, devise, compose, hammer out, formulize, draw up, specify, particularize, designate, determine, denote, indicate, point out, select, itemize, enter into detail, descend to particulars, put in a systematized expression.

FORNICATION, *n.* 1. Voluntary sexual intercourse on the part of an unmarried person, intimate relations, intimacy, coitus, liaison, physical commerce, defloration, stupration, defilement, violation, abuse, debauchery, libertinism, wenching, whoredom, venery, seduction.
2. *(Bible)* Idolatry, idol worship.
3. *(Bible)* Adultery.

FORSAKE, *v.* 1. Desert, leave in the lurch, leave entirely, abandon, quit, cast off, depart, flee, vacate, resign, abdicate, lay down, dispose of, part with, fling away, jettison, maroon.
2. Renounce, have done with, forswear, abandon, repudiate, go back on, give up, relinquish, forego, waive, surrender, drop, revoke, recant, reject, discard, disclaim, disavow, deny, disown, yield.

FORSAKEN, *adj.* Left desolate, deserted, abandoned, destitute, cast off, bereaved, forlorn, solitary, alone, lonely, neglected, isolated, rejected, shunned, ignored, helpless, godforsaken, derelict, marooned.

FORSOOTH, *adv.* In truth, to be sure, in fact, of a truth, indeed, truly, certainly, really, in good truth, verily, yea.

FORSWEAR, *v.* 1. Reject with protestations, renounce upon oath, relinquish, desert, abandon, forsake, quit, leave, drop, give up.
2. Deny with strong asseveration, recant, abjure, retract, repudiate, renounce, disavow.

FORSWEAR ONESELF, *v.* Commit perjury, perjure oneself, swear falsely, take a false oath, bear false witness, play false, break one's word, go back on one's oath, break one's faith, be recreant, lie about.

FORT, *n.* Armed place surrounded by defensive works and occupied by troops, enclosed place possessing bastions, fastness, fortress, citadel, capitol, arx, stronghold, fortification, hold, castle, blockhouse, pill box, keep, donjon, tower, defense, bulwark, refuge, redoubt, stockade, garrison.

FORTE, *n.* That in which one excels, strong point, particular talent, chief excellence, special gift, specialty, masterly faculty, natural turn, genius, bent, unusual aptitude.

FORTH, *adv.* 1. Onward in place, outward in space, ahead, forward, in advance from a given point, on to the end.
2. Away from a place, not at home, abroad, out.
3. Out into notice and view, out from concealment, into view, from confinement, from retirement, into consideration.

FORTHRIGHT, *adj.* 1. Going straight to the point, outspoken, blunt, frank, plain-spoken, calling a spade a spade, not mincing matters, painfully truthful.
2. Proceeding in a straight course, direct, straightforward.

FORTHRIGHT, *adv.* 1. Directly forward, in a direct manner, straight, straightforward, ahead.
2. Straightway, at once, immediately, instanter, forthwith, unhesitatingly, without hesitation.

FORTHWITH, *adv.* Immediately, instanter, instantly, without delay, directly, right off, at once, straightway, instantaneously, quickly, presto, promptly, with reasonable dispatch, within a reasonable time, as soon as can reasonably be expected.

FORTIFICATION, *n.* 1. Science of constructing defensive military works, military architecture, art of furnishing with defensive works.
2. Fortress, fort, fieldwork, fastness, keep, tower, fortified military work constructed to strengthen a position, redan, trench, earthwork, breastwork, redoubt, bulwark, bastion, defense, entrenchment, pill box, parapet, muniment, dugout, stronghold, citadel, arx, stockade, blockhouse, castle.

FORTIFY, *v.* 1. Provide with defensive military works, defend with fortifications, surround with defenses, strengthen against attack, protect by fortifications, circumvallate.
2. Make strong, furnish with resistant power, furnish with a means of resisting force, strengthen, reinforce with a means of standing strain, add strength to, strengthen the construction of, brace, buttress, shore up, stiffen, harden, entrench, give physical strength to.
3. Strengthen mentally or morally, encourage, stimulate, inspirit, embolden, hearten, cheer, assure, reassure, buoy up, instigate, urge on, invigorate, sustain.
4. Corroborate, confirm, bear out, validate, ratify, vindicate, endorse, authenticate, make good, substantiate, uphold, establish, prove, warrant, circumstantiate, make out a case for.

FORTITUDE, *n.* Patient courage under affliction, heroism, manhood, manliness, hardihood, strength of mind, firmness under temptation, bravery, fearlessness, intrepidity, dauntlessness, boldness, valor, moral strength, resoluteness under privation, passive courage, courageous endurance, forbearance, submission, stoicism, patience, resolution, gallantry, prowess, power, pluck, mettle, virtue, nerve, grit, sand, backbone, firmness, spirit, spunk, heart, dash, daring, tenacity.

FORTNIGHT, *n.* The space of fourteen nights and days, two weeks.

FORTRESS, *n.* 1. Large fortified place, fort of magnitude, group of forts including a town, citadel, capitol, arx, hold, stronghold, fortification, fastness, bulwark, castle, blockhouse, muniment, stockade, turret, redan, redoubt, keep, donjon, armory.

2. Any place of security, refuge, sanctuary, asylum, haven, defense, shelter, retreat, covert, hiding place, port in a storm.

FORTUITOUS, *adj.* Occurring without known cause, happening by chance, accidental, chance, not meant, haphazard, stray, random, undesigned, unpremeditated, unexpected, never thought of, unpurposed, undirected, causeless, incidental, casual, unintentional, adventitious, adventive, contingent, unintended, undetermined, uncaused.

FORTUITY, *n.* Chance, coincidence, accidentalness, accidental occurrence, casualty, contingence, casualness, indetermination, fortune, haphazard, hap, hazard, random luck, lucky hit, fluke, *raccroc (Fr.),* happenstance *(colloq.),* chance occurrence, accident, fortuitousness, uncertainty, cast of the dice, lottery, toss up, wheel of fortune, heads or tails, whirligig of chance.

FORTUNATE, *adj.* 1. Receiving good from uncertain or unexpected sources, having good fortune, lucky, successful, favored, flourishing, booming, prosperous, rich, well-off, well-to-do, at one's ease, happy, blessed, prospered, felicitous.

2. Presaging good fortune, portending happiness, auspicious, propitious, favorable, coming by favorable chance, resulting favorably, advantageous, encouraging, providential, promising, redletter, rosy, bright, fair, halcyon, palmy, timely, well-timed, convenient, opportune.

FORTUNE, *n.* 1. Amount or stock of wealth, ample stock of wealth, capital, possessions, substance, estate, property, revenue, income, money, mint of money, treasure, gold mine, means, riches, affluence, opulence, easy circumstances, bonanza, El Dorado, Golconda, Pactolian sands, purse of Fortunatus, *embarras de richesses (Fr.),* windfall.

2. Unforeseen occurrence, fortuity, casualty, happening, accident, chance, hap, luck, chance-medley.

3. Personified power regarded as determining human success, Fortuna, Fors Fortuna, Tyche.

4. Gamble, risk, uncertainty, tossup, hazard, odds, even chance, run of luck, throw of the dice, heads or tails, wheel of Fortune, random shot, fluke, leap in the dark, pig in a poke, grab bag.

5. That which falls to one as his portion in life, condition in life, circumstances, lot, destiny, doom, fate, star, fatality.

6. Future state, prospect, expectation, promise, anticipation.

7. Favorable issue, success, good luck, prosperity, felicity, godsend, issue, result, event.

FORTUNETELLER, *n.* 1. Soothsayer, seer, augur, sibyl, oracle, prophet, mantic, fatiloquist, Cassandra, Pythia.

2. One who professes to tell future events in the life of another, medium, spiritualist, clairvoyant, crystal-gazer, horoscopist, card-reader,

palmist, chiromancer, pedomancer, phrenologist, reader of tea leaves, Gypsy.

FORUM, *n.* 1. Market place of Roman city, public square, agora *(Greece),* mart, bazaar.

2. Court of justice, curia, tribunal, bench, judicatory, bar of justice.

3. Public meeting place for open discussion, popular assembly place, stage, rostrum, platform, hustings, tribune, lecture room, arena, theater.

4. A medium of open discussion, an organization that discusses subjects of current interest, symposium, round-table discussion.

FORWARD, *adv.* 1. Onward, forwards, ahead, before, in advance, in front, in the van, in the foreground.

2. Towards the front, in a frontward direction, frontwards, in a forward direction, toward the future.

3. Into prominence, into view, into consideration, forth, out.

FORWARD, *adj.* 1. Moving ahead, onward, directed toward a point in advance, advancing, progressive, forward-looking, go-ahead, enterprising, up-to-date.

2. Supporting an advanced policy, extreme, ultra, radical, drastic, *outré (Fr.),* left *(Pol.),* revolutionary, rebellious, insurgent, intransigent.

3. Being in a condition of advancement, well-advanced, fore, front, anterior, at the fore part, frontal, foremost, headmost, first, chief, head.

4. Premature, precocious, early, precipitate, anticipatory, inopportune, unseasonable, untimely.

5. Prompt, ready, eager, willing, strongly inclined, disposed in advance, earnest, zealous, alacritous, ardent, **fervent.**

6. Less modest than is proper, immodest, self-assertive, audacious, assuming, presumptuous, overbold, overconfident, presuming, obtrusive, brazen, barefaced, brazen-faced, shameless, fresh, brassy, cheeky, impudent, impertinent, pert, malapert, unabashed, intrusive, meddlesome, unmannerly, officious, insolent, offensive, brash.

FORWARD, *v.* 1. Send toward the place of destination, send forward, send on, transmit, ship, deliver, freight, mail, post, express, dispatch, remit.

2. Help onward, promote, help forward, help on, advance, further, adjuvate, aid, precipitate, lend a hand, support, assist, succor, abet, foster, encourage, **favor.**

3. Hasten, hurry on, expedite, express, speed, accelerate, quicken.

FORWARDNESS, *n.* 1. Overreadiness to push oneself forward, lack of due modesty, immodesty, presumptuousness, presumption, boldness, **over-**confidence, brass, cheek, nerve, pertness, assumption, impertinence, impudence, brashness.

2. Cheerful readiness, promptness, alacrity, eagerness, zeal, enthusiasm, ardor, fervor.

FOSSE, *n.* Defensive ditch in a fortification, trench filled with water, moat, canal, graff, artificial watercourse, trough, channel, gutter, muniment.

FOSSIL, *n.* 1. Prehistoric remains, petrified remains, trace of a former geological age, organic remains, petrified organism, skeleton, *disiecta membra (Lat.),* dry bones, relics, reliquiae, buried records of human activities, petrifaction, lapidescence.

2. Old-fashioned person, fogy, one whose views are extremely antiquated, one whose interests are in the past, person behind the times.

FOSTER, *v.* 1. Promote the growth of, rear, breed, nurture, nourish, nurse, feed, mother, cradle, bring up, rear up, support, sustain, care for, cherish, tend, protect, fondle, coddle, hold dear, treasure.

2. Take up the cause of, abet, work for, promote, forward, advance, help forward, help onward, aid, further, patronize, befriend, smile upon, favor, encourage, advocate, countenance, side with, cultivate, harbor, foment, stimulate, succor, sanction.

FOUL, *adj.* 1. Tainted, putrid, putrescent, decayed, decomposed, fetid, carious, moldy, rancid, feculent, rank, rotten, mephitic, ill-smelling, stinking, noisome, musty, polluted, contaminated, noxious.

2. Dirty, polluted, filthy, soiled, unclean, muddy, grimy, grubby, dusty, soiled, miry, lutose, squalid, smeared, impure, nasty, stained, sullied, tarnished, bedraggled, begrimed, besmeared, defiled, sordid, reeky, black.

3. Grossly offensive to the senses, loathsome, odious, hateful, disgusting, obnoxious.

4. Not conforming to the rules of ethics, unfair, unscrupulous, dishonorable, dishonest, unprincipled, corrupt, shady, slippery, tricky, venal, fraudulent, underhanded, questionable, sinister, knavish, rascally, villainous.

5. Grossly offensive morally, infamous, ignominious, scandalous, base, vile, low, wicked, shameful, sordid, abject, shabby, scurvy, arrant, abominable, contemptible, disgraceful, detestable, heinous, nefarious, flagitious, dark, leprous, ignoble.

6. Obscene, pornographic, profane, smutty, coarse, vulgar, risqué, unchaste, lewd, indelicate, immodest, improper, off-color, suggestive, ribald, Fescennine, salacious, lecherous, lustful, libidinous, blasphemous, indecent.

7. Insulting, abusive, scurrilous, vituperative, derogatory, foul-spoken, reproachful, opprobrious, contumelious.

8. *(Of weather)* Stormy, dirty, squally, bleak, gusty, blasty, blustery, wind-swept, rainy, drizzly, foggy, murky, misty, cloudy, wet.

9. Not favorable, unpropitious, inauspicious, disadvantageous.

10. In obstructing contact, caught, entangled, jammed, tangled, snafu (situated normal: all fouled up), in collision, encumbered, choked, impeded.

FOUL-MOUTHED, *adj.* Given to filthy or abusive speech, vulgar, coarse, obscene, smutty, ribald, indecent, suggestive, risqué, off-color, lewd, pornographic, foul-spoken, foul-tongued, filthy, indecent, dedecorous, ill-bred, ill-mannered, unmannerly, ungenteel, ungentlemanly, impolite, abusive, insulting, scurrilous, defamatory, derogatory, libellous, slanderous, calumnious, blackguard, blasphemous, profane, opprobrious, rude, crude, rough-tongued.

FOUL PLAY, *n.* 1. Unfair conduct, treacherous dealing, dishonesty, secret misdoing, guile, duplicity, inequity, injustice, sharp practice, unfairness, wrong, chicanery, knavery, jobbery, perfidiousness, treachery, perfidy, double-dealing, imposition, roguery, villainy.

2. Crime, outrage, *malum in se (Lat.),* violence, injury, abuse, mistreatment, grievance, tort, offense, insult, indignity, affront, maltreatment, aggravated misdemeanor, hurt, damage, harm, ill, evil, ill-treatment, rape, defilement,

assault, attack, violation, ravishment, constupration, defloration, abduction, kidnapping, white slavery, prostitution, death, murder.

FOUND, *v.* 1. Lay the foundation of, lay the lowest part of, base, fix on a firm base, place on firm ground, ground, set, locate.

2. Construct, rear, build, erect, raise.

3. Set up for enduring existence, institute, give rise to, establish, originate, give origin to, constitute, occasion, bring about, develop, create, set on foot, sow the seeds of.

4. Colonize, settle, people, populate, plant.

5. Melt and pour metal into a mold, cast, make of molten material in a mold, form in a mold, mold.

FOUNDATION, *n.* 1. That on which anything stands and by which it is supported, lowest division of a structure partly below the surface of the ground, substructure, understructure, underbuilding, groundwork, base, *fond (Fr.),* support, bed, footing, ground, bottom, earth, foothold, bed rock, basement, cellar, underpinning.

2. Basis, reason, reason why, cause, purpose, motive, occasion, wherefore, root, source, rationale, underlying principle, origin, commencement.

3. Establishment, setting up, settlement, institution, commencement.

4. The establishment of an institution with provision for its maintenance, gift to a general public use, donation, endowment, legacy.

FOUNDER, *n.* 1. Originator, organizer, establisher, builder, institutor, father, author, generator, maker, creator, producer, mover, discoverer, inventor, architect, introducer, prime mover, planter, settler, colonizer.

2. Caster of metals, molder, foundry man.

FOUNDER, *v.* 1. Fill with water and sink, sink down, capsize, shipwreck, go to the bottom, go to Davy Jones' locker, run aground, split upon a rock, swamp, wallow, welter, roll, toss, tumble about, pitch, take a header, make a plunge.

2. Stumble, trip, fall, go lame, limp, hobble, tumble, break down, lurch, reel, topple, stagger, plunge, come a cropper, sprawl, flounce.

3. Fail utterly, collapse, miscarry, abort, succumb, suffer wreck, come to grief, flounder, meet with disaster, turn out badly, end in smoke, come to nothing, flash in the pan, fall through.

4. Dismay, dumfound, strike with wonder, astonish, astound.

FOUNDLING, *n.* Abandoned infant, waif, orphan, child with a parent or guardian, castaway, derelict, outcast.

FOUNTAIN, *n.* 1. Source of water, head of a stream, well, spring, fount, font, cistern, wellspring, reservoir, fountainhead, springhead, Pieria, Castalia.

2. Jet, *jet d'eau (Fr.),* stream of water made by mechanical means to spout, upwelling.

3. Source, head, rise, beginning, genesis, derivation, origin, *fons et origo (Lat.),* birth, beginning, first principles, cause, reason.

FOUNTAINHEAD, *n.* Primary source, first principle, rise, occasion, cause, origin, place of issue.

FOURFLUSHER, *n.* One who makes pretenses that he cannot bear out, pretender, poseur, *soidisant (Fr.),* boaster, braggart, braggadocio, hot air artist, windbag, blowhard, trumpeter, hornblower, charlatan, Gascon, fanfaron.

FOURFOLD, *adj.* Quadruple, quadruplicate, biquadratic, quadruplex, quadrigeminal, fourscore, four times as much or as many, four-cycle, consisting of four things or parts.

FOUR-HANDED, *adj.* Quadrumanous, involving four hands, requiring two players, rendering a duet.

FOUR HUNDRED, THE, *n.* The exclusive social set, elite, cream of the cream, *crème de la crème,* aristocracy, high life, smart set, world of fashion, silk-stocking set, bon ton, society, *monde (Fr.), beau monde (Fr.),* F.F.V.'s, Vanity Fair, Mayfair, Park Avenue, Newport.

FOUR-SQUARE, *adj.* 1. Square, quadrangular, quadrilateral, rectangular, multilateral, equiangular, having four equal sides and four right angles, in a square form.
2. Firm, steady, with unshakable firmness, immovable, strong like a stone tower, trustworthy, dependable.
3. Frank, blunt, honest, downright, open, without equivocation, presenting a bold front, without ceremony.

FOWL, *n.* 1. Winged animal, birds collectively, large edible bird.
2. Gallinaceous bird of the pheasant family, *Gallus domesticus,* domestic fowl, poultry, domestic hen, barnyard rooster, cock, chanticleer, bantam, Partlet *(Chaucer),* broiler, capon, spring chicken, chicken, chick.
3. Any of other gallinaceous or similar birds, turkey, duck, goose, duckling, gosling, pheasant, quail, partridge, blackcock, plover, rail, snipe, guinea hen, peacock, peahen.

FOXY, *adj.* 1. Foxlike in disposition, vulpine, crafty, artful, sly, stealthy, underhand, subdolous, arch, canny, cunning, wily, tricky, shrewd, astute, shifty, sharp, insidious, designing, intriguing, deceptive, deceitful, subtle, sagacious, discerning, penetrating, politic, wise, intelligent, skilful, knowing, wide-awake, alert, vigilant.
2. Rank, strong-smelling, having a musty taste, sour, unpleasant in taste.
3. Discolored with mildew, foxed, impaired, defective in quality.
4. Reddish-brown, rufous, yellowish-brown, tawny, fuscous, roan, rust-colored.

FOYER, *n.* 1. Lobby of a theater or hotel, reception room, crush-room, green-room.
2. Anteroom, vestibule, antechamber, hall, loggia, entrance porch.
3. *(Italics)* Hearth, fireplace, fireside, ingleside.

FRACAS, *n.* Disorderly noise, uproar, charivari, bombilation, din, clangor, clatter, racket, roar, hubbub, pandemonium, vociferation, hullabaloo, tumult, outbreak, row, noisy quarrel, brawl, discord, *brouillerie (Fr.),* rixation, Donnybrook, broil, breach of the peace, disturbance, commotion, scrimmage, rumpus, imbroglio, riot, squall, squabble, altercation, snip-snap, wrangling, jar, tiff, spat, shindy, fuss, melee, tussle, scuffle, fray, affray, feud, fight, dispute, contention, disagreement, controversy, dissension, vendetta, bickering, jangle.

FRACTION, *n.* 1. Aliquot part of a unit or whole number, ratio between any two numbers, fractional part, subdivision, section, segment.
2. Little part as distinct from the whole of anything, particle, piece broken off, shaving, cutting, chip, chunk, crumb, slice, fragment, bit, portion, scrap, lump, morsel, trifle, mite, moiety.

FRACTIOUS, *adj.* 1. Ill-tempered, irritable, irascible, fretful, peevish, touchy, huffy, peppery, fiery, snappish, waspish, choleric, petulant, splenetic, captious, cantankerous, testy, grouchy, pettish, shrewish, querulous, churlish, perverse, *acariâtre (Fr.).*
2. Disposed to be insubordinate, refractory, rebellious, unruly, recalcitrant, exceptious, contentious, disputatious, bickering, quarrelsome, unmanageable, restive.

FRACTURE, *n.* 1. Severance, cleavage, rupture, breach, division, separation.
2. Split, break, cleft, rift, breach, crack, slit, fissure, rent, cut, flaw, incision, opening, hiatus.

FRAGILE, *adj.* 1. Easily broken, breakable, frangible, easily damaged, brittle, shattery, shivery, splintery, friable, crumbly, crisp, brash, easily destroyed, smashable as an electric light bulb.
2. Weak, slight, frail, feeble, infirm, delicate, soft, tender, discerptible, flimsy, sleazy, unsubstantial, strengthless, rickety, tumbledown, gimcrack, jerry-built, dilapidated.

FRAGILITY, *n.* 1. Breakableness, brittleness, frangibility, frangibleness, frailness, crumbliness, friability.
2. Weakness, softness, delicacy, frailty, infirmity, effeminacy, feminality, infirmness, rope of sand, house of cards, house built on sand, ricketiness.

FRAGMENT, *n.* 1. Part broken off, chip, segment, detached part, fraction, portion, piece, particle, scrap, remnant, bit, morsel, snatch, snip, crumb, shred, driblet, wisp, moiety, modicum.
2. Leavings, debris, rubbish, remains, residue, odds and ends.
3. Section, division, lot, allotment, installment.

FRAGMENTARY, *adj.* Broken, fragmentitious, fractional, sectional, disjunct, detached, odd, separate, scrappy, piecemeal, component, aliquot, incomplete, not entire, disconnected, imperfect, scattered.

FRAGRANCE, *n.* 1. Sweet scent, fragrant odor, fragrancy, sweetness of smell, redolence, perfume, aroma, balminess, bouquet.
2. Incense, frankincense, myrrh, musk, bergamot, attar, civet, balm, potpourri, rose, lily, tuberose, heliotrope, jasmine, hyacinth, violet, carnation, lily of the valley, sweet pea.
3. Eau de cologne, toilet water, cologne, smelling salts, sachet, scent bag.
4. Nosegay, posy, boutonnière, spray, garland, chaplet, wreath, festoon.

FRAGRANT, *adj.* Having a pleasant odor, redolent, aromatic, odorous, odoriferous, sweet-scented, sweet-smelling, olent, spicy, balmy, ambrosial, perfumed, perfumy, incense-breathing, amaranthine, roseate, flower-like.

FRAIL, *adj.* 1. Weak, slight, delicate, weakly, not robust, fragile, thin, svelte, feeble, effeminate, unmanly.
2. Easily destroyed, fragile, brittle, frangible, breakable, brash, readily broken, shivery, shattery, splintery, crumbly, friable, rickety, dilapidated, vulnerable, decrepit, flimsy, sleazy, unsubstantial, not firm, not durable, infirm, perishable.
3. Morally weak, not strong against temptation, easily led astray, lax, loose, liable to err, dissolute, of infirm virtue, unchaste, corrupt, fallible.

FRAILTY, *n.* 1. Weakness, frailness, puniness, fragility, slenderness, thinness, delicacy, tenderness.
2. A fault or sin resulting from weakness, foi-

ble, weak side, failing, imperfection, defect, lapse, deficiency, weak point, blind side, delinquency, moral weakness, proneness to yield to temptation, want of moral fiber, liability to err, fallibility, peccability.

3. Rope of sand, house built on sand, slender reed, silken thread, house of cards.

FRAME, *v.* 1. Form by fitting and uniting parts together, fabricate, build, construct, raise, rear, put together, compose, constitute, make, erect, manufacture, establish, evolve, institute, produce.

2. Fashion, shape, figure, block out, mold, adapt to a particular purpose, adjust.

3. Invent, contrive, forge, plan, devise, conceive, scheme, project, forecast, draft, indite, sketch, hatch, concoct, hit upon, map out, shape out, organize, systematize, formulate, design, coin, excogitate, express, utter.

4. Prearrange fraudulently, incriminate unjustly by a plot.

5. Put into a frame, provide with a frame, encase, enclose.

6. Manage to do something, give promise, prepare, attempt.

7. Betake oneself, resort, repair to, hie to.

FRAME, *n.* 1. Anything composed of parts fitted and joined together, structure, form, fabric, shape, stamp, mold, texture, substance, constitution, order, scheme, system, composition.

2. Skeleton, scaffolding, casing, sustaining parts of a structure fitted and joined together, framing, framework, body, hull, chine, spine, rachis, ridge, backbone, vertebrae, spinal column, vertebral column.

3. Human body with reference to its make or build, shape, figure, physique, *galbe (Fr.),* contour, set, outline, presence.

4. Enclosing border of a picture, case, ornamental border.

5. Particular state of the mind, temper, mood, humor, temperament, disposition, condition, state of feeling, nature, organization, situation, status, circumstance, position.

FRAMER, *n.* Maker, founder, organizer, constructor, former, composer, author, creator, artist, planner, projector, designer, sketcher, inditer.

FRAMEWORK, *n.* Structure composed of parts fitted and joined together, body, chassis, skeleton, frame, fuselage, fabric, construction, composition, shell, scaffold, beam, rafter, girder, lintel, joist, cantilever, travis, trave, cornerstone.

FRANCHISE, *n.* 1. Right to vote, voting power, privilege, prerogative, suffrage, enfranchisement, liberty of choice, freedom.

2. Immunity from some restriction, exemption.

3. Asylum, sanctuary, refuge.

FRANGIBLE, *adj.* Capable of being broken, easily broken, breakable, shatterable, fragile, brittle, discerptible, splintery, shivery, flimsy, friable, fissile, unsubstantial, gimcrack, rickety.

FRANK, *adj.* 1. Unreserved in speech, free in speaking, bold in speech, candid, sincere, outspoken, direct, plainspoken, straightforward, downright, artless, ingenuous, free, open, naive, unsophisticated, guileless, genuine, straight from the shoulder, undissembling, honest, aboveboard.

2. Undisguised, avowed, unequivocal, transparent, patent, obvious, evident, plain, manifest, clear, perspicuous, unambiguous, explicit, lucid, intelligible, distinct, unmistakable.

FRANKINCENSE, *n.* Aromatic gum resin from trees of the genus *Boswellia,* incense, olibanum, perfume.

FRANTIC, *adj.* Wild with excitement, excited, wrought up, overwrought, beside oneself, frenzied, distraught, distracted, nervous, delirious, hectic, agitated, flushed, *bouleversé (Fr.),* raging, phrenetic, rabid, impassioned, transported with passion, raving, mad, furious, violent, infuriate, wild, crazy, insane, ungovernable, deranged.

FRATERNAL, *adj.* Brotherly, related, kindred, akin, consanguineous, agnate, cognate, affiliated, sib, amicable, sympathetic, harmonious, friendly, allied, congenial, banded together, at one with, of one mind, hearty, cordial, warm-hearted, devoted, affectionate, loving.

FRATERNITY, *n.* 1. Society, club, circle, clique, coterie, brotherhood, company, association, union, clan, league, alliance, federation, federacy, confederacy, fellowship, community, united body, coalition, set, pool, combine.

2. Ties of blood, consanguinity, kinship, kindred, sib, propinquity, blood connection, affiliation, brotherhood, brotherliness, brotherly relation.

FRATERNIZE, *v.* Associate in a fraternal way, consort intimately with, keep company with, mingle, hobnob, intercommunicate, club, federate, coalesce, concur, mix with, combine, unite, associate, amalgamate, unionize, federate, federalize, league, confederate, band together, herd, make common cause, sympathize, cooperate, harmonize.

FRAUD, *n.* 1. Breach of confidence to gain some dishonest advantage, sharp practice, duplicity, deception, deceit, imposture, imposition, trickery, artifice, cozenage, stratagem, craft, cheat, guile, trick, subtlety, wile, dodge, subterfuge, chicanery, ruse, shuffle, double-dealing, swindle, falsehood, treachery, cog, gull, fake, hoax, humbug, sham, machination.

2. A person who makes deceitful pretenses, impostor, quack, charlatan, mountebank, rascal, knave, rogue, swindler, chouser, shark.

FRAUDULENT, *adj.* Wily, crafty, deceitful, deceptive, tricky, dishonest, cheating, treacherous, knavish, false, insidious, designing, subtle, subdolous, underhanded, snide, crooked, spurious, guileful, roguish, unprincipled, surreptitious, cunning, imposing, bogus.

FRAUGHT, *adj.* Involving, attended with, full of, laden with, abounding, teeming, pregnant, plethoric, freighted, burdened, weighted, charged, loaded, replete with.

FRAY, *n.* 1. Fracas, spat, tiff, quarrel, row, fuss, brawl, broil, commotion, contention, dispute, disagreement, controversy, bickering, wrangle, jangle, squabble, tussle, rumpus, riot, scuffle, altercation, melee, feud, vendetta, tumult, disturbance, dissension, contest.

2. Fight, skirmish, battle, combat, affray, conflict, warfare.

FRAY, *v.* Wear to loose raveled threads at the edge, shred to fibers at the end, wear by rubbing, ravel, rub, chafe, fret, tatter, frazzle, wear away.

FRAZZLE, *n.* 1. State of being worn out, exhaustion, prostration, enervation, debilitation, disablement, incapacitation, collapse, utter fatigue.

2. Rag, remnant, tag end, tear, fringes, shreds, frayed end.

FREAK, *n.* 1. A sudden causeless change of mind,

capricious notion, caprice, vagary, whim, crotchet, quip, quirk, fit, kink, maggot, humor, fancy, whimsy, *capriccio (It.),* fad, fantasy, craze, crincum *(colloq.),* turn, twist, whimsicality.

2. Caper, prank, antic, gambol, escapade, trick, skylarking, freewheeling.

3. An example of some strange deviation from nature, an irregular or abnormal product, miscreation, monster, monstrosity, abortion, mooncalf, hermaphrodite, sport *(Biol.) lusus naturae (Lat.),* curiosity, oddity, teratism, *rara avis (Lat.),* phoenix, chimera, hydra, harpy, minotaur, sagittary, centaur, cockatrice, kraken, hippocampus, hippogriff, wivern, roc, gargoyle, basilisk, griffin, dragon, Cyclops, mermaid, ogre, two-headed person.

FREAKISH, *adj.* 1. Capricious, eccentric, fitful, whimsical, queer, erratic, full of vagaries, fanciful, humorsome, crotchety, wayward, wanton, maggoty, notional, quixotic, outlandish, curious.

2. Resembling a freak, freaky, grotesque, bizarre, fantastic, strange, wild, incongruous, abnormal, anomalous, unnatural, aberrant, monstrous, preternatural, exceptional, peculiar.

FRECKLE, *n.* 1. A small brownish-yellow spot on the skin, lentil-shaped spot, *lentigo aestiva (Med.),* lenticula, fleck, speck, macula.

2. Any discoloration, blemish, flaw, disfigurement, eyesore, stain, tarnish, blur, patch, mole, blotch, maculation.

FREE, *adj.* 1. Enjoying personal civil rights and political liberty, autonomous, self-governing, enjoying political independence, enfranchised, sovereign, self-directing, freeborn, not subject to regulation, exempt from external authority, immune from restriction, independent, privileged.

2. At liberty, not in bondage, not enslaved, emancipated, manumitted, at large, unrestrained, scot-free, foot-loose, loose, bondless, unconfined, unconstrained, unchained, unshackled, unfettered, unbridled, untrammeled, unimpeded, unentangled, unattached, unhampered, uncurbed, unmuzzled, unbound, released, liberated, delivered, ransomed, uncoerced, freed.

3. Exempted, not liable, favored, allowed, at liberty, able at will to, permitted, open, unrestricted, unlimited, unqualified, plenary, full, absolute, arbitrary, unconditional, unconditioned, discretionary.

4. Unbiased, unprejudiced, dispassionate, impartial, disinterested, uninfluenced.

5. Not attached, loose, not held fast, not in contact with something else, clear from.

6. Candid, frank, unreserved, outspoken, frankhearted, free-spoken, sincere, ingenuous, artless, blunt, direct, unequivocal, downright, communicative, affable.

7. Eager, ready, alacritous, prompt, desirous, willing, spontaneous, voluntary, unforced, freewill.

8. Provided without charge, not subject to a payment, costless, chargeless, gratuitous, for nothing, gratis, for the love of it, for free *(colloq.).*

9. Ready in giving, charitable, munificent, freehanded, liberal, generous, bountiful, not parsimonious, hospitable, open-handed, bounteous, freehearted, handsome.

10. Extravagant, immoderate, lavish, prodigal, copious, profuse, unstinted.

11. Lax, careless, not literal, general.

12. At leisure, unoccupied, idle, otiose, not busy, having nothing else to do.

13. Acting without reserve, open, unceremonious, informal, easy, familiar, overfamiliar, bold, daring, audacious, assured, confident, fearless, overfree, forward, brash, reckless, pushing, impudent.

14. Wanton, licentious, indecent, lax, loose, immoral, improper, incontinent, dissipated, dissolute.

15. Without, devoid, void, lacking, wanting, destitute of, *sans (Fr.).*

FREE, *v.* 1. Set free, make free, liberate, emancipate, manumit, set at liberty, deliver from bondage, release from restraint, rescue from imprisonment, disprison, discharge, parole, enlarge, save, redeem, ransom, enfranchise, disenthrall.

2. Acquit, exonerate, absolve, exculpate, justify, vindicate, clear.

3. Rid of, disengage, loose, relieve of, disencumber, disentangle, extricate, unfetter, unchain, unbind, untie, unmanacle, unshackle.

4. Exempt, immunize, privilege, affranchise, excuse, except.

FREEBOOTER, *n.* 1. Pirate, corsair, viking, buccaneer, rover, ranger, privateer, picaroon, filibuster.

2. One who goes about in search of plunder, member of a predatory band, highwayman, brigand, footpad, depredator, pillager, plunderer, bandit, robber, ladrone, thug, gangster, forager, marauder, rifler, pilferer, burglar, thief, raider, filcher, cutpurse, pickpocket, shoplifter, desperado.

3. Peculator, defaulter, swindler, sharpy, cheat, fraud, forger, embezzler, blackleg, trickster, jockey.

FREEDOM, *n.* 1. Civil liberty, political independence, autonomy, enfranchisement, affranchisement, legal right, self-government, self-determination, latitudinarianism, enlargement, manumission, liberation, emancipation, exemption from restraint.

2. Privilege enjoyed, immunity, franchise, exemption, prerogative, exemption from external control, absence of ties.

3. Facility of action, ease of movement, play, scope, swing, latitude, margin, range, elbowroom, *Lebensraum (Ger.),* wide berth, free play, full swing, rope, unrestricted use.

4. Frankness of manner, absence of reserve, unreservedness, unrestraint, unconstraint, unceremoniousness, overfamiliarity, candor, openness, ingenuousness, outspokenness, downrightness, directness, bluntness, forwardness, informality, naturalness.

5. Disrespect, impropriety, indecorum, unseemliness, impudence, impertinence.

6. Vigorousness, daring, powerfulness, strikingness, effectiveness.

7. Leisure, otiosity, pastime, *dolce far niente (It.),* doux faire rien (Fr.).

8. Divorce, separation, annulment, dissolution of the marriage bond.

9. License, laxity, looseness, indulgence, self-gratification, profligacy, wantonness.

FREE-HANDED, *adj.* Generous, liberal, openhanded, munificent, charitable, bounteous, lavish, prodigal, bountiful, handsome, unstinted, copious, profuse, extravagant.

FREE-HEARTED, *adj.* Having a free heart, lighthearted, spontaneous, unreserved, joyous, blithe, jocund, gladsome, merry, gay, glad.

FREE PLAY, *n.* Freedom, range, latitude, scope, full play, full swing, elbowroom, margin, rope, wide berth, liberty of action, unrestricted use.

FREE-SPOKEN, *adj.* Giving to speaking without reserve, unreserved, frank, communicative, outspoken, plain-spoken, candid, downright, forthright, blunt, direct, unequivocal, ingenuous.

FREETHINKER, *n.* Deist, unbeliever, skeptic, infidel, atheist, pyrrhonist, *esprit fort (Fr.),* one who forms his opinions independently of authority or tradition, rationalist, liberal, latitudinarian, materialist, positivist, nihilist, agnostic, nullifidian, doubter, disbeliever, pagan.

FREE WILL, *n.* 1. Free choice, voluntary decision, power of choice, unrestrained will, volition, velleity, will and pleasure, freedom, discretion, choice, inclination, pleasure, option, wish, mind, desire.
2. Voluntariness, spontaneity, spontaneousness, originality.

FREEZE, *v.* 1. Refrigerate, infrigidate, glaciate, solidify by cold, harden into ice, turn to ice, form ice on the surface of, fix fast in ice.
2. Cause to suffer the effects of intense cold, chill to the marrow, stiffen by cold, benumb, chill, petrify, produce the sensation of extreme cold in, cause loss of feeling in, anaesthetize by cold, pinch, nip, cut, pierce, bite, sting.
3. Make immobile, terrify, chill with fear, dampen the enthusiasm of.
4. Become coldly formal in manner, wither, snub, stand aloof, treat with disdain.

FREIGHT, *v.* Lade with merchandise for transportation, charge, load, burden, ship by freight, transport as freight, embark, mail, post, express, dispatch, send on, transmit, consign, deliver.

FREIGHT, *n.* 1. Shipment, conveyance, transportation, movement, transshipment, cartage, truckage, portage, freightage.
2. Cargo, goods, baggage, luggage, mail, parcel post, traffic, load, burden, contents.

FRENETIC, *adj.* 1. Mentally disordered, deranged, demented, insane, lunatic, mad, unhinged, manic, bereft of reason, *aliéné (Fr.),* off one's head, unsettled in one's mind, crazed, daft, beside oneself, moonstruck, *non compos mentis (Lat.),* raving, stark staring mad, maniacal, loco, delirious, phrenetic, insensate, amuck, berserk.
2. Filled with extreme emotion in religious matters, fanatical, possessed, hipped, rabid, frenzied.

FRENZY, *n.* 1. Violent mental agitation, wild enthusiasm, transport, fanaticism, infatuation, furor, craze, mania, monomania, obsession, distraction, fury, passion, rage, estrus, heat, rut, ecstasy.
2. Violent excitement of a paroxysm of mania, delirium, mental derangement, lunacy, insanity, aberration, madness, raving, wandering, lightheadedness, delusion, hallucination, mental alienation, dissociated mental activity.

FREQUENT, *adj.* 1. Occurring at short intervals, at short distances apart, ofttime, thick-coming, iterative, reiterative, oft-repeated, numerous, recurrent, of frequent occurrence, continual, incessant, perpetual, constant.
2. Customary, wonted, accustomed, usual, habitual, persistent, regular, general, common, familiar, every-day, ordinary, daily, of common occurrence, not rare.

FREQUENT, *v.* 1. Go often to, haunt, resort to frequently, visit and revisit, attend regularly, visit repeatedly, repair to often, resort to habitually, be seen at daily.
2. Infest, overrun, swarm over, throng, beset, take complete possession of.

FREQUENTER, *n.* Regular attendant, frequent visitor, habitual resorter, haunter, habitué, fan, daily customer.

FREQUENTLY, *adv.* 1. At short intervals, in quick succession, many times, oft, ofttimes, oftentimes, often, daily, every day, many a time and oft, again and again, repeatedly, recurrently, continually, constantly, perpetually, incessantly, at all times, every now and then, ever and anon, over and over again, not seldom, sometimes, not rarely, occasionally, at times, once in a while.
2. As a common matter, habitually, commonly, customarily, usually, generally, persistently, familiarly, ordinarily.

FRESH, *adj.* 1. Of recent make, not stale, wholesome, retaining the original properties unimpaired, green, unwilted, not deteriorated, undecayed, unspoiled, unfaded, unwithered, well-preserved, in good condition, unused, unworn, undimmed, untarnished.
2. Not previously met with or known, recent, new, novel, late, modern, neoteric, new-fashioned, newfangled, just out, up-to-date, brand-new, unfamiliar, unaccustomed, unusual, unique, rare, strange.
3. Youthful-looking, ruddy, rosy, fresh-colored, glowing, blooming, bright, flourishing, fair, verdant, gay.
4. Healthy, hearty, sound, euphoric, well, hardy, robust, strong, vigorous, florid.
5. Untired, unwearied, not fatigued, unexhausted, freshened, refreshed, not blown, fit, invigorated, energetic, active, reinvigorated.
6. Retaining the original distinctness, vivid, keen, sharp, bright, shining, clear, lucid, intense, brilliant, not dulled, unfading.
7. Additional, extra, supplementary, further, more, spare, other, to boot, accessory, auxiliary, newly come, just arrived, just received.
8. Not salted, not preserved, unpickled, not brackish, unsalted, uncured, undried, unsmoked, unfired, unmellowed, untanned.
9. Sweet, flavorous, pure, sapid, delicious, bracing, refreshing, health-giving, salubrious, salutary.
10. Unhackneyed, unorthodox, unconventional, unwonted, original.
11. Inexperienced, unskilled, untrained, uninitiated, inexpert, unversed, unacquainted, unpracticed, uncultivated, artless, green, raw, immature, callow.
12. Presumptuous, obtrusive, meddlesome, forward, impudent, smart, cheeky, nervy, brazenfaced, brassy, pert, assuming, bold, lacking propriety, insolent, officious.
13. *(Weather)* Cool, chill, bleak, raw, frigid, algid, gelid, biting, cutting, nipping, piercing, pinching, stinging, stiff, keen, brisk.

FRESHEN, *v.* 1. Remove saltiness from, make less salty, sweeten, make fresher.
2. Freshen up, brighten, tone up, renew, revive, refresh, quicken, stimulate, reinvigorate, renovate, spruce up, repair, refurbish, smarten, dress up, polish, clean up.
3. Grow fresh, liven, rouse, recover strength.
4. Ventilate, deodorize, fumigate, cleanse, purify, disinfect.

FRESHET, *n.* Sudden rise in the level of a stream, spate, flood, overflow, inundation, deluge, profluence, wave, billow, surge, swell, cataclysm.

FRESHMAN, *n.* 1. Beginner, novice, recruit,

greenhorn, apprentice, tyro, neophyte, learner, tenderfoot, inceptor, probationer, catechumen, abecedarian, alphabetarian.

2. First-year student in college, undergraduate, frosh, plebe, pupil of the lowest class.

FRET, *v.* 1. Give oneself up to feelings of irritation, chafe, stew, fume, be discontented, worry oneself, rage, fret and fume, be peevish, be angry, be fretful, be irritated, be vexed, twinge, agonize, writhe, smart, sit on thorns, take to heart, look glum, take ill, grumble, lament, croak, grouse, gripe, haggle, frown, pout, mope, brood over, sulk, pine, repine.

2. Vex, irk, pique, provoke, nettle, rile, displease, irritate, gall, ruffle, try the patience, torment, trouble, bother, pester, plague, harry, harass, incommode, discommode, tire, molest, weary, annoy, tease, make angry, agitate, worry, affront, aggrieve, sting, offend.

3. Cause corrosion, gnaw, wear by friction, abrade, erode, rub, fray, gall, wear away, eat into, grate, bite into.

4. Move *(water)* in agitation, ruffle, ripple, roughen the surface of, agitate.

5. Ornament with fretwork, decorate with raised work, diversify, variegate.

FRET, *n.* 1. Irritated state of mind, fretfulness, peevishness, annoyance, fidgets, sulks, mopishness, chagrin, mortification, grievance, smart, displeasure, malaise, stew, dissatisfaction, discomposure, disquiet, vexation of spirit, disturbance of temper.

2. Burden, load, blow, shock, ordeal, trial, cross, trouble, bother, nuisance, anxiety, solicitude, concern, worry, thorn, bitter pill, plague, care, pest, ache, sore subject, gall and wormwood.

3. Erosion, corrosion, gnawing, cancer, ulcer, abrasion.

4. Ridge set across the fingerboards of a stringed musical instrument to help the fingers stop at the correct points, raised line, wale, welk.

5. Intertwined linear ornament, fretwork, key ornament, meander, arabesque, anthemion, angular design of bands within a border, coquillage, tracery.

FRETFUL, *adj.* Irritable, ill-tempered, ill-humored, sullen, sulky, ill-disposed, captious, peevish, crabbed, testy, pettish, out of sorts, out of temper, grumpy, glum, morose, frumpish, moody, mopish, fidgety, petulant, splenetic, querulous, snappish, touchy, waspish, irascible, surly, sour, ill-natured, angry, snarling, grumbling, cross, fractious, worried, vexed, dissatisfied, troubled, complaining, uneasy, restless, impatient, hasty.

FRIABLE, *adj.* Easily crumbled, crumbly, pulverulent, pulverizable, pulverable, crumbling, easily reduced to powder, triturable, fissile, breakable, brittle, crisp, short, shivery, frangible, deliquescent, fragile, frail.

FRIAR, *n.* Member of a mendicant order not attached to a monastery, monk, Franciscan (Gray Friar), Dominican (Black Friar), Carmelite (White Friar), Augustinian (Austin Friar), brother, father, padre, abbé, curé, mendicant, abbot, prior, beadsman, monastic, cenobite.

FRIBBLE, *adj.* Trivial, trifling, fribbling, slight, flimsy, frothy, inane, ridiculous, frivolous, idle, puerile, airy, shallow, petty, piddling, niggling, fiddle-faddle, wishy-washy, namby-pamby, of little value, paltry, contemptible, silly.

FRIBBLE, *v.* Trifle away, waste foolishly, fritter away, fool away, fiddle-faddle, dillydally, putter, dally, dabble, potter, piddle, idle.

FRICTION, *n.* 1. Rubbing of the surface of one body against that of another, frication, confrication, attrition, abrasion, anatripsis, massage, elbow grease, grinding, grating, chafing, fretting.

2. Resistance to the relative motion of surfaces of bodies in contact, rolling resistance, resistance from roughness, counteraction, interference, opposition.

3. Clash of opinion, discord, dissension, disagreement, conflict, strife, contention, quarrel, antagonism, lack of harmony.

FRIEND, *n.* 1. One attached to another by feelings of personal regard, one on fond terms with another, intimate, companion, comrade, chum, fast friend, bosom friend, beloved companion, confident, buddy, pal, bunkie, crony, sidekick, other self, alter ego, mate, bedfellow, playfellow, playmate, shadow, fidus Achates.

2. Fellow, associate, acquaintance, consort, partner, copartner, co-worker, ally, confrere, brother, frater, colleague, fellow-member, neighbor, shopmate, roommate, schoolmate, schoolfellow, classmate, shipmate, messmate, commensal.

3. Paramour of either sex, lover, sweetheart, concubine, mistress, girl friend, boy friend.

4. Well-wisher, advocate, supporter, backer, favorer, defender, adherent, encourager, patron, Maecenas, partisan, good genius, benefactor, counselor.

FRIENDLINESS, *n.* Cordiality, affability, warmheartedness, amity, amicability, amiability, sociability, kindliness, good will, familiarity, brotherliness, neighborliness, heartiness, benignity, sympathy, considerateness.

FRIENDLY, *adj.* 1. Showing friendship, companionable, amicable, amiable, favorably disposed, benevolent, affectionate, loving, kindhearted, genial, cordial, hearty, warm-hearted, sympathetic, harmonious, ardent, devoted, fond, sincere, gracious, generous, helpful, intimate.

2. Not hostile, not at variance, fraternal, neighborly, sociable, social, affable, accessible, brotherly, familiar, hospitable, on good terms, friends with, at home with, on visiting terms, hail fellow well met, on speaking terms, *sans façon* *(Fr.)*, acquainted with, on a friendly footing, well-disposed toward each other.

3. Favorable, propitious, auspicious, promising, salutary, fair, advantageous, benign, pro.

FRIENDSHIP, *n.* 1. Affection, love, deep regard, fondness, attachment, liking, devotion, esteem.

2. Association as friends, friendly relations, intimacy, close tie, close fellowship, intercourse, companionship, comradeship, companionability, acquaintance, familiarity, brotherhood, fraternity, sodality, sorority, sorosis.

3. Friendliness, good understanding, amicableness, fraternization, amity, harmony, concord, good feeling, neighborliness, kindliness, comity, good-fellowship, cordiality, peace, *entente cordiale* *(Fr.)*.

4. Benevolence, kindness, favor, assistance, consideration, fellow feeling, sympathy, response, good will, help, aid, patronage, partiality, favoritism, agreeableness.

5. Orestes and Pylades, Achilles and Patroclus, Heracles and Iolaus, Theseus and Pirithous, Aeneas and Achates, Damon and Pythias, Castor and Pollux, Epaminondas and Pelopidas, Nisus and Euryalus, David and Jonathan.

FRIGHT, *n.* 1. Extreme fear, sudden terror, fear of danger, alarm, consternation, panic, trepidation, apprehension, perturbation, dread, dismay, affright, horror, scare, cold feet, stampede, funk, pavor, concern, misgiving, anxiety, solicitude, intimidation, flutter, fear and trembling, tremor, quivering, quaking, palpitation, disquietude, reign of terror.

2. Object of shocking appearance, thing of terror, scarecrow, hobgoblin, bugbear, bugaboo, nightmare, ogre, Gorgon, Medusa-head, gargoyle, raw head and bloody bones, skeleton, *bête noire* (*Fr.*), *enfant terrible* (*Fr.*).

FRIGHTEN, *v.* Throw into a fright, raise apprehension, disturb with fear, fright, affright, confound with dread, strike with overwhelming fear, appall, shock, awe, dismay, alarm, scare, terrify, unman, intimidate, bluff, bulldoze, overawe, abash, deter, cow, daunt, bully, threaten, bullyrag, badger, browbeat, agitate, excite, haunt, obsess, beset, prey on the mind, horrify, petrify, strike all of a heap, harrow up the soul, startle, arouse, cry "wolf," disquiet, depress, dispirit, discourage, deject, dishearten, drive away by scaring.

FRIGHTFUL, *adj.* 1. Such as to cause fright, alarming, fearful, dreadful, dread, formidable, redoubtable, appalling, portentous, fell, dire, direful, shocking, horrendous, horrible, horrid, horrific, fearsome, terrible, terrific, awful, eerie, weird.

2. Ugly, hideous, disgusting, abominable, detestable, insufferable, repulsive, revolting, repellent, offensive, loathsome, nasty, grim, ghastly, grisly, gruesome, ogreish, monstrous, freakish, lurid, livid.

3. (*Colloq.*) Very great, extreme, excessive, inordinate, unconscionable.

FRIGID, *adj.* 1. Very cold in temperature, freezing, gelid, algid, glacial, wintry, icy, hiemal, polar, arctic, antarctic, boreal, hyperborean, frore, frozen, frosty, fresh, chill, chilly, chilling, cool, bleak, raw, inclement, bitter, biting, cutting, piercing, nipping, pinching.

2. Without warmth or feeling, without ardor, indifferent, uninterested, destitute of enthusiasm, phlegmatic, passionless, without fervor, unimpassioned, unanimated, reserved, unresponsive, unsympathetic, spiritless, lifeless, apathetic, dull, nonchalant, insouciant, impassive, unmoved, stolid, flat, stoical.

3. Formal, stiff, distant, prim, repellent, forbidding, rigid, strait-laced, austere, aloof.

FRIGIDITY, *n.* 1. Cold, coolness, chilliness, iciness, chill, glaciality, frozenness, gelidity, algidity, gelidness, low temperature, frigidness, winter, zero weather, Arctic, Antarctic, polar front, North Pole, bleakness, inclemency.

2. Want of enthusiasm, indifference, unconcern, pococurantism, insouciance, phlegm, apathy, supineness, disdain, lukewarmness, inattention, inertia, want of animation, lifelessness, tameness, dullness.

3. Formality, primness, stiffness, distance, chilliness, aloofness, repelling manner.

FRILL, *n.* 1. Strip of cloth or lace gathered at one edge and left loose at the other, ruffle, ruche, furbelow, gathering, edging, scollop, scallop, flounce, fringe, jabot, dicky, valance.

2. Showy superfluity, affectation, mannerism, stylism, air, frills and furbelows.

FRINGE, *n.* Ornamental bordering having projecting lengths of thread, edging, trimming, fimbriation, border, margin, skirting, hem, selvedge, welt, fimbria, thrum.

FRINGED, *adj.* Edged, bordered, fimbriate, fimbriated, befringed, laciniate, laciniated (*Bot.*), laciniose, cirrated, cirrate (*Zool.*).

FRIPPERY, *n.* 1. Tawdry finery in dress, trumpery, trappings, trickery, tinsel, spangle, sequin, clinquant, frills and furbelows, gewgaw, gimcrack, knickknack, bauble, baubles bangles and beads, pinchbeck, false ornament, paste.

2. Affected elegance in dress, foppery, manmillinery, equipage, empty display, ostentation, gaud.

3. Trifling, trash, rubbish, stuff, *fatras* (*Fr.*), fribbling, flummery, nonsense.

FRISK, *v.* 1. Romp, spring, skip, leap, jump, bound, hop, vault, cavort, prance, canter, curvet, caracole, bob, bounce, flounce, dance, gambol, frolic, caper, cut capers, ricochet, trip, sport, disport, cut up, jump about.

2. (*Colloq.*) Search a person for concealed articles by feeling his clothing, rummage through, ransack, seek, look for, pickpocket, take from by tricking.

FRISKY, *adj.* 1. Lively, animated, active, coltish, alive and kicking, stirring, nimble as a squirrel, agile, nimble-footed, light-heeled, tripping, jaunty, spry, spirited, vivacious.

2. Frolicsome, full of frolic, playful, gamesome, sportive, in high spirits, in high feather, allegro, gay, rollicking, *folâtre* (*Fr.*), tricksy, jocular, waggish, mirthful, prankish, jocose.

FRITH, *n.* 1. Long narrow indentation of the seacoast, inlet, estuary, firth, arm of the sea, armlet, ostiary, indraught, cove, lagoon, gulf, bay, bight, fiord, creek, opening of a river into the sea.

2. Strait, narrows, roads, roadstead.

FRITTER, *n.* 1. Small cake of batter fried in deep fat or sautéd in a frying pan, pancake, batter cake, apple fritter, corn fritter.

2. Small piece, shred, scrap, fragment, bit, remnant, splinter, ort.

FRITTER, *v.* 1. Cut into small pieces, break into fragments, slice, clip, shred, tear into shreds, shatter, shiver, crumble.

2. Disperse little by little, squander piecemeal, waste bit by bit, reduce to nothing, pare off, scatter.

3. Misuse time, take one's time, poke, dawdle, fool away, drawl, idle away, dillydally, potter, putter.

FRIVOLITY, *n.* Flightiness, volatility, airiness, trifling, levity, lightness, frivolousness, giddiness, emptiness, silliness, puerility, unsteadiness, frippery, fribbling, flummery, triviality, wantonness, folly, thoughtlessness, fickleness, effervescence, jocularity.

FRIVOLOUS, *adj.* 1. Not worthy of serious notice, of little weight, trifling, of no worth, trivial, worthless, unimportant, petty, paltry, insignificant, slight, flimsy, trashy, inconsiderable, piddling, niggling, minor, not worth attention, empty, light, airy, immaterial, idle, nugatory, useless, vain, futile.

2. Characterized by lack of seriousness, given to trifling and levity, light-minded, fickle, volatile, giddy, flighty, flippant, nonchalant, insouciant, pococurante, superficial, unsteady, inconstant, careless, gay, heedless.

3. Senseless, insensate, fatuous, puerile, child-

ish, foolish, witless, shallow-brained, brainless, stupid, inane, nonsensical, silly, foolish.

FRIZZLE, *v.* 1. Curl, friz, crisp, crinkle, crimp, coil, turn in ringlets.

2. Crisp meat by frying, cook with a sizzling noise, sizzle, sputter, fry, broil.

FROCK, *n.* 1. Principal outer garment of women, dress, gown, robe tunic, dolman, mantle, kirtle, cloak, coat, middy, blouse, suit.

2. Clerical garb, clericals, canonicals, stole, soutane, vestments, dalmatic, scapulary, surplice, cassock, alb, cope, chasuble, monk's robe, pallium.

3. Loose outer garment worn by peasants and workmen, smock, smock-frock, sagum.

4. Frock coat, tail coat, morning coat, dress coat, swallow-tailed coat.

FROLIC, *n.* 1. Merriment, gaiety, jollity, pleasantry, fun, joviality, drollery, jocoseness, amusement, recreation, mirth, merrymaking, carousal, festivity, game, laughter, sport, play, entertainment, tomfoolery, buffoonery, mummery.

2. Gay prank, merry play, antic, gambol, romp, skylarking, lark, spree, escapade, vagary, trick, flight of levity, monkey trick, caper.

FROLIC, *v.* Play merrily, have fun, amuse oneself, make merry, play merry pranks, be frolicsome, frisk, romp, caper, dance, gambol, cut capers, act up, wanton, joke, sport, disport, engage in merrymaking, revel, junket, feast, carouse, paint the town red, have one's fling, jest.

FROLICSOME, *adj.* Merrily playful, full of fun, coltish, frisky, roguish, arch, sportive, gay, jocose, festive, gamesome, lively, jovial, jolly, rollicking, sprightly, merry, daft, waggish, skittish, mirthful, vivacious, prankish.

FROM, *prep.* 1. Out of, away from, leaving behind, forth out of, out of contact with.

2. Starting at, beginning with, after.

3. *(Motive)* As, forasmuch as, for the reason that, for, by reason of, for the sake of, on account of, on the score of, out of, because of.

FROM HAND TO MOUTH Consuming at once what is obtained, with provision sufficient only for the needs of the immediate present, by bare subsistence, as chance provides, as want necessitates, without any margin, precariously, in an unsettled state, improvidently, scantily, scarcely, skimpily, jejunely, meagerly, scrimpingly, *in forma pauperis (Lat.).*

FRONT, *n.* 1. Foremost part or surface, forepart, forward part, part directed forward, anterior, foreground, forefront, face, obverse, frontispiece.

2. Front elevation, frontage, façade, face, frontal, proscenium.

3. Foremost line, head, van, vanguard, *avant-garde (Fr.),* advanced guard, fore-rank, front rank, outpost, first lines, line of battle, vedette, outpost, sentry, picket, trenches, No Man's Land.

4. Brow, forehead, face, visage, physiognomy, pan *(slang),* features, countenance.

5. Bow, stem, prow, jib, bowsprit.

6. External appearance, outward impression, demeanor, carriage, port, mien, air, presence, personal bearing.

7. Cool assurance, boldness, audacity, effrontery, impudence, brass, cheek, nerve, face, impertinence, assumption.

8. Movement to achieve a particular end, promotional coalition.

9. Thing attached in front, cravat, necktie, shirt front, dicky, jabot.

FRONT, *v.* 1. Have the front toward, face, stand opposite to, stand over against, breast, look toward.

2. Appear before, stand in front of, encounter, confront, meet face to face.

3. Face in opposition, face in hostility, dare, brave, defy, buck, buffet, withstand.

4. Furnish with a front, fit with a face, make a front for, face, veneer, revet, overlay, cover, adorn in front.

FRONT, *adj.* 1. Anterior, forward, first, chief, lead, fore, previous.

2. Situated at the front, headmost, foremost, frontal.

FRONTIER, *n.* 1. That part of a country which borders another country, boundary, boundary line, bound, border, confine, march, mark, limits, bourn, verge, edge, extreme, pale, *ne plus ultra (Lat.).*

2. That part of a country forming the border of its settled regions, advance region of settlement, backwoods, remote districts, incompletely developed region, outskirts, outlying area, hinterland.

FRONTISPIECE, *n.* Illustrated leaf preceding the title page of a book, illustration in the front of a book, ornament, panel.

FROST, *n.* 1. State of the temperature which occasions the freezing of water, rime, hoarfrost, white frost, frozen dew, covering of minute ice needles, ice crystals, frozen vapor, congelation of moisture, freezing weather, freezing point.

2. Inhospitality, inhospitable attitude toward visitors, austerity of manner, coldness of manner, coolness, frigidity, glaciality, iciness, reserve, aloofness, distance, unfriendliness, want of cordiality, unsociability, snub.

3. *(Colloq.)* A failure, washout, fizzle, fiasco.

FROST, *v.* 1. Cover with frost, congeal, freeze, glaciate, frostbite, nip, pinch, benumb, chill, chill to the marrow, cut, pierce, bite, injure by cold, kill by frost, wither, blight, shrivel, damage by freezing.

2. Chill by formality, be inhospitable to, discourage by cold behavior, snub, stand aloof from.

3. Give a frostlike surface to, cover with frosting, ice a cake.

FROSTING, *n.* 1. Confectioner's preparation for covering cakes, concreted sugar for coating a cake, icing.

2. Lusterless finish of metal or glass, mat.

FROSTY, *adj.* 1. Hoar-covered, rime-laden, wintry, brumal, hiemal, boreal, arctic, antarctic, hyperboreal, Siberian, polar, glacial, icy, niveous, gelid, frigid, algid, bleak, keen, raw, stinging, freezing, bitter, *transi de froid (Fr.),* cutting, biting, chilly, chill, frostbitten, frost-bound, frost-nipped, frozen out.

2. Lacking in warmth of feeling, inhospitable, inimical, uncordial, distant, aloof, reserved, unsociable, cold-hearted, unloving, unaffectionate, indifferent.

FROTH, *n.* 1. Aggregation of bubbles, foam, spume, fume, head, fizz, scum, spray, lather, suds, surf, yeast, barm, spindrift, spoondrift, foamy exudation, effervescence.

2. Something unsubstantial or evanescent, frippery, trumpery, flummery, stuff, *fatras (Fr.),* mere words, idle talk, trivial ideas, triviality, empty show, nonsense, balderdash, trash, bosh,

fudge, fiddlesticks, chaff, minutiae, minor details, idle pleasure, vanity.

FROTH, *v.* 1. Foam, spume, sparkle, effervesce, give out froth, bubble, fizz, ferment, aerate.

2. Emit violent anger, chafe, fume, foam at the mouth, bridle up, flare up, bristle up, boil over, rage, storm.

FROTHY, *adj.* 1. Spumy, foamy, bubbling, bubbly, effervescent, sparkling, *mousseux* (*Fr.*), up, fizzy, with a head on, sudsy, light, spumous.

2. Trivial, trifling, slight, slender, flimsy, shallow, empty, light, frivolous, idle, weak, unsubstantial, petty, airy, fribble, piddling, inane, vain, irresponsible, evanescent, puerile.

FROWARD, *adj.* 1. Reluctant to yield to authority, wilfully contrary, perverse, wayward, refractory, fractious, intractable, exceptious, deaf to reason, contumacious, not easily managed, unmanageable, ungovernable, unyielding, stubborn, obstinate, disobedient, insubmissive, indocile, headstrong, unruly, restive, dogged, wilful.

2. Peevish, irascible, irritable, petulant, querulous, captious, cross-grained, cross, crusty, surly, moody, cantankerous, splenetic, cankered, naughty.

FROWN, *v.* 1. Scowl, glower, lower, look stern, knit the brow, contract the eyebrow, look displeased, have an angry look, glare, fret, sulk, pout, mope, look black.

2. Rebuke with a look, show displeasure, show disapproval, disapprove, look disapprovingly on, view with disfavor, discountenance, look askance, set one's face against.

FROWNING, *adj.* Glowering, scowling, lowering, stern, minatory, threatening, angry, sullen, sulky, grim, glum, moody, gloomy, discourteous, disapproving.

FROWZY, *adj.* 1. Slovenly, slatternly, dirty, unkempt, draggletailed, dowdy, frumpish, disorderly, untidy, disordered, rough and tangled, disheveled.

2. Ill-smelling, fetid, noisome, musty, rank, rancid, stale, strong-smelling, gamy, offensive, stinking, malodorous.

FROZEN, *adj.* 1. Ice-bound, congealed by cold, covered with ice, subjected to severe cold, *transi de froid* (*Fr.*), refrigerated, solidified by cold, not liquid, clogged with ice, obstructed by ice.

2. Very cold, chill, chilly, frigid, glacial, brumal, hiemal, hibernal, wintry, boreal, hyperborean, polar, arctic, antarctic, Siberian, niveous, icy, gelid, algid, injured by frost, benumbed.

3. Chilly in manner, cold-hearted, unsympathetic, distant, aloof, reserved, unfeeling, immovable, obdurate.

FRUCTIFY, *v.* 1. Make productive, make fruitful, fertilize, impregnate, fecundate, spermatize, pollinate.

2. Be fruitful, be productive, bear fruit, bring forth, bear, generate, produce, conceive, beget.

FRUGAL, *adj.* Economical in the use and expenditure of resources, saving expense, prudently sparing, saving, thrifty, unwasteful, economy-minded, parsimonious, penny-conscious, provident, prudent, temperate, abstemious, chary, choice, careful, self-denying, moderate.

FRUGALITY, *n.* Careful management of resources, good husbandry, thrift, economy, savingness, scrimping, parsimony, providence, prudence, parsimoniousness, sparingness, frugalness, thriftiness, economizing, sparing use, temperance,

moderation, abstinence, abstention, miserliness, niggardliness, simplicity, retrenchment, care.

FRUIT, *n.* 1. Produce of the earth, product of vegetable growth useful to men and animals, crop, production, harvest, yield, edible part of a plant developed from a flower, berry, grain, nut, root, tuber, vegetable.

2. Offspring, progeny, young, issue, spawn.

3. Result, outgrowth, upshot, product, consequence, effect, outcome, advantage, good profit, return, revenue, earnings, reward, emolument, remuneration, award.

FRUITFUL, *adj.* 1. Bearing fruit abundantly, abounding in fruit, fructiferous, fruit-bearing, productive, progenerative.

2. Fertile, prolific, fecund, uberous, proliferous, generative, pregnant, enceinte, gravid, parturient, heavy, big with, gestant, life-giving, creative.

3. Bearing results, profitable, advantageous.

4. Copious, exuberant, luxuriant, fructuous, plenteous, plentiful, teeming, abundant, rich, lush, ample, frugiferous, plethoric.

FRUITION, *n.* 1. Attainment of anything desired, realization of results, fulfilment, achievement, possession.

2. Enjoyment of something attained or realized, gratification, usufruct, pleasure, delight, delectation, relish, zest, gusto, satisfaction.

FRUITLESS, *adj.* 1. Without fruit, acarpous, infertile, unprolific, unproductive, unfruitful, infecund, unyielding, arid, sterile, barren, infructuose, *sine prole* (*Lat.*).

2. Without advantage or profit, gainless, without results, unprofitable, useless, inutile, profitless, bootless, ineffectual, unavailing, ineffective, inefficacious, inoperative, without avail, idle, vain, void, abortive, futile, worthless, inept, incompetent, ill-spent, nugatory.

FRUMPISH, *adj.* 1. Slovenly, slatternly, untidy, dowdy, shabby, unkempt, disheveled, ill-dressed.

2. Cross-tempered, grumpy, morose, tart, sour, crabbed, cross-grained, irritable, snappish, waspish, splenetic, irascible, choleric, sulking, sullen, peevish, glum, pouting.

FRUSTRATE, *v.* Prevent from attaining a purpose, disappoint, thwart, circumvent, contravene, counter, baffle, balk, foil, disconcert, check, defeat, checkmate, cross, bring to naught, override, nullify, undo, neutralize, hinder, outwit, antagonize, make of no avail, cancel, confound, render invalid, render null and void, abort, undermine, obstruct, spoil, mar, clip the wings of, cripple, hamstring cut the ground from under one, forestall.

FRUSTRATION, *n.* Thwarting, foiling, balking, circumvention, contravention, counteraction, interference, inhibition, prevention, obstruction, hindrance, preclusion, interception, impedition, defeat, disappointment, baffling, bringing to naught, checkmate, nullification, labor in vain, no-go, nonsuccess, vain attempt, fizzle, fiasco, washout, abortion, failure, abortive attempt, miscarriage, bafflement, discomfiture, slip 'twixt cup and lip.

FRY, *v.* 1. Cook in boiling fat over direct heat, cook in a frying-pan, fricassee, sauté, frizzle, grill, torrefy, seethe, stew, scald, simmer, boil, parboil, singe.

2. Be cooking in fat, undergo cooking, be frying, sizzle, sputter.

FRY, *n.* 1. Fried dish, sautéd dish, fish fry.

2. State of mental excitement, agitation, ferment, tizzy, dither, stew, pother, perturbation, discomposure, flutter, ruffle, flurry, fever, hurry, fret, trepidation.

3. Young of fishes, small fishes, swarm of little fishes, shoal, school of minnows.

4. Young folk, small fry, whelp, cut, pullet, callow, codling, whipster, whippersnapper.

FUDDLE, *v.* 1. Make drunk, intoxicate, inebriate, fuzzle, liquor up, make see double, stupefy with drink, put in one's cups, make the worse for liquor, make mellow, make tight, slip a Mickey Finn, knock out, put under the table.

2. Muddle, confuse, puzzle, pose, confound, perplex, bewilder, nonplus, bother, addle the wits.

FUDDLED, *adj.* 1. Intoxicated, drunk, inebriated, tipsy, corned, crapulous, temulent, pot-valiant, potulent, drunken, bibacious, bibulent, boozy, sottish, groggy, plastered, tight, sozzled, stewed, mellow, beery, merry, elevated, high, primed, screwed, oiled, raddled, maudlin, lush, in one's cups, *inter pocula (Lat.),* three sheets in the wind, half seas over, under the table, one over the eight, the worse for liquor, dead-drunk, blind-drunk.

2. Muddled, confused, perplexed, uncertain, befuddled, puzzled, confounded, bewildered, addled.

FUDGE, *n.* 1. Nonsense, stuff and nonsense, fiddle-faddle, flapdoodle, bosh, hogwash, moonshine, fiddlesticks, twaddle, gibberish, jabber, rubbish, tommyrot, drivel, palaver, jargon, humbug, trash, *fatras (Fr.),* flummery, fribble, frippery, trumpery.

2. Candy composed of sugar, butter, milk and chocolate, confection.

FUEL, *n.* 1. Matter used to produce heat or power by burning, combustible matter used to maintain fire, that which feeds fire, firing material, combustibles, firing, material for burning.

2. Coal, hard coal, anthracite, bituminous coal, soft coal, cannel coal, lignite, carbon, coke, charcoal, wood, kindling, firewood, fagot, brushwood, log, backlog, ember, cinder, touchwood, amadou, punk, tinder, turf, peat, fuel oil, petroleum, kerosene, paraffin oil, gasoline, petrol, coal gas, natural gas, electricity.

3. Means of increasing passion, stimulus, aphrodisiac, cantharides, Spanish fly, incitement, instigation.

FUGITIVE, *adj.* 1. Lasting but a short time, ephemeral, monohemerous, short-lived, caducous, fugacious, deciduous, evanescent, transient, transitory, momentary, passing, fleeting, not durable, elusive, volatile, unstable, uncertain, flitting, impermanent, brief, hasty, hurried, cursory, summary, meteoric, short, temporary, shifting, fading.

2. Running away, escaping, flying, fleeing, evasive.

3. Wandering, roving, roaming, strolling, vagabond, nomadic.

FUGITIVE, *n.* Runaway, refugee, deserter, renegade, runagate, exile, expatriate, displaced person, D. P., wanderer, rover, itinerant, outlaw, apostate, straggler, outcast, vagrant, Okie, vagabond, nomad, loafer, tramp, Gypsy, hobo.

FUGLEMAN, *n.* 1. Well-drilled soldier placed in front of a military company as a model for the others, file-leader.

2. One who leads by example, leader, director, ringleader, conductor, corypheus, precentor, bell-wether, head man.

3. Model, pattern, paragon, standard, criterion, *beau idéal (Fr.).*

FULCRUM, *n.* Point of rest on which a lever turns in moving a body, support of a lever, prop, point d'appui, bearing, caudex, block, rest, stand, fulciment, stay, skid, hold, footing, *locus standi (Lat.).*

FULFILL, *v.* 1. Carry out, accomplish, effect, effectuate, compass, achieve, work out, realize, bring to pass, execute, carry into effect, bring about, establish, consummate, perfect, bring to perfection.

2. Bring to an end, finish, complete, end, terminate, conclude, close, bring to a close, wind up, clinch, seal, put the finishing touch to, crown, cap, round out, dispatch, knock off, dispose of, bring to completion.

3. Obey, follow, observe, heed, keep, perform, discharge, comply with, abide by, live up to, adhere to, be faithful to, redeem, cling to, act up, to, keep faith with.

4. Satisfy requirements, meet, answer, fill the bill, make good, fill out, deliver the goods.

FULFILLMENT, *n.* 1. Accomplishment, effectuation, realization, execution, establishment, perfection, consummation, completion, attainment, achievement, implementation, culmination, crowning of the edifice, finishing touch, *fait accompli (Fr.).*

2. Performance, observance, attention, adhesion, compliance, discharge, acquiescence, obedience, concurrence, acquittal, fidelity.

3. Satisfaction, meeting, answering, filling the bill, making good, delivering the goods.

FULIGINOUS, *adj.* 1. Smoky, sooty, fumid, fumy, muddy, murky, dirty, vaporous, nubiferous, pitchy.

2. Dark, brownish dark-gray, dusky, dull, dim, opaque, lackluster, dingy, darkish, muggy, cloudy, obnubilated, obfuscated, fuscous, turbid, thick, hazy, foggy, swart, black, atramentous, Cimmerian.

FULL, *adj.* 1. Containing all that can be held, filled to utmost capacity, flush, brimful, entirely occupied, brimming over, teeming, replete, abounding, swarming, crammed, fraught, laden, chock-full, saturated, well-supplied, well-stocked, filled up, packed to the gunwales.

2. Abundant, plenteous, plentiful, plenty, enough, adequate, copious, ample, sufficient, lavish, luxuriant, affluent, rich, unstinted, plethoric, liberal.

3. Sated, satiated, gorged, overgorged, overfed, stuffed, glutted, cloyed, soaked, overflowing, swollen, sick of, fed up.

4. Entire, complete, all, total, universal, intact, unabridged, plenary, maximum, perfect, whole, mature, up to the mark, commensurate.

5. Broad, extensive, comprehensive, all-inclusive, capacious, large, wide, rotund, big, round, ample, baggy, voluminous.

6. Exhaustive, thorough, thorough-going, detailed, wholesale, radical, sweeping, widespread.

7. Sonorous, resonant, loud, clear, distinct, strong, deep, orotund, full-toned, rich, mouthfilling, flowing, fluent.

FULL, *n.* 1. To the full, entire extent, full measure, utmost limit, extreme limit, farthest limit, utmost extent, highest degree.

2. In full, no reduction, for the full amount, without abbreviation, without contraction.

FULL, *adv.* 1. Very, quite to the same degree, with the whole force, with the whole effect.

2. Fully, entirely, completely, perfectly, thoroughly.

3. Exactly, directly, precisely.

FULL, *v.* Make full, thicken cloth, gather, pucker, tuck slightly, shirr, sew with gathers.

FULL DRESS, *n.* 1. Style of dress prescribed for occasions of ceremony, ceremonial dress, livery, court dress, knee breeches and silk stockings.

2. Formal attire for evening wear, evening dress, toilette, best bib and tucker, finery, *grande tenue (Fr.),* tail coat, dress suit, swallow-tail, dinner jacket, tuxedo, white tie and tails, white tie and black silk hose, top hat, silk hat, opera hat.

FULL-GROWN, *adj.* Fully developed, fully grown, mature, adult, ripe, full-fledged, grown up, full-blown, out of one's teens, in one's prime, in full bloom, manly, virile, marriageable, nubile, womanly.

FULLNESS, *n.* 1. Abundance, plenitude, amplitude, copiousness, profusion, plenty, galore, lots, affluence, richness, luxuriance, exuberance.

2. Fill, satiety, glut, repletion, saturation, satisfaction, surfeit, enough, *quantum sufficit (Lat.),* sufficiency, no more.

3. Completeness, intactness, entirety, totality, completion, entireness, integrity, wholeness, all, unity, voluminousness, details, minutiae, particulars.

4. Loudness, sonority, orotundity, fluency, clearness, resonance, grandiloquence, magniloquence.

5. Perfection, finish, ripeness, maturity.

6. Enlargement, extension, augmentation, amplification, spread, increment, growth, pullulation, turgescence, tumefaction, swelling, dilation, dilatation, distension, intumescence.

7. Rotundity, roundness, plumpness, chubbiness, buxomness, obesity, stoutness, podginess, embonpoint, puffiness.

FULLY, *adv.* 1. Completely, totally, entirely, wholly, *in toto (Lat.),* altogether, quite, downright, utterly, out and out, positively, at all points, *in extenso (Lat.),* as a whole, all in all, on the whole, substantially, bodily, in all respects, throughout, in every respect, from first to last, from top to toe, from head to foot, cap-a-pie, every inch, every whit, heart and soul, root and branch, perfectly.

2. Abundantly, copiously, plentifully, sufficiently, amply, to the full, richly, full.

FULMINATE, *v.* 1. Explode with a loud noise, detonate, blow up, detonize, burst, rend asunder, displode, go off, pop, flash, flare, erupt, let fly, discharge.

2. Utter menacingly, thunder, proclaim with denunciation, rage, storm, hurl, ejaculate, shout, bellow, snarl, bark, roar, rampage, bluster, flare up, hold up *in terrorem,* intimidate.

3. Declaim against, raise one's voice against, issue denunciations, pour out threats, denounce vehemently, thunder against, inveigh against, curse up hill and down dale, execrate, exprobrate, speak daggers, vituperate, objurgate, rate, berate, upbraid, rail at, anathematize, revile, vilipend, lash with the tongue, load with reproaches.

FULMINATION, *n.* 1. Detonation, explosion, outburst, thunder, burst, dissilience, discharge, blow up, blast, displosion.

2. Hurling of threats, commination, menacing,

minaciousness, minacity, denouncing, threatening, intimidation.

3. Threat, denunciation, malediction, malison, excommunication, thunders of the Vatican, anathema, curse, ban, imprecation, execration, condemnation, violent censure, diatribe, jeremiad, tirade, philippic, invection, obloquy, objurgation, aspersion, vituperation, vilification, scurrility.

FULSOME, *adj.* 1. Nauseous, nauseating, *usque ad nauseam (Lat.),* sickening, fetid, noisome, rank, stinking, rancid, noxious, nocuous, foul, rotten, repulsive, repellent, repugnant, abhorrent, loathsome, unsavory, disagreeable, unpleasant, detestable.

2. Offensive to good taste, excessive, extravagant, immoderate, redundant, gross, inordinate, exaggerated.

3. Flattering, adulatory, sycophantic, parasitic, mealy-mouthed, fair-spoken, servile, specious, blandiloquent, soapy, oily, unctuous, saccharine, sugary, honeyed, smooth-tongued.

4. Tending to obscenity, suggestive, risqué, indelicate, indecent, immodest, loose, questionable, gross, coarse, ribald, lustful, salacious, bawdy, obscene, broad, smutty, free, pornographic, lickerish, prurient, carnal-minded, lewd, lascivious, lecherous, erotic, libidinous.

FULVOUS, *adj.* Dull yellow, yellowish-brown, yellow, dark yellowish-gray, fulvid, tawny, saffron-colored, buff, luteous, flavous, citrine, xanthous.

FUMBLE, *v.* 1. Feel about uncertainly, grope for, grope about, feel one's way, tiptoe, grabble, *tâtonner (Fr.),* flounder, trip, slip.

2. Fish for, angle, try one's fortune, throw out a feeler, send up a pilot balloon, see how the land lies, see how the wind blows, feel the pulse.

3. Muff, bungle, mismanage, handle maladroitly, make awkward attempts, botch, blunder, make a mess of, boggle, make a hash of, spoil, mar, miss, put one's foot in it, not know what one is about.

4. Speak incoherently, mumble, maunder, stutter, stammer, mutter.

5. Fail to catch and hold a ball, fail to handle the ball properly *(Sports).*

FUME, *n.* 1. Vaporous exhalation, vapor, smoke, stream, effluvium, reek, haze, gas, flatus, odor, scent.

2. Irritable mood, angry disposition, huff, tiff, dudgeon, pique, stew, fret, fry, pet, rage, agitation, passion, storm, fit, emotional outburst, tumult, heat, fever, flush, ferment.

FUME, *v.* 1. Send forth fumes, disperse in vapors, send up as vapor, emit, exhale, give out exhalations, vapor, smoke, reek, drive away in smoke, steam, vaporize, transpire, smell.

2. Show irritation, display anger, foam, fidget, fuss, bear ill, chafe, seethe, be hot with anger, flare up, rave, rage, bluster, storm, fret, champ the bit, lose one's temper, get steamed up, fly off the handle, flame up, explode, rant, boil, raise the devil.

FUMIGATE, *v.* Expose to smoke in disinfecting, cleanse by vapor, smoke, disinfect, fume, depurate, purify, sterilize, deodorize, ventilate, perfume, scent.

FUMY, *adj.* Full of fumes, fumelike, fuliginous, smoky, vaporous, full of vapor, reeking, steaming, hazy, fumid, gaseous, flatulent.

FUN, *n.* Mirthful diversion, merry amusement, humor, merriment, gayety, jollity, joviality, jocoseness, waggishness, joking, playfulness, drollery, buffoonery, frolic, enjoyment, pleasantry, play, sport, game, jocularity, facetiousness, wit, mirth, joke, jest, entertainment, cheer, laughter, glee, tomfoolery, mummery, recreation, relaxation, distraction, pastime, cheer, gambol, romp, antic, prank, spree, lark, skylarking, monkey trick, escapade, practical joke, revelry, carnival, Saturnalia, bacchanal, jollification, junket, bat, whoopee, high jinks, wild oats.

FUNCTION, *n.* 1. Business employment, pursuit, occupation, business, calling, vocation, position, post, profession, job, career, métier, line, trade, situation, work, employment, chore, task, service, incumbency, undertaking, assignment, mission, stint, engagement, commission.

2. Affair, concern, interest, capacity, office, activity, duty, role, sphere, province, part, realm, bailiwick, compass, department, scope, field, beat, arena, range, orb, routine, round, billet, berth, station, charge, trust.

3. Ceremonious public occasion, ceremony, elaborate social gathering, grand doings, fête, gala, pomp, rite, festivity, affair, entertainment, reception, party, levée, soirée, afternoon tea, dinner party, banquet, feast, regale.

FUNCTION, *v.* Act, operate, perform, work, go, take effect, avail, serve, answer a purpose, serve one's turn, render a service, benefit, help, do duty, officiate, fill a situation, transact, drive a trade, ply one's task, attend to.

FUNCTIONARY, *n.* Incumbent of an office, office-holder, officer, official, deputy, representative, minister, commissioner, red-tapist, bureaucrat, office-bearer, man-in-office, person in authority, curator, placeman, agent, factor, clerk, secretary, proctor.

FUND, *n.* 1. Supply, stock, stock in trade, reservoir, hoard, stack, heap, treasure, reserve, well, spring, fount, store, mine, vein, lode, quarry.

2. Permanent fund, capital, endowment, accumulation, foundation, nest-egg, savings, *bonne bouche (Fr.),* pool, investment, sum of money.

FUNDAMENT, *n.* 1. The part of the body on which one sits, buttocks, bottom, seat, rump, anus, backside, butt, behind, *derrière (Fr.),* fanny *(slang),* rear end, can *(slang).*

2. Foundation, groundwork, basis, underlying principle.

3. Physical characteristics of a geographical region, terrain, land forms, drainage.

FUNDAMENTAL, *adj.* 1. Serving for the foundation, being a component part of a basis, basic, underlying, basal, bottom, most important, essential, first, primary, necessary, indispensable, elementary, cardinal, inseparable, organic, constitutional.

2. Original, inherent, implanted, native, natural, intrinsic, rooted, innate, inbred, inborn, immanent, ingrained, indigenous, bred in the bone, instinctive.

3. Affecting the foundation, radical, sweeping, revolutionary, thorough, thorough-going.

FUNDAMENTAL, *n.* 1. Leading principle, primary rule, necessary truth, essential part, basis, cornerstone, foundation, groundwork, essential element, grounding, article of faith, creed, credo.

2. Essence, quintessence, elixir, quiddity, gist, keynote, core, pith, kernel, backbone, marrow, soul, heart, lifeblood, substance, flower, essentialness.

FUNDS, *n.* 1. Money and negotiable paper readily convertible into cash, pecuniary resources, revenue, means, substance, capital, assets, finances, wealth, property, ways and means, wherewithal, *de quoi (Fr.),* cash, proceeds, hard cash, currency, specie, stocks and bonds, treasure, money in hand, income, command of money, almighty dollar, coin of the realm, pelf, lucre, shekels, bankroll, jack, dough, spondulics *(slang),* wampum, bank note, treasury note, loose cash, pocket money, pin money.

2. Public funds, thesaurus, treasury, fiscus, fisc, exchequer, bank, almonry, bursary, hanaper, coffer, strongbox, safe, purse, pocketbook, bourse, wallet, money belt, *porte-monnaie (Fr.),* purse-strings.

FUNERAL, *n.* 1. Ceremonies attendant on the disposition of the body of a dead person, obsequies, obit, exequies, burial rites, burial, interment, inhumation, entombment, sepulture, cremation, incineration, funeral solemnities, wake, dirge, coronach, requiem, passing bell, tolling, dead march, muffled drum, funeral procession, cortège.

2. *(Colloq.),* A painful outcome, grievous loss, lookout, personal concern, affair.

FUNEREAL, *adj.* 1. Mortuary, funebrial, sepulchral, funerary, burial, exequial, feral, cinerary.

2. Suitable to a funeral, mournful, doleful, woeful, sepulchral, elegiac, epicedial, Acherontic, adust, dark, triste, somber, dismal, melancholy, lugubrious, gloomy, clouded, woebegone, sad, lachrymose, weepy, cheerless, depressing, dreary, disheartened, long-faced, grave, solemn, lamentable, grim-faced, rueful, pallid, wan, bowed-down, desolate, heart-stricken, broken-hearted.

FUNGOUS, *adj.* 1. Fungus-like, fungal, fungiform, spongy, excrescent.

2. Of the nature of a fungus, ephemeral, parasitic, mushroom, meteoric, upstart, parvenue, transient, sudden, quick-growing, not substantial, wan, pallid, grayish-white.

FUNGUS, *n.* 1. One of a group of thallophytes characterized by lack of chlorophyll and by subsisting on dead or living organic matter, parasite, saprophyte, phycomycete, ascomycete, basidiomycete, mushroom, toadstool, puffball, mold, rust, mildew, smut, lichen, yeast plant, truffle.

2. Morbid growth, spongy excrescence, mass of morbid spongy granulations, proud flesh, carbuncle, wart, polypus, furuncle, bleb, blain, pustule, papula, exostosis, fungosity, adenoid.

FUNICLE, *n.* Fiber, fibril, funiculus, filament, vein, hair, capillament, cilium, tendril, harl, gossamer, stalk, small ligature.

FUNK, *n.* Shrinking back through fear, cowering fear, state of terror, alarm, fright, panic, pavor, terror, horror, dismay, stampede, rout, trepidation, perturbation, tremor, quivering, trembling, shaking, palpitation, cold sweat, cold feet, Dutch courage, white feather, faint heart, consternation, scare, cowardice, poltroonery, recoiling, flinching, pusillanimity.

FUNK, *v.* Shrink back, be frightened, be afraid of, be in fear, have cold feet, break out into a cold sweat, quail in fear, flinch, blench, recoil, cower, crouch, start, wince, turn pale, stand aghast, quake, quiver, quaver, tremble, shake in one's shoes, shudder, show the white feather, show a yellow streak, be cowardly, shrink from, try to shirk, skulk, shy, sneak, turn tail, run away.

FUNNEL, *n.* 1. Cone-shaped utensil with a tube at the apex, duct, channel, shaft, conduit.

2. Smokestack, smokepipe, stovepipe, flue, ventilator, chimney.

FUNNY, *adj.* 1. Affording fun, comic, comical, witty, jocular, jocose, jocund, facetious, waggish, humorous, amusing, diverting, risible, ludicrous, laughable, mirthful, merry, sportive, jesting, farcical, droll, seriocomic, dead-pan, quizzical, absurd, ridiculous, whimsical, salty.

2. *(Colloq.)* Odd, strange, curious, queer, bizarre, peculiar.

FURBELOW, *n.* Plaited or gathered trimming on a woman's gown, fringe, edging, frill, flounce, ruffle, valance, fussy trimming, showy finery.

FURBISH, *v.* Restore to freshness of appearance, polish up, brighten, burnish, scour bright, rub bright, renovate, brush up, touch up, clean, renew, improve, adorn.

FURCATED, *adj.* Fork-shaped, forked, furcular, furcate, bifurcated, crotched, bifurcate, divaricated, branching, forking, branched out, zigzag.

FURFURACEOUS, *adj.* 1. Branlike, granular, mealy, branny, furfurous, made of bran, full of bran, floury, farinaceous, flocculent, gritty, pulverulent.

2. Scaly, squamous, desquamated, scabby, scurfy, lentiginous.

FURIOUS, *adj.* 1. Convulsed with rage, full of violent anger, wroth, wrathful, irate, ireful, furibund, irascible, infuriated, raging, frenzied, fuming, mad, frantic, hot under the collar, *acharné (Fr.)*, rabid, inflamed, fanatical, hot-headed, unbalanced, frenetic.

2. Intensely violent, passionate, vehement, fierce, turbulent, fiery, savage, stormy, tumultuous, boisterous, tempestuous, impetuous, uproarious, rampant, ferocious, ungovernable, unrestrained, impassioned, reckless, heedless.

FURL, *v.* Draw into a compact roll, wrap close about a staff, gather into a roll and secure to a spar or mast, fold up, roll up, stow, wrap up, haul in, take in, reef, fold, curl.

FURLOUGH, *n.* Vacation granted to an enlisted man in the army, extended suspension from duty by executive order, leave of absence, sabbatical leave, ticket of leave, pass, *carte blanche (Fr.)*, license, permit, passport, congé, excuse, warrant, brevet, sanction, authority.

FURNACE, *n.* 1. Enclosed place in which heat is produced by fuel combustion, apparatus in which to generate heat, stove, heater, cupola, retort, calcar, crucible, alembic, still, reverberatory furnace, blast furnace, forge, kiln, smithery, fiery furnace.

2. Place of burning heat, volcano, Vesuvius, desert, Sahara.

3. Place of severe trial, ordeal, test, trying experience, tribulation, misfortune, affliction, visitation, cross.

FURNISH, *v.* 1. Provide, stock, supply, indue, endow, vest, accommodate, render, purvey, cater, administer to, favor with, indulge with, victual, provision, make provision.

2. Equip, arm, man, fit up with necessary appliances, rig, fit out, dress, accouter, array, fit, outfit, appoint, gird, prepare.

3. Present, give, grant, bestow, lend, contribute, lavish, pour on, thrust upon, yield, produce, afford.

FURNITURE, *n.* 1. House fittings, movables, household goods, movable articles of use, chattels, appointments, upholstery, paraphernalia, effects, utensils, contents, garniture, bric-a-brac.

2. Apparatus, fittings, furnishings, equipment, appliances, appendages, gear, tackle, rigging, matériel, necessary accessories, supplies, outfit, equipage, machinery, mechanism, instruments, tools, implements.

FUROR, *n.* 1. General outburst of excitement, unrestrained enthusiasm, to-do, commotion, transport, raptus, towering passion, flush, fever, fanaticism, gusto, fervency, ardor, fervor, zeal, *empressement (Fr.)*, verve.

2. Prevailing mania, craze, vogue, fad, monomania, admiration, inextinguishable desire.

3. Madness, rage, fury, insanity, lunacy, distraction, raving, delirium, frenzy, brain storm.

FURROW, *n.* 1. Narrow trench made in the ground by a plow, track, rut, ditch, dike, fosse, moat, trough, sulcation.

2. Channel, groove, flute, stria, hollow, fluting, canaliculus, drill, line, seam, cut, incision, slit, scratch, streak, score, crack, corrugate.

3. Wrinkle, crow's-foot.

FURROW, *v.* 1. Make furrows in the ground with a plow, plow, trench, ditch, rut.

2. Hollow, groove, channel, chisel, carve, incise, engrave, grave, etch, seam, corrugate, cut, chamfer, flute, cleave, seam, score, drill.

3. Make wrinkles in, wrinkle, knit, pucker, seam, line.

FURROWED, *adj.* 1. Sulcate, plowed, grooved, channeled, canaliculate, canalicular, canaliferous, fluted, ribbed, striated, chamfered, corduroy, ridged, corrugated.

2. Wrinkled, crow's-footed, lined, seamed.

FURTHER, *adj.* 1. More distant, farther, yon, yonder, ulterior, more inaccessible, farther on.

2. More extended, to a greater length, more in advance, going beyond, forward.

3. Additional, extra, more, supplementary, supplemental, spare, new, fresh, other, auxiliary, accessory, contributory, ancillary.

FURTHER, *adv.* 1. More remotely, farther off, more in advance, at a greater distance from, farther on, at a more advanced point, to a greater distance, abroad, yonder, beyond, beyond range, out of range, over the hills and far away, afar off.

2. Additionally, moreover, besides, *au reste (Fr.)*, more, also, likewise, too, furthermore, to boot, again, yet, over and above, as well as, along with, together with, in conjunction with, conjointly, *cum multis aliis (Lat.)*.

FURTHER, *v.* Help forward, forward, promote, advance, assist, help, succor, aid, lend a hand, encourage, strengthen, contribute to, subscribe to, take in tow, abet, facilitate, foster, urge on, push, elevate, exalt, raise, set on one's legs, give new life to, speed, expedite, reinforce, quicken, hasten, oblige, accommodate, favor, stand by, second, back up, work for, take up the cause of, advocate, patronize, countenance, befriend, side with.

FURTHERANCE, *n.* Helping forward, promotion, aid, advance, assistance, succor, help, lift, support, cooperation, coadjuvancy, countenance, patronage, favor, interest, championship, advocacy, defense.

FURTHERMORE, *adv.* In addition, also, and then too, moreover, besides, further, additionally, *au reste (Fr.)*, too, likewise, to boot, withal, over and above, as well as, together with, along with, in conjunction with, again, yet, *cum multis aliis (Lat.)*.

FURTHEST, *adj.* 1. Remotest, farthest, most distant, most remote, uttermost, ultimate, outmost, extreme, remotest, most in advance, latest, wide apart, afar off, out of range.

2. Farthest reaching, greatest, longest, to the ends of the earth, over the hills and far away.

FURTIVE, *adj.* 1. Done by stealth, stealthy, clandestine, surreptitious, secret, feline, hugger-mugger, furaceous, undercover, underhanded, hidden, privy, *in petto (It.)*, behind a screen, in ambush, in hiding, undisclosed, covert, private, mysterious, concealed for a sinister purpose, dissembled, cloaked, unrevealed, underground, collusive, shrouded, veiled, screened, masked, with secret design, arcane, dark, conspiring, conspiratorial, secluded, close, unseen, irrevealable, confidential, not to be spoken of, kept in the dark.

2. Sly, shifty, cunning, crafty, vulpine, evasive, elusive, thievish, shady, secretive, sneaking, skulking.

FURY, *n.* 1. Frenzied violent passion, frenzy, rage, furor, madness, storm of anger, fit, paroxysm, spasm, convulsion of rage, vials of wrath, outburst, explosion, hatred, ill will, malignity, high words, hot blood, *acharnement (Fr.)*, tantrum, pet, huff, sulks, tiff, umbrage, pique, bile, dudgeon, acerbity, gall, virulence, spleen, irascibility, acrimony, exasperation, asperity, indignation, ire, unrestrained wrath, towering rage, choler, animosity.

2. Impetuosity, might, force, brute force, headlong rush, violence, vehemence, fierceness, ferocity, severity, intensity, turbulence, storm, tumult, tumultuousness, bluster, attack, assault, excitement.

3. *(Cap.)* Mythological goddess of Vengeance, avenging deity, Alecto, Megaera, Tisiphone, Erinys, Eumenides, Nemesis, Dirae.

4. Stormy violent person, spitfire, fire-eater, hotspur, berserker, demon, fiend, hellhound, hellcat, wild beast, tiger, dragon, shedevil, hag, shrew, beldam, termagant, vixen, virago, bacchante.

FUSE, *v.* 1. Blend by melting together, liquefy by heat, smelt, melt, dissolve, condense, liquate.

2. Become liquid under the action of heat, be fused, run, thaw.

3. Unite into a whole, merge, consolidate, combine, join, link, embody, incorporate, amalgamate, commingle, blend, intermingle, make homogeneous, intermix, alloy, interfuse, compound, assimilate, cement, centralize, agglutinate, lump together, solidify, federate, confederate, federalize, league, band together, club, associate, fraternize, coalesce.

FUSE, *n.* Firing material, tube saturated with combustible matter for igniting an explosive, igniting tube, ignition, match, light, lucifer, congreve, vesuvian, locofoco, fusee, linstock, spill, wick, brand, torch.

FUSIFORM, *adj.* Rounded and tapering from the middle toward each end, spindle-shaped, wedge-shaped, cuneiform, pointed, tapering, two-edged.

FUSILLADE, *n.* Continuous discharge of arms, hail of bullets, fire, rapid-fire, volley, salvo, simultaneous firing, sharpshooting, *feu d'enfer (Fr.)*, cross fire, broadside, raking-fire, machine gun-fire, sniping, rapid succession of bullets.

FUSION, *n.* 1. Liquefaction accomplished by heat, melting, smelting, dissolving, calefaction, torrefaction, heating, colliquation.

2. Union, amalgamation, merging, conjuncture, centralization, synthesis, unification, coadunation, incorporation, commixture, intermixture, commingling, blending, making homogeneous, coalescence, juncture, federation, confederation, flux, combination, alliance, association, league, order, coalition, guild, club, clique, gang, coterie, set, pool, trust, camarilla, combine.

FUSS, *n.* 1. Excessive display of anxious activity, needless bustle, skurry, ferment, hurly-burly, ado, flurry, flutter, to-do, commotion, disturbance, excitement, fluster, hustle, hubbub, tumult, racket, rout, trepidation, pother, stew, fidget, stir, fret, agitation, worry, hurry, confusion, turbulence, disquiet, turmoil, perturbation, whirl, splutter, scuttle, scramble, bother, much ado about nothing, tempest in a teapot, dispute over a trivial matter, crisis.

2. Person given to fussing, fuss-budget, worry-wart *(colloq.)*.

FUSS, *v.* 1. Bestir oneself, busy oneself, stir about, bustle, peg away, lay about one, raise up a dust, dart to and fro, flutter about, potter.

2. Fret, fume, be in a stew, fidget, be in a pucker, worry.

3. Put into a fuss, disturb with trifles, bother, flurry, fluster, perturb, trouble, rattle, confuse, excite, disconcert, annoy, agitate.

FUSSY, *adj.* 1. Excessively busy with trifles, bustling, pottering, particular about petty details, assiduous, painstaking, finical, pernickety, fastidious, scrupulous, squeamish, over-particular, critical, overnice, crotchety, dealing with details, circumstantial, full of details, operose.

2. Impatient, fidgety, hustling, restless, hurried, hasty, mercurial, excitable, galvanic, quick, untiring, vivacious, active, busy, keen.

FUSTIAN, *n.* 1. Turgid language, bombast, altiloquence, magniloquence, floridness, orotundity, rodomontade, rant, pompous phraseology, pomposity, inflated speech, claptrap, declamation, teratology, flowers of speech, purple passages, prose run mad, rhetoric, euphuism, flourish, high-sounding words, sesquipedalianism, macrology.

2. Jabber, mere words, stuff and nonsense, twaddle, jargon, gibberish, exaggeration, palaver, patter, verbiage, babble, rigmarole, bunkum, moonshine, balderdash, chatter, gabble, flummery, frippery, hocus-pocus, mare's nest, inanity, senselessness, morology.

3. Stout fabric of cotton and flax, stout twilled cotton fabric with a short nap, coarse cotton cloth.

FUSTY, *adj.* 1. Having a stale smell, stuffy, lentiginous, mildewed, musty, mucid, rank, rancid, moldy, reasty, malodorous, ill-smelling, close, without freshness.

2. Old-fashioned, old-fogyish, fogyish, out of date, old-school, antiquated, obsolete, behind the times, passé, moth-eaten.

FUTILE, *adj.* 1. Incapable of producing any result, ineffective, inefficacious, ineffectual, inutile, inoperative, of no effect, not successful, bootless, profitless, fruitless, gainless, useless, worthless, vain, valueless, idle, superfluous, unnecessary, unneeded, ill-spent, to no purpose, unproductive, unprofitable, inept, unavailing, inadequate, unsatisfying.

2. Trifling, nugatory, frivolous, not important, trivial, insignificant, petty, good-for-nothing, not

worth a straw, empty, blind, abortive, inane, not worth powder and shot.

FUTILITY, *n.* 1. Labor in vain, lost trouble, love's labor's lost, fruitlessness, bootlessness, ineffectuality, inefficacy, inutility, uselessness, vanity, idleness, worthlessness, sleeveless errand, unprofitableness, work of Penelope, wild goose chase, carrying water in a sieve, labor of Sisyphus, waste paper, blunt tool, sowing the sand, carrying coals to Newcastle, carrying owls to Athens, beating the air, milking the ram, lowering a bucket into an empty well, preaching to the winds, whistling jigs to a milestone, kicking against the pricks, blind leading the blind, cutting a whetstone with a razor, hurrying toward a dead-end, making bricks without straw, running around in circles.

2. Unimportance, nugacity, frivolity, triviality, nonsense, folly, morology.

FUTURE, *n.* 1. Time to come, futurity, that which is to be hereafter, subsequent time, coming time, events to come, coming events, what is yet to be, morrow, tomorrow, by-and-by, shape of things to come, offing, long pull ahead, new horizon, new vista, life to come, future state, hereafter, womb of Time, the unborn Tomorrow, what will happen in future time, future condition, millennium, doomsday, day of judgment, *dies irae (Lat.)*, crack of doom.

2. Prospect, outlook, anticipation, foresight, expectation, forecast, hope, prescience.

3. Next generation, posterity, offspring, progeny, issue, seed, descendants, children, heirs.

FUTURE, *adj.* Connected with time to come, coming, that is to be hereafter, in prospect, yet to be, to come, that will be, impending, imminent, overhanging, near at hand, next, close at hand, prospective, that will be, eventual, ulterior, hereafter, subsequent, following, succeeding, ensuing, after, later, posterior, latter, sequent, henceforward, unborn.

FUZZ, *n.* Loose light fibrous matter, fine light particles, downy fibers, down, fluff, lint, bloom, pubescence, soft hair.

FUZZY, *adj.* 1. Fluffy, woolly, frizzy, linty, pubescent, curly, downy.

2. Indistinct, blurred, out of focus, not clear, obscure, dim, dark, indistinguishable, shadowy, indefinite, ill-defined, confused, misty.

G

GAB, *n.* Idle talk, small talk, frivolous chatter, prattle, prate, gabble, gift of the gab, twaddle, chatter, glib speech, jabber, babble, patter, clack, jaw, hot air, gossip, *bavardage (Fr.)*, blab, cackle, *caqueterie (Fr.)*, gibber, rattle, gibble-gabble, blather, gush, talkee-talkee, slush, palaver, tittle-tattle, blarney, baloney, blatherskite, balderdash.

GABBLE, *v.* Utter inarticulate sounds rapidly, be loquacious, talk freely, pour forth, talk glibly, patter, gibber, prate, blab, prattle, babble, tattle, tittle-tattle, gibble-gabble, jabber, clack, chatter, cackle, gab, gossip, palaver, prose, maunder, jaw, gush, blather.

GABBLER, *n.* Chatterer, prattler, babbler, chatterbox, gossip, tattler, rattle, prater, driveler, blatherskite, ranter, proser, rattle-pate, windbag, blowhard, empty barrel, jabberer, cackler, magpie, parrot, jay, *moulin à paroles (Fr.)*.

GAD, *v.* 1. Move idly about, ramble without def-

inite purpose, rove about aimlessly, wander, stray restlessly, roam, meander, range widely, gallivant, traipse, prowl, flit, straggle, ramble, foot it, peg on, jog on, circumambulate, peregrinate, nomadize, perambulate, stir one's stumps, plod, wend, promenade, stroll, saunter, go one's rounds, trek, trudge, stalk, tramp, strut, have sand in one's shoes, have an itching foot, bowl along.

2. Run wild, run loose, be uncontrolled, go unrestrainedly, run high, effervesce, be in a ferment, romp, rampage, run riot, tear along, rush about, rush headlong, go pell-mell, raise the dust, run amuck, kick up a row, storm, bluster, riot, bear down, come in like a lion, bounce about.

GADABOUT, *n.* 1. One who gads for curiosity, vagrant, itinerant, peripatetic, rambler, rover, wanderer, loafer, fly-by-night, wastrel, idler, stray, adventurer, straggler, peregrinator, bird of passage, nomad, vagabond, gypsy, *voyageur sur la terre (Fr.)*, Globetrotter, landloper, gadling, scatterling, hobo, tramp, beachcomber.

2. Tattler, one who gads for gossip, gossip, talebearer, chatterer, magpie, parrot, jay, babbler, chatterbox, ranter, rattle, windbag.

GADGET, *n.* Some thing the same of which cannot be recalled, mechanical contrivance, contraption, device, newfangled object, ingenious article, jigger, thing, doohickey, dingus, thingumajig, thingumbob, doodab, gimmick, gimcrack, artifice, wile, invention.

GAFFER, *n.* 1. Goodman, chap, wight, swain, yeoman, fellow, guy.

2. Old fellow, oldster, old rustic, countryman, veteran, dotard, hind, clodhopper, hobnail, hick, yokel, rube, chawbacon, bumpkin, hayseed.

3. Foreman of navvies, overseer of longshoremen, employer of longshore labor.

GAG, *v.* 1. Stop up the mouth so as to prevent sound, silence, muffle, muzzle, stifle, throttle, choke, strangle, garrote, silence by violence, mug, suppress outcry, smother, deaden, still, quiet, hush forcibly.

2. Heave with nausea, retch, keck, be nauseated.

3. Play on one's credulity by false stories, hoax, humbug, deceive, flimflam, spoof, chouse, bluff.

GAGE, *v.* Give as security, pledge, plight, pawn, impawn, offer as a bond, wager, stake, hock, spout, mortgage, hypothecate, impignorate, guarantee, warrant, assure.

GAGE, *n.* 1. Security, guaranty, surety, guarantee, warranty, pawn, earnest, pledge, token, stake, wager, deposit, handsel, mortgage, debenture, pignus, pignoration, lien.

2. Something thrown down in token of challenge to combat, defiance, glove, gauntlet.

GAIN, *n.* 1. Winnings, earnings, wages, salary, income, gainings, emolument, remuneration, lucre, money-making, pelf, velvet, cleanup, bonus, reward, dividend, compensation.

2. Proceeds, avails, produce, return, fruit, crop, harvest, attainment, obtainment, acquirement, acquisition, increase, accretion, increment, accumulation.

3. Advantage, behalf, behoof, interest, service, improvement, profit, benefit, good, weal, boot, good turn, blessing, summum bonum, progress, accomplishment.

GAIN, *v.* 1. Obtain, acquire, get by effort, achieve, come at, net, bag, capture, earn, carry, secure, gather, collect, pick up, light upon, come across, procure, reap, glean, get possession of, reap the fruits of, receive.

2. Acquire as an increase, get a profit, get more, profit, clear, net, realize, make money over and above outlay.

3. Reach by effort, get to, arrive at, attain, win to, come to, approach, hit, make, fetch, overtake, join, rejoin.

4. Avail, serve, help, do good to, advance in interest, boot, benefit, profit, be of advantage to.

5. Make progress, improve, thrive, flourish, prosper, succeed, bloom, blossom.

6. Talk over, persuade, prevail upon, gain over, induce, move, conciliate, get the goodwill of, win over, bring over, enlist, draw, prompt, inspire, lead, sway, influence, urge, lobby, dispose, bias, incline, bring round, overcome, carry, allure, magnetize.

GAINFUL, *adj.* 1. Remunerative, lucrative, money-making, money-grubbing, productive of gain, paying, profitable.

2. Advantageous, beneficial, profitable, useful, desirable, worth-while, valuable.

GAIN GROUND, *v.* 1. Make headway, make progress, move forward, advance, progress, increase, proceed, get on, get along, get nearer, jog on, push on, press on, get ahead, make strides ahead, make up leeway.

2. Improve, get better, rally, pick up, recover, take a favorable turn, turn the corner, be improved by, recuperate.

GAINSAY, *v.* 1. Deny flatly, contradict, controvert, speak contrary to, give denial to, abnegate, negative, shake the head, dispute, forbid, veto, contravene, disown, disaffirm, disclaim, disavow, give the lie to, belie.

2. Act against, speak against, call in question, impugn, rebut, repudiate.

GAIT, *n.* 1. Pace, trot, canter, gallop, single-foot, rack, amble.

2. Manner of walking, carriage of the body in going, mode of stepping, walk, movement of feet, mode of carrying limbs, manner of going, deportment, bearing.

3. Stride, step, tread, footfall, stalk, saunter, jog, run.

4. Rate, clip, speed, velocity.

GAITER, *n.* Covering of cloth or leather for the ankle and instep, legging, spat, spatterdash, puttee, galligaskin, gambado, *chaparajos, chapareras* (*Mex. Sp.*), chaps, leatherstocking, greave (leg armor).

GALA, *adj.* Festive, festal, gay, colorful, splendid, sumptuous, showy, gorgeous, spectacular, dramatic, theatrical, ceremonial, ritualistic, stately, solemn, majestic, formal, magnificent, glittering, flashing, ostentatious, dashing, pretentious, pompous, grand, *en grande tenue (Fr.),* in best bib and tucker, silk-stocking, *ad captandum vulgus* (*Lat.*), with flying colors, with flourish of trumpet, flaunting, pleasing, diverting, entertaining, amusing, sportive, jolly.

GALA-DAY, *n.* Holiday, red-letter day, high holiday, high-day, day of rejoicing, play-day, day of festivity, fête, fiesta, festival, field day, grand function, splendid occasion, festal occasion, festal day, celebration, turnout, demonstration, pageant, flying colors, flourish of trumpets, procession, exhibition.

GALAXY, *n.* 1. Milky Way, *Via Lactea (Lat.),* galactic circle, cosmic system, cosmos, megacosm, macrocosm, creation, universe, starry cope, luminous group of stars, starry host, firmament, heav-

ens, sky, empyrean, constellation.

2. Gathering of notable persons, brilliant company, splendid assemblage, company of celebrities, group of luminaries, élite.

GALE, *n.* 1. Wind with a velocity between 30 and 65 miles per hour, violent wind, strong wind, big blow, windstorm, storm, hard blow, hurricane, tempest, squall, blast of wind, whirlwind, cyclone, tornado, twister, typhoon, monsoon, simoom, sirocco, mistral, gust, capful of wind, northeaster.

2. *(Poetical)* Gentle current of air, breeze, zephyr, light wind, gentle wind.

3. Noisy outburst, flurry, gust, tumult, stir, uproar, agitation, commotion, noise, racket.

GALL, *n.* 1. Bitterness of spirit, malice, spite, malignity, acerbity, asperity, rancor, rankling, venom, pique, dudgeon, umbrage, animosity, spleen, virulence, mordacity, acrimony, anger, envenomed tongue, cynicism, sarcasm, invective, calumny, backbiting, evil-speaking, insult, thorn, irritation, annoyance, resentment, exasperation, exacerbation.

2. Brazen assurance, cheek, brass, impudence, effrontery, brazenness, nerve, hardihood, brashness, audacity, insolence, temerity, high-handedness, sauciness, front, face, haughtiness, bumptiousness.

3. Sore on the skin, excoriation, abrasion, score, blemish.

GALL, *v.* 1. Make sore by rubbing, chafe severely, rub sore, hurt by rubbing, excoriate, abrade, scar, scarify, flay, score, injure.

2. Irritate, provoke, harass, annoy, exasperate, exacerbate, displease, vex, fret, tease, torment, rile, anger, discompose, plague, pester, pique, affront, nettle, harry, badger, incense, persecute, molest, ruffle, enrage, sting, injure, offend.

GALLANT, *adj.* 1. Brave, valiant, valorous, lion-hearted, courageous, manly, manful, stalwart, stout, intrepid, daring, spirited, bold, audacious, fearless, heroic, high-spirited, mettlesome, plucky, dauntless, stout-hearted, resolute, noble, magnanimous, game.

2. Stately in appearance, majestic, imposing, lofty, sublime, august, dignified, princely, imperial, regal, splendid.

3. Showy in dress, spruce, natty, dapper, dashing, elegant, gay in dress, silk-stockinged *(men)*, well-dressed, foppish, dudish, debonair, smartly dressed, chic, jaunty, trim, trig, finical, dandyish.

4. Polite to women, attentive to ladies, chivalrous, chivalric, courteous, courtly, cavalier, suave, urbane, well-bred, deferential, considerate, thoughtful, affable, gentlemanly, mannerly, obliging, complaisant, gentle, kindly.

5. Amorous, erotic, amatory, rakish, sensual, concupiscent, voluptuous, lewd, licentious, libidinous, lustful, salacious, lascivious, carnal, lickerish, wanton, lecherous.

GALLANT, *n.* 1. Man of spirit, mettlesome man, hero, lion, stalwart, warrior, brave, Spartan, Trojan, gamecock.

2. Dashing gentleman, gay dresser, blade, spark, dude, fop, dandy, jack-a-dandy, silk-stocking, swell, cicisbeo, swashbuckler, coxcomb, exquisite, beau, macaroni, man of fashion, male clotheshorse.

3. Man particularly attentive to women, lady's man, lady-killer, swain, sheik, flame, cavalier, amoret, follower, admirer, adorer, suitor, wooer, masher, escort.

4. Paramour, inamorato, lover, lecher, adulterer, seducer, fornicator, voluptuary, gigolo,

libertine, rake, debauchee, satyr, gay deceiver, Lothario, Don Juan, Casanova, roué.

GALLANTRY, *n.* 1. Heroic bravery, heroism, dashing courage, valor, courageousness, contempt of danger, fearlessness, dauntlessness, intrepidity, spirit, daring, mettle, boldness, prowess, resolution, pluck, nerve, sand, grit, derring-do.

2. Courtly attention to women, good manners, mannerliness, good breeding, courtliness, chivalry, polite attention to ladies, politeness, courtesy, deference, thoughtfulness, pink of politeness, suavity, urbanity, gentility, amenity.

3. Flirtation, courtship, wooing, love-making, intrigue, amour, illicit intimacy, liaison, libertinism, debauchery, seduction, venery, lechery.

4. Finery, gay appearance, frippery, foppishness, frills and furbelows, dandyism, coxcombry, man millinery.

5. Gentry, *élite,* aristocracy, upper classes, patricians, cream of society, swells, silk-stockings.

GALLEON, *n.* Large sailing vessel formerly used by the Spaniards, argosy, carrack, galliass, galliot, corsair, tartane, junk, galley, man-of-war, barque, brigantine, barquentine, schooner.

GALLERY, *n.* 1. Underground passage, tunnel, covered walk, corridor, adit, shaft, mine, drift, pit, crosscut, airway.

2. Arcade, portico, colonnade, stoa, loggia, piazza, triforium, veranda, roofed promenade, cloister, ambulatory.

3. Upper balcony in an auditorium, peanut-heaven *(colloq.),* amphitheatre, gallery gods.

4. Bleachers, grandstand, stand for spectators.

5. Art gallery, salon, picture gallery, exhibition hall, art museum.

GALLEY, *n.* 1. Early sea-going vessel propelled by oars and sails, oared ship, trireme, argosy, carrack, galliass, galliot, corsair, catamaran, caravel, barge, barque, brig, brigantine, barquentine, schooner.

2. Page-proof, galley-proof, author's-proof, pull, copy, revise.

3. Cookroom of a ship, caboose, scullery.

GALLIMAUFRY, *n.* 1. Mixture, medley, jumble, hodgepodge, hotchpotch, salmagundi, miscellany, melange, potpourri, olla-podrida, olio, mishmash, farrago.

2. Hash, ragout, mulligatawny, stew, goulash.

GALLING, *adj.* Provoking, irritating, annoying, aggravating, exasperating, exacerbating, chafing, vexing, troublesome, vexatious, oppressive, onerous, distressing, mortifying, stinging, grinding, venomous, maleficent, burning, blistering.

GALLIVANT, *v.* 1. Gad gaily, go about frivolously, roam for pleasure, meander, stray, prowl, range, traipse, travel for pleasure, ramble.

2. Go about with members of the opposite sex, play the gallant, flirt, philander, spark, coquet, dally, court, woo, serenade, ogle, pay one's addresses to, squire, escort.

GALLON, *n.* Measure of capacity, 231 cubic inches *(U. S. A.),* 3.7853 liters, tun.

GALLOP, *v.* 1. Ride at full speed, go at a gallop, trot, canter, amble, prance, frisk, ride at a gallop, rack, move by leaps, lope.

2. Go fast, rush, hurry, scamper, fly, flit, speed, run, race, scud, sprint, hasten, hie, flee, bowl along, spurt, spank, post, scuttle, scurry, cut away, tear along, shoot, whisk, whiz, skim, dash on, bolt, bound, spring, dart, boom, make haste, clap spurs to one's horse.

GALLOWS, *n.* Wooden crossbeam on two upright beams for execution by hanging, gibbet, scaffold, Tyburn tree, drop, noose, halter, rope.

GALORE, *adv.* In abundance, abundantly, more than enough, in large amounts, plentifully, in great plenty, in large numbers, neverendingly, without stint, over and above.

GALVANIZE, *v.* 1. Treat with galvanic current, charge with voltaic electricity, electrify.

2. Stun, astound, petrify, strike dumb, give one a shock, stagger, shock, astonish, shake, fluster, dumfound, stupefy, confound, overwhelm, overpower.

3. Startle into sudden activity, animate, excite, bring to vitality, stimulate, infuse new life into, quicken, stir, arouse, inspirit, inspire, enkindle, wake, spur on, thrill.

GAMBLE, *v.* 1. Play at a game of chance for stakes, risk money on the outcome of anything involving chance, practice gaming, play for money, wager, bet, punt, hazard, dice, game, take a chance at, speculate, chance, venture, stake, back, toss up, draw lots, take a flyer, plunge, go it blind, tempt fortune, shuffle the cards, raffle, try one's luck, put into a lottery.

2. Lose by betting, squander, fritter away.

GAMBLE, *n.* Bet, risk, wager, speculation, plunge, flyer, hazard, jeopardy, tossup, uncertainty, throw of the dice, even chance, heads or tails, stake, pari mutuel, raffle, venture, game of chance, wheel of fortune, sweepstakes, pool, lottery, drawing lots, random shot, leap in the dark, pig in a poke, blind bargain, *rouge et noir (Fr.),* roulette, pitch and toss, the turf, dice box, stock exchange, bourse, curb market, raffle, tombola, turn of the cards, hazard of the die, whirligig of chance.

GAMBLER, *n.* 1. Player for stakes, gamester, dicer, cardsharper, blackleg, plunger, speculator, wagerer, punter, hazarder, adventurer, backer, layer.

2. Bookmaker, bookie, man of the turf, tout, manipulator.

GAMBOL, *v.* Skip about in dancing, romp about in playing, frolic, frisk, caper, caracole, cut capers, hop in sport, leap, spring, bound, disport, sport, cavort, rollick, jump about, vault, prance, dance, gambado, curvet, cut a dido, bounce, bob, buckjump.

GAME, *n.* 1. Play, entertainment, diversion, sport, amusement, pastime, recreation, distraction, relaxation, merriment, frolic, fun, sport, joke, gaiety, jest, festivity, merrymaking, jollity, jollification, drollery, tomfoolery, buffoonery, mummery, gambol, prank, romp, lark, antic, skylarking, spree, escapade, monkeyshine, practical joke, vagary.

2. Contest, match, race, competition, emulation, rivalry, trial, handicap, athletic sports, games of skill, Olympics, agonistics, track events, tournament, gymnastics.

3. Fighting spirit, pluck, mettle, sand, grit, dander, backbone, stamina, nerve, hardihood.

4. Object of pursuit or attack, prey, quarry, fowls, wild fowl, wild animals, gamefish, ravin, victim, kill.

5. Scheme, bit of strategy, project, plan, design, racket, undertaking, measure, stratagem, shift, trick, enterprise, adventure, artifice, coup, stroke.

GAME, *adj.* 1. Having the fighting spirit of a gamecock, plucky, ready, spirited, courageous, brave, fearless, resolute, dauntless, unflinching, valiant, valorous, gallant, intrepid, heroic, in the running, daring, cocky, determined, devil-may-care.

2. Having the will, willing, favorably inclined, disposed, eager, interested, enthusiastic.

3. Lame, limping, crippled, disabled, incapacitated, halt, hobbling, deformed, crooked.

GAME, v. Play games of chance for stakes, gamble, practice gaming, play for money, play cards, play crap, toss dice, play the wheel, play roulette, play poker, draw lots, toss up, chance it, tempt fortune, run the risk, stand the hazard of the die, venture, speculate, take a flyer, risk, hazard, put down stakes, make a bet, wager.

GAMESOME, adj. Playful, sprightly, gay, full of play, frolicsome, sportive, merry, vivacious, frisky, lively, prankish, waggish, tricksy, laughter-loving, rollicking, mirthful, jocular, jocose, folâtre (Fr.), flushed, cock-a-hoop, sparkling, buoyant, debonair, breezy, airy, jaunty, canty, spry, spirited, blithesome, gleeful.

GAMIN, n. Neglected boy left to run about the streets, street Arab, hoodlum, urchin, delinquent, guttersnipe, young rough, roughneck, blackguard boy, waif, derelict, mudlark, rowdy, ruffian, hooligan, toughie.

GAMMON, n. 1. Deceitful nonsense, bosh, hoax, imposition, humbug, jockery, talk intended to deceive, blarney, buncombe, claptrap, cajolery, flimflam, casuistry, cant, jesuitism, pharisaism, lip-homage, eyewash, mouth-honor, window dressing, insincerity, duplicity, hypocrisy, quackery, mealy-mouthedness, charlatanism, pretense, sham, dissimulation, equivocation, prevarication, shuffling, evasion.

2. Cured ham, smoked ham, lower end of a side of bacon, ham of bacon, pork, flitch of bacon salted and smoked or dried, ham haunch for curing.

GAMMON, v. 1. Make pretense, humbug, impose upon, bamboozle, hoax, deceive, gull, dupe, cheat, trick, chouse, outwit, fool, befool, stuff up, bluff, delude, mislead, beguile, inveigle, circumvent, overreach, cozen, take in, jockey, diddle, gyp, cully, pluck, double-cross, victimize, hoodwink, spoof, palm upon, bait the hook.

2. Cure ham by salting and smoking, make bacon of, salt, dry, smoke.

GAMUT, n. 1. Great scale of Guido d'Arezzo including the seven hexachords, whole musical scale, whole series of recognized musical notes, major scale, compass of a voice or instrument.

2. Whole range, sweep, compass, complete sequence, graded series, complete series.

GAMY, adj. 1. Having the flavor of game kept uncooked until slightly tainted, "high," high-flavored, almost tainted, strong, tangy.

2. Amorous, lustful, lecherous, libidinous, lickerish, lewd, licentious, sensual, prurient, lascivious, wanton, concupiscent, salacious, carnal, sexy, "hot," incontinent.

3. Showing unyielding spirit to the last, disposed to fight, showing persistent pluck, plucky, game, high-spirited, spunky, mettlesome, die-hard, courageous.

GANDER, n. 1. Male of the goose, adult male goose, drake.

2. Foolish fellow, stupid fellow, silly fellow, simpleton, nitwit, witling, blockhead, dolt, fool, idiot, tomfool, booby, moron, nincompoop, lout, oaf, dullard, block, dunderhead, numskull, halfwit.

3. (Slang) Sly glance, quick look, once over, scrutiny.

GANG, n. 1. Group of persons working together, squad, shift, crew, team, chain gang, relay, troop, company, posse, phalanx, detachment, side, partnership, guild, corporation, firm, combine, merger, trust, alliance, confederation, association, federation, union, syndicate, league.

2. Crowd, company, band, clique, circle, set, party, coterie, knot, club, brotherhood, fraternity, tribe, clan, sect, society, association, assemblage, gathering, pack, batch, horde, caste, class, faction, cause, denomination, body, community, ring, machine, push, cabal, junto, camarilla.

GANGLING, adj. Awkwardly tall and spindly, spindling, lanky, gangly, lank and loosely built, rangy, slender and long-limbed, straggling.

GANGRENE, n. Dying of tissue from interruption of circulation, mortification, corruption, sphacelus (Med.), necrosis, decay, sphacelation (Med.), canker, cancer, carcinoma, caries, rot, putrefactive fermentation of dead tissue, death of a part of the body from failure in nutrition, partial cessation of vitality in a body part, putrid decay, putrefaction, slough, dry gangrene, mummification, moist gangrene, atrophic gangrene, cutaneous gangrene, embolic gangrene, diabetic gangrene, glycemic gangrene, nosocomial gangrene, pulpy gangrene, senile gangrene, tachetic gangrene.

GANGRENE, v. Become affected with gangrene, be infected with corruption, be mortified, mortify, lose vitality, sphacelate, die, decay, putrefy, shrivel up.

GANGSTER, n. Member of a gang of criminals, ruffian, thug, apache, mobster, desperado, robber, bandit, thief, criminal, freebooter, roughneck, hoodlum, hooligan, footpad, rough, tough, bully, bruiser, racketeer, gunman, bravo, garroter, cutthroat, assassin, slayer, murderer, ruffian, mohock, hijacker, bootlegger, white-slaver, blackguard, miscreant, crook, sharper, swindler, forger, counterfeiter, rowdy, felon, delinquent, malefactor, jailbird, convict, confidence man, blackmailer, extortionist.

GANGWAY, n. Opening in a vessel's bulwarks to afford entrance for passengers and freight, removable section of a ship's rail for the gangplank, platform and stairway slung over the side of a ship, temporary passageway, passage, gangplank, plank, catwalk, drawbridge, gradient, ramp, aisle, alleyway, hatchway.

GAP, n. 1. Opening, mouth, orifice, aperture, rictus, gape, space, interval, vacant space, vacancy, void, vacuum, pause, lacuna, caesura, hiatus, interruption, interim, recess, interlude, intermission, interspace.

2. Crevice, fissure, scissure, cranny, chink, cleft, crack, cut, fracture, flaw, rift, rent, gash, hole, puncture, slit, slot, breach, interstice, cavity, chimney, notch.

3. Deep sloping ravine cutting a mountain ridge, gorge, defile, hollow, canyon, pass, crevasse, couloir (Fr.), barranco (Sp.), gulch, gully, gulf, clough, chasm, abyss, abysm.

GAPE, v. 1. Open the mouth wide, yawn with drowsiness, open the jaws, hiate, inhiate, oscitate, dehisce.

2. Stare in wonder, show astonishment, register admiration, stare open-mouthed, peer, gaze, look intently, regard with awe, strain to look at things, rubberneck (slang), scrutinize closely, be curious.

3. Part widely, crack wide open, split, become wide open, exhibit a fissure, reveal a chasm, show a gap, divaricate, spread out, be separated, fly open, expand, cleave.

GARB, *n.* 1. Mode of dress of a distinctive kind, style of dress, costume, fashion of dress, attire, clothes, habiliments, garments, raiment, habit, vesture, array, accouterments, togs, rig, outfit, vestment, gown, robe, suit, toilette, wardrobe, wearing apparel, finery, trousseau, uniform, regimentals, olive drab, khaki, gear, livery, rigging, harness, trappings, turn out, duds.

2. Appearance, fashion, semblance, guise, form, pretense, disguise, false colors, masquerade, wolf in sheep's clothing, borrowed plumes, mummery.

GARBAGE, *n.* 1. Refuse animal and vegetable matter from a kitchen, offal, carrion.

2. Any foul refuse, vile matter, filthy leavings, rubbish, swill, litter, waste, offensive matter.

GARBLE, *v.* Make unfair selections from statements, make misleading selections from facts, take out of context, falsify, misrepresent, distort, misquote, pervert, mutilate a statement, corrupt, misstate, represent misleadingly, confuse, mix up, color, belie, gloss over, varnish, adulterate, doctor *(colloq.),* exaggerate, embroider.

GARDEN, *n.* 1. Plot of ground devoted to the cultivation of useful or ornamental plants, tract for flowers, flower garden, *jardin (Fr.),* nursery, kitchen garden, potagerie, herbary, horticultural tract, truck garden, grassplot, yard, lawn, orchard, arboretum, shrubbery.

2. Piece of ground with ornamental trees used as a place of public resort, natural park, roof garden, botanical garden.

3. Fertile spot, delightful region, Eden, paradise, Elysium, Elysian fields, Arcadia, garden of the Hesperides, bowers of bliss.

GARDENER, *n.* Person employed to take care of a garden, one who tends a garden, horticulturist, florist, mali *(India),* cultivator, tiller of the soil, agriculturist, husbandman, yeoman, agronomist, granger, farmer, landscape gardener, orchardist.

GARGANTUAN, *adj.* 1. Incredibly huge, unbelievably big, Brobdingnagian, herculean, colossal, enormous, prodigious, immense, gigantic, titanic, tremendous, mammoth, Cyclopean, elephantine, strapping, hulking, vast, towering, massive, huge, monstrous, amplitudinous, stupendous, lubberly, overgrown.

2. Omnivorous, voracious, gluttonous, swinish, ravenous, edacious, insatiable, hoggish, porcine, piggish, greedy, gormandizing, crapulent.

GARGLE, *v.* Wash the throat with a liquid held in the mouth, rinse the mouth with a liquid kept in motion by a stream of air from the lungs, irrigate the throat, swash, use a gargle, make a sound similar to gargling, warble, trill, vibrate, quaver.

GARGOYLE, *n.* 1. Stone spout projecting from the gutter of a building for carrying off rain water, waterspout, projecting conduit, watercourse, canal, trough.

2. Ugly figure of a demon excluded from sacred precincts, grotesque carving, fantastic sculpture.

GARISH, *adj.* Extremely ornate, ostentatious, flashy, gaudy, excessively bright, dazzling, vivid, crudely gay, pretentious, flaunting, tawdry, harsh, meretricious, glaring, "loud," in bad taste, vulgar, showy, pompous, gorgeous, cheaply magnificent, tinsely, brummagem, obtrusive, gimcrack, cheap, trumpery, spangled, pranked out, bedight, tricked out, bedizened, gingerbread, florid.

GARLAND, *n.* 1. String of flowers or leaves worn for ornament, wreath, festoon, chaplet, coronal, bays, crown, coronet, laurel.

2. Collection of short literary pieces, anthology, chrestomathy, florilegium, book of extracts, miscellany, excerpta, spicilegium, flowers of literature, collectanea, analecta, posy.

GARMENT, *n.* Article of clothing, dress, attire, garb, raiment, apparel, habiliment, vestment, habit, mantle, robe, suit, coat, jacket, surcoat. (See GARB.)

GARNER, *n.* Granary, silo, crib, barn, bunker, storehouse, depository, repository, vault, depot, safe deposit.

GARNER, *v.* Gather for preservation, collect, lay in, muster, hoard, accumulate, lay up, treasure up, lay by, store up, save, reserve, husband, deposit, garner up, set by, stock up, gather in, harvest, put away, stow away, cache, amass, bank, fund, stack, preserve, put by for a rainy day.

GARNISH, *v.* 1. Fit out with something that adorns or decorates, embellish, decorate, adorn, beautify, trim, ornament, deck, trick out, bedeck, prank, grace, set out, set off, beset, array, enrich, ornamentalize, bedizen, prink, dress up, polish, furbish, spruce up, smarten, doll up, varnish, gild, paint, enamel, embroider, bespangle, bead, season, emblazon.

2. *(Law)* Attach money due to a debtor while it is in the hands of a third person, attach property by garnishment, garnishee.

3. Warn, give notice, forewarn.

GARNITURE, *n.* Decoration, adornment, trimming, ornament, ornamentation, ornamental appendage, appurtenance, accessory, embellishment, enrichment, tassel, fringe, bow, rosette, plume, feather, brocade, lace, embroidery, scarf, sash, belt, girdle, jewelry, *bijouterie (Fr.),* clinquant, tinsel, spangle.

GARRET, *n.* That part of a building directly under a roof, loft, attic, cockloft, sky parlor, upper story, mansard, clerestory, housetop.

GARRISON, *n.* 1. Body of troops stationed in a fortified place, picket, piquet, detachment, armed forces, militia, soldiery, escadrille, division, brigade, regiment, battery, squadron, corps, platoon, company, squad, guard, phalanx, legion, sentinels, sentry, armed guard.

2. Place where defense troops are stationed, fortification, fort, post, fortress, stronghold, hold, citadel, fastness, barracoon, blockhouse.

GARRISON, *v.* 1. Provide with a garrison, man with troops, fortify, place on duty in a garrison, put on duty in a fort.

2. Occupy a post, defend, guard, watch over, protect, secure, intrench, fence round, mount guard, patrol, spy, scout.

GARROTE, *v.* Execute by the garrote, assault from the rear by locking the forearm around the neck and throttling, mug, strangle, throttle, choke, stifle, stop the breath, smother, asphyxiate, suffocate, seize around the throat from behind.

GARRULITY, *n.* Loquaciousness, talkativeness, loquacity, garrulousness, glibness, volubility, wordiness, diffuseness, longiloquence, multiloquence, verbosity, polylogy, gift of the gab, *copia verborum (Lat.),* flow of words, *flux de paroles (Fr.),* effusiveness, effusion, prattle, gabbling, prate, babbling, chattering, empty talk, hot air *(slang)*, bull *(slang)*, jabber, twaddle, *bavardage (Fr.)*, clack, gibble-gabble, cackle, talkee-talkee, jaw *(slang)*, boloney *(slang)*, blatherskite.

GARRULOUS, *adj.* Given to much talking about trifles, loquacious, wordy, talkative, diffuse, effusive, voluble, verbose, babbling, chattering, prattling, prating, windy *(slang)*, gassy *(slang)*, breezy *(slang)*, self-assertive, polyloquent, multiloquent, declamatory, long-winded, eloquent, fluent, glib.

GAS, *n.* 1. Substance possessing perfect molecular mobility and the property of indefinite expansion, elastic fluid, aeriform fluid, gaseous mixture.

2. Vapor, air, steam, effluvium, ether, fume, flatus, damp, choke damp, fire damp, mephitic air, afterdamp, nitrous oxide, laughing gas, illuminating gas, natural gas, coal gas, acetylene, hydrogen, parahydrogen, carbon monoxide, methane, oxygen, nitrogen, carbon dioxide.

3. Gasoline, petrol.

4. Bombast, empty talk, grandiloquence, rant, fustian, claptrap, highfaluting, eloquence, windbag, idle chatter.

GASCONADE, *n.* Extravagant boasting, boastful talk, proud boast, brag, braggadocio, rodomontade, fanfaronade, bravado, vaunt, vaporing, swagger, bluster, blowhard, balderdash, flourish, vainglory, crow, crake, puffery, swank, bluff, buncombe, highfaluting, rant, jactitation, fine talking, bombast, tall talk, teratology, heroics, magniloquence, hot air *(slang)*, gas *(slang)*, chauvinism, jingoism, egotism, much cry and little wool, *vox et praeterea nihil (Lat.)*, glorification, vanity, exultation, flourish of trumpets.

GASH, *v.* Make a long deep cut in, cut deeply, slit, make an incision in, slash, score, make deep incisions in, nick, incise, lacerate, lance, slice, hew, hack, dissect, carve, anatomize, quarter, tear, crack, split, cleave, rend, rive, nip, snip.

GASH, *n.* Long deep cut in the flesh, slash, gaping wound, incision, slit, cleft, split, crack, rift, scratch, wound, mutilation, slot, fissure, scissure, rent.

GASOLINE, *n.* Volatile inflammable mixture of hydrocarbons used as fluid for internal-combustion engines or as a solvent, gas *(colloq.)*, petrol *(Brit.)*, petroleum, benzine, naphtha.

GASP, *v.* 1. Catch the breath, struggle for breath with open mouth, breathe convulsively, labor for breath, puff, pant, wheeze, blow, choke, have trouble in breathing, have dyspnoea, heave, exhale convulsively, respire laboriously.

2. Exclaim, ejaculate, vociferate, expostulate, blurt, utter in an exclamation, cry hurriedly.

GASSY, *adj.* 1. Gaseous, gas-like, aeriform, gasiform, vaporous, airy, etheric, volatilized, volatile, evaporable, flatulent.

2. *(Colloq.)* Bombastic, boastful, pompous, inflated, windy *(slang)*, breezy *(slang)*, full of talk, prolix, verbose, wordy, garrulous, loquacious, multiloquent, polyloquent, grandiloquent, long-winded, diffuse.

GASTRIC, *adj.* Pertaining to the stomach, digestive, eupeptic, dyspeptic.

GASTRONOMY, *n.* Art of cookery, science of good eating, epicurism, pleasures of the table, gastrology, good living, good cheer, gulosity, pantophagy.

GATE, *n.* 1. Movable barrier in a wall, swinging frame in a fence, opening for passage into an enclosure, gateway, door, wicket, portal, entrance, postern, turnstile, threshold, passageway, doorway, hatch, boom, entrance way, porch, trap door, hatchway, lich gate, *porte-cochère (Fr.)*.

2. Device for regulating the passage of water, sluice, valve, spigot, tap.

GATEKEEPER, *n.* Doorkeeper, janitor, *concierge (Fr.)*, porter, keeper, warder, commissionaire, Cerberus, sentry, guard, beadle, usher, sentinel, ostiary, warden, attendant, ticket taker.

GATHER, *v.* 1. Get together from various places, collect gradually, marshal, muster, cluster, rally, assemble, group, congregate, mobilize, convene, bring together into one aggregate.

2. Pick, cull, pluck, glean, scrape up, get in, bag, net, secure, reap, harvest, garner up, rake up, stack up.

3. Amass, hoard, accumulate, stock-pile, heap up, lump together, bunch together.

4. Learn from observation, infer, deduce, draw an inference, conclude, assume, derive.

5. Draw up cloth on a thread in fine puckers by means of even stitches, pucker, plait, shirr, full, ruffle, rimple.

6. Fester, suppurate, come to a head, putresce, putrefy, rot, rankle, decay.

GATHERING, *n.* 1. Meeting, assembly, crowd, company, assemblage, collection, congregation, concourse, muster, conference, conclave, throng, pack, mob, gang, turnout, forgathering, convocation, aggregation, multitude, convention, conflux, levy, mobilization, ingathering, concentration, meet, convergence, levee, reunion, deluge, flood, rush, host, press, horde, knot, troop, swarm, covey, shoal, herd, flock, roundup, bevy, bunch, drove, galaxy, array, congestion, aggregate.

2. Inflamed and suppurating swelling, abscess, ulcer, sore, carbuncle, imposthume, fester, suppurating tumor, pustule, boil, suppuration, felon, pimple, canker.

GAUCHE, *adj.* 1. Left-handed, awkward, clumsy, heavy-handed, maladroit, bungling, blundering, inexpert, unskilful, inept, unhandy, lubberly, gawky.

2. Lacking the social graces, tactless, ill-bred, ill-mannered, unpolished, ungraceful, inelegant, ungentlemanly, uncourtly, uncouth, plebeian, *contra bonos mores (Lat.)*.

GAUCHERIE, *n.* 1. Lack of social grace, uncouthness, awkwardness, clumsiness, boorishness, ill-breeding, ungentlemanly behavior, want of tact, bad taste, *mauvais goût (Fr.)*, tactlessness, Babbittry, unmannerliness, inelegance, unseemliness, indecorum, incivility, impoliteness, impropriety, rudeness.

2. Unseemly act, *faux pas (Fr.)*, tactless action, awkward action, misbehavior, blunder, bungle, botchery, botch, bad job, act of folly, *étourderie (Fr.)*, *balourdise (Fr.)*.

GAUDY, *adj.* 1. Excessively showy, brilliant, eye-challenging, vivid, colorful, strikingly conspicuous, glittering, glaring, flaunting, flaring, bright, intense, gorgeous, bright-colored, gay, glowing, lustrous, pretentious, ostentatious, over-decorated, obtrusive, sparkling, dazzling, scintillating, florid, striking.

2. Showy without taste, vulgarly showy, "loud," flashy, tawdry, garish, meretricious, tricked out, bespangled, bedizened, trumpery, cheap, worthless, specious, vulgar, barbaric, gimcrack, brummagem, tinsel, sham, flimsy, gingerbread, crude, overly fancy.

GAUGE, *v.* 1. Set a value on, appraise, estimate, judge, form an estimate of, compute, evaluate, value, assess, rate, adjudge.

2. Make conformable to a standard, standardize, adjust, cut to a uniform size, rub to a uniform shape, graduate, calibrate.

3. Measure the dimensions of, ascertain the capacity of, estimate the contents of, determine the quantity of, meter, mete, balance, weigh, scale.

GAUGE, *n.* 1. Standard of measure, standard dimension, standard quantity, extent, scope, size, capacity, limit, degree, amount.

2. Measuring instrument, templet, manometer, level, plumb line, plummet, caliper, compass, dividers, T square, meter.

3. Means of judging, standard, measure, test, criterion, canon, rule, assize, norm, pattern, type, model, scale, trial.

4. *(Ordn.)* Internal diameter of a gun bore, caliber.

GAUNT, *adj.* 1. Abnormally thin, emaciated, haggard, meager, spare, lean, lank, lanky, weedy, spindly, spindle-shanked, spindling, attenuated, slender, bony, rawboned, pinched, peaked, scrawny, scraggy, skinny, starved, withered, shriveled, skeletal, cadaverous, lantern-jawed, hatchet faced, wasted.

2. Bleak, desolate, forbidding, grim, foul, dingy, dirty.

GAUNTLET, *n.* 1. Medieval glove of mail to protect the hand, glove with a cuff-like extension for the wrist, mitten.

2. Cuff, wristlet, muffettee, wristband, sleeve.

3. The gauntlet, a challenge, gage, dare, defiance, daring, cartel.

GAUZY, *adj.* Thin as gauze, filmy, transparent, cobweb, sleazy, flimsy, translucent, sheer, silken, diaphanous, silky, chiffon, voile, lightest-weight, see-through, revealing, vitreous, transpicuous, glassy.

GAVEL, *n.* Mallet used by a presiding officer to signal for attention or order, small hammer, maul, mall, flailer, rammer, tamper, rapper.

GAWK, *n.* Awkward person, ungainly fellow, clumsy wight, swain, clodhopper, lout, boor, clown, booby, bumpkin, bungler, poor hand, all-thumbs, butterfingers, rustic, hind, peasant, oaf, jay, simpleton, lummox, lubber.

GAWKY, *adj.* Clumsy, awkward, maladroit, lubberly, gauche, ungainly, bungling, unhandy, unskilful, green, raw, uncouth, loutish, lumpish, lumbering, hulking, boorish, clownish, clodhopperish, ungraceful.

GAY, *adj.* 1. In a joyous mood, light-hearted, merry, cheerful, jovial, jocund, jocose, hilarious, joyous, joyful, glad, mirthful, gleeful, jolly, happy, frolicsome, gladsome, blithe, genial, sunny, in good spirits, smiling, bright, frivolous, airy, buoyant, dashing, dapper, sportive, skittish, jaunty, debonair, insouciant, nonchalant, chipper, lively, vivacious, effervescent, animated, spirited, frisky, sparkling, sprightly, playful, witty, humorous, jocular, waggish, rollicking, festive, convivial, social, jubilant, cock-a-hoop, flushed, rejoicing, elated, exultant, volatile, coltish, facetious.

2. Brilliant, showy, bright-colored, vivid, fresh, intense, rich, gorgeous, many-colored, parti-colored, variegated, splendid, grand, sumptuous, theatrical, glowing, glittering, lustrous, glaring.

3. Garish, gaudy, tawdry, ostentatious, pretentious, "loud," "splashy," flashy, gimcrack, flaunting, tinsel, meretricious, florid.

4. Licentious, dissipated, loose, profligate, fast, unchaste, wanton, debauched, adulterous, rakish, incontinent, free-living, dissolute, riggish, of easy virtue, lascivious, concupiscent, prurient, lickerish, carnal-minded, lascivious, lewd, lecherous, libidinous, lustful, voluptuous, erotic, salacious, amorous.

GAYETY, *n.* 1. State of being cheerful, gay spirits, sportiveness, cheerfulness, sprightliness, vivacity, exhilaration, high enthusiasm, joyousness, blitheness, joviality, good humor, liveliness, animation, high spirits, happiness, alacrity, mirth, merriment, hilarity, glee, jollity, jollification, delight, frolicsomeness, vivaciousness, festivity, festive spirits, jauntiness, amusement, frolic, celebration, volatility, effervescence, conviviality, jocundity, frivolity, elation, pleasantry, levity, airiness, merrymaking.

2. Showiness, brilliance, garishness, gaudiness, glitter, show, tinsel, brummagem, finery, frippery, frumpery.

GAZE, *v.* Stare steadily, look intently, look fixedly, look long and earnestly, rivet the eyes upon, strain one's eyes, look with curiosity, look with wonder, keep one's look fixed, peer, gape, goggle, glance, pore, peep, watch, view, eye, survey, examine, investigate, scan, inspect, con, peruse, behold, contemplate, cock the eye, witness, observe, peek, scrutinize, blink, squint, regard, pry, glare, lower, glower, leer, ogle, undress with a glance.

GAZETTE, *n.* 1. Newspaper, news sheet, daily, chronicle, journal, tabloid, paper, periodical, public press, fourth estate.

2. Official journal, gazetteer, house organ, trade publication, leaflet, pamphlet, magazine, weekly, monthly.

GAZETTE, *v.* 1. Officially announce, publish officially, chronicle, calendar, record, put upon record, report, put down in writing, print.

2. List in a gazette, enter, post up, insert, register, docket, inscroll, enroll.

GEAR, *n.* 1. Mechanism for transmitting motion, gearing, toothed wheels, cogwheels, flywheels, cams.

2. Mechanical appliances, apparatus, matériel, machinery, implements, instruments, tools, plant, equipment, contrivances, fittings, tackle, rigging.

3. Garb, outfit, array, apparel, dress, clothing, clothes, attire, vestments, garments, livery, turnout, harness, accouterments, suit, trappings, togs, things, duds, caparison, trimmings.

4. Personal baggage, effects, belongings, chattels, property, appointments, appurtenances, goods, accessories, subsidiaries, movables, paraphernalia.

GELATINOUS, *adj.* Having the nature of jelly, jellylike, jellied, gelatinoid, gelatiniform, tremelloid, tremellose, colloidal, glutinous, thick, adhesive, gummy, viscid, viscous, slimy, mucid, mucous, muculent.

GELD, *v.* Deprive of virility, emasculate, unman, castrate, effeminize, eunuchize, spay, caponize, alter, devitalize, glib *(obsolete).*

GELIDITY, *n.* Extreme cold, frigidity, algidity, algor, bitter cold, chill, inclemency, *fresco (It.),* iciness, chilliness, depth of winter, rime, hoarfrost, frost, icicle, snowstorm, blizzard, North Pole, Arctic, Antarctic, Siberia, iceberg, floe, shivering, chattering of teeth, frostbite, chilblain, horripilation, gooseflesh, rigor.

GEM, *n.* 1. Precious stone fashioned to bring out its beauty, jewel, *bijou (Fr.)*, semi-precious stone, brilliant, trinket, ice *(slang for diamond)*, solitaire, ornament, great treasure.

2. Perfection, quintessence, prize, flower, *rara avis (Lat.)*, one in a thousand, wonder, prodigy, marvel, cream, *crème de la crème (Fr.)*, pick, A-1, nonpareil, masterpiece, *chef d'oeuvre (Fr.)*, *coup de maître (Fr.)*, work of art, something prized for great beauty.

GEMINATE, *adj.* Combined in pairs, coupled, twain, doubled, twin, binate, biform, dual, twofold, double, binomial, paired, matched, conjugate, yoked, mated, united, bijugate, duplicate, dualistic, duplex.

GEMINATION, *n.* Doubling, duplication, repetition, reduplication, iteration, renewal.

GENDARME, *n.* French military policeman, *légionnaire (Fr.)*, legionary, detective, cop, dick *(slang)*, flatfoot *(slang)*, constable, *sbirro (It.)*, *alguazil (Sp.)*.

GENDER, *n.* Sex, masculine, feminine, neuter, androgyne, hermaphrodite.

GENEALOGY, *n.* 1. Account of human family pedigrees of ancestors, list of forbears, history of descent, family tree, lineage, ancestry, pedigree, line, house, family, race, stock, tribe, sept, clan, stem, trunk, stirps.

2. Derivation, descent, extraction, birth.

GENERAL, *adj.* 1. Including all members of a class or group, collective, generic, taken as a whole, comprehensive, sweeping, extensive, widespread, nonexclusive, not specific, not partial, not particular, not special, blanket.

2. Universal, pandemic, ecumenical, world-wide, catholic, public, popular.

3. Customary, habitual, wonted, accustomed, usual, common, regular, ordinary, commonplace, conventional, everyday, frequent, current, prevailing, prevalent, rife.

4. Not restricted to one class or field, miscellaneous, panoramic, bird's-eye, encyclopedic, every, all.

5. Vague, unspecified, inexact, ill-defined, abstract, indefinite, inaccurate, undefined, approximate, impersonal.

GENERAL, *n.* (Army) Officer with the rank between lieutenant general and general of the army, full general, brigadier general, major general, lieutenant general, general of the army, general of the armies, generalissimo, commander in chief.

GENERALITY, *n.* 1. General phrase, vague statement, loose statement, general statement.

2. Lack of particularity, indefiniteness, vagueness, uncertainty, inexactitude, inexactness, indeterminateness, looseness.

3. General principle, general law, general rule.

4. Universality, catholicity, ecumenicity, generalness, generic extent.

5. Miscellany, miscellaneousness, collectiveness, indiscriminateness, promiscuity, promiscuousness.

6. Greatest part, bulk, main body, mass, greater part, majority.

7. Average, ruck, ordinary run, common run, run-of-the-mill.

8. Everyone, everybody, *tout le monde (Fr.)*, all hands, anybody.

GENERALLY, *adv.* 1. With respect to the larger part, for the most part, without reference to

particular persons or things, in the main, on the whole, without particularizing, mainly, as a rule, principally, chiefly.

2. Usually, ordinarily, in the usual course of things, in most cases, as a rule, in general, generally speaking, habitually, frequently, often, repeatedly, currently, universally, extensively, always.

GENERALSHIP, *n.* Exercise of the functions of a general, soldiership, leadership, military skill, art of war, military evolutions, word of command, tactics, strategy, strategics, castrametation, course of action, management, plan, game, policy, polity, execution, manipulation, campaign, career, conduct.

GENERATE, *v.* 1. Beget, sire, father, spawn, reproduce, breed, engender, procreate, create, progenerate, impregnate, propagate, proliferate, fructify, fecundate, fertilize.

2. Produce, construct, make, form, fabricate, originate, frame, contrive, invent, fashion, induce, occasion, superinduce, evolve, develop, compose, coin, institute, cause, cause to be, bring into existence, bring about, effect, effectuate.

GENERATION, *n.* 1. Process of generating, engendering, procreation, propagation, fecundation, fertilization, impregnation, proliferation, begetting, breeding.

2. Formation, production, evolution, creation, origination, causation, development, genesis.

3. Mass of beings living at one period, whole body of individuals born about the same time.

4. Average lifetime of a generation, term of years (30) accepted as the average age difference between one generation of a family and the next, single step in natural descent.

5. Century, span, era, age, epoch, eon, cycle.

6. Succession of descendants, progeny, issue, offspring, family, kin, line, lineage, house, clan, tribe, strain, stock, breed, race, stirps, seed, stem.

GENEROSITY, *n.* 1. Readiness in giving, bounteousness, beneficence, munificence, liberality, open-handedness, bounty, benevolence, free giving, philanthropy, hospitality, charity, charitableness, almsgiving, lavishness, goodness.

2. A generous act, a good turn, good Samaritanism, well-wishing, donation, gift, grant, present, gratuity, largess, benefaction.

3. Unselfishness, altruism, humanitarianism, good will, large-heartedness, loftiness of purpose, magnanimity, nobleness, high-mindedness, disinterestedness, freedom from smallness of character, freedom from meanness of mind.

GENEROUS, *adj.* 1. Free-handed, open-handed, liberal, munificent, beneficent, charitable, philanthropic, hospitable, bountiful, princely, free-giving, lavish, unrestricted, unstinted, ungrudging, spare-no-expense, extravagant, effusive, free-hearted, prodigal.

2. Furnished liberally, abundant, rich, plentiful, ample, bounteous, copious, overflowing, plethoric.

3. Unselfish, altruistic, benevolent, indulgent, humane, humanitarian, cordial, obliging, accommodating, considerate, large-hearted, big-hearted, high-minded, magnanimous, noble, honorable, lofty.

GENIAL, *adj.* 1. Sympathetically cheerful, friendly, agreeable, pleasant, happy, cheery, hearty, cordial, kind, kindly, sunny, smiling, optimistic, merry, jovial, mirthful, jocund, jolly, festive, in good spirits, light-hearted, gay, good-natured, joyous, joyful, airy, debonair, chipper, jaunty, lively, dapper, expansive, convivial, social, sociable, congenial, companionable, friendly, bright, agreeable, warm, vivacious, affable, sparkling, complaisant.

2. Favorable to growth or comfort, comfortable, contributing to the enjoyment of life, pleasing, exhilarating, inspiriting, animating, enlivening, supporting life, pleasantly warm, cheering, fostering, nurturing, inspiring, encouraging.

GENIALITY, *n.* Genial quality, sympathetic kindliness, cheerfulness, cordiality, gayety, happiness, gladness, joyousness, joy, light-heartedness, sunniness, buoyancy, optimism, hopefulness, good humor, cheer, high spirits, light heart, liveliness, warmth of disposition, good will, heartiness, good nature, affability, sociability, vivacity, alacrity, animation, airiness, sprightliness, enthusiasm, zeal, earnestness, eagerness, readiness, ready consent, willingness, acquiescence, complaisance, assent, compliance.

GENITALS, *n.* Genitalia, external reproductive organs, sexual organs, organs of generation, private parts, pudenda.

GENIUS, *n.* 1. Exceptional natural capacity for creative and original conceptions, creative power, inspiration, power of invention, mother-wit, intellect, intellectuality, intellectualism, insight, intuition, perception, cognition, ingenuity, invention, sagacity, parts, wit, mind, understanding, percipience, wisdom, judgment, nous, imagination, association of ideas.

2. Master mind, brilliant intellect, mental giant, virtuoso, master spirit, master, proficient, master hand, adept, man of genius, prodigy of learning, walking encyclopedia, whiz *(colloq.)*, mine of information, expert, authority, specialist, connoisseur, past master, dabster, crackajack.

3. Proclivity, penchant, bent, propensity, turn of mind, natural ability, natural capacity, flair, forte, predilection, grain, vein, talent, faculty, endowment, gift, aptitude, aptness.

4. Distinctive character, distinctive spirit, natural disposition, characteristic quality, nature, peculiar constitution.

5. Guardian angel, tutelary genius, tutelar, guardian spirit, familiar spirit, genie, jinni, djinn, demon.

GENRE, *n.* 1. Category of subject matter in painting that represents scenes from ordinary daily life as distinguished from landscapes.

2. Sort, description, style, kind, genus, fashion, school, category, species.

GENTEEL, *adj.* 1. Of gentle blood, well-bred, aristocratic, patrician, thoroughbred, well-behaved, well-spoken, gentlemanly, gallant, ladylike, mannerly, civil, courtly, poised, *distingué (Fr.)*, *dégagé (Fr.)*, decorous, polished, polite, refined, cultivated, cultured, courteous, *bienséant (Fr.)*.

2. Suited to high society, stylish, fashionable, elegant, modish, silk-stocking, delicate, high-toned, tony, *à la mode*, *comme il faut (Fr.)*, swank.

3. Affected in manner, mannered, *maniéré (Fr.)*, high-faluting, hoity-toity *(slang)*, high-hat, up-stage, unnatural, pretentious, ostentatious.

GENTILE, *n.* 1. Nazarene, Christian, non-Jew, uncircumcised, giaour, Aryan.

2. Pagan, heathen, alien, stranger, foreigner.

GENTILITY, *n.* 1. Superior refinement of manners, good-breeding, mannerliness, mannered elegance, urbanity, suaveness, polish, cultivation, culture, presence, amenity, good behavior, savoir-

faire, gentlemanliness, *bienséance (Fr.)*, courtesy, politeness, decorum, propriety, etiquette, conventionality, punctilio, formality, handsome conduct, comity, civility, *prévenance (Fr.)*, gallantry, chivalry, affability, *bon ton (Fr.)*, dignity, quality.

2. Gentle birth, good extraction, superior descent, rank, blood, blue blood, *pur sang (Fr.)*, optimacy, nobility, aristocracy, distinction.

GENTLE, *adj.* 1. Blue-blooded, aristocratic, patrician, high-born, well-born, of good birth, of gentle breeding, of good family, silk-stocking, courtly, princely.

2. Well-bred, courteous, deferential, polite, refined, genteel, civil, mannerly, complaisant, obliging, urbane, well-behaved, of gentle manners, well-mannered, polished, gallant, suave, knightly, chivalrous, fair-spoken, honey-tongued, gracious, genial, respectable, honorable.

3. Kind, kindly, benign, sympathetic, compassionate, tender-hearted, tender, gentle-hearted, considerate, thoughtful, indulgent, tolerant, lenient, clement, merciful, meek, mild, sweet-tempered, affable.

4. Moderate, easy, gradual, soft, light, low, bland, mild, slight, temperate, tranquil, placid, calm, serene, still, quiet, untroubled, smooth, halcyon, zephyr-like, not rough, not violent, not severe, balmy.

5. Easily handled, tame, manageable, domesticated, docile, tractable, pacific, subdued, harmless, broken.

GENTLEFOLK, *n.* Persons of good breeding, gentlefolks, people of good family, ladies and gentlemen, lords and ladies, gentry, gentility, nobility, aristocracy, squirarchy, leisured classes, silk-stockings, upper classes, great folks, fashionable world, *haut monde (Fr.)*.

GENTLEMAN, *n.* 1. Man of good family, man of gentle birth, man of good breeding, man of social position, well-mannered man of delicacy and honor, refined man, aristocrat, patrician, optimate, man of his word, polished man, gent, silk-stocking, swell, esquire, sahib *(India)*, squire, laureate, cavalier, sir, don, hidalgo, caballero, chevalier, *gentilhomme (Fr.)*, *galantuomo (It.)*, *monsieur (Fr.)*, *signor (It.)*, *señor (Sp.)*, *Herr (Ger.)*.

2. Male personal servant, valet, attendant, footman, groom.

GENTLEMANLY, *adj.* Befitting a gentleman, well-bred, well-mannered, well-behaved, genteel, refined, polished, thoroughbred, courtly, polite, civil, courteous, cultivated, cultured, urbane, gallant, *distingué (Fr.)*, poised, *dégagé (Fr.)*, deferential, honorable, delicate, manly, manful, considerate, thoughtful, obliging, accommodating, complaisant.

GENTRY, *n.* Wellborn and well-bred people, upper middle class, people of good position, gentlefolk, quality, aristocracy, *magnates, primates, optimates*, better sort, squirarchy, silk-stockings, high life, *haut monde (Fr.)* upper classes, upper ten-thousand, upper crust *(colloq.)*, elite, cream of society, *crème de la crème (Fr.)*, great folks, fashionable world, peerage, *noblesse (Fr.)*.

GENUFLECT, *v.* Bend the knee in reverence, fall on one's knees, bow the knee, curtsy, kneel, humble oneself, salaam, kowtow, pay homage, prostrate oneself, bow down and worship, pay tribute to, make obeisance, stoop, bob, duck, dip, scrape.

GENUFLECTION, *n.* Bending the knee in worship, kneeling, knee tribute, bow, curtsy, salaam, kowtow, obeisance, homage, prostration, proskynesis, prosternation, abasement, bowing and scraping.

GENUINE, *adj.* 1. Being truly such, real, sterling, pure, Simon-pure, properly so-called, authentic, true, veritable, true-blue, sound, right, valid, all that it purports to be, honest, legitimate, proper, unalloyed, uncorrupt, unadulterated, unfeigned, veracious, bona fide.

2. Free from hypocrisy or pretense, free from affectation, unaffected, frank, sincere, above-board, heartfelt, native, ingenuous, artless, guileless, unsophisticated, candid, open, *ingénu (Fr.)*, simple, plain, naïve, natural, straightforward.

GENUS, *n.* 1. *(Biol.)* Major subdivision of a family usually consisting of more than one species closely related phylogenetically, group subordinate to a tribe or order, assemblage of classes, breed, race, family.

2. Class, kind, order, sort, type, category.

GEOPONICS, *n.* Cultivation of the soil, agriculture, tillage, husbandry, farming, georgics, tilth, agronomy, gardening, rural economy, arboriculture, horticulture, viticulture, citriculture, floriculture, silviculture, landscape, gardening, afforestation, forestry.

GERM, *n.* 1. Disease-producing microorganism, microbe, bacterium, virus, infective agent.

2. Rudiment, origin, first principle, beginning, source, originative cause, prime element, root, spark, fountainhead, rise, radix, radical.

3. That from which anything springs, seed, offshoot, seed-bud, young bud, ovule in plants, ovum in animals, egg, embryo, germ-cell, nucleus, sperm, semen, milt, roe, spawn, stirps, sprout, spore.

GERMANE, *adj.* 1. Sprung from the same father and mother, full, german, closely related, cognate, akin, near of kin, allied.

2. Pertinent, relevant, appertaining, relating, apposite, apropos, applicable, apt, appropriate, to the point, to the purpose, fitting, suitable, fit, adapted, pat, proper, relative.

GERMICIDE, *n.* Agent that kills microorganism, antiseptic, bactericide, disinfectant, antidote, antitoxin, counterpoison, prophylactic.

GERMINATE, *v.* Begin to grow and develop, pullulate, burgeon, vegetate, sprout, put forth shoots, bud, shoot, push up, spring up, burst forth, generate, flower, bloom, develop into a plant, blossom, open out, blow *(of flowers)*.

GESTATION, *n.* Carrying in the womb from conception to delivery, pregnancy, maturation, hatching, incubation, geniture, evolution, development, generation, epigenesis.

GESTICULATE, *v.* Use gestures in an animated manner with speech, make gestures in an excited manner instead of speech, express by gesturing, gesture, signal, motion, indicate, make a sign, signalize, hold up the hand, suit the action to the word, saw the air, hold up the finger, wave the hand, give the cue, nod, nudge, tip the wink, shrug, beckon, wink, pantomime.

GESTURE, *n.* 1. Bodily movement expressive of an idea or an emotion, posture intended to express an attitude, action accompanying oral utterance, gesticulation, pantomime, gesturing, sign, signal, motion, by-play, chironomy, dumb show, dactylology, nudge, touch, shrug, nod, beck, glance, wink, wave.

2. Action intended for effect, proceeding gone through as a formality, demonstration, flourish,

offer made without expectation of its acceptance, *beau geste (Fr.)*.

GET, *v.* 1. Come into possession of, obtain, receive, secure, acquire, procure, come by, meet with, realize, achieve, win, gain, attain, earn, reap, glean, pick up, net, bag, take, succeed to, inherit, pocket.

2. Comprehend, grasp, understand, sense, perceive, take in, catch, fathom, seize, follow.

3. Induce, persuade, prevail upon, influence, dispose, wheedle, coax, elicit, enlist, influence by surreptitious means, suborn, bring round, predispose, incline, bias, carry, talk over, win over, sway, prompt, move.

4. Capture, take, seize upon, snatch, grasp, grab, lay hold of, grip, collar, catch, entrap, ensnare.

5. Overcome, vanquish, worst, floor, overmaster and possess, obtain the mastery over, corner, pen, trap, bring to retribution.

6. Baffle, puzzle, confound, perplex, bewilder, disconcert, upset, annoy, irritate, stagger, nonplus, pose, confuse, mystify.

7. Become, be converted into, grow, fall, turn to, turn into, wax, go, change to, be changed to, come to be, get to be.

GET AHEAD, *v.* 1. Advance, progress, make progress, proceed, get along, move forward, get on, forge ahead, gain ground, press onward, shoot ahead, speed, make up leeway, outdistance, spurt in front of.

2. Prosper, succeed, flourish, thrive, manage well, be successful, turn out well, rise in the world, light on one's feet, feather one's nest, make one's pile.

GET AT, *v.* 1. Get hold of, reach, make way to, gain access to, lay one's fingers on, come across, meet with, fall in with.

2. Acquire knowledge of, ascertain, find out, determine, discover, trace out, evolve, fix upon, worm out, ferret out, root out, fathom, bring to light, unearth, solve, find a clue to, spot, arrive at the truth.

3. Influence by surreptitious means, bribe, tamper with, suborn, influence corruptly.

GET AWAY FROM 1. Disengage oneself from, leave, quit, recede, move from, retire, withdraw, move away, drift away, depart, retreat, stand aside.

2. Pass unobserved, escape, evade consequences, elude.

GET BACK 1. Come back, return, go back, turn back, revisit, come again.

2. Get possession of again, obtain again, retrieve, recover, regain, restore, recruit, recoup, reestablish.

3. Revenge oneself on, slap back at, get even, get quits, retaliate, return like for like, repay, requite, pay back, avenge, match, give *quid pro quo*, give a Roland for an Oliver, give measure for measure.

GET BEHIND 1. Fall in the rear, lag behind, fall behind, drag one's feet, loiter, move slowly.

2. Support actively, put one's shoulder to the wheel, endorse, push, aid, abet, second, further, promote, cultivate, encourage, assist, help.

GET BY HEART Learn by rote, learn by heart, commit to memory, memorize, get into one's head, say one's lesson, repeat as a parrot, have at one's fingers' ends, con over, fix in the memory, impress in the memory, enshrine in the memory, stamp in the memory, store in the memory.

GET DOWN Come down, descend, alight, dismount, drop down, go down, gravitate, fall off, light.

GET FORWARD Advance, progress, make progress, get on, get along, get ahead, proceed, forge ahead, gain ground, step forward, step to the fore, press onward.

GET OFF 1. Start a journey, leave, go away, depart, set out, take one's departure, take oneself off, whip off, pack off, move off, march off, set off, start off, issue, sally forth, go forth, go one's way, take wing, take flight, whip away, take off, hop off, make a getaway.

2. Escape, evade consequences, be acquitted, get free, get clear, be released, be exonerated, be exculpated, wriggle out of, elude, give one the slip, go scot-free, weather the storm, *échapper belle (Fr.)*.

3. Dismount, come down from, descend from, alight from, disembark.

4. Express a joke, quip, jest, wisecrack, banter.

GET ON 1. Don, put on, draw on, slip on, dress in, invest oneself in, assume, wear.

2. Make progress, proceed, advance, progress, get ahead, get along, get forward, forge ahead, gain ground, press onward.

3. Succeed, manage well, thrive, prosper, flourish, be successful, rise in the world, have a run of luck, feather one's nest, make one's fortune, make one's pile.

4. Agree with a person, be congenial.

GET OUT 1. Eject, expel, discard, throw out, push out, sweep out, send away, bundle out, turn out.

2. Come out, clear out, begone, be off, get oneself gone, go away, take oneself off, withdraw, depart, quit.

3. Publish, bring before the public, circulate, spread abroad, emit, give out to the world, hawk about, bruit around.

GET OVER 1. Recover from, recuperate, return to the original state, revive, rally, come round, pull through, weather the storm, get the better of, get well, come to, survive.

2. Succeed, carry all before one, score a success, get the better of, get the best of, surmount an obstacle, overcome a difficulty, win one's cause.

3. Be content, make one's peace with, be reconciled to, take in good part, put up with, take heart, become accustomed to, think of without strong feeling.

GET RID OF 1. Dispose of, cast off, eject, expel, remove, make away with, free, disencumber, disburden.

2. Be freed from, be rid of, get quit of, be relieved from.

GET THE HANG OF Become familiar with, get used to, get acquainted with, get accustomed to, catch on, comprehend, understand, know all about, see into, savvy, get the knack of, latch on to.

GET THE START OF Have the advantage of, have at a handicap, get at a disadvantage, take the lead of, be ahead of, outstrip, outspeed, go beyond, outgo, outrun, outride, outdistance, beat to the jump, have the upper hand.

GET THROUGH 1. Transact, dispatch, execute, discharge, work out, carry out, carry through, carry into effect, enact.

2. Complete, accomplish, finish, do, make,

work out, bring about, polish off, finish off, dispose of, make short work of.

3. Expend, run through, disburse, spend, fritter away, fool away, use up, consume.

GET TOGETHER 1. Collect, gather together, muster, assemble, bring together, levy, convene, marshal, amass, accumulate, heap up, pile up.

2. Congregate, swarm, throng, meet, come together, crowd together.

3. Be reconciled to, be reunited, be restored to friendship, be appeased.

GET UP 1. Rise from bed, arise, spring up, start from bed.

2. Ascend, mount, rise, climb, clamber, scrabble, scramble, scale, escalade, top, surmount, shinny up, shin.

3. Prepare, settle preliminaries, make preparations, arrange, organize, make ready, lay the foundations, prepare the ground.

4. Learn, study, learn by heart, con, pore over, peruse, read through, wade through, bone up on, prime, grind, master, cram.

GEWGAW, *n.* Bit of gaudy finery, gimcrack, trinket, gaud, whim-wham, bauble, bagatelle, fandangle, frippery, trumpery, knickknack, kickshaw, trifle, toy, plaything, fizgig, trickery, fallal, tinsel, spangle, sequin, clinquant, pinchbeck, curio, bric-a-brac.

GEYSER, *n.* Hot spring intermittently sending up fountainlike jets of water and steam into the air, white chimney of water, sporadically eruptive hot spring, seething caldron, volcano.

GHASTLY, *adj.* 1. Deathly pale, ashen, pallid, wan, colorless, pasty, blanched, deathlike, cadaverous, corpselike, pale as death, glassy, lurid, lackluster, ghostly, haggard, bluish-white, livid.

2. Loathsome, ugly, revolting, repulsive, repellent, grisly, gruesome, hideous, odious, spectral, appalling, grim, forbidding, dismal, dreadful, terrifying, horrible, horrid, horrendous, frightful, fearful, terrible, weird, uncanny, awe-inspiring, shocking.

GHOST, *n.* 1. Disembodied spirit wandering among living persons, soul of a dead person haunting living persons, departed spirit, *Doppelgänger (Ger.)*, doubleganger, revenant, apparition, phantom, phantasm, phantasma, wraith, specter, shadow, shade, sprite, spook, supernatural being, materialization, manifestation, banshee, *manes (Rom. Relig.)*, *lemures (Rom. Relig.)*, genie, image, chimera, demon, imp, goblin, hobgoblin.

2. Principle of life, soul, spirit.

3. Any faint shadowy semblance, appearance, vision, delusion, hallucination, mirage, mere shadow.

GHOSTLY, *adj.* 1. Ghostlike, spectral, phantasmal, phantom, phantomlike, spookish, spooky, shadowy, illusive, unearthly, supernatural, haunted, uncanny, weird, unreal, pale, ghastly.

2. Spiritual, not secular, of the soul, not carnal, not fleshly.

GHOUL, *n.* 1. Imaginary evil being who robs graves and feeds upon corpses, vampire, anthropophagus, anthropophagist, man-eater, bloodsucker, succubus, incubus, lamia, werewolf, *loupgarou (Fr.)*, ogre, vulture, harpy, bogie, one who preys upon the dead, grave-robber, body-snatcher.

2. One who revels in what is revolting, monster, demon, fiend, Frankenstein's monster, Jack-the-ripper, slasher, brute, hooligan, savage, ugly customer, evil-eye, cacodemon.

GIANT, *n.* 1. Mythical being of more than human size and strength, mythical manlike being of huge stature, colossus, being of human form but superhuman size and strength.

2. Atlas, Cyclops, Polyphemus, Titan, Antaeus, Briareus, Hercules, Herakles, Goliath, Samson, Gog and Magog, Gargantua, Brobdingnagian, "Triton among the minnows."

3. Monster, mammoth, whale, behemoth, leviathan, megathere, dinosaur, ichthyosaur, elephant, hippopotamus, jumbo, giraffe.

4. Anything of extraordinary size or power, thumper, whopper, mountain, strapper, spanker, tun, clod, block, lump, tower of strength.

GIBBERISH, *n.* Rapid and inarticulate talk, unintelligible language, voluble and foolish talk, unmeaning words, jabber, jargon, babble, gibble-gabble, balderdash, palaver, patter, gabble, prating, verbiage, dog Latin, macaronics, drivel, flummery, stuff and nonsense, bosh, fudge, twattle, twaddle, rigmarole, fiddle-faddle, chatter, double talk, prate, mere words, prattle, tattle, gossip, blab, gibber, flapdoodle, empty sound, idle talk, nonsense, absurdity, inanity, hocus-pocus, *baragouin (Fr.), bavardage (Fr.), niaiserie (Fr.).*

GIBBET, *n.* 1. Gallows with a projecting arm at the top from which criminals' bodies were hung in chains after execution, hangman's tree, lynching tree, Tyburn tree, scaffold, swing.

2. Hanging, drop, noose, rope, halter.

GIBBOUS, *adj.* 1. Humpbacked, hunchbacked, humped, crook-backed, hunched.

2. So viewed as to appear convex on both margins, protuberant, gibbose, rounded, rotund, bowed, arched, bellied, tuberous, bulbous, spherical, spheroidal, globated, globular, globose, globous, swelling, bulging, egg-shaped, ovoid, pear-shaped, *teres atque rotundus (Lat.).*

GIBE, *v.* 1. Utter mocking words, taunt with sarcastic words, jeer, flout, fleer, scoff, mock, scout, mimic, chaff, asperse, tantalize.

2. Ridicule, laugh at, deride, twit, jibe, guy, rag, roast, sneer at, scoff at, rail at, jeer at, taunt, hoot, hiss, boo.

GIBE, *n.* Sarcastic remark, taunting criticism, mockery, derision, ridicule, jibe, thrust, jeer, taunt, fling, flout, scoff, sneer, irony, sarcasm, quip, wisecrack, cutting remark, hiss, hoot, boo.

GIDDY, *adj.* 1. Affected with vertigo, vertiginous, dizzy, light-headed, fainting, faint.

2. Frivolously light, impulsive, flighty, capricious, fickle, volatile, mercurial, notional, humorsome, moody, fitful, inconstant, fanciful, crotchety, whimsical, changeable, mutable, unstable, unsteady, vacillating, inconsistent, irresolute, wanton, hare-brained, heedless, careless, reckless, thoughtless, wild, headlong, giddy-brained, erratic, flyaway, irresponsible, harum-scarum, rattle-brained.

GIFT, *n.* 1. Act of giving, bestowal, conferment, presentation, conferral, dispensation, cession, consignment.

2. Anything given, present, favor, donation, boon, sportula, benefaction, tip, gratuity, *pourboire (Fr.), Trinkgeld (Ger.),* grant, fee, bonus, prize, premium, largess, handout, dole, alms, baksheesh, cumshaw, help, aid, offering, offertory, honorarium, peace offering, douceur, bribe, bait, sop, palm grease, graft, tribute, allowance, pin-money, pittance, consideration, oblation, award, pension, allotment, benevolence, liberality, bounty, legacy, devise, bequest, dot, dower, dowry, subvention, subsidy, endowment, subscription, contribution.

3. Natural endowment, special ability, attribute, virtue, property, qualification, aptitude, aptness, talent, capacity, genius, knack, flair, forte, turn, bent, faculty, quality, power, facility, capability, felicity, *curiosa felicitas (Lat.),* skill, ingenuity, cleverness, expertness, feeling, adroitness, craft, competency, proficiency, efficacy, readiness.

GIFTED, *adj.* Endowed with natural gifts, having a special faculty, talented, clever, able, neat-handed, fine-fingered, felicitous, ingenious, inventive, adroit, slick, handy, deft, quick, resourceful, ready, smart, intelligent, sagacious, cut out for, fitted for, proficient, at home in, good at, master of, accomplished, masterly, *au fait (Fr.),* a good hand at, crack, crackajack, practiced, experienced, skilled, finished, qualified, polished, capable, expert.

GIGANTIC, *adj.* 1. Of great magnitude, gigantean, mammoth, monstrous, colossal, enormous, immense, huge, prodigious, giant, vast, massive, mighty, strapping, spanking, bouncing, hulking, unwieldy, cumbrous, lubberly, overgrown, ponderous, lumpish, large-scale, stupendous, bulky, elephantine, megatherian, megatherine, hippopotamic, jumbo-sized, towering, voluminous, Titanic, Herculean, Cyclopean, Gargantuan, Brobdingnagian.

2. Extraordinary, unusual, out of the normal in some striking way, preternatural, astonishing, extreme, striking, amazing, marvelous.

GIGGLE, *n.* Spasmodic laugh, titter, snigger, snicker, chuckle, crow, chortle, cackle, twitter, guffaw, tehee, cachinnation, simper, grin, smirk, haw-haw.

GIGOLO, *n.* 1. Man who lives upon the earnings of a professional prostitute, pimp, pander, procurer.

2. Paid male dancing partner, professional male escort, cabaret companion.

3. Man supported by a woman, lounge-lizard, lady-killer, playboy, silk-stocking, "silk-sock Sam the sheik from Alabam'," cicisbeo, gallant, paramour, lover, inamorato, leman, *amoroso,* captive, ladies' man.

GILD, *v.* 1. Overlay with gold, coat with gold-colored substance, coat with gold-leaf, plate, electroplate, aureate.

2. Brighten, smarten, furbish, polish, lacquer, enamel, japan, paint, garnish, make bright, make lustrous, adorn, embellish, bedizen, bedeck, bedight, array, make attractive, illuminate, spangle, bespangle, blazon, emblazon, beautify, ornament, make glossy.

3. Give a fair but deceptive outward appearance to, give a bright pleasing aspect to, put a good face upon, sugarcoat, gild the pill, window-dress, make things pleasant, bait the hook.

GIMCRACK, *n.* Showy useless trifle, gewgaw, bagatelle, bauble, trinket, frippery, trumpery, tinsel, sequin, spangle, clinquant, gaud, curio, knick-knack, trifle, kickshaw, thingumajig, thingumbob, jiggumbob, contrivance, ornament, toy, plaything.

GIN, *n.* 1. Pitfall, snare, trap, decoy, toils, net, bird-lime, meshes, springs, noose, *guet à pens (Fr.),* artifice, hook, bait.

2. Alcoholic beverage obtained by redistilling spirits with juniper berries, spirit, liquor.

GINGER, *n.* 1. Pungent spicy rhizome of a reed-like plant of the genus *Zingiber,* flavoring.

2. Tawny color, dull-yellowish color, reddish-yellow.

3. Piquancy, pungency, poignancy, sharpness, raciness, liveliness, sparkle, vivacity, animation, vivaciousness, snap, spirit, mettle, intensity.

GINGERLY, *adv.* 1. With extreme care, very cautiously, carefully, guardedly, circumspectly, vigilantly, watchfully, charily, warily, shrewdly, slyly, leerily, stealthily, cannily, heedfully, prudently, discreetly, sure-footedly, timidly, suspiciously, safely, within bounds, within compass, in reason, moderately, at half speed.

2. Mincingly, daintily, finically, fastidiously, squeamishly, precisely, delicately, tenderly.

GIRD, *v.* 1. Encircle with a belt, bind with a girdle, belt, girdle, strap, lace round, tighten, tie, secure, hitch, truss, fasten, girt.

2. Encircle, surround, hem in, circumscribe, compass, encompass, ensphere, circle, loop, environ, enclose, begird, engird, hedge, pen, confine, embrace, besiege, invest, blockade, lay siege.

3. Prepare oneself mentally for action, gird up, brace, fortify, strengthen, sustain, harden, steel, buttress.

GIRDER, *n.* Main structural horizontal supporting member, principal horizontal timber, main beam, crossbeam, steel section, rafter, lintel.

GIRDLE, *n.* 1. Lightweight undergarment to support the abdominal region of the body, corset, whalebone-stiffened inner garment, corselet, bodice, stays, foundation garment, stomacher.

2. Belt, band for the waist, cingulum, surcingle, cincture, cestus, cord worn about the waist, sash, baldric, cingle, girth, cummerbund, zone, cordon, circlet.

3. Any encircling band, ring, compass, limit, contour, bound, boundary, pale.

GIRDLE, *v.* 1. Gird round, encircle with a corset, bind round, lace up, hitch, truss, strap.

2. Surround, shut in, hem in, circumscribe, enclose, encompass, environ, girt, embrace, circle, encircle, begird, engird, beset, compass, besiege, invest, blockade.

GIRL, *n.* 1. Young female person, maiden, young unmarried woman, virgin, maid, lass, lassie, miss, damsel, damoselle, demoiselle, *Fräulein (Ger.),* daughter, female child, schoolgirl, colleen, girlie, ingenue, nymph, dryad, wench, minx, petticoat, flapper, romp, baggage, hoyden, tomboy, soubrette.

2. Female servant, domestic, maidservant, hired woman, maid, handmaid, lady's maid, abigail, *bonne (Fr.),* help, cook, scullion, Cinderella, maid-of-all-work.

3. Sweetheart, girl friend, lady love, inamorata, darling, angel, mistress, fiancée, betrothed, affianced.

GIRTH, *n.* 1. Measure around anything, circumference, periphery, perimeter, distance around, circuit, bounds, *tournure (Fr.),* boundary, pale, outline.

2. Girdle, bellyband, cinch, cincture, surcingle, belt, vinculum, sash, cummerbund, cestus, zoster, zone.

GIST, *n.* Substance of a matter, essence, essential part, pith, core, marrow, kernel, sum and substance, effect, burden, force, value, sense, drift, spirit, import, tenor, purport, bearing, signification, significance, implication, interpretation, ex-planation, importance, reason, ground, basis, main point.

GIVE, *v.* 1. Bestow voluntarily, present, make a gift, donate, offer, accord, grant, confer, deliver freely, hand over, entrust, commit, award.

2. Apportion, allot, assign, deal, administer, dispense, fork out, hand out, shell out, distribute, subscribe, mete out, contribute.

3. Accommodate with, indulge with, proffer, afford, furnish, spare, supply, provide, equip, help, favor with, lavish, thrust upon.

4. Deliver to another in exchange for something, remunerate, exchange, requite, pay, compensate, bribe, tip, recompense, fee, grease the palm, oil *(slang),* hire, buy, suborn, corrupt.

5. Endow, settle upon, invest, vest in, enrich, bequeath, dower, leave, devise, make over, transfer, entrust.

6. Communicate, impart, announce, notify, describe, portray, render, let know.

7. Pronounce, utter, give vent to, emit, voice, articulate, issue, put forth, convey.

8. Grant permission, permit, vouchsafe, allow, deign, concede, yield, admit, adjudge, enable.

9. Cause, make, do, perform, occasion, inflict.

10. *(Used reflexively)* Apply, devote, addict, attach, surrender, lend, offer.

11. Part with, give up, cede, shed, consign, relinquish, give away, dispose of, sacrifice.

12. Yield to pressure, draw back from strain, give way, loosen, unbend, ease, relax, slacken, abate, relent, become less rigid, bend, sink, recede, move back, retreat, retire, shrink, become soft, deliquesce.

13. Assign as a basis of reasoning, suppose, assume, take for granted.

14. Afford a vista, look out upon, open on, lead on to, afford an entrance.

GIVE AWAY 1. Give as a present, make over gratis, part with freely, dispose of, relinquish, turn over to.

2. Deliver a bride to a groom at a wedding, conduct to the altar.

3. Let a secret be known, let out, let slip, let the cat out of the bag, disclose, divulge, betray.

GIVE BACK Make restitution, return, refund, restore, give up, render up, let go, recoup, reimburse, repay, indemnify, remit.

GIVE CHASE Pursue, chase, run after, make after, follow up, follow the trail, press on the heels of, hound, stalk, hunt, dog, course after.

GIVE EAR Hearken, listen, attend, heed, lend an ear, incline an ear, be all ears, prick up the ears, bend an ear, hark, give attention, pay attention, be attentive.

GIVE IN 1. Acknowledge defeat, cry quits, surrender, give up, yield, cry quarter, submit, lay down one's arms, cede, succumb, capitulate, throw in the towel, throw in the sponge.

2. Announce formally, make known, declare.

GIVE NOTICE 1. Inform, serve notice, put before, lay before, set before, point out, instruct, let one know, give one to understand, acquaint with, inform of, impart to, bring to the ears of, advise, apprise, enlighten, notify, make acquainted with.

2. Caution, warn, forewarn, admonish, give warning, put on one's guard, sound the alarm.

GIVE OFF Emit, exhale, throw off, send out, give out, smell of, reek of, pour out, effuse.

GIVE OUT 1. Emit, send out, send forth, give vent to, pour forth, exhale.

2. Publish, proclaim, report, announce, enunciate, make public, circulate, promulgate, spread abroad, disseminate, rumor, evulgate, bring before the public, bandy about, buzz about, bruit.

3. Present, bestow, give away, dole out, deal out, fork out, shell out, mete out.

4. Become used up, run out, be exhausted, become worn out, come short, fail.

GIVE OVER 1. Cease from, desist from, abandon, quit, discontinue, break off, have done with, surcease.

2. Give up, consider hopeless, relinquish all hope of, consider lost, despair, lose hope, yield to despair, despond, falter.

GIVE PLACE 1. Give ground, make room, give way, recede, retire, retreat, withdraw, abandon one's place, make way for, draw back.

2. Put in the place of, substitute, change for, take the place of, be displaced by, be succeeded by.

GIVER, *n.* Donor, donator, bestower, disposer, contributor, benefactor, granter, deliverer.

GIVE RISE TO Give origin to, give occasion to, originate, occasion, cause, result in, bring about, effect, produce, sow the seeds of, bring on, bring to pass, found, institute, inaugurate, lay the foundation of, lie at the root of.

GIVE UP 1. Lose all hope, abandon as hopeless, consider hopeless, despond, despair, relinquish hope, give over, yield to despair, falter.

2. Not understand, miss, not know what to make of, not be able to account for, be unable to make either head or tail of, be all at sea, be able to make nothing of.

3. Relinquish, abandon, forsake, quit, leave, desert.

4. Surrender, cry quits, capitulate, give in, yield, cry quarter, throw in the sponge, throw in the towel, concede, cease opposition.

GIVE WAY 1. Crumble, totter, drop, tremble, break, snap, crack, shiver, split, burst, splinter, break short, fall to pieces, cave in.

2. Give ground, give in, give up, reel back before, make room, retreat, retire, recede, withdraw, fall back, yield, retire in favor of, concede, cease opposition, capitulate, draw in one's horns.

3. Pine, mourn, grieve, repine, yearn, languish, droop, sink, despair, break one's heart, despond, lose heart.

GLABROUS, *adj.* Having a surface devoid of hair, destitute of pubescence, hairless, bald, smooth.

GLACIAL, *adj.* 1. Icy, frozen, frosty, wintry, freezing, hibernal, brumal, arctic, boreal, antarctic, Siberian, polar, hyemal, hyperboreal, icebound, frozen out, gelid, frigid, algid, raw, inclement, bitter, niveous, biting, piercing, nipping, pinching, cutting, frost-bound.

2. Calm, slow-moving, serene, unmoving.

3. Unfriendly, inhospitable, aloof, remote, distant, hostile.

GLACIATE, *v.* Congeal, freeze, turn into ice, cover with ice, refrigerate, affect by glacial action, produce glacial effects upon.

GLACIER, *n.* Extended mass of ice accumulating over the years and moving very slowly down from high mountains, ice-field, ice-stream, ice-torrent, *névé (Fr.), sérac (Fr.),* floe, berg, ice-floe.

GLAD, *adj.* 1. Delighted, well-contented, pleased, rejoiced, gratified, elated, happy, exhilarated.

2. Showing pleasure, happy, joyful, joyous, jocund, light-hearted, mirthful, jubilant, gleeful, jolly, playful, animated, merry, cheery, cheerful, gladsome, blithe, pleased, ecstatic, blissful, gay, vivacious.

3. Causing joy or pleasure, refreshing, animating, cheering, gratifying, exhilarating, gladdening, felicitous.

GLADDEN, *v.* 1. Make glad, render light-hearted, fill with joy, please highly, fill with pleasure, make joyous, exhilarate, make happy, delight, rejoice, gratify, cheer, bless, encourage, comfort, console, enliven, elate, tickle, amuse, inspire, inspirit, transport, ravish, titillate, animate.

2. Grow happy, become glad, light up, brighten, grow light-hearted, grow bright, smile, beam.

GLADE, *n.* Open space in a forest, open passage through a wood, grassy cleared space in the forest, forest lane, aisle, slade, dingle, vale, dell, dale, combe, strath, grove.

GLADIATE, *adj.* Sword-shaped, ensiform, spiked, cusped, cuspidate, hastate, xiphoid.

GLADIATOR, *n.* (*Rom. Hist.*) Captive slave who fought in public with a sword to entertain the public, swordsman, prize-fighter in Rome, swordplayer, agonistes, secutor, retiarius, fighting-cock, duelist, *sabreur (Fr.),* combatant, belligerent.

GLADNESS, *n.* Joyous satisfaction, cheerfulness, joyfulness, joyousness, joy, gratification, happiness, pleasure, delight, rapture, jubilation, bliss, felicity, cheer, mirth, exhilaration, ecstasy, rejoicing, glee, merriment, gayety, enjoyment, festivity, exultation.

GLADSOME, *adj.* 1. Making joyful, delightful, very agreeable, enchanting, highly pleasing, charming, transporting, rapturous, titillating, thrilling, irresistible, pleasurable.

2. Joyous, joyful, jovial, cheerful, blithe, gay, jocund, jolly, blithesome, glad, gleeful, merry, sportive, lively, vivacious, frolicsome, sprightly, airy, buoyant, jaunty, debonair, insouciant, dapper, light-hearted, delighted, pleased, happy.

GLAMOUR, *n.* 1. Alluring and often illusory charm, making things seem to be what they are not, enchantment, witchery, spell, magic, charm, illusion, glitter, delusion, mirage, ensorcelment, sorcery, obsession, seduction, blandishment, temptation, magnetism, enticement, voice of the Sirens.

2. Allurement, fascination, bewitchment, captivation, attraction, imaginary glory, hocus-pocus, glow, fantastic light.

GLANCE, *n.* 1. Brief look, quick view, transitory glimpse, *coup d'oeil (Fr.),* blink, ken, glint, peek, peep, vision, rapid cast of the eyes.

2. Flash of light, gleam, glitter, beam, flicker, sparkle, shimmer.

3. Rapid oblique movement glancing off after striking, graze, brush, stroke, contact, kiss, lick.

4. Reference in passing, allusion, intimation, hint, insinuation, innuendo, passing mention, implication, suggestion, *soupçon (Fr.).*

GLANCE, *v.* 1. Look quickly, cast the eyes at briefly, catch a glimpse of, cast a brief look at, snatch a glance, look hurriedly, squint, peep, peek, peer, regard hastily, pry, watch for, view, behold, contemplate, observe, witness, scan, see.

2 Go off in an oblique direction from an object struck, dart aside, fly off obliquely, ricochet,

carom, rebound, careen, sweep, brush, lick, kiss, dart, flit, skim, touch, graze.

3. Flash, glint, gleam, glisten, glitter, shine, scintillate, glister, coruscate, reflect.

4. Make passing allusion, allude briefly in passing, hint at, reflect upon, intimate, insinuate, advert, refer to, speak of.

GLAND, *n.* 1. Secreting organ, organ by which certain constituents are separated from the blood for use in the body or for ejection from it, organ by which certain changes are produced in the blood or lymph, secretory, glandule, endocrine organ.

2. Pancreas, kidney, liver, thymus *(in a lamb or calf),* spleen, adrenal, suprarenal capsule, pituitary, carotid, parotid, thyroid, parathyroid, lymph gland, sebaceous gland, sudoriparous gland, sweat gland, lacrimal gland, serous gland, muciparous gland, salivary gland, pineal gland, pyloric gland, mammary gland, seminal gland, prostate, testicle, urethral gland, vaginal gland.

GLARE, *v.* 1. Shine with a strong dazzling light, flare, glitter, glint, dazzle, gleam, glister, glisten, sparkle, coruscate, flame, glow, shine brightly, scintillate, flash, twinkle, radiate, flicker, blaze, shimmer, glimmer.

2. Be intensely bright in color, be vivid, be lustrous, be too brilliantly ornamented, be conspicuous, be ostentatious.

3. Scowl, lower, glower, frown, look with a fierce and piercing stare, look angrily, look black, look threateningly, menace, threaten, goggle.

GLARE, *n.* 1. Brilliant luster, glassy surface, strong dazzling light, flare, glitter, radiance, luminosity, flash, blaze, brightness, radiation, resplendence, effulgence, gloss, shimmer, sheen, gleam, sparkle, glint, coruscation, scintillation, spark, flame, glisten, glance.

2. Showy appearance, showiness, garishness, gaudiness, ostentation, theatricality.

3. Fierce piercing look, glower, scowl, lower, frown, black look, threatening look.

GLARING, *adj.* 1. Dazzling, intense, brilliant, glittering, resplendent, strong, vivid, flaring, piercing, penetrating, bright, deep.

2. Excessively bright, garish, gaudy, showy, gay, ostentatious, florid, flashy, flaunting, tawdry, meretricious, gorgeous, loud.

3. Very conspicuous, open, patent, palpable, overt, flagrant, barefaced, notorious, manifest, extreme, arrant, heinous, audacious, impudent, bold, evident, apparent, shameless, brazen, outrageous, immodest, undisguised, obvious.

GLASS, *n.* 1. Hard brittle transparent substance of silica and silicates, crystal, glazing, crown glass, flint glass.

2. Spectacles, binoculars, eyeglasses, bifocals, lorgnette, louchettes, goggles, specs *(slang),* pince-nez, blinkers, lens, telescope, microscope, spyglass, refractor, opera glass, field-glass, monocle, hourglass, barometer, thermometer, altiscope.

3. Looking glass, mirror, hand mirror, speculum, cheval glass.

4. Glass container for drinking, goblet, beaker, tumbler, chalice, calyx, patella, cup.

GLASSY, *adj.* 1. Vitreous, vitric, crystalline, hyaline, crystal.

2. Transparent, transpicuous, lucid, diaphanous, pellucid, translucent, shimmering, limpid, clear as crystal, gleaming.

GLAUCOUS, *adj.* Light bluish-green, greenish-

blue, sea-green, yellowish-green, cerulean, virescent, olive.

GLAZE, *v.* 1. Produce a vitreous glossy surface on, burnish, furbish, give a gloss to, polish, calender, cover with a smooth lustrous coating, coat with glaze, vitrify.

2. Become glazed, become glassy, become lusterless, grow dim, get a film over.

GLAZE, *n.* Smooth surface, glossy coating, vitreous surface, thin layer of transparency, glazing, enamel, varnish, polish, luster, finish, film, gloss.

GLEAM, *n.* 1. Glow, ray, flash, streak, intermittent stream of light, beam, glimmer, glance, spark, sparkle.

2. Luster, sheen, splendor, effulgence, radiancy, brightness, gleaming, coruscation, glitter, brilliancy.

3. Brief manifestation, slight appearance, flicker.

GLEAM, *v.* Shine, flash, twinkle, flicker, flash, glimmer, glitter, glance, shimmer, glisten, glister, glint, glow, glare, flare, sparkle, coruscate, scintillate, radiate, blink, emit flashes of light.

GLEAN, *v.* 1. Gather grain after the regular reapers, harvest, cull, reap, pick up, scavenge, strip, winnow.

2. Collect little by little, scrape together, accumulate, amass.

GLEBE, *n.* *(Poetic)* Soil, field, turf, earth, sod, ground, clod, land, loam, clay, marl, subsoil, mold, gravel, cledge.

GLEE, *n.* 1. Demonstrative joy, exultation, hilarity, merriment, gayety, mirth, joyousness, jollity, jollification, joviality, jocularity, exhilaration, sportiveness, liveliness, laughter, waggery, cheerfulness, playfulness, sprightliness, ecstasy, festivity, rapture, gladness, delight.

2. Unaccompanied part song for three or more voices, song of interwoven melodies.

GLEEFUL, *adj.* Full of glee, joyous, joyful, merry, glad, exultant, mirthful, jolly, jovial, jocund, elate, happy, gay, light-hearted, cheerful, hilarious, exhilarated, convivial, social, festive.

GLEN, *n.* Secluded and narrow valley, vale, dingle, dale, dell, clough, ravine, bottom, hollow, combe, slade, glade, glen, cove.

GLIB, *adj.* Voluble, fluent, talkative, insincerely nimble of speech, ready of tongue, facile, ready in speech, flippantly smooth, babbling, flowing, smooth-spoken, smooth-tongued, mellifluous, eloquent, bland, oily, suave, easy of manner, unctuous, plausible.

GLIDE, *v.* 1. Move without effort, move smoothly, slide, slip, glissade, skim, float, sail, skate, coast, flow, roll, stream, drift.

2. Pass by gradual change, elapse, roll on, run, steal away, issue, lapse, intervene, proceed, go quietly.

3. Volplane, plane *(colloq.),* drift, hover, soar, climb, zoom.

GLIDE, *n.* Continuous motion, smooth movement, glissade, gliding, lapse, sliding, slip, flight, flowing, drift.

GLIMMER, *v.* Shine unsteadily, flash, twinkle, flicker, glitter, shine faintly, glister, glisten, sparkle, coruscate, scintillate, glow, flare, blink, shimmer, beam, glare.

GLIMMER, *n.* 1. Unsteady beam of light, gleam of faint light, glimmering, ray, scintilla, twinkle, shimmer.

2. Dim perception, glimpse, transitory view, glance, faint inkling, hint, intimation.

GLIMPSE, *n.* 1. Momentary view, brief sight, rapid look, glance, glint, fleeting perception, peep, squint, *coup d'oeil (Fr.),* ken, blink, peek.

2. Vague idea, inkling, faint notion, hint.

GLINT, *n.* Luster, brightness, sheen, glinting brightness, gleaming surface, high polish, shimmer, reflection, gloss, splendor, brilliancy, fulgor, refulgence, effulgence, transplendency, resplendence, luminosity, radiance.

GLISTEN, *v.* Emit a soft scintillating light, shine with a sparkling light, shine with a faint intermittent glow, shimmer, flash fitfully, glitter, sparkle, glint, glister, glimmer, flicker, twinkle, scintillate, coruscate, glow, gleam, beam, radiate.

GLITTER, *v.* 1. Shine with a brilliant light, shine with a sparkling luster, coruscate, scintillate, flash, sparkle, flare, glance, gleam, glister, glisten, glint, twinkle, glimmer, glow, radiate.

2. Make a brilliant show, be striking, be showy, be flamboyant.

GLITTER, *n.* Glittering light, bright luster, splendor, radiance, brilliance, sheen, gleam, shine, glister, sparkle, beaming, coruscation, scintillation, fulgency, refulgence, effulgence, glamour, tinsel, pageantry.

GLOAMING, *n.* Dusk, twilight, eventide, nightfall, fall of evening, crepuscule, going down of the sun, evensong, vespers, close of day, eve, curfew, sunset, sundown, cockshut, bedtime, shades of evening.

GLOAT, *v.* Dwell mentally upon something with intense satisfaction, stare with exultation, look intently, rejoice, exult, triumph, gaze with malignant satisfaction, ogle, vaunt, leer, crow over, contemplate with passionate pleasure, revel, glory over, delight in, take pleasure in, be pleased with, relish.

GLOBATE, *adj.* Shaped like a globe, globated, rotund, round, globose, globular, spheroidal, spherical, bulbous, globous, rounded.

GLOBE, *n.* 1. Sphere on which is depicted a map of the earth or heavens, terrestrial globe, celestial globe, terraqueous globe, terrestrial ball, earth, planet, celestial body, world.

2. Any spherical body, sphere, orb, ball, spheroid, geoid, globoid, ellipsoid, spherule, globule.

3. Lamp shade, glass fish bowl.

GLOBETROTTER, *n.* One who travels widely for sight-seeing, *voyageur sur la terre (Fr.),* voyager, traveler, itinerant, wayfarer, excursionist, tourist, adventurer, wanderer, peregrinator, bird of passage, rover, gadabout, vagrant, beachcomber, nomad, vagabond, gypsy, peripatetic.

GLOBOSE, *adj.* Round as a ball, globelike, globe-shaped, globous, globate, globated, globular, spherical, orbicular, rotundate, rotund, circular, spheroidal, globoid, bulbous.

GLOBULAR, *adj.* Globulous, globe-shaped, globose, globous, globate, globated, spherical, round, rotund, circular, orbicular, orbiculate, pilulous, globoid, cylindroid, bulbous, bell-shaped, campaniform, campanulous, campanulate, campanular, egg-shaped, oviform, ovoid, oval, ovate, elliptical, pear-shaped, pyriform.

GLOBULE, *n.* Small spherical body, spherule, small round particle, little globe, bead, drop, pellet, pill, bubble, bulb, bullet, pea, marble, knob.

GLOOM, *n.* 1. Darkness, obscurity, dimness, gloominess, shadow, shade, cloud, heaviness, cloudiness, dullness, blackness, duskiness, murk, swarthiness, murkiness, dark, dusk, dinginess, opacity, tenebrosity.

2. Low spirits, sadness, melancholy, hypochondria, despondency, depression, dejection, cheerlessness, heaviness of mind, moroseness, the blues, sorrow, hopelessness, pessimism, despair, dolor, grief, distress, doldrums, dumps, mopishness, sullenness, weariness, slough of Despond, disconsolateness, misery, oppression, woe, desolation.

GLOOMY, *adj.* 1. Dark, deeply shaded, obscure, dusky, dim, cloudy, misty, tenebrous, atramentous, fuliginous, Cimmerian, sunless, black, darksome, darkling, swart, swarthy, inky, pitchy, opaque, ebon, nocturnal, dingy, somber, murky, lurid, shadowy, shady, umbrageous, overcast, dull, unilluminated.

2. Cheerless, dismal, dour, grim, funereal, dead, solitary, sad, frowning, sullen, desolate, dreary, comfortless, depressing, heartsick, forlorn, disconsolate, melancholy, despondent, hypochondriacal, unhappy, down in the mouth, in the doldrums, pessimistic, downcast, dejected, crestfallen, disheartened, dispirited, lowspirited, discouraged, heavy-hearted, downhearted, chapfallen, glum, morose, doleful, atrabilious, sorrowful, lugubrious, morbid, lonely, mopish, miserable, saturnine, moody.

GLORIFY, *v.* 1. Magnify with praise, exalt, promote the glory of, extol, celebrate, apotheosize, deify, praise highly, honor greatly, give glory to, laud, canonize, revere, adore, honor, venerate, pay homage to, bow down and worship, sing the praises, hymn, idolize, idolatrize, look up to, elevate, aggrandize, immortalize, enthrone, enshrine, light candles before, burn incense to, consecrate, panegyrize, beatify.

2. Transform into something more splendid, make glorious, add luster to, adorn, brighten, make illustrious, surround with a halo, shed radiance on.

GLORIOLE, *n.* Halo, nimbus, aureola, glory, aura, corona, aureole.

GLORIOUS, *adj.* 1. Brilliantly beautiful, bright, radiant, splendid, resplendent, effulgent, refulgent, brilliant, lustrous, nitid, luminous, shining, sparkling, dazzling, glowing.

2. Full of glory, entitled to great renown, renowned, illustrious, famous, distinguished, celebrated, eminent, far-famed, preeminent, conspicuous, praiseworthy, peerless, *distingué (Fr.),* notable, noted, honored.

3. Conferring glory, excellent, supreme, consummate, sublime, grand, imposing, august, stately, magnificent, solemn, transcendent, majestic.

4. *(Colloq.)* Extremely pleasant, delightful, admirable, ecstatic, marvelous, wondrous, palmy, halcyon.

GLORY, *n.* 1. Exalted praise, honor accorded by common consent, fame, renown, eminence, repute, illustriousness, celebrity, distinction, name, mark, note, figure, éclat, notability, report, vogue, *aura popularis,* popularity, popular favor, esteem, prestige, notoriety.

2. Dignity, stateliness, grandeur, nobleness, gloriousness, exceeding excellence,, exaltation, solemnity, impressiveness, sheer nobility, sublimity, majesty.

3. Pomp, magnificence, state, parade, display, pageantry, show, flourish.

4. Height of prosperity, heyday, prime, zenith, acme, flush, height.

5. Splendor, radiance, brilliancy, brightness, clarity, luster, sheen, effulgence, resplendence, gloss, shimmer, shining, luminosity, glitter, sparkle.

6. Something that makes illustrious, distinguished ornament, object of pride, occasion of pride, boast.

7. Splendor of heaven, celestial happiness, heaven, paradise, Eden, Elysium.

8. Ring of light represented about the head or figure of a heavenly being, halo, nimbus, aureola, corona, aura, aureole.

9. Adoring praise, thanksgiving, gratitude, benediction, benison, blessing, admiration.

GLORY, *v.* Exult with triumph, rejoice proudly, pride oneself, be proud, plume oneself, take pride, pat oneself on the back, take delight, preen oneself, be boastful, boast, vaunt.

GLOSS, *n.* 1. Interlinear note, marginal explanation of an unusual expression in a manuscript text, scholium, commentary, annotation, glossary, comment, interpretation, translation, explanation, elucidation, footnote, exegesis, metaphrase.

2. Luster, sheen, brightness, shimmer, shining, effulgence, splendor, brilliancy, resplendence, radiance, luminousness, refulgency.

3. Polish, glaze, veneer, coat, gloze, varnish.

4. Deceptive appearance, superficial quality, specious representation, speciousness, deceptive show, fair outside, tinsel, paste, scagliola, brummagem.

GLOSS, *v.* 1. Polish, varnish, glaze, veneer, lacquer, japan, enamel, make lustrous, smooth over, give a sheen to.

2 Give a specious appearance to, make plausible, color, explain away, endeavor to excuse, whitewash, cover the defects of, extenuate, apologize for, gloss over, palliate, veil, disguise.

3. Render clear by comments, annotate, comment on, commentate, interpret.

GLOSSARIST, *n.* Annotator, commentator, scholiast, translator, interpreter, expounder, expositor, glossographer, glottologist, glossologist, lexicologist, vocabulist, orismologist, lexicographer, grammarian.

GLOSSARY, *n.* List of basic technical terms in a subject with definitions, dictionary of obscure words, dialectical vocabulary, thesaurus, wordbook, lexicon, clavis, nomenclature, index, *gradus (Lat.)*, concordance, annotation, compilation of marginal notes.

GLOSSY, *adj.* 1. Having a gloss, shiny, lustrous, sheeny, shining, glassy, burnished, polished, glazed, glistening, sleek, smooth, silken, satiny, velvety, elegant, fair.

2. Specious, deceptive, mock, counterfeit, sham, feigned, make-believe, pretended, spurious, pseudo, snide, bogus, fraudulent, meretricious, brummagem, tinsel, factitious, artificial.

GLOVE, *n.* Covering for the hand with a separate sheath for each finger and for the thumb, handwear, gauntlet, mitten, mitt, kids, suedes, mousquetaire.

GLOW, *v.* 1. Emit bright light, be incandescent, shine brightly, gleam, sparkle, glare, glint, glisten, glister, shimmer, flicker, twinkle, flash, scintillate, coruscate, glitter, flare, glance.

2. Burn, blaze, flame, singe, scorch, boil, decoct, kindle.

3. Be hot, flush, blush, feel intensely, be warm, be ardent, be animated, be enthused, be eager, yearn, crimson, change color, mantle, thrill, tingle.

GLOW, *n.* 1. Light emitted by a substance heated to luminosity, incandescence, flame, blaze, white heat, flare, glare, flash, flicker, coruscation, scintillation, shimmer, sparkle, burning.

2. Luminosity, luster, radiation, radiance, phosphorescence, afterglow, effulgence, refulgency, iridescence, splendor, brilliancy.

3. Brightness of color, reddening, vividness, intensity.

4. State of bodily heat, calidity, fever, blush, flush, pyrexia.

5. Warmth of emotion, passion, feeling, ardor, fervor, fervency, vehemence, impetuosity, gusto, eagerness, earnestness, *empressement (Fr.)*, zeal, enthusiasm, ecstasy, thrill, tingling.

GLOWER, *v.* Stare with sullen dislike, look angrily, scowl with discontent, glare, lower, look black, look fierce, frown, sulk, pout.

GLOWING, *adj.* 1. Incandescent, burning, white-hot, candent, luminous, smoldering, flaming, blazing, afire, alight, ablaze, igneous, fiery.

2. Ruddy, flushed, warm in coloring, flame-colored, hectic, blowzy, red-complexioned, red-faced, high-colored, rubicund, florid, erubescent, sanguine, blooming.

3. Thrilling, stirring, fervid, exciting, impressive, heart-moving, soul-stirring, sensational, overpowering, poignant, stimulating.

4. Ardent, impassioned, passionate, vehement, zealous, enthusiastic, eager, earnest, fervent.

GLOZE, *v.* 1. Explain away, cover up, smooth over, apologize, palliate, extenuate, excuse, put a good face upon, mince, varnish, gloss over, whitewash, color, soften, vindicate, exonerate, set right, clear.

2. Humor, flatter, pet, soothe, butter, wheedle, cajole, fawn upon.

GLOZE, *n.* 1. Flattery, adulation, cajolery, blandishment, wheedling, sycophancy, obsequiousness, honeyed words, incense, blarney, buncombe, soft soap, butter, applesauce, flummery, deceit.

2. Gloss, veneer, specious show, plausible covering, pretext, pretense.

GLUE, *v.* Cement with glue, fix firmly, fasten with adhesive, make adhere closely, stick, size, attach with mucilage, paste, agglutinate, gum, lute.

GLUEY, *adj.* Sticky, glutinous, viscid, viscous, cohesive, tenacious, adhering, adhesive, mucilaginous, clinging, tacky.

GLUM, *adj.* Gloomily silent, dejected, moody, down-in-the-dumps, morose, sullen, grumpy, saturnine, gloomy, splenetic, cross, churlish, surly, crabbed, sulky, sour, mopish, grouchy, depressed, crusty, cross-grained, somber, melancholy, pessimistic, cynical, dismal, frowning, glowering, gruff, ill-humored, woebegone, doleful.

GLUT, *v.* 1. Feed to satiety, fill to repletion, gorge, overfeed, gluttonize, cram, stuff, gormandize, overeat, eat one's fill, satiate, raven, gobble up, devour, gulp, bolt, play a good knife and fork, eat out of house and home.

2. Fill to excess, sate, cloy, pall, surfeit, supersaturate, surcharge, load, drug, flood, obstruct, choke up.

GLUT, *n.* 1. Too much, redundance, superabundance, supersaturation, superfluity, nimiety, repletion, *satis superque (Lat.),* more than enough, engorgement, plethora, load, congestion, surfeit, overdose, oversupply, drug, burden, accumulation, excess, surplus.

2. Satiety, saturation, satisfaction, full supply, heart's content, full stomach.

GLUTINOUS, *adj.* Of the nature of glue, viscous, viscid, gluey, gummy, sticky, tenacious, adhesive, smeary, stringy, emplastic, mucilaginous, clammy, albuminous, gelatinous, ropy, tacky, muculent, mucid.

GLUTTON, *n.* One who eats to excess, gourmand, gormandizer, belly-god, cormorant, trencherman, gorger, greedy-gut, crammer, stuffer, gobbler, hog, pig, voracious eater, belly-slave, gourmet, gastronome, epicure, free-liver, excessive indulger, sensualist.

GLUTTONOUS, *adj.* Given to excessive eating, voracious, edacious, gormandizing, swinish, piggish, hoggish, porcine, greedy, ravenous, omnivorous, gross, insatiable, overfed, gorged.

GLUTTONY, *n.* Excess in eating, belly-worship, voraciousness, edacity, voracity, omnivorousness, ravenousness, worship of the palate, gourmandism, gulosity, greed, gormandizing, hoggishness, piggishness, polyphagia *(Med.),* rapacity, gastronomy, epicureanism, greed, high living, bellycheer.

GNAR, *v.* Snarl, growl, gnarr, grumble, murmur, gnarl, complain.

GNARL, *n.* Knotty protuberance *(on a tree),* gnarled lump, hump, hunch, bunch, contortion, twist, knot, snag, protrusion, swelling, gibbosity.

GNARLED, *adj.* 1. *(Of trees)* Full of gnarls, contorted, cross-grained, full of knots, gnarly, knotted, knotty, snaggy, twisted, distorted, nodular.

2. *(Of persons)* Rugged, weatherbeaten, rugous, wrinkled, leathery, rugose.

3. Perverse, cantankerous, captious, peevish, splenetic, waspish, crabbed.

GNASH, *v.* Bite with grinding teeth, strike the teeth together, grind.

GNAW, *v.* 1. Bite persistently, crunch, chew, champ, keep biting, nibble at, masticate, peck, nibble, mumble, graze, browse, crop, munch, ruminate.

2. Remove by persistent biting, eat away, erode, corrode, consume, wear away, induce attrition, exhaust, incapacitate, waste away.

3. Consume with passion, rankle, distress, torment, tantalize, fret, grate, gall, chafe, wrack, harrow.

GNOME, *n.* 1. Diminutive being fabled to inhabit the interior of the earth and to guard the treasures there, shriveled little old man, troll, goblin, imp, sprite, demon, dwarf, elf, fairy, fay, sylph, pixie, brownie, nix, nixie, jinnee, genie, banshee, kobold.

2. Short pithy expression of a general truth, aphorism, saw, maxim, proverb, adage, dictum, saying, apothegm, byword, precept.

GO, *v.* 1. Move, proceed, wend, pass along, advance, go on, stir, make progress, repair, pass from point to point, press onward, make headway, forge ahead, get on, gain ground.

2. Walk, travel, journey, fare, ride, extravagate, go on foot, run, amble, tramp, canter, trot, march, trudge, tread, stalk, peregrinate, tour,

trek, migrate, flit, roam, rove, wander, range, jaunt, prowl, stray, saunter, stroll, ramble, perambulate, gad, straggle, meander, pace, tread, plod, traipse, hike, stride, jog on, shuffle on, bend one's steps, track, promenade, strut, bowl, hie to, betake oneself to, resort to.

3. Move away, move out, depart, set out, disappear, go away, decamp, vamoose, steal away, withdraw, abandon, scram, abscond, make off, steal off, take French leave, show a light pair of heels, give leg bail, make off with oneself, bolt, sneak off, slip away, fly, flee, leave, take one's departure, issue, start, sally forth, take wing, take flight, flit.

4. Operate, be in motion, act, work, run, function, perform.

5. Reach, lead, extend, stretch to, go to, spread to.

6. Elapse, pass, lapse, intervene, flow, slip, glide, slide, drag, crawl, go by, expire, pass by.

7. Vanish, fade, disappear, evanesce, melt away, leave no trace, be gone, pass out of sight, be lost to sight, perish, pass away, cease, fall, die, be lost, be ended, recede, go back, regress, ebb, shrink, withdraw, retire.

8. Contribute to a result, conduce, tend, concur, be of use, have effect, be of service, promote, subserve, forward, advance, serve to, redound, bear a part, be helpful, minister, conspire, cooperate, combine in.

9. Turn out, eventuate, fare, result, come to pass, fall out, take place, terminate.

10. Harmonize, jibe, be compatible, be suited, agree, accord, blend, conform with, tally, comport.

11. Begin, come into action, be about, be destined, be on the point, be intending.

12. Become, grow, get, change to, wax, be converted into, turn to, come to be, assume another state.

13. Be reckoned, be known, be considered, be habitually, be esteemed, be phrased, be expressed, be stated.

14. Tolerate, endure, bear, put up with, stand, brook, abide, bear with, take easily, submit to, take patiently, stomach, withstand, swallow, pocket, permit, accept, take.

15. Wager, risk, hazard, afford, stake, bet, pledge, gamble, plunge.

GO, *n.* 1. Energy, stamina, spirit, animation, verve, vim, pep, endurance, power, go-ahead, perseverance, vigor, intensity, keenness, force, strength, elasticity, high pressure, live wire, mettle, backbone, vivacity, dash, élan, life, enterprise.

2. *(Colloq.)* A try at something, attempt, trial, experiment, endeavor, effort, essay, venture, whirl.

3. Success, something that goes well, lucky hit, prosperous issue, triumph, victory, master stroke, good fortune, ten-strike, good luck, prosperity.

4. Bargain, deal, compact, agreement, covenant, transaction, concordat, wager, contract.

5. Action, business, incident, chance, turn, happening, affair, event, occurrence, circumstance, case, state of facts, doings.

6. Fad, fashion, rage, the thing, vogue, mode, custom, style, prevailing taste, *dernier cri,* mania, furore, craze, fancy, whim, hobby, crotchet, quirk, partiality, blind side, infatuation.

GO, *interj.* Be off, begone, get you gone, get along with you, off with you, avaunt, go along, go away, go your way, away, away with, go about your business, aroynt, beat it, get out, scram, vamoose, on your way with you.

GO ABOUT, 1. Undertake, set about, set oneself about, endeavor, attempt, tackle, take on, essay, try, experiment, strive, tempt, venture, speculate, take a chance, try one's hand, feel one's way, grope one's way, try hard, make a bold push, fall to work, take in hand.

2. *(Naut.)* Change the course by veering, tack, wear, sheer, alter one's course, heel, bear off, yaw, gybe, swerve, curve, bend, turn.

GOAD, *v.* 1. Prick with a goad, drive by a stick with a pointed end, whip, flog.

2. Incite, urge, instigate, stimulate, spur, impel, stir up, arouse, prod, set on, propel, egg on, hurry on, press.

3. Irritate, harass, annoy, badger, needle, worry, inflame, sting, torment, vex, tease.

GOAD, *n.* 1. Stick with a pointed end for driving cattle, prick, point, rowel.

2. Stimulus, incentive, spur, fillip, provocative, whet, incitement, stimulant, driving motive, inducement, instigation, encouragement.

GO AHEAD 1. Go before, go in the van, go in advance, precede, forerun, usher in, herald, introduce, head, take the lead, lead the way.

2. Proceed, push on, advance, press forward, go on, progress, get on, get along, gain ground, jog on, press ahead, press onwards, make one's way, make headway, elbow one's way, push one's way, make rapid strides, shoot ahead, make up leeway.

3. Be active, busy oneself, stir about, stir one's stumps, rouse oneself, stir oneself, peg away, hasten, bustle, fuss, kick up a dust.

GOAL, *n.* That toward which effort is directed, terminal point in a contest, post set to bound a race, mark, mete, home, bound, limit, bourne, butt, terminus, terminal, destination, object, target, objective, design, height of one's ambition, high-water mark, purpose, aim, end, intention.

GOAT, *n.* 1. Agile hollow-horned ruminant animal of genus *Capra,* billy-goat, nanny-goat, kid, buck, Rocky Mountain goat, *Oreamnos montanus.*

2. *(Slang)* Scapegoat, butt of a joke, laughingstock.

3. Lecher, roué, libidinous man, satyr, voluptuary, libertine, rake, debauchee, fornicator, seducer, whoremonger, adulterer.

GOATISH, *adj.* 1. Like a goat, goatlike.

2. Lascivious, wanton, lecherous, licentious, libidinous, lustful, lewd, salacious, voluptuous, lickerish, prurient, concupiscent, carnal, ruttish, erotic, obscene.

GO BACK ON Fail to keep one's word, fail someone, let someone down, give up, desert, abandon, forsake, leave in the lurch, back out of, back down from, go back on one's word, be apostate, beat a retreat, defect from a bargain, renounce, be traitorous, be unfaithful, withdraw from, take leave of, quit, bid a long farewell, have done with, abjure, forego, drop, write off, wash one's hands of, drop all idea of, discard, nolle-pros *(Law).*

GOBBLE, *v.* 1. Make the throaty cry of a turkey cock, gaggle, caw, cackle.

2. Swallow hastily in large pieces, bolt down, gulp, eat greedily, ingurgitate, devour, engorge, gorge, raven, snap up, despatch, fall to, tuck in, champ, munch, cranch, crunch, gormandize, cram, stuff, eat out of house and home, play a good knife and fork.

GOBBLER, *n.* 1. Gallinaceous bird of the genus

Meleagris gallopavo (Greek), turkey-cock, male turkey.

2. Glutton, gormandizer, gourmand, belly-god, cormorant, gorger, greedy-gut, crammer, stuffer, voracious eater, belly-slave.

GO BETWEEN Intervene, intercede, interpose, mediate, arbitrate, referee, mediatize, step in, negotiate, *magnas componere lites (Lat.),* be instrumental, pull the strings.

GO-BETWEEN, *n.* One who acts as agent between persons, interagent, medium, vehicle, intermediary, minister, friend at court, intervener, middleman, broker, negotiator, referee, arbiter, umpire, factor, dealer, procurer, pimp, pander.

GO BEYOND Exceed, surpass, outstrip, outstep, outrival, outdo, beat hollow, distance, leave in the rear, go one better, throw into the shade, shoot ahead of, gain upon, steal a march on, transcend, overstep, transgress, trespass, encroach, infringe, intrude, trench upon, intrench on, stretch a point, pass the Rubicon.

GOBLET, *n.* Drinking glass with a foot and stem, chalice, beaker, bowl-shaped drinking vessel, cup, tumbler, wineglass, tass, rummer, crystal.

GOBLIN, *n.* Grotesque mischievous sprite, imaginary being malevolent to man, hobgoblin, elf, gnome, gremlin, spectre, demon, bogy, bogeyman, evil spirit, playful and mischievous fay, troll, nix, nixie, bugbear, bogle, fairy, ogre, jinnee, genie, brownie.

GOD, *n.* 1. Male deity presiding over some portion of worldly affairs, divinity, divine being, superhuman being, spirit, numen, power, godling, tutelary, *lar familiaris (Lat.),* Olympian, Valhallan.

2. Image of a deity, idol, worshiped image, icon, eikon.

3. The Supreme Arbiter, Creator and Ruler of the Universe, The Fashioner, Artificer of the Universe, The Higher Power, The Almighty, King of Kings, The Supreme Being, Author of all things, First Cause, Sovereign of the Universe, The Most High, The Supreme Goodness, The Eternal and Infinite Spirit, The Omnipotent, The Maker, The Godhead, Ruler of Heaven and Earth, God the Father, The Trinity, Jehovah, The Lord, The Absolute, I AM, The All-Father, Lord of Lords, The All-wise, The Omniscient, The All-knowing, The All-merciful, Triune God.

GODDESS, *n.* 1. Female deity.

2. Good woman, madonna, virgin, Mother of God.

3. Adored woman, inamorata, angel, idol, ladylove, darling, sweetheart.

GODHEAD, *n.* 1. Divinity, Deity, Godship, Omnipotence, Providence, Omniscience, divineness.

2. The Supreme Being, essential being of God.

GODLESS, *adj.* 1. Acknowledging no God, atheistical, agnostic, nullifidian, freethinking.

2. Profane, irreligious, ungodly, wicked, impious, heathen, blasphemous, sacrilegious, unrighteous, impenitent, unhallowed, unsanctified.

GODLIKE, *adj.* Befitting a God, supernal, preëminently good, heavenly, celestial, divine, heaven-born, seraphic, angelic, saintlike, peerless, matchless, exemplary, beyond all praise.

GODLY, *adj.* Conforming to God's laws, pious, God-fearing, devout, heavenly-minded, saintly, holy, religious, righteous, reverent, devoted, pure in heart, spiritual, holy, pietistic, solemn, seraphic, believing, faithful, sanctified, inspired, converted, consecrated, regenerated, unearthly, sacred, humble, hallowed.

GODSEND, *n.* Something unexpected but particularly welcome and timely, unexpected gift, windfall, piece of good fortune, stroke of fortune, piece of good luck, boon, blessing, treasure-trove, lucky find, smile of fortune, run of luck, good turn, benison.

GOGGLE, *v.* Roll the eyes, squint, ogle, glare, stare, cock the eye, look askance, strain one's eyes, leer, look hard at.

GOGGLE, *n.* 1. Goggling look, strained look, squint, owlish look, stare, ogle, glare, leer.

2. *(Pl.)* Spectacles devised to protect the eyes from injury, eyeglasses, glasses, barnacles, giglamps, pince-nez, lorgnettes, sun glasses.

GO HALVES Share equally, go Dutch treat, pay one's own way, divide expenses, split the check.

GO HARD WITH Have serious consequences for, be disastrous to, put to one's shifts, try one, pose, perplex, nonplus, bother, run one hard, try one's patience, go against the grain, put one out, lead a pretty dance.

GO IN FOR Make a thing one's particular interest, go for, engage in, ride one's hobby, court, take to, play with, bend one's course.

GOINGS ON Conduct, actions, behavior, deportment, comportment, manners, deeds, doings, performance, to-do.

GOLD, *n.* 1. Highly malleable and ductile precious yellow metal free from liability to rust, aurum *(Chem.),* Au *(Chem. symbol),* bullion, nugget, ingot, bar.

2. Money, wealth, riches, fortune, affluence, opulence, capital, treasure, mint of money, mine of wealth, bonanza, El Dorado, Pactolus, Golconda, purse of Fortunatus, Midas' touch.

GOLDEN, *adj.* 1. Gold-colored, gold, aureate, gilt, gilded, yellow, resplendent, shining, bright, splendid, xanthous, auriferous.

2. Resembling gold in value, precious, costly, of great price, very valuable, of great worth, priceless, high-priced, expensive, rich.

3. Favorable, opportune, timely, propitious, auspicious, promising, seasonable, "rosy," well-disposed.

4. Happy, halcyon, palmy, blest, glorious, delightful, flourishing, joyous, beatific.

GOLDSMITH, *n.* One who makes and sells articles of gold, jeweler, *orfèvre (Fr.), bijoutier (Fr.).*

GONFALON, *n.* Banner suspended from a crossbar, gonfanon, ensign, flag, standard, pennon, pennant, bandrol, colors, oriflamme, labarum, jack, blue peter, union jack, tricolor, stars and stripes, Jolly Roger, bunting.

GONG, *n.* Oriental bronze disc to be struck with a soft-headed stick, saucer-shaped bell sounded by a hammer, cymbal, peal of bells, carillon.

GOOD, *adj.* 1. Morally excellent, virtuous, righteous, conscientious, pure, moral, pious, devout, religious, dutiful, worthy, honorable, honest, upright, decorous, reliable, exemplary, chaste, innocent, untainted, unsullied, praiseworthy, wholesome.

2. Satisfactory in quality, meritorious, commendable, genuine, sterling, sound, admirable, valuable, excellent, precious, capital, valid, choice, first-rate, first-class, crack, top-hole, tiptop, superfine, select, best, golden, gilt-edged, priceless.

3. Satisfactory for the purpose, serviceable,

useful, beneficial, advantageous, profitable, favorable, competent, reliable, safe, fortunate, auspicious, propitious, commendable.

4. Fit, suitable, right, qualified, proper, adequate, well-adapted, convenient, becoming, appropriate, deserving, proficient, adroit, adapted, skillful, thorough, excellent, admirable, capable, clever, efficient.

5. Kind, gracious, kindhearted, benign, kindly, friendly, benevolent, beneficent, considerate, sympathetic, humane, well-disposed, obliging, complaisant, altruistic, indulgent, well-behaved, well-mannered, proper, seemly.

6. Companionable, agreeable, pleasant, genial, sunny, cheerful, lively, social, sociable, convivial.

7. Considerable, substantial, large, tidy, sizable, ample, full, adequate, fairly great, sufficient.

GOOD, *n.* 1. Advantage, benefit, gain, profit, worth, boon, favor, good turn, good fortune, blessing, windfall, prize, godsend, benison, happiness, service, improvement, behalf, behoof, interest, weal, welfare, prosperity, well-being, enjoyment.

2. Virtue, goodness, moral qualities, righteousness, rectitude, character, excellence, worth, merit, kindness.

3. *(Pl.)* Movable effects, possessions, personal chattels, property, movables, paraphernalia, appurtenances, gear, things, traps, trappings.

4. *(Pl.)* Articles of trade, wares, stock, commodities, stock in trade, merchandise, freight.

5. Textile material, cloth, dry goods, fabrics, stuffs, textiles, materials, woven goods.

GOOD BREEDING Good manners, civility, politeness, urbanity, courtesy, affability, suavity, polish, gentility, refinement, cultivation, chivalry, gallantry, good behavior, *bienséance (Fr.),* comity, presence, culture, amenity, *prévenance (Fr.),* savoir-faire, gentlemanliness, propriety, decorum, dictates of society, etiquette, formality.

GOOD-BY, *n. or interj.* Farewell, Godspeed, valediction, parting, valedictory, adieu, au revoir, *a rivederci (It.),* hasta luego *(Sp.),* hasta mañana *(Sp.),* adiós *(Sp.),* addio *(It.),* auf Wiedersehen *(Ger.),* sayonara *(Jap.),* Lebwohl *(Ger.).*

GOOD FELLOWSHIP Sociability, friendship, camaraderie, cup that cheers, social intercourse, companionship, comradeship, clubbism, esprit de corps, conviviality, company, joviality, jollity, festivity, *savoir-vivre (Fr.),* festive board, merrymaking, loving cup, hospitality, cheer, heartiness.

GOOD-FOR-NOTHING, *n.* Worthless fellow, scapegrace, black sheep, do-little, *vaurien (Fr.), Taugenichts (Ger.),* ne'er-do-well, *mauvais sujet (Fr.),* idle fellow, scamp, careless fellow, loafer, lounger, vagabond, vagrant, "bum."

GOOD FORTUNE Good luck, success, prosperity, well-being, smiles of fortune, blessings, godsend, run of luck, sunny side of the street, fair weather, fair wind, halcyon days, piping times, high tide, full dinner pail, chicken in every pot, two cars in every garage, roaring trade, affluence, Saturnian age, golden age, bed of roses, milk and honey, fat of the land, loaves and fishes, fleshpots of Egypt.

GOOD GRACES Favor, friendship, goodwill, amity, affection, favoritism, partiality, welcomeness, warm friendship, good understanding, intimacy.

GOOD HEED Due caution, great care, solicitous attention, attentiveness, lookout, solicitude, heedfulness, scruple, watchfulness, vigilance, surveillance, watch and ward, *l'oeil du maître (Fr.).*

GOOD HUMOR Amiable mood, geniality, high spirits, good spirits, cheerfulness, gayety, light heart, high glee, flow of spirits, sunshine of the mind, *gaieté de coeur (Fr.),* affability, cheer, benignity, good nature, pleasantry, amiability, jollity, jocularity, joyousness, jocundity, joviality, levity, merriment, mirth, exhilaration, hilarity, rejoicing, heyday, optimism, alacrity, vivacity, *bon naturel (Fr.), allégresse (Fr.), l'allegro (It.).*

GOOD-HUMORED, *adj.* Showing a pleasant mood, cheerful, happy, cheery, of good cheer, smiling, blithe, buoyant, blithesome, in good spirits, in high feather, gay, *allegro (It.),* lighthearted, sparkling, effervescent, vivacious, breezy, jaunty, lively, bright, debonair, free and easy, good-natured, pleasant, good-tempered, mellow, of placid temper, amiable, affable, jovial, genial, merry, joyful, joyous, jocund, jolly, jocose, jocular, mirthful, waggish, sportive, frisky, playful, frolicsome, sunny, palmy.

GOOD-LOOKING, *adj.* Of good appearance, personable, handsome, attractive, well-favored, goodly, well-formed, well-proportioned, well-made, pleasing, bonny, fair, charming, graceful, elegant, seemly, dapper, jaunty, natty, spruce, neat, ruddy-cheeked, bright-eyed, rosy-cheeked, sleek, glossy, glowing, imposing, majestic, *fait à peindre (Fr.),* enchanting, smooth, well-featured, fascinating, captivating, intriguing, inviting, irresistible.

GOOD LUCK Good fortune, run of luck, palmy days, halcyon days, high tide, piping times, prosperity, welfare, success, well-being, affluence, windfall, bonanza, gold mine, roaring trade, full dinner pail, chicken in every pot, two cars in every garage, smiles of fortune, godsend, blessings, golden times, golden age, bed of roses, milk and honey, fat of the land, favorable issue, profit, trump card, prize, coup, hit, go, feather in one's cap.

GOODLY, *adj.* 1. Of good appearance, fine-appearing, good-looking, comely, beautiful, pleasing, bonny, graceful, personable, handsome, well-favored, fair, seemly.
2. Of a good quality, excellent, agreeable, pleasant, desirable, admirable, estimable, first-rate, capital, choice.
3. Of good size or amount, considerable, substantial, tidy, sizable, quite large, ample, immense.

GOOD NATURE Pleasant disposition, cheerful nature, amiability, kindheartedness, kindness, kindliness, fellow feeling, bonhomie, tenderness, warm-heartedness, good will, goodness of heart, sympathy, humanity, brotherly love, good feeling, loving-kindness, unselfishness, benevolence, friendship, consideration, complaisance, affability, geniality.

GOOD-NATURED, *adj.* Having a pleasant disposition, showing a complaisant mood, good-tempered, good-humored, cordial, amiable, kindly, pleasant, jovial, cordial, agreeable, complaisant, obliging, genial, affable, benevolent, kind, well-meaning, accommodating, bland, gracious, considerate, large-hearted, indulgent, helpful, tender-hearted, kindhearted, sympathetic, generous, liberal, unselfish, humane, bountiful, altruistic, beneficent.

GOODNESS, *n.* 1. Moral excellence, integrity, virtue, rectitude, probity, righteousness, upright-

ness, morality, honesty, honorableness, principle, purity, honor, chastity, virginity.
2. Excellence of quality, value, merit, worth, desert, worthiness, credit, account, importance.
3. Kindly feeling, kindness, good will, benevolence, beneficence, generosity, liberality, charitableness, humanity, humaneness, benignity, loving-kindness.
4. Superiority, superexcellence, perfection, masterpiece, *chef-d'oeuvre (Fr.),* supereminence.
5. Best part of anything, essence, quintessence, strength, cream, pick, flower, prime, A-1, nonpareil, gem of the first water, salt of the earth, pillar of the church, flower of the flock, *crème de la crème (Fr.), rara avis (Lat.),* rare bird, pearl, jewel, one in a thousand, treasure.

GOOD OFFICES Assistance, aid, mediation, help, intervention, mediatorship, intercession, interposition, arbitration, parley, negotiation, peace offering, diplomacy, flag of truce, good works, beneficence, generosity, acts of kindness, kind offices, good turn, good treatment.

GOOD OPINION Esteem, estimation, favorable opinion, approbation, regard, nod of approval, golden opinion, admiration, repute, credit, kudos, commendation, laudation, good word, meed of praise, eulogy, panegyric, applause, plaudit, acclamation, blurb, high repute, reputation, prestige, name to conjure with, popularity, *aura popularis (Lat.), succès d'estime (Fr.),* talk of the town, toast of the town, honor, illustriousness, luster, vogue, celebrity, notability.

GOODS, *n.* 1. Property, furniture, effects, chattels, movables, personal estate, personalty, possessions, land, ground, assets, wealth, belongings, resources, means, things, gear, traps, paraphernalia.
2. Cargo, baggage, luggage, freight, mails, consignment.
3. Wares, stock, commodities, merchandise, stock in trade, appurtenances, articles, produce, staples.

GOOD WILL, *n.* 1. Friendly disposition, benevolence, good nature, kindness, favor, amity, countenance, grace, indulgence, charity, philanthropy, unselfish turn, good wishes, kindliness, loving-kindness, brotherly love, benignity, fellow feeling, humanity, bonhomie, goodness of heart, tenderness, amiability, patronage, brotherhood, love, affection, respect.
2. Willingness, willing mind, voluntariness, cordiality, geniality, alacrity, earnestness, readiness, ardor, heartiness, zeal, eagerness, enthusiasm, forwardness.

GOODY-GOODY, *adj.* Affecting goodness, sentimentally good, righteous, moral, pious, sanctimonious, hypocritically devout.

GO OFF 1. Go away, go to a distance, depart, be off, take one's departure, issue forth, set out, go forth, sally forth, take wing, flit, fly, decamp, abscond, take leave, disappear, vacate, withdraw, quit, leave.
2. Explode, detonate, fulminate, let off, let fly, be discharged, blow up, fulgurate, flash, flare, deflagrate, crack, burst, crash, thunder, rumble.
3. Die, pass away, perish, expire, breathe one's last, depart this life, go West, decease, shuffle off this mortal coil, take one's last sleep, pay the debt to Nature, pop off, kick the bucket *(slang),* give up the ghost.
4. Deteriorate, degenerate, fall off, wither, shrivel, fade, run to seed, rot, molder, decay, rankle, go bad, decline, droop, retrograde.

GO ON 1. Continue, last, endure, keep on, persist, hold out, persevere, remain, stay, abide, run, take time, occupy time, hold on, carry on, stick to.

2. Advance, proceed, move forward, go ahead, progress, get along, make progress, gain ground, jog on, press onwards, step forward, make one's way, make headway, make strides, make advances, shoot ahead.

3. Manage, do, handle, hold on, succeed, put over, make a go of, contrive to, come off well.

4. Behave, act, carry on, conduct oneself, acquit oneself, deport oneself.

GOOSE, n. 1. Long-necked web-footed bird of the family *Anatidae, Anser, Branta, Chen.*

2. Tailor's smoothing iron with a curved handle, flatiron.

3. Fool, simpleton, dunce, oaf, moron, numskull, witling, halfwit, dupe, gull, ignoramus, lout, donkey, jackass, loon, nincompoop, dunderhead, blockhead.

GO OUT 1. Go forth, issue forth, egress, emerge, pass out of, emanate, migrate, find vent.

2. Go to social affairs, go out of doors, go abroad, seek entertainment away from home.

3. Cease, come to a standstill, come to a full stop, die away, peter out, wear away, wear off, pass away, be at an end.

4. Be extinguished, expire, become extinct, be quenched, be put out, be doused *(colloq.).*

GO OVER 1. Change sides, pass over, be apostate, defect, apostatize, rat, be a deserter, betray, forswear, jilt, break one's word, sell oneself to the enemy.

2. Penetrate, permeate, thread, enfilade, go through, pass over, cut across, cross, ford, make a passage.

3. Look over, inquire, seek, look for, scan, reconnoitre, sound, explore, ransack, rummage, peer, pry, look through, spy, overhaul, investigate, examine, study, look at, review.

4. Read cursorily, run quickly over, peruse, scrutinize, study, inspect.

5. Repeat, iterate, reiterate, do again, rehearse, recite, tell over.

GORE, n. 1. Clotted blood, shed blood, bloodshed, effusion of blood, carnage, slaughter, butchery, battue.

2. Triangular piece of cloth, insert in a garment to give greater width, gusset.

GORE, v. Pierce with the horns, stab with the tusks, horn, impale, spear, spike, transpierce, pink, spit, lance, puncture, prick, stick, penetrate, hook, poke, gouge, riddle.

GORGE, n. 1. Narrow cleft with steep rocky walls and a stream running through, deep narrow pass, defile, ravine, gully, canyon, abyss, clough, gap, mountain valley, vale, dale, glen, dell, dingle, hollow, bottom, basin, abyss, cavity, crevasse, abysm, chasm, *couloir (Fr.),* gulch, notch, gulf.

2. Throat, esophagus, gullet, muzzle, mouth, orifice.

3. Strong disgust, repulsion, revulsion, nausea.

GORGE, v. Swallow greedily, eat heartily, devour, bolt, gulp, gobble, raven, cram, stuff with food, fill to repletion, surfeit, fill full, satiate, glut, gormandize, sate, gluttonize, overeat, indulge, eat one's fill, play a good knife and fork, eat out of house and home.

GORGEOUS, adj. Splendid in appearance, magnificent, elegant, superb, sumptuous, grand, rich, fine, resplendent, brilliant, bright, dazzling, glit-

tering, showy, shining, princely, florid, august, stately, sublime, imposing, pompous, flamboyant, surpassing, impressive, gaudy, costly, attractive, splendrous, radiant.

GORGON, n. 1. *(Gk. Myth.)* One of three sisters whose heads were covered with snakes instead of hair and whose glance turned the beholder to stone, Medusa, Euryale, Stheno.

2. Hobgoblin, bugaboo, *bête noire (Fr.),* bugbear, scarecrow, demon, daymare, nightmare, mormo, ogre, raw head and bloody bones, frightful object, fright, spectre, terrible creature.

3. Terrible woman, shrew, harridan, vixen, termagant, Amazon, virago, hag, beldam, scold, turbulent woman.

GORGONIAN, adj. Gorgon-like, snaky-haired, Medusan, horrible, paralyzing, petrifying, frightful, terrific, terrible, alarming, redoubtable, formidable, fearful, fearsome, dreadful, fell, dire, ghastly, revolting, repulsive.

GORMANDIZE, v. Eat like a glutton, gluttonize, eat greedily, devour, gorge ravenously, stuff, cram, eat richly, gastronomize, play a good knife and fork.

GORY, adj. Stained with gore, bloody, bloodsoaked, bloodstained, ensanguined, cruentous, sanguinary, sanguinolent, bloodthirsty, redhanded, sanguineous.

GOSPEL, n. 1. Body of doctrine taught by Christ and the apostles, Christianity, revelation by Christ, divine revelation, Christian religion, glad tidings of salvation and the kingdom of God, story of Christ's life and teachings as contained in the first four books of the New Testament, scripture.

2. Something regarded as true and implicitly believed, doctrine of prime importance, principle of action, creed, evangel, credo.

3. Truth, certainty, verity, the whole truth and nothing but the truth, *nuda veritas (Lat.).*

GOSSAMER, n. 1. Floating spider's web, fine filmy web, cobweb, thread, filament, fiber, tendril, feather, down, thistledown, flue, straw.

2. Delicate variety of gauze, thin light fabric, chiffon, tissue.

GOSSAMERY, adj. Filmy, fine, delicate, thin, light, unsubstantial, cobwebby, flimsy, sleazy, transparent, diaphanous, silken, sheer, see-through.

GOSSIP, n. 1. Newsmongering about the affairs of others, whispering gallery, hearsay, rumor, scandal, news, groundless rumor, small talk, prattle, prate, light familiar talk, idle personal talk, clack, tattle, chat, chit, chitchat, grapevine, report, *oui-dire (Fr.),* tittle-tattle, cackle, loquacity, twaddle, comment, babble.

2. Person given to idle tattling, newsmonger, gossipmonger, tattletale, talebearer, busybody, idle talker, sticky-beak *(slang),* long-nose *(slang),* quidnunc, rumormonger, eavesdropper, tattler, scandalmonger, informer, telltale, chatterer, babbler, gadabout, blatherskite, flibbertigibbet, meddler, snoop, snooper, Paul Pry, magpie, chatterbox.

GOSSIP, v. Talk idly about other people's affairs, newsmonger, scandalmonger, gossipmonger, go about tattling, repeat like a gossip, tittle, gabble, prattle, prate, clack, chat, cackle, twaddle, report, confabulate, snoop, pry, peep, take an unwarranted interest in the affairs of others.

GOTHIC, adj. Grotesque, barbarous, barbaric, medieval, rude, antique, horrible, macabre.

GO THROUGH, v. 1. Accomplish, execute, carry

out, complete, do, get through, finish, work out, achieve, effect, compass, consummate, perfect, hammer out, dispatch, polish off.

2. Endure, suffer, put up with, bear with, tolerate, brook, abide, stand, experience, undergo, support, brave, encounter, pass through, meet, find, taste, meet with, be one's lot, fall to the lot of.

3. Have passage, penetrate, cut across, force one's way, thread one's way, make one's way, worm one's way, cross, overpass, traverse, go over, proceed across, thread, ford, permeate, perforate.

GOURD, *n.* 1. Cucurbitaceous plant, *Lagenaria Siceraria,* bottle gourd, calabash, melon, squash, pumpkin, cucumber, muskmelon, watermelon.

2. Dried and excavated gourd shell used as a bottle, cup, dipper, bowl, flask.

GOURMAND, *n.* 1. One fond of good eating, gormand, glutton, gormandizer, greedy-gut, excessive eater, belly-slave, belly-god, cormorant, pig, hog.

2. High liver, Sybarite, voluptuary, man of pleasure, epicurean, sensualist, hedonist, libertine.

GOURMET, *n.* Connoisseur in the delicacies of the table, epicure, gastronome, *bon vivant (Fr.),* Deipnosophist, cultivator of the palate, refined feeder.

GOVERN, *v.* 1. Rule by right of authority, exercise authority, bear sway, have control, reign, wield the scepter, occupy the throne, wear the crown, assume the command.

2. Exercise the function of government, have predominating influence, supervise, have charge of, have the direction of, administer the laws of, regulate, manage, conduct, superintend, oversee, preside over, be at the helm, have jurisdiction over, head, lead, direct, guide, steer, exercise a directing influence over, pilot, pull the strings, be in the chair, hold the portfolio, pull the stroke oar.

3. Hold in check, hold the reins, restrain, bridle, curb, control, sway, command, control, order, dominate, boss, rule the roost, discipline, check, hold in hand, keep under, keep in leading strings, hold in the hollow of one's hand, wear the breeches, play first fiddle.

GOVERNABLE, *adj.* Manageable, controllable, docile, tractable, teachable, amenable, submissive, pliant, tame, domesticated, broken, yielding.

GOVERNESS, *n.* Woman who directs the education of children in their own homes, woman teacher in private household, gouvernante, duenna, tutoress, instructress, mistress, nurse, *bonne (Fr.),* ayah, amah.

GOVERNMENT, *n.* 1. Authoritative direction and restraint over the actions of men in a society or state, direction of the affairs of a state, system of rule by which a state is governed, political rule, political administration, regulation, management, rulership, sway, dominion, guidance, control, command, conduct, autonomy, discipline, law, authority, stewardship, ministry, superintendence, supervision, surveillance, order, charge, statesmanship, statecraft, state management, reins of government, lease of power, jurisdiction, dictation, domination.

2. Executive power, governing body of persons in a state, body of executive officers, ruling power, administration, seat, chair, portfolio, powers that be, regency, ministry, cabinet.

3. Form of sovereignty, state, commonwealth,

body politic, polity, republic, constitution, empire, regime.

GOVERNOR, *n.* 1. Executive head of a state, one charged with the control of a state or society, chief magistrate, regent, dignitary, viceroy, ruler, chief, head, president, director, commandant, potentate, lord, king, emperor, sovereign, monarch, overlord, autocrat, majesty, prefect, consul, proconsul, functionary, administrator, statemonger, statesman.

2. Director, manager, superintendent, supervisor, overseer, master, comptroller, arbiter, rector, monitor, taskmaster, head man.

3. *(Brit.)* Tutor, instructor, guardian, adviser, don, disciplinarian, trainer, teacher, institutor, master, coach.

4. *(Brit.)* One's father, pater, old man.

GOWN, *n.* 1. Dress, robe, garment, frock, costume.

2. Loose flowing outer garment worn as distinctive of office or profession, garb, canonicals, cassock, soutane, academicals, silk.

GRAB, *v.* 1. Snatch suddenly and eagerly, seize violently, grip, clutch, grasp, pluck, nab, gripe, clasp, hold, lay hold of, tackle, bag, embrace, hook, capture, collar, catch, secure, pocket, apprehend, arrest, run away with, kidnap, abduct, abstract, take away, take by storm.

2. Take illegal possession of, seize unscrupulously, commandeer, expropriate, possess oneself of, appropriate, confiscate, usurp, help oneself to, impound, intercept, make free with, dispossess, deprive of, sequestrate, extort, bleed, fleece, strip, despoil, plunder, loot, pillage, sack, strip, rifle, pilfer, purloin, steal, filch.

GRACE, *n.* 1. Attractive endowment, accomplishment, refinement, charm, polish, elegance, propriety, decorum, manners, mannerliness, suavity, urbanity, culture, tact, taste.

2. Attractiveness, beauty, pulchritude, comeliness, symmetry, good looks, gracefulness, suppleness, willowiness, fluidity, fluency, ease.

3. *(Class. Myth.)* One of three sister goddesses presiding over all beauty and charm in nature and humanity, Aglaia ("brilliance"), Euphrosyne ("joy"), Thalia ("bloom").

4. Favor, good will, graciousness, benignity, condescension, kindness, beneficence.

5. Mercy, clemency, lenity, lenience, indulgence, pardon, reprieve, forgiveness, compassion, mildness, mercifulness, fellow feeling.

6. Piety, devoutness, devotion, religion, holiness, sanctity, saintliness, virtue, moral strength, excellence, merit, love, efficacy, felicity, God's favor, divine goodness, God's love, divine influence.

7. Short prayer over food at table, blessing, thanksgiving, thanks, petition, orison, benison, benediction.

8. *(Mus.)* Musical embellishment consisting of a note or notes not essential to the harmony or melody, appoggiatura, trill, shake, turn, inverted mordent.

GRACE, *v.* 1. Beautify, adorn, add grace to, decorate, deck, bedeck, embellish, enhance, garnish, set out, ornament, enrich, smarten, bedizen, bedight, spruce up, dress up, preen, bespangle, polish, furbish, gild, paint, lacquer, enamel, japan, varnish, burnish.

2. Honor, redound to one's honor, dignify, exalt, invest, endue, endow, glorify, aggrandize, nobilitate, elevate.

GRACEFUL, *adj.* 1. Supple, willowy, sinuous, flexible, limber, lissom, lithesome, lithe, easy-moving, light-footed, sylphlike, airy, balletic.

2. Attractive, charming, beautiful, comely, pretty, lovely, handsome, delicate.

3. Flowing, fluent, rounded, natural, unlabored, easy.

4. Tactful, happy, felicitous, befitting, proper, decorous, courtly, suave, refined, urbane, gracious, dignified, fine, polite, courteous, genteel, debonair, agreeable.

GRACELESS, *adj.* 1. Without any sense of right or propriety, corrupt, degenerate, depraved, shameless, dissolute, profligate, lost, abandoned, obdurate, incorrigible, hardened, irreclaimable, worthless, reprobate, seared, impenitent, bad, evil, sinful, wicked, demoralized, evil-minded, sunk in iniquity, iniquitous, accursed, base, ignoble, gross, infamous, vile, nefarious, flagitious, heinous, felonious, flagrant.

2. Awkward, clumsy, maladroit, lumbering, unwieldy, ponderous, uncouth, gauche, inelegant, ungainly, gawky, ungraceful, stiff, rude, gross, rough, boorish, loutish, wooden, rustic, slouching, lubberly, elephantine.

GRACIOUS, *adj.* 1. Disposed to show grace, friendly, favorable, kind, kindly, good-natured, kindhearted, benevolent, benign, benignant, charitable, humane, beneficent, clement, merciful, compassionate, tender, lenient.

2. Courteous, affable, amiable, polite, civil, familiar, mild, easy, obliging, complaisant, debonair, hospitable, urbane, bland, social, cordial, pleasing, pleasant, propitious.

3. Indulgent to inferiors in a condescending way, patronizing, condescending.

GRADATION, *n.* 1. Gradual change taking place through a series of stages or by degrees, gradual advance, regular step-by-step progress, regular progression, succession, series, continuity, sequence, course, continuum, round, suite, unbrokenness, chain, catena, train, scale.

2. Degree, stage, grade, step, rank, extent, measure, amount, rate, ratio, mark, point, height, standard, pitch, plane.

3. Shade, shading, intensity, depth, variation, richness.

GRADE, *n.* 1. Inclined plane, gradient, slope, ramp, obliquity, rising ground, hill, bank, acclivity, declivity.

2. Status, position, station, place, sphere, estate, caste, condition, standing, order, precedence, *pas (Fr.)*, level, stage, step, degree, intensity, brand, class, order, quality, pitch.

GRADIENT, *n.* 1. Degree of inclination, rate of ascent, grade, rate of descent.

2. Inclined surface, slope, ramp, rising ground, inclined plane.

GRADUAL, *adj.* 1. Continuous, progressive, gradational, regular, step-by-step, transitional, by degrees, graduated.

2. Taking place by degrees, changing little by little, slow, gentle, approximate, moderate, deliberate, leisurely, lingering, sluggish, comparative, snail-like, imperceptible, insensible.

GRADUALLY, *adv.* 1. In due succession, progressively, regularly, by degrees, through all the gradations.

2. Little by little, a little at a time, inch by inch, drop by drop, step by step, slowly, imperceptibly, insensibly, bit by bit, *peu à peu (Fr.)*.

GRADUATE, *v.* 1. Change gradually, adjust, modify, adapt, regulate, proportion, accommodate, rectify, correct, square, match.

2. Classify, arrange, place, range, class, file, register, tabulate, list, index, catalogue, alphabetize, sift, sort, range, size, align.

3. Measure, mark with divisions, divide into regular intervals, grade, calibrate, divide with degrees, establish gradation in, arrange in grades or gradations.

4. Confer an academic degree upon, invest with a degree, grant a diploma to, honor with a degree.

5. Receive a diploma upon completing a course of study, take a degree.

GRADUATE, *n.* Recipient of a diploma, bearer of a degree, alumnus, alumna, baccalaureate, licentiate, bachelor of arts, gownsman.

GRADUATION, *n.* 1. Ceremony of conferring of academic degrees following successful completion of a course of instruction, bestowal of diplomas, commencement, promotion.

2. Mark on an instrument or vessel for indicating degree or quantity, division.

GRAFT, *n.* 1. Shoot inserted in another tree so as to become united with it, transplant, scion, sprout, slip, implantation.

2. Unlawful gain, illegal profit, illicit revenue, unjust acquisition, spoil, booty, swag, jobbery, Tammany, plunder, loot, pickings, boodle, prey, racket, bribe, rake-off, kickback, shake-down, blackmail, fraudulent income, lining one's own pockets, hush money, velvet.

GRAFT, *v.* 1. Insert a scion of one plant into another plant, inoculate, ingraft, transplant, implant, inarch, join, bud, plant, inset, infix.

2. Practice graft, bribe, suborn.

GRAIL, *n.* Cup used by Jesus Christ at the Last Supper, vessel preserved by Joseph of Arimathea who received some of Christ's blood in it at the Crucifixion, Holy Grail, Sangreal, Sangraal, Sangrail, emerald patten, chalice, broad bowl, holy dish, platter.

GRAIN, *n.* 1. Small hard seed, kernel, matured ovule, cereal product, grist, cereal, corn, wheat, rye, barley, millet, oat, maize.

2. Smallest possible amount, particle, bit, atom, granule, corpuscle, whit, scrap, jot, iota, ace, mite, trace, pellet, tittle, spark, scintilla, glimmer, shadow, dot, speck, mote, fraction, morsel, fragment, crumb, molecule, ion, monad, electron, magneton, dab, trifle, modicum, touch, dash, pinch, soupçon, suspicion.

3. Texture, contexture, surface, fibre, intertexture, nap, warp and woof, tooth.

4. Natural character, temper, disposition, nature, tendency, humor, temperament, prevailing spirit, frame of mind, qualities, affections, genius, idiosyncrasy, bent, predilection, bias, inclination, predisposition, proclivity, propensity, proneness, vein, aptitude, mood.

5. Coloration, chromatism, tint, tincture, dye, tinge, stain, color, complexion, cast, shade, hue, flush, glow, paint.

GRAMINACEOUS, *adj.* Grassy, grasslike, gramineous, gramineal, resembling grass, belonging to the grass family.

GRAMINIVORUS, *adj.* Grass-eating, feeding on seeds, phytophagous, phytivorous, granivorous, frugiverous, herbivorous.

GRAMMAR, *n.* 1. Features of language considered systematically as a whole, rules of language, accidence, principles, elements, rudiments, laws of language, *jus et norma loquendi (Lat.)*, syntax, orthography, etymology, orthoëpy, inflection, prosody, phonology, linguistics, philology, glossology, lexicology.

2. Parts of speech, noun, pronoun, adjective, verb, adverb, conjunction, preposition, interjection, particle, affix, enclitic, conjugation, declension, parsing, analysis.

3. Treatise on grammar, grammatical handbook, manual of grammar, textbook on grammar.

4. Propriety of speech, speech or writing in accordance with standard usage, art of speaking correctly, right use of language.

GRAMMARIAN, *n.* Specialist in the study of grammar, rhetorician, grammaticaster, adept in grammar, grammatist, grammatical author, writer on grammar, grammatical pedant, philologist, glossologist, chorizontist.

GRANARY, *n.* Repository for grain, storehouse for threshed or husked grain, garner, corn-house, corncrib, silo, grain elevator, grange, barn.

GRAND, *adj.* 1. Of great dignity, distinguished, of great importance, high in power, illustrious, eminent, dignified, great, exalted, lordly, stately, august, princely, majestic, pompous, grandiose, elevated, renowned, kingly, noble, famous.

2. Imposing in appearance or general effect, great, large, palatial, imperial, luxurious, striking, magnificent, superb, splendid, glorious, elegant, royal, gorgeous, lofty, sublime, impressive, pretentious, ostentatious, dashing, showy, glittering, sumptuous.

3. Very high in rank or official dignity, chief, main, principal, superior, preëminent, leading, supreme.

4. Complete, all-inclusive, comprehensive, all-embracing, sweeping, compendious, capacious, wide, extensive, broad, large, full, of great scope, wide-reaching.

5. (*Colloq.*) Very good, first-rate, A-1, excellent, admirable, choice.

GRANDEE, *n.* Nobleman of the highest rank, lord, noble, magnate, aristocrat, hidalgo, peer, magnifico, silk-stocking, don, patrician, prince, duke, marquis, baron, viscount, count, earl, seignior.

GRANDEUR, *n.* 1. Eminence, stateliness, loftiness, distinction, dignity, glory, fame, nobility, importance, exalted rank, sublimity, majesty, augustness, state, pomp, magnificence, splendor, celebrity, solemnity, luster, excellence.

2. Imposing greatness, vastness, elevation, height, immensity, impressiveness, altitude, exaltation.

GRANDFATHER, *n.* Father of one's father or mother, grandsire, grandpapa, grandpa, grandparent, belsire, granddad, patriarch, forefather, ancestor.

GRANDILOQUENCE, *n.* Lofty language, highfalutin style of speech, high-sounding words, sesquipedalianism, high-flown language, altiloquence, magniloquence, fustian, bombast, turgidity of speech, rodomontade, highfaluting, purple patches, euphuism, extravagant diction, lexiphanicism, rant, macrology, Johnsonese, prose run mad.

GRANDILOQUENT, *adj.* Speaking in a lofty style, magniloquent, altiloquent, high-sounding, highfalutin, high-flown, rhetorical, pompous, turgid, bombastic, fustian, declamatory, swollen, tumid, inflated, stilted, grandiose, flowery of speech, spreadeagle, altisonant, turgescent, pedantic,

sonorous, euphuistic, sesquipedalian, big-sounding, Johnsonian.

GRANDIOSE, *adj.* Affectedly grand or stately, pompous, highfalutin, highflown, high-sounding, grandiloquent, magniloquent, altiloquent, declamatory, bombastic, fustian, pompous, pedantic, big-talking, turgid, swollen, tumid, inflated, stilted, euphuistic, florid, flowery, ornate, sesquipedalian, flamboyant, theatrical, imposing.

GRANGE, *n.* 1. Farmhouse, farm, farming establishment, hacienda, ranch, landed estate.

2. Association for promoting agricultural interests, agricultural society, farmers' association, lodge of the "Patrons of Husbandry."

GRANT, *v.* 1. Give, bestow, allot, present, donate, accord, confer, impart, award, offer, dispense, deal out, apportion, fork out, shell out, endow.

2. Furnish, supply, contribute, let, lease, hire, rent, demise.

3. Convey by deed, transfer by writing, make conveyance of, bequeath, dower, devise, leave, consign, assign, will.

4. Consent, concede, admit, permit, allow, cede, agree to, accede to, yield, indulge.

GRANT, *n.* 1. Donation, present, gift, boon, largess, bounty, sportula, benefaction, allowance, indulgence, bestowal, concession, acknowledgment, tribute, endowment, allotment, pension, award, *cadeau (Fr.)*, favor, oblation, offering, contribution, subsidy, subvention, subscription, bequest, devise, legacy, will, dowry, voluntary settlement, dole, alms, gratuity, honorarium, douceur, tip, fee, bribe, stipend.

2. Legal cession, conveyance, transfer, abalienation, devisal, bequeathal.

GRANULATE, *v.* 1. Reduce to grains, powder, comminute, grate, pulverize, levigate, triturate, scrape, abrade, file, grind, pound, rasp, bray, crumble, disintegrate.

2. Be formed into grains, roughen, become granular, dust, flour, bepowder.

GRANULE, *n.* Small particle, little grain, pellet, corpuscle, sporule, crumb, seed, spore, farina, flour, rice, bran, meal, grit, sand, dust, powder, efflorescence.

GRAPH, *n.* Diagram representing a system of interrelations among two or more things by a number of distinctive lines, blueprint, table, drawing, map, picture.

GRAPHIC, *adj.* 1. Pictorial, delineatory, descriptive, diagrammatic, figural, intelligible, expressive, vivid, telling, illustrative, lucid, comprehensible.

2. Forcible, well-delineated, striking, well-drawn, picturesque, lively, realistic, trenchant, clear, distinct, forcible, explicit, precise, unequivocal, cogent, effective, energetic, emphatic.

GRAPHOLOGY, *n.* Study of handwriting as regarded as an expression of the writer's character, chirography, notation, cerography, stelography, stylography, penscript, pencraft, penmanship.

GRAPPLE, *v.* 1. Hold with a grapple, fasten, make fast, clasp, lay hold of, grasp, grip, seize, gripe, catch, clutch.

2. Engage in a close encounter with, close with, lock contest with, struggle with, wrestle with, contend with in close fight, clinch with, seize in a firm grip, sink one's teeth into, try to overcome, tackle, take on, meet, stem, breast, buffet the waves, do battle with, kick against the pricks, encounter, attack.

GRASP, *v.* 1. Seize and hold by clasping with the fingers, clinch, grip, gripe, clutch, clasp, grapple, catch, grab, take, seize upon, lay hold of, hold firmly, try to seize, catch at, snatch, take and hold in possession, apprehend, nab, capture.

2. Lay hold of with the mind, comprehend, understand, catch on, savvy (*slang*), get, take in, fathom, follow, perceive, master, sense, deduce, infer.

GRASP, *n.* 1. Grip of the hand, gripe, clasp, seizure, handclasp, clutches, seizing, gripping.

2. Possession, hold, mastery, retention.

3. Power of seizing, reach, scope, compass, sweep, range.

4. Mental hold, comprehension, thorough understanding, ken, perception, savvy, sense.

GRASPING, *adj.* 1. Rapacious, predatory, plundering, wolfish, ravening, exacting, extortionate, *alieni appetens* (*Lat.*), usurious, sordid, greedy, covetous, avaricious, with itching palm, mercenary, venal, insatiable, hoggish, selfish.

2. Miserly, parsimonious, stingy, close-fisted, strait-handed, niggardly, shabby, mean, near, frugal to excess, pennywise, chary, tight, sparing, grudging, illiberal, griping.

GRASS, *n.* 1. Plant of the family *Gramineae* or *Poaceae* characterized by jointed stems and sheathing leaves.

2. Herbage, plants on which grazing animals pasture, pasturage, pasture, verdure, hay.

3. Turf, sod, sward, greensward, lawn, green, plot, living carpet, grass-covered ground, lea, grounds.

GRASSLAND, *n.* Area in which the natural vegetation consists of perennial grasses, meadowland, pasture, lea, plains, prairie, downs, mead, field, meadow, heath, wold, moor, moorland, pampas, llano, savanna, tundra, campo, playa, steppe, plateau, mesa, uplands, veldt.

GRASSY, *adj.* 1. Grass-like, green, verdant, verdurous, graminaceous, gramineous.

2. Full of grass, grass-covered, swardy, grass-grown.

GRATE, *v.* 1. Rub with noisy friction, abrade, scrape roughly, grit.

2. Reduce to particles by rubbing against a rough surface, comminute, triturate, pulverize, levigate.

3. Make a sound of rough scraping, sound harshly, rasp, grind, creak, scratch, stridulate, screech, screak, shrill, squeak, jar, burr, buzz, jangle, clank, set the teeth on edge, pierce the ears, *écorcher les oreilles* (*Fr.*).

4. Have an unpleasant effect on the feelings, go against the grain, make one shudder, rankle, corrode, gnaw, be disagreeable, be irritating, be offensive, offend, vex, fret.

GRATE, *n.* 1. Frame of metal bars for holding fuel when burning, firebox, firebed, receptacle for fuel, basket, fireplace, stove, hearth, ingle, range, kitchener.

2. Framework of bars used as a partition or guard, latticework, grating, screen, bars, grill.

GRATEFUL, *adj.* 1. Deeply appreciative of benefits received, thankful, indebted to, obliged, obligated, beholden, under obligation, mindful, impressed.

2. Pleasing to the mind or senses, pleasant, gladsome, agreeable, gratifying, genial, acceptable, satisfactory, satisfying, welcome, delightful, charming, restful, comfortable, interesting, lovely,

heartfelt, rapturous, thrilling, felicitous, ecstatic, heavenly.

3. Delicious, sweet, luscious, delectable, savory, palatable, toothsome, nice, refreshing, invigorating.

GRATIFICATION, *n.* 1. Pleasure, enjoyment, delight, laetification, delectation, joy, gladness, exhilaration, glee, jubilation, elation, sunshine, cheer, relish, gusto, zest, kick, thrill, stimulus, titillation, felicity, bliss, beatitude, transport, enchantment, rapture, paradise, ecstasy, heaven, elysium, happiness, well-being, solace, good, comfort.

2. Diversion, entertainment, sport, amusement, jollity, gayety, merriment, hilarity, mirth, treat, refreshment, regale, feast, banquet.

3. Self-gratification, indulgence, dissipation, sensuality, carnal pleasures, hedonism, spree, round of pleasure, creature comforts.

4. Reward, compensation, recompense, requital, guerdon, remuneration, indemnity, pay.

GRATIFY, *v.* 1. Please, charm, delight, pleasure, give pleasure to, make glad, gladden, cheer, tickle, titillate, laetificate, thrill, stimulate, amuse, excite, interest, suit, take one's fancy, transport, entrance, ravish, enthrall, enrapture, enchant, exhilarate, regale, rejoice, refresh, divert, entertain, recreate.

2. Humor inclinations, indulge, coddle, pamper, flatter, compliment, spoil, satisfy desires, give in to, appease, soothe, comply, favor, foster, mollify, fondle.

GRATIFYING, *adj.* Causing pleasure, pleasure-giving, pleasurable, pleasant, pleasing, satisfying, agreeable, delightful, welcome, grateful, nice, attractive, interesting, winning, delectable, good, soothing, indulging, acceptable, glad, lovely, tasteful, luscious, cushy.

GRATING, *adj.* 1. Strident, harsh, jangling, shrill, stridulous, raucous, high-pitched, acute, piercing, cacophonous, discordant, raspy, squeaky, creaky, rusty.

2. Irritating, offensive, disagreeable, displeasing, unpleasant, vexatious, exasperating, exacerbating, annoying.

GRATING, *n.* Frame of parallel or crossing bars, grate, open latticework, gridiron, grille, trellis, tracery, lattice, fretwork, fret, filigree.

GRATIS, *adj.* Gratuitous, for nothing, free of cost, scot-free, for free, without charge, expenseless, costless, unbought, unpaid for, complimentary, free, without compensation, without recompense, for love.

GRATITUDE, *n.* Gratefulness, thankfulness, grateful love, thankful receipt, sense of obligation, feeling of obligedness, beholdenness, recognition, acknowledgment, thanks, thanksgiving, giving thanks, praise, benediction, thank-offering, requital, grace, "a lively sense of favors to come" (Talleyrand).

GRATUITOUS, *adj.* 1. Spontaneous, voluntary, unforced, freewill, unasked, of one's own accord, free, for love, freely bestowed.

2. Costless, expenseless, free of cost, gratis, for nothing, without charge, chargeless, complimentary, honorary, unrecompensed, without compensation.

3. Being without reason or justification, unwarranted, without proof, unfounded, speculative, conjectural, hypothetical, suppositional, theoretical, presumptive, putative, academic, groundless,

not necessitated, wanton, hazarded, uncalled for, baseless, inapplicable, irrelevant, unconnected, impertinent.

GRATUITY, *n.* 1. Gift of money over and above payment due for service, tip, *pourboire (Fr.), Trinkgeld (Ger.), propina (Sp.), mancia (It.),* baksheesh, cumshaw, handout, perquisite.

2. Free gift, present, donation, largess, bounty, benefaction, charity, grant, fee, sportula, douceur, bonus, bribe, bait, peace offering, sop, palm grease, graft, boon, favor, offering, pin money, pittance, alms, dole, help, pension, aid, honorarium, contribution, subsidy, subvention.

GRATULATION, *n.* The expression of joy, best wishes, good wishes, well-wishing, congratulation, gratification, felicitation, thanks, rejoicing, many happy returns of the day, welcome, salute.

GRAVAMEN, *n.* 1. *(Law)* That part of an accusation which weighs most heavily against the accused, burden of a charge, substantial part of a complaint, head and front of one's offense, *argumentum ad hominem (Lat.),* essential point, substance, sum and substance, main point, outstanding feature, gist, principal part, nucleus.

2. Grievance, wrong, outrage, injury, complaint, burden, oppression, crying evil, bad turn, disservice, foul play, spoliation.

GRAVE, *adj.* 1. Involving serious issues, important, serious, weighty, cogent, momentous, of great consequence, pressing, urgent, critical, crucial, vital, outstanding, life-and-death, forcible, consequential, valid, emphatic, significant, instant, exigent, imperative, emergency.

2. Thoughtful in demeanor, staid in appearance, dignified, solemn, sedate, sober, earnest, demure, sage, philosophical, devout, saturnine, grim, grim-visaged, grim-faced, long-faced, rueful, wan.

3. *(Of colors)* Quiet, subdued, somber, dull, plain, lackluster, sad, dark, gloomy, lowering, frowning, obscure, deadened, flat, lifeless, gray, leaden, muddy.

GRAVE, *n.* 1. Excavation made in the earth to receive a dead body in burial, pit for the dead, burial place, sepulture, sepulcher, tomb, mausoleum mastaba *(Egypt),* stupa *(Buddhist),* vault, crypt, catacomb, cenotaph, ossuary, charnel house, barrow, tumulus, cromlech, cairn, place of interment, last home, long home, narrow house, wooden shroud, sarcophagus, coffin, casket, burial chest, last resting place.

2. Death, hell, hades, Great Beyond.

GRAVECLOTHES, *n.* Clothes in which a dead body is interred, winding sheet, shroud, cerements, cerecloth.

GRAVEL, *n.* Mixture of small stones and pebbles with sand, shingle, grit, sand, ballast, rubble, alluvium, small calculi.

GRAVEL, *v.* 1. Spread with gravel, strew gravel on, cover with gravel.

2. Bring to a standstill from perplexity, pose, put out, try one, nonplus, put to one's wit's end, bother, stagger, perplex, puzzle, bewilder, embarrass.

GRAVEYARD, *n.* Burial ground, cemetery, necropolis, polyandrion *(classical),* churchyard, mortuary, ossuary, charnel house, golgotha, God's acre, potter's field, bone yard *(slang),* memorial park.

GRAVITATE, *v.* 1. Move downward under the influence of gravitational force, tend by gravity, incline, descend, tend toward the lowest level, fall, sink, subside, settle down, precipitate, drop.

2. Have a natural tendency, be strongly attracted, incline, be prone to, have a proclivity for, head toward, lean toward, point toward, tend to, bear heavily.

GRAVITATION, *n.* 1. Force of attraction between all bodies, acceleration of one body toward another, fall of bodies to the earth, attraction of gravitation, centripetal force, gravity, statics, ponderosity, heaviness, weight, heft, ponderousness, ballast, burden, load.

2. Sinking, falling, descent, drop, precipitation, subsidence.

3. Natural tendency toward some object of influence, inclination, bent, leaning, penchant, direction, bearing, proclivity, aim, proneness, propensity, predisposition, susceptibility, liability, aptitude, turn, bias, drift.

GRAVITY, *n.* 1. Force of attraction by which terrestrial bodies tend to fall toward the center of the earth, centripetal force, gravitation, attraction of gravitation, statics, pull.

2. Weight, heaviness, heft, ponderosity, ponderousness, pressure, tonnage, mass, ballast, counterpoise, load, burden.

3. Seriousness, solemnity, sobriety, solemnness, sedateness, dignity, poise, serenity, staidness, composure, tranquility, calmness.

4. Critical character, momentousness, moment, importance, significance, greatness, largeness, enormity, magnitude, concern, consideration, import.

GRAY, *n.* Graynes, silveriness, neutral tint, grisaille, pepper-and-salt, dove color, *chiaroscuro (It.).*

GRAY, *adj.* 1. Of a color between white and black, achromatic color, having no definite hue, ash-colored, ashen, griseous, grizzled, devoid of hue, grizzle, grizzly, hoary, pearl-gray, pearly, ashy, cinereous, canescent, hoar, grayish, silvery, silvered, dun, drab, maltese, slate-colored, mouse-colored, dove-colored, stone-colored, dapple-gray, dappled.

2. Cloudy, foggy, misty, clouded, overcast, sunless, frosty, dark, gloomy, dismal, somber.

3. Gray-haired, silver-haired, silver threads among the gold, gray-headed, pepper-and-salt, hoary-headed, grizzly, hoary.

4. Pertaining to old age, ancient, venerable, patriarchal, old.

GRAZE, *v.* 1. Scrape the skin from, abrade, rub, scratch, rasp, grind.

2. Touch lightly in passing over, skim, brush, glance, rub lightly in passing, sweep over, kiss, lick, pass the fingers over, knead, massage, palpate, manipulate, handle.

3. Feed on growing herbage, feed upon growing grass, eat grass, browse, crop.

4. Put cattle to feed on grass, pasture, turn out to pasture.

GREASE, *v.* 1. Put grease on, smear with grease, lubricate, anoint, oil, lard, chrism, balsam.

2. *(Slang)* Grease the palm, bribe, suborn, corrupt with gifts, give a douceur to, give hush money to, cross the palm with silver.

GREASE, *n.* Rendered fat of animals when in a soft state, melted fat, fatty matter, unctuous matter, oily substance, lubricant, drippings, lard, tallow, unguent, unction, ointment, anointment, salve, balm, cerate, nard.

GREASY, *adj.* 1. Composed of grease, containing grease, fatty, fat, adipose, oily, unctuous, sebaceous, oleaginous, slippery, smooth, lubricated, unguinous, smegmatic, pinguid, saponaceous, soapy, lardaceous, butyraceous, buttery, waxy, slithery, greaselike to the touch.

2. Fawning, complaisant, gushing, glib, smooth-tongued, soft-spoken, bland, smooth-spoken, suave.

3. Soiled with grease, slimy, foul, defiled, begrimed, grimy, stained.

GREAT, *adj.* 1. Comparatively large in dimensions, unusually big in size, huge, enormous, immense, vast, bulky, gigantic, Cyclopean, Herculean, Titanic, Brobdingnagian, gross, voluminous, ample, monstrous.

2. Unusual in degree, extreme, excessive, pronounced, high, decided, exorbitant, preposterous, outrageous, unreasonable, undue, extravagant, inordinate, unconscionable, gross, crass, prodigious, towering, stupendous, colossal.

3. Of much consequence, consequential, considerable, weighty, important, momentous, critical, serious.

4. Large in number, numerous, many, countless, abundant, multitudinous, manifold, unlimited, boundless, inexhaustible, illimitable.

5. Principal, leading, chief, main, commanding, preëminent, superior, grand, of high rank, of high official position, of high social standing, august, noble, exalted, elevated, dignified, sublime, majestic, lofty, major, extraordinary.

6. Famous, far-famed, noted, notable, renowned, illustrious, eminent, celebrated, prominent, distinguished, influential, remarkable, noble, supreme, esteemed, conspicuous, signal, glorious.

7. Of lofty character, magnanimous, high-minded, high-souled, chivalrous, generous, philanthropic, altruistic.

8. First-rate, very good, magnificent, fine, fabulous, gorgeous, rich, sumptuous, imperial, precious, goodly.

9. Inexpressible, ineffable, indescribable, unspeakable, unutterable, nameless.

10. Absolute, unequivocal, decided, positive, unconditional, stark, complete, perfect, plenary, thoroughgoing, full, consummate, unqualified, thorough, sheer, arrant, flagrant, downright, glaring, unmitigated, rank, intense, profound, utmost, uttermost.

11. Much addicted, skilful, expert, crack, crackajack, proficient, dexterous, adroit, able, clever, apt.

GREAT, *n.* People of distinction, persons of rank, upper classes, *haut monde (Fr.),* aristocracy, elite, silk-stockings, blue blood, gentility, quality, *pur sang (Fr.),* great folks, world of fashion, peerage, gentry, better sort, squirarchy.

GREAT-BELLIED, *adj.* Big-bellied, tun-bellied, pot-bellied, gor-bellied, large-bellied, paunchy, abdominous, pursy, swag-bellied, distended.

GREATNESS, *n.* 1. Largeness, magnitude, dimensions, bulk, size, immensity, vastness, amplitude, mass, volume, heap, quantity, content, measure, measurement.

2. High degree, abundance, great quantity, sufficiency, deal, store, stock, load, shipload, immensity, fulness, enormity, intensity.

3. Might, strength, force, power, puissance, influence.

4. Distinction, importance, fame, renown, celebrity, elevation, eminence, preëminence, excellence, dignity, grandeur.

5. Nobility, majesty, augustness, loftiness, sublimity, exaltation, stateliness.

6. Magnanimity, nobleness, chivalry, generosity, disinterestedness, high-mindedness, elevation of soul, nobleness of mind, chivalrous spirit.

GREED, *n.* Inordinate desire, rapacious eagerness, lustful longing, craving, avidity, cupidity, avarice, rapacity, covetousness, itch, appetency, hunger, yearning, voracity, itching palm, keenness, appetite, stomach, intemperance, gluttony, gormandism, ravenousness, omnivorousness, insatiableness, edacity, gulosity, selfishness.

GREEDY, *adj.* 1. Very eager for wealth, rapacious, avaricious, grasping, selfish, acquisitive, cupidinous, mercenary, sordid, covetous, stingy, miserly, niggardly, grudging, penny-pinching, extortionate, exacting, predatory.

2. Greatly desiring food, gluttonous, ravenous, voracious, omnivorous, edacious, insatiable, insatiate, devouring, craving, hungry, peckish, sharp-set, ravening, famished, gormandizing, piggish, hoggish, swinish, open-mouthed.

3. Keenly desirous, eager, impatient, anxious, zealous, appetitive, fain, inclined, partial to, burning, fervent, ardent, agog, avid, aspiring, ambitious.

GREEK, *adj.* 1. Of Greece, Grecian, Attic, Hellenic, Dorian, Ionian, Athenian, Spartan, Corinthian.

2. Classic, classical, in the manner of Greece, after the Greek, in the Attic style.

GREEN, *adj.* 1. Between yellow and blue in the spectrum, greenish, emerald, virid, virescent, verdant, olive, aquamarine, olivaceous, pea-green, sea-green, grass-green, blue-green, berylline, glaucous, chlorochrous, citrine, of the color of growing foliage, viridescent.

2. Covered with foliage, covered with herbage, verdurous, grassy.

3. Full of life and vigor, blooming, blossoming, flourishing, fresh, new, recent.

4. Not fully developed in growth, not fully perfected in condition, not fully aged, unripe, immature, unfledged, not grown to prime, undeveloped, crude, unfinished, young, tender.

5. Raw, unseasoned, not dry, not dried, not cured, undried, unmellowed, unsmoked, untanned.

6. Inexperienced, inexpert, callow, crude, untrained, ignorant, unskilful, unskilled, unversed, undisciplined, uninformed, unsophisticated, unacquainted, awkward, neophytic, tyronic, amateurish, dilettantish, immature in judgment, gullible, easily fooled, credulous, simple.

7. Sickly-hued, pale, sickly, wan, livid, peaked *(colloq.),* sickly-looking, unhealthy, nauseous.

GREEN, *n.* 1. Color blended of blue and yellow, terre-verte, ocher, viridian, cobalt green, malachite green, emerald green, sap green, Paris green, celadon, mignonette, emerald, chrysolite, chrysoprase, peridot, chalcedony, jasper, malachite, verdigris, beryl, aquamarine, *crème de menthe,* absinthe, seawater-green, grass-green.

2. Plot of grassy land, lawn, sward, greensward, verdure, common, heath, campus, grassplot, grassplat, turf, putting green, village green, course on which golf is played.

3. Vegetation, verdure, greenery, green plants, verdancy, viridity, virescence, viridescence.

4. Vitality, virility, vigor, stamina, health, lustiness, strength, youth, freshness.

GREENHORN, *n.* 1. Inexperienced youth, novice, tyro, neophyte, amateur, beginner, raw hand, sciolist, tenderfoot, learner, apprentice, probationer, novitiate, initiate.

2. Person easily imposed upon, dupe, sucker *(slang),* fall guy, easy victim, scapegoat, gull, cully, pigeon, April fool, simple Simon, laughing stock, butt, puppet, cat's-paw, stooge.

3. Bungler, blunderhead, blunderer, lubber, fumbler, butterfingers, *blanc-bec (Fr.),* poorhand, bad-shot, oaf, lout, clod, hick, yokel.

GREENHOUSE, *n.* Glass house for the cultivation of tender plants, conservatory, hothouse, nursery.

GREENNESS, *n.* 1. Verdancy, viridity, virescence, verdure, viridescence, greenery.

2. Virility, vigor, lustiness, strength, vitality, health, stamina, freshness, newness, youth.

3. Immaturity, unripeness, inexperience, rawness, sciolism, tyronism, novicehood, novitiate, apprenticeship, dilettantism, amateurism, neophytism.

GREET, *v.* 1. Welcome, accost, hail, salute, address with some form of salutation, give salutations on meeting, hello, bid welcome, nod to, recognize, doff the cap, raise the hat, bow to, smile upon, speak to.

2. Receive with expressions of pleasure, admit, usher in, do the honors, entertain, hold reception, see, introduce, show in, give entrance to, give the entree, initiate.

GREETING, *n.* 1. Salute, salutation, welcome, reception, *accueil (Fr.),* introduction, presentation, respects, regards, *devoirs (Fr.),* friendly "Hello," remembrances, deference.

2. Bow, curtsy, kowtow, salaam, bowing and scraping, obeisance, proskynesis, genuflection, handshake, nod, embrace, kiss, kneeling.

3. *(Pl.)* Friendly message, many happy returns of the day, felicitations, congratulations, gratulations, expressions of joy, best wishes, good wishes, well-wishing, thanks.

GREMLIN, *n.* Mischievous invisible being said by airplane pilots to cause engine trouble and mechanical difficulties, goblin, hobgoblin, imp, elf, bad fairy, demon, bogie, brownie, pixy, urchin, Puck, leprechaun, troll, sprite, oaf, changeling, nixe, pigwidgeon.

GRENADE, *n.* Small explosive shell tossed by hand, hand grenade, explosive missile, shell fired by rifles, rifle-grenade, projectile, pellet, ball, shot, star shell.

GRENADIER, *n.* Tall foot soldier, fusilier, fusileer, sharpshooter, rifleman, yager, carabineer, musketeer.

GRIEF, *n.* 1. Keen mental suffering, sharp sorrow, painful regret, distress over loss, affliction, tribulation, anguish, heartache, heavy heart, heartbreak, broken heart, bleeding heart, misery, agony, dole, woe, bitterness, sadness, bereavement, dolor, wretchedness, desolation, prostration, slough of despond, extremity, lamentation, melancholy, despondency, despair.

2. Cause of sorrow, grievance, trial, hardship, worriment, remorse, rue, trouble, sore, vexation, discomfort, burden, ordeal, blow, shock, anxiety, worry, solicitude, care, concern.

3. Disaster, mishap, misfortune, calamity, catastrophe, evil, failure, miscarriage, casualty, mis-

chance, ruin, ruination, reverse, adversity, illluck, ill-fortune, hardship.

GRIEVANCE, *n.* 1. Wrong considered as grounds for complaint, injustice, injury, hardship, oppression, burden, bone to pick, hurt, iniquity, enormity, damage, outrage, bad turn, atrocity, disservice, foul play, mortal blow, buffet.

2. Cause of sorrow, vexation, annoyance, trial, grief, affliction, woe, bane, distress, trouble, ill, nuisance, irritation, pique, chagrin, mortification, worry, plague, sore subject, thorn in the flesh.

GRIEVE, *v.* 1. Feel grief, mourn, weep, lament, bewail, deplore, sorrow, suffer, be anguished, be heavy-hearted, feel regret, rue, regret, be sad, be in pain of mind, ache, bemoan, take to heart, wail, cry, groan, moan, fret, sob, shed tears, cry one's eyes out, complain.

2. Cause to feel grief, afflict, distress mentally, aggrieve, sadden, make sorrowful, hurt, agonize, pain, discomfort, oppress, wound the feelings of, cut to the quick, torture, harass, vex, cut up, disquiet, depress, deject, make unhappy, cut to the heart, make the heart bleed, break the heart.

GRIEVOUS, *adj.* 1. Hard to bear, sore, severe, intense, excruciating, poignant, harsh, acute, painful, grave, sharp, raw, cutting, agonizing, torturous, bitter, unbearable, intolerable, insufferable, grim, crushing, deplorable, lamentable, oppressive, afflictive, burdensome, distressing, heavy, baneful, detrimental, calamitous, destructive, noxious, injurious, hurtful.

2. Flagrant, atrocious, appalling, flagitious, heinous, outrageous, gross, arrant, iniquitous, violent, nefarious, vexatious, shocking, dire, monstrous, shameful, glaring.

GRILL, *n.* Grated utensil for broiling over a fire, gridiron, griddle, crossbars, broiler.

GRILL, *v.* 1. Broil on a gridiron over a fire, cook on a grill, boil, seethe, simmer, stew, scald, parboil.

2. Subject to severe and intense cross-examination, question, cross-question, put to the third degree, inquisition, interrogate, pump, catechize, cross-examine.

GRIM, *adj.* 1. Stern, unrelenting, unyielding, uncompromising, relentless, merciless, unmerciful, harsh, hard, severe, inflexible, resolute, obstinate, dogged, set, unalterable, irrevocable, deliberate, inexorable, indomitable, iron, strong-willed, determined.

2. Cruel, savage, fierce, ruthless, ferocious, malevolent, pitiless, unfeeling, heartless, brutal, feral, ferine, inhuman, fell, dire, atrocious, barbarous, truculent, fiendish, devilish, demoniac, cold-blooded, vicious, implacable.

3. Of a sinister or ghastly character, of forbidding aspect, repellent, repulsive, appalling, horrible, dire, horrid, frightful, grisly, hideous, ill-looking, ugly, gruesome, dreadful, terrific, cadaverous, haggard, loathsome, odious, foul, revolting, squalid, shocking.

4. Grumpy, cantankerous, saturnine, somber, scowling, sullen, sulky, morose, austere.

GRIMACE, *n.* Facial contortion, ugly facial expression, distortion of countenance, affected contortion of face, wry face, expression of distaste, contemptuous face, mug, mow, mouth, affected face, smirk, *moue (Fr.).*

GRIME, *n.* Foul matter ingrained in a surface, foulness, dirt, smut, filth, soil, smudge, dust, soot.

GRIME, *v.* Cover with dirt, make very dirty, befoul, begrime, soil, defile, sully, ingrain with filth, smudge, spot, smear, smirch, spatter, splash, be- mire.

GRIMY, *adj.* Covered with grime, soiled, filthy, dirty, smutty, foul, defiled, begrimed, full of grime, unclean, besmeared, bedraggled, turbid, squalid, lutose, muddy, grubby, miry, mussy, sooty, dusty.

GRIN, *n.* Act of withdrawing the lips and showing the teeth, broad smile, laugh, grimace, simper, smirk.

GRIND, *v.* 1. Sharpen by rubbing, smooth by friction, whet, file, polish, abrade, scrape, rasp, graze, scour.

2. Reduce to fine particles by pounding or crushing, pulverize, triturate, levigate, bray, grate, bruise, crunch, grit, comminute, powder, mill, granulate, crush, crumble, disintegrate.

3. Rasp, grate together, grit, rub harshly, gnash, stridulate, screak, screech, squeak, shrill, set the teeth on edge.

4. Oppress, persecute, harass, afflict, torment, trouble, plague, be hard upon, dragoon, maltreat, illtreat, hound, harry, bait, molest, worry, annoy.

5. Study laboriously, work hard, burn the midnight oil, drudge, slave.

GRIND, *n.* 1. Laborious work, close study, drudgery, hard job, toil.

2. Student who works hard at his studies, close student, hard student, crammer, burner of midnight oil, drudge.

GRIP, *v.* 1. Seize firmly, grasp, seize hold of, catch hold of, hold fast, hold on to, hold firmly, clutch, seize forcibly, clinch, grab, gripe, snatch, clench, retain, hold tight.

2. Impress deeply, take hold on, hold the interest of, spellbind, hypnotize, mesmerize, rivet, magnetize, take hold on the mind.

GRIP, *n.* 1. Fast hold, firm grasp, seizure, clutch, gripe, clasp, iron grip.

2. Control, hold, domination, keep, retention, custody, detention, clutches.

3. Handclasp, special mode of holding hands, shaking hands, handshake.

4. Mental hold, comprehension, understanding, savvy, perception, sense, ken.

5. Sudden sharp pain, spasm of pain, throe, pang, spasm, fit, agony, anguish, paroxysm.

6. Small suitcase, valise, satchel, traveling bag, gladstone, kit-bag, overnight-bag, carpet-bag, bandbox.

GRIPE, *v.* 1. Seize and hold firmly, clutch, clasp, grasp, lay hold of, snatch, grip, take control, grapple.

2. Pain, distress, produce pain in the bowels by constriction, straighten, give pain to, pinch, twinge, squeeze, compress.

3. Complain constantly, grumble, grouse, grouch, croak, find fault, whine, murmur, lament, repine.

GRIPE, *n.* 1. Firm hold, clutch, grasp, grip, seizure.

2. Intermittent spasmodic pain in the bowels, griping, colic, belly-ache, spasm, distress, affliction, twinge, twitch, pang.

3. Complaint, grousing, grumbling, croaking, faultfinding, whining.

GRISLY, *adj.* 1. Such as to cause shuddering horror, gruesome, ghastly, repugnant, abhorrent, ill-looking, revolting, odious, repulsive, terrible, fear-

ful, fear-inspiring, savage-looking, **forbidding,** horrible, horrid, hideous, appalling, frightful, terrific, dreadful, shocking, abominable, grim, formidable.

2. Gray, gray-haired, griseous, grizzly, hoary.

GRISTLE, *n.* Firm elastic substance of translucent whitish color, cartilage, connective tissue.

GRIT, *v.* Gnash, grate, grind, strike together, scrape, rub, **rasp.**

GRIT, *n.* 1. Gravel, sand, small pebbles, fine stony particles, dirt, dust, shingle, powder.

2. Coarse-grained siliceous rock with sharp and angular grains, gritrock, gritstone.

3. Stamina, pluck, mettle, sand, backbone, game, bottom, bulldog courage, nerve, indomitable spirit, spunk, perseverance, determination, firmness of character, decision, resolution, fortitude, endurance, staying power, vitality, tenacity, doggedness, hardihood.

GRITTY, *adj.* 1. Sandy, arenaceous, calculous, gravelly, sabulous, muddy, arenose, scurfy, dusty, granular, pulverulent, powdery, friable.

2. Plucky, mettlesome, game, spirited, determined, resolute, courageous, indomitable, unyielding, persevering, nervy, spunky, firm, fortitudinous, tenacious, dogged.

GRIZZLED, *adj.* 1. Gray, grayish, grizzly, silvery, steel-gray, iron-gray, leaden, slate-colored, pepper-and-salt, speckled, **whitish-gray.**

2. Gray-haired, hoar, hoary-headed, canescent.

GROAN, *v.* 1. Utter a deep inarticulate sound expressive of grief or pain, moan, whine, murmur, complain, lament, keen, wail, sob, weep, groan, bemoan, bewail, whimper, blubber, snivel, sorrow, fret, heave a sigh, rend the air, vociferate, grumble, grouse, yelp, roar, howl, yammer, grunt, ululate, bellow, bleat.

2. Resound harshly, creak, screech, squeak.

3. Be overloaded, be overburdened, be overladen, overabound, superabound, overflow with, brim over with.

GROATS, *n., pl.* Whole hulled grain, hulled and crushed wheat, hulled oats, parts of oat kernels used as food, grits, coarsely ground hominy.

GROGGY, *adj.* 1. Intoxicated, drunken, fuddled, boozy, plastered, mellow, sozzled, squiffy, potulent, pot-valiant, tight, oiled, screwed, primed, corned, lush, raddled, muddled, in one's cups, *inter pocula (Lat.),* crapulous, the worse for liquor, dead-drunk, three sheets in the wind, halfseas over, bibulous, sottish, bibacious, drunk as an owl, under the table, inebrious, inebriated, temulent.

2. Staggering from blows, punch-drunk, overcome, exhausted, disabled, weak, dizzy, reeling, slap-happy, K.O.'d.

GROGSHOP, *n.* Drinking-house, saloon, dramshop, tavern, ale-house, pot-house, mug-house, bar, gin-mill, speakeasy, bistro.

GROIN, *n.* 1. Fold on either side of the body where the thigh joins the abdomen, crotch.

2. *(Arch.)* Curved edge or line formed by the intersection of two vaults, angle, rib, pier.

GROOM, *n.* 1. Man in charge of horses or the stable, stableboy, hostler, ostler, orderly, jockey, equerry.

2. Valet, servant, lackey, footman, flunky, livery-servant, boots, manservant.

3. Bridegroom, newly married man, man **about** to be married, benedict, neogamist, spouse, **part-** ner, mate, yokemate, husband, consort.

GROOM, v. 1. Currycomb, curry, rub down, comb, brush, tend carefully as to person and dress, make neat, make tidy, tidy up, fettle, freshen, refresh, spruce up.

2. Prepare for a position, train, instruct, familiarize with, drill, exercise, practice, educate, initiate, indoctrinate, inure.

GROOVE, v. 1. Channel, furrow, rut, scoring, cut, rabbet, gutter, cutting, flute, stria, seam, hollow, drill, line, trench, opening, chamfer, canaliculus, sulcation, streak, scratch, crack, slit, score, corrugation.

2. Fixed routine, rut, habitude, habit, wont, beaten path, matter of course, standing order, red tape, convention, precedent, rule, prescription, procedure, second nature, usage, consuetude, practice, use, addiction, custom, run, way.

GROPE, v. Feel about with the hands, feel one's way in the dark, fumble, pass the fingers over, grabble, poke about, pick one's way, move stumblingly, move blindly, walk among eggs, throw out a feeler, paw, finger, see how the land lies, send up a pilot balloon, search blindly, search uncertainly, seek by feeling, hunt, probe, fish for, angle, try one's fortune, venture.

GROSS, adj. 1. Without having been subjected to deduction for charges or loss, entire, whole, total, aggregate.

2. Large, great, big, bulky, huge, prodigious, stupendous, colossal, monstrous, towering, gigantic, terrific, titanic, vast, immense, extreme, enormous, burly, massive.

3. Stupid, dull, ignorant, crass, heavy-witted, Boeotian, obtuse, benighted, dense, thick-skulled.

4. Flagrant, heinous, rank, unmitigated, uttermost, sheer, arrant, downright, outrageous, shameful, grievous, reprehensible, glaring, obvious, plain, manifest, red-handed.

5. Morally coarse, vulgar, earthy, animal, bestial, beastly, carnal, sexual, obscene, licentious, broad, smutty, foul-mouthed, scurrilous, offensive, ribald, pornographic, indecent, indelicate, low, raffish, vile, base, unrefined, unseemly, rough, sensual, lewd, lascivious, libidinous, lecherous, risqué, corrupt, sordid.

GROSS, n. 1. Main body, bulk, mass, gross amount, sum total, lump sum, whole, aggregate, total.

2. Twelve dozen, 144.

GROSSNESS, n. 1. Bigness, bulkiness, largeness, greatness, prodigiousness, vastness, immensity, enormity, burliness, massiveness, obesity, fatness, corpulence.

2. Stupidity, dullness, ignorance, crassness, heavy-wittedness, obtuseness, density, thick-wittedness.

3. Flagrancy, heinousness, rankness, outrageousness, shamefulness.

4. Moral coarseness, vulgarity, earthiness, bestiality, carnality, sexuality, obscenity, licentiousness, broadness, smuttiness, ribaldry, pornography, indecency, indelicacy, lowness, vileness, baseness, sensuality, lewdness, lasciviousness, lechery, corruption.

GROTESQUE, adj. 1. Fantastic, odd in shape, unnatural in appearance, bizarre, strange, fanciful, extravagant, wild, incongruous, queer, eccentric, outré (Fr.), preternatural, out-of-the-way, quaint, sui generis (Lat.), newfangled, exotic, outlandish, baroque, rococo, peculiar.

2. Absurd, ludicrous, whimsical, droll, comical, waggish, antic, ridiculous, burlesque, funny, risible, amusing, farcical, seriocomic, laughable.

3. Misshapen, distorted, deformed, gnarled, crooked, misproportioned, ill-made, humpbacked, hunchbacked, kyphotic.

GROTESQUE, n. 1. Whimsical fantasy, extravagant idea, capricious arabesque, barbarous representation, bold extravagance, vagary, caprice, caricature.

2. Person in fantastic disguise, buffoon, jester, clown, joker, mountebank, zany.

GROTTO, n. 1. Cave, cavern, grot, cove, antrum, retreat, cavernlike recess, burrow, hollow, catacomb, tunnel.

2. Alcove, pergola, summerhouse, kiosk, bower, arbor, hermitage.

GROUCHY, adj. Sullenly discontented, ill-tempered, in a bad temper, out of humor, crabby, sulky, surly, sullen, crabbed, morose, gruff, churlish, boorish, brusque, moody, glum, splenetic, spleeny, cross, irascible, cross-grained, fretful, irritable, waspish, pettish, snappish, petulant, testy, touchy, choleric, shrewish, captious, querulous, quarrelsome, cantankerous, contentious, exceptious, sour, perverse, peevish.

GROUND, n. 1. Earth's solid surface, firm land, terra firma, dry land.

2. Soil, land, mold, glebe, earth, turf, clod, loam, dirt, sod, clay, marl, gravel, subsoil.

3. Land having a special character, terrain, habitat, region, country, territory, domain, sphere, area, realm, tract of land, canton, district, bailiwick, province.

4. Estate, field, acres, farm, real estate, realty, premises, real property, landed estate.

5. Foundation, basis, base, support, groundwork, fond (Fr.), footing, understructure, underbuilding, substructure.

6. Basis on which a theory or action rests, premise, motive, cause, reason, mainspring, pro and con, reason why, wherefore, the why and the wherefore, principle, consideration, call, root, occasion, inducement, rationale, purpose, account, object, excuse, intention, secret motive, ulterior motive.

GROUND, v. 1. Place on the ground, lay on the ground, fell, lay down, floor, knock down, prostrate.

2. (Naut.) Run aground, strand, beach, shipwreck, stick in the mud, founder.

3. Place on a foundation, stabilize, settle, establish, found, fix firmly, base, set, consolidate, institute, organize, secure, confirm, make sure, install.

4. Instruct in first principles, make thorough in the elements, train in rudiments, teach the elements of, inform, initiate, indoctrinate, inure, rear, educate, discipline, prepare, form, qualify, drill, exercise, familiarize with, practice.

GROUNDLESS, adj. Without basis or reason, baseless, without foundation, unfounded, ungrounded, causeless, needless, uncalled for, unsought, gratuitous, idle, unauthorized, unsolicited, unwarranted, unjustifiable, not following, unsubstantial, illogical, unproved, fallacious, erroneous, false, faulty, untrue, apocryphal, imaginary, illusory, tenuous, vague, wanton, chimerical, unreal, cloud-built.

GROUNDS, n. 1. Sediment, dregs, lees, deposit, grouts, settlings, precipitate, sordes, tartar, heeltap, taplash, bottoms.

2. Arguments, pros and cons, whys and wherefores, accounts, considerations, motives, reasons.

3. Premises, estate, land, park, common, campus, lawns, gardens, yard.

GROUNDWORK, *n.* 1. Substratum, foundation, support, basis, base, ground, bottom, footing, foothold, substruction, underpinning, bed, substructure, framework, scaffolding, *échafaudage (Fr.),* background, underbuilding, understructure, bed rock, hardpan, flooring, pavement, sill, cornerstone, basement, keel, deck, stage.

2. First principle, root, fundamental, radical, taproot, origin, source, spring, rise, commencement, cradle, datum.

3. Preparation, training, indoctrination, inurement, novitiate, apprenticeship, first step, first stone, stepping stone.

GROUP, *n.* 1. Collection, aggregation, assemblage, levy, conflux, gathering, concourse, congregation, muster, array, representation, crowd, throng.

2. Troupe, corps, team, posse, squad, crew, band, force, party, gang, knot, clique, circle, set, coterie, faction, guild, league, brotherhood, clan, association, fraternity, sorority, sodality, tribe, sept, family, caste, company, colony, detachment, detail, swarm, covey, shoal, herd, flock, drove, roundup, drive, bevy, galaxy, horde.

3. Classification, class, species, genus, phyle, subdivision, branch, section, variety.

4. Series, cluster, nest, sorus, set, clump, bunch, batch, pack, lot, assortment, packet.

GROUP, *v.* 1. Place in a group, form into groups, arrange in a group, assign places to, dispose, organize, coordinate, rank, range, size, sort, classify, combine, cluster, array, marshal, line up, aline, sift, file, class, catalogue, register, tabulate, alphabetize, index, graduate, grade.

2. Be part of a group, associate, fraternize, consort, keep company, mingle, hobnob.

GROVE, *n.* Small plantation of trees, wood, woodland, copse, coppice, thicket, forest, timberland, greenwood, wildwood, tope, spinney, canebrake, bosk, bosket, boskage, covert, orchard, pinery, shrubbery, wood lot.

GROVEL, *v.* 1. Move with face downward and body prostrate, lie prone, lie low, crouch, crawl, creep, sneak, cringe, slouch, wallow, cower, worm one's way, steal along, stoop, prostrate oneself.

2. Act in an abject manner, humble oneself in mean servility, be servile, demean oneself, behave abjectly, be mean, lick the feet of, kiss the boots of, fawn, truckle, toady, kiss the hem of one's garment, keep time to, bow, stoop, kneel before, lose caste, submit, blandish, butter up *(colloq.),* flatter, sponge, snivel.

GROVELING, *adj.* 1. Crouching, creeping, snaking, lying prone, crawling, sneaking, cringing, slouching, wallowing, cowering, squat, snail-like, tardigrade.

2. Slavish, servile, cringing, abject, abased, prostrate, vile, mean, low, base, beggarly, shabby, paltry, little, contemptible, scurvy, dirty, sniveling, mealy-mouthed, fawning, toadying, truckling, obsequious, sycophantic, parasitical, low-minded, miserable, debased, earthborn, unworthy, undignified.

GROW, *v.* 1. Increase by natural development, swell in substance, expand in size, augment, spread, stretch, fill out, widen, grow taller, become greater, amplify, magnify, aggrandize, extend.

2. Issue from a germ, sprout, vegetate, germinate, bud, shoot, spring up, burgeon, pullulate, shoot up, put forth, flower, blossom, bloom, open, burst forth, arise, develop, mature, ripen, come to fruition.

3. Become by degrees, wax, mount, rise, ascend, swell, gain ground, get to be, come to be.

4. Thrive, flourish, prosper, succeed, be successful, make progress, improve, advance, make improvement, boom, batten.

5. Cause to grow, cultivate, raise, produce, propagate, breed, sow, plant, farm, garden, till, transplant, thin out, bed.

6. Adhere, coalesce, blend, unite, come together, combine, become attached, become consolidated, get fastened.

GROWING, *adj.* Increasing, crescive, crescent, enlarging, augmenting, expanding, waxing, extending, flourishing, thriving, prospering, developing, maturing, booming, mushrooming, spreading like wildfire.

GROWL, *v.* 1. Utter a deep guttural sound of hostility, snarl angrily, rumble, gnarl, howl, bark, yelp, roar, bellow.

2. Murmur, complain, gripe, grouse, grumble, repine, fret, groan, mutter, whine, croak, clamor, grunt.

GROWTH, *n.* 1. Gradual increase, augmentation, extension, expansion, development, increment, enlargement, amplification, aggrandizement, spread, swell, dilatation, dilation, turgescence, distention.

2. Germination, vegetation, sprouting, burgeoning, shooting up, pullulation, excrescence, putting forth, formation.

3. Something that has grown by a natural process, product, produce, crop, herbage, flowerage, plant, vegetable life.

4. Cultivation, propagation, raising, sowing, planting, farming, gardening, production, breeding.

5. Progress, improvement, advancement, development, advance, thrift, vigor.

6. *(Pathol.)* Morbid mass of tissue, tumor, tubercle, excrescence, lump, tuberosity, hump, gnarl.

7. Adulthood, maturity, prime, acme, floruit, flower, bloom, perfection, heyday, best days, ripeness, matureness, completion.

GRUB, *v.* 1. Pluck up by the roots, eradicate, deracinate, uproot, dig up, root up, root out, clear of roots, grub up, extract, draw, tear out, pull out, weed out, averruncate, unroot, extirpate.

2. Drudge, lead a laborious life, work out, moil, toil, slave, fag, plod, grind, hack.

3. Make laborious research, study closely, discover, dig up, unearth, fish up, ferret out, worm out, hunt out.

GRUB, *n.* 1. Bulky larva of insects, maggot, grubworm, caterpillar, entozoon, animalcule.

2. Dull plodding person, drudge, grind, fag, hack, toiler, hard worker, menial, slave, scullion.

3. *(Slang)* Food, victuals, eats, comestibles, fodder, feed, hard tack, edibles, eatables, viands, ingesta, belly timber, regimen, cheer, fare, forage, provision, commons, rations, nutriment, aliment, nourishment, nurture, sustenance, provender, subsistence.

GRUDGE, *v.* 1. Be dissatisfied at seeing the good fortune of another, see with discontent, cast a jaundiced eye, envy, covet, begrudge, feel ill will, resent, take umbrage at, take ill, be offended at, be provoked at, be indignant at.

2. Withhold, stint, pinch, gripe, hold back, screw, grant with reluctance, give unwillingly.

3. Submit to unwillingly, permit reluctantly, murmur, complain, repine, grieve, grumble, grouse, gripe.

GRUDGE, *n.* Feeling of ill will excited by some special cause, sullen malice, long-standing dislike, inveterate hatred, concealed hate, secret enmity, resentment because of some real or fancied wrong, rancor, umbrage, pique, malice, spite, malevolence, hard feeling, persistently entertained aversion, anger, venom, disfavor, spleen, envy, jealousy, animosity, resentment at the good fortune of another, reluctance, enviousness, malignity, covetousness, cupidity, emulation.

GRUESOME, *adj.* Such as to make one shudder, inspiring horror, revolting, horrifying, grisly, ghastly, squalid, repulsive, horrible, macabre, ugly, frightful, terrible, horrible, fearful, hideous, spine-chilling, cadaverous, grim, haggard, foul, repellent, forbidding, odious, repulsive, loathsome, shocking, horrid, horrendous.

GRUFF, *adj.* 1. Low and harsh in sound, hoarse, raucous, coarse, cracked, strident, roupy, gutteral, thick, hollow, ragged.

2. Surly, churlish, blunt, brusque, grumpy, rude, impolite, discourteous, uncivil, ungracious, bluff, rough, abrupt, crabbed, sour, acrimonious, curt, clipped, insulting, snarling, short, crossgrained, stern, boorish, bearish, bristling, thorny, grouchy, peevish, sulky, sullen, caustic, virulent, tart, crusty, crabbed, ill-humored, ill-tempered, sarcastic, trenchant, bitter, contumelious, perverse, sharp.

GRUMBLE, *v.* 1. Utter low indistinct sounds, mutter, gnarl, growl, rumble, roar, thunder, mumble, maunder, muffle, splutter, croak, speak thick, snuffle, whine, snarl, grunt.

2. Complain ill-humoredly, grouse, gripe, murmur in discontent, find fault, repine, take ill, fret, chafe, lament, deplore.

GRUMBLER, *n.* Fault-finder, complainer, growler, griper, grouser, censurer, croaker, murmurer, repiner, malcontent, grouch, irreconcilable, Adullamite, howler, wailer, lamenter.

GRUMBLING, *n.* Faultfinding, querulousness, discontent, dissatisfaction, repining, vexation of spirit, murmuring, complaint, regret, plaint, jeremiad, jobation, muttering, protestation, lament.

GRUMOUS, *adj.* (*Bot.*) Formed of clustered grains, grumose, concreted, clotted, thick, stuffy, knotted, lumpish, gnarled, pultaceous.

GRUMPY, *adj.* Grouchy, ill-tempered, sullen, sulky, surly, sour, glum, irritable, frumpy, disgruntled, resentful, bitter, ill-disposed, ill-humored, out of humor, in a bad temper, crabbed, crusty, moody, splenetic, cantankerous, crossgrained, humorsome, perverse, exceptious, refractory, intractable, unaccommodating, out of sorts, peevish.

GUARANTEE, *v.* 1. Make oneself answerable for, be responsible for, become surety for, answer for, warrant, secure, guaranty, vouch for, assure, insure, sponsor, allege, attest, testify, affirm, avow, undertake, underwrite, indorse, accept.

2. Engage to do something, pledge, promise, be sworn, plight one's word, bind oneself, contract.

GUARANTOR, *n.* Sponsor, voucher, warrantor, insurer, underwriter, bailsman, surety, guarantee.

GUARANTY, *n.* 1. Formal assurance given by

way of security, guarantee, pledge, promise, assurance, surety, security, warrant, agreement, voucher, contract, endorsement, acceptance, undertaking, warranty, insurance, engagement, covenant.

2. Vadium, bail, collateral, stake, earnest, deposit, gage, pawn.

GUARD, *v.* 1. Keep safe from harm, safeguard, defend, protect, shelter, shield, keep in safety, watch over, preserve, save, secure, screen, hedge.

2. Be watchful, take care, beware, be cautious, be vigilant, be on the qui vive, patrol, escort, picket, be on the outlook, attend for protection, supervise, keep under surveillance, keep under close watch.

3. Garrison, man, arm, accouter, harness, secure against attack, stand on the defensive.

GUARD, *n.* 1. Protection, safeguard, security, defense, preservation, shield, screen, fence, bulwark, palladium, rampart, aegis, buckler, stronghold, citadel, fortress, tower, refuge, asylum, fastness, hold.

2. Watchman, sentinel, patrol, picket, watch, sentry, defender, protector, champion, guardsman, guardian, warden, keeper, custodian, watcher, bodyguard, garrison, body of defenders, escort, convoy, guide, warder, watchdog, scout, doorkeeper, janitor, *concierge (Fr.)*, gatekeeper, porter, tyler.

3. Restraining watch, circumspection, vigilance, caution, watchfulness, care, heed, attention, wariness, lookout, discretion, prudence, providence.

GUARDED, *adj.* 1. Circumspect, wary, cautious, vigilant, careful, watchful, attentive, awake, aware, on the lookout.

2. Protected, watched over, under surveillance, in custody, fenced, hedged in.

GUARDIAN, *n.* 1. Protector, preserver, conservator, trustee, keeper, custodian, warden, defender, guard, vigilante, watchdog, curator, superintendent, wardsman, warder, bodyguard, escort, attendant, convoy, safeguard, conductor, picket, sentry, sentinel, patrol, champion, paladin.

2. Tutelary spirit, tutelar, guardian angel, good genius, attendant spirit, patron, benefactor, savior, fairy godmother, *deus ex machina (Lat.)*, special providence, partisan, advocate, champion, friend at court.

GUARDSMAN, *n.* Militiaman, yeoman, beefeater, sentry, sentinel, scout, picket, guard, watchman, garrison.

GUERDON, *n.* Reward, recompense, requital, compensation, remuneration, prize, meed, reguerdon, indemnification, quittance, price, reparation, amends, sop, return, *quid pro quo (Lat.)*.

GUERRILLA, *n.* Independent soldier who harasses the enemy by surprise raids, underground troop, partisan, free shooter, *franc-tireur (Fr.)*, Maquis (*Fr., World War II*), irregular, sniper, Chetnik (*Jugoslavian*), Jayhawker (*U. S., Civil War*), bushwhacker (*U. S., Confederacy*), ladrone, insurgent.

GUESS, *v.* 1. Form an opinion of from evidence admittedly uncertain, risk an opinion regarding something one does not know about, conjecture, presume, surmise, divine, suspect, infer, speculate, theorize, hypothesize, imagine, predicate, hazard a supposition, suggest.

2. Opine, think, fancy, believe, imagine, venture to say, dare say, take it, reckon, judge, deem, conclude, regard, consider, view, conceive, dream, apprehend, feel.

3. Solve, find out, unriddle, fathom, penetrate, arrive at the correct answer to, estimate correctly.

GUESS, *n.* Notion gathered from mere probability, conclusion drawn from imperfect information, supposition, divination, surmisal, conjecture, presumption, hypothesis, shot *(colloq.),* theory, guesswork, assumption, supposal, presupposition, postulation, postulate, speculation, belief, view, suspicion, association of ideas.

GUEST, *n.* Person entertained at the house of another, one who receives hospitality, visitor, caller, company *(collective),* frequenter, *protégé (Fr.),* habitué, parasite, sponge, gate-crasher *(slang),* umbra, shadow, commensal, diner, sojourner, inmate, friend, roomer.

GUFFAW, *n.* Loud coarse burst of laughter, boisterous laugh, horse laugh, cachinnation, hearty laugh, Homeric laughter, peal of laughter, shout of merriment, roar of mirth.

GUIDANCE, *n.* Leadership, direction, conduct, management, lead, government, steering, pilotage, escort, protection, counsel, advice, auspices, clue, information, enlightenment, intelligence, instruction, cue, hint, word to the wise, *verbum sapienti (Lat.),* pointer, tip, orientation.

GUIDE, *n.* 1. Counselor, adviser, instructor, monitor, preceptor, mentor, teacher, tutor, trainer, master, pedagogue, educator, coryphaeus, pioneer.
2. Example, pattern, model, exemplar, rule, last, prototype, original, archetype, paradigm, paragon.
3. Mark to direct the eye, landmark, directory, index, key, clue, thread, rudder, beacon, loadstar, buoy, trail, polestar, regulator.
4. Conductor, pilot, steerer, helmsman, director, cicerone, usher, marshal, attendant, escort, convoy, chaperon, courier, precentor, bellwether, fugleman, mercury, dragoman, *valet de place (Fr.).*

GUIDE, *v.* 1. Show the way to, conduct on the way, escort, pilot, convoy, direct the course of, steer, point out the course to be taken, indicate the route to, orientate, take the helm, be at the helm, lead, attend, accompany.
2. Regulate, direct, control, govern, rule, manage, preside over, superintend, oversee, have charge of, engineer, maneuver, handle, command, manipulate, dispose.
3. Train, instruct, inform, enlighten, show, indoctrinate, rear, ground, discipline, prepare, familiarize with, initiate, inure, qualify.

GUIDEBOOK, *n.* Book of directions and information for travelers, itinerary, handbook, guide, manual, *vade mecum (Lat.),* chart, map, gazetteer, plan, roadbook, Bradshaw, Baedeker, *Guide Bleu (Fr.),* Blue Book, Pausanias *(Greek Antiq.).*

GUILD, *n.* Organization of persons with common professional interests, union, brotherhood, craft, association formed for mutual aid, fraternity, company, society, corporate body, corporation, labor union, federation, confederacy, alliance, coalition, order, league.

GUILE, *n.* Insidious cunning, treachery, deceit, craftiness, duplicity, artifice, wiliness, trickery, wiles, rusefulness, artfulness, craft, subtlety, fraud, deception, slyness, cozenage, rascality, dissimulation, stratagem, strategy, dishonesty, foul play, finesse, astuteness, chicanery, insidiousness, sophistry, imposture, imposition, fraudulence, misrepresentation, hocus-pocus, knavery, hanky-panky, double-dealing, sharp practice.

GUILEFUL, *adj.* Crafty, cunning, fraudulent, artful, treacherous, wily, *rusé (Fr.),* tricky, deceitful, deceptive, designing, subtle, insidious, dishonest, double-dealing, insincere, surreptitious, mendacious, untruthful, false, evasive, disingenuous, *Parthis mendacior (Lat.),* forsworn, hollow, canting, Jesuitical, hypocritical, Machiavellian, pharisaical, double-tongued, tartuffian, two-faced, artful, collusive, perfidious, covinous, smooth-tongued, plausible, crooked, shifty, foxy, vulpine, feline, stealthy, canny.

GUILELESS, *adj.* Free from guile, candid, frank, aboveboard, straightforward, truthful, honest, open, sincere, artless, ingenuous, innocent, pure, simple-hearted, single-minded, simple-minded, undesigning, open-hearted, unsophisticated, unsuspicious, harmless, innocuous, upright, unoffending, naïve, unselfconscious, unaffected.

GUILLOTINE, *n.* Machine for beheading persons, decapitatory device, chopping block, decollation, axe.

GUILT, *n.* 1. Fact of having committed an offense, guiltiness, grave culpability, criminality, blame, blameworthiness, censurability, reprehensibility, censurableness, misbehavior, misconduct, misdoing, turpitude, vice, sinfulness, malpractice, wrongdoing.
2. Misdeed, guilty conduct, wrong, transgression, trespass, vice, sin, crime, offense, viciousness, complicity, misdemeanor, fault, violation, injury, felony, enormity, outrage, infringement, atrocity, delinquency, nonfeasance, malfeasance, misfeasance, negligence, dereliction, corruption, extortion, malefaction, malversation, misconduct, malpractice.
3. Misstep, *faux pas (Fr.),* trip, indiscretion, slip, lapse, blunder, omission, failure, failing, blot, flaw, error, break, peccadillo.

GUILTLESS, *adj.* Free from guilt, innocent, blameless, innocuous, faultless, not guilty, unimpeachable, unblamable, stainless, pure, spotless, sinless, unpolluted, undefiled, unspotted, untainted, immaculate, untarnished, unsullied, unoffending, unerring, above suspicion, irreproachable, virtuous, inculpable.

GUILTY, *adj.* 1. Having incurred culpability by committing an offense, justly charged with guilt, having violated law, actually transgressing, redhanded, self-convicted, condemned, sentenced, doomed, culpable, criminal, wrong, wicked, corrupt, peccant, erring.
2. Remorseful, penitent, hangdog, sheepish, contrite, sorry, repentant, regretful, compunctious, conscience-stricken.

GUISE, *n.* 1. External appearance in general, aspect, semblance, form, figure, shape, mien, look, likeness, complexion, presence, expression, impression, carriage, port, demeanor, air, image, outline, *tournure (Fr.),* contour, silhouette, countenance, profile, visage, face, physiognomy.
2. Habit, wont, practice, manner, custom, mode, disguise, pretense, fashion, tone, wise.

GULCH, *n.* Deep narrow ravine marking the course of a stream, ravine made by running water, gorge, canyon, gully, defile, crevasse, abysm, abyss.

GULF, *n.* 1. Portion of an ocean or sea partly enclosed by land, large bay, inlet, estuary, bight, bayou, arm, fiord, firth, frith, lagoon, cove, natural harbor, mouth, roadstead.

2. Chasm, rift, pit, cleft, canyon, abyss, crevasse, deep abysm, deep hollow, opening.

3. Something that swallows up, whirlpool, eddy, maelstrom, vortex, swirl, Charybdis.

GULL, *v.* Deceive, dupe, trick, cozen, chouse, cheat, circumvent, impose upon, overreach, outmaneuver, beguile, hoodwink, mislead, jockey, delude, bite, victimize, outwit, fool, swindle, cob, defraud, pluck, fleece, bilk, cully, do, diddle, gyp, double-cross, spoof, bluff, throw dust into the eyes, palm upon, foist upon, steal a march upon, bait the hook, decoy, waylay, inveigle, hoax, fool, befool, humbug, bamboozle.

GULL, *n.* One easily deceived, dupe, cat's-paw, victim, greenhorn, sucker, gammon, fall guy, simpleton, goose, gudgeon, cully, cull, April fool, pigeon, simple Simon, puppet, butt, laughing stock.

GULLET, *n.* 1. Tube by which food and drink pass to the stomach, esophagus, pharynx, gorge, throat, neck.

2. Stream, brooklet, rivulet, rill, rillet, runnel, brook, burn, rapids.

GULLIBLE, *adj.* Easily deceived, easily duped, easily cheated, credulous, overtrustful, unsuspicious, confiding, unsophisticated, green, simple, inexperienced, puerile, juvenile, innocent, unsuspecting, trustful, fall-guyish.

GULLY, *n.* Small valley cut by running water, gulch, canyon, ravine, defile, gorge, crevasse, chasm, abyss, abysm, *couloir (Fr.),* gulf, gap, notch, gully, clough.

GULP, *v.* Swallow in large drafts *or* pieces, take in by swallowing eagerly, swallow greedily, bolt, choke back, gobble, engorge, devour, ingurgitate, drink in, quaff, sip, suck up, swig, lap up, tipple, swill, empty one's glass, drink bottoms-up, drain the cup, toss off, wash down.

GUMPTION, *n.* 1. Shrewd practical sense, insight, discernment, shrewdness, penetration, sagacity, astuteness, common sense, acumen, acuteness, mental capacity, *esprit,* quick parts, mother wit, perspicacity, long-headedness, horse sense.

2. Initiative, resourcefulness, inspiration, ingenuity, enterprise, energy, power to originate, inventiveness, imagination.

GUN, *n.* 1. Metallic tube from which missiles are thrown by the force of gunpowder, piece of ordnance, portable firearm, rifle, revolver, pistol, musket, flintlock, matchlock, breechloader, derringer, arquebus, firelock, fowling piece, carbine, shotgun, blunderbuss, muzzle-loader, repeater, automatic, shooting iron, six-shooter, rod.

2. Big gun, cannon, howitzer, field piece, mortar, big Bertha, artillery, machine gun, pompom.

GUNMAN, *n.* Gangster, racketeer, thug, apache, hooligan, hoodlum, roughneck, terrorist, rowdy, ruffian.

GUNPOWDER, *n.* Explosive mixture of sulfur and saltpeter used in gunnery, explosive, smokeless powder, cordite, ammunition, powder and shot, dynamite, high explosive, lyddite, guncotton, melinite, nitrocotton, T.N.T., trinitrotoluene.

GURGLE, *v.* Flow in a broken noisy current, purl, ripple, bubble, guggle, murmur, babble, tinkle, spume, froth, foam, boil, plash, sputter.

GUSH, *v.* 1. Issue with force from confinement, flow suddenly and copiously, pour forth, stream out, spurt, burst forth, rush forth, jet, pour out, eject, emit, well out, squirt, spirtle, trickle, trill, splash, swash, overflow, deluge, inundate, spout.

2. Have a copious flow of words, effuse, talk effusively, be loquacious, prate, prattle, chatter, clack, maunder, blather.

3. Sentimentalize, emotionalize, be carried away by feeling, make too much of.

GUSH, *n.* 1. Sudden violent emission of fluid, rush of liquid, sudden outflow, forceful efflux, discharge, spurt, issue, effusion, torrent, emanation, defluxion, disemboguement, outburst, proruption, outpouring, effluence, jet, squirt, splash, spout, swash, rush, *jet d'eau (Fr.),* sluice, chute.

2. Exaggerated talk, gushing language, fine talking, rodomontade, hot air, gas, bombast, blatherskite, baloney *(slang),* applesauce *(slang),*

3. Sentimentalism, effusive sentiment, mawkishness, emotionalism.

GUSHING, *adj.* 1. Rushing, spouting, flowing copiously, spurting, issuing violently, pouring out, streaming, discharging, emitting.

2. Smooth-tongued, unctuous, suave, bland, soft-spoken, smooth-spoken, complaisant, glib, fervid, fawning, oily.

3. Enthusiastic, demonstrative, effusive, sentimental, exuberantly affectionate, cordial, ebullient, hearty, warm, zealous, ardent, glowing, fervent.

GUST, *n.* 1. Sudden strong blast of wind, squall, wind, breeze, puff, gale, storm, tempest, hurricane, draft, flurry, flaw, blow, blizzard, cyclone, whirlwind, tornado, typhoon, twister, simoom, mistral, sirocco, northeaster.

2. Outburst of passionate feeling, fit, burst, paroxysm, outbreak, explosion, fume, fever, heat, flush, flame, fire, tumult, excitement, ebullition, scene, frenzy.

GUSTABLE, *adj.* Pleasant to the taste, sapid, savory, relishable, toothsome, agreeable, pleasing, delicious, sweet, luscious, palatable, enjoyable, tasty, appetizing, flavorous.

GUSTO, *n.* Keen relish, hearty enjoyment, enthusiasm, zest, delight, pleasure, individual taste, personal liking, appreciation, appetite, savor, style, stimulus, kick, thrill, satisfaction, exhilaration, delectation.

GUSTY, *adj.* Blowing in gusts, squally, windy, stormy, blustering, tempestuous, blustery, breezy, blasty, blowy, typhonic, cyclonic, turbulent, boisterous, raging, violent.

GUT, *n.* 1. Alimentary canal between the pylorus and the anus, intestine, bowel, inward, entrails, viscera, chitterlings, vitals, belly, abdomen.

2. Narrow pass, defile, strait, narrows, sound, kyle, belt.

3. *(Pl., slang)* Courage, stamina, endurance, mettle, pluck, grit, sand, backbone, nerve, fortitude.

GUT, *v.* 1. Take out the entrails of, disembowel, eviscerate, paunch, embowel.

2. Destroy the interior of, consume by fire, lay in ashes, raze, lay in ruins, level with the ground, ravage, lay waste.

3. Plunder of contents, sack, despoil, spoliate, forage, ransack, loot, pillage, rifle, spoil, strip, maraud.

GUTTER, *n.* 1. Channel for leading off surface water, trough for carrying off fluid, conduit, cullis, drain, trench, eaves-trough, watercourse, rindle, duct, race, pantile, flume, main, gully, ditch, sewer, sough, cloaca, culvert.

2. Resort of the lowest class of persons in a community, sink of iniquity, sin-den, haunt.

GUTTERSNIPE, *n.* Street child of the lowest class, street Arab, urchin, gamin, rascal, small fry, tagrag and bobtail, riffraff, vermin, mudlark.

GUTTURAL, *adj.* Hoarse, gruff, low, deep, thick, throaty, harsh, nasal, grum, husky, inarticulate.

GUY, *n.* 1. (*Slang*) Fellow, person, swain, wight, blade, chap, gaffer, goodman, beau, mister, sahib, *monsieur* (*Fr.*), *Herr* (*Ger.*), *signore* (*It.*), *señor* (*Sp.*).
2. (*Brit.*) Person of grotesque appearance, scarecrow, sight, fright, eccentric, dowdy, frump, spectacle.

GUZZLE, *v.* Drink greedily, tipple, carouse, tope, swill, quaff, swig, toss off, lush, bib, sot, soak, booze.

GYMNAST, *n.* Athlete, adept at gymnastics, equilibrist, acrobat, ropewalker, trapeze artist, funambulist, tumbler, muscle-man, weight-lifter.

GYMNASTICS, *n.* (*Pl.*) Athletic exercise, gymnastic drills, calisthenics, athletics, acrobatics, sports, gladiatorship, exercitation, physical education, eurhythmics.

GYPSY, *n.* 1. Wanderer, nomad, vagrant, itinerant, peregrinator, rover, roamer, rambler, bird of passage, gadling, gadabout, Bohemian, Arab, vagabond, beachcomber, tramp, hobo, stray, wastrel, Okie, migrant, peripatetic.
2. Gypsy language, Romany, lingo, broken English, dialect, pidgin English, thieves' Latin, cant, argot, slang.

GYRATE, *v.* Move around a fixed point, rotate, move in a spiral, whirl, revolve, wheel round, spin, move in a circle, turn round, circulate, roll, circumvolve, gyre, wheel, swirl, trundle, twirl, troll.

GYRATION, *n.* Circular motion, spiral motion, circumgyration, circumvolution, rotation, revolution, whirling, spinning, turn, swirl, roll, circulation, circumrotation, volutation, turbination, circination, convolution, pirouette.

GYVE, *n.* (*Usually plural*) Shackle for the leg, fetter, chain, iron, bilbo, iron bar, bolt, pinion, manacle, handcuff, bracelet, trammel, darby.

H

HABERDASHER, *n.* Dealer in men's furnishings (*shirts, ties, gloves, etc.*), clothier, costumer, tailor, outfitter, glover, hosier, hatter.

HABILIMENT, *n.* (*Chiefly in pl.*) Dress, attire, clothes, wearing apparel, gear, vesture, garb, costume, vestment, habit, raiment, wardrobe, clothing, investment, linen, drapery, robes, garmenture, dressing, costumery, covering, array, trim, uniform, frippery, foppery, toilet, guise, feathers, suit, frock, gown, finery, livery, outfit, trappings, accouterments, caparison, adornment, readymades, trousseau, mufti (*coll.*), bib and tucker (*coll.*), shroud, garment, equipage, apparel, toggery (*coll.*), togs (*coll.*), turnout (*coll.*), duds (*coll.*), rags (*derog.*), regalia, tatters, wearables, investiture, bedizenment, rig (*coll.*), things (*coll.*).

HABIT, *n.* 1. Bodily constitution or state, condition, bodily appearance, temperament, characteristic form, aspect or mode of growth, composition, make-up, case, crasis, nature, diathesis, form, fettle, kilter (*coll.*), commission (*coll.*), shape (*coll.*), customary condition, disposition, chronic state, whack (*sl.*).
2. Mental make-up, mental or moral bearing,

disposition or prevailing character of one's thoughts and feelings, customary condition, nature, quality, mien; property, aspect, temper, streak, frame, humor, grain, tone, emotion, rule, principle, wont, way, inclination, cast, proclivity, temperament, tendency, constitution of mind, vein, attitude, mood, cue, crasis, spirit, characteristic, particularity, stripe.
3. Settled tendency of behavior, custom, practice, usage, normal manner of occurrence or procedure, characteristic behavior or tendency, way, wont, fashion, mode, use, system, style, mannerism, form, method, rule of life, consuetude, trait, trick, habitude, principle, second nature, habitual course or practice, pattern, groove, rut, usual procedure, common or ordinary run, one's old way, self-imposed law, regulation, regime, precept, order, convention, repetition, constancy, particularity, distinction, prevalence, peculiarity, proclivity, inclination, observance, institution, prescription, precedent, conduct, deportment, rule, manner, standing order, matter of course, sameness of manner, routine, beaten path, etiquette, customary course, grind (*coll.*), fixed procedure, regularity, quality, clockwork, monotony.
4. Specific aptitude or inclination acquired by repetition, acquired mode of behavior, addiction, proclivity, leaning, weakness, inveterate practice, confirmed way, indulged inclination, pursuit, itch, mania, partiality, fondness, predilection, predisposition, proneness, animus, cacoëthes, bad custom, insatiable desire, addictedness, dilettantism, use, vice, employment, profession, prevailing tendency of action, disposition, propensity, Circean cup.
5. Garb of a particular rank, profession, or religious order, dress, attire, array, apparel, raiment, guise, garment, robe, vesture, suit, clothes, accouterments, costume, clothing, habiliments, lady's riding costume, outfit, gear, uniform, livery, trappings, caparison, investiture, rig (*coll.*), garmenture, investment.

HABIT, *v.* Dress, array, outfit, equip, attire, clothe, accouter, rig, fit out, drape, garb, robe, costume, deck out, caparison, rig out or up, turn out.

HABITABLE, *adj.* Capable of being inhabited, inhabitable, tenantable, fit for dwelling, peopled, supplied with essential physical needs, livable, lodgeable, occupiable, suitable for living in, appropriate for residence, residential.

HABITANT, *n.* Dweller, person or animal that inhabits, resident, inhabitant, resider, sojourner, abider, aborigine, denizen, citizen, occupier, occupant, tenant, incumbent, residentiary, inhabiter, addressee, householder, lodger, settler, colonist, native, indigene, renter, boarder, inmate, townsman, islander, villager, lessee, provincial, colonial, planter, intern (*Med.*), cottager, aboriginal, roomer, homesteader, autochthon, commorant, proprietor.

HABITAT, *n.* 1. Natural locality of a plant or an animal, area of distribution, place, spot, retreat, ground, haunt, refuge, locality, locale, lair, resort, locus, region, vicinity, zone, territory, range, environment, realm, site of residence, demesne, terrain, field, location, domain, background, vivarium, setting, environs, milieu, surroundings, precincts, whereabouts, stamping ground (*coll.*), natural abode, native environment, natural home.
2. Place of abode, habitation, domicile, lodging, abode, dwelling, quarters, inhabitancy, dwelling-place, address, abiding place, seat, native soil,

rooftree *(fig.)*, nest, establishment, fatherland, native land, shelter, homestead, lodgment, colony, roost *(fig.)*, roof *(fig.)*, home, housing.

HABITATION, *n.* 1. Dwelling, abode, place of abode, home, dwelling place, habitat, abiding place, area of distribution, quarters, inhabitancy, lodgment, housing, stopping place, stopover, place where one hangs one's hat *(joc.)*, roost *(fig.)*, joint *(sl., contempt)*, fatherland, native land, seat, native soil, colony, resting place, shelter, nest, dump *(sl., contempt.)*, roof *(fig.)*, homestead, hearth, fireside, diggings *(coll.)*, place of residence, home, lodging, headquarters, settlement, residence, address, site, rooftree *(fig.)*, establishment.

2. Act of inhabiting, occupancy, sojourn, occupation, habitancy, tenancy, possession, dwelling, lodgment, remaining, stop, stay, abode, abiding, continuance, residence, lodging, inhabitancy.

HABITUAL, *adj.* 1. Usual, customary, common, regular, routine, of the nature of a habit, fixed by *or* resulting from habit, according to habit, constant, repeated, prevalent, understood, expected, reiterated, sustained, frequent, methodical, periodical, hackneyed, normal, perpetual, recurrent, inveterate, confirmed, everyday, ordinary, orthodox, iterated, repetitious, faithful, cut and dry *(coll.)*, continual, general, natural, permanent, successive, incessant, reduplicating, retold, stated, accustomed, daily, formal, approved, standard, received, ubiquitous, commonplace, humdrum, trite, innate, spontaneous, oftentime, epochal, seasonal, cyclic, intermittent, thick-coming, universal, conventional, besetting, traditional, rhythmic, established by tradition, isochronal, prescriptive, stock, tautological, ingrained, instinctive, inherent, inbred, recognized, wonted, familiar, inborn, established, settled, reiterative, consuetudinary, orderly, rooted, twice-told, reduplicative, without exception, chronic, uniform, ruling, remittent, set, periodic, serial.

2. Being such by habit, chronic, inveterate, confirmed, continual, permanent, systematic, frequent, iterated, methodical, acting by force of habit, besetting, periodic, constant, repeated, settled, ingrained, recurrent, established, perpetual, iterative, periodical, reiterative, reiterated.

3. Commonly used *(by a given person)*, usual, expected, customary, accustomed, established, regular, wonted, familiar, typical, common, proper, recognized, by force of habit *or* custom, well-trodden, conventional, normal, natural.

HABITUATE, *v.* Accustom *(a person, the mind, etc.)* as to something, make used to, inure, familiarize, train, acclimate, season, initiate, implant, exercise, drill, tame, adapt, discipline, cultivate, foster, penetrate, ground, bring up in, conventionalize, instill, imbue, indoctrinate, inculcate, school, methodize, rear, form, prepare, nurture, develop, caseharden, wont, domesticate, gentle *(coll.)*, addict, harden, break in, naturalize, give to, acclimatize, settle into a groove, engrave, catechize, domesticize, practice, hammer, impress, suffuse with.

HABITUDE, *n.* 1. Customary condition, character *or* habit, settled disposition, settled tendency, habitual attitude, habitual state of mind, usual emotional tone, trait, groove, rut, round, track, nature, constitution, temperament, aspect, mode, composition, make-up, state, case, crasis, bearing, quality, property, mien, temper, frame, grain, humor, wont, inclination, cast, rule, stripe, characteristic, vein, spirit, particularity, form, style, fashion, vogue, regime, order.

2. Custom, practice, wont, way, habit, usage, convention, second nature, mannerism, method, regime, rule, regular course, observance, consuetude, institution, fixed procedure, routine, set form, ordinary run, established rule, usual practice, customary course, beaten path, propriety, convention, characteristic behavior *or* tendency, system, pattern, precept, particularity, peculiarity, inclination, proclivity, precedent, prescription, grind *(coll.)*

HABITUE, *n.* Habitual frequenter, attender, constant guest, adherent, devotee, patron, visitor, resorter, fan, customer, follower, guest, votary, zealot, enthusiast, addict.

HACIENDA, *n.* Landed estate, country house, cultivated farm, productive country seat, gentleman farm, ranch, rural manufacturing works, animal husbandry establishment, dairy farm, manor, holdings, villa, demesne, farmstead, plantation, messuage *(Law)*, grange, range.

HACK, *adj.* 1. Hired, hackney, mercenary, of a hired sort, let out, menial, laboring, drudge, for wages, apprentice, servile, waiting, prosaic, dependent, humble, leased, rented, subservient, engaged, ministering, performed by a hack, hireling, chartered, employed.

2. Hackneyed, trite, commonplace, banal, vapid, fatuous, uninspired, unimaginative, common, stereotyped, old, threadbare, worn, worn-out, stale, stock, platitudinous, regular, bromidic *(coll.)*, humdrum, pedestrian, plodding, matter-of-fact, inane, jejune, insipid, conventional, set, moth-eaten, ordinary, wishy-washy.

HACK, *n.* 1. Notch, cut, nick, cleft, gash, dint, jag, score, slit, slash, incision, gap, fissure, rent, rift, nock *(of an arrow)*, scotch, crena, trench, rupture, rime, breach, scallop, crenature, chasm, crevice, chink, chap, cranny, serration, dent, blaze, split, chop, chip, indentation.

2. Tool for hacking, ax, pick, mattock, hoe, pickax, colter, battle-ax, bill, cleaver, sickle, scythe, tomahawk, billhook, adze hook, sword, hatchet.

3. Act of hacking, cutting blow, dint, stroke, cut, hit, stab, chop, home thrust, slash, rending, cleft, cleaving, splitting, disjunction, parting, severance, slitting, gashing, abrupt punch, chiseling, jab.

4. Short broken cough, dry cough, smoker's hack, rasp, grating cough, cigarette cough *(coll.)*, bark *(coll.)*.

5. A breaking *or* stumbling in speech, hesitation, halting, discontinuity, stammer, unrhythmic speech, stutter, faltering, blundering, hitch, obstruction, suspension, disconnection, pausing, interval, lapse, lull, failing, interruption, speech block, check, arrest, stoppage.

6. Hired horse, worn-out horse, jade, draft horse, dray horse, thill horse, horse for common hire, work horse, plow horse, cart horse, shaft horse, gigster, sumpter, padnag, crock, bidet *(Mil.)*, screw *(coll.)*, rackabones *(coll.)*, rip *(coll.)*, skate *(sl.)*, plug *(sl.)*, pad, thiller, hackney, nag, Rosinante, carriage horse.

7. Writer who hires himself out for general work, author, scribbler, literary drudge, overworked man, penny-a-liner, drone, word-seller, laborer, hodman, jobber, hireling, slave, scribe, creeper *(sl.)*, grubstreet writer, ghost writer, inkslinger *(sl.)*, workhand, wageworker, potboiler *(coll.)*, toiler, moiler, plodder, menial, fagger, flunky, factotum, man of all work, hired man, handy man, ghost, adjective jerker *(sl.)*, quill

driver (*chiefly contempt.*), versifier, day laborer, drudge.

8. Carriage, coach for hire, hackney coach, taxicab, rented vehicle, transport, taxi.

HACK, *v.* 1. Cut clumsily, chop as with heavy blows, cut irregularly, make rough cuts *or* notches, break up the surface of (*the ground*), mutilate, lacerate, notch, deal cutting blows, mangle, hew, haggle, hackle, scratch, disfigure, scar, deface, mar, blemish, incise, sunder, saw, whittle, disjoint, pierce, bayonet, saber, knife, stab, shiver, make mincemeat of, snip, chisel, shear, trim, gash, slit, rend asunder, slice, rip, abscind, claw, bite, rive, lop, fell, prune, cleave, detruncate, amputate, plow, wound, dock, deform, whack (*coll.*), run through, tear, break, chip, botch, injure, quarter, cut to pieces, kick, sever, slash, crop, carve, rend, prod, split, butcher, wedge.

2. Emit short frequent coughs, bark (*coll*), cough dryly and repeatedly.

3. Make trite *or* stale by frequent use, hackney, dull, take the edge from, throw cold water on, deaden, weaken, obtund, overdo, damp, depress, blunt the force of, make less pungent, render prosaic *or* uninteresting, make commonplace, wear threadbare, lay a wet blanket on.

HACKLE, *n.* Neck plumage of the domestic rooster, saddle feathers, long slender feathers, plumage, feathering, mantle, breast feathers, feathers.

HACKLE, *v.* 1. Cut clumsily, chop, hew, hack, mangle, haggle, deal heavy blows, make rough cuts *or* notches, whittle, disjoint, make mincemeat of, chisel, rend asunder, claw, bite, lop, prune, plow, cleave, whack (*coll.*), tear, quarter, cut to pieces, slash, carve, crop, rend, butcher, prod, sunder, abscind, wedge, rive.

2. Hatchel, untangle, cleanse, unravel, heckle, card, comb, dress (*flax*).

HACKNEYED, *adj.* Trite, commonplace, banal, stale, stock, ordinary, moth-eaten, worn, wornout, platitudinous, regular, set, conventional, stereotyped, threadbare, old, bromidic (*coll.*), humdrum, common; (*the following refer largely to language, ideas, etc.*) uninspired, unimaginative, pedestrian, plodding, jejune, insipid, vapid, fatuous, matter-of-fact, inane, wishy-washy.

HADES, *n.* Abode of the dead, underworld, domain of Pluto, hell, hell fire, limbo, inferno, nether regions, lower world, shades below, the abyss, lake of fire, purgatory, Tartarus, Avernus, Sheol, Gehenna, Nastrond (*Norse*), Aralu (*Babylonian*), Amenti (*Egypt.*), Acheron, Abaddon, Pandemonium, Naraka (*Hind. and Budd.*), Avichi (*Budd.*), Lethe (*river*), Cocytus (*river*), Phlegethon (*river*), Styx (*river.*).

HAFT, *n.* Handle (*of a knife, sword, etc.*), hilt, hold, helve, grasp, shaft, grip.

HAG, *n.* 1. Beldam, crone, old witch, Xanthippe, virago, vixen, harridan, shrew, fury, battle-ax (*sl.*), old cat (*coll.*), mean old woman, fishwife, grandmother, hellhag, hellcat, ogress, gorgon.

2. Witch, sorceress, shamaness, hex (*coll.*), Harpy, Circe, lamia, siren, weird sisters (*plur.*).

HAGGARD, *adj.* 1. Tired, weary, exhausted, effete, spent, careworn, worn, wasted, woebegone, heavy-laden, oppressed, crushed, beaten, fatigued, drooping, enfeebled, fagged, tuckered (*coll.*), faint, toilworn, footsore, overwearied, weakened, flagging, dispirited, life-weary, sorry, stricken.

2. Gaunt, hollow-eyed, emaciated, wan, enfeebled, seedy (*coll.*), lean, wasted, thin, harassed, woebegone, drooping, shriveled, fleshless, worn to

a shadow, thin as a rail *or* rake, spare, lanky, scraggy, attenuate, pallid, sallow.

3. Wild, overcome, upset, staring, frenzied, delirious, burning, raging, overwrought, violent, mad, fiery, ranting, demoniac, distracted, wildlooking, harrowed, harassed, raving, fuming, seething, wild-eyed, ebullient.

HAGGLE, *v.* 1. Barter, exchange, higgle, chaffer, truck, transact, drive a bargain, bid for, underbid, negotiate, dicker, beat down, cheapen, stickle, have dealings, make a bargain, strike a bargain, palter.

2. Wrangle, cavil, peck at, blame, disparage, reproach, nag, depreciate, find flaws in, dispute, jibe at, disapprove, censure, reprehend, cast a slur on, deprecate, complain, criticize, decry, pick, find fault, carp, quibble, discredit, pull to pieces, heckle, belittle, faultfind, animadvert, slight, deride, sneer at.

3. Cut (*clumsily*), mangle, hack, cleave, gash, rend asunder, rive, chop, slice, slash, hackle, rip, chip, dissever, rend, abscind, hew, snip.

HAIL, *int.* All hail!, greetings!, welcome!, ahoy!, hello!, hey!, good day!, good morning!, yo-ho!, halloa!, hallo!

HAIL, *n.* 1. Salute, salutation, greeting, wave, nod, hello!, good day!, good morning!, accosting, handshake, salaams, welcome!

2. Hailstones, sleet, snow pellets, frozen rain, graupel.

HAIL, *v.* 1. Salute, greet, welcome, receive, usher in, accost, shake hands with, offer a hand to, make welcome, present arms (*Mil.*), tip the hat to, doff the hat to, touch the hat to, bid one welcome, do the honors.

2. Name, credit, esteem, acclaim, compliment, exalt, prize, honor, clap on the back, sanction, commend, cry up, glorify, magnify, eulogize, cheer, extol, swell, clap, applaud, encore, panegyrize.

3. Call to, accost, shout at, address, cry out to, salute, greet.

4. Sleet, fall as hail.

5. Pour down, snow, rain, fall in profusion, shower, stream, rain down thickly, pelt, flow, swarm.

HAIR, *n.* 1. (*Human*) Locks, ringlets, curls, thatch, crop, crine, kemp, mat, mane, fringe, bangs, down, shock, mop, tresses.

2. (*Animal*) Coat, fur, wool, down, mane, pubescence, fell, pelt, crop, crine, fluff, fleece.

3. (*Singular*) Thread, filament, fiber, villus (*Bot.*), hairlet, filamentule, capillament (*Bot.*), cilia (*eyelash: anat.*), ciliolum (*Biol.*), fibril, fibrilla.

HAIRBREADTH, *n.* Hair, hair's breadth, snip, snippet, shaving, sliver, shred, chip, chipping, shiver, splinter, fraction, skin of one's teeth.

HAIRDO, *n.* Haircut, coiffure, permanent wave, permanent, hair arrangement, hair styling, hair set, hair fashion, marcel, cold wave, finger wave, hairdressing.

HAIRDRESSER, *n.* Haircutter, barber, tonsor, coiffeur, *friseur* (*Fr.*), beautician (*Advertising cant*), hair stylist.

HAIRINESS, *n.* Pilosity, pubescence, hispidity, hirsuteness, crinosity, shagginess, bristliness, furriness, fluffiness, downiness.

HAIRLESS, *adj.* Bald, glabrous, shorn, destitute of hair, tonsured, smooth-faced, clean-shaven, whiskerless, smooth, depilated, depilous, acomous,

smooth-shaven, smooth-chinned, beardless, glabrate *(Bot. and Zool.)*, glabrescent *(Bot. and Zool.)*.

HAIRLESSNESS, *n.* Baldness, depilation, acomia, alopecia, beardlessness, baldpatedness, baldheadedness, smooth-facedness.

HAIRSPLITTING, *adj.* Hypercritical, quibbling, nice, overfine, fussy, fastidious, oversubtle, equivocating, oversensitive, pedantic, meticulous, punctilious, strict, caviling, prevaricating, carping, precise, overconscientious, exacting, overrefined, queasy, squeamish, captious, finicky.

HAIRY, *adj.* Shaggy, nappy, barbigerous, tufted, bristly, pileous, fimbriate *(Bot.)*, lanate, pubescent, piliferous, hirsute, setaceous, comose, comate, strigose *(Bot.)*, hispid *(Bot. and Zool.)*, kempy, fleecy, whiskered, bewhiskered, tomentose *(Anat., Bot., and Entomol.)*, woolly, fluffy, villous, furry, flocculent, crinitory, crinite, bearded, downy.

HALCYON, *adj.* Calm, peaceful, tranquil, unruffled, placid, quiet, serene, happy, golden, halcyonian, untroubled, sunny, pacific, Saturnian, prosperous, temperate, palmy, auspicious, moderate, smiling, gentle, bland, genial, pleasant, smooth, tame, beneficent, tempered, equable, propitious, rosy, halcyonic, mild, merciful, amiable, stormless, clement, soft, lenient, promising, favorable, reposeful, quiescent, felicitous, docile, unperturbed, still, undisturbed, warm, summery.

HALE, *adj.* Free from disease *or* infirmity, sound, healthy, vigorous, robust, well, in good health, strong, hardy, entire, rugged, mighty, whole, strapping, hard as nails, able-bodied, stalwart, brawny, stout, sturdy, doughty, lusty, muscular, sinewy, athletic, virile, stanch, green, blooming, fresh, manly, in fine fettle, flourishing, in the pink *(coll.)*, in good case, in excellent condition, full of vim and vigor, energetic, forceful, spirited, solid, of firm body, fine *(coll.)*, fit as a fiddle *(coll.)*, bursting with health *or* vigor, well-knit, husky *(coll.)*, hearty, fit.

HALE, *v.* 1. Draw with force, tug, haul, pull, tow, lug, drag, heave, cart, jerk, convey, yank *(coll.)*.
2. Bring as by dragging, summon, cite, oblige to appear, force, order, bid, enjoin, charge, conduct, usher, compel, require, convoke, command, subpoena, apprehend, call *or* send for, arraign *(Law)*, constrain, bring up, coerce, challenge, dragoon, strong-arm *(sl.)*, escort.

HALF, *adj.* Partial, incomplete, fractional, fragmentary, shy, short, deficient, inadequate, divided, medium, imperfect, semi-, demi-, hemi-, dichotomous, lesser, sectional, immature, component, limited, moderate, small, slack, truncated, scanty, slight, meager, insufficient, bobtailed, portional, skimpy, one *(of two parts of a thing)*, extending halfway, covering a half, consisting of a moiety, wanting, immature, half-baked, poor, lame, perfunctory, void, jejune, bisected, halved, unripe, moderate, passable, tolerable, middling, halfway.

HALF, *adv.* 1. Partially, imperfectly, to the extent *or* measure of half, in part, partly, somewhat, in some measure, to a degree, to some extent, faintly, weakly, by halves, after a fashion, within bounds, relatively, fairly, middling *(coll.)*, moderately, rather, something *(coll.)*, passably, tolerably, not quite, almost, comparatively, with divided effort, by *or* in half measures, failing, inadequately, in default of, pretty, nearly, all but, insufficiently, in a manner, restrictedly, feebly.
2. *(With* NOT*)* Not at all, not by a great deal,

very little, hardly, not very, scarcely, not completely, not altogether, noway, by no means, in no manner, barely, only just, not a bit, in no wise, not a jot, not in the least, nowise, in no respect, on no account, not by a long shot *(coll.)*.

HALF, *n.* One of two quantitatively *or* numerically equal parts, a part approximately equal to the remainder, moiety, fraction, middle, bisection, fifty percent, fragment, fractional part, portion, mean, mediety *(Law)*, lot, dividend, section, division, hemisphere, one of two shares, considerable segment, quota, semisphere, part.

HALF-BAKED, *adj.* 1. *(Of a plan, proposition, scheme, etc.)* Shallow, superficial, undeveloped, inadequate, rough, crude, uncompleted, premature, cursory, imperfect, ignorant, short-sighted, pointless, foolish, meaningless, harebrained, immature, transitory, partial, inferior, ill-judged, ill-advised, meager, sketchy, unprepared, skimpy *(coll.)*, unfitted, groundless, indifferent, mediocre, unorganized, unformed, undigested, undone, half-cocked *(coll.)*, rudimentary, abortive, embryonic, embryotic, precocious, unfinished, rough-hewn, roughcast, unrefined, coarse, rude, ill-devised, unripe, pretentious, raw, unpolished, previous *(coll.)*, injudicious, impractical, impracticable, not completed, wanting, failing, precipitate, deficient, callow, sciolistic, irrational, in the rough, scanty.
2. *(Of a person)* Shallow, lacking mature judgment *or* experience, untried, superficial, undeveloped, imperfect, unskilled, young, green, unripe, unhatched, unfledged, childlike, leanwitted, harebrained, lack-brained, short-witted, wanting, inadequate, half-learned, sciolistic, lackwitted, unpracticed, unequipped, unfitted, callow, indifferent, unorganized, unformed, unseasoned, half-cocked *(coll.)*, immature, precocious, unpolished, rough, unfinished, uncultivated, unrefined, coarse, rude, rough-hewn, raw, unnurtured, irrational, ill-advised, unprepared, provincial, dilettante, sciolous, ignorant, short-sighted, foolish, naïve, artless, inexperienced, not dry behind the ears *(joc.)*, below par *(coll.)*, below the mark *(coll.)*, windy, pretentious.

HALF-BREED, *n.* 1. Half-caste, crossbreed, half blood, mulatto, hybrid, mestizo *(esp. Sp. Amer. and Philippines)*, mongrel, sambo, zambo *(Sp. Amer.)*, cafuso *(Brazil)*, Eurasian, creole, Ladino *(Sp. Amer.)*, high yellow *(coll.)*, cross, mustee *(West Indies and India)*, Anglo-Indian *(India)*.
2. Hybrid, mongrel, mule, zebrula, zebrass, cattalo, pomato, citrange, tangelo, plumcot *(Hort.)*.

HALF-HEARTED, *adj.* Indifferent, lukewarm, neutral, phlegmatic, timid, perfunctory, unfeeling, inert, insensible, passive, passionless, Laodicean, neither hot nor cold, apathetic, uninquiring, having *or* showing little enthusiasm, cool, sluggish, unstirred, unimpressible, careless, tame, uninterested, cold-hearted, frigid, unconcerned, languid, torpescent, supine, neither one thing nor the other, listless, lackadaisical, easygoing, unambitious, undesirous, disregardful, insouciant, disregardant, numbed, unsolicitous, inappetent, incurious, unmoved, unexcited, unimpressed, unanimated, pococurante, nonchalant, disregarding, obtuse, spiritless, impassive, irresolute, unaspiring, impartial, stolid, depressed, faint, cold, unemotional, dispassionate, devil-may-care, blasé, impassible, unruffled, dull, untouched, numb, benumbed, cold-blooded, cold as charity, torpid, regardless, unmindful, unaffected, uninspired.

HALFWAY, *adj.* Intermediate, middle, medium, midway between two places *or* points, part-way, partial, circumscribed, moderate, conditioned, limited, going *or* covering only half the full extent, mediocre, intermediary, mean, medial, average, neutral, intervening, interposed, middlemost, equatorial, equidistant, interjacent, between two extremes, mediate, mesial, septal, mid, central, midmost, mesne *(Law),* mesian *(Med.),* axial, pivotal, bounded, in the middle of the road, on the fence *(coll.),* portional, half-baked, middling, incomplete, fractional, imperfect, half.

HALFWAY, *adv.* Partially, in the middle, half over the way, to *or* at half the distance, to some degree *or* extent, medially, in the midst, mediumly, in *or* within the mean, in moderation, in part, in some measure, imperfectly, within bounds, fairly, middling *(coll.),* restrictedly, by *or* in half measures, comparatively, rather, moderately, partly, to a degree, to some extent, with divided effort, pretty, nearly, insufficiently.

HALF-WIT, *n.* One who is feeble-minded, dolt, dunce, foolish person, blockhead, simpleton, moron, idiot, lack-wit, crackbrain, incompetent, mental defective, mental deficient, lack-brain, dullard, imbecile, fool, zany, nitwit.

HALF-WITTED, *adj.* Weak-minded, imbecile, feeble-minded, witless, defective, weak-headed, simple-witted, simple-minded, idiotic, moronic, mentally undeveloped, crackbrained, foolish, mentally deficient, dull, stupid, empty-headed, stolid, sluggish, cretinous, anile, senile, incompetent, infantile, unintelligent, incapable of reason, not bright, childish, unteachable, unendowed with intellect, vacant, vacuous, bewildered, nitwitted *(sl.),* weak in the upper story *(sl.),* nutty *(sl.),* balmy *(sl.),* batty *(sl.),* loony *(sl.),* backward, puerile, dull-witted, thick-skulled, doltish, addle-headed, simple, simpletonian, not all there *(coll.),* babbling, driveling.

HALF-YEARLY, *adj.* Semi-annual, biannual, semestral, every six months, occurring twice a year.

HALL, *n.* 1. Entry of a house, entrance room, hallway, lobby, vestibule, corridor, passage, anteroom, antechamber, loggia, propylaeum, threshold, passageway, court.
  2. Large and impressive public *or* semi-public room, assembly room, auditorium, lyceum, meeting-place, lounge, chamber, aula, amphitheater, banquet hall, council chamber, exchange, bourse, mart, club room, concert hall, stoa *(Gk. Antiq.),* sala *(Sp.),* divan *(Orient),* atrium *(Rom. Antiq.),* odeum *(Gk. and Rom. Antiq.),* reception room, drawing room, presence chamber, state room, dining hall, refectory, greenroom, gymnasium, armory, gym *(coll.),* rotunda, waiting room, mess hall *(Mil.),* salon, burse, gallery, casino, lecture room, apartment, durbar *(India).*
  3. Large building for residence, instruction, *etc.,* manor house, public building, college building, mansion, castle, residence, dormitory, lyceum, pantheon, country seat, messuage, villa, concert hall, temple, church, market hall, lodge, guildhall, meeting house, city hall, town hall, student building, chapel, rotunda, hotel, cathedral, pavilion, château, casino, theater, country house, headquarters, place of entertainment, palace, armory.

HALLELUIAH, *interj.* Hosanna! praise ye Jehovah!, alleluia *or* alleluiah!, praise ye the Lord!, praise God!, praise the Lord!, Heaven be praised!, lift up your hearts!, sursum corda!, Deo gratias!, thanks be to God!, praise be!, glory be!, hurrah!, hurray! *(coll.),* huzza!, three cheers!, thank God!, glory be to God in the highest!, bless the Lord!, thank Heaven!.

HALLELUIAH, *n.* 1. Exclamation of "Hallelujah!", spiritual exultation, alleluia *or* alleluja), paean, glory, praise, glorification, laud, magnification, cheer, hosanna, holy rejoicing, hurrah, hurray *(coll.),* shout of praise, cry of jubilation, laudation, huzza, lyric joy.
  2. Musical composition based upon the word *hallelujah,* hymn, psalm, antiphon, Gloria, Gloria Patri, chant, doxology, canticle, carol, Gloria in Excelsis Deo, paean, anthem.

HALLMARK, *n.* Stamp showing conformity to standards, mark of genuineness, indication of quality, purity, *etc.,* certification, symbol, device, emblem, seal, sign, trademark, endorsement, seal of approval, sigil, signet, authentication, ratification, mark of acceptance.

HALLOO, *n.* The cry "Halloo!", shout, call, exclamation to attract attention, cry to incite dogs in hunting, *etc.,* yell, tallyho, yoicks, vociferation, yowl, howl, hoop, hoot, hey, ahoy, hail, hello, hollo, hallo, ho, yo-ho, yoo-hoo, hi, oyez, soho, hist.

HALLOO, *v.* Shout, call with a loud voice, cry out, exclaim, incite *or* chase with shouts and cries, utter with shouts, hollo, yell, whoop, pursue noisily, hail, give cry, sing out, rend the air, clamor, hoot, howl, yowl, hoop, yoick, yo-ho, cry *(as after dogs),* make an outcry, be clamorous, raise a cry, vociferate.

HALLOW, *v.* 1. Consecrate, sanctify, make holy, dedicate, deify, glorify, justify, absolve, exalt, crown, enthrone, signalize, pronounce holy, beatify, canonize, ordain, set apart, invest with solemnity, enshrine, anoint, lay hands on, confirm, celebrate, solemnize, impose, baptize, ritualize, immerse, dip, chrism, shrive, asperge, immortalize, devote, bless, saint, purify, raise, exalt, christen, ennoble, dignify.
  2. Reverence, honor as holy, venerate, pay homage to, observe with reverence, render honor to, revere, adore, glorify, keep holy, believe in, receive, celebrate, memorialize, commemorate, keep hallow, grace, worship, make obeisance to, bend the knee to, esteem, magnify, praise, acclaim, pay tribute to, laud, sing praises to, show honor to, humble oneself before, respect, do service to, bow down to, kneel before, prostrate oneself before, kiss the hem of one's garment, adore.

HALLOWED, *adj.* 1. Holy, sacred, consecrated, made holy, divine, godly, blessed, set apart, dedicated, sainted, pure, sanctified, inviolable, celestial, laudable, saintly, religious, godlike, sacrosanct, devoted, heavenly, devout, pious.
  2. Honored as holy, blessed, held inviolable, sanctified, revered, venerated, lauded, praised, acclaimed, adored, celebrated, rendered tribute, in highest esteem, reverenced, offered homage, bowed to, magnified, respected, adored, observed.

HALLUCINATION, *n.* 1. An apparent perception of sight *or* hearing, illusion, trick of eyesight, deception, delusion, phantasma, wandering of the mind, aberration, phantasm, dream, vision, chimera, infatuation, fancy, afterimage, vapor, phantom, luminescence, false show, ghost, fantod *(sl.),* hobgoblin, bubble, mirage, presence, ghostly form, ignis fatuus, shape, mare's-nest, apparition, seeming, specious appearance, *faux air (Fr.),* fata morgana, specter, imagining, phantasmagoria, will-o'-the-wisp, looming, distortion, figment, false light, goblin, trick, blue devils, snakes, pink elephants (sl.), incubus, pink spiders (sl.), coinage of the brain, Geist (Ger.), myth, fantastic vision, shadow, shade, sprite, wraith, umbra, eidolon, spook (coll.), poltergeist (Folklore and Spiritualism), exteriorized protoplasm (Spiritualism), ectoplasm (Spiritualism), friar's lantern, jack-o-lantern, unsubstantiality, banshee (Ir. and Scot. Folklore), larva (Rom. Rel. and Mediev. Occultism), lemures (Rom. Rel.), Brocken bow, Brocken specter, White Lady (Ger. Folklore).

2. A suffering from illusion or false notions, error, blunder, fallacy, delusion, self-deception, insanity, lunacy, delirium, self-deceit, imagining, misbelief, crotchet, vagary, falsity, philosophastry, speciousness, perversion, false coloring, mirage, dream, distortion, illogicalness, sophistry, misinterpretation, misconception, aberration, false sense of values, misapprehension, misestimation, bubble, fancy, obliquity, warped or distorted impression or idea, mistake, fool's paradise, misconstruction, boggle, fantastic vision, pathological or abnormal illusion, hallucinosis (Psychiatry).

HALO, n. 1. Ring of light, circle, corona, radiance, glory, burr, aureole, aureola, nimbus, aura, anthelion, coma, O, wheel of fire, gloriole, parhelion, vesica piscis (Lat.; Eccl. Art.), aurora, chromosphere (Astron.), halation (Photog.), disk of light, areola.

2. Ideal glory investing an object viewed with feeling or sentiment, luster, glory, limelight, brilliance, beauty, resplendence, sainthood, holiness, sanctity, brightness, glow, luminosity, magnification, praise, luminousness, refulgence, spiritual aura, sublimity, resplendency, illustriousness, radiance, splendor, blaze of glory, effulgence, sparkle, gloss, lucency, fulgidity, elevation, lambency, excellence, solemnity, majesty, exaltation, illumination, refulgency, scintillation, magnificence, beauty of holiness, brilliancy, grandeur, dignity, nobility, honor, lucence.

HALT, n. Stop, lull, cessation, spell, breathing-spell, wait, lapse, time out (coll.), letup (coll.), break, abeyance, rest, desistance, standstill, recess, intermission, leaving off, respite, interval, interlude, stoppage, discontinuance, pause.

HALT, v. 1. Make a temporary stop (as in marching), stop, hold, stand, draw up, wait, cease, rest, tarry, linger, pause, break, abide, cease progress, stay, remain, suspend, stall, stick, interrupt, pull up, quit, windup (coll.), leave off, have done with, call it a day (coll.), refrain, shut down, break off, hang fire, arrest, suspend, be quiescent, repose, come to a stand or standstill, mark time, terminate, relax, end, hang up one's ax or fiddle (coll.), knock off, shut up shop, stop short, come to a stop, desist, intermit, discontinue, cast anchor, become inactive, brake, slacken, rein in, ease up, let up, throttle down, heave to.

2. Cause to halt, check, stay, hold, cut short, bring to a stand or standstill, stem, stall, bring to an end, balk, deter, prevent, curb, arrest, thwart, suppress, interrupt, obstruct, hinder, impede, repress, scotch, undermine, extinguish, cut off, delay, deadlock, checkmate, intermit, intercept, end, defeat, abate, embarrass, frustrate, foil, restrict, clog, hamper, hold in check, stop, block, go or act contrary to, spike one's guns, blockade, estop, choke off, constrain, inhibit, barricade, preclude, discommode, shackle, dam, counteract, contravene, prohibit, restrain, incommode, debar, hedge in, traverse, override, confound, discountenance, baffle, throw a wrench in the works (coll.), stand

in the way of, clip one's wings, tie one's hands, spoil sport, faze (coll.), disconcert, nonplus, overthwart, upset, forbid the banns, dash the cup from one's lips, cut the ground from under one, hang like a millstone round one's neck, scotch the wheel, take the wind out of one's sails, throw or lay a wet blanket on, nip in the bud, vanquish, overthrow, overturn, worst, put to flight, oppose, steal one's thunder, put a spoke in one's wheel, lay by the heels, disallow, forbid, outwit, squelch (coll.) put down, discomfit, subdue, outdo, rout, quell, crush, quash, reduce.

3. Proceed in a faulty way (as in speech, reasoning, etc.), stammer, stutter, falter, hesitate, hobble, stumble, flag, mumble, maunder, speak thickly, snuffle, mouth, mutter, hum or hem and haw, balbutiate, haw, drag, drawl, shake, quaver, elenchize, lisp, reason in a circle, misapply, misjudge, misinterpret, reason illogically, paralogize, distort, shift, shuffle, cavil, quibble, equivocate, pervert, sophisticate, sputter, splutter.

4. Be in doubt, waver, hesitate, be irresolute, debate, be perplexed, hang in doubt or suspense, hang back, scruple, qualm, demur, stick at, boggle, falter, vary, question, wonder, hang fire, back aimlessly, sway, flit, shift, flutter, flicker, back and fill, vacillate, swing from one thing to another, evade the question, show indecision, be of two minds, hum or hem and haw, be afraid to decide, shuffle, have two minds, not know one's own mind, not know which way to turn, be at sea, flounder, stagger, beat about, be changeable, stumble, pause, puzzle over, ponder, fluctuate, dilly-dally, shilly-shally.

HALTER, n. Noose, hangman's noose, rope, bowstring.

HALVE, v. Cut in half, cut in halves, share equally, divide, split, split in two, sever or sunder in two, cleave, dichotomize, bisect, dimidiate, hemisect.

HAM, n. One of the rear quarters of a hog, leg, thigh, hip, butt, gammon, jambon (Fr.), drumstick (of a fowl), popliteal space, buttock, gigot (of lamb, mutton).

HAMADRYAD, n. Wood nymph, dryad, nymphid, tree spirit.

HAMATE, adj. Hooked, hook-shaped, having a hooklike process, hooklike, hamulate, hamulose, incurvate, incurvated, incurved, uncate, rostrate, rostrated, curved, rhamphoid, beaked, uncinate, uncinated, uncinal, unciform, beaklike, crooked, rostroid, rostriform, bent, hamated, hamiform, hamose, hamous, aduncous, adunc, aduncate, aduncated, unguiculate, horned, unguiculated, arciform, arctuated, arctuate, bowed, sickle-shaped, moon-shaped, luniform, falciform, falcate, falcated, aquiline.

HAMLET, n. Village, thorp (Arch. except in compounds), dorp, crossroads, pueblo (Amer. Ind.), jerkwater town (sl.), hick town (sl.).

HAMMER, n. Beetle, tapper, martel (Hist.), helve hammer, steam hammer, tamper, claw hammer, pile driver, sledge, sledge hammer, gavel, marteline (marble work and sculpture), crandall (stone cutting), fuller (blacksmithing), kevel (stone breaking), cock (of a gun), maul, monkey, punch, commander, rammer, mallet.

HAMMER, v. 1. Beat with a hammer, strike, pound, knock, belabor, cudgel, drive, skelp, martellate, ram, martel, pulverize, beetle, pummel, tap, bang, thump, tamp, buffet, rap, baste, punch, whack, slam.

2. *(With* OUT) Form with a hammer, forge, beat out, hew, put together, make, manufacture, construct, form, fashion, pattern, shape, chisel, rough-hew, carve, cut, knock together, knock out *(coll.)*, work out, roughcast, erect, block out, fabricate, contrive.

3. *(With* OUT) Finish, complete, render complete, perform, perfect, make, achieve, culminate, execute, discharge, dispatch, round out, bring to pass, bring to a conclusion, bring to maturity, bring to an end, bring about, effect, produce, compass, do, consummate, fulfill, attain, carry out, carry through.

4. *(Often with* AWAY) Persist, attempt repeatedly, keep on, stay at it, stick to it, hold on, hold out, maintain one's efforts, do frequently *or* often, keep doggedly on, peg away *(coll.)*, plug away *(coll.)*, plod, drudge, labor.

HAMMOCK, *n.* Hanging bed *or* couch, swing, glider.

HAMPER, *n.* Basket, receptacle, hanaper, pannier, punnet, dosser, creel, *corbeille (Fr.)*.

HAMPER, *v.* Hold back, handicap, obstruct, choke, circumscribe, harness, frustrate, thwart, smother, curb, trammel, restrain, impede, shackle, manacle, muzzle, encumber, constrain, bridle, inhibit, brake, gag, cloy, debar, block, rein, withhold, hinder, repress, prevent, fetter, impedite, bar, check, balk, retard, cohibit, circumvent, estop, suppress, hold.

HAMSTRING, *v.* Cripple, disable, maim, lame, hock, incapacitate, becripple, impair, unsinew, disenable, cramp, injure.

HAND, *n.* 1. Palm, fist, manus *(Anat.)*, famble *(sl.)*, extremity *(of animals)*: paw, foot, claw, trotter, hoof, pad, talons, unguis *(pl. ungues)*, pounce *(of bird of prey)*, pincers, nippers.

2. Laborer, worker, employe, man, hired hand, hired man, workman, helper, menial, workingman, aid.

3. Sign *(pointing to something)*, pointer, arrow, finger, guidepost, signpost, direction, finger post.

4. Signature, autograph, endorsement, handwriting, superscription.

5. Handwriting, manuscript, autograph, script, longhand, calligraphy, penmanship, notations, chirography, pencraft, stylography, scrivenery, scrawl, scribble, griffonage *(bad handwriting)*.

6. *(Often plural as In one's* HANDS) Possession, power, hold, grip, governorship, heed, auspices, wardship, control, custody, keeping, care, jurisdiction, guidance, dominion, patronage, command, authority, management, domination, grasp, charge, mastery, clutches, disposal, rule, captaincy, sway, supervision.

7. *(As a master's* HAND) Skill, touch, competency, knowledge, facility, ability, adroitness, proficiency, knack, execution, expertness, mastery, craft, dexterity, cleverness, efficiency, capacity, capability, aptitude, handiness.

HAND, *v.* 1. Deliver, turn over to, reach, pass, hand over, give, forward, put in the hands of, present, furnish with.

2. Help, aid, give a hand to, hold out a helping hand to, do a good turn, expedite, promote, give moral support, come to the aid of, further, speed, back up, upbear, shoulder, abet, pull an oar, stand by, succor, assist, minister to, contribute, bolster, subscribe to, support, serve, prop, second, befriend, give a leg up.

3. *(With* DOWN, *as a legal decision, etc.)*

Transmit, convey, bear, consign, pass down, communicate, impart, deliver.

4. *(With* DOWN) Bequeath, render, impart, allot, apportion, accord, transmit, present, leave to, bestow, cede, communicate, dispense, grant, invest, give, assign, will to, entrust, deliver, transfer, turn over, commit to, confer, award, donate.

HANDBAG, *n.* Bag, pocketbook, purse, wallet.

HANDBILL, *n.* Circular, announcement, advertisement, duplicated communication, bill, notice, follow-up, dodger, broadsheet, broadside, encyclical, form letter, placard, flier, poster, proclamation, bulletin.

HANDBOOK, *n.* Manual, enchiridion, pocket manual, vade mecum *(Lat.)*, bible, basic text, instruction book, book of fundamentals, directory.

HANDCART, *n.* Wagon, pushcart, barrow, handbarrow, wheelbarrow, push car, gocart.

HANDCUFF, *n.* *(Often plural)* Shackles, fetters, chains, bonds, manacles, cuffs, gyve *(for the legs)*, trammels, bilbo.

HANDFUL, *n.* A little, fistful, few, small quantity, tiny amount, scant amount, meager supply, small number, modicum, minimum, mere scattering.

HANDICAP, *n.* 1. Stumbling block, retardment, interference, encumbrance, disadvantage, restriction, penalty, inconvenience, drawback, disability, nuisance, holdback, obstruction, difficulty, weight, inhibition, impediment, barrier, hampering, check, trammel, bridle, stopper, stay, burden, onus, retardation, balk, constraint, impedition, repression, limitation, obstacle.

2. *(Extended sense)* Advantage, edge, allowance, benefit, odds, upper hand, asset, superiority, vantage, jump.

HANDICAP, *v.* 1. Check, hinder, prevent, burden, trammel, hold back, bridle, estop, debar, smother, stop, weigh down, balk, restrain, curb, impede, saddle, bar, obstruct, circumscribe, cohibit, impedite, limit, hold, halt, stall, repress, constrain, retard, block, brake, inhibit, suppress, frustrate, thwart, withhold, muzzle, harness, rein, arrest, encumber, hamper, overburden, overload, shackle.

2. Render equal, equalize, level, balance, nullify, neutralize, counteract, compensate, give points, adjust, offset, square, counterbalance, countervail, counterpoise.

HANDICRAFT, *n.* Hand work, manual skill, craft, handiwork, manual art, industrial art, skilled labor, workmanship, craftsmanship.

HANDICRAFTSMAN, *n.* Craftsman, worker, skilled laborer, artificer, artisan, artifex *(Lat.)*.

HANDILY, *adv.* 1. Dexterously, skillfully, proficiently, cleverly, well, with good technique, facilely, adroitly, expertly, capably, efficiently, competently, readily, quickly, easily, masterfully, artistically, with skill, fluently.

2. Conveniently, easily, without trouble, without difficulty, comfortably, simply, without strain, effortlessly, smoothly, readily.

HANDINESS, *n.* 1. Ability, skill, expertness, adroitness, capacity, knowledge, craft, cleverness, aptitude, facility, proficiency, mastery, knack, efficency, dexterity, competency, capability.

2. Convenience, accessibility, attainability, readiness, workability, availability, practicability, timeliness.

HANDIWORK, *n.* 1. Hand work, manual skill, craftsmanship, skilled labor, workmanship, manual art, handicraft, industrial art, craft.

2. Labor, toil, work, industry, manufacture, manual labor.

3. Workmanship, work, production, origination, invention, creation, fashioning, construction, concoction, formation, fabrication, achievement, manufacture, composition.

HANDKERCHIEF, *n.* Kerchief, neckerchief, sudarium.

HANDLE, *n.* Hilt, haft, lug, bail, trigger, hold, helve, handstaff *(of a flail),* crop *(of a whip),* snath *(of a scythe),* handle bar, rounce *(Print.),* crank, shank, grasp, shaft, withe, pull.

HANDLE, *v.* 1. Touch, hold, pick up, palpate, feel, palm, paw *(coll.),* fumble with, caress, wield, manipulate, thumb, finger, stroke, massage, knead, run the fingers *or* hand over, take in the hands.

2. Use, manipulate, wield, utilize, exercise, avail oneself of, work, employ, turn to account, convert to use, put in operation, put in practice, bring into play, operate, exert, ply.

3. Manage, direct, control, manipulate, command, dispose, maneuver, conduct, dispatch, prescribe, preside over, care for, superintend, engineer, rule, boss, hold the reins, be at the wheel, govern, run, operate, discharge, supervise, head, lead, pilot, take the helm, drive, regulate, guide, steer, administer, execute, transact.

4. Discuss, treat, speak of, take up, deal with, dissertate, discourse upon, comment upon, descant, review, expatiate, write upon *or* about, talk about, go into, touch upon, converse about, dilate, criticize.

5. Deal in, sell, exchange, traffic in, trade, peddle, truck, hawk, realize, barter, vend, dispense, market, retail, merchandise, conduct business in, buy and sell, offer for sale, carry, wholesale, deliver.

HANDSOME, *adj.* 1. Agreeable to the eye *or* to correct taste, comely, fair, tasteful, admirable, elegant, seemly, goodly, sightly, pleasing, shapely, well-favored, good-looking, attractive, lovely, pretty, beautiful, stately, fine-looking, refined, concinnate, artistic, simple, polished, restrained, imposing, impressive, majestic, august, regal, rich, dignified, exquisite, beauteous, grand, splendid, resplendent, manly, queenly, sleek, of noble lineaments, well-composed, well-arranged, proper, in good form, in good taste, chaste, subtle, cultivated, fastidious, well-groomed, showing discrimination, selective, distinctive, *comme il faut (Fr.),* of fine *or* admirable appearance, well-formed, well-proportioned, symmetrical, bonny, fine, nice, smart, neat, well-set, debonair, of fine bearing, easy on the eyes *(sl.),* easy to look at *(sl.),* personable, stunning *(sl.),* dazzling.

2. Evincing a becoming generosity *or* nobleness, generous, liberal, gracious, magnanimous, munificent, princely, unselfish, ungrudging, unstinting, bounteous, humane, free, unsparing, bighearted, open-handed, great-hearted, beneficent, hospitable, philanthropic, humanitarian, almsgiving, charitable, bountiful, benignant, lavish, benevolent, benign, good, kind, chivalric, merciful, elevated, compassionate, lofty, high-minded, pitying, courteous, supererogatory, eleemosynary, abounding, noble-minded, altruistic, chivalrous, sublime, noble, impartial, disinterested.

3. Ample, sufficient, considerable, liberal in amount, sizeable, goodly, large, plentiful, bountiful, veteran, seasoned, able, *au fait (Fr.),* versed, abundant, tidy *(coll.),* satisfactory, moderately large, full, equal to all demands.

HANDWRITING, *n.* Writing done with the hand, a kind *or* style of writing, hand, script, chirography, style of penmanship, longhand, shorthand, engrossment, fist *(coll.),* writing, penmanship, scrawl, scribble, manuscript, scrabble, scratch *(coll.),* autograph, signature, autography, scription, penscript, scrivening, griffonage, scrivenery, pencraft, calligraphy.

HANDY, *adj.* 1. Dexterous, ready with the hands, skillful with the hands, expert, adroit, deft, inventive, apt, ingenious, versatile, accomplished, practiced, trained, gifted, experienced, endowed, nimble-fingered, capable, up in, at home in, well-versed in, fine-fingered, a good hand at, conversant with, familiar with, adept, proficient, quick, masterly, crack *(coll.),* crackerjack *(sl.),* masterful, veteran, seasoned, able, *au fait (Fr.),* versed, efficient, felicitous, good at, strong in, competent, facile, helpful, skilled, clever.

2. Convenient, ready to hand, easily accessible, available, close at hand, at hand, on call, nigh, near, obtainable, adjacent, waiting, attending, at one's call, on tab, in readiness, on hand, prepared, at one's elbow, present, propinquous, bordering, proximate, proximal, furnished, vicinal, neighboring, contingent, contiguous, adjoining, propinquant, ready-made, ready-mixed, fitted, well-stocked, well-supplied, well-provided, at one's beck and call, juxtapositional, juxtapositive, equipped, on the table.

3. Convenient to handle, easily manipulated, maneuverable, manageable, governable, compliant, yielding, ductile, compact, portable, wieldy, flexible, plastic, limber, tractable, simple, light, supple, facile, docile, submissive, toward, pliant, responsive, sensitive.

4. Convenient, useful, commodious, serviceable, fitting, applicable, adaptable, beneficial, instrumental, conducive, adjuvant, efficacious, effective, timely, all-round *(coll.),* of all work, expedient, advantageous, good to have, desirable, recommendable, profitable, worth-while, helpful, utilitarian, practical, contributory, practicable, cooperative.

HANDY MAN, *n.* Do-all, factotum, jack-of-all-trades, general servant, man of all work, man Friday, office boy, servant of all work, hired man, doer-of-all-work.

HANG, *v.* 1. Fasten from above, suspend, attach so as to swing, append, balance, swing, fasten into position, fix, affix, string up, fasten up, sling, make pendulous, hinge, hook up, make pendent, fix at a proper angle, attach to a wall *(of wallpaper).*

2. Fasten *(a person)* on a cross as capital punishment, execute by hanging, gibbet, truss, kill by hanging, suspend by the neck until dead, bring to the gallows, garrote, noose, neck, suspend *(a person)* on the gallows, bowstring, impale, string up, crap *(thieves' slang),* crucify, lynch, strangle, throttle, choke.

3. Incline *(the head),* decline, drop, droop, let droop, bend forward *or* downward, nod, swag, sag, descend, lower, tend downward, lean over, trail, flow, slope, stream, lop, draggle, bedraggle, daggle, flap.

4. Adorn, *(with hangings, draperies, tapestries, pictures, etc.),* furnish *or* decorate with something suspended, drape, deck, bedeck, cover, array, trim, garnish, enrich, embellish, ornament.

5. Depend, dangle, be suspended, swing freely, pend, impend, be pendent.

6. Depend, rely, be dependent, hang in the balance, hang on or upon, repose in, rest in, lie in, lean upon, be contingent, hang in suspense, tremble in the balance, revolve around, turn upon, hinge on, be conditioned by, pend, rest, be subject to.

7. Be doubtful, waver, hesitate, be uncertain, doubt, be undecided, be undetermined, change, debate, dubitate, question, wonder, pause, falter, hang fire, vacillate, hang back, hold back, remain unfinished, have one's doubts, be on the fence, lose one's way, wander aimlessly, hang in the balance, be at sea, toss and turn, ponder, swing from one thing to another, flounder, back and fill, puzzle over, boggle, qualm, have qualms, be irresolute, show indecision, not know one's own mind, not know where one stands, wait to see how the wind blows, stop to consider, have two minds, be of two minds, swerve, veer, chop and change, shuffle, shift, blow hot and cold, be capricious, dodge, deviate, aboutface, straddle, shift one's ground, be changeable, tergiversate, dally with, weigh one thing against another, think twice about, fluctuate, consider both sides, hum or hem and haw, wait to see how the cat jumps, tremble in the balance, hang in doubt.

8. Stick, stay, delay, prevent from reaching a decision, check, keep (a jury) from rendering a verdict, impede, nonplus, hinder, demur, retard, hold up, block, refuse to agree, bring to a standstill, obstruct, preclude, blockade, curb, cramp, hamper, inhibit, embarrass, deadlock, take exception, hold back, stalemate, hang up, restrict.

9. (With ABOUT) Frequent, loiter, linger, resort to frequently, haunt, revisit constantly, hover about, repair to habitually, go to often, bend one's steps to, beat a path to, direct one's course to, dance attendance upon, stick around (sl.), hang out at (sl.), hang around (sl.).

10. (With BACK) Hesitate, shy at, stick at, hold back, be fearful, resist advance, pull back, avoid, shirk, recoil, shy, flinch, wince, be reluctant, falter, have qualms, qualm, vacillate, quail, retire, dodge, swerve, duck, sheer off, shrink back, cower, crouch, fear, take fright or alarm, freeze, shrink, hang, blink, blench, waver, be backward, tremble in the balance.

11. (With BACK) Resist advance, be reluctant to proceed, take one's time, loiter, linger, stroll, inch along, drag, lag, trail, saunter, halt, refrain from action, hang fire, procrastinate, dillydally, pull back, temporize, shirk, tarry, shamble, delay, dawdle, be leisurely, poke, be inactive, do nothing, consume time, idle, mosey (sl.), fiddle-faddle, fuss with trifles, watch and wait, stall (sl.), stall for time (sl.), hang a leg, be dilatory, gain or make time, talk against time, play for time, hold off, be unproductive, fold one's arms, twiddle one's thumbs, mark time, bide one's time, tie up with red tape, filibuster, potter, piddle, withhold (decision, etc.), coquet, flag, dally, dam the stream, hold back, hang fire.

12. (With BACK) Abstain, refrain, forbear, hold, be passive, ignore, have nothing to do with, take no part in, refuse, stand, be at a standstill, stop short, be quiescent, be inert, drift with the current, desist, discontinue, sleep, slumber, leave undone, leave unfinished, not complete, do nothing, idle, consume time, refrain from action, let slide, let go, let it ride, not stir, let be, leave or let well enough alone, let things take their course, have no hand in, watch and wait, repose, rest, stop, stay, halt, smolder, laissez faire (Fr.), stall (sl.), fail to

attain, decline, stall for time (sl.), be unproductive, fold one's arms, twiddle one's thumbs, be neutral, bide one's time, mark time, hang fire, withhold (decision, etc.), cease, be inactive, wait.

13. (With BACK) Scruple, boggle, stick at, protest, raise objections, carp, ergotize, cavil, stickle, argue sophistically, wrangle, dissent, oppose, object, take exception.

14. (With ON) Continue, remain in force or existence, last, persevere, be persistent, be protracted, adhere, stay, stick, endure, persist, extend, stretch out, be prolonged, remain, wear on, drag on, linger, crawl, linger on.

15. (With ON or ONTO) Keep hold, hold fast, cling, stick, adhere, cleave, clinch, rest for support, hold on or onto, hold tight, follow, grip, gripe, clench, lean on, cohere, clutch, rest on, keep a firm hold on, grasp, put one's weight on, hold for support, keep close.

16. (With ON or UPON) Attend closely, hang upon the skirts of, stick like a leech, follow close upon, follow persistently, tread on the heels of, be in constant attendance, dance attendance to, hang about, linger in one's presence, pander to, minister to, work for, do service to, work in the service of, serve, dog, wait upon, tend, hang on the sleeve of, be doormat to, fawn, truckle, toady, toadeat, lickspittle, kowtow, bow and scrape, follow at heel, be obsequious, bend the knee to, prostrate oneself, kneel to, stoop before, creep, crawl, grovel, black one's boots, worm oneself, creep into the good graces of, ingratiate or insinuate oneself, pay court to, court or curry favor, adhere, be servile, handshake (sl.), pin or fasten oneself upon, stick closer than a brother, cling like ivy, cling like a bur, be sycophantic, be a hanger-on, heel, shadow, fetch and carry, sponge on (coll.), be a timeserver, adulate, flatter, be a parasite, be a clinging vine.

17. (With ON or UPON, of one's words) Attend admiringly, regard with passionate admiration, be spellbound, listen devotedly, absorb, attend closely, be in a state of rapt attention, be charmed by, rivet the mind on, devote oneself to, heed, mind, give ear, hang upon the lips of, be entranced by, be bewitched by, wait upon eagerly.

18. (With ON or UPON) Rest in, depend upon, rely upon, hang in the balance, hinge on, be conditioned by, pend, be subject to, be contingent upon, revolve around, turn upon, repose in, lie in, lean upon.

19. (With OUT) Display, be displayed, project, protrude, be suspended in open view, stand out, traject, extend, jut out, be posted, bulge.

20. (With OUT) Hold out, offer resistance, not submit, be unyielding, resist, be obstinate, hinder, thwart, counteract, stickle, stand out, not yield an inch, die hard, be wedded to an opinion, persist in one's way, resist to the end, fight to the last ditch, reluct, reluctate, kick against the pricks, stand fast, make a stand against, take one's stand, stand or hold one's ground, countervail, stultify, obstruct, never say die, breast or stem the tide, oppose, sell one's life dearly, play or work at cross-purposes, protest, embarrass, restrict, impede, be contrary to, run counter to, cross, take issue with, die fighting, go down fighting, hug a belief, clog or scotch the wheels, stand up against, fly in the face of, make a determined resistance, withstand.

21. (With OVER) Overhang, impend, project, beetle, jut, rise above, overlie, overlap, abut, command, surmount, arch over, imbricate, overarch, overlook.

22. *(With* OVER*)* Hover, float, be in the air, impend, be near at hand, be imminent, lie over, threaten, hang over one's head, stare one in the face, lower, be in store for, menace, loom, approach, await, come on, come near, advance, draw near, be in the wind, near.

HANGDOG, *adj.* Sneaking, base, mean, ashamed, having a mean *or* sneaking appearance, degraded, contemptible, ignoble, cringing, fawning, groveling, shifty, furtive, guilty, shamefaced, outcast, abject, scurvy, villainous, blackguard, low, lowbred, lowborn, baseborn, lowly, inglorious, infamous, petty, little, dirty, scabby, scrubby, shabby, paltry, recreant, caitiff, cowardly, poltroon, wretched, pusillanimous, dastardly, dastard, dunghill, cowering, skulking, beggarly, despicable, dunghilly, evil-faced, ill-contrived, obsequious, servile, slinking, spiritless, unwholesome, sinister, evil-eyed, pettifogging, deplorable, reptilian, quailing, evil-affected, currish, spineless, white-livered, disingenuous, ignominious.

HANGER-ON, *n.* One who clings to a person, place *or* service, follower, parasite, dependent, vassal, minion, tagtail, fawner, toady, votary, toad-eater, sponger, sycophant, snob, tufthunter, groveler, spaniel, truckler, lickspit, appendant, handshaker *(sl.),* apple-polisher *(sl.),* sidekick *(sl.),* yes man *(sl.),* henchman, appendage, bootlicker, footlicker, lackey, shadow, flunky, sectary, disciple, dangler, courtier, carpet knight, partisan, adherent, satellite, retainer, wheedler, bur, heeler *(sl.),* client, lickspittle.

HANGING, *n.* 1. Act of one who *or* that which hangs, pendency, droop, hang, dangling, clinging, inclination, poise, pensility, pendulousness, dependence, declining, inclining, suspension, overhanging, drooping, pendulosity, suspensation, pensileness, overhang.

2. Capital punishment by suspension with strangling on a gallows, death by the halter, death on the gallows, execution by hanging, the noose, the rope, strangling, the gallows, garrote, strangulation, the scaffold, floorless jig *(coll.),* necktie party *or* sociable *(coll.).*

3. *(Often plural)* Something that hangs *or* is hung on the walls of a room, drapery, tapestry, curtain, dorsal, arras, blind, lambrequin, valance, Venetian blind, jalousie, portière, dosser, canopy, tester, sash curtain, window shade, window curtain, veil.

4. *(Theater)* Drop, backdrop, back cloth, back scene, act drop, drop screen, teaser, cloth, drop curtain, teaser curtain.

HANGMAN, *n.* One who hangs persons condemned to death, public executioner, Jack Ketch, garroter, topsman *(sl.).*

HANK, *n.* Skein *(as of thread or yarn),* loop, coil *(of hair, etc.),* twist, knot, roll, definite length *(of thread or yarn).*

HANKER, *v. (Often foll. by* AFTER, FOR, *or an infinitive)* Have a restless *or* incessant longing for *or* after, long for, covet, yearn, crave, wish, hunger, desire ardently, set one's heart upon, itch after, be bent upon, have a fancy for, set one's cap for *(coll.),* grasp at, die for, pant for, cry for, gasp for, pine for, languish for, raven for, run mad after, aspire after, be fervently desirous of, thirst, lust, cast sheep's eyes upon, ogle, court, woo, jump at, look sweet upon *(coll.),* yen for *(coll.),* sigh for, have an eye to, take into one's head.

HANKERING, *n.* Longing, strong desire, burning want, craving, appetite, itching, importunate craving, passion, cupidity, wish, weakness, insatiable desire, craze, mania, prurience, breathless impatience, ardor, eagerness, aspiration, coveting, vaulting ambition, zeal, *empressement (Fr.),* sheep's eyes, frenzy, irresistible urge, cacoëthes, greed, covetousness, extreme *or* inordinate desire, voracity, keenness, grasping, rapacity, libido *(Psychol.),* ravenousness, greediness, avarice, yearning, lust, teasing desire, impatience, appetence, itch, yen *(coll.),* appetency.

HAPHAZARD, *adj.* Chance, random, without order *or* purpose, unsystematic, aimless, slapdash, careless, accidental, without choice, scratch, sudden, casual, arbitrary, capricious, stray, nonchalant, fortuitous, unconsidered, chancy *(coll.),* hit or miss, unexpected, incidental, lawless, chaotic, cursory, unpurposed, undesigned, uncertain, mercurial, fluctuating, inconstant, undirected, adventitious, undeterminate, never thought of, fitful, wavering, anarchic, unintended, indiscriminate, unwitting, disorganized, sporadic, determined by chance, orderless, offhand, driftless, unforeseen, extemporaneous, spontaneous, promiscuous, occasional, contingent, risky, spasmodic, dependent on mere chance, catch-as-catch-can, disorderly, disordered, unarranged, desultory, unthinking, unmethodical, irregular, coincidental, straggling, undetermined, unintentional, unpremeditated, fluky *(sl.).*

HAPLESS, *adj.* Luckless, unlucky, unfortunate, wretched, ill-fated, jinxed, Jonahed, disastrous, ill-starred, unhappy, miserable, fortuneless, unblest, unprosperous, out of luck, woebegone, bereft, hopeless, evil-starred, under a cloud, clouded, down on one's luck *(coll.),* thwarted, born with a wooden ladle in one's mouth, scotched, foiled, crossed, victimized, stultified, balked, woeful, forlorn, hoodooed *(coll.),* in ill luck, born under an evil star, cursed, dashed *(coll.),* infelicitous.

HAPPEN, *v.* 1. Occur, take place, come to pass, take effect, come off, betide, befall, come, fall out, supervene, go, pass, bechance, rise, fall, intervene, go wrong, miscarry, present itself, prevail, crop up, come into existence, take its course, come around, spring up, prove, ensue, fare, result, come after, evenuate, arise, issue, come about, appear.

2. Come to pass by chance, happen without apparent reason *or* design, chance, fall out, turn up, bechance, befall, betide, exist, be the case, appear, occur providentially, be one's lot, be one's fortune.

3. Have the fortune *or* lot *(to do or be as specified),* chance, be so fortunate as, be by chance, exist fortuitously, be opportunely.

4. *(With* TO*)* Befall *(as to a person or thing),* betide, fall to one's lot, be one's fate, be suffered by, be endured by, grip, have one in its grip, become of, be undergone by, be borne by, be one's fortune *or* misfortune, be supported by, be experienced by.

5. *(Foll. by* ON *or* UPON*)* Come on by chance, discover unexpectedly, stumble on, fall upon by chance, meet with, blunder upon, hit upon, light upon, hit.

HAPPENING, *n.* Event, occurrence, proceeding, case, transaction, incident, chance, affair, episode, coming, mishap, doing, fact, particular, occasion, phenomenon, experience, circumstance, incidence, contingency, matter, business, pass, crisis, vicissitudes of fortune, job *(coll.),* happenstance *(humorous)*, adventure, eventuality, contretemps, coincidence, concern, accident, casualty, venture, advent, fortune, fortuity, emergency, hazard, lot.

HAPPILY, *adv.* 1. With pleasure, in a happy manner, contentedly, gladly, zestfully, with open arms, of one's own accord, freely, delightfully, delightedly, with relish, willingly, graciously, with a good will, with all one's heart, sincerely, joyously, with good grace, nothing loath, fain, without demur, merrily, as lief, without reluctance, *con amore (It.)*, tactfully, with zeal, *de bonne grâce (Fr.)*, lovingly, devotedly, agreeably, elatedly, blithely, buoyantly, with willingness, with right good will, *de bonne volonté (Fr.)*, heart and soul, heartily, *ex animo (Lat.)*, joyfully, in happy circumstances.

2. Luckily, fortunately, favorably, easily, opportunely, swimmingly, by good fortune, as luck would have it, auspiciously, propitiously, seasonably, providentially, prosperously, expediently, at a critical moment *(or period or point)*, in the nick of time, conveniently, advantageously.

3. Aptly, appropriately, skillfully, dexterously, gracefully, with skill, felicitously, fitly, with credit, commendably, pertinently, apropos, well, tactfully, excellently, aright, with fine technique, easily, suitably, properly, artfully, cleverly, neatly, admirably.

HAPPINESS, *n.* 1. Quality *or* state of being happy, joy, delight, pleasure, cheerfulness, ecstasy, elation, gladness, rejoicing, felicity, bliss, enjoyment, satisfaction, well-being, blitheness, high spirits, jubilation, merrymaking, mirth, rapture, ravishment, joyance, gusto, peacefulness, delectation, festivity, jollity, gaiety, good, serenity, fullness of the heart, Elysium, sunshine, cheeriness, geniality, oblectation, intoxication, clover, transport, exultation, paradise, brightness, lightheartedness, heaven, complacence, welfare, beatitude, third *or* seventh heaven, merriment, relish, mirthfulness, cheer, enchantment, glee, blessedness, exaltation, jubilation, hedonism, exuberance.

2. Good fortune, good luck, prosperity, content, blessedness, well-being, affluence, the smiles of fortune, comfort, satisfaction, triumph, success, luck, advance, progress, achievement, fair wind, high tide, providence, blessings, windfall, godsend, millennium, golden age, bright clouds, Saturnian time, silver lining, thriving condition, halcyon days, fat of the land, bed of roses, pleasure, gladness, contentment, welfare, gratification, satisfaction, fair weather.

3. Felicity *(as of expression)*, aptness, graceful aptitude, felicitous elegance, deftness, ingenuity, technique, faculty, knack, trick of thought, turn of phrase, art, mastery, address, discrimination, harmonious simplicity, pertinence, appositeness, harmony, euphony, facility, dexterity, balance, beauty, grace, craft, taste, the right word in the right place, refinement, propriety, relevancy, compatibility, wit, aptitude, ease, execution, finish, gift, unstudied grace.

HAPPY, *adj.* 1. Characterized by *or* indicative of pleasure, content *or* gladness, joyous, lighthearted, contented, gay, merry, cheerful, blissful, sunny, blithe, buoyant, rapturous, ecstatic, delirious, enrapt, charmed, radiant, mirthful, zestful, captivated, in good *or* high spirits, in high feather, happy as a king, happy as the day is long, happy as a lark, cloudless, unalloyed, blessed, blest, beatific, jocund, smiling, exultant,

content, glad, pleased, delighted, gratified, rejoiced, gladdened, vivacious, jovial, gleeful, comfortable, satisfied, gladsome, laughing, relieved, congenial, transported, boon, bonny, tickled, rhapsodic, intoxicated, hearty, expressing happiness, enraptured, entranced, exuberant, debonair, carefree, elated, rejoicing, joyful, jolly, overjoyed, riant, hilarious, jubilant, flushed with excitement *or* pleasure, merry as a cricket *or* grig, Elysian, peaceful, in third *or* seventh heaven, blithesome, light, cheery, well, halcyon, primrose, sparkling, exhilarated.

2. Lucky, fortunate, favored by fortune, favored by luck, propitious, of good omen, promising, palmy, auspicious, favorable, bright, judicious, golden, sunny, timely, seasonable, prosperous, successful, goodly, flourishing, providential, profitable, worth-while, Saturnian, cheering, convenient, opportune, red-letter *(day)*, rosy, primrose, halcyon, prospering, thriving, expedient, advantageous.

3. Ready, apt, felicitous, fitting, dexterous, adroit, skilful, able, expert, neat, strong, graceful, clever, lively, pleasing, delightful, apropos, suitable, meet, idoneous, euphonious, fluent, flowing, easy, facile, appropriate, sprightly, becoming, pleasurable, politic, pleasant, agreeable, gratifying, harmonious, congenial, pertinent, well-timed, apposite, appurtenant, pat, semly, decorous, beguiling, germane, proper, in point, to the point *or* purpose, bearing upon, relevant, applicable, entrancing, enchanting, gladsome, exhilarating, adapted, mellifluous, tasteful, comely, expedient, ravishing, befitting, seasonable, opportune, timely, advisable, desirable, well put *or* expressed, *ad rem (Lat.)*.

HAPPY-GO-LUCKY, *adj.* Easygoing, casual, unthrifty, improvident, careless, slack, lax, remiss, thoughtless, thriftless, loose, indifferent, unconcerned, imprudent, nonchalant, slothful, lazy, indolent, supine, unenterprising, irresponsible, unmindful, negligent, heedless, shiftless, perfunctory, inadvertent, inattentive to practical matters, neglectful, offhand, apathetic, impassive, unfaithful, unthinking, improvident, vagrant, derelict, wasteful, prodigal, slovenly, disorderly, allowing luck to decide, unguarded, listless, preoccupied, self-absorbed, sluggish, trusting to luck, undiscerning, flighty, scatterbrained, harebrained, delinquent, faithless, unreflecting, harum-scarum *(coll.)*, insouciant, unemployed, culpose *(Law)*, pococurante, oblivious, giddy.

HARANGUE, *n.* 1. Speech addressed to a large popular assembly, public address, discourse, formal address, popular oration, declamation, loud address to a multitude, rhetorical discourse, disquisition, lecture, prelection, sermon, dissertation, peroration, allocution, homily, preachment, exhortation, recital, spiel, eloquence, public utterance.

2. Passionate and vehement speech, noisy and intemperate address, diatribe, noisy ranting speech, tirade, declamatory speech, bombastic performance, screed, strain of invective, spouting, strain of railing language, boisterous declamation, effusion, ranting, Philippic, dilation, bitter *or* abusive speech, bombast, angry exuberance, verbosity, expatiation, rodomontade, long-windedness, longiloquence, cloud of words, prolixity, rigmarole, amplification, loquacity, grandiloquence, verbiage, diffuseness, profuseness, rhetorical discourse *or* argument, wordiness, flow of words.

HARANGUE, *v.* 1. Make a declamatory speech, speak to a large assembly, continue long upon, make a formal address, expound, exposit, lecture, hold forth, utter, prelect, spiel, discourse, descant, preach, plead, proclaim, deliver, address, declaim, sermonize, pronounce, dwell on, spellbind.

2. Declaim vehemently, make a declamatory speech, diatribe, rail at, hold forth, rant, perorate, expand, dilate, rodomontade, maunder, argue tediously, expatiate angrily, be copious in speech *or* writing, soapbox, scold, tirade, inveigh against, flourish, gush, mouth, ramble, enlarge, harp on *or* upon, spout *(coll.),* indulge in a tirade, stump *(coll.).*

HARASS, *v.* 1. Fatigue, tire with repeated and exhausting efforts, weary by importunity, exhaust, wear down, torment, disturb persistently as with troubles, vex, plague, worry, distress, keep assaulting, drive from pillar to post, annoy, harry, tease, gall, badger, molest, heckle, bullyrag, abuse, chafe, grate, haunt, huff, baffle, provoke, sting, pique, aggrieve, ruffle, weigh upon, puzzle, gripe, get *(coll.),* keep in alarm, jade, fag, tire out, wear out, tucker *(often with* OUT, *coll.),* bleed white, nettle, gnaw, roil, bate, prick, prostrate, disarm, buffalo *(sl.),* intimidate, cow, browbeat, terrorize, trouble, tantalize, infest, enrage, hound, embarrass, persecute, harrow, nag, fret, pester, disquiet, macerate, pother, rack, haggle, hector, toss, goad, distract, wring, perplex, grind, pain, squeeze, bother, mortify, egg, revile, mock, grieve, fool, ruffle, irritate, cut up, injure persistently, discompose, displease, pursue, oppress, inflame, beset, irk, gibe, overrun, upbraid, bulldoze *(sl.),* scourge, banter, delude, confuse, flout, distract, disconcert, exercise, arouse, infuriate, afflict, reproach, fleer, twit, vilify, calumniate, incense, ridicule, dispirit, dragoon, discommode, incommode, deride, traduce, exacerbate, anger, excite, agitate, exasperate, taunt, jeer, defame, bully, disturb.

2. Harry, raid, lay waste, subdue by wearying, trouble by repeated attacks, incursions, *etc. (as in war or hostilities),* confuse, confound, dispirit, tire out, wear down, weary, besiege, mortify, overrun, discompose, disconcert, embarrass, beset, lay siege to, assault continually, plague, worry, distress, keep in alarm, harrow, hound, grind, perplex, destroy, terrorize, impede, oppress, discommode, threaten, coerce, weaken, corrode, grind away at, dragoon, disarm, disquiet, baffle, scourge.

HARBINGER, *n.* One who *or* that which goes before and makes known the approach of another, forerunner, precursor, herald, messenger, usher, omen, foregoer, augur, marshal, avant-courier, predecessor, prophecy, crier, portent, prodromus, scout, pioneer, indication, indicator, proclaimer, premonitor, premonitory sign, dawn, forecast, prognostic, augury, prediction, paver, type, emblem, antecedent, precedent, sign, pointer, token, runner, stormy petrel, handwriting on the wall, Mother Carey's chickens, clue, symbol, auspice, divination, annunciator, teller, enlightener, signaler, trumpeter, evangel, bearer of tidings, tipper, enunciator, intelligencer, prediction, prefiguration, soothsay, courier, presage, halcyon birds, prefigurement, foretoken, informant, preparer, nunciate, announcer, adviser.

HARBOR, *n.* 1. Safe shelter for ships, port, haven, anchorage, dock, basin, navigable bay, cove, creek, bight, gulf, lagoon, arm of the sea, moorings, breakwater, mole, pier, wharf, landing, quay, landlocked and navigable water, harborage, roadstead, road *(often in pl.),* bourn, goal, terminal point, portlet, inlet, destination.

2. Asylum, refuge, shelter, cover, sanctuary, hideaway, hiding, safety, protection, security, safekeeping, care, anchorage, haven, safehold, concealment, resting place, lodging, resort, kennel, fastness, journey's end, fortress, mew, keep, ward, stronghold, covert, citadel, tower, rock, pillar, home, ark, cloister, hermitage, port in a storm, refuge in time of need, hide-out, den, lair, nest, subterfuge, cell, storm blown over, hold, retreat, place of shelter, tower of strength, bourn, safety zone, fasthold, castle, sanctum, harborage, resource.

HARBOR, *v.* 1. Shelter, lodge, protect, conceal, give hiding place to, ensconce, keep, aid, hide, screen, take in, defend, quarter, billet, bed, room, render safe, give safekeeping, flank, foster, maintain, conserve, keep safe, watch over, guard, safeguard, shield, preserve, cover, garrison, care for, circumscribe, fence round, nurse, secure, house.

2. Entertain in the mind, cherish, indulge *(feelings, esp. unfavorable or evil),* hold stubbornly, embrace, nurture, foster *(a notion),* cling to, bear in mind, hold dear, retain, treasure, maintain, clasp, feel, receive, be certain of, apprehend, assume, believe, suppose, imagine, fancy, picture, create, speculate, conceive, dream over, hold in view, regard, be convinced of, imbibe, adopt, possess, hold, contemplate, brood over, muse over, covert, deem.

HARD, *adj.* 1. Impenetrable, inflexible, adamantine, flinty, rigid, unyielding, not soft, compact, solid, firm, indurated, resistant, stony, implastic, stubborn, insoluble, steely, concrete, condensed, repelling, irresilient, dintless, intractile, inelastic, unbending, unmalleable, stiff, thick, heavy, stark, stout, substantial, ossified, oaky, resisting, steady, inextensile, hardened, stable, cement, impregnable, lapideous, stonelike, rocklike, lithoid, unimpressible, infrangible, dense, strong, fixed, dry, horny, rugged, tight, leathery, coriaceous, leatherlike, schirrous *(Med.),* sclerotic, unpliable, renitent, marble, granite, stiff, compressed, pressed, unrelenting, not easily cut *or* separated, immutable, unalterable, glassy, vitreous, petrified, unlimber, fossilized, crystallized, unextendible, rocky, tense, proof, tough, sound, impervious, solid, solidified, osseous.

2. Physically fit for endurance *or* exertion, tough, hardy, seasoned, inured, in good condition, robust, vigorous, strong, hefty *(coll.),* rugged, hale, burly, lusty, able-bodied, muscular, brawny, Herculean, Atlantean, mighty, sinewy, wiry, solid, beefy, leathery, strapping, resilient, sturdy, stout, puissant, enduring, acclimatized, husky *(coll.),* powerful, tough as leather, strong as a lion *(horse, or an ox),* stanch, staminal.

3. Firmly joined *or* formed, tight, unyielding, firm, secure, tough, fast, set, sound, fixed, taut, close, reliable, impregnable, unassailable, indivisible, inseverable, inseparable, indiscerptible.

4. Carried on *or* performed with great exertion, energy *or* persistence, laborious, arduous, toilsome, exacting, burdensome, exhausting, tiresome, oppressive, wearying, fatiguing, rigorous, wearisome, onerous, operose, distressing, heavy, draining energy, uphill, strenuous, full of obstacles, painstaking, tedious, boring, requiring

skill *or* special effort, not easy, requiring great endurance, difficult to do *or* accomplish, resistant, unrelenting, unmitigating, Herculean, wicked *(coll.)*.

5. Difficult to deal with, manage, control, overcome *or* understand, perplexing, knotty, baffling, puzzling, trying, requiring skill *or* sagacity, bewildering, distressing, insoluble, troublesome, incomprehensible, dense, intricate, complicated, thorny, ticklish, exacting, nice, risky, critical, difficult to decide *or* explain, entangled, mazy, complex, tangled, crabbed, involved, perplexed, gnarled, irreducible, obscure, labyrinthine, inextricable, full of obstacles, resisting, uphill, delicate, spiny, not easily apprehended, tortuous, convoluted, ambiguous, imperspicuous, enigmatic, deep, tough, unintelligible, beyond *or* past comprehension *or* understanding, impenetrable, inscrutable, vague, unfathomable, paradoxical, confusing, inexplicable, undecipherable, acroamatic, esoteric, profound, recondite, nebulous, dark, abstruse, uncontrollable, ungovernable, unwieldy, tedious, problematic, riddling, cryptic, wicked *(coll.)*, unyielding, perverse, wayward, trackless, pathless, rebellious, balky, stubborn, obstinate, unliable, ponderous, awkward, clumsy, refractory, untoward, cross-grained, unruly, unbending, intractable, unmanageable, painstaking.

6. Energetic, persevering, hearty, active, vigorous, earnest, violent, diligent, conscientious, determined, industrious, forcible, dynamic, strenuous, pushing, tenacious, aggressive, resolute, assiduous, sedulous, persistent, constant, untiring, unremitting, plodding, unflagging, intent, ardent, zealous, indefatigable, enduring, relentless, unfaltering, keen, emphatic, intense, profound, studious, steadfast, unswerving, indomitable, acute, strong, brisk, quick, animated, fast, stirring, spirited, eager, avid, forward, enterprising, mettlesome, strong-willed, unwearied, up-and-coming *(coll.)*, plucky, gritty *(coll.)*, relentless, undeviating, not to be swayed, hard-working, stanch, faithful.

7. *(Of weather, the elements, etc.)* Vigorous, severe, violent, stormy, bad, intense, **cutting, piercing,** biting, inclement, incisive, raging, heavy, tempestuous, fuming, rigorous, sharp, penetrating, turbulent, tumultuous, persevering, unremitting, persistent, furious, fierce, pitiless, ruthless, demoniac, rampant, overpowering, overwhelming, amuck, rampaging, uproarious, boisterous, ravening, frantic, wild, mad, unruly, boiling, seething, ebullient, disturbed, blustering, acute, trenchant, savage, frenzied.

8. Oppressive, grievous, harsh, merciless, rough, heavy, severe, afflictive, rigorous, disastrous, strict, cruel, distressing, painful, disagreeable, unpleasant, afflicting, calamitous, unfavorable, stringent, unsparing, stern, searching, peremptory, absolute, stark, stiff, Spartan, unremitting, inexorable, exacting, exigent, uncompromising, poignant, unwelcome, intolerable, bitter, searing, grating, consuming, caustic, insupportable, insufferable, rueful, injurious, unbearable, noxious, corroding, excruciating, disheartening, melancholy, lamentable, mournful, sad, devastating, unendurable, unprofitable, austere, ironhanded, tyrannical, overbearing, grinding, extortionate, inflexible, grim, unrelenting, coercive, relentless, inquisitorial, withering, pressing, despotic, arrogant, hurtful, baleful, grave, sharp, piercing, biting, racking, agonizing, torturous, tormenting, sore, cutting, dolorous, dismal, de-

pressing, distressful, abusive, woeful.

9. Incapable of being denied *or* explained away, cold, inescapable, undeniable, necessary, inevitable, irrevocable, inexorable, uncontrollable, final, necessitous, inevasible, irresistible, unavoidable, irrefragable, irrefutable, incontrovertible, incontestable, indisputable, unquestionable, ineluctable, unanswerable, inappealable, indefeasible, leaving no choice, undeniable, conclusive, ultimate, intrusive, compelling, inalterable.

10. Harsh *or* unpleasant to the eye, ear *or* aesthetic sense, grating, coarse, unrefined, blatant, crude, strident, jarring, repellent, unattractive, ungraceful, repelling, sharp, rigid, stiff, cacophonous, dissonant, discordant, raucous, gaudy, garish, flashy, forbidding, grim, ostentatious, fulsome, low, offensive, brazen, repugnant, uncouth, provincial, vulgar, grotesque, barbarous, gross, abrupt, flaunting, distasteful, screaming *(coll.)*, glaring, Gothic, brutish, loud *(coll.)*, stridulating, stridulous, hoarse, stertorous, raw, rustic, crass.

11. Brave, courageous, difficult, rigorous, heavy, arduous, against odds, valiant, valorous, gallant, intrepid, plucky, mettlesome, resolute, doughty, stout, hardy, gritty *(coll.)*, stouthearted, game, spirited, manly, carried on *or* performed with great exertion, energy *or* perseverance, unabashed, unflinching, unblenched, unawed, unrelenting, with great endurance, not easy, bold, daring, undaunted, unappalled, undismayed, audacious, unshrinking, heroic, soldierly, defiant, undespairing, herolike, unalarmed, fearless, exhausting, wearisome, exacting, toilsome, weary, Herculean, demanding, tough.

12. Not swayed by sentiment *or* sophistry, shrewd, hard-headed, smart, sagacious, calm, resourceful, firm, tough, cool, unswaying, argute, astute, subtle, sharp-witted, wily, crafty, cagey *(sl.)*, artful, level-headed, discreet, well-advised, cool-headed, calculating, long-headed, clear-headed, keen-witted, politic, prudent, sound, sensible, discriminating, knowing, apperceptive, discerning, piercing, perceptive, perspicacious, penetrating, undeceived, unruffled, Machiavellian, deft, adept, adroit, canny, accurate, nobody's fool *(sl.)*, not born yesterday *(sl.)*, no dumbbell *(sl.)*.

13. Difficult to impress, unfeeling, insensible, unkind, severe, exacting, untender, austere, unsympathetic, unyielding, callous, obdurate, hardhearted, reprobate, mean, close, grasping, harsh, remote, soulless, obtuse, untouched, incompliant, incorrigible, unimpressible, unaccommodating, unstirred, stringent, unemotional, cold, unreasonable, implacable, unresponsive, cruel, frigid, passionless, indifferent, hostile, unkindled, inexorable, unjust, unforgiving, impervious, pitiless, vengeful, stingy, impenitent, insentient, unrelenting, unrepentant, haughty, chill, icy, unmoved, acrimonious, stern, forbidding, bitter, relentless, heartless, unrepenting, indurate, dour, stoical, stolid, unconcerned, not easily moved, unfriendly, strict, unsparing, merciless, inflexible, shameless, stony, flinty, steely, insensitive, thick-skinned, deadened, numbed, pachydermatous, inured, hardened, remorseless, punitive, avenging, revengeful, ruthless, bowelless, inclement, uncompassionate, brutal, unnatural, unaffected, uncaring, dull, infrangible, unapproachable, inaccessible, not to be trifled with, not to be infringed upon, uncontrite, recusant, supercilious, unsub-

missive, recalcitrant, hard-boiled *(coll.)*, seared, hard-shell *(coll.)*, disdainful, contemptuous, brazen, unbending, steeled against, proof against, casehardened, abusive, nonchalant, pococurante, aweless, unabashed, bloodless, cold-blooded, cold of heart, cold-hearted, unmerciful, grim-faced, vindictive, bloodthirsty, inhumane, inhuman, bestial, brutish, grim-visaged, incompassioned, vengeful.

HARD, *adv.* 1. With great exertion, laboriously, incessantly, steadily, diligently, energetically, unyieldingly, arduously, toilsomely, exactingly, perseveringly, heartily, actively, tediously, ardently, strenuously, dynamically, untiringly, vigorously, persistently, unweariedly, indomitably, emphatically, unfalteringly, indefatigably, unflaggingly, studiously, lustily, with might and main, with all one's might, by the sweat of one's brow, conscientiously, heart and soul, pluckily, spiritedly, unswervingly, keenly, enduringly, zealously, ploddingly, steadfastly, exhaustingly, determinedly, with strain, earnestly, stubbornly, tenaciously, pertinaciously, undeviatingly, avidly, eagerly, manfully, with high heart *or* courage, strongly, wearisomely, painstakingly, industriously, constantly, unremittingly, with inspiration, with vigor *or* violence, ardently.

2. With difficulty, not easily, with resistance, slowly, reluctantly, under protest, upstream, arduously, heavily, laboriously, not readily, stiffly, tensely, hardly, uphill, unwillingly, in spite of oneself, loathly, against the stream, against the grain, in spite of difficulties, grudgingly, with much ado, *malgré lui (Fr.)*.

3. Vehemently, violently, forcibly, relentlessly, severely, piercingly, pitilessly, unremittingly, turbulently, furiously, tumultuously, fiercely, ruthlessly, rampantly, rampageously, seethingly, blusteringly, savagely, madly, raveningly, wildly, frenziedly, fumingly, ragingly, bitingly, persistently, constantly, forcefully, emphatically, cuttingly.

4. So as to be solid *or* firm, tightly, fast, firmly, soundly, closely, solidly, securely, tautly, close, impregnably, inseparably, indiscerptibly, indivisibly.

5. Harshly, severely, gallingly, painfully, rigorously, distressfully, raising difficulties, producing strain, unpleasantly, sternly, peremptorily, inexorably, searchingly, afflictively, disagreeably, involving pain *or* trouble, relentlessly, oppressively, grievously, cruelly, abusively, dismally, agonizingly, balefully, inflexibly, sorely, depressingly, woefully, wearisomely, tediously, heavily, stringently, unsparingly, bitterly, gratingly, consumingly, searingly, intolerably, unfavorably, mercilessly, roughly, arduously, operosely, insupportably, excruciatingly, injuriously, unendurably, overbearingly, tyrannically, austerely, lamentably, unbearably, insufferably, onerously, censoriously, with a high (strong, tight *or* heavy) hand.

6. Intently, earnestly, scrutinizingly, fixedly, ardently, intensely, keenly, penetratingly, sharply, searchingly, unblenchingly, unashamedly, unflinchingly, defiantly, seriously, inquiringly, closely, resolutely, fearlessly, piercingly, urgently.

7. *(With* BY *or* UPON) Close, near, nigh, close upon, about, on every side, at close quarters, but a step, in an inch of, at no great distance, near by, not far from, within an ace of, within call *or* hearing, within a whoop, bordering upon, on the brink *or* verge of, at one's door, at one's feet *or* elbow, next door to, on the threshold of, within a stone's throw, within earshot, within reach *or*

range, at one's finger's end *or* tip, in sight of, beside, against, around, in the presence of, under one's nose.

HARD-BITTEN, *adj.* Tough, dogged, pertinacious, obdurate, hard-set, immovable, unpitying, headstrong, opinionated, bulldogged, not to be moved, hard-bit, casehardened, mulish, pigheaded, hard-boiled *(coll.)*, obstinate, self-willed, uninfluenced, unyielding, rigid, unpliable, hard, unaffected, bulletheaded *(coll.)*, strong-willed, willful, unbending, hard as nails *or* a rock, hardened, thick-skinned, impervious, callous, hard-hearted, resistant, adamantine, stubborn, bulldog, tenacious, bullheaded, *entêté (Fr.)*.

HARDEN, *v.* 1. Indurate, make hard *or* harder, toughen, make callous, convert to stone, congeal, ossify, petrify, consolidate, make firm, freeze, cake, encrust, set, caseharden, temper, lapidify, amalgamate, compress, densify, coagulate, clot, granulate, precipitate, hornify, glacify, vitrify, cement, fix, concrete, deposit, anneal, braze, make compact, make tight, incrassate, candy, inspissate, fossilize, lithify *(Geol.)*, desiccate, dry, callous, thicken, mineralize, crystallize, cornify, Harveyize, starch, vulcanize, bake, solidify.

2. Make hardy, robust *or* capable of endurance, inure, season, accustom, discipline, train, form, familiarize, adapt, acclimatize, exercise, ground, potentiate, ripen, anneal, wean, key up, screw up, mellow, prime, bind, use, caseharden, equip, addict, foster, cultivate, prepare, break in, nurture, develop, habituate, temper, toughen, put in trim, wont, strengthen, steel, brace, stiffen, nerve, fortify, invigorate, quicken, empower, invest, endue, braze, endow, arm, enable, reinforce, restore, buttress, wind up, vivify, sustain, set up, refresh, energize, gird, dynamize.

3. Strengthen *or* confirm in disposition, feeling *or* actions, set, bear out, support, reassure, make permanent, fix, stabilize, establish, verify, substantiate, habituate, season, inure, accustom, make habitual, corroborate, maintain, ground, prove, ratify, warrant, uphold, retain, indorse, give assurance, toughen, buttress, make certain, keep alive, fortify, reinforce, sustain, affirm, arm.

4. Sear, make callous, make unfeeling, render unimpressible, embitter, make obdurate, confirm in wickedness, blunt, hebetate, deaden, paralyze, dull, numb, benumb, stun, brutify, envenom, stupify, obtund, callous, brutalize, render insensible.

HARDENED, *adj.* 1. Indurated, made hard, solidified, annealed, casehardened, tempered, inured, sclerosed, impervious, fossilized, crystallized, fixed, dried, compressed, condensed, implastic, concrete, stony, steely, flinty, impenetrable, ossified, made compact, rigid, adamantine, firm, inflexible, unyielding, insoluble, hard.

2. Confirmed in error *or* vice, habituated, seasoned, impious, cold, seared, inured, deadened, steeled, unfeeling, callous, reprobate, obdurate, inveterate, impenitent, unrepenting, impenetrable, unyielding, remorseless, shameless, acclimated, obstinate, irreligious, inexorable, cruel, graceless, profane, unsusceptible, bad, hard, unmerciful, irreclaimable, incorrigible, lost, abandoned, irredeemable, depraved, insensible, benumbed, accustomed, blasphemous, unhallowed, unregenerate, chronic, habitual, irreverent, tough, hard-hearted, untouched, obtuse, not amenable, implacable, unrelenting, indurate, unashamed, un-

caring, inaccessible, uncontrite, recusant, unsubmissive, seared, hard-boiled (coll.), disdainful, contemptuous, unbending, sacrilegious.

HARD-FAVORED, adj. Having a hard, unpleasant countenance, ugly, ill-favored, uncomely, unprepossessing, unbeautiful, forbidding, unlovely, unseemly, hard-featured, hard-visaged, homely, evil-favored, ill-looking, gruesome, hideous, frightful, grim, grim-faced, grisly, cadaverous, plain, ordinary, severe, monstrous, haggard, ghastly, grim-visaged, uncouth-looking, vulgar-looking, beautiless, deathlike, evil-looking, macabre, ghostlike, grotesque, fearful-looking.

HARD-FEATURED, adj. Having hard or harsh features, having coarse, unattractive or stern features, rugged, rough, gross-featured, austere, severe, granite-faced, hatchet-faced, marble-faced, forbidding, hard-favored, stern-looking, steely-faced, fearful-looking, rude-countenanced, grim, grotesque, stony-faced, flint-faced, ill-favored, vulgar-looking, uncouth-looking, frightful, harsh-looking, grim-faced, of coarse features, homely, ugly, grim-visaged.

HARD-FISTED, adj. Close-fisted, stingy, miserly, niggardly, penurious, mercenary, venal, tight-fisted, pinching, gripping, stinting, scrimping, churlish, moneygrubbing, mean, shabby, covetous, parsimonious, peddling, sordid, cheeseparing, meager, selfish, rapacious, illiberal, ungenerous, grudging, sparing, chary, usurious, greedy, extortionate, close-handed, close, near, penny-wise, hidebound, avaricious, tight (coll.), save-all, skimping (coll.).

HARD-HANDED, adj. Ruling with a strong or cruel hand, severe, oppressive, heavy, rigid, exacting, ironhanded, peremptory, inclement, coercive, pitiless, stiff, austere, arbitrary, uncompassionate, absolute, unsparing, stern, imperious, Procrustean, grievous, onerous, arrogant, harsh, exigent, obdurate, inexorable, rigorous, stringent, burdensome, ponderous, weighty, galling, inhuman, unkind, brutal, malign, unfeeling, grinding, inquisitorial, dictatorial, tyrannical, domineering, unsympathetic, despotic, high-handed, extortionate, merciless, ruthless, bowelless, hard-hearted, remorseless, trying, sanguinary, relentless, heartless, unpitying, overbearing.

HARDHEAD, n. 1. A shrewd, practical person, unfeeling person, skinflint, curmudgeon, hard bargainer, sharp bargainer, deceiver, swindler, extortionate person, adventurer, churl, niggard, miser, skin (sl.), gouge (sl.), cheat, harpy, viper, juggler, crimp, rogue, quack, Hessian, knave, sharper, cozener, Shylock, spieler (coll.), fourflusher (sl.), usurer, shark, diddler (coll. or sl.), tightwad (sl.), shyster, bunco steerer (sl.), medicaster, screw, jockey, greek, pretender, defrauder, impostor, fraud (coll.), rook, humbug, crafty person, thimblerigger, trickster, charlatan, mountebank, faker (coll.), empiric, blackleg (coll.), magsman (sl.), gull (sl.), gyp (sl.), flimflammer (coll.), land shark, confidence man, defaulter, cunning person, fox, pettifogger, grifter (sl.), welsher (sl.), carpetbagger (sl.), con man (cant), Artful Dodger, land pirate, jackleg (sl.), coin ringer (sl.), bamboozler (coll.), bilker.

2. Blockhead, dolt, stupid fellow, dunce, ignoramus, dullard, clod, numskull, oaf, dunderhead, clodpate, blunderhead, thickskull, ninny, woodenhead (coll.), lunkhead (coll.), moron, simpleton, idiot, lack-wit, imbecile, lack-brain, crackbrain,

fool, zany, nitwit, squarehead (sl.), bonehead, thickhead (coll.), chowderhead, nincompoop, muddlehead, loggerhead, juggins (sl.), tomfool, goose, ninnyhammer, gawk, driveler, loony (sl.), noddy, noodle, witling, gump (sl.), softhead, bumpkin, dotard, dullhead, ass, dunderpate, jolterhead, noodlehead, bullhead, cabbagehead (coll.), loon, lout, harebrain, addlebrain, featherbrain, fathead (coll.), half-wit, clod, clodpole, pumpkin head, jolthead, addlepate, Simple Simon, dummy, illiterate, saphead (coll.), sap (sl.), chump (coll.), asshead, donkey, dumbbell (sl.), thickwit, chucklehead (coll.), mutt (sl.), muttonhead (coll.), boob, booby, dumbhead (sl.).

HARD-HEADED, adj. 1. Shrewd, practical, not easily moved or deceived, sagacious, intelligent and firm, of strong sense, cool, sensible, astute, sound, judicious, wise, well-balanced, not to be imposed upon, having sound judgment, sharp-witted, keen, long-headed, clear-headed, clear-thinking, lucid, discerning, cognitive, unperturbed, unruffled, unshaken, steady, poised, self-possessed, comprehending, resourceful, right-minded, acute, perspicacious, penetrating, luminous, perceptive, cool-headed, rational, clear-witted, undeceived, subtle, discriminating, prudent, argute, accurate, sane, undisturbed, self-controlled, sage, sharp, in possession of one's faculties, knowing, strong-minded, of sound mind, thinking, placid, serene, unnervous, unexcited, level-headed, composed, alert, aware, nobody's fool (sl.), not born yesterday (sl.), no dumbbell (sl.), percipient, apperceptive, appercipient, piercing.

2. Stubborn, obstinate, perverse, self-willed, willful, wayward, cross-grained, balky, arbitrary, intractable, untoward, unaffected, contumacious, resistant, indocile, dogged, refractory, recalcitrant, ungovernable, unruly, pigheaded, contrary, unsubmissive, unmanageable, sullen, immovable, unbending, unresigned, heady, mulish, firm, inexorable, rigid, strict, determined, obstreperous, pervicacious, incorrigible, froward, inflexible, unyielding, not amenable, headstrong, not to be moved, strong-willed, pertinacious, bulldogged, tenacious.

HARD-HEARTED, adj. Cruel, unfeeling, unpitying, ruthless, pitiless, heartless, unsympathetic, obdurate, marble-hearted, inhuman, stony, unrelenting, implacable, merciless, uncompassionate, fell, unmerciful, relentless, inexorable, remorseless, savage, unkind, obstinate, stern, cold, unsparing, barbarous, callous, unforgiving, insensible, brutal, adamantine, apathetic, unresponsive, distant, aloof, hard, frigid, unsusceptible, passionless, indifferent, unconcerned, cold-blooded, adverse, hostile, supercilious, unkindled, disdainful, uninterested, withering, scathing, stiff, forbidding, unimpassioned, unimpressible, unmindful, insensible, flinty, half-hearted, Laodicean, irreligious, supine, unsolicitous, stony, indurated, uncaring, untouched, unmoved, unstirred, impervious, insentient, sharp, hardened, soulless, insensitive, thick-skinned, ironhearted.

HARDIHOOD, n. 1. Firmness, resolution, mettle, boldness, daring, spirit, self-reliance, hardiness, stoutness, courage, manhood, aplomb, dash, gallantry, chivalry, stamina, bottom, game, decision, grit, nerve, resistance, fearlessness, coolness, constancy, stability, strength, heroism, vigor, prowess, temerity, sand (sl.), perseverance, will power, virtue, might, vitality, pith, devotion to purpose, ardor, strength of mind, self-possession, doughtiness, moral fiber, doggedness, élan (Fr.), intransigency, self-control, contempt of danger, heart of oak, guts (sl.), spunk (coll.), crest, morale, sinew, sturdiness, endurance, virility, lustiness, heart, audacity, bravery, hardy spirit or character, determination, intrepidity, pluck, fortitude, backbone, manliness, vigor, valor, confidence, derring-do, resoluteness, self-mastery.

2. Audacity, boldness, temerity, impudence, impertinence, presumption, barefacedness, audaciousness, effrontery, assurance, overweening confidence, procacity, pertness, contumely, flippancy, overbearance, arrogance, front, haughtiness, unmannerliness, incivility, rudeness, airs, brass (coll.), ill breeding, disrespect, scoffing, insolence, petulance, brazen assurance, brazenness, cheek (coll.), face (coll.), gall (sl.), abuse, discourtesy, malapertness, offensiveness, sauciness, crust (sl.), nerve (sl.), impoliteness, shamelessness, disdain, self-assertion, sauce (coll.), lip (sl.).

HARDLY, adv. 1. Scarcely, barely, merely, little, not quite, not much, scantly, uncommonly, no more than, sparsely, not often, infrequently, only just, here and there, rarely, almost inconceivably, only arduously, only against the grain, rather, somewhat, simply, faintly, comparatively, miserably, slightly, with little likelihood, with difficulty or trouble, by the skin of one's teeth, imperceptibly, once in a blue moon, once in a coon's age (coll.), sporadically, only laboriously, with much ado, only in spite of difficulties, almost not at all, seldom, but just, not by a great deal, noway, in no manner, by no means.

2. Severely, harshly, rigorously, unkindly, roughly, cruelly, painfully, distressfully, gallingly, sternly, inexorably, unpleasantly, peremptorily, afflictively, relentlessly, censoriously, austerely, injuriously, roughly, heavily, sorely, abusively, oppressively, grievously, agonizingly, depressingly, woefully, stringently, searingly, arduously, unendurably, overbearingly, operosely, unsparingly, balefully, wearisomely, bitterly, gratingly, onerously, insufferably, unsupportably, excruciatingly, unfavorably, mercilessly, intolerably, with a high (strong, tight or heavy) hand, unbearably.

HARDNESS, n. 1. State or quality of being hard, firmness, solidity, impenetrability, compactness, stiffness, steel, adamant, renitency, callosity, rigor, durity, strength, rigidity, ossification, imperviousness, immutability, impliability, want of elasticity, petrifaction, density, glaciation, inextensibility, rigidness, imporosity, induration, insolubility, sclerosis, unmalleability, intractability, unalterability, irresilience, toughness, inelasticity, resistance, inflexibility, temper.

2. Severity, rigor, harshness, acerbity, pitilessness, induration, obduracy, want of pliancy, want of feeling, arrogance, strictness, rigidity, austerity, stringency, bitterness, insensibility, unfeelingness, formalism, precisianism, resistance, gall, badness, vice, rancor, insensitivity, inclemency, Puritanism, intractability, immorality, impenitence, deaf ears, irrepentance, apathy, iciness, criminality, spite, wickedness, sinfulness, acridness, cruelty, acrimony, impassiveness, unconcern, callosity, indifference, obtundity, stoicism, unimpressibility, callousness, uncontriteness, seared conscience, inflexibility, impiety, ruthlessness, abuse, barbarity, persecution, venom, malice, irreligion, disdain, hard-heartedness, ungodliness, hardness of heart, coldness, carelessness, acidity, virulence, vindictiveness, ill-usage, bloodthirstiness, want of compassion, renitency, truculence, mercilessness, relentlessness, inhumanity, coldness, unkindness,

heart of stone, overbearance, lofty bearing, hauteur, haughtiness, high horse, malevolence, uncharitableness, uncharity.

3. Hardship, tribulation, perplexity, difficulty, trial, suffering, affliction, oppressiveness, misery, grief, austerity, privation, severity, sadness, unhappiness, distress, bitter cup, purgatory, evil, cloud, curse, dead weight, travail, adverse circumstances, bitter pill, hell, bitter draft, woe, severe toil, sorrow, destitution, neglect, regrettableness, pinch, ordeal, pain, hard case, rub, pressure, desolation, want, trouble, arduousness, hard life, hard row to hoe (coll.), Herculean task, Sisyphean labor, Augean task, uphill work or going, difficult task, heavy sledding, hard road to travel, disconcertion, dilemma, frowns of fortune, ups and downs, bad fortune or luck, hard luck, tough luck (coll.), extremity, hopelessness, worry, throes, discomfort, excruciation, martyrdom, discomfiture, anguish, agony, smart, wretchedness, gall, strait, plight, adversity, bitterness, ache, prostration.

HARDSHIP, n. 1. Suffering, affliction, oppression, severe toil, trial, misery, severity, privation, tribulation, distress, grief, trouble, sorrow, hardness, need, adverse circumstances, purgatory, bitter cup, evil, cloud, curse, travail, woe, difficult task, heavy sledding, hard life, ordeal, pain, pressure, neglect, destitution, want, desolation, rub, stress, unhappiness, sadness, oppressiveness, austerity, hell, bitter draft, difficulty, arduousness, bitter pill, dead weight, Sisyphean labor, Augean task, Herculean labor, uphill work or going, pinch, regrettableness, hard case, hard row to hoe (coll.), hard road to travel, disconcertion, ups and downs, quandary, dilemma, confoundment, passion, smart, pang, ache, plight, adversity, frowns of fortune, strait, predicament, wretchedness, anguish, agony, cancer, bitterness, canker, gall, martyrdom, discomfiture, mourning, discomfort, excruciation, worm at the heart of the rose, worry, throes, hopelessness, straitened circumstances, hard luck, ill luck, peck or sea of troubles, bad fortune or luck, evil fortune, prostration, bewilderment, extremity, depth of misery, broken fortunes, tough luck (coll.).

2. Grievance, suffering, trial, misfortune, trouble, burden, calamity, stumbling block, obstacle, care, cross, load, scourge, infliction, embarrassment, rub, injury, oppression, disaster, catastrophe, visitation, mischance, casualty, accident, aggravation, misery, injustice, reverse, stroke, hard lines, shock, blow, pestilence, torment, bad fortune or luck, ill luck, pressure, curse, blight, ordeal, wreck, fatal mischief, setback, wrong, distress, regret, grief, harm, misadventure, bitter pill, bane, bitter cup, backset, check, bitter draft, affliction, contretemps, mishap, evil fortune, tribulation, adversity, sorrow, bother, stress, hamper, impediment, plight, pickle, quandary, confoundment, ill, humiliation, undoing, overthrow, comedown, unhappy lot, ill wind, impasse, trying condition, downfall, hitch, millstone round one's neck, failure, handicap, hindrance, onus, fix (coll.), pass.

HARDWARE, n. Metalware, implements, household utensils, kitchenware, tools, housewares, fixtures, appointments, accouterments, fittings (as handles, knobs, etc.).

HARDY, adj. 1. Strong, robust, stout, enduring, sturdy, tough, rugged, hearty, sound, hale, vigorous, firm, lusty, rigorous, inured to fatigue hardship, *etc.*, healthy, cast-iron, fresh, able, powerful, mighty, wiry, seasoned, in good case, sinewy, brawny, burly, leathery, well, fit, in good condition, in fine fettle, capable of endurance, with bottom, able to withstand winter *(of plants)*, green, stanch, blooming, flourishing, buxom, florid, youthful, adapted, staminal, puissant, beefy, resilient, strapping, husky *(coll.)*, acclimatized, Herculean, Atlantean, muscular, substantial, hefty *(coll.)*, stalwart, flush, virile, able-bodied, physically fit, substantial, solid.

2. Requiring great physical endurance, rugged, laborious, difficult, exacting, strenuous, operose, arduous, brisk, uphill, fatiguing, tiring, vigorous, wearisome, tough, toilsome, hard, violent, producing strain, steep *(coll.)*, stiff, heavy, hefty *(coll.)*, Herculean, wearying.

3. Bold, intrepid, brave, daring, courageous, stout, resolute, manly, virile, game, stout-hearted, rigorous, austere, audacious, aweless, masculine, indomitable, enduring, unyielding, stubborn, continuing, undaunted, dogged, firm, lasting, spirited, unapprehensive, determined, heroic, chivalric, soldierly, hero-like, frugal, mettlesome, plucky, gallant, adventurous, enterprising, venturesome, dashing, doughty, strong-willed, lion-hearted, high-spirited, manful, tenacious, resisting, Spartan, fearless, dauntless, resistant, confident, mighty, valorous, defiant, hard, unshrinking, unalarmed, unblenched, unappalled, high-mettled, undismayed, unflinching, stalwart, invincible, irresistible, unabashed, dreadless, forcible, valiant, vigorous, energetic, forceful, gritty, cogent, masterly, vehement, capable, formidable, dynamic, intense, powerful, impetuous, spunky *(coll.)*, potent, redoubtable *(usually in contempt or burlesque)*, indefatigable.

4. Confident, assured, rash, unduly bold, foolhardy, wild, full of assurance, impudent, bluff, reckless, wanton, audacious, presumptuous, temerarious, overweening, arrogant, temeritous, imprudent, injudicious, incautious, headstrong, unabashed, brazen, unblushing, barefaced, hot-headed, precipitous, aweless, insolent, indiscreet, contemptuous, heedless, shameless.

HARE, *n.* Rabbit, jack rabbit, cottontail, bunny, leveret, pika, tapeti, bawd *(Scot.)*.

HAREBRAINED, *adj.* Reckless, giddy, headlong, rash, careless, wild, light, volatile, flighty, harum-scarum *(coll.)*, changeable, unsteady, foolish, thoughtless, vagrant, capricious, puerile, foolhardy, distracted, flustered, without ballast, unsettled, changeful, quixotic, insouciant, uncircumspect, heedless, unwary, silly, unstable, frivolous, inconstant, variable, crazy *(coll.)*, slap-happy *(sl.)*, scatterbrained *(coll.)*, rattlebrained, rattleheaded, undependable, giddy-brained, giddy-pated, addlepated, unruly, defiant, impulsive, erratic, unreliable, shatterbrained, rattlepated, bird-witted, harebrain, giddy-headed, giddy-witted, rampant, regardless of consequences, light-minded, barmybrained, empty-headed, empty-noddled, witless, fickle, feverish, brainless, bemused, woolgathering, befuddled, frothy, mercurial, irresponsible, rantipole, empty-skulled, empty-pated, featherbrained, barmy, hasty, punch-drunk, extravagant, incautious, improvident, imprudent, uncalculating, indiscreet, wanton, madcap, death-defying, desperate, devil-may-care, daring, hot-headed, impetuous, precipitate, absent-minded, confused, muddleheaded, bewildered, preoccupied.

HAREM, *n.* The women in an Oriental household, seraglio, concubines, gynaeceum *(Gk. and Rom. Antiq.)*, zenana *(Ind. and Persia)*, purdah (Ind.).

HARK, *v.* 1. *(Chiefly in imperative)* Hear, listen, attend, hearken, give ear, lo, heed, give heed, oyez, hark ye, hear ye, attention, mind, mind you, mark, notice, harkee, behold, prick up one's ears, 'tention *(Mil. coll.)*, mark you, mark my words, harken *(Poetic)*, hear he.

2. *(With BACK)* Revert, return to previous point or subject, recall, resume, retrovert, go back, reverse, begin again, iterate, repeat, echo, rehearse, say over, revivify, review, recount, retell, revive, renew, reanimate, regress, go over the same ground, recapitulate, recur, rehash, reiterate, rejuvenate, rekindle, resuscitate.

HARELQUIN, *adj.* Having the characteristics of a harlequin *(esp. in appearance)*, fancifully varied in color or decoration, *etc.*, checkered, kaleidoscopic, multicolor, variable, parti-color, versicolor, mottled, mixed, motley, bicolored, many-hued, mosaic, tricolor, rainbow, spangled, whimsically adorned, tesselated, begilt, variegated, many-colored, polychromatic, divers-colored, dichromatic, trichromatic, heterogeneous, of frolicsome appearance, droll, fantastic, bizarre, playful, merry, glittering, antic, comic, ludicrous, laughable, hilarious, ridiculous, gelogenic, diverting, amusing, curiously ornamented, facetious, clownish, burlesque, grotesque, jocose, jocund, sportive, humorous, funny, comical, farcical, jolly, gay, colorful, jocular, waggish, vivid, jesting, mirthful, buffo *(It.)*.

HARLEQUIN, *n.* Buffoon, jester, droll, clown, zany, antic, fool, Punch, comedian, funnyman, farceur, Pierrot, pantaloon, grimacer, mountebank, Scaramouch, merry-andrew, Punchinello, comic, buffo *(It.)*, wearer of the cap and bells, mummer, mime, pantomimist, joker, caricaturist, mimic, mimer, wit, wag, Jack Pudding, Pickelhering *(Ger.)*, motley fool, wearer of the motley, Hanswurst, pickle-herring, farcist, tumbler.

HARLEQUINADE, *n.* Masking, buffoonery, mummery, foolery, comedy, waggery, masquerade, tomfoolery, fun, waggish trickery, fooling, frolic, frisk, romp, revel, horseplay, burletta, hilarity, gambol, merrymaking, antic, prank, slapstick, roguishness, jocoseness, waggishness, pantomime, jesting, play featuring a harlequin, good humor, merriment, farce, travesty, sock, mime, lampoon, caricature, mimicry, wit, skit, pleasantry, drollery, comicality, whimsicality, humor, shenanigans *(coll.)*, jocosity, facetiousness, monkeyshines *(sl.)*, jocularity, roguery, burlesque, joking.

HARLOT, *n.* Whore, prostitute, streetwalker, strumpet, lewd woman, bawd, jade, trull, wanton, drab, procuress, doxy, lewd reprobate, Cyprian, demirep *(sl.)*, trollop, loose woman, grisette, harridan, adventuress, bitch *(vulgar)*, Paphian, temptress, woman of easy virtues or morals, tart *(sl.)*, fornicatress, adulteress, hussy, pander, quean, slut, fallen woman, daughter of joy, courtesan, cocotte, stew, bat *(sl.)*, woman of the profession *(euphemistic)*, Lais, madam *(coll.)*, conciliatrix *(Fr.)*, Mrs. Warren, Delilah, harlotry, unfortunate woman, white slave, woman of the town, erring sister, baggage, frail sister, Sadie Thompson, Jezebel, abandoned woman, chippy *(sl.)*, pickup, demimondaine, broad *(sl.)*, scarlet woman, meretrix, cat *(sl.)*, Messalina, painted woman, hetaera *(Gk. Antiq.)*, Thais.

HARLOTRY, *n.* Practice *or* trade of prostitution, whoredom, bordel, whoremastery, fornication, adultery, illicit sexual intercourse, meretricious traffic, streetwalking, Mrs. Warren's profession, whoremongering, free love, cuckoldom, criminal conversation *(Law)*, cuckoldry.

HARM, *n.* 1. Injury, hurt, misfortune, damage, loss, mishap, ill, detriment, mischief, prejudice, blemish, pain, havoc, devastation, destruction, adversity, wound, defilement, deterioration, foul play, abuse, hardship, offense, impairment, lesion, infliction, disaster, nuisance, vitiation, gall, enormity, agony, ache, woe, abomination, forfeiture, deprivation, grievance, vexation, cross, burden, curse, bugbear, torment, ruin, bane, want, trauma, *bête noire*, imprecation, defacement, plague, atrocity, poisoning, persecution, malediction, anathema, debasement, pollution, desolation, breakdown, collapse, inroad, ravage, outrage, disadvantage, ill consequence, suffering, trial, calamity, scourge, catastrophe, mischance, accident, reverse, blow, stroke, injustice, pestilence, blight, ordeal, setback, contretemps, handicap, hindrance, onus, impediment, confoundment.

2. Evil, wrong, wickedness, badness, moral injury, outrage, sin, blight, hurtfulness, destructive force, malevolence, the Adversary, the Devil, cankerworm, depravity, venom, deterioration, malice, ill blood, malignancy, ill-disposedness, poison, worm at the heart of the rose, the archenemy, the archfiend, the serpent, pestilence, affliction, maleficence, ill will, improbity, virulence, bad blood, acerbity, despite, rancor, scourge, plague, cancer, worm, moth and rust, evil spirits, host of hell, vice, canker, mischief, hate, Satan, spite, mordacity, peccancy, damnability, peccability, error, sinfulness, obduracy, reprobacy, iniquity, immorality, obliquity, machinations of the devil, malignity, gall, powers of darkness, evil eye, bitterness, hostility, corruption, .vindictiveness, perversion, maliciousness, breakdown, impurity, guilt, deviation from rectitude, scurrility, perniciousness, reprehensibility, dishonor, demerit, want of principle, carnality, obscenity, impiety, culpability, rascality, roguery, alloy, perversity, bawdry, unregeneracy, unrighteousness, contamination, laxity, scoundrelism, turpitude, villainy, knavery, ribaldry, dishonesty, hardness of heart.

HARM, *v.* Do harm to, injure, hurt, damage, blemish, mar, impair, maim, spoil, ruin, bane, wound, wrong, deface, corrupt, infect, taint, attack, inflict harm *or* injury, oppress, grind, aggrieve, persecute, do a mischief, do an evil office to, tread on, victimize, bring *or* lead into trouble, put upon, bear hard upon, weigh down, break, maul, molest, destroy, pain, defame, misuse, waste, abuse, maltreat, tear, rack, stab, buffet, pierce, mangle, do violence to, outrage, ravage, devastate, desolate, labefy, cripple, hock, lame, hamstring, disfigure, lacerate, play the very devil with *(coll.)*, play havoc with, weigh heavy on, desecrate, ill-treat, deprave, defile, pollute, adulterate, rust, tarnish, alloy, leaven, stain, envenom, disserve, distress, demolish, canker, undo, contaminate, deflower, eat away, denaturalize, ulcerate, tamper with, disorder, sicken, incapacitate, grieve, gnaw, brutalize, consume, harrow, enervate, disease, derange, pervert, warp, smite, dishonor, demoralize, subvert, prejudice, alter, doctor *(coll.)*, degrade, ill-use, debase, damnify, scratch, torture, labefact, mutilate, play the deuce (devil *or* mischief) with *(coll.)*, batter, bruise,

break on the wheel, crucify, afflict, agonize, debauch, vitiate, corrode, sophisticate, poison, prostitute.

HARMFUL, *adj.* Fraught with *or* doing harm, injurious, detrimental, deleterious, pernicious, mischievous, noxious, baneful, hurtful, prejudicial, evil, ruinous, malefic, deadly, destructive, demolitionary, nocent, internecine, adverse, fraught with evil, inimical, harassing, sinister, painful, subversive, catastrophic, incendiary, virulent, sore, poignant, griping, cataclysmic, corroding, corrupting, disserviceable, baleful, menacing, disastrous, ill-omened, dire, fell, satanic, insalubrious, unwholesome, morbific, putrefactive, extirpatory, distressful, afflictive, rancorous, septic, toxic, engulfing, fatal, lethal, malevolent, diabolic, unhealthful, bad, morbiferous *(Med.)*, extirpative, distressing, afflicting, malignant, demoniac, grievous, mortal, devouring, mephitic, venomous, cruel, disadvantageous, damaging, unfortunate, pestiferous, destructive, felonious, vicious, aching, pricking, ill, brutal, objectionable, poisonous, sinistrous, wide-wasting, maleficent, annihilative, unlucky, devilish, noisome, malign, corrosive, unpropitious, fiendish.

HARMLESS, *adj.* Without power *or* tendency to harm, innoxious, not hurtful, innocent, disarmed, peaceable, gentle, unhurtful, effete, inoffensive, safe, sinless, good, blameless, spotless, unarmed, unobnoxious, impotent, out of operation, mild, out of gear, inoperative, disabled, constrained, confined, incorrupt, obedient, guiltless, simple, unblemished, unoffending, good-natured, irreproachable, easygoing, innocuous, dovelike, virtuous, undespotic, sterile, spent, inefficacious, clean, clement, moderate, lenient, soft, broken, domesticated, tame, uninjurious, crippled, uncorrupting, pure, faultless, undefiled, artless, childlike, docile, unobjectionable, manageable.

HARMONIC, *adj.* 1. *(Music)* Pertaining to harmony *(as distinguished from melody and rhythm)*, melodious *(of old music)*, pertaining to melody *(as apart from rhythm; old music)*, harmonized, harmonistic, mathematically perfect, major *(of triads)*, common *(of triads)*.

2. Harmonious, consonant, forming a pleasingly consistent whole, marked by harmony, concordant, in harmony, agreeing, in accord, concerted, in concord, symphonious, concentual, congruous, correspondent, compatible, cooperating, fitting, similar, like, suitable, congenial, having like sounds, symphonic, in concert, harmonical, in tune, accordant, conformable, symmetrical, parallel, euphonious, consistent, harmonizing, consonous, proportionate, orderly, unified, sympathetic, musical, pleasant-sounding, in unison, undiscordant, cooperative, attuned, concinnous, related.

HARMONICA, *n.* Small reed wind instrument, mouth organ, mouth harp, musical glasses, harmonicon, harp, French harp *(dial.)*.

HARMONIOUS, *adj.* 1. Correspondent, harmonic, congruent, orderly, symmetrical, uniform, parallel, sympathetic, suitable, fitting, like, congruous, compatible, similar, proportionate, unanimous, conformable, consistent, consonant, forming a pleasingly consistent whole, concordant, agreeing, in harmony, concerted, symphonious, concentual, in accord, attuned, concinnous, unified, harmonizing, consonous, cooperating, congenial, symphonic, accordant, commensurate, answerable, in concord, having like sounds (*colors, ideas, etc.*), euphonious, musical, in unison, related, adaptable, apt, coordinated, consentaneous, apposite, of a piece, in synchronization, to the point, bearing upon, pertinent, relevant, synchronous, consentient, blended, equal, even, becoming, equable, regular, methodical, systematic, neat, usual, in order, arranged, seasonable, timely, coincident, isotonic, smooth, trim, well-regulated, synchronal, synchronized.

2. Friendly, amicable, in rapport, in harmony, fraternal, agreeable, in unison, compatible, adaptable, peaceable, pleasant, congenial, agreeing, brotherly, cordial, at one, cemented, like-minded, of one mind, equable, loving, on good terms, at peace, allied, united, affectionate, at home, of the same mind, in accordance, neighborly, in step, conjoined, amiable, acquiescent, cooperating, in accord, mutually sympathetic, amical, hand and glove, hand-in-hand, sociable.

3. Melodious, agreeable to the ear, tuneful, vocally *or* musically concordant, agreeably consonant, aesthetically pleasing, attuned, euphonious, peaceful, marked by harmony, symphonic, assonant, amiable, gratifying, felicitous, regaling, clear-toned, mellifluent, mellow, songlike, symphonious, round, sweet-sounding, subtle, beautiful, delightful, charming, lovely, winning, enchanting, ravishing, empyreal, celestial, seraphic, entrancing, bewitching, prepossessing, engaging, exquisite, cosmic, melodious in movement, accordant, consonous, liquid, Orphean, rhythmic, restful, paradisaic, heavenly, lyric, soothing, bland, mellisonant, harmonizing, soft, genial, gladsome, tunable, rich, mellifluous, smooth, musical, dulcet, in concord, canorous, delectable, sweet, of the spheres, spheral, undiscording, rhythmical.

HARMONIZE, *v.* 1. Make harmonious, unite, adapt, accord, temper, reconcile, adjust to each other, put in tune, modulate, meet, regulate, methodize, coordinate, make symmetrical, balance, adjust, order, bring to terms, placate, make peace, bring together, patch up, intercede, negotiate, attune, coapt, fix up (*coll.*), settle differences, accommodate, set straight, restore harmony, pour oil on the waters, mediate, tranquilize, arbitrate, render accordant, heal the breach, conciliate, pour balm into, restore to friendship, pacify, systematize, attune, bring into harmony, negotiate a peace between, moderate, attemper.

2. (*Music*) Accompany with appropriate harmony, set accompanying parts to, complete, score, fit with harmony, instrumentate, orchestrate, fill out, add corresponding parts (*to a melody*), make an instrumentation for.

3. Be in harmony, accord *or* agreement, be in agreement in action, sense *or* feeling, accord, agree, correspond, blend, sympathize, chime, comport, tally, square, conform with, be harmonious, suit, concur, match, quadrate, fraternize, console, heal, sort, jibe, consist, accommodate, be in unison, tune, accord, acquiesce, assent, reciprocate, hold with, comply, gee (*sl.*), consent, dovetail, accede, come to terms, combine, work together, pull together, team, fit, fall in together, symphonize, consonate.

HARMONY, *n.* 1. Concord (*of sound, color, line, etc.*), accord, order, consent, agreement, chime, beauty, melody, music, tune, chorus, compatibility, cadence, concentus, organum (*Mediev. Mus.*), polyphony, collation, conformity, minstrelsy, sympathy, uniformity, symphony, symmetry, unity, agreeableness, sweetness, tuneful-

ness, relation, blending, unison, accordance, consonance, concert, concordance, concinnity, euphony, attunement, symphoniousness, chord.

2. A consistent, orderly *or* pleasing arrangement of parts, congruity, agreement between things, ideas, *etc.*, consistency, suitableness, fitness, congruence, smoothness, correspondence, concurrence, propriety, coherence, proportion, mutual fitness, accord, unison, compatibility, affinity, fusion, consonance, agreement, connaturalness, Homoöusia, correlation, conformation, adaptability, synchronization, congeniality, keeping, coincidence, concinnity, assonance, synthesis, amalgamation, organic totality, coalescence, aptitude, relevancy, conjunction, parallelism, apposition, integrality, concomitancy.

3. Peace, amity, friendship, agreement, accord, harmonious relations, kind feeling, good understanding, unanimity, communion, tranquillity, amicableness, amity, good feeling, concord, concurrence in opinions, sentiments, *etc.*, unity, love, sympathy, fraternity, congeniality, assent, amicability, oneness, union, accordance, mutual regard, rapprochement (*Fr.*), comradeship, affinity, acclamation, consentaneity, good will, rapport (*Fr.*), like-mindedness, brotherhood, compliance, cordiality, neighborliness, consensus, compatibility, fellowship, cooperation, one voice.

HARNESS, *n.* 1. Working gear of a draft animal, tackle, equipment, halter, bridle, lines, cavesson, reins, traces, tugs, straps, caparison, trappings, paraphernalia, oxbow and bar, hackamore (*Western U. S.*), accouterments, gear.

2. Routine of work, restraint, bond, chains, yoke, shackle, fetter, thralldom, confinement, control, groove, rut, beaten track, clockwork, tedium, undeviation, sameness, round, trammel, even tenor, heaviness, humdrum, regularity, beaten path, grind, trot, jog, run, cycle, monotony, unvariability, repression.

HARNESS, *v.* 1. Tackle, put in harness, yoke, rein in, domesticate, saddle, accouter, hitch up (*coll.*), equip, inspan, fit out for work, strap, tame, gentle, break in, cinch (*Western U. S.*), gear, rig up *or* out, furnish, collar.

2. Bring under conditions for working, control as a source of power, moderate for use, direct to a useful purpose, channel, restrain, curb, manacle, secure, utilize, rein, shackle, govern, muzzle, bridle, arrest, capitalize on, render useful, make productive, turn to account.

HARP, *n.* Lyre, langspiel (*Shetland I.*), tamboura (*Asia*), claviharp, cithara (*Gk. Antiq.*), aeolian harp.

HARP, *v.* 1. Play on the harp, strike the lyre, sweep the chords *or* strings, twang, pluck, strum, thrum, touch the strings.

2. Dwell tediously, iterate, utter incessantly, refer to repeatedly, battologize, tautologize, insist upon, rehearse, reiterate, harp on one *or* the same string, sing the same old song *or* tune, reëcho, recur, go on, repeat, bore, buttonhole, mount *or* ride a hobby, persist, ding, parrot, drill, hammer, weary, tire, jade, pound, palaver, din *or* drum in the ear.

HARPOON, *n.* Barbed spearlike missile, harpagon, gaff, eelspear.

HARPOON, *v.* Strike, catch *or* kill with *or* as with a harpoon, peg, lance, spear, spike, stab, fix, pierce, hook, stick, transfix, impale, fire a harpoon at.

HARPY, *n.* 1. (*Cap.; Mythol.*) Defiling monster (half bird, half woman), Celaeno, Pello, demon, eagle, vulture, vampire, siren, hag, ghoul, unclean spirit, bird of prey, sorceress, lamia.

2. Rapacious, grasping person, extortioner, sharper, oppressor, snatcher, miser, vampire, bloodsucker, seductive, mercenary person, swindler, shark, cozener, despoiler, robber, ravisher, temptress, ogress, spoiler, falcon, depredator, fleecer, peculator, vamp (*sl.*), hawk, usurper, purloiner, thief, dispossessor, ghoul, siren, vulture, plunderer.

HARRIDAN, *n.* Disreputable violent woman, mean old woman, jade, beldam, rip (*coll.*), fishwife, witch, shrew, fury, vicious old woman, old hag, battle-axe (*sl.*), old cat (*coll.*), grandmother, vixen, crone, virago, gorgon, hell cat, hellhag, ogress, scarecrow, Xanthippe.

HARROW, *v.* 1. Draw a harrow over, till with a harrow, break up (*soil*), refine, cultivate, plow, roll, smooth, comminute, crush, rake, hoe, disintegrate, pulverize, powder, granulate.

2. Disturb keenly *or* painfully, sting *or* cut to the quick, rend, wound, torture, lacerate, distress, afflict, burden, horrify, appall, scarify, grind, gnaw, cut, stab, prick, pierce, weigh on, hurt, plague, excruciate, wring, haunt, crucify, agonize, chafe, grate, rack, prey on, buffet, kill by inches, flay, flog, convulse, batter, corrode, put on the rack, martyr, shock, offend, prolong the agony, break on the wheel, plant a dagger in the breast, unman, turn the screw, twist the knife, disquiet, frighten, startle, put a thorn in one's side, abash, make one's blood run cold, daunt, disconcert, make one's hair stand on end, dismay, harry, tear, torment, harass, aggrieve, oppress, inflict pain on, prostrate.

HARRY, *v.* 1. Pillage, plunder, ravage, waste, lay waste, devastate, strip, lay about one, drive *or* press one hard, rob, raid, make harassing incursions, sack, hound, hector, despoil, subdue by wearying, trouble by repeated attacks, wear down, besiege, overrun, discompose, disconcert, embarrass, beset, assault continually, worry, plague, scourge, disquiet, grind away at, disarm, discommode, weaken, corrode, perplex, terrorize, keep in alarm, distress.

2. Worry, annoy, molest, torment, agitate, plague, tease, harass, incommode, disturb, harrow, gall, fret, chafe, trouble, bother, afflict, vex, cut up, persecute, distress, badger, lacerate, hector, pique, bait, pester, egg, hurt, drive from pillar to post, bully, intimidate, irritate, exhaust, wear down, heckle, bullyrag, haunt, huff, provoke, ruffle, gripe, get (*coll.*), irk, gibe, inflame, discompose, goad, distract, macerate, pother, haggle, hound, buffalo (*sl.*), cow, roil, nettle, bleed white, fag, jade, tantalize.

HARSH, *adj.* 1. Harsh-sounding, grating, jarring, twanging, atonal (*Mus.*), grinding, out of tune, clashing, sour, stertorous, rasping, dissonant, strident, hoarse, cacophonous, scratching, untuneful, discordant, husky, shrill, croaking, unharmonious, unmusical, gruff, raucous, absonant, stridulatory, squawking, acute, jangling, ear-piercing, piercing, grum, guttural. (*The following do not esp. pertain to sound*): unrefined, blatant, gaudy, offensive, flaunting, barbarous, glaring, crude, repellent, garish, brazen, Gothic, flashy, brutish, loud (*coll.*), crass, raw, rustic, inartistic, ungraceful, forbidding, distasteful, rude, vulgar, repelling.

2. (*As relating to punishment or treatment, etc.*) Ruthless, pitiless, exacting, cruel, ungentle, afflictive, unkind, unfavorable, unsparing, unremitting, inexorable, uncompromising, merciless, heavy, bitter, exigent, unreasonable, severe, stringent, strict, inhuman, hard, rough, stern, unpleasant, afflicting, stiff, drastic, stark, austere, rigorous, distressing, painful, Spartan, caustic, insufferable, devastating, baleful, despotic, dismal, inquisitorial, iron-handed, iron-fisted, uncharitable, rueful, obdurate, insupportable, tyrannical, mean, unbearable, extortionate, biting, relentless, woeful, sore, noxious, grinding, abusive, overbearing, inflexible, racking, dolorous, grim, draconian, depressing, cutting, uncompassionate, unrelenting, torturous, pressing, coercive, agonizing, distressful, tormenting, brutal, unfeeling, implacable, unconcerned, insensitive, remorseless, inclement, punitive, uncontrite, unbending, hard-boiled (*coll.*), cold-blooded, vindictive, vengeful, savage, soulless, heartless, hard-hearted.

3. (*As relating to one's nature, temperament, etc.*) Currish, short, ungraceful, cankered, curt, iracund, testy, mean, vulgar, bestial, unhandsome, grouty (*coll.*), acetose, insolent, ill-mannered, choleric, rude, morose, reptilian, coarse, splenetic, peppery, rough, caviling, resentful, callous, crude, crass, offensive, mordant, acrid, discourteous, dastardly, base, ill-tempered, fractious, spiteful, sour, snarling, uncivil, petulant, abrupt, unmannerly, obnoxious, bristling, quarrelsome, snappish, waspish, brutish, impolite, churlish, gruff, acerbic, ill-bred, insulting, sullen, growling, thorny, uncouth, bearish, crabbed, sarcastic, sharp, grouchy, irascible, tart, acrimonious, surly, brusque, grim, swinish, unamiable, unkind, shrewish, ugly, doggish, glum, blunt, sulky, crusty, boorish, beastly, peevish, rancorous, cross-grained, touchy, moody, bitter, cynical, miserable, saturnine, jaundiced, vengeful, bilious, irritable.

4. Rough (*as a surface*), jagged, uneven, coarse, rough-grained, gnarled, coarse-grained, prickly, raw, scraggy, choppy, unsmooth, rugose, rugate, flaky, scabrous, rugged, unpolished, bumpy, lumpy, irregular, scaly, scabby, broken, asperous (*Bot.*), scurfy, nodose, knotted, wrinkled, roughened, knurled.

HARUM-SCARUM, *adj.* Rash, reckless, harebrained, volatile, precipitate, chance, aimless, indiscreet, giddy, wild, irresponsible, headlong, flighty, unsteady, thoughtless, capricious, puerile, distracted, unsettled, quixotic, heedless, silly, frivolous, scatterbrained (*coll.*), impulsive, absentminded, muddleheaded, bewildered, confused, devil-may-care, hotheaded, impetuous, desperate, wanton, punch-drunk, incautious, imprudent, death-defying, madcap, careless, light, changeable, foolish, unsteady, vagrant, foolhardy, flustered, changeful, insouciant, without ballast, unwary, unstable, uncircumspect, unruly, rattlebrained, undependable, giddy-pated, defiant, erratic, shatterbrained, unreliable, giddy-brained, addlepated, rattleheaded, bird-witted, giddy-headed, light-minded, barmybrained, empty-noddled, fickle, witless, empty-headed, rattlepated, giddy-witted, regardless of consequences, brainless, bemused, frothy, rantipole, mercurial, inconstant, crazy (*coll.*), variable, slap-happy (*sl.*), daring, feverish, woolgathering, befuddled featherbrained, hasty, barmy, empty-skulled, uncalculating.

HARVEST, *n.* 1. The gathering of crops, ingathering, harvesting, reaping, picking, mowing, cutting, amassment, accumulation, cropping, assemblage, harvest home.

2. Season of gathering crops, harvest time, harvest home, harvest festival, autumn, harvest tide, harvest feast, fall of the year, Thanksgiving, Indian summer.

3. Produce, crops, yield, vintage, that which is reaped *or* gathered, gleanings, gathering, windfall, second crop, grain, fruitage, return, increase, fruition, intake, storage, season's growth, amassment, hoard, collection, accumulation, fruit, second-growth crop, second mowing, rowen.

4. Product *or* result of any labor *or* process, proceeds, receipts, take, intake, reward, gain, gleaning, reaping, return, benefit, fruit, fruition, flower, blossom, yield, collection, offspring, outgrowth, creature, issue, child, production, aftermath, produce, pickings, profit, wages, output, perquisite, winnings, earnings, creation, offshoot, avails, increase, accumulation, amassment.

HARVEST, *v.* Gather in, reap, garner, store, glean, gather the harvest, mow, cut, pick, pluck, cull, hoard, amass, accumulate, crop, take the yield, put in barns, strip the fields *(orchards, etc.),* gather the first fruits, take the second crop.

HASH, *n.* 1. Hashed meat, fricandeau, minced meat, mash, ragout, chow-chow, gallimaufry, salmagundi, réchauffé, olio, ollapodrida.

2. Jumble, muddle, confusion, imbroglio, olla-podrida, litter, gallimaufry, mess, disarray, chaos, mishmash, topsy-turvy, salmagundi, réchauffé, mixture, tumble, olio, hodgepodge, farrago. omnium-gatherum, mix-up, tangle.

HASH, *v.* Chop *(into little pieces),* mince, make mincemeat of, cut up small, grind up, granulate, dice, triturate, comminute, mangle, disintegrate, pulverize, crumble.

HASP, *n.* Hook, clasp, fastening, holdfast, catch, latch, fastener, snap, clinch, clamp.

HASSOCK, *n.* Footstool, footrest, cushion, kneeling stool, squab, taboret, cricket, musnud *(Orient.),* ottoman.

HASTATE, *adj.* *(Bot.)* Spear-shaped, halberd-shaped, triangular, with spreading lobes at the base, spearlike.

HASTE, *n.* 1. Celerity of motion, dispatch, quickness, nimbleness, speed, hurriedness, velocity, rapidity, alacrity, expedition, fleetness, briskness, fastness, agility, swiftness, bustle, rapidness, urgency, liveliness, instantaneity, race, flight, tall stepping, sprint, round pace, exertion, burst of speed, precipitation, smartness, readiness, energetic *or* vigorous action, instantaneousness, immediateness, alertness, promptness, promptitude, acceleration, career, expeditious performance.

2. Undue celerity, precipitance, unthinking quickness of action, rush, hurry, impetuosity, unconsidered zeal, rashness, impetuousness, leaping, precipitancy, press, foolhardiness, recklessness, want of caution, hastiness, prematurity, precocity, untimeliness, inexpedience, impatience, testiness, excitation, petulance, abruptness, ebullition, violent display, fretfulness, inopportunity, precipitation, vehemence, temerity, jumping *(to conclusions),* intempestivity, outburst, unwise *or* rash rapidity, unrestraint, hurriedness, impulsiveness, prematureness, anticipation, impulse of the moment, irascibility, incautiousness, imprudence, indiscretion, presumption, heedlessness, carelessness, leap in the dark, folly, gamble, infatuation, irrationality, unwisdom, bungle, blunder, giddiness,

plunge, blind bargain, audacity, overconfidence, thoughtlessness.

3. Obligation *or* eagerness to act quickly, hustle, dash, bustle, scurry, intentness, impulse, drive, alarm, hurry, impatience, scramble, excitation, precipitancy, disquiet, uneasiness, eagerness, fretfulness, pressure, furor, fuss, splutter, whirl, agitation, perturbation, ruffle, hurly-burly, ferment, flutter, stir, readiness, feeze *(coll.),* pother, helter-skelter, scamper, scud, wakefulness, unrest, restlessness, turbulence, zeal, nervousness, turmoil, commotion, dither, jitters *(sl.),* tremor, panting, tremble, twitter, trepidation, fire, enthusiasm, ardor, avidity, fervor, fear of being late, no time to be lost, sweat *(coll.),* cold sweat *(coll.),* disquietude, hurry-skurry, ado, fidget *(often pl.),* necessity, worry, urgency, trepidity, concern, press, vehemence, hubbub, scuttle, stew *(coll.),* fidgetiness, inquietude, sleeplessness, push, spurt, passion.

HASTEN, *v.* 1. Move *or* act with haste, proceed with haste, hurry, move speedily, be in a hurry, make haste, lose no time, race, scurry, flee, skip, spurt, push on, whisk, run, sprint, rush, make time, ride hard, shoot, tear, fly, scour, scoot *(coll.),* bolt, dart, skedaddle *(sl.),* outstrip the wind, fly on the wings of the wind, bowl along, cut along *(coll.),* clap spurs to one's horse, wing one's way, crowd sail *(Naut.),* mend one's pace, spank, post, hie *(often reflexive with personal pronoun),* scuttle, trip, flit, be on the run, scamper, hustle, pace, swoop, career, bestir oneself, be quick, move quickly, haste *(Lit.),* rip *(coll.),* whiz, sweep, cover ground, get over the ground, dash off *or* on, go on the double *(coll.),* beat a retreat, not lose a moment, stir one's stumps, work against time, spin, leap, go like lightning *or* greased lightning *(coll.),* go like a shot *(coll.),* go hell-bent *(coll.),* clip, bound, boom, spring, bustle, make forced marches *(Mil.),* burn up the road *(sl.),* press on, zip *(coll.),* skim, brush, whip off *or* away, go like a bat out of hell *(coll.),* get out and dig *(coll.),* jump, make the best of one's time, make short work of, bundle, hump it *(sl.),* step *(coll.),* step along *(coll.),* step on the gas *(coll.),* crack on, speed up, work under pressure, go at full blast, run like mad, march in double-quick time, put on more speed, hurry up, quicken, give her the gas *(coll.),* take wing, go all out, pack off *or* away, carry sail *(Naut.),* canter, trot, gallop, lope, make strides *or* rapid strides, go *or* run wide open, do some tall stepping, step on it *(coll.),* step lively *(coll.),* take to flight, hie one's way.

2. Cause to hasten, accelerate, give a shove *or* impulse to, stimulate, vivify, animate, press, urge, festinate, rouse, bring speedily, push forward, urge on, goad, whip, help, aid, assist, precipitate, dispatch, urge forward, spur, quicken, speed, press on, promote, drive on, scorch, express, prick, hurry on, send away quickly, bring on, set on one's legs, lend wings to, make easier *or* less difficult, advance, whisk, railroad *(coll.),* facilitate, pack *(sometimes foll. by* OFF *or* AWAY*),* put on one's feet, forward, free from difficulty *or* impediment, send off summarily, hound on, egg on, impel, propel, set on, incite, expedite, post, push on, send express, drive, precipitate, hustle, lubricate, give full play, lighten the labor, disencumber, deobstruct, free, clear, kindle, lash, encourage, force, inflame, disembarrass, disburden, lighten, give the reins to, give an impetus, thrust, boost, jog, hurtle, prompt, jolt, prod, shove, move, motivate, inspire, exhort, instigate, bestir, flog, zip up *(coll.),* excite, inspirit, provoke.

HASTILY, *adv.* 1. With speed *or* quickness, speedily, nimbly, quickly, hurriedly, presto, apace, slightly, all at once, with haste, in no time, amain, posthaste, with great *or* all haste, promptly, instantly, straightway, with breathless speed, pronto *(coll.),* double quick, in a wink, in an instant, trippingly, whip and spur, like greased lightning *(coll.),* like all possessed *(coll.),* like a shot, like a thunderbolt, like mad *(coll.),* lickety-split *(sl.),* lickety-cut *(sl.),* lickety-brindle *(sl.),* on the double *or* double-quick *(coll.),* P.D.Q. *(sl.),* by leaps and bounds, like a bat out of hell *(sl.),* readily, full tilt, full pelt, hotfoot, pell-mell, head over heels, headforemost, heels over head, at once, right away, without further delay, straight, straightforth, in less than no time, before you can say "Jack Robinson," before the ink is dry, under press of sail *(or canvas, sail and steam; Naut.),* for all one is worth *(coll.),* as fast as one's legs *or* heels will carry one, fast, all out *(sl.),* wide open, at full blast, in high gear, breathlessly.

2. Rashly, hurriedly, headlong, abruptly, precipitately, slapdash, slapbang, unexpectedly, pell-mell, in haste, recklessly, in confusion, carelessly, in disorder, summarily, head over heels, heels over head, headforemost, smack *(coll.),* pop *(coll.),* plunk *(coll.),* too quickly, without due reflection, on the spur of the moment, at *or* on sight, at short notice, incontinently, extempore, lightly, by surprise, prematurely, too soon, at half cock, without notice *or* warning, like a bolt from the blue, like a thunderbolt, unpreparedly, like a thief in the night, heedlessly, thoughtlessly, superficially, cursorily, fleetingly, impatiently, feverishly, helter-skelter, incautiously, unadvisedly, foolishly, unwarily, injudiciously, inopportunely, passionately, immaturely, aimlessly, impulsively, impetuously, without due caution, plop *(coll.).*

HASTY, *adj.* 1. Moving *or* acting with haste, quick, speedy, swift, rapid, fleet, fast, rushing, expeditious, running, prompt, urgent, sudden, hasteful, brisk, hurried, winged, mercurial, agile, nimble, snappy, extempore, active, sprightly, lively, dynamic, bustling, immediate, instant, telegraphic, electric, extemporaneous, light-footed, light-legged, eagle-winged, quick as lightning, instantaneous, quick as thought, swift as an arrow, spirited, quick as a wink, light of heel.

2. Made *or* done with haste *or* speed, cursory, slight, hurried, superficial, passing, transient, with limited time, brief, mortal, volatile, meteoric, flying, urgent, temporal, impermanent, short-lived, ephemeral, feverish, momentary, peevish, pushed, breathless, shifty, slippery, techy, fugacious, diurnal, evanescent, temporary, short, rapid, fugitive, cometary, impatient, preterient, deciduous, perishable, fleeting, transitory, caducous, pressed for time.

3. Unduly quick in movement *or* action, rash, precipitate, headlong, reckless, pell-mell, helter-skelter, foolish, incautious, heedless, without deliberation, indiscreet, brash, unwary, eager, unadvised, careless, ill-advised, unmeditated, unbridled, abrupt, boisterous, unchecked, furious, pressing, brusque, frantic, heady, hotspur, adventurous, daredevil, passionate, foolhardy, immature, hurried, irrepressible, turbulent, inopportune, premature, too forward, injudicious, excited, aimless, breakneck, unexpected, regardless, harum-scarum, scrambling, subitaneous, impulsive, **impetuous,** snap, thoughtless, madcap, mad-**brained,** uncontrolled, ungoverned, precipitous,

impassioned, without due caution, feverish, precipitant.

4. Done with *or* characterized by thoughtless *or* angry haste, easily excited to anger, irritable, touchy, testy, waspish, petulant, peevish, choleric, fiery, fretful, passionate, spleenful, acerbic, jaundiced, bristling, fractious, quick-tempered, cantankerous, pettish, blunt, irascible, excitable, hot-headed, peppery, headstrong, heady, unconsidering, unthinking, desultory, warm, impulsive, impetuous, skittish, hot, cross, startlish, ill-humored, brusque, captious, querulous, high-strung, fierce, quick, ungovernable, simmering, volcanic, crusty, explosive, huffy, churlish, bearish, cross-grained, burning, snappish, mettlesome, high-mettled, intolerant, bilious, iracund, splenetic, abrupt, quarrelsome, angry, brash, startish *(coll.),* uncontrollable, moody, hostile, contentious, shrewish, sensitive, boorish, neurotic, inflammable, nervous, like a barrel of gunpowder, like touchwood *or* tinder, vindictive, thin-skinned, resentful.

HAT, *n.* Shaped cover for the head, bonnet, headpiece, cap, haberdashery, millinery, headgear, chapeau, derby, castor, billycock *(Brit.),* bowler *(Brit.),* beaver, sun hat, sunbonnet, dicer *(sl.),* lid *(sl.),* tile *(coll.),* fedora, silk hat, top hat, crush hat, turban, sundown, shovel, hood, miter, caubeen *(Anglo-Ir.),* poke bonnet, jerry *(sl., Eng.),* benny *(sl., Brit.),* topper *(sl.),* plug hat *or* plug *(sl.),* stovepipe hat *or* stovepipe *(coll.),* opera hat, felt hat, cocked hat, scraper *(sl.),* fore-and-after, pith hat *or* helmet, picture hat, ten-gallon hat *(Western U. S.),* sombrero, kelly *(sl.),* wide-awake *or* wide-awake hat, cloche, sailor, beret, sun helmet, topee *(Ind.),* sou'wester, fantail *(Eng.),* pugree *(Ind.),* straw hat, Dutch cap, kepi, forage cap, overseas cap, casque, tam, calotte, service cap *or* hat, casquetel, steel helmet, tin hat *(Soldiers' sl.),* gibus, toque, sallet, zucchetto, calash, capote, coif, fez, tarboosh, shako *(Brit.),* leghorn, bearskin, Panama hat *or* panama, straw basher *(sl., Brit.),* boudoir cap, mobcap *(chiefly Hist.),* skullcap, nightcap, tam-o'-shanter, coonskin cap, rumal *(Ind.),* benjy *(sl., Brit.).*

HATCH, *n.* 1. That which is hatched, brood, offspring, young of a fowl, progeny, flock, covey *(of partridge, etc.),* aerie *(of birds of prey and other large birds),* nide *(of pheasants).*

2. Cover for an opening in a ship's deck *(or floor or roof, etc.),* door flush with floor or ceiling, hatchway-grating, trap door *(often in pl.),* hatchway, wicket, sluice gate, floodgate, frame for catching fish, weir, cellarway, scuttle, barway, booby hatch *(Naut.).*

HATCH, *v.* 1. Bring forth young from the egg, breed *(from eggs),* generate, brood, cover, set, sit, incubate, cause young to emerge from *(the egg),* give being to.

2. Be hatched, emerge, come forth, break through the shell, appear, pip, see the light of day.

3. Concoct, devise, contrive, plot, plan, design, scheme, think out, produce, lay out, brew, project, excogitate, frame, invent, prepare, fabricate, make up, formulate, compound, form, imagine, construct, create, originate, fashion, evolve, elaborate, perfect, mature, compose, shape, forge, spin, get up, cast, innovate, trump up, cook up *(coll.),* coin, build, develop, manufacture, bring forth, give birth to, hammer out, block out, hatch up, dream up, conceive.

4. Mark with lines *(as for shading, drawing or engraving),* engrave, enchase, cut, carve, scratch,

tool, gouge, stipple, scrape, bite, channel, flute, furrow, groove, score, etch, incise, ornament by engraving, crosshatch, mezzotint, chase.

HATCHERY, *n.* Place for hatching eggs of poultry, fish, *etc.,* incubator, brooder, fish hatchery, breeding place.

HATCHET, *n.* Small short-handled ax, machete, dolabra, tomahawk, adz, billhook, bill, mattock, poleax *(Nav.),* celt *(Archaeol.),* pickax, cutlass, cleave, cleaver, battle-ax, bushwhacker.

HATCHWAY, *n.* Doorway in a floor *or* ceiling, hatch, trap door, cellarway, scuttle, hatches, opening to another level.

HATE, *n.* 1. Hatred, intense aversion, strong dislike, abhorrence, detestation, enmity, hostility, antipathy, animosity, venom, rancor, malice, spite, odium, bad blood, malevolence, envy, jealousy, horror, repugnance, distaste, ill will, coldness, loathing, phobia, aversion, conflict, nausea, inimicality, clashing, oppugnancy, discord, execration, displacency, alienation, bitterness, dissension, disrelish, estrangement, irreconciliation, heartburning, inimicalness, abomination, disaffection, vials of hate *or* wrath, coolness, disfavor, averseness, vindictiveness, implacability, resentment, dudgeon, wrath, anger, virulence, harshness, contumely, acerbity, acrimony, ire, revengefulness, misogyny, misanthropy, hardness, heartlessness, ruthlessness, asperity, disdain, spleen, animus, scorn, derision, caustic mordacity, evil, cruelty, rankling, rage, fury, grudge, maliciousness, malignity, causticity, obduracy, avoidance, contempt, immitigability, pitilessness, hardheartedness.

2. Object of hatred, dislike, anathema, aversion, enemy, abomination, annoyance, *bête noire,* bugbear, gall, bane, damnation, plague, pestilence, grievance, curse, offense, antipathy, open enemy, bitter enemy, foe, evil, execration, bitter pill, thorn in the flesh, provocation, horror, detestation, irritation, affront, sore subject, umbrage.

HATE, *v.* 1. Regard with a strong *or* passionate dislike, have *or* possess hatred for, bear malice to be hostile to, dislike intensely, disdain, despise, detest, envy, anathematize, have (entertain, conceive, take) an aversion to, shudder at, not care for, not be able to bear (endure, abide), spurn, shun, avoid, denounce, curse, execrate, shrink from, abhor, abominate, nauseate, loathe, recoil from, misprize, tread *or* trample underfoot, spit upon, think nothing of, disparage, sicken at, have enough of, resent, be sick *(or* tired) of, set at naught, esteem slightly, be repelled by, feel repulsion from, reject, deride, disfavor, disrelish, mislike, have no use for, view with horror, revolt against, have no taste *or* stomach for, look down upon, hold cheap, contemn, feel malice toward, bear a grudge, hold aloof from, set one's face against, be malevolent, be disgusted with, hold in contempt, owe a grudge to, keep a grudge against, object to.

2. *(With infinitive, participle, or clause with* THAT) Feel great aversion for, dislike exceedingly, be unwilling, be extremely sorry, regret deeply, abhor, abominate, loathe, detest, mind, reluctate, reluct, resist, object to, not care to, would rather not, wish to avoid, shun, demur, put off, not have the heart to, shrink from, recoil from, wish to evade, blench from, pull *or* draw back from, struggle against, hang fire, hesitate, feel sick at, eschew, nauseate, wish to abstain from, keep clear of, feel disinclined to, turn from, shy away from, wince from, flinch from, quail from,

make a mouth (wry face, grimace) at, stick at, regard as distasteful (unpleasant, difficult, *etc.),* have no taste *or* stomach to, be reluctant.

HATEFUL, *adj.* Exciting *or* deserving great dislike (aversion *or* disgust), detestable, odious, abhorrent, accursed, abominable, execrable, repugnant, loathsome, nauseous, offensive, repulsive, cursed, annoying, ignominious, ugly, heinous, corrupt, invidious, monstrous, confounded, shocking, horrid, foul, obnoxious, opprobrious, hideous, rotten, distasteful, sinister, tainted, evilgotten, wicked, sinful, blameworthy, nasty, contemptible, diabolic, despicable, coarse, frightening, grotesque, gross, misshapen, insufferable, nauseating, forbidding, vulgar, putrid *(fig.),* villainous, atrocious, infamous, base, nefarious, flagrant, reprehensible, vile, sickening, beastly, evil-fashioned, evil-favored, evil-savored, devilish, infernal, bloody *(vulgar),* fulsome, scurvy, rank, peccant, evilshaped, evil-eyed, evil-affected, hellish, revolting, damnable, horrible, evil, disgusting, unendurable, nameless, abject, intolerable, ignoble, low, unworthy, mawkish, deplorable, discourteous, mean, unpleasant, unbearable, unpalatable, objectionable, dishonorable.

HATRED, *n.* The feeling of one who hates, intense dislike, animosity, detestation, malignity, rancor, malevolence, hostility, enmity, settled ill will, strong aversion, acrimony, umbrage, abhorrence, abomination, execration, loathing, disgust, evil, revulsion, repugnance, horror, disfavor, ignominy, despite, prejudice, feeling, wrong, malignance, invidiousness, spite, malice, resentment, anger, pique, bad blood, spleen, grudge, odium, bitterness, revenge, hate, antipathy, venom, envy, distaste, coldness, pitilessness, contempt, obduracy, avoidance, immitigability, hard-heartedness, causticity, maliciousness, mordacity, asperity, scorn, animus, ruthlessness, derision, disdain, inimicality, oppugnancy, discord, displacency, alienation, dissension, estrangement, inimicalness, heartburning, disaffection, coolness, dudgeon, wrath, virulence, harshness, vindictiveness, implacability, contumely, misogyny, misanthropy, cruelty, rankling.

HAUBERK, *n.* Mail, armor, coat of mail, armature, corselet, tunic of mail, brigandine, panoply, habergeon *(loosely).*

HAUGHTY, *adj.* Arrogant, disdainful, supercilious, proud, lofty, big, stiff, aristocratic, swelledheaded, contemptuous, aloof, cold, unsympathetic, unfeeling, hard, contumelious, distant, hoitytoity, assuming, overbearing, uppish *(coll.),* fastuous, pompous, puffed up, high and mighty, consequential, conceited, snobbish, pretentious, boastful, condescending, bloated with pride, distended with self-esteem, ostentatious, presumptuous, arbitrary, domineering, absolute, self-sufficient, commanding, self-assertive, high-hat *(sl.),* overweening, imperious, egotistical, cynical, pedantic, dictatorial, swollen, affected, cavalier, patronizing, high-headed *(sl.),* stiff-necked, high-minded, highflown, vain, magisterial, high-handed, sniffy *(coll.),* toplofty *(coll.),* uppity *(coll.),* impudent, audacious, highfalutin *(coll.),* snooty *(coll.),* overproud, stuck-up *(coll.),* self-important, lordly, insolent, defamatory, vilifying, derogatory, detracting, vainglorious, prideful, high, bumptious, chill, chesty *(sl.),* peacockish, wise in one's own conceits, self-glorious, self-satisfied, windy, disparaging, grandiloquent, derisive, scornful, inflated, bombastic, belittling, slighting, gasconading, withering, fanfaronading, thrasonical, braggart, flaunting, gassy *(coll.)*, self-complacent, self-applauding, self-lauding, insulting, self-flattering, self-praising, intolerant, oppressive, vilipenditory, cocky *(coll.)*, priggish, abusive, self-opinionated, know-it-all, unresponsive, cruel, unconcerned, frigid, unapproachable, unfriendly, inaccessible, forbidding, remote, impassive, unsolicitous, callous, stony, obdurate, unmoved, unstirred, impervious, untouched, uncaring, unkind, insensible, untender, icy, unbending, ruthless, bowelless, bragging.

HAUL, *n.* 1. Act of hauling, haulage, pull, wrench, yank *(coll.)*, tug, heave, drag, jerk, lug.

2. *(Esp. of fish)* Catch, take, yield, creel, quantity *(of fish caught)*, bag, capture, seizure, gain.

3. *(Coll.)* Booty, spoils, prey, steal, gains, loot, swag *(coll.)*, acquisitions, acquirements, bag, capture, takings, plunder, pilferage, pickings, gain, pelf, reward.

HAUL, *v.* 1. Carry, bear, tow, lug, bring, trail, take, convey, tote, portage, transmit, tug, move, drag, fetch, transfer, convoy, transplant, conduct, truck, wagon, snake.

2. Pull at, heave, wrench, snake, trawl, twitch, drag, yank *(coll.)*, draw, jerk, lug, tug.

3. *(With* UP. *Coll.)* Call to account, summon, have on the carpet *(coll.)*, have up, reprimand, take to task, roast *(coll.)*, remonstrate, discipline, call down, berate, send for, arraign *(Leg.)*, bawl out *(coll.)*, bring to justice, bring into court, reprehend, upbraid, indict, reprove, chide, rate, serve with a writ *(Leg.)*, dress down, admonish, objurgate, cite, bring forward, rebuke, scold, bring to book, censure, subpoena.

4. *(With* UP *or* OFF. *Esp. Nautical)* Change course, turn, veer, yaw, change bearing, wear, swerve, alter course, shift, go about, haul to, break, tack, turn aside, jibe, cast, turn tail, draw off, draw away, pull away.

HAUNCH, *n.* Hip, fleshy part about the hip, hind quarter of an animal, leg and loin *(of an animal, as for food)*, rump, buttocks, croup, butt, huckle, round *(of beef)*, breech, hind end, backside, nates, seat, posterior *(sometimes pl.)*, thigh, fundament, posteriority, hinder parts, quarter, podex *(Zool.)*, crupper *(of a horse)*, dorsal *or* lumbar region, bottom, gluteal region.

HAUNT, *n. (Often in plur.)* Retreat, resort, place to which one often resorts, home, haven, frequented place, usual vicinity, meeting place, rendezvous, shelter, abode, realm, arbor, bower, cloister, hermitage, chimney corner, hearth, anchorage, inglenook, ingleside, asylum, locality, purlieu, habitat, tryst, hideaway, hide-out *(coll.)*, whereabouts, environs, moorings, sanctuary, territory, demesne, stamping ground *(coll.)*, hangout *(sl.)*, repose, gathering place. *(The following usually refer to animals):* den, lair, nest, cave, hole, covert, habitat, burrow, dugout, range, vivarium, environs, natural home, native environment, natural abode, watering place, mew, water hole, kennel.

HAUNT, *v.* 1. Reappear frequently to after death, visit habitually as a supposed spirit *or* ghost, hover about, frequent, manifest itself, materialize, recur, rise, walk, return from the dead, float before the eyes, be disclosed, inhabit, dwell in, take up abode in.

2. Intrude upon continually, be ever present, recur to persistently, obsess, harass, infest, worry, plague, pester, tease, disquiet, disturb, torment,

molest, trouble, beset, annoy, vex, terrify, besiege, cause nostalgia, frighten, cause regret *or* sorrow, agitate, sting, agonize, harrow, rack, hang over one's head, nettle, unman, appall, overrun, possess one's mind, terrorize, weigh *or* prey on.

3. Frequent, resort to, visit, repair to, go to repeatedly, return often to, revisit, remain at, sojourn, stay at, bend one's steps to, direct one's course to, hie to, affect, betake oneself to, loiter, linger, hover about, beat a path to, hang around *or* about at *(sl.)*, hang out at *(sl.)*, migrate to, retire to.

4. Frequent the company of, be often with, hang upon, attend, court, hang about, buttonhole, follow importunately, insinuate, ingratiate oneself, accompany, seek out, trail, intrude upon, worm *or* work in, foist oneself upon, meddle, impose oneself, encroach, shadow, appear like the Cheshire cat, tail *(coll.)*, pursue, run after, press in, break in upon, trespass, wedge in, stick like a leech, dance attendance to, pander to, hang on the sleeve of, truckle, toady, pay court to, court *or* curry favor, adhere, cling like ivy *or* a bur, be a hanger-on, heel, be sycophantic, be a clinging vine.

HAUTEUR, *n.* Haughtiness, haughty manner *or* spirit, vanity, contempt, loftiness, lordliness, imperiousness, contumely, pomposity, toploftiness *(coll.)*, pretentiousness, unwarrantable pride, haughty airs, snobbery, domineering, swelled head, high horse, self-importance, superciliousness, contemptuousness, disdain, insolence, hardihood, self-esteem, self-conceit, self-approbation, self-applause, priggishness, condescension, snobbism, inordinate confidence, peacockery, impertinence, arrogance, altitudes *(coll.)*, peacockishness, self-content, self-satisfaction, self-praise, overweeningness, priggism, egoism, vainglory, highmindedness, effrontery, overbearance, gall, presumption, pretension, egotism, scoffing, affectation, oppression, detraction, belittling, disparagement, derision, magniloquence, conceit, bumptiousness, conceitedness, assumption, selfsufficiency, pretense, parade, fanfaronade, display, audacity, self-love, ostentation, inflation, scorn, despisal, contemptuousness, sovereign contempt, despect, grandiloquence.

HAVE, *v.* 1. Hold for use, be in possession of, possess, own, keep, exercise *(as a right, privilege)*, be in control of, retain, maintain, comprise, harbor, command, control, inherit, tie up, detain, grip, clutch, embody, number, count, grasp, accommodate, entertain, consist of, comprehend, embrace, subsume, enclose, include, contain, hold *or* keep back, keep close, withhold, involve, support, cherish, carry.

2. Obtain, acquire, receive, get, gain, take, come into possession of, procure, secure, be informed of, glean, accept, take in, be granted, catch, learn, come in for, pick up, imbibe, be given, be in receipt of, have fall to one, get hold of, come by, gather, collect, be accorded, be vouchsafed, have come one's way, be proffered *or* offered, discover, get possession of, find out.

3. *(Foll. by infinitive)* Be obliged, be under necessity, be compelled, must, acknowledge as something to be done, be forced, be made, be under pressure, be pressed, be driven, have no choice *or* alternative, be destined, be called upon, be bound, be coerced, feel constrained, be drawn irresistibly, need, stand in need, be caused, be pushed to the wall, be in for, be impelled, be

unable to avoid or refuse, be swept, find it necessary, be required.

4. Experience, enjoy, suffer, undergo, sustain, bear, catch, endure, taste, support, respond to, be possessed of, encounter, meet with, go or pass through, smart under, thrill to, savor, receive, meet, find, be subjected to, submit to, brave.

5. Hold in mind, sight, etc., entertain, permit oneself, maintain, cherish, feel, think, attend to, observe, mark, receive an impression of, be impressed by or with, harbor, bear in mind, accept, be filled with, foster, nurture, believe, nurse, imagine, devote oneself to, fix the mind on, be obsessed with, give ear to, take cognizance of, adopt, embrace, trust, turn over in the mind, assume, recognize, take into consideration or account, allow, heed, mind, occupy the mind with, hold in view, credit, approve, consider, find room for.

6. Require (to do something, be done, or as specified), cause, oblige, effect, bring, exact, get, make, prevail on (or with or upon), bring pressure to bear on, coerce, bind, bid, order, direct, kindle, incite, contrive, command, desire, enjoin, persuade, bear upon, press, drive, procure, induce, motivate, necessitate, put under a necessity, expect, lead, move, coax, compel, force, engage, constrain, ask, request.

7. Show in action, exhibit, take, use, exercise, display, give expression to, set forth, reveal, disclose, express, evidence, manifest, prove, indicate, evince, employ, exert, practice, apply, avail oneself of, do with, demonstrate, utilize.

8. Engage in, perform, indulge in, take part in, participate in, enter into, share, join in, hold, be a party to, undertake, pursue, unite in, carry on, execute, enact, prosecute, be employed in, partake of, be about, lend oneself to, do together.

9. (Usually with negative) Permit, allow, support, bear, endure, tolerate, countenance, approve, let, admit, recognize, favor, take, bear with, humor, indulge, give the reins to, submit to, consent, sustain, bide, brook, disregard, put up with, make light of, wink at, digest, swallow, stomach, pocket, reconcile oneself to, resign oneself to, suffer, stand, abide, connive at.

10. (Usually with IT) Assert, maintain, hold, affirm, say, hint, suggest, state, voice, put, phrase, word, present, style, render, speak, bespeak, signify, declare, aver, claim, allege, predicate, protest, pronounce, put forward, propound, tell, impart, advance, insinuate, imply, propose, intimate, insist, point to, offer, contend, broach, stress, divulge, emphasize, make known, express, couch (in terms), clothe (in words), designate, enunciate, set forth, assever, asseverate.

11. Know well, understand, comprehend, embrace, apprehend, fathom, be trained in, have profited by instruction in, possess, grasp, penetrate, seize, interpret correctly, be expert in, memorize, be proficient in, be apprised of, be master of, be conversant with, have knowledge of, remember.

12. Give birth to, engender, bear, beget, bring forth, deliver, procreate, reproduce, gestate, bring into being, carry, breed.

13. (Foll. by ON) Wear, be dressed in, assume, be clothed in, sport (coll.).

HAVEN, n. 1. Port, harbor, anchorage, dock, harborage, portlet, destination, base, moorings, inlet, landing, wharf, quay, pier, bay, cove, creek, bight, gulf.

2. Sanctum, asylum, refuge, harbor, castle,

fasthold, shelter, tower of strength, bourn, retreat, place of safety, cell, subterfuge, hide-out, den, lair, nest, port in a storm, hermitage, cloister, ark, home, pillar, rock, citadel, stronghold, keep, fortress, fastness, kennel, resort, lodging, resting-place, concealment, safehold, anchorage, care, safekeeping, security, protection, safety, hiding, hideaway, sanctuary, cover.

HAVERSACK, n. Provision bag, bag, kitbag, saddlebag, shoulder bag, ditty bag, knapsack, satchel, case, rucksack, reticule, sabretache (Mil.).

HAVOC, n. Devastation, ravage, disruption, debacle, inundation, tragedy, dissolution, cataclysm, catastrophe, extirpation, fatality, breakup, wash-out, obliteration, disaster, ruinous damage, wrack and ruin, upheaval, consumption, extinction, collapse, extermination, desolation, deluge, wreck, destruction, alluvion, annihilation, elimination, ruination, crash, waste, flood, gutting, smashing, razing, demolition, disaster, eradication, decimation, pillaging, rooting out or up, laying waste, unbuilding, undoing.

HAVOC, v. Work or wreak havoc upon, play havoc with, ruin, destroy, deluge, annihilate, waste, eliminate, blast, flood, cut down, trample in the dust, break up, break down, root up or out, inundate, extirpate, exterminate, stamp out, disable, despoil, squash, overturn, decimate, trample out, overthrow, quell, cut out root and branch, sweep away, level, overwhelm, tumble, gut, undo, unbuild, disintegrate, shatter, topple, fell.

HAW, v. Hesitate (in speech), stutter, hem and haw, stammer, falter, halt (in speech), stumble (in speech), balbutiate, titubate.

HAWK, n. Falcon, buzzard, kite, harrier, caracara, goshawk, kestrel, osprey, saker (Old World), lanner (Old World), brancher (Falconry), haggard (Adult. Falc.), eyas (Young. Falc.).

HAWK, v. 1. Cry, vend, peddle, sell in the streets, dispense, market, huckster, higgle, chaffer.

2. Clear the throat, cough noisily, raise phlegm.

HAWKER, n. Huckster, peddler, vender, monger, street seller, higgler, colporteur, sutler, cheap-John (coll.), cheap-Jack (coll.).

HAWK-EYED, adj. Having keen eyes, sharp-sighted, quick-sighted, keen-eyed, eagle-eyed, lynx-eyed, Argus-eyed, with penetrating vision, cat-eyed, scrutinizing, percipient, piercing, scrutinous, clear-eyed, ferret-eyed, farseeing, farsighted, discerning, gimlet-eyed, with acute vision, examining closely.

HAY, n. Harvest of grasses and other forage plants, grass mowed or ready for mowing, forage grass, fodder, feed, provender, clover, timothy, lucerne, alfalfa, tall fescue, meadow fescue, silage, ensilage, fescue (Bot.).

HAYCOCK, n. Hayrick, haystack, conical pile or heap of hay, haymow, rick, cock, sheaf, stack, mow, temporary storage for hay, bundle, heap, mass, shock.

HAYFIELD, n. Field used for hay grass, pasture, meadow, mead (chiefly poetic), grassland.

HAYLOFT, n. Haymow, loft in barn or stable for storage of hay, hayrack, mow, scaffold for hay, mass of hay stored in a barn or stable.

HAYMOW, n. 1. Hayloft, hayrack, mow, scaffold for hay, mass of hay stored in barn or stable, loft in barn or stable for storage of hay.

2. Haycock, mow, cock, hayrick, conical pile or

heap of hay, haystack, rick, sheaf, stack, shock, heap, mass, bundle.

HAYSEED, n. 1. Bits of hay such as cling to the clothes, straw, grain, grass seed, chaff, wisp, hull, bur, shuck, pod, bran, husk, palea (Bot.), locusta (Bot.), episperm (Bot.), testa (Bot.), bract (Bot.), spikelet (Bot.).

2. (Slang) Rustic, countryman, churl, bumpkin, lout, hind, clodhopper, peasant, farmer, hick (sl.), swain, boor, plowman, drone, clown, son of the soil, lubber, hobnail, yokel, greenhorn, Tony Lumpkin, hodge (coll.), son of Martha, cuddy, tiller of the soil, gaffer, looby, clod, country bumpkin, chuff, kern, joskin (sl.), rube (coll.), lumpkin, jake (coll.), galoot (sl.).

HAZARD, n. 1. Exposure to danger or harm, risk, peril, danger, unsafety, jeopardy, insecurity, source of risk, crisis, strait, plight, endangerment, imperilment, vulnerability, liability, openness to danger, susceptibility, threat, contest with evil, race with death, nonplus, pitfall, predicament, hole, dilemma, heel of Achilles, breakers ahead, storm brewing, clouds gathering, susceptivity, clouds on the horizon, instability, precariousness.

2. Chance, casualty, accident, fortuitous event, lot, game, scratch hit or shot (coll.), contingency, stake, odds, risk, random shot, adventure, fluke, stroke, fortune, casual event, unforeseen occurrence, contretemps, doom, misfortune, fortuity, absence of assignable cause, gamble, Lady Luck, break (coll.), haphazard, potluck, venture, portion, cup, fatality, kismet, destiny, ups and downs, vicissitudes of fortune, mishap, mischance, dispensation, wheel of fortune or chance, coincidence, draw, plunge (sl.), fall of the cards, cast or throw of the dice, flip of the coin, heads or tails, turn of the table or cards, planets, stars, happenstance (humorous), happening, chance-medley (Law).

3. Uncertainty of the result (as when throwing a die), risk, insecurity, fortune, probability, possibility, likelihood, presumption, speculation, fortuity, random, tossup, doubtfulness, fearfulness, suspense, doubt, fallibility, gamble, precariousness, lot, fate, odds, luck, fortune, anxiety, apprehension, run of luck, contingency, errability, dependence on chance, variability.

4. Something risked or staked, that which is wagered, security, bet, potshot, wager, guarantee, warranty, ante (Poker), stake (in gaming and fig.), deposit, pledge, gage, pawn, bond, surety, pot, bail, play, pool, assurance, investment, guaranty.

HAZARD, v. 1. Venture (a statement, conjecture, etc.), offer, throw out, submit, proffer, advance, presume, dare say, volunteer, risk, dare, chance, attempt, suppose, infer, gather, guess, take a liberty, make free, theorize, hypothesize, run the risk, expect (coll.), conjecture, experiment.

2. Take or run the risk of (a misfortune, penalty, etc.), undertake against odds, risk, adventure, experiment, bet, punt, lay, venture upon, venture to incur, conjecture, wage, take a chance, speculate, back, sport, game, play, defy, wager, enter upon blindly, dare, gamble, take potluck, practice gaming, try one's fortune, take one's chance, take a pig in a poke, chance it (coll.), be rash, take a leap in the dark, play a desperate game, tempt fate, tempt fortune, tempt Providence, shuffle the cards, toss up, leave or trust to chance or luck, trust to the chapter of accidents, call heads or tails, call the coin, mock

or despise danger, plunge (sl.), toss or flip the coin, ante up (Poker).

3. Put to the risk of being lost, expose to the operations of chance, peril, imperil, endanger, put in danger, hit, jeopard, stake, venture, expose to risk, pawn, bait, jeopardy, threaten, danger, compromise, set at hazard, adventure, subject to menace, involve, invest, embark, sink, lead on, entangle, ensnare, lay a trap for, lure, strand, decoy, jeopardize, put at hazard, risk.

HAZARDOUS, adj. 1. Perilous, full of danger, full of risk, unsafe, fraught with danger, unprotected, attended or beset with danger, dangerous, unreliable, unsound, adverse, evil, bad, infirm, unhealthy (coll.), risky, precarious, alarming, threatening, ominous, menacing, portentous, ill-omened, shaky, tottery, unsteady, ticklish, slippery, sinister, dismaying, appalling, inauspicious, foreboding, minatory, minacious, disquieting, trembling in the balance, hanging by a thread, serious, grave, dire, arduous, untrustworthy, dark, insecure, critical, unstable, built upon sand.

2. Dependent on chance, risked, precarious, unpredictable, venturesome, speculative, uncertain, gambled, up in the air, unsure, doubtful, dubious, rash, undecided, undetermined, fortuitous, tentative, casual, accidental, random, pending, in suspense, contingent on circumstances, of obscure outcome, undemonstrable, debatable, enigmatic, unstable, questionable, problematical, adventitious, conjectural, at stake, controvertible, unsettled, disputable, fluky, haphazard, unforeseeable, ambiguous, equivocal, obscure, dark, an open question, conditional, subject to chance, in question, irregular, ticklish, insecure.

HAZE, n. 1. Aggregation of minute suspended water or dust particles, fog, mist, cloud, gauze, vapor, steam, film, nebula, pall, fume, miasma, nebulosity, lack of transparency or clarity, exhalation, scud, veil, screen, drisk, smog, shadow, puff, cloak, mantle, frost, smoke.

2. (Fig.; a mental state) Obscurity, vagueness, dimness, fog, confusion, indecisiveness, ambiguity, pall, oppression, nebulosity, fogginess, grogginess, befuddlement, obscuration, discomposure, mistiness, dejection, depression, lack of clarity, indefiniteness, unintelligibility, indistinctness, mystification, benighted state, clouded condition, haziness, fume, fuddle (sl.), daze, bewilderment, muddle.

HAZE, v. Subject a newcomer (as in college, etc.), to abusive or ridiculous tricks, abuse, tease, hector, bully, worry, make fun or game of, chaff, poke fun at, annoy, rally, initiate, taunt, bullyrag, jolly (coll.), jest, twit, stultify, badger, bait, joke with, make a fool of, rag (sl.), make practical jokes, victimize, joke at one's expense, send on a fool's errand, make merry with, smoke, get the laugh on (sl.), make a goat of (sl.), show up (coll.), banter, harass.

HAZEL, adj. Light brown, reddish brown, tan, acorn, citrine, fawn, cinnamon, burnt umber, red-yellow, khaki, Algerian, tanbark, meadowlark, rhubarb, fuscous, tawny, beige.

HAZY, adj. 1. Characterized by the presence of haze, misty, foggy, unclear, overcast, steaming, cloudy, screened, nebulous, opaque, fuliginous, fumy, dull, obscure, dim, murky, rimy, gauzy, vaporous, frosty, veiled, shadowy, wavering, dusky, thick, bleared, filmy, obfuscated, lowering, obfuscous, semitransparent, blurred, blurry, glimmering, crepuscular, shadowed forth, faint, pale, bleary, smoky, spraylike.

2. Confused, uncertain, indistinct, vague, nebulous, dim, obscure, clouded, shrouded, lacking distinctness, muddy, mazy, enigmatic, muddled, puzzling, impenetrable, unclear, equivocal, nubilous, obfuscous, invisible, hidden, veiled, bleared, unknown, blurred, undisclosed, caliginous, clear as mud (joc.), in eclipse, inconspicuous, unexplored, untraced, ill-marked, ill-defined, undefined, indefinite, indiscernible, unrevealed, obfuscated, mysterious, faint, unknowable, untracked, unsolved, unexplained, blank, dreamy, variable, inexplicable, paradoxical, undistinguishable, unexpressed, unsettled, imperspicuous, indeterminate, fitful, capricious, inarticulate, evanescent.

HEAD, *adj.* 1. Situated at the head, top *or* front, fore, first in order *or* position, front, leading, highest, top, tiptop, topmost, lofty, culminating, summital, vertical, acmic, polar, uppermost, topgallant, meridian, capital, in advance, in superior position, most prominent, in the foreground, primary, elevated, anterior, forward, cardinal, in front, in the van, in the lead, frontal, apical, radical, overhead, preceding, headmost, precedent, precursory, preliminary, protruding, projecting, salient, eminent, previous, antecedent, protuberant, acmatic, meridional, foremost.

2. Being in a position of leadership, chief, principal, superior, main, leading, grand, primary, foremost, prime, supreme, first in importance, ruling, highest, preëminent, paramount, autocratic, prepotent, best, executive, imperial, suzerain, sovereign, administrative, eminent, ascendant, major, matchless, peerless, hegemonic, predominant, exalted, distinguished, elevated, prominent, monarchal, regal, overruling, second to none, authoritative, commanding, preponderant, imperious, prepollent, regnant, august, big (coll.), governing, dominant, prevailing, managerial, proctorial, supervisory, omnipotent, overwhelming, controlling.

3. (Of the wind) Coming from in front, adverse, contrary, opposing, counter, impeditive, dead against, checking progress, impeding, hindering, slowing, deterrent, obstructive, counteractive, in one's face, in one's teeth, resistant.

HEAD, *n.* 1. Upper *or* anterior part of human *or* animal body (joined by neck to trunk), seat of the brain, headpiece, cephalon (Zool.), mazard, headmold, skull, poll, sensorium (Physiol. and Psychol.), sensory (Physiol. and Psychol.), sconce (coll.), pate, brain, nob (sl.), noodle (sl.), bean (sl.), upper story (sl.), cap, jowl (of a fish), coxcomb (hum.), costard (contempt or humorous).

2. Seat of thought, memory, understanding, etc., intellect, mind, thought, cognition, reasoning power, wisdom, proficiency, capacity, aptitude, talent, potentiality, sense, knowing, apprehension, instinct, faculty, comprehension, perception, grasp, keenness, sconce (coll.), mentality, wits, sensibility, brain *or* brains, percipience, parts, headpiece, discernment, mental balance, reception, quickness, cleverness, qualification, endowment, penetration, bent, gift, reason, acuteness, ken, gray matter (coll.), cognitative faculties, sharpness, ability, judgment, genius, poise, presence of mind, receptivity.

3. Source, rise, beginning, origin, fountainhead, genesis, inception, spring, fountain, springhead, wellhead, well, wellspring, reservoir, derivation, commencement, birthplace, font.

4. Chief part, position of leadership, chief command, reins, place of honor, greatest authority, priority, control, lead, front part, chief position, directorship, prepotency, government, charge, supervision, eminence, dictatorship, regality, imperiality, primacy, premiership, dominion, first place, precedence, stewardship, lordship, magistracy, cap, fore part, helm, guidance, rudder, power of rule, kingship, seigniory, headship, prevalence, captaincy, prefecture, suzerainty, oversight, prepollency, superintendence, predominance, supremacy, chieftaincy, leadership.

5. One to whom others are subordinate, chief, leader, master, director, superintendent, superior, general, manager, premier, overseer, president, cardinal, guide, dean, provost, foreman, boss (coll.), chief official, captain, supervisor, chairman, impresario, ruler, commandant, admiral, coryphaeus, king, regent, suzerain, top, functionary, seignior, commodore, kingpin (coll.), patriarch, matriarch, headmaster, champion, chief magistrate, executive, potentate, proprietor, lord, protector, entrepreneur, speaker, person in authority, controller, ringleader, overman, sovereign, governor, commander, administrator, principal, conductor, dictator, senior.

6. Foremost part *or* end of anything, top, upper part, acme, summit, pinnacle, peak, tip, height, front, fore, van, capital, knob, headpiece, lintel, headboard, front part, part opposite the foot, opening (of a bottle, keg, etc.), cap, jetty, jutty, breakwater, mole, projecting part, apex, upper end, uppermost extremity, topmost, headpost, fascia, dentil (Archit.), abacus (Archit.), zenith, crown, brow, crest, cornice, coxcomb, protuberance, forehead, face, bracket capital (Archit.), corbel (Archit.), cymatium (Archit.), blunt end (of a pin), foreground, vertex, meridian, vanguard, proscenium, frontispiece, façade, bowsprit, prow, first line, forerank, front rank, elevation.

7. One of the chief divisions of a discourse, topic, subject, section, title, term, order, point, heading, capital, grouping, inscription (at the beginning of a page or section), theorem, headnote, syllabus, chapter, item, motif, text, category, class, division, separate part, caption, classification, indication of contents, resolution, distinction, specification, designation.

8. Culmination, crisis, end, flowering, fruition, limit, term, crown, windup, cap, ultimate, fulfillment, acme, extremity, summit, highest degree, utmost extent, crowning event, issue, realization, turning point, perfection, fructification, florescence, unfolding, turn of the tide, inevitable result, height, zenith, maximum, termination, conclusion, consummation.

9. Rounded *or* compact part of a plant, flower buds (cauliflower), leafstalks (celery), ear, sessile florets (Bot.), leaves (cabbage and lettuce), close fructification (of grain), cluster of blossoms, bunched foliage.

10 Projecting point of a coast (esp. when high), eminence, headland, cape, promontory, foreland, point, naze, ness, tongue, spur, neck, bluff, cliff, ridge, height, hill, peninsula, mole, breakwater, reef, dune, chine, ledge, shelf, chersonese, precipice, palisade, steep, vantage point *or* ground, bill, crag.

11. Representation of a head, obverse of a coin (opposed to tail), likeness, study, image, profile, portrait, bust, cameo.

12. Cream, foam, froth, scum, lather, fizz, suds, first runnings.

13. (Often with plural **HEAD**) Person *or* animal considered as one of a number, each one among a

number, individual, unit, living being *or* thing, mortal, soul, body, one, hand, each, creature.

HEAD, *v.* 1. Go at the head of *or* in front of, lead, precede, van, be first in, be at the top of, antecede, come first, begin, stand first, stand at the head, lead the way, initiate, instigate, pioneer, prevene, break ground, break the ice, have the start, outrank, go in advance, forerun, announce, go before, precurse, dawn, take the first step, lay the first stone, incept, introduce, set up, usher in, ring in, open the door, originate, take the decisive step, forego, be prior, proclaim, herald, go in the van, go ahead, set going, lead off, open fire, launch, set a precedent, inaugurate, institute, install, preface, prelude, premise, take precedence, take the lead, be previous, rank.

2. Be head *or* chief of, act as leader to, take the lead, have precedence, have authority, supervise, conduct, escort, usher, lead, direct, command, guide, rule, control, govern, manage, be at the helm, take charge of, take care of, watch over, engineer, instruct, manipulate, rank, dispose, sway, boss *(coll.)*, steer, pilot, preside over, be master of, have the portfolio, convoy, chaperon, protect, reign, exert *or* wield authority, administer, occupy the chair, regulate, show the way, hold the reins, pull the stroke oar, keep in order, crack the whip, wield the scepter, superintend, officiate.

3. Outdo, excel, surpass, lead, rise above, overtop, outstrip, top, outrank, pass, be ahead of, steal a march upon, outgo, exceed, outrun, overtake, pass in front of, be superior, outplay, get *or* shoot ahead of, throw into the shade, beat, outride, come to the front of, preponderate, prevail, predominate, transcend, leave in the lurch *or* rear, outdistance, play first fiddle, take the cake *(coll.)*, eclipse, rank first, bear the palm, overrun, outrival, outstep, distance, crown, surmount, cap, tower above, leave behind, get a head start, outdo.

4. Turn the head *or* front of *(in a specified direction)*, give a start *or* impulse to, forward, put *or* set in motion, direct, steer, shape the course *or* progress of, force, drive, wave, run, trend, determine, turn, bend, pilot, helm, guide, push, assist, coxswain, aim at, commit, start off, conduct, set going, start, dispatch, incline, launch, relegate, set.

5. Tend, be pointed, aim, be aimed, be directed, drift, make for, work towards, gravitate, trend, dispose, lean, incline, bend to, move forward toward a specified point, go in a certain direction, direct one's course, push, press, make one's way, work one's way, make strides, make headway, make progress, proceed, stream, run, hie, flow, roll, be attracted, nose, strive, steer for, advance, be bound for, course, forge, make a bee line for.

6. Behead, take the head off, decapitate, decollate, poll *(of trees and plants)*, pollard.

7. Get in front of *(in order to stop)*, intercept, hinder, impede, interrupt, obstruct, curb, cut off, turn aside, avert, deflect, detain, check, block, fend off, repel, divert, sidetrack, obviate, keep off, hamper, inhibit, counteract, withstand, restrict, stand in the way of, repulse, constrain, stand against, scotch, thwart, blockade, cut short, stem, stay, stall, keep at bay, ward off, stave off, embarrass, resist, drive back, turn back, restrain, oppose.

HEADACHE, *n.* Migraine, megrim, cephalalgy, hemialgia, hemicrania, sick headache.

HEADDRESS, *n.* 1. Cover for the head, headgear, cap, bonnet, helmet, cowl, turban, hat, headpiece,

capuche, hood, millinery, coiffure, haberdashery, capote.

2. Coiffure, hairdo, pompadour, bun, hair-arrangement, upsweep, bangs, pigtails, braids, plaits, tresses, curls, chignon.

HEADFIRST, *adv.* 1. With the head foremost, headlong, headforemost, heels over head, diving, plunging, overset, overturned, on one's head, in a header *(coll.)*, in a tail spin *(Aviat.)*, in a dive, head-on, ducking, ducked, pitching, keel *or* heels over, in a nose dive.

2. Rashly, precipitately, hastily, headlong, pell-mell, recklessly, in confusion, head over heels, heels over head, headforemost, without deliberation, at half cock, heedlessly, without due reflection, abruptly, in disorder, carelessly, summarily, on the spur of the moment, at *or* on short notice, thoughtlessly, cursorily, impatiently, feverishly, incautiously, foolishly, injudiciously, passionately, impulsively, without due caution, impetuously, immaturely, unwarily, unadvisedly, helter-skelter, superficially, at *or* on sight, slapdash, hurriedly, full tilt, full pelt.

HEADING, *n.* 1. Something that serves as a head, top *or* front, face, front, headpiece, lintel, prow, bowspirit, façade, frontal, frontispiece, fascia, summit, pinnacle, tip, fore, van, headboard, cap, projecting part, upper end, topmost, crest, coxcomb, forehead, protuberance, cornice, vertex, dentil *(Archit.)*, corbel *(Archit.)*, cymatium *(Archit.)*, bracket capital *(Archit.)*, elevation, first line, proscenium, meridian, foreground, abacus *(Archit.)*, crown, brow, zenith, topmost, uppermost extremity, jetty, breakwater, apex, capital, knob, height, acme, peak.

2. Title *(of page, chapter, etc.)*, caption, head, headline, overline, banner, superscription, banner head, docket, frontispiece, ticket, display line, label, banner line, topic, subject, section head, capital, headnote, preface, prologue, preamble, title page, imprint, streamer *(Jour.)*, screamer *(Jour. cant)*, spearhead *(Jour.)*, scarehead *(Jour.)*, inscription, designation, specification, indication of contents.

3. Section of a subject *or* discourse, topic, subdivision, division, title, order, point, group, term, syllabus, chapter, motif, category, text, item, classification, caption, distinction, resolution.

HEADLAND, *n.* Promontory extending into a large body of water, cape, cliff, foreland, bluff, reach, strip, head, spit, tongue, projection, naze, ness, reef, point, escarpment, neck, isthmus, eminence, bill, spur, peninsula, breakwater, palisade, vantage point *or* ground, chersonese.

HEADLESS, *adj.* 1. Without a head, acephalous, beheaded, decapitated, decollated, guillotined.

2. Without leader *or* chief, leaderless, undirected, chaotic, disorganized, acephalous, straggling, orderless, disordered, anarchic, anarchical, stray, erratic, lawless, confused, ungoverned, unbridled, unconstrained, unguided, reinless, wandering, vagrant, roving, loose, desultory, driftless, rudderless, aimless, anarchal, anarchial, disorderly, unruly.

3. Destitute of brains *or* prudence, foolish, stupid, rash, senseless, silly, irrational, empty-minded, empty-noddled, empty-pated, rattle-brained, rattleheaded, vacant, vacuous, injudicious, harebrained, empty-headed, empty-skulled, heedless, unwise, unthinking, giddy, thoughtless, incogitant, half-witted, simple-witted, simple-minded, scatterbrained, foolhardy, imprudent, unreason-

able, inconsistent, absurd, inane, bungling, madcap, wild, misguided, fatuous, idiotic, impolitic, not bright, unintelligent, indiscreet, lackwit, weak in the upper story *(sl.)*, not all there *(coll.)*, dull, impulsive, blundering, undiscerning, blind, purblind, obtuse, dullard, short-sighted, blunt, dense, dumb *(coll.)*, doltish, dizzy, sappy *(sl.)*, barmy, barmybrained, asinine, foolheaded, insensate, incapable of reason, impetuous, inobservant, witless, flighty, brainless, mindless, reckless, unmindful, forgetful, insensible, confused, bewildered, imbecile, wanton, hot-headed, unconsidering, inadvertent, neglectful, unreflecting, thick-witted, addleheaded, addlepated, addlebrained, nearsighted, lacking in foresight, prone to mistakes, feather-brained.

HEADLINE, *n.* Title, caption, head, overline, superscription, banner, streamer *(Jour.)*, screamer *(Jour. cant)*, spearhead *(Jour.)*, banner head, banner line, scarehead *(Jour.)*, indication of contents.

HEADLONG, *adj.* 1. Done *or* going with the head foremost, head-on, diving, pitching, plunging, overturned, overset, ducking, tumbling, nose diving, swooping down, pouncing, prone, toppling.
2. Hasty, quick, speedy, swift, fleet, fast, rushing, running, urgent, sudden, brisk, winged, rapid, expeditious, prompt, hasteful, hurried, mercurial, nimble, extempore, snappy, agile, sprightly, immediate, instant, extemporaneous, quick as lightning, instantaneous, swift as an arrow, spirited, quick as a wink, quick as thought, eagle-winged, light-footed, telegraphic, electric, dashing.
3. Rash, impetuous, unduly quick, precipitate, reckless, pell-mell, helter-skelter, incautious, without deliberation, brash, eager, careless, unmediated, abrupt, unchecked, furious, brusque, scrambling, impulsive, snap, madcap, thoughtless, subitaneous, unexpected, harum-scarum, regardless, extravagant, injudicious, aimless, breakneck, excited, premature, turbulent, hurried, irrepressible, inopportune, immature, foolish, dare-devil, adventurous, passionate, foolhardy, hotspur, frantic, heady, pressing, boisterous, unbridled, unadvised, ill-advised, unwary, indiscreet, mad-brained, ungoverned, precipitous, impassioned, feverish, uncontrolled, precipitant, inconsiderate, perilous, dangerous, ruinous, over-confident, giddy, dashing, quixotic, desperate, uncircumspect, blindfolded, hot-headed, hare-brained, wanton, silly, wild, light, flighty, volatile, distracted, frivolous, erratic, unreliable, rampant, regardless of consequences, fickle, irresponsible, rantipole, punch-drunk, imprudent, uncalculating, death-defying, devil-may-care, prodigal.
4. Steep, precipitous, sheer, bluff, abrupt, bold, sloping, sharp, oblique, stiff, inclined, arduous, falling, rapid, breakneck, heavy, straight-up, vertical, plumb, declining, perpendicular, prone *(Poetic)*, sheer downward, decurrent, decursive, descending, declivitous, dropping away, steepy *(Poetic)*.

HEADLONG, *adv.* 1. Headforemost, headfirst, heels over head, diving, on one's head, head-on, keel *or* heels over, in a dive, plunging, overturned, in a header *(coll.)*, overset, pitching, ducking, in a tail spin *(Aviat.)*, sheer downward, in a nose dive.
2. Hastily, speedily, fast, quickly, hurriedly, apace, nimbly, with haste, amain, posthaste, promptly, instantly, breathlessly, with great *or* all haste, straightway, pronto *(coll.)*, trippingly, like a shot, like mad *(coll.)*, like a thunderbolt, on the double *or* double-quick *(coll.)*, hotfoot, full tilt, pell-mell, head over heels, headforemost, at once, in less than no time, without further delay, straight, for all one is worth *(coll.)*, before you can say "Jack Robinson," straightforth, wide open, in high gear, at full blast, all out *(sl.)*, as fast as one's legs *or* heels will carry one, under press of sail *(or canvas, sail and steam)*, full pelt, readily, heels over head, presto, all at once, with breathless speed, double quick, in a wink, whip and spur, in an instant, like greased lightning *(coll.)*, like all possessed *(coll.)*, lickety-split *(sl.)*, lickety-cut *(sl.)*, lickety-brindle *(sl.)*, by leaps and bounds, like a bat out of hell *(sl.)*, right away, before the ink is dry, without pause, without respite, unceasingly, untiringly, at a rush, hurry-skurry, helter-skelter.
3. Rashly, precipitately, without deliberation, headforemost, hastily, thoughtlessly, confusedly, hurriedly, abruptly, slapdash, unexpectedly, pell-mell, in haste, recklessly, heedlessly, carelessly, summarily, heels over head, head over heels, helter-skelter, incautiously, feverishly, impatiently, unpreparedly, without notice *or* warning, on the spur of the moment, at *or* on sight, unadvisedly, unwarily, inopportunely, immaturely, impulsively, without due caution, impetuously, aimlessly, passionately, foolishly, injudiciously, like a bolt from the blue, by surprise, like a thunderbolt, at *or* on short notice, lightly, smack *(coll.)*, pop *(coll.)*, plunk *(coll.)*, plop *(coll.)*, slap-bang, in confusion, in disorder, incontinently, prematurely, at half cock, like a thief in the night, superficially, cursorily.

HEADMAN, *n.* One to whom others are subordinate, head, master, leader, ruler, chief, director, superior, manager, superintendent, president, guide, dean, foreman, chief official, captain, general, admiral, coryphaeus, king, regent, top, speaker, senior, conductor, administrator, governor, overman, controller, protector, proprietor, executive, champion, patriarch, kingpin *(coll.)*, dictator, principal, commander, sovereign, ringleader, person in authority, entrepreneur, lord, potentate, chief magistrate, headmaster, commodore, functionary, suzerain, commandant, impresario, seignior, boss *(coll.)*, chairman, provost, cardinal, premier, overseer.

HEADMASTER, *n.* Principal of a school, principal master, dean, head, senior, administrator, superintendent, director, superior.

HEADMOST, *adj.* Foremost, most advanced, preceding, outriding, fore, anterior, leading, outstanding, projecting, initial, most forward, highest, frontal, utmost, predominant, antecedent, uppermost, paramount, dominant, ruling, precessional, precedent, principal, anticipatory, commanding, imposing, exalted, lofty, most mature, advance, best developed, head, main, grand, supreme, maximal, prime, cardinal, overruling, controlling, maximum, over, major, superior, preëminent, surpassing, ascendant, eminent, topmost, champion, crowning, capital, hegemonic, topnotch *(coll.)*, exceeding, precocious, prevenient.

HEADPIECE, *n.* 1. Helmet, armor for the head, morion, casque, heaume, cabasset, visor, beaver, face guard, sallet, crest, casquetel, casquet, bard *(for horses)*, chamfron *(for horses)*.
2. Covering for the head, hat, headdress, headgear, cap, millinery, coiffure, haberdashery, capote, capuche, hood, turban, cowl, bonnet.

3. *(Radio, teleph., etc.)* Headset, headphones, receivers with band over head, earphone *(coll.)*.

4. Seat of intellect, understanding, judgment, head, brain, top, skull, sconce, thought, cognition, sharpness, mind, proficiency, aptitude, potentiality, sense, talent, capacity, knowing, instinct, comprehension, perception, grasp, wits, mentality, keenness, faculty, apprehension, sensibility, faculty, parts, percipience, discernment, reception, bent, gift, penetration, qualification, cleverness, endowment, quickness, mental balance, reason, ken, cognitative faculties, ability, genius, poise, gray matter *(coll.)*, receptivity, reasoning power.

5. Top piece *or* part, lintel, headboard, summit, pinnacle, tip, peak, front, fore, height, capital, front part, knob, apex, projecting part, uppermost extremity, headpost, fascia, crown, zenith, brow, crest, protuberance, forehead, face, coxcomb, cornice, vertex, meridian, elevation, proscenium, façade, prow.

6. *(Print.)* Engraved ornament at head of chapter *or* page, decorative piece, colophon, emblem, cipher, cut.

HEADQUARTERS, *n.* 1. Offices from which orders are issued, chief office, center of operations, center of authority, post, base, quarters, cantonment, military station, military town, H. Q.

2. Military unit consisting of commander, staff and assistants, administrators of a command, personnel of headquarters, high command, administration, admiralty, superior officers, H. Q.

HEADSHIP, *n.* Position of chief *or* head, chief authority, leadership, supremacy, control, dominion, primacy, royalty, regality, imperiality, command, sway, rule, jurisdiction, judicature, preponderance, prepotency, prepollence, prestige, prefecture, premiership, matriarchy, patriarchy, dictatorship, mastery, mastership, administration, government, predominance, superintendence, supervision, oversight, charge, domination, protectorate, paramountcy, the highest degree, potency, power, strength, magistracy, mayoralty, direction, guidance, regulation, highest position, presidentship, lordship, sovereignty, suzerainty, prerogative, seigniory, legislation, rudder, helm, reins, surveillance, steerage, pilotage, ministry, agency, conduct, stewardship, kingship, the throne, the crown.

HEADSMAN, *n.* One who beheads condemned persons, hangman, beheader, public executioner, executionist, decapitator, Jack Ketch, topsman *(sl.)*.

HEADSTONE, *n.* Stone set at the head of a grave, gravestone, memorial, tombstone, marker, cross, slab, tablet, stone, obelisk, monument, pillar, monolith, shaft, column.

HEADSTRONG, *adj.* Bent on having one's own way, not easily restrained, obstinate, ungovernable, dogged, stubborn, intractable, self-willed, cantankerous, cross-grained, restive, perverse, wanton, impetuous, bigoted, hasty, foolhardy, headless, unruly, heady, violent, wayward, rash, vehement, bullheaded, pigheaded, contrary, froward, tough, strong-willed, bulldogged, tenacious, daring, resisting, bold, audacious, contemptuous, casehardened, disobedient, untoward, contumacious, peremptory, hard-bitten, reckless, willful, determined, impulsive, unyielding, refractory, uncontrollable, indocile, mulish, obdurate, hotheaded, regardless of consequences, peevish, stiffnecked, rampant, immovable, hard, firm, unhesitating, self-assured, not amenable, resolute, resistant, unaffected, sulky, sullen, balky, unsub-

missive, unmanageable, recalcitrant, incorrigible, obstreperous, unpliable, pervicacious, rebellious, resistive, renitent, defiant, incautious, venturesome, pertinacious, imprudent, heedless, temerarious, temerous, temeritous, overconfident, overweening, careless, thoughtless, giddy, wild, madcap, madbrain, desperate, harebrained, Quixotic, rakish, rantipole, precipitate, headlong, feverish, furious.

HEADWAY, *n.* 1. Motion *or* rate of motion in a forward direction, advance, progress, rate of progress, way, onward course, betterment, improvement, progression, furtherance, ongoing, advancement, increase, lift, upsurgence, upswing, growth, climb, extension, accretion, enlargement, accumulation, speed, march, boost *(coll.)*, revival, restoration, ascent, rise, perfection, promotion, melioration, mend, preferment, procession, passage, expansion, refinement, course, emendation, amendment, enrichment, enhancement, procedure, development, recovery.

2. Clear space *(under an arch, girder, etc.)*, headroom, clearance, passage, room to spare, margin, leeway *(coll.)*, height, altitude, free scope.

HEADY, *adj.* 1. Rash, violent, impetuous, impulsive, precipitate, hasty, thoughtless, rushing, stubborn, inflexible, contumacious, hot-headed, headstrong, forcible, obstinate, refractory, headlong, reckless, inconsiderate, willful, giddy, careless, wild, volatile, harum-scarum *(coll.)*, unsteady, light, flighty, changeable, foolish, vagrant, capricious, foolhardy, distracted, without ballast, changeful, insouciant, heedless, silly, frivolous, variable, slap-happy *(sl.)*, crazy *(coll.)*, inconstant, unstable, unwary, uncircumspect, quixotic, unsettled, flustered, puerile, scatterbrained *(coll.)*, rattleheaded, giddy-brained, addlepated, defiant, unreliable, rattlepated, harebrained, giddy-witted, regardless of consequences, lightminded, rampant, giddy-headed, bird-witted, shatterbrained, erratic, unruly, giddy-pated, undependable, rattlebrained, barmybrained, emptynoddled, fickle, brainless, bemused, befuddled, mercurial, rantipole, irresponsible, frothy, woolgathering, feverish, witless, punch-drunk, incautious, imprudent, improvident, extravagant, barmy, empty-pated, empty-skulled, featherbrained, indiscreet, uncalculating, wanton, death-defying, devil-may-care, daring, desperate, madcap, muddle-headed, without deliberation, pell-mell, helter-skelter, unadvised, unmeditating, unchecked, frantic, hotspur, feverish, febrile, excited, subitaneous, injudicious, ungoverned, uncontrolled, impassioned, passionate, precipitant, precipitous, not amenable to reason, pervicacious, defiant, obstreperous, unmanageable.

2. Intoxicating, apt to affect the head, highly spirituous, strong, exciting, inflaming, effervescent, perfumed, tangy, exhilarating, stimulating, disquieting, discomposing, inviting, alluring, provocative, ambrosial, maddening, pungent, stirring, piquant, breathtaking, thrilling, seducing, tempting, sensuous, attractive, quickening, fiery, enravishing, agitating, swelling, seductive, tantalizing, going to the head, enchanting, sparkling, entrancing.

HEAL, *v.* 1. Make sound *or* whole, free from ailment, restore, cure, remedy, repair, amend, cicatrize, medicate, incarn, help to get well, cause to heal up, work a cure, renew, improve, purge, bring round, recruit, effect a cure, treat, make hale, minister to, revive, revivify, reanimate, knit, resuscitate, rebuild, rehabilitate, dress *(a wound)*, set, meliorate, stay the course of *(a disease)*, foment, purify, recall to life, rejuvenate, reinvigorate, make clean, ameliorate, physic, break off *(a habit)*, set on one's feet *or* legs, snatch from the jaws of death, salve.

2. Free from anything evil *or* distressing, amend, harmonize, reconcile, compose, settle, make up, soothe, put *or* set to rights, correct, redress, relieve, rectify, improve, right, mitigate, palliate, alleviate, assuage, allay, soften, modify, pour oil on, pour balm onto, salve, subdue, ease, pacify, fix up *(coll.)*, fix *(coll.)*, make good *or* right, make all square, put *or* set straight, bind up wounds, repair, remedy, temper, meliorate, restore good relations, make harmonious, accord, adjust, regulate, order, placate, adapt, put in tune, bring to terms, make peace, patch up, attune, accommodate, negotiate, coapt, tranquilize, conciliate, attune.

3. *(Often foll. by UP or OVER)* Become sound *or* whole, get well, be cured, recover, be healed, incarn, come round, pull through, improve appreciably, knit, mend, heal over, skin over, revive, right itself, progress, gain strength, meliorate, advance, make progress, recruit, renew *or* regain one's strength, perk up, take a new *or* fresh lease on life, convalesce, return to health, weather the storm, come to oneself, come to life again, rise from the grave *or* ashes, recuperate, get over, get the better of one's ills, make headway, rally, be oneself again, cicatrize, get round, live again.

HEALING, *adj.* That cures *or* heals, curative, curing, sanative, restorative, favorable *or* conducive to health, healthful, mild, composing, assuasive, assuaging, remedial, medicinal, lenitive, comforting, soothing, healthy, therapeutic, therial, theriacal, corrective, emollient, salutary, salutiferous, mollifying, wholesome, cleansing, salubrious, balmy, anodyne, paregoric, palliative, mitigative, demulcent, balsamic, abirritant, alexipharmic, alexiteric *(Med.)*, restitutive, vulnerary, reparative, reparatory, revivatory, recuperatory, roborant, recuperative, corroborant, febrifugal, purifying, antidotal, invigorating, bracing, tonic, calming, sedative, revivescent, beneficial, benign, good, prophylactic, easing, unctuous, regenerative, regeneratory, restoring, restitutory, gentle, sanatory, promoting health.

HEALTH, *n.* 1. Soundness of body, freedom from disease *or* ailment, physical condition, healthfulness, tone, sanity, strength, well-being, vigor, haleness, clean bill of health, vitality, lustiness, stamina, energy, hardiness, robustness, bloom, fine fettle, fine *or* high feather, full bloom, rosy cheeks, salubrity, eupepsia *(Med.)*, euphoria *(Psychol.)*, robustfulness.

2. Polite *or* complimentary wish for a person's health, happiness, *etc.*, toast, pledge, bumper.

HEALTHFUL, *adj.* Conducive to health, salubrious, salutary, beneficial, wholesome, invigorating, bracing, nutritious, health-giving, healthy, nourishing, salutiferous, hygienic, sanatory, healing, disease-free, life-giving, sanative, hygeian, uninjurious, innoxious, harmless, innocuous, favorable, advantageous, hurtless, preventive, clean, aseptic, pure, cleanly, untainted, unpolluted, unadulterated, desirable, good for one, sustentative, sustaining, nutritive, digestible, substantial, promoting health, tonic, keeping, restoring, regenerative.

HEALTHY, *adj.* Possessing *or* enjoying health, sound, hale, hearty, strong, healthful, pertaining to *or* characteristic of health, well, in good health,

in sound condition, in good case, in trim, unfaded, salubrious, unimpaired, undecayed, good, cured, fit, robust, hardy, firm, stout, buxom, flourishing, sane, ruddy, benignant, fresh, untainted, whole, of a sound constitution, vigorous, lusty, hygienic, florid, flush, staminal, sound of wind and limb, sound as a roach *or* bell, in fine fettle, in fine *or* high feather, blooming, green, lively, clear-eyed, virile, plump, hearty as a buck, rosy-cheeked, fit as a fiddle, in fine whack *(sl.)*, fine *(sl.)*, in the pink, in the pink of condition, spirited, chipper *(coll.)*, bobbish *(sl.)*, like a giant refreshed, made of iron, full of life and vigor, fresh as a daisy *or* rose, robustious *(hum.)*, restored, free from disease *or* infirmity, able-bodied, sturdy, tough, burly, youthful.

HEAP, *n.* 1. Assemblage of things lying one on another, pile, mass, mound, stack, huddle, cumulus, fagot, load, cargo, packet, cluster, bale, bundle, gathering, mow, bulk, harvest, deposit, cock, jumble, confused mass, accumulation, clump, hoard, bunch, stock, budget, barrow, driven mass, cartload, carload, wagonload, congeries, pyramid, rouleau, shock, batch, block, hillock, swell, pyre, hill, drift, tumulus, cumulation, lump, aggregation, amassment, conglobation, concentration, acervation *(Bot.)*, funeral pyre, collection, bank, mountain, rick, agglomeration.

2. *(Coll.)* Great quantity *or* number, large amount, abundance, multitude, throng, array, legion, scores, heaps *(coll.)*, sum, raft *(coll.)*, bulk, volume, plenty, profusion, total, crowd, lot *(coll.)*, fullness, quantities, pack *(coll.)*, quite a little, considerable, wad *(sl.)*, deal, host, lump, hunk *(coll.)*, gob *or* gobs *(sl.)*, scad *or* scads *(sl.)*, numbers, chunk, mess, batch, storm, shower, swarm, slew *or* slews *(coll.)*, lots *(coll.)* peck, mint, ocean *or* oceans *(coll.)*, sea, world *or* worlds *(coll.)*, bounty, hoard, store, neat *or* tidy sum, barrels, bags, budget, myriad, power *(coll.)*, swad *(sl.)*, oodles *(sl.)*, tons *(coll.)*, full supply, rabble, rout, mob, sight *(coll.)*, press, crush, cloud, good *or* great deal, horde, load *(coll.)*, pot *(sl.)*.

HEAP, *v.* 1. *(Often fol. by UP, ON, TOGETHER, etc.)* Pile, gather in a heap, throw *or* cast in a heap, group, rake together, dredge, coacervate, get in, gather, load, ruck, collect, batch together, bunch together, draw together, garner, deposit, reposit, lump, bundle, amass, harvest, glean, cram, truss, pack, shock, whip in, concentrate, bank, mound, mow, barrow, dump, lump together, mass.

2. *(Often fol. by UP)* Amass, accumulate, acquire, gather, save, husband, reserve, assemble, get *or* bring together, aggregate, hoard, overfill, build up, cumulate, increase, collect, add, augment, expand, treasure up, reservoir, file away, take in, stash *(sl.)*, salt down *or* away *(coll.)*, store *or* stow away, colligate, lump together, muster, collocate, agglomerate, unite, compile, rake up, garner, concentrate, feather one's nest, deposit, bank, cache, reposit, put by for a rainy day, put up, intreasure, lay up, get in, glean, scrape together.

3. Cast *or* bestow in great quantity, load *or* supply abundantly with something, deal out, give in profusion, confer, grant, vouchsafe, apportion, mete out, pour upon, encumber, embarrass, favor with, indulge with, shower upon, lavish, lay, pile, flood, inundate, engulf, deluge, allow, accord, award, render, present, assign, shed.

4. Become heaped *or* piled, mass, rise in a heap *or* heaps, deposit, collect, bank, cluster, come together, accumulate, swarm, drift, abound,

pile up, teem, flourish, stream, join, surge, concentrate, foregather, flock together, assemble, be blown together, aggregate, lie close.

HEAR, *v.* 1. Perceive by the ear, have perception of sound by the ear, have the sense of hearing, listen, apprehend *or* take in (by the ear), take cognizance of, strain one's ears, become aware of, detect, descry, auscultate, listen in *(coll.),* eavesdrop, overhear, hark, get *(sl.),* catch, hearken, listen with both ears, keep one's ears open.

2. Listen to, give audience to, heed, regard, mind, hear out, hearken to, attend to, notice, give attention, give a hearing to, audition, recognize, have regard to, incline one's ear, pay attention to, advert to, be attentive, be all ears *(coll.),* hang upon the lips of, lend *or* bend an ear, grant access to oneself, give ear, shrive.

3. Learn by the ear *or* by being told, be informed, have an account, gather, hear say *(coll.),* get scent of, discover, receive information, find out, overhear, gain knowledge *or* appreciation of, hear of, understand, be led to believe, be made aware of, be told, come across, ascertain, descry, obtain *or* receive knowledge of, glean knowledge of, learn, hear tell of *(coll.),* get wise to *(sl.),* get an earful *(sl.),* pick up knowledge of.

4. Be among the audience at *or* of, attend *(as hearer or worshipper),* be present at, witness, be a spectator, look on, be an auditor, audit, appear at *(a performance),* listen to.

5. Listen to with favor, assent *or* compliance, regard, heed, give heed to, obey, accede to, favor, bow, bend, kneel, hearken, permit, listen to, admit, grant, concede, agree, acknowledge, acquiesce, comply, yield, defer to, esteem, reverence, have no objection, not refuse, satisfy, incline, succumb, resign, give way, give assent, be willing, concur, approve, consent, submit, respect, entertain the idea of, hear of *(coll.),* hear to *(coll.),* be of a favorable disposition, think good *or* proper, see *or* think fit, hold with, subscribe to, receive.

6. Give a formal, official *or* judicial hearing to, sit in judgment, try, examine judicially, judge, conduct a trial, investigate judicially, adjudicate, inquire into, interrogate.

HEARING, *n.* 1. Faculty *or* sense by which sound is perceived, sense of hearing, discovery by ear, act of perceiving sound, audition, attending, auscultation, listening, perception, ear *(as for music).*

2. Opportunity to be heard, audience, interview, audition, conference, performance, audit, admittance, attention, consultation, attendance, presentation, reception, congress, council, tryout *(coll.),* notice.

3. *(Law)* Presentation of testimony and arguments *(as in a suit at law),* trial, judicial examination, adjudication, review, investigation, representation, judgment, grilling, questioning, interrogation, cross-examination, cross-questioning, inquest, assize, inquisition, inquirendo, percontation, inquiry, probe, third degree *(sl.),* cross-interrogation.

4. Earshot, range, hearing distance, earreach, reach, sound, carrying distance.

HEARKEN, *v.* Listen, hear, hark, eavesdrop, give heed, give ear, attend, pay regard, be attentive, be of a favorable disposition, take notice, incline one's ear, prick up the ears, be all ears, strain one's ears, keep the ears open, have no objection, lend *or* bend an ear, be receptive, be acquiescent, see *or* think fit, give assent, pay attention.

HEARSAY, *n.* Rumor, gossip, news, scandal, common voice, town *or* village talk, fame, report, whisper, cry, talk, by-talk, topic of the day, idea afloat, news stirring, idle talk, mere talk, small talk, apocrypha, the grapevine, fabricated report, *on-dit,* groundless rumor, broadcast, common talk, legend, babble, babblement, canard, dirt *(sl.),* tattle, tittle-tattle, chat, chit-chat, unreliable report, buzz, hoax, hearsay evidence *(Law),* scuttlebutt *(sl.).*

HEARSE, *n.* Funeral vehicle, undertaker's limousine, funeral van, conveyance for a coffin, meat wagon *(sl.),* dead wagon *(sl.),* funeral coach.

HEART, *n.* 1. Bosom, breast, seat of life, vitals, mainspring of life, vital spot, center *or* organ of circulation, ticker *(sl.).*

2. Inner feelings, emotion, response, feeling, sentiment, mood, deep sense, soul, humor, sensibility, passion, spirit, nature, disposition, temperament.

3. Sympathy, pathos, soft-heartedness, placability, liberality, leniency, tenderness, altruism, benignity, samaritanism, pity, gentleness, benevolence, compassion, grace, kind offices, kind treatment, mercy, forbearance, humanity, charity, kindness, magnanimity, mitigation, clemency, lenity, mercifulness, indulgence, forgivingness, toleration, brotherly love.

4. Bravery, courage, braveness, pluck, valor, doughtiness, fearlessness, lion-heartedness, stoutheartedness, spirit, manfulness, firmness, boldness, daring, heroism, dauntlessness, resoluteness, audaciousness, audacity, stoutness, daring, gameness, resolution, awelessness, stalwartness, gallantry, grit *(coll.),* stanchness, sand *(coll.),* backbone *(coll.),* spunk *(coll.),* mettle, unappalledness, guts *(sl.),* fortitude.

5. Core, center, hub, kernel, axis, radiant, middle, marrow, navel, inside, gist, focus, interior, nucleus, omphalos, focal point, bull's-eye.

6. Essence, elixir, radical, ground, source, origin, life, marrow, gist, nucleus, soul, substance, foundation, hypostasis *(Philos.),* principle, rudiments, inmost nature, pith, kernel, center, vital principle, quintessence, core, spirit, base, fundamentals, midst, quiddity, root, elements, essentials.

HEARTACHE, *n.* Sorrow, misery, mental anguish, wretchedness, mental pain, mental torment, heartbreak, infelicity, affliction, distress, grief, prostration, dole, woe, desolation, mental suffering, heavy heart, bleeding heart, bitterness, agony, regret, sadness.

HEARTBEAT, *n.* Throb of the heart, pulsation of the heart, systole *(Anat.),* diastole *(Anat.),* pulse.

HEARTBREAK, *n.* Distress, grief, prostration, affliction, dole, woe, desolation, heavy heart, bleeding heart, regret, agony, mental anguish, bitterness, sadness, sorrow, misery, mental pain *or* torment, wretchedness, heartache, infelicity.

HEARTBREAKING, *adj.* Tragic, sad, pitiful, lamentable, depressing, heart-rending, melancholy, affecting, moving, appalling, desolating, grim, shocking, pitiful, dolorous, dismal, unbearable, piteous, distressing, crushing, disheartening, withering, rueful, intolerable, woeful, mournful, tearful, touching, insufferable, insupportable, oppressive, heavy, cruel, bitter, acute, painful, harsh, biting, burdensome, hard, hurtful, heart-sickening, afflictive, excruciating, consuming, rending, harrowing, sharp, dire, grave, torturous, poignant, agonizing, heart-wounding, aching.

HEARTBROKEN, *adj.* Dejected, desolate, inconsolable, woebegone, crushed, downcast, forlorn, miserable, heartsick, unmanned, bowed-down, weighted, comfortless, disconsolate, broken-hearted, heavy-hearted, doleful, overcome, cheerless, wretched, downfallen, grieving, dashed, sorrowing, sorrowful, lamenting, in despair, bemoaning, bewailing, mourning, mournful, melancholy, sad, saddened, discouraged, sorry, dispirited, joyless, dampened, burdened, sorrow-stricken, grief-stricken, sobbing, crying, cut to the heart.

HEARTBURN, *n.* Indigestion, stomach upset, cardalgia, pyrosis, water brash, water qualm.

HEARTBURNING, *n.* Envy, jealousy, rancor, discontent, animosity, antagonism, resentment, causticity, maliciousness, venom, malice, acrimony, hostility, vindictiveness, odium, asperity, disdain, hate, spleen, malignity, rankling, grudge, anger, bitterness, rage, virulence, antipathy, hatred, derision, dudgeon, spite, pique, wrath.

HEART DISEASE, *n.* Heart failure, weak heart, heart ailment, angina pectoris, myocarditis, valvular lesion, ischemia of the heart, heart attack, carditis, pyopericarditis, heart murmur, endocarditis, hypertrophy of the heart, heart palpitation.

HEARTEN, *v.* Cheer, gladden, reassure, console, revitalize, quicken, comfort, give hope, brighten, exhilarate, uplift, encourage, fortify, inspirit, buoy up, stimulate, revivify, nerve, enliven, inspire, animate, restore, invigorate, elate, strengthen, enhearten, warm, refresh, embolden, regale, give courage, urge, assure, rally.

HEARTFELT, *adj.* Ardent, impassioned, warm, genuine, zealous, extreme, keen, unalloyed, gushing, deep, veritable, deepest, avid, fervent, wholehearted, glowing, hearty, whole-souled, enthusiastic, devout, responsive, profound, profuse, earnest, exuberant, sincere, intense, deep-felt, cordial, congenial, complete, unfeigned, glad, eager, passionate, authentic, bona fide.

HEARTFREE, *adj.* Not in love, unattached, foot loose and fancy free, free and easy, on the loose, unspoken for, heartwhole, unplighted, without romantic entanglements, without serious intentions.

HEARTH, *n.* 1. Fireplace, ingle, hearthstone, inglenook, chimney corner, ingleside.
2. *(Fig.)* Home, family, family circle, abode, domestic circle, fireside, homestead, ménage, household, castle *(coll.)*.

HEARTLESS, *adj.* 1. Brutal, callous, cruel, adamantine, unfeeling, unforgiving, insensible, ironhearted, thick-skinned, insensitive, soulless, unmoved, unstirred, impervious, sharp, hardened, untouched, uncaring, supine, stony, indurated, Lacdicean, flinty, unimpressible, irreligious, stiff, uninterested, disdainful, hostile, adverse, coldblooded, passionless, indifferent, unconcerned, frigid, aloof, distant, unresponsive, apathetic, barbarous, unsparing, cold, stern, unkind, pitiless, ruthless, unpitying, hard-hearted, unsympathetic, obdurate, insentient, marble-hearted, inhuman, unrelenting, implacable, savage, remorseless, inexorable, relentless, unmerciful.
2. Having *or* showing little enthusiasm, unstirred, lukewarm, passive, passionless, insouciant, phlegmatic, perfunctory, inert, unmindful, unaffected, torpid, untouched, numb, benumbed, blasé, dispassionate, unemotional, impartial, stolid, faint, cold, spiritless, obtuse, unimpressed, unanimated, pococurante, nonchalant, disregarding, inappetent,

undesirous, unambitious, easygoing, lackadaisical, listless, torpescent, frigid, unconcerned, languid, cool, sluggish, unimpressible, apathetic, Laodicean, indifferent.
3. Cowardly, timid, fearful, afraid, unheroic, unwarlike, irresolute, frightened, scared, timorous, unmanly, shrinking, yellow *(sl.)*, jittery *(sl.)*, wavering, unspirited, unsoldierly, dastardly, pusillanimous, easily alarmed, unvalorous, unvaliant, nervous, faint-hearted, hesitating, uncourageous, halting, unbrave, apprehensive, undoughty, uneasy, restive, shaky.

HEART-RENDING, *adj.* Sad, pitiful, lamentable, depressing, poignant, agonizing, melancholy, mournful, torturous, dire, grave, sharp, harrowing, rending, consuming, affecting, moving, appalling, desolating, intolerable, woeful, hard, hurtful, afflictive, excruciating, biting, painful, harsh, burdensome, acute, bitter, insufferable, insupportable, rueful, intolerable, disheartening, withering, crushing, distressing, piteous, dolorous, shocking, grim.

HEARTSICK, *adj.* 1. Cheerless, wretched, grieving, dashed, sorrowing, sorrowful, in despair, bemoaning, bewailing, lamenting, melancholy, sad, saddened, discouraged, sorry, dispirited, joyless, dampened, burdened, sorrow-stricken, grief-stricken, sobbing, crying, cut to the heart, brokenhearted, heavy-hearted, doleful, overcome, disconsolate, comfortless, weighted, miserable, heartbroken, forlorn, downcast, dejected, desolate, inconsolable, woebegone, crushed, unmanned.
2. Tired, weary, haggard, sorry, effete, dispirited, life-weary, stricken, worn, harassed, drooping, fatigued, woebegone, spent, careworn, overwearied, weakened, flagging, crushed, beaten, toilworn, heavy-laden.

HEARTY, *adj.* 1. Cordial, wholehearted, friendly, neighborly, genial, well-meant, glad, eager, cheerful, deep-felt, fervent, congenial, amicable, heartfelt, sincere, genuine, deepest, deep, intense, unalloyed, happy, warmhearted, avid, passionate, glowing, brotherly, ardent, exuberant, gushing, unfeigned, enthusiastic, authentic, devout, profuse, frank, impassioned, responsive.
2. Vigorous, keen, zealous, complete, thorough, avid, hot, burning, eager, zestful, enthusiastic, fervent, fiery, glowing, red-hot, flaming, impassioned, fervid, willing, ready, earnest, sincere, absolute, wholehearted.
3. Healthy, hale, sound, sturdy, virile, stalwart, lusty, rigorous, strong, well, stout, hardy, fresh, buxom, able, enduring, vigorous, resilient, capable of endurance, burly, in fine fettle, tough, robust, brawny, stanch, flourishing, rugged, blooming, physically fit, powerful, mighty.

HEAT, *n.* 1. Warmth, temperature, hotness, warmness, tepidity, sultriness, torridity, torridness, caloric, calidity, incandescence, incandescency, calefaction, cauma *(Med., of body temperature)*, incalescence, red heat, white heat, tropical heat.
2. Heat wave, warm weather, swelter, dog days, roasting weather, summer, simmering weather, broiling weather, canicular days.
3. Zeal, eagerness, excitement, verve, ardor, enthusiasm, animation, rapture, ravishment, warmth, fire, fervor, violence, furor, impetuosity, flush, desperation, distraction, ecstasy, intensity, thrill, transport, fervency, intoxication, blush, agitation, earnestness, fever, enchantment.
4. Hot temper, rage, anger, frenzy, wrath, outburst, fury, furor, eruption, exasperation, fit, fierceness, bluster, temper, hot blood, hate, ha-

tred, vehemence, hot words, scene, storm, explosion, indignation, violence, blind rage, simmering, seething, ranting.

5. Race, run, dash, lap, relay race.

HEAT, *v.* 1. Make hot *or* warm, raise the temperature, calorify, burn, mull, chafe, bask, melt, sun, fire, cook, recalesce *(Physics)*, incandesce, foment, digest *(Chem.)*, scorch, singe, sear, bake, cauterize, oxidize, oxidate, char, carbonize, smelt, cupel, cremate, calcine, incinerate, reheat, simmer, stew, seethe, boil, flush, fume, scald, ignite, thaw, superheat, roast, toast, set fire to, scorify, fricassee, steam, fry, braze, recook, heat up, warm up, warm over, brew, ferment, fuse, broil, deflagrate *(Chem.)*.

2. Excite in mind *or* feeling, flush, make feverish, inflame with passion, animate, rouse, stir, incense, impassion, ferment, agitate, exacerbate, foment, set in motion, kindle, whet, glow, make glowing, fluster, stimulate, warm, inspirit, affect, play upon the feelings, quicken, disquiet, awaken, encourage, infuriate, madden, provoke, discompose, arouse, add fuel to the flame, feed the fire, fan the flame, intoxicate, motivate, raise to a fever heat, fire *or* warm the blood, set on fire, instigate, enkindle, make one's blood boil, shake, jolt, jar, chafe, exasperate, aggravate, needle, enrage, try one's temper.

HEATED, *adj.* Inflamed, warmed, emotional, vehement, angry, hot, fiery, fuming, violent, mad *(coll.)*, wrought-up, bitter, rabid, ireful, irate, foaming, harsh, boiling, sharp, savage, worked up, raging, intense, stormy, rigorous, tempestuous, caustic, frenzied, emphatic, passionate, impassioned, rackety, furious, obstreperous, infuriated, disturbed, loud, loud-sounding, unquiet.

HEATER, *n.* Apparatus for heating, stove, furnace, calefactor, range, reverberatory, blowpipe, kiln, salamander, athanor, oven, forge, toaster, iron, blowtorch, radiator, register, warmer, cooker, boiler, broiler, incinerator.

HEATHEN, *n.* 1. Pagan, savage, barbarian, idolist, infidel, polytheist, sun worshiper, paynim *(Hist.)*, demonolater, pyrolater, heliolater, zendik, unconverted person, henotheist, fetishist, idolater, Parsee, Sabaist, gentile, giaour *(Mohamm.)*.

2. Atheist, heretic, skeptic, disbeliever, unbeliever, secularist, apostate, idolater, nullifidian, Pyrrhonist, materialist, antichrist, gentile, dubitant, worldling.

HEATHEN, HEATHENISH, *adj.* 1. Pagan, paganish, ethnic, polytheistic, fetishistic, fetishic, infidelic, paynim *(Hist.)*, chthonian, henotheistic, idolatrous, demonolatrous, idolistic, sun-worshiping, gentile.

2. Atheistic, skeptical, disbelieving, secular, secularistic, heretic, heretical, materialistic, worldly, apostate, antichristian, nullifidian, dubitant, infidel.

3. Savage, barbaric, slaughterous, untamed, demoniacal, hellish, ferocious, brutish, brutal, fell, merciless, rough, uncivilized, gothic, outlandish, bloodthirsty, ruthless, relentless, pitiless, barbarous, barbarian, sanguinary, devilish, vandalic, feral, ferine, inhuman, atrocious, cold-blooded, callous, soulless, unmerciful, remorseless, stony, fierce, bloody, murderous, malignant, unfeeling, wicked, diabolical, satanic, fiendish, infernal.

HEAVE, *v.* 1. Lift *or* raise with effort *or* force, hoist, raise with exertion, elevate with difficulty, erect, raise up, upraise, rear, boost *(coll.)*, uphoist, dredge, lever, pry, rear up, fish up, drag up, upheave, uprear, uplift, buoy.

2. Lift and throw *(often with effort or force)*, throw, toss, hurl, send, cast, pitch, fling, put *(as a shot)*, sling, launch, bung, dart, lance, dash, let fly, pelt, peg *(coll.)*, chuck, stone, rock *(coll.)*, pitchfork, bowl, trundle, hurtle, impel, ram, precipitate, ejaculate, traject, tilt, eject, propel, expel, propulse, drive, fire, project, shy.

3. Utter laboriously *or* painfully, breathe, force from the breast, utter with effort, exhale, raise, sigh, moan, sob, groan, expire, suspire, blow, puff, strain, eject, burst, discharge, emit, sough, give *(a sigh)*, draw *(a sigh)*, fetch *(a sigh)*, disembogue.

4. Rise and fall with a swelling motion, swell, dilate, wave, throb, billow, sough, expand, sob, toss, surge, roll, palpitate, be full of emotion, pant, puff, waft, slosh, swirl, wash, ebb and flow, undulate, swell with emotion, be choked with emotion, draw a deep breath, wax and wane, breathe with effort.

5. Vomit, retch, try to vomit, spew, puke *(an offensive term)*, regurgitate, disgorge, cast *or* heave the gorge, bring *or* cast up, be seasick, disembogue, throw up *(coll.)*, chuck up *(sl.)*, keck.

6. Raise *or* force up in a swelling movement, force to bulge, buckle, warp, rise as if thrust up *(as a hill)*, swell, be thrown upward *(as by frost)*, rear, tilt up, lever, bulge, bilge, bouge, vault, arch.

7. Struggle, labor, make an effort to raise, throw *or* move anything, work against odds, strive, wrestle, contend, grapple, toil, moil, strain to do something difficult, pull, push, tug, put forth one's strength, tax one's energies, sweat, fag, ply, buckle to, endeavor, work *or* fight one's way, do one's utmost, put one's hand to the plow, put *or* lay one's shoulder to the wheel, flounder, scramble, exert oneself, try hard.

8. *(Naut.)* Haul *(as at a cable)*, draw, pull, drag, lug, wrench, tug, snake, hitch, jerk, yank *(coll.)*, bouse, twitch, move a ship by heaving action, move ahead, go about.

HEAVEN, *n.* 1. *(Chiefly plur.)* Firmament, sky, welkin, empyrean, ether, infinity, universe, expanse of space surrounding the earth, creation, blue, blue sky, aerosphere, air, space, azure, celestial expanse, canopy of heaven, vault of heaven, starry heaven, celestial sphere, the wild blue yonder, aerial region, stratosphere, interplanetary space, interstellar space, intercosmic space, ozone *(coll.)*, hyaline *(Poetic.)*.

2. Abode of God and angels, abode of spirits of the righteous after death, place of existence of the blessed after mortal life, paradise, bliss, abodes of bliss, our eternal home, our Father's house, Abraham's bosom, the Divine abode, the New Jerusalem, the city of our God, heavenly kingdom, heavenly city, happy hunting grounds *(N. Amer. Ind.)*, Zion, Elysium, the Eternal Rest, the house not built with hands, the abode of saints, Valhalla, Arcadia, Olympus, Holy City, Land of Beulah, Happy Isles, Fortunate Isles *or* Islands, Islands *or* isles of the Blessed, Elysian fields, kingdom of heaven, life *or* world beyond the grave, world to come, next world, afterworld, welkin, Bower of Bliss, Beulah, Beulah Land, inheritance of the saints in light, throne of God, the great white throne, City Celestial, home, Nirvana *(Hind. & Buddh.)*.

3. State of existence of the blessed after mortal life, paradise, bliss, life everlasting, afterlife, future existence, hereafter, life to come, life be-

yond the grave, never-ending day, eternal *or* unending bliss, glory, release from cares, presence of God, celestial *or* heavenly bliss, postexistence, object of this life, eternity.

4. *(Cap., often plur.)* The Deity, God, the Almighty, the celestial powers, the Supreme Being, Lord, Jehovah, the Divinity, the Infinite, the Absolute Being, the Eternal, the First Cause, the All-powerful, the All-wise, the All-knowing, the All-merciful, the All-holy, Demiurge, I Am, the Preserver, the Maker, the Creator, the Lord of Lords, the King of Kings, Providence, the Supreme Soul, Omnipotence, Omniscience, Author and Creator, universal life force, world spirit *or* soul, world principle, world-self, archeus, anima mundi *(Philos.)*, oversoul.

5. Place *or* state of supreme bliss, exalted state, great felicity, seventh heaven, supreme happiness, ecstasy, transport, pleasure, providence, glory, elysium, paradise, rapture, transcendent delight, utopia, nirvana, Eden, delight, heaven on earth, dreamland, cloudland, millennium, delectation, ravishment, fairyland, Shangri-La, beatitude, gladness, beatification, enchantment, unalloyed happiness, Promised Land, kingdom come.

HEAVENLY, *adj.* 1. Of *or* in the heavens, celestial, ethereal, empyreal, of the firmament, of the visible heavens, sky, empyrean, cosmic, universal, uranic, solar, heliacal, lunar, supernal, sidereal, planetary, stellar, starry, astronomical, astral, space, sphery *(Poet.)*, nebular, asteroidal, extraterrestrial.

2. Of, belonging to *or* coming from the heaven of God, divine, angelic, godlike, celestial, blessed, holy, pure, glorified, beatific, beatified, hallowed, from on high, infinite, unearthly, sublime, godly, sacrosanct, sacred, extramundane, supramundane, archangelic, seraphic, cherubic, elysian, blest, saintly, sainted, supernal, spiritual, Olympian, heaven-born, supernatural, superhuman, matchless, superphysical, empyreal, empyrean, unworldly, paradisiac, elysiac, Olympic.

3. Resembling *or* befitting heaven, enrapturing, ravishing, ecstatic, transporting, celestial, divine, angelic, blissful, beatific, golden, glorious, mystical, seraphic, delightful, sublime, ambrosial, fine, pleasing, blessed, unblemished, fadeless, ideal, bright, radiant, superb, pure, majestic, unalloyed, righteous, shining, brilliant, exalted, utopian, perfect, consummate, never-fading, immortal, deathless, flawless, faultless, Olympian, Elysian, Arcadian, Edenic, paradisiacal, splendorous, resplendent, dazzling, rapturous, enravishing, captivating, felicitous, exquisite, imperishable, excellent in the highest degree, supremely admirable.

HEAVINESS, *n.* State *or* quality of being heavy, weight, burden, gravity, impediment, sluggishness, oppression, ponderousness, ponderosity, poundage, pressure, heft *(coll.)*, freight, cargo, imposition, obligation, inertness, depression, sinking, dead weight, specific gravity, relative density *or* weight, counterweight, inertia, torpor, stupor, inactivity, dullness, coarseness, massiveness, ballast, incumbency, languidness, stolidity, weightiness, load, cumbrance, lethargy, encumbrance, lump, tonnage, mass, burden, onus, incubus, gravitation, ponderance, thickness.

HEAVY, *adj.* 1. Of great weight, hard to lift *or* carry, ponderous, stout, weighty, heaved *or* lifted with labor, having much weight in proportion to bulk, being of high specific gravity, cumbersome, cumbrous, burdensome, elephantine, unwieldy,

big, large, portly, corpulent, fat, substantial, massive, dense, abundant, ample, bulky, hefty *(coll.)*, overweight.

2. Bearing hard upon, not easy to bear, hard to endure, accomplish *or* fulfil, burdensome, harsh, distressing, onerous, grievous, afflictive, hard to deal with, heavy-handed, intolerable, unbearable, harmful, hurtful, cruel, severe, hard, difficult, wearying, trying, oppressive, noisome, malefic, prejudicial, disastrous, wasting, corrosive, malignant, damaging, corroding, nocent, noxious, baleful, baneful, injurious, deleterious, pernicious, detrimental, excessive, outrageous, monstrous, unconscionable, ruinous, arduous, toilsome, laborious, tiring, wearing, destructive, painful, deadly, wearisome, fatiguing, overbearing, uphill, malevolent, mortal *(coll.)*, operose, tough, strenuous, hefty *(coll.)*, herculean, hard-fought, hard-earned, strained, troublesome, exorbitant *(of expenses, etc.)*, irksome, rugged, crabbed, formidable, knotty, unmanageable, intractable, unruly, ungovernable, unyielding, devouring, engulfing, exhausting, crushing, taxing, evil, wrong, villainous, exacting, spiny, thorny, full of difficulties, embarrassing, encompassing *or* beset with difficulties, balky, refractory, perverse, awkward, stubborn, obstinate, untoward, unpliable, resistant, vexatious, unendurable, harrowing.

3. Serious, intense, momentous, weighty, grave, of great import, consequential, sad, hard, harsh, of great consequence, important, solemn, unpleasant, rueful, critical, requiring deliberation and careful judgment, imposing, notable, striking, eventful, significant, noteworthy, salient, earnest, tragic, extraordinary, exceptional, stirring, memorable, commanding, impressive, outstanding, desperate, unnerving, crushing, overbearing, pessimistic, tormenting, deplorable, painful, ruinous, irreparable, irreversible, irrevocable, hopeless, distressing, dire, dreadful, dismal, lamentable, woeful, adverse, unfortunate, sinister, evil, black, untoward, calamitous, regrettable, disagreeable, melancholy, bitter, inauspicious, ominous, not to be overlooked *or* despised, dolorous, mournful, overwhelming, engulfing, decisive, determinative, grim, conclusive, ponderous, crucial, marked.

4. Deep, profound, intense, solemn, expectant, weighted, laden, burdened, oppressive, fraught with meaning, pregnant, ponderous, significant, vast, immense, infinite, appalling, absolute, great, engulfing, overwhelming, utter, awed, awe-inspiring, impressive, ominous, terrifying, startling, absorbed, awful, prominent, frightening, immeasurable, unfathomable, fathomless, conspicuous, fearful, boundless, emphatic, brown (study).

5. Depressed with trouble *or* sorrow, laden with that which is weighty, showing sorrows, serious, solemn, grave, gloomy, sad, wan, rueful, tearful, plaintive, grief-stricken, pained, encumbered, burdened, bowed down, full of care, troubled, heavyhearted, weary, broken, depressed, melancholy, aching, suffering, harassed, stricken, crushed, woebegone, somber, woeful, hard-pressed, heavy-laden, elegiac, cut up *(coll.)*, morose, pessimistic, heartbroken, brokenhearted, racked, afflicted, distressed, hurt, under the harrow, agonized, grieved, wounded, lugubrious, wretched, miserable, infelicitous, sorrowful, saturnine, pensive, joyless, cheerless, tristful, doleful, despondent, downhearted, downcast, careworn, lamenting, despairing, dejected, dispirited, in low spirits, soul-sick, heartsick, desolate, comfortless, forlorn, inconsolable, disconsolate, mournful, long-faced,

funereal, prostrated, unmanned, discouraged, crestfallen, chapfallen, down in the mouth (coll.).

6. Slow in movement or action, sluggish, clumsy, ponderous, dull, weary, without vivacity, without vitality, lifeless, not resilient, inactive, stupid, leaden, lazy, dronish, drony, indolent, snaillike, torpescent, torporific, listless, lusterless, lacking mirth or gaiety, soulless, exanimate, lentitudinous, doleful, stolid, bovine, elephantine, cumbersome, unwieldy, inert, lethargic, lumpish, loutish, crass, sottish, doltish, obtuse, dense, hebetate, idle, hippopotamic, motionless, quiescent, apathetic, blunt, torpid, passive, static, supine, lymphatic, languid, phlegmatic, otiose, hebetudinous, undiscerning, lumbering.

7. Clumsy, infelicitous, prolix, humdrum, tiresome, tedious, wearisome, gross, lumbering, indiscreet, insipid, dreary, unfunny (humor), exanimate, soulless, without vivacity or interest, boring, laborious, monotonous, flat, torpid, dead, stagnant, prosy, prosaic, static, tumid, turgid, bombastic, diffuse, inflated, pedantic, flatulent, dry, arid, tasteless, vapid, jejune, stupefying, benumbing, dull, undiscerning, stolid, crass, elephantine, ham (Theat. sl.), hammy (Theat. sl.), soporific.

8. Overcome with weariness, dulled, drowsy, sleepy, languid, sleep-drunk, sleep-drowned, utterly relaxed, bedimmed, somnolent, sleep-filled, sleepful, sleep-desiring, soporose, lusterless (of eyes), with half-shut eyes, half asleep, Morphean, dozy, fighting sleep, languorous, somnolescent, slumberous, comatose.

9. (Of food and drink) Exceptionally dense in substance, insufficiently raised or leavened, not raised or made light, not easily digested, indigestible, solid, rich, of high fat content, flatulent, dark and rich (beer and ale), of high alcohol content (liquors), strong (liquors), thick, like a rock (coll.), concentrated, compact, lumpy, causing discomfort.

10. Pregnant, great with child, big, parturient, gravid, laden, gestant, travailing, great, with child or young, enceinte (Fr.).

11. (Of weather, the sea, cannonade, etc.) Of great force or momentum, strong, violent, tempestuous, boisterous, stormy, roaring, hard, mountainous, severe, vigorous, bad, cutting, inclement, raging, fuming, incisive, rigorous, sharp, tumultuous, penetrating, turbulent, unremitting, furious, pitiless, demoniac, overpowering, amuck, uproarious, rampaging, overwhelming, rampant, ruthless, fierce, persisting, persistent, savage, acute, frenzied, ebullient, boiling, mad, frantic, ravening, wild, unruly, seething, disturbed, blustering, trenchant, persevering, harsh, biting.

12. (Of sky, clouds, air, etc.) Dense, gloomy, overcast, lowering, cloudy, humid, moist, oppressive, murky, dark, glowering, dreary, dismal, clammy, umbrageous, saturated, supersaturated, musty, close, foggy, gray, muggy, madid, leaden, dull, vaporous, pea-soup (coll.), soupy (slang), lurid, steamy, dingy, caliginous, overshadowed, nubilous.

13. (Of soil, roads, etc.) Cloggy, clayey, impeding motion, boggy, miry, soggy, deterrent, hindering, rain-soaked, poachy, uliginose, mucky, lutose, sodden, sticky, muddy, soft, pasty, inhibitive, obstructive, waxy, gumbo, oozy, quaggy, squashy, argilliferous (Petrog.), argillaceous (Petrog.), marshy, swampy, clammy, fenny, fennish.

14. (Of sounds) Grave, loud, deep, thundering, blatant, stentorian, full, blaring, fulminating, roaring, sonorous, resonant, deafening, powerful,

stertorous, booming, tonitruous, big-voiced, imposing, tonant.

15. (Of hair, undergrowth, foliage, etc.) Abundant, copious, dense, overgrown, thick, impenetrable, extravagant, teeming, luxuriant, bounteous, profuse, full, excessive, plentiful, shadowed, shady, umbrageous.

16. (Of lines, features, scars, etc.) Broad, massive, thick, coarse, gross, rough, rugged, grim, large, big, extensive.

17. (Of odors, etc.) Oppressive, producing languor, soporific, toxic, lush, balmy, soothing, demulcent, softening, morbific, overcharged, somnolent, somnifacient, sedative, mesmeric, hypnotic, on one's hands (of time), unwholesome, baleful, insalubrious, somnorific, narcotic, overladen, deadly, mortal, somnific, somniferous, sleep-inducing, poisonous, envenomed.

18. (Of a grade, hill, etc.) Steep, sheer, declivitous, precipitous, bluff, abrupt, bold, sharp, headlong, stiff, arduous, breakneck, straight-up, vertical, steepy (Poetic), sloping, inclined.

19. (Of drinking, spending, etc.) That is such to an exceptionally great degree, inordinate, undue, prodigal, undisciplined, unrestrained, immoderate, unwarranted, extravagant, excessive, preponderant, unstinting, intemperate, out of bounds or all bounds, incontinent, overindulgent, habitual, hardened, hard, inured, steep (coll.), stiff (coll.), seasoned, habituated, inveterate, chronic.

20. (Of vote, attendance, influence, etc.), Plenary, full, large, considerable, influential, impressive, imposing, thronged, populous, numerous, crowded, strong, powerful, forceful, formidable, telling, weighty, potent, preponderant.

21. (Of bounty, endowments, etc.) Generous, liberal, abundant, substantial, full, munificent, sumptuous, copious, profuse, affluent, ample, rich, lavish, replete, bountiful, bounteous, inexhaustible, plentiful, sufficient, extensive, unstinting, wellprovided.

22. (Of fabrics, other goods, etc.) Above usual weight, winter-weight, warm, protecting, thick, bulky, dense, close-woven, enduring, tough, heavyduty, strong, rugged, sturdy, serviceable, insulated, interlined (of a coat, etc.), toasty (coll.).

HEAVY-HANDED, adj. 1. Oppressive, harsh, ruthless, exacting, ungentle, unkind, unsparing, bitter, inexorable, merciless, unreasonable, stringent, inhuman, strict, severe, exigent, heavy, uncompromising, unremitting, unfavorable, afflictive, cruel, pitiless, hard, stern, afflicting, distressing, drastic, austere, insufferable, iron-fisted, uncharitable, iron-handed, baleful, inquisitorial, despotic, painful, caustic, rigorous, stark, stiff, tyrannical, extortionate, biting, relentless, noxious, abusive, racking, grim, draconian, overbearing, grinding, uncompassionate, torturous, pressing, tormenting, brutal, implacable, insensitive, unconcerned, unfeeling, coercive, remorseless, punitive, cold-blooded, unbending.

2. Clumsy, awkward, unskillful, maladroit, blundering, unhandy, inapt, bungling, uncouth, slovenly, without skill, ungraceful, inelegant, unpolished, graceless, uncourtly, without dexterity, inept, like a bull in a china shop, clownish, rough, gauche (Fr.), dull, dense, thick (coll.) insensitive, untoward, insulse, obtuse, stiff, left-handed, bovine, doltish, all thumbs (coll.), oafish, inexpert, butterfingered (coll.), stolid.

HEAVY-HEARTED, adj. Comfortless, cheerless, heartbroken, dejected, desolate, heavy, forlorn, downcast, crushed, woebegone, miserable, bowed-down, disconsolate, doleful, overcome, wretched, grieving, inconsolable, heartsick, weighted, sorrowing, lamenting, in despair, sorrowful, grief-stricken, burdened, joyless, melancholy, saddened, sorry, discouraged, sad, dispirited, dampened, mourning, bemoaning, mournful, unhappy, woeful, rueful, prostrated, depressed.

HEBETATE, *v.* Make *or* become blunt, render insensible, numb, benumb, callous, obtund, dull, impair in keenness, muddle, besot, fuddle, brutify, brutalize, harden, stupefy, stun, deaden, inure, hypnotize, caseharden, steel, sear, take off the point *or* edge, chloroform, anesthetize, drug, dope *(sl.)*, narcotize.

HEBETUDE, *n.* State of being dull, lethargy, stupidity, imbecility, slowness, dullness, obtundity, deadness, obtuseness, torpidity, sluggishness, lassitude, apathy, phlegm, languor, supineness, numbness, anesthesia, analgesia, stupefaction, stupor, drowsiness, sleepiness, torpor, lentitude, density, insulsity, stolidity, oafdom, dullardism, kef *(Arab)*, doltishness, somnolence, oscitancy, somnolescence, induration, insensibility, insentience, unfeeling, impassibility, inappetence, impassivity, torpescence, bluntness, poor head, blockhead, numskullism *(coll.)*, numskullery *(coll.)*, numskulledness *(coll.)*, dull understanding, clouded perception, indifference, unconcern.

HECATOMB, *n.* Slaughter, sacrifice, mactation, slaying, killing, carnage, butchery, bloodshed, trucidation, manslaughter, murder, massacre, internecion, warfare, battle, pogrom, destruction, saturnalia of blood, immolation, fusillade, lapidation, martyrdom.

HECKLE, *v.* 1. Badger, torment, harass, shout *or* cry out *or* yell in contempt, inflame, question loudly, incommode, pique, hoot, wear down, torment, disturb persistently, exhaust, plague, vex, annoy, harry, molest, bullyrag, grate, provoke, sting, chafe, tease, worry, gripe, nettle, bait, roil, disarm, intimidate, hound, persecute, harrow, nag, pester, fret, embarrass, cow, browbeat, goad, perplex, bother, egg, mock, ruffle, discompose, irk, gibe, distract, hector, pother, confuse, twit, taunt, bully, jeer, fleer, banter.

2. Hackle, hatchel, untangle, card, comb, cut, unravel, dress *(flax)*.

HECTIC, *adj.* 1. Characterized by great excitement, passions, *etc.*, flushed, rabid, fanatical, wild, heated, furious, mad, ravening, delirious, feverish, febrile, frenzied, frantic, blustering, fiery, flaming, breathless, tumultuous, raging, turbulent, overwrought, passionate, reckless, stormy, tempest-tossed, excited, precipitous, tempestuous, harum-scarum *(coll.)*, unruly, rampant, impetuous, impulsive, disturbed, boisterous, uproarious, agitated, riotous, rampageous, ranting, infuriate, maniacal, raving, wrought up, beside oneself, violent, amuck, frenetic, fitful, haggard, wild-looking, wild-eyed, hysterical, out of one's wits, foaming at the mouth, upset, madcap, hotheaded, desperate, distracted, distraught, mazed, possessed, bewildered, infatuated, headlong, breakneck, overzealous, tense, hasty.

2. Feverish, hot, heated and emaciated, fevered, flushed, red, burning, inflamed, febrile, hot-skinned, feverous, wasted, exhausted, pyretic *(Med.)*, pyrexic *(Med.)*.

3. Pertaining to *or* affected with hectic fever, consumptive, phthisical, pneumonic, pulmonic, malarial, wasting, wasted.

HECTOR, *n.* Bully, blusterer, swaggerer, swashbuckler, domineering fellow, bluffer, pretender, blowhard, windbag *(sl.)*, gasbag *(sl.)*, impostor, blatherskite, braggadocio, brag, bucko, desperado, braggart, fanfaron, boaster, noisy fellow, roisterer, intimidator, coercer, tough, ruffian, browbeater, despot, tyrant, ranter, hard master, terror, inquisitor, oppressor, raver, vaporer, rowdy, bulldozer, ruffian, blusterer, gascon.

HECTOR, *v.* Bully, treat with insolence, threaten, menace, harass, heckle, provoke, irritate, plague, torment, badger, huff, cow, browbeat, act in a blustering, domineering way, brag, boast, be a bully, gasconade, vapor, bluff, overbear, lord it over, bulldoze *(coll.)*, domineer, molest, nag, fanfaronade, swagger, pester, bluster, persecute, intimidate, worry, harry, fret, vex, buffalo *(sl.)*, tease, beat down, annoy, talk big, puff, trumpet, vaunt, blow *(coll.)*, carry with a high hand, inflame, pique, incommode, wear down, exhaust, bullyrag, grate, gripe, nettle, bate, sting, chafe, roil, hound, harrow, goad, mock, discompose, gibe, jeer, fleer, fatigue, disturb persistently, distress, gall, abuse, bleed white, gnaw, prostrate, terrorize, rack, pursue, beset, scourge, arouse, infuriate, exasperate.

HEDGE, *n.* 1. Fence of bushes *or* shrubs, hedgerow, boundary-marking bushes, fringe, quickset, edge, border, thicket, weir, protecting enclosure, trellis, espalier, hawthorne, avenue, bed.

2. Barrier, boundary, circumference, protection, margin, wall, confine, paling, limit, cincture, circuit, line, fence, outline, periphery, compass, bound, extent, border, hem, ambit, circumscription, skirt, frame, orbit, delineation, lineaments, girth, zone, contour, rim, extremities.

HEDGE, *v.* 1. *(Often foll. by IN OFF, ABOUT, etc.)* Enclose with a hedge, separate by a hedge, bound, limit, edge, border, mark a boundary, delineate, delimitate, define, divide, mark off, demarcate, delimit, outline, encircle, section, isolate, cut off, set off, determine, plant hedge around.

2. *(Often fol. by IN or UP)* Obstruct, hinder, surround, limit, circumscribe, hem, encumber, prevent escape *or* free movement, restrain, restrict, proscribe, bind, curb, lash, trammel, keep within bounds, incarcerate, intern, hold in check, shackle, beleaguer, collar, imprison, blockade, impede, stay, hinder, constrain, bridle, repress, debar, deny, disallow, cage, besiege, hobble, inhibit, harass, impound, prohibit, immure, check, circumvent, fetter, tie one's hands, pen in, interdict, cloister, preclude.

3. Fortify, protect, offset, balance, give and take, cancel, neutralize, nullify, compensate, counteract, square, shield, secure, counterbalance, defend, safeguard, guard.

4. Turn aside, swerve, avoid an open *or* decisive course, evade, dodge, temporize, hide, skulk, take refuge in a hiding place, duck *(coll.)*, be cowardly, disregard, recoil, shrink back, hang back, give the slip, throw off the scent, circumvent, double, parry, wriggle out of, shift *or* put off, give the go-by, pass up *(sl.)*, flinch, fight shy of, keep clear of, shuffle, fence, palter, prevaricate, cavil, trifle, escape, quibble, hold aloof, eschew, take no part in, haggle, proceed stealthily, change the subject, split hairs, subtilize, blow hot and cold, beg the question, pettifog, refine, elude, get around *(coll.)*, give the runaround, shun, equivocate, beat about the bush.

HEDONISM, *n.* 1. *(Philos.)* Eudemonism, utilitarianism, theory of pleasure *or* happiness as the supreme good, Epicureanism, hedonic school, ehoistic hedonism, psychological hedonism, universalistic hedonism *(Ethics),* Benthamism. 2. Devotion to pleasure, pleasure-seeking, sensualism, gratification, satisfaction, free living, dissipation, delight, titillation, excitement, enjoyment, rapture, thrill, ravishment, delectation, enchantment, captivation, transport, well-being, gluttony, debauchery, oblectation, libertinism, profligacy, licentiousness, fascination, bewitchment, zest, intemperance.

HEDONIST, *n.* 1. Adherent of hedonism, eudemonist, Epicurean, Benthamite, utilitarian. 2. Sensualist, pleasure-seeker, voluptuary, dissipater, glutton, rake, debauchee, libertine, profligate, free liver, Sybarite, epicure, high liver *(coll.),* gourmand, Heliogabalus, votary *or* swine of Epicurus, hard liver.

HEED, *n. (Usually with* GIVE *or* TAKE*)* Notice, attention, care, regard, heedfulness, watchfulness, observation, carefulness, caution, mindfulness, consideration, vigilance, wariness, solicitude, oversight, cognizance, forethought, devotion, concern, attentiveness, precaution, supervision, anxiety, advertence, diligence, discrimination, circumspection, thought, respect, pains, note, ear, scrutiny, prudence, deliberation, reflection, cautiousness, discretion, surveillance, application, concentration, conscientiousness, particularity, scrupulousness, fastidiousness, meticulousness, absorption, study, perusal, examination.

HEED, *v.* Regard, notice, pay attention to, take notice of, mind, mark, consider, give heed to, take heed, hearken to, obey, listen to, observe, attend to, glance at, pay respect to, be ruled by, take to heart, be conscious of, appreciate, look into, incline one's ear, perceive, give a thought to, trouble one's head about, give the mind *or* attention to, be attentive, be concerned about, make *or* take note of, take into consideration *or* account, bear in mind, hold in view, watch, pay regard, give ear to, respect, note, guard, follow, seek *(opportunity),* move warily, pick one's steps, keep a weather eye open, feel one's ground, mind one's P's and Q's, have all one's eyes *or* wits about one, take care, beware, take it easy *(coll.),* think, have a care, be on one's guard, look sharp, remark, advert to, bow to, hear, be guided by, be cautious, accede to, acknowledge, acquiesce, comply, defer to, yield, reverence, incline, concur, be willing, approve, consent, see *or* think fit, receive, hold with, be of a favorable disposition, submit, agree, favor.

HEEDFUL, *adj.* Mindful, attentive, careful, observant, regardful, wary, watchful, observing, cautious, circumspect, provident, discreet, alert, thoughtful, scrupulous, considerate, alive to, vigilant, prudent, solicitous, conscientious, on guard, open-eyed, politic, precautionary, precautious, precautional, on the qui vive *(Fr.),* awake, all ears, wakeful, all eyes and ears, on the watch *or* lookout, painstaking, wide-awake, advertent, open-eared, meticulous, exact, on the job *(coll.),* judicious, concerned, discerning, percipient, discriminative, discriminating, expedient, guarded, deliberative, particular, deliberate, perspicacious, calculating.

HEEDLESS, *adj.* Careless, thoughtless, unmindful, regardless, reckless, precipitate, headlong, headless, inattentive, unobservant, negligent, neg-

lectful, inconsiderate, unwatchful, rash, forgetful, listless, slovenly, mindless, dizzy, secure, loose, oblivious, unobserving, unsolicitous, slack, remiss, shiftless, happy-go-lucky, indolent, unconcerned, hasty, abstracted, unwary, wild, harebrained, uncircumspect, unthinking, unreflecting, improvident, insouciant, deaf, blind, unaware, imprudent, impulsive, indifferent, scatterbrained, disregardant, inadvertent, insensible, not on the job *(coll.),* unheeding, unthoughtful, lax, nonchalant, indiscreet, unheeding, absent, not attending to, giddy, culpose *(Rom. Law),* foolish, fickle, witless, irresponsible, preoccupied, hasty, distracted, incautious.

HEEL, *n.* 1. Lower back part *(of foot, shoe or stocking),* spur *(of birds; loosely),* lower palm of the hand *(near the wrist),* part of a tool near the handle, projection, knob, lift, heeltap, heelpiece, support for the heel *(on a shoe),* hock *(in digitigrade animals and birds),* calcaneus *(Anat.),* protuberance. 2. Foot *(esp. in ref. to kicking or running away),* hoof, hind foot, kicker, back, rear. 3. Latter *or* concluding part, fag end, remnant, rind *(as of cheese),* crust *(of bread),* balance *(coll.),* leavings, remainder, butt, stump, rump. 4. *(Naut.)* Cant, yaw, tilt, sheering, veering, turning, deviation, inclination, tipping, wearing, shift.

HEEL, *v.* 1. Follow at the heels of, chase closely, dog, bedog, shadow, trail, prowl after, track, pursue, hound, tag *or* tag after *(coll.),* tail *(coll.),* hang on the skirts of, tread close upon. 2. Arm with spurs *(a gamecock),* fit gaffs upon, fit out, rig, gear, equip, accouter, furnish with a heel, mend, cobble, heelpiece, put a heel on *(as a shoe),* repair *(shoes).* 3. Perform with the heels, use the heels *(as in dancing),* caper, cut capers, leap, jump, spring, capriole, curvet, buck, prance, gambol, antic, cavort *(coll.),* caracole. 4. *(Naut.)* Incline, lean, cant, tilt, veer, sheer, shift, turn, tip, wear, jib, swing, haul off, deviate, yaw, careen, list, keel, turn aside, swerve, put in an oblique position.

HEGEMONY, *n.* Leadership, command, sway, rule, government, dominion, grasp, headship, paramountcy, authority, dominance, predominance, mastery, masterdom, influence, mastership, lordship, preponderance, supremacy, ascendancy, control, presidency, directorship, chieftainship, captaincy, superintendence.

HEGIRA, *n.* Escape, flight, exodus, fleeing, sudden departure, withdrawal, retreat, evasion.

HEIGHT, *n.* 1. Extent upward, highness, altitude, elevation, prominence, tallness, pitch, stature, loftiness, procerity. 2. Hill, peak, mound, bluff, mountain, crag, summit, plateau, precipice, tableland, eminence, promontory, acclivity, alp, ascent, pinnacle, vantage point, steep, palisade, cliff, escarpment. 3. Utmost degree, flowering, fruition, limit, term, zenith, exaltation, prime, supremacy, peak, extremity, grandeur, intensity, culmination, maximum, ne plus ultra *(Lat.),* extent, pink, crisis, consummation, heyday, turning point, crowning event, crown, meridian, ultimate, head, acme, fructification, pinnacle, climax, summit, florescence, realization, perfection, cap. 4. Top, uttermost extremity, acme, summit, peak, crest, climax, tiptop, pinnacle, tip, head, cap, apex, topmost, zenith, ceiling, crown, brow, vertex, meridian, culmen.

HEIGHTEN, v. 1. Make more vivid, add color, intensify, add to, increase, augment, aggrandize, enlarge, reinforce, magnify, deepen, embroider, touch up, enhance, extend, hyperbolize, stretch, aggravate, strengthen, color, amplify, overpicture, exaggerate, improve, overdraw, tone up, vivify, maximize, develop, widen, broaden.

2. Make higher, increase the height of, elevate, raise, lift up, exalt, rear, upraise, uplift, upthrust, thrust up, uphoist, erect, upheave, hoist, heave up.

HEINOUS, adj. Objectionable, unbearable, odious, offensive, repugnant, abominable, accursed, detestable, execrable, abhorrent, nauseous, loathsome, cursed, annoying, repulsive, ugly, hateful, horrid, shocking, confounded, monstrous, invidious, corrupt, foul, opprobrious, hideous, rotten, wicked, sinful, sinister, blameworthy, reprehensible, diabolic, nasty, contemptible, vulgar, forbidding, nauseating, insufferable, frightening, coarse, distasteful, despicable, mean, deplorable, unworthy, low, ignoble, intolerable, abject, unendurable, evil, disgusting, obnoxious, revolting, damnable, hellish, peccant, fulsome, infernal, devilish, vile, sickening, beastly, nefarious, base, infamous, villainous, atrocious, forbidding, nasty, blameworthy, bad, flagrant, black, iniquitous, shameful, felonious, notorious, arrant, outrageous, immoral, sinful, awful, profligate, facinorous, vicious, satanic, disgraceful, dire, terrible, ill, flagitious, scandalous, ghastly, noisome, woeful, pitiable, grievous, lamentable, regrettable, baneful, baleful, pernicious, beggarly, shabby, petty, unmentionable, derogatory, uncommendable, improper, unpraiseworthy, culpable, illaudable, despiteful, ill-intentioned, evil-disposed, ill-contrived, malefic, venomous, harmful, scurvy, unprincipled, malfeasant, wrong.

HEIR, n. One who inherits, heiress (fem.), inheritress (fem.), inheritrix (fem.), beneficiary, heir of the body, heir apparent, heir presumptive, heir expectant, heir general, heir at law, coheir, inheritor, donee, relessee, grantee, devisee.

HEIRLOOM, n. Inheritance, hereditament, bequest, heritage, legacy, birthright, patrimony, reversion.

HELICAL, adj. Pertaining to or having the form of a helix, spiral, winding, helicoid, spiroid, screwlike, coiled, screw-shaped, cochleated, screwy, tortuous, corkscrew, sinuous, corkscrewy, cochleate, cochlear (Anat.) cochleous, anfractuous, turbinate (Zool.), turbinal (Anat. and Zool.), turbinoid (Zool.), turbiniform (Zool.).

HELIX, n. Spiral, spiral object or part, coil, circumvolution, spiral line (Geom.), spiral ornament (Archit.), volute (of Corinthian capital), screw thread, twist, tendril, whorl, corkscrew, curlicue, curl, curved fold (of external ear; Anat.).

HELL, n. 1. Place or state of punishment of the wicked after death, place of departed spirits, abode of the damned, infernal regions, shades below, the lower world, the grave, purgatory, perdition, inferno, underworld, realms of Pluto, everlasting fire, bottomless pit, place of torment, abyss, limbo, nether world, hell-fire, lake of fire and brimstone, place of the lost, habitation of fallen angels, Gehenna (Jew. Hist.), Tartarus (Myth.), Sheol (Heb.), Pandemonium, Tophet (Lit.), Avernus, Satan's kingdom, Naraka (Hind. and Buddh.), Styx, Abaddon, Erebus (Gr. Myth.),

Malebolge, Avichi (Buddh.), Acheron (Class. Myth.), abode of the dead, Hades (Gr. Myth.).

2. Place or state of misery or torment, misery, moral agony, unassuaged remorse, utter chaos, confusion of soul, darkness of spirit, depths, mental suffering, spiritual agony, stings of conscience, inward torment, sense of curse, rack, intense pain, passion, pang, anything that causes distress, martyrdom, crucifixion, cruciation, purgatory, cruelty, wretchedness, anguish, desolation, grief, despair, hopelessness, prostration of soul, broken heart, extremity, Avichi (Buddh.), fiery ordeal.

3. The powers of evil, fiends, devils, demons, fallen angels, unclean spirits, inhabitants of Pandemonium, Mammon, evil spirits, host of hell, rulers or powers of darkness, demonkind, demoniac forces, satanic beings, Belial, Beelzebub.

4. Gambling establishment, gambling or gaming house, gambling den, casino, prison, jail, dungeon, black hole, betting house, gambling hell, Domdaniel, limbo, sink or den of iniquity or corruption, hole (sl.), joint (sl.), dive, brothel, the underworld, opium den.

HELLENIC, adj. Pertaining to the Greeks, Grecian, Greek, Koine (Lang.), classical, Periclean, pure, elegant, in the character or spirit of the Greeks, of ancient Greek culture or ideals, Hellenistic, of exquisite proportion, chaste, simple, serene, severe, Attic, refined, restrained, concinnate, concinnous, symmetrical.

HELLENIST, n. One who admires or studies Greek civilization, classicist, classicalist, purist, stylist, precisian.

HELLISH, adj. Of, like or befitting hell, infernal, satanic, devilish, sinful, iniquitous, Plutonian, fiend-like, fiendish, diabolical, evil, heinous, evil-fashioned, evil-favored, evil-eyed, evil-faced, bestial, malevolent, brutal, sinister, infamous, flagitious, vile, accursed, atrocious, abominable, execrable, nefarious, diabolic, black, inhuman, profligate, reprobate, notorious, wicked, demoniac, cursed, damned, monstrous, evil-affected, evil-savored, detestable, shameless, Stygian, Tartarean, vicious, malignant, damnable, invidious, bewitched, ghoulish, cruel, ruthless, fierce, fell, pitiless, treacherous, venomous, envenomed, Plutonic, chthonian, demonic, demonish, hellborn, recreant, wrong, bad, impious, flagrant, villainous.

HELM, n. 1. Steering apparatus, steering gear, tiller, wheel, rudder, handle, telemotor.

2. Post of command, direction, control, reins, rule, rudder, authority, steering, management, supremacy, kingship, throne, sway, leadership, helmsmanship, presidency, mastery, guidance, conduct, government, care, charge, steerage, ministry, jurisdiction, superintendence, dominion, administration, command, legislation, supervision, surveillance, pilotry, pilotship, pilotage, regulation, hegemony, chieftaincy, sovereignty, mastership, reins of government.

HELMET, n. Morion, casque, headpiece, heaume, cabasset, sallet, crest, armor for the head, casque, beaver, visor, face guard, casquetel, basinet.

HELOT, n. Slave, serf, bondsman, one in servitude, peasant, thrall, vassal, bond-slave, bondman, bondmaid, bondwoman, bondswoman, odalisque, villein, peon, man, ryot (Ind.), churl (Hist.).

HELP, n. 1. Act of helping, relief, assistance, succor, support, aid, patronage, fosterage, advocacy, interest, backing, encouragement, altruism, philanthropy, humanitarianism, charity, subvention, contribution, benefit, service, favor, countenance, cooperation, benefaction, advancement, hand, maintenance, ministry, ministration, advance, protection, useful office, restoration, subsidy, facilitation, friendship, championship, almsgiving, benevolence, blessing, furtherance, sustenance, abetting, upholding, promotion, auspices, care, good offices, welfare, kind regard, advantage, grace, helping hand, service, use, means, good turn, lift, boost (sl.), speed, boon, good or kind deed, gift, kindness, utility.

2. Person or thing that helps, assistant, ally, coadjutor, aider, abettor, helpmate, partner, colleague, collaborator, supporter, helpmeet, acolyte, co-aid, companion, subsidiary, adherent, handmaiden, co-worker, right-hand man, right hand, man Friday, helping hand, aid, confrere, consort, consociate, benefactor, backer, adjunct, auxiliary, angel (sl.; sometimes contempt.), second, advocate, comforter, patron, associate, accomplice, tutelary deity or spirit, familiar spirit, familiar, fairy godmother, special providence, good genius, friend in need, friend in deed, succorer, befriender, good Samaritan, benefactress, benefiter, champion, friend, attendant, accessory, confederate, workfellow, ministering angel, deputy.

3. Helper, assistant, servant, menial, employee, hired helper, domestic servant, farm laborer, hand, personnel, group of helpers, worker, workman, workhand, staff, man, girl, retainer, domestic, apprentice, servantry, inferior, underling, gang, force, crew, wage worker, maid, factotum, adjunct.

4. Means of remedying, stopping or preventing, remedy, cure, relief, corrective, healing, restorative, aid, step, measure, shift, artifice, resort, contrivance, subterfuge, stopgap, expedient, way, device, avail, working proposition, resource, makeshift, turning back, going back, retrieving, preventive, analeptic, returning, alterative (Med.).

HELP, v. 1. Assist, aid, cooperate with, collaborate, lend a hand, support, second, back, serve, subserve, give aid, render a service, contribute, bear a part, be of service or advantage, have a hand in, have a finger in, give a lift, have a share in, put one's shoulder to the wheel, put one's hand to the plow, be hand in glove with, unite, side with, go with, go along with, synergize, coact, combine, pull an oar, conspire, stand by, concur, do one's part, exert oneself, be auxiliary, give moral support to, enlist under the banners of, perform or discharge a function, hitch horses (coll.), render assistance, coadunate, sustain, take part with, wait upon, stick by, chip in (coll.), abet.

2. (Sometimes with ON) Lend or furnish aid, contribute assistance, give a lift, contribute means or strength, assist in doing, intercede for, profit, advantage, subsidize, befriend, better, incite, encourage, advance, tide over, stand in good stead, bring forward, guide, foster, maintain, nourish, advise, do good to, prosper, benefit, contribute, serve, uphold, facilitate, smooth or pave the way, render easy, ease, be the making of, endorse, do a world of good, tend, avail, prevail in one's behalf, advocate, lift, instigate, speed, improve, favor, stand by, conduce, stand for, further, prop, promote, incline, bend, turn, perfect, forward, bolster, quicken, hasten, lend wings to, expedite, cultivate, enhance, bestead, clear the way, lighten the labor, disburden, open the way, disencumber, disembarrass, deobstruct, set up, set agoing, put on one's feet, give a shove or impulse to, go to bat for (sl.), stick up for (coll.), take up the cudgels

for, take the part of, espouse the cause of, give moral support to, use one's influence for, smile upon.

3. Succor, save, relieve, come to the aid of, take in tow, deliver, rescue, free, release, retrieve, redeem, ransom, extricate, liberate, come to the rescue of, snatch from danger, bring off or through, pull back from the brink, emancipate.

4. Relieve (someone) in need, sickness, pain or distress, remedy, restore, improve, better, alleviate, mend, cure, emend, rectify, correct, lift, uplift, make whole, inspire, rehabilitate, reinstate, reinvigorate, refresh, recreate, minister, meliorate, comfort, minister to the convenience of, nurture, bring through, ameliorate, heal, bring round, do a world of good for, accommodate, set on one's feet, revive, revivify, recondition, rejuvenate, amend, solace, soothe, encourage, gladden, allay, quiet one's fears, console, sustain, hearten, calm, palliate, assuage, bear up, put at ease, salve, enhearten, reassure, inspirit, mitigate, speak peace, provide easement.

5. (With CAN or CANNOT) Avoid, forbear, refrain from, abstain, cease, evade, shun, spare, resist, let pass, eschew, let slip, turn away from, turn one's back on, get around (coll.), dodge, circumvent, keep clear of, fight shy of, keep from, escape, stop, stay, halt, break loose, get away from, discontinue, let alone, put off.

6. Remedy, prevent, stop, withstand, resist, control, hinder, deflect, gainsay, put or set straight, right, correct, rectify, redress, put or set right, countervail, hold in check, arrest, keep within bounds, adjust, fix, hold back, keep back, regulate, square, stay, halt, be proof against, confront, stand against, hold out against, bear up against, keep off, ward off, fend off, turn aside, stave off, keep at bay, repulse, repel, counteract, avert, circumvent, contravene, thwart, check, curb, balk, deal with, cope with, grapple with, breast or stem the tide (current, flood, stream).

7. (Reflex., with ONESELF) Take at will, appropriate, adopt, assume, usurp, arrogate, possess oneself of, make use of, make free with, take liberties with, annex (sl.), borrow, steal, lift (coll.), pirate, plagiarize, take for oneself, take possession of, commandeer (coll.), lay under contribution.

HELPER, n. Person or thing that helps, assistant, aider, partner, abettor, colleague, helpmate, auxiliary, coadjutor, adjunct, backer, supporter, co-aid, help, co-worker, right hand, consociate, benefactor, workfellow, confrere, man Friday, right-hand man, accomplice, confederate, patron, adjuvant, comforter, advocate, second, friend, ministering angel, benefactress, good Samaritan, succorer, friend in need, good genius, fairy godmother, familiar spirit, tutelary deity or spirit, ally, help-fellow, coöperator, companion, acolyte, deputy, collaborator, maidservant, recruit, adherent, aid, helping hand, consort, angel (sl.; sometimes contempt.), benefiter, befriender, champion, special providence, familiar, accessory, associate, contributor, attendant, friend in deed, helpmeet, subsidiary, handmaiden, worker, hand, apprentice.

HELPFUL, adj. Useful, beneficial, advantageous, giving or affording help, full of help, coöperative, inclined to aid others, assistant, constructive, adjuvant, subsidiary, aiding, munificent, propitious, ministrant, kind, neighborly, comfortable, attendant, well-disposed, edifying, efficacious, effective, beneficial, utilitarian, good for, valuable, serving, practical, sympathetic, charitable, synergetic, wholesome, salubrious, ancillary, benign, handy, instrumental, contributory, favorable, serviceable, aidful, profitable, available, subservient, favoring, conducive, salutary, philanthropic, auxiliary, accessory, coalitional, commodious, applicable, healthful, well-affected, merciful, friendly, benevolent, ready to help, effectual, adjunct, helping.

HELPLESS, adj. 1. Unable to help oneself, weak, dependent, feeble, infirm, imbecile, disabled, prostrate, paralyzed, palsied, lame, crippled, spent, exhausted, enervated, debilitated, faint, incurable, effete, flaccid, strengthless, devitalized, halt, powerless, impotent, at the end of one's rope, laid on one's back, atonic *(Pathol.)*.

2. Without help (aid, succor), exposed, outcast, destitute, abandoned, defenseless, friendless, pregnable, forsaken, rudderless, done for, unmanned, unnerved, unarmed, vincible, conquerable, vulnerable, weaponless, unguarded, aidless, guideless, resourceless, fatherless, naked, neglected, unprotected, deserted, unaided, forlorn, waterlogged, adrift, unsupported, unstrengthened, open to attack, expugnable, unfortified, at the end of one's wits, on one's beam ends.

3. Shiftless, inadequate, spineless, incapable, incompetent, inefficient, unendowed, unqualified, unfit, impotent, without initiative, unresourceful, without backbone, inane, empty, fatuous, sinewless, inept, inapt, effete, barren, sterile.

HELPMATE, n. 1. Wife or husband, consort, companion, helpmeet, spouse, better half, mate, partner, wife of one's bosom, benedict, wedded wife, bride, bridegroom, yokefellow, matron, rib *(hum.),* squaw *(Amer. Ind.),* hubbie *(coll.),* old woman *(joc.),* little woman *(joc.),* old man *(joc.).*

2. Helper, companion, aider, associate, assistant, partner, comrade, mate, consort, confrere, attendant, colleague, aid, adjunct, participant, workfellow, accessory, auxiliary, ally, accomplice, coadjutor, consociate, abettor, confederate, man Friday, right-hand man, help, cooperator, collaborator, helping hand, contributor, co-worker.

HELTER-SKELTER, adv. Pell-mell, irregularly, in confusion, in headlong, disorderly haste, precipitately, headforemost, headlong, at a rush, untidily, heels over head, confusedly, hurry-skurry, with precipitancy, in disorder, rashly, hastily, hurriedly, abruptly, thoughtlessly, recklessly, carelessly, head over heels, prematurely, at or on short notice, like a thunderbolt, injudiciously, without due caution, impetuously, aimlessly, on the spur of the moment, unwarily, impulsively, foolishly, passionately, unpreparedly, higgledy-piggledy, huggermugger, harum-scarum, in a ferment, topsy-turvy, upside down, every which way *(coll.).*

HEM, n. 1. Edge (folded back and sewed) of cloth or garment, finished edge, picoted edge, hemstitched edge, rolled hem or edge.

2. Border, margin, rim, edge, verge, brim, brink, selvage, boundary, pale, curb, limit, bounds, perimeter, frame, fringe, skirt, bordure *(Her.),* circumference, periphery, confines, confine, outline, compass, girdle, contour, circuit, girth, zone, delineation, lineaments, extent, orbit, purlieus, ambit, circumscription.

HEM, v. 1. Form an edge or border to or about, border, sew, skirt, edge, fringe, margin, circle, encircle, marginate, ring, hemstitch, fold back and sew down the edge of *(cloth, a garment, etc.),* double (fold, turn) under, environ, rim, enclose, envelop.

2. *(Fol. by* IN, AROUND *or* ABOUT*)* Surround, confine, enclose, circumscribe, shut in,

hedge in, encircle, encompass, environ, beset, limit, proscribe, restrain, hold in check, blockade, imprison, impede, constrain, repress, hobble, bridle, inhibit, impound, immure, bound, delimit, delimitate, restrict, embrace, picket, cage, preclude, debar, harass, circumvent, fetter, check, demarcate, keep within bounds, trammel, cloister, pen in, beleaguer, incarcerate.

3. *(Imit.)* Hesitate in speaking, falter, halt, hum or hem and haw *(coll.),* stutter, stammer, stumble, balbutiate, titubate, proceed in a faulty way, hobble, delay, quaver, drag, haw, mumble, maunder, snuffle, mouth, mutter.

HEMISPHERE, n. Half of the terrestrial globe or celestial sphere, map or projection of a hemisphere, half-globe, half-sphere, semiglobe, semisphere, half-orb.

HEMORRHAGE, n. Discharge of blood *(as from ruptured blood vessel),* profuse or violent bleeding, emission of blood, hemorrhea, bloody flux, dysentery, effusion, extravasation, issue *(Med.).*

HEMP, n. Tough fiber of the hemp plant, jute, oakum, sennit, rope, aloe hemp, bowstring hemp, burlap, hop sacking, gunny or gunny cloth, sacking, sackcloth.

HEN, n. Female of the domestic fowl *(and other similar birds),* setting hen, bantam, poulard, pullet, Partlet, biddy, chicken, banty *(coll.),* guinea hen, peahen, chickabiddy.

HENCE, adv. 1. As an inference from this fact, therefore, for this reason, as a consequence, from this cause, on account of this, ergo, accordingly, consequently, that being the case, such being the case, under the circumstances or conditions, logically, whence, so, as matters stand, wherefore, in consequence, as a natural result, naturally, inevitably, to that end, on that ground, on that account, thus, then, because of this, for which reason, that being so.

2. From this source or origin, herefrom, from this, from here.

3. From this time, henceforth, henceforward, from this time forth or forward, in future, in time to come, hereafter, at the end of a given period, from now on, anon, in aftertime, at a later or subsequent date or time, after a time or while, after this.

4. From this place, from here, away, elsewhere, outward-bound.

HENCEFORTH, adv. Henceforward, from this time, in future, from now on, hence, hereafter, in time to come, from this time forth or forward.

HENCHMAN, n. 1. Follower, trusty attendant, supporter, retainer, servant, assistant, liege, disciple, votary, apostle, subject, slave, aider, acolyte, helper, dependent, adherent, proselyte, shadow, satellite, puppet, tool, instrument, accessory, partisan, copartner, colleague, adjunct, ally, companion, backer, supporter, right-hand man, champion, friend, advocate, man Friday, right hand.

2. Servile and unscrupulous follower, political follower, sycophant, hanger-on, heeler *(coll.),* minion, vassal, tagtail, toady, toad-eater, tufthunter, spaniel, truckler, fawner, votary, sponger, groveler, lick-spit, yes man *(sl.),* lick-spittle, carpet knight, flunky, lackey, bootlicker, footlicker, appendage, sidekick *(sl.),* apple-polisher *(sl.),* handshaker.

HENPECK, v. *(Of a wife toward her husband)* Domineer over, subjugate, nag, browbeat, bully, keep under one's thumb, oppress, overbear, tyrannize, lay a heavy hand on, bear hard upon, subdue, suppress, hold *or* keep at one's beck and call, dictate, have at one's apronstrings, lay down the law to, lord it over, intimidate, subject, keep at heel, hold in leash *or* leading strings.

HENPECKED, *adj.* *(Of a husband)* Wife-ridden, browbeaten, obedient, in subjection, dependent, without freedom *or* independence, in bondage, timid, compliant, acquiescent, at one's beck and call, tied to one's apron strings, in leading strings, under one's thumb, constrained, yielding, resigned, submissive, subject, subordinate, in harness, meek, docile, passive, under the lash, led by the nose, unresisting, unassertive, cringing.

HERALD, *n.* 1. Forerunner, harbinger, precursor, foreshadower, usher, predecessor, envoy, foregoer, pioneer, scout, antecedent, prefigurement, omen, premonitor, sign, token, warning, indicator, indication, prodromus, symptom, foretoken, augury, soothsay, symbol, clue, auspice, divination, handwriting on the wall, stormy petrel, Mother Carey's chickens, prognostic, forecast, portent.

2. One who proclaims *or* announces, proclaimer, publisher, crier, informant, messenger, informer, reporter, trumpeter, annunciator, envoy, ambassador, outrider, runner, announcer, prophesier, circulator, intimater, prophetess, diviner, prophet, augur, harbinger, deputy, vaticinator, evangel, Gabriel, adviser, notifier, enlightener, appriser, soothsayer, prognosticator, avantcourier, marshal, enlightener, tipper, enunciator, intelligencer, nunciate.

HERALD, *v.* 1. Give tidings of, proclaim, announce, inform, report, sound, promulgate, publish, circulate, publicize, air, communicate, reveal, enlighten, foretell, trumpet, tell, spread, notify, preannounce, vent, express, disseminate, advertise, circumfuse, rumor about, bruit abroad, make known, divulge, issue, disperse, scatter, bestrew, blow, put about, hawk about, noise abroad, ventilate, give to the world, give out, emit, put forward, put *or* lay before the public, blaze, blazon, give voice to, divulgate, bandy about, evulgate, enunciate, declare, utter, placard, diffuse, whisper about.

2. Usher in, foreshadow, inaugurate, dawn, foreshow, forerun, betoken, be prior, presage, prognosticate, anticipate, prevene, divine, omen, auspicate, typify, ·pretypify, signify, promise, shadow forth, prophesy, bode, intimate, lead the way, precede, pave the way, prepare a passage for, pre-exist, proclaim, hold out expectation *or* hope of, foretoken, prefigure, augur, antecede, precurse.

HERALDRY, *n.* 1. Art, practice *or* science of recording genealogies and emblazoning arms *or* ensigns, registry, authority in and care of armorial bearings, blazonry, emblazonry, the herald's office, marshaling *(at processions, public ceremonies, etc.).*

2. Proclaiming, announcing, publishing, publication, issuance, announcement, proclamation, broadcasting, declaration, notification, setting forth of decrees, evulgation, propagation, advertisement.

3. Heraldic bearing *or* symbol *(or* a collection of them), emblazonment, insignia, ensign, symbol, crest, shield, scutcheon, escutcheon, arms, hatchment, armorial bearings, coat of arms.

4. Heraldic pomp, ceremony, festivity, magnificence, state, solemnity, splendor, formality, circumstance, convention, ritual, pageantry, glitter, flourish, display.

HERB, *n.* Soft, succulent seed plant, plant of economic value *(for medicine, scent, or flavor, etc.),* wort.

HERBAGE, *n.* Nonwoody vegetation, herbs, grass, plants, vegetation of the fields, succulent parts of herbaceous plants, flora, stand, crop, flowerage, verdure, herbal vegetation.

HERBAL, *adj.* Pertaining *or* relating to herbs, herbaceous, consisting of herbs, vegetal, vegetable, vegetative, herby, herbous, herbose, grassy, grasslike, verdant, floral, turfy, turflike.

HERBALIST, *n.* Collector of herbs, dealer in medicinal plants, herborist, plant-collector, botanist.

HERBARIUM, *n.* Herbary, hortus siccus, botanic garden, herb garden, room, building *or* institution housing an herbarium.

HERCULEAN, *adj.* 1. Difficult, laborious, arduous, resistant, painstaking, toilsome, burdensome, onerous, wearying, fatiguing, rigorous, heavy, distressing, uphill, strenuous, full of obstacles, requiring great effort, difficult to accomplish, hard, wicked *(coll.).*

2. Robust, tough, sturdy, rugged, enduring, hale, vigorous, firm, lusty, substantial, solid, burly, brawny, physically fit, able-bodied, virile, stalwart, hefty *(coll.),* healthy, powerful, mighty, sinewy, stanch, strapping, husky *(coll.),* Atlantean, hardy, muscular, athletic, sound, staminal, puissant, fit, in good condition, in fine fettle.

3. Stalwart, unflinching, brave, bold, intrepid, undismayed, unshrinking, high-mettled, hard, dreadless, indefatigable, valiant, gritty, unalarmed, unappalled, valorous, dauntless, fearless, manful, high-spirited, lion-hearted, doughty, dashing, venturesome, plucky, soldierly, daring, courageous, stout, resolute, stout-hearted, game, audacious, aweless, manly, indomitable, unyielding, firm, spirited, unapprehensive, spunky *(coll.),* gallant, herolike.

4. Gigantic, monumental, ponderous, huge, large, big, gigantean, Antaean, titanic, colossal, monstrous, imposing, extreme, terrible *(coll.),* tall, immense, grand, enormous, elephantine, overwhelming, vast, prodigious, stupendous, mammoth, gross, towering, staggering, great, massive, Brobdingnagian, awe-inspiring, overpowering, Cyclopean, commanding, lofty, Gargantuan, massy, bulky, Atlantean, dinotherian, dinosaurian, strapping *(coll.),* jumbo, megatherine, leviathan, magnitudinous.

HERCULES, *n.* Strong man, Titan, giant, tower of strength, Goliath, muscle man *(coll.),* Samson, Gargantua, mountain, leviathan, pillar of strength, man mountain *(coll.),* Atlas, Antaeus, Cyclops, Tarzan, Superman, athlete, gymnast, Polyphemus, palaestrian, wrestler, pancratiast.

HERD, *n.* 1. *(Of animals, etc.)* Group, gathering, pack, drove, tribe, swarm, colony, bunch, covey, bevy, flock, cluster, school *(of fish),* shoal *(of fish),* flight *(of birds),* gaggle *(of geese).*

2. Assemblage, assembly, band, party, meeting, gathering, troop, set, team, collection, company, string, array, legion, body, multitude, crowd, host, ruck, circle, gang, crew, concourse, convention, cavalcade, mob, lot, number, entourage, congregation, confluence, conflux, levy, muster, tribe, congress, bunch *(coll.),* caravan, posse, cohort, drove, covey, brood, mess, conclave.

3. Rabble, the many, riffraff, rank and file, the multitude, the crowd, mob, the masses, commonage, commonalty, proletariat, every Tom, Dick and Harry, hoi polloi (*Gk.*), rout, ragtag and bobtail, vulgar herd, the populace, the million, the great unwashed.

HERD, *v.* 1. Assemble, call together, group, convene, summon, gather, muster, congregate, bring together, rally, convoke, come together, flock together, round up (*coll.*), cluster, join, unite, meet, gang up (*coll.*), foregather, crowd, swarm, bunch, collect, concentrate, center around, throng, associate, go into a huddle, get together, convocate.

2. Drive (*as cattle, etc.*), guide, spur, prick, goad, corral, round up.

HERDER, *n.* Cowkeeper, cowboy, cowpuncher, drover, herd, cowherd, oxherd, goatherd, gooseherd, shepherd, swineherd, pasturer, vaquero (*South West, U. S.*).

HERE, *adv.* 1. In this place, in this spot, in this locality, in attendance, hereabouts, in this vicinity, on the spot, present, herein, internally, on this occasion, on the present occasion, at this moment, at this time, inside, nearby, not far away.

2. To *or* toward this place, hither, hitherward, herein, within, to the speaker, from elsewhere.

3. At this point, at this juncture, then, there, at this place, at this time, now, at this moment, before going on *or* continuing, after this section (phase, unit, *etc.*).

4. Nigh, close at hand, close by, near, nearby, present, beside one, adjacent, proximal, contiguous, in proximity, in juxtaposition, at one's side, in one's presence, within reach (sight, call), in direct contact.

5. In the present life *or* state, in the flesh, alive, in life, existing, prevalent, current, afloat, on the face of the world, immanent, existent, subsistent, actual, instant, today, in these days, that is, under the sun, extant, hereadays.

HEREAFTER, *adv.* 1. After this in time *or* order, in time to come, henceforth, hence, in some future time, farther along, subsequently, coming, henceforward, afterwards, then and by, then, now, after this, from now on, at a later *or* subsequent date *or* time, after a time *or* while, in the course *or* process of time, in the fullness of time, in due time, prospectively, in course of time, tomorrow, sooner or later, all in good time, one of these days, sometime or other, ultimately, eventually, approaching, anon, from this time forth.

2. In the world to come, in a future state, in the next life, in the millennium, beyond the grave, in paradise, in heaven, in glory, eternally, in afterlife.

HEREAFTER, *n.* 1. Future life, world to come, future state *or* existence, world without end, the grave, world *or* life beyond, afterlife, postexistence, next world, afterworld, heaven, Day of Wrath, Day of Judgment, doomsday, crack of doom, millennium, heaven, hell, place of departed spirits, abode of the dead, the lower world, perdition, purgatory, infernal regions, heavenly kingdom, heavenly city, paradise, bliss.

2. Coming events, what is yet to be, time to come, what may occur, prospect, afteryears, womb of time, events to come, time drawing on, expectation, eventuality, by-and-by, the morrow, tomorrow, posterity, anticipation, probability, certainty, likelihood, subsequent time, coming time, future, advent.

HEREBY, *adv.* By this, as a result of this, here-

with, through, per, by, by this means, by the agency of this, by the aid of this, by virtue of, helped by, by dint of.

HEREDITABLE, *adj.* Capable of being inherited, inheritable, heritable, transmissible, hereditary, innate, inborn, inbred, ingrained, ingenerate, inwrought, intrinsic, native, inherent, indwelling, infixed, connate, essential, lineal, genealogical, ancestral, spontaneous, constitutional, in the grain, instinctive, intrinsic, congenital.

HEREDITARY, *adj.* 1. Passing *or* capable of passing naturally to offspring, pertaining to inheritance *or* heredity, by inheritance, inherited, transmitted from ancestors, maternal, paternal, inbred, inheritable, hereditable, heritable, innate, inborn, connate, essential, genealogical, constitutional, instinctive, congenital, intrinsic, in the grain, inherent, indwelling, infixed, ingenerate.

2. Having title *or* possession through inheritance, held through inheritance, traditional, age-old, ancient, established, landed, propertied, manorial, seigniorial, passed down, inherited, by inheritance, patrimonial, ancestral, real, feudal, allodial (*Law*), allodian (*Law*), freeholder (*Law*).

HEREDITY, *n.* 1. (*Biol.*) Transmission of genetic characters from parents to progeny, fixation of genes by selection (*natural or induced*), bequest, bestowal, transmittal, passing on of qualities, eugenics, mutation.

2. Genetic characteristics transmitted to an individual by its parents, instinct, heritage, inheritance, inbeing, birthright, lineage, ancestry, extraction, descent, line, succession, origin, birth, temperament, endowment, constitution, nature, pedigree, family, character, genealogy.

HEREIN, *adv.* 1. In *or* into (*this place*), inside (*this place*), within, internally, withinward, inly.

2. In this, in this respect *or* regard, in this fact *or* circumstance, in view of this, in this matter, in reference to this.

HEREOF, *adv.* Concerning this, about this, on this subject, in this regard, in this connection.

HERESY, *n.* 1. Opinion *or* doctrine at variance with orthodoxy (*esp. Theol.*), heterodox belief, error, false doctrine, heterodoxy, fallacy, irreligion, delusion, paganism, agnosticism, idol worship, unscripturality, unchristianity, superstition, iconoclasm, unorthodoxy, unsound doctrine, apostasy, idolatry.

2. Maintaining of heretical beliefs, heterodoxy, recusancy, dissent, apostasy, disbelief, misbelief, unbelief, infidelity, atheism, delusion, irreligion, idolatry, agnosticism, free thought, freethinking, sectarianism, dissension, nonconformity, superstition, unorthodoxy, skepticism, paganism, iconoclasm, schism.

HERETIC, *n.* One at variance with doctrine of his professed religion, sectary, separatist, skeptic, apostate, antichristian, atheist, agnostic, recreant, dissenter, deserter, protester, protestant, seceder, heathen, deist, theophobe, latitudinarian, nullifidian, free thinker, infidel, misbeliever, backslider, irreligionist, nonjuror, sectarian (*Hist.*), heterodox, pervert, pagan, iconoclast, Lollard, recusant, schismatic, unbeliever, nonconformist, dissentient, heresiarch.

HERETICAL, *adj.* Of, pertaining to *or* like heretics *or* heresy, heterodox, schismatic, sectarian, idolatrous, infidel, heretic, doubting, unsound, unscriptural, uncanonical, skeptical, faithless, erroneous, deistic, theistic, pagan, unchristian, deluded, defective, fallacious, erring, untrue, disbelieving, delusory, unbelieving, contrary to accepted standards, schismatical, false, faulty, backsliding, delusive, wrong, nonjuring, anti-Scriptural, iconoclastic, misbelieving, irreligious, nullifidian.

HERETOFORE, *adv.* Formerly, previously, beforetime, before this, past, of old, up to this time, in days of yore, before the present time, bygone, till now, ere now, aforetime, long ago, anciently, hitherto, in times past, in past ages, earlier, once.

HEREUPON, *adv.* Upon this, hereafter, from now on, from this time, hereon, forthwith, as a consequence of this, following from this, next, afterwards, on this, in future, close upon this, immediately upon this, shortly, presently, early, betimes, subsequently, now.

HEREWITH, *adv.* 1. Along with this, in company with, together with, coupled with, included, in addition, enclosed, herein, attached, in conjunction with.

2. By means of this, with, by, per, by way of, by virtue of, by the aid of this, by the agency of this, through, by dint of, helped by, hereby.

HERITAGE, *n.* 1. That which comes *or* belongs to one by reason of birth, inherited lot *or* portion, inheritance, patrimony, legacy, bequest, birthright, heritance, lot, condition, status, endowment, reversion, descent, lineage, dotation, estate, possession, hereditament *(Law),* portion.

2. Something reserved for one, reward, due, promise, deserts, measure, prospect, right, merits, inheritance, expectation.

HERMAPHRODITE, *n.* Gynandroid, bisexual, homosexual, Lesbian, epicene, androgyne, intersex, sex-intergrade.

HERMAPHRODITE, HERMAPHRODITIC, *adj.* Androgynous, partaking of both sexes, composed of two opposing elements, epicene, androgynic, bisexual, Lesbian, monoclinous *(Bot.),* gynandroid *(Med.),* gynandrous, intersexual.

HERMENEUTIC, *adj.* Interpretive, explanatory, elucidative, definitive, annotative, scholiastic, paraphrastic, explicatory, explicative, amplificatory, explaining, expository, exegetic.

HERMENEUTICS, *n.* Interpretation *(esp. of the Scriptures),* that branch of theology which treats of the principles of exegesis, exegetics, annotation, commentary, critique, explanation, exegesis.

HERMETIC, *adj.* 1. Airtight *(by fusion or sealing),* shut fast, snug, closed, impervious to air, unventilated, watertight, impermeable, sealed.

2. Pertaining to occult science *(esp. alchemy),* secret, occult, obscure, cryptic, dark, arcane, abstruse, recondite, hidden, symbolical, magical, mystical, mystic, mysterious, anagogical, containing doctrines clothed *or* concealed in symbols, Masonic, Freemasonic, Rosicrucian, cabalistic, transcendental, alchemic, theosophic, esoteric, emblematic, metaphysical.

HERMIT, *n.* One living in seclusion *(sometimes for religious reasons),* anchorite, anchoret, solitarian, anchoress, ascetic, hermitress, eremite, recluse, solitary, Marabout *(Moham.),* santon *(Moham.),* stylite *(Eccl. Hist.),* pillarist *(Eccl.),* pillar saint, Hieronymite *(Eccl. Hist.).*

HERO, *n.* 1. Man of distinguished valor *or* performance, brave man, god, demigod, man of courage *or* mettle, brave, warrior, lion, combatant, victor, champion, master, saint, celebrity, star, knight-errant, fearless soldier, dauntless flier, paladin, great man, worthy, idol, popular figure,

exemplar, a man among men, model, intrepid warrior, conqueror, man of the hour *or* day.

2. Principal male character *(of story, play, etc.),* protagonist, leading man, male lead, male star, actor, matinee idol.

3. *(Mythol.)* Being of godlike prowess and beneficence, demigod, divinity, god-man, halfgod, deity, immortal, warrior chieftain of superior strength, courage *or* ability, godling, godkin, godlet, man of superhuman achievements.

HEROIC, *adj.* 1. Of *or* pertaining to heroes, suitable to the character of a hero, intrepid, daring, noble, courageous, valiant, brave, fearless, dauntless, valorous, chivalrous, plucky, doughty, manful, stout-hearted, hardy, princely, soldierly, mettlesome, unflinching, unblenching, chivalric, handsome, sublime, aweless, high-minded, unshrinking, splendid, virile, resolute, spirited, enterprising, undaunted, spartan, game, firm, large, bold, illustrious, magnanimous, lion-hearted, determined, unappalled, undismayed, herolike, gallant, great, masculine, meritorious.

2. Dealing with *or* applicable to heroes *(as in lit.),* epic, Homeric, of *or* pertaining to the heroes of antiquity, classic, mythical, fabulous, legendary, idealistic, romantic, mythological.

3. *(Chiefly Med.)* Having *or* involving recourse to bold, daring *or* extreme measures, violent, extreme, intense, rigorous, drastic, large, extravagant, potent, powerful, desperate, great.

4. *(Of style, language, etc.)* Resembling heroic poetry, grand, magniloquent, of a size between life and colossal *(Arts),* high-flown, bombastic, classic, dignified, august, elevated, huge *(hum.),* sublime, exalted, epopoeia, extravagant, high, enormous *(hum.).*

HEROIC, *n.* 1. *(Often pl.)* Epic, heroic verse, heroic poem, epos, epopee.

2. *(Pl.)* Bombast, extravagance of expression, braggadocio, excess, exorbitance, bluster, bravado, ostentation, pretense, rant, gasconade, puffery, bragging, boasting, rodomontade, much cry and little wool, exaggeration, magniloquence, much ado, jactation, overpraise, inflation, overestimation, stretch, embroidery, coloring, extravagation, intemperance, turgidity, grandiosity, high-flown diction, orotundity, pomposity, pretension, grandiloquence, inordinacy, overlaudation, hyperbole, immoderacy, bluff, braggartism, tall talk *(coll.).*

HEROINE, *n.* 1. Intrepid woman, supremely courageous woman, woman of heroic character, demigoddess, resourceful woman *(as in a crisis),* woman of the hour *or* day, celebrity.

2. Principal female character *(of story, play, etc.),* actress, female star, female lead, leading lady, diva, prima donna.

HEROISM, *n.* Qualities of a hero *or* heroine, valor, gallantry, prowess, intrepidity, fearlessness, boldness, bravery, courage, spirit, contempt *or* defiance of danger, hardihood, stout heart, grit, nerve, pluck, backbone, knight-errantry, elevation of spirit *or* purpose, dauntlessness, manliness, fortitude, endurance, daring, great-heartedness, mettle, heroic conduct, game, heart, resoluteness, sublimity, exaltation.

HESITANCY, *n.* Hesitance, hesitation, indecisiveness, infirmity of purpose, fluctuation, constraint, irresoluteness, reserve, vacillation, uncertainty, halting, half-heartedness, irresolution, unsettlement, reluctance, indetermination, doubtfulness, doubt, demurity, dubitation, misgiving, shillyshally, scruple, demur, suspension, wavering, boggle, diffidence, qualm, dubiousness, indecision, equivocation, timidity.

HESITANT, *adj.* Lacking confidence, hesitative, dubious, infirm of purpose, fidgety, inconstant, irresolute, half-hearted, tremulous, undecided, vacillating, wavering, quibbling, fickle, uncertain, timid, unsure, doubtful, fluctuating, unresolved, dallying, unsettled, faltering, demurring, debating, pausing, shilly-shallying, sitting on *or* straddling the fence, hanging back, hovering, wobbling, considering, seesawing, variable, alternating, halting, oscillating, oscillatory, equivocating, constrained, reserved.

HESITATE, *v.* 1. Be uncertain, irresolute, *etc.*, falter, demur, pause, not know what to do, shy at, pull back, tergiversate, oscillate, hang back, hover, debate, shilly-shally, seesaw back and forth, stick at, weigh and consider, ponder, recoil, swerve, shrink, vacillate, fluctuate, scruple, think twice, dally, waver, shift, change one's mind, straddle the fence, equivocate, stickle, wait, balk, balance, linger, deliberate, dilly-dally, blow hot and cold, trim, alternate.

2. Stutter, stammer, hem and haw, haw, falter, halt *or* stumble in speech, balbutiate, titubate.

HETEROCLITE, *adj.* Irregular, abnormal, exceptional, unconventional, unusual, anomalous, anomalistic, erratic, nonconformable, deviative, unorthodox, divergent, aberrant, out of tune, out of line, out of keeping, heteromorphic.

HETERODOX, *adj. (Esp. Theol.)* Not in accordance with established beliefs, heretical, skeptical, unscriptural, unorthodox, uncanonical, dissenting, nonconformist, unbelieving, recusant, schismatic, Pyrrhonistic, iconoclastic, incredulous, anti-Scriptural, apocryphal, doubting, misbelieving.

HETERODOXY, *n.* Unorthodoxy, heresy, schismatism, misbelief, iconoclasm, doubt, dissent, recusancy, skepticism, Pyrrhonism, nonconformity, nonconformance.

HETEROGENEITY, *n.* Disparateness, inconsistency, dissimilitude, variance, variation, disconformity, inharmoniousness, nonuniformity, dissimilarity, diversity, variegation, heteromorphism, multifariousness, unevenness, polymorphism.

HETEROGENEOUS, *adj.* Unlike, dissimilar, incongruous, discrepant, incompatible, composite, mongrel, unallied, independent, mixed, multiplex, miscellaneous, inharmonious, amalgamate, mingled, compounded, unrelated, diversified, variegated, conglomerate, motley, unmatched, disaccordant, mosaic, assorted.

HEW, *v.* 1. Cut, hack, cleave, rive, rend, sever, sunder, chop, hackle, slash, whittle, whack *(coll.)*, haggle, chip, gash, carve, dissever, split, abscind, slice, lacerate, notch, incise, disjoint, shear, lop, prune, detruncate, amputate, quarter, trim, dismember, dislimb.

2. Fell by cutting, hew down, cut down, chop down, drop, raze, level, mow down, crop, whack down *(coll.)*, bring down.

3. Form, make, shape, fashion, figure, pattern, carve, mold, chisel, hew out, cut out, hammer *or* knock out, roughhew, frame, devise, forge, weave, work up, construct, fabricate, produce, build, lick *or* put into shape, sculpture, model, formulate, roughcast.

HEYDAY, *n.* 1. Stage *or* period of highest vigor *or* fullest strength, flush, acme, bloom, crest, crown, cap, top, tiptop, height, pinnacle, apex, climax, peak, culmination, spire, crowning-point, merid-

ian, prime, zenith, summit, uttermost, culmen, perfection, florescence, fructification, flowering, fruition, term, prime, maximum, extent, pink, consummation, ultimate, realization, triumph.

2. High spirits, frolic, rejoicing, jubilee, reveling, revels, frolicsomeness, pleasure, prosperity, bloom, youth, play, revelry, merrymaking, skylarking, conviviality, joviality, merriment, triumph, happy day, exultation, excitement, jollity, jubilation, celebration.

HIATUS, *n.* Opening, rift, chasm, interval, scissure, aperture, fissure, interspace, interstice, gulf, slot, foramen, crevice, chink, crack, chap, incision, trench, hole, gash, cut, rent, rime, slit, breach, caesura, synapse *(Physiol.)*, furrow, vacancy, blank, lacuna, break, disruption, separation, cleft, split, channel, orifice, gap, space, cranny, interruption, groove, cavity, score, rupture.

HIBERNATE, *v.* 1. Winter, lie torpid for the winter, vegetate, lie dormant, sleep.

2. Lie torpid, remain in seclusion, hide oneself, lie hid *or* hidden, suffer an eclipse, be concealed, retire from the world, lie perdu, lie snug *or* close, rusticate, hermitize, dissocialize, live in retirement, shut oneself up, seclude oneself, stand *or* hold oneself aloof, hide out *(coll.)*, conceal oneself, lie low *(coll.)*, retire from sight.

HIDDEN, *adj.* Concealed, clouded, covered, cloaked, veiled, close, sealed, withdrawn, unobserved, lying hid, out of view, secreted, disguised, unavowed, overlaid, cloistered, blotted, snug, deep, impenetrable, eclipsed, unseen, screened, unsuspected, opaque, in ambuscade, intercepted, secluded, subterranean, lurking, latitant, clandestine, private, suppressed, blind, covert, occult, latent, abstruse, unrevealed, unsolved, untold, imperceivable, indiscernible, out of sight, delitescent, inert, incomprehensible, paradoxical, undecipherable, undisclosed, unknown, oracular, cryptic, hermetic, esoteric, inward, dark, unexposed, arcane, underground, underhand, potential, unheard of, surreptitious, sequestered, unsearchable, camouflaged, secret, masked, enshrouded, withheld, secured, in ambush, invisible, undetected, perdu, buried, symbolical, illegible, inexplicable, unintelligible, reticent, inscrutable, obscure, cabalistic, mystical, mysterious, recondite, mystic, imperceptible, imperspicuous, dim, vague, shrouded, shadowy, dormant, quiescent, caliginous, unapparent, enigmatical, supernatural, inconceivable, puzzling, hieroglyphic.

HIDE, *n.* Skin of the larger animals, pelt, coat, leather, fell, fur, jacket, integument *(Anat. and Zool.)*.

HIDE, *v.* 1. Prevent from being seen *or* discovered, conceal from sight, secrete, cover, suppress, store, hush, inter, stow away, overlay, couch, keep under a bushel, hoard, ensconce, closet, put in concealment, dissemble, harbor, seclude, entomb, cache, cavern, den, withhold, obstruct the view of, eclipse, bury, keep out of sight, protect, hush up, enwomb, shroud, shadow, hood, curtain, throw a veil over, darken, obscure, cloud, mask, disguise, screen, veil, shelter, adumbrate, wrap, envelop, camouflage, render invisible, keep in the shade, latentize, hugger-mugger.

2. Conceal from knowledge, keep secret, veil, obscure, mask, cloak, dissemble, secrete, keep clandestine, hoodwink, gloze, suppress, eclipse.

3. Lie hid, lie *or* be concealed, hibernate, conceal oneself, keep oneself out of sight, avoid notice, skulk, lie in wait, take refuge in a hiding

place, lie low, keep in the background, go underground, burrow, hedge, abscond, be withdrawn from view, lie in ambush, suffer eclipse, hide out (coll.), lie perdu, lie snug or close, dissocialize, rusticate, shut oneself up, stand or hold oneself aloof, seclude oneself, couch, lurk, keep out of the way, occultate, retire from sight, lie hid or hidden, go or stay in hiding, hermitize.

HIDEBOUND, adj. Conservative, narrow in opinion, rigid, bound, illiberal, stiff, creed-bound, stiff-necked, intolerant, insular, provincial, ultraconservative, prejudiced, dogmatic, strict, shackled, pedantic, pragmatic, zealotic, puritanical, smug, firm, rooted, settled, opinionated, immovable, parochial, oracular, self-assured, austere, deaf to advice or reason, arrogant, obdurate, impervious to reason, wedded to an opinion, obstinate, bigoted, intractable, uncompromising, arbitrary, prudish, opposed to change, absolute, fanatical, strait-laced, positive, hyperorthodox.

HIDEOUS, adj. 1. Frightening to the senses, horrible, repellent, offensive, homely, grotesque, ugly, shocking, grim, ghastly, horrid, dreadful, frightful, appalling, awful, repulsive, fell, odious, ogreish, abortive, terrifying, forbidding, monstrous, vile, loathsome, foul, sickening, disgusting, repugnant, unshapely, detestable, unsightly, gorgonian, putrid, fierce, gorgonesque, pestilential, grisly, mephitic, abhorrent, terrific, abominable, revolting, tremendous, cadaverous.

2. Shocking or revolting to the moral senses, detestable, odious, contemptible, execrable, damnable, dreadful, despicable, loathsome, unnatural, beastly, demoniac, ghastly, appalling, accursed, monstrous, foul, abominable, grim, grisly, vile, harrowing, sickening, horrifying, heinous, hateful, cruel.

HIDING, n. Place or means of concealment, refuge, concealment, corner, retreat, hideaway, ambuscade, secret place, seclusion, den, lair, cave, asylum, hermitage, cloister, act of concealing, recess, secretion, haven, mew, shelter, safehold, cover, sanctuary, rendezvous, hiding-place, hideout, hangout (sl.), retirement, covert, isolation, hole, ambush.

HIE, v. (Often reflexively with the personal pronoun) Hurry, run, hasten, speed, scamper, whisk, go in haste, go, scud, make haste, proceed with haste, lose no time, scurry, skip, flee, rush, fly, scoot (coll.), ride hard, scour, bolt, dart, bustle, clip, leap, go like lightning, spin, get over the ground, go on the double (coll.), scuttle, flit, hustle, career, bestir oneself, move quickly, rip (coll.), whiz, post, mend one's pace, spank, wing one's way, clap spurs to one's horse, cut along (coll.), bowl along, fly on the wings of the wind, skedaddle (sl.), outstrip the wind, skim, bundle, step (coll.), step along (coll.), take wing, pack off or away, trot, lope, make strides, make rapid strides, step on it (coll.), step lively (coll.), gallop, do some tall stepping.

HIERARCHY, n. Ecclesiastical government or governing body, hierocracy, theocracy, ecclesiastical officialdom.

HIERATIC, adj. Pertaining to priests or the priesthood, priestly, sacred, clerical, pastoral, divine, holy, devoted to sacred uses or office, consecrated, sacerdotal, ecclesiastic, ministerial, hierarchical.

HIEROGLYPH, HIEROGLYPHICS, n. 1. Hieroglyphic writing or symbol, hieratic writing, demot-

ic writing, ideograph, ideogram, rune, futharc or futhorc (Teut.).

2. Code, stenogram, cryptogram, cryptograph, secret symbol.

HIEROLOGY, n. Literature or learning regarding sacred things, sacred lore, hierography, hagiology, hagiography, theology, scriptures, saints' lives, church writing.

HIEROPHANT, n. Interpreter of sacred mysteries or esoteric principles, expounder of religious mysteries, explainer, minister, priest, presbyter, clergyman, revealer, discloser, expositor, teacher, preacher, divine, ecclesiastic, clerk, cleric, theologian.

HIGGLE, v. Haggle, bargain in a petty way, chaffer, be tedious in a bargain, cavil, cheapen, stickle for advantage, negotiate, hawk, peddle, underbid, drive a bargain, dicker, palter, truck, bid for, beat down, depreciate, discredit, find fault, disparage, peck at, belittle, quibble.

HIGH, adj. 1. Having a great or considerable reach or extent upward, lofty, tall, elevated, of great altitude, soaring, towering, extending to or from an elevation, supernal, cloud-topped, capital, alpine, peak, arduous, heaven-kissing, high-reaching, skyscraping, at its height or apex, in its zenith, long, far, uplifted, steep, imposing, aerial, mountained, cloud-touching, cloud-capped, remote from the equator.

2. Situated above the ground or some base, elevated, exalted, lofty, overlying, hovering, surmounting, perched, towering, eminent, uplifted, superior, raised, high-set, overlooking, commanding, upland, prominent, overtopping.

3. Intensified, exceeding the common degree or measure, strong, intense, energetic, extreme, full, of great amount (degree, force, etc.), violent, boisterous, inflamed, vehement, turbulent, powerful, intemperate, excessive, undue, beyond expectation, inordinate, unrestrained, uncurbed, unsuitable, inappropriate, unbridled, exorbitant, extravagant, unreasonable, exaggerated, immoderate, tumultuous.

4. Expensive, dear, costly, high-priced, exorbitant, precious, fancy, stiff (coll.), steep (coll.), extortionate, unreasonable, priceless, extravagant, inestimable, of great price, invaluable, valuable, excessive.

5. Produced by relatively rapid vibrations, a little sharp (above desired pitch; Mus.), acute in pitch (Mus.), sharp, shrill, high-toned, high-pitched, ear-piercing, ear-splitting, in the upper registers (Mus.), piercing, intense.

6. Elevated, eminent, distinguished, chief, principal, main, capital, mighty, proud, worshipful, princely, head, lordly, great, lofty, admirable, noble, exalted, dignified, preëminent, prominent, heaven-born, peerless, august, stately, strong, sublime, illustrious, important, rank-bearing, high-born, kingly, sovereign, queenly, titled, reputable, well-bred, thoroughbred, majestic, of the best, excellent, aristocratic, of rank, patrician, wellborn, aspiring, magnanimous, superior, glorious, imposing, grand, of exalted character or quality, ascendant, top, uppermost, leading, dominant, ruling, prime, cardinal, primary, handsome, first, foremost, paramount, imperial, prepotent, major, hegemonic, predominant, authoritative.

7. Of great consequence, important, grave, serious, urgent, signal, sad, significant, momentous, consequential, stirring, capital, stern, heavy, deep, far-reaching, importunate, essential, telling, sub-

stantial, considerable, notable, paramount, fundamental, earnest, ponderous, supreme, radical, crucial, clamorous, crying, pressing, vital, exigent, weighty, pregnant, insistent, trenchant, eventful, conspicuous, critical.

8. Haughty, arrogant, lofty, proud, proudhearted, swollen, lordly, supercilious, arbitrary, vain, tyrannical, ambitious, conceited, boastful, bloated, condescending, toplofty, flaunting, egotistical, forward, overweening, vainglorious, pretentious, puffed up, high-swelling, fastuous, ostentatious, bumptious, assuming, pompous, self-assertive, high-hat, stiff, purse-proud, high-handed, disdainful, contemptuous, stuck-up (coll.), stiff-necked, patronizing, wise in one's own conceits, insolent, proud-minded, boastful, inflated, self-glorious, blown, pretentious, swelled-headed.

9. Elated, merry, hilarious, flushed, rollicking, jolly, gleeful, mirthful, joyous, jovial, jocose, playful, waggish, cock-a-hoop, cheerful, jubilant, sportive, exultant, joyful, light-hearted, gay, ecstatic, delirious, in good or high spirits, in high feather, happy as a king, happy as a lark, rejoiced, transported, rhapsodic, hearty, enraptured, exuberant, overjoyed, riant, exhilarated; (the following in a coll. sense) excited with drink, intoxicated, foolish, fuddled, in liquor, in one's cups, inebriated, tipsy, merry, gay, happy, muddled, flustered, bemused, addled, bacchic, nappy, dizzy, mellow, tight (sl.), under the influence of liquor, unsteady.

10. Extreme in opinion or doctrine (esp. religious or political), unwavering, unbending, orthodox, conformable, doctrinal, standard, creedal, wonted, dogmatic, ex cathedra (Lat.), cathedral, received, unequivocal, uncompromising, undeviating, canonical, authoritative, of the faith, of the true faith, sound, firm, traditional, catholic, faithful, strict, reserved, fixed, established, prescriptive, conventional.

HIGHBORN, adj. Of high rank by birth, noble, well born, exalted, of good birth or family, royal, highbred, princely, patrician, aristocratic, thoroughbred, blue-blooded, of rank, of gentle blood, genteel, prince-like, gentle, silk-stocking.

HIGH-FLOWN, adj. 1. Elevated, proud, lofty, extravagant in aims or pretensions, etc., bloated, presumptuous, swollen, vain, haughty, magisterial, condescending, boastful, flaunting, grandiose, quixotic, ostentatious, conceited, inflated, highflying, overweening, consequential, swank or swanky (sl.), puffed up, assuming, contumelious, patronizing, uppish (coll.), highfalutin (coll.), precocious, would-be, arrogant, high, blown, mighty, blustering, self-important, supercilious, contemptuous, cavalier, toplofty, egotistic, pretentious, vainglorious, lordly.

2. (Of style, language, etc.) Extravagant, overdrawn, strained, pretentious, high-colored, bombastic, overdone, inflated, overwrought, hyperbolic, intemperate, extreme, rhapsodical, bizarre, fantastic, monstrous, gross, flagrant, egregious, magniloquent, orotund, fustian, showy, tumid, highflying, exaggerated, ecstatic, altisonant, mouthy, flaunting, flatulent, florid, affected, pompous, outré (Fr.), sesquipedalian, high-sounding, big-sounding, lexiphanic, highfalutin (coll.), glittering, flamboyant, Johnsonian, grandisonant, rhetorical, magisterial, grandiose, declamatory, outrageous, sententious, grandiloquent, turgid, overstrained, lofty, ornate.

HIGH-HANDED, adj. Overbearing, arbitrary, despotic, self-willed, harsh, oppressive, stringent, rig-

orous, arrogant, dictatorial, withering, grinding, pressing, imperious, disdainful, contemptuous, headstrong, self-assured, peremptory, saucy, tyrannical, autocratic, pompous, domineering, wilful, violent, inquisitorial, brash, high and mighty, ironhanded, inexorable, insolent, extortionate, assuming, severe, magisterial, contumacious.

HIGHLAND, n. 1. Elevated region, plateau, height, eminence, mountain, headland, tableland, spine, chine, crest, down, table, hill, ridge, vantage point or ground.

2. (Pl.) Mountainous region, uplands, heights, tableland, hilly country.

HIGH LIGHT, HIGHLIGHT, n. Conspicuous or striking part, important event (scene, etc.), focal point, memorable part, point of concentration, key, cream, gist, salt, keynote, outstanding or distinctive feature, cardinal point, prominent part or detail, spot of most intense light (Art), essence, salient point, issue, significant feature, essential, moment, principle, pith, kernel, fundamental, elixir, substance, cynosure, quintessence, trump card, central point, nucleus, core, sum and substance, basics, convergence.

HIGHLIGHT, v. Emphasize or make prominent, accentuate, accent, stress, give emphasis to, lay emphasis or stress upon, underline, punctuate, mark, make light or bright (Art), make the focal point, focus attention on, give (attach, ascribe) importance to, center attention on, make outstanding, feature (coll.), give prominence to, write in letters of gold, underscore.

HIGHLY, adv. 1. In or to a high degree, extremely, in a great degree, greatly, much, well, largely, vastly, quite, intensely, immensely, very much, exceedingly, incomparably, by far, eminently, immeasurably, supremely, considerably, fully, in great measure, acutely, extraordinarily, plenty (coll.), tremendously, no little, preëminently, very, richly, transcendently.

2. With high appreciation or praise, commendingly, well, with regard, with esteem, respectfully, with approbation, with deference, with respect, with credit, graciously, favorably, approvingly, flatteringly, lavishly, in favor of, appreciatively, deferentially.

HIGH-MINDED, adj. 1. Having or showing high, exalted principles or feelings, noble, honorable, magnanimous, lofty, gallant, princely, upright, righteous, reputable, manly, worthy, estimable, guileless, veracious, uncorrupt, respectable, open, pure, sans peur et sans reproche (Fr.), moral, tolerant, just, conscionable, fair, principled, unselfish, philanthropic, scrupulous, conscientious, spiritual, firm in principle, high-toned, dispassionate, square-dealing, even-handed, heroic, liberal, disinterested, uninfluenced, truthful, sincere, candid, trustworthy, praiseworthy, sterling, meritorious, aboveboard, law-loving, law-abiding, equitable, square-shooting, charitable, clean, impartial, admirable, square, good, reasonable, true-dealing, right-minded, creditable, ethical, elevated, great-minded, chivalrous, generous, stately, refined, straightforward, straight-shooting.

2. Proud, arrogant, lofty, haughty, fastuous, big, puffed up, supercilious, stiff, contemptuous, aloof, distant, hard, hoity-toity, overbearing, assuming, pompous, high and mighty, grandiloquent, inflated, wise in one's own conceits, self-satisfied, self-glorious, peacockish, prideful, high, vainglorious, lordly, self-important, overproud, high-flown, high-handed, vain, magisterial, stiff-

necked, egotistical, swollen, imperious, overweening, toplofty *(coll.)*, uppity *(coll.)*, high-hat *(sl.)*,
domineering, arbitrary, presumptuous, ostentatious, consequential, conceited, boastful, pretentious, snobbish, condescending, self-sufficient,
snooty *(coll.)*, belittling, gasconading, flaunting,
bragging, intolerant, vilipenditory, oppressive,
priggish, cocky *(coll.)*, remote, inaccessible, unapproachable, know-it-all, self-opinionated.

HIGH-PRESSURE, *adj.* 1. Having *or* involving
a pressure above the normal, under compression,
high-powered, forceful, powerful, potent, dynamic, vigorous, puissant, strong, compressed.

2. Vigorous, persistent, intense, strenuous, energetic, forcible, compelling, peremptory, compulsive, powerful, importunate, high-powered, high-
geared, enterprising, dynamic, vigorous.

HIGH-PRICED, *adj.* High, costly, dear, expensive, exorbitant, precious, fancy, valuable, excessive, of great price, inestimable, priceless, extravagant, invaluable, extortionate, stiff *(coll.)*, steep
(coll.), unreasonable.

HIGHROAD, *n.* 1. Main road, thoroughfare, highway, avenue, artery, street, boulevard, turnpike,
causeway, royal road, coach road, state highway,
King's or Queen's highway, speedway, route, expressway, public road, place, beaten way, broad
way, parkway.

2. Easy *or* certain course, broad road, wide
gate, comfortable way, certainty, inevitability,
line of least resistance, inside track *(coll.)*, cinch
(sl.), conformity, the way of submission, laissez
faireism, idleness, apathy.

HIGH SCHOOL, *n.* Secondary school, upper
grades, intermediate school, preparatory school,
trade school, vocational school, seminary, academy, high *(coll.)*, junior high *(coll.)*, junior high
school, lycée *(Fr.)*, Gymnasium *(Central Europe,
esp. Germany)*.

HIGH-SOUNDING, *adj.* Having an imposing *or*
pretentious sound, artificial, swelling, high-flown,
stilted, grandiloquent, declamatory, pompous,
pretentious, altisonant, big-sounding, bombastic,
unctuous, self-righteous, canting, pharisaical, hypocritically devout *or* pious, sanctimonious, theatrical, insincere, unnatural, ostentatious, flashy-
mannered, affected, pedantic, tartufian, extravagant, overdrawn, strained, magniloquent, orotund,
tumid, showy, fantastic, rhapsodical, inflated,
overwrought, high-colored, hyperbolic, intemperate, flagrant, gross, monstrous, ecstatic, flatulent,
florid, lexiphanic, glittering, magisterial, sententious, turgid, grandisonant, Johnsonian, grandiose,
sesquipedalian, exaggerated, lofty, flamboyant,
highfalutin *(coll.)*, mouthy, flaunting, ornate.

HIGH-SPIRITED, *adj.* Having a high, proud *or*
bold spirit, mettlesome, brave, resolute, high-mettled, fiery, daring, bold, valiant, doughty, game,
courageous, plucky, gritty, lion-hearted, persevering, bent on, resolved, enterprising, earnest, stout,
hardy, stout-hearted, unalarmed, unblenching, confident, heroic, high-strung, ardent, proud, unfaltering, passionate, vehement, headstrong, quick,
sensitive, hasty, unawed, undismayed, rash, wilful, fervent, keen, zealous, eager, avid, venturesome, strong-willed, audacious, fearless, spirited,
intrepid, gallant, jubilant, tenacious, unflinching,
adventurous, undaunted, unappalled.

HIGH-STRUNG, *adj.* At *or* of great tension, nervous, strung to a high pitch, in a state of high tension, sensitive, startlish, quick, impatient, neurot-

ic, unquiet, moody, skittish, agitated, intolerant,
uneasy, restless, peevish, mettlesome, febrile, feverish, tremulous, jittery *(sl.)*, irritable, irascible,
wrought-up, passionate, easily frightened, high-
mettled, excitable.

HIGH-TONED, *adj.* 1. High in tone *or* pitch,
high-pitched, piercing, shrill, treble, clarion-
voiced, ear-rending, trumpet-toned, ear-splitting,
ear-piercing, sharp, acute.

2. Having high principles, dignified, lofty, noble, august, honorable, stately, magnanimous, estimable, ingenuous, creditable, high-minded,
princely, superior, majestic, ennobled, elevated,
elegant, respectable, ethical, right-minded, gallant,
upright, reputable, worthy, veracious, uncorrupt,
pure, open, moral, just, fair, conscionable, spiritual, truthful, uninfluenced, candid, praiseworthy,
meritorious, sterling, clean, good, square, great-
minded, elevated, straightforward, straight-shooting, aboveboard, equitable, law-abiding, law-loving, sincere, disinterested, dispassionate, scrupulous, principled.

HIGHWAY, *n.* Highroad, main road, public way,
street, place, course, waterway, fairway, channel,
track, thoroughfare, way, broad way, artery,
route, beaten way, seaway, canal, communication,
speedway, parkway, expressway, boulevard, turnpike, causeway, coach road, royal road, King's *or*
Queen's highway, state highway, public road,
avenue, road, path, ocean *or* sea lane.

HIGHWAYMAN, *n.* Robber on the highway *(esp.
on horseback)*, brigand, footpad, hijacker, pillager,
highway robber, holdup *(sl.)*, stick-up *(sl.)*, holdup man *(sl.)*, strong-arm man, tramp, filibuster,
desperado, road agent *(coll., chiefly Western U.
S.)*, knight of the road, outlaw, marauder, bandit,
freebooter, nighthawk *(coll.)*, thief, picaroon,
stick-up man.

HIKE, *v.* 1. Tramp, march, journey, travel on
foot, ramble, hoof it *(coll.)*, leg it *(coll.)*, walk,
wander, roam, rove, trudge, peripateticate.

2. *(Sometimes with UP)* Move with a jerk,
raise suddenly, draw spasmodically, hitch, tug,
limp, hobble, twitch, halt, inch along, jack up
(coll.).

HILARIOUS, *adj.* Gay, cheerful, merry, noisy,
boisterous, mirthful, lively, jolly, in high spirits,
sportive, jocund, effervescent, jovial, joyful, exhilarated, joyous, elated, playful, gleeful, excited,
frolicsome, highly amusing, riotous, jubilant, vociferous, gamesome, larking, convivial, droll, rollicking, sprightly, uproarious, cock-a-hoop, exuberant, blithe, vivacious, exultant, felicitous.

HILARITY, *n.* Gaiety, cheerfulness, merriment,
jollity, exhilaration, high spirits, jocundity, levity,
jubilation, heyday, revelry, boisterousness, merrymaking, jubilee, rejoicing, exultation, festivity,
vivacity, felicity, sport, noise, liveliness, celebration, ecstasy, jollification, pleasantry, enthusiasm,
joviality, mirth, glee, joyousness, laughter, racket,
amusement, playfulness, blithesomeness, Homeric laughter, sportiveness, fun, noisy sport.

HILL, *n.* Eminence, elevation, rising ground, ascent, mount, rise, hillock, incline, vantage point
or ground, hummock, knap, barrow, dune, protuberance, mountain, heap *(of earth, etc.)*, monticle, bluff, mound, acclivity, upland, knoll, spine,
chine, slope, climb, grade, foothill, steep, ridge,
down, upgrade, downgrade, declivity, bank, tor,
pitch, ramp, kop *(S. Afr.)*, kopje *(S. Afr.)*, Acropolis, monadnock *(Phys. Geog.)*, esker *(Geol.)*,

butte (*West. U. S. and Can.*), summit, anthill, highland, cliff, talus (*Geol.*), monticule, promontory, holt (*chiefly Poet.*), hillside, hilltop, swell, height.

HILLOCK, *n.* Mound, small hill, slight elevation, rise, swell, dune, knoll, knob, bank, barrow, knap, monticle, heap (*of earth, etc.*), hummock, esker (*Geol.*), kopje (*S. Afr.*).

HILT, *n.* Handle (*of a weapon*), haft, shaft, shank, grip, grasp, hold, helve.

HIND, *adj.* Situated in the rear *or* at the back, back, hinder, after, posterior, hindmost, posterial, dorsal, last, aft (*Naut.*), aftermost, rearmost, aftmost (*Naut.*), stern (*Naut.*), postern, hindermost, posticous (*Bot.*), caudal, gluteal, rearward, rear, hindhand, astern (*Naut.*), terminal, ultimate, abaft (*Naut.*), posteriormost, final, behind.

HINDER, *adj.* Situated at the rear *or* back, posterior, rear, hind, back, seat, rump, fundamental (*hum.*), after, hindmost, dorsal, posterial, rearmost, aftermost, hindermost, posteriormost, hindhand, gluteal, caudal, rearward.

HINDER, *v.* Prevent (*from acting or taking place*), interrupt, retard, check, thwart, delay, bar, restrain, hamper, arrest, trammel, obstruct, encumber, deadlock, clash with, antagonize, hold from *or* back, be an obstacle *or* impediment to, control, save, frustrate, inhibit, shorten, exclude, counterwork, slacken, clog *or* scotch the wheels, snub, hamstring, cross, embarrass, oppose, counteract, curb, defer, postpone, repress, foil, block, incommode, choke off, slow down, stem, stall, traverse, conflict with, shackle, bring to a stand *or* standstill, be *or* play at cross-purposes, discommode, limit, keep in *or* within bounds, circumscribe, filibuster, go against, hold up, dam, forestall, cramp, deter, resist, belate, prohibit, withhold, hedge, baffle, balk, preclude, checkmate, clog, stop, impede, forbid, hang fire, handicap, cause to delay, smother, keep under, stanch, set one's face against, repulse, repel, rein in, tie one's hands, bind *or* tie hand and foot, restringe, occlude, pinion, trap, throttle, countervail, disappoint, keep down, spike, disallow, silence, spoil, invalidate, annul, cancel out, neutralize, offset, vitiate, put a spoke in one's wheels, gag, muzzle, hobble, bridle, fetter, constrict, cage, deprive, choke, suspend, clip one's wings, set *or* pit against, fly in the face of, stalemate, keep back, render difficult, taboo, contravene, detain, stay, obviate, put back, interfere, cut off.

HINDMOST, *adj.* Hind, rear, last, aftermost, hindermost, last-minute, eleventh-hour, back, ultimate, terminal, posterior, rump, rearward, gluteal, caudal, posteriormost, after, rearmost, tail, hindhand, hinder, aft (*Naut.*), stern (*Naut.*), astern (*Naut.*), abaft (*Naut.*), behind, final.

HINDRANCE, *n.* Impedition, stoppage, restriction, cohibition, retardation, retardment, forbiddance, oppilation, snag, catch, disallowance, enjoining, stopper, constraint, balk, injunction, limitation, trammel, bridle, proscription, embargo, prohibition, preclusion, barricade, obstruction, curb, difficulty, ban, stop, impediment, barrier, bar, estoppel (*Leg.*), prevention, stumbling block, block, obstacle, repression, restraint.

HINGE, *n.* Articulated joint, articulation, pivot, knee, elbow, flap, joint.

HINGE, *v.* Be occasioned by, be produced by, turn upon, be due to, germinate from, result from, follow from, accrue from, sprout from, depend,

pivot, bud from, arise from, spring from, originate in, come from, hang, hang upon, rest on, flow from, emanate from, revolve around, issue from, turn upon, ensue from.

HINT, *n.* Suggestion, implication, intimation, inkling, clue, tip, trace, suspicion, innuendo, allusion, symptom, sign, jog, mark, evidence, prompter, supposition, implied warning, idea, notion, reminder, insinuation, signification, tinge, connotation, bare suggestion, impression, word in the ear, vague knowledge, glimmering, scent, gleam, token, omen, prefigurement, broad hint, gentle hint, inference, flea in the ear, monition, cue, reference, whisper, taste, memorandum, premonitor, denotation, augury, foretoken, tip-off (*coll.*), pointer (*coll.*), smattering, premonition, word to the wise, mnemonic device, subtle communication, memento, touch, observation, manifestation, indirection, slight knowledge, indication, subaudition.

HINT, *v.* (*Sometimes fol. by* AT) Suggest, give a hint of, make indirect suggestion, intimate, allude to, imply, insinuate, refer to, signify, indicate, infer, make an allusion to, connote, breathe, whisper, jog the memory, notice, tip off (*coll.*), warn, fish for, angle for, cause to remember, advise, apprise, remind, prompt, broach, advert to, wink, tip the wink (*coll.*), prefigure, foreshadow, adumbrate, mention, give an inkling of, inform by indirection, put a flea in one's ear, implicate, glance at, impart, acquaint one with.

HIP, *n.* Haunch, coxa (*Anat.*), huckle, innominate (*of the bones ilium, ischium and pubis*), lumbar region, fundament, posterior, rump, buttocks, ham, gluteal region, crupper, croup, hindquarters, butt, breech.

HIPPODROME, *n.* Circus, arena, structure for equestrian performances, stadium, bowl, turf, coliseum, big top, lists, tiltyard, racecourse (*Gk. Antiq.*), gymnasium, palaestra, Colosseum.

HIRE, *n.* Wages, salary, pay, rent, bribe, remuneration, fee, stipend, compensation, cost, charge, quotation, fare, income, receipts, profit, gain, toll, perquisite, payment, reward, allowance, freight, emolument, price of corruption, recompense, cartage, salvage, porterage, haulage, dockage (*Naut.*), freightage, ferriage, ballastage (*Law*), earnings, amount, figure, scot (*Hist.*).

HIRE, *v.* 1. Engage the services of for hire, employ, take into service, take into one's employ, contract with, give employment to, retain, engage, enlist, appoint (*to a position*).
2. Engage the temporary use of for hire, rent, take a lease, sublease, subrent, charter, get, buy, lease, occupy, secure temporarily for pay, take (*by stated periods of time*).
3. (*Often fol. by* OUT) Grant the temporary use of *or* services of for a compensation, rent *or* rent out, charter, hack, lease, ship, let, grant a lease, sublease, sublet, subrent, demise (*Law*).
4. Pay for the desired action *or* conduct of, reward, bribe, obtain one's services by corruption, suborn, buy up, tip, palm (*sl.*), oil, grease (*sl.*), corrupt, buy off, graft, secure, square (*sl.*), fix (*coll.*), bring one round by bribery, grease the palm of (*sl.*).

HIRELING, *n.* One serving for hire (*usually in contempt*), mercenary, hired servant, hack, tool, venal henchman, flunky, instrument, myrmidon, hired soldier, employee, victim, parasite, pensionary, menial, adventurer, wageworker, toady, puppet, jackstraw, jackal, minion, Hessian, hired man *or* hand, condottiere *(It.)*, servant, factotum.

HIRSUTE, *adj.* Hairy, bristly, of, pertaining to *or* of the nature of hair, bushy, nappy, ciliated, pileous, downy, bearded, pubescent *(Bot., Zool.)*, hispid *(Bot., Zool.)*, whiskered, filamentose, filamentoid, bargate *(Bot.)*, bewhiskered, pilose, pappose, pappous, barbigerous, trichoid, strigate, cirrose, cirrous, setaceous, setarious, strigose *(Bot.)*, setose, setal, barbate, crinal, crinated, crinose, bristling, hispidulate, bristlelike, filiform, rough, coarse, villous, tomentose, tomentous, shaggy, awny, tufted, spiny, woolly, prickly, spiked, bristled, shagged, unshaven, unshorn, ciliate, crinate *(Bot., Zool.)*, hispidulous *(Bot., Zool.)*, filamentous, cirrate *(Zool.)*.

HISS, *n.* 1. Hissing *(esp. in disapproval)*, sibilation, sibilance, buzz, rasp, wheeze, fizzle, aspiration, sizzle, utterance of prolonged S-sound, whisper, sibilant sound, siffle *(Med.)*.

2. Expression of disdain *or* contempt, scoffing, ridicule, mockery, catcall, mock, taunt, scoff, flout, twit, jeer, fling, gibe, fleer, sneer, snicker, razz *(sl.)*, outcry, clamor, hue and cry, hoot, derision, raspberry *(sl.)*, Bronx cheer *(sl.)*.

HISS, *v.* 1. Make *or* emit sharp prolonged sound of the letter S, rasp, buzz, wheeze, whiz, whir, shrill, fizzle, sizzle, utter with a hiss, aspirate, sibilate, seethe, boil, fizz, whistle.

2. Express disapproval *or* contempt by a hissing sound, flout, snort, cry down, laugh to scorn, give the raspberry *or* Bronx cheer *(sl.)*, point the finger of scorn, scoff, point at, disdain, ridicule, scout, condemn by hisses, snicker, jeer, gibe, twit, taunt, mock, niggle, deride, revile, catcall, gird, fling, razz *(sl.)*, show dislike, spit, hoot, fleer, damn, sneer, goose *(Theatr. sl.)*.

HISTORIAN, *n.* Expert in *or* authority on history, writer of history, chronicler, annalist, compiler, recorder, reporter, historiographer, biographer, chronographer, paleologist, archaeologist, medievalist, Egyptologist, Assyriologist, archivist, scribe, antiquary, sagaman, memorialist, storyteller, narrator, antiquarian, logographer *(Gk. Antiq.)*.

HISTORICAL, *adj.* Relating to *or* concerned with history *or* historical events, well-known as, part of the past, important in history, historic, actual *(as opposed to legendary or fictional)*, pertaining to *or* of the nature of history, constituting history, verifiable, confirmed, dealing with *or* treating of history, narrated *or* mentioned in history, belonging to the past, archival, factual, traditional, recorded, reliable, real, past, true, prior, authentic, former, obsolete, bygone, extinct, storied, narrative, descriptive, depictive, biographical, autobiographical, delineatory, memorable, commemorated, documented, ancient, chronicled, supported by evidence.

HISTORY, *n.* 1. Branch of knowledge dealing with past events, record and explanation of the steps of human progress, study of the character and significance of events, record of past events *(esp. human)*, relation of growth and development of human life, chronology, interpretation of human events.

2. Continuous systematic written narrative of the past of a particular people, country, period, person, *etc. (actual or fictional)*, account, relation, narration, record, story, recital, chronicle, biography, memoirs, saga, novel, legend, tale, yarn, romance, journal, epic, fortunes, experiences, confessions, minutes, yearbook, annual, auto-

biography, genealogy, register, review, summary, ana, retelling, recapitulation, depiction, delineation, ledger, narrative, annals, anecdote, rehearsal, transactions, adventures, historiette, exposition, proceedings, daybook, public record, archive, portrayal, diary, log, résumé, memorabilia, representation, unfolding of events.

3. The aggregate of past events, tradition, former times, yesterday, old days, race memory, bygone days *or* times, unalterable fact, water over the dam, water under the bridge, days *or* times of old *or* yore, old *or* olden times, yesteryear, the past, *fait accompli (Fr.)*.

4. A past worthy of record *or* out of the ordinary, saga, tale, fabulous past, notoriety, striking memories, perilous journey, extraordinary series of experiences.

5. Systematic account of natural phenomena, record of observations, scientific treatise, life story, life cycle, monograph, report, thesis, dissertation.

HISTRIONIC, *adj.* 1. Of *or* pertaining to actors *or* acting, histrionical, stagelike, dramatic, theatrical, tragic, comic, tragicomic, vaudevillian, legitimate, operatic, farcical, scenic, make-believe, Thespian, buskined, cothurned, melodramatic, dramaturgic.

2. Artificial, affected, theatrical, deceitful, histrionical, pompous, mannered, spectacular, extravagant, claptrap, theatric, stagy, false, insincere, overacted, spurious, pretentious, unnatural, fustian, orotund, mouthy, ostentatious, grandiloquent, high-sounding, melodramatic, forced, showy, overwrought.

HISTRIONICS, *n., pl.* 1. Dramatic representation, theatricals, acting, the stage, the theater, dramatic art, dramaturgy, dramatism, performing, Thespian art, theatercraft, histrionicism, stagecraft, melodramatics, dramaticism.

2. Artificial behavior (speech, *etc.*) for effect, theatricism, affectation, show, false show, display, pretension, parade, front *or* false front *(coll.)*, theatricalism, airs, dissembling, ostentation, fanfaronade, veneer, gloss, lip homage *or* service, humbug, fake, make-believe, gaudery, acting, glitter, inflation, orotundity, pretense, pomposity, hypocrisy, melodramatics, uncontrolled emotion.

HIT, *n.* 1. Impact, stroke, blow, shock, brunt, bump, clash, collision, fillip, buffet, cuff, box, tap, carom, prick, slug, dint, thwack, rap, slam, thump, jab, pelt, punch, bang, chop, cut, clip *(coll.)*, bat *(coll.)*, whack, smack, plunk *(coll.)*, spank, paste *(sl.)*, wallop *(coll.)*, plug *(sl.)*, lick *(coll.)*, stab, swat *(coll.)*, smash *(coll.)*, clout *(coll.)*, crack *(coll.)*, crash, appulse, douse *(sl.)*, poke, dig, belt *(sl.)*, whop *(coll.)*, sock *(sl.)*, slap.

2. Successful stroke, performance *or* production, fortune, boon, hazard, lucky stroke, lucky venture, success, find, providence, godsend, profit, gain, luck, coincidence, prosperity, sensation, chance, good stroke, windfall, felicity, piece of good luck *or* fortune, master stroke, trump card, feat, go, coup, blessing, opportunity, striking *or* sensational success, ten-strike *(coll.)*, smiles of fortune, fluke *(sl.)*, bold stroke, triumph, victory, smash *(sl.)*, sellout, best seller.

3. Stroke of satire *or* censure, *etc.*, effective *or* telling expression *or* saying, happy remark, home thrust, pertinent *or* appropriate remark, coup, gibe, comeback *(sl.)*, sarcasm, apt expression, felicity, trump card, indignity, outrage, brickbat, quip, cut, slap, fling, verbal thrust, master stroke, well-chosen words, short answer, back answer,

slap in the face, aspersion, caustic remark, animadversion, wipe *(coll.)*, stricture, reprehension, insinuation, rude reproach, rap *(sl.)*, slam *(coll.)*, knock *(sl.)*, insult, cutting remark, adverse criticism, dig *(coll.)*.

HIT, *v.* 1. Deal a blow *or* stroke, bring forcibly into collision, strike, knock, come against with an impact, slap, smite, touch, cane, birch, strike together, impinge on (upon, against), collide with, slug, thump, bump, smash, shatter, devastate, pound, beat, cudgel, pat, buffet, clap, poke, whack, slam, club, cuff, box, bang, clout *(coll.)*, bat, belt *(sl.)*, jab, whop *(coll.)*, douse *(sl.)*, plug *(sl.)*, thrash, whip, spank, lace, lash, whale *(coll.)*, strap, scourge, flog, thresh, batter, pelt, larrup, lambaste *(sl.)*, paste *(sl.)*, soak *(sl.)*, sock *(sl.)*, tamp, baste, pommel, tan *(coll.)*, bastinado, trounce, swinge, flail, drub, flagellate, strike against, clip *(coll.)*, punch, dash, sway *(coll.)*, wallop *(coll.)*, switch, hurt, fustigate.

2. Succeed in striking, reach *(with missile, weapon, blow, etc.)*, shoot, stone, plug *(sl.)*, fell, kill, sink, pepper, pelt, riddle, bring down, drop, pour a broadside into, aim true, go straight, steer a straight course, make a beeline for, make a bull's-eye, go *or* send to the mark, cut down.

3. Touch effectively, affect severely, strike, abash, accuse, condemn, assail effectively and sharply, overwhelm, attack, vilify, revile, put in one's place, deal a deathblow to, baste, overcome, damn, strike at the root of, make an inroad into, rouse, blackball, arouse, kindle, provoke, smite, stir, shatter, fire, inflame, denounce, heat, foment, warm, boycott, quicken, pierce, hamstring, prostrate, quash, upset, crush, reproach, impugn, undo, quell, cripple, wound, knock *(coll.)*, rap *(sl.)*, criticize adversely, black-list, incite, blow the coals, stimulate, move, touch, thrill, blame, bring to bay, strike home, censure, devastate, impress, foil, thwart, discomfit, frustrate, assault, assail, charge.

4. Succeed in representing *or* producing exactly, bring off successfully, capture, find the key to, arrive at, discern, penetrate, arrest, seize, perfect, reproduce, effect, attain, execute, apprehend, articulate, catch, achieve, realize.

5. Agree with, suit exactly, concur, delight, touch agreeably, be concordant with, tally with, meet, dovetail with, gratify, tickle, be suitable to, be conformable to, fit, accord with, please, strike, appeal, correspond with, sympathize with, coincide with, square with, harmonize with, blend in with, be at one with, fall *or* chime in with, elicit a response, jibe with *(coll.)*.

6. *(Sometimes with* ON *or* UPON) Come *or* light upon, meet with, find, discover, chance upon, stumble on, encounter, learn, pitch upon, blunder upon, guess correctly, come in contact with, make out, espy, spy, descry, pick up, fall upon, detect, distinguish, recognize, spot *(coll.)*, find out, come across, burst upon.

7. *(With* OFF) Imitate, mimic, mock, depict, set forth, ape, mime, take off, impersonate, personify, caricature, simulate, represent, reproduce, personate, burlesque, travesty, pose as, characterize, portray, parody.

8. *(With* OFF) Improvise, invent, contrive, create, produce, strike off, originate, coin, fabricate, frame, devise, concoct, hatch, dream up *(sl.)*, think up *(sl.)*, turn out, make up.

HITCH, *n.* 1. A making fast as to something *(esp. temporarily)*, joining, fastening, connection, articulation, knot, elbow, hinge, joint, connective, coupling, copula, cable, chain, holdfast, suspend-

ers, garter, anchorage, moorings, clinch, clamp, hasp, buckle, coupler, guy, tie, bond, link, clasp, yoke, juncture, knee, pivot, bend *(Naut.)*.

2. Obstruction, obstacle, hindrance, catch, impediment, mishap, mischance, contretemps, check, interruption, complication, node, curb, stay, stop, brake, estoppal, intricacy, nodus, vexed question, knotty point, brunt, snag, crux, stress, rub, clog, paradox, hard nut to crack, barrier, hamper, drag, spoke, enigma, poser, thin ice, delicate ground, pinch, problem, puzzle, nonplus, restraint, disconcertion, stumbling block *or* stone, grit in the oil, spoke in one's wheel, Gordian knot, holdback, difficulty, dilemma, halt, quandary, involvement, perplexity, limitation, complexity, handicap, restriction, obstruction.

3. Hitching movement, jerk, hobble, hitching gait, jerking motion, faltering, twitching, limp, spasm, drag, haul, tug, strain, fidgeting, snaking *(coll.)*, staggering, pull, yank *(coll.)*, halt.

HITCH, *v.* 1. Make fast *(esp. temporarily)*, strap, fix, secure, string, lash, leash, truss, hook up *(coll.)*, bracket, clasp, clamp, couple, chain, shackle, fetter, hook, put in harness, yoke, bind, colligate, fasten together, attach, connect, tie, fasten, unite, clinch, string, pinion, moor, tether, harness, picket.

2. Move *or* draw something with a jerk, go by jerks, pull, hobble, limp, hop, tug, stop, strain, jog, pause, jolt, totter, haul, drag, shuffle, scuttle, raise with jerks, fidget, yank *(coll.)*, jerk, falter, stagger, flounce, snake *(coll.)*, halt, lag, shamble, linger.

3. *(Sometimes with* ON *or* UP) Become fastened *or* caught, catch, fasten oneself *or* itself to something, trap, snare, snag, become impaled, hook, ensnare, illaqueate, sniggle, get impeded, stick, get stopped.

HITHER, *adj.* 1. On *or* toward this side, nearer, closer, vicinal, adjacent, contiguous, adjoining, neighboring, nigh, proximal, propinquant.

2. Earlier, more remote, fore, anterior, antecedent, former, more ancient, previous, prior, precursory, preëxistent, foregoing.

HITHER, *adv.* To *or* toward this place, here in this place, this way, hitherward, forward, onward, on, to this vicinity, from elsewhere.

HITHERTO, *adv.* Till now, yet, until this time, up to this time, before this, beforetime, in time past, aforetime, ere now, then, once, once upon a time, already, some time ago *or* back, anciently, formerly, heretofore, latterly, before, to this *or* the present day, to this time, thus far.

HIVE, *n.* 1. Beehive, apiary, alvearium *(Lat.)*, alveary.

2. Swarm of bees, cloud of bees, swarm, colony, cluster of bees.

HOAR, HOARY, *adj.* 1. Gray *or* white with age, grizzly, ancient, elderly, advanced in years, venerable, aged, gray-haired, patriarchal, senile, anile *(fem.)*, declining, senescent, time-worn, canescent, vetust, superannuated, old, grizzled.

2. Frosty, frost-covered, frosted, rime-frosted, frost-riven, frost-bound, rime-damp, rime-laden, rimed, rime-covered, pruinous, pruinose.

HOAR, *n.* Hoarfrost, frost, rime frost, rime, pruinescence, hoariness.

HOARD, *n.* Hoarding, accumulation, heaping, gathering, store, wealth, garner, cumulation, repository, stockpile, pile, fund, provisions, reserve, supply, gleaning, crop, saving, collection, mass, harvest, quantity, profusion, abundance, amassment.

HOARD, *v.* Accumulate, lay up, acquire, husband, aggregate, cumulate, treasure up, agglomerate, collect, store, stow away, save, garner, reposit, harvest, get in, reservoir, bank, gather, pile, heap, stack, mass, amass, file away, cache, glean.

HOARSE, *adj.* 1. Shrill, husky, gruff, breathy, indistinct, throaty, croaking, dry, cracked, whispering.

2. Raucous, rough, grating, blatant, harsh, jarring, squawking, scratching, shrill, absonant, rasping, gruff, guttural, unmusical, discordant, piercing, strident.

HOAX, *n.* Humorous *or* mischievous deception, cheat, imposture, fraud, canard, ruse, absurd story, exaggerated tale, quiz, scheme, wile, device, false alarm, extravagant report, flam, bilk, counterfeit, fabrication, bunko, forgery, chouse *(coll.)*, flimflam, nonsense, cry of wolf, chicanery, hocuspocus, fake *(coll.)*, trepan, stratagem, swindle, bam *(sl.)*, gyp, bite, fob *(sl.)*, farfetched story, bunk, bull *(sl.)*, claptrap, fish story *(coll.)*, bubble, practical joke, humbug, trick, sell *(sl.)*, imposition, cock and bull story, fictitious story, take-in *(coll.)*, string, bosh *(coll.)*, fable, gloss, fiction, yarn *(coll.)*, concoction, thimblerig, sleight-of-hand trick, juggle, legerdemain, spoof *(sl.)*.

HOAX, *v.* Deceive, swindle, fool, hoodwink, beguile, cozen, sharp, defraud, gudgeon, bluff, guy *(coll.)*, spoof *(sl.)*, trepan, counterfeit, bunko, bunk, bilk, fob, mump, muzzle, dupe, thimblerig, pass off, fake *(coll.)*, put over *(sl.)*, chouse *(coll.)*, bite, impose on *or* upon, practice upon, play with, put on *or* upon, delude, betray, mock, chaff, gull, bam *(sl.)*, gouge *(coll.)*, do *(coll.)*, hocus-pocus *(coll.)*, gyp *(sl.)*, flimflam *(coll.)*, take in, kiddy *(sl.)*, kid *(sl.)*, sell *(sl.)*, come over *(coll.)*, come it over *(sl.)*, befool, victimize, mislead, bamboozle *(coll.)*, hocus, cheat.

HOBBLE, *n.* 1. Act of hobbling, uneven gait, hitch, jerk, drag, pull, hitching movement *or* gait, snaking *(coll.)*, stagger, toddle, retardation, jerking motion, spasm.

2. Rope (strap, *etc.*) used to hobble an animal, fetter, shackle, clog, check, curb, brake, drag, trammel, bond, gyve *(usually pl.)*.

HOBBLE, *v.* 1. Limp, walk lamely, lag, falter, proceed irregularly and haltingly, hitch, halt, jog, jolt, toddle, scuttle, stop, lumber, claudicate, shuffle, stagger, strain, flounce, snake *(coll.)*, pause, drag, tug, linger, shamble, hop.

2. Cause to limp, fasten together the legs of *(a horse, etc.)* to prevent free motion, trammel, lame, restrain, shackle, fetter, gyve, lash, strap, leash, truss, secure, hopple, stake out, tie, tie up, peg down *or* out, make fast, entrammel, gravel, pinion, picket, tether, bind, chain, hogtie.

3. Embarrass, impede, perplex, confuse, bewilder, nonplus, confound, detain, delay, baffle, disconcert, daze, block, addle, bar, disable, hock, hamstring, put out, barricade, deadlock, disqualify, clog *or* scotch the wheels, maim, unfit, invalidate, counteract, hinder, restrict, inhibit, interfere with, snub, hold in leash, hold *or* keep in check, hold *or* keep back, check, slacken, retard, cripple, clog, restrain, trammel, cramp, hamper, obstruct, interrupt, discommode, filibuster, undermine, unsinew, silence, weaken, depotentiate, muzzle, incapacitate, gravel *(coll.)*, curb, constrain, shackle, incommode.

HOBBY, *n.* 1. Favorite occupation (topic, *etc.*) pursued for amusement, avocation, leisure-time activity, diversion, relaxation, play, sport, craft, art, side line, pastime, caprice, whim, favorite pursuit, pet topic, specialty, whimsy, craze, bias, vagary, labor of love, fancy, divertissement, amusement, fun, game, entertainment, quest.

2. Hobbyhorse, stick with a horse's head, wooden horse, rocking horse.

HOBGOBLIN, *n.* Anything causing superstitious fear, bogy, specter, sprite, goblin, imp, ghost, ghoul, troll, spook, bad fairy, bugaboo, banshee, gnome, poker, *bête noire (Fr.)*, fetish, boggart, elf, ogre, gorgon, demon, Puck, Robin Goodfellow, bugbear, frightful apparition, mischievous sprite, Mumbo Jumbo, pygmy, bad peri *(Persian)*, kobold *(Ger. folklore)*, leprechaun *(Irish folklore)*, feefaw-fum.

HOBNOB, *v.* Associate on very friendly terms, be jolly companions, keep close company, drink together, be pot companions, be inseparable, fraternize, club together, consort with, be close friends, confabulate, collaborate, commune, coöperate, team, concur, gossip, chat, confab *(coll.)*, clink glasses, hit it off *(coll.)*, cotton to *(coll.)*.

HOBO, *n.* Wandering worker, tramp, vagrant, vagabond, wanderer, itinerant, nomad, roamer, rover, loafer, gypsy, stray, bum *(sl.)*, progger, outcast, wastrel, Romany, refugee, migrant, trekker, fugitive, drifter *(coll.)*, floater *(coll.)*, landlouper, turnpiker, stiff, bo *(sl.)*, Arab, street Arab, vagabondager, prodigal, sponger, knight of the road, beachcomber, idler, rambler, Wandering Jew, vag *(sl.)*, Okie.

HOCUS, *v.* 1. Cheat, deceive, hoax, play a trick on, swindle, hoodwink, sharp, cozen, defraud, bluff, spoof *(sl.)*, gouge *(coll.)*, bamboozle *(coll.)*, victimize, fool, befool, mislead, sell *(sl.)*, gyp *(sl.)*, flimflam *(coll.)*, take in, come over *(coll.)*, come it over *(sl.)*, put on *or* upon, gull, practice upon, chaff, mock, betray, bite, chouse *(coll.)*, impose on *or* upon, fob, bunk, bunko, counterfeit, bilk, mump, dupe, gudgeon, guy *(coll.)*, trepan, thimblerig, fake *(coll.)*, hocus-pocus *(coll.)*, beguile, muzzle, pass off, put over *(sl.)*, delude, bam *(sl.)*, do *(coll.)*, kid *(sl.)*, kiddy *(sl.)*.

2. Drug, adulterate, stupefy with drugged liquor, dope *or* dope up *(sl.)*, corrupt, treat, alter, contaminate, doctor *or* doctor up *(coll.)*, deacon, numb, benumb, narcotize, deaden, paralyze, render insensible *or* incompetent, sophisticate.

HOCUS-POCUS, *n.* 1. Formula used in conjuring *or* incantation, chant, charm, spell, magic spell, bewitchment, mumbo jumbo, philter, magic words *or* formula, glamour, demonifuge, Open sesame!, voodooistic charm, abracadabra, invocation, conjuration, wanga *(W. Indies and South. U. S.)*.

2. Juggler's trick, sleight of hand, legerdemain, sorcery, conjuring, conjuration, magic, glamour, deception of the eye, jugglery, feint, shift, dodge, blind, hokey-pokey *(coll.)*, spoof *(sl.)*, hankypanky *(coll.)*, prestidigitation.

3. Cheat, deception, hoax, trick, delusion, artifice, sham, imposture, imposition, juggle, trickery, deceit, humbug, stuff, trash, fudge, gyp, swindle, stuff and nonsense, rant, bosh *(coll.)*, jargon, hogwash *(coll.)*, tommyrot *(sl.)*, thimblerig, cardsharping, bunko, confidence game, stratagem, moonshine, twiddle-twaddle, twaddle, trumpery, flummery, balderdash, rubbish, poppycock *(coll.)*, fraud, buncombe, dishonesty, sell *(coll.)*, fake *(coll.)*, cunning, con game *(sl.)*, circumvention,

chouse *(coll.)*, piece of finesse, empty talk, fiddle-de-dee, fiddle-faddle *(coll.)*, flapdoodle, *(coll.)*.

HOCUS-POCUS, *v.* Play tricks on *or* with, trap, trip up, fool, befool, dupe, practice on one's credulity, gull, philter, snare, take in, cheat, hoax, swindle, deceive, cozen, bluff, gouge *(coll.)*, delude, gudgeon, chaff, come it over *(sl.)*, gyp *(sl.)*, bamboozle *(coll.)*, sharp, hoodwink, defraud, victimize, flimflam *(coll.)*, put on *or* upon, mock, betray, fob, bunk, guy *(coll.)*, beguile, bam *(sl.)*, do *(coll.)*, muzzle, bam *(sl.)*, pass off, trepan, thimblerig, bunko, counterfeit, betray, chouse *(coll.)*, bite, practice upon, come over *(coll.)*, bluff, spoof *(sl.)*, mislead, sell *(sl.)*, impose on *or* upon, bilk, dupe, mump, fake *(coll.)*, kiddy *(sl.)*, put over *(sl.)*.

HOD, *n.* Portable trough *or* tray for carrying *(mortar, bricks, etc.)*, coal scuttle, small bucket, supporter, carrier, temporary container.

HODGEPODGE, *n.* Heterogeneous mixture, medley, jumble, mixture, stew, gallimaufry, salmagundi, farrago, olio, mess, mélange, confused mass, potpourri, ollapodrida, hotch-potch, miscellany, combination, commixture, concoction, intermixture, conglomeration, varied assortment, aggregate, compilation, composite, accumulation, mosaic, confusion, hash, mix, chowchow, patchwork, omnium-gatherum, Noah's ark, salad, what the cat brought in *(coll)*, tumble, muddle.

HOE, *v.* Use a hoe, dig, cultivate, scrape, harrow, weed, rake, scratch, till, scuffle.

HOG, *n.* Swine, sow, pig, boar, peccary, grunter, porker, barrow, piggy, shoat, shote, babirusa, hoggerel, razorback.

HOGGISH, *adj.* 1. Like *or* befitting a hog, swinish, piggish, porcine, beastly, filthy, omnivorous, dirty, unclean, unwashed, foul, offensive, besmirched, besmeared, drabbled in the mud, defiled, squalid, all-devouring, brutish.

2. Gluttonous, selfish, sordid, mean, greedy, open-mouthed, rapacious, vile, sensual, crapulous, covetous, insatiable, voracious, grasping, ravenous, devouring, overfed, overgorged, intemperate, Apician, gormandizing, edacious, overindulged.

HOGTIE, *v.* Tie as a hog is tied *(all four feet together)*, hobble, trammel, restrain, fetter, lash, shackle, gyve, truss, tie up, make fast, entrammel, bind, strap, prevent motion, chain, pinion.

HOGWASH, *n.* 1. Refuse given to hogs, swill, garbage, waste, draff, offal.

2. Any worthless stuff, scourings, scum, rubbish, trash, debris, refuse, waste, litter, shoddy, leavings, sweepings, lees, slag, chaff, rags, bones, dregs, scraps, orts, offal, garbage, riffraff, truck *(coll.)*, dross.

HOI POLLOI, *n.* *(Gr.)* The mob, the vulgar herd, the herd, ragtag and bobtail, rout, proletariat, riffraff, the multitude, commonalty, commonage, rabble, every Tom, Dick and Harry, the crowd, the many, rank and file, the masses.

HOIST, *n.* 1. Apparatus for hoisting, elevator, derrick, dredge, sling, crane, lift, tackle, lifter, gin, winch, capstan, jackscrew, jack, windlass, lever, dumbwaiter, erecter.

2. Act of hoisting, lift, boost, elevation, erection, rearing, weighing, heave, exaltation, upcast, upthrust, upheaval, raising.

HOIST, *v.* Raise *(esp. by mechanical appliance)*, lift, raise up, elevate, boost, upraise, uplift, sway, sling, whip, weigh, heave, bear up, take up, set up, stick up, uprear, uphoist, mount, crane, jack,

winch, windlass, exalt, bear aloft, unfurl *(a flag, banner, etc.)*, break out *(a flag, banner, etc.)*, rear, erect.

HOLD, *n.* 1. Act of holding fast *(physical)*, manner of holding, grasp, grip, clutch, embrace, bite, retention, clasp, anchorage, foothold, seizure, fulcrumage, leverage, stance, strangle hold, stand, iron grip, viscidity, viscosity, stickiness, tenacity, cohesiveness, glutinousness, adhesiveness, purchase, prehension, gripe.

2. Something to hold by *or* grasp for support, stay, prop, handle, anchor, grasp, staff, cane, crutch, rod, stave, brace, support, pole, shaft, hilt, hasp, column, fence, wall, pillar, crook, rail, railing, banister, balustrade *(Archit.)*.

3. That which holds something, receptacle, support, bracket, lock, container, utensil, enclosure, urn, bowl, box, case, crate, carton, rack, crib, sheath, socket, chest, till, coffer, casket, treasury, keg, jar, bursary, pot, basin, vault, tank, sconce, vat, crypt, safe-deposit box, cash register, money box, strongbox, strongroom, vessel, stronghold.

4. Nonphysical bond *or* force, restraint, constraint, control, possession, dominating influence, clutches, custody, tenure, talons, fangs, ascendancy, preponderance, reign, sway, potency, persuasive force, influence, mastery, dominion, grip, gripe, sovereignty, keeping, weight, pressure, authority, dominance, headship, leadership, hand, detention, claim, standing, rooting, supremacy, corner, monopoly, upper *or* whip hand, inside track *(coll.)*, tenancy, attachment, edge *(coll.)*, power, strangle hold, stable position, footing, advantage, vantage-ground, command, rule, interest.

5. Prison, place of confining, cellar, jail, keep, tower, confinement, prison cell, custody, bastille, black hole, dungeon, pound, limbo, den, cell, brig *(Naut.)*, penitentiary, guardhouse *(Mil.)*.

6. *(Naut.)* Interior of ship below decks, storage, cargo space, cavity, below, hole, brig, stokehold, bilge, compartment, below decks, bin.

HOLD, *v.* 1. Have *or* keep in the hand, cause to remain in a given situation *(position, relation)*, keep fast, grasp, clutch, seize, grip, gripe, clasp, retain, keep *or* maintain a grasp on, bear, support, sustain, hug, hold fast *or* tight, embrace, keep, corner, monopolize, tie, fasten, fix, keep close, palm, bind, pin, lock, nail, unite, hog *(sl.)*, rein, take, catch, clinch, clench, handle, carry, cling, keep a firm hold on, have an iron grip on, fasten upon, stay, mainstay, uphold, upbear, brace, buttress, prop, underset, bottom, base, found, shore up, bear up, shoulder, bolster up, underpin, underprop, pillow, cradle, riprap *(Masonry)*, ground, underbrace.

2. *(Sometimes with OFF)* Keep in specified state, relation, *etc.*, contain, keep from advance *or* attack, stop, stay, check, forestall, avert, deflect, hinder, prevent, repel, curb, arrest, withhold, halt, resist, suspend, keep at bay, foil, checkmate, obstruct, stave off, ward off, keep off, balk, scotch, circumvent, traverse, confound, fend off, repulse, oppose, counteract, sidetrack, turn aside, keep from gaining advantage, stand one's ground against, keep at arm's length, parry, stand siege, nip in the bud, thwart, draw off, frustrate, drive back, anchor, defeat, disconcert, neutralize, cancel, confuse, bewilder, baffle, annul, vitiate, exclude, proscribe, nullify, restrain, restrict, taboo, ban, forbid, disallow, interdict, shut out, warn off, stultify, run counter to, veto, prevail against, bar, blockade, block, deadlock, flummox *(sl.)*, faze

(coll.), filibuster, counterbalance, oppugn, withstand, be *or* play at cross-purposes, slam the door in one's face, barricade, contradict.

3. Assemble, call together, muster, gather, carry on, preside over, direct, administer, manage, discharge, officiate at, observe, celebrate, have, join in, take, call, meet with, conduct, convene, execute, bring about, pursue, bring together, engage in, prosecute.

4. *(Sometimes with* BACK *or* IN) Keep back from action, hinder, restrain, smother, check, curb, repress, suppress, detain, confine, control, hem in, cramp, enchain, limit, compel, impede, counteract, hold in check, restrict, restringe, inhibit, forbid, cohibit, disallow, embarrass, interrupt, interfere with, delay, deny, bar, table, shut up, shut in, imprison, bind, constrain, forbear, oppose, keep under, retain, contain, prohibit, hold in leash *or* leading strings, keep within bounds, pull *or* rein in, clip the wings of, hang like a millstone round one's neck, hobble, trammel, shackle, preclude, debar, cage, thwart, frustrate, strap, pinion, bridle, bind one hand and foot, jail, leash, manacle, tie one's hands, act as a drag, scotch, balk, cut the ground from under one, stand in the way of, take the wind out of one's sails, incarcerate, lock up *or* in, enthrall, hold in thrall, intern, impound, immure, entomb, pen, cloister, fetter, coop up, stop, block, slacken, retard, snub, hedge in, dam, keep under lock and key, circumscribe, discommode, incommode, interdict, embargo, hamper, handicap, encumber, hogtie, lash.

5. Have the ownership *or* use of, possess, have, occupy, keep as one's own, enjoy, derive title to, have by tenure *or* inheritance, maintain, tie up, fill, be in *(office),* own, reserve, retain, keep in possession, bear the responsibility of, be the possessor of, be possessed of, hold down *(sl.).*

6. Contain *or* be capable of containing, have a capacity for, take in, bear, comprehend, enclose, include, carry, stow, accommodate, compose, involve, incorporate, cover, comprise, subsume, take into consideration *or* account, entail, enumerate *or* number among, encircle, embody, reckon among, refer to, admit, receive, encompass, retain.

7. Have *or* keep in the mind, think, believe, entertain, bear in mind, assert, conceive, nurture, foster, be convinced of, receive, cherish, embrace, advocate, find congenial, be sure of, take in, accept, maintain, admit, harbor, presume, surmise, assume, posit, predicate, submit, propound, propose, take it, have it, bring forward, argue, concur in, affirm, persist in, trust, accredit, give faith to, give credence to, have *or* repose confidence in, confide *(hope, trust)* in, attach weight to, bet on, swear by, bank on *(coll.),* rely on, profess, be wedded to, apprehend, realize, rest assured in, see, find compatible, take as true, postulate.

8. Have *or* form an estimate of, regard, consider, judge, think, count, esteem, decide legally, observe, apprehend, infer, fear, realize, conceive, dare say, conjecture, view as, understand, be of the opinion, be afraid *(coll.),* suppose, assume, guess, surmise, imagine, fancy, suspect, be sure, be convinced, affirm, know, repute, reckon, account, deem, believe, entertain, conclude, deduce, think likely, gather, venture, take to be, look upon, set down as *or* for, see.

9. Regard with affection, retain in love *or* affection, love, like, think worlds *or* the world of, cherish, value, treasure, dote on, idolize, care for, bear love to, prize, fancy, adore.

10. *(Sometimes with* TOGETHER *or* UP) Remain *or* continue in a specified state, relation, *etc.,* stand, hold true *or* good, prove good, be valid, continue to exist, hang together, last, go on, be consistent, be in force, make sense, be permanent, not change, take its course, follow, be on foot, run, stand the test *or* trial, be tenable, perendinate, be sound, be common sense, be logically evident, hold water *(coll.),* remain, bear up, be confirmed *or* supported, be demonstrated *or* substantiated, prove its worth *or* merit, prove itself, abide, endure, be manifest *or* evident, linger on, be worthy *or* worth while, remain constant, spin out, be open, obtain, occur, be true, stand to reason.

11. *(Sometimes with* TOGETHER) Remain fast, adhere, cling, cleave, hang *or* grow together, grasp, hug, join, take hold of, stay affixed, cement, keep hold, attach, hang on, stick, be joined, cling like ivy, stick closer than a brother, cling like a bur, stick like wax, agglomerate, conglutinate, agglutinate, glue, stay put, close with, go with, remain attached, cohere, hold fast, stick like a wet shirt, stick like the paper on the wall, march with.

12. *(Sometimes with* OUT *or* ON) Maintain one's position against opposition, endure test *or* trial, stand, continue, persist, remain unbroken and unsubdued, carry on, keep on, resolve, will, manage, hold out, remain steadfast, purpose, be resolute, not fail, persevere, not give way, continue in resistance *or* action, steel oneself, grit one's teeth, set one's jaw, be firm, be fast, determine, go ahead, take one's stand, stand firm, stick to one's guns, stick at nothing, mean business, be obstinate, adhere resolutely, fight to the last ditch, die fighting, nail one's colors to the mast, take the bit in one's mouth *or* teeth, stand pat *(coll.),* oppose successfully, commit oneself to, not stick at trifles, not yield an inch, never say die, not give up, peg away *or* along, plod, plug *(coll.),* devote oneself to, keep at, stick out, hang on, not give way, set one's back against the wall, hold one's ground, set one's mind *or* heart upon, stand no nonsense, put one's foot down, die hard, keep to *or* maintain one's course, put (lay, set) one's shoulder to the wheel, buckle to.

13. Retain in keeping, not relinquish, defend, secure, refuse to give up, fight for, conceal, hide, reserve, guard, protect, care for, take care of, man, fortify, safeguard, cherish, screen, shelter, give (furnish, afford, supply, lend) support to, watch over, mind, nurse, foster, conserve, save, maintain, circumscribe, house, ensconce, support, shield, harbor, preserve.

14. Bind legally *or* morally, oblige, compel, drive, press, require, force, make, expect of one, constrain, make incumbent on, make one responsible, bring pressure to bear upon, place upon, coerce, dragoon, strong-arm *(coll.),* bind, make answerable, call for, bear upon.

15. *(Sometimes with* IN) Restrain *or* withhold oneself, cease *or* forbear intended *or* threatened action, stall, halt, stand, stop, stay, desist from, stick, quit, resist temptation, refrain, give up, rest, repose, pause, abandon, relax, leave off, discontinue, submit, renege *(coll.),* yield, waive, stay one's hand, spare, forgo, give over, not do *or* act, abstain, hang fire, pull up *or* stop short, break off, let alone, mark time, suspend action, let well enough alone, relinquish, stand aloof, let things take their course, live and let live, come to a

stand *or* standstill, slacken, throw in the sponge *(coll.)*.

16. *(Sometimes with* ON *or* TO) Maintain in being *or* action, push forward, prosecute, believe in, be resolute, sustain, be firm in, prolong, persist in, keep up, support, upbear, uphold, back up, follow, advance, adhere to, drag out, draw out, protract, go on with, conduct, be tenacious, be wont, discharge, execute, move *or* travel in a rut *or* groove, stick to, see through *(coll.)*, stay with, carry on, continue, justify, lead on, guide, head, steer, govern, help, aid, endorse, regulate, keep alive, keep going, assert, perpetuate, extend, follow through *or* up, plod, rest in, remain steadfast, be faithful to, direct, dispatch.

17. *(With* OUT *or* FORTH) Offer, propose, extend, present, proffer, tender, submit, invite, overture, stretch forth, propound, hold forth, put *or* place at one's disposal, advance, volunteer, broach, put forth *or* forward, make a motion, lay at one's feet, put in one's power, make possible, exhibit, represent.

18. *(With* FORTH; *often implying contempt)* Harangue, speak in public, lecture, make *or* deliver a speech, rant, spout *(coll.)*, sermonize, prelect, discourse, exposit, declaim, expound, preach, orate *(chiefly hum.)*, perorate, flourish, soapbox, stump *(coll.)*, elocutionize, go on *or* take the stump, recite, demagogue *(coll.)*, give or read a lesson.

19. *(With* UP) Keep erect, brace, hold, prop, bear, shore up, stay, underset, found, base, ground, bottom, shoulder, underpin, underprop, mainstay, sustain, enable to stand, carry, maintain, underbrace, buttress.

20. *(With* UP) Present to notice, display, proffer, offer, set forth, flaunt, visibilize, make visible, show off, overture, exhibit, dangle before the eyes, brandish, wave, trot out *(coll.)*, put forward *or* forth, unfurl, unveil, unmask, lay open, bring to light, submit, advance, tender, show forth, make an example of, bring *or* call into notice, unshroud, unroll, bare, expose.

21. *(With* UP) Stop, stop forcibly in order to rob, delay, impede, hinder, retard, hold *or* keep back, slacken, bar, check, hamper, curb, clog, interfere with, choke off, detain, restrain, block, slow down, embarrass, trammel, obstruct, stick up *(sl.)*, rob, hijack *(sl.)*, intercept, inhibit, cut off, incommode.

22. *(With* UP) Support, uphold, countenance, lend one's name *or* favor to, underwrite, sustain, stand by, give moral support to, back up, endorse, aid, assist, reinforce, abet, prop, stand behind *or* back of, work for, go to bat for *(sl.)*, advocate, take the part of, expedite, advance, forward, give a lift, concur in, bolster up, shoulder, befriend, further, second, boost, stick up for *(coll.)*, facilitate, sanction, approbate, maintain, agree to lend (give, afford, furnish, supply) support to, approve, speed, promote, patronize, subscribe to, nourish, nurture, foster, serve, hold a brief for *(coll.)*, set up, lend oneself to.

23. *(With* UP) Keep up *or* on, endure, maintain one's position (condition, *etc.*), persevere, keep one's courage, support oneself, bear up, last, stand the test, wear *or* wear well, stick out, remain true, ring true, stand *or* hold up in the wash *(sl.)*, prove true, be resolute, continue, be steadfast, never say die, keep to *or* maintain one's course, not give up, see it through *(coll.)*, be constant, perpetuate, go on, hang on, stick to one's guns, carry on, stick at nothing, mean business, work at doggedly, plug away *(coll.)*, die at one's post, have determination, die in harness, be in at the death, persist.

HOLDBACK, *n.* Restriction, barrier, impediment, hitch, limitation, prohibition, trammel, retardment, retardation, restraint, stumbling block, stop, cohibition, dam, barricade, stay, bridle, hindrance, oppilation, forbiddance, repression, prevention, ban, stoppage, impedition, preclusion, proscription, embargo, injunction, obstacle, block, difficulty, curb, obstruction, balk, constraint, stopper, enjoining.

HOLDER, *n.* Owner, proprietor, occupant, possessor, landlord, tenant.

HOLDFAST, *n.* Catch, clamp, hook, clip, hasp, fastener, vise, grip, clinch.

HOLDINGS, *n.* 1. Property, assets, possessions, interests, chattels, vested interests, investments, tenements, goods, belongings, estate, effects, legal estate, seizin *(Law)*, wealth, resources, circumstances, stock, means, bonds.

2. Real estate, land owned, tenements, stake, claim, allodium, freehold, property, estate, dominions, landed property, demesne, territory, realty.

HOLE, *n.* 1. Aperture, opening, breach, crevice, crack, break, space, cranny, gash, rent, cut, scission, orifice, leak, gap, cleft, rift, fissure, venthole, vent, incision, slot, slit, chink, rupture, chasm, nick, fracture, scissure, interstice, notch, foramen *(Anat.)*, fenestra *(Zool.)*, puncture, eye, rime, spiracle *(Anat. and Zool.)*, perforation, scupper *(Naut.)*, acupuncture *(of the skin)*.

2. Excavation, hollow, cavity, concavity, cave, cavern, depression, pit, shaft, abyss, deep, crater, impression, crevasse, indentation, dent, dint, cup, cell, chamber, mine, scoop, burrow, cistern, pit, ingate, niche, mouth, tunnel, defile, valley, gorge, ravine, cutting, crypt *(Anat.)*, fossa *(Anat.)*, alveolus *(Anat. and Zool.)*, hiatus, sinus, pore.

3. Burrow *(of an animal)*, den, lair, dugout, refuge, cave, retreat, excavation, lodge, shelter, furrow.

4. Mean cottage, hovel, shack, hut, shanty, dump *(sl.)*, dive *(sl.)*, joint *(sl.)*, lean-to, shed, abode, box.

5. Dungeon, prison, cell, pound, brig *(Naut.)*, cage, keep, donjon.

6. *(Colloq.)* Quandary, precarious position, difficult situation, bad position, dilemma, predicament, perplexity, scrape, pretty pass, tight place, fix *(coll.)*, pucker *(coll.)*, stew *(coll.)*, squeeze *(coll.)*, pinch, mess, hitch, difficult straits, plight, hobble *(coll.)*, pickle *(coll.)*, jam *(coll.)*, muddle, trouble, bother.

7. Cove, small harbor, creek, inlet, anchorage, lagoon, little bay, basin, portlet.

HOLE, *v.* 1. Put holes in, bore, perforate, puncture, stab, drill, pierce, spike, penetrate, pink, stick, punch.

2. *(With* UP) Winter, lie torpid, hide oneself, be concealed, retire, seclude oneself, vegetate, hibernate, sleep, hide out *(coll.)*, lie low, lie dormant, retire from sight, conceal oneself.

HOLIDAY, *adj.* Festival, joyous, glad, festive, anniversary, celebrating, gala, commemorative, vacational, memorial, recreational, jubilant, sabbatical.

HOLIDAY, *n.* 1. Cessation of work, vacation, time off, furlough, leave, leave of absence, congé *(Fr.)*, breathing spell, leisure time, red-letter day, recess, anniversary, fete day, respite, jubilee, time out, sabbatical.

2. Feasting, spree, fete, merrymaking, bacchanal, gala, jamboree (sl.), heyday, carousal, carnival, festival, celebration, revelry, jollification, carousing, frolic, junket, Mardi gras.

HOLINESS, n. Quality of being holy, sanctity, devotion, devoutness, piety, sacredness, religionism, righteousness, purity, religiosity, saintliness, consecration, reverence, unction, sanctitude, goodness, spirituality, theopathy, virtue, virtuousness, spiritual-mindedness, charism (Theol.), grace, saintship, divineness.

HOLLO, v. Call with a loud voice, be clamorous, raise an outcry, shout, vociferate, clamor, call, yo-ho, hoop, yell, cry out, rend the air, halloo, exclaim, yoick, hoot, yowl, whoop, hail, give cry, sing out, hallo, halloa, holla, holloa, hullo.

HOLLOW, adj. 1. Empty, void, excavated, unfilled, vacant, vacuous, blank, dry, drained, devoid, cannulate, fistulous or fistulatous (both of pipes, reeds, etc.).

2. Rounded inward, curving inward, hollowed out, indented, sunken, incurved, cupped, concave, calathiform, cyathiform, poculiform, incurving, incurvate, trough-like.

3. Nonresonant, rumbling, dull, muffled, low, sepulchral, plangent, resounding, clangorous, deep-mouthed, deep-toned, deep, vibrating, muffled, vibrant, sordine, reverberating, booming, mute, muted, thunderous, ringing.

4. Vain, fatuitous, fatuous, unavailing, ineffective, useless, worthless, gainless, futile, invalid, hopeless, idle, pointless, unsubstantial, empty, unsatisfactory, nugatory, trifling, inefficacious, ineffectual, inane, inutile, Pyrrhic (of battles, etc.), bootless, valueless, fruitless, profitless, unprofitable.

5. Insincere, false, deceptive, double-handed, underhanded, two-faced, double-tongued, serpent-tongued, treacherous, mealy-mouthed, dissembling, lying, double-dealing, faithless, idle, empty, pharisaic, specious, hypocritical, unsound, artificial, Janus-faced, deceitful, perjured, counterfeit, disingenuous, forsworn, untruthful, sham, sly, cunning, fabricated, unveracious, fraudulent, mendacious, wily, feigned, tricky, recreant, sophistical, perfidious, tartufian, tartufish.

6. With an empty stomach, hungry, famished, ravening, starved, peckish (coll.), lickerish, esurient.

HOLLOW, n. 1. Indentation, furrow, cavity, dip, sink, concavity, dimple, crevasse, dint, cutting, bowl, cup, vacancy, impression, pit, crater, antrum (Anat.), sinus, ditch, hole.

2. Valley, glen, vale, dell (Lit.), basin, dingle, dale, ravine, gulch, gorge, notch, gap, cutting, canyon, cut, chasm, divide.

HOLLOW, v. Make hollow, scoop out, furrow, gouge out, dish, indent, dent, dig out, depress, excavate, groove, channel, dint.

HOLOCAUST, n. 1. Vast slaughter, wholesale destruction of life (esp. by fire), bloodshed, hecatomb, decimation, demolition, ruin, fire, gore, conflagration, butchery, carnage, war to the finish or end, devastation, fusillade, trucidation, internecion, extirpation, havoc, waste, saturnalia of blood, pogrom, massacre, noyade, fight to the last ditch or the death, immolation, killing, mass murder, shambles, incendiarism, annihilation, ravage, extinction.

2. Burnt-offering (wholly consumed), sacrifice, oblation, mactation, idolothyte, whole offering, whole burnt offering, immolation, suttee, self-immolation, hecatomb, sacrificial pyre, offering.

HOLY, adj. 1. Specially recognized as or declared sacred, consecrated, hallowed, set apart, solemn, fast, feast, religious, blessed, sanctified, sacred, devoted, devotional, sacrosanct.

2. Dedicated or devoted to the service of God, church or religion, saintly, godly, pious, devout, religious, pure, righteous, moral, just, heavenly-minded, profoundly good, perfect, sainted, saint-like, sinless, angelic, chaste, faithful, believing, inviolable, immaculate, reverent, spiritual, devotional, virtuous, unstained, guileless, upright, unworldly, uncorrupted, pure in heart, zealous, pietistic, sanctified, heaven-sent, seraphic, right-minded, dedicated, unspotted.

3. Of religious purity or solemnity, otherworldly, exalted, pure, innocent, guileless, reverent, godlike, virtuous, spiritual, laudable, perfect, saintlike, platonic, sacred, faultless, childlike, uncorrupt, undefiled, untainted, heaven-born, unworldly, lamblike, dovelike, hallowed, heavenly, spotless, unearthly, clean, sinless, blameless, clear, sainted, immaculate.

4. Entitled to worship or profound religious reverence, of divine character or origin, pertaining to God or divinity, divine, heavenly, revered, seraphic, angelic, celestial, heaven-sent, heaven-born, from above, sinless, hallowed, perfect, sacred, revealed, canonical, prophetic, venerable, Biblical, scriptural, theopneustic, divinely inspired, ecclesiastical, faultless.

HOLY GHOST, n. Third Person of the Trinity, the Spirit of God, Holy Spirit, the Comforter, the Spirit, the Dove, the Intercessor, the Spirit of Truth, the Sanctifier, Paraclete.

HOLY WRIT, n. Bible, Scriptures, Holy Scriptures, the Good Book, the Word, the Word of God, the Gospel, Old and New Testaments, the Book of Books, inspired or sacred writings, Sacred Scriptures.

HOMAGE, n. 1. Respect paid or rendered, reverence, honor, regard, esteem, veneration, exaltation, glorification, praise, genuflection, bowing, kneeling, prostration, bending the knee, consideration, humility, service, duty, court, obeisance, devotion, worship, adoration, ascription, adulation, apotheosis, obsequiousness, latria (Rom. Cath. Theol.), dulia (Rom. Cath. Theol.), deference, incense.

2. Something done or given in acknowledgment of vassalage, relation of vassal to lord, fealty, loyalty, devotion, service, servitude, yielding, submission, allegiance, bondage, adherence, servility, abasement, subservience, lowliness, meekness, obedience, deference, humility, constancy, singleness of heart, faithfulness, duty, fidelity.

HOME, adj. 1. Of, pertaining to or connected with one's home or country, domestic, native, indigenous, familiar, natal, one's own, interior, within the country, internal, autochthonous, domiciliary, home-born, home-grown, native-grown, aboriginal, vernacular, accustomed, rooted, ingrained, garden, established, homemade, family, acclimated, homebred.

2. That strikes home or to the mark aimed at, close, direct, to the point, incisive, sharp, effective, penetrating, intimate, home-reaching, that goes to the core, poignant, summary, curt, neat, clear, terse, pithy, decided, acute, deep-felt, emphatic, razor-edged, barbed, marked, biting, caustic, rough, stinging, harsh, deep, profound, cutting,

keen, edged, astringent, arrowlike, spearlike, knife-edged, indelible, pregnant, severe, trenchant, piercing, pointed.

HOME, *adv.* 1. *(Sometimes with* AT*)* To, toward *or* at one's home, indoors, in the bosom of one's family, within doors, to one's house *or* abode, homebound.

2. Deep, to the mark, with telling effect, with a vengeance, to the heart, pointedly, closely, completely, effectively, to the core *or* inmost core, with force, to the vital center *or* seat, incisively, trenchantly, decidedly, indelibly, tersely, harshly, profoundly, keenly, directly, poignantly, piercingly, summarily, where it hurts, to good account, to the quick, severely, to the inmost feeling *or* sensibility.

3. *(With* AT*)* In a situation familiar to one, at ease, comfortable, contented, at rest, unperturbed, content, familiar with, proficient in, inured, habituated, used to, on home territory, easy, skilled, accustomed, versed in, snug, cozy, peaceful, congenial, conversant with, fixed, established, master of, good at, in smooth water, well-grounded, acquainted with, acclimated, naturalized, unconstrained in manner, *dégagé (Fr.),* unvexed, unmolested, in one's own *or* proper element, up in, strong in, well-read in, satisfied.

HOME, *n.* 1. Shelter, fixed residence, place of existence *or* refuge, native land, abiding place, abode, dwelling, domicile, living quarters, address, country, place of dwelling *or* residence, rooftree, place, lodgings, retreat, resort, haunt, roof over one's head, farm, deanery, parsonage, vicarage, manse, teacherage *(chiefly West. U. S.),* rendezvous, stamping ground *(coll.),* hangout *(sl.),* seat, habitat, place of abode, house, dwelling place, apartment, habitation, lodgment.

2. Place of one's domestic affections, one's native place *or* own country, bosom of one's family, hearth, fireside, family, domestic circle, family circle, household, ingle, ingleside, retreat, roof, hearthstone, resort, haunt, home roof, inglenook, chimney corner, homestead, place where one hangs one's hat *(joc.),* home sweet home, stamping ground *(coll.), ménage (Fr.).*

3. Institution for homeless, sick, *etc.,* asylum, hospital, retreat, haven, poorhouse, orphanage, almshouse, hospice, refuge for the destitute, sanitarium, sanatorium, nursing home.

4. Dwelling place *or* retreat of an animal, place *or* region where something is native *or* most common, habitat, native environment *or* locality, vicinity, region, mew, haunt, shelter, stamping ground *(coll.),* watering hole, nest, lair, den, hole, cave, purlieu, covert, resort, retreat.

5. Goal, destination, journey's end, terminus, harbor, port, last stop, anchorage, basin, dock, bourn, refuge, eternal home, cemetery, grave, heaven, rest, haven, moorings, terminal point, retreat, asylum.

HOMEBRED, *adj.* 1. Bred at home, native, indigenous, home-raised, domestic, natural, homeborn, not foreign, internal, homemade, garden, native-grown, interior, one's own, from available stock, cared for at home.

2. Unpolished, unsophisticated, unrefined, rude, plain, artless, vulgar, homespun, gross, indecorous, ill-bred, coarse, sorry, indelicate, inelegant, base, low, homely, uncouth, rural, inurbane, barbarous, bucolic, rowdy, wild, beggarly, uncultivated, improper, unseemly, unpresentable, uncivil, ill-mannered, discourteous, impolite, uncourtly,

ungenteel, ungentlemanlike, unladylike, uncultured, crude, raw, crass, clownish, loutish, boorish, cloddish, lumpish, churlish, in bad taste, impudent, ill-behaved, unmannerly, graceless, unconventional, ignoble, rustic, provincial, unceremonious, rough.

HOMELESS, *adj.* Having no home, exiled, vagabond, outcast, forsaken, unhoused, friendless, houseless, disinherited, desolate, left to shift for oneself, abandoned, derelict, estranged, unwelcome, unsettled, unplaced, unharbored, dispossessed, unestablished, outside the gates.

HOMELIKE, *adj.* Like *or* suggestive of home, comfortable, domestic, friendly, unpretentious, congenial, cordial, familiar, common, warm, normal, customary, wonted, homespun, cheerful, simple, intimate, cozy, unpretending, plain, natural, informal, hospitable, accustomed, agreeable, pleasant, concordant, unsophisticated, homely, homey *(coll.),* peaceful, restful, artless, snug, easeful.

HOMELY, *adj.* 1. Proper *or* suited to the home *or* to ordinary domestic life, homelike, domestic, plain, unpretentious, informal, commonplace, matter-of-fact, everyday, familiar, simple, unpretending, unassuming, free from affectation, unsophisticated, peaceful, friendly, snug, easy, cozy, convenient, restful, comfortable, natural, artless, native, common, homebred, ordinary, workaday, unaffected, prosaic, homespun, easeful, homey *(coll.),* usual.

2. Not good-looking, plain, of plain features, rather ugly, hard-favored, unlovely, hard-featured, unhandsome, artless, unsightly, unshapely, unbeautiful, uncomely, forbidding, unattractive, not fit to be seen, misshapen, evil-favored, ill-favored, plain-looking, hideous, frightful, monstrous, displeasing to the eye, beautiless, unpretty, ordinary, gawky, graceless, ungraceful, unprepossessing, grotesque, repellent.

3. Unrefined, inelegant, uncultivated, vulgar, rustic, barbaric, barbarous, artless, unseemly, coarse, doltish, tasteless, inartistic, gross, cloddish, graceless, crude, crass, churlish, ungentlemanly, unladylike, plebeian, loutish, humble, untitled, common, proletarian, upstart, unmannerly, clownish, ignoble, uncouth, uncourtly, unpretentious, ungainly, rude, rough, awkward, thick, mean, lowly, blunt, ill-favored, unceremonious, base, low, in poor taste, ungenteel, offensive, indelicate, illbred, objectionable, Philistine, low-minded, unpolished, unadorned, tramontane, homespun, uncomely, plain, boorish, lumpish, ill-mannered, parvenu, raw.

HOMEMADE, *adj.* Made at home, homespun, of domestic manufacture, home-loomed, self-made, native, home, indigenous, home-wrought, home-worked, domestic, not foreign.

HOMERIC, *adj.* 1. Epic, epopoean, lyrico-epic, heroic, grand, magniloquent.

2. *(Of laughter)* Loud, cheerful, vigorous, hearty, full, jovial, powerful, booming, deafening, vociferous, bursting, passionate, thundering, sonorous, vehement, warm, enough to wake the dead.

HOME RULE, *n.* Political independence, self-government, autonomy, self-determination, freedom from interference *or* domination (on the part of higher government levels).

HOMESICK, *adj.* Ill *or* depressed from a longing for home, pining for friends and kindred, nostalgic, lamenting, unhappy, malcontent, discontented, plaintive, wretched, grieving, languishing, infelicitous, heartbroken, woebegone, miserable, drooping, disconsolate, dispirited, dejected, melancholy, downcast, heartsick, inconsolable, comfortless, forlorn, desolate, mournful.

HOMESPUN, *adj.* 1. Spun *or* made at home, homemade, native, of domestic manufacture, made of homespun cloth, home-loomed, home-wrought, home-worked, self-made.

2. Plain, rude, unpolished, simple, modest, rough, rustic, vulgar, homely, household, workaday, plebeian, informal, uncultivated, rough hewn, roughcast, unpretending, unassuming, inelegant, unsmooth, uneven, unadorned, natural, prosaic, common, everyday, workday, unpretentious, unaffected, ungenteel, uncouth, lowly, humble, uncultured, homebred, indelicate, unfeigning, linsey-woolsey, provincial, boorish, artless, garden, untutored, guileless, blunt, candid, direct, forthright, straightforward, sincere, open, frank, inurbane, backwoods, bucolic, hick *(sl.),* coarse, unkempt, rugged, uncourtly, unsophisticated, unvarnished, unornamented, ordinary.

HOMESTEAD, *n.* Dwelling with its lands and buildings, farm, grange, manor, country house, country seat, messuage *(Law),* house and grounds, farmstead, ranch, plantation, estate, demesne, hacienda *(Sp. Amer.).*

HOMEWARD, *adv.* Toward home, homewards, home, back home, homewardly, homeward bound, to one's family *or* native land.

HOMICIDAL, *adj.* Pertaining to homicide, having a tendency to homicide, patricidal, bloody, murderous, maniacal, sanguinary, violent, raving, cutthroat, killing, bloodthirsty, parricidal, matricidal, fratricidal, regicidal, slaughterous, dangerous, frenzied, maniac.

HOMICIDE, *n.* 1. Killing of one human being by another, murder, slaying, manslaughter, patricide, regicide, trucidation, foul play, lapidation, matricide, fratricide, infanticide, parricide, strangling, feticide, aborticide, assassination, bloodshed, uxoricide, vaticide, thuggism, slaughter.

2. Murderer, manslayer, Cain, assassin, cutthroat, slayer, bloodshedder, gorilla *(sl.),* apache, strangler, infanticide, bravo, thug, burker, vaticide, feticide, aborticide, tryannicide, uxoricide, matricide, patricide, parricide, fratricide, cannibal, head-hunter, poisoner, hatchet man, man-eater, man-killer, regicide, garroter, gunman, killer.

HOMILETIC, *adj.* Of homilies *or* sermons, relating to sermons, sermonic, of the nature of a homily, hortatory, persuasive, edifying, instructional, doctrinal, educational, preaching, expository, disquisitional, admonitory, teaching, instructive, moralizing, disciplinary, didactic, propagative, of *or* pertaining to homiletics.

HOMILETICS, *n.* Branch of practical theology that treats of homilies *or* sermons, art of preaching *or* sermonizing, art of making homilies, sermonizing, preaching, didactics, sermon-writing, preachment, rhetorical religious discourse, training in preaching technique, creation of edifying discourse, composition and delivery of sermons *or* homilies.

HOMILY, *n.* Religious discourse addressed to a congregation, sermon, tract, preaching, exhortation, dissertation, lesson, admonitory *or* moralizing discourse, treatise, disquisition, exposition, declamation, discursus, prelection, discussion, reasoning, expounding, discipline, doctrine, edifica-

tion, preachment, address, lecture, propagation, persuasion, teaching, speech, instruction, apologue, parable.

HOMOGENEITY, *n.* Composition from like parts, congruity of constitution, purity, uniformity, consonance, accordance, unity, evenness, identity, comparability, agreement, likeness, resemblance, similitude, semblance, rapport, affinity, equivalence, oneness, sameness, parallelism, correspondence, analogy, simplicity, congruity, continuity, approximation, correlation, parity, conformity, alliance, cognation, homology, homogeneousness.

HOMOGENEOUS, *adj.* 1. Composed of similar particles, uniform, all alike, of the same nature throughout, of uniform structure, the same, unvarying, of consistent texture, single, pure, unmixed, unalloyed, unadulterated, of a piece, unsophisticated, emulsified, constant, homogeneal, homogenized.

2. Of the same kind *or* nature, essentially alike, similar, closely akin, alike, kindred, congenial, comparable, uniform, homogenetic, relative, regular, cognate, the same, twin, equivalent, congeneric, congenerous, correlative, parallel, analogous, connatural, homogenous *(Biol.),* corresponding, Homoiousian *(Eccl. Hist.),* proportionate, approximative, unigenous *(Biol.).*

HOMOLOGATE, *v.* Approve, ratify, endorse, assent to, establish, accredit, confirm, affirm, support, uphold, validate, accept, sign, sanction, subscribe to, visa, agree to, recognize, concur, approbate, be in favor of, underwrite, undersign, lend one's support to, give one's voice for, verify, certify, vote for, bear out, advocate, recommend, commend, corroborate, settle firmly, warrant, vouch for, acquiesce, vouchsafe, countenance, substantiate.

HOMOLOGOUS, *adj.* Of the same ratio *or* proportion, in the same relation, corresponding in structure *or* position, relative, alike, correspondent, similar, akin, kindred, comparable, parallel, cognate, homogenous *(Biol.),* analogous, homogenetic, of the same type, equivalent, regular, connatural.

HOMOLOGY, *n.* State of being homologous, homologous relation *or* correspondence, relation, relative position, applicability, affinity, rapport, homogeneity, kinship, affiliation, alliance, cognation, comparability, proportion, ratio, concern, bearing, reference, mutuality, similarity, balance, commensurability, apposition, connection, association, correlation, relevance, parallelism.

HOMOPHONIC, *adj.* 1. Of the same sound, of like pitch, homophonous, unisonous, unisonant, in unison, attuned, assonant, consonant, accordant.

2. Having one part *or* melody predominating, monodic, melodic, monophonic.

HOMOSEXUAL, *adj.* Hermaphrodite, hermaphroditic, androgynous, epicene, monoclinous *(Bot.),* gynandrous *(Bot.),* Lesbian, perverted, effeminate, queer *(sl.).*

HOMUNCULUS, *n.* Little man, dwarf, atomy, mite, runt, shrimp, pygmy, Tom Thumb, midget, manikin, dapperling, hop-o'-my-thumb, Lilliputian.

HONE, *n.* Oilstone, fine whetstone, sharpening stone, sharpener, grindstone, rubstone, emery, emery wheel, carborundum, novaculite *(Petrog.).*

HONE, *v.* Whet, sharpen on a hone, edge, file, grind, acuminate, put a fine edge upon.

HONEST, *adj.* 1. Honorable in principles, intentions and actions, upright, virtuous, reputable, truth-telling, truth-loving, faithful, reliable, sound, square, impartial, just, true, trusty, trustworthy, unprejudiced, observant of obligations, ethical, uncorrupted, equitable, conscientious, standing by one's word, principled, law-abiding, law-loving, undissembling, moral, true-blue, righteous, truthful, rightful, dispassionate, downright, true-hearted, high-minded, tried and true, unbribed, scrupulous, good, veracious, single, as good as one's word, true-dealing, *sans peur et sans reproche (Fr.),* veridical, decent, fair, straight, dependable, unperjured, unbiased, reasonable, uninfluenced, unbought, white *(coll.),* disinterested.

2. Showing uprightness and fairness, gained fairly, honorable, equitable, open, free from fraud, proper, legal, suitable, aboveboard, in open sight, reputable, impartial, estimable, scrupulous, worthy, disinterested, dispassionate, unbiased, licit, lawful, rightful, laudable, open and aboveboard, valid, even-handed, right, fair, fair and square, foursquare, unfeigned, on the up-and-up *(coll.),* on the level *(coll.),* legitimate, according to agreement, faithful to contract, just as represented, free from tricks, creditable, round, reasonable, satisfactory.

3. Sincere, open, ingenuous, clear, unclouded, unfeigning, artless, incapable of deceit, forthright, pure, guileless, childlike, wholesome, simple-hearted, clear-cut, aboveboard, undisguised, rustic, plain, innocent, guiltless, unsophisticated, bona fide, single-hearted, unaffected, direct, frank, candid, unreserved, trustful, harmless, confiding, with clean hands, lamblike, dovelike, straightforward, clean-cut, open-hearted, undissimulating, undissembling, undepraved, unflattering, unromantic, outspoken, direct, blunt, downright, plain-spoken.

4. Genuine, unadulterated, unalloyed, reliable, good, true, real, faithful, untainted, undiluted, undistorted, valid, fair and square, intrinsically sound, authentic, pure, free from shams, straight, honorable, round, full *(measure, strength, etc.),* bona fide, sterling, unmixed, unperjured, unexaggerated, baker's *(dozen),* unvarnished, undefiled, solid, true to claims, thorough, just.

5. Chaste, virtuous, faithful, pure, undefiled, unfallen, spotless, sinless, holy, clean, uncorrupted, immaculate, innocent, decorous, celibate, modest, virgin, decent, unsullied, virginal.

HONESTY, *n.* 1. Quality *or* fact of being honest, integrity, uprightness, veracity, fairness, rectitude, probity, honor, fidelity, truthfulness, scrupulousness, virtue, right, reputability, merit, morality, principle, goodness, faithfulness, equity, veraciousness, impeccability, uncorruptibility, veridity, straightforwardness, trustworthiness, trustiness, justice, faith, freedom from fraud, truth-telling, truth-loving, respectability, honorableness, conscientiousness.

2. Truthfulness, sincerity, frankness, candor, artlessness, simplicity, innocence, plain-speaking, veracity, unreserve, openness, truth, purity, guiltlessness, impeccability, simple goodness, bonhomie, good-heartedness, straightforwardness, inartificiality, immaculacy, clean hands, pure heart, clear conscience, unsophistication, naïveté, inerrability, forthrightness.

3. Freedom from deceit *or* fraud, genuineness, earnestness, righteousness, good faith, observance of one's word, repute, fidelity, just dealing, plain dealing, responsibility, disinterestedness, fair play,

self-respect, thoroughness, reputation, honest behavior, square dealing *(coll.),* square *or* straight shooting *(coll.),* conscientiousness, reputability, scrupulousness, loyalty to principle, good *or* fair name, impartiality, faithfulness.

HONEY, *n.* 1. Sweet viscid fluid produced by bees, insect product resembling bees' honey, nectar.

2. Something sweet, delicious *or* delightful, sweetness, delight, pleasure, delectation, felicity, bliss, rapture, lovableness, flattery, good word, benediction, honeyed words, oblectation, beatitude, ravishment, ecstasy, manna, jewel, gem, posy, peach, nosegay, bouquet, unction, taffy *(coll.),* flummery, puff, blarney, blandishment, adulation, encomium, cajolery, blessing, eulogy, panegyric, compliment, cream, pearl, pure gold.

HONEYCOMB, *n.* Cellular wax housing *(of bees)* for honey, pollen and eggs, structure of open cells *(resembling that of bees),* sieve, strainer, cribble, net, riddle, filter, sifter, screen, pierced metal plate, perforated surface.

HONEYCOMB, *v.* Reduce to the structure of a honeycomb, pierce with many holes *or* cavities, perforate, puncture, stick, prick, pit, cribble, shoot through, penetrate in all parts, enfilade *(Mil.),* riddle.

HONEYCOMBED, *adj.* Having structure *or* appearance of honeycomb, pierced through with many holes *or* cavities, perforated in every direction, penetrated in all parts *or* many directions, porous, eaten through in every part, alveolate, cellular, riddled, sievelike, spongy, punctured, cribbled, pitted, shot through, pricked, pierced, cribriform, lacy, favose, faveolate, faviform, foraminate, favaginous, undermined, flawed.

HONEYED, *adj.* 1. Dulcet, mellifluous, sweet, ingratiating, bland, amiable, smooth-tongued, soft-spoken, suave, smooth, flattering, saccharine, entrancing, seductive, fine-spoken, smooth-spoken, cloying, mellow, candied, mellisonant, winsome, bewitching, enchanting, taking, ravishing, winning, inviting, music to one's ears, alluring, dainty, delicious, smoothly flowing, sugary, nectared, melleous, musical, pleasing, gratifying, agreeable, pleasurable, melodious, mellifluent, luscious, engaging, unctuous.

2. Consisting of, containing *or* resembling honey, candied, sugary, nectared, cloying, sweetened, luscious, rich, sweet, saccharine, melleous.

HONOR, *n.* 1. High public esteem, reputation, credit, fame, glory, good name, repute, acclaim, recognition, figure, note, luster, brilliance, laurel, notability, radiance, splendor, kudos, consideration, renown, merit, name, account, elevation, exaltation, resplendence, good report, reputability, popularity, popular report *or* favor, éclat, eminence, greatness, bay, worth, halo, respect, glorification, blessing, commendation, blaze of glory, mark, primacy, superiority, illustriousness.

2. Source of credit *or* distinction, boast, pride, credit, glory, jewel, gem, flower, cream, diamond, joy, hope, hero, grace, blessing, tribute, pearl, ornament, feather in the cap.

3. High respect, reverence, esteem, homage, approbation, credit, worship, adulation, celebration, adoration, laudation, trust, praise, account, regard, laud, good report, popularity, eulogium, wreath, laurel, bay, feather in the cap, trophy, prize, mark of approval, deference, veneration,

fealty, admiration, dignification, canonization, glorification, need of praise, tribute, elevation, exaltation, apotheosis, lionization, immortalization, deification, aggrandizement, confidence.

4. Special privilege *or* favor, pleasure, permission, grant, warranty, authorization, sanction, leave, power, right, compliment, trust, liberty, vouchsafement.

5. *(Usually pl.)* Dignity, distinction, high rank, recognition for eminence *or* success, distinguished position, elevation, excellency, consequence, prestige, nobility, majesty, standing, footing, station, status, place, degree, greatness, illustriousness, grandeur, importance, supremacy, sublimity, superiority, preeminence, notability, eminence, prominence, nobleness.

6. High-minded character *or* principles, fine sense of one's obligations, sense of honor, sense of right *or* justice, integrity, honesty, probity, uprightness, constancy, decency, honorableness, morality, good faith, principle, truth, grace, sincerity, nobleness of mind, magnanimity, right, veracity, rectitude, fidelity, fairness, scrupulousness, reputability, merit, goodness, equity, faithfulness, truthfulness, justice, impeccability, uncorruptibility, trustworthiness, conscientiousness, veridity, self-respect, chivalry.

7. Virtue, chastity, delicacy, virginity, modesty, purity, innocence, pudicity, pucelage, continency, womanly honor, decorum, chivalry.

HONOR, *v.* 1. Hold in respect, esteem, venerate, respect, admire, hail, approve, have regard for, regard, reverence, approbate, look up to, set store by, hold, countenance, think much of, value, show courtesy to, defer to, show deference to.

2. Glorify, praise, exalt, raise, lionize, magnify, toast, elevate, laud, extol, compliment, celebrate, salute, eulogize, cheer, aggrandize, immortalize, deify, ennoble, reverence, enthrone, revere, panegyrize, belaud, applaud, bless, blazon, venerate, acclaim, pay homage to, puff, swell, clap.

3. Solemnize, signalize, memorialize, commemorate, observe, keep, ceremonialize, consecrate, dedicate, hallow, celebrate, ritualize.

4. Worship, reverence, idolize, venerate, revere, lift up one's heart to, pay homage, praise, bow down before, laud, magnify, pray to, pay divine honors to, adore, deify, kneel before.

5. Make payment on, make good, pay, redeem, cash, credit, take, acknowledge, refund, defray, accept.

HONORABLE, *adj.* 1. *(Of persons)* Trustworthy, reliable, reputable, upright, trusty, sound, gentlemanly, faithful, ethical, noble, just, good, candid, conscientious, admirable, praiseworthy, uncorrupted, high-minded, righteous, fair, worthy, straight, unprejudiced, laudable, equitable, principled, *sans peur et sans reproche (Fr.)*, dependable, disinterested, truthful, scrupulous, veracious, unperjured, white *(coll.)*, dispassionate, uninfluenced, downright, true-dealing, unbiased, unbought, sincere, open, undissembling, forthright.

2. *(Of dealings, affairs, etc.)* Aboveboard, legitimate, equitable, reputable, licit, lawful, rightful, laudable, valid, fair, fair and square, on the level *(coll.)*, on the up and up *(coll.)*, according to agreement, estimable, faithful to contract, free from tricks, just as represented, creditable, round, reasonable, sound, satisfactory, worthy, ethical, open.

3. *(Of persons)* Of superior bearing, of high rank, noble, high, great, *distingué (Fr.)*, preemi-

nent, outstanding, lordly, important, grand, august, respectable, popular, marked, celebrated, famous, far-famed, elevated, honored, illustrious, renowned, eminent, reputable, estimable, magnificent, noteworthy, worthy, glorious, reverenced, splendid, revered, distinguished, prominent, conspicuous, foremost, noted, of note.

HONORARIUM, *n.* Fee, reward, compensation, gratuity, largess, handsel, remuneration, consideration, bonus, emolument.

HONORARY, *adj.* 1. Without fee, emolument, etc., verbal, nominal, titular.

2. Free, gratis, for nothing, for love, costless, expenseless, scot-free, donated, without charge, voluntary, gratuitous, complimentary, contributory, given, no strings attached *(coll.)*.

HOOD, *n.* Cowl, capuche, coif, mantilla, calash, chaperon *(Hist.)*, mozzetta *(Eccl.)*, capuchin, camail *(Hist.)*, amice *(Eccl.)*, wimple, fascinator, cap, kerchief, snood, capote, bonnet.

HOODLUM, *n.* Petty gangster, rowdy, tough, plug-ugly, larrikin, miscreant, desperado, thug, gunman, sandbagger, crook, hooligan *(sl.)*, Apache, strongarm-man, footpad, ruffian, gamin, gorilla *(coll.)*, cutthroat, mobster. (See also BANDIT, *n.*)

HOODWINK, *v.* 1. Blind *(by covering the eyes)*, blindfold, cover the eyes, bandage the eyes, put blinkers *or* blinders on, blinker.

2. Hide, conceal, dissemble, veil, curtain, obscure, mask, cache, disguise, ensconce, cover, cloak, camouflage, shelter, blind, cover, bury, keep out of sight, make invisible, make inconspicuous, render indiscernible.

3. Delude, gammon, cheat, bamboozle, impose upon, humbug, fleece, foist upon, play upon, gyp, diddle, cozen, do, lure, rook, mulct, ensnare, entrap, cheat, hoax, play false, jockey, cajole, mislead, bilk, entice, baffle, gouge *(coll.)*, take *(coll.)*, wheedle, cog, chouse *(coll.)*, flam, betray, palm upon, pluck *(sl.)*, bunko, victimize, outwit, practice upon, defraud, befool, circumvent, overreach, trick, gull, inveigle, abuse, fraud, beguile, dupe, swindle, deceive.

HOOF, *n.* *(Of animals)* Foot, trotter, ungula, unguis *(pl.* ungues*)*, ungual cloot, coffin *(Veterinary)*, cloven foot.

HOOFED, *adj.* Having hoofs, having cloven feet, ungulate, unguled, unguligrade, ungulous, clovenfooted *(esp. of ox, sheep, etc.)*, cloven-hoofed.

HOOK, *n.* 1. Crook, bill, bill hook, grappling, cleek, grapnel, agraffe, grapple, uncus *(Zool. and Anat.)*, peavey *(Lumbering)*, fluke, tenaculum, pothook, trammel, sling dog *(usually in pairs)*, gaff, crotchet, crampon *(usually pl.)*, hamus *(Zool.)*, hamulus *(Zool.)*, uncinus *(Zool.)*.

2. Any curved cutting instrument, scythe, sickle, falchion *(Hist.)* reaper, cutter, cutlass, scimitar, saber.

3. Angle, curve, crook, bend, arc, arch, inflection, warp, semicircle, fork, crimp, circumflex, horseshoe, curl, crescent, buckle, meniscus, bow, bifurcation, loop.

4. Trap, snare, snap, gin, springe, noose, sniggle.

HOOK, *v.* Catch, seize, take, capture, nab, trepan, snare, snag, grab, net, ensnare, noose, collar *(coll.)*, bag, get, cop, clasp, grip, entrap, grapple.

HOOKED, *adj.* Hook-shaped, hook-like, hooky, bent, aquiline, curved, falculate, falcate, uncinate, adunc, aduncous, hamate, hamiform, hamulate, hamulose, arcuate, hamose.

HOOKUP, n. Assemblage, connection, junction, union, joining, meeting, conjunction, accouplement, tie-up (coll.), link, linking, combination, conjoining.

HOOK UP, v. Join, hitch, tether, couple, connect, fuse together, conjoin, unite, splice, tie-up (coll.), yoke, assemble, put together, fasten together, attach, combine, lay together, piece together, clinch, link, link up, bracket, bring together.

HOOP, n. 1. Band, ring, circlet, wheel, ringlet, loop, annulet, grommet, collar, hoople (for play).
2. Hoop skirt, hoop petticoat, farthingale, crinoline.

HOOP, v. Circumscribe, spiral, surround, hedge in, curve around, lie around, beset, crook, hem in, be circumjacent, coil, encircle, wind about, round, encompass, enclose or inclose, gird, twine around, compass about, cincture, ring, envelop, belt, ensphere, loop, girdle, environ, compass, embrace.

HOOP SKIRT, n. Hoop petticoat, farthingale, crinoline, hoop.

HOOT, v. 1. Howl, screech, bellow, bawl, caterwaul, hullo, halloa, holla, hollo, holloa, hallo, yowl, call, squawk, clamor, vociferate, shout, scream, whoop, roar, jeer, boo, yoick, yo-ho, hail, sing out, yelp, proclaim, ejaculate, squall, babble, chorus, din.
2. Screech (as an owl), ululate, pipe, shrill, screak, scream, howl, shriek, wail, honk, whoop.

HOOT, n. Tumult, disturbance, uproar, hullabaloo, bellow, clangor, storm, bray, fracas, catcall, caterwauling, shouting, wild chorus, hubbub, noise, outcry, agitation, vociferation, brawling, babble, commotion, rumpus, Babel, war cry, jangle, racket, Bedlam, Dutch concert (coll.), cat's concert (coll.).

HOP, v. 1. Leap, jump, bound, bounce, buck, buckjump, prance, gambol, leapfrog, frisk, spring, skip, romp, caper, dance, saltate, curvet, bob, upleap, vault, upspring, trip.
2. Proceed haltingly, hobble, jolt, scuttle, lumber, claudicate, limp, halt, lag, falter, hitch, jog, shuffle, shamble, toddle.

HOPE, n. 1. Faith, reliance, belief, expectancy, presumption, expectation, assumption, anticipation, affiance, assurance, security, optimism, confidence, prospect, conviction.
2. Hopeful longing for some desired thing, desire, wish, want, fancy, eagerness, ambition, craving, yearning, aspiring, hankering, yen (sl.), coveting, dream, daydream, aspiration, longing.
3. Cheerfulness, optimism, good spirits, sprightliness, jocundity, brightness, jauntiness, breeziness, animal spirits, exhilaration, geniality, aspiration, good humor, playfulness, cheer, hopefulness, good cheer, sunniness, joyousness, joy, glee, blithesomeness, jocularity, joviality, jollity, merriment, hilarity, mirth, levity, airiness.

HOPE, v. 1. Look forward to, expect, anticipate, presume, foresee, count upon, suppose, reckon on, think to, believe, promise oneself, aspire, rely upon, contemplate, watch for, depend upon, bank on, deem likely, doubt not, surmise, suspect, calculate on, hold.
2. Have faith, take heart, rest assured, trust, believe, presume, assume, feel confident, be reassured, be assured, rest assured, look on the bright or sunny side, rely on, be hopeful.

3. (With FOR) Desire, long for, be bent upon, be ambitious for, have an eye to, have one's heart set on, aspire to, yearn for, wish, hanker for, covet, dream of, crave, have a fancy for, pine for, hunger for, thirst for, languish for, pant for, cry for, sigh for.

HOPEFUL, adj. 1. Full of hope, optimistic, expectant, faithful, cheerful, enthusiastic, assured, confident, sanguine, buoyant, anticipative, anticipating, trusting.
2. Promising, auspicious, of good omen, fair, favorable, propitious, pleasant, bright, rosy, inspiriting, encouraging, assuring, reassuring, heartening, roseate, cheering, uplifting, consoling, fortifying, gladdening, revivifying, elating, animating.

HOPELESS, adj. 1. Without hope, despairing, despondent, dejected, gloomy, desperate, downcast, crushed, forlorn, melancholy, morose, comfortless, tearful, sorrowful, grieving, lamenting, woeful, woebegone, heartbroken, funereal, disconsolate, spiritless, joyless, rueful, dreary, dolorous, lugubrious, doleful, heavy-hearted, downhearted, dispirited, sullen, glum, miserable, unhappy, depressed, sorrow-stricken, plaintive, sorrow-laden, sick at heart, down in the mouth (coll.), lachrymose, in despair, grief-stricken, discouraged, broken-hearted, overcome, downfallen, wretched, burdened, dampened, sobbing, cut to the heart, inconsolable, bowed-down, weighted, unmanned, dashed, bemoaning, bewailing, sorry, mourning.
2. Beyond recall, past hope, past cure, impossible, desperate, lost, forlorn, incurable, abandoned, helpless, unreclaimable, remediless, irredeemable, irretrievable, futile, irrevocable, vain, unmitigable, irreversible, irreparable, irreclaimable, recidivous, relapsing, gone, irrecoverable, useless, valueless, unavailing, to no avail, empty, idle, incorrigible, worthless, cureless, unserviceable, ineffective, pointless.

HOP-O'-MY-THUMB, n. Little man, diminutive person, mite, pygmy, midget, dapperling, Lilliputian, elf, bantam, shrimp, runt, homunculus, Tom Thumb, manikin, dwarf.

HOPPLE, v. Fasten together (the legs of an animal, etc.), cause to limp, secure, gravel, pinion, tether, bind, chain, trammel, lame, lash, hobble, truss, tie up, peg down, make fast, hogtie, restrain, leash, strap, gyve, fetter, shackle, entrammel.

HORDE, n. Crowd, crew, multitude, host, tribe, gang, assemblage, assembly, party, congregation, concourse, confluence, conflux, band, lot, number, entourage, bunch, bevy, caravan, posse, cohort, drove, gathering, troop, throng, cavalcade, mob, muster, covey, legion, company.

HORIZON, n. 1. Line or boundary between earth and sky, skyline, apparent horizon, visible, horizon, azimuth (Geol. and Astron.), range of vision or sight, eyereach, eyeshot, level.
2. Limit of perception, thought, etc., range, extent, area, vista, scope, distance, realm, bounds, demesne, sweep, play, field, orbit, compass, arena, ambit, spread, frontier, swing, verge, stretch, latitude, zone, sway, domain, sphere, expanse, confines.

HORIZONTAL, adj. Parallel to the horizon, level with the ground, flat, level, plane, lying, supine, prone, reclining, recumbent, incumbent, decumbent (Bot.), procumbent, prostrate, couchant, homaloidal (Math.).

HORN, *n.* 1. *(Of animals, etc.)* Tusk, antler, quill, spine, point, spike, corniculum *(dim. Anat. and Zool.)*, cornu, cornule *(Zool.)*, cornicle, corniplume *(of bird's feathers, tufts, etc., resembling horn).*

2. *(Musical instruments)* Trumpet *(loose)*, trombone *(loose)*, cornet, alto horn, clarion, cornopean, *cornet-à-pistons*, tuba, shophar, mellophone, French horn, English horn, conch *(Art.)*, lure, bugle, baritone, althorn, ballad horn, tromba, euphonium, lituus *(Rom. Antiq.)*, corno *(It.)*.

3. Noisemaker, alarm, klaxon, siren, megaphone, fog horn, hooter, buzzer.

4. Horn-shaped container, cornet, cone, pyramid, funnel, cornucopia *(horn of plenty).*

5. *(Of saddles)* Pommel, nubbin.

HORNY, *adj.* 1. Horn-like, callous, hard, hardened, cornified *(Anat.)*, indurate, ceratoid, bony, ossified, bone-like, firm, tough, toughened, corneous.

2. Having horns, horned, horn-bearing, corniculate, cornigerous, cornuted, cornupete *(Rom. Antiq.)*, bicorn, bicornous, bicornute, cornific.

3. Horn-shaped, corniform, crescent-shaped, cornute, bicorn, sigmoid, crescentiform.

HOROLOGE, *n.* Any instrument for telling time, timepiece, watch, clock, isochron, sundial, horologium, chronometer, clepsydra, water clock, *ghurry (Ind.)*, chronograph, chronoscope, dial, metronome, hourglass, gnomon.

HOROSCOPY, *n.* Casting the ascendant, calculating nativities, astrology, genethlialogy, judicial astrology, mundane astrology, natural astrology.

HORRIBLE, *adj.* Terrible, abhorrent, detestable, alarming, sickening, fell, odious, unsightly, appalling, frightful, terrifying, horrific, hideous, harrowing, revolting, repulsive, monstrous, awful, fearful, grim, ghastly, bloodcurdling, shocking, grotesque, horrid, forbidding, ugly, ogreish, execrable, atrocious, ghoulish, vile, loathsome, disgusting, gorgonesque, abominable, grisly, beastly, unbearable, insufferable, hellish, teratoid, heinous, hateful, damnable, dreadful, nocuous, unspeakable, gruesome, evil-looking, noxious, unseemly, unpleasant, base, evil-shaped, obnoxious, despicable, noisome, misshappen, unutterable, revolting, nauseating, sinister, evil, develish, rank, Satanic, foul, misproportioned, fulsome, macabre, displeasing, astounding, terror-bringing, portentous, ill-looking, evil-looking, cadaverous, ghostlike, distasteful, unsavory, dismaying, disagreeable, disconcerting, terror-breathing, startling, creepy, scaring, formidable, awe-inspiring, disquieting, unmanning, terror-breeding, lurid, redoubtable, crushing, repellent, baleful, malevolent, maleficent, harmful, demoniac, diabolical, infernal, Stygian, Tartarean, evil-fashioned, black, hellish, fiendish, bestial.

HORRIFY, *v.* Strike terror into, shock, appall, unman, startle, daunt, make tremble, strike awe into, prostrate, dishearten, harass, disconcert, harrow, petrify, haunt, terrify, dismay, scare, alarm, fill with horror, disquiet, sicken, disgust, freeze the blood, nauseate, repel, revolt, offend, make one's hair stand on end, intimidate, frighten, make one sick, turn one's stomach, make the flesh creep.

HORROR, *n.* 1. Feeling of horror, repugnance, dread, *etc.,* fear, terror, loathing, pain, abhorrence, fright, antipathy, awe, dread, dismay, phobia, abomination, trepidation, aversion, detestation.

disgust, execration, fearfulness, panic, nightmare, hatred, apprehension.

2. Monster, monstrosity, malignity, fiend, beast, Gorgon, phantom, banshee, evil-spirit, ghoul, demon, cacodemon, vampire, terror, fright, nightmare, nightmarish creature, ghost, troll, hellhound, ogre, ogress, devil, lamia.

3. Malevolent act, atrocity, outrage, offense against humanity, evil deed, crime, cruelty, barbaric act, inhumanity, terror, bestial behavior, malefaction, enormity, sin, monstrous act.

HORS D'OEUVRE, *n.* Relish, appetizer, antipasto.

HORSE, *n.* 1. Mount, steed, charger, courser, bronco, mule, hunter, filly *(fem.)*, palfrey, stallion *(masc.)*, ambler, gelding *(emasculated horse)*, mare *(fem.)*, bayard, nag *(derog.)*, barb, cob, dobbin, hackney, hinny *(hybrid)*, stud *(for breeding)*, trotter, runner, galloper, equine, jade *(usually derog.)*, sumpter, roan, sorrel, plug *(sl., derog.)*, screw *(coll., worn out horse)*, geegee *(coll.)*, pacer, garran, mustang, centaur *(Gr. Myth., half-human)*, pinto *(West. U.S.)*, warragal *(wild horse, Austral.)*, bat horse *(Mil.)*, clicker *(Forging)*, grizzle, punch, pintado *(U.S. and Mex.)*, draft horse, thoroughbred, thiller, tarpan, Hambletonian, American Standard, Clydesdale, Belgian, Galloway, Arab, Turk, jennet. *YOUNG:* yearling, colt, weaner, foal.

2. Stand, frame, trestle, support, clotheshorse, buck, sawbuck, sawhorse.

HORSELAUGH, *n.* Hoot, guffaw, cackle, shriek, cachinnation, bellow, lough, laugh.

HORSEMAN, *n.* 1. Rider, equestrian, equestrienne *(fem.)*, jockey, gaucho, pricker *(Hist.)*, broncobuster *(West. U.S.)*, cowboy, buckaroo *(West. U.S.)*, postilion.

2. Mounted soldier, cuirassier, lancer, knight *(Hist.)*, hussar, Cossack, cavalier, trooper, dragoon, horse soldier, horse marine *(Hist.)*, cavalryman.

3. One who tends horses, stableman, stableboy, trainer, groom, equerry, hostler, ostler, tiger *(Hist. sl.).*

HORSEPLAY, *n.* Boisterous play, clowning, fooling, foolery, monkeyshines *(sl.)*, buffoonery, tomfoolery, shenanigans *(coll.)*, capers, practical jokes, monkey tricks, jests, antics, pranks, sprees, larks.

HORTICULTURE, *n.* Care *or* cultivation of gardens, olericulture *(vegetables)*, floriculture, viniculture *(grape vines)*, arboriculture *(trees and shrubs, etc.).*

HOSANNA, *n.* Cry of praise, cry of jubilation, cry of hosanna, paean, laudation, glory, huzza, cheer, magnification, hallelujah, allelujah, hurrah, laud, spiritual exaltation, glorification.

HOSE, *n.* 1. Garments for the leg, etc. (See HOSIERY, *n.* **below.**)

2. Pipe, tubing, tube, tubulation, tubulure *(Chem.)*, tap, catheter *(Med.)*, siphon.

HOSIERY, *n.* Garments for the leg, hose, stockings, socks, leggings, gaiters.

HOSPITABLE, *adj.* Friendly, neighborly, cordial, kind, open, gregarious, unhostile, welcoming, companionable, gracious, cooperative, receptive, sociable, warm, approachable, convivial, amicable.

HOSPITAL, *n.* Institution for the physically *or* mentally sick, asylum, sanatorium, sanitarium, infirmary, sick bay, clinic, policlinic, polyclinic, medical center, valetudinary, valetudinarium *(Rom. Antiq.)*, lazaretto, pesthouse *(largely Hist.).*

HOSPITALITY, *n.* Receptiveness, friendliness, neighborliness, sociability, warmth, conviviality, amicability, cordiality, kindness, openness, gregariousness, graciousness, welcome, hospitableness, reception, greeting.

HOST, *n.* 1. Entertainer, hostess *(fem.)*, Amphitryon.

2. Hotel keeper, landlord, hotel manager, master, mistress, manager, proprietor, innkeeper, restaurateur, Boniface, hotelier, owner, hosteler *(Hist.)*, proprietress *or* proprietrix *(fem.)*.

3. Great number, band, party, circle, group, assembled body, gathering, meeting, gang, crew, troop, concourse, convention, throng, congregation, company, cohort, convocation, multitude, cavalcade, mob, lot, entourage, legion, confluence, conflux, levy, muster, tribe, congress, drove, covey, brood, mess, conclave, swarm, array, posse.

4. *(Eccl., capitalized)* Bread of the Lord's *or* Last Supper, wafer, Eucharist, Communion bread *or* loaf, altar bread, sacramental bread.

HOSTAGE, *n.* Person *or* thing held as pledge, pledge, pawn, gage, earnest, surety, security, guarantee, guaranty, vadium *(Leg.)*, warrant, tie, bond, token, collateral, bail, deposit.

HOSTEL, *n.* Lodging place *(usually)* for young tourists, inn, hospice, caravansary, lodging place, resting place, *khan (Near East.)*.

HOSTILE, *adj.* 1. At war, warring, contesting, skirmishing, tilting, jousting, bickering, opposing, opposed, quarreling, feuding, belligerent, contending, militant, fighting, combative, wrangling, enemy, discordant, disaccordant, oppositional, battling, broiling, dueling, attacking, countering, disputing, clashing, jarring, at odds, at outs, up in arms, with crossed swords, at loggerheads, with daggers drawn, at enmity, on bad terms, factious, discrepant, incompatible, dissident, disagreeing.

2. Antagonistic, unfriendly, unsympathetic, ugly, mean, estranged, haughty, contentious, inimical, cold, unsociable, inhospitable, antipathetic, bristling, disdainful, ill-willed, quarrelsome, bellicose, belligerent, fractious, contrary, snappish, disputatious, harsh, cranky, sullen, cantankerous, disobliging, splenetic, crabbed, huffy, ill-natured, argumentative, froward, iracund, touchy, testy, bearish, crusty, bitter, unkind, spiteful, malevolent, malicious, virulent, acrimonious, malignant, maleficent, ill-disposed, venomous, treacherous, vicious, rancorous, truculent.

HOSTILITY, *n.* 1. Antagonism, unfriendliness, enmity, hatred, hate, dislike, animosity, malevolence, inimicality, antipathy, spite, odium, bad blood, ill will, malice, grudge, venom, rancor, phobia, aversion, rankling, coldness, loathing, conflict, clashing, bitterness, oppugnancy, discord, harshness, alienation, displacency, dissension, estrangement, irreconciliation, inimicalness, disaffection, coolness, disfavor, averseness, vindictiveness, implacability, resentment, dudgeon, wrath, anger, virulence, contumely, acerbity, acrimony, ire, revengefulness, misanthropy, misogyny, hardness, contempt, rage, fury.

2. *(Often Plural)* Fighting, battling, contention, conflict, fight, engagement, encounter, rencounter, tourney, action, concussion, military operation, arms, scrimmage, bloodshed, the sword, onslaught, feud, duel, embroilment, clash, match, impact, action, counteraction, confrontation, controversy, dispute, impingement, charge, assault, resistance, fisticuffs, collision, fracas, militancy, bombardment, tussle, belligerence, struggle, affray, strife, set-to, fray, tournament, warfare, bout, tilt, joust, affair, brush, percussion, scuffle, combat, siege, altercation, disputation.

HOT, *adj.* 1. Warm, red hot, white hot, at high temperature, roasting, calescent, torrid, boiling, heated, incandescent, searing, blazing, scorching, scalding, fiery, broiling, grilling, parching, flaming, burning, candent, thermal, igneous, piping-hot, molten, calid, ovenlike, toasting, baking, smoldering, sizzling, simmering, thermogenic *(producing heat)*, recalescent *(Phys. and Chem.)*, decalescent *(Phys. and Chem.)*.

2. *(Of weather, climates, etc.)* Sultry, tropical, oppressive, sweltering, steaming, blazing, warm, boiling, simmering, heat-laden, summery, scorching, blistering, broiling, roasting, canicular, torrid, baking, sizzling, toasting, sweltry, oven-like.

3. *(Of electric wires, etc.)* Electrified, live, carrying current, powered, high-powered, charged, galvanic.

4. *(Of spices, foods, etc.)* Burning to the tongue, peppery, mustard-like, sharp, highly-seasoned, nippy, biting, piercing, caustic, keen, acrid, pungent, piquant, tart.

5. Ardent, passionate, fervid, excited, agitated, furious, desperate, violent, hectic, zealous, intense, feverish, warm, intoxicated, frenzied, fierce, vehement, stormy, inflamed, emotional, wrought-up, foaming, disturbed, boiling, unquiet, perturbed, animated, kindled, burning, glowing, delirious, rigorous, tempestuous, raging, seething, simmering, ebullient.

6. Lustful, salacious, animalistic, lecherous, carnal, sensual, prurient, concupiscent, voluptuous, theroid, physical, bestial, wanton, brutish, lickerish, sexual, libidinous, lascivious, lewd, ruttish.

7. Fresh, strong, new, warm, recent, late, latest.

HOTBED, *n.* Den, sink, breeding ground, breeding place, nest, cradle, incubator, nidus.

HOT-BLOODED, *adj.* Wild, rash, quick, impetuous, madcap, venturesome, dashing, indiscreet, excitable, giddy, reckless, breakneck, harebrained, brash, headlong, foolhardy, devil-may-care, daring, helter-skelter, foolish, heedless, hasty, careless, impulsive, unwary, unadvised, injudicious, regardless, snap, precipitous, precipitate, rantipole, over-eager, unbridled, unchecked, hotspur, thoughtless, mad-brained, uncontrolled, ungoverned, adventurous.

HOTEL, *n.* Inn, house, tavern, caravansary, hospice *(esp. one kept by a religious order)*, lodging place, rooming house, motel, *khan (Near East.)*, hostel *(esp. for young travelers)*.

HOT-HEADED, *adj.* See HOT-BLOODED, *adj.* above.

HOTHOUSE, *n.* Artificially heated place for growing plants, *etc.*, greenhouse, glasshouse, conservatory.

HOTSPUR, *n.* Hellcat, blood, rantipole, hothead, madcap, harebrain, daredevil, harum-scarum.

HOUGH, *v.* Hamstring, disable, lame, incapacitate, impair, injure, cramp, disenable, unsinew, hock, maim, becripple, cripple.

HOUND, *n.* Dog, canine, cur, tyke, pooch *(sl.)*, mutt *(sl.)*. YOUNG: whelp, pup, puppy.

HOUND, *v.* Pursue unrelentingly, track, follow, chase, hunt, trail, dog, bedog, pursue, stalk, tag after, try to overtake, shadow, keep after, drive, fly after, go after, tail *(coll.)*, make after.

HOUR, *n.* Period, time, fixed time, short time, an instant or two, a few minutes, term, while, interval, a second or two, moment, span, stretch, space, little bit, spell.

HOUSE, *n.* 1. Building for human habitation, dwelling, residence, home, place of lodgment *or* rest, residential hall for students, lodgings, quarters, abode, habitation, seat, place, shanty, domicile, mansion, cottage, ranch, rancho, hut, hall, shed, bungalow, barracks, apartment house, cabin, parsonage, duplex, den, igloo, kennel, box, tenement, messuage, barn, tupek, dump *(sl.),* joint *(sl.),* coop, stable, hotel, palace, hovel, booth, lodge, villa, manse, lair, address, inn, country residence, château, hutch, court, cot, cote, pavilion, diggings *(coll.),* kiosk, shack, castle, shelter, dwelling-place.

2. Building for public gatherings, people assembled, edifice, place of entertainment, temple, theater, convent, hall, audience, opera house, congregation, spectators, fabric, monastery, headquarters, concert hall, tavern, conventicle, odeum, hippodrome, auditorium, dome *(Poetic),* church.

3. Family, household, members *or* residents of a hall *(as in colleges),* fraternity, domestic establishment, garrison, crew, ménage.

4. Lineage, kindred, tribe, ancestry, extraction, pedigree, ancestors, descent, blood, race, strain, stock, root, people, clan, stem, nation, sept, line, birth, derivation, family tree, stirps, gens *(Rom. Hist. or Anthrop.),* dynasty.

5. Legislative body, advisory *or* deliberative group, congress, council, legislature, lower chamber, Commons, gemot *(Hist.),* quorum *(of legislative or deliberative body),* assembly.

6. Firm, concern, commercial establishment, company, stock, partnership, co-partnership, business, trading concern, corporation, shop, enterprise, store, undertaking.

HOUSE, *v.* Put *or* receive into a house, give shelter to, lodge, protect, harbor, remove from exposure, guard, safeguard, enclose in a house, confine, cover, roof, shelter, put under cover, furnish with a house, put in a safe place, billet, quarter, shield, bed, ensconce, procure a house *or* home for, put up.

HOUSEBREAKER, *n.* Thief, rascal, burglar, prowler, robber, felon, yegg *(sl.),* second-story worker *(coll.),* cracksman *(sl.).*

HOUSEHOLD, *n.* Family, house, home, family circle, establishment, ménage, hearth, home roof, ingleside, chimney corner, homestead.

HOUSEHOLDER, *n.* Occupier of a house, head of a family, property owner, proprietor, cottager, cotter, patriarch, landlord, landlady, master, mistress, proprietress, innholder, host, hostess, innkeeper, hotel keeper, lord of the manor, hôtelier *(Fr.),* landowner.

HOUSEKEEPER, *n.* Woman who does *or* directs the work of a household, housewife, matron, chief maid, manager of domestic details, home economist, female servant, maid-servant.

HOUSEWIFE, *n.* Mistress of a family, homemaker, wife, housekeeper, home economist, family manager.

HOUSING, *n.* 1. Something serving as a shelter, covering, *etc.,* abode, house, home, roof, dwelling, domicile, lodgment, lodging, shelter, protection, covering, cantonment, headquarters, quarters, diggings *(coll.),* stopping place, stopover, accommodations, shield, box, residence, habitation,

case, cask, enclosure, wrapper, sheath, jacket, envelope, capsule, receptacle.

2. Providing of houses, act of one who houses *or* shelters, quartering, billeting, making room for, accommodation, harboring.

3. *(Often plural)* Covering of cloth for back and flanks of animals, horsecloth, horse blanket, caparison, saddle blanket, pad, trappings, saddle cloth, tilpah *(Southwestern U. S.),* apishamore *(Northwestern U. S.).*

HOVEL, *n.* Small mean dwelling-house, wretched hut, open shed *(as for sheltering cattle, tools, etc.),* cabin, cot, hole, den, mean habitation, cottage, hutch, dump *(sl.),* lean-to, chalet, shanty, dugout, shack *(coll.),* ramshackle building.

HOVER, *v.* 1. Hang suspended in the air, flutter, flit, soar, wing, be buoyed up, drift, be wafted, rise, float, volitate, play, fly.

2. Linger about, hang over, be imminent, impend, haunt, trouble, plague, await, loom, obsess, be ever-present, accompany, frequent, menace, lower, threaten, be often with, hang upon, court, heel, shadow, trail, attend, vex, harass, be sycophantic, truckle, toady, be a hanger-on, follow importunately, ingratiate oneself, impose oneself, hang *or* lie over, hang about, wait near at hand, intrude upon continually, worry, molest.

3. Remain in an uncertain *or* irresolute state, show indecision, vacillate, hang, compromise, hesitate, not know one's own mind, pause, demur, falter, pendulate, oscillate, vary, shift, shuffle, palter, hang fire, hang in doubt, hang back, debate, be of two minds, think twice about, seesaw, shilly-shally, fluctuate, consider, dally, ponder, wobble, back and fill, straddle *(coll.),* be uncommitted, blow hot and cold, hum *or* hem and haw, sit on the fence *(coll.),* wait to see how the wind blows, wait to see how the cat jumps.

HOW, *adv.* 1. In what manner, after what fashion, by what mode, in what way, from what source, whence, by virtue of what, wherewith, by what aid, through what agency *or* medium, by whose help, by what means, whereby.

2. To what extent, to what degree, at what price, in what quantity *or* abundance.

3. In what state, by what name, in what plight, in what condition.

4. For *or* from what cause, why, by what justification, how comes it, wherefore, why ever, for what purpose, on what account, for what reason.

5. To what effect, with what meaning, with what efficacy, by what recommendation, by what standard, in what context, by what explanation, with what qualification.

HOWEVER, *adv.* Howsoever, in whatever manner, by any means, in any way *or* respect, anywise, to any degree, to whatever extent *or* degree, no matter how *(far, much, etc.),* in whatever degree, by any manner of means.

HOWEVER, *conj.* Yet, still, nevertheless, in spite of that, at any rate, notwithstanding, though, despite that, at all events, albeit, regardless of, for all that, just the same *(coll.),* although such be the case, after all, anyway, anyhow, rather, excepting that only, on the other hand, in consideration of that, but, howbeit, in any case, even so, at the same time, be that as it may, all the same *(coll.).*

HOWL, *n.* Cry *(as of a dog, wolf, etc.),* wail, yell, hoot, roar, yowling, howling, wailing, vociferation, moan, groan, complaint, plaint, ululation, loud mournful sound, challenge (*Hunting*), hub-bub, ecphonesis, lament, chorus, loud scornful laugh *or* yell, call, ululu (*imit.*), bawling, bellow, weeping, tumult, crying, uproar, clamor, outcry, yawl, caterwaul, lamentation, mourning, hue and cry, song (*coll.*), hullabaloo, exclamation.

HOWL, v. Utter a loud prolonged mournful cry, cry (*as a dog or wolf*), lament, wail, yell, cry out in distress (pain, rage, *etc.*), bay, moan, groan, scream, squall, yelp, mourn, weep, call, shout, rend the air, whistle (*of wind*), bellow, cry out, hoot, exclaim, roar, ejaculate, shriek, rail, yawl (*coll.*), vociferate, yowl, bawl, ululate.

HOYDEN, adj. Boisterous, hoydenish, romping, tomboyish, sportive, termagant, rambunctious (*coll.*), wild, unruly, noisy, perverse, reckless, un-tamed, ill-behaved, ill-mannered, rough, inelegant, rustic, roistering, ungovernable, obstinate, uncon-trollable, tumultuous, uncivilized, unrepressed, un-gentle, unsuppressed, unbridled, uncultivated, up-roarious, pert, saucy, sly, impudent, obstreperous, harum-scarum, irrepressible, playful, turbulent, youthful, uncouth, ungenteel.

HOYDEN, n. Rude *or* ill-bred girl, tomboy, romp, hussy, minx, lively young girl, roughneck (*sl.*), baggage (*fam. or playful*), termagant.

HUB, n. 1. Central part of wheel (*in which spokes are inserted*), axle, nave, gudgeon, journal (*Mach.*).
2. Central part around which all else revolves, axis, center, fixed point, focal point, pivot, core, kernel, basis, heart, focus, nucleus, backbone, nex-us, middle, foundation, hinge, radiant, marrow, gist, interior, navel.

HUBBUB, n. Loud confused noise, uproar, tu-mult, sound of many voices, pandemonium, fo-mentation, din, racket, hullabaloo, disorder, clam-or, riot, disturbance, commotion, hurly-burly, perturbation, lamentation, quarrel, ferment, ado, storm, to-do (*coll.*), agitation, bluster, hue and cry, rumpus (*coll.*), ruckus (*sl.*), pother, squall (*coll.*), fuss, rowdydow (*coll.*), row (*coll.*), excita-tion, bobbery (*coll.*), charivari, bedlam, shindy (*sl.*), callithump, babble, turmoil, rout, fluster, noise, outcry, confusion, babel, bustle, riot, stir.

HUCKSTER, n. 1. Retailer of small articles, street peddler, hawker, vender, higgler, colporteur, cheap-Jack (*coll.*), cheap-John (*coll.*), cadger, petty dealer, hucksterer, sutler, *vivandier (Fr.)*, *vivandi-ère (fem., Fr.)*, faker (*coll.*), *camelot (Fr.)*.
2. Cheaply mercenary person, miser, churl, niggard, faker, monger, tightwad (*sl.*), pinchfist, skinflint, codger, harpy, hunks, scrimp (*coll.*), pinchpenny, skate, muckworm, lickpenny, skin (*sl.*), curmudgeon, moneygrubber, screw.

HUDDLE, n. Confused mass, crowd, jumble, dis-order, confusion, heap, disarray, topsy-turvy, lit-ter, lumber, imbroglio, mess, medley, farrago, hugger-mugger, mix-up, mix (*coll.*), rummage, chowchow, odds and ends, olla-podrida, unassort-ed collection, tangle, wilderness, mixture, muddle, accumulation, pother, turmoil, jungle, disturbance, tumult, tumble, hash, hodgepodge, holy mess (*coll.*).

HUDDLE, v. 1. Throw together in confusion, gather in disorder, muddle, tumble, shove, round up, push, cram, pack, litter, shuffle, herd, hurry, throw in a heap, crowd confusedly, toss at ran-dom, disarrange, bunch, mass, heap, hustle (*coll.*).
2. (*Often foll. by* UP) Draw (*oneself*) closely together, nestle, hug, snuggle, curl up, make one-self small, cuddle.

3. (*Often foll. by* UP, OVER *or* TOGETHER) Do hastily *or* carelessly, hustle, rush through, scramble, scamper, bustle, hurry, plunge, be pre-cipitate, work against time, work under pressure, make short work of.
4. (*Often foll. by* ON) Put on (*clothes*) with careless haste, toss on, slip on, dash on, wrap, grab.
5. Crowd together, collect in a small space, gather closely, shrink, swarm, stream, converge, concentrate, throng, herd, cluster, bunch, surge, flock together, press together in confusion.

HUE, n. 1. Distinct region of the spectrum, color, tint, blush, chroma, dye, tone, cast, shade, tinc-ture, tinge, half tint (*Fine Arts*), demitint (*Fine Arts*), flush.
2. Outcry (*as of pursuers*), alarm, tumult, rack-et, clamor, uproar, hullabaloo, hurly-burly, fo-mentation, callithump, bustle, stir, fluster, babel, hue and cry, disturbance, whoop, cry, hoot, call, din, fuss, charivari, ado, Bedlam, agitation, com-motion, turbulence.

HUFF, n. Sudden swell of anger, fit of resentment, tiff, rage, pet, dudgeon, words, wrangle, run-in (*sl.*), falling out, rupture, breach, set-to (*coll.*), dispute, high words, bickering, squall (*coll.*), al-tercation, offense, peevishness, quarrel, passion, fume, petulance, indignation, squabble, spat, di-vision, pucker (*coll.*), cat fit (*hum.*), duck fit (*hum.*), ferment, scene, storm, explosion, out-burst, fury, flare-up (*coll.*), burst of anger, stew (*coll.*), disruption, pique, conniption (*coll.*), tan-trum (*coll.*), miff (*coll.*).

HUFF, v. 1. Give offense to, make angry, incense, inflame, incite, provoke, vex, roil, ruffle, anger, offend, stir one's bile, chafe, nettle, sting, affront, infuriate, have a falling out, pick a quarrel, pique, kindle wrath, excite to anger, tiff, spat, miff (*coll.*), put one out of countenance *or* humor, make one hot under the collar (*coll.*), envenom, embitter, raise one's gorge *or* choler, raise one's dander (*coll.*), put *or* get one's back up (*coll.*), put *or* get one's Irish up (*coll.*), irritate, exasperate, fall out, annoy, enrage, throw *or* fling down the gauntlet, insult, arouse.
2. Treat with arrogance *or* contempt, bluster at, storm at, slight, vilipend, vilify, disrespect, intimidate, bully, rage at, hector, affront, insult, trifle with, traduce, snub, desecrate, dishonor, speak evil of, point at, set down, humiliate, dis-parage, hold cheap, scorn, look down upon, in-dulge in personalities, contemn, despise, disdain, esteem slightly, snap one's fingers at, bite the thumb, scold, call names, spit upon, rebuff, keep at arm's length, revile, detract, derogate, decry, browbeat, cow, cut (*coll.*), taunt, underestimate, lord it over, cold-shoulder, blaspheme, ridicule, mock, jeer, gibe, calumniate, libel, defame, ma-lign, slander, cast aspersions, belittle, run down (*coll.*), flout, scout, scoff, heckle, harass, badger, bait, goad, gripe, scourge, abuse, gall, bullyrag, treat high-handedly, domineer, threaten, overbear, torment.

HUFFISH, adj. 1. Angry, impatient, petulant, irascible, peevish, touchy, churlish, easily offend-ed, irritable, waspish, resentful, ill-humored, quar-relsome, pettish, crabbed, choleric, thorny, bris-tling, sharp, acerbic, tart, acrimonious, peppery, splenetic, crusty, unamiable, perverse, morose, fractious, testy, caviling, curt, short, captious, jaundiced, rancorous, bilious, cross-grained, vengeful, defiant, arbitrary, self-willed, willful, contumacious.

2. Swaggering, blustering, insolent, intimidating, bullying, harassing, browbeating, cowing, overbearing, hectoring, bold, high-flown, puffed up, vain, proud, full of sound and fury, disdainful, cavalier, brazen, bluff, brash, audacious, impudent, haughty, supercilious, presumptuous, magisterial, pompous, lofty, imperious, arbitrary, scornful, withering, sarcastic, derisive, patronizing, high-headed, contumelious, contemptuous, arrogant, noisy, boisterous, toplofty (coll.), overweening, high-handed.

HUFFY, adj. 1. Easily angered, touchy, easily offended, petulant, impatient, churlish, ill-humored, resentful, irascible, pettish, waspish, quarrelsome, arbitrary, rancorous, fractious, peppery, thorny, angry, bristling, splenetic, testy, bilious, self-willed, wilful, cross-grained, caviling, crusty, sharp, peevish, crabbed, choleric, acrimonious, unamiable, morose, jaundiced, captious, defiant, contumacious, vengeful, short, curt, perverse.

2. Offended, sulky, obstinate, sullen, surly, wounded, hurt, stung, mumpish, glum, moping, scowling, morose, willful, cross, discontented, glowering, growling, dismal, bitter, rancorous, resentful, disgusted, disgruntled, fretful, displeased, irate, fiery, sore, unforgiving, splenetic, spleenful, furious, angered, perturbed, bearing a grudge, up in arms, out of humor, virulent, nauseated, sickened, infuriated, in high or deep dudgeon, in a pucker (coll.), ireful, set against, troubled, disturbed, cross-grained, moody, vindictive, acrimonious, injured, grumpy.

HUG, v. 1. Embrace, clasp tightly in the arms, fold in the arms, cling, hold, seize, enfold, envelop, embosom, cuddle, snuggle, lock, strain, caress, press, clutch, grasp, nestle, welcome, press to the bosom, throw oneself into the arms of, receive with open arms, cling together, lie close, fold to the breast or heart, receive warmly.

2. Cling firmly or fondly to, retain, nurse in the mind, cherish, nurture, nourish, persist in, refuse to give up, hold fast, foster, cultivate, be wedded to, keep hold of, be obstinate in, not yield an inch, be resolute, hold one's ground, stand pat in (coll.), doubt not, clench, clutch, assume, die hard, stick fast, adhere to, grip, maintain against opposition, swear by, embrace, have confidence in, trust in, attach weight to, entertain, harbor, hang on to, continue in, be determined, cradle, keep, clinch.

3. Keep close to (as in sailing or going along), go near, follow closely, hold, hover near, keep in sight of, trail, trail, shadow, coast, stay near, lie along (the shore), range (the shore).

HUGE, adj. Extraordinarily large in bulk (quantity or extent), vast, enormous, stupendous, colossal, herculean, very great, giant, excessive, titanic, mighty, ample, capacious, massive, main, mammoth, prodigious, egregious, tremendous, bulky, immense, gigantic, elephantine, Cyclopean, very large, mountainous, monstrous, massy, imposing, terrible (coll.), big, tall, grand, colossus-size, overwhelming, gross, towering, staggering, commanding, lofty, Gargantuan, dinotherian, dinosaurian, strapping (coll.), Atlantean, jumbo, leviathan, magnitudinous, extravagant, megatherine, spectacular, wonderful, exorbitant, ponderous, Antaean, monumental, inordinate, incredible, exceeding, gigantean, megatherian.

HUGGER-MUGGER, adj. 1. Secret, clandestine, concealed, sly, hidden, covered, screened, unrevealed, masked, dissembled, obscured, buried, delitescent, disguised, camouflaged, unseen, secreted, private, underhanded, secluded, feigned, evasive, dark, arcane, sneaking, ensconced, covert, veiled, taciturn, with secret design, shrouded, undisclosed, collusive, underground, cunning, confidential, skulking, dissembled, furtive, crafty, stealthy, surreptitious, undercover, privy.

2. Disorderly, confused, untidy, slovenly, messy, orderless, chaotic, dowdy, tousled, uncombed, slouchy, grubby, unkempt, frowzy, aimless, perplexed, sloppy (coll.), anarchic, sluttish, bedlamitish, helter-skelter, slatternly, topsy-turvy, frumpish, draggletailed, haphazard, disordered, disorganized, disarranged, all balled up (sl.), drabbletailed, wild, unsystematic, jumbled, pell-mell, littered, askew, awry, desultory, ramshackle, casual, scattered, straggling, deranged, discomposed, slipshod, muddled, careless.

HUGGER-MUGGER, n. Disorder, confusion, muddle, confused mass, jumble, heap, disarray, litter, imbroglio, mess, lumber, topsy-turvy, hodgepodge, pother, unassorted collection, rummage, medley, farrago, chow-chow, tangle, turmoil, holy mess (coll.), jungle, wilderness, odds and ends, mix-up, olla-podrida, mix (coll.), mixture, accumulation, disturbance, tumult, hash, tumble, huddle, ferment, scramble, upheaval, convulsion, discomposure, bustle, fuss, flurry, discord.

HULK, n. 1. Hull (of an old vessel), skeleton, shell, ruin, dismasted ship, derelict, body (of ship).

2. Prison ship.

HULKING, adj. Hulky, big, cumbersome, bulky, heavy, clumsy, unwieldy, awkward, overgrown, ugly, lubberly, oafish, lumpish, blockish, blundering, maladroit, gawky, gawkish, ungainly, uncouth, ungraceful, graceless, inelegant, cumbrous, loutish, unskillful.

HULL, n. 1. Husk, shell, covering, rind, coating, coat, crust, cortex, skin, integument, tegument, tegmentum, tegmen, protective covering, cuticle, cuticula, bark, fell, epidermis, ecderon, scarfskin, ectoderm, scale, calyx, bract, dermis, derma, corium, epithelium, pellicle, putamen, pod, case, membrane, pericarp, shuck, testa, episperm, cornhusk, cornshock, legume, legumen, peasecod, peapod, follicle, spore case, capsule, theca, bur, burr, glume, gluma, lemma, chaff, bran, palea, peel, peeling, epicarp, cortical tissue, peridium, periderm, dermatogen, carapace.

2. Body of ship.

HULL, v. Pare, peel, skin, flay, excoriate, bark, strip, decorticate, strip from, strip the hull from, strip the skin (peel, shell, bark) from, scalp, shell, shuck, pod, unstrip, exfoliate, desquamate, expose, denude, exuviate, uncover, bare, lay bare.

HULLABALOO, n. Noise, racket, din, outcry, vociferation, clamor, gaff, exclamation, ejaculation, ecphonesis, chorus, hue and cry, hubbub, roar, uproar, tumult, brouhaha, ballyhoo (coll.), bobbery, pandemonium, bedlam, brawl, fracas, rumpus, ruckus, ruction, alarm, alarum, clang, clangor, charivari, shivaree (dial. U. S.), babel, jangle, turmoil, turbulence, disturbance, ado, to-do, stir, row, fuss, trouble, bother, pother, riot, embroilment, melee, scramble, Donnybrook Fair.

HUM, *v.* 1. Buzz, make a buzzing sound, murmur, drone, bombinate, thrum, bum, whir, purr, vibrate, bombilate, zoom.

2. Sing, carol, lilt, troll, utter, croon, intone, tone, solmizate, drone, purr, warble.

HUM, *n.* Low noise, faint noise, faint sound, murmur, muration, bombination, bombilation, buzzing, buzz, zooming, zoom, whir, whirring, drone, droning, whiz, whizzing, purr, purring, vibration, vibrating, bombus.

HUMAN, *adj.* 1. Anthropoid, manlike, humanistic, hominine *(rare),* mortal, personal, individual, man's, of man, belonging to man, proper to man, hominal.

2. Fleshly, mortal, in the flesh, earthborn, physical, carnal, perishable, bodily, ephemeral, transient, transitory, transeunt, corporal, corporeal, short-lived, diurnal, fugacious, fleeting, transitive, passing, flying, evanescent, impermanent, temporary, temporal.

3. Erring, defective, culpable, faulty, faultful, at fault, peccant, wrong, wrongful, straying, errant, aberrant.

HUMAN, *n.* Creature, man, fellow creature, fellow man, person, personage, homo *(pl.* homines*),* anthropos, individual, mortal, soul, fellow *(coll.),* member of human race, fellow mortal, living soul, body, somebody, one, someone, guy *(sl.),* worldling.

HUMANE, *adj.* 1. Human, kind, kindly, benevolent, good-natured, amiable, genial, cordial, helpful, indulgent, well-natured, nonselfish, unselfish, magnanimous, warm-hearted, large-hearted, big-hearted, soft-hearted, sympathetic, sympathizing, forbearing, salutary, lenient, charitable, liberal, freehearted, bounteous, forgiving, benign, generous, gracious, pitying, beneficent, good, gentle, merciful, clement, compassionate, tender, accommodating, obliging, benignant.

2. Edifying, hortatory, humanistic, instructional, instructive, elevating, rational, refining, cultural, culturine, spiritual, humanizing, cultivating.

HUMANIST, *n.* Student of literature, philosopher, classicist, scholar, thinker, linguist, pundit, wise man, sage, scholiast, gownsman, Latinist, Hellenist, Graecist, Hebraeist, philomath, glossologist, glossolalist, man of letters, man of learning, commentator, annotator, classicalist, *littérateur (Fr.),* literatus *(pl.* literati*),* pantologist, bookworm, bibliophile, savant, bibliomaniac, authority, expert, specialist, mentor, connoisseur, philologer, philologist, philologian, philologue, grammarian, grammatist, lexicographer, lexicographist, lexicographologist, glossarist, glossarian, vocabulist, vocabularian.

HUMANITARIAN, *n.* 1. Benevolist, friend of man, friend to man, salt of the earth, good fellow, well-wisher, favorer, sympathizer, good samaritan, public servant, philanthropist, altruist, lover of mankind, almsgiver, almoner, benefactor, benefactress, benefiter, befriender, succorer, helper, helpmate.

2. *(Philosophy)* Philosopher, eudaemonist, Benthamite, utilitarian, socialist, communist.

3. *(Theology)* Theologist, theologian, Homoiousian, Heterousian, Arianist.

HUMANITIES, *n., pl.* (with prefix THE) Belles-lettres, polite literature, the classics, classics, humane studies, classical languages, learned languages, liberal arts, (the) muses, letters, litterae humaniores.

HUMANITY, *n.* 1. Human nature, mankind, the human race, humankind, man, manhood, the world, brotherhood of man, mortality, people, flesh, flesh and blood, race of man, homo, homo sapiens, mortals, anthropos.

2. Fellowship, brotherliness, benevolentness, benevolence, kindness, benignity, philanthropy, tenderness, amiability, grace, goodness, warmth of heart, sympathy, charity, charitableness, good will, bonhommie *(or* bonhomie*),* compassion, love for mankind, brotherly love, fraternal feeling, humaneness, kindheartedness, good-heartedness, big-heartedness, soft-heartedness, fellow feeling, good nature, milk of human kindness, kindliness, bounty, clemency, lenity, mercy, sensibility, altruism, ruth, forbearance, consideration, toleration, knight-errantry, chivalry, magnanimity, eudaemonism, brotherhood, fraternity, beneficence, Christian charity, unselfishness, generosity, humanitarianism.

HUMANIZE, *v.* 1. Make humane, soften, temper, attemper, polish, rub off the corners, rub off the rough edges, cultivate, tranquilize, modulate, mitigate, lenify *(rare),* dulcify, subdue, chasten, mellow, make polite.

2. Civilize, cultivate, refine, polish, improve, enlighten, educate, meliorate, ameliorate, develop, advance, forward, enrich, lift, raise, uplift, inspire.

HUMBLE, *adj.* 1. Meek, modest, unassuming, unpretending, biddable, cessionary, consentient, ductile, manageable, slavish, subsidiary, subservient, obsequious, lowly, submissive, unambitious, free from pride, without arrogance, godly, supplicatory, unpresuming, broken, contrite, reverential, docile, obedient, broken in spirit, restrained, reserved, yielding, unostentatious, mild, hesitant, timid, diffident, unimportant, of little importance, of small importance, inconsequential, insignificant, small, little, minute, ordinary, commonplace, meek-minded, meek-spirited, meek-hearted, low, unresisting, tolerant, enduring, tame, gentle, clement, peaceful, placid, peaceable, longanimous, passive, stoic, stoical, resigned, subdued, content, shy, bashful, demure, timorous, compliant, acquiescent, deferential, complaisant, tractable, sedate.

2. Low, small, poor, unpretending, undistinguished, meek, obscure, mean, plain, ignoble, inglorious, inferior, earthborn, base, little, of low birth, simple, low in rank, of low rank, low-ranking, common, plebeian, proletarian, of low parentage, of mean parentage, lowbred, baseborn, homely, homespun, uncouth, ignominious, measly, contemptible, ordinary, humdrum, ill-bred, inferior, menial, miserable, ordinary, paltry, peddling, petty, puny, scrubby, shabby, sordid, trivial, underbred, unfit, unequal, unrefined, vulgar, wretched.

HUMBLE, *v.* 1. Humiliate, shame, mortify, abash, abase, make ashamed, put out of countenance, strike dumb, confuse, confound, meeken, put to shame, put to the blush, snub, deny, disgrace, take down a peg, discomfit, embarrass.

2. Degrade, crush, break, subdue, bring down, put down, take down, take down a peg *(coll.),* demean, dishonor, depress, bring low, conquer, pull down, debase, cast down, stigmatize, brand, stain, tarnish, defile, reduce, derogate, tread *(or* trample) underfoot, expose *(to infamy),* cast dishonor upon, make lowly, make humble, chasten.

HUMBUG, *n.* 1. Hoax, imposture, imposition, fraud, deceit, trickery, deception, trick, cheat, gammon, dodge, gouge, blind, feint, chouse, gull, sham, stuff, spoof, bunk, buncombe, hokum (*sl.*), bamboozlement, misrepresentation, counterfeit, cheating, wile, cog, shift, blind, swindle, gyp (*sl.*), fake, make-believe, guise, disguise, disguisement, false colors, camouflage, mockery, mock, forgery, pretense, flam, flimflam, fabrication, invention, pretension, affectation, grandiosity, orotundity, pomposity, inflation, bombast, bombastry, rant, fustian, rodomontade, balderdash, Barnumism, duplicity, double-dealing, stratagem, artifice, brummagem, canard, bull (*sl.*), fable, story, tale, fiction, yarn, whopper, tall-story (*coll.*), tall-tale (*coll.*).

2. Quackery, mummery, hypocrisy, charlatanism, charlatanry, charlatanship, cant, fraudulence, trumpery, bosh (*sl.*), flummery, jargon, cajolery, jockery, nonsense, fraudulency, spoofery, humbuggery, humbuggism, bamboozling, trickery, pettifoggery, dishonesty, pretension, pretentiousness, hocus-pocus, equivocation, quackism, quackishness, fourflushing, bluffery, bluffing, affectation, affectedness, airs, display, show, putting on airs, putting on a front (*both coll.*), fanfaronade, pomposity, veneer, surface, Pharisaism, mendacity, untruth, untruthfulness, fib, fibbing, lie, lying, falsehood, falsifying, falsification, perjury, puffing, flattery, trumpeting, absurdity, babble, babbling, nonsense, blather, chatter, chitchat, wind, windiness, flatulence, folderol, rabble, rattle, claptrap, stuff, tergiversation.

3. Impostor, charlatan, quack, cheat, fop, knave, deceiver, rascal, mountebank, hypocrite, fake, fraud, deluder, dissimulator, dissembler, pharisee, sophist, cheater, sharper, trickster, rogue, swindler, perjurer, cozener, faker, fourflusher, liar, prevaricator, equivocator, romancer, fibber, storyteller (*coll.*), fibster, pretender, malingerer, adventurer, adventuress, huckster, duffer, gouger, shyster, necromancer, chameleon, coxcomb, dandy, puppy, snob, upstart, parvenu, puffer, flatterer, sycophant, adulator, trumpeter.

HUMBUG, *v.* Cheat, deceive, swindle, trick, hoax, cozen, impose upon, chouse, befool, fool, mystify, bamboozle, deride, affect, mislead, invent, attitudinize, counterfeit, dissemble, dissimulate, fox (*coll.*), doctor, pose, sham, mask, soldier, beguile, brag, bluster, roister, bluff, belie, bias, canard, chicane, delude, diddle, distort, dogmatize, equivocate, exaggerate, fable, fib, fabricate, fabulize, falsify, feign, flare, foist, forswear, fudge, gammon, hyperbolize, illude, imp, lie, magnify, malinger, misrepresent, misguide, perjure, pervert, prejudice, pretend, prevaricate, quibble, romance, simulate, babble, blather, cackle, chatter, puff, hoodwink, sell (*sl.*), cajole, conjure, juggle, Machiavellize, cog, sharp, let in, take in (*both coll.*), bilk, bite, betray, play false, divert, lead astray, outwit, practice upon, gull, victimize, palm off, overreach, outreach, steal a march on, ensnare, entrap, dupe, play a trick on, throw off the scent, misstate, blindfold, pass off, play possum, conceal, bemask, hide under *or* put on a false front, twist, garble, stretch, strain, maneuver, disarm, mulct, bilk, palter.

HUMDRUM, *adj.* Monotonous, dull, prosy, tedious, tiresome, dry, wearisome, stupid, dreary, slow, prosaic, prosaical, irksome, uneventful, ordinary, unchanged, unchanging, undeviated, undeviating, unvaried, unvarying, undiversified, worn-thin, wearying, weariful, boring, boresome, uninteresting, unlively, lifeless, bald, jejune, flat, insipid, drearisome, trite, trivial, stereotyped,

stock, set, banal, common, commonplace, familiar, everyday, household, household-variety, garden-variety, matter-of-fact, platitudinous, threadbare, thin, hackneyed, dismal, cheerless, doleful, stolid, stagnant, sluggish, listless, inert, inanimate, dead, conventional, Philistine, usual, regular, unexciting, uninspired, uninspiring, mediocre, middling, passable, fair, fairish, indifferent, average, unobjectionable, unexceptionable, wishy-washy, unanimated, unruffled, arid, unentertaining.

HUMID, *adj.* Damp, moist, dank, wet, waterish, sultry, aqueous, dewy, liquid, pluvial, watery, rainy, steamy, moisty, dampish, wettish, muggy, sticky, madid (*rare*), sweaty, perspiry, sudatory, sudorous, sudorific, sudoric, sudoriferous, sudoriparous, stifling, oppressive, humectant, humectating, hydrous, vaporous, vaporose, vaporish, vapory, vaporific, vaporiferous, vaporescent.

HUMIDITY, *n.* Moisture, dampness, wet, sultriness, mugginess, vaporization, evaporation, humectation, humidification, steaminess, steam, dankness, sweatiness, dewiness, liquidity, stickiness, madidity, sudorificness, oppressiveness, wetness, moistness.

HUMILIATE, *v.* Humble, mortify, shame, abash, strike dumb, confuse, confound, meeken, put to shame, put to the blush, snub, deny, disgrace, take down a peg, discomfit, embarrass, cast into the shade, fill with shame, chagrin, lower, make subdue, bring down, put down, take down humble, make lowly, degrade, crush, break, abase, make ashamed, put out of countenance, a peg (*coll.*), demean, dishonor, depress, bring low, conquer, vanquish, pull down, cast down, stigmatize, debase, chasten, brand, stain, tarnish, defile, reduce, derogate, tread (*or* trample) underfoot, expose (*to infamy*), cast dishonor upon.

HUMILIATION, *n.* Dishonor, meekness, submission, reduction, humbling, dishonoring, putting to shame, crushing, degradation, mortification, abasement, disgrace, baseness, abuse, shame, downfall, ingloriousness, ignominy, abjection, depression, obloquy, self-abasement, disrepute, disreputation, ill repute, bad repute, lowliness, lowlihood, humbled pride, letdown, setdown, depreciation, disparagement, derogation, detraction, execration, impeachment, imputation, indictment, fall, humbleness, humility, indignity, vilification, infamy, renunciation, recrimination, reproach, reproof, slander, libel, scandal, scurrility, scurrilousness, stigma.

HUMILITY, *n.* Humbleness, meekness, self-abasement, submission, abasement, diffidence, modesty, lowliness of mind, lowliness of spirit, timidity, resignation, confusion, mortification, reserve, diffidence, shyness, bashfulness, demureness, unobtrusiveness, inferiority, commonalty, subjection, subservience, obsequiousness, obedience, lowliness.

HUMMOCK, *n.* 1. Hillock, knoll, knob of soil, barrow, bump, dune, hump, knob, kopje, mount, mound, prominence, protuberance, swelling, bulge, protrusion, excrescence, excrescency, gibbosity, boss, hammock, butte, convexity, convexness, convexedness, intumescence, tumescence, swell, knurl, elevation, eminence, knap, monticule, monticle.

2. Ridge, pile, hump, knob, protuberance, hub, raised rim, hog's back, esker, fillet, ridgelet, ridge, inion, crest, spine, seam, convexity, chine, kame, comb, horseback, hogback.

HUMOR, *n.* 1. Fluid (*of animal bodies*), moisture, vapor, phlegm, choler, bile, lymph, eyewater, pus, fluid matter, liquid, blood, juice, rheum, sanies, liquor, sap, latex, flatulence, milk, serous fluid, serum, plasma, ichor, chyle, mucus, melancholy, gas, volatility, gaseity, gaseousness, flatulency, ether, fume, mist.

2. Disposition, bent, temper, turn of mind, frame of mind, bias, propensity, predilection, vein, tendency, quality, spirit, prevailing spirit, qualities, character, nature, grain, mood, tendency, disposedness, inclination, predisposition, proneness, diathesis, proclivity, sympathy, soul, heart, bosom, zeal, force, élan *(Fr.)*, ardor, fire, verve, aptness, temperament, habit, cast, stripe, mould, crasis, propensitude, propenseness, readiness, penchant, turn, warp, leaning, gravitation, course, trend, tenor, drift, set, idiocrasy, conduciveness, nisus, conatus, conation, susceptibility, liability, susceptivity, idiosyncrasy, animus, mettle, characteristics, desire, wish, desideration, like, liking, love, fondness, relish, partiality, weakness.

3. Fancy, whim, caprice, wrinkle, crotchet, freak, vagary, whimsey, maggot, pet, whimsicality, affections, idiosyncrasy, cacoethes, pruriency, prurience, itch, hankering, notion, whim-wham, boutade, flimflam, fad, fantastic notion, fancy notion, quirk, crank, kink, bee in the bonnet *(coll.)*, fit, capriciousness, coquetry, eccentricity, erraticism, queerness, oddity, peculiarity, twist, mental twist, quip, conceit, craze, mania, fanaticism, infatuation, obsession, fascination, enthusiasm, passion, fixed idea, idée fixe *(Fr.)*, faddishness, changeableness, changeability, inconstancy, instability, vacillation, variability, fluctuation, tergiversation, fickleness.

4. Jocosity, jocularity, facetiousness, fun, wit, comedy, pleasantry, jocoseness, sense of the ludicrous, burlesque, joke, banter, quip, jest, caprice, capriciousness, satire, waggery, shenanigans, comicality, drollery, raillery, jesting, wittiness, salt, Attic salt, Atticism, ready wit, buffoonery, buffoonism, fooling, foolery, tomfoolery, waggish trickery, waggishness, harlequinade, monkeyshines, witticism, capital joke, gag, wisecrack *(both coll.)*, play of wit, quirk, conceit, quiddity, mot, fantasy, badinage, repartee, bon mot *(Fr.)*, happy thought, bright idea, bright saying, smart saying, story, yarn, tale, funny story, flash of wit, anecdote, scintillation, persiflage, retort, sally, clever sally, snappy comeback *(coll.)*, ready reply, witty reply, quips and cranks, wordplay, play on words, pun, punning, old joke, trite joke, chestnut, hoary chestnut, bromide *(coll.)*, Joe Miller, Joe Millerism, prank, trick, waggish trick, practical joke, ridiculousness, ludicrousness, ridiculosity, farcicality, amphigouri *or* amphigory, nonsense, nonsense verse, doggerel, doggerel verse, malapropism, spoonerism, Partingtonism, farce, comedy, broad humor, low humor, low comedy, raw comedy, slapstick, polite comedy, ridicule, derision, mockery, raillery, twitting, chaffing, chaff, asteism, sarcasm, humoresque, parody, travesty, caricature, espièglerie *(Fr.)*, cleverness, brightness, brilliance, smartness.

HUMOR, *v.* 1. Gratify, give way to, indulge, comply with *(the wishes of)*, pamper, coddle, wheedle, satisfy, wink at, satiate, grant, cajole, cue, fondle, spoil, appease, caress, placate, soothe, mollify, coax, flatter, baby, turn, temporize, foster, please, permit, let, allow, admit, suffer, tolerate, stretch a point, cosset, overindulge, accede to, be lenient, let one have his own way, be lax with, laisser faire *(Fr.)*, laisser aller *(Fr.)*, give free rein

to, tickle another's fancy, hit another's fancy, flatter, adulate, pet, coquet, suit, accommodate, do another proud, slaver, beslaver, beslubber, puff, fawn, truckle, toady, toadeat, lick another's shoes, lick the dust off another's shoes (boots), grovel before, crawl before, creep before, throw oneself at the feet of, kowtow to, bow and scrape to, ingratiate oneself with, insinuate oneself with, be in the good graces of, court, curry favor with, pay court to, follow at the heels of, serve time for, sate.

2. Favor, suit the nature of, meet the requirements of, satisfy, fit, accommodate, oblige, consult the wishes of, cheer, encourage, meet, adapt to, follow, conform to, provide for, make provision for, indulge with, favor with, comply with, submit, submit to, yield to, yield before, comply, acquiesce, accede, relent, give way, give place to, resign oneself, stoop to, bend *(the neck)*, bow, knuckle to, knuckle under, bend to another's yoke, kneel to, bend the knee to, fall on one's knees before, obey, bear obedience to, do one's bidding, attend to orders, serve, serve faithfully, serve loyally, serve devotedly, play second fiddle to, consent, give consent, admit, allow, yield assent, concede, concede to, grant to, give in to, close with, deign, vouchsafe.

HUMORIST, *n.* Wit, wag, comedian, droll fellow, joker, jokester, jester, reparteeist, banterer, persifleur *(Fr.)*, wisecracker *(sl.)*, epigrammatist, punster, bel-esprit *(Fr.)*, life of the party, droll, buffoon, merry-andrew, mime, tumbler, mountebank, harlequin, pantaloon, punch, clown, punchinello, motley, fool, caricaturist, grimacer, antic, pierrot, scaramouche, buffo, jokesmith, puck, satirist, lampoonist, lampooner, comique, comic, comedian, comedienne, cutup, zany, witling, wagwit, galliard, spark, punner, madcap, burlesquer, Joe Miller, funnyman, farcist, farcer, farceur *(Fr.)*, farceuse *(Fr.)*, mummer, mimer, mimic, mimologist, motley fool, wearer of motley, Punch, Pulcinella, Polichinelle, Columbine, light comedian, low comedian, slapstick artist, slapstick comedian, comedist, genteel comedian.

HUMOROUS, *adj.* Jocular, jocose, pleasant, facetious, droll, funny, witty, ludicrous, comical, comic, sportive, playful, arch, mirthful, rich, rib-tickling, risible, side-splitting, waggish, lively, vivacious, sprightly, amusing, paronomastic, punning, pungent, brilliant, laughable, whimsical, epigrammatic, smart, sparkling, quizzical, serio-comic, absurd, nonsensical, extravagant, preposterous, burlesque, ironical, satirical, mock-heroic, Hudibrastic, mock-epic, mock-epical, entertaining, diverting, recreative, festive, festal, jovial, jolly, playful, cheering, cheerful, merry, merry-and-wise, drollish, clever, smart, scintillating, sprightly, keen-witted, nimble-witted, quick-witted, pointed, sharp, ridiculous, farcical, screaming, screamingly funny, rompish, pranky, cute *(coll.)*, subtle, bizarre, convulsing, convulsive, Falstaffian, Rabelaisian, sarcastic, scurrilous, gelogenic.

HUMORSOME, *adj.* 1. Petulant, peevish, snappish, crusty, crotchety, fretful, touchy, perverse, wayward, cross-grained, fitful, freakish, morose, contrary, irascible, irritable, churlish, bearish, testy, fiery, techy, tetchy *(both coll.)*, huffy, pettish, querulous, captious, fractious, cantankerous, bristling, doggish, currish, impatient, bad-humored, ill-humored, galvanic, excitable, reckless, hasty, overhasty, quick, quick-tempered.

crabbed, cranky, choleric, huffish, cross, splenetic, peppery, moody, waspish.

2. Odd, capricious, fantastic, whimsical, fitful, fanciful, volatile, vaporish, eccentric, unconventional, irregular, heteroclite, informal, deviative, deviating, deviationist, diverging, divergent, straying, errant, aberrant, wandering, lawless, anomalous, anomalistic, full of whims, kinky, skittish, fanciful, fantastic, freakish, faddish, fadmongering, vagrant, wanton, unrestrained, undisciplined, uncontrolled, fast-and-loose, hysterical, contrary, unreasonable, not amenable, arbitrary, erratic, fickle, frivolous, giddy, light, lightminded, lightsome, frothy, mercurial, without ballast, irresponsible, unreliable, not to be relied upon, not to be depended upon, coquettish, flirtatious, variable, inconstant, unpredictable, unforeseeable, unstable, abnormal, abnormous, protean, proteiform, changeful, changeable, unstaid, unsteady, vacillating, idiocratic, idiosyncratic, queer, flighty, vertiginous.

HUMP, *n.* 1. Protuberance, hummock, convexity, convexedness, bulge, prominence, eminence, projection, barrow, bump, dune, kopje *(So. Africa),* mound, swelling, protrusion, excrescence, excrescency, gibbosity, boss, butte, convexness, tumescence, swell, knurl, knob, elevation, knap, monticle, hunch, lump.

2. Kyphosis *(Med.),* deformity, deformation, malformation, malconformation, monstrosity, misshape, humpback, hunchback, hunch, bunchback, crook-back, crooked-back, camel-back, round shoulders, stoop-shoulders, stoop, gibbosity, gibboseness, gibbousness.

HUMP, *v.* *(To move by strenuous exertion)* Convey, carry, heave, bear, shoulder, lug *(coll.),* tote *(coll.),* pack, haul.

HUMPBACK, *n.* Crooked back, kyphosis *(Med.),* hunch, hunchback, bunchback, crook-back, round shoulders, deformity, malformation, monstrosity, misshape, gibbus, stoop-shoulders, gibbosity, gibbousness, gibboseness, camel-back, malconformation.

HUMPBACKED, *adj.* Deformed, gibbous, kyphotic, crook-backed, camel-backed, hunched, malformed, malconformed, misshapen, hunchbacked, round-shouldered, stoop-shouldered, stooped, bowed, humped.

HUMUS, *n.* Soil, compost, dirt, earth, mold, loam, ground, glebe, clay, marl, subsoil, clod, sod, till, loamy soil, leaf mold, gumbo, mud, gumbo soil.

HUNCH, *n.* 1. Hump, protuberance, knob, lump, bunch, convexity, convexness, convexedness, bulge, prominence, projection, barrow, bump, kopje *(So. Africa),* mound, swell, swelling, protrusion, excrescence, excrescency, gibbosity, boss, hummock, butte, tumescence, knurl, knob, elevation, monticle, monticule, dune.

2. Impulse, impulsion, impetus, momentum, push, pulsion, thrust, shove, jog, jolt, jostle, propulsion, stroke, nudge, punch, buffet, blow, hit.

3. Lump, hunk, large piece, thick slice, chink, piece, bit, snatch, snack, cut, cutting, rasher, gob.

4. Premonition, intuition, foreknowledge, forewisdom, precognition, prescience, presage, presagement, preconceived notion, preapprehension, foreboding, forebodement, boding, presentiment, augury, portent, forewarning, clue *or* clew, omination, auguration *(both obs.),* prenotice, prenotation, apprehension, misgiving, qualm, idea, hint, suspicion, inkling, glimmer.

HUNCH, *v.* Punch, push, shove, jostle, nudge, elbow, jolt, bump, buffet, actuate, propel, thrust, goad, prod, poke, jog, shoulder, propulse, bunt, strike, hit, smite, impel.

HUNCHBACK, *n.* Humpback, crook-back, kyphosis *(Med.),* hunch, hunched-back, bunchback, camel-back, round shoulders, crooked back, deformity, stoop-shoulders, malformation, malconformation, monstrosity, misshape, gibbus, gibbosity, gibbousness, stoop.

HUNDRED, *n.* 1. Century, one C *(U. S.Crim. sl.),* centennium, centennial, centenary, central, centigram, centiliter, centimeter, centiare, centistere, hundredweight *(cwt.),* C-note *(sl.),* hecatomb, centipede, centumvir, centumvirate, centurion, bicentenary, bicentennial, tercentenary, tercentennial, long hundred, great hundred *(both for 120).*

2. Land, territory, division, ward, wapentake.

HUNGER, *v.* 1. Feel hungry, feel hunger, starve, famish, crave food, thirst for, pant for, crave (want) nourishment, hunger for, hunger after, have a good appetite, lick one's chops *(coll.),* thirst after.

2. Long for, hanker, feel desire, desire eagerly, pine for, feel a drive for, feel compelled, desire, be desirous, desiderate, wish, want, would fain, burn for, set one's heart on, have an eye to, take a fancy to, covet, thirst after, crave, crave for, crave after, lust after, itch for, itch after, aspire after, run madly after, yearn for, have a yen for *(sl.),* raven for, have a hankering for, cry for, gape for, gasp for, pant for, die for.

HUNGER, *n.* Desire for food, famine, malnutrition, hungriness, appetite, appetition, appetence, appetency, greed, greediness, bulimia *(Med.),* want, craving, panting, longing, ravenousness, peckishness *(coll.),* gluttony, canine appetite, a stomach for *(coll.),* sweet tooth *(coll.),* polydipsia *(Med.),* drought, chasm, gulf, starvation, vacancy, void, bottomless pit *(coll.).*

HUNGRY, *adj.* 1. Starving, voracious, famishing, of keen appetite, craving *(for food),* edacious, insatiate, famished, hungered, starved, half-starved, supperless, dinnerless, ravening, omnivorous, covetous, greedy as a hog, peckish, half-famished, piggish, hoggish.

2. Avid, greedy, covetous, eagerly desirous, desirous, predatory, in painful desire, voracious, rapacious, itching, with itching fingers, openmouthed, grasping, exacting, insatiate, insatiable, desiring, desiderative, desiderant.

3. Poor, barren, unfertile, fallow, depleted, meager, unproductive, unfruitful, infertile, stunted, unprolific, starved, issueless, fruitless, impaired, otiose, sterile, acarpous, arid, addle, jejune, deteriorated, deteriorating, worn, worn to a shadow, worn thin, wasted, wilted, emaciated, gaunt, needful, needy, teemless, spare, sparing, thin, lean, puny, slender, slight, slim, underfed, faminestricken, undernourished, stinted.

HUNK, *n.* Chunk, piece, large piece, quantity, portion, slice, thick slice, lump, gob, collop, bunch, morsel, hank, bulk, block, loaf, mass, clod, nugget, a lot, lots, a pile, loads, batch, wad *(all colloq.).*

HUNKS, *n.* 1. Mean fellow, miser, niggard, pinchpenny, skinflint, curmudgeon, screw, muckworm, lickpenny, codger *(coll.),* scrimp, sordid wretch, earthworm, gripepenny, churl, tightwad, moneygrub, moneygrubber, pinchfist, harpy, usurer, extortionist, extortioner.

2. Grouch, dragon, crosspatch *(coll.),* old

grouch, tartar, spitfire, bear, bruin, hothead, fury, hotspur, ugly customer (sl.), grizzly bear, codger, scold, common scold, termagant, shrew, vixen, virago, frump (coll.), beldame, beldam, she-wolf, tigress, Xanthippe, catamaran, harridan, wasp.

HUNT, v. 1. Chase, stalk, track, snare, run, hawk, grouse, ride, ferret, drag, drive, seek, look for, hound, trail, trace, shadow, fish, fish for, give chase, course, beagle (coll.), start game, poach, shoot, gun.

2. Follow the chase, ride to hounds, fox hunt.

3. Search, seek, wander in search of, forage, refer, inquire, question, query, probe, try to find, rummage, ransack, look, peer, pry, scan, look around, look round, make inquiry, reconnoiter, explore, leave no stone unturned, turn everything upside down, . . . inside out, gun for, go gunning, pry, spy, nose, nose out, hunt out, fish out, ferret out, unearth, seek a clue (clew), mouse, dodge, race, pursue, trace, dig for, delve for, prowl after, quest, follow, go in quest of, go in search of, follow up, follow the trail of, follow the scent of, track down, sniff out, search out, hunt up, look up, rake, scour (look, peer, pry) into every (hole, corner), look high and low.

HUNT, n. 1. Chase, course, sport, game, hunting, shooting, gunning, pursuit, field-sport, race, steeplechase, fox hunt, fox-hunting, riding to hounds, coursing, shikar (India), angling, fishing, venery, sporting, hawking, beagling, still hunt, piscation, piscatology, halieutics.

2. Inquiry, quest, seeking, investigation, inquisition, interrogation, research, hue-and-cry, looksee (sl.), frisking (sl.), rummage, pursuing, following, prosecution, reconnaissance.

HUNTER, n. 1. Huntsman, gunner, trapper, sportsman, falconer, pigsticker, huntress, chaser, pursuer, stalker, deerstalker, Nimrod, pursuant, shikari, shikaree (India), courser, sportswoman, horseman, horsewoman, equestrian, equestrienne, fisher, fisherman, angler, piscator, piscatorian, piscatorialist, Waltonian, shooter, archer, toxophile, toxophilite, toxophilist, bowman.

2. Hound, hounddog, foxhound, rabbit hound, hunting dog, hunting horse, hunting nag, chaser, courser, steed, equine, garran, stalking horse, saddle horse, riding horse, mount.

HUNTING, n. Hunt, venery, chase, field, pursuit, sport, falconry, venatics, hawking, steeplechase, fox hunting, riding to hounds, chevy, chivy, coursing, beagling (coll.), shikar (India), angling, fishing, still-hunt, fishery, piscation, shooting, gunning, halieutics.

HUNTSMAN, n. Hunter, manager of chase, master of fox hounds, horseman, horsewoman, equestrian, equestrienne, horseback rider, horsebacker, pursuer, pursuant, foxhunter, sportsman, Nimrod, shikari, shikaree (India), stalker, courser, sportswoman, huntress, trapper, trappist, fisher, fisherman, angler, piscator, piscatorialist, piscatorian, Waltonian.

HURDLE, n. 1. Fence, boundary, confine, paling, palisade, picketing, picket fence, rail, rail fence, railing, balustrade, balustrading, ring fence, zigzag fence, garden wall, stone wall, hedge, hedgerow, espalier, trellis, barrier, grating, wattle, network, meshwork, screen, wicker, wickerwork, lattice, latticework.

2. Obstacle, difficulty, hindrance, hampering, impediment, embarrassment, stoppage, deadlock, obtrusion, interference, interception, interruption, checkmate, check, arrest, blockage, setback,

counteraction, obstruction, barrier, handicap, stumbling block, stumbling stone, snag, snags and sawyers (U. S.), lion in the path.

HURL, v. 1. Cast, throw, sling, pitch, fling, send, project, propel, throw violently, send whirling, throw suddenly, precipitate, launch, dash, toss, chuck, cast down, cast forth, cast headlong, shoot, drive, lance, let fly, shy, peg (coll.), bung, flirt, cant, jerk, tilt, reject, throw by, pelt, rush, send away quickly, heave, jaculate, ejaculate, catapult, strike, hit, put, put the shot, lapidate, stone, bowl, trundle, pitchfork, pistol, fire off, discharge.

2. Speak violently, utter violently, fulminate, emit, thunder, storm, rage, hiss, rant, rave, spit, sputter, snap, snort, blare, bellow, blast, resound, deafen, stun, boom, detonate, explode, blast the ear, thunder, trumpet, trumpet forth, thunder against, curse, hurl curses, rail at.

HURLY-BURLY, n. Agitation, perturbation, perturbance, unrest, restlessness, disquiet, disquietude, inquietude, turbulence, hubbub, brouhaha, huggermugger, fomentation, fuss, fluster, flurry, bustle, racket, ferment, pother, stew, bother, distraction, disturbance, confusion, ado, stir, to-do, whirl, hurry, hurry-scurry, commotion, tumult, turmoil, pandemonium, convulsion, discomposure, disorganization, furor, huddle, imbroglio.

HURRAH, interj. Cheer, ha!, hoity-toity, shout, exclamation, ejaculation, interjection, hip, hip, hurrah!, hurray!, three cheers!, banzai! (Jap.), viva! (It.), vive, vivat! (Fr.), yell, tiger, exultance, exultation, elation, hoch! (Ger.), one cheer more!, aha!, hail!, hail, hail, the gang's all here!, tra-la-la!, hallelujah!, halleluiah!, alleluia, alleluiah, alelluja!, hosanna!, praise the Lord!, Heaven be praised!, glory be!, glory be to God!, glory to God!, glory to God in the highest!

HURRICANE, n. High wind, storm, squall, blast, tempest, uproar, tornado, cyclone, gale, violent gale, wild storm, gust, rush of wind, monsoon, windstorm, typhoon, baguio (Philippines), twister, samiel, simoom, sirocco, harmattan, northeaster, nor'easter, northeast gale, blow, big blow, big wind, ill wind, tempestuous winds, blizzard, rotary storm, waterspout, rainspout, whirlblast, whirlicane, bayamo, levant, levanter, southeaster, sou'easter, southwester, sou'wester, easter, wester, easterly, westerly, wind eddy.

HURRIED, adj. 1. Driven, pressed for time, flying, urgent, helter-skelter, pushing, scrambling, expeditious, breakneck, furious, boisterous, feverish, precipitate, precipitant, hustling, bustling, rushing, scurrying, scuttling, scampering, fluttering, darting, pressing, plunging.

2. Hasty, cursory, superficial, passing, slapdash, hastish, shallow, rushed, careless, thoughtless, heedless, reckless, unthinking, lax, loose, slack, perfunctory, perfunctory, offhand.

HURRY, v. 1. Jump at, speed, move, move quick, move quickly, move swiftly, move double-quick, move in double-quick time, move on the double, move apace, move with speed, move in haste, move with celerity, move with rapidity, move with dispatch, move at a great rate, move at railway speed, move on eagle's wings, move at a good clip (coll.), move posthaste, move PDQ (slang), move headlong, move hell-bent for leather, move hell-bent for election, trip, hie, hasten, make haste, bolt, dart, bowl along, cut along, run along, sprint, post, run, charge, charge along, spank, scud, scuttle, scurry, scoot, scamper, scour, fly, flit, go it, come it (both coll.), wing one's way, fly on the wings of the wind, outstrip the wind, breeze, breeze along, hit the breeze, whiz, whisk, zip, clip, dash, dash on, chase *(coll.)*, burn the breeze, make time, make tracks, race, shoot, tear, tear along, hop, hop along, brush, cover the ground, get over the ground, bundle, bundle along, stir one's stumps *(sl.)*, step on it *(sl.)*, step on the gas *(sl.)*, step out, step along, pour it on *(sl.)*, go like lightning, go like the wind, go like a bat out of hell, go like a shot, hump, hump along, gallop, lope, trot, jog, jig, canter, go all out, hustle, bustle, plunge, scramble, dash off, rush, fly, wing *(one's way)*, push on, press on, be in haste, be in a hurry, have no time, have no time to lose, have no time to spare, have not a moment to lose, work against time, work under pressure, plunge headlong, flurry, fidget, spurt, mend one's pace, lose no time, rush headlong, rush pellmell.

2. Hasten, rush, accelerate speed, excite, stir, speed up, quicken, expedite, dispatch, precipitate, forward, urge, whip, lash, flog, spur, goad, prod, push, prick, press, drive, drive on, hound, egg on *(coll.)*, set on, hustle, motivate, move, propel, impel, push on, provoke, animate, actuate, instigate, put up to *(sl.)*, incite, urge on, bring pressure to bear upon, rouse, arouse.

HURRY, *n.* 1. Scurry, rush, scampering, dash, drive, precipitation, flurry, flutter, fuss, bother, pother, stew, agitation, confusion, flutter, bustle, perturbation, perturbancy, hurry-skurry, fidgeting, urgency, impetuosity, impetuousness, precipitance, precipitancy, *brusquerie (Fr.)*, ebullition, fume, disquiet, movement, inquietude, disquietude, ruffle, turmoil, tumult, turbulence, commotion, to-do *(coll.)*, ado, stir. whirl, hurly-burly, ferment, effervescence, impatience, nonendurance, intolerance, irritability.

2. Velocity, haste, rapidity, dispatch, despatch, celerity, quickness, lightning speed, promptitude, expedition, hastiness, zeal, pace.

HURRY-SKURRY, *n.* *(Coll.)* Hurry, perturbation, perturbancy, perturbance, disturbance, agitation, fluster, flutter, ruffle, fuss, flurry, stir, hurlyburly, fume, haste, ebullition, ado, turmoil, to-do *(coll.)*, pother, bother, stew, commotion, tumult, whirl, ferment, effervescence, fluttering, confusion, row, rowdydow, hubbub, racket, convulsion, bluster, rumpus, ruckus, embroilment, melee, scramble, pandemonium.

HURRY-SCURRY, *adv.* Hurriedly, confusedly, precipitately, helter-skelter, slapdash, holus-bolus, full drive, full tilt, hotfoot, hop, skip, and jump, slap-bang, pell-mell, headlong, headforemost, posthaste, 'scrambling, ramble-scramble, slam-bang, head-over-heels, heels-over-head, head-and-shoulders, hand-over-hand, hand-over-fist, hastily, heedlessly, recklessly, hugger-mugger, riotously, troublously, tumultuously, agitatedly, turbulently.

HURT, *v.* 1. *(To give injury)* Harm, bane, injure, wound, scathe, damnify, inflict harm, inflict injury, do evil, do an ill office to, do a mischief, maltreat, ill-treat, ill-use, misuse, abuse, outrage, do violence to, torture, agonize, crucify, buffet, batter, strike, bludgeon, club, sandbag, sap *(coll.)*, hammer, bruise, scratch, cut, maul, manhandle, cripple, becripple, maim, lame, disable, hamstring, prick, stab, lancinate, pierce, scratch, mangle, mutilate, disfigure, blemish, deface, scar, sprain, strain, blight, blast.

2. *(To give pain)* Give pain, inflict pain, wound, afflict, burn, sting, bite, nip, tweak, punch, pinch, pierce, gnaw, grind, gripe, gall, fret, chafe,

rasp, grate, torment, torture, rack, agonize, harrow, crucify, excruciate, wring, convulse, martyr, martyrize, prolong the agony, whip, beat, thrash, spank, chastise, flog, punish, lace, flag, scourge, blackjack, flagellate, flail, pommel, swinge, buffet, smite, drub, trounce, baste, lambaste, bastinado, belabor, lay on, lash, strap, belt, cudgel, birch, cane, switch, sandbag, cause pain, occasion pain, bring pain, anguish, distress, displease, discompose, commode, incommode, put out, faze *(coll.)*.

3. *(To cause damage)* Mangle, mutilate, disfigure, deface, bruise, blemish, scar, sprain, strain, blight, blast, lay waste, pillage, devastate, desolate, dilapidate, dismast, dismantle, impair, make waste, damage, break, bust *(coll.)*, smash, fragmentize, worsen, make worse, injure, harm, spoil, mar, burst, crack, craze, break up, break apart, break (smash) to smithereens *(coll.)*, shatter, ravage, despoil, disable, disarm, incapacitate, disqualify, unfit, invalidate.

4. *(To corrupt)* Corrupt, debase, prostitute, defile, debauch, degrade, contaminate, canker, deflower, taint, pollute, infect, vitiate, alloy, adulterate, tamper with, doctor *(coll.)*, pervert, subvert, warp, weaken, enfeeble, make weak, deprive of strength, debilitate, extenuate, devitalize, shake, unstring, sap the strength of, impair, reduce, exhaust, spend, impoverish, take it out of *(coll.)*, take the starch out of *(coll.)*, blunt, dull, take the edge off *(coll.)*.

5. *(To injure the feelings)* Faze, cut to the heart, cut to the quick, wound the feelings, sting, cut, bite, snap at, assail, bite the hand that feeds one, anger, cause anger, give anger, make angry, madden *(coll.)*, excite to anger, incite, arouse, rouse, kindle wrath, aggrieve, affront, get one's goat *(coll.)*, burn up *(sl.)*, exasperate, try one's patience, pique, roil, rile *(coll.)*, enrage, ruffle, stir the temper, incense, make hot under the collar *(coll.)*, inflame, stir into flame, get one's dander up *(coll.)*, get one's back up *(coll.)*, put out of humor, put out of countenance, envenom, embitter, huff, provoke, annoy, irritate, fret, chafe, nettle, insult, outrage, give umbrage, give offense.

HURT, *n.* 1. *(Pain)* Pain, malady, physical pain, bodily pain, suffering, ordeal, misery, malaise, discomfort, cut, ache, laceration, distress, nip, sore, soreness, aching, torment, torture, painful trial, agony, anguish, pang, dolor, bale, woe, affliction, infliction, tribulation.

2. *(Harm)* Evil, injury, wrong, bad, badness, scathe, woe, mischief, abomination, nuisance, annoyance, bad turn, cruelty, foul play, vexation, accident, mishap, mischance, grievance, ruin, disaster, catastrophe, tragedy, ill treatment, ill usage, misuse, abuse, molestation, oppression, persecution, outrage, atrocity, ravage, ravagement, ravaging, torture, ill service, disservice, ill turn, brutality, inhumanity, fatal mischief, loss, enormity, foul play, trauma, blow, shock, misadventure, contretemps *(Fr.)*, collision, block, crash, wreck, stroke.

3. *(Damage)* Wound, impairment, impediment, harm, scathe, labefaction, loss, detriment, outrage, havoc, destruction, breakage, breaking, ravagement, ravaging, inroad, devastation, laying waste, desolation, corruption, vitiation, pollution, contamination, defilement, adulteration, perversion, subversion, labefaction.

4. *(Affliction)* Bane, curse, cause of harm, thorn in the flesh, pest, pestilence, affliction, visitation, evil, cross, burden, burthen, blight, blast,

rust, smut, worm in the apple, nuisance, vexation, canker, cancer, scourge, plague, woe, infestation, trouble, troublement, bother, pother, botherment (coll.), annoyance, aggravation, grievance, sting, thorn in the side, crown of thorns, load, trial, cares, bitter pill, bitter draft, sore subject, rub, fly in the ointment (coll.), pressure, stress, strain, sea of troubles, hell on earth, ordeal, distress, misery, bad fortune, bad luck, hard times, bad times, evil days, adversity, reversal, setback, comedown, plight, strait, predicament, malediction, anathema.

HURT, adj. 1. (Offended) Mortified, annoyed, sorry, resenting, resentful, indignant, wounded, bitter, stung, injured, acrimonious, rancorous, virulent, crushed, unhappy, distressed, sorrowful, disappointed, disillusioned, crestfallen, dismayed, mournful, dismal, dreary, afflicted, spiritless, disheartened, grieved, aggrieved, harrowed, tortured, mortified, chagrined, pained, racked, on the rack, convulsed, agonized, shocked, appalled, melancholy, gloomy, morose, concerned, cut up (coll.), displeased, discomposed, discommoded, disquieted, disturbed, perturbed, troubled, aching, griped, sore, excoriated, raw, galled, chafed, stricken, horrified, heartbroken, heart-stricken, infelicitous, wretched, miserable, woebegone, woeful, comfortless, piqued, miffed, dejected, heavy-laden, rueful, cheerless, heartsick.

2. (Damaged) Hurting, tormented, in pain, in a state of pain, pained, suffering, torminous, torminal, impaired, deteriorated, injured, altered for the worse, the worse for wear, all the worse (for wear), worn, tattered, shabby, shopworn, shelfworn, worn to a frazzle, worn to a thread, worn to a shadow, worn to rags, worn to a stump, timeworn, seedy, tacky, threadbare, deteriorating, crumbling, ruined, declining, dilapidated, reduced, wasted, wilted, tabid, withered, shrunken, broken, out of repair, in disrepair, out of whack (coll.), sprung, shaken, done up, done in, done for (all coll.), infirm, lame, crippled, unsound, feeble, enfeebled, unsteady, decayed, decomposed, wounded, corrupt, corrupted, ailing, unwell, dying, fading, indisposed, diseased, rotten, rotting.

HURTFUL, adj. 1. Baneful, baleful, harmful, deleterious, malignant, malefical, malefic, scatheful, injurious, noisome, prejudicial, disserviceable, disadvantageous, mischievous, widewasting, disastrous, full of mischief, mischief-making, damaging, corrupting, pernicious, noxious, impairing, undermining, blighting, shattering, sapping, shaking, spraining, straining, strainful, worsening, deteriorating, endamaging, spoiling, marring, crippling, becrippling, wounding, mangling, mutilating, defacing, scarring, breaking, bursting, cracking, splintering, splitting, tearing, shattering, crushing, spoiling, despoiling, wasteful, wasting, decimating, depraving, debauching, defiling, contaminating, dismantling, polluting, vitiating, infecting, afflicting, tainting, perverting, prostituting, brutalizing, ulcerating, decadent, degenerate, degenerating, crumbling, insalubrious, unhealthful, unhealthy, unwholesome, bad, evil, disease-ridden, sickening, morbid, morbidical, morbiferous, septic, venomous, toxic, envenomed, poisonous, mephitic, mephitical, toxiferous, toxicant, intoxicating, intoxicant, all-engulfing, all-devouring, disarming, disqualifying, invalidating, deadening, cramping, prostrating, paralyzing, muzzling, maiming, laming, strangling, throttling, choking, enervating, emasculating, unnerving, fa-

tal, lethal, mortal, deadly, internecine, malign, malignant, dissolute, iniquitous, base, low, vile, foul, abominable.

2. Paining, painful, harrowing, torturing, aching, hurting, wounding, distressing, afflicting, shocking, stunning, convulsing, agonizing, crucifying, racking, sore, raw, harsh, irritated, hard, poignant, sharp, piercing, biting, severe, cruel, caustic, inflamed, burning, hot, tender, consuming.

HURTLE, v. Crack up, smash, smash into, smash up, hurt, collide, come into collision with, enter into collision with, bump, butt, meet, encounter, thrust, push, shove, bear down upon, rush headlong, meet headforemost, tear, tear along, plunge, plunge headlong, jump at, lunge, clash, foul, jog, jostle, strike, rush, precipitate.

HUSBAND, n. Married man, man, bridegroom, groom, goodman (arch.), benedict, monogamist, bigamist, monogynist, polygynist, consort, spouse, hubby (sl.), mate, cuckold, common-law husband, common-law spouse, lord (coll.), head-of-the-house (coll.).

HUSBAND, v. Save, retain, preserve, hold in reserve, keep in reserve, put aside, save for a rainy day, set aside, stash, stash away, lay aside, conserve one's resources, keep a nest egg, feather one's nest, stow, hoard, treasure, amass, garner, secure, keep intact, spare, make provision for, invest, make investments, save up, lay in a supply, lay in a store, lay in a stock, cache, nurse, maintain, economize, keep, retrench, make both ends meet, cultivate, spend frugally, accumulate, manage wisely, manage frugally, conserve.

HUSBANDMAN, n. Farmer, planter, agriculturist, agriculturalist, yeoman, tiller, tiller of the soil, grower, raiser, plantation owner, agronomist, gardener, truck gardener, landscaper, horticulturist, reaper, plowman, sower, viniculturist, viticulturist, vinegrower, winegrower, vintager, vintner, arboriculturist, silviculturist, forester, woodsman, woodchopper, rustic, clod, countryman, yokel (coll.), peasant, son of the soil.

HUSBANDRY, n. 1. Farming, agriculture, cultivation, market-gardening, gardening, agronomy, culture, tillage, tilth, georgics, geoponics, field management, field culture, horticulture, olericulture, flower gardening, viniculture, viticulture, arboriculture, silviculture, agronomics, forestry, farm management, stock-raising, cattle-raising, cattle-farming, animal-farming, kitchen-gardening.

2. Thrift, frugality, conservationism, economy, thriftiness, care, caution, savingness, sparingness, economizing, management, managership, stewardship, good housekeeping, good housewifery, retrenchment.

HUSH, v. 1. (To be still) Quiet down, quiet, quieten, pipe down (coll.), lay off, soft-pedal (coll.), quiesce, become silent, grow silent, keep mum, keep to one's self, keep a secret.

2. (To make silent) Quiet, quieten, still, shush, silence, quell, subdue, soft-pedal, stifle, gag, choke, muffle, quench, stop, put a stop to, squelch, squash, muzzle, mute, soften, deaden, dull, repress, suppress, dampen, damp, smother, stifle, throttle, render mute, strike dumb, dumfound.

3. (To placate) Quell, quiet, assuage, placate, appease, pacify, lull, put to sleep, put at rest, assure, becalm, calm, still, stay, allay, tranquilize, console, mollify, dulcify, mellow, relax, compose, soothe.

4. *(To suppress)* Keep secret, keep dark, hide, suppress, stifle, smother, conceal, put down, deny, hugger-mugger, breathe not a word, keep one's own counsel.

HUSH, *interj.* Shut up!, hold your tongue, silence, shush, sh, tush, hist, tut, *pax tibi (Lat.), pax vobiscum (Lat.),* be still, keep still, softly, softly now, quiet please, hold your whist, pipe down *(coll.),* there now, belay that, stow it, can it, shut your mouth, mum, mum's the word, keep quiet, don't make a sound.

HUSH, *n.* Soundlessness, stillness, silence, quiet, quiescence, q.t. *(sl.),* shush, lull, rest *(Mus.),* solemn hush, intense hush, intense quiet, awful silence, dead silence, deadly silence, deathlike silence, inaudibility, muteness, aphonia, aphony, voicelessness, dumbness, mutism, mutescence, peace, peacefulness, tranquility, taciturnity, inarticulateness.

HUSH MONEY, *n.* Bribe, graft, subornation, corruption, purchase, sop, palm oil *(sl.),* oil of palms *(sl.),* bonus *(coll.),* boodle *(coll.),* buying, blackmail, extortion.

HUSK, *n.* Hull, shell, covering, rind, coating, coat, crust, cortex, integument, skin, tegument, tegmentum, tegmen, protective covering, cuticle, cuticula, bark, fell, epidermis, ecderon, scarfskin, ectoderm, scale, calyx, bract, dermis, derma, corium, epithelium, pellicle, putamen, pod, case, membrane, pericarp, shuck, testa, episperm, cornhusk, cornshock, legume, legumen, peasecod, peapod, follicle, spore case, capsule, theca, bur, burr, glume, gluma, lemma, chaff, bran, palea, peel, peeling, epicarp, cortical tissue, peridium, periderm, dermatogen, carapace.

HUSK, *v.* Pare, peel, skin, flay, excorticate, excoriate, bark, strip, decorticate, strip from, strip the hull from, hull, strip the skin (peel, bark, shell, covering) from, scalp, shuck, pod, unstrip, exfoliate, desquamate, expose, denude, exuviate, uncover, bare, lay bare, shell.

HUSKY, *adj.* **1.** Corky, shrivelled, dry, desiccated, siccated, sapless, withered, shrunken, juiceless, sear, sere, seared, dried-up, parched, mummified.

2. Grating, hoarse, strident, strident-voiced, stridulant, stridulous, harsh, harsh-sounding, coarse, rasping, croaking, guttural, dry, thick, throaty, gruff, rude, grum, raucous, cracked.

3. Strong, vigorous, big, robust, robustious, hale, sturdy, hardy, muscular, brawny, well-knit, mighty, powerful, sinewy, strapping, stalwart, lusty, able-bodied, athletic, doughty, powerful, puissant, potent, strong as an (ox, horse, lion), Herculean, Titanic, Titanesque, Atlantean, Cyclopean, Briarean, Brobdingnagian, stout, tough, solid, firm, sound, stanch, stable, resistant, capable, rugged, hard, hard as nails, adamantine, broad-shouldered.

HUSSAR, *n.* Cavalryman, cavalry soldier, fighter, mounted soldier, cavalry trooper, mounted trooper, horse soldier, horseman, dragoon, light dragoon, heavy dragoon, cuirassier, lancer, rider, armed rider.

HUSSY, *n.* Malapert, saucebox *(coll.),* minx, smarty *(coll.),* boldface, brazenface, worthless woman, adulteress, fornicatress, loose woman, woman of easy virtue (morals), trollop, wench, trull, baggage, drab, bitch *(coll.),* jade, quean, slut, harridan, wanton, *cocotte (Fr.),* grisette *(Fr.),* demirep, tart, broad *(U.S.),* chippy

(U.S.), piece *(U.S.),* prostitute, courtesan, demimondaine, scarlet woman, harlot, whore, fallen woman, erring sister, *fille de joie (Fr.),* daughter of joy, woman, woman of the streets, girl of the streets, streetwalker, white slave, pickup, Sapphist, Lesbian, Jezebel, Messalina, Delilah, Thais, Phryne, Aspasia, Lais, Sadie Thompson, Mrs. Warren.

HUSTLE, *v.* **1.** Put in motion, goad, prod, poke, shove, push, jog, jolt, jostle, hurtle, elbow, nudge, shoulder, bunt, butt, urge, prompt, animate, actuate, motivate, forward, drive, jounce, jar, bounce, buffet, bump, joggle, be busy, keep busy, stir about, bustle, rustle, stir one's stumps, keep moving, carry on, keep on the go, leave no stone unturned, work, labor, toil, slave, sweat, plug away *(coll.).*

2. Hurry, speed, move quick, move quickly, move swiftly, move double-quick, move in double-quick time, move on the double, move apace, move with speed, move in haste, move with celerity, move with rapidity, move with dispatch, move at a great rate, move at railway speed, move on eagle's wings, move at a good clip *(coll.),* move posthaste, move PDQ *(coll.),* move headlong, move hell-bent for leather, move hell-bent for election, trip, hie, hasten, make haste, bolt, dart, bowl along, rush, cut along, run, run along, sprint, dash, charge, charge along, spank, scud, scuttle, scurry, scoot, scamper, scour, flit, go it, come it *(both coll.),* bundle, wing one's way, fly on the wings of the wind, outstrip the wind, breeze, breeze along, hit the breeze, whiz, whisk, zip, clip, dash on, chase *(coll.),* burn the breeze, make time, make tracks, race, shoot, tear, tear along, hop, hop along, skip and jump, brush, cover the ground, get over the ground, rush pellmell, bundle along, stir one's stumps, step on it *(sl.),* step out, step along, pour it on *(sl.),* go like lightning, go like the wind, go like a bat out of hell, go like a shot, hump, hump along, gallop, lope, trot, canter, jig, jog, go all out, bustle, plunge, plunge ahead, scramble, fly, push on, press on, be in haste, be in a hurry, have no time, have no time to lose, have no time to spare, have not a moment to lose, work against time, work under pressure, plunge, plunge headlong, flurry, fidget, spurt, mend one's pace, lose no time, jump at, rush headlong.

3. Hasten, rush, accelerate, speed, speed up, hurry, quicken, expedite, precipitate, forward, urge, whip, lash, flog, spur, goad, prod, push, prick, press, drive, drive on, drive forward, hound, egg on *(coll.),* set on, motivate, move, propel, push on, provoke, animate, actuate, instigate, put up to *(sl.),* incite, arouse, rouse, bring pressure to bear upon, stir, dispatch, impel.

HUSTLE, *n.* Energetic action, vigorous action, brisk action, bustle, stir, agitation, splutter, ferment, movement, activity, zeal, excitement, fuss, scurry, flutter, hurry, hurrying, hurly-burly, hurry-skurry, hubbub, ado, to-do *(coll.),* bother, pother, haste, scramble, scrambling, rush, dispatch, no time to be lost, no time to lose, precipitance, precipitancy, precipitation, celerity, alacrity, eagerness, avidness, avidity, ardor, passion, enthusiasm, quickness, promptness, intensity.

HUSTLER, *n.* Man of action, busy bee, go-getter, live wire, human dynamo, zealot, fanatic, enthusiast, advocate, follower, worker, cohort, devotee, bug *(sl.),* nut *(sl.),* supporter, pusher.

HUT, *n.* Hutch, dump *(sl.),* hovel, shack, shanty, cabin, cot, cote, cottage, shed, lean-to, hogan, wigwam, tepee, wickiup, tupek, tupik, igloo, jacal, dugout, log house, log cabin, crib, mean dwelling, poor cottage.

HUTCH, *n.* 1. Box, chest, bin, crate, coffer, coffin, casket, caddie.

2. Enclosure, closure, close, pen, fold, coop, yard, corral, paddock, pound, dog pound, pinfold, sheepfold, sty, pigsty, pigpen, hogpen, chicken coop, hen coop, hen cote, dovecote, pigeoncote, shed, trap, dwelling, house.

HUZZAH, *int.* Hurrah!, hurray!, hoch! *(Ger.)*, one cheer more!, three cheers!, hip, hip, hooray!, aha!, hear! hear!, hail!, all hail!, alleluia!, alleluiah!, hallelujah!, halleluia!, hosanna!, praise be!, praise the Lord!, Heaven be praised!, glory be!, glory be to God!, Glory to God!, Glory to God in the highest!, well done!, viva! *(It.)*, vive! *(Fr.)*, vivat! *(Fr.)*, evviva! *(It.)*.

HYALINE, *adj.* Transparent, translucent, lucent, watery, crystal, crystalline, glassy, lucid, pellucid, vitreous, vitreal, tralucent, limpid, clear, hyalescent, crystal-clear, clear as crystal, clear as glass, glass-like, vitriform, diaphanous, diaphane, sheer, thin, gossamer, gossamered, gossamery, cloudless, gauzy, flimsy, filmy.

HYBRID, *n.* Crossbreed, cross, mixture, halfbreed, half-caste, half-blood, mestizo, mestiza, mustee, Eurasian, mulatto, quadroon, outcross, mule, mongrel, high yellow *(coll.)*, quarteroon, quarteron, quinteroon, quintroon, quinteron, octoroon, octoon, sambo, zambo, cafuzo, ladino, marabou, sacatra, griffe, griffin, mameluco, mustafino.

HYBRID, *adj.* Mongrel, amphibious, crossbred, crossed, half-blooded, half-bred, half-caste, composite, half-and-half, variegated, heterogeneous, commingled, intermingled, alloyed, impure, mutated.

HYDRANT, *n.* Discharge pipe *(from the main or service pipe)*, water plug, water outlet, stop valve, tap, cock, fireplug, faucet, spigot.

HYDRAULICS, *n.* Science of liquids in motion, hydrodynamics, hydrostatics, hydromechanics, hydrokinetics, hydrography, hydrology, hydrometry, fluviology, pegology.

HYDROPATHY, *n.* Treatment of disease by water, water cure, hydrotherapy, hydrotherapeutics, physiotherapy *(by means of water)*.

HYDROUS, *adj.* Watery, containing water, fluid, liquid, aqueous, wet, lymphatic, juicy, succulent, sappy, serous, streaming, flowing, fluent, hydrated *(Chem.)*, chylifactive *(Physiol.)*, chyliferous *(Physiol.)*.

HYGIENE, *n.* The science which deals with the preservation of health, hygienics, hygiastics, hygiology, hygienization, sanitation, regimen *(Med.)*, preventive medicine, public health, cleanliness, healthful living, hygiantics, sanitary measures *or* provisions.

HYGIENIC, *adj.* Pertaining to health *or* hygiene, sanitary, clean, cleanly, spotless, disinfected, hygienal, hygiantic, hygiastic, germ-free, sterile, conducive to health, disease-free, sanative, hygeian, harmless, aseptic, pure, unpolluted, wholesome, salubrious, uninjurious, innoxious.

HYMENEAL, *adj.* Pertaining to marriage, nuptual, wedded, bridal, connubial, conjugal, spousal, marital, marriage, conjugial, matrimonial, epithalamic, epithalamial, married.

HYMENEAL, *n.* Marriage song, wedding song, epithalamy, hymen, nuptual song, epithalamium.

HYMN, *n.* Song *or* ode in praise *or* honor of God (deity, nation, *etc.*), song of praise, spiritual song, psalm, sacred song, paean, exaltation, alleluia, hallelujah, hosanna, chant, triumph, anthem, carol, praise, Gloria, Sanctus *(Liturgy)*, laud, prose *(Liturgy)*, canticle, sacred lyric, devotional song, motet, choral, chorale, Te Deum, Gloria Patri, Gloria in Excelsis Deo, Miserere *(Lat.)*, introit *(Eccles.)*, Nunc Dimittis, response *(Eccles.)*, answer, antiphon *(Eccles.)*, offertory *(Eccles.)*, Magnificat, Benedicte *(Eccles.)*, Agnus Dei *(Eccles.)*, Passion music *or* oratorio, Exultet *(R. C. Church)*, sequence *(R. C. Church)*, spiritual *or* Negro spiritual, doxology, glorification, responsory *(Eccles.)*, Trisagion *(Eccles.)*.

HYMN, *v.* 1. Praise *or* celebrate in a hymn, extol, express in a hymn, laud, magnify, bless, sing praises, psalm, doxologize, carol, exalt, praise, glorify.

2. Sing hymns, intone, chant, descant, psalm, deacon, carol, cantillate.

HYPERBOLE, *n.* *(Rhet.)* Exaggeration for effect, excessive statement *(not intended to be understood literally)*, extravagant statement, overstatement, stretch of the imagination *or* truth, excess, amplification, figure of speech, expansion, metaphor, gloss, enlargement, caricature, distortion, irony, trope, tralatition, bombast, rant, flight of fancy, embroidery, coloring, strain, metalepsis, antonomasia, metonymy, synecdoche, imagery, image, fish story *(coll.)*, whopper *(coll.)*.

HYPERBOREAN, *adj.* Of the far north, arctic, frigid, very cold, most northern, wintry, boreal, icy, remote, distant, far-off, ulterior, transalpine, tramontane, transmontane, brumal, hiemal, frosty, heatless, frozen, unthawed, unmelted, sunless, glaciated, frostbitten, glacial, gelid, algid, chill, snowy, hibernal, hoary, hyperboreal, Siberian, stern, harsh, biting, stinging, intense, sharp, keen, polar, icicled, cutting, piercing, rimy, frost-fettered.

HYPERCRITICAL, *adj.* Overcritical, faultfinding, captious, scrupulous, critical, hair-splitting, prone to find fault, trenchant, hard upon, difficult to please, discontented, exacting, fussy, dainty, precise, calumnious, defamatory, detracting, derogatory, carping, caviling, sparing of *or* grudging praise, finical, strict, nice, delicate, fine, overnice, oversubtle, cynical, sarcastic, abusive, denunciatory, disparaging, scurrilous, maledictory, overparticular, overscrupulous, severe, biting, sharp, withering, cutting, oversensitive, malcontent, disgruntled, censorious, querulous, captiously critical, exigent, complaining, finicky, subtle, blameful, dissatisfied, fastidious.

HYPERSENSITIVE, *adj.* Excessively sensitive, oversusceptible, oversensitive, thin-skinned, without skin, excitable, hyperirritable, hyperaphic *(Med.)*, hyperalgesic *(Pathol.)*, unduly responsive, high-strung, startlish, skittish, fastidious, squeamish, queasy, tremblingly alive, emotional, allergic *(Pathol.)*, easily affected, tender, impatient, irritable, feverish, volcanic, finicky, finical, febrile, quick, hasty, overhasty, meticulous, difficult, querulous, waspish, hot-tempered, like touchwood *or* tinder, testy, touchy, intolerant of pain, mettlesome, unduly sensible, pettish, petulant, like a barrel of gunpowder, huffy, high-mettled, easily excited, higly impressible, irascible, oversensible.

HYPERTROPHY, *n.* Excessive growth *or* accumulation, overexpansion, overgrowth, overdistention, superfluity, redundance, profusion, excess, superabundance, enlargement of a part *or* organ *(Pathol., Bot.),* overfullness, oversupply, plethora, surfeit, prolixity, prodigality, affluence, exuberance, amplitude, copiousness, overflow, exaggeration, overplus, surplus, nimiety, overdevelopment, enough and to spare.

HYPNOSIS, *n.* Sleep-like state *(artificially produced),* stupor, sleep, hypnotism, sleepiness, insentience, hypnotic sleep, slumber, insensibility, trance, lethargy, somnolism, swoon, dazed state, languor, drowsiness, anesthesia, mesmeric sleep, somnipathy, catalepsy *(Med. and Physiol.),* cataplexy *(Physiol.),* spell, animal hypnosis, animal magnetism, twilight sleep, coma, narcosis, induration, numbness, sopor *(Pathol.),* narcotization, hypnoidal state.

HYPNOTIC, *adj.* 1. Pertaining to hypnosis *or* hypnotism, soporific, mesmeric, opiate, narcotic, anesthetic, sleep-producing, anodyne, soothing, sleep-inducing, lenitive, soporiferous, soperose, somnolent, somnific, somnifacient, somniferous, calmative *(Med.).*

2. Susceptible to hypnotism *(as a person),* sensitive, under magic influence, spellbound, sleepy, drugged, doped *(sl.),* hypnotized, impressionable, responsive, vulnerable, easily affected, impressible.

HYPNOTIC, *n.* 1. Agent *or* drug that produces sleep, narcotic, opiate, anesthetic, anesthetic agent, dope *(sl.),* soporific, gas, sleep-inducer, sleeping draught, somnifacient, sleep-producer, hypnotist, mesmerist, sedative.

2. One subject to hypnotic influence, person under the influence of hypnotism, subject, object, patient, victim.

HYPNOTISM, *n.* Induction of hypnosis, mesmerism, hypnotherapy, deep sleep, spell-casting, suggestion, sleep-production, hypnotic suggestion, autohypnosis, fascination, psychokinesis, bewitchment, hypnoanalysis, self-hypnosis.

HYPNOTIZE, *v.* Place in a trance *or* hypnotic state, stupefy, dope *(sl.),* drug, narcotize, magnetize, charm, anesthetize, dominate, overpower, mesmerize, put to sleep, sopite, soothe, entrance, subject to suggestion, place under control, indurate, make drowsy *or* sleepy, fascinate, psychologize, cast a spell over.

HYPOCHONDRIA, *n.* *(Psychiatry)* Morbid condition of mind characterized by a sense of physical ailment, imagined ill-health, neurosis, melancholy, depression, melancholia *(Psychiatry),* hyp *(coll.),* despondency, doldrums, lachrymals, megrims, psychoneurosis, low spirits, dejection, hypochondriasis *(Med.),* anxiety neurosis, valetudinarianism.

HYPOCHONDRIAC, *adj.* Melancholy, depressed, sad, psychoneurotic, disconsolate, valetudinary, hypochondrial, listless, malingering, undone, cheerless, vaporish, mopish, spiritless, melancholic, dejected, dispirited, hippish *(coll.),* hipped *(coll.),* unnerved, hypochondriacal *(Med.).*

HYPOCHONDRIAC, *n.* One subject to hypochondria, victim of melancholy *or* hypochondria, melancholiac, hypochondriast, malingerer, mope, dispirited person, self-tormentor, sourbelly *(joc.).*

HYPOCRISY, *n.* 1. Pretending to have a character (beliefs, principles, *etc.*) one does not possess, dissimulation, counterfeit, insincerity, guile, false profession, imposture, deceit, imitation, fraud, quackery, charlatanry, cajolery, lip service, make-believe, dissembling, mockery, mere show, hollowness, mealy-mouthedness, front *(coll.),* false front *(coll.),* ambiguity, flattery, malingering, hypocrisis, Judas kiss, flam, duplicity, pretense, fake *(coll.),* fakement *(coll.),* simulation, crocodile tears, feigning, sham, pretension, humbug, humbuggery, mummery, cant, disguise, affectation, doubleness of heart *or* speech, double-dealing, pretext, sophistry, two-facedness, speciousness, concealment.

2. Pretense of virtue *or* piety, false goodness, formalism, pharisaism, sanctimoniousness, false *or* assumed piety, lip homage, lip service, tartufism, tartufery, solemn mockery, empty ceremony, lip reverence, false profession, pietism, cant, sanctimony.

HYPOCRITE, *n.* 1. One who feigns virtue *or* piety, pharisee, canter, pietist, tartufe, puritan, formalist, lip server, religionist, Holy Willie, saint abroad and a devil at home, pious fraud, lip worshiper.

2. One given to hypocrisy, dissembler, deceiver, quack, sharper, casuist, sophist, malingerer, attitudinarian, impostor, crimp, mountebank, confidence man, adventurer, informer, traitor, humbug, empiric, charlatan, bunko steerer *(sl.),* Judas, knave, swindler, rascal, fraud *(coll.),* Uriah Heep, wolf in sheep's clothing, tartufe, crook *(coll.),* fourflusher *(sl.),* Pecksniff, spieler *(coll.),* masquerader, pretender, cheat, attitudinizer, actor, stool pigeon *(sl.),* decoy, rogue, faker *(coll.),* dissimulator, ass in lion's skin, jackdaw in peacock's feathers.

HYPOCRITICAL, *adj.* 1. Pharisaical, sanctimonious, pharisaic, unctuous, squeamish, pietistic, puritanical, tartufish, canting, self-righteous, tartufian.

2. Dissembling, canting, false, caviling, lying, demure, smooth-spoken, bland, deceptive, artificial, spurious, tartufian, unctuous, double-dealing, shuffling, dissimulating, tartufish, two-faced, captious, insincere, deceitful, dishonest, deluding, assuming, feigning, truthless, double-faced, faithless, smooth-tongued, pretentious, affected, unnatural, mannered, plausible, Janus-faced, mealy-mouthed.

HYPOSTATIC, *adj.* Elementary, fundamental, real, tangible, essential, actual, first, supporting, corporeal, material, substantive.

HYPOTHECATE, *v.* 1. Pledge to a creditor as security without delivery, bail, mortgage, plight, impignorate, insure, certify, assure, guarantee, bottomry, warrant.

2. Put in pledge by delivery, give as security, handsel, pawn, hock *(sl.).*

HYPOTHESIS, *n.* 1. Proposition offered as explanation of phenomena, theory, unproved theory, working hypothesis, antecedent *(of conditional proposition),* assignment *(of cause),* rule, law, reason, starting point, basis, ground, apriority, inference, position, derivation, term, foundation, presumption, system, scheme, postulate, proposal, belief, assumption, conjecture, premise *(in an argument),* attribution, data, interpretation, axiom, philosopheme, conclusion drawn from accepted truths *or* facts, tentative law, principium, demonstration, deduction, principle, explanation, lemma, rationale, sumption *(Logic),* accounting for, theorem, suggestion, thesis, condition, speculation, philosophy, supposition.

2. Mere assumption, guess, hint, supposition, chance, surmise, conjecture, inference, rationale, reason, intimation, interpretation, suspicion, inkling, idea, notion, thought, shot (coll.), rough guess, impression, attribution, hazard, explanation, argument, speculation, suggestion, accounting for.

HYPOTHESIZE, v. Form a hypothesis, suppose, assume by hypothesis, conjecture, derive from data, predicate, postulate, presume, offer, submit, theorize, believe, suggest, deduce, propose, conceive, set forth at the beginning, surmise, assume, conclude, find, premise, hold tentatively, guess, posit (Logic).

HYPOTHETICAL, adj. Assumed by hypothesis, conditional (Logic), uncertain, of the nature of hypothesis, involving hypothesis, possible, debatable, imaginary, conjectural, theoretical, speculative, provisory, casual, supposed, pretending, hypothetic, vague, refutable, controvertible, moot, open, disputable, doubtful, contestable, postulational, assumptive, presumptive, based on incomplete knowledge, contingent, theoretic, assumed, suppositional, questionable, indefinite, imagined, equivocal, indeterminate, postulated, supposititious, imaginary.

HYSTERIA, n. Hysterics, loss of emotional control, psychoneurotic disorder, violent agitation, delirium, emotional frenzy, nervousness, convulsion, storm, paroxysm, brain storm, furor, fit, frenzy, emotional instability, morbid excitement or emotionalism, lata, perturbation.

HYSTERICAL, adj. Resembling or suggesting hysteria, spasmodic, emotionally disordered, morbidly excited, tempest-tossed, amuck, distraught, uncontrolled, unrestrained, irrepressible, convulsive, seething, carried away, possessed, out of one's wits, beside oneself, harrowed, wild-eyed, affected with or suffering from hysteria, turbulent, mad, rampant, frothing, uncontrollable, emotional, distracted, rabid, fuming, fanatical, delirious, frenzied, confused, blazing, agitated, uproarious, tempestuous, raging, incensed, maddened, impetuous, crazy, foaming, violent, furious, crazed, boiling, high-wrought, impassioned, nervous, overwrought, passionate, raving, vehement, panic-stricken, overmastered, fiery.

I

I, pron. Nominative case of the singular pronoun of the first person, pronoun by which a speaker or writer designates himself, first person singular, myself.

I, n. (Metaph.) The pronoun I represented as a person, the spiritual personality, the ego, the sentient self-conscious subject, second self, alter ego (Lat.), that which apprehends its own existence.

IAMBIC, n. 1. Dissyllabic metrical foot consisting of a short (or unaccented) followed by a long (or accented) one, iambic verse, iambus, iamb.

2. Invective poem, satirical poem, satire, lampoon, pasquinade, squib, burlesque, skit, parody, travesty, caricature, take-off, farce.

IBIDEM, adv. In the same place, in the same book, in the same chapter, on the same page, ibid. (abbrev.).

ICE, n. 1. Solid form of water produced by freezing, frozen water, congealed water, crystal, icicle, hail stone, sleet, rime, frost, hoarfrost, iceberg, ice floe, floe, glacier.

2. Frozen dessert made of sweetened water and fruit juice, sherbet.

3. Reserve, formality, stiffness, constraint, restraint, coldness, aloofness, distance, uncommunicativeness, reticence, unresponsiveness.

4. Icing, frosting, concreted sugar for coating cake.

ICE, v. 1. Change into ice, convert to ice, congeal, freeze, glaciate.

2. Cool with ice, make icy, chill, refrigerate, make cool, refresh, infrigidate.

3. Ice over, cover with ice, make slippery, glaze over.

4. Cover with icing, frost.

ICHOR, n. 1. (Mythol.) Ethereal fluid supposed to flow in the veins of the gods, blood of the gods, celestial cruor.

2. (Med.) Watery fluid, acrid watery discharge, serous humor, serosity, sanies, rheum, serum, lymph, acrid liquid.

ICHOROUS, adj. Serous, watery, liquid, fluid, thin, lymphatic.

ICING, n. Preparation made with sugar and egg whites for covering cakes, concreted sugar for coating cake, frosting, ice.

ICON, n. Representation in painting of some sacred personage, holy image, religious picture, eikon, ikon, likeness, holy portrait.

ICONOCLAST, n. 1. Destroyer of images set up for religious veneration, image-breaker, vandal, antichrist, pagan, heathen, abdal, dervish, fanatic, assailant.

2. Attacker of cherished beliefs as based on superstition, nonconformist, dissenter, skeptic, agnostic, atheist, freethinker, esprit fort (Fr.), nullifidian, misbeliever, apostate, radical, heretic.

ICONOCLASTIC, adj. 1. Destructive of holy images, image-breaking, vandalic, antichristian, heathenish, pagan, fanatical.

2. Nonconforming, dissentient, skeptical, agnostical, atheistic, freethinking, radical, realistic, recusant, dissident, schismatic, heretical.

ICONOLATRY, n. Adoration of religious idols, image worship, idolatry, worship of the Golden Calf, idolism, demonolatry, idol worship, zoolatry, fetishism, adoration of graven images, Baalism.

ICTUS, n. 1. Rhythmical stress, metrical accent, accentuation, pulsation.

2. (Med.) Fit, seizure, raptus, stroke, convulsion.

ICY, adj. 1. Frozen, freezing, glacial, frore, ice-bound, frost-bound, slippery, glassy, glazed, sleeted, frosty.

2. Intensely cold, gelid, frigid, algid, chilly, chill, wintry, hiemal, arctic, boreal, hyperborean, bitter, raw, biting, cutting, nipping, piercing, shivering, frostbitten, fresh, stinging, keen, bleak.

3. Without warmth, unfeeling, aloof, distant, reserved, cool, indifferent, undemonstrative, unemotional, unsympathetic, unresponsive, cold-hearted, apathetic, phlegmatic, unimpassioned.

IDEA, n. 1. Conception existing in the mind as the result of mental apprehension, concept, notion, thought, mental impression, apprehension, perception, reflection, observation, consideration.

2. Opinion, view, theory, doctrine, supposition, belief, sentiment, judgment, conjecture, guess.

3. Plan of action, intention, purpose, regulative

principle, design, intent, aim, object, objective, end, goal.

4. Viewpoint, standpoint, point of view, angle, aspect.

5. Image in the mind, fantasy, fancy, conceit, object of thought, fiction, imagination, generic image, recept *(Psychol.)*, eidolon, mental representation of an object, memory, image in reflection, phantom, form, creation, phantasm, mental picture.

6. *(Platonic)* Archetype of which individual objects are imperfect copies, pattern existing from eternity, prototype, eternal model, exemplar, everlasting ideal, essence shared by all individual things, form.

7. *(Hegelian)* The realized ideal, supreme principle, Absolute Idea, the Absolute, the Self-determined, the Self-existent.

8. *(Kantian)* The supreme principle of pure reason, *das Ding an Sich (Ger.)*, highest unitary principle of thought.

9. *(Music)* Theme, phrase, figure, *Leitmotiv (Wagner)*, motif.

IDEAL, *adj.* 1. Conceived as constituting a standard of excellence, regarded as perfect in its kind, meeting one's utmost conception, consummate, complete, perfect, exemplary, supreme, absolute, model, faultless, excellent, transcendental.

2. Existing only in idea, abstract, intellectual, mental, psychological, metaphysical, spiritual, idealistic, not real, imaginary, unreal, fancied, visionary, theoretical, unsubstantial.

3. Imaginative, fanciful, fantastic, chimerical, illusory, shadowy, delusive, aerial, speculative, fictitious, romantic, poetic, quixotic, fabulous, legendary, mythical, mythological, notional, whimsical, figmental, dreamy, cloud-built, elfin, fairylike, extravagant, preposterous, high-flown, not practical, impracticable, Utopian.

IDEAL, *n.* 1. Something conceived in its highest perfection, ideal model, imaginary standard, standard of perfection, standard of excellence, model for imitation, *beau idéal (Fr.)*, *ne plus ultra (Lat.)*, acme of perfection, pink, nonpareil, nonesuch, flower, phoenix, queen, mirror.

2. Prototype, archetype, exemplar, original, pattern, type, model, precedent, norm, criterion, test, rule, example, paradigm, design, copy, die, mold, matrix, last, mint, text.

3. Ultimate aim of endeavor, goal, objective, aim, height of one's ambition, end, destination, design, purpose, target, butt, mark.

IDEALISM, *n.* 1. Idealistic philosophy, theory that the real is of the nature of thought, belief that matter is the phenomenon of the mind, immateriality, theory that mind alone is absolute, spiritualism, transcendentalism, metaphysics.

2. Romanticism, utopianism, castle-building, dreaming, rose-colored glasses, *la vie en rose (Fr.)*.

3. Pursuing of ideals for attainment, cherishing of ideals, perfectionism, ideality.

4. Imaginative treatment of subjects in art on a high ethical plane, opposite of realism.

IDEALIST, *n.* 1. One who cherishes ideals, pursuer of ideals for attainment, perfectionist.

2. Metaphysicist, philosopher, transcendentalist, spiritualist, ideologist.

3. Visionary, romancer, romanticist, poet, dreamer, castle-builder, ivory-tower planner, millenarian, unpractical person.

4. One who represents things as they might be

rather than as they are, imaginative artist, impressionist, Pollyanna, Pippa.

IDEALITY, *n.* 1. Capacity to idealize, invention, conception, imagination, fancy, divine afflatus, fine frenzy, poetic frenzy, inspiration, flight of fancy, stretch of the imagination, creation of the brain.

2. Ideal character, cloudland, dreamland, fairyland, illusion, phantom, vision, chimera, shadow, fantasy, phantasm, myth, dream, figment, conceit, maggot, vagary, whimsy, rhapsody, extravaganza, romance.

3. Existence only in idea and not in actuality, *ignis fatuus (Lat.)*, will-o'-the-wisp, Fata Morgana, air-drawn dagger, bugbear, nightmare, man in the moon, castle in the air, *châteaux en Espange (Fr.)*, Utopia, Atlantis, flying Dutchman, daydream, golden dream, dream of Alnaschar, Arabian nights.

IDEALIZATION, *n.* Representation in ideal form or character, exaltation to ideal excellence, glorification, apotheosis, magnification, ennoblement, deification.

IDEM, *adj., pron. (Lat.),* The same as previously mentioned, as before, ditto, likewise, selfsame, the same as that given above, *id. (abbr.)*.

IDENTICAL, *adj.* Agreeing exactly, exactly the same, one and the same, same, very same, selfsame, identic, not different, alike, like, one, ditto, similar, indistinguishable, equal, coinciding, coincidental, coincident, corresponding, synonymous, equal, equivalent, tantamount, convertible, coalescent, interchangeable.

IDENTIFICATION, *n.* 1. Recognition, realization, verification, discovery, ascertainment, disclosure, find, invention, detection, revelation.

2. Comparison, collation, contrast, simile, similitude.

3. Sign, hallmark, badge, criterion, tab, label, ticket, cachet, stamp, credentials, signature, identity book, passport, *carte d'identité (Fr.)*, password, *mot de passe (Fr.)*, shibboleth, *mot du guet (Fr.)*, *passe-parole (Fr.)*, attestation, trademark, monogram, mark, seal, sigil, signet, superscription, endorsement, autograph.

IDENTIFY, *v.* 1. Establish as being a particular person or thing, recognize, place, determine, know, perceive, name, nominate, designate, specify, call by name, term, dub, denominate, style, tell the name of, notice as already known, remember as formerly known, verify, tell the identity of.

2. Prove to be identical, prove to be as purported, attest to be as asserted, ascertain to be the same, prove the same.

3. Regard as the same, treat as identical, make identical, take for identical, consider the same.

4. Associate oneself with, unite, combine, incorporate, coalesce, coincide.

IDENTITY, *n.* 1. Identicalness, sameness, selfsameness, exactness, exactitude, correspondence, exact likeness in nature or qualities, resemblance, similarity, alikeness, absolute sameness, parallelism, equality, coincidence, coalescence, unity, connature, convertibility, homogeneity.

2. Facsimile, duplicate, copy, replica, reflection, reprint, reproduction, counterpart, ditto.

3. Self, oneself, personality, individuality, person, credentials, name, identity, appellation, denomination, title, designation.

IDEOLOGY, *n.* 1. Science that treats of the history and evolution of human ideas, doctrine of the development of ideas, theory of the origin of ideas.

2. Philosophical system which derives ideas exclusively from sensation, sensationalism, sensuous theory of the origin of ideas, empiricism, theory that all ideas are evolved from elementary sensations.

3. Theorizing of an unstable nature, idle theorizing, fanciful speculation, forming of impracticable theories.

4. Systematic scheme of ideas about life, moral philosophy, abstract principles, subjective interpretation of social phenomena.

5. Body of doctrine of a social group, manner of thinking characteristic of a class.

IDIOCY, *n.* 1. Extreme degree of mental deficiency, congenital imbecility, feeble-mindedness, cretinism, native irrationality, hopeless deficiency from birth in the ordinary mental powers, lack of the capacity to develop beyond the mental level of three or four years, feebleness of mind, dementia, derangement.

2. Senseless folly, senselessness, fatuity, foolishness, stupidity, shallowness, unintelligence, silliness, absurdity, asininity, poverty of intellect, hebetude, inanity, stolidity, puerility, senility, dotage, second childhood, anility.

IDIOM, *n.* 1. Form of expression peculiar to a language, expression peculiar to itself in grammatical construction, set phrase, locution, expression, phrase, turn of phrase, turn of expression, phraseology, wording.

2. Language peculiar to a class of people or a community, variety or form of a language, dialect, brogue, patois, provincialism, colloquialism, localism, regionalism, vernacular, tongue, jargon, cant, lingo, argot, slang, flash.

3. Peculiar character of a language, characteristic linguistic quality, genius of a language, distinct linguistic style, elegant expression, classicism, atticism.

IDIOMATIC, *adj.* Peculiar as respects mode of expression, containing idiom, full of idiom, peculiar to idiom, vernacular, dialectal.

IDIOSYNCRASY, *n.* 1. Mode of expression peculiar to an individual, peculiarity of temperament, idiocrasy, eccentricity, distinctive characteristic, quality, nature, attribute, feature, property, mark, trait, mettle, cast, vein, grain, humor, drift, cast of mind, diathesis, tendency peculiar to a person, proneness, bent, proclivity, penchant, propensity, predisposition, inclination, leaning to, warp, set, turn.

2. Constitutional susceptibility toward food or drugs, allergy, sensitivity, hypersensitivity, abnormal sensitivity, hypersensitiveness, anaphylaxis.

IDIOT, *n.* 1. One hopelessly deficient from birth in the ordinary mental powers, one lacking the capacity to develop beyond the mental level of three or four years, cretin.

2. Utterly senseless person, fool, congenital imbecile, blockhead, booby, simpleton, dunce, half-wit, nitwit, witling, tomfool, Simple Simon, moron, ninny, dolt, hoddy-doddy, ass, donkey, goose, noodle, nincompoop, dullard, dunderhead, loon, lout, oaf, block, thickskull, numskull, crank, nut, crackpot, mooncalf, driveler.

IDIOTIC, *adj.* 1. Marked by idiocy, born imbecile, imbecilic, moronic, cretinous, feeble-minded.

2. Senselessly foolish, fatuous, asinine, stupid, sottish, insulse, brainless, *non compos mentis (Lat.),* weak-headed, fat-witted, weak-minded,

rattlebrained, irrational, nit-witted, dull-witted, shallow-pated, weak in the upper story, half-witted, thick-skulled, vacant, senseless, obtuse, daft, moon-struck, nutty, sappy, crackbrained, insensate, nonsensical, inept, blockish, blunt, stolid, doltish, oafish, Boeotian, bovine, puerile, senile, anile, driveling.

IDLE, *adj.* 1. Doing nothing, not kept busy, unemployed, unoccupied, inactive, unbusied, out of work, out of employment, workless, jobless, truant, vagrant, slack, disengaged.

2. Not in use, vacant, empty, not in operation, unused, fallow, uncultivated, waste, untilled, barren, shallow, void, unfilled, vacuous.

3. Indolent, slothful, inert, lazy, sluggish, dronish, supine, dawdling, listless, do-nothing, shiftless, loafing, otiose, recumbent, remiss, at leisure, *fainéant (Fr.),* languid, dilatory, laggard, motionless, stagnant, passive, torpid, heavy, dull, leaden, lifeless, dormant, comatose, lethargic.

4. Of no real worth, worthless, trashy, unimportant, trivial, trifling, frivolous, fiddling, not worth a straw, good-for-nothing, valueless.

5. Useless, bootless, unavailing, futile, ineffective, ineffectual, vain, foolish, unprofitable, abortive, unsuccessful, inutile, inefficacious, inept, incompetent, ill-spent, gainless, profitless, unproductive, unserviceable, uncalled for, superfluous, unnecessary, unneeded, fruitless, purposeless.

IDLE, *v.* 1. Pass time in idleness, loaf, dally, drone, vegetate, dillydally, loll, lounge, laze, while, trifle, do nothing, be inactive, fritter, fool away time, putter, potter, dabble, drowse, doze, slumber, nap, snooze, hibernate, take it easy, loiter, slouch, move idly, saunter, dawdle, lag, drawl, wait, delay, procrastinate.

2. *(Mach.)* Operate at minimum speed while the transmission is disengaged.

IDLER, *n.* Loafer, lounger, lazy fellow, drone, laggard, sluggard, slowback, trifler, dawdler, truant, good-for-nothing, do-nothing, *fainéant (Fr.), Taugenichts (Ger.),* do-little, loiterer, no-account, inefficient person, snail, gadabout, *flâneur (Fr.),* dreamer, slow-coach, afternoon farmer, lazybones, *lazzarone (It.),* tramp, hobo, bum, Weary Willie, lotus-eater, ne'er-do-well, *vaurien (Fr.).*

IDOL, *n.* 1. Material object representing a deity to which religious worship is addressed, effigy, graven image, simulacrum, icon, pagan deity, false god, golden calf, fetish, mumbo-jumbo, joss, Lares et Penates *(Rom.),* Baal, Dagon, Moloch, Juggernaut, Buddha, Guatama, Siddhartha, teraphim, figurine, statue.

2. Blindly adored person, pet, beloved, favorite, darling, fondling, spoiled child, *enfant gâté (Fr.),* jewel, apple of one's eye.

3. Incorporeal phantom, mere image of something visible but without substance, image in a mirror, reflection, apparition.

4. Cause or source of error, misleading habit of reasoning, fallacious tendency, idolon, figment of the mind, false notion, fallacy, falsity, delusion, illusion, delusive assumption.

IDOLATER, *n.* 1. Worshiper of idols, adorer of graven images, idolist, idolizer, fetishist, pagan, iconodulist, iconolater.

2. Extravagant lover, great admirer, devotee, fan, blind adorer, enthusiast, zealot, *aficionado (Sp.).*

IDOLATROUS, *adj.* 1. Idol-worshiping, worshiping idols, pagan, idolistic, fetishistic, chthonian, prone before, at the feet of, prostrate before, in the dust before.

2. Blindly adoring, excessive in adoration, ardent, impassioned, loving, infatuated, attached to, enamored, lovesick.

IDOLATRY, *n.* 1. Worship of idols, idolism, idolatrousness, idolization, fetishism, idol-worship, deification, demonology.

2. Blind adoration, excessive fondness, extravagant love, inordinate devotion, extreme reverence, infatuation, rapture, transport of love, enthusiasm, fervor, ardency, enchantment, ensorcelment, close attachment, hero worship.

IDOLIZE, *v.* 1. Worship idols, idolatrize, make an idol of, worship, glorify, put on a pedestal, canonize, deify, apotheosize, make sacrifice to, prostrate oneself before, kiss the feet of.

2. Regard with blind devotion, adore, love excessively, love to distraction, *aimer éperdument (Fr.),* dote upon, be stuck on, look sweet upon, feast one's eyes on, treasure, prize, set one's affections on, lose one's heart to, wear one's heart on the sleeve, be extravagantly fond of.

IDYLL, *n.* Pastoral composition consisting of a "little picture" of rustic life, eclogue, bucolic, georgic, pastoral, short but highly finished poem.

IF, *conj.* 1. In case that, supposing that, granting that, on the supposition that, provided, allowing that, in the event that, on condition that, admitting that, grant that, though, if so be, whenever.

2. Whether, whether or not, in case.

3. Even though, for all that, although.

IGNEOUS, *adj.* 1. Fiery, incandescent, incalescent, on fire, candent, glowing, blazing, ablaze, afire, in flames, red hot, white hot, volcanic, isothermal, plutonic.

2. Produced under the action of fire, produced under conditions involving intense heat, molten, melted, smelted, fluxed, fused, vitrified.

IGNIS FATUUS, *n. (Lat.)* 1. Flitting phosphorescent light seen at night over marshy ground and due to spontaneous combustion of gas from decomposed organic matter, will-o'-the-wisp, phosphorescent light, *feu follet (Fr.),* friar's lantern, jack o'lantern, firedrake, Fata Morgana, corposant, St. Elmo's fire.

2. Misleading influence, something deluding, *deceptio visus (Lat.),* false light, refraction, illusion, mirage, spectrum, phantasm, vision, phantom.

IGNITE, *v.* 1. Set on fire, set fire to, kindle, apply the match to, fire, enkindle, inflame, light, touch off, burn, cause to explode, blow up, relume.

2. Catch fire, take fire, flare up, fire up, begin to burn, blaze, glow, incandesce, flame, smolder.

3. Heat intensely, roast, singe, grill, scorch, torrefy, bake, fry, parch, toast, scorify, smelt, cook, boil, stew, scald, parboil, seethe, simmer.

IGNOBLE, *adj.* 1. Not noble, vulgar, plebeian, lowborn, baseborn, lowbred, of low station, lowly, common, obscure, untitled, of humble birth, servile, menial, humble, inglorious, rustic, peasant, ungenteel, uncouth, underbred, cottonstockinged, uncultivated, boorish, raffish, ragtag and bobtail, sorry, scrubby, beggarly, proletarian, underling, subaltern, dunghill, mushroom, of low extraction.

2. Of low character, contemptible, shameful,

disgraceful, dishonorable, degraded, infamous, base, vile, mean, depraved, scurrilous, ribald, despicable, discreditable, debased, abject, degenerate, unmanly, indecent, unworthy, cowardly, pusillanimous, craven.

3. Of low quality or grade, inferior, worthless, insignificant.

IGNOMINIOUS, *adj.* 1. Marked by ignominy, shameful, inglorious, disgraced, blown upon, discreditable, disgraceful, disreputable, unworthy, despicable, opprobrious, infamous, dishonorable, humiliating, dedecorous, degrading, *infra dignitatem (Lat.),* scandalous.

2. Deserving ignominy, contemptible, base, in bad repute, loaded with shame, ill spoken of, out of repute, under a cloud, down in the world, foul, arrant, vile, base, blackguard, low, abject, shabby, mean, sneaking, paltry, scurvy, dirty, scrubby, rascally, heinous, atrocious, disgusting, wicked, abominable, offensive, revolting, hateful, flagrant, flagitious, nefarious, execrable, low-lived, outrageous, treacherous, notorious, abusive, ribald, mean.

IGNOMINY, *n.* 1. Public contempt, odium, opprobrium, obloquy, disgrace, dishonor, disrepute, discredit, infamy, scandal, shame, turpitude, perfidy, stain, stigma, brand, blot, badge of infamy, ingloriousness, disapprobation, derogation, debasement, abjectness, degradation, dedecoration, disfavor, ill repute, bad odor, bad name, abjection.

2. Base conduct, deviation from rectitude, improbity, dishonesty, bad faith, fraudulency, Punic faith, deception, faithlessness, infidelity, betrayal, breach of faith, disloyalty, prodition, villainy, shabbiness, debasement, laxity, double-dealing, roguery, knavery, foul play, rascality, sharp practice, depravity, degeneracy.

IGNORAMUS, *n.* 1. Ignorant person, illiterate, know-nothing, blockhead, numskull, dullard, simpleton, dunce, fool, bonehead, duffer, dumbbell, dolt, thickhead, lowbrow, idiot, imbecile, moron, cretin.

2. Novice, sciolist, greenhorn, smatterer, dabbler, charlatan, fourflusher, mountebank, quack, wiseacre, bluffer, plebe, beginner, bungler, amateur.

IGNORANCE, *n.* 1. Lack of learning, illiteracy, illiterateness, nescience, unenlightenment, darkness, benightedness, blindness, unawareness, want of knowledge, inerudition, unlearnedness, ineducation, unacquaintance, incomprehension, unconsciousness, simplicity, inexperience, know-nothingism, denseness, thickness, stolidity, dumbness, stupidity, cretinism, moronism, virgin soil, sealed book, *terra incognita (Lat.),* unexplored ground, Dark Ages.

2. Imperfect knowledge, sciolism, superficiality, smattering, half-learning, bewilderment, perplexity, maze, incapacity, shallowness, glimmering, vagueness, haze, fog, ambiguity, obscurity, confusion.

3. Pretense of knowledge, charlatanism, charlatanry, bluff, quackery, four-flushing, mountebankism, empiricism, pedantism.

IGNORANT, *adj.* 1. Destitute of knowledge, knowing nothing, illiterate, uneducated, unlearned, uninformed, unenlightened, uninstructed, untaught, untutored, unlettered, unread, inerudite, unacquainted, benighted, unschooled, uncultivated, empty-headed, unintelligent, nescient, blind, in the dark, unaware, unwitting, unapprised, unknowing, unconversant, unconscious, uninitiated, witless, lowbrow, shallow-brained, obtuse, dense, thick, cretinous, moronic, imbecilic, unbookish, *au bout de son Latin (Fr.)*.

2. Superficial, green, tyronic, sciolistic, shallow, rude, half-learned, unscholarly, half-baked, misinformed, at fault, charlatanic, quackish.

IGNORE, *v.* Refrain from noticing, abstain from recognizing, not recognize, slight, disregard, utterly overlook, neglect, cut, pass over, snub, shut one's eyes to, blink, pay no heed to, pretend not to see, brush aside, turn one's back on, take no notice of, give the cold shoulder, pass by, pass over, skip, not take into account, omit, leave out of view, be inattentive to, pass without notice, turn a blind eye on, look down upon, wink at, connive, turn a deaf ear to, hold in contempt, ostracize, push aside, slur over, not trouble oneself with, be blind to.

ILL, *adj.* 1. In poor health, physically disordered, sick, indisposed, ailing, diseased, out of health, unwell, on the sick list, valetudinarian, nauseated, qualmish, under the weather, invalid, weak, feeble, below par, poorly, morbid, laid up, bedridden, confined.

2. Harmful, evil, bad, maleficent, malignant, iniquitous, wicked, baneful, wrong, sinful, corrupt, depraved, vicious, reprehensible, injurious, detrimental, deleterious, pernicious.

3. Peevish, out of sorts, crabbed, cross, surly, sullen, cantankerous, splenetic, complaining, malevolent, malicious, unkind, acrimonious.

4. Ill-favored, ugly, homely, unsightly, unprepossessing, unlovely, uncomely.

5. Unfavorable, adverse, unlucky, unpropitious, inauspicious, sinister, malominous, unfortunate, calamitous.

ILL, *n.* 1. Disease, ailment, sickness, illness, malady, affection, infirmity, complaint, indisposition, disorder, qualm, nausea.

2. Wickedness, evil, depravity, badness, vice, malignancy, abomination, virulence, mischief.

3. Ill-treatment, abuse, outrage, molestation, annoyance, oppression, harm, injury, scathe, damage, misusage, affliction, pain, grievance, distress.

ILL, *adv.* 1. In an ill manner, wickedly, evilly, hurtfully, banefully, mischievously, malignantly.

2. With difficulty, not easily, with inconvenience, with trouble, not well, badly, poorly, unsatisfactorily, faultily, improperly.

3. With displeasure, with offense, in an unfriendly manner, hostilely, inimically.

4. Unfavorably, unfortunately, inauspiciously, unpropitiously, sinisterly.

ILL-ADVISED, *adj.* Acting without due consideration, unwise, injudicious, ill-judged, imprudent, rash, reckless, foolish, unseemly, miscounseled, hasty, inconsiderate, misadvised, headlong, wild, infelicitous, inexpedient, inadvisable, impolitic, undesirable, inopportune, inappropriate, disadvantageous, inconvenient, inadmissible, unsuitable, unfit, misguided.

ILLAPSE, *n.* Ingress, entrance, introgression, entry, influx, inroad, intrusion, invasion, incursion, irruption, infiltration, penetration.

ILL-AT-EASE, *adj.* Anxious, uneasy, uncomfortable, disturbed, concerned, solicitous, restless, apprehensive, unquiet, restive, troubled, fearful, distrustful, afraid, suspicious.

ILLATIVE, *adj.* Expressing a conclusion, deductive, inferential, deducible, consectary, consequential, following, consectaneous, consequent, indirect, by implication, latent.

ILL-BRED, *adj.* Showing lack of good breeding, unmannerly, ill-mannered, ill-behaved, badly brought up, uncouth, unpolished, rude, uncourtly, discourteous, impolite, uncivil, uncourteous, churlish, boorish, lowbred, vulgar, indecorous, undignified, ungentlemanly, misbehaved, gross, raffish, clownish, disrespectful, unseemly, not *comme il faut, contra bonos mores (Lat.)*, caddish, snobbish, ungracious, coarse, offensive, awkward, countrified, provincial, rustic, uncultured, unrefined, homespun, gauche, clumsy.

ILLEGAL, *adj.* 1. Not legal, illicit, unlawful, illegitimate, unauthorized, unlicensed, prohibited, unwarranted, unconstitutional, lawless, actionable, contraband, *verboten (Ger.), défendu (Fr.)*, banned, proscribed, outlawed, interdicted, criminal.

2. Autocratic, tyrannical, tyrannous, despotic, arbitrary, discretionary, irresponsible, summary, undue, irregular, unofficial, extrajudicial.

ILLEGIBLE, *adj.* Impossible to read, unreadable, hard to decipher, indecipherable, undecipherable, unintelligible, puzzling, baffling, enigmatical, obscure, indefinite, clear as mud, crabbed, hieroglyphical, scribbled.

ILLEGITIMATE, *adj.* 1. Not legitimate, unlawful, illicit, illegal, unauthorized, unconstitutional, unwarranted, contraband, prohibited, actionable, lawless, extrajudicial, unofficial, unlicensed, unsanctioned.

2. Born out of wedlock, bastard, misbegotten, natural, unlawfully begotten, hedgeborn, unfathered, baseborn, adulterine, mongrel.

3. Not genuine, spurious, bogus, artificial, forged, counterfeit, simulated, falsified, factitious, deceitful, deceptive, sham, brummagem, fraudulent, pinchbeck, make-believe, feigned, delusory, surreptitious, trumped up, mock, snide, false, disguised, insidious.

ILL-FATED, *adj.* 1. Destined to an unhappy fate, ill-starred, ill-omened, planet-struck, born under an evil star, unpropitious, doomed, ominous, inauspicious, luckless, unfortunate, unlucky, improsperous, hapless, out of luck, in a bad way, in trouble, in an evil plight, clouded, under a cloud, ill-off, on the road to ruin, on the wane, on its last legs.

2. Bringing bad fortune, disastrous, calamitous, catastrophic, adverse, untoward, ruinous, baleful, baneful, dire.

ILL-FAVORED, *adj.* 1. Not pleasant in appearance, ill-looking, homely, ugly, plain, hard-featured, hard-favored, unlovely, unprepossessing, uncomely, beautiless, unbeauteous, hard-visaged.

2. Offensive, unpleasant, objectionable, obnoxious, undesirable, odious, repellent, repulsive, unpleasing.

ILL-HUMOR, *n.* Disagreeable mood, ill-temper, petulance, peevishness, testiness, fretfulness, irritability, irascibility, asperity, pique, spleen, bile, chagrin, sullenness, morosity, moroseness, churlishness, moodiness, spinosity, crabbedness, dudgeon, sulks, mumps, doldrums, *bouderie (Fr.)*, fit of the sulks, scowl, black looks, huff, crossness, procacity, temper, tartness, protervity, acerbity, crow to pluck, grudge, offense, red rag to a bull, tantrums, passion, pet, tiff, choler, ire, pucker, fume, dander.

ILL-HUMORED, *adj.* Crabbed, petulant, morose, cross, fretful, irritable, irascible, sour, bitter, sulky, sullen, tart, snappish, waspish, cantankerous, perverse, virulent, bitter, acrimonious, acerbous, irate, boiling over, fuming, foaming, worked up, peeved, peevish, sore, hurt, in a huff, in high dudgeon, ill-tempered, susceptible, thin-skinned, fidgety, touchy, testy, peppery, choleric, shrewish, captious, querulous, moody, restive, churlish, fractious.

ILLIBERAL, *adj.* 1. Not generous in giving, stingy, parsimonious, niggardly, miserly, ungenerous, narrow, penurious, close-fisted, mean, sordid, selfish, covetous, greedy, near, shabby, stinting, tight-fisted, tight, scrimping, sparing, grudging, venal, mercenary, avaricious, grasping.

2. Narrow-minded, biased, bigoted, prejudiced, uncharitable, intolerant, insular, provincial, exclusive, inhospitable, hidebound, reactionary, conservative, parochial, narrow-hearted, shortsighted, purblind, one-sided, partial, interested, warped, fanatical, dogmatic, *opiniâtre (Fr.)*, opinionated, *entêté (Fr.)*.

ILLICIT, *adj.* 1. Not permitted, illegal, unlawful, illegitimate, unlegalized, unauthorized, unsanctioned, unlicensed, lawless, contraband, prohibited, barred, banned, extrajudicial, unofficial, actionable, unwarranted, unconstitutional.

2. Immoral, improper, adulterous, *contra bonos mores (Lat.)*, unseemly, misbecoming, not the thing, wrong, sinful, criminal, guilty, bad, iniquitous, wicked, naughty, scandalous, shameful, facinorous, nefarious, felonious, vile, base, gross, infamous, heinous, villainous, flagrant, demoralizing, degrading, flagitious.

ILLIMITABLE, *adj.* Infinite, endless, boundless, unbounded, immense, immeasurable, vast, indefinite, interminable, unlimited, measureless, interminate, limitless, incalculable, unfathomable, inexhaustible, without end, termless.

ILLITERACY, *n.* Lack of ability to read and write, lack of education, want of learning, ignorance, benightedness, nescience, illiterateness, unenlightenment, ineducation, darkness, unlearnedness, blindness, incomprehension, *tabula rasa (Lat.)*, unacquaintance, inexperience, simplicity, *terra incognita (Lat.)*, unexplored ground, virgin soil, sealed book, Dark Ages.

ILLITERATE, *adj.* Unable to read or write, uninstructed, untaught, unlearned, untutored, unschooled, unlettered, ignorant, uninformed, unacquainted, uneducated, unenlightened, lacking education, nescient, witless, unwitting, unversed, unbookish, in the dark, benighted, belated, dense, dumb, dull, unscholarly, inerudite, empty-headed.

ILL-MANNERED, *adj.* Exhibiting bad manners, ill-behaved, impolite, rude, ill-bred, uncouth, discourteous, ungentlemanly, uncourteous, unmannerly, uncivil, uncourtly, ungainly, unpolished, boorish, clownish, gauche, awkward, blunt, carlish, disrespectful, caddish, snobbish, indecorous, ungracious, uncultivated, uncultured, unrefined, countrified, rustic, provincial.

ILL-NATURED, *adj.* 1. Having an unpleasant disposition, showing an unkindly nature, unamiable, unkind, unfriendly, inimical, unaccommodating, disobliging, hateful, malicious, malevolent.

2. Ill-tempered, cantankerous, morose, crabbed, crusty, sullen, cross-grained, petulant, cross, sulky, spiteful, ill-willed, wayward, perverse, acrimonious, acerbous, bitter, surly, peevish, irritable, irascible, quarrelsome, contentious, exceptious, sour, acidulous.

ILLNESS, *n.* State of bad health, sickness, disorder, indisposition, ailment, disease, complaint, malady, ailing, distemper, poor health, infirmity, invalidism, valetudinarianism, loss of health, affection.

ILLOGICAL, *adj.* Contrary to the rules of logic, fallacious, specious, preposterous, irrational, untenable, inconsequent, inconsistent, inconclusive, unsound, sophistical, absurd, unsubstantial, invalid, unreasonable, incorrect, casuistic, Jesuitical, paralogistic, paralogical, plausible, false, groundless, hollow, fallible, unproved, unscientific, self-contradictory, incongruous, irrelevant, unconnected, having the cart before the horse.

ILL-OMENED, *adj.* Attended by bad omens, malominous, unpropitious, inauspicious, ominous, unpromising, sinister, ill-starred, clouded over, threatening, lowering, portentous, ill-boding, unfavorable, untoward, unfortunate, unlucky, adverse, minatory, minacious, frowning.

ILL-PROPORTIONED, *adj.* Misproportioned, misshapen, shapeless, unsymmetrical, asymmetric, ill-shaped, disproportionate, ill-made, out of shape, wry, irregular, askew, crooked, anamorphous, not straight, deformed, grotesque, crooked, bandy, twisted, distorted, unsightly.

ILL-SMELLING, *adj.* Putrid, fetid, malodorous, foul-smelling, rank, stinking, rancid, gamy, offensive, rotten, fusty, moldy, musty, stale, stuffy, noisome, strong-smelling, mephitic, tainted, sour, bad, sickening, nauseous, putrefied, carious, putrescent.

ILL-SOUNDING, *adj.* Strident, raucous, grating, cacophonous, inharmonious, unmusical, unmelodious, harsh, stridulous, hoarse, coarse, metallic, horrisonous, gruff, rough, shrill, sharp, cracked, discordant, dissonant, absonant, out of tune, jarring.

ILL-STARRED, *adj.* Under the influence of an evil star, ill-fated, luckless, unhappy, hapless, unlucky, unfortunate, disastrous, calamitous, catastrophic, untoward, unprosperous, adverse, abortive, frustrated, vain, futile, sad, grievous, deplorable, wretched.

ILL-TEMPER, *n.* Bad disposition, ill-nature, crabbedness, sullenness, petulance, irritability, crossness, sulkiness, moroseness, bad temper, irascibility, acerbity, asperity, bitterness, virulence, grouchiness, sourness, tartness, acrimony, perverseness, procacity, protervity, exasperation, vexation, displeasure, ill-humor, churlishness, animosity, indignation, wrath, anger, ire, hot blood, *genus irritabile (Lat.)*, irritation, resentment, huff, miff, dudgeon, umbrage, pique, soreness, choler, gall, spleen, bile, tiff, pet, pucker, fume, dander, tantrum, fit, ferment, fiery temper, towering passion, angry mood, rage.

ILL-TEMPERED, *adj.* Ill-natured, ill-humored, acrimonious, acerbous, exacerbated, exasperated, virulent, sullen, bitter, cross, sulky, irritable, irascible, testy, fretful, touchy, hasty, petulant, huffy, pettish, snappish, waspish, peppery, fiery, choleric, wrathful, angry, irate, raging, fuming, foaming at the mouth, grumpy, frumpish, lowering, glaring, scowling, glowering, growling, in high dudgeon, in a fume, in a huff, in a pucker, in a stew, up in arms, rabid, infuriate, furious, relentless, savage, sore, worked up, peeved, hurt, offended, indignant, shrewish, captious, quarrelsome, cantankerous, contentious, disputatious, exceptious, querulous, fractious, restive, peevish, churlish, *acariâtre*

(Fr.), splenetic, tart, snarling, spleeny, cross-grained, perverse, unamiable, moody, resentful, vindictive, cankered, refractory, wayward, intractable, humorsome, recalcitrant, unobliging, unaccommodating, froward, crusty, vinegarish, morose, crabbed, corrosive, sharp-tongued, surly, sour, *acharné (Fr.).*

ILL-TIMED, *adj.* Badly timed, inopportune, untimely, mistimed, intempestive, unseasonable, premature, immature, unpunctual, late, tardy, dilatory, out of place, *mal à propos (Fr.),* inconvenient, inexpedient, inapposite, untoward, irrelevant, wrong-timed, unsuited, inauspicious, unpropitious, ill-omened, ill-fated, ill-starred, unlucky, unfortunate, unfavorable.

ILL-TREAT, *v.* 1. Treat badly, maltreat, ill-use, abuse, mishandle, misuse, wrong, aggrieve, oppress, persecute, victimize, wreak one's malice on, grind, weigh down, overburden, trample upon, tyrannize, bully, domineer, intimidate, annoy, vex, browbeat, hound, dragoon, ride roughshod over, tread under foot, deal hardly with, lay a heavy hand on, put on the screw, castigate, crush, force down the throat, coerce, show no mercy, harry, harass, badger.

2. Be cruel to, manhandle, maul, scratch, buffet, bruise, contuse, batter, whip, flagellate, bastinado, trounce, thrash, pommel, smite, do violence to, torture, torment, hurt, harm, wound, pain, scathe.

3. Rape, molest, deflower, outrage, violate, assault, attack, defile, debauch, constuprate, force, ravish, commit rape upon.

ILLUMINATE, *v.* 1. Supply with light, light up, illumine, light, lighten, illume, brighten, irradiate, cast luster upon, turn light upon.

2. Throw light on a subject, make lucid, make clear, elucidate, explain, interpret.

3. Fill with knowledge, make wise, enlighten, instruct, teach, inform, give insight into, inspire.

4. Adorn with colored letters, illustrate with pictures, ornament with color, emblazon, blazon, emblaze, miniate, rubricate, color, imbue, decorate with gold.

ILLUMINATION, *n.* 1. Luminescence, florescence, electroluminescence, ray, flash, light, gleam, flame, beam.

2. Light-giver, gasolier, chandelier, electrolier, electric light, gas light, ceiling light, spotlight, limelight, lamplight, lantern, coal oil light, lamp, candle, taper, rushlight, night lamp, *veilleuse (Fr.),* candelabrum, sconce, luster, fire, torch, flambeau, brand, link, fireworks, pyrotechnics, rocket, flare, beacon, lighthouse, Pharos.

3. Intellectual enlightenment, instruction, information, education, culture, learning.

4. Painted decoration of a page or manuscript, miniation, rubrication, emblazonment, illustration, ornamentation, embellishment.

ILLUMINE, *v.* 1. Supply with light, illuminate, illume, light, enlumine, irradiate, brighten.

2. Enlighten, throw light upon, explain, clarify, elucidate, make clear.

ILLUSION, *n.* 1. False impression, false belief, error, fallacy, false mental image, fancy, delusion, misconception, misbelief, heresy, aberration, mistake, falsehood, myth, sophism, unreality, monomania, wild conceit, wandering of the mind.

2. Something that deceives by producing a false impression, phantasm, fantasy, phantom, ghost, revenant, spook, spirit, image, apparition, specter, manes, shade, sprite, fairy, vision, wraith, will-o'-the-wisp, ignis fatuus, Fata Morgana, mirage, vapor, chimera, daydream, air castle, dream, bubble, fool's paradise.

3. Camouflage, disguise, false colors, masquerade.

ILLUSORY, *adj.* Causing illusion, deceitful, deceptive, false, fallacious, delusive, illusive, illusionary, spurious, misleading, elusory, untrustworthy, fraudulent, counterfeit, sham, make-believe, mock, Barmecidal, tantalizing, imaginary, unsubstantial, unsatisfying, unreal, unfounded, ideal, visionary, dreamlike, dreamy, phantasmal, cloud-built, fancied, chimerical, quixotic, air-built, air-drawn, Utopian, shadowy, fantastic, fanciful, vain, wild, romantic, Laputan, impractical, unpractical, absurd, hallucinatory, mythical, supposititious.

ILLUSTRATE, *v.* 1. Make clear by examples, make intelligible, exemplify, explain, elucidate, make plain, define, throw light upon, interpret, clarify, demonstrate, teach, make evident, expound, instance, bring forward an example, comment upon, expound, gloss, margin, annotate.

2. Supply with pictorial representations for adornment, represent, delineate, depict, portray, picture, furnish with drawings, adorn with pictures.

ILLUSTRATION, *n.* 1. Explanation, exemplification, elucidation, clarification, explication, definition, exposition, commentary, reflection, deduction, inference, animadversion, exegesis, annotation, scholium, gloss, note.

2. Comparison intended for corroboration, example meant for explanation, analogy, symbol, simile, metaphor, case, instance, sample, exponent.

3. Delineation, representation, depictment, portrayal, illumination, ornature, decoration, enrichment, embellishment, ornamentation.

4. Illustrative picture, drawing, cartoon, vignette, sketch, cut, frontispiece, figure, image.

ILLUSTRATIVE, *adj.* 1. Explanatory, explicative, explicatory, expository, elucidative, exemplificative, interpretative, definitive, definitional, graphic, throwing light upon, descriptive, illuminative, representative, annotative, inferential, scholiastic, hermeneutic, interpretational, constructive.

2. Typical, normal, true-to-type, exemplary, emblematic, emblematical, figurative, indicative, symbolic.

ILLUSTRIOUS, *adj.* 1. Famous, talked of, famed, far-famed, renowned, eminent, celebrated, noted, *distingué (Fr.),* distinguished, notable, of note, conspicuous, popular, honored, remarkable, signal, eximious, applauded, acclaimed, widely known, memorable.

2. Brilliant, radiant, bright, resplendent, transplendent, splendid, glorious, lustrous, grand, time-honored, heroic, sublime, *aere perennius (Lat.).*

ILL WILL, *n.* Unfriendly feeling, dislike, animosity, rancor, venom, malignity, hatred, hate, malice, hostility, malevolence, enmity, bad blood, antipathy, aversion, invidiousness, malignance, resentment, cankeredness, bitterness, hardness of heart, dudgeon, grudge, spite, spleen, envy, unkindness, ill-nature, uncharitableness, ill-blood, bad intent, malice aforethought, maliciousness, malice prepense, despite, acrimony, rankling, gall, virulence.

IMAGE, *n.* 1. Material representation of a person, similitude of a human being, statue, effigy, bust, herm, imago, simulacrum, figure, cast, icon, likeness, portrait, resemblance, facsimile, reproduction, statuette.

2. Idol, icon, fetish, object of worship, graven image, teraphim, puppet.

3. Form, aspect, phase, shape, guise, semblance, likeness, mien, look, color, complexion, cast, air, port, contour, silhouette, *tournure (Fr.),* countenance, face, profile, visage, physiognomy, appearance.

4. Phantom, apparition, ghost, specter, phantasm, vision, illusion, fantasy, wraith.

5. Idea, conception, mental picture, reflection, eidolon, reflection, counterpart, embodiment.

IMAGE, *v.* 1. Represent in the mind, picture mentally, fancy, imagine, conceive, envision, envisage.

2. Make an image of, represent, delineate, portray, depict, picture, make a likeness of, shadow forth, adumbrate, describe, paint, copy, form, fashion, concoct.

3. Reflect the likeness of, mirror, throw back, reproduce, imitate, bring before one's eyes, show to one's face, unveil.

IMAGERY, *n.* 1. Representation, portraiture, illustration, depictment, delineation, portrayal, iconography.

2. Fanciful forms, fanciful dreams, visions, phantasms, phantoms, chimeras, myths, figments, conceits, maggots.

3. Use of rhetorical images, word pictures, word painting, tropes, figurative language, tropical speech, figures of speech, metaphors, metonymy, tralatition, figurativeness, similes, allusions.

IMAGINABLE, *adj.* Capable of being imagined, conceivable, supposable, thinkable, possible, within reach, believable, credible, within the bounds of possibility, *in posse (Lat.),* on the cards.

IMAGINARY, *adj.* 1. Existing only in the fancy, fanciful, fantastic, fancied, not real, fictitious, invented, unreal, visionary, shadowy, chimerical, illusive, illusory, dreamy, fabulous, mythical, legendary, mythological, figmental, notional, quixotic, Utopian, wild, romantic, poetic, idealistic, ideal, extravagant, high-flown, preposterous, unsubstantial, pictured, aerial, non-existent, phantasmal, abstract, cloud-built, air-drawn.

2. Conceivable, supposed, hypothetical, assumed, supposititious, speculative, groundless, baseless.

IMAGINATION, *n.* 1. Formation of mental images of what is not actually present to the senses, flight of fancy, invention, production of ideal creations consistent with reality, faculty of original conception, creative power, fantasy, rhapsody, fancy, imagining power, anticipative perception, reproductive perception, imaginative faculty, imaging power, envisaging of the past as present, envisionment of the possible as actual, imaginativeness, inspiration, creative thought, originality, creation, fiction, mind's eye, imagery, idealized creation, castle-building, romanticism, utopianism, ideality, dreaming, reverie, daydream, ecstasy, golden dreams.

2. Mental image, mental creation, conception, idea, notion, reflection, thought, impression, perception, conceit, fancy, vagary, whim, myth, figment, extravaganza, romance, vision, dream, chimera, shadow, phantom, illusion, phantasm, nightmare, bugbear, man in the moon, castle in Spain,

castle in the air, fairyland, Atlantis, Utopia, supposition, delusion.

IMAGINATIVE, *adj.* 1. Given to imagination, having exceptional powers of imagination, creative, inventive, original, pictorial, originative, constructive, fictive, plastic, fertile, productive, ingenious, intellectual, ideal, romantic, poetic, quixotic, dreamy, visionary.

2. Fanciful, imaginary, legendary, mythical, mythological, fabulous, chimerical, fantastical, fictitious, notional, whimsical, figmental, unreal, shadowy.

IMAGINE, *v.* 1. Form a mental image of, envision, image, picture, dream, dream up, dream of, figure to oneself, picture to oneself, conceive, idealize, conjure up, summon by enchantment, form an image of, visualize, indulge in reverie, feign, form a conception of, realize, create, rhapsodize, envisage.

2. Originate, invent, devise, make up, plan, fabricate, coin, hatch, improvise, scheme, excogitate.

3. Think, suppose, opine, apprehend, deem, believe, assume, guess, conjecture, esteem, surmise, opinion, conclude, judge, regard, suspect, make the hypothesis, infer, deduce, have a notion, take into one's head, take for granted, ween, take it, presume.

IMBECILE, *n.* 1. Person of defective mentality above the grade of idiocy, person of feeble mind, half-wit, natural, congenital, cretin, moron, mooncalf, witling, nitwit, oaf, nidget, blockhead, fool.

2. Senile person, one in second childhood, dotard, driveler, old woman, one in his caducity.

IMBECILE, *adj.* 1. Having the mental powers not fully developed, feeble-minded, weak-minded, showing mental incapacity, idiotic, moronic, cretinous, witless, half-witted, mentally debilitated, defective, mentally deficient, mentally infirm, irrational, *non compos mentis (Lat.),* half-baked *(colloq.),* unreasoning, mindless, brainless, vacant, nutty.

2. Superannuated, senile, doting, driveling, simple, anile, old-womanish, credulous.

3. Silly, fatuous, absurd, inane, asinine, crackbrained, crazy, senseless, stupid, foolish, giddy, flighty, addle-headed, muddle-headed, sottish, Boeotian, bovine, thick-skulled, obtuse, purblind, hebetudinous, doltish, inapt, sluggish, blockish.

IMBECILITY, *n.* 1. Mental weakness that falls short of absolute idiocy, feebleness of mind, feeble-mindedness, mental infirmity, mental deficiency, defectiveness of intellect, idiocy, moronism, cretinism, irrationality.

2. Foolishness, silliness, fatuity, inanity, asininity, stupidity, senselessness, folly, brainlessness, hebetude, stolidity, shallowness, puerility, juvenility, childishness, infantilism.

3. Senility, anility, dotage, second childhood, old-womanishness, incompetency, alienation, ineptitude, incapacity, unfitness, inability, incapability, impotence, inadequacy, disability.

IMBIBE, *v.* 1. Absorb liquid, take in fluid, drink in, drink, ingest, suck in, swallow up, suck up, assimilate, gulp, guzzle, tope, englut, sip, quaff, tipple, booze, carouse, ingurgitate, snuff up, engorge, drink freely, bolt down, swill, lap, swig, toss off, drain the cup, wet one's whistle, wash down.

2. Gather learning, receive into the mind, drink in, learn, acquire, pick up, glean knowledge, gain, get.

IMBRICATED, *adj.* Bent and hollowed like a roof tile, decorated with overlapping tiles, under cover, cowled, hooded, loricated.

IMBROGLIO, *n.* 1. Perplexing state of affairs, difficult situation, embarrassing fix, intricate involvement, complication, complexity, impasse, checkmate, stymie, quandary, dilemma, pickle, jam, predicament.
2. Complicated misunderstanding, disagreement of a complicated nature, discord, babel, bedlam, Donnybrook, rumpus, riot, tumult, melee, fracas, row, disturbance, commotion, trouble, turmoil
3. Confused heap, welter, disorder, network, labyrinth, maze, knot, tangled skein, Gordian knot, coil, jungle, wilderness, chaos.

IMBRUE, *v.* Wet with something that stains, stain, soak, steep, drench, moisten, humectate, dampen, infiltrate, saturate, impregnate, ensteep, infuse, instill, imbue.

IMBRUTE, *v.* Debase to the level of a brute, embrute, brutalize, brutify, degrade completely, debase, pervert, vitiate, corrupt, deprave, make bestial.

IMBUE, *v.* 1. Tinge, tint, stain, color, tincture, dye, impregnate with color, steep, bathe, suffuse, infuse, diffuse, saturate, pervade, permeate.
2. Inspire with feelings, impress, instill, ingrain, fill with, inject with, teach, endow, train, indoctrinate, inculcate, implant.

IMITATE, *v.* 1. Copy in manner, pattern after, do like, follow, emulate, reflect, mirror, echo, follow suit, repeat, parrot, reproduce, model after, take after, follow as an example, parallel, match, simulate, tread in the steps of.
2. Make a copy of, reproduce closely, counterfeit, forge, duplicate.
3. Assume the appearance of, personate, represent, impersonate, mock, ape, mimic, take off, act.
4. Parody, burlesque, travesty, take off, caricature.

IMITATION, *n.* 1. Imitating, copying, apery, mimicking, parrotry, mockery, parrotism, simulation, echo, representation, impersonation, masquerade, disguise, pretense, semblance, reproduction, repetition, duplication, quotation, reduplication, mimesis.
2. Counterfeit, fake, forgery, sham, Brummagem, make-believe, tinsel, fraud, plagiarism, facsimile.
3. Mocking, mimicry, parody, burlesque, travesty, take-off, adaptation, paraphrase.

IMITATIVE, *adj.* 1. Mimetic, mimic, copying, reflective, following, echoic, apish, mock, parrotlike, reflecting, mimical.
2. Counterfeit, forged, sham, imitation, pretended, modeled after, feigned, molded on, second-hand, Brummagem, borrowed, flashy, false,

IMITATOR, *n.* Copyist, copier, mimic, follower, near, imitational, pseudo, spurious. impersonator, ape, parrot, cuckoo, catbird, mocking bird, monkey, echo, feigner, pretender, counterfeiter, forger.

IMMACULATE, *adj.* 1. Free from spot or stain, unspotted, spotless, unstained, stainless, unblemished, undefiled, unsoiled, unsullied, untarnished, untainted, unpolluted, spotlessly clean, snowy, spick and span, impeccable.
2. Free from moral impurity, pure, virginal,

faultless, saintly, holy, sinless, guiltless, innocent, flawless, blameless, chaste, vestal, irreproachable, virtuous, irreprehensible, perfect, incorrupt, inculpable, unimpeachable, unerring, unoffending, above suspicion.

IMMANENT, *adj.* 1. Indwelling, intrinsic, inherent, remaining within, internal, inner, implanted, natural, essential, innate, ingenerate, native, inbred, inborn, ingrained, inwrought.
2. Taking place within the mind of the subject and having no effect outside of it, subjective, nonobjective, empirical, belonging to the world of sense, staying within the bounds of experience.

IMMANITY, *n.* Ferocious cruelty, ferocity, barbarity, inhumanity, savageness, savagery, atrocity, brutality, ferity, truculence.

IMMATERIAL, *adj.* 1. Not material, bodiless, incorporeal, unsubstantial, unbodied, incorporate, impalpable, intangible, metaphysical, spiritual, superphysical, hyperphysical, extramundane, unearthly, transcendental, supersensible, animistic, spiritistic, ethereal, aerial, unfleshly, ghostly, insensible, mental, spectral, disembodied, discarnate, bodiless, asomatous, shadowy, immaterialized.
2. Of no essential consequence, inconsequential, unimportant, unessential, nonessential, insignificant, of no importance, trifling, trivial, inconsiderable, diminutive, small, inferior, piddling, worthless, indifferent, of little account, irrelevant, beside the mark, of no moment, slight, minor, inessential, petty, light, inappreciable.

IMMATURE, *adj.* Unripe, crude, raw, green, undeveloped, unfinished, tender, unfledged, young, inexperienced, callow, unsophisticated, fresh, new, unmellowed, unacquainted, gullible, ignorant, unversed, unprepared, unformed, imperfect, rudimental, youthful, infantile, half-grown, puerile, juvenile, childish, boyish, beardless, impuberal, not fully grown, embryonic.

IMMATURITY, *n.* 1. Youthfulness, youth, nonage, boyhood, minority, childishness, juvenility, puerility, impuberty, leading strings, juvenescence, boyishness, juniority, adolescence, childhood, infancy, incunabula, nursery, cradle, wardship, tender age, teens, pupilage, bloom, virginity.
2. Undevelopedness, unripeness, greenness, crudity, crudeness, imperfection, rawness, rudimentariness, incompleteness, incipiency.

IMMEASURABLE, *adj.* Incapable of being measured, immensurable, measureless, limitless, illimitable, boundless, immense, unbounded, infinite, fathomless, unfathomable, vast, unlimited, inexhaustible, endless, interminable, incalculable, indefinite.

IMMEDIATE, *adj.* 1. Present, instantaneous, prompt, instant, occurring without delay, having no time intervening, sudden, speedy, alacritous, swift, timely, early, punctual, unhesitating, extempore, momentary, subitaneous, hasty, quick as a flash.
2. Having no space intervening, close, near, nearest, next, proximate, approximate, nigh.
3. Direct, continuous, unmediated, without intervening medium, uninterrupted, unbroken, unintermitted.
4. *(Metaphy.)* Primary, indemonstrable, intuitive.

IMMEDIATELY, *adv.* 1. At once, straightway, now, forthwith, speedily, summarily, instantly, instantaneously, this instant, right off, right away, anon, directly, suddenly, in a trice, presto, pronto, this moment, *instanter (Lat.),* quickly, promptly, presently, on the moment, eftsoons, without delay, betimes, shortly, readily, before one can say "Jack Robinson," in a flash, in the twinkling of an eye, plump, apace, on the spot, on the spur of the moment, offhand, at sight, straight, by and by, on a moment's notice, on the instant, in no time, in a jiffy, in the same breath, without hesitation, posthaste, in double-quick time.

2. Without intervening medium or agent, affecting directly without any intervention.

3. With no space intervening, closely, proximately.

IMMEMORIAL, *adj.* 1. Extending back beyond memory, remote, ancient, that cannot be remembered, olden, primitive, hoary, antique, primeval, reaching back beyond tradition, prehistoric, primordial, antediluvian, aboriginal, dateless, archaic, patriarchal, old as the hills.

2. Traditional, unwritten, prescriptive, rooted, inveterate.

IMMENSE, *adj.* 1. Enormous, gigantic, vast, very great, prodigious, colossal, huge, stupendous, tremendous, cyclopean, titanic, elephantine, extremely large, herculean, monstrous, mountainous, mighty, bulky, of great size, very big, massive, Gargantuan, huge, beyond belief, mammoth, behemoth, towering, hulking, megatherian, Brobdingnagian.

2. Boundless, immeasurable, immensurable, illimitable, unbounded, interminable, infinite, measureless, unlimited, incalculable.

3. *(Slang)* Very good, very fine, wonderful, fabulous, marvelous, superfine.

IMMENSITY, *n.* 1. Enormousness, hugeness, immenseness, giganticness, monstrousness, bigness, greatness, vastness, stupendousness, massiveness, sizableness, bulkiness.

2. Vast expanse, infinite extension, boundless space, infinity, eternity, gulf, abyss, abysm.

3. Pile, heap, lump, lot, hunk, stack.

IMMERSE, *v.* 1. Place under a liquid, plunge into a liquid, dip, immerge, submerge, bathe, douse, duck, souse, sink, cover with water, baptize, drown, thrust under, drench, steep, soak.

2. Involve deeply, absorb, engage, engross, occupy, bury in.

IMMERSION, *n.* 1. Plunging, dipping, immersing, mersion, submerging, submersion, submergence, washing, humectation, spargefaction, bathing, baptism.

2. State of being deeply engaged, absorption, engagement, engrossment, brown study, occupation, deep involvement.

3. *(Astron.)* Disappearance of a celestial body by passing either behind another or into its shadow, occultation, eclipse.

IMMIGRANT, *n.* Person who migrates into a country for permanent residence, newcomer, incomer, settler, comeling, colonist, migrant, migrator, visitor, stranger, foreigner, *Auslandsmann (Ger.),* expatriate.

IMMIGRATE, *v.* Come into a new place of residence, pass into a new habitat, come into a country of which one is not a native for permanent residence, migrate, colonize, emigrate, set foot on strange soil, become an expatriate.

IMMINENT, *adj.* 1. Likely to occur at any moment, impending, near at hand, coming, threatening, near, instant, hanging over, about to happen, drawing near, at hand, approaching, going to happen, in store, impendent, destined, overhanging.

2. Threatening harm, portentous of disaster, ominous, malominous, inauspicious, unpropitious, dangerous, alarming, perilous, menacing, minatory, brewing, lowering, clouded over.

IMMITIGABLE, *adj.* That cannot be mitigated, unalleviable, unassuageable, unallayable, unappeasable, implacable, hopeless, incurable, immedicable, remediless, irremediable.

IMMOBILE, *adj.* 1. That does not move, motionless, static, stable, quiescent, immovable, fixed, stationary, inflexible, steadfast, unmovable, still, at rest, at a standstill, stock-still, riveted, rooted, statuesque.

2. Inscrutable, sphinx-like, inexpressive, frozen-faced, imperturbable, apathetic.

IMMOBILITY, *n.* 1. Stability, unmovableness, immovableness, immovability, immutability, stable equilibrium, constancy, stabilization, fixedness, fixity, steadfastness, movelessness, motionlessness, steadiness, resistance to motion, rest, quietus, quiescence, stagnation.

2. Lack of facial expression, inscrutability, inscrutableness, Sphinx-like expression, lack of play in features, statue-like repose, inflexibility, stiffness, rigidity, stolidity, dullness, resistance to emotion, imperturbability, apathy, inertia.

IMMODERATE, *adj.* Exceeding just or reasonable limits, excessive, inordinate, extreme, intemperate, exorbitant, unreasonable, extravagant, rank, unbridled, lavish, prodigal, profligate, unrestrained, unlimited, undue, preposterous, outrageous, unconscionable, crass, monstrous, gross, prodigious, unbounded.

IMMODEST, *adj.* 1. Not modest in conduct, indecorous, indelicate, gross, shameless, lewd, coarse, obscene, smutty, indecent, impure, broad, filthy, dirty, unchaste, lascivious, wanton, suggestive, loose, risqué, pornographic, bawdy, ribald, salacious.

2. Not modest in assertion, impudent, forward, bold, brazen, cheeky, nervy, brassy, brazen-faced, assuming, overweening, unblushing, assured, destitute of proper reserve.

IMMODESTY, *n.* 1. Indecorum, indelicacy, coarseness, grossness, impudicity, shamelessness, impurity, obscenity, unchastity, lewdness, smuttiness, pornography, indecency, filthiness, bawdiness, ribaldry, salacity.

2. Boldness, impudence, cheek, nerve, forwardness, brass, brazenness, want of proper reserve.

IMMOLATE, *v.* Kill as a sacrificial victim, offer up in sacrifice, sacrifice, mactate, slaughter, butcher, put to death, shed blood, slay, victimize.

IMMORAL, *adj.* 1. Unethical, wrong, antisocial, vicious, wicked, evil, bad, unprincipled, corrupt, sinful, iniquitous, infamous, unrighteous, heinous, nefarious, flagitious, criminal, pernicious, illicit, unlawful, illegal, irregular, unseemly, dirty, shocking, lax.

2. Impure sexually, unchaste, loose, dissolute, profligate, licentious, dissipated, lewd, lecherous, libidinous, prurient, salacious, adulterous, promiscuous, concupiscent, debauched, degenerate, perverted, rotten, reprobate, rakish, wanton, depraved, indecent, abandoned, pederastic, homosexual, Lesbian, whoremongering, smutty, pornographic, risqué, suggestive.

IMMORALITY, *n.* 1. Immoral action, antisocial act, wrong, vice, sin, evil, knavery, depravity, enormity, excess, brutality, atrocity, obliquity, recidivism, iniquity.

2. Wickedness, sinfulness, corruption, impurity, corruptness, criminality, want of principle, demoralization, profligacy, irregularity, badness, viciousness, contamination, rottenness, dissipation, delinquency.

3. Sexual impurity, unchastity, lewdness, debauchery, lechery, venery, whoremongering, lasciviousness, wantonness, sexual promiscuity, brutal appetite, salacity, lubricity, libertinism, dissoluteness, concupiscence, looseness, incontinence, depraved sensuality, bestial carnality, licentiousness, act of lust, rape, fornication, adultery, buggery, sodomy, unnatural copulation, pederasty, homosexuality, Lesbianism, sexual perversion, indecency, pornography.

IMMORTAL, adj. Deathless, undying, not liable to death, having unlimited existence, everlasting, everliving, imperishable, indissoluble, indestructible, never-dying, unfading, amaranthine, incorruptible, undecaying, lasting, destined to live in all ages of this world, never ceasing, enduring, abiding, permanent, lasting through all time, continuing as long as the world endures, sempiternal, never-ending, perpetual, endless, eternal, ceaseless, perdurable, constant, perennial, superior to time, interminable, remembered and celebrated through all time, *aere perennius (Lat.).*

IMMORTALITY, n. 1. Unending life, exemption from death, athanasia, deathlessness, incorruptibility, indestructibility, unceasingness, perpetuity, continuity, endlessness, perdurability, everlastingness, perpetuation, sempiternity, eternity, infinity, imperishability, aye, everness, unlimited existence, eternal continuance, endless life.

2. Enduring celebrity, undying repute, perpetual fame, exemption from oblivion, gloriousness, niche in the temple of fame, commemoration, glorification, enshrinement, canonization, beatification, immortal name, *magni nominis umbra (Lat.),* posthumous fame.

IMMORTALIZE, v. 1. Render deathless, exempt from death, endow with immortality, deify, apotheosize, canonize, beatify, exempt from oblivion, eternify, eternize, perpetuate, make everlasting, signalize, enthrone, exalt to the skies.

2. Bestow unending fame upon, make forever famous, perpetuate in memory, reflect honor upon, confer luster on, ennoble.

IMMOVABLE, adj. 1. Incapable of being moved, fixed, stationary, immobile, stable, set, not to be moved, motionless, settled, fast, irremovable, unmovable, secure.

2. Incapable of being moved from one's purpose, stubborn, dogged, obdurate, inflexible, inexorable, unyielding, unchangeable, stolid, determined, resolute, adamantine, stern, persistent.

3. Incapable of being affected with feeling, emotionless, impassive, imperturbable, steely.

IMMUNE, adj. Exempt, not liable, not subject, safe, free, protected, unsusceptible, privileged, at liberty, clear, unrestrained, scot-free, unbound, released, unrestricted, irresponsible, not accountable.

IMMUNITY, n. 1. Exemption from any usual liability, exoneration, release, freedom, emancipation, respite, reprieve, exculpation, pardon, acquittal, clearance, discharge, compurgation, quittance, disengagement, excuse, absolution, exception.

2. Special privilege, dispensation, prerogative,

liberty, right, franchise, charter, safety, impunity, irresponsibility, license.

IMMURE, v. Enclose within walls, wall up, shut in, confine, shut up, build into a wall, inclose, entomb, imprison, incarcerate, lock up, wall in, impound, pen up, coop up, encage, clap under hatches, cast into prison, commit to prison.

IMMUTABLE, adj. ˙ Not mutable, unchangeable, unalterable, changeless, invariable, inflexible, undeviating, steadfast, stable, constant, fixed, permanent, perpetual, irreversible, irrevocable, abiding, persistent, durable, perennial, fast, steady, confirmed, immovable, irremovable, rooted, riveted.

IMP, n. 1. Evil spirit, little demon, goblin, hobgoblin, malignant spirit, little devil, sprite, elf, flibbertigibbet, gnome, djinn, bogie, kobold, fairy, brownie, pixy, leprechaun, dwarf, troll, oaf, changeling, banshee.

2. Mischievous child, pert child, rascal, urchin, gamin, street Arab, Puck.

IMPACT, n. 1. Striking of one body against another, collision, contact, impinging, forcible encounter, crash, clash, smash, charge, élan, onset, concussion, impetus, momentum.

2. Shock, brunt, impulse, slam, blow, bump, push, shove, thrust, boom, stroke, knock, smack, bang, clip, hit, whack, thwack, thump, impression, touch.

IMPACT, v. Drive firmly into something, force in, wedge in, cram, press close together, pack close, pack in, pack together.

IMPAIR, v. 1. Injure, damage, deface, mar, blemish, spoil, ruin, harm, deteriorate, vitiate, make worse, cripple, corrupt, demoralize, defile, blight, corrode, degrade, shatter, debauch, pollute, crush, debase, wear away, waste, decay, alloy, contaminate, adulterate, despoil, taint, mutilate, disfigure, stain.

2. Make less, lessen, weaken, decrease, diminish, reduce, enervate, enfeeble, debilitate.

IMPALATABLE, adj. Unfit to be eaten, unsavory, not pleasant tasting, inedible, uneatable, rank, loathsome, nauseous, sickening.

IMPALE, v. Pierce with a sharpened stake thrust up through the body, pierce through with anything pointed, transfix, empale, spike, spear, gore, pink, spit, stab, puncture, lance, prick, stick, riddle, bore, drill, empierce, perforate, run through, thrust upon a stake, kill by impaling, fix upon a sharpened stake, crucify.

IMPALPABLE, adj. 1. Incapable of being perceived by the sense of touch, intangible, not palpable, not to be felt, not perceptible by the touch, delicate, very fine, attenuated, efflorescent.

2. Imperceptible, incorporeal, unsubstantial, inapprehensible, indistinct, shadowy, evanescent, invisible, inappreciable, infinitesimal, molecular, atomic, corpuscular, embryonic, rudimentary, least, small, microscopic.

IMPART, v. 1. Grant, confer, bestow, give, share, lend, present, render, contribute, deal, apportion, allot, allocate, commit, entrust, deliver, hand over, assign, turn over, consign, part with, cede, offer, accord, donate, award, hand out, fork out, shell out, dispense, distribute.

2. Tell, communicate, divulge, make known, reveal, disclose, inform, confide, relate, apprise, report, uncover, pass on, hint, acquaint, intimate, mention, specify, advise, enlighten, notify, signify, publish, instruct, proclaim, promulgate, tip off.

IMPARTIAL, *adj.* Equitable, fair, just, even-handed, not partial, dispassionate, candid, disinterested, honorable, neutral, upright, without favoritism, uninfluenced, unprejudiced, unbiased, unwarped, unbigoted, unimpassioned, taking no part with either side, fair-minded, fair and square, equal, equable, true, even, incorrupt, unobjectionable, justifiable, right, level, rational, correct, liberal, tolerant, conscientious, aboveboard, scrupulous, punctilious, moderate, average.

IMPARTIALITY, *n.* Equity, fairness, justness, even-handedness, evenness, dispassion, disinterest, probity, liberality, candor, tolerance, toleration, veracity, justice, disinterestedness, dispassionateness, impartialness, fair play, neutrality, equal division, fifty-fifty, two-way split.

IMPASSABLE, *adj.* 1. That cannot be passed over or along, impenetrable, pathless, untraversable, impermeable, impervious, unpassable, invious, wayless, untrodden, unnavigable, inaccessible, insuperable.

2. Closed, airtight, watertight, hermetically sealed, tight, snug, unventilated, hermetic.

3. Impossible, unachievable, impracticable, unfeasible, insurmountable, unattainable.

IMPASSE, *n.* Position from which there is no escape, deadlock, blind alley, cul-de-sac, blocked road, bottleneck, log jam, stop, detour, road that has no outlet, barrier, stile, dead end, snag, quandary, predicament.

IMPASSIBILITY, *n.* Insensibility, insensibleness, insusceptibility, indifference, inertness, inertia, impassibleness, apathy, hebetude, phlegm, indifference, unimpressibility, stoicism, *sang froid (Fr.),* imperturbation, coolness, callousness, torpidity, lethargy, coma, obstupefaction, numbness, impassivity.

IMPASSIBLE, *adj.* Incapable of feeling, insensible, unmoved, unaffected, unimpressible, apathetic, phlegmatic, dull, frigid, cold, impassive, unconscious, unfeeling, dead to, obtuse, inert, sluggish, numb, supine, torpid, comatose, anaesthetic, insusceptible, stupefied, indifferent, unmoved, impervious, thick-skinned, pachydermatous, callous, inured, hardened, proof against, imperturbable.

IMPASSIONED, *adj.* Filled with passion, passionate, glowing, ardent, fervent, warm, fervid, intense, vehement, spirited, demonstrative, animated, zealous, excited, impetuous, mettlesome, vivacious, expressive, lively, mobile, eager, sparkling, enthusiastic, vigorous, impassionate, earnest, burning, amorous, erotic, loving, tender, impulsive, fiery, wild, violent, furious, inflammable, fierce, overzealous, hot-headed, frantic, raging, fanatical, devoted, mad, rabid, flaming, fuming, overwrought, frenzied, thrilling, stirring, ranting, clamorous, boisterous, turbulent, tumultuous, tempestuous, uproarious, rampant, agitated, roused, shaken, hysterical, pathetic, disturbed, perturbed, stirred up, worked up, in a ferment, stormy, *acharné (Fr.),* tremulous, feverish, fretful, impatient.

IMPASSIVE, *adj.* 1. Not showing emotion, without emotion, emotionless, passionless, inexcitable, imperturbable, unemotional, cold-blooded, dispassionate, stoical, philosophic, philosophical, apathetic, unmoved, phlegmatic, sober, staid, grave, frigid, unfeeling, obdurate, stony, indifferent, passive, lukewarm, unconcerned, nonchalant, unimpassioned, stolid, unmoved, immovable, immobile, inexpressive.

2. Calm, tranquil, serene, cool, quiet, undemonstrative, unperturbed, unruffled, composed, collected, steady, level-headed, sedate.

3. Unconscious, insensate, insensible, insensitive, dead, insusceptible, deaf to, blind to, dull, unimpressible, supine, inert, obtuse, sluggish, languid, torpid, comatose, sleepy, stupefied, numb, anaesthetic, callous, impervious, unsusceptible, inured, hardened, pachydermatous, thick-skinned, lackadaisical, listless.

IMPASSIVITY, *n.* 1. Passionlessness, dispassion, calmness, serenity, tranquillity, placidity, coolness, composure, sobriety, gravity, staidness, equanimity, sang-froid, self-possession, philosophy, stoicism, equability, quietude.

2. Unfeelingness, impassibility, insensitiveness, insensibility, passiveness, inertia, indifference, lukewarmness, imperturbation, unimpressionableness, apathy, dullness, insusceptibility, unconcern, callousness, callosity, hardness, torpidity, hebetude, coma, lethargy, stupor, stupefaction, daze.

IMPATIENCE, *n.* 1. Lack of patience, eager desire for relief or change, restlessness, disquietude, uneasiness, disquiet, restiveness, fidgets, itchy feet.

2. Haste, precipitancy, precipitation, eagerness, impetuosity, excitability, vehemence, turbulence, agitation, perturbation, trepidation, ruffle, hurry, flurry, fuss, flutter, fluster, whirl, ferment, pother, stew.

3. Intolerance, non-endurance, lack of forbearance, irritability, shortness of temper, heat, irritableness, irascibility, anger, sharpness, inability to bear, nervousness.

IMPATIENT, *adj.* 1. Uneasy, unquiet, not composed, restless, restive, agitated, nervous, neurotic, high-strung, fidgety, excitable, skittish, fussy, uncomposed.

2. Eagerly desirous, agog, overzealous, enthusiastic, anxiously awaiting, impetuous, eager, vehement, hasty, precipitate, feverish, demonstrative, fanatical, impassioned, rampant, rabid, impulsive, quick, rash, passionate, uncontrollable, uncontrolled, reckless, heedless, madcap, irrepressible, ungovernable, volcanic, galvanic, turbulent, tempestuous, hurried, clamorous, ardent, curious.

3. Irritable, peevish, irascible, moody, mercurial, fretful, choleric, testy, violent, hot-headed, quick-tempered, explosive, seething, chafing, dissatisfied, intolerant, without forbearance.

IMPEACH, *v.* 1. Accuse of misconduct in office, arraign for malfeasance, indict for maladministration, charge, incriminate, impugn, reprobate, reprimand, castigate, chastise, condemn, denounce, slate, censure, criminate, asperse, brand, berate, blame.

2. Impute fault to, challenge the credibility of, cast an imputation upon, call in question, call to account, bring to book, take to task, discredit, bring to order, object to, take exception to, raise a hue and cry against, exclaim against, inveigh against, raise one's voice against, cry out against, fulminate against, anathematize, deprecate, view with disfavor, rebuke, exprobrate, vituperate, upbraid, disapprove, disparage, chide, reprehend.

IMPECCABLE, *adj.* 1. Immaculate, free from imperfection, perfect, unblemished, spotless, stainless, unspotted, undefiled, clean, clear, faultless.

2. Not liable to sin, sinless, incapable of wrong, exempt from the possibility of doing wrong, unerring, innocent, virtuous, guiltless, inculpable, blameless, impeccant, incorrupt, *sans peur et sans reproche (Fr.),* unblamable, inerrable, above sus-

picion, irreproachable, irreprovable, unimpeachable, pure, perfect, harmless, inoffensive, innocuous.

IMPECUNIOUS, *adj.* Having no money, poverty-stricken, needy, beggarly, out of pocket, insolvent, poor, bankrupt, destitute, impoverished, penurious, indigent, ill-off, poorly-off, poor as a church mouse, poor as Job's turkey, flat, broke, out of money, short, minus, hard up, beggared, strapped, in want, pinched, necessitous, unable to keep the wolf from the door, unable to make both ends meet, embarrassed, cleaned out, in straitened circumstances.

IMPEDE, *v.* Retard in movement by means of obstacles, stop in progress by hindrances, obstruct, hinder, thwart, block, encumber, check, interrupt, delay, restrain, prevent, restrict, inhibit, preclude, debar, detain, slacken, balk, frustrate, foil, contravene, clog, arrest, barricade, choke, dam up, bar, put on the brake, clip the wings, cripple, undermine, spike, incapacitate, cut the ground from under one, take the wind out of one's sails, stay, put a stop to, intercept, interfere, oppose, stave off, avert, obviate, ward off, forestall, turn aside, nip in the bud, countercheck, counteract, cramp, hamper, cumber, handicap, overburden, saddle with, entrammel, incommode, tree, corner, stymie, checkmate, offset, neutralize, confound, baffle, deter, make hazardous, entangle, repress, fetter, put back, cross, hold back, embarrass, shackle, hitch, hamper.

IMPEDIMENT, *n.* 1. Hindrance, obstruction, embarrassment, hampering, interruption, counteraction, prevention, stoppage, delay, retardation, interception, inhibition, restraint, restriction, preclusion, interference, determent, obtrusion, stay, stop, opposition, discouragement, check, blockage, prohibition, oppilation, restriction, retardment.

2. Obstacle, encumbrance, stumbling block, bar, barrier, difficulty, drawback, objection, disadvantage, knot, hitch, trammel, snag, drag, holdback, block, rub, setback, load, burden, onus, dead weight, bit, curb, tether, clog, brake, head wind, ill wind, setback, damper, wet blanket, old man of the sea, kill-joy, crape-hanger, embargo, stricture, blockade, red tape.

3. Physical defect, speech disorder, balbuties, stammer, stutter, hesitation, aphasia, titubancy, traulism, tardiloquence, lisp, hemming and hawing.

IMPEDIMENTA, *n. (pl.)* Military supplies carried with an army, matériel, equipment, gear, equipage, baggage, luggage, things, encumbrances, trappings, tackle, rigging, paraphernalia, traps, accouterments, harness, rigging, apparatus, goods, effects, movables, parcels, appurtenances.

IMPEL, *v.* 1. Drive forward, push, put in motion, urge forward, impart motion to, propel, move forward, thrust, boost, press on, prod, force, start going, set in motion.

2. Constrain to action, induce, instigate, persuade, prompt, goad, spur, quicken, incite, influence, stimulate, compel, enforce, whet, provoke, motivate, actuate, prick, egg on, bring round, sway, prevail on, bias, incline, dispose, talk over, arouse, rouse, animate, inspire, advocate, abet, necessitate, inspirit, oblige, embolden.

IMPEND, *v.* 1. Draw near, be near, be at hand, approach, stare one in the face, be in store, be in the wind, be in prospect, be imminent, hover,

await, loom, brew, be near at hand, threaten, menace, be oncoming, be forthcoming.

2. Hang, be suspended, overhang, project, jut out, protrude, bulge.

IMPENDING, *adj.* 1. About to happen, near at hand, coming, oncoming, forthcoming, imminent, impendent, brewing, looming, in store, to come, at hand, instant, in prospect, in the wind, on the lap of the gods, prospective, staring one in the face, menacing, threatening.

2. Hanging, suspended, overhanging, projecting, jutting out, protruding, bulging.

IMPENETRABLE, *adj.* 1. That cannot be entered, not to be penetrated, impervious, invious, impermeable, closed, shut, unopened, unpierced, trackless, wayless, untrodden, pathless, impassable, inaccessible, tight, snug, hermetic, hermetically sealed, inperforable, solid, imperviable, compact, hard, adamantine, flinty.

2. Inaccessible to ideas or influences, dull, crass, obtuse, Boeotian, stolid, dense, impassive, insensible, senseless, indifferent, cold to, proof against.

3. That keeps his own counsel, reticent, taciturn, inscrutable, incomprehensible, unfathomable, not to be found out, insoluble, inexplicable, past comprehension, hidden, mysterious, puzzling, enigmatic, obscure, intricate, nebulous, dim, undecipherable, incognizable, inextricable, abstruse, unaccountable, occult, supernatural.

IMPENITENT, *adj.* Not penitent, hard, callous, seared, uncontrite, irrepentant, unrepentant, unrepenting, relentless, remorseless, recusant, graceless, insensible, unfeeling, incorrigible, hardened, obdurate, flinty, indurate, reprobate, lost, unconverted, godless, abandoned, irreclaimable, unreclaimed, unreformed, wayward, irreligious, unsusceptible, refractory.

IMPERATIVE, *adj.* 1. Authoritative, imperious, peremptory, commanding, dictatorial, magisterial, overruling, absolute, decretory, jussive, final, decisive, departmental, bureaucratic, ministerial, official, executive, administrative, gubernatorial, domineering, decretive, dominant.

2. Obligatory, binding, not to be avoided, not to be evaded, essential, urgent, necessary, exigent, needful, requisite, called for, pressing, in demand, crying, instant, insistent, indispensable, compulsory, mandatory, positive, paramount, inexorable.

3. Despotic, haughty, dogmatical, dictative, severe, strict, harsh, austere, arbitrary, coercive, obdurate, iron-handed, hard, hard-headed, tyrannical, masterful, inflexible, unsparing, stringent, exacting, strait-laced, stern, dour, relentless, rigorous, Spartan, Draconian.

4. Obligated, beholden, obliged by, under obligation, tied by, bound by, saddled with, incumbent on.

IMPERCEPTIBLE, *adj.* 1. Not affecting the perceptive faculties, unperceptible, unperceivable, undiscernible, unnoticeable, invisible, unapparent, unseen, latent, hidden, inconspicuous, concealed, screened, veiled, enshrouded, out of sight, out of hearing, inaudible, faint, indistinct, obscure, dim, shadowy, darksome, blurred, muted, ill-defined, hazy, misty, nebulous, impenetrable, vague.

2. Very slight, minute, minuscule, picayune, infinitesimal, comminuted, pulverized, triturated, atomic, molecular, minimal, miniature, minikin, wee, pygmy, Lilliputian, slender, evanescent, inconsiderable, inappreciable, very small, microscopic, scanty, scant, unappreciable, inconsequen-

tial, very subtle, fine, impalpable, intangible, very gradual, slow.

IMPERFECT, *adj.* 1. Incomplete, not entire, unfinished, undeveloped, rudimentary, abortive, inadequate, unsuitable, below par, insufficient, scanty, partial, short, limited, deficient, frail, feeble, unsound, crude, poor, inferior, immature, rough, bad, inexact, inelegant, bad, vicious, corrupt, peccable, transient.

2. Faulty, defective, out of order, not running, done for, ruined, *kaput (Ger.),* impaired, warped, disfigured, injured, flawed, broken, rickety, mutilated, decrepit, lame, crippled.

3. Mediocre, indifferent, ordinary, middling, passable, so-so, average, fair, tolerable, moderate, superficial, not bad, decent, not amiss, second-rate, secondary, milk-and-water, one-horse, two-by-four, petty, small, picayune, mean, unsatisfactory.

IMPERFECTION, *n.* 1. Incompleteness, imperfectness, want of perfection, faultiness, weakness, defectiveness, deficiency, infirmity, frailty, inadequacy, inferiority, badness, unsoundness, immaturity, shortcoming, failing, drawback, fallibility, default, error, omission, failure, transgression, misdeed, offense, vice, viciousness, wrong, sinfulness, foible, limitation, weak point, screw loose.

2. Imperfect detail, defect, snag, catch, tear, run, ladder, rent, cut, scratch, break, flaw, blemish, cloud, shot, fly, spot, rift, taint, stain, fault, lack, disfigurement, deformity.

IMPERIAL, *adj.* 1. Pertaining to an emperor or empress, regal, royal, kingly, sovereign, princely, queenly, monarchical, imperialistic, sceptered, imperatorial, monarchal.

2. Ruling, regnant, dominant, supreme, predominant, paramount, in the ascendant, hegemonic, hegemonal, absolute, overruling, imperious, authoritative, administrative, executive, clothed with authority, ministerial, official, bureaucratic, gubernatorial.

3. Of a commanding manner or aspect, magnificent, august, grand, stately, imposing, majestic, exalted, sublime, noble, great, consummate, dignified, lofty, splendid.

IMPERIALISM, *n.* Policy of extending the authority of a nation over foreign countries, rod of empire, acquisition and holding of dependencies, colonialism, foreign expansion, monarchism, sovereignty, empire, command, dominion, protectorate, province, military despotism, extraterritorial tyranny.

IMPERIL, *v.* Endanger, put in peril, put to hazard, jeopardize, jeopard, expose, risk, venture, chance, compromise, stake, peril, sail too near the wind, go out on a limb, stick one's neck out, fly in the face of fate, take a gamble, gamble, set at hazard.

IMPERIOUS, *adj.* 1. Despotic, dictatorial, tyrannical, lordly, baronial, princely, regal, overbearing, arrogant, haughty, contumelious, supercilious, high-handed, iron-fisted, high and mighty, proud, disdainful, overweening, consequential, arbitrary, toplofty, swaggering, bumptious, bullying, assertive, dogmatic, presumptuous, insolent, exacting, commanding, authoritative, dominant, masterly, masterful, peremptory, bossy, pompous, nervy, cheeky, brazen-faced, stern, magisterial.

2. Urgent, imperative, compelling, pressing, binding, compulsory, irresistible.

IMPERISHABLE, *adj.* Not perishable, indestructible, undying, unfading, amaranthine, everlasting,

enduring, never-ending, perennial, eternal, immortal, ever-living, deathless, undecaying, endless, sempiternal, perpetual, permanent, never-dying, incorruptible.

IMPERMEABLE, *adj.* 1. Impenetrable, impassable, impervious, invious, unpenetrable, pathless, wayless, untrodden, close, shut, operculated, unpierced, imporous, caecal.

2. Proof against, airtight, watertight, waterproof, hermetic, hermetically sealed.

3. Dense, solid, thickset, close, compact, lumpish, tight, snug.

IMPERSONAL, *adj.* Without personal reference or connection, general, objective, dispassionate, disinterested, neuter, indefinite, unselfish.

IMPERSONATE, *v.* 1. Assume the character of, pretend to be, act the part of, take the part of, enact, personate, play, pose as, dress as, represent.

2. Imitate, mimic, ape, parrot, copy, take off, mock.

3. Represent in bodily form, invest with personality, embody, incarnate, personify, typify, body forth, delineate, depict, portray, picture.

IMPERSONATION, *n.* 1. Personation, imitation, enactment, mimicry, simulation, acting, dramatic performance, role.

2. Investment with personality, personification, representation, bodily manifestation, incarnation.

IMPERTINENCE, *n.* 1. Incivility, unmannerliness, rudeness, impudence, audacity, insolence, presumption, presumptuousness, bumptiousness, intrusiveness, unmannerly intrusion, forwardness, freshness, brazenness, self-assertion, boldness, effrontery, malapertness, sauciness, pertness, impoliteness, unscrupulous smartness, hardihood, flippancy, shamelessness, gall, sauce, nerve, cheek, lip, front, face, brazen face, brass, impertinent action, insult, outrage, indignity.

2. Irrelevancy, irrelevance, impropriety, unfitness, impertinency, inapplicability, irrelation, unrelatedness, unconformity, incongruity, inappropriateness, heterogeneity, inconsequence, disagreement.

IMPERTINENT, *adj.* 1. Uncivil, unmannerly, disrespectful, bold, forward, impudent, insolent, presumptuous, officious, rude, intrusive, meddlesome, meddling, arrogant, pert, malapert, saucy, flippant, fresh, audacious, assuming, shameless, unabashed, barefaced, brazen, self-assertive, brazenfaced, lippy, cheeky, impolite, insulting, contumelious, contemptuous, insubordinate, abusive, offensive, vulgar, coarse, gross, ill-mannered, underbred.

2. Not pertinent, not to the point, beside the mark, not pertaining to the matter in hand, malapropos, inapposite, irrelevant, inapplicable, unrelated, inappropriate, inconsequent, unessential, unsuitable, alien, gratuitous, incongruous, out of place, unseemly.

IMPERTURBABLE, *adj.* Incapable of being agitated, not easily disturbed, not readily excited, level-headed, cool, cool as a cucumber, calm, collected, composed, unmoved, unruffled, undisturbed, inexcitable, tranquil, serene, stoical, philosophic, cold-blooded, philosophical, staid, sedate, placid, sober-minded, grave, dispassionate, unsusceptible, unimpassioned, unperturbed, steeled against, proof against, casehardened, hardened, inured, untroubled, immovable, undiscomposed, impassive, nonchalant, patient, resolute, stoic, meek, mild.

IMPERVIOUS, *adj.* 1. Impassable, impermeable, impenetrable, closed, shut, operculated, unpierced, unopened, imporous, imperforate, caecal.

2. Inaccessible, pathless, wayless, invious, untrodden, uncome-at-able, unnavigable, unapproachable.

3. Airtight, unventilated, watertight, waterproof, hermetic, hermetically sealed, tight, snug, close.

4. Thick-skinned, pachydermatous, callous, hard, hardened, inured.

IMPETUOSITY, *n.* 1. Sudden rash energy, great impetus, impelling force, forceful movement, momentum, impulsion, impulse, élan, dash.

2. Hastiness in action, unreasoned action, heedlessness, impulsiveness, precipitancy, precipitation, eagerness, rashness, brashness, temerity, ardency, ardor, passion, heat, fire, glow, scurry, reckless speed.

3. Ferocity, rage, fury, fierceness, furiousness, *acharnement (Fr.),* ferociousness, malignity, violence, vehemence, might, brute force, severity, acuteness, intensity, sharpness, frenzy.

IMPETUOUS, *adj.* 1. Acting with sudden energy, characterized by rash energy, hasty, headlong, temerarious, precipitate, quick, rash, breakneck, headlong, dashing, pell-mell, helter-skelter, quick, swift, slapdash.

2. Impulsive, irrestrainable, ungovernable, uncontrollable, heedless, incautious, rash, brash, hotheaded, passionate, fiery, ardent, headstrong, overzealous, capricious, mercurial, fickle, abrupt, unreasoned, excitable, impatient, intractable, fervid, perfervid, burning, heady, hot-brained, foolhardy, madcap, demonstrative.

3. Violent, rampant, forcible, wild, frantic, unruly, furious, fierce, ferocious, vehement, raging, fiery, savage, merciless, cruel, stormy, acute, extreme, intense, sharp, severe, angry, quarrelsome.

IMPETUS, *n.* 1. Moving force, impelling force, impulsion, momentum, propulsive force, moment, propulsion, energy, pressure, push, thrust, boom, shove, boost, drive, kick, start, send-off, jog, jolt, dynamics, kinetics, brunt.

2. Impulse, stimulus, incentive, actuation, motive, encouragement, influence, call, instigation, abetment, spur.

IMPIETY, *n.* 1. Lack of reverence for God, ungodliness, godlessness, irreverence, irreligionism, irreligion, apostasy, recusancy, nonconformity, backsliding, recidivism, tergiversation, recreancy, lapse, reprobation, profaneness.

2. Unrighteousness, sinfulness, unholiness, iniquity, wickedness, hypocrisy, pietism, cant, lipservice, pious fraud, sanctimoniousness, sanctimony, sabbatarianism, pharisaism.

3. Act of impiety, sin, wrong, transgression, trespass, offense, sabbath-breaking, profanity, profanation, desecration, sacrilege, blasphemy, malediction, cursing.

4. Lack of filial devotion, lack of dutifulness, want of respect for one's parents, unfilial character, undutifulness.

IMPINGE, *v.* 1. Run against, knock against, butt against, bump against, collide with, strike against, dash against, clash upon, fall against, strike, hit, jog, jolt, push, thrust, prod, shove, come in collision, crash.

2. Infringe, encroach, trespass, make inroad, intrude, invade, trench, usurp.

IMPIOUS, *adj.* Lacking reverence for God, not pious, irreverent, ungodly, godless, irreligious, blasphemous, sacrilegious, profane, unholy, unsanctified, unhallowed, desecrative, iniquitous, unrighteous, pharisaical, canting, pietistical, sanctimonious, unctuous, unregenerate, sinful, wicked, hardened, perverted, reprobate, recusant, satanic, diabolic, deceitful, double-faced, two-faced, disobedient, undutiful, disrespectful, unethical, immoral, ribald.

IMPISH, *adj.* Like an imp, elfish, elfin, puckish, mischievous, malignant, malicious, vexatious, troublesome, annoying, naughty, destructive, hurtful, pernicious, injurious, detrimental, demoniac, fiendish.

IMPLACABILITY, *n.* Vindictiveness, ruthlessness, cruelty, revenge, malice, hatred, rancor, revengefulness, vengefulness, rancorousness, malevolence, malignancy, spitefulness, inexorableness, inexorability, relentlessness, mercilessness, pitilessness, deadliness, hard-heartedness, virulence, savagery, bitterness, remorselessness, grimness, direness, wrathfulness.

IMPLACABLE, *adj.* Not to be appeased, not able to be pacified, unappeasable, vindictive, unforgiving, relentless, unrelenting, irreconcilable, inflexible, inexorable, unpacifiable, unyielding, immitigable, hard-hearted, uncompassionate, rancorous, wrathful, remorseless, ruthless, pitiless, merciless, deadly, lethal, malevolent, malicious, invidious, unpitying, grim, spiteful, severe, cruel, fiendish, fell, bitter, savage, virulent, dire, inexpiable, stiff, hard.

IMPLANT, *v.* 1. Plant in something, ingraft, graft, bud, infix, put, set, place, introduce, insert, put into, inject, imbed, inlay, set out, root.

2. Indoctrinate, imbue, instill, impregnate, infuse, teach, inculcate, beat into, drum in, train, impress, open the eyes, enlarge the mind.

IMPLAUSIBLE, *adj.* Not having the appearance of truth, not worthy of credibility, not deserving of credence, unworthy of belief, unbelievable, unreasonable, contrary to all reasonable expectation, specious, unheard of, unimaginable, inconceivable, incredible, more than doubtful, improbable, unlikely, doubtful, disputable, questionable, suspect, open to doubt, hard to believe, staggering.

IMPLEMENT, *n.* 1. Article of equipment, tool, instrument, utensil, contrivance, device, machine, engine, motor, mechanism, appliance, apparatus.

2. Means, agent, channel, medium, wherewithal, wherewith, machinery.

3. *(Pl.)* Arms, ammunition, munition, matériel, outfit, paraphernalia, tackle, gear, equipment, rigging, plant, harness, fittings, trappings, accouterments, appointments.

IMPLICATE, *v.* 1. Show to be privy to, testify to be an abettor of, prove to be participant in, incriminate, criminate, charge, accuse, tax, inculpate, impute, inform against, denounce, indict, impeach, arraign, charge with, cite, draw into, compromise.

2. Involve as concerned in a matter, bring into connection with, imply as something to be inferred or understood, associate, connect.

3. Imply, connote, import, contain, mean, allude to, signify, represent, typify, emblematize, symbolize.

4. Fold together, infold, twist together, intertwine, entangle, interlace.

IMPLICATION, *n.* 1. Suggested meaning, suggestion, tacit inference, allusion, hint, intimation, innuendo, insinuation, reference, assumption, indication.

2. Intent, purpose, significance, sense, signification, purport, import, connotation, denotation, acceptation, interpretation, drift, bearing, force, upshot, value, substance, effect, gist, burden, sum and substance, pith, spirit, essence.

3. Involvement, involution, entanglement, intertwining, interlacing, connection.

IMPLICIT, *adj.* 1. Implied rather than expressly stated, understood, inferred, deduced, tacit, not expressed, virtually contained, latent, indirect, inferential, deducible, by implication, by inference, allusive, in the background.

2. Unquestioning, unhesitating, unreserved, firm, unshaken, undoubting, certain, assured, sure, steadfast, cocksure, positive, confident, satisfied, absolute, convinced, secure, complete.

IMPLICITLY, *adv.* 1. Tacitly, by implication, by inference, impliedly, inferentially, deducibly, virtually, between the lines, by mutual understanding, on the tip of one's tongue, in the background, secretly.

2. Without hesitancy, unhesitatingly, unreservedly, with full confidence, to the best of one's belief, completely, sure enough, rest assured, depend upon it, I'm sure, I doubt not, beyond the shadow of a doubt.

IMPLIED, *adj.* Tacitly understood, suggested by implying, involved by implication, tacit, assumed, inferential, undeclared, latent, virtual, potential, indirectly meant, implicit, connoted, involved, inferred, significative, allusive, indicative, eloquent, clear, explicit, pregnant with meaning.

IMPLORE, *v.* Call upon in urgent supplication, beseech, entreat, pray, solicit, beg, adjure, conjure, invoke, obtest, obsecrate, ask, importune, pray to, supplicate, petition for, canvas, plead, make urgent supplication for, crave, request, press, urge, address, solicitate, besiege, dun, sue, cry to, appeal to, invoke, evoke.

IMPLY, *v.* 1. Involve as a necessary circumstance, indicate as something naturally to be inferred, include by implication, entail, presuppose, devolve as a necessary consequence, assume, presume, surmise, take for granted, suppose, infer.

2. Import, mean, signify, denote, connote, betoken, evidence, express, bespeak.

3. Insinuate, hint, allude to, suggest, intimate, breathe, whisper, tip off, let fall, tip the wink, give a pointer to, prompt, give the cue, confide to, give the low-down, give inside information.

IMPOLICY, *n.* Ill-judgment, bad policy, indiscretion, imprudence, inexpediency, folly, improvidence, inconsiderateness, incaution, carelessness, incautiousness, heedlessness, rashness, unwiseness, injudiciousness, temerity.

IMPOLITE, *adj.* Not courteous, unmannerly, uncourteous, uncivil, ungentlemanly, unrefined, unpolished, rough, rude, boorish, bearish, insolent, impudent, disrespectful, ill-bred, discourteous, inurbane, churlish, ill-mannered, unamiable, ungracious, impertinent, saucy, malapert, vulgar, indecorous, coarse, savage, gruff, brusque, bluff, blunt, surly, ungentle, unhandsome, unladylike, misbehaved, clownish, unpolite, respectless, uncourtly, undignified, ill-behaved, unceremonious, unaccommodating, ungallant, pert, obtrusive, forward, fresh *(sl.),* flippant.

IMPOLITIC, *adj.* Ill-judged, ill-advised, unwise, injudicious, imprudent, indiscreet, inexpedient, incautious, temerarious, rash, reckless, foolish, senseless, stupid, careless, heedless, inconsiderate, hasty, headlong, harebrained, giddy, uncircumspect, unwary.

IMPONDERABLE, *adj.* That cannot be weighed, imponderous, light, subtle, airy, astatic, ethereal, aerial, weightless, volatile, buoyant, floating, unweighable, unsubstantial, weightless, light as thistle down, light as a feather.

IMPORT, *v.* 1. Bring into a country from abroad, give entrance to, introduce, carry, ship from overseas, convey.

2. Convey as a meaning or implication, make known, denote, imply, signify, purport, mean, betoken, express, indicate, argue, connote, suggest, point to, allude to, intimate, symbolize, drive at, declare, involve, affirm, manifest, utter, state, tell of, touch on.

3. Concern, be of consequence to, matter, be of importance to, be of interest to, carry weight, weigh, count, be influential, be potent.

IMPORT, *n.* 1. Importation, imported commodity, foreign-made article, merchandise from abroad.

2. Meaning, signification, significance, implication, purport, sense, interpretation, drift, spirit, tenor, gist, intention, bearing, intent, essence, pith, suggestion, allusion, upshot, substance, effect, burden, sum and substance.

3. Importance, force, moment, matter, weight, consequence, value, interest, effect, materialness, concern.

IMPORTANCE, *n.* 1. Consequence, moment, weightiness, weight, significance, concern, momentousness, import, materialness, interest, emphasis, standing, caliber, distinction, influence, usefulness, value.

2. Outstanding feature, salient point, essential matter, cardinal point, gist, gravamen, heart, core, nucleus, kernel, salt, cream, substance, sum and substance.

3. Self-importance, pomposity, greatness, superiority, self-estimation, dignity, magnitude, high self-regard, notability, self-sufficiency.

4. Solemnity, seriousness, gravity, urgency, press, pressure, stress, matter of life and death.

IMPORTANT, *adj.* 1. Of much significance, of great consequence, mattering much, momentous, of moment, serious, grave, weighty, ponderous, of great weight, considerable, significant, valuable, material, importunate, urgent, big, substantial, influential, marked, salient, critical, instant, imperative, exigent, crucial, pressing, vital, earnest.

2. Prominent, esteemed, of high standing, of social distinction, of high station, of influence, high-level, powerful, dignified, magnitudinous, top-flight, solid, remarkable, mighty, formidable, outstanding, majestic, grand, signal, noteworthy, grave, impressive, solemn, imposing, commanding.

3. Leading, foremost, first, principal, main, prime, chief, primary, cardinal, capital, paramount, superior, supreme, preëminent, essential.

4. Telling, significant, emphatic, positive, decided, trenchant, pregnant, forceful, powerful, effective.

5. Self-important, pompous, consequential, blustering, swaggering, gasconading, pretentious, boastful, conceited, egotistical, toplofty, cock-a-hoop, grandiose, high-flown, vainglorious, in-

flated, overweening, self-admiring, self-flattering, puffed up, ostentatious, flaunting, dashing.

IMPORTATION, *n.* 1. Bringing in of merchandise from foreign countries, importing, foreign trade.

2. Merchandise imported, foreign-made article, imported commodity.

IMPORTUNATE, *adj.* Earnestly solicitous, persistent in solicitation, clamorous, pressing, insistent, urgent, instant, exigent, eagerly desirous, cap in hand, on bended knees, on one's knees, pestering, bothering, teasing, harassing, carking, tormenting, worrying, pertinacious.

IMPORTUNE, *v.* Beset with solicitation, solicit insistently, ply persistently, ask urgently, press by entreaty, entreat, beg urgently, dun, urge, beg hard, sue, beseech, supplicate, plead, implore, apostrophize, adjure, conjure, obtest, kneel to, appeal to, imprecate, impetrate, invoke, clamor for, tax, throw oneself at the feet of, besiege, make requisition, prefer a petition, address a prayer, call upon for, apply to, beg a boon, make bold to ask, petition, pray, crave, request, plague, pester, harass, annoy, vex, bother, heckle, badger, persecute, cajole, inveigle, coax, entice, push, hound, require, peck at, tease, woo, insist, haunt, cry to.

IMPORTUNITY, *n.* Persistence in solicitation, pressing entreaty, persistent solicitation, insistence, urgency, requisition, request, petition, suit, overture, prayer, apostrophe, canvas, appeal, orison, imprecation, impetration, appeal, address, canvass, rogation, postulation, begging, supplication, instance, obsecration, imploration, invocation, obtestation, interpellation.

IMPOSE, *v.* 1. Lay on as something to be borne, set as something to be fulfilled, put by authority, place on, set on, lay upon, saddle, encumber, burden, superpose.

2. Enjoin, prescribe, dictate, appoint, force, subject to some penalty, inflict, levy, tax, charge, ordain, order, command, decree, enact, give orders, direct, set, mark out, bid, call upon, require, exact, demand, task.

3. Obtrude one's requirements upon others, presume upon good nature, thrust oneself upon others, intrude, apply, bully, domineer over.

4. Palm off deceptively, foist, pass fraudulently, victimize, put upon, mislead, defraud, counterfeit, adulterate, cajole, deceive, beguile, sham, delude.

IMPOSE ON, *v.* Act with a delusive effect, produce a false impression, deceive, chouse, cheat, befool, trick, circumvent, overreach, play upon, impose upon, victimize, dupe, hoax, bamboozle, abuse, put upon, cozen, gull, delude, defraud, palm off, take in, jockey, do, diddle, swindle, bilk, gyp, play one false, doublecross, spoof, practice upon, foist upon, outreach, outwit, humbug.

IMPOSING, *adj.* Making an impression on the mind, impressive, stately, majestic, pompous, illustrious, inspiring, dignified, august, grand, exalted, grandiose, magnificent, lofty, commanding, noble, supreme, superlative, striking, eminent, towering, capital, surpassing, regal, royal, massive, gorgeous, elaborate, splendid, superb, sublime, notable, palatial, solemn, paramount, foremost, overruling, leading, chief, principal.

IMPOSITION, *n.* 1. Laying on of something as a burden or obligation, imposing by authority, placing, putting on, encumbrance, infliction.

2. Exaction, encroachment, seizure, usurpation, assumption, breach, demand, requisition, reclamation, claim, revendication, request.

3. Oppression, constraint, charge, burden, unusual task, extraordinarily burdensome requirement, levy, tax, injunction, ultimatum, toll, duty.

4. Taking undue advantage of a person's good nature, presumption, forwardness, obtrusion, intrusion.

5. Deception, imposture, trickery, cheating, artifice, fraud, fake, gammon, hocus-pocus, stratagem, deceit, forgery, take in, wile, dissimulation, humbug, delusion, hoax, quackery, falsehood, beguilement, trick, swindle.

IMPOSSIBLE, *adj.* 1. That cannot be done or effected, unachievable, unattainable, unfeasible, impracticable, unobtainable, inaccessible, insuperable, insurmountable, hopeless, out of the question, impassable, innavigable, impervious.

2. That cannot exist or happen, unthinkable, inconceivable, that cannot be, incapable of occurring, unimaginable, improbable, impractical, incredible, unreasonable, contrary to reason, visionary, unlikely, not possible, that cannot be true, self-contradictory, incompatible, paradoxical, absurd, preposterous.

3. Stubborn, intractable, indocile, unmanageable, unyielding, intransigent, inflexible.

4. Hopelessly undesirable, highly objectionable, incurable, irredeemable.

IMPOST, *n.* Customs duty, excise, tax, toll, custom, tribute, assessment, rate, levy, tariff, *octroi (Fr.),* taxation, exactment.

IMPOSTOR, *n.* One who imposes fraudulently upon others, one who practices deception under an assumed name or character, charlatan, quack, mountebank, pretender, cheat, empiric, humbug, dissembler, hypocrite, pharisee, trickster, sharper, rogue, knave, deceiver, counterfeiter, faker, cozener, swindler, malingerer, medicine man, juggler, jockey, usurper, rascal, shyster, Judas, wolf in sheep's clothing, dissimulator, ass in the lion's skin.

IMPOSTUME, *n.* Abscess, pustule, fester, gathering, sore, ulcer, imposthume, whitlow, canker, carbuncle, boil.

IMPOSTURE, *n.* Instance of fraudulent imposition, deception, fraud, trick, artifice, stratagem, wile, chouse, ruse, crafty device, deceit, delusion, hoax, cheat, hocus-pocus, guile, quackery, charlatanry, cozenage, sham, gammon, circumvention, jugglery, trumpery, swindling, machination, fake, falsehood, humbug, bosh, chicane, sharp practice, knavery, duplicity, trickery, shift, subterfuge, finesse, flimflam, swindle, bunco, gold brick, confidence game, trap, net.

IMPOTENCE, *n.* 1. Powerlessness, feebleness, weakness, frailty, infirmity, decrepitude, debility, impuissance, inanition, exhaustion, atony, helplessness, inefficacy, inefficiency, incapability, inability, incapacity, incompetence, disability, ineptitude, disablement, disqualification, washout *(slang),* failure, imbecility, superannuation, senility, anility, paralysis, prostration, collapse.

2. Complete failure of sexual power, lack of procreative power, frigidity, sterility, barrenness.

IMPOTENT, *adj.* 1. Powerless, helpless, weak, feeble, frail, infirm, lacking bodily strength, physically unable, impuissant, exhausted, disabled, incapacitated, nerveless, enfeebled, enervated, debilitated, paralyzed, palsied, valetudinary, prostrate, crippled, senile, superannuated, decrepit, paralytic, done for, spent, all in, dead-beat, shattered, demoralized.

2. Without effectiveness, ineffective, ineffectual, inefficient, incompetent, incapable, unfitted, unfit, unqualified, disqualified.

3. Unarmed, weaponless, defenseless, unprotected, harmless, *hors de combat (Fr.)*.

4. Inoperative, unsound, invalid, nugatory, inadequate, futile, inefficacious, null and void, good for nothing, useless, fruitless, vain.

5. Wholly lacking in sexual power, incapable of begetting offspring, unable to procreate, sterile, barren, frigid.

IMPOUND, *v.* 1. Shut up a stray animal in a pound, put into a pound, coop up, confine within an enclosure, imprison, encage, shut up within limits, pen, pen up, rail in, cage.

2. Take summarily, seize, appropriate, retain in custody of the law.

IMPOVERISH, *v.* 1. Reduce to poverty, make poor, pauperize, beggar, bring to want, reduce to indigence, ruin, bankrupt, send to the dogs, break, undo, depauperate, fleece, ruinate, bring to rack and ruin.

2. Deplete the strength of, exhaust, drain the richness of, exhaust the fertility of, render barren, make sterile, make poor in quality, weaken, stint, drain of resources.

IMPRACTICABILITY, *n.* Impracticableness, infeasibility, impossibility, infeasibleness, hopelessness.

IMPRACTICABLE, *adj.* 1. That cannot be put into practice with the available means, not practicable, unfeasible, impossible, unachievable, unattainable, unobtainable, out of the question, hopeless, unsuitable for practical use or purposes, not be effected, not to be done.

2. Obstinate, obdurate, stubborn, hard to get along with, recalcitrant, fractious, unmanageable, thorny, untractable, hard to deal with, inflexible, immovable, inexorable, unyielding, impervious, unpersuadable.

IMPRACTICAL, *adj.* Not practical, un-matter-of-fact, chimerical, quixotic, wild, absurd, starry-eyed, romantic, ideal, visionary, theoretical, useless, ill-adapted to use, speculative, ill-adjusted to facts, unqualified, unefficacious.

IMPRECATE, *v.* Call down evil upon, invoke a curse upon, maledict, curse, anathematize, execrate, proscribe, excommunicate, denounce, thunder against, fulminate, damn, accurse, call down curses on the head of, devote to destruction.

IMPRECATION, *n.* Denunciation, execration, invocation of evil, malediction, curse, malison, fulmination, commination, anathema, proscription, ban, excommunication, thunders of the Vatican, aspersion, swearing, vindictive oath, blasphemy, profanity, scurrility, vituperation, vilification, abuse, foul language.

IMPRECATORY, *adj.* Conveying curses, execratory, maledictory, cursing, precatory, invocatory, denunciatory, comminatory, excommunicatory, blasphemous, fulminatory, proscriptive.

IMPREGNABLE, *adj.* Unconquerable, invincible, indomitable, inexpugnable, invulnerable, proof against, adamantine, immovable, unattackable, imperdible, unassailable, not to be overthrown, not to be overcome, not to be stormed, not to be taken by assault, not to be shaken by force, tenable against all odds, irresistible, irrefragable, secure from assault, unable to be captured, stout,

strong, mighty, powerful, puissant, potent, sturdy, hardy, robust, fast, formidable, redoubtable, founded on a rock, inextinguishable.

IMPREGNATE, *v.* 1. Make pregnant, cause to conceive, get with child, get with young, make fruitful, fructify, fecundate, make prolific, fertilize, spermatize, progenerate, beget, procreate, generate, create, propagate, engender.

2. Charge with something suffused throughout, surcharge, saturate, infuse, instill, imbue, fill, permeate, pervade, soak, imbrue, drench, whelm, deluge, inundate, flood, tincture, tinge, dye, transfuse into, steep, ingrain.

3. Teach, implant, indoctrinate, inculcate, ingraft, infix, sow the seeds of, open the eyes to, disseminate, propagandize.

IMPRESARIO, *n.* Manager of a concert company, organizer of an opera company, personal manager of concert artists, one who is responsible for a public musical performance, producer, director, business manager, press agent, entrepreneur, publicist of artistic productions, backstage driver of art.

IMPRESS, *v.* 1. Make an impression on, affect deeply in mind, act upon, move strongly in feelings, strike, influence in opinion, work upon, touch, interest, excite, inspire, stir, reach, rouse, arouse, touch to the quick, go to one's heart, possess the soul, rivet the attention, galvanize, electrify, prey on the mind, inculcate firmly in the memory, fix deeply on the mind.

2. Produce a mark by pressure, press into, imprint, stamp, engrave, leave a mark, indent, crimp, earmark, seal, sign, nick, blaze, print.

3. Force into public service, enlist, levy, draft, requisition, recruit.

IMPRESS, *n.* 1. Imprint, print, stamp, mark made by pressure, impression, seal.

2. Device upon a seal, emblem, symbol, cachet, characteristic, cognizance, mark of distinction, motto, token, sign, signum, note, indicium, cipher, figure, type, star, asterisk, hallmark, trademark, insigne *(pl.,* insignia*)*.

IMPRESSIBILITY, *n.* Susceptibility to impression, sensibility, susceptibleness, susceptivity, sensitivity, sensitiveness, emotionality, impressionability, perceptivity, affectibility, feeling, tenderness, sentimentality, softness, pliableness, plasticity, flexibility, pliancy.

IMPRESSIBLE, *adj.* Impressionable, sensitive, easily affected, susceptible to impression, soft, tender, emotional, facile, sensible, sensuous, sentient, alive to impressions, susceptive, perceptive, responsive, sympathetic, empathic, amenable, excitable, waxen, plastic, movable, impulsive, penetrable, thin-skinned.

IMPRESSION, *n.* 1. Strong effect produced on the feelings or intellect, first and immediate effect upon the mind in perception, sensation, feeling, effect produced by an influence, influence, deep sense, emotion, affection, pathos, sense, subconscious perception, cryptaesthesia, hyperaesthesia, delicacy of feeling, discernment, susceptibility, impact.

2. Mental view, image in the mind produced by something external to it, idea, notion, thought, apprehension, opinion, vague belief, indistinct recollection, hazy remembrance, fancy, sentiment, conception, concept, observation, consideration, reflection, surmise, conviction, position, persuasion, creed, judgment, conclusion.

3. Mark produced by pressure, impress, stamp, brand, indentation.

4. Total number of copies of a book printed at one time, edition, printing, imprint, circulation, indiction, stamping.

5. Copy, proof, page proof, galley proof, revise, print, pull, reprint.

IMPRESSIONABLE, adj. Easily influenced, capable of being impressed, easily affected, sensitive, sensible, sensuous, aesthetic, with tender feeling, perceptive, conscious, sentient, responsive, alive to, susceptible, susceptive, soft, impressible, impassionable, sentimental, excitable, mobile, thin-skinned, keen, acute, sharp, vivid, lively.

IMPRESSIVE, adj. 1. Such as to impress the mind, arousing definite feelings, touching, affecting, moving, absorbing, penetrating, pervading, deepfelt, heartfelt, soul-stirring, heart-rending, thrilling, electrifying, exciting, sensational, pathetic.

2. Ecstatic, rapturous, rapt, fervent, enthusiastic, zealous, ardent, glowing, rabid, burning, fanatical, enraptured.

3. Awe-inspiring, stately, imposing, lofty, formidable, grand, splendid, majestic, noble, magnificent, ostentatious, dignified, lordly, princely, regal, royal, imperial, imperious, sublime, solemn, grave, sage, oracular, wise-looking, solemn-faced, sober, venerable, revered, reverenced, authoritative, erudite, sapient, sagacious, deep, profound.

4. Striking, commanding, overpowering, powerful, telling, speaking, vigorous, trenchant, emphatic, incisive, mordant, forcible, vehement, eloquent, piquant.

5. Notable, prominent, outstanding, salient, signal, eximious, egregious, important, weighty, momentous, remarkable, memorable, paramount, vital, cardinal, essential, main, chief, foremost, first-rate, A-1, superior, significant, marked, leading, principal, primary, capital, in the front rank.

IMPRIMATUR, n. Formula of license to print or publish, license, sanction, voucher, approval, warrant, permit, charter, certificate, dispensation, authorization, permission.

IMPRIMIS, adv. First in order, in the first place, first and foremost, first of all, especially.

IMPRINT, v. 1. Make an imprint upon, print, mark by pressure, stamp, impress, surprint, put a mark on, tick, blaze.

2. Linotype, stereotype, electrotype, engrave.

3. Label, ticket, docket, earmark, set one's seal upon.

4. Fix firmly on the mind, impress on the memory, fix deeply, inculcate, fix in mind, memorize, rivet in the memory, store up in the memory, engrave in the memory, enshrine in the memory.

IMPRISON, v. 1. Cast into prison, incarcerate, immure, jail, lock up, put in durance, confine in a prison, detain in custody, put behind bars, put in duress, place in confinement, put in irons, clap under hatches, enchain, shackle, fetter, trammel, manacle, pinion, hobble, handcuff, secure, tie up, hold captive, put in the jug.

2. Hold in restraint, impound, put into a cage, encage, coop up, pen, inclose, entomb, restrain, circumscribe, constrain.

IMPRISONMENT, n. Incarceration, immurement, placing in confinement, commitment, detention, constraint, restraint, durance vile, duress, arrest, custody, safekeeping, captivity, enthrallment, thralldom, bondage.

IMPROBABILITY, n. Unlikelihood, bare possibility, inconceivableness, inconceivability, implausibility, incredibleness, incredibility, doubtfulness, shadow of a doubt, unbelievability, questionableness, rarity, questionability.

IMPROBABLE, adj. Not probable, unlikely to be true, unlikely to happen, rare, unheard of, inconceivable, unimaginable, implausible, incredible, unbelievable, questionable, unplausible, doubtful, fishy (slang).

IMPROBITY, n. 1. Reverse of probity, dishonesty, unrighteousness, unfairness, lack of integrity, breach of trust, faithlessness, bad faith, falseness, falsity, wickedness, badness, crookedness, corruption, disingenuousness, disingenuity, fraudulence, lying, fraud, wrongdoing, evil behavior, malpractice, professional misconduct, disrepute, dishonor, disgrace, turpitude, degradation, laxity.

2. Rascality, villainy, knavery, roguery, scoundrelism, shuffling, trimming, reprobacy, baseness, foul play, graft, venality, sharp practice, jobbery.

3. Infidelity, apostasy, treason, Judas kiss, Iscariotism, perfidy, perfidiousness, betrayal, treachery, double-dealing.

IMPROMPTU, adj. Having the character of an improvisation, done without previous preparation, offhand, extempore, extemporaneous, unprepared, hastily made, improvised, makeshift, extemporary, unpolished, rough-cast, fait à loisir (Fr.), on the spur of the moment, natural, spontaneous, unguided, unprompted, improvisé (Fr.), improvisatory, untutored, undrilled, impulsive, indeliberate.

IMPROPER, adj. 1. Unfit, unsuitable, unfitting, unsuited, inappropriate, unapt, unbefitting, unmeet, incongruous, inapposite, malapropos, unadapted, irregular, abnormal, inexpedient, unadvisable, out of place, unseasonable, untimely, inopportune, imprudent, unwarranted, undue, preposterous.

2. Not in accordance with propriety of behavior, indecorous, not conforming to the standards of conventional morality, immoral, indecent, indelicate, unseemly, unbecoming, offensively contrary to standards of modesty, immodest, gross, risqué, contra bonos mores (Lat.), naughty, corrupt, illicit, off-color, illegitimate, reprehensible, sinful, wicked.

3. Incorrect, wrong, inaccurate, erroneous, faulty, inexact, false, amiss, unjustified, unsound, illogical, untrue, mistaken, wide of the mark.

IMPROPRIETY, n. 1. Unsuitableness, unsuitability, inappropriateness, inappositeness, unaptness, unfitness, incongruousness, incongruity, irregularity, abnormality, inexpediency, unadvisability, unseasonableness, untimeliness, inopportuneness, imprudence, undueness.

2. Indecorum, indecorousness, unseemliness, indecency, immorality, indelicacy, immodesty, grossness, naughtiness, lewdness.

3. Incorrectness, inaccuracy, erroneousness, faultiness.

4. Slip, blunder, solecism, barbarism, absurdity, ineptitude, mistake.

IMPROVE, v. 1. Bring into a more desirable condition, make better, meliorate, better, ameliorate, mend, amend, correct, rectify, repair, restore, reform, enhance, touch up, polish, make improvements, doctor, enrich, elaborate, mellow, develop, refine, purify, elevate, humanize, civilize, modernize, retouch, remodel, reconstruct, reorganize, refashion, reclaim, uplift, ennoble, regenerate, redeem.

2. Revise, edit, review, make corrections, emend, rewrite.

3. Become better, get better in health, mend, convalesce, recuperate, gain, gain ground, pick up, get on, recover, brighten, grow better, rally, recruit one's strength, thrive.

4. Make good use of, turn to good account, employ advantageously, avail oneself of, use, utilize, profit by, make productive, cultivate.

5. Take a step forward, make progress, promote, advance, forward, further, push, speed, bring forward, foster, aid, benefit, forge ahead, go onward, progress.

6. Increase, rise, flourish, prosper, make gain, get on, grow bigger, mount.

IMPROVEMENT, *n.* 1. Betterment, enrichment, advancement, amelioration, melioration, amendment, reform, reformation, revision, correction, development, elaboration, repair, reconstruction, reclamation, purification, edification, rectification.

2. Progress, advance, promotion, preferment, increase, elevation, profit, upswing, proficiency, gain, growth, advantage.

3. Recovery, recuperation, mending, restoration, cure, recruital, convalescence, recruitment.

4. Cultivation, culture, refinement, menticulture, civilization, polish, march of intellect, race culture, eugenics, euthenics.

IMPROVIDENCE, *n.* 1. Lack of foresight, thoughtlessness, heedlessness, carelessness, negligence, unwariness, incautiousness, imprudence, want of forethought, short-sightedness.

2. Negligence in providing for future needs, unthriftiness, unthrift, thriftlessness, wastefulness, prodigality, extravagance, squandering, lavishness, shiftlessness, unpreparedness, unguardedness, neglect of preparation, carelessness of future needs, loselism.

IMPROVIDENT, *adj.* 1. Lacking foresight, thoughtless, heedless, careless, unwary, incautious, happy-go-lucky, easy-come easy-go, caught napping, unguarded, rash, imprudent, indiscreet, temerarious, injudicious, reckless, brash, hasty, headlong.

2. Negligent in providing for future needs, unthrifty, thriftless, wasteful, prodigal, extravagant, profuse, lavish, losel, dissipated, overliberal, careless of the future, without foresight, spendthrift, squandering, unfrugal, penny-wise and pound-foolish, with money burning a hole in one's pocket, shiftless.

IMPROVISATION, *n.* 1. Extemporaneous composition, extemporization, extemporizing, improvising, rough copy, impromptu, sudden thought, hunch, spurt, flash, impulsive creation.

2. Imagination, invention, originality, inspiration, fancy, divine afflatus, conception, fantasy, rhapsody, flight of fancy.

IMPROVISE, *v.* Invent offhand, compose extempore, make up, improvisate, prepare hastily, provide offhand, ad-lib, extemporize, compose on the spur of the moment, execute extemporaneously, strike out something new, coin, fabricate impulsively, devise, create offhand, originate, give play to the imagination, rise to the occasion, express in spurts.

IMPRUDENCE, *n.* Want of caution, incautiousness, incaution, rashness, temerity, brashness, indiscretion, foolhardiness, inconsiderateness,

thoughtlessness, carelessness, recklessness, heedlessness, impolicy, short-sightedness, foolishness, folly, fatuity, absurdity, desperation, fire-eating, improvidence, gambling, blind bargain, leap in the dark, quixotism, fool's paradise, too many eggs in one basket.

IMPRUDENT, *adj.* Lacking prudence, wanting discretion, indiscreet, incautious, temerarious, ill-judged, unadvised, ill-advised, reckless, brash, rash, inconsiderate, ill-considered, short-sighted, impolitic, thoughtless, injudicious, uncalculating, heedless, careless, giddy, impulsive, wanton, precipitate, over-hasty, uncircumspect, inexpedient, unwise, wrong-headed, unwary, unguarded, heels over head, madcap, wild, desperate, devil-may-care, hot-headed, breakneck, headlong, hazardous, foolhardy, venturous, adventurous, venturesome, quixotic, impulsive, hare-brained, fire-eating, inexpectant, overconfident, foolish, shiftless, silly.

IMPUDENCE, *n.* Audacity, effrontery, boldness, brazenness, forwardness, freshness, cheekiness, cheek, sauce, nerve, jaw, lip, brass, gall, front, face, sauciness, malapertness, pertness, brashness, impertinence, rudeness, incivility, unmannerliness, insolence, shamelessness, presumption, assumption, self-assertion, assurance, hardihood, flippancy, swagger, bluster, airs, toploftiness, arrogance, overbearance, braggartism, braggadocio, intrusiveness, officiousness, procacity, defiance, contempt, disdain, insult, abuse, protervity, bumptiousness, contumely, superciliousness, haughtiness.

IMPUDENT, *adj.* Characterized by shameless boldness, brazen, brazen-faced, bold-faced, shameless, bold, forward, impertinent, presumptuous, rude, pert, malapert, saucy, cheeky, lippy, nervy, fresh, brassy, galling, brash, uncivil, insulting, insolent, contumelious, swaggering, blustering, hectoring, arrogant, caustic, sarcastic, bumptious, overbold, glaring, unabashed, unblushing, immodest, flippant, cool, self-assured, officious, meddlesome, intrusive, obtrusive, domineering, high-hat, upstage, toplofty, haughty, supercilious, self-assertive, audacious, contumacious, overconfident, procacious, offensive, obnoxious.

IMPUGN, *v.* Call in question, challenge as false, gainsay, contradict, assail by argument, attack by words, controvert, dispute, impeach, charge, contravene, rebut, join issue upon, give denial to, deny peremptorily, refuse to believe, doubt the truth of, be skeptical as to, throw doubt upon, raise a question as to, question, query, object to, take exception to, frown upon, shake the head at, not speak well of, condemn, slate, bring to book, censure, pass censure upon, reproach, reprobate, recriminate, raise a hue and cry against, reprimand, reprehend, inveigh against, declaim against, raise one's voice against, make a fuss about, pick holes in, reflect upon, animadvert upon, find fault with, criticize, pick to pieces, peck at, carp at.

IMPULSE, *n.* 1. Impelling force driving onward, impetus, momentum, pressure, impulsion, propulsion, push, thrust, shove, boost, boom, kick, drive, start, send-off, get-up-and-go, energy, wave of vibration, stroke, shock.

2. Sudden involuntary inclination prompting to action, propensity, proclivity, penchant, taste, liking, appetite, itch, tendency, instinct, passion, mania, cacoëthes, desire, proneness, set, bias, bent, leaning, predisposition, twist, turn.

3. Sudden feeling, quick emotion, influence, hunch, impression, inducement, instigation, incitement, stimulus, incentive, spur, encouragement, abetment, call, urge, actuation, motive, inspiration, flash, spurt, effusion, improvisation, impromptu.

IMPULSIVE, *adj.* 1. Characterized by impulsion, moving, impelling, propulsive, impellent, dynamic, driving, forcible.

2. Extemporaneous, spontaneous, unpremeditated, improvised, unprompted, inspirational, extemporary, snap, offhand, unguarded, natural, instinctive.

3. Rash, passionate, impetuous, quick, hasty, precipitate, capricious, heedless, madcap, devil-may-care, ungovernable, incautious, hot, careless, headlong, rampant, reckless, hot-headed, headstrong, fiery, temperamental, high-strung, impatient, imprudent, indiscreet, wild, excitable, foolhardy, wayward, wanton, fitful, quixotic, heady, temerarious, vehement, violent, clamorous, boisterous.

IMPUNITY, *n.* Exemption, immunity, privilege, prerogative, respite, reprieve, pardon, dispensation, quietus, release, absolution, discharge, clearance.

IMPURE, *adj.* 1. Unclean, filthy, foul, dirty, polluted, defiled, fetid, feculent, maculate, contaminated, infected, tainted, rancid, unwholesome, nasty, muddy, turbid, soiled.

2. Unchaste, immoral, lewd, obscene, licentious, indecent, bawdy, coarse, immodest, gross, loose, indelicate, smutty, ribald, pornographic, risqué, improper, off-color, shameless, suggestive, Fescennine, dissolute, vile, libidinous, incontinent, sensual, lascivious, lustful, lecherous, salacious, concupiscent, Paphian, vulgar, nasty, prurient, adulterous, sexy, carnal, depraved, degenerate.

3. Mixed with extraneous matter of an inferior kind, combined with something else, admixed with foreign elements, adulterated, debased, deteriorated, doctored, vitiated, drugged, spurious, alloyed, hybrid.

IMPURITY, *n.* 1. Uncleanness, filthiness, foulness, dirtiness, filth, pollution, feculence, defilement, unwholesomeness, corruption, contamination, infection, rancidity, turbidity.

2. Unchastity, indecency, indelicacy, immodesty, grossness, obscenity, ribaldry, lewdness, carnality, concupiscence, lust, incontinence, salacity, salaciousness, immorality, sensuality, libertinism, dissipation, looseness, coarseness, impudicity, smuttiness, depravity, bawdiness, suggestiveness.

3. Admixture with foreign matter, adulteration, vitiation, deterioration, debasement, taint, adulterated condition, alloy.

IMPUTABLE, *adj.* Attributable, ascribable, traceable, referable, chargeable, owing to, due to, derivable from, putative.

IMPUTATION, *n.* 1. Ascription, attribution, reference to, accounting, derivation from.

2. Accusation, charge, reproach, blame, censure, inculpation, delation, exprobration, crimination, incrimination, accrimination, denouncement, challenge, arraignment, citation, impeachment, indictment.

3. Slur, insinuation, innuendo, reflection, stigma, brand, stain, spot, blot, blur, badge of infamy, scandal, slander, libel, aspersion, defamation, detraction, obloquy, calumny, vilification, backbiting, traducement, detraction, opprobrium, odium, ignominy, disrepute, dishonor, disgrace.

IMPUTE, *v.* 1. Attribute something discreditable to a person, ascribe to some evil cause, consider as due to, refer, charge, derive from, point to, set down to, trace to, invest with, lay at the door of, saddle with, father upon, account for, tax with, call to account, assign to.

2. Accuse, blame, censure, inculpate, criminate, incriminate, accriminate, denounce, challenge, arraign, cite, impeach, indict, allege, implicate.

3. Slur, twit, taunt with, reproach for, denounce, brand, stigmatize, post, defame, vilify, hold up to shame, drag through the mire, show up, heap dirt upon, reprehend, tarnish, sully, discredit, debase, degrade, defile, cause shame to, shame, disgrace, cast dishonor upon, derogate from, traduce, backbite, calumniate, cast aspersions on, slander, reflect upon, make insinuations.

IN, *prep.* 1. Enclosed within the bounds of, enveloped by, surrounded by, restrained by, within, on the inside of.

2. In the time of, inside of, during, pending, up to the time of, during the continuance of.

3. Among, amid, midst, amidst, existing as one of a group.

4. In regard to, respecting, with respect to, as to, by means of, conformably to.

5. Within the scope of, within the reach of, within the influence of, because of, with the purpose of, in order to.

6. In office, in power, on the inside track, in possession, in occupancy.

INABILITY, *n.* 1. Weakness, feebleness, impuissance, impotence, powerlessness, frailty, helplessness, disablement, disability, paralysis, exhaustion, collapse, infirmity, decrepitude.

2. Incapability, incapacity, ineptitude, inefficiency, incompetency, incompetence, inefficacy, inaptitude, clumsiness, inexperience, disqualification, unskillfulness, failure, washout *(slang)*.

3. Blunder, botch, bungle, botchery, *gaucherie (Fr.)*, bad job, hash, mess, flounder, stumble, trip, fumble, mistake.

INACCESSIBLE, *adj.* 1. Not to be reached, inapproachable, unapproachable, distant, far away, remote, far off, unreachable, telescopic, ulterior, yonder, yon, transmarine, transatlantic, transpontine, tramontane, transalpine, ultramontane, antipodean, hyperborean, out of the way, impassable, impervious, innavigable.

2. Unattainable, unobtainable, uncome-at-able, out of reach, unachievable, insurmountable, impracticable.

INACCURACY, *n.* 1. Inexactness, inexactitude, erroneousness, incorrectness, impropriety, fallaciousness, *non sequitur (Lat.)*, deception, misinterpretation, misconstruction, miscalculation, misjudgment, misstatement, aberration, misunderstanding, misapprehension, misconception, obliquity, anachronism, metachronism, illusion, delusion, false impression, hallucination, dream, mirage, falsification, gloss, exaggeration, invention.

2. Error, mistake, blunder, slip, boner *(slang)*, fault, fallacy, oversight, erratum, misprint, corrigendum, trip, flaw, blot, break, stumble, bungle, *lapsus linguae (Lat.)*, slip of the tongue, *lapsus calami (Lat.)*, slip of the pen, solecism, bull, spoonerism, malapropism, fable, cock-and-bull story, myth, bosh, moonshine, canard.

INACCURATE, *adj.* Erroneous, incorrect, wrong, improper, inexact, faulty, amiss, wide of the mark, mistaken, blundering, untrue, false, erring, fallacious, unfounded, illogical, unsound, groundless, in error, out in one's reckoning, deceived, at fault, illusory, deceptive, unreal, untrustworthy, incomplete, partial, latitudinous, ungrammatical, solecistic.

INACTIVE, *adj.* 1. Not active, without inherent energy, having no inherent power of motion, destitute of activity, lifeless, inanimate, stagnant, vegetant.

2. Not on active duty, not on active status, inoperative, not in force, not in action, unoccupied, unbusied, unemployed, disengaged, resting.

3. Quiet, dormant, quiescent, motionless, silent, restful, resigned, indifferent, impassable, impassive, apathetic, unresisting, nonresistant, patient, noninterfering.

4. Idle, sluggish, indolent, loafing, vacant, inert, slothful, lazy, do-nothing, torpid, supine, passive, sleepy, heavy, drowsy, dull, lumpish, dronish, dilatory, Fabian, slumbering, listless, languid, recumbent, lackadaisical, slow, sedentary, easygoing, otiose.

INACTIVITY, *n.* Inaction, torpor, sluggishness, torpidity, inertness, passivity, passiveness, noninterference, *laissez-faire (Fr.),* nonresistance, Fabianism, Fabian policy, dilatoriness, watchful waiting, idleness, neglect, supineness, indolence, otiosity, sloth, laziness, vegetation, stagnation, *dolce far niente (It.),* loafing, rest, unemployment, want of activity, inactiveness, lethargy, dormancy, latency, drowsiness, inertia, motionlessness, repose, paralysis, dullness, heaviness, do-nothingness, faineancy, inexertion, lull, languor, quiescence, peace, somnolence, stupor, siesta, doze, catnap, snooze, reverie, coma, trance, catalepsy, hypnosis, hibernation, aestivation.

INADEQUACY, *n.* 1. Inadequateness, insufficiency, shortage, shortness, scarcity, shortcoming, stint, paucity, poverty, meagerness, need, necessity, exigency, dearth, short allowance, exhaustion, depletion, reduction, low water, ebb tide, want, lack, scantiness, deficiency.

2. Incompleteness, imperfection, defectiveness, inaptness, incompetence, disability, incommensurability, inferiority, inefficacy, uselessness, ineptitude, inefficiency, unskillfulness.

INADEQUATE, *adj.* 1. Insufficient, scanty, lacking, deficient, short of, wanting, meager, bare, scant, scarce, infrequent, incommensurate, ill-provided, thin, slight, slim, scurvy, slender, stinted, in want, unsupplied, unprovided, empty-handed, vacant, empty, at low ebb, penurious, indigent, minus.

2. Imperfect, incomplete, defective, incompetent, incapable, inefficient, unfit, disqualified, unable, perfunctory, ineffectual, inept, ineffective, helpless, powerless, inapt, unfitted, unworthy, failing, unqualified.

INADMISSIBLE, *adj.* Not admissible, not to be admitted, not to be allowed, unallowable, not to be received, ineligible, inappropriate, unfit, unsuitable, inconsonant, inexpedient, inadvisable, undesirable, objectionable, inapt, inconvenient, troublesome, unsatisfactory, inopportune, untimely, unseasonable, out of place, unseemly, improper, impracticable, unfeasible.

INADVERTENCE, *n.* 1. Thoughtlessness, heedlessness, carelessness, inconsiderateness, inattention, negligence, remissness, non-observance, neglect, neglectfulness, disregard, indifference, dereliction, absence of mind, woolgathering, unconcern, absent-mindedness, want of thought, inconsideration, preoccupation, abstraction, *étourderie (Fr.),* reverie, brown study, daydream.

2. Act of inattention, oversight, blunder, slip, error from inattention, omission, fault, boner, misprint, erratum, corrigendum, flaw.

INADVERTENT, *adj.* 1. Thoughtless, heedless, careless, inconsiderate, inattentive, negligent, unobservant, unconscious, unmindful, unreflecting, preoccupied, undiscerning, regardless, unheeding, neglectful, absent-minded, *distrait (Fr.),* abstracted, woolgathering, in a reverie, daydreaming.

2. Unintentional, accidental, unintended, undesigned, fortuitous, chance, unmeant, unthinking, unpurposed, unpremeditated, spontaneous, involuntary, casual.

INADVERTENTLY, *adv.* 1. Thoughtlessly, heedlessly, inconsiderately, in an unguarded moment, unguardedly, off guard, negligently, remissly, inattentively, with one's wits gone a-woolgathering, carelessly.

2. Without thinking, by inattention, without intention, by accident, unintentionally, accidentally, fortuitously, by a slip, unwittingly, without knowing.

INADVISABLE, *adj.* Imprudent, unwise, injudicious, undesirable, inexpedient, impolitic, ill-advised, disadvantageous, inopportune, unprofitable, inappropriate, unfit, objectionable, unsuitable, unsatisfactory, unseemly, improper, inconvenient, inadmissible, discommodious, ineligible.

INALIENABLE, *adj.* That cannot be transferred to another, untransferable, incommunicable, inviolable, prescribed, absolute, imprescriptible, unimpeachable, sacrosanct, lawful, legal, legitimate, unforfeitable, indeprivable, inherent.

INAMORATO, *n.* 1. Male lover, beau, swain, suitor, admirer, wooer, amoret, adorer, sweetheart, flame, paramour, gallant, sheik, *amoroso (It.),* leman, Lothario, *cavaliere servente (It.),* ladies' man, Don Juan.

2. Inamorata, female lover, goddess, enchantress, ladylove, darling, idol, angel, mistress, concubine.

INANE, *adj.* 1. Vacuous, vacant, void, empty, blank, unintelligent, unintellectual, dull, unreasoning, void of intelligence, void of reason, shallow, stupid, inexpressive, incogitant, incogitative, irrational, thoughtless, unthinking, expressionless.

2. Silly, senseless, idiotic, foolish, fatuous, imbecile, absurd, asinine, laughable, ridiculous, frivolous, nonsensical, puerile, empty-headed.

INANIMATE, *adj.* 1. Inorganic, mineral, azoic, unorganized.

2. Dead, deceased, breathless, extinct, deprived of life, exanimate, lifeless, demised, stone dead, exanimous, defunct, clay-cold.

3. Inert, soulless, spiritless, passive, sluggish, torpid, dull, dormant, flat, heavy, vapid, inactive, stagnant, insipid, mawkish, indolent, apathetic, listless.

INANITION, *n.* 1. Vacuity, void, emptiness, vacuum, inanity, vacancy, empty space.

2. Exhaustion from lack of nourishment, starvation, innutrition, collapse, prostration, famishment, extreme hunger.

INANITY, *n.* Lack of sense or ideas, silliness, foolishness, folly, stupidity, fatuity, fatuousness, unwisdom, senselessness, irrationality, levity, frivolity, absurdity, foolery, ineptitude, trifling, asininity, extravagance, giddiness, light-headedness, rashness, madness.

INAPPLICABLE, *adj.* Unsuitable, unfit, irrelevant, impertinent, inapposite, inapt, incompatible, unsuited, strange, inconsistent, alien, inappropriate.

INAPPOSITE, *adj.* Not pertinent, impertinent, inapplicable, irrelevant, out of place, not to the point, not to the purpose, unessential, extraneous, inappropriate, out of keeping, unsuitable, unfit, incongruous, wrong, unapt, ill-timed, improper, inexpedient, incompetent.

INAPPRECIABLE, *adj.* Not appreciable, imperceptible, trifling, impalpable, very small, infinitesimal, very little, tiny, microscopic, minuscule, minute, insignificant, trivial, atomic, inconsiderable, molecular, homoeopathic, evanescent, unimportant, inconsequential, slight, paltry, petty, wee, minikin.

INAPPROPRIATE, *adj.* Not appropriate, improper, unsuitable, unfit, unsuited, unbecoming, unadapted, out of place, out of keeping, out of character, inapt, inept, inapplicable, unbefitting, unseasonable, inopportune, ill-timed, malapropos, irrelevant, infelicitous, uncongenial, incompatible, displeasing, in bad taste, incongruous, alien, inconsistent, unapt, amiss, unadvisable, wrong, unseemly, unfortunate, odd.

INAPT, *adj.* 1. Not apt, not fitted, unsuited, inappropriate, unsuitable, unfit, inapplicable, unsuited, inexpedient, irrelevant, unseasonable.

2. Without aptitude, without capacity, unskillful, awkward, clumsy, not handy, not ready, inexpert, bungling, ungainly, unseemly, inadequate, indocile, backward, inhabile, unteachable, unhandy, gauche, maladroit.

INAPTITUDE, *n.* 1. Unsuitableness, inappropriateness, unfitness, inapplicability, irrelevancy, impertinency, inexpediency, undesirableness, impropriety, unsuitability, incompatibility, incongruity.

2. Unskillfulness, ineptitude, incompetency, infelicity, inability, inexperience, want of dexterity, unproficiency, clumsiness, gaucherie, disqualification, heavy-handedness.

INARTICULATE, *adj.* 1. Unable to use articulate speech, mute, dumb, silent, speechless, voiceless, aphonic, nonvocal, mum, reticent, taciturn, wordless, noiseless, tongue-tied.

2. Blurred, indistinct, confused, thick, muttering, mumbling, throaty, guttural, harsh, husky, lisping, muffled, obscure, indistinguishable, inaudible.

3. (*Zool.*) Having no joint, not joined, inarticulated, jointless, unjointed, unsegmented.

INARTIFICIAL, *adj.* 1. Not artificial, not factitious, not made by art, natural, plain, simple.

2. Sincere, naive, artless, guileless, ingenuous, unaffected, simple-minded, unsophisticated, untutored, candid, honest, innocent, unreserved, straightforward, undesigning, aboveboard, frank, downright, direct, matter-of-fact.

INASMUCH AS 1. In view of the fact that, considering that, seeing that, since, forasmuch as, whereas, because.

2. Insofar as, to such a degree as, to the extent that.

INATTENTION, *n.* 1. Wandering of mind, want of attention, idle exercise of the imagination, straying of attention, abstraction, detachment, absorption, preoccupation, engrossment, reverie, brown study, distraction, daydream, woolgathering.

2. Absent-mindedness, unmindfulness, inconsiderateness, inadvertence, thoughtlessness, carelessness, heedlessness, inapplication, disregard, unobservance, negligence, neglect, remissness, unconcern, inconsideration, oversight, forgetfulness, slackness, indifference, apathy, oscitance.

INATTENTIVE, *adj.* 1. Not attentive, wandering, abstracted, detached, absorbed, preoccupied, engrossed in a reverie, distracted, *distrait (Fr.),* woolgathering, daydreaming, musing, rapt, lost, faraway, dazed, dreamy, in the clouds.

2. Absent-minded, thoughtless, unmindful, unobservant, heedless, careless, inadvertent, regardless, inconsiderate, absent, negligent, unwatchful, oscitant, remiss, off one's guard, caught napping, forgetful, neglectful, unmindful, listless, unheeding, undiscerning, indifferent, apathetic, deaf, blind, scatterbrained, volatile, mercurial, flighty, harebrained, giddy, unreflecting, harum-scarum, wild, reckless, unsteady, disregardful, incurious, supine, unaware.

INAUDIBLE, *adj.* Unhearable, too low to be heard, imperceptible, indistinct, faint, muffled, dull, stifled, out of earshot, whispered, muttered, mute, muted, soft, gentle, still, silent, noiseless, quiet, not audible, not heard.

INAUGURATE, *v.* 1. Make a formal beginning of, set in action, set going, commence, originate, institute, launch, initiate, undertake, start, open, introduce, conceive, embark upon, lay the first stone, break ground, usher in, forerun, lead the way, set on foot, lay the foundations, set up, found, broach, open the door to.

2. Introduce into an office, invest with office, induct into office with formal ceremonies, install, instate, chair, induct, coronate.

3. Celebrate the institution of, introduce into public use with fitting ceremonies, commemorate, signalize, solemnize, observe.

INAUGURATION, *n.* 1. Formal opening, debut, commencement, initiation, beginning, institution, origination, inception, start, dawn, outset, opening, prologue, prelude, preface, introduction.

2. Installation, investiture, ceremony of induction, instatement, coronation, presentation.

3. Commemoration, signalization, observance, celebration, jubilation, triumph, ovation.

INAUSPICIOUS, *adj.* Ill-starred, ill-omened, ill-fated, ill-boding, ominous, portentous, premonitory, unpropitious, untoward, unfavorable, unpromising, augural, unfortunate, unlucky, sinister, doomed, hostile, disastrous, calamitous, catastrophic, dark, gloomy, threatening, lowering, menacing, minatory, infelicitous, untimely, unhappy.

INBORN, *adj.* Innate, implanted by nature, inbred, ingrained, inherent, in the grain, congenital, bred in the bone, connate, constitutional, ingenerate, chronic, natural, native, instinctive, organic, essential, intrinsic, deep-rooted, inveterate, dyed-in-the-wool, blown-in-the-bottle.

IN BRIEF Briefly, tersely, concisely, laconically, pithily, curtly, crisply, succinctly, summarily, in a word, in short, in epitome, in substance, in a few words, in a nutshell, for shortness sake, abridgedly, compendiously, condensedly, synoptically, it comes to this, the long and the short of it is, to come to the point, to be brief, to cut the matter short, to make a long story short.

INCALCULABLE, *adj.* 1. That cannot be calculated, beyond calculation, beyond computation, not to be reckoned, beyond estimate, inestimable, very great, enormous, unnumbered, incomputable, countless, numberless, untold, unmeasured, sumless, measureless, immense, immeasurable, innumerable, illimitable, illimited, unlimited, unbounded, infinite, uncountable, innumerous, interminable, unfathomable, inexhaustible, indefinite, without limit, limitless, endless, boundless, without number, without end.

2. That cannot be forecast, unpredictable, unforeseen, uncertain.

INCALESCENCE, *n.* Incipient heat, warmth, calefaction, calidity, temperature, recalescence, decalescence, incandescence.

INCANDESCENCE, *n.* Glowing whiteness, white heat, luminescence, illumination, luminosity, glow, effulgence, refulgence, fulgor, incandescency, resplendence, transplendency, glimmering, phlogiston, fire, glint, spark, flash, scintillation, blaze, flame, flood of light, lambent flame, sheet of fire, coruscation, emication, phosphorescence, conflagration, fulguration, radiation, irradiation, reflection, renitency, sparkling, luster, shimmer, light, ray, gleam, brilliancy, brightness, splendor, radiance.

INCANDESCENT, *adj.* 1. Glowing white, whitehot, white with heat, self-luminous, luminescent, blazing, ablaze, relucent, lambent, luciferous, phosphorescent, phosphoric, fluorescent, illuminating, rutilant, aglow.

2. Intensely bright, splendent, resplendent, transplendent, radiant, scintillant, effulgent, refulgent, shining, beamy, sheeny, shiny, lustrous, nitid, brilliant, vivid, glassy, sunny.

INCANTATION, *n.* 1. Chant purported to have magical power, magic formula, rune, weird, invocation, cantrap, exsufflation, abracadabra, open-sesame, mumbo-jumbo, hocus-pocus, fee-fawfum, charm, Ephesian letters, counter-charm.

2. Occult art, black magic, spell, sorcery, witchcraft, witchery, enchantment, conjuration, exorcism, necromancy, fetishism, hoodoo, voodoo, *Hexerie (Ger.),* divination, sortilege, oracle, obsession, possession, evil-eye, *malocchio (It.).*

INCAPABILITY, *n.* 1. Inability, incapableness, incapacity, inaptitude, ineptitude, incompetence, inefficiency, invalidity, disability, disqualification.

2. Impotence, impuissance, helplessness, prostration, caducity, paralysis, collapse, palsy, ataxia, emasculation, inanition, decrepitude.

INCAPABLE, *adj.* 1. Not having the capacity for a specified function, inherently lacking in ability, incompetent, inept, inapt, ineffective, inefficient, unfit, unfitted, unable, unqualified, disqualified, inadequate, not up to, unequal to.

2. Impotent, impuissant, powerless, prostrate, decrepit, helpless.

INCAPABLE OF 1. Without ordinary ability, without capacity for, incompetent for, unable to, not capable of, without qualification for, inefficacious, ineffectual, inadequate, good for nothing, disqualified for.

2. Not open to the influence of, not admitting of, not susceptible of, impervious to.

3. Too good to, not base enough for, utterly above, too great for, above suspicion, inoffensive, harmless, innocuous, innoxious, unimpeachable, blameless, inerrable, irreproachable, innocent.

INCAPACIOUS, *adj.* Not capacious, not ample, not amplitudinous, of small capacity, narrow, close, contracted, limited, scant, slim, circum-

scribed, confined, pinched, cramped, straitened, scanty, slight.

INCAPACITATE, *v.* Deprive of capacity, make unfit, make incapable, disable, render powerless, disenable, debilitate, weaken, enervate, devitalize, render helpless, cripple, maim, lame, hamstring, unman, emasculate, castrate, spay, geld, effeminize, caponize, enfeeble, shake, shatter, exhaust, deprive of strength, unbrace, disarm, disqualify, unfit, invalidate, undermine, tie the hands, hogtie, spread eagle, muzzle, prostrate, cramp, paralyze, clip the wings of, render *hors de combat,* spike the guns, put out of gear, break the back of, draw the teeth of, put a spoke in the wheel, sabotage, unhinge, deprive of power to perform acts with legal consequences *(Law).*

INCAPACITY, *n.* 1. Lack of capacity, incapability, inability, impotence, impuissance, incompetence, unfitness, inaptitude, ineptitude, inefficiency, inefficacy, disablement, disenablement, disqualification, invalidity, disability.

2. Decrepitude, infirmity, helplessness, failure, asthenia, adynamy, prostration, paralysis, ataxia, palsy, exhaustion, collapse, caducity, inanition, deliquium, feebleness.

3. Ignorance, nescience, unacquaintance, incomprehension, unconsciousness, inexperience.

4. Stupidity, idiocy, imbecility, vacancy of mind, poverty of intellect, hebetude, dull understanding, stolidity, clouded perception, desipience, irrationality, poor head, simplicity, puerility, dotage, senility, anility, second childishness.

INCARCERATE, *v.* 1. Cast into prison, imprison, immure, send to jail, put in duress, put in the hoosegow, put in the jug, put in the clink, place in durance, put in confinement, hold in custody, confine, lock up, commit to prison, jail, engaol, prison, clap under hatches, put in irons, arrest, take into custody, enchain, fasten, fetter, shackle, entrammel, pinion, manacle, handcuff, hobble, tie up, secure, make prisoner.

2. Enclose, impound, hem in, pen up, coop up, constrict closely, bolt in, rail in, wall in, restrain, shut away, put under restraint, check, restrict, cage, encage, repress, suppress.

INCARNATE, *adj.* 1. Invested with a human bodily form, embodied in flesh, carnal, clothed with flesh, fleshly, somatic, bodily, corporeal, corporal, human, physical, personified, material, materialized, substantial, palpable, tangible, ponderable, objective, typified.

2. Flesh-colored, incarnadine, pale red, crimson, peaches-and-cream *(colloq.).*

INCARNATE, *v.* 1. Invest with a human bodily form, clothe with flesh, embody, incorporate, personate, impersonate, animate, materialize, vitalize, substantialize, materiate, exteriorize, substantiate, externalize.

2. Be the embodiment of, personify, typify, represent.

3. Put into concrete form, represent concretely, give concrete form to.

INCARNATION, *n.* 1. Assumption of human form, bodily manifestation, embodiment, bodily presentation, personification, impersonation, incorporation, incarnification, somatic exemplification.

2. Incarnate form, flesh and blood, corporeity, corporality, bodiliness, substantiality, material existence, living being embodying a spirit, body, materialness, matter, substance, protoplasm.

INCAUTIOUS, *adj.* 1. Indiscreet, injudicious, impolitic, improvident, imprudent, unsuspecting, unguarded, unwary, uncircumspect, uncautious, uncalculating.

2. Rash, temerarious, impulsive, reckless, headlong, precipitate, hasty, overconfident, overhasty, foolhardy, venturesome, venturous, adventurous, quixotic, madcap, wild, devil-may-care, desperate, intrepid, breakneck, harebrained, hot-headed, brash, foolish, ill-advised, unthinking.

3. Careless, heedless, unconcerned, negligent, remiss, neglectful, thoughtless, inconsiderate.

INCENDIARY, *adj.* 1. Adapted for setting property on fire, inflammable, combustible, ignitible, burnable.

2. Tending to arouse strife, inflammatory, seditious, dissentious, factious, subversive, destructive, malevolent, malicious, maleficent, demagogical, rebellious, recalcitrant, turbulent, refractory, rancorous, virulent, treacherous, invidious, fell, ruthless, truculent, deletory, ruinous, anarchistic, iconoclastic, communistic, provocative, inciting, instigating, spellbinding, excitative, agitative.

INCENDIARY, *n.* 1. One who maliciously sets fire to property, burner of buildings, arsonist, pyromaniac, firebug, fire-setter, firer, *pétroleur (Fr.).*

2. One who stirs up sedition, political agitator, firebrand, *agent provocateur (Fr.),* instigator, rabble-rouser, mutineer, rebel, rioter, insurgent, revolter, brawler, demagogue, anarchist, bolshevik, communist, fifth-columnist, iconoclast, mischief-maker, ringleader, soapbox orator, spellbinder, lobbyist, prompter.

INCENSE, *v.* 1. Inflame with wrath, excite hatred, make angry, provoke, irritate, nettle, pique, exasperate, exacerbate, anger, enrage, chafe, enkindle, inflame, envenom, rile, excite, embitter, estrange, alienate, huff, heckle, vex, annoy, fret, ruffle, infuriate, madden, stir up bile, make one's blood boil, raise one's dander, fire, heat, displease, aggravate, burn up *(slang),* gall, give offense, give umbrage, offend, affront, insult, incite, sting to the quick, hurt the feelings, wound, rankle, add fuel to the flame, harass.

2. Perfume with incense, burn incense for, offer incense, thurificate.

INCENSE, *n.* 1. Aromatic gum producing a sweet odor when burned, fragrance, perfume, fragrancy, scent, censery, frankincense, sweet aroma, thurification.

2. Oblation, sacrifice, libation, burnt offering, votive offering.

3. Adulation, homage, laudation, adoration, worship, admiration, applause, plaudits, gloze, blandishment, blandiloquence, cajolery, flattery, honeyed words, mouth-honor, lip-homage, blarney, applesauce *(slang),* soft soap *(slang),* butter *(slang),* buncombe, flummery, rose water.

INCENSED, *adj.* Wrathful, angry, irate, wroth, ireful, raging, boiling, fuming, convulsed with rage, *acharné (Fr.),* infuriated, worked up, overwrought, excited, hysterical, indignant, offended, cross, bitter, embittered, waxy, hurt, sore, peeved, furious, flushed with anger, in a huff, in a fume, in a stew, in a pucker, on one's high ropes, in high dudgeon, on one's high horse, up in arms, at daggers drawn, at swords points, not on speaking terms.

INCENTIVE, *n.* Inducement, instigation, incitement, stimulus, spur, fillip, whip, whet, goad, provocative, provocation, urge, impulse, motive, reason, cause, ground, mainspring, reason why,

occasion, object, excuse, purpose, encouragement, press, insistence, inspiration, exhortation, persuasion, consideration, enticement, allurement, lure, bait, bribe, sop, grease *(slang),* graft, decoy, magnet, charm, temptation.

INCEPTION, *n.* Beginning, commencement, inauguration, initiation, incipience, installation, embarkation, starting point, dawn, opening, outset, debut, start, exordium, outbreak, onset.

INCERTITUDE, *n.* Uncertainty, dubiety, doubtfulness, dubitancy, indecision, hesitancy, hesitation, doubt, ambiguity, vagueness, haze, fog, obscurity, insecurity, perplexity, quandary, dilemma, bewilderment, indetermination, vacillation, embarrassment, suspense, puzzle, enigma, riddle, poser.

INCESSANT, *adj.* Continuing without interruption, uninterrupted, continuous, continual, unremitting, unceasing, ceaseless, endless, unending, without ceasing, unintermitting, constant, perpetual, interminable, perennial, untiring, indefatigable, everlasting, eternal, unwearied, habitual, persistent, recurrent, thick-coming, frequent, repeated, unbroken, redundant, pleonastic, tautological, monotonous, iterative, harping.

INCEST, *n.* Sexual intercourse between persons related by blood, abuse, fornication, defilement, rape, seduction, defloration, carnality, stupration, lechery, adultery, debauchery, depravity, bestiality, lust, concupiscence, pruriency, lewdness, lasciviousness.

INCESTUOUS, *adj.* Adulterous, bestial, debauched, depraved, voluptuous, licentious, lascivious, unclean, impure, covetous, lewd, libidinous, lecherous, wanton, salacious, dissolute, degenerate, fornicative, carnal, lustful, concupiscent, prurient.

INCHOATE, *adj.* Just begun, incipient, rudimentary, embryonic, initial, nascent, inceptive, initiatory, preliminary, preparative, preparatory, provisional, commencing, beginning, elementary.

INCIDENCE, *n.* Range of occurrence of a thing, extent of an influence's effects, scope, direction, course, bearing, drift, set, tenor, tendency, trend, line, aim.

INCIDENT, *adj.* 1. Liable to happen, happening, occurring, apt to happen, likely, possible, on the cards, contingent, within range of, in the wind.

2. Naturally appertaining, pertaining, belonging, accessory, relating, natural.

INCIDENT, *n.* 1. Occurrence, event, circumstance, episode, affair, distinct piece of action, happening, phenomenon, fact, proceeding, transaction, particular, experience, adventure, contingency, eventuality, emergency, pass, crisis, casualty, accident, issue, passage.

2. Anecdote, tale, story, legend, fiction, romance, narrative, fable, yarn, parable, apologue.

INCIDENTAL, *adj.* 1. Happening in fortuitous conjunction with something else, casual, accidental, fortuitous, chance, contingent, subordinate, possible, haphazard, random, stray, causeless, uncaused, unintentional, dependent on, unintended, not meant.

2. Extraneous, adventitious, adventive, nonessential, parenthetical, occasional, non-pertinent, superfluous, irrelevant, indifferent, immaterial, not vital, secondary, collateral, episodic, accessory, adscititious, supplementary.

INCIDENTALLY, *adv.* Inappositely, irrelatively, parenthetically, disconnectedly, by the by, by the way, *en passant (Fr.)*, in passing, in that connection.

INCINERATE, *v.* Reduce to ashes, burn to ashes, cremate, char, calcine, carbonize, scorify, smelt, burn to a cinder, torrefy, bake, parch.

INCIPIENT, *adj.* Beginning to exist, inchoate, commencing, just begun, in an initial state, nascent, initial, inchoative, elementary, rudimentary, embryonic, inceptive, in the blueprint stage, initiative, prefatory, introductory, initiatory, prime, inaugural, primal, primordial, primitive.

INCISE, *v.* Cut into, cut marks upon, notch, engrave, carve, sculpt, chase, enchase, grave, etch, furrow, groove.

INCISED, *adj.* Made by cutting, cut, cut into, graved, engraved, carved, graven, furrowed, grooved, notched, sulcated, canaliculated.

INCISION, *n.* Cut, gash, notch, nick, scratch, slash, slit, score, incisure, insection, crack, streak, rut, furrow, groove.

INCISIVE, *adj.* Penetrating, biting, piercing, cutting, acute, sharp, keen, severe, vivid, intense, trenchant, vigorous, brisk, caustic, corrosive, harsh, mordant, piquant, poignant, sarcastic, satirical, mordacious, going straight to the heart, sharp-cut, distinct, clear, impressive, forcible, powerful, sensational, lively, spirited, sparkling, glowing, racy, slashing, bold, pungent, pithy, pointed, antithetical, sententious, vehement, impassioned, graphic, telling, effective, moving, galvanic, electric, impelling.

INCISOR, *n.* Tooth in the anterior part of the jaw adapted for cutting, cutting tooth, canine-tooth, eye-tooth *(upper jaw)*, stomach-tooth *(lower jaw)*, cusp, tusk.

INCITE, *v.* Rouse to action, constrain, actuate, induce, instigate, animate, arouse, inflame, urge, prod, egg on, provoke, sic on, push, prompt, impel, foment, fire, spur, goad, encourage, stimulate, spur on, work up, stir up, excite, inspirit, drive, hound, prick, entice, persuade, sway, wheedle, influence, coax, tempt, lure, exhort, abet, enkindle, kindle, agitate, embolden, touch off, quicken, whet, prevail upon, awaken, force, motivate, advocate, inveigle.

INCITEMENT, *n.* Actuation, inducement, instigation, press, insistence, solicitation, provocative, abetment, influence, call, kindling, provocation, quickening, excitement, fomentation, egging, incitation, persuasion, spurring, incentive, impulse, stimulus, spur, urge, fillip, goad, whip, encouragement, motive, prompting, dictate, instance, allurement, seduction, cajolery, siren song, exhortation, inspiration, enticement, temptation, magnetism, fascination, blandishment.

INCIVILITY, *n.* Uncivil behavior, bad manners, unmannerliness, ill-manners, ill breeding, uncouthness, uncourtliness, uncourteousness, inurbanity, rudeness, impoliteness, discourteousness, coarseness, discourtesy, incomity, churlishness, boorishness, *brusquerie (Fr.)*, rusticity, tactlessness, barbarism, vulgarity, conduct unbecoming a gentleman, ungentlemanliness, indecorum, misbehavior, disrespect, impudence, slight, insult, affront, impertinence, roughness, harshness, unkindness, bluntness, acerbity, acrimony, contumely, hard words, procacity, *grossièreté (Fr.)*, gaucherie, want of tact, awkwardness.

INCLEMENCY, *n.* 1. Bitterness, severity, harshness, rigor, coldness, violence, boisterousness,

tempestuousness, storminess, roughness, rawness, vehemence, windiness, gustiness, blustering.

2. Mercilessness, unmercifulness, cruelty, pitilessness, unfeelingness, unkindness, remorselessness, ruthlessness, stoniness, implacableness, obdurateness, ferociousness, savagery, hard-heartedness, callousness, barbarity, malevolence, stringency, inexorableness.

INCLEMENT, *adj.* 1. Bitter, severe, cold, violent, harsh, rigorous, raw, stormy, tempestuous, boisterous, rough, not mild, unfavorable, vehement, squally, penetrating, windy, rainy, gusty, blustering.

2. Merciless, unmerciful, pitiless, cruel, devoid of clemency, remorseless, unkind, hard-hearted, unfeeling, ungenial, inexorable, unpitying, ruthless, grim-visaged, stony, implacable, obdurate, unrelenting, barbarous, ferocious, savage, Draconian, Spartan.

INCLINATION, *n.* 1. Liking, fondness, partiality, preference, taste, desire, appetite, appetency, relish, wish, fondness, fancy, notion, whim, stomach, attachment, love, wish, affection, attraction, animus, pleasure, gratification, zeal, aim, purpose, willingness, allurement, fascination, longing, hunger, hankering, ardor, craving, avidity, voracity, concupiscence, itch, pruriency.

2. Propensity, proclivity, predilection, penchant, proneness, leaning, tendency, bent, turn, bias, twist, mind set, disposition, predisposition, aptitude, set, trend, drift, liability, susceptibility, temperament, idiosyncrasy, humor, cast, grain, mood, readiness, willingness.

3. Inclined surface, slant, slope, incline, obliquity, rake, tilt, diagonal, bevel, cant, gradient, acclivity, rise, pitch, ascent, grade, inclined plane, ramp, bank, hill, declivity, fall, dip, downhill, descent.

4. Deviation from a normal position or direction, divergence, declination, droop, turn, swing, fall, angle, list, sag, zigzag, twist, curve, bend, lurch.

5. Nod, bow, obeisance, salaam, kowtow, proskynesis, curtsy, genuflection, scrape, bowing and scraping, kneeling, prostration.

INCLINE, *v.* 1. Have a mind to, have an eye to, have a desire for, desire, wish for, like, want, take to, have a fancy for, be bent upon, crave, covet, hanker after, yearn for, long for, be disposed to, have a disposition for, prefer, have liefer, relish, favor.

2. Have a tendency toward, tend, exhibit a leaning to, have a proclivity, have a propensity, have a predisposition, be predisposed, have a bent, have a bias, show inclination.

3. Dispose, predispose, influence, affect, tempt, persuade, actuate, direct the mind to, prompt, induce, lead, conduce.

4. Slant, slope, cant, shelve, lean, descend, decline, bend, careen, heel over, lurch, reel, slouch, roll, sidle, sag, tilt, veer, sheer, dip, droop, stoop, pitch.

5. Tend obliquely, verge, trend, bend forward, gravitate, hang, sway, take an oblique direction, turn, incurvate, crook, bend, zigzag, stagger.

6. Bow the head, bend, nod, curtsy, kowtow, salaam, bow and scrape, make obeisance, genuflect, kneel.

INCLINE, *n.* Inclined surface, slope, cant, gradient, inclination, grade, ramp, rise, ascent, rising ground, pitch, hill, bank, declivity, descent, fall, dip, downhill.

INCLINED, *adj.* 1. Prone, disposed, predisposed, fain, desirous, mindful, zealous, apt, addicted, given, willing, caring, susceptible, liable, partial to, appetitive, longing, wishful, ardent, keen, eager, fervent, avid, hungry, craving, thirsty, athirst.

2. Deviating from the horizontal or vertical, sloping, leaning, sideling, aslant, slant, askew, skew, oblique, zigzag, tilted, supine, bias, diagonal, acclivous, ascending, rising, precipitous, uphill, abrupt, steep, shelving, declivitous, declining, downhill, descending, declivous, falling.

INCLUDE, *v.* 1. Contain the parts of a whole, involve parts of a whole, comprehend, comprise, take in, subsume, embrace, cover, incorporate, embody, admit, hold, inclose, receive, encircle, encompass, subjoin, reckon among, number among, count, number.

2. Place in an aggregate, put in a class, classify, categorize, place under a group, arrange under, tabulate, index, file, list, catalogue, register, graduate, grade, range.

3. Involve as a factor, contain as a subordinate element, implicate, refer to, take into account.

INCLUSIVE, *adj.* 1. Enclosing, embracing, incorporating, embodying, encircling, surrounding, inclusory, comprehending, taking in, embracing.

2. Both being included, including both, including everything concerned.

3. Comprehensive, extensive, large, wide, full, all-embracing, compendious, sweeping, general.

INCOGITABLE, *adj.* Inconceivable, not to be thought of, unthinkable, not cogitable, unintelligible, incapable of being made coherent, unthought of, unconsidered, undreamt of.

INCOGNITO, *n.* 1. Concealment of real identity, disguise, masquerade, domino, cloak, veil, mask, false appearance, cover, counterfeit dress, visor, muffler, screen, blind, curtain, secrecy, privacy, secretness, camouflage, alias, pseudonym, false name, fictitious name, pen name, *nom de plume (Fr.),* assumed name.

2. One who is incognito, person under an assumed name, person with an alias, disguised person, masquerader.

INCOGNITO, *adj.* and *adv.* Having one's identity concealed, in an assumed character, with the real identity concealed, veiled, cloaked, masked, muffled, screened, secreted, camouflaged, disguised, in masquerade, in disguise, unknown in one's true character, unrecognized, with an alias, privy, private, *in petto (It.),* clandestine, inviolate, behind a screen, under cover, incommunicado, mysterious, irrevealable, inviolable, confidential, secretive, noncommittal, uncommunicative, secretly, in secret, undisclosed.

INCOGNIZABLE, *adj.* Indistinguishable, incognoscible, unrecognizable, unperceivable, unobservable, unnoticeable, unknowable, inexplicable, inscrutable, incomprehensible, inapprehensible, insoluble, impenetrable, unintelligible, unaccountable, undiscoverable, unfathomable, undecipherable, unexplained, undiscernible, inconceivable.

INCOHERENCE, *n.* 1. Looseness of parts, laxity, relaxation, want of cohesion, non-adhesion, immiscibility.

2. Inconsistency, incongruity, unsuitableness, incompatibility, disagreement, impropriety, dissonance, irreconcilableness, discordancy, disconnection, disjunction, want of connection, inconsequence, illogicality, absurdity.

INCOHERENT, *adj.* 1. Without physical cohesion, non-cohesive, non-adhesive, immiscible, loose, detached, lax, slack, relaxed, unconsolidated, broken, uncombined, segregated, ununified, without unity of elements.

2. Inconsistent, incongruous, inharmonious, uncoordinated, unsuitable, incompatible, improper, unfit, unsuitable, discordant, disagreeing, dissonant, contradictory, variant, unconnected, disconnected, disjointed, without connection, rambling, irreconcilable, incongruent, discrepant, antagonistic, contrary, incoordinate, illogical, absurd, irrational, unintelligible, wild, confused, discursive, digressive.

INCOMBUSTIBLE, *adj.* Incapable of being burned, fireproof, uninflammable, indestructible by fire, unburnable, that will not burn, asbestine, asbestic, unflammable.

INCOME, *n.* Periodic returns from property or labor, revenue, earnings, receipts, gains, profits, emoluments, perquisites, interest, salary, wages, annuity, fruits of labor, proceeds, remuneration, winnings, avails, benefits.

INCOMMENSURABLE, *adj.* Having no standard of comparison, without a common measure, having no common measure, not measurable by the same factor, not measurable by the same aliquot part, not to be measured by the same standard, disproportionate.

INCOMMENSURATE, *adj.* Having less than the proper effect, having less than the desired value, insufficient, inadequate, unequal, disproportionate, scanty, deficient, incompetent.

INCOMMODE, *v.* Put to inconvenience, discommode, inconvenience, discomfort, trouble, bother, disturb, molest, annoy, vex, harass, harry, pester, disquiet, badger, embarrass, hinder, impede, discompose, put out, obstruct, interrupt, intercept, hamper, cramp, encumber, handicap, saddle with.

INCOMMODIOUS, *adj.* 1. Not affording sufficient room, small, cramped, restricted, not large, not capacious, incapacious, narrow, confined, contracted.

2. Inconvenient, burdensome, onerous, cumbrous, cumbersome, awkward, unwieldy, inhabile, unhandy, unmanageable, unsuitable.

3. Troublesome, provoking, harassing, vexatious, irritating, annoying, disadvantageous.

INCOMMUNICABLE, *adj.* Not to be told to others, that cannot be communicated, not to be divulged, unrevealable, inexpressible, unutterable, ineffable, top-secret, confidential, inviolable, not to be spoken of, esoteric, private, privy.

INCOMMUNICATIVE, *adj.* Reticent, taciturn, uncommunicative, secretive, noncommittal, evasive, reserved, buttoned up, mum, silent, mute, sparing of words, close-mouthed, close-tongued, inconversable, laconic, curt, unsocial, unsociable, exclusive, of few words, dumb.

INCOMPARABLE, *adj.* Matchless, unequaled, unrivaled, unparalleled, peerless, transcendent, surpassing, inimitable, unmatchable, unmatched, unsurpassed, rare, exceptional, without an equal, superlative, pluperfect, without a parallel, beyond compare, unexampled, uncommon, supreme, unapproachable, superior, exquisite, unique.

INCOMPATIBILITY, *n.* Irreconcilable opposition, contrariety, contrast, variance, contradictoriness, difference, discongruity, incongruity, inconsistency, want of agreement, want of adaptation, antipathy, repugnance, intolerance, uncongeniality, discordancy, inharmoniousness, irreconcilableness, irreconcilability, intransigence, divergence, disunion, dispute, discord, misunderstanding, dissent, wrangle, dissidence, conflict, dissension, division, controversy, antagonism, dissent, quarrel, disparity, unlikeness, diversity, unconformity, discrepancy, dissonance, nonconformity, dissimilitude, disagreement, disparity, inequality, irrelevancy, disproportion.

INCOMPATIBLE, *adj.* 1. Inconsistent, unsuitable, contradictory, incongruous, inappropriate, disagreeing, opposite, jarring, discordant, incoherent, inadmissible, inapplicable, contrary, opposed, unadapted, clashing, factious, inconsonant, inaccordant.

2. Incapable of existing together in harmony, incapable of coexistence, antipathetic, constitutionally opposed, intolerant, antagonistic, repugnant, uncongenial, irreconcilable, adverse, inharmonious, unsympathetic, mismatched, ill-assorted, unaccommodating, displeasing, hostile, dissentient, unpleasant, disagreeable, offensive, distasteful, unamiable.

INCOMPETENCE, *n.* Inability, incapability, incapacity, incompetency, inefficiency, disability, inadequacy, insufficiency, unfitness, disqualification, impotence, ineptitude, disablement, weakness, feebleness, inefficacy, failure, washout *(slang)*, fiasco, botch, fizzle, muff, flash in the pan, collapse, breakdown.

INCOMPETENT, *adj.* 1. Unfit, inefficient, incapable, unable, unapt, unsuitable, inffectual, inept, unskillful, inadequate, lacking qualification, unqualified, unfitted, incapacitated, disqualified, inadmissible, deficient, unequal, insufficient, ineffective.

2. Inexpert, unskilled, awkward, bungling, maladroit, gauche, gawky, clumsy, unhandy, lubberly, ungainly, stupid, benighted, stumbling, ignorant, floundering.

INCOMPLETE, *adj.* 1. Unfinished, unaccomplished, uncompleted, unexecuted, left undone, not completed, inexhaustive, imperfected, crude, sketchy, rough, perfunctory, meager, hollow, scarce, undeveloped, immature, inchoate, abortive.

2. Lacking some part, defective, deficient, short of, partial, not total, not entire, failing, wanting, in arrear, containing omissions, fragmentary, elliptic, inaccurate, garbled, broken, mutilated, defaced, distorted, mangled, butchered, maimed, hashed, truncated, docked.

INCOMPREHENSIBLE, *adj.* Impenetrable, unfathomable, inscrutable, not to be comprehended, unimaginable, unconceivable, past finding out, inexhaustible, inconceivable, incogitable, unintelligible, not understandable, unaccountable, enigmatic, beyond comprehension, inexplicable, obscure, occult, deep, infinite, supernatural, mysterious, unsearchable, undiscoverable, measureless, fathomless, boundless, meaningless, hard, nebulous, hidden, concealed, mystic, mystical, esoteric, abstruse, metaphysical, unknowable, incognoscible, crabbed, insoluble, intricate, puzzling, acroamatic, recondite, dark, dim, muddy, latent, apocalyptic, vague, ambiguous, indefinite.

INCOMPRESSIBLE, *adj.* Not compressible, not to be compressed, solid, dense, solidified, cohesive, compacted, compact, close, lumpish, massive, impenetrable, imporous, impermeable, concrete, gnarled, thick, grumous.

INCOMPUTABLE, *adj.* Beyond estimate, past calculation, incalculable, innumerable, enormous,

prodigious, immense, astronomical, staggering, unnumbered, numberless, countless, untold, unmeasured, sumless, measureless, immeasurable, illimitable, illimited, unlimited, infinite, unbounded, uncountable, innumerous, interminable, inexhaustible, indefinite, limitless, without limit, boundless, endless, without end, without number.

INCONCEIVABLE, *adj.* Unthinkable, unimaginable, unbelievable, incomprehensible, incredible, impossible, beyond the bounds of reason, not to be thought of, out of the question, improbable, unlikely, contrary to all reason, implausible, unheard of, incogitable, unthought of, undreamed of, hard to believe, staggering, open to doubt, suspect, suspicious, questionable, doubtful, disputable, inexpressible, undefinable, ineffable, monstrous, prodigious, extraordinary, indescribable, stupendous, marvelous, strange, passing strange, overwhelming, striking, wondrous, surprising, miraculous.

INCONCLUSIVE, *adj.* Not conclusive, not such as to settle a question, indecisive, unconvincing, indefinite, untenable, incorrect, unproved, unscientific, fallible, fallacious, hollow, invalid, unwarranted, weak, feeble, flimsy, loose, frivolous, quibbling, absurd, inconsequent, illogical, lame, without final results, still open.

INCONGRUITY, *n.* 1. Unsuitability, unsuitableness, inaptitude, inappropriateness, unfitness, inapplicability, inconsistency, incoherence, irrelevancy, incompatibility, impropriety, inharmony, irreconcilableness, discrepancy, discordancy, dissonance, variance, dissimilitude, difference, unconformity, nonconformity, unlikeness, diversity, disparity, divergence, inequality, disproportion, incongruousness, contrast.

2. Contradictoriness, contradiction, contrariety, absurdity, nonsense, illogicality, inconsequence, abnormality.

INCONGRUOUS, *adj.* 1. Inappropriate, unsuitable, unfit, out of keeping, out of place, inapt, unbecoming, improper, inapplicable, disagreeing, incoherent, incongruent, illogical, absurd, incoordinate, contradictory, grotesque, mismated, heterogeneous, incommensurable, mismatched, ill-matched, different, divergent, disparate, inconformable, unconformable, inapposite, inapropos, untimely, unseasonable, inopportune, inconsonant, inharmonious, discordant, dissonant, inconsistent.

2. Conflicting, inconsequent, incompatible, variant, irreconcilable, repugnant, antagonistic, hostile, dissentient, clashing, jarring, factious, discrepant, contrary.

INCONSEQUENT, *adj.* Lacking sequence in thought, lacking logical sequence, disconnected, detached, apart, forced, illogical, inconsecutive, unconnected, unrelated, unallied, independent, separate, heterogeneous, irrespective, divergent, inconsistent, fragmentary, discontinuous, loose, desultory, irrelevant, *à propos de bottes (Fr.),* inapplicable, inappropriate, unessential, inapposite, beside the point, not in keeping with the general character, not following from the premises, unwarranted, inconclusive.

INCONSEQUENTIAL, *adj.* Worthless, trifling, of no account, of minor importance, insignificant, picayune, slight, light, slender, flimsy, frothy, idle, airy, shallow, weak, frivolous, niggling, petty, fribble, namby-pamby, wishy-washy, of no consequence, trivial, of no moment, mean, little, unimportant, unessential, immaterial, nondescript, inane, puerile.

INCONSIDERABLE, *adj.* Not worthy of notice, minute, inappreciable, attenuated, nominal, meager, modest, shallow, slight, small, unimportant, so-so, nugatory, dispensable, of no moment, of no consequence, nonessential, immaterial, petty, trifling, piddling, trivial, frivolous, insignificant.

INCONSIDERATE, *adj.* 1. Without due regard for the rights or feelings of others, unthoughtful, uncharitable, roughshod, intolerant, harsh, unkind, severe, censorious, illiberal, unaltruistic, selfish, self-centered, rude, blunt, bluff, brusque, churlish, bearish, gruff, ungracious, uncivil, unamiable, disobliging.

2. Acting without consideration, indiscreet, impolitic, imprudent, unthinking, thoughtless, inattentive, negligent, inadvertent, unobservant, undiscerning, unheeding, unmindful, neglectful, indifferent, listless, apathetic, regardless, deaf, blind, heedless, careless, uncircumspect, unwary, unwatchful, off guard, hasty, rash, headlong, scatterbrained, light-headed, harebrained, giddy, volatile, flighty, unreflecting, *écervelé (Fr.),* harumscarum, wild, giddy-brained, offhand, flippant, unwise, nonchalant, pococurante, ill-advised.

INCONSISTENCY, *n.* 1. Incoherence, incompatibility, incongruity, unsuitableness, impropriety, variance, disagreement, difference, inconsonance, inharmony, dissonance, discordance, repugnance, antagonism, discrepancy.

2. Contradiction, contrariety, illogicality, antilogy, alogy, absurdity, nonsense, paradox, nugacity, irrationality, desipience, antithesis.

3. Instability, vacillation, inconstancy, changeableness, mercurialness, unsteadiness, capriciousness, fitfulness, flightiness, volatility.

INCONSISTENT, *adj.* 1. Incoherent, incompatible, incongruous, unsuitable, improper, different, inconsonant, inharmonious, dissonant, discordant, repugnant, antagonistic, discrepant, irreconcilable, inconsequent, at variance, incongruent, inimical, jarring, divergent, inappropriate, unbefitting, disagreeing.

2. Contradictory, contrary, illogical, fallacious, unwarranted, unconnected, absurd, nonsensical, paradoxical, antilogistic, preposterous, senseless, antithetical, conflicting, irrational, desipient, nugacious.

3. Inconstant, unstable, changeable, mercurial, volatile, unsteady, capricious, fitful, flighty, erratic, eccentric, fanciful, whimsical, wayward, freakish, wanton, giddy, notional, moody, humorsome, mutable, frivolous, indecisive, irresolute, variable, vacillating, hot and cold.

INCONSOLABLE, *adj.* Woebegone, broken-hearted, heartbroken, disconsolate, forlorn, comfortless, cheerless, hopeless, crushed, desolate, *désolé (Fr.),* despondent, unhappy, inconsolate, wretched, despairing, sad, downcast, downhearted, down in the mouth, heavy-hearted, in the doldrums, in the dumps, mopish, glum, moody, in low spirits, low-spirited, disheartened, discouraged, heartsick, sick at heart, soul-sick, bowed-down, overcome, in despair, *au désespoir (Fr.),* heart-stricken, doleful, tristful, pensive, lugubrious, lachrymose, melancholic, in tears, hypochondriacal.

INCONSPICUOUS, *adj.* Not noticeable, not prominent, unnoticeable, unobtrusive, unostentatious, modest, unpretentious, retiring, unassuming, shy, behind the scenes, behind the curtain, indistinguishable, obscure, non-apparent, imperceptible, undiscernible, unapparent, unseen, covert, hidden, latent, concealed, veiled, shrouded, suppressed, dim, indistinct, blurred, shadowy, misty, feeble, hazy, nebulous, faint, vague, confused.

INCONSTANT, *adj.* 1. Fickle, capricious, mercurial, volatile, flighty, giddy, erratic, unsteady, changeable, fitful, unsteadfast, faithless, wavering, vacillating, hot-and-cold, like a weathercock, unsettled, fluctuating, changeful, restless, irresolute, indecisive, skittish, desultory, spasmodic, rambling, roving, unmethodical, irregular, vagrant, wayward, wanton, fanciful, unreliable, fancy-free.

2. Unfixed, variable, mutable, unstable, uncertain, mobile, slippery, tremulous, vibratory.

INCONTESTABLE, *adj.* Not admitting of dispute, indubitable, undeniable, incontrovertible, irrefragable, unquestionable, past dispute, beyond a shadow of a doubt, indubious, beyond all question, indefeasible, irrefutable, unequivocal, uncontradictable, proof against, unimpeachable, conclusive, certain, assured, sure, reliable, trustworthy, official, authoritative, genuine, authentic, valid, patent, clear as day, overt, palpable, clear, plain, self-evident, unmistakable, evident, obvious, indisputable.

INCONTINENCE, *n.* Lack of sexual restraint, indulgence of lust, lechery, lasciviousness, lewdness, licentiousness, libidinousness, lustfulness, concupiscence, prurience, carnality, pornography, indecency, grossness, impudicity, unchastity, debauchery, libertinism, libertinage, lubricity, dissipation, venery, harlotry, bawdry, wenching, fornication, seduction, whoredom, concubinage, adultery, cuckoldry, rakishness, obscenity, smuttiness, orgies, excess, flesh pots of Babylon, eroticism, amorousness, voluptuousness, bestiality, animalism, dissoluteness, salacity, ribaldry.

INCONTINENT, *adj.* Lacking in sexual restraint, uncontrolled, unrestrained, bestial, salacious, lecherous, licentious, lustful, lewd, lascivious, libidinous, erotic, amorous, voluptuous, prurient, concupiscent, bawdy, ribald, lickerish, dissolute, loose, of easy virtue, wanton, debauched, rakish, ruttish, rampant, carnal, obscene, smutty, pornographic, coarse, gross, shameless, unchaste, indecent, impure, immoral, incestuous, adulterous, promiscuous, riggish, gay, frail, meretricious, dissipated, gallant, on the loose, fast.

INCONTROVERTIBLE, *adj.* 1. Undeniable, incontestable, indisputable, irrefutable, unquestionable, past dispute, beyond contradiction, unchallengeable, irrefragable, uncontradictable, indubitable, beyond a shadow of a doubt, indubious, undisputed, unimpeachable, indefeasible.

2. Vested, settled, established, authoritative, official, authentic, apodictic, positive, peremptory, stereotyped, indeclinable.

INCONVENIENCE, *n.* 1. Disturbance, molestation, nuisance, vexation, trouble, annoyance, derangement, agitation, commotion, unsettlement, perturbation, discomposure, fuss, distraction, hindrance, harassment, worriment, infliction, discommodity.

2. Disadvantage, inadvisability, inutility, inexpediency, unsuitableness, inopportuneness, unseasonableness, untimeliness, unfitness, impropriety, undesirability, troublesomeness, disadvantageousness.

3. Encumbrance, impediment, dead weight, millstone around one's neck, drag, check, stumbling block, unwieldiness, cumbersomeness, awkwardness, incommodiousness, clumsiness.

INCONVENIENT, *adj.* 1. Inopportune, ill-timed, untimely, unseasonable, come-amiss, inexpedient, inadvisable, ill-advised, improvident, impolitic, discommodious, unsatisfactory, inapt, improper, unseemly, inappropriate, objectionable, obnoxious, inadmissible, ineligible, unsuitable, unfit, incommodious, troublesome, disadvantageous, unprofitable.

2. Unhandy, awkward, unwieldy, uncomfortable, unmanageable, cumbrous, cumbersome, ponderous, ungainly, clumsy, lumbering, hulky, vexatious, annoying.

INCONVERTIBLE, *adj.* 1. Not transmutable, incapable of being converted, unchangeable, unalterable, immutable, invariable, changeless, inflexible, constant, permanent, stable.

2. Continuing, uninterrupted, unremitting, unintermitting, unshifting, unvarying, unrevoked, irrevocable, unstopped, unreversed, sustained, unvaried, undying, incessant, interminable.

INCORPORATE, *v.* 1. Introduce into a body as an integral part, consolidate, compound, amalgamate, blend, fuse, interfuse, mix, merge, intermix, alloy, link, join, combine, unite, concentrate, centralize, center, coalesce, associate, assimilate, mingle.

2. Create a corporation, form into a society, federate, affiliate, organize, unionize. federalize, league, confederate.

3. Embody, materialize, incarnate, personify, substantialize, materiate, externalize, exteriorize, substantiate.

INCORPORATE, *adj.* 1. Intimately united, combined into one mass, blended, consolidated, merged, coadunate, conjoint, amalgamated, allied, corporated, federate, incorporated, confederate.

2. Not embodied, incorporeal, spiritual, supernatural, immaterial, insubstantial, bodiless, impalpable.

INCORPORATION, *n.* 1. Combination, consolidation, amalgamation, mixture, blending, union, unification, coadunation, centralization, synthesis, conjuncture, fusion, coalescence, organization, inclusion.

2. Association, alliance, league, coalition, order, federation, federacy, confederacy, guild, club, trust, pool, combine, cartel.

INCORPOREAL, *adj.* Bodiless, asomatous, incorporal, incorporate, immaterial, immateriate, impalpable, unsubstantial, unextended, unembodied, unbodied, disembodied, supernatural, spiritual, extramundane, unearthly, supersensible, psychical, pneumatoscopic.

INCORRECT, *adj.* 1. Not correct as to fact, inexact, erroneous, inaccurate, untrue, false, fallacious, wrong, mistaken, in error, unsound, amiss, out in one's reckoning, unveracious, wide of the mark, untrustworthy, unreliable.

2. Faulty, improper, defective, imperfect, corrupt, illogical, unbecoming, ungrammatical, solecistic, barbarous, malapropian.

INCORRECTNESS, *n.* 1. Inaccuracy, mistake, error, misrepresentation, untruth, faultiness, inexactness, falsity, falseness, falsehood, inveracity, erroneousness, fallaciousness, fallacy, obliquity, aberration, fault, blunder, misprint, corrigendum, erratum, slip, bungle, oversight.

2. Solecism, barbarism, bull, boner, impropriety, malapropism, spoonerism.

INCORRIGIBLE, *adj.* 1. Past mending, past cure, incurable, cureless, past hope, hopeless, irreclaimable, irredeemable, immedicable, irremediable, remediless, irremedicable, irreparable, irrecoverable, beyond help, helpless.

2. Firmly fixed, inveterate, inured, irrevocable, intractable, obstinate, stubborn, uncontrollable, indocile, inflexible, hardened, toughened, chronic, deep-seated, habituated, ingrained, accustomed, confirmed, willful.

3. Bad beyond reform, past praying for, obdurate, unregenerate, depraved, lost, shameless, abandoned, recreant, reprobate, recidivous, irreformable, corrupt, vicious, iniquitous, degenerate, steeped in iniquity, uncontrite, impenitent, recusant, remorseless, relentless, seared, wicked, unrepentant, impervious to reason, deaf to advice.

INCORRUPTIBILITY, *n.* 1. Indestructibility, incorruptibleness, imperishableness, deathlessness, immortality, eternal perpetuity, incorruption, unlimited existence, eternal continuance.

2. Incorruptible integrity, impermeability to corruption, inflexible honesty, probity, rectitude, purity, principle, uprightness, unvenality, unpurchasableness, unmercenariness, imperviousness to bribery, impeccability, guiltlessness, innocence, faith, good faith, honorableness, honor, clean hands, justice, fair play, equity, grace, impartiality, fidelity, constancy, veracity, loyalty, candor, trustworthiness, clear conscience, singleness of heart.

INCORRUPTIBLE, *adj.* 1. Incapable of decay, unfading, amaranthine, deathless, undying, imperishable, everlasting, immortal, indestructible, everliving, indissoluble, eternal, continuing, perdurable, sempiternal, perpetual, endless.

2. That cannot be perverted, of inflexible honesty, upright, not to be bribed, unvenal, unmercenary, faultless, sinless, guiltless, blameless, spotless, immaculate, impeccable, unblemished, innocent, unerring, inculpable, inerrable, irreproachable, above suspicion, unimpeachable, inoffensive, harmless, innocuous, virtuous, honorable, constant, true-blue, faithful, loyal, sincere, scrupulous, stanch, trusty, trustworthy, conscientious, high-principled, jealous of honor, as good as one's word.

INCREASE, *v.* 1. Enlarge, make larger, make greater, greaten, augment, aggrandize, magnify, superadd to, amplify, supplement, inflate, broaden, double, lengthen, deepen, heighten, extend, exalt, thicken, redouble, strengthen, develop, maximize, stretch out, prolong, protract, double, treble, triple, quadruple.

2. Raise, boost, reinforce, add to, enhance, advance, step up, elevate, build up, improve, upturn, revise upward, accumulate, amass.

3. Multiply by propagation, propagate, fructify, engender, beget, breed, procreate, produce, originate, bring into being, generate, be fruitful, be prolific, proliferate.

4. Intensify, aggravate, exaggerate, deepen, concentrate.

5. Rise, ascend, swell, wax, mount, grow, become, accrue, enlarge, augment, intensify, become greater, become larger, advance, extend, greaten, shoot upward, accresce, burgeon, pullulate, sprout, vegetate, protuberate, tumefy, dilate, distend, expand, widen, spread, germinate, branch out, thrive, shoot up, gain ground, pile up.

INCREASE, *n.* 1. Augmentation, growth, development, accretion, extension, enlargement, expansion, dilation, dilatation, amplication, distension, turgescence, intumescence, swelling, inflation, accumulation, accession, spread, addition, reinforcement, increment, heightening, multiplication, aggrandizement, accruement, accrual, enhancement, improvement, step-up, rise, addendum, appendage, upsurge, crescendo, upswing, upgrading, pickup, upward trend, advance.

2. Profit, gain, benefit, advantage, interest, produce, product, gettings, cleanup, bunce, bonus, velvet, graft, plunder, swag, rake-off, booty, return, harvest.

3. Production of offspring, multiplication by propagation, progeneration, progeny, issue, offspring, descendants, brood, posterity, children, litter, "seed" *(Biblical),* reproduction, proliferation, prolification, procreation, begetting, generation.

4. Intensification, aggravation, exaggeration, concentration, deepening, exacerbation, exasperation, heightening, quickening.

INCREDIBLE, *adj.* Seeming too extraordinary to be possible, unbelievable, beyond belief, hard to believe, inconceivable, not credible, that cannot be believed, inadmissible, disputable, questionable, suspicious, suspect, unthinkable, improbable, surpassing belief, doubtful, mythical, absurd, preposterous, fabulous, false, astounding, astonishing, miraculous, marvelous, strange, amazing, prodigious, monstrous, fictitious, legendary, fabricated, unreal, apocryphal, invented, romancing.

INCREDULITY, *n.* Refusal of belief, unbelief, indisposition to believe, disbelief, miscreance, distrust, incredulousness, skepticism, nullifidianism, Pyrrhonism, doubt, doubtfulness, doubting, agnosticism, infidelity, suspicion, suspiciousness, amazement, astonishment.

INCREDULOUS, *adj.* Indisposed to believe, unbelieving, disposed to doubt, doubtful, distrustful, mistrustful, withholding belief, disbelieving, skeptical, agnostic, nullifidian, Pyrrhonic, dubious, suspicious, dissenting, heretical, heterodox, doubting.

INCREMENT, *n.* 1. Increase, augmentation, enlargement, addition, accretion, accumulation, aggrandizement, enhancement, reinforcement, development, amplification, extension, expansion, growth, spread, swell, dilation, dilatation, pullulation, germination, burgeonment, accrescence, sprout, vegetation, protuberance, tumefaction, accession, upgrowth.

2. Profit, gain, benefit, advantage, interest, produce, product, bonus, velvet, bunce, perquisite, cleanup, rake-off, graft, swag, plunder, booty, loot, spoil, pillage.

INCRIMINATE, *v.* Charge with a crime, involve in an accusation, accuse of a fault, indict, criminate, inculpate, call to account, take to task, impeach, tax, impute, blame, involve in guilt, appeach, denounce, challenge, cite, lodge a complaint, prosecute, bring an action against, charge with, saddle with, lay to one's charge, arraign, implicate.

INCRUST, *v.* Line with a hard coating, cover with a crust, coat over, cover with a scale, scab, superpose, superimpose, overspread, overlay, face, case, pave, veneer, encrust, paint, stucco, varnish, dab, cement, plaster, besmear, tar, bedaub, gild, japan, plate, lacquer, enamel, whitewash, line, wad, stuff, pad, fill.

INCUBATE, *v.* Sit upon for the purpose of hatching, hatch, brood, develop, breed, keep at an even temperature, keep in an incubator.

INCUBUS, *n.* 1. Evil spirit supposed to descend upon sleeping persons, nightmare-fiend, demon of nightmare, night hag, cacodemon, succubus, succuba, harpy, vampire, ghoul, ogre, goblin, hobgoblin, werewolf, *loup-garou (Fr.),* banshee, gremlin, evil eye, ephialtes.

2. Dead weight, drag, load, onus, burden, hindrance, impediment, oppression, encumbrance, weight, clog, obstacle, obstruction, break, stay, stop, drag-weight, fardel, millstone around one's neck, old man of the sea, lumber, pack.

INCULCATE, *v.* Impress by repeated statement, instill persistently, infuse earnestly, teach, infix, enforce, implant, ingraft, inspire, preach, train, enlighten, indoctrinate, propagandize, beat into, instruct, imprint, insinuate.

INCULPABLE, *adj.* Not culpable, blameless, unblamable, irreproachable, irreprovable, unimpeachable, irreprehensible, innocent, faultless, guiltless, sinless, not guilty, unguilty, stainless, spotless, clear, *rectus in curia (Lat.),* unerring, unblamed, inerrable, above suspicion, harmless, innocuous, innoxious, inoffensive, virtuous.

INCULPATE, *v.* Charge with fault, implicate in a charge, incriminate, criminate, accuse, impute guilt to, impeach, involve in guilt, censure, blame, reprove, arraign, indict.

INCULPATORY, *adj.* Imputing blame, involving in guilt, tending to inculpate, serving to establish guilt, incriminatory, criminatory, implicating, accusatory, accusative, imputative, denunciatory, recriminatory.

INCUMBENT, *adj.* 1. Lying on something, overlying, superincumbent, supernatant, superimposed, overhanging, weighing down, pressing down, bearing down, leaning, superjacent, reclining, prone.

2. Resting on one, binding, obligatory, chargeable on, imperative, behooving, stringent, peremptory, necessary, imposed on, coercive, indispensable, pressing, persistent, urgent, unavoidable, inescapable, ineluctable, in duty bound, devolving, tied down, saddled with, tied by, obliged by, bound by, beholden, under obligation, chargeable to.

INCUMBENT, *n.* 1. Tenant, occupant, occupier, dweller, indweller, habitant, inhabitant, resident, residentiary, denizen, inmate, renter, *locum tenens (Lat.),* commorant, sojourner, settler, squatter, colonist, indigene, native.

2. Occupant of a benefice, holder of an office, beneficiary, officer, functionary, parson, minister, chaplain, curate, deacon.

INCUR, *v.* Run into some consequence, bring upon oneself, fall into, bring on, expose oneself to, be liable, lie under, enter into, assume, acquire, become subject to, become liable for, contract, bargain for, covenant, undertake.

INCURABLE, *adj.* Cureless, remediless, beyond medical aid, beyond recovery, past cure, irremediable, immedicable, insanable, unhealable, irremediable, irrecoverable, ruined, undone, moribund, desperate, hopeless, helpless, not to be got rid of, irredeemable, irreclaimable, irretrievable, irreparable, irrevocable, incorrigible.

INCURIOUS, *adj.* 1. Devoid of curiosity, not curious, uninquiring, uninquisitive, uninterested, inattentive, careless, unobservant, heedless, disregardful, bored, blasé, apathetic, impassive, indifferent, nonchalant, insouciant, pococurante, adiaphorous, Laodicean, lukewarm, unconcerned, *sans souci (Fr.).*

2. Deficient in novelty, devoid of interest, wonted, everyday, accustomed, usual, common, ordinary, run-of-the-mill, garden-variety, regular, familiar, habitual, general, prevailing, prevalent, frequent, normal, unexciting, unexceptional, tedious, humdrum, routine, prosy, dull, monotonous, tiresome, wearisome, dreary, dry, boring.

INCURSION, *n.* Hostile entrance into a place, sudden invasion, intrusion, illapse, irruption, forced entry, inroad, descent, attack, assault, rushing in, ingress, infiltration, penetration, insinuation, harmful onset, onslaught, fell swoop, sally, sortie, raid, foray, *camisade (Fr.,* night attack), storming, aggression, influx.

INCURSIVE, *adj.* Making incursions, aggressive, hostile, invasive, raiding, predatory, predacious, preying, looting, pillaging, foraging, plundering, attacking, assaulting, storming, offensive, obsidional, ingressive, on the warpath.

INCURVATE, *v.* Make curved, turn from a straight line or course, curve inward, inflect, deflect, curve, bow, bend, crook, make crooked, incline, round, arch, arcuate, concamerate, curl, coil.

INCURVATE, *adj.* Curved inward, arcuate, curviform, aduncous, bowed, hooked, crooked, bent, inflected, deflected, awry, vaulted, falciform, falcated, semicircular, crescentic, luniform, lunular, meniscal.

INDEBTED, *adj.* 1. Obliged, obligated, under obligation, beholden, bound, bounden, in duty bound, liable, responsible, answerable for, chargeable, accountable.
2. Due, unsettled, unliquidated, in arrear, unsatisfied, outstanding, owing, unpaid.
3. In debt, in embarrassed circumstances, out of pocket, in difficulties, straitened, encumbered, involved, insolvent, bankrupt.
4. Appreciative, thankful, grateful.

INDEBTEDNESS, *n.* 1. State of being indebted, owing, obligation, beholdenness, incumbency, bond of duty, compulsion, accountableness, responsibility.
2. Debt, obligation, liability, debit, score, due, claim, account.
3. Amount owed, outstandings, arrears, deficit, deferred payment, default, insolvency, bankruptcy, failure.
4. Gratitude, thankfulness, gratefulness, sense of obligation, acknowledgment, thanksgiving, recognition.

INDECENCY, *n.* 1. Impropriety, indecorum, unseemliness, indecorousness, ill breeding, ill manners, violation of propriety, transgression of convention, incivility, impoliteness, rudeness, outrageousness, offensiveness.
2. Immorality, bawdiness, lewdness, lechery, ribaldry, carnality, lust, salacity, incontinence, concupiscence, dissipation, libertinism, sensuality, pruriency, lubricity, bawdry, debauchery, venery, whoredom, stupration, pollution, defilement, unchastity, uncleanness, unwholesomeness, dirtiness, vulgarity, filthiness, smuttiness, pornography, corruption, vileness, impurity, foulness, grossness, coarseness, indelicacy, impudicity, immodesty, obscenity, double-entendre, shamelessness, nastiness, suggestiveness, bestiality, scurrilousness, broadness.

INDECENT, *adj.* 1. Offending against recognized standards of propriety, indecorous, unbecoming, unseemly, improper, *contra bonos mores (Lat.),* outrageous, offensive, obnoxious, bold, impudent, ignoble, impolite, rude, vulgar, ill-bred, ill-mannered, uncivil.
2. Immoral, bawdy, lewd, lecherous, ribald, carnal, lustful, salacious, incontinent, concupiscent, dissipated, libertine, dissolute, licentious, sensual, prurient, lickerish, debauched, unchaste, unclean, unwholesome, dirty, filthy, smutty, pornographic, foul-mouthed, corrupt, depraved, degenerate, vile, impure, gross, coarse, indelicate, immodest, obscene, shameless, nasty, suggestive, risqué, off-color, Fescennine, broad, scurrilous, bestial, libidinous, lascivious, Paphian, shameful, profligate, unblushing, evil-minded.

INDECIPHERABLE, *adj.* 1. Illegible, unreadable, hieroglyphical, steganographic, cryptographic, cryptic, cramped, blotted, blurred, deleted, effaced, rubbed out, undecipherable.
2. Impossible to make out, as Greek to one, puzzling, baffling, enigmatic, clear as mud, dark, obscure, dim, misty, hidden, latent, indefinite, loose, vague, undetermined, ambiguous, recondite, occult, abstruse, crabbed, esoteric, unaccountable, unintelligible, unfathomable, unknowable, incognizable, inscrutable, inexplicable, incomprehensible, insoluble, insolvable, impenetrable, undiscoverable, incapable of interpretation, hopeless.

INDECISION, *n.* Fluctuation of the power of the will in which no choice resulting in action is made, want of settled purpose or determination of the mind, inability to decide, uncertainty, incertitude, irresolution, instability, unsteadiness, vacillation, oscillation, hesitancy, hesitation, indetermination, irresoluteness, faltering, shilly-shally, inconstancy, suspense, doubt, wavering, abeyance, fickleness, changeableness, caprice, tergiversation, weakness, levity, pliancy, lukewarmness, demur, timidity, cowardice.

INDECISIVE, *adj.* 1. Irresolute, dubious, hesitating, undecided, hesitant, vacillating, oscillating, wavering, unsettled, without any backbone, weak, fluttering, changeable, fickle, mercurial, changeful, variable, unsteady, unstable, mutable, capricious, vacillant, inconstant, half-hearted, lukewarm, irresponsible, uncertain, unreliable, blowing hot and cold, undetermined, volatile, light-minded, frivolous, giddy, featherbrained, frail, spineless, pliant, cowardly, timid, infirm of purpose, unresolved, shilly-shally, at a loss.
2. Not decisive, inconclusive, dubious, doubtful, unsettled, open to question, questionable, open to discussion, controvertible, insecure, fallible, debatable, disputable, slippery, ticklish, precarious, unconfirmed, unascertained, undemonstrated.

INDECOROUS, *adj.* Violating good manners, *contra bonos mores (Lat.),* ill-bred, ill-mannered, impolite, gross, coarse, rude, uncivil, unbecoming, unseemly, offending propriety, improper, indecent, shocking, undignified, vulgar, reprehensible, impudent, impertinent, in bad taste, ribald, unpresentable, ungraceful, ungentlemanly, unladylike, underbred, uncourtly, unchivalrous, ungenteel, uncouth, plebeian, unpolished, uncultivated, uncultured, boorish, clownish, countrified, provincial, rustic, indelicate, immodest, indecent, loose, risqué, suggestive, broad, bad, naughty, disorderly, unprincipled, uncommendable, blameworthy, disreputable, discreditable, disgraceful.

INDECORUM, *n.* 1. Violation of propriety, improper behavior, impropriety, indecorousness, want of decorum, impoliteness, grossness, indecency, unseemliness, incivility, rudeness, *grossièreté (Fr.),* ill manners, unmannerliness, ill breeding, inurbanity, misbehavior, coarseness, vulgarity, bad taste, *mauvais goût (Fr.),* gaucherie, ungentlemanliness, boorishness, misconduct, laxity, immorality, scandal, looseness of morals, indecency, indelicacy, ribaldry, obscenity, bawdry, smut, double-entendre.

2. Breach of propriety, unseemly act, breach of decorum, faux pas, indiscretion, misdeed, transgression, error, fault, lapse, trip, slip, delinquency, dereliction, peccadillo, trespass, offense, misdemeanor, outrage, enormity, atrocity, unpardonable sin, intrigue, incontinence, amour, amourette, liaison, gallantry, false step, wrong step, slip of the tongue, bull, boner.

INDEED, *adv.* 1. In truth, truly, verily, veritably, really, in reality, certainly, genuinely, in good truth, actually, forsooth, to be sure, certes, of course, assuredly, precisely, exactly, absolutely, positively, yea, aye, yes, affirmatively, in the affirmative, marry, you may be sure, upon my word, on my honor, by my troth, I assure you, of a truth, pardi, in all conscience, be assured, on my oath.

2. As a matter of fact, strictly speaking, in point of fact, strictly, to tell the truth, in fine, in fact, in effect, joking apart, not to mince the matter.

INDEED, *interj.* Who'd have thought it, you don't say, is it possible, is it so, really, *mirabile dictu (Lat.),* lo and behold, what, good gracious, good heavens, by jove, good lord, gad so, egad, only to think, dear me, by heaven, my stars, goodness gracious, my goodness, heavens and earth, mercy on us, God bless us, gadzooks, by jiminy, Heaven bless the mark, zounds, what in the world, what on earth, fancy, you don't say so, did you ever, well I'll be blowed, what do you say to that.

INDEFATIGABLE, *adj.* Incapable of being tired out, not yielding to fatigue, tireless, untiring, unwearied, never-tiring, unflagging, unfaltering, inexhaustible, unremitting, unfailing, never-failing, untired, indomitable, persevering, industrious, assiduous, sedulous, persistent, diligent, laborious, zealous, patient, unyielding, agile, alert, steadfast, unwavering, unflinching, unsleeping, unintermitting, strenuous, plodding, pertinacious, unconquerable, stanch, game to the last, hard-working, bustling, pottering, restless.

INDEFEASIBLE, *adj.* Not to be annulled, not forfeitable, irreversible, irrevocable, unalterable, immutable, indissoluble, that cannot be abrogated, unable to be made void, that cannot be thwarted, incommutable, intransmutable, irretrievable, irresoluble, reverseless, irreducible, inextinguishable, indestructible, insusceptible of change, incontrovertible, irrefutable, incontestable, absolute, inalienable, inviolable, imprescriptible, unimpeachable, reliable, sacrosanct, unchallenged, legitimate, binding, obligatory, inevitable.

INDEFENSIBLE, *adj.* 1. That cannot be defended by force of arms, defenseless, unfortified, weaponless, unarmed, *sine ictu (Lat.),* pregnable, vincible, untenable, surrendering, submissive, weakkneed, nonresisting, unresisting.

2. That cannot be justified, unjustifiable, inexcusable, unpardonable, unwarrantable, insupportable, imputable, irremissible, inexpiable, accusable.

INDEFINITE, *adj.* 1. Illimitable, measureless, infinite, unlimited, endless, indesignate, unbounded, immeasurable, incalculable, unfathomable, inexhaustible, limitless, boundless.

2. Undefined, indeterminate, undetermined, confused, indistinct, indecisive, indefinable, dim, dark, indistinguishable, shadowy, ill-defined, ill-marked, fuzzy, blurred, out of focus, misty, delitescent, veiled, opaque, obfuscated, hazy, cloudy, nubiferous, fuliginous.

3. Doubtful, vague, inexplicit, unsettled, uncertain, unfixed, equivocal, obscure, nondescript, general, inexact, loose, lax, inconclusive, hypothetical, questionable, puzzling, ambiguous, evasive, problematic, cryptic, oracular, abstruse, apocryphal, enigmatic, mysterious, mystic, transcendental, recondite, occult, esoteric.

INDELIBLE, *adj.* Incapable of being deleted, not to be obliterated, ineffaceable, not to be blotted out, unerasable, ingrained, deep-dyed, fast, fixed, permanent, unforgettable, not to be forgotten, enduring, present to the mind, unforgotten, still vivid, green, deep, profound, impressive.

INDELICACY, *n.* 1. Unseemliness, indecorum, impropriety, offensiveness, rudeness, impertinence, intrusiveness, lack of refinement, unrefinement, impudence, want of delicacy, shame.

2. Obscenity, impudicity, ribaldry, pornography, indecency, immodesty, lewdness, bawdiness, bawdry, Aretinism, double-entendre, grossness, filthiness, vulgarity, coarseness, smuttiness, smut, pruriency, lechery, concupiscence, carnality, salacity, lasciviency, lubricity.

INDELICATE, *adj.* 1. Unbecoming, indecorous, unseemly, improper, offensive to a sense of modesty, immodest, rude, impertinent, intrusive, unreserved, deficient in regard for the feelings of others, wanting in refinement, unrefined, blunt, impudent, rough.

2. Indecent, off-color, suggestive, risqué, broad, coarse, vulgar, gross, obscene, unchaste, lewd, foul, smutty, pornographic, ribald, shameless, nasty, filthy, bawdy, prurient, lustful, lickerish, concupiscent, carnal, lascivious, erotic, salacious, lecherous, libidinous.

INDEMNIFICATION, *n.* Compensation, remuneration, reimbursement, recompense, restitution, reparation, satisfaction, redress, atonement, restoration, indemnity, quits, quittance, expiation, amends, retribution, requital, reckoning, return, *quid pro quo (Lat.).*

INDEMNIFY, *v.* 1. Compensate for loss sustained, make restitution to, pay, make good, requite, remunerate, reimburse, recompense, reward, repay, pay one's footing, make amends, atone, satisfy, acknowledge, expiate, propitiate, render up, recoup, remit, pay back.

2. Make good against anticipated loss, secure against injury, guarantee, insure, answer for.

INDEMNITY, *n.* 1. Compensation, recompense, reparation, remuneration, reimbursement, restitution, indemnification, reward, redress, atonement, retribution, amends, damages, restoration, quittance, quits, expiation, propitiation, reckoning, acknowledgment, requital, sop, atonement, consideration, *quid pro quo (Lat.),* return.

2. Security against damage, protection against loss, insurance, pledge.

INDENT, *v.* 1. Form deep recesses in, make dents in, jag, dint, dent, score, notch, make notches in, scallop, pink, serrate, make bruises in, bruise, dimple, recess, pit, nick, denticulate, toothmark, perforate, depress, scarify, cut, gash, crimp, crenelate.

2. Set in from the margin, begin farther in.

3. Make a compact, bind by indenture, indenture, enter into an agreement by indenture.

4. Requisition, order, call for, make application, make a request, demand, claim, beg a boon, beg leave, call to, apply to.

INDENTATION, *n.* Deep recess, depression, dent, dint, jag, notch, nick, pit, impression, cavity, scallop, cut, incision, crenel, crenellation, serrature, engrailment, concavity, dimple, intaglio, pocket, hollow, dip, sinus, antrum, honeycomb, furrow, trough, bruise, score, serration, denticulation, indention, serrulation.

INDENTURE, *v.* Bind by indenture, apprentice, article, indent, engage, contract, undertake, volunteer, embark in, engage in, launch in, devote oneself to, take upon oneself.

INDENTURE, *n.* 1. Deed executed in several copies with edges indented as a means of identification, written contract, legal instrument, document, sealed agreement, official certificate authenticated for use as a voucher, article, stipulation, bargain, contract by which an apprentice is bound to service, covenant, bond, compact, affidation, deal.

2. Indentation, indented state.

INDEPENDENCE, *n.* 1. Self-government, autonomy, liberty, freedom, emancipation, exemption from external arbitrary control, self-direction, self-determination, noninterference.

2. Liberation, unconditioned state, non-dependence, manumission, release, exemption, enfranchisement, immunity, franchise, prerogative, privilege, right.

3. Boldness, unrestraint, confidence, outspokenness, downrightness, directness, unreservedness, unconstraint, license, laxity.

4. Affluency, affluence, sufficiency, competence of income, competency, ease, easy circumstances, opulence, prosperity, wealth, money, livelihood, abundance.

INDEPENDENT, *adj.* 1. Self-governing, autonomous, self-directing, unfettered, free, self-reliant, uncoerced, unrestrained, unrestricted, exempt from external arbitrary control, not subject to another's authority, uncontrolled, sovereign.

2. Not influenced by others, free-thinking, thinking for oneself, individualistic, unbiased, unprejudiced, free from party commitments in voting, nonpartisan, dispassionate, impartial, disinterested, voluntary, absolute.

3. Separate, distinct, unattached, disjunct, disjoined, irrespective of, exclusive of, unallied, unrelated, unconnected, disconnected, segregate.

4. Bold, confident, at large, scot-free, free-lancing, loose, unconstrained, foot-loose, free and easy, unconventional, unceremonious, careless, Bohemian, informal, quite at home, *dégagé (Fr.),* self-willed, headstrong, irrepressible, assured.

5. Affluent, well-to-do, in easy circumstances, rich, wealthy, opulent, moneyed, well-off, flush, rolling in riches, not relying on another for support, declining others' financial aid.

INDEPENDENT, *n.* Nonpartisan, one who votes without blind loyalty to any organized party, liberal, free lance, freethinker, free trader, freeman, adventurer.

INDESCRIBABLE, *adj.* That cannot be described,

inexpressible, ineffable, beyond words, above speech, that beggars description, unutterable, nameless, unmentionable, indefinable, unspeakable, unnamable, inconceivable, incredible, prodigious, astonishing, marvelous, strange, stupendous, miraculous, *foudroyant (Fr.),* staggering, wondrous, wonderful, unheard of, nondescript, overwhelming, striking, extraordinary, remarkable, astonishing, amazing, singular, unprecedented, unwonted, signal, unusual.

INDESTRUCTIBLE, *adj.* Imperishable, undecaying, inextinguishable, indissoluble, adamantean, durable, undying, indeciduous, indelible, insusceptible of change, everlasting, immortal, amaranthine, permanent, enduring, abiding, unfading, fadeless, endless.

INDETERMINATE, *adj.* Not fixed in extent, not precise, not settled, undetermined, unfixed, indefinite, uncertain, not clear, vague, obscure, wavering, undistinguishable, enigmatic, undefined, ambiguous, questionable, equivocal, doubtful, problematic, hypothetic, suspenseful, mysterious, mystic, confused, veiled, oracular, cryptic, perplexing.

INDEX, *n.* 1. Detailed alphabetical key to topics in a book with reference to their page location, alphabetical list of matters in a book, table of references in alphabetical order, catalogue, concordance.

2. Something serving to point out, guide, indication, sign, token, mark, indicant, cue, clue, hint.

3. Pointer, director, indicator, tracer, hand, arm, forefinger, index finger.

INDIA RUBBER, *n.* Highly elastic substance obtained from the milky juice of various tropical plants, caoutchouc, rubber, gutta-percha, latex, gum elastic.

INDICATE, *v.* 1. Be a sign of, denote, show, manifest, evince, designate, register, signify, make known, reveal, exhibit, present, bespeak, evidence, tell, reveal, display, disclose, point out, mark, connote, express, point to, mean, demonstrate, notify, betoken.

2. Shadow forth, be the sign of, foreshadow, prefigure, presage, portend, augur, prognosticate, give notice of, symptomatize, adumbrate.

3. Typify, symbolize, represent, stand for, designate, particularize, specify, express briefly, state in a general way.

4. Stamp, imprint, impress, sign, label, earmark, seal, blaze, nick, ticket.

5. Gesticulate, nudge, signal, shrug, wave, nod, beckon, wink, glance, leer, saw the air.

6. Hint, suggest, intimate, imply, insinuate, allude to, let fall, whisper, breathe, tip off, tip the wink, give a pointer to, give the cue, prompt, cue.

INDICATION, *n.* 1. Indicating, signifying, mention, implication, telling, showing, pointing, designation.

2. Manifestation, symptom, diagnosis, prognostic, intimation, suggestion, hint, allusion, omen, presage, portent, prognostication, boding, foretoken, warning, foreboding, foreshowing, adumbration, augury, prefigurement, premonition, straw in the wind, clue, signal, evidence, proof, demonstration.

3. Symbol, sign, token, note, mark, signum, emblem, device, type, cipher, star, asterisk, reference, impression, line, imprint, dash, stroke, tick, score, dot, streak, nick, hachure, notch, blaze.

4. Feature, trait, lineaments, peculiarity, property, quality, earmark, cast.

5. Gesticulation, gesture, motion, beck, shrug, nudge, glance, wink, nod, high sign, pantomime, touch, watchword, *mot de passe (Fr.)*, *mot d'ordre (Fr.)*, shibboleth, cue, catchword, password, grip, sign, countersign.

6. Track, spoor, scent, footprint, vestige, trail, footstep, step, trace, footmark.

7. Beacon, signal, flate, watch fire, rocket, fiery cross, watchtower, lighthouse, Pharos, semaphore.

8. Alarm, tocsin, alarum, siren, whistle, hooter, horn, beat of the drum, tattoo, bugle call, reveille, summons, taps, command, call.

9. Insignia, badge, emblem, device, trademark, countermark, hall mark, countercheck, voucher, stub, tally, ticket, label, slip, check, stamp, credentials, seal, monogram, signet, autograph, signature, endorsement, signum, cross, frank, subscription, crest, coat of arms, escutcheon, armorial bearings, scutcheon, hatchment, shield, epaulet, chevron, uniform, livery, flag, pennant, ensign, standard, banner, colors, streamer, oriflamme, eagle, jack, blue peter, tricolor, union jack.

10. Signpost, signboard, sign, waypost, guidepost, landmark, milestone, beacon, milepost, cairn, cresset, pointer, hand, flagstaff, weathercock, vane, weathervane, cock.

11. Stigma, brand, mark of Cain, stripes, fool's cap, stain, scarlet letter, badge of infamy, bar sinister.

INDICATIVE, *adj.* That indicates, pointing out, indicatory, significatory, significative, significant, indicant, expressive, evidential, suggestive, connotative, denotative, characteristic, symptomatic, diagnostic, symptomatical, premonitory, typical, representative, symbolic, emblematic, distinctive, telling, meaningful, demonstrative.

INDICT, *v.* Accuse of a crime, charge with an offense, arraign, bring to the bar, bring to trial, bring to justice, put on trial, prosecute, cite, serve with a writ, sue, bring a formal accusation against, file a claim, bring to book, call to account, denounce, impeach, lodge a complaint, inculpate, implicate, incriminate, tax with, impute.

INDICTABLE, *adj.* 1. Open to prosecution, liable to indictment, accusable, arraignable, chargeable, deserving of being brought to the bar, prosecutable, accountable, impeachable, inculpatory, incriminatory.

2. Indefensible, inexcusable, unpardonable, unallowable, unjustifiable, illegal, unlawful, illicit, criminal, felonious, vicious.

INDICTMENT, *n.* 1. Indicting, citation, denunciation, denouncement, imputation, inculpation, exprobration, crimination, accrimination, incrimination, implication, challenge, impeachment, appeachment.

2. Formal accusation presented by a grand jury, presentment, true bill, bill of indictment, prosecution, arraignment, charge, gravamen of a charge.

INDIFFERENCE, *n.* 1. Lack of concern, unconcernedness, want of interest, unconcern, impassiveness, impassivity, absence of feeling, coldness, coolness, frigidity, aloofness, lukewarmness, phlegmaticness, phlegmatism, phlegm, sang-froid, insouciance, nonchalance, callousness, heedlessness, carelessness, disdain, apathy, inattention, negligence, neglect, incuriosity, listlessness, insensibility, stoniness, iciness, hebetude, inertia, supineness, sluggishness, dullness, impassibility, impassible-

ness, stoicism, Laodiceanism, adiaphorism.

2. Neutrality, impartiality, dispassionateness, dispassion, equality, disinterestedness, freedom from prejudice, freedom from bias.

3. Insignificance, inconsiderableness, unimportance, paltriness, inferiority, triviality, levity, immaterialness.

4. Mediocre quality, mediocrity, ordinariness, passableness, tolerableness, commonplaceness.

INDIFFERENT, *adj.* 1. Without interest, uninterested, not caring, unconcerned, apathetic, stoical, impassive, phlegmatic, listless, incurious, stolid, insensible, lukewarm, cool, cold, frigid, icy, stony, insensate, insusceptible, distant, aloof, frosty, dull, dead, perfunctory, unambitious, halfhearted, easygoing, regardless, inattentive, unmindful, careless, heedless, insouciant, nonchalant, pococurante, destitute of enthusiasm, Loadicean, adiaphoristic, undesirous, unsolicitous, passive, supine, sluggish, otiose, indolent, negligent, neglectful, abstracted, asleep at the switch, inconsiderate, impassible, unimpressible, impenetrable, Spartan.

2. Having no feeling favorable or unfavorable to some thing or person, neutral, impartial, disinterested, dispassionate, unprejudiced, unbiased, making no distinction between.

3. Ordinary, moderate, middling, medium, mediocre, so-so, neither good nor bad, fair, not very good, rather poor, commonplace, tolerable, passable.

4. Falling short of any standard of excellence, average, equal, reasonable, modest, temperate, betwixt and between, all one, all the same, the same thing, not making a difference either way.

5. Insignificant, unimportant, immaterial, inconsiderable, trifling, inconsequential, paltry, petty, picayune, slight, small, inferior, inappreciable.

6. Plain, unattractive, unprepossessing, unalluring, undesirable, uncoveted, undesired, unvalued, unwished, unwanted, homely, not personable, uncomely.

INDIGENCE, *n.* Poverty, impecuniosity, penury, pauperism, empty pocket, light purse, bare cupboard, straitened circumstances, reduced circumstances, slender means, need, want, neediness, necessity, destitution, distress, privation, lack, difficulties, wolf at the door, straits, hand-to-mouth existence, pauper state, *res angusta domi (Lat.)*, pennilessness, necessitude, stint, dearth, scarcity, beggary, mendicancy, mendicity, beggarliness, bankruptcy, insolvency, broken fortune, down-at-the-heels existence, insufficiency, scantiness, misery, starvation, hunger, famine, threadbareness, pinch of poverty.

INDIGENOUS, *adj.* 1. Originating in a particular country, home-bred, native, original, aboriginal, autochthonous, autochthonal, endemic, homegrown, domestic, not exotic, naturalized, domiciled, vernacular, characterizing a particular region.

2. Congenital, connate, hereditary, in the grain, incarnate, bred in the bone, ingenerate, inbred, innate, inborn, running in the blood, ingrained, in the grain, inured.

INDIGENT, *adj.* Poverty-stricken, impecunious, penniless, unmoneyed, moneyless, out of cash, out of pocket, short of money, without a sou, *qui n'a pas le sou (Fr.)*, broke, flat, insolvent, bankrupt, without resources, embarrassed, strapped, unable to make both ends meet, unable to keep the wolf from the door, at the end of one's tether, put to one's last shifts, down-at-heels, out-at-elbows, threadbare, necessitous, destitute, poor, needy, reduced, pinched, distressed, fleeced, straitened, stripped, in want, in need, poor as Job's turkey, ill-off, lacking the necessaries of life, beggarly, beggared, badly off, hard-up, seedy, barefoot, ragged, shirtless, *descamisado (Sp.)*, mendicant.

INDIGESTED, *adj.* 1. Not digested, undigested, unconcocted, unboiled, uncooked, raw, green, unleavened, unmellowed.

2. Crude, coarse, rough-cast, shapeless, unformed, rough-hewn, unpolished, in the rough, unwrought, unhewn, uncut, unfashioned.

3. Without arrangement, disorderly, out of order, unorderly, out of place, disorganized, ill-arranged, confused, in disorder, immethodical, in confusion, unmethodized, unsystematic, chaotic, irregular, hugger-mugger, careless, topsy-turvy, slip-shod, untidy, slovenly, messy.

4. Ill-advised, impolitic, ill-judged, not duly considered, ill-considered, imprudent, improvident, unguarded, unpremeditated, thoughtless, reckless.

INDIGESTIBLE, *adj.* Not digestible, not easily digested, undigestible, that cannot be digested, not nourishing, innutritious, unnutrient, indigestive, heavy, disagreeing, dyspeptic.

INDIGESTION, *n.* Difficulty in digesting food, dyspepsia, difficult digestion, dyspepsy.

INDIGNANT, *adj.* Affected with indignation, peeved, provoked, exasperated, resentful, irascible, wrathful, irate, wroth, ireful, choleric, incensed, roused, angry, touchy, offended, huffy, riled, sore, piqued, bitter, virulent, acrimonious, up in arms, hurt, on one's high horse, fighting mad, foaming at the mouth, raging, in high dudgeon, fuming, infuriated, hot under the collar, furious, *acharné (Fr.)*, wrought up, worked up, pettish, petulant, shrewish, captious.

INDIGNATION, *n.* Displeasure at something deemed unworthy or unjust, righteous anger, resentment, exasperation at injustice, irascibility, irritation, annoyance, vexation, dudgeon, tiff, pet, huff, pique, animosity, umbrage, sulks, spleen, gall, bile, ferment, rage, ire, wrath, choler, fury, temper, virulence, bitterness, soreness, acrimony, acerbity, asperity, contempt, disdain, scorn, agitation, tempestuousness, tantrum, hot blood, vials of wrath, high words, explosion, paroxysm, outburst, passion, excitement, *acharnement (Fr.)*.

INDIGNITY, *n.* Humiliating affront, contemptuous treatment, mistreatment, abuse, outrage, insult, injury to dignity, offense, provocation, *casus belli (Lat.)*, buffet, slap in the face, rap on the knuckles, box on the ear, dishonor, discourtesy, disrespect, slight, irreverence, disparagement, contemptuous rudeness, obloquy, vituperation, contumely, opprobrium, scurrility, reproach, sore subject, crow to pluck, red rag to a bull, hooting, scoffing, mocking, jeering, taunt, mockery, blasphemy.

INDIRECT, *adj.* 1. Not direct in space, deviating from a straight line, oblique, circumambient, devious, ambagious, tortuous, sidelong, roundabout, circuitous, winding, turning, zigzag, crablike, askew, curving, meandering.

2. Not directly to the point, circumlocutory, periphrastical, discursive, periphrastic, excursive, desultory, rambling, wandering, roving, cursory, digressive, aberrant, deviating.

3. Not straightforward, crooked, dishonest, deceitful, unfair, dishonorable, underhand, covert, sneaky, undercover, clandestine, underground, evasive, secretive, stealthy, furtive, surreptitious, backhanded, ulterior.

4. Mediate, subordinate, secondary, inferential, implicative, circumstantial, collateral, distant, remote, implied, implicit, understood, tacit, unexpressed, allusive.

INDISCERNIBLE, *adj.* Not to be discerned, imperceptible, undiscernible, unapparent, nonapparent, not in sight, undiscoverable, out of sight, invisible, *à perte de vue (Fr.)*, behind the scenes, behind the curtain, inconspicuous, indistinguishable, unperceivable, unseen, covert, eclipsed, veiled, indistinct, in a dark corner, delitescent.

INDISCIPLINE, *n.* Absence of discipline, laxity, slackness, license, disobedience, insubordination, unrestraint, disorder, lawlessness, contumacy, infringement, infraction, violation, recreancy, noncompliance, nonobservance, backsliding, mutinousness, anarchy.

INDISCREET, *adj.* Lacking prudence, wanting discretion, imprudent, impolitic, improvident, injudicious, incautious, hasty, rash, reckless, temerarious, headlong, headstrong, foolhardy, harebrained, heedless, lacking sound judgment, unwise, ill-judged, ill-advised, inconsiderate, impulsive, impetuous, inexpedient, inopportune, uncircumspect, unwary, unadvised, off one's guard, foolish, light-headed, giddy, wanton, wild, madcap, devil-may-care, pococurante, hot-blooded, hot-brained, precipitate, unreasonable, improper, lax, weak, infirm, frail, short-sighted, without judgment, uncalculating, thoughtless, careless, harum-scarum.

INDISCRETION, *n.* 1. Lack of discretion, imprudence, improvidence, impoliticness, impolicy, unwisdom, foolishness, folly, short-sightedness, rashness, temerity, precipitancy, impulsiveness, impetuosity, carelessness, levity, incautiousness, injudiciousness, hastiness, recklessness, foolhardiness, heedlessness, ill-judgment, inconsiderateness, inexpediency, uncircumspection, light-headedness, giddiness, wantonness, unreasonableness, laxity, thoughtlessness.

2. Act of indiscretion, indiscreet act, faux pas, misstep, mistake, blunder, slip, lapse, trip, error, fault, impropriety, peccadillo, omission.

3. Slip from virtue, loss of chastity, misconduct, misbehavior, misdeed, misdoing, wrongdoing, transgression, offense, misdemeanor, trespass, violation, injury, infringement, infraction, crime, sin, outrage, felony, enormity, atrocity, dereliction, delinquency.

INDISCRIMINATE, *adj.* 1. Undiscriminating, undistinguishing, indiscriminative, promiscuous, not selective, not choosing, casual, random, common.

2. Mixed, confused, mingled, jumbled, chaotic, higgledy-piggledy, messy, hugger-mugger, undistinguishable, diverse, omnigenous, turbid, topsy-turvy, heterogeneous, motley, miscellaneous, variegated, mongrel, hybrid, manifold, diversified, of every description, varied, undistinguished.

INDISPENSABLE, *adj.* Not to be dispensed with, obligatory, imperative, called for, needed, needful, vital, requisite, compulsory, binding, essential, urgent, exigent, instant, pressing, insistent, crying, fundamental, required, prerequisite, basic, expedient, absolutely necessary, incumbent, unavoidable, ineluctable, inevitable, inexorable, inevasible, irresistible, that cannot be disregarded, that cannot be neglected.

INDISPOSE, *v.* 1. Put out of the proper condition, disqualify, make unfit, unfit, disenable, incapacitate, disable, make incapable.

2. Make slightly ill, sicken, disease, nauseate, make qualmish.

3. Render unwilling, disincline, render averse, make unfavorable, dissuade, render reluctant, dispirit, discourage, dishearten, hold back, deter, turn aside, repel, wean from, act as a drag, throw cold water on, cool, dampen.

INDISPOSED, *adj.* 1. Slightly sick, ill of, ailing, unwell, taken ill, seized with, out of health, squeamish, qualmy, queasy, out of sorts, afflicted, affected with, poorly, under the weather, on the sick list, unhealthy, laid up, confined, bedridden, invalided, unsound, valetudinary, sickly, drooping, infirm, weakly.

2. Reluctant, unwilling, averse, disinclined, loath, not disposed, disliking, not in the vein, backward, unfavorable, not in favor of, unfriendly, inimical, hostile, adverse, shy of, not content, slow to, demurring, renitent, unconsenting, opposed, repugnant, grudging.

INDISPOSITION, *n.* 1. Slight illness, ailment, sickness, poor health, infirmity, disorder, complaint, malady, visitation, seizure, attack, delicacy, valetudinarianism, queasiness, qualmishness, nausea, indigestion, dyspepsia, common cold, rheum, headache, migraine, invalidism, cachexia, dysphoria.

2. Indisposedness, disinclination, reluctance, unwillingness, averseness, aversion, aversation, backwardness, nolleity, nolition, slowness, renitency, want of readiness, indifference, irresolution, hesitancy, opposition, unfriendliness, hostility, adverseness, repugnance, dislike, loathness.

INDISPUTABLE, *adj.* Indubitable, incontestable, undeniable, incontrovertible, beyond a shadow of a doubt, beyond all question, beyond dispute, unquestionable, irrefragable, beyond peradventure of a doubt, above all contradiction, apodictic, demonstrable, infallibly so, assured, sure, certain, categorical, demonstrated, proven, well-founded, conclusive, solid, demonstrably evident, unequivocal, invincibly reliable, irresistibly cogent, obvious, axiomatic, self-evident, indubious, final, decided, decisive, absolute, positive, definite, clear, authoritative, official, unassailable, unmistakable, impregnable, indefeasible, irrefutable, uncontradictable, unimpeachable.

INDISSOLUBLE, *adj.* 1. Never to be sundered, impossible to be broken, infrangible, irrefrangible, indiscerptible, not to be unraveled, indissolvable, insoluble, that cannot be dissolved, undissolvable, infusible.

2. Indivisible, irreducible, ineradicable, inextinguishable, irrevocable, irremovable, perpetually binding, obligatory, *de rigueur (Fr.).*

3. Indestructible, unchangeable, immutable, imperishable, undying, indeciduous, unalterable, not to be changed, incorruptible, indelible, not to be broken, abiding, constant, permanent, stable, lasting, firm, fixed, fast, steady, enduring, incommutable, intransmutable.

INDISTINCT, *adj.* 1. Not clearly marked off, ill-defined, indefinite, undefined, inarticulate, not clearly perceptible, undistinguishable, inaudible, muffled, too low to be heard, imperfectly distinguished, muttered, mumbled, undecipherable, illegible, out of focus, weak, feeble, faded, unintelligible.

2. Vague, obscure, faint, dim, cloudy, nebulous,

nebular, *sfumato (It.)*, smoky, filmy, bleary, shadowy, misty, hazy, blurred, dusky, dull, overcast, lowering, murky, muddy, darksome, dark, darkened, pale, thick, clouded, caliginous, fuliginous, atramentous.

3. Confused, doubtful, uncertain, ambiguous, equivocal, puzzling, perplexing, enigmatic, dubious, indeterminate, mysterious, recondite, hidden, incomprehensible.

INDISTINGUISHABLE, *adj.* 1. That cannot be distinguished from another, that cannot be differentiated, identical, same, self-same, similar, identic, equivalent, equal, coinciding, coincident, coalescent, one, like, ditto.

2. Unnoticeable, undiscernible, unobservable, not capable of being made out, nonapparent, imperceptible, invisible.

3. Indistinct, obscure, vague, confused, chaotic, mysterious, dark, shadowy, clouded.

INDITE, *v.* Draw up in words, compose, redact, draft, formulate, pen, write, dictate, inscribe, dash off, write out, throw on paper, concoct, write down, transcribe, copy, scrawl, scribble, record, type, typewrite, stain paper, dip one's pen in ink, commit to words, frame, couch in language.

INDIVIDUAL, *adj.* 1. Existing as a distinct entity, separate, one, single, particular, special, sole.

2. Peculiar to a single person, one's own, personal, singular, peculiar to one alone, proper, specific, especial, exclusive, private, restricted, intimate, intended for the use of one person only, custom.

3. Exhibiting individuality, distinguished by marked characteristics, different from others, original, unconventional, unique, *sui generis (Lat.)*, exceptional, extraordinary, uncommon, rare, characteristic, typical, decided, positive, definite, representative, distinct.

INDIVIDUAL, *n.* 1. Single human being, person, creature, personage, fellow creature, mortal, character, body, being, soul, living soul, earthling, somebody, party, head, hand, chap, fellow, man, self, self-determined being, autonomous being.

2. Distinct indivisible entity, single item, unit, one, ace, monad, monas, integer, particular object, single instance.

INDIVIDUALITY, *n.* 1. Distinct existence, identity, oneness, unity, singleness, undividedness, integrality, selfsameness, definiteness, particularity, state of oneness, distinction, finality, final character.

2. Peculiar character distinguishing one person from others, personality, ego, temperament, selfness, peculiarity, singularity, originality, specialty, characteristic, feature, trait, diagnostic, trick, mannerism, idiosyncrasy, *je ne sais quoi (Fr.)*, differentia.

3. Person of distinctive character, eccentric, bohemian, original, queer, nonsuch, nonpareil, *rara avis (Lat.)*, curiosity, oddity, *lusus naturae (Lat.)*, freak, sport *(Biol.)*, nondescript, crank, crackpot, monomaniac, connoisseur, specializer, virtuoso, technicist, expert, specialist, sharp.

INDIVIDUALIZE, *v.* 1. Consider individually, singularize, name with exactness, formulate, specify, designate, determine, mention, indicate, denote, point out, itemize, descend to particulars, enter into detail, select, single out, define, particularize.

2. Give a distinctive character to, make individual, specialize, render unique, make original, individuate, differentiate, set apart, exhibit dif-

ferentiation, invest with fullness of character, render self-directing.

INDIVISIBLE, *adj.* Incapable of being divided, inseparable, indissolvable, infrangible, impartible, that cannot be separated into parts, undividable, unpartible, indissoluble, unsunderable, unbreakable, indiscerptible, insoluble, infusible.

INDOCILE, *adj.* Not amenable to teaching, unteachable, inapt, unmanageable, intractable, ungovernable, froward, inflexible, immovable, unchangeable, unaffected, uninfluenced, wilful, self-willed, perverse, refractory, wayward, restive, unruly, heady, headstrong, *entêté (Fr.),* obstinate, stubborn, obdurate, tenacious, mulish, dogged, pigheaded, inexorable, unsubmissive, cross-grained, contumacious, disobedient, opinionated, arbitrary, prejudiced, bigoted, prepossessed, stiff-necked, stiff-backed, hidebound, impervious, unyielding, unpersuadable, incorrigible, deaf to advice.

INDOCTRINATE, *v.* Instruct in a doctrine, imbue with learning, teach, give instruction to, ground in doctrine, inculcate, initiate, proselytize, discipline, train, ground, infuse, instill, school, enlighten, educate, exercise, drill, qualify, prepare, familiarize with, break in, habituate, inure, beat into the head, brainwash, impress upon the memory, give new eyes to, open the eyes, propagandize, disseminate, sow the seeds of.

INDOCTRINATION, *n.* Propagandism, proselytism, grounding, preparation, qualification, training, instruction, schooling, initiation, inculcation, instillation, teaching, education, edification, tutelage, tutorage, guidance, telling people what to think, direction, brainwashing, persuasion, propaganda, gentle introduction, drill, exercitation, exercise, discipline, practice.

INDOLENCE, *n.* Inaction, do-nothingness, faineance, inexertion, ergophobia, inactivity, otiosity, inapplication, deedlessness, *dolce far niente (It.), doux faire rien (Fr.),* ease, idleness, sloth, laziness, slothfulness, sluggishness, apathy, inertness, stagnation, languor, torpor, stupor, somnolence, lethargy, indiligence, pottering, dawdling, remissness, neglect.

INDOLENT, *adj.* Having a disposition to avoid exertion, habitually idle, do-nothing, fainéant *(Fr.),* shiftless, sluggish, lazy, otiose, slothful, inactive, slack, easygoing, inert, supine, listless, remiss, languid, lethargic, comatose, torpid, dozing, dormant, lumpish, heavy, leaden, logy, dull, passive, stagnant, drowsy, dronish, sleepy-eyed, somnolent, soporific, indifferent, lackadaisical, careless, unoccupied, disengaged, dawdling, pottering, procrastinating, dilatory, flagging, laggard, slow.

INDOMITABLE, *adj.* That cannot be overcome, unconquerable, invincible, impregnable, insuperable, not to be subdued, unyielding, resistless, irresistible, indefatigable, redoubtable, overpowering, overwhelming, all-powerful, omnipotent, solid, stout, firm, sound, tough, stanch, in the plenitude of power, masterful, potent, forcible, puissant, energetic, forceful, vehement, vigorous, stiff, stable, virile, manly, manful, hardy, gutty, persevering, cast-iron, stalwart, doughty, valiant, formidable, insurmountable, unwavering, unshrinking, plucky, resolute, undaunted, dauntless, bold, game, resolved, courageous, resolute, determined, fearless, unflinching, defiant, self-reliant, brave, intransigent, irrepressible.

INDUBITABLE, *adj.* That cannot be doubted, undeniable, indisputable, irrefragable, unquestionable, incontrovertible, incontestable, indefeasible, unimpeachable, irrefutable, beyond a shadow of a doubt, indubious, beyond peradventure of a doubt, past dispute, beyond all question, self-evident, axiomatic, obvious, certain, sure, clear as day, undoubted, unquestioned, positive, assured, disputeless, infallible, official, authentic, authoritative, conclusive, final, unequivocal.

INDUCE, *v.* 1. Move by persuasion to some action, influence, lead by influence, prompt, impel, actuate, instigate, provoke, persuade, urge, lobby, spur, egg on, incite, act upon, allure, entice, tempt, inveigle, coax, wheedle, incline, bias, dispose, predispose, seduce, lure, decoy, enlist, engage, invite, court, elicit, excite, attract, bring, draw, drive, inspire, rouse, stimulate, sway, win over, prevail on, prevail upon, talk over, weigh with, set on, bring round, carry, advocate, encourage, whet, quicken, gain, get, bribe, suborn.

2. Give rise to, bring about, cause, effect, produce, motivate, occasion, bring on, set on foot, entail, sow the seeds of, originate, develop, make, create, procure, obtain, acquire.

INDUCEMENT, *n.* 1. Reason, motive, ground, reason why, wherefore, purpose, object, principle, call, secret motive, occasion, sake, cause, consideration.

2. Incentive, incitement, spur, stimulus, fillip, goad, provocative, whet, enticement, instigation, temptation, allurement, solicitation, incitation, attraction, persuasion, drawing, decoy, bait, impulse, dictate, press, urge, prompting, influence, inspiration, insistence, encouragement, exhortation, advice, cajolery, blandishment.

INDUCT, *v.* 1. Introduce formally into office, inaugurate, initiate, install, invest, instate, chair, ordain, frock, consecrate, translate, lead in, bring in, usher in.

2. Draft, conscript, levy, enroll, enlist.

INDUCTION, *n.* 1. Formal introduction into office, inauguration, installation, institution, investiture, appointment, initiation, ordination, consecration, preferment, presentation, translation.

2. Selective service, draft, conscription, enrollment, enlistment, levy.

3. *(Psychol.)* Conclusion from many facts, generalization, inference, inductive method, Baconianism, dialectics, reasoning, syllogization, dialecticism, demonstration.

INDULGE, *v.* 1. Pamper the whims of, yield to the wishes of, humor to excess, gratify the desires of, allow to satisfy one's caprices, humor, spoil, baby, cater to, coddle, pet, cosset, pander to, cocker, fondle, favor, flatter, caress, nurse, make much of.

2. Indulge oneself, yield to an inclination, gratify, give loose rein to, give oneself up to, satisfy, appease, satiate, license, give way to, treat oneself, revel, wallow, be intemperate, be excessive, exceed, live high, carouse, regale, wine and dine, run riot, live hard, paint the town red, sow one's wild oats, plunge into dissipation, go on a spree, hit the booze, luxuriate.

3. Grant by favor, bear with, suffer, tolerate, brook, endure, permit, allow, be mild, be gentle, show mercy, give quarter, *parcere subiectis (Lat.),* spare, forbear to censure, excuse.

INDULGENCE, *n.* 1. Gratification of desire, appeasement, satisfaction, coddlement, pampering, humoring, fostering.

2. Liberality, favor, kindness, lenience, tenderness, lenity, clemency, patience, gentleness, fondness, courtesy, privilege, grant, license.

3. Indulgent allowance, sufferance, tolerance, quarter, toleration, considerateness, forbearance, humanity, compassion, mildness, mercy, moderation, temperateness, forgiveness, excuse.

4. Self-indulgence, self-gratification, dissipation, free living, high living, prodigalism, pleasure, fast living, luxury, fastness, dissoluteness, inebriety, drunkenness, tragalism, sensuality, voluptuousness, animalism, crapulence, debauchery, sybaritism, epicureanism, orgy, debauch, revelry, spree, carousal, hot time, saturnalia, drinking bout, intemperance, immoderation, excess, unrestraint, flesh pots, extravagance, riotousness.

5. *(Theol.)* Remission of temporal punishment still due to sin after it has been forgiven, absolution from canonical penance.

INDULGENT, *adj.* 1. Gentle, mild, easy, tender, kind, not severe, gracious, amiable, obliging, complaisant, easygoing, benign, lenient, merciful, fond, compassionate, humane, tolerant, clement, moderate, soft, forbearing, conciliatory, considerate, pacific, genial, temperate, meek, bland, suave, humoring, pampering, favoring, benevolent, yielding, forgiving, sparing, tender-hearted, patient, good-natured, favorably disposed.

2. Self-indulgent, self-gratifying, intemperate, immoderate, excessive, unbridled, inordinate, unrestrained, extravagant, fast, wild, dissolute, dissipated, lax, profligate, crapulous, prodigal, licentious, luxurious, sybaritic, pampered, epicurean, carnal, sensual, voluptuous, gross, lascivious, fleshly, lecherous, lewd, libidinous, concupiscent, lustful, goatish, wanton, salacious, gluttonous, gourmandizing, inebrious, drunken, bibacious, sottish, boozy, crapulent, carousing, reveling, winebibbing.

INDURATE, *v.* 1. Make harden, harden, inure, callous, stiffen, temper, petrify, ossify, vitrify, toughen, inlapidate, strengthen, thicken.

2. Make unfeeling, make obdurate, sear, make callous, steel the heart, harden the heart, make impenitent.

INDURATE, *adj.* 1. Hardened, inured, callous, hard, rigid, flinty, adamantine, adamantean, lithic, stony, concrete, granitic, rocky, horny, vitreous, corneous, bony, gritty, crystalline, osseous.

2. Impenitent, uncontrite, obdurate, recusant, seared, unrepentant, remorseless, relentless, graceless, irreclaimable, incorrigible, lost, unfeeling, unsusceptible, inflexible, tense, proof, unbending, unyielding, stubborn, obstinate.

INDURATION, *n.* 1. Hardness, hardening, petrification, lapidescence, lapidification, ossification, vitrification, cornification, durity, callosity, rigidity, adamantineness, inflexibility.

2. Hardness of heart, obduracy, impenitence, irrepentance, seared conscience, recusancy.

INDUSTRIALIST, *n.* 1. One who owns an industrial enterprise, big business man, lord of industry, tycoon, businessman having great wealth and power.

2. Foreman, overseer, boss, superintendent, supervisor.

INDUSTRIOUS, *adj.* Hard-working, diligent, painstaking, indefatigable, sedulous, busy as a bee, assiduous, operose, laborious, busily engaged, plodding, businesslike, unwearied, pertinacious, persevering, expeditious, up and stirring, diligent-

ly employed, intent, occupied, officious, aggressive, brisk, persistent, prompt, wide-awake, go-ahead, up and coming, live wire, snappy, lively, active, spirited, alive, nimble, agile, alert, spry, instant, bustling, hurried, rushing, fussy, energetic, restless, sleepless, vigorous.

INDUSTRY, *n.* 1. Diligence, activity, assiduity, sedulousness, sedulity, assiduousness, laboriousness, habitual devotion to labor, assiduous activity, application, wakefulness, vigilance, bustle, fuss, stir, hustle, ado, flurry, movement, turmoil, press of business, enterprise, energy, vim, vigor, go, snap, liveliness, dispatch, expedition, perseverance, persistence, constancy, pursuit, indefatigability, intentness, devotedness, zeal, attention, patient plodding, busy vigor.

2. Systematic work, toil, labor, efforts, endeavors, exercise, occupation, task, stint, job, chore, business, employment, undertaking, vocation, pursuit, profession, matter in hand, what one is doing, irons in the fire.

3. Commerce, trade, line, metier, craft, handicraft, manufacture, busy hum of men.

4. Workshop, factory, foundry, mill, shop, manufactory, works, forge, hive of industry.

INEBRIATE, *v.* 1. Make drunk, intoxicate, stupefy with drink, fuddle, befuddle, fuzzle, liquor up, lift one's elbow, make see double, give a drop too much, tipple, tope, swill, booze, guzzle, lush, sot, carouse, swig, drink hard, drain the cup, take a hair of the dog that bit you, wet one's whistle, toss off, sacrifice at the shrine of Bacchus.

2. Intoxicate emotionally, exhilarate, enliven, cheer, animate, stimulate, make merry, elate, thrill, excite, give a kick to.

INEBRIATE, *n.* Intoxicated person, habitual drinker, drunk, alcoholic, alky *(slang)*, dipsomaniac, sot, tippler, toper, bibber, winebibber, bar fly, lush, lushington, elbow-bender, boozer, hard-drinker, sponge, soak, soaker, toss-pot, love-pot, carouser, reveler, thirsty soul, wet, antiprohibitionist, devotee to Bacchus, drunkard.

INEBRIATED, *adj.* Under the influence of liquor, drunken, drunk, intoxicated, intemperate, tipsy, boozy, maudlin, crapulous, lush, bibacious, bibulous, toping, sottish, wet, inebrious, fuddled, lip up, full, overcome, elevated, groggy, tight, screwed, primed, sozzled, stupefied, muddled, oiled, three sheets to the wind, half seas over, dead drunk, alcoholic, drunk as a lord, spirituous, in one's cups, *inter pocula (Lat.)*, temulent, plastered, mellow, piflicated, beery, pot-valiant, corned, potulent, the worse for liquor, raddled, under the table, one over the eight.

INEBRIETY, *n.* Drunkenness, intoxication, inosbriety, inebriation, intemperance, oinomania, dipsomania, befuddlement, alcoholism, temulency, bibacity, winebibbing, compotation, flowing bowl, drop too much, spree, carousing, libations, bacchanalia.

INEFFABLE, *adj.* Beyond expression, incommunicable, undefinable, indescribable, unspeakable, inexpressible, unutterable, that cannot be spoken, unpronounceable, mysterious, strange, marvelous, unmentionable, wonderful, miraculous, unheard of, *foudroyant (Fr.)*, prodigious, inconceivable, stupendous, incredible, unimaginable, staggering, overwhelming, striking.

INEFFACEABLE, *adj.* 1. Ingrained, indelible, inexpungeable, inerasable, indestructible, not effaceable, ineradicable, deep-dyed, inextinguishable, imperishable, indissoluble, insoluble, irrevocable.

2. Inveterate, bred in the bone, deep-rooted, congenital, inherent, inbred, inborn, innate.

IN EFFECT 1. In reality, in fact, really, in truth, veritably, truly, actually, in actuality, absolutely, positively, genuinely.

2. In operation, operative, working, active, acting, in action.

INEFFECTUAL, *adj.* 1. Without satisfactory effect, lacking decisive effect, ineffective, inefficacious, inutile, inadequate, profitless, gainless, bootless, useless, fruitless, vain, abortive, futile, unavailing, unprofitable, unproductive, unserviceable, ill-spent, worthless, idle, good-for-nothing, without avail, nugatory, unsuccessful.

2. Weak, feeble, powerless, impotent, inefficient, inadequate, inept, incompetent, barren, effete, sterile, worn out, obsolete, unsatisfactory, lame, unoperative, indolent, blank, empty.

INEFFICACY, *n.* Lack of power to produce the desired effect, ineffectualness, inefficaciousness, inutility, uselessness, unprofitableness, futility, worthlessness, inefficiency, ineptitude, inadequacy, unskillfulness, incompetence, labor in vain, nullity, weakness, impotence, incapacity, inability, nugacity, failure, unfruitfulness, wild goose chase, sleeveless errand, work of Penelope.

INEFFICIENT, *adj.* Unable to accomplish in a capable way, lacking in efficiency, ineffective, inefficacious, ineffectual, unable, incapable, incompetent, inept, inapt, unendowed, unfit, unqualified, disqualified, inadequate, weak, unsound, feeble, impotent, nugatory, inoperative, good for nothing, dud, sloppy, indifferent, haphazard, slipshod, slack, remiss, shiftless, futile, lame, deficient, defective, unsuitable, unproductive, unfitted.

INELASTIC, *adj.* Lacking elasticity, irresilient, inductile, flaccid, flabby, inflexible, unyielding, inextensible, stiff, rigid.

INELEGANT, *adj.* 1. Awkward, uncouth, ungainly, gauche, clumsy, crude, rude, graceless, ungraceful, without taste, coarse, homely, tawdry, vulgar, rough.

2. Not refined, unrefined, uncourtly, unpolished, uncultivated, uncultured, undignified, unfinished, barbarous, common, plain.

3. Constrained, stiff, formal, forced, harsh, bald, abrupt, cramped, labored, halting, dry.

4. Turgid, tumid, inflated, bombastic, ponderous, fustian, euphuistic, swollen, affected, artificial, mannered.

INELIGIBLE, *adj.* 1. Not suitable for choice, unqualified, not eligible, disqualified, unentitled, unmerited, undeserved, undeserving, unearned, forfeited, unbefitting, unmeet, seemless, not to be thought of, not the thing, out of the question, preposterous.

2. Inadvisable, imprudent, unwise, ill-advised, impolitic, inadmissible, undesirable, inexpedient, inopportune, objectionable, inappropriate, unfit, disadvantageous, unsuitable, inconvenient, discommodious, improper, inept, unsatisfactory, unseasonable, untimely.

INEPT, *adj.* 1. Not apt, not fitted, not suitable, unfit, unsuitable, unapt, inapposite, improper, disqualified, unqualified, inefficient, incompetent, ineffective, unendowed, inapt, awkward, puerile, bungling, unseemly, ungainly, raw, inadequate, unskillful, without dexterity, unadroit, obtuse, good for nothing, inappropriate, out of place.

2. Valueless, worthless, useless, inutile, inefficacious, bootless, unavailing, insubservient, inef-

fectual, of no avail, void, null, unprofitable, dispensable, inane, idle.

3. Foolish, absurd, nonsensical, silly, stupid, senseless, pointless, futile, petty.

INEPTITUDE, *n.* 1. Unsuitableness, unfitness, incapacity, inability, inaptitude, inappositeness, inappropriateness, impropriety, inefficiency, incompetence, inefficacy, disqualification, *telum imbelle (Lat.), brutum fulmen (Lat.)*, flash in the pan, blank cartridge, dud, *vox et praeterea nihil (Lat.)*, bit of waste paper, dead letter, dummy.

2. Uselessness, worthlessness, inutility, nullity, emptiness, futility, unsubservience, inadequacy, unfruitfulness, labor in vain, nugacity.

3. Folly, inanity, nonsense, stupidity, foolishness, silliness, pointlessness, senselessness, imbecility.

INEQUALITY, *n.* 1. Lack of equality, imparity, disparity, diversity, difference, unevenness, disproportion, irregularity, roughness, variableness, inconstancy, changeableness, divergence, dissimilarity, unlikeness, dissimilitude, odds, contrariety.

2. Unfairness, injustice, partiality, bias, prejudice, inequitable character.

3. Insufficiency, shortcoming, inferiority, inadequacy, deficiency, incompetency.

INEQUITABLE, *adj.* Not equitable, unfair, unjust, destitute of equity, wrongful, one-sided, partial, bigoted, biased, prejudiced, iniquitous, unrighteous, unwarrantable, wrong, bad.

INERT, *adj.* 1. Having no inherent power of motion or action, motionless, inactive, still, quiet, passive, quiescent, dead, comatose, lifeless, inanimate, spiritless.

2. Latent, hidden, concealed, dormant, slumbering, smoldering, unexerted.

3. Indolent, sluggish, slothful, lazy, leaden, logy, idle, lumpish, heavy, dull, slack, slow, tame, dronish, torpid, supine, lethargic, phlegmatic, apathetic, pococurante, listless, sleepy, languid.

INERTIA, *n.* 1. Passiveness, passivity, inertness, want of activity, lack of motion, inactivity, stagnation.

2. Indisposition to move, inertness, sluggishness, torpor, laziness, sloth, inaction, indolence, languor, quiescence, supineness, apathy, negligence, inexcitability, indecision, irresolution, lethargy, apathy, languor, dullness, lassitude, vegetation, weariness.

3. *(Phys.)* Tendency to continuance of rest, standing still, *vis inertiae (Lat.)*, lack of movement, property of matter by which it tends to stand at rest, resistance to change.

INESTIMABLE, *adj.* Too great to be estimated, incalculable, of incalculable value, priceless, above all price, of great price, precious, invaluable, extremely valuable, costly, worth its weight in gold, worth a king's ransom, peerless, matchless, eximious, *recherché (Fr.)*, rare, select, unparalleled, unparagoned, superfine, superlative, superexcellent, exquisite, crack, tiptop, prime, gilt-edged, cardinal, capital, inimitable.

INEVITABLE, *adj.* That cannot be avoided, unavoidable, avoidless, not to be escaped, inescapable, that must be suffered, ineluctable, irresistible, unpreventable, necessary, needful, fated, fateful, written in the book of Fate, destined, sure to happen by the very nature of things, assured, certain, unfailing, without fail, that must be, ineludible, it must needs be, one's fate is sealed, the die is cast, *alea est iacta (Lat.), nolens volens*

(Lat.), willy-nilly, *che sará sará (It.), ex necessitate rei (Lat.), Fata obstant (Lat.),* compulsory, irrevocable, uncontrollable, inexorable, binding, resistless, unchangeable, unerrable, incontrovertible, indubitable, irrefragable, undoubted, irrefutable, involuntary, blind, automatic, mechanical, it is written, it cannot be helped, decisive, final, ultimate, fixed.

INEXACT, *adj.* 1. Incorrect, false, faulty, mistaken, erroneous, inaccurate, erring, fallacious, untrue, in error, out in one's reckoning, unsound, without precision, wide of the mark, unsubstantial, ungrounded.

2. Indefinite, loose, vague, rough, ambiguous, approximate, general, crude, partial, careless.

INEXCUSABLE, *adj.* Incapable of being justified, unjustifiable, unpardonable, inexpiable, indefensible, incapable of excuse, accusable, irremissible, unallowable, reprehensible, blameworthy, reprovable, imputable, censurable, unwarrantable, unatonable, nefarious, delinquent, lax.

INEXHAUSTIBLE, *adj.* 1. Incapable of being exhausted, exhaustless, unlimited, unfailing, unstinted, boundless, infinite, limitless, endless, replete, flush, intarissable, affluent, chock-full, cornucopian, well-provided, plenteous, plentiful, copious, abundant, full, plethoric, ample.

2. Indefatigable, untiring, tireless, weariless, unwearied, never tired, unsleeping, unremitting, unfaltering, unwavering, unflagging, plodding, undrooping, persevering, game to the last, indomitable.

INEXORABLE, *adj.* 1. Unmoved by entreaties, not to be persuaded by prayers, obdurate, immovable, unyielding, intransigent, uncompromising, inflexible, iron-handed, sternly just, strict, severe, hard, dour, stern, harsh, stiff, rigorous, unbending, unrelenting, exacting, stringent, austere, peremptory, remorseless, unmerciful, merciless, unfeeling, unpitying, pitiless, uncompassionate, relentless, cruel, cold-hearted, unsympathetic, hardened, unforgiving, unsparing, ruthless, inclement, tyrannical, coercive, Draconian, Spartan, hard-hearted, grim-faced, adamantine, stony, implacable, bigoted, unalterable.

2. Irrevocable, inevitable, ineluctable, unavoidable, binding, uncontrollable, fated, compulsory, destined, necessary, imperative.

INEXPEDIENT, *adj.* 1. Imprudent, impolitic, ill-judged, injudicious, unwise, indiscreet, ill-advised, inadvisable, objectionable, inadmissible, ineligible, discommodious, inconvenient, inopportune, untimely, unseasonable, inapposite, malapropos, inappropriate, improper, inapt, unsuitable, undesirable, unsatisfactory, unseemly, inept, unfit, unprofitable, disadvantageous.

2. Awkward, clumsy, gauche, cumbrous, cumbersome, ungainly, hulky, unwieldy, unmanageable, unhandy, unskillful, ungraceful.

INEXPENSIVE, *adj.* Costing little, low-priced, reasonable, nominal, moderate, popular-priced, cheap, dirt-cheap, of small value, reduced, marked down, half-price, good at the price, well worth the money, light on the pocketbook, unexpensive, *magnifique et pas cher (Fr.),* catchpenny.

INEXPERIENCE, *n.* Lack of skill gained from experience, unskillfulness, inexpertness, inaptitude, incompetence, inability, disqualification, clumsiness, untrainedness, rawness, callowness, greenness, verdancy, freshness, ignorance, apprenticeship, novitiate, tyronism, noviceship, neophytism, want of experience.

INEXPERIENCED, *adj.* Without knowledge or skill gained from experience, unskilled, untrained, unpracticed, undisciplined, untried, unschooled, uninformed, uninitiated, unacquainted, ignorant, unconversant, unversed, undrilled, unseasoned, untutored, unaccustomed, unfamiliar, unused, unsophisticated, unfledged, without experience, green, verdant, callow, fresh, raw, young, new at, impractical, unbusinesslike, inexpert, ill-qualified, in one's salad days.

INEXPERT, *adj.* Unskillful, awkward, gauche, unhandy, maladroit, clumsy, lacking dexterity, lubberly, heavy-handed, inhabile, gawky, bungling, inapt, unskilled, unpracticed, incompetent, green, unexperienced, without experience, fumbling, unbusinesslike, blundering.

INEXPIABLE, *adj.* 1. Admitting of no atonement, not to be expiated, not to be atoned for, admitting of no satisfaction, unatonable, irredeemable, irremissible, unpardonable, indefensible, unjustifiable, unforgivable, inexcusable, incorrigible, irreclaimable, reprobate, past praying for.

2. Vicious, depraved, corrupt, sinful, iniquitous, base, criminal, black, wicked, grave, vile, facinorous, flagitious, nefarious, felonious, infamous, villainous, shameful, heinous, accursed, lost to virtue.

3. Not to be appeased by expiation, unappeasable, implacable, inexorable, vindictive, unrelenting, unforgiving, rancorous, relentless, merciless, pitiless, unpropitiating, irreconcilable.

INEXPLICABLE, *adj.* Incapable of being explained, unfathomable, incognizable, unaccountable, unintelligible, insolvable, insoluble, impenetrable, inscrutable, undiscoverable, incomprehensible, undecipherable, strange, shrouded in mystery, mysterious, enigmatical, paradoxical, baffling, puzzling, occult, dark, recondite, abstruse, unexplainable, hidden, indefinable, esoteric.

INEXPRESSIBLE, *adj.* 1. That cannot be represented in words, ineffable, indescribable, incommunicable, indefinable, unspeakable, unutterable, unpronounceable, unnamable, beyond expression, nameless.

2. Infinite, boundless, surpassing, unbounded, illimitable, immeasurable, interminable.

3. Marvelous, wondrous, fabulous, miraculous, stupendous, amazing, astonishing, prodigious, incredible, surprising.

INEXPRESSIVE, *adj.* Devoid of expression, unexpressive, inscrutable, poker-faced, dead-pan, blank, dull, vacant, empty, vacuous, void, impenetrable, impassive, unemotional, cold, unmoved, unaffected, impervious, unanimated, callous, vegetative, imperturbable, hardened.

INEXPUGNABLE, *adj.* 1. That cannot be taken by force, impregnable, not to be taken by assault, unassailable, unattackable, imperdible, proof against, tenable against all odds, secure from capture, invulnerable, invincible, unconquerable, not to be stormed, defensible, founded on a rock, bombproof, fireproof, bulletproof, safe and sound, out of danger, protected, panoplied, armed cap-à-pie, armed to the teeth, fully accoutered, ironclad, iron-plated.

2. Incontrovertible, incontestable, indisputable, irrefragable, unimpeachable, unerring, infallible, unquestionable, undeniable, indefeasible, irrefut-

able, uncontested, undisputed, unquestioned, indubitable.

INEXTINGUISHABLE, *adj.* That cannot be extinguished, unquenchable, quenchless, that cannot be quenched, ever-burning, simmering, volcanic, unsuppressible, not to be brought to an end, indestructible, irreducible, imperishable, undying, vehement, fiery, rampant, violent, ungovernable, uncontrollable, irrepressible, insatiable, voracious, omnivorous.

IN EXTREMIS *(Lat.)* 1. In the very act of death, at the point of death, moribund, near death, at death's door, in one's last moments, receiving extreme unction, morient, dying, Acherontic, *in articulo (Lat.),* in the jaws of death, passing away, expiring, near one's end, with one foot in the grave, on one's death bed, given over, booked, life hangs by a thread, one's hour is come, fey.

2. In extremity, in difficulty, in a scrape, in hot water, in a pickle, in a pinch, in a jam, between Scylla and Charybdis, surrounded by shoals, in a quicksand, straitened, pinched, at a loss, hard up, at the end of one's tether, nonplused, graveled, stuck fast, stranded, aground, up a tree, driven into a corner, at bay, *aux abois (Fr.),* driven to the wall.

INEXTRICABLE, *adj.* 1. That cannot be disentangled, not to be unraveled, entangled, not to be loosed, raveled, knotted, tangled, complex, hopelessly intricate, involved, confused, turbid, topsyturvy, disordered, disorderly, chaotic, disheveled, perplexed, labyrinthine, mazy, daedal.

2. Inaccessible, out of one's reach, out of one's grasp, too much for, insurmountable, insuperable, uncome-at-able, impervious, impassable.

IN FACT 1. In truth, in reality, in actuality, truly, actually, really, of a truth, de facto.

2. In point of fact, as a matter of fact, forsooth, indeed, to tell the truth, joking apart, pardi, be assured, upon my honor, by my troth, you may be sure, in faith, marry, so help me God, in sober earnest, not to mince the matter, in all conscience, upon oath, I'll answer for it, I'll warrant.

INFALLIBILITY, *n.* 1. Infallibleness, incapability of error, exemption from liability to err, complete perfection of judgment.

2. Certainty, certitude, certainness, reliability, surety, sureness, assurance, dead certainty, assuredness, confidence, indubitableness, gospel, scripture, positive fact, positiveness.

INFALLIBLE, *adj.* 1. Exempt from liability to error, not liable to err, incapable of error, perfect in judgment, free from mistake, inerrable, inerrant, incontestable, unquestionable, incontrovertible, irrefragable, irrefutable, undisputed, unquestioned, indubitable.

2. Not liable to fail, unfailing, sure, certain, absolutely trustworthy, dependable, reliable, confident, unhesitating, assured, oracular, well-founded, solid, positive, absolute, unequivocal, definite, categorical.

INFAMOUS, *adj.* Of evil fame, of ill repute, disreputable, ill spoken of, dishonorable, notorious, disgraceful, scandalous, shameful, discreditable, ignominious, shameless, outrageous, ignoble, opprobrious, blackguard, villainous, shameless, vile, base, foul, arrant, low, abominable, atrocious, damnable, wicked, heinous, dark, odious, nefarious, flagitious, facinorous, scelerate, scelerous, felonious, iniquitous, rascally, recreant, knavish,

shocking, unmentionable, perfidious, treacherous, sneaking, dirty, detestable, shamefully bad, contumelious, sordid, despicable, abject, venal, corrupt, of a deep dye, satanic, sinister, offensive, scurrilous, black, reprehensible, abhorrent, immoral, depraved, dissolute, sinful, profligate, flagrant, execrable, vicious, abandoned, malevolent, maleficent, malicious.

INFAMY, *n.* 1. Evil fame, shameful notoriety, public reproach, ill-repute, ill-name, ill-odor, ingloriousness, discredit, disgrace, disrepute, dishonor, obloquy, ignominy, opprobrium, shame, degradation, abasement, scandal, odium, stigma, brand, stain, spot, badge of infamy, blot on the escutcheon, bar sinister, defilement, pollution, taint, tarnish, abjectness, baseness.

2. Infamous conduct, infamous act, obliquity, atrocity, depravity, knavery, immorality, turpitude, impropriety, indecorum, flagrancy, corruption, demoralization, extreme vileness, wickedness, villainy, shamefulness, disgracefulness, odiousness, dishonorableness, scandalousness, detestableness, baseness.

INFANCY, *n.* 1. Babyhood, babyism, cradlehood, infanthood, cradle, nursery, early childhood, first part of life, incunabula *(pl.).*

2. Early period of existence, commencement, beginning, first age, youthfulness, juvenescence, Juventas *(Roman),* Hebe *(Greek),* boyhood, girlhood, adolescence, flower of youth, seedtime of life, springtide of life, golden season of life, heyday of youth, schooldays.

3. Period of life to the age of majority (to the end of the 21st year), minority, nonage, immaturity, pupilage, wardship, juvenility, juniority, teens, tender age, leading strings, bloom, puberty, virginity, pucelage.

INFANT, *n.* 1. Child during the earliest period of its life, baby, babe in arms, *bambino (It.),* suckling, nursling, weanling, foundling, papoose, *enfant (Fr.),* little one, tot, bairn, chit, chick, kid *(slang),* mite, bantling, brat, pickaninny, young one, lambkin, cub, whelp, urchin, imp, elf, cherub.

2. *(Law)* One who has not attained the age of 21 years, person who is not of full age, minor, juvenile, ward, teen-ager, pupil, youngster, adolescent, stripling, scion, sprig, slip, cadet.

3. Beginner, neophyte, tyro, greenhorn, apprentice, novice, learner.

INFANTICIDE, *n.* Killing of an infant, childmurder, feticide, aborticide, filicide, puericide.

INFANTILE, *adj.* 1. Being in the earliest stage, newborn, tender, unfledged, new-fledged, in swaddling clothes, in the cradle, at the breast.

2. Characteristic of an infant, babyish, childish, weak, infantine.

3. Childlike, puerile, boyish, girlish, kittenish, juvenile.

INFANTRY, *n.* Military units that fight on foot, foot soldiers, riflemen, infantry soldiers, foot, rifles, privates, doughboys, frontline troops, infantrymen, G.I.'s, Tommy Atkinses, Poilus, Froggies, Sammies, rank and file, cannon fodder.

INFATUATE, *v.* 1. Affect with folly, make fatuous, addle the wits, besot, befool, dupe, gull, delude, deceive, stultify, deprive of reason, make foolish, deprive of common sense, turn the head, madden, craze, dementate.

2. Inspire with a blind love, possess with an unreasoning passion, captivate, charm, bewitch, enrapture, entrance, spellbind, ensorcel, intoxicate,

enamor, inflame with love, secure the affection of, endear, ensnare, entrap, lure, seduce, allure, beguile, entangle.

INFATUATION, *n.* 1. Foolishness, besottedness, gullibility, gullibleness, credulity, credulousness, self-deception, self-delusion, blindness, blind side, mote in the eye, partiality, *idée fix (Fr.)*, fool's paradise, senseless prepossession, passionate absorption, stupefaction, fatuity, hallucination, intoxication, craze, mania, monomania, arrant folly, fanaticism, *tête monté (Fr.)*.

2. All-absorbing passion, captivation, love, enchantment, enthusiasm, flame, fervor, tender passion, devotion, rapture, gallantry, yearning, idolization, adoration, idolatry, excessive love, fascination.

INFEASIBLE, *adj.* That cannot be accomplished, unfeasible, not to be done, impracticable, unachievable, insuperable, insurmountable, out of reach, unobtainable, out of the question, not to be thought of, impossible, contrary to reason, unreasonable, beyond the bounds of possibility, inconceivable, visionary, unimaginable, unthinkable.

INFECT, *v.* 1. Impregnate with disease-producing germs, affect with contagious matter, taint with disease, inoculate, vaccinate.

2. Imbue with something that affects unfavorably, contaminate, pollute, poison, vitiate, defile, inquinate, taint, empoison, canker, envenom, exulcerate, corrupt, embase, debauch, blight, spoil, impair.

3. Influence feeling, prompt to action, excite, impassion, animate, inspire, interest, intrigue, strike, move, impress, affect, touch, smite, provoke, call forth, arouse, rouse, kindle, fire, enkindle, stimulate, quicken, whet, sharpen, work upon, fan the flame, stir the embers, heat, foster, foment, warm, play on the feelings.

INFECTION, *n.* 1. Morbific matter by means of which a communicable disease is transmitted from the sick to the well, living organism that causes the spread of an infectious disease, virus, contagium, poison of an infectious disease, infective transmissible poison, toxic bacillus.

2. Contagion, contamination, epidemic, affection, pollution, taint, vitiation, corruption, defilement, disease, plague, pest, bane, miasm, pestilence, poisoning, septicity, septicaemia, murrain, pox, death in the pot.

3. Influence passing from one to another, impulse affecting feeling or action, suscitation, excitation of feeling, galvanism, provocation, stimulation, calling forth, inspiration.

INFECTIOUS, *adj.* 1. Communicable by infection, virus-borne, bacterium-transmissible, contagious, morbiferous, morbific, inoculable, toxiferous.

2. Epidemic, zymotic, epizootic, toxic, poisonous, virulent, venomous, deleterious, azotic, septic, mephitic, noxious, noisome, pestilential, pestiferous, pandemic, endemic.

3. Tending to spread from one to another, catching, sympathetic.

INFECUND, *adj.* Infertile, unfruitful, unproductive, sterile, arid, barren, unprolific, effete, fruitless, addle, unfertile, acarpous, *sine prole (Lat.)*, childless, without offspring, fallow, issueless, impotent, sexually weak.

INFECUNDITY, *n.* Unfruitfulness, unproductiveness, infertility, sterility, barrenness, aridity, impotence, sexual weakness.

INFELICITOUS, *adj.* 1. Miserable, wretched, unhappy, poor, woebegone, cheerless, concerned, sorrowful, chagrined, pained, afflicted, worried, prey to grief, unfortunate, hopeless, heavy-laden, steeped in misery, brokenhearted, on the rack, in limbo.

2. Inauspicious, unpropitious, malominous, inopportune, untimely, unseasonable, premature, unlucky, unfavorable, calamitous, disastrous, adverse, untoward, unprosperous.

3. Unfitting, inappropriate, inapt, malapropos, ill-chosen, in bad taste, clumsy, gauche, maladroit, ill-advised, misadvised, inhabile, ill-judged, ill-imagined, ill-contrived, not well expressed, fumbling, awkward, misguided, wild, random.

INFER, *v.* 1. Draw a conclusion by reasoning, conclude from evidence, derive by reasoning, judge from premises, deduce, gather, glean, collect, presume, guess, consider probable, opine, suppose, reckon, esteem, think, believe, deem, imagine, regard, form an opinion, construe.

2. Involve as a conclusion, imply, indicate, intimate, hint, insinuate.

INFERENCE, *n.* 1. Process of reasoning, a priori reasoning, process of inferring from the general to the particular, illation, derivation, induction, generalization, assumption.

2. That which is inferred, conclusion, consequence, deduction, proposition reached by a process of inference, corollary, implication.

INFERIOR, *adj.* 1. Smaller, lesser, less, reduced, lower, nether, subordinate, secondary, minor, junior, deficient, humble, second-class, lower in the scale, of less importance, subsidiary, ancillary, tributary, subservient, subject, menial.

2. Second-rate, of comparatively low grade, poor, petty, paltry, shabby, base, mean, bad, imperfect, indifferent, puny.

3. Insignificant, unimportant, two-by-four, one-horse, mediocre, tolerable, poorer, less valuable, less good, not up to snuff.

INFERIORITY, *n.* 1. Subordination, subordinacy, juniority, subservience, subjection, submission.

2. Imperfection, deficiency, shortcoming, inadequacy.

3. Littleness, smallness, poorness, baseness, meanness, shabbiness, indifference, mediocrity, lower quality, lower worth, degeneracy, low estate.

INFERNAL, *adj.* 1. Pertaining to the lower world of classical mythology, Stygian, Acherontian, Tartarean, Lethean, Plutonian, Avernian, Hadean.

2. Devilish, diabolical, satanic, Mephistophelean, demoniacal, hell-born, hellish, fiendish, fiendlike.

3. Atrocious, damnable, nefarious, accursed, dark, malicious, abominable, iniquitous, detestable, horrible, heinous, flagitious, scelerate, scelerous, inhuman, black, sinister, felonious, foul, gross, vile, infamous, monstrous, flagrant, villainous, dire, horrendous, execrable, confounded, feral, truculent, ferocious, bloodthirsty, facinorous, incarnate.

INFERTILITY, *n.* Unfruitfulness, sterility, barrenness, aridity, infecundity, unproductiveness, effeteness, aridness, sexual weakness, impotency.

INFEST, *v.* 1. Overrun in a troublesome manner, throng, swarm in, teem, beset, be numerous in, take complete possession of, frequent, haunt, spread like wildfire, meet at every turn, run through, overspread, permeate, pervade, fill, be diffused throughout, creep with, bristle with.

2. Plague, harass, torment, molest, vex, disturb, tease, annoy, badger, trouble, worry, pester, importune, persecute, heckle, harry, bother, irk, rag, discommode, incommode, discompose.

INFIDEL, *n.* 1. Unbeliever, denier of religious obligation, atheist, disbeliever in God, heathen, agnostic, skeptic, heretic, nullifidian, irreligionist, giaour *(Turkish)*, gentile, alien, zendik *(Arabic)*, pagan.

2. Freethinker, *esprit fort (Fr.)*, rationalist, positivist, materialist, nihilist, Pyrrhonist, Comtist, dissenter, deist.

INFIDELITY, *n.* 1. Lack of religious faith, unbelief, disbelief, atheism, agnosticism, nullifidianism, Pyrrhonism, irreligion, ungodliness, godlessness, irreverence, impiety, skepticism, incredulity, doubt, freethinking, antichristianism.

2. Faithlessness, breach of trust, bad faith, disloyalty, treachery, perfidy, improbity, betrayal, perfidiousness, apostasy, divided allegiance, treason, Iscariotism, Judas kiss, *Punica fides (Lat.)*, Punic faith.

3. Marital unfaithfulness, adultery, cuckoldry, violation of the marriage bed, advoutry, breaking of the marriage vows, criminal conversation *(Law)*.

INFILTRATE, *v.* 1. Pass by filtration, pervade, permeate, soak into, be absorbed, penetrate, pass in through a substance, filter into, percolate, imbrue, imbue, saturate, humectate, moisten, seep through.

2. Penetrate into the enemy's line at weak or unguarded points, intrude, invade, slip into, creep into, break in upon, insinuate oneself into, interpenetrate, find one's way into, worm oneself into, wriggle oneself into.

3. Indoctrinate, inculcate, infuse, inoculate, instill, sow the seeds of, propagandize, disseminate, implant, imbue, enlighten, teach.

INFINITE, *adj.* 1. Countless, numberless, untold, incalculable, innumerable, unnumbered, limitless, illimitable, knowing no limit, unlimited, boundless, unbounded, interminable, all-embracing, inexhaustible.

2. Immeasurable, measureless, unmeasured, endless, perpetual, without end, unfathomable, immense, vast, enormous, stupendous.

3. Eternal, perfect. self-determined, absolute, self-existent, unconditioned, omnipotent.

INFINITESIMAL, *adj.* Exceedingly tiny, immeasurably small, less than an assignable quantity, minute, microscopic, atomic, molecular, corpuscular, homeopathic, inappreciable, imperceptible, evanescent, diminutive, inconsiderable, wee, puny, exiguous, minikin, pigmy, miniature, elfin, Lilliputian, petty, picayune.

INFINITESIMAL, *n.* Variable having zero as a limit, quantity whose limit is zero, quantity converging to zero, infinitely small amount, infinitely diminishing amount, vanishing fluxion.

INFINITUDE, *n.* Infiniteness, interminateness, endlessness, boundlessness, immensity, illimitability, immeasurability, immeasurableness, inexhaustibility, inexhaustibleness, vastness, immensity, illimitable expanse, boundless multitude, infinite number, illimitableness.

INFIRM, *adj.* 1. Feeble in body or health, decrepit, unsound, failing, weak, enfeebled, weakened, ailing, frail, debilitated, emaciated, doddering, trembling, sickly, poorly, ill, drooping, spent, languid, wasted, worn, tottering, asthenic, enervated,

languishing, faint, weakly, exhausted, strengthless, impotent, laid low, helpless, powerless, sapless.

2. Irresolute, not steadfast, faltering, wavering, vacillating, unstable, inconstant, undecided, fickle, undetermined, changeable, easily led, pliable.

3. Not solid, not strong, precarious, insecure, unsound, rotten, decayed, seedy, worn, deteriorated, withered, the worse for wear, on its last legs, tumbledown, shaky, rickety, unsubstantial, jerrybuilt, gimcrack, sleazy, frail, fragile, shattery, frangible, flimsy.

INFIRMARY, *n.* Place for the care of the infirm or sick, hospital, dispensary, clinic, lazaretto, valetudinarium, sanitarium, sanatorium, asylum, pesthouse, leprosarium, leprosery, *maison de santé (Fr.)*, nursing home.

INFIRMITY, *n.* 1. Physical weakness, lack of strength, debility, feebleness, frailness, infirmness, languor, debilitation, enervation, asthenia, atony *(Med.)*, adynamy *(Med.)*, decrepitude, impotence, attenuation, disability, malady, ailment, invalidism, fragility, delicacy, faintness, prostration, disease, cachexia, sickness, illness, affection, disorder, delicate health, complaint, loss of health, indisposition, disorder, collapse, decline, breakdown.

2. Moral weakness, frailty, failing, fault, foible, defect, peccability, deficiency, imperfection, defect, lapse.

3. Instability, irresolution, vacillation, indecision, unstableness, irresoluteness, wavering, changeability, inconstancy, fickleness.

INFIX, *v.* 1. Drive in, plant, fasten, fix, set, lodge, imbed.

2. Fix in the mind or memory, impress, inculcate, instill, implant, infuse, indoctrinate, inoculate, ingraft, rivet.

INFLAME, *v.* 1. Set aflame, set afire, light with flames, kindle, accend, ignite, set fire to.

2. Excite inflammation in, redden with inflammation, raise to a feverish heat, affect morbidly, cause suppuration.

3. Arouse to a high degree of feeling, stimulate desires, excite passions, intensify, fire, incite, enkindle, rouse, heat up, animate, work up, inspirit, set on, stir up, fan, craze, madden, energize, invigorate, strengthen, potentialize, activate, sharpen, enliven, electrify, galvanize, magnetize, pep up.

4. Irritate, exasperate, exacerbate, aggravate, infuriate, incense, enrage, anger, nettle, provoke, pique, enchafe, heckle, ruffle, taunt, embitter, harass, goad, pester, vex, tease, envenom, foment, convulse, add fuel to the flame, lash into fury.

INFLAMMABILITY, *n.* Combustibility, inflammableness, combustibleness, flammableness, flammability, accendibility, ignitibility.

INFLAMMABLE, *adj.* 1. Capable of being set on fire, ignitible, combustible, flammable, accendible, burnable.

2. Easily roused to passion, excitable, irritable, irascible, choleric, inflammatory, high-strung, nervous, hasty, impatient, wrathful, temperamental, precipitous, impetuous, impulsive, frantic, furious, frenzied, fiery, vehement, passionate.

INFLAMMATION, *n.* 1. Setting on fire, burning, ignition, kindling, firing, conflagration, fire, lighting, accension, combustion, adustion, flagration, deflagration.

2. *(Pathol.)* Reaction of the body to injurious agents promoting redness and swelling or pain and

disturbed function, suppuration, causoma, hyperemia, phlogosis, erysipelas, eruption, exanthema, rash, calenture, fever.

3. Excitement, animosity, anger, wrath, ire, wrathfulness, turbulence, rage, violence, heat, irritation, rankling, exasperation, exacerbation, vexation, virulence, acerbity, choler, bile, gall, pucker, fume, dander, ebullition, ferment, tiff, pet, passion, tantrum, fit, explosion, outburst, paroxysm, storm, fury, fire and fury, vials of wrath, hot blood.

INFLAMMATORY, *adj.* 1. Fiery, flaming, scorching, red-hot, ebullient, explosive, inflammable, burnable, combustible, volcanic.

2. Incendiary, dissentious, seditious, mutinous, rebellious, rabble-rousing, demagogic, rabid, insurgent, lawless, riotous, revolutionary, restive, recalcitrant.

INFLATE, *v.* 1. Swell by blowing, sufflate, distend, expand, blow up, bloat, puff out, dilate, tumefy, pump up, fatten, stretch, aerate.

2. Enlarge, increase, magnify, wax, grow, fill out, spread out, augment, mount, rise.

3. Puff up, elate, make conceited, render vain, swell, turn one's head, give one a swell head, blow up one's ego.

4. (*Econ.*) Expand currency unduly, raise above the proper value.

INFLATED, *adj.* 1. Swollen, distended with air, bloated with gas, full-blown, puffy, ballooning.

2. Bombastic, turgid, tumid, pedantic, high-blown, overblown, artificial, grandiloquent, magniloquent, altiloquent, pompous, declamatory, stilted, rhetorical, altisonant, fustian, sesquipedalian.

3. Puffed up with pride, elated, cock-a-hoop, vain, egotistic, conceited, toplofty, exultant.

INFLATION, *n.* 1. Blowing up, swelling by air, sufflation, distention, expansion, bloatedness, puffiness, intumescence, tumefaction, vesiculation.

2. Accretion, increment, dilatation, dilation, spread, extension, accession, increase, augmentation, enlargement, reinforcement, growth, development, aggrandizement, enhancement, intensification, exaggeration.

3. Conceit, vanity, vainglory, vaingloriousness, conceitedness, self-sufficiency, self-importance, self-complacency, self-glorification, self-praise, self-applause, self-laudation, self-esteem, self-love, *amour propre (Fr.),* self-admiration, pretentiousness, pretension, affected manner, airs, egotism, pride, arrogance, ostentation.

4. Bombast, sesquipedalianism, altiloquence, magniloquence, grandiloquence, altisonance, fustian, rodomontade, mouthing, rant, turgid talk, pompous phraseology.

5. (*Econ.*) Undue expansion of currency by the issuing of paper money not redeemable in specie, overenlargement of currency, runaway prices, upward revaluations, credit runaway, swollen purchasing power, upturn in prices, false prosperity, substantial rise of prices caused by an undue expansion in paper money or bank credit.

INFLECT, *v.* 1. Turn from a direct line, curve, bow, bend, deflect, recurve, arch, crook, hook, round, incurve, coil, curl.

2. Modulate the voice, vary the tone, diversify, temper, vary, alter, change, moderate, vocalize, accentuate.

3. Vary the terminations of a word, decline a noun or an adjective, conjugate a verb, parse, grammaticize, analyze.

INFLECTION, *n.* 1. Curvature, bending, curvity, bend, crook, angle, flexure, deflexion, aduncity, deviation, curvation.

2. Modulation of the voice, change in pitch or tone of voice, cadence, accentuation, expression, intonation, vocalization, enunciation, articulation, ecphonesis, delivery.

3. Variation in declension or in conjugation, accidence, grammar, syntax, phonology.

INFLEXIBILITY, *n.* 1. Rigidity, stiffness, inflexibleness, flintiness, adamantineness, solidity, toughness, callosity, induration, ossification, petrifaction, fossilization, glaciation, crystallization, vitrification, vitrescence, renitence, temper, durity, cornification, lapidification, lapidescence.

2. Stubbornness, obstinacy, doggedness, mulishness, pertinacity, tenacity, immovability, obduracy, contumacy, perversity, pervicacity, opinionativeness, intractability.

3. Resolution, perseverance, firmness, steadfastness, determination, will, unconquerable will, iron will, decision, backbone, strength of mind, grit, resolve.

4. Rigor, stringency, austerity, severity, strictness, pitilessness, inclemency, hardness of heart, inexorability, relentlessness, implacability, sternness.

INFLEXIBLE, *adj.* 1. Not flexible, rigid, stiff, unbending, hard, solid, implastic, taut, adamantine, rocky, stony, steely, flinty, callous, horny, indurate, brassy, corneous, stark, tense, concrete, lithic, granitic, bony, vitreous, osseous, cartilaginous, stiff as a poker.

2. Unyielding in temper, stubborn, obstinate, dogged, mulish, pigheaded, headstrong, refractory, wilful, intractable, indocile, cantankerous, cross-grained, perverse, contumacious, unpliant.

3. Resolved, determined, resolute, strong-willed, self-possessed, tenacious, decided, firm, cast iron, indomitable.

4. Unmoved by prayer, relentless, implacable, obdurate, stern, inexorable, immovable by entreaties, unrelenting, uncompromising, intransigent, grim, unchangeable, unmoved, unaffected, uninfluenced, stony-hearted, impervious, impersuasible, harsh, dour, strict, severe, rigorous, exacting, austere, Spartan, Draconian, strait-laced, stringent, tyrannical, despotic, inclement, oppressive, pitiless, ruthless, merciless, uncompassionate, cruel.

5. Unyielding in purpose, adhering to a set plan, *tenax propositi (Lat.),* resolute, steadfast, persevering, upright.

INFLICT, *v.* Impose as something that must be borne or suffered, lay on anything unwelcome, bring to bear, visit upon, cause to suffer, administer a penalty, put upon, wreak, execute, put on the screw, be hard upon, perpetrate, commit, transact, enact.

INFLICTION, *n.* 1. Imposition, perpetration, commitment, committal, execution, transaction, enactment, exercitation, exercise, performance, administration, visitation.

2. Punishment, punition, castigation, chastening, chastisement, correction, judgment, trial, discipline, retribution, penalty, requital, Nemesis, harshness, austerity, stringency, severity, inclemency, arbitrary power, undoing.

3. Affliction, irritation, annoyance, worry, mortification, ordeal, trouble, blow, shock, load, burden, vexation.

4. Scourge, harm, pest, misfortune, abomination, torment, hurt, calamity, disaster.

INFLORESCENCE, *n.* 1. Blossoming, flowering, blooming, florescence.

2. Arrangement of flowers on the axis, flower cluster, mode of flowering.

INFLUENCE, *n.* 1. Power, potency, influentiality, capability, ascendancy, weight, importance, bias, favor, domination, control, dominance, sway, authority, supremacy, prevalence, mastery, upper hand, predominance, rule, reign, pressure, drag *(slang),* pull *(slang),* hold, interest, lobby, inducement, patronage.

2. Prestige, credit, reputation, repute, standing, footing, auspices.

3. Vantage ground, support, advantage, leverage, play, foundation, stable position, foothold, *pou sto (Greek), locus standi (Lat.),* base of operation.

4. Protection, championship, aid, encouragement, guidance.

5. Insensible action exerted by one thing on another, power of producing effects by invisible means, exercise of occult power by the stars *(Astrol.),* mysterious agency, spell, magnetism, magic, unseen power.

INFLUENCE, *v.* 1. Persuade, induce, work upon, impel to, move, incite, instigate, prevail upon, arouse, rouse to, prompt, compel, stimulate, act upon, urge, actuate.

2. Be potent, be influential, make one's influence felt, carry weight, tell, weigh, count, take hold.

3. Dominate, master, control, govern, manage, rule, sway, overpower, subject, override, wield, overbear, predominate, gain the upper hand, take the lead, get control of, pull the strings, set the fashion, turn the scale, lead the dance, command.

4. Exercise influence on, direct, regulate, guide, determine, affect, modify, bias, incline, lead, drive, play a decisive role, have a bearing, magnetize.

5. Impregnate, infiltrate, pervade, penetrate, permeate, run through, prevail, be rife, fill, spread like wildfire.

INFLUENTIAL, *adj.* 1. Having great influence, weighty, important, potent, powerful, puissant, effective, substantial, dominant, authoritative, predominant, strong, recognized, controlling, forcible, great, cogent, effectual, efficacious, telling, momentous, leading.

2. Rife, rampant, prevalent, prevailing, abundant, current, common, general, well supplied, abounding in, numerous, plentiful.

INFLUENZA, *n.* Acute contagious epidemic disease characterized by general prostration and symptomized by nasal catarrh and bronchial inflammation, flue, la grippe.

INFLUX, *n.* 1. Flowing in, inflow, inpouring, inundation, introduction, introgression, ingress, entrance, entry, infiltration, penetration, inroad.

2. Place at which one stream flows into another or into the sea, mouth of a stream.

INFORM, *v.* 1. Notify, advise, enlighten, apprise, give information, acquaint, make known to, tell, disclose to, mention to, signify to, give notice to, send word to, tip, warn, flag, teach, instruct, post, forewarn, serve notice on, reveal, tattle, divulge, impart, communicate, report, intimate, affirm, express, assert, state, declare, represent, specify, signify, describe, retail, confide to, explain, give

inside information, announce, give the low-down, proclaim, enunciate, publish, broadcast, promulgate, disseminate, insinuate, hint, indicate, allude to, suggest, whisper, let fall, imply, breathe a word of, give a pointer to, tip off, give the cue, prompt, set right, correct, open the eyes of, undeceive, disabuse.

2. Furnish incriminating evidence to a prosecuting officer, delate, inform against, accuse, denounce, report an offense, charge, tax.

3. Give character to, shape, give shape to, pervade with determining effect on the character.

INFORMAL, *adj.* 1. Irregular, arbitrary, lawless, stray, peculiar, egregious, eccentric, peccant, exclusive, out of the common run, out of the beaten path, out of the usual course, uncustomary, unofficial.

2. Not according to prescribed forms, unconventional, unorthodox, unceremonious, bohemian, original, *sui generis (Lat.),* without formality, off-the-cuff, nonconforming, noncompliant.

3. Easy, natural, casual, familiar, lax, simple, colloquial, extemporaneous, unconstrained, free, free-and-easy.

INFORMALITY, *n.* 1. Irregularity, lawlessness, peccancy, eccentricity, unusualness.

2. Want of conformity to prescribed forms, absence of ceremony, unceremoniousness, unconventiality, want of formality, unorthodoxy, Bohemianism, originality, nonconformity, disconformity, noncompliance.

3. Ease, naturalness, casualness, familiarity, laxity, simplicity, extemporaneousness, unconstraint, freedom.

INFORMANT, *n.* 1. One who gives information, teller, appriser, adviser, notifier, exponent, spokesman, mouthpiece, newsmonger, intelligencer, relator, narrator, authority, advertiser, messenger, harbinger, reporter, herald, warner, divulger, communicant, proclaimer, announcer, instructor, enlightener, tipster, tipper, interpreter, translator.

2. Accuser, informer, delator, spy, stool pigeon, eavesdropper, peacher, squealer, *mouchard (Fr.),* spotter, detective, shadow, sleuth, dick, undercoverman, complainant, whistle guy *(slang),* tattler.

INFORMATION, *n.* 1. Knowledge received or communicated concerning some circumstance, tidings, news, report, intelligence, instruction, enlightenment, advice, notice, tip, pointer, acquaintance, advertisement, counsel, communication, message, word, proclamation, announcement, intimation, inkling, innuendo, insinuation, hint, suggestion, recital, account, telling, mention, statement, whisper, cue, word to the wise, *verbum sapienti (Lat.),* monition, warning, communiqué, tale, publicity, spotlight, notoriety, limelight, notification, rumor, hearsay, gossip, grapevine *(coll.).*

2. Knowledge on various subjects, learning, wisdom, lore, erudition, edification, reading, book learning, scholarship, letters, education, attainments, accomplishments, culture, proficiency, omniscience, pantology, study, reading, perusal, rudiments, elements, dilettantism, dossier.

3. *(Law)* Official criminal charge, delation, complaint, accusation, denunciation, declaration, affidavit, *procès-verbal (Fr.),* corpus delicti, bill of right, indictment, arraignment, crimination, impeachment, true bill.

INFRACTION, *n.* 1. Infringement, violation, trespass, overstep, transgression, transilience, transcursion, extravagation, transcendence, encroachment, breaking, breach, intrusion, invasion, illapse, contravention.

2. Nonobservance, disobedience, insubordination, concompliance, inobservance, evasion, omission, laxity, neglect, laches, failure.

3. Revolt, sedition, mutiny, rebellion, revolution, secession, defection, uprising, outbreak, *émeute (Fr.)*, riot, insurrection, tumult, Putsch, strike, sabotage, defiance.

INFRANGIBLE, *adj.* 1. Unbreakable, indivisible, inseparable, indiscerptible, indissoluble, indissolvable, insoluble, infusible, dense, thickset, solid, cohesive, close, compact, substantial, impenetrable, impermeable, imporous, concrete, crystalline, adamantean, hard.

2. That may not be infringed, not to be violated, inviolable, sacramental, sacred, sacrosanct, hallowed, holy.

INFREQUENCY, *n.* Uncommonness, infrequence, rareness, rarity, seldomness, sparseness, scantness, scantiness, meagerness, scarceness, scarcity, unusualness, uniqueness, irregularity, sporadicalness, occasionalness, unwontedness, fewness.

INFREQUENT, *adj.* Happening at long intervals, unfrequent, occurring not often, not constant, not regular, not habitual, unwonted, occasional, sparing, now and then, sporadic, few, not plentiful, scarce, sparse, scant, uncommon, rare, unusual, unique, unheard of, unprecedented.

INFRINGE, *v.* 1. Commit an infraction of, commit a breach of, violate, break, contravene, transgress, set at naught, treat as of no importance, repudiate, resist, discard, disobey, break through, infract.

2. (With UPON) Encroach, invade, impinge, overstep, trespass, intrude, trench on, usurp, arrogate, exact, aggress.

INFRINGEMENT, *n.* Violation, breach, infraction, transgression, trespass, encroachment, inroad, invasion, attack, usurpation, assumption, dispossession, seizure, tort, exaction, imposition, nonobservance, disobedience, nonacquiescence, contravention, nonperformance, noncompliance, evasion, omission, neglect, laxness, laxity, laches, slackness, failure, insubordination, lawlessness.

IN FULL, 1. In its entirety, complete, entire, total, whole, integral, full, at length, unabridged, unabbreviated, uncontracted.

2. For the full amount, without reduction, owning nothing, out of debt, all straight, clear of debt, clear of encumbrance, unindebted, unowing.

INFURIATE, *v.* Kindle wrath, make angry, enrage, inflame, provoke, irritate, aggravate, exasperate, exacerbate, rile, sting to the quick, stir up bile, envenom, embitter, harass, madden, make furious, fan into flame, incense, chafe, wound, huff, nettle, pique, ruffle, fret, discompose, give umbrage, give offense, offend, affront, put out of humor, try one's temper, raise one's dander, work up into a passion, excite, disturb a hornet's nest, make one's blood boil, lash into a fury, throw into a ferment, anger.

INFURIATED, *adj.* Flushed with anger, carried away by passion, enraged, incensed, infuriate, angry, furious, raving, frantic, mad, maddened, raging, towering, boiling over, foaming at the mouth, fuming, amuck, berserk, demoniacal, purple-faced, convulsed with rage, worked up, *acharné (Fr.)*, fiery, savage, explosive, irate, wrathful, rabid, rampant, savage, violent, wild, fierce,

ungovernable, wrought-up, bitter, acrimonious, virulent, rageful, indignant, set against, in high dudgeon, in a passion, in a huff, up in arms, paroxysmal.

INFUSE, *v.* 1. Introduce by pouring, diffuse, cause to penetrate, instill, shed, tinge, imbue, saturate, pour into, mingle, steep, soak, plunge, bathe, impregnate, inoculate, lace *(a beverage)*, fortify, flavor, tincture, entincture, season, macerate.

2. Infix, implant, ingraft, inspire with, inculcate, insinuate, breathe into, impart.

INFUSION, *n.* 1. Steeping, infusing, macerating, soaking, immersion, submersion, submergence, plunge, dip, tincture, tinge, dash, touch, vein, *soupçon (Fr.)*, suspicion, strain, shade, spice, smack, seasoning.

2. Inculcation, introduction, instillation, inoculation, injection, implantation, insinuation, infiltration, impregnation, transfusion.

3. Liquid extract obtained from a substance by steeping or soaking it in water, steeped liquor.

INFUSORIA, *n., pl. (Zool.)* Microscopic aquatic protozoans having vibratile cilia, minute animal and vegetable organisms developed in infusions of decaying organic matter, animalcula, animalcules, bacilli, microbes, microorganisms, bacteria.

INGATHERING, *n.* 1. Collecting, gathering, bringing in, garnering, scraping together, accumulating, amassing, amassment, conglomeration, accumulation, acquisition.

2. Harvest, produce, fruit, return, crop, aftermath, gleanings, profit, winnings, earnings, cleanup, pickings.

IN GENERAL 1. With respect to the whole class referred to, for the most part, with few exceptions, in the main, in most cases, generally speaking, in the ordinary course of things, as times go, as things go, as the world goes, as it may happen, as it may turn out.

2. On the whole, as a general rule, to speak summarily, speaking generally, to sum up, upon the whole.

INGENIOUS, *adj.* 1. *(Of persons)* Having inventive faculty, skillful in contriving, inventive, resourceful, clever at constructing, able, ready, adroit, sagacious, bright, felicitous, neat, gifted, capable, proficient, apt, talented, neat-handed, scientific, artistic, fine-fingered, dexterous, feat, deft, artful, quick, expert, handy, slick, subtle, smart, good at, crack, masterly, master of, facile, *au fait (Fr.)*.

2. *(Of things)* Artful in construction, original, cunning, cute *(colloq.)*, showing cleverness of invention, exhibiting ingenuity.

INGENUITY, *n.* Inventive talent, keen perception, inventiveness, ingeniousness, skill, resourcefulness, skillfulness, sharpness, ability, readiness, acuteness, capacity, capableness, aptitude, faculty, intelligence, inspiration, felicity, *curiosa felicitas (Lat.)*, cleverness, aptness, proficiency, competence, endowment, attainment, acquirement, accomplishment, trick, adroitness, expertness, address, dexterity, efficiency, mastery, excellence, deftness, qualification, featness, adeptness, finish, facility, craft, technique, cunning, sleight, turn, knack, genius, gift, forte, flair, parts, brightness, sagacity, discernment, wit, astuteness, artifice.

INGENUOUS, *adj.* 1. Free from reserve, open, sincere, unreserved, unrestrained, plain, downright honest, simple, unsophisticated, unaffected, natural, genuine, unsuspicious, straightforward, aboveboard, single-minded, truthful, open-hearted, simple-minded, transparent, truthful, outspoken, blunt, frank, candid, unselfconscious, *ingénu (Fr.).*

2. Devoid of dissimulation, guileless, undesigning, artless, innocent, childlike, naive.

INGENUOUSNESS, *n.* Singleness of purpose, single-mindedness, openness, simplicity, candor, frankness, honesty, artlessness, sincerity, truthfulness, guilelessness, innocence, *épanchement (Fr.),* unsophistication, naivete, childlikeness, openheartedness, plain-dealing, veracity, veraciousness, straightforwardness, unselfconsciousness, uprightness.

INGLORIOUS, *adj.* 1. Disgraceful, dishonorable, disreputable, shameful, discreditable, humiliating, despicable, unbecoming, questionable, shady, unworthy, infamous, opprobrious, ignominious, scandalous, arrant, outrageous, shocking, notorious, ignoble, abject, base, vile, mean, under a cloud, in bad repute, in bad odor.

2. Not famous, unknown to fame, nameless, unnoted, unnoticed, unhonored, unmarked, unglorified, undistinguished, lowly, obscure, humble.

INGLORIOUSNESS, *n.* 1. Dishonor, disrepute, disgrace, disfavor, disesteem, discredit, ill-repute, ill favor, ill fame, ignominiousness, ignominy, infamy, obloquy, opprobrium, shame, abasement, odium, derogation, degradation, debasement, humiliation, baseness, scandal, turpitude, vileness, reproach, stigma, brand, stain, slur, spot, blot on the escutcheon, taint, tarnish, badge of infamy, byword. bar sinister.

2. Lack of distinction, want of fame, obscurity, nonentity, lowliness, humbleness, meanness, namelessness.

INGOT, *n.* 1. Cast metal mass formed by smelting and casting to shape, casting obtained when melted metal is poured into a mold with the expectation that it be further processed.

2. Bullion, nugget, bar.

INGRAIN, *v.* Fix deeply, implant firmly, impregnate, imbue, dye in the grain.

INGRAINED, *adj.* Firmly fixed, infixed, inherent, rooted, inborn, inbred, innate, intrinsic, ineffaceable, indelible, inveterate, deep, thorough, radical, essential.

INGRATE, *n.* Ungrateful person, one who returns evil for good, bad investment *(colloq.),* black sheep, one who enjoys another's good services without intent to repay, bounder, cad, thankless wretch, self-seeker, ungrateful opportunist.

INGRATIATE, *v.* Establish oneself in the favor or good graces of others, insinuate oneself, get into favor, worm oneself, curry favor with, *faire l'aimable (Fr.),* pay one's court to, set one's cap at, make a date with, coquet, flirt, take the fancy of, engage the affections of, wind round the heart of, propitiate, conciliate, win the confidence of, flatter, cajole, wheedle, take the fancy of, attach, attract, captivate, seduce, fascinate, bewitch.

INGRATIATING, *adj.* Attractive, winning, charming, adorable, lovable, sweet, lovely, engaging, seductive, captivating, enchanting, fascinating, bewitching, intriguing, interesting, amiable, tactful, congenial, suave, urbane, smooth, cordial, good-humored, affable, gracious, friendly, genial, familiar, obliging, good-mannered, courteous, chivalrous, gallant.

INGRATITUDE, *n.* Thanklessness, unthankfulness, ungratefulness, "benefits forgot," indisposi-

tion to reciprocate or return favors, ill return for favors, insensibility to kindness, feeling of inobligation for favors received.

INGREDIENT, *n.* Element in a mixture, component part, constituent, component, integral part, contents, feature, member.

INGRESS, *n.* 1. Entrance, entrée, introgression, début, influx, entry, incoming, penetration, interpenetration, insertion, insinuation, infiltration, incursion, intrusion, invasion, inroad, illapse, importation, admission.

2. Means or place of going in, door, doorway, portal, opening, aperture, inlet, orifice, porch, ostiary, gate, wicket, postern, arcade, gangway, hatch.

INHABIT, *v.* Live in, dwell in, occupy, reside in, abide, stay, sojourn, domicile, take up one's abode, room, lodge, roost, tenant, bunk, nest, populate, nestle, perch, people.

INHABITANT, *n.* 1. Permanent resident, residentiary, dweller, inhabiter, inmate, occupant, occupier, indweller, householder, addressee, incumbent, tenant, lodger, boarder, roomer.

2. Denizen, citizen, townsman, burgher, burgess, cottager, villager, cotter, colonist, habitant, planter, squatter, settler, backwoodsman, aborigine, native, autochthon, aboriginal, indigene.

3. Inhabitants, population, community, folk, people, race, nation, state, settlement, colony.

INHALATION, *n.* Breathing, respiration, inspiration, exhalation, eupnoea *(Med., opposite of* dyspnoea*),* pant, puff, wheeze, gasp, sniffle, snuffle, sigh, indraught, snuff, sniff, breath, expiration.

INHALE, *v.* Inbreathe, draw into the lungs by breathing, breathe in, inspire, respire, pant, puff, blow, wheeze, gasp, sniff, snuff, sniffle, snuffle, sigh, aerate, sufflate, suck in.

INHARMONIOUS, *adj.* 1. Inharmonic, unharmonious, unmusical, out of tune, cacophonous, unmelodious, tuneless, harsh, jangling, dissonant, absonant, jarring, strident, raucous, horrisonous.

2. Gaudy, garish, flamboyant, florid, flashy, showy, crude, glaring, motley, incongruous.

3. Discordant, conflicting, incompatible, quarrelsome, litigious, disputatious, factious, disagreeing, dissentient, contradictory, inconsistent, discrepant, unreconciled, controversial, embroiled.

INHARMONIOUSNESS, *n.* 1. Unharmoniousness, unmusicality, cacophony, dissonance, caterwauling, harshness, unmelodiousness, tunelessness, absonance, jangling, stridency, raucousness, cat's concert, pandemonium, babel.

2. Gaudiness, floridity, flamboyancy, garishness, flashiness, showiness, crudeness, incongruousness.

3. Discord, disagreement, disaccord, dissidence, clash, jarring, division, disunion, breach, difference, variance, dissension, split, cross purposes, rupture, disruption, rift, schism, faction, feud, dispute, quarrel, tiff, spat, squabble, words, altercation, wrangling, litigation, polemics, brawl, broil, hubbub, racket, fracas, imbroglio. rumpus, disturbance, commotion, riot.

INHERE, *v.* Exist permanently and inseparably in, belong intrinsically, exist as a part, be inherent, reside, be fixed as a quality, be immanent, belong, lie, abide, pertain, be part of, enter into, appertain to, make up, constitute.

INHERENT, *adj.* Existing in something as a permanent and inseparable element, inborn, innate, inbred, immanent, essential, indwelling, inseparable, intrinsic, subsistent, ingrained, native, inwrought, infixed, bred in the bone, congenital, deep-rooted, inveterate, ineffaceable, inalienable, proper, natural.

INHERIT, v. Receive property or a right as the heir of the former owner, receive by succession from predecessors, receive as one's portion, come into possession of as an heir, obtain by inheritance, acquire from ancestors, possess by inheritance, come into, succeed to, fall heir to, have succession as heir, come in for, devolve upon.

INHERITANCE, n. Property passing at the owner's death to the heir, legacy, heritage, patrimony, birthright, portion, peculiar possession, anything received by succession from predecessors, jointure, dower, dot, bequest, gift, endowment, estate and effects.

INHERITOR, n. Heir, heritor, parcener, coheir, heiress, heritress, inheritrix, beneficiary, devisee, legatee, legatary, reversioner, remainder-man, possessor, successor.

INHIBIT, v. 1. Restrain an action, check an impulse, arrest, suppress, repress, hold back, strangle, smother, keep under, stop short, pull in, muzzle, bridle, gag, harness, constrain, rein in, curb, check, debar, restrict, hinder, coerce, control, compel, govern, hold in leash, prevent, obstruct, stop, bar.

2. Forbid, prohibit, interdict, veto, ban, proscribe, taboo, disallow, annul, nullify, rescind, suspend, abolish.

INHIBITION, n. 1. Restraint of action, coercion, arrestation, restriction, arrest, obstruction, hindrance, repression, cohibition, constraint, check, obstacle, impediment, stricture, coarctation, impedition, stoppage, preclusion, interclusion, interception, constriction, retardation, oppilation, blockade, interposition, obtrusion, stay, stop, encumbrance, handicap.

2. (Psychol.) The blocking of any psychological process by another psychological process, mental block.

3. Prohibition, injunction, proscription, prevention, ban, embargo, interdict, interdiction, veto, taboo, disallowance, verboten (Ger.), forbiddance.

INHOSPITABLE, adj. 1. Not inclined to hospitality, unfriendly to strangers, unsociable, unsocial, inconversable, eremetic, unclubbable, dissocial, cynical, sauvage (Fr.), unreceptive, ungenerous, unkind, illiberal, intolerant, narrow, prejudiced, bigoted.

2. Not offering shelter, not affording favorable conditions, desolate, wild, barren, isolated, solitary, lonesome, unfrequented, uninhabitable, uninhabited, untenanted, deserted, abandoned, forlorn, unvisited, sequestered, secluded, retired, in a backwater, forbidding, cool, desert, arid, parched, dry, droughty, infertile, infecund, sterile, bare, poor, unfruitful.

INHOSPITALITY, n. 1. Inhospitable attitude toward visitors, unfriendliness, unsociableness, inconversability, unkindness, illiberality, intolerance, narrowness, dissociability, reclusion, solitariness, solitude, anchoritism, aloofness.

2. Desolation, desolateness, wildness, barrenness, isolation, lonesomeness, desertion, abandonment, forlornness, seclusion, coolness, aridity, aridness, dryness, droughtiness, infertility, infecundity, sterility, bareness, unfruitfulness, poverty.

INHUMAN, adj. Lacking natural human feeling for others, unsympathetic, unfeeling, cold-hearted, cruel, merciless, pitiless, ruthless, remorseless, heartless, harsh, cold-blooded, brutal, ferocious, barbarous, savage, fell, atrocious, bloodthirsty, rancorous, venomous, satanic, devilish, infernal, fiendish, malevolent, truculent, fierce, stony-hearted, hard-hearted, grim, feral, ferine, brutish, diabolical, demoniac, maleficent, malicious, malignant, vicious.

INHUMANITY, n. Barbarity, brutality, ferocity, cruelty, savageness, savagery, bloodthirstiness, ferity, fiendishness, atrocity, outrage, enormity, hard-heartedness, persecution, ill-usage, mercilessness, pitilessness, ruthlessness, ruffianism, truculence, torture, unkindness, cold-heartedness, indignity, affront, virulence, rancor, venom, hardness of heart, heart of stone, malignity, maliciousness, malice.

INHUME, v. Bury, deposit in the earth, inhumate, inter, lay in the grave, put to bed with a shovel, shovel under, entomb.

INIMICAL, adj. 1. Unfriendly, hostile, antagonistic, at enmity, at war with, at swords points with, at daggers drawn, on bad terms with, not on speaking terms, cool, alienated, estranged, irreconcilable, disaffected, antipathetic, cross, offended, angry, up in arms.

2. Adverse in tendency or effect, harmful, hurtful, pernicious, noxious, unfavorable, contrary, opposed, repugnant, prejudiced, opposing, ambivalent, unpropitious, resistant, detrimental.

INIMITABLE, adj. Incapable of being imitated, surpassing imitation, peerless, matchless, beyond compare, unmatched, unrivaled, unparagoned, incomparable, unparalleled, unexampled, unequaled, faultless, perfect, model, consummate, ideal, crack, prime, very best, superfine, superexcellent, superlative, eximious, rare, recherché, tiptop, estimable, admirable, supreme, transcendent, preeminent.

INIQUITOUS, adj. Wicked, wrong, sinful, criminal, heinous, nefarious, flagitious, scelerate, scelerous, facinorous, vicious, bad, immoral, atrocious, infamous, accursed, vile, gross, inequitable, unrighteous, unjust, unfair, unprincipled, worthless, profligate, dissolute, recreant, reprehensible, flagrant, shameful, scandalous, felonious, black, foul, base, scurvy, villainous, knavish, disreputable, corrupt, depraved, evil-minded, malevolent, abandoned, sunk in iniquity, incorrigible, obdurate, irreclaimable, reprobate, culpable, lawless.

INIQUITY, n. Violation of right, unjust action, sin, wickedness, sinfulnes, evildoing, wrongdoing, vice, viciousness, peccability, unrighteousness, gross injustice, error, transgression, depravity, abomination, profanity, infamy, immorality, obliquity, brutality, backsliding, demoralization, corruption, knavery, roguery, villainy, improbity, malevolence, profligacy, lust, flagrancy, atrocity, enormity, outrage, crime, felony, criminality.

INITIAL, adj. At the beginning, first, at the head, commencing, introductory, opening, beginning, inchoate, incipient, initiatory, primary, elementary, in the first stages, rudimentary, embryonic, original, nascent, prime, capital, prefatory, initiative, inaugural, primal, pristine, foremost.

INITIATE, v. 1. Enter upon, start, inaugurate, institute, commence, begin, set going, originate, open, propose, set afoot, start the ball rolling, blaze the trail, break ground, lay the first stone, undertake, lead the way, usher in, take the lead, lay the foundation, set up, broach, launch, found, open the door to.

2. Indoctrinate in the knowledge of some subject, ground, instruct, prime, teach, train, coach, tutor, enlighten, direct, give lessons in, inculcate, instill, imbue, implant, open the eyes, discipline, qualify, prepare, practice, drill, inure, familiarize with, graduate.

3. Admit with formal rites into some secret society, take in, introduce, induct, give entrance to, bring in, haze.

INITIATION, *n.* 1. Beginning, commencement, opening, start, outset, inception, incipience, introduction, preface, preamble, foreword, prologue, inauguration, installation, coming out *(colloq.),* début, embarkation, curtain raiser, rising of the curtain, exordium, onset, outbreak.

2. Indoctrination, instruction, enlightenment, inculcation, qualification, preparation, inurement, familiarization, training, discipline, schooling, edification, guidance, direction.

3. Formal admission into a society, introduction, entrance, reception, admittance, entrée.

INITIATIVE, *n.* 1. First step, introductory act, beginning, lead, leading movement, first move, fresh start, new departure, thin end of the wedge, onset, brunt, outbreak, first blow.

2. Readiness and ability in initiating action, power to originate, enterprise, energy, creativity, leadership, power to begin.

INITIATORY, *adj.* Indroductory, initiative, inceptive, initial, incipient, preliminary, preparatory, rudimental, opening, precursory, prime, prefatory, inaugural, rudimentary, embryonic, primary, primal, original, foremost, first, leading, head, principal, front, chief, maiden.

INJECT, *v.* Insert, introduce, force in, interject, lug in, throw in, intromit, instill, impregnate, inoculate, vaccinate, immit, put into, infuse, infix, imbue, thrust in, ram in, stick in, drive in, pierce, press in.

INJECTION, *n.* Insertion, implantation, introduction, infusion, impregnation, inoculation, vaccination, hypodermic, hypo *(colloq.),* clyster, enema, lavement, immission.

INJUDICIOUS, *adj.* Showing lack of judgment, inconsiderate, ill-advised, ill-judged, imprudent, impolitic, improvident, indiscreet, unwise, unreasoned, blind, inexpedient, incautious, rash, hasty, foolish, temerarious, unreasonable, stupid, silly, asinine, heedless, uncalculating, wild, wanton, madcap, devil-may-care, hot-headed, headlong, precipitate, foolhardy, impulsive, impetuous, harebrained, breakneck.

INJUNCTION, *n.* Judicial order restraining from action, command, precept, admonition, mandate, imposition, bidding, requirement, direction, behest, exhortation, regulation, ordinance, commandment, dictation, ruling, instructions, charge, act, fiat, exaction, demand, dictate, decree, writ, rescript, caveat, prescript, ordination, decretal, prescription, enactment.

INJURE, *v.* 1. Cause harm to, damage, hurt, harm, wound, impair, spoil, mar, do harm to, disfigure, sully, stain, blemish, deface, maim, lame, bruise, cripple, mangle, deform, mutilate, leave a scar, lacerate, scathe, despoil, stab, pierce, hamstring, warp.

2. Maltreat, abuse, misuse, ill-treat, wrong, outrage, dishonor, degrade, vitiate, molest, violate, do wrong to, treat unjustly, do an ill office to,

affront, insult, slander, offend, calumniate, defame, vilify, malign, blacken, denigrate, brand, asperse, libel, traduce, disparage, detract from, debase, deprave, adulterate, tamper with, doctor, subvert, pervert, brutalize, demoralize, taint, corrupt, infect, poison, contaminate, canker, pollute, blight, defile, endamage, aggrieve, grind, oppress, persecute, harass, harry, overrun, ravage, pillage.

INJURIOUS, *adj.* 1. Harmful, hurtful, destructive, baneful, deleterious, detrimental, pernicious, deadly, lethal, noxious, fatal, damaging, ruinous, evil, prejudicial, disadvantageous, mischievous, pestiferous, pestilential, felonious, facinorous, malefic, dire, fell, maleficent, malign, disastrous, calamitous, perverse, grievous.

2. Iniquitous, wrong, wrongful, unjust, inequitable, abusive, adverse, corrupt, vicious, depraved, nefarious, bad, villainous, sinister.

3. Slanderous, libelous, detractory, derogatory, defamatory, offensive, insulting, abusive, contumelious, false and malicious.

INJURY, *n.* 1. Harm done or sustained, damage, hurt, detriment, wound, contusion, mutilation, bruise, blemish, cut, scar, defacement, disfigurement, lesion, scratch, gash, stab, laceration, mortal blow, deformation, havoc, ravage, inroad, discoloration, contamination, canker, corruption, pollution, wear and tear, disintegration, dilapidation, decay, decomposition, corrosion, erosion, dry rot, atrophy, blight.

2. Wrong done, injustice, outrage, enormity, atrocity, foul play, evil, ill, calamity, bale, woe, bane, misfortune, adversity, fatal mischief, disaster, catastrophe, ruin, ruination, undoing, abuse, ill-treatment, misuse, violation, indignity, vitiation, insult, affront, grievance, perversion, depravation, debasement, degradation, violence, offense, felony, rape, molestation, assault, attack, ravishment, defilement, defloration, constupration, devirgination, tort, iniquity.

3. Mischief, trouble, disadvantage, impairment, prejudice, calamity, slander, defamation, detraction, aspersion, calumny, vilification, obloquy, libel, scandal.

INJUSTICE, *n.* 1. Unfairness, inequity, unjust character, inequitable character, partiality, onesidedness, prejudice, bigotry, bias, favoritism, inequality, nepotism, unrighteousness, partisanship, leaning, prepossession.

2. Piece of injustice, injury, foul play, wrong, infringement, hardship, grievance, oppression, persecution, tyranny, cruelty, encroachment, imposition, offense, iniquity, sin, evil, guilt, misdoing, malpractice, obliquity, tort, crime, villainy, rascality, roguery, transgression.

INKHORN, *n.* Small container of horn used to hold writing ink, inkwell, inkpot, inkstand, inkbottle.

INKLING, *n.* Slight suggestion, hint, whisper, intimation, suspicion, soupçon, glimmering, innuendo, insinuation, vague idea, faint notion, supposition, cue, tip, pointer, surmise, association of ideas, glimpse.

INKY, *adj.* Black as ink, atramentous, swart, swarthy, murky, raven, ebon, pitchy, jetty, jetblack, sable, fuliginous, sooty, coal-black.

INLAID, *adj.* Made with a design set in the surface, decorated with inlaid work, mosaic, tessellated, vermiculated, chequered, daedal, enameled, worked, ornamental.

INLAND, *adj.* 1. Interior, upcountry, midland, hinterland, backwoods, internal.

2. Carried on within a country, domestic, native, not foreign, homebred, home, intraterritorial.

INLAY, *v.* Decorate with veneers of fine materials set in the surface of an object, adorn with inserted material, apply layers of fine materials in a surface, arrange in mosaic pattern, checker, tessellate, vermiculate, hatch, embed, enchase, marquet, execute buhlwork, tool, emboss, fret, work, damascene, tattoo.

INLET, *n.* 1. Long and narrow indentation of a shore line, arm, channel, bay, waterway, cove, bight, watercourse, arm of the sea, estuary, frith, fiord, bayou, creek, gulf, narrow passage between islands, strait, recess, nook, firth.

2. Entrance, place of ingress, orifice, opening, mouth, path, door, way.

INMATE, *n.* 1. One who dwells within, dweller, occupant, occupier, denizen, guest, intern, inhabitant, residentiary, resident, indweller, boarder, lodger, paying guest, tenant, incumbent, renter, sojourner, commorant, roomer, habitant.

2. One confined in a hospital or prison, patient, valetudinary, bedlamite, prisoner, jailbird, captive, case, subject, sufferer, invalid.

INMOST, *adj.* 1. Situated furthest within, deepest, innermost, most inward, visceral, intestinal, deep inside.

2. Most intimate, close, bosom, confidential, secret, esoteric, deep-seated, deep-rooted, to the inmost core, to the quick, ingrained, inherent, intrinsic, intraregarding, deep-musing, introspective.

INN, *n.* 1. Small hotel, public house for travelers, hostelry, hostel, lodging house, rest house, caravansary, khan, serai, dak bungalow, choultry, hospice.

2. Tavern, bar, cabaret, pub, saloon, roadhouse, barroom, speak-easy, bistro, alehouse, public house, house of entertainment, *auberge (Fr.)*, *posada (Sp.)*, *albergo (It.)*, *Wirtshaus (Ger.)*, *Gasthof (Ger.)*, café, eating house, chophouse, restaurant, grill room, coffeehouse, buffet, canteen, *estaminet (Fr.)*, night club.

INNATE, *adj.* Existing in one from birth, congenital, inborn, inbred, indigenous, constitutional, natural, native, instinctive, inherent, inherited, organic, ingenerate, ingrained, essential, immanent, radical, intrinsic, interior, transcendental, inward, indwelling, subsistent, inwrought, infixed.

INNER, *adj.* 1. Situated farther within, interior, internal, inside, inward, within, intestinal, visceral.

2. More intimate, more secret, more private, not obvious, esoteric.

3. Mental, spiritual, psychic, psychological.

INNERMOST, *adj.* Farthest inward, inmost, most inward, deepest, deep-seated, ingrained, deep-rooted, to the inmost core, to the quick, inwoven, infixed.

INNKEEPER, *n.* Mine host, tavern keeper, host, innholder, landlord, hotel keeper, hosteler, victualer, *restaurateur (Fr.)*, khansamah, boniface.

INNOCENCE, *n.* 1. Harmlessness, innocuousness, inoffensiveness, innoxiousness, blamelessness, guilelessness, artlessness, simplicity, naiveté, ingenuousness, lack of sophistication.

2. Chastity, purity, freedom from sin or moral wrong, sinlessness, guiltlessness, stainlessness, spotlessness, impeccability, immaculateness, incorruption, clear conscience, clean hands.

INNOCENT, *adj.* 1. Harmless, innocuous, inoffensive, innoxious, safe, hurtless, inculpable, inerrable, unoffending, unerring.

2. Free from moral wrong, not tainted with sin, sinless, virtuous, chaste, virginal, pure, spotless, clean, immaculate, impeccable, blameless, guiltless, faultless, clear, upright, unblemished, exemplary, irreproachable, righteous, undefiled, uncorrupted, unstained, stainless, unsullied, unimpeachable, above suspicion.

3. Having the naiveté of an unworldly person, naive, unsophisticated, guileless, artless, ingenuous, simple, open, frank, childlike, sincere, honest, candid, unsuspicious.

4. Legal, legitimate, lawful, permitted, warrantable, rightful, unprohibited, right, not contraband.

5. Destitute, devoid, lacking, wanting, unprovided, void.

INNOVATE, *v.* Make changes in anything established, make innovations, introduce novelties, break from precedent, modernize, turn over a new leaf, introduce new blood, revolutionize, depart from the old, make a drastic change, neoterize, neologize.

INNOVATION, *n.* Introduction of novelty, breaking of precedent, violent departure from the old, radically new measure, novelty, introduction of new things, drastic change, variation, alteration, diversion, novation, deviation, shift, neoterism, renovation, modernism, modernization, latest fashion, *dernier cri (Fr.)*, latest thing.

INNUENDO, *n.* Indirect derogatory intimation about a person, remote allusion, insinuation, oblique hint, defamatory words, sly suggestion, implication, whisper, inkling, word in the ear, passing word, cue, gentle hint, broad hint, *verbum sapienti (Lat.)*, word to the wise, animadversion, stricture, reflection, criticism, sardonic grin, left-handed compliment.

INNUMERABLE, *adj.* Countless, numberless, very numerous, myriad, incapable of being counted, that cannot be numbered, legionary, incalculable, untold, incomputable, infinite, very many, unnumbered.

INOCULATE, *v.* 1. Implant a disease in a person by the introduction of virus in order to produce a mild form of the disease and thus secure immunity, vaccinate, infect, immunize, introduce microorganisms into surroundings suited to their growth.

2. Imbue a person with ideas, instill, infuse, impregnate, imbrue, inculcate, indoctrinate, implant.

INOCULATION, *n.* 1. Insertion of virus in order to produce immunity, vaccination, injection, infection, ovination.

2. Infusion, impregnation, imbruement, inculcation, indoctrination, implantation.

INOFFENSIVE, *adj.* Doing no harm, harmless, innocuous, innoxious, unoffending, not being a cause of offense, unobjectionable, innocent, peaceable, non-provocative, quiet, offenseless, unobnoxious.

INOPERATIVE, *adj.* 1. Not operative, not in operation, not in effect, not in force.

2. Without effect, ineffectual, inefficacious, ineffective, of no effect, useless, inutile, futile, unavailing, effectless, bootless, null and void, nuga-

tory, defunct, dud, good for nothing, abortive, issueless, fruitless, unproductive, addle, barren, arid, sterile, unprolific, infecund, unfruitful, fallow.

INOPPORTUNE, *adj.* Not opportune, unseasonable, out of season, untimely, mistimed, ill-timed, badly timed, unpunctual, too late for, premature, too soon for, wise after the event, inexpedient, inconvenient, malapropos, inappropriate, untoward, unseemly, unfavorable, unfortunate, unpropitious, inauspicious, unlucky, ill-starred, inadvisable, undesirable, unsuitable, unfit, unsuited, objectionable, amiss, inapt, ineligible, inadmissible, disadvantageous, troublesome, discommodious, incommodious, ill-advised, impolitic.

INORDINATE, *adj.* Not within proper limits, excessive, overmuch, undue, superfluous, unnecessary, intemperate, immoderate, exorbitant, extravagant, prodigal, lavish, exuberant, nimious, superabundant, profuse, overflowing, replete, overcharged, redundant, crammed, supersaturated, drenched, filled to overflowing, in excess, to spare, over and above, *de trop (Fr.),* supernumerary, supervacaneous, adscititious, supererogatory, needless, unreasonable, uncalled for, unrestrained, *un peu fort (Fr.),* overweening, fabulous, unlimited, on one's hands.

INORGANIC, *adj.* 1. Not having the organization which characterizes living bodies, unorganized, disorganic, mineral, lithoidal, lithoid.

2. Not characterized by vital processes, dead, inanimate, azoic.

3. Not fundamental, unessential, extraneous, irregular, abnormal.

INQUEST, *n.* Judicial inquiry before a jury, legal investigation by a coroner, search into facts, examination, prosecution, trial, interrogation, inquisition, quest, questioning, percontation, quiz, catechism, cross-examination, cross-interrogation.

INQUIETUDE, *n.* Restlessness, uneasiness, restiveness, impatience, nervousness, trepidation, flutter, perturbation, disturbance, anxiety, solicitude, concern, care, apprehension, misgiving, disquietude, disquiet, fear and trembling, palpitation, heart-sinking, funk, qualm, suspicion, mistrust, vexation of spirit, discontent, querulousness, heartburning, unrest, discomposure, annoyance, trouble, brooding, calm before the storm, malaise, dysphoria, fidgeting, dissatisfaction.

INQUIRE, *v.* 1. Make inquiry about, seek information by questioning, ask about, seek to learn by asking, interrogate, catechize, query, question, pump, cross-question, grill, put through the third degree, cross-interrogate, interpellate, cross-examine, quiz, address another to obtain information, solicit, demand.

2. Study, look over, inspect, investigate, examine, scrutinize, look into, explore, probe, seek, search, cast about, dip into, sound, fathom, scan, reconnoiter, scour, rummage, pry, ransack, overhaul, rake, look round, peer, spy, survey, pursue, look behind the scenes, hunt out, track down, ferret out, nose out, unearth, angle for, fish out, trace, trail, shadow, leave no stone unturned, sift, thresh out, winnow.

INQUIRY, *n.* 1. Interrogation, enquiry, query, question, quiz, catechism, third degree, cross-examination, cross-interrogation, interpellation, interrogatory, request, problem, point in dispute, issue, poser, moot point, question at issue.

2. Examination, investigation, scrutiny, explo-

ration, search, quest, pursuit, hunt, research, percontation, trial, study, test, assay, inspection, review, survey, reconnaissance, consideration, analysis, inquest, ventilation, titration, lantern of Diogenes.

INQUISITION, *n.* 1. Act of inquiring, research, search, exploration, examination, investigation, inquest, inquiry.

2. Roman Catholic tribunal for the judgment of heresy and the application of canonical punishment, the Holy Office.

INQUISITIVE, *adj.* 1. Given to inquiring, eager for knowledge, research-minded, given to research, scholarly, searching, scrutinizing, inquisitorial, inquiring, curious, fond of investigation, analytic, investigative, interrogative, zetetic, percontatorial, questioning.

2. Unduly curious, burning with curiosity, overcurious, nosey, meddling, intrusive, meddlesome, prying, peeping, eavesdropping, mousing, peering, agape, expectant.

INROAD, *n.* 1. Forcible encroachment, serious infringement, forcible entry, hostile ingress, predatory incursion, invasion, irruption, illapse, intrusion, introgression, raid, foray, sally, *camisade (Fr.),* sortie, drive, offensive, attack, assault, onslaught, aggression, charge, infiltration, interpenetration.

2. Havoc, outrage, scath, ravage, injury, damage, detriment, impairment, loss.

INSALUBRIOUS, *adj.* Unhealthful, unhealthy, unfavorable to health, innutritious, indigestible, uncongenial, unwholesome, toxic, poisonous, narcotic, virulent, envenomed, venomous, deleterious, pestilential, pestiferous, pestilent, mephitic, noxious, noisome, foul, morbiferous, morbific, septic, azotic, pernicious.

INSANE, *adj.* Not of sound mind, mentally deranged, crazy, demented, crazed, mad, maniacal, lunatic, disordered, daft, cracked, touched, bereft of reason, *non compos mentis (Lat.),* unsound, out of one's mind, out of one's wits, maddened, moonstruck, stark staring mad, paranoiac, psychotic, manic, schizophrenic, beside oneself, off one's rocker *(slang),* out of one's head, unhinged, frenzied, frenetic, wandering, delirious, distracted, rambling, light-headed, incoherent, driveling, raving, off one's head, wild, rabid, fanatical, crackbrained, crackpot, infatuated, mad as a March hare, mad as a hatter, having bats in one's belfry, nutty *(slang),* queer, insensate, idiosyncratic, eccentric, wild-eyed, utterly senseless, fatuous, imbecile, idiotic, foolish, simple-minded, unusual, bizarre, quixotic, absurd.

INSANITY, *n.* Derangement of psychical function due to disease of the mind, dementia, paranoia, mania, monomania, psychosis, schizophrenia, lunacy, madness, dissociated mental activity, mental alienation, aberration of mind, loss of reason, craziness, mental illness, mental unsoundness, fugue *(Psychol.),* delirium, frenzy, hallucination, amentia, bellamism, delirium tremens, oenomania, *mania a potu (Lat.),* blue devils, pink spiders, snakes in the boots, gallon distemper, the horrors, bats in the belfry, idiocy, imbecility, raving, wandering, light-headedness, delusion, obsession, craze, infatuation, fanaticism, eccentricity, quixotism, oddity, twist, jimjams, extreme folly, fatuousness.

INSATIABLE, *adj.* Incapable of being satisfied, insatiate, unsatisfied, unsated, unappeasable, ravenous, voracious, omnivorous, hungry, famished, ravening, sharp-set, peckish, craving, thirsty, unquenchable, dry, athirst, droughty, parched, arid, greedy, rapacious, covetous, grasping, avaricious, avid, exacting, sordid, extortionate.

INSCRIBE, *v.* 1. Mark with characters in a durable way, letter, write words, engrave signs, emblaze, imprint, impress, indorse, pen, scrawl, scribble, scratch, scrabble, scriven, write down, set down, note down, write on, pen, delineate, take pen in hand, take up the pen, dash off, dedicate informally by a handwritten note, address as a literary work, autograph, sign.

2. Enroll on an official list, enter, register, record, tally, list, inventory, tabulate, catalogue, schedule, calendar, index, file, book, docket, slate, post, manifest, draft, bill, invoice, census, poll.

INSCRIPTION, *n.* Indorsement, engrossment, dash of the pen, stroke of the pen, *coup de plume* (*r.r.*), autograph, signature, handwriting, dedication, legend, record, address, writing, entry, memorandum, testimonial, deposition, memento, memorial, epitaph, exergue.

INSCRUTABLE, *adj.* Incapable of being searched into, not able to be scrutinized, impenetrable to investigation, inexplicable, incognizable, incomprehensible, unfathomable, unsearchable, undiscoverable, unknowable, above comprehension, past comprehension, not to be understood, enigmatic, puzzling, baffling, ambiguous, hidden, insoluble, mysterious, unintelligible, occult, unaccountable, unrevealed, concealed, poker-faced, dead-pan, sphinx-eyed.

INSCRUTABLENESS, *n.* Incomprehensibleness, incomprehensibility, inscrutability, impenetrability, inexplicability, imperspicuity, unintelligibility, unsearchableness, unfathomableness, inconceivableness, obscurity, vagueness, uncertainty, perplexity, spinosity, mystification, mystery, mysteriousness, ambiguity, doubtful meaning, confusion, latency, transcendentalism, poker face, dead-pan, sphinx, Mona Lisa smile.

INSECT, *n.* 1. Animal of the subphylum or class *Insecta,* small air-breathing arthropod with a body clearly divided into three parts (head, thorax and abdomen) and with three pairs of legs and two pairs of wings, ephemerid, ephemera, bug, hexapod, winged creature, horrid little thing (*colloq.*).

2. Fly, gnat, flea, mosquito, bee, queen bee, honeybee, worker, drone, wasp, locust, cricket, grasshopper, beetle, moth, butterfly, arachnid, spider, ant, termite, emmet, pismire, weevil, louse, vermin, earwig, cockroach, bedbug, thousandlegger, silverfish, water bug, bluebottle fly, dragonfly, mite, grub, larva, caterpillar, worm.

INSECTICIDE, *n.* Preparation used for killing insects, insect powder, poison spray, Pyrethrum flowers, cyanide, hydrocyanic acid, strychnine, arsenic, DDT.

INSECURE, *adj.* 1. Not free from doubt, not sure, uncertain, not confident, doubtful, dubious, undecided, unsettled, in question, problematical, ambiguous, enigmatic, perplexing, apocryphal, hypothetical, indefinite, vague, Q. E. D., unauthenticated, unauthoritative, not guaranteed, unconfirmed, in a state of uncertainty, on the horns of a dilemma, at a nonplus, puzzled, astray, *désorienté (Fr.)*, adrift, at sea, at a loss.

2. Not free from fear, perilous, dangerous, hazardous, risky, parlous, at stake, precarious, aleatory, ticklish, risky, critical, on the verge of a precipice, on slippery ground, under fire, between two fires, not out of the wood, between Scylla and Charybdis, in the lion's den.

3. Endangered, unprotected, defenseless, guardless, unshielded, expugnable, open to, at bay, *aux abois (Fr.)*, vulnerable, unsheltered, exposed, unsafe, in danger, ill-protected.

4. Weak, infirm, shaky, tumbledown, ramshackle, dilapidated, crumbling, shaking, wobbly, tottering, frail, rickety, not firm, topheavy, unstable, untrustworthy, unsteady, unreliable, built upon sand, slippery, waterlogged, hanging by a thread, in a bad way, nodding to its fall.

INSECURITY, *n.* 1. Uncertainty, incertitude, lack of sureness, lack of assurance, doubt, doubtfulness, dubiety, dubiousness, dubitancy, hesitation, perplexity, puzzlement, bewilderment, quandary, dilemma, indecision, indetermination, vacillation, vagueness, ambiguity, obscurity, fog, haze, open question, contingency, instability, leap in the dark, pig in a poke, blind bargain, something or other, *onus probandi (Lat.)*, fallibility, untrustworthiness, unreliability.

2. Danger, peril, risk, jeopardy, venture, hazard, stakes, endangerment, precariousness, slipperiness, exposure, defenselessness, vulnerability, heel of Achilles, hairbreadth escape, storm brewing, gathering clouds, clouds on the horizon, breakers ahead, source of danger, cause for alarm.

INSENSATE, *adj.* 1. Not endowed with sensation, insensible, insentient, non-percipient, destitute of perception, unperceiving, unconscious, inanimate, insusceptible, impassive, unimpressible, unimpressionable.

2. Indifferent, torpid, dull, unfeeling, without feeling, callous, hardened, hard, thick-skinned, pachydermatous, proof, casehardened, inured, lethargic, apathetic, numb, dead to.

3. Without understanding, without judgment, stupid, foolish, heavy, obtuse, insulse, destitute of sense, doltish, Boeotian, asinine, prosaic, fatuous, fat-headed, irrational, inept, unwise, senseless, brutish, thoughtless, nonsensical, sottish.

INSENSIBILITY, *n.* 1. Suspension of consciousness, unconsciousness, stupor, sleep, coma, narcosis, anaesthesia, hypnosis, anaesthetization, senselessness.

2. Unfeelingness, insensibleness, insentience, insensitiveness, numbness, induration, absence of feeling, absence of sensation.

3. Dullness, obtuseness, torpor, torpidity, inactivity, sluggishness, stolidity, apathy, lethargy, torpor, stupidity, incuriosity, indifference, callousness, impassibility, insusceptibility.

INSENSIBLE, *adj.* 1. Incapable of feeling or perceiving, deprived of sensation, unconscious, sleeping, asleep, anesthetized, hypnotized, numb, unfeeling, insentient, comatose, stupefied.

2. Void of feeling, not susceptible of emotion, unresponsive in feeling, not subject to a particular feeling, insensate, torpid, apathetic, indifferent, phlegmatic, insensitive, callous, hard, hardened, pachydermatous, thick-skinned, case-hardened, obtuse, proof, lethargic, dull, cold, frigid, coldhearted, cold-blooded, unemotional, stolid, brutish, stupid, unsusceptible, unimpressible, impassive, unmoved, untouched, unaffected, obdurate.

INSENTIENT, *adj.* Without feeling, destitute of sensation, without perception, insensate, unperceiving, insensible, non-sentient, senseless, inert, inanimate, unconscious, non-percipient, unsusceptible.

INSEPARABLE, *adj.* 1. Incapable of being parted, that cannot be disjoined, not to be separated, indivisible, indissoluble, indissolvable, unsunderable, not to be severed, inseparable.

2. Constantly together, extremely intimate, bosom, always in each other's company, inveterate, devoted, attached, dear, close, confidential, chummy, special, faithful, trusty, ever present.

INSERT, *v.* 1. Put in, introduce, inlay, imbed, inweave, inject, interpolate, interject, parenthesize, intercalate, inset, interlineate, interpage, infix, impregnate, imbue, inoculate, instill, infuse, intrude, intervene, set in, place in, put between, intromit, wedge in, intersperse, interlard, slide in.

2. Thrust in, obtrude, ram in, stick in, press in, stuff in, drive in, tuck in, pierce, pop in, whip in, hammer in, impact, empierce.

3. Ingraft, graft, implant, bud, inarch, plant, dovetail, splice, mortise, ingrain, infiltrate, insinuate.

4. Make an entry of, book, list, enroll, docket, inscroll, file, enter.

INSIDE, *n.* 1. Inner space within something, interior part, interior, inner part, interspace, inner side, inner surface.

2. Contents, pith, substance, marrow, inward parts, heart, breast, bosom, abdomen, vitals, entrails, viscera, bowels, intestines, belly, chitterlings, guts, womb, cell, gland, internal organs, endocrines, penetralia, innermost recesses, concavity.

3. Inward nature, internal thoughts, private feelings.

INSIDE, *adj.* 1. Situated on the inside, being in the inside, internal, interior, intimate, inner, inward, inmost, innermost, deep-seated, endocrinal, endocrinic, endocrinous, visceral, intestinal, subcutaneous.

2. Indoor, home, intramural, domestic, vernacular, enclosed, inwrought.

3. Derived from the inner circle of those having private knowledge of a case, confidential, esoteric, private.

INSIDE, *prep.* Inside of, in the interior of, within, into the interior of, within the interior of.

INSIDIOUS, *adj.* 1. Intending to entrap or beguile, stealthily treacherous, wily, crafty, sly, cunning, arch, artful, guileful, subtle, subdolous, deceitful, designing, treacherous, intriguing, foxy, tricky, crooked, snaky, Machiavellian, covinous, delusive, feline, vulpine, contriving, politic, diplomatic, strategic, underhand, double-tongued, shrewd, pawky, canny, false-hearted, dark, slippery, shady, fishy, questionable, perfidious, disingenuous.

2. Proceeding inconspicuously but with grave effect, stealthy, furtive, surreptitious, sneaking, undetected.

INSIGHT, *n.* Penetrating mental vision, faculty of seeing into inner character or underlying truth, discernment, perception, penetration, perspicuity, intuition, spontaneous understanding, penetrating judgment, quick vision, clairvoyance, sagacity, introspection, acumen, immediate apprehension, immediate cognition, *Anschauung (Ger.),* innate knowledge, intuitiveness, instinctive knowledge, perceptivity, perspicacity, perceptiveness, presentiment, inspiration, divination, cryptaesthesia.

INSIGNIA, *n., pl.* 1. Insigne *(sing.),* distinguishing marks of honor, badges of office, marks of authority, regalia, decorations, ensigns of royalty, emblems, signs, symbols, tokens, signa, castemark, tilka *(Hindu),* paraphernalia.

2. Oak leaf, bar, star, Sam Browne belt, eagle, shoulder knot, shoulder strap, aiguillette, *fourragère (Fr.),* crown *(Brit.),* epaulet, stripe, chevron, medal.

INSIGNIFICANCE *n.* 1. Unimportance, nullity, paltriness, pettiness, nonentity, triviality, worthlessness, meanness, contemptibleness, trashiness, vileness, poorness, smallness, emptiness, nothingness, immateriality, matter of indifference, side issue, no object, nothing particular, nothing worth speaking of, nothing to boast of, nothing to write home about, nothing to speak of, trifling matter, no great matter, mere nothing, *peu de chose (Fr.),* no great shakes, cipher, figurehead, child's play, small beer, joke, jest, snap of the fingers, fiddlestick, nine days' wonder, flash in the pan, *ridiculus mus (Lat.),* storm in a teacup, much ado about nothing, mole hill, fleabite, drop in the ocean, drop in a bucket, feather in the scale, dust in the balance.

2. Plaything, bagatelle, toy, popgun, gimcrack, bauble, gewgaw, trinket, knicknack, kickshaw, whimwham, trifle, trash, trumpery, rubbish, frippery, stuff, froth, chaff, bubble, pin, straw, fig, continental, feather, button, halfpenny, farthing, rap, jot, iota, pinch of snuff, minutiae, finglefangle, small fry.

INSIGNIFICANT, *adj.* 1. Petty, small, unimportant, trivial, paltry, inconsiderable, contemptible, trifling, of little account, of no moment, of no consequence, unessential, immaterial, inferior, picayune, picayunish, worthless, vile, base, mean, trashy, sorry, pitiable, scurvy, flashy, tawdry, gaudy, flimsy, gimcrack, two-by-four, one-horse, third-rate, second-rate, small potatoes, piddling, puny, nominal, meager, humble, unpretentious, modest, so-so, inappreciable, nugatory, non-essential, not vital, incidental, irrelevant, indifferent, frivolous, niggling, twopenny-halfpenny, cheap, catchpenny, not worth the pains, not worth mentioning, not worth speaking of, not worth a rap, not worth a straw, beneath consideration.

2. *(Of persons)* Of no influence or distinction, nonentitative, nonentitive, nondescript, without weight of character.

INSINCERE, *adj.* Not honest in the expression of actual feeling, disingenuous, hypocritical, dishonest, two-faced, evasive, pharisaical, double-tongued, dissembling, dissimulating, deceitful, false, untrue, faithless, uncandid, hollow, guileful, double-hearted, lying, smooth-tongued, empty, fraudulent, untruthful, mendacious, treacherous, perfidious, perjured, forsworn, canting, tartuffish, mealy-mouthed.

INSINCERITY, *n.* Deceitfulness, hypocrisy, disingenuousness, duplicity, falseness, dissimulation, dishonesty, bad faith, faithlessness, pretense, lip service, guile, hollowness, emptiness, double-dealing, cant, pharisaism, Machiavellism, casuistry, mere show, mealy-mouthedness, flattery, buncombe, perfidy, Judas kiss, cunning, flimflam, dissembling, sham, profession, malingering, false coloring, prevarication, untruthfulness, mendacity, perjury, guilefulness, deception, misrepresentation, untruthfulness, perversion, exaggeration, distortion, suppression, mental reservation, equivocation, evasiveness, evasion.

INSINUATE, *v.* 1. Hint slyly, intimate, suggest something unfavorable or discreditable, allude remotely to, whisper, imply, indicate, breathe, let fall, give a pointer to, tip off, let out of the bag, prompt, tip the wink, give the cue, give the lowdown, give inside information.

2. Curry favor with, ingratiate, push artfully, propitiate, worm one's way into the favor of, bring into a position by indirect methods, fool to the top of one's bent, butter up, soft-soap, jolly, fawn upon, humor, court, truckle to, pander to.

3. Instill artfully, infuse subtly, introduce gently, insert, inculcate, inject, import, implant, infiltrate.

INSIPID, *adj.* 1. Without sufficient taste to be pleasing, tasteless, unsavory, savorless, stale, gustless, flat, vapid, mawkish, unflavored, weak, *fade (Fr.),* watery, milk-and-water, wishy-washy, aqueous.

2. Without interesting or attractive qualities, uninteresting, prosaic, pointless, prosy, dull, tame, dead, lifeless, spiritless, stupid, heavy, unentertaining, monotonous, jejune, barren, arid, sterile, meager, thin, lean, characterless, wearisome, unanimated, banal, trite, commonplace, hackneyed.

INSIPIDITY, *n.* 1. Tastelessness, insipidness, unsavoriness, vapidness, staleness, mawkishness, flatness, lack of zest, weakness, wateriness.

2. Dullness, monotonousness, prosiness, tameness, heaviness, uninteresting character, lifelessness, lack of interest, platitudinousness, banalness, stupidity, triteness.

INSIST, *v.* Urge, demand persistently, maintain, hold, be pertinacious, be firm, be emphatic, stress, emphasize, lay stress on, enforce, lay down the law, assert positively, dwell with earnestness, contend, pronounce, claim, press earnestly, pound the table, take a firm stand, persist, stick to one's colors, stand one's ground, require, enforce, command, solicit, importune, push, preach, repeat, persevere.

INSISTENCE, *n.* Persistent urgency, importunity, urging, solicitousness, pertinacity, persistency, contention, determination, solicitation, asseveration, assurance, swearing, emphasis, positiveness, peremptoriness, determination, iron will, resolution, firmness, intransigence, perseverance, tenacity, obstinacy, continuance, tenacity of purpose, iteration, harping, repetition, ding-dong, enforcement, compulsion, pressure, constraint, coercion, necessity, necessitation, obligation.

INSISTENT, *adj.* Earnest in dwelling upon something, emphatic in making a demand, peremptory, importunate, compelling attention, insisting on notice, bent upon, serious, intent upon, tenacious, not to be put down, contentious, inexorable, coercive, coactive, not to be trifled with, emphatic, positive, absolute, confident, assertive, trenchant, categorical, decided, marked, dogmatic, solemn, formal, argumentative, polemical, commanding, imperative, decretive, jussive, decisive, iterative, repeated, repetitional, recurrent, incessant, harping, monotonous, habitual, resurgent.

INSOBRIETY, *n.* Drunkenness, inebriety, intemperance, crapulousness, intoxication, inebriation, drinking, inebriosity, temulency, befuddlement, bibacity, winebibbing, compotation, dipsomania, oenomania, alcoholism, libations.

INSOLENCE, *n.* 1. Overbearing contempt, overbearance, haughty disrespect, insulting rudeness, arrogance, haughtiness, airs, domineering, swagger, bluster, bumptiousness, toploftiness, intrusiveness, presumption, assumption, insult, contumely, disdain, oppression, abuse, affront.

2. Pertness, impertinence, malapertness, sauciness, incivility, flippancy, unmannerliness, sauce, cheekiness, cheek, lip, impoliteness, gall, nerve, front, face, hardihood, effrontery, impudence, shamelessness, boldness, brazenness, freshness, audacity, assurance, self-assertion, brass, forwardness, insulting disobedience, insubordination, contumacy.

INSOLENT, *adj.* 1. Arrogant, haughty, toplofty, magisterial, overbearing, high and mighty, imperious, arbitrary, dictatorial, high-handed, domineering, overweening, blustering, intolerant, bumptious, swaggering, supercilious, hectoring, devil-may-care, pococurante, roistering, rollicking, abusive, oppressive, insulting, foul-mouthed, scurrilous, ribald, opprobrious.

2. Impudent, impertinent, pert, malapert, cheeky, saucy, nervy, fresh, rude, flippant, intrusive, unmannerly, impolite, meddlesome, disrespectful, audacious, self-assertive, assuming, presumptuous, immodest, brazen-faced, bold, brazen, shameless, barefaced, lost to shame, unabashed, unblushing, outrageous, defiant.

INSOLUBLE, *adj.* 1. Incapable of being dissolved, that cannot be liquefied, not able to be melted, irreducible, indissolvable, indissoluble, irresoluble, unthawable, infusible.

2. That cannot be solved, inexplicable, insolvable, not to be explained, unintelligible, incomprehensible, enigmatic, puzzling, riddling, undecipherable, unaccountable, unfathomable, unknowable, undiscoverable, incognizable, inscrutable, impenetrable, paradoxical, unexplained, shrouded in mystery, ambiguous, undetermined, mysterious.

INSOLVENCY, *n.* Bankruptcy, involuntary liquidation, failure, overdrawn account, run upon a bank, dishonored bills, non-payment, default, deferred payment, deficit, arrears, indebtment, score, obligation, liability, pauperism, impecuniosity, loss of fortune, destitution, poverty, penury, indigence, wolf at the door, distress, straits, mendicancy, mendicity, broken fortune, empty pocket.

INSOLVENT, *adj.* Unable to satisfy creditors, incapable of discharging liabilities, not able to pay debts as they mature, bankrupt, ruined, broken, failed, defaulting, destitute, penniless, moneyless, beggared, reduced, straitened, stripped, impoverished, impecunious, in debt, not paying, in arrear, behindhand, worse than nothing, unable to make both ends meet, minus, in the gazette, gazetted, in difficulties, in embarrassed circumstances, plunged head over ears in debt, fast tied up, out of money, flat, broke, involved.

INSOMNIA, *n.* Chronic inability to sleep, sleeplessness, wakefulness, indisposition to sleep, counting sheep, restlessness, *pervigilium (Lat.).*

INSOUCIANCE, *n.* Nonchalance, indifference, unconcern, apathy, recklessness, phlegm, supineness, lukewarmness, sang-froid, dry eyes, callousness, thoughtlessness, heedlessness, negligence, passivity, lackadaisicalness, carelessness, laxness, laxity, pococurantism.

INSOUCIANT, *adj.* Free from concern, without anxiety, nonchalant, passive, lackadaisical, heedless, careless, harebrained, phlegmatic, negligent, lax, carefree, fancy-free, pococurante, indifferent, respectless, harum-scarum, deaf, blind, flighty, giddy, offhand, casual, thoughtless, scatterbrained, apathetic, indifferent, unconcerned, *sans souci (Fr)*, cool as a cucumber, easygoing, devil-may-care, unambitious.

INSPECT, *v.* 1. Look carefully at, view closely and critically, investigate, scrutinize, look into carefully, examine, pry into, regard carefully, scan, reconnoiter, eye, glance over, peer at, pry into, keep watch, pore over, rivet the eyes upon, look intently, gaze, watch, peruse, observe, explore, ransack, search, probe, take stock of.
2. Superintend, survey formally, oversee, supervise, review, regulate.

INSPECTION, *n.* 1. Careful inspecting, critical viewing, examination, investigation, scrutiny, inquiry, perusal, review, regard, survey, contemplation, observation, view, reconnaissance, lookout, watch.
2. Supervision, superintendence, surveillance, oversight.

INSPECTOR, *n.* 1. Observer, beholder, viewer, spectator, looker-on, onlooker, bystander, witness, passer-by, eyewitness, sightseer, caller, visitor.
2. Inquisitor, investigator, inquirer, experimenter, querist, examiner, catechist, scrutineer.
3. Inspecting officer, arbiter, arbitrator, umpire, judge, referee, censor, assessor, reviewer, critic, connoisseur.
4. Superintendent, supervisor, intendant, overseer, overlooker, foreman, boss, surveyor, curator, warden.

INSPIRATION, *n.* 1. Creative impulse, imagination, genius, flight of fancy, creation, imaginativeness, creative thought, invention, originality, imagery, ideality, castle-building, dreaming, golden dream, fire, mind's eye.
2. Divine influence directly and immediately exerted upon the mind of a man, afflatus, theopneusty, frenzy, ecstasy, rhapsody, reverie, revelation, prophecy, flash of truth.
3. Stimulation, uplift, persuasion, encouragement, exhortation, solicitation, dictate, instance, influence, impulse, incitement, incentive, spur, stimulus, goad, whip, fillip, whet, provocative.
4. Lofty mood, exaltation, felicity, enthusiasm, ennobling sentiment, bliss.
5. Breathing, eupnoea, respiration, inhalation, exhalation, expiration.

INSPIRE, *v.* 1. Infuse a quickening or exalting influence into, stimulate to aspiration, exalt, elevate, ennoble, illumine, endow with extraordinary insight, light the torch, fill with genius.
2. Guide or control by divine influence, fill with preternatural knowledge, affect by supernatural influence, instill, infuse, inform, imbue.
3. Influence, prompt, instigate, give rise to, occasion, cause, impel, quicken, animate, embolden, prompt.
4. Inspirit, cheer, enliven, stir, move, arouse, stimulate, exhilarate, rouse, encourage, gladden, interest, impress, excite, affect, reach, touch, strike, fire, enkindle, possess the soul.
5. Take air into the lungs, respire, inhale, exhale, breathe in, draw in the breath, sigh.

INSPIRIT, *v.* Infuse new life into, enliven, quicken, fire, animate, incite, invigorate, stimulate, arouse, rouse, instigate, persuade, cheer, embolden, encourage, hearten, urge, impel, move, console, comfort, solace, gladden, relieve, revive, refresh, strengthen.

INSPISSATE, *v.* Thicken by evaporation, make thick, make dense, make stiff, incrassate, condense, compress, coagulate, congeal, clot, gelatinize, gelatinify, emulsify, jell.

INSPISSATE, *adj.* Inspissated, incrassated, thick, stiffened, condensate, condensed, emulsive, curdled, uliginous, muculent, mucid, gelatinous, mucilaginous, glutinous, albuminous.

IN SPITE OF In disregard of, in defiance of, in the face of, in the teeth of, against the grain, against the current, counter to, in conflict with, *malgré (Fr.)*, despite, nevertheless, nothwithstanding.

INSTABILITY, *n.* Lack of firmness, weakness, liability, insecurity, mutability, fluctuation, irresolution, inconstancy, wavering, vacillation, vicissitude, indecision, uncertainty, oscillation, alternation, changefulness, changeability, unsteadiness, alterableness, alterability, unstableness, fickleness, capriciousness, changeableness, inconsistency, tergiversation, mobility, variability, volatility, mercurialness, fitfulness, flightiness, veering, lubricity, slipperiness, modifiability.

INSTALL, *v.* 1. Place in a position for service or use, fix, set, embed, lodge, insert, locate, station, establish, situate, emplace, localize, arrange, orientate, dispose, plant, root, engraft, allocate, deposit, lay, put, post, quarter, billet, accommodate.
2. Establish in an office, introduce into office, induct, invest, inaugurate, set up, initiate, solemnize, instate, chair, seat, enthrone, crown, coronate, ordinate, ordain, admit.

INSTALLATION, *n.* 1. Placement, placing, location, stationing, establishment, fixation, emplacement, localization, disposition, orientation, arrangement, settlement, lodgement, accommodation, billeting, posting, quartering, deposition, allocation, plantation, planting.
2. Ceremony of induction into an office, inauguration, presentation, installment, induction, solemnization, ordination, crowning, coronation, enthronement, accession.

INSTALLMENT, *n.* Any of several parts in which a sum payable is divided for payment at successive fixed times, part payment, money payable, partial payment, amount due, remittance, stake, successive portion, earnest, handsel, kist *(E. India)*, advance payment, deposit, single portion of something issued by parts at successive times, following chapter, quota, proportion, share, quantum, allotment, section, segment, fragment, division, fraction, subdivision, dividend.

INSTANCE, *n.* 1. A case of anything, example put forth in proof or illustration, exemplification, exemplar, illustration, representative, occasion, specimen, pattern, sample, precedent, object lesson, antecedent, prototype, archetype, criterion, paradigm, guide, canon, type, rule, standard, norm, model.
2. Influence, press, prompting, impulsion, dictate, impulse, exhortation, incitement, importunity, entreaty, impetration, supplication, obtestation, imploration, urgent solicitation, persistent pressure, urgency, instigation, request, suggestion, motive.

INSTANCE, *v.* Cite as an example, exemplify, elucidate, illustrate, explain, quote, bring forward as an example, mention as an instance, adduce, specify, point out, call to attention.

INSTANT, *adj.* 1. Succeeding without any interval of time, direct, abrupt, sudden, prompt, quick, immediate, instantaneous, pronto, subito, subitaneous, rapid, fast, hasty, swift, spry, extempore, forthwith, outright, alert, ready, sharp, slick, smart, lickety-split, expeditious, go-ahead, wide-awake, speedy, pushing.

2. Present, current, now passing, actual, latest, existing, momentary, that is.

3. Pressing, critical, urgent, exigent, importunate, crying, earnest, absorbing

4. Impending, imminent, destined, coming, about to happen, going to happen, to come, in store, at hand, overhanging, near, forthcoming, brewing, that is to be, looming in the distance, in reserve.

INSTANT, *n.* 1. Infinitesimal space of time, split second, moment, smallest conceivable point of time, twinkling, minute, flash, breath, trice, crack, jiffy, twinkling of an eye, *coup (Fr.),* burst, flash of lightning, flick.

2. Point of time now present, specific moment, stroke of time, particular time, moment, hour, epoch, time of day, very minute, very hour, present time.

INSTANTANEOUS, *adj.* Occurring or done in an instant, prompt, immediate, instant, quick, abrupt, sudden, subitaneous, momentary, in a flash, extempore, hasty, speedy, quick as thought, swift, rapid, hurried, precipitate, headlong, cursory, expeditious.

INSTANTANEOUSLY, *adv.* Immediately, at once, promptly, instantly, now, on the instant, on the moment, right away, forthwith, instanter, in a trice, in a jiffy, in no time, in a moment, at a stroke, in less than no time, presto, in a fraction of a second, without delay, anon, straightway, straightaway *(Brit.),* directly, without hesitation, forthright, suddenly, subito, on the spur of the moment, extempore, on the spot, quick as thought, like greased lightning, quick as lightning, like a shot, in the twinkling of an eye, in the same breath, at one jump, *uno saltu (Lat.), per saltum (Lat.),* pronto, eftsoons, all at once, plump, slap, in one's tracks, at the same instant, at one fell swoop, slapdash, full-tilt, just then, on the dot, before you could say Jack Robinson, before you could turn around, amain, apace, posthaste, with speed, in haste, urgently, presently.

INSTATE, *v.* Put into a certain position, establish, induct, install, invest, inaugurate, chair, seat, enthrone, crown, coronate.

INSTAURATION, *n.* Restoration, restoral, replacement, repair, renovation, reparation, reconstruction, reconstitution, rehabilitation, redintegration, reorganization, renewal, reinstatement, reestablishment, resuscitation, revival, revivescence, revivification, rejuvenation, rejuvenescence, renascence, regeneration, resurgence, reconversion, resurrection, reclamation, recovery, reproduction, rectification.

INSTEAD, *adv.* In the stead, in the place, in the room, in lieu, as proxy for, as a substitute for, as an alternative, rather, *faute de mieux (Fr.).*

INSTEP, *n.* Arched upper surface of the human foot between the toes and the ankle, arch on the upper surface of the foot, acrotarsium, metatarsus, metatarsal arch.

INSTIGATE, *v.* Prompt to some course, incite to some action, bring about by incitement, foment, induce, actuate, stir up, provoke, agitate, arouse, rouse, set on, impel, urge, tempt, move, influence, prevail upon, persuade, stimulate, encourage, spur on, egg on, goad, predispose, animate, press, sway, entice, exhort, pique, abet, inspire, lobby, bias, incline, carry, whet, motivate, advocate, inveigle, coax, wheedle, suborn, tamper with, whip up, prick, orate from a soap-box, practice demagoguery, use honeyed words.

INSTIGATION, *n.* Incitement to wrongdoing, solicitation, urgency, instance, fomentation, temptation, actuation, motivation, prompting, encouragement, influence, incitation, press, provocation, persuasion, exhortation, advocacy, lobbying, suscitation, galvanism, stimulation, calling forth, inspiration, agitation, animation, perturbation, interest, infection, impressiveness, emotional appeal, soap-box oratory, rabble-rousing, demagoguery, sensationalism, inducement, attraction, magnetism, enticement, *agacerie (Fr.),* allectation, allurement, honeyed words, siren song, voice of the tempter, incentive, spur, stimulus, goad, fillip, whet, provocative.

INSTILL, *v.* Infuse slowly or by degrees into the mind, inject into the feelings, impart gradually, insinuate, disseminate, inspire, diffuse, indoctrinate, impregnate, beat into, teach, train, qualify, coach, prime, infix, ingraft, implant, inculcate, enforce, impress, imbue, instruct, school, tutor, infiltrate, sow the seeds of, propagandize, give an idea of, enlarge the mind, give new ideas, educate, exercise, drill, habituate, familiarize with, impress into the mind.

INSTILLATION, *n.* Insinuation, inculcation, indoctrination, persuasion, propagandism, proselytism, instruction, teaching, edification, education, tutelage, tutorage, preparation, training, schooling, exercitation, implantation, gentle introduction, infusion, injection, importation, inoculation, forcible ingress, insertion.

INSTINCT, *n.* Inborn pattern of activity and response common to a given biological stock, particular natural tendency, innate inclination, natural impulse, prompting, blind impulse, inborn proclivity, native aptitude for something, intuition, association, presentiment, percipience, apperception, intellection, flair, judgment, conception, reason, faculty, natural sense, knowledge, mind, capacity, gift, feel, talent, propensity, penchant, natural intuitive power.

INSTINCT, *adj.* Infused with some active principle, animated from within, informed, imbued, pregnant with, charged with, actuated, inspired, alive, alert, quick, smitten with, stirred, moved.

INSTINCTIVE, *adj.* Prompted by instinct, resulting from instinct, intuitive, intuitional, impulsive, automatic, spontaneous, involuntary, not deliberate, unreflecting, perceptive, inspirational, natural, inherent, innate, inborn, bred in the bone, in the grain, constitutional, running in the blood, characteristic, congenital, indigenous, native, incarnate, immanent, indwelling, ingenerate, ingrained, subjective, idiosyncratic.

INSTITUTE, *v.* 1. Start, begin, inaugurate, initiate, commence, set going, set in operation, set on foot, introduce, bring into use, bring into practice, found, lay the foundation of, broach, occasion, bring on.

2. Originate, found, organize, establish, settle, appoint, set up, uphold, fix, constitute.

3. Enact, formulate, put into effect, systematize, ordain, pass, prescribe.

4. Produce, cause, constitute, compose, get up, accomplish, achieve.

5. Invest with a spiritual charge, establish in a position, invest with the care of souls, consecrate, translate, prefer, call, induct.

INSTITUTE, *n.* 1. Society for carrying on a particular work of educational or scientific character, scientific body, literary association, philosophical society, fraternity, sodality, confraternity, fellowship, unit within a university organized for advanced instruction in a specialized field.

2. The building occupied by such a society, institution devoted to instruction in technical subjects, place of education, academy, institution of learning, seminary, conservatory, gymnasium *(European)*, school, Lyceum, college, alma mater, university, *palaestra (European)*, technical school, polytechnic.

INSTITUTION, *n.* 1. Act of setting up, establishment, foundation, enactment, commencement, beginning, inception, incipience, opening, introduction, inauguration, installation.

2. Organized pattern of group behavior accepted as a fundamental part of a culture, custom, familiar practice, established usage, law, permanent rule, prevalent practice, code, canon, regulation, ordinance, standing order, bylaw, rescript, decree, statute.

3. Organization for the promotion of a particular object, organized society, association, league, alliance, union, fellowship, fraternity, confraternity, sodality, brotherhood.

4. Building devoted to public or educational work, institute, place of education, academy, school, college, university, gymnasium *(European)*, seminary, alma mater, Lyceum, conservatory, *conservatoire (Fr.)*, technical school, polytechnic.

INSTRUCT, *v.* 1. Order, direct, furnish with directions, prescribe to, command, bid, enjoin, charge, dictate, decree, ordain, issue a command, give orders, demand, require, exact, impose, appoint, set, lay out, set to work.

2. Notify, tell, apprise, furnish with information, impart, acquaint, advise, enlighten, communicate, mention, intimate, declare, state, affirm, assert, express, represent, specify, signify, give the low-down, admonish, announce, brief, counsel, convey.

3. Furnish with knowledge by a systematic method, educate, teach, enlighten, inform, tutor, coach, drill, exercise, school, train, indoctrinate, discipline, show how, open the eyes, prime, guide, give lessons in, instill, inculcate, impregnate, disseminate, expound, explain, interpret, lecture, preach, hold forth, ground, qualify, prepare, familiarize with, initiate, practice, catechize.

INSTRUCTION, *n.* 1. Command, order, charge, injunction, precept, advice, counsel, mandate, direction, word to the wise, *verbum sapienti (Lat.)*, recommendation, suggestion, message, bidding, commission, dictate, precept, writ.

2. Practice of instructing, act of teaching, guidance, education, information, indoctrination, tuition, schooling, training, tutoring, coaching, drill, discipline, cultivation, breeding, nurture, propaedeutics, enlightenment, inculcation, tutelage, tutorship, pedagogics, pedagogy, initiation, preparation, qualification, practice, lecture, lesson, harangue, explanation, disquisition, interpretation, imposition, assignment.

INSTRUCTIVE, *adj.* Serving to instruct or inform, doctrinal, didactic, educational, preceptive, edifying, informative, informational, informatory,

conveying knowledge or information, mentorial, academic, scholastic, disciplinary, pedagogical, homiletic, propaedeutic, humanistic, cultural, scientific, naturalistic, psychological, eclectic, vocational, practical, pragmatic, utilitarian.

INSTRUCTOR, *n.* Teacher, pedagogue, tutor, master, preceptor, educator, schoolmaster, trainer, dominie, director, guru *(India)*, lecturer, professor, coryphaeus, coach, don, catechist, counselor, guide, mentor, adviser, propagandist, expounder, expositor, demonstrator, explainer, exponent, spokesman, conductor, director, leader, pilot, cicerone, dragoman, monitor, sage, Solon, Nestor, wise man, arbiter, referee, pundit, Brahmin.

INSTRUMENT, *n.* 1. Agency, agent, medium, means, channel, wherewithal, wherewith, machinery, *matériel (Fr.)*, material supplies, vehicle, equipment, gear, plant, outfit, rigging, tackle, trappings, harness, appointments, accouterments, fittings, furniture, paraphernalia.

2. Thing with which something is effected, mechanical device, machine, implement, tool, appliance, utensil, apparatus, contrivance, mechanism, convenience, engine, motor, automaton, robot, lathe, gin.

3. Formal legal document, charter, writing, indenture, deed, contract, grant, record, paper, note, bond, mortgage, bill, muniment, title, testament, will, codicil, settlement.

4. One who is used by another, cat's-paw, hireling, stooge, puppet, dupe, gudgeon, gull, cully, sucker, victim, pigeon, April fool, simple Simon, stepping stone, go-between, handmaid, servant, dependent, jackal, creature, right hand, tool, satellite, parasite, *âme damnée (Fr.)*.

INSTRUMENTAL, *adj.* Serving as an instrument or means, useful, helpful, conducive, contributory, subservient, serviceable, ministrant, mediatorial, ministerial, contributive, subsidiary, auxiliary, assisting, ancillary, helping, utilitarian, utile, assistant, furthering, good for, efficacious, effective, expedient, effectual, valuable, advantageous, applicable, adaptable.

INSTRUMENTALITY, *n.* 1. Agency, means, assistance, help, contribution, aid, subservience, intervention, action, working, mediation, operation, procurement, pull *(slang)*, influence, drag *(slang)*, go-between, friend at court, good angel, Maecenas, patronage, intermediary, interagent, handmaid, minister, servant, tool, cat's-paw, stooge, right-hand man, medium, instrument, vehicle, helping hand, stepping stone, passkey, masterkey, open sesame, *passe-partout (Fr.)*, passport, wherewithal, resources.

2. Measure, stroke, step, master stroke, trump card, *coup (Fr.)*, clever move, bright idea, expedient, device, artifice, stratagem, shift.

INSUBORDINATE, *adj.* Not submitting to authority, disobedient, ungovernable, intractable, refractory, disorderly, unruly, indocile, contumacious, turbulent, defiant, riotous, mutinous, rebellious, seditious, undutiful, unsubmissive, lawless, fractious, uncompliant, uncomplying, impatient of control, restive, recusant, recalcitrant, insurgent, revolutionary, resistant.

INSUBORDINATION, *n.* Disobedience, contumacy, non-compliance, infraction, infringement, revolt, mutiny, rebellion, outbreak, insurgency, defiance, turbulence, sedition, riotousness, insurrection, revolution, unruliness, uprising, *émeute (Fr.)*, Putsch, resistance, mutinousness, mutineering, *lèse-majesté (Fr.)*, indiscipline, intractableness, indocility, refractoriness, disorderliness, rebelliousness, undutifulness, restiveness, recusancy, recalcitrance.

INSUBSTANTIAL, *adj.* 1. Spiritual, incorporeal, immaterial, ethereal, supersensible, ghostly, psychical, bodiless, impalpable, intangible, unreal, without reality.

2. Slight, modest, petty, picayune, inconsiderable, small, trifling, trivial, of no consequence, unimportant.

INSUFFERABLE, *adj.* 1. Not to be endured, unendurable, insupportable, intolerable, unbearable, that cannot be borne, past bearing, more than flesh and blood can bear, grim, appalling, crushing, excruciating, agonizing, harrowing, frightful, dreadful, grievous, terrific, fearful, dire, tremendous, rending, acute, sore, severe, harsh, cruel, cutting, racking, searing, painful, afflictive, poignant, raw, consuming, corroding, torturous.

2. Detestable, outrageous, execrable, disgusting, abominable, contemptible, egregious, offensive, repugnant, repulsive, repellent, abhorrent, horrid, nauseous, fulsome, unsavory, caddish, boorish, hateful, odious, objectionable, unpopular, obnoxious, vile, loathsome, revolting.

INSUFFICIENCY, *n.* Deficiency in amount of force, inadequacy, inadequateness, incompetence, shortage, dearth, lack, paucity, defectiveness, straitness, want, poverty, indigence, destitution, scantiness, scarcity, pittance, scantness, sparseness, shortcoming, imperfection, stint, bare subsistence, meagerness, need, exigency, famine, starvation, drought, depletion, emptiness, exhaustion, vacancy, reduction, low water, ebb tide, half rations, short allowance, mite, dole, modicum, trifle.

INSUFFICIENT, *adj.* 1. Deficient in quality or amount, inadequate, defective, incompetent, incommensurate, scanty, meager, poor, lean, lacking, thin, incapacious, penurious, destitute, scarce, scant, unequal, rare, infrequent, lacking, wanting, incomplete, ill-provided, short of, ill-furnished, out of, bereft of, devoid of, at low ebb, slack, denuded of, vacant, empty, bare, dry, drained, empty-handed, unfed, spare, slim, barren, stinted, emaciated, underfed, undernourished, half-starved, famished, famine-stricken, in want, without resources, at the end of one's tether.

2. Unfit, incapable, unfitted, unsuited, incompetent, unqualified, unsatisfactory, inefficient, disqualified, unable, superficial, cursory, perfunctory, careless.

INSULAR, *adj.* 1. Dwelling or situated on an island, surrounded by water, detached, standing alone, isolated, insulated, seagirt, archipelagic.

2. Characteristic of inhabitants of an island, narrow-minded, prejudiced, bigoted, biased, narrow, illiberal, petty, provincial, limited, restricted, opinionated, parochial, circumscribed, hidebound, self-centered, uncharitable.

INSULATE, *v.* 1. Place in an isolated situation, detach, isolate, disjoin, dissociate, disconnect, separate, part, sunder, divorce, divide, cut off, sever, segregate, dissever, keep apart, quarantine, disunite, disengage, sequestrate.

2. Surround with non-conducting material, separate by the interposition of non-conductors.

INSULATION, *n.* Isolation, segregation, detachment, insularity, severance, divorce, disconnection, disjunction, disunion, dissociation, parting, disengagement, rupture, cleavage, disruption, separation, quarantine, sequestration.

INSULATOR, *n.* *(Elect.)* Material of such low conductivity that the flow of current through it can usually be neglected, non-conductor.

INSULT, *v.* Treat with contemptuous rudeness, offer an indignity to, display insolence toward, offend, affront, treat with insolence, commit an indignity upon, be rude to, treat with discourtesy, make free with, take a name in vain, take a liberty, put to the blush, turn one's back upon, cut, snub, give the cold shoulder to, look coldly upon, show the door to, give umbrage to, hurt the feelings, discompose, nettle, ruffle, heckle, pique, huff, sting to the quick, stir up bile, provoke, rile, wound, inflame, chafe, incense, aggravate, widen the breach, exasperate, raise one's dander, make one's blood boil, make one's ears tingle, hold in disrespect, slight, disregard, overlook, push aside, pass by, laugh in one's sleeve, be disrespectful, be discourteous, treat with disrespect, outrage, dishonor, disparage, speak slightingly of, call names, vilipend, fling dirt, point at, drag through the mud, indulge in personalities, hold in derision, sneer, scoff, deride, twit, taunt, fleer, flout, jeer, mock, burlesque, guy, laugh to scorn, make a fool of, rag, scout, boo, hiss, hoot, catcall, cheek, cold shoulder, keep at arm's length, turn on one's heel.

INSULT, *n.* Contemptuously rude action, act which injures another's honor, deeply humiliating insolence of manner, open disrespect, insolent speech, offense, affront, indignity, insolence, outrage, contumely, abuse, rudeness, scoffing, derision, sly dig, slap in the face, cold shoulder, mockery, sneer, impudence, impertinence, sauce, cheek, taunt, hoot, hiss, catcall, jibe, jeer, fling, quip, wipe, vilipendency, dishonor, discourtesy, sibilation, scurrility, sarcasm, disparagement, slight, cut, neglect, contempt, high words, provocation, crow to pluck, *casus belli (Lat.),* ill breeding, bad manners, uncourteousness, incivility, procacity, conduct unbecoming a gentleman, *brusquerie (Fr.), grossièreté (Fr.),* vulgarity, obscenity, blasphemy, profanity, virulence, tartness, acerbity, acrimony, hard words, rebuff, short answer, personality, unparliamentary language, impoliteness, misbehavior, ungentlemanliness, blackguardism.

INSULTING, *adj.* Disrespectful, discourteous, impolite, rude, derisive, uncivil, disparaging, disdainful, irreverent, supercilious, scurrilous, sarcastic, insolent, contemptuous, opprobrious, abusive, arrogant, vituperative, contumelious, grossly overbearing, impudent, impertinent, saucy, ribald, foul-mouthed, calumnious, outrageous, offensive, irritating, provoking, invidious, obnoxious, ungentlemanly, ill-mannered, ill-bred, fresh, forward, flippant, malapert, vulgar, obscene, blasphemous, profane, unrefined, ungracious, ungallant, unmannerly, blunt, gruff, churlish, boorish, brusque, harsh, bristling, surly, snarling, caustic, trenchant, ill-tempered, venomous, acrimonious, ill-behaved, cool, icy, obtrusive, mocking, taunting, jeering, flouting, fleering, twitting, hissing, catcalling, booing.

INSUPERABLE, *adj.* Incapable of being passed over, too great to be overcome, insurmountable, that cannot be got over, impassable, unattainable, impossible, unachievable, out of reach, not to be had, inaccessible, uncome-at-able, impervious, innavigable, too much for, indomitable, invincible, unconquerable, unbeatable.

INSUPPORTABLE, *adj.* Not endurable, unendurable, intolerable, insufferable, not to be borne, past bearing, more than flesh and blood can bear, enough to provoke a saint, enough to try Job's patience, obnoxious, disagreeable, painful, aggravating, annoying, provoking, irritating, galling, importunate, tormenting, pestering, dreadful, frightful, fearful, hateful, odious, execrable, cruel, excruciating, racking, harrowing, unbearable.

INSUPPRESSIBLE, *adj.* That cannot be suppressed, irrepressible, uncontrollable, that cannot be held in check, not to be kept down, inextinguishable, unquenchable, ungovernable, unappeasable, unmitigable, unconcealable, incapable of being covered up, troublous, turbulent, tumultuous, blustering, riotous, uproarious, obstreperous, boisterous, rampant, vehement, violent, explosive, volcanic, meteoric, stormy, unruly, headstrong, determined.

INSURANCE, *n.* 1. Assurance of property or life against loss or harm in consideration of a payment proportioned to the risk involved, security against loss, financial umbrella, indemnity, amount for which anything is insured, premium paid for insuring a thing.

2. Guarantee, warranty, obligation, stipulation, covenant, contract, earnest, promise, word, pledge, plight, troth, security, gage, indenture.

INSURE, *v.* 1. Guarantee against risk of loss or harm, secure against loss, agree to indemnify for loss, secure indemnity on in case of damage or death, indemnify, cover, underwrite, furnish insurance on, issue an insurance policy on.

2. Make certain or sure, make secure, secure, warrant, guarantee, endorse, contract, vouch, assure, clinch.

INSURGENCY, *n.* Condition of insurrection against an existing government by a group not recognized as a belligerent *(Internat. Law)*, rebellion, revolt, sedition, mutiny, insubordination, defiance, infraction, noncompliance, outbreak, uprising, Putsch, *émeute (Fr.)*, strike, walkout, sitdown, tumult, mutinousness, mutineering, treason, high treason, *lèse-majesté (Fr.)*, secession, defection, revolution, bolshevism, sabotage.

INSURGENT, *n.* One who engages in armed resistance to a government or to the execution of laws, one who rises in forcible opposition to lawful authority, rebel, mutineer, revolter, traitor, insurrectionist, radical, rioter, *sans-culotte (Fr.)*, *carbonaro (It.)*, Fenian, communist, bolshevik, *frondeur (Fr.)*, anarchist, brawler, seceder, demagogue, suffragette, Jack Cade, Spartacus, striker, malcontent, Red, Sinn Feiner, secessionist, nihilist, renagade, apostate.

INSURGENT, *adj.* Rising in revolt, seditious, rebellious, revolutionary, mutinous, malcontent, disobedient, insubordinate, tumultuous, turbulent, unruly, lawless, riotous, insurrectionary, ungovernable, refractory, unmanageable, defiant, restive, contumacious, recusant, recalcitrant, dissentient, nihilistic, bolshevistic, anarchistic, Red.

INSURRECTION, *n.* Act of rising up in arms, open resistance against established authority, revolt, rebellion, insurgence, sedition, mutiny, uprising, outbreak, turbulence, revolution, insubordination, mob-law, riot, storm, tumult, turbulence, street fighting, rioting, commotion, fighting at the barricades, mutineering, treason, violation of law, Putsch, *émeute (Fr.)*, defiance, *lèse-majesté (Fr.)*, bolshevism, sabotage, oppugnation, opposition, recalcitrance, renitence, disobedience, reluctation,

strike, lockout, *levée en masse (Fr.)*, disorder, Jacquerie *(Fr.)*.

INSURRECTIONARY, *adj.* Given to insurrection, seditious, rebellious, mutinous, anarchistic, nihilistic, resistant, restive, unruly, refractory, disobedient, insubordinate, renitent, recalcitrant, repellent, up in arms, ungovernable, contumacious, refractory, recusant, lawless, insurgent, revolutionary, riotous, Red bolshevistic.

INSUSCEPTIBLE, *adj.* 1. (Followed by TO) Not susceptible, insusceptive, unimpressible, insensible, insensate, unsusceptible, not sensitive, not accessible, impassive, unconscious, impassible, deaf to, blind to, unimpressionable, dead to, unfeeling, apathetic, unconcerned, phlegmatic, unemotional, frigid, cold-hearted, numb, indifferent.

2. (Followed by OF) Not admitting, incapable of receiving, incapable.

INTACT, *adj.* Remaining unaltered, whole, complete, integral, entire, untouched, unbroken, undiminished, sound, without fracture, unaffected by injury, hale, unimpaired, flawless, scathless, unharmed, unhurt, uninjured, healthy, safe and sound, unblemished, perfect, unabridged, total, all, universal, plenary, full, undivided, solid, unmarred, without a scratch, with a whole skin.

INTAGLIO, *n.* Gem cut with an incised design, seal with a sunken design, piece of jewelry with incised carving, engraving, engravure, insculpture, carving, *rilievo (It.)*, bas relief, *basso-rilievo (It.)*, anaglyph, the opposite of a cameo.

INTAKE, *n.* 1. Contraction, narrowing, constriction, drawing together, drawing in, reduction, diminution, shortening, lessening, furling.

2. Quantity taken in, take, harvest, ingathering, yield, produce, profit, gain, boot, gleanings, crop, vintage, mow, rick, stack, hoard, accumulation, store.

INTANGIBLE, *adj.* Incapable of being perceived by the sense of touch, that cannot be touched, unable to be felt, untouchable, impalpable, imperceptible, incorporeal, immaterial, intactile, spiritous, aerial, phantom, bodiless, insubstantial, airy, ethereal, transcendental, metaphysical, spiritual, superphysical, hyperphysical, discarnate, spiritistic, asomatous, nonobjective, subjective, psychical, invisible, evanescent, vague, shadowy, dim, indefinite, imponderable, not definite or clear to the mind, infinitesimal, inappreciable, homoeopathic.

INTEGER, *n.* Whole number, not a fraction, a complete entity, integral, complete unity, unit.

INTEGRAL, *adj.* Pertaining to a whole, necessary for the completeness of the whole, belonging as a part of the whole, made up of parts which together constitute a whole, integrant, integrate, component, constituent, aggregate, agglomerate, entire, whole, complete, total, gross, undivided, unbroken, intact, undiminished, perfect, indivisible.

INTEGRATION, *n.* 1. Combination into an integral whole, compages, organic unity, compaction, assemblage, complexus, collectiveness, completion, integrality, omnitude.

2. Individual behavior in harmony with the environment, orientation, adaptation, conformity, accommodation, harmonization, adjustment.

INTEGRITY, *n.* 1. State of being entire or undiminished, unimpaired condition, entirety, wholeness, completeness, entireness, soundness, totality, integrality, omnitude, allness, *tout ensemble (Fr.)*, complexus, collectiveness, undividedness, intactness, universality, indiscerptibility, indivisibility.

2. Soundness of moral principle, rectitude of character, probity, goodness, moral soundness, purity, uprightness, principle, virtue, honor, honesty, clean hands, good faith, *bona fides (Lat.)*, constancy, morality, respectability, fidelity, faithfulness, trustworthiness, veracity, loyalty, singleness of heart, candor, truth, equity, justice, fairness, point of honor, scrupulousness, scrupulosity, square shooting, righteousness, sincerity, piety, chastity, goodness, justness.

INTEGUMENT, *n.* Covering, casing, envelope, skin, tegument, coat, shell, rind, peel, bark, cortex, crust, husk, sheath, cod, pod, involucrum, wrapping, vesicle, capsule.

INTELLECT, *n.* Power of the mind by which one knows, faculty of the mind by which one understands, understanding, brains, intelligence, reasoning faculty, cognitive powers, thinking principle, mental capacity of a high order, intellectual powers, rational faculty, mind, reason, sense, mentality, apprehension, comprehension, perception, cognition, intuition, insight, consciousness, percipience, judgment, wisdom, genius, *nous (Greek)*, *mens (Lat.)*, wit, parts, *penetralia mentis (Lat.)*, soul, spirit, ego, subconscious, brain, cranium, skull, sensorium, headpiece, gray matter, brain pan, cerebrum, cerebellum.

INTELLECTION, *n.* Process of understanding, cognition, cognizance, apprehension, knowing, percipience, perception, cerebration, lucubration, cogitation, reflection, meditation, study, speculation, consideration, deliberation, pondering, brainwork, mentation, contemplation, abstraction, brown study, musing, workings of the mind, depth of thought, self-consultation, association of ideas, retrospection, examination, thoughtfulness, invention, excogitation.

INTELLECTUAL, *adj.* 1. Engaging the intellect, appealing to the intellect, mental, relating to the understanding, rational, cerebral, spiritual, subjective, metaphysical, nooscopic, psychical, psychological, abstract, transcendental, ideal, moral.

2. Inclined toward things that involve the intellect, possessing a high degree of mental capacity, characterized by a predominance of intellect, of marked intellect, full of intellect, highly intelligent, imaginative, thoughtful, learned, egghead, highbrow, long-haired, cultured, accomplished, sagacious, acute, discerning, talented, gifted, brainy, scholarly, clever, profound, literate, well-informed, smart, quick, bright, quick-witted, keen, inventive, sharp, ingenious, percipient.

INTELLECTUAL, *n.* A member of a class professing enlightened judgment and opinions with respect to public or political questions, an intellectual person, cognoscent, connoisseur, long-hair, egg-head, savant, pundit, scholarly person, Einstein, metaphysician, philosopher, philomath, Ph. D., scholar, academician, *littérateur (Fr.)*, bibliophile, bookworm, bibliomaniac, blue-stocking, *bas-bleu (Fr.)*, *homo multarum literarum (Lat.)*, literary man, man of learning, intelligentsia, highbrow, saga, pedant, pantologist, know-it-all, *doctrinaire (Fr.)*.

INTELLIGENCE, *n.* 1. Capacity for understanding, aptitude in grasping truths, good mental capacity, intellectuality, mentality, brain-power, reason, counsel, wisdom, judgment, brains, intellect, acumen, sagacity, insight, intuition, penetra-

tion, wits, shrewdness, discernment, quick understanding, clear apprehension, brightness, imagination, subtlety, comprehension, cognition, apperception, understanding, mother wit, parts, *esprit (Fr.)*, gumption, hard-headedness, common sense, acuteness, smartness, keeness, longheadednes, perspicacity, good judgment, refinement, discrimination, sapience.

2. Information, notification, advice, notice, instruction, news, report, tip, pointer, dope *(slang)*, low-down *(slang)*, tidings, communication, knowledge.

INTELLIGENT, *adj.* 1. Having knowledge, enlightened, educated, instructed, well-informed, well-read, sapient, intellectual, well-schooled.

2. Having a good mental capacity, quick to understand, showing distinctive comprehension, sagacious, understanding, sensible, knowing, astute, shrewd, brainy, clever, discerning, alert, acute, quick, bright, apt, keen-sighted, sharpsighted, clear-sighted, quick-sighted, sharp-witted, keen-eyed, clear-headed, wise, foxy, judicious, thoughtful, observant, *au fait (Fr.)*, rational, smart, penetrating, discriminating, percipient, perceptive, ingenious, quick-witted, gifted, aware, subtle, wide-awake, knowing, hard-headed, longheaded, calculating, farsighted, perspicacious, sharp as a needle.

INTELLIGENTSIA, *n.* Group of persons claiming special enlightenment in views or principles, the intellectuals, egg-heads, highbrows, long-haired crowd, freethinkers, Bohemians, cognoscenti, savants, the learned, connoisseurs, *literati, illuminati*.

INTELLIGIBILITY, *n.* Capability of being understood, comprehensibility, clarity, intelligibleness, perspicuity, lucidness, lucidity, clearness, coherence, explicitness, plainness, precision, simplicity, plain-speaking, comprehensibleness.

INTELLIGIBLE, *adj.* Capable of being understood, comprehensible, clear, lucid, coherent, explicit, plain-spoken, precise, simple, distinct, plain, manifest, perspicuous, evident, obvious, patent, transparent, apprehensible by the mind, cognoscible, articulate, understandable, palpable, legible, positive, clear-cut, definite, to the point, unmistakable, unambiguous, unequivocal, vivid, expressive, graphic, picturesque, pictorial, delineatory, telling, descriptive.

INTEMPERANCE, *n.* 1. Excessive indulgence of a natural passion, immoderate gratification, immoderation, unrestraint, excessiveness, excess in any indulgence, lack of due restraint, extravagance, overabundance.

2. Free-living, self-indulgence, sybaritism, epicureanism, epicurism, dissipation, self-gratification, high living, prodigality, prodigalism, luxuriousness, pleasure-seeking, dissoluteness, license, fastness, looseness, tragalism, animalism, sensuality, lewdness, wantonness, lechery, venery, voluptuousness, debauchery, licentiousness, libidinousness, lustfulness.

2. Habitual excess in drinking alcoholic beverages, alcoholism, dipsomania, oenomania, drunkenness, inebriety, intoxication, crapulence, saturnalia, drinking bout, spree, carousal, orgy, revels, debauch, jollification.

INTEMPERATE, *adj.* 1. Immoderate, unrestrained, excessive, extravagant, inordinate, unbridled, ungovernable, uncurbed, extreme, nimious, uncontrolled.

2. Dissipated, dissolute, prodigal, self-gratify-

ing, self-indulgent, fast, loose, wild, lax, profligate, crapulous, epicurean, sybaritic, pampered, indulged, luxurious.

3. Carnal, sensual, gross, voluptuous, fleshly, bestial, gluttonous, brutish, piggish, hoggish, porcine, swinish, beastlike, animal, lecherous, lustful, lascivious, lewd, licentious, libidinous, concupiscent, salacious, goatish, wanton.

4. Given to excess in drinking, sottish, drunken, bibacious, inebrious, crapulent, boozy, wine-bibbing, alcoholic, dipsomaniacal, oenomaniacal, pifflicated, tight, pickled, bibulous, stewed, three sheets in the wind *(colloq.),* maudlin, obfuscated, unsteady, tipsy, half-seas over, mellow, muddled, lush *(slang),* muzzy.

INTEND, *v.* Have in mind as something to be done or brought about, mean for a particular purpose, design for a particular use, determine, purpose, contemplate, propose to one's self, meditate, think of, have in view, drive at, aim at, know what one wishes to do, set as a goal, bid for, desire, labor for, pursue, aspire to, talk of, dream of, destine, premeditate, plan, project, calculate, will, devise, resolve, scheme.

INTENDANT, *n.* One who has the direction or management of the affairs of an established public business, supervisor, superintendent, inspector, overseer, overlooker, monitor, curator, watchman, watchkeeper, boss, foreman, taskmaster, rector.

INTENSE, *adj.* 1. Existing in an extreme degree, very great, acute, intensified, deep, dark, rich, concentrated, poignant, grievous, exquisite, profound, extreme, forced, highest, grave, sharp, flaming, vivid.

2. Susceptible to strong emotion, fervent, ardent, perfervid, vehement, passionate, earnest, emotional, fiery, temperamental, highstrung, high-mettled, impassioned, zealous.

3. Energetic, strenuous, forcible, powerful, vigorous, potent, sharp, violent, strong.

INTENSIFY, *v.* Strengthen, make more intense, heighten, deepen, concentrate, quicken, enhance, aggravate, sharpen, whet, pique, exacerbate, inflame, increase, raise, step up, accelerate, augment, extend, warm, tone up, darken, thicken, advance, exaggerate, reinforce, extend, boost, magnify.

INTENSITY, *n.* 1. Extreme degree, high degree, excess, extremity, extravagance, immoderation, inordinateness, inordinacy, magnitude.

2. Ardor, earnestness, warmth, fervency, perfervidness, enthusiasm, passionateness, devotion, zeal, spirit, fervor, pitch, eagerness.

3. Great energy, potency, puissance, power, strength, vigor, force, activity, pep, ginger, white heat, fever point.

INTENT, *adj.* 1. Steadfastly directed upon, firmly fixed on, earnestly set on, bent upon, set upon, bent, aspiring, ambitious, vaulting.

2. Earnest, eager, avid, keen, burning, fervent, ardent, open-mouthed, breathless, agog, closely fixed, close, on duty, at work, in action, assiduous, engaged, industrious.

3. Attentive, having the eyes glued on, mindful, heedful, observant, regardful, observing, alert, occupied with, taken up with, engrossed, absorbed, interested, rapt, wrapped up in, watchful, preoccupied, steadfast, on the watch, undistracted, open-eyed.

INTENT, *n.* Intention, purpose, design, end, aim, ambition, project, *cui bono (Lat.),* destination, point, goal, *quo animo (Lat.),* target, bull's-eye,

butt, quarry, prey, game, mark, purview, object, objective, mind, animus, contemplation, view, resolve, wish, resolution, ultimatum, motive, *arrière pensée (Fr.),* predetermination, frame of mind, pleasure, desire, discretion, velleity, volition, will, inclination, choice, option, predilection, penchant, propensity, bent, leaning, point, tenor, spirit, diligence, scope, import, drift, purport, plan, meaning.

INTENTION, *n.* Act of determining mentally upon some action, settled determination to achieve something, end intended, a wish which one means to carry out, objective, goal, purpose, design, plan, intentionality, determination, resolve, decision, resolution, fixed purpose, object, aim, intent, tendency, drift, end, inclination, bent, set, destination, point, mark, target, bull's-eye, butt, quarry, prey, game, project, undertaking, final cause, *raison d'être (Fr.),* ambition, view, proposal, contemplation, end in view, idea, wish, direction, counsel, meaning, significance, purport, import, upshot, connotation, implication, signification, force, denotation.

INTENTIONAL, *adj.* Done on purpose, designed, purposive, purposed, purposeful, premeditated, intended, contemplated, predetermined, studied, preconcerted, pointed, deliberate, voluntary, willing, wilful, free, spontaneous, bent upon, minded, advised, inclined, express, witting, determinate, in cold blood, prepense, calculated, meditated, determined, aimed at, projected, aforethought.

INTER, *v.* Lay in the grave, deposit in a grave, commit to the earth, consign to the tomb, bury with funeral rites, inhume, inhumate, sepulcher, ensepulcher, sepulture, inearth, tomb, inurn, entomb.

INTERCALATE, *v.* Put between, interpolate, interpose, insert, intromit, introduce, interject (see INTERPOLATE).

INTERCEDE, *v.* 1. Interpose in behalf of one in difficulty, plead for one in trouble, petition for, make intercession for, deprecate, enter a protest, expostulate, entreat, pray for.

2. Make peace between, act as go-between, arbitrate, mediate, intermediate, intervene, step in, negotiate, mediatize, meet halfway, propitiate, reconcile, *magnas componere lites (Lat.).*

INTERCEPT, *v.* 1. Seize on the way from one place to another, cut off from the intended destination, stop on the way, check passage, seize in passage, catch, expropriate, scramble for, make free with, help oneself to, impound, confiscate, commandeer, possess oneself of, dispossess, take away, wrest from, run away with, pounce upon.

2. Interrupt, stop the natural course of, obstruct, prevent the effect of, cut off the operation of, put a stop to, interfere, interpose, intermeddle, debar, stay, preclude, restrain, inhibit, check, prevent, detain, delay, retard, impede, hinder, shut off, arrest, head off, frustrate, thwart, foil.

INTERCESSION, *n.* 1. Pleading in behalf of one in trouble, entreaty, supplication, prayer, plea, solicitation, petition, request, invocation, obstestation, interpellation.

2. Mediation, mediatorship, intervention, instrumentality, agency, intermediation, interposition, peace offering, peacemaker, good offices, arbitration, negotiation, parley, diplomacy, compromise, propitiation, reconciliation, reconcilement.

INTERCESSOR, *n.* Interceder, mediator, reconciler, pacificator, make-peace, negotiator, go-between, middleman, interagent, medium, intermediary, intermedium, arbitrator, diplomatist, moderator, umpire, peacemaker, propitiator, reconciler, intermediator.

INTERCHANGE, v. 1. Put each of two in the place of the other, cause one thing to change places with another, transpose, exchange, change, counterchange, substitute, convert, trade, traffic, truck, swap, bandy, barter, dicker, swap, give and take, commute, requite, retaliate, retort, return, reciprocate, give and receive reciprocally, give in return.

2. Cause to follow one another alternately, alternate, occur by turns, happen in succession, change reciprocally, vary, shuttle, gig, seesaw, correspond, correlate, change places with another.

INTERCHANGE, n. 1. Reciprocal exchange, shuffling, shuffle, tit for tat, barter, swap, *quid pro quo (Lat.)*, reciprocation, reciprocity, correlation, correspondence, equivalence, mutuality, give-and-take, commerce, intercourse, retaliation, reprisal, retort, requital, cross fire, commutation, permutation, transmutation, intermutation, transposition, transposal, substitution, interchangeability, commutability.

2. Alternate succession, changing of places of one with another, alternation, occurrence by turns, reciprocal change, varying, variation, conversion, alternative, vicissitude.

3. Traffic circle, cloverleaf, crossroad, intersection.

INTERCHANGEABLY, adv. In succession, alternately, by turns, turn about, turn and turn about, reciprocally, by interchange, mutually, by reciprocation, in exchange, *vice versa (Lat.)*, conversely, equivalently, correspondently.

INTERCOMMUNICATION, n. Mutual communication, relation, intercourse, liaison, communicativeness, outpouring, acquainting, mention, instruction, notification, notice, announcement, circular letter, round robin, manifesto, placard, advertisement, poster, *affiche (Fr.)*, bill, presentment, report, representation, monition, advice, account, news, enlightenment, statement, information, knowledge, acquaintance, promulgation, pronouncement, publicity, propagation.

INTERCOURSE, n. 1. Dealings between individuals, communication, commerce, connection, truck, mutual exchange, congress, communion, intercommunion, reciprocity, correspondence, union, liaison, association, congress.

2. Sociability, sociality, companionability, fellowship, friendship, friendliness, comradeship, fraternity, familiarity, intimacy, association, consociation, clubbism, esprit de corps, urbanity, circle of acquaintance, family circle, reunion, social gathering, levee, matinée, soirée, congregation, reception.

3. Converse, conversation, colloquy, collocution, discourse, talk, interlocution, conference, parley, *pourparler (Fr.)*, *conversazione (It.)*, tête à tête, causerie (Fr.), interview, appointment, date, rendezvous, assignation, tryst, audience, powwow, palaver.

4. Sexual relations, coitus, coition, fornication, stupration, seduction, abuse, violation, rape, adultery, incest, sodomy, buggery, copulation, sexual congress, venereal act, venery, defloration, defilement, debauchery, wenching, sexual attack, assault.

INTERDEPENDENCE, n. Mutual dependence, dependence on each other, reciprocal trust, lean-

ing upon, reliance, confidence, *uberrima fides (Lat.)*, sheet, anchor, mainstay.

INTERDICT, v. Cut off authoritatively from, prohibit, forbid, inhibit, put one's veto upon, veto, place under an interdiction, place under a ban, disallow, forefend, bar, debar, embargo, censor, exclude, taboo, excommunicate, unchurch, anathematize, exile, ostracize, banish, restrain, withhold, cohibit, restrict, clip the wings of, circumscribe.

INTERDICT, n. Prohibition, veto, interdiction, forbiddance, ban, taboo, proscription, excommunication, unchurching, anathematization, exile, banishment, ostracism, censure, stricture, exclusion, embargo, disallowance, injunction, *verboten (Ger.)*, restriction, forbidden fruit, index, expurgatorius, suspension of religious privileges, punishment by which the faithful are prohibited from participation in certain religious acts.

INTEREST, v. 1. Engage the attention of, rivet the attention, attract, grip, magnetize, galvanize, hypnotize, mesmerize, electrify, possess the soul, animate, arouse, awake, wake, smite, inspire, absorb, hold, occupy, excite the curiosity of, pierce, infect, move, imbue, reach, impress, strike, rouse, fire, stir, inflame, kindle, quicken, whet, instigate, spur, incite, provoke, evoke, entertain, delight, please, enliven, divert, amuse, cause to sit up and take notice.

2. Concern in something, involve, be of importance to, relate to, affect, touch.

INTEREST, n. 1. Good, gain, boon, benefit, advantage, weal, improvement, profit, behoof, behalf, service, good fortune, blessing, benison, happiness, enrichment, self-interest.

2. Concern, absorption of mind, regard, intentness, attentiveness, consideration, engrossment, heed, attention, once-over, notice, scrutiny, study, inspection, pleased attention, feeling, concernment, sympathy, inquisitiveness, curiosity.

3. Importance, emphasis, gravity, seriousness, urgency, pressure, consequence, materialness, significance, import, moment, weight.

4. Hold, domination, control, sway, authority, power, dominance, mastery, upper hand, supremacy, rule.

5. Portion, share, participation, part, stake, possession, holding, credit, right of ownership in, title, claim, demand, due, estate, copyright, patent, vested interest, use, prerogative, trust, dowry, dower, dot, inheritance, jointure, patrimony, bequest, legacy, endowment, privilege, droit (Law), license, grant, exemption, immunity.

6. Revenue, proceeds, receipts, salary, wages, annuity, payment, sum.

7. Sum paid for the use of money borrowed, rate percent per unit of time represented by such payment, premium for the use of money, profit from money loaned, usury, business advantage, discount, investment.

INTERESTED, adj. 1. Attentive, mindful, occupied, engrossed, observant, heedful, regardful, awake to, alert, taken up with, wrapped up in, absorbed, preoccupied, rapt, breathless, open-eyed, wide-eyed, agog, intent on.

2. Having an interest in something, concerned, involved, participating, partial, prejudiced, biased, in favor of.

3. Influenced by personal motives, self-seeking, self-interested, self-centered, egoistic, egocentric, self-indulgent, wrapped up in oneself, selfish.

4. Mercenary, venal, avaricious, sordid, corrupt,

vendible, purchasable, hireling, covetous, worldly-minded, time-serving.

INTERESTING, *adj.* Arousing a feeling of interest, holding the attention, attracting the curiosity, satisfying to the mind, gratifying, pleasing, engaging, entertaining, attractive, exciting, occupying the mind, charming, sweet, lovely, winning, seductive, enchanting, fascinating, captivating, intriguing, bewitching, amiable, agreeable, amusing, eventful, readable, racy, piquant, funny, beloved, precious, dear, pet, popular, favorable, loved.

INTERFERE, *v.* 1. Oppose, be opposed, be in opposition, collide, come in collision, conflict, clash, be at variance, contravene, counter.

2. Take a part in the affairs of others, meddle, intermeddle, interpose, horn in, butt in, put in one's oar, come between, intervene, intrude, obtrude, thrust in, intercede, interrupt, intercept.

3. Obstruct, hinder action, hamper, encumber, bar, cumber, cramp, handicap, entrammel, act as a drag, play the deuce with, put a crimp in, inhibit, frustrate, thwart, foil, balk, clip the wings, cut the ground from under one, cripple, spike the guns, sabotage, throw out of gear, put on the brake, put a stop to, stay, dam up, barricade, block.

INTERFERENCE, *n.* 1. Clashing, opposition, collision, conflict, contravention, disapproval, discouragement, disapprobation, censure, stricture.

2. Interposition, intermeddling, interposal, intervention, horning in, butting in, meddling, coming between, intrusion, obtrusion, intercession, interruption, interception, meddlesomeness.

3. Impediment, obstruction, obstacle, objection, difficulty, stumbling block, snag, knot, hitch, illwind, head-wind, setback, check, brake, clog, tether, trammel, drag, curb, load, burden, encumbrance, impedimenta, onus, pack, deadweight, damper, wet blanket, handicap, disturbance.

INTERIM, *n.* 1. An intervening time, intermediate time, interval, while, meantime, bit, pendency.

2. Intermission, intermittence, interlude, interregnum, respite, pause, intervention.

3. Unity of time, concomitance, concurrence, coincidence, conjuncture.

4. Temporary arrangement, provisional status, stopgap, makeshift, *pis aller (Fr.)*.

INTERIOR, *adj.* 1. Inside of anything, being within, inner, internal, inward, inmost, innermost.

2. Intrinsic, innate, inbred, inborn, inherent, deep-seated, implanted, ingrained, inwoven, inwrought, infixed, immanent, indwelling.

3. Inland, remote from the frontier, at a distance from the coast or border, midland, up-country, hinterland.

4. Domestic, home, home-grown, not foreign, native, homebred, intraterritorial.

5. Inner, private, secret, esoteric, intimate, confidential.

6. Mental, spiritual, subjective, personal, individual, special.

7. Abdominal, ventral, visceral, splanchnic, intestinal, duodenal, celiac, stomachic, rectal.

INTERIOR, *n.* 1. The internal part, inside part, interior part, inner part, inside, center, interspace.

2. Heart, womb, belly, bosom, breast, bowels, entrails, intestines, viscera, splanchna, inner parts, guts, marrow, pith, substance, core, spirit, soul, essence.

3. Inland parts of a country, hinterland, inland,

in-country, midland, up-country, backwoods, the sticks.

4. Innermost recesses, penetralia, alcove, hollow, niche, nook.

5. Domestic affairs of a country.

INTERJACENT, *adj.* Intervening, intervenient, interplane, interposed, parenthetical, interjectional, episodic, intercalary, intermediary, intermediate, intrusive, medial, mean, mesial, middle.

INTERJECT, *v.* 1. Throw in abruptly between other things, put between, insert, interpolate, interpose, inject, intromit, introduce, import, insinuate, implant, force in, interjaculate, parenthesize, interlard, infiltrate, intersperse, infuse, ingrain, intercalate, dovetail, splice, mortise.

2. Comment, exclaim, ejaculate, vociferate, utter in an exclamation, blurt, utter suddenly.

INTERJECTION, *n.* 1. Act of throwing between, interjecting, interpolation, intercalation, insertion, insinuation, interlocation, intrusion, obtrusion, interjacence, interposition, parenthesis.

2. Utterance of ejaculations expressive of emotion, exclamation, ejaculation, vociferation, brief and sudden utterance, ecphonesis.

3. Part of speech that constitutes utterances without grammatical connection, exclamatory particle.

INTERLACE, *v.* Cross one another as if woven together, interweave, intertwine, entwine, inweave, twine together, weave, plait, twist, braid, raddle, blend intricately, bind, unite, intersperse, intermingle, mix, mingle, mat, tie, knot, complicate, entangle, interlock, interknit, pass alternately over and under, dispose so as to intercross one another.

INTERLARD, *v.* Diversify with something intermixed, interweave, intersperse, intertwine, vary, mix, interdigitate, put in, interpose, intercalate, interject, interpolate, interleave, interline.

INTERLINE, *v.* Insert words between the lines of writing, write between the lines of print, mark between the lines, put between lines, interscribe, interpolate, commentate, make marginalia, make scholia, gloss.

INTERLINEAL, *adj.* Inserted between lines, situated between the lines, interlinear, having interpolated lines, scholiastic, having the same text in various languages set in alternate lines.

INTERLINK, *v.* 1. Link with one another, concatenate, connect, join closely together, interchain, interrelate, interlace, intertwine, intertwist, interdigitate, interweave, decussate, cross, twine, entwine, weave, dovetail, splice.

2. Interlock, lock together, engage with each other, lock with one another, fit into each other, fit the parts of together so that all must move together.

INTERLOCUTION, *n.* Interchange of speech, collocution, colloquy, confabulation, converse, discourse, talk, verbal intercourse, conversation, dialogue, oral communication, communion, commerce, *causerie (Fr.)*, chitchat, tattle, chat, babble, gossip, palaver, conference, interview, *tête à tête (Fr.)*, powwow, *pourparler (Fr.)*, *conversazione (It.)*, parley, audience.

INTERLOCUTOR, *n.* Minstrel in the middle of a line of performers who carries on a conversation with the end men, one who takes part in a conversation, speaker in a dialogue, dialogist, companion in conversation, respondent, prolocutor, speaker, spokesman, conversationalist, elocutionist, mouthpiece, platform orator, tub-thumper, patterer, *improvisatore (It.)*, interlocutrix, interlocutrice, interlocutress.

INTERLOPER, *n.* Unlicensed intruder into some field or trade, obtruder, meddler, interferer, one who thrusts himself into the affairs of others, buttinsky *(slang)*, bodkin, intermeddler, invader, trespasser, poacher, interrupter, hinderer, marplot.

INTERLUDE, *n.* 1. Intervening episode, intervening period, intervening time, intervening space, interspace, interval, recess, pause, respite, interruption, intermission, interregnum.

2. Short light or farcical dramatic piece, *entr' acte (Fr.)*, intermezzo, *divertissement (Fr.)*, intermediate entertainment between the acts of a play, *comedietta (It.)*, curtain-raiser, afterpiece, extravaganza, farce, harlequinade, burlesque, pantomime, ballet, spectacle, tableau, charade, masque, vaudeville.

matter, interpose, interfere, intrude, intervene, intercede, obtrude, intercept, mediate, meddle,

INTERMEDDLE, *v.* Take part officiously in a butt in, horn in, chime in, thrust in.

INTERMEDIARY, *n.* Mediator, intermediate agent, interagent, intermedium, go-between, middle-man, intervener, interposer, peacemaker, emissary, agent, vehicle, medium, means, agency.

INTERMEDIATE, *adj.* Being between two stages, situated between two points, acting between two persons, intervening, intermediary, intervenient, interjacent, interposed, interfering, inserted, medium, halfway, median, medial, mesial, mean, mesne *(Law)*, middle, transitional.

INTERMENT, *n.* 1. Act of interring, burial, sepulture, entombment, inhumation, obsequies, funeral rites, obit, funeral, exequies, passing bell, knell, tolling, death-bell, dirge, wake, coronach, elegy, requiem, epicedium, muffled drum, dead march.

2. Burial place, grave, tomb, sepulcher, mausoleum, vault, crypt, catacomb, cromlech, cairn, tumulus, barrow, graveyard, God's acre, burial ground, necropolis, cemetery, polyandrion, ossuary, churchyard, potter's field.

INTERMEZZO, *n.* Short light dramatic or musical entertainment introduced between the acts of a drama or opera, *entr' acte (Fr)*, *divertissement (Fr.)*, afterpiece, short musical composition between main divisions of an extended musical work, independent musical composition.

INTERMINABLE, *adj.* 1. That cannot be terminated, without termination, having no limitation, unlimited, inexhaustible, illimitable, unbounded, boundless, immeasurable, endless, unending, infinite, limitless, indefinite, without end, without measure, without limit, ceaseless, unceasing, incessant, termless, uninterrupted, indesinent, unremitting, having no end, everlasting, eternal.

2. Wearisomely protracted, long-drawn, no end of, tediously long, prolix, long-winded, that seems as if it would never end.

INTERMINGLE, *v.* Mingle one with another, commingle, blend, mix together, commix, intermix, compound, fuse, interweave, combine, intersperse, confound, incorporate, amalgamate.

INTERMISSION, *n.* Period during which action temporarily ceases, interval between periods of activity, interim, interval, intermediate time, pendency, abeyance, suspension, remission, stop, halt, stoppage, rest, pause, respite, lull, suspense, cessation, interruption, intervention, intermittence, interregnum, interlude, discontinuance, desistance,

desinence, recess, quiescence, break, leaving off, truce, armistice, cease-fire.

INTERMIT, *v.* 1. Break off operations for a time, discontinue temporarily, interrupt, suspend, stop for a while, hold for the time, desist, stay, leave off, cease, give over, have done with, surcease, give up, stay one's hand, repose on one's laurels, rest on one's oars, pull up, stop short, stall, check, halt, rest, pause, put a period to, put an end to, bring to a stand, cut short, switch off, pull the check string, interpel, intromit.

2. Abate, subside, wane, decline, fall away, ebb, sink, peter out, die away, be at an end, remit, cease for a time.

INTERMITTENT, *adj.* That ceases for a time, alternately ceasing and beginning again, discontinuous, remittent intermitting, alternate, every other, on-again off-again, fitful, capricious, spasmodic, recurrent, recurring, periodic, cyclic, cyclical, epochal, termly, serial, rhythmic, seasonal, pulsatile, pulsating, flickering, broken, irregular.

INTERN, *n.* Resident member of the medical staff of a hospital, recent medical graduate acting as assistant on a medical staff, resident physician, newly graduated doctor.

INTERN, *v.* Oblige enemy aliens to reside within prescribed limits under prohibition to leave them, imprison combatant troops who take refuge in a neutral country, hold within a country until the termination of a war, disarm and quarter, confine prisoners of war, restrict freedom, shut in, impound, keep within, internalize, circumscribe.

INTERNAL, *adj.* 1. Situated or existing in the interior of something, interior, inmost, innermost, inside, inward, inner, deepest, away from the surface, not superficial.

2. Innate, inborn, inbred, deep-seated, inveterate, implanted, ingrained, inwoven, inwrought, indwelling, immanent, infixed, inherent, intrinsic.

3. Existing or occurring within a country, domestic, pertaining to the domestic affairs of a country, intraterritorial, native, homebred, indigenous, autochthonous, home, not foreign, inland.

4. Pertaining to the mind, mental, in the mind, being within the soul, spiritual, psychic, psychological, incorporeal, in the heart, subjective.

5. Esoteric, occult, higher, deeper, inner, hidden, secret, confidential, personal.

INTERNATIONAL, *adj.* Common to nations, pertaining to the relations between nations, among nations, worldwide, interracial, cosmopolitan, gregarious, ecumenical.

INTERNECINE, *adj.* Characterized by great slaughter, involving bloodshed on both sides, mutually destructive, internecive, internecinal, interneciary, exterminatory, slaughterous, murderous, deadly, lethal, mortal, fatal, suicidal, sanguinary, sanguinolent, bloodstained, gory, homicidal, bloody, ensanguined, sanguineous, mortiferous, lethiferous.

INTERPELLATE, *v.* 1. Call formally upon in interpellation, question imperatively and officially, put to the question, interrogate, catechize, pump, grill, put through the third degree, cross-question, cross-examine.

2. Speak to, accost, address, appeal to, apostrophize, invoke, bid, enjoin, instruct, charge, cite, subpoena, summon.

INTERPELLATION, *n.* 1. Official interrogation of a minister by the legislative body, demand for an official statement or an explanation, legislative procedure of calling upon a member of the government to explain some official act or policy, challenge, cross-examination, catechism, leading question, close inquiry, inquest, examination, inquisition, investigation.

2. *(Law)* Summons, citation, subpoena, mandamus, *duces tecum (Lat.), nisi prius (Lat.).*

3. Interruption in a debate, verbal interference, oral intercession, interposition in speaking.

4. Apostrophe, allocution, alloquy, speech, address, appeal, salutation, obtestation, imploration, obsecration, impetration, entreaty, solicitation, postulation, importunity, instance, supplication.

INTERPLAY, *n.* Play between the parts of something, reciprocal play, reciprocal influence, reciprocal movement, mutual influence, contrasting action, reciprocal action, interaction, reciprocal effect.

INTERPOLATE, *v.* 1. Alter by the insertion of new matter, introduce additional or extraneous matter between things, interpose, interject, interjaculate, throw in, intercalate, insinuate, foist in, import, implant, inject, force in, interlard, parenthesize, intersperse, infuse, put in.

2. Insert deceptively or without authorization, falsify, adulterate, corrupt, scramble, garble, doctor, alloy, mingle with, commingle, intermingle.

INTERPOLATION, *n.* 1. Act of putting in between, insertion, introduction, addition, interlocation, intervention, interjection, intercalation, interspersion, interlarding, insinuation, obtrusion, interlineation, parenthesis, immixture, intermixture, commingling, minglement, adulteration, corruption, alteration, admixture, interposition.

2. Supplement, addendum, codicil, postscript, rider, tag, appendage, prefix, suffix, subscript, affix, adjunct, passage introduced into a text, gloss, scholium, marginal notes, marginalia, postfix.

INTERPOSE, *v.* 1. Put a barrier between, put an obstacle in the way, come between things, assume an intervening position, interfere, interrupt, intercept, oppose, tamper, meddle, intermeddle, butt in, horn in, intrude, obtrude.

2. Insert, put in, place between, sandwich, interject, cause to intervene, introduce, thrust in, intercalate, import, insinuate, implant, interpolate, inject, interjaculate, intersperse, interlard, parenthesize.

3. Bring influence to bear between parties, step in between parties at variance, offer by way of mediation, bring to bear by way of mediation, bring in by way of mediation, mediate, intercede, negotiate, arbitrate, intermediate, be a go-between, adjudicate, intervene, meet halfway, mediatize, reconcile, propitiate.

INTERPOSING, *adj.* 1. Coming between, intervening, intervenient, intermediate, interjacent, medial, mesial, intercalary, interjectional, parenthetical, episodic.

2. Meddlesome, meddling, officious, interfering, intrusive, obtrusive, opposing, hindering.

3. Mediatory, mediating, mediatorial, intermedial, intercessory, interventional, intermediary, reconciliatory, propitiatory, diplomatic, instrumental.

INTERPOSITION, *n.* 1. Interlocation, interjacence, interpenetration, intercurrence, interpolation, introduction, insertion, interjection, intercalation, insinuation, interspersion, parenthesis, interlineation.

2. Interference, obtrusion, intrusion, meddlesomeness, officiousness, meddling, tampering.

3. Mediation, intermediation, intercession, intervention, mediatorship, interpellation, instrumentality, ministry, agency, arbitration, good offices, negotiation, parley, compromise, reconciliation.

INTERPRET, *v.* 1. Set forth the meaning of, expound, explain, explicate, elucidate, make clear, clear up, explain the meaning of, account for, define, make out, spell out, read between the lines, unfold, unravel, disentangle, decode, decipher, solve, throw light upon, lay open, reveal.

2. Understand in a particular way, read significance into, construe, render, literalize, synonymize, express by a synonym, paraphrase, rephrase, reword, restate, state differently, repeat, rehash, express broadly, describe, comment upon, commentate, annotate, margin, gloss, illustrate, illuminate, exemplify, simplify, popularize.

3. Bring out the meaning of *(a dramatic work, music, etc.)* by performance or execution, enact, portray, depict, play, perform, dance, choreograph.

INTERPRETATION, *n.* 1. Act of interpreting, explanation, explication, exposition, definition, elucidation, diagnosis, solution, rendition, reddition, unfoldment, decipherment, unravelment, disentanglement, revelation, hermeneutics, description.

2. Construction, construal, understanding, version, reading, rendering, paraphrase, translation, commentary, note, comment, scholium, annotation, exegesis, *éclaircissement (Fr.),* exemplification, illustration, rewording, metaphrase, signification, reflection, deduction, inference, animadversion, equivalent, synonym, analogue, meaning, sense, answer, clue, key, *mot de l'énigme (Fr.),* clavis, gloss, crib, pony, trot.

3. Rendering of (a dramatic work, music, dance, etc.) so as to bring out the meaning or to indicate one's particular conception, enactment, portrayal, depiction, performance, execution, choreography.

INTERPRETER, *n.* Expounder, exponent, demonstrator, expositor, explainer, guide, conductor, leader, director, teacher, *cicerone (It.),* steerer, pilot, dragoman, *valet de place (Fr.),* translator, commentator, annotator, scholiast, oracle, oneirocritic *(dreams),* spokesman, mouthpiece, speaker, prolocutor, foreman *(jury),* chairman, representative, ambassador, delegate, plenipotentiary, mediator, advocate, intercessor, pleader.

INTERREGNUM, *n.* 1. Interval of time between the close of a sovereign's reign and the accession of his successor, period during which a state has no ruler or only a temporary executive, suspension of authority, dethronement, abdication, deposition, usurpation, temporary arrangement, period of derangement, anarchy, freedom, laxity, laxness.

2. Any pause in continuity, interruption, discontinuance, cessation, remission, pendency, abeyance, interim, while, interlude, interval, intermission, recess, respite, rest, lull, intermediate time.

INTERROGATE, *v.* Ask a person questions, examine by questions, catechize, ask, question, inquire of, make inquiry of, interpellate, put questions to, put to the question, query, quiz, pump, grill, cross-examine, cross-interrogate, cross-question, subject to examination, investigate, put through the third degree, prosecute an inquiry of, require an answer, demand, dispute, controvert, doubt, challenge, accuse, charge, roast, badger, heckle.

INTERROGATION, *n.* 1. Interrogating, interpellation, examination, catechizing, questioning, examining, quiz, third degree, catechism, investigation, query, asking, Socratic method, cross-interrogation, cross-examination, cross-questioning, challenge, demand, request.

2. Question, query, inquiry, problem, poser, moot point, question at issue, interrogatory.

INTERROGATIVE, *adj.* Conveying a question, questioning, interrogatory, quizzical, inquisitive, inquisitorial, inquiring, investigative, prying, curious, percontatorial, analytic, zetetic.

INTERRUPT, *v.* 1. Stop in the midst of, cause a discontinuance, cause to cease, put a stop to, cause to delay, interfere with, hinder from proceeding, interpose, intercept, disturb, clog, obstruct, check, hinder, break, oppose, pretermit, thwart, frustrate, balk, foil, retard, cut short, arrest, dam up, cut in on, infringe upon, break in upon, butt in.

2. Cease in the midst, suspend, intermit in the course of, cease for a while, leave off, break off, come to a standstill, come to an end, remit, desist, discontinue, quiet down.

3. Disconnect, punctuate, intersect, disjoin, divide, disunite, sunder, sever, dissever, dissolve, break, cut.

INTERRUPTION, *n.* 1. Retardation, inhibition, prevention, restriction, restraint, interception, counteraction, hampering, preclusion, determent, delay, impediment, embarrassment, obstruction, stoppage, obstacle, hindrance, punctuation, closure, remission, relinquishment, cancellation, annulment, caesura.

2. Pause, intermission, discontinuance, discontinuation, cessation, respite, suspension, standstill, deadlock, dead stop, checkmate, end, halt, rest, lull, armistice, truce, cease-fire, interval, abeyance, break, recess, interval, hitch, stop, arrest, check, block, stay, interregnum.

3. Disconnection, disunion, dissolution, disjunction, severance, division, sunderance, separation, break, rift, gap, hiatus.

INTERSECT, *v.* 1. Cut by passing through, divide by lying across, decussate, cross, interrupt, thwart, crosscut.

2. Cross each other, interlace, crisscross, lace, cut each other, interweave, intertwine, interlink.

INTERSECTION, *n.* 1. Crossing, decussation, meeting place, dividing point, crisscross, crossway, crossroad, crosswalk, crosspath, network, interlacement, interconnection, complex system, reticulation.

2. *(Highways)* Traffic circle, interchange, cloverleaf.

INTERSPACE, *n.* Space between things, opening, gap, interstice, break, crevice, crack, cleft, slit, fissure, cranny, chink, chimney *(mountaineering)*, rift, puncture, hole, fracture, gash, rent, fault, flaw, breach, hiatus, rime, chasm, cut, mesh, lacuna, scissure, slot, chap.

INTERSPERSE, *v.* Scatter here and there among other things, sprinkle, intermingle, introduce here and there, interlard, interpose, diversify with something scattered, pepper, distribute, intercalate, interpolate, interdigitate, interpose, work in, wedge in, put between.

INTERSTICE, *n.* Intervening space, small or narrow space between parts, interspace, space between, interval, small opening, break, fissure, gap, crevice, hole, cranny, mesh, crack, chap, slot, slit, cleft, creek, lacuna, rime, chasm, hiatus, interruption, leak, cut, fracture, gash, rent, breach, rift, flaw, scissure.

INTERSTITIAL, *adj.* Pertaining to interstices, forming interstices, intervenient, intermediate, intervening, intermediary, interjacent, intercurrent, intercostal, intercalary, intermural, embolismal, embolismic, parenthetical, episodic.

INTERTEXTURE, *n.* 1. Intertwining, interweaving, interlacement, intertwinement, intersection, convolution, transversion, decussation, inosculation, anastomosis, interdigitation, reticulation, network, meshwork.

2. Interwoven mass, tissue, netting, web, net, mesh, plexus, skein, plait, wicker, twill, trellis, matting, wattle, grille, lattice, fretwork, reticle, tracery, filigree.

INTERTWINE, *v.* Interlace, twine together, intwine, interweave, inweave, tangle, entangle, braid, fret, cross, decussate, intersect, intertwist, interdigitate, entwine, interlink, wreathe, weave, twist, inosculate, anastomose, splice, dovetail, plait, plat, mat, ravel, knot, net, dishevel, raddle.

INTERVAL, *n.* 1. Space intervening between things, interspace, interstice, intermediate space, space between, gap, skip, distance, hiatus, break, lacuna, separation, division, void, vacuum, vacancy, crevice, fissure, cleft, crack, opening, cranny, rift, hole, fracture, flaw, puncture, breach, rent, cut, gash, fault, difference, stretch, degree, way between, chasm, snap, gorge, defile, ravine, pass, canyon, abyss, crevasse, abysm, notch, clough, gulf, gully, *couloir (Fr.),* barranco *(Sp.),* gulch.

2. Intervening period of time, intermediate time, interim, meantime, pause, recess, respite, interlude, interregnum, space of time, term, spell, season, period, vacation, reprieve.

INTERVENE, *v.* 1. Come between in action, interpose, mediate, intercede, step in, arbitrate, negotiate, use one's influence, meet halfway, mediatize, propitiate, reconcile.

2. Fall between other events, happen in the meantime, befall, betide, occur, happen between other periods, occur incidentally so as to modify a result, take place, transpire, chance, eventuate, come to pass, turn out, take effect, fall out, present itself, supervene, crop up, turn up, ensue, arrive, result, start, arise, take its course, elapse, lapse, run, flow, proceed, advance, fly, pass, slip, slide, expire, go by, drag, crawl, glide, pass by, be past.

3. Interfere, intrude, obtrude, intermeddle, butt in, horn in, come in as something not belonging, interrupt, break in.

4. Discontinue, pause, break off, part, drop, stop, suspend, cease, disconnect, disjoin, separate, dissever, disunite.

INTERVENING, *adj.* 1. Intermediate, intercurrent, interjacent, intervenient, intermediary, intercalary, interjectional, medial, interposing, interfering, coming between.

2. Interstitial, intercostal, intermural, interplanetary, interstellar.

3. Incidental, parenthetical, episodic, happening, intrusive, occurring, current, prevailing, doing.

4. Instrumental, ministerial, useful, subservient, mediatory, mediating, intercessory, intermedial, interventional, conciliatory, pacificatory, propitiatory, diplomatic, reconciliatory.

INTERVENTION, *n*. 1. Interposition, interpolation, interference, interjacence, interlocation, interjection, interpenetration, intercalation, interspersion, insertion, insinuation, parenthesis, intercurrence, intrusion, obtrusion.

2. Mediation, mediatorship, intermediation, agency, instrumentality, intercession, arbitration, peacemaking, ministry, good offices, hand, negotiation, compromise, parley.

3. Occurrence, eventuality, emergency, contingency, crisis, pass, experience, episode, adventure, phenomenon, circumstance, proceeding, transaction, incident, affair, fact, event, scene, happening.

4. Lapse, passage, march, tide, flow, sweep, progress. passing, course, flight, duration, termination, expiration, end, age, lifetime, eon.

INTERVIEW, *n*. 1. Conversation with a person from whom information is sought, parley, colloquy, collocution, consultation, conference, meeting of persons face-to-face for formal conference, discussion, *tête-à-tête (Fr.)*, oral communication, confabulation, audience, *conversazione (It.)*, reception, powwow, converse, palaver, *causerie (Fr.)*, *pourparler (Fr.)*, discourse, communion, intercourse, commerce, chitchat, chat, dialogue, duologue, appointment, date, call, rendezvous, assignation, tryst, interlocution.

2. Gathering, congregation, assembly, assemblage, conclave, congress, social gathering, reunion, levee, soirée, matinée.

INTERWEAVE, *v*. Weave together one with another, interlace, intertwine, inweave, cross, decussate, intersect, interdigitate, intertwist, twine, interlink, entwine, twist, wreathe, intermingle, combine as if by weaving, commingle, confound, commix, splice, mat, tangle, plait, plat, braid, twill, felt, entangle, ravel, knot, net, dishevel, raddle.

INTESTINE, *adj*. 1. Internal, interior, inner, inside, inward, inmost, innermost.

2. Domestic, homebred, native, indigenous, autochthonous, civil, home, indoor, intramural, inland, vernacular, endemic, intraterritorial.

3. Innate, inborn, inbred, intrinsic, inherent, ingrained, deep-seated, implanted, infixed, inwrought.

4. Visceral, intestinal, splanchnic, abdominal, celiac, ventral, stomachic, duodenal, rectal.

INTESTINES, *n., pl*. Lower part of the alimentary canal extending from the pylorus to the anus, inwards, entrails, bowels, viscera, splanchna, insides, guts, chitterlings, vitals, belly.

INTIMACY, *n*. 1. Close acquaintance, intimate association, warm friendship, familiarity, fellowship, mutual affection, companionship, fraternization, brotherliness, brotherhood, fraternity, friendliness, neighborliness, fellow feeling, sociability, amity, cordiality, chumship, chumminess, comradeship, fast friendship, close attachment, nearness 'and dearness, close physical contact, close personal knowledge, close personal relationship.

2. Nearness, closeness, propinquity, proximity, contiguity, adjacency, adherence, connection.

3. Illicit sexual relations, clandestine sexual commerce, intercourse, liaison, amour, amourette, love affair.

INTIMATE, *adj*. 1. Associated in close personal relations, involving personally familiar association, on intimate terms with, bosom, close, confidential, very dear, inseparable, chummy, companionly, comradely, fraternal, brotherly, fast, thick, hearty, hand-and-glove, friendly, affable, confiding, at home with, companionable, warmhearted, near and dear.

2. Pertaining to the inner character or essential nature of a thing, springing from the inmost self, deep-seated, innermost, from within, internal, inward, interior, deep within, intrinsic, inherent, indwelling, immanent.

3. Connected, related, close, near, contiguous, adjacent.

4. Detailed, deep, direct, thorough.

5. Private, closely personal, exclusive, special, especial, peculiar, restricted, individual, unique.

6. Maintaining illicit sexual relations, amorous, amatory, erotic, voluptuous, sensual, carnal, fleshly, lascivious, lewd, lecherous, concupiscent, lustful, licentious, wanton, libidinous, salacious, dissolute, adulterous, fornicative, prurient, debauched, unchaste, loose, of easy virtue, rakish, libertine, *in flagrante delicto (Lat.)*.

INTIMATE, *n*. 1. Bosom friend, fast friend, close associate, intimate acquaintance, familiar, confidant, crony, chum, comrade, mate, pal, buddy, sidekick, shadow, bedfellow, bunkie, boon companion, man Friday, devoted follower, alter ego, other self, *fidus Achates (Lat.)*.

2. Pylades and Orestes, Theseus and Pirithous, Nisus and Euryalus, Heracles and Iolaüs, Damon and Pythias, Castor and Pollux, Epaminondas and Pelopidas, Achilles and Patroclus, David and Jonathan.

INTIMATE, *v*. Make known indirectly, hint, mention briefly, insinuate, allude to, suggest, make allusion to, give an inkling of, indicate, put in mind of, drop a hint, tip off, throw out a hint, give a pointer, breathe in the ear, let fall, imply, prompt, give the cue, communicate, tell, inform of, acquaint with, bring to the ears of, impart to, advise, apprise, point out, put into one's head, report, disclose, announce, notify, signify, refer to.

INTIMATELY, *adv*. 1. Familiarly, confidentially, closely, inseparably, personally, chummily, companionably, fraternally, brotherly, thickly, confidingly, nearly and dearly.

2. Closely, nearly, hand-in-glove, side-by-side, cheek-by-jowl, cheek-to-cheek.

3. Thoroughly, fully, deeply, in detail, through and through, to the bottom, *au fond (Fr.)*, fundamentally, to the core.

INTIMATION, *n*. Passing word, word in the ear, word to the wise, *verbum sapienti (Lat.)*, insinuation, hint, innuendo, allusion, suggestion, reference, inkling, implication, wrinkle, indication, subaudition, gentle hint, monition, warning, whisper, by-play, cue, gesture, communication, notice, notification, representation, clue, annunciation, reminder.

INTIMIDATE, *v*. Make timid, inspire with fear, affright, frighten, terrify, put in fear, scare, alarm, appall, dismay, astound, awe, daunt, cow, overawe, bulldoze, bully, bullyrag, abash, terrorize, threaten, startle, stampede, panic, subdue, browbeat, badger, unman, petrify, make afraid, undomineer, bluster, bluff, dishearten, deter from some action by inducing fear, discourage, dispirit, damp.

INTIMIDATION, *n.* 1. Intimidating, daunting, bullying, browbeating, overawing, bulldozing, terrorizing, threatening.

2. Fright, affright, terror, fear, alarm, dismay, dread, terrorism, panic, reign of terror, consternation, perturbation, scare, cold feet funk, trepidation, stampede, fear and trembling, flutter, tremor, disquietude, nervousness.

3. Bugbear, bogy, nightmare, incubus, hobgoblin, bugaboo, *bête noire (Fr.),* scarecrow, specter.

INTOLERABLE, *adj.* 1. That cannot be borne, not to be put up with, not to be endured, unendurable, insupportable, insufferable, unbearable, unsustainable, not tolerable.

2. Painful, grievous, cruel, sore, excruciating, agonizing, harrowing, rending, cutting, torturous, tormenting, racking, acute, raw, maddening.

3. Terrific, grim, appalling, frightful, dire, fearful, dreadful, shocking, horrifying, horrible, terrible.

4. Unpleasant, unwelcome, disagreeable, displeasing, distasteful, irritating, annoying, provoking, aggravating, odious, obnoxious, offensive, execrable, hateful, abominable, revolting, loathsome.

INTOLERANCE, *n.* 1. Indisposition to tolerate contrary beliefs or opinions, lack of toleration, bigotry, narrow-mindedness, narrowness, illiberality, dogmatism, fanaticism, persecuting spirit, want of forbearance, opinionativeness, zealotry, prejudice, fixed idea, *idée fixe (Fr.),* monomania, warped judgment, onesidedness, jingoism, chauvinism, proscriptive spirit, persecution.

2. Incapacity to bear or endure, non-endurance, rejection, disallowance, refusal, impatience.

INTOLERANT, *adj.* 1. Not tolerating contrary opinions, narrow-minded, illiberal, bigoted, prejudiced, one-sided, fanatical, proscriptive, narrow, confined, parochial, provincial, insular, besotted, warped, infatuated, cracked, *entêté (Fr.),* rabid, dogmatic, positive, opinionated, opinionative, *opiniâtre (Fr.),* unreasonable, arbitrary, sectarian, denominational, heterodox, schismatic, recusant, protestant, negative, dissentient, prepossessed.

2. Stiff-necked, hide-bound, stiff-backed, hard-mouthed, strait-laced, puritanical, ascetic, strict, rigorous, rigid, prim, prudish, severe.

3. Impatient, excitable, high-strung, irritable, feverish, unquiet, restless, fussy, fidgety, hurried, hasty, chafing, skittish, mettlesome, vehement, violent, fiery, hot-headed, fierce, wild, furious, overzealous, impassionated, clamorous, rampant, turbulent, tempestuous, boisterous, tumultuary, volcanic, burning, simmering, irrepressible, ungovernable.

4. Indisposed to tolerate, inhospitable, unforbearing, uncharitable, misanthropic, cynical, incompatible, inconsiderate, disobliging, unfriendly.

5. Imperious, overbearing, dictatorial, supercilious, arrogant, magisterial, haughty, high-handed, contumelious, high and mighty, overweening, domineering, bold-faced, barefaced, presumptuous, officious.

INTONATION, *n.* Melody of pitch changes revealed in connected speech, pitch pattern of a sentence distinguishing speakers of different nationalities, manner of producing musical tones, relation in pitch of tones to their key or harmony, accent, twang, cadence, tone, modulation of voice, inflection, pronunciation, musical recitation, utterance, enunciation, vocalization, prolation, articula-

tion, accentuation, pitch, overtone, tune, sonority, resonance, timbre, sonorousness.

INTONE, *v.* 1. Utter with a particular tone, intonate, phonetize, phonate, prolate, articulate, enunciate, pronounce, accentuate, give voice, aspirate, mouth, deliver, emit, whisper, murmur, vocalize, modulate, give variety of tone to.

2. Utter in a singing voice, chant, sol-fa, chaunt, warble, chirp, hum, carol, lilt, trill, purl, croon, twitter, quaver.

3. Recite in monotone, singsong, drawl.

IN TOTO *(Lat.)* Wholly, in the whole, entirely, outright, in all, at all points, quite, utterly, altogether, completely, totally, entirely, as a whole, all, *in extenso (Lat.),* fully, in the aggregate, *en masse (Fr.), en bloc (Fr.),* collectively, substantially, from top to toe, cap-a-pie, from head to foot, from first to last, every inch, every whit, out and out, in all respects, throughout, root and branch, heart and soul, lock, stock and barrel.

INTOXICANT, *n.* 1. Intoxicating agent, strong drink, stimulant, liquor, alcohol, John Barleycorn, blue ruin, booze, moonshine, firewater, rot-gut, spirits, *spiritus frumenti (Lat.),* whiskey, brandy, rum, vodka, gin, wine, beer, ale, grog, porter, stout, cider, champagne, liqueur, cordial, absinthe, toddy, punch, aperitif, cocktail, highball.

2. Drug, narcotic, dope, opium, morphine, morphia, cocaine, heroin, hashish, snow *(slang),* bhang, marijuana, reefer *(slang),* hop *(slang).*

INTOXICATE, *v.* 1. Affect temporarily with loss of control over physical and mental powers by means of liquor (or a drug), make drunk, inebriate, fuddle, make tipsy, besot, muddle, befuddle, stupefy, stew, fuzzle, mellow, cause intoxication, make see double, give a drop too much, liquor one up, go to one's head, sozzle, overcome, put under the table, cause to be three sheets in the wind, make drunk as a lord, send half seas over, hop up, pifflicate, light up, pickle.

2. Excite mentally beyond self-control or reason, elate, exhilarate, infatuate, animate, stimulate, enliven, incite, rouse, goad, arouse, inflame, spur, foment, whet, stir up, kindle, work up, prepossess, enrapture, captivate, fascinate, enchant, entrance, ensorcel, bewitch, charm, get *(slang),* fire.

INTOXICATED, *adj.* 1. Drunk, drunken, inebriated, three sheets to the wind, tipsy, tight, in one's cups, *inter pocula (Lat.),* lush, mellow, befuddled, boozy, stewed, muddled, maudlin, half-seas-over, fuddled, muzzy, screwed, oiled, primed, temulent, inebrious, inebriate, squiffy, plastered, sozzled, flushed, red-nosed, topheavy, groggy, pot-valiant, potulent, overcome, corned, sewed up, pickled, pifflicated *(slang),* nappy, bosky, the worse for liquor, crapulous, blind-drunk, dead-drunk, one over the eight, under the table, drunk as a lord, sottish, bibulous, bibacious, full *(slang),* lit up, stupefied, elevated.

2. Excited mentally beyond self-control, infatuated, exhilarated, prepossessed, ecstatic, rapt, beside oneself, captivated, fascinated, enchanted, ensorceled, bewitched, charmed, enraptured, rapturous, entranced, absorbed, enamored, rhapsodic.

INTOXICATION, *n.* 1. Drunkenness, inebriation, inebriety, insobriety, tipsiness, crapulousness, stupefaction, cups, intemperance, winebibbing, oenomania, libations, bacchanalia, dipsomania, alcoholism, debauchery, befuddlement, bibacity, temulency, deep potations, spree, jollification, orgy, revel, carousal, saturnalia, drinking bout.

2. Overpowering effect upon the mind, extreme

exhilaration, infatuation, uncontrollable excitement, ecstasy, frenzy, elation, madness, excitation of feeling, stimulation, galvanism, infection, subjugation, fascination, enravishment, ensorcelment, emotional transport, thrill, ferment, whirl, madness, distraction, delirium, raving, brain storm, tearing passion, *tête montée (Fr.)*, enchantment.

INTRACTABILITY, *n.* 1. Stubbornness, intractableness, dogged resolution, obstinacy, obduracy, inflexibility, perverseness, indocility, pervicacity, contumacy, perversity, spinosity, sternness, torvity, ticism, zealotry, infatuation, monomania, cacoëthes, opinionativeness, dogmatism, bigotry, incorrigibility, fixed idea, *idée fixe (Fr.).*

2. Sullenness, morosity, churlishness, crabbedness, moodiness, sulkiness, sulks, dudgeon, doleful dumps, doldrums, *bouderie (Fr.)*, huff.

INTRACTABLE, *adj.* Hard to deal with, not docile, stubborn, indocile, unmanageable, uncontrollable, obstinate, cross-grained, ungovernable, refractory, recalcitrant, restive, contrarious, perverse, contrary, fractious, unyielding, obdurate, headstrong, wilful, dogged, stiff-necked, wrongheaded, contumacious, pervicacious, inflexible, wayward, froward, difficult, rampant, wild, unbridled, rebellious, not pliable, hard to handle, not easily governed, incorrigible, impetuous, impossible, sullen, grim, torvous, churlish, uncompromising, intransigent, irreconcilable, resolved, unruly, cantankerous, tough, mulish, pigheaded, pertinacious.

INTRANSIGENT, *adj.* Uncompromising, irreconcilable, not to be shaken, *tenax propositi (Lat.)*, inflexible, unbending, unyielding, firm as a rock, stand-pat, determined, resolved, strong-willed, strong-minded, tenacious, die-hard, cast-iron, firm-minded, indomitable, inexorable, obdurate, obstinate, intent upon, bent upon, steeled against, rigorous, rigid, exacting, exigent.

INTREPID, *adj.* Not alarmed, fearless, bold, brave, valiant, valorous, doughty, courageous, daring, heroic, undaunted, dauntless, undismayed, lion-hearted, audacious, stalwart, manful, virile, gallant, adventurous, venturesome, game, soldierly, manly, chivalrous, nervy, plucky, stout, hardy, unshrinking, unfaltering, unappalled, unterrified, unawed, aweless, unafraid, firm, self-reliant, Spartan, high-spirited, mettlesome, resolute, stout-hearted, iron-hearted, bold-spirited, confident, bold as brass, enterprising, dashing, hardy, indomitable.

INTREPIDITY, *n.* Fearlessness, contempt of danger, courage, boldness, bravery, spirit, dauntlessness, daring, valor, mettle, nerve, pluck, grit, sand, spunk, prowess, heroism, gallantry, hardihood, resolution, assurance, audacity, fortitude, chivalry, firmness, resoluteness, derring-do, defiance of danger, dash, self-reliance, confidence, manliness, virility, gameness, virtue, backbone, heart of oak.

INTRICACY, *n.* Intricateness, entanglement, complexity, involution, convolution, complication, maze, labyrinth, network, tangled skein, jungle, Gordian knot, coil, tortuosity, anfractuosity, meandering, windings and turnings, ambages, snarl, confusion, difficulty, perplexity, obscurity, dilemma, involvement, quandary, nonplus.

INTRICATE, *adj.* Complicated, perplexingly involved, confusingly complex, mazy, labyrinthine, chaotic, knotty, daedalian, meandering, anfractuous, tortuous, confused, winding, bending in and out, flexuous, twisted, wreathed, circuitous, obscure, entangled, convoluted, tortile, sinuous, difficult, puzzling, highly wrought, arduous, hard to understand, unintelligible, not easy, troublesome, irksome, laborious, operose, onerous, formidable, plaguy, thorny, trying, embarrassing, ticklish, delicate, beset with difficulties.

INTRIGANT, *n.* 1. One who carries on intrigue, plotter, schemer, intriguer, conspirator, man of cunning, trickster, sly boots, shifter, fox, reynard, Machiavelli, Ulysses, Greek, sharp fellow.

2. Busybody, meddler, snooper, snoop, Paul Pry, kibitzer, pickthank, intermeddler, gossip, tattler, talebearer.

3. Libertine, rake, roué, debauchee, fast man, rip, rakehell, voluptuary, silk-stocking, gallant, lecher, satyr, fornicator, seducer, adulterer, *paillard (Fr.)*, whoremonger, Don Juan, Lothario, Casanova, gay deceiver, sensualist.

INTRIGUE, *n.* 1. Underhand machination to accomplish some design, scheme, ruse, wile, stratagem, finesse, maneuver, wirepulling, conspiracy, racket, plan, plot, cabal, connivance, deception, craftiness, Machiavelianism, cunning, circumvention, dodge, duplicity, chicanery, collusion, trickery, diplomacy, behind-the-scenes manipulations, artifice, subtlety, jugglery, complot, double-dealing, frame-up, knavery, sharp practice, guile, jobbery, backstairs, influence, shift, subterfuge, *espièglerie (Fr.)*, trap, net.

2. Clandestine love affair, liaison, amour, illicit intimacy, tryst.

3. Licentiousness, gallantry, coquetry, flirtation, debauchery, libertinism, fornication, venery, wenching, dissipation, seduction, harlotry, whoremongering, concubinage, stupration, adultery, cuckoldom, incontinence, pruriency, lasciviousness, lechery, concupiscence.

INTRIGUE, *v.* 1. Use underhand machinations, plot craftily, maneuver, conspire, machinate, scheme, complot, cabal, counterplot, mine, undermine, contrive, live by one's wits, finesse, circumvent, stoop to conquer, temporize, overreach, steal a march upon, throw off one's guard, surprise, get the better of, outdo, waylay, have all one's eyes about one, be sharp, seize the opportunity, have fish to fry, have an iron in the fire, have a finger in the pie, tamper with, meddle.

2. Engage in an illicit love affair, carry on an amour, have a liaison, keep trysts with, make an assignation.

3. Excite the interest of, take the fancy of, beguile by appeal to the interest, captivate, fascinate, enamor, carry away, bewitch, allure, charm, enrapture, give pleasure, rivet the attention, absorb, intoxicate, transport, ravish, please, delight, take, entrance, seduce.

INTRIGUING, *adj.* 1. Crafty, insidious, cunning, subtle, wily, *rusé (Fr.)*, sly, artful, tricky, foxy, vulpine, designing, arch, scheming, deceitful, crooked, slippery, tortuous, diplomatic, Machiavellian, politic, underhand, feline, double-faced, deceptive, shifty, strategic.

2. Attractive, exciting, inviting, engaging, prepossessing, taking, winning, captivating, fascinating, seductive, enticing, alluring, bewitching, enchanting, interesting, ravishing, absorbing, entrancing, delightful, charming, beguiling.

INTRINSIC, *adj.* 1. Belonging to a thing by its very nature, innate, inborn, inbred, inherent, ingrained, inward, internal, inner, interior, implanted, native, natural, congenital, immanent, indwelling, inherited, ingenerate, inwrought, fundamental, incarnate, radical, hereditary, indigenous, connate, bred in the bone, constitutional, in the grain, running in the blood, inseparable, ineradicable, characteristic, fixed, constituent, subjective.

2. Genuine, sterling, real, authentic, legitimate, orthodox, pure, sound, true, essential, actual, true, veritable, veracious, unimpeachable.

INTRODUCE, *v.* 1. Start, commence, begin, institute, initiate, inaugurate, be the first to take up, broach, originate, conceive, open, embark in, break ground, undertake, lay the foundations, set on foot, set up, launch, bring into use, bring before the public, bring into notice.

2. Usher in, lead into a place, conduct, lead the way, forerun, precede, head, take the lead, herald.

3. Present formally, bring into relations, bring into the acquaintance of another, make known to, acquaint with.

4. Preface, prelude, premise, preamble, make introductory remarks, M.C.

5. Place in, insert, import, inject, bring into, induct, interpolate, put in, cast in, obtrude, interpose, intercalate, implant, infuse, interject, insinuate, interjaculate, interlard, intersperse.

INTRODUCTION, *n.* 1. Formal presentation of one person to another, acquaintanceship, acquaintance, ceremonial, greeting, salutation, welcome, reception, *acceuil (Fr.)*, *bienvenue (Fr.)*.

2. Material given at the front of a book to explain it to the reader, foreword, preface, prolegomenon, proem, prelude, exordium, prologue, preamble, prelusion, prolepsis, protasis, overture, frontispiece, heading, groundwork, elementary treatise, rudiments, primer, formal preliminary guide, preliminary part.

3. Preliminary remarks, first appearance, debut, admittance, initiation, opening, insertion, introception, receiving, **recipience.**

INTRODUCTORY, *adj.* Preliminary, introductive, opening, precursory, initiative, preparatory, initiary, prelusive, initiatory, preludial, antecedent, prevenient, preceding, initial, prefatory, prolegomenal, proemial, inaugural, incipient, rudimentary, basic, embryonic, leading, inauguratory.

INTROSPECTION, *n.* Observation of one's own mental states, examination of one's own mental processes, self-examination, self-contemplation, introversion, looking within oneself, consideration of one's own internal feelings, self-study, self-scrutiny, self-absorption, direction of interest inward upon the self, self-counsel, self-communion, abstraction, musing, brown study, reverie, inmost thoughts, self-consultation.

INTROSPECTIVE, *adj.* Inward-looking, pensive, self-communing, thoughtful, subjective, rapt in, deliberative, reflective, meditative, museful, cogitative, contemplative, wistful, self-speculative, deep-musing, in a brown study, self-absorbed, engrossed in self, lost to the outside world, brooding, self-examining, introversive, woolgathering.

INTROVERT, *n.* Person concerned chiefly with his thoughts, self-observer, self-communer, muser, self-scrutinizer, self-absorbed person, self-counselor, self-inspector, brooder, woolgatherer, *heautontimoroumenos (Gk.)*, self-tormentor.

INTRUDE, *v.* Enter where one is not welcome, thrust oneself in, force oneself in, obtrude, interlope, come uninvited, impose, muscle into *(slang)*, bring in without reason, encroach without permission, foist in, worm oneself in, interfere, interpose, intermeddle, invade, take part officiously, trespass, infringe, trench on, transgress, overstep, horn in, butt in, intervene, break in upon, be ill-timed, mistime, crash.

INTRUDER, *n.* Intermeddler, interloper, obtruder, interrupter, interferer, meddler, buttinsky *(slang)*, trespasser, imposer, invader, stranger, newcomer, parvenu, upstart, transgressor.

INTRUSION, *n.* 1. Forced entrance, uninvited attendance, intruding, obtrusion, interloping, imposition, interference, interposition, intermeddling, meddlesomeness, intervention, horning in, butting in.

2. Infringement, encroachment, trespass, transgression, overstepping, overrunning, transilience, transcendence, advance, overture, aggression, invasion, infraction, attack, inroad, incursion, irruption, illapse.

3. Unseasonableness, inopportuneness, intempestivity, improper time, contretemps, evil hour.

INTRUSIVE, *adj.* Coming without welcome, entering unbidden, ill-timed, mistimed, inopportune, unseasonable, untimely, inexpedient, ingressive, invasive, obtrusive, trespassing, transgressive, irruptive, irreptitious, meddlesome, meddling, officious, pushing, impertinent, presumptuous, troublesome, disturbing, interfering, importunate, annoying, inquisitive.

INTUIT, *v.* Receive knowledge by insight, know by intuition, apprehend, hazard a feeling, judge intuitively, have a presentiment, know by instinct, be conscious of, feel instinctively, realize, sense, have insight, feel in one's bones, have a hunch, be clairvoyant, have second sight.

INTUITION, *n.* 1. Direct perception independent of any reasoning process, immediate perception by the intellect, direct cognition, instinctive knowledge, apprehension at first sight, insight, instinctive comprehension, pure untaught noninferential knowledge, *Anschauung (Ger.)*, innate knowledge.

2. Extrasensory perception, perceptivity, penetration, sagacity, discernment, inspiration, perspicacity, clairvoyance, hunch, presentiment, divination, second sight.

INTUITIVE, *adj.* 1. Resulting from intuition, perceived at once without any rational process, apprehended immediately, intuitional, instinctive, inherent, natural, innate, inborn, inbred, ingrained, bred in the bones, transcendental, knowing, presentient, augural, percipient, apperceptive, cognitive, independent of reason, anterior to reason, inspirational, impulsive, automatic, involuntary, perceptive.

2. Immediate, on the spot, direct, clear, full, distinct, plain.

INTUMESCE, *v.* Swell up, dilate, incrassate, expand, become larger, become tumid, grow, enlarge, extend, increase, gather, spread, stretch, magnify, puff, inflate, blow up, fatten, augment, bloat, bag, bulge, belly, protrude.

INTUMESCENCE, *n.* Swelling up with congestion, turgescence, tumefaction, inturgescence, bloating, protuberance, protrusion, excrescency, tuberosity, tumor, increase, expansion, enlargement, augmentation, growth, increment, dilation, dilatation, turgidness, turgidity, distension, inflation, amplification.

INUNDATE, *v.* 1. Overspread with a flood, deluge, overflow, flood, submerge, drown, overwhelm, engulf, immerse, drench, irrigate, stream over, flow over.

2. Fill to superfluity, glut, surcharge, gorge, supersaturate, load, drug, cloy, choke, lavish, lay on thick.

INUNDATION, *n.* 1. Deluge, flood, cataclysm, overflow, floodtide, springtide, irrigation, freshet, cataract, waterspout, current, race, tide, torrent, rapids, spate, swash, high tide, indraught, reflux, wave, surge, swell, roller, breaker, surf, comber.

2. Oversupply, superfluity, redundance, superabundance, supersaturation, superfluence, engorgement, surfeit, load, congestion, overdose.

INURBANE, *adj.* Lacking in courtesy, wanting suavity, uncouth, unpolished, uncourteous, uncourtly, uncomplaisant, impolite, harsh, discourteous, surly, rude, rough, ill-mannered, ill-bred, ill-behaved, unmannerly, ungentlemanly, ungenteel, vulgar, uncivil, unceremonious, ungracious.

INURBANITY, *n.* Discourtesy, impoliteness, uncourtliness, ungentlemanliness, incivility, indecorum, boorishness, rusticity, bad manners, ill breeding, insuavity, uncourteousness, tactlessness, misbehavior, conduct unbecoming a gentleman, *brusquerie (Fr.), grossièreté (Fr.),* vulgarity.

INURE, *v.* Accustom, habituate, familiarize, discipline, harden by exercise, train, toughen, indurate, acclimatize, acclimate, season, wont, addict, caseharden, indoctrinate, strengthen.

INURN, *v.* Put into a funerary urn, inter, inhume, entomb, bury, consign to the grave, lay in the grave, consign to earth, inhumate.

INUTILE, *adj.* 1. Of no use, of no service, useless, bootless, unprofitable, ineffectual, inoperative, unavailing, futile, inefficacious, inefficient, inadequate, incompetent, inept, unproductive, unserviceable, fruitless, ill-spent, gainless, profitless.

2. Trashy, valueless, not worth a straw, unsalable, worthless, meritless, dear at any price, good for nothing, idle, vain, inane, empty, barren, impotent, effete, sterile, obsolete, worn out, not worth powder and shot.

INUTILITY, *n.* 1. Uselessness, unserviceableness, unprofitableness, futility, worthlessness, inefficacy, inadequacy, ineptitude, inefficiency, unfitness, unskillfulness, incompetence, labor in vain, flash in the pan, pouring water into a sieve, carrying coals to Newcastle, casting pearls before swine, beating the air, kicking against the pricks, baying the moon, nugacity, frivolity, triviality.

2. Trash, rubbish, litter, junk, refuse, leavings, rags, odds and ends, waste, dross, sweepings, dregs, scum, offscourings, garbage, rubble, stubble, tares, chaff, weeds, debris.

INVADE, *v.* 1. Go into with hostile intent, enter as an enemy, march into, enter with an army, enter in force, assail, attack, harry, overrun, make aggression, make an assault upon, fall upon, take the offensive, thrust at, strike at, be the aggressor, advance against, march upon, march against, cross the frontier, cross the Rubicon, set foot on.

2. Intrude upon, encroach upon, violate, infringe upon, trench upon, trespass, make inroad, raid, butt in, horn in, break in upon.

INVADER, *n.* Intruder, trespasser, interloper, violator, infringer, encroacher, aggressor, assailant, attacker, overrunner, frontier-crosser, enemy, foe, raider.

INVALID, *adj.* (In-val'id) 1. Null, void, null and void, of no binding force, inoperative, unsound, nugatory, weak, of no weight, ineffectual, inefficacious, inadequate, futile, useless, good for nothing, dud.

2. Illogical, that does not hold true, untrue, unfounded, fallacious, baseless, unreasonable, unwarranted, false, not following, unscientific, untenable, fallible, unproved, incorrect, irrational, flimsy, irrelevant.

INVALID, *adj.* (In'va-lid) Deficient in health, infirm, ailing, sick, sickly, valetudinary, feeble, weak, weakly, frail, debilitated, unwell, ill, indisposed, disabled, laid up, bedridden, confined, on the sick list, unhealthy, unsound, morbose, chlorotic, crippled, lame, flagging, halt, drooping, in declining health, prostrate, moribund, helpless, decrepit, superannuated, senile, paralyzed, paralytic, under doctor's care.

INVALID, *n.* Sickly person, infirm person, feeble person, valetudinarian, convalescent, patient, case, cripple, bedridden person, martyr to disease, paralytic.

INVALIDATE, *v.* Render of no binding effect, nullify, make void, cancel, annul, abrogate, reverse, quash, overthrow, undo, repeal, unmake, vitiate, disprove, refute, abolish, overrule, disannul, vacate, revoke, rescind, retract, reverse, recall, withdraw, set aside, override, nol-pros *(Law)*, declare null and void, dissolve, countermand, disclaim, repudiate, discard, dismiss, deprive of legal force, deprive of efficacy, render invalid.

INVALIDATION, *n.* Abolishment, abolition, vacation, annulment, cancellation, abrogation, rescission, revocation, countermand, repeal, recantation, retractation, repudiation, counterorder, recall, defeasance, *nolle prosequi (Law),* vacatur .*(Law),* undoing, vitiation, nullification.

INVALIDISM, *n.* Chronically prolonged ill health, valetudinarianism, loss of health, delicacy, cachexy, cachexia, decline, prostration, paralysis, palsy, ataxia, syncope, collapse, deliquium, debility, infirmity, sickness, feebleness, illness, morbosity, indisposition, complaint.

INVALIDITY, *n.* Want of validity, voidness, unsoundness, nullity, fallacy, fallaciousness, falsity, erroneousness, speciousness, flaw in an argument, lame and impotent conclusion, weak point, antilogy, inconsistency, sophism, paralogism, false refutation, elenchus, false teaching, perversion, falseness.

INVALUABLE, *adj.* That cannot be appraised, above appraisal, above all value, priceless, of inestimable value, above all price, very precious, costly, incapable of being paid, impayable, gilt-edged, capital, inimitable, first-class, first-rate, matchless, peerless, unequaled, unparalleled, rare, golden, unusual.

INVARIABLE, *adj.* Not capable of being varied, not changing, unchanging, changeless, unchangeable, immutable, always the same, unalterable, unvarying, uniform, regular, constant, permanent, stable, unbroken, flat, even, smooth, level, dead, stereotyped, cliché, undeviating, unvaried, symmetrical, homogeneous, correspondent, of a piece, monotonous, dreary, irreversible.

INVARIABLENESS, *n.* Invariability, unchangeableness, changelessness, immutability, regularity, unalterability, uniformity, constancy, unvarying character, uniformness, sameness, evenness, consistency, continuity, stability, permanence, even tenor, monotony, routine.

INVARIABLY, *adv.* Perpetually, everlastingly, eternally, evermore, forever, always, ever, universally, without exception, in all cases, in every instance, unceasingly, constantly, uniformly, regularly.

INVASION, *n.* 1. Predatory incursion, hostile ingress, irruption, illapse, inroad, aggression, attack, foray, assault, raid, drive, offensive, sally, sortie, investment, siege, bombardment, air raid, infiltration.

2. Infringement by intrusion, encroachment, intrusion, violation, trespass, transgression, infraction, breach.

INVASIVE, *adj.* Ingressive, incoming, intrusive, incursive, irruptive, aggressive, on the offensive, attacking, obsidional, up in arms, on the warpath, frontier-crossing, over the top, assailing, assaulting, assailant, invading.

INVECTIVE, *n.* 1. Vehement denunciation, utterance of violent censure, railing, abuse, vituperation, contumely, sarcastic attack, reproach, billingsgate, denouncement, condemnation, disapprobation, disparagement, reprehension, accusation, remonstrance, reprimand, depreciation, reproach, obloquy, opprobrium, expostulation, reprobation, increpation, rebuke, castigation, dressing down, rating, rebuff, home thrust, objurgation, personal remarks, hard words, cutting words, tirade, tongue-lashing.

2. Diatribe, philippic, lampoon, pasquinade, fling, satire, sarcasm, jeremiad, outcry, abusive harangue, squib.

INVECTIVE, *adj.* Censoriously abusive, railing, vituperative, denunciatory, censorious, reproachful, scolding, captious, harsh, disparaging, condemnatory, objurgatory, damnatory, defamatory, satirical, sardonic, sarcastic, assailing, sharp, biting, cutting, withering, virulent, trenchant, severe, carping, hypercritical, hard upon.

INVEIGH, *v.* Attack vehemently in words, vituperate, censure, score, denounce, declaim against, exclaim against, reproach, blame, condemn, rail at, thunder at, fulminate, blast, abuse, exprobrate, objurgate, raise a hue and cry against, disparage, impugn, remonstrate, recriminate, expostulate, chide, reprehend, admonish, lecture, call to account, rebuke, castigate, reprimand, blow up, lash, impeach, accuse, cry shame upon, execrate, speak daggers, scold, rate, upbraid, anathematize, call names, vilify, revile, lash with the tongue, raise one's voice against, cry down, satirize, lampoon.

INVEIGLE, *v.* Draw by artful inducements, allure, entice, beguile, cajole, lure, decoy, win, ensnare, entangle, seduce, lead astray, coax, wheedle, tempt, persuade, mislead, illaqueate, involve, attract, bamboozle, importune, gammon, defraud, delude, cozen, chouse, victimize, gull, cheat, swindle, catch, waylay.

INVEIGLER, *n.* Tempter, prompter, seducer, coaxer, seductor, wheedler, suggester, instigator, *agent provocateur (Fr.).*

INVENT, *v.* 1. Be the first to devise, contrive something new, discover, produce what did not before exist, originate as a product of one's own contrivance, create, compose, fashion.

2. Produce with the imagination, imagine, fancy, concoct something fictitious, idealize,

realize, dream of, give play to the imagination, design something false, improvise, picture, rhapsodize, indulge in reverie, conceive, excogitate, hatch, make up, project, sketch, conjure up a version, romance, plot, scheme, hit upon, visualize, draft, outline.

3. Fabricate, make up, forge, hammer out, mint, coin, cast, counterfeit, sham, fake.

4. Lie, trump up, prevaricate, humbug, feign, falsify, misrepresent, simulate, fib, distort, pervert, equivocate, mince the truth, varnish, embroider, dress up, exaggerate, cant, malinger.

INVENTION, *n.* 1. Act of inventing, origination, discovery, creation, production, concoction, formation, making, conception of an idea and the means by which the result is obtained *(Patent Law).*

2. Contrivance, expedient, design, device, artifice, gadget, thingumagig *(slang)*, stratagem, nostrum, receipt, bright idea, coup, master stroke, step, measure, great gun, trump card, maneuver.

3. Exercise of imagination or creative power, creating by the exercise of the imagination, power of inventing, ingenuity, originality, fancy, inspiration, verve, mind's eye, figment, excogitation, genius, conception, romanticism, ideality, dreaming, castle-building, rhapsody, reverie, daydream, whim, fantasy, romance, myth, vision, fairyland.

4. Fabrication, counterfeit, forgery, coinage, dissimulation, sham, fake, fiction, untruth, falsehood, mendacity, lie, fib, equivocation, prevarication.

INVENTIVE, *adj.* Apt at devising, imaginative, original, fertile, fictive, productive, creative, quick at contrivance, ingenious, originative, concoctive, gifted, clever, able, felicitous, talented, endowed, sharp, strategic, intellectual, adroit, expert, handy, slick, deft, apt, ready, resourceful, accomplished *au fait (Fr.).*

INVENTOR, *n.* One who devises some new process or article, originator, contriver, deviser, designer, creator, founder, father, author, generator, architect, mover, constructor, maker, grower, producer.

INVENTORY, *n.* Detailed descriptive list of number and value of articles, value of a stock of goods, list of the goods of a merchant, contents, index, table, account, invoice, bill, manifest, register, record, catalogue, enumeration, document, roll, schedule, rota, muster, panel, beadroll, poll, roster, ticket, slate, docket, ballot, bulletin, calendar, canon, score, file, tally, row, census, statistics, *cadre (Fr.)*, directory, ledger, book, gazetteer, atlas.

INVERACITY, *n.* 1. Mendacity, untruthfulness, falseness, deception, subterfuge, evasion, fraud, imposture, fraudulence, deceit, covin, guile, misrepresentation, trickery, jugglery, chicanery, sharp practice, cozenage, circumvention, collusion, ingannation, falsification, perversion, exaggeration, distortion, dissembling, sham, pretense.

2. Untruth, lie, falsehood, fib, prevarication, forgery, fabrication, fable, fiction, fairy tale, tall story, romance, trumped up tale, yarn, canard, cock-and-bull story, myth, claptrap, bosh, moonshine, equivocation.

INVERSE, *adj.* 1. Inverted as respects order, indirect, reversed in position, reverse, converse, opposite to in nature or effect, antipodal, antithetical, contrary, transposed, hyperbatic, palindromal, palindromic.

2. Turned upside down, wrongside up, inside

out, upside down, on one's head, bottom-upward, topsy-turvy, *sens dessus dessous (Fr.).*

INVERSION, *n.* 1. Reversal of the usual or natural order, placing in contrary order, subversion, reversion, contraposition, eversion, transposition, transposal, conversion.

2. Turning upside down, upsetting, capsizal, upset, capsize, somersault, overturn, *culbute (Fr.),* revulsion, turn of the tide, revolution.

3. Contrariety, contradiction, opposition, polarity, antithesis.

4. *(Rhet.)* Transposition of words, hyperbaton, anastrophe, hypallage, hysteron proteron, metathesis, palindrome.

5. *(Psychiatry)* Assumption of the sexual role of the opposite sex, homosexuality, homoeroticism, lesbianism, tribadism, pederasty, sodomy, buggery.

INVERT, *v.* 1. Reverse in position or direction, place in contrary order, turn about, transpose, turn to the opposite, change to the contrary, introvert, subvert, put the cart before the horse.

2. Turn upside down, capsize, upset, overturn, upturn, overbalance, topple, turn topsy-turvy, *culbuter (Fr.),* overthrow, turn the tables, *bouleverser (Fr.).*

3. Be inverted, turn about, wheel about, veer about, tilt over, turn over, turn turtle.

INVERTEBRATE, *adj.* 1. *(Zool.)* Destitute of a backbone, not vertebrate, without vertebrae, invertebral.

2. Without strength of character, lacking in resolution, spineless, weak, irresolute, infirm of purpose, half-hearted, lukewarm, shilly-shally, hesitant, undecided, vacillating.

INVEST, *v.* 1. Put money to use, place out to interest, let out, lend on security, loan, intrust, advance, lay out, subsidize, embark, risk, venture, sink, fund, venture capital.

2. Cover as an article of attire does, dress, clothe, array, drape, attire, robe, gown, adorn, rig out, deck, fit out, apparel, enclothe, bedight, accouter, equip, harness, caparison, muffle, enwrap, shroud, sheathe, swathe, swaddle, vest, pall, enrobe.

3. Surround a place with military works so as to prevent escape, beleaguer, besiege, beset, lay siege to, enclose, blockade, compass, encompass, environ, circumscribe, confine, hem in, hedge, girdle, pen, gird, belt, engird.

4. Endow with authority, empower, indue, confer, enable, commission, license, authorize, sanction, delegate, legalize, arm, strengthen, permit, privilege.

5. Clothe with the insignia of office, install in a position, furnish with rank, induct, inaugurate, instate, institute, chair, seat, settle a power in a person, vest a right in.

INVESTIGATE, *v.* Examine into the particulars of, study in detail, scrutinize, scrute, look into, search into, look over, probe, sound, fathom, dip into, inspect, explore, consider, dissect, overlook, analyze, sift, winnow, thresh out, subject to investigation, overhaul, look up, seek, look for, reconnoiter, scan, rake, rummage, scour, look around, pry, ransack, nose out, survey, ferret out, unearth, track, seek a clue, leave no stone unturned, trace out, follow up, discuss, canvass, question, inquire into, ask, interrogate, catechize, pump, grille, cross-examine, put through the third degree, seek information regarding,

make inquiry about, observe narrowly, research, look into a matter, see how the land lies.

INVESTIGATION, *n.* Searching inquiry in order to ascertain facts, careful study, formal scrutiny, scrutation, official inquiry, detailed examination, active effort to find out something, minute and thorough attempt to learn the facts of something complex or hidden, systematic search, exploration, research, sifting, overhauling, inquisition, cross-examination, quest, questioning, interrogation, quiz, third degree, Socratic method, catechism, interpellation, discussion, debate, survey, reconnaissance, reconnoitering, lantern of Diogenes, espionage, percontation, trial, analysis, dissection, consideration, calculation, ventilation, test, assay, review, probe, pursuit, inquest.

INVESTIGATOR, *n.* Examiner, searcher, inquirer, scrutator, querist, researcher, inquisitor, inspector, questioner, catechist, questionist, scrutinizer, peeker, analyst, experimenter.

INVESTITURE, *n.* Formal bestowal of a possessory right, habitation, installation, ordination, induction, inauguration, endowment, vestment, institution, assumption, admission, appointment.

INVESTMENT, *n.* 1. Investing of capital in order to secure profitable returns, money invested, mortgage, advance, loan, accommodation, lending on security, venture, risk.

2. Siege, blockade, beleaguerment, enclosement, encompassment.

3. *(Biol.)* Integument, covering, coating, outer layer, shell, rind, hull, husk, bark, peel, crust, cortex, coat.

4. Habiliments, garments, clothes, dress, vestment, robe, clothing, raiment, costume, drapery, guise, attire, toilette, vesture, garb, palliament, wardrobe, apparel, garniture, accouterment, caparison, rigging, trappings, togs, suit, toggery, livery, harness, gear.

INVETERACY, *n.* Chronic state, lingering obstinacy, tradition, prescription, deep-rootedness, customariness, immemorialness, habitude, assuefaction, assuetude, matter of course, beaten track, usage, consuetude, one's old way, confirmed habit, addiction, cacoethes, inurement, hardening, *veteris vestigia flammae (Lat.).*

INVETERATE, *adj.* Firmly established by long continuance, besetting, ingrained, chronic, confirmed in a habit or feeling, accustomed, habituated, hardened, inured, deep-seated, long-standing, habitual, dyed-in-the-wool, deep-rooted, obstinate, prescriptive, customary, traditional, of every-day occurrence, wonted, conventional, fixed, ingraffed, permanent, wedded to, never free from, in the habit of, *habitué (Fr.),* addicted to, used to, seasoned, devoted to, immemorial, time-honored, riveted, irremovable, vested, settled, ineradicable, stubborn, tenacious, ineffaceable.

INVIDIOUS, *adj.* Such as to bring envious dislike, likely to excite ill will, calculated to provoke resentment, offensive, odious, hateful, unpopular, objectionable, obnoxious, spiteful, malicious, irritating, annoying, provoking, malignant, rancorous, virulent, vexatious, unaccommodating, implacable.

INVIGORANT, *n.* Tonic, bracer, pick-me-up, restorative, stimulant, cordial, eye opener, panacea, elixir, theriac, ptisan.

INVIGORATE, *v.* Give vigor to, fill with life and energy, energize, stimulate, animate, enliven, refresh, fortify, strengthen, vivify, quicken, give a lift to, raise, inspirit, make vigorous, revive, brace, pep up, perk up, nerve, embolden, vitalize, tone up, steel, sustain, buttress, set on one's legs, reman, restore, confirm, reinforce, reflect, give new life to, fire, exhilarate, encourage.

INVIGORATING, *adj.* Invigorative, refreshing, energizing, restorative, analeptic, strengthening, animating, bracing, salutary, healthful, salubrious, wholesome, nourishing, healthy, salutiferous, benign, tonic, good for, nutritious, reparative, remedial.

INVINCIBLE, *adj.* 1. That cannot be vanquished, incapable of being overcome, unconquerable, unsubduable, indomitable, unyielding, unable to be subjugated, irresistible, impregnable, unassailable, not to be taken by storm, powerful, iron, firm, resistless, strong, sovereign, fast, formidable, irrepressible, ineradicable, tough, stanch, solid, stable, resistant, in the plenitude of power, powerful, potent, puissant, herculean, strong as a lion, mighty, sturdy, hardy, stalwart, doughty, heroic, manly, manful, virile, all-powerful, indefatigable, tenacious, uncompromising.

2. Too great to be overcome, insurmountable, insuperable, overpowering, overwhelming, immovable, inexpugnable, impermeable, secure from capture, tenable against all odds, that cannot be taken by assault, repellent.

INVIOLABILITY, *n.* 1. Sanctity, sacrosanctness, sacredness, inviolacy, incorruptibility, solemnity, purity, holiness, goodness, religiousness, grace, saintliness.

2. Secrecy, secretness, privacy, *incognita (Lat.)*, confidentialness, hiddenness.

INVIOLABLE, *adj.* 1. That must not be violated, to be kept free from violence, not to be injured, unbroken, uncorrupt, undefiled, unstained, untarnished.

2. Inalienable, imprescriptible, unimpeachable, prescriptive, unchallenged.

3. Sacrosanct, sacred, sacramental, holy, inviolate, hallowed, taboo.

INVIOLATE, *adj.* 1. Unbroken, intact, integral, unviolated, undisturbed, perfect, whole, not infringed, complete, entire.

2. Free from outrage, sound, unaffected by injury, without fracture, uninjured, unhurt, untouched, unimpaired, unharmed, scatheless, stainless, pure, unstained, unblemished, unpolluted, undefiled, unprofaned.

3. Free from desecration, inviolable, sacred, sacrosanct, hallowed, consecrated, holy, divine, sanctified, set apart, devoted, blessed.

INVIRILITY, *n.* Effeminacy, softness, sexual weakness, unmanliness, femininity, womanishness, muliebrity, impotence, fragility, flaccidity, debility, languor, enervation, timidity, cowardliness, pusillanimity.

INVISIBILITY, *n.* Indistinctness, imperceptibility, invisibleness, obscurity, indefiniteness, concealment, delitescency, seclusion, latency, mystery, smoke screen, mystification, suppression, cloudiness, haziness, fogginess, mistiness, duskiness, nebulousness, darkness, gloominess, gloom, secretion, camouflage, retirement.

INVISIBLE, *adj.* 1. Not perceptible by the eye, imperceptible, that cannot be seen, undiscernible, unseen, incapable of being seen, indistinguishable, unnoticeable, unapparent, latent, covert, inconspicuous, concealed, hidden, enshrouded, masked, shrouded, screened, cloaked, veiled, suppressed,

not in sight, out of sight, evanescent, unseeable, microscopic, atomic, impalpable, aerial, supernatural, preternatural.

2. Indistinct, dim, dark, shadowy, obscure, ill-defined, indefinite, out of focus, blurred, hazy, nebulous, cloudy, overclouded, misty, faint, feeble, uncertain, vague, confused, mysterious, occult.

INVITATION, *n.* 1. Solicitation, postulation, entreaty, impetration, imploration, obtestation, bidding, summons, challenge, call, request, bid, requisition, petition, suit, motion, overture, appeal, address, apostrophe, rogation, proposal, proposition, offer, proffer, tender, bid, overture.

2. Inducement, attraction, allurement, magnetism, allectation, enticement, temptation, *agacerie (Fr.)*, bewitchment, spell, charm, blandishment, fascination, seducement, honeyed words.

INVITE, *v.* 1. Ask in a courteous or complimentary way to attend, summon formally, bid, offer a bid for, solicit, ask, request politely, call, challenge, call for, order, command, make application, sue, crave, pray, beg, petition, canvass, beseech, entreat, implore, supplicate, adjure, apostrophize, appeal to, invoke, urge, press, importune, dun.

2. Tempt, lure, allure, attract, entice, persuade, prevail upon, draw on, lead, leave the door open to, court, induce, ask for, act so as to bring on, give occasion for, inveigle, incite, whet, provoke, motivate, instigate, encourage, actuate, inspire, prompt.

INVITING, *adj.* 1. Tempting, attractive, seductive, fascinating, captivating, alluring, engaging, winning, bewitching, enchanting, pleasing, enticing, provocative, suasive, appetizing, mouth-watering, irresistible.

2. Prepossessing, auspicious, promising, persuasive, hortative, propitious, favorable, rosy, golden, bright, opportune, seasonable.

INVOCATION, *n.* Entreaty for guidance, request, conjuration, prayer, supplication, orison, petition, calling upon for aid or protection, summoning, attestation, summons, suit, address, apostrophe, imploration, conjuration, evocation, solicitation, beseechment, obtestation, obsecration, importunity, impetration, intercession.

IN VOGUE In fashion, fashionable, modish, stylish, the rage, having a run, popularly favored, accepted, fashionably current, à la mode, *comme il faut (Fr.)*, high-toned, toney, *recherché (Fr.)*, in the latest style, newfangled, talk of, in every one's mouth, in high favor, in the ascendant.

INVOICE, *n.* 1. Written list of articles of merchandise with prices shipped or sold, itemized bill containing the prices comprising the total charge, inventory, bill of lading, manifest, itemized list, schedule, account.

2. Merchandise, shipment, goods, stock, articles, wares, commodities, effects, produce, cargo, freight.

INVOKE, *v.* Call for with earnest desire, make prayer for, implore, entreat, solicit, beseech, supplicate, make orison, pray, call upon, pray to, importune, beg, call on, appeal to, adjure, direct a request to, conjure, summon, evoke, ask for, request, sue, crave, petition, canvass, bid, beg a boon, call to, apply to, plead, apostrophize, kneel to, cry to, cry for help, cry aloud, commune with a divine spirit, call for by incantation, address, attest, obtest, invocate.

INVOLUNTARY, *adj.* 1. Done without one's own volition, occurring without conscious control, mechanical, reflex, instinctive, spontaneous, independent of volition, blind, unintentional, unconscious, unwitting, unthinking, automatic.

2. Against one's will, reluctant, unwilling, compulsory, necessary, binding, not in the vein, disinclined, loath, averse, indisposed, grudging, unconsenting.

INVOLUTION, *n.* 1. Folding in upon itself, inwrapping, rolling in, infolding, envelopment, inclusion, infolded state, retrograde development, immanent, degeneration.

2. Complication, complexity, intricacy, entanglement, engagement, perplexity, confusion, involved character, circumvolution.

3. *(Med.)* Bodily changes involving a lessening of sex-organ activity in late middle age, resorption.

INVOLVE, *v.* 1. Involve as a necessary circumstance or consequence, comprehend within itself, entail, comprise, contain, embrace, hold, incorporate, include, embody, admit.

2. Roll in something that surrounds, inwrap, envelop, surround, cover, wrap, infold, shroud, engulf, swallow up, overwhelm.

3. Roll upon itself, twine, intwine, interlace, intertwist, interweave, intertwine, twist together, inweave, wind spirally, coil, wreathe, enmesh.

4. Combine inextricably, connect, join, mingle, conjoin, blend, unite, merge.

5. Bring into difficulties, get one into a position from which it is difficult to extricate himself, bring deeply into something troublesome, inculpate, implicate in guilt, entangle in crime, incriminate, embarrass, compromise, embroil.

6. Imply, mean, signify, betoken, denote, connote, allude to, import, represent, typify, symbolize.

INVOLVEMENT, *n.* Embarrassment, entanglement, imbroglio, ticklish situation, quandary, dilemma, nonplus, strait, pinch, pass, crisis, exigency, scrape, pickle, stew, hot water.

INVULNERABILITY, *n.* Invulnerableness, security, safety, impregnability, safeguard, invincibleness, inexpugnability.

INVULNERABLE, *adj.* 1. Incapable of being hurt or damaged, unable to be wounded, secure from harm, unwoundable, woundless, scatheless.

2. Proof against attack, invincible, inexpugnable, unassailable, irrefragable, defensible, unattackable, tenable, imperdible, impregnable, bombproof, safe and sound, secure.

INWARD, *adj.* 1. Internal, interior, inner, situated within, inside, inmost, innermost, most inward.

2. Inherent, intrinsic, inbred, innate, inborn, deep-seated, ingrained, implanted, immanent, indwelling, inwoven, infixed, inwrought, essential.

3. In the mind or soul, mental, spiritual, psychological, psychic, private, secret, hidden, intimate.

4. Located within the body, intestinal, visceral, splanchnic, duodenal, ventral, abdominal, stomachic, celiac, rectal.

INWARD, *adv.* 1. Toward the inside or interior, inwardly, within, interiorly, inly, internally, *ab intra (Lat.),* inwards.

2. In the mind or soul, mentally, spiritually, psychologically, privately, secretly, confidentially.

INWARDS, *n., pl.* Intestines, entrails, viscera, splanchna, bowels, guts, insides, chitterlings, inner parts.

INWEAVE, *v.* Introduce into a fabric in weaving, weave in, weave together, combine with something woven in, interweave, intwine, intertwine, interlace, twine, wreathe, twist, diversify, variegate.

INWROUGHT, *adj.* 1. Closely combined with something worked in, worked with something by way of decoration, wrought in, worked into, having figures worked in, figured, patterned, diapered.

2. Inherent, innate, inborn, inbred, indwelling, immanent, indispensable, infixed, ingrained, inseparable, internal, intrinsic, essential, congenital, native, natural, subjective.

ION, *n.* Substance resulting from electrolytic dissociation, electrically charged radicle, anion, cation, electron, atom, molecule, particle.

IOTA, *n.* Very small quantity, bit, jot, tittle, whit, particle, scrap, speck, glimmer, spark, scintilla, mite, atom, grain, trace, soupçon, shadow, suspicion, mote, dot, fleabite, corpuscle, molecule, electron, drop, dab, sprinkling, dash, nip, tinge, pinch, snack, morsel, snatch, crumb, droplet, fragment, shred, trifle, sliver, chip, snip, splinter, paring, peeling, hair, shaving.

IPSE DIXIT, *Lat.* "He himself said it" *(literally),* assertion without proof, mere assertion, dogmatic assertion, dictum, sentence, saying, word, declaration, affirmation, statement, remark, observation, position.

IRASCIBILITY, *n.* Irritability, acrimony, ill temper, asperity, testiness, touchiness, crossness, bad temper, irritation, anger, grouchiness, petulance, irascibleness, tartness, huffishness, churlishness, acerbity, excitability, pugnacity, waspishness, spleen, gall, temper, cantankerousness, fieriness, indignation, procacity, susceptibility, protervity, contentiousness, hot blood, *genus irritabile (Lat.),* ill humor, sullenness, a word and a blow, crabbedness, dudgeon, sulks, black looks, *bouderie (Fr.),* virulence, pique, animosity, wrathfulness.

IRASCIBLE, *adj.* Easily provoked to anger, hot-blooded, choleric, irritable, petulant, peevish, snappish, waspish, testy, nettlesome, quick, impatient, huffy, cranky, touchy, splenetic, huffish, easily riled, pettish, quick-tempered, hasty, like touchwood, hot, peppery, like tinder, irritated, moody, resentful, edgy, cross, inflammable, angry, querulous, fractious, ireful, fretty, crabbed, hot-tempered, fiery, quarrelsome, excitable, perverse, passionate, unamiable, bad-tempered, thin-skinned, spleeny, fretful, warm, hot under the collar, captious, sensitive, cross-grained, ill-natured, ill-humored, grouchy, churlish, shrewish, cantankerous, contentious, pugnacious, factious, belligerent, disputatious, hostile, wrangling, dissentious.

IRATE, *adj.* Angry, enraged, envenomed, embittered, venomous, virulent, *acharné (Fr.),* incensed, irritated, ireful, piqued, provoked, in a passion, wrathful, choleric, infuriated, hostile, mad *(slang),* vexed, indignant, furious, excited, passionate, impassioned, in the tantrums, wroth, cross, bitter, violent, acrimonious, boiling over, foaming at the mouth, fuming, convulsed with rage, raging, waxy, offended, worked up, wrought, sore, set against, hurt, peeved, fierce, rageful, wild, fiery, savage, rabid, flushed with rage, in a huff, up in arms, on one's high ropes, in high dudgeon.

IRE, *n.* Anger, choler, passion, wrath, fury, exasperation, exacerbation, resentment, bitterness, indignation, dudgeon, dander, umbrage, pique, towering rage, vexation, animosity, displeasure, acerbity, huff, miff, virulence, soreness, acrimony, gall, rankling, speen, asperity, bad humor, illtemper, irascibility, irritation, bile, fume, warmth, pucker, ferment, excitement, angry mood, *acharnement (Fr.),* vials of wrath, passion, tantrums, tiff, fit, pet, fury, storm, explosion, paroxysm, outburst, violence, fieriness, gnashing of teeth, high words, hot blood, sore subject, crow to pluck, *casus belli (Lat.),* red rag to a bull.

IREFUL, *adj.* Full of ire, wrathful, irate, raging, incensed, passionate, furious, angry, choleric, waspish, irascible, provoked, cross, virulent, bitter, envenomed, venomous, violent, burning, warm, hot under the collar, fuming, foaming at the mouth, *acharné (Fr.),* offended, nursing a grudge, sore, hurt, peeved, miffed, huffy, infuriate, nettled, rabid, fierce, fiery, wild, in a huff, in a pucker, in high dudgeon, heated, worked up, overwrought, steamed up *(slang),* acrimonious, riled.

IRENIC *adj.* Tending to promote peace, peaceful, peacemaking, pacificatory, promotive of peace, conciliatory, intercessory, intermediary, propitiatory, appeasing, placating, mollifying, diplomatic, mediatory, pacific.

IRIDESCENCE, *n.* Display of colors like those of the rainbow, iridization, play of lustrous changing colors, opalescence, changeableness, versicolor, irisation, variegation, polychrome, spectrum, mother-of-pearl, nacre, peacock feathers, butterfly wings, tortoise shell, nacreousness, kaleidoscope.

IRIDESCENT, *adj.* Changeable in color, versicolor, varicolor, parti-colored, variegated, rainbow-like, opalescent, nacreous, irisated, prismatic, pavonine, pearly, opaline, many-hued, polychromatic, kaleidoscopic, shot, *chatoyant (Fr.), gorge de pigeon (Fr.),* pied, motley, dappled, iridian, irised, cymophanous, tortoise-shell, nacred, marmoraceous.

IRISHISM, *n.* Irish idiom, Celticism, Hibernianism, Hibernism, Hibernicism.

IRK, *v.* Fatigue, weary, fag, tire, bore, harass, jade, knock up, prostrate, exhaust, wear out, tax, strain, go against the grain, try one's patience, vex, displease, incommode, annoy, discompose, disturb, discommode, trouble, worry, bother, plague, harry, pester, badger, beset, persecute, tease, molest, rag, provoke, irritate, nettle, rile, pique, chafe, fret, gall, ruffle, aggrieve, cut to the quick, sour the temper.

IRKSOME, *adj.* 1. Fatiguing, wearisome, tiring, tiresome, burdensome, wearying, laborious, operose, onerous, troublesome, trying, exhausting, fagging, taxing, tasking, difficult, uphill, arduous, tough, toilsome, toilsome, formidable.

2. Irritating, annoying, galling, provoking, aggravating, exasperating, exacerbating, vexatious, plaguy.

3. Dull, monotonous, tedious, devoid of interest, humdrum, uninteresting, jejune, dry, arid, flat, bald, stupid, prosy, soporific, slow.

IRON, *adj.* 1. Ferrous, ferric, chalybeate, ferruginous.

2. Stern, harsh, severe, unyielding, obdurate, inexorable, unfeeling, cruel, ironclad, adamantine, rigid, stubborn, hard, stark, unbending, inflexible, proof, firm, irresistible.

3. Indomitable, resolved, determined, decided, game, obstinate, tenacious, invincible, grim.

4. Heroic, manly, manful, virile, stalwart, mighty, strong, potent, puissant, vigorous, forcible, robust, stout, hardy, sturdy, powerful.

IRONICAL, *adj.* Expressing irony, full of irony, mocking, sarcastic, satirical, derisive, cynical, burlesque, quizzical, mock, derisory, scurrilous.

IRONS, *n.* Fetters, shackles, gyves, manacles, chains, pinions, trammels, handcuffs, bracelets, darbies.

IRONSMITH, *n.* Worker in iron, blacksmith, forger, smithy, Vulcan, Hephaestus, farrier.

IRONWORKS, *n.* Blacksmith's shop, forge, smithy, farriery, foundry, fiery furnace, hearth.

IRONY, *n.* 1. Saying one thing and implying another, speech understood by the audience but not grasped by the speakers on the stage *(Theat.),* contradiction between the literal and the intended meaning, locution that understates the effect intended, outcome of events contrary to what was expected.

2. Ridicule, mockery, satire, sarcasm, derision, parody, travesty, persiflage, jeering, scoffing, buffoonery, burlesque, banter, skit, gibe, taunt, sneer, raillery, disparagement, squib, quip, badinage, chaff, asteism, farce, mimicry, caricature.

3. Mental reservation, *arrière-pensée (Fr.),* hidden motive, half truth, white lie, shuffle, shift, pretense.

IRRADIATE, *v.* Shed rays of light upon, illuminate, brighten with light, radiate light, illumine, illume, make bright, light up, emit rays, shine upon, cast luster upon, throw light upon, adorn with light, emanate in rays, lighten, enlighten, give out a light, relume, heat with radiant energy.

IRRADIATION, *n.* Radiance, radiation, illumination, luminescence, phosphorescence, radiant heat, infrared rays, ultraviolet rays, actinic rays, actinism, reflection, shimmer, brightness, brilliancy, splendor, refulgence, effulgence, fulgidity, fulgor, resplendence, transplendency, luminousness, luminosity, renitency.

IRRATIONAL, *adj.* 1. Not endowed with reason, void of reason, brute, brutish, unthinking, unreasoning, without judgment, unintelligent, unwise, stupid, belluine, mindless.

2. Utterly illogical, not in accordance with reason, preposterous, unreasonable, false, invalid, unsound, unwarranted, not following, untenable, unscientific, inconclusive, fallible, unproved, groundless, feeble, weak, poor, loose, flimsy, vague, foolish, pettifogging, short-sighted, injudicious, paralogistic, absonant.

3. Silly, absurd, extravagant, nonsensical, vacuous, fatuous, ridiculous, asinine, insensate, crackbrained, addlepated, brainless.

4. Alienated in mind, demented, crazed, crazy, insane, lunatic, aberrant, *non compos mentis (Lat.),* idiotic, imbecile, off, odd, queer, touched, unhinged, nutty *(slang),* feeble-minded, daft.

IRRATIONALITY, *n.* 1. Want of reason, brutishness, lack of judgment, unintelligence, stupidity, mindlessness, brainlessness, desipience.

2. Utter illogicality, unreasonableness, preposterousness, invalidity, unsoundness, *non sequitur (Lat.),* untenableness, fallibility, weakness, feebleness, looseness, vagueness, short-sightedness, injudiciousness, paralogism, absonance.

3. Silliness, absurdity, extravagance, nonsensicality, foolishness, folly, fatuity, preposterousness,

vacuousness, asininity, ineptitude, trifling, nugacity, giddiness.

4. Mental alienation, incoherence, dementia, craziness, insanity, lunacy, aberrancy, idiocy, imbecility, oddness, feeble-mindedness, delusion, hallucination, aberration.

IRRECLAIMABLE, *adj.* 1. Incapable of being reclaimed, hopeless, incurable, remediless, beyond hope, beyond cure, irremediable, irreparable, irrecoverable, past mending, unimprovable, irredeemable, irreversible, irretrievable, undone, ruined, irrevocable.

2. Impenitent, uncontrite, hardened, recusant, seared, unrepentant, remorseless, incorrigible, lost, graceless, abandoned, shameless, obdurate, recreant, profligate, reprobate, past praying for.

IRRECONCILABLE, *adj.* 1. That cannot be harmonized, unadjustable, uncomformable, heterogeneous.

2. That cannot be brought to acquiescence, unwilling, loath, disinclined, indisposed, reluctant, averse, renitent, demurring, restive, unconsenting, intransigent, uncompromising, unappeasable, inexpiable.

3. Implacably opposed, inexorable, hostile, disaffected, estranged, alienated, at variance.

IRRECOVERABLE, *adj.* 1. Never to be regained, past, lost forever, gone by, over with, bygone, lapsed, elapsed, expired, that has been, whilom, no more, extinct, run out, forgotten, never to return, exploded, irretrievable, irrevocable.

2. That cannot be rectified, irreparable, not to be repaired, unrestorable, hopeless, irremediable, remediless, incurable, irreversible, irredeemable, irreclaimable.

IRREDEEMABLE, *adj.* 1. Incapable of being bought back or paid off, irreclaimable, irrevocable, unregenerate, beyond redemption, irretrievable, incorrigible, unrepentant, impenitent, reprobate.

2. Hopeless, irreparable, irremediable, incurable, remediless, cureless, beyond remedy, ruined, undone.

IRREDUCIBLE, *adj.* Unchangeable, intransmutable, irresoluble, incommutable, irreversible, irrevocable, reverseless, inextinguishable, indissoluble, indestructible, imperishable, indeciduous, indelible, insusceptible of change, incapable of being diminished.

IRREFRAGABLE, *adj.* 1. Unassailable, impregnable, inexpugnable, invincible, insurmountable, irresistible.

2. Irrefutable, indisputable, disputeless, incontestable, incontrovertible, undeniable, unanswerable, indubitable, unquestionable.

IRREFUTABLE, *adj.* Proven, demonstrated, unanswered, unconfuted, evident, unanswerable, conclusive, final, incontrovertible, indubious, past dispute, beyond all question, unimpeachable, undeniable, incontestable, indisputable, indefeasible, indubitable.

IRREGULAR, *adj.* 1. Without even shape, asymmetric, unsymmetrical, uneven, unlevel, rough, humpy, jagged, bunchy, lumpy, rugged, broken, hilly, hummocky, unequal, pitted, holey, knotty, hillocky, devious, crooked, tortuous.

2. Not characterized by any fixed principle, unmethodical, disordered, immethodical, improper, unsystematic, unparliamentary, uncanonical, desultory, confused, disarranged, amorphous.

3. Unnatural, abnormal, heteroclite, hetero-morphous, anomalous, anomalistic, unconformable, unusual, exceptional, aberrant, illegitimate, heteromorphic, singular, odd.

4. Changeable, erratic, capricious, fitful, desultory, spasmodic, uncertain, variable, unpunctual, unsettled, rambling, flickering, mutable.

5. Not conforming to rules of justice or morality, lawless, disorderly, loose, dissolute, immoral, unruly, wild, turbulent, vicious, intemperate, excessive, inordinate, extravagant, promiscuous, wanton, licentious, lax.

IRREGULARITY, *n.* 1. Lack of symmetry, asymmetry, unevenness, roughness, jaggedness, humpiness, lumpiness, bunchiness, ruggedness, deviousness, crookedness.

2. Lack of order, want of method, disorderliness, immethodicalness, unsystematicalness, confusion, disarrangement.

3. Abnormality, abnormity, aberration, anomaly, singularity, unnaturalness, unconformity, unusualness, exceptionalness, aberrancy, oddness.

4. Changeableness, erraticism, capriciousness, fitfulness, desultoriness, spasmodicalness, uncertainty, unpunctuality, variableness, mutability.

5. Immorality, laxity, lawlessness, disorderliness, looseness, dissoluteness, unruliness, wildness, turbulence, viciousness, intemperance, wantonness, promiscuousness, licentiousness, inordinacy, extravagance.

IRREGULARLY, *adv.* Intermittently, by fits and starts, fitfully, at intervals, by jerks, by snatches, periodically, by turns, at irregular intervals, off and on.

IRRELEVANT, *adj.* Not to the point, impertinent, unapropos, inapplicable, inapposite, aside from the point, inconsequent, inappropriate, extraneous, foreign, unrelated, unessential, beside the mark, inconsistent, illogical, unwarranted, gratuitous, self-contradictory, incongruous, out of place, unsuitable, absurd, not significant, unconnected, alien, inapt, malapropos.

IRRELIGION, *n.* Disregard of religion, godlessness, ungodliness, impiety, irreverence, laxity, skepticism, unbelief, doubt, disbelief, freethinking, agnosticism, atheism, nullifidianism, infidelity, antichristianity, materialism, Pyrrhonism, positivism, rationalism, worldliness, profaneness, paganism, iniquity, sinfulness, wickedness, heathenism, unholiness, nihilism.

IRRELIGIOUS, *adj.* 1. Undevout, ungodly, godless, graceless, profane, irreverent, blasphemous, impious, unsanctified, unholy, unhallowed, worldly, worldly-minded, carnal, mundane, earthly, unregenerate, unspiritual, sacrilegious, iniquitous, wicked.

2. Freethinking, skeptical, incredulous, agnostic, atheistic, Pyrrhonic, materialistic, unbelieving, positivistic, faithless, nullifidian, unconverted, unchristian, antichristian, heathenish, pagan.

IRREMEDIABLE, *adj.* 1. Hopeless, beyond hope, past cure, cureless, immedicable, remediless, irremedicable, incurable, irrecoverable, unremediable, beyond remedy, beyond correction, past mending, irreparable, beyond redress, past help, not to be repaired, irreversible, irretrievable, malignant.

2. Not to be atoned for, inexpiable, wrong, evil, shocking, reprehensible, abominable, execrable, detestable, accursed, damnable.

IRREMISSIBLE, *adj.* That cannot be remitted, not to be forgiven, inexpiable, unpardonable, unatonable, unforgivable, indefensible, inexcusable, unjustifiable, that admits of no satisfaction, irredeemable.

IRREMOVABLE, *adj.* Immovable, rooted, riveted, fixed, unmovable, established, settled, fast, firm, steadfast, stable, not to be changed, permanent, constant, unchangeable, anchored, moored, tethered, ineradicable, deep-rooted, stuck fast, transfixed.

IRREPARABLE, *adj.* Incapable of being rectified, unable to be made good, not to be repaired, remediless, irremediable, beyond redress, past mending, irreclaimable, incorrigible, irrecoverable, irreversible, irretrievable, irredeemable, irrevocable, hopeless, helpless, undone, ruined, incurable.

IRREPREHENSIBLE, *adj.* Undeserving of censure, innocent of wrong, unblamable, inculpable, blameless, irreproachable, faultless, irreprovable, unimpeachable, unobjectionable, impeccable, unassailable, above suspicion, inerrable, unexceptionable, venial, salvable, harmless, innoxious, innocuous, inoffensive, harmless, immaculate, unchallengeable, guiltless, unsullied, unblemished, not guilty, guiltless, spotless, stainless, sinless, unerring.

IRREPRESSIBLE, *adj.* Not to be repressed, insuppressible, uncontrollable, ungovernable, unruly, unquenched, unquenchable, unsmotherable, inextinguishable, unbridled, free, unconstrained, unrestrained, untrammeled, unbound, unfettered, unchained, unimpeded, unrestricted, mercurial, unquiet, galvanic, electric, restless, rampant, turbulent, tempestuous, tumultuary, impetuous, impulsive, passionate, stanchless, simmering, burning, volcanic, ready to burst forth, impassioned, vehement, violent, demonstrative, fiery, fierce, hot-headed, enthusiastic, rabid, fanatical, overzealous, high-strung, mettlesome, skittish, feverish, febrile, impatient, excitable, wild, boisterous, uproarious, riotous, raging, obstreperous, ebullient.

IRREPROACHABLE, *adj.* Free from fault, without blame, faultless, blameless, inculpable, unblamable, inerrable, above suspicion, irreprovable, irreprehensible, unobjectionable, unexceptionable, unimpeachable, venial, salvable, inoffensive, harmless, innocuous, innoxious, innocent, virtuous, spotless, stainless, guiltless, faultless, impeccable, immaculate, undefiled, unblemished, unerring, unspotted, unstained, untarnished, pure, perfect, upright.

IRRESISTIBLE, *adj.* 1. That cannot be withstood, incapable of being successfully resisted, overwhelming, overpowering, that carries all before it, overmastering, puissant, potent, powerful, vigorous, unconquerable, indomitable, invincible, formidable, cogent, energetic, forceful, forcible, masterful, vehement, violent, intense, concentrated, acute, keen, passionate, ardent, extreme, seductive, enticing, tempting, alluring, enchanting, ensorceling, bewitching.

2. Compulsory, necessary, needful, destined, fated, fateful, inevitable, irrevocable, unavoidable, inexorable, binding, written in the book of fate, in the lap of the gods.

3. Involuntary, automatic, instinctive, mechanical, blind, unconscious, unwitting, undesigned, impulsive, impetuous.

4. Irrefragable, irrefutable, undeniable, apodictic, unanswerable, conclusive, proven, incontestable, demonstrated, valid, unconfuted, unre-

futed, evident, indisputable, incontrovertible, unassailable, indubitable, unquestionable.

IRRESOLUTE, *adj.* 1. Undecided, uncertain, undetermined, inconstant, vacillating, oscillating, vacillant, hesitant, hesitating, faltering, changeable, unstable, mutable, unsettled, doubtful, wavering, unsteady, infirm of purpose, fickle, capricious, mercurial, irresponsible, unreliable, half-hearted, changeful, variable, volatile, frivolous, giddy, light-headed, lightsome, feather-headed, feather-brained, notional, indecisive, lukewarm, shilly-shally, double-minded, erratic, vagrant, neutral, fluctuating, unsteadfast, restless.

2. Spineless, invertebrate, weak, frail, timid, cowardly, pusillanimous, feeble-minded, pliant, soft, pliable, yielding, weak-kneed, passive, faint.

IRRESOLUTION, *n.* Lack of decision or purpose, indecision, uncertainty, indetermination, vacillation, oscillation, fluctuation, instability, irresoluteness, shilly-shallying, hesitancy, hesitation, changeableness, capriciousness, mercurialness, fickleness, caprice, notionality, whimsicalness, levity, lightheadedness, lukewarmness, weakness, pliancy, pliability, timidity, demurral, cowardice, pusillanimity, suspense, inconstancy, wavering.

IRRESPECTIVE, *adj.* Without regard to something specified, regardless, independent, unassociated, apart from, separate, distinct.

IRRESPONSIBLE, *adj.* Not capable of responsibility, untrustworthy, not answerable, unaccountable, devil-may-care, light-minded, infirm of purpose, fly-by-night, capricious, unreliable, fickle, mercurial, irresolute, inconstant, changeable, unstable, mutable, unsteady, variable, undecided, half-hearted, volatile, giddy, frivolous, feather-brained, wavering, vacillating, fluctuating, unsettled, flighty, thoughtless, arbitrary, lawless, summary, unauthorized, foot-loose and fancy-free, harum-scarum.

IRRESPONSIVE, *adj.* Not responding readily in speech, taciturn, reticent, habitually silent, uncommunicative, reserved, unconversable, close-mouthed, of few words, laconic, close-tongued, sparing of words, mum, mute, secretive, unsociable, cool, aloof, distant.

IRRETRIEVABLE, *adj.* 1. Lost forever, long lost, irrecoverable, never to be regained, hopeless, past recall, given up, out of the question, irreclaimable, irreversible, irredeemable, irrevocable, indefeasible, intransmutable, incommutable.

2. That cannot be restored, beyond repair, past reparation, irreparable, incurable, remediless, irremediable, immedicable, beyond remedy, incorrigible, ruined, undone.

IRREVERENCE, *n.* 1. Lack of religious reverence, impiety, profanity, profaneness, blasphemy, sacrilege, sacrilegiousness, profanation, desecration, cursing, apostasy.

2. Lack of respect, disrespect, disesteem, slight, rudeness, indignity, disfavor, disestimation, neglect, affront, insult, dishonor, discourtesy.

IRREVERENT, *adj.* 1. Profane, sacrilegious, blasphemous, impious, irreligious, unholy, undevout, ungodly, wicked, graceless, unhallowed.

2. Lacking in respect, disrespectful, slighting, uncivil, aweless, insulting, disparaging, rude, contemptuous, derisive.

IRREVERSIBLE, *adj.* That cannot be reversed, unalterable, unchangeable, irrevocable, reverseless, irrepealable, incommutable, immutable, invariable, hopeless, remediless, irrecoverable, irremediable, irreparable, irretrievable, irreclaimable, irredeemable.

IRREVOCABLE, *adj.* 1. Not to be recalled, incapable of revocation, admitting of no return, incommutable, irresoluble, intransmutable, irretrievable, reverseless, irreversible, indissoluble, indestructible, indelible.

2. That cannot be repealed or annulled, necessary, fated, needful, destined, fateful, compulsory, inevitable, unavoidable, inexorable, irresistible, written in the book of fate, binding, not to be put down, unyielding.

IRRIGATE, *v.* Supply with water by means of streams, water, moisten, immerse, submerge, inundate, deluge, drench, swash, douse, soak.

IRRIGATION, *n.* Supplying of land with water from artificial channels, watering, immersion, submergence, humectation, spargefaction, affusion.

IRRITABILITY, *n.* 1. Bad temper, irascibility, irritation, irascibleness, crossness, grumpiness, touchiness, grouchiness, petulance, huffishness, peevishness, fretfulness, snappishness, testiness, acerbity, tartness, asperity, acrimony, churlishness, pugnacity, excitability, choler, anger, ill nature.

2. Susceptibility to the influence of some stimulus, responsiveness, sensitivity, hypersensitivity.

IRRITABLE, *adj.* 1. Ill-humored, irascible, fretful, petulant, peevish, touchy, testy, captious, waspish, peppery, fiery, excitable, high-strung, hot, snappish, passionate, pettish, grumpy, splenetic, choleric, moody, out of humor, angry, readily excited, impatient, crabbed, hasty, cross, ill-tempered, sour, grumpy, edgy, hot-blooded, cantankerous, short-tempered, wrathful, sore *(slang)*, quarrelsome, huffy, fractious, querulous, thin-skinned, resentful, out of sorts, quick-tempered, cross-grained, shrewish, grouchy, crabby, contentious, like touchwood.

2. Susceptible to the influence of some stimulus, responsive, sensitive, hypersensitive, inflammable.

IRRITANT, *n.* 1. Source of irritation, sore subject, wound, thorn in the flesh, gall and wormwood, where the shoe pinches, skeleton in the closet, grievance, annoyance, nuisance, vexation, bitter pill, cross, trial, mortification, trouble, care, burden, blow, load.

2. Therapeutic agent producing irritation, poison, toxin.

IRRITATE, *v.* 1. Stir to anger, excite to wrath, provoke, incense, pique, nettle, exasperate, exacerbate, chafe, rile, anger, infuriate, enrage, gall, ruffle, annoy, fret, vex, rasp, jar, offend, grate, discompose, put out of humor, pester, tease, nag, wound, rankle, aggravate, torment, rub the wrong way, hector, arouse, inflame, incite, madden, plague, goad, rack, persecute, displease, affront, agitate, disturb, irk, fluster, tantalize, embitter, harass, harry, badger, aggrieve, sting.

2. *(Med.)* Bring to an abnormally sensitive condition, inflame by friction, make sensitive.

IRRITATING, *adj.* Irksome, exasperating, exacerbating, annoying, grating, galling, obnoxious, aggravating, incommodious, offensive, vexatious, provoking, disquieting, bothering, pestering, plaguy, tormenting, harassing, worrying, teasing, nagging, maddening, disturbing, tantalizing, infuriating.

IRRITATION, *n.* 1. Exasperation, provocation, annoyance, exacerbation, ire, wrath, anger, indignation, passion, resentment, excitement, animosity,

displeasure, choler, vexation, irascibility, ferment, ebullition, acrimony, asperity, bitterness, spleen, gall, bile, virulence, soreness, acerbity, pique, dudgeon, huff, umbrage, tiff, sulks, pet, tantrum, angry mood, hate, hatred, enmity, malignity, ill will, rage, fury, vehemence, hot blood, impatience, fume, temper, temperamentalism, stew, mortification, chagrin, discomfort, dissatisfaction, discomposure, infliction, botheration.

2. *(Med.)* Inflammation by friction, burning, itching, pruritus, smart, aching, soreness, chafing.

IRRUPTION, *n.* Bursting in, intrusion, breaking in, invasion, incursion, inroad, introgression, forcible entry, ingress, illapse, penetration, infiltration, aggression, outbreak, foray, raid, sally, sortie.

ISHMAELITE, *n.* Descendant of Ishmael, Arab, wanderer, vagrant, nomad, gypsy, vagabond, outcast, castaway, loafer, land-louper, beggar, tramp, hobo.

ISLAM, *n.* 1. Religious system of Allah according to Mohammed, Islamism, Mohammedanism, Mahometanism, Moslemism, the Koran.

2. Whole body of Mohammedan believers, Moslems, Mahometans, Mussulmans, Mohammedans.

ISLAND, *n.* Tract of land completely surrounded by water, isle, atoll, islet, reef, ait, holm, bar, key, ridge, archipelago, calf, eyot.

ISLANDER, *n.* Inhabitant of an island, insulary, islesman, islandman, *insulaire (Fr.).*

ISM, *n.* Distinctive practice, system, theory, doctrine, tenet, belief, dogma, opinion, teaching, precept, principle, article of faith, philosophy.

ISOLATE, *v.* Keep from contact with others, dissociate, separate, detach, set apart, put by itself, insulate, segregate, quarantine, cut off, dissever, part, disengage, disjoin, disunite, divorce, disconnect, seclude, keep in solitude, lock up, pen up, boycott, exclude, banish, outlaw, exile, expatriate, ostracize, excommunicate, blacklist, sequester.

ISOLATED, *adj.* Solitary, detached, single, separate, segregated, secluded, alone, forlorn, forsaken, lonely, parted, desolate, exiled, retired, private, sequestered, secret, hidden, outlying, remote, aloof, covert, godforsaken, unfrequented, inhospitable, eremetical, troglodytic, hermitical, anchoretical, insular.

ISOLATION, *n.* 1. Complete separation from others, dissociation, disconnection, detachment, segregation, sequestration, insulation, quarantine, *cordon sanitaire (Fr.),* insularity, aloofness.

2. Loneliness, solitude, solitariness, seclusion, retirement, privacy, withdrawal, delitescence, rustication, *villeggiatura (It.),* concealment, obscurity, reclusion, anchoretism, retreat, cloister, hermitage, convent, monastery, cell, sanctum sanctorum, unsociableness, inhospitality.

ISRAEL, *n.* The people traditionally descended from Israel or Jacob, Jewish people, Jewry, Hebrews, God's chosen people, the elect.

ISRAELITE, *n.* Descendant of Israel or Jacob, one of God's chosen people, Jew, Hebrew.

ISSUE, *n.* 1. Means of egress, outlet, exit, vent, way out, passage out, mouth, door, opening, conduit, escape, sortie, sally.

2. Discharge, outflow, drainage, oozing, suppuration, emanation, eruption, outbreak, leakage, outpour, gush, effluence, efflux, effusion, emission, flux, stream, debouchment, issuance.

3. Result, outcome, upshot, effect, consequence,

resultant, aftergrowth, catastrophe, afterclap, development, aftermath, outgrowth, denouement, conclusion, end, consummation, termination, finale, final event, winding up, finishing stroke.

4. Point in question, question, matter the decision of which is of special or public importance, topic, problem, poser, matter in dispute, question at issue, moot point, subject, bone of contention, debatable point, political football, knotty point, desideratum.

5. Offspring, progeny, children, lineal descendants, posterity, line of descendants, family, brood, seed, fruit, breed, spawn, heirs, rising generation, scion, offshoot, son, daughter, bantling, papoose, baby, infant, pickaninny, kid, chip of the old block.

ISSUE, v. 1. Go out, leave, depart, set out, sally forth, start, take one's departure, go off, go away, march out, go forth, debouch, take wing, take flight, leave, vacate, remove, evacuate, withdraw, fly, flee, run away, make off, escape, emerge, exit, egress.

2. Flow out, emanate, spurt, gush, stream, pour forth, exude, leak, discharge, sweat, perspire, drain, seep, ooze, spout, well out, effuse, find vent, trickle, emit.

3. Be the effect of, proceed from, follow, be due to, originate from, be owing to, spring from, rise from, result from, accrue, arise as a consequence, ensue, take rise, come about, grow out of.

4. Distribute, give out, put into circulation, print for sale or distribution, circulate, publish, put out, promulgate, edit, get out, divulgate, bring out.

ISTHMUS, n. Narrow strip of land bordered on both sides by water, peninsula, delta, promontory, neck of land, tongue of land.

ITALICISM, n. Italian idiom, Italianism, Romanism, Latinism, Dagoism (slang).

ITALICIZE, v. Print in italics, underscore with a single line, underline, distinguish by italics, draw a line under, give importance to, emphasize, lay stress on, draw attention to.

ITCH, v. 1. Feel an irritation of the skin which causes a desire to scratch the part affected, feel itchy, tingle, prickle, prick, tickle, creep, thrill, sting, formicate, titillate.

2. Desire, hanker after, crave, long for, yearn for, wish for, covet, lust after, hunger for, run mad after, raven for, burn to, die for, desiderate, pine for, sigh for, languish for, aspire after, set one's heart upon, look sweet upon, have an eye to, have an itching palm, grasp after, grab for.

ITCH, n. 1. Sensation of itching, titillation, tickling, tingling, formication, prickling, paraesthesia.

2. Contagious disease caused by the itch mite which burrows into the skin, psora, prurigo, scabies, pruritus, eczema, scab, mange.

3. Uneasy desire, restless longing, importunate craving, hankering, yearning, cacoethes, orexis, propensity, penchant, pruriency, mania, inclination, proclivity, predilection, burning passion, animus, leaning, concupiscence, lust, cupidity, relish, appetency, appetite.

4. Grasping disposition, itching palm, greed, covetousness, greediness, ravenousness, rapacity, avidity, avarice, tenacity, cupidity, selfishness, *auri sacra fames (Lat.).*

ITCHY, adj. 1. Itching, tingling, tickling, formicative, creepy, crawly, prickly, thrilling, stinging,

goose flesh *(colloq.)*, sensitive, ticklish, tickly, titillative.

2. Mangy, scabious, psoroid, psoric, pruritic, pruriginous, eczematous.

3. Lustful, prurient, concupiscent, longing, appetitive, desirous, ardent, fervent, keen, eager, burning, impatient, avid, hot, passionate.

4. Greedy, covetous, voracious, avaricious, grasping, rapacious, insatiable, extortionate, sordid, unsatisfied, insatiate.

ITEM, n. Detail, particular, article, entry, separate piece of information or news, separate paragraph, detail, member, component, element, ingredient, constituent, individual, unit, ace, monad, integer, circumstance, feature, particularity.

ITEMIZE, v. Mention in detail, descend to particulars, detail, particularize, set down as an item, enter as an item, state by items, give the particulars of, make a note of, make a memorandum of, enter into detail, specify, formulate, individualize, denote, designate, select, point out, indicate, mention, determine.

ITERATE, v. Utter repeatedly, say again, reiterate, repeat, harp on, dwell on, emphasize, do over again, echo, parrot, drum on, battologize, hammer away at, revert to, recur to, return to, ring the changes on, din in the ear, conjugate in all its tenses and moods, go over the same ground, begin again, recapitulate, reword, never hear the last of.

ITERATION, n. Repetition, reiteration, ding-dong, harping, battology, tautology, tautophony, monotony, redundancy, pleonasm, diffuseness, echo, chimes, *ritornello (It.),* refrain, burden of a song, encore, recapitulation, *rifacimento (It.),* *réchauffé (Fr.),* drumming in, twice-told tale, chestnut, old story, new edition, second edition, return match, reappearance, reproduction, periodicity, recurrence, renewal.

ITINERANCY, n. Traveling from place to place, going about, wandering, roaming, roving, peregrinating, wayfaring, peripateticism, nomadism, pilgrimage, vagrancy, *wanderlust (Ger.),* vagabondism, hoboism, migration, flitting, gadding, pererration, itineracy, periegesis.

ITINERANT, adj. Traveling from place to place, itinerating, journeying, roving, roaming, wandering, nomadic, peripatetic, going to here and there, wayfaring, strolling, ambulatory, perambulating, migratory, rambling, flitting, straying, gadding, vagrant, wayworn, weather-beaten, travel-stained, gypsylike, unsettled, periegetic, having itchy feet, having sand in one's shoes.

ITINERANT, n. One who travels from place to place, traveler, wayfarer, vagrant, nomad, gypsy, migrant worker, Okie, wanderer, migrant, rambler, rover, roamer, pilgrim, walker, voyager, trekker, tourist, tripper, excursionist, peripatetic, globetrotter, adventurer, peregrinator, straggler, gadling, gadabout, bird of passage, landloper, stray, scatterling, hobo, tramp, beachcomber, vagabond, Arab, bohemian, pilgrim, periegete.

ITINERARY, n. 1. Route, course, circuit, order of march, road, plan, path, way, passage, line of travel.

2. Guidebook, guide, handbook, book describing routes of travel, *vade mecum (Lat.),* periegesis, Pausanias, Baedeker, Bradshaw, *Guide Bleu (Fr.),* blue book, map, chart, gazetteer, timetable, *cicerone (It.),* manual, pilot.

3. Detailed account of a journey, record of travel, diary, logbook, log.

IVORY, *n.* Hard white substance composing the main part of the tusks of elephants and walruses, variety of dentine, tusk, teeth *(pl., slang)*, piano keys *(pl.)*, billiard ball, dice *(pl.)*.

IVORY TOWER, *n.* 1. Place withdrawn from the world and worldly things, region of reverie, castle-in-the-air, *château en Espagne (Fr.)*, dreamland, *tour d'ivoire (Fr.)*, cloudland, retreat, sanctuary, *sanctum sanctorum (Lat.)*, haunt, shrine.

2. Attitude of aloofness, reserve, stand-offishness, taciturnity, reticence, unresponsiveness, uncommunicativeness, distance, concealment.

IVY, *n.* Climbing vine with smooth shiny evergreen leaves, *Hedera helix (Bot.)*, English ivy, Japanese ivy, ground ivy, trailing plant.

J

JAB, *n.* Poke *(as with end or point of something)*, sharp *or* smart thrust, thump, cut, pelt, dig, punch, blow, hit, pass, lunge, stroke, bayonet, swing, stab, clout *(coll.)*, paste *(sl.)*, swat *(sl.)*, lick *(coll.)*, clip *(coll.)*, sock *(sl.)*, plug (sl.).

JAB, *v.* Stab, poke smartly, thrust sharply, strike, hit, wallop, tap, rap, prod, jog, lunge, fetch a blow, attack, bayonet, punch, feint, assault, cuff, box, dig, soak *(sl.)*, sock *(sl.)*, hit a clip *(coll.)*, plug *(sl.)*, belt *(coll.)*, paste *(sl.)*, clout *(coll.)*.

JABBER, *n.* Jabbering talk *or* utterance, gibberish, chatter, babble, prattle, confabulation, clack, rattle, prating, gabble, patter, drivel, blather, twattle, gushing, blabber, idle talk, chitter-chatter, blab, twaddle, maundering, nonsense, palaver, chit-chat, gossip, buzzing, babblement, tattle, raving, bosh *(coll.)*, hot air *(sl.)*, rant, bombast, fustian, rodomontade, claptrap, scribbling, cackle, gas *(sl.)*.

JABBER, *v.* Prattle, chatter, babble, confabulate, palaver, buzz, prate, rattle, clack, gossip, gabble, patter, drivel, blather, twattle, gush, blab, twaddle, chitter-chatter, gibble-gabble, talk aimlessly *or* idly, chaffer, fiddle-faddle, smatter, trifle, gas *(sl.)*, ramble, maunder, talk rapidly, mumble, gibber, tattle, clatter, utter nonsense, rant, rodomontade, utter drivel, talk incoherently, mutter, splutter, sputter, stammer, spout *(coll.)*, pour forth, talk *or* run on like a mill race, be loquacious.

JABOT, *n.* Frill *(at front of a dress)*, falling ruffle, pleated trim, sash, scarf, fringe, lace, ruche, tassel, flounce, furbelow, cascade (of lace, embroidery, etc.).

JACK, *n.* 1. *(Cap.)* Man, fellow, sailor, gob *(sl.)*, tar *(coll.)*, chap *(coll.)*, mister *(coll.)*, guy *(sl.)*, *hombre (Span.)*, knave, rustic, yokel, lout, swain, gaffer, drone, duffer, oaf, Jacky *(often l.c.)*, Jack Tar.

2. Mechanical device for raising great weights small distances, device for turning a spit, windlass, jackscrew, lifter, rotator.

3. Small ensign used by a ship, flag, union, pennon, bunting, colors, signal flag, pennant, burgee, blue peter, banneret, standard.

JACK, *v.* *(Usually fol. by* UP*)* Hoist, lift *or* move with a jack, raise, boost, increase (prices; *coll.*), elevate, upraise, heave, rear, erect, hold up, uplift, uphoist, bear up.

JACK-A-DANDY, *n.* Man excessively concerned about clothes and appearance, coxcomb, exquisite, fop, popinjay, macaroni, dude, buck, fine gentleman, beau, ladies' man, man about town, blade,

Beau Brummell, swell *(sl.)*, dandy, silk-stocking, silk-sock Sam.

JACKAL, *n.* One who does drudgery for another, one who meanly serves the purpose of another, instrument, puppet, cat's-paw, flunky, satellite, jackstraw, hand, follower, drudge, fag, drone, tool, creature, yes man *(sl.)*, minion, heeler *(coll.)*, sycophant, tagtail, toadeater, spaniel, fawner, sponger, lickspit, groveler, votary, truckler, tuft-hunter, toady, vassal, lickspittle, lackey, carpet knight, footlicker, bootlicker, toiler, laborer, hack, hired man, plodder, slave.

JACKANAPES, *n.* Pert presuming man, whipper-snapper, puppy, coxcomb, impertinent fellow, smart aleck, wiseacre, blade, boldface, malapert, insolent, wise guy *(sl.)*, popinjay, swell *(sl.)*, cock of the walk, brazen face, pretender.

JACKASS, *n.* 1. Male ass, male donkey, jack, dickey, Jerusalem pony, moke *(chiefly sl.)*, burro *(Southwest. U.S.)*, longear *(coll.)*, neddy *(often cap.)*.

2. Very stupid *or* foolish person, blockhead, dolt, fool, bungler, imbecile, moron, boggler, clodpole, oaf, clod, idiot, booby, witling, boob *(sl.)*, ninny, tomfool, dunce, ninny-hammer, donkey, nincompoop, goose, tomnoddy, noddy, nitwit, dimwit *(sl.)*, looby, loon, saphead *(sl.)*, sap *(sl.)*, chump *(coll.)*, simpleton, ignoramus, jerk *(sl.)*, mutt *(sl.)*, softhead, asshead, stupid, silly *(coll.)*, dullard, dummy *(coll.)*, dumbbell *(sl.)*, numskull *(coll.)*, woodenhead *(coll.)*, bonehead, thickwit, thickhead, lunkhead *(coll.)*, dunderhead, dunderpate, squarehead *(sl.)*, jolterhead, chowderhead, chucklehead *(coll.)*, beetlehead, loggerhead, jolthead, blunderbuss, bullhead, cabbagehead *(coll.)*, noodlehead, doughhead *(sl.)*, bullethead, fathead, muttonhead *(coll.)*, noodle, clodpoll, clodpate, pumpkin head.

JACKET, *n.* 1. Jerkin, short coat, blouse, camisole, bolero, sack, doublet, blazer, cardigan, garibaldi, dressing jacket, shooting jacket, Eisenhower jacket, pilot jacket, shadbelly, Mackinaw coat, sack coat, coatee, *chaqueta (Sp.)*, polka, sweater, reefer, grego *(Gk. and Levantine)*, vareuse *(Southern U.S.)*, pea jacket, spencer, temiak *(Eskimo)*, sontag, jumper, cassock, sports coat *or* jacket, monkey jacket, dinner coat *or* jacket, smoking jacket, jersey.

2. Outer covering, envelope, casing, hide, coat, wrapper, enclosure, tube, case, binding, involucre, involucrum, sheath, sheathing, integument, bark, leather, pelt, fur, capsule, wrapping, cover.

JACKKNIFE, *n.* Large pocketknife, clasp knife, penknife, blade, folding knife.

JACK-OF-ALL-TRADES, *n.* Handy man, factotum, doer of all work, hack, servant of all work, man Friday, general servant, do-all, man of all work, office boy, versatile person.

JACKSTRAW, *n.* 1. Straw-stuffed figure of a man, scarecrow, straw man, effigy.

2. Insignificant person, nobody, nonentity, puppet, nullity, straw man, obscurity, naught, nothing, inferior, underling, man of straw, lightweight *(coll.)*, John Doe, man in the street, Tom, Dick, and Harry, cipher, scrub, layman, lay figure, heeler, tagtail, tinhorn *(sl.)*, dummy, mediocrity, small fry, cat's-paw, creature, satellite, follower, tool, servant, whiffet *(coll.)*, whippersnapper, hanger-on, shadow, no great shakes *or* catch, small beer.

JADE, *n.* 1. Green gem stone, jadestone, nephrite,

jadeite, true jade, Imperial jade, nephritic stone, kidney stone.

2. Jade green, emerald green, turquoise green, terre-verte, chrysoprase green, variscite green, sulphate green, shamrock green, emerald green, Egyptian green.

3. Hack, tired or worn-out horse, nag, plug (sl.), horse of inferior breed, vicious horse, worthless horse, padnag, crock, screw, rackabones (coll.), rip (coll.), skate (sl.), rosinante.

4. Disreputable woman, wench, whore, street walker, lewd woman, bawd, prostitute, trull, drab, doxy, lewd, procuress, wanton, strumpet, reprobate, demirep (sl.), trollop, grisette, hussy, Cyprian, temptress, woman of easy virtues or morals, tart (sl.), harridan, bitch (vulgar), fornicatress, pander, slut, adulteress, daughter of joy, cocotte, stew, courtesan, fallen woman, woman of the profession (euphemistic), Delilah, white slave, erring sister, frail sister, Sadie Thompson, baggage, woman of the town, Lais, bat (sl.), Jezebel, chippy (sl.), demimondaine, scarlet woman, cat (sl.), Thais, hetaera (Gk. Antiq.), meretrix, Messalina, broad (sl.), pickup, abandoned woman, harlot.

JADE, v. Tire, weary, faint, swoon, wilt, sink, fail, give out, flag, prostrate, dispirit, worry, strain, overwork, irk, exhaust, fatigue, crush, trample, distress, harass, bore, be fatigued, dull, become weary, succumb, do up (coll.), bleed white, frazzle, overtax, satiate, cloy, surfeit, gorge, accloy, saturate, glut, peg out (sl.), fag, droop, be ready to drop, tucker (often with OUT, coll.), poop (sl.), tire out.

JADED, adj. 1. Worn-out, exhausted, fatigued, tired, dog-tired, dead-tired, done, all in (coll.), played out, drooping, spent, fagged, overfatigued, overspent, overwearied, worn, prostrate, toilworn, ready to drop, dead (coll.), beat (coll.), tuckered out (coll.), bushed (sl.), pooped (sl.), wearied, harassed, tired out, dead-beat (coll.), pegged out (sl.).

2. Sated, satiated, saturated, overful, bored, dulled, cloyed, glutted, gorged, surfeited, satiate, fed up (coll.), drugged, obtuse, obtundent, narcotized, numbed, stupefied, blunted, sickened, incurious, indifferent, impassive, unfeeling, inured, hardened, insensible, insensitive, deadened, wearied.

JAG, n. Sharp projection on edge or surface, notch, protuberant point, knob, dent, sprocket, dentil (Archit.), ratchet, cog, score, crena, blaze, scotch, crenel, dint, jog, nub, cleft, protuberance, barb, tooth, gash, cut, nick, comb, indent, indentation, slit, snag, saw tooth, groove, crenation, crenelation, crenature, serration, serrulation, picot edge, rickrack, Vandyke edge, dentation (Bot., Zool.), projection, denticulation, nock (Archery).

JAG, v. Cut in points or pendants along the edge, form notches (teeth, ragged points) in, slash, notch, nick, gash, dint, dent, score, indent, tooth, crenelate, crenulate, pink, groove, mill (of coins), Vandyke, blaze, scotch, serrate.

JAGGED, adj. Having notches (teeth, ragged edges), notched, serrated, dentiform, crenate, serriform, jaggy, ragged on the edges, uneven, cleft, indented, zigzag, rough, abrupt, slashed, rugged, sharp, slit, cragged, erose, Vandyke-edged, gnawed, saw-toothed, toothed, snaggy, studded, nicked, rocky, rugose, ridged, broken, irregular, craggy, spiny, thorny, bristly, spiculate, acute, spinous, hooked, crotched, pointed, squarrose (Biol.), crenelated, dentate (Bot., Zool.), barbed, angular, furrowed.

JAIL, n. Prison, lockup, dungeon, gaol, detention house or cell, place of confinement, pound, penal institution, prisonhouse, state prison, station house, police station, guardhouse (Mil.), guardroom (Mil.), hoosegow (sl.), can (sl.), boobyhatch (sl.), cooler (sl.), reform school, limbo, calaboose (coll.), workhouse, penitentiary, brig (Naut.), keep (Mediev.), pinfold, cage, coop (sl.), panopticon, reformatory, cell, black hole (Mil.), bastille, rattle (Naut. sl.), pen (sl.), clink (coll.), bridewell (coll.), house of correction, jug (sl.), stir (sl.), big house (sl.).

JAIL, v. Take into or hold in custody, lock up, confine, imprison, impound, entomb, pen, coop, immure, gaol, incarcerate, pen in, shut in, intern, jug (sl.), place in confinement, commit to prison, clap or lay under hatches, subjugate, put into bilboes, shut up, clap up, seize, capture, bag (sl.), pinch (sl.), nab (coll.), run in (sl.), apprehend, collar (sl.), lay by the heels, arrest, throw or cast into prison, consign, put under arrest, take or make prisoner.

JAILBIRD, n. One who is or has been confined in jail, criminal, prisoner, outcast, offender against society, convict, ex-convict, felon, delinquent, reprobate, miscreant, parolee (Penol.), lag (sl.), lagger (sl.), trusty (Penol.), rascal, malefactor.

JAILER, n. Keeper of a jail, warden, gaoler, jailkeeper, guard, custodian, screw (sl.), turnkey, warder, sheriff.

JALOUSIE, n. Slatted window covering, shutter, blind, Venetian blind.

JAM, n. 1. Thick preserve, conserve, preserve of crushed fruit, jelly, marmalade, confiture, confection, (apple, peach, etc.) butter.

2. Mass of objects or persons pushed together, state of being jammed, crowd, block, crush, blockade, host, horde, swarm, dense mass of people, rabble, drive, drove, storm, cloud, herd, mob, sea, push, shove, amassment, conglomeration, agglomeration, thrust, throng, press, accumulation, pack, multitude, army, legion, flock, cram (coll.).

JAM, v. 1. Press into a small space, crowd, crush, bind, ram, cram, stuff, fill up by crowding, push or thrust violently, make inextricable, wedge, sandwich, intercalate, insert forcefully, work in, foist in, put between, squeeze, bruise, mortise, rabbet, dovetail, miter, worm in, edge in, overcrowd, block, force in.

2. Cause to become wedged (caught, displaced), become or make unworkable, interfere with the operation of, interrupt, stop, stall, cease, stick, arrest, block, deadlock, break, suspend, gum (sl.), obstruct.

JAMB, n. Side of an opening (fireplace, door, window, etc.), doorjamb, upright, column, lintel support, vertical piece, post, block, pillar, gatepost, doorpost.

JAMBOREE, n. Rally (as of Boy Scouts), gathering, festival, celebration, convention, investiture ceremony, jubilee, fete, observance, ceremony.

JANGLE, n. 1. Harsh sound, discord, clangor, clang, rattle, percussion, cacophony, stridor, diaphony, jumble of sound, clutter, clatter, concussion, dissonance, din, clank, uproar, tumult, racket, clashing, crash, jarring, wild pealing, reverberation, raucity, confusion of noise.

2. Altercation, quarrel, clashing, jangling, wrangle, wrangling, skirmish, fight, encounter, collision, concussion, crash, shock, appulse, ruction, conflict, joust, scuffle, brush, jar, impinge-

ment, smashup, engagement, affray, tilt, battle, dogfight, combat, argument, *mêlée (Fr.),* bout, fray, row, jolt, imbroglio, scrap *(sl.),* set-to *(coll.),* free-for-all *(coll.),* smash *(coll.),* run-in *(sl.),* percussion, meeting, bump, cannon, disagreement, antagonism, friction, discord, feud, cross fire, dispute, disceptation, tiff, contention, squabble, faction, controversy, dissention, contrariety, hostility, strife, litigation, rupture, enmity.

JANGLE, *v.* 1. Clash, clang, sound harshly *or* discordantly, vibrate harshly, clank, crash, rattle, make a racket, percuss, clatter, hurtle, din.

2. Speak angrily, wrangle, spat *(coll.),* spar, quarrel, squabble, bicker, tiff, have words, disagree, conflict, clash, altercate, brawl, dispute, jar, dissent, controvert, litigate, lock horns, collide, differ violently, pick a bone with, take issue, argue, broil, contend, feud, fall foul of, disceptate, strive.

JANITOR, *n.* Person employed to care for a building, offices, *etc.,* porter, doorkeeper, gatekeeper, sentinel, janitress *(fem.),* sexton, custodian, caretaker, concierge *(in France),* ostiary, usher, sentry, watchdog, Cerberus, beefeater *(Eng.),* tiler *(Freemasonry),* keeper, guardian, beadle *(Eccles.).*

JAPE, *n.* Joke, jest, gibe, jeer, caper, banter, chaff, twit, quiz, lampoon, burlesque, waggery, whimsicality, buffoonery, satire, raillery, badinage, ridicule, derision, squib, conceit, quip, crank, quirk, witticism, gag *(coll.),* detraction, fleer, antic, prank, scoffing, disparagement, wisecrack *(sl.),* persiflage, personality, mockery, horseplay, macaronic, caricature, parody, travesty, play of wit, sarcasm, flout, bite, fling.

JAR, *n.* 1. Broad-mouthed earthen *or* glass vessel, crock, cruse, pot, cylindrical receptacle, jug, pitcher, ewer, can, mug, bottle, flask, carafe, flagon, decanter, cruet, caster, canteen, canister, stein, urn, tankard, cask, carboy, demijohn, amphora *(Gr. and Rom.).*

2. Vibrating movement, concussion, agitation, jolt, shake, shock, harshly unpleasant effect *(on mind or feelings),* start, jog, quake, jostle, jounce, bump, jerk, bounce, lurch, sway, rock, surprise, twitch, turn *(coll.),* jiggle, joggle, tremble, shiver, quaver, yank *(coll.),* staggerer, thunderclap, thunderbolt, blow, eye opener, bolt out of *or* from the blue, clash, crash, collision, brunt, smash, smashup, impact, percussion, encounter, quiver.

3. Harsh grating sound, discordant sound *or* combination of sounds, cacophony, discord, clang, percussion, stridor, jumble of sound, clatter, dissonance, clank, tumult, clashing, jarring, clangor, rattle, diaphony, clutter, concussion, din, uproar, racket, crash, wild pealing, raucity, reverberation, chink, rasp, buzz, blast, harsh resonance, blare, bong, knell.

4. Conflict of opinion, quarrel, altercation, jangle, wrangling, wrangle, skirmish, litigation, rupture, strife, dissension, percussion, friction, discord, fight, collision, crash, shock, clash, combat, bout, row, fray, jolt, scrap *(sl.),* imbroglio, set-to *(coll.),* run-in *(sl.),* dispute, contention, tiff, bump, encounter, concussion, appulse, conflict, ruction, scuffle, brush, impingement, engagement, tilt, battle, affray, dogfight, smash *(coll.),* free-for-all *(coll.),* meeting, cannon, feud, cross fire, disceptation, squabble, faction, hostility.

JAR, *v.* 1. Produce a harsh grating sound, vibrate audibly, grate, rattle, sound discordantly, clash,

clang, clank, make a racket, clatter, din, percuss, hurtle.

2. Be at variance, conflict, clash, differ, be uncongenial, not correspond, quarrel, contend, wrangle, tiff, dispute, oppose, disagree, have an altercation, have words, squabble, jangle, spar, spat *(coll.),* bicker, tiff, altercate, brawl, dissent, controvert, litigate, collide, lock horns, take issue, strive, argue, broil, disceptate, fall foul of, pick a bone with.

3. Vibrate harshly, shake, agitate, jounce, bump, jolt, jiggle, joggle, bounce, jerk, buffet, trouble, disturb, stir, hustle, cause to quiver, disquiet, perturb, foment, flurry, convulse.

4. Have a harshly unpleasant effect upon (feelings, nerves, *etc.),* jangle, rankle, surprise, grate, startle, disquiet, discompose, disturb, pierce, aggravate, irritate, shock, annoy, disaccord, prey on the mind, touch a sore spot *or* place, give one a turn *(coll.),* stun, stupefy, take aback, give one a shock, flurry, sting, cut, chafe, nettle, irk, vex, stir, perturb, unsettle, upset, go against the grain, get on one's nerves, gall, ruffle, fluster, flutter, trouble, shake up, astound, disconcert, toss, convulse, bother, faze *(coll.),* discomfit, daunt, confuse, bewilder, muddle, flummox *(sl.),* distract, daze, befuddle, put out.

JARDINIERE, *n.* Ornamental receptacle *(for flowers, plants, etc.),* vase, pot, flower bowl, epergne, urn, plant stand, tazza *(It.),* amphora *(Gk. and Rom. Antiq.).*

JARGON, *n.* 1. Drivel, prattle, rigmarole, piffle, gibberish, flapdoodle, bunk, tommyrot, rot, fiddle-faddle, blabber, rubbish, stuff and nonsense, nonsense, stuff, absurdity, prating, bosh, wishwash, balderdash, clatter, jabberwocky, gab, flummery, hocus-pocus, inanity, abracadabra, gobbledegook *(sl.),* babble, hogwash, moonshine *(coll.),* twaddle, clack, blather, trash, froth, meaningless talk, bibble-babble, prate, patter, hooey *(sl.),* rattle, fudge *(coll.),* poppycock *(coll.),* bavardage *(Fr.),* kibosh *(sl.),* piffle *(sl.).*

2. Specialized *or* professional language, cant, idiom, slang, lingo, usage, vocabulary, vernacular, tongue, argot, phraseology.

3. Simplified *or* conventional language, patois, dialect, tongue, parlance, diction, brogue, vernacular, "pidgin."

JAUNDICE, *n.* Yellow jaundice, icterus, xanthochromia, xanthochroia.

JAUNDICED, *adj.* 1. Distorted, prejudiced, biased, warped, twisted, unjust, intolerant, narrowminded, bigoted, one-sided, prepossessed, partial, unfair, unbalanced.

2. Suspicious, distrustful, mistrustful, greeneyed, doubting, covetous, yellow, envying, jealous, spiteful, feeling ill-will, envious, resentful.

3. Tart, rude, acetous, petulant, sullen, crabbed, surly, brusque, choleric, acrimonious, bearish, insulting, abrupt, ill-mannered, uncouth, illbred, unmannerly, insolent, gross, obnoxious, acerbic, irascible, acetose, sharp, grouchy *(coll.),* thorny, bluff, bristling, grouty *(coll.),* sarcastic, growling, harsh, uncivil, rough, impolite, brutish, snarling, waspish, peppery, snappish, quarrelsome, sour, splenetic, crusty, sulky, unamiable, unhandsome, coarse, boorish, blunt, glum, swinish, bestial, beastly, vulgar, perverse, ugly, doggish, ungallant, morose, ill-tempered, spiteful, fractious, mean, sordid, base, discourteous, dastardly, testy, recreant, lowbred, resentful, caviling, iracund, acrid, mordant, curt, currish, short, ungraceful,

cankered, captious, churlish, moody, cynical, irritable, thin-skinned, touchy, churlish, saturnine, mordacious, bitter, rancorous, peevish, bilious, cross-grained, shrewish, gruff.

JAUNT, *n.* Short journey, short trip, ramble, excursion, spin *(coll.),* adventure, promenade, tour, stroll, airing, outing, voyage, peregrination.

JAUNTY, *adj.* 1. Happy, gay, debonair, gladsome, blithe, cheery, light-hearted, winsome, jolly, jovial, genial, merry, mirthful, buoyant, joyous, joyful, animated, elated, sprightly, lively, pleasant, vivacious, jocund, airy, sportive, brisk, gleeful, sunny, hopeful, optimistic, resilient, volatile, jubilant, carefree, free and easy, in high humor, in high spirits, bright, breezy, cheerful, chipper *(coll.),* frisky, pert.

2. Dapper, trim, spruce, chic *(coll.),* smart, neat, sleek, spic and span, natty *(coll.).*

JAVELIN, *n.* Spear, dart, lance, harpoon, gaff, pike, shaft, jereed, assagai, spontoon, eelspear, weet-weet *(Austral.).*

JAW, *n.* 1. Bony framework of mouth, jawbone, mandible, maxilla, maxillary bone, mandibular bone, jawbone with teeth and soft tissues *(Dentistry).*

2. *(Often pl.)* Mouth parts *(collectively),* mouth, chaps, chops, bill *(of a bird),* muzzle *(of an animal),* maw *(of an animal),* trap *(sl.),* mug *(sl.),* bazoo *(sl.).*

3. *(Often pl.; fig.)* Opening, entrance, mouth, portal, ingress, yawning *or* gaping hole, orifice, access, adit, gate, door, gateway, doorway, aperture, maw, inlet, enclosing crag, craggy opening, throat, wall *(of a pass),* crater, grasping parts *(of a machine),* cheeks *(of a machine).*

JAZZ, *n.* Dance music ("hot" and improvisatory), syncopation, swing, hot jazz, rag *(coll.),* ragtime *(coll.),* jitterbug music, jive *(sl.),* rock-and-roll, Dixieland, blues, boogie-woogie.

JEALOUS, *adj.* 1. Envious, resentful, suspicious, distrustful, mistrustful, characterized by *or* proceeding from suspicions *or* fears, spiteful, feeling ill will, grudging, envying, jaundiced, yellow, covetous, doubting, green-eyed.

2. Solicitous in maintaining *or* guarding something, anxious, vigilant, watchful, suspicious, careful, concerned, wary, wakeful, sleepless, unsleeping, advertent, heedful, prudent, regardful, painstaking, mindful, scrupulous, alert, on the watch *or* lookout, lynx-eyed, Argus-eyed, apprehensive, cautious, on guard, precautious.

JEALOUSY, *n.* Suspicion, envy, distrust, solicitude, resentment, vexation, misgiving, hatred, qualm, scruple, fearfulness, care, spite, ill will, grudging, watchfulness, bitterness, heartburn, misdoubt, green-eyed monster, jaundiced eye, foreboding, mistrust, chagrin, mental uneasiness (from suspicion *or* fear of rivalry), doubt, sense of injury *or* deprivation, anxiety, want of confidence, apprehension, humiliation, vigilance.

JEER, *n.* Jeering utterance, sneer, taunt, hoot, derisive *or* rude gibe, sarcasm, flout, aspersion, yell of contempt, disparagement, fleer, defamation, derogation, obloquy, invective, slur, pasquinade, pasquil, roorback, evilspeaking, malediction, cut, scurrility, verbal thrust, insult, indignity, retort, brickbat *(coll.),* caustic remark, insolence, contempt, abuse, offense, affront, backbiting, calumniation, contumely, quirk, banter, fling, jest, biting, rub, slander, assault, rap *(sl.),* slam *(sl.),* knock *(sl.),* dig *(coll.),* provocation, slap in the face, depreciation, vilification, scoff, quip, burlesque, wipe *(coll.),* rude reproach, back answer, short answer, comeback *(sl.),* derision, parody, travesty, mockery, persiflage, detraction, wisecrack *(sl.),* raillery, lampoon, twit, quiz, chaff.

JEER, *v.* Speak *or* shout derisively, sneer, flout, mock, fleer, jape, hiss, banter, scorn, scout, twit, revile, aggravate, throw mud at, cry out against, taunt, ridicule, catcall, whistle at, knock *(sl.),* have a fling at, spurn, rebuff, give the raspberry *or* Bronx cheer *(sl.),* slander, backbite, satirize, lampoon, run down, traduce, malign, defame, vilify, cast aspersions, curl up one's lip, scoff, derogate, decry, be contemptuous, disparage, calumniate, point the finger of scorn, hold up to scorn, gibe rudely, jest, hoot, rail, laugh at, hold in derision, razz *(sl.),* slur, deride, chaff, contemn, gird at, poke fun at, harass, treat with insolence, make game *or* sport of, cavil at, shame.

JEJUNE, *adj.* 1. Lacking in nourishment, innutritious, unnutritious, deficient, unsatisfying.

2. Tame, insipid, meager, arid, empty, wanting, prosaic, insulse, worthless, deficient, lean, hollow, flat, barren, devoid, uninteresting, inefficacious, vacant, vapid, inadequate, puerile, poor, colorless, unsatisfying, fruitless, addle, otiose, unfertile, uninspiring, weak, unprofitable, inept, stale, lame, unfruitful.

JELLIFY, *v.* Become *or* make jelly, thicken, congeal, set, gel, solidify, gelatinize, gelatinate, jell *(coll.),* jelly.

JELLY, *n.* 1. Jellied preserve, aspic, gelatin, blancmange, gelée *(Fr. cookery),* jujube, jello *(trade name often used generally).*

2. Jellylike substance, gelatin, glutin, gluten, gelatinoid.

JELLYFISH, *n.* Medusa, hydrozoan, coelenterate, Scyphozoa *(Zool.).*

JELLYLIKE, *adj.* Gelatinoid, glutinous, glutose, glutinose, gelatose, tremellose *(Bot.),* tremelloid *(Bot.),* muculent *(Bot.).*

JEOPARDIZE, *v.* Imperil, risk, endanger, peril, jeopard, compromise, venture, chance, stake, hazard, expose, put in danger, threaten, subject to menace, gamble.

JEOPARDY, *n.* Openness to danger, danger, risk, peril, unsafety, insecurity, chance, hazard, accident, casualty, precariousness, endangerment, liability, threat, vulnerability, predicament, imperilment, uncertainty.

JEREMIAD, *n.* Prolonged lamentation, lamentation, lament, sobbing, moan, moaning, wail, wailing, murmur, obloquy, plaint, cry, complaint, whine, whimper, outcry, "weeping and gnashing of teeth."

JERK, *n.* Twist, pull, shake, trembling, agitation, bump, lurch, sway, quiver, quaver, blow, clash, crash, start, thrust, yank *(coll.),* pull, twitch, buffet, jog, jiggle, wrench, tweak, twang.

JERK, *v.* Twist, pull, yank *(coll.),* shake, agitate, bump, flurry, convulse, thrust, jiggle, bounce, lurch, sway, disturb, perturb, buffet, jog, twitch, tweak, pluck, twang, jounce, stir, ruffle, jostle, joggle, jolt.

JERRY-BUILT, *adj.* Poorly *or* cheaply built, flimsy, shaky, defective, faulty, unsubstantial, weak, poor, inferior, shoddy, ill-designed, ill-constructed, rickety, puny, thin, stinted, frail, gimcrack, crude, unstable, inadequate, unsound, wobbly, below par, meager, second *or* third *or* fourth rate.

JEST, *n.* Humorous story *or* deed, joke, quip, bon mot, prank, trick, farce, mot, crank, quirk, game, witticism, pleasantry, quiz, sally, carri-witchet, jape, crack, gag *(coll.)*, wisecrack *(sl.)*, *jeu d'esprit (Fr.)*, pun, paronomasia.

JEST, *v.* Crack jokes, bandy jokes, play the fool, josh *(sl.)*, banter, joke, pun, fool, laugh, scoff, flout, burlesque, rally, quip, quiz, gibe, snigger, tease, wisecrack *(sl.)*, gag *(coll.)*, sally, jig, twit, caper, mock, chaff.

JESTER, *n.* Comedian, funnyman, farceur, fool, antic, zany, clown, harlequin, droll, buffoon, Punch, Pierrot, pantaloon, grimacer, comic, pun-chinello, merry-andrew, Scaramouch, mounte-bank, buffo *(It.)*, wearer of the cap and bells, mummer, mime, pantomimist, joker, caricaturist, mimic, mimer, wit, wag, fool, motley fool, Jack Pudding, Pickelhering *(Ger.)*, wearer of the mot-ley, Hanswurst, pickle-herring, farcist, tumbler, humorist, madcap, jack-a-dandy, card *(coll.)*.

JESTING, *n.* Banter, chaff, buffoonery, fooling, whimsicality, wit, humor, disparagement, badi-nage, ridicule, fun, derision, persiflage, parody, horseplay, scoffing, lampoon, waggery, raillery, laughing, joshing *(sl.)*, wisecracking *(sl.)*, joking, quipping, quizzing, mocking, twitting, teasing, wordplay, nonsense, clowning, antics, jocularity, facetiousness, drollery, comicality, pranks, farce, farcicality, larks, sprees, capers, tomfoolery, har-lequinade, monkey tricks *(sl.)*, shenanigans *(coll.)*, pantomime, frisk, romp, hilarity, gambol, roguish-ness, mimicry, jocosity, mime, caricature, slap-stick, jocoseness, travesty, merriment, good humor, levity, revel, burletta, repartee.

JESUS, *n.* The Saviour, the Christ, the Son of Man, the Messiah, the Lord, the Redeemer, King of the Jews, Son of David, Son of Mary, the Anointed, the Son of Righteousness, God the Son, the Prince of Peace, the Nazarene, the Galilean, the Good Shepherd, Emmanuel, Immanuel, the Man of Sorrows, the Lamb, the Lamb of God, Lord of Lords, the Word Incarnate, the Door, King of Kings, the Way, the Truth, the Life, the Way of Life, the Light of the World, the God-head, the Crucified, the Bread of Life. *(As a Child)* The Babe, the Holy Infant, the Infant Re-deemer, the Child of Bethlehem, the Christ Child.

JET, *adj.* Black, coal-black, jet-black, pitch-dark, black as midnight, black as the ace of spades, sable, ebony, ebon *(Poet.)*, pitchy, raven, jetty, inky, nigrine, nigrous, atramentous.

JET, *n.* 1. Stream of liquid, stream, spurt, sparge, spout, shoot, squirt, rush, fountain, swash, spray, flush, gush.
  2. Tip *(for squirting liquid, etc.)*, nozzle, spout, sprayer, sprinkler, nose, atomizer, syringe, rose, sparger, rosehead.

JET, *v.* Break *or* burst forth *(as a liquid)*, stream, spurt, rush up, shoot, squirt, flow, surge, emanate, issue, fountain, spray, gush, well, spout, discharge, vomit forth, exude, disembogue, effuse, extrava-sate.

JETSAM, *n.* Goods thrown overboard to lighten a ship in distress, jettison, flotsam and jetsam, castoff.

JETTISON, *v.* Throw overboard *(to lighten a ship in distress)*, discard, throw off ballast, eliminate, throw out, throw over, cast off, toss overboard.

JETTY, *n.* Pier, wharf, embankment, sea wall, dock, wall, mole, breakwater, key, quay, jutty, landing, landing place.

JEW, *n.* Hebrew, Israelite, Judaist, rabbinist, Kar-aite *(one who rejects Talmud)*, Talmudist *(one who accepts Talmud)*, Sadducee *(chiefly Hist.)*.

JEWEL, *n.* 1. Cut and polished stone, brilliant, gem, precious stone, bijou, stone, diamond, pearl, ice *(sl.)*, pivot *(Watchmaking)*, bearing *(Watch-making)*.
  2. Fashioned ornament for personal adorn-ment, trinket, brooch, bauble, bracelet, curio, necklace, earring, torque, tiara, chatelaine, ring, article of virtu, diadem, bangle, coronet, crown, locket, lavaliere, pendant, badge *(as of an order)*.
  3. Precious possession, thing *or* person of great worth *or* rare excellence, favorite, gem, treasure, work of art, pure gold, bijou, diamond, pearl, honey, prize, flower, pearl of great price, pink, paragon, cream, salt of the earth, one in a thou-sand *or* ten thousand, man after one's own heart, apple of one's eye, idol, pet, find, pip *(sl.)*, trump *(coll.)*, pippin *(sl.)*, humdinger *(sl.)*, crackerjack *(sl.)*, prodigy, wonder, loved one, champion, first-rater, topnotcher *(coll.)*, winner *(sl.)*, brick *(coll.)*, knockout *(sl.)*, ace, masterpiece, darling, fondling, saint, angel, queen, goddess, god, worthy, nature's nobleman.

JEWELER, *n.* One who makes *or* deals in jewels *or* jewerly, lapidary, artist, artificer, watchmaker, craftsman.

JEWELRY, *n.* Jewels, bijouterie, virtu *or* articles of virtu, gems, finery, costume jewelry, personal adornment, precious stones, filigree, trinkets, craftsmanship, fine workmanship, fashioned orna-ments, ice *(sl.)*.

JEWISH, *adj.* Hebrew, Hebraic, Israelite, Israelit-ish, Judaic, Hebraistic, Hebraistical, Yiddish *(of Yiddish language, etc.)*, rabbinistic *(adhering to Talmud)*.

JEZEBEL, *n.* Shameless abandoned woman, street walker, whore, jade, wanton, lewd, reprobate, demirep *(sl.)*, loose woman, harridan, Paphian, woman of easy virtues *or* morals, adulteress, pander, slut, daughter of joy, cocotte, woman of the profession *(euphemistic)*, conciliatrix *(Fr.)*, harlot, erring sister, frail sister, pickup, broad *(sl.)*, painted woman, meretrix, scarlet woman, hussy, quean, bawd, trull, drab, doxy, procuress, strumpet, prostitute, Cyprian, trollop, grisette, adventuress, bitch *(vulgar)*, tart *(sl.)*, temptress, fornicatress, courtesan, stew, bat *(sl.)*, Lais, Thais, hetaera *(Gk. Antiq.)*, baggage, Sadie Thompson, chippy *(sl.)*, demimondaine, white slave, madam *(coll.)*, Mrs. Warren, unfortunate woman, Delilah, woman of the town, cat *(sl.)*.

JIG, *n.* Rapid springy dance, lively irregular rhythm, piece of jig music, reel, hornpipe, riga-doon, strathspey.

JIG, *v.* Dance *(a jig or other lively dance)*, hop, bob, jerk, jog, flip, hitch, flounce, joggle, move with a jerky motion, bounce, bound, leap, prance, gambol, frisk, skip, caper, trip, vault, saltate, romp, leapfrog, buck, curvet, upleap, upspring.

JIGGLE, *v.* Move *(up and down, to and fro)* with short quick jerks, wiggle, jog, trot, dance, shake, fidget, jolt, wriggle, twitch, joggle, jigget *(coll.)*, dangle, rock, quake, wag, bounce, bob, jump, bobble *(coll.)*, jounce, convulse, waggle, vibrate, agitate, yank *(coll.)*, jerk, hitch.

JILT, *v.* Cast off *(a lover or sweetheart),* deceive, leave, cheat, desert, be faithless, leave in the lurch, betray, forsake, break one's heart, break one's word *or* promise, let one down, humiliate one, not keep faith with, go back on *(coll.),* go back on one's word *or* promise *(coll.),* reverse oneself, break an engagement, double-cross *(sl.).*

JINGLE, *n.* 1. Harsh sound, tinkle, raucity, reverberation, jarring, crash, clashing, racket, tumult, uproar, din, dissonance, concussion, clatter, clutter, jumble of sound, diaphony, cacophony, percussion, discord, stridor, clang, clangor.

2. Burlesque poem *or* verse, comic poem, crude verse, halting verse, jog-trot verse, trivial verse, doggerel, crambo *(contempt.),* Hudibrastic verse, mock-heroic verse, limerick.

JINGLE, *v.* Vibrate harshly, dingle, rattle, clash, cling, clatter, twang, jangle, ding, click, clack, tinkle, clank, clink, ting, tink, hurtle, din.

JINGOISM, *n.* Chauvinism, exaggerated patriotism, vainglorious patriotism, overpatriotism, spread-eagleism, patriolatry.

JINX, *n.* *(Colloq.)* Person (thing, influence) supposed to bring bad luck, bogy, bugbear, hoodoo *(coll.),* bugaboo, hobgoblin, voodoo, imp, sprite, evil eye, evil star, evil genius, Jonah, devil, incubus, succubus, ghoul, barghest, possession, sorcery, demon, black magic, hocus-pocus, ill wind, ogre, ogress, devilkin, bad fairy, evil spirit, poker, Fury, undoing, spell, pixy, ouphe, puck, goblin, Flibbertigibbet, vampire, fee-faw-fum, werewolf *(Folklore),* bête noire, bewitchment, jinn *(Mohammedan Myth.),* Loki *(Scand. Myth.),* Lorelei *(Ger. Legend),* siren, Harpy *(Gk. Myth.),* troll *(Scand. Folklore),* lamia *(Class. Myth.),* afreet *(Myth.).*

JITTERBUG, *n.* Hepcat, cat, jive enthusiast, swing enthusiast, hot music fan, boogie-woogie fan.

JOB, *n.* 1. Piece of work, chore, business, handiwork, matter in hand, anything one has to do, concern, affair, venture, commission, trust, mission, assignment, enterprise, duty, care, charge, grind, task, handicraft, stint, work, business affair, undertaking, role, function, part, doings, achievement, exercise, effort, performance, contribution, project, plan, transaction, proceeding, dealings, errand, share, pursuit, composition, activity, accomplishment.

2. Situation, post of employment, position, employment, living, business, province, trade, craft, livelihood, occupation, kind of work *(for a living),* vocation, calling, line of business, profession, station, billet, career, berth, field, part, role, capacity, means of support, office, sinecure, pursuit, métier, engagement, incumbency, appointment, place, function.

3. Unit of material being worked upon *(finished or unfinished),* lot, consignment, piece, pack, parcel, opus, sum, bunch, batch, division, output, turnout, contingent, portion, quota, quantity, composition, amount, allotment, assignment, share, product.

4. Public *or* official business conducted for improper private gain, scheme, game, steal, fraud, sinecure, racket *(sl.),* extortion, blackmail, graft *(coll.),* corruption, jobbery, swindle, fraudulence, sharp practice, chicanery, dishonesty, pettifoggery, exploitation.

JOB, *v.* 1. Do job work, work at jobs *or* odd pieces of work, operate, hire oneself out, do piecework, do miscellaneous jobs, service *(of automobiles),* work by the piece, perform a job.

2. Do business as a jobber, act as a middleman, distribute *(goods),* buy in large quantities and sell in smaller lots, buy and sell, dispense, wholesale, disperse, allocate, apportion, maintain a wholesale establishment, consign *(Commerce),* supply retailers.

3. Turn public business improperly to private gain, scheme, use to one's own purposes, carry out sharp practice, steal, pettifog, swindle, exploit, blackmail, extort, maneuver, cheat the taxpayer, machinate, gerrymander, manipulate office, hold a sinecure, engage in graft *(coll.) or* corruption, pull wires *or* strings.

4. Let out *(work)* among different contractors *or* workmen, sublet, employ specialists, hire workers, underlet, commission, farm out, lease, purchase the services of, send out, consign, procure the services of, relegate.

JOBBER, *n.* 1. Wholesale merchant *(esp. one selling to retailers),* agent, salesman, broker, wholesaler, regrater, dealer, middleman.

2. Piece worker, hack, day laborer, employee, hired hand, hand, help, migrant, wageworker, workman, workwoman, hireling, drone, drudge, man of all work, workhand, plodder, menial, toiler, fagger, handy man, hodman, laborer.

3. One who perpetrates corrupt public *or* official jobs, one who practices jobbery, grafter *(coll.),* carpetbagger *(contemptuous),* schemer, strategist, intriguer, wirepuller, machinator, tactician, Machiavellian, gerrymanderer, swindler, politician, betrayer of the public trust, sharper, bunco steerer *(coll.).*

JOBBERY, *n.* Practice of making improper private gains from public business *or* trust, perpetration of corrupt public *or* official jobs, sharp practice, political cunning, politics, graft *(coll.),* Machiavellianism, deception of the public, gerrymandering, corruption, undue profiting from public funds, pettifogging, fraudulence, betrayal of the public trust.

JOCKEY, *n.* One who professionally rides horses in races, rider, equestrian, horseman, trainer, horseback rider, jock *(coll.).*

JOCKEY. *v.* 1. Ride *(a horse)* as a jockey, race on horseback, run a horse race, participate in a Derby, sweepstakes, steeplechase, *etc.*

2. Bring (put, *etc.*) by skillful maneuvering, navigate, manage skillfully, maneuver, steer into position, ease, coax, adjust, induce, guide gently and carefully, control in close quarters.

3. Cheat, trick, gull, get the better of one, perplex, outwit, dupe, overreach, delude, mislead, beguile, humbug, chouse *(often fol. by* OF *or* OUT OF*),* entrap, trap, hoodwink, cozen, deceive, bamboozle, inveigle, impose upon, beggar, victimize, bite, gammon *(coll.),* circumvent, manipulate trickily, swindle, hoax, fraud, abuse, defraud, practice upon, befool, do, diddle, play upon, fleece, lure, mulct, ensnare, rook, foist upon, gyp, entice, cajole, play false, wheedle, gouge *(coll.),* flam, betray, pluck *(sl.),* bunco *(coll.),* take *(coll.),* cog, bilk, palm upon.

4. Act trickily, seek advantage by trickery, aim at an advantage by skillful maneuvering, pull a fast one, court favor, woo, misrepresent oneself, fish for, solicit, bid for, curry favor, fawn upon, flatter, be a sycophant, dance attendance upon, polish up *(sl.),* butter up *(coll.),* kneel, bend the knee, be a hypocrite, toady, be servile, toadeat,

bootlick (sl.), lick the dust, bow and scrape, kowtow, cajole, dupe, gull, practice on one's credulity, make a fool of, grovel, cringe, lickspittle, lay it on thick, fawn, truckle, prostrate oneself, pander to, lay it on, soft-soap, ingratiate or insinuate oneself, pull one's leg, adulate, take in.

JOCOSE, adj. Given to or characterized by joking, humorous, jesting, comical, merry, sportive, jocular, gay, jolly, arch, jocund, entertaining, amusing, absurd, full of fun, playful, provoking laughter, comic, lusory, rompish, risible, prankish, facetious, waggish, witty, funny, laughable, hilarious, joyous, rich, ludicrous, fantastic, ridiculous, mirthful, diverting, doggerel, light, mimic, screaming, gleeful, jovial, joyful, nonsensical, whimsical, keen-witted, quick-witted, burlesque, slapstick, farcical, Attic, full of point, gamesome, tricksy, sparkling, frolicsome, scintillating, sprightly, mirth-loving, laughter-loving, pungent, keen, droll, roguish, playful, ·nimble-witted, quizzical.

JOCOSITY, n. 1. State or quality of being jocose, wittiness, playfulness, joking, jesting, jollity, mirth, levity, hilarity, drollery, pleasantry, comicality, merriment, nonsense, fooling, waggishness, farcicality, merrymaking, amusement, jocularity, whimsicality, ridiculousness, waggery, facetiousness.

2. Joking, joke, jest, banter, whimsy, chaff, fancy, fun, facetiousness, humorous exchange, caricature, prank, pun, drollery, comedy, wit, farce, comic element, parody, caper, horseplay, badinage, mimicry, foolery, repartee, Attic salt, Attic wit, wordplay, buffoonery, playful raillery, nonsense, trick, monkeyshine (sl.), harlequinade, shenanigan (often pl., coll.), waggery, humor, pleasantry, whim, amphigory, fooling, antic, persiflage.

JOCULAR, adj. Given to, characterized by, intended for or suited to joking or jesting, humorous, jesting, comical, merry, sportive, jocose, gay, jolly, arch, jocund, entertaining, amusing, absurd, full of fun, playful, provoking laughter, comic, lusory, rompish, risible, prankish, facetious, waggish, witty, funny, laughable, hilarious, joyous, rich, ludicrous, fantastic, ridiculous, mirthful, diverting, doggerel, light, mimic, screaming, gleeful, jovial, joyful, nonsensical, whimsical, keen-witted, quick-witted, burlesque, slapstick, farcical, Attic, full of point, gamesome, tricksy, sparkling, frolicsome, scintillating, sprightly, mirth-loving, laughter-loving, pungent, keen, droll, roguish, playful, nimble-witted, quizzical.

JOCULARITY, n. 1. State or quality of being jocular, jocoseness, wittiness, playfulness, joking, jesting, jollity, mirth, levity, hilarity, drollery, pleasantry, comicality, merriment, nonsense, fooling, waggishness, farcicality, merrymaking, amusement, jocosity, whimsicality, ridiculousness, waggery, facetiousness, sportiveness.

2. Jocular speech or behavior, jocular remark or act, joke, jest, banter, whimsy, chaff, fancy, fun, facetiousness, humorous exchange, caricature, prank, pun, drollery, comedy, wit, farce, comic element, parody, caper, horseplay, badinage, mimicry, foolery, repartee, Attic salt, Attic wit, wordplay, buffoonery, playful raillery, nonsense, trick, monkeyshine (sl.), harlequinade, shenanigan (often pl., coll.), waggery, humor, pleasantry, whim, amphigory, fooling, antic, persiflage.

JOCUND, adj. Merry, cheerful, gay, lively, glad, debonaire, jovial, jocose, sportive, playful, frolicsome, joyful, joyous, blithesome, jolly, airy, facetious, pleasant, sprightly, hilarious, light-hearted, blithe, happy, mirthful, buoyant, vivacious, volatile, gladsome, jocular, cheery, winsome, genial, elated, animated, sunny, optimistic, jubilant, carefree, in high spirits, bright, jaunty, pert, frisky, chipper (coll.), breezy, blissful, rapturous, radiant, ecstatic, zestful, smiling, exultant, rejoiced, tickled, riant, sparkling, exhilarated, scintillating.

JOCUNDITY, n. State of being jocund, joyousness, cheerfulness, gaiety, sportiveness, merriment, high glee, spirits, buoyancy, good humor, mirth, jocularity, blitheness, light heart, rejoicing, levity, laughter, delight, felicity, gladness, joy, happiness, pleasure, vivacity, sprightliness, joyfulness, hilarity, exhilaration, cheeriness, delectation, sunshine, exultation, hopefulness, breeziness, jubilance, jubilation, conviviality, joviality, high spirits, glee, fun, festivity, joyance, jollity, animation.

JOG, n. 1. Bump, lurch, nudge, twist, pull, shake, trembling, quiver, quaver, blow, clash, crash, start, thrust, yank (coll.), pull, twitch, buffet, jiggle, jerk, wrench, tweak, twang, jostle, joggle, jolt.

2. Sharp projection on edge or surface, notch, protuberant point, knob, dent, sprocket, dentil (Archit.), ratchet, cog, score, crena, blaze, scotch, crenel, dint, jag, nub, cleft, protuberance, barb, tooth, gash, cut, nick, comb, indent, indentation, slit, snag, saw tooth, groove, crenation, crenelation, crenature, serration, serrulation, picot edge, rickrack, Vandyke edge, dentation (Bot., Zool.), projection, denticulation, nock (Archery).

JOG, v. Jiggle, bounce, jounce, jar, shake, jigget (coll.), flick, flip, bob, bobble, jump, fidget, agitate, vibrate, nudge, wag, waggle, rock, jostle, convulse, hitch, joggle, wiggle, wriggle, twitch, tweak, jerk, serrate.

JOGGLE, v. Move (up and down or to and fro) with short quick jerks, wiggle, jog, trot, dance, shake, fidget, jolt, wriggle, twitch, jiggle, dangle, rock, quake, wag, bounce, bob, jump, bobble (coll.), jounce, convulse, waggle, vibrate, agitate, yank (coll.), jerk, hitch, jigget (coll.).

JOG TROT. n. Slow pace, halting pace, creeping pace, monotonous pace, easy-going pace, slow gallop, dawdling, lingering, loitering, crawling.

JOIN, v. 1. Bring together, fasten together, connect, inosculate, mix, coalesce, commingle, bridge, span, yoke, link, chain, marry, band, splice, converge, fasten, pool, coadunate, piece together, fuse, unite, bind, couple, alloy, anastomose, combine, commix, compound, tie together, merge, co-ordinate.

2. (As groups, forces, etc.) Unite, league, associate, combine, federate, merge, club together, ally, cooperate, pool efforts, form a union, unify, meet, amalgamate, consolidate, agglomerate, confederate, fraternize, co-ordinate, synergize, conglomerate, get together, hold together, syndicate.

3. Cohere, stick, stick together, hold fast, cleave, be attached, hold to, hold together, be connected, clasp, cement, cling, concrete, be spliced, be clinched, be bound, be tacked together, be fastened, be glued, be made fast, fuse, fasten, attach, seal, fix, bind, unite, conjoin, affix, unify, weld, compress, solder, paste, glue.

4. Join up, become a member of, sign up with, enlist in, become connected with, unite with, enroll in, enter, associate oneself with.

5. Be contiguous with, touch, meet, adjoin, hug, fringe on, verge on, connect, scrape, graze, border on, abut, append, conjoin, reach, skirt, margin, marginate, brush.

JOINER, *n.* 1. That which joins, link, bond, coupling, knot, miter, mortise, weld, nexus, coupler, clasp, hasp, clip, hook, dowel, rabbet, copula, buckle, dash, hyphen, universal woodworking machine, connective, clamp, cinch, latch, holdfast, ligature, butt, raphe (*Anat.*), seam, closure, stitch, suture, tie, hinge, hitch, splice, dovetail.

2. Carpenter, woodworker, craftsman, artisan, cabinetmaker, chips (*Naut. sl.*), door *or* window maker.

JOINT, *adj.* Shared by *or* common to two *or* more, sharing *or* acting in common, united, combined, corporate, conjunct, common, mutual, leagued, consentual, consentaneous, consentient, allied, conjoint, conjugate, coadunate, compact, inseparable, shared, converging, parallel, unified, coordinate, consilient, joined in relation (interest *or* action), associated, agreed, synergetic, synergistic, consensual (*Law*), participating, co-operative, collaborative, coalitional, consolidated, cohesive, in conjunction, conjunctive, associate, reciprocal, in common, communal, collective, commutual, corporative, conjoined, incorporated, federate, confederate, confederated, communistic, unanimous, community, assenting, concordant, like-minded, twin, fellow, accompanying, attendant, concomitant, amalgamated, in league, correal (*Civil Law*), concerted, concurrent, coequal, hand in hand, solidary.

JOINT, *n.* Place of joining, part where joining occurs, junction, juncture, connection, hinge, splice, link, connexus, knot, nexus, articulation, elbow, knee, knuckle, mortise and tenon, communication, hock, butt, atlas (*Anat.*), overlapping, pivot, weld, suture, joiner, joining, commissure, seam, hitch, coupling, ligature, decussation, osculation, bond, dovetail, intersection, point of contact, node (*Bot.*), raphe (*Anat.*), closure, union.

JOINT, *v.* 1. Unite by a joint *or* joints, form *or* provide with a joint *or* joints, couple, hook, link, solder, secure, attach, tack together, connect, conjoin, suture, wedge, fuse, fix, nail, screw, graft, glue, cement, mortise, rabbet, affix, dovetail, rivet, clasp, pin, weld, miter, dowel, joggle, join, fit together, bracket, brace, braze (*Metall.*), fay, pivot, scarf, fit, bolt, hasp.

2. Disjoint, divide at the joints, dismember, separate into pieces, sunder, sever, segment, dissect, carve, dislimb, cleave, hew, hack, chop, section, detach, cut up (*as meat*), cut, dissever, part.

JOINTLY, *adv.* In common, together, by combined action *or* effort, with, in conjunction, conjointly, in union, hand in hand, side by side, arm in arm, in a body, collectively, mutually, in unison, in close harmony, by agreement, along with, coupled with, by mutual consent *or* assent, cheek by jowl, conjunctly, unitedly, in association, in company with.

JOIST, *n.* Timber to which floor boards, ceiling laths, *etc.*, are fastened, beam, rafter, sleeper, stringer, floor timber, tie beam, support, scantling, stud, upright, post, prop, stringpiece (*Archit.*), corbel (*Archit.*), binding joist, bridging joist, ceiling joist, trimming joist, girder, batten, balk, crossbeam, summer, traverse, trave (*Archit.*).

JOKE, *n.* 1. Something said *or* done to excite laughter *or* amusement, jest, quip, frolic, playful *or* mischievous trick *or* remark, play of wit, funny story, prank, crank, sally, witticism, bon mot, irony, wit, humor, gag (*coll.*), jocosity, fun, rig, hoax, sarcasm, burlesque, mimicry, caricature, macaronic, parody, satire, squib, lampoon, caper, antic, pun, drollery, scoffing, comic (*coll.*), funnies (*sl.*), amusing *or* ridiculous circumstance, jeu d'esprit (*Fr.*), pleasantry, practical joke, quiz, nonsense, sportive trick, Joe Miller, chaff, whimsy, banter, facetiousness, farce, badinage, repartee, foolery, Attic salt, Attic wit, buffoonery, jape, carriwitchet, paronomasia.

2. Object of joking *or* jesting, thing *or* person laughed at rather than taken seriously, object of scorn, reproach, *or* derision, fool, butt, byword, jester, Punch, laughingstock, scorn, game, fair game, victim, dupe, clown, bumpkin, buffoon, monkey, jestingstock, gazingstock, village idiot, town fool, incompetent, derision.

3. (*Often used in negative*) A matter of joking about, trifle, nothing, straw, hair, fig, insignificant, something done easily, triviality, paltry affair, no great matter, insignificancy, pin, button, bubble, peanut, bean, hill of beans, a little thing, hardly *or* scarcely anything, inconsequential, nothing to speak of *or* worth speaking of, matter of no importance *or* consequence, matter of indifference, feather, prune, rap, hoot, shucks (*coll.*), mite, cent, farthing, picayune, curse, roll of pins, fleabite, pinprick, farce, fiddlestick, nullity, snap of the fingers, child's play, tinker's dam *or* damn, iota, tinker's curse *or* cuss, two cents, mere nothing, thing of naught, mote, doit.

JOKE, *v.* 1. Speak *or* act in a playful *or* merry way, say something in mere sport rather than in earnest, jest, banter, rally, sport, mock, frolic, crack jokes, josh (*sl.*), pun, laugh, gag (*coll.*), play the fool, chaff, caper, burlesque, gibe, twit, quiz, wisecrack (*sl.*), gambol, retort, flash back, come back at.

2. Make merry with, make jokes upon, chaff, banter, rally, hoax, subject to jokes, scoff at, laugh at, grin at, stultify, mock, twit, taunt, make ridiculous, make a fool of, expose, show up, laugh to scorn, make game of, poke fun at, lampoon, pooh-pooh, deride, snicker, gibe at, gird, scout, flout, fleer, gull, dupe, take in, spoof (*sl.*), play tricks upon, send on a fool's errand, play a practical joke upon, laugh in one's sleeve, make a goat (*sl.*), disparage, tease, jeer at, fool, haze, rag (*sl.*), roast (*sl.*), jolly (*coll.*), guy (*sl.*), bully, bullyrag, badger, abuse, smile at, jest, ridicule.

JOKER, *n.* 1. One who jokes, jester, funnyman, humorist, clown, punster, banterer, reparteeist, punner, caricaturist, wagwit, spark, burlesquer, parodist, comedian, zany, epigrammatist, madcap, extra card in the pack, wag, wit, life of the party, quiz, wisecracker (*sl.*), mimic, monkey, humorous fellow.

2. Hidden clause in a paper *or* document, *etc.*, changing its apparent nature, rider, adjunct, additament, codicil, affix, appendage, addendum, supplement, nigger in the woodpile (*coll.*), concealed motive, obscure factor, snake in the grass, masked battery, rocks, reef, hidden danger, snag, catch, hitch, impediment, obstruction, ambush, snare, pitfall, trap, mine, gin, springe (*fig.*).

3. Device *or* expedient for getting the better of another, ruse, artifice, trick, extortion, fraud, cheat, wile, hoax, feint, blind, craft, foul play, machination, gyp (*sl.*), game, trap, snare, stratagem, sell (*sl.*), swindle, deceit, plot, racket (*sl.*), duplicity, subterfuge, bunco (*coll.*), blackmail, confidence game, squeeze (*coll.*), sharp practice, falsification, flimflam, humbug, misrepresentation, flam (*coll.*).

JOLLIFICATION, *n.* Jolly merrymaking, jolly festivity, conviviality, revelry, joviality, jubilation, revels, carouse, wassail, jolly time, spree, merriment, carnival, celebration, feast, heyday, romp, caper, gambol, gay time, gaiety, levity, junket, mirth, high old time *(sl.)*, frisk, hilarity, jocundity, sport, merry frolic, potation, compotation, carousal, blowout *(coll.)*, recreation, escapade, jollities, jamboree *(sl.)*, skylarking, party, laughter, festival, rejoicing, fete, bacchanals.

JOLLITY, *n.* Jolly state, mood *or* proceedings, jolly festivities, conviviality, revelry, merrymaking, gaiety, geniality, fun, vivacity, merriment, jocundity, levity, jubilance, enjoyment, delectation, gusto, rejoicing, gleefulness, jubilation, exuberance, hedonism, pleasure, frolic, hilarity, sport, wassail, compotation, potation, carousal, recreation.

JOLLY, *adj.* In good spirits, gay, cheerfully festive *or* convivial, happy, convivial, merry, joyful, mirthful, jocund, funny, sportive, gamesome, cheerful, blithe, elated, carefree, festal, rollicking, hilarious, in high spirits, good-natured, sparkling, animated, sunny, genial, jaunty, light-hearted, jubilant, mirth-loving, breezy, glad, joyous, jovial, playful, facetious, waggish, lively, blithesome, mellow, spirited, congenial, fun-loving, jocose, gleeful, vivacious, chipper *(coll.)*, airy, boon, bright, laughing, debonair, buoyant, volatile, cheery, jocular, frolicsome, sprightly.

JOLT, *n.* Jolting shock *or* movement, jar, jounce, shaking, shock, concussion, bump, lurch, sway, bounce, quake, rock, jog, start, jiggle, tremble, joggle, quiver, quaver, blow, encounter, percussion, smash, brunt, impact, clash, crash, collision, staggerer, shiver, jostle, jerk, agitation, twitch, thunderbolt.

JOLT, *v.* Jar, shake as by a sudden rough thrust, shake up, jog, jump, shock, jerk, joggle, jounce, jiggle, bounce, disquiet, perturb, convulse, buffet, disturb, agitate, bump, toss, startle, discompose, stun, jostle, hitch, bob, bobble *(coll.)*, quake.

JOSTLE, *v.* 1. Strike against, push roughly *or* rudely against, jar, clash, elbow roughly, hustle, collide, hit against, jolt, jerk, run against, butt against, bounce, batter, lunge against, justle, hunch, press against, shock, shove, joggle, shake, tussle, perturb, stir, jounce, charge, bear down upon, run full tilt against, run at, have at, attack, assault, assail, rush at, dash at, disturb, agitate, bump, bombard, tilt, battle, cross, conflict, shoulder.

2. Drive by pushing *or* shoving, force, rush, hurry, herd, goad, shove, thrust, push, impel roughly, hurtle, hustle, boot, propel, urge, jolt, jog, kick, throw, cant, bunt, prod, poke.

3. Strive *(as with collisions, pushing, etc.)* for place *or* advantage, scramble, lunge, fight, rampage, rush, contest, push, war, contend, scuffle, strain, tussle, tear, bear down, browbeat, romp, ride roughshod, trample down opposition, make a bold push, slash one's way, proceed unconcerned, lay about one, thrust oneself, be ruthless, struggle, battle, scrap *(sl.)*.

JOT, *n.* The least part of something, iota, a little bit, trace, speck, grain, atom, mite, mote, whit, tittle, corpuscle, trifle, point, microbe, minim, hair, scintilla, scrap, minutia, molecule, speckle, nothing, pin, straw, cent, farthing, two cents, doit, scratch, snippet, micron, snip, pinprick, pinpoint, spot, particle, bit, ace, hairsbreadth, modicum, flyspeck, ion, rap, insignificance, note, freckle.

JOT, *v.* *(Usually fol. by* DOWN*)* Write *or* mark down briefly, note, record, state, list, mark down, set down, note down, make a memorandum of, make a note of, scribble, tally, enter, notice, indicate, observe, register, chronicle, put down, take down.

JOTTING, *n.* Something jotted down, brief note, memoir, indication, item, entry, memorandum, memorabile, excerpt, minute, memo *(coll.)*, record, tally.

JOUNCE, *n.* A jouncing movement, jolt, jar, jiggle, bounce, concussion, shake, shock, lurch, jerk, bump, jostle, jog, quake, rock, vibration, joggle, tremble, impact, encounter, brunt, clash, blow, collision, crash, smash, percussion, thunderbolt, thunderclap, yank *(coll.)*, tilt, fray, jog, sway.

JOUNCE, *v.* Move violently up and down, bounce, jolt, jar, shock, shake, bump, jostle, jiggle, joggle, buffet, jerk, stir, hustle, agitate, vibrate harshly, wiggle, yank *(coll.)*, rock, quake, dance, trot, bob, bobble *(coll.)*, jigget *(coll.)*, batter, shove, heave, waggle.

JOURNAL, *n.* 1. Daily record *(as of occurrences, experiences or observations)*, daily register, diary, record, almanac, chronology, registry, log *(Naut.)*, logbook *(Naut.)*, annals, notebook, memoir, catalogue, ledger, yearbook, account-book, history, chronicle, narrative, story, album, scrapbook, chartulary, calendar, cadastre, calends, bulletin, memorandum book, record book, commentaries, commonplace book, memory book, register of transactions *(of public or legislative body)*, daybook *(Bookkeeping)*, autobiography.

2. Newspaper, magazine, serial, sheet, daily, weekly, monthly, quarterly, annual, chronicle, paper, publication, gazette, periodical, adversaria, tabloid, rag *(contemptuous or humorous)*.

JOURNALESE, *n.* Style of writing *or* expression supposed to characterize newspapers, edited style, jargon, journalistic cant, newspaper idiom, reporter's language, editorial style.

JOURNALISM, *n.* Writing for, editing and conducting newspapers and other journals, newspaper work, reporting, recording, authorship, preparation for press, composition, preparation of copy, pencraft, penship, the press, public press, fourth estate, editing, reporting, hack work.

JOURNALIST, *n.* One engaged in journalism, editor, columnist, author, publisher, newsman, newspaperman, reporter, publicist, gazetteer, writer for the press, gentleman *or* representative of the press, subeditor, news editor, copy editor, reviser, rewriter, rewrite man, correspondent, interviewer, copyman, editorial writer, leader writer, paragrapher, ghostwriter, hack writer, leg man *(sl.)*, gentleman of the fourth estate, diaskeuast.

JOURNALISTIC, *adj.* Of, pertaining to *or* characteristic of journalists *or* journalism, reportorial, newspaper, hack, editorial, press, published, publishing, circulated, of the public press, printed.

JOURNALIZE, *v.* 1. Enter *or* record in a journal, record, register, inscribe, jot down, set down, note, chronicle, keep *or* make entries, tell *or* relate *(as done in a journal)*, keep *(diary, record, etc.)*, enter.

2. Engage in journalism, write for the press, publish, report, editorialize, ghostwrite, correspond *(with a newspaper)*.

JOURNEY, *n.* 1. Course of travel from one place to another *(esp. by land)*, tour, trip, ride, drive, walk, run, junket, movement, way, passage, peregrination, expedition, safari, trek, flight, sail, voyage *(usually by water or air)*, wandering, roving, migration, meander, itinerary, route, transit, traverse, cruise *(by water)*, jornada *(Sp.)*, circuit, odyssey, excursion, pilgrimage, jaunt, sightseeing trip, hop *(coll.)*, ramble, quest.

2. Distance traveled *or* suitable for traveling, trip, leg, lap, trek, beat, round, circuit, ambit, stretch, march, orbit, extent, reach, range, scope, number of miles, jornada *(Sp.)*.

JOURNEY, *v.* Make a journey, travel, take *or* make a tour, voyage *(by water)*, cruise, sail, betake oneself, direct one's course, bend one's steps *or* course, go on a journey, tour, transit, proceed, go, go on a sightseeing trip, sightsee, go for an outing *or* airing, range, meander, jaunt, vagabond, migrate, emigrate, march, take the road, wayfare, fly, course, itinerate, peregrinate, run, drive, tramp, wander, ride, take a trip, roam, rove, ramble, make an excursion, trek, wend, junket, progress, go for a walk *or* ride, navigate, circumnavigate, transmigrate, pilgrimage, hike, hit the trail *(coll.)*.

JOURNEYMAN, *n.* One who has completed his apprenticeship, handicraftsman, artificer, craftsman, tradesman, artisan, craftworker, mechanic, skilled laborer, worker.

JOURNEYWORK, *n.* The work of a journeyman, trade, craft, skill, vocation, handicraft.

JOUST, *n.* Combat of two armored knights on horseback using lances, conflict, just, tilt, jostle, brush, clash, fight, skirmish, tournament, match, encounter, game of skill at arms, passage at *or* of arms, tourney.

JOUST, *v.* Contend in a joust *or* tournament, contest, just, fight, strive, tourney, jostle, encounter, enter the lists, collide, tilt, break a lance with, run a tilt *or* a tilt at, couch one's lance, skirmish, combat, clash.

JOVIAL, *adj.* Endowed with *or* characterized by a hearty, joyous manner, having a spirit of good-fellowship, merry, joyous, joyful, gay, sunny, buoyant, cheerful, mirthful, in good *or* high spirits, zestful, jocund, exultant, delighted, vivacious, gleeful, sparkling, light, riant, jubilant, hilarious, jolly, elated, exuberant, hearty, laughing, congenial, cordial, convivial, festive, sportive, gamesome, festal, rollicking, genial, waggish, playful, fun-loving, jocular, jocose, frolicsome, good-natured, cheery.

JOVIALITY, *n.* State *or* quality of being jovial, merriment, jollity, glee, jolly mood, conviviality, merrymaking, geniality, gaiety, revelry, gusto, gleefulness, jubilation, pleasure, levity, carousal, hilarity, wassail, exuberance, rejoicing, vivacity, sport, cheerfulness, festivity, liveliness, mirth, joy, gladness, animation, jocundity, jocularity, exuberance, relish, high spirits, good humor, frolic, fun, sportiveness, celebration, buoyancy.

JOWL, *n.* Jaw *(esp. the under jaw)*, cheek, chops, wattle, mandible, chaps, mouth parts, muzzle *(of an animal)*, mug *(sl.)*, flesh of the lower face.

JOY, *n.* 1. An emotion of keen *or* lively pleasure, exultant satisfaction, delight, great gladness, exultation, ecstasy, triumph, mirth, gaiety, cheerfulness, happiness, relish, content, elation, gratification, cheer, thrill, rapture, glee, enjoyment, exhilaration, excitement, oblectation, hedonism, jubilance, contentment, kick *(sl.)*, peace, well-being, sweetness, comfort, pleasure, delectation, felicity,

serenity, light-heartedness, enchantment, entrancement, rejoicing.

2. Source *or* cause of gladness *or* delight, pleasure, charm, jewel, gem, thing of beauty, treat, refreshment, feast *or* banquet of the soul, manna in the wilderness, kick *(sl.)*, sight for sore eyes, pleasurableness, delectability, wonder, treasure, precious possession, prize, find, flower, thing *or* person of great worth *or* rare excellence, one in a thousand *or* ten thousand.

3. State of happiness *or* felicity, bliss, beatitude, ecstasy, blessedness, ravishment, rapture, transport, heaven, Eden, Arcadia, Utopia, paradise, felicity, beatification, happiness, third *or* seventh heaven, unalloyed happiness, heavenly joy, ecstasy, delight, peace, serenity, fullness of heart, transport, exaltation.

4. Manifestation of glad feeling, outward rejoicing, jubilation, festive gaiety, exultation, mirth, enthusiasm, cheer, glee, merriment, festivity, hilarity, cheerfulness, high spirits, light heart, jocundity, jocularity, jocoseness, laughter, rejoicing, merrymaking, levity, jollity, high glee, zest, sunshine, blitheness, celebration, glorification, triumph, jubilee.

JOY, *v.* Feel joy, be glad, rejoice, be joyful, be in heaven, delectate, fall *or* go into raptures, bask in the sunshine, relish, jubilate, chuckle, gloat, make merry, triumph, celebrate, lilt, carol, chirp, clap hands, dance *or* skip for joy, be delighted, exult, tread on enchanted ground, glory, be in clover, bless *or* thank one's stars, revel, delight, take pleasure.

JOYFUL, *adj.* 1. Full of joy *(as a person, the heart, etc.)*, glad, delighted, merry, happy, exultant, blissful, cheerful, blessed, elated, rejoicing, rapturous, overjoyed, entranced, enchanted, content, light-hearted, ecstatic, jubilant, beatified, in paradise, in third *or* seventh heaven, in a transport of delight, carefree, sunny, pleased, tickled, gratified, beside oneself with joy, carried away, buoyant, joyous, in heaven, gladsome.

2. Showing *or* expressing joy *(as looks, actions, speech, etc.)*, genial, merry, happy, blithe, airy, jocund, jolly, gay, elated, jubilant, buoyant, shouting with joy, sunny, cheerful, jovial, exultant, carefree, riant, sparkling, light-hearted, debonair, jaunty, mirthful, hilarious, bright, flushed, in good *or* high spirits, in high feather, jubilant, jocose, blithesome.

3. Causing *or* bringing joy *(as an event, a sight, news, etc.)*, delightful, heart-warming, exulting, happy, felicitous, festive, encouraging, gratifying, desirable, looked-for, hoped-for, promising, cheery, reassuring, enravishing, entrancing, uplifting, propitious, auspicious, bright, of good omen, rosy, sanguine, hopeful, cheerful, blessed, heartening, inspiriting, exhilarating, pleasing, pleasurable, gladsome, festal.

JOYLESS, *adj.* 1. Destitute of joy *or* gladness, gloomy, cheerless, dismal, melancholy, sad, mournful, dejected, spiritless, disconsolate, unhappy, pitiful, dark, funereal, forlorn, depressed, glum, woebegone, downcast, miserable, desolate, heartbroken, rueful, dolorous, lugubrious, dreary, doleful, downhearted, heavy-hearted, dispirited, sullen, sorrow-worn, sorrow-laden, morose, comfortless, down in the mouth *(coll.)*, lachrymose, sick at heart, sorrow-burdened, solemn, grim, saturnine, plaintive, tearful, sorrowful, grieving, woeful, hopeless, despondent, lamenting.

2. Causing no joy *or* pleasure, depressing, dejecting, unwelcome, gloomy, lonely, desolate,

bleak, uninviting, dingy, sunless, grim, austere, somber, dismal, barren, lightless, bitter, comfortless, heartbreaking, dispiriting, saddening, distressing, afflictive, unpleasant, deplorable, pitiable, lamentable, pathetic, cheerless, grievous, woeful.

JUBILANCE, *n.* **JUBILATION,** Joy, delight, pleasure, cheerfulness, ecstasy, elation, gladness, rejoicing, felicity, bliss, enjoyment, satisfaction, well-being, blitheness, high spirits, jubilation, happiness, merrymaking, mirth, rapture, ravishment, gusto, peacefulness, delectation, festivity, jollity, gaiety, good, serenity, fullness of heart, Elysium, sunshine, cheeriness, geniality, oblectation, intoxication, clover, transport, exultation, paradise, blitheness, light-heartedness, heaven, complacence, beatitude, third *or* seventh heaven, mirthfulness, cheer, enchantment, glee, blessedness, exaltation, exuberance, exhilaration.

JUBILANT, *adj.* Rapturous, buoyant, blithe, sunny, blissful, cheerful, merry, gay, contented, lighthearted, joyous, ecstatic, delirious, enrapt, charmed, radiant, mirthful, zestful, captivated, in good *or* high spirits, in high feather, happy as a king, happy as the day is long, happy as a lark, jocund, smiling, exultant, glad, pleased, delighted, gratified, rejoicing, gladdened, vivacious, jovial, gleeful, satisfied, gladsome, laughing, congenial, transported, tickled *(coll.),* rhapsodic, intoxicated, hearty, enraptured, entranced, exuberant, debonair, carefree, elated, joyful, jolly, overjoyed, riant, hilarious, happy, flushed with excitement *or* pleasure, merry as a cricket, blithesome, light, cheery, exhilarated.

JUBILATE, *v.* Be jubilant, happy, gay, delighted, *etc.,* rejoice, exult, crow, delight, dance *or* sing, *etc.,* with joy, glory, make merry, revel, hug oneself, clap hands, rollick.

JUBILEE, *n.* Festival, celebration, ovation, frolic, carousal, libation, junket, holiday, festivity, carnival, jollification, wassail, compotation, Saturnalia, feast, fete, gala, bacchanal, potation, conviviality, spree, revelry.

JUDAIC, *adj.* Jewish, Hebrew, Hebraic, Israelite, Israelitish, Hebraistic, Hebraistical, Yiddish *(of Yiddish language, etc.),* rabbinistic *(adhering to Talmud).*

JUDAIST, *n.* Hebrew, Israelite, Judaist, rabbinist, Jew, Karaite *(one who rejects Talmud),* Talmudist *(one who accepts Talmud),* Sudducee *(chiefly Hist.).*

JUDAS, *n.* Betrayer, deceiver, traitor, informer, false friend, turncoat, cat's-paw, trepan, squealer *(coll.),* archtraitor, beguiler, hypocrite, serpent, double-dealer, quisling, telltale, renegade.

JUDGE, *v.* 1. Pass sentence, try *(a case),* conduct judicator, justice of the peace, probate judge, surrogate, police judge, presiding judge, puisne *(Junior),* judge advocate, judiciary *(plur.),* judicature *(plur.).*

2. Arbiter, critic, judicator, censor, intermediary, moderator, umpire, referee, adjudicator, juror, censurer, abitrator, intermediate, referendary.

3. Critic, connoisseur, criticaster *(contempt.),* commentator, reviewer, criticule *(petty),* critickin *(petty).*

JUDGE, *v.* 1. Pass sentence, try *(a case),* conduct tice, hear *(a case),* pronounce judgment, announce *(a trial),* adjudicate, adjudge, test, administer justice, deliver *or* render a verdict, determine, settle, sit in judgment, decide, rule.

2. Estimate, decide, interpret, find, resolve, consider, surmise, conjecture, pronounce, suppose, measure, regard, glean, guess, deduce, reckon *(coll.),* gather, infer, believe, suspect, ascertain, distinguish, weigh, determine, assume, hold, divine, deem, decree, gauge, perceive, conclude, derive, fancy, imagine.

3. Comment upon, appraise, examine, test, diagnose, criticize, survey, weigh, rate, gauge, appreciate, value, size up, assess, investigate, censure, censor, review.

JUDGMENT, *n.* 1. Verdict, view, upshot, decree, award, opinion, adjudication, ruling, resolution, order, result, sentence, declaration, finding, doom, determination.

2. Estimate, estimation, interpretation, opinion, ratiocination, thought, resolution, illation, surmise, supposition, inference, guess, decision, deduction, assumption, understanding, persuasion, conjecture, consideration, conviction, conclusion, perception, view, choice, belief, fancy.

3. Wisdom, sagacity, shrewdness, perspicacity, mental faculty, brain, acumen, diagnosis, apperception, perception, sharpness of mind, sense, intuition, taste, ability, perceptiveness, penetration, shrewdness, reasoning, reasoning power, acuteness, percipience, skill, level-headedness, acumen, power, common sense, grasp, keenness, mind, discernment, sapience, judiciousness, understanding, discrimination, insight.

4. Criticism, notice, critique, censure, comment, diagnosis, appraisal, report, review, opinion, commentary, appreciation.

JUDICATORY, *adj.* Judicial, judiciary, jurisdictional, offical, juridical, legal, juristic, jurisdictive.

JUDICATORY, *n.* Judgment seat, court of justice, tribunal, bench, seat of justice, court, bar, Areopagus.

JUDICATURE, *n.* Primacy, administration, supervision, jurisdiction, supremacy, control, authority, suzerainty, magistracy, rule, mayoralty, dominion, sovereignty, sway, command.

JUDICIAL, *adj.* 1. Judiciary, jurisdictional, official, juridical, legal, juristic, judicatory, jurisdictive.

2. Becoming *or* fitting a judge, judgelike, magisterial, magistral.

3. Just, impartial, equitable, fair, well-judged, sage, unprejudiced, dispassionate, disinterested, unwarped, unbigoted, unswayed, uninfluenced, unbiased, rational, discerning, sagacious, discriminating, critical, acute, sapient, perspicacious, understanding, perceptive, percipient, level-headed.

JUDICIOUS, *adj.* Discreet, wise, expedient, sensible, well-advised, guarded, astute, diplomatic, keen-sighted, circumspect, discerning, discriminating, sagacious, apperceptive, cautious, politic, knowing, perspicacious, thoughtful, sober, reflecting, considered, calculating, percipient, sound, level-headed, tactful, shrewd, acute, sober-minded, perceptive, prudent, clear-sighted, vigilant, wary.

JUDO, *n.* "The gentle art," jujitsu, jujutsu.

JUG, *n.* Vessel for holding liquids, pitcher, stein, carafe, flask, bottle, ewer, flagon, toby, pot, decanter, crock, urn, jar, flasket, pipkin, gallipot, canister, cruse, tankard, demijohn.

JUGGLE, *v.* 1. Perform conjuring tricks, conjure, practice jugglery, perform feats of skill *(esp. keeping objects in motion in the air),* deceive the eye, hocus-pocus, keep *(objects)* in play, practice legerdemain.

2. Manipulate by artifice *or* trickery, practice artifice *or* imposture, cheat, hocus-pocus, trick, outwit, dupe, delude, deceive, cozen, beggar, victimize, hoax, swindle, abuse, defraud, gammon *(coll.)*, humbug, trap, hoodwink, overreach, perplex, gull, bamboozle, bite, take *(coll.)*, bilk, palm upon, cog, betray, flam *(coll.)*, wheedle, gouge *(coll.)*, bunco *(coll.)*, pluck *(sl.)*, fraud, do *(sl.)*, play upon, mulct, rook, gyp *(sl.)*, cajole, fleece, foist upon, diddle *(coll.)*, lure, play false.

JUGGLER, *n.* 1. One who performs juggling tricks, trickster, entertainer, acrobat, sleight-of-hand man, magician, conjurer, tumbler, jongleur *(Hist.)*, legerdemainist, contortionist, prestidigitator.

2. One who deceives by trickery, trickster, swindler, cozener, cunning person, impostor, gypper *(sl.)*, cardsharp, sharper, sharp, bilker, fleecer, gammoner *(coll.)*, deceiver, cheat, charlatan, quacksalver, quack, humbug, bamboozler, hoaxer, jockey, crimp, bunco steerer *(coll.)*, fourflusher *(sl.)*, trepan, beguiler, carpetbagger *(Hist.)*, fake *(coll.)*, faker *(coll.)*, fox, con man *(sl.)*, confidence man, diddler *(coll.)*, flimflammer *(coll.)*, coin ringer *(sl.)*, magsman *(sl.)*, spieler *(coll.)*, decoy duck, come-on man *(sl.)*, capper *(sl.)*, jobber, fraud *(coll.)*, deluder, dissembler, traitor, Judas, Janus, double-dealer, empiric, mountebank, bluff.

JUGGLERY, *n.* 1. Art *or* practice of a juggler, juggling, hocus-pocus, magic, conjuring, conjury, sleight of hand, legerdemain, prestidigitation, performance of juggling feats.

2. Trickery, imposture, cunning, subtlety, fraudulence, knavery, guile, craftiness, cheating, deceit, wirepulling, politics, sharp practice, chicanery, dodgery, rascality, jobbery, intrigue, maneuvering, pettifoggery, duplicity, graft *(coll.)*, treachery, hocus-pocus, slyness, swindling, hoax, flam *(coll.)*, humbug, flimflam, gyp *(sl.)*.

JUICE, *n.* Drink, fluid, extract, serum, liquor, sap, secretion, liquid, lymph, water, grume, must, soup, watery element, broth, nectar, potable, lush, fluid part, serous fluid, latex *(Bot.)*, ichor *(Path.)*, beverage, blood.

JUICY, *adj.* 1. Succulent, full of juice, watery, fluid, wet, serous, damp, spongy, bibulous, lush, flowing, fluent, rheumy, madid, lymphatic, ichorous, deliquescent, rainy, luscious, sappy, moist, liquid, melted, molten, bloody.

2. Interesting, tantalizing, colorful, exciting, vivacious, provocative, irresistible, spicy, captivating, amusing, alluring, entrancing, attractive, enchanting, thrilling, electric, galvanic, piquant, sensational, killing *(coll.)*, pithy, imaginative, suggestive, zestful, picturesque, racy, vibrant, bright, tangy, rich, compelling, savory, spirited.

JUMBLE, *n.* Disorder, hodgepodge, Noah's ark, confused mixture, olla-podrida, confusion, gallimaufry, hotchpotch, chaos, farrago, mess, mixture, potpourri, puzzle, miscellany, medley, disarray, mélange, huddle, stew, salmagundi, olio, commixture, concoction, intermixture, conglomeration, aggregate, composite, accumulation, hash, chowchow, omnium-gatherum, patchwork, mix, muddle, tumble, salad, what the cat brought in *(coll.)*.

JUMBLE, *v.* Mix confusedly, mix up, complicate, tangle, muddle, mess, discompose, press together in confusion, huddle, throw together, shuffle,

botch, muss, clutter, mingle, entangle, disarrange, displace, confuse, litter, strew about, upset, derange, dishevel, scatter, lumber, turn topsy-turvy, disorganize, cram, toss at random, bunch, heap.

JUMP, *n.* 1. Act of jumping, sudden upward *or* other movement, leap, hop, skip, pounce, dancing, caper, vault, bound, buckjump, fall, spring, leapfrogging, hurtling *(of oneself)*, precipitation, casting *(of oneself)* down, bound, saltation, upleap, upspring, gambol, curvet, prance, frolic.

2. Space, obstacle *or* apparatus cleared in a leap, hurdle, buck, obstruction, chasm, rail, fence, opening, leap, wall, handicap, horse *(Gymnastics)*.

3. Sudden rise *(in amount, price, etc.)*, increase, upsurge, ascent, leap, uprise, mounting, raising, inflation, up, hike *(sl.)*, dilation, intensification, accumulation, advance, enlargement, boost, augmentation, extension, appreciation *(in value)*, aggrandizement, redoubling, magnification, increment, upleap, doubling (trebling, *etc.*).

4. Abrupt transition from one point *or* thing to another *(with omission of what intervenes)*, gap, hiatus, synapse *(Physiol.)*, chasm, scissure, fissure, gulf, breach, disruption, rupture, channel, interruption, break, lacuna, split, cleft, blank.

5. Sudden start *(as from nervous excitement)*, twitch, jolt, shock, jerk, jiggle, quiver, shake, dance, tic *(Pathol.)*, quaver, pull, wrench, tweak.

JUMP, *v.* 1. Leap, spring, bound, hop, saltate, bounce, start, start up, buck, buckjump, pounce, vault, skip, bob, prance, gambol, leapfrog, curvet, frisk, upspring.

2. Leave a gap, skip, miss, pretermit, fail, circumvent, pass, evade, shun, neglect, omit, avoid, keep clear of, turn away from, fight shy of.

3. Cause to break cover *(as game, etc.)*, surprise, startle, frighten, spring upon, pounce upon, rouse, start, flush.

JUMPY, *adj.* Nervous, fidgety, excited, fussing, fretting, unsteady, unquiet, apprehensive, diffident, restless, agitated, chafing, in a stew, timid, shaky, frightened, fluttering, startled, panicky, disquieted, afraid, skittish, shy, restive, scared, jittery *(sl.)*, alarmed, panic-stricken, frenzied.

JUNCTION, *n.* 1. Juncture, coincidence, union, joining place, joining, accouplement, contingence, tie-up *(coll.)*, coadunation, contiguity, commissure, confluence, connection, assemblage, congregation, coalescence, congress, convergence, concentralization, concourse, concurrence, concurrency, concentration, gathering, contiguousness, conjugation, hookup, correlation, conflux, union, corradiation, joinder, focalization.

2. Railroad station *(where lines meet, cross, etc.)*, center, main station, terminal.

JUNCTURE, *n.* 1. Concurrence *(of circumstances, events, etc.)*, occasion, conjuncture, contingency, advent, incident, moment, eventuality, event.

2. Crisis, emergency, quandary, extremity, plight, dilemma, strait, crux, zero hour, critical moment, critical point, exigency, contingency, predicament, squeeze *(coll.)*, scrape *(coll.)*, push *(coll.)*, hole *(coll.)*, pinch *(coll.)*.

3. Seam, articulation, junction, connection, hinge, splice, link, weld, suture, joiner, joining, joint, overlapping, connexus, knot, nexus, elbow, knee, knuckle, mortise and tenon, pivot, hock, butt, communication, commissure, osculation, bond, intersection, closure, union, hitch, coupling, ligature, decussation, dovetail, point of contact, raphe *(Anat.)*, node *(Bot.)*.

4. Place where things join *or* meet, joining

place, joining, coincidence, union, coadunation, tie-up (coll.), contingence, accouplement, contiguity, commissure, confluence, connection, convergence, congress, coalescence, congregation, assemblage, concentralization, junction, concourse, concurrence, concurrency, concentration, gathering, contiguousness, conjugation, hookup, correlation, conflux, union, corradiation, joinder, focalization.

JUNGLE, n. Wild, unpenetrable land, virgin forest, woodland, wilderness, forest, wild, swampy forest, bush, undergrowth, dense vegetation.

JUNIOR, adj. 1. Younger, minor, later, more recent.

2. Lower, inferior, subordinate, minor, secondary, puisne (Leg.), subaltern, lesser, smaller.

JUNK, n. Old or discarded material (as metal, paper, rags, etc.), trash, rubbish, debris, lumber, oddments, wastements, litter, leavings, refuse, truck (coll.), scrap iron (paper, tin, etc.), shoddy, castoffs, ruins, rummage, waste.

JUNKET, n. 1. Sweetened curded milk dessert, rennet custard, curds and cream, pudding, jelly.

2. Social gathering (esp. outdoors), feast, picnic, spread, pleasure excursion, merriment, jollity, festival, fete, meal, barbecue, airing, outing, jaunt, larking, wayzgoose, fish fry, clambake, merrymaking, festivity, feed (coll.), carousal, wassail, frolic, spree, jollification, caper, gambol, party, sport, hayride.

JUNKET, v. 1. Feast, picnic, make merry, go on a pleasure excursion (esp. at public cost), spree, carouse, sport, revel, have a fling, be on pleasure bent, disport, make or keep holiday, divert oneself, play, game, eat, drink and be merry.

2. Entertain, treat, make welcome, regale, feast, fete, celebrate, give a party, kill the fatted calf, play host to.

JUNTA, n. Meeting, council, committee, convention, board, gathering, cabinet, congress, judicature, commission, conclave, convocation, quorum, syndicate, parley, divan, Sanhedrin (Jewish Antiq.), chamber, court, tribunal, junto, palaver, muster, powwow (coll.), session, consultation, privy council, caucus, plenum, durbar (India), congregation, assembly, deliberative or administrative council (esp. in Spain), synod, concourse, amphictyonic council (Gk. Antiq.).

JUNTO, n. Clique, coterie, faction, league, camarilla, band, plot, ring, confederacy, combination, cabal, party, set, secret council, gang, club, knot, side, class, circle, cell, alliance, conclave, fraternity, coalition, body of partisans, machine, sodality, brotherhood, interest, clan, lodge, outfit (coll.), sect, division, union, Bund (Ger.), association, members of a conspiracy.

JURISDICTION, n. 1. Right, power or authority to administer justice by hearing and determining controversies, judicature, magistracy, justice, legal right, power or authority, judgeship, judicatory, equity (Law), cognizance (Law), original or appellate jurisdiction, exclusive or concurrent jurisdiction, civil or criminal jurisdiction, common law or equitable jurisdiction, in rem or in personam jurisdiction.

2. Power, authority, control, supervision, superintendence, rule, oversight, magistracy, judgment, sway, liberty, charge, controlment, care, sovereignty, supremacy, government, reign, suzerainty, dominion, hegemony, lordship, directorship, right of control, headship, leadership, surveillance,

presidency, patronage, protection, auspices, ministry, administration, direction, command.

3. Extent or range of judicial authority, compass, territory over which authority is exercised, dominion, province, circuit, round, orbit, judicature, range, ambit, sphere, reach, district, court, scope, precinct, circle, bounds, area, zone, field, latitude, vicinage, purlieu, capacity, purview, domain, bailiwick, quarter, beat.

JURISPRUDENCE, n. 1. Philosophy or science of law, moral principles, legal philosophy, law, doctrines of lawmaking, legislation, nomology, nomography, codification (Law).

2. Body or system of laws, the law, legal code, canon or ecclesiastical law, corpus juris, pandects, charter, digest (Law), equity (Law), canon, common law, statute, civil law, international law, unwritten law, written or statute law, mercantile law, criminal law, constitution.

JURIST, n. One who professes the science of law, one versed in the law, one who writes on the subject of law, lawyer, civilian, counselor, judge, justice, attorney, attorney at law, jurisprudent, Romanist, jurisprudentialist, counsel, legal adviser, advocate, legislator, barrister (coll.), publicist, legist, Justinianist, jurisconsult (Civil Law), judiciary (collectively), legislature (collectively).

JUROR, n. 1. One of a body of persons sworn to deliver a verdict in a case submitted to them, jurat, juryman, one of a jury or the panel from which it is selected, jurywoman, foreman (of a jury), grand juror, petty juror, talesman, recognitor (Hist.).

2. One who has taken an oath or sworn allegiance, covenanter, swearer, party to an agreement, pledger, covenantor (Law).

JURY, n. Body of persons sworn to render a verdict or true answer on questions officially submitted to them, body of persons chosen to adjudge prizes, etc., twelve men in a box, inquest, talesmen, grand jury, petty jury, coroner's jury, body of jurors, panel, committee, country (Law).

JUST, adj. 1. (Of a person, his actions, dealings, etc.) Actuated by truth, justice and lack of bias, fair, moral, honest, upright, conscientious, uncorrupt, even-handed, impartial, equitable, good, uninfluenced, truthful, open to reason, blameless, sincere, distinterested, even, unbiased, ethical, principled, impersonal, unwarped, scrupulous, veracious, unswayed, unbigoted, aboveboard, upstanding, straightforward, true-dealing, candid, fairminded, straight, high-minded, unprejudiced, righteous, honorable, dispassionate.

2. (Of an award, claim, etc.) In accordance with true principles, equitable, rightful, lawful, legitimate, valid, legal, fair, well-advised, sane, sound, sensible, logical, solid, strong, firm, meet, balanced, wise, within the law, licit, ethical, regular, reasonable, right, constitutional, of real worth or value, defensible, warrantable, as it should or ought to be, unmistakable, unquestionable, conscionable, substantial, well-founded, reputable, befitting, justified, justifiable, well-grounded, based on right, even-handed, judicious.

3. (Of a statement, etc.) Agreeable to truth or fact, true, correct, factual, accurate, well-founded, acceptable, rational, truthful, plausible, defensible, careful, scrupulous, inferential, deducible, justifiable, justified, credible, logical, proper, well-grounded, precise, constant, unerring, faithful, undeniable, meticulous, veracious, reliable, tangible, tenable, unquestionable, apparent, bona fide, un-

perjured, literal, believable, undistorted, religious, fastidious, unexaggerated, unimpeachable, conscientious, unflattering, admissible, straight.

4. Given *or* awarded rightly *or* deservedly (*as a sentence, punishment, reward, etc.*), deserved, condign, suitable, expected, reasonable, moral, worthy, justified, fitting, meet, proper, in accordance with duty, owing, owed, deserving, ascribable, attributable, as it should *or* ought to be, merited, due, adequate, justifiable, logical, befitting, acceptable.

5. (*Of proportions, etc.*) In accordance with standards *or* requirements, proper, right, pleasing, seemly, sound, suitable, fit, classic, harmonious, agreeing closely *or* exactly (*with a pattern, copy, model, etc.*), tasteful, sortable, idoneous, seasonable, decorous, timely, apropos, expedient, conformable to, adapted, becoming, appropriate, happy.

JUST, *adv.* 1. Within a brief preceding time, but a moment before, a moment ago, not long ago, a short time ago, recently, only now, lately.

2. Exactly, precisely, accurately, in all respects, quite, square, fully, completely, perfectly, in every respect, verbatim, to the letter, entirely, neither more nor less, straight, absolutely, to a hair (tittle, turn, T, *or* nicely), ad unguem (*Lat.*).

3. By a narrow margin, barely, by a hair's-breadth, by a little, closely, hardly, only just, scarcely, within an inch, within an ace, no more than, barely, scantly, faintly, somewhat, by no means, in no manner.

4. Only, merely, no more than, at most, simply, but, nothing but.

JUSTICE, *n.* 1. Quality of being just, equitableness, right, righteousness, form of moral rightness, moral principle determining just conduct, justness, truth, integrity, honor, honorableness, merit, honesty, rectitude, uprightness, virtue, goodness, equity, fitness.

2. Rightfulness, lawfulness, legality, justification, justness (*of ground or reason*), fairness, legitimacy, constitutionality, reasonableness, reason.

3. Conformity to moral principle of just conduct, just conduct (dealing *or* treatment), fair play, integrity, reasonableness, honor, candor, virtue, honesty, uprightness, equitable action *or* treatment, plain dealing, probity, impartiality, rectitude, conscientiousness, fair-mindedness, honorableness, fairness, freedom from bias, right *or* just view, equity, square dealing (*coll.*).

4. Requital of desert (*as by punishment or reward*), compensation, due, return, retribution, merits, just deserts, punition, due reward *or* punishment, all that is coming to one (*sl.*), recompense, solatium, guerdon, meed, atonement, satisfaction, amends, redress, quittance, retaliation, payment, discipline, remuneration, nemesis, penalty, ferule, castigation, chastisement, chastening, square deal (*coll.*), correction, comeuppance (*coll.*), reparation, revenge.

5. Judgment of persons *or* causes by judicial process, maintenance *or* administration of law (*as by judicial proceedings*), judicature, the law, trial, jurisdiction, jurisprudence, magistracy, judicatory, judgeship, equity (*Law*), cognizance (*Law*).

6. Judicial officer, magistrate, judge, justiciary (*Hist.*), justiciar (*Hist.*), judicator, adjudicator, probate, surrogate, judge advocate, justice of the peace, police judge, puisne (*Law*), presiding judge.

JUSTIFIABLE, *adj.* Capable of being justified, defensible, that can be shown to be just *or* right,

logical, just, well-founded, well-grounded, warrantable, valid, allowable, legitimate, excusable, venial, pardonable, right, rational, plausible, sound, sensible, sane, inferable, inoffensive, unobjectionable, inculpable, unblamable, expiable, legal, inferential, remissible, condign (*chiefly of punishment, etc.*), vindicable, fit, proper, defendable, suitable, reasonable, believable, tenable, unimpeachable, admissible, acceptable, truthful, deducible, credible, justified, proper, undeniable, reliable, unquestionable, fitting, meet, owing, deserving, merited, befitting, due.

JUSTIFICATION, *n.* 1. Something that justifies, defensive plea, excuse, warrant, justice, defense, argument, exonerating fact *or* circumstance, justifying fact *or* circumstance, extenuation, mitigation, palliation, forgiveness, impunity, apologia, salvo, alibi (*coll.*), apology, explanation, rationalization, pretext, apologetic, immunity, amnesty, indemnity, compurgation, pardon, vindication, reason.

2. Act of justifying, acquittal, absolution, exculpation, exoneration, release from guilt, standing up for, disculpation, quittance, pleading, clearance, defense, vindication, explanation, approval, righting, warranty, forgiveness, rationalization, remission of sin *or* blame, excusing, compurgation.

3. State of being justified, absolution, freedom from guilt *or* blame, redemption, regeneration, adoption, new birth, rebirth, birth from above, acquittal.

JUSTIFICATORY, *adj.* Serving to justify, affording justification, justificative, apologetic, defending, defensive, upholding, sustaining, supporting, palliative, extenuating, extenuative, exculpatory, excusing, justifying, vindicating, vindicatory, vindicative.

JUSTIFIER, *n.* Defender, vindicator, justificator, advocate, apologete, defendant, apologizer, apologist, supporter, upholder, proponent.

JUSTIFY, *v.* 1. Prove *or* show to be just, right *or* warranted (*as an act, claim, statement, etc.*), vindicate, defend, support, approve, warrant, explain, make legitimate, legalize, account for, legitimate, maintain *or* defend as conformable to law (right, justice *or* duty), sustain, make defense for, plead for, be apologist for, bolster up, stand up for, authorize, stand by, apologize for, endorse, bear out, corroborate, establish as truth, prove fit, strengthen, deraign (*Law*), prove the truth of, give sufficient grounds *or* good reason for, confirm, make explanation of, advocate, uphold.

2. Pronounce free from guilt *or* blame, declare guiltless, acquit, absolve, excuse, allow, forgive, discharge, set free, set right, extenuate, gloss over, legitimate, clear, exonerate, make allowance for, purify, liberate, release, exempt, relieve of imputation, palliate, exculpate, countenance, let off (*coll.*).

JUSTLE, *v.* 1. Strike against, push roughly, jar, clash, elbow roughly, hustle, collide, hit against, jolt, jerk, run against, butt against, bounce, batter, lunge against, jostle, hunch, press against, shock, shove, joggle, shake, tussle, stir, jounce, charge, bear down upon, run full tilt against, run at, have at, attack, assault, assail, rush at, dash at, disturb, agitate, bump, bombard, tilt, battle, cross, conflict, shoulder, perturb.

2. Drive by pushing *or* shoving, force, rush, hurry, herd, goad, shove, thrust, push, impel

roughly, hurtle, hustle, boot, propel, urge, jolt, jog, kick, throw, cant, butt, prod, poke.

3. Strive *(as with collisions, pushing, etc.)* for place *or* advantage, scramble, lunge, fight, rampage, rush, contest, push, war, contend, scuffle, strain, tussle, tear, bear down, browbeat, romp, ride roughshod over, trample down, make a bold push, slash one's way, proceed unconcerned, lay about one, thrust oneself, be ruthless, struggle, battle, scrap *(sl.)*.

JUT, *v.* Jut out, project, stick out, protrude, beetle, thrust forward, impend, protuberate, overhang, stand out, poke out, shoot out, shoot forward.

JUVENILE, *adj.* Young, youthful, immature, childly, adolescent, kiddish *(coll.),* beardless, babyish, youthlike, girlish, boyish, budding, callow, unfledged, unfeathered, childlike, puerile, infantile, tender, infantine.

JUVENILE, *n.* Youngster, youth, boy, minor, stripling, girl, youngling, child, urchin *(contempt.),* kid *(sl.),* whippersnapper, shaver *(coll.),* mite, pickaninny, cherub, innocent, chickabiddy, cub, pubescent, chit, young *or* small fry *(coll.),* tad, chick, tot.

(For contemptuous terms see BRAT, *n.)*

JUXTAPOSE, *v.* Place side by side, juxtaposit, put alongside, place in juxtaposition, place near, place parallel.

K

KALEIDOSCOPIC, *adj.* Kaleidoscopical, variegated, changeable, protean, daedal *(Poet.),* many-sided, ever-changing, variable, alterable, proteiform, checkered, varying, mutable.

KEEL, *n. (Of a ship)* Board *(for balancing ship),* keelson *(attachment),* centerboard.

KEEL, *v.* Keel over *(coll.),* turn over, capsize, overset, turn turtle, overturn, upset, tip over, be reversed.

KEEN, *adj.* 1. Sharp, pointed, edged, sharp-edged, acute, needle-sharp, razor-edged, cutting, razor-like, thin, sharp as a needle, sharp as a razor, sharp as a bayonet, sharp as a butcher knife.

2. Eager, ardent, diligent, enterprising, animated, assiduous, high-spirited, intense, violent, impetuous, aspiring, fierce, active, fervid, fervent, heated, impassioned, excited, enthusiastic, sedulous, impatient, earnest, spirited, vehement, feverish, perfervid, zealous, sharp, excitable, ambitious, avid, high-mettled, persevering, unfaltering.

3. Bitter, cutting, caustic, biting, trenchant, mordant, harsh, severe, acrid, stringent, poignant, sharp, cruel, unkind, hurtful, unbenevolent, unamiable, uncharitable, uncordial, invidious, envenomed, rancorous, spiteful, ill-natured, maleficent, malicious, galling, lashing, insulting, derisory, crusty, excoriating, derisive, mordacious, crabbed, malignant, venomous, malevolent, satirical, mocking, scathing, unmannerly, ungracious, bitter, ungentle, uncivil, ill-bred, inaffable, impolite, churlish, bearish, discourteous, virulent, stern, austere, short, tart, drastic, curt, brash, gruff, rude, blunt, abrupt, brutal, acrimonious, mean, brusque, stinging.

4. Shrewd, discerning, sagacious, astute, cunning, sly, crafty, foxy, wily, artful, Machiavellian, diplomatic, politic, hawk-eyed, knowing, calculating, designing, intelligent, acute, sharp, bright, smart, quick-witted, clear-headed, long-headed,

discriminating, subtle, wise, clever, ingenious, wide-awake, sharp-sighted, quick-sighted, clear-sighted, far-sighted, lynx-eyed, hard-headed, open-eyed, aware, penetrating, argute, gimlet-eyed, ferret-eyed, sapient, imaginative, quick of apprehension, judicious, comprehending, prudent, provident, Argus-eyed, forehanded, prepared, discretional.

KEEN-EYED, *adj.* Open-eyed, far-seeing, sagacious, discriminating, critical, clear-eyed, discretional, prudent, sharp-sighted, far-sighted, gimlet-eyed, lynx-eyed, hawk-eyed, Argus-eyed, discerning, level-headed, cool-headed, clear-witted, ferret-eyed, quick of apprehension, sharp-eyed.

KEENNESS, *n.* 1. Vehemence, sharpness, feverishness, intensity, excitement, warmth of feeling, intense desire, ardor, fervency, fervor, perfervor, fierceness, impetuosity, mettle, animation, verve, élan, vigor, zeal, eagerness, enthusiasm, earnestness, spirit, heartiness, soul, cordiality, good will, *empressement (Fr.).*

2. Clear-wittedness, sagacity, penetration, perspicacity, perspicuity, sensitivity, penetration, discernment, subtlety, astuteness, acumen, clear-sightedness, long-headedness, sapiency, quick-wittedness, shrewdness, sharpness, acuteness, ingenuity, smartness, brightness, intelligence, esprit *(Fr.),* cleverness, dexterity, wit, capacity, inventiveness, deftness, brilliance, alertness, intellect, resourcefulness, cleverness, cunning, ingeniousness, clear-headedness.

3. Malevolence, malignity, choler, acerbity, acrimony, bitterness, sharpness, satire, asperity, harshness, severity, virulence, animosity, crabbedness, sarcasm, moroseness, rudeness, churlishness, rancor, roughness, unkindness, abusiveness, venom, ill temper, irascibility, anger, spitefulness, resentment, malice, grudge, spleen, bile, gall, brusqueness, acid, bluntness, abruptness, gruffness, insolence, mordacity, causticity, tartness, mordancy, testiness, curtness, iracundity, effrontery, audacity.

KEEP, *n.* Fortification, fortress, stronghold, castle, chateau, tower, donjon, citadel, fort, acropolis, fasthold, safehold, fastness, hold.

KEEP, *v.* 1. Observe, celebrate, hold, solemnize, ceremonialize, consecrate, ritualize, commemorate, memorialize, hallow, dedicate, signalize.

2. Preserve, maintain, retain, secure, conserve, sustain, keep alive, hold, embrace.

3. Guard, defend, watch over, protect, screen, care for, take care of, safeguard, shelter, cover, look after, keep an eye on, mind, shield.

4. Continue, maintain, carry on, stay, be constant, abide, last, persevere, keep up, preserve, remain, endure, persist, be steadfast, stand.

5. Supply with necessaries of life, support, sustain, maintain, pay for.

6. Detain, hold, keep back, delay, encumber, obstruct, stall, retain, restrain, retard, hinder, shackle, impede, bar, hamper, inhibit, hamstring, hold up, arrest, tie up, cramp, deter, belate, clog, hobble, withhold, secure, constrain, restringe, grasp, clench, clasp, gripe, clutch, clinch, block, grip.

7. Keep in the background *or* shade, conceal, hide, bury, veil, curtain, camouflage, becloud, cloud, befog, ensconce, dissemble, latentize, secrete, cache, disguise, obscure, shelter, cover, blind, cloak, mask.

8. Have, carry, furnish, stock, heap, trade in, store, stack, accumulate, deal in, keep in stock,

save up, treasure up, amass, hoard up, lay in, garner, pile.

KEEP AFTER, *v.* Follow, follow up, pursue, go after, camp on the trail of, trail, shadow, dog the steps of, trail after, trail behind, track, follow the track of, tread close upon, follow in the tread (track) of, fly after, follow on the heels of, tail *(coll.),* seek, search, seek for, search for, look, look for, pry, pry into, peer, hunt, dig for, root for, fish for, delve for, quest, query, trace, search out, ferret out, scout out, prosecute, take to, go in for, run after, take a course, adopt a course.

KEEP AN EYE ON, *v.* Watch, scrutinize, observe, scrutinate *(rare),* look at, regard, look closely at, gaze on, gaze upon, fasten the gaze upon, look hard at, stare, examine, gape, goggle, gawk *(coll.),* observe, perceive, eye, ogle, perlustrate, review, contemplate, give the once-over *(sl.),* scan, inspect, notice, attend, pay attention to, heed, mind, have regard to, investigate, view, mark, note, pay heed to, heed, peruse, study, consider, survey, try, take stock of, overhaul, explore, remark.

KEEP AT, *v.* Persist, persevere, endure, stick, stick to, stick it out *(coll.),* see it through, never say die, follow to a conclusion, follow to a finish, prosecute to a conclusion, cling to, adhere to, hold fast, hold on, keep going, die at one's post, die with one's boots on, die in one's shoes, go down trying, go down with flying colors, keep doggedly at, plod, peg, plug, peg away, peg along, forge ahead, move heaven and earth, keep the ball rolling, keep it up, hang on, hang on for dear life, be resolute, be tenacious, be determined, have determination, stick at nothing, stop at nothing, mean business, stickle, hold out, hold out for, take no denial, brook no opposition, not take 'no' for an answer, be unyielding, die hard, be stubborn, be mulish, be obstinate, die fighting, have one's own way, insist on one's own way, drudge, grind, toil, moil, labor, work, slave, sweat, dig, grub, go all out, go through fire and water, go through hell and high water, work like a dog, work like a drudge, coalheaver, horse, ox, animal), sweat and slave, hammer at, wade through, finish, complete, do thoroughly, stick to one's post, be a slave of duty, stick by one's guns, bear up under, go to any lengths, exhaust one's opportunities, exhaust oneself, spend oneself.

KEEP BACK, *v.* 1. *(Delay)* Retard, push back, push aside, slacken, slow down, detain, suspend, waive, hold, stave off, hold up *(coll.),* shift off, put off, postpone, stop, block, stay.

2. *(Keep secret)* Keep in ignorance, huggermugger, keep dark, conceal, keep it a secret, keep it a deep dark secret, keep close, keep a close mouth, keep to oneself, withhold, let it go no farther, not tell, not breathe a word, keep one's own counsel, make no sign, suppress, stifle, hush up, smother, gag, throttle, muffle, keep snug.

3. *(Reserve)* Save, retain, put by, put by for a rainy day, hold back, husband, husband one's resources, save up, hold as a nest egg, save as a nest egg, feather one's nest.

4. *(Not use)* Do without, reserve, hold in reserve, hold back, withhold, dispense with, not touch, abstain, abstain from, neglect, waive, spare, save, forbear, put away, lay up, lay aside, cast aside, put aside, shelve, set by, set aside, push aside, ignore, disregard, repudiate, repulse, reject.

5. *(Hinder)* Interfere, inhibit, impede, restrict, hamper, trammel, entrammel, interrupt, intercept, obstruct, clog, cram, snub, curb, constrain, brake, put the brakes on, countercheck, check, keep from, hold back, hold up *(coll.),* keep in check, hold in check, keep in leash, hold in leash, clog the wheels, oppose, impede the progress of, retard, block, block the way of, block up, blockade, slacken, delay, detain, stop, estop, stop up, put a stop to, put an end to, end, terminate, finish, suspend, bring to a stop, deadlock, checkmate, bar, barricade, bolt, lock, trap, hedge in, surround, hedge round, inconvenience, filibuster *(U.S.),* shackle, chain, enchain, bind, discommode, incommode, choke, choke off, cut off, preclude, debar, dam, stem *(the tide of),* slow, slow down, decelerate, thwart, repel.

6. *(Restrain)* Constrain, restrict, put under restraint, lay under restraint, check, curb, prohibit, smother, inhibit, keep a tight hand on, keep a tight rein on, control, master, dominate, hold back, hold in check, hold in abeyance, manage, enleash, keep within bounds, hold, limit.

7. *(Prohibit)* Forbid, interdict, withhold, disallow, deny, inhibit, debar, circumscribe, cohibit, preclude, exclude, forefend *(arch.),* embargo, ban, veto, proscribe, taboo, tabu, shut out, prevent, restrict, enjoin.

8. *(Retain)* Keep, withhold, reserve, maintain, hug, clasp, grasp, clench, embrace, detain, restrain, gripe, grip, hold fast, hold tight, keep a firm grip, keep an iron grip, hold one's ground, hold one's own, secure, hold back, entail, tie up, husband, save, preserve, have in stock, keep in stock.

KEEP COMPANY WITH, *v.* 1. *(Accompany)* Attend, guard, usher, chaperon, conduct, escort, bear company, companion *(rare),* companionize *(coll.),* hang on, hang around with *(coll.),* couple with, associate with, consort with, flock together with, herd together *(coll.),* row in the same boat, go with, go hand in hand with, chum *(sl.),* pal *(sl.),* buddy *(sl.),* buddy up with *(sl.),* pal up with *(sl.),* pal around with *(sl.),* take up with *(coll.),* gang with *(coll.),* mob with *(coll.).*

2. *(Consort)* Associate with, intercommunicate, fraternize, mingle with, join, have intercourse with, walk hand in hand with, eat off the same trencher, club together, bear one company.

KEEP DARK, *v.* Suppress, stifle, keep secret, smother, muffle, conceal, hide, hush, hush up, silence, eclipse, seal, lock, keep under lock and key, bottle up, hugger-mugger, keep in the dark, keep hidden, keep close, keep snug, keep back, keep to oneself, not let it go farther, not breathe a word about, not breathe a syllable, not let the left hand know what the right hand is doing, cache, plant, secrete, cover, cover up, blind, shroud, curtain, cloak, enshroud, screen, veil, bury, mask, disguise, camouflage, obscure, cloud, becloud, draw the veil, draw the curtain, render invisible, keep unseen, keep out of sight, keep out of view, put up a front, befog, hoodwink, bamboozle, deceive, keep in the shade, cover one's tracks, hide one's light under a bushel.

KEEP DOWN, *v.* 1. *(Subdue)* Subjugate, take captive, repress, hold down, subject, make captive, hold in bondage, keep in bondage, hold in slavery, hold in captivity, enslave, enthrall, inthrall, bethrall, quell, suppress, restrain, temper, chasten, weigh down, quash, squash, trample, put down, trample underfoot, trample in the dust, tame, gentle, hold in leash, enleash, master, dominate.

2. *(Conquer)* Subdue, quell, vanquish, worst,

master, get the better of, get the best of, overwhelm, overcome, overpower, overmaster, overreach, overset, upset, trip, trip up, trample, subjugate, put down, suppress, crush, reduce, beat, drub, floor, break the neck of, break the back of, prevail, overlord.

3. *(Muffle)* Reduce the volume of, muffle, mute, deaden, soften, damp, dampen, damp the sound of, deaden the sound of, dull, drown, soft-pedal, smother, subdue, repress, throttle, stifle, hush, silence, quiet.

KEEPER, *n.* 1. *(Of animals)* Gamekeeper, cowkeeper, cowboy, cowpuncher *(coll.),* cowgirl, drover, herder, herdsman, herdboy, grazier, cowherd, swineherd, neatherd, goatherd, gooseherd, shepherd, shepherdess, sheepherder, sheeprancher, stockman, pigman, stablemen, husbandman, gooseboy, goosegirl, stableboy, groom, ostler, hostler, breeder, trainer, equerry, horsebreeder, horsebreaker, broncobuster *(coll.),* horseshoer, farrier, beekeeper, apiculturist, apiarist.

2. (Guardian): custodian, caretaker, protector, protectoress, patron, warder, curator, ranger, range-rider, rangeman, castellan, escort, convoy, retainer, bodyguard, lifeguard, chaperon, duenna, nurse, governess, wet nurse, dry nurse, nurserymaid, lifesaver *(coll.),* guardian angel, amah *(Oriental),* mammy *(U.S.),* conservator, doorkeeper, watchman, janitor, concierge *(Fr.),* sentry, sentinel, picket, outpost, vanguard, rear guard, coastguard, nursemaid.

3. *(Jailer)* Gaoler, custodian, guard, warder, warden, turnkey.

KEEP FROM, *v.* Abstain, forbear, desist, desist from, withhold, eschew, refrain, hold aloof from, keep aloof from, stay aloof from, spare, refrain from indulgence in, have no hand in, take no part in, want no part of, have nothing to do with, want nothing to do with, let alone, let well enough alone, deny oneself, know oneself, avoid, shun, fight shy of, evade, elude, steer clear of, exercise self-control, exercise self-denial, exercise self-restraint, take the pledge, get on the wagon *(coll.),* stay on the wagon *(coll.),* swear off, renounce, repudiate.

KEEPING, *n.* 1. Upkeep, safekeeping, safeguard, protection, maintenance, sustenance, protectorship, tutelage, guidance, ward, custody, guardianship, guardiancy *(rare),* care, auspices, heed, charge, wardenship, watch and ward, salvation, saving, holding, protectorship, protectorate, detention, retention, attendance.

2. Accordance, uniformity, harmony, consistency, performance, observance, observation, satisfaction, acknowledgment, concurrence, accommodation, conformance, conformity, conformation, line, symmetry, correspondence, proportion, proportionality, balance, congruity, regularity, evenness, parallelism, adaption, adaptation.

KEEP OFF, *v.* 1. *(Keep distant)* Keep away from, stand clear of, keep clear of, remain at a distance, remain aloof, remain remote, be removed from, keep one's distance, stand away from, keep far off, stay far off, stand afar, be inaccessible, be unapproachable, view from far off, view from afar.

2. *(Forbear! - interjection)* Hands off!, cease!, enough!, hold!, stop!, hold on!, whoa!, stay!, halt!

3. *(Forbear)* Retire, shrink, recoil, desist, shy, shy away from, keep shy of, flinch, wince, refrain from, recede, withdraw, stand back, stand

away from, go back, retreat, move away, go away, swerve away, stand off, sheer off, veer off, veer away from.

4. *(Avert)* Stave off, fend off, repel, repulse, drive back, avoid, evade, elude, obviate, sidetrack, draw aside, resist, defend against, stand one's ground, put to flight, ward off, fight off, keep at bay, hold at bay, hold at arm's length, keep at arm's length, deflect, divert, prevent.

5. *(Interjection)* Hands off!, Don't touch!, Noli-me-tangere! *(Lat),* Stay off! Stay away!

KEEP ON, *v.* 1. *(To persist)* Repeat, recur, reiterate, duplicate, reproduce, ditto *(coll.),* harp on, hammer at, tautologize, recapitulate, hammer away at, insist upon, do nothing but, beat, drum, sing the same old tune, din, do over again, go over the same ground.

2. *(Continue)* Persevere, persist, be steady, work steadily, endure, go on, hold, be steadfast, hold on, hold to one's course, remain, abide, perpetuate, keep alive, prolong, protract, maintain the course, drag on, work doggedly, proceed, keep the pot boiling, keep the ball rolling, keep at it, plug away, plug along, see it through, keep it up.

3. *(Persevere)* Continue, endure, persist, hold out, hold up, keep on, adhere to, cling to, plod, plod along, plod ahead, keep on one's course, hold one's ground, stick tenaciously, be tenacious, bear up, be steady, work doggedly, work persistently, be stubborn, be obstinate, be determined, be pertinacious, be firm, be constant, be unswerving, be loyal, be aggressive, be unflagging, be plucky, sink or swim, stick to, stick it out.

KEEPSAKE, *n.* Memento, souvenir, representation, reminder, emblem, token, symbol, relic, token of remembrance, remembrance, memorandum, reliquiae, remains, relic of the past.

KEEP UNDER, *v.* 1. *(Dominate)* Predominate, prevail, preponderate, subdue, suppress, quell, mortify, repress, govern, rule, have superiority over, wield authority over, be superior to, gain ascendancy over, get the upper hand, get the whip hand, control, master, overrule, override, overreach, overmaster, overawe, overbear, hold down, boss *(coll.),* oppress, hold sway, head, lead, manage, superintend.

2. *(Restrain)* Check, curb, constrain, cohibit, hold back, keep within bounds, keep within limits, limit, control, withhold, suppress, inhibit, smother, throttle, prohibit.

KEEP UP, *v.* 1. *(Continue)* Protract, sustain, maintain, perpetuate, go on, carry on, keep alive, keep the ball rolling, keep on foot, keep at it, plug away *(sl.),* hold to one's course, stay with it, stick it out *(sl.),* stay the distance *(sl.),* die in harness, die with one's boots on, go down fighting, follow through, see it through, hold on, stay.

2. *(Support)* Sustain, carry, shoulder, uphold, bear, maintain, shore up, brace, brace up, bolster, bolster up, back up, bear up, hold up, upbear, buttress, prop, stay, base, ground, bottom, found, bed, underbrace, underpin, underset, cradle, pillow, cushion, give support, furnish support, provide support, lend support.

3. *(Keep pace)* Keep pace with, march alongside of, run abreast of, run neck and neck, run alongside, stay in step with, maintain the pace, share the pace.

4. *(Persevere)* Continue, endure, persist, hold out, hold up, keep on, adhere to, cling to, plod, plod along, plod ahead, keep to one's course, hold one's ground, stick tenaciously, be tenacious, bear

up, work doggedly, work persistently, be stubborn, be obstinate, be mulish, be determined, be pertinacious, be firm, be loyal, be unswerving, be constant, be aggressive, be unflagging, be plucky, be steady, sink or swim, stick to, stick it out.

5. *(Preserve)* Keep, keep safe, keep secure, keep sound, keep intact, take care of, look after, safeguard, guard, sustain, keep alive, condition, support, spare, sustain, nurse.

KEG, *n.* Container, barrel, tun, hogshead, butt, cask, vat, tank, firkin, kilderkin, puncheon, harness cask, harness tub, rundlet, tub.

KELTER (var. of *kilter*), *n.* Kilter, shape *(coll.),* case, condition, lot, form, state, order, commission *(coll.),* whack *(coll.),* fashion, style, mode, constitution, mood, temper, disposition, character, modality, fettle, make-up *(coll.).*

KEN, *n.* 1. (Vision): vision, perception, view, discernment, field of view, field of vision, field of observation, visibility, eyeshot, eyereach, range of vision, sight, eyesight, eye view, perspective, outlook.

2. (Knowledge): knowledge, cognizance, acquaintance, acquaintanceship, cognition, savvy *(U. S.),* sabe *(U. S.),* awareness, perception, appreciation, appreciativeness, consciousness, conscience, recognition, privity, familiarity, understanding, apperception, sensibility.

KENNEL, *n.* 1. Doghouse, doghole, pound, breeding farm, breeding ground, dog pound.

2. Pack of hounds.

3. Hole, den, covert, burrow, lair, confine, haunt, cave, habitat.

KEPT-MISTRESS, *n.* Kept-woman, paramour, mistress, sweetheart, sweetie *(coll.),* demimondaine, ladylove, madam, girl, woman, concubine, doxie, spiritual wife, common-law wife, demirep, adultress, *petite amie (Fr.),* bachelor's wife.

KERCHIEF, *n.* Handkerchief, neckerchief, neckercher, headkerchief, coverchief, neckcloth, cloth, neckwear, neckpiece, neckband, scarf, muffler.

KERNEL, *n.* 1. Seed, grain, nucleus, pith, germ, marrow, center, nut, nutlet, nutmeat, meat, core, central body, essence, jet, germinal matter, mast, inside.

2. Essence, gist, essential matter, essential part, important part, substance, gravamen, core, heart, heart of the matter, principal part, principal portion, quintessence, fundamental, vital part, nub *(coll.),* nucleus, flower, backbone, marrow, sine qua non *(Lat.),* main point, main thing, key, keystone, cornerstone, foundation, basis, keynote, sum and substance, basic facts, brass tacks *(coll.),* turkey *(coll.),* cases *(coll.),* cardinal point, outstanding feature, salient point.

KEROSENE, *n.* Fuel oil, petroleum derivative, hydrocarbon, mineral oil, rock oil, coal oil, petroleum product, lamp oil.

KETTLE, *n.* Crucible, pot, caldron (cauldron), boiler, tureen, pan, vat, tub, saucepan, stewpan, teapot, teakettle, kitchen boiler.

KETTLEDRUM, *n.* Tympanum, percussion instrument, percussion, drum, atabal, naker, *caisse (Fr.),* tympano, tympani, timpani, kettle, timbal.

KEY, *n.* 1. (Opening device): opener, opening device, clavis, latchkey, skeleton key, master key, housekey.

2. (Means of admission): pass, safe-conduct, passport, open-sesame, agency, intermediary, go-between, agent, instrument, tool, means, medium.

3. (Indication): point, pointer, solution, cue, clew, clue, indicant, indicator, indication, index, sign, symbol, emblem, token, interpretation, exegesis, explanation, elucidation, explication, exposition, resolution, answer, finding, light, diagnosis, prognosis, *éclaircissement (Fr.),* illumination, meaning, significance, pony *(coll.),* crib *(coll.),* trot *(coll.),* translation, rendering, rendition, version, reading, construction, paraphrase, comment, commentary, dissertation, illustration.

4. (Music): pitch, tone, clef, note, tonality, keynote, tonic, key, major key, minor key, tonic major, tonic minor, leading note, color, coloration, coloring, tone color, *Klang (Ger.),* pervading note, dominant note, dominant tone, modulation, inflection, supertonic, submediant, dominant, subdominant, subtonic, stop, hole, lever, manual, finger board, fundamental, fundamental note, scale, mode.

5. (Cotter): cotter, pin, cotter pin, bolt, screw, dowel, wedge, fastening, fastener, binder, binding, plug, feather, plug-and-feather, wrest, wrest-pin, coin, quoin, clamp.

6. (Fruit): samara, seed, key fruit, fruit, maple-seed, ash-seed, elm-seed, maple-key, ash-key, elm-key.

7. (Var. of *quay*): dock, anchorage, pier, landing, bank, embankment, bankside, mooring, wharf, jetty, jutty, quay, landing place.

KEYBOARD, *n.* Manual, bank of keys, row of keys, clavier, claviature.

KEYNOTE, *n.* 1. (Music): key, leading note, fundamental, fundamental note, tonic key, tonic major, tonic minor.

2. (Principle): key, cornerstone, substance, principal point, salient point, cardinal point, theme, essence, essential feature, essential point, gravamen, sine qua non *(Lat.),* rule, criterion, model, paradigm, standard, outstanding feature, sum and substance, substance, gist, important part, important feature, important idea, fundamentals.

KEYSTONE, *n.* Ground, basis, occasion, call, principle, key, root, spring, mainspring, prime mover, motive, salient point, essence, essentials, sine qua non *(Lat.),* cardinal point, outstanding feature, distinctive feature, important feature, basic principle, fundamentals, fundamental idea, fundamental principle, rule, criterion.

KHAKI, *n.* Uniform, drill, twill, regimentals, cloth, fabric, textile, woven fabric, textile fabric, material, goods, dry goods, color, hue, dye, shade.

KHAKI, *adj.* Brown, brownish, khaki-colored, brownish-yellow, yellowish-brown, mustard-colored, dun-colored, mud-colored, earth-colored, clay-colored, tan, yellowish-tan, clay-tan, earth-brown.

KHAN, *n.* 1. (Title): dignitary, potentate, ruler, sovereign, chief, chieftain, autocrat, despot, prince, tyrant, oligarch, dictator, monarch, governor, ruling prince.

2. (Inn): caravansary, caravanserai, rest house, inn, hospice, hostel, hotel, tavern, roadhouse, wayside inn.

KICK, *v.* 1. (Strike with the foot): punt, calcitrate, boot, hit, strike, thump, bang.

2. (Recoil): fly back, recalcitrate, rebound, kick back, react, spring back, resile.

3. (Eject): turn out, cast out, throw out, boot out, give the boot to, send packing, send about one's business, bow out, show the door, show the gate, give the gate, give the bum's rush *(U.S. sl.),* remove, exclude, check out.

4. (Object): oppose, protest, take on *(coll.)*, disfavor, find fault, spurn, fret and fume, fuss, cause a fuss, stir up a fuss, clamor, croak, grouse, grouch, beef *(coll.)*, complain, murmur, mutter, grumble, grump, growl, grunt, make a fuss.

KICK, *n.* 1. *(Sl.:* zest): punch, pepper, ginger, pep, vim, vigor, pungence, pungency, intensity, force, verve, snap, sparkle, dash, piquancy, relish, flavor, high seasoning, tang.

2. *(Sl.:* protestation): protest, protestation, veto, remonstrance, remonstration, expostulation, boggle, exception, rejection, objection, opposition, resisting, resistance, complaint, grievance.

3. *(Sl.:* thrill): thrill, pleasure, gratification, enjoyment, great satisfaction, excitement, hedonics, hedonism, relish, fun, amusement, enjoyment.

4. (Act): calcitration, kick, boot, stroke.

5. (Recoil): recoil, rebound, recoilment, backlash, return, recalcitration, reaction.

KICK IN, *v.* *(Slang)* Contribute, render, give, donate, give out, bestow, chip in *(coll.)*, subscribe, pay over, pay, make payment, honor a bill, pay one's way, pay one's footing, lay the money down, hand out, hand over, ante up *(coll.)*, ante *(coll.)*, shell out, fork out, fork over, cough up, come through with, plank down.

KICK ONE'S HEELS, *v.* *(Sl.)* Wait, delay, bide, stay, tarry, bide one's time, dawdle, linger, dillydally, take time, take one's time, loiter, stay, hang around *(coll.)*, hang about *(coll.)*, stick around, cool one's heels, not move a foot, not move a hand, kill time, beguile the time, while away the time, while away the hours, pass time, temporize, not stir, not lift a finger, lie on one's oars, rest on one's oars, procrastinate, wait around, wait about, hang fire, hesitate, gain time, stall for time, play for time, stall off, hang back, idle, laze, loaf, lounge, loll, dabble, lie fallow, poke, twiddle one's thumbs, lag, slouch, fold one's arms, whistle for want of thought, putter, piddle, peddle, potter, fritter away time, let grass grow underfoot.

KICK OVER THE TRACES, *v.* *(Sl.)* Mutiny, mutineer, revolt, rebel, insurrect, rise, arise, rise against, riot, run riot, rise up in arms, disobey the law, transgress the law, violate the law, break the law, trespass, infringe the law, offend against the law, commit a crime, set the law at naught, trample the law underfoot, ride roughshod over the law.

KICKSHAW, *n.* Goody, dainty, delicacy, marchpane, marzipan, choice bit, sweetmeat, titbit, savory, trifle, triviality, thing of little value, thing of little (no) importance, trifling matter, small matter, trivia, morsel, obscurity, bagatelle, knickknack, gimcrack, gewgaw, bauble, toy, trinket, whimwham, inconsequential, inconsequentiality, plaything, feather, fig, jot, iota, tittle, gaud, bric-a-brac, fribble, frippery, doit.

KICK THE BEAM, *v.* *(Sl.)* Want, lack, miss, require, be unequal, be found wanting, —unbalanced, —ill-matched, —different, —variant, —irregular, —overbalanced, —outweighed, —topheavy, —lopsided, —disquiparant, —incongruous, —unmatched, —skimpy, —unharmonious, —discrepant, —discordant, —irreconcilable, —small, —below the mark, —under par, —scanty, —inferior, fall short of, come short of, be lesser, —lower, —subordinate, —unimportant, —secondary,—minor, play second fiddle, decline, lose ground, slump, miss, be imperfect.

KICK THE BUCKET, *v.* *(Sl.)* Die, expire, perish,

breathe one's last, quit the world, lay down one's life, give up one's life, depart, fade, cease to live, pass away, give up the ghost, yield up the ghost, lose one's life, succumb. See DIE.

KICK UP A DUST, *v.* *(Sl.)* Roar, rage, storm, fume, fret, fuss, raise a fuss, romp, rant, rampage, make a disturbance, create a disturbance, raise a ruckus *(coll.)*, run wild, go on a rampage, run amuck, run amok, make a row, kick up a row *(both coll.)*, raise a breeze, raise a squall, raise Cain, raise Ned, raise hell, raise hail Columbia, raise the roof, whoop it up, roughhouse, cut up, take on *(coll.)*, be noisy, make a noise, noise, uproar, fulminate, shout, make a racket, flutter, scramble, quarrel, dispute, altercate, squabble, tiff, spat, roister, scrap, swagger, rollick, swashbuckle, wrangle, rant, rave, boil with indignation, stew, be angry.

KID, *n.* 1. Young goat, yearling, kiddy, she-goat, he-goat, billy goat *(coll.)*, nanny goat *(coll.)*, Angora goat, Cashmere goat, ibex, bezoar goat, mountain goat, gnu goat, great antelope, markhor, Rocky Mountain goat.

2. Child, urchin, tad, tot, little tot, imp, brat, bratling, elf, scrap, scrap of a child, little one, gamin, *gamine (Fr.)*, squirt *(sl.)*, shaver, little shaver, punk, punk kid, pickaninny, moppet, darling, cherub, angel, duckling, pup, chickabiddy, kitten, lamb, lambkin, bud, innocent, chick.

3. Leather, goatskin, hide, tanned hide.

KID, *v.* *(Sl.)* Jest, banter, make fun of, make sport of, make game of, mock, chaff, deceive, hoodwink, bamboozle, humbug, ridicule, laugh at, twit, fool, beguile, tease, delude, toy, hoax, bilk, bluff, trick, cozen, flam, flimflam, play upon, impose upon, bluff, befool, gull.

KIDDISH, *adj.* Youthful, childish, childlike, youthlike, young, juvenile, juvenescent, immature, green, puerile, unripe, callow, sappy.

KIDNAP, *v.* Carry off, bear off, steal, abduct, convey, take away, make off with, impress, lay hands on, lay hold of, make away with, spirit away, shanghai, crimp *(sl.)*, hold for ransom, lift, snatch, seize, steal away with.

KIDNAPPER, *n.* Crimp, crimper, felon, criminal, thief, depredator, interloper, abductor, shanghaier, marauder, bandit.

KIDNAPPING, *n.* Abduction, felony, crime, depredation, stealing, child stealing, defiliation.

KIDNEY, *n.* 1. Organ, excretory organ, reins, urinary organ.

2. Type, kind, sort, stripe, character, disposition, stamp, ilk, designation, manner, style, description, temper, temperament, habit, mood, humor, color, grain, the like of, the likes of, form, quality, constitution, spirit, streak, variety, species, group, family, breed, blood.

KILL, *v.* 1. Slay, slaughter, dispatch, put to death, end the life of, deal out death, blot out, erase *(sl.)*, give the business to *(sl.)*, put an end to, take one's life, get rid of, do to death, victimize, murder, commit murder, assassinate, send west, do for, fix, settle, do in, lay out, kick into the beyond, bump off, polish off, take for a ride, croak, put one out of his misery *(all coll.)*, give the works, put the kibosh on, wipe out *(all sl.)*, annihilate, shed blood, spill blood, butcher, decimate, silence, give the quietus to, bloody one's hands with, dye one's hands with blood, cut off, nip in the bud, shoot down, riddle, pump full of lead *(sl.)*, blackjack, knock one's brains out, dash out one's brains, knock on the head, beat one's brains out, lapidate, stone, throttle, choke, strangle, asphyxiate, burke, garrote, smother, suffocate, stop the breath of, drown, club, poison, hang, electrocute, execute, behead, decapitate, guillotine, decollate, gibbet, cut to pieces, cut the throat of, jugulate, lynch, finish, finish off, immolate, sacrifice, inflict capital punishment, burn, burn to death, bring to the gallows, bring to the block, axe *(coll.)*, dismember, hew, hack, hack to pieces, chop, chop to pieces, mutilate, wound mortally, wound fatally, wound lethally, injure mortally, injure fatally, injure lethally, tear limb from limb, hang, draw and quarter, impale, shoot, execute by fire, put to the sword, put to the edge of the sword, put to the knife, knife to death, stab fatally, break on the wheel, commit to the flames, string up, stretch *(sl.)*, neck *(coll.)*, scrag *(coll.)*, gibbet *(coll.)*, noose *(coll.)*, bayonet, saber, run through, pierce, let the daylight into *(coll.)*, cut, cut down, give no quarter, show no mercy, wade in blood, pick off, knock off *(sl.)*, snipe (at), spear, lance, stick, disembowel.

2. Interrupt, extinguish, quench, quell, put a stop to, break, stay, halt, stem the tide, check, check in full career, arrest, stall.

KILL., *n.* 1. Prey, victim, meat, carcass, spoor.

2. Channel, river, stream, creek, crick *(coll.)*, brook, run, branch *(coll.)*, gill, bourn, burn, brook, brooklet, rill, rivulet, rillet, feeder, tributary, race, runlet, streamlet, watercourse.

KILLER, *n.* Slayer, murderer, strangler, slaughterer, butcher, bloodletter, bloodshedder, shedder-of-blood, assassin, Cain, cutthroat, bravo, *apache (Fr.)*, manslayer, thug, gorilla *(sl.)*, garroter, gunman, gun *(sl.)*, triggerman *(sl.)*, torpedo *(sl.)*, burker, burkist, hatchetman, cannibal, man-eater, regicide, parricide, patricide, fratricide, matricide, homicide, infanticide, uxoricide, vaticide, insecticide, aborticide, matador, destroyer, executioner, decapitator, headsman, beheader, vandal, exterminator, annihilator, executionist, lyncher, sniper, fungicide, germicide, sororicide.

KILLING, *n.* 1. Slaying, butchery, murder, slaughter, trucidation, bloodshed, massacre, homicide, foul play, bloody murder, murder most foul, violent death, death by violence, pogrom, carnage, saturnalia of blood, fusillade, thuggism, thuggery, execution, electrocution, hanging, lynching, decapitation, decollation, guillotining, shooting, burning, burning at the stake, martyrdom, lapidation, stoning to death, organized murder, mass murder, capital punishment, judicial murder, garroting, necktie party *(coll.)*, impalement, crushing to death, beating to death, flogging to death, flaying, breaking on the wheel, strangling, strangulation, crucifixion, patricide, parricide, matricide, uxoricide, vaticide, regicide, suicide, infanticide, aborticide, poisoning, elimination, annihilation, holocaust, extermination, immolation, fatality, fratricide, sororicide.

2. *Coup (Fr.)*, stroke of luck, stroke of fortune, fluke *(sl.)*, feat, hit, smash hit *(sl.)*, big hit *(sl.)*, tenstrike *(sl.)*, master stroke, *coup de maître (Fr.)*, piece of luck, piece of good luck, piece of good fortune.

KILLING, *adj.* 1. (Murderous): lethal, deadly, death-dealing, withering, devastating, slaughterous, bloodthirsty, bloody-minded, sanguinary, sanguine, sanguinolent, sanguineous, annihilating, deathly, internecine, lethiferous, destructive, mortal, gory, ensanguined, bloody, bloodstained, fatal.

2. (Captivating): captivating, engaging, arresting, beguiling, alluring, seductive, seducing, fascinating, attractive, attracting, charming, enrapturing, entrancing, enchanting, enravishing, ravishing, winsome, winning, inviting, tantalizing, provocative, mouth-watering, prepossessing, taking, exciting, arousing, stimulating, bewitching, felicitous, exquisite, rapturous, thrilling, empyrean, beatific, beatifical, seraphic, ecstatic, exalting, lovely, delightful.

3. *(Sl.: beautiful)*: brilliant, sparkling, glowing, shining, dazzling, beaming, effulgent, refulgent, rich, gorgeous, fine, superb, magnificent, grand, stunning, devastating, sublime, glorious, radiant, splendorous, splendid, splendiferous.

4. (Ludicrous): ludicrous, ridiculous, comic, comical, farcical, laughable, risible, funny, amusing, foolish, rich, screaming, screamingly funny, too funny for words, too funny for anything, quizzical, droll, drollish, absurd, nonsensical, outrageous, outlandish.

KILT, *n.* Article of clothing, skirt, petticoat, garment, apparel, wearing apparel, philibeg, filibeg.

KILTER, *n.* Kelter, shape, case, condition, lot, form, state, order, commission *(coll.)*, whack *(coll.)*, fashion, style, mode, constitution, mood, temper, temperament, disposition, character, modality, fettle, make-up *(coll.)*.

KIMONO, *n.* Negligee, morning gown, article of clothing, wearing apparel, tea gown, bath robe, robe, *robe de chambre (Fr.)*, wrapper, lounging robe, dressing gown, smoking gown.

KIN, *n.* 1. Kindred, consanguinity, relation, relationship, blood relation, blood relationship, blood, blood ties, family ties, connection, alliance, cognation, agnation, filiation, affiliation, nationality, lineage, stock, descent, extraction, gentility.

2. Kinsman, kinfolk, folks, kith, kith and kin, relatives, relations, kinsfolk, people, blood, blood relatives, blood relations, near relations, near relatives, distant relatives, one's own flesh and blood, race, tribe, family, house, clan, nation, caste, brood.

KIN, *adj.* Consanguine, consanguineous, consanguinean, agnate, cognate, kindred, related, akin, of the same blood, of the same family, of the same nature, of the same kind, allied, fraternal, german, germane, affinal, intimately related, closely related, affiliated.

KIND, *adj.* Kindly, forbearing, patient, understanding, forbearant, easygoing, benign, benignant, good, amiable, indulgent, lenient, obliging, considerate, thoughtful, generous, charitable, warm-hearted, tender-hearted, good-hearted, big-hearted, soft-hearted, amiable, cordial, accommodating, gracious, tender, mild, warm, compassionate, pitying, merciful, good-humored, good-natured, sympathizing, sympathetic, kindly-meant, kindly-intended, well-meant, well-intended, well-meaning, well-affected, well-disposed, kindly-disposed, chivalrous, chivalric, courteous, polite, devoted, fraternal, paternal, maternal, brotherly, sisterly, fatherly, motherly, friendly, friendlike, amicable, amiable, neighborly, gentle, courtly, gallant, good-mannered, well-mannered, mannerly, civil, unhostile, bounteous, generous, helpful, obliging, tactful, conciliatory, winsome, merciful, clement, ruthful, humane, philanthropic, humanitarian, soft, tender-hearted, unhardened, temperate, helpful, easygoing, touched, moved, complaisant, fond, affectionate, devoted, well-intentioned.

KIND, *n.* 1. Strain, family, race, brood, breed, clique, coterie, sect, clan, phylum, sept, genus, subgenus, subspecies, subfamily, tribe, caste, set, suit, persuasion, progeny, antecedents, ancestors.

2. Sort, type, lot, stamp, stripe, streak, brand, designation, style, description, constitution, character, disposition, habit, frame, color, feather, connection, the like, the likes, kidney, make, cast, vein, mold, cue, mood, mode, humor, spirit, tone, grain, nature, genus, *genre (Fr.),* diathesis, aspect, temper, temperament.

KINDHEARTED, *adj.* Kind, kindly, benign, benignant, amiable, cordial, good, good-hearted, great-hearted, warm-hearted, big-hearted, soft-hearted, tender-hearted, obliging, indulgent, understanding, compassionate, thoughtful, considerate, good-humored, good-natured, sympathizing, sympathetic, chivalrous, chivalric, well-meaning, well-affected, well-disposed, kindly disposed, well-intending, well-intentioned, charitable, generous, humane, humanitarian, altruistic, philanthropic, brotherly, fatherly, sisterly, motherly, paternal, fraternal, maternal, loving, clement, lenient, amicable, amiable, gentle, courtly, courteous, polite, tactful, conciliatory, winsome, patient, easygoing, forbearing, forbearant, gracious, mild, warm, pitying, merciful, accommodating, mannerly, well-mannered, unhostile, bounteous, ruthful, temperate, unhardened, helpful, devoted, touched, moved, complaisant, fond, affectionate.

KINDHEARTEDNESS, *n.* Kindness, kindliness, generosity, bounty, benevolence, beneficence, benignity, charity, charitableness, grace, graciousness, philanthropy, altruism, humaneness, humanitarianism, goodness of heart, warmth of heart, Christian charity, Christian love, love for mankind, love for one's fellow man, good will to man, good will toward man, brotherly love, sympathy, toleration, forbearance, patience, understanding, compassion, friendly feelings, good feelings, warm feelings, kind feeling, kindly feeling, good will, good wishes, best wishes, magnanimity, consideration, considerateness, chivalry, chivalrousness, goodness, favor, service, good deed, act of kindness, act of generosity, act of humanity, good works, almsgiving, good treatment, boon, benefaction, good turn, mercy, disinterestedness, unselfishness, humanity, bonhomie, bonhommie, philanthropism, good nature, kindly nature.

KINDLE, *v.* 1. Set on fire, light, ignite, rekindle, relight, calefy, build a fire, put the torch to, apply a match to, fire, light up, strike a light, conflagrate, fuel, stoke, coal, coal up, fuel up, fan the flame, feed the flame, blow up a fire, add fuel to the flames, supply with fuel, burn, inflame.

2. Stir, excite, arouse, rouse, waken, awake, wake, call forth, enkindle, illumine, illuminate, inflame, incite, stir up, agitate, sharpen, invigorate, intensify, induce, quicken, step up, animate, set astir, urge, lash, goad, prod, accelerate, whet, sharpen, foment, stimulate, provoke.

3. Sting, render violent, make violent, pique, madden, enrage, infuriate, exacerbate, arouse, provoke, irritate, exasperate, lash, lash into fury, lash into rage, lash into anger, fan the flame, inspirit, inspire, work up, stir up, act upon, blow up, pour oil on the fire, excite, affect, interest, impassion, actuate, motivate, animate, strike, anger, bite, make one's blood boil, make one's blood race.

KINDLINESS, *n.* Kindness, altruism, generosity, bounty, benevolence, beneficence, benignity, charity, charitableness, grace, graciousness, philanthropy, altruism, humaneness, humanity, humanitarianism, goodness of heart, warmth of heart, Christian charity, Christian love, love for mankind, love for one's fellow man, good will to man, good will toward man, brotherly love, sympathy, toleration, forbearance, patience, understanding, compassion, friendly feeling, good feeling, warm feeling, kind feeling, kindly feeling, good will, good wishes, best wishes, magnanimity, consideration, considerateness, chivalry, chivalrousness, goodness, favor, service, good deed, good turn, act of kindness, act of charity, act of generosity, act of humanity, good works, almsgiving, good treatment, boon, benefaction, mercy, disinterestedness, unselfishness, bonhomie, bonhommie, philanthropism, good nature, kindly nature.

KINDLING, *n.* 1. Lightwood, firewood, scrapwood, tinder, fuel, fagots, brushwood, driftwood, stovewood, brush, log, timber, coals, paper, shavings, leaves.

2. Ignition, inflammation, burning, setting fire to, lighting, firing, calefaction, torration, oxydation, oxidation, combustion, enkindling.

KINDLY, *adj.* Kind, forbearant, forbearing, patient, understanding, easygoing, benign, benignant, good, amiable, indulgent, lenient, obliging, considerate, thoughtful, generous, warm-hearted, charitable, tender-hearted, big-hearted, large-hearted, soft-hearted, great-hearted, amiable, cordial, accommodating, tender, mild, warm, compassionate, pitying, merciful, good-humored, good-natured, sympathizing, sympathetic, kindly-meant, kindly-intended, kindly-done, well-meaning, well-intentioned, well-intended, well-affected, well-disposed, chivalrous, chivalric, courteous, polite, devoted, fraternal, maternal, paternal, brotherly, sisterly, motherly, fatherly, friendly, friendlike, amicable, neighborly, gentle, courtly, gallant, good-mannered, well-mannered, mannerly, civil, unhostile, bounteous, generous, helpful, conciliatory, winsome, merciful, clement, ruthful, humane, philanthropic, humanitarian, soft, unhardened, temperate, touched, moved, complaisant, fond, affectionate, devoted, kindly-disposed.

KINDLY, *adv.* Kindlily, forbearingly, patiently, understandingly, comprehendingly, benignly, benignantly, amiably, indulgently, leniently, obligingly, considerately, thoughtfully, generously, warmly, warm-heartedly, charitably, tender-heartedly, big-heartedly, large-heartedly, soft-heartedly, great-heartedly, magnanimously, cordially, accommodatingly, tenderly, mildly, compassionately, pityingly, mercifully, good-humoredly, good-naturedly, sympathizingly, sympathetically, well-meaningly, done with kind intentions, well-affectedly, well-disposedly, chivalrously, courteously, politely, devotedly, paternally, maternally, amicably, neighborly, gently, courtly, gallantly, good-manneredly, well-manneredly, civilly, bounteously, generously, helpfully, obligingly, conciliatorily, winsomely, mercifully, handsomely, clemently, ruthfully, humanely, philanthropically, softly, temperately, easily, complaisantly, fondly, affectionately, devotedly, friendlily.

KINDNESS, *n.* 1. Kindliness, benevolence, generosity, bounty, beneficence, benignity, charity, charitableness, grace, graciousness, philanthropy, altruism, humaneness, humanitarianism, goodness, goodness of heart, warmth of heart, Christian charity, Christian love, love for mankind, love for one's fellow man, good will to men, good will toward men, brotherly love, sympathy, toleration, forbearance, patience, understanding, compassion, friendly feelings, good feelings, warm feelings, kindly feeling, good will, best wishes, good wishes, magnanimity, consideration, considerateness, chivalry, chivalrousness, goodness, favor, service, good deed, benefaction, mercy, disinterestedness, unselfishness, humanity, bonhomie, bonhommie, philanthropism, good nature, kindly nature.

2. Kind act, kindly gesture, humane gesture, gift, donation, good deed, generosity, benefaction, favor, service, act of charity, act of generosity, kind office, bounty, accommodation, good turn, good act, good treatment, philanthropies, beneficences, almsgiving, act of grace, benison, labor of love, help, assistance, grace, patronage, protection, guidance, interest, backing, sustenance, support, maintenance, aid, help, succor, ministration, munificences.

KINDRED, adj. Cognate, agnate, related, consanguine, consanguineous, consanguinean, akin, allied, of the same blood, connate, collateral, fraternal, intimately related, closely related, affinal, affiliated, germane, german, connatural, associated, congeneric, congenerical, corresponding, correspondent, allied to, congenerous, tarred with the same brush, matching, alike, resembling, resemblant, parallel to, paronymous, sympathetic, consonant, in accord, cemented, congenial, agreeing, homologous, of a piece, consimilar, united, friendly, harmonious, analogous.

KINDRED, n. 1. Consanguinity, blood relation, kinship, connection, blood relationship, relationship, ties of blood, blood ties, agnation, cognation, filiation, affiliation, alliance, connection, family, family ties.

2. Lineage, descent, race, stock, cousinage, cousinry, tribe, sept, clan, strain, line of descent, birth, kin, kinfolk, kinfolks (coll.), kinsfolk, kinspeople (U.S.), kith, folks, relatives, relations, people, near relations, near relatives, kith and kin, connections, distant relatives, distant relations, german, germane, consanguinean, generation, blood relative, blood relation, ancestor, ancestry, progeny, forbears, next of kin, issue, offspring, children, seed, brood, fathers, sons, forefathers, posterity, parentage, parents, progenitors, heirs, descendants, daughters.

KINE, n. Cows, cattle, milk cows, dairy cows, dairy cattle, bovine, bovine animal, beef, beeves, beefs, milcher, beef cattle, meat cattle, bossy (U.S.), bull, bullock, castrate, gelding, heifer, calf, steer, ox, dogie (coll.), leppy (coll.), shorthorn, longhorn, muley-cow, muley-head, zebu, Alderney, Guernsey, Jersey, Brahma bull, Galloway, belted Galloway, Angus, Aberdeen Angus, Holstein, yearling, maverick, butt head, redpoll, Red Polled.

KINETIC, adj. Motor, motile, moving, in motion, transitional, metabatic (Phys.), motiferous, motific, motary, motorial, motive.

KING, n. Ruler, anointed ruler, sovereign, monarch, tyrant, despot, oligarch, master, lord, overlord, liege, potentate, suzerain, liege lord, emperor, crowned head, imperator, protector, autocrat, the anointed, majesty, royal person, royal personage, paramount lord, overking, tsar, czar, Kaiser, Caesar, chieftain, usurper, regulus, rex.

KINGDOM, n. State, country, nation, realm, territory, dominion, domain, empire, land, fatherland, motherland, homeland, monarchy, power,

supreme power, absolute monarchy, limited monarchy, constitutional monarchy, imperiality, kingship, kinghood, sovereignty, suzerainty, aristarchy, oligarchy, tyranny, despotism, dynasty.

KINGLINESS, n. Courtliness, gorgeousness, magnificence, splendor, augustness, sublimity, magnanimity, regality, exaltedness, highness, nobility, stateliness, supremacy, imperiality, sovereignty, dominance, dominancy, authority, honorableness, authoritativeness, imposingness, munificence, generosity, glory, grandness, greatness, gallantry, dignity.

KINGLY, adj. 1. Princely, autocratic, of high birth, of high rank, of exalted birth, of exalted rank, of princely bearings, despotic, monarchical, princelike, royal, regal, sovereign, imperial, kinglike, palatine, powerful, puissant, strong.

2. August, noble, dignified, exalted, stately, elevated, imposing, splendid, grand, majestic, regal, imperial, gallant, courtly, generous, munificent, magnanimous, sublime, honorable, great, glorious.

KINGSHIP, n. Majesty, kinghood, the throne, the crown, dominion, dominance, dominancy, domination, supremacy, sway, power, rule, royalty, regality, command, authority, government, state, sovereignty, reign, regime, regimen.

KINK, n. 1. Twist, crimp, coil, curl, spiral, volute, helix, twirl, ringlet, fizz, frizzle, frizz, crinkle, curlicue, screw, corkscrew.

2. Complication, complexity, Gordian knot, involvement, involution, tangle, knot, intricacy, perplexity, tangled skein, gnarl, twist.

3. Eccentricity, singularity, peculiarity, twist, mental twist, quirk, quip, crank, idiocrasy, idiosyncrasy, idiocrasis, queerness, crotchet, conceit, whim, whimsey, freak, whimwham, flimflam, notion, vagary, fad, fancy, humor, fit, bee, bee in one's bonnet (coll.), prank, escapade.

4. Pain, pang, twitch, twinge, sharp pain, stabbing pain, crick, stitch, shooting pain, nip, pinch, flash, hot flash, charley horse (coll.), knot, stiffness.

KINKY, adj. 1. Snarled, entangled, twisted, curly, knotted, wiry, winding, meandering, wandering, complex, complicated, turning, spiraling, coiling, curling, meandrous, intricate, tortuous, tortuose, sinuous, sinuose, wavy, sinuate, flexuous, flexuose, sigmoid, sigmoidic, frizzed, frizzy, frizzly, mazy, labyrinthine, labyrinthical, ruffled, ambagiatory, ambagious, gnarled, tangly, daedal, Daedalian, Daedalic.

2. Odd, peculiar, idiosyncratic, idiocratic, strange, bizarre, outlandish, butre (Fr.), erratic, queer (coll.), twisted, unnatural, whimsical, full of whims, capricious, crotchety, fanciful, fantastic, wanton, vagrant, errant, wayward, contrary, skittish, fitful, captious, unreasonable, inconsistent, changeful, changeable, chimerical, protean, undisciplined, uncontrolled, spasmodic, volatile, irregular, unsteady, unstaid, vacillating, unreliable, fluctuating, undependable, unfixed, vicissitudinous, vicissitudinary, alternating, wavering, vibratory, desultory.

KINSFOLK, n. Lineage, race, descent, people, stock, cousinage, cousinry, tribe, sept, clan, strain, line of descent, birth, kin, kinfolk, kinfolks, kinspeople (U.S.), kindred, kith, kith and kin, folks, relatives, relations, near relatives, near relations, distant relatives, distant relations, german, germane, consanguinean, generation, blood relatives, blood relations, ancestors, ancestry, progeny, forbears, forefathers, next of kin, issue, offspring, children, seed, brood, sons, daughters, fathers, mothers, posterity, parentage, parents, progenitors, heirs, descendants.

KINSHIP, *n.* Consanguinity, blood, blood relationship, kindred, cognation, agnation, alliance, connection, affiliation, family, family tie, association, blood ties.

KINSMAN, *n.* Relative, relation, blood relative, blood relation, brother, father, mother, sister, cousin, sib, people, cousinry, cousinage, clan, tribe, sept, kith and kin, german, germane, consanguinean, ancestor, forefather, forbear, next of kin, issue, offspring, child, children, son, daughter, seed, progeny, parent, heir, descendant, landman, countryman, fellow-man, fellow-citizen, kith.

KIOSK, *n.* Pavilion, building, house, outhouse, outbuilding, structure, edifice, erection, bandstand, newsstand, summerhouse, pergola, arbor.

KIPPER, *v.* Cure, dry, salt, smoke, pickle, split, preserve, marinate, season, smoke-cure, smoke-dry, can.

KIRK, *n.* Church, temple, place of worship, house of God, house of prayer, house of worship, meeting house, tabernacle, shrine, bethel, sanctuary, basilica, chapel.

KIRKMAN, *n.* Ecclesiastic, churchman, divine, clergyman, cleric, clerk, clerk in holy orders, parson, pastor, minister, minister of the gospel, preacher, missionary, proselyte, man of God, servant of God, shepherd, black coat *(coll.),* sky pilot *(sl.),* sermoner, sermonizer, sermonist, reverend *(coll.),* priest, chaplain, hierophant, presbyter, father, father in Christ, spiritual Father, padre, abuna, curé, confessor, parish priest, father confessor, spiritual director, schoolman, canonist, theist, theologian, theologist, theologizer, theologician, theologue, scholastic, monotheist.

KIRTLE, *n.* Mantle, coat, petticoat, frock, dress, gown, skirt, garment, covering.

KISMET, *n.* Destiny, fate, fortune, lot, portion, doom, fatality, fatalism, cup, dispensation, will of Heaven, will of Allah, God's will, book of fate, handwriting on the wall, Fortune's wheel, wheel of Fortune, destination, wheel of chance.

KISS, *v.* 1. Salute (with a kiss), accolade, greet, give salutation to, buss, embrace, squeeze, osculate, hail, bid welcome, say hello, kiss hands, kiss the cheek, bid good day.

2. Caress, pat, pet, fondle, osculate, cosset, cherish, embrace, hug, clasp, dandle, cuddle, nuzzle, buss, smack, lip, take in one's arms, enfold in one's arms, pat on the head, pat on the cheek.

KISS, *n.* 1. Salute (with a kiss), accolade, buss, smack, mark of welcome, mark of greeting, mark of recognition, hail, sign of welcome.

2. Embrace, touch, lip, osculation, caress, fondling, dalliance, smack, buss, token of affection.

KIST, *n.* Chest, box, coffin, casket, receptacle, container, enclosure, basket, treasury, coffer, caddie, caddy, trunk.

KIT, *n.* 1. Tools, equipment, apparatus, implements, utensils, appliances, devices, contrivances, outfit, gear, necessaries, tackle, rig, rigging, traps, trappings, appurtenances, accouterments, things, impediments, furniture, paraphernalia, supplies, fittings, provisions, furnishings.

2. Wardrobe, clothing, uniform, apparel, livery, caparison, turnout, rig *(coll.),* wear, dress.

3. Violin, violette, kit violin, violino piccolo,

instrument, fiddle, kit fiddle, musical instrument, stringed instrument.

4. Kitten, cat.

KITCHEN, *n.* Cookroom, *cuisine (Fr.),* scullery, cookhouse, galley, caboose, camboose, bakehouse, bakery, cookery.

KITE, *n.* 1. Bird, bird of prey, hawk, elanet, swallowtail.

2. Toy, plaything, bauble, gewgaw, gimcrack.

3. Sharper, cheat, embezzler, swindler, cozener, cheater, confidence man, bilker, flimflammer, juggler, con man *(cant),* fraud *(coll.),* defrauder, diddler, gypper, gypster *(coll.),* gyp artist *(sl.),* humbug, bamboozler, welsher, loan shark, peculator, land pirate, land shark, jockey.

4. Counterfeit, bad check, worthless check, false money, bad money, fancy stocks, bad instrument, fictitious instrument, forgery, rubber check, fictitious check.

KITTEN, *n.* Cat, domestic cat, young cat, catling, pussy cat, puss, feline, house cat, kit, kitty, kitling, grimalkin, gib, tomcat, tabby cat, mouser.

KITTENISH, *adj.* Playful, sportive, childish, childlike, babylike, kittenlike, playsome, full of play, frolicsome, gamesome, frisky, waggish, rollicking, rollicksome, tricksy, playful as a kitten, infantile, infantine.

KLEPTOMANIA, *n.* Neurosis, dementia, disorder, mental disorder, nervous disorder, nervous derangement, compulsion, compulsion neurosis, thievishness, rapacity, predacity, mania for stealing, propensity for stealing.

KLEPTOMANIAC, *n.* Neurotic, thief, stealer, kleptomanist, dement, disordered person, deranged person, demented person, morbid person, pilferer.

KNACK, *n.* Skill, skillfulness, adroitness, expertness, facility, genius, ability, faculty, dexterity, cleverness, finesse, address, proficiency, efficiency, talent, gift, endowment, competence, dexterousness, dextrousness, natural endowment, capacity, forte, bent, aptness, aptitude, qualification, art, trick, hang, sleight, felicity, turn for, capacity for, genius for, talents, parts, propensity, quickness, readiness, ingenuity.

KNAP, *n.* Summit, hill, knoll, height, elevation, prominence, protuberance, top, crest, rise, swell, swelling, knob, convexity, hillock, convexedness, eminence, projection, barrow, dune, kopje *(Africa),* mound, excrescence, gibbosity, boss, hammock, butte, convexness, tumescence, knurl, monticle, monticule, hunch, lump.

KNAPSACK, *n.* Rucksack, pack, kit, kit bag, war bag, war sack, duffel bag, haversack, yannigan bag *(U.S.),* holdall, grab-all *(sl.),* bag.

KNAVE, *n.* 1. Rascal, scoundrel, bad man, blackguard, rogue, villain, reprobate, cheat, caitiff, miscreant, colluder, accomplice, reptile, snake, viper, rodent, rat, dog, cur, hound, whelp, mongrel, snake in the grass, wolf in sheep's clothing, mischief-maker, scamp, scalawag, sharper, trickster, shyster *(U.S.),* betrayer, traitor, Judas, plotter, complotter, renegade, recreant, rascalion, rapscallion, rep, rip, scapegrace, evildoer, ruffian, backslider, black sheep, rotter, cad, bounder, budmash *(Ind.),* ne'er-do-well, good-for-nothing, good-for-naught, devil, devil incarnate, devil in human shape, hellhound, fallen angel, delinquent, rakehell, rake, roué, wrongdoer, malefactor, sinner, transgressor, felon, pharisee, misfeasor, malfeasor, culprit, offender, criminal, crook *(coll.),* convict, jailbird, gaolbird, desperado, calumniator, ragamuffin, vagabond, quack, humbug, bamboozler, fake, faker, phony (coll.), hypocrite, grafter, liar, detractor, pretender, perjurer, adventurer, confidence man, con man (cant), bunco artist, mountebank, charlatan, double-dealer, sneak, backbiter, trimmer (sl.), impostor, shark, falsifier.

2. Picture card, face card, court card, varlet, jack, bower, pam.

KNAVERY, n. Rascality, villainy, cunning, cunningness, deceit, deceitfulness, deception, fraud, dishonesty, wrongdoing, artfulness, craftiness, malefaction, craft, sharp practice, roguery, fraudulence, fraudulent skill, maneuvering, dishonor, venality, graft, corruption, laxity, chicanery, chicane, hanky-panky, hocus-pocus, intrigue, trickery, trimming, swindling, tergiversation, apostasy, confidence game, cheating, scoundrelism, jobbery, dodgery, disloyalty, disaffection, treason, treachery, guile, chouse, turpitude, criminality, crime, felony, malfeasance, misfeasance, misdemeanor, pettifoggery.

KNAVISH, adj. Dishonest, dishonorable, unconscionable, unprincipled, roguish, felonious, reprobate, scampish, lawless, venal, corrupt, sinister, illegal, criminal, crooked, tortuous, insidious, Machiavellian, rascally, villainous, blackguard, fraudulent, tricky, trickish, cunning, unjust, shameful, slippery, cunning, foxy, sneaking, pettifogging, dark, fishy (coll.), uningenuous, disingenuous, scheming, plotting, designing, questionable, doubtful, dubious, recreant, dead to honor, deceitful, deceptive, lost to shame, false, mendacious, lying, untruthful, hypocritical, conniving, collusive, bad, evil, sinful.

KNAVISHNESS, n. Rascality, villainy, cunning, cunningness, deceit, deceitfulness, deception, fraud, dishonesty, wrongdoing, artfulness, craftiness, malefaction, craft, sharp practice, roguery, fraudulence, fraudulent skill, maneuvering, dishonor, venality, graft, corruption, laxity, chicanery, chicane, hanky-panky, hocus-pocus, intrigue, trickery, trimming, swindling, tergiversation, apostasy, confidence game, cheating, scoundrelism, jobbery, dodgery, disloyalty, disaffection, treason, treachery, guile, chouse, turpitude, criminality, crime, felony, feloniousness, malfeasance, misfeasance, misdemeanor, pettifoggery.

KNEAD, v. Mix, stir, mix thoroughly, form, shape, work, work into shape, work thoroughly, manipulate, mingle, wield, massage, petrie, rub, rub down, stroke, caress.

KNEE, n. Joint, patellar region, juncture, articulation, pivot, hinge, bend, angle, connection.

KNEE, v. 1. Yield, submit, accede, defer to, bow down to, submit to, bend the neck to, comply, acquiesce, succumb, be submissive, stoop, bend, knuckle to, fall at one's feet, fawn, grovel, yield obsequiously, bend obsequiously, give up, kowtow, bow and scrape, surrender, cede, give up, give way.

2. Implore, beseech, entreat, beg, supplicate, pray, appeal, urge, importune, press, kneel to, throw oneself at the feet of, throw oneself at the mercy of.

3. Truckle, toady, fawn, be servile, grovel, stoop, lick one's shoes, lick the boots of, creep, crawl, cringe, kowtow, do service, wait upon, fetch and carry, pander to, be menial, ingratiate oneself, be slavish, be subservient, be obeisant, be abject, be base, be obsequious, kiss the hem of one's garment.

4. Be grateful, show gratitude, be obliged, be thankful, be indebted, be beholden, make obeisance, nod, salaam, incline one's head, bow one's head, bend the neck, bob, curtsey, make a curtsey, fall down before, prostrate oneself.

KNEE BREECHES, n. Pants, pantaloons, pantalettes, knickers, plus fours, breeches, britches, knickerbockers, trouserettes, small clothes, smalls.

KNEECAP, n. Patella, kneepan, knee-bone.

KNEEL, v. Bow, bend the knee, make obeisance, kowtow, salaam, bow down, incline one's head, fall on one's knees, bob, bob down, curtsey, bow and scrape, genuflect, bow the knee, get down on one's knees, throw oneself on one's knees, fall at the feet of, prostrate oneself, kiss the hem of one's garment.

KNELL, n. Passing bell, death bell, tolling, tolling of the knell, funeral bell, funeral ring, death signal.

KNELL, v. Peal, toll, ring, chime, tintinnabulate, sound, resound, herald, proclaim, betoken, sound with doom, sound the doom of, ring portentously, ring ominously, announce.

KNICKERBOCKER, n. Knee breeches, small clothes, smalls, knickers, knee pants, pants, trousers, trouserets, pantalets, pantaloons, plus fours, culottes.

KNICKNACK, n. Kickshaw, gimcrack, gewgaw, bauble, thingumajig, trinket, trifle, knack, plaything, toy, triviality, thing of little value, thing of small value, thing of no value, bagatelle, whimwham, inconsequential, inconsequentiality, gaud, tittle, feather, frippery, bric-a-brac.

KNIFE, n. Tool, cutting tool, cutting edge, edged tool, cutlery, blade, cutter, jackknife, steel, cold steel (coll.), naked steel (coll.), paring knife, pocket knife, clasp knife, switchblade knife, pen knife, bread knife, butcher knife, case knife, bowie knife, cane knife, farrier's knife, linoleum knife, skinning knife, scalping knife, surgical knife, scalpel, hunting knife, table knife, goldbeater's knife, palette knife, carving knife, woodcarver's knife, corn knife, machete, putty knife, felt knife, paperhanger's knife, hacking knife, oyster knife, chopping knife, belduque, drawing knife, drawknife, spokeshave, drawshave, razor, safety razor, bistoury, pruning knife, billhook, kris, creese, stiletto, barong, poniard, dagger, bolo, misericord, chive, parang, lance, kukri (India), basilard, dirk, katar (India), skean, skean dhu (Scotland), bayonet, sword, saber, épée, foil, cutlass, rapier, scimitar poignard, lancet.

KNIFE, v. Cut, cut down, cut apart, stab, wound, mutilate, lacerate, slash, cut to ribbons, pierce, bayonet, run through, cut the throat, jugulate, hack, hack to pieces, cut to bits, mangle, scar. deface, prune, lop off, whittle, shave.

KNIGHT, n. 1. Soldier, horseman, brave, fighter, man-at-arms, equestrian, warrior, warfarer, fighting man, armiger, arms-bearer, Templar, Ritte (Ger.).

2. Defender, champion, advocate, paladin, protector, hero, demigod, brave man, brave person, brave, vindicator, guardian.

3. Courteous man, gallant, the pink of courtesy, cavalier, knight-errant, flower of courtesy, flower of chivalry, Lancelot, Galahad, Sidney, Chesterfield, Bayard.

KNIGHT-ERRANTRY, n. 1. Quixotism, heedlessness, irresponsibility, precipitancy, idealism, impracticality, impracticability, impetuosity, impetuousness, recklessness, temerity, audacity, imprudence, indiscretion, foolhardiness, foolhardihood, rashness.

2. Benevolence, philanthropy, altruism, kindliness, nobility, good will to men, charity, love of mankind, sympathy.

3. Heroism, chivalry, knightly skill, knighthood.

KNIGHTHOOD, *n.* Chivalry, knight-errantry, gallantry, knightly skill, baronetcy, donship, peerage, title.

KNIGHTLY, *adj.* Heroic, gallant, doughty, courageous, audacious, brave, courteous, intrepid, hardy, stout, steadfast, strong, polite, considerate, gentle, compassionate, urbane, civilized, good-mannered, well-bred, stout, stout-hearted, lion-hearted, cordial, amiable, affable, gentlemanly, gentlemanlike, gracious, obliging, plucky, mettlesome, valiant, civil, chivalrous, chivalric, devoted, devout, humble, temperate, mild, good, virtuous.

KNIT, *v.* Weave, twist, interweave, intertwist, interlace, interthread, intertwine, intertissue, intertie, interentwine, draw in, corrugate, draw together, wrinkle, intort, plait, plat, braid, knot, stitch, intangle.

KNOB, *n.* 1. Handle, grip, hold, hand-hold.

2. Hump, protuberance, protuberancy, gibbosity, boss, tumescence, knot, bunch, knurl, snag, excrescence, appendage, protrusion, tumidity, bulge, swelling, swell, tumefaction, knur, gnarl, stud, lump, pommel, horn, bulb, tubercle, tuberosity, tubercule, hummock, geniculate, dune, whelk, monticle, monticule, mound, node, nub, finial, barrow, projection, prominence, eminence, extumescence, intumescence, convexity, convexness, excurvature, excurvation, nubble, croche, knop, kopje *(Africa),* knosp.

KNOBBY, *adj.* Bumby, lumpy, nodose, nodiform, nodulous, nodular, nodulated, noduled, nodulate, nodulose, torose, knotty, knobbed, gibbous, gibbose, bulbous, bulbose, caruncular, carunculous, carunculose, carunculated, caruncule, embossed, bossy, bossed, chased, raised, in relief, *repoussé (Fr.),* warty, verrucated, verrucate, papulous, papulose, papulated, papillous, papillate, papillar, papillary, papillulate, tuberous, tuberculous, tumorous.

KNOCK, *n.* 1. Blow, clap, slap, stroke, hit, bang, crack, whack, smack, buffet, fillip, rap, box, bat *(coll.),* clout *(coll.),* squash, jab, cut, thump, chop, clip *(coll.),* dig, poke, bunt, swat, punch, soak *(coll.),* sock *(coll.),* lick *(coll.),* tap, rap, dab, slap, spank, whip, stripe, pat, thrust, pass, clash, impact, appulse, impulse, shock, smash, side blow, glancing blow, swing, collision, bump, crash, impact.

2. Criticism, censure, reprehension, blame, hit *(coll),* rap *(coll.),* faultfinding, adverse criticism, stricture, obloquy, animadversion, hostile criticism, slam, rap, reflection, insinuation, imputation, home thrust, reprobation, denouncement, denunciation, censorship, boycott, reprimand, reproof, reproach, rebuke, condemnation, innuendo, castigation.

KNOCK, *v.* 1. Smash, stroke, crack, bang, rap, tap, bump, jolt, jostle, slam, slap, thump, smite, strike, hit, pound, hammer, drum, pummel, dash, rattle, crash.

2. Jolt, hit, strike, smite, cuff, buffet, box, crack *(coll.),* belt *(coll.),* bat *(coll.),* slam, dash, bounce, slap, swat, wallop *(coll.),* tamp, plug, push, jab, thump, soak *(sl.),* sock *(sl.),* lam-

baste *(sl.),* clout *(coll.),* pummel, thrash, lay on, rap, tap, pound, flap, slap, pat, dab, strike a blow, carom, kick, fetch a kick, boot, beat, calcitrate, lash, whip, cane, thwack, larrup *(coll.),* sideswipe.

3. Censure, criticize, inveigh against, cry out against, decry, deplore, reprehend, rap *(sl.),* find fault, cut up, cut to pieces, animadvert, annihilate, belittle, minimize, deprecate, reflect upon, clamor, cavil, peck at, abuse, condemn, damn, damn with faint praise, carp at.

KNOCK ABOUT, *v.* Wander, peregrinate, range, rove, gad, gad about, traipse, trapes, haze, haze around, haze about, jaunt, ramble, go about, travel, run about, go one's round, roam, go on the gad, gallivant, knock around, kick around, mooch, mosey *(coll.),* saunter, stroll, bat, bat around, prowl, stray, tramp, go on the bum *(coll.),* hobo *(coll.),* hover about.

KNOCK DOWN, *v.* 1. Lay level, lay low, fell, raze, raze to the ground, down, hew down, cut down, bring down, cast down, throw down, pull down, fling down, dash down, bowl down, bowl over, drop, floor, precipitate, prostrate, throw prostrate, trample, supinate, lay in ruins, ravage, devastate, desolate, wreck, destroy, break up, break apart, batter, smash, demolish, ruin, ruinate, crush, crumple up, pull to pieces, pick to pieces.

2. Auction, sell at auction, sell by auction, put up at auction, sell to the highest bidder, bring under the hammer, assign to a bidder, put on the block, auction off, auctioneer, sell.

3. Sadden, deject, depress, depress the spirits, make unhappy, render dejected, dispirit, dishearten, dismay, lower, dull, sink, damp, damp one's spirits, cast a damp on, dash one's hopes, wither one's hopes, cast a gloom upon, cast a shade upon, frown upon, grieve, aggrieve, sorrow, plunge into sorrow, plunge into gloom, cut up *(coll.).*

KNOCK OFF, *v.* *(Coll.)* 1. Stop, quit, terminate, close, conclude, finish, stay, halt, hold, belay, leave off, drop it, suspend, discontinue, shut up shop, shut down, call it a day, break off, pull up stakes, stop short.

2. Do carelessly, do superficially, toss off, hammer out, do recklessly, do a slapbang job, do perfunctorily, skimp, pass over lightly, do hastily, do inattentively, do a slipshod job, toss off, toss out, toss together, slap together, throw together.

3. Die *(q.v.),* kill *(q.v.).*

4. Write, compose, draft, indite, produce, knock out, throw together, draw up, dash off, scribble, scrawl, throw onto paper, toss onto paper.

KNOLL, *n.* Hillock, knob of soil, knob, barrow, bump, dune, hump, kopje, mount, mound, prominence, protuberance, protuberancy, swell, swelling, bulge, protrusion, excrescence, excrescency, gibbosity, boss, hummock, butte, convexity, convexness, convexedness, intumescence, tumescence, knurl, elevation, eminence, knap, monticule, monticle.

KNOLL, *v.* Peal, toll, knell, ring, chime, tintinnabulate, sound, resound, herald, proclaim, sound with doom, sound the doom of, ring portentously, ring ominously, announce.

KNOT, *n.* 1. Interlacement, meshwork, tissue, reticulum, web, lacework, webwork, lace, lacery, net, netting, plexus, twist, intertwist, braid, plait, square knot, granny's knot, hawser fastening, half-crown knot, half hitch, hitch, bend, tie, slipknot, slide knot, hawser bend, running knot, anchor—, weaver's—, becket—, wall—, timber—, bow-line—, surgeon's—, builder's—, stopper—, steve-dore's—, diamond—, figure-eight—, flat—, Flem-ish—, French shroud—, German—, single—, shroud—, rope-yarn—, reef—, prolonge—, over-hand—, lanyard—, loop—, manrope—, open hand—, netting—, mesh—, Matthew Walker—, harness—, Blackwall—, clove—, double—, round turn and half—, rolling—, magnus—, midship-man's—, marling—, carrick bend, cat's paw, stud-ding sail, halyard bend, tack—, fisherman's—, sheet—, heaving-line—, reeving-line—, bowknot, clinch, clinch inside, clinch outside, cuckold's neck, sheepshank, round-seizing.

2. Ornament, frog, star, badge, rosette, cock-ade, shoulder knot, epaulette, aiguillette, aglet, loop, tag, cord, braid.

3. Cluster, gathering, tuft, topknot, bun, braid, plait, chignon, clique, coterie, circle, junto, band, club, camarilla, bunch, cabal, outfit, group, mob, gang, body, collection, assemblage, aggregation, accumulation, cluster, pack, clump, bundle, cu-mulation, agglomeration, glomeration, conglom-eration, lump, mass, heap, pile.

4. Protuberance, node, lump, bump, block, cake, solid, mass, body, gob, convex, convexity, bow, bulge, swell, swelling, rise, tumescence, hump, knob, knur, knurl, gnarl, bulb, nodule, nodulus, nodulation, nodosity, button, boss, stud, excrescence, excrescency.

5. Woody formation, burl, joint, juncture, junc-tion, flaw, blemish, fault.

6. Linear measure, measure of distance, meas-ure of speed, nautical speed, nautical-mile-per-hour.

7. Problem, intricacy, dilemma, complication, involvement, involution, complexness, complexus, entanglement, perplexity, labyrinth, tangled skein, problem, puzzle, raveling, Gordian knot, gnarl, twist, kink, snare, trap, coil, tangle, horns of a dilemma, difficulty, vexation, trouble, tough nut to crack, crux, hitch, delay, stress, rub, pinch, ob-scurity, unintelligibility, inscrutability, enigma, mystery, bafflement, poser, question, conundrum, sphinx, riddle of the sphinx.

8. Bond, tie, joint, joining, ligature, jointure, juncture, junction, connection, articulation, bind-ing, link, weld, hitch, fastening, fastener, attach-ment.

KNOT, *v.* 1. Attach, fix, tie, bind, fasten, affix, secure, tighten, clinch, make fast, make secure, make taut, make tight, make set, make insepara-ble, pinion, string, lash, leash, bandage, swathe, wrap, truss, girth, girdle, moor, tether, hogtie *(coll.),* weave, interweave, knit, crochet, entangle.

2. Tangle, entangle, entwine, twine, twist, ravel, mat, intertwist.

3. Distort, contort, disfigure, twist, warp, gnarl, deform, misshape, blemish, mar.

KNOTTED, *adj.* Nodose, nodular, nodiform, nod-ulated, gnarled, gnarly, knurled, knurly, inextrica-ble, snarled, tangled, complex, complicated, in-tricate, raveled, entangled, tangly, involved, in-volute, dense, grumose, grumous, compact, mat-ted, interwoven, woven, difficult, not easy, trouble-some, tricky, hard, tough *(coll.),* problematic, problematical, irksome, toilsome, baffling, formi-dable, puzzling, enigmatic, obscure, unintelligible, perverse, refractory, thorny, Herculean, cross-grained, convolute, convoluted, kinky, jointed, distorted, knuckled, knaggy.

KNOTTY, *adj.* 1. Embossed, bossed, bossy, raised, chased, knobby, protuberant, gibbous, gibbose, gnarled, nodulous, nodulated, nodulose, nodose, carunculous, carunculated, carunculate, rough, un-smooth, unfinished, flawed, blemished, defective, unpolished, uneven, coarse, rugged, rugous, rugu-lose, bumpy, knurled, knurly, rough-grained, coarse-grained, knaggy, snaggy, torose, caruncular.

2. Formidable, difficult, Herculean, thorny, puzzling, obscure, not easy, insoluble, unsolvable, tricky, problematical, problematic, baffling, irk-some, arduous, full of difficulty, entangled with, deep, perplexing, troublesome, hard, tough, intri-cate, embarrassing.

KNOW, *v.* 1. Comprehend, recognize, realize, perceive, see, notice, have knowledge, understand, have comprehension of, have apprehension of, be cognizant of, be conscious of, be aware, be appre-ciative of, have appreciation for, have awareness, be sensible of, be perceptive of, have perception of, be acquainted with, have acquaintance of, be enlightened about, have information about, per-ceive, be perceptive, apprehend, ken, cognize, dis-cern, get sight of, make out, conceive, savvy *(U.S.),* sabe *(U.S.),* have in mind, possess, keep in mind, wit, wot, weet, ween, trow, have experience of, be conversant with, have knowledge of, be knowing, be cognitive, be understanding, be intelligent, be wise, have wisdom, be hep *(sl.),* be percipient, be apperceptive, be shrewd, be saga-cious, become informed, be informed, be wise to, get wise to *(coll.),* gather information.

2. Be friendly, be acquainted with, be friends with, have the ear of, be intimate with, enjoy intimacy with, enjoy the friendship of, be com-municative with, have dealings with, fraternize, understand, be sympathetic to, sympathize with, be amiable with, be on intimate terms with, be on good terms with, be on a good footing with, be close to, be in one's good graces, be thick with, be a friend of.

3. Know how to, know what's what *(coll.),* know a thing or two *(coll.),* know the time of day *(coll.),* have *savoir-faire (Fr.),* be worldly-wise, be worldly, know which side one's bread is but-tered on, have the knack, have the hang, have a turn for, have a bent for, have an aptitude for, have a capacity for, have a genius for, have talent, have art, have accomplishment in, be experienced in, have sophistication, be sophisticated, have wit, have the wits for, have wisdom, have poise, have skill, have mastery of, show mastery of.

4. Identify, distinguish, make out, perceive, dis-cern, discriminate, recognize differences, per-ceive differences, know which is which, know a hawk from a handsaw *(coll.).*

5. Know the ropes *(coll.),* know well, know full well, have thorough knowledge of, have down pat, have down cold *(both coll.),* have in one's head, have by heart, have at one's fingertips, know by rote, know inside out, know backwards, know backwards and forwards, know down to the ground, know one's stuff *(coll.),* know one's on-ions *(coll.).*

6. Be intelligent, have the capacity for, be knowing, be clever, be sagacious, be perceptive, be informed, be well-informed, be well-read, be deeply-read, be canny, be alert, be awake, be alive, be wide-awake, be bright, be percipient, be apperceptive, be seeing, be sapient, be wise be-yond one's years, be prudent, be well-advised, be in the know, have information, be enlightened, have the dope *(sl.),* have the goods *(sl.),* be in-structed, be conversant with.

7. Be sure, be certain, feel certain, be positive, be absolutely sure, be definite, be unequivocal, be categorical, be decided, be decisive, be deadsure, be sure as death, be sure as death and taxes, be sure as fate, be assured, be convinced, be confident, be ascertained, be settled, rest assured doubt not, have no doubt.

KNOWABLE, *adj.* Ascertainable, discoverable, discernible, perceptible, distinguishable, cognizable, recognizable, cognoscible, comprehensible, understandable, explicable, accountable, conceivable, penetrable, easily understood, easy to understand, clear, clear as day, clear as crystal, lucid, pellucid, perspicuous, transpicuous, transparent, translucent, luminous, plain, distinct, clear-cut, definite, precise, explicit, unequivocal, unambiguous, unconfused, legible, decipherable, readable, intelligible, popularized, exoteric, obvious, evident, apparent, manifest, defined, palpable, patent, ostensible, avowed, acknowledged, express, visible, seeable, observable, noticeable, bare, naked, uncovered, unclouded, unconcealed, unobscure, revealed, disclosed, undisguised, unshaded, uncloaked, unscreened, undraped, unshrouded, uncurtained, unveiled, unmasked, demonstrable, unmistakable.

KNOW-ALL, *n.* Quidnunc, Sir Oracle, know-it-all, humbug, egoist, egotist, pretender, phony *(coll.).*

KNOW-HOW, *n.* Faculty, skill, ability, capability, capableness, capacity, adequacy, competence, what it takes *(sl.),* proficiency, endowment, practical knowledge, knowledge, technical knowledge, professional knowledge, special knowledge, gift, turn, bent, aptitude, knack, art, hang, trick, turn for, genius, skillfulness, expertness, adroitness, dexterousness, dexterity, dextrousness, facility, ingenuity.

KNOWING, *adj.* 1. Solid, deep, profound, abstruse, perceptive, percipient, apperceptive, shrewd, sagacious, wise, highbrow *(sl.),* intelligent, intellectual, cognitive, understanding, comprehending, knowledgeable, astute, sharp, reasonable, rational, bright, sage, sapient, judicious, judicial, discreet, sound, philosophical, prudent, politic, considerate, circumspect, thoughtful, brainy, aware of, cognizant, conscious, acquainted with, privy to, in on the secret, alive to, apprised of, informed of, undeceived, widely read, deeply read, lettered, literary, cultured, cultivated, bookish, scholastic, academic, sensible, cognitive, educated, schooled, instructed, enlightened, taught, erudite, learned, well-posted, posted, well-informed, well-educated, well-grounded, well-versed, self-taught, self-instructed.

2. Shrewd, sharp, acute, mindful, heedful, watchful, keen, argute, cute *(coll.),* alive, canny *(coll.),* astute, quick-witted, nimble-witted, sharp-witted, needle-witted, keen-minded, clear-headed, awake, penetrating, perceptive, piercing.

3. Deliberate, intentional, by design, planned, conscious, willed, witting, on purpose, meant, meaningful, purposeful, intended, cunning.

KNOWINGLY, *adv.* Intentionally, deliberately, advisedly, expressly, determinedly, willfully, determinately, mindfully, meaningfully, wittingly, studiously, pointedly, purposely, on purpose, by design, designedly, with intent, by intent, with one's eyes open, with malice aforethought, with premeditation, in cold blood, ruthlessly, studiedly, calculatedly, by calculation, premeditatedly.

KNOWLEDGE, *n.* 1. Learning, erudition, lore, scholarship, science, letters, literature, book learning, bookishness, general information, information, education, culture, cultivation, attainments, intellectual attainments, accomplishments, intellectual accomplishments, proficiency, higher education, liberal education, light, enlightenment, revelation, intelligence, communication, intercommunication, news, tidings, telling, account, declaration, statement, word, report, mention, specification, notice, notification, intimation, monition, presentment, representation, indirect inference, incidental information, sidelight, instruction, facts, data, lowdown *(sl.),* tip, tipoff, pointer, point *(sl.),* advice, hint, intimation, glimmer, glimmering, divulgement, exposure, exposé, discovery, detection, philosophy, etiology, doctrine, pandect, sophistry, physics, mathematics, epistemology, theory of knowledge, logic, chronometry, evolutionism, ambiogenesis, micrology, enterology, dermatology, malacology, kinetics, ecrinology, astronomy, koniology, oceanography, zoology, biology, botany, acoustics, dynamics, skiagraphy, navigation, aeronautics, actinology, anthropology, Assyriology, bryology, climatology, conchology, criminology, demonology, Egyptology, ethnology, geology, gynecology, histology, horology, ideology, immunology, mineralogy, morphology, neurology, ontology, paleology, pathology, pharmacology, philology, phonology, phrenology, phytology, psychology, semasiology, sociology, theology, admission, avowal, publication, pronouncement, announcement, manifesto, advice, reading, schooling, tuition, lesson, example, bacteriology.

2. Cognition, cognizance, apperception, perception, comprehension, apprehension, recognition, appreciation, judgment, understanding, intention, cryptaesthesia, consciousness, awareness, perceptiveness, impression, discovery, insight, privity, ken, familiarity, acquaintance, experience, savvy *(U.S.),* sabe *(U.S.),* appreciativeness, conscience, abstract knowledge, intellective knowledge, representative knowledge, intuitive knowledge, realization, conception, intuition, intuitiveness, intuitive reason, intuism, omniscience, polymathy, sense, subconscious perception, direct perception, innate knowledge, immediate perception, instinct, second sight, discernment, foreknowledge, forewisdom, precognition, prescience, presentiment, presage, preapprehension, premonition, sciolism, imperfect knowledge, slight knowledge, smattering, half-learning, superficial learning, shallowness.

KNOWN, *adj.* Perceived, apprehended, scanned, cognized, recognized, discerned, seen, understood, fathomed, made out, comprehended, conceived, realized, appreciated, had, well-known, possessed, received, well-kenned, widely known, commonly known, universally recognized, familiar, household, common, commonplace, popular, current, proverbial, notorious, celebrated, famous, noted, general, prevalent, hackneyed, trite, outmoded, out *(coll.),* public, revealed, determined, come to light, disclosed, divulged, unconcealed, unhidden, uncovered, manifest, exposed, confessed, acknowledged, told, imparted, communicated, made known, mentioned, let fall, expressed, announced, apparent, evident, obvious, plain, perspicuous, clear, definite, distinct, patent, ostensible, avowed, expressed, explicit, exoteric, visible, perceptible, perceivable, discernable, seeable, observable, noticeable, self-evident, self-evidencing, open, uncovered, unveiled, unmasked, unclouded, unconcealed, conspicuous, published, aired, vented, blown, propagated, promulgated, circulated, spread, disseminated, broadcast, diffused, noised about, bruited about, noised abroad, made public, publicized, put forward, put forth, issued, got out, told, declared, voiced, spoken of, talked of, talked about, announced, proclaimed, blazoned, reported, heralded.

KNOW-NOTHING, *n.* Ignorant, dunce, duffer, greenhorn, greeny *(coll.)*, greener *(coll.)*, lowbrow, ignoramus, moron, illiterate, clod, clodpoll, clodpate, unintelligentsia, bonehead *(sl.)*, numskull, dumbbell, dumbhead, dummy, dumb-bunny, galoot, gawk, gowk, oaf, lout, loon, lubber, swab, slob *(sl.)*, fool, booby, sap *(sl.)*, chump *(sl.)*, gull, dupe.

KNUCKLE, *v.* Submit, yield, yield to, truckle, defer to, comply, acquiesce, accede, resign oneself, relent, give way, succumb, yield resignedly, be submissive, stoop, bend the neck, bend to, bow to, kowtow, bend to one's yoke, kneel, kneel to, yield obsequiously, cringe, cringe to, bow and scrape, eat humble pie, eat crow, eat dirt, obey, surrender, capitulate, cede, give up, give way, give ground, give in.

KNUCKLE, *n.* 1. Angle, bend, crook, joint, hook, geniculate, projection.

2. Meat, joint, cut of meat, joint of meat, knee joint, hock joint, soup bone, soup meat.

KNUCKLE TO, *v.* 1. Knuckle, yield, yield to, truckle, defer to, comply, acquiesce, accede, resign oneself, relent, give way, succumb, yield resignedly, be submissive, stoop, bend, bend the neck, bend to, bow to, kowtow, bend to one's yoke, kneel to, yield obsequiously, cringe, cringe to, bow and scrape, eat humble pie, eat crow, eat dirt, obey, surrender, capitulate, cede, give up, give way, give ground, give in, kneel.

2. Set to work, fall to work, get busy, fall to, buckle down to, turn to, set to, set about, enter upon, enter on, start in, start to work, launch into, launch upon, pitch in, pitch into, fire away, tackle, get going, put one's shoulder to the wheel, put one's hand to the plow, bend the bow, take the bull by the horns.

KNURL, *n.* Ridge, projection, elevation, prominence.

KNURLED, *adj.* 1. Ridged, corrugated, milled.

2. Bumpy, lumpy, nodose, gnarled, nodiform, nodulous, nodular, nodulated, noduled, nodulate, nodulose, torose, knotty, knobbed, gibbous, gibbose, bulbous, caruncular, carunculous, carunculose, carunculated, caruncule, embossed, bossy, bossed, chased, raised, in relief, *repoussé (Fr.)*, warty, verrucated, verrucate, papulous, papulated, papulate, papillous, papillate, papillar, papillary, papillulate, tuberous, tuberculous, tumorous.

KOBOLD, *n.* Fairy, fairyman, fay, pixy, elf, dwarf, cluricane, brownie, gnome, nisse, peri, hobgoblin, goblin, leprechaun, shee, sidhe, little people, little men, troll, sprite.

KODAK, *n.* *(Trade name)* Photograph, hand camera, photographic apparatus, camera lucida, motion-picture camera, cinematograph, kinematograph, candid camera.

KOSHER, *adj.* Clean, pure, ritually clean, lawful, edible, permitted, allowed, fit, acceptable.

KOUMISS, *n.* Liquor, fermented beverage, fermented liquor, milk-product, alcoholic beverage, drink, libation, potion, potation, liquid, fluid, potable, intoxicant, inebriant, hard liquor, hard drink, strong drink, spirits, ardent spirits, toxicant, alcohol, booze *(coll.)*.

KUDOS, *n.* Fame, glory, repute, reputation, renown, distinctive mark, famousness, celebrity, report, *éclat (Fr.)*, popularity, popular repute, esteem, honor, account, high account, regard, high regard, illustriousness, luster, brilliance, resplendence, resplendency, celebratedness, good repute.

L

LABEL, *n.* Identification, identification tag, sign, superscription, inscription, brand, countermark, stamp, counterstamp, seal, cachet, trademark, copyright mark, hallmark, mark, earmark, ticket, docket, tally, name, designation, specification, impress, sticker, band, fillet, tassel, lappet, infula.

LABEL, *v.* Mark, put a mark on, mark off, note, earmark, tick, tag, dot, spot, score, dash, tally, ticket, docket, name, denominate, call, characterize, describe, define, title, entitle, nickname.

LABILE, *adj.* Changeable, unstable, permutable, alterable, alterative, modifiable, eversible, versatile, variable, checkered, kaleidoscopic, protean, proteiform, transitional, mobile, moveable, plastic, inconstant, changeful, uncertain, unstaid, unsteady, unsteadfast, unreliable, unstable, unfixed, unsettled, vicissitudinous, vicissitudinary, fluctuating, alternating, vacillating, wavering, vibratory, irregular, unregular, fitful, vagrant, wanton, volatile, undependable, fickle, irresponsible, unreliable, fallible, errable, erratic, erring, undemonstrable, untrustworthy, slippery, insecure, unsubstantial, insubstantial, chancy, speculative.

LABIUM, *n.* Lip, fold, ridge, crease, protection, covering.

LABOR, *n.* 1. Labor, work, employment, occupation, job, industry, toil, moil, travail, fatigue, sweat of one's brow, grind, drudgery, slavery, plodding, hammering, hard work, hard labor, manual labor, menial work, struggle, laboriousness, operoseness, operosity, industry, industriousness, exercise, exertion, effort, strain, task, business, pursuit, activity, affair, concern, means of support, livelihood, living, task, job, chore, function.

2. Birth, parturition, genesis, delivery, nativity, childbirth, confinement, childbed, *accouchement (Fr.)*, birth throes, birth pangs, travail.

3. Workers, manpower, employees, employes, laborers, slaves, slave power, toilers, tillers, craftsmen, artisans, operator, servants, plodders, drudges, hacks, proletariat, working classes, laboring classess, skilled labor.

LABOR, *v.* 1. Work, toil, sweat, fag, grind, toil and moil, drudge, grub, plod, slave, pull, ply, ply the oar, ply one's trade, peg, peg away, plug, plug at it *(sl.)*, plug away, work one's fingers to the bone, work like a slave, work like a galley slave, busy oneself with, occupy oneself with, employ one's time, burn the midnight oil, overwork, overdo, work day and night.

2. Feel, be impressed with, be affected by, experience, pass through, undergo, smart under, suffer, bear up under, be the victim of, suffer affliction, pain, ache, hurt, bleed, agonize, writhe, wince, be burdened, be troubled.

3. Bear, give birth, drop, calf, spring, throw,

pup, whelp, cub, kitten, foal, calve, lamb, fawn, spawn, miscarry, travail, be in labor, be in travail.

LABORATORY, *n.* Workroom, workshop, working place, atelier, studio, lab *(coll.),* testing place, proving ground, experimental room.

LABORED, *adj.* Ponderous, forced, mannered, cramped, over-elaborate, stiff, formal, affected, artificial, halting, Gongoresque, Gongoristic, elaborate, difficult, strained, heavy.

LABORER, *n.* Workman, worker, workingman, hand, doer, employee, employe, slave, lackey, hireling, underling, laboring man, day laborer, wage earner, navvy *(Eng.),* workhand, man, workwoman, working woman, working girl, toiler, moiler, drudge, hack, plodder, fag, fagger, hired man, hired hand, wage earner, help *(coll.),* menial, tool, mere tool, roustabout, stevedore, apprentice, craftsman, artisan, handicraftsman, artificer, skilled laborer, journeyman, builder, coolie, peon, fellah, breadwinner, peasantry.

LABORIOUS, *adj.* 1. Industrious, persevering, assiduous, persistent, pertinacious, dogged, constant, steady, steadfast, diligent, hard-working, sedulous, painstaking, plodding, energetic, indefatigable, untiring, never tiring, sleepless, unsleeping, businesslike, unflagging, energetic, tenacious, unflinching, unswerving, relentless, unrelenting, patient, unremitting, unintermitting, undeviating.
2. Wearisome, arduous, toilsome, burdensome, irksome, uphill, heavy, hard, hefty *(coll.),* onerous, fatiguing, tiring, tiresome, wearying, wearisome, wearing, troublesome, strenuous, strained, operose, difficult, thorny, Herculean, risky, critical, nice, hard-fought, hard-earned, oppressive, knotty, spiny, cruel, intricate, exacting.

LABORIOUSLY, *adv.* Strenuously, arduously, operosely, painfully, persistently, diligently, fatiguingly, irksomely, troublesomely, wearyingly, tiresomely, tiringly, wearisomely, with much ado, with might and main, in spite of difficulties, in the teeth of adversity, hammer and tongs, hardly, uphill, upstream, onerously, heftily, mightily, pertinaciously, tenaciously, constantly, steadfastly, steadily, unflaggingly, doggedly, industriously, assiduously, sedulously, sleeplessly, relentlessly, ploddingly, wakefully, patiently, unremittingly, undeviatingly, unintermittingly, unflinchingly, energetically, indefatigably.

LABYRINTH, *n.* 1. Maze, intricacy, puzzle, perplexity, riddle, complication, involution, winding path, conundrum, enigma, mystery, arcanum, poser, wilderness, webwork, meander, jungle, winding course, difficulty, confine, complexity.
2. Inner ear.

LABYRINTHIAN, *adj.* Tortuous, twisted, complex, complicated, mazy, gnarled, tangled, tangly, involved, involute, convolute, raveled, meandering, wandering, baffling, circuitous, circumlocutory, insoluble, unsolvable, confusing, perplexing, ambagious, tortuose, labyrinthine, labyrinthic, labyrinthical, mystifying, confounding, bewildering, labyrinthiform.

LACE, *n.* 1. Fancywork, openwork, network, mesh, netting, braid, braiding, trimming, ornament, fabric, tissue, needlework, embroidery, point-lace, pillow-lace, needle-point, petit point, guipure, tatting, crochet, crocheting, decoration, insertion, Valenciennes, Mechlin (lace), edging, frill, frilling, frillery, cording, binding, web, weave, lacery, lacing, braid, plait, textile, veil, veiling.

2. Binding, cord, gut, thong, fastening, bond, fastener, lashing, tie, leash, string, rope, twine, holdfast.

LACE, *v.* 1. Knot, bend, tie, hitch, sew, attach, tack, fasten, bind, splice, affix, secure, make fast, clinch, make secure, make tight, tighten, make taut, make firm, make fixed, set, make set, make close, close, tether, strap, pinion, truss, girth, string, leash, lash, tie up, braid, wrap.
2. Punish, whip, flog, beat, give a beating, chastise, give a whipping, spank, flagellate, flail, bastinado, horsewhip, lash, stripe, administer the lash, cane, switch, thrash, thresh, scourge.
3. Add, infuse, pour into, mix, mingle, suffuse, instill, fortify, flavor, tincture, entincture, spike *(coll.),* dope *(sl.),* dope up *(sl.),* adulterate, add spirits.

LACERATE, *v.* Mangle, hurt, tear, cut, slice, slash, distress, wound, stab, pain, give pain, deface, scar, mutilate, scratch, blemish, inflict pain, harrow, agonize, torture, torment, crucify, excruciate, convulse, scarify, wring, rend, lancinate, laniate, claw, gash, harry, distress, sever.

LACERATION, *n.* Tearing, tear, rent, cut, scratch, gash, slash, wound, scar, scarring, delaceration, cleft, cleavage, cutting, wounding, scratching, slashing, incision, mutilation, laniation, torture, harrowing, pain, distress, rent, rip, ripping, clawmark, gouge.

LACHES, *n.* Neglect, neglectfulness, negligence, laxity, laxness, carelessness, remissness, disregard, indifference, nonobservance, omission, malfeasance, nonfeasance, inobservance, unobservance, default, slight, oversight, delay, dilatoriness, procrastination, noncompliance, nonperformance.

LACHRYMAL, *adj.* Tearful, weeping, crying, melting, lachrymose, lachrymatory, with tears in the eyes, almost in tears, on the point of tears, with brimming eyes, with overflowing eyes.

LACHRYMATION, *n.* Weeping, crying, sobbing, blubbering, sniveling, yammering, squalling, wailing, shedding tears, dropping tears, whimpering, flood of tears, fit of crying, crying jag *(coll.),* a good cry *(coll.),* tearful eyes, tearful overflow.

LACHRYMOSE, *adj.* Tearful, weeping, crying, melting, lachrymal, lachrymatory, with tears in the eyes, almost in tears, on the point of tears, with brimming eyes, with overflowing eyes, sobbing, blubbering, sniveling, yammering, squalling, wailing, dropping tears.

LACHRYMATORY, *n.* 1. Vase, receptacle, bottle, tear-bottle, vessel.
2. Tear-producer, irritant.

LACING, *n.* 1. Tie, bond, fastening, fastener, knot, hitch, stitch, splice, attachment, tightening, pinion, string, strap, twine, cord, thong, lashing, leash, truss, girth, tether, mooring, braid, ornament, gold lace, silver lace.
2. Chastisement, punishment, beating, flogging, whipping, thrashing, threshing, spanking, scourging, flagellation, flailing, lashing, horsewhipping, caning, switching, birching.
3. Infusion, mixture, admixture, suffusion, instillation, fortification, flavoring, tinge, tincture, tincturing, entincturing, spiking *(coll.),* doping *(sl.).*

LACK, *n.* Requirement, need, want, needfulness, neediness, essential, exigency, urgency, stress, pinch, case of need, case of life or death, privation, deprivation, indigence, poverty, penury, pennilessness, want, hunger, famine, malnutrition, distress, hardships, difficulties, wolf at the door, straits, impecuniosity, impecuniousness, pauperism, insolvency, deficiency, shortage, scarcity, paucity, dearth, wantage, omission, deletion, ullage, defalcation, inanition, starvation, drought, drouth, stint, scantiness, scantness, depletion, exhaustion, vacancy.

LACK, *v.* 1. Fall short, fall short of, come short, come short of, want, be found wanting, not reach the mark, fail to reach the mark, kick the beam, be deficient, be short, be caught short, be inadequate, be wanting, fall down, fall flat, come to nothing, come to naught, flat out *(coll.),* fizzle out, go up in smoke, be insufficient.

2. To be poor, —stricken, —poverty-stricken, —embarrassed, —poorly off, —bad off, —badly off, —hard up, —down and out, —on one's uppers, —reduced, —indigent, —on Queer Street, —needy, —needful, —destitute, —penurious, —pinched, —necessitous, —straitened, —down to rock bottom, —at the end of one's rope, —on the edge, —on the ragged edge, —unable to make both ends meet, —down to bedrock, —impecunious, —impecuniary, —penniless, —broke, —flat broke, —moneyless, —insolvent, —in the gazette, —gazetted, —fortuneless, —unmoneyed, —dowerless, —poor, —short of funds, —out of funds, —out of pocket, —impoverished, —stone-broke, —stony-broke, --pauperized, —beat, —beaten, —ruined, —bankrupt.

3. Want, need, require, find necessary, miss, be on short allowance, feel the want of, stand in need of.

LACKADAISICAL, *adj.* Lazy, indolent, shiftless, do-nothing, fainéant, slothful, remiss, slack, lax, dilatory, maudlin, idle, idlish, laggard, inactive, loafing, languid, supine, lentitudinous, torpid, torpescent, torpedinous, torporific, dronish, indifferent, cold, frigid, cool, icy, lukewarm, sluggish, hebetudinous, phlegmatic, otiose, lymphatic, heavy, dull, dopey *(sl.),* leaden, dead, lethargic, lethargical, apathetic, listless, lifeless, soulless, exanimate, inanimate, inert, neuter, neutral, unconcerned, insouciant, nonchalant, blasé, pococurante, pococurantish, uninterested, easygoing, devil-may-care, mindless, unmindful, dispassionate, unambitious, unaspiring, undesiring, unsolicitous, unattracted, impassive, dilatory, delaying, Micawberish, procrastinating, procrastinative, procrastinatory, cunctatious, cunctative, cunctatory, dillydallying, negligent, neglectful, careless, heedless, unheeding, disregardful, disregardant, regardless, respectless, forgetful, perfunctory, perfunctionary, cursory, imperturbable, passionless, spiritless, heartless, unexcited, unexcitable, insensible, unfeeling, numb, numbed, unemotional, unimpressed, uninspired, untouched, unaffected, unmoved, unruffled, unanimated, unstirred, nonchalant, melancholy, atrabilious, dreamy, soulful, pensive, preoccupied, somnolent, woolgathering, mopish, abstracted, distracted, desponding, despondent, sullen, oscitant, languorous.

LACKADAY, *int.* Alas!, ah me!, wellaway!, alack!, O dear!, alas the day!, heigh-ho!, woe is me!, lackadaisy!, that I had never been born!, *O tempora, o mores! (Lat.),* what a pity!, sad but true!, too true!, welladay!

LACKEY, *n.* Attendant, waiter, servant, servitor, follower, retainer, employee, employe, hireling, mercenary, flunkey, assistant, help, helper, slave, slavey, menial, pensionary, pensioner, boy, *garçon (Fr.),* usher, bearer, office boy, page, footman,

footboy, squire, gillie, ghillis, steward, house steward, bootblack, caddie, bellboy, bellhop, trainbearer, cupbearer, groom, livery, liveried servant, stableboy, butler, major-domo, valet, *valet de chambre (Fr.),* scullion, dishwasher, domestic servant, domestic *(coll.),* household servant, household assistant, kitchenman, ostler, hostler, groomsman, vassal, thrall, helot, factotum, apprentice, hired man, servant of all work, bondman, bondsman, bondslave, underling, inferior, tool, puppet, creature, instrument, dupe, gull, stableman.

LACKING, *adj.* Wanting, needing, absent, not present, minus *(coll.),* away, gone away, gone, omitted, deleted, missing, nowhere to be found, void, null, null and void, unoccupied, devoid, hollow, empty, vacuous, clear, blank, out of sight, uninhabited, untenanted, slight, sketchy, skimpy *(coll.),* in arrears, shy *(coll.),* meager, incomplete, free from, in want of, in default of, dry, short, inadequate, insufficient, deficient, desolate, deprived of, scanty, destitute of, out of, bereft of, out of pocket, denuded of, divested of, imperfect, unfinished, undone, perfunctory, failing, crude, immature, undeveloped, underdeveloped, jejune.

LACKLUSTER, *adj.* Dim, dimmish, pale, ashy, shadowed, dark, darkish, faint, ashen, livid, indistinct, clouded, obscure, nebulous, dusky, dusk, dull, leaden, dun, dun-colored, dingy, tarnished, blurry, blurred, blear, bleary, bleared, glassy, glazed, grimy, sooty, smoky, dirty, fuliginous, muddy, weak, colorless, anemic, lifeless, drab, cold, dead, inanimate, pallid, faint, wan, sallow, lusterless.

LACK-WITTED, *adj.* Lean-witted, unintelligent, unsophisticated, stupid, doltish, foolish, unendowed, unreasoning, senseless, insensate, insensible, witless, lack-brained, lean-minded, short-witted, dumb *(coll.),* unwise, imprudent, thoughtless, ungifted, mindless, cloddish, clodlike, reasonless, brainless.

LACONIC, *adj.* Short, concise, succinct, economical of words, untalkative, unloquacious, ungarrulous, brief, short and sweet, terse, pithy, crisp, trenchant, summary, epigrammatic, epigrammatical, close, compact, condensed, compressed, sententious, elliptic, elliptical, curt, curtate, decurtate, pointed, blunt, to the point, compendious, compendiary, epitomized, pregnant, abridged, taciturn, not loquacious, not talkative, not talky, not garrulous, word-bound, secretive, reticent, reserved, quiet, uncommunicative, close-mouthed, pauciloquent, sparing of words, silent, mum, mute, like a mummy.

LACONISM, *n.* Conciseness, compendiousness, laconicism, succinctness, briefness, brevity, shortness, curtness, curtativeness, terseness, pithiness, neatness, closeness, compactness, sententiousness, condensation, pregnancy, trenchancy, trenchance, trenchantness, crispness, ellipsis, syncope, uncommunicativeness, taciturnity, reticence, shyness, reserve, reservedness, pauciloquency, pauciloquence, silence, muteness, dumbness.

LACQUER, *n.* Resin, pyroxylin, lac, synthetic lac, Chinese lac, Chinese lacquer, shellac, color, coat, coating, finish, varnish, coloring matter, japan, oleoresin, color, hue, tint, tincture, tinct, dye.

LACQUER, *v.* Coat, brush, paint, gloss, shellac, do over, varnish, cover, face, finish, color, japan, resinize, resinate, resinify, protect, apply lacquer, apply lac, apply varnish.

LACTEAL, *adj.* 1. Milky, milk-like, lactean, lacteose, lacteous, lactescent, lactiferous, liquid, fluid, emulsive.

2. Chyliferous.

LACTESCENCE, *n.* Whiteness, whitishness, fluidness, fluidity, chalkiness, chalky-whiteness, milkiness.

LACUNA, *n.* Interstice, space, interval, pit, cavity, air space, interspace, intervening space, gap, hiatus, interruption, follicle.

LACY, *adj.* Transparent, translucent, lace-like, diaphane, diaphanous, perforate, perforated, sheer, thin, gossamer, gossamered, gossamery, filigree, filigreed, woven, braided, twisted, web-like, webby, cobwebby, cobweb-like, crocheted, knitted, tangled, matted.

LAD, *n.* Boy, young man, youth, laddie, youngster, schoolboy, stripling, sprout, cadet, hobbledehoy, master, sonny, slip, sprig, sprout, sonnyboy, pup, puppy, fellow, colt, whelp, cub, feller *(coll.),* whippersnapper *(coll.),* chap, chappie *(coll.),* guy *(coll.),* Jack *(coll.),* scout *(coll.),* comrade, companion, friend, chum *(coll.),* confrere.

LADE, *v.* 1. Load, burden, fill, charge, weight down, wad, pad, stuff, freight, pile, pack, ship, stevedore, place a load on, encumber, stow, bag.

2. Dip, draw, bucket, scoop, shovel, spade, drain, decant, lift out, take out, remove.

LADEN, *adj.* Full, loaded, replete, charged, full to the brim, running over, good, plenary, plump, ample, flush, saturated, full-laden, fraught, freighted, weighted, weighted down, burdened, heavy-laden, brimming, brimful, brimming over, bursting, ready to burst, topfull *(coll.),* chock-full *(coll.),* cram-full *(coll.),* pregnant, full-fraught, burthened.

LADING, *n.* Cargo, load, burden, freight, burthen, haul, haulage, baggage, luggage, mail, bale, cumber, cumbrance, encumbrance, incumbrance, impedimenta, shipload, carload, cartload, deposition, packing, stowing, reposition, shipment, goods, lug *(coll.),* weight, wagonload.

LADLE, *n.* Dipper, spoon, scoop, bail, vessel, utensil, bucket, device, carrier, receptacle.

LADLE, *v.* Lade, bail, bucket, dip, scoop, shovel, spade, pour, fill, convey, transport, carry.

LADRONE, *n.* Rogue, blackguard, robber, thief, cutpurse, footpad, highwayman, marauder, highway robber, holdup man, stealer, larcenist, larcener, picaroon, thug, crook *(coll.),* desperado, bandit, guerrilla, outcast, renegade, escapist.

LADY, *n.* 1. Woman of rank, noblewoman, sultana, queen, princess duchess, countess, marchioness, archduchess, maharani, rani, ranee, senhora *(Port.),* begum *(Moslem),* viscountess, empress, tsarina, czarina, czarevna, aristocrat, peeress, margravine, Shazadi, kumari, kunwari, rajwari, margriesa.

2. Woman of refinement, well-bred woman, *madame (Fr.), mademoiselle (Fr.), Dame (Ger.),* gentlewoman, woman, milady, matron, dame, dowager, mistress, *Senhora (Port.), Señora (Sp.), Signora (It.), señorita (Sp.), signorina (It.),* mistress, khanum, *doña (Sp.), dona (Port.), donna (It.),* memsahib *(Ind.).*

3. Wife, goodwife, goodwoman, spouse, married woman, wife of one's bosom, rib *(coll.),* Adam's rib *(coll.),* helpmate, helpmeet, better half *(coll.),* the little woman, mate, wifey *(coll.).*

LADYLIKE, *adj.* 1. Woman-like, womanly, feminine, effeminate, muliebrous, muliebrile, womanish, womanlike, unmanly, sissy, sissyish, female, gynecic.

2. Well-bred, well-behaved, well-mannered, good-mannered, courteous, polite, considerate, gentle, mild, dignified, stately, courtly, queenly, matronly, gentlewomanly, gentlewomanlike, matronal, matronlike, respectable, estimable, proper, seemly, noble, worthy, highly respectable, civil, human, mannerly, well brought up, well-spoken, gently bred, polished, refined, genteel, cultured, cultivated.

LADYLOVE, *n.* Love, beloved, girl, girl friend, truelove, sweetheart, idol, darling, inamorata, mistress, kept-woman, best girl, favorite, paramour, doxy, concubine, dido, flame *(coll.).*

LAG, *v.* Delay, hang back, fall behind, linger, tarry, loiter, drag, drag behind, procrastinate, move slowly, dally, dillydally, inch one's way, inch along, inch, saunter, stroll, trail, dawdle, take one's time, mosey *(coll.),* poke, falter, halt, limp, totter, stagger, get behind, fall behind, vacillate, temporize, slow down, decelerate, slacken, stay, bide one's time, wait, be late, be tardy, be behind, be overdue, idle, be idle, trudge, drawl.

LAGGARD, *n.* Slowfoot, poke *(coll.),* slowpoke *(coll.),* lingerer, dawdler, dawdle, loiterer, drone, sluggard, stick in the mud *(coll.),* dead one *(sl.),* idler, lounger, dallier, moper, mope, clockwatcher, lubber, do-little, do-nothing, fainéant, indolent, loller, snail, truant, idle fellow.

LAGGER, *n.* 1. Slowfoot, poke *(coll.),* slowpoke *(coll.),* lingerer, dawdler, dawdle, loiterer, drone, sluggard, stick in the mud *(coll.),* dead one *(sl.),* idler, lounger, dallier, moper, mope, clockwatcher, lubber, do-little, do-nothing, fainéant, indolent, loller, snail, truant, idle fellow, procrastinator.

2. Prisoner, convict, con *(sl.),* captive, culprit.

LAGOON, *n.* Channel, lake, pool, pond, sound, inlet, cove, bay, gulf, fjord, fiord, loch, harbor, natural harbor, tarn, pondlet, water lake, millpond, fishpond, bayou, fen, marsh, lough, mere.

LAICAL, *adj.* Lay, congregational, secular, secularist, popular, civil, nonreligious, nonecclesiastical, nonministerial, nonpastoral, temporal, profane, worldly.

LAIR, *n.* Hole, burrow, cave, cell, cavern, dugout, nest, den, kennel, tunnel, covert, retreat, hideout, hideaway, haunt, purlieu, mew, cell, sanctuary, anchorage, house, couch, sty, lie.

LAIRD, *n.* Tenant-in-chief, landholder, lord, lord of the manor, landed proprietor, lord paramount, vavasor, vavasour, planter, peer, nobleman, gentleman, master, landlord, freeholder, landowner.

LAISSEZ FAIRE, *n. and v.* Conservation, conservatism, laisser-aller, laisser-faire, opposition to change, Toryism, laisser-faireism, unconcern, indifference, let pass, let slip, let things take their course, leave well enough alone, live and let live, noninterference, nonintervention let-alone principle, let-alone doctrine, let-alone policy.

LAITY, *n.* Laymen, flock, congregation, fold, assembly, people, parish, society, class, sheep, nonecclesiastics, temporality.

LAKE, *n.* 1. Loch, lough, mere, tarn, basin, reservoir, lagune, lagoon, pond, lakelet, pondlet, pool.

2. Color, red, crimson, dye, pigment, hue, mineral pigment, carmine, tincture, tinct, tint, coloring matter, coloring, stain, carmine lake,

carminette, burnt lake, crimson lake, burnt carmine.

LAMASERY, *n.* Monastery, convent.

LAMB, *n.* 1. Young sheep, lambkin, kid, ewe lamb, weanling, cosset, yearling, yearling lamb.

2. Innocent, unsophisticate, naive, naif, mere child, child, dove, tenderfoot, ingenue, newborn babe, babe unborn, greenhorn, greenie *(coll.)*, meek person.

3. Meat, mutton, spring lamb, *mouton (Fr.)*, saddle of mutton, saddle of lamb, lamb chops, mutton chops, rack of lamb, rack of mutton, lamb fries, lamb cutlet, lamb roast, leg of lamb, leg of mutton, mountain oysters *(coll.)*, baked sheep's head, jimmy.

LAMBASTE, *v.* Strike, whip, hit, beat, bludgeon, cudgel, chastise, punish, thump, thwack, slam, wallop *(coll.)*, baste, clout, belabor, sock *(coll.)*, club, buffet, pummel, batter, bang, thrash, flog, scourge, drub, horsewhip, lash, beat black and blue, bruise, cane, switch, birch, maul, manhandle.

LAMBENT, *adj.* 1. Touching, touching lightly, delicate, gliding, wavering, flickering, licking, tonguing, tangent.

2. Luminous, luminant, bright, radiant, effulgent, fulgent, fulgurant, fulgurous, glowing, shining, lustrous, nitid, nitidous, refulgent, rutile, rutilous, rutilant, coruscant, coruscating, fulgid.

LAMBLIKE, *adj.* 1. Tolerant, unresisting, resigned, long-suffering, meek, mild, patient, tame, gentle, clement, subdued, submissive, chastened, passive, longanimous, content, complacent.

2. Innocent, ingenuous, unworldly, guiltless, free from guilt, blameless, unerring, sinless, childlike, undefiled, naif, naive, dovelike, unbought, unsullied, stainless, spotless, immaculate, uncorrupted, unfallen.

LAME, *adj.* 1. Crippled, halt, maimed, disabled, hamstrung, hobbled, hobbling, limping, spavined, infirm, unsound, game, deformed, faltering, halting, feeble, weak, jejune.

2. Inadequate, incomplete, deficient, insufficient, unconvincing, perfunctory, wanting, failing, short, short of, scarce, meager, paltry, inconsiderable, ineffectual, ineffective, feeble, unsatisfactory, unsatisfying, inconclusive, poor, imperfect, inefficient.

LAMELLA, *n.* Leaf, layer, lamination, sheet, foil, scale, plate, lap, fold, ply, plait, stratum, foliation, stratification, flake, exfoliation, coating, coat, veneer, skin, integument, pellicle, peel, film.

LAMELLAR, *adj.* Filmy, filmlike, stratified, stratiform, scaly, flaky, scabby, scurfy, membranous, membranaceous, foliated, foliate, exfoliate, exfoliated, exfoliaceous, laminated, laminate, laminous, laminose, laminiferous, lamellated, lamelliform, lamellate, lamelliferous.

LAMENT, *v.* 1. Mourn, grieve, wail, keen, sorrow, fret, regret, moan, groan, rend the air, yell, yelp, scream, roar, howl, sigh, inspire, cry, weep, sob, blubber, snivel, whimper, shed tears, burst into tears, cry one's eyes out, pine, ululate.

2. Deplore, bewail, console, regret, commiserate, commiserate with, bemoan, condole with, express pity for, mourn, sympathize with, complain about.

LAMENT, *n.* 1. Lamentation, mourning, plaint, complaint, wail, wail of woe, whimper, sob, moan, cry, outcry, bawl, howl, jeremiad, yell, ululation,

scream, sigh, deep sigh, suspiration, ejaculation, whine.

2. Music, slow music, slow movement, dirge, Lydian mode, Lydian measures, adagio, adagietto, andante, andantino, dead march, funeral march, *marcia funebre (It.)*, threnody, monody, song of lamentation, elegy, requiem, epicedium, funeral music, pibrock, coronach, dead song, death song, song of lament.

LAMENTABLE, *adj.* 1. Distressing, woeful, unhappy, miserable, awful, wretched, sad, grievous, saddening, dismal, grave, horrid, mournful, sorrowful, pitiful, pitiable, depressing, depressive, joyless, uncomfortable, comfortless, dreadful, touching, pathetic, moving, piteous, doleful, melancholy, discouraging, dreary, disheartening, distressful, rueful, affecting.

2. Paltry, poor, shabby, mean, wretched, meager, sorry, pitiful, miserable, vile, scrubby, trashy, weedy, contemptible, beneath contempt.

LAMENTATION, *n.* Lamenting, mourning, lament, plaint, complaint, murmur, mutter, grumble, groan, moan, whine, whimper, sob, wail of woe, ululu, ululation, cry, outcry, scream, howl, bawl, wail, jeremiad, dolorous tirade, weeping, keening, crying, lachrymation, lachrymals, tears, fit of crying, floods of tears, regret, regretfulness, deploring, deploration, rue, ruefulness, repining, condolence, consolation, commiseration, sympathy, repentance, remorse, contrition, compunction, self-reproach, self-accusation, self-condemnation, resipiscence, dirge, threnody, monody, ejaculation.

LAMENTING, *adj.* Mourning, keening, crying, weeping, lachrymose, sorrowing, sorrowful, sad, doleful, wailing, moaning, bemoaning, deploring, complaining, mournful, plaintive, plaintful, ululant, clamorous, crying to high heaven, querulous, querimonious, in mourning, in sackcloth and ashes, tearful, in tears, regretting, regretful, rueful, remorseful.

LAMINA, *n.* Layer, flake, stratum, substratum, stage, coat, coating, peel, peeling, pellicle, skin, integument, course, lamination, lamella, lamellation, level, zone, tier, sheet, foil, scale, plate, veneer, film, membrane, cut, slice, fold, cap, flap, ply, plait, overlay, blade.

LAMINATE, *v.* Form in layers, divide in layers, cut into layers, stratify, delaminate, desquamate, exfoliate, flake, scale, plate, coat, veneer, overlay, superpose, superimpose, lay over, overspread, foliate.

LAMINATED, *adj.* Laminate, laminous, laminose, laminiferous, lamellar, lamellated, lamellate, lamelliform, stratified, stratiform, scaly, flaky, scabby, squamous, squamoid, squamose, squamosal, squamate, squamiferous, micaceous, micacious, membranous, membranaceous, foliate, foliated, foliaceous, leafy, covered, loricate, loricated, lamelliferous, scurfy.

LAMP, *n.* Illuminant, battery lamp, electric lamp, gas lamp, oil lamp, light, glim *(sl.)*, luster, lantern, candle, taper, torch, lamplet, gaslight, flash, flasher, headlight, headlamp, taillight, tail lamp, side light, side lamp, stop light, stop lamp, Carcel lamp, flame lamp, sunlight lamp, sunlamp, heat lamp, moderator lamp, Argand lamp, petane lamp, aphlogistic lamp, glow lamp, bridge lamp, floor lamp, ceiling lamp, ceiling light, ceiling fixture, chandelier, wall light, wall lamp, wall fixture, miner's lamp, safety lamp, carbide lamp, carbide lantern, night lamp, night light, bull's-eye lantern, dark lantern, policeman's lantern, lanthorn (arch.), barn lantern, railroad lantern, electrolier, magic lantern, Chinese lantern, Japanese lantern, electric lantern, incandescent lamp, incandescent bulb, glow lamp, carbon lamp, carbon-arc lamp, flaming arc-lamp, electric arc lamp, mercury-arc lamp, mercury-vapor lamp, mercury lamp, neon lamp, neon tube, magnetite-arc lamp, open-arc lamp, closed-arc lamp, spotlight, spot, klieg light, sun spot, sun arc, floodlight, floodlamp, footlight, searchlight, searchlight lantern, bougie, beacon, landmark light, airport light, airway light, code light, radio marker, radi-range beacon light, navigation light, position light, course light, boundary light, obstruction light, anchor light, fixed light, blinker light, flambeau, brand, gasolier.

LAMPOON, *n.* Personal satire, burlesque, satire, skit, pasquil, pasquinade, squib, derision, ridicule, libel, raillery, mockery, parody, travesty, caricature, macaronic, macaronic composition, farce, comedy, tirade, denunciation, diatribe, invective, insinuation, defamation, reflection.

LAMPOON, *v.* Satirize, attack, ridicule, lambaste, abuse, defame, degrade, bring down, take down a peg, libel, detract, discredit, disparage, asperse, cast aspersions on, traduce, belittle, denigrate, slur, cast a slur upon, calumniate, speak ill of, expose, expose to infamy, debase, throw dirt at, fling dirt at, sling mud (coll.), vilify, bring low, blacken, censure, scandalize, revile, dishonor, throw in the mud, drag through the mud, bespatter, besmirch, backbite, malign, sneer, reproach, belabor, drub, chasten.

LANATE, LANATED, *adj.* Nappy, shaggy, velutinous, downy, pily, fluffy, woolly, wooly, flocculent, floccose, lanuginous, lanuginose, villose, villous, velvety.

LANCE, *n.* 1. Spear, pike, sponton, javelin, assegai, jereed, jerrid, dart, shaft, bolt, reed, harpoon, gaff, eelspear, weetweet, womera, throwing stick, throw stick, lancegay.
2. Perforator, lancet, knife, scalpel, surgical knife.

LANCE, *v.* 1. Throw, fling, cast, hurl, pitch, toss, shy, put forth, chuck, heave, let fly, launch, dart, tilt, jaculate, fling.
2. Stick, prick, cut, incise, drain, irrigate, open, slit, perforate, puncture, penetrate, spear, stab, lay open, cut open, cut with a lancet.

LANCE-SHAPED, *adj.* Spear-shaped, spearlike, hastate, hastiform, lanceolate, lanceolated, lanciform, lance-like.

LANCINATE, *v.* 1. Tear, rend, sever, cut, slash, incise, sunder, pierce, prick, stick, cleave, rive, slit, puncture, penetrate, stab, slice, carve, circumcise, abscise, discerpt, dirempt, lacerate, mangle, tear, claw.
2. Pain, cause pain, give pain, bring pain, inflict pain, hurt, wound, scathe, afflict, distress, scath, cut up (coll.), cut to the heart (coll.), lacerate, dilacerate.

LANCINATION, *n.* 1. Sunderance, sundrance, disseverance, severance, severing, discerption, diremption, scission, cleavage, abscission, rescission, disjunction, laceration, dilaceration, circumcision, tearing, rending, cutting, incision, piercing, pricking, sticking, cleaving, slitting, slit, puncturing, puncture, penetration, stabbing, stabwound, slice, slicing, carving, mangling, tearing, clawing.
2. Torment, affliction, pain, torture, anguish,

suffering, dolor, discomfort, distress, agony, anguish, rack, cruciation, crucifixion, martyrdom, affliction, infliction, visitation, passion, vivisection.

LAND, *n.* 1. Zone, territory, area, ground, soil, section, district, terrain, country, nation, quarter, part, department, compartment, division, purlieus, vicinity, vicinage, neighborhood, sphere, hemisphere, realm, demesne, domain, dominion, circuit, compass, orb, orbit, ambit, circle, range, province, precinct, confines, field, pale, location.
2. Country, nation, state, republic, commonwealth, realm, dominion, polity, domain, body politic, empire, empery, principality, archduchy, duchy, palatinate, chiefdom, chieftainry, kingdom, protectorate, colony, settlement, toparchy, power, monarchy, democracy, fatherland, motherland, homeland, *Vaterland (Ger.),* native soil, native land, God's country, God's own country, the old country.
3. Ground, dry land, terra firma, continent, subcontinent, mainland, main, midland, inlands, interior, shore, coast, strand, beach, waterside, foreshore, bank, embankment, seashore, seacoast, littoral, seaside, seaboard, sea beach, sea bank, sea margin, coastland, coastal region, scar, loom of the land, derelict, innings, reclamation, reclaimed land, made land, alluvium, alluvion, height, rise, rising ground, mount, mountain, alp, hill, knap, kopje, down, moor, brae, kop, fell, hillock, hump, knoll, mound, barrow, kame, spine, ridge, dune, sand dune, chime, comb, esker, horseback, hogback, plateau, table, tableland, table mountain, butte, promontory, mull, point, crag, ledge, shelf, pinnacle, pike, crest, tor, range, mountain range, chain, watershed, divide, continental divide, heights, uplands, highlands, precipice, cliff, steep, bluff, wall, scarp, scar, escarpment, inland, palisade, palisades, incline, slope, rise, grade, climb, rising ground, declivity, downward slope, descent, dip, drop, downgrade, decline, glacis, hillside, side, shelf, talus, point, point of land, foreland, headland, head, naze, ness, peak, cape, tongue, bill, spur, neck, neck of land, reef, coral reef, breakwater, mole, jetty, jutty, peninsula, chersonese, delta, isthmus, prairie, plains, pampas, flat, flats, flatland, level, level land, open country, wide open spaces, champaign, champaign country, reach, stretch, expanse, lone prairie, steppe, savanna, tundra, vega, campo, sebkha, common, wold, weald, veld, veldt, moor, moorland, down, downs, heath, basin, saltpan, saltmarsh, alkali plain, desert, barren, barrens, waste, wastes, wild, wilds, wilderness, brush, bush, canebrake, marsh, marshland, swamp, swampland, fen, fenland, bog, peat bog, quagmire, mire, slough, dump (U.S.), wash, baygall, jhebl, vlei, bottom, bottoms, bottomland, holm, island, islet, isle, eyot, ayot, ait, calf, bar, key, quay, reef, cay, archipelago, Sahara, karroo, defile, pass, passage, valley, vale, jungle, dell, dingle, coomb, scad, strath, gill, glade, glen, grove, gorge, ravine, gap, notch, cut, close, canyon, gulch, clough, chasm, abyss, abysm, gulf, crevasse, wood, woods, woodland, timberland, timber, forest, forestland, tropical forest, rain forest, virgin forest, copse, coppice, copsewood, hurst, spinney, clump of trees, thicket, covert, boscage, bosk, bosket, brake, motte, chamisal, chaparral, hanger, orchard, bosch.
4. Realty, real property, property, real estate, chattels real, tenement, landed property, lands, grounds, acres, ground, hereditaments, heritage, corporeal hereditaments, incorporeal hereditaments, acquest, messuage, toft, hacienda, manor,

mesestead, homestead, domain, demesne, zamindari, plant, fixtures, farm, plantation, farmstead, grange, ranch, range, rancho, rancheria, location, mains, pen, demesne farm, barton, homecroft, free land, freehold, alod, alodium, frankalmoign, tenure in the alms, tenure by alms, mortmain, dead hand.

5. Canton, country, county, shire, province, precinct, ward, *arrondissement (Fr.)*, *mufussil (Ind.)*, parish, diocese, township, commune, wapentake, hundred, riding, lathe, tithing, bailiwick, acreage, acres, field, fields, tract, plat, plot, patch, piece of land, parcel of land, cultivated land, croft, lot, cleared land, wheatfield, cornfield, grassland, grass, meadow, mead, pasture, pastureland, pasturage, lea, park, *maidan (Ind.)*, grassplot, grassplat, green, greenyard, lawn, campus, common, village green, putting green.

6. Soil, earth, loam, clay, marl, shale, ground, terrain, mold, mould, subsoil, clod, clot, glebe, cledge, residual clay, sedimentary clay, boulder clay, fill, indurated clay, metal, clunch, shale, cloam, chalk, shell marl, greensand marl, loamy soil, gumbo, gumbo soil, humus, leaf mold.

LAND, *v.* 1. Alight, land, set her down *(coll.)*, light, descend, come down, fly down, level off, come in for a landing, flatten out, up-wind, downwind, overshoot, undershoot, pancake, pancake a landing, make a dead-stick landing, settle down, balloon in, nose up, nose over, make a three-point landing.

2. Arrive, come to land, anchor, tie up, put into port, put into the harbor, set foot on dry land, reach land, make land, close with the land, run in with the land, put in shore, go ashore, debark, disembark, unboat, unship, cast anchor, drop anchor, anchor, come to anchor, lay anchor, let go the anchor, carry out the anchor, moor, run out a warp, run out a rope, lash, tie.

3. Catch, capture, collar, grasp, snatch, grab, snag, lay by the heels, lay hold of, catch hold of, lead one to, get, take, secure, gain, sell, bag, net, snare, take prisoner, pocket, seize, fasten upon, grip, grapple, grasp, clutch, clasp, clinch, nab *(coll.)*, induce, persuade, sell one on, bring round, prevail upon, win over, overcome, move, move one to, influence.

LANDING, *n.* 1. Platform, floor, estrade, stage, dais, landing stage, landing place.

2. Arrival, landing run, ballooning in, parachute approach, blind landing, instrument landing, glide landing, stall landing, crash landing, deadstick landing, fishtail landing, sideslip landing, emergency landing, level landing, two-point landing, three-point landing, normal landing, nose over, pancake landing, landing field, airport, airport runway, runway, aerodrome, airdrome, airline terminal.

3. Disembarkment, disembarkation, debarkation, arrival, coming, advent, homecoming, coming home, reëntry, reëntrance, alighting, docking, tying up, return.

4. Anchorage, haven, harbor, seaport, port, moorings, roadstead, roads, bund, bunder, dock, basin, landing place, pier, wharf, waterfront, jetty, jutty, quay, key, embankment.

LANDLADY, *n.* 1. Owner, landowner, lessor, proprietress, proprietrix, improprietrix, mistress, landholder, freeholder, householder, possessor, holder, occupant, occupier, renter.

2. Hostess, innkeeper, innholder, hotelkeeper.

LANDLORD, *n.* 1. Proprietor, proprietary, owner, master, lord, laird, landholder, landowner, freeholder, *zamindar (Ind.)*, laird of the manor, lord paramount, vavasour, mesne lord, mesne, planter, plantation owner, householder, possessor, holder, lessor, occupant, occupier, renter, vavasor.

2. Host, mine host, innholder, innkeeper, publican, pub-owner, restaurateur, hôtelier, Amphitryon, boniface.

LANDMARK, *n.* Boundary, bounds, line of demarcation, boundary line, turning point, milestone, Rubicon, seamark, cairn, menhir, milepost, line of circumvallation, guide, guidepost, familiar object, catstone, event, happening, occurrence, incident.

LANDSCAPE, *n.* View, scene, spectacle, sight, perspective, outlook, prospect, vista, lookout, scenic view, scape, delineation, picture, painting, tableau, panorama, scenograph, exterior, rural scene, representation, scenic representation, aspect, *paysage (Fr.)*, scenery, riverscape, seascape, waterscape, cityscape, townscape, airscape, skyscape, cloudscape.

LANE, *n.* Alley, passage, footpaths, thoroughfare, way, passageway, cut, course, road, roadway, pass, alleyway, approach, aisle, access, line of way, track, trail, run, route, footpath, bypath, byway, channel.

LANGUAGE, *n.* 1. Speech, vocabulary, tongue, idiom, *lingua (Lat.)*, patter, locution, lingo *(coll.)*, parole, prattle, colloquialism, colloquial expression, patois, jargon, slang, slangism, provincialism, palaver, gaff *(sl.)*, guff *(sl.)*, lip *(sl.)*, chin music *(sl.)*, vulgate, vulgar tongue, cant, argot, billingsgate, back slang, rhyming slang, pig latin, barbarism, gibber, gibberish, jabber, dialect, localism, isogloss, accent, brogue, twang, Anglicism, Briticism, Gallicism, Scottism, Americanism, Hibernicism, Irishism, cockney, cockneyese, vernacular, native tongue, mother tongue.

2. Specific Languages: Austroasiatic, Austronesian, Bantu, Dravidian, Dravido-Munda, Hamitic, Indian, American Indian, Indochinese, Sino-Tibetan, Tibeto-Burman, Tibeto-Chinese, Indo-European, Indo-Germanic, Aryan, Ural-Altaic, Finno-Tatar, Ugro-Altaic, Turanian, Ugrian, Ugro-Finnic, Finno-Ugric, Finnic, Uralian, Semitic.

Achinese, Afghan, Aka, Albanian, Algonquin, Amharic, Annamese, Arabic, Aramaic, Araucan, Assamese, Armenian, Austral, Avestan, Aymara, Balinese, Baluchi, Bashkir, Batan, Battak, Bengali, Bihari, Bikol, Brahui, Breton, Bugi, Bulgarian, Buriat, Burmese, Caroline, Castilian, Catalan, Cham, Chamoro, Cheremiss, Chibcha, Chin, Chinese, Chuvash, Coman, Coptic, Czechoslovak, Dafla, Danish, Dutch, Dyak, Egyptian, English, Eskimo, Estonian, Ethiopian, Fiji, Finnish, Flemish, Formosan, French, Frisian, Gadaba, Gaelic, Galcha, Garo, German, Gilbertese, Gold, Gondi, Greek, Gujarati, Gypsy, Hawaiian, Hebrew, Hindustani, Ho, Ibanag, Icelandic, Igorot, Ilokano, Irish, Italian, Jagatai, Jakun, Japanese, Javanese, Juang, Kabyle, Kachin, Kafiri, Kalmuck, Kamasin, Kanarese, Kara-Kalpak, Karen, Kashmiri, Kasubian, Kavi, Kazan-Tatar, Kharia, Khasi, Khmer, Khond, Khovar, Kiranti, Kirghiz, Kodagu, Kohistani, Koibal, Kongoese, Korwa, Kuki, Kumyk, Kurdish, Kurukh, Lahnda, Lampong, Land, Languedoc, Lapp, Latin, Lettish, Limbu, Lithuanian, Livonian, Low German, Madurese, Magyar, Makassar, Malagasy, Malay, Malayalam, Maltese, Malto, Manchu, Mangar, Manobo, Manx, Maori, Marathi,

Marquesan, Marshall, Maya, Meithi, Mishmi Mon, Mongolian, Montes, Mordvinian, Moro, Mru, Muong, Murmi, Muskogee, Naga, Newari, Niasese, Nicobarese, Niue, Nogai, Norwegian, Oraon, Oriya, Osmanli, Ossetic, Ostyak, Pahari, Palau, Palaung, Pali, Pampango, Pangasinan, Panjabi, Permian, Persian, Phrygian, Plattdeutsch, Polish, Portuguese, Prakrit, Provençal, Quechuan, Rajasthani, Rejang, Rhaeto-Romanic, Romany, Ronga, Rumanian, Russian, Sakai, Samoan, Sanskrit, Santali, Sassak, Savara, Selung, Semang, Serbo-Croatian, Shan, Shilha, Shina, Siamese, Sindhi, Singhalese, Slovenian, Sorbian, Soyot, Spanish, Sudanese, Swahili, Swedish, Syriac, Syryenian, Tagalog, Tahitian, Tamashek, Tamil, Tavghi, Teluet, Telugu, Tibetan, Tigré, Tigriña, Tino, Tupura, Toda, Tongan, Tuamotuan, Tulu, Tungus, Tupi, Turkoman, Uigur, Ukrainian, Uzbek, Veps, Visayan, Vote, Wa, Welsh, Yenisei, Yurak, Zenaga, Zula-Kaffir.

Universal language, international language, world language, auxiliary language, interlingua, pasilaly, lingua franca, Esperanto, Volapuk, Ido, lingua internaciona, Antido, Lingvo Kosmopolita, Latinesce, Esperantido, Nov-Esperanto, Nov-Latin, Monario, Novial, Arulo, Europan, Optez, Occidental, Latino, Latino sine flexione, Idiom Neutral; pidgin English, pidgin Malay.

3. Power of speech, faculty of speech, utterance, discourse, verbal intercourse, spoken language, elocution, oral communication, word of mouth, words, accents, cant.

4. Wording, vocabulary, phrasing, phraseology, verbiage, speech, talk, dialect, parlance, expression, locution, grammar, rhetoric, style, manner, mode, strain, vein, manner of speaking, manner of writing, mode of expression, style of expression, idiologism, use of words, idiom, diction, accent.

5. Cursing, profanity, swearing, execration, vilification, malediction, imprecation, reviling, profane swearing, profane talk, evil-speaking, invective, ribaldry, billingsgate, cussing (coll.), name calling.

LANGUID, adj. 1. Sickly, valetudinary, faint, infirm, valetudinarian, shaky, rickety, unstable, feeble, tottery, doddering, totterish, unsound, frail, delicate, unhealthy, on the decline, drooping, flagging, weak, watery, declining, wishy-washy (coll.), poor, poorly (coll.), exhausted, spent, wan, pale, pallid, trembling, debilitated, worn-out, fatigued.

2. Lentitudinous, supine, sluggish, listless, lifeless, inanimate, lethargic, spent, spiritless, phlegmatic, lymphatic, otiose, heavy, dull, lethargical, inert, torpid, exanimate, torpescent, torporific, dronish, slow, weary, wearied, leisurely, bored, blasé (Fr.), spiritless, world-weary, uninterested, indifferent, insensitive, unfeeling, unemotional, sleepy, somnolent, somnolescent, lackadaisical, lukewarm, cold, cool, inactive, pensive, indolent, vapid, dispassionate, frigid, passionless, unconcerned, indifferent, uninterested, insouciant, careless, comatose, blind, imperturbable, incurious, hebetudinous, leaden.

LANGUIDNESS, n. 1. Inertness, weakness, weakliness, feebleness, decrepitude, asthenia, adynamia, lassitude, strengthlessness, infirmity, debility, debilitation, infirmness, frailty, frailness, faintness, atony.

2. Inertness, dullness, torpidity, torpor, stupor, sluggishness, apathy, stolidity, languor, lethargy, inertia, inactivity, inaction, supineness, lassitude, kef, phlegm, hebetude, hebetation, lentitude, tor-

pescence, torpidness, statuvolence, statuvolism, somnolence, somnolescence, leisureliness.

LANGUISH, v. 1. Flag, droop, decline, go into decline, give way, faint, fail, drop, break down, despair, decrease, wane, ebb, bate, abate, waste away, diminish, sicken, sink, wither, decrease, let up, dwindle, die away, fall off, drop off, erode, waste, fizzle (coll.), take sick, become ill, die, decay, wilt, fizzle out.

2. Desire, be desirous of, covet, yearn for, pine for, hunger, hunger for, hunger after, thirst, thirst for, thirst after, run madly after, raven for, long for, pine for, sigh for, gape for, gasp for, pant for, die for, have a yen for (coll.).

3. Pine, grieve, mourn, pine for, repine, lament, sorrow, despond, lose heart, droop, sink, brood over, brood, fret, fuss (coll.), take on (coll.), mope, ache, hurt, bemoan, bewail.

LANGUISHING, adj. Frail, slight, sluggish, debilitated, inanimate, lifeless, torpid, weak, weakly, sick, sickly, declining, drooping, fading, failing, delicate, dull, slack, stagnant, leaden, torpescent, logy, flat, lingering, apathetic, leisurely, dilatory, indolent, supine, otiose, lentitudinous, lymphatic, phlegmatic, torporific, heavy, hebetudinous, lumpish, listless, dronish, drony, soulless, inanimate, exanimate, inert, drooping, pining, lovesick, amatory.

LANK, adj. Lanky, slim, skinny (coll.), gaunt, meager, spare, tall, gawky, gaunted, weedy (coll.), spindling, spindly, scraggy, rawboned, bony, skeletal, gangling, gangly, spindle-shanked, attenuated, attenuate, starved, starving, slender, shriveled, emaciated, poor, marcid, angular, bony, awkward, uncouth, ungraceful, ungainly.

LANOSE, adj. Lanate, wooly, nappy, lanuginous, velvety, velutinous, shaggy, downy, pily, floccose, flocculent, lanuginose, villose, villous, woolly.

LANTERN, n. Lanthorn, barn lantern, searchlight lantern, railroad lantern, jack-o'-lantern, Japanese lantern, Chinese lantern, magic lantern, dark lantern, bull's-eye lantern, lamp, light (coll.), covered lamp.

LANYARD, n. Cord, rope, string, tie, bond, binding, thong, strap, line, lace.

LAP, v. 1. Wrap, clothe, sheathe, cover, enwrap, enfold, fold, case, encase, envelop, garb, dress, array, enclothe, attire, circumvest, swathe.

2. Drink, tongue, drink in, drink up, quaff, sip, imbibe, swig (coll.), swill (coll.), suck, guzzle, tipple, nip, soak, sot, crack a bottle, slake one's thirst, refresh the inner man, drown one's sorrows, drown one's troubles, lick.

3. Contact, touch, adjoin, border, come into contact with, meet, overlap, hit, neighbor, impinge, laminate.

4. Dribble, trickle, plash, murmur, babble, splash, drip, drop, spurtle, percolate, bubble, ripple, gurgle, guggle, purl, trill, slosh, swash, wash, lick.

LAPIDARY, n. Jeweller, jeweler, glyptologist, glyptographer, engraver, lapidist, lapicide, stonecutter, carver, etcher, stoneworker, gemologist, inscriber, glyptician.

LAPIDATE, v. Stone, throw rocks at, throw stones at, pelt, hurl, hurl at, hurl against, brickbat (coll.).

LAPIDIFICATION, n. Petrification, petrifaction, fossilization, lapidescence, hardening, petrescence, petrescency, lapidity, fossilification, fossilation, lithification.

LAPPET, *n.* Bib, apron, flap, fold, tab, tag, lug, lapel, fly, tuck, lap, band, lobe, streamer, pendant, skirt.

LAPSE, *n.* 1. Course of time, process of time, interval, sweep of time, interim, respite, interruption, break, intermission, pendency, interregnum, pause, stay, drop, lull, hesitation, caesura, interlude, recess, remission, hiatus, hitch.

2. Decline, subsidence, descent, catabasis *(Med.)*, slump, wane, ebb, expiration, expiry, termination, end, downfall, sinkage, drop, ebb tide, neap tide, reflux, devolution, deviation, default, falling off, declension.

3. Error, flaw, slip, fault, peccadillo, slight mistake, negligence, misadventure, inadvertence, fall, fall from grace, backslide, recidivation, recidivism, forfeiture, loss, failing, delinquency, shortcoming, offense, transgression, sin, dereliction, secession, recreancy, miscreancy, miscarriage, apostasy, relapse, reversion, declension, perversion, retrogression, regression, regress, retreat, reflux, devolution, retrogradation, degeneration, degeneracy, depravation, depravement, depravedness, defection, desertion, infidelity, improbity, unreliability, faithlessness, inconstancy, falsity, disloyalty, breach of faith, decadence, deterioration, misdeed, misdoing, crime, wrongdoing, malfeasance, misfeasance, nonfeasance, sin, misdemeanor, wrong, evil, peccancy, violation, trespass, infringement, infraction, breach, dereliction, failure, slip, laxity, laxness, laches, *gaucherie (Fr.)*.

LAPSE, *v.* 1. Fail, slip, deteriorate, backslide, secede, fall, decline, grow worse, worsen, fall off, retrograde, retrogress, degenerate, wane, ebb, droop, sink, go down, go downhill, collapse, go to waste, go to seed, fall into disuse, go to pot *(coll.)*, wither, recidive, recidivate, fall from grace, misbehave, misstep, misdo, sin, commit sin, transgress, offend, do wrong, err, trespass, misdemean, stray, apostatize, tergiversate, go over, be found wanting, lack, kick the beam *(coll.)*, turn cloak, desert, forsake.

2. Slip by, slip away, pass by, run out, expire, run its course, elapse, proceed, flow, advance, roll on, press on, end, terminate, glide, go.

3. Go down, decline, come down, fall, drop, slump, sag, droop, sink, fall down, slump down, decelerate, slow down, pause, hesitate, stop, falter, fail.

LAPSED, *adj.* Past, gone, bypast, bygone, elapsed, expired, gone by, ago, agone *(arch.)*, over, passed, passed away, late, no more, extinct, run out, never to return, irrecoverable, exploded, forgotten, obsolete, antiquated, superannuated, old, former, outdated, out of date, old-fashioned, old-style, *passé (Fr.)*, disused, stale, old-hat *(coll.)*.

LARCENY, *n.* Theft, thievery, stealing, robbery, burglary, swindling, cheating, fleecing, bilking, fraud, forgery, extortion, highway robbery, direption, rapacity, plagiarism, plunder, rapine, sack, sacking, looting, embezzlement, embezzling, absconding, thievishness, depredation, appropriation, misappropriation, peculation, pilfer, pilfering, hijacking, housebreaking, kleptomania, purloining, shoplifting, cattle theft, cattle stealing, cattle rustling *(coll.)*, stealage, second-story work, safecracking, safebreaking, bank robbery, highway robbery, holdup, stickup *(sl.)*, petit larceny, grand larceny, petty larceny, pilferage, pocketpicking.

LARD, *v.* Dress, dress with grease, dress with bacon, dress with tallow, oil, grease, smear, daub, lubricate, baste.

LARDER, *n.* Room, store room, storage room, chamber, pantry, scullery, buttery, spence, food room, cooler, refrigerator room, stillroom, supply room.

LARDY, *adj.* Fat, fatty, sebaceous, oleaginous, oleic, oily, greasy, adipose, lardaceous, lardiform.

LARGE, *adj.* Big, great, bulky, spacious, comprehensive, massive, sizeable, substantial, considerable, immense, enormous, gigantic, elephantine, hippopotamic, ample, voluminous, mighty, towering, capacious, fine, magnificent, huge, enormous, gigantean, titanic, vast, vasty, monster, monstrous, megatherian, grand, colossal, hulky, cumbrous, cumbersome, lubberly, Gargantuan, Brobdingnagian, Cyclopean, mammoth, ponderous, lumpish, goodly, massive, massy, strapping, rotund, heavy, portly, fat, obese, corpulent, plump, chubby, brawny, fleshy, burly, imposing, intense, strong, sound, plenary, deep, high, lusty, stalwart, monumental, stupendous, giantlike, jumbo *(coll.)*, prodigious, whopping, whacking, thumping, bumping, thundering, banging; spacious, roomy, extensive, inclusive, expansive, ample, wide, widespread, far-reaching, far-flung, unlimited, unbounded, boundless, infinite, limitless, illimitable, immeasurable, measureless, liberal, copious, unstinted, gross, wholesale, sweeping, prevalent, world-wide, far spreading, far-flying, unending, broad, wide, astonishing, appalling, terrific, horrible, inordinate, excessive, outsized, overgrown, hypertrophied, overwrought, overdone, monstrous, exorbitant, outrageous, extravagant, preposterous, puffy, largish, king-sized *(coll.)*, magnificent, tumid, swollen, potbellied, bloated.

LARGE-HEARTED, *adj.* Kind, forbearant, forbearing, patient, understanding, easygoing, benign, benignant, good, amiable, indulgent, lenient, considerate, thoughtful, generous, warmhearted, charitable, tender-hearted, big-hearted, soft-hearted, kindly, cordial, accommodating, tender, mild, warm, compassionate, pitying, merciful, good-humored, good-natured, sympathizing, sympathetic, kindly-meaning, well-meaning, well-intentioned, well-intended, well-affected, well-disposed, kindly-disposed, chivalrous, chivalric, courteous, polite, devoted, fraternal, maternal, paternal, brotherly, sisterly, motherly, fatherly, friendly, friendlike, amicable, neighborly, gentle, courtly, gallant, good-mannered, well-mannered, mannerly, civil, unhostile, bounteous, generous, helpful, obliging, conciliatory, winsome, clement, ruthful, humane, philanthropic, humanitarian, soft, unhardened, temperate, touched, moved, complaisant, fond, affectionate.

LARGENESS, *n.* Greatness, vastness, great size, bigness, tallness, extensiveness, fullness, immensity, giganticness, enormity, might, strength, intensity, magnitude, dimensions, proportions, area, expanse, expansiveness, spread, range, scope, extent, measurements, sizeableness, bulk, bulkiness, comprehensiveness, substantialness, volume, voluminousness, ampleness, amplitude, capaciousness, massiveness, mightiness, magnificence, hugeness, stupendousness, hypertrophy, monstrousness, cumbersomeness, clumsiness, awkwardness, puffiness, obesity, corpulence, fat, fatness, girth, weightiness, adiposity, cumbrousness, swollenness, fattiness, plumpness, chubbiness, burliness, huskiness, brawn, brawniness, fleshiness, strength, soundness, heaviness, plenariness, height, width, length, depth, highness, rotundity, lustiness, copiousness, roominess, spaciousness, wideness, infinity, infiniteness, boundlessness, limitlessness, immeasurability, endlessness.

LARGESS, *n.* Gift, donation, benefaction, generosity, kindness, gratuity, grant, offering, bounty, bestowal, sportula, tip, fee, baksheesh, dash *(Africa), douceur (Fr.),* lagniappe *(Louisiana),* dole, favor, act of mercy, act of charity, act of generosity, act of kindness, help, assistance, benevolence, amiability, benignity, philanthropy, remuneration, payment, solatium, honorarium, extra pay, reward.

LARIAT, *n.* Lasso, rope, thong, *riata (Sp.), reata (Sp.),* lass rope, throw rope, ketch rope *(coll.),* lazo *(coll.).*

LARK, *n.* 1. Bird, songbird, meadowlark, skylark, titlark, songster, warbler, feathered songster.

2. Frolic, gambol, trick, sportiveness, revel, revelry, frisk, spree, bout, bust, tear, bender, hellbender, toot, bat, bun, carouse, carousal, prank, mischief, antic, caper, caprice, game, tease, escapade, high old time *(coll.),* fling.

LARRIKIN, *n.* Rowdy, street arab, street urchin, ruffian, hoodlum, hood *(sl.),* bully, bravo, hooligan, apache, gorilla, desperado, Mohock, street loafer, idler, loiterer, loafer, tough, vagrant, thug, plug-ugly.

LARVA, *n.* Chrysalis, cocoon, nymph, caterpillar, maggot, grub, aurelia, worm, apple worm, fruit worm.

LASCIVIOUS, *adj.* Incontinent, immoral, lewd, lustful, dirty-minded, sensual, wanton, impure, unclean, obscene, smutty, indelicate, unchaste, ribald, filthy, gross, vulgar, coarse, licentious, dissolute, depraved, Fescennine, shameless, indecent, lubricious, improper, libidinous, lecherous, concupiscent, salacious, Paphian, unclean, foul, dirty, fetid, sordid, feculent, polluted, nasty, unwholesome, defiled, voluptuous, satyrical, erotic, lubricous, animalistic, beastlike, beastly, brutish, swinish, bestial, theroid, goatish, lickerish, prurient, bawdy, unblushing, pornographic, rakish, profligate, aphrodisiacal, loose, nymphomaniacal, incestuous, masochistic, sadistic, sexy, sex-ridden, lurid, carnal, fornicative, coprophilic.

LASCIVIOUSNESS, *n.* Carnality, impurity, wantonness, grossness, indelicacy, impropriety, impudicity, immodesty, shamelessness, vulgarity, scurrility, Fescenninity, bawdiness, bawdry, pornography, coprophilia, unchastity, vileness, offensiveness, incontinence, adulterousness, dissipation, dissoluteness, venery, dissolution, wildness, wenching, fornication, debauchery, uncleanness, salaciousness, foulness, filthiness, nastiness, sensuality, lewdness, animality, animalism, voluptuousness, lustfulness, prurience, incestuousness, sexual desire, lechery, lecherousness, erotism, eroticism, satyriasis, nymphomania, brutishness, swinishness, lubricousness, lubriciousness.

LASH, *n.* 1. Scourge, whip, knout, cat, cat-o'-ninetails, flagellum, cowhide, rawhide, bullwhip, blacksnake whip, bullwhacker *(coll.),* rope's end, strap, thong.

2. Incentive, provocation, urging, motive, motivation, inducement, impulse, impulsion, spur, rowel, prick, goad, prod, fillip, whet, dram, whip, actuation.

3. Eyelash, cilium, blinkers *(coll.).*

LASH, *v.* 1. Thrash, beat, chastise, whip, baste, lambaste, bastinado, flagellate, flog, lace, thresh,

punish, flail, smite, trounce, administer the lash, horsewhip, strike.

2. Correct, lecture, vilify, bring to book, bring to task, rail at, satirize, lampoon, punish, scold, castigate, admonish, chide, upbraid, exprobrate, reprove, rebuke, reprehend, reprimand, objurgate, rate, berate, trounce, fulminate against, revile, slander, execrate, denounce, censure, call down, rag, swear at, curse, anathematize.

3. Goad, stir up, provoke, rouse, arouse, kindle, foment, incite, spur, sharpen, quicken, animate, stimulate, rile, urge, accelerate, whet, exasperate, exacerbate, irritate, anger, madden, infuriate, motivate, egg on *(coll.),* evoke, call up, summon, hasten, actuate, move, propel, prompt, prod, urge on, push, press, impel.

4. Tie, affix, fix, attach, fasten, bind, lace, rope, belay, batten, secure, clinch, hitch, pinion, string, strap, make fast, leash, truss, swathe, gird, tie up, tether, moor, brace, grapple, lash and tie, run out a line, run out a rope, run out a warp.

LASS, *n.* Girl, maiden, demoiselle, damoiselle, damosel, damsel, female, lassie, lassy, maidservant, wench, miss, maid, colleen, girleen, hussy, tart, hoyden, tomboy, virgin, schoolgirl, schoolmaid, schoolmiss, youth, nymph.

LASSITUDE, *n.* Weariness, lethargy, indolence, inertia, debility, weakness, weakliness, feebleness, faintness, asthenia, supineness, apathy, kef, phlegm, indifference, dullness, hebetude, hebetation, torpor, lentitude, torpidity, torpescence, stupor, stupefaction, statuvolence, statuvolism, drowsiness, oscitance, oscitancy, oscitation, heavy eyelids, fatigue, tiredness, wearisomeness, enervation, oppression, prostration, languor, languidness, drooping, droopingness.

LASSO, *n.* Lariat, reata, riata, lass rope, throw rope, ketch rope *(coll.),* lazo *(coll.),* rope, thong.

LAST, *n.* 1. Model, shape, pattern, form, original, prototype.

2. End, ending, finality, termination, ultimate, terminal, terminus, term, conclusion, consummation, closing, finish, finis, finale, windup, doom, doomsday, crack of doom, fate, Day of Judgment, goal, limit, Omega.

LAST, *adj.* 1. Rearmost, hindmost, hindermost, hinder, hind, behind, at the end, at the tail end, tailing, tagging along, final, ultimate, aftermost, posteriormost, aftmost.

2. Conclusive, conclusory, eventual, final, ultimate, terminal, terminative, determinative, definitive, caudal, farthest, extreme, settled, over, decided, ended, all over, decisive, utmost, uttermost, ulterior.

LAST, *adv.* 1. Finally, conclusively, definitely, decidedly, eventually, ultimately, terminally, determinatively, in fine, at last, at the last, once and for all, extremely.

2. Behind, in the rear, astern, astern of, in back of, in the background, behind the back, back to back, after, aft, abaft, baff, baft, rearwards, hindwards, tailwards, back, backwards.

LAST, *v.* Survive, perdure, endure, subsist, bide, abide, extend, continue, persist, exist, stay, remain, stand, stand up, wear, carry on, hold out, hold up, stick, maintain, keep, live, hold good, outlive, outwear, remain valid.

LASTING, *adj.* Permanent, prolonged, chronic, durable, abiding, drawn-out, extended, extensive, interminable, long, boundless, limitless, illimitable, continual, continuous, of long duration, lifelong, livelong, long-lived, longeval, longevous, perdurable, perennial, sempervirent, evergreen, unchanging, unchangeable, immutable, firm, steadfast, constant, reliable, dependable, persistent, intransient, protracted, intransitive, lingering, long-continued, eternal, never-ending, incessant, unceasing, sempiternal, dateless, ageless, infinite, endless, unremitting, unflagging, unrelenting, never-fading, uninterrupted, imperishable, static, fixed, immovable, immortal, undying, unmodifiable, indissoluble, indissolvable, indestructible, indelible, ineradicable, indeciduous, intransmutable, established, firmly established, long-established, solid, deep-seated, deep-rooted, reliable, alone, unfading.

LASTLY, *adv.* Finally, at length, at last, in the end, after all, on the whole, all things considered, in fine, taking one consideration with another, in conclusion, taking everything into consideration.

LATCH, *n.* Catch, snap, fastening, fastener, hook, clamp, lock, bolt, loop, button, latchet, buckle, clip, tie, clinch, hasp.

LATCHET, *n.* Tie, fastening, fastener, thong, lace, loop, buckle, strap.

LATE, *adj.* 1. Slow, behindhand, tardy, delayed, cunctatory, dilatory, backward, overdue, moratory, unpunctual, procrastinating, postponed, delayed, stayed, put off, reserved, waived, cunctative, retarded, slack, behind time, languid, leisurely, lingering, slow-going, slow-moving, slow-running, slow-sailing, slow-paced, slow-crawling.

2. New, recent, fresh, raw, green, evergreen, immature, newfledged, of yesterday, newborn.

3. Former, far, *ci-devant (Fr.),* dead, defunct, deceased, gone, passed on, passed over, quondam, erstwhile, erst, whilom, sometime, previous, antecedent, pristine, ancient, ancestral.

LATE, *adv.* 1. Backward, behind time, tardily, behind hand, after time, late in the day, at the eleventh hour, lately, recently, slowly, cunctatorily, languidly, leisurely, lingeringly, slackly.

2. Untimely, unseasonably, ill-timedly, ill-seasonedly, too late, timelessly, out of time, inopportunely, inconveniently, untowardly, inapropos, unfavorably, inauspiciously, unpropitiously.

LATELY, *adv.* Lately, recently, a short time ago, not long ago, the other day, once upon a time, of late, only yesterday, just now, right now, formerly, latterly, before, ere now, ere this, before now, heretofore, therefore, hitherto, erst, whilom, ago, no longer, a way back, some time back, years ago, ages ago, once, one day, time was.

LATENCY, *n.* Dormancy, dormantness, inertness, latence, latentness, abeyance, possibility, potentiality, secrecy, tacitness, insinuation, implication, inference, latitancy, quiescence, inactivity, passivity, inertia, obscuration, obscurity, adumbration, darkness, hidden meaning, obscure meaning, undercurrent, suggestion, indication, hint, imperceptibility, lethargy, torpor, concealment, inaction, languidness, languor.

LATENESS, *n.* Procrastination, delay, slowness, backwardness, delation, deferral, adjournment, adjournal, prorogation, prolongation, tardiness, tarriance, tarrying, dilatoriness, dilly-dallying, loitering, lagging, lapse, deferment, respite, reprieve, truce, suspension, moratorium.

LATENT, *adj.* Quiescent, inert, latitant, static, passive, dormant, suspended, sleeping, slumbering, in abeyance, in suspension, in suspense, smolder-

ing, stagnant, lurking, inert, inactive, potential, possible, delitescent, hidden, secret, cryptic, occult, arcane, esoteric, implied, implicated, meant, inferred, insinuated, intimated, hinted, adumbrated, insinuatory, insinuative, implicatory, implicative, implicational, inferential, allusive, allusory, constructive, construed, suggestive, indirect, indicative, involved, unexpressed, unmentioned, unspoken, unbreathed, untalked-of, unsung, unpublished, unproclaimed, unacknowledged, unwritten, unexposed, invisible, unapparent, unsuspected, steganographic, cryptographic, cryptographical, anagogic, anagogical, mystic, mystical, veiled, recondite, symbolic, emblematic, emblematical, figurative, tacit, covert, undercover, concealed, underground, underhand, underhanded, crooked, tortuous, devious, clandestine, undiscernible, indiscernible, imperceptible, inconspicuous, abstruse, profound, unclear, dim, vague, indefinite, arcanal, cabalic, cabalistic, dark, cloudy, hazy, nebulous, nebulose, mysterious, acroamatic, acroamatical, unsuggested, unindicated, unintimated, unintended.

LATER, *adj.* Subsequent, posterior, following, succeeding, successive, sequent, consequent, postdiluvial, postdiluvian, posthumous, after-death, after, attendant, consecutive, ensuing.

LATER, *adv.* Subsequently, thereafter, since, afterwards, at a late time, after a while, next, from that time, whereupon, upon which, from that moment, thereupon, hereupon, hereon, in process of time, in sequel, successively, consecutively.

LATERAL, *adj.* Bordering, oblique, sidelong, edging, flanking, fringing, skirting, sideling, marginate, sided, flanked, verging, edgeway, edgeways, sloping, indirect, abreast, sideways, sidewise, collateral, ancillary, minor, incidental, sideward, edgewise, askance, askant, asquint, edgelong, marginal.

LATERALLY, *adv.* Laterad *(Anat.),* sidewise, sideways, abreast, alongside, neck and neck, cheek to cheek, side by side, broadside, broadside on, beside, by the side of, right and left, to windward, to leeward, toward, on her beam ends, edgelong, askance, askant, asquint, edgewise, edgeways, windward, leeward, in juxtaposition, tête à tête, obliquely, slopingly, to one side, slantwise, slantways, slopewise, askew, awry, transversely, crosswise, crossways, athwart, athwartships, across, aside.

LATH, *n.* Strip, slat, wood, lumber, groundwork, single lath, double lath, stave.

LATHER, *n.* Foam, suds, soapsuds, froth, fizz *(coll.),* bubbles.

LATHERY, *adj.* Soapy, sudsy, frothy, foamy, bubbly, fizzy.

LATIN, *n.* Tongue, language, Roman language, classical language, speech, Early Latin, Late Latin, Medieval Latin, Low Latin, Vulgar Latin, Vulgate, New Latin, Old Latin.

LATITANT, *adj.* Quiescent, inert, lying, static, passive, suspended, sleeping, slumbering, somnolent, somnolescent, in abeyance, in suspense, in suspension, smoldering, stagnant, lurking, inactive, potential, possible, delitescent, hidden, secret, cryptic, occult, arcane, esoteric, implied, implicated, implicatory, implicational, implicit, meant, inferred, inferential, insinuated, intimated, hinted, adumbrated, profound, insinuatory, insinuative, allusive, allusory, constructive, construed, suggestive, indirect, indicative, involved, unexpressed, unmentioned, unspoken, unbreathed, untalked-of, unsung, unpublished, unproclaimed, unacknowledged, unwritten, unexposed, invisible, unapparent, unsuspected, steganographic, dark, cryptographic, cryptographical, anagogic, anagogical, mystic, mystical, veiled, recondite, symbolic, emblematic, emblematical, figurative, tacit, covert, undercover, concealed, underground, underhand, underhanded, crooked, tortuous, devious, clandestine, undiscernible, indiscernible, unapparent, imperceptible, inconspicuous, abstruse, unclear, dim, vague, indefinite, arcanal, cabalic, cabalistic, cloudy, nebulous, nebulose, mysterious, acroamatic, acroamatical, unsuggested, unindicated, unintimated, unintended, dormant.

LATITUDE, *n.* 1. Amplitude, stretch, range, scope, liberality, free play, free scope, elbow room, full swing, margin, rope, enough rope, extensiveness, room, capacity, extent, wide berth, play, field, sphere.

2. Liberty hall, free use, indulgence, unrestricted use, range, room, play, free scope, free swing, reach, swing, elbowroom, margin for error, leeway, wide berth, license, unrestraint, looseness.

3. Meridian, zone, longitude, equator, bearing.

LATITUDINARIAN, *adj.* Unprejudiced, unsettled, lenient, indulgent, unbiased, unwarped, unrooted, unswayed, unaffected, disaffected, liberal, ecumenical, catholic, unprovincial, unbigoted, unpositive, undogmatic, unprepossessed, unjaundiced, tolerant, amenable, broad-minded, broad, undazzled, undeceived, unperplexed, unpragmatic, unpragmatical, uninfatuated, unfanatical, accessible, openminded, disinterested, dispassionate, impartial, unrestricted, uncurbed, unbridled, unconstrained, unrestrained, unshackled, uninfluenced, freethinking, forbearing, forbearant, persuadable, persuasible, unchecked, untrammeled, unfettered, unreined, just, fair, equitable, balanced.

LATRINE, *n.* Water closet, W. C., toilet, comfort station, rest room, rest station, lavatory, cloaca, privy, jakes, john, johnny, bathroom, backhouse, outhouse, necessary, can, Mrs. Jones, locus *(sl.),* head, roundhouse, men's room, lady's room, women's room, washroom.

LATTER, *adj.* Posterior, following, consequent, subsequent, second-mentioned, last-mentioned, more recent, ensuing, successive, succeeding, after, later.

LATTERLY, *adv.* Lately, recently, not long ago, a short time ago, just the other day, right now, just now, any more *(coll.),* only yesterday, hitherto, of late.

LATTICE, *n.* Frame, framework, skeleton, arbor, fretwork, screen, network, reticulum, trellis, grill, grating, grate, window, lattice, framing.

LAUD, *v.* Applaud, praise, compliment, commend, congratulate, approve, esteem, respect, admire, honor, clap, cheer, acclaim, encore, accolade, eulogize, extol, glorify, exalt, root for *(coll.),* boost *(coll.),* puff, appreciate, indorse, recommend, panegyric, panegyricize, magnify, swell, make much of, bless, bepraise, belaud, value, sing the praises of, chant the praises of, shout, shout the praises of, celebrate, venerate, pay honor to, pay tribute to, hymn, worship, adore, revere, reverence.

LAUDABLE, *adj.* Good, excellent, praiseworthy, virtuous, worthy of praise, worthy of estimation, estimable, commendable, admirable, deserving, deserving of praise, meritorious, creditable, unimpeachable, beyond praise, *sans peur et sans*

reproche, just, righteous, right-minded, nice, exemplary, noble, sterling, holy, saintly, correct, right, healthful, wholesome, salubrious, true, hallowed, kind-hearted, kind, kindly, true-hearted.

LAUDATION, *n.* Renown, praise, commendation, approval, sanction, esteem, advocacy, estimation, favor, admiration, appreciation, regard, affection, love, credit, repute, compliment, encomium, congratulation, eulogy, eulogium, panegyric, benediction, blessing, benison, kudos, adulation, honor, celebration, fame, extolment.

LAUDATORY, *adj.* Approbatory, approbative, approving, acclamatory, uncritical, flattering, uncensorious, benedictory, complimentary, commendatory, panegyrical, panegyric, encomiastical, encomiastic, eulogistical, eulogistic, praising, praiseful.

LAUGH, *n.* Titter, giggle, snigger, snicker, guffaw, horselaugh, roar, scream, screech, shriek, cackle, cachinnation, burst of laughter, fit of laughter, peal of laughter, laughter, crow, risibility, risibilities, risibles, laughing, merriment, mirth, glee, gaiety.

LAUGH, *v.* Laugh, burst out laughing, bust out laughing *(coll.),* giggle, titter, snigger, snicker, cackle, cachinnate, shriek, roar, shake with laughter, be convulsed, horselaugh, split one's sides, chortle, teehee, sniggle, haw-haw, guffaw, chuckle.

LAUGHABLE, *adj.* Risible, funny, amusing, ridiculous, outrageous, trivial, nonsensical, pathetic, quaint, silly, stupid, dumb *(coll.),* frivolous, useless, vain, waggish, asinine, inane, grotesque, fantastic, fantastical, absurd, unreasonable, extravagant, preposterous, bombastic, inflated, burlesque, outlandish, freakish, prankish, sportive, merry, entertaining, diverting, pleasant, facetious, droll, quizzical, drollish, ludicrous, recreative, pleasant, side-splitting, witty, comic, comical, playful, roguish, jocose, jocund, festal, tragicomical, serio-comical, mock-heroic, satirical, odd, eccentric, bizarre.

LAUGH AT, *v.* Ridicule, scoff, jeer, mock, grin at, smile at, snicker, snigger, chuckle, be amused at, deride, banter, chaff, jest, joke, make jokes at one's expense, laugh up one's sleeve, revile, flout, scout, scorn, hold up to scorn, point at, point the finger of scorn, laugh to scorn, taunt, haze, twit, rag, rally, sneer.

LAUGHING, *adj.* Merry, gay, jesting, jocular, jocund, sportive, joking, funny, smiling, grinning, rejoicing, jubilant, shaking, convulsed with laughter, gleeful, elated, exultant, giggling, tittering, snickering, sniggering, chortling, chuckling, cachinnating, cackling, bubbling.

LAUGHINGSTOCK, *n.* Jesting stock, joke, butt, dupe, gull, gullible person, fool, ass, game, fair game, figure of fun, byword, easy mark, April Fool, victim, sucker, cull, cinch, pushover *(sl.),* mark *(sl.),* greenhorn, babe, babe in the woods, puppet, cat's paw, tool, monkey.

LAUGHTER, *n.* Mirth, merriment, joy, gaiety, glee, laughing, cachinnation, chuckling, chortling, sniggering, snickering, tittering, giggling, guffawing, roaring, crowing, horselaugh, shouting, shrieking, jollity, jocularity, jocundity, jocundness, joviality, hilarity, levity, exhilaration, amusement, entertainment.

LAUNCH, *v.* 1. Propel, impel, drive, hurl, cast, throw, project, push, send, send off, fire, fire off, let off, dash, pitch, force, shoot, discharge, send forth, let fly, expel, eject, start, start off, set in motion, launch forth, dart, lance, thrust.

2. Set afloat, set into the water, float, slide from the stocks.

3. Begin, start, inaugurate, initiate, break ground, institute, found, establish, start in, enter upon, embark, embark upon, set in, set forth on, set in motion, set forward, turn to, fall to, undertake, venture into, venture upon, launch into, launch forth.

LAUNDER, *v.* Elute, wash, lave, lavate, clean, cleanse, purify, rinse, scour, scrub, soap, iron, do up *(coll.)*, press, soak, tub *(coll.)*, wash out, dryclean, dry-cleanse.

LAUNDRESS, *n.* Washer, washerwoman, washwoman, washlady, wash maid, washing maid, *blanchisseuse (Fr.)*, worker, servant, servant girl, cleaning woman, cleaning lady, domestic servant, domestic worker, domestic *(coll.)*, maid.

LAUNDRY, *n.* Washery, washroom, wash house, wash shed, laundry room.

LAUREL, *n.* Decoration, festoon, badge of honor, mark of honor, badge, wreath, reward, award, honor, honorary crown, chaplet, trophy, prize, distinction, coronal, garland, palm.

LAVA, *n.* Volcanic rock, volcanic residue, ash, cinder, rock, molten rock, liquid rock, igneous rock, basalt, rhyolite, pumice, pumice stone.

LAVATION, *n.* Washing, cleansing, cleaning, ablution, abstersion, detersion, lustration, washup, balneation, natation, bathing, purification, lavage, scrubbing, scouring.

LAVATORY, *n.* Washroom, wash basin, balneary, shower bath, shower, bath tub, washbowl, washery, wash house, toilet, bathroom, bathhouse, water closet, W. C., cloaca, latrine, privy, outhouse, backhouse.

LAVE, *v.* Bathe, clean, cleanse, purify, purge, absterge, deterge, edulcorate, decrassify, tub, launder, wash out, elute, rinse, scrub, scour, mop, wipe, full, wring, sponge, soap, shampoo.

LAVISH, *adj.* Profuse, thriftless, unthrifty, improvident, bounteous, bountiful, generous, liberal, in profusion, wasteful, squandering, extravagant, plenty, plenteous, plentiful, superabundant, prodigal, myriad, unsparing, unmeasured, limitless, copious, very many, abundant, stintless, unstinting, unstinted, without stint, luxuriant, wholesale, prolix, full, munificent, hospitable, free-hearted, big-hearted, large-hearted, great-hearted, openhanded, sumptuous, sumptuary, handsome, intemperate, overliberal, ample, unselfish, ungrudging, princely, in excess, overabundant. flush. superfluous, redundant, abounding, gorgeous, immoderate, effusive, exhaustive, rich, costly, dear, overmuch, wild.

LAVISH, *v.* Prodigalize, drain, spend, spend recklessly, spend freely, shower, spill, be prodigal, be thriftless, accommodate with, be generous, be extravagant, be unthrifty, be improvident, dissipate, be over liberal, be wasteful, pour on, drain, exhaust, deluge, squander, give much, give overmuch, load, deplete, scatter, disperse, run riot, run over the limit, consume, bestow, give in profusion, carry to excess, carry too far, overindulge, misspend, gorge, flood, inundate, rain benefactions, brim over.

LAVISHNESS, *n.* Plenty, plenitude, affluence, handsomeness, generosity, bounty, bountifulness, amplitude, fullness, improvidence, plenteousness, copiousness, ampleness, abundance, prodigality,

extravagance, repletion, fulsomeness, unthriftiness, wastefulness, kindness, unselfishness, liberality, ungrudgingness, freedom, luxuriance, sumptuousness, openhandedness, hospitality, waste, wastefulness, dissipation, intemperance, immoderateness, immoderation.

LAW, *n.* 1. Formula, rule, edict, dictate, dictum, principle, governing principle, governing law, prescribed form, settled rule, established rule, Procrustean rule, Law of the Medes and Persians, regulation, maxim, authoritarian rule, standing order.

2. Truth, truism, instruction, direction, directive, charge, unwritten law, command, commandment, decalogue, standard, criterion, rule, canon, code, dogma, principle, principium, injunction, dogmatic precept, code, convention, rule of conduct, working rule, regulation, model, formula, formulary, precept, recipe, receipt, general truth, universal truth, golden rule, form, prescription.

3. Constitution, statute, ordinance, *ordonnance (Fr.)*, enactment, act, dictate, dictum, pronouncement, edict, pronunciamento, form, formulary, standing order, rubric, institution, bylaw, byelaw, habeas corpus, code, code of laws, body of laws, Corpus Juris, capitulary, pandect, digest, charter, precept, ukase, decision, judgment.

4. International law, law of nations, nomology, nomography, jurisprudence, local law, federal law, state law, civil law, criminal law, mercantile law, contract law, crown law, canon law, ecclesiastical law, equity, divine law, divine revelation, common law.

5. The Law, Mosaic Law, Biblical Law, Pentateuch, Decalogue.

6. Litigation, lawsuit, suit at law, suit in law, dispute, contention, action, legal action, proceedings, legal proceedings, prosecution, case, cause.

7. Custom, usage, convention, codification, legality, legitimacy, lawfulness, legislation, constitutionality, constitutionalism, legal process, justice, due process of law.

LAWBREAKER, *n.* Malfeasor, misfeasor, nonfeasor, criminal, convict, felon, crook, miscreant, parolee, captive, jailbird, gaolbird, offender, culprit, delinquent, desperado, fugitive, outlaw, misdemeanant, misdemeanist, sinner, transgressor.

LAWBREAKING, *n.* Offense, crime, violation, breach, transgression, felony, misdemeanor, malfeasance, misfeasance, nonfeasance, vice, sin, evil, criminality, misdeed, wrongdoing, delict, error, fault, lapse, slip, omission, commission, delinquency, dereliction, capital crime, outrage, atrocity, enormity, infraction, infringement, trespass, contravention.

LAWFUL, *adj.* 1. Legal, legitimate, rightful, licit, according to law, in accordance with the law, constituted, constitutional, authorized, sanctioned, vested, statutable, statutory, legislated, legislational, judicial, juridical, jurisprudential, jurisprudent, legalized, lawlike, legitimized, enacted, ordained, conformable to law, within the law, nomistic, nomothetical, jural, canonical.

2. Permissive, recognized, acknowledged, vouchsafed, favored, permitted, granted, licensed, chartered, empowered, authorized, conferred, admitted, admissory, unprohibited, unforbidden, legitimate, patent, facultative, optional, entitled, titled, conceded, warranted, prescribed, ordained, allotted, patented, allowed, enabled, admissive.

3. Licit, just, fair, right, rightful, optional,

equitable, proper, good, fitting, regular, in order, as it should be, valid, in force, balanced, sound.

LAWFULNESS, *n.* 1. Licitness, legality, legalization, legitimacy, sanction, judiciousness, judiciality, rightness, rightfulness, constitutionality, right, conformity to law.

2. Permissiveness, allowableness, allowability, recognition, vouchsafement, favor, entitlement, right, sanction, privilege, warrant, authorization, ordination, prescription, allotment, patent, permission.

LAWGIVER, *n.* Statesman, congressman, congresswoman, senator, senatress, senatrix, representative, solon, adviser, counselor, legislator, elder statesman, politico, politician, elected representative, boss *(coll.),* Member of Congress, M.C., Member of Parliament, M.P., assemblyman, assemblywoman, selectman, councilman, commissioner, elder.

LAWLESS, *adj.* Rebellious, mutinous, insurrectionary, insurgent, nonconformable, nonconformist, unconventional, disorderly, nihilistic, anarchic, anarchical, anarchistic, eccentric, deviative, divergent, ungoverned, licentious, disorganized, chaotic, terroristic, unruly, stray, straying, unsubmissive, transgressive, insubordinate, uncontrollable, refractory, contumacious, criminal, reprobate, revolutionary, disobedient, intractable, corrupt, riotous, knavish, rascally, roguish, villainous, defiant, noncompliant, felonious, scampish, venal, crooked, insidious, miscreant, recreant, uningenuous, unrestrained, disingenuous, recalcitrant, wayward, slack, dishonest, unscrupulous, unprincipled, remiss, secessionist, evasive, recusant, piratical, wanton.

LAWLESSNESS, *n.* Nihilism, terrorism, irresponsibility, despotism, tyranny, anarchy, anarchism, violence, reign of terror, reign of violence, disobedience, sedition, treason, overthrow, revolt, revolution, uprising, insurrection, riot, chaos, sabotage, licentiousness, mob rule, mob law, ochlocracy, mobocracy, license, misrule, disorder, disorganization, felony, lynch law, Lydford law, martial law, club law, insubordination, rebellion, mutiny, barratry, mutineering, rising, racketeerism, crime, criminality, feloniousness, abandon.

LAWN, *n.* 1. Grass, grasslands, mead, meadow, meadowland, park, field, green, greensward, greenyard, yard, campus, grassplot, grassplat, sward, grounds.

2. Cloth, textile, texture, fabric, textile fabric, linen, cotton, woven fabric, material, goods, dry goods.

LAWSUIT, *n.* Debate, contention, dispute, litigation, legal action, legal proceedings, trial, process, legal process, due process of law, suit, suit in law, suit at law, prosecution, case, cause, pleadings, debate, argument, legal argument, argumentation, disceptation, disputation.

LAWYER, *n.* Attorney, attorney-at-law, counselor, councilor, barrister, solicitor, pleader, special pleader, counsel, advocate, counselor-at-law, legal adviser, proctor, procurator, bencher, jurist, judge, justice, justice of the peace, J. P., magistrate, jurisconsult, jurisprudent, jurisprudentialist, patent attorney, attorney in fact, prosecutor, prosecuting attorney, District Attorney, public prosecutor, attorney general, civilian, civil lawyer, cursitor, sergeant-at-law, conveyancer, criminal lawyer, notary, judicator, scrivener, writer, green bag *(coll.),* shyster *(sl.),* ambulance chaser *(sl.),* mouthpiece,

law agent, King's Counsel, K. C., Queen's Counsel, Q. C., gownsman, leader, tubman, moderator, umpire, arbiter, arbitrator, referee, jurat.

LAX, *adj.* 1. Loose, slack, careless, negligent, remiss, nonadhesive, noncohesive, incoherent, detached, flapping, baggy, streaming, relaxed, flaccid, disheveled, unbridled.

2. Weak, unexacting, soft, bendable, pliable, flexible, lenient, mild, moderate, easy, tolerant, indulgent, long-suffering, forbearing, forbearant, complaisant, unconcerned, easygoing, pliant, pliable, yielding, elastic, relaxed, mellow, tender, malleable, tractable, flexile, flexuous, ductile.

3. Neglectful, negligent, neglective, unheeding, inadvertent, shiftless, improvident, indolent, slack, loose, thoughtless, heedless, careless, lazy, slovenly, sloppy, slipshod, happy-go-lucky, thriftless, unguarded, unthrifty, do-nothing, slothful, laggard, lackadaisical, indifferent, languid, supine, casual, unobservant, unretentive, undutiful, unconscientious.

4. Dissolute, immoral, depraved, licentious, slack, loose, wanton, corrupt, venal, characterless, unvirtuous, virtueless, sinful, lewd, debauched, wicked, vicious, recreant, wrong, wrongdoing, unrighteous, unsteady, unsteadfast, wild, reckless, indecent, of easy virtue, of loose morals, infirm, weak, dishonorable, dishonest, deceitful, sly, devious, deceptive, profligate.

LAXATIVE, *n.* Cathartic, purgative, purge, purgation, salts, dose, deobstruent, aperient, carminative, physic.

LAXITY, *n.* 1. Softness, plasticity, flaccidity, flaccidness, pliableness, pliability, flexibility, ductility, ductibility, tractability, tractility, elasticity, looseness, incoherence.

2. Remission, remissness, negligence, inattentiveness, lenity, lenience, lenitence, mildness, tolerance, license, indulgence, nonobservance, unobservance, inobservance, nonfulfillment, noncompliance, omission, failure, default, oversight, slackness, casualness, inattention, carelessness, recklessness, disobedience, unruliness, insubordination, contumacy, contumaciousness, neglect, indolence, laziness, supineness, lethargy, languor, languidness, slovenliness, sloppiness, perfunctoriness.

3. Delinquency, dereliction, moral failure, weakness, moral weakness, turpitude, immorality, looseness of morals, improbity, venality, faithlessness, unconscientiousness, trickery, knavery, roguery, dishonor, deviation.

LAY, *n.* 1. Song, poem, verse, lyric, metrical composition, poetic composition, descant, refrain, air, melody, tune, strain, canto, measure, carol, ballad, art song, verses, ditty, rhyme, rime.

2. Form, array, arrangement, disposition, conformation, condition.

LAY, *adj.* Lay, laic, civil, secular, nonecclesiatic, nonreligious, secularist, secularistic, congregational, nonclerical, popular, profane, temporal, nonprofessional, worldly.

LAY, *v.* 1. Ovulate, produce eggs.

2. Bet, wager, gamble, hazard, risk, make a bet, stake, lay odds on, bet upon, take a flyer *(coll.),* plunge, back, play.

3. Set, set down, prostrate, supinate, fell, bring down, sink, knock down, floor, mow down, cut down, drop, ground, bowl over, hew down.

4. Locate, place, set, settle, repose, seat, put, situate, establish, pitch, plant, camp, deposit, station.

5. Allay, assuage, deaden, lull, modify, moderate, temper, dull, take the edge off, make temperate, make mild, make bland, attemper, soften, obtund, mollify, appease, blunt, sheathe, subdue, make gentle, make soft, compose, cool, quiet, still, sober, pacify, make tame, quell, limit, weaken, check, curb, lessen, diminish, damp, dampen, sober down, make smooth, make unruffled, make untroubled, lenify, dulcify, abate, palliate, tame, tone down, restrain, limit, quell, put down, chasten, tranquilize, mitigate.

6. Attribute, assign, impute, put down to, set down to, account for, ascribe, charge, charge to, lay to.

7. Flatten, level, align, lay down, lay level, lay out, raze, smooth, even, equalize, aline.

8. Demand, ask, charge, exact, assess, assess a tax on, impose, fine, impost, levy, require, lay a duty on, put a duty on.

LAY ABOUT ONE, *v.* 1. Act, be active, act rapidly, act vigorously, move, keep busy, labor, struggle, fall to with a will, strive, strain, sweat, pull, tug, peg away at, plug, plug away at, ply, work, drive, go at it with a will.

2. Attack, assault, charge, charge one's enemy, assault vigorously, assail, charge at, saber, bayonet, cut and slash, cut and thrust, harry, drive hard, drive one's enemy before him, press hard.

LAY ASIDE, *v.* 1. Reject, disregard, repudiate, disclaim, disown, renounce, pay no attention to, pay no mind (*coll.*), ignore, dismiss, discount, overlook, pass over, except, exclude, abjure, repel, repulse, discard, relinquish, wash one's hands of, set aside, cast aside, push aside, throw aside, stand over, let stand, delay, table, place on the table, lay on the table, pigeonhole, shunt, postpone, put off, stave off, reserve, defer, cast aside, sneeze at, forego, abandon, drop, resign.

2. Lay by, set aside, put aside, reserve, preserve, set by, retain, store up, store, stockpile, separate, isolate, weed out, segregate, pick out, winnow, sift, part, divide, store, lay up a supply, lay in a stock.

LAY AWAY, *v.* Warehouse, preserve, conserve, set aside, put aside, lay aside, reserve, store, stockpile, save, save up, save for a rainy day, garner, garner up, pile, stack, stash away, heap, collect, accumulate, amass, hoard, deposit, shelve, reposit, reservoir, file away.

LAY BARE, *v.* Divest, reveal, disclose, denude, unclothe, lay open, bare, strip, undress, undrape, ungarment, doff, cast off, take off, dismantle, put off, disrobe, unapparel, peel, pare, shuck, hull, reveal, discover, unconceal, uncover, unveil, unscreen, uncloak, unshroud, make a clean breast of, admit, acknowledge, unfold, unroll, tell, say, narrate, recount, divulge, make known, publish, broadcast, breathe, whisper, utter, vent, admit, concede, grant, own, betray, confess, confirm.

LAY BY, *v.* 1. Reserve, save, preserve, set aside, lay aside, accumulate, hoard, conserve, garner, stock, stockpile, collect, amass, pile up, put away, treasure, retain, reserve for future use, husband.

2. Postpone, delay, put off, stave off, defer, waive, suspend, hang up, table, keep off.

LAY BY THE HEELS, *v.* 1. Defeat, destroy, demolish, lay waste, devastate, desolate, lay in ruins, lay in ashes, prostrate, quell, put down, sink, rout, vanquish, get the better of, floor, drub, overcome, overwhelm, override, overthrow, overpower, over-

master, overmatch, overreach, suppress, quash, scuttle, ruinate, ruin, undo, master, lick (*coll.*).

2. Apprehend, arrest, catch, capture, make captive, take prisoner, seize, collar (*coll.*), wrest, get one's hands on, nab (*coll.*), lay hold of, grab, grasp, clutch, pick up (*coll.*), take into custody.

LAY CLAIM TO, *v.* Claim, arrogate, assert a right, claim as one's due, exact, demand, take one's due, revindicate, revendicate.

LAY DOWN, *v.* 1. Resign, yield, give up, capitulate, surrender, succumb, yield one's life, sacrifice one's self, die, be killed, submit, bend to the yoke.

2. Make level, make horizontal, flatten, smooth, smooth out, align, aline, even, equalize, raze, lay level, lay out.

3. (*Nautical*): Careen, heave down, heel, keel, lie along, list.

LAY DOWN THE LAW, *v.* Dominate, dictate, dogmatize, emphasize, stress, lay stress on, assert roundly, assert positively, predominate, preponderate, direct, command, arrogate, instruct, enjoin, lord it over (*coll.*), exact, domineer, prescribe, proscribe, charge, forbid, interdict, decree, enact, overrule, overbear, overawe, override, order, ordain, lay down, rap out, reaffirm, repeat, reassert, have the last word, enunciate, announce, assert, get the upper hand, rule the roost (*coll.*), insist upon.

LAYER, *n.* 1. Shoot, twig, branch, growth, propagation, graft.

2. Stratum, bed, couch, substratum, post (*Geol.*), measure (*Geol.*), magma (*Geol.*), stage, story, tier, course, coping, rasher, shive, plate, platter, sheet, foil, lamination, lamella, lamina, slab, flag, flagstone, cast, coating, veneer, film, membrane, pellicle, peel, skin, cuticle, slice, cut, pane, board, plank, zone, level, wafer, disc, fold, lap, flap, ply, plait, eschar, stratification, foliation, lamellation, delamination, cover, shaving, flake, piece, scale, integument, tegmentum, tegument, tegmen, cortex, ledge, floor, belt, panel.

3. Atmospheric layer, —stratum, stratosphere, ionosphere, Heaviside layer, isothermal region, substratosphere, ozone layer, ozone blanket, Heaviside region, tropopause, troposphere.

LAY EYES ON, *v.* See, look, behold, observe, perceive, gaze, stare, view, discern, make out, descry, sight, distinguish, discover, spy, espy, have in sight, get in sight, hold in view, take in, cast the eyes upon, cast one's gaze upon, clap the eyes on, get a glimpse of, glimpse, witness, notice, command a view of, obtain a view of, spot (*coll.*), describe.

LAY FIGURE, *n.* 1. Pattern, model, mannequin, mannekin, puppet, doll, marionette, icon, ikon, image, prototype, original, paradigm, archetype, artist's model, figurine, figure.

2. Nobody, nonentity, nullity, nihility, unimportant person, zero (*coll.*), nothing, jackstraw, puppet, dummy, mediocrity, lightweight (*coll.*), insignificancy, naught, nought, cipher, man of straw.

LAY FOR, *v.* 1. Approach, draw near, near, draw nigh, move toward, advance toward, draw close to, draw closer.

2. Sail for, make for, put into port, lay a course, bear up to, bear down upon, lay in, lie in, lie into, make at, run for, head for, steer for, sail for, stand for, steer toward. (*All Nautical.*)

LAY HANDS ON, *v.* 1. Anoint, chrism, confirm, impose, lay on the hands.

2. Get, obtain, acquire, come by, secure, procure, win, catch, wrest, get into one's hands, get one's hands on, collar, apprehend, seize, arrest, intercept, capture, take prisoner, make captive, glean, gather, collect, accumulate, pick, pick up, fasten upon, grab, grasp, grapple, nab, snatch, snag, snare, come into possession of.

LAY HOLD OF, *v.* Catch, get hold of, catch hold of, seize, wrest, grab, nab, clap hands on, set hands on, grasp, grapple, clasp, clutch, nip, claw, clinch, embrace, snag, snare, trap, entrap, pluck, pick, adopt, usurp, take by the throat, throttle, hold fast, hug, fasten upon, appropriate, assume, hook *(coll.)*, apprehend, take prisoner, lay by the heels.

LAY IN, *v.* 1. Garner, treasure, hoard, store, lay in a supply, stockpile, stock, keep in stock, save, reserve, conserve, put away, save for a rainy day, stow away, store away, lay up, put up, accumulate, amass, stack, stash *(coll.)*, pack away, provide, fund, collect, keep in supply, heap up.

2. *(Nautical):* See LAY FOR.

LAY IT ON, *v.* 1. Barnumize, talk big, exaggerate, overcharge, overload, pile it on *(coll.)*, prevaricate, euphuize, buncomize, be pompous, —swelling, —grandiloquent, —showy, —boastful, —mouthy, —windy, —ostentatious, —flaunting, —altiloquent, —altiloquious, —magniloquent, —flatulent, —inflated, —high-sounding, —grand-sounding.

2. Commend lavishly, flatter, cajole, wheedle, coax, gloze, pet, cosset, oil the tongue *(coll.)*, soothe, slaver, beslaver, pat on the back, butter up *(coll.)*, honey, soft-soap, fawn upon, truckle.

LAYMAN, *n.* Laity, congregation, public, people, nonecclesiastic, sheep, flock, assembly, class, society, brethren, parishioner, secular, members, church members, communicants, believers, laywoman, parish, churchman.

LAY OFF, *v.* 1. Lie idle, be idle, loaf, idle.

2. *Command:* Stop, withhold, desist, hold, cease, hold on, can it *(coll.)*, cut it out *(coll.)*, avast, stay, halt, chuck it *(coll.)*, let up, belay it, enough, whoa!, come off it, quiet, quiesco, quieten, grow silent, be silent, grow quiet, pipe down *(sl.)*, soft-pedal, silence!, hush!, shh!, hist!, list!, listen!, hark!

LAY ON, *v.* Beat, chastise, thrash, flog, flail, lash, whip, drub, knock, thump, pummel, buffet, batter, belt, box, cuff, trounce, belabor, lace, scourge, chasten, castigate, smite, punish, slap, fetch a blow.

LAY OPEN, *v.* Cut, incise, knife, slash, slice, lacerate, wound, stab, gash, dissect. See also LAY BARE.

LAY OUT, *v.* 1. Pay out, spend, disburse, fork out, shell out, go through, run through, hand over, hand out, get through.

2. Kill, slay, lay low, bring down, cut down, level, raze, demolish, ruin, ruinate, lay waste, devastate, desolate, ravage, wreck.

3. Flatten, make horizontal, smoothe, raze, lay down, lay level, lay low, align, equalize, even, aline.

4. Upbraid, reprove, rebuke, chastise, castigate, cuss *(coll.)*, curse, abuse, reprimand, reprehend, objurgate, tongue, betongue, lash, lecture, rail at, trounce, chide, admonish, scold, rate, berate, exprobrate, take to task, bawl out *(coll.)*, tell a thing or two *(coll.)*.

5. Prepare for burial, embalm, mummify, lay in state.

6. Plan, map out, lay in order, design, project, forecast, set forth, arrange, draw up a plan, chalk out, stake out, chart, map, devise, plan ahead, outline.

LAYOVER, *n.* Stop, stopping place, terminal, depot, stopover, station, railroad station, railroad depot, railway station, railway depot, station house, terminus, delay, interruption, pause, break, lapse, postponement, deferment.

LAY OVER, *v.* Be slow, —behindhand, —tardy, —late, —overdue, —unpunctual, reserve, hold back, detain, delay, stave off, table, place on the table, suspend, hang fire, postpone, defer.

LAY TO, *v.* 1. Ascribe, assign, attribute, put down to, credit to, explain by, fix the burden of, impute, account for by.

2. *(Nautical):* Lay by, lie near, head to windward, lie offshore, lie off the land, lay up, lie up, lie close to the wind, lie to.

LAY UP, *v.* 1. Put away, store, store up, conserve, preserve, save, save for an emergency, save for a rainy day *(coll.)*, lay in a supply, storehouse *(coll.)*, stockpile, treasure, hoard, garner up, heap up, pile up, accumulate, collect, amass, stack up, stash away *(coll.)*, table, put on the shelf, lay aside, pigeonhole.

2. Ail, be ill, fall ill, come down with sickness, fall victim to an ailment, droop, languish, fail, wilt, pine, peak *(coll.)*, feel ill, be sick, weaken, lose strength, take sick, catch an illness, catch a disease.

3. See LAY TO (2).

LAZAR HOUSE, *n.* Hospital, lazaret, lazaretto, pesthouse, sick bay, quarantine, asylum, hospice, sick house.

LAZINESS, *n.* Inertia, indolence, remissness, neglectfulness, dilatoriness, sloth, slothfulness, somnolence, somnolency, somnolescence, laggardliness, shiftlessness, maudlinity, fainéance, faineancy, inexertion, indiligence, unindustriousness, procrastination, ergophobia, supineness, sluggishness, torpor, torpitude, otiosity, otioseness, lethargy, slackness, want of effort, idleness, lackadaisicality, lackadaisicalness, laxness, do-nothingness.

LAZY, *adj.* Indolent, shiftless, unindustrious, do-nothing, slothful, sluggish, torpid, supine, slack, lax, fainéant, remiss, sleepy, somnolent, dilatory, dronish, lumpish, inert, sluggard, lymphatic, hebetudinous, lethargic, lethargical, soulless, lifeless, exanimate, maudlin, lackadaisical, nonchalant, insouciant, languid, slow, lentitudinous, heavy, dull, torpid, torpescent, drowsy, yawny, comatose, oscitant, flagging, phlegmatic, apathetic, good-for-nothing, worthless, spineless.

LEA, *n.* Meadow, meadowland, pasture, pasturage, pastureland, grass, grassland, green, greensward, pen, field, park, common, lawn, plain, prairie, maidan *(India)*, lay *(coll.)*, greenyard, grassplot, pampas.

LEACH, *v.* Lixiviate, dissolve, dissolve out, percolate, remove, wash out.

LEAD, *v.* 1. Affect, weigh with, sway, bias, control, rule, bend to one's will, attract, dominate, control, carry weight with, tell, count, incline, influence, assume mastery over, command, have the upper hand, overrule, override, dispose, magnetize, draw, attract, rule the roost, gain ascendancy over, prompt, have superiority over.

2. Hold the reins, direct, manage, drive, head,

show the way, guide, steer, take the helm, pilot, regulate, conduct, handle, run *(coll.)*, crack the whip, preside over, administer, administrate, occupy the chair, rule, reign, wield the scepter, wear the crown, hold office, counsel, advise, superintend, govern, actuate, prescribe.

3. Precede, antecede, go before, go ahead, blaze the trail, pioneer, usher in, go in the van, stand at the head of, forego, come first, go ahead of, go in advance of, stand first, rank, outrank, proclaim, herald, get a head start, introduce, take the lead, take precedence.

4. Outstrip, outrun, excel, exceed, transcend, outride, overdo, overleap, outjump, outdo, outstep, outrival, outstrip, outmarch, leave in the lurch, steal a march on, bear the palm, surpass, come first, rank first, bring home the bacon, beat, vanquish, defeat, cap, top, overtop, outpoint, outplay, eclipse, throw in the shadow, overshadow.

5. Seduce, lure, allure, charm, attract, fascinate, titillate, entice, induce, bewitch, enrapture, beckon, lead on, draw on, draw, bait, offer bait to, tantalize, appetize, entrap, trap, snare, court, invite, wheedle, cajole, coax, captivate, persuade, tempt, vamp, inveigle, carry away.

6. Conduct, direct, wield the baton *(Musical)*.

7. Rule, command, govern, head, be master, hold the authority, wield power, wield authority, boss, sway, hold sway, captain, pilot, be in command, be at the head of.

8. Tend, conduce, work towards, dispose, lean, contribute, show a tendency, look, verge, incline, bend to, warp, turn, head, serve, gravitate, trend, affect, carry.

LEAD, *n.* 1. Direction, guidance, indication, sign, suggestion, leadership, example, exemplum, precedent, pointer.

2. Antecedence, antecedency, anteriority, anteposition, priority, epacme *(Zool.)*, precedency, precedence.

3. Role, leading role, part, piece, cue, lines, side *(cant)*, actor, leading actor, leading actress, leading man, leading lady, performer, player, playactor, protagonist, heavy lead *(cant)*, juvenile lead, ingenue lead, star, headline player, headline attraction, featured player, headliner, matinee idol.

4. Connection, line, electric wire, electric cable, conductor, power line, terminal, connecting wire, connecting cable, pole.

5. Pantile, top, housetop, thatch, roof, covering, shelter, roofing.

LEAD, *n.* 1. Element, mineral, ore, metal, graphite, plumbago, red lead, white lead.

2. Plummet, plumbum, plumb line, plumb bob.

3. Fathomer, sounding lead, sounding line, sounding rod, sounding bottle, sound, plumb line, plumb, plummet, bob, dipsey line, deep sea line, dipsey lead, deep sea lead.

LEADEN, *adj.* 1. Dun, dun-colored, glassy, somber, dull, ashen, pale, livid, lurid, ghastly, dim, dimmish, dimmed, dismal, dreary, obscure, gloomy, flat, sad, dead, deadened, grave, sober, cold, lackluster, anemic, bloodless, gray, grayish, dingy.

2. Listless, inanimate, torpid, languid, exanimate.

LEADER, *n.* 1. *(Music):* Conductor, coryphaeus leader, Kapellmeister *(Ger.)*, orchestra leader, band leader, band major, drum major, concertmaster, Konzertmeister *(Ger.)*, choirmaster, chorister, song leader, choir chaplain, cantor, precentor, musical director, musical supervisor.

2. Chief, ringleader, ruler, captain, supervisor, superintendent, commander, commandant, director, manager, head, rector, dictator, administrator, controller, comptroller, intendant, overseer, overlooker, foreman, boss, flugelman, fugleman, agitator, fomenter, lord, master, patron, *padrone (It.)*, seigneur, cynosure, pilot, courier, cicerone, guide, shepherd, chairman, chair, speaker, demagogue, head man, headmaster, superior, senior, dean, principal, despot, monarch, king, prince, liege, suzerain, sovereign, patriarch, champion, chieftain, bellwether.

3. Forerunner, pioneer, precursor, outrider, bellwether, bell mare, predecessor, antecedent, precedent, advance guard, vanguard, pathfinder, paver of the way, trail blazer, trainer, teacher, harbinger, scout.

4. Tendon, sinew, thew, line, ligament.

5. *(Mainly English):* Commentary, editorial, leading article, article, piece, writing.

LEADERSHIP, *n.* 1. Managership, proctorship, governorship, directorship, administratorship, generalship, stewardship, statesmanship, mastery, mastership, masterhood, lordship, headship, captaincy, captainship, hegemony, superintendency, superintendentship, seigniory, seignior-alty, chieftainship, kingship, presidency, premiership.

2. Primacy, superiority, supremacy, supremeness, paramountcy, sway, influence, legal power, potency, puissance, authority, right, prerogative, authorization, sovereignty, suzerainty, reign, predominance, domination, hegemony, headship.

LEADING, *adj.* Supreme, greatest, foremost, second to none, transcendent, transcendental, *facile princeps (Latin)*, ne plus ultra *(Latin)*, best, sovereign, suzerain, uppermost, highest, maximal, maximum, cardinal, prime, ruling, primary, preeminent, supereminent, eminent, overruling, peerless, matchless, incomparable, unrivalled, unparalleled, unmatched, unequalled, unapproached, inimitable, beyond compare, principal, dominant, hegemonic, hegemonical, main, chief, top, topmost, paramount, first, essential, outstanding, prominent, prime, capital, precedent, precedentary, headmost, advanced, superlative.

LEAF, *n.* 1. Leaf, frond, cotyledon, lamina, lamella, blade, needle, pine needle, bract, bractlet, bracteole, phyllome, pad, flag, leaflet, foliole, caulis, leafstalk, petiole, sepal, petal, lithophyll, stipe, stipule, seed leaf, calyx leaf, caulome.

2. Lamina, lamella, sheet, foil, page, folio, insert, inset, leaflet.

3. Scale, flake, sheet, lamination, lamella, lamina. See LAYER.

LEAFAGE, *n.* Verdure, greenery, foliage, foliation, vernation, ramage, frondescence, praefoliation, leafery, growth, leafy growth.

LEAFLET, *n.* 1. Foliage, leaf, frond, cotyledon, blade, needle, pine needle, bract, bractlet, bracteole, phyllome, pad, flag, foliole, caulis, leafstalk, petiole, sepal, petal, lithophyll, stipe, stipule, seed leaf, calyx leaf, caulome.

2. Handbill, brochure, pamphlet, throwaway, flyer, flier, dodger, folder, broadside, booklet, chapbook, tract, advertisement, ad *(coll.)*, broadsheet, bill, circular.

LEAFY, *adj.* Laminate, foliate, leaved, bowery, bosky, foliaceous, woody, frondent, green, verdant.

LEAGUE, *n.* 1. Alliance, association, partnership, corporation, incorporation, cartel, agreement, concord, compact, conspiracy, cabal, plot, complot, collusion, collaboration, participation, copartnership, confraternity, fraternity, fraternization, clanship, partisanship, accord, deal, covenant, treaty, convention, guild, union, trade union, labor union, combination, confederacy, federation, confederation, unification, combine, combination, fusion, conjugation, conjunction, consolidation, network, tieup, hookup, complicity, society, sodality, institute, institution, ring, gang, tong, machine, concordat, connection, cooperative, cooperation.

2. Linear measure, distance, length, lineal measure, measurement of length, measure of distance.

LEAGUED, adj. Cooperative, enleagued, allied, conjoined, confederate, federated, amalgamated, coadjuvant, coadjutant, coadjutive, coactive, coalitional, synergetic, synergistic, fraternal, fraternized, associated, consolidated, clubbed together, federal, corporate, related, organized, unionized, linked, banded, consociated, concurrent, concurring, teamed, collusive, conspirational, collaborating, coalescent, unified, united, incorporated, compound, compounded, partners, coupled, agreed, merged, covenanted.

LEAK, n. 1. Chink, gash, crevice, puncture, hole, scissure, fissure, cleft, cranny, chap, cut, perforation, slit, break, fracture, rupture, fault, flaw, rift, rent.

2. Egress, leakage, leaking, seepage, seeping, oozing, ooze, outflow, effusion, efflux, effluxion, defluxion, effluence.

LEAK, v. 1. Ooze, ooze out, escape, filter, exfiltrate, pour out, well out, exude, exudate, discharge, find vent, run out, drip, dribble, run to waste, go to waste, run dry, dry up, reek.

2. Blurt out, reveal, divulge, evulgate, disclose, let out, vent, give vent to, publish, spill, spill the beans (coll.), give away, inform, tell tales out of school, let fall, let drop, let on (coll.), breathe, whisper, make known, utter, give utterance to, come out with, let slip, let the cat out of the bag (coll.), divulgate.

LEAKPROOF, adj. Rainproof, dampproof, wetproof, moisture proof, waterproof, watertight, raintight, floodproof, dripproof, stormproof, weathertight, impervious.

LEAKY, adj. 1. Forgetful, indiscreet, talkative, garrulous, loquacious, rash, incautious, reckless, heedless, thoughtless, voluble, talky, injudicious, blabber-mouthed (coll.).

2. Percolative, pervious, damaged, imperfect, injured, defective, porous, exudatory.

LEAN, v. 1. Gravitate, be attracted to, incline toward, tend, point, careen, slouch, cant, slant, slope, lead, head toward, propend, crook, bend, sag, sway, deviate, totter.

2. Lie on, recline on, repose on, be sustained by, be supported by, be based on, bear on, abut on, rest on.

3. Contribute, conduce, point, lead, dispose, look, trend, work, warp, incline, verge, bend, serve, tend, have a tendency, —propensity, —proclivity, —leaning, —liking, —twist, —proneness, —predilection, —penchant, —bias, —bent, —turn.

4. Depend on, rely on, have faith in, confide in, presume, trust, pin one's hopes on, pin one's faith on, rest assured, swear by, set store by, believe in, give credence to, place confidence in, rest on, count on, reckon on, build on.

5. Prefer, show preference for, regard, incline towards, have preference for, set before, honor before, set above, choose rather, see fit, think best, please, had as lief, would as lief, propend, lean towards, be willing.

LEAN, adj. 1. Peaked, slender, thin, skinny, emaciated, gaunt, slim, bony, skeletonlike, skeletal, angular, meager, lanky, lank, starved, starveling, famished, scraggy, withered, shriveled, pinched, poor, haggard, wizened, wizen, tabid, tabetic, spare, rawboned, weedy (coll.), delicate, slight, attenuated, attenuate, thin as a rail, tabic, fallen away, spindly, spindle-shanked, lathy, hatchet-faced, lantern-jawed, puny, weak, weakling, stunted, famine-stricken, famine-racked, underfed, undernourished.

2. Spare, sparse, meager, scanty, scant, skimpy, stinted, few, of small number, scarce, exiguous, few and far between, inconsiderable, not to be had, rare, not plentiful, in short supply, wanted, not ample, not enough, inadequate, insufficient, pitiful, slender.

3. Free from fat, not fat (Meat).

LEANING, n. Aptness, aptitude, tendency, preference, weakness, itch, prurience, disposition, temper, temperament, inclination, gravitation, propensity, propenseness, propensitude, propension, proclivity, predilection, predisposition, proneness, turn, bent, bias, warp, twist, liking, animus, feeling, diagonality, course, trend, list, cant, slope, pitch, idiosyncrasy, idiocrasy, predisposition, diathesis, attitude, mind, frame of mind, streak, desire, want, fancy, love, partiality, weakness, inexorability, inflexibility, susceptibility, incumbency, readiness.

LEAN-TO, n. Annex, shanty, shed, pen, shelter, structure, building, addition, hutch, hut, hovel, sty, shack, afterthought.

LEAP, v. 1. Pounce, jump, bound, pounce on, pounce upon, leapfrog, hop, spring, skip, dive upwards, hurdle, clear, negotiate, start, start up, vault, saltate, upleap, upspring, bounce.

2. Caper, gambol, capriole, buckjump, flounce, bounce, prance, dance, spring, buck, frisk, curvet, romp, cut a dido, cavort, caracole, demivolt, gambado, bob, sally, go.

3. Overleap, overjump, leap over, jump over, bound over, bound across, cross, vault, hop, jump, hurtle over.

LEAP, n. 1. Steeplechase, leap, saltation, bound, jump, spring, hop, upleap, upspring, standing jump, flying jump, running jump, standing broad jump, running broad jump, broad jump, high jump, standing high jump, hurdle, hurdle race, vault, pole vault, demivolt, pounce.

2. Caper, dido, buck, frisk, buckjump, falcade, hop, skip and jump, frolic, dance, cavort, prank, caracole, curvet, antic, capriole, prance, gambade (Fr.).

LEARN, v. 1. Get knowledge, take in—, acquire—, pick up—, drink in—, obtain—, receive—, secure—, imbibe—, collect—, gather—, glean—, acquaint oneself with, master, learn by heart, memorize, commit to memory, fix in one's mind, grave in one's memory, get the hang of (coll.), learn by rote, learn word for word, store in one's mind, treasure in one's mind, engrave in one's mind.

2. Discover, determine, bring to light, disclose, hit upon, find, find out, root up, dig up, disinter, uncover, worm out, ferret out, fish out, hunt

down, trace, uncover, ascertain, make out, catch, smoke out, evolve, drag forth, elicit, stumble upon, pitch upon, fall upon, light upon, be informed of, become aware of, become alive to, overhear, get scent of, understand, detect, spot, spy, espy, descry, discern, read, study, peruse, research, investigate, pursue, follow up, exhaust the subject, hunt.

LEARNED, *adj.* 1. Knowing, wise, informed, well-read, enlightened, well-taught, instructed, educated, erudite, lettered, literate, aware, cognitive, cognizant, acquainted with, alive to, informed of, intelligent, sagacious, sage, apprised of, omniscient, sapient, deeply read, widely read, oracular, well-posted, well-educated, well-grounded, well-versed, well-trained, well-conned.

2. Deep, profound, solid, abstruse, acroatic, acroamatic, bookish, booky, book-minded, book-loving, bibliophilic, bibliophilist, bibliophagic, scholastic, scholarly, bluestocking, intellectual, rational, thoughtful, reasoning, brainy, cognitive, percipient, appercipient, scholarlike, academic, monitorial, studious, diligent, assiduous, sedulous, industrious, accomplished, able, proficient, sagacious, talented, expert, experienced.

LEARNER, *n,* Tyro, neophyte, beginner, pupil, student, scholar, scholarian, scholastic, freshman, frosh *(sl.),* freshie *(coll.),* sophomore, soph *(coll.),* junior, senior, upperclassman, underclassman, lowerclassman, undergraduate, postgraduate, graduate, graduate student, alumnus, alumna, schoolboy, schoolgirl, schoolchild, schoolmaid, schoolmiss, classmate, questionist, questioner, monitor, prefect, disciple, follower, apostle, apprentice, 'prentice, articled clerk, probationer, probationist, proselyte, college student, grade-school student, grammar-school student, colleger, collegian, collegiate, college boy, college man, college girl, college woman, coed, co-ed, sophister, grad, novice, novitiate, entrant, matriculate, newcomer, greenhorn, tenderfoot, initiate, catechumen, greenie *(coll.),* recruit, rookie *(coll.),* raw recruit, abecedarian, alphabetarian, commoner, pensioner, charity student, honor man, Phi Beta Kappa.

LEARNING, *n.* 1. Acquisition of knowledge, acquirements, attainment, edification, study, mental cultivation, culture, reading, perusal, inquiry, search, research, quest, hunt, exploration, scrutiny, survey, analysis, questioning, query, pursuit of knowledge, education.

2. Refinement, proficiency, enlightenment, information, body of knowledge, store of knowledge, lore, scholarship, erudition, letters, literature, reading, book learning, book knowledge, pedantry, experience, liberal education, practical knowledge, practical learning, profound knowledge, solid knowledge, extensive knowledge, wide knowledge, vast knowledge, encyclopedic knowledge, infinite knowledge, universal knowledge, wisdom, sagacity, sagaciousness.

LEASE, *v.* 1. Let, demise, hire, rent, subrent, sublet, sublease, underlet, rent out, grant a demise, grant a lease.

2. Hire, rent, lease, take a lease, sign a lease, take a demise, hire by the hour, — by the day, — by the year, sublet, sublease.

LEASH, *n.* Cord, strap, bond, fastening, lead, string, rope, harness, thong.

LEASH, *v.* Secure, fasten, tie, hitch, bind, restrain, curb, keep in check, restrict, check, string, hold, lash, strap, tie up, tether, hook up, pinion.

LEATHER, *n.* Hide, tanned hide, tanning, pelt, fell, scarfskin, skin, covering material, epidermis, integument, tegmentum, dermis, derma, cuticle, kid, capeskin, goatskin, alligator, crocodile, pigskin, peccary, ostrich, suede, glacé kid, mocha, shagreen, chamois, cordovan, horsehide, rawhide, cowhide, buffalo hide, snakeskin, sharkskin, lizard, shoe leather, glove leather.

LEATHER, *v.* Thrash, flog, chastise, whip, beat, punish, lash, flagellate, horsewhip.

See LASH.

LEATHERY, *adj.* Tough, horny, durable, strong, resistant, long-wearing, wrinkled, dried-out, dry, rugged, coarse, resisting, leatherlike, coriaceous, tough as leather, alutaceous.

LEAVE, *n.* 1. Allowance, permission, liberty, license, sanction, sufferance, exemption, authorization, warranty, warrant, exemption, favor, special favor, vouchsafement, tolerance, toleration, grace, concession, indulgence, indulgency.

2. Retirement, departure, farewell, *congé (Fr.),* retreat, going, leave-taking, leaving, evacuation, removal, withdrawal, adieu, parting, debouchment, takeoff *(coll.),* exit, egress, valediction, going away.

3. Furlough, vacation, rest, respite, holiday, excursion, trip, recess, time off *(coll.).*

LEAVE, *v.* 1. Part, part company, separate from, take leave, quit, depart, go away, take one's leave, go along, get along, be off, get off, go, go out, exit, make an exit, make off, be gone, start out from, push off, shove off, embark, entrain, emplane, embus, weigh anchor, hoist anchor, set sail, go forth, sail forth, evacuate, vacate, pull up stakes, fly, flee, flit, say goodbye, bid farewell, bid adieu, bid godspeed, withdraw, remove, retreat, take oneself away, check out *(coll.),* break camp, pull up stakes, take ship, go on board, hotfoot it *(sl.),* hurry away, run away, sally forth, move on, hasten away.

2. Forsake, abandon, quit, withdraw from, relinquish, surrender, yield, drop, wash one's hands of, secede from, evacuate, desert, vacate, leave behind, take leave of, leave in the lurch, turn one's back on, give up, jettison, cast away, forgo, have done with, drop like a hot potato *(coll.),* renege, renig *(coll.).*

3. Disuse, disutilize, give up, cease, desist, abandon, drop, supersede, refrain, shut up shop *(coll.),* call it a day *(coll.),* surrender, resign, renounce, throw up, let slip, let go, release, quit one's hold, discontinue, desist, give over, expropriate, demit, give away.

4. Bequeath, bequest, endow, dow, dower, hand down, assign dower, devise, will, will to, endow with, dot, bless with, intermit, leave behind, give by will, commit, consign, refer.

LEAVE IN THE COLD, *v.* Snub, neglect, overlook, ignore, let slip, let slide, forget, slight, shun, gloss over, put aside, give the go-by *(coll.),* highhat *(coll.),* refuse to recognize, refuse to acknowledge, rebuff, turn from, turn away from, turn one's back on, not take care of, disregard, be heedless of, be neglectful, be negligent, be disregardful, be disrespectful, be thoughtless, be careless, be heedless, slight, blink at, wink at, dodge, pass by, by-pass, **pass up.**

LEAVE IN THE LURCH, *v.* Beat, surpass, outmarch, outdistance, outrun, outrival, cast in the shade, outstrip, outstep, overrun, overshadow, get ahead of, overreach, give the runaround *(coll.),* take the lead, lead, excel, exceed, distance, outdo, outgo, circumvent, abandon, forsake.

LEAVEN, *n.* 1. Leavening, barm, ferment, yeast, enzyme, zyme, diastase, pepsin, fermenting substance, fermenting agent.

2. Cause, motive, component, constituent, integrant, ingredient, source, reason, agent, producer, impulse, power, influence, generator, part and parcel, aspect, contents, appurtenance, makings *(coll.),* element, factor, determinant, determining agent, determining factor.

LEAVEN, *v.* 1. Work, raise, ferment, effervesce, pepsinate, lighten.

2. Tinge, qualify, affect, limit, narrow, restrict, modulate, abate, assuage, temper, soften, mitigate, lenify, reduce, diminish, color, adjust, permeate, imbue, pervade, inspire, lift, elevate.

3. Taint, maculate, corrupt, debase, infect, denaturalize, alloy, adulterate, tarnish, blemish, defile, smear, besmear, befoul, foul, vitiate, soil, spatter, bespatter, sully, pollute, blot, contaminate, degrade, deprave, blotch.

LEAVE NO STONE UNTURNED, *v.* Persevere, persist, seek, search, pry, peer, hunt, fish for, dig for, delve for, hunt after, pursue, track, trail, nose out, smell out, sniff, sniff out, look high and low, turn everything upside down, turn everything inside out, carry on, hold on, endure, stay, stick with it *(coll.),* do one's best, hustle, bustle, keep busy, keep moving, keep the pot boiling, stir about, stir one's stumps *(coll.),* rummage, ransack, peep, pry into every hole, quest, try everything, exhaust every possibility.

LEAVE OFF, *v.* Stick, stall, hold, stay, cease, discontinue, stop, desist, hold one's hand, belay *(Naut.),* refrain, have done with, drop it *(coll.),* halt, pause, rest, hang fire, disuse, disutilize, quit.

LEAVE OUT, *v.* Eliminate, reject, throw out, excise, cut, cut out, expurgate, omit, delete, elide, pass over, slide over, slur, eradicate, extirpate, exclude, bar, count out, repudiate, abridge, cast aside, expunge, erase, discard, remove.

LEAVE-TAKING, *n.* Goodbye, farewell, adieu, valediction, last look, departure, going, retreat, withdrawal, removal, embarkation, takeoff, leave, leaving, going, quittance, debouchment, debouching, debouch, start, outset, setoff, parting, evacuation, abandonment, decampment, decamping.

LEAVINGS, *n.* Leftovers *(coll.),* residue, residuum, remains, balance, remainder, sediment, lees, precipitation, rest, oddments, odds and ends, rags, sawdust, shavings, offal, garbage, waste, chaff, stubble, rubble, straw, detritus, parings, fossil, skeleton, shadow, scobs, filings, raspings, settlings, bottoms, deposit, heel tap, alluvium, alluvion, diluvium, moraine, silt, loess, soot, carbon, charcoal, lava, ash, ashes, cinder, embers, coals, clinker, sinter, scourings, sweepings, dregs, fag end *(coll.),* butt, stump, sordes, mother, dross, sprue, offscourings, froth, scum, wastage, wastements, rubbish, droppings, offaling, slough, draff, carrion, raff, riffraff, bones, junk, rummage, crap *(coll.),* litter, swill, dishwater, bilge, bilgewater, rinsings, scurf, furfur, truck, ordure, manure, excrement, fertilizer, muck, guano, lientery, lienteria, feculence, feces, faeces, spoor.

LECHER, *n.* Wanton, dissipater, rip, rake, rakehell, libertine, adulterer, fornicator, cad, seducer, rapist, raper, violator, ravisher, wolf *(coll.),* fast man, whoremonger, whoremaster, gigolo, silkstocking, fancy man, debaucher, debauchee, intri-

gant, sensualist, voluptuary, sybarite, free liver, immoralist, hard liver, rounder, gay deceiver, gay dog, defiler, satyr, goat, old goat, pederast, sodomite, hedonist, reprobate, pleasure-seeker.

LECHEROUS, *adj.* Carnal, voluptuous, sensual, passionate, libidinous, oversexed, fleshly, animalistic, swinish, brutish, bestial, prurient, lustful, lascivious, concupiscent, salacious, satyric, satyrical, erotic, erotical, lubricous, lubricious, ruttish, rutty, sexy *(coll.),* dissipated, lickerish, lewd, dirty, dirty-minded, goatish, oestrous, oestral, beastlike, theroid, incontinent, desirous, incestuous, unchaste, libertine, musty, burning, beastly.

LECHERY, *n.* Concupiscence, carnality, aphrodisia, carnal passion, fleshliness, lewdness, sexual desire, lust, sexual lust, bodily desire, lustfulness, lasciviousness, bodily appetite, animal nature, lubricity, salaciousness, salacity, prurience, pruriency, debauchery, heat, rut, must, incest, sodomy, masochism, sadism, pederasty, satyrism, satyriasis.

LECTERN, *n.* Reading table, reading desk, table, desk, dais, platform, stage, pulpit, rostrum, ambo.

LECTURE, *n.* 1. Discussion, dissertation, disquisition, talk, speech, screed, oration, preachment, preaching, sermon, spiel *(coll.),* address, public address, declamation, prelection, discourse, allocution, narration, reading, lection, exposition.

2. Reproof, reprimand, censure, harangue, scolding, berating, rating, talk, sermon, preachment, castigation, chastisement, remonstrance, tongue-lashing, dressing, dressing-down, speaking-to, talking-to, objurgation, rebuke, upbraiding, admonishment, exprobration, bawling-out, reproach, chiding.

LECTURE, *v.* 1. Recite, expound, exposit, discourse, preach, address, speak, talk, make a speech, deliver a speech, spiel *(sl.),* hold forth, perorate, mouth, spout *(coll.),* rant, prelect, orate, read, take the stump *(coll.),* stump *(coll.),* state, present, declaim.

2. Rebuke, reprobate, reprehend, reprove, reprimand, call down, give what-for *(coll.),* harangue, trounce, lash, rail at, remonstrate, bring to book, take to task, upbraid, exprobrate, scold, give a lesson to, rate, berate, admonish, chide, give a tongue-lashing, betongue, jaw *(sl.),* objurgate.

LECTURER, *n.* Reader, prelector, prolocutor, speaker, talker, speechmaker, speechifier, reciter, instructor, professor, teacher, tutor, faculty member, orator, spokesman, public speaker, rhetorician, lector, expositor, expounder, staff member.

LEDGE, *n.* 1. Narrow horizontal surface, flat protrusion from a cliff *or* slope, shelf, shelve, sill, mantel, mantelshelf, mantelpiece, shoulder, hob, predella, gradin *(Eccles.),* retable *(Eccles.),* corbel *(Archit.).*

2. Line of rocks *(in the sea or other water bodies),* ridge, reef, layer *or* mass of rock underground *(Mining),* mound, jetty, mole, bar, shoal, flat, vein *(Mining),* lode *(Mining),* stratum *(Mining),* breakwater.

LEDGER, *n.* 1. *(Bookkeeping)* Account book, books, daybook, yearbook, journal, inventory, register, registry, record book, annual, record.

2. Horizontal timber of a scaffolding beam, tie, crosstie, cross-beam, tie-beam, truss, sleeper, corbel, stringpiece.

3. Flat slab of stone over a grave *or* tomb,

marker, tombstone, gravestone, stone, slab, tablet, headstone, footstone, monument.

LEE, *adj.* Pertaining to, situated in *or* moving toward the quarter *or* region toward which the wind blows, leeward *(opposed to weather)*, quiet, sheltered, safe, protected, out of *or* away from the wind.

LEE, *n.* Leeward, lee side, point (quarter, region, shore, place, *etc.*) toward which the wind blows *(chiefly Naut.)*, side sheltered *or* turned away from the wind, shelter, protection, haven, refuge, quiet harbor, safe moorings, asylum, retreat, cover, resort, place out of the wind and weather.

LEECH, *n.* Person who clings to another with a view to gain, adherer, sycophant, parasite, bloodsucker, minion, vassal, tagtail, toady, sponger, toadeater, fawner, truckler, appendant, handshaker *(sl.)*, lickspit, spaniel, tufthunter, snob, groveler, apple-polisher *(sl.)*, barnacle, bur, lickspittle, heeler *(sl.)*, carpet knight, wheedler, courtier, sectary, shadow, flunky, footlicker, lackey, bootlicker, henchman, sidekick *(sl.)*, appendage, dangler, satellite, yes man *(sl.)*.

LEER, *n.* Side glance of sly *or* insulting suggestion, look of malicious significance, sly look *or* glance, sidelong look, evil eye, wink, scoffing *or* derisive look, weasel-like look, smirk, grin, fleer, malign eye *or* look, blighting glance, ogle, squint, basilisk, cockatrice.

LEER, *v.* Look askance (in contempt), glance sideways, look slyly, ogle, gloat, fleer, give the evil eye, smirk, grin, look obliquely, look with insulting familiarity, look significantly, wink, cut one's eye *(sl.)*, eye, squint, give a sidelong look.

LEERY, LEARY, *adj.* Cautious, circumspect, shy of, guarded, careful, wary, suspicious, shrewd, sharp, acute, hesitant, unsure, uncertain, unconvinced, chary.

LEES, *n., pl.* That which settles from a liquid *(esp. from wine)*, dregs, draff, sediment, bottoms, remains, deposit, residue, refuse, grounds, precipitate, settlings, dunder *(West Indies)*, waste, dross.

LEEWARD, *adv.* Toward the lee, alee, to leeward, in the shelter of, away from the wind.

LEEWAY, *n.* 1. *(Navigation):* Way, progress, lateral drift, drifting, deviation from course, lateral movement.

2. *(Aeronautical):* Drift, lateral drift, drift angle.

3. Room, space, room to spare, headway, scope, range, full swing, play, free play, full scope, free scope, latitude, margin, elbow room, wide berth, reach, swing.

4. Delay, cunctation, pause, prolongation, protraction, postponement, demurrage, deferment, dilatoriness, respite, reprieve, tarriance.

LEFT, *adj.* 1. Spare, to spare, left over, remaining, remainder, supplementary, remnant, remanent, surplus, residuary, sedimentary, sedimental, exceeding, over and above, superfluous, over, odd, surviving, unused, uneaten, unconsumed, residual.

2. Sinister, sinistral, sinistrous, sinistrose, sinister-handed, left-handed, sinistrodextral, dextrosinistral, sinistromanual, sinistrocerebral, sinistrocular, leftward, near *(animals)*, sinistrogyrate, sinistrogyric, larboard, port *(Naut.)*.

3. Departed, gone, gone away. (See LEAVE.)

LEFT, *n.* 1. Left hand, left side, near side *(animals)*, port *(Naut.)*, portside, larboard, gospel side *(Eccl.)*, cantorial side *(Eccl.)*, port tack, verso,

left-hand side, wrong hand *(coll.)*, sinistrality, sinistration.

2. Radicals, liberals, democrats, left-wingers.

LEFT-HANDED, *adj.* 1. Having the left hand more serviceable than the right, preferably using the left hand, sinistromanual, sinistral, sinistrodextral, dextrosinistral.

2. Adapted to *or* performed by the left hand, situated on the side of the left hand, sinistral, left-hand, morganatic.

3. Ambiguous, doubtful, opposite, uncertain, obscure, questionable, disputable, equivocal, dubitable, backhand, backhanded, insulting, disparaging, paradoxical, enigmatic, tactless, contrary, disdainful, sardonic, ironic, indefinite, indistinct, veiled, withering, mock, quizzical, irreverent, disrespectful, controvertible, contestable, open to question, speculative, vague, indeterminate, unclear, double, derisive, sarcastic, dubious, contradictory, ill-omened, debatable, mysterious, oracular, cryptic, perplexing, puzzling, bewildering, recondite, abstruse, nebulous, imperspicuous.

4. Clumsy, awkward, fumbling, lubberly, bungling, oafish, blockish, blunderheaded, cumbersome, cumbrous, careless, graceless, gawky, crude, artless, floundering, fudgy, maladroit, gauche, heavy-handed, clumsy-fisted, unhandy, butter-fingered *(coll.)*, ungainly, undexterous, ungraceful, unproficient, inexpert, lumpish, undeft, unadept, inapt, unapt, unskillful, all thumbs *(joc.)*.

LEFTIST, *n.* Socialist, radical, reformer, progressive, red, dissenter, anarchist, Bolshevik, Bolshevist, nonconformist, democrat, liberal, agitator for reform, extremist, left wing *(collectively)*, the left *(collectively)*.

LEFTOVER, *n.* Remainder, residue, residuum, stump, butt, parings, shaving, dust, ashes, cinder, clinker, sinter, carbon, charcoal, embers, planing, shavings, chaff, straw, stubble, rubble, remanent, fragments, scraps, shards, odds and ends, oddments, surplusage, surplus, ruins, detritus, overage, balance, rest, survivor, superfluity, orts, candleends, debris, carry-over, relic, leavings. (See LEAVINGS.)

LEG, *n.* 1. Member, limb, hindquarters *(pl.)*, hind leg, foreleg, lower limb, tibia *(Zool. and Anat.)*, stump *(coll.)*, underpinnings *(coll.)*, epipodiale *(Bones, incl. radius, ulna, tibia & fibula)*, shank, shin, gam *(sl.)*, peg *(coll.)*, pin *(coll.)*.

2. Support, post, column, pillar, prop, brace, upright, trestle, standard.

LEGACY, *n.* Gift left in one's will, bequest, inheritance, devise, heriditament, heritance, patrimony, heirloom, bestowal, reversion.

LEGAL, *adj.* 1. Pertaining to the law, lawful, judiciary, judicatory, official, jurisdictive, jurisdictional, juridical, juristic, vested, constitutional, statutory.

2. According to law, permitted, permitted by law, accordant with the law, prescribed, permissible, unprohibited, allowed, valid, ordained, rightful, licit, legitimate, allowable, admissible.

LEGALITY, *n.* Accordance with law, lawfulness, legitimacy, permissibleness, permissibility, validity, admissibility, admissibleness, rightfulness, constitutionality.

LEGALIZE, *v.* Make lawful, enact, sanction, sanction by law, legitimate, legitimize, legitimatize, legislate, constitute, formulate, enact, pass as law, decree by law, order, order by law, command, ordain, dictate, enjoin, charge, instruct, fix, set, establish, charter, authorize, codify, formulate, bring into conformity with the law, make conformable.

LEGATE, *n.* Diplomat, emissary, minister, minister plenipotentiary, chargé d'affaires, diplomatist, diplomatic agent, ambassador, attaché, vice-legate, nuncio, internuncio, consul, proconsul, representative, diplomatic representative, envoy.

LEGATEE, *n.* Legal heir, beneficiary, donee, recipient, receiver, feoffee, legatary, heir, heiress, inheritor, inheritrix, heir at law, beneficiary heir, heir of provision, devisee, grantee, transferee, indorsee, assignee.

LEGATION, *n.* Commission, delegation, representation, deputation, mission, ministry, embassy, consulate, diplomatic residence, proconsulate.

LEGEND, *n.* 1. Folk tale, fable, fantasy, myth, account, epic, old wives' tale, adventure tale, chronicle, romance, tale, story, saga, yarn, tradition, fairy tale, lay, history, fiction, annal.

2. Motto, device, inscription, writing, jottings, superscription, imprint, impression, annotation, cipher.

LEGENDARY, *adj.* Pertaining to *or* of the nature of legend, celebrated *or* described in legend, fabulous, mythical, mythological, uncanonical, traditional, fanciful, imagined, imaginary, figmental, storied, narrative, epic, fancy-formed, heroic, apocryphal, supernatural, fictional, fictitious, romantic, idealistic.

LEGERDEMAIN, *n.* 1. Sleight of hand, jugglery, trickery, magic, prestidigitation, juggle, thaumaturgy, conjury, hocus-pocus, juggling.

2. Trickery, deception, artful tricks, imposture, fraudulence, guile, cheating, knavery, subtlety, cunning, sharp practice, dodgery, chicanery, jobbery, maneuvering, duplicity, treachery, hocus-pocus, humbug, gyp *(sl.)*, jugglery, swindling, graft *(coll.)*, wirepulling, politics, rascality, deceit, intrigue, pettifoggery, slyness, hoax, flimflam, flam *(coll.)*.

LEGERDEMAINIST, *n.* Artist, artiste, theatrical performer, theater artist, juggler, magician, sleight of hand artist, trickster, tricker, wizard, conjurer, prestidigitator.

LEGGINGS, *n., pl.* Extra outer covering for the leg, gaiters, puttees, gambados, antigropelos, leg armor, greaves, spats, galligaskins, chaps *(Western U. S.)*, spatterdashes, chaparajos *(Sp. Amer.)*, chivarras *(Mexico & Southwest U. S.)*.

LEGIBILITY, *n.* Neatness, cleanness, readability, plainness, clarity, decipherability, lucidity, lucidness, intelligibility, distinctness, explicitness, distinguishability, discernibility, unmistakability.

LEGIBLE, *adj.* 1. That may be read *or* deciphered *(esp. with ease)*, clear, distinct, precise, regular, uniform, careful, even, tidy, plain, fair, orderly, neat, painstaking, definite, methodical, unmistakable, decipherable, readable, clear-cut, comprehensible, graphic, understandable, well-marked, intelligible.

2. That may be discerned *or* distinguished, apparent, evident, manifest, discoverable, visible, recognizable, graphic, self-evident, straightforward, express, unquestionable, prominent, pronounced, plain, certain, unhidden, patent, uncloaked, unconcealed, revealed, palpable, salient, comprehensible, understandable, vivid, decisive, positive, decided, articulate, well-marked, undis-

guised, perspicuous, clear-cut, clear, unmistakable, distinct, intelligible.

LEGION, *n.* 1. Military *or* semi-military unit, large body of armed men, corps, military force, troops, battalion, brigade, regiment, phalanx, force, soldiery, host, army.

2. Multitude *(of persons or things)*, host, horde, myriad, army, party, gathering, congregation, cohort, mob, levy, tribe, great number, conclave, swarm, convention, throng, lot, band, troop, gang, concourse, company, cavalcade, muster, conflux, confluence, drove, array.

LEGIONARY, *n.* Legionnaire, soldier, foot soldier, infantryman, infantry soldier, fighting man, warrior, combatant, fighter, rifleman, light infantryman.

LEGISLATE, *v.* Exercise the function of legislation, enact laws, pass laws, make laws, constitute laws, prescribe *or* formulate laws, set *or* establish laws, ordain, effect by legislation, create *or* annul by law *or* legislation, bring about by legislation.

LEGISLATION, *n.* 1. Act of making *or* enacting laws, lawmaking, codification, government, regulation, guidance, legislature, conduct, congressional statesmanship, constitution-making.

2. A law *or* body of laws enacted, system of rules, polity, canon, legal code, constitution, regulation, ordinance, statute, ruling, enactment, act, digest, edict, charter, capitulary, prescript, dictate, corpus juris, pandect.

LEGISLATIVE, *adj.* 1. Having the function of making laws, judicial, lawmaking, juridical, jurisdictive, nomothetic, legific, vested, jurisprudential, lawgiving, legal, official, jurisdictional, judiciary.

2. Of *or* pertaining to legislation *or* a legislature, legislatorial, judicial, council, congressional, juridical, judicatory, curule, senatorial, synodical, parliamentary, jurisdictive.

3. Ordained by legislation, lawful, legitimate, legal, licit, decreed, statutory, authorized, ordained, chartered, constituted, within the law, conformable to law, licensed, rightful, according to law, permitted, constitutional, judicial, legalized, synodical, prescribed, valid, allowed, allowable, admissible, official.

LEGISLATOR, *n.* One who gives *or* makes laws, lawgiver, member of a legislative body, statesman, lawmaker, congressman, senator, congresswoman, congressist, congressionist, assemblyman, senatress, Member of Congress, M. C., Member of Parliament, M. P., congressionalist, statist, politician, representative, filibuster, politico *(often derog.)*.

LEGISLATURE, *n.* Parliament, Senate, House of Representatives, The House, House of Commons, House of Lords, Assembly, General Assembly, State Senate, reins of government, caucus, convention, States-General, diet *(Japan)*, Duma *(Imperial Russia)*, Soviet *(USSR)*, National Congress, Chamber of Deputies *(France)*, Upper House, Lower House, Reichstag *(Germany)*, Bundestag *(West Germany)*, Riksdag *(Sweden)*, Storthing *(Norway)*, Bundesversammlung *(Austria, Switzerland)*, Rigsdag *(Denmark)*, Oirechtas *(Eire)*, Cortes *(Spain)*, Cortes Geraes *(Portugal)*.

LEGITIMATE, *adj.* 1. Lawful, in accordance with law, permitted, legalized, rightful, constitutional, licit, right, proper, born in wedlock *or* of parents legally married, resting on *or* ruling by the principle of hereditary right, ordained, statutory, warranted, allowable, equitable, indefeasible, statutable, enfranchised, prescribed, unimpeachable, permissible, chartered, licensed, sanctioned, vested.

2. In accordance with established rules, principles *or* standards, of the normal *or* regular type *or* kind, pure, authentic, true, natural, standard, fair, real, not spurious, genuine, normal, unqualified, constant, faithful, all wool and a yard wide *(coll.)*, trustworthy, scrupulous, reliable, unadulterated, orthodox, eighteen-carat, sterling, bona fide, rightful, accurate, statutable, authoritative.

3. In accordance with the laws of reasoning, logical, logically inferrible, admissible, sound, tenable, valid, plausible, inferential, well-grounded, justifiable, rational, reasonable, fairly deduced, correct, credible, reliable, just.

LEGITIMATE, LEGITIMIZE, *v.* Make *or* pronounce lawful, legalize, make legitimate, show *or* declare to be legitimate *or* proper, justify, authorize, establish as lawfully born, sanction, allow, validate, establish, entitle, approve, certify, defend, vindicate, support, endorse, give sufficient grounds *or* good reason for.

LEGUME, *n.* Edible seed of leguminous plants, pea, bean, lentil, leguminosal, vegetable, pod of leguminous plants, pulse, legumen *(Bot.)*.

LEISURE, *adj.* Free from demands, unoccupied, disengaged, spare, free, one's own, unrestricted, independent, unhampered, unhindered, uncurbed, optional, unburdened, scot-free, at liberty, clear, unobstructed, unencumbered.

LEISURE, *n.* Free time, unoccupied time, holiday, recess, ease, freedom from business, time to spare, vacant time, liberty, rest, pause, inoccupation, loafing, stay, halt, lull, convenience, breather, spell, letup *(coll.)*, intermittence, breathing spell, respite, break, time out *(coll.)*, time on one's hands, disengagement, vacation, time of one's own, interval, intermission, interlude, interruption of work, spare time, spare hours.

LEISURELY, *adj.* Acting, proceeding *or* done without haste, unhurried, deliberate, idle, slack, creeping, long-continuing, showing *or* suggesting ample leisure, inactive, idling, unemployed, lymphatic, phlegmatic, heavy, listless, drawn-out, protracted, restful, peaceful, languid, tardy, slow-going, slow-moving, easy, gradual, gentle, moderate, dilatory, quiescent, torpid, inert, poking, poky, drony, weary, spun-out, snail-like, acting slowly, hasteless, indolent, tortoiselike, extended, torpescent, apathetic, lethargic, dillydallying, at one's leisure, at one's convenience, at one's own sweet time, lazy, supine, exanimate, lax, otiose, disengaged, lingering, unoccupied, dronish, prolonged, slow, leisured, reposing, loafing.

LEISURELY, *adv.* In a leisurely manner, without haste, unhurriedly, at snail's pace, slowly, deliberately, at one's own sweet time, idly, tardily, at one's leisure, at slow tempo, at one's convenience.

LEITMOTIF, *n.* *(Music, drama)* Motif associated throughout with a particular person, situation *or* idea, statement, motive, theme, suggestive melody.

LEMON, *n.* 1. Fruit, citrus fruit.

2. Color, hue, tint, yellow, lemon yellow, citron yellow, lemon chrome, chrome lemon.

LEND, *v.* Advance, accommodate, trust with, extend credit, lend on security, let out, put out at interest, invest, come across with *(coll.)*, accredit, intrust.

LEND A HAND, *v.* Do a good turn, assist, help, pitch in *(coll.)*, pull an oar, succor, boost, come

to the aid of, relieve, rescue, give support, lend sustenance, bear up, shoulder, sustain, cooperate, aid, render a service, extend a helping hand, give a lift, chip in *(coll.)*, subscribe, support.

LENDER, *n.* Moneylender, moneychanger, Shylock, usurer, banker, moneymonger, loanshark, pawnbroker, creditor, credit man, creditress, creditrix, debtee, mortgagee, grantor, bestower, my uncle *(sl.)*, money broker, lessor.

LEND ONESELF TO, *v.* Consent, assent, concur, agree with, agree to, participate in, give assent, yield assent, hold with, accede, accept, abet, go to work for, countenance, give support to, second, endorse, stand behind, stand back of, be a party to, act as an accessory to, have a hand in, bear a hand, pull an oar.

LENGTH, *n.* 1. Longitude, extent, measure, distance, mileage, range, reach, fly, span, longness, remoteness, compass, stride, measurement, magnitude, size, limit.

2. Lengthiness, elongation, prolixity, amplification, long-windedness, endlessness, tediousness, interminableness, boringness, tedium, wearisomeness, discursiveness, ramblingness, talkiness, verbosity, longiloquence, desultoriness, digressiveness, wordiness.

3. Accent, stress, prolongation, quantity.

4. Duration, stretch, extent, continuance, space, period, term.

5. Piece, coil, roll, run, section.

LENGTHEN, *v.* Make long, extend, elongate, stretch, prolong, protract, draw out, let out, spin out, aggrandize, make larger, increase in length, eke out, produce *(Geom.)*, drawl, tarry, dawdle, temporize, delay.

LENGTHWISE, *adv.* Longitudinally, crosswise, from end to end, along, endways, endlong, lengthways, from stem to stern.

LENGTHY, *adj.* 1. Verbose, talky, prolix, discursive, long-winded, digressive, garrulous, loquacious, longiloquent, rambling, maundering, wandering, errant, interminable, boring, tedious, tiresome, wearisome, inflated, over-inflated, without end, endless, sesquipedalian, drawn-out, extended, over-extended, diffuse, roving, desultory, wordy.

2. Elongated, lengthened, extended, prolonged, protracted, elongate, great, far-reaching, far-distant, far-seeing, faraway, extensive, outstretched.

3. Prolonged, accented, accentuated, stressed, sustained, lengthened.

4. Tall, rangy, lanky, gangling *(coll.)*, lofty, high, long-legged, spindle-shanked, spindle-legged, long-limbed, spare, gaunt, big.

LENIENCE, LENIENCY, *n.* Lenitude, mercy, mildness, tolerance, toleration, lenity, gentleness, patience, pity, flexibility, forbearance, indulgence, clemency, compassion, grace, readiness to spare, forgivingness, charity, humanity, disposition to mercy, freedom from vindictiveness, exorability, favor, benevolence, liberality, longanimity, consideration, ruth, moderation, mercifulness, placability, quarter, kindness, mitigation, soft-heartedness, laxity.

LENIENT, *adj.* Merciful, tender, tender-hearted, clement, mild, kind, indulgent, forgiving, tolerant, benevolent, liberal, kindhearted, soft, moderate, charitable, free from vindictiveness, sympathetic, pitiful, ready to spare, placable, ruthful, exorable, pardoning, pitying, magnanimous, longanimous, compassionate, temperate, soft-hearted, considerate, patient.

LENITIVE, *adj.* Palliative, soothing, mitigating, assuaging, alleviating, assuasive, lenient, emollient, lubricative, easing, balmy, mitigative, relieving, demulcent, sedative, softening.

LENITIVE, *n.* Demulcent, ointment, salve, embrocation, liniment, balm, lotion, palliative, cerate, anodyne, unguent, opiate, lenient, nard, emollient, pomade, pomatum, calmative.

LENITY, *n.* Mercifulness, moderation, ruth, consideration, longanimity, placability, quarter, kindness, mitigation, soft-heartedness, laxity, exorability, favor, benevolence, liberality, freedom from vindictiveness, disposition to mercy, humanity, forgivingness, readiness to spare, grace, compassion, lenience, charity, clemency, gentleness, patience, pity, flexibility, forbearance, indulgence, toleration, tolerance, leniency, mercy, mildness.

LENS, *n.* Eyeglass, optic, optical, ocular, loupe, spectacles, eyeglasses, glasses, eyepiece, lorgnette, magnifier, magnifying glass, spyglass, converging lens, reducing lens, diverging lens, concave lens, convex lens, periscopic lens, meniscus, hand lens, telescope, telescopic lens, field glasses, monocular, binocular, opera glasses, microscope, anamorphic lens, panoramic lens, achromatic lens.

LENTICULAR, *adj.* 1. Of *or* pertaining to a lens, convexo-convex, lentoid, meniscal, meniscoid, menisciform, bulging, swelling, excurved, lentiform, protuberant, gibbous, gibbose, gibberose, arched, bowed, bellied, lens-shaped.

2. Resembling a lentil (seed) in form, seed-like, pod-like, pea-shaped, bean-shaped, lentiform.

LENTITUDE, *n.* Sluggishness, slowness, tardiness, leisureliness, lentor, languor, deliberateness, loginess, sleepiness, pokiness (*coll.*), dullness, lassitude, stagnancy, inactivity, lethargy, torpor, torpitude, oscitance, oscitancy, apathy, kef, inertness, lumpishness, hebetude, heaviness, dilatoriness, slackness, easiness.

LEONINE, *adj.* Belonging to a lion *or* lions, pertaining to the lion, lionlike, powerful, bold, kingly, courageous, brave, mighty, aweless, imperial, lion-hearted. (The following pertain to physical description): shaggy, tawny, maned, mane-like, heavy with hair.

LEOPARD, *n.* 1. Fur, leopard skin, Baltic Leopard, Coney Leopard.

2. Felidae (*Zool*), Felinae (*Zool*), cat, feline, wild cat, jungle cat, spotted cat, *Panthera Pardus* (*Zool*), jaguar, American Leopard, cheetah, hunting leopard, ounce, snow leopard, black leopard, panther.

LEPER, *n.* Outcast, pariah, social outcast, derelict, castaway, Ishmael, man without a country.

LEPRECHAUN, *n.* Shee, sidhe, cluricaune, fairy, fairyman, fay, sprite, elf, dwarf, goblin, hobgoblin, gnome, the little people, the little men, the good folk, the good people, elfenfolk, banshee, pixy, brownie.

LEPROSY, *n.* Disease, infection, virus infection, ailment, affliction, malady, sickness, disorder, affection.

LEPROUS, *adj.* Affected with leprosy, diseased, of *or* like leprosy, cankered, ulcerated, tainted, morbid, scabby, scaly, scabious, syntectic, consumptive, tubercular, phthisical, palsied, mortified, sphacelate (*Med.*), anesthetized (of skin areas), gangrened, gangrenous, lepidote (*Bot.*).

LESE MAJESTE (Lese Majesty), *n.* Revolt, disloyalty, sedition, treachery, treason, duplicity, treacherousness, perfidy, misprision, petty treason, high treason, betrayal, Iscariotism, defection, disaffection, outbreak, rebellion, insurrection, riot, double-dealing, revolution.

LESION, *n.* 1. Injury, wound, break, ill, cut, scratch, puncture, contusion, stab, scuff, burn, disfiguration, sore, pock, blister, scar, mutilation, incision, trauma, harm, hurt, gash, bruise, laceration, impairment, blemish, damage, scrape, defect, flaw, labefaction.

2. (*Pathol.*) Localized morbid structural change in the body, disorder, growth, failure, tumor, swelling, excrescence, ravage, inroad, abnormality, derangement, breakdown.

LESS, *adj.* 1. Smaller in size, amount *or* degree, *etc.*, not so large, great *or* much, inconsiderable, compressed, narrower, contracted, trivial, slighter, shorter, deficient, lower, abated, reduced, dwarfed, briefer, scarce, meager, puny, insufficient, inappreciable, diminutive, minute, lessened, subsided, immaterial, modest, little, limited, abated, moderate, scant, skimpy, infinitesimal, fewer, shortened, fainter, stinted, shrunk, diminished, inferior.

2. Lower in consideration, dignity *or* importance, unessential, insignificant, inferior, unaspiring, secondary, minor, lesser, ignoble, junior, commonplace, humble, indifferent, fair, frail, in the shade, subaltern, subordinate, suppressed, found wanting, imperfect, below par, simple, of little *or* no consequence, of no account, mediocre, immaterial, second-rate, unimportant, least, mere, ineffectual, under.

LESS, *adv.* To a smaller extent, amount, *etc.*, not so much, in a less degree, under par, not so well, below the mark, short of, under, below.

LESS, *n.* Not so much, smaller quantity *or* amount, deficiency, minimum, decrease, decline, lower degree, subtraction, contraction, decrement, lesser amount, inferiority, abridgment, reduction, shortening, abbreviation, curtailment, diminishment, little, loss, inadequacy, disappointment.

LESSEE, *n.* Roomer, tenant, lodger, renter, underlessee, sublessee, holder, possessor, property holder, relessee, tenant at will, tenant from year to year, person in possession, boarder, room-and-boarder, occupant, occupier.

LESSEN, *v.* 1. Become less, wither, fall, ebb, bate, shrivel, fail, decline, reduce, abate, mitigate, erode, tail off, run low, dwindle, let up, languish, crumble, fall to a low ebb, waste *or* wear away, remit, wane, melt *or* die away, drop off, deliquesce, attenuate, diminish, moderate, subside, decrease, grow less, consume, contract, shrink, fall off *or* away.

2. Make less, shrink, pare, mitigate, remit, minify, cut, prune, truncate, take the edge off, attenuate, extenuate, allay, crop, take from, take away, contract, assuage, modify, lenify, quell, lop, relax, deplete, appease, blunt, deaden, soothe, palliate, slake, dull, alleviate, constrict, temper, thin out, decimate, discount, soften, weed out, stunt, boil down, deduct, shorten, curtail, reduce, narrow, dock, ease, subtract, qualify, liquidate, retrench, render less, take in, relieve, clip, abbreviate, minimize, moderate, condense, abridge, cut down, fritter away, compress, epitomize.

3. Represent as less, disparage, lower, put in one's place, detract, belittle, dwarf, debase, call into question, blacken, reprehend, disvalue, denounce, blame, reflect upon, pass censure upon, derogate, undervalue, depreciate, discommend, dis-

praise, decry, cry down, despise, misprize, slight, scorn, underestimate, decimate, discount, discredit, slander, malign, vilify, vilipend, libel, speak slightingly *or* ill of, gibbet, give a bad name, muckrake, minimize, calumniate, make light of, attach too little importance to, not do justice to, extenuate, set at naught, bear false witness against, defame, stigmatize, expose to infamy, fling *or* throw mud at, bespatter, weaken one's position, make little of, asperse, slur, run down, traduce, cast aspersions, underrate, cast doubt upon, deride, impeach, censure.

LESSER, *adj.* Less (*as in size, amount, importance, etc.; esp. of two*), smaller, inferior, lower, secondary, junior, minor, subaltern, simple, under, second-rate, subordinate, slighter, less considerable, more modest, humbler, simpler, less perfect, mediocre.

LESSON, *n.* 1. Something to be learned *or* studied, part of a book assigned for study, exercise, task, teaching, assignment, study, homework, instruction, stint, lecture, reading, recitation.

2. Useful *or* salutary piece of practical wisdom, something from which one learns *or* should learn, example, parable, apologue, prelection, sermon, moral fable, allegory, precept, discourse, advice, teaching, disquisition, harangue, forewarning, word to the wise, flea in the ear, word in one's ear, notification, didactive narrative, preachment, instruction.

3. Reproof intended to teach one better ways, punishment, warning, scolding, caution, denunciation, reproval, exprobration, reproach, talking-to, jobation (*coll.*), lecturing, rebuke, censure, tirade, deterrent example, sharp hint, caveat, blackball, boycott, reprimand, correction, set down, chastisement, remonstrance, piece *or* bit of one's mind, calling-down (*sl.*), tongue-lashing (*coll.*), hit (*coll.*), hint, threat, castigation, bawling out (*sl.*), expostulation, curtain lecture, admonishment, rap on the knuckles, slap in the face, philippic, dressing-down (*coll.*), raking down, ragging (*sl.*), trimming (*coll.*), roasting (*coll.*), chiding, lecture, slam (*coll.*), slap, injunction. example, admonition, reprehension, upbraiding, objurgation.

LESSOR, *n.* One who grants a lease, lender, owner, rent receiver, landlord, landlady, creditor, mortgagee, holder.

LEST, *conj.* That . . . not, in order to avoid *or* prevent, so that . . . not, if perhaps . . . not, if perchance . . . not, for fear that, that (*after words expressing fear, danger, etc.*).

LET, *v.* 1. Allow, permit, give leave to, give permission to, sanction, authorize, give power *or* full power, entitle, suffer, license, facultate, recognize, vouchsafe, grant, favor, wink at, consent to, commission, empower, concede, tolerate, warrant, give the reins to, approve, yield to, give franchise to, affranchise, liberate, not interfere, give one rope, render free, concur, not refuse, assent, give one his head, have no objection, leave it to one, give *carte blanche* (*Fr.*), give one leeway (*coll.*), privilege, entrust, bear with, enable, open the door to.

2. Allow to pass, go, come *or* escape, liberate, loose, uncork, let out, spill, pour, let go, let loose, set free, discharge, unimprison, uncage, give entree, open the door to, open the gates *or* floodgates, give passage to, receive, take in, release, unloose, admit, free from restraint, grant passage.

3. Grant the occupancy *or* use of for rent *or* hire (*occas. fol. by* OUT), lend, loan, sublet, sub-

lease, lease, put to hire, charter, farm, rent *or* hire out, underlet, subrent, hire.

4. (*As in the phrase "to let one know"*) Cause, make, enable, permit, allow, make it possible for, not refuse, grant, suffer, warrant, contrive, bring about, bring to pass, empower, facultate.

5. (*Fol. by* DOWN) Disappoint, depress, drop, lower, fail, crush, be found wanting, fall short of expectation, not keep faith, be faithless, be deficient, sell out (*sl.*), renege, withdraw one's support, pull out, bolt, abandon, forsake, desert, jilt, double-cross (*sl.*), cross up (*sl.*), play one false, go back on (*coll.*), abjure, recant, prove treacherous to, repudiate, renounce, mortify, humiliate, abash, put out, change sides, back out, leave in the lurch, break one's word *or* promise, go back on one's word *or* promise (*coll.*), apostatize, betray.

6. (*Fol. by* ON) Allow to be known, announce, come out with, let fall *or* drop, let slip, blurt out, utter, whisper, leak out, spill (*sl.*), reveal, tell, breathe, publish, give away (*sl.*), tattle, blab, betray *or* reveal a secret *or* confidence, make public, break the news, divulge, let the cat out of the bag (*coll.*).

7. Be rented *or* leased, be for hire, be on loan, be put out, be offered, be available.

LETDOWN, *n.* (*Coll.*) Disappointment, blighted hopes, dashed expectations, failure, flop (*coll.*), drubbing, beating, setback, frustration, balk, check, foil, comedown, comeuppance (*coll.*), blow, buffet, licking (*coll.*), undoing, overthrow, discomfiture, rout, defeat, collapse, adversity, blow to one's pride, deflation, deflating, disillusionment, disillusioning, humbling, humiliation, disgrace, shame, shaming, set down, mortification.

LETHAL, *adj.* Deadly, lethiferous, mortal, suicidal, murderous, fatal, slaughtering, nocuous, poisonous, malefic, noxious, venomous, baneful, killing, destructive, mortuous, deathful, internecine, internecive, annihilative, harmful, pernicious, hurtful, injurious, nocent, toxic, septic.

LETHARGIC, LETHARGICAL, *adj.* Spiritless, indifferent, inanimate, drowsy, weary, torpid, heavy, inert, inactive, comatose, lackadaisical, dull, stupefied, supine, impassive, idle, lifeless, obtuse, phlegmatic, soporific, slumbrous, somnolent, listless, languid, sleepy, sluggish, indolent, dormant, insouciant, slothful, fainéant.

LETHARGY, *n.* Stupor, languor, supineness, insouciance, obtuseness, dullness, apathy, sleepiness, weariness, slowness, somolence, coma, torpor, inactivity, oscitancy, tiredness, torpescence, phlegm, drowsiness, sluggishness, inactivity, laziness, torpidity, stupefaction, stupidity, indolence, inertia, insensibility, latency, lassitude, heaviness, doze, inertness.

LETTER, *n.* 1. Communication in writing *or* printing, epistle, note, line, dispatch, missive, answer, reply, billet, message, bulletin, favor, rescript, encyclical, business letter, billet-doux, bull, acknowledgment, circular, drop letter, form letter, fan letter, round robin, monitory, pastoral (*Eccles.*), hieroglyphic, letteret, loveletter.

2. Mark *or* sign conventionally used to represent speech sound, alphabetic character, symbol, subscript, superscript, digraph, monogram, vowel, consonant, capital, majuscule, minuscule, ligature (*Print.*), ABC's (*pl.*), lower-case (*Print.*), upper-case (*Print.*).

3. Actual terms *or* wording (*as distinct from general meaning or intent*), literality, strict meaning, minuteness, nicety, fastidiousness, literal in-

terpretation, exact sense, rigor, austerity, preciseness, scrupulousness, literalness.

LETTER, *v.* Mark *or* write with letters, initial, inscribe, sign, mark, outline, stencil, trace, draft, block in, character.

LETTER CARRIER, *n.* Mail carrier, postman, mailman, postboy, postal clerk, public servant, government employee, civil servant, civil service employee, carrier, bearer, transporter, courier.

LETTERED, *adj.* 1. Informed, educated, instructed, enlightened, wise, sagacious, book-wise, book-fed, book-taught, book-learned, book-read, bookish, scholastic, literate, cultivated, cultured, learned, erudite, highbrow *(coll.),* accomplished, literary, well-informed, well-posted, well-educated, well-grounded, well-versed, well-read, deeply read, widely read, polished, refined.
2. Literal, spelled, spelt, spelled out, spelt out, acristic, syllabic, polysyllabic, dissyllabic, monosyllabic, majuscular, minuscular, uncial, half-uncial, rubricated, alphabetical, abecedarian, transliterated, monogrammed, traced, traced out, orthographic, orthographized, ciphered, encoded, coded.

LETTERS, *n., pl.* 1. Literature, writing, books, scholarship, study, studies, *belles lettres (Fr.),* polite literature, muses, humanities, litterae humaniores *(Lat.),* republic of letters, world of letters, field of letters, field of literature.
2. Alphabet, ABC, ABC's, abecedary.

LETUP, *n. (Coll.)* Abatement, time out, abeyance, lessening, interim, retard, diminution, diminishing, interval, retardation, decrease, interlude, slackening, decrescence, recess, slowing down, diminishment, rest, slowdown, alleviation, pendency, ease off, mitigation, spell, easing up, curtailment, breathing, breath, deceleration, decline, cut, lull, wane, reduction, lapse, vacation, pause, termination, hesitation, stay, intermission, respite, remission, interruption, relief, break, subsidence, suspense, suspension, caesura.

LEVEE, *n.* 1. Porch, ridge, stoop, embankment, dike, river bank, veranda, terrace.
2. Party, ceremony, assembly, entertainment, ceremonious party, soiree, social gathering, gathering, foregathering, get-together, reception.

LEVEL, *adj.* 1. With even *or* flat surface, smooth, uniform, plane, even, flat, horizontal, flush, complanate, homaloidal *(Math.).*
2. Quiet, restrained, nonchalant, composed, serene, placid, imperturbable, quiescent, level-headed, tranquil, inexcitable, unruffled, self-controlled, self-assured, self-possessed, inirritable, unruffled, balanced, sane, poised, even-tempered, undisturbed, untroubled, cool-headed, steady, recollected, dispassionate, collected, peaceful, at ease, *degagé (Fr.),* unstirred, undemonstrative, temperate.

LEVEL, *n.* 1. Horizontal plane, horizontal, flat, plane, homaloid.
2. Rank, grade, class, place, position, estate, station, footing, status, standing, degree, situation, sphere.

LEVEL, *v.* 1. Flatten, smooth, even out, roll, align, plane, horizontalize, planish, equalize, levigate.
2. Raze, wreck, lay waste, dissolve, unmake, tumble, obliterate, gut, lay in ruins, root out, blast, efface, pull down, knock down, annihilate, expunge, reduce to nothing, ravage, eradicate, extirpate, ruin, consume, devour, shatter, shiver, topple.

LEVEL-HEADED, *adj.* Calm, cool, cool-headed, sober, sober-minded, self-possessed, steady, wise, sagacious, prudent, considerate, circumspect, dispassionate, dependable, sedate, self-controlled, self-restrained, unruffled, solid, peaceful, placid, judicious, judicial, politic, calculating, unimpassioned, thoughtful, philosophical, composed, poised, discreet, discretionary, collected, indisturbable, imperturbable, reflecting, reasonable, sensible, sound, cool as a cucumber, nerveless, inexcitable, discriminative, discriminating.

LEVER, *n.* Bar acted upon by two forces and rotating on a fulcrum, device for mechanical advantage, pry, crowbar, crow, prying bar, jimmy, handspike, oar, wing, limb, arm.

LEVER, *v.* Raise by use of mechanical advantage, pry, force, raise, hoist, lift, boost.

LEVERAGE, *n.* Action of a lever, mechanical advantage *or* power gained by using a lever, increased power of action, foothold, pry, purchase, fulcrumage, elevation, lift, lifting power, vantage, advantage, support, hold, sublevation.

LEVIGATE, *v.* Reduce to a fine powder *(with or without liquid),* rub, grind, smooth, powder, pulverize, crumble, bray, mix, crush, commix, triturate, comminute, atomize, contriturate, grate, granulate, disintegrate, mash, smash.

LEVITATE, *v.* 1. Rise in the air by reason of lightness *or* alleged supernormal power, float, hover, swim, soar, rise, plane, glide, be buoyed up, be light as a feather.
2. Cause to rise *or* float in the air, lighten, raise, inflate, render light, make buoyant, buoy up, uplift.

LEVITY, *n.* Lightness of mind, character *or* behavior, lack of proper seriousness *or* earnestness, fickleness, frivolity, hilarity, triviality, foolishness, folly, silliness, jollity, waggery, jocundity, merriment, inanity, tomfoolery, fatuity, ninnyism, futility, imprudence, frivolousness, fribble, inconstancy, giddiness, buffoonery, variability, jocularity, horseplay, waggishness.

LEVY, *n.* 1. Raising *or* collecting *(as of money or troops)* by authority *or* force, mobilization, muster, draft, conscription, exaction, extortion, assessment, taxation, collocation, impressment.
2. That which is raised *(as a tax assessment or body of troops),* recruits, army, draft, troops, militia, armed forces, duty, dues, revenue, reserves, tax, reward, excise, custom, fee, tariff, toll, tribute, contribution, impost, assessment.

LEVY, *v.* 1. Make a levy of, collect *(taxes, contributions, etc.),* extort, seize, require, demand, wrest, commandeer, take by force, distrain *(Law),* impose as an assessment on, tax, assess, charge, lay *(a duty)* on, put *(a duty)* on.
2. Raise *(troops, etc.)* for service, enlist, conscript, force, compel, dragoon, impress, draft, coerce, press, constrain.
3. Make *(war),* start, instigate, begin, wage, carry on, combat, harry, strike the first blow, bombard, open fire, invade, lift a hand against, march on, advance against, do *or* give battle, engage in hostilities, campaign, declare, fight, storm, attack, charge, draw *or* unsheathe the sword, take up the cudgels *or* sword, take up arms, take the field, lay at, set *or* fall upon, make an inroad, raid, besiege, harass, ravage, go on the warpath, assault, assail.

LEWD, *adj.* Inclined to, characterized by *or* inciting to lust *or* lechery, incestuous, concupiscent, impure, ruttish, bawdy, lascivious, ribald, lubricious, obscene, pornographic, Cyprian, light, fast, loose, whorish, scarlet, dissolute, dissipated, debauched, adulterous, lurid, smutty, unclean, dirty, coarse, gross, foul, filthy, unchaste, unvirtuous, incontinent, wanton, vile, offensive, fulsome, Fescennine, indecent, immodest, lustful, beastly, bestial, swinish, animalistic, theroid, prurient, lickerish, lecherous, libidinous, foul-spoken, foul-mouthed, licentious, suggestive, fleshly, carnal, salacious, shameless, abandoned, scurrilous, profligate, of easy virtue, satyric, goatish, erotic, free, of loose character *or* morals, streetwalking, Paphian, sensual, brutish.

LEWDNESS, *n.* Carnality, sensuality, voluptuousness, salaciousness, salacity, prurience, pruriency, lechery, lecherousness, lubricity, lasciviousness, carnal passion, sensuous desire, sexual desire, bodily appetite, aphrodisia, sapphism, fleshly lust, lustfulness, concupiscence, eroticism, erotism, nymphomania, satyriasis, unnatural desires, incest, incestuousness, sodomy, pederasty, sadism, masochism, Lesbianism, profligacy, indecency, smut, smuttiness, evil, evil-mindedness, impurity, debauchery, obscenity, unchastity, incontinence, fleshliness. (See also LEWD, *adj.*)

LEXICOGRAPHER, *n.* Dictionary maker, compiler, editor, author, dictionarist, scholar, lexicologist, lexicographist, glossarist, glossarian, glossologist, glossographer, glottologist, vocabulist, phonologer, phonologist, orthoëpist, linguist, linguistic scholar, etymologist, etymologer, orismologist, dialectician, dialectologist, philologist, philologian, philologer, phonetician, pohoneticist.

LEXICOGRAPHY, *n.* Derivation, etymology, origin, genesis, glottogony, glossology, glossography, lexigraphy, lexicology, philology, phonology, terminology, orismology.

LEXICON, *n.* Dictionary *(esp. of Greek, Latin or Hebrew),* wordbook, list of words belonging to a particular subject, field *or* class, vocabulary, glossary, thesaurus, polyglot, atlas, idioticon, onomasticon, synonymicon, gradus, gloss, index.

LIABILITY, *n.* 1. Obligation *(esp. for payments),* debt, duty, score, due *or* dues, indebtment, debit, pledge, contract, onus, burden, responsibility, accountability, indebtedness.

2. Something disadvantageous, drawback, hindrance, inconvenience, discommodity, disadvantage, obstacle, inutility, unfitness, inopportunity, incommodity, impropriety, unsuitability, barrier, difficulty, hamper, obstruction, undesirability, check, block, bar, hitch, catch, curb, holdback, stumbling block, weight, millstone 'round one's neck, cross, encumbrance, spoke in one's wheel, load, shackle, impediment, fetter, objection, infelicity, handicap, drag, clog.

3. State *or* fact of being liable, proneness, tendency, aptness, exposure, susceptivity, obligation, state of being subject, disposition, inclination, proclivity, aptitude, propensity, predisposition, predilection, penchant, readiness, vulnerability, susceptibility.

LIABLE, *adj.* 1. Subject to something possible *or* likely *(esp. something undesirable),* exposed, open, unprotected, obnoxious, pregnable, susceptive, susceptible, vulnerable, in danger, amenable.

2. Under legal obligation, responsible, chargeable, answerable, unexempt from, amenable, obnoxious *(chiefly Legal).*

LIAISON, *n.* 1. Contact between units *or* bodies maintained to ensure concerted action, close relationship, correlation, alliance, association, connection, bond, nexus, link, tie, coherence, kinship, affiliation, vinculum, junction, coalition, union, coöperation, consolidation, privity *(Law).*

2. Illicit intimacy between a man and a woman, intrigue, entanglement, amour, amourette, affair.

LIAR, *n.* One who lies *or* tells lies, prevaricator, storyteller, falsifier, fabricator, prologue, perjurer, false witness, fibber, romancer, fabulist, untruther, misleader, equivocator, pseudologist *(hum.),* fibster *(coll.),* mytholomaniac *(Psychopathol.),* Ananias *(coll.).*

LIBATION, *n.* Drink, offering, wine offering, sacrifice, oblation, propitiation, gift.

LIBEL, *n.* Defamation, slander, commination, malicious falsehood, invective, aspersion, disparagement, abuse, slur, calumny, denunciation, revilement, depreciation, obloquy, denigration.

LIBEL, *v.* Slur, cast a slur upon, vilipend, vilify, malign, detract, defame, derogate, run down *(coll.),* disparage, discredit, decry, debase, degrade, bring low, muckrake, throw mud on, blacken, dishonor, insult, slander, revile, pull to pieces, besmirch, bespatter, spatter, calumniate, bear false witness against, speak ill of, speak evil of, give a bad name to, satirize, lampoon, asperse, cast aspersions, belittle, traduce, cry down, anathematize, brand, scandalize, abuse, accuse, denigrate.

LIBELANT, (LIBELLANT, *Brit.),* *n.* Accuser, accusant, accusatrix, complainant, appellant, delator, party, party to a suit, suitor, plaintiff.

LIBELOUS, *adj.* Derogatory, vilifying, maledictory, slanderous, detracting, scurrile, scurrilous, abusive, vilipenditory, contumelious, disparaging, defamatory, calumnious, calumniatory, traducent, critical, insulting, dishonoring, discreditable, discrediting, satirical, sarcastic, backbiting, acrimonious.

LIBERAL, *adj.* 1. Favorable to progress *or* reform *(as in religious or political matters),* radical, reforming, advanced, progressive, modern, enlightened, humanitarian, latitudinarian, libertine *(derog.),* not conservative, open-minded, forward-looking.

2. Advocating freedom for self-expression *or* self-fulfillment, opposed to restriction of the individual, broad-minded, modern, up-to-date, favoring enlightened ideas, progressive, liberalistic, informal, unconventional, bohemian.

3. Of representative forms of government *(rather than aristocracies and monarchies),* republican, democratic, federal, of the people, self-ruling, autonomous, independent, self-governing.

4. Free from prejudice *or* bigotry, tolerant, unprejudiced, broad-minded, unprepossessed, dispassionate, disinterested, broad, free-thinking, not strict *or* rigorous, unbigoted, unwarped, unbiased, lenient, charitable, indulgent, catholic, responsive, emancipated, amenable, nonsectarian, unprovincial, open-minded, of broad sympathies, forgiving, unhidebound, unopinionated, liberated, uninfluenced, unperplexed, unjaundiced, impartial, unswayed, big, latitudinarian.

5. Giving freely *or* abundantly, generous, openhanded, free, lavish, beneficent, altruistic, humane, benevolent, almsgiving, ungrudging, unsparing, free-handed, big-hearted, bounteous, bountiful, munificent, princely, unstinting, prodigal, indulgent, charitable, extravagant, handsome, humani-

tarian, eleemosynary, unselfish, magnanimous, great-hearted.

6. Given freely *or* abundantly, plentiful, bountiful, extensive, copious, free, abundant, ample, profuse, prodigal, full, wholesale, far-reaching, widespread, sweeping, replete, unstinted, prevalent, inexhaustible, unsparing, unmeasured, rife, enough and to spare, rich, affluent, plenteous, lavish, bounteous, wide, broad.

7. Not strict *or* rigorous, broad, loose, not confined to the literal sense, not close, free, extended, casual, inexact, unprecise, departing from the original *or* intended, unrestricted.

8. Befitting a freeman, gentleman *or* nonprofessional person, educated, cultured, gentlemanly, kind, kindly, elevated, indulgent, not servile, princely, high, lofty, gracious, gallant, gentle, well-mannered, well-bred, genteel, courteous, courtly, cultivated, self-respecting, unsubmissive, charitable, chivalrous, sublime, exalted, noble, proud, mild, queenly, handsome, magnanimous, broad-minded, big-hearted, heroic, generous, humane.

LIBERALISM, *n.* Liberal principles *(as in religion or politics)*, freedom from tradition and authority *(modern Protestantism)*, open-mindedness, emancipated view, radicalism, free thought, freethinking, progressivism, catholicity, universality, lack of bigotry *or* prejudice, breadth of mind, liberality, forward view, broad-mindedness, latitudinarianism.

LIBERALITY, *n.* 1. The quality of being liberal in giving, bounty, generosity, charitableness, magnanimity, beneficence, philanthropy, open *or* free hand, large *or* free heart, good *or* kind offices, chivalry, elevation of spirit *or* purpose, altruism, largess, kindness, hospitality, liberalness, unselfishness, munificence.

2. Liberal gift, largess, donation, gratuity, reward, bounty, large tip, premium, bonus, handsel, benefaction, labor of love, generous offering, sportula, lagniappe.

3. Breadth of mind, liberalism, broad-mindedness, free thought, freethinking, universality, catholicity, open-mindedness, latitudinarianism.

LIBERALIZE, *v.* Make *or* become liberal, broaden, extend one *or* oneself, widen, grow, develop, increase *or* enlarge one's view, expand, bud, outgrow, grow out.

LIBERATE, *v.* 1. Set free *(as from bondage)*, release, extricate, deliver, emancipate, acquit, give liberty to, ransom, redeem, let go, manumit, let loose, let out, set at large, affranchise, dismiss, discharge, absolve, clear, unfetter, loose, disenthrall, vindicate, exonerate, untie, unshackle, unchain, unbind, exculpate.

2. Disengage, set free from combination *(as a gas)*, release, volatilize, drive off *or* out, vaporize, extricate, purify, gasify, evaporate, make volatile, render gaseous, extract, sublime *(Chem.)*, sublimate *(Chem.)*, aerify, etherify *(Chem.)*, distill.

LIBERATION, *n.* Rescue, liberating, freeing, setting free, emancipation, manumission, escape, deliverance, loosing, release, enfranchisement, disenthrallment, disimprisonment, dismissal, discharge, absolution, extrication, acquittance, acquittal, redemption, disengagement, liberty, freedom, getaway *(coll.)*, jail break, elusion, flight, immunization, salvation, exemption, reprieve, reprieval, exculpation, exoneration, remission, compurgation, clearance, pardon, vindication, ransoming, ransom.

LIBERATOR, *n.* Freer, rescuer, savior, emancipator, preserver, manumitter, redeemer.

LIBERTINE, *adj.* Characteristic of a libertine, free from moral restraints, dissolute, freethinking, uncontrolled, unconstrained, unchecked, licentious, unrestrained, sensual, debauched, lewd, light, fast, wanton, easy, prostitute, voluptuous, dissipated, free-living, luxurious, excessive, saturnalian, inordinate, incontinent, ungoverned, loose, lax, slack, unbridled, weak-willed, lawless, inabstinent, bacchic, rakish, orgiastic, immoderate, unchaste, epicurean, crapulous, corybantic, lenient, intemperate, licensed, self-indulgent, unself-disciplined, prodigal, profligate.

LIBERTINE, *n.* One free from restraint *or* control, one free from moral restraints, dissolute man, rake, profligate, sensualist, fast man *or* woman, lecher, debauchee, voluptuary, hedonist, sybarite, carpet knight, epicurean, gourmand, free liver, epicure, glutton, bon vivant, man of pleasure, Lothario, rip *(coll.)*, rounder *(sl.)*, Don Juan, Casanova, Heliogabalus, prodigal, dissipater, roué.

LIBERTINISM, *n.* Libertine practices *or* habits of life, licentiousness, dissipation, intemperateness, inabstinence, intemperance, debauchery, incontinence, wantonness, unrestraint, orgy, luxury, gluttony, saturnalia, prodigality, epicureanism, sensuality, sensualism, unchastity, wild living, high living, crapulence, profligacy, laxity, looseness, immoderation, excessive indulgence, self-indulgence.

LIBERTY, *n.* 1. Freedom from arbitrary *or* despotic government, absence of external *or* foreign rule, independence, power *or* right of choice *(in doing, thinking, speaking, etc.)*, chance, scope, room, place, one's own initiative, license, self-determination, wide berth, elbowroom, margin, free course, immunity, full swing, exemption, franchise, space, latitude, freedom from hampering conditions *(as control, interference, obligation, restriction, etc.)*.

2. Freedom from captivity, confinement *or* physical restraint, emancipation, exoneration, exculpation, vindication, liberation, release, deliverance, dismissal, acquittal, absolution, ransom, escape, reprieve, pardon, respite, excuse, disenthrallment, disengagement, affranchisement, manumission, discharge.

3. Leave granted to a sailor to go ashore, shore leave, time off, congé *(Fr.)*, pass *(Mil.)*.

4. Freedom *or* right of frequenting *or* using a place, *etc.*, opportunity, permission, run, range, leave, favor, due, free passage, vouchsafement, prerogative, sanction, authorization, admission, privilege, grant, power.

5. Unwarranted *or* impertinent freedom in action *or* speech, laxity, brazenness, forwardness, impudence, audacity, temerity, boldness, presumptuousness, arrogance, gall *(sl.)*, malapertness, complacency, brass *(coll.)*, self-assurance, assumption, shamelessness, overconfidence, presumption, sauce *(coll.)*, sauciness, cheek *(coll.)*, effrontery, nerve *(sl.)*, crust *(sl.)*.

LIBIDINOUS, *adj.* Full of lust, lustful, lewd, licentious, incestuous, vile, wanton, whorish, lubricious, obscene, concupiscent, ruttish, foul, unchaste, incontinent, unvirtuous, filthy, fast, loose, bawdy, lascivious, impure, pornographic, debauched, dissipated, dissolute, scarlet, Cyprian, adulterous, smutty, dirty, gross, coarse, fulsome, indecent, immodest, offensive, Fescennine, bestial, animalistic, prurient, theroid, beastly, swinish, lickerish, lecherous, fleshly, carnal, satyric, scurrilous, profligate, goatish, free, Paphian, sensual, brutish, erotic, suggestive, unclean.

LIBIDO, *n.* The innate actuating *or* impelling force in living beings, vital impulse, urge, all instinctual energies and desires derived from the id *(Psychoanal.),* dynamic, life, spirit, intensity, animus, breath, energy, divine spark, life principle, vital force *or* energy, life force *or* energy, Promethean spark, animating principle, psyche, soul, heart, *vis vitae (Lat.).*

LIBRARIAN, *n.* Person trained in library science and engaged in library service, officer in charge of a library, curator, bibliothec, bibliosoph, bibliognost, bibliothecary.

LIBRARY, *n.* Room *or* building containing books and other literary materials *(for reading, study or reference),* lending library, collection of manuscripts, publications, *etc.,* public organization maintaining books, study, book room, public library, bibliothec, bibliotheca, book club, circulating library, bookery, athenaeum.

LIBRETTIST, *n.* Lyrist, lyricist, author, playwright, poet, writer, dramatist, dramatizer, dramatic author, dramatic writer, stagewright.

LIBRETTO, *n.* Text *or* words of an opera *or* other extended musical composition, book *or* booklet containing text, score, part, song book, opera.

LICENSE, *n.* 1. Formal permission *or* leave to do *or* not do something, authorization, power, grant, charter, patent, sanction, copyright, furlough, warrant, safe-conduct, imprimatur, carte blanche *(Fr.),* admission, free passage, vouchsafement, privilege, prerogative.

2. Certificate of permission, permit, charter, pass, warrant, passport, safe-conduct, safeguard, imprimatur.

3. Freedom of action, speech, thought, *etc.,* permitted *or* conceded, absence of external restraint, liberty, free choice, self-determination, immunity, franchise, exemption, privilege, independence, margin, free course, latitude.

4. Intentional deviation from rule, convention *or* fact *(as for the sake of literary or artistic effect),* divergence, aberration, nonconformity, irregularity, disregard of conventional concepts, the law in one's own hands, nonobservance of laws, noncompliance, evasion, nonperformance.

5. Excessive *or* undue freedom *or* liberty, licentiousness, libertinism, laxity, audacity, forwardness, temerity, presumptuousness, gall *(sl.),* malapertness, brass *(coll.),* assumption, overconfidence, presumption, effrontery, crust *(sl.),* nerve *(sl.),* cheek *(coll.),* boldness, arrogance, complacency, self-assurance, shamelessness, sauce *(coll.),* sauciness, brazenness, impudence, wantonness, prodigality, self-indulgence, looseness, immoderation, profligacy, epicureanism, wild living, high living, debauchery, incontinence, intemperateness, dissipation, inabstinence, unrestraint, orgy, sensuality, saturnalia, gluttony.

LICENSE, *v.* Grant authoritative permission *or* license to, warrant, allow, permit, authorize, enable, charter, accredit, invest with authority, entitle, privilege, enfranchise, empower, sanction, commission.

LICENTIOUS, *adj.* 1. Sensually unbridled, lewd, libertine, incestuous, concupiscent, impure, ruttish, bawdy, lascivious, ribald, lubricious, obscene, pornographic, Cyprian, loose, whorish, scarlet,

dissolute, dissipated, debauched, adulterous, lurid, smutty, unclean, dirty, coarse, gross, foul, filthy, unchaste, unvirtuous, incontinent, wanton, vile, offensive, Fescennine, indecent, immodest, lustful, beastly, bestial, swinish, animalistic, theroid, prurient, lickerish, lecherous, libidinous, fleshly, carnal, salacious, shameless, abandoned, scurrilous, profligate, of easy virtue, satyric, goatish, erotic, free, of loose character *or* morals, streetwalking, brutish, sensual, Paphian.

2. Going beyond customary *or* proper bounds *or* limits, unrestrained by law *or* morality, lawless, immoral, unruly, anarchic, criminal, irresponsible, ungoverned, unrestrained, disorderly, chaotic, unchecked, freethinking, fast, light, loose, intemperate, prodigal, licensed, immoderate, unconstrained, unconformable, irregular, deviative, divergent, aberrant, straying, wanton, anomalous, unorthodox, egregious, flagrant, eccentric, heteroclite, exceptional, ungoverned, wayward, transgressive, slack, lax, disobedient, unprincipled, unconscienced, unconscionable, unscrupulous.

LICIT, *adj.* Lawful, permitted, legal, accordant with the law, prescribed, unprohibited, valid, ordained, allowed, legitimate, admissible, allowable, rightful, permissible, sound, inferrible, just, reasonable, justifiable, legalized, right, proper, statutory, indefeasible, warranted, licensed, enfranchised, constitutional.

LICK, *n.* 1. Stroke of the tongue over something, light touch, brush, kiss, taction, contact, glance, graze, lambency.

2. Small quantity, bit, particle, modicum, scrap, jot, touch, dab, snatch, cut, chip, snip, crumb, soupçon, tinge, splinter, shred, suspicion, shade, tittle, speck, point, dot, mote, iota, hoot, ace, whit, spark, morsel, sip, bite, hint, suggestion, dash.

LICK, *v.* 1. Touch lightly, brush, graze, glance, sweep, tongue, wash, play, pass the tongue over, ripple.

2. Drink, drink in, drink up, suck, suck in, suck up, sup, bib, swig *(coll.),* swill *(coll.),* guzzle *(coll.),* quaff, sip, lap, lap up, take up, take in, consume.

3. *(Coll.)* Defeat, beat, conquer, vanquish, subdue, put down, worst, get the better of, overthrow, overturn, upset, overcome, drub, floor, get the best of, overpower, overmaster, overmatch, override, thrash, whip, discomfit, rout, put to flight, beat up *(coll.),* crush, quell, flog, scourge, punish, chastise, slap, buffet, pummel, spank, smack.

LICKERISH, *adj.* Lascivious, concupiscent, obscene, licentious, bawdy, coarse, gross, filthy, pornographic, salacious, lurid, shameless, smutty, libidinous, indecent, lustful, lecherous, prurient, fulsome, vile, Fescennine, unchaste, unclean, dirty, wanton, ribald, erotic, debauched, Paphian, dissipated, goatish, suggestive, satyric, carnal, fleshly, brutal, bestial, animalistic, ruttish.

LICKING, *n.* *(Coll.)* Beating, drubbing, chastising, chastisement, defeat, vanquishment, conquerment, overthrow, overturn, rout, discomfiture, flogging, thrashing, lashing, punishment, whipping, conquest, undoing, flogging, castigation.

LICKPENNY, *n.* Miser, niggard, pinchpenny, harpy, curmudgeon, tightwad *(sl.),* skinflint, save-all *(dial.),* moneygrubber, moneygrub, codger, pinchfist, scrimp, muckworm, churl, screw.

LICKSPITTLE, *n.* Sycophant, toady, toad-eater, hanger-on, parasite, timeserver, bootlicker, footlicker, back-slapper, yes-man, back-scratcher, clawback, tufthunter, groveler, adherent, henchman, appendage, follower, dependent, reptile, leech, barnacle, satellite, tagtail, sponger, sponge, flatterer, cringer, teacher's pet, apple-polisher, wardheeler, sucker, snob, flunky, dead beat.

LID, *n.* 1. Cover, operculum, cork, cap, top, bottle cap, stopper, stopple, stop, plug, covercle. 2. Eyelid. 3. Hat, head covering, headdress, cap, headgear, headpiece, headclothes, castor, bonnet, *etc.* (See HAT.)

LIE, *n.* Falsehood, deception, prevarication, dissimulation, lying, falsification, untruth, untruthfulness, falseness, subterfuge, tall story, tale, fib, white lie, romance, fiction, taradiddle, flam, untruism, fabrication, forgery, story, yarn *(coll.),* invention, concoction, mendacity, false statement, false story, perjury, guile, dishonesty, misstatement, cock-and-bull story, far-fetched story, incredible tale, myth, fable, deception, deceptiveness, monstrous lie, whopper *(coll.),* perversion, suppression, false coloring, mental reservation, simulation, concealment, exaggeration, hyperbole, distortion, evasion, fraud, fraudulence, deceit, gloss, barefaced lie, dirty lie, inaccuracy, fish story.

LIE, *v.* 1. Falsify, prevaricate, distort, misstate, invent, spin, concoct, coin, fabricate, fake, fake up, cook up, doctor, varnish, gloss over, pervert, equivocate, fib *(coll.),* bull, perjure oneself, utter a falsehood, tell a falsehood, be untruthful, forswear, be a liar, bear false witness, speak falsely, delude, draw the long bow, exaggerate, misteach, misinform, misguide, misinstruct, miseducate, dupe, fool, cozen, magnify, enlarge, hyperbolize, color too highly, trifle with the truth, mince the truth, hoax, victimize, betray, play false, deceive, beguile, trick, cheat, misrepresent, pervert, overdraw, stretch, strain, wrench the truth, pile up. 2. Be horizontal, be supine, recline, repose, rest, sprawl, loll, laze, be level, be flat, be smooth, be even, be plane, be plain, be flush. 3. Inhere, be present, exist, remain, stand, consist, abide, obtain, exist in space, be, prevail, endure, last, consist, occur, fall in the way of, nestle in. 4. Be situated, be placed, range, run, stay, be located, have place in.

LIEGE, *n.* Overlord, superior, lord, ruler, chief, chieftain, master, lord paramount, sovereign, liege lord.

LIEGEMAN, *n.* Vassal, inferior, subject, subordinate, henchman, underling, servant, man.

LIEN, *n.* Charge, security on property, real security, hold on property.

LIEUTENANT, *n.* 1. Commissioned officer, first lieutenant, second lieutenant, lieutenant junior grade, commander, leader, platoon leader, sublieutenant, military man, soldier, fighter, naval officer, army officer, navy man, army man. 2. Subordinate, *alter ego (Lat.),* representative, deputy, employee, assistant, second, delegate, agent, factor, tool, surrogate, secondary, aid, aide, helper, aide-de-camp, vicar.

LIFE, *n.* 1. The condition which distinguishes animals and plants from inorganic organisms and dead objects, existence, being, presence, substantiality, viability, flesh and blood, animateness. 2. Term of animate existence of an individual, span, life expectancy, term of existence (activity,

effectiveness) of something inanimate *(as a machine or lease),* lifetime, generation, one's born days, one's natural life, period of existence, duration of life. 3. A living being, soul, person, individual, human, creature, man, woman, child, homo, mortal, anthropos, member of the human race, people *(pl.),* folk *or* folks *(pl.),* personage. 4. Living things collectively, creation, kingdom, fauna, flora, denizens, native growth, wild life, fish of the sea, beasts of the field, fowls of the air, stock, game. 5. Course *or* mode of existence, way of life, manner of life, function, part, scope, field, walk, course, cue, role, pattern, capacity, province, sphere, routine, race, line, career, position, situation. 6. Biography, autobiography, journal, letters, life story *or* history, fortunes, adventures, experiences, confessions, personal narrative. 7. Animation, liveliness, vitality, energy, vivacity, spirit, sprightliness, intensity, fire, drive, kick, pep, verve, vigor, mettle, dynamic, vim, alacrity, activeness, snap *(coll.),* briskness, go *(coll.).* 8. That which makes *or* keeps alive, vivifying *or* quickening principle, universal life force, world spirit *or* soul, oversoul, God, nature, archeus, logos, the Absolute, impelling force, vital impulse, urge, animus, breath, life principle, breath of life, divine spark, Promethean spark, psyche, soul, heart, *vis vitae (Lat.),* animating principle. 9. Existence in the world of affairs *or* society, *etc.,* the world, state of affairs, doings, concerns, the times, march of events, ups and downs, chapter of incidents, course *or* tide of events, circumstances, vicissitudes of fortune. 10. One who *or* that which enlivens, effervescence, freshness, sparkle, wit, spark, animation, pungency, refreshment, enlivenment, invigoration, exhilaration, dynamic, spirit, vigor, stimulation, vivification. 11. Living form *or* model *(as the subject or representation in art),* prototype, original, posed subject, the object itself, action, motion, figure.

LIFE-GIVING, *adj.* Vitalizing, revitalizing, vivifying, fecundative, energizing, animating, quickening, generative, procreative, progenerative, procreant, propagative, animative, Promethean, productive, spermatic, fertilizing, inceptive.

LIFELESS, *adj.* 1. Dead, without life, bereft of life, defunct, gone, stone-dead, azoic *(Biol.),* deceased, inanimate, demised, dead as a doornail *(coll.),* dead as mutton *(coll.),* departed *(euphem.),* asleep *(euphem.),* at rest *(euphem.).* 2. Dead, dull, empty, barren, devoid, inadequate, insipid, arid, hollow, flat, effete, inefficacious, worthless, tame, meager, wanting, prosaic, uninteresting, insulse, lean, vapid, deficient, vacant, uninspiring, poor, weak, puerile, unsatisfactory, unsatisfying, fruitless, colorless, unprofitable, stale, flat, unfruitful, otiose, lame, unfertile, inept.

LIFELIKE, *adj.* Speaking, true, faithful, graphic, exact, imitative, natural, descriptive, well-drawn, realistic, strict, close, conscientious.

LIFEWORK, *n.* The work, labor *or* task of a lifetime, profession, line, following, job, vocation, activity, pursuit, work, walk, life, employment, career, livelihood, occupation, business, calling.

LIFT, *n.* 1. Act of lifting, raising, elevation, sublevation, upthrow, ascension, escalade, ascent, mounting, uplift, upheaval, rising, erection. 2. Extent of rise, distance through which anything is lifted, ascent, climb, rise, height, altitude, range upward, space upward.

3. 'Helping hand upward *or* onward, assistance, advancement, chance, aid, betterment, backing, sustenance, nurture, interest, advance, help, service, succor, boost, hand, promotion, headway, encouragement, heart, ease *(coll.),* patronage, good turn, guidance, ministration, ride, support, *deus ex machina (Lat.),* championship, relief, reinforcement, maintenance, easement, fosterage, auspices, subvention, enhancement, improvement, furtherance, ministry, accommodation.

4. Exaltation, uplift in feeling, elation, transport, rapture, ecstasy, inspiration, rhapsody, bliss.

5. Device *or* apparatus for lifting, elevator, crane, derrick, winch, tackle, capstan, erecter, windlass, pulley, jack, jackscrew, escalator, dumbwaiter, dredge.

6. Rise of ground, elevation, upgrade, knoll, dune, ridge, chine, bank, climb, grade, vantage point, mountain, slope, height, hillock, hummock, incline, acclivity, monticule, mound, hill, eminence, spine.

LIFT, *v.* 1. Move something from the ground *or* other support to a higher position, raise, leaven, rear, erect, elevate, hoist, heave, upraise, set up, uplift, uprear, buoy, mount, pick up, pitch, heighten, set on its feet, dredge up, stand up, fish up, direct upward, sublevate, take up.

2. Hold up, display on high, manifest, show, wave, trumpet, present, proclaim, unveil, unfold, set forth, blazon, bear aloft *or* up, put forward, proclaim from the housetops, put in the limelight, flaunt, brandish, post, herald, publicize, unmask, publish, exhibit, unfurl, uphold.

3. Raise *(in rank, condition, estimation, etc.),* exalt, improve, elevate, extol, honor, promote, better, meliorate, profit, ameliorate, place *or* set on a pedestal, ennoble, benefit, help, enthrone, signalize, enshrine, be the making of, deify, celebrate, uplift, distinguish, aggrandize, aid, sublimate, immortalize, dignify, advance, avail, do a good turn to.

4. Send up audibly *or* loudly by utterance, raise, give voice to, bawl, brawl, call, heave, plead, roar, bellow, weep, shriek, shrill, entreat, cheer, beg, invoke, importune, carol, pipe, screech, beseech, vociferate, supplicate, rend the air, wail, howl, clamor, implore, caterwaul, cry.

5. Go up, give to upward pressure, rise, rise and disperse, ascend, come up *or* off, wind *or* curl upward, float away, be dispelled, vaporize, soar, be driven off *or* away, mount, release, move upward, evaporate.

6. Pull in the effort to lift something, strain, pull, tug, ply, struggle, heave, exert oneself, strive, draw, drag, haul, put forth one's strength, tow.

7. Rise to view above the horizon *(when approached),* grow, appear gradually, heave in sight, open to view, materialize, approach, draw nearer, come closer, loom, be disclosed, emerge.

LIFTER, *n.* Hoist, jack, derrick, erector, erecter, windlass, capstan, winch, pulley, block, block and tackle, dredge, dredger, dredging machine, cone pulley, jackscrew, chute, lever, crowbar, jemmy, jimmy, elevator, elevator dredge.

LIGATURE, *n.* Anything that serves for binding *or* tying up, band, bond, cord, ligament, link, nexus, connection, vinculum, bandage, stroke *or* bar connecting two letters *(Print.),* string, line, cable, strap, strand, rope, thong, funiculus *(Anat.),* bridge, ligation, slur *(Music),* hitch, thread *or* wire used for constriction *(Surg.).*

LIGATURE, *v.* Bind with a ligature, tie up, ligate, strap, hobble, hitch, secure, pinion, fasten, cinch, shackle, fetter, couple, leash, lash, truss, fix.

LIGHT, *adj.* 1. Not heavy or burdensome, weightless, feathery, gossamery, light as a feather, light as air, levitative, buoyant, imponderous, floaty, ethereal.

2. *(Of food, etc.)* Easily assimilated, digestible, digestive, frugal, of light texture, peptic, moderate, scanty, slight, fluffy.

3. Not hard *or* difficult, easy, slight, trivial, facile, simple, manageable, soft, cushy *(sl.),* convenient, handy.

4. Frivolous, airy, gay, spry, carefree, lighthearted, flimsy, trivial, frothy, sprightly, trifling.

5. Gleeful, in high spirits, debonair, bright, sportive, breezy, optimistic, jaunty, sunny, laughing, smiling, riant, happy-go-lucky, elastic, airy, jubilant, mirthful, free and easy, gay, light-hearted, jolly, elated, unworried, jovial, jocular, careless, happy, resilient, cheerful, glad, nonchalant, sprightly, joyous, buoyant, brisk, easygoing.

6. Well-lighted, bright, illuminated, luciform, lucid, brilliant, scintillating, fulgid, orient, scintillant, sparkling, floodlit, blazing, luciferous, shining, gleaming, sunny, beamy, luminous, radiant, rutilous, rutilant, lustrous, lambent, vivid, luculent, garish, glowing, aglow, effulgent.

7. Light-colored, pale, white, fair, whitish, ivory, creamy, bleached, light-hued, light-toned, pearly, blond, pearl-white.

8. Thin, paltry, little, skimp, skimpy *(coll.),* sparse, trivial, modest, slight, superficial, inappreciable, inconsiderable, moderate, petty, scanty, minute, small, slender, cursory.

LIGHT, *n.* 1. Flood of light, brightness, blare, nitency, illumination, radiance, irradiation, glare, shine, brilliance, effulgence, emanation, incandescence, fulgor, luster, radiation, gleam, refulgence, lucency.

2. Day, daylight, dawn, foredawn, aurora, daybreak, sunrise, sunup, dayspring.

3. Intelligence, understanding, information, elucidation, wisdom, enlightenment, learning, education, culture, civilization, rationalism, refinement, freedom of thought, sapience, knowledge, insight, perception.

4. Luminary, model, precept, mirror, archetype, paragon, example, guide, *beau idéal (Fr.).*

LIGHT, *v.* 1. Set burning *(candle, lamp, pipe, etc.),* kindle, ignite, fire, set fire to, inflame, strike a light, apply the match *or* torch to, conflagrate.

2. Give light to, illuminate, illumine, shine upon, irradiate, furnish with light *or* illumination, luminate, supply with light, cast *or* throw light upon, strike a light, flood with light, turn *or* switch on a light, brighten, overshine, floodlight.

3. *(Usually with* UP) Make bright *(as with light or color),* lighten, brighten, glow, beam, flash, shine, glimmer, radiate, flare, blaze, glitter, become dazzling, phosphoresce, effulge, illuminate, luminesce, scintillate, blaze, shimmer, break into a smile *(of a face),* flicker, take on radiance.

4. Conduct with a light, guide, make the path *or* way clear, escort, usher, clear, elucidate, clarify, direct, pilot, shed *or* throw light upon, explain, make plain, lend a helping hand, make intelligible, illuminate.

5. Get down *(as from a horse or vehicle),* alight, descend, unhorse, detrain, drop, settle, sit down,

disemplane, dismount, debus *(Mil. sl.)*, come to rest *(as on a spot or thing)*, perch, land, fall *(as a stroke, weapon, vengeance, choice, etc.)* on a place *or* person.

6. *(Fol. by* ON *or* UPON) Come by chance, happen, hit, meet with, find, discover, stumble on, learn, encounter, blunder upon, make out, spy, descry, fall upon, come across, burst upon, find out, spot *(coll.)*, distinguish, detect, guess correctly, pitch upon, pick up.

LIGHTEN, *v.* 1. Become lighter *or* less dark, brighten, shine, light up, be bright, enlighten, glow, supply with light, irradiate, luminesce, phosphoresce, give light to, reveal by light, gleam, illuminate, illumine, luminate, flood with light, make bright, effulge.

2. Flash as *or* like lightning, glint, flare, glance, blaze, fulgurate, dazzle, glitter, glimmer, sparkle, glisten, scintillate, flicker, blink, shimmer, twinkle, play.

3. Make lighter, lessen the weight of, reduce the load of, ease, uplift, buoy up, mitigate, facilitate, levitate, unload, relieve, palliate, alleviate, unburden, make less burdensome, assuage, disencumber, allay, take off a load, leaven, disburden, upraise, make buoyant.

4. Cheer, gladden, brighten, buoy up, uplift, invigorate, refresh, hearten, inspirit, elate, encourage, enliven, make rejoice, exhilarate, regale, inspire, stimulate, quicken, restore, revivify, comfort, warm, revive, reassure, animate.

LIGHTER, *n.* 1. One who *or* that which ignites, igniter, sparker, torch, incendiary, firebrand, flint, lucifer, match, fusee, detonator, flint and steel, fuse, cap, spill, taper, pyromaniac, fire bug *(coll.)*, brand, vesuvian.

2. Flat-bottomed, unpowered vessel, loading vessel, barge, raft, float, catamaran, canal boat, hoy *(Naut.)*.

LIGHT-FINGERED, *adj.* Having nimble fingers *(esp. in picking pockets)*, thievish, larcenous, thieving, sly, furacious, furtive, stealthy, pilfering, filching, stealing, slick, cunning, adroit, wily, crafty, lifting *(coll.)*.

LIGHT-FOOTED, *adj.* Stepping lightly *or* nimbly, light-foot *(Poetic)*, agile, fast, swift, airy, lightsome, nimble, buoyant, speedy, rapid, winged, quick, brisk, spry, peppy, active, light of heel, sprightly, fleet, nimble-footed.

LIGHT-HEADED, *adj.* 1. Having *or* showing a frivolous *or* volatile disposition, fickle, whimsical, giddy, fitful, fanciful, light-minded, trivial, foolish, frothy, lightsome, silly, wavering, vacillating, light, airy, inane, erratic, irresponsible, mercurial, variable, trifling, inconstant, flirtatious, capricious, unreliable, tergiversating, changeable, unstable, shallow, superficial, adrift, afloat, without ballast, undependable, coquettish.

2. Giddy, dizzy, delirious, phrenetic, raving, wandering, mazed, rambling, incoherent, vertiginous, off one's head, bewildered, distracted, hazy, foggy, confused.

LIGHT-HEARTED, *adj.* Cheerful, carefree, lightsome, gay, happy, blithe, debonair, jolly, gladsome, cheery, winsome, genial, joyous, mirthful, buoyant, jovial, merry, pert, joyful, elated, animated, sprightly, pleasant, jocund, sportive, gleeful, sunny, brisk, in high spirits, in high humor, bright, chipper *(coll.)*, sans souci *(Fr.)*, lively, vivacious, airy, hopeful, free and easy, optimistic, volatile, jubilant, frisky, jaunty, breezy.

LIGHTHOUSE, *n.* Tower *or* other structure displaying lights for the guidance of mariners, beacon, signal light *or* lamp, lookout, lightship, watchtower, observation post, Pharos.

LIGHTING, *n.* Enlightenment, light-making, radiation, irradiation, gas lighting, electric lighting, incandescent lighting, fluorescent lighting, arc lighting, direct lighting, indirect lighting, decorative lighting, stage lighting, flood lighting, overhead lighting, diffuse lighting, illumination.

LIGHTLESS, *adj.* Without light, receiving no light, darksome, giving no light, dark, black, night-clad, night-mantled, night-filled, night-veiled, gloomy, murky, dismal, dusky, lowering, starless, moonless, sunless, pitch black, pitch dark, unilluminated, unlighted, obscure, darkling, penumbral, tenebrous, pitchy, nocturnal, shady, dim, tenebrific, clothed *or* shrouded in darkness, caliginous, funereal, somber, stygian.

LIGHT-MINDED, *adj.* Having *or* showing a light mind, characterized by levity, frivolous, erratic, mercurial, unreliable, capricious, variable, fickle, light-headed, giddy, trifling, undependable, without ballast, coquettish, inconstant, wavering, vacillating, lightsome, foolish, trivial, fitful, whimsical, fanciful, frothy, silly, light, inane, airy, irresponsible, flirtatious, tergiversating, unstable, shallow, changeable, superficial, unintelligent, unconsidering.

LIGHTNING, *n.* Flash of lightning, stroke of lightning, streak of lightning, bolt from the blue, thunderbolt, firebolt, thunderball, thunderstroke, thunderlight, fulguration, fulmination, levin, levin bolt, levin brand, forked lightning, fork lightning, chain lightning, summer lightning, heat lightning, globular lightning, ball lightning, sheet lightning, Jupiter Fulgur, Jupiter Fulminator.

LIKABLE, LIKEABLE, *adj.* Such as to be liked, pleasing, taking, lovable, adorable, admirable, lovely, sweet, attractive, charming, winsome, pleasurable, pleasant, amiable, agreeable, gratifying, acceptable, to one's liking, mind *or* taste, engaging, inviting, welcome, genial, desirable.

LIKE, *adj.* 1. Resembling, similar, much the same, of the same form (appearance, kind, character amount, *etc.*), comparable, identical, bearing resemblance, analogous, alike, twin, relevant, cognate, allied to, equivalent, of a piece, much at one, uniform, parallel, proportional, in the same category, congeneric, congenerous, lifelike, approximative, the picture *or* image of, like as two peas, cast in the same mold, speaking, faithful, quasi, near, close, assonant, rhyming, alliterative, agreeing *(in general or some noticeable respect)*, corresponding, Homoiousian.

2. Characteristic of, typical of, in character, representative, peculiar to, in a class with, common to, illustrative, distinctive to, idiosyncratic, usual with, unique with, figurative, symbolic, depictive, imitative, exemplary, expected of one.

3. Giving promise *or* indication of, as though it might, suggestive of, indicative of, tending to, ready to, hinting, signifying, implying, implicatory, insinuative, inferential, significative of.

4. *(After* FEEL) Disposed, inclined, equal to, minded to, in the mood to, up to, able to, interested in, willing to, fain, ready to, eager, agreeable, predisposed, intending to, in the humor to, content to, enthusiastic, consenting, assenting, nothing loth, warm toward, keen about, avid about, accordant with, acquiescent with, dispositional to, prone to, compliant.

LIKE, *n.* 1. (*Prec. by* THE) Something of a similar nature, a like person *or* thing, kind, sort, such, type, genus, kin, class, match, equal, counterpart, variety, stamp, brand, color, stripe, kidney, strain, grain, description, denomination, suchlike, similar, species, feather.

2. (*Usually pl.*) Favorable feeling, partiality, inclination, desire, wish, fancy, prejudice, favorite, choice, preference, desideration, predilection, predisposition.

LIKE, *v.* 1. Take pleasure in, find agreeable to one's taste, relish, fancy, care for, savor, enjoy, love, appreciate, prefer, delight in, degust, admire, take to, regard with favor, be fond of, be attracted to, take in good part, have a liking for, hail, welcome, feel satisfied with, get a kick out of (*sl.*), hold in regard *or* affection, be glad of, prize, esteem, take an interest in, hold dear, think good, think well (much, highly) of, have a kindly *or* friendly feeling for (*a person, etc.*), would fain do *or* have.

2. Feel inclined, wish, desire, see *or* think fit, prefer, see *or* think best, rather, please, care to, choose, want, desiderate, be willing, find convenient, have a mind to.

LIKELIHOOD, *n.* Liability, liableness, conceivability, good chance, the possible, possibility, the attainable, attainability, reasonableness, reasonability, logicality, logicalness, chance, contingence, contingency, favorable chance, good prospect, favorable prospect, appearance, hazard, potentiality, plausibility, the plausible.

LIKELY, *adj.* 1. (*With* TO) Apt, probable, liable, tending, inclined, prone, subject.

2. Believable, acceptable, credible, plausible, trustworthy, conceivable, satisfactory, tenable, well-founded, reliable.

3. Suitable, acceptable, qualified, fit, appropriate, meet, proper, befitting, seasonable, adapted, worth-while, idoneous, advantageous, profitable, sortable.

LIKE-MINDED, *adj.* Having a like opinion *or* purpose, in accordance with, agreeing, harmonious, in rapport, at one with, in step, accordant, hand in hand with, hand in glove with, consonant, concordant, correspondent, compatible, conformable, united, assenting, affirming, willing, congenial, acquiescent, consenting, of one mind, of the same mind.

LIKEN, *v.* Represent as like, compare, set side by side, relate, collate, match, show to be alike, bring into comparison, simile, similize, juxtapose, parallel, parallelize, draw a parallel, place in juxtaposition, point out similarities between, link, allegorize, put alongside.

LIKENESS, *n.* 1. Representation, picture, image, icon, effigy, painting, portrait, cast, study, sketch, drawing, reproduction, facsimile, transfer, print, ectype, duplicate, delineation, illustration, head, profile, portrayal, personification, fair copy, faithful copy, model, replica, tracing, photograph, snapshot, canvas, statue, tableau, adumbration, reflection, reflex, echo, shadow, double, copy, depiction, counterpart, mirrored image, ringer (*sl.*).

2. State *or* fact of being like, similarity, resemblance, alikeness, equivalence, approximation, consimilarity, agreement, comparability, identity, affinity, similitude, parallelism, analogy, correspondence, Homoiousia, uniformity, homogeneity, semblance, appearance, guise, perfect likeness, striking resemblance, very image, very picture.

LIKEWISE, *adv.* Moreover, also, too, to boot, into the bargain, in like manner, in addition, furthermore, similarly, as well, beyond, more, further, over and above, besides, and also, additionally.

LIKING, *n.* Preference, pleasure, taste, fancy, favor, inclination, proclivity, predilection, mind, temper, relish, penchant, propensity, sympathy, bias, bent, like, humor, weakness, leaning, disposition, affinity, attraction, partiality.

LILLIPUTIAN, *adj.* Elfin, pygmy, little, small, diminutive, midget, dwarfed, stunted, slight, tiny, minute, miniature, petite, bantam, banty (*coll.*), pint-sized (*coll.*), pocket-sized (*coll.*), dwarfish, puny, teeny, teeny-weeny (*coll.*), runty (*U.S.*), minikin, wee.

LILT, *n.* 1. Rhythmic swing, cadence, beat, pulsation, swing, measure, wave, rhythm, lyricism, sway.

2. Lilting song *or* tune, lively music, swing, fast *or* spirited music, light and playful music, scherzo (*Mus.*), allegretto (*Mus.*), allegro (*Mus.*).

LIMB, *n.* 1. Part *or* member of an animal body (*as distinct from head and trunk*), arm, leg, wing, large *or* main branch of a tree, projecting part *or* member, shank, shin, extension, bough, spur, joint, sail (*of a windmill*), peg (*coll.*), gam (*sl.*), stump (*coll.*), pin (*coll.*).

2. Person *or* thing regarded as a part of something, member, offshoot, descendant, heir, scion, son, offspring, child, chip off the old block.

LIMBER, *adj.* Impressionable, flexible, malleable, tensile, pliable, pliant, adaptable, plastic, lissome, lithe, fictile, tractile, bendsome, lithesome, supple, flexuous, bendable.

LIMBO, *n.* 1. Limbus, purgatory, domain of Pluto, underworld, Phlegethon, nether world, Lethe, pandemonium, abode of the dead, inferno, Hades, lake of fire, Cocytus, Styx, Acheron.

2. Oblivion, neglect, outer darkness, obliteration, relegation.

3. Exile, banishment, internment, incarceration, imprisonment, entombment, bondage, duress, servitude, confinement, durance, thrall, thralldom, impoundment, captivity, slavery.

LIMELIGHT, *n.* Public gaze, public scrutiny, publicity, notoriety, celebrity, spotlight, flagrancy, report, light, public notice, public eye.

LIMIT, *n.* 1. Final *or* furthest bound *or* point, extent, length, span, proportions, reach, compass, area, measure, swing, stretch, limitations, expanse, breadth, width, confines, circuit, distance, dimensions, term, period, latitude, duration, gauge, gamut (*Mus.*), field, territory, scope.

2. Boundary, bound, border, periphery, enclosing line, ring, fringes, zone, horizon, belt, ambit, orbit, margin, enclosure, circumference, circumscription, round, rim, perimeter.

LIMIT, *v.* Lay down limits, mark off, bound, confine, demarcate, delimit, delimitate, define, circumscribe, fix, check, bar, specify, proscribe, determine, restrain, restrict, condition, qualify, constrain.

LIMITATION, *n.* That which limits, bound, limiting condition *or* circumstance, impediment, hindrance, restriction, curb, limit, restraint, disadvantage, proscription, stay, block, bond, qualification, disallowance, injunction, veto, condition, hitch, catch, cincture, halt, obstruction, discipline, opposition, repression, determent, detention, stricture, setback, cohibition, embarrassment, stoppage, check, bar, taboo, circumscription, inhibition, handicap, counteraction, confinement, constriction, enclosure, control, modification.

LIMITATIVE, *adj.* Lenitive, restrictive, modificatory, modifying, provisional, provisory, extenuating, mitigating, limiting, delimiting, qualifying, qualificatory, qualificative.

LIMITED, *adj.* Esoteric, confined, special, especial, conditioned, circumscribed, bounded, finite, halfway, part-way, express, explicit, singular, individual, personal, private, intimate, fine, finite, fixed, definite, determinate, moderate, little, small, inadequate, incompetent, inexpert, unable, unproficient, maladroit, temperate, modulated, moderate, tiny, minute, certain, exclusive, partial, narrow, narrowing, insular, strait, reduced, diminished, limital, terminal, terminable, conterminal, conterminate, clear-cut, exact, shallow, shallow-pated, shallow-minded, shallow-witted, not deep, prejudiced, bigoted, mediocre, medium, average, run-of-mine *(coll.)*, run-of-the-mill *(coll.)*, fair-to-middling *(coll.)*, commonplace, arrested, checked, stopped, constrained, ordinary, common, modest, meager, controlled, short, brief, held back, withheld.

LIMITLESS, *adj.* Without end, having no conclusion, infinite, unlimited, untold, never-ending, eternal, unmeasurable, boundless, unending, unfathomable, perpetual, illimitable, measureless, incalculable, termless, indeterminable, unending, numberless, sempiternal, endless, unnumbered, perdurable, countless, perpetual.

LIMN, *v.* Paint, design, draw, delineate, depict, represent, depicture, picture, portray, illustrate, picturize, set forth, describe, sketch, pencil, scratch, catch, capture, seize.

LIMNER, *n.* Depicter, artist, delineator, portrayer, portrait artist, cartoonist, sketcher, caricaturist, draftsman, draughtsman.

LIMP, *adj.* 1. Lacking stiffness or firmness *(as of substance, fiber, structure or bodily frame)*, limber, flexible, relaxed, slack, bending readily, lax, pliable, pliant, flexile, flaccid, soft, supple, ductile, plastic, flimsy, fictile, yielding, impressible, susceptible, formative, responsive, flabby.

2. Without proper firmness, force, energy, *etc. (as of character)*, bloodless, spineless, slack, effete, formative, flaccid, sapless, impressionable, impressible, infirm, weak, frail, shaky, light, receptive, easily influenced, irresolute, lightweight *(coll.)*, loose-moraled, pithless, lethargic, marrowless, sinewless, nerveless, impotent, colorless, powerless, unsteady, unstable, lame, invertebrate, easily swayed, susceptible, tractable, adaptable, of easy virtue, flexile, flabby, wishy-washy, characterless, lukewarm, ineffective, spiritless, insipid, jejune, sickly, anemic, weak-kneed.

LIMP, *n.* Halt, lame movement *or* gait, hobble, hitch, shuffle, limping gait, totter, claudication.

LIMP, *v.* Walk with a labored jerky movement *(as when lame)*, proceed in a lame *or* faulty manner, halt, walk lamely, lag, stagger, claudicate, flag, falter, shuffle, teeter, totter, hop, hitch, hobble.

LIMPID, *adj.* 1. *(Of water, crystal, air, etc.)* Clear, pellucid, transparent, lucid, transpicuous, serene, fair, crystal, bright, pure, crystalline, translucent, hyaline, pervious, glassy, vitreous, crystal-clear, diaphanous.

2. *(Of style, etc.)* Free from obscurity, lucid, sane, logical, rational, intelligible, pervious, unim-

peded, untrammeled, clear, clear-cut, unobstructed, unburdened, self-evident, manifest, straightforward, comprehensible, salient, plain, pronounced, patent, distinct, visible, palpable, unhidden, disclosed, unconcealed, revealed, articulate, unquestionable, well-marked, sharply outlined, precise, exact, direct, graphic, well-formed, overt, pellucid, unequivocal, conspicuous, clean-cut, explicit, unambiguous, luminous, transparent, transpicuous, translucent.

LINE, *n.* 1. Cord, thread, string, lanyard, twine, fiber, cordage, strand, whipcord, strap, fishline, ribbon, inkle, filament, rope, cable, strop, wire, thong, cotton, hemp rope, braid, towline, tape, gut.

2. *(Often pl.)* Limit, confine, border, edge, enclosure, pale, line of demarcation, frame, frontier, compass, extremity, circumference, purlieus, periphery, side, hem, fringe, curb, circuit, skirt, brim, rim, end, march, verge, girdle, termination, margin, boundary, perimeter.

3. Scratch, score, mark, stroke, dash, stripe, streak, gash, notch, cut, nick, nitch, scotch, jag, slash, slit, slice.

4. Row, series, rank, file, string, procession, queue, succession, column, range, chain, train, tier, parade, cavalcade.

5. *(As along lines of: often pl.)* Plan, scope, purpose, form, intention, arrangement, direction, nature, sort, scheme, order, drift, system, method, idea, tendency, policy, trend.

6. Course, direction, route, beat, path, bend, track, road, trail, channel, avenue, lane, way, trend.

7. Transportation system, transportation company, transit company, railroad, bus line, air line, truck line, *etc.*

8. Letter, note, communication, epistle, billet-doux, card, post card, missive, dispatch.

9. Parentage, progeniture, lineage, stock, descent, heredity, birth, genealogy, people, sept, clan, house, extraction, race, family tree, family, strain, ancestry, root, blood, race, trunk, breed, dynasty, stirps, caste, stem, gens *(Rom. Hist.)*.

10. Occupation, business, calling, trade, profession, racket *(sl.)*, craft, employment, job, work, pursuit, vocation, office, forte, specialization, specialty, activity, means of support, living, livelihood, venture, undertaking, enterprise, avocation, walk of life.

11. *(Railroading; pl.)* Track, roadbed, rails.

12. *(Plural; Art)* Contours, brushstrokes, mark, lineation, lineaments, outlines, dash of the pen.

LINE, *v.* 1. Take a position in a line, line up, align, bring into a line with others, arrange, order, fix, place, rank, fall in, list, group, set out, space, fall into line, range, array.

2. Mark with a line *or* lines, mark, wrinkle, crease, scratch, score, rule, engrave, draw, furrow, abrade, inscribe, etch, incise, cut, chisel, carve, flute, pencil, groove, chase, gash, crack, slit, crackle, channel, tool, hatch.

3. Sketch verbally *or* in writing, trace by *or* as by a line *or* lines, outline, delineate, portray, limn, draw, design, describe, draw up, lay out, define, block out, rough in, chart, draft, mark out, project, devise, plot, frame, determine, profile, circumscribe, plan, represent, dash off, carve, engrave, map out, chisel, contour, character, depict, shape, diagram, cast, demarcate, cut.

4. Arrange a line along, spread, sprinkle, edge, dot, border, rim, fringe, bound, margin, hem, form a line along.

5. Measure *or* test with a line, plumb, sound, take soundings, make a sounding, fathom, probe, mark, span, heave (cast *or* sling) the lead.

6. Cover *or* fit on the inner side with something, interline, face, provide with an inner layer, coat, cover, sheathe, reinforce the back of, wainscot, panel, back up, inlay, incrust, bush *(Mach.)*.

7. Furnish, fill, provide, stuff, load, stow, provision, fund, equip, arm, lay in, stock, store, supply.

LINEAGE, *n.* Parentage, progeniture, line, stock, descent, heredity, clan, sept, people, genealogy, birth, house, extraction, race, family tree, family, strain, ancestry, root, blood, trunk, breed, dynasty, stirps, caste, stem, gens *(Rom. Hist.)*.

LINEAL, *adj.* In a direct line *(from an ancestor)*, direct, ancestral, straight, inherited, racial, family, parental, patriarchal, tribal, hereditary, running, direct in descent, phyletic *(Biol.)*, phylogenetic *(Biol.)*.

LINEAMENT, *n.* Feature *(of a face, body, or figure, with respect to its outline or contour)*, outline *(particularly of the face)*, line, form, figure, shape, detail, contour, relief, profile, front, bounds, boundary, cut, visage, circumference, periphery, aspect, delineation, silhouette.

LINEAR, *adj.* 1. Extended in a line, lineal, resembling a thread, narrow, elongated, long, continuous, slender, threadlike, straight, pertaining to length, of *or* pertaining to a line *or* lines, in the direction of a line, undeviating, unbent, direct, sequential, successive, true, right, rectilinear, rectilineal, unswerving, endless, looking like a line, unintermitting, unbroken, continuing.

2. Involving measurement in one dimension only, horizontal, lengthwise, longitudinal, in a line, direct, perpendicular, between two points.

3. Consisting of *or* involving lines, etched, lined, scored, furrowed, crackled, ruled, incised, lineate, lineolate *(Biol.)*, hatched.

LINEN, *n.* Fiber, thread *or* yarn of linen, cloth of flax, flaxen fabric, lingerie, flax, linen cloth, crash, huck, huckaback, harl, sheets and pillowcases, sheeting, bedding, bed linen, table linen, bedclothes, bedcovers, damask, napery, linsey-woolsey, holland.

LINER, *n.* One of a commercial line *(of steamships or airplanes)*, ship, steamship, ocean liner, passenger vessel, floating hotel *or* palace, ocean greyhound *(coll.)*, airplane, plane, transport, air liner, air cruiser, aircoach, steamer.

LINESMAN, *n.* Official, umpire, referee, field judge.

LINGER, *v.* 1. Delay, tarry, idle, trifle, potter, fritter away time, lounge, shilly-shally, dawdle, crawl, dillydally, hang back, loll, procrastinate, vacillate, be irresolute, loiter, lag, loaf, take one's time, wait, putter, pause, hover, wobble, boggle, falter, waver, let the grass grow under one's feet, dabble.

2. Die slowly, persist, endure, continue, remain, hold, hang on, abide, stand, stick.

3. Amble, stroll, jaunt, ramble, saunter, shamble, shuffle, totter, traipse, lope, slouch, limp, drag, toddle.

LINGERIE, *n.* Undergarments, underwear, linen, undies *(coll.)*, underclothing, unmentionables *(hum.)*.

LINGO, *n. (Often contempt.)* Dialect, language, brogue, idiom, talk, speech, slang, tongue, lingue,

lingua franca *(of hybrid speech)*, jargon, patois, vernacular, twang, cant.

LINGUAL, *adj.* 1. Of *or* pertaining to the tongue *or* some tonguelike part, linguiform, tongue-shaped, lingulate, ligulate.

2. Pertaining to languages, philological, glossological, semantic, linguistic, bilingual, diglot, glottologic, hexaglot, polyglot, colloquial, jargonal, dialectical, vernacular, semasiological.

LINGUIST, *n.* Person skilled in foreign languages, one adept at languages, polyglot, philologist, philologer, philologue, philologian, linguistician, etymologist, etymologer, glossarist, glossarian, glottologist, lexicographer, lexiconist, colloquialist, dialectician, phonologist, vocabulist, interpreter, translator, grammarian, grammatist, glossographer, glossologist, polyglottist, linguistic scholar.

LINGUISTIC, *adj.* Lingual, pertaining to languages, philological, glossological, semantic, bilingual, diglot, glottologic, hexaglot, polyglot, colloquial, jargonal, dialectical, vernacular, semasiological.

LINGUISTICS, *n.* Science of language, phonetics, phonemics, morphology, syntax, philology, linguistic science, semantics, semasiology, descriptive linguistics *or* philology, comparative linguistics *or* philology, historical linguistics *or* philology, glossology, accidence *(Gram.)*, speechcraft, pronunciation, lexicology, lexigraphy, terminology, grammar, lexicography, etymology, speechlore, translation, orismology, paleography, glottology.

LINIMENT, *n.* Liquid preparation (usually oily) for rubbing on *or* applying to the skin as for sprains, bruises, *etc.*, soft ointment, lotion, soothing substance, salve, balm, demulcent, curative, sedative, unguent, anodyne, emollient *(Med.)*, remedy, lenitive, embrocation, wash, medicament, healing application, alleviative, palliative, abirritant *(Pathol.)*.

LINING, *n.* That with which something is lined, layer of material on the inner side of something, inner coating *or* covering, facing, wadding, wall, filling, stuffing, interlining, reinforcement, sheathing, inlayer, doublure, doubling, packing, padding, brattice, partition, incrustation, wainscot, wainscoting, bush *(Mach.)*, bushing *(Mach.)*.

LINK, *n.* One of the separate pieces *or* rings of which a chain is composed, bond, connective, vinculum, coupler, ring, loop, bond of union, fastening, splice, anything serving to connect one part *or* thing to another, hitch, knot, intersection, nexus, fastener, clinch, catch, bridge, interconnection, dash, peg, rung, bar, lock, joint, joiner, copula, coupling, elbow, hinge, seam, articulation, alliance, unifier, association, connection, weld, tie, juncture, ligation, hyphen, knee, single constituent part.

LINK, *v.* Connect, conjoin, unite, tie, band, yoke, couple, associate, knot, loop, catenate, fix, fasten, bind, join, inosculate, span, bridge, splice, chain, marry, fuse, anastomose, merge, combine, syndicate, consolidate, cement, clasp, seal, weld, meet, touch.

LINT, *n.* Soft material for dressing wounds, *etc.*, soft down, cotton, bits of thread, flue, compress, pledget, gauze, sponge, fibers, filaments, bandage, absorbent cotton, fluff, dressing, dossil *(Surg.)*.

LION, *n.* 1. Man of great courage, strength, *etc.*, brave, hero, man of mettle, paladin, demigod, Achilles, Theseus, Hector, strong man, Perseus, Hercules.

2. Person of note *or* celebrity who is much sought after, notable, object of interest *or* note, prodigy, wonder, phenomenon, nabob, magnate, sensation, marvel, gazing stock, figure, worthy, great man, celebrity, notability, personage, man of mark *or* note, hero, curiosity, somebody, mogul, bigwig *(coll.).*

LION-HEARTED, *adj.* Courageous, brave, valiant, hardy, mettlesome, doughty, valorous, plucky, spartan, bold, intrepid, manly, gallant, daring, dauntless, resolute, stout, game, stout-hearted, audacious, aweless, enduring, indomitable, unyielding, firm, spirited, heroic, adventurous, unapprehensive, dashing, tenacious, fearless, confident, mighty, defiant, unappalled, unalarmed, unshrinking, undismayed, invincible, dreadless, unabashed, irresistible, tenacious, strong-willed, enterprising, dogged, masterly, powerful, formidable, rugged, sinewy, staunch, herculean, stalwart.

LIONIZE, *v.* 1. Treat *(a person)* as a celebrity, confer distinction on, honor, dignify, praise, pay tribute, acclaim, exalt, blazon, elevate, signalize, deify, commemorate, sound the praises of, admire, laud, eulogize, panegyrize, pledge, aggrandize, enshrine, cheer, flatter, magnify, glorify, make much of, drink to, applaud, esteem, run after, raise, throne, celebrate, enthrone.

2. Visit *or* exhibit the objects of interest *(of a place),* exploit, sightsee, rubber, rubberneck *(sl.),* promote, present to view, take in, take an interest in, demonstrate, be spectator at, set forth, trot out, bring out, bring to view, display, inspect, hold open house.

LIP, *n.* 1. Either of two fleshy parts forming the margins of the mouth, edge *or* border of the mouth, liplike part *or* structure, labrum, labium, mouth *(pl.).*

2. *(Plural)* Speech *(as passing between the lips),* talk, discourse, utterance, expression, accents, voice, tongue, oral communication, pronunciation, enunciation, remarks, articulation, words.

3. Margin *or* edge of a container, rim, edge of an opening *or* cavity, margin, brim, projecting edge *(as of a pitcher),* flange, brow, edge, brink, curb, perimeter, bulge, frame, portal, periphery, threshold, verge, nozzle.

LIQUEFY, *v.* Make *or* become liquid, liquesce, fuse, dissolve, flux, run, fluidize, fluidify, condense, put into solution, resolve, solubilize, soak, liquate *(Metall.),* chylify *(Physiol.),* reduce to a liquid state, liquidize, deliquesce, melt, thaw.

LIQUEUR, *n.* Cordial, stimulant, appetizer, curaçao, ratafia, absinthe, benedictine, *crème de moka (Fr.), crème de cacao (Fr.),* cassis, *crème de noyau (Fr.),* chartreuse, *crème de menthe, crème (Fr.),* anisette, maraschino, Cointreau, cherry *or* apricot *or* blackberry, *etc.* brandy.

LIQUID, *adj.* 1. Fluid, fluidic, liquefied, liquiform, molten, sappy, rheumy *(Med.),* damp, wet, serous, fluent, hydrous, deliquescent, aqueous, moist, sanious *(Med.).*

2. *(Of sounds, etc.)* Mellifluous, sweet, dulcet, melodious, tuneful to the ear, vocally *or* musically concordant, agreeable, aesthetically pleasing, attuned, euphonious, marked by harmony, symphonic, assonant, gratifying, felicitous, clear-toned, mellifluent, mellow, song-like, symphonious, round, sweet-sounding, subtle, beautiful, delightful, charming, lovely, winning, enchanting, ravishing, entrancing, empyreal, celestial, seraphic, consonous, Orphean, rhythmic, restful, lyric, sooth-

ing, bland, mellisonant, harmonizing, soft, genial, gladsome, tunable, smooth, musical, in concord, canorous, delectable, sweet, of the spheres, spheral, undiscording, rhythmical.

LIQUID, *n.* Fluid, water, potable, juice, sap, extract, secretion, beverage, latex *(Bot.),* lymph *(Anat.),* soup, broth, nectar, liquor.

LIQUIDATE, *v.* 1. Discharge (debts, *etc.*), pay, clear, dispose of, defray, settle, square accounts, cancel debts, wipe off, satisfy, meet payments.

2. Turn into money, realize in cash, change into cash, cash.

3. Dispose of, do away with, get rid of, kill, quell, bring to naught, abolish, unbuild, wipe out, stifle, snuff out, suppress, remove, take away, cancel, erase, strike out, expunge, delete, quash, blight, finish, end, put down, annihilate, exterminate, extinguish, cause to vanish, obliterate, efface.

4. Murder, assassinate, kill, cut down, garrote, strangle, choke, shoot, decapitate, smother, choke off, hang, knife, extirpate, eradicate, root out, eliminate, slay, take the life of, give a deathblow to, mow down, rub out *(sl.),* blot out, throttle, mug *(slang).*

LIQUOR, *n.* 1. Fluid, water, drink, extract, sap, secretion, beverage, juice, latex *(Bot.),* lymph *(Anat.),* soup, broth, nectar, potable, liquid.

2. Alcoholic beverage, alcohol, hard liquor, drink, strong drink, inebriants, spirits, grog, intoxicants, tipple, booze *(coll.),* the demon rum *(coll.).*

LISP, *v.* Hiss, sputter, sibilate, speak indistinctly, speak with an impediment, mispronounce, misspeak, missay, talk incoherently, splutter, falter.

LISSOM, LISSOME, *adj.* 1. Spry, nimble, deft, sprightly, dexterous, easy-moving, fast, tripping, mentally quick, dapper, expeditious, lively, bustling, quick, alert, light-footed, swift-footed, alive, active, winged, ready, prompt, rapid, swift, fleet, brisk, supple, lithe.

2. Limber, flexible, lithe, ductile, bendsome, pliable, pliant, impressionable, adaptable, tractile, lithesome, supple, flexuous, plastic, malleable, bendable, fictile, tensile.

LIST, *n.* 1. Register, record, schedule, inventory, cartulary, muster roll, gazette, slate, archive, gazetteer, terrier, docket, classification, directory, screed, bulletin, roll, prospectus, draft, panel, brief, syllabus, table, file, catalogue, beadroll, enumeration, index.

2. Band, edge, border, bordering strip, slip, spill, fascia, shred, fillet, tape, ribbon, cummerbund, taenia *(Gr. Antiq.),* selvage, selvedge.

3. Stripe, streak, fascia *(Zool.),* band, mark, line.

4. Border, margin, rim, edge, verge, brim, brink, selvage, boundary, pale, curb, limit, bounds, perimeter, frame, fringe, skirt, bordure, circumference, periphery, confines, confine, outline, compass, girdle, contour, circuit, girth, zone, delineation, lineaments, extent, orbit, purlieus, ambit, circumscription.

LIST, *v.* 1. *(Naut.)* Tilt, careen, heel, incline, slope, slant.

2. Arrange, list, file, record, codify, alphabetize, group, register, summarize, rank, tabulate, docket *(Legal),* ticket, graduate, segregate, digest, calendar, enroll, chronicle.

3. Form an edge *or* border to, border, edge, fringe, margin, circle, encircle, marginate, ring, hemstitch, fold back and sew down the edge of,

double *or* fold *or* turn under, environ, rim, enclose, envelop.

LISTEN, *v.* Hark, catch, strain one's ears, be all ears *(coll.)*, be attentive, eavesdrop, keep one's ears open, listen in, give ear, incline an ear, prick up the ears, pick up, overhear, auscultate.

LISTLESS, *adj.* Feeling no inclination toward *or* interest in anything, heedless, unconcerned, indifferent, laggard, faint, absent, lacking zest, thoughtless, torpid, indolent, slack, mopish, languid, insipid, inattentive, dreamy, apathetic, lukewarm, uninterested, sluggish, supine, abstracted, careless, lackadaisical, idle, drowsy, inactive, comatose, heavy, inanimate, spiritless, dull, phlegmatic, soporific, lethargic, fainéant, dormant, insouciant, obtuse, lifeless, stupefied, impassive, cool, inert, dilatory, nonchalant, lazy, recumbent, shilly-shally, leaden, forgetful.

LISTLESSNESS, *n.* State of being listless, languid inattention, torpor, fatigue, indifference, disinclination, indolence, abstraction, coolness, lack of zeal, thoughtlessness, heedlessness, unconcern, forgetfulness, dormancy, dullness, nonchalance, lack of spirit, insipidity, absence of mind, recumbency, passivity, inertia, sloth, ennui, dreaminess, inactivity, remissness, lassitude, lentitude, hebetude, slowness, oscitancy, supineness, vacancy, languor, apathy, carelessness, idleness, heaviness, kef *(Arab.)*, faintness, lack of interest, dilatoriness.

LITANY, *n.* Ceremonial *or* liturgical form of prayer, supplication, petition, invocations with responses, rite, entreaty, imploration, impetration, importunity, prayer, worship, collect, praise, adoration, intercession, liturgy, canonical prayers, beseechment, obsecration, obtestation, rogation *(Eccles.)*.

LITERACY, *n.* State of being literate, possession of education, mental cultivation, proficiency in the basic skills of writing and reading, edification, articulateness, ability to read and write, learning, developed intelligence, culture, enlightenment, scholarship, erudition.

LITERAL, *adj.* 1. *(Of words, translations, etc.)* According to the exact meaning, faithful, precise, true, direct, undeviating, verbatim, strict, following the exact words *or* the letter, near, close, word for word, critical, unerring, authentic, undisputed, orthological, fine, nice, explicit, metaphrastic, natural, transcribed, veracious, scrupulous, veritable, conformable, plain, not metaphorical, accurate, exact.

2. *(Of persons)* Tending to construe in the strict sense *or* in an unimaginative way, matter-of-fact, prosaic, simple-minded, sober, precise, unromantic, unimaginative, obtuse, blunt, unpoetic, prosy, ponderous, heavy, slow, colorless, simple, boring, stereotyped, elephantine, dull, unentertaining.

3. True to fact, not exaggerated, actually such, real, correct, factual, without exaggeration *or* inaccuracy, bald, primary, scriptural, truthful, naked, actual, unerring, realistic, unrefutable, unconfuted, exact, veritable, undeviating, authentic, categorically true, veracious, verifiable, true, religious, strict, just, undeniable, meticulous, accurate, scrupulous, right, unimpeachable, orthodox, conscientious, unbiased, honest, reliable, scientific, mathematical, particular, careful, textual, trustworthy, unfeigned, dependable, bona fide, uncorrupted, authoritative, unperjured, undistorted, undisputed.

4. Of *or* pertaining to the letters of the alphabet, of the nature of letters, as regards letters, written, expressed by letters, alphabetic, scriptory, longhand, affecting a letter *or* letters, lettered, runic, uncial, capital, syllabic, hieroglyphic, manuscript, vocabular, majuscular, minuscular, upper-case *(Print.)*, lower-case *(Print.)*, inscribed in writing, in black and white, acrostic, textual, demotic, hieratic, verbal, cuneiform, abecedarian, by letter.

LITERALLY, *adv.* 1. In a literal manner, exactly, strictly, word for word, scrupulously, to the letter, accurately, faithfully, verbatim, rigorously, precisely, straight.

2. In the literal sense, at face value, unimaginatively, plainly, in plain words *or* terms, at one's word, without reading between the lines, point-blank, in plain English, unsympathetically.

3. Actually, without exaggeration *or* inaccuracy, really, indeed, truly, verily, veritably, in reality, to be exact, completely, utterly, in every respect, in all respects, in fact, beyond question *or* doubt.

LITERARY, *adj.* 1. Pertaining to literature *or* belles-lettres, poetic, stylistic, bookish, artistic, literate.

2. Erudite, academic, scholarly, well-informed, intellectual, scholastic, literate, learned, bookish, widely read, lettered, well-read, cultured, enlightened, studious.

LITERATE, *adj.* 1. Able to read and write, educated, informed, schooled, proficient in writing.

2. Well-informed, scholarly, *etc.* See LITERARY, *adj., above.*

LITERATURE, *n.* 1. Belles-lettres, literary works, letters, writings, lore, classics, polite literature, republic of letters.

2. Store of knowledge (on a given subject, *etc.*), books, teaching, lore, reading, learning, erudition, scholarship, treatises, information, culture, theses, works, papers, dissertations.

LITHE, LITHESOME, *adj.* Bendsome, pliant, flexible, limber, ductile, impressionable, pliable, adaptable, tractile, lissom, supple, flexuous, plastic, malleable, bendable, fictile, tensile.

LITHIC, *adj.* Pertaining to *or* consisting of stone, lapidose, lithoidal, adamantine, flinty, fossilized, petrified, stony, rocky, lapideous, lithoid, cement, concrete, cemental, calculous *(Med.)*.

LITIGANT, *adj.* Taking legal action, litigating, engaged in a lawsuit, accusing, defending, prosecuting, pressing suit.

LITIGANT, *n.* One engaged in a lawsuit, disputant, suitor, party, opponent, litigator, litigationist, prisoner, libelee, claimant, libelant, appellee, appellant, accusant, complainant, correspondent, respondent, controversialist, contender, contestant, accused.

LITIGATE, *v.* 1. Contest at law, defend in a lawsuit, make the subject of a lawsuit, charge, open, claim, protect, justify, preserve, sustain, maintain, plead for, assert, bring up, uphold, contend for.

2. Dispute *(a point, etc.)*, quarrel, argue, debate, contend, wrangle, come to blows, join issue, contest, agitate, altercate, squabble, jangle, clash, spar, discept, logomachize, pick a bone with, pluck a crow with, brawl, make the fur fly, have words with, lock horns, fall out, brabble, huff, row, strive, battle, jostle, jar, conflict, tiff, spat *(coll.)*, scrap *(sl.)*, polemize.

3. Carry on a lawsuit, prosecute, sue, go into litigation, take up a side *or* case, bring suit, seek justice *or* legal redress, seek in law, put on trial,

take to court, take up the cudgels, take one's stand upon, prefer *or* file a claim, bring an action against, take *or* institute legal proceedings against, prefer charges, implead, impeach, bring before the court *or* bar, appeal to the law, institute a lawsuit.

LITIGATION, *n.* The process of litigating, lawsuit, judicial contest, polemics, rivalry, controversy, quarrel, case, legal contest, law, action, prosecution, proceedings, wrangling, disceptation, altercation, contention, suit at law, spat *(coll.),* scrap *(sl.).*

LITIGIOUS, *adj.* 1. Overly inclined to litigate, contentious, quarrelsome, polemical, controversial, dissentious, argumentative, combative, bellicose, warlike, discordant, hostile, aggressive, wrangling, antagonistic, militant, belligerent, litigatory, disputatious, pugnacious.

2. Of *or* pertaining to litigation, controvertible, litigant, causidical, litigable, actionable, disputable, *coram judice (Lat.), sub judice (Lat.).*

LITTER, *n.* 1. Things scattered about, scattered rubbish, waste matter, confused mass, motley collection, mess, tumble, fragments, shreds, odds and ends, mix-up, hodgepodge, hash, tangle, minglement, muddle, mishmash, rummage, lumber, huddle, topsy-turvy, ollapodrida, gallimaufry, disorderly heap *or* assemblage, orts, leavings, slag, sweepings, debris, refuse, dross, junk *(sl.),* trash, oddments, rubbish.

2. Disorder, untidiness, confusion, disarray, chaos, lack of system, irregularity, muss, mess, disarrangement, disorganization, want of order, hugger-mugger, topsy-turvy, disheveled state, derangement, disorderliness, jumble, accumulation.

3. Number of young brought forth at one birth, issue, offspring, young, flock, farrow, brood, seed, spawn, progeny.

4. Vehicle with a bed *(borne by hand),* framework of canvas' stretched between parallel bars *(for transportation of sick and wounded),* bier, sedan chair, palanquin, stretcher, portable couch, handbarrow, horse litter, camel litter, hammock, swing, carriage, bed, brancard, cacolet *(Fr.),* tonjon *(Ceylon),* jampan *(India),* dooly *(East Indies),* muncheel *(India),* norimon *(Japan),* sedan.

5. Bedding of straw, hay, *etc. (used for animals or protection for plants),* mulch, dead leaves and twigs on a forest floor, horse litter, pallet, winter covering.

LITTER, *v.* 1. Strew *(a place)* with scattered objects, scatter *(objects)* in disorder, be strewed about *(a place)* in disorder *(fol. by* UP*),* cover with things negligently scattered, clutter, disorder, muddle, jumble, derange, mess up *(coll.),* disturb, upset, dishevel, agitate, toss, turn topsy-turvy, disarrange, shuffle, discompose, encumber with useless articles, confuse, tumble, huddle.

2. Supply *(an animal)* with litter for a bed, bed down, cover with straw, hay, *etc.,* for bedding, cradle.

3. Give birth to *(chiefly of animals),* bear, drop, spring, pup, cub, kitten, foal, lamb, fawn, calve, whelp, spawn, yean, spat, farrow, throw, bring forth.

LITTLE, *adj.* 1. Small in size, not big or large, minute, tiny, wee, diminutive, stunted, dwarfish, light, slight, short, limited, cramped, weazened, breviped, scrubby, scraggy, shrunk, inappreciable, imperceptible, undersized, puny, Lilliputian, pygmy, atomic, elfin, runty, invisible, microscopic, petite, bantam, dumpy, squat, pint-sized, pocket-sized, embryonic, shriveled, miniature, sear, amoebic,

microzoic, vestigial, animalcular, stocky, pug, pugged, stubby, truncated, snub, half-pint, molecular, microbic, infinitesimal, toy, child's, minikin, Tom Thumb, pollard, neat.

2. Small in extent *or* duration, short, brief, compact, curt, elliptical, terse, ephemeral, succinct, laconic, clipped, decurtate, curtate, momentary, compendious, passing, truncate, temporary, fugacious, fugitive, summary, circumscribed, concise, short-lived, perishable, mortal, transitory, hasty, abbreviatory, fleet, volatile, quick, brisk, cursory, compacted, short and sweet, condensed, precarious.

3. Small in number, composed of few, deficient, skimpy, scant, slim, stinted, meager, stunted, sparse, short, insufficient, thinly scattered, to be counted on one's fingers, few and far between, hardly *or* scarcely any, scrimpy, thin, slender.

4. Small in amount *or* degree, not much, paltry, scant, impalpable, imperceptible, evanescent, insufficient, meager, feeble, faint, poor, fading, inappreciable, infinitesimal, intangible.

5. Being such on a small scale, small *(in dignity, power or importance),* small *(in consideration or consequence),* insignificant, feeble, trivial, exiguous, of little *or* no consequence, of no account, lightweight, middling, mediocre, ordinary, common, not vital, immaterial, piddling, mincing, nugatory, mean, shallow, niggling, humble, imperfect, inconsequential, weak, slight, petty, unimportant, inconsiderable, one-horse *(coll.),* poor, indifferent, picayune, no great shakes *(coll.),* slender, moderate, scanty, trifling, faint, flimsy, unworthy, unworthy of serious consideration, inferior, tin-horn *(sl.),* nameless, renownless, unnoticed, unknown, obscure, lowly, second-rate, third-rate, fourth-rate, foolish, pitiful, dime-a-dozen, two-by-four *(sl.),* downtrodden, ignoble, tin-pot *(sl.),* uncouth, worthless, negligible.

6. Small in force *or* efficiency, weak, feeble, faint, frail, inefficient, strengthless, unclear, delicate, quiet, hushed, fragile, puny, colorless, low, soft, effeminate, childlike, baby, gentle, faint-sounding, indistinct, whispered, murmured, subdued, muted, stifled, inaudible, scarcely *or* barely audible, muffled.

7. Mean, narrow, illiberal, bigoted, miserly, close, chary, contemptible, selfish, small, scrimping, grudging, sordid, penurious, superficial, stinting, stingy, meager, paltry, pinching, churlish, hidebound, inflexible, limited, provincial, insular, intolerant, prejudiced, purblind, unreasonable, narrow-minded, stiff, stiff-necked, stiff-backed, near-sighted, short-sighted, immovable, uncompromising, incapable of breadth in thought *or* action, opinionated, deaf, parsimonious, beggarly, shabby, poverty-stricken, tight *(coll.),* niggard, niggardly, near, unwilling to learn.

LITTLE, *adv.* In only a small amount *or* degree, not at all *(before a verb),* not much, never, by no means, in a small compass, merely, hardly, scarcely, limitedly, in some degree, in a small degree, in a nutshell, small, not in a thousand years, in miniature, not quite, uncommonly, only just, rarely, somewhat, rather, faintly, slightly, noway.

LITTLE, *n.* 1. That which is little, small quantity (amount, degree), manageable amount, pittance, trifle, jot, smack, some, minimum, bite, scrap, small degree, small scale, piece, miniature, whit, handful, modicum, pennyworth, triviality, dash, few, suspicion, atom, dot, spot, tittle, shade, bit, trace, next to nothing, touch, somewhat, driblet.

snatch, snack, patch, scantling, sprinkling, grain, mite, lick, inch, tinge, smell, crumb, morsel, gobbet, soupçon, hint, suggestion, drop in the bucket *or* ocean, fragment, fraction, splinter, sliver, mere nothing, thimbleful, snip, snippet, chip, tatter, speck, taste, shred, pinch, particle, point, negligible amount.

2. A short distance *or* way, step, stone's throw, ace, bit, few steps, brief space, earshot.

3. A short time, while, minute, moment, trice, bit, wink, instant, second, brief time, limited space of time, spurt, less than no time *(coll.)*, shake of a lamb's tail *(coll.)*, two shakes *(coll.)*.

LITURGICAL, *adj.* Of *or* pertaining to public worship, having to do with liturgies *or* forms of public worship, of *or* pertaining to the liturgy *or* eucharistic service, liturgic, formal, solemn, ritualistic, high, formulary, sacramental, ceremonious, ceremonial, communion, Eucharist, ritual.

LITURGY, *n.* Ritual, form of public worship, rite, ceremony, particular arrangement of services, collection of formularies for public worship, formality, litany, ceremonial, communion, Eucharist, sacrament, Mass, solemnity, symbolism, ordinance.

LIVABLE, *adj.* 1. Suitable for living in, inhabitable, satisfactory, fitting, usable, unexceptionable, acceptable, desirable, adequate, equal to the requirement *or* purpose, adaptable, habitable, convenient, decent, comfortable, unobjectionable.

2. That can be lived with, companionable, good-natured, comfortable, easygoing, sociable, affable, conversable, friendly, amicable, well-affected, gracious, cordial, warm, communicative, harmonious, well-disposed.

3. Worth living, bearable, endurable, tolerable, good enough, acceptable, not bad, worth-while, pretty good, satisfactory, unobjectionable, so-so, profitable, passable, middling, supportable.

LIVE, *adj.* 1. Being in life, of *or* pertaining to life of living beings, vital, alive, living, breathing, in the flesh, subsistent, existent, animate, palpable, substantial, bodily, fleshly, real, under the sun, on the face of the earth, quick, sensible, embodied, incarnate, this side the grave, physical, corporeal, material, zoetic *(Biol.)*, vivified, extant, viable, existing, tangible, motile *(Biol.)*.

2. Characterized by *or* indicating the presence of living creatures, bustling, restless, busy, teeming, fraught, swarming, thronged, abounding, full, overflowing, rife, replete.

3. Full of life, energy *or* activity, lively, alert, active, brisk, stirring, sparkling, energetic, glowing, bright, dynamic, frisky, eager, ardent, industrious, enterprising, spirited, intense, sharp, peppy *(sl.)*, snappy *(coll.)*, effervescent, breezy, attentive, wide-awake, vigorous, brilliant, vivid, keen, vivacious, vive.

4. Glowing, burning, fiery, blazing, aflame, afire, incandescent, living, red-hot, white-hot, inflamed, scorching, ignited, igneous, aglow, smoldering, alight, candent, hot, ablaze, flaming.

5. Flowing freely *(as water)*, fresh *(as air)*, moving, fluent, streaming, circulating, revolving, in motion, unquiet, restless, fluctuating, windy, blowing, breezy, coursing, traveling, whirling, rushing, profluent, swirling, blowy, gusty, airy, running, affluent.

6. Loaded, combustible, explodable, detonating, unexploded, fulminant, explosible, explosive, fulminating.

7. Still in use *or* to be used, up-to-date, current, extant, existing, afloat, in the air, of present interest, active, at hand, at issue, happening, going on, in the wind, prevailing, prevalent, in question, instant, latest, on foot.

LIVE, *v.* 1. Be capable of vital functions, have life, be alive, be, act, begin, draw breath, receive life, subsist, walk the earth, arise, rise, be animated, have being, breathe, quicken, come forth, appear, see light, originate, come into the world, take birth, come into existence, exist, see the light of day, respire.

2. Remain alive, continue in existence, operation, memory, *etc.*, last, continue to live, survive, persist, cling to life, obtain, abide, stand, keep a hold on, stick out, stick to, outlive, hold on *or* onto, escape destruction, prevail, endure, be permanent, stay, tarry, sojourn.

3. *(Fol. by* ON *or* BY) Maintain life, rely for maintenance, subsist, support oneself *or* one's family, acquire a livelihood, provide for one's needs, make one's living, earn money, get ahead, follow *(an occupation)*, perform.

4. *(Fol. by* ON *or* UPON) Feed, subsist, be nourished, be supported, thrive, increase, wax, get along, nourish oneself, augment, multiply, flourish, grow, fare.

5. *(Often with* IN *or* AT) Dwell, reside, occupy, remain, tenant, room, hang out *(sl.)*, take up one's abode, take quarters, bunk, people, populate, take *or* strike root, anchor, moor, take residence, establish oneself, billet, settle, cohabit, pass one's life, stay, lodge, abide, inhabit, have lodgings, nest.

6. Lead, be *(as specified; happy, frugal, etc.)*, acquit oneself, behave, follow, play one's part, direct *or* regulate one's life, carry on, govern, guide, control, comport oneself, carry out, demean oneself, steer one's course, play the game, make one's habit, conduct oneself, practice, put in practice, pilot, steer, handle.

7. Experience life to the full, enjoy life, make a splash, have rich experiences, live abundantly, make the most of life, live high, live fast, be happy, take the earth's bounty, make every moment count, have a meaningful existence, make *or* cut a figure, flourish.

LIVELIHOOD, *n.* Means of maintaining life, maintenance, occupation, calling, trade, business, pursuit, living, vocation, job, situation, line of work, profession, source of income, métier, post, incumbency, walk, office, place, career, function, work, capacity, employment, position, support, subsistence, sustenance, enterprise, venture, undertaking, activity, specialty, specialization, forte, craft, racket *(sl.)*.

LIVELINESS, *n.* 1. Vivacity, spark, ardor, warmth, vigor, brightness, energy, fire, dash, élan, vitality, zeal, briskness, animation, speed, spirit, spiritedness, sprightliness, elasticity, promptitude, airiness, alertness, swiftness, force, alacrity, eagerness, enthusiasm, buoyancy, celerity.

2. Gaiety, merriment, jollity, high spirits, jocundity, exhilaration, revelry, exultation, pleasantry, fun, sportiveness, laughter, blithesomeness, playfulness, amusement, glee, mirth, joviality, celebration, ecstasy, jollification, sport, felicity, vivacity, festivity, rejoicing, jubilee, merrymaking, boisterousness, heyday.

LIVELONG, *adj.* *(Of time)* Whole, entire, undivided, total, full, lifelong, solid, complete, unbroken.

LIVELY, *adj.* Alive, glowing, spirited, zealous, alert, mettlesome, earnest, breezy, sanguine, vigorous, hearty, fervent, ardent, buoyant, airy, sprightly, vivacious, brisk, full of life, full of spirit, full of action, elated, jocund, sportive, quick, animated, active, bright, vivid, heated, keen, excitable, eager, intense, violent, zealous, sharp, enthusiastic, excited.

LIVER, *n.* Resident, inhabitant, dweller, resider, abider, sojourner, habitant, denizen, occupier, occupant, tenant, incumbent, residentiary, inhabiter, addressee, householder, lodger, settler, renter, boarder, inmate, lessee, homesteader, commorant, indigene, autochthon, islander, villager, townsman.

LIVERY, *n.* Uniform, garb, clothing, suit, vestments, costume, regimentals, guise, attire, regalia, raiment.

LIVESTOCK, *n.* Cattle, domestic animals, dairy cattle, bovine cattle, farm animals, barnyard animals, flocks, herds, droves.

LIVID, *adj.* 1. Black and blue, dull, discolored, cyanotic *(Med.)*, cyanopathic *(Med.)*, plum-colored, purple, ecthymosed *(Med.)*, bruised.
2. Lead-colored, dirty white, ashy, ashen, ashy pale, grayish, gray, leaden.

LIVING, *adj.* 1. Breathing, in the flesh, live, alive, subsistent, existent, animate, palpable, substantial, bodily, fleshly, real, under the sun, on the face of the earth, quick, sensible, embodied, incarnate, this side of the grave, corporeal, material, vivified, extant, viable, existing, tangible, motile *(Bot.)*.
2. Blazing, fiery, aflame, flaming, ablaze, hot, candent, alight, smoldering, aglow, igneous, scorching, inflamed, white-hot, red-hot, incandescent, live, afire, burning, glowing.
3. Still in use, current, active, operative, extant, existent, up-to-date, in the air, afloat, alive, of present interest, live, at issue, happening, going on, in the wind, prevalent, in question, instant, latest, on foot.

LIVING, *n.* 1. Being, existing, existence, moving, having life, animation, drawing breath, crawling, subsisting, subsistence, vitality, life.
2. Profession, work, job, employment, craft, racket *(sl.),* trade, occupation, business, calling, vocation, specialization, means of support, livelihood, walk of life, undertaking, enterprise, venture, office.
3. *(Eccl.)* Benefice, curacy, deanery, bishopric, canonry, ministry, manse, tithes, diocese, emoluments, advowson, subdeanery, rectorate, rectorship, prelateship, charge, care of souls, vicariate, church, rectory, pastorate, parish, preferment, incumbency, glebe, chaplaincy, abbacy, deanship, subdeanship, pastorship.

LIVING ROOM, *n.* Parlor, lounge, front room, drawing room, best room *(coll.).*

LIZARD, *n.* Saurian, hardim, iguana, gecko, skink, chameleon, dragon, Gila monster; *(the following used incorrectly):* eft, newt, salamander.

LOAD, *n.* 1. Cargo, shipment, shipload, bale, parcel, contents, package, goods, weight, pack, wagonload, haul, lading, charge, capacity, carload, freight.
2. *(Heavy object)* Burden, onus, impediment, encumbrance, gravity, weight, lump, heaviness, mass, ponderance, ballast, burthen, pressure, dead weight.
3. Millstone, holdback, obstruction, scourge, disability, bane, hindrance, unhappy lot, handicap, nuisance, care, trouble, oppressiveness, oppression, restraint, misfortune, worry, hamper, unhappiness, bad fortune, impediment, austerity, pressure, stress, misery, extremity, penalty, in-

justice, trail, cumbrance, sadness, anguish, onus, heaviness, depression, hardship, affliction, sorrow, agony, adversity, gravamen, burden, strain, difficulty, privation, tribulation, impedition, bitter cup.
4. Amount of work, duty, agenda *(sing.,* agendum), tour of duty, assignment, stint, schedule, task, job, chore, turn, routine.

LOAD, *v.* 1. Put goods, merchandise, contents, *etc.,* in, freight, lade, weight, pack, stack, pad, pile, heap, implete, stow, fill, burden, stuff, wad, lumber.
2. Weigh down, handicap, strain, pile, overwhelm, surcharge, hinder, trouble, cumber, tax, burden, task with, hamper, lade, drag, saddle with, overtask, afflict, overcharge, press down, obligate, encumber, vex, try, oppress, overlay, overload.
3. Heap with *(as honors, gifts, etc.),* bestow, award, deal out, give lavishly, shower upon, lavish, pile, render, give in profusion, accord, pour upon, flood, inundate, encumber, embarrass, assign generously, shed, apportion, engulf, mete out, favor with, present.

LOADSTONE, *n.,* **LODESTONE** Magnetic ore *or* stone, magnet, magnetite, siderite.

LOAF, *n.* Brick, block, slab, cake, lump, nugget.

LOAF, *v.* Waste time, idle, slack off, fritter away time, laze, twiddle the thumbs, shirk, not lift a finger, goldbrick *(sl.),* be lazy, loll, lounge, goof off *(sl.),* bum *(sl.),* be indolent, kill time, malinger, take it easy, do nothing, vegetate, dally.

LOAFER, *n.* Ne'er-do-well, bum *(sl.),* good-for-nothing, wastrel, lazybones, idler, sluggard, malingerer, fainéant, dead beat *(sl.),* lingerer, lounger, lounge lizard *(sl.),* drugstore cowboy *(sl.),* shirker, goldbrick *(sl.),* drone, laggard.

LOAN, *n.* 1. Act of lending, lending, advance, advancing, permission to borrow, accommodation, giving credit.
2. Thing *or* sum of money lent *or* borrowed, advance, credit, allowance, mortgage.

LOAN, *v.* Permit to borrow, advance, lend, allow, credit, mortgage.

LOATH, *adj.,* **LOTH** Averse, renitent, counter, against, recalcitrant, restive, reluctant, afraid of, disinclined, unfavorable, unwilling, laggard, hostile, adverse, shy of, shrinking, inimical, rankled, indisposed, revolted, shocked, opposed, squeamish, resenting, hating, abhorrent, repelled, demurring, mortified, backward, disgusted, horrified, set against, disquieted, remiss, pained, resisting, bitter, nauseated, queasy, virulent, sickened, grieved, harrowed, rancorous.

LOATHE, *v.* Have a strong aversion to, not be able to endure *or* bear, disdain, recoil from, abhor, contemn, object to, despise, abominate, sicken at, disrelish, view with horror, detest, anathematize, misprize, shrink from, recoil from, have hatred for, reluctate, scorn, mind, shun, hate, have no stomach for, eschew, execrate, feel sick at, blench from, draw back from, deprecate, keep clear of, shy away from, flinch from, quail from, reluct.

LOATHFUL, LOATHSOME, *adj.* Exciting great dislike, abominable, accursed, unbearable, unpalatable, objectionable, unpleasant, mean, deplorable, intolerable, abject, unendurable, disgusting, evil, hellish, revolting, evil-shaped, evil-affected, fulsome, rank, peccant, reprehensible, base, atrocious, nauseating, insufferable, blameworthy, nasty, distasteful, contemptible, hateful, opprobrious, obnoxious, foul, shocking, heinous, invidious, annoying, nauseous, offensive, execrable, repugnant, odious, detestable.

LOATHING, *n.* Feeling of one who loathes, intense dislike, detestation, rancor, hostility, enmity, aversion, rankling, contumely, scorn, contempt, virulence, inimicalness, estrangement, oppugnancy, asperity, mordacity, ill will, distaste, venom, antipathy, bitterness, hate, hatred, odium, rankling, spleen, grudge, bad blood, spite, invidiousness, disfavor, horror, repugnance, revulsion, abhorrence, abomination, execration, disgust, umbrage, malevolence, acrimony.

LOB, *v.* Throw, pitch, heave, toss, chuck, shy, fling, put *(as a shot, discus, etc.)*, loft *(Golf.)*, hurtle, bowl, trundle.

LOBATE, *adj.* Having a lobe *or* lobes, having the form of a lobe, lobular, lobed, pendulous, rounded, pendant, sectional, lobelike, lobated, lobulate, divided.

LOBBY, *n.* 1. Corridor, vestibule *(as of a public building)*, anteroom, court, porch, hallway, gallery, portal, foyer, entrance hall, passage, waiting room, reception room *or* hall, antechamber, portico, narthex *(Archit.)*.

2. Persons who frequent a legislative lobby *or* chamber *(esp. to influence its members)*, pressure group.

LOBBY, *v.* Frequent the lobby of a legislative chamber *(to influence the members)*, solicit votes *(of members of a legislative body)*, influence, promote, exercise *or* exert influence, urge *or* procure *(passage of a bill by lobbying)*, bring pressure to bear, affect, sway, weigh with, politic, wirepull, pull strings (wires, ropes), carry by solicitation.

LOBE, *n.* Roundish projection or division *(as of an organ, leaf, etc.)*, wing, convexity, protuberance, ear, lobule, wattle, pendant, knob, bulge, excurvation, nodule, node, tubercle, fluke, lappet, division.

LOCAL, *adj.* Pertaining to *or* characterized by place *or* position in space, pertaining to, characteristic of *or* restricted to a particular place *or* places, locational, limited, circumscribed, confined, nearby, neighborhood, divisional, of a town *or* small district, pertaining to *or* affecting a particular part *or* parts *(as of a system or object)*, regional, sectional, insular, adjacent, close, positional, epichorial, topical, circuit, adjoining, surrounding, circumjacent, small-town, territorial, county, district, parochial, situal, provincial.

LOCALE, *n.* Place *(esp. with reference to events or circumstances connected with it)*, locality, situation, habitat, quarter, zone, field, vicinity, territory, point, province, compass, situs, circle, area, neighborhood, pale, precinct, realm, district, whereabouts, spot, location, region, site, ambit, circuit, section, post.

LOCALISM, *n.* 1. Manner of speaking (pronunciation, usage *or* inflection) peculiar to one locality, dialect, provincialism, phrase characteristic of a district *or* people, brogue, accent, twang, patois, peculiar expression, idiom.

2. Local custom, habit, way, practice, observance, institution, tradition, folklore, usage.

3. Attachment to a particular locality, regional pride, provincialism, patriotism, allegiance, tie, bond, loyalty, adherence, faithfulness, nostalgia, devotion to *or* affection for home.

LOCALITY, *n.* Position, location, territory, quar-

ter, spot, site, ground, lôcale, situation, environment, bearings, terrain, purlieus, demesne, range, orbit, environs, soil, latitude and longitude, habitat, station, district, place, venue *(Law)*, vicinage, region, neighborhood, abode, province, whereabouts, pale, zone, area.

LOCALIZE, *v.* Make local, confine, fix in *or* assign *or* restrict to a particular place *or* locality, locate, situate, surround, bound, limit, compass, restrict, concentrate, keep from spreading, quarantine, circumscribe, consign to a place, territorialize, cut off, set, restrain, contain, encompass, proscribe, bind, define, hem in, pen in, beset, imprison, delimit, immure, impound.

LOCATE, *v.* 1. Discover the place *or* location of, search out, uncover, detect, get at, find, ferret out, reach, hit upon, come upon, fix upon, stumble on *or* upon, discern, lay one's finger *or* hands upon, unearth, track down, expose, reveal, bring to light, fish out, root up *or* out, disinter, light upon, meet with, descry, trace, come across.

2. Place, establish, settle, fix, situate, seat, deposit, lay down, set down, reposit, put, quarter, set, assign *or* consign to a place *or* locality, establish in a charge *or* office, localize, post, park, station.

3. Enter a claim to *(a tract of land)*, take up *(land)*, designate, survey, define, outline, demarcate, establish right to, map out, mark off *or* out, circumscribe, delineate.

4. Refer *(something)* as by opinion *or* statement to a particular place, consider to be, appoint, assign, believe, conjecture, agree upon the location of, find the place of, trace, ascribe, attribute, find to have been.

5. Establish oneself in a place, settle, reside, take up one's abode *or* quarters, take *or* strike root, take residence at, cast anchor, pitch camp, moor, squat, plant oneself, alight, settle down, place oneself, get a footing, establish one's home, hang up one's shingle *(coll.)*, pitch one's tent, move to, set up housekeeping, put up at, anchor, camp.

LOCATION, *n.* 1. Place of settlement *or* whereabouts, tract of land, space within designated limits, locale, locality, situation, colony, plot, quarter, position, patch, station, settlement, bailiwick, state, territory, spot, site, ground, environment, terrain, bearings, demesne, latitude and longitude, district, vicinage, region, province, whereabouts, zone, area, purlieus, range, neighborhood.

2. Locating, placing, placement, localization, marking out the limits *or* boundaries, establishing, lodgment, disposition, collocation, deposition, reposition, settlement, colonization, insertion, fixation, installation, exposure, stand, allocation.

LOCK, *n.* 1. Device for securing something in position, fastening, bolt, padlock, brake, gear, fixture *(Mach.)*, valve, stopper, plug, safety catch, hook, catch, clamp, clasp, latch, clinch, bar, bond, holdfast.

2. Grapple *(as in wrestling)*, hold, grasp, clasp, clamp, grip, cinch *(coll.)*, clinch, clutch, hug, embrace, strangle hold, gripe, seizure.

3. Portion of hair, tuft, flock (of wool, cotton, flax, *etc.*), bang, elflock, ringlet, curl, tress, lovelock, heartbreaker *(hum.)*, hair of the head *(plur.)*.

4. Device to control the flow of water *(as in a canal, river, etc.)*, floodgate, dam, canal gate, sluice gate, flood-hatch, penstock, weir.

LOCK, *v.* 1. Fasten with a lock, secure, padlock,

bolt, catch, screw, hasp, seal, button, bar, attach, close fast, zip up, snap.

2. *(Fol. by UP, IN, etc.)* Confine, shut up, shut in a locked place, close, trap, put behind bars, shackle, hold, encircle, close the door on, manacle, take into custody, coop up, pen, cage, entomb, immure, incarcerate, imprison, jail, cover, intern, secrete, hide, bind, impound, keep under lock and key, enthrall, arrest, clap up, put in irons, handcuff, cloister, conceal, circumscribe, fetter, enclose, restrain.

3. *(Usually fol. by OUT)* Exclude *(by or as by a lock)*, shut out, interdict, preclude, forbid entrance, ostracize, exile, banish, bar, debar, turn one's back upon, excommunicate, proscribe, snub, spurn, blackball, outlaw, embargo, shut the door upon, ignore, neglect, slam the door in one's face, keep at arm's length, overlook, slight.

4. Make fast *or* immovable *(by or as by a lock)*, clog, stop, occlude, blockade, dam, hinder, block, immobilize, keep back, constrain, inhibit, hamper, check, deadlock, tie one's hands, cut off, bar, barricade, entrammel, curb, prevent motion, impede, obstruct, cramp, restrict, choke off, snub.

5. *(Often fol. by UP)* Fasten *or* fix firmly *(as by engaging parts)*, seal, unite, conjoin, attach, close, consolidate, band, link, belay, brace, pinion, make inseparable, truss, cinch, graft, set, mortise, weld, dovetail, fuse, cement, solder, cohere, miter, braze *(Metall.)*, girdle, immobilize, glue, jam, lash, league, connect, press together, attach.

6. Join firmly *(by interlinking or intertwining)*, get a strangle hold on, grapple, grasp, clinch, entwine, seize, fasten, hold, grip, grab, hug, embrace, wrestle with, unite, clasp.

LOCOMOTION, *n.* Forward motion, progression, movement, progress, travel, advancement, furtherance, headway.

LODGE, *n.* 1. Hunting cottage, chalet, box, country seat, country house.

2. *(Of animals)* Den, lair, excavation, dugout, hole, retreat, furrow, nest, covert, refuge, mew, haunt, shelter, nidus.

3. *(Of American Indians, etc.)* Wigwam, tent, tepee, wickiup, hogan *(Navaho)*, tupek *(Eskimo)*, igloo *(Eskimo)*.

LODGE, *v.* 1. Quarter, ensconce, shelter, house, harbor, protect, put up, shield, roof, bed, furnish with lodgings, billet, guard, remove from exposure.

2. Establish oneself, settle, settle down, take root, abide, sojourn, stay, take possession, occupy, plant oneself, bunk, stop, dwell, inhabit, room, camp, remain, encamp, tenant, squat, reside, set up housekeeping.

3. Deposit, place, put, bank, lay, file, set, cache, park, station, reposit, stow.

LODGER, *n.* Roomer, tenant, occupant, renter, guest, paying guest, lessee, inmate, incumbent, boarder.

LODGMENT, *n.,* **LODGEMENT** 1. Lodging place, lodgings, diggings *(coll.)*, address, rooms, quarters, abode, chambers, place, apartment, domicile, dwelling, habitation, residence.

2. Accumulation, collection, amassing, aggregation, accretion, conglomeration, gathering, hoarding, pile, compilation, stock, gleaning, mass, agglomeration, assemblage, amassment, heap, bulk, fund, stockpile, accruement, acervation, concentration, harvest, profusion, coacervation, garner, quantity, supply, store, reserve.

LOFT, *n.* Upper room *or* chamber, attic, gallery, belfry, balcony, garret, mansard, cockloft, hayloft, clerestory.

LOFTY, *adj.* 1. Towering, soaring, arduous, elevated, raised, of great altitude *or* height, high-reaching, heaven-kissing, tall, high-set, prominent, overtopping, cloud-capped, supernal, high, peak, alpine, skyscraping, aerial, mountained, cloud-topped.

2. Distinguished, preëminent, predominant, leading, uppermost, top, ascendant, glorious, imposing, grand, dominant, ruling, prime, hegemonic, of exalted character, superior, patrician, wellborn, aristocratic, excellent, of the best, majestic, well-bred, reputable, thoroughbred, kingly, sovereign, queenly, noble, titled, important, illustrious, ranking, of high rank, peerless, sublime, stately, great, honorable, high, exalted, dignified, mighty, chief, elevated, eminent.

3. Proud, disdainful, mighty, aloof, arrogant, big, stiff, inflated, scornful, self-satisfied, self-glorious, peacockish, prideful, high, haughty, grandiloquent, insolent, lordly, self-important, stuck-up *(coll.)*, overproud, impudent, highfalutin *(coll.)*, sniff *(coll.)*, snooty *(sl.)*, vain, high-handed, stiff-necked, patronizing, affected, swollen, egotistical, imperious, overweening, self-assertive, high-hat *(sl.)*, ostentatious, boastful, condescending, bloated with pride, distended with self-esteem, snobbish, overbearing, uppish *(coll.)*, contumelious, distant, hoity-toity, supercilious, cold, conceited, pompous, puffed up, high and mighty, bombastic, self-opinionated, gasconading, braggart, self-complacent, self-flattering, self-praising, priggish, cocky *(coll.)*, know-it-all, unapproachable, unfriendly, forbidding, remote.

LOG, *n.* 1. Trunk, chunk, piece, stump, block, beam, puncheon, yule log.

2. *(Chiefly Nautical)* Record, schedule, account, logbook, journal, book, ship's diary, daybook.

LOG, *v.* Record, chart, tally, set down, register, enter, book, tabulate, mark off, note, catalogue, keep score, report.

LOGE, *n. (Chiefly of the theater)* Box, stall, parterre, circle, family circle, parquet circle.

LOGGERHEAD, *n.* Simpleton, idiot, clod, lunkhead *(coll.)*, lack-wit, woodenhead, dolt, dunce, chowderhead *(coll.)*, knucklehead *(coll.)*, crackbrain, pighead, blockhead, imbecile, numbskull, incompetent, pigsconce, dullard, lack-brain, fool, zany, loon, clodpoll, lout, tyke, bumpkin, oaf, thickskull, goon, goof *(coll.)*, looby, clodpate, ninny, dunderhead, jackass, ignoramus, blunderhead, wiseacre *(sl.)*.

LOGGING, *n.* Felling trees, lumbering, woodchopping, woodcutting, lumberjacking.

LOGIC, *n.* 1. Science of reasoning, science of inference, deduction, induction, syllogization, dialectics, epistemology, epagoge, syllogistic reasoning.

2. Train *or* chain of reasoning, reason, sense, synthesis, sound thought, inference, deduction, rationalizing, rationalization, dialectics, analysis, ratiocination.

LOGICAL, *adj.* 1. Deducible, consistent, coherent, valid, sound, close, cogent, legitimate, relevant, germane, pertinent.

2. Skilled in reasoning, discriminating, versed in logic, syllogistic, ratiocinative, disputatious, polemical, dialectic, argumentative, rational, analytical, inductive.

LOGICIAN, *n.* Reasoner, sophist, dialectician, casuist, epistemologist, ratiocinator, logistician, logicalist, logicaster, syllogist, syllogizer.

LOIN, *n.* (*Usually pl.*) Part of the body between the false ribs and hipbone, side lower *or* rear end of vertebral area, flank, saddle (*of mutton, venison, etc.*).

LOITER, *v.* Linger idly *or* aimlessly in *or* about a place, move *or* go in a slow *or* lagging manner, pass time in idleness, dally, dawdle, delay, waste time, halt, idle, tarry, potter, fritter away time, let the grass grow under one's feet, dabble, hover, wait, pause, boggle, loaf, lag, loll, procrastinate, hang back, dillydally, shilly-shally, limp, slouch, lope, traipse, shuffle, ramble, amble, stroll, shamble.

LOLL, *v.* 1. Recline in a relaxed *or* indolent manner, lounge, lean, slouch, lie around, slump, flop, sprawl, relax, repose, languish, doze, loiter, loaf, take it easy, vegetate.
2. Hang loosely *or* droopingly, be pendent, swing, droop, drop, sag, fall, flow, flap, trail, draggle, dangle.

LONELY, *adj.* 1. Being alone, unaccompanied, solitary, by oneself, lone, apart, single, unattended, without company, companionless, anchoritic, unsocial, hermitic, secluded, reclusive, withdrawn, troglodytic, self-contained.
2. Destitute of sympathetic companionship *or* relationships, exiled, cut off, lonesome, friendless, deserted, unwelcome, kithless, depressed by solitude *or* a sense of being alone, unaided, desolate, forsaken, lorn, unfriended, abandoned, estranged, uninvited, outcast, derelict, unpopular, unreceived, homeless, marooned, stranded.
3. Remote from men *or* from places of human habitation *or* resort, standing apart, isolated, private, separate, secluded, uninhabited, apart, deserted, desert, waste, desolate, wilderness, seagirt, depopulated, unpopulated, hidden, hid, buried, in a backwater, unfrequented, sequestered, unvisited, concealed, cut off, far between, shrouded, obscured, withdrawn, barren, insular, retired, privy.

LONG, *adj.* 1. Prolonged, protracted, copious, tautological, exuberant, wordy, verbose, prolix, lengthy, battological, unending, meandering, long-winded, circumlocutory, windy (*coll.*), pleonastic, discursive, spun out, redundant, rambling, interminable, padded, ambagious, sesquipedalian (*of words*).
2. Tall, stringy (*coll.*), protracted, outstretched, far-reaching, elongated, lengthy, gangling (*coll.*), extended, lanky (*coll.*).

LONG, *v.* Have a prolonged *or* unceasing desire, have an earnest and strong desire, yearn, hunger, thirst, covet, lust, crave, wish desperately, hope ardently, sigh, cry, pine for, languish, be bent upon, die, grasp, pant, want, have at heart, feel the want of, set one's heart *or* mind upon, have one's heart set on, set one's cap at *or* for, desiderate, look sweet, cast sheep's eyes, hanker, aspire, yen (*coll.*), gasp.

LONGEVITY, *n.* Length *or* duration of life, long life, durability, continuance, survival, endurance, years, elderliness, oldness, persistence, perpetuity.

LONG-LIVED, *adj.* Having a long life, longevous, macrobiotic, long-lasting, perdurable, lasting, diuturnal, longeval.

LONG-SIGHTED, *adj.* Far-seeing, sharp-sighted, piercing, subtle, argute, quick-witted, clear-headed, clear-sighted, open-eyed, Argus-eyed, penetrating, discriminating, undeceived, keen, shrewd, discretional, clear-headed, lynx-eyed, sagacious, judicious, acute, wise, apprehensive, clear-witted, gimlet-eyed, discerning, ferret-eyed, percipient, prepared, sapient, imaginative, provident, prudent, eagle-eyed, forehanded.

LONG-SPUN, *adj.* Long-winded, meandering, unending, battological, circumlocutory, windy (*coll.*), pleonastic, discursive, spun out, redundant, rambling, interminable, padded, ambagious, lengthy, long, prolix, verbose, wordy, tautological, copious, protracted, prolonged, exuberant, extended, diffuse.

LONG-SUFFERING, *adj.* Patient, easygoing, lax, tolerant, lenient, clement, forbearing, indulgent, enduring, forgiving, uncomplaining, longanimous, resigned, mild.

LONG-WINDED, *adj.* Talking *or* writing at tedious length, continued tediously, garrulous, longiloquent, voluble, rambling, verbose, long, prolix, meandering, battological, windy (*coll.*), pleonastic, spun out, redundant, gushy, effusive, wordy, diffuse, extended, exuberant, prolonged, protracted, copious, unending, circumlocutory, discursive, interminable, ambagious, padded, lengthy, tautological, talkative, loquacious, gabby, gassy (*coll.*).

LOOK, *n.* 1. Act of looking, visual search *or* examination, sight, observance, gaze, glower, once-over (*sl.*), reconnaissance, lookout, introspection, glimpse, scrutiny, stare, glare, speculation, quick cast of the eyes, survey, contemplation, watch, ogle, gloat, bird's-eye view, glance, flicker *or* twinkle of an eye, view, peek, leer, regard, inspection, peep, squint, espionage.
2. (*Sometimes pl.*) Way of looking *or* appearing to the eye *or* mind, general aspect, appearance, revelation, sight, vision, ostent, complexion, countenance, quality, bearing, port, cast, color, mien, favor, guise, turn, air, presence, condition, demeanor, expression, fashion, figure, shape, phase, front, show, impression, effect, semblance, seeming.

LOOK, *v.* 1. See, fix the eye on, cock the eye, give attention, visualize, squint, turn the eyes upon, watch, survey, scrutinize, examine, glance, stare, scan, peer, ogle, have an eye on, study, peep, regard, gape, spy, peek, contemplate.
2. Have an appearance, present an appearance, have the expression, appear, carry the appearance, cut a figure, present, seem, show, evidence, wear the aspect, exhibit, strike one as being, manifest.
3. (*With* TO) Expect, anticipate, prepare oneself for, wait for, look forward to, reckon upon, calculate on, count on, long for, pin hope on.
4. (*With* TO) Care for, pay attention, heed, hearken, listen, give ear, mark, be attentive, give heed to, mind, notice, be attentive to, observe, consider, hearken to.

LOOM, *v.* Appear indistinctly, rise gradually and appear huge, bulk, figure, show, tower, emerge, be imminent, hover, soar, ascend, impend, mount, hang over, come *or* draw on, break through the clouds, glare, lower, menace, lie over, threaten, darkle, move slowly, stand out, stand forth.

LOOP, *n.* Noose, circle, spiral, convolution, coque, whorl, eye, twirl, loophole, ring, bow, coil, eyelet, aureole, crupper (*of harness*), circuit, bend, curve, twist, opening.

LOOP, *v.* Make a loop, twist, turn, circle, bend, roll, furl, hoop, wind, round, kink, curve around, whirl, curl, spiral, twirl, coil, curlicue, plait, braid, plat.

LOOSE, *adj.* 1. Unbound, unconnected, disconnected, unlocked, unlatched, unattached, unfastened, untethered, untied, unbuttoned, unshackled, unpinned, unhasped, unclasped, unhooked.

2. Free, liberated, freed, unchained, unfettered, unyoked, unimprisoned, at large, uncaged, scot-free, untethered, unshackled, unhandcuffed, unmanacled, unhooked.

3. *(Of information, etc.)* Detached, roundabout, inaccurate, stray, discursive, deviative, vague, irrelevant, circuitous, desultory, roving, rambling, wandering, obscure, erratic, prolix, abstruse.

4. Lax, relaxed, slack, cursory, remiss, weak, careless, easy, unexacting, offhand, heedless, negligent, neglectful, perfunctory.

5. Immoral, rakehell, rakehelly, rampant, lawless, prodigal, wanton, licentious, profligate, abandoned, fast, debauched, lewd, incontinent, wild, dissolute, dissipated, libertine, uncontrolled, unconstrained, unself-disciplined, unchaste, free-living, unbridled, immoderate.

LOOSE, LOOSEN, *v.* 1. Set free, free, let go, release, unchain, unbridle, unshackle, unmanacle, unhandcuff, manumit, liberate, untie, deliver, unbind, extricate.

2. *(Of restrictions, regulations, etc.)* Relax, slacken, ease, mitigate, extenuate, reduce, soften, diminish, ameliorate, attenuate, lessen, step down *(coll.),* weaken.

3. (LOOSE *only*) Shoot (a bullet, arrow *etc.*), discharge, hurl, catapult, fire off, emit, eject, throw off *or* out, project.

LOOT, *n.* Anything dishonestly and ruthlessly appropriated, plunder taken by pillaging, spoils, pillage, taking, illegal gain, booty, stolen goods, piece of plunder, prey, grab, take, filch, haul *(coll.),* stealings, boodle *(sl.),* stealage, prize, swag *(sl.),* steal *(coll.).*

LOOT, *v.* Take, carry off, plunder, rob, despoil, depredate, appropriate illegally, lay waste, raid, harry, sack, steal, spoliate, ransack, gut, maraud, ravage, spoil, strip, seize, rifle, make off with, fleece, swindle, forage.

LOP, *v.* 1. Cut, sever, obtruncate, trim, detach, amputate, dock, crop, mutilate, detruncate, pollard, clip, top, dissever, shear, poll, truncate, cut off, curtail, cut short, mow, chop, prune.

2. Hang loosely *or* limply, droop, be suspended, move in a drooping *or* heavy way, draggle, dangle, flap, sway awkwardly, swing aimlessly, depend, be pendent.

LOPE, *v.* Go with long easy strides, canter leisurely, move *or* run with bounding steps, coast, skim, sweep, cut along, glide, run easily, gallop, trundle, course, fly, wheel, soar, stroll, saunter, amble, slide, cruise *(coll.),* glissade, drift, flit, roll along.

LOPSIDED, *adj.* Lopping *or* inclining to one side, one-sided, unsymmetrical, larger *or* more developed on one side than the other, uneven, ill-balanced, overbalanced, disproportioned, unbalanced, unequal-sided, irregular, asymmetrical, unequal.

LOQUACIOUS, *adj.* Disposed to talk freely, talkative, voluble, wordy, profuse, copious in speech, tonguey, babbling, chattering, prattling, babblative, fluent, gushy, long-winded, gabbling, jabbering, windy, gabby, diffusive, effusive, prolix, di-

gressive, longiloquent, exuberant, flatulent, gassy *(sl.),* glib, diffuse, discursive, multiloquent, polyloquent, prating, blabbing, tattling, bombastic, multiloquous, rambling, verbose, garrulous.

LORD, *n.* One who has dominion over others, master, chief, ruler, monarch, superior, commander, overlord, noble, one who exercises authority from property rights, owner *or* possessor of houses *or* land *etc.,* feudal superior, proprietor, baron, seignior, earl, count, duke, grand duke, aristocrat, sachem, landholder, landowner, prince, liege, governor, sovereign, lording *(often contempt.),* peer, grandee, marquis, archduke, king, suzerain, magnate, signor *(Ital.),* lordling, nobleman, magnifico, gentleman, viscount, mogul, silk-stocking.

LORDLY, *adj.* 1. Suitable for a lord, magnificent, befitting a lord, high, great, having the attributes of a lord, regal, eminent, noble, majestic, exalted, lordlike, princely, royal, august, formal, sublime, worshipful, radiant, suzerain, imperial, supreme, baronial, authoritative, stately, magisterial, princely, liberal, grand, dignified, large, sovereign, imposing, glorious, lofty, absolute, silk-stockinged.

2. Imperious, insolent, domineering, overbearing, stiff, proud, despotic, contemptuous, overweening, arbitrary, brazen, bold, pretentious, puffed up, condescending, pompous, lofty, saucy, patronizing, disdainful, contumelious, audacious, insulting, bumptious, forward, brash, unabashed, bluff, barefaced, uppish *(coll.),* dominant, high and mighty, toplofty, stilted, stiff-necked, tyrannical, haughty, swollen *or* bloated with pride, arrogant, supercilious, impertinent, self-assertive, aweless, high-handed, magisterial, presumptuous, cavalier, flippant, cocky *(coll.),* nervy *(sl.),* fresh *(sl.).*

LORE, *n.* Traditional knowledge, body of knowledge, learning, teaching, doctrine, literature, wisdom, craft, science, knowledge.

LOSE, *v.* 1. Miss, misplace, be deprived of, incur loss, suffer loss, mislay.

2. Be the loser, miss, be defeated, have the worst of it, fail, succumb, fall.

LOSS, *n.* 1. Wreck, wreckage, destruction, ruin, extermination, eradication, extinction, extirpation, annihilation, perdition, bane, end, undoing, dissolution, removal, abolition, breaking up, disruption, disorganization, suppression, sacrifice, immolation.

2. Act of losing, losing, mislaying, misplacing, privation, bereavement, forfeiture, deprivation, expenditure, riddance.

3. Wastage, waste, leakage, shrinkage, decrement, deterioration, wear and tear, depletion.

4. Defeat, failure, undoing, rout, beating, vanquishment, licking *(coll.),* overthrow, subjugation, overturn.

LOST, *adj.* 1. Destroyed, wrecked, ruined, effaced, undone, obliterated, abolished, wiped out, taken, finished, ended, put down, annihilated, exterminated, quenched, dissolved, extinguished, perished, vanished, extirpated, eradicated, killed, murdered, eliminated, quelled.

2. Gone out of one's possession, mislaid, misplaced, astray, missing, forfeited, vanished, strayed, absent, lacking, stray.

3. Irreclaimable, irretrievable, irrevocable, irrecoverable, irredeemable, irreversible, destroyed, beyond hope *or* call.

4. Incorrigible, irreformable, incurable, unreformed, debauched, degenerate, unreclaimed, **gone**

to the dogs (coll.), hopeless, dissolute, abandoned, profligate, prodigal, recidivous.

5. Bewildered, bemuddled, distracted, mystified, désorienté (Fr.), puzzled, baffled, befogged, befuddled, disoriented, perplexed, confused, nonplused, confounded, obfuscated.

LOT, n. 1. Object used to determine a question by chance, counter, check, die, chip, bone, straw.

2. Casting or drawing of lots to reach a decision, impartial choice, chance, luck, haphazard, shot, fortune, hazard, accident, fluke, stroke, fortuity, Fortune's wheel, hit, contingency, flip of the coin, draw, tossup, toss, fate, potluck, gamble, random.

3. What comes to or befalls one, allotted portion, share, meed, apportionment, measure, allowance, pittance, proportion, quota, ration, dose, dole, piece, part, contingent, commission, whack (sl.), percentage, cut (coll.), allotment.

4. Portion in life, fortune, plight, state, estate, condition, luck, status, destiny, walk, cup, doom, stars, situation, planets, kismet, predestination, predicament, fate, case.

5. Distinct portion or parcel of land, plot, division, plat, property, patch, tract, clearing, field, piece of ground, part.

6. Number of associated persons or things taken collectively, collection, company, package, set, parcel, bundle, pack, batch, shipment, multitude, bunch, host, troop, packet, budget, cluster, group, body.

LOTION, n. Liquid preparation, wash, medicine, lenitive, embrocation, abirritant (Pathol.), solution, liniment, salve, balm, demulcent, curative, unguent, emollient, medicament, alleviative, palliative.

LOTTERY, n. Game of chance, chance, raffle, draw.

LOUD, adj. Intense, fulminating, resounding, loudmouthed, booming, clarion-voiced, thunderlike, noisy, stentorian, blatant, tonant, tonitruous, deafening, vociferous, roaring, thundering, clamorous, ear-splitting, ear-rending, ear-piercing.

LOUNGE, n. 1. Sofa, seat to recline on, davenport, day bed, divan, couch, ottoman.

2. Large room for resting, lobby, vestibule, waiting room, reception hall or room.

LOUNGE, v. 1. Recline indolently, stretch out, loll, relax, lie around, laze, slumber, sleep, rest, repose, lie at ease, take one's ease, sprawl, couch, lean, languish, take it easy, slouch, slump, flop.

2. Pass time idly or indolently, live lazily, do nothing, dally, loaf, waste time, trifle away time, fritter away time, laze, dillydally, dawdle, twiddle one's thumbs, fold one's arms, vegetate, stagnate, mark time, relax, let the grass grow under one's feet, not lift a finger or hand, lie around, drift with the current, lie down, eat the bread of idleness, be inert, bum (coll.), burn daylight, kill time, idle.

3. Move or go in a leisurely indolent manner, dawdle, saunter, lag, stroll, slouch, poke, dally, take one's time, dillydally, take one's own sweet time (coll.), linger, loiter, drag, amble, ramble, shuffle, toddle, limp, jaunt, traipse, shamble, crawl, delay, tarry, idle, pause, hang back, halt.

LOUSY, adj. Infested with lice, pedicular.

LOUT, n. Awkward stupid person, boor, churl, rustic, clodhopper, hobnail, hind, peasant, yokel, farmer, countryman, bumpkin, hick (sl.), greenhorn, swain, Tony Lumpkin, country bumpkin,

clown, plowman, drone, son of the soil, hayseed (sl.), hodge (coll.), lumpkin, lubber, son of Martha, chuff, kern, galoot (sl.), clod, joskin (sl.), looby, jake (coll.), rube (coll.), gaffer, tiller of the soil, booby, dunce, lummox, bungler, gawky, blunderbuss.

LOUTISH, adj. Like or characteristic of a lout, boorish, churlish, awkward, stupid, uncouth, illmannered, abrupt, gross, rough, ungainly, rustic, blunt, vulgar, ill-bred, cloddish, lowbred, clownish, lubberly, rude, gawky, ungentlemanly, obtuse, ungraceful, gauche, uncourtly, unpolished, indelicate, inelegant, untoward, unrefined, bungling, lacking dexterity, maladroit, inept, clumsy, blundering, like a bull in a china shop, dull, dense, oafish, insulse, stolid, heavy-handed, insensitive, doltish, dumb (coll.), thick (coll.).

LOVABLE, LOVEABLE, adj. Of such a nature as to attract love, amiable, winning, sweet, charming, attractive, taking, engaging, delightful, lovely, winsome, lovesome, adorable, enchanting, worthy of love, endearing, estimable, likable.

LOVE, n. 1. Sexual attachment or desire, gratification of desire, amour, the tender passion, amativeness, infatuation, craving, longing, coveting, sentiment, transport, emotion, flame, amorousness, passionate affection, heat, ardor, heart, rapture, crush (sl.), yearning.

2. Object of love or affection, dear, dearest, darling, beloved, inamorata, paramour, precious, jewel, truelove, well-beloved, angel, mistress, goddess, idol, light of one's eyes or life, dearly beloved, sweetie (coll.), lover, loved one, girl (coll.).

3. (Cap.) Personification of sexual affection, Cupid (Rom.), Eros (Gk.), Venus (Rom.), Aphrodite (Gk.), amorino, amoretto, cupidon, Amor (Rom.), Kama (Hind), Freya (Scand. Myth.), Astarte (Phoenic).

4. Feeling of warm personal attachment, deep affection, devotion, affectionate regard, tenderness, fondness, endearment, rapport, amity, brotherhood, solicitude, Christian charity, good will, favoritism, benevolence, affinity, concord, congeniality, fellow feeling, fervor, idolism, attraction, admiration, esteem, delight, friendship, partiality, compatibility, grace, sympathy, cordiality, adoration.

5. Strong predilection or liking for anything (as for books), fondness, devotion, strong attachment, weakness, relish, penchant, taste, mania, mind, turn, bent, leaning, regard, partiality, proclivity, warm feeling, inclination, liking, absorption.

LOVE, v. 1. Have love or affection for, regard with affection, hold dear, hold in affection or love, prize, esteem, regard, think worlds or the world of, take joy in, feast one's eyes on, take an intense interest in, treasure, be drawn to, care for, be fond of, delight in, cherish, admire.

2. Have a strong or passionate affection for (one of the opposite sex), be enamored of, idolize, lose one's heart to, set one's affections on, adore, honor, yearn for, be in love with, hold in affection, hold dear or precious, cling to, pine for, sigh for, be infatuated, have a crush on (sl.), court, pant for, look sweet on, pay court to, set one's cap at or for, be swept off one's feet, make love to, burn, desire, treasure, dote on or upon, make much of, languish for, long for, cherish.

3. Have a strong liking for, take great pleasure in, fancy, delight in, relish, bask in, riot in, rejoice in, savor, find irresistible, receive or derive

pleasure from, indulge in, revel in, treat oneself to, enter into the spirit of, take in good part, wallow in, enjoy, approve, get a kick out of *(sl.)*, luxuriate in, be drawn to, appreciate, like immensely, applaud.

LOVELESS, *adj.* 1. Receiving no love, devoid of *or* unattended with love, disliked, forlorn, unfriended, hated, unvalued, unloved, unpopular, forsaken, lovelorn, lonely, cut off, exiled, out of favor, uncared-for, undeplored, unlamented, friendless, unmissed, unbeloved, jilted, rejected, deserted, unwelcome, desolate, uninvited, unreceived, out in the cold.

2. Feeling no love, cold, indifferent, unresponsive, without natural feeling, heartless, unsympathetic, hard, cruel, unfeeling, aloof, without heart, lukewarm, supercilious, icy, unimpassioned, remote, harsh, insensible, impassive, numb, callous, unsolicitous, stony, flinty, hostile, insensitive, soulless, hardened, obtuse, unmoved, unstirred, untouched, uncaring, cold-blooded, cold-hearted.

LOVELY, *adj.* Engaging, rapturous, elegant, beautiful, transporting, exquisite, diverting, alluring, winsome, winning, fair, magnetizing, diverting, delightful, pleasing, inducing, catching, tantalizing, handsome, irresistible, enthralling, likable, delectable, electrifying, titillating, enamoring, intriguing, engrossing, absorbing, fetching, seductive, graceful, tempting, charming, prepossessing, sweet, enchanting, fascinating, attractive, entrancing, thrilling.

LOVER, *n.* 1. Sweetheart, admirer, infatuate, beau, paramour, fiancé, suitor, swain, flame *(coll.)*, inamorato, wooer, courter.

2. Lothario, Casanova, Don Juan, Romeo, amorist, gallant, lion among ladies, philanderer, vampire *(fem.)*, cicisbeo, cavalier, ladies' man, coquette *(fem.)*, flirt, squire *(coll.)*.

LOVING, *adj.* Amatory, benign, benevolent, friendly, amiable, solicitous, fond, kind, affectionate, tender, enamored, amorous, ardent, warmhearted, attached, earnest, passionate, cordial, devoted, warm, lovesick, fervent, sympathetic, doting, caring.

LOW, *adj.* 1. Situated *or* occurring not far above the ground, floor *or* base, not far above the horizon, low-lying, lower, unelevated, low-hanging, lowering, knee-high, ankle-high, scudding *(of clouds)*.

2. Lying below the general level, near sea level, coastal, nether, under, flat, ebb, neap, concave, deep, depressed, sunken, buried, underground, underwater, bottom, undersea, submerged, submarine, unelevated.

3. Prostrate, dead, near death, sick, ill, supine, prone, flat, horizontal, strengthless, pithless, upset, downcast, downthrown, unstrung, sapless, unnerved, enervated, wasted, devitalized, demoralized, recumbent, listless, drooping, flaccid, faint, sinewless, nerveless, detruded, crippled, disabled, incompetent, exhausted, helpless, powerless, defenseless, done for, on the shelf, languid, slack, dull, effete, impotent, spent, wilted, infirm, debilitated, worn out, at low ebb.

4. Deep, profound, respectful, reverential, prostrate, obeisant, on one's knees, venerative, obsequious, on bended knee, devout, adorant, submissive, humble, at the feet of, pious, worshipful, ceremonious, reverent, prone, in the dust before.

5. Of small extent upward, not high *or* tall, rising but slightly from a surface, having little

elevation, short, small, stumpy, low-lying, truncated, knee-high, scrubby, dumpy, stubby, squat, crouched, little, snubbed, crouching, couchant.

6. Of less than average *or* normal height *or* depth *(as a liquid, stream, etc.)*, lacking in strength *or* vigor, in inadequate supply, shallow, feeble, weak, spent, short, used up, expended, drained, impoverished, at low ebb *or* tide, decreased, consumed, depleted, exhausted, reduced, dried up.

7. Assigning *or* attributing no great amount, value *or* excellence, unflattering, minimum, meager, poor, sorry, slender, slight, paltry, niggardly, damning, pitiful, uncharitable, contemptible, underrating, condemning, underestimated.

8. Depressed, dejected, cast down, miserable, crestfallen, disheartened, downcast, in the dumps, heavy-hearted, despondent, discouraged, unhappy, sad, down in the mouth *(coll.)*, in the doldrums, out of spirit, forlorn, weary, mopish, glum, low-spirited, disconsolate, chapfallen, heartsick, dispirited, downhearted, cheerless, gloomy, melancholy, woebegone, sullen, doleful, lugubrious, dolorous, dreary, joyless, spiritless, desolate, funereal, woeful, lamenting, grieving, sorrowful, mournful, plaintive, tearful, sorrow-worn, sorrow-laden, morose, comfortless, rueful.

9. Far down in the scale of rank *or* estimation, lowly, humble, inferior, obscure, vulgar, common, servile, lacking in dignity *or* elevation, destitute, pitiful, plain, simple, frugal, baseborn, plebeian, menial, mean, poor, paltry, slave, meek, inglorious, lowborn, insignificant, inconsequential, homely, unknown, homespun, inconsiderable, lewd, contemptible, wretched, niggling, of inferior breed, ignominious, abject, lesser, mediocre, nameless, renownless, base, small fry, puny, ineffectual, unworthy of notice *or* serious consideration.

10. Of inferior quality *or* character, ignoble, groveling, degraded, foul, filthy, obscene, scurvy, low-minded, base-minded, corrupt, sunken, rattish, dirty, fallen, reprobate, reptilian, inglorious, scoundrelly, blackguardly, profligate, abandoned, debauched, demoralized, wicked, sorry, sneaking, hangdog, dishonorable, unmanly, mean, abject, offensive, disgraceful, derogatory, unbecoming, unhandsome, base, depraved, uncouth, coarse, vulgar, discreditable, shameless, lamentable, despicable, dastardly, cowardly, ribald, sordid, common, gross, raffish, disreputable, dishonorable, ignominious, earthy, cheap, yellow, rascally, beggarly, mean-spirited, petty, infamous, odious, execrable, dissipated, earth-born, fulsome, rank, peccant, rotten, degenerate, opprobrious, notorious, outrageous, scandalous, arrant, heinous, nefarious, tainted, abominable.

11. Not loud, quiet, grave *(Phonet.)*, not high-pitched, subdued, dampened, produced by relatively slow vibrations *(Mus.)*, deep, whispered, dim, feeble, murmured, weak, stifled, scarcely *or* barely audible, hushed, muffled, toneless, hoarse, flat, faint, soothing, muted, indistinct, hollow, soft, gentle, *sotto voce (It.)*.

LOW, *v.* Utter the sound characteristic of cattle, bellow, moo, bawl, blare.

LOWBORN, *adj.* Of humble birth, vulgar, baseborn, plebeian, ignoble, common, lesser, nameless, inferior, undistinguished by high birth, insignificant, without rank, obscure, mediocre, bourgeois, unheard of, unnoticed, unknown, renownless, base, average, of little *or* no account, humble, small fry, lowly, ordinary, untitled, uncouth, simple, little, mean.

LOWBRED, *adj.* Rude, ill-bred, unrefined, coarse, vulgar, rustic, boorish, churlish, lacking delicacy of feeling *or* manner, uncivil, unpolished, ill-mannered, rough, unhandsome, clownish, loutish, gruff, impolite, bluff, ungentlemanly, offensive, barbaric, harsh, cloddish, brazen, bestial, indecent, ungraceful, improper, bold, crass, crude, sordid, lubberly, indelicate, broad, mean, ignorant, vile, plebeian, gross, ignoble, inelegant, degraded, insensitive, brutish, lacking taste, indecorous, common.

LOWER, *v.* 1. Lessen, diminish, reduce in amount, price, degree, force, *etc.,* slacken, weaken, decrease, ease, restrain, cut, remit, curtail, abbreviate, shorten, mitigate, pare, deduct, abate, bate, make less, minify, minimize, flatten, render less, detract from, subtract from, moderate, temper, prune, truncate, attenuate, extenuate, allay, crop, take from, assuage, contract, lenify, quell, lop, relax, blunt, appease, soothe, deaden, deplete, slake, dull, palliate, discount, stunt, boil down, deduct, qualify, retrench, dock, narrow, relieve, compress.

2. Make less loud, deepen, muffle, modify, quiet, hush, damp, tone down, soft-pedal, subdue, modulate, reduce, dull, mute, throttle, suppress, repress, soften, stifle, deaden.

3. Bring down in rank *or* estimation, sacrifice one's dignity, degrade, humble, humiliate, dishonor, detract from, debase, disgrace, misprize, hold cheap, belittle, prostrate, unman, reduce, put in one's place, chasten, depreciate, subvert, cheapen, make subject, abash, undermine, sully, taint, blot, stigmatize, defile, blacken, unfrock, disbar, malign, put to shame, cry shame upon, drag through the mire, stain, brand, vilipend, vilify, tarnish, bespatter, discredit, blackball, blacklist, give a bad name, take down a peg *(coll.),* abase, decry, demean, derogate, deteriorate, disparage, dwarf, reprehend, disvalue, denounce, blame, reflect upon, pass censure upon, discommend, dispraise, despise, slight, scorn, underestimate, decimate, slander, libel, speak slightly *or* ill of, gibbet, muckrake, minimize, calumniate, set at nought, bear false witness against, expose to infamy, fling *or* throw mud at, asperse, slur, run down, traduce, cast aspersions, impeach, deride, weaken one's position, censure, make little of.

4. Cause to descend, let down, drop, dip, thrust down, bury, sink, send to the bottom, submerge, engulf, plunge, souse, douse, raze, put down, let fall *or* drop, push down, level, bring down, take down, fell, overthrow, detrude, immerse, couch, depress, duck, pull down.

5. Become lower *or* less, diminish, decrease, lessen, abate, grow less, slacken, weaken, ebb, bate, recede, decline, wane, subside, let up, languish, fall away, fall off, drop off, tail off, shrink, contract, fall to a low ebb, melt *or* die away, dwindle, run low.

6. Descend, come down, drop, fall, stoop, slump, decline, depreciate, lose altitude, collapse, gravitate, pitch *or* plunge downward, droop, swag, set, settle, slip, slide, souse, swoop, mire, submerge, nose-dive, dive, dip, flop, founder, pitch, precipitate, tumble, sag, lapse, sink.

LOWER, *v.* 1. Be dark and threatening, be clouded, blacken, cloud over, overhang, darkle, dusk, loom, gloom, menace, grow dim, threaten, appear gloomy *or* stormy, darken, impend.

2. Frown, scowl, look sullen, sulk, knit the brow, glower, look black, look black as thunder, look daggers, mope, pout, pull *or* make a long face.

LOWERING, *adj.* 1. Dark and threatening, cloudy, dark, murky, sullen, black, gloomy, heavy, lurid, overcast, clouded, overclouded, somber, moonless, sunless, starless, gray, leaden, dull, dreary, caliginous, overshadowed, dismal, depressing, under a pall, dun, oppressive, glowering, umbrageous.

2. Frowning, sullen, black, ominous, minatory, threatening, somber, sinister, glowering, gloomy, scowling, dismal, saturnine, lugubrious, funereal, menacing, defiant.

LOWLAND, *n.* Land low with respect to neighboring country, swamp, flat, valley, marsh, seacoast, dell, dale, depressed area, plain, bottom.

LOWLY, *adj.* 1. Humble in station, condition, nature *or* spirit, belonging to a low rank, modest, meek, unassuming, simple, obscure, lowborn, vulgar, common, unpretending, plebeian, mean, low, subject, servile, bowed-down, content, lamblike, homely, proletarian, mild, inglorious, submissive, untitled, uncouth, unobtrusive, unimportant, cockney, unpretentious, baseborn, homespun, subdued, unresisting, lowbred, chastened, dependent, renownless, unknown, unaspiring, unassertive, docile, pliant, subordinate, conformable, mediocre, ordinary, average, little, forbearant, tractable, dutiful, obedient, subjected, gentle, ignoble, base, insignificant.

2. Low in growth, position *or* development, poor, puny, lesser, small, inferior, humble, modest, mean, secondary, second-rate, insignificant, inconsiderable, garden variety, petty, paltry, indifferent, diminutive, trivial, slight, plain, commonplace, common, little, simple, limited.

LOW-MINDED, *adj.* Having *or* showing a low, coarse *or* vulgar mind, mean, base, abject, low, slavish, servile, sordid, vulgar, mean-spirited, base-minded, groveling, foul, filthy, scurvy, obscene, degraded, ignoble, inferior, corrupt, rattish, dirty, fallen, sunken, reprobate, reptilian, inglorious, scoundrelly, blackguardly, profligate, abandoned, debauched, demoralized, wicked, sorry, sneaking, dishonorable, unmanly, offensive, depraved, uncouth, coarse, shameless, despicable, dastardly, sordid, common, gross, cowardly, ribald, ignominious, cheap, rascally, beggarly, odious, execrable, dissipated, infamous, rank, rotten, degenerate, opprobrious, peccant, beneath contempt.

LOYAL, *adj.* Faithful, true, steadfast, trustworthy, reliable, honest, sincere, unwavering, unswerving, scrupulous, uncorrupted, as good as one's word, conscientious, incorruptible, unbought, unbribed, at one's command, punctilious, devoted, constant, dependable, inviolable, tried and true, trusty, unperfidious, unfalse, single-hearted, single-minded, unpurchased, upright, true-blue, allegiant, fast, incorrupt, true-hearted, dutiful, stanch, firm, obedient, reputable.

LOYALIST, *n.* One who is loyal, supporter *(of sovereign or existing government),* patriot, adherent, admirer, follower, zealot, sustainer, maintainer, upholder, disciple, die-hard, conservative, partisan, one of the old guard, champion, devotee, votary.

LOYALTY, *n.* State *or* quality of being loyal, faithfulness, adherence to duty, singleness of heart, bond, attachment, tie, constancy, fidelity, fealty, group feeling, *esprit de corps (Fr.),* homage, probity, uprightness, faith, honor, good faith, reliability, scrupulousness, incorruptibility, firmness, conscientiousness, trustworthiness, singlemindedness, obedience, sincerity, inviolability, dependability, allegiance.

LOZENGE, *n.* Small flavored cake *or* confection *(often medicated),* tablet, pill, pastille, drop, electuary, comfit, bonbon, sweet, sweetmeat, sugarplum, jujube, bolus, troche *(Pharm.).*

LUBBER, *n.* Lout, awkward person, boor, churl, rustic, clodhopper, hobnail, hind, peasant, yokel, farmer, countryman, bumpkin, hick *(sl.),* greenhorn, swain, Tony Lumpkin, country bumpkin, clown, plowman, drone, son of the soil, hayseed *(sl.),* hodge *(coll.),* lumpkin, lummox, bungler, gawk, gawky, blunderbuss, dunce, booby, gaffer, rube *(coll.),* jake *(coll.),* looby, chuff, kern, galoot *(sl.),* clod, joskin *(sl.).*

LUBBERLY, *adj.* Loutish, boorish, churlish, awkward, stupid, clumsy, uncouth, ill-mannered, abrupt, gross, rough, ungainly, rustic, blunt, vulgar, ill-bred, cloddish, low-bred, clownish, rude, gawky, obtuse, ungraceful, gauche, unpolished, indelicate, inelegant, untoward, unrefined, bungling, lacking dexterity, maladroit, inept, blundering, like a bull in a china shop, dull, dense, oafish, insulse, stolid, heavy-handed, insensitive, doltish, dumb *(coll.),* thick *(coll.).*

LUBRICANT, *n.* Lubricating material, oil, lubricator, grease, slush, ointment, glycerin, jelly, salve, synovia *(Physiol.),* graphite, plumbago, black lead, unguent, balm, emollient.

LUBRICATE, *v.* Apply an oily *or* greasy substance to *(to diminish friction),* smooth, oil, grease, anoint, daub, soap, wax, slush, dress, pinguefy, smear with grease, make slippery *or* smooth.

LUBRICITY, *n.* 1. Smoothness, slipperiness, gloss, glaze, oiliness, sleekness, greasiness, shine, polish, pinguefaction, unctuousness, oleaginousness.

2. Shiftiness, instability, treachery, defection, desertion, fluctuation, unreliability, uncertainty, unsteadiness, unctuousness, duplicity, suavity, undependability, fickleness, capriciousness, slipperiness, tergiversation, mutability, changeableness, vacillation, inconstancy, variableness, infidelity, deceptiveness, infirmity of purpose, unfaithfulness, erraticism, mouth honor, faithlessness, falsity, disloyalty, guile, deceitfulness, Punic faith, perfidy, bad faith.

3. Lasciviousness, carnality, passion, pruriency, nymphomania, satyrism, aphrodisia, salacity, salaciousness, sensuality, concupiscence, lust, lewdness, lechery, unchastity, venery, intemperance, debauchery, dissipation, wantonness, licentiousness, fornication, wenching, libertinism.

LUBRICOUS, *adj.* 1. Of an oily smoothness, slippery, lubricious, oily, slick, sleek, greasy, lubric, lubricated, soapy, unctuous, glossy, slimy, waxy.

2. Unstable, uncertain, shifty, elusive, inconstant, unsteady, indecisive, unreliable, unsteadfast, erratic, unsettled, changeful, lubric, wavering, slick, sly, irresolute, tergiversating, fickle, slippery, vagrant, wayward, mercurial, fitful, spasmodic, vacillating, timeserving, trimming, deceitful, ambidextrous, light, loose, undependable, irresponsible, double-dealing, afloat, shilly-shally, irregular, changeable, evasive, untrustworthy, capricious, vicissitudinous, vicissitudinary, lubricious, adrift,

wanton, volatile, fluctuating, alternating, sporadic, desultory.

3. Lascivious, lewd, licentious, incestuous, concupiscent, impure, ruttish, bawdy, ribald, lubricious, obscene, pornographic, Cyprian, light, fast, loose, whorish, scarlet, dissolute, dissipated, debauched, adulterous, lurid, smutty, unclean, dirty, coarse, gross, foul, filthy, unchaste, unvirtuous, incontinent, wanton, vile, offensive, fulsome, Fescennine, indecent, immodest, lustful, beastly, bestial, swinish, animalistic, theroid, prurient, lickerish, lecherous, libidinous, carnal, salacious, abandoned, shameless, scurrilous, profligate, of easy virtue, satyric, goatish, erotic, free, of loose character *or* morals, Paphian, sensual, brutish.

LUCID, *adj.* 1. Shining, bright, clear, transparent, radiant, beaming, beamy, gleaming, lambent, glowing, vivid, illuminated, enlightened, illumined, flashing, glistening, sparkling, scintillating, flaming, brilliant, luminous, lustrous, light, effulgent, refulgent, resplendent, twinkling, coruscating, dazzling, luminiferous, blazing, irradiant, luciferous, nitid, sheeny, glossy, sunny, fulgid, limpid, incandescent, burnished, translucent, crystalline, fair, pure, pellucid, diaphanous, luculent, hyaline, vitreous, glassy, orient *(Poetic.).*

2. Clear to the mind, distinct, easily understood, plain, intelligible, rational, obvious, graphic, transparent, manifest, crystal clear, luculent, explicit, indisputable, understandable, perspicuous, self-evident, comprehensible, straightforward, apparent, express, well-marked, unquestionable, vivid, decided, undisguised, downright, decisive, articulate, positive, certain, clear-cut, salient, prominent, pronounced, palpable, visible, unmistakable, unhidden, revealed, disclosed, point-blank, uncloaked, patent, precise, direct, to the point, specific, sharply outlined, striking, open, determinate, clearly discernible, overt, bare, naked, concise, sharply defined, unconcealed, pointed, unequivocal, accurate, conspicuous, marked, bald, unambiguous, luminous, transpicuous, translucent, categorical *(Log.).*

3. Possessing clear perception *or* understanding, characterized by a normal state of the faculties, sane, responsible, reasonable, sound in mind, sober, stable, rational, serene, compos mentis *(Law),* clear-minded, clear-headed, clear-thinking, untroubled, discerning, clear-sighted, clear-eyed, cognitive, calm, unperturbed, collected, unruffled, composed, unshaken, unexcited, unnervous, levelheaded, steady, tranquil, self-possessed, poised, placid, comprehending, fully conscious, rightminded, perspicacious, shrewd, acute, penetrating, sagacious, luminous, of sound judgment, strongminded, knowing, sage, astute, sharp, sensible, self-controlled, prudent, undeceived, undisturbed, discriminating, argute, cool-headed, clear-witted, perceptive.

LUCK, *n.* 1. That which happens in the course of events *(as if by chance),* fortune, hap, fate, casualty, fortuity, random, adventure, gamble, potluck, happening, destiny, kismet, accident, chance, hazard, haphazard, venture, Fortuna *(Rom. Myth.),* Tyche *(Gk. Myth.),* Lady Luck, draw, lot, wheel of fortune.

2. Good fortune, success, advantage, windfall, piece of luck, prosperity, favorable issue *or* outcome, fluke, Midas touch, well-being, run of luck, streak of luck *(coll.),* profit, gain, triumph, victory, master stroke, trump card, smiles of fortune, fair wind and no favor, godsend, velvet *(sl.),* wel-

fare, stroke of luck, break (*sl.*), walkover (*coll.*), pushover (*coll.*).

3. Object on which good fortune is supposed to depend, lucky piece, charm, amulet, talisman, phylactery, philter, specific, periapt, fetish, voodoo, rabbit's foot.

LUCKILY, *adv.* Fortunately, by good luck *or* fortune, opportunely, happily, swimmingly, beyond all expectation *or* hope, auspiciously, advantageously, to advantage, by mere chance, by one's guardian angel, rosily, successfully, as good luck would have it, in the nick of time, beyond one's fondest dreams, appropriately, aptly, fitly, pertinently, suitably.

LUCKLESS, *adj.* Unfortunate, unsuccessful, ill-fated, unhappy, cursed, hapless, unprosperous, infelicitous, ill-starred, unlucky, unpropitious, calamitous, poor, wretched, jinxed, Jonahed, disastrous, miserable, fortuneless, unblest, out of luck, woebegone, bereft, hopeless, evil-starred, under a cloud, clouded, down on one's luck (*coll.*), thwarted, born with a wooden ladle in one's mouth, scotched, foiled, crossed, victimized, stultified, balked, woeful, forlorn, hoodooed (*coll.*), in ill luck, born under an evil star, dashed (*coll.*).

LUCKY, *adj.* 1. Having *or* attended with good luck, fortunate, blessed, favored, flourishing, gaining, in luck, in a good way (*sl.*), successful, happy, thriving, victorious, palmy, rewarded, benefiting, overcoming, wealthy, healthy, born under a lucky star, born with a silver spoon in one's mouth, winning, triumphant.

2. Happening fortunately, producing *or* resulting in good, propitious, fortunate, felicitous, opportune, happy, providential, timely, memorable, expedient, rosy, charmed, seemly, halcyon, palmy, beneficial, of good omen, red-letter, favorable, enchanted, promising, well-timed, conquering, prosperous, auspicious.

LUCRATIVE, *adj.* Profitable, productive, valuable, fruitful, gainful, paying, moneymaking, advantageous, fertile, rich, fat, remunerative, beneficial.

LUCRE, *n.* Gain *or* money (*as the object of sordid desire*), profit, mammon, riches, spoils, filthy lucre (*coll.*), plunder, root of all evil, almighty dollar, booty, loot, take, winnings, greed, pelf (*usually contempt.*), steal (*coll.*), pillage, grab, haul (*coll.*), swag (*sl.*), muck, wealth.

LUCUBRATE, *v.* 1. Study, work *or* write laboriously (*esp. at night*), slave, toil, moil, fag, burn the midnight oil, hit the books (*sl.*), labor, drudge, hammer away, grind (*coll.*), plod, cram (*coll.*), beat *or* cudgel the brains, apply oneself, do some tall head work (*coll.*), peg away (along, on), work one's head to the bone (*joc.*), sweat (*coll.*), exert oneself strenuously, plug (*coll.*).

2. Write learnedly, dissertate, discourse, expound, exposit, dissert, review, criticize, critique, treat a subject, report one's findings.

LUCUBRATION, *n.* 1. Laborious work *or* study (*esp. at night*), deep thought, close application, labor, toil, headwork, brain work, grind (*coll.*).

2. Learned *or* carefully written production, discourse, treatise, writing, work, thesis, dissertation, inditement, monograph.

3. (*Often pl.*) Literary effort, composition, piece, essay, product of one's pen, work, opus, production, jottings, brain child, screed, article, draft, manuscript, paper, letters, book, writing, theme, potboiler.

LUCULENT, *adj.* 1. Clear (*as explanations*), lucid,

luminous, explicit, plain, distinct, easily understood, intelligible, rational, obvious, graphic, transparent, manifest, crystal clear, indisputable, understandable, perspicuous, self-evident, comprehensible, straightforward, apparent, express, well-marked, unquestionable, vivid, decided, undisguised, downright, decisive, articulate, positive, certain, clear-cut, salient, prominent, pronounced, palpable, visible, unmistakable, unhidden, revealed, disclosed, unconcealed, uncloaked, patent, precise, direct, to the point, specific, sharply outlined, striking, open, determinate, clearly discernible, overt, bare, naked, concise, sharply defined, point-blank, pointed, unequivocal, accurate, conspicuous, marked, bald, unambiguous, transpicuous, translucent, categorical (*Log.*).

2. Convincing, conclusive, ultimate, final, indisputable, irrefutable, unanswerable, decisive, undeniable, indubitable, probative, irresistible, demonstrable, proven, evidential, apodictic, unimpeachable, unappealable, determinative, unquestionable, irrefragable, incontrovertible, evident, manifest.

LUDICROUS, *adj.* Such as to cause laughter *or* derision, laughable, ridiculous, absurd, amusing, comic, odd, droll, funny, comical, strange, farcical, diverting, senseless, foolish, egregious, gross, flagrant, asinine, imbecile, crazy, antic, doggerel, slapstick, nonsensical, quizzical, inane, fatuous, fantastic, irrational, eccentric, burlesque, bizarre, mirthful, high-flown, risible, waggish, childish, screaming, grotesque, quaint, bombastic, rich, sophistical, outlandish, queer, lamentable, amphigoric, incongruous, extravagant, preposterous, monstrous, screwy (*sl.*), poppycockish (*coll.*), outré (*Fr.*), stultiloquent.

LUG, *n.* Projecting piece for holding *or* support, loop, ear, tab, tag, handle, pull, grasp, hold, trigger, crank, arm, flap, rounce (*Print.*).

LUG, *v.* Carry with force *or* effort, pull, tug, tow, bear, heave, draw, drag, haul, handle with difficulty, tote, convey, wrench, snake, yank (*coll.*), trawl, portage, transport.

LUGUBRIOUS, *adj.* Mournful, doleful, dismal, sad, woeful, saturnine, depressed, dark, dejected, downcast, weary, dreary, rueful, melancholy, piteous, morose, woebegone, frowning, plaintive, grieving, low-spirited, heavy-hearted, dispirited, despondent, tearful, cheerless, wretched, disconsolate, forlorn, elegiac, wailing, disheartened, chapfallen, crestfallen, glum, pensive, dirgelike, wearisome, drear, sorrowful, gloomy, complaining, unhappy, depressing, funereal, somber, glowering, flat, dull, lamenting, discouraged, joyless, miserable, desolate.

LUKEWARM, *adj.* 1. Tepid, moderately warm, mild, cool, blood-warm, chill, chilly, of skin temperature.

2. Having *or* showing little ardor *or* zeal, indifferent, cold, cool, languid, apathetic, half-hearted, listless, unconcerned, torpid, dead, irresolute, spiritless, unaffected, insipid, vapid, lifeless, uninspired, uninspiring, lacking in fervor, without savor, unconvincing, tame, weak, mediocre, bloodless, drab, uncompelling, lackluster, unprepossessing, pallid, colorless, etiolated, unimpassioned, passive, undemonstrative, unresponsive, phlegmatic, sluggish, supercilious, unkindled, chill, inaccessible, nonchalant, unimpressionable, listless, insensible, impassive, adamantine, numb, unexcited, calculous, comatose, supine, inert, unsolicitous, unfeeling, soulless,

lethargic, insentient, unmoved, unstirred, untouched, incurious, impervious, uncaring, uninterested, cold-blooded, antipathetic, insouciant, hardened, indurated, pococurante.

LULL, *n.* 1. Lulled condition, temporary stillness, temporary quiet, cessation, respite, hush, stay, lapse, break, truce, repose, recess, remission, interlude, intermittence, caesura, inactivity, idleness, quiescence, placidity, stupor, peace, short rest, intermission, fall of the wind, pause, halt, suspension, breather, breathing time *or* spell, abatement, time out *(coll.)*, interruption, letup *(coll.)*, abeyance, calm, calmness, interval, drop, brief silence, tranquillity, subsidence.

2. Soothing sound, murmur, soft *or* muffled sound, drone, thrumb, drowsy hum, sigh, whisper, patter *(as of raindrops)*, gurgle, rustle, purr, whir, soporific, bombilation, susurration.

LULL, *v.* 1. Put to sleep *or* rest by soothing means, quiet, soothe, calm, hush, pacify, compose, assuage, subdue, sober, cool, stay, deaden, settle, cause to relax, pour oil on the waves *or* troubled waters, remove one's fears *or* anxieties, induce forgetfulness, mitigate, mollify, appease, rock, tranquilize, still, ease one's mind, quell, stupefy.

2. Become lulled, quieted *or* stilled, subside, let up, slacken, weaken, diminish, become calm, relax, lessen, decline, bate, abate, ebb, decrease, cease, recede, slake, languish, dwindle, moderate, temper, fall off *or* away, allay, wane.

LULLABY, *n.* Cradlesong, soft music, siren strains, berceuse *(Mus.)*.

LUMBER, *n.* 1. Miscellaneous useless articles, trash, truck, junk *(sl.)*, rubbish, refuse, waste, motley collection, tumble, mess, shreds, odds and ends, hodgepodge, hash, muddle, mishmash, rummage, tangle, minglement, mix-up, fragments, huddle, topsy-turvy, ollapodrida, gallimaufry, disorderly heap *or* assemblage, orts, slag, sweepings, debris, dross, oddments, jumble, accumulation, litter.

2. Timber *(sawed or split)*, boards, planks, log, wood, lath, beam, post, hardwood, softwood, siding, wallboard, clapboard.

LUMBER, *v.* 1. Cut timber, prepare logs for market, log, fell trees, operate a sawmill.

2. Heap together in disorder, clutter, litter, huddle, disarrange, muddle, tumble, jumble, confuse, strew, discompose, derange, disorganize, muss up *(coll.)*, shuffle, turn topsy-turvy, dishevel, agitate, upset, pile at random, batch, bunch, lump, cram, dump, shove, huddle, hustle *(coll.)*, crowd confusedly, herd, toss.

3. Fill with miscellaneous useless articles, obstruct, encumber, crowd, choke, overload, overburden, engulf, satiate, saturate, glut, overlade, fill to overflowing, smother, inundate, envelop, constrict, flood, gag, deluge, surcharge, block, bar, blockade, congest, barricade, make impassable.

4. Move heavily *or* clumsily *(esp. from great or ponderous bulk)*, plod, trudge, stamp, drag, stump, lunge, lump, barge, jog, peg, drag one's freight *(sl.)*, clump, shamble, stumble, fumble, shuffle, hobble, waddle, flounder.

5. Make a rumbling noise, roll, rumble, boom, bombilate, thunder, peal, roar, resonate, drum, thrumb, beat, pound, pulsate, thump, throb, resound, reverberate, bombinate, bellow, shake the rafters, vibrate.

LUMBERMAN, *n.* One who works at lumbering, lumberjack, one who deals in lumber, forester, woodsman, logger, wood chopper, wood cutter, silviculturist, arboriculturist.

LUMINARY, *n.* 1. Celestial body, body *or* thing that gives light, moon, sun, star, source of light, illuminator, illuminant, beacon, lamp, orb, sphere, searchlight, flood lamp, flashlight, fire, match, flame, arc light, spotlight, torch, taper, lantern, glim *(sl.)*, candle, light.

2. Person who enlightens mankind *or* makes some subject clear, wise man, sapient, mahatma, philosopher, authority, thinker, expositor, annotator, exegete, definer, commentator, expounder, explainer, interpreter, savant, pundit, oracle, sage, teacher, guide, exponent, diviner, seer, prophet, adviser, spokesman, preceptor.

LUMINESCE, *v.* Exhibit luminescence, fluoresce, phosphoresce, shine, shimmer, twinkle, blink, glisten, radiate, scintillate, flicker, glimmer, glint, beam, gleam, glow.

LUMINESCENCE, *n.* Emission of light *(at temperatures below that of incandescence)*, phosphorescence, fluorescence, photoluminescence *(Physics)*, noctilucence *(Biol.)*, bioluminescence *(Biol.)*, nebula, corona, aureole, halo, nimbus, aurora, northern lights, aurora borealis, southern lights, aurora australis, will-o'-the-wisp, ignis fatuus, friar's lantern, corposant, jack-o'-lantern, St. Elmo's fire, ectoplasm *(Spiritualism)*, Fata Morgana.

LUMINESCENT, *adj.* Characterized by *or* pertaining to luminescence, aglow, lambent, fulgid, luminous, glowing, shimmering, luciform, gleaming, radiant, glistening, twinkling, glimmering, flickering, glinting, rutilous, rutilant, phosphorescent, fluorescent, photoluminescent *(Physics)*, bioluminescent *(Biol.)*, noctilucent *(Biol.)*, neon *(Physics)*.

LUMINOSITY, *n.* Quality of being luminous, illumination, effulgence, irradiation, brilliance, shine, nitency, refulgence, glow, glare, radiance, light, sparkle, brightness, splendor, luminousness, lucency, lucidity, glory, luster, fire, incandescence, luminescence, dazzle, lightness, fulgor, radiation, emanation, gleam, flood of light, stream of light.

LUMINOUS, *adj.* 1. Radiating *or* reflecting light, lighted up, shining, illuminated, incandescent, glowing, resplendent, effulgent, aglow, sunny, ablaze, luminiferous, phosphorescent, relucent, sparkling, rutilous, rutilant, fulgid, clear, brilliant, lucid, orient *(Poetic)*, radiant, refulgent, shiny, lambent, lit, irradiated, fulgent, lucent, alight, luminescent, lighted, blazing, light, bright, radiative, nitidous.

2. Brilliant intellectually, highly intelligent, learned, percipient, quick, bright, gifted, profound, deep, sage, knowing, sapient, understanding, apprehending, of keen penetration, cerebral, cognitive, erudite, widely read, well-read, educated, scholarly, wise, sagacious, shrewd, argute, acute, subtle, judicious, long-headed, hard-headed, clear-headed, nimble-witted, sharp-witted, keen-witted, perspicacious, percipient, perceptive, clever, sound, philosophical, penetrating, discerning.

3. Clear, readily intelligible, lucid, perspicuous, vivid, plain, luculent, self-evident, comprehensible, graphic, straightforward, understandable, apparent, express, well-marked, unquestionable, manifest, decided, undisguised, articulate, clear-cut, salient, palpable, patent, disclosed, revealed, distinct, unmistakable, unhidden, unveiled, uncloaked.

LUMP, *n.* Shapeless mass *or* piece, chunk, agglomeration, swelling, protuberance, knob, hunch, concentration, gobbet, gob, bump, bulk, pile, node, dab, nugget, mass, portion, pat, clod, excrescence, swad, wad, growth, protrusion, aggregation, concretion, knot, lot, heap, nodulosity, amassment, congestion, hump, block, loaf, nodule, bulb, gnarl, prominence, knurl, tumor, tumescence, bulge, convexity, projection, rising, wen, tubercle, tuberosity, condyle *(Anat.)*, welt *(coll.)*, process *(Biol.)*, apophysis *(Anat., Biol.)*, brick, heap, hunk *(coll.)*, clump, accumulation, cake.

LUMP, *v.* 1. Unite into an aggregation *or* mass, throw together, collect, join, combine, amass, make into a lump *or* lumps, assemble, gather, aggregate, accumulate, heap, compile, congregate, get in, pile, batch together, mass, bunch, agglomerate, group, store, deposit, reposit, cache, stow away, stash *(sl.)*, pool, blend, mix, commix, scramble, fuse, compound, merge.

2. Deal with in the lump *or* mass, take in the gross, treat as one, consider to be a unit, combine, take jointly, total, conjoin, regard collectively, associate, pool, consolidate, coördinate.

3. Raise into *or* cover with lumps, form *or* raise a lump *or* lumps, swell, bulge, buckle, heave, dilate, expand, clot, clobber, form welts, precipitate, thicken unevenly, cake, crystallize, hump, granulate, become rough *or* uneven, deposit, curd, curdle, coagulate, bouge, bilge.

LUMPISH, *adj.* 1. Like a lump, heavy, bulky, lumpy, hulky, stodgy, slow, gross, dull, languid, stolid, ponderous, weighty, cumbrous, leaden, massive, cumbersome, bovine, exanimate, lifeless, listless, dense, weary, big, large, elephantine, unwieldy, sluggish, lazy, dronish, indolent, solid, onerous, inert, supine, inactive, torpescent, torporific, sottish, lethargic, static, torpid, passive, apathetic, lymphatic, phlegmatic, otiose, hebetudinous, lumbering, hefty *(coll.)*, burdensome, dull, languid, obese, ponderable.

2. Stupid, clumsy, loutish, doltish, gross, heavy, ignorant, obtuse, dullard, sluggish, blunt, dull, incumbent, slow, oafish, bovine, bungling, lubberly, uncivil, churlish, barbaric, boorish, cloddish, dumb *(coll.)*, thick *(coll.)*, dull-headed, dull-pated, crass, witless, hebetudinous, undiscerning, uncomprehending, clodpated, thick-headed, addleheaded, addlepated, dull-witted, numskull *(coll.)*, dronish, dense, awkward, rough, gawky, uncouth, ungainly, heavy-handed, insulse, stolid, blundering, unrefined, inept, maladroit, lacking dexterity, inelegant, unpolished, gauche, rustic, vulgar, clownish.

LUMPY, *adj.* 1. Full of lumps, covered with lumps, knotty, lumpish, cloddy, clotted, clabbered, caked, welted, thick, caseous, bulging, raised in places, granulated, grumose *(Bot.)*, grumous *(Bot.)*, coagulated, flaky, cloggy, knobby, protuberant, uneven, curdled, crystalline.

2. Like a lump, clumsy, heavy *(see LUMPISH, above)*.

LUNACY, *n.* 1. Insanity, madness, mental aberration, derangement, insaneness, diseased *or* unsound mind, psychopathic condition, paranoia, psychosis, schizophrenia, mental dissociation, delusion, frenzy, hallucination, distraction, possession, delirium, crack, mania, craziness, dementia *(Pathol., Psychiatry)*, alienation *(Psychiatry)*, dementia praecox *(Pathol., Psychiatry)*, disordered mind *or* reason, fugue *(Med.)*.

2. Extreme foolishness, folly, foolhardiness, absurdity, irrationality, imprudence, giddiness, morology, sottage, imbecility, asininity, sophistry, futility, idiocy, stupidity, inanity, fatuity, fallacy, sciamachy, illogicality, ineptitude, unreasonableness, antilogy, speciousness, contradiction in terms *or* ideas, nonsense, infatuation, rashness, indiscretion, moonshine, silliness, want of good sense, simpletonianism, ninnyism, stuff, fudge, trash, stuff and nonsense, balderdash, meaninglessness, senselessness, twaddle, farce, hogwash, trumpery, rubbish, poppycock *(coll.)*, tommyrot *(sl.)*, bosh *(coll.)*, truck *(coll.)*, hokum *(sl.)*.

LUNATE, *adj.* Crescent-shaped, moon-shaped, lunar, crescent-like, crescentiform, semicircular, horned, horny, meniscoid, crescentic, semilunar, sigmoid, Cynthian, lunular, moon-like, bicorn, horn-like, lunulate *(Bot., Zool.)*, lunated, convexoconcave.

LUNATIC, LUNATICAL, *adj.* Insane, mad, crazy, of unsound mind, unhinged, unbalanced, daft, demented, deranged, mentally ill, psychotic, psychopathic, raving, ranting, non compos mentis *(Law)*, indicating lunacy, characteristic of a lunatic, irrational, moon-struck, wandering, schizophrenic, touched in the head, off one's head *(coll.)*, out of one's mind (head, senses, wits), not all there *(coll.)*, far-gone, rabid, frenzied, off, touched, loco *(sl.)*, foolish, amuck, wild, beside oneself, foaming *or* frothing at the mouth, cracked *(coll.)*, queer *(coll.)*, crack-brained, off one's base *or* rocker *(coll.)*, brainsick, possessed, bereft of reason, reasonless, senseless, crazed, nutty *(sl.)*, loony *(sl.)*, screwy *(sl.)*, not right in one's head, not in one's right mind, maniacal, unsettled, balmy *(sl.)*, bughouse *(sl.)*, cuckoo *(sl.)*, batty *(sl.)*.

LUNATIC, *n.* Madman, insane person, crazy person, deranged person, crackbrain, dement, demoniac, energumen, phrenetic, non compos, psychopath, schizophrenic, bedlamite, manic-depressive, paranoiac, loon, nut *(sl.)*, screwball *(sl.)*, crackpot *(sl.)*, maniac.

LUNCH, *n.* Light meal between breakfast and dinner, luncheon, tiffin, bite, collation, morsel, slight repast, refection, refreshment, snack, brunch *(coll.)*, déjeuner.

LUNGE, *n.* Sudden forward movement, thrust, plunge, pass, jab, swing, cut, coup, home thrust, charge, carte *(Fencing)*, tierce *(Fencing)*, assault, lightning attack, rush, jump, tilt, stab.

LUNGE, *v.* Thrust, cause to move with a lunge, barge, jab, attack, pitch, lay at, charge, set *or* fall on *or* upon, pounce, cut and thrust, run a tilt, ride full tilt, stab, dash, dive, go headfirst, make a pass, let drive, punch, strike at, plunge, hit at, poke.

LUPINE, *adj.* Pertaining to *or* resembling the wolf, wolfish, savage, ravenous, allied to the wolf, rapacious, predatory, plundering, ferocious, raptorial, predacious, cruel, ravening, devouring, preying.

LURCH, *n.* 1. Sudden leaning *or* rolling to one side, sudden swaying *or* staggering movement, swing, sway, tilt, swag, rock, shift, pitch, cant, sag, inclination, slope, shuffle, list, jolt *(sideward)*, roll, swerve, slant, stagger.

2. Position of one discomfited *or* in a helpless plight, misfortune, predicament, state, reverse, hole, exigency, backset, setback, pass, pickle *(coll.)*, comedown, fix, scrape, strait, trouble, desertion, bereavement, kettle of fish, embarrassment, pinch, impasse, nonplus, crisis, perplexity, jam *(coll.)*.

LURCH, *v.* Make a lurch, move with lurches, roll suddenly, stagger, swag, topple, pitch, incline, cant, careen, stumble, totter, hitch, sag, tilt, sway, swing, reel, tumble, rock, roll, rear, toss, sprawl, welter, wallow, flounder, slant, keel, list, slope, lunge, plunge.

LURE, *n.* Anything that attracts, entices *or* allures, enticement, bait, decoy, temptation, pitfall, siren song, baited hook, attraction, allurement, trap, bribe, snare, gin, hook, magnet, loadstone, trepan, springe, forbidden fruit, inducement, cajolery, toils, meshes, net, pit, deadfall, trapfall, stratagem, charm, come-on *(sl.),* stool pigeon, red herring, witchery, bewitchment, ambush, attractor, enchantment, soap *(sl.),* oil *(sl.),* draw *(coll.),* pull *(Trade sl.),* soft *or* honeyed words, sop, source of temptation, voice of the tempter, blandishment, drawing card.

LURE, *v.* Draw as by a lure, entice, allure, decoy, captivate, enrapture, lead on, carry away, enravish, draw on, invite, inveigle, seduce, tempt, attract, bewitch, charm, coax, cajole, fascinate, deceive, persuade, induce, delude, wheedle, tantalize, hold out temptation *or* allurement, spread the toils, troll, beguile, fish, trick, trip, titillate, entangle, enmesh, provoke desire, make one's mouth water, excite desire, magnetize, entrap, trap, snare, beckon, vamp *(sl.),* whet the appetite, ensnare, bait.

LURID, *adj.* 1. Lighted up *or* shining with an unnatural *or* wild *(esp. red or fiery)* glare, glowing, inflamed, rubicund, bloody, sanguine, scarlet, flaming, flamelike, carmine, brazen, brick-colored, blood-red, ruddy, flushed, coppery, gory.

2. Glaringly vivid *or* sensational, harshly *or* ominously vivid, grimly terrible, terrible in fiery intensity, fierce, fulsome, wild, hot, unrestrained, passionate, nervous, graphic, overwhelming, vigorous, powerful, salacious, trenchant, biting, forcible, impressive, strong, prurient, voluptuous, bestial, foul, smutty, vulgar, coarse, broad, filthy, dirty, pornographic, mordant, gross, ribald, sultry, intemperate, low, indelicate, indecorous, bawdy, lewd, obscene, vile, lustful, immoral, galvanic, electric, stimulating, provocative, nippy, racy, poignant, pungent, overmastering, overpowering, melodramatic, snappy *(coll.),* with a kick *(sl.),* alluring, tantalizing, sensual, scurrilous, spicy, piquant, yellow, zippy *(coll.),* risqué.

3. Wan, pale, ghastly in hue, sallow, dun, crepuscular, dull, dismal, gloomy, murky, yellowish, dingy, dusky, misty, gray, somber, sullen, funereal, caliginous, leaden, under a pall, umbrageous, hueless, colorless, stygian, etiolated, washed-out, ghostly, corpse-like, weak, faint, pallid, achromatic, shadowy, looming, glowering, lowering, drab, cold, glassy, sickly, haggard, cadaverous, lackluster, anemic, tallow-like, overcast.

LURK, *v.* Remain in *or* about a place secretly *or* furtively, lie hid, lie concealed, lie in wait, exist unperceived *or* unsuspected, be latent, go furtively, slink, skulk, keep out of the way, keep out of sight, darkle, steal, ambush, ambuscade, keep snug *or* close, seclude oneself, prowl, go into eclipse, eclipse, lie in ambush, couch, lie perdu, lie low *(coll.),* escape notice (observation, detection, recognition), hide, sneak, keep in the background, smolder, gumshoe *(sl.).*

LUSCIOUS, *adj.* 1. Highly pleasing to the taste *or* smell, sweet to the senses *or* the mind, dainty, ambrosial, pleasing, delightful, grateful, savory, delicious, agreeable, delectable, exquisite, melli-

fluous, dulcet, pleasant, mellifluent, appetizing, satisfying, tasty *(coll.),* juicy, tangy, heady, toothsome, succulent, to one's taste, amiable, tempting, balmy, spicy, mouth-watering, piquant, delicate, refreshing, odorous, cordial, genial, titillative, essenced, perfumed, fragrant, scented, nectareous, aromatic, saporous, sapid, flavorsome, scrumptious *(sl.),* sensuous, creamy, rich, palatable, sweet, good, nice, fit for a king, redolent.

2. Excessively sweet, cloying, sugary, candied, sickening, rich, oversweet, saccharine, honeyed, nectareous.

LUSH, *adj.* 1. Juicy and tender, succulent, luxuriant, fresh, moist, sappy, watery, soft, pulpy, mellow, pliant, supple, spongy, pithy, fleshy, full of juice, delicate.

2. Characterized by luxuriant vegetation, tropical, jungly, jungled, wild, overgrown, flourishing, rank, dense, overrun, excessive, prolific.

LUST, *n.* Desire, bestiality, bodily appetite, salaciousness, passion, pruriency, lewdness, impurity, concupiscence, sexuality, grossness, satyrism, lasciviousness, libidinousness, venery, ruttishness, lechery, sensuality, bawdiness, lubricity, incontinence, brutishness, fleshly desire, impurity.

LUSTER, *n.* Brightness, gleam, radiance, refulgence, glitter, irradiance, radiation, illumination, incandescence, brilliance, luminosity, dazzle, burnish, effulgence, opalescence, glare, glow, gloss, sheen, shine, gleam, glimmer, glint, nitency, lucidity, resplendence, blare, lambency, luminousness.

LUSTERLESS, *adj.* Dull, flat, dingy, lackluster, pale, wan, muddy, smoky, sooty, pallid, dun, besmirched, faded, dim, gray, weak, lifeless, lurid, somber, dark, colorless, drab, murky, sallow, gloomy, overcast, leaden, umbrageous, dismal, hueless, dreary.

LUSTFUL, *adj.* Impure, bawdy, lascivious, ruttish, concupiscent, ribald, Cyprian, obscene, lubricious, debauched, gross, coarse, dirty, unclean, smutty, lurid, unchaste, unvirtuous, incontinent, wanton, vile, beastly, bestial, swinish, theroid, animalistic, lickerish, lecherous, libidinous, licentious, fleshly, carnal, salacious, shameless, scurrilous, profligate, satyric, goatish, Paphian, sensual, brutish.

LUSTROUS, *adj.* Flaming, bright, polished, shiny, gaudy, irradiant, radiant, beamy, glittering, brilliant, garish, effulgent, glistening, twinkling, scintillating, lambent, luminous, beaming, shining, gleaming, resplendent, shimmering, coruscating, sparkling, flashing, refulgent, illuminated, incandescent, spangled, nitid, glossy, silvery, argent, burnished, sheeny, fulgid, fulgurant, fulgent, shiny, sunny, orient, rutilant.

LUSTY, *adj.* 1. (See LUSTFUL above)

2. Strong, robust, stout, enduring, tough, rugged, firm, youthful, vigorous, hale, sound, hearty, solid, substantial, buxom, physically fit, able-bodied, virile, muscular, hefty, flourishing, stalwart, flush, herculean, Atlantean, husky *(coll.),* puissant, beefy, resilient, strapping, staminal, blooming, stanch, in fine fettle, in good condition, sinewy, hardy, brawny, powerful, mighty, seasoned, wiry, able, healthy, rigorous, inured to fatigue.

LUXURIANT, *adj.* 1. Exuberant in growth, overgrown, rank, abundant, jungly, jungled, dense, lush, tropical, flourishing, wild, overrun, teeming, rich, copious.

2. Florid, garish, vivid, extravagant, profuse, adorned, flowery, ornamented, gaudy, fancy,

showy, flashy, elegant, splendrous, magnificent, ornate.

LUXURIATE, *v.* 1. Grow exuberantly, grow rank, grow wild, grow lush, flourish, overgrow, overrun.

2. Live in luxury, wallow, bask, live in comfort, live extravagantly, be in clover *(coll.),* live in comfort, take it easy *(coll.),* live off the fat of the land, have a good time, live lavishly.

3. Overindulge, overdo, go too far, carry to excess, be intemperate.

LUXURIOUS, *adj.* 1. Characterized by luxury, ministering *or* conducing to luxury, rich, costly, comfortable, delicious, dainty, nice, luscious, refined, enjoyable, grand, voluptuous, pleasurable, silken, elegant, agreeable, amiable, pleasure-giving, titillative, gratifying, carnal, sensual, easeful, delectable, hedonic, delicate, Lydian, sumptuous, epicurean, excessive, inordinate, immoderate, easy, fleshly.

2. Given *or* inclined to luxury, voluptuous, sensual, self-indulgent, intemperate, overindulged, gluttonous, insatiable, gormandizing, pampered, indulged, crapulous, inabstinent, hedonistic, immoderate, epicurean, effeminate, sybaritic, silk-stocking.

LUXURY, *n.* 1. Free indulgence in things which gratify the appetite *or* tastes, mode of living characterized by material abundance, epicureanism, voluptuousness, sensuality, high living *(sl.),* profuseness, rioting, repletion, ease, well-being, sufficiency, bed of ease, velvet, bed of roses *or* down, gluttony, unrestraint, immoderation, purple and fine linen, prodigality, extravagance, elegance, wealth, richness, comfort, effeminacy, animalism, epicurism, pleasure, enjoyment, delight, clover, excessiveness, nimiety, exorbitance, intemperance, intemperateness, self-indulgence, sensualism, crapulence, inabstinence, inordinacy, luxuriousness, sybaritism.

2. Anything which pleases the senses *(and is costly or difficult to obtain),* expensive rarity, treat, delicacy, nonessential, bauble, accessory, embroidery, frill, choice bit, trinket, trifle, ornament, adornment, trappings *(pl.),* finery *(pl.),* dainty.

LYCEUM, *n.* 1. Association for discussion and popular instruction, academy, assembly, seminar, institute, chautauqua.

2. Building devoted to instruction by lectures, hall, theater, school, auditorium, assembly room, exchange, bourse, chamber, amphitheater, gallery, lecture room *or* hall, phrontistery *(often disparaging).*

LYDIAN, *adj.* *(Of music)* Softly sweet, voluptuous, sensuous, emotive, soothing, titillative, sensual, dulcet, easing, emotional, assuaging, anodyne, comforting, luxurious, exciting desire, mitigative, mollifying, mellifluous, mellifluent, enravishing, alluring, enchanting, seductive, entrancing, effeminate.

LYING, *adj.* 1. That lies, false, untruthful, mendacious, deceptive, truthless, unveracious, dissembling, deceitful, dishonest, insincere, evasive, hypocritical, equivocating, untrue, sophistical, hollow, fabricating, surreptitious, casuistic, uncandid, crooked, disingenuous, perfidious, treacherous, faithless, fraudulent, tartufian, canting, bland, two-faced, Janus-faced, mealy-mouthed, erroneous, Jesuitic, unconscioned, unconscionable, pharisaical.

2. Recumbent, couchant, supine, reclining, crouching, jacent, prone, prostrate, resting, horizontal, flat, procumbent, decumbent, accumbent, stretched out, resupine, reposing.

LYING, *n.* The telling of lies, falsehood, mendacity, invention, fiction, untruthfulness, prevarication, deceit, guile, fraud, subtlety, fibbery, falsity, falseness, storytelling *(coll.),* cunning, artfulness, false coloring *or* construction, deception, flattery, improbity, misstatement, misconstruction, dishonesty, duplicity, exaggeration, pseudology, falsification, calumny, fabling, equivocation, subreption, forgery, perjury, casuistry, bad faith, Jesuitism, false swearing, counterfeiting, misrepresentation, perfidy, deceitfulness, dissimulation, dissembling, evasion, lip homage, Judas kiss, double-dealing, hypocrisy, mythomania *(Psychiatry).*

LYMPHATIC, *adj.* 1. Pertaining to (containing *or* conveying) lymph, watery, fluid, hydrous, lymphoid, ichorous *(Pathol.),* chylous *(Physiol.),* weak, aqueous, dilute, serous, liquid, rheumy.

2. Of a temperament characterized by sluggishness of action and thought, phlegmatic, dronish, drowsy, lethargic, languid, listless, stupid, sluggish, faint, absent, torpid, indolent, zestless, mopish, slack, insipid, dreamy, apathetic, indifferent, supine, stupefied, lifeless, obtuse, soporific, dormant, fainéant, dull, inanimate, spiritless, heavy, comatose, inactive, leaden, slumbrous, somnolent, sleepy, slothful, weary.

LYNCH, *v.* Put to death (by concerted action) without authority *or* process of law, murder, hang, burn, rack, tar and feather, gibbet, noose, tear limb from limb, garrote, kill by inches, lapidate, torture, martyrize, string up, pelt, stone, break on the wheel, crucify, neck, scrag *(sl.),* beat up *(sl.),* gang up on *(coll.).*

LYNCH LAW, *n.* Administration of summary punishment without authority of law, mob law *or* rule, anarchy, nihilism, violence, club law, coercion, constraint, high-pressure methods, brute force, terrorism, lawlessness, the law in one's own hands.

LYNX-EYED, *adj.* Sharp-sighted, keen-eyed, clear-sighted, gimlet-eyed, alert, wakeful, observing, all eyes, open-eyed, attentive, unsleeping, on the lookout, farsighted, keen-sighted, ferret-eyed, vigilant, Argus-eyed, hawk-eyed, eagle-eyed, on the *qui vive (Fr.),* sleepless, watchful, broad *or* wide awake, critical, far-seeing, discriminating, shrewd, acute, piercing, astute, aware, penetrating, argute, undeceived, discerning, perceptive, percipient, perspicacious.

LYRIC, *adj.* Having the form and musical quality of song, characterized by a songlike outpouring of thoughts and feelings, melic, melodious, moving, feeling, musical, suggestive of song, choral, choric, dulcet, tunable, melodic, poetic, lilting, elegiac, iambic, singing, spontaneous, ardent, lyrical, warm, deep-felt, earnest, expressive, cantabile *(Mus.),* sweet-tongued, flowing, mellifluent, mellifluous, mellisonant, pure, tempered, rhapsodic, concordant, consonant, harmonious, symphonious, symphonic, ariose, silvery, clear, canorous, passionate, impassioned, fervid, in chorus, mellow, tuneful, dithyrambic, sweet-sounding, fervent, impulsive, euphonious.

LYRICISM, *n.* 1. Lyric character in style *(as in poetry),* musicalness, feeling, lilt, melody, rhapsody, expressiveness, mellifluence, consonance, melodiousness, tunefulness, song.

2. Lyric outpouring of feeling, emotionally expressed enthusiasm, fervency, fervor, eagerness, eloquence, expressiveness, warmth, lightness of heart, feeling, zeal, ardor, passion, vehemence.

LYRIST, *n.* Lyric poet, versifier, musician, lyricist, composer, bard, muse, versemaker, imagist, symbolist, minstrel, laureate, sonneteer, idylist, rhapsodist, elegiast, bucolic, rhymer, dithyrambic, vers librist *(Fr.)*.

M

MACABRE, *adj.* Deathlike, grim, gruesome, gaunt, ghastly, horrible, haggard, cadaverous, ghostlike, repellent, frightful, horrid, wan, pallid, pale, shroud-wearing, alarming, fearful, dreadful, fell, horrific, dire, weird, eerie.

MACARONI, *n.* 1. Italian paste, Genoese paste.
2. 18th century English dandy affecting foreign ways, fop, jackanapes, coxcomb, exquisite, beau, man milliner, blade, blood, buck, toff, man about town, spark, silk-stocking, silk-sock Sam, fribble, popinjay, jack-a-dandy, carpet-knight, *petit maître (Fr.)*, dude, fine gentleman, dandiprat, swell, masher, man of dress, man of fashion, vain fellow, sheik *(colloq.)*.
3. Something fanciful, extravaganza, medley, burlesque, farce, rhapsody, galimatias, gibberish, jargon, amphigory, rigmarole, nonsensical parody, farrago, romance, twaddle, mummery.

MACE, *n.* 1. Clublike weapon of war with a spiked metal head, truncheon, cudgel, club, bludgeon, shillelagh, halberd, tomahawk, battleaxe, poleaxe, sprig.
2. Staff borne by certain officials as a symbol of office, scepter, baton, wand, verge, rod, warder, fasces.

MACERATE, *v.* 1. Separate the parts of a substance by steeping in a liquid, break up by action of a solvent, reduce to a soft mass by soaking, soften up, soak, steep, digest, saturate, drench, dissolve, douse, swash, affuse.
2. Cause to grow thin, make lean, emaciate, waste away, wear away.
3. Mortify, do penance, purge, expiate, atone for, make amends, shrive, repent in sackcloth and ashes, flagellate, fast.

MACERATION, *n.* 1. Softening by infusion, soaking, steeping, saturation, reduction to a soft mass by soaking, drenching, dousing, affusion, dilution.
2. Emaciation, wasting away, wearing away.
3. Mortification, penance, fasting, flagellation, sackcloth and ashes, lustration, shrift, white sheet, purgation, asceticism, austerity.

MACHETE, *n.* Heavy Spanish-American knife used as a tool and a weapon, heavy cutlass used by natives of tropical America, cleaver, hatchet, broadsword, cane-cutter, path-clearer.

MACHIAVELLIAN, *adj.* Cunning, artful, sly, subtle, intriguing, designing, crafty, insidious, arch, tricky, wily, shrewd, diplomatic, astute, politic, Jesuitical, subdolous, scheming, crooked, unscrupulous, deceitful, fraudulent, dishonest, untruthful, *Parthis mendacior (Lat.)*, disingenuous, evasive, insincere, double-tongued, two-faced, double-dealing, perfidious, collusive, feline, vulpine, strategic, time-serving, stealthy, foxy, shifty, underhand, canny, knavish, false-hearted, slippery, tortuous, treacherous, blackguard, corrupt.

MACHIAVELLIANISM, *n.* Machiavellism, double-dealing, trickery, duplicity, artifice, cunning, chicane, dissimulation, stratagem, chicanery, insidiousness, guile, guilefulness, shifting, circumvention, craft, deception, roguery, knavery, deceit, quibbling, hocus-pocus, subtlety, foxiness, improbity, perfidiousness, perfidy, treachery, roguery, knavery, jobbery, fishiness, sharp practice, maneuvering, jugglery, duplicity, diplomacy, politics, backstairs, influence, machination, wile, dodge, trickery, ruse, subterfuge, tour de force, imposture, *espièglerie (Fr.)*.

MACHINATE, *v.* Contrive artfully, plot, devise with evil purpose, scheme, plan, intrigue, conspire, cabal, maneuver, finesse, design, concoct, frame, lay a trap for, spread the toils, forelay, bait the hook, inveigle, waylay, decoy, beguile, ensnare, benet.

MACHINATION, *n.* Conspiracy, plot, cabal, complot, intrigue, artifice, trick, contrivance, stratagem, design, scheme, crafty plan, finesse, ruse, dodge, project, maneuver, device, artful dodge, frame-up, wile.

MACHINATOR, *n.* Conspirator, schemer, plotter, intriguer, strategist, *intrigant (Fr.)*, trickster, sly boots, reynard, fox, Catiline, Guy Fawkes.

MACHINE, *n.* 1. Engine, mechanism, apparatus used in the performance of some kind of work, mechanical contrivance, instrument of force, tool, device, appliance, implement, lathe, gin, loom, die, lever, wheel and axle, screw, pulley, wedge, inclined plane, treadle, pedal, wheelwork, clockwork, crank, cam, winch, flywheel, capstan, cogwheel, gear, derrick, crane, belt, propeller, screw, worm.
2. Person acting like a mechanical apparatus, mechanical man, robot, automaton, drudge.
3. Body of persons controlling the activities of an organization, gang, ring, organization, push, junto, camarilla, cabal, clique, inner circle, coterie, set, combine, cartel, pool, trust, faction.
4. Vehicle, car, automobile, auto, motorcar, conveyance, sedan, limousine, touring car, roadster, speedster, coupé, runabout, convertible, hardtop, station wagon, brougham, victoria, landaulet, cabriolet, hot rod.

MACHINERY, *n.* 1. Mechanical apparatus, enginery, industrial equipment, *matériel (Fr.)*, production facilities, factory equipment, material supplies, appliances, contrivances, tackle, tools, gear, wherewithal, mechanism.
2. System of agencies by which action is maintained, organization, system, setup, wheels within wheels, clockwork, wheelwork.

MACHINIST, *n.* Skilled operator of machine tools, mechanic, mechanist, mechanician, engineer, one who makes and repairs machines, operative.

MACROCOSM, *n.* The great world, universe, megacosm, wide world, cosmos, terraqueous globe, earth, sphere, nature, creation, heavenly bodies, nebulae, stars, milky way, galaxy, firmament, starry heaven, empyrean, welkin, sky, heavens, canopy of heaven, vault of heaven, galactic circle, celestial spaces, *via lactea (Lat.)*.

MACULA, *n.* Spot, speck, freckle, blur, patch, mole, blotch, blain, smudge, blot, stain, slur, birthmark, maculation, bruise, wen, scar, pustule, pimple, excrescence, blemish, flaw, defect, injury, eyesore.

MACULATE, *v.* 1. Mark with a spot, speckle, stain, blotch, spot, blur, blemish, disfigure, splash, smudge, smear, daub, blot, besmear, spatter, draggle, drabble, begrime, bemire, beslime, befoul.

2. Sully, pollute, contaminate, defile, taint, debase, corrupt, smirch.

MACULATE, *adj.* 1. Spotted, freckled, spotty, blotted, maculose, blotched, blurred, stained, fleabitten, studded, flecked, brindled, pitted, pimply, scarred.

2. Impure, defiled, unclean, contaminated, corrupt, polluted, sullied.

MAD, *adj.* 1. Insane, demented, lunatic, crazy, lunatical, crazed, disordered in intellect, deranged, distracted, maniacal, bughouse *(slang)*, screwy *(slang)*, nutty *(slang)*, moon-struck, daft, unhinged, delirious, maniac, cuckoo *(slang)*, addlepated, out of one's mind, cracked *(slang)*, touched, non compos mentis *(Lat.)*, bereft of reason, off one's rocker *(slang)*, aliéné *(Fr.)*, not all there, not quite right, balmy *(slang)*, loco *(slang)*, not right in one's upper story.

2. Frenzied, wildly excited, frantic, frenetic, distracted, corybantic, bacchic, dithyrambic, giddy, rabid, dizzy, wild, mazed, distraught, bewildered, flighty, fanatical, eccentric, beside oneself, out of one's wits, *bouleversé (Fr.)*, ready to burst, hysterical, quixotic, fatuous, fiery, hot, red-hot.

3. Furious in violence, raging, enraged, berserk, amok, fierce, violent, reckless.

4. Mad with rage, angry, irate, wrathful, incensed, exasperated, enraged, provoked, furious, stormy, ireful, foaming at the mouth, fuming, boiling over, convulsed with rage, *acharné (Fr.)*, worked up, wrought up, infuriate, flushed with anger, in a huff, up in arms, in high dudgeon, on one's high ropes.

5. Wild with desire, impassioned, infatuated, passionate, ardent, fervent, impatient, avid, burning, all agog, mad after, devoured by desire, dying for, covetous.

MADAM, *n.* 1. Woman of rank or authority, lady, mistress, dame, ma'am *(colloq.)*, madonna, matron, dowager, Mrs., *madame (Fr.)*, *Frau (Ger.)*, *Vrouw (Dutch)*, signora *(It.)*, señora *(Sp.)*, senhora *(Port.)*.

2. Woman in charge of a brothel, bawd, procuress, mackerel, *conciliatrix (Lat.)*, jade, hustler.

MADCAP, *n.* 1. Wildly impulsive person, hotheaded person, hotspur, blood, hot-brained fellow, daredevil, rashling, desperado, bravo, bully, fire-eater, *enfant perdu (Fr.)*, scrapegrace, adventurer, Don Quixote, Icarus, knight-errant.

2. Fury, beldame, tiger, demon, dragon, Tisiphone, Alecto, Megaera, virago, tremagant, harridan, beldam, spitfire.

MADDEN, *v.* Excite to frenzy, drive mad, make insane, craze, irritate, exasperate, enrage, provoke, infuriate, lash into fury, inflame, make one's blood boil, turn one's head, envenom, anger, enchafe, incense, exacerbate, derange, vex, embitter, offend, affront, give offense, discompose, ruffle, fret, nettle, insult, pique, huff, heckle, stir up bile, rile, sting to the quick, aggravate, add fuel to the flame, kindle wrath, rankle, stick in one's gizzard, put one's back up, put out of humor, raise one's dander, throw into a ferment, work up into a passion, set by the ears.

MADDENING, *adj.* Driving to frenzy, irritating, provoking, exasperating, exacerbating, galling, vexatious, annoying, unmitigated, outrageous, aggravating, enraging, infuriating, offensive, discomposing, riling.

MADE-UP, *adj.* 1. Put together, finished, prepared, in readiness, ready-made, cut-and-dried, hand-me-down, ready for use, made to order.

2. Artificially produced, fabricated, invented, concocted, devised, counterfeit, sham, artificial, false, brummagem, elaborate, smelling of the lamp, make-believe, fake, pseudo, mock, spurious, bogus, factitious, meretricious, pinchbeck, tinsel.

MADHOUSE, *n.* Lunatic asylum, bedlam, hospital for the insane, state hospital, clinic for the insane, infirmary for mental cases, lock hospital, *maison de santé (Fr.)*.

MADMAN, *n.* 1. Insane person, lunatic, crazy person, bedlamite, maniac, deranged person, mooncalf, moonling, paranoiac, schizophrenic, manicdepressive, megalomaniac, psychotic, monomaniac, automaniac, pyromaniac, dipsomaniac, kleptomaniac, one with a persecution complex.

2. Crank, crackpot, enthusiast, eccentric, *fanatico (It.)*, dreamer, *exalté (Fr.)*, seer, rhapsodist, highflier, Don Quixote.

3. Idiot, half-wit, witling, tomfool, simpleton, fool, nitwit, moron, hoddy-doddy, imbecile, lackwit, changeling.

MADNESS, *n.* 1. Insanity, lunacy, mental aberration, distraction, craziness, derangement, mania, mental alienation, dementia, lyssa, rabies, lyssophobia, paranoia, schizophrenia, psychosis, psychoneurosis, megalomania, persecution-complex, delusion of grandeur, monomania, automania, pyromania, dipsomania, kleptomania, disordered reason, diseased mind, unsoundness, unsound mind, amentia, dementation, dementia praecox, morosis, phrenitis, hallucination, delusion, delirium, wandering, calenture of the brain, delirium tremens, D.T.s, hypochondriasis, melancholia, screw loose, bats in the belfry *(sl.)*.

2. Frenzy, rabies, furor, fury, franticness, rage, raving, perturbation, hysteria, passion, indignation, ire, wrath, anger, choler, resentment.

3. Infatuation, possession, fascination, intoxication, enravishment, ecstasy, bliss, entrancement, thrill, craze, fanaticism, inextinguishable desire, fatuity, senseless folly.

MAELSTROM, *n.* Whirlpool, vortex, eddy, gurge, swirl, whirl, whir, surge, Charybdis, indraught, undertow, reflux, regurgitation, overflow, rapids, bore.

MAENAD, *n.* Female attendant of Bacchus, bacchante, nymph, female reveler, devotee to Bacchus, frenzied and raging woman.

MAGAZINE, *n.* 1. Place for keeping gunpowder and explosives, building for keeping military stores, repository for war munitions, supply chamber, storehouse, warehouse, depository, entrepot, receptacle, arsenal, armory, *étape (Fr.)*, depot.

2. Periodical pamphlet, seasonal publication containing miscellaneous articles or stories, journal, ephemeris, slick *(sl.)*, weekly, monthly, quarterly.

MAGENTA, *n.* Reddish purple color, fuchsia, damask, crimson, carmine, maroon, cardinal, vermilion.

MAGGOT, *n.* 1. Legless larva of a fly, entozoon, worm, grub, footless insect-larva, beet-leaf maggot, corn-seed maggot, corn-stalk maggot, fir-bark maggot, head maggot, red maggot.

2. Fantastic notion, odd fancy, caprice, vagary, whim, quirk, whimsy, crotchet, humor, freak, wrinkle, conceit, whim-wham, *capriccio (It.)*, fad,

fit, prank, flimflam, kink, *boutade (Fr.),* figment, fantasy, rhapsody, romance.

MAGGOTY, *adj.* 1. Infested with maggots, wormy, flyblown, tainted, putrid, purulent, putrescent, feculent, carious, stercoraceous, excrementitious, rotting, rotten, high, corrupt.

2. Capricious, full of whims, whimsical, fanciful, having queer notions, freakish, crotchety, odd, fantastic, strange, fantastical, eccentric, erratic, inconsistent, fitful, humorsome, hysterical, wayward, wanton, skittish, frivolous, volatile, giddy.

MAGIC, *n.* 1. Pretended art of producing preternatural effects through command of occult forces in nature, sorcery, witchcraft, the black art, voodoo, thaumaturgy, necromancy, conjury, Magianism, wonderworking, black magic, conjuration, wizardry, shamanism, theurgy, legerdemain, prestidigitation, sleight, demonology, witchery, fetishism, hoodoo, obiism, voodooism, incantation, conjuration, divination, invocation, sortilege, hocuspocus, occultism, jugglery, alchemy, genethlialogy, genethliacism, goety, superstition, *diablerie (Fr.),* exorcism, mysticism, evil eye, jinx, hex.

2. Irresistible influence, glamorous attraction, witchery, fascination, charm, enchantment, spell, bewitchment, ensorcelment, glamor, possession, obsession, captivation, seduction, allurement, entrancement, mesmerism, animal magnetism.

3. Fortunetelling, prognostication, soothsaying, horoscopy, presage, forecast, foreboding, omen, presagement, auguration, portent, astrology, augury, second sight, clairvoyance, spiritualism, table-rapping, telepathy, thought-reading, automatic writing, crystal gazing, oracle.

4. Abracadabra, open sesame, wand, phylactery, amulet, philter, fetish, merrythought, wishbone, rabbit's foot, swastika, scarab, gammadion, triskelion, caduceus, divining rod, magic ring, Aladdin's lamp, magic carpet, Fortunatus's cap, wishing cap, Tarnhelm, cap of darkness, sevenleague boots.

MAGIC, *adj.* 1. Thaumaturgic, wonder-working, necromantic, occult, druidic, talismanic, shamanistic, Magian, theurgical, fetishistic, alchemical, alchemistic, magical, incantatory, witching, cabalistic, weird, canny.

2. Mysteriously enchanting, Circean, charming, irresistible, seductive, alluring, mesmeric, hypnotic, glamorous, bewitching, fascinating, ensorceling, spell-weaving, spell-binding, obsessive, captivating, entrancing, magnetic.

MAGICIAN, *n.* 1. Sorcerer, wizard, magus, necromancer, enchanter, shaman, theurgist, warlock, witch, incantator, evocator, wonder-worker, thaumaturgist, diviner, Magian, charmer, pellar, exorcist, witch doctor, medicine man, seer, fairy, lamia, voodoo, dowser, medium, clairvoyant, mesmerist, hypnotist, astrologer, soothsayer, fortuneteller, Merlin, Cagliostro, Katerfelto, Mesmer, Comus, siren, witch of Endor, Circe, hex, powwow-doctor.

2. Juggler, conjurer, prestidigitator, trickster, sleight-of-hand artist.

MAGIC LANTERN, *n.* Projector of illusive images, phantasmagoria, megascope, *ombres chinoises (Fr.),* dissolving views, pageantry.

MAGISTERIAL, *adj.* Befitting a master, domineering, dictatorial, despotic, imperious, lofty, lordly, arrogant, pompous, authoritative, proud, haughty, toplofty, consequential, high-flown, disdainful, assuming, assertive, dogmatical, bluster-

ing, swaggering, swashbuckling, self-important. masterly, judicial, overbearing, supercilious, commanding, grand, ex cathedra, oracular, high-toned, majestic, noble, masterful, puffed up, jingoistic, presumptive, bumptious, high-handed, presumptuous, arbitrary, insolent, saucy, august, stately, dignified, proud-crested, baronial, high-plumed, swollen, blown, vainglorious, high and mighty, overweening, stiff-necked, stuck-up, on one's high horses, on stilts, *en grand seigneur (Fr.),* contumelious, intolerant, audacious, vaporing, fireeating, thrasonic.

MAGISTRATE, *n.* Civil officer charged with the administration of the law, minor judicial officer having jurisdiction to try minor criminal cases and to conduct preliminary examinations of persons charged with serious crimes, justice of the peace, police justice, officer in civil service, prefect, consul, judge, bencher, ephor, doge, authority, governor, minister, dignitary, mayor, chancellor, provost, syndic, archon, alcalde, seneschal, burgomaster, constable, warden, *corregidor (Sp.),* alderman, sheriff, lord mayor, portreeve, high commissioner, bailiff, beadle.

MAGNANIMITY, *n.* Nobleness of mind, greatmindedness, high-mindedness, elevation of spirit, chivalry of soul, generosity, forbearance, disinterestedness, impartiality, unselfishness, liberality, nobility, great-heartedness, largeness of mind, altruism, toleration, tolerance, benevolence, loftiness of purpose, exaltation, self-forgetfulness, large-heartedness.

MAGNANIMOUS, *adj.* Generous in forgiving, free from petty resentfulness, free from vindictiveness, disinterested, impartial, liberal, altruistic, large-hearted, great-hearted, noble-minded, greatsouled, high-minded, unselfish, generous, philanthropic, beneficent, princely, chivalrous, lofty, noble, exalted, elevated, honorable, great, courageous, heroic, sublime, self-forgetful, self-sacrificing, devoted, dispassionate, unbiased, just, unprejudiced, charitable, gallant, handsome.

MAGNATE, *n.* Nobleman, grandee, aristocrat, distinguished person, man of rank, noble, mogul, lord, celebrity, bigwig, personage, man of distinction, notable, notability, great man, star, grand Panjandrum, seignior, swell, silk-stocking, three-tailed bashaw, peer, magnifico, hidalgo, patrician, gentleman, optimate, squire, person of eminence in a field, dominant person, big shot *(colloq.),* figure, somebody, great gun, big gun, big boy *(colloq.),* nabob, pasha, his nibs, top sawyer, cock of the walk.

MAGNET, *n.* 1. Body which possesses the property of attracting certain substances, loadstone, loadstar, siderite, magnetite.

2. Attraction, allurement, temptation, lure, fancy, seduction, fascination, whim, whimsy, maggot, height of one's ambition, desideratum.

3. Person that attracts by some inherent charm, idol, siren, sorceress, darling, apple of one's eye, sweetheart, flame, tempter, seducer.

MAGNETIC, *adj.* Exerting a strong attractive power, attractive, attrahent, adductive, adducent, electric, electrical, irresistible, potent, powerful, multipotent, omnipotent, inviting, tempting, seductive, fascinating, persuasive, protreptical.

MAGNETISM, *n.* Magnetic power, attractive charm, attraction, spell, magic, allurement, glamor, power of attraction, fascination, electrification, galvanism, *vis viva (Lat.),* attractiveness, pull, drawing to, adduction, pulling towards, lure, decoy, bait, allectation, temptation, *agacerie (Fr.)*, enticement, witchery, seduction, sorcery, mesmerism, hypnotic influence, siren song, voice of the tempter, forbidden fruit, honeyed words, golden apple.

MAGNETIZE, *v.* Exert a compelling influence upon, have a hold upon, bear upon, work upon, sway, actuate, rivet the attention, galvanize, electrify, mesmerize, hypnotize, attract, move, influence, lure, allure, charm, enchant, ensorcel, bewitch, entrance, fascinate, cast a spell, spellbind, seduce, tempt, entice, captivate, intrigue, carry away.

MAGNIFICENCE, *n.* Grand appearance, grandeur, stateliness, state, pomp, splendor, majesty, impressiveness, sumptuousness, sublimity, glory, gorgeousness, radiance, show, ostentation, nobility, éclat, brilliancy, bloom, polish, gloss, elegance, grace, pulchritude, beauty, swank, style, display, flourish, *étalage (Fr.)*, *coup d'oeil (Fr.)*, glitter, splash, pageantry, solemnity, parade, flying colors, spectacle, foppery, frippery, fancy dress, luxuriousness, court dress, equipage.

MAGNIFICENT, *adj.* Making a splendid show, grand in appearance, majestic, noble, sublime, superb, sumptuous, splendid, gorgeous, ostentatious, august, beautiful, princely, extraordinarily fine, garish, gallant, glorious, royal, regal, kingly, surpassing, transcendent, pompous, imposing, stately, showy, grandiose, proud, palatial, radiant, brilliant, gaudy, flashy, spectacular, flashing, glittering, gleaming, refulgent, commanding, handsome, elegant, graceful, lovely, beauteous, exquisite, swanky, sparkling, resplendent, dazzling, sleek, glossy, rich, ornamental, pretentious, jaunty, flaming, gay, colorful.

MAGNIFICO, *n.* Great personage, aristocrat, patrician, grandee, lord, nobleman, peer, hidalgo, don, swell, personage, man of distinction, three-tailed bashaw, bigwig, silk-stocking, magnate, celebrity, man of note, gentleman, squire, chevalier, courtier, seignior, knight, prince.

MAGNIFY, *v.* 1. Make greater in size, enlarge, increase the apparent size of, amplify, augment, make great, expand, add to, aggrandize, greaten, raise, boost *(colloq.)*, extend, deepen, double, duplicate, heighten, incrassate, lengthen, thicken, redouble, inflate, dilate, stretch, puff up, distend, maximize, gigantize.

2. Cause to seem more important, exalt, extol, glorify, elevate, celebrate, praise, laud, bless, eulogize, acclaim, dignify, applaud, adore, worship, revere, reverence, panegyrize.

3. Exaggerate, overstate, overrate, enlarge upon, overcolor, embroider, strain, overstrain, color too highly, depict extravagantly, romance.

MAGNILOQUENCE, *n.* Grandiose speaking style, grandiloquence, altiloquence, bombast, fustian, turgidity, pomposity, flourish, inflation, orotundity, floridness, turgescence, well-rounded periods, euphuism, flowers of rhetoric, macrology, high-sounding words, sesquipedalianism, rant, prose run mad, fine writing, jactitation, highfalutin, rodomontade, teratology, heroics.

MAGNILOQUENT, *adj.* Speaking in a lofty style, altiloquent, grandiloquent, bombastic, declamatory, high-flown, highfalutin, tumid, inflated, turgid, orotund, swelling, stilted, pompous, thrasonic, gasconading, pretentious, periodic, florid, ornate, flowery, sonorous, euphuistic, big-sound-

ing, turgescent, pedantic, highflowing, rhetorical, sententious, grandiose, sesquipedalian, fustian, mouthy, Johnsonian, Ciceronian, figurative.

MAGNITUDE, *n.* 1. Size, bigness, bulk, mass, dimension, extent, volume, amplitude, measure, expanse, enormity, proportions, largeness, extension, space, immensity, vastness, measurement, capacity, corpulence, plumpness, obesity, embonpoint, hugeness, monstrosity.

2. Great amount, quantity, abundance, lot, heap, much, great deal, content, multitude, sufficiency, stock, load, store, shipload, infinity, fullness, intensity, might, strength.

3. Importance, consequence, eminence, distinction, greatness, dignity, grandeur, fame, nobility, loftiness, sublimity.

MAGPIE, *n.* 1. Noisy, mischievous corvine bird of the genus *Pica*.

2. Chattering person, chatterbox, babbler, talker, rattle, ranter, windbag, blatherskite, gossip, jay, poll, parrot, *moulin à paroles (Fr.)*.

MAID, *n.* 1. Young unmarried woman, virgin, lass, lassie, damsel, maiden, girl, miss, nymph, celibate, bachelor girl, spinster, old maid, *femme sole (Fr.)*, vestal, sister, nun, damozel, demoiselle, colleen, schoolgirl, flapper, tomboy, hoyden, baggage, minx, wench, soubrette, ingenue.

2. Female servant, maidservant, lady's maid, handmaid, *ancilla (Lat.)*, handmaiden, abigail, domestic, girl, help, *bonne (Fr.)*, nurse, nursemaid, ayah *(India)*, amah *(Oriental)*, maid-of-all-work, general servant, upstairs girl, chambermaid, parlor maid, waitress, cook, scullion, Cinderella, hired girl, laundress.

MAIDEN, *adj.* 1. Of virgins, unmarried, girlish, daughterly, youthful, virgin, virginal, chaste, pure, undefiled, unpolluted.

2. Appearing for the first time, making its debut, fresh, first, new, untried, unused, initial, prime, introductory, initiatory, inaugural, initiative, primal, pristine, original.

MAIDENHOOD, *n.* 1. Virginity, virginal purity, pudicity, pudency, *pucelage (Fr.)*, chastity, delicacy, modesty, virtue, pure-mindedness, pureness, innocence, continence, cleanness, decency, celibacy, singleness, single blessedness.

2. Freshness, newness, bloom, rosiness, novelty.

MAIDENLY, *adj.* Girlish, maidenlike, virginal, chaste, modest, reserved, gentle, single, celibate, soft, artless, vestal, unsullied, pure.

MAIDSERVANT, *n.* Maid, lady's maid, female servant, abigail, biddy, handmaid, *ancilla (Lat.)*, housemaid, *confidente (Fr.)*, soubrette, *bonne (Fr.)*, nursemaid, chambermaid, *fille de chambre (Fr.)*, *femme de chambre (Fr.)*, *camarista (It.)*, scullion, cook, Cinderella, waitress, hired help, cleaning woman, charwoman, maid-of-all-work, upstairs girl, tweeny, girl, slavey, goody, laundress, bedmaker, domestic, parlor maid.

MAIL, *n.* 1. Postal service, system of transmission of letters, conveyance for mailed matter, post-office service, mailer, mail train, post boat, mail boat, air mail, aerial mail.

2. Letters, packages arriving by post, mailed matter, post.

3. Flexible armor of interlinked rings, defensive armor, coat of mail, arms, harness, breastplate, aegis, cuirass, habergeon, plastron, hauberk, brigandine, lorication.

MAIL, *v.* Put in the post office for transmission, put in the mail, send by post, drop in a letter box, post, send by mail, dispatch, forward, ship, express, transmit, consign, freight, embark.

MAILMAN, *n.* One who carries mail, postman, letter carrier, mail carrier, *facteur (Fr.),* courier.

MAIM. *v.* Deprive of the use of some bodily member, inflict severe injuries on the body, give a disabling wound, mutilate, cripple, lacerate, obtruncate, mangle, disable, amputate, detruncate, hamstring, bemaim, truncate, cut to pieces, commit mayhem on, wound, despoil, deface, lame, cut off, castrate, emasculate, unman, geld, spay, caponize, surbate, hough, scotch, disfigure, impair, mar, injure, hurt, scathe.

MAIN, *adj.* 1. Primary, principal, chief, leading, capital, cardinal, prime, paramount, head, first, predominant, staple, foremost, preëminent, supreme, superior.
2. Essential, important, radical, indispensable, requisite, vital, necessary, urgent, pressing, instant, exigent, imperative, critical, crucial, consequential, substantial, big *(colloq.),* material, notable, outstanding, marked, signal, salient, remarkable, memorable, unusual, particular, noteworthy, special.

MAIN, *n.* 1. Principal duct in a system used to distribute water or gas, main pipe, main conduit, main channel, main tube, drain, sewer, gutter, culvert, cloaca, moat.
2. Strength, force, might, power, violent effort, potency, puissance, efficacy, efficiency.
3. Chief part, principal point, the gross, the greater part, the bulk, majority, preponderance, the mass, gist, substance, sum and substance, gravamen, kernel, core, nucleus, keynote, key, cornerstone.
4. Open ocean, high sea, great sea, deep, briny deep, vasty deep, watery waste, bounding main. Davy Jones' locker.
5. Continent, mainland, chersonese, peninsula, tongue of land, isthmus, promontory, cape, highland, neck of land, delta.

MAINLAND, *n.* Principle land as distinguished from islands or peninsulas, continent, main, tongue of land, neck of land, promontory, highland, dry land, *terra firma (Lat.).*

MAINLY, *adv.* Principally, for the most part, in the main, chiefly, mostly, most of all, above all, in great measure, *par excellence (Fr.),* to crown all, first and foremost, on the whole.

MAINSPRING, *n.* 1. Principal spring in a mechanism, wheelwork, clockwork, inner part, wheels within wheels, heart.
2. Chief motive power, impelling cause, agent, prime mover, *primum mobile (Lat.), vera causa (Lat.),* source, origin, principle, producer, author, generator, dynamo.

MAINSTAY, *n.* Principle support, final resource, main dependence, chief reliance, prop, staff, strength, pillar, anchor, sheet anchor, refuge, hope.

MAINTAIN, *v.* 1. Claim, declare, assert, affirm, allege, contend, insist, state, asseverate, aver, avouch, set forth, swear, avow, annunciate, propound, predicate, acknowledge, profess, protest, broach.
2. Provide for, take care of, provide with the means of existence, support, supply with means of living, care for, keep, preserve, sustain, uphold, keep up, conserve, keep alive, make safe, protect, secure, guard, shield, cherish, nurture, nourish, feed, finance, grubstake.
3. Keep, retain, keep up, continue, carry on,

hold up, bolster up, brace, shore up, truss, buttress, prop, stay, underset, underprop, upbear, hold, carry.
4. Support in argument, defend, justify, vindicate, advocate, plead for, champion, back up, patronize, second, help, back, countenance, succor, aid, assist.
5. Abide by, persist in, adhere, be firmly fixed, stand by, not give up, keep possession of, hold on to, stand one's ground, be firm, persevere, keep one's ground, hold one's own with, hold against attack, bear up against, weather, keep one's course, stand firm, hold out, keep unimpaired.

MAINTENANCE, *n.* 1. Means of subsistence, upkeep, livelihood, living, nourishment, provisions, victuals, food, bread and butter, room and board, sustentation, sustainment, support, necessaries, keep, nutriment, grubstake, stores, stock, sustenance.
2. Safekeeping, preservation, saving, conservation, economy, protection, defense, deliverance, salvation.
3. Advocacy, assistance, aid, help, succor, countenance, favor, patronage, backing, championship, encouragement, vindication, justification.

MAJESTIC, *adj.* Of lofty dignity, imposing in aspect, dignified, stately, august, noble, regal, princely, royal, imperial, magnificent, grand, splendid, sublime, gorgeous, glorious, superb, impressive, distinguished, illustrious, kingly, eminent, renowned, affecting, solemn, famous, prominent, conspicuous, signal, noted, esteemed, supreme.

MAJESTY, *n.* Imposing character, regal grandeur, lofty dignity, loftiness, stateliness, augustness, noble bearing, magnificence, splendor, dignity of mien, distinction, eminence, nobility, glory, honor, luster, illustriousness, sublimity, solemnity, sovereignty, supreme authority.

MAJOR, *adj.* Greater, higher, larger, superior, over, upper, ultra, above, exceeding, extreme.

MAJOR-DOMO, *n.* Man in charge of a great household, chief steward, seneschal, castellan, chamberlain, bailiff, groom of the chambers, vizier, housekeeper, factotum, butler.

MAJORITY, *n.* 1. Greater part, greater number, more than half, bulk, preponderance, mass, plurality, excess, number greater than half of the total, lion's share, Benjamin's mess.
2. Full legal age, adulthood, manhood, virility, full bloom, flower of age, seniority.

MAKE, *v.* 1. Put into definite form, construct, manufacture, combine parts, fashion, shape, frame, mold, figure, form, build, erect, cast, mint, stamp, devise, invent, bring into being, create, produce, contrive, effect, forge, conceive, prepare, compose, organize, embody, beget, engender, develop, fabricate, be productive of, constitute, compound.
2. Draw up, appoint, render, fix, establish, enact, legislate, pass.
3. Bring into a certain form, convert, alter, transform, change, turn.
4. Do, perform, practice, execute, accomplish.
5. Earn, win for oneself, gain, get, acquire, secure, obtain, take, get a profit, profit by.
6. Compel, induce, constrain, require, force, coerce, cause, occasion, dragoon, press, drive, impel, necessitate, enforce, oblige, drag into, force upon, exact, pin down, bind, insist upon, impress, conscript, draft, commandeer.

7. Serve for, serve as, answer for, do the part of, oblige.

8. Judge, infer, deduce, estimate, reckon.

9. Accomplish by traveling, reach, arrive at, attain.

10. Go toward, journey, move, approach, tend, travel, proceed, traverse, travel over.

11. Be of effect, have effect, operate, conduce, contribute, favor, be of advantage.

MAKE, *n.* Style of being made, construction, structure, form, shape, mark, kind, brand, stamp, texture, composition, fabric, constitution, build, character, disposition, nature, formation, make-up, quality, grade, sort, stamp, cachet.

MAKE BELIEVE, v. Pretend, act as if, feign, make as if, seem to, appear to, simulate, put on, assume, personate, affect, counterfeit, sham, act a part, pass off for, fake, make a show of, fabricate, invent, romance, hatch, forge, concoct, malinger, trump up.

MAKE-BELIEVE, *n.* Pretense, sham, counterfeit, pretext, feint, simulation, pretending, malingering, mere show, window dressing, crocodile tears, disguisement, buncombe, charlatanism, flimflam, quackery, false colors, wolf in sheep's clothing, mummery, masquerade, borrowed plumes, brummagem, pinchbeck, ormolu, scagliola, paste jewelry, tinsel, forgery, invention, fabrication, romance, fiction, subterfuge, shuffle, shift, evasion.

MAKE-BELIEVE, *adj.* Sham, mock, unreal, counterfeited, pretended, claptrap, simulated, meretricious, spurious, false, supposititious, assumed, buncombe, quack, charlatanic, flimflam, brummagem, paste, tinsel, fabricated, fictitious, pseudo, faked, trumped up, feigned, fraudulent, bogus, pinchbeck, invented, factitious.

MAKE FOR, *v.* 1. Move toward, head for, strike for, go toward, aim at, steer for, hold a course, level at, be bound for, direct one's course, bend one's steps towards, align one's march, go straight.

2. Tend to the advantage of, favor, be favorable to, conduce, be propitious to, ease, facilitate, make easier, promote, subserve, contribute towards, have a tendency, forward, advance, redound.

MAKE GOOD, 1. Redintegrate, make whole, rectify, recoup, set right, put right, set straight, put to rights, correct, put in order, mend, repair, retouch, put in repair, patch up, reclaim, redeem, restore, return to the original state, reconstruct, regenerate, recondition, rejuvenate, renew.

2. Make up for, compensate for, supply by an equivalent, make compensation for, make restitution for, satisfy, indemnify, make amends, offset, square, requite, recompense, repay, remunerate.

3. Establish, circumstantiate, verify, prove, confirm, substantiate, authenticate, make out a case, demonstrate, evince, show, have the best of the argument, prove one's point.

4. Defend, vindicate, maintain, justify, uphold, stand by, avenge, advocate.

5. Be as good as one's word, carry into effect, carry out, put in force, fulfill, discharge, realize, perform, complete, accomplish, make short work of, polish off, dispatch, finish off, knock off, do thoroughly, go the whole hog, not do by halves, carry through, drive home, fill the bill, deliver the goods, crown, cap.

MAKE KNOWN, Proclaim, inform of, tell, acquaint with, bring to the ears of, impart to, apprise, advise, let fall, communicate, mention, publish, declare, cry in the streets, announce, send word, report, bruit about, disclose, tip off, whisper in the ear.

MAKE MERRY, Feast, banquet, carouse, revel, disport, wanton, sport, junket, drown care, drive dull care away, amuse oneself, play pranks, gambol, frolic, caper, romp, frisk, sow one's wild oats, paint the town red, have one's fling, take one's pleasure, keep holiday.

MAKE MUCH OF, 1. Exaggerate, magnify, amplify, hyperbolize, overstate, make the most of, draw a long bow, strain a point, go great lengths, overcolor, spin a long yarn, embroider, heighten, color.

2. Treat with fondness, cherish, fondle, coddle, pet, foster, humor, pamper, nurse, indulge, cocker, caress, cosset.

3. Make a stir about, make much ado about, make a thing of, attach great importance to, set store by, underline, print in large letters, print in italics, emphasize, accentuate, lay stress on.

MAKE OF, 1. Interpret, understand, construe, find the meaning of, make out, spell out, decipher, unravel, decode, puzzle out, read between the lines, find the key of, account for, elucidate, clear up, understand by.

2. Consider, esteem, account, reflect upon, weigh, ponder, contemplate, deem, regard, judge, adjudge, reckon, view, look upon.

MAKE OFF WITH, 1. Carry off, take away, kidnap, abduct, shanghai, convey away, spirit away, spirit off, snatch, lay violent hands on, crimp.

2. Steal, purloin, filch, pilfer, cabbage, lift, bag, thieve, rob, abstract.

MAKE OUT, 1. See, discern, perceive, behold, descry, espy, sight, distinguish, ken, recognize, have in sight, catch a glimpse of.

2. Get a clear understanding of, discover, learn, ascertain, determine, decipher, interpret, decode, read between the lines, construe, define, explain, render, translate, find the meaning of, figure out, spell out, puzzle out, disentangle, unravel, resolve, solve, comprehend, understand, take in, grasp, catch, follow.

3. Prove, evince, establish, substantiate, circumstantiate, verify, demonstrate, settle the question, prove one's point, have the best of the argument.

4. Get along, manage, be able at last, succeed, make a shift, fare, prosper, thrive, come off well, come off with flying colors, carry all before one, have the best of, drive a roaring trade, reap the fruits of, turn to good account.

MAKE OVER, 1. Make anew, alter, mend, amend, improve, emend, render better, better, ameliorate, correct, rectify, improve upon, touch up, refine upon, brush up, brighten up, furbish up, polish, restore, repair, remodel, reform, reorganize.

2. Hand over into the possession of another, transfer, convey, sign over, alienate, assign, transmit, hand down, pass, deliver over, turn over, put into the hands of, bequeath, devise, leave, settle upon.

MAKE PEACE, Bring to terms, restore harmony, heal the breach, reconcile, conciliate, placate, propitiate, meet halfway, pacify, hold out the olive branch, pass the peace pipe, make up a quarrel, settle matters, come to an understanding, bury the hatchet, turn swords into plowshares, lay down one's arms, sheathe the sword, close the temple of Janus, mediate, mediatize, intervene, intercede, negotiate, arbitrate, *magnas componere lites (Lat.)*.

MAKER, *n.* 1. God, Creator, Father, Author of all things, Author of our being, The Almighty, The First Cause, The Supreme Being.

2. Artificer, architect, manufacturer, wright, artist, builder, constructor, former, producer, framer, mason, smith, forger, carpenter, tailor, seamstress, needleworker, cordwainer, artisan, craftsman, handicraftsman, hand, hack, perpetrator, doer, agent, operator, executor, writer, composer, author, scribe, amanuensis, scrivener.

MAKESHIFT, *n.* Temporary expedient, tentative substitute, succedaneum, stopgap, shift, provisional excuse, apology, alternative, *pis aller (Fr.), locum tenens (Lat.),* mere pretext, understudy, pinch hitter, scapegoat, *quid pro quo (Lat.)*.

MAKE SPORT OF, Deride, mock, ridicule, scoff at, laugh at, scout, jeer at, snigger, twit, laugh in one's sleeve, poke fun at, rally, chaff, jolly, rag, roast, play tricks upon, make a fool of, fleer, caricature, satirize, travesty, parody, burlesque, turn to ridicule, gibe, niggle, guy, laugh to scorn, lead one a dance, hoot, hiss, speak slightingly of, call names, disparage, toss in a blanket.

MAKE SURE OF, 1. Secure, fasten, make certain, stabilize, stabilitate, establish, settle, fix, set.

2. Consider as certain, find out for sure, see how the wind blows, watch how the cat jumps.

MAKE-UP, *n.* 1. Manner of being put together, structure, formation, composition, arrangement, texture, constitution, compounding, nature, make, caliber, temperament.

2. Articles used to paint a person's face, cosmetics, rouge, powder, mascara, eyeshadow, eyebrow pencil, lipstick, pancake.

MAKE UP, *v.* 1. Put together, construct, fabricate, weave, form, constitute, compose, compile.

2. Concoct, invent, hatch, coin, forge, devise, contrive, design, project, frame, brew.

3. Apply cosmetics to the face, powder, rouge, pencil the eyebrows, use mascara, apply eyeshadow, use lipstick.

4. Settle amicably, reconcile, bury the hatchet, smoke the peace pipe, sheathe the sword, settle differences, come to an understanding, come to terms, shake hands.

5. Make up for, compensate for, offset, counterbalance, counterpoise, balance, equalize, recoup, square, redeem.

MAKE WAY, *v.* 1. Advance, progress, proceed, get on, gain ground, get along, jog on, hold on one's course, move forward, press on, push forward, forge ahead, make headway, make strides, make advances.

2. Open a passage, clear a way, elbow one's way, clear the path.

MAKING, *n.* 1. Construction, formation, fabrication, manufacture, composition, compounding, constitution, combination, conjunction, synthesis, blending, production.

2. Structure, texture, make-up, form, workmanship, craftsmanship, brand, stamp, cachet, grade, sort, quality, kind, mark.

MALADMINISTRATION, *n.* Inefficient management, misgovernment, misrule, malversation, misconduct, impolicy, misapplication, misdirection, misfeasance, bungling, blunder, incompetency, unproficiency, disqualification.

MALADROIT, *adj.* Lacking in adroitness, inexpert, inapt, unskilled, unskillful, awkward, gauche, clumsy, lubberly, unhandy, bungling, incompetent, heavy-handed, butter-fingered, inhabile, unfit.

MALADY, *n.* Chronic bodily disorder, deep-seated ill, ailment, illness, sickness, complaint, disease, indisposition, distemper, infirmity, affliction, affection, invalidism, delicate health, virus, infection, contagion, poison, taint, pollution, pestilence, plague, nausea, qualm, malnutrition, consumption, tuberculosis, phthisis, T.B., paralysis, palsy, stroke, paresis, polio, infantile paralysis, poliomyelitis, malaria, ague, fever, pyrexia, calenture, febricity, typhoid, typhus, scarlet fever, yellow fever, cancer, diphtheria, pneumonia, head cold, asthma, allergy, hypersensitivity, carcinoma, jaundice, hepatitis, hypertension, hypotension, arteriosclerosis, dystrophy, arthritis, lumbago, gout, sciatica, neuralgia, migraine.

MALAISE, *n.* Indefinite bodily weakness, discomfort marking the onset of a disease, dysphoria, dolor, pain, suffering, ache, smart, disquiet, discomposure, uneasiness, inquietude, gripe, twitch, twinge, stitch, spasm, throe, pang, throb.

MALAPERT, *adj.* Unbecomingly bold, impudent, impertinent, forward, saucy, flippant, rude, insolent, presumptuous, pert, cavalier, supercilious, disdainful, fresh, assuming, bumptious, brazenfaced, bare-faced, unabashed, audacious, devilmay-care, free and easy, swaggering, jaunty.

MALAPROPOS, *adj.* Inappropriate, unbecoming, unseemly, unfit, unsuitable, inexpedient, unseasonable, untimely, inopportune, mistimed, ill-timed, untoward, unpropitious, unfortunate, infelicitous, inauspicious, unlucky, not to the point, inapposite, out of place, out of keeping.

MALARIA, *n.* 1. Intermittent febrile disease carried by infected anopheline mosquitoes, chills and fever, ague, malaria fever, aestivo-autumnal fever, pernicious fever, tertian malaria, quartan malaria.

2. Unwholesome poisonous air, miasma, noxious exhalation, foul air, bad air, miasm, floating effluvia, mephitis, sewer gas, azote.

MALARIOUS, *adj.* Insalubrious, unwholesome, miasmatic, mephitic, azotic, unhealthy, unfavorable to health, noxious, noisome, fetid, foul, poisonous, pestilential, baneful, morbific, morbiferous, septic, malarial.

MALCONTENT, *adj.* 1. Unsatisfied, dissatisfied, discontented, uneasy, restive, hard to please, displeased, faultfinding, morose, sullen, glum, sour, irritable, grouchy, grumpy, dissentient, regretful, dejected, downcast, exacting, disconsolate, despondent.

2. Inclined to rebellion, rebellious, mutinous, insurgent, fractious, unruly, refractory, recalcitrant, seditious, defiant, contumacious, intractable, insubordinate, disobedient, ungovernable, unsubmissive, impatient of control, recusant, riotous, revolutionary.

MALCONTENT, *n.* 1. Faultfinder, grumbler, repiner, growler, grouch, irreconcilable, croaker, *laudator temporis acti (Lat.),* complainer, censurer, murmurer, Adullamite.

2. Rebel, agitator, radical, anarchist, nihilist, demagogue, agitator, reactionary, reactionist, *frondeur (Fr.),* seditionist, revolutionary, Red,

seditionary, revolutionist, bitter-ender, diehard, extremist, obstructionist.

MALE, *adj.* Belonging to the sex which begets young, masculine, virile, he-man, manly, manlike, mannish.

MALE, *n.* 1. Male human being, man, boy, *homo, homo sapiens (Lat.),* he, chap, guy, fellow, swain, wight, yeoman, gentleman, beau, blade, spark, gaffer, esquire, sir, sahib *(India),* don, hidalgo, husband, boy friend, mister.

2. Male animal, he, tom- (in compounds), stallion, buck, gelding, stag, boar, dog, hart, cock, gander, drake, bullock, bull, steer, ox, ram, billygoat, he-goat, tomcat, capon, rooster.

MALEDICTION, *n.* 1. Curse, malison, execration, imprecation, anathema, proscription, fulmination, commination, denunciation, thunders of the Vatican, excommunication, ban, ostracism, banishment, bell, book and candle.

2. Aspersion, vilification, obloquy, revilement, vituperation, invective, tongue-lashing, contumely, diatribe, libel, slander, defamation, calumniation, backbiting, disparagement, traduction, scandalization, dispraise, evil-speaking, scurrility, expletive, oath, ribaldry, billingsgate, foul language, profanity, swearing, blackguardism, damnation.

MALEFACTOR, *n.* 1. Offender against the law, criminal, felon, culprit, outlaw, convict, *condamné (Fr.),* jailbird, lawbreaker, murderer, assassin, crook *(slang),* thief, robber, footpad, burglar, cutthroat, mugger, rapist, adulterer, pervert, bandit, *ladrone (It.),* highwayman, brigand, gallowsbird, kidnapper, abductor, pickpocket, shoplifter, swindler, peculator, counterfeiter, forger, fence, housebreaker, cracksman, rumrunner, bootlegger, hijacker, blackmailer.

2. Evil-doer, ruffian, roughneck, thug, apache, gunman, gangster, racketeer, hoodlum, tough, hooligan, black sheep, ne'er-do-well, scapegrace, scamp, scalawag, rapscallion, scoundrel, rascal, villain, rogue, reprobate, miscreant, blackguard, wretch, caitiff, trickster, sharper, hellhound, *âme damnée,* monster, demon, devil, mischief-maker, wrong-doer, knave, brute, desperado, larrikin, rowdy, delinquent, rakehell, varlet, transgressor, misdoer, vagabond.

MALEFICENT, *adj.* Doing evil, harm-doing, harmful, injurious, mischievous, baleful, baneful, pernicious, deleterious, detrimental, mischief-making, malefic, noxious, oppressive, malign, destructive, villainous, evil, depraved, grinding, cold-blooded, hard-hearted, ruthless, relentless, cruel, savage, brutal, ferocious, feral, barbarous, inhuman, truculent, fell, atrocious, bloodthirsty, fiendish, devilish, diabolical, demoniacal, hellish, murderous, homicidal, lethiferous.

MALEVOLENCE, *n.* 1. Wishing of harm to others, corrosive hatred, implacable resentment, smoldering ill will, animosity, malignity, enmity, antipathy, rancor, spitefulness, hate, venom, spite, maliciousness, bitterness, pique, grudge, gall, virulence, ill nature, bad intention, uncharitableness, unkindness, bad blood, malice, malignancy, malice prepense, malice aforethought, heart of stone, evil eye, affront, bad turn, indignity, acerbity, acrimony.

2. Ferocity, brutality, bloodthirstiness, cruelty, savagery, fiendishness, ferity, atrocity, outrage, barbarity, ruthlessness, persecution, inhumanity, ill-usage, pitilessness, hard-heartedness, trucu-

lence, mercilessness, ruffianism, torture, inquisition.

MALEVOLENT, *adj.* 1. Wishing evil to others, showing ill will, evil-minded, spiteful, malignant, ill-natured, ill-disposed, malicious, mischievous, invidious, envious, rancorous, resentful, acrimonious, bitter, ill-intentioned, evil-disposed, malign, venomous, envenomed, maleficent, treacherous, perfidious, vicious, faithless, virulent, disobliging, harsh, unkind, grinding, galling, unfriendly, churlish, ungracious, sullen, surly, sinister, pernicious, revengeful, implacable.

2. Hard-hearted, cold-blooded, cruel, unnatural, grim, brutal, ruthless, ferocious, pitiless, savage, bloodthirsty, merciless, unfeeling, feral, inhuman, ferine, truculent, diabolical, hellish, devilish, fiendish, demoniac, infernal, fell, dire, barbarous, murderous, homicidal, infamous, hateful, baleful, baneful, lethal.

MALFEASANCE, *n.* Wrongful performance of a deed which the actor has no right to perform, wrongdoing, misbehavior, malversation, misfeasance, impropriety, unfitness.

MALFORMATION, *n.* Faulty formation, anomalous structure, deformity, disfigurement, distortion, misproportion, monstrosity, kyphosis, anamorphosis, asymmetry, ugliness, crookedness, twist, grimace, obliquity, contortion, twisting, screw, warp, teratology, knottiness.

MALFORMED, *adj.* Faultily formed, misshapen, distorted, awry, crooked, askew, anamorphous, unsymmetric, irregular, not straight, deformed, crump, misbegotten, ill-proportioned, misproportioned, grotesque, ill-made, round-shouldered, scalene, hunchbacked, humpbacked, bowlegged, bandy-legged, knock-kneed, clubfooted, splayfooted, taliped, snub-nosed, stumpy, dwarfed.

MALICE, *n.* Desire to inflict suffering on another, evil intent, ill will, malevolence, malignity, maliciousness, hate, rancor, animosity, enmity, venom, spite, pique, bitterness, spitefulness, grudge, malignancy, gall, implacableness, spleen, dudgeon, hatred, abhorrence, dislike, umbrage, resentment, evil disposition, ill feeling, bad blood, detestation, virulence, uncharitableness, unkindness, unfriendliness, evil eye, *Hexerei (Ger.), malocchio (It.),* ferity, hard-heartedness.

MALICIOUS, *adj.* Spiteful, vicious, ill-natured, ill-disposed, envious, bitter, invidious, malignant, malevolent, rancorous, resentful, vindictive, pernicious, evil-minded, mischievous, malign, revengeful, implacable, virulent, wanton, hateful, treacherous, slanderous, libelous, defamatory, calumnious, false-spoken, disparaging, venomous, scurvy, felonious, infernal, satanic, hellish, devilish, diabolical, demoniac, cold-blooded, hard-hearted, inhuman, merciless, unfeeling, grim, ruthless, relentless, stony-hearted, brutal, ferocious, feral, bloodthirsty, cruel, savage, fell, barbarous, truculent, caustic, acrimonious.

MALIGN, *adj.* 1. Evil in effect, baneful, baleful, pernicious, injurious, harmful, pestilential, pestiferous, unfavorable, unpropitious, malominous, extremely bad, detrimental, deleterious, noxious, malefic, sinister, unlucky, disastrous, untoward, obnoxious, inauspicious, destructive, arrant, rank, dire, foul, vile, depraved.

2. Showing an evil disposition, ill-disposed, spiteful, malevolent, malicious, malignant, fiendish, devilish, demoniac, hellish, satanic, rancorous, envenomed, bitter, acrimonious, maleficent,

virulent, cold-blooded, stony-hearted, inhuman, unnatural.

MALIGN, *v.* Speak ill of, disparage, calumniate, traduce, slander, revile, abuse, defame, vilify, asperse, scandalize, blacken, denigrate, depreciate, decry, lampoon, inveigh against, vituperate, detract, derogate, run down, belittle, minimize, damn with faint praise, pull to pieces, criticize, cast aspersions, pick a hole in one's coat, vilipend, bespatter, blow upon, backbite, brand, libel, fling dirt, anathematize.

MALIGNANCY, *n.* 1. Extreme malevolence, ill will, virulence, hatred, malice, animosity, malignity, malignance, rancor, bitter enmity, spite, pique, dudgeon, umbrage, grudge, heinousness, deadliness, evilness, destructiveness, deleteriousness, fatality, poisonousness, peccancy, badness, heart of stone, hardness of heart, cruelty, obduracy, ferity, brutality, ferocity, savagery, inhumanity, barbarity, truculence, immanity, cloven foot, evil eye, venom, gall, hate, bad blood, ill turn, atrocity, outrage, persecution, affront, ill usage.
2. Unpropitiousness, inauspiciousness, unfavorableness, untowardness, sinisterness, untimeliness, ominousness.

MALIGNANT, *adj.* 1. Disposed to cause distress, virulently inimical, hostile, resentful, invidious, envious, rancorous, spiteful, malicious, bitter, malign, malevolent, revengeful, pestilential, pestiferous, hellish, sullen, hateful, unkindly, impish, evil-minded, fell, fiendish, satanic, venomous, inhuman, vicious, vindictive, sardonic, mischievous, devilish, scurrilous, acrimonious, nefarious, treacherous, perfidious, traitorous.
2. Threatening great danger, harmful in influence *or* effect, sinister, ominous, unpropitious, inauspicious, unfavorable, minatory, portentous, unlucky, untoward, unpromising, unfortunate, ill-starred, ill-omened, boding ill.
3. *(Med.)* Tending to produce death, deadly, lethal, fatal, pernicious, virulent, poisonous, toxic.

MALIGNER, *n.* Vilifier, traducer, backbiter, slanderer, calumniator, defamer, libeler, detractor, disparager, evil-speaker, lampooner, inveigher, censurer, carper, critic, knocker, satirist, dawplucker, dearest foe, vituperator, reviler, castigator, Zoilus, Thersites.

MALIGNITY, *n.* 1. Hatred, hate, animosity, rancor, ill will, spite, grudge, pique, dudgeon, acrimony, hostility, envy, invidiousness, bitterness, gall, spleen, despite, malevolence, malignancy, malice, maliciousness, venom.
2. Violence, rage, ferocity, fury, berserk, exacerbation, exasperation, paroxysm, fit, brute force, passion.
3. Virulence, deadliness, fatality, destructiveness, deleteriousness.

MALISON, *n.* Curse, malediction, denunciation, imprecation, oath, execration, anathema, fulmination, commination, profane swearing, foul invective, expletive, tongue-lashing, revilement, obloquy, vituperation, diatribe, vilification, aspersion, evil-speaking.

MALL, *n.* Shaded public walk, promenade, square, piazza, circus, colonnade, arcade, cloister, peristyle, esplanade, parade, lane, alley, street, road, quadrangle, court, yard, close, terrace, parade.

MALLEABLE, *adj.* 1. Capable of being shaped by hammering, able to be extended by pressure with rollers, extensile, sequacious, ductile, plastic,

tractile, pliable, flexible, pliant, flexile, supple, extensible, yielding, readily wrought.
2. Adaptable, tractable, docile, teachable, governable, manageable, submissive, impressionable, sensitive.

MALLET, *n.* Hammerlike tool with a head used for driving another tool with a handle, wooden hammer, rammer, ram, pile driver, tamper, sledge-hammer, flail, maul, mall, gavel, beetle, wooden implement used to strike the balls in croquet, stick used to drive the ball in polo.

MALNUTRITION, *n.* Lack of proper nutrition, imperfect nutrition, undernourishment, exhaustion from hunger, inanition, emaciation, wasting away, starvation, famishment, tabes, tabefaction, consumption, phthisis, marasmus, cachexia, decline, prostration.

MALODOROUS, *adj.* Having a bad odor, ill-smelling, stinking, smelling, fetid, strong, strong-smelling, rotten, rancid, noisome, rank, putrid, foul, putrescent, graveolent, bad, high, spoiled, gamy, moldy, musty, fusty, tainted, mephitic, miasmal, miasmatic, miasmic, offensive, noxious, unclean, unwashed, disgusting, sickening, frowzy, nauseating.

MALPRACTICE, *n.* Improper professional action, reprehensible conduct, illegal treatment, professional negligence, wrongdoing, misdoing, misconduct, dereliction, misbehavior, malversation, evil practice, misdeed, wrong, violation, transgression, improbity, laxity, jobbery, jobbing, graft, corruption, venality, sharp practice, knavery, rascality, scoundrelism, roguery, villainy, misdoing, obliquity, delinquency, crime, tort, felony.

MALTREAT, *v.* Treat ill, mistreat, ill-treat, handle roughly, maul, manhandle, abuse, ill-use, injure cruelly, batter, buffet, pommel, bruise, contuse, scratch, molest, smite, violate, outrage, rape, deflower, attack, assault, ravish, constuprate, devirginate, defile, pollute, do violence to, debauch, hurt, harm, wound, oppress, trample upon, persecute, aggrieve, wrong, victimize, misuse, tamper with, beat, smash, damage, strike, castigate, punish, hit, torment, torture, put on the rack, martyrize, spank, thump, cuff, wham, thump, thrash, lash, cowhide, scourge, flog, horsewhip, cane, birch, switch, beat black and blue, pelt, lambaste, trounce, lace, belabor, strafe, tar and feather, drub, pervert, prostitute.

MALTREATMENT, *n.* Mistreatment, ill-usage, ill-treatment, bad treatment, abuse, outrage, pollution, prostitution, perversion, defilement, misusage, constupration, ravishment, violation, devirgination, deflowerment, debauchery, rape, molestation, oppression, enslavement, persecution, victimization, castigation, punishment, torture, torment, mauling, manhandling, rough treatment, misuse.

MALVERSATION, *n.* Corrupt behavior in office, fraudulent conduct, misconduct in office, misbehavior, malpractice, fraudulency, wrongdoing, malfeasance, peculation, embezzlement, misdemeanor, misfeasance, misprision, tort, malefaction, misdoing, misdeed, dereliction, transgression, delinquency, trespass, offense, crime, felony.

MAMMON, *n.* Wealth, riches, material goods, pelf, lucre, money, opulence, fortune, affluence, filthy lucre, well-lined purse, Pactolus, El Dorado, bonanza, Golconda.

MAMMONIST, *n.* Greedy pursuer of riches, mammonite, worldling, rich man, man of substance, millionaire, capitalist, silk-stocking, materialist, Babbitt, Philistine, Croesus, nabob, Midas, Dives.

MAMMOTH, *adj.* Huge, very large, elephantine, behemothistic, hippopotamic, gigantic, immense, colossal, vast, enormous, monstrous, mighty, amplitudinous, vasty, stupendous, hulking, whopping, spanking, thundering, whacking, thumping, unwieldy, heavy, clumsy, hulky, bulky, massive, great, big, towering, mighty, strapping, Brobdingnagian, Cyclopean, Gargantuan, titanic, mountainous, tremendous, of great size.

MAN, *n.* 1. Member of the genus *Homo,* individual at the highest level of animal development and mainly characterized by exceptional mentality, *Homo sapiens,* person, personage, living soul, soul, human being, body, one, some one, anyone, somebody, biped, primate, human.
2. Male, masculine, he, swain, chap, fellow, yeoman, gaffer, wight, beau, blade, sir, gentleman, squire, sahib. hidalgo, don. husband, married man, spouse.
3. Mister, Mr., *signor (It.), señor (Sp.), Monsieur (Fr.), M., senhor (Port.), Herr (Ger.).*
4. The human race, mankind, humanity, human beings, lords of creation, mortals, humankind.
5. Vassal, male follower, subordinate, subject, liegeman, liege, dependent, attendant, henchman, retainer, male servant, valet, train-bearer, cupbearer, page, equerry, hostler, jockey, groom, servitor, assistant, helper, manservant, orderly, aide-de-camp, butler, boots, steward, lackey, flunky, footman, waiter, boy, hireling, satellite, puppet, mercenary, bondsman, thrall, drudge, churl, employee, workman, man-of-all-work, jack-of-all-trades, handyman, factotum, right-hand man, hired hand, day laborer, hack.
6. One having many qualities or virtues, hero, man of courage, brave man, lion, paladin, warrior, soldier, man of mettle, demigod, game cock, gentleman, chevalier, man of his word, man of honor, trump, square shooter, brick.

MAN, *v.* 1. Furnish with men for defense or service, supply with hands, staff, people, garrison, station, provide, equip, arm, array, appoint, fit out, gird, outfit.
2. Fortify, strengthen, brace, buttress, reinforce, prime, forearm, stiffen, give strength to, prop, shore.

MANACLE, *n.* Handcuff, shackle for the hands, hand-fetter, bracelets *(slang),* trammel, gyve, pinion, darbies, irons, bonds, chains for the hands, wristlet.

MANACLE, *v.* 1. Handcuff, fetter, shackle, pinion, gyve, trammel, put bracelets on, enchain, immanacle, entrammel, hobble, bind hand and foot, tie one's hands, tie up, put in irons, put in chains, put into bilboes.
2. Restrain, hamper, bind, tie, confine, curb, check, put under restraint, constrain, control, keep within bounds, hold in leading strings, fasten.

MANAGE, *v.* 1. Take care of, direct, take charge of, superintend, regulate, supervise, oversee, control, order, engineer, conduct, administer, carry on, rule, dominate, influence, treat, guide, master, sway, have control, preside, boss, instruct, command, maneuver, steer, dispose, prescribe, lead, head, orientate, pilot, steer, be at the helm, take the helm, see to, look after, hold the reins, run, officiate, watch over, govern.

2. Handle, wield, manipulate, operate, run, work, make go, use, ply, brandish.
3. Contrive to get along, get on, keep one's head above water, survive, cope with, deal with, accomplish against opposition, weather the storm, work out, succeed, arrange, eke out, economize, save, husband, help oneself.

MANAGEABLE, *adj.* Controllable, governable, tamable, docile, tractable, amenable, pliant, flexible, facile, sequacious, yielding, wieldy, submissive, ductile, compliant, obedient, complaisant, conformable, gentle.

MANAGEMENT, *n.* 1. Direction, guidance, supervision, director, superintendence, surveillance, administration, regulation, conduct, charge, control, regime, regimen, government, stewardship, organization, husbandry, economy, treatment, disposal, policy, managery, agency, ministry, oversight, order, command, eye of the master, orientation, steerage, pilotage, leadership, plan, menage, housekeeping, thrift, frugality, strategy, tactics, generalship, diplomacy, manipulation, operation, transaction, dealing, negotiation.
2. Skill, address, finesse, savoir-faire, aptitude, aptness, genius for, discretion, mother wit, self-help, tact, capability, capacity, qualification, accomplishment, disposition.

MANAGER, *n.* One charged with the direction of something, director, superintendent, supervisor, overseer, administrator, executive, proctor, controller, comptroller, factor, agent, steward, *entrepreneur (Fr.),* organizer, governor, enterpriser, surveyor, inspector, master, taskmaster, pilot, guide, helmsman, adviser, cicerone, foreman, seneschal, major-domo, bailiff, housekeeper, wire-puller, power behind the throne, head, chief, boss, king pin, bigwig, coryphaeus, leader, precentor, fugleman, bellwether, press agent, producer, impresario.

MANDATE, *n.* 1. Order, command, precept, decree, edict, injunction, charge, instruction, ordinance, regulation, fiat, act, dictation, commandment, ruling, dictate, rescript, caveat, prescript, ordination, writ, decretal, bull, firman, ukase, direction, authorization, commission, warrant, authority, requisition, demand, bidding, behest, ultimatum.
2. Mandated territory, province, protectorate, colony, dependency, subject territory.

MANDATORY, *adj.* Obligatory, binding, coercive, permitting no option, imperative, preceptive, directory, requisite, required, necessary, needful, prerequisite, indispensable, instant, in demand, called for, exigent, urgent, essential, pressing, authoritative, decretive, jussive, final, decisive.

MANDIBLE, *n.* Lower jaw, jaws, mouth, chops, mazard.

MANDUCATE, *v.* Masticate, chew, eat, devour, feed, bolt, gulp, snap, swallow, dispatch, fall to, tuck in, gormandize, champ, crunch, bite, munch, nibble, gnaw, feed upon, play a good knife and fork.

MANE, *n.* Long hair growing on the back of the neck of some animals, brush, shag, fringe, flowing mane.

MAN-EATER, *n.* 1. Cannibal, anthropophagus *(pl.,* anthropophagi*),* eater of human flesh, bloodsucker, ghoul, ogre, vampire.
2. Animal that eats men, wild beast, lion, tiger, hyena.

MAN-EATING, *adj.* Cannibal, cannibalistic, anthropophagous, anthropophagistic, bloodthirsty, bloodstained, homicidal, sanguinary, murderous, sanguinolent, bloody-minded, ensanguined, gory, deadly, feral, ferine, ferocious, brutish, inhuman.

MANES, *n., pl.* Deified souls of the dead, lemures, benevolent infernal deities, lares, shades, apparitions, ghosts, blessed spirits, specters, shadows, phantoms, souls of the departed.

MANEUVER, *n.* 1. Planned and regulated movement of troops or war vessels, series of tactical exercises carried out in the field by bodies of troops, evolution, deployment, marching, figure.

2. Artful proceeding, adroit move, artful management, stratagem, tactic, artifice, ruse, plot, scheme, finesse, plan, trick, intrigue, machination, device, wile, art, chicane, artful dodge, shift, subterfuge, tour de force, juggle, *espièglerie (Fr.),* circumvention, temporization, hoax, flimflam, trickery, white lie.

MANEUVER, *v.* 1. Change the position of troops or vessels by a maneuver, perform evolutions, turn the flank of, flank, deploy, swerve, form figures.

2. Plan with art, contrive, manage with address, plot, intrigue, machinate, finesse, scheme, pull strings, pull wires, live by one's wits, surprise, gerrymander, circumvent, temporize, throw off one's guard, get the better of, outdo, play a deep game.

MANEUVERER, *n.* Strategist, tactician, wirepuller, adroit manager, intriguer, *intrigant (Fr.),* schemer, fox, sly boots, Machiavelli, trickster, politician, machinator, promoter, projector, mastermind, cunning fellow, jobber, diplomat, power behind the throne.

MANFUL, *adj.* Having manly spirit, daring, intrepid, bold, heroic, courageous, undaunted, dauntless, brave, resolute, manly, hardy, gallant, indomitable, strong, stout, vigorous, valiant, virile, masculine, mighty, plucky, self-possessed, cast-iron, game, high-spirited, mettlesome, lion-hearted, spirited, audacious, confident, self-reliant, adventurous, enterprising, chivalrous, dashing, soldierly, doughty, robust, forcible, powerful, puissant, unconquerable, invincible, able-bodied, muscular, athletic, well-built, brawny, husky, wiry, stalwart, broad-shouldered, strapping, sinewy.

MANGE, *n.* Skin disease characterized by loss of hair and scaly eruptions, psoriasis, rash, exanthema, erysipelas, eruption, breaking out.

MANGER, *n.* Box in a stable from which animals eat, feeding-trough, crib, *crèche (Fr.),* rack.

MANGLE, *v.* 1. Cut so as to disfigure, tear in cutting, hack, lacerate, mutilate, maim, slash, commit mayhem, hamstring, truncate, lancinate, detruncate, obtruncate, slit, rend, butcher, cripple, dismember, lame, hock, wound, stab, pierce, blemish, disfigure, deface, mar, spoil, destroy, warp, hurt, scathe, harm, impair, damage, injure, maul, carve, slice, hackle.

2. Iron, press with a mangle, calender, smooth, polish, glaze, crease.

MANGY, *adj.* 1. Infected with mange, scabby, itchy, erupted, broken out, exanthematous, exanthematic, erysipelatous, psoriatic.

2. Contemptible, base, mean, scurvy, low, despicable, vile, dirty, sneaking, abject, unfair, dishonorable, caitiff.

3. Squalid, shabby, foul, dirty, unclean, mucky,

unkempt, slovenly, sordid, seedy, threadbare, ragged, poor.

MANHANDLE, *v.* Handle roughly, maul, rough up, trample upon, tread upon, maltreat, abuse, molest, ill-treat, ill-use, buffet, smite, bruise, do violence to, torment, torture, pommel, thrash, drub, trounce, slap, cuff, smack, wallop, beat black and blue, beat to a jelly, sandbag.

MAN-HATER, *n.* Misanthrope, hater of mankind, misanthropist, cynic, egotist, Diogenes, Timon, hermit, recluse, solitary, anchorite, ascetic, eremite.

MANHOLE, *n.* Hole with a cover through which a man may enter a sewer or drain to make repairs, scuttle, hatch, small passage for ingress and egress, grating.

MANHOOD, *n.* 1. Maturity, majority, adulthood, man's estate, virility, full age, full bloom, flower of age, prime of life.

2. Manliness, manly qualities, fortitude, bravery, courage, resolution, manfulness, firmness, hardihood, mettle, pluck, nerve, sand, grit, backbone, spirit, energy, force, daring, indomitableness, determination, valor, heroism, strength of will, force of character.

MANIA, *n.* 1. Form of insanity characterized by great excitement, madness, lunacy, dementia, violent derangement, delirium, aberration, frenzy, alienation, distraction, raving, hallucination, delusion.

2. Great enthusiasm, vehement desire, craze, exaggerated love for, obsession, fixation, passion, monomania, fad, infatuation, fanaticism, furor, rage, estrus, rut, heat.

MANIAC, *n.* Raving lunatic, madman, insane person, bedlamite, crazy person, raver, paranoiac, manic-depressive, psychotic, schizophrenic, pyromaniac, kleptomaniac, monomaniac, megalomaniac, dipsomaniac, nut, crack, crackpot, fanatic.

MANIACAL, *adj.* Raving with madness, insane, maniac, mad, deranged, delirious, demented, unbalanced, unhinged, manic-depressive, psychotic, schizophrenic, paranoiac, incoherent, wandering, frantic, berserk, amuck, moonstruck, maddened, lunatic, non compos mentis *(Lat.),* aliéné *(Fr.),* touched, cracked, bereft of reason, daft, frenetic, frenzied, far gone, balmy *(slang),* bughouse *(slang),* nuts *(slang),* loco *(slang),* of unsound mind, out of one's mind, not right in one's upper story, not all there, off one's rocker, mad as a hatter, possessed, rabid.

MANIFEST, *adj.* Readily perceived by the eye or the understanding, obvious, evident, apparent, patent, open, plain, clear, overt, tangible, palpable, bare, visible, striking, naked, salient, conspicuous, prominent, pronounced, in the foreground, glaring, unmistakable, distinct, discernible, indubitable, avowed, ostensible, notable, undisguised, bald, literal, plain-spoken, frank, candid, unreserved, downright, conclusive, indisputable, definite, express, explicit, perceptible, self-evident, lucid, intelligible, notorious, flagrant, arrant, glaring, flaunting, in flagrante delicto *(Lat.),* shameless, bold, brazen, barefaced, transparent, unconcealed, insuppressible, unquestionable, perspicuous, diaphanous, axiomatic, proverbial.

MANIFEST, *v.* Show plainly, make manifest to the eye or the understanding, disclose, reveal, exhibit, display, expose to view, make known, bring to light, hold up to view, set forth, discover, evidence, declare, evince, express, speak out, publish, proclaim, uncover, demonstrate, unveil, undrape, bare, unroll, lay open, betray, disinter, elicit, bring out, produce, hold up, expose, show up, show forth, make visible, embody, materialize, represent, point out, indicate, prove, put beyond doubt or question, certify, divulge, attest, explain.

MANIFESTATION, *n.* 1. Demonstration, showing, exhibition, presentation, revelation, display, unfoldment, parade, show, expression, production, indication, evincement, exposition, disclosure, revealment, showdown, exposé, divulgence, divulgation, publication, divulgement, publicity, uncovering, unveiling, plain speaking, candor, frankness, *épanchement (Fr.),* openness, plainness, saliency, prominence, conspicuousness, declaration, representation, performance, staging.

2. Sign, phenomenon, testimony, apparition, materialization, séance, theophany, epiphany, token, appearance, vision, phantom.

MANIFESTO, *n.* Public statement of intentions or objectives, proclamation, declaration of a government, public protestation, manifest, decree, promulgation, publication, pronouncement, pronunciamento, encyclical, bull, circular letter, announcement, edict, broadside, poster, advertisement, placard, *affiche (Fr.),* bill, notice.

MANIFOLD, *adj.* 1. Numerous, multitudinous, many, multiplex, multifold, made up of many, multiform, myriad, innumerable, multiplied.

2. Of many kinds, multifarious, diverse, divers, sundry, miscellaneous, diversified, complex.

MANIKIN, *n.* 1. Little man, homunculus, dwarf, pygmy, Lilliputian, midget, atomy, Pigwiggen, chit, elf, urchin, Hop-o'-my-Thumb, Tom Thumb, Humpty-Dumpty, fingerling, dapperling, dandiprat, cock sparrow, mannikin, manakin.

2. Figure employed to wear clothing to exhibit to customers, mannequin, model, clotheshorse, puppet.

MANIPLE, *n.* 1. Subdivision of a Roman legion consisting of 60 or 120 men, small band, handful, company of soldiers, division.

2. Eucharistic vestment, ornamental band worn on the left arm near the wrist, stole, fanon, scarf.

MANIPULATE, *v.* 1. Handle, wield, work with the hands, operate, ply, work, adhibit, apply, employ, utilize, use, put into operation, set to work, put in action, set in motion, drive.

2. Maneuver, engineer, manage, command, control, preside, rule, influence, direct, govern, conduct, dispose, regulate, orientate, take the helm, be at the wheel, pilot, steer, guide, head, lead.

3. Pass the fingers over, finger, feel, touch, grabble, paw, thumb, twiddle, rub, massage, knead, stroke, fondle, caress, palpate, titillate, milk.

MANIPULATION, *n.* 1. Appliance, adhibition, utilization, employment, use, exercise.

2. Direction, guidance, government, management, administration, agency, order, control, charge.

3. Fingering, feeling, touch, palpation, contact, graze, brush, titillation, massage, rubbing, kneading, caress, stroke.

MANKIND, *n.* Mankind, humankind, man, the human race, human species, flesh, mortality, humanity, persons, people, society, public, world, folk, community, nation, body politic, common-

alty, the masses, proletariat, crowd, multitude, commons, populace, lords of creation.

MANLIKE, *adj.* 1. Resembling a man, anthropoid, having a manlike form, human, primatial, apelike, simian.

2. Becoming or proper to a man. (See MANLY.)

MANLINESS, *n.* 1. Strength, potency, vigor, energy, power, puissance, force, stamina, brawn, muscle, thews, sinews, physique, nerve, vitality, grit, virility, prowess.

2. Bravery, heroism, courage, firmness, intrepidity, valor, daring, spirit, gallantry, mettle, pluck, hardihood, fortitude, resolution, boldness.

MANLY, *adj.* 1. Possessing qualities proper to a man, strong, robust, vigorous, hardy, husky, hale, sturdy, muscular, sinewy, well-knit, stalwart, strapping, able-bodied, powerful, mighty, puissant, athletic, virile, masculine, male, brawny, wiry.

2. Brave, courageous, valiant, valorous, undaunted, determined, resolute, daring, stout-hearted, fearless, intrepid, bold, heroic, noble, mettlesome, gallant, chivalrous, indomitable, self-reliant, audacious, firm, lion-hearted, plucky, stanch.

MANNA, *n.* 1. Food miraculously supplied the children of Israel in the wilderness, wafers made with honey, divine food, spiritual nourishment.

2. Sustenance, sustentation, alimentation, maintenance, nourishment, aid, help, assistance, succor, lift, support.

MANNER, *n.* 1. Kind, sort, type, nature, class, classification, genre, character, sex, gender, description, color, denomination, category, grouping, caste, sept, clan, grade, rank, race, party, tribe, sect, feather, breed, strain, kidney, stamp, brand, family, order, genus, species, variety, subspecies, phylum, cast, make, form, mold, turn.

2. Mode, style, fashion, method, way, form, wise, mien, guise, aspect, look, appearance, character.

3. Conduct, behavior, customary way of doing, practice, habit, deportment, comportment, address, carriage, demeanor, bearing, presence, *prestance (Fr.),* line of action, air, way of addressing and treating others, distinctive social attitude toward others, tone, ways of behaving with reference to polite standards, courtesy, civility, politeness, etiquette.

MANNERISM, *n.* Mannered style, habitual peculiarity of manner, characteristic style, distinctive trait, marked adherence to an unusual manner, air of distinction, affectation, idiosyncrasy, artificiality, affectedness, insincerity, pretension, pretense, side, frill, modishness, airs, dog *(slang),* formality, stiffness.

MANNERLY, *adj.* Showing good manners, well-mannered, well-behaved, well-bred, respectful, ceremonious, civil, courteous, courtly, refined, urbane, suave, complaisant, decorous, gentlemanly, genteel, polite, polished, poised, thoroughbred, *distingué (Fr.),* obliging, kindly, gentle, cultivated, chivalrous, gallant, gracious, cordial, amiable, affable, diplomatic, tactful, bland, fair-spoken, mild, smooth.

MANNERS, *n., pl.* 1. Habits, morals, mores, morality, decalogue, ethics, virtuousness, virtue, integrity.

2. Breeding, politeness, savoir-faire, decorum, gentility, *bienséance (Fr.),* propriety, conventionality, convention, Mrs. Grundy, punctilio, formality, etiquette, form, courtesy, urbanity, breeding,

refinement, polish, culture, amenity, civility, chivalry, gallantry, courtliness, pink of courtesy, respect, complaisance, affability, behavior, bearing, deportment, comportment, air, demeanor, carriage.

MANNISH, *adj.* 1. Masculine, virile, male, manlike, manly, bold, vigorous, forceful.

2. (*Of women*) Unfeminine, amazonian, hoidenish, unwomanly, rough, coarse.

MAN - OF - ALL - WORK, *n.* Jack-of-all-trades, handy man, factotum, do-all, caretaker, employee, male servant, seneschal, major-domo, general servant, shaft horse, laboring oar, beast of burden, fag, drudge, working bee.

MAN OF MEANS, *n.* Plutocrat, rich man, millionaire, financier, capitalist, man of wealth, man of substance, moneyed gentleman, made man, independent gentleman, stockholder, *rentier (Fr.),* fundholder, annuitant, coupon-clipper, nouveau riche, silk-stocking, aristocrat, banker, profiteer, moneybags, multimillionaire, billionaire, nabob, Midas, Croesus, Dives, Plutus, Fortunatus, mushroom, parvenu, industrialist, magnate, tycoon, baron of business, bigwig, great gun, squire, swell, somebody, grandee, mogul, his nibs, captain of industry.

MAN-OF-WAR, *n.* Warship, armed vessel, dreadnought, battleship, cruiser, capital ship, destroyer, torpedo boat, submersible, submarine, U-boat, gunboat, corvette, mine sweeper, mine layer, aircraft carrier, flattop, troopship, transport, ironclad, line-of-battle ship, war vessel, monitor, submarine chaser, flagship, tender.

MANOR, *n.* Territorial unit originally of the nature of a feudal lordship, landed estate, lord's demesne, mansion of a lord with the lands pertaining to it, countryseat, rural domain.

MANOR HOUSE, *n.* House of the lord of a manor, hall, mansion, manor-seat, mansion-house, chateau, lodge, castle, court, capital messuage, palace, country seat, villa, place, hermitage.

MAN POWER, *n.* 1. Power supplied by the physical exertions of a man, unit equal to the rate at which a man can do mechanical work (1/10 horsepower), normal rate at which a man does mechanical work, unit of power assumed to be the rate at which a man can work.

2. Power, collectively, of all the men of a community, power in terms of men available as required, resources, reserves.

3. Strength of a nation expressed in terms of the number of men available for military service, conscriptive might, men at arms.

MANSE, *n.* House and land occupied by a minister, parsonage, clergyman's residence, rectory, parsonage-house, deanery, vicarage.

MANSERVANT, *n.* Male servant, flunky, lackey, footman, butler, valet, man Friday, *valet de chambre (Fr.),* man, boots, orderly, waiter, steward, groom, servitor, yeoman, attendant, page, squire, trainbearer, cupbearer, jockey, equerry, hostler, employee, caddie, buttons.

MANSION, *n.* Imposing dwelling, stately residence, impressive house, villa, lodge, place, hermitage, castle, chateau, palace, court, hall, *rus in urbe (Lat.),* folly, pavilion, tower, rotunda, country seat, messuage, domicile, abode, habitation, manor house, manor-seat, manor.

MANSLAUGHTER, *n.* Killing of a human being by a human being, homicide, murder, assassination, occision, trucidation, spilling of blood, bloodshed, carnage, butchery, massacre, shooting, garroting, choking, strangulation, stabbing, running over, hit-and-run, thuggism, suffocation, killing of a human being unlawfully but without malice aforethought *(Law).*

MANSLAYER, *n.* One who kills a human being, homicide, murderer, man-killer, slayer, assassin, slaughterer, killer, Cain, butcher, garroter, cutthroat, thug, gunman, gangster, executioner, parricide, regicide, infanticide, aborticide, fratricide, sororicide, patricide, matricide, tyrannicide, uxoricide, Juggernaut, Moloch.

MANTILLA, *n.* 1. Lace head scarf arranged over a high comb and falling over the back, draped silk head covering, hood, back veil.

2. Light cloak, small mantle, light cape. (See MANTLE.)

MANTLE, *n.* 1. Loose sleeveless cloak, cape, shawl, covering, pelisse, wrap, pallium, toga, tunic, chiton, robe, burnoose, cardinal, cope, pelerine, dolman, sari, chuddar, chasuble, kirtle, drape, paletot, gown, frock, sagum, mantua, mantlet, veil, yashmak, chlamys, negligee, peignoir, wrapper, kimono, dishabille, dressing gown.

2. Something that covers, envelope, covering, cover, pall, cloud, screen, shade, film, curtain, mask, disguise.

MANTLE, *v.* 1. Cover, cloak, invest, envelop, enwrap, muffle up, sheathe, swathe, shroud, circumvest, conceal, disguise, obscure, shade, veil.

2. Be suffused with red, flush, blush, color up, redden, incarnadine, rubricate, warm, glow, change color, crimson.

3. Become covered with a coating, foam, effervesce, sparkle, bubble, cream, froth, spume, gurgle, ferment, fizzle.

MANTOLOGY, *n.* Prophecy, vaticination, soothsaying, forecasting, prediction, premonstration, prognostication, augury, auguration, foreboding, hariolation, omination, horoscopy, divination, fortunetelling, necromancy, crystal gazing, astromancy, astrology, presage, premonition, sorcery, oracle, sortilege.

MANUAL, *n.* Small book giving information or instructions, handbook, enchiridion, vade mecum, reference book, guidebook, gazetteer, textbook, abecedary, primer, rudiments, grammar, treatise, livret, tract, brochure, codex, pamphlet, monograph.

MANUFACTURE, *v.* 1. Make by hand, produce by machinery, work up material into form for use, fabricate, produce, build, make by mechanical industry, construct, turn out by industrial process, build, form, put together, assemble, contrive, frame, weave, carve, chisel, run up, organize, compose, create, develop.

2. Produce artificially, invent fictitiously, romance, tell tall stories, lie, make up.

MANUFACTURE, *n.* Large-scale making of goods or wares by manual labor or by machinery, fabrication, production, assembling, assembly line, construction, workmanship, handiwork, industry, handicraft, creation, formation, putting together, craftsmanship, industry.

MANUMISSION, *n.* Freedom from bondage, liberation, emancipation, deliverance, enfranchisement, release, disenthrallment, enlargement, extrication, redemption, discharge.

MANUMIT, *v.* Set free, free from slavery, release from servitude, liberate, enfranchise, emancipate, unfetter, unmanacle, unshackle, extricate, disengage, disenthral, redeem, rescue, set at liberty, enlarge, affranchise, dismiss, discharge, let go, deliver, loose, unharness, disentangle, unchain.

MANURE, *v.* Treat soil with fertilizing matter, apply manure to, fertilize, enrich, dress the ground, cultivate.

MANURE, *n.* Natural *or* artificial substance for fertilizing the soil, fertilizer, fertilizing mixture, dressing, compost, guano, night soil, muck, animal residue, ordure, tankage, waste products, dung, stable refuse, animal droppings, marl, lime, bone dust, phosphate, chemicals, coprolite, excrement.

MANUSCRIPT, *n.* Author's copy of his work which is used as the basis for typesetting, typescript, copy, written document, original, MS. *(abbr., pl.* MSS.), script, writing, deed, holograph, instrument, *litterae scriptae (Lat.),* codex, opisthograph, codex rescriptus, palimpsest.

MANY, *adj.* Constituting a very large number, numerous, multitudinous, innumerable, myriad, multifold, manifold, multifarious, multiplied, not few, countless, multiple, various, divers, sundry, frequent, galore, endless, several, profuse, crowded, prevalent, rife, thick, abundant, alive with, teeming, studded.

MANY, *n.* Considerable number, a liberal quantity of, myriad, lot, lots, scores, numbers, array, aggregation, host, assemblage, legion, army, cloud, galaxy, heap, swarm, flock, shoal, drove, bevy, school, covey, brood, hive, multiplicity, profusion, amassment, accumulation, stock, store, congestion, lump, pile, mass, litter, snowdrift, sands, sheaf, stack, shower, volley, assortment, bunch, pack, batch, packet, series, cluster, set, group, medley, miscellany, congregation, concentration, muster, mobilization, levy, collection, concourse, conflux, gathering, convergence, abundance, deal, sight *(colloq.),* shipload, infinity, immensity, multitude, crowd, numerous company, hoi polloi, press, throng, mob.

MANY-COLORED, *adj.* Multicolored, polychromatic, polychrome, variegated, parti-colored, showy, many-hued, versicolor, tricolor, rainbowlike, kaleidoscopic, opalescent, iridescent, nacreous, prismatic, shot, *chatoyant (Fr.),* gorge de pigeon (Fr.), irisated, pearly, piebald, pied, motley, skewbald, dappled, marbled, plaid, tesselated, mosaic, chequered *(Brit.),* speckled, spotted, flecked, striated, veined, brindled.

MANY-SIDED, *adj.* 1. Having many sides, multilateral, polyhedral, polyhedrous, polyhedrical, bilateral, dihedral, trilateral, triquetrous, quadrilateral, tetrahedral.

2. Having many capabilities, versatile, adaptable, protean, varied, ready, plastic, malleable, talented, gifted, dexterous, deft, capable, able.

MAP, *n.* Representation on a flat surface of all or part of the earth's surface or of the heavens, graph, chart, plot, diagram, plan, projection, elevation, outline, view, atlas, gazetteer, itinerary, cartography.

MAP, *v.* 1. Represent in a map, picture, delineate, draw, outline, depict, trace.

2. Map out, sketch, project, plan, devise, scheme, design, contrive, frame, lay out, cut out, chalk out, lay down a plan, mark out a course, preëstablish, predetermine, prepare, plot, hatch a plot, organize, arrange, systematize.

MAR, *v.* 1. Damage, injure, impair. hurt, harm, spoil, ruin, scathe, waste, destroy, sully, stain, corrupt, contaminate, infect, taint, canker. pollute, blight, degrade, defile, vitiate, alloy, tamper with, subvert, pervert, adulterate, overshadow, sadden, detract from, reduce, decrease, diminish.

2. Disfigure, deface, maim, mutilate, mangle, deform, hamstring, nick, lacerate, blemish, warp, hock, cripple, lame, stab, wound, pierce, hack, truncate, foul, scar.

MARASMUS, *n.* Gradual loss of flesh and strength from malnutrition, emaciation, cachexia, consumption, wasting away, phthisis, tuberculosis, T.B., decline, malnutrition, atrophy, collapse, deterioration, tabefaction, attenuation.

MARAUD, *v.* Make a raid for booty, rove in quest of plunder, ravage, overrun, prey, depredate, make depredations, pillage, sack, loot, despoil, pirate, plunder, rifle, ransack, spoliate, gut, strip, forage, rustle, poach, lift cattle, snatch and run, seize, spirit away, carry off, thieve, pilfer, steal, purloin, lift, filch, bag, appropriate, hijack, hold up, stick up, burgle.

MARAUD, *n.* Spoliation, depredation, sack, brigandage, rapine, pillage, plunder, ravage, holdup, stickup, piracy, foray, raid, privateering, hijacking, plundering expedition, *razzia (It.).* buccaneering, cattle rustling, cattle stealing, poaching, filibustering, housebreaking, burglary, thieving, stealing.

MARAUDER, *n.* Plunderer, depredator, pillager, freebooter, spoiler, ravager, filibuster, highwayman, brigand, bandit, desperado, outlaw, picaroon, pirate, thief, robber, harpy, crook, stickup man, holdup man, privateer, hijacker, buccaneer, bushranger, thug, nighthawk, footpad, strong-arm man, intruder, burglar, housebreaker, sneak thief, cracksman, yegg, rustler, poacher, cattle thief, rifler, filcher, ugly customer.

MARAUDING, *adj.* Plundering, predatory, predacious, ravaging, pillaging, rapacious, living by prey, raptorial, pilfering, thieving, piratical, freebooting, hijacking, larcenous.

MARBLE, *n.* 1. Crystalline limestone capable of taking a polish and much used in architecture and sculpture, metamorphosed limestone, rock composed mainly of calcium carbonate.

2. Carrara marble, Florentine marble, Parian marble, Pentelic marble, Hymettian marble, Egyptian marble, Palombino marble, bird's-eye marble, peacock marble, forest marble.

3. Work of art carved in marble, sculptured piece, sculpture, statue, bust, bas relief, tombstone, epitaph, monument, statuary.

4. Hardness, lapidification, lapidescence, crystallization, cornification, vitrification, rigidity, smoothness, coldness.

5. Insensibility, inflexibility, heart of stone, callousness, deadness, stock and stone, unimpressibility, insusceptibility, frigidity.

MARBLE-HEARTED, *adj.* Hard-hearted, cold-hearted, stony-hearted, flint-hearted, hard of heart, cruel, ruthless, merciless, remorseless, unmerciful, unrelenting, relentless, savage, fell, barbarous, unsusceptible, unfeeling, harsh, unfriendly, unkind, ungracious, disobliging.

MARCH, *v.* 1. Walk with regular and measured tread, advance in step in an organized body, move forward in a deliberate manner, file, parade, goosestep, defile, tread, step, pace, trudge, stump, tramp, traipse, strut, stride, shuffle on, jog on, patrol, file off, jaunt, ramble, plod, shuffle, shamble, amble, saunter, stroll, tread, trek, promenade, perambulate, peregrinate.

2. Proceed, advance, forge ahead, make progress, make headway, continue onward, go on.

MARCH, *n.* 1. Military movement, deploy, file, countermarch, transit of soldiers, military parade, procession, cavalcade, caravan, column, cortege, train, retinue.

2. Deliberate walk, pace, tread, gait, goose step, trudge, tramp, strut, stride, shuffle, patrol, jaunt, ramble, stroll, trek, promenade, perambulation, peregrination, constitutional, course, hike, saunter, turn, jog trot, stalk, ambulation, circuit, tour, expedition, trip, excursion, journey, pererration, migration, itinerary, route.

3. Forward movement, advance, progression, progress, advancement, progressive development, progressiveness, headway, ongoing, rise, improvement.

4. Piece of music with a rhythm suited to accompany marching, military tune, martial music, funeral march, dead march, dirge.

5. Region, tract of land along a border of a country, frontier, border, pale, corridor, district, beat, circuit, domain, precinct, arena, enclosure, enclave, boundary, confine, limit, close.

MARE, *n.* Female horse, filly, foal, jennet, jenny, roe, doe.

MARE'S-NEST, *n.* Something purporting to be an unusual discovery, hoax, delusion, myth, moonshine, fiction, invention, fabrication, canard, cock-and-bull story, traveler's tale, claptrap, fairy tale, absurdity, twaddle, practical joke, monkeyshine.

MARGIN, *n.* Edge, border, brink, rim, limit, verge, skirt, brim, confine, curb, brow, frame, ledge, side, flange, lip, mouth, featheredge, hem, welt, strand, beach, coast, shore, seashore, bank, waterside, extremity, boundary, fringe.

MARINE, *adj.* 1. Pertaining to the sea, pelagian, pelagic, thalassic, oceanic, salt-water, aquatic, sea.

2. Pertaining to navigation, naval, maritime, nautical, seagoing, seafaring, seaworthy, oceangoing.

MARINE, *n.* 1. Soldier of a ship of war, seasoldier, naval troop serving both on shipboard and on land, leatherneck *(slang)*, man-of-war's man, bluejacket, devil dog, jolly *(British)*.

2. Seagoing vessels collectively, shipping in general, navy, fleet, squadron, flotilla, armada.

3. Picture with a marine subject, marine painting, seascape, seapiece, coastal scene.

MARINER, *n.* One who assists in the navigation of a ship, sailor, seafaring man, seafarer, seaman, ablebodied seaman, tar, salt, sea dog, *matelot (Fr.), Matrose (Ger.), marinaio (It.), marinero (Sp.),* shellback, bluejacket, Jack, limy, gob, middy, midshipman, hand, skipper, navigator, mate, boatswain, coxswain, helmsman, pilot.

MARIONETTE, *n.* Puppet moved by the strings or the hands, manikin, *fantoccini (It.),* lay figure, figurine, doll, model, Punch and Judy, string figure.

MARITAL, *adj.* Pertaining to marriage, matrimonial, conjugal, connubial, husbandly, wedded, hymeneal, nuptial, spousal, bridal.

MARITIME, *adj.* 1. Connected with the sea in relation to navigation, naval, nautical, marine, seafaring, seagoing, coasting, navigable, natatory, aquatic, afloat, seaworthy, oceanic, thalassic, pelagian, pelagic, hydrographic, Neptunian.

2. Bordering on the sea, littoral, near the sea.

MARK, *n.* 1. Measure, degree, extent, step, grade, gradation, stage, height, pitch, scale, rate, ratio, point, amount, standard, plane.

2. Impress, line, impression, streak, score, stroke, scratch, bruise, cut, dent, scar, cicatrix, stain, dot, tick, notch, blaze, hachure, nick.

3. Token, indication, symbol, proof, evidence, sign, badge, device, figure, emblem, note, signum, type, cipher, hallmark, countermark, trademark, signet, monogram, signature, seal, cross, fingerprint, caste mark, brand, indorsement, autograph, frank, ticket, label, stamp.

4. Track, trace, vestige, trail, footprint, step, spoor, scent, footmark, footstep.

5. Earmark, trait, characteristic, feature, quality, diagnostic, property, peculiarity, cast, lineament.

6. Object aimed at, target, bull's-eye, goal, objective, desideratum, end striven for, butt, aim, intent, point, destination.

7. Note, notability, eminence, reputation, distinction, consequence, preëminence, importance, eminent position, prominence, repute, name, éclat, renown, public esteem, report, fame, honor, popularity, glory, prestige, regard, credit, respect, account, rank, celebrity, standing, exaltation.

MARK, *v.* 1. Put a mark upon, distinguish by a mark, impress, stamp, imprint, earmark, seal, autograph, sign, countersign, indorse, blaze, nick, notch, scratch, cut, score, bruise, stain, streak, scar, dent, dot, spot, underline, label, docket, ticket, brand, blemish, deface, crease.

2. Designate, denote, betoken, indicate, signify, imply, connote, evidence, disclose, manifest, display, reveal, evince, register, exhibit, show, specify, read, symbolize, typify, represent, prefigure, stand for, note.

3. Characterize, destine, point out, single out, stigmatize, distinguish, differentiate.

4. Notice, give attention to, remark, regard, observe, note, take notice of, keep an eye on, witness, watch, mind, heed, pay heed to, perceive, see, be aware of, contemplate.

MARKED, *adj.* Strikingly noticeable, prominent, conspicuous, unique, exceptional, singular, extraordinary, uncommon, peculiar, special, particular, especial, specific, definite, certain, pointed, salient, intense, distinguishable, to be recognized immediately, individual, decided, typical, characteristic, representative.

MARKER, *n.* Something used as a mark or indication, pointer, sign, symbol, indicator, token, signal, guidepost, hand, vane, weathercock, post, beacon, Pharos, lighthouse, buoy, cairn, tombstone, signpost, gravestone, recorder, milestone, landmark, polestar, lodestar, guide, cynosure, signboard.

MARKET, *n.* 1. Marketplace, mart, place of traffic, fair, emporium, exchange, market house, bazaar, entrepot, store for the sale of commodities, grocery, grocer's shop, staple, exposition, rialto, curb market, the street, stock exchange, bourse, financial center.

2. Current price, value, worth, cost, valuation, charge, rate, appraisement.

MARKET, *v.* Bring to market, hawk, peddle, vend, sell, retail, dispense, sell off, turn into money, dispose of, offer for sale, put up for sale, traffic in.

MARKETABLE, *adj.* Readily salable, merchantable, vendible, having a ready sale, in demand, interchangeable, staple, for sale, in the market, retail, wholesale.

MARKSMAN, *n.* One skilled in shooting at a target, one who shoots well, sharpshooter, rifleman, crack shot, dead shot, good shot, William Tell, Annie Oakley.

MAROON, *v.* Leave on a desolate island by way of punishment, put ashore, abandon, cast off, cast behind, isolate, seclude, turn one's back upon, outlaw, banish, proscribe, ostracize, cut off from, excommunicate, exclude, exile, expatriate, blackball, repel, relegate.

MARRIAGE, *n.* 1. Legal union of a man and a woman, legal relation of spouses to each other, conjugal union, wedlock, matrimony, nuptial knot, nuptial tie, *vinculum matrimonii (Lat.),* match, formal declaration by which a couple join in wedlock.

2. Marriage ceremony, wedding, nuptial rites, nuptials, spousals, espousals, hymeneals, bridal, hymen, leading to the altar, tying the knot, nuptial benediction, confarreation, wedding bells, honeymoon, *lune de miel (Fr.),* marriage song, epithalamium, nuptial ode, hymeneal, wedding song.

3. Intermarriage, miscegenation, remarriage, morganatic marriage, common-law marriage, lefthanded marriage, shotgun marriage, marriage of convenience, *mariage de convenance (Fr.),* trial marriage, companionate marriage, levirate *(ancient Jewish),* hierogamy, lobolo *(by purchase, Africa),* exogamy *(outside the clan),* endogamy *(inside the clan),* polygyny *(plurality of wives),* Mormonism, polyandry *(plurality of husbands),* monogamy, monandry, monogyny, bigamy, deuterogamy, digamy, second marriage, trigamy, polygamy.

MARRIAGEABLE, *adj.* Old enough for marriage, ripe for marriage, mature, marriable, nubile, fullblown, full-grown, in full bloom, manly, virile, adult, womanly.

MARRIED, *adj.* 1. Wedded, spliced, one bone and one flesh, united in wedlock, mated, yoked.

2. Matrimonial, connubial, conjugal, spousal, nuptial, bridal, hymeneal.

MARROW, *n.* 1. Soft fatty vascular tissue in the interior cavities of bones, medulla.

2. Essential part, essence, quintessence, pith, best part, substance, core, nucleus, kernel.

MARRY, *v.* 1. Join in marriage, unite in holy wedlock, tie the knot, splice, make one.

2. Take in marriage, wed, wive, espouse, lead to the altar, take for better or for worse, bèstow one's hand upon, take for husband or for wife, slip the ring around the finger of, take to oneself a spouse.

3. Unite intimately, make one, couple, match, pair, join together, mate, yoke, tie together.

MARRY, *interj.* Exclamation of surprise, indeed, in truth, i'faith, I must say, forsooth, egad, upon my word, upon oath, let me tell you, joking apart, I'd have you to know, give me leave to say, be assured, so help me God, you may be sure, why, by my troth, I'll venture to say, truly, of a truth, in fact, I'll warrant, in all conscience.

MARSH, *n.* Tract of low wet land, swamp, bog, slough, morass, mire, quagmire, fen, marsh-land, peat bog, slush, mud, quag, lagoon, wash.

MARSHAL, *n.* 1. Military officer of high rank, commander in chief, chief officer of arms, field marshal, *maréchal (Fr.),* generalissimo.

2. Herald, harbinger, pursuivant, flag bearer, apparitor, trumpeter, crier, bellman.

3. Person charged with the arrangement of ceremonies, master of ceremonies, regulator, director, manager, supervisor, intendant, monitor, moderator, corypheus, precentor, functionary.

MARSHAL, *v.* 1. Arrange in due or proper order, set in order, draw up, gather, rank, range, array, place, put in order, muster, dispose in order, group, align, line up.

2. Usher, herald, prepare the way, lead, escort, guide, conduct, introduce, forerun, precede.

MARSHY, *adj.* Soft and wet, swampy, morassy, fenny, paludal, palustral, palustrine, paludine, paludous, quaggy, fennish, boggy, poachy, miry, muddy, spongy, squashy, sloughy.

MART, *n.* Trading center, market, bazaar, entrepôt, emporium, commercial resort, place of traffic, rialto, market place, exposition, fair, curb market, exchange, stock exchange, bourse, curb.

MARTIAL, *adj.* 1. Under arms, in arms, armed, sword in hand, armed to the teeth, in full panoply, panoplied, in battle array, embattled, armorbearing, bristling, armigerous.

2. Disposed to war, warlike, belligerent, bellicose, pugnacious, combative, hostile, brave, courageous, soldierly, military-minded, militant, chivalrous, contentious.

3. *(Of music)* Stirring, rhythmic, measured, blaring, brassy, drum-beating.

MARTINET, *n.* Severe disciplinarian, rigid formalist, strict precisian, stickler, hard master, tyrant, despot, bashaw, drill-sergeant, taskmaster, oppressor, drillmaster.

MARTYR, *v.* 1. Put to death as a martyr, sacrifice because of faith, throw to the ·lions, put to a violent death, put to the rack, stretch on the wheel, nail to the cross, crucify, burn at the stake, immolate, victimize, impale.

2. Persecute, torture, torment, agonize, rack, excruciate, afflict, scourge, flagellate.

MARTYRDOM, *n.* 1. Crucifixion, impalement, burning at the stake, immolation, the rack, victimization, gladiatorial combat, judicial murder, massacre, *noyade (Fr.),* pogrom, auto-da-fé, suttee.

2. Extreme suffering, agony, anguish, throe, torment, torture, cup of misery, bitter cup, crown of thorns, affliction, ordeal.

MARVEL, *n.* 1. Wonderful thing, miracle, wonder, portent, prodigy, phenomenon, rarity, *rara avis (Lat.),* curiosity, curio, oddity, eye opener, spectacle, flash in the pan, nine days' wonder, freak, monstrosity, sport *(Biol.), lusus naturae (Lat.),* genius.

2. Feeling of wonder, astonishment, amazement, amazedness, wonderment, wonder, surprise, admiration, fascination, stupor, awe, stupefaction, bolt out of the blue.

MARVEL, *v.* Wonder at, be curious about, feel surprise, be astonished, be surprised, be amazed, be taken aback, regard as strange, stare, start, hold one's breath, gape, stand aghast, be staggered, be flabbergasted, be fascinated, be awed.

MARVELOUS, *adj.* Such as to excite wonder, most extraordinary, amazing, astonishing, surprising, surpassing belief, stupendous, miraculous, prodigious, wonderful, wondrous, wonder-working, thaumaturgic, mirifical, monstrous, mysterious, striking, most strange, remarkable, signal, singular, unusual, unwonted, unprecedented, unexpected, incredible, inconceivable, improbable, preternatural, supernatural, portentous, fabulous, phenomenal, ineffable, inexpressible, indescribable, unspeakable, overwhelming, thrilling, astounding, *foudroyant (Fr.).*

MARVELOUSLY, *adv.* Wonderfully, wondrously, strange to relate, *mirabile dictu (Lat.), mirabile visu (Lat.),* to one's great surprise, astonishingly, exceedingly, unexpectedly, like a bolt from the blue, strangely. ·

MASCOT, *n.* Being or thing supposed to bring good luck, talisman, amulet, phylactery, periapt, philter, merrythought, wishbone, fetish, scarab, swastika.

MASCULINE, *adj.* 1. Of the male sex, male.

2. Having manlike qualities, strong, powerful, robust, vigorous, muscular, husky, sturdy, hardy, wiry, brawny, stalwart, sinewy, strapping, lusty, athletic, puissant, potent, mighty, virile, manly, forceful, energetic, resolute, brave, courageous, manful, daring, intrepid, stout-hearted, bold, heroic, fearless.

3. Unwomanly, unfeminine, mannish, coarse, forward, hairy, hirsute, amazonian, aggressive.

MASCULINITY, *n.* Manliness, strength, power, force, vigor, stamina, sinew, muscle, muscularity, lustihood, physique, nerve, vitality, virility, athleticism, brawn, grit, puissance, potency, energy, drive, aggressiveness.

MASH, *v.* 1. Reduce to a soft pulpy mass, pulp, pulpify, squash, beat up, churn, knead, massage, crush, bruise, beat, mix, compound.

2. Flirt with, make advances, ogle, annoy unescorted women, make overtures to, leer at, set one's cap at, *faire l'aimable (Fr.),* pay one's court to, make a date with, feast one's eyes on, give a wolf-whistle, look sweet upon, philander, *faire les yeux doux (Fr.),* cast sheep's eyes upon.

MASH, *n.* 1. Soft pulpy mass, dough, pudding, clay, wax, squash, slush, ooze, pulp, paste, sponge, pap, jam, mush, grume.

2. Mess of boiled grain or meal fed warm to livestock.

MASK, *n.* 1. Cover for the face, false face, visor worn for disguise, face guard, piece of cloth or silk to cover the face, vizard, mascaron, grotesque face, maskoid, *mascherone (It.).*

2. Fancy-dress ball, masquerade, *bal masqué,* mummery, revel, carnival, Mardi gras, merry-making, *fête galante (Fr.), bal paré (Fr.), bal costumé (Fr.), ballo in maschera (It.),* harlequinade.

3. Person wearing a mask, domino, masker, masquerader, mime, mummer, guiser, incognito.

4. Likeness of a face molded in plaster after death, death mask.

5. Disguise, cover, camouflage, cloak, screen, veil, blind, curtain, shade, blinker, shroud.

6. Subterfuge, feint, guise, trick, pretense, shift, evasion, ruse, pretext, plea, expedient, excuse, artifice, shuffle, sophistry, quirk, equivocation, quibble, chicane.

MASK, *v.* 1. Cover with a mask, put a mask on, masquerade.

2. Hide, cover, conceal, camouflage, screen, veil, cloak, disguise, shroud, curtain, secrete, suppress, dissemble, keep from, keep secret, keep to oneself, withhold, blindfold, blind, hoodwink.

MASON, *n.* Builder in stone or brick, stonemason, brickmason, bricklayer, stonecutter, cowan *(Scot.).*

MASONRY, *n.* That which is built of regularly

arranged stones or bricks, stonework, rubble, rubblework, brickwork.

MASQUERADE, *n.* 1. Assembly of persons wearing fancy-dress and masks, masked ball, *bal masqué, bal paré (Fr.), bal costumé (Fr.),* mask, revel, mummery, mime, *fête galante (Fr.), ballo in màschera (It.),* harlequinade, carnival, Mardi gras.

2. Disguise, cover, veil, mask, camouflage, screen, cloak, blind, shade, curtain, blinker.

3. Subterfuge, guise, feint, pretense, shift, trick, ruse, pretext, expedient, plea, excuse, artifice.

MASQUERADER, *n.* One who takes part in a masquerade, masker, domino, mime, mummer, mask, guiser, guisard, person in disguise, incognito.

MASS, *n.* 1. Body of coherent matter of considerable size, lump, clot, cake, concretion, block, nugget, bullion, coagulum, hunk, curd, grume.

2. Heap, pile, accumulation, conglomeration, collection, aggregation, assemblage, congeries, combination, amassment, cumulation, stock, congestion, pyramid, litter, drift, snowdrift, cluster, group, set, nest, lot, batch, pack, assortment, parcel, bunch, bundle, bale, tuft, shock, tussock, clump, stack, sheaf, array, galaxy, shoal, school, swarm, flock, gaggle, drove, herd, bevy, muster, concentration, concourse, convergence, conflux, gathering, mobilization, congregation, medley, miscellany, throng, crowd, rush, flood, deluge, horde, troupe, knot, corps, band, party, multitude, host, body, crush, press, covey.

3. Amount, quantity, portion, quantum, share, allotment, quota, dole, proportion, measure, spoonful, mouthful, dose, handful, armful.

4. Bigness, bulk, dimension, magnitude, size, expanse, measurement, weight, ponderosity, density, fullness, largeness, area, extent, amplitude, greatness, content, capacity, cordage, tonnage, plumpness, embonpoint, obesity, corpulence, stoutness, fatness, pinguitude, polysarcia *(Med.),* immensity, massiveness, sizableness, bulkiness, hugeness.

5. Main body, greater part of anything, majority, almost all, lion's share, Benjamin's mess, great number.

6. Whole, sum total, aggregate, totality, all, everything, gross amount.

7. Eucharist, Eucharistic rite, Holy Communion, celebration of the Lord's Supper, Communion service in the Roman Catholic Church, the holy sacrament, celebration of the sacrament, consecration of the elements, offering of bread and wine.

MASSACRE, *v.* Kill human beings indiscriminately, decimate, butcher in a general slaughter, slay a great number of human beings, murder by mass, perpetrate genocide, slaughter at random, mow down, wallow in an orgy of bloodshed, put large groups to death, wade knee-deep in blood, pour out blood like water, give no quarter, run amuck, go berserk.

MASSACRE, *n.* Unnecessary and indiscriminate killing of a number of human beings, general slaughter, mass murder, genocide, decimation, butchery, carnage, pogrom, fusillade, *noyade (Fr.),* bloodletting, effusion of blood, shambles, slaughterhouse, abattoir.

MASSAGE, *v.* Make supple, knead, rub, stroke, finger, palpate, shampoo, fricate, chafe, pass the fingers over, touch lightly, twiddle, manipulate, handle, palm.

MASSAGE, *n.* Rubbing, stroking, kneading, shampoo, frication, manipulation, anatripsis *(Med.)*, friction, attrition, palpation, handling.

MASSES, *n., pl.* The common people, commons, the humbler classes, working classes, lower social orders, commonalty, proletariat, rabble, vulgus, the many, hoi polloi, the multitude, riffraff, rabble, common herd, humbler orders, rank and file, the crowd, the men in the street, the million, king mob, great unwashed, rout, chaff, *canaille (Fr.)*, horde, *hoc genus omne (Lat.)*, *fruges consumere nati (Lat.)*, dregs of society, *faex populi (Lat.)*, *profanum vulgus (Lat.)*, tagrag and bobtail, Tom, Dick and Harry.

MASSIVE, *adj.* Huge, immense, great, imposing, solid, substantial, gigantic, Brobdingnagian, cyclopean, elephantine, ponderous, heavy, bulky, weighty, beamy, cumbrous, cumbersome, enormous, titanic, gigantean, vast, mighty, monstrous, stupendous, megatherine, mammoth, colossal, giant, Gargantuan, unwieldy, hulking, hippopotamic, lubberly, lumpish, obese, corpulent, fat, portly, fleshy, brawny, burly, stout, voluminous, amplitudinous, towering, magnificent, spacious, capacious, large, big, thickset, dense, extensive, solid, burdensome, strapping, bouncing, lusty, full, spanking, whopping, whacking, thundering, thumping.

MAST, *n.* Tall pole rising vertically from the deck of a ship, yard-support, spar, mizzen, topmast, mainmast, flagstaff, topgallant mast.

MASTER, *n.* 1. Director, governor, ruler, overseer, superintendent, supervisor, boss, manager, controller, superior, authority, big shot, leader, kingpin, margrave, dictator, paterfamilias, patriarch, senior, head, chieftain, captain, commander, lord, commandant, chief, sirdar, sahib *(India)*, sachem, emir, sheik, aga, sovereign, potentate, liege lord, overlord, monarch, suzerain, emperor, imperator, majesty, king, protector, despot, autocrat, tyrant, Caesar, czar, kaiser, caliph, sultan, shah, imaum, khan, mikado, mogul, doge, rajah, maharajah, viceroy, regent, mandarin, satrap, tetrarch, bey, khedive, pasha, presiding officer, skipper, prefect, mayor, archon, magistrate, seneschal, generalissimo, commander-in-chief, corregidor, provost, chancellor, constable, warden, commodore, admiral, marshal.

2. Victor, conqueror, subjugator, defeater, subduer, winner, vanquisher, champion, cock-of-the-walk.

3. Proprietor, owner, possessor, holder, *padrone (It.)*, employer, landowner, landholder, landlord, patroon.

4. Instructor, teacher, pedagogue, preceptor, tutor, schoolmaster, mentor, don, magister, guru *(India)*, dominie *(Scot.)*, maestro *(It.)*, principal, educator, trainer, corypheus, professor, adviser, counselor, guide, mentor, pedant, rabbi, mystagogue.

5. Man eminently skilled in something, adept, proficient, master hand, whiz *(colloq.)*, wizard, genius, expert, pundit, savant, virtuoso, skilled hand, skillful artificer, specialist, technician, crack *(colloq.)*, connoisseur, crackajack, top sawyer, past master, medalist, prizeman.

6. Young gentleman, youth, lad, boy, male child, scion, minor, cadet, hopeful, schoolboy, whippersnapper, whipster, hobbledehoy, unlicked cub, youngster, sprig, slip, stripling.

MASTER, *v.* 1. Vanquish, conquer, overcome, subjugate, subdue, overpower, defeat, reduce to subjection, triumph over, overthrow, overwhelm, bring under subjection, subject, surmount, tame, reduce, enslave, dominate, control, rule, govern, superintend, regulate, direct, manage, boss, get the upper hand of, get the better of, worst.

2. Learn thoroughly, acquire thoroughly, become an adept in, make oneself master of, become proficient, acquire skill in, get, attain, grasp.

MASTER, *adj.* 1. Main, principal, leading, chief, cardinal, prime, most important, great, especial, grand, controlling, commanding, dominating, predominant, state.

2. Domineering, masterful, dictatorial, high-handed, overbearing, autocratic, arrogant, bossy, haughty, imperious, self-willed, arbitrary, authoritative, magisterial, commanding, lordly.

3. Eminently skilled, proficient, dexterous, adroit, deft, skillful, accomplished, finished, talented, gifted, able, apt, crack *(colloq.)*, slick *(slang)*, feat, good at, artful, masterly, *au fait (Fr.)*.

MASTER HAND, *n.* Expert, nice hand, good hand, proficient, adept, dabster *(colloq.)*, crack *(colloq.)*, ace, virtuoso, specialist, connoisseur, authority, crackajack *(colloq.)*, past master, old hand, veteran, genius, tactician, strategist, topsawyer, first fiddle, professional, prizeman, medalist, wizard.

MASTERLY, *adj.* 1. Expert, skillful, dexterous, deft, adroit, clever, proficient, workmanlike, artistic, able, admirable, finished, excellent, gifted, accomplished, talented, *au fait (Fr.)*, skilled, apt, crack *(colloq.)*.

2. Domineering, masterful, dictatorial, despotical, imperious, magisterial, arbitrary, self-willed, arrogant, haughty, bossy, overbearing, commanding, autocratic, lordly, high-handed, pompous, self-important.

MASTER MIND, *n.* Master spirit, brilliant intellect, genius, prodigy of learning, mine of information, walking encyclopedia, sage, wise man, longhead, pundit, savant, oracle, authority, shining light, luminary, man of learning, *esprit fort (Fr.)*, wizard, pantologist.

MASTERPIECE, *n.* Masterwork, *chef-d'-oeuvre (Fr.)*, prize winner, prize, *tour de force (Fr.)*, *coup de maître (Fr.)*, gem of the first water, tidbit, jewel, treasure, good thing, one in a thousand, *rara avis (Lat.)*, nonesuch, nonpareil, *crème de la crème (Fr.)*, pick, elite, A-1, flower of the flock, phoenix, *beau idéal (Fr.)*, paragon, pink, acme of perfection, *ne plus ultra (Lat.)*, black tulip, *cygne noir (Fr.)*, model, trump.

MASTERSHIP, *n.* 1. Office or authority of a master, headship, leadership, principate, kingship, presidency, primacy, hegemony, predominance, ascendancy, sovereignty, jurisdiction.

2. Supreme power, dominion, imperium, control, sway, rule, mastery, upper hand, supremacy, superiority, preëminence, predominating influence, direction, domination, command, government, domain.

3. Masterly knowledge, mastery, ability, skill, talent, cleverness, adroitness, dexterity, skillfulness, deftness, facility, readiness, expertness, quickness, address, aptitude, ingenuity, knack, flair, forte.

MASTER STROKE, *n.* Masterly achievement, stroke, hit, success, coup, *coup d'état (Fr.)*, feat, hit, *coup de maître (Fr.)*, ten strike *(colloq.)*, trump card, killing, go, prize, checkmate, feather in one's cap, home run, great gun, bold move, bright idea, best seller, triumph.

MASTERY, *n.* 1. Power of command or control, upper hand, whip hand, supreme power, ascendancy, headship, leadership, preëminence, superiority, victory, supremacy, conquest, mastership, command, dominion, hegemony, sway, rule, dominance, domination, government, control, subjugation, palm, advantage, walkover, triumph.
2. Expert skill, expert knowledge, grasp, cleverness, acquisition, attainment, acquirement, accomplishment, ability, great proficiency, dexterity, adroitness, deftness, achievement, successfulness, favorable issue.

MASTICATE, *v.* Chew, reduce to a pulp by crushing, Fletcherize, manducate, eat slowly, bite, munch, champ, crunch, gnaw, nibble, epulate, gulp, ruminate.

MASTICATION, *n.* Chewing food until it is reduced to a finely divided mass, manducation, reducing to a pulp by crushing, Fletcherism, deglutition, epulation, rumination.

MASTURBATION, *n.* Sexual self-gratification, onanism, self-abuse, manustupration, self-defilement, self-pollution, unnatural excitation of the genitalia, secret vice, self-love, narcissism, narcism, chiromania, edeogargalismus.

MAT, *v.* Twist together, interweave, interwine, entangle, plait, interlink, interlace, entwine, inweave, plat, braid, twill, felt.

MATADOR, *n.* Toreador, killer of bulls, bullfighter, tauromachist.

MATCH, *n.* 1. Competition, contest, game, trial, tournament, meet, joust, handicap, race, tourney, regatta, scrimmage, duel, athletics, emulation, rivalry, scuffle, bout, tussle, combat, fight, engagement, event, *concours (Fr.),* agonism, field day, gymnastics, fisticuffs, pugilism, boxing, scrap, gladiatorship, prize fighting, wrestling, luctation, colluctation, shoot.
2. One able to cope with another, mate, equal, tally, companion, peer, compeer, brother, fellow, colleague, counterpart, equivalent, parallel, congener, pair, double, twin, sister, alter ego.
3. Matrimonial compact, marriage, alliance, union, matrimony, intermarriage, wedlock, nuptial knot, nuptial tie, *vinculum matrimonii (Lat.),* wedding, espousals, Hymen, nuptials.
4. Safety match, lucifer, locofoco, fusee, vesuvian, Congreve, light, lighter, *allumette (Fr.), fiammifero (It.),* wax-match, *cerino (It.).*

MATCH, *v.* 1. Rival, complete with, race with, vie with, emulate, strive to excel, enter the lists, challenge, invite to contest, dare, defy, join issue, take up the gauntlet, couch one's lance, measure swords, contend, strive, contest, oppose, antagonize, grapple, spar, scramble, tilt, wrestle, box, tussle, fence, oppose, pit oneself against, encounter as an adversary with equal power, cope with.
2. Equal, be equal to, keep pace with, come up to, run abreast, compare to, duplicate, tie, balance, parallel, imitate, approximate, look like, resemble, reproduce, echo, follow, take after, favor *(colloq.),* smack of, savor of.
3. Make correspond, suit, adapt, fit, make harmonize, comport, tally, proportion, make proportionate.
4. Fit together, combine, pair off, couple, join, sort, conjoin, unite, connect, yoke, link together.
5. Take oneself a wife, marry, be married, wed, be spliced, wive, espouse, lead to the altar, be made one, be united in marriage, procure a matrimonial alliance, ally oneself in marriage, mate.

MATCHABLE, *adj.* Comparable, tantamount, equivalent, correspondent, like in kind, equal, similar, resembling, duplicate, twin, homologous, parallel, of a piece, analogous, allied to, akin to, cognate, correlative, kindred, something like, approximate, synonymous, identical.

MATCHLESS, *adj.* Supreme, unsurpassed, superior, inimitable, having no equal, unrivaled, unequaled, unparalleled, incomparable, unmatched, peerless, consummate, excellent, unmatchable, unapproached, second to none, *nulli secundus (Lat.),* transcendent, *sans pareil (Fr.),* superlative, sovereign, preëminent, paramount, foremost, principal, chief, utmost, crowning, unparagoned, inestimable, invaluable, rare, priceless, eximious, choice, best, elect, *recherché (Fr.),* precious, gilt-edged, first-class, exquisite, superfine, of the first water, prime, cardinal, capital, sterling, exemplary, unique, unexampled, perfect.

MATCHMAKER, *r.* Marriage arranger, match promoter, matrimonial agent, marriage broker, marriage schemer, schatchen *(Yiddish),* lonely-hearts expert.

MATE, *n.* 1. Associate, comrade, companion, intimate, fellow, partner, consort, compeer, boon companion, pal, buddy, chum, crony, confederate, yokemate, confrere, ally, bunkie *(colloq.),* bedfellow, roommate, messmate, bosom friend, confidant, other self, *alter ego (Lat.),* colleague, co-partner, side kick *(slang),* playfellow, fast friend, *fidus Achates (Lat.).*
2. Husband, spouse, benedict, lord and master, hubbie *(colloq.),* man, helpmate, helpmeet, better half, wife, rib, wedded wife, squaw.
3. Match, equal, peer, counterpart, equivalent, half of a pair, twin, duplicate, parallel, fascimile, copy, pair, double.
4. Officer of a merchant vessel who ranks below the captain or master; skipper, midshipman, master mariner, shellback, sea dog, tar, able seaman, A.B., salt, jack, gob, bluejacket, boatswain, coxswain, helmsman, navigator, pilot, steersman, petty officer, warrant officer, first mate, chief mate, second mate, gunner's mate, machinist's mate, mate of the deck, mate of the watch, mate of the hold, navigating mate.

MATE, *v.* 1. Join suitably, pair off, associate, couple, sort, match, combine, conjoin, group.
2. Take oneself a spouse, marry, be married, wed, be spliced, unite in holy wedlock, wive, be made one, espouse.
3. Have sexual relations with, be joined in sexual companionship, have coitus with, copulate, fornicate, deflower, constuprate.
4. Match oneself against, pit oneself against, oppose, rival, vie with, compete with.

MATERIAL, *adj.* 1. Formed of matter, physical, bodily, corporeal, somatic, incarnate, corporal, embodied, materialized, palpable, tangible, ponderable, sensuous, sensibly real, substantial, somatological, hylozoistic.
2. Pertaining to the physical rather than the spiritual, worldly, mundane, secular, temporal, earthly, earthy, materialistic, carnal, external, objective.
3. Of substantial importance, of much consequence, important, consequential, essential, vital, momentous, weighty, significant, serious, indispensable, grave.

MATERIAL, *n.* 1. Raw matter, constituent element, stuff, substance, substratum, body, principle, protoplasm, tissue, *corpus (Lat.), hyle (Greek)*, entity.

2. Material thing, article, object, something, means, dry goods, textile fabrics, building materials, bricks and mortar, timber, stores, stocks, supplies, equipment, stuff, staple, grist, fabric, ore.

MATERIALLY, *adv.* 1. With reference to matter or material things, physically, somatically, in substance, substantially, not in form only, ponderably, tangibly, palpably, sensibly, corporeally.

2. In the main, above all, significantly, importantly, consequentially, vitally, momentously, essentially, to an important degree, considerably, memorably, emphatically, tellingly, not to be overlooked, indispensably, not to be sneezed at, not to be despised.

MATERIEL, *n.* 1. Aggregate of things needed in any operation, equipment, materials, supplies, tools, utensils, implements, essentials, stores, provisions, gear, machinery, apparatus, instruments, contrivances, machine, plant, tackle, rigging, means.

2. *(Mil.)* Arms, munitions, ammunition, weapons, guns, explosives, powder and shot, firearms, ordnance, artillery, fieldpieces, cannon, battery.

MATERNAL, *adj.* Having the qualities of a mother, motherly, motherlike, parental, sympathetic, loving, doting, caring, sheltering, shielding, protective, holding in leading strings, tender, kind, affectionate, fond, devoted, warm-hearted.

MATERNITY, *n.* 1. Child-bearing, gestation, geniture, confinement, parturition, lying-in, delivery, labor, travail, accouchement, obstetrics.

2. Motherliness, motherhood, tenderness, kindness, warm-heartedness, devotion, affectionateness, warm attachment, loving kindness.

MATHEMATICAL, *adj.* 1. Pertaining to mathematics, arithmetical, statistical, numerative, numerical, algebraic, geometrical, calcular, trigonometrical, logarithmic, equational, quantitative, fractional, divisional, multiplicational, additive, subtractive, differential, analytical.

2. Precise as mathematics, exact, definite, well-defined, scientific, strict, accurate, correct, right, positive, unerring, rigid, rigorous, particular, meticulous, punctilious, scrupulous, literal.

MATIN, *n.* 1. One of the canonical hours of the breviary, first of the canonical hours, canonical hour immediately preceding lauds.

2. Solemn chorus service sung between midnight and dawn, service beginning at daybreak, order for public morning prayer, public Sunday service preceding the first Mass.

3. Morning song, aubade, morning serenade.

MATINEE, *n.* 1. Daytime theatrical performance, afternoon dramatic show, entertainment held in the afternoon.

2. Afternoon party, tea party, *thé dansant (Fr.),* garden party, *fête champêtre (Fr.),* outdoor festival, reception, at home, levée, cocktail party, picnic.

3. Gymkhana, track meet, field day, regatta, derby, races.

MATRIARCH, *n.* 1. Female head of a family or tribal line, mother and ruler of a race, female chieftain, wife of a patriarch.

2. Stately old woman, materfamilias, dowager, matron, grandmother, dame, dignified elderly lady.

MATRICULATE, *v.* Admit to membership in a college or society, grant privileges by enrolling,

enroll, register, enter, put upon record, list, catalogue, file, inscroll, attest, inscribe, book, insert, post.

MATRICULATION, *n.* 1. Enrollment in a college or society, registration, tabulation, entry, registry, booking, inscrollment.

2. Novitiate, tutelage, pupilage, apprenticeship, groundwork, first steps, preparation, training.

MATRIMONIAL, *adj.* Nuptial, conjugal, connubial, marital, hymeneal, spousal, sponsal, wedded, bridal, betrothed, spoken for, plighted, affianced, engaged.

MATRIMONY, *n.* Sacrament of marriage, nuptial state, holy wedlock, marriage, Hymen, nuptial knot, wedding ring, nuptial tie, *vinculum matrimonii (Lat.),* confarreation, union, match. (See MARRIAGE)

MATRIX, *n.* That which gives form to thing it encloses, mold, die, prototype, mint, last, punch, seal, stamp, intaglio, cast, make, form, womb, turn, type, outline, impression, frame, pattern, contour, fashion, cut, *galbe (Fr.),* format, form, figure.

MATRON, *n.* 1. Married woman of ripe years, dame of established position, woman of staid character, dowager, elderly woman, matriarch, stately lady.

2. Woman in charge of the domestic affairs of an institution, housekeeper, house mother, supervisor, overseer, directress, female head, head nurse, stewardess, forelady, curatrix, executrix, governess, superintendent, mistress, mother superior.

MATRONLY, *adj.* 1. Motherly, maternal, matronal, matron-like, womanly, wifely, in one's prime, elderly, anile, ripe, mature, mellow, venerable, advanced in years.

2. Having the characteristics of a matron, sedate, staid, grave, serious, sober, dignified, dowager-like.

MATTED, *adj.* Covered with a dense and tangled mass, entangled in a thick mass, snarled, interlaced, tangled, tousled, disheveled, raddled, rumpled.

MATTER, *n.* 1. That of which physical objects are composed, substance, material, stuff, body, content, brute matter, element, protoplasm, *corpus (Lat.), hyle (Greek), soma (Greek),* tissue, parenchyma, plasma, whatever occupies space, anything perceived to be occupying space.

2. Cause of distress, trouble, difficulty, embarrassment, quandary, predicament, dilemma, fix *(colloq.),* pass, rub, strait, pinch, trial, crisis, crux, exigency, push, emergency, imbroglio, rub, hot water, scrape, stew, pickle, snag, stumbling-block, hitch, quagmire, slough, obstruction, bar, impediment, obstacle, muddle, mess, botch, hard nut to crack, poser, knot, intricacy, perplexity, knotty point, puzzle, concern, question at issue, concernment, distress, maze.

3. Business, affair, thing, event, doings, occurrence, happening, episode, incident, phenomenon, fact, transaction, adventure, circumstance, experience, eventuality, proceeding.

4. Subject matter, content, topic, theme, subject, text, gist, essence, motif, thesis, moot point, field of inquiry, argument, sum and substance.

5. Importance, significance, consequence, moment, import, intent, connotation, implication, signification, real meaning, drift, tenor, spirit, force, sense, purport.

6. Pus, purulent matter, purulence, bioplasm, putrescence, decay, peccant humor, suppuration.

MATTER, *v.* 1. Import, signify, be of importance, carry weight, be of consequence, weigh, have influence, be an object, be worthy of notice, mean, express, denote, connote, bespeak, purport, import, imply, convey, indicate, touch on, drive at, involve.

2. Fester, suppurate, maturate, come to a head, draw, gather, rankle, putresce, rot.

MATTER-OF-FACT, *adj.* Adhering to actual facts, prosaic, prosy, literal, unimaginative, sober, pragmatical, objective, practical, plain, sensible, dry, jejune, unsentimental, unpoetic, free from introversion, plain-spoken, workaday, ordinary, commonplace, dull, insipid, unentertaining, uninteresting, heavy-gaited, banal, stereotyped, plodding, stolid, flat, humdrum, blunt, downright, direct, outspoken.

MATTOCK, *n.* Instrument for loosening the soil in digging, pickax with one end broad instead of pointed, grub-ax, grubbing-hoe, pick, adze.

MATTRESS, *n.* Quilted case filled with straw or cotton used on a bed, pallet, bedding, *paillasse (Fr.),* litter, shakedown.

MATURATE, *v.* Fester, ulcerate, suppurate, matter, gather, come to a head, draw, rankle, putresce, decay, rot.

MATURE, *adj.* 1. Complete in natural growth, fully developed, full-grown, ripe, full-blown, of age, pubescent, adolescent, of full age, out of one's teens, grown up, marriageable, nubile, adult, virile, manly, womanly, in one's prime, middle-aged, *entre deux âges (Fr.),* practiced, experienced.

2. Perfected, completed, ready, elaborated in full, seasoned, mellow, prepared, well-considered.

3. Having reached the limit of its time, payable, due, owing, to be paid, owed.

MATURE, *v.* 1. Bring to maturity, make mature, mellow, ripen, season, nurture.

2. Come of age, grow up, come to man's estate, attain one's majority, come to years of discretion, assume the toga virilis, be old enough to vote, leave one's nonage behind.

3. Bring to full development, bring to perfection, advance toward perfection, perfect, elaborate, develop, complete, bring to full bloom, bring to a head, bring to its peak, put the finishing touch to, consummate, finish, crown.

4. Fall due, become payable, be owing.

MATURITY, *n.* 1. Adulthood, prime of life, full age, majority, full bloom, flower of age, virility, manhood, womanhood, full growth, matureness, age of discretion.

2. Completion, perfected condition, perfection, full development, maturation, ripeness, fulfillment, accomplishment, consummation, culmination, elaboration, evolution, readiness, mellowness, preparedness, refinement.

MATUTINAL, *adj.* Occurring in the morning, early in the day, matin, morning, matinal, happening before noon.

MAUDLIN, *adj.* 1. Tearfully emotional, lachrymose, weakly sentimental, lackadaisical, tearfully affectionate, supersentimental, gushing, overemotional, oversentimental.

2. Made foolish by drinking intoxicating liquor, drunk, befuddled, besotted, inebriated, intoxicated, muddled, fuddled, tipsy, lush, mellow, boozy, drunken, sottish, inebrious, in one's cups, in... ... plastered, sozzled,

screwed, groggy, flustered, pot-valiant, topheavy, potulent, tight, oiled, pifflicated, crapulous, half seas over, under the table, three sheets in the wind, one over the eight, bibulous, bibacious.

MAUL, *n.* Heavy wooden hammer for driving piles, sledge hammer, beetle, heavy mallet, mace, heavy club, truncheon, cudgel, battering ram, rammer, tamper.

MAUL, *v.* 1. Pound, beat, buffet, belabor, pelt, batter, baste, whack, slam, thwack, bang, dash, punch, bash, thump, strike, hit, knock, hammer, whip, pommel, lambaste, thrash, cudgel, club, smite.

2. Handle roughly, maltreat, abuse, manhandle, ill-treat, ill-use, do violence to, persecute, oppress, aggrieve, trample upon, tread upon, molest, assail, bully, injure grossly, do much harm to, damage seriously, shatter.

MAULING, *n.* Severe beating, drubbing, clubbing, whipping, manhandling, fustigation, pommeling, cudgeling, thrashing, thumping, pounding, flagellation, fustigation, bastinado, strappado, rain of blows, misusage, ill-treatment.

MAUNDER, *v.* Utter in an incoherent manner, talk in a foolish way, drivel, mutter, murmur, grumble, mumble, ramble on, mince, lisp, gibber, snuffle, splutter, sputter, speak thick, croak, talk inarticulately, twaddle, blather, blubber, snivel, whimper, grunt, speak in an aimless and confused way.

MAUNDERER, *n.* Incoherent speaker, inarticulate talker, murmurer, driveler, mutterer, grumbler, croaker, growler, mumbler, twaddler, blubberer, sniveler.

MAUSOLEUM, *n.* Stately and magnificent tomb, tomb of more than ordinary size, sepulchral monument, grand monumental structure, Taj Mahal, sepulcher, house of death, tholos, memorial, shrine, tower of silence, charnel house, crypt, catacomb, repository for the dead, tumulus, barrow.

MAUVE, *adj.* Pale bluish purple, lilac, violet, bluish red, puce, lavender, plum-colored.

MAVERICK, *n.* 1. An animal found without an owner's brand, a calf separated from its dam, yearling, motherless calf.

2. A dissenter, nonconformist, dissident, malcontent, recusant.

MAW, *n.* 1. Crop of a fowl, first stomach of a bird, craw.

2. Stomach of animals, fourth stomach of ruminants, ingluvies, gizzard, ventricle, venter.

3. Gullet as concerned in devouring, jaws, throat, mouth, muzzle, orifice.

MAWKISH, *adj.* 1. Slightly sickening, nauseating, sick, nauseous, disgusting, loathsome, squeamish, unsavory.

2. Characterized by sickly sentimentality, lackadaisical, lacking strength or vigor, insipid, vapid, flat, stale, tasteless, void of taste, jejune, gustless, savorless, milk and water, namby-pamby, *fade (Fr.),* weak, wishy-washy, lifeless, spiritless.

MAXIM, *n.* 1. Aphoristic expression, aphorism, apothegm, sententious saying, proverb, adage, saw, byword, dictum, axiom, precept, *mot (Fr.),* cliché, commonplace, moral, reflection, sentence, epigram, truth, truism, self-evident truth, formula, motto, *bon mot (Fr.),* witticism.

2. Principle of conduct, golden rule, standard, recipe, canon, commandment, code, regulation.

MAXIMIZE, *v.* 1. Increase, magnify, extend, maximate, expand, aggrandize, amplify, widen, deepen, heighten, lengthen, broaden, enlarge, incrassate, fill out, swell, dilate, stretch, spread, blow up, inflate, puff out, cram, stuff, pad, elongate, protract, draw out, tighten, strain.

2. Exaggerate, overrate, overstrain, boost, extol, panegyrize, gush, embroider, hyperbolize, overdraw, overcolor.

MAXIMUM, *adj.* Utmost, greatest, highest, supreme, most, maximal, optimal, paramount, unparalleled, matchless, unequaled, unsurpassed, unapproached, preëminent, chief, foremost, crowning, principal, excellent, peerless, dominant, transcendent, superlative, sovereign, incomparable, supernal, capital.

MAYBE, *adv.* Perhaps, mayhap, possibly, it may be, haply, *peut-être (Fr.)*, *vielleicht (Ger.)*, *forse (It.)*, *quizá (Sp.)*, perchance, peradventure, by possibility, if possible, God willing, *deo volente (Lat.)*, wind and weather permitting, as luck may have it, for aught one knows, as the case may be.

MAYHEM, *n.* Wilful mutilation of another's body, violent bodily injury, harm, gash, slashing, ripping, wounding, *immedicable vulnus (Lat.)*, hurt, laceration, dilaceration, impairment, outrage, havoc, ravage, scath, disfigurement, deformation, defacement.

MAYOR, *n.* Principal officer of a municipality, chief magistrate of a city or borough, city manager, proctor, lord mayor, prefect, provost, chancellor, burgomaster, syndic, alcalde, sheriff, portreeve, constable, warden, alderman, seneschal, archon.

MAZE, *n.* 1. Confusing network of intercommunicating paths, labyrinth, winding course, meander, coil, ambages, circuit, spiral, corkscrew, helix, volute, twist, convolution, undulation, tortuosity, winding, contortion, tangle, entanglement, torsion, sinuosity, complex, crookedness, intricacy, knot.

2. State of confusion, perplexity, embarrassment, poser, puzzle, quandary, dilemma, paradox, riddle, enigma, fix, predicament, trouble, vexed question, strait, critical situation, crux, imbroglio, mizmaze, uncertainty.

MAZY, *adj.* 1. Full of intricate windings, labyrinthine, labyrinthian, ambagious, anfractuous, devious, tortuous, daedal, winding, sinuous, serpentine, snaky, convoluted, twisted, involved, circuitous, vermiculate, turbinate, coiled, spiral, cochleate, helical, screw-shaped, complex.

2. Confusing, confused, embarrassing, perplexing, trying, crabbed, critical, crucial, thorny, ticklish, awkward, delicate, puzzling, disconcerting, enigmatical, knotty, perverse, obscure, arduous, abstruse.

MEADOW, *n.* Grassland, lea, mead, pasture, field, plain, sward, savanna, green, bottom, pratal land, grazing land, flat, lowland, champaign, prairie, heath, moor, wold, pampas, llano, tundra, campo, steppe, basin, downs, mesa, plateau, veldt, bush, haugh, pasturage.

MEAGER, *adj.* 1. Deficient in quantity, little, sparing, bare, slight, scanty, poor, slim, slender, moderate, sparse, scrimpy, spare, stingy, scurvy, stinted, inadequate, insufficient, scarce, rare, infrequent, lacking, ill-provided, slack, short of, destitute of, wanting, penurious, poverty-stricken, indigent, niggard, beggarly, shabby.

2. Having little flesh, thin, lean, skinny, lank, emaciated, scraggy, gaunt, scrawny, starveling, haggard, starved, slim, underfed, undernourished, half-starved, withered, hungry.

3. Barren, unproductive, arid, sterile, unfertile, infertile, unyielding, acarpous, unprolific, fallow, unfruitful.

4. Deficient in quality, vapid, insipid, tame, jejune, uninteresting, dry, bald, feeble, prosy, prosaic, monotonous, tedious, wishy-washy, watery, milk-and-water, sketchy, rambling, dull, faint, trivial, petty, nugatory, inconsiderable.

MEAGERNESS, *n.* 1. Deficiency, bareness, scantiness, slimness, slenderness, moderateness, sparseness, spareness, scrimpiness, inadequacy, insufficiency, rarity, scarceness, infrequency, slackness, destitution, want, lack, need, penury, indigence, niggardliness, poverty, shabbiness, beggarliness, poorness, scarcity, shortage, paucity, stint, bare subsistence, dearth, famine, starvation, drought, desiccation, dehydration.

2. Thinness, leanness, skinniness, lankness, emaciation, gauntness, scrawniness, haggardness, slimness, undernourishment.

3. Barrenness, aridity, aridness, sterility, infertility, unproductivity, unfruitfulness.

4. Tediousness, dullness, tameness, insipidity, vapidity, jejuneness, baldness, dryness, monotonousness, faintness.

MEAL, *n.* '. Repast, collation, refection, board, victuals, dinner table, food, snack, refreshment, nutriment, nourishment, pabulum, sustenance, nurture, provender, ration, provision, commissariat, cheer, dietary, diet, regimen, fare, staff of life, cuisine, table, bill of fare, menu, spread, feast, picnic, junket, banquet, potluck, breakfast, *déjeuner (Fr.)*, luncheon, lunch, tiffin, dinner, supper, afternoon tea, manna, eats *(colloq.)*, grub *(slang)*, viands, foodstuffs, comestibles.

2. Edible part of any grain or pulse ground to a coarse powder, flour, grits, groats, corn meal, Indian meal, farina, pinole, bran, sporule.

MEALY, *adj.* Farinaceous, branny, granular, pulverulent, powdery, floury, furfuraceous, flocculent, gritty, efflorescent, crumbly, friable.

MEALY-MOUTHED, *adj.* Avoiding the use of plain terms from excessive delicacy, using soft words, honeyed, smooth-tongued, adulatory, unctuous, oily, soapy, blandiloquent, fine-spoken, specious, servile, fulsome, sycophantic, obsequious, fawning, cringing, sniveling, slavish, groveling, insincere, hollow, mendacious, *Parthis mendacior (Lat.)*, affected, artful, smooth-spoken, two-faced, Janus-faced, double-tongued, canting, hypocritical, pharisaical, Jesuitical, tartuffish, tartuffian, euphuistic.

MEAN, *v.* 1. Have in mind, intend, purpose, propose, contemplate, design, aim at, determine upon, have in view, labor for, bid for, desire, aspire to, pursue, think of, meditate, dream of, project, destine, calculate, reckon, plan, premeditate, resolve, drive at.

2. Express, signify, imply, indicate, convey, import, purport, denote, connote, symbolize, suggest, argue, allude to, intimate, point to, declare, involve, insinuate, hint at, betoken, affirm, state, manifest, utter, tell of, touch on, stand for.

MEAN, *adj.* 1. Stingy, penurious, close-fisted, parsimonious, miserly, pinch-penny, illiberal, mercenary, sordid, skinflinty, tight-fisted, ungenerous, narrow, unhandsome, selfish, niggardly, meager, cheap, self-seeking, avaricious, rapacious, extortionate, greedy, hoggish, shabby, tight, scrimping, cheese-paring, grudging, sparing, grasping, venal, covetous, beggarly.

2. Shameful, abject, contemptible, vile, base,

ignominious, notorious, opprobrious, infamous, outrageous, scandalous, shocking, arrant, flagrant, unworthy, despicable, questionable, shady, disreputable, degrading, disgraceful, discreditable, dishonorable, groveling, servile, sneaking, scurvy, dirty, unfair, villainous, knavish, rascally, caitiff, roguish, pusillanimous, base-minded, disingenuous, low-minded, time-serving, churlish, hangdog, degenerate, shameless, debased, corrupt, filthy, foul, vicious, offensive, nasty, unaccommodating, scoundrelly, worthless, malicious, malignant, malign, scurrilous.

3. Ignoble, low-born, plebeian, vulgar, coarse, common, ordinary, humble, earth-born, inglorious, proletarian, undistinguished, inconsequential, obscure, scrubby, sorry, baseborn, untitled, boorish, loutish, rude, clodhopping, countrified, rustic, backwoods, bourgeois.

4. Petty, picayune, small, of little importance, insignificant, paltry, piddling, little, diminutive, wretched, trivial, frivolous, trifling, unimportant, slender, fribbling, flimsy, idle, shallow, trashy, rubbishy, cheap, gimcrack, sleazy, catchpenny, trumpery, second-rate, jerry-built, squalid.

5. Average, medium, moderate, middling, mediocre, run-of-the-mill, indifferent, commonplace, tolerable, passable, fair, so-so.

6. Occupying a middle position, occupying an intermediate place, coming between, intervening, intermediate, medial, interjacent, mid, midmost, central, intermediary.

MEAN, *n.* 1. Average, medium, normal, balance, rule, golden mean, run, mean proportion, middle state, mediocrity, measure, moderation, neutrality, compromise, middle course, *juste milieu (Fr.), aurea mediocritas (Lat.), ariston metron (Greek),* middle term, *mezzo termine (It.),* midst, midmost.

2. Core, nucleus, center, kernel, umbilicus, omphalos, navel, hub, heart, bull's-eye, diaphragm, midriff, equator, halfway house, equidistance, interjacence, bisection.

MEANDER, *n.* Winding path, maze, labyrinth, ambages, circuition, anfractuosity, tortuousness, circumambulation, turning, spiral, corkscrew, coil, helix, evagation, zigzag, detour, circumvolution, sinuosity, twirl, twist, windings and turnings, bypaths and crooked ways, indirect course, circuitous journey, intricate fret, fretwork.

MEANDER, *v.* 1. Proceed by a winding course, turn in a serpentine manner, flow 'round, wind, turn, be tortuous, zigzag, stray, deviate, digress, undulate, wave, turn and twist, twine, be convoluted, twirl, coil, twist, contort, curve, bend.

2. Wander aimlessly, circumambulate, stroll, ramble, peregrinate, straggle, rove, circulate, *battre la campagne (Fr.).*

MEANDERING, *adj.* 1. Serpentine, winding, anfractuous, labyrinthine, meandrian, flexuous, tortuous, circuitous, devious, crooked, zigzag, mazy, sinuous, vermicular, circumfluent, roundabout, circumforaneous, circumambient, aberrant, excursive, erratic, stray, vagrant, convoluted, tortile, undulatory, wavy, snaky, circling, sigmoidal, spiral, ambagious.

2. Diffuse, discursive, desultory, rambling, loose, disjointed, spun out, prolix, protracted, periphrastic, circumlocutory, digressive, episodic, rhapsodic.

MEANING, *n.* 1. That which is intended to be expressed, significance, sense, signification, purport, import, force, denotation, connotation, tenor, drift, gist, trend, acceptation, interpretation,

explanation, implication, bearing, sum and substance, essence, pith, spirit, allusion, insinuation, suggestion, effect, upshot, value, burden, content, argument, subject matter, text, subject.

2. Intention, purpose, intent, aim, design, object, scheme, end, plan, view.

MEANINGFUL, *adj.* Significant, expressive, full of meaning, significatory, meaning, significative, indicative, explicit, eloquent, suggestive, allusive, intelligible, pregnant with meaning, boding, portentous, ominous, pithy, prognostic, implied, connoted, tacit, exact, verbatim, literal, word for word, declaratory, definitive, emphatic, affirmative, certain, pointed, distinct, decided, marked, assertive, peremptory, insistent, solemn, dogmatic, trenchant, categorical.

MEANINGLESS, *adj.* Without meaning or significance, senseless, nonsensical, unmeaning, inexpressive, vague, unintelligible, incomprehensible, empty, hollow, blank, inane, insignificant, unimportant, trite, trivial, twaddling, worthless, trashy, rubbishy, unfathomable, insoluble, inexplicable, unaccountable, impenetrable, inscrutable, enigmatical, puzzling, ambiguous, indefinite, illegible, undecipherable, incognizable, obscure, nebulous, dim, abstruse, recondite, irrational, frivolous, vain, useless, stupid, absurd, foolish, fatuous, idiotic, imbecile, unreasonable, preposterous, paradoxical, silly, asinine, fantastic, farcical, without rime or reason.

MEANINGLY, *adv.* Significantly, ominously, portentously, prognostically, bodingly, darkly, threateningly, minatorily, admonishingly, monitorily, significatively, warningly, menacingly, frowningly, minaciously, expressively, emphatically, pointedly, pithily, suggestively, eloquently, explicitly, distinctly, markedly, peremptorily, solemnly, trenchantly, tellingly, knowingly, impressively, persuasively, fluently, vigorously.

MEANLY, *adv.* 1. In a mean manner, poorly, basely, stingily, parsimoniously, sordidly, squalidly, niggardly, selfishly, penuriously, ungenerously, mangily, closely, shabbily, miserably, wretchedly, meagerly, close-fistedly, from hand-to-mouth, scrimpingly, grudgingly, sparingly.

2. Dishonorably, disrespectfully, unworthily, scurvily, villainously, churlishly, knavishly, shadily, ignobly, vilely, abjectly, contemptibly, despicably, ignominiously, disreputably, shamefully, unworthily, questionably, infamously, scandalously, dishonestly, unscrupulously, corruptly.

MEANNESS, *n.* 1. Stinginess, closeness, parsimoniousness, penuriousness, niggardliness, close-fistedness, avarice, illiberality, rapacity, avidity, selfishness, cupidity, cheeseparing, economy, frugality, miserliness, sordidness, ungenerousness.

2. Vileness, despicableness, baseness, abjectness, contemptibleness, churlishness, scurviness, corruptness, ignominiousness, degradation, debasement, ingloriousness, disesteem, disrepute, odium, opprobrium, disgrace, infamy, turpitude.

MEANS, *n., pl.* 1. Pecuniary resources, money, wealth, income, revenue, property, estate, substance, ways and means, the wherewithal, capital, riches, possessions, funds, cash, finance, money to burn, millions, dollars, dough *(slang),* long green, jack *(slang),* shekels, bucks, velvet *(slang),* easy circumstances, independence, lucre, pelf, command of money.

2. Agency used to attain an end, instrumentality, instrument, agent, measure, medium, aid, factor, contributing force, expedients, conven-

iences, appliances, devices, apparatus, faculty, resort, contrivance, process, method, way, mode, course, alternative.

MEAN-SPIRITED, *adj.* Base, beggarly, servile, despicable, groveling, abject, obsequious, low-minded, vile, cowardly, pusillanimous, recreant, timid, shrinking, caitiff, sneaking, ignoble, cringing, slavish, fawning, truckling, mealy-mouthed, sniveling, abased.

MEANTIME, *adv.* In the intervening time, in the interim, during the interval. meanwhile, at the same time, *ad interim (Lat.)*, in the meantime, *pendente lite (Law)*, in the course of, for the time being, *de die in diem (Lat.)*, day by day, for the time being, for the season, till, until, up to, to the time of, throughout, all along, whilst, while, pending, during.

MEASURABLE, *adj.* That may be measured, mensurable, computable, reckonable, fathomable, gaugeable, determinable, appraisable, assessable, admeasurable, surveyable, estimable.

MEASURE, *n.* 1. Standard of measurement, rule, gauge, meter, graduated rod, vessel of standard capacity, scale, level, plummet, plumb line, compass, calipers, square, T square, tape, line, quadrant, vernier, theodolite, balance, weighing machine, ell, yardstick.

2. Size, dimensions, extent, degree, amount, quantity, stage, mark, scale, rate, point, pitch, ratio, plane, limit, determined length, height, width, depth, breadth, magnitude, amplitude, capacity, bound, scope, reach, caliber, range, strength, intensity, shade, bulk, mass, volume, abundance, extension, substance, weight, content, aggregate, sum, duration.

3. Definite quantity measured out, share, allotment, due proportion, portion, quota, quantum, dole, pittance, driblet, dose, batch, stock, lot, handful, armful, spoonful, mouthful, division, allowance.

4. Extent not to be exceeded, moderation, limitation, limit, reasonable bound, just degree, temperance, sobriety, golden mean, *aurea mediocritas (Lat.)*, *ne quid nimis (Lat.)*, forbearance, frugality, restraint, mid-course, *juste milieu (Fr.)*, *mezzo termine (It.)*.

5. Standard of comparison, criterion, norm, canon, pattern, type, model, touchstone, test, rule.

6. Action intended as a means to an end, step, procedure, course, plan, proceeding, means, bill, enactment, law, act, proposal, outline, scheme, design, proposition, project.

7. Rhythm, meter, cadence, numbers, verse, poesy, poetry, metrical unit, tune, melody, short rhythmical movement, air, slow stately dance movement, versification, prosody, orthometry, scansion, scanning.

MEASURE, *v.* 1. Ascertain the dimensions of, mete, meter, calibrate, caliper, inch, span, step, pace, space, divide, graduate, plumb, weigh, balance, scale, dial, survey, graph, plot, delimit, lay out, trace, rule, block out, mark out, lay off, size.

2. Estimate, compute, calculate, assess, gauge, appraise, value, judge of, determine, rate, form an estimate, estimate relatively, compare, bring into comparison, adjudge.

3. Deal out, mete out, distribute, apportion, allot, allocate, dole, share, assign, portion out, admeasure, set apart.

4. Travel over, traverse, pass over, pass through, overpass, cross, itinerate, track, travel through, range, wander over, trek, ply, ford.

MEASURED, *adj.* 1. Steady, uniform, rhythmical, regular, metrical, moderated, equal, graduated, progressive, gradual, moderate.

2. Deliberate, studied, prepense, premeditated, calculated, weighed, thought out, reasoned, purposed, aforethought, intentional, cold-blooded.

MEASURE FOR MEASURE. Retaliation, requital, reprisal, repayment, retribution, counterstroke, punishment, revenge, vengeance, eye for an eye, Roland for an Oliver, tit for tat, boomerang, backfire, *lex talionis (Lat.)*, reciprocation, desert, blow for blow, *quid pro quo (Lat.)*, the biter bit, diamond cut diamond, give and take, game at which two can play.

MEASURELESS, *adj.* Without bounds, boundless, unbounded, unlimited, limitless, endless, immeasurable, immense, infinite, vast, countless, sumless, numberless, innumerable, illimitable, incalculable, unfathomable, interminable, exhaustless, inexhaustible, untold, indefinite, termless, unending, fathomless, eternal, perpetual.

MEASUREMENT, *n.* 1. Act of measuring, mensuration, admeasurement, metage, valuation, survey, assessment, appraisement, appraisal, estimation, estimate, gauging, reckoning.

2. Horsepower, foot-candle, candle power, erg, foot-pound, foot-ton, dinamode, magnifying power.

3. Latitude and longitude, altitude and azimuth, declination and right ascension, surveying, triangulation, cadastration, cartography, topography, hypsography, geodesy, altimetry, stereometry, geometry, hypsometry, micrometry, autometry.

4. Ascertained dimension, area *or* content, size, bulk, quantity, extent, capacity, limitation, mass, volume, extension, substance, weight, aggregate, ponderosity, amplitude, magnitude, breadth, depth, width, height, length.

MEAT, *n.* 1. Flesh of animals for food, flesh-meat, animal food, muscle and fat of animal bodies, edible animal organs.

2. Food in general, nutriment, aliment, viands, victuals, nourishment, regimen, diet, cheer, provision, sustenance, subsistence, feed, fare, rations, comestibles, edibles, dietary, pabulum, sustentation, nurture, provender, board, commons, keep, commissariat, forage, belly timber, proteins, grub, hard tack, fleshpots, contents of the larder, creature comforts.

3. Edible part of anything, pulp, kernel, nut, fruit, pith, substance, marrow, heart.

MEATY, *adj.* Fleshy, muscular, fatty, full of substance, pithy, pulpy.

MECHANIC, *n.* Skilled worker with tools *or* machines, operative, artisan, craftsman, artificer, handicraftsman, hand, workman, worker, laborer, mechanician, machinist, tradesman, navvy, day laborer, journeyman, grease monkey, engineer, plumber, electrician, wright, forger, smith, bricklayer, mason, carpenter, platelayer, ganger, gasfitter.

MECHANICAL, *adj.* 1. Self-acting, automatic, motor-driven, power-driven, electric, machinal, labor-saving, ingenious, useful, efficient.

2. Machine-like, robotian, perfunctory, involuntary, blind, instinctive, unthinking, unconscious.

3. Subordinating the spiritual to the material, materialistic, hylozoistic, somatologic, temporal, worldly, worldly-minded, Philistine, mundane, carnal, earthly, mercenary, unspiritual.

MECHANICALLY, *adv.* Automatically, blindly, perfunctorily, instinctively, involuntarily, unconsciously, unthinkingly, willy-nilly, *nolens volens (Lat.),* by rote, by heart.

MECHANICS, *n.* Branch of knowledge concerned with mechanical appliances, science dealing with the action of forces on bodies and with motion, statics, kinetics, kinematics, dynamics, technology, industrial science, mechanical powers.

MECHANISM, *n.* 1. Agency by which a particular effect is produced, machinery, apparatus, works, mechanical appliances, engineering, gear, instruments, tools, organs, implements, contrivances, utensils, motors, machines, engines, lathes, mills, gins, pumps, rigging, matériel, plant, equipment, clockwork.

2. Mechanical execution, technology, technical skill, technography, brilliant performance, bravura.

MECHANIZE, *v.* Make mechanical, operate by machinery, industrialize, introduce machinery into, equip with rolling stock, motorize, put on the assembly line.

MEDAL, *n.* Inscribed flat circular piece of metal issued to commemorate an event, badge to reward for merit, testimonial, order, citation, decoration, insignia, award of honor, medallion, trophy, emblem, prize, contorniate, medalet, cross, reward, Distinguished Service Cross, Congressional Medal, Medal of Honor, Victoria Cross, Iron Cross, Croix de Guerre.

MEDDLE, *v.* Busy oneself with something without warrant, concern oneself without necessity, interfere, interpose, intermeddle, obtrude, put in one's oar, have a finger in the pie, pry into, horn in, butt in, dip one's nose in, tamper with, have a hand in, dabble, take an active part in, come between, mix oneself up in, be inquisitive, peep, inspect, pry, snoop, kibitz, intrigue, trouble one's head about, have many irons in the fire, have fish to fry, moil, have to do with, be a party to, intrude.

MEDDLER, *n.* Busybody, intermeddler, officious person, sticky beak *(slang),* quidnunc, newsmonger, gossip, eavesdropper, Paul Pry, snooper, intriguer, intrigant, talebearer, kibitzer, pickthank, intruder, obtruder.

MEDDLESOME, *adj.* Given to meddling, interfering, intrusive, obtrusive, officious, intermeddling, inquisitive, curious, prying, pushing, forward, impertinent, busy, overcurious, mousing, kibitzing, audacious, interposing.

MEDIAL, *adj.* 1. Pertaining to the middle, median, intermediate, intervenient, intercurrent, intercalary, intermediary, interstitial, middle, midmost, mid.

2. Mean, average, medium, median, ordinary.

MEDIATE, *v.* Bring about an agreement between parties, settle a dispute by mediation, arbitrate, intercede, interpose, make peace between, effect an agreement, reconcile, step in, intervene, negotiate, mediatize, interfere, propitiate, moderate, referee, umpire, pacify, compromise, use one's good offices, *magnas componere lites (Lat.),* arrange differences, placate, meet halfway, heal the breach, hold out the olive branch, restore harmony, bring to terms, bring to an understanding.

MEDIATION, *n.* Intercession, intervention, interposition, mediate agency, arbitration, instrumentality, mediatorship, intermediation, interference,

negotiation, good offices, parley, compromise, mediatization, peace offering, flag of truce, olive branch, diplomacy, peace pipe, pacification, conciliation, reconciliation, reconcilement, adjustment, terms, settlement of difficulties, good understanding, amnesty, calumet, armistice.

MEDIATIVE, *adj.* Mediatory, intermediary, interfering, mediatorial, intercessory, intermedial, interventional, reconciliatory, propitiatory, diplomatic, irenic, peacemaking, pacificatory, arbitrative, conciliatory, pacific, intercessive.

MEDIATOR, *n.* 1. One who mediates between parties at variance, intercessor, interceder, propitiator, reconciler, pacificator, peacemaker, interagent, intermedium, intermediary, negotiator, arbitrator, moderator, diplomatist, umpire, referee, go-between.

2. Christ, The Messiah, The Advocate, The Savior, The Redeemer, The Intercessor, The Judge, The Anointed.

MEDICABLE, *adj.* Susceptible of medical treatment, remediable, curable, recoverable, restorable, healable, retrievable.

MEDICAL, *adj.* Pertaining to medicine, of the medical art, healing, curative, therapeutic, therapeutical, sanatory, medicative, medicinal, remedial, restorative, sanative, prophylactic, salutiferous, health-bringing, salutary, palliative, corrective, tonic, analeptic, corroborant, balsamic, sedative, narcotic, demulcent, lenitive, emollient, detersive, depuratory, disinfectant, alterative, febrifugal, peptic.

MEDICAMENT, *n.* Curative substance, healing application, medicine, remedy, physic, tonic, balm, panacea, antidote, antiseptic, prophylactic, corrective, stimulant, restorative, sedative, febrifuge, palliative, alterative, specific, carminative, emetic, narcotic, cure-all, potion, drug, dose, draught, bolus, pill, lozenge, capsule, tablet, linctus, electuary, nostrum, catholicon, elixir, balsam, theriac, cordial, ptisan, ointment, salve, lenitive, oil, cerate, cosmetic, lotion, plaster, embrocation, epithem, liniment, traumatic, cataplasm, poultice.

MEDICATE, *v.* Treat with medicine, impregnate with something medicinal, tincture with medicaments, drug, dose, physic, attend, dress, cure, heal, remedy, relieve, restore, palliate, doctor *(colloq.).*

MEDICINAL, *adj.* Having the properties of a medicine, remedial, curative, sanatory, healing, medicative, medical, therapeutic, therapeutical, salutiferous, corrective, restorative, recuperatory, sanative, prophylactic, sedative, tonic, lenitive, palliative, homeopathic, allopathic, laxative, aperient, purgative, aseptic, antiseptic, antidotal, alexipharmic, anodyne, corroborant, demulcent, emollient, narcotic, balsamic, analeptic, depuratory, febrifugal, disinfectant, alterative.

MEDICINE, *n.* 1. Substance used in treating disease, physic, nostrum, medicament, remedy, drug, remedial agent, specific, tonic, potion, simples, dose, draft, lozenge, pill, bolus, electuary, lincture, prescription, cordial, balm, elixir, balsam, ptisan, sedative, dope, narcotic, anodyne, painkiller, lenitive, palliative, emollient, lotion, liniment, embrocation, poultice, ointment, salve, oil, antidote, counteractive, emetic, febrifuge, antitoxin, antipoison, antiserum, antibody, antiseptic, prophylactic, disinfectant, germicide, restorative, stimulant, bracer, panacea, cure-all.

2. Healing art, leechcraft, therapeutics, practice of medicine, allopathy, homeopathy, materia med-

ica, pharmaceutics, pharmacology, pathology, aetiology, nosology, symptomatology, medical treatment.

MEDICO, *n.* Physician, doctor of medicine, M.D., doctor, medic *(colloq.),* leech *(archaic),* general practitioner, medical man, specialist, consultant, surgeon, diagnostician, sawbones *(slang),* Asclepius, Galen, Hippocrates, healer.

MEDIEVAL, *adj.* Middle-Age, Dark-Age, post-Classical, pre-Renaissance, unenlightened, benighted, barbarous, Gothic, rude, grotesque.

MEDIOCRE, *adj.* Of only moderate excellence, average, middling, medium, ordinary, indifferent, neither good nor bad, betwixt and between, mean, commonplace, run-of-the-mill, second-rate, fair to middling, tolerable, so-so, passable, normal, everyday, respectable, presentable, admissible, undistinguished, bourgeois, middle-class, neutral, modest, reasonable, temperate, inconsiderable, inappreciable, inferior, rather poor, unimportant, common, slight, paltry, petty, inconsequential, immaterial, insignificant, trifling, limited, lesser, meager, picayune, negligible.

MEDIOCRITY, *n.* 1. Moderate degree, middle state, middle course, mean, golden mean, *aurea mediocritas (Lat.), mezzo termine (It.), juste milieu (Fr.),* balance, mean proportion, rule, run.

2. Average capacity, ordinariness, commonplaceness, moderation, normality, average standard, lower quality, passableness, tolerableness, indifference, insignificance, unimportance, inferiority, inconsiderableness, immaterialness, paltriness, triviality, neutrality.

3. Middle classes, persons of but moderate ability, bourgeoisie, nonentities.

MEDITATE, *v.* 1. Consider in the mind as something to be effected, plan, intend, design, scheme, purpose, devise, concoct, contrive, speculate, project, resolve, have in view, mean, bid for, aim at, propose, destine, calculate, aspire to, dream of.

2. Engage in thought, contemplate, muse, reflect, ruminate, revolve in the mind, study, think of, turn over in the mind, chew the cud upon, reason, dwell intently upon, ratiocinate, concentrate, ponder, cogitate, excogitate, cudgel one's brains, advise with one's pillow, collect one's thoughts, focus on, deliberate, brood over, mentalize, weigh, cerebrate, set one's wits to work, mull over, con over, take into consideration, consult, apply the mind.

MEDITATION, *n.* Continued thought, reflection, close attention, contemplation, deep thought, musing, brown study, pondering, rumination, brooding, consideration, deliberation, excogitation, cerebration, thoughtfulness, cogitation, mental exercitation, thinking, revolving a subject in the mind, speculation, lucubration, brainwork, mentation, train of thought, application, reverie, self-consultation, self-communion, introversion, retrospection, second thought, reconsideration, headwork, abstraction.

MEDITATIVE, *adj.* Given to meditation, thoughtful, pensive, contemplative, ruminative, studious, speculative, reflective, lucubrative, excogitative, considerative, musing, wistful, thinking, cogitative, deliberative, museful, introspective, philosophical, metaphysical, abstract, absorbed, engrossed in, rapt, intent, lost in thought, attentive, occupied with, taken up with, wrapped in.

MEDIUM, *adj.* Intermediate in degree or quality, middling, middle, mediocre, mean, ordinary, commonplace, between the extremes, so-so, half-and-half, moderate, average, mezzo, middle-class, normal, standard, neutral, mediate, median.

MEDIUM, *n.* 1. Middle, mean, mean average, middle state, mean proportion, average, rule, balance, happy medium, run, golden mean, *aurea mediocritas (Lat.), ne quid nimis (Lat.),* measure, moderation, neutrality, compromise, mid-course, middle way, *juste milieu (Fr.), mezzo termine (It.), ariston metron (Greek),* temperateness.

2. Intermediary, interagent, instrumentality, agency, means, instrument, channel, interagency, wherewithal, machinery, matériel, material supplies, wherewith, mechanism, mediation, action, intervention, aid, help, assistance, vehicle, tool, go-between, intermediate, expedient, representative, handmaid, friend at court.

3. Environment, surroundings, condition of life, atmosphere, influences, milieu, external circumstances, neighborhood, *entourage (Fr.).*

4. Person instrumental in the manifestation of some alleged supernatural agency, spiritualist, clairaudient, telepathist, oracle, necromancer, conjurer, wizard, warlock, diviner, exorcist, ecstatica, mesmerist, soothsayer, fortuneteller, astrologist, crystal-gazer, Sibyl, clairvoyant, seer, psychic.

MEDLEY, *n.* Mixture of heterogeneous elements, jumble, miscellany, hodgepodge, potpourri, confused mass, farrago, gallimaufry, salmagundi, olio, mish-mash, mélange, miscellaneous collection, intermixture, mixed assemblage, pastiche, macaroni, hash, mess, olla-podrida, mingle-mangle, omnium-gatherum *(humorous), pasticcio (It.),* patchwork, crazy quilt, chowchow, motley, mosaic, Noah's ark, charivari.

MEED, *n.* Reward for desert, recompense for service, prize, guerdon, award, premium, remuneration, reguerdon, indemnification, compensation, quittance, return, consideration, *quid pro quo (Lat.),* douceur, emolument, pay, stipend, fee, honorarium, dividend, dole, pittance, portion, allotment, share, divvy, split, allowance, gratuity, gift, present, donation, contribution, offering, benefaction, bounty, boon, sportula, grant, bonus, tribute, largess.

MEEK, *adj.* Humble, submissive, gentle, soft, patient, yielding, lowly, docile, modest, mild, pacific, forbearing, unassuming, unpretentious, compliant, serene, placid, retiring, reserved, imperturbable, subdued, deferential, complaisant, long-suffering, free from pride, tender-hearted, lamblike, demure, stoical, enduring, tolerant, clement, unresisting, spiritless, tame.

MEEKNESS, *n.* Humility, humbleness, submissiveness, lowliness, submission, forbearance, gentleness, mildness, modesty, abasement, self-abasement, patience, tolerance, toleration, endurance, sufferance, long-suffering, longanimity, serenity, docility, compliance, deference, complaisance, tameness.

MEET, *adj.* Fitting, proper, befitting, fit, appropriate, suitable, qualified, suited, apposite, adapted, decorous, congruous, expedient, admissible, pertinent, relevant, condign, applicable, rightful, becoming, seemly, commensurate, harmonious, consistent, convenient, apt, right, conformable, opportune, agreeable, compatible.

MEET, *v.* 1. Come upon, confront, come face to face with, encounter, come across, light upon, come into contact with, face, eye directly, come into the presence, come into personal acquaintance with, be introduced to, welcome, speak with, be presented to, greet.

2. Congregate, collect, gather, forgather, assemble, convene, muster, rally, come together, parley, hold a session, cluster, swarm, flock, mass, herd, throng, crowd, associate, huddle, resort, concentrate.

3. Unite, join, converge, come together, intersect, transect, cross, concur, conjoin.

4. Equal, match, come up to, keep pace with, tie, parallel, cope with, deal effectively with, counter in opposition, oppose.

5. Fulfill, satisfy, settle, discharge, gratify, comply with, answer, redeem, keep one's pledge, keep faith with, carry out, execute, perform, acknowledge, respect, observe, abide by, heed, adhere to, be faithful to, follow, obey, act up to, recompense, pay, defray, liquidate.

MEETING, *n.* 1. Encounter, presentation, introduction, salutation, greeting, welcome, reception, tryst, rendezvous, assignation.

2. Assemblage, assembly, gathering, concourse, convention, conference, get-together, collection of persons, company, council, reunion, session, congress, synod, caucus, muster, conventicle, convocation, séance, sitting, hearing, auditory, durbar, palaver, powwow, conclave.

3. Union, conflux, junction, confluence, intersection, joining, convergence, juncture, concurrence, connection.

4. Hostile encounter, collision, duel, opposition, combat, concussion, conflict, impact, clash.

MEETING HOUSE, *n.* 1. Hall, auditorium, assembly room, pump room, club, chamber, public room.

2. Building for religious worship, church, house of worship, temple, house of God, cathedral, chapel, house of prayer, place of worship, minster, kirk, bethel, tabernacle, basilica, holy place, fane, oratory, chantry, synagogue, sanctuary.

MEET WITH, *v.* 1. Find, fall in with, fall upon, light on, meet, come to, happen upon, come across, bump into, stumble upon, hit upon.

2. Experience, encounter, undergo, suffer, be exposed to, be subjected to, fall to the lot of, be one's lot, be one's chance, pass through, endure, brook, tolerate, stand.

MELANCHOLIA, *n.* Mental disease characterized by great depression of spirits and gloomy forebodings, hypochondriasis, mental derangement accompanied by excessive gloominess, insane brooding, barythymia *(Med.)*, stuporous melancholia, low-spiritedness, the blues, the blue devils, panphobic melancholy, melancholia attonita, involution melancholia, melancholia agitata, hysteria, monomania, blank despondency.

MELANCHOLY, *adj.* 1. Disposed to melancholy, depressed, low-spirited, hypochondriac, melancholic, hypochondriacal, dejected, dispirited, blue, despondent, downhearted, sad, discouraged, heavyhearted, down in the mouth, sick at heart, cheerless, disconsolate, unhappy, forlorn, heartsick, doleful, woebegone, sorrowful, lachrymose, lugubrious, moody, mopish, downcast, in the dumps, atrabilious, lackadaisical, languishing, chapfallen, crestfallen, saturnine, morose.

2. Depressing, somber, mournful, gloomy, dismal, unpromising, dark, dreary, overcast, desolate, funereal, lamentable, dreadful, unfortunate, calamitous, dull, overcast, plaintive, joyless, deplorable, sorry, heavy.

3. Soberly thoughtful, pensive, wistful, grave, earnest, solemn, rueful, demure, long-faced, grimvisaged, staid, serious, sedate, dreamy, quiet.

MELANCHOLY, *n.* 1. Habitual *or* prolonged gloomy state of mind, depression, dejection, despondency, gloominess, hypochondria, low spirits, moodiness, blues, disconsolateness, melancholia, heaviness of spirits, blue devils, megrims, sadness, gloom, dumps, vapors, hopelessness, pessimism, dolefulness, sorrow, despair, desperation, mopishness, grief, dolor, doldrums, distress, disgust of life, Slough of Despond, prostration, weariness, broken-heartedness.

2. Sober thoughtfulness, pensiveness, wistfulness, reverie, demureness, sobriety, soberness, seriousness, solemnity, grave face, gravity.

MELANGE, *n.* Mixture of heterogeneous elements, miscellany, jumble, potpourri, hodgepodge, confused mass, gallimaufry, farrago, olio, salmagundi, medley, mishmash, miscellaneous collection, intermixture, pastiche, hash, macaroni, mess, mingle-mangle, olla-podrida, *pasticcio (It.),* patchwork, omnium-gatherum *(humorous),* crazy quilt, mosaic, chowchow, motley, charivari, Noah's ark.

MELEE, *n.* Confusedly mixed fight, general affray, broil, fray, hand-to-hand conflict, riotous contest, mellay, scuffle, brawl, set-to, row, Donnybrook, fracas, pandemonium, rumpus, riot, tumult, commotion, altercation, shindy, tussle, scrap, scrimmage, skirmish, brush, battle royal, pitched battle, fisticuffs, mill, spar, bout.

MELIC, *adj.* Intended to be sung, suitable for singing, lyrical, choral, monodic, musical, melodious.

MELIORATE, *v.* Improve, make better, ameliorate, better, amend, mend, emend, reform, correct, rectify, revise, edit, doctor, ease, mitigate, palliate, promote, advance.

MELIORATION, *n.* Improvement, betterment, amelioration, mend, emendation, amendment, promotion, preferment, advancement, reformation, revision, rectification, correction, repair, recovery, mitigation, palliation.

MELLIFLUENCE, *n.* Sweet flow, smoothness, euphoniousness, euphony, silver tongue, concinnity, fluency, sweetness, mellowness, softness, eloquence, facundity, flow of words, *copia verborum (Lat.).* melodiousness, musicalness.

MELLIFLUOUS, *adj.* Flowing like honey, mellifluent, euphonious, silver-tongued, fluent, eloquent, euphonic, silver-toned, silvery, dulcet, sweet, soft, smooth, mellow, nectared, honeyed, melodious, harmonious, musical, liquid, sweettoned, sublime, impassioned, graceful, easy, rhythmical, felicitous, canorous, clear as a bell, fulltoned, resonant, ringing.

MELLOW, *adj.* 1. Ripe, mature, full-flavored, seasoned, luscious, delicious, tender, sweet.

2. Delicate, soft, rich, softened, pearly, subtle, pure, full, subdued, toned down, creamy, smooth, mild.

3. Mellifluous, silver-toned, melodious, musical, canorous, dulcet, silvery, sweetly flowing, orotund, euphonious, mellifluent, clear as a bell.

4. Tipsy, inebriated, drunk, intoxicated, drunken, tight, boozy, lush, muddled, maudlin, half seas over, screwed, oiled, primed, pifflicated, three sheets in the wind, in one's cups, *inter pocula (Lat.),* elevated, plastered, squiffy, sozzled, potulent, bibulous, bibacious, toping.

MELLOW, *v.* 1. Ripen, mature, wax, be converted into, become, grow, undergo a change into, age, run to seed.

2. Perfect, improve, bring to perfection, elaborate, dry, cure, season, salt, smoke.

3. Smooth down, soften, tone down, make gentle, subdue, temper.

MELODEON, *n.* 1. Small reed organ, harmonium, parlor organ, harmoniphon, wind instrument.

2. Accordion, concertina, seraphina.

MELODIOUS, *adj.* Tuneful, musical, melodic, euphonious, lyric, lyrical, singing, canorous, ariose, harmonious, ringing, resonant, full-toned, Orphean, sweet-sounding, euphonic, symphonious, dulcet, mellifluous, mellisonant, mellifluent, soft, rich, mellow, clear, silvery, agreeable, accordant, pleasing, silver-toned, deep-toned, tunable, melic.

MELODRAMA, *n.* A play which does not observe the dramatic laws of cause and effect but which intensifies and exaggerates, sensation drama, emotional drama, *drame larmoyant (Fr.),* soap opera *(colloq.),* tragicomedy, thriller.

MELODRAMATIC, *adj.* Sentimental and exaggerated, dramatic, sensational, stagey, theatrical, spectacular, histrionic, buskined, overacted, ham *(sl.),* soap opera *(colloq.),* hysterical, agonizing, thrilling, high-wrought, frantic, raving, flaming, overwrought.

MELODY, *n.* 1. Succession of single tones in musical composition, musical sounds in agreeable succession, pleasing succession of sounds as distinguished from harmony or rhythm, melodiousness, tunefulness, sweetness of sound, musicalness, mellifluence, euphony, musical quality, timbre, *Klangfarbe (Ger.),* tone color.

2. Tune, air, aria, ariette, chant, plainsong, theme, measure, cantilena, canticle, song, cantabile, strain, lay, carol, *chanson (Fr.), Lied (Ger.),* canzonet, ditty, ballad.

3. Chief voice part, descant, soprano, treble.

MELT, *v.* 1. Liquefy, dissolve, fuse, thaw, deliquesce, liquate, smelt, scorify, eliquate, flux, reduce to a liquid state by heat, colliquate, sweat, make lose substance, cause to become liquid.

2. Blend, shade, merge into, grow into, pass into.

3. Disappear, fade, evanesce, vanish, evaporate, pass away, sink, dwindle, waste away, dissipate, scatter.

4. Make gentle, soften in feeling, mollify, make susceptible, relax, subdue, touch, affect, move, incline, excite pity, disarm, propitiate.

MELTING POT, *n.* Pot in which metals are melted or fused, caldron, crucible, alembic, mortar, matrix, retort.

MEMBER, *n.* 1. Limb, organ, leg, arm, digit, finger, toe, *membrum virile (Lat.),* phallus, penis, ala, wing, pinion, appendage, tail, extremity.

2. Constituent, element, component, integral part of a larger body, subordinate part of a composite whole, portion, ingredient, radicle, subdivision.

MEMBERSHIP, *n.* Total number of persons belonging to a body, persons composing a society, body of members, personnel, community, roster, society, association, company, fellowship, club, fraternity, sodality, brotherhood.

MEMBRANE, *n.* Thin pliable layer of tissue serving to line and connect parts, integument, pellicle, skin, film, peel, sheet, envelope, chorion, perisarc, pericarp, endocarp, endocardium, tympan, web, drumhead, meninx.

MEMENTO, *n.* 1. Reminder of what is past or gone, remembrancer, memorial, token, souvenir, keepsake, relic, trophy, emblem, trace, vestige, monument, sign, mark, record.

2. Memento mori, death's head, skull and crossbones, skeleton at the feast, warning.

MEMOIR, *n.* Intimate biography, personal narrative, autobiography, personal history, biographical sketch, annals, letters, journal, diary, ana, recollections, reminiscences, experiences, life, adventures, memorials, memories, chronicles, first person singular, confessions.

MEMORABLE, *adj.* Worthy to be remembered, remarkable, significant, signal, notable, red-letter, historic, momentous, crucial, critical, vivid, eminent, illustrious, prominent, extraordinary, distinguished, celebrated, conspicuous, noticeable, particular, great, famous, important, uncommon, striking, unforgettable, noteworthy, full of incidents, eventful, solemn, marked, outstanding, salient, rare, special, unusual, stirring, impressive, consequential.

MEMORANDUM, *n.* A note made of something to be remembered, memo, entry, remembrancer, commemorative record, minute, jotting, file card, slip, document, list of agenda, list of items, reminder.

MEMORIAL, *adj.* Preserving the memory of a person or thing, commemorative, immortalized, time-honored, monumental, reverent, devotional, solemn, celebrated.

MEMORIAL, *n.* 1. Something designed to preserve the memory of a person or event, monument, mausoleum, cenotaph, tombstone, headstone, shaft, obelisk, monolith, column, dolmen, cromlech, menhir, pillar, slab, trophy, tablet, inscription, hatchment, escutcheon, reliquary, shrine, sacred place, sacred object, altar.

2. Commemorative record, memento, memorandum, remembrancer, reminder, souvenir, note, minute, entry.

MEMORIZE, *v.* Commit to memory, learn by heart, learn by rote, fix in the mind, con over, impress upon the memory, engrave in the memory, master, have at one's fingers' ends, learn, get, retain, keep in mind, retain the memory of, remember, dwell upon, brood over, hold in remembrance.

MEMORY, *n.* 1. Mental faculty of retaining and reviving impressions, capacity of recalling or recognizing previous experiences, recollection, reminiscence, remembrance, retentive memory, mental reproduction, readiness of memory, tenacious memory, retrospection, retrospect, recognition, retention, retentiveness, art of memory, *memoria technica (Lat.),* mnemotechny, mnemonics, mnemotechnics, mnemonization.

2. Commemorative record, commemoration, memorial, memento, token, reminder, suggestion, hint, memorandum, keepsake, souvenir, relic, remembrancer, testimonial, jubilee, anniversary.

3. Reputation, fame, renown, celebrity, repute, notoriety, glory, eminence, distinction, mark, name, account, note, esteem, estimation, honor, prestige, éclat, report, regard, respect.

MENACE, *v.* Direct a threat against, intimidate, threaten, alarm, exhibit hostile intentions, show hostility, terrify, bulldoze, browbeat, bully, snarl, growl, defy, shake a fist at, thunder at, fulminate, look daggers, bluster, inspire fear, raise apprehensions, scare, affright, strike terror into, haunt, beset, obsess, put in bodily fear, terrorize, cow, daunt.

MENACE, *n.* Threat, minacity, intimidation, abuse, defiance, fulmination, commination, gathering clouds, warning, dehortation, admonition, handwriting on the wall, foghorn, monitor, siren, warning voice, signs of the times, Cassandra, bird of ill omen, clouds on the horizon, brewing storm, stormy horizon.

MENACING, *adj.* Threatening, fatidical, oracular, minatory, minacious, comminatory, premonitory, ominous, portentous, prophetic, vaticinal, sibylline, haruspical, presageful, augural, monitory, prescious, pregnant with, significant of, warning, cautionary, lowering, frowning, impending, imminent, dangerous, formidable, hanging over, predictive.

MENAGE, *n.* 1. Domestic establishment, household, family, kin, near and dear ones.

2. Household management, housekeeping, housewifery, stewardship, regimen, regime, economics, economy.

MENAGERIE, *n.* Collection of wild animals for exhibition, zoological garden, *jardin zoologique (Fr.), Tiergarten (Ger.),* zoo, vivarium, terrarium.

MEND, *v.* 1. Make whole or sound, repair, restore, put in repair, retouch, refit, touch up, patch, darn, stitch, redintegrate, recondition, renovate, renew, reconstruct, rehabilitate, rejuvenate, regenerate, set to right, put in order, tinker, cobble, revamp, fix, recover, freshen, refresh, revivify, recreate, strengthen, reinforce, refashion, reform, remodel, reclaim, cure, heal, remedy.

2. Better, meliorate, improve, ameliorate, make better, correct, remove defects in, rectify, amend, reform, emend, revise, doctor, make improvements, polish, uplift, civilize, raise, ennoble, promote, advance, cultivate, further, forward, enhance, benefit, profit, foster, aid, help.

MENDACIOUS, *adj.* Lying, untruthful, false, deceitful, untrue, unveracious, fictitious, made up, pseudological, prevaricative, falsified, distorted, fabricated, invented, trumped up, fraudulent, evasive, insincere, disingenuous, forsworn, *Parthis mendacior (Lat.),* hypocritical, two-faced, doubletongued, Janus-faced, perfidious, collusive, spurious, sham, mock, make-believe, faked, counterfeit, pseudo, so-called, feigned, pretended, bogus, void of foundation, far from the truth, unfounded, *ben trovato (It.),* forged, exaggerated, fabulous, mythological, *outré (Fr.),* hyperbolical, colored, embroidered, highflying, extravagant, mythical, misrepresented, misstated, perverted.

MENDACITY, *n.* 1. Quality of being mendacious, disposition to lie, habitual lying, untruthfulness, deception, deceit, duplicity, falsehood, pseudology, falsification, falsity, misrepresentation, bad faith, guile, perjury, false swearing, perversion of truth, suppression of truth, false coloring, distortion, prevarication, exaggeration, equivocation, fencing, shuffling, fraudulency, fraud, evasion, dissimulation, dissembling, pretending, lip service, windowdressing, mere show, eyewash, double-dealing, hypocrisy, insincerity, humbug, cant, jesuitism, casuistry, pharisaism, crocodile tears, quackery, buncombe, charlatanism, Judas kiss, flimflam, perfidy, imposture, chicanery, cozenage, circumvention, collusion, ingannation, sharp practice.

2. Lie, falsehood, untruth, fabrication, invention, misstatement, tall story, fib, whopper, fable, fiction, canard, yarn, traveler's tale, cock-and-

bull story, Canterbury tale, claptrap, fairy tale, moonshine, myth, bosh, white lie.

MENDICANCY, *n.* Beggary, mendicity, beggarliness, begging life, mendication, begging, pauperism, impecuniosity, insolvency, indigence, poverty, pennilessness, penury, neediness, want, necessity, need, destitution, lack, privation, *res angusta domi (Lat.),* wolf at the door, difficulties, straits, broken fortune, exigency, dole-seeking, alms-begging, necessitude, panhandling, needy circumstances, hand-to-mouth existence, empty pocket.

MENDICANT, *n.* One who lives by begging, beggar, panhandler, pauper, starveling, *pauvre-diable (Fr.),* alms-seeker, cadger, mumper, tramp, hobo, vagabond, beachcomber, knight of the road, vagrant, *lazzarone (It.),* mudlark, ragamuffin, tatterdemalion, pariah, weary Willie, bum, ragpicker, *chiffonier (Fr.),* palmer, parasite, begging friar, mendicant monk, ascetic, fakir.

MENIAL, *adj.* Proper to domestic servants, servile, slavish, subservient, obsequious, fawning, cringing, truckling, groveling, sycophantic, parasitical, prostrate, abject, mean, base, timeserving, low, lowly, humble, lowborn, ignoble, common, vile, scrubby, sorry, beggarly, proletarian, plebeian, underling, subaltern.

MENIAL, *n.* 1. A domestic servant, lackey, flunky, footman, valet, attendant, domestic, waiter, drudge, fag, factotum, slavery, maid of all work, servitor, buttons, manservant, boots, orderly, butler, steward, boy, footboy, retainer, yeoman, henchman, page, squire, cupbearer, trainbearer, equerry, jockey, groom, helper, subordinate, assistant, underling, agent, understrapper, apprentice, employee, maidservant, handmaid, abigail, ancilla, nursemaid, *bonne (Fr.),* scullion, Cinderella, laundress, washerwoman, charwoman, cleaning woman, chambermaid.

2. A servile person, sycophant, bootlicker, toady, doer of dirty work, hanger-on, parasite, yes-man, lickspittle, stooge, timeserver, tool, flatterer, courtier, truckler, sponge.

MENSURABLE, *adj.* That may be measured, measurable, computable, fathomable, reckonable, gaugeable, appraisable, determinable, assessable, surveyable, admeasurable, estimable.

MENSURATION, *n.* Determination of area and volume, surveying, survey, measuring, measurement, admeasurement, valuation, assessment, appraisement, assize, estimate, gauging, reckoning, estimation.

MENTAL, *adj.* 1. Existing in the mind, intellectual, psychological, psychic, metaphysical, psychical, subjective, ideal, rational, spiritual, subliminal, inward, abstract.

2. Gifted, brainy, clever, talented, learned, scholarly, quick-witted, smart, bright, well-informed, intelligent, keen, inventive, imaginative, percipient, knowing, long-headed, astute, shrewd, thoughtful, discerning, perspicacious, penetrative, pensive, reflective, cogitative, deliberative, speculative, contemplative, wistful, studious, introspective.

MENTALITY, *n.* Mental endowment, thinking capacity, intellectuality, mind, brains, acumen, penetration, keenness of mind, intelligence, understanding, judgment, gray matter, comprehension, perception, intuition, insight, cognition, rationality, reason, intellectual faculties, intellectualism, percipience, wisdom, wit, parts, sagacity, mother wit, long-headedness, smartness, perspicacity, discernment, mental power.

MENTALLY, *adv.* In *or* with the mind, intellectually, psychically, psychologically, inwardly, rationally, thoughtfully, pensively, perspicaciously, brainily.

MENTION, *v.* Refer to briefly, declare incidentally, specify, state, remark, tell, name, impart, cite, allude to, make mention of, make known, speak of, disclose, report, communicate, divulge, hint at, broach, animadvert upon, touch upon, insinuate, intimate, reveal, advert to, adduce, observe, inform, acquaint with, apprise, recite, enumerate, recount, note, quote, narrate, utter, report, suggest, tell of, advise, notify, enlighten, affirm, assert, express, mention, retail, signify, describe, confide to, explain, give inside information, give the low-down, promulgate, disseminate, publish, broadcast, indicate, imply, let fall, give a pointer to, tip off.

MENTION, *n.* Passing reference, cursory allusion, a speaking of, noting, notification, notice, designation, citation, rehearsal, indication, recitation, recital, statement, relation, intimation, insinuation, hint, suggestion, acquaintance, enlightenment, communication, annunciation, announcement, representation, specification, report, monition, advice, advisement, account, acquainting, instruction, outpouring, innuendo, passing word, inkling, word in the ear, cue, *verbum sapienti (Lat.),* word to the wise.

MENTOR, *n.* Wise and trusted counselor, instructor, adviser, guide, monitor, master, teacher, trainer, tutor, director, proctor, pedagogue, preceptor, Nestor, wise man, sage, pundit, authority, luminary, oracle, *esprit fort (Fr.),* shining light, example, man of learning, longhead, expert.

MENU, *n.* List of the dishes served at a meal, bill of fare, *carte (Fr.),* cuisine, table, *à la carte (Fr.),* cover, *prix fixe (Fr.),* ordinary, spread, meal, repast, course.

MEPHITIC, *adj.* Offensive to the smell, foul-smelling, fetid, stinking, noxious, noisome, pestilential, miasmic, poisonous, baleful, malodorous, putrid, rancid, morbiferous, morbific, septic, deleterious, azotic.

MEPHITIS, *n.* Noxious exhalation, noisome stench, miasma, poisonous emanation, pestilential smell, azote, sewer gas, stink, fetor, fume, black damp, choke damp, malodor, fetidness, reek, effluvium.

MERCANTILE, *adj.* Pertaining to merchants or trade, commercial, trading, engaged in commerce, jobbing, mercatorial, marketable, staple, for sale, in the market, wholesale, retail.

MERCENARY, *adj.* 1. Working merely for gain, serving in a foreign army, hireling, hired, paid, purchased, auxiliary, venal, in the train of, in one's pay, at one's call, in one's employ.

2. Parsimonious, acquisitive, avaricious, grasping, sordid, greedy, rapacious, selfish, penurious, niggardly, pennywise, ungenerous, illiberal, covetous, usurious, extortionate, hidebound, close-fisted, peddling, mean, stingy, self-seeking, self-interested, egocentric, worldly-minded, timeserving.

MERCENARY, *n.* Professional soldier serving in a foreign army, hireling, myrmidon, Hessian, hired soldier, auxiliary, legionary, legionnaire, campaigner, janissary, Mameluke, condottiere, irregular.

MERCHANDISE, *n.* Manufactured goods, wares, effects, commodities, stock, articles, vendibles, goods for sale, produce, cargo, stock in trade, staples.

MERCHANT, *n.* One who buys and sells commodities for profit, wholesale trader, tradesman, dealer, storekeeper, shopkeeper, retailer, trafficker, monger, shopman, chandler, salesman, peddler, costermonger, huckster, hawker, *vivandier (Fr.),* sutler, colporteur, duffer *(sl.),* street vendor, faker, seller, jobber, packman, chapman, commercial traveler, drummer.

MERCHANTABLE, *adj.* Salable, marketable, vendible, staple, in demand, popular.

MERCHANTMAN, *n.* Merchant ship, trading vessel, argosy, galleon, freight steamer, freighter, coaster, cargo boat.

MERCIFUL, *adj.* Exercising mercy, compassionate, clement, pitiful, lenient, forgiving, ruthful, forbearing, sparing, exorable, pitying, piteous, sympathetic, gracious, indulgent, kind, benignant, tender, humane, tender-hearted, gentle, kind-hearted, soft-hearted, feeling, soft, beneficent, moderate, touched, humanitarian.

MERCILESS, *adj.* Hard-hearted, cruel, harsh, pitiless, inhuman, savage, fell, barbarous, unrelenting, severe, relentless, unsparing, unmerciful, unfeeling, inexorable, uncompassionate, callous, stony-hearted, brutal, hardened, unkind, ruthless, heartless, implacable, remorseless, unforgiving, unpitying, brutish, marble-hearted, fierce, stony, ferocious, unyielding, inclement, grim-visaged, Draconian, obdurate, inflexible.

MERCURIAL, *adj.* Changeable, flighty, inconstant, fickle, mobile, erratic, restless, touch-and-go, capricious, whimsical, notional, irresolute, feverish, wavering, unstable, unsteady, fluctuating, highly strung, excitable, electric, hurried, hasty, quick, impassioned, enthusiastic, galvanic, impetuous, impulsive, irrepressible, ungovernable, active, sprightly, spirited, vivacious, ebullient, lively, nimble, prompt, giddy, light-hearted, cheerful, gay.

MERCURY, *n.* 1. Heavy silver-white metallic element remarkable for its fluidity at ordinary temperatures, hydrargyrum, Hg *(symbol),* quicksilver.

2. Roman deity, messenger of the gods, carrier of news, Hermes *(Greek),* courier, nuncio, emissary, envoy, herald, god of dexterity and eloquence, god of commerce.

MERCY, *n.* 1. Kindly forbearance shown toward an offender, clemency toward an enemy in one's power, lenience, mildness, leniency, lenity, benevolence, compassion, pity, gentleness, kindness, tenderness, ruth, bowels of compassion, sympathy, soft-heartedness, tolerance, toleration, humaneness, humanity, loving-kindness, indulgence, charity, forgiveness, pardon, quarter, favor, benignity, fellow feeling, commiseration, tender-heartedness, grace, long-suffering.

2. Discretionary power, disposal, discretion, *manus (Lat.),* rule, control, domination, dominion, puissance, command, influence, management, direction, regulation, ordering.

MERE, *n.* Lakelet, pool, pond, tarn, loch, plash.

MERE, *adj.* 1. Pure and simple, plain, bare, stark, sheer, bald, naked, sole, nothing else but, utter, blank, such, unqualified, unmixed, unmitigated, entire, absolute.

2. Common, uneventful, ordinary, commonplace, tolerable, so-so, inconsiderable, inappreciable, insignificant, nugatory, trifling, slight,

flimsy, slender, idle, shallow, petty, piddling, niggling, paltry.

MERELY, *adv.* Only as specified and nothing more, purely, simply, solely, alone, only, barely, just, hardly, scarcely, plainly, unqualifiedly, absolutely, entirely, utterly.

MERETRICIOUS, *adj.* Alluring by a show of false attractions, showily attractive, gaudy, tawdry, brummagem, pinchbeck, spurious, sham, flashy, loud, tinsel, spangled, theatrical, showy, vulgar, make-believe, gingerbread, bedizened, tricked out, obtrusive, garish, mock, counterfeit, bogus, factitious, artificial, cheap, false, valueless, worthless, dissolute, licentious, gallant, rakish, riggish.

MERGE, *v.* 1. Mingle, blend, fuse, assimilate, amalgamate, consolidate, compound, centralize, concentrate, agglutinate, center, solidify, cement, lump together, impregnate, coalesce, absorb, incorporate, combine, join, unite, link, embody, intermix, alloy, interfuse, federate, league, band together, mass, confederate, associate, pool.
2. Cause to be swallowed up or absorbed, sink the identity of by combination, lose, bury, immerge, immerse, submerge, involve, insert.

MERGER, *n.* Statutory combination of several corporations, union of two or more business enterprises, trust, incorporation, amalgamation, pool, combine, cartel, syndicate.

MERIDIAN, *n.* 1. Noon, noonday, noontide, midday, high noon, broad daylight.
2. Zone, climate, clime, latitude.
3. Meridian of life, prime, flower of age, *floruit (Lat.),* manhood, virility, adulthood, maturity.
4. Summit, point of highest development, zenith, acme, apex, culmination, pinnacle, height, top, vertex, *ne plus ultra (Lat.),* utmost height, apogee, maximum, pitch, climax, crowning point, peak, crown, tiptop, crest, brow.

MERIDIONAL, *adj.* 1. Meridian, midday, noon, noonday, noontide, sunny, blazing, resplendent, fulgent, relucent, ablaze, aglow, bright as noonday, beamy, radiant.
2. Southern, southerly.

MERIT, *n.* 1. Claim to commendation, good desert, credit, due, right, meed, prerogative, prescription, privilege, title.
2. Worthiness, worth, excellence, goodness, virtue, quality, value, uprightness, rectitude, morality, integrity, morals, probity, nobleness, honor, welldoing, good behavior, good actions, wellspent life, temperance, justice, fortitude, prudence, purity, innocence, chastity, strength, efficacy, potency, force, energy, effectiveness, efficiency, perfection, stability, truthfulness, honesty, righteousness, character.

MERIT, *v.* Deserve, be worthy of, be entitled to, have a right to, earn, have claim to, discharge one's duty, be virtuous, fight the good fight, practice virtue, fulfill one's duty, keep in the right path, acquit oneself well, set a good example, richly deserve, be on one's best behavior, keep straight, redeem one's pledge, do good, excel, transcend, pass muster, stand the test, be good.

MERITED, *adj.* Deserved, due, condign, rightful, fitting, suitable, fit, adequate, proper, just, right, correct, appropriate, meet, befitting, seemly.

MERITORIOUS, *adj.* Deserving of reward or commendation, commendable, possessing merit, worthy, excellent, good, laudable, estimable, praiseworthy, fine, creditable, plausible, deserv-

ing, exemplary, righteous, high-principled, conscientious, honest, admirable, heroic, manly, honorable, chivalrous, unselfish, magnanimous, disinterested, charitable, philanthropic, generous, sacrificing, noble, self-denying.

MERMAID, *n.* Imaginary female marine creature having the tail of a fish and the head and trunk of a woman, water spirit, undine, marine sprite, nymph, merrow, seamaid, sea nymph, siren.

MERRIMENT, *n.* Merry gaiety, hilarity, jocularity, mirth, joviality, jollity, liveliness, sportiveness, frolic, laughter, happiness, monkeyshine, light-heartedness, cheer, pleasantry, amusement, jocundity, playfulness, enthusiasm, entertainment, conviviality, enjoyment, gladness, festivity, celebration, cheerfulness, fun, tomfoolery, buffoonery, joyousness, jollification, merrymaking, exhilaration, recreation, mummery, levity, gleefulness, glee, joy, joyfulness, geniality, good humor, good spirits, light heart, rejoicing, reveling, jubilation, flush, whoopee, drollery, romp, gambol, antic, prank, lark, skylarking, spree, round of pleasures.

MERRY, *adj.* Full of cheer and gaiety, cheerful, gay, joyous in disposition, jovial, gladsome, blithe, vivacious, light-hearted, jocund, gleeful, mirthful, facetious, sportive, hilarious, lively, blithesome, frolicsome, buxom, wanton, jolly, sprightly, airy, high-spirited, genial, arch, cheery, waggish, droll, comical, gamesome, skylarking, rejoicing, reveling, happy, festive, laughing, convivial, jocular, bonny, sporting, jubilant, buoyant, lightsome, rollicking, devil-may-care, jesting, full of fun, playful, sunny, hearty, debonair, jaunty, saucy, chipper, dashing, racy, dapper, social, sparkling, animated, tricksy, skittish, elated, flushed, exultant, cock-a-hoop, frisky.

MERRY-ANDREW, *n.* Clown, zany, harlequin, buffoon, fool, scaramouch, jester, mountebank, droll, pickle-herring, jack-pudding, mimic, court jester, wag, humorist, wit, *farceur (Fr.),* punch, mime, wearer of the cap and bells, pantaloon, madcap, *grimacier (Fr.),* jokesmith, spark, *drôle de corps (Fr.), gaillard (Fr.), bel espirt (Fr.),* life of the party.

MERRYMAKING, *n.* Merry festivity, frolic, lark, funmaking, gambol, gratification, pleasure, delectation, entertainment, amusement, diversion, recreation, pleasure-making, whoopee, jollification, conviviality, highjinks, revel, revelry, festival, jubilee, feast, celebration, blowout *(colloq.),* carnival, sport, gaiety, festive board, cheer, bacchanal, saturnalia, carousal, debauch, drinking bout, wassail, orgies, dissipation, free living, indulgence, epicureanism, licentiousness, crapulence, debauchery.

MESA, *n.* Flat-top land form bounded wholly or in part by steep rock walls, plateau, elevated plain, tableland, heath, veld, moor, uplands, downs, tundra, steppe, prairie, pampas, champaign.

MESH, *n.* 1. Open space of network, interstice, meshwork, network, reticulation, net, web, cobweb, plexus, silk lace, netting, embroidery, openwork, dropstitch clock, fishnet.
2. Meshes, toils, pitfall, gin, trap, snare, decoy, noose, birdlime, ambush, maze.

MESH, *v.* Catch in the meshes of a net, enmesh, entangle, ensnare, snare, spread the toils, forelay, lay a trap for, lime, hook in, entrap, entoil, benet, springe, sniggle, illaqueate.

MESMERIC, *adj.* Hypnotic, spellbinding, soporific, somniferous, trance-laying, dormitive, magnetic, odylic, telepathic, psychometric.

MESMERISM, *n.* Hypnotism, animal magnetism, hypnotic suggestion, hypnosis, spellbinding, trance-laying, mesmeric trance, hypnotic sleep.

MESMERIZE, *v.* Hypnotize, magnetize, induce hypnosis, spellbind, lay a trance, place under control, place in a trance, put to controlled sleep, weigh down the eyelids, rivet the eyes upon.

MESS, *n.* 1. Jumble, confused mass, litter, conglomeration, medley, miscellany, hodgepodge, mixture, farrago, olio, salmagundi, mishmash, mélange, gallimaufry, potpourri, stew, olla-podrida, hash, mingle-mangle, omnium-gatherum, pastiche, patchwork, chow-chow, motley.

2. State of embarrassing confusion, muddle, difficult situation, plight, predicament, pickle, perplexity, botch, difficulty, trouble, quandary, dilemma, fix, pass, strait, pinch, hot water, scrape, imbroglio, emergency, crisis, trial.

3. Group regularly taking meals together, set who eat together, sitting, table, set who habitually take their meals together, chief master-at-arms' mess, midshipmen's mess, steerage mess, wardroom mess, warrant officers' mess.

MESSAGE, *n.* Communication, notice, dispatch, word, news, missive, letter, intimation, account, tidings, report, note, intelligence, advice, bulletin, cable, cablegram, telegram, wire, marconigram, radiogram, telephone call, radiophone, radiotelegram, wireless.

MESSENGER, *n.* 1. Forerunner, harbinger, herald, precursor, pursuivant, apparitor, evangel, crier, trumpeter, angel, nuncio, legate, emissary, envoy, intermediary, delegate, go-between, marshal, Hermes, Mercury, Gabriel, Ariel, Iris, representative, nuntius, internunciary.

2. Express courier, carrier, runner, express, intelligencer, commissionaire, dispatch rider, errand boy, bell hop, mailman, postman, letter carrier, *facteur (Fr.),* informer, scout, secret agent, spy, stool pigeon, stoolie *(slang),* informant, reporter, newsmonger, spokesman, mouthpiece, tipster.

MESSIAH, *n.* Expected deliverer, savior, redeemer, mediator, advocate, intercessor.

MESSMATE, *n.* Associate in a ship's mess, commensal, buddy, comrade, friend, mate, partner, companion, confrere, partner, fellow, consort, pal, chum, side kick *(colloq.),* bedfellow, bunkie, shipmate, roommate, colleague, intimate, neighbor, fast friend, alter ego.

MESSY, *adj.* Untidy, disheveled, bedraggled, disordered, turbid, out of place, slovenly, confused, sloppy, dirty, chaotic, topsy-turvy, knotted, entangled, raveled, tangled, inextricable, unkempt, frowzy, dowdy, grubby, slatternly, slipshod.

METAL, *n.* 1. Elementary substance that is crystalline when solid, ore, bullion, pig, element that forms a base by combining with a hydroxyl group, alloy.

2. Gold, silver, copper, tin, iron, lead, mercury.

METALLIC, *adj.* 1. Of the nature of metal, metalline, ory, golden, aureate, silvery, argentine, tinny, iron, leaden, stannic, mercurial.

2. *(Of sound)* Harsh, piercing, shrill, trumpet-toned, raucous, rough, gruff, horrisonous, stridulous, strident, hoarse.

METAMORPHIC, *adj.* Characterized by change of form, variable, changeable, mutable, protean, modifiable, alterative, changeful, changing, versatile, kaleidoscopic, mobile, plastic.

METAMORPHOSE, *v.* Change the form of, subject to metamorphosis, transform, transfigure, transmute, vary, alter, diversify, modulate, modify, revamp, convert, transmogrify, reshape, recast, remodel, change the face of.

METAMORPHOSIS, *n.* 1. Complete change in appearance, transfiguration, transmutation, change of form, transformation, metaphysis, mutation, alteration, variation, permutation, metastasis, modification, transubstantiation, metagenesis, catalysis, transmogrification, conversion.

2. Proteus, moon, avatar, kaleidoscope, chameleon, quicksilver.

METAPHOR, *n.* Figure of speech to suggest a resemblance of one thing to another, figurative expression, trope, analogy, similitude, comparison, likening, parallel, collation, identification, metonymy, tralatition, enallage, imagery, personification, anagoge, simile, allegory, apologue.

METAPHORIC, *adj.* Figurative, metaphorical, parabolic, tropical, allegorical, allusive, symbolical, emblematical, typical, descriptive, pictorial, catachrestical, tralatitious, anagogical, referential.

METAPHYSICAL, *adj.* Concerned with abstract thought, relating to first principles and ultimate grounds, transcendental, ontological, immaterial, incorporeal, spiritual, unsubstantial, Platonistic, superphysical, intangible, impalpable, psychical, speculative, abstract, visionary, philosophical, highly abstruse, oversubtle, intellectual, ideal, supersensible, incomprehensible, hyperphysical.

METAPHYSICS, *n.* Branch of philosophy that treats of first principles, ontology, epistemology, science of existence, speculative philosophy, cosmology.

METE, *v.* Apportion by measure, measure out, allot, dispense, allocate, distribute, deal, divide, dole out, fork out, dispose of, give away, present, divvy, administer, detail, share, cast, assign, appropriate.

METE, *n.* Limiting mark, bound, measure, term, limit, terminus, boundary, butt, goal, bourn, destination.

METEMPSYCHOSIS, *n.* Passage of the soul from one body to another, rebirth of the soul at death in another body, reincarnation, transmigration, metagenesis, transanimation, avatar.

METEOR, *n.* Transient fiery streak in the sky produced by a meteoroid passing through earth's atmosphere, bolide, meteoroid, meteorite, aerolite, falling star, shooting star, fireball.

METEORIC, *adj.* 1. Flashing like a meteor, transiently brilliant, phosphorescent, rutilant, aglow, ablaze, blazing, relucent, effulgent, luminiferous, luciferous, flaming, fiery.

2. Swift, rapid, speedy, ephemeral, transitory, transient, fast, instant, sudden, unexpected, short-lived, evanescent, fugacious, fugitive, brief, momentary.

METEOROID, *n.* Remnant of a comet heated to luminosity while traveling through space, falling stone, shooting star, meteor, meteorite.

METEOROLOGY, *n.* Science dealing with the atmosphere and its phenomena, weather, climate, rise and fall of the barometer, climatology, climatography, aerology, aerography, aeroscopy.

METHOD, *n.* 1. Orderly and systematic mode of procedure, way of doing something in accordance with a definite plan, manner of doing, modus operandi, course, process, settled procedure, rule, means, technique, usage, program, form, fashion, formula, routine.

2. Arrangement, order, scheme, system, design, plan, orderly disposition, classification, categorization.

METHODICAL, *adj.* Systematic, orderly, systematical, methodic, well-regulated, formal, exact, businesslike, regular, step by step, tidy, precise, neat, orderly, *en règle (Fr.),* uniform, shipshape,

METHODIZE, *v.* Reduce to method, arrange with method, systematize, organize, classify, regulate, systemize, digest, coordinate.

METICULOUS, *adj.* Solicitous about minute details, minutely careful, finical, scrupulous, particular, precise, exact, punctilious, literal, accurate, strict, severe, rigorous, rigid, scientific, mathematical, nice, fine, delicate.

METROPOLIS, *n.* Mother city, capital, chief city, big city, megalopolis.

METTLE, *n.* Pluck, stamina, spirit, sand, grit, backbone, nerve, spunk, courage, hardihood, valor, resoluteness, fearlessness, resolution, heart, boldness, derring-do, daring, élan, dash, intrepidity, audacity, self-reliance, gallantry, heroism, prowess, rashness, chivalry, confidence, fortitude, manliness, firmness, tenacity, manhood, vigor, fire, ardor, enthusiasm, animation, bravery, determination, vim, earnestness, go, energy, intensity, temper, character, characteristic disposition.

METTLESOME, *adj.* Courageous, brave, spirited, high-spirited, mettled, valiant, valorous, heroic, gallant, chivalrous, fiery, ardent, vivacious, sprightly, brisk, gay, lively, lion-hearted, unafraid, resolute, manly, virile, plucky, dashing, animated, nervy, self-reliant, self-confident, energetic, vigorous, dauntless, active, forceful, daring, venturesome, rash, bold, keen, spunky, game *(colloq.).*

MEW, *v.* 1. Shed feathers, molt, change, cast the skin, exfoliate, desquamate, peel, pare, doff, shed, cast off.

2. Shut up in a mew, encase, enclose, confine, coop, cage, imprison, stable, immure, impound, pen, corral, rail in, lock up.

MEW, *n.* 1. Seamew, seagull, gull, cob.

2. *(Pl.)* A set of stables around a court, pen, barn, kennel, byre, hutch, coop, shed.

MEWL, *v.* Cry, bawl, squall, caterwaul, whine, miaul, pule, purr.

MEZZANINE, *n.* Low story between two other stories of greater height, entresol.

MEZZO, *adj.* Middle, half, medium, mean, medial, mid, intermediate, mediate, middlemost, intermediary.

MEZZOTINT, *n.* Copper or steel engraving made by burnishing or scraping away a uniformly roughened surface, half-tone, black and white, line engraving, plate engraving.

MIASMA, *n.* Noxious exhalations from putrescent organic matter, floating effluvia, mephitis, azote, malaria, sewer gas, stench, toxic fume, fetor, black damp, choke damp, reek, mofette, empyreuma, bad air, haze, poisoned air, infection, contagion.

MIASMATIC, *adj.* Mephitic, pestilential, malarious, noxious, noisome, insalubrious, morbific, foul, septic, morbiferous, deleterious, azotic, poisonous, virulent, toxic, infectious, contagious, catching, toxiferous, deadly, lethal, injurious, unwholesome, pernicious.

MICROBE, *n.* Microscopic being of the animal or vegetable kingdom, disease-causing bacterium, microorganism, germ, bacillus, micrococcus, microparasite, microzyme, spirochete, spirillum, vibrio, streptococcus, diplococcus, planococcus, staphylococcus, meningococcus, microphyte, zoogloea, schizomycete, zygote, spore, zygospore, zoospore, arthrospore, gamete.

MICROSCOPE, *n.* Optical instrument having a magnifying lens for inspecting objects too small to be seen in detail by the naked eye, magnifier, magnifying glass, meniscus, teinoscope, megascope, micrometer.

MICROSCOPIC, *adj.* So small as to be invisible without the use of a microscope, minute, infinitesimal, tiny, wee, minikin, very little, imperceptible, molecular, atomic, evanescent, microbic, embryonic, animalcular, microbial, homeopathic, exiguous, diminutive, exceedingly fine, inappreciable.

MID, *adj.* At or near the middle point, occupying a middle position, middle, intervening, mean, medial, midmost, middlemost, central, intermediate, equidistant, intermediary, mediate, midway, interjacent, halfway.

MIDDAY, *n.* The middle of the day, noon, noontime, noontide, high noon, noonday, meridian.

MIDDLE, *adj.* Equally distant from extremes or limits, equidistant, halfway, central, axial, intermediate, intermediary, pivotal, equatorial, mediate, midmost, mid, middlemost, medial, mean, midway, median, interjacent.

MIDDLE, *n.* 1. Central part, center, midst, midmost, medium, mean, thick.

2. Navel, omphalos, umbilicus, nucleus, kernel, core, nave, hub, bull's-eye, heart, axis, pivot, midriff, diaphragm, waist.

3. Equal distance, equidistance, interjacence, half distance, equidivision, bisection, equator, medial line, halfway house.

MIDDLE AGE, *n.* Period between youth and old age, maturity, prime of life, full age, floruit, prime, virility, manhood, adulthood, majority, flower of age, full bloom, meridian of life.

MIDDLE-AGED, *adj.* Intermediate in age between youth and old age, in one's prime, mature, *entre deux âges (Fr.),* graying, of ripe age, matronly.

MIDDLE CLASSES, *n., pl.* Classes intermediate between the classes of higher and lower social rank, class socially intermediate between the aristocracy and the laboring class, bourgeoisie, classes in average circumstances.

MIDDLEMAN, *n.* Intermediary who distributes goods from producer to consumer on his own account, agent, factor, broker, jobber, salesman, commissioner, go-between, medium, intermedium, interagent.

MIDDLING, *adj.* Moderately large or good, moderate, ordinary, passable, average, mediocre, tolerable, medium, betwixt and between, so-so, *comme ci comme ça (Fr.), cosi cosi (It.),* fair, indifferent, milk and water, run of the mill, pretty good, well-enough, not bad, decent, admissible, unobjectionable, bearable, second-rate, secondary, inferior.

MIDGET, *n.* Very small person, little man, pygmy, dwarf, hop-o'-my-thumb, Tom Thumb, homunculus, manikin, runt, Lilliputian, pigwidgeon, chit, elf, dapperling, fingerling, cock-sparrow, dandiprat.

MIDMOST, *adj.* Middlemost, middle, halfway,

central, midway, medial, median, intermediate, equidistant, interjacent.

MIDNIGHT, *n.* Dead of night, 12 P.M., stroke of midnight, witching hour, noon of night.

MIDSHIPMAN, *n.* Sailor, mariner, seaman, middy, reefer, navigator, tar, gob, salt, bluejacket, skipper, mate, naval cadet, ensign, sublieutenant.

MIDST, *n.* Middle, bosom, heart, thick, dead center, kernel, core, nucleus, axis, nucleolus, bull's-eye, navel, hub, umbilicus, midriff, diaphragm.

MIDWAY, *adj.* To the middle of the distance, halfway, equidistant, intermediate, intermediary, mediate, equatorial.

MIDWIFE, *n.* Woman who assists in childbirth, *accoucheuse (Fr.)*, obstetrician, Lucina.

MIDWIFERY, *n.* Art of assisting women in childbirth, tocology, obstetrics, gynaecology, travail, *accouchement (Fr.)*, parturition, delivery, geniture.

MIEN, *n.* Air, aspect, appearance, countenance, look, expression, visage, demeanor, manner, deportment, bearing, carriage, port, conduct, behavior, guise, presence, gait, feature, contour, attitude, action, gesture, style, semblance.

MIFF, *n.* (*Colloq.*) Petulant displeasure, petty quarrel, pique, dudgeon, umbrage, slight resentment, tiff, huff; animosity, indignation, acerbity, soreness, acrimony, bitterness, asperity, rankling, bad humor, ill temper, choler, dander, fume, pucker, angry mood, pet, tantrum, fit, sulks, scowl.

MIFF, *v.* (*Colloq.*) 1. Give offense to, displease, affront, offend, vex, provoke, give umbrage, hurt the feelings, nettle, discompose, pique, huff, rile, irritate, incense, chafe, embitter, envenom, wound, put out of humor, raise one's dander.

2. Take offense, have a petty quarrel, boil with indignation, lose one's temper, stamp the foot, rear on one's hind legs, fly off the handle, pout, scowl, frown, crab, grouch.

MIGHT, *n.* Strength, potency, puissance, power, vigor, energy, force, prowess, main, ability, efficacy, efficiency, cogency, vehemence, intensity, robustness, sturdiness, stamina, muscle, toughness, durability, competence, capability, capableness, lustihood, brawn, sinews, physique, thews, virility, grit.

MIGHTILY, *adv.* 1. In a mighty manner, strongly, vigorously, powerfully, strenuously, with might and main, tooth and nail, hammer and tongs, by main force, potently, forcibly, *vi et armis (Lat.)*.

2. (*Colloq.*) To a great extent, in large degree, greatly, very much.

MIGHTY, *adj.* 1. Strong, robust, powerful, sturdy, hardy, lusty, potent, puissant, stalwart, strapping, husky, muscular, brawny, herculean, manful, virile, forcible, vigorous, adamantine, stout, hard, invincible, unconquerable, irresistible, indomitable, overpowering, broad-shouldered, sinewy, able, bold, valiant, courageous, valorous.

2. Of great size, extremely large, immense, enormous, vast, huge, titanic, gigantic, Brobdingnagian, massive, towering, stupendous, amplitudinous, monstrous, elephantine, colossal, Gargantuan, ponderous, majestic, imposing.

3. Haughty, high and mighty, overweening, lofty, insolent, puffed up, vainglorious, swollen, flushed, blown, bumptious, supercilious, high-handed, imperious, magisterial, arrogant, consequential.

MIGRATE, *v.* Go from one place of abode to settle in another, immigrate, emigrate, move periodically, wander, trek, transmigrate, peregrinate, journey, roam, rove, nomadize.

MIGRATORY, *adj.* Roving, nomadic, migrating, transmigratory, wandering, unsettled, emigrant, transient, roaming, vagrant, itinerant, wayfaring, peregrinating, roaming, rambling, gypsy.

MILD, *adj.* 1. Amiably gentle, temperate in behavior toward others, kind, clement, lenient, compassionate, merciful, tender, gentle, indulgent, good-tempered, pacific, genial, civil, docile, moderate, easy, calm, tranquil, bland, placid, suave, pleasant, gracious, considerate, complaisant, tolerant, easygoing, benign, conciliatory, humane, forbearing, unassuming, submissive, meek.

2. Not severe, not extreme, not sharp, not pungent, not strong, not acute.

3. (*Of weather*) Warm, balmy, summery, temperate, sunny.

4. Lenitive, soothing, mollifying, demulcent, assuasive, emollient, healing, tranquilizing, palliative.

5. Insipid, tame, jejune, vapid, flat, unsavory, feeble, dull, half-hearted, spiritless, unanimated, unenthusiastic.

MILDEW, *n.* Plant disease characterized by a whitish coating on the surface and caused by various parasitic fungi, discoloration due to fungi, blight, rust, mold, blast, smut, must, mustiness, dry-rot, rubigo.

MILDNESS, *n.* Gentleness, lenity, tenderness, humanity, humaneness, clemency, quarter, temperateness, mercy, compassion, forbearance, moderation, tolerance, indulgence, toleration, considerateness, favor, kindness, kindliness, lenience, meekness, placidity, suavity, sweetness, affability, blandness.

MILESTONE, *n.* 1. Stone set up to mark distance by miles, milliary, signpost, milepost.

2. Event regarded as marking a stage in the journey of life, anniversary, birthday, jubilee, red-letter day, centenary.

MILITANCY, *n.* Militarism, warfare, saber-rattling, jingoism, chauvinism, combativeness, pugnacity, aggressiveness, aggression, bellicosity, belligerency, appeal to the sword, flag-waving, arbitrament of the sword, war to the death, *guerre à mort (Fr.)*.

MILITANT, *adj.* Inclined to warfare, engaged in warfare, warring, combative, contending, fighting, belligerent, pugnacious, martial, warlike, aggressive, bellicose, jingoistic, chauvinistic, saber-rattling, war-mongering, flag-waving, contentious, armigerous, sword in hand, embattled.

MILITARISM, *n.* Military spirit, martial policy, tendency to regard military efficiency as the supreme ideal of the state, principle of maintaining a large military establishment, jingoism, chauvinism, saber-rattling, flag-waving, goose-stepping, preparedness, mobilization.

MILITARIST, *n.* One imbued with militarism, one skilled in the art of war, warlord, military expert, saber-rattler, jingoist, chauvinist, war advocate, warmonger.

MILITARY, *adj.* Martial, warlike, belligerent, bellicose, militant, armigerous, combative, hostile, soldier-like, soldierly, armed to the teeth, under arms, embattled, in battle array, sword in hand, in the field.

MILITARY, *n.* Body of soldiers, soldiery, militia, soldiers, army, troops, armed forces, Sabaoth, standing army, regulars, troops of the line, yeomanry, auxiliary forces, reserves, national guard, trainband.

MILITIA, *n.* Body of men enrolled for military service in emergencies, trainband, national guard, organized reserves, body of citizen soldiers, yeomanry, volunteers, reserve forces, posse comitatus.

MILK, *n.* 1. Opaque white liquid secreted by the mammary glands of female mammals, lactage, strippings, kumiss, cream, buttermilk, skim, beestings, foremilk, colostrum, clabber, bonnyclabber, whey, curd, casein, posset.

2. Any liquid resembling milk, latex, sap, juice, emulsion, serum.

MILK, *v.* Draw from, press from, extract, manipulate, lactate, drain from, exploit.

MILK-LIVERED, *adj.* Cowardly, pusillanimous, craven, timorous, white-livered, fearful, timid, spiritless, skittish, effeminate, shy, weak, yellow, milksop, faint-hearted, frightened, unmanned.

MILKSOP, *n.* Soft unmanly fellow, effeminate man, mollycoddle, sissy, milquetoast, poltroon, coward, dastard, dunghill cock, white-liver, coistril, nidget, craven.

MILKY, *adj.* 1. Lacteal, lactic, lacteous, lactescent, lactiferous, emulsive.

2. Whitish, pearly, cloudy, frosted, nacreous, opaline, semiopaque, semipellucid, filmy, hazy, clouded, milk-white, chalky, snowy, niveous, hoar, creamy, ivory, albescent.

3. Timorous, craven, pusillanimous, weak, effeminate, womanish, soft, unmanly, frail, spineless, spiritless, tame, meek, mild, gentle.

MILKY WAY, *n.* Luminous band in the heavens composed of innumerable stars too faint for unassisted vision, galaxy, Via Lactea, galactic circle, starry host, nebulae.

MILL, *n.* 1. Establishment with machinery in which various forms of manufacture are carried on, workshop, manufactory, factory, foundry, hive of industry.

2. Machine for crushing or pulverizing, crusher, roller, gin.

3. Establishment with appliances for grinding grain into flour, windmill, *moulin (Fr.).*

MILL, *v.* 1. Grind, pulverize, comminute, levigate, powder, beat, granulate, reduce to powder, triturate, grate, rasp, bray, crush, crunch.

2. Move confusedly in a circle, jostle, push, impel, shoulder, elbow, shove, bump against.

MILLENNIUM, *n.* 1. Period of a thousand years, chiliad, millenary, *annus magnus (Lat.).*

2. Period of general righteousness and happiness, golden age, Utopia, Atlantis, happy valley, golden dream, *le pot au lait (Fr.),* castles in the air, *châteaux en Espagne (Fr.), annus mirabilis (Lat.).*

MILLINER, *n.* 1. One who makes or sells hats for women, modiste, hatter.

2. Man milliner, fop, dandy, fine gentleman, swell, dandiprat, beau, coxcomb, silk-stocking, toff, exquisite, buck, macaroni, blade, blood, silk-sock Sam, man about town, spark, fribble, popinjay, *petit maître (Fr.),* jack-a-dandy, dude, masher, Johnnie, carpet-knight.

MILLION, *n.* 1. One thousand times one thousand, thousand thousand units.

2. *(With the definite article)* The masses, the multitude, the public, the great body of the people, the populace, general public, community at large, common herd, lower classes, rank and file, the peasantry, *hoc genus omne (Lat.),* proletariat, king Mob, horde, rabble, *canaille (Fr.), faex populi (Lat.), profanum vulgus (Lat.),* tagrag and bobtail, riffraff, small fry, dregs of society.

MILLIONAIRE, *n.* Very rich man, person of great wealth, nabob, Croesus, Dives, old potentate, moneyed man, man of substance, Midas, capitalist, Plutus, silk-stocking, financier, coupon-clipper, money bags, profiteer, plutocrat, billionaire, multimillionaire.

MILLSTONE, *n.* 1. Grindstone, quern, mill, muller, kern, grinder, grater, pestle and mortar, molar, chopper, grinder.

2. Heavy burden, load, lead, mountain, onus, staggering responsibility, old man of the sea, incubus, fardel, dead weight, Ephialtes, heavy affliction, pack of troubles.

MIME, *n.* 1. Comedian, mimic, jester, *farceur (Fr.),* clown, imitator, impersonator, actor, player, pantomimist, harlequin, *grimacier (Fr.),* buffoon, pantaloon, punchinello, mummer, strolling player, merry-andrew, scaramouch, zany.

2. Farce, caricature, burlesque, parody, travesty, low comedy, after-piece, *divertissement (Fr.),* extravaganza, harlequinade, burletta, pantomime, mimodrama.

MIMESIS, *n.* Imitation, mimicry, mimicking, copying, aping, apery, impersonation, parrotry, simulation, representation, echo, adaptation, parody, paraphrase, reproduction.

MIMETIC, *adj.* Exhibiting mimicry, mimic, imitative, mimical, apish, mock, make-believe, echoic, copying, reflective.

MIMIC, *adj.* Apt at imitating, simulating, reproductive of the real thing, imitative, mimetical, mimetic, mimical, mock, apish, echoic, copying, reflective, imitated, modeled after, second-hand, counterfeit, molded on, pseudo, false, imitational, near-, brummagem.

MIMIC, *n.* Imitator, copyist, pretender, copier, burlesquer, parodist, pretender, feigner, mocking bird, cuckoo, parrot, echo, catbird, monkey, ape.

MIMIC, *v.* Imitate, copy, ape, simulate, parrot, echo, reflect, mirror, repeat, reproduce, follow after, do like, follow suit, emulate, model after, reëcho, follow the example of, parallel, take after, counterfeit, forge, take off, represent, impersonate, travesty, burlesque, parody, caricature, mock, make sport of, deride, personate, ridicule, gibe, play.

MIMICRY, *n.* Imitation, simulation, mimesis, representation, reproduction, copying, apery, mockery, mimicking, parrotry, impersonation, echoing, masquerade, disguise, pretense, semblance, adaptation, parody, paraphrase, burlesque, travesty.

MINACIOUS, *adj.* Threatening, minatory, menacing, comminatory, threatful, attempting to terrify, warning, lowering, premonitory, cautionary, monitory, ominous, admonitory.

MINARET, *n.* Lofty slender tower from which the muezzin calls to prayer, turret of a Mohammedan mosque, steeple, spire, belfry.

MINATORY, *adj.* Menacing, threatening, minacious, comminatory, premonitory, admonitory, monitory, lowering, frowning, ominous, unpropitious, discouraging, unfavorable.

MINCE, *v.* 1. Subdivide minutely, cut into small pieces, chop fine, hash, dice, reduce to particles, grate, comminute.

2. Moderate one's words to a milder form, be mealy-mouthed about, be euphuistic, be euphemistic, soften one's speech, speak in euphemistic terms, be reserved in speaking about, palliate, extenuate, qualify, apologize for, excuse, mitigate, gloss.

3. Move with short dainty steps, affect delicacy, toddle, waddle, step short, attitudinize, simper, lisp, pose, strike a pose.

MINCING, *adj.* Affected, full of affectation, stilted, not natural, *maniéré (Fr.)*, artificial, overnice, euphuistic, prudish, priggish, coxcombical, dandified, pussyfooting, conceited, foppish, finicky, simpering, milquetoast, namby-pamby.

MIND, *n.* 1. That which exercises perception in a human being, intellect, reason, consciousness, judgment, understanding, thinking principle, intellectual powers, ratiocinative ability, intellectual faculties, intelligence, brains, gray matter, sense, rationality, mentality, insight, comprehension, cognition, perception, intellectuality, percipience, wit, nous, association of ideas, apperception, *esprit (Fr.)*, headpiece, sensorium, head, cranium.

2. Spirit, psyche, soul, inner man, conscience, the I, ego, *penetralia mentis (Lat.)*, subliminal consciousness, subconscious self, genius.

3. Intent, inclination, intention, wish, desire, pleasure, craving, longing, leaning, proclivity, penchant, propensity, disposition, liking, bent, proneness, humor, affection, temper, will, choice, purpose.

4. Opinion, sentiment, belief, thought, notion, conception, impression, consideration, reflection, judgment, contemplation.

5. Memory, recollection, commemoration, remembrance, retentiveness, tenacity, tablets of the memory, reminiscence, recurrence, rememoration, retrospection, retrospect.

MIND, *v.* 1. Perceive, take notice of, note, mark, notice, regard, give heed to, heed, attend to, fix the mind on, pay attention to, advert to, listen, take cognizance of, watch, observe, obey, be obedient to, apply oneself to, look after, tend, take care of, be careful concerning, be wary about, be cautious about.

2. Object to, feel inconvenienced by, disrelish, dislike, disfavor, disapprove, look askance at, turn up the nose at, have no taste for, shudder at, shrink from, have an aversion to, shun, recoil from, eschew, avoid, detest, loathe, abhor, abominate, despise, hate.

MINDED, *adj.* Disposed, inclined, willing, desirous, fain, partial, favorably minded, nothing loth, in the vein, in the humor, bent upon, propense, predisposed, ready, enthusiastic, forward, eager, determined, resolved.

MINDFUL, *adj.* Keeping in mind, attentive, heedful, aware, observant, watchful, cautious, regardful, alert, alive to, wary, thoughtful, reminiscent, thankful, grateful, awake to, taken up with, engrossed in mind, occupied with, absorbed in, intent on, undistracted, open-eyed, on the watch, careful.

MINDLESS, *adj.* 1. Destitute of mind, imbecile, brainless, witless, feeble-minded, idiotic, moronic, vacant, not all there *(colloq.)*, not bright, unreasoning, unintelligent, reasonless.

2. Stupid, insensible, insulse, heavy, obtuse, doltish, fatuous, asinine, blunt, blockish, Boeotian,

sluggish, dull, unthinking, torpid, comatose, stupefied.

3. Inattentive, unobservant, unheeding, listless, absent-minded, regardless, heedless, careless, negligent, neglectful, forgetful, oblivious.

MINE, *n.* 1. Excavation in the earth, burrow, trench, tunnel, sap, pit, shaft, colliery.

2. Deposit of ores, lode, vein, quarry.

3. Abounding store, source of supply, heap, treasure, reserve, hoard, stack.

4. Large charge of explosive, land mine, infernal machine, booby trap.

MINE, *v.* 1. Dig in the earth, excavate, burrow, sap, make subterranean passages, tunnel, delve, scoop out, extract.

2. Remove the foundations of, subvert, undermine, ruin slowly, destroy secretly, attack covertly, desolate, devastate, blast, eradicate.

MINERAL, *n.* Natural product of inorganic origin, substance neither animal nor vegetable, inorganic body, ore.

MINGLE, *v.* 1. Put together in a mixture, blend, combine, join, merge, intermix, intermingle, commix, compound, commingle, mix, interfuse, amalgamate, fuse, agglutinate, cement, lump together, incorporate, interweave, intertwine.

2. Mix in company, hobnob, keep close company with, fraternize, associate, band together, club, have social intercourse, socialize, consort, see one's friends, hang out, keep open house.

MINGLE-MANGLE, *n.* Mixture, mélange, medley, hodgepodge, salmagundi, hash, olla-podrida, olio, pastiche, farrago, miscellany, chow-chow, omnium-gatherum, potpourri, gallimaufry, jumble, ragout, réchauffé, stew, concoction, commixture, mosaic, patchwork, Noah's ark, mishmash, salad.

MINIATURE, *adj.* Diminutive, small-scale, little, tiny, in a greatly reduced form, bantam, vestpocket-size, minute, microscopic, wee, exiguous, Lilliputian, pollard, elfin, pygmy, stunted, sawed-off, runty.

MINIKIN, *adj.* Dainty, delicate, mincing, namby-pamby, simpering, finical, exquisite, lovely, pretty, elegant, graceful, trim, neat, tidy, dapper, petite, slender, svelte.

MINIMIZE, *v.* 1. Reduce to the lowest possible degree, lessen, decrease, diminish, make less, abridge, abbreviate, decimate, curtail, attenuate, cut down, prune, contract, compress, condense, epitomize, shorten, summarize.

2. Represent at the lowest possible estimate, underestimate, understate, undervalue, gloss over, soft-pedal, whitewash, belittle, disparage, depreciate, not do justice to, slur over, ridicule, make light of, run down, make little of, set at naught, make no account of, decry, derogate, detract.

MINIMUM, *n.* Smallest amount possible, least part, lowest quantity, least, modicum, particle, drop in the bucket, thimbleful, shaving, splinter, fragment, chip, paring, sliver, snip, sprinkling, dash, mite, minim, grain, bit, tinge, dab, crumb, morsel, mouthful, pinch, nip, dot, speck, jot, iota, shred, scrap, fraction, fragment, trifle.

MINION, *n.* Base favorite of a patron, favorite creature, servile dependent, hanger-on, parasite, crony, fondling, *enfant gâté (Fr.)*, cosset, pet, spoiled child, idol, *persona grata (Lat.)*, apple of one's eye, darling, honey, moppet, duck, deary, sweet love.

MINISTER, *n.* 1. One authorized to conduct religious worship, clergyman, pastor, parson, preacher, cleric, ecclesiastic, rector, vicar, curate, chaplain, divine, evangelist, priest, clerk in holy orders, shepherd of his flock, sky pilot, curé, abbé, padre, father, reverend, missionary, revivalist, rabbi, hierophant, dominie, liturgist, incumbent, sin-shifter (*slang*), pulpiteer.

2. Diplomatic representative accredited by one government to another, ambassador, consul, plenipotentiary, envoy, diplomatist, legate, delegate, chargé d'affaires, magistrate, diplomatic agent.

3. One appointed by the executive head of government to some high office of state, official, deputy, administrator, executive officer, chancellor, premier, prime minister, provost.

4. One acting as the agent or instrument of another, underling, subordinate, assistant, agent, servant, employee, proxy, surrogate, *locum tenens* (*Lat.*).

MINISTER, *v.* 1. Help, aid, succor, assist, lend assistance, lend a hand, give a lift, relieve, tender to, pander to, tend, attend, wait on, take care of, accommodate, oblige, stand by, second, back up, abet, support, patronize, befriend, favor, doctor, nurse, heal, cure, remedy, care for.

2. Do service, serve, perform, officiate, service, attend, preside.

3. Give, contribute, supply, furnish, favor with, indulge, lavish, shower down upon, thrust upon, offer, present, dole out, put into the hands of, render.

MINISTERIAL, *adj.* 1. Clerical, priestly, sacerdotal, pastoral, ecclesiastical, prelatical, capitular, canonical, hierarchical.

2. Ambassadorial, consular, diplomatic, plenipotentiary, official, representative, executive.

3. Subsidiary, subservient, assistant, ancillary, conducive, attendant, auxiliary, instrumental, clerkly.

MINISTRATION, *n.* 1. Accommodation, aid, subministration, subvention, aidance, help, assistance, succor, opitulation, coadjuvancy, support, promotion, advance, furtherance, favor, countenance, patronage, advocacy, auspices, championship.

2. Administration, stewardship, agency, proctorship, supervision, superintendence, regulation, direction, management, conduct, government.

3. Ecclesiastical function, service, rite, sacrament, ceremonial, ceremony, liturgy, preachment, predication, holy sacrament, communion, Lord's supper, Eucharist, visitation of the sick, last rites, extreme unction, viaticum.

MINISTRY, *n.* 1. Body of ministers of religion, profession of a minister of religion, clergy, cloth, priesthood, presbytery, the pulpit, clericals, clergymen, the desk, clerical order, prelacy, pastorate, frock, rectorship, vicarage.

2. Agency, instrumentality, aid, ministration, service, intervention, interposition, subvention, subsidy, relief, rescue, deliverance, mitigation, alleviation.

3. Administration, government, policy-forming executive officials of a country, administrative department, agency.

MINOR, *adj.* 1. Lesser of two, secondary, subordinate, less, smaller, lower, inferior, junior, *cadet* (*Fr.*), under legal age.

2. Petty, inconsiderable, unimportant, insignificant, small, paltry, picayune, second-rate, two-by-four, one-horse, trivial, trifling, niggling, piddling, slight, idle, not worth mentioning, beneath consideration, nugatory, inconsequential, ordinary, common, mere.

MINOR, *n.* 1. Person under legal age, youth, child, youngster, scion, adolescent, teen-ager, stripling, lad, boy, cub, whippersnapper, hopeful, hobbledehoy, cadet, schoolboy, schoolgirl, lass, lassie, maiden, small fry.

2. One of inferior rank or importance, subordinate, inferior, subject, underling, commoner, plebeian, menial, nonentity, cipher, nobody, man of straw, whiffet (*colloq.*).

3. Subordinate course of study, subject for which less credit than a major is granted.

MINORITY, *n.* 1. Period of being under legal age, pupilage, nonage, childhood, teens, teen-age, wardship, tender age, youthhood, bloom, immaturity, puberty, pucilage, juvenility, juvenescence, adolescence, juniority, boyhood, girlhood, flower of youth, heyday of youth.

2. Number forming less than half of the whole, smaller part, the less, the smaller, the smaller number, splinter group, handful.

MINSTREL, *n.* 1. Musician reciting to the accompaniment of instruments, bard, singer, poet, jongleur, minnesinger, player, troubadour, meistersinger, laureate, lyrist, *trouvère (Fr.)*, *trovatore (It.)*, scald, versifier, *improvisatore (It.)*, rhapsodist, balladmonger.

2. Comedian made up as Negro, blackface, gleeman, jester, entertainer, end man, interlocutor, song-and-dance man, vaudevillian.

MINSTRELSY, *n.* Music, song, strain, air, melody, rhapsody, dithyramb, serenade, canticle, recitative, carol, ditty, measures, poesy, Muse, verses, versification, afflatus, Pierian spring, Parnassus, Calliope, Helicon, singing, harmony.

MINT, *v.* 1. Make coins by stamping metal, stamp money, mold into a required form, convert into money by stamping, cast, punch, impress with a die, coin, strike.

2. Invent, fabricate, produce, fashion, originate, create, devise, make, forge, counterfeit.

MINUS, *adj.* Less, diminished, negative (*Math.*), lacking, short, missing, wanting, nonexistent, deducted, deficient, devoid of, short of, made smaller.

MINUTE, *adj.* 1. Extremely small, diminutive, little, tiny, wee, slender, fine, exiguous, tenuous, delicate, miniature, puny, infinitesimal, imperceptible, microscopic, inappreciable, inconsiderable, slight, petty, trifling, atomic, corpuscular, elfin, pocket-size, undersized, minikin, dwarf, runty, pygmy, nanoid, Lilliputian, stunted, molecular, evanescent, microbic, embryonic, animalcular, homuncular, petite, comminuted, pulverized, triturated, homeopathic, narrow.

2. Accurate, exact, precise, meticulous, punctilious, particular, detailed, concerned with very small particulars, scrupulous, conscientious, strict, nice, pinpointed, careful, neat, tidy.

MINUTE, *n.* 1. Sixtieth part of an hour, sixty seconds.

2. Indefinitely short space of time, instant, moment, trice, second, twinkling, flash, jiffy, crack, breath, *coup (Fr.)*, burst.

3. Rough draft of a document, written summary, record, note, memorandum, entry, deposition.

4. (*Pl.*) Official record of the proceedings at a meeting of a society, transactions, proceedings, agenda, compendium, epitome, abstract, digest, brief, sum and substance, summary, abridgment, aperçu, synopsis, conspectus.

MINUTE, v. Enter in the minutes of a society, record in a memorandum, take a note of, note, jot down, place upon record, chronicle, set down in writing, calendar, report, put on paper.

MINUTIAE, n. Particulars, minor details, trifling circumstances, trivial details, trivia, counts, items, small fry.

MINX, n. Pert or flirtatious girl, impudent lass, baggage, jade, hussy, quean, wanton, strumpet, malapert, saucebox, trollop, wench, trull, slut, harridan, demirep, bitch, drab.

MIRACLE, n. Supernatural effect in the physical world, wonderful thing, marvel, prodigy, wonder, portent, phenomenon, sign, wonderwork, curiosity, rarity, *rara avis (Lat.),* spectacle, *coup de théâtre (Fr.),* omen.

MIRACULOUS, adj. Supernatural, thaumaturgical, wonderworking, preternatural, mirific, marvelous, beyond the powers of nature, hyperphysical, superhuman, unnatural, extraordinary, incredible, wonderful, unaccountable, passing strange, prodigious, astonishing, astounding, stupefying, inexpressible, bewildering, monstrous, freakish, fearful, awesome, unimaginable, spectacular, curious, surprising, overwhelming, amazing, stupendous, enormous, wondrous, striking, unexpected, mysterious, inconceivable, unprecedented, remarkable, unwonted, singular, unusual, signal.

MIRAGE, n. Reflection of images of distant objects, optical illusion, imposition, will-o'-the-wisp, *feu follet (Fr.),* ignis fatuus, *deceptio visus (Lat.),* refraction, false light, phantasm, Fata Morgana, firedrake.

MIRE, n. Wet swampy ground, slimy soil, slough, filth, ooze, slime, mud, quagmire, muck, sludge, slush, marsh, fen.

MIRROR, n. 1. Glass reflecting surface, reflector, looking glass, hand mirror, hand glass, pier glass, cheval glass.
2. *(Optics)* Surface for reflecting rays of light, speculum. ·
3. Something that gives a true picture of something else, pattern for imitation, exemplar, model, example, paragon, archetype, prototype, precedent, criterion, standard, original, ideal.

MIRROR, v. 1. Reflect, show, exhibit, manifest, display, bring into view, expose to view, put before one's eyes, bring into notice, disclose, indicate.
2. Imitate, reproduce, copy, repeat, take after, echo, reëcho, catch, ape, mimic, take off, simulate, personate, represent.

MIRTH, n. Humorous amusement, joyous gaiety, festive jollity, merriment, rejoicing, joviality, hilarity, glee, frolic, merry-making, joyousness, fun, sport, gladness, laughter, festivity, *gaîté de coeur (Fr.),* sociality, vivacity, conviviality, jovialness, sociability, cheerfulness, enthusiasm, celebration, pleasure, good spirits, liveliness, felicity, jocularity, delight, joyfulness, happiness, cheer, wit, jocundity, exhilaration, sportiveness, playfulness, blithesomeness, high spirits, light heart.

MIRTHFUL, adj. Full of mirth, laughingly gay, jovial, merry, joyous, joyful, jolly, jocund, jocose, jocular, sportive, vivacious, frolicsome, playful, lively, festive, hilarious, cheery, cheerful, blithe, genial, festal, sprightly, laughing, happy, glad, gladsome, gleeful, comic, funny, droll, facetious, witty, ludicrous, waggish, smiling, sunny, in good spirits, debonair, light-hearted, saucy, chipper, convivial, social, animated, sparkling, spirited, frisky,

tricksy, rollicking, larky, jubilant, elated, cock-a-hoop.

MIRY, adj. Bespattered with mire, slimy, muddy, oozy, sloughy, filthy, squalid, unclean, dirty, lutose, grimy, grubby.

MISADVENTURE, n. Piece of ill fortune, stroke of ill luck, mischance, calamity, misfortune, disaster, mishap, reverse, cross, infelicity, contretemps, miscarriage, hardship, accident, catastrophe, affliction, adversity, undoing, evil, ruination, frowns of fortune, curse, evil dispensation, casualty, check, setback, pinch, rub, comedown, downfall, extremity.

MISANTHROPE, n. Hater of mankind, manhater, misanthropist, cynic, egotist, egoist, Timonist, Timon, Diogenes, woman-hater, misogynist.

MISANTHROPIC, adj. Man-hating, misanthropical, antisocial, egoistical, selfish, egotistical, morose, Diogenic, sullen, woman-hating, misogynistic, unsociable, discourteous, surly, unaccommodating, cynical.

MISANTHROPY, n. Hatred or distrust of mankind, misanthropism, cynicism, moroseness, cynicalness, sullenness, egotism, egoism, selfishness, incivism, incivility, want of patriotism, unpatriotism, hatred of women, misogyny.

MISAPPLY, v. 1. Misinterpret, misunderstand, misconstrue, misjudge, misrepresent, put a false construction on, distort, pervert, garble.
2. Make a wrong use of, misuse, abuse, misemploy, misappropriate, profane, prostitute, desecrate, squander, waste, overtax, embezzle, expropriate, mismanage, misdirect, misconduct.

MISAPPREHEND, v. Mistake, misunderstand, misconstrue, misjudge, misconceive, err, deceive oneself, be mistaken, be in error, be deceived, miscount, misreckon, miscalculate, slip up, blunder, receive a false impression, be in the wrong, misinterpret.

MISAPPREHENSION, n. Misunderstanding, misconception, fallacy, error, erroneousness, misinterpretation, misconstruction, miscalculation, misjudgment, false impression, delusion, self-deception, hallucination, false belief, misbelief, mirage, misacceptation, misapplication, cross purposes, mistake, false coloring, misrepresentation, exaggeration, perversion, distortion, falsification, inexactness, warped notion.

MISAPPROPRIATE, v. Put to a wrong use, misemploy, misuse, misapply, abuse, desecrate, profane, prostitute, overtax, squander, apply dishonestly to one's own use, steal, peculate, embezzle, expropriate, pervert.

MISBEGOTTEN, adj. Unlawfully begotten, illegitimate, bastard, misbegot, miscreated, illicit, unlawful.

MISBEHAVE, v. Behave badly, misconduct, do amiss, transgress, misdemean oneself, forget oneself, misdo, lapse, err, trespass, offend, fall, slip, deviate from the path of virtue, stray from the path of propriety, sow one's wild oats, sin, demoralize, corrupt, be vulgar, show poor manners.

MISBEHAVED, adj. Unmannerly, discourteous, rude, ill-behaved, ill-mannered, ill-bred, impolite, ungentlemanly, ungracious, uncivil, forward, imprudent, insolent, reprehensible, censurable, blameworthy, objectionable, disorderly, unrighteous, bad, iniquitous, undutiful, criminal, wicked, lawless, discreditable, unprincipled, recreant, facinorous, nefarious, felonious, infamous, shameful, scurvy, gross, foul, scandalous, villainous, flagrant, flagitious, heinous, malevolent, unconscionable, reprobate, incorrigible, culpable, inexcusable, unjustifiable, unpardonable, indecorous.

MISBEHAVIOR, *n.* Ill behavior, ill conduct, misdoing, misdeed, fault, transgression, trespass, delinquency, dereliction, lapse, indiscretion, faux pas, slip, peccadillo, failing, omission, offense, misdemeanor, naughtiness, malpractice, malefaction, tort, malfeasance, malversation, fraudulent conduct, felony, crime, outrage, enormity, corpus delicti, blackguardism, brutality, *grossièreté (Fr.),* impudence, procacity, disrespect, discourtesy, ill breeding, rudeness, bad manners, misconduct.

MISBELIEF, *n.* Erroneous belief, false opinion, unbelief, discredit, disbelief, miscreance, dissent, skepticism, doubt, demur, misgiving, mistrust, distrust, suspicion, incredulity, delusion, pyrrhonism, incredulousness, nonconformity, heterodoxy, heresy, recusancy, schismaticism, backsliding, apostasy, iconoclasm, atheism.

MISBELIEVE, *v.* Disbelieve, doubt, not believe, discredit, refuse to admit, be doubtful, be skeptical, doubt the truth of, mistrust, diffide, distrust, smell a rat, suspect, harbor doubts, question, dispute, challenge, deny, demur, scruple, hesitate, stop and consider, raise a question, be incredulous, turn a deaf ear to, shut one's eyes to, ignore.

MISBELIEVER, *n.* Unbeliever, disbeliever, skeptic, cynic, aporetic, heretic, agnostic, atheist, pyrrhonist, infidel, apostate, backslider, heathen, pagan, antichrist, giaour, iconoclast, recusant, schismatic, seceder, dissenter, separatist, nonconformist.

MISCALCULATE, *v.* Calculate wrongly, miscompute, misestimate, misreckon, miscount, miscast, fly in the face of facts, be wide of the mark, overestimate, underestimate, jump to a conclusion, blunder, err, be in the wrong, go astray.

MISCALL, *v.* Call by a wrong name, misname, misterm, call by a misnomer, use a pseudonym, call by an alias.

MISCARRIAGE, *n.* 1. Failure to attain the desired result, nonsuccess, defeat, frustration, miss, botch, shipwreck, accident, casualty, failing, nonfulfillment, no-go, labor in vain, vain attempt, fizzle, fiasco, inefficacy, disappointment, washout, slip, mishap, mischance, misfortune, collapse, deathblow, rebuff, repulse, overthrow, rout, checkmate, downfall, wreck, crash, ruination, flash in the pan.

2. Failure of a letter to reach its destination, nondelivery.

3. Premature expulsion of a fetus from the uterus, premature birth, untimely birth, abortion, premature delivery.

MISCARRY, *v.* 1. Fail of an intended effect, go wrong, be defeated, be unsuccessful, abort, come to grief, run aground, flounder, meet with disaster, founder, shipwreck, come to nothing, turn out badly, go to the wall, labor in vain, make vain efforts, fall short of, miss the mark, slip, stumble, lick the dust, lose the day, fall through, end in smoke, fizzle, flat out, flash in the pan, hang fire, go to wrack and ruin.

2. Be carried by a wrong route, go astray, be carried to a wrong place, be lost in transit.

MISCELLANEOUS, *adj.* Of mixed character, heterogeneous, mingled, varied, diversified, various, indiscriminate, promiscuous, compound, farraginaceous, commixed, commingled, assorted, of various kinds, multifarious, composite, blended, variegated, motley, mongrel, hybrid, polyglot, polychromatic, half-and-half, versatile, many-sided, diverse, multiphase, protean, manifold, of every description, mosaic, multiform, multifarious, variform, multiplex, polymorphous, omnifarious, diversiform.

MISCELLANY, *n.* 1. Medley, jumble, blend, mixture, miscellaneous collection, conglomeration, mélange, variety, combination, diversity, concoction, gallimaufry, hash, goulash, stew, mishmash, hodgepodge, olio, olla-podrida, farrago, potpourri, salmagundi, mingle-mangle, omnium-gatherum, mess, pastiche, chow-chow, patchwork, crazy quilt, mosaic, motley, Noah's ark.

2. Anthology, miscellanea, collectanea, compilation, ana, florilegium, extracts, symposium, compendium, flowers, spicilegium, analecta, fugitive pieces, excerpta.

MISCHANCE, *n.* Ill luck, ill fortune, misfortune, misadventure, miscarriage, mishap, disaster, calamity, catastrophe, adversity, undoing, infelicity, reverse, accident, contretemps, woe, bale, ruin, tragedy, devil to pay, buffet, blow, evil, harm, hurt, failure, frown of fortune, evil dispensation, jinx, evil day, ill wind, dark cloud, gathering clouds, bitter pill, trial, infliction, visitation, affliction, losing game, downfall, comedown, ruination.

MISCHIEF, *n.* 1. Hurt, damage, trouble, harm, detriment, injury, evil, wrong, ill, vexation, annoyance, disadvantage, injustice, prejudice, disservice, nuisance, drawback, outrage, enormity, bad turn, foul play, atrocity, mortal blow, ill-consequence, misfortune, adversity, bale, woe, bane, calamity, catastrophe, disaster, ruination, casualty, mishap.

2. Wrongdoing, villainy, roguery, deviltry, devilment, bedevilment, ill-treatment, molestation, abuse, misuse, persecution, oppression, knavery, rascality, arch trick.

MISCHIEF-MAKER, *n.* 1. One who stirs up discord by talebearing, tattletale, gossip, gadabout, tattler, busybody, idle talker, talebearer, quidnunc, rumormonger, newsmonger, meddler, stickybeak *(sl.),* rabble-rouser, incendiary.

2. Rogue, rascal, villain, blackguard, reprobate, knave, worker of iniquity, bad man, wrongdoer, evildoer, scoundrel, miscreant, urchin, scamp, scapegrace, blacksheep, *vaurien (Fr.),* rowdy, rough, hooligan, hoodlum, malefactor, culprit, delinquent, misdemeanant, felon, marplot, iconoclast, anarchist.

MISCHIEVOUS, *adj.* 1. Injurious, hurtful, harmful, pernicious, noxious, detrimental, destructive, pestiferous, ruinous, prejudicial, grievous, disadvantageous, baleful, baneful, deleterious, malefic, noisome, malignant, disserviceable, obnoxious, untoward, corrupting, virulent, corrosive, venomous, poisonous, morbific, lethal, deadly, pestilential, sinister.

2. Vicious, sinful, wicked, malicious, villainous, iniquitous, base, vile, wrong, evil, depraved, nefarious, maleficent, criminal, felonious, immoral, scampish, unprincipled, reprehensible, blameworthy, scurvy, facinorous, scelerous, infamous, flagitious, flagrant, heinous, atrocious, evil-disposed, evil-minded, malevolent, unconscionable, incorrigible.

3. Playfully annoying, maliciously teasing, vexatious, fond of mischief, roguish, arch, impish, naughty, elfish, elfin, frolicsome, sportive, prankish, tricksy, waggish, meddlesome, intrusive, interfering.

MISCONCEIVE, *v.* Conceive wrongly, interpret incorrectly, misinterpret, misunderstand, mistake, misapprehend, misjudge, misconstrue, misreckon, miscount, be in the wrong, be in error, be mistaken, receive a false impression, deceive oneself, fall into an error, blunder, put a false construction on, misconjecture, overestimate, underestimate, prejudge, presuppose, have a bias, jump to a conclusion, run away with the notion.

MISCONCEPTION, *n.* Erroneous conception, mistaken notion, misapprehension, mistake, misunderstanding, misconstruction, misjudgment, warped judgment, hasty conclusion, misinterpretation, miscomputation, miscalculation, prejudgment, preconceived idea, obsession, fixed idea, *idée fixe (Fr.),* delusion, fallacious notion, fallacy, mispersuasion, error, false light, hallucination.

MISCONDUCT, *n.* 1. Improper conduct, wrong behavior, misbehavior, bad conduct, ill conduct, misdeed, wrongdoing, trespass, transgression, delinquency, misdemeanor, offense, fault, sin, crime, peccadillo, misdoing, vice, turpitude, depravity, violation, infringement, felony, outrage, atrocity, enormity, faux pas, indiscretion, slip, blot, lapse, trip, misstep, flaw, failing, blunder, error.
2. Unlawful conduct by an official in regard to his office, mismanagement, misgovernment, ill management, evil practice, malpractice, malfeasance, malversation, dereliction, negligence, nonfeasance, corruption, extortion, graft, venality, malefaction, misfeasance.

MISCONDUCT, *v.* 1. Mismanage, misapply, misdirect, mishandle, misrule, manage ill, fumble, botch, make a mess of, begin at the wrong end, make sad work of, be unskillful, bungle, blunder, muff, stumble, make a hash of, put one's foot in it, act foolishly, do things by halves, play at cross purposes, not know what one is about.
2. Misbehave oneself, do amiss, transgress, err, commit sin, forget oneself, misdo, lapse, trespass, offend, trip, slip, deviate from the path of virtue, hug a sin, go astray, take a wrong course, sow one's wild oats, paint the town red, be vicious.

MISCONSTRUCTION, *n.* Wrong construction, misinterpretation, misunderstanding, misapprehension, misacceptation, misapplication, cross reading, catachresis, mistake, misrepresentation, exaggeration, distortion, perversion, false coloring, falsification, hyperbole, high coloring, stretch, strain, embroidery, stretch of the imagination, flight of fancy.

MISCONSTRUE, *v.* 1. Construe wrongly, take in a wrong sense, misrender, mistranslate, misinterpret, turn out of its meaning, pervert, distort, garble, give a false coloring to, wrest from its sense, misrepresent, strain the sense, play upon words, put a false construction on.
2. Misunderstand, misapprehend, misjudge, misconceive, misreckon.

MISCOUNT, *v.* Compute erroneously, miscalculate, miscompute, misreckon, misjudge, misstate, misestimate, fly in the face of facts, overestimate, overreckon, estimate too highly, magnify, exaggerate, underestimate, underrate, underreckon, not do justice to.

MISCREANT, *n.* Vile wretch, villain, rascal, knave, rogue, scamp, scoundrel, caitiff, reprobate, base fellow, evildoer, worker of iniquity, bad man, sinner, wrongdoer, scapegrace, runagate, rip, ne'er-do-well, good-for-nothing, *vaurien (Fr.),* rake, roué, *âme damnée (Fr.),* rowdy, roughneck, ugly customer, hoodlum, hooligan, ruffian, delinquent, malefactor, criminal, culprit, misdemeanant, outlaw, felon, jailbird, convict, blackguard, sneak, mean wretch, varlet, vagabond, outcast, riffraff, scum of the earth, conspirator, traitor, snake in the grass, mischief-maker, squealer, renegade, recreant, truant, larrikin, rapscallion, scalawag, tough, racketeer, gangster, gunman, bootlegger, hijacker, bully, apache, pickpocket, thief, robber, safecracker, highwayman, footpad, desperado, marauder, bandit, brigand, freebooter, plunderer, murderer, assassin, cutthroat, killer, thug, bravo, slayer, assailant, assaulter, rapist, rakehell, loose fish, libertine, debauchee.

MISDATE, *v.* Date incorrectly, anachronize, mistime, antedate, predate, postdate, overdate, anticipate, violate the calendar, take no note of time.

MISDEED, *n.* Wicked action, crime, misdemeanor, offense, trespass, transgression, misconduct, ill behavior, misbehavior, fault, misdoing, iniquity, wrong, malpractice, violation, injury, infringement, sin, felony, atrocity, outrage, delinquency, enormity, blunder, error, faux pas, peccadillo, lapse, dereliction, corpus delicti.

MISDEMEANOR, *n.* Offense defined by law as less serious than a felony. malefaction, trespass, transgression, misdeed, offense, thievery, petty larceny, burglary, breach of peace, delinquency, tort, malfeasance, malversation, fault, crime, wrong, lawbreaking, misconduct, misbehavior.

MISDOER, *n.* Malefactor, criminal, offender, felon, wrongdoer, transgressor, delinquent, trespasser, worker of iniquity, evildoer, sinner, culprit, misdemeanant, convict, outlaw, jailbird, blackguard, rogue, rascal, villain, scamp, no-good. (See **MISCREANT.**)

MISDOING, *n.* Evildoing, wrongdoing, iniquity, malpractice, vice, wickedness, knavery, rascality, villainy, roguery, turpitude, foul play, improbity, dishonesty, deviation from rectitude, fraud, bad faith, betrayal, infidelity, breach of promise, treason, perfidy, treachery, double-dealing, nepotism, venality, graft, sharp practice, trespass, offense, crime, felony, malfeasance, malversation, malefaction, tort, immodesty, indecency, impudicity, obscenity, lust, carnality, concupiscence, lewdness, lechery, lubricity, debauchery, libertinism, fornication, dissipation, venery, seduction, violation, rape, abuse, defilement, defloration, incest, perversion, whoredom, harlotry, stupration, cuckoldom, adultery, solicitation.

MISEMPLOY, *v.* Employ improperly, make an ill use of, abuse, misuse, misapply, misappropriate, profane, desecrate, prostitute, overtax, overwork, squander, waste, mistreat, exhaust, dissipate, misspend, run through, burn the candle at both ends, fritter away, maltreat.

MISER, *n.* Avaricious person, skinflint, curmudgeon, niggard, money-grubber, pinchpenny, pennypincher, hoarder, harpy, nickle-snatcher, dime-squeezer, screw, churl, pinchfist, extortioner, extortionist, usurer, scrimp, hunks, mean fellow, sordid wretch, skimper, muckworm, cheeseparer, codger, tightwad, Harpagon, lickpenny.

MISERABLE, *adj.* 1. Wretched in mind, unhappy, disconsolate, distressed, forlorn, doleful, lachrymose, heartbroken, brokenhearted, comfortless, afflicted, crushed, sorrowful, gloomy, desolate, woebegone, cheerless, dejected, depressed, downhearted, melancholic, hypochondriac, infelicitous, heartsick, careworn, heavy-laden, grieved, sad, mournful, chagrined, cut up *(colloq.),* mortified, worried.

2. Attended with misery, pitiable, deplorable, lamentable, unfortunate, calamitous, ill-starred, unlucky, hapless, disastrous.

3. Of wretched character, abject, mean, low, contemptible, despicable, sordid, arrant, base, degraded, venal, mercenary, groveling, servile, menial.

4. Worthless, valueless, very poor, of poor quality, scrubby, sorry, trashy, scurvy, rubbishy, meager, niggardly, shabby, beggarly, catchpenny, cheap, two-by-four, gimcrack, second-rate, inferior, one-horse, trumpery, sleazy, jerry-built, not worth a rap, piddling, insignificant, flimsy, petty.

5. Being in poor health, ailing, sickly, valetudinarian, invalid, unwell, poorly, confined, laid up, bedridden, on the sick list, out of sorts, chlorotic, infirm, in declining health, indisposed.

MISERLY, *adj.* Avaricious, penurious, parsimonious, illiberal, close-fisted, niggardly, stingy, mean, sordid, covetous, rapacious, curmudgeonly, selfish, grasping, pinching, narrow, excessively frugal, ungenerous, churlish, near, shabby, tight-fisted, close-handed, cheeseparing, meager, scrimping, grudging, sparing, mercenary, greedy, venal, extortionate, hard-fisted, beggarly.

MISERY, *n.* Extreme unhappiness, wretchedness, grief, heartache, broken heart, sorrow, bleeding heart, desolation, heavy heart, bereavement, affliction, tribulation, suffering, distress, agony, anguish, woe, trial, torment, torture, dolor, infelicity, despair, despondency, prostration, extremity, anxiety, worry, solicitude, concern, ordeal, trouble, load, burden, fret, adversity, oppression, depression, mortification, vexation, irritation, chagrin, care, hardship, need, indigence, destitution, privation, penury, mendicancy, beggary, misfortune, bale, calamity, disaster, catastrophe, evil.

MISFEASANCE, *n.* Wrong (actual or alleged) arising from affirmative action, wrongful performance of a normally legal act, injurious exercise of lawful authority, misapplication, misdirection, misgovernment, misdemeanor, misprision.

MISFIT, *n.* A badly adjusted person, person ill adjusted to his environment, round peg in a square hole, sorry figure.

MISFORTUNE, *n.* Calamity, disaster, catastrophe, adverse fortune, adversity, ill fortune, ill luck, reverse, accident, trouble, affliction, infliction, blow, visitation, mischance, distress, trial, stroke, mishap, casualty, misadventure, hardship, harm, ill, scourge, evil day, ill wind, gathering clouds, curse, evil, blight, sorrow, setback, check, comedown, downfall, ruin, failure, fall, wreck, crash, undoing, losing game, extremity, frowns of fortune, tragedy, infelicity, damage, loss, frustration, chastening, contretemps, disappointment, misery, gloom, ruination, grief, bereavement, tribulation, wretchedness.

MISGIVING, *n.* Feeling of apprehension, want of confidence, doubt, hesitation, mistrust, distrust, suspicion, foreboding, evil premonition, alarm, dread, dismay, worry, disquiet, fear, anxiety, suspense, indecision, demur, scruple, qualm, uncertainty, dubiety, skepticism, dubiousness, doubtfulness, misdoubt, discredit.

MISGUIDED, *adj.* Misdirected, misled, misadvised, ill-advised, ill-judged, ill-conducted, unguided, misconducted, led astray, adrift, inexperienced, green, raw, fallacious, erroneous, faulty, in error, mistaken, out in one's reckoning, aberrant, wide of the mark, on a false scent, at sea,

on the wrong scent, at cross purposes, lost, *désorienté (Fr.),* adrift, at a nonplus, precarious, questionable, ticklish, slippery, misinformed, deceived.

MISHANDLE, *v.* Handle badly, mismanage, illtreat, abuse, maltreat, manhandle, molest, outrage, injure, wrong, harm, ill-use, bungle, blunder, muff, fumble, botch, make a mess of, make sad work of, make hash of.

MISHAP, *n.* Unfortunate accident, mischance, misfortune, misadventure, ill luck, disaster, calamity, catastrophe, casualty, reverse, adversity, stroke, blow, buffet, trouble, grief, harm, loss, miscarriage, contretemps, ill fortune, hurt, mischief, affliction, collapse, tragedy, bale, woe, ruin, ruination, injury, foul play, outrage, evil dispensation, cross, check, setback, downfall, comedown, infliction, bitter pill, rainy day, failure, nonsuccess, no go, labor in vain, fizzle, fiasco, washout, slip, trip, stumble, faux pas, mess, scrape, muddle, beating, drubbing, checkmate, rout, defeat, overthrow, repulse, discomfiture, rebuff, crash, break, wreck, shipwreck, explosion, smash-up, crack-up, blowout, flat, breakdown, flash in the pan.

MISHMASH, *n.* Jumble, hodgepodge, mélange, miscellany, potpourri, salmagundi, olla-podrida, pastiche, farrago, olio, gallimaufry, mingle-mangle, hash, mulligatawny, chutney, omnium-gatherum, chow-chow, patchwork, crazy quilt, Noah's ark, charivari, mosaic, motley, intermixture, miscellaneous collection, medley, mess.

MISINTERPRET, *v.* Understand incorrectly, explain wrongly, misconstrue, give a false coloring to, put an incorrect construction on, put a wrong construction on, mistranslate, misunderstand, misapprehend, misrender, misjudge, mistake, misspell, misexplain, misapply, misstate, misrepresent, distort, pervert, falsify, garble, wrest the sense of, strain the meaning of, twist the significance of, caricature, travesty, burlesque.

MISINTERPRETATION, *n.* Misrendering, misconstruction, misapprehension, misexplication, misexplanation, misapplication, misunderstanding, misconception, mistake, misrepresentation, misstatement, distortion, abuse of terms, perversion, exaggeration, catachresis, misuse of words, cacology, falsification, travesty, burlesque.

MISJUDGE, *v.* 1. Judge wrongly, miscalculate, misconceive, misconstrue, misconjecture, misunderstand, underestimate, think too little of, overestimate, exaggerate, twist, warp, bias.

2. Presuppose, prejudge, presume, forejudge, have a bias, dogmatize, jump to conclusions, run away with a notion, blunder, err.

MISJUDGMENT, *n.* 1. Warped judgment, misconception, hasty conclusion, misinterpretation, miscalculation, misconstruction, miscomputation, preconception, preconceived idea, foregone conclusion, fixed idea, *idée fixe (Fr.),* obsession, prepossession.

2. Partiality, bias, prejudice, one-sidedness, favor, twist, warp, craze, crotchet, whim, cult, fad.

3. Partisanship, partisanism, clannishness, esprit de corps, party spirit, class consciousness, class prejudice, race prejudice, provincialism, insularity.

MISLAY, *v.* Put in a place later forgotten, misplace, lose, disorganize, disorder, displace, dislocate, jumble, muddle, confuse, scatter, let slip, allow to slip through the fingers, miss.

MISLEAD, *v.* Guide wrongly, lead into error, lead

astray, misdirect, misguide, delude, beguile, deceive, misinform, betray, gammon, seduce, dazzle, circumvent, take in, outwit, overreach, throw dust into the eyes, take advantage of, trick, hoax, gull, bamboozle, cozen, chouse, victimize, inveigle, allure, waylay, decoy, play false, fool, hoodwink, trifle with, cajole, bluff, humbug, sham, counterfeit, juggle, conjure, palm off, play off, foist off, bilk, diddle, bunko *(slang)*, dupe, enmesh, misrepresent, jerry *(slang)*, ensnare, defraud, entangle, bait, distract, impose.

MISLIKE, *v.* Dislike, disapprove of, disrelish, object to, mind, not care for, have rather not, entertain an aversion to, take a dislike to, have no taste for, eschew, shrink from, look askance at, turn up the nose at, make a wry face, grimace.

MISMANAGE, *v.* Manage badly, misconduct, misrule, misdirect, mishandle, misapply, act foolishly, fumble, bungle, botch, manage ill, blunder, make a mess of, muff, boggle, make sad work of, make a hash of, spoil, mar, stumble, flounder, trip.

MISMATCHED, *adj.* Matched unsuitably, uncongenial, unsympathetic, incompatible, incongruous, ill-assorted, displeasing, inharmonious, discordant, inconsistent, inaccordant, inconsonant, inappropriate, inapt, unsuited, unbefitting, unsuitable, infelicitous.

MISNAME, *v.* Call by a wrong name, miscall, misterm, mistitle, misstyle, nickname, misdenominate, label incorrectly.

MISNOMER, *n.* 1. Mistaking of the true name of a person, misnaming, malapropism.

2. Wrong name, misapplied name, wrong designation, error in naming, inapplicable, title, sobriquet, assumed name, nickname, pet name, byname, alias, pseudonym, stage name, *nom de théâtre (Fr.)*, pen name, *nom de plume (Fr.)*, *nom de guerre (Fr.)*.

MISOGYNIST, *n.* Hater of womankind, womanhater, misanthrope, bachelor, celibate, agamist, misogamist, cynic.

MISPLACE, *v.* Put in a wrong place, place unsuitably, place improperly, set wrongly, displace, misset, mislay, disturb, disarrange, dislocate, confuse, disorder, derange.

MISPRINT, *n.* Mistake in printing, erratum, errata *(pl.)*, error in printing, corrigendum, corrigenda *(pl.)*, oversight, blunder, boner, fault, miss, bloomer, slip, flaw, blot.

MISPRISION, *n.* 1. Offense, trespass, official transgression, wrongful action of a public official, misdemeanor, misfeasance, malfeasance, malversation, malefaction, tort, deviation from rectitude, criminality, culpability, guilt, misconduct, misdeed, malpractice, delinquency, dereliction.

, 2. Neglect, oversight, mistake, slip, lapse, trip, indiscretion, faux pas, peccadillo.

MISPRIZE, *v.* Hold cheap, underestimate, undervalue, slight, underrate, depreciate, disregard, set at naught, overlook, push aside, disparage, speak slightingly of, not do justice to, disprize, ridicule, make nothing of, belittle, minimize, run down, contemn, despise, scorn.

MISPRONOUNCE, *v.* Pronounce incorrectly, missound, misspeak, missay, misaccentuate, slur over, murder the language, mangle, pronounce incoherently, speak thickly, clip one's words, hesitate, splutter, falter, balbutiate, commit cacology.

MISPRONUNCIATION, *n.* Incorrect pronunciation, balbutiation, cacology, cacoepy, misaccentuation.

MISQUOTE, *v.* Quote incorrectly, miscite, misstate, misreport, misrepresent, misrecite, misrepeat, falsify, distort, pervert, garble, varnish, dress up, embroider, stretch, overstate, understate, overdraw, exaggerate, wrest the sense.

MISRECKON, *v.* Reckon incorrectly, miscalculate, miscount, miscompute, misestimate, misjudge, fly in the face of facts.

MISREPORT, *v.* Report incorrectly, state falsely, misstate, misrelate, misquote, miscite, misrepresent, falsify, distort, pervert, play fast and loose, mince the truth, garble, give a color to, varnish, embroider, dress up, bear false witness, trim, fence with words, beat about the bush.

MISREPRESENT, *v.* 1. Represent incorrectly, falsify, belie, misstate, distort, understate, minimize, overstate, exaggerate, overdraw, wrest the sense, stretch, put a false construction on, give a false coloring to, embroider, dress up, doctor, garble, miscolor, color, disguise, mislead, torture the sense.

2. Mock, mimic, parody, burlesque, ridicule, buffoon, caricature, satirize, travesty.

MISREPRESENTATION, *n.* 1. Misstatement, distortion, falsification, anamorphosis, exaggeration, bad likeness, daub, inexact copy, poor likeness.

2. Take-off, parody, ridicule, mimicry, caricature, travesty, burlesque, burletta, mockery, mock tragedy, paratragedia, mock heroic.

MISRULE, *n.* Bad rule, misgovernment, mismanagement, maladministration, misdirection, misguidance, impolicy, confusion, anarchy, lawlessness, tumult, disorder, riot, *émeute (Fr.)*, nihilism, laxity, lynch law.

MISS, *v.* 1. Fail to catch, fail to light upon, fail to receive, fail to obtain, fail to accomplish, fail to attain, fail to perform, fail to attend to, fail to perceive, fail to see, fail to hear, fail to understand, fail to be present, fail to reach, fail to hit, fail to find, lose, miscarry, muff, fall short, misfire, prove abortive, miss aim, fly wide, not succeed, prove unsuccessful, come to nothing, end in smoke, founder, run aground, go on the rocks, come to grief, flounder, fall, break down, meet with disaster, collapse, succumb, fall through, go to wrack and ruin, flash in the pan.

2. Omit, overlook, skip, forego, pass by, go without, leave out, dispense with, let slip, neglect, cut, slight, disregard, forget, gloss over, let pass, ignore, *laisser aller (Fr.)*, let go, not trouble oneself about, push aside, slur over, overpass.

3. Perceive the absence of with regret, feel the want of, desiderate, feel the loss of, want, require, lack, long for, desire, pine for, need.

MISS, *n.* 1. Oversight, omission, neglect, error, slip, mistake, fault, failure, blunder, trip, default, negligence, false step, faux pas, delinquency.

2. Felt absence, loss, want, hankering, yearning, pining for, longing, requirement.

3. Young unmarried woman, maiden, lass, damsel, girl, young lady, maid, mademoiselle, demoiselle, lassie, damazel, nymph, virgin, colleen, schoolgirl, spinster, old maid.

MISSAL, *n.* Prayer book, mass book, service book, breviary, beadroll, book of common prayer.

MISSHAPEN, *adj.* Ill-formed, ill-shaped, badly shaped, deformed, disfigured, crooked, misformed, misproportioned, unshapely, ungainly, ugly, shapeless, amorphous, distorted, ill-made, humpbacked, hunchbacked, kyphotic, grotesque, bowlegged, bandylegged, knock-kneed, splayfooted, taliped, clubfooted.

MISSILE, *n.* Object that can be thrown or shot, projectile, arrow, dart, boomerang, spear, lance, flechette, bullet, shell, shot, grenade, ball, bomb, javelin, harpoon, assagai, pike, tomahawk.

MISSING, *adj.* Wanting, lacking, absent, not found, gone, lost, astray, abstracted, invisible, minus, parted with, strayed, stray, displaced, misplaced, *spurlos versenkt (Ger.)*, melted away, evanescent, nowhere to be found.

MISSION, *n.* 1. Business with which an agent is charged, errand, commission, charge, duty, trust, office, assignment, stint, work, chore, task, job, appointment.

2. Calling, vocation, profession, metier, trade, line, occupation, employment, pursuit, undertaking, activity, venture, concern, affair, interest, office, position.

3. Permanent diplomatic establishment abroad, body of persons sent to a foreign country to conduct negotiations, legation, delegation, deputation, embassy, missionary post.

MISSIONARY, *n.* Propagator of religious faith among the heathen, evangelist, apostle, colporteur, propagandist, proselytizer, moonshee, interpreter, pioneer, padre, revivalist, Jesuit, field preacher, evangelical, missioner, clergyman.

MISSISH, *adj.* Prudish, prim, fastidious, affected, artificial, *maniéré (Fr.)*, formal, unnatural, demure, smug, priggish, finical, mincing, delicate, meticulous, straitlaced, overparticular.

MISSIVE, *n.* Written message, letter, communication, epistle, note, dispatch, billet, postcard, billet-doux, bulletin, post.

MISSPEND, *v.* Spend foolishly, squander, fool away, misuse, fritter away, waste, dissipate, exhaust, be prodigal, lavish, pour forth like water, drain, pay through the nose, outrun the constable, overdraw, throw good money after bad, burn the candle at both ends, make ducks and drakes of one's money, spend money like water, pour water into a sieve.

MISSTATE, *v.* Make a wrong statement about, state misleadingly, misrepresent, garble, falsify, misreport, misrelate, misquote, miscite, misword, distort, invent, misinform, give a false impression, deceive, pervert.

MISSTATEMENT, *n.* Wrong statement, misrepresentation, untruth, garbled version, mistake, distortion, perversion, false coloring, misreport, falsification, gloss, exaggeration, malapropism, blunder, howler, boner, bloomer, slip of the tongue, *lapsus linguae (Lat.).*

MISSTEP, *n.* Wrong step, false step, faux pas, false movement, slip, lapse, stub, stumble, trip, lurch, nose dive, titubation, error, weak side, failing.

MIST, *n.* 1. Cloud, cloudiness, haze, haziness, dimness, fog, vapor, steam, smog, film, smoke screen, fine rain, drizzle, mizzle.

2. Obscurity, perplexity, bewilderment, confusion, vagueness, imperspicuity, uncertainty, ambiguity, mystification.

MIST, *v.* Cover with mist, cloud, rain in very fine drops; drizzle, mizzle, fog, befog, envelop.

MISTAKE, *v.* 1. Take one for another, confound, take in error, mischoose, confuse with each other,

identify incorrectly, name inaccurately, mix up, misidentify.

2. Err, slip, misapprehend, stray, blunder, miscalculate, sin, misjudge, misconceive, misunderstand, be at fault, make a mistake, be wide of the mark, be on the wrong scent, fall into error, bark up the wrong tree, take the shadow for the substance, lose one's way, deceive oneself, slip up, miscount, misreckon, miscalculate, misinterpret.

MISTAKE, *n.* 1. Misunderstanding, misapprehension, mistaking, misconception, misjudgment, misstatement, miscalculation, misinterpretation, misconstruction, fallacy, error, mispersuasion.

2. Blunder, slip, oversight, trip, fault, break, misprint, erratum, corrigendum, slip of the pen, *lapsus calami (Lat.)*, slip of the tongue, *lapsus linguae (Lat.)*, bungle, solecism, bull, clerical error, spoonerism, malapropism, anachronism, parachronism, metachronism, boner, howler, faux pas, misstep, impropriety, false step, sour note, flaw.

MISTAKEN, *adj.* In error, wrong, incorrect, erroneous, inaccurate, wide of the mark, astray, on the wrong scent, faulty, false, untrue, fallacious, erring, unfounded, illogical, groundless, ungrounded, inexact, unsound, out in one's reckoning, deceived, at sea.

MISTER, *n.* Conventional title of respect for a man, Mr., *monsieur (Fr.)*, *Herr (Ger.)*, *signor (It.)*, *señor (Sp.)*, *senhor (Port.)*, *sahib (India)*, sir.

MISTERM, *v.* Misname, miscall, mistitle, give an alias to, use a misnomer, commit a malapropism, give a sobriquet to, give a pseudonym.

MISTIMED, *adj.* Ill-timed, untimely, unseasonable, intrusive, out of season, inopportune, predated, anachronistic, inauspicious, untoward, unfavorable, unpropitious, unsuited, unpunctual, premature, too late for, too soon for, wise after the event, postdated.

MISTINESS, *n.* Fogginess, nebulosity, cloudiness, obscurity, haziness, dampness, dimness.

MISTRANSLATE, *v.* Misinterpret, misrender, misconstrue, misunderstand, misapprehend, misconceive, misrepresent, garble, pervert, distort, wrest the sense, put a false construction on, give a false coloring.

MISTREAT, *v.* Ill-treat, maltreat, misuse, abuse, treat unjustly, wrong, injure, buffet, maul, manhandle, smite, do violence to, harm, outrage, aggrieve, persecute, oppress, trample upon, bully, assail, torture, torment, rack, wreak one's malice on, molest, harass, harry, grind, prostitute, violate, rape, attack, assault.

MISTREATMENT, *n.* Maltreatment, abuse, wrong, ill-treatment, misuse, injury, manhandling, mauling, violation, outrage, harm, persecution, oppression, torture, torment, molestation, prostitution, rape.

MISTRESS, *n.* 1. Mrs., lady, madam, *madame (Fr.)*, *Frau (Ger.)*, *Vrouw (Dutch)*, *signora (It.)*, *donna (It.)*, *señora (Sp.)*, *doña (Sp.)*, *senhora (Port.)*, *memsahib (India)*, squaw, dowager, *femme (Fr.)*, dame, weaker vessel, matron, belle, wife.

2. Miss, maiden, damsel, maid, damosel, girl, nymph, virgin, colleen, *mademoiselle (Fr.)*, *Fräulein (Ger.)*, *signorina (It.)*, *señorita (Sp.)*, *senhorita (Port.)*, flapper, skirt *(slang)*, petticoat *(slang)*, female, she.

3. Woman who has authority or control, female head, woman who has the power of disposing of something at pleasure, female owner, female

sovereign, woman employing servants, matron, head, executrix, headwoman, materfamilias, mother superior, housekeeper, sultana, maharani.

4. Female teacher, schoolmistress, instructress, governess.

5. Woman illicitly occupying the place of a wife, kept woman, paramour, concubine, doxy, demimondaine, demirep, cocotte, lorette, grisette, hetaera, leman, *bona roba (It.),* courtesan, harlot, strumpet, jade, broad *(slang),* prostitute, tart, chippy, hustler, streetwalker, wanton, wren *(slang),* pickup, *fille de joie (Fr.),* woman of easy virtue, white slave, Cyprian, trull.

6. Sweetheart, ladylove, flame, dulcinea, inamorata, sweetie, beloved, darling, idol, favorite, queen, goddess, angel.

MISTRUST, *n.* Lack of trust, want of confidence, distrust, misgiving, suspicion, doubt, skepticism, demur, misdoubt, qualm, jealousy, uncertainty, scruple.

MISTRUST, *v.* Regard with mistrust, be distrustful, distrust, suspect, be suspicious of, be jealous of, believe to be guilty, doubt, doubt the truth of, be skeptical, diffide, scent, smell a rat, entertain doubts, harbor suspicions, stop and consider, scruple, demur, question, throw doubt upon, challenge, discredit, disbelieve, misbelieve.

MISTRUSTFUL, *adj.* Distrustful, suspicious, jealous, apprehensive, full of forebodings, anxious, watchful, suspiciously vigilant, inclined to suspect, doubtful, incredulous, skeptical as to, shy of, doubting.

MISTY, *adj.* 1. Abounding in mist, hazy, foggy, caliginous, clouded by mist, steamy, vaporous, brumous, murky, overcast, nubiferous, frosted, turbid, fuliginous, cloudy, muggy, smoky, spraylike.

2. Appearing as if seen through mist, indistinct in form, vague in outline, obscure, dim, dark, shadowy, gloomy, confused, nebulous, dusky, opaque, gray, thick, semitransparent, opacous, obfuscated.

MISUNDERSTAND, *v.* Understand wrongly, take in a wrong sense, misapprehend, misconstrue, mistake, misconceive, misinterpret, misjudge, misapply, misreckon, miscount, miscalculate, take the shadow for the substance, miss the point, misperceive, put a false construction on.

MISUNDERSTANDING, *n.* 1. Failure to understand, mistake as to meaning, misapprehension, error, misconception, miscomprehension, mispersuasion, misinterpretation, blunder, fallacy, misconstruction, miscalculation, misjudgment, fault, oversight, bungle, false impression, delusion.

2. Disagreement, difference, variance, quarrel, spat, tiff, dispute, dissension, difficulty, breach, disunion, discord, wrangle, dissent, conflict, dissidence, division, controversy.

MISUSAGE, *n.* 1. Improper use of words, cacology, barbarism, catachresis, solecism, archaism, corruption, caconym, antiphrasis.

2. Abuse, exploitation, maltreatment, perversion, outrage, ill usage, bad treatment, wrong.

MISUSE, *v.* 1. Use wrongly, use improperly, misemploy, put to a wrong use, misapply, misappropriate, exploit, profane, desecrate, prostitute, pervert, debase, squander, waste.

2. Abuse, ill-treat, maltreat, ill-use, wrong, harm, mistreat, injure, hurt, maul, manhandle, molest.

3. Tire, overwork, overtask, exhaust, overtax, overburden, fatigue, overlabor, overstrain, harass, jade.

MISUSE, *n.* 1. Wrong use, improper usage, erroneous use, misapplication, misemployment, misappropriation, solecism, barbarism.

2. Abuse, ill-usage, ill-treatment, ill-use, maltreatment, prostitution, perversion, molestation, desecration, profanation.

MITE, *n.* 1. Small contribution, all that one can afford, very small sum of money, coin of very little value, lepton, centime, sou, ha'penny, farthing, bob.

2. Particle, piece, bit, morsel, scrap, crumb, fragment, atom, molecule, corpuscle, monad, scintilla, fraction, iota, tittle, whit, pittance, speck, grain, jot.

3. Small arachnid, animalcule, insect, gnat, midge.

MITIGATE, *v.* Moderate in severity, abate in intensity, lessen in force, assuage, alleviate, palliate, remit, relieve, lighten, deaden, weaken, reduce, soften, soothe, hush, appease, pacify, mollify, still, quiet, quell, calm, allay, tranquilize, meliorate, ameliorate, subdue, ease, smooth over, temper, attemper, diminish, propitiate, compose, lull, cool, sober, slacken, decrease, smother, blunt, curb, check, restrain, tame.

MITIGATION, *n.* Moderation, diminution, alleviation, abatement, relief, palliation, remission, subdual, allayment, melioration, amelioration, assuagement, tranquilization, pacification, composure, relaxation, sedation, easement, deliverance, softening, soothing, comfort, appeasement, extenuation.

MITIGATIVE, *adj.* Lenitive, emollient, soothing, lenient, mollifying, assuasive, assuaging, relieving, alleviative, palliative, meliorative, ameliorative, anodyne, mild, balmy, mitigatory, softening, consolatory, balsamic, sedative, demulcent, moderative, bland, extenuative.

MIX, *v.* 1. Put together, combine, unite, commix, mingle, commingle, blend, interlard, compound, interfuse, amalgamate, alloy, incorporate, intermingle, pour into, jumble, scramble, confuse, confound, knead, interpolate, interweave, intertwine, cross, intersperse, infiltrate, adulterate, intermix, fuse, immix.

2. Saturate, impregnate, imbue, diffuse, transfuse, infuse, suffuse, tinge, season, lace, flavor, entincture, tincture, dash.

3. Associate in company, socialize, fraternize, consort, hobnob, have intercourse, conjoin, join.

MIXED, *adj.* 1. Composed of different constituents, put together, formed by mixing, blended, mingled, associated, joined, fused, amalgamated, adulterated, alloyed, intermingled, composite, united, combined, immixed, interwoven.

2. Of various kinds, heterogeneous, variegated, motley, promiscuous, miscellaneous, indiscriminate, hybrid, half-and-half, mongrel, diversified, conglomerate, pepper-and-salt, piebald, involved, confounded, jumbled, confused.

MIXTURE, *n.* 1. Minglement, admixture, intermixture, association, union, combination, amalgamation, compound, blend, immixture, junction, commingling, alloyage, composite, complexus, compositeness, infusion, impregnation, instillation, infiltration, interpolation, interlarding, adulteration.

2. Hodgepodge, miscellany, medley, mélange, potpourri, mingle-mangle, omnium-gatherum, olio,

olla-podrida, hash, farrago, pastiche, mess, sal-magundi, goulash, mulligatawny, gallimaufry, chow-chow, motley, mosaic, crazy quilt, patch-work, Noah's ark, commixture, mishmash, minced meat, variety, diversity.

3. Hybrid, mongrel, half-breed, half-blood, half-caste, crossbreed, cross, Eurasian, mestee, quadroon, mulatto, octoroon, androgyne, herma-phrodite.

4. Tinge, touch, soupçon, seasoning, dash, tinc-ture, spice, smack, strain, shade, vein.

MIX-UP, *n.* 1. Confused state of things, imbroglio, complicated misunderstanding, muddle, mess, jumble, disorder, disarrangement, confusion, litter, muss, farrago, clutter, complexity, entanglement, complication, perplexity, intricacy, maze, network, labyrinth, jungle, wilderness, Gordian knot, tan-gled skein, coil, dilemma, quandary, embarrass-ment, involvement, vexed question, puzzle, poser.

2. Fracas, melee, shindy, fight, rumpus, pande-monium, commotion, uproar, row, tumult, disturb-ance, Donnybrook, ferment, bustle, trouble, con-vulsion, riot, babel, bedlam, breach of the peace, scrimmage, broil, hubbub, racket, embranglement, embroilment.

MIZZLE, *v.* Rain in small drops, drizzle, mist, sprinkle, shower lightly, dribble, drip, spirtle, plash, trickle, ooze.

MNEMONIC, *adj.* Pertaining to mnemonics, of the memory, intended to assist the memory, for the help of the memory, mnemotechnic, reminiscen-tial.

MOAN, *v.* Make lamentation, utter in lamentation, groan, lament, mourn, deplore, bewail, bemoan, grieve for, weep for, wail, whimper, sob, keen, whine, complain, ululate, rend the air, snivel, mut-ter, whinny, pipe, grumble, pule, yaup, cry, blub-ber, mew, yammer, murmur, grunt, croak, maun-der, sigh.

MOANING, *n.* Prolonged inarticulate sound from physical or mental suffering, lamentation, plaint, wailing, mourning, sighing, susurration, complaint, murmur, groan, whimper, suspiration, whine, sob-bing, heaving, wail of woe, outcry, weeping, lan-guishment.

MOAT, *n.* Deep wide trench surrounding a forti-fied place, fosse, ditch, graff, dike, channel, trough, gutter, gully, bulwark, entrenchment.

MOB, *n.* 1. Disorderly assemblage of persons, horde engaged in lawless violence, riotous throng, tumultuous rabble, lawless crowd, excitable dis-orderly gathering, hostile concourse, disorderly element.

2. Common mass of people, rabble, common people, populace, vulgar herd, *profanum vulgus* (*Lat.*), riffraff, canaille, scum of society, ragtag and bobtail, lower orders, dregs of the people, rude multitude, rank and file, proletariat, hoi polloi, hewers of wood, drawers of water, lower classes, filthy crew, the great unwashed, masses, common sort, commonalty, plebeians, small fry, *faex pop-uli* (*Lat.*), vermin, rabblerout, king Mob, the mil-lion, chaff, residuum of the people.

3. Throng, crowd, great number, press, legion, assembly, array, aggregation, army, host, assem-blage, scores, profusion, galaxy, herd, flock, swarm, drove.

MOBBISH, *adj.* Vulgar, tumultuous, disorderly, mean, lowborn, ignoble, common, vile, base, beg-garly, scrubby, sorry, proletarian, plebeian, of low origin, baseborn, lowbred, obscure, unpolished,

uncivilized, boorish, loutish, raffish, brutish, churl-ish, rude, barbarous, cockney, riotous, violent, rude, rough, wild, impetuous, boisterous, bluster-ing, turbulent, troublous, tumultuary, frenzied, obstreperous, hysteric, ravening, frantic, desperate, ferocious, excited, fierce, savage, headstrong, un-governable, unruly, explosive.

MOBILE, *adj.* 1. Moving readily, movable, motile, motory, unquiet, mercurial, shifting, restless, flow-ing freely, liquid.

2. Changing easily in expression, quickly re-sponding to impulses, sensitive, expressive, emo-tional, excitable, temperamental, high-strung, im-pressionable, susceptible, spirited, enthusiastic, mettlesome, lively, vivacious, impassioned, impas-sionable.

3. Fickle, changeable, volatile, inconstant, vari-able, unsettled, unstable, protean, erratic, irreso-lute, wayward, capricious, maggoty, whimsical, vagrant, plastic, alterable, inconsistent, fitful, crotchety, skittish, giddy, frivolous.

MOBILIZE, *v.* 1. Put armed forces into readiness for active service, organize for government ser-vice in time of war, call to arms, muster troops, summon to the colors, arm, raise troops, draft, conscript, take up the cudgels.

2. Render mobile, mechanize, put in motion, put into active use.

MOB-LAW, *n.* Lynch-law, lawlessness, antinomy, arbitrariness, brute force, violence, club-law, drumhead-law, *le droit du plus fort* (*Fr.*), illegal-ity, unlawfulness, *argumentum ad baculum* (*Lat.*).

MOBOCRACY, *n.* Political control by a mob, mob rule, ochlocracy, ergatocracy, *vox populi* (*Lat.*).

MOCK, *v.* 1. Treat with derision, assail with ridi-cule, deride, ridicule, laugh at, make fun of, tease, make game of, insult, jeer, scoff, flout, gibe, scout, taunt, defy, chaff, treat with scorn, treat with con-tempt, scorn, make a butt of, sneer, treat with raillery, spurn, poke fun at, twit, trifle with, treat with disrespect, make sport of, rag, make a fool of, guy (*colloq.*), roast (*colloq.*).

2. Imitate, take off, mimic, ape, counterfeit, burlesque, simulate, impersonate, personate, trav-esty, parody, caricature, act.

MOCK, *adj.* Having merely the semblance of, counterfeit, sham, make-believe, spurious, false, claptrap, feigned, pretended, assumed, imitational, bogus, specious, glossy, pseudo, so-called, unreal, assumed, snide, base, alloyed, fraudulent, mere-tricious, tinsel, brummagem, factitious, artificial.

MOCKER, *n.* 1. Derider, scoffer, scorner, despiser, railer, jeerer, insulter, flouter, hooter, giber, taunt-er, ridiculer, sniggerer.

2. Impostor, charlatan, mountebank, quack, pretender, cheat, deceiver, trickster, sharper, mis-leader.

MOCKERY, *n.* 1. Derision, ridicule, jeering, con-temptuous mimicry, scorn, persiflage, irrision, sardonic smile, snigger, disrespect, scoffing, ban-ter, raillery, irony, chaff, badinage, burlesque, travesty, parody, caricature, take-off, satire, quip, squib, grin, buffoonery, practical joke.

2. Imitation, sham, counterfeit, make-believe, brummagem, fraud, forgery, fake, snare and a delusion, whited sepulcher, painted sepulcher, paste, tinsel, scagliola, ormolu, masquerade, false colors, borrowed plumes, mummery, wolf in sheep's clothing.

MOCKING, *adj.* Derisive, jeering, scoffing, disrespectful, disdainful, discourteous, rude, uncivil, disparaging, irreverent, supercilious, insulting, sarcastic, ironic, scurrilous, insolent, contemptuous, contumelious, withering, scornful, cynical, arrogant, derogatory, detractory, biting, impudent, sardonic, pert, fresh, forward.

MODE, *n.* 1. Prevailing style, fashion, vogue, custom, *dernier cri (Fr.),* the rage, the latest thing, the go, bon ton, fad, craze, prevailing taste, usage, habit, *haut ton (Fr.),* dress, taste, cut, trim, appearance.

2. Method, manner, procedure, *modus operandi (Lat.),* way, means, process, course, practice, system, form, agency, plan, rule.

MODEL, *n.* 1. Pattern, miniature representation to show the construction of, design, prototype, archetype, protoplast, mold, original, type, example, plan, precedent, representation, tracing, cast, imitation, similitude, facsimile, copy, duplicate, replica, dummy.

2. Standard for imitation or comparison, criterion, paragon, *beau idéal (Fr.),* ideal, pink, nonpareil, nonesuch, flower, phoenix, mirror, ne plus ultra, worthy, paradigm, sample, exemplar, gauge.

3. Manikin, dummy, clotheshorse, figure, puppet, marionette, waxwork, fantoccini, doll, lay figure, statuette, bust.

MODEL, *v* 1. Form according to a model, give shape to, shape, design, mold, fashion, plan, sketch, cast, outline, adapt, build, make a representation of.

2. Display articles of apparel to customers, wear clothes for exhibit, be a manikin.

MODERATE, *adj.* 1. Temperate, gentle, mild, lenient, reasonable, calm, tranquil, peaceful, pacific, irenic, halcyon, unruffled, quiet, cool, sober, untroubled, still, peaceable, reasonable, deliberate, judicious, steady, clement, lenient, rational, dispassionate, chaste, tolerant, compassionate.

2. Keeping within due bounds, sparing, frugal, economical, provident, saving, careful, chary, thrifty, unwasteful, abstemious, abstinent, parsimonious, nonindulgent, conservative, regulated, measured, continent.

3. Of medium quantity or extent, mediocre, fair, medium, average, mean, passable, middling, ordinary, modest, cheap, low-priced, meager, inexpensive.

MODERATE, *v.* 1. Reduce the excessiveness of, make less severe, temper, attemper, slacken, diminish, qualify, soften, palliate, alleviate, mitigate, assuage, mollify, soothe, quell, allay, appease, still, lessen, blunt, dull, quiet, subdue, repress, abate, pacify, compose, calm, tranquilize, sober, smooth, hush, cool, smother, deaden, restrain, tame, chasten, curb, check, weaken, tone down, mute.

2. Preside over, govern, regulate, control, act as moderator, direct, manage, act as chairman.

MODERATION, *n.* 1. Avoidance of extremes, quality of being moderate, temperance, sobriety, restraint, forbearance, frugality, abstinence, abstemiousness, continence, temperateness, thriftiness, economy, self-control, moderateness, golden mean, *aurea mediocritas, ne quid nimis (Lat.),* measure.

2. Equanimity, composure, mental calmness, pacification, tranquilization, deliberateness, mildness, coolness, calmness, sedateness, gentleness, lenity, quiet.

3. Mitigation, remission, abatement, diminu-

tion, palliation, alleviation, assuagement, relaxation.

MODERATOR, *n.* 1. One who presides over a deliberative body, presiding officer over a public forum, conductor of a public meeting, chairman, president, manager, regulator, mediator, arbitrator, umpire, referee.

2. Sedative, opiate, balm, palliative, lenitive, demulcent, mitigator.

MODERN, *adj.* Pertaining to present time, existing in the present age, new, present, recent, novel, fresh, late, up-to-date, neoteric, newfangled, newfashioned, brand-new, just out, advanced, *fin de siècle (Fr.),* newfledged, twentieth-century, newborn, unhandled, spick-and-span, young, green, modernized, present-day, latest, of our time, fashionable, streamlined, current, untried, improved, up-to-the-minute, having the new look.

MODERNISM, *n.* 1. Modern character, modernness, modernity, sympathy with what is modern, up-to-dateness, freshness, modernization, neoterism, innovation, renovation, novelty, novelness, lateness, newness.

2. The latest thing, the go, the rage, *dernier cri (Fr.),* prevailing style, fashion, vogue, modishness, bon ton, streamlining, new-look, surrealism, cubism, futurism, vorticism, postimpressionism.

3. Movement in thought which interprets past teachings in the light of modern conceptions, liberalism, opposite of fundamentalism.

MODERNIST, *n.* Modern, neoteric, neologist, neoterist, pathfinder, innovator, pioneer, trailblazer, *Bahnbrecher (Ger.),* surrealist *(Art),* cubist, futurist, vorticist, postimpressionist.

MODERNISTIC, *adj.* Pertaining to modernism or modernists, up-to-date, surrealistic, cubist, futurist, vorticist, postimpressionist.

MODERNIZE, *v.* 1. Make modern, give a modern character or appearance to, refurbish, streamline, endow with the new look, refresh, rejuvenate, renovate, revamp, regenerate, bring up to date.

2. Become modern, adopt modern ways and views, get on the ball *(slang).*

MODEST, *adj.* 1. Having a humble estimate of one's merits, free from vanity, devoid of egotism, unpretentious, unobtrusive, unpretending, unostentatious, unassuming, retiring, verecund, meek, free from pride, unpresumptuous, keeping in the background, humble, demure, diffident, timorous, timid, coy, bashful, blushing, sheepish, shy, backward, shrinking, reserved, undemonstrative, lowly, quiet, constrained.

2. Showing regard for the decencies of behavior or dress, decent, decorous, becoming, seemly, pure, chaste, virtuous, proper, conforming to propriety, sober, continent, chaste, delicate, innocent.

MODESTY, *n.* 1. Lack of boastfulness, freedom from vanity, unobtrusiveness, freedom from presumption, retiring disposition, diffidence, timidity, shyness, demureness, bashfulness, humility, meek humbleness, reserve, coyness, sheepishness, backwardness, constraint.

2. Regard for decency, propriety, decency, moderation, sobriety, continence, purity, chastity, delicacy, honor, innocence, viriginity, virtuousness, virtue, pudicity, decorum, decorousness.

MODICUM, *n.* Small quantity, little, minimum, trifle, dash, mite, dab, tinge, nip, bit, dole, sprinkling, drop, snatch, pinch, crumb, morsel, slip, fragment, fraction, snip, peeling, chip, splinter, sliver, paring, shaving, mouthful, handful, thimbleful, minim, grain, jot, tittle, iota, speck, particle, atom, corpuscle, electron, molecule.

MODIFICATION, *n.* 1. Alteration, change, variation, inflection, modulation, mutation, commutation, permutation, transposition, substitution, qualification, deviation, innovation, shift, conversion, reduction, metastasis, transition, metabolism, resolution, overthrow, overturn, revolution, vicissitude, inversion, reversal, transfigurement, transfiguration, transformation, metamorphosis, transmutation, transubstantiation.

2. Limitation, restriction, condition, qualification, proviso, provision, stipulation, arrangement, saving clause, exception, exemption.

MODIFY, *v.* 1. Make somewhat different, alter, change, give a new form to, vary, shape anew, reshape, transform, moderate, temper, modulate, diversify, inflect, shift, patch, piece, transfigure, transmute, translate, reduce, convert, resolve, innovate, revolutionize, ring the changes, metamorphose, transmogrify, shift the scene, shuffle the cards, turn over a new leaf, remold, recast, remodel, reconstruct, overturn, reverse, invert, upset, transpose, exchange, reorganize, reform, adapt, adjust, rectify, correct, revise.

2. Qualify, restrict, condition, limit, narrow, soften, restrain, lower, tone down.

MODISH, *adj.* In accordance with the prevailing mode, stylish, fashionable, high-style, in vogue, elegant, chic, smart, nobby, *à la mode (Fr.)*, *distingué (Fr.)*, jaunty, dapper, dashing, tony, *recherché (Fr.)*, *bien soigné (Fr.)*, well-groomed.

MODISTE, *n.* Maker of articles of fashionable attire, dressmaker, designer, *couturier* (man), *couturière* (woman), milliner, *costumier (Fr.)*, seamstress.

MODULATE, *v.* 1. Vary in tune and accentuation, inflect the voice, diversify, moderate, temper, qualify, change.

2. Harmonize, attune, tune, pitch, accord, symphonize, chime.

MODULATION, *n.* Voice inflection, variation, accentuation, cadence, pitch, timbre, intonation, tone, overtone, tonality.

MODUS OPERANDI (*Lat.*) Manner of operating, way of doing, process, method, mode of operation, procedure, system, order of the day, line of conduct, wise, mode, fashion, practice.

MOGUL, *n.* An important person, personage, magnate, bigwig, big shot, big wheel, tycoon, czar, celebrity, three-tailed bashaw, baron, notable, man of distinction.

MOHAMMEDAN, *n.* Moslem, Mussulman, Mahometan, Saracen, Islamite, Osmanli.

MOIETY, *n.* 1. Half, mediety, hemisphere, semisphere, fifty per cent.

2. Indefinite portion, share, fraction, piece, fragment, section, morsel, measure, ration, allotment, dividend, dole, dose, pittance, need, modicum, crumb, particle, sample, scrap, slice, chunk, chip, cut, bit, part.

MOIL, *v.* Work hard, toil, drudge, labor, plod, grub, tax one's energies, exert oneself, fag, sweat, slave, strain, wade through, strive, drag a lengthened chain, tug, pull, ply, take the laboring oar, put forth a strong arm, fall to work, buckle to, keep one's nose to the grindstone, set one's shoulder to the wheel, work like a cart horse, be a galleyslave, work like a coal-heaver.

MOIST, *adj.* Wet, damp, dank, humid, vaporous, muggy, wettish, watery, rainy, dewy, sopping wet, soaked, saturated, sodden, juicy, perspiring, sweated, soggy, sloppy, soft, dripping, reeking, wringing wet, soaking, wet through, oozy, marshy, swampy, misty, tearful, lachrymose, aqueous.

MOISTEN, *v.* Dampen, damp, humidify, bemoist, bedew, soak, irrigate, water, wash, imbrue, wet, sponge, drench, sop, sodden, seethe, infiltrate, saturate, baste *(cooking)*, dabble, lick, pass the tongue over, tongue.

MOISTURE, *n.* Wetness, dampness, damp, dankness, humidity, moistness, wet, mugginess, sweat, perspiration, teardrops, tears, drip, fog drip, dew, exudation, exhalation, humidification, vapor, water, wateriness.

MOLD, *n.* 1. Stamp, kind, cast, make, form, brand, frame, set, construction, contour, cut, outline, configuration, format, get-up, conformation, shape, figure, formation, *galbe (Fr.)*, build, type, turn, pattern, structure, fashion, impression, sculpture, architecture.

2. Matrix, last, die, punch, seal, mint, intaglio, negative.

3. Carious growth of minute fungi, furry coating, mildew, mucor, mustiness, blight, smut, rust.

MOLD, *v.* 1. Turn, convert, form, render, make, reform, remodel, reorganize, resolve into, convert into, transmute, transfigure, transform, influence, affect, work upon.

2. Create, shape, fashion, cast, model, trim, pattern, knead, stamp, mint, sculpture, carve, figure, chisel, cut, hew, construct.

MOLDY, *adj.* Musty, stale, rancid, tainted, putrescent, putrefactive, carious, foul, putrid, rotten, gamy, strong, bad, high, strong-smelling, rank, noisome, malodorous, fetid.

MOLE, *n.* 1. Massive stone structure set up in the water, jetty, breakwater, pier, dike, mound, embankment, anchorage, harbor.

2. Birthmark, naevus, spot, blemish, macula, freckle, blotch, maculation, pimple, pustule, excrescence, protuberance.

MOLECULAR, *adj.* Extremely small, very little, corpuscular, atomic, microbial, microbic, embryonic, animalcular, imperceptible, microscopic, invisible, evanescent, homeopathic, infinitesimal, minikin, minute, exiguous, diminutive, fine, wee, tiny, elfin, inconsiderable, insignificant, slight, pulverized, comminuted, triturated, inappreciable.

MOLECULE, *n.* 1. Ultimate particle, monad, atom, ion, magneton, corpuscle, electron, smallest physical unit of an element or compound.

2. Any very small particle, speck, iota, dot, fragment, fraction, mote, jot, scrap, mite, crumb, scintilla, spark, dab, modicum, trifle, whit, bit, tinge, dash, pinch, animalcule, microbe, microorganism, germ, bacterium, bacillus, proton, primordium, grain.

MOLE-EYED, *adj.* Near-sighted, short-sighted, myopic, blind, purblind, dim-sighted, presbyopic, astigmatic, blear-eyed, half-blind.

MOLEST, *v.* Annoy, disturb, bother, plague, harass, harry, discommode, disquiet, inconvenience, incommode, pester, trouble, hector, badger, tease, vex, fret, worry, torment, irritate, chafe, oppress, harm, ill-treat, abuse, affront, misuse, maltreat, interfere with injuriously, attack, assault, rape, deflower, violate, constuprate, devirginate, ravish, defile, aggrieve, outrage, wrong, persecute, torture, damage, hurt, injure, hound, bait, dragoon.

beset, importune, heckle, irk, mortify, rag, thwart, afflict, distress.

MOLLIFICATION, *n.* Appeasement, softening, alleviation, mitigation, assuagement, pacification, tranquilization, remission, relaxation.

MOLLIFY, *v.* 1. Soften, make soft, mellow, temper, relax, knead, squash, massage, mash.

2. Pacify, appease, compose, tranquilize, quiet, calm, soothe, propitiate, ameliorate, reconcile.

3. Mitigate, palliate, assuage, allay, ease, relieve, abate, moderate, attemper, temper, dull, restrain, lull, quell, repress, lessen, blunt, alleviate, still, hush, sober, smooth, cool, decrease, slacken, smother, deaden, subdue, weaken, check, curb, chasten, tone down, qualify.

MOLLIFYING, *adj.* Mitigative, assuasive, palliative, alleviative, bland, mild, softening, healing, gentle, cooling, tranquilizing, pacific, lenitive, demulcent, anodyne, sedative, soft.

MOLLYCODDLE, *n.* Man who is used to being coddled, milksop, effeminate man, pampered boy, sissy, mama's boy, molly, muff, betty, silk-sock, old woman.

MOLT, *v.* Shed feathers, slough, cast, exuviate, mew, moult.

MOLTEN, *adj.* Melted, fused, smelted, liquefied, liquated, fluxed, vitrified, igneous, volcanic, inflammatory, combustible, heated, red-hot, white-hot.

MOMENT, *n.* 1. Point of time, minute, second, instant, flash, trice, twinkling, jiffy, eyewink, *coup d'oeil (Fr.),* wink, crack, split second, breath, spurt, stroke of time, flash of lightning, burst.

2. Importance, weight, consequence, gravity, force, significance, signification, consideration, import, avail, value, materiality, weightiness, concern, prominence, mark, materialness, ponderosity, emphasis, influence, interest, caliber, distinction, standing, usefulness, greatness.

MOMENTARILY, *adv.* Instantaneously, instanter, presto, instantly, forthright, in no time, at once, in a trice, eftsoons, in a jiffy, in the twinkling of an eye, suddenly, immediately, promptly, now, any moment now, in the same breath, on the spur of the moment, extempore, plump, without hesitation, speedily, apace, quickly.

MOMENTARY, *adj.* 1. Instantaneous, abrupt, sudden, immediate, prompt, hasty, instant, quick as a flash, quick as lightning, quick as thought.

2. Transient, evanescent, transitory, ephemeral, fleeting, temporary, passing, fugitive, fugacious, fading.

MOMENTOUS, *adj.* Of great consequence, consequential, of much importance, important, grave, weighty, serious, significant, considerable, material, big, substantial, ponderous, impressive, critical, urgent, pressing, crucial, imperative, instant, exigent, signal, memorable, outstanding, salient, marked, influential, prominent, notable, remarkable, special, noteworthy, particular, unusual, rare, eventful, full of incident, of vital interest, essential, epochal, earthshaking.

MOMENTUM, *n.* Energy, impetus, moment, force, drive, impulse, impelling force, impulsion, thrust, pressure, boom, push, shove, send-off, start, kick, propulsion, jolt, jog, brunt, boost, projection, *vis a tergo (Lat.).*

MONACHAL, *adj.* Monkish, monastic, monastical, eremitic, cenobitic, mendicant, canonical, secluded, sequestered, solitary, anchoritic, celibate.

MONACHISM, *n.* Monasticism, monkery, monastic life, monarchy, monkhood, holy orders, cenobitism, priestcraft, mendicancy, anchoritism, estrangement from the world, seclusion, reclusion, retirement, celibacy.

MONAD, *n.* 1. *(Chem.)* Element having a valence of one, atom, molecule, radicle, indivisible particle, ultimate particle.

2. *(Zool.)* Simple single-celled organism, minute animalcule, amoeboid flagellate.

MONARCH, *n.* Absolute ruler, hereditary sovereign, autocrat, king, queen, emperor, empress, potentate, czar, kaiser, prince, dynast, lord, rajah, crown, sultan, shah, Pharaoh, regent, viceroy, bey, khedive, khan, calif, amir, pasha, doge, satrap, imperator, chief, dictator, tyrant, despot, liege, suzerain, crowned head, overlord, majesty, mogul, mikado, mandarin, sirdar, tetrarch, sheik, aga, chieftain, commander, commandant, consul, caesar.

MONARCHAL, *adj.* Having the status of a monarch, kingly, regal, royal, imperial, princely, autocratic, sovereign, supreme, ruling, monarchial, preëminent, monocratic, absolute, dictatorial, despotic, tyrannical, lordly, commanding, authoritative, domineering, masterful, regnant, dominant.

MONARCHISM, *n.* Advocacy of monarchical principles, Caesarism, autocracy, absolutism, autocratism, imperialism, divine right, kaiserism, czarism, despotism, tyranny, rod of empire, iron sway, sovereignty, suzerainty, dictatorship.

MONARCHY, *n.* Supreme power wielded by a single person, monocracy, absolute monarchy, despotic monarchy, limited monarchy, constitutional monarchy, kingship, princedom, principate, autocracy, sovereignty, divine right, dynastic rights, authoritativeness, suzerainty, lordship, regnancy, regime, protectorate, caliphate, proconsulship, empire, dominion, prerogative, command, primacy, supremacy.

MONASTERY, *n.* Community of monks, cloister, priory, abbey, friary, lamasery, convent, monkery, charterhouse, cenoby, nunnery, hospice, vihara *(Buddhist),* khankah *(Moham.).*

MONASTIC, *adj.* Monkish, cenobitic, monachal, conventual, cloistral, abbatical, canonical, capitular, clerical, ecclesiastical, eremitic, anchoritic, secluded, solitary, sequestered, recluse, devout, pious, humble, celibate.

MONASTICISM, *n.* Monastic life, monachism, monkhood, monkism, monkery, friarhood, cloistered life, celibacy.

MONDE, *n.* *(Fr.)* The world, people of the world, society, mankind, public, folk, community at large, general public, commonalty, masses, human race, humanity.

MONETARY, *adj.* Pertaining to coinage or currency, fiscal, pecuniary, financial, numismatic, nummulary, nummular, sterling.

MONEY, *n.* 1. Medium of exchange, measure of value, circulating medium, standard of value, currency, specie, hard cash, coin, government certificate, banknote, greenback, paper money, bill, long green *(sl.),* precious metal, gold, silver, bullion, nickle, copper, dollar, dollar sterling, pound, note, legal tender, small change, chicken feed *(sl.).*

2. Ready money, bankroll, purse, wallet, dough, spondulics, mazuma, jack, simoleons, bucks, wad, shekels, velvet, pelf, lucre, wampum, wampum-

peag, gingerbread, tin, brass, boodle, rhino, kale, hay, chips, rocks, clinkers, bones, moss.

3. Funds, capital, assets, resources, property, finances, stocks and bonds, buying power, ways and means, wherewithal, revenue, substance, affluence, opulence, treasure, wealth, riches, almighty dollar, mint of money, fortune, easy circumstances, financial independence, income, bonanza, El Dorado.

MONEYBAGS, *n.* A wealthy person, rich man, moneyed man, man of substance, millionaire, billionaire, capitalist, Midas, Croesus, Plutus, Dives, plutocrat, profiteer, tycoon, captain of industry, financier, banker.

MONEYED, *adj.* Rich, well-to-do, wealthy, opulent, well off, well-heeled *(colloq.),* in easy circumstances, independent, rolling in riches, flush, worth a great deal, well provided for, made of money, rich as Croesus, pecunious, in cash, in funds.

MONEYLESS, *adj.* Penniless, destitute, indigent, poverty-stricken, poor as a churchmouse, impecunious, short of cash, broke, flat, hard up, strapped, needy, necessitous, straitened, pinched, unable to keep the wolf from the door, unable to make both ends meet, insolvent, bankrupt, out of pocket, beggared, minus, *qui n'a pas le sou (Fr.),* out at the elbows, down at the heels, seedy, beggarly, reduced, in want, put to one's shifts, under hatches, embarrassed.

MONGREL, *adj.* Of mixed breed, hybrid, crossbred, half-blooded, crossbreed, crossed.

MONITION, *n.* 1. Warning, admonition, caution, remonstrance, expostulation, reprehension, rebuke, reproach, censure, reprimand, reproof, caveat, dehortation, word to the wise, *verbum sapienti (Lat.).*

2. Legal notice, information, advice, indication, notification, hint, intimation, announcement, communication, acquaintance, enlightenment, report, mention.

MONITOR, *n.* Adviser, admonisher, mentor, counselor, Nestor, prompter, teacher, guiding star, tutor, instructor, preceptor, warner, admonitor, reminder, overseer, director, superintendent.

MONITORY, *adj.* Warning, admonitory, admonishing, exemplary, preceptive, mentorial, dissuasive, dehortatory, expostulatory, monitive, cautionary, ominous, minatory, portentous.

MONK, *n.* Religious recluse, holy man, monastic, cenobite, eremite, friar, conventual, padre, abbé, lama, anchorite, prior, abbot, religious, caloyer *(Eastern Church),* pillar saint, stylite, beadsman, lay brother, mendicant, hospitaler, palmer, hermit, Jesuit, Franciscan, Loyolite, Minorite, Gray Friar, Capuchin, Observantine, Black Friar, Dominican, White Friar, Carmelite, Augustinian, Benedictine, Trappist, Carthusian, Cistercian, cloisterer, ecclesiastic, knight of Onan *(humorous),* Sarabaite, Mekhitarist, Marabout, fakir, Cluniac.

MONKEY, *n.* 1. Member of the mammalian order *Primates,* simian, ape, gorilla, orang-utan, chimpanzee, baboon, gibbon, lemur, macaques, guenon, capuchin, langur, marmoset, tamarin, chacma, tota, kahau, hoolock, grivet, marimonda, mangabey, sagoin, guariba, marikina, sapajou, lar, entellus, jackanapes, teetee.

2. Laughingstock, gazing-stock, butt, April fool, dupe, fair game, game, sucker, victim, fool.

3. Buffoon, jester, merry-andrew, *farceur (Fr.),* clown, zany, *grimacier (Fr.).*

4. Imitator, mimic, copier, copyist, pretender, feigner, actor, mime, pantomimist.

MONKEYSHINE, *n.* Mischievous trick, clownish prank, tomfoolery, practical joke, escapade, *boutade (Fr.),* skylarking, *gambade (Fr.), espièglerie (Fr.),* antic, romp, gambol, horseplay, frolic, whoopee, buffoonery, mummery, fun, vagary, amusement, entertainment, diversion, pastime, sport, fooling.

MONOCRACY, *n.* Government by a single person, monarchy, autocracy, dictatorship, despotism, tyranny, aristarchy, demagogy, absolutism.

MONODY, *n.* Ode sung by a single voice, elegy, lament, threnody, coronach, dirge, nenia, keen, epicedium, requiem, threne, deathsong.

MONOLOGUE, *n.* Prolonged talk by a single speaker, solo discourse, soliloquy, apostrophe, lengthy aside, dramatic entertainment by a single speaker, monodrama.

MONOMANIA, *n.* Insanity in which the patient is irrational on one subject only, partial madness, self-deception, delusion, hallucination, illusion, obsession, infatuation, aberration, delirium, lunacy, fanaticism, furor, mania, craze, eccentricity, twist, oddity, fetishism, kleptomania, dipsomania, screw loose, bee in one's bonnet, bats in the belfry, dotage, zealotry, opinionativeness, fixed idea, *idée fixe (Fr.),* brain storm, distraction, *tête montée (Fr.),* raging passion, consuming passion.

MONOPOLIZE, *v.* Obtain exclusive possession of, keep entirely to oneself, engross the whole of, corner, hog *(sl.),* bag, commandeer, control, dominate, own, absorb, appropriate, exercise a monopoly of.

MONOPOLY, *n.* Sole control of a commodity in a market, exclusive possession of, exclusive privilege to carry on a traffic, monopolism, exclusive control, retention, corner, preoccupancy, restriction, limitation, protection, economic pressure, manipulation of prices.

MONOTONE, *n.* Single tone without variation in pitch, drone, uniformity of tone, sameness of pitch, singsong, tattoo, ding-dong, want of modulation, dead sound, non-resonance, sameness of style, uniform intonation.

MONOTONOUS, *adj.* 1. Unvarying in any respect, lacking in variety, tiresomely uniform, unvaried, tedious, humdrum, tiresome, dreary, repetitious, recurrent, iterative, undiversified, wearisome, dull, dry, prosy, uneventful, uninteresting, dead, flat, vapid, insipid, colorless, commonplace, irksome, tame, jejune, languid, weak, wishy-washy, bald, stupid, arid, mortal, soporific, unimaginative, unlively, heavy-gaited, prosaic, banal, pointless, ponderous, sluggish, stolid, plodding, routine, dread, jog trot, bleak, fatiguing.

2. Limited to a narrow pitch range, having a sound continuing on one note, having very little inflection, singsong, harping, ding-dong, drawling.

MONOTONY, *n.* 1. Wearisome uniformity, sameness, selfsameness, tedium, lack of variety, changelessness, tediousness, repetition, iteration, duplication, recurrence, reiteration, redundance, tautology, wearisomeness, dreariness, humdrum routine, boredom, ennui, tedium vitae, lassitude, satiety, dull work, rut, groove, twice-told tale, heavy hours, time on one's hands, matter of fact, want of originality, dearth of ideas, old stuff, chestnut, old story.

2. Continuance of an unvarying sound, sameness of tone or pitch, monotone, harping, ding-

dong, singsong, droning, drone, whirr, buzz, rub-a-dub, tattoo, drumming, pitapat.

MONSOON, *n.* 1. Seasonal rain wind of the Indian Ocean and southern Asia, harmattan, trade wind, sirocco, simoon, typhoon, cyclone, tornado, samiel, hurricane, tempest, whirlwind, gale, squall, mistral.

2. Heavy rains, deluge, downpour, cloudburst, driving rain, inundation, rainy season.

MONSTER, *n.* 1. Fabulous animal compounded of brute and human shape, gorgon, centaur, griffin, sphinx, harpy, satyr, hippogriff, gargoyle, minotaur, chimaera, dragon, leviathan, hydra, hircocervus, merman, behemoth, bucentaur, wivern, manticore, phoenix, sagittary, cockatrice, kraken, basilisk, roc, sea serpent, unicorn, hippocamp.

2. Monstrosity, miscreation, cacogenesis, teratogeny, freak, mooncalf, abortion, unnatural production, oddity, freak, curiosity, sport (*Biol.*), *rara avis* (*Lat.*), *lusus naturae* (*Lat.*), two-headed calf, sight, spectacle, phenomenon, prodigy, wonder, miracle, marvel, enormity, abnormity, deformity, anomaly.

3. Giant, Cyclops, Antaeus, Colossus, Polyphemus, Briareus, Titan, Gog and Magog, Hercules, Goliath, Gargantua, Brobdingnagian.

4. Fiend, devil, beast, Frankenstein, demon, devil incarnate, vampire, bloodsucker, succubus, ogre, cannibal, man-eater, anthropophagite, werewolf.

5. Person that excites horror by wickedness or cruelty, miscreant, demon, villain, wretch, ruffian, hoodlum, hooligan, scoundrel, desperado, knave, rascal, apache, gunman, tough, cutthroat, evildoer, firebrand, incendiary, nihilist, anarchist, destroyer, savage, barbarian, Hun, Goth, vandal, terrorist.

6. Gorilla, alligator, octopus, crocodile, tiger, lion, hyena, leopard, catamountain, panther, jaguar, lynx, puma, cougar, boa constrictor, rattlesnake, cobra, viper, asp, cockatrice, vulture, hippopotamus, elephant, whale, mammoth, jumbo, dinosaur, ichthyosaur.

MONSTROUS, *adj.* 1. Abnormal, unnatural, preternatural, anomalous, teratological, teratoid, teratogenetic, grotesque, bizarre, *outré* (*Fr.*), *tombé des nues* (*Fr.*), crossbred, hybrid, mongrel, hermaphroditic, androgynous, androgynal, bisexual, monoclinous, gyandrous, epicene, aberrant, miscreated, freakish, misshapen, teratogenic.

2. Huge, enormous, titanic, immense, prodigious, gigantic, colossal, vast, stupendous, mammoth, tremendous, bulky, towering, strapping, mighty, elephantine, megatherian, giant, Brobdingnagian, Gargantuan, cyclopean, hippopotamic, lubberly, hulking, cumbrous.

3. Ugly, unsightly, revolting, gross, ill-made, unprepossessing, ill-favored, grisly, gruesome, ghastly, cadaverous, frightful, repellent, repulsive, hideous, forbidding, odious, foul, loathsome, horrible, horrid, shocking, terrible, dreadful, dire, awful, hellish.

4. Flagrant, outrageous, atrocious, villainous, heinous, flagitious, facinorous, diabolical, fiendish, devilish, satanic, infernal, demoniacal, shameless, accursed, depraved, degenerate, corrupt, recreant, immoral, iniquitous, vicious, evil, wicked, sinful, criminal, bad, unprincipled, abandoned, infamous, ignoble, base, scurvy, foul, black, vile, gross, felonious, opprobrious, shameful, unconscionable, unspeakable.

MONTH, *n.* Period of a complete revolution of the moon with regard to some point, lunation, interval from one new moon to the next, lunar month, synodic month, twelfth division of the year, period of four weeks, period of thirty days.

MONUMENT, *n.* 1. Testimonial, memorial, record, remembrancer, enduring evidence, notable example, exemplar, memento, token, souvenir, reminder, memorandum, commemoration, relic, trace, vestige, remains, footprint, mark, track, trail, spoor, wake, scent, *piste* (*Fr.*), register, document, record, memorabilia, note, minute, paper, deed, bulletin, archive, scroll, log, journal, ephemeris, diary, calendar, daybook, gazetteer, almanac, account, report, proceedings, transactions, chronicle, history, annals.

2. Gravestone, cenotaph, tombstone, tomb, vault, mausoleum, slab, headstone, sepulcher, cromlech, shrine, shaft, dolmen, monumental tablet, obelisk, pillar, column, crypt, catacomb, cairn, barrow, mastaba, tumulus, cross, footstone, marker, inscription, epitaph, statue, bust.

MONUMENTAL, *adj.* Of a size larger than that of life, conspicuously great, massive, colossal, lofty, tall, gigantic, exalted, big, towering, soaring, beetling, large, spacious, mighty, immense, huge, enormous, stupendous.

MOOD, *n.* 1. Frame of mind, state of feeling, temper, humor, disposition, temperament, vein, proclivity, propensity, inclination, susceptibility, turn of mind, prevailing spirit, nature, character, constitution, predilection, idiosyncrasy, bent, genius, grain, tendency, predisposition, bias, proneness, diathesis, sympathy.

2. (*Pl.*) Fits of uncertainty, gloominess, sullenness, melancholia, hypochondria, moodiness, vapors, depression of spirits, dejection, heaviness of heart, sadness, mumps, dismals, mopes, dumps, blues, blue devils, megrims, doldrums, pessimism, despondency, moroseness.

MOODY, *adj.* 1. Changeable, humorsome, variable, capricious, inconstant, mercurial, volatile, erratic, fickle, fitful, spasmodic, vagrant, wavering, wayward, desultory, mobile, plastic, full of whims, maggoty, crotchety, whimsical, impulsive, impetuous, passionate, ungovernable, irrepressible.

2. Gloomy, sad, melancholy, despondent, hypochondriacal, pensive, saturnine, abstracted, blue, in the dumps, mumpish, brooding, morose, depressed, mopish, cheerless, unhappy, dismal, somber, triste, lugubrious, downcast, downhearted, heavy-hearted, down in the mouth, in the doldrums, moping, glum, low-spirited, long-faced.

3. Sullen, ill-humored, perverse, sulky, spleeny, cross-grained, grumpy, surly, atrabilious, ill-disposed, out of humor, crabbed, captious, cantankerous, splenetic, crusty, torvous, cankered, restive, intractable, refractory, exceptious, deaf to reason, sinistrous, unaccommodating, dogged, grim, frumpish, glowering, scowling, peevish.

4. Petulant, angry, irascible, irritable, snappish, sour, pettish, waspish, snarling, testy, fretful, hot, incensed, furious, raging, high-strung, excitable, choleric, irate, volcanic, simmering, burning, ready to burst forth, turbulent, rampant, violent, vehement, wild, fiery, hot-headed, fierce, offended, worked up, indignant, sore, infuriate, rabid, in high dudgeon, in a fume, in a pucker, in a huff, on one's high ropes, up in arms.

MOON, *n.* 1. Celestial body which revolves around the earth monthly, secondary planet, planetary satellite.

2. New moon, increscent moon, crescent, me-

niscus, sickle, decrescent moon, half moon, demilune, harvest moon, full moon, plenilune, hunter's moon, old moon, waxing moon, waning moon.

3. Luna, Selene, Cynthia, Diana, Phoebe, Hecate, Artemis, Astarte, Queen of the Night, moon goddess, silver-footed queen.

4. Month, lunation, lunar month, twelfth division of the year, period of four weeks, period of thirty days.

MOONCALF, *n.* Congenital imbecile, fool, tomfool, idiot, simpleton, witling, nitwit, dolt, moron, ninny, booby, nincompoop, *niais (Fr.)*, natural, dullard, oaf, blockhead, addlehead, dunderhead, numskull, fathead, bullcalf, sot, changeling, jobbernoll, dunce.

MOONLIGHT, *n.* Light of the moon, *clair de lune (Fr.)*, moonbeams, moonshine, lunar, luminosity.

MOON-SHAPED, *adj.* Luniform, lunar, crescentshaped, meniscoid, sickle-shaped, falciform, crescentiform, crescentic, meniscal, lunated, lunular, lunulate, semilunar, bicorn, bicornuous, sigmoid.

MOONSHINE, *n.* Empty talk, foolish ideas, nonsense, balderdash, fudge, stuff, trash, twaddle, flummery, fiddle-de-dee, bosh, fustian, jargon, mare's nest, tomfoolery, jabber, gibberish, mere words, rant, hocus-pocus, palaver, bombast, verbiage, *bavardage (Fr.)*, babble, *baragouin (Fr.)*, rigmarole, drivel, rot, rubbish, flapdoodle, fiddlefaddle, myth, fiction.

MOON-STRUCK, *adj.* Injuriously affected in mind, dazed, crazed, lunatic, deranged, mad, delirious, rabid, insane, rapt, moon-stricken, hazy, bewildered, silly, idiotic, foolish, simple-minded, *non compos mentis (Lat.)*, *aliéné (Fr.)*, cracked, touched, not all there, bereft of reason, beside oneself, unhinged, daft, demented, phrenetic, possessed, frenzied, maddened, far gone, shatterpated, crackbrained, bughouse, barmy, loco, light-headed, rambling, incoherent, wandering, raving, frantic, berserk, amok, infatuated.

MOOR, *n.* Tract of open peaty waste land, heath, moorland, waste, wold, downs, reach, champaign, expanse, prairie, pampas, savanna, tundra, steppe, campo, mesa, plateau, veldt, fell, desert, wild, bush, wilderness, upland, llano *(Sp.-Amer.)*, campagna *(It.)*.

MOOR, *v.* Secure by cables and anchors, berth, fix firmly, tie fast, fasten, anchor, tether, picket.

MOORY, *adj.* Marshy, boggy, fenny, swampy, campestrine, paludal, poachy, plashy, soft, quaggy, squashy, muddy, sloppy, campestral, campestrian, open, flat, champaign, expansive, extensive, vast, boundless, far-flung, pathless, trackless.

MOOT, *v.* Bring forward for discussion, debate, discuss, argue a case, dispute, agitate, ventilate, contend, put forth, propound, propose, hypothesize, submit, put a case, reason, wrangle, bandy arguments, chop logic, carry on an argument, join issue, come to the point, stir a question, torture a question, try conclusions, take up a side, take one's stand upon, investigate, look into, sound, probe, fathom, scrutinize, dissect, analyze, winnow, sift, thresh out, view in all its phases, go into a question, grapple with a question.

MOOT, *adj.* Subject to argument, open to discussion, debatable, disputed, open to question, disputable, questionable, in question, doubtful, unsettled, undecided, arguable, controvertible, controversial, disputatious, in issue, in dispute, under discussion, *sub judice (Lat.)*, conjectural, hypothetical.

MOPE, *v.* Be sunk in listless apathy, look downcast, be dejected, be gloomy, wear a long face, look blue, repine, languish, brood, pine, fret, sulk, pout, yearn, despond, droop, grieve, lose heart, take on, lay to heart, look grave, look down in the mouth, take no interest in anything, eat one's heart out, be spiritless, be dull.

MOPISH, *adj.* Long-faced, down in the mouth, in the dumps, out of sorts, cast down, glum, saturnine, dumpish, gloomy, chapfallen, blue, dejected, hipped, melancholy, sad, hypochondriacal, despondent, downhearted, depressed, sullen, moody, sulky, crusty, morose, sour, ill-humored, gruff, splenetic, jaundiced, bilious, lachrymose, woebegone, doleful, lackadaisical, spiritless, dull, listless, lifeless, languid.

MOPPET, *n.* Doll, rag-doll, child, young girl, dear, darling, mopsey, honey, duck, pet, favorite, minion, cosset, apple of one's eye.

MORAL, *adj.* 1. Concerned with right conduct, pertaining to the distinction between right and wrong, concerned with the principles of right conduct, conforming to the rules of right conduct, ethical, virtuous, good, upright, righteous, just, honorable, honest, morally excellent, noble, whole-souled, right-minded, deserving, meritorious, dutiful, worthy, laudable, duteous, creditable, exemplary, commendable, praiseworthy, innocent, chaste, saintly, pure, spotless, godly, conscientious, fair and square, clean, high-minded, aboveboard, principled, responsible, bound to do what is right, accountable, decorous, fit, correct, proper, meet, becoming, seemly, suitable, befitting, appropriate.

2. Probable, presumable, likely, presumptive, hopeful, verisimilar, apparent, in a fair way.

MORAL, *n.* Moral teaching, practical lesson, maxim, dictum, aphorism, apothegm, saying, adage, gnome, epigram, saw, proverb, mot, byword, motto, sentence, word, phylactery, precept, reflection, conclusion, judgment, intent, significance, meaning, *envoi (Fr.)*.

MORALE, *n.* Mental condition toward something, moral state, spirit, esprit de corps, moral courage, cheerfulness, confidence, hope, hopefulness, zeal, self-assurance, aplomb, self-command, self-possession, self-reliance, self-control, moral strength, moral fiber, tenacity, perseverance, resoluteness, pluck, manliness, firmness, resolve, strength of will, grit, backbone, sand, spunk, resolution, unconquerable will, iron determination.

MORALITY, *n.* 1. Moral philosophy, ethics, morals, code of ethics, ethical philosophy, decalogue, Ten Commandments, sense of duty, inward monitor, conscience, still small voice, bounden duty, moral obligation.

2. Virtue, rectitude, probity, uprightness, righteousness, goodness, honor, honesty, integrity, nobility, propriety, decorum, seemliness, fitness decorousness, correctness, *bienséance (Fr.)*, good behavior, responsibility.

MORALS, *n. pl.* Principles with respect to right or wrong conduct, standards of practice, generally accepted customs of conduct and right living in a society, mores, ethics, morality, conscientiousness, accountableness, onus, cardinal virtues, course of life, behavior, habits, manners, conduct, comportment, deportment, manner of life, actions.

MORASS, *n.* Low soft wet ground, marsh, swamp, bog, slough, quagmire, fen, sump, wash, moss, squash.

MORBID, *adj.* 1. Diseased, tainted, unhealthy, vitiated, contaminated, peccant, septic, poisoned, cankered, leprous, mangy, tabid, rotten, malignant, toxic, poisonous, pathological, tubercular, consumptive, cancerous, carcinomatous.

2. Suggesting an unhealthy mental state, unwholesomely gloomy, morose, drooping, somber, pessimistic, despondent, hypochondriacal, melancholic, blue, depressed, low-spirited, lugubrious.

MORBIFIC, *adj.* Causing disease, deleterious, pestilential, noxious, unwholesome, poisonous, toxic, baneful, unhealthy, pestiferous, morbifical, pernicious, insalubrious, noisome, foul, mephitic, morbiferous, azotic, septic, venomous, virulent, contagious, infectious, communicable, zymotic, epidemic, catching, deadly, lethal.

MORDACITY, *n.* Malevolence, unkindness, acrimony, malignity, malice aforethought, spite, despite, maliciousness, uncharitableness, venom, gall, rancor, virulence, acerbity, asperity, churlishness, sarcasm, satire, sharp tongue, irony, invective, ridicule, diatribe, philippic, lampoon, squib.

MORDANT, *adj.* Biting, keen, trenchant, mordacious, bitter, corrosive, acrimonious, sharp, severe, acute, incisive, virulent, caustic, stringent, harsh, double-edged, sarcastic, satirical, nipping, slashing, sharp-tongued.

MORE, *adj.* Greater degree of, greater amount of, greater quantity of, greater measure of, greater number of, superior, added, additional, supplementary, supplemental, spare, extra, further, other, auxiliary, accessory, contributory, new, fresh.

MORE, *adv.* To a greater degree, in a greater extent, beyond, over, in addition to, over and above, further, longer, besides, again, additionally, *au reste (Fr.),* also, likewise, too, furthermore, to boot, as well as, along with, together with, in conjunction with, conjointly.

MORE, *n.* Additional number, additional amount, greater degree, greater quantity, addition, accession, supplementation, reinforcement, annexation, increment, increase, adjunct, appendage, supplement, addendum, accompaniment, extension.

MOREOVER, *adv.* Beyond what has been said, besides, further, furthermore, more than that, over and above that, too, likewise, also, additionally, in addition, *au reste (Fr.),* and likewise, to boot, withal, together with, as well as, along with, conjointly, in conjunction with, and then too.

MORESQUE, *adj.* Moorish, Berber, Arab, Mohammedan, Saracen, Arabic, Arabian, Morisco.

MORGUE, *n.* 1. Place for identification of persons found dead, dead house, charnel house, mortuary.

2. *(Journal.)* Reference library of clippings kept by a newspaper, clipping room, files, *bibliothèque (Fr.).*

MORIBUND, *adj.* In a dying state, at the point of death, at death's door, on one's deathbed, at the last gasp, with one foot in the grave, *in extremis (Lat.),* morient, *in articulo (Lat.),* in the jaws of death, on one's last legs, near one's end, tottering on the brink of the grave, in declining health, incurable, prostrate.

MORIGEROUS, *adj.* Obedient, obsequious, sequacious, submissive, compliant, duteous, deferential, dutiful, respectful, subservient, slavish, servile, sycophantic, fawning, cringing, flattering, truckling, crouching, cringing, sneaking, timeserving, obliging, agreeable, complaisant.

MORNING, *n.* Forenoon, early part of the day, daybreak, dawn, sunrise, aurora, break of day, first blush of day, prime of day, peep of day,

morn, morningtide, matins, cockcrow, *ante meridiem (Lat.),* A.M., dayspring, sunup, daylight.

MORNING STAR, *n.* Bright planet seen in the east before sunrise, Lucifer, Phosphor, Phosphorus.

MORON, *n.* Feeble-minded person, person of arrested intelligence, person with mentality limited to that of 8 to 12 year old child, oaf, nut *(slang),* loony, gawk, softy, dunderhead, imbecile, calf, dunce, muttonhead, lunkhead, chowder head, lubber, mutt, bonehead, dullard, addlepate, boob, simpleton, Simple Simon, lout, goose, saphead, numskull, fool, tomfool, thickhead, chucklehead, ignoramus, illiterate, dunce, wooden spoon, idiot, nitwit, witling, dizzard, ass, donkey, ninny, dolt, booby, ninnyhammer, hobby-dobby, noddy, noodle, owl, nizy, goosecap, nincompoop, *badaud (Fr.),* babbler, zany, *niais (Fr.),* natural, dullard, loon, doodle, block, numps, blockhead, thickskull, shallow-brain, lackwit, halfwit, fathead, dunderpate, jobbernoll, mooncalf, driveler.

MOROSE, *adj.* Sullen, crabbed, perverse, crossgrained, gruff, surly, crusty, waspish, splenetic, spleeny, spleenish, churlish, sulky, sour, glum, grumpy, dumpish, moody, gloomy, ill-humored, pessimistic, despondent, hypochondriacal, melancholic, long-faced, humorsome, wayward, ill-natured, saturnine, mumpish, austere, severe, low-spirited, scowling, doggish, cross, discourteous, harsh, unamiable, acrimonious, petulant, acerbous, frowning, snappish, bitter, frumpish, ill-tempered, grouchy, cantankerous, fretful, lugubrious, mournful, dolorous, unsociable, peevish, acetous, funereal, grum, glowering, growling, ill-disposed, refractory, restive, intractable, cussed, cynical, caustic, soured, sour-tempered, vinegary, snappish, testy, misanthropic, acidulous.

MOROSENESS, *n.* Sullenness, crankiness, crabbedness, churlishness, sulkiness, spleen, sulks, ill-temper, sourness, vinegariness, moodiness, pessimism, asperity, acerbity, gloominess, acrimony, acrimoniousness, crossness, perverseness, harshness, contumacy, morosity, melancholy, unsociability, unsociableness, unamiableness, unamiability, irascibility, perversity, spinosity, glumness, dudgeon, doldrums, dumps, black looks, huff, scowl, grouch.

MORROW, *n.* Tomorrow, the next day, the day after the present, *mañana (Sp.), demain (Fr.), domani (It.), morgen (Ger.).*

MORSEL, *n.* Bit, bite, mouthful, tidbit, scrap, crumb, fragment, morceau, little piece, segment, speck, grain, mite, whit, iota, jot, tittle, scintilla, mote, section, share, taste, *bonne-bouche (Fr.),* particle, atom, shaving, paring, fleabite, molecule, corpuscle, electron, grain, minim, sprinkling, drop, dash, dab, nip, tinge, snack, pinch, snatch, trifle, slip, sliver, snip, chip, splinter, peeling, thimbleful, sample, sip, soupçon, suspicion, streak, suggestion, hint, shade.

MORTAL, *adj.* 1. Subject to death, perishable, destined to die, deathbound, short-lived, temporal, transient, evanescent, ephemeral, fleeting, passing, transitory, fugitive, caducous, temporary, impermanent, monohemerous, diurnal, deciduous, precarious.

2. Human, terrestrial, corporeal, anthropoid, hominine, humanistic, earthborn, earthly, mundane.

3. Deadly, lethal, fatal, mortiferous, destructive, lethiferous, tragic, slaughterous, sanguinary,

homicidal, bloodthirsty, gory, bloody, murderous, internecine, death-bringing, final, death-dealing.

4. Wearisome, long, irksome, tiresome, wearing, uninteresting, dry, bald, stupid, dull, monotonous, tedious, arid, flat, humdrum, soporific, slow, jejune.

MORTAL, *n.* Human being, man, earthling, body, person, creature, individual, somebody, living soul, wight, gaffer, chap, yeoman, swain, guy, fellow, sir.

MORTALITY, *n.* 1. Condition of being mortal, necessity of dying, subjection to death, mortalness, impermanence, evanescence, transientness, transitoriness, fugacity, caducity, volatility, temporary existence, flash in the pan, May fly, nine days' wonder, bubble.

2. Destruction on a large scale, death, fatality, Angel of Death, doom, king of terrors, casualty, carnage, holocaust, trucidation, occision, effusion of blood, slaughter, bloodshed, butchery, juggernaut, gore, *battue (Fr.),* massacre, pogrom, *fusillade (Fr.),* genocide, extermination.

3. Mortal beings collectively, humanity, flesh, generation, human species, human race, mankind, man, people, folk, persons, world, society, community at large.

4. Relative death rate, number of deaths, frequency of death.

MORTAR, *n.* 1. Material for binding stones into a compact mass, mixture for binding bricks, cement, stucco, plaster, grout.

2. Bowl-shaped vessel for reducing drugs to powder with a pestle, pulverizer, muller.

3. Piece of ordnance for throwing bombs, mortar-piece, cannon, gun, artillery, heavy gun, field gun, field piece, trench mortar, howitzer, carronade, *bouche à feu (Fr.).*

MORTGAGE, *n.* Conditional conveyance of a property to a creditor as security, pledge for the payment of a debt, guaranty, security, warranty, gage, bond, debenture, hypothecation, lien, pignoration, pignus, floating capital, paper credit.

MORTIFICATION, *n.* 1. Humiliation in feeling by some wound to pride, vexation, displeasure, dissatisfaction, discontent, chagrin, shame, disappointment, trouble, pique, embarrassment, confusion, grievance, annoyance, irritation, nuisance, bother, worry, pest, plague, sore subject, thorn in the flesh, discomfort, disapprobation, discomposure, dislike.

2. Practice of asceticism by penitential discipline to overcome desire for sin, self-abasement, penance, austerity, self-denial, total abstinence, maceration, flagellation, sackcloth and ashes, fasting, anchoritism, purgation, lustration.

3. Death of one part of the body while the rest is alive, gangrene, necrosis, sphacelus, death of a circumscribed piece of tissue, corruption, cancer, carcinoma, canker, rot.

MORTIFY, *v.* 1. Shame, crush, disgrace, send away with a flea in one's ear, confuse, put to the blush, put out of countenance, take down a peg, teach one his place, make one sing small, abash, abase, tread down, render humble, humiliate, humble, make change color, make blush, make eat humble pie, cause discontent, put out, dissatisfy, disconcert, disappoint, displease, harass, vex, plague, disquiet, worry, annoy, chagrin, trouble, depress, embarrass, offend, wound.

2. Bring the body into subjection by asceticism, practice rigorous austerities, discipline, flagellate,

wear a hair shirt, sit in sackcloth and ashes, do penance, fast, abstain.

3. Affect with necrosis, gangrene, necrose, sphacelate, rot, putrefy, fester, suppurate.

MORTUARY, *n.* 1. Morgue, dead house, charnel house, funeral chapel, funeral home.

2. Cemetery, necropolis, burial ground, burial place, graveyard, city of the dead, churchyard, bone yard *(slang),* polyandrion, God's acre, mausoleum, crypt, catacomb, tomb, sepulcher, vault, tumulus, barrow, cairn, cromlech.

MOSAIC, *adj.* Composed of divers elements combined, inlaid, tessellated, variegated, marquetry-like, buhlwork, parquetry, vermiculated, varied, checkered, motley, plaid, daedal, marbled, pepper-and-salt, many-colored, parti-colored.

MOSLEM, *n.* Mohammedan, Mohometan, Mussulman, Muslem, Muslim, Saracen, Turk, Arab, Islamite, dervish, heathen, pagan, Osmanli.

MOSS, *n.* 1. Cryptogamic plant belonging to the class *Musci,* bryophyte, leafy-stemmed plant growing on moist ground, lichen, Iceland moss, lycopod, club moss, conferva, mold.

2. Swamp, peat bog, marsh, morass, fen, quagmire, sump, slough, wash.

MOSSBACK, *n.* Person attached to antiquated notions, extreme conservative, reactionary, Tory, old-fogy, square-toes, stick-in-the-mud, old-fashioned person.

MOST, *adj.* Greatest in quantity, greatest in number, greatest in degree, most numerous, maximum, greatest in size, greatest in extent, largest, greatest in amount, nearly all.

MOST, *adv.* In the greatest degree, to the greatest extent, in the highest degree, extremely, very.

MOST, *n.* Majority of a class specified, greatest number, greatest part, largest quantity, greatest amount, preponderating portion, most persons, the general.

MOSTLY, *adv.* 1. In the main, for the most part, for the greatest part, as a rule, generally, most frequently, most often.

2. Specially, especially, particularly, primarily, principally, chiefly.

MOT, *n.* 1. Witty remark, witticism, bon mot, flash of wit, atticism, retort, repartee, quip, witty sally, smart saying, *jeu d'esprit (Fr.),* word play, *jeu de mots (Fr.),* double-entendre, pun, conundrum.

2. Pithy saying, shrewd observation, epigram, proverb, aphorism, maxim, apothegm, gnome, dictum, saw, saying, adage, sentence, byword, motto, moral, precept, truism, axiom.

MOTE, *n.* Speck, spot, particle, mite, iota, jot, tittle, dot, fraction, fragment, scrap, grain, scintilla, crumb, spark, modicum, dab, trifle, bit, atom, corpuscle, ion, magneton, monad, electron, whit, tinge, pinch, dash.

MOTHER, *n.* Female parent, mater, mamma, progenitress, mater familias, mammy, ma, matriarch, progenitrix, venter *(Law),* mother-in-law, adoptive mother, stepmother, foster mother, the hand that rocks the cradle, mistress of a family, matron, housewife, dam.

MOTHER, *v.* 1. Be the mother of, give birth to, bring forth, create, beget, conceive, bring into being, breed, produce, spawn.

2. Care for, protect, nurture, raise, watch over, take care of, shelter, look after, keep a sharp eye

on, keep in leading strings, tie to one's apron strings, watch and ward.

MOTHERHOOD, *n.* Mothership, maternity, motherhead, maternal love, motherliness.

MOTHERLY, *adj.* Befitting a mother, maternal, motherlike, parental, kind, affectionate, tender, protective, sheltering, shielding, loving, fond, devoted, indulgent, obliging, accommodating, considerate, warm-hearted, soft-hearted, beneficent.

MOTHER WIT, *n.* Common sense, native wit, sagacity, quick parts, grasp of intellect, acumen, perspicacity, discernment, good judgment, long-headedness, discrimination, gray matter, long head, wisdom, sapience, clear thinking, prudence, tact, foresight, aplomb, mental balance, intelligence, comprehension, capacity, undersanding.

MOTIF, *n.* Theme for treatment, subject for development in art or music, dominant feature, prevailing idea, salient element, distinctive figure, *Leitmotiv (Ger.),* theme song.

MOTION, *n.* 1. Process of changing place, change of position in space, power of movement, motive power, mobility, drift, stir, movement, passage, direction, driftage, tendency, inclination, flow, stream, flux, course, set, transit.

2. Manner of moving the body in walking, gait, port, tread, step, stride, footfall, stalk, amble, canter, rack, walk, trot, pace, gallop, jog, run, carriage, clip, rate, velocity, speed, dash, rush.

3. Journey, excursion, expedition, pilgrimage, travel, progress, locomotion, cruise, voyage, sail.

4. Bodily movement, gesture, gesticulation, action, agitation, sign, indication, pantomime, shrug, nod, beck, nudge, touch, dactylology, dumb show, by-play, hint, cue, signal.

5. Proposition formally made in a deliberative body, proposal, suggestion, recommendation, submission, application for a ruling, amendment.

MOTIONLESS, *adj.* Stationary, still, immobile, quiescent, inert, immovable, quiet, at rest, at a stand, standing still, stock-still, unmoved, becalmed, stagnant, at a standstill, moveless, fixed, stable, dormant, slumbering, sleeping, resting, reposeful, calm, tranquil, hushed, silent, idle, inactive, inoperative, lifeless, dead, defunct, bereft of life, unmoving, sedentary, torpid, benumbed.

MOTIVATE, *v.* Provide with a motive, incite, quicken, impel, drive, propel, goad, egg on, spur, induce, move, stimulate, prompt, arouse, rouse, sway, urge, dispose, influence, persuade, incline, bring 'round, carry, whet, instigate, provoke, fire, actuate, encourage, advocate, set in motion, trigger, be at the base of, underlie, occasion, cause, give rise to.

MOTIVE, *n.* 1. Reason, cause, ground, *raison d'être (Fr.),* wherefore, reason why, the why and the wherefore, occasion, object, root, purpose, basis, excuse, rationale, intention, ulterior motive, secret motive, principle, mainspring, call, pro and con.

2. Incentive, inducement, spur, stimulus, provocation, consideration, goad, whet, fillip, whip, magnetism, enticement, attraction, temptation, allurement, witchery, fascination, spell, charm, cajolery, blandishment, voice of the Sirens, seduction, glamor, loadstone, prompting, influence, instance, dictate, impulse, urge, instigation, insistence, press, incitement, persuasion, exhortation, encouragement, inspiration, advice, power, solicitation, control, pressure, actuation, abetment, sudden thought.

3. Bribe, graft, venality, sop, grease *(slang),* bait, decoy, reward, prize, recompense, compensation, guerdon, remuneration, pay, indemnity, requital, bonus, premium, meed.

4. Goal, destination, target, objective, bull's-eye, butt, point, aim, end, quarry, prey, game, ambition, contemplation, view, project, proposal, plan, design, intent, intention, resolution.

5. Predisposition, proclivity, inclination, tendency, itch, propensity, penchant, cacoëthes, desire, leaning, proneness, set, bias, passion, taste, liking, bent, twist, turn.

MOTLEY, *adj.* 1. Exhibiting great diversity of elements, heterogeneous, composite, diversified, mixed, mingled, jumbled, half-and-half, miscellaneous, variegated, promiscuous, indiscriminate, mongrel, hybrid, varied.

2. Being of different colors combined, dappled, parti-colored, varicolored, mottled, spotted, polychrome, speckled, checkered, piebald, shot, pied, marbled, skewbald, pepper-and-salt, flecked, striated, veined, brindled, watered, tabby, grizzled, many-hued, polychromatic, bicolor, tricolor, versicolor, kaleidoscopic, rainbow-colored, iridescent, opalescent, nacreous, irisated, pearly, *gorge de pigeon (Fr.), chatoyant (Fr.).*

MOTTLE, *v.* Diversify with spots of a different color, spot, maculate, bespot, stipple, checker, variegate, fleck, streak, striate, polychromatize, opalesce, iridize, speckle, marbleize, dot, sprinkle, inlay, tessellate, water, damascene.

MOTTLED, *adj.* Parti-colored, dappled, speckled, variegated, spotted in coloring, blotched, motley, piebald, pied, flecked, dotted, diversified, multicolor, many-hued, many-colored, varicolored, versicolor, daedal, kaleidoscopic, polychromatic, pleochroic, irised, iridescent, rainbowy, irisated, opalescent, pavonine, nacreous, pearly, cymophanous, prismatic, *chatoyant (Fr.), gorge de pigeon (Fr.),* nacred, tortoise shell, shot, skewbald, marmoraceous, marbled, marmoreal, watered, clouded, pepper-and-salt, freckled, striped, veined, barred, tabby, brindled, striated, streaked, checkered, checked, tessellated, mosaic, tartan, plaid.

MOTTO, *n.* Maxim expressive of a guiding principle, appropriate phrase inscribed on something, aphorism, apothegm, proverb, saw, adage, saying, dictum, axiom, truism, precept, principle, rule, law, byword, epigram, mot, sentence, cliché, commonplace, reflection, moral, golden rule, guide, formula, canon, model, precedent, criterion, standard, hard and fast rule, formulary, recipe.

MOUND, *n.* 1. Natural elevation of earth, hillock, hill, knoll, rise, eminence, hummock, dune, rising ground, butte, ridge, hog's back, monticle, barrow, tumulus, mole.

2. Artificial elevation for defense, rampart, bulwark, embankment, parados, parapet, muniment, earthwork, entrenchment.

MOUNT, *n. (Poetic)* High hill, peak, tor, craig, pike, clough, cliff, bluff, steeps, kopje, butte, monticle, knap, hog's back, ridge, height, mountain, alp, knoll, hummock, hillock.

MOUNT, *v.* 1. Climb, go up, ascend, scale, escalade, shin *(colloq.),* scramble, clamber, scrabble, work one's way up, start up, scale the heights, surmount.

2. Get upon, get up on the back of a horse, bestride.

3. Provide with appurtenances, set off, have framed and glazed, prink, emblazon, fix in a setting, set, frame, display, prepare as a specimen,

make ready, put into position for use, raise upon something.

4. Rise, grow, uprise, arise, soar, rise on high, tower, swell, increase, surge, augment, grow, shoot up, become, wax, intensify, multiply.

MOUNTAIN, *n.* Natural elevation of the earth's surface, high hill, mount, vast eminence, height, range, chain, highland, sierra, ridge, craig, tor, peak, pike, alp, butte, kopje, cliff, bluff, headland, watershed, *arête (Fr.),* upland, monticle, knap, steeps, clough, escarpment, brae, dizzy height.

MOUNTAINOUS, *adj.* 1. Full of mountains, hilly, rolling, alpine, upland, heaven-kissing, cloud-topt, cloud-touching, cloud-capt, aerial, towering, soaring, beetling, elevated.

2. Large, huge, vast, enormous, bulky, tremendous, mighty, immense, stupendous, gigantic, colossal, massive.

MOUNTEBANK, *n.* Quack doctor, charlatan, pretender, quack, impostor, fraud, fourflusher, humbug, faker, confidence man, ringer *(slang),* swindler, cheat, spieler *(slang),* empiric, hot air artist, Cagliostro, deceiver, capper, *soi-disant (Fr.),* adventurer, saltimbanco, medicaster, quacksalver, crimp, trickster, knave, rogue, carpetbagger, bunko-steerer *(slang),* rascal, hypocrite.

MOURN, *v.* Feel sorrow, express grief, display tokens of sorrow, lament, grieve, be sorrowful, sorrow, wail, bewail, bemoan, deplore, be grieved, look downcast, feel regret, lay to heart, weep over, repine, elegize, keen, besigh, ululate, rue, whimper, groan, take to heart, yearn, pine, languish, give way, despair, break one's heart, break down, shed tears, sob, cry, wear mourning, wear the willow, put on sackcloth and ashes, give sorrow words, *infandum renovare dolorem (Lat.),* melt into tears, *fondre en larmes (Fr.),* cry one's eyes out, show pity, commiserate, compassionate, condole, share one's misery, feel for.

MOURNER, *n.* Lamenter, keener, weeper, wailer, mute, pallbearer, willow-wearer, sorrower, griever, bewailer, bemoaner, elegizer, repiner, whimperer, groaner, commiserator, condoler.

MOURNFUL, *adj.* 1. Attended with sorrow, sad, afflicting, distressing, afflictive, calamitous, grievous, melancholy, lamentable, deplorable, woeful, cheerless, joyless, disheartening, dismal, depressing, dreary, piteous, pitiable, affecting, pathetic, touching, heartbreaking, tragic, disastrous, somber, dark, gloomy, Acherontic, elegiac, epicedial, threnetic.

2. Full of sorrow, showing grief, lugubrious, lachrymose, tearful, doleful, dolorous, rueful, triste, heavy-hearted, sorrowful, sepulchral, funereal, melancholic, plaintive, threnodic, lamentatory, wailful, woebegone, prostrate, forlorn, broken-hearted, heartsick, disconsolate, shedding tears, unhappy, plangorous, solemn, dirgeful, low-spirited, pensive, despairing, blue, downhearted, downcast, in mourning, in sackcloth and ashes, wearing the willow, sorrowing, crying, querulous, bathed in tears, discouraged, disheartened, desponding, tristful, *penseroso (It.),* long-faced, solemn, wan, grim-visaged, overcome, bowed-down, dashed, cut up.

MOURNING, *n.* 1. Lamentation, sorrow, grief, bereavement, wail, plaint, jeremiad, complaint, murmur, whimper, groan, sob, moan, suspiration, sigh, outcry, tears, lachrymation, weeping, sobbing, fit of crying, flood of tears.

2. Conventional manifestation of sorrow for a

person's death, wearing of black, black garments, weeds, sackcloth and ashes, crape, widow's weeds, armozeen, hanging of flags at half-mast, dirge, death song, keen, coronach, ullalulla *(Irish),* elegy, requiem, epicedium, threnody, nenia, taps.

MOUSE, *n.* Small rodent of the family *Muridae,* murine, house mouse, *Mus musculus,* harvest mouse, *Micromys minutus,* meadow mouse, field mouse, vole, jumping mouse, pocket mouse, rat, water rat.

MOUSE, *v.* Catch mice, hunt out, track down, watch for slyly, pursue diligently, pry about on the lookout, move about softly, peer, search watchfully, prowl about, look closely, seek stealthily, ferret out, unearth, pry into every hole and corner, look behind the scenes, trail, shadow, follow the scent.

MOUTH, *n.* 1. Cavity containing the masticating apparatus, oral opening, jaws, chops, chaps, muzzle, maxilla, mandible, gorge, throat, fauces, gullet, kisser *(slang).*

2. Aperture for receiving or discharging, opening, orifice, entrance, hole, sucker, crater, nozzle, windpipe, faucet, outlet, inlet, gap, chasm, cleft, fissure, dehiscence, oscitance, yawning, perforation, venthole, foramen, pore, interstice, spout, ostiole.

3. Mouth of a river, embouchure, estuary, outfall, embouchement, firth, frith, fiord, bayou, bight, gulf, bay.

4. Grimace made with the lips, wry face, pucker, *moue (Fr.),* smirk, contortion of countenance, mop, mow.

5. Utterance, expression, pronouncement, pronunciation, delivery, articulation, speech, declaration, voicing, communication, emission, assertion.

6. Mouthpiece, spokesman, speaker, oracle, prolocutor, representative, interpreter, expositor, explainer, exponent.

MOUTH, *v.* 1. Utter in a sonorous or pompous manner, declaim oratorically, vociferate, rant, give utterance, ejaculate, vocalize, prolate, enunciate, articulate, accentuate, deliver, emit, murmur, croon, whisper, mumble, mutter, maunder, lisp, mince, gabble, jabber, drawl, snuffle, vent, utter, spout, rave, exclaim.

2. Take into the mouth, ingest, imbibe, swallow, suck, devour, gulp, bolt, tuck in, lick, peck, champ, bite, munch, cranch, crunch, masticate, fletcherize, chew, gnaw, nibble, sip, sup, lap, swill, swig, tipple.

MOUTHFUL, *n.* As much as a mouth can hold, morsel, bite, bit, snack, sop, gobbet, bolus, sippet, tidbit, kickshaw, *bonne bouche (Fr.),* crumb, pinch, scrap, drop, sprinkling, mite, dash, dab, nip, snick, sliver, peeling, paring, spoonful, forkful, driblet, portion, dose, taste, swallow, piece, gob.

MOUTHPIECE, *n.* Speaker in behalf of other persons, spokesman, person that voices the sentiments of others, advocate, prolocutor, Hermes, exponent, proponent, reporter, interpreter, expositor.

MOUTHY, *adj.* Loud-mouthed, bombastic, fustian, ranting, magniloquent, altiloquent, grandiloquent, sesquipedalian, declamatory, rhetorical, grandiose, high-flown, stilted, pompous, pedantic, tumid, turgid, inflated, big-sounding, ornate, sonorous, flowery, euphuistic, Johnsonian.

MOVABLE, *adj.* 1. Capable of being moved, not fixed in one place, portable, transportable, not permanent in place, portative, transferable.

2. Changeable, shifting, mobile, restless, mer-

curial, nomadic, unstable, unsettled, erratic, irresolute, capricious, fitful, touch-and-go, spasmodic, wayward, alternating, wavering, plastic, fickle.

MOVABLES, *n., pl.* Articles of personal property not attached to land, goods, chattels, effects, movable property, furniture, wares, things, gear, possessions, belongings, assets, personal effects, personalty, traps, paraphernalia.

MOVE, *v.* 1. Pass from one place to another, change position, stir, change place, budge, change one's abode, change residence, remove, go, repair, hie, flit, pass, proceed, advance, progress, walk, march, peg along, sweep along, lob, wander, ramble, skip, hop, rush, glide, slide, drift, start off, step, tread, pace, trudge, plod, stump, traipse, wend, tramp, hike, stride, stalk, bowl along, strut, paddle, jog on, promenade, shuffle on, defile, bend one's steps, stroll, stray, peregrinate, perambulate, saunter, straggle, meander, nomadize, gad about, jaunt, prowl, rove, roam, range, flit, migrate, emigrate, trek, tour, travel, journey, betake oneself, bustle, keep going, lope, lumber, get on, locomote, circulate, dance, waltz, pirouette, caper, frisk, chassé, sashay *(colloq.)*, mince, toddle, gyrate, rotate.

2. Transfer, transport, carry, convey, tote, bear, hand over, forward, pass, shift, change, relegate, dislodge, displace, transpose, transplant, dispatch, send, transmit, deliver, conduct, escort, lead.

3. Put in motion, cause to act, stir, shake, drive, propel, start, jiggle, twirl, fan, lash, swing, whip, jerk, whisk, bounce, vibrate, turn, operate.

4. Induce, influence, persuade, impel, prevail upon, prompt, instigate, incite, actuate, rouse, arouse, stimulate, inspire, urge, dispose, incline, whet, motivate, goad, egg on, spur, prick, hurry on, stir up, awaken, magnetize, inspirit, tempt, wheedle, lure, coax, inveigle, entice, force, enforce.

5. Affect with emotion, excite the feelings of, touch, stir, impress, play on, catch at the heart strings, sway, touch a chord, interest, strike, impassion, infect, smite, fire the blood, set astir, quicken, work upon, fan the flame, stir the embers, touch the soul, bring home to, touch to the quick, possess the soul, absorb, rivet the attention, electrify, galvanize, intoxicate, overpower, *bouleverser (Fr.)*, overwhelm, upset, enrapture, fascinate, bewitch, ensorcel, ravish, perturb, agitate, shake, ruffle, disturb, flutter, startle, faze, stagger, shock, strike dumb, astound, stun, petrify.

6. Propose formally to a deliberative body, offer for consideration, submit a formal request, recommend, bring forward, suggest, urge, prescribe, exhort, advocate, prompt, counsel, advise, call upon, request, put forth, propound, make a motion.

MOVE, *n.* Agitation, gesture, action, stroke, blow, maneuver, step, measure, proceeding, turn, play, round, gyration, revolution, rotation, change, alteration, vicissitude, shift, spell, inning, opportunity, bout.

MOVEMENT, *n.* 1. Exercise, performance, labor, operation, perpetration, action, work, exertion, task, execution, process, working, mechanism, procedure, maneuver, transaction, job, enterprise, *coup (Fr.)*, step, measure, effort.

2. Gesture, agitation, move, step, gait, tread, stalk, stride, amble, walk, canter, trot, pace, gallop, run, jog, rack, rate, velocity, clip *(colloq.)*, speed,

carriage, port, progress, journey, locomotion, travel.

3. Transportation, transport, conveyance, moving, carriage, transvection, shipment, truckage, cartage, portage, carry, freightage, freight, ferriage, transit, transference, shift, removal, change, dislodgment, translocation, displacement, transplantation, conduction.

4. Rapid progress of events, course of tendency, trend of affairs, series of actions directed toward a particular end, drive, crusade, operation, march, undertaking.

5. Distinct portion of a mechanism, works, wheels within wheels.

6. *(Music)* Rhythm, tempo, time, rhythmical character, principal division of a symphony or concerto, strain, part.

MOVIES, *n. (Colloq.)* Moving picture, motion picture, silver screen, biograph, cinema, kinematograph, photodrama, talkies *(colloq.)*, flickers *(colloq.)*, photoplay, bioscope, film, cosmorama, cinerama, kinescope, 3-D.

MOVING, *adj.* 1. Motile, traveling, motive, mobile, motor, movable, shifting, transitional, nomadic, erratic, changeable, restless, erratic.

2. Touching, stirring, pathetic, affecting, appealing, impressive, exciting the feelings, tender, sensuous, pitiful, piteous, poignant, thrilling, overpowering, overwhelming.

MUCH, *adj.* Plenteous, abundant, considerable, a great quantity of, a great deal of, a great amount of, ample, sufficient, full, plenty, plentiful, copious, well-provided, chock-full, replete, lavish, unstinted, inexhaustible, exuberant, excessive, profuse, prodigal, fulsome, overflowing, brimful, brimming, crammed, fraught, saturated, plenary.

MUCH, *adv.* 1. To a great degree, greatly, to a large extent, far, freely, in abundance, without stint, with no sparing hand, to one's heart's content, *ad libitum (Lat.)*.

2. Frequently, often, repeatedly, many times, ofttimes, oftentimes, not seldom.

3. Almost, approximately, nearly, about the same, well-nigh, toward, towards, all but, for the most part, within a little, not quite.

MUCH, *n.* Great quantity, great deal, great amount, abundance, plenty, plenitude, amplitude, copiousness, profusion, repletion, full measure, surfeit, fill, satiety, horn of plenty, cornucopia, horn of Amalthaea, sufficiency, sufficientness, enough, *quantum sufficit (Lat.)*, exuberance, plethora, deluge, avalanche, *embarras de richesses (Fr.)*, heaps, lot, swarm, flock, drove, shoal, hive, legion, host, army, array, scores, numbers, great number, crowd, galaxy, aggregation, cloud, flood, rush, lump, pile, mass, litter, snowdrift, accumulation, conglomeration, amassment, stock, store, congestion, shower, volley, flight.

MUCILAGE, *n.* Preparation of gum for causing adhesion, glue, paste, size, beeswax, adhesive, lute, rubber cement, sticker.

MUCILAGINOUS, *adj.* Secreting mucilage, viscid, sticky, glutinous, ropy, gummy, adhesive, viscous, clinging, tenacious, gluey, mucid, moist, soft, slimy, mucous.

MUCK, *n.* Foul matter, filth, ordure, excrement, manure, dung, faeces, coprolite, compost, guano, *merde (Fr.)*, excreta, night soil, slime, mud, mire, sludge, slush, sewerage, sewage.

MUCKWORM, *n.* Miser, niggard, curmudgeon, skinflint, sordid wretch, lickpenny, pennypincher, scrimp, screw, money-grubber, churl, hunks, codger, tightwad, crib, pinchfist.

MUCKY, *adj.* Filthy, dirty, stercoraceous, excrementitious, fecal, feculent, foul, nasty, offensive, reeky, fetid, putrid, slimy.

MUCUS, *n.* Viscid secretion of the mucous membranes, excrementitious humor, phlegm, snot *(vulgar)*.

MUD, *n.* Wet soft earth, earthy matter on the ground after rain, mire, ooze, slime, muck, dirt, silt, lute, gumbo, drenched soil, slush, sludge, slosh, moya, filth, slop, quagmire, slough, morass, swamp, fen, bog.

MUDDLE, *v.* 1. Mix up in a confused way, jumble in a bungling way, confound, confuse, litter, disarrange, derange, disorder, disturb, muss, ruffle, entangle, ravel, rumple, enmesh.

2. Make a mess of, muff, spoil, botch, mull, bungle, boggle, fumble, make a hash of, put one's foot in it, mismanage, act foolishly, begin at the wrong end, put the cart before the horse, not know what one is about, mistake, put a square peg into a round hole, go further and fare worse, miss one's way, fail, not succeed, labor in vain, lose one's labor, bring to naught, do by halves, flunk, fall short, miss the mark, stumble, trip, slip, blunder, bitch it.

3. Stupefy with drink, render unable to think clearly, render confused mentally, fuddle, inebriate, make half drunk, make tipsy, intoxicate, befog, bewilder.

MUDDLE, *n.* 1. Jumble, mess, botch, imbroglio, pickle, hot water, stew, scrape, exigency, strait, pinch, pass, rub, critical situation, knotty point, paradox, poser, puzzle, maze, Gordian knot, entanglement, perplexity, intricacy, hard nut to crack, vexed question, quandary, dilemma, predicament, fix, trouble, embarrassment, embarrassing state of affairs, confusion, labyrinth.

2. Disorder, disarrangement, untidiness, derangement, disarray, muss, litter, hodgepodge, medley, clutter, wilderness, jungle.

MUDDLED, *adj.* 1. The worse for liquor, fuddled, potulent, inebriated, intoxicated, tipsy, mellow, in one's cups, *inter pocula (Lat.),* screwed, primed, tight, corned, addled, half seas over, half drunk, maudlin, temulent, bemused, addleheaded, muddle-headed, inebrious, plastered, squiffy, sozzled, befuddled, groggy, topheavy, pot-valiant, oiled, lushy, muzzy, bosky, obfuscated, three sheets in the wind, drunken, sottish.

2. Stupefied, confused, foggy, thick-skulled, muddy-headed, puzzle-headed, blunder-headed, rattle-brained, fat-witted, stupid, insulse, obtuse, doltish, asinine, fatuous, blockish, Boeotian.

MUDDY, *adj.* 1. Miry, slimy, oozy, mucid, lutose, unclean, filthy, dirty, grubby, grimy, sodden, soft, soggy, sloppy, marshy, boggy, moist, damp, turbid, foul, sludgy, slushy.

2. Obscure, vague, dim, indistinct, faint, misty, muggy, fuliginous, overcast, obnubilated, lurid, leaden, dun, opaque, obfuscated, smoky, fumid, murky, dingy.

3. Stupid, dull-witted, heavy, muddy-brained, muddy-headed, confused, brainless, witless, not bright, feeble-minded, rattle-brained, blunt-witted, shallow-pated, thick-skulled, *borné (Fr.),* weak, wanting, insulse, obtuse, doltish, fatuous, imbecilic, idiotic, moronic, sottish, bewildered, blockish, unteachable, bovine.

MUFF, *v.* Perform clumsily, fumble, bungle, make a muff, miss, blunder, be unskilful, boggle, botch,

flounder, bitch, make sad work of, fail to hold a ball that comes into one's hands *(baseball).*

MUFFLE, *v.* 1. Wrap, conceal, cloak, cover, envelop, shroud, veil, mask, bemuffle, swaddle, swathe, hide, hood, disguise, involve.

2. Hush, stifle, gag, throttle, strangle, garrote, choke, silence, still, quiet, muzzle, put to silence, suppress, quell, stop.

3. Deaden sound, mute, damp, damper, soft-pedal, tone down.

MUFFLED, *adj.* Softened, toned down, subdued, deadened, suppressed, quiet, low, dull, faint, noiseless, inaudible, stifled, indistinct, dim, feeble, pale, not clear.

MUFFLER, *n.* 1. Heavy neck scarf, tippet, ascot, neckerchief, stock, cravat, ruff, boa, collar, neckcloth, guimpe, chemisette.

2. Device for deadening sound, silencing device, silencer, mute, sordino, soft pedal, damper.

MUG, *n.* 1. Cylindrical drinking cup with a handle, tankard, pot, toby, pipkin, chalice, goblet, glass, tumbler, beaker, tass.

2. *(Slang)* Face, map, physiognomy, visage, phiz, countenance, features, cast of countenance, kisser.

3. Grimace, wry expression, *moue (Fr.),* pout, distortion of countenance, smirk, mop, mow, mouth, black look, sulk.

4. Person easily imposed upon, dupe, gull, gudgeon, sucker, victim, fall guy, April fool, *gobemouche (Fr.),* pigeon, cully, simple Simon, greenhorn, cat's-paw, puppet.

MUG, *v.* 1. Assault from the rear by throttling, strongarm, strangle, choke, stifle, garrote, throttle, stop the breath, smother, suffocate, asphyxiate, lock the forearm around the neck.

2. Grimace, make a wry face, make a *moue, (Fr.),* pout, smirk, distort the countenance, screw up the face, look sullen, show ill temper, sulk, make a face, frown.

MUGGY, *adj.* Damp, moist, sultry, wet, close, humid, uncomfortable, oppressive, dank, vaporous, sodden, steaming, sweaty, hot, stuffy, stifling, sweltering, sudorific, canicular, tropical, estival, reeking.

MULCT, *n.* Fine, pecuniary penalty, amercement, forfeiture, forfeit, exaction, escheat, damages, confiscation, sequestration, deodand, scot, praemunire, estreat, sconce.

MULCT, *v.* Impose a fine upon, deprive of something as a penalty, penalize, fine, amerce, punish by forfeiture, sconce, confiscate, sequestrate, escheat, exact by way of fine, estreat.

MULE, *n.* 1. Offspring of a male donkey and a mare, hinny, hybrid, mongrel, sumpter mule, ass, jackass, donkey, jack, burro, Jerusalem pony, jenny.

2. Obstinate person, stubborn fellow, recalcitrant, incompatible, bitter-ender, irreconcilable, bigot, opinionist, stickler, opinionatist, die-hard.

MULISH, *adj.* Headstrong, obstinate, intractable, stubborn, cross-grained, refractory, recalcitrant, indocile, obdurate, pertinacious, dogged, wilful, perverse, stiff-necked, restive, wrong-headed, tenacious, inflexible, unbending, irreconcilable, intransigent, immovable, inexorable, balky, determined, persistent, pigheaded, hard-set, unyielding, hard-bitten, wayward, untoward, self-willed, opinionated, opinionative, hidebound, heady, unruly, ungovernable, contumacious, bigoted, dogmatic, prejudiced, arbitrary, incorrigible, sulky, sullen.

MULL, v. 1. Study over, ruminate, brood over, cogitate, excogitate, ponder, meditate, consider, muse, think, deliberate, reflect, reason out, bestow thought upon, contemplate, speculate, con over, animadvert, weigh, take counsel, bethink oneself, commune with oneself, turn over in the mind, chew the cud, advise with one's pillow, set one's wits to work.

2. Make a mess of, make a failure of, botch, muff, bungle, muddle, blunder, boggle, fumble, bitch, trip, make a hash of, make sad work of.

3. Spice for drinking, sweeten, render sweet, edulcorate, saccharize, sugar, candy.

MULTI-COLORED, adj. Many-colored, multi-hued, parti-colored, variegated, divers-colored, many-hued, polychromatic, versicolor, tricolor, kaleidoscopic, of all the colors of the rainbow, opalescent, iridescent, prismatic, shot, nacreous, irisated, pearly, *chatoyant (Fr.), gorge de pigeon (Fr.),* piebald, pied, motley, skewbald, marbled, mottled, paned, pepper-and-salt, dappled, checkered, mosaic, tessellated, plaid, tortoiseshell, freckled, speckled, flecked, barred, striated, veined, brindled, watered, tabby, daedal, pavonine, cymophanous, tartan, multicolor, varicolored, pleochroic, florid, gaudy, garish.

MULTIFARIOUS, adj. Diversified, divers, various, different, of all sorts and kinds, of every description, diverse, manifold, varied, indiscriminate, heterogeneous, mixed, variegated, motley, mosaic, of many sorts, manifold, of various kinds, miscellaneous.

MULTIFORM, adj. Of many shapes, many-shaped, of many forms, polymorphous, polymorphic, metamorphotic, diversiform, variform, multiphase, multifold, multiplex, multiple, manifold, omniform, protean, proteiform, many-sided, amoebiform.

MULTILOQUENCE, n. Talkativeness, loquacity, garrulity, garrulousness, loquaciousness, largiloquence, volubility, volubleness, facundity, grandiloquence, *copia verborum (Lat.), flux de paroles (Fr.),* gift of gab, flow of language, burst of eloquence, effusion, much speaking, wordiness, fluency, flowing tongue, *cacoethes loquendi (Lat.),* verbosity, verboseness, gibble-gabble, *bavardage (Fr.),* verbiage, cloud of words, polylogy, tautology, exuberance, redundance, prolixity, ambages, circumlocution, periphrasis, padding.

MULTIPLICATION, n. 1. Increase, production, begetting, procreation, breeding, generation, propagation, prolification, reproduction, proliferation, histogenesis, progeneration, germination, fructification, pullulation.

2. Enlargement, addition, augmentation, extension, spread, accession, reinforcement, expansion, accretion, increment, growth, inflation, accumulation, aggrandizement, enhancement, exaggeration, intensification, rise.

MULTIPLY, v. 1. Increase the number of, make manifold, make more, take by addition a given number of times, find the product of by multiplication, double, reduplicate, triple, quadruple, quintuple, sextuple, septuple, octuple, decuple.

2. Augment, enlarge, aggrandize, magnify, add to, enhance, spread, boost, raise, extend, redouble, reinforce, intensify, exaggerate, inflate, heighten.

3. Produce by propagation, increase by procreation, make fruitful, fecundate, make prolific, generate, propagate, procreate, proliferate, engender, get, beget, impregnate, progenerate, hatch, breed, sire, father.

4. Be fruitful, bring forth, usher into the world, give birth to, evolve, drop, calf, whelp, pup, kitten, farrow, yean, ean, pullulate, spawn, teem, bear fruit, mother, flower, sprout, blossom, burgeon.

MULTITUDE, n. 1. Crowd, mob, host, legion, a great many, throng, press, concourse, array, aggregation, assemblage, assembly, conflux, great number, numbers, scores, army, horde, posse, human sea, gathering, ingathering, collection, congregation, crush, gang, corps, troupe, team, squad, force, band, pack, ruck, rabble, the populace, mass, commonalty, hoi polloi, profanum vulgus, mobilization, muster, levy.

2. Swarm, flock, shoal, drove, herd, covey, roundup, drive, bevy, bunch, school, hive, litter, brood, farrow, galaxy, cloud, flight, series, cluster, group, nest, batch, pack, lot, assortment, thicket, clump, shock, stack, rick, swath, sheaf, shower, volley, heap, conglomeration, amassment, accumulation, cumulation, stock, store, heap, pile, lump, mass, pyramid, drift, flood, stream, deluge.

3. Profusion, multitudinousness, multiplicity, mass, magnitude, vastness, largeness, greatness, bulk, quantity, size, volume, amplitude, abundance, power *(colloq.),* deal *(colloq.),* load, immensity, shipload, enormity.

MULTITUDINOUS, adj. Occurring in great numbers, very numerous, crowded, studded, rife, alive with, teeming, outnumbering, thick, abundant, populous, profuse, prevalent, manifold, widespread, many, divers, galore, sundry, various, several, endless, thickset, serried, dense, tight, compact, close, solid, swarming, supernumerary, mushroom.

MUM, adj. Not saying a word, mute, silent, dumb, speechless, still, reticent, taciturn, tight-lipped, tongue-tied, voiceless, wordless, muzzled, inarticulate, close-mouthed, laconic, sparing of words, inconversable, evasive, secretive, noncommital, reserved, uncommunicative, buttoned up.

MUMBLE, v. Speak inarticulately, mutter low indistinct sounds, utter indistinctly, murmur, maunder, mouth, babble, mump, patter, grumble, gabble, jabber, gibber, croak, snuffle, lisp, mince one's words, talk incoherently, splutter, hem and haw, sputter.

MUMMER, n. One who wears fantastic disguise, masker, guiser, guisard, masque, harlequin, farceur, pantaloon, columbine, clown, buffoon, *grimacier (Fr.),* Pierrot, Pierrette, punchinello.

MUMMERY, n. 1. Masquerade, harlequinade, masking, tomfoolery, foolery, diversion, sport, merriment, masquing, gambol, drollery, recreation, divertissement, entertainment, amusement, frolic, jocosity, buffoonery.

2. Empty spectacular pretense, mere theatrical performance, vain parade, empty show, vain ceremony, flourish of trumpets, dash, strut, swagger, swank, pomposity, showing off, glitter, display, *étalage (Fr.),* pageantry, gala, fete, equipage, borrowed plumes, false colors, mockery.

MUMMIFY, v. Dry into a mummy, prepare for burial, embalm, lay out, preserve, fossilize.

MUMMY, n. Dead body preserved by embalming, withered and shrunken corpse, dried carcass, corse, reliquiae, mortal remains, dry-bones, dust, carrion, ashes, clay, earth, fossil.

MUMPISH, adj. Sulky, sullen, morose, spleenish, sour, spleeny, moody, heavy, dull, unamiable, ill-humored, ill-tempered, ill-disposed, out of humor, crabbed, crusty, surly, cankered, splenetic, cantankerous, exceptious, unaccommodating, sinistrous, intractable, refractory, humorsome, cross-grained, glum, grumpy, out of sorts, frumpish, peevish, touchy, testy, petulant, irritable, irascible, waspish, snappish, choleric, shrewish, captious, querulous, contentious.

MUNCH, *v.* Chew with steady and vigorous working of the jaws, masticate audibly, nibble, craunch, gnaw, cranch, champ, crunch, bite.

MUNDANE, *adj.* 1. Worldly, earthly, terrestrial, terrene, terraqueous, sublunary, temporal, secular, earthy, cosmical, subastral, telluric, under the sun, here below, on the face of the globe, of this life, down-to-earth, possible, conceivable.

2. Unspiritual, not heavenly, irreligious, undevout, godless, unholy, ungodly, atheistic, skeptical, freethinking, faithless, unbelieving, worldly-minded, carnal, pleasure-loving, fleshly, money-grubbing, selfish, timeserving, interested, worldly-wise.

MUNICIPAL, *adj.* Pertaining to the local government of a town or city, civic, civil, administrative, executive, judicial, juridical, gubernatorial, authoritative, official, departmental.

MUNICIPALITY, *n.* District possessing corporate existence, town, city, borough, bailiwick, shrievalty, polity, township, parish, village, hamlet, thorp, kraal, burgh, county seat.

MUNIFICENCE, *n.* Generosity, beneficence, liberality, bounteousness, bountifulness, bounty, benevolence, benefaction, philanthropy, kindness, kindliness, benignity, charitableness, alms-giving, good works, good turn, altruism, humanitarianism.

MUNIFICENT, *adj.* Extremely liberal in giving, very generous, bountiful, beneficent, bounteous, free-handed, free-hearted, princely, open-handed, philanthropic, lavish, royal, kingly, gracious, profuse, unsparing, prodigal, unselfish, hospitable, charitable, sportulary, eleemosynary, handsome, ungrudging, full-handed, large-hearted, open-hearted, unstinting, kindly, extravagant, replete.

MUNIMENT, *n.* 1. Document by which rights are defended, charter by which privileges are maintained, record, title deed, credential, warrant, docket, voucher, warranty, deed, affidavit, certificate.

2. Defense, protection, propugnation, safeguard, shelter, screen, fortification, munition, bulwark, dike, parapet, palisade, stockade, battlement, rampart, breastwork, bastion, redan, redoubt, stronghold, hold, fastness, fortress, citadel, castle, capitol, keep, donjon, blockhouse, turret, fort, arx, acropolis.

MUNITION, *n.* Materials used in war, ordnance, matériel, military stores, ammunition, supplies, provision, armaments, military weapons, arms, gunpowder, explosives, firearms, artillery, guns, cannon, bombs, bullets, shot, sinews of war.

MURDER, *n.* Unlawful killing of a human being with malice aforethought, homicide, manslaughter, assassination, bloodshed, slaying, effusion of blood, dispatch, massacre, strangulation, suffocation, thuggee, garrote, shooting, knifing, hit-and-run, stifling, choking, throttling, asphyxiation, poisoning, lynching, burking, running through, stabbing, drowning, smothering, decapitation, beheading, hanging, burning.

MURDER, *v.* 1. Kill with malice, put to death, assassinate, massacre, slaughter, put an end to, deal the deathblow, make away with, destroy, slay, smite down, shed blood, butcher, poison, finish, lynch, dispatch, take for a ride, do to death, bump off, burke, brain, shoot, run through, knife, stab, put to the sword, bayonet, garrote, strangle, asphyxiate, smother, choke, throttle, suffocate, stifle, hang, drown, decapitate, behead, burn, deprive of life, victimize, immolate, stop the breath, cut down, cut the throat, jugulate, knock on the head, blow one's brains out, stone, lapidate, give the coup de grâce, nip in the bud, cut off from life, send to one's last account, launch into eternity, rub out, pour out blood like water.

2. Violate grossly, abuse, mangle, solecize, murder the King's English, commit a solecism, use bad grammar, break Priscian's head, mispronounce, misuse, spoil, mar.

MURDERER, *n.* Manslayer, homicide, assassin, killer, slayer, slaughterer, cutthroat, butcher, bloodshedder, Cain, garroter, thug, bravo, gunman, racketeer, gangster, mobster, matador, Moloch, executioner, lyncher, strangler, apache, bandit, hatchet man, poisoner, knifer, parricide, regicide, tyrannicide, fratricide, matricide, sororicide, infanticide, uxoricide, aborticide, vaticide, Bluebeard, Jack the Ripper, criminal, ruffian, malefactor, hit-and-run driver.

MURDEROUS, *adj.* Bloodthirsty, bloody, sanguinary, blood-guilty, lethal, destructive, deadly, cutthroat, homicidal, criminal, slaughterous, ferocious, savage, cruel, fell, fatal, brutal, bloodstained, mortal, lethiferous, gory, red-handed, bloody-minded, berserk, deathly, mortiferous, death-dealing, assassinative, sanguinolent, ensanguined, sanguineous, cannibalistic, anthropophagous, fiendish, barbarous, amuck.

MURKY, *adj.* Obscure with mist, thick with haze, foggy, cloudy, misty, hazy, vaporous, nubiferous, fuliginous, overcast, clouded, dusky, dark, dim, gloomy, lurid, lowering, caliginous, umbrageous, tenebrous, dreary, darkling, sombrous, somber, murksome, dingy, nigrescent, dismal, lugubrious, intensely cheerless.

MURMUR, *n.* 1. Low continuous sound, undertone, whisper, susurrus, susurration, hum, rustle, buzz, sough, purl, souffle, drone, lap, plash, babble, moan, purr, sigh, tinkle.

2. Mumbled expression of discontent, mutter, complaint, plaint, whimper, sigh, grumble, snuffle, wail, lament, groan, whine, sob, suspiration, heaving.

MURMUR, *v.* 1. Make sounds not fully intelligible, speak in a low tone, utter indistinctly, mumble, mutter, make a low continued sound, rustle, hum, whisper, susurrate, buzz, purl, plash, lap, sough, souffle, drone, babble, moan, gurgle.

2. Grumble, complain, whimper, sigh, snuffle, lament, wail, groan, whine, suspire, sob, heave, mourn, keen, fetch a sigh, croak, maunder, grunt, growl, fret.

MURMURER, *n.* Complainer, repiner, grumbler, fault-finder, objector, censurer, growler, malcontent, croaker, *laudator temporis acti (Lat.),* diehard, Adullamite, bitter-ender.

MURMUROUS, *adj.* 1. Low and indistinct, faint, muttered, gentle, whispered, soft, purling, stifled, muffled, rustling, droning, humming, buzzing, hissing, susurrant, swishing, babbling.

2. Voicing complaints, repining, complaining, peevish, grumbling, faultfinding, querulous, captious, discontented, dissatisfied, malcontent, regretful, disappointed.

MURRAIN, *n.* Cattle-disease, epizootic disease, cattle-plague, murr, anthrax, hoof-and-mouth disease, Texas fever, pox, pestilence.

MUSCLE, *n.* 1. Discrete bundle of contractile fibers with the function of producing movement in the body, thew, sinew, tendon.

2. Muscular strength, brawn, physique, lustihood, puissance, potency, power, force, energy, stamina, vigor, virility, nerve, grit, iron grip, steel, adamant.

MUSCULAR, *adj.* 1. Musculous, fibrous, sinewy, thewy.

2. Having well-developed muscles, brawny, stalwart, strong, strapping, powerful, vigorous, lusty, sturdy, able-bodied, herculean, stout, athletic, sound, potent, puissant, mighty, hard, hale, robustious, husky, wiry, well-knit, virile, manly, tough, stanch, firm, solid, doughty.

MUSE, *n.* Silent meditation, deep thought, reverie, reflection, brown study, abstraction, preoccupation, contemplation, rumination, absorption, engrossment, musing, self-communing, depth of thought, self-consultation, cogitation, thoughtfulness, consideration, speculation, deliberation, cerebration, lucubration, train of thought, association of ideas, stream of consciousness, daydreaming, woolgathering.

MUSE, *v.* Meditate, mull, contemplate, ponder, cogitate, ruminate, reflect, deliberate, brood over, think, lucubrate, speculate, reason, consider, be in a reverie, be in a brown study, daydream, dream, fancy, conceive, con over, weigh, mentalize, woolgather, cerebrate.

MUSES, *n., pl.* 1. The tuneful Nine, sacred Nine, sister goddess presiding over the arts, tuneful quire *(archaic).*

2. Calliope, Clio, Erato, Euterpe, Melpomene, Polyhymnia, Terpsichore, Thalia, Urania.

MUSEUM, *n.* Building for the exhibition of art works and scientific specimens, exhibition hall, gallery, pinacotheca, repository, pantechnicon, zoological gardens, zoo, *Tiergarten (Ger.), jardin des plantes (Fr.),* menagerie, aquarium, conservatory, hothouse.

MUSHROOM, *n.* 1. Fleshy fungus, toadstool, coral fungus, meadow mushroom, *Agaricus campestris (Lat.),* puffball, morel, chanterelle, champignon, truffle.

2. Upstart, parvenu, nouveau riche, skipjack, made man, *bourgeois gentilhomme (Fr.), novus homo (Lat.),* gent, snob.

3. Modernism, modernity, latest fashion, *dernier cri (Fr.),* last word.

MUSHROOM, *adj.* 1. Of rapid growth, of brief duration, short-lived, ephemeral, transitory, transient, diurnal, flitting, fleeting, fugacious, evanescent, fugitive, momentary, occasional, cursory, deciduous, passing, temporal, temporary, provisional, quick, brief, meteoric, cometary.

2. Risen from the ranks, parvenu, upstart, self-made, *nouveau riche (Fr.),* dunghill, unknown to fame, of low origin, baseborn, newborn, fresh, green, recent.

MUSHROOM, *v.* Grow quickly, spread quickly, overrun, be ubiquitous, crop up everywhere, spring up fast, rise in the world, get on in the world, make one's way, thrive, prosper, flourish, superabound, overabound, run riot, spread like wildfire, shoot up overnight.

MUSIC, *n.* 1. Art of sound in time expressing ideas and emotions in significant forms, sweet pleasing sounds, harmoniously effective sound, melody, strain, tune, air, harmony, symphony, polyphony, measure, minstrelsy, contrapuntal composition, refrain, burden.

2. Nocturne, serenade, serenata, aubade, morning song, caprice, rondo, pastoral, toccata, cavatina, adagio, largo, andante, berceuse, cradle song, lullaby, coronach, dirge, pavane, canon, fugue, fantasia, psalm, hymn, canticle, chant, song, *chanson (Fr.), Lied (Ger.),* canzonet, carol, lay, recitative, arietta, aria, ditty, ballad, cantata, oratorio, opera, music drama, operetta.

3. Waltz, valse, minuet, gavotte, galop, mazurka, cotillion, bolero, hornpipe, polka, jig, reel, march, allegro, jazz, ragtime, syncopation, two-step, foxtrot, blues, jitterbug.

4. Orchestral score, opus, composition, concert piece, sonata, concerto, symphony, tone poem, symphonic poem, chamber music, program music, prelude, overture, *Vorspiel (Ger.),* movement, scherzo, accompaniment, voluntary, incidental music, potpourri, medley, orchestration, harmonization, instrumentation.

5. Part song, madrigal, glee, descant, round, catch, chorale, antiphon, chorus, solo, duet, trio, quartet, quintet, sextet, octet, double quartet, inside part, vocal score, soprano, alto, contralto, tenor, baritone, bass, septet.

6. Tone, pitch, timbre, tonality, intonation, overtone, harmonics, figuration, modulation, resolution, phrasing, coloratura, suspension, cadenza, variation, run, roulade, cadence, *fioritura (It.),* bravura, virtuosity, trill, turn, shake, arpeggio, slur, phrase, passage, theme, tonic, keynote.

7. Scale, gamut, clef, key, chord, note, natural, flat, sharp, character, grace note, *appoggiatura (It.),* whole note, semibreve, breve, half note, minim, quarter note, crotchet, eighth note, quaver, sixteenth note, semiquaver, thirty-second note, demisemiquaver, undertone, sustained note, bourdon, drone, interval, step, half tone, half step, semitone, melodic interval, harmonic interval, solfeggio, solfa, solmization.

MUSICAL, *adj.* 1. Tuneful, melodious, canorous, harmonious, sweet-sounding, symphonious, dulcet, melic, melodic, euphonious, symphonic, contrapuntal, unisonant, homophonous, euphonic, harmonic, rhythmical, rhythmic, orotund, mellifluous, mellisonant, mellow, silver-toned, full-toned, Orphean, resonant, ringing, pleasant-sounding.

2. Orchestral, instrumental, vocal, lyric, choral, operatic.

MUSICAL, *n.* Program of music forming part of a social occasion, concert, musical entertainment, *soirée musicale (Fr.), matinée musicale (Fr.),* morning concert, *aubade (Fr.),* musical, recital, popular concert, pops *(colloq.),* chamber concert, open air concert, sing, singsong.

MUSICAL INSTRUMENTS, 1. Concert orchestra, symphony, philharmonic, band, brass band, string band, jazz band, dance orchestra, military band.

2. Strings, violin, fiddle, Stradivarius, Guarnerius, Cremona, viola, cello, violoncello, contrabass, double bass, contrabasso, bass viol, viola da gamba, viola da braccio, viola d'amore, rebec, viol, tenor viol.

3. Harp, lute, lyre, zither, cither, cithara, theorbo, psaltery, archlute, balalaika, samisen, banjo, guitar, mandolin, mandola, ukelele, steel guitar.

4. Pianoforte, piano, clavichord, clarichord, harpsichord, manichord, clavier, virginal, spinet, celesta.

5. Wind instruments, pipe organ, reed organ,

harmonium, organ, seraphine, melodeon, parlor organ, concertina, accordion, mouth organ, harmonica, syrinx, pipes, Pandean, Panpipe, bagpipes, doddlesack.

6. Reed instruments, wood winds, clarinet, clarionet, oboe, flageolet, piccolo, flute, fife, bassoon, double bassoon, contrafagotto, serpent, saxophone.

7. Percussion instruments, drum, kettledrum, timpano, bass drum, timbal, snare drum, side drum, taboret, tambour, tom-tom, timbrel, tambourine, glockenspiel, bells, carillon, cymbals, xylophone, vibraphone, triangle, marimba, castanets.

8. Brass, cornet, trumpet, horn, bugle, bugle horn, French horn, saxhorn, post horn, trombone, slide trombone, saxtuba, bass tuba, bombardon, euphonium, ophicleide, lituus, conch, tuba.

9. Mechanical instruments, player piano, automatic piano, player, street piano, hurdy-gurdy, calliope, barrel organ, hand organ, music box, phonograph, gramophone, graphophone, victrola.

MUSICIAN, *n.* 1. One who makes music a profession, one skilled in music, performer on an instrument, virtuoso, *artiste (Fr.),* minstrel, player, *maestro (It.),* composer, contrapuntist, harmonist.

2. Instrumentalist, pianist, accompanist, organist, violinist, fiddler, flautist, flute player, harpist, lutanist, lutist, fifer, cornetist, trumpeter, bugler, piper, cellist, bass fiddler, violist, harpsichordist, clavichordist, accordionist, bagpiper, clarinetist, oboist, drummer, timpanist.

3. Singer, bard, songster, songstress, *chanteuse (Fr.), cantatrice (It.),* vocalist, melodist, songbird, warbler, diva, soprano, contralto, tenor, baritone, basso, bass, caroler, chanter, chorister, choral singer, chorus, choir, Apollo, Orpheus, Linus, The Muses, tuneful Nine, sacred Nine, Polyhymnia, Euterpe, Erato, nightingale, thrush, lark, philomel, oriole, bulbul, mavis.

4. Leader, conductor, *maestro (It.),* director, *Kapellmeister (Ger.),* concert master, bandmaster, choirmaster, drum major, precentor, song leader, cantor.

MUSING, *adj.* Absorbed in thought, dreamy, preoccupied, meditative, absent-minded, woolgathering, daydreaming, pensive, wistful, ruminative, contemplative, abstracted, in a brown study, in a reverie, reflective, thoughtful, cogitative, deliberative, museful, studious, introspective, speculative, rapt, absorbed, intent, engrossed in, tense, lost in thought, philosophical, metaphysical.

MUSING, *n.* Reverie, meditation, abstraction, reflection, deep thought, brown study, contemplation, rumination, daydreaming, woolgathering, preoccupation, engrossment, absorption, self-consultation, self-communing, train of thought, stream of consciousness, association of ideas, speculation, lucubration, deliberation, weighing, cogitation, cerebration.

MUSKET, *n.* Hand gun for infantry soldiers, predecessor of the modern rifle, flintlock, firelock, fowling piece, *fusil (Fr.),* carbine, caliver, musketoon, blunderbuss, matchlock, harquebus, petronel, breechloader, small bore, muzzleloader.

MUSKETEER, *n.* Rifleman, carabineer, yager, sharpshooter, fusileer, grenadier, skirmisher, chasseur, mounted rifle, hussar, dragoon.

MUSS, *v.* Put into disorder, make untidy, make messy, rumple, crumple, ruffle, dishevel, jumble, confuse, disarrange, disturb, mess up, tousle, tangle, entangle.

MUSSY, *adj.* Messy, rumpled, crumpled, tousled, disheveled, untidy, disarranged, disordered, ruffled, jumbled, confused, disturbed, messed up, tangled, straggling, slovenly, frowzy, grubby, unkempt, dowdy, frumpish, slatternly, sloppy.

MUST, *v.* Be bound by some imperative requirement to, be under the necessity of, be obliged to, be necessitated to, be required to, be compelled to by some constraining force, have to, have no choice, have no alternative, should, ought to.

MUST, *n.* 1. Mold, dry rot, mildew, rubigo, mucor, mustiness, fustiness, sourness, rust, fungus.

2. Unfermented grape-juice, new wine, fresh wine.

MUSTACHE, *n.* Hair growing on the upper lip, bristles growing near the mouth, whiskers, mustachio, moustache, handlebar.

MUSTANG, *n.* Small wild horse of the American plains, bronco, unbroken pony, roan, filly, colt, foal.

MUSTER, *v.* 1. Gather, collect, convene, assemble, congregate, marshal, array, convoke, call together, bring together, summon, muster up, get together, levy, convocate, gather together, round up, call the roll of.

2. Be assembled, rally, meet together, flock, cluster, swarm, stream, surge, crowd, mass, herd, throng, associate, huddle, forgather, resort, concentrate.

MUSTER, *n.* 1. Assemblage, gathering, collection, conflux, ingathering, concourse, levy, mobilization, concentration, forgathering, meet, convergence, congregation, focalization, concurrence, confluence.

2. Assembly, meeting, séance, sitting, conference, hearing, convention, session, palaver, durbar, powwow, caucus, congress, levee, council, audience.

MUSTY, *adj.* 1. Moldy, fusty, stale, sour, spoiled, mildewed, lentiginous, rusty, mucid, rancid, gone bad, reasty, corrupt, rotten, tainted, flyblown, high, fetid, foul, rank, frowzy, maggoty, putrescent, putrid, carious, reeky, strong-smelling, noisome, damp, dirty, dusty, filthy, smudged, stuffy, close.

2. Staled by time, hackneyed, threadbare, trite, cliché, stereotyped, old, antiquated, obsolete, proverbial, familiar, commonplace, conventional, banal, bromidic, stock, set, traditional, prescriptive, customary, dull, heavy, insipid, vapid.

MUTABILITY, *n.* Changeableness, variableness, mutableness, instability, inconstancy, unsteadiness, mobility, versatility, vacillation, fluctuation, alternation, volatility, fickleness, changeability, alterability, irresolution, indecision, vicissitude, oscillation, alteration, changefulness, uncertainty.

MUTABLE, *adj.* Subject to change, liable to alteration, changeable, alterable, variable, inconstant, ever-changing, vacillating, irresolute, wavering, unsettled, fickle, mercurial, protean, unstable, unsteady, changeful, mutatory, fitful, capricious, fast-changing, commutable, fluctuating, giddy, undecided, unsteadfast, uncertain, kaleidoscopic, versatile, erratic, touch-and-go, desultory, vagrant, wayward, plastic, alternating, mobile, volatile, spasmodic.

MUTATION, *n.* 1. Change, alteration, variation, permutation, modification, qualification, innovation, shift, deviation, divergence, inversion, turn, reversal, transformation, transfiguration, transmutation, metamorphosis.

2. (*Biol.*) Sudden departure from the parent type, individual or species resulting from such a departure, sport.

MUTE, *adj.* 1. Unable to speak, obmutescent, dumb, incapable of speech, aphonic, voiceless, nonvocal, noiseless, still.

2. Refraining from utterance, silent, speechless, inarticulate, mum, tight-lipped, taciturn, reticent, wordless, tongue-tied, close-mouthed, reserved, close-tongued, uncommunicative, hushed.

3. Unpronounced, unarticulated, unuttered, surd.

MUTE, *n.* 1. One unable to utter words, deaf-mute, dummy.

2. Actor whose part is confined to dumb show, supernumerary, walk-on, extra, *figurante (Fr.),* pantomimist, mime, mimist.

3. Device for muffling tone, sordino, sourdine, damp, soft pedal, damper, silencer.

MUTILATE, *v.* 1. Deprive of an important part, amputate, detruncate, excise, lop off, cut away, cut off, truncate, dislimb, dismember, hack off, butcher, cut to pieces, commit mayhem, dock.

2. Disfigure, maim, cripple, hamstring, hough, scotch, mangle, lame, surbate, deface, deform, foul, blemish, scar, mar, spoil, injure, harm, damage, hurt, labefy, impair, distort.

MUTILATED, *adj.* 1. Maimed, dismembered, mangled, butchered, amputated, truncated, detruncated, obtruncated, excised, dislimbed, lopped off, cut off, hacked off, cut to ribbons, docked, defaced, disfigured.

2. Distorted, garbled, hashed, incomplete, misrepresented, expurgated, bowdlerized.

MUTINEER, *n.* Insurgent, rebel, revolter, subversive, revolutionary, revolutionist, insurrectionist, bolshevik, rioter, sansculotte, *carbonaro (It.),* traitor, Fenian, *frondeur (Fr.),* seceder, anarchist, brawler, demagogue, runagate, Spartacus, Jack Cade, Wat Tyler.

MUTINOUS, *adj.* Disposed to revolt against constituted authority, insurgent, seditious, insurrectionary, rebellious, restive, defiant, disaffected, discontented, disorderly, turbulent, refractory, contumacious, unruly, riotous, insubordinate, lawless, ungovernable, tumultuary, disobedient, revolutionary, recalcitrant, unsubmissive, resistant, resistive, uncompliant, impatient of control, recusant, intransigent, radical, Red, bolshevistic.

MUTINY, *v.* Revolt against constituted authority, rise up in arms, rebel, resist authority, defy, disobey, set authority at naught, fly in the face of, run riot, kick over the traces, take the law into one's own hands, turn restive, champ the bit, secede, not submit, reluctate, repugn, stand up against, take a stand against, kick against the pricks, recalcitrate, oppose, lift the hand against.

MUTINY, *n.* Insurrection, sedition, rebellion, revolt, uprising, outbreak, riot, disobedience, insubordination, revolution, *bouleversement (Fr.),* rising, debacle, subversion, political upheaval, coup d'état, bolshevism, overthrow, insurgency, disaffection, turbulence, resistance, defiance, oppugnation, opposition, reluctation, renitence, recalcitration, *levée en masse (Fr.),* riot, strike, lockout, sit-down, passive resistance, contumacy, non-compliance, putsch, *émeute (Fr.),* tumult, secession, defection, sabotage.

MUTTER, *v.* 1. Mumble, maunder, mump, gibber, snuffle, clip one's words, lisp, mince, talk incoherently, speak thickly, croak, drawl, sputter,

hem and haw, muffle, talk to oneself, say in one's sleeve, grunt.

2. Grumble, complain, lament, repine, find fault with, growl, murmur, grouse, whine, clamor, make a fuss about, deprecate, disapprove.

MUTTER, *n.* Indistinct utterance, murmur, whine, whimper, moan, groan, grumble, rumble, suspiration, sigh, jeremiad, plaint, complaint, lament, lamentation, wail.

MUTUAL, *adj.* Possessed or experienced by each of two or more with respect to the other, pertaining to each of two or more, having the same relation each toward the other, reciprocal, reciprocally given and received, interchanged, interchangeable, correlative, common, interactive, commutual, joint, coincident, correspondent, intermutual, give-and-take, complementary, interchanging, equivalent, identical, similar, analogous.

MUTUALITY, *n.* Mutual dependence, reciprocation, reciprocalness, alternation, reciprocity, give-and-take, correspondence, correlation, equivalence, *quid pro quo (Lat.),* exchange, interchange, intermutation, shuffle, swap, intercourse, barter, commerce, interchangeableness, tit for tat, substitution, commutability, interchangeability, reprisal, retaliation.

MUZZLE, *v.* 1. Silence, hush, quiet, deaden, muffle, mute, subdue, throttle, damp, repress.

2. Gag, bridle, bind, restrain, coerce, harness, govern, control, hold back, snub, pull in, repress, strangle, suppress, inhibit, keep under, smother, curb, check, rein in, constrain, restrict, fasten, trammel, confine, keep within bounds, stifle, stop.

MYOPIA, *n.* Near-sightedness, short-sightedness, purblindness, presbyopia, lippitude, astigmatism, strabismus, dim-sightedness, half-sightedness, dull-sightedness, nystagmus.

MYOPIC, *adj.* Near-sighted, short-sighted, dimsighted, dull-sighted, half-sighted, purblind, myopy, presbyopic, lippitudinous, astigmatic, strabismic, blear-eyed, moon-eyed, mole-eyed, mope-eyed, goggle-eyed.

MYRIAD, *adj.* 1. Ten-thousand, of an indefinitely great number, multitudinous, innumerable, uncounted, manifold, extremely many, countless, boundless, infinite, immense, measureless, sumless, immeasurable, illimitable, incalculable, unfathomable, interminable, inexhaustible, without number, limitless, endless, without measure, unnumbered, untold, unlimited, unbounded, illimited.

2. Having innumerable aspects, protean, kaleidoscopic, versatile, variable, mutable, checkered, ever changing, proteiform.

MYRMIDON, *n.* One who executes without scruple his master's commands, mercenary, hireling, henchman, retainer, janissary, Mameluke, dependent, led captain, puppet, liegeman, subject, follower.

MYSTERIOUS, *adj.* Of obscure nature or meaning, puzzling, inexplicable, not easily comprehended, not readily explained, enigmatical, recondite, cryptic, esoteric, occult, secret, cabalistic, abstruse, mystical, mystic, inscrutable, unfathomable, unintelligible, unknown, dark, hidden, obscure, incomprehensible, sphinxlike, oracular, concealed, transcendental, ambiguous, equivocal, unrevealed, covert, impenetrable, clandestine, surreptitious, mystifying, hermetical, darkling, ineffable, inexpressible, inconceivable, incredible, unaccountable, latent, shadowy, nebulous, dim, supernatural, preternatural, unexplainable, cloudy, nubiferous, dusky, caliginous, strange, unexplained, shadowy, umbrageous, tenebrous, nocturnal, undisclosed, untold, privy, veiled, masked, screened, cloaked, disguised, confidential, circuitous, mazy, labyrinthine, meandrous, furtive, underhand, stealthy, insidious, reticent, taciturn, silent, uncommunicative, tight-lipped, close-mouthed, secretive, indistinct, indistinguishable, confusing, indefinite, ill-defined, skulking, feline, evasive, noncommittal, buttoned up, irrevealable, inviolable, not to be spoken of, undercover, buried, underground, secluded, undecipherable, coded, incognizable, insoluble, insolvable, impenetrable, indecipherable, as Greek to one, baffling, in suspense, indeterminate, vague, perplexing, apocryphal.

MYSTERY, *n.* 1. Something unexplained or unknown, enigma, puzzle, riddle, secret, arcanum, maze, labyrinth, tangle, poser, problem, *terra incognita (Lat.),* closed book, rebus, conundrum, charade, logograph, Sphinx, oracle, *crux criticorum (Lat.),* hidden meaning, occultness, mysticism, cabala, symbolism, latency, concealment, taciturnity, reticence, silence, more than meets the eye, *le dessous des cartes (Fr.),* hard nut to crack, Hercynian wood, unexplored ground, dark ages, virgin soil, ambiguity, equivocalness, doubtful meaning, *dignus vindice nodus (Lat.),* Gordian knot, steganography, Freemasonry, Greek, Hebrew, imperceptibility, screen, disguise, masquerade, code, cipher, cryptography, invisible ink, seclusion, secrecy, secretiveness, suspense, dilemma, quandary, vagueness, fog, haze, obscurity.
2. Sacramental rite, eucharist, Lord's supper, Holy Communion, Holy Sacrament, transubstantiation, mass.

MYSTIC, *adj.* 1. Esoteric, occult, cabalistic, symbolical, allegorical, symbolic, emblematical, mystical, dark, cryptic, recondite, inviolate, confidential, close, undisclosed, secretive, clandestine, privy, hidden, concealed, secret, *in petto (It.),* apocalyptic, hermetical, figurative, anagogical, veiled.
2. Mysterious, unknowable, inscrutable, steganographic, cryptographic, enigmatical, obscure, abstruse, transcendental, puzzling.

MYSTICISM, *n.* Doctrine of an immediate spiritual intuition of truths believed to transcend ordinary understanding, direct and intimate union of the soul with the Divinity through contemplation and love, Orphism, cabala, quietism, pietism, enthusiasm, divine afflatus, ontologism, occultism, cabalism.

MYSTIFICATION, *n.* Bewilderment, perplexity, confusion, obfuscation, puzzlement, uncertainty, incertitude, doubtfulness, dubiancy, dubiety, suspense, hesitation, dilemma, quandary, indecision, indetermination, vacillation, vagueness, ambiguity, double meaning, leap in the dark, something or other, blind bargain, pig in a poke.

MYSTIFY, *v.* Impose upon a person by playing upon his credulity, bewilder purposely, pose, puzzle, perplex, befog, obfuscate, involve in obscurity, embarrass, confuse, deceive, dupe, delude, fool, hoodwink, take in, dissemble, confound, mislead, misguide, misrepresent, equivocate, humbug, befuddle, trick, bamboozle, nonplus, distract, pervert, equivocate, elude, evade, blindfold, keep in the dark, throw off the scent, put on a false scent, spoof, throw dust into the eyes, draw a herring across the trail.

MYTH, *n.* 1. Legendary story concerning some superhuman being or alleged event, legend, fable,

tradition, fairy tale, epic, parable, allegory, romance, fabulous story, fiction.
2. Fantasy, fancy, conceit, vagary, whim, notion, figment, extravaganza, vision, dream, chimera, illusion, shadow, phantasm, man in the moon, castle in the air, *château en Espagne (Fr.),* great sea serpent, Utopia, fairyland, Atlantis, land of Prester John, flying Dutchman, golden dream, daydream, reverie, rhapsody.
3. Falsehood, untruth, lie, prevarication, tall story, fib, whopper, fabrication, canard, yarn, traveler's tale, cock-and-bull story, moonshine, bosh, Canterbury tale, claptrap, mare's nest, invention, forgery, taradiddle, crammer, bounce.

MYTHICAL, *adj.* Existing only in myth, having no foundation in fact, fabled, fabulous, imaginary, fanciful, fictitious, mythological, traditional, preposterous, untrue, false, trumped up, void of foundation, unfounded, invented, *ben trovato (It.),* forged, fabricated, supposititious, factitious, illusory, *soi-disant (Fr.),* theoretical, hypothetical, chimerical, visionary, notional, fantastic, unreal, ideal, in the clouds, *in nubibus (Lat.),* romantic, unsubstantial, utopian, quixotic, rhapsodical, extravagant, imagined, air-built, air-drawn, high-flown.

MYTHOLOGICAL, *adj.* Fabulous, legendary, mythical, mythic, imaginary, fairy-like, fanciful, imaginative, fictitious, supposititious, unreal, untrue, traditional, chimerical, supernatural, preternatural, fantastic, visionary, idealistic, dreamy, delusive, illusory, false, invented.

MYTHOLOGY, *n.* Body of myths of a particular people, myths collectively, tradition, folklore, mythical lore, fairy mythology, fairyism, fairyology, heathenology, paganism, animism, superstition, polytheism.

N

NAB, *v.* *(Coll.)* Lay hold of, get hands on, lay hands on, seize, catch, apprehend, capture, take into custody, lay by the heels, collar, wrest, grasp, grab, take possession of, seize possession of, grip, grapple, gripe, clutch, clap hands on, claw, clinch, hook *(sl.),* snag, snare, snap up, snatch, arrest.

NACREOUS, *adj.* Pearly, pearl-like, pearl-white, glistening, iridescent, iridial, irisated, pearlish, iridian, iridal, nacrous.

NADIR, *n.* Low point, depression, lowest point, base, lowest position, lowest ebb, zero, minimum, nothing, scratch *(coll.),* bottom, starting point, foot.

NAG, *n.* Horse, small horse, pony, steed, mount, garran, jade, hoss *(coll.),* equine, dobbin, hack, hobby.

NAG, *v.* Torment, pester, harass, worry, badger, plague, fret, scold, harp at *(coll.),* bicker, importune, peck at, hector, gall, nettle, chafe, harry, tease, complain, molest, grouse *(coll.),* persecute, remonstrate, devil, bedevil, haunt, rail at, irritate, annoy, twit.

NAIAD, *n.* Nereid, water nymph, water sprite, undine, ondine, nix, nixie, kelpie, fairy, sprite, mermaid, siren, sea nymph, sea maid, limniad, Oceanid, ocean nymph.

NAIL, *n.* 1. Spike, brad, pin, hardware, fastening, peg, skewer, rivet, staple, tack, point, treenail.
2. Fingernail, unguis, claw, talon.

NAIL, *v.* Attach, fix, join, unite, fasten, pin, hammer, hold, clinch, secure, firm.

NAIVE, *adj.* Gullible, credulous, innocent, unsophisticated, unspoiled, artless, ingenuous, unsuspecting, unsuspicious, uninitiate, uninitiated, stupid, foolish, unwise, imprudent, plain, simple, natural, overcredulous, overtrustful, infatuated, green, childish, void of suspicion, inexperienced, unseasoned, amateurish, unripe, immature, unconversant, wet behind the ears *(coll.)*, not dry behind the ears *(coll.)*, unaffected, unassuming, frank, open, candid, simple-hearted, simple-minded, unversed in, unused to.

NAIVETE, *n.* *(Fr.)* Artlessness, simplicity, ingenuousness, modesty, innocence, candor, sincerity, veracity, plain speaking, naturalness, unartificiality, unsophistication, unaffectedness, honesty, immaculateness, trustfulness, credulity, stupidity, foolishness, imprudence, plainness, simplicity, overcredulity, greenness, inexperience, amateurishness, unripeness, frankness, simple-mindedness, childishness.

NAKED, *adj.* 1. Unclothed, nude, undraped, exposed, laid bare, bare, denuded, bald, raw *(sl.)*, in the buff, in one's birthday suit *(coll.)*, divested, without a stitch, disrobed, in dishabille, stripped, in a state of nature, ungarmented, unappareled, stark-naked, bared.

2. Palpable, patent, clear, plain, apparent, perceptible, perceivable, evident, manifest, obvious, unmasked, uncurtained, unveiled, undraped, uncovered, uncloaked, visible, in plain view, in plain sight, seeable, observable, evident, self-evident, definite, unmistakable, certain, ostensible.

3. Uncorrupted, undefiled, uncolored, unalloyed, pure, simon-pure, natural, unadulterated, unmixed, unexaggerated, stark, unqualified.

4. Unarranged, undecked, unornamented, unadorned, undecorated, untrimmed, ungarnished, unenriched, bare, barren, plain, simple.

NAKEDNESS, *n.* Nudity, bareness, exposure, baldness, birthday suit *(coll.)*, the buff *(coll.)*, dishabille.

NAMBY-PAMBY, *adj.* Wishy-washy, watery, insipid, insubstantial, mawkish, sentimental, mediocre, vapid, simpering, affected, insincere, milk-and-water, mushy, sickly, weak.

NAME, *n.* 1. Denomination, cognomen, compellation, appellation, title, titulus, moniker *(sl.)*, handle *(coll.)*, designation, style, prenomen, eponym, epithet, appellative, proper name, Christian name, first name, surname, family name, last name, middle name, nickname, soubriquet, signature, autograph, antonym, synonym, trademark, trade name, by-name, byword, patronymic, alias, false name, dionym, cognomination, pseudonym, *nom de guerre (Fr.)*, *nom de plume (Fr.)*, vocable, euphemism, trionym, toponym, pet name, pen name, stage name, forename, imprint, anonym, cryptonym, cipher, misnomer, metronymic, caconym, noun, word, substantive, colophon, inscription, bookplate.

2. Fame, reputation, celebrity, notoriety, repute, worth, good repute, famousness, renown, kudos *(coll.)*, popularity, importance, consequence, mark, distinction, eminence, éclat, popular repute, popular esteem, popular estimation, good odor, honor, regard, reputability, high repute, glory, report, note, notability, praise, label, mark.

NAME, *v.* 1. Entitle, denominate, characterize, describe, cite, specify, tag, title, designate, term,

style, dub, call, christen, baptize, cognominate, nickname, give appellation to.

2. Commission, delegate, nominate, ordain, deputize, authorize, empower, accredit, appoint, employ, engage, hire, entrust, consign, commit, assign, charge, send out, return, cite, commit to hand of, depute.

3. Mention, denote, indicate, select, point out.

NAMELESS, *adj.* 1. Anonymous, anonymal, undesignated, unnamed, unacknowledged, undefined, without a name, having no name, pseudonymous, unspecified.

2. Inglorious, obscure, humble, renownless, unheard-of, unnoted, unhonored, ignoble, unknown to fame.

3. Abominable, unspeakable, indescribable, repulsive, indefinable, ineffable, unnamable, inexpressible, unutterable.

NAMELY, *adv.* i. e., *id est (Lat.)*, to wit, viz., *videlicet (Lat.)*, in other words, specifically, in plain words, strictly speaking, to explain, nominally, *scilicet (Lat.)*, *scil.*, that is, that is to say, as much as to say.

NAP, *v.* Take a sleep, doze, doze off, drowse, snooze *(coll.)*, drift off, fall asleep, take forty winks, catnap, pound the ear *(coll.)*, drop off *(coll.)*, go to sleep, rest, recline, lie down, repose, sleep soundly, sleep heavily, take a short sleep, take a short snooze.

NAP, *n.* 1. Siesta, repose, rest, sleep, doze, drowse, slumber, arms of Morpheus, shut-eye *(sl.)*, snooze, *(coll.)*, wink, wink of sleep, forty winks *(coll.)*, cat nap, beauty sleep.

2. Pile, shag, wool, fleece, fuzz, fiber, velvet, surface, texture, villosity, villi, fluff.

NAPE, *n.* Hindhead, scruff, scruff of the neck, back of the neck, occiput, back of the head, poll.

NAPKIN, *n.* Serviette, doily, cloth, bib, linen, table linen, towel.

NAPPY, *adj.* Pily, shaggy, velvet, velvety, velutinous, downy, woolly, flocculent, lanate, villous, fleecy, napped, rough.

NARCOTIC, *adj.* Assuasive, anaesthetic, narcotinic, lenitive, pharmaceutical, medicinal, balsamic, calmative, stupefying, hypnotic, anodyne, palliative, analgesic.

NARCOTIC, *n.* Opiate, nepenthes, laudanum, atropine, heroin, loco weed, marijuana, hashish, hyoscyamine, dope *(sl.)*, morphine, cocaine, snow *(sl.)*, drug, hop *(sl.)*, hops *(sl.)*, cannabis, Indian hemp, soporific, hypnotic, therapeutic, pharmaceutical, medication, medicine, remedy.

NARRATE, *v.* Tell, set forth, describe, historize, relate, recount, render, report, analyze, give words to, give a report of, give an account of, sum up, review, run over, rehearse, storify, tell a story, recapitulate, particularize, detail, historicize, romance, novelize, epitomize, chronicle, disclose, reveal, state, proclaim, repeat, mention, circumstantiate, dilate.

NARRATION, *n.* 1. Annals, journal, description, account, story, tale, fable, report, myth, legend, history, chronicle, brief, summary, memoir, ana, experience, letters, biography, autobiography, adventures, life, telling, epic, saga, communication, record, recitation, relation, rehearsal, statement.

2. See NARRATIVE.

NARRATIVE, *n.* (See NARRATION.) Writing, piece of writing, book, story, volume, publication, script, scrip, chronicle, register, composition, work, output, opus, production, scripture, novel, romance, short story, anecdote, tale, yarn *(coll.)*, mystery story, thriller *(coll.)*, dime novel, detective story, whodunit *(coll.)*, fable, parable, allegory, fairy tale, myth, horse opera *(coll.)*, epic, saga, description, account, recital, rehearsal, episode, theme, paper.

NARRATOR, *n.* Author, teller, teller of tales, storyteller, spinner of yarns, writer, fabulist, fabler, romancer, romanticist, sagaman, bard, skald, scop, troubadour, minstrel, prose writer, poet, epic poet, autobiographer, biographer, recorder, relater, chronicler, interviewer, raconteur, annalist, historian, chronographer, novelist, anecdotist, memorialist.

NARROW, *adj.* 1. Slender, attenuated, drawn out, slim, strait, close, tight, thread-like, tapered, scant, scanty, pinched, cramped, spare, sparse, diminished, reduced, emaciated, fine, finespun, coarctate, restricted, confined, limited, incapacious.

2. Bigoted, narrow-minded, provincial, insular, isolationist, opinionated, opinionate, opinionative, self-opinionated, isolated, mean-spirited, narrow-spirited, dogmatic, arbitrary, orthodox, hyperorthodox, petty, little, parochial, confined, shallow, ungenerous, positive, positivistic, impersuadable, shortsighted, nearsighted, intolerant, illiberal, stiff, stiff-backed, stiff-necked, rooted, settled, set in one's ways, immovable, uncompromising, intransigent, irreconcilable, strait-laced, fanatical, fanatic, parsimonious, stingy, mean, crabbed, tight, selfish, self-centered, inhospitable, smug, complacent, prim, priggish, mincing, puritanical, covetous, grasping, unyielding, adamant, hard, hard-hearted, cold, cold-blooded, unfeeling, unsympathetic, exacting, demanding.

NARROW, *v.* Pinch, constrain, contract, lessen, diminish, modify, change, limit, qualify, alter, cramp, compact, restrict, reduce, draw in, taper, draw together, compress, squeeze, squeeze together, dwindle, confine, tighten, straiten, make smaller.

NARROWING, *n.* Attenuation, shrinkage, shrinking, emaciation, defalcation, stricture, reduction, lessening, constriction, contraction, constringency, curtailment, limitation, limiting, circumscription, angustation.

NARROW-MINDED, *adj.* (See NARROW.) Bigoted, prejudiced, partial, one-sided, positive, positivist, positivistic, dogmatic, arbitrary, superficial, fanatic, fanatical, orthodox, hyperorthodox, obstinate, stubborn, mulish, sanctimonious, faddish, besotted, obsessed, infatuated, puritanical, absolute, doctrinary, doctrinaire, boorish, illiberal, insular, uncatholic, short-sighted, mean, warped, biased, categorical, categoric, creed-bound, overreligious, prepossessed.

NARROW-MINDEDNESS, *n.* Monomania, prejudice, bigotry, warp, bias, uncatholicity, illiberality, opinionatedness, insularity, intolerance, stiff-neck, short-sightedness, purblindness, pedantry, positivism, prudery, sanctimony, sanctimoniousness, hyperorthodoxy, obstinacy, stubbornness.

NARROWNESS, *n.* Hair's-breath, slenderness, exiguity, exiguousness, closeness, straitness, incapaciousness, coarctation, scantiness, slightness, circumscription, slimness, confinement, restriction, restrictedness.

NARROWS, *n.* Strait, neck, isthmus, ravine, defile, channel, canal, pass, passage.

NASCENT, *adj.* Beginning, commencing, introductory, elementary, prime, primary, primal, primi-

tive, primigenial, inchoate, inaugural, proemial, incipient, initial, initiatory, aboriginal, original, starting, dawning, evolutionary, evolving, rudimentary, rudimental, embryonal, embryonic, developing, opening.

NASTY, *adj.* 1. Offensive, repulsive, repellent, foul, filthy, dirty, sullied, maculate, blotched, smudged, dirtied, bespotted, begrimed, bemired, smutty, besmutted, besmirched, smeared, daubed, blotted, blemished, tainted, stained, corrupt, contaminated, putrid, putrescent, putrefied, high, rank, foul-smelling, evil-smelling, nauseous, nauseant, nauseating, sickening, abominable, beastly, vile, obnoxious, noxious, noisome, fulsome, loathsome, odious, coarse, revolting, disgusting, distasteful, stercorous, stercoral, stercoraceous, excrementitious, dungy, mucid, slimy, fecal, feculent, purulent, impetiginous, lentiginous, scurfy, maggoty, decayed, rotted, rotten, rotting, saprogenic, flyblown, putrefactive, reeking, sloppy, horrible, ugly, unsightly, mucky, polluted, squalid, hateful, unclean, impure.

2. Dirty, unclean, immoral, distasteful, impure, unpure, foul, obscene, vile, fulsome, foul-mouthed, foul-minded, dirty-minded, prurient, lascivious, lecherous, foul-spoken, brazen, bold-faced, brazen-faced, shameless, loose, ribald, coarse, sluttish, mean, vulgar, lewd, indecent, indecorous, indelicate, gross, impudent, unblushing, fescennine, bawdy, pornographic, immodest, low, risqué, lurid, unseemly.

NATATORIAL, *adj.* Swimming, detergent, washing, bathing, abstergent, lavatory, balneal, purifying, watering, lavational, balneatory, cleansing, cleaning, natatory.

NATION, *n.* 1. Land, country, kingdom, republic, polity, body politic, empire, empery, land, realm, commonwealth, domain, principality, protectorate, colony, settlement, toparchy, monarchy, democracy, dominion, state.

2. Population, habitancy, inhabitation, inhabitants, people, folk, public, race, stock, tribe, commonweal, commonwealth, generation, family, house, nationality, gentility, lineage, strain, extraction, family tree, pedigree, ancestry, line, bloodline, descent, birth.

NATIONAL, *adj.* Public, general, state, provincial, federal, common, social, societal, civil, civic, tribal, family, racial, political, lineal, gentile, gentilitian, gentilitial, gentilitious, communal.

NATIONALISM, *n.* Patriotism, chauvinism, national loyalty, love for one's country, isolationism, insularity, provincialism, dogmatism, jingoism, love of country, *amor patriae (Lat.)*, civism, public spirit.

NATIONALIST, *n.* Patriot, isolationist, jingoist, jingo, chauvinist, loyal citizen.

NATIONWIDE, *adj.* Overall, countrywide, widespread, general, national, federal, universal, wide, interstate, cross-country, transcontinental, transnational, extensive, broad, far-reaching, inclusive.

NATIVE, *adj.* 1. Indigenous, locally born, indigenal, natal, vernacular, original, home-grown, aboriginal, primitive, endemic, endemical, domestic, home-born, garden, garden-variety, naturalized, acclimated, acclimatized, domiciliary, home, homespun, autochthonal, autochthonous.

2. Simple, commonplace, uncomplicated, unborrowed, inland, endemic, unsophisticated, plain, natural, pure, not foreign, not alien, unpretending, unfeigning, undissembling, undissimulating, guile-

less, undesigning, untutored, unaffected, genuine, real, sincere, primeval, unacquired, vulgar, wild, artless, guileless, ordinary, common, matter-of-fact, everyday, plebeian, household, workaday.

3. Syngenetic, syngenic, genetous, connate, innate, inborn, inbred, immanent, inherent, intrinsic, incarnate, inwrought, ingenerate, implanted, indwelling, infixed, ingrained, ingenite, congenital, normal, essential, bred-in-the-bone, hematobious, hereditary, instinctive, radical, original, basal, underlying, elementary, fundamental, primary.

NATIVE, *n.* Dweller, citizen, inhabitant, habitant, countryman, landsman, countrywoman, indigena, original, aboriginal, aborigine, old-timer *(coll.),* sourdough *(coll.),* primitive, autochthon, indigene.

NATIVITY, *n.* Birth, development, parturition, genesis, hatching, childbirth, incubation, *accouchement (Fr.),* travail, labor, act of God *(coll.),* blessed event *(U.S.),* origin, nationality, citizenship.

NATTY, *adj. (Coll.)* Trim, trig, tidy, well-dressed, well turned-out, smart, chic, smartly dressed, smartly appareled, well-tailored, well-clothed, classy *(coll.),* glossy, sleek, dapper, spruce, jaunty, finical, finicky, foppishy, dandified, silk-socked.

NATURAL, *adj.* 1. See NATIVE, 3.
2. Instinctive, intuitive, inherent, intuent, animal, intuitional, knowing by intuition, perceiving by intuition, automatic, unintended, unintentional, unalloyed, unmixed, uncolored, unvarnished, unqualified, unaffected, unmodified, unrestrained, habitual, normal, usual, regular, native, impulsive, pure, naked, involuntary, untutored, uneducated, spontaneous, artless, simple, plain, simple-hearted, simple-minded, unartificial, childlike, naive, unsophisticated, unassuming, unpretending, undissimulating, undissembling, undesigning, guileless, ordinary, unstudied, informal, unconscious, unwitting, ingenuous, frank, open, open-hearted, candid, straight, straightforward, unreserved, outspoken, plain-spoken, blunt, downright, direct, unpretentious, inexperienced, matter-of-fact, unpoetical, unflattering, innocent, unguided, uncontrolled, unguarded, rash, snap, everyday, commonplace, workaday, homely, garden, garden-variety, prosy, prosaic, unimaginative, household.

NATURAL, *n.* 1. Fool, idiot, simpleton, half-wit, dunce, dunderhead, imbecile, moron, dimwit, natural idiot, natural-born fool, born fool, blockhead, dolt, ninny, tomfool, numskull, clod, lout, clodpole, oaf, loon, nitwit, dullard.
2. Note, musical note, tone, musical tone.

NATURAL CHILD, *n.* Bastard, love-child, illegitimate offspring, illegitimate child, son of nobody, bantling.

NATURALIZE, *v.* Adopt, domesticate, adapt, admit, endow with rights of citizenship, swear in as citizen, confer rights of citizenship, acclimatize, familiarize, acclimate, habituate, inure, accustom, season, adopt as a citizen.

NATURE, *n.* 1. World, wide world, creation, all creation, sphere, globe, vale of tears, vale, earth, natural forces, universe, cosmos, macrocosm, macrocosmos, megacosm, megacosmos, system, natural system, system of nature, system of creation.
2. Character, essence, characteristic, feature, trait, quality, property, peculiarity, singularity, particularity, identity, synthesis, getup *(coll.),* setup *(coll.),* embodiment, formation, construction, composition, spirit, quiddity, constitution, vitality.
3. Kind, type, stamp, feather, stripe, color, species, variety, kin, kidney, style, manner, denomi-

nation, brand, designation, strain, form, mold, cast, genus.
4. Habit, frame, mood, spirit, tone, vein, temper, temperament, affections, frame of mind, qualities, leaning, bias, animus, inclination, disposition, disposedness, predisposition, diathesis, proneness, crasis, proclivity, propensity, idiocrasis, aptitude, propensitude, sympathy, propension, tendency, turn of mind, warp, twist.
5. Universal force, life force, creator, creating principle, universal life force, *élan vital (Fr.),* world spirit, oversoul, logos, archens, world principle, nous, the Absolute, God, the creator, supreme soul, supreme ruler, principle, Truth, soul of the universe, author of all things, supreme being.

NAUGHT, *n.* Zero, cipher, nothing, nullity, nil, nought, none, none whatever, nothing whatever, nothing at all, no part, no degree, no quantity, no such thing, zip *(sl.),* goose egg *(sl.).*

NAUGHTY, *adj.* 1. Bad, evil, wicked, obscene, iniquitous, sinful, reprobate, recreant, graceless, wanton, prodigal, defective, faulty, virtueless, arrant, wayward, unrighteous, unvirtuous, good for nothing, good for naught, corrupt, worthless.
2. Disrespectful, froward, refractory, disobedient, mischievous, full of mischief, unmindful, unheedful, unheeding, harmful, recalcitrant, stubborn, obstinate, willful.

NAUSEA, *n.* 1. Sickness, biliousness, throwing up, emesis, vomiting, qualm, upset stomach, queasiness, sickness of the stomach, squeamishness, seasickness, travel sickness, motion sickness, airsickness, planesickness, trainsickness, carsickness.
2. Disgust, loathing, repugnance, abomination, hatred, revulsion, detestation, antipathy, execration, aversion, averseness, abhorrence.

NAUSEATE, *v.* Sicken, disgust, repel, revolt, repulse, pall, offend, turn one's stomach, make one sick, make one's gorge rise, stink in one's nostrils, stick in one's throat.

NAUSEATED, *adj.* Sick, sick at one's stomach, sick to one's stomach, ill, unwell, sickened, queasy, qualmish, squeamish, under the weather, offended, repelled, repulsed, digusted, qualmy.

NAUSEATING, *adj.* Nasty, offensive, odious, hateful, repellent, repugnant, repulsive, noxious, noisome, obnoxious, bad, foul, loathsome, disgusting, unsavory, execrable, fulsome, vile, nauseant, detestable, sickening, revolting, loathful.

NAUTICAL, *adj.* Marine, maritime, seafaring, seagoing, ocean-going, aquatic, oceanic, coasting, rowing, boating, yachting, natatory, natatorial, nautic.

NAVE, *n.* Hub, center, central part, central structure, hubble.

NAVEL, *n.* Pit, depression, umbilicus, central point, centrum, centroid, centy, center, omphalos.

NAVIGABLE, *adj.* Boatable, sailable, negotiable, watertight, seaworthy, open to navigation, waterproof, snug, tight, passable, unobstructed.

NAVIGATE, *v.* 1. Sail, cruise, ship, go by ship, go on a voyage, voyage, journey, journey by water, take a trip, take an ocean trip, carry sail, bear sail, carry canvas, perinavigate, circumnavigate, sail round, fly, plow the waves, ride the waves, gather way, make sail, coast, put to sea, scud, boom, ride, sail over, sail on.
2. Sail a course, steer a course, manage, plot a course, chart a course, direct, con, conn.

NAVIGATION, *n.* Navigating, seamanship, ocean

travel, seafaring, piloting, pilotage, pilotship, shipping, steerage, celestial navigation, circumnavigation, cruising, sailing, voyaging, boating, yachting, aquatics, spherical navigation, plane sailing, traverse sailing, great-circle sailing, parallel sailing, middle sailing, latitude sailing, mercator sailing.

NAVIGATOR, *n.* Sailor, mariner, seaman, seafarer, pilot, course plotter, sea dog, waterman, bluejacket, old salt, tar, Jack tar, common seaman, ordinary seaman, able seaman, marine, boatman, salt, man-o'-war's-man, gob (*sl.*), seafaring man, flier, aeronautical pilot.

NAVY, *n.* 1. Naval forces, first line of defense, defensive forces, attack forces, offensive forces, fleet, flotilla, task force, argosy, armada, squadron, division, mosquito fleet, naval militia, naval brigade, naval establishment, marine establishment.

2. Color, hue, shade, blue, marine blue, navy blue.

NEAR, *adj.* 1. Vicinal, in the vicinity of, approximate, contiguous, contingent, adjacent, adjoining, nigh, nearby, intimate, neighboring, propinquent, osculatory (*Geom.*), juxtapositional, juxtaposed, proximal, proximate, bordering, bordering on, close, close-at-hand, at hand, handy, near-at-hand, close by, by, around (*coll.*), about (*coll.*), in the neighborhood of, warm (*coll.*), hot (*coll.*), tangent, tangential, contactual, touching, connecting, conjoining, conterminous.

2. Imminent, momentary, impending, overhanging, lowering, menacing, looming, threatening, in the distance, approaching, expected, anticipated, looked for, future, brewing, preparing, immediate, instant, at hand, in store, in reserve, in the wind, to come, about to be, forthcoming, foreseen, eventual, coming.

3. Intimate, close, related, dear, familiar, brotherly, sisterly, fraternal, paternal, maternal, parental, neighborly, cordial, hearty, acquainted, on good terms with, devoted, thick (*coll.*), consanguineous, hand-in-hand, hand-in-glove, friendly, friendlike, amicable, sympathetic.

4. Short, straight, quick, close, immediate, ready, a stone's throw away, at close range, beside, alongside.

5. Resembling, literal, approximate, imitation, factitious, fraudulent, mock, mimic, imitative, representational, suggestive of, quasi, borrowed, second-hand, trumped-up, spurious, trick, tricky, fictive, counterfeit, purported, sham, bogus, false, feigned, simulated, forged, stamped, jerry-built, illusory, artificial, deceptive, misrepresentational, misrepresentative.

6. Penurious, parsimonious, close, tight (*coll.*), tight-fisted, pinching, penny-pinching, grasping, covetous, mean, skinflint, hard, hard-hearted, miserly, close-fisted, moneygrubbing, shabby, peddling, petty, selfish, mercenary, sordid, avaricious, greedy, venal, extortionate, rapacious, stinting, skimping, scrimping, grudging, sparing, illiberal, ungenerous, churlish, gripping, hard-headed, niggardly, penny-wise, stingy, careful.

NEAR, *adv.* Almost, nearly, most (*coll.*), nigh, well nigh, nigh onto, hereabout, approximately, approximatively, generally, in round numbers, roughly, roundly, close to, next door to, hard upon, within call, within view, within sight, within hearing, within earshot, within aid, within range, at the heels of, at close quarters, on the verge of, on the brink of, closely, near the mark, in juxtaposition, side by side, cheek to cheek, within an

ace of, thereabout, thereabouts, hardly, scarcely, barely, as good as, all but, about, within an inch of, not more than, fast by, verging on, bordering on, but a step, no distance from, *tête à tête* (*Fr.*), alongside, alongside of, on the threshold of.

NEAR, *v.* Move toward, approach, draw on, draw near, proximate, approximate, draw nigh, verge, come close to, anear, advance, advance nearer, come to close quarters, accede, steer for, hit for (*coll.*), light out for (*coll.*), set in toward, make for, meet, unite, come together, converge, close in upon, close with.

NEARING, *adj.* Approaching, convergent, converging, approximate, coming, approximating, next, oncoming, imminent, impending.

NEARLY, *adv.* Closely, approximately, almost, most (*coll.*), well nigh, nigh upon, nigh onto, nigh, about, not quite, all but, near the brink of, on the verge of, approximatively, barely, hardly, scarcely, say (*coll.*), thereabouts, somewhere about, somewhere near, all but, as good as, roughly, in round numbers, generally.

NEARNESS, *n.* Closeness, propinquity, proximation, proximateness, proximity, vicinity, vicinage, contiguity, contiguousness, neighborhood, precinct, adjacence, adjacency, contact, contingence, contingency, taction, touch, tangence, tangency, abuttal, abutment, touching, meeting, union, approach, approachment, access, brief span, a stone's throw, short step, environs, gunshot, purlieus, confines, consanguinity, relationship.

NEAR-SIGHTED, *adj.* 1. Short-sighted, myopic, myopical, mope-eyed.

2. Imperceptive, short-sighted, unperceptive, impercipient, unobservant, obstinate, stubborn, arbitrary, opinionated, dogmatic, hidebound, blind, purblind, dim-sighted, bigoted, prejudiced.

NEAR-SIGHTEDNESS, *n.* Myopia, myopy, short-sightedness, near sight, short sight.

NEAT, *adj.* 1. Clean, cleanly, orderly, regular, well-regulated, methodical, correct, uniform, tidy, shipshape, shapely, well made, well constructed, well turned out, untainted, unsoiled, unblemished, washed, immaculate, faultless, systematic, trim, trig, spruce, harmonious.

2. Felicitous, pat, apt, apposite, in point, to the point, applicable, pertinent, relevant, admissible, suitable, well put, well expressed, neatly put, neatly expressed, to the point, happy, germane, appurtenant.

3. Clever, adroit, deft, dexterous, dextrous, skillful, adept, apt, handy, quick, ready, Daedalian, ingenious, resourceful, neat-handed, fine-fingered, capable, competent.

4. Pure, simple, uniform, unalloyed, unadulterated, unmixed, straight, unblended, uncombined, uncompounded, undiluted, unwatered, clear, unmingled.

5. Commonplace, plain, simple, unvarnished, unornamented, natural, severe, chaste, pure, prosaic, homely, unadorned.

6. Epigrammatic, epigrammatical, concise, compendious, brief, short, economical, succinct, summary, compressed, elliptic, elliptical, crisp, sententious, curt, curtate, decurtate, to the point, pregnant, pointed, compact, condensed.

NEB, *n.* 1. Bill, tip, beak, olfactory organ, nose, smeller (*coll.*), snout, snoot (*coll.*), muzzle, proboscis, trunk, nib, pecker, breather (*coll.*), beezer (*coll.*), bugle (coll.).

2. Tip, point.

3. Mouth, Q. V.

NEBULA, *n.* 1. Film, fog, opacity, opaqueness.

2. Luminous vapor, planetary nebula, diffuse nebula, spiral nebula, bark nebula, nimbus, galactic nebula, anagalactic nebula.

NEBULOUS, *adj.* 1. Nebular, nebulose.

2. Obscure, hazy, indistinct, cloudy, cloudlike, dark, darkish, murky, ambiguous, indeterminate, muddy, faint, pale, uncertain, dim, vague, foggy, clouded, nubiferous, nubilated, shadowed, inchoate, confused.

NECESSARILY, *adv.* Naturally, as a result, it follows that, of course, accordingly, willy-nilly, will-he-nill-he, whether or no, by force of, without choice, compulsorily, inexorably, unpreventably, inescapably, ineluctably, irresistibly, fatefully, instinctively, automatically, mechanically, unwittingly, needs must, grudgingly, unconsciously, blindly.

NECESSARY, *adj.* 1. Unavoidable, inexorable, necessitous, necessitative, unevasible, ineluctable, indefeasible, irrevocable, inescapable, inevitable, uncontrollable, avoidless, irresistible, perforce, urgent, fateful, fit, fitting.

2. Requisite, essential, needful, indispensable, occasioned, wanted, needed, called for, in demand, desiderated, vital, requisitioned, desired, exigent, incumbent.

3. Peremptory, required, requisite, overbearing, binding, coercive, obligatory, obliging, choiceless, compulsory, compulsive, compelling, constraining, driving, imperative, pressing, importunate, coercitive, destined, fateful, elect, devoted, axiomatic, axiomated.

NECESSARY, *n.* 1. Prerequisite, prerequirement, requisite, requirement, essential, demand, want, need, essentiality, *sine qua non (Lat.),* desideratum, indispensable factor.

2. Water closet, toilet, rest room, W. C., men's room, ladies' room, lady's room, washroom, bathroom, latrine, backhouse, outhouse, john *(coll.),* johnny *(coll.),* jakes *(coll.),* comfort station, lavatory, privy, cloaca.

NECESSITATE, *v.* 1. Cause, require, force, drive, insist on, make, press, bring pressure to bear upon, enforce, coerce, dragoon, make a point of, say something must be done, constrain, oblige, impel, concuss.

2. Need, want, desiderate, lack, have occasion for, create a need for, create a necessity for, call for, make necessary, stand in need of, find indispensable, be incumbent upon, pertain to, make unavoidable.

3. Destine, foredoom, appoint, predetermine, foreordain, preordain.

NECESSITOUS, *adj.* 1. See NECESSARY, 1-3.

2. Needy, poor, destitute, indigent, pinching, pinched, narrow, in dire straits, in need, in want, poverty-stricken, short, short of funds, short of cash, short of goods, reduced, in reduced circumstances, moneyless, impoverished, out of pocket.

NECESSITY, *n.* 1. Compulsion, obligation, necessitude, obligement, inevitability, inevitableness, uncontrollability, irrevocability, unavoidability, inescapability, ineluctability, indefeasibility, spur of necessity, inevasibility, destiny, destination, Hobson's choice, portion, dispensation, fatality, fate, kismet, fortune, lot, doom, press, pressure, urgency, duress, constraint, coercion, choicelessness, inexorability, unpreventability, necessitation.

2. Demand, requirement, need, *sine qua non (Lat.),* necessaries, necessities, essential, want, desideratum, prerequisite, prerequirement, desideration, stress, pinch, needfulness, matter of life and death, case of life and death, the least one can do, prerequisition, essentiality, exigency, necessitativeness, necessitousness, requisition, last resort.

3. Poverty, need, want, impecuniosity, impecuniousness, indigence, difficulties, straits, straitened circumstances, privation, neediness, penury, pauperism, bad circumstances, poor circumstances, reduced circumstances, slender means, hand-to-mouth existence, broken fortune, extreme need, extreme want, extremity.

NECK, *n.* Isthmus, cervix, nape, scruff, narrowing, constriction, junction, narrows, kill, gullet, hals, cut, jugulum, channel.

NECKBAND, *n.* Neckcloth, neckpiece, collar, choker, collar band, band, cloth, cravat.

NECKCLOTH, *n.* Scarf, neckpiece, neckband, necktie, cravat, jabot, tie, neckerchief, bandanna, choker, stock, collar, ruff, tucker, guimpe, chemisette, soubise, four-in-hand, bow tie, ascot.

NECKLACE, *n.* Chaplet, beads, locket, bauble, jewelry, lavaliere, chain, sultana, gorget, ornament, decoration, encirclement, band, carcanet, riviere.

NECROLOGY, *n.* Register, registrar of deaths, death registry, death record, record, obituary, chronicle, account, death notice.

NECROMANCER, *n.* Magician, diviner, medium, witch doctor, spiritualist, conjuror, mage, magus, sorcerer, wizard, warlock, thaumaturge, thaumaturgist, bewitcher, enchanter, enchantress, witch, exorcist, dowser, theurgist, seer, soothsayer, charmer, wonderworker, miracleworker.

NECROMANCY, *n.* Sorcery, thaumaturgy, thaumaturgia, thaumaturgics, thaumaturgism, incantation, exorcism, exorcisation, conjuring, conjuration, conjurement, divination, gramarye, glamour, rune, magic, feats of magic, wizardry, enchantment, witchery, witchcraft, fetishism, voodoo, voodooism, shamanism, bewitchery, bewitchment, black magic, demonry, demonism, diabolism, demonianism, Black Mass, entrancement, obi.

NECROMANTIC, *adj.* Magic, magical, talismanic, cabalistic, sorcerous, witchy, witchlike, shaman, shamanic, telesmatic, telesmatical, phylacteric, phylacterical, magian, weird, Circean.

NECROPOLIS, *n.* Mausoleum, sepulcher, burying place, cemetery, graveyard, burial ground, boneyard, polyandrium, golgotha, memorial park, city of the dead, village of the dead, God's acre, potter's field, tomb.

NECROPSY, *n.* Post-mortem, autopsy, necroscopy, post-mortem examination.

NECROSIS, *n.* Decay, decomposition, morbid condition, putrefaction, putridity, death, dead tissue, gangrene, sphacelus, corruption, enantheme, mortification, caries, slough, rot, rotting, disintegration, dissolution, rottenness, cariosity, exenthema, sphacelation.

NECTAREOUS, *adj.* Nectareal, sweet, dulcet, sugary, oversweet, cloying, sugared, honied, saccharine, honey-sweet, sugar-sweet, candied, savory, rich, luscious, melliferous, delectable, delicious, toothsome, tasty, good, nice, honeyed.

NEED, *v.* Demand, require, have occasion for, have use for, call for, requisition, lack, want, desiderate, necessitate, stand in need of, exact, force, make a demand of, covet, hunger for, crave, thirst for, yearn for, claim, find necessary, find indispensable, not be able to do without.

NEEDLE, *n.* 1. Pin, bodkin, dibble, tool, implement, device, probe, trocar, piercer, perforator, punch, puncturer, darner.

2. Style, stylus, etching point, engraver, engraving tool, engraver's point, dry point, tracer.

3. Pine needle, foliage, leaf, leafage, verdure, foliation.

4. Pointer, hand, indicator, compass hand.

NEEDLE-SHAPED, *adj.* Needle-like, aciculated, aciform, acicular, aciculate, spiculate, spiculated, pointed, sharp, keen, long, slender, thin.

NEEDLESS, *adj.* Superfluous, unnecessary, redundant, excessive, *de trop (Fr.)*, uncalled for, supererogatory, useless, disposable, dispensable, unavailing, pleonastic, tautological, wordy, periphrastic, circumlocutory, ambagious, wanton, unrequired, supervaneous, duplicate, duplicated, superabundant, overabundant.

NEEDLEWOMAN, *n.* Dressmaker, *modiste (Fr.)*, needleworker, seamstress, sempstress, couturiere, stitcher, sewer, knitter, Tricoteuse.

NEEDLEWORK, *n.* Stitching, sewing, lacework, tapestry, needlepoint, petit point, grospoint, embroidery, tatting, fancywork, point lace, crochet, crocheting, trimming, insertion, ornamentation, knotwork, broidery, broider.

NE'ER-DO-WELL, *n.* Scamp, scalawag, rogue, rascal, knave, loafer, scapegrace, blackguard, losel, good-for-nothing, black sheep, recreant, miscreant, reprobate, rake, rakehell, bad example, spendthrift, roué, lost sheep, defaulter, vagrant, rover, outcast, wastrel.

NEFARIOUS, *adj.* Evil, bad, abominable, atrocious, confounded, deplorable, vile, foul, peccant, infernal, base, iniquitous, wicked, hellish, outrageous, devilish, odious, obnoxious, wrong, arrant, grievous, lamentable, execrable, diabolical, unmentionable, unspeakable, ungodly, sinister, detestable, despicable, regrettable, contemptible, disreputable, felonious, discreditable, malignant, insidious, hateful, grave, black, rank, depraved, vicious, disgraceful, scurvy, fulsome, noisome, cursed, accursed, damned, damnable, damnatory, damnific, beastly, ghastly, infamous, shameful, scandalous, heinous, villainous, shocking, flagitious, flagrant, gross, indecent, dishonorable, mean, low, ignoble, ignominious, incorrigible, immoral, demoralized, recreant, miscreant, unpardonable, unforgivable, dreadful, horrible, horrific, unrighteous, improper, criminal, unhallowed, unblessed, reprehensible, mischievous, profligate, opprobrious, brazen, enormous.

NEGATE, *v.* Deny, forswear, abrogate, refute, rebut, negative, contradict, contravert, contravene, disaffirm, disavow, disallow, revoke, refuse, protest, grudge, begrudge, renounce, abjure, doubt, retract, recant, confute, set aside, quash, prohibit, traverse, oppose, gainsay, dispute, impugn, nullify, veto, repeal, disclaim, disown, belie, give the lie to, join issue upon, repudiate, invalidate, answer, defeat, confound, vanquish, quell, squash, silence, squelch, settle, floor, overthrow, overwhelm, answer, reply to, parry, dismiss.

NEGATION, *n.* 1. Disaffirmation, recusance, recusancy, recusation, rebuttal, refutation, confutation, disproof, counterevidence, recantation, retraction, withdrawal, rejection, gainsaying, gainsay, traversal, contradiction, contraversion, contravention, forswearing, denial, abnegation, dis-

avowal, disowning, disownment, disclaimer, disclamation, abjuration, abjurement, dissent, refusal, nonagreement, disagreement, protest, protestation, prohibition, veto, repeal.

2. Nonexistence, oblivion, nullity, nothingness, existlessness, nonentity, nonbeing, nonsubsistence, nihility, nihilism, negativeness, abeyance, abeyancy, vacuity, blank, blankness.

NEGATIVE, *n.* 1. Print, picture, photograph, snapshot, exposure, frame, shot.

2. Die, mold, impression, matrix, last, intaglio, stamp, punch, seal, mint.

NEGATIVE, *adj.* 1. Nonexistent, void, null, nonsubsistent, inexistent, minus, missing, absent, blank, omitted, deleted, existenceless, null and void.

2. Opposite, contradictory, contrary, converse, reverse, contrasted, contrasting, inverse, dead against, anti-, opposed, opposing, antipodal, antipodean, antipodic, clashing, conflicting, inimical, repugnant, antagonistic, abjuratory, abnegative, denied, denying, inconsistent, recusant, at issue, at odds with, revocatory, dissentient, confutative, dissident, protestant, nonjurant, unconvinced, unconverted. See NEGATE, v.

NEGLECT, *v.* 1. Blink at, ignore, let (it) ride, overlook, disregard, forget, omit, pass over, slight, pass by, pass up, connive at, lose sight of, take no notice of, let slip, let slide, let go, fail, skimp *(coll.)*, scamp, make light of, shirk, cut, be inattentive, be heedless, abandon, be remiss, gloss over, wink at, blink at, take no note of, shake off.

2. Do without, not use, dispense with, abstain from, waive, leave undone, disregard, forbear, not touch, leave alone, shun, renounce, repudiate, default, despise, disesteem, contemn, slight.

NEGLECT, *n.* Neglectfulness, inattention, cut, cold shoulder, inactivity, uncompletion, unfulfillment, unachievement, unactivity, inaction, inertness, snub, indolence, nonchalance, imprudence, laches, laxity, laxness, negligence, negligency, remissness, inadvertence, inadvertency, disregard, *laisser-faire (Fr.), laisser-aller (Fr.),* abandonment, default, omission, oversight, slight, disregard, disregardance, delay, deferment, procrastination, noncompletion, nonpreparation, recklessness, improvidence, inaccuracy, rashness, slovenliness, inexactitude, inexactness, dormancy, idleness, stasis, passivity, passiveness, passivism, stagnation, stillness, unfitness, unreadiness, unpreparedness, nonpreparation, indifference, dilatoriness, quiescence, repose, rest, laziness, sloth, indiligence, inexertion, inertia, ergophobia, otiosity, languor, languidness, truancy, insolence, dereliction, incautiousness, incaution, slackness, noncompliance.

NEGLECTFUL, *adj.* Slack, remiss, forgetful, indifferent, heedless, perfunctory, sloppy, dilatory, cursory, negligent, neglective, unheeding, unthinking, unmindful, forgetful, unsolicitous, lax, inconsiderate, thoughtless, respectless, disregardful, disregardant, offhand, imprudent, procrastinating, procrastinative, cunctatious, cunctatory, indolent, lazy, slothful, inattentive, unobservant, oblivious, unmindful, shiftless, improvident, inadvertent, happy-go-lucky, insouciant, careless, devil-may-care, unguarded, thriftless, offhand, donothing, fainéant, laggard, lackadaisical, maudlin, inconstant, unfaithful, indiscreet, injudicious, temerarious, untrue, loose, slipshod, unwatchful.

NEGLIGEE, *n.* Dishabille, undress, nightdress, nightgown, robe, house coat, hostess coat, kimono, wrapper, bathrobe, peignoir, morning dress, *décolleté (Fr.), robe de chambre (Fr.),* dressing gown.

NEGOTIATE, *v.* 1. Bargain, transact, contract, mediate, intercede, intermediate, arrange, intervene, interpose, propitiate, submit, agree to arbitration, arbitrate, arrange, parley, confer, meet, umpire, bid for, dicker *(coll.),* haggle, make terms, come to terms, straighten out, adjust, adjust difference, meet halfway, stipulate, referee, treat, patch up, interfere, step in.

2. Placate, accommodate, settle, settle differences, settle disputes, put in tune, pacify, conciliate, appease, propitiate, adjust, bring to terms.

3. Transfer, convey, transmit, pass, pass over, deliver, make over, sign over, consign, hand over, hand down, turn down.

4. Leap, jump, jump over, vault, spring, bound, upleap, upspring, clear, hurdle, make (a hurdle) *(coll.).*

NEGOTIATION, *n.* 1. Mediation, arbitration, arbitrament, diplomacy, diplomatics, intervention, interposition, interference, intercession, intermediation, diplomatism, parley, conciliation, pacification, treaty, deal.

2. Transaction, treaty, compact, agreement, understanding, parley, contract, dicker *(coll.),* bond, covenant, convention, engagement, stipulation, barter, bargain, bargaining, trade, trading, collective bargaining, transfer.

NEGOTIATOR, *n.* Delegate, peacemaker, mediator, intermediator, intermediary, moderator, arbiter, arbitrator, make-peace, envoy, ambassador, emissary, representative, agent, prolocutor, prolocutrix, spokesman, pacifier, pacificator, propitiator, reconciler, diplomat, diplomatist, diplomatic agent, negotiant, negotiatrix, referee, referendary, umpire, middleman, medium, go-between, intercessor, interceder, internuncio, interpleader, plenipotentiary.

NEGRESS, *n.* Negro, colored woman, black, mammy *(coll.),* wench, auntie *(coll.).* See NEGRO.

NEGRO, *n.* Colored man, man of color, negress, colored woman, nigger *(contemp.),* darky, black, Ethiopian, black fellow, blackamoor, Moor, Bantu, Sudanese, Negrito, Negrillo, Hottentot, Melanesian, Papuan, Senegambian, Mandingo, Krooman, buck *(coll.),* quadroon, octoroon, mestee, mestizo, zambo, Sambo, Afro-American, Afro-European, Afro-Asiatic, mulatto, Congo, pygmy, Nigritian, melanian, bushman.

NEGRO, *adj.* Negroid, racial, negrous, negrine, negricant, negritic, negritudinous.

NEIGH, *v.* 1. Whinny, nicker, hinny, cry, call.

2. Exult, triumph, joy, rejoice, jubilate, chuckle, cackle, gloat, cheer, glory, crow, crow over.

NEIGHBOR, *n.* Bystander, acquaintance, associate, friend, borderer.

NEIGHBOR, *v.* Conjoin, be near, touch, meet, adjoin, abut, border, border on, impinge, lap, append, connect, come into contact, meet, verge upon, stand by.

NEIGHBORHOOD, *n.* 1. Purlieus, vicinity, vicinage, sphere, quarter, precincts, region, part, locality, presence, confines.

2. Surroundings, environs, environment, suburbs, borderlands, outskirts, circumjacencies, circumambiences.

3. See NEARNESS.

NEIGHBORING, *adj.* Close, near, nearby, adjacent, contiguous, juxtapositional, at hand, to hand,

near at hand, circumjacent, circumambient, circumfluent, surrounding, proximal, proximate, approximate, bordering, bordering on, propinquant, adjoining, around, lying close to, nigh, vicinal, in proximity, attiguous, contiguous, abutting.

NEIGHBORLY, *adj.* 1. Friendly, warm-hearted, generous, kind, kindly, intimate, well-disposed, kindly-disposed, amiable, affable, agreeable, considerate, helpful, unhostile, close, near, cordial, hearty, amicable, amical, brotherly, sisterly, chummy *(coll.),* courteous, thoughtful, polite, civil, obliging, gracious, harmonious.

2. Sociable, solicitous, familiar, attentive, accessible, companionable, gregarious, hospitable, convivial.

NEITHER, *pron. and adj.* Not one or the other, not either, none.

NEMESIS, *n.* Retribution, revenge, vengeance, punishment, justice, retributive justice.

NEOLOGISM, *n.* Coinage, coinage of words, coinage of phrases, neology, neoterism, new word, neonism, new term, new phrase, nonce word, vogue word, manufactured word, synthetic word.

NEOLOGIST, *n.* Modernist, linguist, modernizer, neoterist, neoteric, word coiner, innovator, coiner of words or phrases.

NEOLOGY, *n.* 1. Introduction, innovation, new words, coinage, novelty, invention, devising.

2. New doctrine.

NEOPHYTE, *n.* Convert, beginner, tyro, proselyte, disciple, catechumen, learner, novice, novitiate, probationer, apprentice, entrant, newcomer, tenderfoot, pupil, student.

NEOTERIC, *adj.* Neological, new, modern, novel, recent, late, neologic, fresh, newfangled *(coll.),* new-fashioned, up-to-date.

NEOTERISM, *n.* 1. See NEOLOGY.

2. Recentness, newness, novelty, modernity, up-to-dateness.

NEPHALISM, *n.* Prohibitionism, soberness, sobriety, teetotalism, teetotalitarianism, temperance, abstention, abstainment, abstemiousness, eschewal, total abstinence, abstinence, avoidance.

NEPHALIST, *n.* Abstainer, prohibitionist, hydropot, Rechabite, temperance advocate, teetotaller, abstainer, water-drinker.

NEPOTISM, *n.* Partisanship, partiality, family patronage, favoritism, warp, bias, inclination, tendency, prejudice, leaning, injustice, inequity, unfairness, inequitableness, partisanism.

NEPTUNE, *n.* Poseidon, sea god, Oceanus, Triton, old man of the sea, god of the sea.

NEREID, *n.* Oceanid, sea nymph, water sprite, ocean sprite, sea maid, water nymph, mermaid, siren, undine.

NERVE, *n.* 1. Vigor, strength, force, grit, puissance, power, might, lustiness, stalwartness, physical strength, physical force, brute strength, brute force, robustness, vitality.

2. Courage, intrepidity, dash, daring, boldness, bravery, resolution, resoluteness, fearlessness, valor, spunk *(coll.),* gallantry, audacity, derring-do, prowess, chivalry, pluck, grit, mettle, backbone *(coll.),* stamina, endurance, guts *(coll.),* hardihood, fortitude, virtue, heart, bulldog courage, stout-heartedness, mettlesomeness, doughtiness, gameness, boldness, spirit, confidence, self-assurance, self-reliance, heroism, coolness, steadiness, hardiness.

3. Assumption, presumption, gall, insolence, impudence, arrogance, impertinence, procacity, assurance, flippance, flippancy, petulance, petulancy, effrontery, brass (coll.), cheek (coll.), shamelessness, cheekiness (coll.), crust (coll.), brazenness, brass (coll.), malapertness, contemptuousness, sauciness, sauce (coll.), sass (coll.).

NERVE, v. Embolden, invigorate, hearten, cheer, encourage, rally, inspirit, harden, vitalize, revitalize, innervate, brace, bolster, fortify, strengthen, inspire, inspirit, inspire courage, instill courage, put on one's mettle.

NERVELESS, adj. 1. Soft, flaccid, drooping, languid, powerless, impotent, debilitated, marrowless, listless, sinewless, unmanned, unnerved, enervated, demoralized, unhardened, feeble, asthenic, weak, weakly, emasculate, forceless, paralyzed, palsied, enfeebled.

2. Controlled, self-controlled, courageous, fearless, brave, intrepid, doughty, inexcitable, unexcitable, imperturbable, undisturbable, placid, peaceful, unruffled, calm, unimpassioned, impassive, dispassionate, undemonstrative, philosophical, steady, steady-nerved, steady-handed, sure-handed, deft, cool, cool-headed, level-headed, self-possessed, collected.

NERVOUS, adj. 1. Vigorous, mordant, mettlesome, impressive, incisive, trenchant, biting, forceful, powerful, strong, energetic, nervy, robust, graphic.

2. Disquieted, unquiet, disturbed, ruffled, excited, excitable, feverish, mercurial, volatile, fussy, alarmed, startled, jumpy, scared, scary, uneasy, disquieted, moody, intolerant, fear-struck, fear-stricken, apprehensive, timid, timorous, fearful, shy, diffident, anxious, jittery, tremulous, shaky, skittish, restless, fidgety, high-strung, peevish, neurotic, irritable, impatient, appalled, horrified, dismayed, restive, restless, unquiet, trembling, shaking, palsied, irascible, clamorous, chafing, febrile, galvanic, electric, chafed, delirious, wild, furious, rampant, rabid, mad, enthusiastic, overzealous, fierce, demonstrative, inflammable, impassioned, fanatic, fanatical, fiery, hot-headed, violent, hysterical, shaking, perturbed, quivering, turbulent, roiling, boiling, riled (coll.), boisterous, ungovernable, irrepressible, volcanic, fulminating, rash, impetuous, quick, madcap, unstrung, panic-stricken, tense.

NERVOUSNESS, n. 1. Strength, sinew, brute force, might, main, vigor, lustiness, lustihood, forcibleness, robustness, stoutness, vitality, physical strength, muscle, beef (coll.), brawn, brawniness, puissance, stamina, thews, grit, fortitude, guts (sl.), nerve, spring, power, energy, elasticity, pith, pithiness.

2. Excitability, fear, trembling, timorousness, fear, the shakes (coll.), vehemence, perturbation, disturbance, flutter, panting, agitation, disquiet, irritability, turbulence, impatience, fluster, trepidation, trepidity, ferment, fuss, flurry, fidgets (coll.), fidgetiness, irascibility, intolerance, restlessness, ruffle, perturbance, perturbancy, pother, bother, stew (coll.), distraction, effervescence, panic, tension, hysteria, tremor, unrest, inquietude, ebullition, fume, stage fright, shaking, quivering, quavering, buck fever (coll.), twitching, tic, panting, heaving, the shakes (coll.), floccilation, vellication, chorea, St. Vitus' dance, megrims, the creeps (coll.).

NERVY, adj. (Slang) 1. Insolent, disrespectful, impolite, brash, importunate, presumptuous, mala-

pert, impertinent, insulting, audacious, impudent, cheeky (coll.), procacious, flippant, flip (coll.), fresh (sl.), saucy, precocious, bodacious, cocky (coll.), smart, assured, overconfident, cocksure, ungentlemanly, unladylike, unceremonious, uncourtly, unmannerly, ill-bred, ill-behaved, ill-conditioned, rude, unbred, unpolished, contumelious, improper, unseemly, crass, crude, coarse, vulgar, unrefined, indelicate, tasteless, in bad form, in bad taste, indecorous.

2. Energetic, sinewy, strong, pithy, mighty, powerful, puissant, vigorous, forceful, brawny, gutsy (sl.), stout, stalwart, robust, beefy (coll.), muscular, lusty, vital.

3. Brave, courageous, intrepid, daring, plucky, venturesome, valiant, valorous, gallant, mettlesome, gritty (coll.), stout, stout-hearted, bold, bold-spirited, high-spirited, audacious, fearless, dreadless, dauntless, dreadnought, undaunted, unappalled, unabashed, unflinching, unshrinking, unblenching, unapprehensive, assured, confident, game, doughty, heroic, chivalrous, enterprising, adventurous, venturous.

NESCIENCE, n. Perplexity, ignorance, unenlightenment, unacquaintance, want of knowledge, unscience, illiterateness, darkness, benightedness, benightment, unlearnedness, uninformedness, uncomprehension, uncognizance, greenness, blindness, naivete, newness, dullardism, stolidity, numskullery (coll.), crass ignorance, inexperience, unintelligence, obtuseness, unwisdom.

NESS, n. Promontory, point, point of land, headland, cape, foreland, naze, bill, spur, mull, tongue, neck, neck of land.

NEST, n. 1. Multitude, shoal, swarm, group, crowd, bevy, horde, large number, abundance, batch, pack, lot, set, series, assemblage, cluster, clutch, scores, quantities, members, cloud, herd, flock, covey, drove, brood, litter, farrow, fry.

2. Nursery, birthplace, cradle, womb, breeding place, hotbed, incubator, venter (Legal).

3. House, home, habitation, dwelling, domicile, retreat, resting place, perch, refuge, anchorage, hermitage, cloister, cell, aerie, eyrie, roost, covert, hole, hiding place, arbor, bower, asylum, dugout, den, purlieu, hangout (sl.), haunt, resort, mew, cavern, grotto.

NESTLE, v. Snuggle, inhabit, occupy, nest, tenant, remain, stay, reside, clasp, enfold, embrace, coddle, nuzzle, fondle, pet, cosset, caress, cuddle, lie snug, lodge, live, abide, dwell, lie, be, exist.

NESTLING, n. Birdling, fledgling, chick, child, infant, weanling, babe, baby, nursling, suckling.

NET, n. 1. Mesh, meshwork, network, web, webwork, lattice, latticework, tissue, reticulum, lace, lacing, lacery, riddle, sieve, sifter, seine, screen, screening, weave, cloth, textile, fabric, woven fabric, cheesecloth, butter muslin, lace, reticella, reticello, tapestry, wicker, wickerwork, mat, matting, trellis, tracery, fretwork, fret, plexus, plexure, filigree, braid, plait, plat (coll.), intertwist, twist, grid, gridiron, veiling, mosquito netting, grate, grating, grille, grillwork, interweave.

2. Trap, snare, spring, meshes, bobbinet, toils, spider web, cobweb, gin, fyke.

NET, v. 1. Gain, realize, profit by, gather, gather in, collect, bag, sack, take in, accumulate, secure, pocket, obtain, pick, pick up, collect, earn, win, acquire, come by, receive, be in receipt of, bring, bring in, clear above expenses, clear a profit of, take along.

2. Snare, ensnare, enclose, capture, take, seize,

apprehend, lay hold of, lay by the heels, snap, snap up, catch, sack, pocket, hook, snag, clutch, clasp, grip, grapple, get hold of, take prisoner, take captive, make captive, dragnet, enmesh, entangle, trawl, seine, dredge.

NETHER, *adj.* Lower, downward, inferior, underlying, basal, bottom, basic, fundamental, subjacent, under, subordinate, less advanced *(Biol.),* earlier *(Geol.),* nadiral, low.

NETTED, *adj.* 1. Webbed, weblike, retiform, reticular, reticuled, reticulated, reticulose, reticulate, acrolar, acrolate, acrolated, latticed, grated, woven, textile, retiary, plexiform, plexal, complex, complicated, webby, meshed, meshlike, interwoven, woven.

2. Caught, captured, ensnared, enmeshed, caught in the toils, brought up, enclosed, seized, apprehended, laid hold of, laid by the heels, snapped, snapped up, sacked, bagged, pocketed, snagged, clutched, clasped, gripped, grappled, taken prisoner, made captive, taken captive, entangled, seined, trawled.

NETTING, *n.* Mesh, meshwork, network, web, webwork, lattice, latticework, tissue, reticulum, lace, lacing, lacery, riddle, sieve, sifter, seine, screen, screening, weave, cloth, textile, fabric, woven fabric, cheesecloth, butter muslin, lace, reticella, reticello, tapestry, wicker, wickerwork, mat, matting, trellis, tracery, fret, fretwork, plexus, plexure, filigree, braid, plait, plat *(coll.),* interweave, intertwist, twist, grid, gridiron, veiling, mosquito netting, grate, grating, grille, grillwork.

NETTLE, *v.* Discomfort, annoy, pester, harass, irritate, vex, plague, beset, throw into a ferment, tweak one's nose, persecute, badger, harry, heckle, bait, get *(sl.),* get one's goat *(coll.),* gripe, chafe, grate, enchafe, provoke, sting, gall, bait, tease, bullyrag, tantalize, infest, enrage, affront, aggravate *(coll.),* burn up *(coll.),* try one's patience, try the patience of Job, worry, molest, offend, sour, ruffle, aggrieve, roil *(coll.),* rile *(coll.),* pique, incense, incite, excite, discompose, make one's gorge rise, make one's choler rise, madden, make one's blood boil, hurt one's feelings, stir up, wound, irk, anger, kindle, enkindle, displease, kindle wrath, make one hot under the collar *(coll.),* insult, drive one mad, exasperate, burn.

NETTLED, *adj.* Vexed, angered, angry, irate, irked, piqued, annoyed, fazed, feazed *(coll.),* hot, hot under the collar *(coll.),* ruffled, wrathful, ireful, mad *(coll.),* sore, disturbed, dismayed, discomforted, offended, perturbed, tormented, worried, harried, harassed, chafed, enchafed, galled, riled *(coll.),* roiled *(coll.),* wounded, stung, injured, bitter, acrimonious, rancorous, virulent, querulous, soured, sour, sullen, acerb, acerbic, hurt, resentful, uneasy, disquieted, displeased, troubled, bothered, annoyed, irritated, irascible, grouchy, testy, wrathful, peevish, petty, huffy, petulant, illhumored, ill-tempered, bad-tempered, out of humor, out of sorts, cross, grumpy, pestered, plagued, beset, badgered, heckled, baited, griped, provoked, teased, bullyragged, tantalized, infested, aggravated *(coll.),* burned up *(coll.),* impatient, molested, offended, soured, aggrieved, incensed, incited, aroused, excited, discomposed, maddened, stirred up, agitated.

NETLIKE, *adj.* Webbed, weblike, webby, woven, interwoven, textile, retiary, meshed, enmeshed, meshlike, complex, complicated, plexal, plexiform, grated, latticed, fretted, cancellate, cancelled,

acrolar, acrolate, acrolated, retiform, reticulate, reticulated, reticule, reticuled, reticulose.

NETWORK, *n.* Tissue, webwork, mat, matting, reticulum, net, netting, mesh, sieve, cobweb, spider web, filigree, reticle, reticule, complex, complexus, maze, meander, labyrinth, wilderness, jungle, tangle, interconnection, ramification, gridiron, openwork, fretwork, system, plait, plat *(coll.),* braid, cancellation, plexure, intertexture, grid, tracery, structure, fabric, weave, ganglion *(Med.),* intercement, interlacing, grillwork, grille, wattle, trellis, latticework, lattice, grate, grating, organization, screening, screen, lace, lacery, lacing.

NEURAL, *adj.* Posterior, posterial, dorsal, gluteal, lumbar, back, tergal, nerve.

NEUROSIS, *n.* Psychoneurosis, mental disorder, emotional disorder, emotional disturbance, mental disturbance, aberration, neurasthenia, emotional instability, compulsion neurosis, anxiety neurosis, pathoneurosis, neurotic condition, disorder, psychoneurotic condition, disorientation, psychasthenia, nervous disorder, myoneurosis, acroneurosis, neuroticism.

NEUROTIC, *adj.* Emotionally unstable, psychoneurotic, neurasthenic, manic-depressive, unstable, disoriented, emotionally unstable, aberrant, pathoneurotic, compulsive neurotic, disturbed, psychasthenic, acroneurotic, myoneurotic, sick, disturbed, upset.

NEUTER, *adj.* Asexual, neutral, sexless, fallow, barren, impotent, unfertile, sterile.

NEUTRAL, *adj.* 1. Middle, neuter, in the middle, center, impartial, mean, fifty-fifty *(sl.),* neither one nor the other, even, evenly balanced, average, normal, intermediate, intermediary, medial, indefinite, without choice, undistinguished, indistinct, half-and-half.

2. Irresolute, undecided, undetermined, unsettled, vague, colorless, nonchalant, doubleminded, vacillating, hesitating, hesitant, shillyshallying, wobbly, inert, unconcerned, indifferent, middling, of two minds, nonpartisan, noncombatant, pacific, pacifistic, impartial, peaceful, peaceable, nonparticipating, nonparticipant, unbelligerent, noninterfering, noninterventionist, disinterested, unbiased, unaffected, disaffected, aloof, remote, Olympian, unimplicated, withdrawn, dispassionate.

NEUTRALITY, *n.* Peacefulness, peace, peaceability, nonpartisanship, aloofness, disinterestedness, noninterference, nonintervention, inertness, unconcern, indecision, indecisiveness, nonchalance, freedom from war, quiescence, noncombatance, truce, nonbelligerence, dispassionateness, unaffectedness, disaffectedness, unconcernedness, midcourse, middle of the road, middle state, indetermination, happy medium, pacifism, irresolution, indetermination, vagueness, colorlessness, vacillation, hesitation, hesitancy, shilly-shallying, impartiality, nonparticipance, nonparticipation, Olympian indifference, withdrawal.

NEUTRALIZATION, *n.* Counteraction, opposition, incapacitation, disabling, nullification, counterpoise, countervailing, compensation, ballast, ballasting, counterbalance, counterbalancing, disenabling, deadening, depotentiation, equalization, contravention, contradiction, refutation, rebuttal, countermand, countermanding, clash, collision, check, frustration, hindrance, undoing, cancellation, bafflement, resistance, balancing, invalidation, repression, suppression, setoff, counterpoise, killing, liquidation, counterblast, check, checkmate, impasse, stymie, reaction, annulment.

NEUTRALIZE, *v.* Compensate, prevent, resist, impede, stop, halt, kill, oppose, clash, countervail, withstand, overpower, overcome, defeat, interfere, interfere with, frustrate, oppose, annul, negate, contradict, contravene, undo, offset, antagonize, baffle, balance, counterbalance, react, nullify, repress, restrain, overcome, refute, rebut, militate against, react, cancel, incapacitate, disable, disenable, deaden, equalize, depotentiate, suppress, checkmate, stymie, block.

NEVER, *adv.* At no time, under no circumstances, *sine die (Lat.),* at no period, nevermore, on no occasion, never in the world, never in one's born days *(coll.),* at all, not at any time, not at all, none, ne'er, to no degree, on the Greek calends.

NEVER-CEASING, *adj.* Perpetual, timeless, dateless, incessant, unceasing, unstopping, continuous, continued, consecutive, unrelenting, unremitting, endless, perennial, constant, unintermitting, unbroken, uninterrupted, infinite, unending, sustained, unstopped, customary, wonted, regular, accustomary, persistent, chronic, boundless, illimitable, limitless, never-ending, repeated, repetitive, recurrent, recurring, steady, habitual, ever-living, long-lived, ever-flowing, enduring, eternal, sempiternal, sempiternous.

NEVER-DYING, *adj.* Illimitable, incessant, long-lived, lasting, steadfast, steady, stable, abiding, longeval, longevous, deathless, immortal, undying, sempiternal, sempiternous, everlasting, perdurable, enduring, coeternal, timeless, permanent, continual, sempervirent, unfading, never-fading, imperishable, never-ceasing, unceasing, unstopped, unstopping, consecutive, endless, perennial, sustained, persistent, chronic, limitless, never-ending, never-stopping, ever-flowing.

NEVER-ENDING, *adj.* Perpetual, timeless, dateless, incessant, unceasing, unstopping, continuous, continued, consecutive, unrelenting, unremitting, endless, perennial, constant, unintermitting, unbroken, uninterrupted, infinite, unending, sustained, unstopped, customary, wonted, steady, regular, accustomary, persistent, chronic, boundless, illimitable, limitless, never-ceasing, repeated, repetitive, recurrent, recurring, habitual, everliving, long-lived, longevous, ever-flowing, enduring, perdurable, eternal, sempiternal, sempiternous, imperishable, stable, steady, steadfast, abiding, sempervirent, unfading, never-fading, lasting.

NEVERTHELESS, *adv.* Nonetheless, natheless *(Arch.),* after all, on the other hand, by any manner of means, in spite of, despite, in the face of, in the teeth of, excepting, anyway, anyhow, regardless, in any way, notwithstanding, all the same, yet, still, however, howbeit, albeit, although, though, at all events, in any event, be that as it may, for all that, even so, after all is said and done, in defiance of, contrarily, otherwise, contrariwise, taking one consideration with another, by any means.

NEVER-TIRING, *adj.* Unfaltering, unflagging, unremitting, unhesitating, persevering, unwavering, untiring, unintermitting, unhesitant, assiduous, industrious, diligent, studious, attentive, businesslike, energetic, never idle, unsleeping, sleepless, ever-waking, intent, stanch, unyielding, solid, steadfast, steady, unbending, inflexible, strongminded, strong-willed, uncompromising, indomitable, intransigent, unswerving, unflinching, undrooping, unwearying, unwearied, indefatigable,

game, game to the last, relentless, unrelenting, sedulous, plodding, mettlesome, plucky, painstaking, dogged, tenacious, pertinacious, persisting, resolute.

NEW, *adj.* 1. Recent, modern, up-to-date, fresh, green, vernal, maiden, advanced, newborn, newfledged, of yesterday, neoteric, neoterical, virgin, immature, young, youthful, untouched, intact, untried, fresh as a daisy, late, raw, later, unusual, extraordinary, immature, abreast of the times, brand-new, brand-spanking-new, hot, just out, newly issued, lately issued, hot off the griddle *(coll.),* up-to-the-minute, up-to-date, unfledged, unripe, sappy, budding, novel, newfangled *(derog.),* of recent make, of recent period, spick and span, spanking, spanking new, ultra-modern, modernistic, futuristic, modernized.

2. Unheard-of, further, fresh, additive, additory, supplemental, strange, unused, bizarre, different, supplementary, annexed, affixed, added, superposed, superimposed, adscititious, extra, subjunctive, subjoined, auxiliary, ulterior, more, suppletory.

3. Unessayed, untried, unventured, unused, unhackneyed, original, untrodden, unexercised, unapplied, unaccustomed, unseasoned, unfamiliar, unprecedented, unread, unconsumed, ungathered, uncollected, unculled, untouched, unexpected, undescribed, uncharted, unexplored, unparalleled, out-of-the-way, remote, curious, peculiar, unexampled.

4. Renewed, restored, repaired, fixed, reinvigorated, redivivus, renascent, reborn, recreated, modernized, remedied, refreshed, reconstructed, regenerate, regenerated, rebuilt, remodeled, resumed, reopened.

5. Spruce, chic, fashionable, stylish, in style, in the latest style, modish, in the mode, swell *(sl.),* à la mode *(Fr.),* the latest thing, all the rage, all the go.

NEWBORN, *adj.* Regenerate, regenerated, new, recent, infant, infantile, infantine, babyish, baby, in the cradle, in swaddling clothes, newfledged, young, in long clothes, unweaned.

NEWCOMER, *n.* Immigrant, comer, entrant, alien, stranger, recruit, rookie *(coll.),* Johnny-come-lately, tenderfoot *(coll.),* ultramontane, barbarian, outlander, foreigner, outsider, colonist, settler, naturalized citizen, intruder, obtruder, interloper, maverick *(sl.),* trespasser, interferer, intermeddler, interrupter, visitor, colonizer, immigrator, guest, novice, neophyte, beginner, tyro, probationer, greenhorn, greenie *(coll.),* catechumen, novitiate.

NEWFANGLED, *adj.* Novel, unique, unusual, newly invented, newly devised, recent, new, unimitated, unfamiliar, progressive, unparalleled, unexampled, unaccountable, altered, changed, unexpected, uncommon, unprecedented, new-wrinkled *(sl.),* newfandangled *(sl.),* unheard-of, undescribed, strange, foreign.

NEW-FASHIONED, *adj.* Fashionable, stylish, modish, of recent period, up-to-date, modernistic, modernized, futuristic, ultra-ultra, ultramodern, *chic (Fr.),* in fashion, in style, à la mode *(Fr.),* neologic, neological, neoteric, neoterical, abreast of the times, up-to-the-minute, being done, the latest thing, the thing, just the thing.

NEWLY, *adv.* Recently, latterly, lately, just now, of late, not long ago, a short time ago, a short while ago, only yesterday, right now, freshly, neoterically, immaturely, youthfully, rawly, unusually, extraordinarily, modernistically, futuristically, supplementally, strangely, bizarrely, differently, adscititiously, subjunctively, subjoinedly, ulteriorly, curiously, remotely, unexpectedly, peculiarly, sprucely, fashionably, stylishly, anew, afresh, again, repeatedly, modishly.

NEWLYWED, *n.* Bride, bridegroom, groom, husband, wife, benedict, plighted bride, spouse, blushing bride, wife of one's bosom, helpmeet, married man, helpmate, squaw, goodwife, better half.

NEWNESS, *n.* Novelty, recentness, immaturity. newfangledness, unusualness, futurism, modernization, modernity, lateness, youthfulness, greenness, unaccustomedness, freshness, renovation, restoration, youth, juvenility, originality, bizarreness, difference, singularity, tender age, neology, neologism, the last word, *le dernier cri (Fr.),* the latest thing, the latest fashion, uniqueness, stylishness, modishness, fashion, fashionableness, swellness *(sl.),* lateness, unripeness, ultramodernness, ultramodernity, differentness, strangeness.

NEW-RICH, *n.* Upstart, parvenu, *nouveau riche (Fr.), bourgeois gentilhomme (Fr.),* adventurer, newly rich, mushroom, skipjack, sprout, jack-in-the pulpit, bounder *(sl.),* pig in clover *(sl.),* codfish aristocrat *(sl.).*

NEWS, *n.* Message, tidings, dispatch, report, talk, rumor, by-talk, word, information, advice, copy *(cant),* piece, article, story, news article, news story, intelligence, letterpress, scandal, gossip, letter, telegram, tittle-tattle, cry, bruit, noise, hearsay, evangel, announcement, communication, communiqué, release, news release, intermessage, cablegram, wireless message, wire *(coll.),* flash *(coll.),* bulletin, wireless telegram, wireless *(coll.),* radiogram, radio telegram, flying rumor, village talk, village gossip, telephone call, call, phone call, telephone message, buzz, slander, detraction, defamation, libel, babble, chatter, common talk, malicious, rumor, malicious gossip, dirt *(sl.),* newsmongery, jouralism, aviso, advice, advisement, glad tidings, good news, hoax, gossipry, disclosure, exposure, publication, publicity, advertisement, account, declaration, statement, dope *(sl.),* confidential information, lowdown*(coll.),* inside facts, mention, enlightenment, discovery, exposé, divulgation, divulgence, revelation.

NEWSCAST, *n.* Broadcast, radio broadcast, telecast, talk, commentary, review of the news, news roundup *(coll.),* announcement, publicity, publication, disclosure, reporting, reportage, announcement, enlightenment, communication, communiqué, intelligence, rumor, account, story, news story, scoop *(cant),* beat *(cant).*

NEWSMONGER, *n.* 1. Inquirer, questioner, scandalmonger, busybody, quidnunc, talebearer, Paul Pry, nosy poke *(coll.),* pry, snooper, informant, teller, relater, reporter, chatterer, chatterbox, witness, gossip, tattletale, telltale, tattler, tittle-tattler, mumble-news, magpie, enlightener, notifier, informer, teller.

2. Journalist, newsman, newspaperman, reporter, columnist, leg man, publisher, gentleman of the press, representative of the press, member of the fourth estate, pressman, correspondent, informant, informer, reportress, woman reporter, female reporter, war correspondent, foreign correspondent, special correspondent, publicist, editor, copy editor, news editor, city editor, editorial writer, leader writer, sports editor, sports reporter, sports writer, theatrical reporter, theatrical writer, theater critic, critic, reviewer, book reviewer, book critic, book editor, rewrite man, rewriter, writer

for the press, newspaperwoman, pundit, sage, news analyst, news commentator, commentator, national affairs expert, foreign affairs expert.

NEWSPAPER, *n.* The press, journal, daily, weekly, monthly, tabloid, tab *(cant),* publication, sheet, yellow journal, yellow sheet, periodical, gazette, news, organ, house organ, Sunday edition, bulldog edition, quarterly, gazetteer, intelligencer, serial.

NEXT, *adj.* Succeeding, ensuing, successive, adjacent, adjoining, close, closest, attendant, after, neighboring, propinquant, propinquous, sequential, consequent, sequacious, proximate, approximate, proximal, nearest, near, nearby, immediate, proximo, contiguous, nigh, later, bordering.

NEXT, *adv.* Subsequently, consequently, after that time, from that time, thereafter, whereupon, whereat, whereafter, upon which, since, later, at a later date, at a later time, following, successively, sequentially, close upon, following upon, in the sequel, in sequence, hereon, from that time, from that moment, sequaciously, closely, at a later time, at a subsequent time.

NIB, *n.* 1. Nose, beak, bill, pecker, beezer *(sl.),* snoot *(coll.),* nozzle, muzzle, trunk, proboscis, olfactory organ, smeller *(sl.),* nostrils, snout, breather, neb, noseholes, antlia.

2. Peak, point, tip, extreme, end, apex, culmen, vertex, summit, height, top, tiptop, pinnacle, upper end, extremity.

NIBBLE, *v.* 1. Masticate, chew, nip, crunch, munch, peck, peck at, eat, consume, chaw *(coll.),* ground, bite off, eat sparingly, scrunch.

2. Carp, murmur, complain, growl, grump, grunt, fret, fuss, find fault, nag, wrangle, quibble, peck at, clamor, cavil, accuse, badger, harry, harass.

NICE, *adj.* 1. Unerring, exact, precise, clean-cut, accurate, correct, all right *(coll.),* just right, careful, painstaking, constant, well-defined, mathematically exact, delicate, ticklish, meticulous, positive, sure, skillful, strict, rigorous, critical, valuable, punctual, methodical, discriminative.

2. Fastidious, squeamish, particular, demanding, exacting, queasy, overrefined, difficult, querulous, scrupulous, punctilious, overconscientious, overcritical, hypercritical, oversubtle, overnice, hairsplitting, dainty, oversensitive, censorious.

3. Acute, discriminating, astute, choosy, choiceful, choicy *(coll.),* fine, delicate, discriminatory, discretional, discretionary, tactful, distinctive, perceptive, perspicacious, finicky, finical, peculiar, discreet, keen, differentiative, tasteful, discerning, perceptive, percipient, scrupulous, particular, subtle, differentiating, distinguishing.

4. Elegant, proper, tasteful, in good taste, correct, appropriate, fine, delicate, formal, euphemistic, refined, cultured, cultivated, good-looking, chaste, seemly, proper, polished, simple, pure, finished, felicitous, classic, classical, artistic, artistical, graceful, dainty, comely, restrained.

5. Appetizing, luscious, delicious, delectable, fit for a king, flavorful, nectareous, savory, palatable, to one's taste, flavorsome, flavorous, exquisite, toothsome, good-tasting, high-flavored, highly flavored, piquant, dainty, sweet, ambrosial, good, scrumptious *(coll.),* tasty *(coll.),* mouth-watering, tempting, succulent, enjoyable, rich, rich-flavored, lickerish, liquorish, tender, lean, soft.

6. Fascinating, taking, winning, enchanting, entrancing, ravishing, bewitching, captivating,

gracious, gratifying, well-favored, pleasant, agreeable, delightful, winsome, fair, good, kindly, generous, warm-hearted, benevolent, charitable, kind, amiable, friendly, sympathetic, understanding, compassionate, chivalrous, attractive, interesting, charming, pleasing, cordial, pleasurable, comfortable, comforting, satisfying, satisfactory, lovely, felicitous, happy, luxurious, genial, congenial, voluptuous, sensuous, likeable, pleasuregiving, cheering, cheerful, amusing, humorous, desirable.

7. Good, fine, excellent, great, dandy, jim-dandy, crackerjack, swell, rum, keen, tops, wonderful, O.K. *(slang-usage)*, bully.

NICENESS, *n.* 1. Exactness, exactitude, precision, accuracy, correctness, care, caution, carefulness, constancy, definition, clear definition, definitiveness, mathematical exactitude, meticulousness, positiveness, surety, sureness, skill, skillfulness, strictness, rigor, rigorousness, criticalness, value, punctuality, method, methodicalness, discrimination.

2. Fastidiousness, squeamishness, particularity, exactingness, queasiness, overrefinement, refinement, difficulty, querulousness, scrupulousness, scrupulosity, punctilio, punctiliousness, overconscientiousness, overcriticalness, hypercriticalness, oversubtlety, overniceness, daintiness, oversensitiveness, censoriousness.

3. Acuity, acuteness, discrimination, astuteness, choosiness, choicefulness, choiciness *(coll.)*, fineness, delicacy, discretion, tact, perception, perceptiveness, perspicaciousness, perspicacity, finickiness, finicalness, peculiarity, keenness, differentiativeness, tastefulness, discernment, percipiency, percipience, scrupulousness, scrupulosity, particularity, subtlety, distinction.

4. Elegance, propriety, properness, tastefulness, correctness, appropriateness, fineness, delicacy, formality, euphemism, refinement, culture, cultivation, handsomeness, chastity, seemliness, polish, simplicity, finish, finesse, felicity, classicism, artistry, artisticality, grace, gracefulness, daintiness, comeliness, restraint.

5. Lusciousness, deliciousness, delectableness, fitness, flavor, flavorsomeness, nectareousness, savor, savoriness, palatability, palatableness, flavorfulness, flavorousness, exquisiteness, toothsomeness, good taste, good flavor, high flavor, piquancy, daintiness, sweetness, goodness, scrumptiousness *(coll.)*, tastiness *(coll.)*, mouth-watering goodness, temptingness, succulence, succulency, enjoyability, richness, lickerishness, liquorishness, tenderness, juiciness, leanness, softness.

6. Fascination, winsomeness, enchantment, entrancement, ravishment, captivation, graciousness, gratification, gratifyingness, pleasantness, agreeability, agreeableness, delightfulness, fairness, goodness, kindness, kindliness, charity, charitableness, generousness, generosity, warm-heartedness, benevolence, amiability, friendliness, sympathy, understanding, compassion, chivalrousness, attractiveness, interestingness, charm, pleasingness, pleasurability, graciousness, cordiality, pleasurableness, comfort, satisfactoriness, loveliness, felicity, happiness, luxury, luxuriousness, geniality, congeniality, voluptuousness, sensuousness, likability, cheer, cheerfulness, humor, humorousness, desirability.

NICETY, *n.* 1. Particularity, discrimination, circumstantiality, attention, minute attention, precision, preciseness, minuteness, rigidity, subtlety, subtleness, accuracy, correctness, finicality, finicki-

ness, finicalness, care, caution, pedantry, pedanticism, pedantism, delicacy, exactness, exactitude, meticulosity, meticulousness, punctuality, punctualness, punctiliousness, punctilio, elaborateness, elaboration, attention to detail, rigor, rigorousness, distinguishment, differentiationism, acumen, insight, penetration, percipiency, percipience, acuteness, cuteness *(coll.)*, sensibility, sensitivity, perspicacity, perspicaciousness, squeamishness.

2. Fastidiousness, good taste, taste, tastefulness, particularity, culture, cultivation, tact, feeling, fine feeling, refinement, refined taste, refined feeling, cultivated taste, cultivated feeling, grace, tact, flair, polish, finesse, elegance, delicacy, subtlety.

NICHE, *n.* Hole, hole in the wall, depression, recess, nook, corner, cranny, alcove, small place, snug place, cramped place, cantle, cove, coign, dugout, cavity, excavation, cubbyhole, cubby.

NICK, *v.* 1. Indent, cut, notch, injure, scar, scarify, dint, dent, damage, mark, mar, deface, mitch, gash, score, blaze, jag, scotch, scratch, touch, lacerate.

2. Humbug, cheat, deceive, swindle, trick, hoax, cozen, impose upon, chouse, befool, fool, mystify, doctor, pose, sham, mask, soldier, beguile, bamboozle, deride, affect, mislead, invent, attitudinize, counterfeit, dissemble, dissimulate, brag, bluster, roister, bluff, belie, bias, chicane, delude, diddle, distort, dogmatize, equivocate, exaggerate, fable, fib, fabricate, fabulize, falsify, feign, flare, foist, forswear, fudge, gammon, hyperbolize, imp, elude, illude, lie, disarm, malinger, misrepresent, misguide, perjure, pervert, prejudice, pretend, prevaricate, quibble, romance, simulate, babble, blather, cackle, chatter, drool, puff, hoodwink, sell *(sl.)*, cajole, conjure, juggle, Machiavellize, cog, sharp, let in, take in *(both coll.)*, bilk, bite, betray, play false, divert, lead astray, outwit, practice upon, gull, victimize, palm off, overreach, outreach, steal a march on, ensnare, entrap, dupe, play a fast one, play a trick on, throw off the scent, misstate, blindfold, pass off, play possum, conceal, bemask, hide under a false front, put on a false front, pretend, twist, garble, stretch, strain, mulct, palter.

NICK, *n.* 1. Notch, cut, scratch, score, scoring, indentation, dent, dint, mark, mar, scar, injury, wound, marking, jag, incision, blaze, blazoning, cleft, depression, record, trace, crena, crenel.

2. Crisis, critical point, the right moment, moment of crisis, the turning point, psychological moment, zero hour, high time, crucial point, fortunate conjuncture.

NICKEL, *n.* 1. Metal, element, chemical element, plating, electroplating.

2. Coin, coinage, five-cent piece, one-twentieth of a dollar, legal tender, money, five cents, five pennies.

NICKNAME, *n.* Soubriquet, sobriquet, cognomen, name, title, diminutive, familiar name, moniker *(sl.)*, first name, given name, school name, handle *(sl.)*, pet name, little name, appellation, babyism, baby name, childhood name, byword, byname, appellative, epithet, nomination, designation, term.

NICTATE, *v.* Wink, blink, bat the eyes, bat the eyelashes, flutter the eyelashes, nictitate.

NIGGARD, *n.* Miser, churl, curmudgeon, skinflint, Scrooge, screw, tightwad *(coll.)*, skin *(sl.)*, muckworm, scrimp *(coll.)*, pinchfist, pinchpenny, pinchgut, harp, Hessian, save-all, codger, moneygrub, moneygrubber, stint, carl, pincher, nipper, lickpenny, hunks (coll.), mean man, mean fellow, meanie (coll.), sordid fellow.

NIGGARDLINESS, n. 1. Miserliness, parsimony, stinginess, graspingness, covetousness, shabbiness, penury, nearness, close-fistedness, closeness, close-handedness, hard-fistedness, hard-heartedness, u-suriousness, venality, stintingness, scrimping, stint, skimpiness, grudgingness, chariness, sparingness, moneygrubbing, mercenariness, illiberality, ungenerosity, misanthropy, churlishness, avarice, avariciousness, greed, greediness, extortion, economy, saving, thrift, thriftiness, frugality, sordidness.

2. Meanness, poorness, wretchedness, paltriness, scrubbiness, measliness (coll.), sorriness, pitifulness, trumpery, scurfiness, scurviness, cheapness, tawdriness, flimsiness, beggarliness, miserableness, contemptibleness, meagerness, scantiness, spareness, unworthiness.

NIGGARDLY, adj. 1. Miserly, parsimonious, stingy, grasping, covetous, shabby, penurious, save-all, peddling, penny-wise, near, close-fisted, close, close-handed, hard-fisted, hard-handed, hardhearted, cheeseparing, usurious, venal, stinting, scrimping, skimping (coll.), grudging, chary, sparing, hidebound, lickpenny, pinchpenny, moneygrubbing, shabby, mercenary, illiberal, ungenerous, misanthropic, churlish, avaricious, greedy, extortionate, economical, saving, thrifty, frugal, sordid, niggard, grudging.

2. Mean, poor, wretched, paltry, scrubby, measly (coll.), sorry, pitiful, trumpery, scurfy, scurvy, cheap, tawdry, flimsy, beggarly, second-rate, thirdrate, fourth-rate, miserable, contemptible, meager, scanty, spare, unworthy.

NIGGLE, v. Trifle, potter, putter, idle, fribble, fritter, piddle, fiddle, fool around (coll.), amble, poke about.

NIGGLING, adj. Finicking, trifling, piddling, peddling, fribbling, puny, insignificant, amateurish, idle, petty, fidfad, fiddle-faddle, slight, poky, picayunish, picayune, meager, pitiful, mean, sorry, poor, inane, frivolous, contemptible, shabby, beggarly, worthless, wretched, trashy, weedy, scrubby, scurvy, scurfy, nugatory, finical, finikin, finicky, trivial, slender, nugacious.

NIGH, adv. Closely, approximately, almost, most (coll.), well nigh, nearly, nigh upon, nigh onto, about, not quite, all but, near the brink of, on the verge of, barely, hardly, scarcely, say (coll.), thereabouts, somewhere about, somewhere near, all but, as good as, roughly, in round numbers, generally, close upon, pretty near, near the mark, near upon.

NIGH, adj. 1. Vicinal, in the vicinity of, approximate, contiguous, contingent, adjacent, adjoining, nearby, intimate, neighboring, propinquent, osculatory (Geom.), juxtapositional, juxtaposed, proximal, proximate, bordering, bordering on, close, close-at-hand, at hand, to hand, handy, near-at hand, at a convenient distance, close by, by, around (coll.), about (coll.), in the neighborhood of, warm (coll.), hot (coll.), tangent, tangential, contactual, touching, connecting, conjoining, conterminous.

2. Imminent, momentary, impending, overhanging, lowering, menacing, looming, threatening, in the distance, not far away, approaching, expected, anticipated, looked for, future, brewing, preparing, immediate, instant, at hand, in store, in reserve, in the wind, to come, about to be, forthcoming, forseen, eventual, coming.

3. Intimate, close, related, dear, familiar, brotherly, sisterly, fraternal, paternal, maternal, parental, neighborly, cordial, hearty, acquainted, on good terms with, devoted, thick (coll.), consanguineous, related, hand-in-hand, hand-in-glove, friendly, like, amicable, sympathetic.

4. Short, straight, quick, close, immediate, ready, a stone's throw away, at close range, beside, alongside, remaining.

5. Resembling, literal, approximate, imitation, factitious, fraudulent, mock, mimic, imitative, representational, suggestive, suggestive of, quasi, borrowed, second-hand, trumped up, spurious, trick, tricky, fictive, counterfeit, purported, sham, bogus, false, phony, feigned, simulated, jerry-built, illusory, artificial, deceptive, misrepresentational, misrepresentative.

NIGHT, n. Nighttime, dark, darkness, the dark hours, obscurity, murkiness, bedtime, Stygian darkness, Cimmerian darkness, dead of night, tenebrity, tenebrosity, tenebrousness, the witching hour, midnight, slumber time, nighttide, hush of night.

NIGHT CLOTHES, n. Nightgown, nightdress, pajamas, sleeper (coll.), nightie (coll.), night robe, robe de nuit (Fr.), night gear, night wear, sleeping garments, sleeping clothes, nightshirt, bedgown.

NIGHTFALL, n. Evening, dusk, twilight, decline of day, vespers, evensong, crepuscule, crepuscle, fall of day, sunset, sundown, shank of the evening, gloaming, last light of day, close of day, shut of day, the eleventh hour, candlelight, curfew, bedtime, night, darkness, eve, even, eventide, owl-light, duskingtide.

NIGHTINGALE, n. Bird, singing bird, songbird, songster, warbler, singer, fowl, night fowl, feathered songster, philomel.

NIGHTLY, adj. Night, nocturnal, night-dark, night-cloaked, night-mantled, night-veiled, night-black, night-hidden, dark, obscure, darkling, darksome, noctivagant, noctivagous, black as night.

NIGHTLY, adv. Nights, nocturnally, through the night, at night, by night.

NIGHTMARE, n. Hallucination, bad dream, horrid dream, incubus, dream, vision, ephialtes, night hag, horror, cacodemon.

NIGHTTIME, n. Night, dark, darkness, hours of darkness, obscurity, blackness, murkiness, bedtime, stygian darkness, Cimmerian darkness, dead of night, tenebrity, tenebrousness, tenebrosity, the witching hour, midnight, slumber time, nighttide, hush of night.

NIGHTWALKER, n. 1. Noctambulist, somnambulist, noctambule, sleepwalker, somnambulator, somnambule.

2. Trull, whore, courtesan, prostitute, streetwalker, meretrix, trollop, hussy, baggage, drab, harridan, strumpet, wench, scarlet woman, fallen woman, cat, bag (sl.), old bag, pickup, Cyprian, Paphian, slut, quean, burglar, vagabond, wanderer, cutpurse, footpad, robber, knave, rogue, housebreaker, assassin, killer, murderer, slayer, strangler, attacker, lurker, prowler, highwayman, holdupman, second-story man (cant), thief, brigand, stealer, marauder, plunderer.

NIGRIFICATION, n. Blackening, shadowing, smudging, darkening, bedarkening, denigration, infuscation, obfuscation, blotting.

NIHILISM, n. 1. Nonexistence, negativeness, nullity, nothingness, nihility, blank, void, oblivion, negation, existencelessness, existlessness, nonsubsistence, inexistence, insubstantiality, unsubstantiality, insubstantialness, incorporeality, incorporality, incorporeity, negation of being, abeyance, abeyancy, nonentity, nonbeing.

2. Anarchy, force, lawlessness, lynch law, anarchism, misrule, mob rule, destructive force, disorder, chaos, license, licentiousness, revolt, revolution, insurgence, insurgency, insurrection, uprising, rising, rebellion, mutiny, insubordination, mutineering, outbreak, riot, sedition, *lèse majesté (Fr.)*, mobocracy, ochlocracy, terrorism, reign of terror, violence, *émeute (Fr.)*, revolutionism, Lydford law, club law, overthrow, upset, irresponsibility.

3. Skepticism, doubtism, agnosticism, atheism, disbelief, ethical nihilism, nullifidianism, doubt.

NIHILIST, *n.* Revolutionary, revolutionist, traitor, insurgent, insurrectionist, mutineer, anarchist, rebel, insubordinate, terrorist, destroyer, iconoclast, idoloclast, agitator, seditionist, nullifier, nullificator, atheist, agnostic, doubter, skeptic, doubting Thomas, nullifidian, ruiner, exterminator.

NIHILISTIC, *adj.* Terroristic, seditious, revolutionary, revolutionist, rebellious, insurgent, insurrectionary, riotous, anarchic, anarchical, anarchistic, ungoverned, unruly, licentious, disorderly, disorganized, lawless, mutinous, mutineering.

NIHILITY, *n.* Nonexistence, negativeness, nullity, nothing, nothingness, nihilism, blank, void, oblivion, vacuum, negation, existencelessness, existlessness, nonsubsistence, inexistence, insubstantiality, unsubstantiality, insubstantialness, incorporality, incorporeity, negation of being, abeyance, abeyancy, nonentity, nonbeing.

NIL, *n.* Nothing, no part, not a one, no degree, no quantity, zero, cipher, zip *(coll.)*, scratch, goose egg, duck egg, not a blessed thing *(coll.)*, nixie, nary, never a one, nary a one, no such thing, *nichts (Ger.)*, *nihil (Lat.)*, *rein (Fr.)*, naught, none, nothing whatever, none whatever, nothing at all, nothing on earth, nothing under the sun, none in the world.

NIMBLE, *adj.* Fast, swift, quick, speedy, mercurial, electric, snappy *(coll.)*, agile, rapid, eagle-winged, expeditious, nimble-footed, nimble-fingered, light-footed, fleet-footed, light-fingered, light-legged, light of heel, quick as lightning, alert, lively, smart, smart as a whip, smart as a steel trap, spry *(coll.)*, instant, ready, prompt, quick as a thought, swift as an arrow, on the alert, wide-awake, fleet, active, tripping, deft, skillful, dexterous, easy, sly, on the *qui vive (Fr.)*, light, quick-moving, busy, expert, proficient, vivacious, full of life, animated, spirited, graceful.

NIMBLE-FINGERED, *adj.* Skillful, expert, qualified, proficient, dexterous, dextrous, apt, trained, accomplished, fitted, efficient, sure-handed, fine-fingered, sure-footed, neat-handed, crack *(coll.)*, slick *(coll.)*, cute *(coll.)*, handy, quick, ready, clever, adept, adroit, deft, capable, competent, good *(coll.)*.

NIMBLE-FOOTED, *adj.* Fast, swift, quick, speedy, mercurial, electric, snappy *(coll.)*, agile, rapid, eagle-winged, expeditious, light-fingered, light-footed, fleet-footed, light of heel, quick as lightning, alert, lively, smart, spry *(coll.)*, instant, ready, prompt, quick as thought, quick as an arrow, on the alert, fleet, active, tripping, easy, sly, on the *qui vive (Fr.)*, light, quick-moving,

busy, vivacious, full of life, animated, spirited, graceful.

NIMBLENESS, *n.* Skill, animation, quickness, smartness, alertness, rapidity, agility, alacrity, briskness, liveliness, expedition, dispatch, readiness, fleetness, fleet-footedness, haste, speed, celerity, spirit, vivacity, energy, adroitness, dexterousness, dexterity, aptness, aptitude, cleverness, competence, adequacy, efficacy, efficientness, efficiency, proficiency, facility, address, ease, expertness, skillfulness, velocity, capacity, sufficiency, finesse.

NIMBLE-WITTED, *adj.* Sparkling, witty, sharp, shrewd, acute, cute *(coll.)*, canny, sly, argute, astute, subtle, clever, brilliant, smart, quick-witted, clear-witted, clear-headed, keen-witted, sharp as a tack, sharp as a needle, hard-headed, long-headed, thoughtful, pungent, alert, incisive, smart as a whip, smart as a steel trap, wide-awake, awake, on the alert, alert, on the *qui vive (Fr.)*, quick as lightning.

NIMBLY, *adv.* Fast, swiftly, speedily, mercurially, electrically, snappily, agilely, rapidly, expeditiously, fleet-footedly, light-footedly, light-fingeredly, light-leggedly, alertly, lively, smartly, spryly, instantly, readily, promptly, fleetly, actively, trippingly, deftly, skillfully, dexterously, dextrously, easily, slyly, lightly, busily, expertly, proficiently, vivaciously, animatedly, spiritedly, gracefully.

NIMBUS, *n.* Glow, shining, effulgence, refulgence, emanation, halo, circle, circle of light, aura, aureole, aureola, light, glory, radiance, aurora, luminousness, luminosity, nebulous light, gloriole, cloud.

NIMIETY, *n.* Excess, surplus, surplusage, redundance, overplus, overage, redundancy, superabundance, superfluity, superfluousness, exorbitancy, exorbitance, inordinacy, inordinateness, exuberance, inundation, flood, deluge, diffuseness, prolixity, verbosity, tautology, verbiage, wordiness, circumlocution, engorgement, swelling, swell, surcharge, overset, oversupply, overmeasure, pleonasm, plethora, enough, more than enough, congestion, glut, enough and to spare, too much, too many, too much of a good thing, repletion, supersaturation, overdose, sickener, the last straw, the straw that broke the camel's back, overflow, overrunning, overrun, drug, drug on the market, padding, embroidery, frills, supererogation, overpraise, overcommendation, overlaudation, extravagance, embarrassment of riches, surfeit.

NINCOMPOOP, *n.* Fool, tomfool, mutt *(sl.)*, dope *(sl.)*, jerk *(sl.)*, ninny, ninnyhammer, dunce, dolt, clod, lout, shatterbrain, shatterpate, harebrain, featherbrain, chump *(sl.)*, prize sap *(sl.)*, scatterbrain, loon, loony, simpleton, blockhead, witling, wiseacre, ass, jackass, donkey, bonehead *(coll.)*, imbecile, idiot, moron, calf, colt, gawk, halfwit, goose, rube *(sl.)*, clown, dotard, simp *(sl.)*, juggins *(coll.)*, owl, gander, lunkhead *(sl.)*, rattlebrain, rattlepate, rattlehead, knucklehead, lubber, clodhopper, softy *(coll.)*, noodle, gabby, noddy, tomnoddy, dumbbell, dummy, zany, stick, sop, asshead, mooncalf, bull calf *(coll.)*, silly, silly ass, duffer *(coll.)*, dumbhead, dumb bunny, dunderhead, dunderpate, square *(sl.)*, numskull, dimwit, thickwit, woodenhead, squarehead, clodpoll, clodpate, lummox, yokel, lackbrain, halfwit, dimwit, driveling, idiot, lackwit, ditzy, addlepate, addlebrain, chucklehead, chowderhead, blunderhead, bullhead, fathead, jolthead, mutton-head, pumpkinhead, beetlehead, blubberhead, doughhead, bakehead, noodlehead, Boeotian, Gothamite, wise man of Gotham, nitwit.

NINE, *adj.* Novenary, enneatic, nonage *(Eccl.),* novena *(Eccl.),* nonagon, ennead, nonary, thrice three, three threes, three times three, nonuplet *(Music),* the Muses, the Nine Muses, the sacred Nine.

NINEFOLD, *adj.* Ninth, nonuple, novenary, thrice three, three threes, three times three, enneahedral, novenahedral, nonahedral, nonary, enneastyle *(Arch.).*

NINEPINS, *n.* Tenpins, bowling, game, sport, skittles, play, competition, relaxation, recreation, pastime.

NINTH, *adj.* Ninefold, nonuple, novenary, thrice three, three threes, three times three, enneahedral, novenahedral, nonahedral, nonary, enneastyle *(Arch.).*

NIP, *v.* 1. Seize, clutch, snare, snap, snag, snatch, grab, compress, tweak, pinch, get one's fingers on, finger, clasp, grip, grasp.
2. Shorten, curtail, cut off, cut, retrench, lop, snip, abbreviate, cut short, snap, crack, sunder, cleave, shave, shave off, truncate, snub, crop, dock, shear, clip.
3. Put down, destroy, put an end to, blight, crush, thwart, blast, ruin, ruinate, knock out, suppress, quash, squelch, put the kibosh on, stunt, nip in the bud, finish, finish off, demolish, deal a blow to, deal a knockout blow.
4. Cut, pierce, bite, freeze, chill, chill to the bone, chill to the marrow, make one's teeth chatter, make one shiver.
5. Tweak, pinch, sting, smart, throb, pain, give pain, pierce, bite, vex.
6. Tipple, liquor, liquor up *(coll.),* toss off, tope, swill *(coll.),* guzzle, bib, sot, grog, drink, tun, quaff, imbibe, sup, sip, crack a bottle, wet one's whistle, slake one's thirst, drown one's sorrows, drown one's troubles, drink deep, booze, swig, moisten one's clay, soak, toss the pot, bend the elbow, bun, swack, crook the elbow, drink like a fish, empty one's glass, drain one's glass, drain the cup, toss it down, tank up, get drunk.

NIP, *n.* 1. Race, raciness, pungency, pungence, piquance, piquancy, strong taste, tang, twang *(coll.),* punch *(coll.),* smack *(coll.),* zest, tartness, zip *(coll.),* high relish, strong seasoning, high seasoning, high flavor, poignance, poignancy, savor.
2. Discomfort, pain, twitch, twinge, pang, shooting pain, sharp pain, piercing pain, kink, crick, stitch.
3. Morsel, nibble, gulp, swig, sip, sup, guzzle *(vulg.),* particle, bit, drink, potion, portion, draught, lap, drop, shot, dram, draft, swill *(coll.),* peg.

NIPPERS, *n.* 1. Eyeglasses, spectacles, pince-nez, reading glasses, glasses, specs *(coll.),* corrective lenses *(slang usage).*
2. Pincers, tweezers, pliers, forceps, grippers, tongs, grip, clinchers, clinch, vise, *pincette (Fr.),* holders, hemostat *(Surg.),* haemostat.

NIPPING, *adj.* Cold, freezing, frosty, rigorous, cutting, piercing, pinching, icy, icy-cold, ice-cold, blasting, stinging, hiemal, wintry, wintery, winter-like, hibernal, mordant, freezing-cold, numbing, chilling, chilly, fresh, keen, sharp, inclement, severe, bitter, raw, chill, ice-like.

NIPPLE, *n.* Protuberance, papilla, teat, dug, pap, mammary, mammilla, tit *(vulgar),* titty.

NITID, NITIDOUS, *adj.* Shining, luminous, luminescent, shiny, glossy, glassy, lustrous, luminiferous, fulgurant, refulgent, effulgent, fulgent, bright, lambent, beaming, lucid, lucent, glaring, glary, brilliant, vivid, splendid, fulgid, splendrous, sheeny, burnished, luculent, rutilant, rutilous, niveous, irradiated, irradiate, alight, lucific, luciferous, relucent, lamping, orient.

NIVEOUS, *adj.* White, pure white, whitish, pearly, pearl-white, frosted, hoar, hoary, snow-white, white as snow, snowy, bright, shining, shiny white, grozzled, grizzly, grizzled, lint-white, milk-white, milky, milky-white, albescent, albinistic, lily-white, white as a lily, lactescent, marmoreal, marmorean, albificative, albicant, canescent, silver, silvery, argent, argentous, chalky, cretaceous.

NIX, NIXIE, *n.* 1. Water sprite, water creature, fairy, siren, Oceanid, ocean nymph, Nereid, sea nymph, sea maid, mermaid, undine, kelpie, water nymph, naiad, limniad, fresh-water nymph, sylph, sea maiden.
2. Nothing, no part, not a one, no degree, no quantity, zero, cipher, zip *(coll.),* scratch, goose egg, duck egg, not a blessed thing *(coll.),* nary, nary a one, never a one, no such thing, *rien (Fr.),* *nichts (Ger.),* *nihil (Lat.),* naught, none, nothing whatever, none whatever, nothing at all, nothing on earth, nothing under the sun, none in the world.
3. No one, nobody, not a soul, not a one, never a person *(coll.),* nobody on earth, nobody present, no man, nobody under the sun.

NO, *adv.* 1. Nope *(coll.),* nowise, noway, no-ways, no siree *(coll.),* no indeed, none *(coll.),*
2. Never, to no extent, not, not a bit, not so, no such thing, not by a long shot, not on your life, not for the world, far from it, anything but, by no manner of means, *tout au contraire (Fr.),* on the contrary, contrariwise, nothing of the kind, nothing of the sort, in no respect, on no account, not much.

NO, *adj.* Not one, none, not any.

NO, *v.* Negate, say no to, deny, give the lie to, abjure, abrogate, repudiate, refuse, take issue with, impugn, gainsay, contradict, contravene, oppose, traverse, controvert, negative, belie, abjure, disown, disallow, forswear, renounce, refuse permission, reject, not consent, refuse assent, turn down, disfavor, view with disfavor, disapprove, refuse point blank, refuse out of hand, reject out of hand, grudge, begrudge, withhold one's assent, withhold one's consent, veto, revolt at, frown, frown down, spurn, demur, scruple, boggle at, be scandalized at, not hear of, object to, take exception to, protest, abnegate, rebut, refute, confute, shake the head at, nod at, turn up one's nose at, discountenance, not countenance.

NOB, *n.* 1. Head, pate, poll, knob, noodle, garret, attic, upper story, top, sconce, conk, crumpet, nut, noggin, skull, cranium, think tank, bun, cocoa, belfry, bean, dome.
2. Personage, celebrity, bigwig, great card, V.I.P. (very important person), nabob, great personage, person of importance, somebody *(coll.),* something, figure, great man, notable, man of mark, man of distinction, man of merit, grandee, magnifico, noble, worthy, panjandrum, mogul, magnate, sachem, chief, head man, captain, leader, cynosure, blue blood, upper-cruster *(coll.),*

member of the four-hundred, lion, elite, hero, social lion, thoroughbred, swell *(coll.)*, aristocrat.

NOBILITATE, *v.* Ennoble, honor, confer honor on, confer distinction upon, distinguish, dignify, aggrandize, pay honor to, pay homage to, render honor to, show honor toward, do honor to, look up to, signalize, crown, crown with laurel, hold in esteem, esteem, respect, elevate, raise, exalt to the skies.

NOBILITY, *n.* 1. Eminence, distinction, importance, significance, majesty, prestige, grandeur, splendor, sublimity, supremacy, preëminence, name, primacy, headship, elevation, leadership, exaltedness, exaltation, figure, consequence, prominence, dignity, note, notability, loftiness, paramountcy, supereminence, highness, high-and-mightiness, impressiveness, stateliness, magnificence.

2. Rank, condition, state, nobleness, aristocracy, gentility, birth, high birth, royalty, quality, noble birth, blood, breeding, high breeding, blue blood *(coll.)*, rank, distinction, order, upper classes, ruling classes.

3. The nobility, optimates, the elite, the ruling classes, *noblesse (Fr.)*, aristocracy, the noble classes, the upper classes, upper crust *(coll.)*, upper cut *(coll.)*, the four hundred *(coll.)*, *haut monde (Fr.)*, great folks, House of Lords, House of Peers, peerage, patriciate, high society, *samurai (Japanese)*, world of fashion, F.F.V. (First Families of Virginia) *(coll.)*, Vanity Fair, Mayfair, the Court, the elite, baronage, notabilities, lords temporal, lords spiritual, knightage, royalty, optimates, peerdom, earldom, dukedom, gentility.

NOBLE, *adj.* 1. Grand, great, tall, large, mighty, precious, goodly, full, strong, intense, heavy, sound, plenary, imposing, high, deep, elevated, magnanimous, illustrious, lofty, majestic, dignified magisterial, august.

2. Reputable, honorable, respectable, worthy, estimable, creditable, highly respectable, in good favor, in good order, honorific, favored, trustworthy, reverend, superior, elevated, punctilious, trusty, trustful, scrupulous, sure, reliable, tried and true, right-minded, excellent, nice, well-intentioned, well-meaning, exemplary, sterling, meritorious, whole-souled, noble-minded, correct, right, upright, estimable, honest, manly, reputable, uncorrupt, ethical, uncorrupted, truehearted, law-abiding, true-spirited, open, open-hearted, principled, high-principled, faithful, constant, loyal, staunch, steady, steadfast, unerring, unfailing, firm, resolute, true, true-blue, dependable, incorruptible, good, moral, virtuous, just, righteous.

3. Righteous, of rank, of high rank, high-born, patrician, exalted, aristocratic, aristocratical, thoroughbred, well-bred, blue-blooded, pure-blooded, of gentle blood, princely, genteel, princelike, gentlemanly, gentlemanlylike, distinguished, distingué, ladylike, kingly, titled, queenly, honored, well-mannered, superior, royal, high.

4. Grand, dignified, stately, baronial, lordly, majestic, impressive, stiff, stiff-minded, imposing, courtly, skilled, awful, awesome, awe-inspiring, free, liberal, eminent, candid, incorrupt, loyal, generous, first-rate, faithful, truthful, splendid, distinguished, magnificent, glorious, high-minded, manful, lofty, handsome, supreme, lordlike, renowned, regal, famous, preëminent, famed, imperial, imposing, distinguished, sublime, superb, gentilitial, generous.

NOBLE, *n.* Countess, baronet, baroness, nobiliary,

viscount, count, baron, duke, earl, noblewoman, nobleman, peer, magnifico, grandee, *hidalgo (Sp.)*, *daimio (Jap.)*, blue blood, don, patrician, thoroughbred, lord, upper-cruster, aristocrat, *laird (Scot.)*, squire, lordling, Signior, gentleman, *Signor (It.)*, peeress, notable, gentlewoman, notability, duke, archduke, grand duke, earl, marquis, count, notability, silk-stocking, knight, cavalier, chevalier, boyar, thane, banneret, armiger, palgrave, margrave, waldgrave, landgrave, duchess, marchioness, viscountess, lady, *dona (Sp.)*, Signora *(It.)*, notable, prince, atheling, khan, sheik, princeling, princelet, rajah, princess, empress, maharajah, maharani, begum, ranee (rani), person of importance, personage, man of mark, great man, man of merit, man of distinction.

NOBLEMAN, *n.* Baronet, nobiliary, viscount, count, baron, duke, earl, peer, magnifico, grandee, *hidalgo (Sp.)*, *daimio (Jap.)*, blue blood, silk-stocking, don, patrician, thoroughbred, lord, upper-cruster, aristocrat, *laird (Scot.)*, squire, lording, signior, gentleman, *Signor (It.)*, notable, notability, archduke, grand duke, marquis, knight, cavalier, chevalier, boyar, thane, banneret, knight banneret, armiger, palgrave, margrave, waldgrave, landgrave, prince, khan, sheik, princeling, princelet, rajah, maharajah, begum, ranee (rani), person of importance, personage, man of mark, great man, man of merit, man of distinction.

NOBLE-MINDED, *adj.* Magnanimous, generous, princely, great, handsome, high, lofty, elevated, sublime, exalted, high-hearted, high-minded, large-hearted, great-hearted, free-hearted, heroic, chivalrous, benevolent, altruistic, good, virtuous, righteous, moral, right, right-minded, well-meaning, well-intentioned, nice, excellent, creditable, exemplary, laudable, meritorious, sterling, praiseworthy, worthy, fine, whole-souled, correct, saintlike, saintly, estimable, noble, admirable, just, benign, good, kind, kindly, open-handed, free-handed, free, unselfish, benignant, munificent, unsparing, unstinting, ungrudging, hospitable, charitable, forbearant, forbearing, patient, understanding, easygoing, benign, amiable, indulgent, lenient, obliging, considerate, thoughtful, generous, warm-hearted, well-affected, well-disposed, kindly-done, kindly-intended, chivalrous, chivalric, courteous, polite, courtly, gallant, good-mannered, well-mannered, mannerly, philanthropic, humanitarian, civil, well intended.

NOBLENESS, *n.* 1. Eminence, distinction, importance, significance, majesty, prestige, grandeur, splendor, sublimity, supremacy, preëminence, name, primacy, headship, elevation, leadership, exaltedness, exaltation, figure, consequence, prominence, grandeur, dignity, note, notability, loftiness, paramountcy, supereminence, highness, high-and-mightiness, impressiveness, stateliness, magnificence.

2. Rank, condition, state, nobleness, aristocracy, gentility, birth, high birth, royalty, quality, noble birth, blood, breeding, high breeding, blue blood *(coll.)*, rank, distinction, royalty, quality, order, upper classes, ruling classes.

3. The nobility, optimates, the elite, the ruling classes, *noblesse (Fr.)*, aristocracy, the noble classes, upper crust *(coll.)*, upper cut *(coll.)*, the four hundred *(coll.)*, *haut monde (Fr.)*, great folks, House of Lords, House of Peers, Peerage, patriciate, high society, *manurai (Jap.)*, world of fashion, F.F.V. (First Families of Virginia) *(coll.)*, Vanity

Fair, Mayfair, the Court, the elite, baronage, notabilities, lords temporal, lords spiritual, knightage, royalty, optimates, peerdom, earldom, dukedom, gentility.

NOBLESSE, *n. (Fr.),* Nobleness, nobility, aristocracy, quality, gentility, high birth, birth, noble birth, high descent, blood, blue blood, distinction, rank, the nobility, *ancien régime (Fr.),* elite, optimates, upper class, upper classes, aristocratic class, upper cut, The Four Hundred, upper crust, haut monde, high life, great folks, notables, royalty, lords temporal, lords spiritual, lords, house of peers, House of Lords, baronage, peerage, notabilities.

NOBLEWOMAN, *n.* Countess, baroness, peeress, gentlewoman, marchioness, viscountess, lady, *dona (Sp.), Signora (It.),* princess, empress, maharani.

NOBLY, *adv.* 1. Grandly, greatly, largely, mightily, preciously, fully, strongly, intensely, heavily, soundly, imposingly, highly, deeply, magnanimously, illustriously, loftily, majestically, magisterially, augustly.

2. Reputably, honorably, respectably, worthily, creditably, highly respectably, honorifically, trustworthily, favoredly, reverendly, punctiliously, trustily, trustworthily, trustfully, scrupulously, surely, reliably, dependably, morally, virtuously, justly, righteously, right-mindedly, excellently, nicely, meritoriously, noble-mindedly, correctly, rightly, honestly, reputably, uncorruptly, ethically, uncorruptedly, true-heartedly, law-abidingly, truespiritedly, openly, open-heartedly, faithfully, constantly, loyally, staunchly, steadily, steadfastly, unerringly, unfailingly, firmly, resolutely, truly.

3. Righteously, highly, exaltedly, aristocratically, genteelly, well-manneredly, royally.

4. Grandly, baronially, majestically, impressively, stiffly, imposingly, awfully, stiff-mindedly, awe-inspiringly freely, faithfully, liberally, truthfully, splendidly, magnificently, gloriously, high-mindedly, manfully, loftily, handsomely, supremely, regally, famously, imperially, imposingly, sublimely, superbly, generously.

NOBODY, *n.* 1. No one, not a soul, not a one, not a blessed one *(coll.),* no man, *nemo (Lat.),* never a one, ne'er a one, nary a one *(coll.),* nobody on earth, nobody under the sun.

2. Unimportant person, nonentity, nullity, obscurity, naught, nought, cipher, insignificancy, nobody one knows, nihility, whippersnapper, no great shakes *(coll.),* lightweight, mediocrity, nix *(sl.),* man of straw, jackstraw, lay figure, puppet, nixie *(sl.),* zero.

NOCENT, *adj.* Harmful, hurtful, injurious, deleterious, scatheful, baneful, baleful, noisome, malefic, malefical, malignant, prejudicial, disserviceable, disadvantageous, mischievous, full of mischief, mischief-making, damaging, corrupting, disastrous, insalubrious, unhealthful, unhealthy, unhealthsome, noxious, bad, septic, virulent, venomous, pernicious, morbific, morbifical, morbiferous, poisonous, ruinous, destructive, internecine.

NOCTAMBULIST, *n.* Noctambule, somnabulist, sleepwalker, somnambulator, somnambule.

NOCTURNAL, *adj.* Night, night-dark, night-cloaked, nightmantled, night-veiled, night-black, night-hidden, dark, obscure, darkling, darksome, noctivagant, noctivagous, black as night.

NOCTURNE, *n.* Piece, musical piece, composition, piece of music, work, opera, production, serenata,

serenade, night music, night piece, evening song, *Nachtmusik (Ger.), Abendmusik (Ger.).*

NOCUOUS, *adj.* Harmful, hurtful, injurious, deleterious, scatheful, baneful, baleful, noisome, malefic, malignant, prejudicial, disserviceable, disadvantageous, mischievous, full of mischief, mischief-making, damaging, corrupting, disastrous, insalubrious, unhealthful, unhealthy, unhealthsome, noxious, bad, septic, virulent, venomous, pernicious, morbific, morbifical, morbiferous, poisonous, ruinous, destructive, internecine.

NOD, *v.* 1. Express, show, signal, give a signal, motion, indicate, reveal, signify, make a sign, sign, signalize, make a motion, beckon, acquiesce, show acquiescence, assent, consent, show assent, show consent, agree, show agreement, concur, show concurrence, recognize, acknowledge, shrug, move.

2. Go to sleep, fall asleep, be sleepy, drowse, drop off *(coll.),* be inactive, be torpid, be languid, doze, fall off *(coll.).*

3. Greet, hail, salute, touch the forelock, give salute, give salutation, say hello, bid hello, acknowledge, bow, smile at, smile upon, make obeisance, incline the head, bend the neck, bow down, bow one's head, scrape, bob, curtsey, curtsy, courtesy, give courtesy.

4. Err, fall into error, be mistaken, go astray, deviate, wander, mistake, make a mistake, go wrong, be wrong, be in the wrong, miscalculate, stumble, falter, bungle, make a botch, make a blunder, slip, slip up, trip, trip up, misreckon, sin, misconstrue, deviate from the right, deviate from the truth.

5. Incline, droop, yield, give, subside, dip, slump, sag, decline, descend, bend, sink, drop, drop down, relax, unbend, pitch down.

NOD, *n.* 1. Sign of assent, recognition, acknowledgment, assentation, accession, acquiescence, agreement, concurrence, sanction, approval, approbation, sign of approval.

2. Cue, indication, show, gesture, shrug, movement, move, sign, signal, gesticulation.

3. Call, beck, beckoning, direction, command, order, commandment, hest, behest, word of command, word, demand, exaction, ordinance.

4. Greeting, mark of recognition, sign of recognition, acknowledgment, wave, salute, hail, hello, bow, curtsey, curtsy, good day, salutation, good morrow, good morning, good evening, salaam, obeisance, bob, welcome, welcoming, bowing and scraping, kowtow, kowtowing, homage, reverence, inclination.

NODE, *n.* 1. Protuberance, knot, lump, bump, block, cake, solid mass, body, gob, convex, convexity, bow, bulge, swelling, rise, tumescence, hump, knob, knur, knurl, hill, nodule, nodulus, nodulation, nodosity, button, boss, stud, excrescence, excrescency, gnarl.

2. Woody formation, burl, joint, juncture, junction, knot, bud, joint, connection, articulation, splice, splicing, suture, stitch, raphe, binding, link, attachment.

3. Problem, intricacy, dilemma, complication, involvement, involution, complexness, complexity, complexus, entanglement, perplexity, labyrinth, tangled skein, problem, puzzle, raveling, Gordian knot, gnarl, twist, kink, snare, trap, coil, tangle, horns of a dilemma, difficulty, vexation, trouble, tough nut to crack, crux, hitch, delay, stress, rub, pinch, obscurity, unintelligibility, inscrutability.

enigma, mystery, riddle, bafflement, poser, question, conundrum, sphinx, riddle of the Sphinx.

NODOSE, *adj.* Knotty, nodular, nodiform, nodulated, gnarled, gnarly, knurled, knurly, knuckled, knaggy, embossed, bossy, bossed, raised, knobby, protuberant, gibbous, gibbose, caruncular, carunculous, carunculated, carunculate, rough, unsmooth, unfinished, uneven, coarse, rugged, rugous, bumpy, convex, convexed, excurvate, excurvated, excurved, nodiferous, torose, nubby, projecting, prominent, bulging, protuberous, protuberantial, protrusive, protrusile, furuncular, furunculate, furunculated, furunculoid, papulous, papillose, papillary, papillulate, tuberculous, papulated.

NODOSITY, *n.* 1. Protuberance, knot, lump, bump, block, cake, solid mass, body, gob, convex, convexity, bow, bulge, swelling, rise, tumescence, hump, knob, knur, knurl, gnarl, hill, nodule, nodulus, nodulation, button, boss, stud, excrescence, excrescency, gibbosity, caruncle, ruga, rugosity, excurvation, torosity, nub, projection, prominence, protrusion, furuncle, furuncule, papule, papilla, papillary, tuber, tuberosity.

2. Woody formation, burl, joint, juncture, junction, knot, bud, connection, articulation, splice, splicing, suture, stitch, raphe, binding, link, attachment.

NODULAR, *adj.* Knotty, nodose, nodiform, nodulated, gnarled, gnarly, knurled, knurly, knuckled, knaggy, embossed, bossy, bossed, raised, knobby, protuberant, gibbous, gibbose, caruncular, carunculous, carunculated, carunculate, rough, unsmooth, unfinished, uneven, coarse, rugged, rugose, rugulous, bumpy, convex, convexed, excurved, excurvated, excurvate, nodiferous, torose, nubby, projecting, prominent, bulging, protuberous, protuberantial, protrusive, protrusile, furuncular, furunculate, furunculated, furunculoid, papulous, papulated, papulose, papillose, tuberous, papillary, papillulate, tuberculous.

NODULATION, *n.* 1. Protuberance, knot, lump, bump, block, cake, solid mass, body, gob, convex, convexity, bow, bulge, swelling, rise, tumescence, hump, knob, knur, knurl, knarl, hill, nodule, nodulus, node, button, boss, stud, excrescence, excrescency, gibbosity, caruncle, ruga, rugosity, excurvation, torosity, nub, projection, prominence, protrusion, furuncle, furuncule, papule, papilla, papillary, tuber, tuberosity.

2. Woody formation, burl, joint, juncture, junction, knot, bud, connection, articulation splice, splicing, suture, stitch, raphe, binding, link, attachment.

NODULE, *n.* 1. Protuberance, knot, lump, bump, block, cake, solid mass, body, gob, hump, convex, convexity, bow, bulge, swelling, rise, tumescence, knob, knur, knurl, gnarl, hill, node, nodulus, button, boss, stud, excrescenc, excrescency, gibbosity, caruncle, ruga, rugosity, excurvation, torosity, nub, projection, prominence, protrusion, furuncle, furuncule, papule, papilla, papillary, tuber, tuberosity.

2. Woody formation, burl, juncture, knot, bud, joint, connection, articulation, splice, splicing, suture, raphe, stitch, binding, link, attachment.

NOISE, *n.* Sound, sonant, ringing, roll, rumbling, rumble, ecphonesis, peal, bell, cacophony, clang, clangor, cry, outcry, ejaculation, babel, babble, babbling, drumfire, barrage, cannonade, rolling, thunder, exclamation, hue and cry, sonancy, blare, din, racket, ado, hubbub, discharge, conclamation,

loudness, boom, riot, rowdydow, alarm, alarum, vociferation, roar, uproar, charivari, shivaree (*U.S.*), rattle, rattling, clatter, clutter, chatter, chattering, clacking, clack, clacket, ruction, ruckus (*dial.*), fracas, pandemonium, bedlam, brawl, hell let loose, bedlam let loose, bobbery, hullabaloo, tumult, bruit, tinkling, caterwauling, bluster, blare, blast, detonation, tintinnabulation, ranting, talk, gabble, brawling, rattle, hum, shouting, resonance, stir, hilarity, gabbling.

NOISELESS, *adj.* Silent, quiet, mute, soundless, still, hushed, muted, peaceful, solemn, deathly, deathlike, stilly, hushful, uncommunicative, speechless, tongueless, reserved, laconic, soft, calm, serene, quiescent, taciturn, voiceless, inarticulate, dumb, toneless, inaudible, aphonic, echoless, aphonous, unsounding, unsounded, nonsonant, unuttered, atonic, atonal, unvocal, dead, muffled, gagged, lulled, smothered, stifled.

NOISOME, *adj.* 1. Harmful, nocent, hurtful, deleterious, injurious, scatheful, baneful, baleful, malefic, malefical, malignant, prejudicial, disserviceable, disadvantageous, mischievous, full of mischief, mischief-making, damaging, corrupting, disastrous, insalubrious, unhealthy, unhealthful, unwholesome, unhealthsome, bad, noxious, septic, virulent, venomous, pernicious, morbific, morbifical, morbiferous, poisonous, ruinous, destructive, internecine.

2. Offensive, repulsive, repellent, foul, filthy, dirty, sullied, maculate, blotched, smudged, dirtied, bespotted, begrimed, bemired, smutty, besmutted, besmirched, smudged, smeared, daubed, blotched, blotted, blemished, tainted, stained, corrupt, contaminated, putrid, putrescent, putrefied, high, rank, foul-smelling, evil-smelling, ill-smelling, nauseous, nauseating, nauseant, sickening, abominable, beastly, loathsome, odious, coarse, revolting, disgusting, distasteful, stercorous, stercoral, stercoraceous, excrementitious, dungy, mucid, slimy, fecal, feculent, purulent, impetiginous, lentiginous, scurfy, maggoty, decayed, rotten, rotted, rotting, saprogenic, flyblown, putrefactive, reeking, stinking, sloppy, horrible, ugly, unsightly, mucky, polluted, squalid, hateful, unclean, impure, obnoxious, fulsome, strong, strong-tasting, fetid, rancid, sour, spoiled, gone bad (*coll.*), odorous, unpleasantly scented, bad-scented, odorific, odoriferous, stenchy, whiffy (*coll.*), graveolent, olid, olidous, peccant, scurvy, suffocating, unbearable, contemptible, ghastly, atrocious, dreadful, horrid, horrible, evil, saprogenic, saprogenous.

NOISY, *adj.* Rackety, piercing, shrill, loud, cacophonous, obstreperous, blustering, clamorous, clamoring, clamant, exclamant, chattering, ear-splitting, deafening, enough to wake the dead, clarion-voiced, stentorian, big-voiced, loud-voiced, sonorous, tonant, clangorous, uproarious, blatant, turbulent, noiseful, dinsome, riotous, hilarious, braying, blattering, blaring, bacchanalian, sharp, acute, trumpet-voiced, trumpet-toned, strident, thunderous, thundering, thundrous, tonitrous, crepitating, crepitant, discordant, dissonant, unharmonious, jarring, grating, coarse-sounding, harsh-sounding, stridulant, stridulent, stridulous, fremescent, fulminating, boisterous, tumultuous, pandemoniacal, unmelodious, unmusical, unsmothered, absonant, turbulent, out of tune, tuneless, raging, stormy, tempestuous, riled, roiled, rampageous, furious, disturbed, unquiet, unstilled, unhushed, non-silent, unmuted, unstill, unpeaceful, lively, animated, communicative, talkative, chattering, garrulous, loquacious, excited, agitated, articulate, echoing, resounding, sonant, tonal, vocal, voluble, alive, unmuffled, unstifled.

NOMAD, *n.* Wanderer, traveler, bohemian, Arab, pilgrim, renegade, runaway, *émigré (Fr.),* immigrant, emigrant, hobo, vagabond, tramp, bum *(sl., U.S.),* straggler, bird-of-passage, itinerant, mover, rambler, strayer, roamer, landlouper, gipsy, *Zigeuner (Ger.),* turnpiker, knight of the road *(sl.),* stray, wastrel, migrator, migrant, refugee, palmer, stroller, Okie *(sl. U.S.).*

NOMADIC, *adj.* Traveling, wandering, peripatetic, peregrinating, vagrant, vagabond, mundivagant, footloose, footloose-and-fancy-free, migratory, migrational, itinerant, ambuling, ambulant, ambulatory, ambulational, ambulative, roving, strolling, discursive, landlouping, perambulating.

NOM DE PLUME *(Fr.), n.* Pseudonym, *nom de guerre (Fr.),* name, assumed name, false name, alias, pen name, writing name.

NOMENCLATURE, *n.* Naming, nuncupation, terminology, technology, baptism, christening, appellation, compellation, cognomen, cognomination, nomination, phraseology, orismology, glossology, terms, expression, vocabulary, designation, denomination, title, titulus, locution, name, naming.

NOMINAL, *adj.* 1. Unsubstantial, insignificant, so-called, in name only, titular, cognominal, known as, nuncupatory, nuncupative, pretended, purported, represented, ostensible, professed, suggested, baseless, groundless.

2. Cheap, low, low-priced, a bargain, dirt-cheap, cheap as dirt, marked down, inexpensive, moderate, moderately priced, of low cost, reasonable, worth the money, reduced, on sale.

NOMINATE, *v.* 1. Name, label, tag, designate, appellate, call, term, style, dub, define, describe, distinguish, distinguish by name, nickname, entitle, title, christen, baptize, cognominate, characterize, call.

2. Commission, appoint, present, offer, propose, place, accredit, designate, delegate, depute, deputize, name, entrust, commit, authorize, set over, place in authority, place in command, intrust, employ, elect, choose, vote, vote into office, select, ordain, send out, call, invite, bid, install, induct, invest, chair, place in the chair, engage, hire, bespeak, consign.

NOMINATION, *n.* 1. Orismology, technology, terminology, phraseology, term, style, name, naming, nuncupation, cognomination, designation, appellation, compellation, denomination, baptism, christening, toponymy, glossology, antonomasia.

2. Election, selection, choice, return, appointment, designation, deputation, deputization, installation, investiture, investing, accession, choosing, ballot, inauguration.

NOMINEE, *n.* 1. Consignee, assignee, trustee.

2. Candidate, suitor, aspirant, bidder, asker, seeker, office-seeker, runner, canvasser, competitor, contestant, supplicant, suppliant, solicitor, petitioner, claimant, solicitant.

NONACCEPTANCE, *n.* Refusal, declining, declination, declension, negativing, negation, refusing, denial, disallowing, disallowance, abnegation, abjuring, renunciation, unwillingness, discountenancing, discountenance, renouncement, begrudging, repulse, rebuff, disapprobation, disapproval, dissent, noncompliance, incompliance, disclaimer, disclamation, recusance, recusancy, recusation, protest, nonconcurrence, nolition, renitence, reni-

tency, reluctance, schism, nonassent, disaffection, dissidence, discordance.

NONAGE, *n.* Youth, immaturity, juvenility, infancy *(Legal),* juniority, tender age, childage, childhood, boyhood, girlhood, minority, adolescence.

NONAPPEARANCE, *n.* Avoidance, absence, absentation, default, invisibility, invisibleness, cut *(coll.),* hooky *(coll.),* French leave *(coll.),* absenteeism, truancy, truantism, nonattendance, truantry, shirking, imperceptibility, defaulting.

NONCE, *n.* This day, the present, today, now, actual time, at the moment, present day, present time, present moment, present hour, this moment, the particular occasion, this occasion, the one occasion, the present juncture, the present occasion, the times, the age, this day, this day and age, this hour, right now, the time being.

NONCHALANCE, *n.* Laziness, indifference, shiftlessness, do-nothingism, fainéance, sloth, slothfulness, slackness, laggardliness, laxness, laxity, dilatoriness, maudlinity, idleness, inactivity, loafing, languor, languidness, supineness, lentitude, torpor, torpidness, torpidity, dronishness, indifference, coldness, frigidity, coolness, iciness, lukewarmness, sluggishness, hebetude, phlegm, otosity, lymph, heaviness, dullness, dopiness *(sl.),* leadenness, deadness, lethargy, apathy, listlessness, soullessness, exanimation, exanimateness, inertness, inertia, neutrality, unconcern, insouciance, blaséness, pococurantism, uninterest, easygoingness, mindlessness, unmindfulness, dispassionateness, dispassion, unambitiousness, undesirousness, unsolicitude, unsolicitousness, impassivity, impassiveness, Micawberishness, procrastination, cunctatiousness, cunctativeness, cunctatoriness, dilly-dallying, dallying, dalliance, negligence, neglectfulness, carelessness, heedlessness, unheedingness, disregard, disrespect, forgetfulness, perfunctoriness, cursoriness, imperturbability, passionlessness, spiritlessness, heartlessness, unexcitability, insensibility, unfeelingness, numbness, unemotionality, unaffectedness, disaffectedness, disaffection, melancholy, atrabiliousness, dreaminess, soulfulness, preoccupation, languorousness, equanimity, insentience, insusceptibility, calm, serenity, inappetence, inappetency, anorexia, disdain, contempt, contemptuousness.

NONCHALANT, *adj.* Lazy, indolent, shiftless, do-nothing, fainéant, slothful, remiss, slack, lax, dilatory, maudlin, idle, idlish, laggard, inactive, loafing, languid, supine, lentitudinous, torpid, torpescent, torpidinous, torporific, dronish, indifferent, cold, frigid, cool, icy, frosty, lukewarm, tepid, sluggish, hebetudinous, phlegmatic, otiose, lymphatic, heavy, dull, dopey *(sl.),* leaden, dead, lethargic, lethargical, apathetic, listless, lifeless, soulless, exanimate, inanimate, inert, neuter, neutral, blasé, unconcerned, insouciant, pococurantist, pococurante, uninterested, easygoing, withdrawn, devil-may-care, mindless, unmindful, dispassionate, unambitious, unaspiring, undesiring, unsolicitous, unattracted, impassive, delaying, Micawberish, procrastinating, procrastinative, procrastinatory, cunctatious, cunctatory, cunctative, dilly-dallying, dallying, negligent, neglectful, careless, heedless, incautious, unheeding, disregardful, disregardant, regardless, respectless, disrespectful, forgetful, perfunctory, perfunctionary, cursory, imperturbable, passionless, spiritless, heartless, unexcited, unexcitable, insensible, insentient, unfeeling, numb, numbed, benumbed, unemotional, unimpressed, unimpressionable, uninspired, untouched, unmoved, unaffected, disaffected, unruffled, unanimate, unanimated, unstirred, preoccupied, languorous, oscitant, abstracted, removed, unimpassioned.

NONCOMMITTAL, *adj.* Cautious, unspeaking, reserved, careful, wary, watchful, on the safe side, safe, playing it safe, playing it cool, cool, gingerly, politic, reserved, laconic, taciturn, vigilant, canny *(dial.)*, prudent, wise, smart *(coll.)*, neutral, guarded, reticent, circumspect, discreet, precautious, precautionary, cautionary, on guard, alert, mum, mute, dumb, unspeaking.

NON-COMPLETION, *n.* Deficiency, nonaccomplishment, scantiness, unfulfillment, nonfulfillment, nonexecution, nonperformance, immaturity, incompleteness, Sisyphean labor, default, shortcoming, fizzle *(sl.)*, dud *(sl.)*, laxity, laxness, remissness, inadequacy, shortage, neglect, negligence, disregard, omission, abandon, abandonment, imperfectness, imperfection, flaw, fault, faultiness.

NONCOMPLIANCE, *n.* Nonconformity, nonconformance, disconformity, nonobservance, nonconventionality, unconventionality, originality, informality, dissent, bohemianism, disagreement, recusancy, recusance, violation, breach of custom, usage, infraction of custom, usage, infringement of custom, usage, violation of custom, usage, trespass, unorthodoxy, uniqueness, strangeness, disobedience, unruliness, mutinousness, insubordination, contumacy, obstinacy, refusal, refusing, nonacceptedness, declining, declination, declension, incompliance, nonconsent, rejection, nonacceptance, denial, negation, protest, abnegation, disclamation, disclaimer, renouncement, renunciation, dissentience, dissidence, nonassent, nonagreement, discordance, disaffection, disapproval, disapprobation, opposition, objection, exception, veto, nonobservance, nonperformance, nonfulfilment, inconventionality, waywardness, intractability, intractableness, breachiness, impatience, recalcitrance, refractiousness, contumaciousness, lawlessness, transgressiveness, heresy, heterodoxy.

NONCOMPLIANT, *adj.* Heterodox, heterodoxical, unconverted, unconvinced, nonjuring, dissenting, dissentious, unconsenting, nonconsenting, uncomplaisant, inacquiescent, negative, negatory, protestant, declinatory, refusing, transgressive, lawless, wayward, recalcitrant, refractory, impatient, restive, insubordinate, contumacious, breachy, intractable, ungovernable, unruly, unsubmissive, uncomplying, uncompliant, disobedient, free and easy, bohemian, original, outlandish, exotic, quaint, funny *(coll.)*, queer, strange, odd, anamalous, anomalistic, wanton, erratic, wandering, stray, straying, aberrant, divergent, deviative, informal, heteroclite, irregular, eccentric, nonobservant, unconventional, nonconformant, nonconforming, nonconformist, heretical.

NON COMPOS MENTIS, *adj.* Insane, unsane, not sane, mad, mentally unsound, maddened, crazy, crazed, lunatic, maniacal, deranged, demented, unhinged, unbalanced, unsettled, loco *(coll.)*, daft, psychopathic, psychotic, psychopathological, tetched *(dial.)*, touched *(coll.)*, touched in the head, off, off one's head, off one's rocker, out of one's mind, out of one's senses, reasonless, insensate, dumb, stupid, not right, not quite right, not in one's head, not in one's mind, mad as a hatter, mad as a March Hare, mad as a weaver, crazy as a bedbug, crazy as a loon, batty, crazy as a coot, stark-raving mad, stark-staring mad, dopey

(sl.), loony *(sl.)*, nuts *(sl.)*, nutty *(sl.)*, **screwy** *(sl.)*, daffy *(sl.)*, dippy *(sl.)*, bats, buggy, bughouse, balmy, barmy, cuckoo, off one's base, off one's nut, off one's track, off one's trolley, infatuated, disordered, disturbed, beside oneself, frenzied, giddy, dizzy, vertiginous, distraught, distracted.

NONCONFORMIST, *n.* Orginal, bohemian, eccentric, character *(coll.)*, card *(coll.)*, case *(sl.)*, crank *(sl.)*, crackpot *(sl.)*, nut *(sl.)*, screwball *(sl.)*, nonjuror, protestant, protester, curiosity, rarity, *rara avis (Lat.)*, rare bird, exception, abnormality, recusant, radical, dissenter, abnormality, dissentient, noncontent, malcontent, seceder, apostate, recreant, bolter, mugwump *(U.S.)*, deserter, renegade, runaway, schismatist, schismatic, secessionist, recidivist, backslider, reversioner, insurgent, mutineer, rebel, revolutionary, revolutionist, iconoclast, skeptic, heretic, heterodox.

NONCONFORMITY, *n.* Noncompliance, nonconformance, disconformity, nonobservance, nonconventionality, unconventionality, originality, informality, dissent, bohemianism, disagreement, recusancy, recusance, violation, breach of custom, usage, infraction of custom, usage, infringement of custom, usage, violation of custom, usage, unorthodoxy, uniqueness, strangeness, disobedience, unruliness, mutinousness, insubordination, contumacy, obstinancy, refusal, refusing, nonacceptedness, declining, declination, declension, incompliance, nonconsent, rejection, nonacceptance, denial, negation, protest, abnegation, disclamation, disclaimer, renouncement, renunciation, dissent, dissentience, dissidence, nonassent, nonagreement, disaffection, discordance, disapproval, disapprobation, opposition, objection, exception, veto, nonobservance, nonperformance, nonfulfillment, inconventionality, waywardness, intractability, breachiness, impatience, recalcitrance, refractiousness, contumaciousness, lawlessness, transgressiveness, heresy, heterodoxy.

NONDESCRIPT, *adj.* Unusual, odd, nonconformist, unconformist, indescribable, unclassifiable, queer, quaint, original, *sui generis (Lat.)*, unorthodox, singular, unaccustomed, uncustomary, uncommon, rare, unwonted, unique, curious, extraordinary, eccentric, bohemian, strange, funny *(coll.)*, outlandish, exotic, fantastic, fanciful, grotesque, freakish, bizarre, weird.

NONE, *pron. sing. and pl.* No, not one, not any, no one, nothing, nil, *nihil (Lat.)*, nix *(sl.)*, naught, nought, nothing whatever, none whatever, nothing at all, none at all, nothing on earth, nothing under the sun, none in the world, no such thing, never a one, nary a one *(coll.)*, nothing, no thing, no degree, no part, no quantity, not a blessed one *(coll.)*, not a particle, nobody, not a soul.

NONENTITY, *n.* 1. Nonexistence, inexistence, existlessness, existenceless, nonsubsistence, nonbeing, nullity, nothingness, oblivion, nirvana, nihility, nihilism, negativeness, negation, negation of being, abeyance, abeyancy, vacuity, blank, void, absence, insubstantiality, unsubstantiality, unsubstantialness, incorporeity, immateriality.

2. Nullity, thing of naught, nihility, obscurity, cipher, nothing, lay figure, dummy, puppet, all talk, phantom, illusion, dream, phantasy, moonshine, flash in the pan, blank, dud *(sl.)*, shadow, mockery, bubble.

3. Nobody, unimportant person, nihility, nullity, nothing, obscurity, naught, nought, cipher, insignificant, insignificance, nobody much *(coll.)*, no great shakes, whippersnapper, scrub, runt, little

fellow, John K. Spelvin, John Q. Public, man in the street, mediocrity, jackstraw, small one, small fry, John Doe, second fiddle, Tom, Dick and Harry.

NONESSENTIAL, *adj.* Extrinsical, extrinsic, adventitious, adscititious, accidental, incidental, fortuitous, casual, unessential, supervenient, accessory, contingent, subsidiary, modal, extraneous, irrelevant, inconsequent, impertinent, inapplicable, inappropriate, inapposite, unconnected, beside the point, beside the mark, aside from the purpose, disquiparant, not equiparant, inapt, unimportant, inconsequential, immaterial, insignificant, inappreciable, inconsiderable, ineffectual, small, little, minute.

NONESUCH, *n.* Elite, choice, pick, select, best, very best, prize, flower, cream, *crème de la crème*, gem, champion, wonder, prodigy, paragon, phenomenon, wonderment, marvel, miracle, amazement, astonishment, sensation, exception, one in a thousand, curiosity, spectacle, sight, monstrosity, freak, original, bohemian, eccentric, character *(coll.)*, card *(coll.)*, case *(sl.)*, crank *(sl.)*, crackpot *(sl.)*, nut *(sl.)*, screwball *(sl.)*, nonjuror, protestant, protester, curiosity, rarity, *rara avis (Lat.)*, rare bird, exception, abnormality, dissentient, noncontent, malcontent, revolutionary.

NONEXISTENCE, *n.* Nihility, negativeness, nullity, nothing, nothingness, nihilism, blank, void, oblivion, vacuum, negation, existencelessness, existlessness, nonsubsistence, inexistence, insubstantiality, insubstantialness, incorporeality, incorporality, incorporeity, negation of being, abeyance, abeyancy, nonentity, nonbeing.

NONEXISTENT, *adj.* Fictitious, fabulous, legendary, mythical, mythological, phantasmic, phantasmagorical, unreal, inexistent, nonsubsistent, existless, null, void, null and void, minus, missing, omitted, negative, blank, not present, away, gone, out of sight, missing, wanting, lacking, omitted, nowhere to be found, dead, imaginary, illusory, nil, chimerical, fanciful, visionary, utopian, quixotic.

NONFULFILLMENT, *n.* Disappointment, failure of hope, failure of expectation, blighted hope, frustration, buffet, check, balk, fail, bafflement, comedown *(coll.)*, letdown *(coll.)*, noncompletion, nonaccomplishment, nonachievement, unfulfillment, nonexecution, inexecution, nonperformance, failure, unsuccessfulness, unsuccess, ill success, flop *(sl.)*, fiasco, washout *(coll.)*, abortion, miscarriage, misfire, flash in the pan, dud *(sl.)*, vain attempt, miss, nonobservance, inobservance, unobservance, nonperformance, noncompliance, omission, default, slight, oversight, laxity, laxness, neglect, negligence, nonchalance, casualness, disobedience, evasion, avoidance, avoidment.

NONHUMAN, *adj.* Cruel, brutal, brutish, bestial, savage, ferocious, ferine, feral, barbarous, barbaric, truculent, vicious, fell, atrocious, unhuman, inhuman, inhumane, fiendish, fiendlike, demoniac, demoniacal, diabolic, diabolical, satanic, devilish, unfeeling, heartless, bloodless, unnatural, hard, hard-hearted, stony-hearted, ghoulish, hellish.

NONINTERFERENCE, *n.* Inaction, passivity, passiveness, laissez-faire, stand-stillism, Fabian policy, do-nothingness, do-nothingism, laissez-faire policy, apathy, quiescence, dormancy, immobility, neutrality, procrastination, nonintervention, let-alone principle, Monroe Doctrine, calmness, nonresistance.

NONINTERVENTION, *n.* Noninterference, passivity, passiveness, laissez-faire, stand-stillism, Fabian policy, do-nothingness, do-nothingism, laissez-faire policy, apathy, quiescence, dormancy, immobility, neutrality, procrastination, let-alone principle, Monroe Doctrine, calmness, nonresistance, inaction.

NONJUROR, *n.* Original, bohemian, eccentric, character *(coll.)*, card *(coll.)*, case *(sl.)*, crank *(sl.)*, crackpot *(sl.)*, nut *(sl.)*, screwball *(sl.)*, noncontent, protestant, protester, curiosity, rarity, *rara avis (Lat.)*, rare bird, exception, abnormality, recusant, radical, dissenter, heterodox, dissentient, malcontent, seceder, apostate, recreant, bolter, mugwump *(U.S.)*, deserter, renegade, runaway, schismatist, schismatic, secessionist, recidivist, backslider, reversioner, insurgent, mutineer, rebel, revolutionary, revolutionist, iconoclast, skeptic, heretic.

NONLEGAL, *adj.* Illegal, illegitimate, unconstitutional, informal, unwarranted, unauthorized, on the index, nonlicit, illicit, unlawful, against the law, criminal, criminalistic, unchartered, impermissible, criminous, wrong, wrongful, actionable, unallowed, disallowed, extrajudicial, outside the law, contraband, outlaw, outlawed, interdicted, proscribed, forbidden, prohibited, null, null and void, voided, invalid, canceled, ineffectual, fraudulent, spurious, false, forged, unauthentic, unlicensed, unwarrantable, unofficial, tabu, taboo, banned, under the ban.

NONOBJECTIVE, *adj.* Subjective, infixed, intrinsic, intrinsical, inborn, innate, inbred, congenital, personal, individual, inherent, incarnate, indwelling, native, immanent, ingrained, inwrought, ingenerate, personal, individual.

NONOBSERVANCE, *n.* Nonconformity, noncompliance, inobservance, unobservance, neglect, inattentiveness, oversight, overlooking, heedlessness, thoughtlessness, insubordination, mutiny, mutinousness, mutineering, laxity, laxness, laches, inconsiderateness, slight, unruliness, disregard, nonperformance, nonfulfilment, failure, omission, default, slackness, casualness, nonpayment, infraction, faithlessness, infidelity, disloyalty, falsity, perfidy, inconstancy, informality, non-cooperation, uncooperativeness, relaxation, truancy, truantism, shunning, evasion, avoidance, procrastination, shirking, malingering, malingery, breach, trespass, violation, lackadaisicality, lackadaisicalness, indolence, laziness, supineness, negligence, neglectfulness, neglect, apostasy, backsliding, breach of trust, breach of faith, faithlessness, infringement.

NONPAREIL, *n.* Nonesuch, elite, choice, pick, select, best, very best, prize, flower, cream, crème de la crème, gem, champion, wonder, prodigy, paragon, phenomenon, wonderment, marvel, miracle, amazement, astonishment, sensation, exception, one in a thousand, curiosity, spectacle, sight, monstrosity, freak, original, bohemian, eccentric, character *(coll.)*, card *(coll.)*, case *(sl.)*, crank *(sl.)*, crackpot *(sl.)*, nut *(sl.)*, screwball *(sl.)*, nonjuror, protestant, deviationist, protester, curio *(coll.)*, rarity, *rara avis (Lat.)*, rare bird, exception, abnormality, dissentient, dissident, noncontent, malcontent, revolutionary, rebel.

NONPARTISAN, *adj.* Unwarped, unbiased, unprejudiced, neutral, impartial, independent, freelance, uninfluenced, unswayed, unaffected, disinterested, equitable, fair, just, unperplexed, unimplicated, uninvolved, unbigoted, unprepossessed, impersonal, objective, unjaundiced, undazzled, dispassionate, freethinking.

NONPAYMENT, *n.* Arrears, default, debt, defalcation, evasion, the skip *(sl.)*, runaround *(sl.)*, collapse, crash, arrear, arrearage, deficit, insolvency, bankruptcy, avoidance, delinquency, delinquence, shirking.

NONPLUS, *n.* Puzzle, perplexity, quandary, dilemma, horns of a dilemma, baffle, bafflement, confusion, confounding, confoundment, deadlock, stalemate, botheration, bother, botherment, nonplusment, nonplusation, impasse, predicament, blind alley, deadlock, deadset, standstill, halt, cul-de-sac, corner, hole, stop, check, checkmate, vexation, trouble, difficulty, plight, pickle *(sl.)*, pass, howdedo, how-do-you-do, slough, quagmire, bog, embarrassment, disconcertion, difficulty, kettle of fish *(coll.)*, mess *(coll.)*, fine mess *(coll.)*, holy mess *(coll.)*, plight, poser, tangle, straits, trouble.

NONPLUS, *v.* Confuse, beat *(coll.)*, muddle, stop, halt, disturb, bother, bring to a standstill, addle the wits, baffle, mystify, stump, ground, perplex, bewilder, lick *(coll.)*, floor *(coll.)*, make the head swim, thwart, frustrate, keep one guessing, try one's wits, check, checkmate, stalemate, deadlock, corner, back into a corner, run into a corner, pose, put out, disconcert, embarrass, dismay, puzzle, abash, scotch, balk, foil, try one's patience, drive to the wall, flummox *(sl.)*, run up a tree, discountenance, override, upset, faze *(coll.)*, tree, astound, astonish, dumfound, flabbergast, trump, bewilder, blanken.

NONPREPARATION, *n.* Neglect, neglectfulness, carelessness, insouciance, unpreparedness, unreadiness, undevelopment, immaturity, unmaturity, unfitness, disorganization, disqualification, unqualification, rawness, roughness, unrefinement, uncultivation, unculture, unculturedness, undeveloped condition, unexploitation, unexploitedness, natural state, state of nature, coarseness, greenness, rudimentariness, incipience, incipiency, inadvertence, negligency, improvidence, unrefinement, abortiveness, abortion, improvision, improvisation, extemporization, extempore.

NONPRODUCTIVE, *adj.* Unproductive, unfruitful, sterile, unfertile, nonfertile, fallow, barren, unprolific, otiose, acarpous, addled, jejune, arid, unfecund, teemless, issueless, inoperative, forceless, unforceful, inane, vain, futile, childless, ineffectual, of no avail, of no effect, powerless, worked-out, exhausted, spent, crippled, unable, incapable, incompetent, weak, inept, inefficacious, ineffectual, senile, disabled, decrepit, nugacious, nugatory, inutile, doddering, superannuated. unserviceable, useless, unuseful, unavailing. bootless, worthless. valueless, profitless, null and void.

NONPROFIT, *adj.* Eleemosynary, charitable, philanthropic, public-service, public-spirited, beneficent, altruistic. humane, humanitarian, almsgiving.

NONRESISTANCE, *n.* Submission, yielding, complaisance, tolerance, toleration, subjection, patience, submissiveness, conformity, unresistance, impassiveness, subjugation, subordination, conformance, compliance, acquiescence, deference, adjustment, accommodation, subordination, subordinacy. impassivity, humility, humbleness, dependence. dependency, sufferance, longanimity, stoicism, long-suffering, forbearance, endurance, resignation, obedience, passivity, passiveness, reconcilement, reconciliation, conciliatoriness, conciliation, line, keeping, obediency.

NONRESISTANT, *adj.* Submissive, yielding, complaisant, tolerant, subjected, patient, in line, passive, conforming, conformant, conformist, conformable, unresisting, unresistant, impassive, subjugated, subordinate, subordinated, compliant, complying, acquiescent, deferent, deferential, adjusted, adjusting, accommodated. accommodating, subordinated, humble, dependent, sufferant, suffering, long-suffering, longanimous, stoic, stoical, forbearing, forbearant, enduring, resigned, obedient, reconciled, conciliatory, in keeping.

NONSENSE, *n.* Jargon, waggery, folly, foolishness, guff *(sl.)*, rigmarolery, fooling, buffoonery, buffoonism, tomfoolery, harlequinade, clowning, joking, jokery, comedy, comicality, pothooks, hangers, daubs, scrawl, scratchings, henscratchings, chickentracks, hentracks, rodomontade, claptrap, drool, drivel, triviality, trifles, scrabble, dribble, trickery, horseplay, chaff, gimcrackery, bubble, smoke, cobweb, small beer, small fry, monkey-shines, monkey business *(coll.)*, jocosity, jocularity, shenanigans, jocoseness, facetiousness, whimsicality, waggishness, quip, word play, play on words, pun, prank, antic, antics, vagary, *boutade (Fr.)*, ridiculousness, ridiculosity, farcicality, foam, froth, absurdity, futility, absurdness, asininity, foolery, imbecility, fatuity, fatuousness, sciamachy, stultiloquence, stultiloquation, stultiloquy, paradox, contradiction, incongruity, self-contradiction, nonsensicality, stuff, stuff and nonsense, stupidity, nugacity, egregiousness, monstrousness, monstrosity, craziness, screwiness *(sl.)*, silliness, insensateness, senselessness, poppycock, ludicrousness, bathos, ineptitude, trumpery, rigmarole, prattle, babble, amphigoury, amphigory, prate, prating, chatter, chattering, blather, babbling, babblement, bushwa *(sl.)*, gabble, jabber, jabbering, jabberwocky, patter, hot air *(sl.)*, gammon *(coll.)*, gas *(sl.)*, bull, palaver, jargon. mere words, clack, clacking, noise, wild and whirling words, just talk, airy talk, bizarreness, ninnyism, levity, conceit, doltishness, stupidity, dumbness, frivolity, ninny-ship, simpletonism, morology, sottage, infatuation, bombast, extravagance, flagrancy, flagrance, sappiness *(coll.)*, foolheadedness, maudlinity, obtuseness, dullardry, dullness, irrationality, unreasonableness, insignificance, insignificancy, balderdash, crap *(sl.)*, illogicality, illogic, illogicalness, invalidity, faultiness, meaninglessness, inconclusiveness, flapdoodle, flummery, *niaiserie (Fr.)*, twattle, twaddle, twiddle, twiddle-twaddle, rubbish, rot, fudge, refuse, trash, truck *(coll.)*, bosh *(coll.)*, moonshine, fiddle-faddle, fiddle-de-dee, bunk, buncombe, humbug, hocus-pocus, applesauce, baloney *(sl.)*, tommyrot, blah, blurb, eyewash, hogwash, nonsensification, piffle, kibosh, flap, drollery, rant, inscrutability, undiscoverability, doggerel verse, doggerel, nonsense verse, malaprop, malapropism, spoonerism, farce, comedy, unintelligibility, unintelligibleness, incomprehensibility, inapprehensibility, illegibility, unrecognizability, unclarity, obscurity, Dutch, double Dutch *(sl.)*, Greek, Choctaw, Hebrew, haver, bragging, braggadocio, fustian, puerility, juvenility, childishness, brimborion.

NONSENSICAL, *adj.* Waggish, foolish, buffoonish, tomfool, clownish, joking, in jest, comic. comical, scrawled, scrawling, daubed, scratched. drooling, driveling, trivial, trifling, scrabbling. dribbling. trick, chaffing, gimcrack, bubble-like. bubbly, smoky, cobwebby, small, insignificant, jocose, jocular, facetious, playful, sportive, whimsical, quippish. punning, punned, prankish, antic, vague, ridiculous, farcical, foamy, frothy, absurd, futile, asinine, fool, imbecilic, fatuous, sciamachous, stultiloquent, paradoxical, contradictory, incongruous, self-contradictory, stupid, nugacious, nugatory, egregious, monstrous, crazy, dizzy *(coll.)*, screwy *(coll.)*, silly, insensate, senseless, ludicrous, bathetic, trumpery, prattling, babbling, amphigorious, prating, chattering, blathering, blatherskite, gabbling, jabbering, pattering, gassy *(sl.)*, palavering, clacking, talky, voluble, bizarre, noisy, nincompoopish, light, doltish, dumb, frivolous, simple, sottish, infatuated, bombastic, extravagant, flagrant, sappy *(coll.)*, fool-headed, maudlin, obtuse, dull, irrational, unreasonable, crappy *(sl.)*, illogical, invalid, faulty, meaningless, inconclusive, rubbishy, trashy, humbug, ranting, droll, inscrutable, undiscoverable, doggerel, malaprop, unintelligible, incomprehensible, illegible, unrecognizable, unclear, obscure, braggart, bragging, fustian, puerile, juvenile, childish.

NONSENTIENT, *adj.* Apathetic, unfeeling, insensible, numb, benumbed, dead, deadened, senseless, insensitive, insentient, insensate, callous, heartless, soulless, cold-blooded, unconscious, impercipient, unperceiving, imperceptive, unperceptive, pachydermatous, thick-skinned, hard, hardened, case-hardened, inured, proof, impervious, anaesthetized, narcotized, drugged, doped, phlegmatic, stony-hearted, languid, torpid, unconcerned, nonchalant, indifferent, cool, frigid, cold.

NONSPIRITUAL, *adj.* Material, corporeal, corporal, bodily, worldly, earthly, materiate, substantial, fleshly, hylic, corporified, incarnate, parenchymatic, parenchymal, sensible, palpable, tangible, ponderable, embodied, materialistic, substantive, substantialistic, irreligious, actual, factual, human, temporal, concrete, practical, existent, living, personal, parenchymatous.

NONSUBJECTIVE, *adj.* Objective, external, outside, impersonal, nonpersonal, scientific, disinterested, unimpassioned, dispassionate.

NOODLE, *n.* 1. Fool, tomfool, mutt *(sl.)*, dope *(sl.)*, jerk *(sl.)*, ninny, ninnyhammer, dunce, dolt, clod, lout, shatterbrain, shatterpate, harebrain, featherbrain, chump *(sl.)*, prize sap *(sl.)*, scatterbrain, loon, loony, simpleton, blockhead, witling, wiseacre, ass, jackass, donkey, bonehead *(coll.)*, imbecile, idiot, moron, calf, colt, numskull, gawk, halfwit, goose, rube, clown, dotard, simp *(sl.)*, juggins, owl, gander, lunkhead *(sl.)*, rattlebrain, rattlepate, rattlehead, knucklehead, lubber, clodhopper, softy *(coll.)*, gabby, noddy, tomnoddy, dumbbell, dummy, zany, stick, sop, duffer *(coll.)*, dumb bunny, dunderhead, dunderpate, square *(sl.)*, dimwit, yokel, thickwit, woodenhead, squarehead, clod, clodpoll, clodpate, lummox, lackbrain, nitwit, driveling idiot, lackwit, ditzy *(coll.)*, addlepate, addlebrain, chucklehead, chowderhead, blunderhead, dunderhead, bullhead, fathead, jolthead, muttonhead, pumpkinhead, beetlehead, blubberhead, doughhead, bakehead, noodle-head, Boeotian, Gothamite, wise man of Gotham.

2. Head, headpiece, poll, pate, cranium, pericranium, brainpan, brain case, think tank, think box, skull, crown, top, sconce, knob *(coll.)*, garret *(coll.)*, attic *(coll.)*, loft *(coll.)*, upper story *(coll.)*, belfry *(coll.)*, bun *(coll.)*, cocoa *(coll.)*, crumpet *(coll.)*, nut *(coll.)*, knob *(coll.)*, bean *(coll.)*, dome *(coll.)*, conk *(coll.)*.

NOOK, *n.* Hole, hole in the wall, depression, recess, corner, niche, cranny, alcove, small place, hiding place, place of concealment, snug place,

cramped place, cantle, cove, coign, dugout, cavity, excavation, cubbyhole, cubby.

NOONDAY, *n.* Noon, noontide, noontime, midday, nooning, meridian, twelve o'clock, zenith.

NO ONE, *pron.* No man, nobody, not a soul, nary a one, not a one, nobody alive, not one, never a one, nobody under the sun, nobody in the world, nix *(sl.)*, nobody present.

NOOSE, *n.* 1. Tie, fastening, hemp, rope, hangman's noose, hangman's knot, ligature, lasso, running noose, loop.

2. Snare, springe, sniggle, gin, trap.

3. The noose, capital punishment, the gallows, the rope, the gibbet, garrote, strangling, halter, necktie party *(sl.)*, garroting, strangulation, hanging.

NORM, *n.* Check, norma, measure, standard, criterion, yardstick, pattern, gauge, model, type, prototype, canon, test, scale, rule.

NORMAL, *adj.* Sane, reasonable, ordinary, standard, regular, average, middle, methodical, rational, right-minded, mean, medium, middling, uniform, unchanging, unchanged, mediocre, neutral, natural, mid, midmost, medium, even, standardized, illustrative, homogeneous, unvarying, unvaried, conforming, conformable, exemplary, model, typical, invariable, representative, ideal, emblematic, general, orderly, figurative, prefigurative, symbolic, consistent, unintermitting, unremitting, unceasing, incessant, conventional, well-regulated, in good order, in good shape, in shape, in usual condition, in good form, constant, continuous, continual, uninterrupted, steady, steadfast, dependable, reliable, unchanging, unstopped, unstopping.

NORTH, *adj.* Northerly, northern, norther, northernmost, boreal, polar, high, septentrional, arctic.

NORTH, *adv.* Northward, northerly, northwardly, northwards.

NORTHERLY, *adj.* North, northern, norther, northernmost, boreal, polar, arctic, high, septentrional.

NORTH STAR, *n.* Pole star, Polaris, polar star, northern star, Cynosure, guiding star, lodestar, guide, *l'Etoile du Nord (Fr.)*.

NOSE, *n.* 1. Prow, bow, bowsprit, jib, jib boom, beak, stem.

2. Olfactory organ, organ of smell, snoot, snout, smeller, nozzle, muzzle, neb, nib, beak, bill, pecker *(coll.)*, breather, nose holes, blow holes, proboscis, trunk, antlia, beezer, bugle, olfactories.

NOSEGAY, *n.* Posy, posey, bouquet, corsage, flowers, blooms, blossoms, boutonniere, buttonhole, spray, wreath garland, boughpot, bunch of flowers.

NOSEY, *adj.* 1. Curious, inquisitive, quizzical, quizzish, gaping, staring, prying, prurient, burning, itching, burning with curiosity, curious as a cat, overcurious, supercurious, snooping, snoopy, agape, agog, all agog.

2. *(Coll.)* High, ill-smelling, evil-smelling, fetid, stinking, reeking, gamey, ripe, smelly, smellsome, malodorous, odorous, stenchy, whiffy *(sl.)*, graveolent, mephitical, mephitic, strong, strong-smelling, noisome, fulsome, repulsive, unbearable, reeky, suffocating.

NOSTALGIA, *n.* Homesickness, regret, remorse, lonesomeness, loneliness, regretfulness, solitude, longing for home, *Heimweh (Ger.)*, *mal du pays (Fr.)*, nostalgy, pining, languishing.

NOSTALGIC, *adj.* Lonely, lonesome, homesick, regretful, remorseful, languishing, pining.

NOSTRIL, *n.* Nosehole, breathing hole, nare, nares, blowhole, spiracle, breather.

NOSTRUM, *n.* Remedy, contrivance, invention, recipe, receipt, formula, physic, proprietary, medicine, drug, potion, pill, bolus, embrocation, electuary, lincture, linctus, tincture, scheme, quack remedy, patent medicine, medicament, treatment, draft, draught, dose, prescription, cure, panacea, arcanum, balm, elixir, balsam.

NOTABILITY, *n.* Interest, importance, eminence, consequence, precedence, distinction, paramountcy, primacy, supereminence, preëminence, repute, reputation, nobility, superiority, significance, import, fame, famousness, concern, salience, mark, moment, weight, value, note, sublimity, grandeur, figure, name, majesty, dignity, prestige, splendor, popularity, credit, respect, report, réclame, glory, éclat, celebrity, high repute, good repute, esteem, regard, account, remarkableness.

NOTABLE, *n.* Celebrity, man of distinction, man of mark, great card, panjandrum, somebody, rare bird, *rara avis (Lat.),* worthy, name, big name, figure, important figure, V.I.P. (Very Important Person), cynosure, pillar of the community, pillar of the state, pillar of the church, pillar of society, lion, social lion, great man, hero, heroine, the great, sachem, bigwig, big gun *(sl.),* personage, great personage, something, nabob, great mogul, grand mogul, notability, person of consequence, big shot *(sl.),* high muck-a-muck, magnate, tycoon, noble, baron, baronet, countess, count, baroness, nobiliary, viscount, viscountess, earl, lady, noblewoman, nobleman, peer, peeress, magnifico, grandee, blueblood, don, patrician, thoroughbred, aristocrat, lord, upper-cruster *(sl.),* squire, lordling, prince, princeling, princelet, gentleman, silk-stocking, gentlewoman, duke, duchess, archduke, archduchess, grand duke, grand duchess, marquis, marchioness, marquise, marchesa, knight, banneret, knight banneret, armiger, palgrave, landgrave, margrave, waldgrave, lady, princess, atheling, kahn, sheik, rajah, rani, ranee, maharajah, maharani, maharanee, begum.

NOTABLE, *adj.* 1. Majestic, reputable, renowned, notorious, celebrated, famed, famous, dignified, well-known, eminent, grand, marked, of mark, remarkable, noteworthy, extraordinary, unusual, august, distinguished, sublime, unordinary, unaccustomed, unparalleled, unwonted, singular, unique, undescribed, indescribable, rare, curious, peculiar, unexampled, unheard-of, unprecedented, uncustomary, unaccustomed, illustrious, unexpected, great, popular, known, conspicuous, radiant, brilliant, lustrous, glorious, much-touted, touted, acclaimed, much-acclaimed, outstanding, egregious, consequential, of consequence, peerless, splendid, splendrous, exalted, lofty, imposing, impressive, stately, prominent, big *(coll.),* at the top of the tree, of the first water, unmatched, matchless, preëminent.

2. Conspicuous, striking, prominent, in bold relief, in high relief, in strong relief, notorious, glaring, flagrant, marked, pronounced, particular, outstanding, salient, striking, bold, noticeable, defined, clear, clearly defined, definite, plain, showy, flaunting, daring, evident, manifest, apparent, seeable, visible, observable, ostensible, ostentatious, showing, discernible, perceptible, perceivable, distinct, patent, unconcealed, unhidden, unveiled, un-

covered, disclosed, naked, bare, barefaced, overt, open, revealed, exposed, remarkable, noteworthy, momentous, signal, relevant, to the point, in point, unmistakable, important, uncurtained, unshrouded, unscreened, uncloaked, material.

NOTABLY, *adv.* 1. Majestically, reputably, renownedly, notoriously, famously, eminently, grandly, markedly, remarkably, noteworthily, extraordinarily, unusually, augustly, distinctively, sublimely, unaccustomedly, unwontedly, singularly, uniquely, undescribably, indescribably, rarely, curiously, peculiarly, unprecedentedly, uncustomarily, unaccustomedly, illustriously, unexpectedly, grandly, lustrously, greatly, popularly, conspicuously, radiantly, brilliantly, lustrously, gloriously, outstandingly, egregiously, consequentially, peerlessly, splendidly, splendrously, exaltedly, loftily, imposingly, impressively, stately, prominently, matchlessly, preëminently.

2. Conspicuously, strikingly, prominently, notoriously, glaringly, flagrantly, markedly, pronouncedly, particularly, outstandingly, saliently, strikingly, boldly, noticeably, definitely, clearly, plainly, showily, flauntingly, daringly, evidently, manifestly, apparently, seeably, visibly, observably, ostensibly, ostentatiously, discernibly, perceptibly, perceivably, distinctly, patently, disclosedly, nakedly, barely, barefacedly, overtly, openly, revealingly, exposedly, remarkably, noteworthily, momentously, signally, relevantly, pertinently, pointedly, unmistakably, importantly, materially.

NOTARY, *n.* Functionary, official, recorder, recordit, prothonotary, writer, clerk, scribe, scrivener, record-maker, register, registrar, stenographer, notary public, writer, record-keeper, greffier.

NOTATION, *n.* 1. Arithmetical operations: addition, subtraction, multiplication, division, logarithms, proportion, rule of three, practice, reduction, involution, approximation, interpolation, differentiation, integration, equation, extraction of roots, proportions, progressions.

2. Character, signs, notes, musical notes, scale, notes of the scale, signature, symbol.

3. Inscription, record, register, registry, minute, entry, item, marginalia, single entry, double entry, scription, endorsement, annals, chronicle, memorabilia, note, notes, jottings, minutes, memorandum, reminder.

NOTCH, *n.* 1. Rank, position, standing, degree, grade, round, rung, mark, peg, hole, term, rank, gradation, scale, link, place, position, stair, peg, pitch, precedence, condition, caste, footing, standing, station, status, locus, point.

2. Fracture, rupture, crena, fault, flaw, gorge, gap, canyon, cañon, defile, pass, cut, ravine, gulch, gully, passage, abysm, abyss, rent, break, breach, fissure, nick, nitch, cut, dimple, depression, indentation, dent, indention, nock, jag, score, scoring, scotch, blaze, chasm, clough, close, split, rift, incision, scissure, slit, crevasse.

NOTCH, *v.* Nick, cut, mark, tick, indent, score, scratch, serrate, tooth, scotch, scar, scarify, crimp, jag, cleave, gash, scallop, scollop, escollop, pink, mill, crenelate, crenulate, earmark, label, escallop.

NOTCHED, *adj.* Nicked, scalloped, escallop, escalloped, dentate, dentated, dentelated, sharp, rough, bumpy, edgy, crenelated, crenulated, earmarked, labeled, serrate, serratic, serrilate, serrulated, serriform, jagged, jaggy, palmate, palmated, sawtoothed, pinked, milled, marked, ticked, crimped, cut, cleft, scotched, scored, blazed, scarred, scarified, incised.

NOTE, *n.* 1. Voucher, record, recordation, recording, memorandum, memorabilia, annals, memoirs, factum, certificate, credential, warrant, item, entry, inscript, inscription, endorsement, indorsement, notes, notation, jottings, minutes, memorial.

2. Footnote, comment, commentary, explanation, illumination, illustration, illustrative matter, auxiliary matter, explication, exegesis, documentation, commentation, explanatory note, explanatory comment, marginal note, marginalia, marginal annotation, scholium, gloss, scholion, exemplification, criticism, critique.

3. Entry, item, credit, debit, minute, notation, single entry, double entry.

4. Letter, epistle, communication, message, missive, correspondence, errand, communiqué, dispatch, despatch, white paper, memorandum, word, bulletin, news, tidings, billet, *billet doux (Fr.)*, love note, mash note, information, line, chit, fan letter *(sl.)*, love letter, paper, formal note, advice.

5. Attention, attentiveness, regard, mindfulness, heedfulness, thought, consideration, mind *(dial.)*, observance, scrutiny, watching, concentration, respect, advertence, application, intentness, devotion, care, exactness, diligence, observation.

6. Interest, gravity, seriousness, importance, import, consequence, prominence, notability, eminence, significance, celebrity, éclat, good name, credit, solemnity, reputation, distinction, figure, fame, notoriety, famousness, notedness, respectability, renown, account, report, glory, kudos *(coll.)*, respect, reputability, good odor, good report, popular favor, popular repute, popularity.

7. Money, currency, instrument, legal paper, legal tender, paper money, voucher, certificate, bill, banknote, paper, parchment, document, deed, silver certificate, gold certificate, negotiable instrument, commercial paper, warrant, draft, banker's draft, promissory note, sight draft, mortgage note, Federal Reserve note, Treasury note, national bank note, order, draft, greenback, folding money *(sl.)*, check, checque, debenture, bill of exchange, letter of credit, postal note, note of hand.

8. Musical note, musical notation, tone, enharmonic note, enharmonic, grace note, ornament, figure, interval, stop, degree, patent note, shaped note, held note, sustained note, report, staccato, spiccato, responding note, sound, sound quality, tonal quality, tonation, intonation, pitch, tune, tonality, key, pervading note, dominant, subdominant, burden, strain, tenor, vein, sharp, flat, natural, half-tone, quarter tone, incidental, accidental, whole note, half-note, quarter-note, eighth-note, sixteenth-note, thirty-second-note, sixty-fourth-note, double whole note, minim, crochet, quaver, semiquaver, hemisemiquaver, hemisemidemiquaver, percet, triplet, drone, dominant, tonic, bourdon, semibreve.

9. Color, tone, hue, tint, tinge, tincture, tinct, shade, cast, complexion.

NOTE, *v.* 1. Notice, mark, remark, realize, take cognizance of, perceive, see, look at, regard, give attention to, attend, heed, sight, spot *(coll.)*, observe, mind, animadvert, make note of, take notice of, attend to, advert to, give thought to, rivet the thoughts to, pay attention to, be aware of, become aware of, appreciate, be conscious of, become conscious of, look at, look into, look after, look to, look over, view, hold in view, lend an ear to, incline one's head toward, apply oneself to, mind one's business, tend to, examine, scrutinize, inspect.

2. Record, mark down, put down, make a note of, take a minute, memorandize, set down, put down, make an entry, enter, book, insert, inscribe, indite, write, write in, catalogue, catalog, chronicle, write out, write up, post, post up, annotate, list return, make a memorandum, jot down, inscroll, docket, place on record, put on record, register, enregister, commit to writing, pencil, scribble, scrawl, calendar.

3. Keep accounts, invoice, indent, bill, post, enter, account, balance, balance accounts, balance the books, credit, debit, book, docket.

4. Document, annotate, footnote, append, affix, attach, explain, account for.

NOTEBOOK, *n.* Record book, memorandum book, reminder, pocketbook, memo book *(coll.)*, engagement book, promptbook, scrapbook, memory book, album, birthday book, address book, tablet, calendar, pad, memorandum pad, memo pad, blankbook, reminder, daily reminder, adversaria, memoir, memorial, commonplace book, logbook, log, journal, diary, daybook, account book.

NOTED, *adj.* 1. Noticed, marked, remarked, seen, observed, realized, perceived, looked at, regarded, attended, attended to, given attention, heeded, sighted, spotted *(coll.)*, observed, minded, animadverted, made note of, appreciated, viewed, looked at, looked into, scrutinized, examined, inspected.

2. Recorded, marked down, marked, put down, memorandized, set down, entered, booked, docketed, inserted, inscribed, written, indited, catalogued, cataloged, logged, chronicled, written out, posted, annotated, footnoted, documented, appended, affixed, attached, listed, inserted, included, returned, jotted, jotted down, inscrolled, registered, enregistered, penciled, scribbled, scrawled, calendared.

3. Invoiced, billed, debited, credited, posted, entered, accounted, balanced, booked.

4. Notable, celebrated, famous, illustrious, brilliant, glorious, renowned, notorious, famed, well-known, eminent, marked, of mark, remarkable, noteworthy, extraordinary, unusual, august, distinguished, sublime, unordinary, unaccustomed, unparalleled, unwonted, singular, unique, grand, great, popular, known, conspicuous, radiant, lustrous, glorious, much-touted, touted, acclaimed, much-acclaimed, outstanding, egregious, consequential, exalted, lofty, preëminent, prominent.

NOTEWORTHY, *adj.* Singular, unusual, great, grand, distinguished, famed, famous, celebrated, honored, necessary, urgent, august, noble, big, outstanding, commanding, exceptional, prominent, preëminent, eminent, odd, strange, stupendous, prodigious, marvelous, salient, important, significant, substantial, considerable, to the point, relevant, pertinent, material, signal, momentous, unimaginable, unimagined, unexpected, unaccountable, unparalleled, unprecedented, wonderful, rare, unimaginable, unordinary, extraordinary, unaccustomed, uncustomary, unwonted, uncommon, unfamiliar, unknown, noticeable, special, unexampled, undescribed, indescribable, especial, special, of mark, remarkable, astonishing, astounding, notable.

NOTHING, *n.* 1. Triviality, trivia, inconsequentials, bauble, trinket, minor details, nihility, bagatelle, gimcrack, gewgaw, small beer, small fry, foam, bubble, froth, air, stuff, trash, truck *(coll.)*, rubbish, chaff, fiddle-faddle, fidfad, fiddlestick, whimwham, trumpery, frippery, insignificancies, insignificance, mere nothing, naught, nought, nullity, obscurity, illusion, phantom, ghost, wraith.

2. Void, oblivion, blankness, nonexistence, negation, negativeness, nullity, nothingness, nihilism, vacuum, existencelessness, existlessness, nonsubsistence, inexistence, insubstantiality, unsubstantiality, insubstantialness, incorporeality, incorporality, incorporeity, negation of being, abeyance, abeyancy, nonentity, nonbeing.

3. Zero, nought, naught, cipher, nil, *nichts (Ger.)*, none, scratch, nix, nixie, goose egg, duck egg, zip *(coll.)*, *rien (Fr.)*.

NOTHINGNESS, *n.* 1. Oblivion, void, blankness, nothing, nullity, nihility, nonexistence, negation, negativeness, nihilism, vacuum, existencelessness, existlessness, nonsubsistence, inexistence, insubstantiality, unsubstantiality, unsubstantialness, incorporeality, incorporality, incorporeity, negation of being, abeyance, abeyancy, nonentity, nonbeing.

2. Unimportance, idleness, nugacity, nugaciousness, paltriness, triviality, inconsequentialness, inconsequentiality, immateriality, ineffectuality, inappreciableness, inconsiderableness, littleness, smallness, minuteness, insignificance, poverty, worthlessness, beggarliness, niggardliness, cheapness, trumpery, scurviness, shabbiness, pitifulness, meagerness, meanness, weediness, badness.

NOTICE, *n.* 1. Prominence, note, eminence, celebrity, éclat, good name, credit, reputation, distinction, attention, regard, cognizance, recognition, notoriety, fame, renown, figure, report, glory, kudos *(coll.)*, praise, laudation, adulation, respect, popularity, popular favor, popular repute.

2. Information, report, mention, enlightenment, lights, light, specification, notification, acquaintance, intelligence, intimation, monition, admonition, warning, admonishment, knowledge, know *(sl.)*, dope *(sl.)*, goods *(sl.)*, info *(sl.)*, presentment, representation, communication, intercommunication, disclosure, account, declaration, statement, word, publication, publicity, propagation, teaser *(sl.)*, literature *(coll.)*, poster, bill, handbill, throwaway, circular, bulletin, broadside, pamphlet, folder, sheet, leaf, leaflet, dodger, broadsheet, circular letter, promulgation, encyclical, broadcast, report, manifest, manifesto, advertisement, announcement, pronunciamento, edict, decree, divulgation, enunciation, annunciation, notoriety, limelight, spotlight, flagrancy, dissemination, evulgation, public notice, diffusion, circulation, pronouncement.

3. Caution, caveat, warning, admonition, tipoff, pointer, steer *(sl.)*, dehortation, tip *(coll.)*, suspicion, lesson, intimation, hint, indication, suggestion, forewarning, prewarning, premonition, allusion, implication, portent, portention, portendment, portendance, notification, telling, advisement, aviso, caution, cautioning, sign, monition.

4. Critique, criticism, review, critical review, critical article, piece, column, article, adverse criticism, report, comment, commentary.

NOTICE, *v.* See, behold, take sight of, catch sight of, perceive, look at, regard, heed, observe, recognize, ken, witness, discern, get a load of *(sl.)*, espy, spy, spot *(coll.)*, make out, describe, descry, sight, cognize, eye, hear, find, take in, mind, command a view of, animadvert, take notice, take notice of, attend to, advert to, give heed to, discover, have in sight, mark.

NOTICEABLE, *adj.* Unhidden, in sight, in plain sight, in plain view, open, unconcealed, exposed, manifest, well-marked, of mark, remarkable, pointed, staring, flagrant, observable, perceivable, perceptible, discernible, seeable, beholdable, visible, visual, apparent, in evidence, evident, starkstaring, well-defined, definite, unshaded, plain, clear, unclouded, unconcealed, distinct, open, revealed, recognizable, obvious, showing, showy, prominent, conspicuous, patent, autoptic, autoptical, unmistakable, clear as day, palpable, plain as day, glaring, stark, perspicuous, ostensible, avowed, explicit, express, exoterical, exoteric, self-evident, open, naked, bare, uncovered, uncurtained, bold, flagrant, arrant, glaring, salient, unobscure, unmasked.

NOTIFICATION, *n.* 1. Information, report, mention, enlightenment, light, specification, acquaintance, intelligence, intimation, monition, admonition, admonishment, warning, knowledge, presentment, representation, communication, message, intercommunication, disclosure, account, declaration, statement, word, publication, publicity, propagation, teaser, literature, poster, bill, handbill, throwaway, circular, bulletin, broadsheet, broadside, pamphlet, folder, sheet, leaf, leaflet, dodger, circular, circular letter, encyclical, promulgation, broadcast, report, manifest, manifesto, advertisement, announcement, pronouncement, pronunciamento, edict, decree, divulgation, evulgation, enunciation, public notice, diffusion, dissemination, circulation.

2. Caution, caveat, warning, admonition, tipoff, pointer, steer, dehortation, tip, suspicion, lesson, intimation, hint, indication, suggestion, forewarning, portent, portending, portention, allusion, implication, portendment, portendance, advisement, advice, aviso, caution, cautioning, sign, monition.

NOTIFY, *v.* 1. Tell, relate, inform, present, put forth, publish, give to understand, put into one's head, acquaint, represent, express, impart, communicate, mention, impart to, acquaint with, divulge, tell of, make known, apprise, advise, bring word, send word, write word, write to, give notice of, lay before, let one know, give word.

2. Make allusion, herald, report, proclaim, imply, announce, insinuate, cable, wire, telegraph, telephone, phone, intimate, indicate, hint, suggest, signify, publish, whisper, tip, tip off, jog, remind, air, vent, divulge, divulgate, evulgate, bruit, bruit about, rumor, make known, declare, prompt, put in mind of, tell, enunciate, publicize, announce, cue, give a cue, prompt, voice.

NOTION, *n.* 1. Idea, eidolon, concept, conception, suspicion, abstract idea, abstraction, vague idea, supposition, presupposition, presumption, image, mental image, picture, mental picture, sentiment, observation, reflection, consideration, rough guess, apprehension, impression, conceit, thought.

2. Kink, quirk, caprice, whim, whimwham, whimsey, whimsicality, conceit, quip, crank, fantastic idea, fantastic notion, fad, *boutade (Fr.)*, maggot in the brain, bee in the bonnet, prank, trick, escapade, fit, humor, fancy, vagary, flimflam.

3. Merchandise, trifle, knickknack.

NOTIONAL, *adj.* Imaginary, abstract, chimerical, imaginal, imagined, fantastic, phantasmic, phantasmagorical, conjured up, pictured, envisioned, fanciful, fancied, conceived, conceptual, dreamed, dreamt, idealistic, fabled, fabulous, phantasmal, romantic, romantical, unreal, illusory, unsubstantial, baseless, groundless, ungrounded, unfounded, figmentary, maggoty, figmental, utopian, quixotic, visionary, whimsical, irresponsible, unreasonable, faddish, faddy, fadmongering, capricious, freaky, freakish, fanciful, fitful, humorsome, sportive, playful, crotchety, skittish, fast, uncontrolled, unrestrained, contrary, wanton, wayward, erratic, changeable, fickle, frothy, frivolous, volatile, mercurial, frolicsome, arbitrary, giddy, dizzy, unreliable, tergiversating, unstable, inconstant, coquettish, undependable, flirtatious, variable.

NOTORIETY, *n.* 1. Bad publicity, publicity, limelight, spotlight, public gaze, public notice, *réclame (Fr.),* flagrancy, bruit, report, currency, publicness, ballyhoo.

2. Prominence, notability, eminence, significance, celebrity, éclat, reputation, distinction, fame, famousness, notedness, renown, account, glory, popularity, popular repute.

NOTORIOUS, *adj.* 1. Known, apparent, advertised, obvious, recognized, widely known, commonly known, sure, unconcealed, glaring, flagrant, in the public eye, notable, open, manifest, plain, unmistakable, arrant, common, commonplace, avowed, visible, in plain sight, in plain view, palpable, distinct, conspicuous, outstanding, talked-of, talked-about, in everyone's mouth, on everyone's lips, celebrated, renowned.

2. Disreputable, discreditable, scandalous, shameful, dishonorable, ignominious, opprobrious, inglorious, disgraceful, unseemly, ignoble, infamous.

NOTWITHSTANDING, *prep.* However that may be, however, yet, still, withal, albeit, all the same, at all events, in any event, even so, despite, in spite of, howbeit, for all that, on the other hand, at the same time, without regard for, after all, when all is said and done, in disagreement with, taking one consideration with another.

NOUN, *n.* Name, proper name, proper noun, common noun, substantive, part of speech, word, noun adjective, verbal noun, gerund, adverbial noun, adherent noun, term.

NOURISH, *v.* Feed, dine, sustain, nurture, strengthen, gratify, regale, put out to pasture, graze, pasture, supply with food, supply with nourishment, cultivate, maintain, provision, provender, cater, victual, purvey, serve, minister, care for.

NOURISHING, *adj.* Eatable, edible, wholesome, healthsome, healthy, nutritious, salutary, salubrious, gustable, good for you, drinkable, potable, health-giving, digestible, assimilable, corroborant, roborant, good for what ails you *(coll.),* tonic, bracing, invigorating, alimentary, nutritive, esculent, comestible.

NOURISHMENT, *n.* Victuals, viands, food, nutriment, wholesome food, sustenance, subsistence, nurture, nutrition, board, table, comestibles, refection, feeding, eating, consumption, consumption of food, ingestion, digestion, assimilation, alimentation, keep, meat, food and drink, provender, pabulum, bread, daily bread, provisions, supplies, eats *(vulg.),* foodstuffs, subsidy, feed, mash, eatables, plant food, animal food, fodder, swill, grain, hay, oats, manna, bounty.

NOVEL, *adj.* Singular, exceptional, unusual, new, new-fangled, unique, recent, late, unfamiliar, unheard-of, extraordinary, unordinary, uncustomary, unhandled, untried, untouched, late, neoteric, neoterical, fresh, virgin, virginal, original, uncopied, unparalleled, unexampled, new-fashioned, modern, modernistic, strange, different, peerless,

uncommon, unaccustomed, unwonted, unfamiliar, unprecedented, rare, out of the ordinary, off the beaten track.

NOVEL, *n.* Book, fiction, story, work, work of fiction, literature, work of literature, literary production, novella, *nouvelle (Fr.),* novelet, romance, chronicle, yarn, tale, narrative, writing, composition, opus, work, brainchild, volume, dime novel, penny dreadful, shilling shocker, dreadful, science novel, science fiction, epistolary novel, psychological novel, novel of manners, satirical novel, historical novel, mystery novel, whodunit *(sl.).*

NOVELIST, *n.* Writer, author, storyteller, teller of tales, spinner of yarns, *littérateur (Fr.),* authoress, bookman, bookwright, novel writer, chronicler, man of letters, romancer, romancist, storier, novelettist, word painter, writer of fiction, fictioneer, relater, *raconteur (Fr.).*

NOVELTY, *n.* Originality, uniqeness, newness, neology, neologism, radicalness, radicality, *dernier cri (Fr.),* the last word, the latest word, the latest thing, the newest thing, contraption, modernity, modernism, innovation, change, new measure, recency, recentness.

NOVICE, *n.* Convert, beginner, proselyte, tyro, disciple, neophyte, catechumen, learner, pupil, student, novitiate, probationer, apprentice, entrant, newcomer, tenderfoot, greenhorn, schoolboy, schoolgirl, *débutant (Fr.),* amateur, blunderer, newcomer.

NOVITIATE, *n.* Tutelage, novitiation, apprenticeship, prenticeship, learning period, trial period, tyronism.

NOW, *adv.* At present, at this moment, immediately, on the moment, on the spur of the moment, at this time, today, at this time of day, even now, just now, right now, but now, for the nonce, nowadays, for the time being, at the present time, at this day and age, at the present, straightaway, at this instant, on the instant, instantly, instanter, right away, presently, without delay, here.

NOWADAYS, *adv.* In these times, at this time, at present, at this moment, at this moment in time, today, now, just now, but now, for the nonce, in this day and age, at the present time.

NOW AND THEN, *adv.* Sometimes, occasionally, intermittently, infrequently, every so often, often, at various times, on occasion, on divers occasions, at times, every once in a while, once in a blue moon *(coll.),* once in a coon's age *(coll.),* sporadically, *toties quoties (Lat.),* at intervals, in jumps and starts, by fits and starts, by jerks, discontinuously.

NOWAY, NOWAYS, NOWISE, *adv.* No, not a bit, not at all, not in the least, on no account, by no means, by no manner or means, not by a long shot, not by a damn site, in no wise, in no respect, not much.

NOXIOUS, *adj.* 1. Offensive, repulsive, noisome, repellent, foul, filthy, dirty, sullied, maculate, blotched, smudged, dirtied, bespotted, begrimed, bemired, smutty, besmutted, besmirched, smeared, daubed, blotted, blemished, tainted, stained, corrupt, contaminated, putrid, putrescent, putrefied, high, rank, foul-smelling, strong-smelling, ill-smelling, nauseating, nauseous, nauseant, sickening, abominable, beastly, loathsome, odious, coarse, revolting, disgusting, distasteful, stercorous, stercoral, stercoraceous, excrementitious, dungy, mucid, slimy, fecal, feculent, purulent, impetiginous, maggoty, lentiginous, scurfy, decayed, rotted, rotten, rotting, saprogenic, flyblown, putrefactive, reeking, sloppy, horrible, ugly, unsightly, mucky, squalid, hateful, unclean, impure, evil-smelling.

2. Harmful, nocent, hurtful, deleterious, injurious, scatheful, baneful, baleful, malefic, maleficial, malignant, malign, prejudicial, disserviceable, disadvantageous, mischievous, full of mischief, mischief-making, damaging, corrupting, disastrous, insalubrious, unhealthy, unhealthful, unwholesome, bad, septic, virulent, venomous, pernicious, morbific, morbifical, morbiferous, poisonous, ruinous, destructive, dilatory, internecine, unhealthsome.

NOZZLE, *n.* 1. Nose, snout, snoot *(coll.)*, proboscis, trunk, olfactory organ, breather, nib, bill, pecker, neb.

2. Mouth, jaws, mouthpiece, maxilla, mandibles.

3. Rose, rosehead, sprinkler.

NUANCE, *n.* Refinement, delicacy, subtlety, nicety, distinction, nice distinction, delicate distinction, refined distinction, differentia, differential, shade of difference.

NUB, *n.* 1. Core, essence, pith, kernel, substance, essential part, fundamental part, fundamentals, quid, quiddity, inner reality, gist, nucleus, salient point, important part.

2. Hump, protuberance, protuberancy, gibbosity, boss, tumescence, knot, bunch, knurl, snag, excrescence, appendage, protrusion, tumidity, bulge, swelling, swell, tumefaction, knur, gnarl, stud, lump, pommel, horn, bulb, tubercle, tuberosity, tubercule, hummock, geniculate, dune, whelk, monticule, monticle, mound, node, finial, barrow, knob, projection, prominence, eminence, extumescence, intumescence, convexity, convexness, excurvature, excurvation, nubble, croche, knop, kopje *(Africa)*, knosp.

NUBILATE, *v.* Cloud over, becloud, overshadow, shadow, darken, shade, adumbrate, fog, befog, mist, obfuscate, dim, bedim, encloud, overcast, darken over, make dim, render dim, make shadowy, obscure.

NUBILOUS, *adj.* Nebulous, nebulose, cloudy, clouded, beclouded, nubilated, nubiferous, obnubilated, misty, hazy, foggy, befogged, fogged, steamed, obscure, indistinct, vague, obfuscous, obfuscated, opaque, murky, murkish, smoky, fumy, vaporous, cirrose, cirrous, nimbose, overcast.

NUCLEUS, *n.* Seed, pith, core, semen, essence, marrow, sap, gist, nub, quintessence, elixir, essential, fundamental, blood, lifeblood, essential quality, quid, quiddity, center, heart, jet, central point, centrum, central body, centrosphere, centrosome, germ, egg, sperm, roe, milt, spawn, source, radix, origin, heart, root, rudiment, focus, radicle, embryo, fetus, foetus, wellspring, bud.

NUDE, *adj.* Naked, bare, unclothed, exposed, divested, stark-naked, undressed, unclad, uncovered, unapparelled, ungarmented, denuded, laid bare, revealed, shown, raw *(coll.)*, stripped to the buff, in one's birthday suit *(coll.)*, in a state of nature, *au naturel (Fr.)*, wearing nothing, without a stitch, unarrayed.

NUDGE, *v.* Push, touch, elbow, jog, poke, motion, nod, signal, signalize, indicate, jostle, bump, punch.

NUDGE, *n.* Push, jostling, bump, jog, touch, poke, indication, gesture, gesticulation.

NUDITY, *n.* Undress, nakedness, bareness, unadornedness, nudation, denudation, divestiture, divestment, the nude, the buff *(coll.)*, birthday suit, the raw *(coll.)*, natural garb, nature's garb, dishabille, bare skin.

NUGACITY, *n.* Triviality, frivolity, futility, trifling, ineptitude, absurdity, foolishness, folly, fatuity, inanity, morology, sottage, silliness, tomfoolery, tomfoolishness, levity, levity of mind, ninnyism, ninnyship, simpletonianism, infatuation, irrationality, unintelligence, witlessness, senselessness, brainlessness, stultiloquence, unimportance, insignificance, immateriality, irrelevance, irrelevancy, inconsequentiality, ineffectuality, paltriness, trivialism, fribblery, uselessness, inutility, inefficacy, inaptitude, incompetence, unserviceability, unprofitability, unfruitfulness, inadequacy, worthlessness, vanity.

NUGATORY, *adj.* Nugacious, trifling, trivial, piddling, peddling, fribbling, slight, flimsy, superficial, frivolous, frothy, worthless, vain, futile, absurd, petty, jejune, inept, foolish, fatuous, inane, morologistic, sottish, silly, tomfoolish, light, airy, infatuated, irrational, unintelligent, witless, senseless, brainless, stultiloquent, unimportant, insignificant, immaterial, irrelevant, inconsequential, ineffectual, paltry, ineffective, useless, inefficacious, inapt, incompetent, unserviceable, unprofitable, unfruitful, inadequate, worthless, vain, unproductive, abortive, unavailing, void, inoperative, null, bootless, feckless, to no purpose, purposeless, picayune, picayunish, niggling, finicking, finicky, superficial, shallow, slender, fatuitous, insubstantial, unsubstantial, baseless, groundless, fragile, frail, slight, impotent, invalid, barren, sterile, effete, inutile, inefficacious, unprofitable, unremunerative, valueless, good-for-nothing, unsalable, idle, empty, dispensable, disposable, no-good, no-account *(coll.)*.

NUGGET, *n.* Lump, mass, chunk *(coll.)*, hunk *(coll.)*, piece, clod, gold nugget, gold, precious metal.

NUISANCE, *n.* Annoyance, vexation, evil, grievance, inconvenience, bother, scourge, affliction, hurt, thorn in the side, botheration, trouble, pest, plague, handicap, cross, abomination, mortification, visitation, misfortune, bane, torment, torture, burden, blight, curse, woe, aggravation *(coll.)*, pestilence, worry, gall, fret, bore, irritation, pique, sore subject, cares, thorn, sting.

NULL, *adj.* Blank, annihilated, nothing, negative, obliterated, nonexistent, null and void, existless, minus, omitted, blank, inexistent, nonsubsistent, jejune, empty, bare, clear, hollow, vacuous, invalid, inoperative, nugatory, trifling, trivial, piddling, worthless, valueless, vain, futile, inept, foolish, insignificant, immaterial, senseless, unproductive, abortive, unavailing, bootless, purposeless, insubstantial, unsubstantial, baseless, groundless, impotent, barren, sterile, inutile, inefficacious, unprofitable, unremunerative, good-for-nothing, unsalable, empty, disposable, dispensable, no-account *(coll.)*, no-good.

NULLIFICATION, *n.* Neutralization, invalidation, repeal, abolition, abrogation, repudiation, cancellation, annihilation, commutation, rescission, revocation, revoking, defeasance, renege, countermand, countermanding, cancel, abolishment, dissolution, recantation, annulment, retractation, retraction, forswearing, disavowal, withdrawal, renunciation, abjuration, disclaimer, disclamation, renouncement.

NULLIFY, *v.* Repudiate, dishonor, default, abrogate, rescind, retract, recant, renege, cancel, cancellate, reverse, repeal, void, make void, invalidate, declare null and void, sweep away, cast aside, cast behind, renounce, disown, countermand, override, overrule, counterorder, abolish, annul, dissolve, quash, nol-pros (*Legal*), recall, frustrate, neutralize, compensate, undo, vitiate, counterbalance, counterpoise, overbalance, outweigh, counteract, conflict, annihilate, obliterate, destroy.

NULLITY, *n.* Nothingness, nihilism, oblivion, nonbeing, nonexistence, nihility, negation, negativeness, abeyance, abeyance, vacuity, blank, blankness, void, naught, thing of naught, nonentity, obscurity, cipher, zero, insignificance, insignificancy, nobody, nonentity, bagatelle, frippery, fribble, fribblery, triviality, thing of naught, blankness, obliteration, annihilation, mere nothing, trinket, bauble, gewgaw, whimwham, knickknack.

NUMB, *adj.* Insensible, insensate, insensitive, unfeeling, senseless, imperceptive, dead, deadened, anaesthetized, insentient, thick-skinned, hardened, case-hardened, unsensitive, unconscious, unperceiving, obtuse, dull, benumbed, narcotic, narcotized, dazed, passionless, unimpassioned, insusceptible, spiritless, dispassionate, impassive, heartless, soulless, indifferent, unconcerned, insouciant, languid, lethargic, stupefied, comatose, imperturbable, indifferent.

NUMB, *v.* Dull, deaden, render numb, make numb, obtund, paralyze, stun, hebetate, stupefy, brutify, brutalize, blunt, drug, anesthetize, narcotize, torpify, petrify, freeze, chill, nip, freeze to death, glacify, glaciate, make cold, render cold, render frigid, refrigerate, put to sleep, chloroform, hypnotize, magnetize, mesmerize.

NUMBER, *v.* Numerate, enumerate, count, tell, tell off, tally, figure, cipher, figure up, tot, reckon, reckon up (*coll.*), compute, calculate, score, total, cast up, sum up, sum, add, estimate, make an estimate, make an account, make an accounting, render an accounting, paginate, muster, foliate, recite, mark, run over, recapitulate, foot up, tottle (*coll.*), call over, run over, call the roll, poll, subtract, multiply, divide, extract roots, algebraize, page, affix numbers to, check, tick, audit, balance, take stock, take inventory, overhaul, prove, demonstrate, include, comprise, comprehend, contain, reckon among, number among, encircle, encompass.

NUMBER, *n.* 1. Figure, numeral, character, symbol, integer, digit, folio, round number, cipher, numero, No., Nos. (*abbreviation*), sum, difference, aggregate, tally, score, total, tale, amount, quantity, product, company, collection, assemblage, multitude, many, problem, example (*Arith.*), power, root, logarithm, index, modulus, exponent, progression, arithmetical progression, geometrical progression, proportion, quota, ratio, function, series, counter, formula, complement, subtrahend, minuend, multiplier, multiplicand, multiple, submultiple, quotient, fraction, decimal, numerator, denominator, mixed number, mixed decimal, common measure, differential, integral, radix, modulus, logarithm, repetend, circulating decimal.

2. Part, section, portion, division, chapter, verse, phrase, paragraph, article, clause, book, passage, edition, issue.

3. Plurality, few, multitude, quantity, preponderance, preponderancy, preponderation, several, indefinite number, indeterminate number, abundance, quantities, scores, array, bevy, galaxy, bags, barrels, tons, pounds, acres, bunch, a good many, a great number, herd, covey, shoal, school, swarm, hive, cloud, gaggle, pride, brood, litter, farrow, fry, nest, mob, crowd, assemblage, host, army, legion, collection, company, amount, pack, force, troop, majority, mass, aggregate, total, sum.

4. Cadence, expression, modification, modulation, inflection, rhythm, meter, rhyme, rime, measure, rhythmical flow, lilt, swing.

NUMBERING, *n.* Enumeration, numeration, count, computation, tally, score, reckoning, summation, calculation, adding, footing, totaling, casting, account, estimate, estimation, tale, roll, roll call, muster, poll, census, statistics.

NUMBERLESS, *adj.* Myriad, countless, incalculable, innumerable, many, multitudinous, infinite, illimitable, immeasurable, incomprehensible, measureless, without measure, without bound, boundless, termless, endless, unbounded, unlimited, illimited, indefinite, indeterminate, unapproachable, unfathomable, unnumbered, uncountable, unnumberable, numerous, plentiful, thick, teeming, outnumbering, rife, abundant, widespread, crowded, profuse, populous, various, galore (*coll.*), manifold, sundry.

NUMBERS, *n., pl.* 1. Quantity, bulk, strength, force, amount, mass, amplitude, sum, measure, portion, multitude, large numbers, abundance, scores, a number, an array, bevy, galaxy, loads (*sl.*), gobs (*sl.*), buckets full (*coll.*), bags, barrels, tons, pounds and pounds, a profusion, a bunch, quite a few, a good number, a good many, legion, army, no end of, no small amount, host.

2. Verse, rhyme, meter, rhythm, rhythmic flow, metrical composition, poetry, stanzas, song, cadence, expression, lilt, swing.

NUMBNESS, *n.* Insensibility, insensateness, insensitiveness, insensitivity, unfeelingness, senselessness, imperceptience, deadness, morbidity, anaesthesia, insentience, thick skin, thick-skinnedness, hardness, unsensitiveness, unconsciousness, obtuseness, dullness, narcosis, dazedness, daze, passionlessness, unimpassionedness, insusceptibility, spiritlessness, dispassion, dispassionateness, impassivity, impassiveness, heartlessness, soullessness, indifference, unconcernedness, insouciance, nonchalance, languor, languidness, lethargy, stupefaction, coma, imperturbability, coldness, frigidness, frigidity, chill, chilliness, painlessness, imperceptiveness.

NUMERAL, *n.* Number, numero, No. (*abbreviation*), character, symbol, cipher, digit, figure, figger (*coll.*), integer, round number, cardinal number, Arabic numeral, Roman numeral.

NUMERARY, *adj.* Numeral, pecuniary, numerical, numerative, figural, figurative, arithmetical, analytic, algebraic, statistical, aliquot, submultiple, logometric, differential, prime, fractional, exponential, integral, totitive, positive, negative, irrational, rational, surd, radical.

NUMERATE, *v.* Reckon, count, enumerate, number, call over, tell, tell off, compute, assess, rate, appraise, measure, value, valuate, evaluate, gauge, meter, measure out, tally, figure, figure up, tot, compute, cipher, calculate, score, total, cast up, sum up, sum, add, estimate, make an estimate, make an account, make an accounting, render an accounting, paginate, muster, recite,

NUMERICAL, *adj.* Numerary, numeral, numerative, figural, figurative, arithmetical, analytic, algebraic, statistical, aliquot, submultiple, multiple, logometric, differential, integral, prime, fractional, exponential, totitive, positive, negative, irrational, rational, surd, radical.

NUMEROUS, *adj.* Many, various, multitudinous, myriad, countless, innumerable, numberless, divers, several, sundry, multifold, manifold, multiple, bounteous, bountiful, plentiful, plenteous, not a few, no few, multitudinal, multitudinary, multiferous, multifarious, copious, abundant, abounding, very many, quite a few, ever so many, considerable, rife, superabundant, generous, teeming, profuse, thronged, alive with, thick, in profusion, prodigal, countless, incalculable, infinite, illimitable, immeasurable, incomprehensible, measureless, without measure, without bound, boundless, endless, unlimited.

NUMSKULL, *n.* Fool, tomfool, mutt *(sl.)*, dope *(sl.)*, jerk *(sl.)*, ninny, ninnyhammer, dunce, dolt, clod, lout, shatterbrain, shatterpate, harebrain, featherbrain, chump *(sl.)*, prize sap *(sl.)*, scatterbrain, loony, loon, simpleton, blockhead, witling, wiseacre, ass, jackass, donkey, bonehead, imbecile, idiot, moron, calf, gawk, halfwit, goose, rube *(sl.)*, clown, dotard, simp *(sl.)*, juggins *(coll.)*, owl, gander, lunkhead *(sl.)*, rattlebrain, rattlepate, rattlehead, knucklehead, lubber, clodhopper, softy *(coll.)*, noodle, gabby, noddy, tomnoddy, dumbbell, dummy, zany, stick, sop, ass-head, mooncalf, bull calf, silly, silly ass, duffer *(coll.)*, dumb head, dumb bunny, dunderhead, dunderpate, square *(sl.)*, dimwit, thickwit, woodenhead, squarehead, clodpoll, clodpate, lummox, yokel, lackbrain, halfwit, nitwit, driveling idiot, lackwit, ditzy *(sl.)*, addlepate, addlebrain, chucklehead, chowderhead, blunderhead, bullhead, fathead, jolthead, muttonhead, pumpkinhead, noodlehead, Boeotian, Gothamite, wise man of Gotham.

NUMSKULLED, *adj.* Obtuse, stolid, thickwitted, doltish, dumb *(coll.)*, stupid, oafish, cloddish, clodlike, dull, dullard, slow, uncomprehending, hebetate, hebetudinous, undiscerning, unapprehending, dull-witted, foolish, fatuous, silly, rattlebrained, rattleheaded, barmy *(coll.)*, goosy, asinine, inane, sappy, dizzy, maudlin, apish, empty-headed, empty-minded, vacant, vapid, vacuous, thoughtless, giddy, dead from the neck up, unteachable, blind, purblind, unenlightened, uncognizant, not bright, unendowed, short-witted, lack-brained, mindless, thick, bovine, lumpish, sottish, crass, Boeotian, Boeotic, blunder-headed, blunt-witted, addlepated, thickbrained, pigheaded, muttonheaded, chuckleheaded, chowderheaded, pumpkinheaded, addleheaded, addlebrained, sappy *(sl.)*, sapheaded, clodpated, clodpolled, beefheaded, foggy, foggy in the head, beetleheaded, cabbage-headed, driveling, dull-headed, dull-pated, dull-brained.

NUN, *n.* Sister, religious woman, anchorite, conventual, abbess, prioress, mother superior, lady superior, superioress, reverend mother, canoness, secular canoness, postulant, novice, maiden, bride of Christ.

NUNCIO, *n.* 1. Messenger *(obsolescent)*, intelligencer, emissary, dispatch bearer, runner, nunciate, enunciator, annunciator, commissionaire, announcer, proclaimer, proclamator, proclaimant.

2. Papal legate, Papal emissary, Papal ambassador, diplomat, diplomatist, diplomatic agent, representative, envoy, minister, internuncio.

NUNCUPATIVE, *adj.* Oral, uttered, verbal, spoken, hearsay, vocal, unwritten, parol, acroamatic, acroamatical.

NUNCUPATORY, *adj.* Oral, uttered, verbal, spoken, hearsay, unwritten, nondocumentary, acroamatic, acroamatical.

NUNNERY, *n.* Convent, cloisters, abbey.

NUPTIAL, *adj.* Bridal, hymeneal, spousal, matrimonial, epithalamial, marital, conjugal, epithalamic, connubial, wedded.

NUPTIALS, *n., pl.* Marriage, wedding, espousing, matrimony, matrimonials, hymeneals, hymen, bridals, epithalamium, epithalamy, espousals, espousement, nuptial benediction, hymeneal rites, leading to the altar, confarreation *(Roman)*, wedlock, union, marital union, nuptial tie, nuptial knot.

NURSE, *n.* Trained nurse, registered nurse, male nurse, practical nurse, sister, monthly nurse, private nurse, graduate nurse, district nurse, public health nurse, probationer, probe *(sl.)*, nurserymaid, nursegirl, dry nurse, wet nurse, lady with the lamp, servant, servant girl, body servant, serving girl, serving maid, nursemaid, guardian, attendant, helper, caretaker, governess.

NURSE, *v.* 1. Suckle, succor, feed, feed at the breast, nourish, give suck to, wet nurse, dry nurse, nurture, foster, cultivate, cherish, put out to nurse, cradle.

2. Guard, protect, foster, cherish, pamper, succor, aid, assist, coddle, wait upon, attend, care for, take care of, attend to, support, take charge of, ride herd on *(U.S., sl.)*, safeguard, watch over, ward, shield, screen, shelter, keep watch over.

3. Harbor an idea, nurse an idea, entertain an idea, nurture an idea, bear in mind, keep in mind, have in mind.

4. Remedy, treat, attend to, minister to, doctor.

NURSERY, *n.* 1. Cradle, nest, nidus, breeding place, incubator, hotbed, schoolroom, children's room, garden, garden patch, botanical garden, greenhouse, cold frame, forcing house, forcing pit, stovehouse, conservatory.

2. Infant school, kindergarten, nursery school, day school, day nursery.

NURSLING, *n.* Infant, baby, babe, suckling, baby bunting, babykins, *bambino (Italian)*, papoose, fondling, child, nurse-child, bantling, bottle-baby.

NURTURE, *n.* 1. Nutriment, nourishment, refection, provender, provisions, keep, board, subsistence, sustenance, sustentation, meat, bread, daily bread, table, food, eats *(coll.)*, diet, nutrition, rations, alimentation, maintenance.

2. Breeding, training, care, fostering, tutelage, education, rearing, schooling, teaching, tuition, instruction, discipline, support, cultivation, preparation, development, drill, practice.

NURTURE, *v.* 1. Feed, nourish, sustain, foster, strengthen, victual, cater, provision, purvey, provender, mess, forage, pasture, graze, provide with food, provide with sustenance, provide with nourishment, regale, satisfy, gratify.

2. Train, foster, discipline, take in hand, tutor, teach, educate, breed, cultivate, rear, form, guard, bring up, fetch up, raise, develop, put to nurse,

dry-nurse *(coll.)*, habituate, familiarize with, prepare.

NURTURING, *n.* 1. Feeding, nourishment, nutrition, fostering, strengthening, victualing, provisions, provender, mess, forage, foraging, pasturage, grazing, sustenance.

2. Training, fostering, discipline, tutelage, teaching, education, breeding, cultivation, rearing, formation, guarding, bringing up, fetching up *(coll.)*, upbringing, raising, development, nursing, habituation, familiarization, preparation.

NUT, *n.* 1. *(Slang)* Crackpot, nonconformist, original, eccentric, bohemian, one in a thousand, crank, screwball *(sl.)*, queer one, queer specimen, rare bird, *rara avis (Lat.)*, odd one, oddity, dissenter, radical, recusant, heretic, fanatic, enthusiast, character *(coll.)*, card *(coll.)*, case *(coll.)*, devotee, zealot, follower, fan *(coll.)*, energumen, bug *(sl.)*, rooter *(sl.)*.

2. Kernel, seed, meat, vegetable, mast, almond, walnut, black walnut, English walnut, peanut, cashew, coconut, hazlenut, chestnut, buckeye *(coll.)*, Brazil nut, filbert.

3. *(Slang)* Head, pate, poll, skull, cranium, noodle, sconce. See HEAD.

4. *(Slang)* Madman, loon, loony, dement, crackbrain, screwball, bedlamite, candidate for bedlam, cracked wit, psychopath, psychopathic case, energumen, demoniac, demon, maniac, raving maniac, lunatic, goof *(sl.)*, bat *(sl.)*, coot *(sl.)*, crackpot *(sl.)*, monomaniac, megalomaniac, kleptomaniac, kleptomanist, dipsomaniac, idiot, phobe, phobic, paranoiac.

NUTATION, *n.* Vibration, nodding, nod, circumnutation, inequal motion, libration, libratory motion, oscillation, vibratility, vibratiunculation.

NUTBROWN, *adj.* Brown, brownish, reddish-brown, brown-red, red-brown, toast-brown, cinnamon, cinnamon-brown, roan, sorrel, henna, chestnut, chestnut-brown, coppery, copperish, copper-brown, chestnut-colored, castaneous, mahogany, mahogany-brown, brown as a berry, sunburned, sunburnt, tan, tanned, golden-brown, bronze, bronzed, bronze-colored, terra-cotta, rufous, coffee, coffee-colored, coffee-brown. seal-brown, umber, umber-brown.

NUTRIMENT, *n.* Aliment, nourishment, food, sustenance, nutrition, meat, bread, board, diet, pap, papulum, support, foodstuff, eatables, eats *(coll.)*, supplies, provisions, provender, rations, mess, forage, fodder, fare, cheer *(coll.)*, grub, grubbery, chow, chuck, refection, provisions, provision, keep, subsistence, sustentation, daily bread, table, groceries, feed, pasturage, pasture, grain, oats, barley, corn, silage, ensilage, hay, straw, mash, swill, grass.

NUTRITION, *n.* Food, diet, nourishment, sustenance, sustentation, meat, bread, aliment, alimentation, board, pap, papulum, support, foodstuff, eatables, eats *(sl.)*, supplies, provisions, provender, rations, mess, forage, fodder, fare, cheer *(coll.)*, grub, grubbery, chow, chuck, refection, provision, keep, subsistence, daily bread, table, groceries, feed, pasturage, pasture, grain, oats, barley, corn, ensilage, silage, hay, straw, swill, grass, eutrophy, dystrophy, malnutrition, denutrition, innutrition, mash.

NUTRITIOUS, *adj.* Esculent, eatable, edible, alimentary, gustable, comestible, nutritive, dietetic, succulent, culinary, wholesome, healthful, health-giving, healthy, beneficial, good, good for you,

good for what ails you *(coll.)*, digestive, digestible, salutary, peptic, peptical.

NUTRITIVE, *adj.* Esculent, eatable, edible, succulent, alimentary, gustable, comestible, nutritious, dietetic, culinary, wholesome, good, healthful, health-giving, healthy, beneficial, good for you, good for what ails you *(coll.)*, salutary, digestive, digestible, peptic, peptical.

NUZZLE, *v.* Cuddle, caress, kiss, coddle, snuggle, nestle, buss, smack, dandle, cosset, cherish, cocker, pet, pat.

NUTTY, *adj.* Irrational, abnormal, unhinged, insane, deranged, unsane, out of one's mind, unbalanced, unsettled, of unsound mind, *non compos mentis (Lat.)*, daft, loco, locoed *(coll.)*, touched in the head, tetched *(coll.)*, reasonless, bereft of reason, out of one's head, not right, not quite right, not right in the head, mad, mad as a hatter, cuckoo, off one's nut *(sl.)*, buggy, beany *(sl.)*, maddened, crazed, crazy, lunatic, moonstruck, befuddled, befooled, insensate, pixilated, off in the upper story *(sl.)*, monomaniac, monomaniacal, maniac, psychopathic, psychopath, imbecile, idiotic, mentally deficient, with bats in the belfry *(sl.)*, batty *(sl.)*, psychopathological, fargone, cracked *(sl.)*, brainsick, addled, mixed-up, sick, ill, unwell, mentally ill, mentally sick.

NYMPH, *n.* 1. Larva, chrysalis, pupa, aurelia, cocoon, grub, maggot, caterpillar, worm.

2. Dryad, nymphid, fairy, hamadryad, wood nymph, alseid, nymphet, nymphlin, oread, mountain nymph, limoniad, meadow nymph, flower nymph, Napaea, Hyads, Pleiades, Atlantides, water nymph, peri, water sprite, undine, ondine, nix, nixie, kelp, kelpie, naiad, limniad, fresh-water nymph, ocean nymph, Nereid, seamaid, mermaid, seamaiden, siren, Hyades.

3. *(Poetic)* Girl, maid, maiden, damsel, lass, woman, sprite, sylph, child.

O

OAF, *n.* Booby, dullard, simpleton, dolt, blockhead, beetlehead, addlehead, mutt, imbecile, bullhead, fool, lummox, gawk, idiot, dunce, numbskull, boneheaded, screwball *(sl.)*, nut *(sl.)*, nitwit, thickskull, ninny, witling, thickhead, ass, lout, clod, moron, dunderhead, shallow-brain, sap, halfwit, ignoramus, jackass, nincompoop, donkey, loon, fathead, jerk *(sl.)*.

OAR, *n.* Paddle, scull, sweep, pole, punt.

OAR, *v.* Move *(as a boat, etc.)*, row, propel, scull, punt, pull, paddle, ply the oars.

OARSMAN, *n.* Boatman, ferryman, rower, boater, gondolier, waterman, bencher.

OASIS, *n.* Fertile *or* green spot, island, resting place *(in the desert, etc.)*, watering place *(in the desert, etc.)*.

OAT, *n.* Grain *(of a cereal grass)*, corn, barley, meal, maize, rye, fodder, cereal.

OATH, *n.* 1. Solemn avowal, affirmation, pledge, vow, plight, invocation, covenant, affidavit *(written)*, swearing, attestation, averment, adjuration, avouchment, guarantee, warrant, troth.

2. Swearing, blasphemy, profanity, curse, cuss *(coll.)*, imprecation, malediction, expletive.

OATMEAL, *n.* Hot cereal, porridge, mush, farina.

OBDURATE, *adj.* 1. Stubborn, unyielding, obstinate, unimpressible, uninfluenced, unaffected, intractable, pervicacious, unmanageable, inflexible, unbending, unmalleable, mulish, firm, immovable, refractory, uncontrollable, self-willed, bullheaded, pigheaded, wilful, bullethead (coll.), ungovernable, recalcitrant, opinionated, bigoted, headstrong.

2. Callous, unpitying, cold-blooded, harsh, averse, unyielding, unbending, tough, dogged, unsympathetic, stiff, unfeeling, unconcerned, supercilious, inhuman, hardened, uncompassionate, unmerciful, unsparing, unforgiving, hard-hearted, unimpassioned, unimpressible, untouched, unmoved, insentient, insensitive, stony, merciless, relentless, remorseless, iron-hearted, stern, unresponsive, hard-bitten, indifferent, flinty, Laodicean, unstirred, thick-skinned, unrelenting, implacable, inexorable, cold, hard, disdainful, supine, indurated, uncaring, impervious.

OBEDIENCE, *n.* Compliance, yielding, acquiescence, dutifulness, obeisance, subjection, submissiveness, submission, deference, morigeration, ductility, allegiance, tractability.

OBEDIENT, *adj.* Submissive, deferential, devoted, duteous, dutiful, law-abiding, rule-abiding, compliant, governable, observant, morigerous, morigerate, supple, ductile, tractable, acquiescent, loyal, pliant, faithful.

OBEISANCE, *n.* 1. Bodily expression of deep respect *or* deferential courtesy (*as before a superior*), salutation, curtsy, greeting, inclination, genuflection, prostration, kneeling, scrape, nod, kowtow, salaam, bow.

2. Deference, homage, worship, adoration, reverence, submission, obedience, service, respect, veneration, duty, honor, estimation, piety, awe, yielding, ceremony, prayer, meekness, humility, humbleness, lowliness, self-abasement, complaisance, subjection, resignation, service, self-mortification, dulia (*Rom. Cath. Theol.*), latria (*Rom. Cath. Theol.*), hyperdulia (*Rom. Cath. Theol.*).

OBELISK, *n.* Tapering four-sided shaft of stone, column, tower, pillar, tombstone, quadrangular pillar, needle, memorial, shaft, guglia, monolith, monument.

OBESE, *adj.* Excessively fat, corpulent, tubby, portly, stout, gross, puffy, well-fed, thickset, chubby, rounded out, round, paunchy, moonfaced, pudgy, strapping, big-bellied, bulky, burly, large, rotund, swollen, unwieldy, potbellied, abdominous, whopping (*coll.*), fleshy, plump, lumpish, full, brawny.

OBEY, *v.* Comply with, fulfill the commands *or* instructions of, respond conformably in action to, submit to, be ruled by, mind, heed, yield, follow, fall in with, bow to, discharge, satisfy, keep, observe, respect, serve, please, be regulated by, be faithful to, abide by, conform to, defer to, listen, fall under, pay attention to, acknowledge, prostrate oneself before, humble oneself to, perform, surrender to, concur with, knuckle (down *or* under), succumb, accede, acquiesce, carry out, give way, resign, stoop to, get into line, toe *or* mark the line, keep in step, be guided by, walk the chalk mark *or* line, kneel to, bend the knee to, be subject, attend to, execute, do one's bidding, crouch before, keep faith with, carry into execution, bend to, regard with submission, be governed by.

OBFUSCATE, *v.* 1. Confuse, stupefy, bewilder, muddle, mystify, perplex, complicate, mix up, daze, blind, disconcert, throw into confusion, faze (*coll.*), perturb, upset, unsettle, make one's

head swim, addle the wits, confound, fluster, rattle (*coll.*), befuddle, baffle, puzzle, embarrass, dismay, fog, nonplus, disturb, keep one guessing, put off the track, throw off the scent, keep one in suspense, dazzle.

2. Darken, obscure, adumbrate, obtenebrate, shade, dim, darkle, becloud, cloud, eclipse, gloom, somber, murk, hide, overshadow, shroud, shadow, dull, blur, blacken, bedim, encompass with shadow, occult, blind, curtain, shade, begloom, benight, veil, conceal, cover, cloak, screen, blear, smoke, fog, nubilate, hide.

OBITUARY, *n.* Notice of the death of a person, brief biographical sketch (*as in a newspaper*), necrology, death notice *or* announcement, obit.

OBJECT, *n.* 1. Visible *or* tangible thing, substantiality, reality, phenomenon, thing perceived by the senses (*esp. by sight or touch*), existence, stuff, chemical, element, creation, body, percept, particular, materiality, individuality, article, lump of matter, device, contrivance, protoplasm, substance, person, creature, being, something, external reality.

2. Thing *or* person to which attention *or* action is directed, mark, butt, target, spectacle, cynosure, vision, sight, recipient, testee, victim, subject, fair game, gazing-stock, dupe, point, monkey, guinea pig, joke, game, prey, quarry, bull's-eye, quintain (*Mediev.*).

3. Thing that is presented to the mind, matter, issue, subject, thought, vision, significant, argument, idea, affair, concern, item, particular, challenge, phenomenon, study, subject matter.

4. End toward which effort is directed, aim, intent, intention, view, motive, desire, objective, reason, cause, substance, essence, gist, marrow, meat, pith, point, determination, ambition, use, design, purpose, drift, goal, final cause, prospect, proposal, project, hope, search, sense, significance, heart, core, meaningfulness, implication, denotation, connotation, import, purport, eye, plan, will, scheme, resolution, spirit, tenor, bearing, force, effect, ground, rationale, standard, tendency, coloring, contemplation, resolve, decision, basis, occasion, mainspring, keystone, principle, call, wish, explanation, root, prime mover, meaning, thing wanted, desideration.

5. Person *or* thing which arouses feelings of pity, disgust, *etc.*, eyesore, gorgon, fright, figure, ugly duckling, specter, monster, hag, harridan, blemish, scarecrow, sight (*coll.*), frightful thing, laughingstock, jecting-stock, byword, quiz.

OBJECT, *v.* 1. Offer (*a reason or argument*) in opposition, adduce in opposing *or* dissenting, protest, attest, cite, submit against, present, evidence, appeal, call to witness, bring forward, instance, allege, plead.

2. Express *or* feel disapproval, be averse, state *or* declare opposition, remonstrate, expostulate, detest, take exception, protest, demur, disapprove, cavil, complain, loathe, sicken, resist, carp, shrink from, contravene, controvert, find fault, nauseate, call in question, kick (*coll.*), impeach, counter, reject, dislike, obstruct, spurn, reluct, counteract, abhor, abominate, oppose, animadvert on *or* upon, challenge, except, eschew, be at variance, quarrel, make objections to, scruple, execrate, dispute, impugn, stick at, shy at, differ, dissent, disagree, disfavor, disrelish, renounce, have no use for, be hostile, refuse to admit, doubt, deny, contradict, look askance at, discountenance, revolt at, frown on, shudder at, quibble, deprecate, repudiate.

OBJECTIFY, v. Present as an object (esp. of sense), realize, make objective, externalize, exteriorize, make realistic, actualize, visualize, embody, body, substantiate, incarnate, personify, make corporeal or physical, corporealize, substantialize, envisage, materialize.

OBJECTION, n. 1. Something adduced or said in disagreement or disapproval, adverse reason, exception, doubt, protest, demur, demurrer, drawback, complaint, stricture, imputation, charge, detraction, boycott, obstacle, veto, disparagement, scruple, remonstrance, difficulty, expostulation, dispute, halt, hitch, stop, stay, hindrance, hamper, obstruction, impediment, contradiction, handicap, barrier, counter argument, contrary principle, accusation, stumbling block, catch, snag, block, check, reproach, disadvantage, rebuke, reproof, reprimand, kick (sl.), challenge.
2. Act of objecting, protest, protestation, opposition, dissent, denial, hesitation, hesitancy, reproof, censure, objectation, blaming, carping, cavil, demur, demurrer, kick (coll.), blame, faultfinding, disparagement, contradiction, remonstrance, negation, rejection, disapprobation.
3. Feeling of disapproval or dislike, disrelish, disfavor, prejudice, animadversion, distaste, displacency, reluctance, execration, aversion, offense, mental reservation, odium, antipathy, hatred, disinclination, disaffection, exception, opposition, discountenance, disesteem, disapprobation, phobia, resentment, dissatisfaction, repugnance, abhorrence, loathing, detestation, disgust, protest, dissent, refusal, indisposition, vexation, irritation, annoyance, indignation, renunciation, renouncement, abnegation, nonacceptance.

OBJECTIONABLE, adj. That may be objected to, offensive, obnoxious, displeasing, horrid, unacceptable, invidious, culpable, unseasonable, amiss, unseemly, unadvisable, undesirable, unfit, ineligible, revolting, exceptionable, harmful, repugnant, rank, disgusting, impalatable, nasty, foul, peccant, nefarious, noxious, execrable, abominable, unbearable, intolerable, unendurable, gross, unpleasant, vile, odious, heinous, deplorable, fulsome, insufferable, loathsome, obscene, sickening, evil, filthy, dirty, unsavory, base, despicable, scurvy, hateful, noisome, pernicious, nauseating, annoying, unwholesome, shocking, detestable, disagreeable.

OBJECTIVE, adj. 1. Final, destined, end, eventual, intended, strategic, desired, ultimate.
2. Not subjective, impersonal, nonsubjective, candid, open-minded, judicial, neutral, detached, sober, uncolored, disinterested, impartial, uninfluenced, unwarped, unprejudiced, unswayed, unbiased, dispassionate, just, fair, equitable, unbigoted.
3. (Gramm.) Accusative.

OBJECTIVE, n. 1. Aim, goal, target, intent, design, end, purpose, butt, mark, destination.
2. (Gramm.) Object, accusative.

OBJURGATE, v. Execrate, denounce, reprehend, admonish, reprimand, reprove, fulminate against, curse, scold, damn, chide, upbraid, revile, rebuke, berate, anathematize, accuse, lash, trounce, vituperate, throw stones at, recriminate, vilipend, overhaul, roast, haul over the coals, rail at, abuse, vilify, thunder against, denunciate.

OBLATION, n. Gift (to a religious establishment, etc.), offering, alms, offertory, donation, collection, present.

OBLIGATE, v. Bind, elicit, coerce, constrain,

oblige, force, press, compel, necessitate, make, impel, require, command, restrict.

OBLIGATION, n. 1. Covenant, agreement, commitment, deal, acknowledgment, indenture, promise, bond, contract, compact, treaty, cartel, stipulation, warranty, understanding, transaction, pact, word, oath, arrangement, guaranty.
2. That which is owing, indebtedness, debt, a favor owed, liability, charge, due, debit.
3. Duty, responsibility, charge, care, onus, liability.

OBLIGATORY, adj. 1. That which binds or compels, binding, obligating, importunate, imperative, commanding, demanding, forcing, compelling, restrictive, compulsatory, constrictive, cohibitive, imperious, coercive, constraining, forcible, mandatory, compulsive, limitary, requisite, peremptory.
2. That which is compulsory, mandatory, required, essential, compulsory, imperative, necessary, requisite.

OBLIGE, v. 1. Put under obligation, require, impel, make, command, press, force, constrain, obligate, bind, elicit, coerce, compel, necessitate.
2. Do a favor for, help, aid, put oneself out for, accommodate, do a service for, favor, provide, assist, convenience, serve, furnish, tender to.

OBLIQUE, adj. 1. Inclined, slanting, inflected, aslant, skew, slanted, sloping, diagonal, transverse, acclivous, tilted.
2. Not straightforward, surreptitious, indirect, cloaked, sly, underhand, disingenuous, crafty, covert, underground, huggermugger, conspiring, ensconced, stealthy, sneaking, clandestine, masked, furtive, privy, arcane, veiled, obreptitious.

OBLITERATE, v. 1. Render imperceptible, erase, blot out, efface, delete, rule out, sponge out, wipe out, cancel, omit, expunge, render illegible, strike out, dele, write out.
2. Destroy, extirpate, desolate, swamp, engulf, blast, deracinate, annihilate, ruin, abolish, snuff out, stamp out, finish, quell, dispel, tear down, gut, crash, nullify, exterminate, blight, unbuild, pull up by the roots, suppress, topple, quash, squash, dissolve, break up, devour, consume, swallow up, smash, remove, sweep away, beat down, raze, fell, level, blow down, mow down, dissipate.

OBLIVION, n. 1. Forgetfulness, obliviousness, insensibility, insensibleness, obscurity, blankness, effacement, blotting out, darkness, amnesty, lethe, unconsciousness.
2. Nonexistence, nothingness, nirvana, nothing, nonsubsistence, nullity, existlessness, nihility, abeyance, void, negativeness.

OBLIVIOUS, adj. (Often with OF) Not mindful, forgetful, heedless, insensible, unconscious, forgetting, amnemonic, amnesic, blank.

OBLONG, adj. (Of a circle or square) Elongated, oblongated, rectangular, elliptical, prolonged, oblongitudinal.

OBLOQUY, n. 1. Reproach, animadversion, execration, berating, anathema, admonishment, imprecation, abuse, calumny, censure, denunciation, accusation, scolding, disparagement, commination, malison, aspersion, lashing, defamation, stricture, imputation, libel, chiding, slander, malediction, backbiting, curse, revilement, upbraiding, rapping, scurrility, slur, contumely, remonstrance, exprobration, castigation, tongue lashing, dressing down (coll.), traducement, derision, jeremiad, objurgation, tirade, chastisement, vituperation, invective, diatribe.

2. State of being in disgrace, disgrace, dishonor, odium, degradation, disrepute, bad graces, bad books *(coll.)*, humiliation, shame, disesteem, ignominy, infamy, ill favor, disfavor, ingloriousness, contempt, debasement.

OBNOXIOUS, *adj.* Repugnant, rank, disgusting, impalatable, objectionable, offensive, nasty, foul, peccant, nefarious, noxious, execrable, abominable, unbearable, intolerable, unendurable, gross, unpleasant, vile, odious, heinous, deplorable, fulsome, insufferable, loathsome, loathful, evil, obscene, sickening, filthy, dirty, unsavory, hellish, disagreeable, base, despicable, blameworthy, scurvy, hateful, noisome, invidious, pernicious, revolting, displeasing, nauseating, nauseous, distasteful, annoying, unwholesome, shocking, detestable.

OBSCENE, *adj.* 1. Filthy, unpleasant, disgusting, etc. See OBNOXIOUS, *adj.* above.

2. Lascivious, foul-mouthed, foul-spoken, lewd, ruttish, lubricious, ribald, lustful, salacious, shameless, lickerish, satyric, lecherous, impure, smutty, unclean, dirty, filthy, indecent, disgusting, pornographic, adulterous, lurid, coarse, gross, vile, offensive, bestial, goatish, libidinous, indelicate, swinish, Cyprian, sensual, brutish, Fescennine.

OBSCURANT, OBSCURANTIST, *n.* Opponent of culture, hinderer of knowledge, anti-intellectual, barbarian, vandal, yahoo. *Words used in this sense derogatively:* plebeian, bourgeois, proletarian, Philistine.

OBSCURE, *adj.* 1. Lightless, dark, overcast, nubilous, umbrageous, blurred, turbid, thick, gloomy, murky, shadowy, somber, cloudy, dim, lowering, funereal, filmy, dusky, black, rayless, nebulous, misty, foggy, moonless, smoky, shady, starless, sunless, tenebrous, caliginous, viscid, dirty, dingy, unilluminated, soupy *(sl.)*, overshadowed, muggy, unlighted.

2. Not easily understood, vague, unclear, enigmatic, indefinite, nebulous, impenetrable, abstruse, confusing, confused, recondite, indistinct, ambiguous, cryptic, equivocal, unfathomable, difficult, perplexing, puzzling, imperspicuous.

3. Low, mean, unknown, insignificant, unhonored, unsung, out-of-the-way, unheard of, inglorious, nameless, unnoted, unrenowned, hidden, inconspicuous.

4. Pale, hard to see *or* read, faint, misty, invisible, vague, hazy, imperceptible, undefined, weak, inconspicuous, hardly noticeable, indistinct, illegible, blurred, fuzzy, indiscernible, bleared.

OBSCURE, *v.* Make dim, pale, *or* indistinct, darken, conceal, hide, cloud, cover, dim, dusk, overcast, overshadow, obfuscate, gloom, befog, mask, shadow, shroud, eclipse, disguise, curtain, adumbrate, shade, haze, darkle, becloud, fog, mist, nubilate, begloom, benight, screen, dull, bedim, obtenebrate, veil, blacken, blur, occult, cloak, frost.

OBSEQUIOUS, *adj.* Fawning, sycophantic, servile, subservient, slavish, whining, toadying, scraping, menial, truckling, ingratiating, bootlicking *(sl.)*, prostrate, vernile, footlicking *(sl.)*, cringing, unassertive, docile, tractable, unctuous, mealymouthed, honey-mouthed.

OBSEQUY, *n.* *(Used only in plural:* OBSEQUIES*).* Funeral rites, burial, entombment, burial ceremonies, exequy *(pl.* exequies*)*, funeral oration *or* sermon, interment, inhumation, sepulture, wake.

OBSERVABLE, *adj.* Capable of being observed, discernible, perceptible, detectible, manifest, distinct, patent, visible, seeable, plain, noticeable, evident, obvious, apparent, revealed, in plain view *or* sight, perceivable, unhidden, clear, unconcealed, perspicuous, well-defined, well-marked, appreciable, recognizable.

OBSERVANCE, *n.* 1. Eyeing, act of observance, paying attention to, observation, ascertainment, inspection, descrying, reconnaissance, apprehension, noticing, heeding, attention, regarding, espial, apperception, eyeshot, notice, perception, discernment, examination, regard.

2. Religious rite, ordinance, function, invocation, formality, commemoration, formulary, ceremony, ritual, rituality, celebration, service, remembrance, keeping, memorialization, duty, dedication, solemnity, ceremonial, ceremonialism, practice, cult, custom.

3. Custom, practice, form, habit, wont, trait, particularity, prevalence, customary course, fixed procedure, institution, style, mannerism, convention, use, mode, fashion.

OBSERVANT, *adj.* Attentive, careful, awake to, sharp, heedful, considerate, thoughtful, intent, on the lookout, wary, vigilant, regardful, mindful, listening, on the alert, watchful, conscious, circumspect.

OBSERVATION, *n.* 1. Act of noticing *or* perceiving, act of regarding attentively *or* watching, noting, seeing, eyeing, perlustration, observing, advertence, espial, cognizance, heed, cognition, absorption, once-over *(sl.)*, reconnaissance, espionage, note, lookout, sightseeing, consideration, speculation, study, deliberation, concentration, interest, application, intentness, mindfulness, attentiveness, perception, watchfulness, heedfulness, search, probe, check, investigation, analysis, thought, dissection, scrutiny, inspection, examination, survey, exploration, vision, sight, attention, regard, view, ken, glance, research.

2. Information gained by observing, remark, annotation, gloss, finding, report, account, sketch, detail, review, explanation, comment, discovery, delineation, depiction, ascertainment, illustration, revelation, description, clue, fact, light, commentary, idea, note, scholium, particular, elucidation, recapitulation.

3. Utterance *(by way of remark or comment)*, comment, remark, saying, thought, hint, commentary, opinion, view, conviction, criticism, expression of opinion *or* point of view, declaration, consideration, assertion, judgment, mind, sentence, phrase, word, say, announcement, affirmation, dictum, animadversion, reflection, statement, sentiment, mention, pronouncement, allegation.

OBSERVATORY, *n.* Place *or* building fitted up for making observations *(of the heavens, etc.)*, place *or* structure with an extensive view, watchtower, lookout, observation post, belvedere, gazebo, crow's-nest *(Naut.)*.

OBSERVE, *v.* 1. See, notice, perceive, behold, eye, mark, detect, find, discern, descry, catch sight of, make out, recognize, distinguish, sight, be aware of, be conscious of, take notice of, have in sight, spot *(coll.)*, peruse, discover, look on, glimpse, set *or* lay eyes on.

2. Regard with attention *(to see or learn something)*, note, watch, make *or* take an observation of, examine, stare at, peruse, ogle, eye, remark, pay attention to, scan, heed, notice, take a look at, contemplate, consider, witness, cognize, regard, take into consideration *or* account, peer at, investigate, explore, overlook, audit, dissect, re-

connoiter, glance over, keep watch, take in the sights, peek, peep, be a spectator, be vigilant, perlustrate, cast the eye over, take note *or* cognizance of, see to, look sharp, keep an eye on, direct the mind to, do research, size up, search through, take stock of, scrutinize, recognize, delve *or* pry into, study, attend, inspect, view, mind, look, survey, review, pore over, probe, inquire into.

3. Comment, remark, advert to, put into words, say, mention, pronounce, state, aver, give tongue *or* voice to, declare, tell, communicate, relate, convey, put *or* set forth, blurt out, offer, allege, impart, divulge, phrase, express, enunciate, give expression to, exclaim, vocalize, announce, put, present, breathe, notice, couch in terms, let fall, come out with, utter, give utterance to, proclaim, break in with, articulate, assert, recite, make known, voice.

4. Keep *or* maintain in one's action, conduct, *etc.,* fulfill, obey, conform to, comply with, be faithful to, discharge, execute, abide by, chime *or* fall in with, perform, respect, adhere to, act up to, cling to, accede, acknowledge, adjust to, adapt to, tally with, be guided *or* regulated by, satisfy, be resigned *or* submissive to, bow before *or* to, acquiesce, yield *or* defer to, submit to, hold, meet, accommodate, follow, carry out.

5. Show regard for *(by appropriate procedure, ceremonies, etc.),* solemnize, sanctify, hallow, perform duly, do honor to, signalize, minister, ceremonialize, attend service, communicate, commemorate, remember, keep, celebrate, regard, honor, perform *(a rite, service, etc.),* memorialize, consecrate.

OBSERVER, *n.* One who observes, beholder, looker-on, onlooker, spectator, viewer, witness, inspector, eyewitness, bystander, looker, lookout, scrutinizer, watcher, examiner, sightseer, hearer, attendant, frequenter, patron, rubberneck *(sl.),* excursionist, perceiver, attender, theater-goer, gallery *(pl.),* house *(pl.),* audience *(pl.),* sidewalk superintendent *(joc.),* listener.

OBSESS, *v.* Haunt, trouble, dominate, beset, run in one's head, control, craze, madden, dement, weigh *or* prey on the mind, bedevil, loco, derange, unhinge, shatter, unbalance, diabolize, possess, overpower, demonize, harass, besiege, pervade, lay siege to, recur, addle the wits, confound, discompose, disconcert, plague, distress, hound, grind, perplex, oppress, terrorize, disarm, baffle, pursue, rack, goad, hector, toss, nag, prostrate, gnaw, nettle, bleed white, abuse, badger, harry, vex, torment, unman, afflict, hold in power, enthrall, hold captive, seize.

OBSESSION, *n.* 1. Besetting *or* dominating action *or* influence *(of a persistent feeling, idea, etc.),* besetting fear *or* idea, *etc.,* fancy, phantom, craze, fixation, delusion, fixed conviction, spell, charm, quirk, siege, fetish, twist, mania, fascination, infatuation, passion, witchery, evil eye, enchantment, delirament, enthusiasm, fixed idea, *idée fixe (Fr.),* faddishness, ruling whim, phobia, incubus, nightmare, bad dream, monomania, hallucination, illusion, crotchet, crank, preoccupation, imagining, caprice, warp, bias, prepossession, misconception, maggot on the brain, bee in the bonnet *(coll.),* compulsion, distortion, self-deceit, fallacy, specter, bewitchment, exaggeration.

2. State of being obsessed, possession, delusion, fixation, siege, trance, bewitchment, monomania, insanity *(on one subject),* subjection, fool's paradise, infatuation, fanaticism, preoccupation.

OBSOLESCENT, *adj.* Becoming obsolete, passing

out of use, tending to become out of date, disappearing, dying, disused, archaic, old-fashioned, worn out, done with, out of use, effete, exhausted, passé, past its prime, antiquated, waning, archaical, fading, declining, timeworn, aging, out of fashion, rusty, deteriorating, moth-eaten, elderly, rare, obscure, moldering, crumbling, mildewed, fusty, stale, aged, decrepit, fossilized, unproductive, senectuous, hoary, superannuated, faded, ancient, grown unfamiliar, old.

OBSOLETE, *adj.* Fallen into disuse, no longer in use, out of date, effaced by wearing down *or* away, disused, neglected, ancient, antique, gone to seed, retired, gone by, lapsed, elapsed, irrecoverable, extinct, past, archaic, fallen into desuetude, dead, hoary, outworn, timeworn, discarded, exploded, expired, bygone, effete, forgotten, never to return, desuete, out of use, outdated, primitive, antediluvian, discredited, rejected, dismissed, prehistoric, former, refuted, antiquated, passé.

OBSTACLE, *n.* Impediment, ban, difficulty, curb, preclusion, limitation, disallowance, impedition, block, stumbling block, estoppel *(Leg.),* check, stop, barricade, barrier, prohibition, dam, snag, catch, stoppage, balk, embargo, injunction, trammel, constraint, enjoining, obstruction, bar, foreclosure *(Leg.),* stay, barrage, retardment, snag, cohibition, bridle, stopper, proscription, oppilation, remora, restraint, restriction, repression, forbiddance, hindrance, retardation, embarrassment, obstruent *(chiefly Med.).*

OBSTETRICS, *n.* Science of pregnancy, midwifery, tocology.

OBSTINACY, *n.* Stubbornness, firmness, unwillingness, reluctance, self-will, pertinacity, persistence, perversity, inflexibility, intractability, impersuasibility, unchangeableness, determination, tenacity, unyielding, obduracy, immovability, renitence, resolve, resolution, perseverance.

OBSTINATE, *adj.* Dogged, stubborn, intractable, pertinacious, immovable, resolved, resolute, firm, unmoving, unyielding, unbending, inflexible, headstrong, unimpressible, obdurate, pervicacious, unaffected, unmanageable, unmalleable, opinionated, bigoted, ungovernable, self-willed, uncontrollable, recalcitrant, bullheaded, refractory, mulish, willful, pigheaded.

OBSTREPEROUS, *adj.* Loud, noisy, vociferous, boisterous, ear-splitting, clamorous, rackety, blatant, turbulent, blustering, loud-voiced, unruly, rambunctious, rampaging, hot-headed, uproarious, tempestuous, hilarious, unrestrained, riotous, excited, raving, raging, loud-mouthed, ear-piercing, stentorian, resounding, ear-rending, deafening, tonant, booming, fulminating.

OBSTRUCT, *v.* 1. Block, barricade, trammel, occlude, bridle, retard, hedge in, curb, obviate, impede, shut off, restrain, foreclose, debar, stop, dam up, oppilate, ban, choke off, embar, prohibit, estop, plug up.

2. Hinder, balk, cohibit, forbid, embarrass, circumvent, impedite, gag, check, circumscribe, restrain, bridle, handicap, retard, control, trammel, brake, rein, harness, inhibit, delay, suppress, hold, thwart, arrest, halt, cramp, withhold, muzzle, limit, frustrate, smother, stay, stall, hamstring, shackle, deter, bring to a standstill, preclude, bind, restringe, trap, countervail, spike, suspend, hobble, tie hand and foot, throttle, pinion, counterwork, offset, vitiate, fetter, clog the wheels, put a spoke in one's wheel, hang fire, cause to delay,

checkmate, set one's face against, keep back, encumber, harass, deadlock, keep within bounds.

OBSTRUCTION, *n.* Impediment, impedition, retardation, catch, balk, check, retardment, disallowance, obstacle, hindrance, restriction, restraint, cohibition, forbiddance, oppilation, snag, enjoining, injunction, limitation, prohibition, block, repression, remora, stopper, hitch, trammel, embargo, preclusion, curb, difficulty, barrier, bar, constraint, stay, bridle, proscription, barricade, ban, stop, block, stumbling block, obstruent, (*chiefly Med.*).

OBTAIN, *v.* 1. Gain possession, procure, take possession, take, acquire, attain, achieve, come to have, gain for oneself, pick up, get one's hands on, come by, get, secure, realize, glean, earn, receive, gather.
2. Exist, be, be customary, hold, be usual, stand, prevail, be the case.

OBTEST, *v.* 1. Beseech, entreat, ask, supplicate, petition, urge, obsecrate, pray for, beg, importune, implore, plead, request, appeal to, adjure, enjoin, impetrate, obtestate, solicit.
2. Call to witness, summon as witness, invoke as witness, ask evidence of *or* from, call to the stand, place in the witness box.

OBTRUDE, *v.* 1. Thrust out, expel, repudiate, force away, force out, put away, drive away, cast away, reject, discard, oust, eject, evict, dispossess, extrude, repulse, fling away.
2. Thrust forward, intrude, interlope, break in, burst in, insinuate, barge in (*coll.*), intermeddle, interfere, interrupt, butt in, impose, invade, interpose, encroach, intervene, trespass, horn in (*sl.*).

OBTRUSION, *n.* Thrusting forward, intrusion, intermeddling, interruption, invasion, encroachment, trespassing, insinuation, breaking in, inroad, incursion, interference.

OBTRUSIVE, *adj.* 1. Jutting out, sticking out, protruding, projecting, beetling, impending, protuberant, protrusive, overhanging, prominent, bulging, salient.
2. Intrusive, forward, pushing, aggressive, busybody, audacious, officious, intruding, presumptuous, interfering, prying, encroaching, brash, meddling, meddlesome, trespassing, impertinent, familiar, interrupting.

OBTUND, *v.* Make less violent, pungent, *etc.*, take the edge off, impair the force of, dull, blunt, deaden, moderate, lenify, allay, alleviate, benumb, numb, soften, stupefy, modulate, stun, mitigate, abate, assuage, palliate, dulcify.

OBTUSE, *adj.* 1. Blunt, blunted, dull, bluff, without a sharp point, unedged, unpointed, unsharpened.
2. Insensitive, passionless, spiritless, callous, thick-skinned, insentient, insensate, heartless, insensible, hard-hearted, uncaring, inured, senseless, sluggish, unfeeling, unimaginative, impercipient, unconscious, apathetic, lethargic, languid, leaden, torporific, torpescent, phlegmatic, indifferent, listless, passive, supine, lymphatic, undiscerning, lentitudinous, otiose, hebetudinous.
3. Stupid, doltish, clumsy, loutish, incumbent, oafish, bovine, bungling, gross, heavy, sluggish, blunt, dull, slow, slow-witted, lubberly, churlish, cloddish, ignorant, lumpish. dumb (*coll.*), uncomprehending, moronic, idiotic, imbecilic, dull-witted, thick (*coll.*), dull-pated, crass, gawky, uncouth, ungainly, insulse, gauche, stolid, blundering, thick-headed, witless, addleheaded, addlepated, clodpated, numbskull (*coll.*), dronish, dense, awk-

ward, unrefined, inelegant, inept, simple, simpleminded, asinine, maladroit, lacking dexterity, unpolished, rustic, vulgar, clownish, mutton-headed (*coll.*), beetle-headed (*coll.*), muddle-brained, fatheaded (*coll.*), shallow-witted, fatuous.

OBVERSE, *n.* 1. Principal surface, front, face, façade, forefront, frontage, head (*of a coin.*).
2. That which completes *or* complements, impletion, remainder, rest, supplement, complement.

OBVIATE, *v.* Prevent, forestall, debar, sidetrack, avert, preclude, ward off, stave off, fend off, nip in the bud, parry, divert, shield, forefend, avoid.

OBVIOUS, *adj.* Plain, distinct, conspicuous, manifest, palpable, apparent, unconcealed, discernible, bald, notable, unquestionable, visible, lucid, patent, unequivocal, unmistakable, ostensible, undeniable, overt, perspicuous, glaring, recognizable, prominent, disclosed, plain as a pikestaff, plain as the nose on one's face, unhidden, uncamouflaged, open, undoubted, decided, pronounced, explicit, revealed, undisguised, unscreened, unmasked, clear.

OCCASION, *n.* 1. Particular time, occurrence, event, situation, advent, juncture, point, phase, conjuncture, episode, accident, crisis, emergency, instance, happening, casualty, incident, contingency, exigency, circumstance, place, critical time, important time, function, gala time, experience, adventure, venture, affair, mishap, case, transaction.
2. Convenient *or* favorable juncture *or* time, chance, liberty, freedom, opportune time, convenience, opportunity, scope, space, show (*coll.*), clear stage, fair field, season, room, time, place, leisure, suitable time, opening, conjuncture, contingency, timeliness, golden opportunity.
3. Cause, ground, reason, motive, inducement, influence, inception, origin, source, birth, beginning, wherefore, factor, base, call, basis, impulse, determinant, determining condition, leaven, provocation, principle, rationale, explanation, rise, agent, genesis, derivation.

OCCASION, *v.* Give occasion *or* cause for, lie at the root of, bring about, cause, breed, originate, bring to pass, raise, call forth, provoke, make, give, engender, invent, causate, sow the seeds of, develop, bring in its train, set on foot, elicit, persuade, induce, move, found, broach, instill, establish, install, constitute, erect, rear, raise, build, bring into being *or* existence, turn, bring on, produce, create, give rise to, be the cause of, beget, generate, set afloat, set up, give birth to, institute, evolve.

OCCASIONAL, *adj.* 1. Occurring *or* appearing on one occasion *or* another, now and then, infrequent, unexpected, chance, incidental, accidental, capricious, periodic, provisional, conditional, unreliable, indefinite, seldom, fragmentary, extemporaneous, extemporary, contingent, spasmodic, irregular, rare, uncertain, uncommon, casual, scattered, few, scarce, sparse, unsystematic, erratic, fitful, intermittent, variable, sporadic.
2. Intended for use whenever needed, side, on call, auxiliary, spare, assistant, standing in, annexed, extra, extraneous, surplus, supplementary, supplemental, subsidiary, ancillary, additional, useful, serviceable, accessory, added.
3. Pertaining to, arising out of *or* intended for the occasion, solicited (*by a patron, committee, etc.*), inspired by an occasion, celebrating, festive, special, memorial, jubilant, honoring, commemorative.

4. Serving as the occasion *or* incidental cause, causative, causing, constitutive, institutive, productive, germinal, seminal, formative, propulsive, prompting, causal, promoting, at the bottom of, creative, influential, influencing, impelling, motivating, fabricative, persuasive, potent, telling, weighty, effective, aiding, helping, dynamic.

OCCASIONALLY, *adv.* At times, now and then, sporadically, by snatches, by fits and starts, sometimes, periodically, intermittently, fitfully, seldom, hardly ever, once in a while, at intervals, irregularly, once and again, once in a blue moon, once in a coon's age, from time to time, discontinuously, casually, every now and then.

OCCLUDE, *v.* Close, obstruct, shut in (out, off, up), stop up, bar, debar, block, prohibit, choke off, oppilate, dam up, foreclose, curb, bridle, barricade, trammel, retard, hedge *or* hem in, estop, plug up, impede, obviate, cover, cork, stanch, seal, trap, throttle.

OCCULT, *adj.* Beyond the bounds of ordinary knowledge, secret, hidden, mysterious, not disclosed, revealed only to the initiated, private, unknown, unknowable, unrevealed, recondite, abstruse, shrouded, veiled, cabalistic, covert, hieroglyphical, supernatural, ambiguous, latent, undiscoverable, invisible, inscrutable, magic, dark, arcane, profound, enigmatic, hermetical, magical, transcendental, impenetrable, metempirical, obscure, cryptic, esoteric, concealed, sealed, cloaked, secreted, clouded, unavowed, cloistered, screened, impenetrable, suppressed, clandestine, untold, delitescent, withheld, oracular, paradoxical, sequestered masked, symbolical, baffling, puzzling.

OCCULTATION, *n.* Disappearance from view *or* notice, state of being occulted, evanescence, vanishment, eclipse, departure, concealment, darkness, retirement, retreat, reclusion, ambush, burial, disguise, latency, obscuration, obscurity, delitescence, clusion, secretion, withdrawal, retreat, adumbra nonappearance, invisibility, imperceptibility, setion, fade-out.

OCCULTISM, *n.* Doctrine *or* study of the occult, magic, esoteric sciences, esoterics, transcendentalism, metaphysics, supernaturalism, cabalism, spiritism, hyperphysics, mysticism, theosophy, Masonry, Freemasonry, symbolism, Rosicrucianism, spiritualism, mediumism, transphysical science, diabolism.

OCCUPANCY, *n.* 1. Act of taking possession, inhabitance, habitation, tenancy, retention, monopoly, possessorship, proprietorship, tenure, holding, occupation, enjoyment, use, possession, sojourn, lodgment, stop, stay, abode, abiding, continuance, lodging, inhabitancy, habitancy.

2. Term during which one is a tenant, time one remains in a place, duration, retention, tenancy, tenure, lease, continuance, allotted period.

OCCUPANT, *n.* One who occupies, possessor, tenant, holder, owner, lessee, lodger, inmate, resident, incumbent, roomer, occupier, inhabitant, interne, dweller, resider, sojourner, citizen, residentiary, addressee, householder, settler, colonist, native, indigene, renter, colonial, cottager, homesteader, proprietor.

OCCUPATION, *n.* 1. Employment, business, living, livelihood, walk of life, trade, craft, concern, province, function, work, line, pursuit, calling, lifework, vocation, profession, station, place, capacity, job, sphere, berth, duty, charge, situation, career, industry, metier, office, enterprise, activity, specialty, specialization, forte, racket *(sl.)*.

2. That in which one is engaged, activity, engagement, pastime, pursuit, hobby, amusement, enterprise, preoccupation, absorption, craft, project, venture, adventure, commission, mission, undertaking, handicraft, exercise, avocation.

3. Possession, holding, tenure, occupancy, use, habitation, billet, seizure, inhabitation, inhabitancy, incumbency, tenancy, care, retention, possessorship, proprietorship, enjoyment, sojourn, continuance, abode, stay, stop, lodgment, lodging, abiding.

4. State of being occupied, supervision, foreign rule *or* domination, possession, constraint, subjection, coercion, enthrallment, control, subjugation, thrall, slavery, bondage, enslavement, protectorate, oppression, repression, subordination, defeat, submission, subdual, thralldom, conquest, seizure *(as by invasion)*.

OCCUPATIONAL, *adj.* Of *or* pertaining to an occupation (trade, calling, *etc.*), vocational, workday, workaday, industrial, connected *or* involved with one's work, resulting from an occupation, functional, official, professional.

OCCUPY, *v.* 1. Employ, engage *(the mind, attention, etc., or the person)*, fill, take, busy, entertain, pervade, beguile, interest, possess, cover, use, charge, stuff, weight, pile, pack, saturate, load, monopolize, arrest, absorb, engross, interpenetrate, overrun, run through, penetrate, permeate, exercise, concern, be on one's mind, take up *(space, time, etc.)*, be diffused through, be uppermost, amuse, run in the head.

2. Take possession of *(as by invasion)*, seize, take by force, commandeer, restrain, assume, usurp, hold in thrall, coerce, control, subject, subjugate, protect, repress, oppress, defeat, subdue, force to submission, enslave, dominate, arrogate.

3. Be resident *or* established in, hold, have possession of, keep, maintain, own, dominate, prevail, be possessed of, move into, fill, be in, retain, enjoy, command, control, possess, have, derive title to, have by tenure *or* inheritance, be in (office), reserve, bear the responsibility of, hold down *(sl.)*.

OCCUR, *v.* 1. Happen, come to pass, come about, take place, transpire, fall out, befall, crop up, turn up, come, pass, chance, ensue, supervene, eventuate, take effect, come off, go, bechance, rise, fall, prevail, spring up, fare, result, issue, appear.

2. Appear, arise, present itself, rise, spring up, be found, be met with, meet the eye, open to the view, show itself, become visible, turn up, crop up, be revealed, be exposed, loom, rear, materialize, emerge, issue, arrive, offer, become manifest, manifest itself, come into view.

3. *(Commonly foll. by* TO*)* come to one's mind, suggest itself, impress one, catch one's attention, appear, flash on the mind, come into one's head, suggest itself in thought, arrest the thoughts, pass through one's head *or* mind, enter one's mind, strike the mind, strike one, present itself, cross one's mind.

OCCURRENCE, *n.* Action *or* fact of occurring, something that occurs, incident, event, happening, incidence, doing, casualty, falling, chancing, passage, phenomenon, fact, thing, transpiration, emergence, pass, business, issuance, scene, sight, view, phantom, phantasm, apparition, unfolding, manifestation, revelation, materializing, situation, advent, eventuality, circumstance, conjuncture, juncture, contingency, exigency, instance, coming, precedent, opportunity, episode, case, supervention, crisis, chance, passing, emergency, experience, occasion, fall, arising, rise, issue, accident, landmark, enterprise, scene, proceeding, transaction, adventure, affair, mishap, matter, venture, contretemps.

OCEAN, *n.* 1. Vast body of salt water, sea, main *(Poetic),* deep *(Poetic),* high sea, flood *(Poetic),* briny deep, brine, Davy Jones's locker, waterway, seaway, depths.

2. Vast expanse *or* quantity, immense expanse, infinity, abundance, volume, profusion, quantities, flood, numbers, scads *(sl.),* mass, mint, peck, pack, multitude, sea, world *or* worlds, stock, store, hoard, lot *(coll.),* accumulation, collection, slew *(coll.),* sight *(coll.),* loads *(coll., pl.),* waste, prodigality, raft *(coll.),* pile *(coll.),* stack *(coll.).*

OCEANIC, *adj.* Of *or* pertaining to the ocean, pelagic, marine, maritime, nautical, Neptunian, ocean, naval, ocean-going, seagoing, seaworthy, bathysophical, hydrographic, oceanographic, bathyorographical, bathybic *(Biol.),* benthonic.

OCULAR, *adj.* Visual, seen, observed, discerned, noticed, viewed, apparent, manifest.

OCULIST, *n.* Eye doctor, eye specialist, ophthalmologist.

ODD, *adj.* 1. Without a mate, single, sole, remaining one *(of a pair),* remaining.

2. *(Of numbers)* Indivisible by two, uneven.

3. *(Of pairs)* Not matching, unlike, disparate, divergent, dissimilar, unalike, nonidentical, unequal, ill-matched, unmatched, irregular, different, disquiparant.

4. Unusual, unique, strange, *outré (Fr.),* curious, outlandish, unfamiliar, uncommon, freakish, bizarre, peculiar.

5. *(Of time, minutes, etc.)* Extra, spare, surplus, extraneous.

6. *(Coll.)* Eccentric, notional, abnormal, crotchety, unusual, unconventional, faddish, whimsical, unstable, changeful, flighty, volatile, wayward, weird, erratic, quirked, giddy, fanciful, fickle, aberrant, frivolous, inconsistent, capricious, impulsive, irresponsible, variable.

ODDITY, *n.* Quality of being odd, strange, *etc.,* singularity, exceptionality, individuality, bizarreness, outlandishness, freakishness, peculiarity, strangeness, unusualness, uniqueness, abnormality, unnaturalness, queerness.

ODDMENT, *n.* Scrap, leaving, paring, modicum, patch, gobbet, snip, chip, tag, piece, remnant, snippet, odds and ends, fragment, discard, sliver, chunk, shred, crumb.

ODDS, *n.* 1. Advantage *or* disadvantage *(as the case may be),* partiality, superiority *or* inferiority, difference, balance, unevenness, inequality, edge *(for one side or another),* preëminence, lead, ascendancy, predominance *or* deficiency, inadequacy, subordination *(as the case may be).*

2. Difference, inequality, disparity, variation, variance, dissimilarity, incongruity, discrepancy, irregularity, divergence, diversity, discordancy.

3. *(Usually in expressions as* AT ODDS) Dispute, conflict, impugnation, broil, brawl, jangle, controversy, quarrel, bickering, difference, strife, disagreement, disturbance, discord, altercation, clash, dissension, wrangle, tiff, spat, argument, feud, litigation, imbroglio, scrimmage, faction, antipathy, open rupture, fracas, strife, disputation, enmity, squabble, hostility, outbreak, row, rumpus, contravention, antagonism, contrariety, jar, dissidence, contention.

ODDS AND ENDS, *n.* Particles, remnants, scant-

lings, snatches, cantlets, scraps, chunks, cuttings, fragments, shavings, patches, clippings, gobbets, modicums, specks, morsels, parings, bits, snippets, crumbs, snips, flakes, splinters, shreds, slivers, tags, pieces, chips.

ODE, *n.* Lyric, song, epode, eclogue, palinode, Olympionic, epinician, epicedium, genethliacon, pro-ode *(Gr. Dram. Poetry).*

ODIOUS, *adj.* Exciting *or* deserving great dislike, objectionable, unpalatable, mean, unbearable, unpleasant, unworthy, low, ignoble, obnoxious, hateful, abject, intolerable, unendurable, evil, disgusting, horrible, damnable, evil-shaped, evil-eyed, evil-affected, hellish, revolting, infernal, fulsome, scurvy, sickening, beastly, rank, peccant, evil-fashioned, evil-favored, evil-savored, devilish, infamous, base, putrid *(fig.),* nauseating, forbidding, vulgar, insufferable, despicable, coarse, frightening, grotesque, diabolic, contemptible, nasty, blameworthy, sinister, tainted, foul, opprobrious, hideous, rotten, horrid, distasteful, shocking, confounded, monstrous, invidious, corrupt, repulsive, heinous, ugly, ignominious, annoying, cursed, execrable, repugnant, loathsome, nauseous, offensive, abominable, accursed, abhorrent, detestable.

ODIUM, *n.* 1. Feeling against one who is hated, dislike, hostility, malevolence, rancor, malignity, detestation, enmity, ill will, strong aversion, acrimony, umbrage, animosity, abhorrence, abomination, execration, loathing, disgust, revulsion, despite, ignominy, disfavor, horror, repugnance, bad feeling, malice, resentment, anger, pique, bad blood, spleen, grudge, grudging, rankling, hatred, implacability, bitterness, revenge, hate, antipathy, venom, envy, distaste, coldness, pitilessness, contempt, obduracy, avoidance, immitigability, hardheartedness, causticity, maliciousness, mordacity, asperity, scorn, animus, ruthlessness, derision, alienation, dissension, estrangement, inimicalness, heartburning, disaffection, coolness, dudgeon, wrath, virulence, harshness, vindictiveness, contumely, misogyny, misanthropy, cruelty, rankling.

2. State of being in disgrace, disrepute, degradation, dishonor, disgrace, obloquy, bad favor, bad books *(coll.),* humiliation, shame, disesteem, ignominy, infamy, ill favor, disfavor, ingloriousness, contempt, debasement, bad odor.

ODOR, *n.* Smell, scent, perfume, aroma, fragrance, stink, redolence, essence, effluvium, stench, nidor, emanation, bouquet, odoriferousness, exhalation, aura, savor, fetor, incense, pungence.

ODORIFEROUS, ODOROUS, *adj.* Agreeable in smell, sweet-smelling, fragrant, perfumed, redolent, essenced, scented, spicy, aromatic, nidorulent, heady, olent.

OF, *prep.* 1. From, belonging to, coming from, pertaining to, hailing from.

2. By, produced by, written, composed, engendered, *etc.,* by.

3. Composed of, made of, consisting of, formed of, filled with.

OFF, *adj.* 1. At a distance, removed, remote, distant, further, far-off, far, afar, faraway, outlying.

2. Inaccurate, irregular, below standard, inferior, improper, incorrect.

OFF, *prep.* From, away from, out of, out.

OFFAL, *n.* 1. Putrefying meat *or* flesh, remains, carrion, rotten carcasses.

2. Garbage, refuse, rubbish, waste, sweepings, castoffs, rags and bones, dung, recrement, scoria, excreta, sordes, sewage, trash, slag, junk, defeca-

tion, bilgewater, grounds, scourings, faeces, scurf, lees, refuse, draff, leavings, residue, chaff, stubble, dross, ordure, scum, dregs, feculence.

OFFEND, *v.* 1. Sin, commit sin, commit a misdemeanor, lapse, stray from the straight and narrow, fall from grace, disobey the moral code, transgress, trespass, misdemean, err, go wrong, go to the dogs *or* devil, misbehave, fall, commit a crime, go against the law, slip, trip.

2. Wound, displease, anger, rattle, chafe, ruffle, discommode, discompose, aggravate, vex, annoy, incense, slight, gall, embarrass, affront, injure, roil, irk, irritate, pique, madden, disturb, distress, chagrin, exasperate, humiliate, rankle, miff, rile, smart, nettle, disgruntle, inflame, fret.

OFFENSE, *n.* 1. Injury, hurt, slap, gibe, snub, contumely, indignity, insult, outrage, twit, flout, taunt, insolence, damage, wound, annoyance, slight, embarrassment, affront, humiliation, disrespect, abuse.

2. Sin, crime, misdemeanor, breach *(of conduct, law, etc.),* misdeed, evil deed, wickedness, transgression, erring, going astray, malefaction, violation, peccancy, fault, delict *(Civil Law),* felony, delinquency, atrocity, malfeasance, infringement, infraction, peccadillo *(dim.),* slip, lapse, shortcoming, dereliction, outrage, enormity.

3. Resentment, umbrage, pique, dudgeon, rage, huff, petulance, indignation, tiff, fury, miff *(coll.).*

4. Onslaught, offensive, inroad, assailment, onset, push *(sl.),* expedition, attack, aggression, incursion, sally, thrust, sortie, bombardment, escalade, dragonnade, attempt, assault, raid, assailment, storming, jab, besetment, charge, encounter, surprisal, lunge.

OFFENSIVE, *adj.* 1. Attacking, combative, aggressive, bellicose, belligerent, invasive, contentious, irruptive, martial, hostile, quarrelsome, pugnacious, assailant, assault, incursive, provoking, obsidional, warlike, provocative, antagonistic, thrusting, assailing, pushing, raiding, lunging, charging, truculent.

2. Insulting, rude, offending, discourteous, disrespectful, insolent, contumelious, uncivil, inaffable, ungallant, disdainful, impudent, ungracious, harsh, unmannered, unmannerly, ill-bred, unceremonious.

3. Exciting great dislike, unpleasant, unbearable, intolerable, unendurable, evil, disgusting, obnoxious, unpalatable, objectionable, ignoble, horrible, evil-shaped, evil-flavored, evil-savored, hellish, peccant, rank, beastly, abominable, sickening, scurvy, fulsome, infernal, revolting, infamous, evil-fashioned, devilish, base, putrid *(fig.),* nauseating, insufferable, despicable, contemptible, nasty, blameworthy, tainted, foul, bad, opprobrious, hideous, rotten, distasteful, horrid, monstrous, invidious, corrupt, repulsive, heinous, ugly, ignominious, annoying, cursed, excerable, repugnant, loathsome, nauseous, odious, abhorrent, detestable.

OFFENSIVE, *n.* Attack, assault, onslaught, etc. *(See* OFFENSE, *n.* 4 above)

OFFER, *n.* Proposal, invitation, advancement, proffer, suggestion, submission, motion, overture, proposition, advance, presentation.

OFFER, *v.* 1. *(With* UP) Sacrifice, make an oblation, make an offering.

2. Offer to give, present, *or* donate, *etc.,* tender, proffer, award, donate, grant, allow, submit, hold out, put forth, advance, present, make a present.

place at one's disposal, vouchsafe, extend, **bestow,** volunteer, accord.

3. Suggest, bid, bring forward, propose, propound, advance, move, submit, put forward, extend, make a motion.

4. Give *(as resistance, etc.),* make, do, create, produce, cause, execute, carry through, bring, bring about.

5. Offer to pay, allow, bid, grant, give, pay, tender, proffer.

OFFERING, OFFERTORY, *n.* Gift *(to a religious establishment, etc.),* alms, donations, collection, oblation, present.

OFFHAND, *adj.* 1. Accidental, chance, fortuitous, unforeseen, unlooked-for, unplanned, random, involuntary, undesigned, unexpected, **unpremeditated,** casual, contingent, incidental, adventitious, unpurposed.

2. Careless, desultory, haphazard, casual, irregular, occasional, thoughtless, unsystematic, vague, aimless, unmethodical, indiscriminate, disorganized, disorderly, undirected, orderless, straggling, unarranged, equivocal, ambiguous, dubious, questionable, uncertain, unsure, unsettled, unfixed.

3. Unconcerned, nonchalant, inconstant, blasé, indifferent, insouciant, uninterested, pococurante, apathetic, inattentive, lackadaisical, casual, listless, careless.

OFFHAND, *adv.* Without preparation, suddenly, without notes, without references, instantly, at one's finger tips, unpremeditatedly, unexpectedly, extemporaneously, extempore, impromptu, by improvisation.

OFFICE, *n.* 1. Something done for another *(as a service, duty, etc.),* service, duty, function, occupation, assigned task, position, appointment, role, billet, place, situation, station, charge, berth, engagement, commission, post, incumbency, business, job, capacity, province.

2. *(Usually plural)* Rites, ceremonies, obsequies, exequies, formalities, functions, solemnities, ceremonialisms, invocations, celebrations, observances, rituals, practices, ordinances, services, sacraments, customs, incantations.

3. Room for conducting business, place of business, desk *(fig.),* In some meanings: workroom, studio, library, workshop, shop, plant.

4. Bureau, agency, commission, department, secretariat *(Polit.),* portfolio *(Polit.),* legation, mission, embassy, delegation, deputation, authority.

5. *(Eccl.)* Divine service, worship, ceremony, exercises, meeting, mass, vespers, compline, complin, sacraments, rite, duty, fellowship, litany, angelus, evensong, matins, Eucharist, communion.

OFFICER, *n.* 1. One holding official powers, office-holder, functionary, executive, official, agent, minister, dignitary, officiant *(Eccl.).*

2. *(Mil. & Nav.)* Commissioned officer, noncommissioned officer, commander, staff officer, orderly officer, field officer, officer of the day, commandant, master *(Nav.),* mate *(Nav.),* warrant officer, petty officer.

3. Constable, policeman, sheriff, bailiff, deputy, shrieve, marshal, patrolman, cop *(sl.),* gendarme *(largely Fr.).*

OFFICER, *v.* 1. Give orders to, dictate to, bid, head, oversee, command, direct, hold office, officiate, order, superintend, control, preside over, have charge of, boss, charge, instruct, rule, govern, supervise, lead, exercise power over.

2. See to, manage, head, look after, drive, be at the helm, guide, conduct, regulate, engineer.

handle, pilot, sway, steer, maneuver, officiate, run *(coll.)*.

OFFICIAL, *adj.* 1. Formal, functional, professional.

2. Authorized, authoritative, licensed, sanctioned, approved, certified, ex cathedra, warranted, ordained, ex officio, accredited, allowed.

3. Valid, factual, trustworthy, reliable, dependable, authoritative, authentic, authenticated, standard, accepted, attested, credible, unquestionable, from competent sources, from official data, worthy of belief, bona fide, accurate, accordant with the facts, orthodox, canonical, genuine, of reputed origin, real, sure, true, veritable, legitimate, veridical, not spurious, not false, not apocryphal, uncorrupted, what it purports to be, literal, faithful.

OFFICIAL, *n.* One holding official powers, officeholder, functionary, executive, officer, agent, minister, dignitary, officiant *(Eccl.)*.

OFFICIATE, *v.* Act one's part, perform the duties of an office *or* position, fill an office, fulfill one's office *or* duties, minister, carry on *or* out, do duty, serve in the office *or* capacity of, execute, exercise, hold an office, regulate, govern, discharge functions, guide, order, hold the reins, direct, treat, overlook, oversee, handle, look after, administer, see to, preside, have the portfolio, be in a position of authority, occupy the chair, enact, dispatch, transact, manage, forward, maintain, superintend, supervise, boss *(coll.)*, steer, pilot, hold down a job *(sl.)*, run *(coll.)*.

OFFICIOUS, *adj.* Forward in tendering *or* obtruding one's service upon others, marked by *or* proceeding from forwardness, prying, meddling, meddlesome, interfering, importunate, pushing, intrusive, overkind, overbold, curious, inquisitive, offering gratuitous services, aggressive, overzealous, busybody, tampering, keeping one's finger in the pie, poking one's nose in, killing one with kindness, butting in *(coll.)*, busy, intermeddling, obtrusive, pragmatic, impertinent.

OFFING, *n.* More distant visible part of the sea, position at a distance from shore, background, offshore waters, horizon, skyline.

OFFPRINT, *n.* Copy in separate form of an article *(originally appearing as part of a larger publication)*, reproduction, reprint, duplicate, facsimile, reissue.

OFFSCOURING, *n.* *(Often plural)* That which is scoured off, refuse, filth, dirt, rubbish, waste, dregs, leavings, wastage, scurf, orts, draff, slag, sprue, offal, sordes, lees, scoria, grounds, residue, settlement, silt, scourings, smut, precipitate, deposit, bottoms, incrustation, feculence, offscum, trash, dross, sweepings, scum, sediment, settlings, soot, ash, tartar *(dent.)*.

OFFSET, *n.* 1. Something that offsets *or* counterbalances, counterpoise, balance, compensation, substitute, recompense, atonement, makeweight, counterbalance, counteractant, counterweight, indemnification, indemnity, neutralizer, antidote, counterblast, satisfaction, amends, hindrance, impediment, counteragent, expiation, composition, retribution, *quid pro quo (Lat.)*, equivalent, setoff, ballast, reparation.

2. Start, outset, commencement, beginning, opening, setout, outstart, inception, inauguration, installation, embarkment, first step, infancy, initial, prime, alpha, egress, exit, leave-taking, going, dawn, front, prelude, take-off, withdrawal, decampment, exodus, outgoing, outcoming, on-

set, outbreak, first, send-off *(coll.)*, departure, incipience, leave, embarkation.

3. Offshoot, branch, scion, descendant, *etc.* (See OFFSHOOT (2) below.)

OFFSET, *v.* 1. Balance by something else as an equivalent, counterbalance, square, compensate for, make up for, countervail, counteract, counterpoise, neutralize, nullify, cancel, run counter, resist, withstand, annul, frustrate, vitiate, thwart, hinder, impede, be *or* play at cross purposes, provide security for *(a risk, etc.)*, hedge *(of bets, etc.)*, overbalance.

2. Project *(as an offset or branch)*, protrude, branch, fork, jut out, poke out, stick out, stand out, impend, beetle, overhang.

OFFSHOOT, *n.* 1. Shoot from a main stem *(as of a plant)*, lateral shoot, sprout, offset, branch, bough, twig, branchlet, switch, runner, petiole, limb, sprig, leafstalk, tendril, bine, bud, ramification, spurgeon, outgrowth, sarmentum *(Bot.)*, tigella *(Bot.)*.

2. Descendant of a family *or* race, heir, scion, offspring, child, daughter, son, offset, branch, sprout, heiress, progeny *(pl.)*, issue *(pl.)*, house *(pl.)*, line *(pl.)*.

3. Anything received as springing *or* proceeding from a main stock, spur, side line, division, subdivision, byway, adjunct, bypath, offset, limb, wing, annex, addition, branch, supplement, extension, ramification, section, member, colony, sprit *(Naut.)*, dependency, daughter country, satellite.

OFFSPRING, *n.* 1. Children, descendants, young, lineage, issue, progeny, family, succession, successors, increase, seed, posterity, litter, brood, tribe, progeniture, blood, race, people, nation, clan, line, dynasty, kindred, hatch, stirps, stock, younger generation, rising generation, fry, pullulation, spawn *(Zool., or of humans usually disparaging)*.

2. Child *or* animal *(in relation to its parents)*, descendant, young, heir, heir apparent, heir presumptive, offset, offshoot, minor, juvenile, lineal descendant, chick, lamb, colt, cub, cadet, chip off the old block, brat *(contempt.)*, kitten, puppy, pup, yearling, scion.

3. Effect of something, product, byproduct, result, consequence, sequence, creation, upshot, outcome, issue, derivative, fruit, subscript, postscript, spawn, rider, pendant, corollary, side issue, appendix, appendage, episode, digression, supplement, outgrowth, aftermath, wake, train, trail, aftereffect, eventuality.

OFTEN, *adv.* Frequently, many times, in many cases, as a common thing, generally, constantly, habitually, continually, sometimes, ever and anon, many a time, every now and then, every once in a while, regularly, periodically, commonly, at short intervals, oft *(chiefly Poetic)*, repeatedly, usually, much, daily, over and over, time and again, day by day, in many instances.

OGLE, *n.* Ogling glance, leer, side glance, goggle, gaze, fleer, gibe, jeer, smirk, wink, squint, grin, sheep's eyes, scrutiny, gloat, impertinent *or* insulting look, once-over *(sl.)*.

OGLE, *v.* Eye with amorous (ingratiating *or* impertinently familiar) glances, stare, fleer, glance sideways, look at, look slyly, look significantly, leer, smirk, coquet, flirt, point at, gape, wink, squint, give a sidelong look, cut one's eye *(sl.)*, gawk *(coll.)*, cast sheep's eyes at, give the once-over *(sl.)*, scrutinize, goggle.

OGRE, *n.* Monster, hideous giant, hobgoblin, specter, scarecrow, fiend, hellhound, nightmare, incubus, bugbear, bugaboo, chimera, beldam, ghoul, vampire, harpy, Grendel, succubus, witch, barghest, tigress, dragon, she-wolf, fright, cannibal, frightful object, goblin, devil, Minotaur *(Gk. Myth.)*, afreet *(Arabic Myth.)*, hellhag, hag, *bête noire (Fr.)*, demon, ogreish person, Frankenstein's monster, lamia *(Class. Myth.)*, Gorgon *(Gr. Legend)*.

OIL, *n.* Lubricant, ointment, petroleum, grease, liniment, fuel, pomade, pomatum, mineral oil, vegetable oil, animal oil, illuminant, unction *(Relig.)*, olein *(Chem.)*, fat, balm, salve, ungent.

OIL, *v.* Smear *or* supply with oil, lubricate, grease, salve, anoint, lard, daub, pomade, pinguefy.

OILSTONE, *n.* Hone, whetstone, oiled wheel *(for sharpening knives, etc.)*, sharpener, grindstone, rubstone.

OILY, *adj.* 1. Containing oil, of oily texture, oillike, unctuous, oleaginous, oleoresinous, pinguid, sebaceous, fatty, oleous, lardaceous, buttery, emulsive, butyraceous, unguentary, unguentiferous, unguentous, lardy, lardiform.

2. Covered with oil, slippery, greasy, lubricated, smeared with oil, lubricous, synovial *(Anat.)*.

3. Suave, glib, suaviloquent, honey-tongued, smooth-tongued, mealy-mouthed, blandiloquous, flattering, servile, compliant, buttery *(coll.)*, bland, ingratiating, fawning, sycophantic, wheedling, bootlicking *(coll.)*, toadying.

OINTMENT, *n.* Unguent, salve, pomade, pomatum, balm, palliative, malabathrum, collyrium *(for the eyes)*, emollient, demulcent, aromatic oil, cerate, lotion, liniment, embrocation, abirritant *(Pathol.)*, nard, spikenard *(Bibl.)*.

OLD, *adj.* 1. Gray *or* white with age, elderly, aged, hoary, veteran, venerable, antiquated, timeworn, declining, grizzled, grizzly, canescent, vetust, senile *(masc.)*, anile *(fem.)*, superannuated, senescent, patriarchal, decrepit, gray-headed, venerable, ancient.

2. Of long standing, ancient, antique, longestablished, old-fashioned, vintage, of great age, of yore, time-honored, traditional, olden *(Poet.)*.

3. *(Of very old, prehistoric, etc., things)* Prehistoric, primeval, primordial, primitive, pristine, primigenial, aboriginal, preadamite.

4. Worn-out, used, decrepit, dilapidated, weathered, much-used, mildewed, moldy, moth-eaten, deteriorated, rusty, stale, weather-beaten, decayed, crumbling, battered, ramshackle, tumble-down, decadent, run-down, wasted, disintegrated, brokendown.

5. *(As in the expression "Five years old.")* Of age, at the age of, having lived for, aetatis suae *(L.)*.

OLD AGE, *n.* Age, senility *(masc.)*, anility *(fem.)*, agedness, senescence, senectitude, second childhood *(fig.)*, decrepitude, caducity, decline of life, declining years, oldness, dotage, antiquity, superannuation, dotardism.

OLDER, *adj.* Elder, senior, coming before, preceding, prior, former, earlier, less recent.

OLDEST, *adj.* First, first-born, senior, primordial, primogenous, pristine, primogenitary, original, initial, incipient, primeval.

OLD-FASHIONED, *adj.* 1. Old-fangled, of great age, traditional, antiquated, archaic, of long standing, long established, time-honored, ancient, oldtime, venerable, olden *(poet.)*.

2. Out-of-date, behind the times, out-of-fashion,

unfashionable, extinct, obsolete, passé, dead, gone by, disused, outmoded.

OLD MAN, *n.* Graybeard, sexagenarian, octogenarian, nonagenarian, centenarian, patriarch, Methuselah, grandfather *(coll. in this sense.)*, Nestor *(fig.)*, old codger *(sl. contempt.)*, dotard, grisard, oldster *(coll.)*, old-timer *(coll.)*, gaffer *(contempt.)*, geezer *(sl.)*.

OLD-TIME, *adj.* Belonging to *or* characteristic of old *or* former times, old, late, early, previous, prior, old-fashioned, antecedent, *ci-devant (Fr.)*, foregoing, bygone, gone-by, passed away, antiquated, out-of-date, expired, extinct, hoary, venerable, outmoded, outdated, forgotten, ancient, obsolete, erstwhile, sometime, ancestral, antique, of yore, rooted, traditional, superannuated, immemorial, time-honored, of long standing, timeworn, mildewed, moldy, dead, disused, passé, crumbling, fusty, stale, old-world, archaic, of other times, of the old school, former, quondam, preëxistent, rusty.

OLD-WOMANISH, *adj.* Of *or* like an old woman, excessively fussy, doting, superannuated, doddering, childlike, in one's second childhood, oldmaidish *(coll.)*, prim, prudish, spinsterish, dotardly, fastidious, timid, mincing, demure, bustling, fidgety, strait-laced, decrepit.

OLD-WORLD, *adj.* Of *or* pertaining to the ancient world *or* to a former period of history, archaic, European, classical, academic, Mediterranean, Aegean, Roman, Greek, medieval, Attic, Ciceronian.

OLEAGINOUS, *adj.* Having the nature *or* qualities of oil, containing oil, producing oil, oily, oleic, sebaceous, unctuous, oleoresinous, pinguid, fatty, lardaceous, buttery, emulsive, butyraceous, unguentary, unguentiferous, lardiform, lardy, greasy, lubricous, slippery, synovial *(Anat.)*.

OLFACTION, *n.* Act of smelling, sense of smell, scent, sniff, nose, perception of odors, olfactory sense.

OLIGARCHY, *n.* Form of government in which power is vested in a few *or* in a dominant class *or* clique, triumvirate, diarchy, duarchy, triarchy, theocracy.

OLIO, *n.* Hash, jumble, miscellany, mess, potpourri, oglio, compound, farrago, medley, gallimaufry, mélange, hotchpotch, hodgepodge, salmagundi, mixture, variety, heterogeneous mixture, stew, confusion, ollapodrida, mishmash, concoction, intermixture, conglomeration, aggregate, compilation, composite, commixture, accumulation, mosaic, mix, chow-chow, patchwork, omnium-gatherum, Noah's ark, salad, what the cat brought in *(coll.)*, tumble, muddle, litter, minced meat, fracabdeau, mash, ragout, réchauffé, imbroglio, dishevel, huddle.

OMEN, *n.* Anything regarded as indicating the future, prognostic, augury, presentiment, divination, portent, sign, presage, premonition, handwriting on the wall, foreshadowing, boding, soothsay, sunspot, forecast, foreknowledge, indication, token, foretoken, harbinger, prophecy, vaticination, herald, prelude, hint, symptom, promise, hariolation, bird of omen, assurance, clouds on the horizon, Mother Carey's chickens, stormy petrel, straw in the wind, precursor, foreboding, auspice, prediction, warning, prognostication, message from the dead, reading of the palm, bodement, prefiguration, prefigurement, implication, prodrome *(Pathol.)*, prophetic significance.

OMEN, *v.* 1. Be an omen of, portend, herald, proclaim, foreshadow, signify, shadow forth, announce, promise, foretoken, threaten, point to, auspicate, forerun, typify, pretypify, preindicate, augur, premise, presignify, prefigure, forebode, bode, betoken, forewarn.

2. Divine *(as if from omens)*, prognosticate, augur, prophesy, foretell, foresee, forewarn, haruspicate, hariolate, ascertain by divination, annunciate, premonish, prewarn, tell fortunes, vaticinate, forecast, predict.

OMINOUS, *adj.* 1. Portending evil, portentous, inauspicious, unpropitious, menacing, minatory, dangerous, perilous, fell, direful, doomed, evil-starred, ill-starred, ill-fated, impending, minacious, premonitory, unpromising, unlucky, disastrous, hopeless, fearful, bad, unblest, luckless, clouded, dire, hapless, unprosperous, planet-struck, planet-stricken, sinister, threatening, alarming, fateful, ill-boding, jinxed *(coll.)*, Jonahed, under a cloud, fortuneless, lowering, frightening, fear-inspiring, disquieting, disturbing, dismaying, hoodooed *(coll.)*, comminatory.

2. Having the significance of an omen, oracular, predictive, indicative, prophetic, precursory, precursive, presaging, indicating, significant, foreboding, predictory, presentient, prescient, presageful, fatidic, premonitory, prognostic, prognosticatory, sibyllic, sibylline, augural, pythonic, vaticinal, haruspical, divinatory, fatiloquent, boding, suggestive.

OMISSION, *n.* 1. Act of leaving out *or* neglecting, neglect, nonfulfillment, failure, preclusion, exclusion, exception, noninclusion, negligence, laches *(Leg.)*, apocope *(Gramm.)*, inadvertence, oversight, noncompliance, breach, elision, forgetfulness, nonadmission, delinquency, laxity, expulsion, elimination, debarment, lockout, ejection, pretermission, omittance.

2. Gap, mistake, fault, flaw, error, hiatus, slip, miss, break, interval, rift, rupture, lacuna, separation, blank, vacancy, caesura, hole, gulf, interspace.

3. Anything omitted *or* left out, thing overlooked, neglected fact, *etc.*, paralipomena *(Plur.)*.

OMIT, *v.* 1. Leave out, forget about, abstain from inserting, except, not include, bar, elide, jump, drop, skip, pass over, exclude, ignore, delete, set aside, miss, preclude, pretermit, repudiate.

2. Neglect, forget, fail, evade, not heed, let slip, skim, be careless of, not think of, pay no attention, ignore, dodge, leave undone, let ride, overlook, not trouble oneself with, shirk, shun, avoid, steer clear of, elude, decline, eschew, balk at, avert, malinger.

OMNIBUS, *n.* 1. Bus, motorbus, motor coach.

2. Volume of reprinted works by a single author *or* related in interest *or* nature, collected works, anthology, spicilege, delectus, corpus, posy, album, gleanings, ana, analects, garland, chrestomathy, treasury, thesaurus, miscellany, collectanea, compilation, reader.

OMNIFARIOUS, *adj.* Of all forms, varieties *or* kinds, multiform, multifarious, multifold, manifold, variegated, many-sided, diversified, divers, varied, protean, proteiform, motley, heterogeneous, diversiform, variform, multiplex, omniform, polymorphous, polymorphic, omnigenous, metamorphotic, metamorphic, multiphase, mixed.

OMNIFIC, *adj.* Creating all things, all-creating, before all things, prime, eternal, from eternity, original, primary, protogenic, aboriginal, primordial, procreative, seminal, germinal, institutive, originative, causal, causative, formative, constitutive, essential, generative, progenitive, possessing the life-force, life-giving.

OMNIPOTENCE, *n.* The quality of being omnipotent, almightiness, supreme power, undisputed sway, supremacy, dominion, prerogative, divine right, infinite authority, sovereignty, majesty, imperiality, rule, preponderance, prepotency, prepollency, lordship, mastership, predominance, empery *(Poetic)*, carte blanche *(Fr.)*, unlimited power, mastery, control, domination, godlikeness, primacy, suzerainty, jurisdiction.

OMNIPOTENT, *adj.* Almighty *(as God or a deity)*, all-powerful, infinite in power, puissant, dynamic, ruling, highest, preëminent, plenipotent, plenipotentiary, multipotent, having unlimited *or* very great authority, cogent, supreme, irresistible, cunctipotent.

OMNIPRESENT, *adj. (In strict sense applied only to the Supreme Being)* Present everywhere, ubiquitous *(loose)*, almighty, infinite, all-seeing.

OMNISCIENT, *adj. (Usually applied only to Supreme Being)* Having infinite knowledge, all-wise, infinite, all-knowing, preëminent, supreme.

OMNIUM-GATHERUM, *n.* Medley, mishmash, imbroglio, réchauffé, ragout, muddle, litter, fracabdeau, mash, tumble, jumble, hash, mess, potpourri, compound, farrago, gallimaufry, mélange, hotchpotch, hodgepodge, stew, heterogeneous mixture, variety, mixture, salmagundi, olio, ollapodrida, commixture, concoction, intermixture, aggregate, compilation, conglomeration, patchwork, chow-chow, mix, mosaic, accumulation, salad.

OMNIVOROUS, *adj.* Eating everything, pamphagous, existing *or* living on a mixed diet, pantophagous.

OMPHALOS, *n.* 1. *(Anat.)* Navel, umbilicus, nave, nombril.

2. Central point, radiant, point of convergence, focus, core, heart, navel, marrow, centrality, centriole *(Biol.)*, center, cynosure, axis, pivot, middle point, focal point, nucleus, hub, focalization, gist, point of concentration, kernel.

ON, *adv.* 1. *(On a thing, place, person, or oneself)* Upon, about, over, round, around, abroad *(a vehicle)*.

2. Fast to a thing *(as for support)*, onto, close, firm, securely, firmly, tightly, for dear life *(coll.)*.

3. With continuous procedure, without interruption, along, perseveringly, steadily, without ceasing, unceasingly, progressively, forth, under way, under sail, in transit, en route, in a line, from beginning to end, continually, continuously, onward, ahead, doggedly.

4. Forward, onward, toward, along, beyond, ahead, forth, before one, in the direction one is going, to the horizon (goal, destination, *etc.*).

ON, *prep.* Upon, by, above and in contact with, beside, onto.

ONCE, *adv.* 1. Single time, one time, on one occasion, once for all, for the nonce.

2. At a time in the past, formerly, long ago, before *or* ere now, in times past, long since, erenow, some time back, at one time, heretofore, previously, time was, once upon a time, aforetime, hitherto, in the old *or* good old days, in other days, years *or* ages ago, in the memory of man, time out of mind, some time ago *or* since.

3. Even a single time, ever, possibly, by chance,

by a fluke, in the realm of possibility, just, only, merely, barely, simply, but, at least, nothing but, no more than.

ONCOMING, *adj.* Approaching, advancing, on-rushing, coming, close, expected, looming, bearing down, in prospect, nearing, impending, imminent, on the horizon, immediate.

ONE, *adj.* 1. Being a single unit *(rather than two or more)*, single, individual, singular, a, an, unique, odd, only, unrepeated, being a person, thing, *or* individual instance *(of a number or kind indicated)*, one and only, sole, solitary, lone, complete, whole, entire, each, azygous *(Zool., Bot.)*.

2. Some, any, a particular, to come, coming, past, foregoing, recent, previous, prior, antecedent, former, hereafter, to be, eventual, future, such and such, prospective.

3. Single through union, agreement, *or* harmony, united, whole, wedded, married, bonded, complementary, unified, undivided, inseparable, concordant, joined, indissoluble, in accord, like-minded, of one mind, allied, cemented, corporate, one bone and one flesh, agreeable, congenial, compatible, accordant, integrated, bound, harmonious.

4. The same, of a single kind, nature, *or* character, common, identical, one and the same, alike, analogous, all one, coinciding, coalescent, inseparable, equal, equivalent, undistinguishable, synonymous, homoöusian, coincident, tantamount.

ONE, *n.* Single person *or* thing, unit, ace, monad, mortal, soul, body, creature, item, integer, member, entity, person, somebody, someone, man, human, individual, each *(Pron.)*.

ONENESS, *n.* 1. Quality of being one, unity, singleness, sameness, identity, integrality, un-dividedness, solidarity, totality, wholeness, compages, compaction, entirety, isolation, solitude, coherence, coalescence, coincidence, identicalness, completeness, consistency, equivalence, homoöusia, union, individuality, unification.

2. Agreement, unity of thought, belief, aim, *etc.*, union, unanimity, chime, concord, single-ness of mind, accord, amity, concordance, concurrence in opinions *or* sentiments, *etc.*, friendship, harmony, good understanding, sympathy, consensus, congeniality, brotherliness, fellowship, brotherhood, cordiality, consentaneity, consentaneousness, *rapport (Fr.)*, concert, conformance, compatibility, understanding, coöperation, one voice, joint assent, affinity, comradeship, acquiescence, amicability, accordance, reconciliation.

ONEROUS, *adj.* Burdensome, oppressive, heavy, troublesome, bearing hard upon one, not easy to bear, hard to endure, accomplish *or* fulfill, harsh, distressing, grievous, afflictive, hard to deal with, heavy-handed, intolerable, unbearable, harmful, hurtful, cruel, severe, hard, difficult, wearying, wearing, trying, noisome, malefic, prejudicial, wasting, corrosive, malignant, corroding, nocent, noxious, baleful, baneful, injurious, deleterious, pernicious, detrimental, arduous, toilsome, laborious, tiring, painful, wearisome, fatiguing, over-bearing, malevolent, operose, strenuous, irksome, rugged, crabbed, formidable, knotty, unmanageable, intractable, ungovernable, unyielding, devouring, engulfing, exhausting, crushing, taxing, exacting, thorny, full of difficulties, balky, refractory, perverse, awkward, stubborn, obstinate, untoward, resistant, vexatious, unendurable, harrowing, weighty, cumbrous, cumbersome, over-powering, galling, grinding.

ONE-SIDED, *adj.* 1. Having but one side, existing *or* occurring on one side only, unilateral, unsymmetrical, irregular, unbalanced, unequal, having one side larger *or* more developed than the other, lopsided, uneven, ill-balanced, overbalanced, dis-proportioned, unequal-sided, asymmetrical.

2. Considering but one side of a matter *or* question, partial, unfair, partisan, bigoted, lopsided, inequitable, warped, contorted, distorted, prepossessed, intolerant, biased, shortsighted, un-candid, interested, unbalanced, unjust, prejudiced, influenced, narrow-minded, *ex parte (Lat.)*.

ONE-TIME, *adj.* Having been *(as specified)* at one time, former, ancient, preceding, precedent, prior, prevenient, earlier, anterior, foregoing, precursive, quondam, old, late, preëxistent, sometime, *ci-devant (Fr.)*, previous, antecedent.

ONLOOKER, *n.* One who looks on *or* observes, observer, beholder, looker-on, spectator, viewer, witness, inspector, eyewitness, bystander, looker, lookout, scrutinizer, watcher, examiner, sight-seer, attendant, rubberneck *(sl.)*, perceiver, frequenter, patron, theater-goer, attender, gallery *(pl.)*, house *(pl.)*, audience *(pl.)*, sidewalk, super-intendent *(joc.)*.

ONLY, *adj.* Being the single one *or* the relatively few of the kind, sole, alone, single, exclusive, unique, solitary, individual, one and only, lone, singular, odd one, unrepeated, unparalleled, un-matched.

ONLY, *adv.* 1. Without others *or* anything further, as the only one, by oneself *or* itself, singly, exclusively, alone, solely, apart.

2. No more than, just, but, at least, barely, merely, simply, nothing but, to such an extent, to the last extent, purely.

ONLY, *conj.* But, excepting that, but for the fact that *or* of, if it were not that.

ONOMATOPOEIA, *n.* Formation of a word by imitating a sound associated with the thing designated, onomatopoësis, onomatopoesy, correspondence of sound *(between word and object)*, echoism *(Philol.)*.

ONRUSH, *n.* Strong onward rush, flow, *etc.*, plunge, assault, attack, storm, push, run, dash, drive, onset, onslaught, flux, flight, freshet, stream, wall of water, millrace, wave, tidal wave, flood, deluge, niagara, surge, race, tide, career, current, torrent, swift course, mill run, charge.

ONSET, *n.* 1. Attack, assault, storm, attempt, raid, incursion, onslaught, aggression, dash, rush, shock, encounter, onrush, sortie, besetment, sur-prisal, thrust, sally, expedition, inroad, dragon-nade, opening, gambit *(of war, battle, etc.)*, brunt, offense, push *(sl.)*, charge, storming, access, concussion, smash, offensive, invasion.

2. Start, beginning, commencement, inception, outset, opening, birth, genesis, threshold, initiation, origination, dawn, head, spring, inauguration, incipience, foundation, inchoation, incubation, first move, outbreak, rise of the curtain, infancy, coming, take-off *(coll.)*, rise, embarkation, first step.

ONSHORE, *adj., adv.* Ashore, off the sea, on dry land, on terra firma, aground, on land (dock, pier, *etc.*).

ONSLAUGHT, *n.* Onset *(esp. a vigorous or furious one)*, assault, attack, *etc.* (See ONSET *above.*)

ONTOLOGY, *n.* Science of existence *or* being, metaphysics, philosophy, cosmology.

ONUS, *n.* Burden, responsibility, impediment, duty, care, obligation, handicap, encumbrance, cross, weight, load, pack, lumber, millstone 'round one's neck, liability, hamper, debt.

ONWARD, *adj.* Directed *or* moving onward *or* forward, moving ahead, progressing, approaching, profluent, ongoing, forward-looking, advancing, flowing, forward-moving, progressive, forward.

ONWARD, ONWARDS, *adv.* Toward a point ahead *or* in front, forward, on ahead, along, on, in advance, at a position *or* point in advance, beyond, before one, to *or* toward a goal *or* destination, fronted, headward *or* headwards, frontward, on the way, en route, in transit, on one's way, under way, under sail, ahead, *en avant (Fr.),* on the wing.

OOZE, *n.* 1. Calcareous mud *(covering parts of the ocean bottom),* that which oozes, soft mud, slime, slush, slosh, slop, leakage, seepage, silt, gumbo, alluvium, secretion, squash, sludge, transudation, transudate, excretion, clay, muck, mire, exudation.

2. Marsh, bog, fen, morass, mire, moor, quagmire, slough, wash, quicksand, swamp, bottom *(Phys., Geog.).*

OOZE, *v.* Percolate, exude *(as through pores or small openings),* drain, strain, filter, sweat, seep, bleed, exudate, discharge, emit, filtrate, trickle, distil, pass slowly *or* gradually, pass out slowly *or* imperceptibly, leach, extravasate *(Pathol.),* shed, drop, drip, dribble, effuse, weep, lixiviate, transpire, leak, transude.

OOZY, *adj.* 1. Exuding moisture, damp with moisture, moist, washy, weepy, seepy, watery, hydrous, infiltrative.

2. Of *or* like ooze, soft mud *or* slime, miry, slimy, fenny, muddy, marshy, sloppy, boggish, uliginose, soft, spongy, swampish, splashy, quaggy, clayey, slushy, sloshy, mucky, gumbo, sludgy, lutose, plashy, wet, paludal, slimy, squashy, alluvial.

OPACITY, *n.* State of being opaque, want of transparency, opaqueness, intransparency, nubilousness, obfuscation, darkness, cloudiness, filminess, nubilation, fuliginosity, nontransparency, nontranslucency, dullness.

OPALESCENT, *adj.* Exhibiting a play of colors *(like that of the opal),* nacreous, irisated, iridescent, opaline, pearly, nacrous, nacry, opaloid, translucent, milky, irised, iridic, iridal, iridical, polychromatic, variegated, shaded, mottled.

OPAQUE, *adj.* 1. Impenetrable to light, not transmitting light (radiation, sound, heat, *etc.*), filmy, nubilous, opacous, intransparent, thick, shady, misty, smokey, nontransparent, nontranslucent, impervious to light, turbid, murky, hazy, obscure, clouded, dirty, muddy, obfuscated, unclear, frosted, dense, fuliginous, sooty, adiaphanous.

2. Not shining *or* bright, dark, dull, mat, tarnished, dim, dusky, unglazed, lusterless, fuliginous, blurred, smoky, nacreous, frosty, dirty, dingy.

3. Hard to understand, not clear *or* lucid, obscure, vague, unclear, enigmatic, indefinite, impenetrable, abstruse, confusing, confused, recondite, ambiguous, cryptic, equivocal, unfathomable, difficult, perplexing, puzzling, imperspicuous.

4. Unintelligent, stupid, ignorant, crass, dense, thick, unenlightened, lumpish, simple, doltish, obtuse, witless, empty-headed, nescient, dullwitted, dumb *(coll.),* unteachable, benighted, incompetent, heavy, bungling, cloddish, uncomprehending, imbecilic, moronic, stolid, thick-headed, dronish, maladroit.

OPEN, *adj.* 1. Not shut *(as a door, gate, etc.),* not closed, covered, *or* shut up *(as a house, box, drawer, etc.),* unclosed, uncovered, unsealed, unshut, lidless, coverless, ajar, agape, ringent, dehiscent, yawning, gaping, unconfined, perforated.

2. Not enclosed *(as by barriers),* that may be entered, used, shared, competed for, *etc.,* by all, available, accessible, public, unenclosed, not engaged *(as time),* unfilled *(as a position),* optional, unqualified, elective, unbarred, unfenced, passable, unbounded, not circumscribed, volitional, voluntary, unconditional, without prohibition, unrestricted, free to all, unobstructed.

3. Undetermined, debatable, undecided, doubtful, uncertain, questionable, tentative, disputable, speculative, moot, mooted, controvertible, undemonstrated, unfixed, unsettled, indefinite, experimental, uncounted, untold, yet to be decided, vague, dubious, contestable, unconfirmed.

4. *(Foll. by* TO) Liable or subject to, susceptive to, in danger of, incident to, dependent on, exposed to, obnoxious to.

5. Accessible *(to appeals, ideas, offers, etc.),* willing, hospitable, conversable, open-minded, unswayed, unbigoted, unprejudiced, unbiased, impartial, dispassionate, broad, disinterested, unwarped, broad-minded, unprepossessed, tolerant, impersonal, candid, fair, just, square, evenhanded, responsive, persuadable, easy, amenable, equitable, uninfluenced.

6. Not covered *or* protected, bare, exposed, unprotected, uncovered, unsheltered, vulnerable, unfortified, pregnable, defenseless, weaponless, unguarded, undefended, unshielded, expugnable, unwarmed.

7. Unobstructed, clear, passable, exposed, windswept, fit for travel, navigable, unchecked, free, unhampered, unhindered, unimpeded, wide, extensive, broad, not built up, uncrowded, uncluttered.

8. *(Of weather, esp. winters, waterways, etc.)* Mild, moderate, free from ice *(of water),* free from fog *(Naut.),* free from frost, equable, not extreme, not violent, harsh, *or* intense, temperate, unfrozen.

9. Exposed to general view *or* knowledge, existing *or* carried on without concealment, plain, apparent, laid bare, naked, frank, explicit, genuine, glaring, undisguised, revealed, noticeable, discernible, perceptible, unconcealed, unhidden, rife, unclouded, published, notorious, observable, in sight *or* view, naïve, aboveboard, reported, barefaced, arrant, flagrant, demonstrable, disclosed, unmasked, overt, express, defined, unmistakable, investigable, in broad daylight, in circulation, avowed, perspicuous, public, manifest, in evidence, perceivable, conspicuous, conversable, visible, patent, obvious, evident, artless, bonafide.

10. Acting publicly *or* without concealment, frank, candid, unreserved, honest, sincere, fair, undissembling, undesigning, foursquare, naïve, plain-spoken, downright, open-hearted, single-minded, ingenuous, simple-minded, artless, aboveboard, blunt, truthful, direct, clear-eyed, unfeigning, incapable of deceit, innocent, guiltless, unsophisticated, bona fide, lamblike, straightforward, clean-cut, outspoken.

11. Liberal, generous, bounteous, bountiful, open-handed, munificent, free, lavish, beneficent, benevolent, almsgiving, ungrudging, unsparing, free-handed, big-hearted, princely, unstinting, prodigal, indulgent, charitable, extravagant, handsome, humanitarian, eleemosynary, unselfish, magnanimous, great-hearted.

12. Perforated, porous, loose, riddled, spongy, airy, pierced, leachy, not compact *or* dense, foraminous, honeycombed, cribriform, sievelike, alveolate, cellular, punctured, pitted, shot through, pricked, lacy, favose, faveolate, faviform, favaginous.

13. Extended, spread out, wide, unfolded, unfurled, opened out, distended, fanned, expanded, unclose, dilated, made larger, patulous, stretched out, wide-open.

OPEN, *v.* 1. Move something from shut *or* closed position, unclose, make open, become open, be unclosed *or* parted, be sundered *or* severed, render *(an enclosed space)* open to passage *or* access, cut *or* break into, come apart *or* asunder, lay open, cut through, unstop, unseal, rend, unbar, gape, throw open, separate, unlock, undo, unwrap, uncork, incise, lance, slit, tear, crack, split, uncover, uncase, dehisce, cleave, cut, gap, yawn, unclutch, unclench, dissect, bud, part.

2. Give access to, make accessible *or* available *(as for use)*, establish for the entrance *or* use of the public, customers, *etc.*, afford entrance, be ready to receive *or* do business, *etc.*, offer one's services, provide, found, institute, create.

3. Clear of obstructions, make clear, cut a passage through, flush out, clean out, let flow, make passable, remove obstacles, unclog, deobstruct, cleanse, purge, unstop, sweep out, rout out, expurgate, deterge, defecate, elute.

4. Lay bare, expose to view, unconceal, unhide, lay open, uncover, reveal, exhibit, disclose, display, set forth, manifest, make evident *or* manifest, unscreen, uncloak, hold up to view, bring to light, unmask, bare, show up, unshroud, uncurtain, unbosom, evince, unveil, produce.

5. Bring to knowledge, disclose, divulge, reveal, tell, breathe, whisper, utter, give utterance to, show, make known, explain, come out with, publish, inform, proclaim, let fall *or* drop, give vent to, interpret, enunciate, decipher, elucidate, enlighten, exposit, expound, decode, expatiate upon, speak out, announce, present, make plain, expand upon, divulgate.

6. Spread out, expand, extend, dilate, unfurl, diverge, branch, augment, inflate, blow up, untwine, untwist, uncoil, unwind, unroll, burst forth, lengthen, enlarge, broaden, increase, bud, develop, divaricate, unfold, unravel.

7. Make less compact, less close together, *etc.*, set at intervals, separate, dispart, part, interspace, space, interval, perforate, puncture, pierce, punch, prick, riddle, honeycomb, cribble, shoot through, penetrate, pit, enfilade *(Mil.)*.

8. Set in action, begin, commence, start, inaugurate, enter upon, initiate, give a first performance *(Theat.)*, broach, begin to appear, originate, engage upon, undertake, set in operation, take the first step, embark upon, inchoate, go ahead with, lay the first stone, put the ball in motion, introduce, incept, be off, venture forth, take up, plunge into, put in execution, open fire, set up, launch, usher in, break ground, break the ice, set on foot, ring in *(coll.)*, set forward, institute.

9. Afford access *(into, to, etc.)*, have an opening, passage, *or* outlet *(into, upon, etc.)*, lead, take one, meet, adjoin, neighbor on, converge upon, join, abut on *or* upon, connect with, border on, reach, verge upon.

OPEN-AIR, *adj.* Existing in, taking place in *or* characteristic of the open air, outdoor, outside, out-of-doors, alfresco, exposed, airy, plein-air, hypoethral.

OPEN-EYED, *adj.* 1. Having the eyes wide open *(as in wonder)*, wide-eyed, receptive, surprised, amazed, bewildered, astonished, wondering, astounded, aghast, breathless, open-mouthed, agape, inquiring, ingenuous, agog.

2. Watchful, vigilant, alert, awake, sharp-eyed, eagle-eyed, keen, critical, far-seeing, expectant, regardful, all eyes, observant, on the lookout, cognizant, heedful, mindful, attentive, on guard, unsleeping, Argus-eyed, lynx-eyed, ready, anticipative, on the job *(coll.)*, on the qui vive *(Fr.)*.

3. Done *or* experienced with the eyes open, aware, knowing, conscious, anticipated, intentional, willful, voluntary, understood, perceptible, cognizable, express, free, determinate, willing, independent, self-determined, volitional, predetermined.

OPEN-HANDED, *adj.* Liberal, generous, bountiful, munificent, beneficent, benevolent, ungrudging, unsparing, free-handed, big-hearted, bounteous, princely, unstinting, indulgent, prodigal, charitable, extravagant, handsome, humanitarian, eleemosynary, unselfish, magnanimous, great-hearted.

OPEN-HEARTED, *adj.* 1. Unreserved, candid, frank, open, sincere, honest, truthful, veracious, upright, plain, undissembling, artless, guileless, ingenuous, open, fair, undesigning, foursquare, plain-spoken, naïve, downright, aboveboard, unfeigning, direct, clear-eyed, guiltless, bona fide, unsophisticated, straightforward, outspoken.

2. Kindly, benevolent, benignant, good, kind, obliging, gracious, indulgent, complacent, considerate, tender, kindhearted, good-natured, well-affected, loving, helpful, liberal, humane, charitable, unselfish, well-meaning, sympathetic, accommodating.

OPENING, *adj.* Initial, beginning, commencing, introductory, prefatory, proemial, inaugural, initiatory, incipient, primary.

OPENING, *n.* 1. Rent, gap, cleft, slit, slot, crack, cranny, chink, rime, crevice, rift, scissure, gash, chasm, gulf, fissure, hole, perforation, dent, indentation, breach, bore, caliber, interstice, vent, pore, eye, break, eyelet, pinhole, pigeonhole, loophole, outlet, entrance, inlet, mouth, embouchure, orifice, vomitory, postern, gate, wicket, hatch, door, trap door, portal, window, dormer, lattice, spiracle, oriel, open passage, dehiscence *(Biol.)*, patefaction, puncture, hiation, foramen *(Anat.)*, fenestra *(Zool.)*, scupper *(Naut.)*, acupuncture *(of the skin)*.

2. Beginning, act of commencing, start, inception, genesis, birth, outset, commencement, threshold, initiation, origination, dawn, head, spring, incipience, first cause, inauguration, source, rudiments, foundation, onset, first beginning, inchoation, incubation, first move, prelude, preface, introduction, preliminary, proem, overture, morning, first attempt, outbreak, raising of the curtain, first stage, infancy, installation, coming out *(coll.)*, debut, take-off *(coll.)*, send-off *(coll.)*, kick-off *(coll.)*, rise, derivation, embryo, embarkation, the first step.

3. Opportunity, chance, occasion, advantage, time, place, means, moment, possibility.

4. Vacancy, place, chance, opportunity, unfilled place, open position, available job.

OPEN-MINDED, *adj.* Receptive, amenable, unprejudiced, tolerant, unbiased, broad-minded, undogmatic, impartial, tractable, persuadable, reasonable, liberal, unjaundiced, unwarped, unswayed, open to suggestions, acquiescent, compliant, pliant.

OPERA, *n.* Musical drama *or* play, operetta (*light*), *opéra bouffe* (*Fr.*), *opéra comique* (*Fr.*), *dramma per musica* (*It. Hist.*).

OPERATE, *v.* 1. Perform a work *etc.*, work, act, function, do, exert effort, achieve, commit, perpetrate, behave, manage.

2. Have a desired effect (*as a medicine, etc.*), behave, function, have influence, act, be effective, be operative.

OPERATION, *n.* 1. Act of operating, doing, performance, action, activity, labor, performance, procedure, exercise, execution, deed, consummation, turn, course, step, conduct, handiwork, working, work.

2. Means of producing effects, exertion of influence, *etc.*, agency, exertion, efficiency, influence, instrumentality, activity, medium, appliance, means, action, force.

3. (*Commerce*) Transaction, deal, business deal, speculation, negotiation, agreement.

4. (*Mil.* and *Naval*) Mission, military (*or* naval) errand, military project, military task, assignment, consignment.

5. (*Medicine*) Surgery, the knife (*coll.*).

OPERATIVE, *adj.* 1. Exerting influence *or* force, in force, influential, active, in harness, performing, functional, employed, functioning, in operation, instrumental, acting, in play, engaged.

2. Producing the desired results, effective, efficient, efficacious, effectual, adequate, sufficient, ample, helpful, beneficial, useful, advantageous.

OPERATOR, *n.* 1. Actor, doer, agent, performer, executor, maker, perpetrator, worker, artificer, author, practitioner.

2. Doctor, surgeon.

OPEROSE, *adj.* 1. Hard-working, zealous, earnest, diligent, plodding, industrious, steady, assiduous, unflagging, painstaking, sedulous, persistent, active, pertinacious, persevering, studious, ardent, unsleeping, deeply-engrossed, untiring.

2. Laborious, difficult, toilsome, hard, fatiguing, wearisome, exhausting, heavy, tough, onerous, burdensome, troublesome, deadly, herculean, formidable, trying, intricate, taxing, thorny, wearing, uphill, irksome, rugged, tiring.

OPHTHALMOLOGIST, *n.* Oculist, eye-specialist, eye doctor.

OPIATE, *n.* 1. Narcotic, drug, dope (*sl.*), snow (*sl.*), opium, morphine, cocaine, heroin, marijuana, laudanum.

2. Soporific, somnifacient, analgesic, assuasive, lenitive, hyoscyamine, belladonna, sedative, mydriatic, stupefacient, nepenthe, calmative, palliative, mandrake, febrifuge, mitigative, demulcent, mandragora.

OPINION, *n.* 1. Belief, conviction, sentiment, view, persuasion, faith, tenet, mind, conclusion, surmise, notion, plerophory, idea, impression, conception, assumption, apprehension, presumption, supposition, putation, fancy, inference, conceit, theory, judgment, conjecture, resolve, reflection, speculation.

2. Professional decision *or* advice, verdict, diagnosis, judgment, finding, inference, determination, deduction, estimate, estimation, illation.

OPINIONATED, *adj.* Bullheaded, bigoted, stubborn, conceited, wilful, mulish, self-willed, unmanageable, unmalleable, ungovernable, pervicacious, obdurate, unimpressible, headstrong, inflexible, unbending, unyielding, unmoving, dogged, pertinacious, egotistical, self-important, overbear-

ing, lordly, cocky, vain, peacockish, pompous, self-esteeming, inflated, lofty, opinionative.

OPINIONATIVE, *adj.* 1. Conceited, bigoted, self-important, *etc.* See OPINIONATED, adj., *above.*

2. Doctrinal, creedal, canonical, generally held *or* believed, recognized, standard, accepted.

OPPONENT, *adj.* 1. Opposite, facing, vis-à-vis, contrary, antithetical, antonymous (*of words*), reverse, oppositional, contrapositive, antipodal, opposed, counter, diametrically opposed.

2. Battling, contending, bickering, opposing, opposed, quarreling, feuding, disagreeing, dissident, incompatible, discrepant, factious, on bad terms, at enmity, with daggers drawn, with crossed swords, at loggerheads, up in arms, at outs, jarring, clashing, broiling, disputing, countering, attacking, dueling, battling, oppositional, wrangling, enemy, discordant, disaccordant, combative, fighting, militant, belligerent, antagonistic, unfriendly, contentious, antipathetic, quarrelsome, on bad terms, adverse, contrary, renitent, uncongenial, bellicose, disputations, at variance, oppugnant.

OPPONENT, *n.* One who opposes, one who is unfriendly, enemy, foe, assailant, contender, opposer, antagonist, oppugnant, oppositionist.

OPPORTUNE, *adj.* Seasonable, timely, right, fit, fitting, suitable, auspicious, appropriate, expedient, favorable, propitious, profitable, fortunate, proper, advantageous, lucky.

OPPORTUNISM, *n.* Taking advantage, striking while the iron is hot, making the most of circumstances, timeliness, expediency, making hay while the sun shines.

OPPORTUNITY, *n.* Favorable time, good chance, opening, place, occasion, advantage, time, means, moment.

OPPOSE, *v.* 1. Counterbalance, set over against, balance, countervail, equate, parallel, face, confront, match, neutralize, correspond.

2. Resist, withstand, contest, strive, contend, struggle, tourney, counteract, act in opposition to, repulse, repel, make a stand against, draw sword against, take one's stand, confront, face, march against, fight, war, battle, tilt, joust, jostle, clash, fall foul of, close with, join issue, collide, break lance with, bandy blows with, skirmish, scuffle, enter the lists, cross swords, come to blows, box, fence, thrust and parry, duel, wrestle, spar, make warfare, engage in hostilities, go to battle against, measure swords with, contend against, encounter, attack, engage, cope with, struggle with, assault, assail, grapple with.

3. Contradict, defy, withstand, reluct, antagonize, obstruct, check, thwart, block, interdict, embargo, be contrary to, hinder, proscribe, impede, restrict, veto, play at cross purposes, oppugn, resist, restrain, inhibit, constrain, interfere, curb, barricade, bar, preclude, blockade, debar, prohibit, foil, cross, confound, act in opposition to, traverse, repel, frustrate, recalcitrate, repulse, militate against, contravene, protest.

OPPOSITE, *adj.* Facing, vis-à-vis, contrary, antithetical, antonymous, reverse, oppositional, contrapositive, antipodal, opposed, counter, diametrically opposed.

OPPOSITION, *n.* 1. Resistance, constraint, impediment, hindrance, contravention, oppugnation, counteraction, contrary action, restriction, cross purposes, debarment, frustration, preclusion, defiance, disagreement, restraint, inhibition, prohibition, contradiction, interference, antagonism, obstruction, barricade, blockade.

2. One who opposes, one who is unfriendly, enemy, foe, assailant, contender, opposer, antagonist, oppugnant, oppositionist.

OPPRESS, *v.* 1. Trouble, hinder, vex, drag down, overtask, burden, weigh down, handicap, overload, overcharge, obligate, hamper, strain, lade, encumber, overwhelm, overlay, surcharge, load, press down, saddle, try, harness, bridle, suppress, smother.

2. Depress, wrong, grieve, rack, grind, gall, overburden, overcharge, subdue, tyrannize, burden, encumber, wound, plague, afflict, fret, gnaw, worry, abuse, chafe, grate, haunt, harass, try, beset, infest, hound, embarrass, macerate, disquiet, scourge, punish, chasten, gall, roil, trouble, pursue, irk, harrow, threaten, wring, squeeze, pain, crush.

OPPRESSIVE, *adj.* Overpowering, cumbersome, cumbrous, weighty, harrowing, galling, grinding, vexatious, unendurable, exhausting, crushing, taxing, exacting, onerous, thorny, laborious, arduous, devouring, engulfing, unyielding, irksome, rugged, formidable, fatiguing, overbearing, operose, strenuous, wearisome, painful, tiring, toilsome, burdensome, heavy, troublesome, hard to endure, not easy to bear, harsh, distressing, grievous, afflictive, intolerable, unbearable, harmful, hurtful, cruel, severe, hard, difficult, wearing, trying, wasting, pernicious, detrimental.

OPPRESSION, *n.* 1. Cruelty, severity, tyranny, abuse, brutality, coercion, heavy-handedness, maltreatment, suppression, subjection, subjugation, compulsion, persecution, ill-treatment, misuse, inhumanity, ruthlessness, unkindness, ferocity, truculence, ferity, barbarity, savagery, conquest, enslavement, repression, hard-heartedness, harshness.

2. Unhappiness, anxiety, incubus, trouble, care, anguish, concern, sadness, solicitude, stress, cross, heartache, sorrow, pressure, affliction, vexation, grief, charge, desolation, hardship, misery, wretchedness, gravamen, despair, tribulation, concernment, annoyance.

OPPROBRIOUS, *adj.* 1. Disparaging, querulous, vitriolic, damnatory, reproachful, derogatory, abusive, crabbed, defamatory, rude, complaining, censorious, critical, scurrilous, contemptuous, petulant, condemnatory, vituperative, contumelious, calumniatory, calumnious, faultfinding, upbraiding, chiding, uncharitable, acrimonious, injurious, satirical, insulting, scolding, fulminating, objurgatory, denunciatory, hurtful, thersitical, vilificatory, invective, blackguard, carping.

2. Disgraceful, dishonorable, infamous, heinous, nefarious, low, inglorious, scandalous, villainous, ignominious, despicable, indecent, ignoble, outrageous, shameful, base, shocking, disreputable, discreditable, mean, unworthy, reprehensible, contemptible, facinorous, blameworthy, flagitious, uncommendable, scandalous, inquitous, wicked, corrupt, dastardly, sneaking, execrable, sinister, immoral, black, diabolic, infernal, arrant, despicable, deplorable, unmanly, objectionable, illaudable, sinful, proflifiate, fulsome, felonious.

OPPROBRIUM, *n.* 1. State of being in disgrace, discredit, ill-favor, debasement, disrepute, bad graces, bad books *(coll.),* inglorious, disesteen, contempt, degradation, dishonor, humiliation, baseness, disfavor, obloquy, infamy, odium.

2. That which causes disgrace, slur, reproach, disparagement, attaint, tarnish, ignominy, scandal, smirch, stain, blot, stigma, brand, ill-repute, defilement.

OPPUGN, *v.* Call in question, bring to question, assail, question, wrangle, contradict, refute, confute, object, challenge, quibble, impute, denounce, disagree, take exception, remonstrate, controvert, dispute, protest, attack, charge, retort, dissent, gainsay, demur, cavil.

OPTICAL, *adj.* Relating to vision, visual, ocular.

OPTIMISM, *n.* Disposition to hope for the best, tendency to look on the bright side of things, hopefulness, cheerfulness, anticipation, happy expectancy, security, aspiration, assurance, confidence, presumption, assumption, certainty, fond hope, enthusiasm, golden dream, fool's paradise, bright hope, buoyancy, sunshine, blitheness, reliance, trust, conviction, faith, sanguineness, overestimation, pipe dream *(coll.).*

OPTIMIST, *n.* One given to optimism, visionary, hoper, enthusiast, dreamer, utopian, Candide, hopeful, daydreamer, romancer, romantic, castle-builder.

OPTIMISTIC, *adj.* 1. Disposed to take a favorable view of things, hopeful, optimistical, heartened, assured, sunny, blithe, in hopes, full of hope, happily expectant, comforted, enthusiastic, sanguine, exultant, flushed, dauntless, bright, undespairing, carefree, in good heart *or* spirits, buoyant, utopian, jubilant, buoyed up, cheerful, sunny, elated, confident.

2. Of *or* pertaining to optimism, hopeful, promising, lifting, palmy, favorable, auspicious, propitious, cheering, heartening, inspiriting, encouraging, bright, rosy, roseate, sunny, of good omen, full of promise, prosperous, flourishing, utopian, assuring, comforting, looking up.

OPTIMUM, *adj.* Best, most favorable, prime, choice, select, elect, first-rate, first-class, superlative, extremely good, A-one *(also* A-1; *coll.),* picked, unexcelled, preferable, ideal, quintessential, paramount, supreme, unsurpassed, with a minimum of imperfections, capital, most nearly perfect.

OPTIMUM, *n.* The best *or* most favorable point (degree, amount, etc.) for the purpose, height, acme, perfection, cream, pink, preference, prize, pick, prime, flower, choice, standard, ideal, pattern, faultlessness, perfectness, quintessence.

OPTION, *n.* 1. Power *or* liberty of choosing, right *or* freedom of choice, will, election, volition, voice, license, decision, vote, leave, sanction, range, scope, free rein, latitude, permission, discretion, selection, franchise, privilege, grant, warranty, authorization, prerogation, interest, title, claim, eclecticism, coöption, suffrage, free will, self-determination, vouchsafement.

2. Something which may be *or* is chosen, choice, preference, partiality, predilection, selection, liking, preoption, alternative, mind, will, desire, will and pleasure.

OPTIONAL, *adj.* Left to one's choice, elective, non obligatory, free, volitional, volitionary, conative, permissive, volitive, unrestricted, unqualified, facultative, unforced, arbitrary, voluntary, discretional, unlimited, unconditioned, independent, coöptive, not required.

OPULENCE, *n.* Wealth, riches, abundance, affluence, plenty, sufficiency, opulency, easy circumstances, fortune, prosperity, comfort, enough and to spare, luxury, complacency, bed of roses, copiousness, plenteousness, plenitude, full measure, satiety, repletion, lucre, money, mammon, long purse, fat of the land, fleshpots of Egypt, prodigality, profusion, exuberance, horn of plenty, creature comforts, ample means, financial independence, richness, well-being, overflow, fullness, cornucopia, lavishment, amplitude, elegance, clover, excessiveness.

OPULENT, *adj.* 1. Wealthy, rich, pecunious, well provided for, prosperous, comfortable, flourishing, well-to-do, in clover, on a bed of roses, well-off, affluent, rich as Croesus, moneyed, set up *(coll.),* on velvet *(sl.),* rolling *or* wallowing in wealth *or* riches.

2. Richly supplied, profuse, rife, brimming, flush, plentiful, abundant, bounteous, affluent, lavish, copious, generous, superabundant, in large measure, exuberant, plenteous, abounding, excessive, inordinate, luxuriant, rich, elegant.

OPUS, *n.* Composition, work, writing, creation, brain child, draft, script, invention, offspring, handiwork, piece, production, magnum opus, effort, attempt.

OR, *conj.* Otherwise, else, or else, contrarily, in other words, in paraphrase, elsewise, alternatively, conversely, on the other hand.

ORACLE, *n.* 1. Utterance, divine communication, revelation, wise saying, foretelling, decree, law, dictate, dictum, answer, truth, scripture, maxim, precept, judgment, injunction, divine sanction, commandment, prescript, adjudication *(Law).*

2. Agency of divine communication, medium, sage, prophet, wise man, interpreter, adviser, luminary, authority, sapient, prophet, predictor, magian, forecaster, augur, seer, soothsayer, diviner, divinator, sibyl.

ORACULAR, *adj.* 1. Resembling *or* suggesting an oracle, prophetic, foretelling, Delphian, Delphic, foreknowing, fatidic, prognostic, sibylline, Pythonic, Dodonaean, vatic, predictive, indicative, precursory, precursive, presaging, significant, predictory, presentient, sibylic, augural, divinatory, fatiloquent, haruspical, boding, suggestive, vaticinal.

2. Giving forth utterances *or* decisions as if by special inspiration *or* authority, sage, wise, vaticinal, sapient, knowing, dogmatic, opinionated, self-assured, imperious, grave, magisterial, pragmatic, arbitrary, absolute, positive, wise in one's own conceits, dictatorial, infallible.

3. Uttered *or* delivered as if divinely inspired *or* infallible, significant, presageful, sage, wise, judicious, judicial, authentic, sound, philosophical, profound, dogmatic, magisterial, authoritative, discreet, cathedral, official, imperative, prescriptive, irrevocable, commanding, *ex cathedra (Lat.),* mandatory, sapient, positive.

4. Obscure, enigmatic, ambiguous, dark, hidden, arcane, mystic, clouded, Orphic, Delphic, Delphian, mysterious, indefinite, questionable, equivocal, blind, not easily understood, vague, unclear, nebulous, impenetrable, abstruse, confusing, recondite, cryptic, unfathomable, perplexing, puzzling, imperspicuous, difficult.

5. Portentous, ominous, foreboding, inauspicious, unpropitious, menacing, minatory, direful, premonitory, unpromising, sinister, threatening, alarming, fateful, ill-boding, lowering, frightening, fear-inspiring, disquieting, disturbing.

ORAL, *adj.* Uttered by the mouth, employing speech, vocal, verbal, spoken, nuncupative, acroamatic, viva-voce, expressed in words, unwritten, parol *(Law).*

ORATION, *n.* Formal speech *(as for a special oc-*

casion), discourse, declamation, address, lecture, panegyric, disquisition, prelection, peroration, monologue, valedictory, tirade, rhetoric, bombast, sermon, harangue, allocution, recital, spiel, preachment, homily.

ORATOR, *n.* One who delivers an oration, eloquent speaker, talker, rhetorician, demagogue, speechmaker, rhetor, preacher, lecturer, prelecter, reciter, elocutionist, stump orator, soapbox orator, declaimer, spellbinder *(coll.).*

ORATORICAL, *adj.* 1. Of, pertaining to, *or* characteristic of an orator *or* oratory, rhetorical, eloquent, studied, heightened, elocutionary, Ciceronian, Demosthenean, Tullian, declamatory, verbal, classical.

2. Given to oratory, fluent, diffuse, digressive, roving, altiloquent, magniloquent, bombastic, grandiloquent, long-winded, wordy, verbose, exuberant, lengthy, rambling, loquacious, Johnsonian, pedantic, maundering, discursive, effusive, tumid, inflated, declamatory, pedantic, garrulous, pretentiously rhetorical, gassy *(coll.),* windy *(coll.),* voluble.

ORATORY, *n.* 1. Exercise of eloquence, art of public speaking, rhetoric, art of delivery, declamation, pleading, loftiness (elevation, sublimity, grandeur) of style, wordcraft, speechcraft, elocution.

2. Place of prayer, small room for private devotions, chapel, cubicle, proseuche.

ORB, *n.* Round object, ball, sphere, orbit, spherule, globule.

ORBICULAR, *adj.* Like an orb, spherical, ringlike, rounded, round, orbic, globular, spheroid, spheriform, spherular, spherelike, orblike, orbiculate, cycloidal, annular, discoid, globose, globous, globated, circular, rotund, orbed.

ORBIT, *n.* 1. Elliptical *or* curved path of a celestial body, elliptic, path, course, track, trajectory.

2. Course regularly pursued *(as in life),* round, walk, ambit, sphere, circle, circuit, beat, way, routine, traversal, road, compass, bounds, tour, lap, area, track, circumference, route, course, itinerary, travel, peregrination.

3. Orb, sphere, ball, round object, spherule, globule.

ORCHARD, *n.* Collection of fruit trees *or* the area in which they are cultivated, grove, orangery, peachery.

ORCHESTRA, *n.* 1. Company of musical performers *(who play symphonies, operas, etc.),* symphony orchestra, chamber group, string orchestra, ensemble.

2. *(Theater)* Space reserved for musicians, orchestra pit, pit, parquet, main floor *(for spectators).*

ORCHESTRAL, *adj.* Pertaining to, composed for, *or* performed by an orchestra, symphonic, accompaniment, concert, philharmonic, operatic, scored for orchestra.

ORCHESTRATE, *v.* Compose *or* arrange *(music)* for performance by an orchestra, instrumentate, harmonize, set, adapt for orchestra, instrument, score *(Mus.).*

ORDAIN, *v.* 1. Appoint authoritatively, call, elect, destine, devote, name, nominate, deputize, depute, consign, frock, confer holy orders upon *(Eccles.),* install, set apart, consecrate, command, direct, assign, commission, preordain, foreordain, delegate, invest, instate.

2. Give orders for, decree, pass judgment, prescribe, will, adjudge, rule, charge, instruct, bid.

call on *or* upon, judge, pronounce, dictate, pass sentence, award, enjoin, legislate, warrant, order, enact, determine.

ORDEAL, *n.* 1. Severe experience, harrowing experience, trial, trouble, desolation, mental suffering, mental torment, sorrow, misery, grief, anguish, pangs, tragedy, affliction, infliction, tribulation, oppression, vexation, calamity, distress, wrack, throes, agony, adversity, scourge, pressure, purgatory.

2. Severe trial, trial by fire, trial by water, trial by combat.

ORDER, *n.* 1. Society, organization, brotherhood, fraternity, lodge, team, sisterhood, sorority, confederacy, guild, house, junto, sodality, body, group, alliance, club, coterie, cabal, combine, federation, trust, affiliation, company.

2. Religious order, denomination, church, schism, cult, communion, brotherhood, fellowship.

3. Rank of society, family, influence, prestige, title, hierarchy, caste, station, breed, sphere, circle, coterie, condition, position, status, degree, connection, precedence, company, stirps, class, derivation, descent, extraction, estate, ancestry, stock, lineage, connection.

4. Kind, category, species, group, nature, distinction, denomination, kidney, sort, type, stamp, designation, breed, stripe, the like *(coll.)*, selection, sphere, range, grade, brood, genus, genre, constitution, brand, aspect, temper, disposition, spirit, school, form, set, kind, classification, class, head, order, province, character, origin, variety, feather, grain, make, cast, mold, suit, sect.

5. Method, organization, system, arrangement, disposal, classification, codification, grouping, allocation, disposition, graduation, categorization, designation, form, structure, tabulation.

6. Customary mode of procedure, regularity, normal procedure, uniformity, rules and regulations.

7. Peace and quiet, quiet, calm, equanimity, silence, law and order, peacefulness, control, discipline, tranquillity, harmony, good behavior, concord, placidity, serenity.

8. Demand, direction, command, charge, injunction, bidding, dictation, ordinance, precept, dictum, decree, imperative, notification, citation, summons, dictate, fiat, caveat, beck, nod, ultimatum, prescript, dispensation, word of command, hest, requirement, edict, writ, rule, regulation, warrant, mittimus *(Law)*, mandamus *(Law)*, proclamation, mandate, request, bull, will, say-so *(coll.)*, call, act, imposition, claim, commandment.

9. Request for supplies, merchandise, *etc.*, requisition, purchase of merchandise, authority to purchase merchandise.

ORDER, *v.* 1. Put in order, regulate, arrange, organize, tabulate, dispose, coördinate, classify, marshal, systemize, methodize, codify, digest, ticket, label, assort, docket, rate, arrange, catalogue, size, number, segregate, range, grade, rank, class, categorize.

2. Bid, direct, dictate, compel, appoint, adjure, task, call for, enjoin, instruct, decree, inflict, cite, charge, call upon, prescribe, require, ordain, enact, authorize, summon.

3. Put in an order for merchandise, supplies, *etc.*, contract for, purchase merchandise, indicate a desire to buy, authorize purchase of, call for, require, ask for.

ORDERLY, *adj.* 1. Arranged *or* disposed in order *or* regular sequence, regular, systematic, tidy, trim, disposed, classified, filed, even, spruce, uniform,

formal, harmonious, neat, shipshape, in place, consistent, proportioned, balanced, coördinate, in meaningful order, patterned, following a pattern, homogeneous, classified, methodic, methodical, unconfused, symmetrical, cosmic, planned, designed, businesslike, tabular, arranged, constant.

2. Observant of system *or* method *(as persons, the mind, etc.)*, adjusted, regulated, well-regulated, well-conducted, efficient, methodical, systematic, working smoothly, thorough, businesslike, tidy, clear, unhampered, unobstructed, unencumbered, meticulous, fastidious, straightforward, wide-awake, discriminating, perceptive, level-headed, clear-witted, clear-headed, rational, perspicacious, judicious, steady, tranquil, serene, self-possessed, self-controlled, poised, collected, free from confusion.

3. Characterized by *or* observant of order, rule, *or* discipline, peaceable, well-behaved, settled, normal, prudent, well-mannered, quiet, polite, civil, mannerly, neighborly, honest, law-abiding, dutiful, gentle, decorous, civilized, well-bred, well-brought-up, moral, restrained, reputable, self-controlled, compliant, ethical, careful, honorable, obedient, upright, harmonious, conscientious, acquiescent, obliging, tractable, mild.

ORDERLY, *n.* Soldier appointed to carry orders, *etc. (Mil.)*, hospital attendant who maintains order, cleanliness, *etc.*, servant, menial, man, dispatch bearer, runner, errand boy, chore boy, assistant, adjutant, attendant, courier, messenger, batman, steward, medic *(coll.)*.

ORDINANCE, *n.* 1. Authoritative rule *or* law, decree, command, statute, regulation, order, prescript, edict, enactment, proclamation, precept, maxim, law, act, constitution, declaration, fiat, injunction, demand, direction, charge, bidding, dictum, imperative, caveat, ultimatum, dispensation, requirement, writ, mandate, bull, commandment, mandamus *(Law)*, mittimus *(Law)*.

2. *(Eccles.)* Established rite, ceremony, sacrament, the communion, ritual, ceremonial, formulary, formality, institution, service, function, form, observance, solemnity, Eucharist, Lord's Supper, Holy Communion.

ORDINARILY, *adv.* Commonly, usually, customarily, habitually, for the most part, as a rule, generally, in the usual course of things, in the ordinary way, familiarly, by and large, normally, as a matter of course, on an average, in most instances, day by day, from habit, regularly, daily, constantly, conventionally.

ORDINARY, *adj.* 1. Such as is commonly met with, of the usual kind, prevalent, everyday, usual, common, commonplace, conventional, household, universal, popular, prevalent, general, rife, prevailing, predictable, familiar, habitual, plentiful, current, customary, daily, average, wonted, normal, accustomed, domestic, native, natural, unexceptional, homespun, middle-class, pat *(coll.)*, known, expected, garden-variety, stock, vernacular, set, indiscriminate, well-trodden, regular, routine, repeated, established, consuetudinary, standard, recurrent, cut and dried, received, acknowledged, dime-a-dozen, workday, unassuming, Philistine, traditional, understood, approved, anticipated, fixed, predetermined, recognized, stereotyped, generally practiced, typical.

2. Not above but rather below the average level of quality, somewhat inferior, mean, commonplace, undistinguished, medium, mediocre, run-of-the-mill, humdrum, middling, so-so, passable, giftless, tolerable, fair, second-rate, indiffer-

ent, colloquial, trivial, insignificant, unrefined, cheap, deficient, insipid, wishy-washy, ignoble, inadequate, pedestrian, discreditable, stale, trite, hackneyed, unimpressive, prosaic, tame, dry, dull, banal, tedious, homely, stereotyped, unimaginative, uninspiring, uninspired.

ORDINARY, *n.* Ordinary condition, degree, run, *or* the like, something regular, customary *or* usual rule, convention, usual rut, groove, expected routine, beaten track *or* path, wont, round, fixed practice, habit, settled way, conventional usage, fashion, usual run.

ORDINATION, *n.* 1. Act *or* ceremony of ordaining *(Eccles.)*, fact of being ordained, consecration, investiture, installation, empowering, orders, ecclesiastical office, induction, charging *(with duties, responsibilities, etc.)*, qualification, accrediting, election, calling, institution, presentation, conferment, instatement.

2. Decreeing, ordaining, commandment, exaction, requirement, bidding, behest, decreement, dictation, instruction, judgment, enjoinment, prescription, notification, declaration, ruling.

3. Act of arranging, result of arranging, settlement, disposition, arrangement, distribution, organization, order, system, grouping, classification, collocation, allocation, method, disposal, codification, graduation, categorization, designation, structure, form, tabulation, scheme, construction, organism, coördination, composition.

ORDNANCE, *n.* 1. Military supplies, quartermaster's stores, provisions, materials of war, army supplies.

2. Arms, guns, artillery, cannon, firearms, battery, mortars, machine-guns, howitzers, culverins *(chiefly Hist.)*, carronade *(Hist.)*.

3. Ammunition, explosives, high explosives, missiles, shells, bullets, munitions, shot, powder, cartridges, rockets, torpedoes, shrapnel, grenades, bombs.

ORDURE, *n.* Dung, filth, excrement, sewage, droppings, feculence, stercoration, soil, compost, manure, muck, refuse, offal, guano, coprolite, excreta, slime, stool, faeces, lientery *(Pathol.)*.

ORE, *n.* Metal-bearing mineral *or* rock, non-metallic natural product, lodge, metallic vein, prill, float, slimes, chats.

ORGAN, *n.* 1. Musical instrument, pipe organ, barrel organ, hand organ, reed organ, harmonium, melodion, seraphine, hurdy-gurdy.

2. *(In plant or animal)* Vital part essential to life, part having some specific function, member, vital component, integrant, integral part, constituent.

3. Means *(as of performance)*, instrument, medium, implement, tool, agent, resource, vehicle, apparatus, appliance, step, measure, shift, provision, contrivance, utensil, servant, subterfuge, aid, device, expedient, ways and means, way.

4. Means *or* medium of communicating thoughts, opinions, *etc.*, mouthpiece, vehicle, periodical, newspaper, sheet, circular, daily, weekly, monthly, quarterly, paper.

ORGANIC, *adj.* 1. Characteristic of, pertaining to, *or* derived from living organisms, living, animate, vital, alive, quick, zoöidal, biotic, biothical, breathing, responding, visceral, splanchnic, of *or* pertaining to the organs of an animal *or* plant.

2. Characterized by the systematic arrangement of parts, formal, organized, systematized, systematic, regular, arranged, in sequence, disposed, classified, neat, shipshape, consistent, tabular, de-

signed, planned, cosmic, unconfused, symmetrical, methodical, methodic, patterned, ordered, meaningfully laid out, balanced, filed, tidy, spruce, trim, smooth, working, harmonious, efficient.

3. Of *or* pertaining to the constitution *or* structure of a thing, constitutional, structural, essential, innate, textural, inherent, intrinsic, ingrained, architectural, original, skeletal, elementary, fundamental, radical, vital, primary, elemental, rudimentary, morphological, anatomical, basic, basal, indigenous, rooted.

ORGANISM, *n.* 1. Any form of animal *or* plant life, individual composed of mutually dependent parts, organized being *or* existence, individual, animal, plant, body, cell, physiological unit, organic structure, living being, metabolic being, morphon *(Biol.)*, bion *(Biol.)*, bacterium, germ.

2. Any organized body *or* system analogous to a living being, organization, institution, cosmos, group, union, corps, machinery, federation, confederation, corporation, order, society, association, community, fraternity, league, functioning whole, macrocosm, microcosm.

ORGANIZATION, *n.* 1. Act *or* process of organizing, state *or* manner of being organized, arrangement, association, formation, making, ordering, construction, institution, systematization, constitution, disposal, disposition, composition, adjustment, formulation, distribution, preparation, categorization, combination, division, separation, unionization, establishment, regimentation, analysis, discipline, incorporation, coördination, classification.

2. That which is organized, organized being *or* existence, organism, organized whole *or* structure, order, scheme, file, collection, table, being, machine, machinery, union, society, system, economy, framework, setup, arrangement, structure, settlement, array, physique, body, force, outline, plan, compact, construction, bond, contract, method, adjustment, agreement, covenant, government, constitution, association, polity.

3. Body of persons organized for some end *or* work, administrative apparatus *or* personnel of a business, functionaries of a political party *(with the offices, committess, etc., which they fill)*, association, machinery, force, band, party, gang, club, corps, army, group, union, kingdom, sect, society, order, school, fellowship, incorporation, alliance, collusion, league, fraternity, coalition, combination, federation, affiliation, communion, outfit, faction, interest, company, confederation.

ORGANIZE, *v.* 1. Form as *or* into a whole *(esp. for harmonious or united action)*, constitute *(by assignment of parts)*, compose, initiate, set afoot, formulate, form into a body, make, shape, construct, put into systematic form, institute, set up, fix, found, put in action, develop, originate, establish, frame, form, bring into being, brigade, regiment, plot, promote, produce, regulate, settle, incorporate, embody, order, create, erect, adjust, set on foot, lay the foundation of, put together.

2. Arrange, coördinate, methodize, put into systematic form, separate into categories, classify, marshal, systematize, establish, order, adjust, regulate, harmonize, index, codify, file, alphabetize, group, grade, standardize, tabulate, catalogue, class, form into classes, district, correlate, align, divide, graduate, categorize, place.

3. Combine in an organized company *or* party, *etc.*, assume organic structure, take shape, regiment, brigade, unite, join, league, associate, federate, incorporate, merge, club together, ally, co-

öperate, pool effort, unify, meet, amalgamate, consolidate, confederate, coördinate, synergize, hold together, band together.

ORGY, *n.* Wild, drunken, *or* licentious festivities *or* revelries; bacchanalia, drinking bout, spree, proceedings marked by unbridled indulgence of passions, saturnalia, dissipation, carousal, carouse, debauch, bestial indulgence, bacchanal, fling, bust, tear, revelry, drunken frolic, jag *(sl.),* binge *(sl.),* bender *(sl.),* bat *(sl.),* toot *(sl.),* hellbender *(sl.),* riot.

ORIENT, *n.* 1. *(Cap.)* The East, eastern regions, sunrise, Levant, Asia.

2. Luster peculiar to the pearl, luminosity, luminousness, luster, sheen, gloss, opalescence, iridescence, nacrine, *essence d'orient,* nacre, pearliness.

ORIENT, ORIENTATE, *v.* 1. Place so as to face the east, place *(in any definite position)* with reference to the points of the compass *(or other points),* turn, face, front, relate, render true, square, situate, set, collimate, collineate, fix, ascertain *or* get the bearings, locate, direct.

2. Adjust with relation to surroundings *(circumstances, facts, etc.),* make to feel at home *or* at ease, familiarize, reconcile, settle, accommodate, straighten out, habituate, adapt, conform, compromise, get one's bearings, relearn, make used to, acclimate, acclimatize, domesticate, reëvaluate, naturalize, reassess.

ORIENTAL, *adj. (Usually cap.)* Eastern, orient, auroral, Asian, Levantine.

ORIENTATION, *n.* 1. Act *or* process of orienting, state of being oriented, placing, placement, straightening out, course, habituation, domestication, bearings, familiarization, collineation, collimation, acclimatization, acclimation, naturalization.

2. Ascertainment of one's true position with reference to new ideas, *etc.,* adjustment, adaptation, reconcilement, conformity, compromise, assimilation, accommodation, bending, yielding, understanding, open-mindedness, reassessment, relearning, reëvaluation, settlement, accustoming.

ORIFICE, *n.* Hole, aperture, mouth, vent, opening, perforation, cavity, jaws, cleft, gap, crack, cranny, pore, fissure, chasm, gulf, breach, bore, caliber, eye, break, eyelet, pinhole, outlet, entrance, inlet, embouchure, window, door, portal, passage, hiation, puncture, foramen *(Anat.),* fenestra *(Zool.),* scupper *(Naut.),* interstice, gash, rift, rime, crevice, slot, slit, scissure.

ORIGIN, *n.* 1. That from which anything arises *or* is derived, source, spring, rise, tap, taproot, head, cause, alpha, first occasion. base, basis, first cause, prime mover, father, mother, matrix, element, creator, rudiment. womb, nucleus, reason, bud, well, root, foundation, derivation, beginning, fountain, fountainhead, starting point, cradle, dawn, germ, prime, ultimate cause, impulse, author, agent, leaven, stem, stock, fetus *(Embryol.),* provocation, motivation, primogenitor, producer, generator, fount, ground, principle, seed.

2. Rise *or* derivation from a particular source. origination, springing, evolution, evolving, inception, incipience, birth, growth, unfolding, development, incubation, genesis, etymology. commencement, emergence, descent.

3. First stage of existence, beginning, original embryo, embryonic stage, egg, germ, shoot, ovum, sprout, bud, fetus, commencement, rudiment. first

flowering, Anlage *(Embryol.),* primordium *(Embryol.).*

4. Parentage, birth, extraction, native land, nativity, descent, stock, sept, stirps, breed, stem, trunk, race, strain, line, lineage, family, house.

ORIGINAL, *adj.* 1. Belonging *or* pertaining to the origin *or* beginning of something, primitive, first, pristine, primary, earliest, elementary, native, root, prime, incipient, prefatory, radical, basic, initiative, prior, fundamental, initial, causal, causative, initiatory, introductory, inaugural, inchoate, rudimentary, head, front, foremost, creative, maiden, nascent, natal, embryonic, germinal, seminal, formative, primal, precedent, formational, productive, underlying, aboriginal, primeval, primordial, antecedent, essential, generative.

2. Novel, new, fresh, untried, underived, uncommon, unconventional, unexampled, imaginative, unimitated, unusual, unique, different, odd, unborrowed, rare, unknown, unthought-of, whimsical, fanciful, daring, unorthodox, out of the ordinary, unexpected, unheard-of, extraordinary, curious, singular, ingenious.

3. Arising *or* proceeding from a thing itself, independent of anything else, basic, underived, unborrowed, endemic, intrinsic, peculiar, unique, characteristic, *sui generis (Lat.),* indigenal, indigenous, aboriginal, vernacular, indwelling, infixed, inborn, innate, inward, native, natural, root, inherent, inbred, autochthonous, congenital, subjective, instinctive, inherited, ingenerate, connate, ingrained, idiosyncratic, documentary, documental, inwrought, primary, radical, basic, first-hand, proceeding from a person as the inventor (composer, author, *etc.).*

4. Capable of *or* given to thinking *or* acting independently in self-suggested and individual ways, inventive, imaginative, creative, unorthodox, unconformable, self-contained, fertile, freethinking, self-determining, bohemian, originative, informal, self-reliant, constructive, self-sufficient, daring, having the courage of one's convictions, fruitful, strong-minded, unique, unconventional, ingenious.

5. Being that from which a copy *or* translation, *etc.,* is made, manuscript, first, genuine, author's authentic, written, true, textual, holographic.

ORIGINAL, *n.* 1. Primary form *or* type from which varieties are derived, archetype, precedent, pattern, type, model, first copy, example, standard, rule, criterion, source, beau idéal, ancestor, module, measure, exemplar, protoplast, prototype, first, paragon, mirror, foreshadowing, paradigm.

2. Original work *or* writing, *etc. (as opposed to a copy or imitation),* person *or* thing represented by a picture *or* description, *etc.,* subject, composition, manuscript, document, canvas, draft, author's copy, first copy, true copy, text.

3. One who is original in his ways of thinking *or* acting, oddity, eccentric person, bohemian, nonconformist, dissenter, heretic, freethinker, isolationist. nonpartisan, free lance, radical, independent, one in a thousand, sectarian, sulphite *(sl.),* eccentric, character *(coll.).*

ORIGINALITY, *n.* 1. State *or* quality of being original, newness, invention, dissimilarity, variation, variance, unlikeness, uniqueness, authenticity, bohemianism, unorthodoxy, individuality, unusualness, unconventionality, nonimitation, novelty, nonconformity, difference, divergence, disparity, diversity.

2. Ability to think *or* act in an independent *or* individual way, inventiveness, individuality, self-

reliance, independence, fertile *or* pregnant imagination, self-determination, strength of mind, imaginative power, constructiveness, productiveness, imaginativeness, creativeness.

3. Freshness *or* novelty *(as of an idea, method, or performance)*, newness, innovation, change, dissimilarity, nonimitation, freedom, newfanglement, introduction, break with tradition, imaginativeness, unexpectedness, surprise.

ORIGINATE, *v.* 1. Take its origin *or* rise, arise, spring, come into existence, come into the world, become, emanate, flow, rise, begin, proceed, start, commence, stem, derive, break out, burst forth, see the light, sprout, germinate, ensue, spring *or* crop up, issue, descend, come, bud, grow, accrue, result, follow, take birth.

2. Give origin *or* rise to, bring into existence, create, initiate, invent, devise, improvise, author, write, hatch, compose, undertake, formulate, lay the foundation of, start, conceive, draw up, give birth to, launch, breed, institute, occasion, form, be the cause of, cause to be, produce, construct, inaugurate, found, establish, set on foot, beget, fashion, usher in, introduce, inchoate, coin, raise, begin, broach, fabricate, design, dream up, contrive, concoct, evolve, bring about, sow the seeds of, lie at the root of, develop, generate, get up, rear, engender, envision, draft, chisel, hew, carve, think out, organize, forge, block out, open, make, propagate.

ORIGINATIVE, *adj.* Having *or* characterized by the power of originating, creative, productive, inventive, imaginative, fertile, constructive, fruitful, ingenious, fabricative, demiurgic, generant, generative, genetic, formational, visionary.

ORNAMENT, *n.* 1. Accessory, article used to beautify the appearance *or* general effect, detail, adornment, trim, trimming, gloss, enrichment, finery, embossing, drapery, knickknack, jewel, flounce, fancy work, beautification, design, embroidery, elaboration, furbelow, trappings, flowers *(of speech or rhetoric)*, motif, border, plume, bric-a-brac, embellishment, bedizenment, garnish, ornamentation, decoration.

2. Person who adds luster *(as to surroundings, society, etc.)*, idol, favorite, worthy, notable, colorful figure, star, celebrity, lion, bright addition, luminary.

3. Mere outward display, ostentation, show, gilding, glitter, tinsel, spangle, frill, pinchbeck, sham, gaudiness, parade, gloss, veneer, pretense, showiness, frippery, superfluity, gilt, gingerbread, floridity.

ORNAMENT, *v.* Furnish with ornaments, be an ornament to, decorate, adorn, brighten, dress, titivate, bedeck, bedizen, grace, emboss, festoon, bejewel, trim, elaborate, illumine, glorify, furbish, chase, tool, carve, engrave, embroider, figure, drape, gild, befeather, bespangle, set off, illustrate, enrich, trick out, deck, illuminate, embellish, beautify, emblazon.

ORNAMENTAL, *adj.* Used *or* serving for ornament, embellishing, decorative, adorning, becoming, agreeable, pleasing, sightly, colorful, enhancing, adding interest, fair, attractive, curious, picturesque, rich, ravishing, graceful, artistic, beautifying, garnishing.

ORNAMENTATION, *n.* That with which a thing is ornamented, decoration, adornment, trim, embellishment, embroidery, garnishment, frills, design, fancy work, fretwork, border, fringe, illus-

tration, garnish, ornament, elaboration, rhetoric, flourish, trappings, figure *(of speech)*.

ORNATE, *adj.* Elaborate, sumptuously *or* showily splendid *or* fine, flashy, richly wrought, decorated, adorned, bedecked, rich, fancy, flamboyant, overwrought, overdone, peacockish, glittering, elegant, gorgeous, festooned, begilt, gilt, tawdry, affected, garish, conspicuous, meretricious, gaudy, bespangled, bejewelled, ostentatious, orotund *(of style)*, figurative *(of speech, writing, etc.)*, flowery, florid, figured, highly wrought, beautified, rhetorical, frilly, ornamented, embellished, showy, baroque, rococo.

ORNITHIC, *adj.* Of *or* pertaining to birds, ornithological, ornithoid, bird-like, avicular, avian *(Zool.)*.

OROTUND, *adj.* 1. *(Of the voice or utterance)* Characterized by strength, fullness, richness, and clearness, resonant, resounding, deep, rolling, full, round, rich, booming, big, ringing, vibrant, vibrating, mellifluous, reverberating, reverberant, soul-stirring, clear, mellow, musical, sonorous, strong, powerful, loud, heavy.

2. *(Of style of utterance)* Pompous, bombastic, high-flown, overdrawn, extravagant, strained, pretentious, high-colored, inflated, hyperbolic, extreme, rhapsodical, magniloquent, fustian, showy, tumid, altisonant, ornate, mouthy, flatulent, florid, affected, sesquipedalian *(hum.)*, high-sounding, lexiphanic, flamboyant, Johnsonian, grandisonant, rhetorical, grandiose, declamatory, sententious, grandiloquent, turgid, lofty, glittering, highfalutin *(coll.)*.

ORPHAN, *n.* Child bereaved of parents *(or of one parent)*, twice-bereaved child, parentless *(motherless, fatherless)* child, foundling, waif.

ORPHREY, *n.* Ornamental band *or* border *(esp. on ecclesiastical vestment)*, embroidery, piece of richly embroidered stuff, medallion, tapestry, galloon, fringe, edging, trimming.

ORRERY, *n.* Apparatus for representing the motions and phases of the planets, *etc.,* planetarium, eidouranion.

ORTHODOX, *adj.* 1. Sound *or* correct *(in religious or theological opinions or doctrines)*, of the true faith, faithful, catholic, rigid, strict, conventional, standard, traditional, doctrinal, cathedral, *ex cathedra (Lat.)*, authoritative, official, firm, true, dogmatic, textual, scriptural, hyperorthodox, Christian, authentic, canonical, accurate, puritanic, uncompromising, creedal, established, unschismatic, hard-shell *(coll.)*, received, accepted.

2. Approved, conventional, according to use *or* custom, fixed, established, prescriptive, standard, accurate, wonted, received, accustomed, recognized, admitted, customary, prevailing, right, correct, proper, acknowledged, understood, conformable to rule, in line, usual, regular, according to Hoyle, traditional, cut and dried.

ORTHODOXY, *n.* 1. Orthodox belief *or* practice, true faith, principle *or* article of faith, doctrine, gospel, teaching, creed, canon, dogma, tenet, form, truth, authority, credo, tradition, church, custom, observance, formality, etiquette.

2. Orthodox character, soundness of doctrine, authenticity, validity, conformity, conformance, canonicity, decorum, strictness, etiquette, formality, observance, conventionality, tradition, faithfulness, adherence.

ORTS, *n.* *(Usually pl.)* Fragments of food left at a meal, scraps, bits, leftovers, waste, garbage, crumbs, morsels, leavings, remnants, refuse, relics, odds and ends, remains.

OSCILLATE, *v.* 1. Swing *(as a pendulum does)*, move to and fro, vibrate, sway, come and go, pendulate, nutate, librate, nod, alternate, fluctuate, pulsate, beat, come *or* occur in turn, return, rock, roll, pitch, lurch, ebb and flow, undulate, agitate, wave, move backward and forward, seesaw, wigwag.

2. Fluctuate between states (opinions, purposes, *etc.*), waver, be in suspense, vary, vacillate, scruple, alter, dodge, shift, reel, veer, shuffle, be doubtful, hang, hesitate, be uncertain, be undecided *or* undetermined, change, debate, falter, be on the fence, hang in the balance, back and fill, be irresolute, not know one's own mind *or* where one stands, have *or* be of two minds, swerve, chop and change, blow hot and cold, deviate, about-face, tergiversate, hum *or* hem and haw, straddle *or* be on the fence.

OSCILLATION, *n.* 1. Act *or* fact of oscillating, swinging, pendulation, change, vibration, fluctuation, undulation, pulse, vacillation, alternation, rhythm, coming and going, flux, nutation, libration, waving, ebb and flow, swing and return.

2. Single swing *or* movement in one direction of an oscillating body, *etc.*, stroke, beat, sway, wave, measure.

OSCITANT, *adj.* Gaping, yawning, agape, sleep-filled, heavy with sleep, sleep-drunk, half asleep, somniferous, drowsy, sleepy, somnific, inattentive, supine, lentitudinous, sluggish, lazy, slack, lax, dull, shiftless, lethargic, indifferent, slothful, lumpish, leaden, heavy, hebetudinous, laggard, lymphatic, phlegmatic, slow, weary, dronish, torpid, inert, exanimate, stupefied, listless, lackadaisical, dopey *(sl.)*.

OSCULATE, *v.* 1. Kiss, buss *(coll.)*, smack.

2. Come *or* bring into close contact *or* union, be contiguous, anastomose, inosculate, contact, meet, touch, conjoin, rub, graze, adhere, skim, brush, join, clasp, hug, nuzzle, blend, cohere, merge, adjoin, articulate, connect.

OSCULATION, *n.* 1. Kiss, caress with the lips, kissing, smack, buss *(coll.)*.

2. Close contact, contiguity, articulation, inosculation, anastomosis, meeting, clasp, grasp, touch, grip, graze, brush, hug, hinge, merging, intersection, lick, impact, taction, tangency, union, conjugation, lambency, bond, connection, conjunction, junction, link, glance, adhesion, cohesion.

OSIER, *n.* Willow, willow twig, wicker, withe, switch, sprig.

OSSEOUS, *adj.* Composed of, containing, *or* resembling bone, bony, hard, rigid, ossified, inflexible, skeletal, ossiferous, stiff, inextensile, inextensible, callous, supported, unyielding, impliable, unbending.

OSSIFICATION, *n.* Bone formation, hardening, fossilization, induration, ostosis *(Pathol.)*.

OSSIFY, *v.* Convert into bone, harden, stiffen, indurate, callous, fossilize, cornify, hornify.

OSTENSIBLE, *adj.* Given out *or* outwardly appearing as such, shown, avowed, declared, pretended, deceptive, offered, presented, visible, apparent, manifest, feasible, evident, likely, probable, nominal, exoteric, reasonable, perceivable, surface, alleged, pretexed, observable, seeable, excusing, feigned, fictitious, used *or* serving as a pretext, professed, plausible, specious, colorable, trumped-up, artificial, seeming, plain, assigned, outward, exhibited.

OSTENTATION, *n.* Pretentious show, display intended to impress others, parade, pretense, flourish, flaunting, pomposity, pompousness, vanity, flashiness, gaudery, gaudiness, superfluity, frills, tinsel, gilt, gilding, effect, figure, strut, glitter, peacockery, spectacle, exhibition, speciousness, veneer, splash, affectation, coxcombery, foppery, inflation, pose, swagger, orotundity, dog *(coll.)*, showiness, pageantry, vaunting, pretension, pomp, dash, front *(coll.)*, trappings, swank *(sl.)*.

OSTENTATIOUS, *adj.* Characterized by *or* given to ostentation *or* pretentious show, fond of display, boastful, pompous, vainglorious, elaborate, affected, egotistical, spectacular, orotund, raw, crude, florid, garish, grandiloquent, gaudy, loud, intended to attract notice, conspicuous, daring, overdone, dandified, theatrical, turgid, extreme, ornate, fancy, overwrought, glittering, meretricious, foppish, coxcombish, artificial, mannered, tawdry, sententious, magisterial, grandiose, high-sounding, high-flown, swelling, fustian, bombastic, showy, flashy, thrasonical, obtrusive, pretentious, dashing, flaunting, vain, lofty, specious.

OSTRACISM, *n.* Act of ostracizing, fact *or* state of being ostracized, banishment, expulsion, relegation, excommunication, expatriation, ejection, deportation, repudiation, shunning, ousting, rejection, transportation, exilement, exile, exclusion, proscription, segregation, boycott, blackball, Coventry, disfellowship, snub, cut *(coll.)*.

OSTRACIZE, *v.* Banish, exclude *(by general consent, from society, privileges, etc.)*, shut out, exile, repudiate, excommunicate, expatriate, isolate, proscribe, boycott, refuse to associate with, snub, cast aside, oust, shun, bar, eject, segregate, put under the ban, turn one's back upon, shut the door upon, blacklist, blackball, keep at arm's length, set one's face against, deport, transport, drum out, disinherit, disown, send to Coventry, disregard, maroon, debar, cold shoulder, high-hat *(sl.)*, leave out in the cold *(coll.)*, discard, expel, cut *(coll.)*, disapprove, outlaw, throw out, reject, bounce *(sl.)*, discharge, cut out.

OTHER, *adj.* 1. Further, another, additional, being the remaining one of two *or* more, alternate, remaining, last, second, spare, auxiliary, extra, surplus, added, annexed, more, supplementary.

2. Different *(in nature or kind)*, distinct *(from ones mentioned or implied)*, not the same, another, otherwise, contrary, dissimilar, contrasted, differentiated, inverse, reverse, opposite, unlike, else, converse.

3. Former, earlier, past, prior, previous, antecedent, anterior, sometime, gone, bygone, ancient, quondam, foregoing, passed away.

OTHERWISE, *adv.* 1. Under other circumstances, elsewise, if not, things being other, on the other hand.

2. In another manner, differently, contrarily, inversely, in reverse, contrariwise, conversely, nay rather, in defiance, in disagreement, in opposition, at cross-purposes, regardless, in contempt, not so.

3. In other respects, apart from this, without, besides, save, excluding, with the exception of, barring, exclusive, excepting.

OTHERWORLDLY, *adj.* Of, pertaining to, *or* devoted to another world *(as the world of imagination or the world to come)*, supernatural, immaterial, transcendental, spiritual, unworldly, unearthly, psychical, ghostly, religious, decarnate, incorporeal, incorporal, extramundane, future, unsubstantial, impalpable, dreamlike, hyperphysical, disembodied, bodiless, intangible, absent, detached, phantom, chimerical.

OTIOSE, *adj.* 1. At leisure, idle, indolent, lazy, slow, heavy, dull, sluggish, lymphatic, phlegmatic, lentitudinous, languid, unemployed, supine, inanimate, spiritless, torpid, inert, inactive, comatose, lackadaisical, stupefied, impassive, lifeless, obtuse, soporific, slumbrous, somnolent, listless, dormant, slothful, fainéant, insouciant.

2. Ineffective, unproductive, futile, barren, fruitless, unfertile, inadequate, deficient, unavailing, profitless, sterile, arid, jejune, unprolific, inefficient, powerless, fallow, impotent, null and void, forceless, incompetent, insufficient, vain, empty, inane, fatuous, effete, lame, worthless, bootless, unserviceable, unprofitable, useless, superfluous, acarpous *(Bot.)*, unfruitful, unfit, inept, weak, exhausted, inefficacious.

OTTOMAN, *n.* Divan *(with or without a back)*, sofa, footstool, low cushioned seat *(without back or arms)*, hassock, squab, taboret.

OUGHT, *v. aux.* Am (are, is, *etc.*) bound in duty *or* moral obligation, must, should, find it obligatory *or* expedient, feel it incumbent upon one, feel called upon, had best *or* better, find it fitting *or* right, find it honorable *or* ethical.

OUST, *v.* Expel *(from a place or position occupied)*, eject, evict, throw *or* drive out, cast away, put out, dispossess, turn out, dismiss, unseat, unhouse, discard, disown, chase out, give the air, send packing, kick out, reject, extrude, bar, turn adrift, displace, depose, dethrone, discharge, banish, ostracize, eliminate, remove, supersede, bounce *(sl.)*, fire *(sl.)*, dislodge.

OUT, *adj.* 1. Outside, without, beyond, outdoor.

2. Absent, away, elsewhere, abroad, gone, flown, not at home, forth, wanting, not present, missing, non-attendant.

3. Fallen into disuse, passé, antiquated, no longer· in use, out of date, disused, neglected, antique, ancient, obsolete, elapsed, lapsed, dead, hoary, gone by, retired, extinct, past, archaic, outworn, timeworn, discarded, expired, bygone, effete, forgotten, desuete, outdated, primitive, antediluvian, former, unfashionable, not in vogue, finished.

4. Brought into the open, unfolded, revealed, disclosed, apparent, evident, unhidden, in the open, brought to light, transpired, manifest, published, patent, exposed, made known, bared, overt, discovered, exhibited, obvious, broadcast, visible.

5. Erring, wide of the mark, false, erroneous, wide, stray, aberrant, at odds, off, distorted, perverted, inaccurate, faulty, off the mark, short, short of the mark, wrong, incorrect, missing the mark.

6. Out of the ordinary, unusual, singular, exceptional, strange, outré *(Fr.)*, bizarre, abnormal, peculiar, off the beaten track, quaint, grotesque, outlandish, freakish, weird, curious, extraordinary.

OUT-AND-OUT, *adj.* Complete, thoroughgoing, decided, total, full, outright, whole, entire, absolute, altogether, exhaustive, pronounced, arrant, sheer, unrestricted, unqualified, consummate, extreme, flagrant, downright, unequivocal, unmitigated, thorough.

OUTBALANCE, *v.* Have the edge on, outweigh, exceed, overbalance, preponderate, outrank, outdo, outbear, turn the tables, top, overtop, tip the scales, transcend, overmatch, eclipse, outstrip, predominate over, outpoint, gain the ascendancy.

OUTBREAK, *n.* 1. Uprising, insurrection, revolt,

riot, rebellion, *coup d'état (Fr.)*, sedition, rising, insurgence, mutiny.

2. Noisy strife, embroilment, imbroglio, scrap, struggle, jolt, fray, set-to *(colloq.)*, ruction, appulse, concussion, clash, skirmish, fracas, racket, uproar, stir, hubbub, flurry, hullabaloo, turbulence, fight, encounter, contest, concussion, brush, turmoil, tumult, disorder, upheaval, pother, ado, to-do *(colloq.)*, altercation, ruckus, violence, bustle, furor, fuss, clatter, row.

3. Eruption, blow up, outburst, burst, breaking out, explosion, volley, displosion, dissilience, temblor, cataclysm, upheaval, detonation, proruption, ebullition, discharge, outpouring.

4. Sudden appearance and spread of a disease, epidemic, plague, pandemic, contagion, infection, visitation, septicity, endemic, pestilence, murrain, pest.

OUTBUILDING, *n.* Outhouse, outside building, backhouse, stable, barn, shed, storehouse.

OUTBURST, *n.* Eruption, explosion, cataclysm, ebullition, blow up, burst, breaking out, proruption, detonation, upheaval, discharge, outpouring, dissilience, temblor, outbreak, displosion, volley.

OUTCAST, *adj.* Rejected, thrown out, expelled, thrust out, cast away, ejected, driven out, discarded, disowned, excommunicated *(Eccl.)*, ousted, ostracized, deported, expatriated, dismissed, outlawed, banished.

OUTCAST, *n.* Vagabond, hobo, destitute person, pariah, outlaw, exile, tatterdemalion, bum, wanderer, rover, human wreck, derelict, castaway, leper, waif, stray, foundling, vagrant, beggar, renegade.

OUTCLASS, *v.* Be superior to, lead, excel, surpass, outstrip, outweigh, cap, overtop, outdistance, tower above, outstep, go beyond, outrival, overbear, outrank, prevail, predominate, attain superiority, throw into the shade, beat, outplay, outdo, eclipse, outshine, exceed, outdistance.

OUTCOME, *n.* Result, end, aftereffect, issue, consequence, fruit, outgrowth, development, flower, eventuation, pay-off *(coll.)*, aftermath, effect, blossom, upshot, culmination, consummation, sequel, offshoot, yield.

OUTCROP, *n.* *(Usually Geol.)* Part of a stratum appearing on the surface, basset, outcropping, exposure, bared rock *or* soil.

OUTCRY, *n.* Cry for alarm *or* distress, hue and cry, shout, clamor, racket, hullabaloo, wild chorus, jangle, shouting, blast, loud protest, caterwauling, hissing, yelling, rumpus, catcall, fracas, brawl, pandemonium, commotion, vociferation, broil, bray, tumult, disturbance, uproar, cry, hubbub, agitation, noise, clangor.

OUTDISTANCE, *v.* Exceed, excel, outdo, throw into the shade, beat, outplay, outweigh, cap, overtop, outclass, go beyond, outstrip, prevail, outshine, eclipse, attain superiority, predominate, outrival, outstep, surpass.

OUTDOOR, *adj.* Open, open-air, exterior, outside, extramural.

OUTDOORS, *n.* The open, the open air, the wide-open spaces, the field, field and stream, the woods, the highways and byways, under the sky, hill and plain, out-of-doors.

OUTER, OUTERMOST, *adj.* External, exterior, outlying, surface, peripheral, extraneous, outward, outside, extramural, superficial.

OUTFACE, *v.* Defy, stare down, put on a bold face, stand up to, march up to the cannon's mouth, outbrazen, snap the fingers at, dare, affront, face, stare out of countenance, confront, brave, outbrave, buck *(coll.)*, outstare, meet, oppose.

OUTFIT, *n.* Assemblage or set of articles, equipment, wardrobe, dress, clothing, ensemble, fittings, livery, trousseau, caparison, accouterments, gear, rig *(coll.)*, trappings, equipage, turnout, getup, appointments, appurtenances, appliances, impedimenta, things, furnishings, furniture, tackle, paraphernalia, habit, goods, plant, provisions, supplies, fixtures.

OUTFIT, *v.* Furnish with an outfit, equip, clothe, gear, array, dress, rig up *or* out *(coll.)*, appoint, fit up *or* out, accouter, provision, munition, arm, caparison, habit, costume, turn out, supply, deck.

OUTFITTER, *n.* One who outfits, clothier, costumer, hosier, glover, couturier, dressmaker, draper, haberdasher, tailor.

OUTFLOW, *n.* Act of flowing out, outward movement, that which flows out, effusion, efflux, effluence, ebb, outgo, outflowing, outgush, outpour, outstream, outwell, flow, outpouring, escape, issue, drainage, extravasation, emanation, leakage, discharge, springing, flush, spout, spurt, gush, jet, eruption, outburst.

OUTGO, *v.* Outstrip in going, go beyond, go faster than, excel, surpass, exceed, outdo, leave behind, take the lead, outrun, outride, outrival, overleap, distance, overtake, get *or* shoot ahead of, leave in the lurch *or* rear, top, be superior to, beat, outvie, transcend, predominate, prevail, pass, cap, eclipse, be ahead of, take precedence, lead, throw into the shade, precede.

OUTGOING, *adj.* Going out, outbound, departing, leaving, outward bound, emergent, withdrawing, retiring, extending.

OUTGROW, *v.* Grow too large for, discard, grow beyond, abandon, reject as useless, leave behind *or* lose in the changes incident to development *or* the passage of time, turn one's back on, renounce disclaim, repudiate, mature beyond, lay aside, relinquish.

OUTGROWTH, *n.* 1. Natural development, offshoot, result, product, effect, outcome, aftermath, consequence, aftergrowth, upshot, issue, eventuation, sequel, offspring, fruit, development, end, consummation, derivative, conclusion, culmination, pay-off *(coll.)*, blossom, yield, flower, aftereffect.

2. Offshoot, that which grows out, excrescence, projection, protuberance, convexity, node, knob, sprout, shoot, process *(Biol.)*, caruncle *(Biol.)*, burgeon, bulge, apaphysis *(Biol.)*, enation *(Bot.)*, outcropping.

OUTHOUSE, *n.* Outbuilding, outside privy, subordinate building, latrine, backhouse, barn, stable, shed.

OUTING, *n.* Excursion, pleasure trip, picnic, junket, promenade, turn, hike, field day, regatta, ramble, tramp, spin, ride, drive, airing, tour, walk, sport, hayride, jaunt.

OUTLANDER, *n.* Foreigner, alien, stranger, visitor, newcomer, settler, intruder, barbarian, outsider, colonizer, immigrant, untramontane, tramontane.

OUTLANDISH, *adj.* 1. Barbarous, strange, bizarre, grotesque, freakish, odd, unusual, ridiculous, barbaric, eccentric, ludicrous, clownish, irregular, fantastic, incredible, inconceivable, unheard-of, unnatural, rare, fanciful, original, singular, ex-

ceptional, extraordinary, curious, peculiar, weird, baroque, rococo, comical, monstrous, nondescript, indescribable, unexampled, unimaginable, unprecedented, wild, rustic, rude, abnormal, preposterous, unconventional, bohemian, capricious, unaccepted, crotchety, maggoty, idiosyncratic, erratic, teratological *(Biol.)*, queer, uncouth, out-of-the-way, unparalleled.

2. Foreign-looking, exotic, strange, alien, unfamiliar, from abroad, oversea, different, tramontane, ultramontane.

3. Out-of-the-way, remote, distant, inaccessible, concealed, secluded, faraway, far-off, ulterior, ultramontane, tramontane, unvisited, unfrequented, lonely, solitary, hidden, deserted, forsaken, God-forsaken *(coll.)*, in a backwater, isolated.

OUTLAST, *v.* Last longer than, outlive, remain after, endure beyond, outwear, survive.

OUTLAW, *n.* One excluded from the benefits and protection of the law, proscript, miscreant, fugitive, offender against society, expellee, man without a country, Ishmael, pariah, criminal, outcast, habitual criminal, pirate, brigand, bandit, robber, marauder, highwayman, freebooter, desperado, felon, reprobate, Robin Hood.

OUTLAW, *v.* 1. Deprive of the benefits and protection of the law, ban, ostracize, proscribe, banish, isolate, seclude, exile, oust, shun, repudiate, expatriate, excommunicate, bar, deport, transport, expel, cut out, cast aside, blacklist, blackball, reject.

2. Prohibit, ban, stop, repress, suppress, smother, forbid, interdict, preclude, embargo, circumscribe, boycott, limit, shut out, exclude, bar, deny, disallow, keep under, keep within bounds, hold back, check, withhold.

OUTLAY, *n.* Amount expended, expenditure, disbursement, expense, cost, charge, outgo, payment, price, investment, spending.

OUTLET, *n.* Passage *(by which anything is let out)* exit, egress, opening, valve, gate, door, hatch, trap, floodgate, escape, spout, mouth, sluice, race, main, emunctory, gully, gorge, ravine, cut, port, penstock, loophole, vent, spigot, faucet, drain, scupper, sewer, cloaca, gutter, cock, stopcock, channel, duct, chasm, flume, blowhole, way of escape, trough, culvert, pore, postern, portal, porthole, conduit.

OUTLINE, *n.* 1. Line by which a figure *or* object is bounded *or* defined, contour, silhouette, boundary, horizon, coast, lineaments, delineation, brim, profile, periphery, configuration, conformation, circumference, perimeter, *tournure (Fr.)*, external form.

2. Outline drawing *(without shading)*, sketch, draft, plan, lines, skeleton, diagram, graph, framework, map, study, layout, features, design, tracing, suggestion, cast, rough draft, blocking in, delineation, penciling.

3. General sketch indicating only the main features *(as of a book, subject, project, facts, events, etc.)*, rough account, sketchy report, synopsis, syllabus, argument, prospectus, program, compendium, summary, plot, basis, abridgment, review, recapitulation, condensation, abstract, protocol, pattern, schedule, roster, agenda, slate, pandect, skeleton, analysis, résumé, conspetcus, principles, epitome, brief, scheme, thumbnail sketch, digest, plan, idea.

OUTLINE, *v.* 1. Draw the outline of, contour, silhouette, profile, determine, demarcate, circumscribe, define, block, pencil, trace, sketch, indicate, delineate, fashion, skeletonize, draft, bound, diagram, shape.

2. Give an outline of *(a subject, etc.)*, sketch the main features of, indicate, plan, draft, describe, delineate, shape, define, block out, draw up, design, devise, frame, summarize, project, digest, lay out, abridge, cast, chart, mark out, lay down a plan, review, map, give an idea of, epitomize, analyze, reconstruct, recapitulate, prepare, predetermine, trace.

OUTLIVE, *v.* 1. Survive, live longer than, outlast, endure beyond, remain after.

2. Outlast, survive, come through, rally, live *or* last through, weather, pull through, recuperate, get over, rise from, recover from, resurge, resume, endure.

OUTLOOK, *n.* 1. View from a place, prospect, sight, perspective, vista, exposure, aspect, scene, picture, panorama, spectacle.

2. Mental view, perspective, attitude, point of view, frame of mind, position *(from which one regards or judges),* standpoint, spirit, mettle, disposition, affectation, emotional tone, temper, cast, vein, mood, humor, grain.

3. Prospect of the future, expectation, anticipation, probability, likelihood, chance, certainty, assumption, presumption, promise, foresight, hope, speculation.

4. Place from which an observer looks out, watchtower, lookout, observatory, observation post, gazebo, belvedere, crow's-nest *(naut.).*

OUTLYING, *adj.* Lying at a distance from the center *or* the main body, lying outside the boundary *or* limit, exterior, external, detached, distant, remote, outer, outermost, extraneous, extraterritorial, ulterior, far-off, peripheral, frontier, tramontane, ultramontane, out-of-the-way, Godforsaken *(coll.),* circumferential, secluded, provincial.

OUTMODE, *v.* Cause to be out of style, obsolete, disuse, cease to use, discontinue, have done with, discard, supplant, succeed, substitute *(a new model)* for, replace, supersede, abandon, give up, drop, antiquate.

OUT-OF-DATE, *adj.* Of a previous style *or* fashion, outmoded, obsolete, old-fashioned, antiquated, antique, gone by, fallen into desuetude *or* disuse, anachronous, anachronistic, behind time, archaic, neglected, retired, lapsed, elapsed, extinct, past, hoary, dead, timeworn, discarded, expired, forgotten, desuete, outdated, discredited, rejected, former, refuted, passé.

OUT-OF-THE-WAY, *adj.* 1. Remote, unfrequented, outlying, outlandish, secluded, distant, inaccessible, faraway, far-off, ultramontane, ulterior, tramontane, unvisited, concealed, off the beaten track, lonely, hidden, forsaken, in a backwater, isolated, solitary.

2. Unusual, uncommon, singular, strange, rare, odd, eccentric, irregular, unheard-of, original, exceptional, extraordinary, peculiar, curious, unparalleled, unexampled, unprecedented, abnormal, unconventional, unaccepted, outlandish, queer, idiosyncratic, bohemian, informal, capricious.

3. Improper, inelegant, untasteful, indecent, indecorous, vulgar, unbecoming, unseemly, uncommendable, discreditable, indiscreet, untoward, inexpedient, unpraiseworthy, reprehensible, disreputable, inappropriate, wrong, unlawful, unmeet, unsuitable, rude, in bad taste, ungenteel, uncivil, discourteous, unfitting, undue, injudicious, unwise, imprudent, ill-advised, out of place, fool-

ish, impolite, incorrect, ungrammatical, solecistic, inaccurate, faulty, unseasonable.

OUTPLAY, *v.* Play better than, outpoint, outdo, defeat, exceed, trump, prevail, beat, outshine, overtop, outstrip, surpass, lead, be superior to, outrival, go beyond, overbear, outdistance, tower above, eclipse, throw into the shade, preponderate, predominate over, excel above, top, cap.

OUTPOST, *n.* Station at a distance from the main body of an army, outskirt, guard, border, fringes, scout, forerunner, Cossack post, sentinel box, flanker, security detachment, frontier settlement, picket, forward line, flank.

OUTPOURING, *n.* Effusion, outflow, efflux, issue, outgushing, burst, expulsion, emission, ejection, eruption, outburst, jet, gushing, escape, effluence, evacuation, issuance, exodus, egress, emanation, extravasation, outbreak, spurting, spouting, flush, rushing out, overflow, discharge.

OUTPUT, *n.* Act of turning out, production, quantity *or* amount produced, yield, product, produce, harvest, crop, circulation, printing, issue, publication, dispatch, discharge, achievement, accomplishment, realization, fulfillment, result *(of work),* outturn.

OUTRAGE, *n.* Act of wanton violence, gross violation of law *or* decency, anything that outrages the feelings, offense, crime, atrocity, barbarism, malignity, indignity, affront, maleficence, evil action *or* deed, contumely, devastation, injury, transgression, insult, foul play, rapine, rape, pillage, seizure, malice, enormity, plunder, misusage, maliciousness, ravage, felony, disservice, cruelty, maltreatment, ill-treatment, barbarity, grievance, perversion, prostitution, destruction, infringement, slap in the face, infraction, blow, buffet, peccancy, desecration, oppression, rudeness, profanation, hurt, harm, brutality, damage, last straw, scurrility, provocation, inroad, havoc, detriment, abuse, flout, excess.

OUTRAGE, *v.* Subject to grievous violence *or* indignity, affect with a sense of offended decency *or* right, shock, offend against grossly *or* shamelessly, insult, maltreat, abuse, injure, harm, hurt, persecute, ravage, ravish, violate, incense, illtreat, humiliate, anger, kindle wrath, provoke, vex, make one's blood boil, huff, desecrate, envenom, embitter, inflame, assault, wrong, rape, set down, excite to anger, sting, affront, give umbrage, do violence, rack, break on the wheel, buffet, do one's worst, take *or* pluck by the beard, add insult to injury, slap in the face, crucify, agonize, raise one's gorge *or* choler, add fuel to the flames, madden, infuriate, enrage, lash into fury, hurt the feelings, treat with contempt, ill-use, stir up.

OUTRAGEOUS, *adj.* 1. Of the nature of *or* involving gross injury *or* wrong, grossly offensive to the sense of right *or* decency, atrocious, villainous, scandalous, disgraceful, vile, opprobrious, virulent, envenomed, insulting, rank, invidious, acrimonious, treacherous, scurrilous, notorious, nefarious, heinous, revengeful, despicable, ignominious, shabby, petty, venomous, little, low, mean, base, beggarly, incendiary, foul, galling, deplorable, treasonous, dishonorable, infamous, contemptible, gravely reprehensible, questionable, wicked, rancorous, bitter, malevolent, mordant, malicious, ill-intentioned, despiteful, spiteful, humiliating, malign, malignant, detestable, peccant, shocking, hateful, perfidious, odious, black.

2. Passing reasonable bounds, excessive, ex-

travagant, enormous, flagrant, vehement, monstrous, wanton, conspicuous, amazing, astonishing, immoderate, extreme, undeserved, unwarranted, gross, unreasonable, unbearable, preposterous, notorious, glaring, grievous, shameful, atrocious, arrant, exaggerated, inordinate, hyperbolical, fulsome, overdone, undue, immense, unconscionable, exorbitant, intolerable, shocking, egregious, *outré (Fr.).*

3. Violent in action *or* temper, furious, abusive, mad, wild, disorderly, fierce, ferocious, raging, frantic, frenzied, raving, ranting, maniacal, seething, fuming, fiery, hot-headed, vehement, madcap, rampant, passionate, amuck, beside oneself, frenetic, tempestuous, turbulent, distracted, ebullient, boiling over, overwrought, overmastered, overpowered, out of one's wits, carried away, clamorous, infuriate, rabid, tumultuous, uproarious, foaming at the mouth.

OUTRANK, *v.* Rank above, precede, excel, be superior to, transcend, overtop, take precedence, come *or* rank first, lead, hold authority over, prevail, rank, rival, top, cap, have the upper *or* whip hand, preponderate.

OUTREACH, *v.* Reach beyond, exceed, outstretch, overreach, surpass, gain the ascendancy, prevail over, predominate, outplay, cap, rival, beat, top, outdo, overtop, outmaneuver, circumvent, outstrip, triumph over, distance, have the advantage.

OUTRIDER, *n.* Mounted attendant riding beside *or* before a carriage, escort, accompanier, bodyguard, defender, patrol, protector, guardian.

OUTRIGHT, *adj.* Complete, total, entire, utter, downright, full, comprehensive, unqualified, unmitigated, absolute, consummate, out-and-out, sweeping, radical, thorough, thoroughgoing, sheer, veritable, dead, unreserved, unconditional, undiminished, exhaustive, solid, undivided, perfect.

OUTRIGHT, *adv.* Completely, wholly, utterly, straight, unconditionally, in one transaction, in a single act, to the limit, totally, altogether, all at once, to the utmost, to the full, in the mass *or* aggregate, one and indivisible, *in toto (Lat.),* bodily, collectively, absolutely, clean, thoroughly, entirely, for all, as a whole.

OUTSET, *n.* Beginning, commencement, start, origin, first, threshold, opening, entrance, startingpoint, birth, inception, genesis, initiation, dawn, head, spring, incipience, inauguration, source, foundation, inchoation, incubation, first move, prelude, preface, overture, morning, outbreak, infancy, installation, debut, take-off *(coll.),* kickoff *(coll.),* rise, embryo, embarkation, first step, onset.

OUTSHINE, *v.* Surpass in shining, excellence, splendor, *etc.,* outluster, overshadow, eclipse, bedim, becloud, extinguish, make to fade *or* pale by comparison, adumbrate, transcend, obscure, blind, obfuscate, outblaze, outdo, outsparkle, outglow, outglitter, take the limelight, outdazzle, throw into shadow *or* the shade.

OUTSIDE, *adj.* 1. Being, acting, done, *or* originating beyond an enclosure, boundary *etc.,* not belonging to *or* connected with *(an institution, society, etc.),* exterior, external, outer, on the surface, abroad, peripheral, extraneous, alien, outdoor, outlying, foreign, fringe, exotic, tramontane, ultramontane, exclusive, excluded, not included, left *or* shut out, aloof, extrinsic, contingent, accessory, unrelated, nonessential, objective, incidental, unassociated, oversea, outland, ulterior, adventitious, adscititious, exoteric, additional, supplemental, superficial, outward.

2. Extreme, utmost, final, top, highest, terminal, farthest, making all allowance, circumscribed, limitary, limiting, uttermost, absolute, ultimate, unequivocal, last.

OUTSIDE, *n.* 1. Outer side, surface, *or* part, space without *or* beyond *(an enclosure, boundary, etc.),* exterior, surface, overlayer, sheath, external, periphery, external aspect *or* appearance, covering, cast, unenclosed parts, outline, visage, physiognomy, countenance, superstratum, case, superficies, externality, skin, face.

2. Something merely external, face, image, simulacrum, appearance, show, superficies, effect, looks, ostent, fashion, figure, front, mien, guise, apparent, character, impression, superficial aspect, semblance, ostentation.

OUTSIDER, *n.* One not within an enclosure, boundary, *etc.,* one not belonging to a particular group, set, party, *etc.,* one unacquainted *or* unconnected with the matter in question, alien, nonmember, foreigner, interloper, uninitiated, immigrant, uninformed newcomer, tenderfoot, guest, outlander, intruder, visitor, ultramontane, tramontane, trespasser, extern, outlier, exoteric, stranger, crasher *(coll.),* uninvited.

OUTSKIRT, *n.* *(Usually pl.)* Outer *or* bordering part *or* district, distant point *or* region, suburb, precinct, edge, frontier, confines, rim, remote region, perimeter, bounds, surroundings, periphery, borderland, boundary, circumambiencies, circumjacencies, circumference, outlying districts, neighborhood, environs, vicinage, purlieu, outpost, fringe, verge, border.

OUTSPOKEN, *adj.* Uttered *or* expressed with frankness *or* lack of reserve, free *or* unreserved in speech, plain, plain-spoken, frank, blunt, direct, straightforward, open, unflattering, candid, unconcealed, downright, unfeigning, honest, undissembling, free, bold, guileless, undisguising, unpretending, undissimulating, unvarnished, untrimmed, artless, bluff, ingenuous, sincere, aboveboard, inartificial, forward *(in expressing opinions, etc.),* unsparing, truthful, forthright.

OUTSPREAD, *adj.* Spread *or* stretched out, extended, diffused abroad, widespread, outstretched, wide-open, welcoming, wide, extensive, fanlike, fanned out, fan-shaped, ample, unfolded, unfurled, expanded, flabellate *(Biol.).*

OUTSTANDING, *adj.* 1. Striking, prominent, conspicuous, salient, glaring, paramount, principal, primary, eminent, leading, signal, essential, impressive, memorable, significant, great, notable, marked, momentous, stirring, august, grand, eventful, egregious, consequential, celebrated, famed, notorious, burning, famous, particular, imposing, commanding, distinguished, noteworthy, unforgettable, renowned, exceptional, extraordinary, chief, foremost, exceeding, overruling, considerable, substantial.

2. That continues in existence, that remains unsettled, unpaid, *etc.,* surviving, in arrears, owing, unsettled, uncollected, ungathered, due, payable, unpaid.

3. Standing out, projecting, detached, overhanging, beetling, jutting, protrusive, bulging, prominent, salient, bold, exterior, external, protuberant.

4. That resists *or* opposes, dissenting, dissident, dissentient, schismatic, discordant, rebellious, protestant, uncovered, unconsenting, disagreeing, recusant, obstinate, nonjuring, refusing, at odds, negative, negatory, incompliant, uncomplaisant, refractory, restive, declinatory, at cross purposes, hostile, contrary, deviative, jarring, inaccordant.

antagonistic, contentious, irreconcilable, factious, differing, divergent.

OUTSTRETCH, *v.* Stretch forth *or* out, extend, expand, sprawl, widen, broaden, spread, stretch beyond, outreach, strain, outspread, exceed, open wide, fan out, diffuse, unfold.

OUTSTRIP, *v.* Excel, surpass, outdo, outgo, outrun, outdistance, beat, exceed, overtake, lead, get ahead of, forespeed, forereach, top, cap, overtop, precede, take precedence, get the start of, outride, outspeed, go beyond, outwing, eclipse, best, pass, leave behind, distance, steal a march on, transcend, outvie, take the lead over, outclass, outweigh, predominate over, outplay, outshine.

OUTWARD, *adj.* 1. Being *or* pertaining to what is seen *or* apparent, external, visible, apparent, superficial, surface, ostensible, seeming, showing, appearing, formal, given out, shown, avowed, declared, pretended, manifest, evident, exoteric, perceivable, alleged, observable, seeable, feigned, professed, colorable, assigned, exhibited.

2. Pertaining to the body *(as opposed to the mind or spirit)*, carnal, corporeal, belonging to the external world, unspiritual, secular, physical, worldly, profane, temporal, mundane, fleshly, terrestrial.

3. Belonging *or* pertaining to what is external to oneself, extrinsic, extraneous, objective, impersonal, alien, foreign, adventitious, public, civil.

4. Proceeding *or* directed toward the outside, diverging, radial, radiant, divergent, dispersing, spreading, fanning, emanating, effluent, eliminative, eruptive, outgoing, outbound, exudative, centrifugal.

5. Of *or* pertaining to the outside *or* outer surface, outer, exterior, external, exoteric, outermost, outside, that lies toward the outside, on the outer side, surface, fringe. outlying, perimetric, peripheral, exomorphic *(Petrog.).*

OUTWARD, OUTWARDS, *adj.* 1. Toward the outside, out, away, thence, without, from here.

2. Visibly, openly, outwardly, externally, manifestly, evidently, in the open, overtly, aboveboard, in the market place, at the crossroads, in plain sight, apparently, unreservedly, on the table, in broad daylight, *prima facie (Lat.),* to one's face.

OUTWEAR, *v.* 1. Wear *or* last longer than, outlast, outlive, survive, outgrow, surpass in durability, endure beyond.

2. Wear out, exhaust, spend, expend, tire out, waste away, deteriorate, dissipate, deplete, weary, jade, harass, weaken, fag, flag, fatigue, erode, destroy, consume *(by wearing).*

OUTWEIGH, *v.* Exceed in value. importance, influence, *etc.,* have *or* take precedence over, come first, rise above, surpass, prevail, outbalance, overbalance, overweigh, override, overpower, preponderate, eclipse, be of greater significance than. hold all the trumps.

OUTWIT, *v.* 1. Get the better of by superior ingenuity *or* cleverness, outmaneuver, trip up, take advantage of, trick, trap, snare, ensnare, evade fool, make game of, play a trick *or* practical joke upon, practice on one's credulity, give the runaround *(sl.),* baffle, jockey, steal a march upon.

2. Overreach, work around, deceive, circumvent, dupe, cheat, swindle, victimize, impose upon, gammon, mislead, throw off the scent, lead a merry chase, thwart, undo. worst, humbug, defraud, cozen, gull, diddle *(coll.),* confuse, elude, bewilder. betray, give the slip, outflank, checkmate, double-cross *(sl.),* flummox *(sl.),* frustrate, confound, kid *(sl.).*

OUTWORN, *adj.* 1. Outgrown *(as opinions),* exploded, discarded, refuted, rejected, discredited, obsolete, archaic, dismissed, no longer valid, passé, effete, antiquated, past, dead.

2. Obsolete, out of date, ancient, exhausted, fallen into desuetude *or* disuse, past, antiquated, effaced by time, disused, neglected, antique, gone to seed, retired, gone by, lapsed, elapsed, extinct, dead, hoary, timeworn, expired, bygone, forgotten, effete, outdated, primitive, discredited, prehistoric, former, antediluvian.

3. Worn out *(as clothes),* discarded, unfit for use, ragged, shopworn, faded, shabby, second-hand, ramshackle, broken, decrepit, battered, dilapidated, weather-beaten, frayed, the worse for wear, deteriorated, threadbare, tumbledown, run-down, washed-out.

4. Exhausted in strength *or* endurance, worn out, tired, fatigued, utterly weary, fagged out, prostrate, drooping, enfeebled, spent, played out, all in, ready to drop, tuckered out *(coll.),* on one's last legs, haggard, footsore, beat *(coll.),* bushed *(coll.),* dog-tired, dead-tired, pooped *(sl.),* faint, more dead than alive, pegged out *(sl.).*

OVAL, *adj.* Having the general form, shape, *or* outline of an egg, elliptical, elliptic, curved, ellipsoidal, egg-shaped, obovate, obovoid, oviform, ovoid, ovate, rounded.

OVATION, *n.* Enthusiastic public reception of a person, enthusiastic applause, cheering, triumph, acclamation, cheers, fanfare, laudation, demonstration, hand-clapping, acclaim, loud greeting, huzza, hurray, hurrah, flourish of trumpets, jubilee, tumultuous pleasure.

OVEN, *n.* Chamber *or* receptacle for baking and heating *or* for drying by heat, kiln, dryer, stovehouse, stove, limekiln, brickkiln, Dutch oven.

OVER, *adj.* 1. Covering, upper, outer, superior, taller, above, topmost, greater, higher, towering, overhanging, overlying, outermost, outside, uppermost.

2. Superior, higher in authority, station, *etc.,* better, greater, major, surpassing, outranking, head, above, leading, ascendant, exceeding, supreme, primary, prepotent, executive, predominant, sovereign, foremost, elevated, prominent, overruling, authoritative, commanding, preponderant, prepollent, dominant, governing, prevailing, proctorial, supervisory, controlling, managerial.

3. In excess *or* addition, additional, extra, surplus, left, excessive, remaining, too great, supplementary, surviving, odd, residual, unused, spare. outstanding, sedimentary, superfluous, unconsumed.

4. At an end, done, past, gone, gone-by, ended, concluded, done with, bygone, elapsed, lapsed, expired, no more, finished, set at rest, completed, passed away, run out, all off *(coll.).*

OVER, *adv.* 1. Above the top *or* upper surface *or* edge of, so as to cover the surface, on top of, above, aloft, overhead, higher than.

2. Through a region, area, *etc.,* from end to end, from beginning to end, all through, from stem to stern, all over, over all, here and there in, along the length *or* course of, from cover to cover, from top to bottom, from head to foot.

3. Across any intervening space, from one side to the other, from side to side, athwart, at some distance.

4. From one person, party, *etc.*, to another, by transfer, from hand to hand, on, by assignment, by bequest, by agreement, by negotiation.

5. On the other side, upside down, in reverse, head over heels, inversely, vice versa, wrong side up, to the opposite (reverse, obverse, *etc.*).

6. Once more, again, afresh, anew, twice, a second time, repeatedly, in repetition, often, encore, time and again.

7. In excess, in addition, remaining, beyond a certain amount, additional, into the bargain, to boot, overly, overmuch, too far, too much, extra, on the side, beyond, in advance of, upwards of, over and above, too, else, also, plus, on top of, across the brim.

8. Beyond (*a period of time*), throughout, on longer, in continuance, subsequently, thereafter, later, more, after, afterward.

OVER, *prep.* 1. Above in place *or* position, higher up than, at a height, reaching higher than, on, upon, so as to cover *or* rest on, in charge of, in command of, beyond, ascendant, above, superior to.

2. Above and to the other side of, across, athwart, upon, beyond, from side to side of, on the other side of, from one side of to the other.

3. Here and there on *or* in, through all parts of, all through, throughout, to and fro, about in *or* on, from end to end, back and forth, from side to side of, across, around, in all places, everywhere, through the whole extent of.

4. In excess of, above in degree, *etc.*, upward of, more than, over and above, as well as, in addition, along *or* together with, further, besides, not to mention, let alone.

5. Until after the end of, for the duration of, during, through the interval of, pending, throughout, in the time *or* course of, for the period of, through.

6. In preference to, rather than, first before, before, sooner than.

7. In reference to, concerning, about, in relation to, regarding, in respect to *or* of, apropos of, as regards, on the subject of, in point of, as for, as respects, touching, in connection with.

8. While engaged on *or* concerned with, in the midst of, in the middle of, midway in, in the thick of, halfway through.

OVERABOUND, *v.* Abound to excess, superabound, exceed, overrun, run riot, swarm, overwhelm, be profuse, bristle with, exist prodigally, choke, surfeit, gorge, know no bounds, be superfluous, inundate, overproduce, engulf, flood, drench, surcharge, well (run, flow, brim) over.

OVERABUNDANCE, *n.* Excessive abundance, surfeit, redundance, superfluity, oversupply, glut, overplus, overmeasure, plethora, excess, inordinancy, exorbitance, surcharge, overdose, deluge, flood, overflow, drug on the market, satiety, diffuseness, luxury, supererogation, extravagance, profusion, too much, exuberance, prodigality, embarrassment of riches, superabundance, nimiety, surplus, supersatuation, pleonasm (*Dict.*).

OVERACT, *v.* Act (*a part*) in an exaggerated manner, overdo, rant, spout, ham (*Theat. sl.*), lay it on thick (*sl.*), pose, overplay, affect, put on, assume, counterfeit, sham, make a show of.

OVERALL, *adj.* From one extreme limit to the other, total, general, all-inclusive, widespread, panoramic, sweeping, universal, comprehensive, compendious, extensive, long-term, long-range, exhaustive, thorough, catholic, all-embracing, complete.

OVERAWE, *v.* Restrain *or* subdue by inspiring awe, intimidate, daunt, cow, awe, browbeat, abash, bully, appall, keep under, lord it over, make a puppet of, lead by the nose, keep under one's thumb, dominate, frighten into submission, impose upon, huff, bluster out of *or* into, lay down the law to, domineer, grind, oppress, threaten, override, rule with a rod of iron, harass, terrorize, dragoon, hector, bend to one's will, bulldoze (*sl.*), buffalo (*sl.*), ride roughshod over, compel, coerce, dismay, disconcert, faze (*coll.*), carry with a high hand.

OVERBALANCE, *n.* More than necessary, extra quantity, excess, abundance, superfluity, surplusage, profusion, repletion, overabundance, surfeit, outbear, turn the tables, preponderate.

OVERBALANCE, *v.* 1. Gain the ascendancy, outpoint, predominate over, outstrip, eclipse, overtop, outweigh, exceed, transcend, overmatch, top, have the edge on, outdo, tip the scales, outrank, outbear, turn the tables, preponderate.

2. Cause to lose balance, cause to keel over, push over, tip over, tilt, unseat, knock over *or* down, turn turtle, overturn, overset, capsize, upset, topple.

OVERBEAR, *v.* 1. Rule with an iron hand, domineer, tyrannize, lay down the law, be overbearing, govern despotically, ride roughshod over, coerce, oppress, have control over, lord over, sway, dominate, command.

2. Bear fruit *or* offspring excessively, be parturient, be fruitful, breed prolifically.

OVERBEARING, *adj.* Stiff, disdainful, contumelious, self-assertive, high-hat (*sl.*), overweening, arrogant, haughty, supercilious, puffed up, boastful, high and mighty, proud, swelled-headed, aloof, hoity-toity, patronizing, uppish (*coll.*), conceited, bloated with pride, pompous, imperious, egotistical, high-handed, snotty (*sl.*), sniffy (*coll.*), fanfaronading, swollen, vain, toplofty (*coll.*), uppity (*coll.*), highfalutin (*coll.*), overproud, stuck-up (*coll.*), gasconading, affected, self-important, magisterial, lordly, peacockish, strutting, prideful, high, self-glorious, cocky (*coll.*), priggish, know-it-all, self-opinionated.

OVERBLOWN, *adj.* Excessive, exuberant, superabundant, plenteous, superfluous, immoderate, overgrown, lavish, fulsome, overflowing, copious, profuse, prolific, surplus, extravagant.

OVERBOARD, *adj.* Over the side (*of a ship, etc.*), in the water, in the drink (*sl.*), fallen in, washed overboard.

OVERCAST, *v.* Overshadow, cloud, eclipse, darken, nubilate, shade, fog, mist, haze, pale, dim, dusk, gloom, promise rain, adumbrate, murk, becloud, darkle, befog, smoke, obfuscate, lower, hide.

OVERCHARGE, *v.* 1. Charge *or* fill beyond normal capacity, charge to excess, crowd, overfill, overburden, strain, overtax, stretch, overstretch, overstrain, overdo.

2. Delineate extravagantly, magnify, exaggerate, embroider, heighten, overdraw, overdo, overpicture, overshoot, amplify, increase, enhance, overstate, hyperbolize, augment, overcolor, color, strain, overvalue, overestimate, misrepresent.

OVERCOAT, *n.* Topcoat, greatcoat, surtout, ulster, cloak, Inverness, surcoat (*Hist.*), paletot, raglan, wraprascal (*Hist.*).

OVERCOME, *v.* Overwhelm, crush, quell, subdue, squash, master, smash, discomfit, reduce, humble, conquer, beat, floor, rout, triumph over, whip, drub, get the better of, put down, surmount, get the upper hand of, vanquish, worst, overpower, defeat, checkmate, prevail over, be victorious over, outmaneuver, trample on, overmaster, subjugate, thrash, trim, trample in the dust, overturn, subject, break.

OVERCOME, *adj.* Weakened, fagged, tuckered, impoverished, enervated, exhausted, emasculated, depleted, weary, worn out, emptied, tired, jaded, done in *(coll.),* fatigued, debilitated, used up, expended, drained, oppressed, weighed down, drooping, faint, spent, haggard, wayworn, ready to drop, played out, footsore, enfeebled, sickly, sick at heart, unsteady, groggy.

OVERCONFIDENT, *adj.* Too confident, brash, overweening, assured, reckless, adventurous, hasty, careless, hotspur, presumptuous, incautious, secure, temerarious, venturesome, rash, hot-headed, foolhardy, overcredulous, injudicious, giddy, quixotic, unsuspecting, overtrustful, not amenable to reason, blind, deaf, regardless, thoughtless, death-defying, devil-may-care, indiscreet, daring, heedless, impudent, positive, precipitate, headlong.

OVERCRITICAL, *adj.* Critical to excess, too critical, hypercritical, nice, subtle, precise, exacting, complaining, carping, censorious, fastidious, querulous, disapprobatory, condemnatory, hard upon, disparaging, finical, fussy, finicky, finicking, captious, faultfinding, caviling, hairsplitting, oversensitive, dainty, hard *or* difficult to please, overnice, oversubtle, overparticular, overscrupulous, sparing *or* grudging of praise, harsh, sharp, severe, withering, squeamish.

OVERCROWD, *v.* Crowd to excess, jam, congest, pack, stuff, wedge, ram, press, surcharge, overfill, fill to overflowing, drug, choke, supersaturate, overburden, overload, overlade.

OVERDO, *v.* 1. Do to excess, not know when to stop, carry too far, carry beyond the proper limit, indulge, be intemperate, run riot, luxuriate in.

2. Overact *(a part),* exaggerate, overstate, heighten, magnify, stretch *or* strain a point, overcharge, overdraw, enlarge, hyperbolize, expand, amplify, embroider, overestimate, color highly, out-Herod Herod, rant, spout, ham *(Theat. sl.),* put on, overplay, affect, sham, pose, lay it on thick *(sl.).*

3. Overtax the strength of, exhaust, fatigue, do too much, overexert, tire, task, strain, overwork, drive, weary, overlabor, burn the candle at both ends, wear out, jade, bleed white, tire to death, fag, prostrate.

OVERDUE, *adj.* Past due, tardy, back, in arrear, behind time, belated, delayed, unpunctual, backward, behindhand, slow, accrued, late.

OVEREAT, *v.* Eat too much *or* more than is good for one, engorge, overindulge, surfeit, gorge, glut, have a ravenous appetite, eat one's fill, guzzle, gormandize, be gluttonous, gluttonize, stuff, cram, eat like a horse, raven, worship the palate, satiate.

OVERESTIMATE, *v.* Estimate at too high a value, amount, rate, *etc.,* make too much of, exaggerate, overprize, overpraise, overcount, stretch, overmeasure, overweigh, set too high an estimate *or* value on, magnify, enhance, heighten, flatter, puff, adulate, make a mountain of a molehill, at-

tach too much importance to, overesteem, overrate, overvalue.

OVEREXCITE, *v.* Overstimulate, quicken, incite, inflame, stir up, arouse, add fuel to the flame, pour oil on the fire, irritate, foment, madden, infuriate, whip, intoxicate, goad, spur, prick, provoke, fan the flame, lash, urge on, exasperate, impassion, fan into flame, raise to fever heat, kindle, exacerbate.

OVEREXERT, *v.* Strain, overtax, exhaust, fatigue, do too much, overdo, task, overwork, weary, drive, tire, prostrate, fag, bleed white, jade, wear out, burn the candle at both ends, overlabor, push oneself too hard, not spare oneself.

OVERFEED, *v.* Feed to excess, surfeit, glut, overfill, cloy, choke, pamper, stuff, satiate, gorge, feed to satiety.

OVERFILL, *v.* Fill too full, fill to overflowing, become too full, heap, swell, overload, overlade, overburden, crowd, cram, fatten, overweight, inundate, engulf, gorge, oversupply, bloat, stuff, inflate, dilate, distend, stretch, supersaturate, overfeed, pile up, bulge, flood, overstock, overcharge, surcharge, satiate, glut.

OVERFLOW, *n.* 1. Overflowing, flooding, that which flows *or* runs over, inundation, wash, flood, alluvium, washout, freshet, debacle, avalanche, deluge.

2. Superabundance, excess, luxuriance, exuberance, satiety, amplitude, prolixity, prodigality, opulence, repletion, overplus, abundance, avalanche, superfluity, engorgement, ebullience, copiousness, full measure, cornucopia, horn of plenty, more than enough, lavishment, affluence, surcharge, exorbitance, inordinacy, nimiety, overproduction, oversupply, surplus, profusion, redundancy, overflowing, plenty, congestion, plethora, enough and to spare.

OVERFLOW, *v.* Flow *or* run over, overrun, pass from one place *or* part to another *(as if flowing from an overfull space),* emigrate, overspread, flood, deluge, exundate, slop over, overbrim, teem, have the contents overflowing *(as a vessel),* discharge a flow, be filled *or* supplied in overflowing measure *(fol. by* WITH*),* superabound, overabound, submerge, glut, overwhelm, overstream, overspill, spill, inundate, abound, engulf, drown, cover.

OVERGROW, *v.* 1. Grow over, cover with a growth of something, outdo in growing, choke *or* supplant by a more exuberant growth, overrun, overspread, infest, flourish, luxuriate, grow rank *or* lush, run riot, overwhelm, obstruct.

2. Grow beyond, grow too large for, outgrow, grow to excess, expand, *or* swell beyond, mature beyond.

OVERGROWTH, *n.* Growth overspreading *or* covering something, excessive *or* too exuberant growth, rank growth, luxuriance, redundance, hypertrophy, overdevelopment, denseness, overdistention, wild *or* uncontrolled growth, jungle, excess.

OVERHANG, *n.* Overhanging, projection, extent of projection, brow, eave, pendency, suspension, bow, salient, protuberance.

OVERHANG, *v.* 1. Extend over, hang *or* be suspended over, overlie, overtop, impend, shoot out, beetle, jut, stand out, tower above, command, arch, vault, overarch, stick out, protrude, project.

2. Impend, threaten, be imminent, portend, hang *or* lie over, forebode, lower, hover, endanger,

menace, approach, omen, stare one in the face, loom, await one, jeopardize.

OVERHAUL, v. 1. Examine *(as for repair)*, investigate thoroughly, search, haul *or* turn over, take account of, pore over, look over, peruse, review, explore, inventory, take stock, study, scan, audit, overlook, scrutinize, look into, contemplate, service, revamp, renovate, give the once-over *(sl.)*, inspect, reconstruct, ransack, probe.

2. Overtake, gain upon, come up with *or* to, overpass, overstride, overshoot, go by, pass.

OVERHEAD, adj. Upper, over, topmost, superior, overhanging, uppermost, overlying, outermost, roof, ceiling.

OVERHEAD, adv. Aloft, above, above one's head, atop, aloof, skyward, above the top, on top of.

OVERHEAR, v. Hear what one is not intended to hear, catch, get, hear, become aware of, descry, detect, get an earful *(sl.)*.

OVERLAP, v. Cover by extension, overlie, extend over, extend beyond, reach over, overlay, imbricate, superimpose, overspread.

OVERLAPPING, adj. Obvolute, overlying, coincidental, convolute, imbricated, superimposed, clinker-built *(of ship's planks, etc.)*, lapstreak *(of ship's planks, etc.)*, equitant *(Bot.)*.

OVERLAY, v. 1. Weigh down, oppress, load, press down, burden, overburden, encumber, saddle, overtask, overcharge, overload, lade, strain, harness, bridle.

2. Cover by extension, superimpose, overlap, overlie, extend over, extend beyond, reach over, imbricate.

OVERLEAP, v. 1. Ignore, leave out, miss, pass up, not trouble oneself with, delete, set aside, preclude, forget, omit, forget about, except, elide, skip, exclude, overlook, pretermit, bar, jump, drop, leave undone, let ride.

2. Jump over, skip over, spring over, pass, hop, bound, vault, leapfrog.

3. Overjump, go too far, overskip, miss (by going too far), overstep, overstride, shoot beyond, overshoot, overrun, overreach.

OVERLIE, v. *(Often used of infants)* Suffocate, smother, choke, stifle, stop the breath of, strangulate.

OVERLIVE, v. Live longer than, survive, remain, remain after, endure beyond, outlast, outlive.

OVERLOOK, v. 1. View from a higher position, look over, overtop, tower above, command, command a view of, crown, beetle over, top, cap, surmount, jut over, survey.

2. Inspect, survey, look at, glance at, scrutinize, study, examine, take stock of, scan, peruse, contemplate, overhaul, consider, peer at, review.

3. Supervise, direct, oversee, watch over, look after, hold the reins, pilot, steer, guide, superintend, boss *(coll.)*, see to, administer, preside, conduct, govern, be at the helm, navigate.

4. Forget, neglect, omit, miss, pass up, except, skip, pretermit, not trouble oneself, set aside, preclude, leave out, drop, leave undone, let ride, jump, bar, overpass,

5. Forgive, forget about *(coll.)*, excuse, pass over, regard indulgently, let bygones be bygones, bear with, pardon, condone, think no more of, overpass, disregard, wink at, blink at.

OVERMASTER, v. Overwhelm, crush, master, squash, subdue, smash, discomfit, reduce, humble, conquer, beat, floor, rout, triumph over, whip, drub, get the better of, put down, surmount, get

the upper hand of, vanquish, worst, overpower, defeat, checkmate, overcome, prevail over, be victorious over, outmaneuver, trample on, subjugate, overmatch, thrash, trim, trample in the dust, overturn, subject, break.

OVERMUCH, adj. Too much, unnecessary, lavish, exuberant, profuse, copious, disproportionate, surplus, uncalled for, excess, excessive, superfluous, extra, too great, overflowing, superabundant, fulsome, overplus, needless.

OVERMUCH, n. More than necessary, surplusage, profusion, repletion, surfeit, plethora, oversupply, overplus, excess, extra quantity, superfluity, overabundance, overweight, glut, fulsomeness.

OVERPASS, n. Bridge, viaduct, span, overbridge, grade crossing, culvert.

OVERPLUS, n. More than necessary, excess, superfluity, repletion, extra quantity, overabundance, overweight, glut, fulsomeness, oversupply, plethora, overmuch, profusion, surfeit, surplusage.

OVERPOWER, v. 1. Get the upper hand of, vanquish, surmount, put down, overwhelm, smash, subdue, squash, master, overmaster, overmatch, overcome, discomfit, reduce, humble, conquer, beat, floor, worst, defeat, checkmate, prevail over, be victorious over, outmaneuver, trample on, subjugate, thrash, trim, trample in the dust, overturn, break, subject.

2. Stir emotionally, move, incite, influence, move to tears, affect, incline, touch, excite, sway, work upon, electrify, magnetize, bias, infect, stimulate, smite, inspirit, impassion, animate.

OVERPOWERING, adj. All-powerful, irresistible, overwhelming, subduing, crushing, conquering, resistless, prevailing, mastering, overmastering, inexorable, inescapable, inevitable, uncontrollable.

OVERRATE, v. Rate too highly, overestimate, make too much of, overprize, overvalue, overreckon, expect too much of, exaggerate, overcount, magnify, heighten, enhance, stretch, overesteem, attach too much importance to, puff, embroider, color, overlaud, amplify, flatter, dilate, strain.

OVERREACH, v. 1. Reach *or* extend over *or* beyond, reach too far, exceed, outreach, overshoot, outstretch, overtop, overextend, outdo.

2. Defeat *(oneself)* by overdoing matters, be excessively eager *or* cunning, overdo, defeat one's own purpose, undo, nullify one's gains, annul, offset, vitiate, frustrate, cut one's own throat, try too hard, overleap, have one's plans backfire *or* boomerang, be caught in one's own trap, negate *or* wipe out one's accomplishments, have things rebound *or* recoil.

3. Get the better of, beguile, fool, cheat, trick, gull, swindle, take in *(coll.)*, impose upon, diddle *(coll.)*, dupe, circumvent, outwit, deceive, undermine, gammon, hoodwink, overextend, thwart, mislead, victimize, defraud, work around, worst, humbug, cozen, betray, outflank, double-cross *(sl.)*, confound, kid *(sl.)*, frustrate, flummox *(sl.)*.

OVERRIDE, v. 1. Pursue one's course in desregard of, not consider, disobey, snub, not heed, dismiss, ignore, disregard, act despite, overlook, dismiss from one's mind, pay no attention to, turn a deaf ear to, slight, defy, neglect, turn one's back on, rebel against, violate, flout, cold shoulder, fly in the face of, treat with disdain *or* contempt, elude, evade, refuse to hear, snap one's fingers at, close one's eyes *or* mind to.

2. Prevail over, surpass, repudiate, balk, exceed, overbear, outweigh, upset, reverse, do away with, quell, annul, be superior to, take precedence

over, have the advantage *or* ascendancy over, overpower, overwhelm, overcome, thwart, overmatch, obsolete, supersede, nullify, make null and void, set aside, come to the fore, trample down, transcend, preponderate, lead, revoke, retract, dissolve, invalidate, make ineffectual, put down, crush, subdue, overturn, control, overrule, subjugate, dominate, abrogate, cancel, countermand, counteract.

OVERRULE, *v.* 1. Rule against, disallow, decide against, obsolete, recall, supersede, obviate, prevail over, invalidate, rescind, revoke, cancel, annul, upset, crush, override, counteract, countermand, balk, overturn, do away with, abolish, make null and void, prevent, abrogate, thwart, nullify, trample down, transcend, preponderate, retract, repudiate, do away with.

2. Prevail over so as to change the purpose *or* action, have *or* carry weight with, lead by the nose, keep under one's thumb, overbear, induce, influence, control, overawe, manipulate, domineer, rule with a rod of iron, hold the reins, call the plays for, lay down the law to, bend to one's will, usurp authority over, be master of.

3. Control, govern, have control of, rule, have the upper *or* whip hand, command, lead, head, predominate, sway, master, officiate over, preponderate, administer, dominate, compel, domineer, conduct, exercise power over, supervise, manage, direct, prevail over.

OVERRUN, *v.* 1. Rove over *(as hostile or ravaging invaders)*, infest, swarm over in great numbers, overspread, crowd, people, occupy, populate, pervade, teem, penetrate, permeate, run riot, be diffused *or* disseminated over *or* through, pour in *or* over, assume possession of, mount.

2. Run over *(as plants, esp., vines, weeds, etc.)*, overspread, overgrow, mantle, grow *or* spread over, luxuriate, flourish, grow rank *or* lush, run riot over, overwhelm, spread like wildfire, choke, engulf, fill to overflowing.

3. Run over so as to injure *or* overwhelm, ravage, devastate, overwhelm, harass, oppress, despoil, lay waste, infest, invade, trample, subdue, scour, scourge, plunder, pillage, strip, lay about one, raid, rob, sack, hector, hound, beseige, beset, assault, plague, worry, terrorize, distress, maraud.

4. Run beyond, exceed, be too long for, outstrip, outrun, overshoot, overpass, overreach, overextend.

5. Overflow, run over, exundate, spill, overspill, overbrim, slop over, have the contents overflowing, discharge a flow, overstream.

OVERSEAS, OVERSEA, *adj.* Of *or* pertaining to passage over the sea, situated beyond the sea, foreign, barbarian, exotic, external, alien, ultramarine, colonial, immigrant, emigrant.

OVERSEAS, OVERSEA, *adv.* Over *or* across the sea, beyond the sea, abroad, in foreign parts, in foreign service.

OVERSEE, *v.* 1. Supervise, direct, manage, superintend, overlook, have charge of, attend to, see to, look after, lead, run, administer, take care of, control, be the guiding force, boss, govern, regulate, rule, command, guide, handle, be at the helm, steer, pilot, carry on, conduct, preside over.

2. Survey, overlook, inspect, watch, observe, note, regard with attention, examine, peruse, ogle, eye, remark, pay attention to, scan, notice, heed, take a look at, contemplate, witness, cognize, peer at, investigate, explore, reconnoiter, be a spectator,

keep an eye on, scrutinize, study, attend, view, look.

OVERSEER, *n.* One who oversees, supervisor, governor, master, overman, foreman, inspector, director, provost, censor, head, surveyor, overlooker, officer, chief, chairman, ranger, executive, monitor, proctor, captain, president, keeper, guard, superintendent, boss *(coll.)*, magistrate, matron.

OVERSET, *v.* 1. Overturn, upset, overthrow, throw into confusion, disorder, reverse, tip over, knock down, capsize, invert, derange, ruffle, rumble, spill, litter, scatter, disorganize, disarrange, precipitate, pull down, scuttle, subvert, level, prostrate, discomfit, rout, tumble, shuffle, huddle, jumble, muddle, disturb, agitate, turn topsy-turvy, confuse, dishevel, toss.

2. Become overturned, overthrown, *or* upset, keel *or* heel over, turn a somersault, capsize, upturn, upend, fall, turn turtle, be upside down, overturn, tilt *or* topple over, turn *or* go over, flounder, upset.

OVERSHADOW, *v.* 1. Tower above *(so as to cast a shadow over)*, overtop, dominate, diminish the importance of, render insignificant in comparison, outshine, minimize, reduce, eclpse, belittle, surpass, be superior to, dwarf, detract from, steal the limelight from, override, overrule.

2. Cast a shadow over, make dark *or* gloomy, overshade, overcloud, shade, cover, darken, shroud, eclipse, hide from view, outshine, adumbrate, screen, cloud, obscure, bedim, begloom, obtenebrate, murk, benight, veil, conceal, blear, fog, nubilate, dim.

3. Shelter, protect, safeguard, harbor, foster, defend, keep safe, shield, screen, cover, secure, cloak, watch over, hover over, guard.

OVERSHOE, *n.* Shoe worn over another *(for protection, etc.)*, waterproof shoe, rubber, galosh, arctic, gum, rubber boot.

OVERSHOOT, *v.* Shoot *or* go over *or* beyond, shoot above, miss *(by shooting too high or too far)*, exceed the limit, exaggerate, overreach, overact, overplay, overdo, overleap, overjump, override, go too far, try too hard, overextend, overstretch, outreach.

OVERSIGHT, *n.* 1. Failure to notice *or* consider due to negligence *or* inadvertence, error, omission, slight, slip, mistake, blunder, neglect, inadvertency, miss, inattention, disregard, thoughtlessness, carelessness, heedlessness, stumble, accident, default, laxness, laxity, remissness, fault, nonobservance, inconsideration, aberration, trip, negligence.

2. Watchful care, supervision, charge, surveillance, ministry, ministration, jurisdiction, protection, patronage, heed, overlooking, watchfulness, watch, dominion, auspices, inspection, direction, management, superintendence, control, care, administration, command, guidance, regulation.

OVERSPREAD, *v.* Extend over, spread over, cover, film, overflow, wrap, enwrap, bespread, overlie, overlay, overcast, pervade, mantle, shroud, immantle, envelop, sheathe, encase, perfuse, coat, cloak.

OVERSTATE, *v.* Depict extravagantly, state extravagantly, hyperbolize, strain, aggravate, maximize, exaggerate, enlarge, overcolor, heighten, misrepresent, enhance, touch up *(coll.)*, overpicture, expand, magnify, color, stretch, overcharge, overdraw, overestimate, amplify.

OVERSTEP, *v.* Advance beyond proper limits,

encroach, infringe, transgress, violate, overrun, break in upon, accroach, trespass, intrude, invade, impinge, obtrude, usurp.

OVERSTOCK, *v.* Glut, overcharge, overfill, flood, surcharge, satiate, heap, overload, cram, crowd, overburden, overlade, oversupply.

OVERSTRUNG, *adj.* Highly strung, emotional, neurotic, nervous, over-sensitive, temperamental, hysterical, excitable.

OVERT, *adj.* In plain sight, easily seen, in full view, plain, manifest, public, open, noticeable, distinct, apparent, visible, patent, evident, palpable, disclosed, uncovered, undisguised, perspicuous, perceptible, seeable, revealed, unhidden, unconcealed, clear.

OVERTAKE, *v.* 1. Catch up with, come up beside, gain upon, attain, pass, overhaul, approach, arrive at, go *or* pass by, reach, run down, catch by chasing.

2. Come upon suddenly *(of night, storm, death, etc.)*, fall, befall, betide, beset, engulf, overwhelm, take by surprise, take off guard, astonish, strike, catch unprepared, surprise.

OVERTAX, *v.* Make too great demands on, impose too heavy a burden on, overdo, strain, fatigue, oppress, overtask, overwork, overlabor, overburden, bleed white, misuse, harass, flag, jade, wear out, drive, prostrate, fag, ill-use, abuse, weary, tire, exhaust, overweigh.

OVERTHROW, *n.* Deposition, destruction, ruin, defeat, downfall, rout, demolition, desolation, discomfiture, dispersion, undoing, prostration, subversion, debacle, collapse, perdition, reversal, confusion, beating, drubbing, consumption, havoc, ravage, wreck, waste, cataclysm, extinction, rebellion, mutiny, reverse, revolt, uprising, breakdown, breakup, upset, revolution, overset, overturn, eruption, upheaval, derangement, coup d'état, disestablishment, deathblow, crackup, catastrophe, insurgence, convulsion, insurrection, vanquishment, ruination, *bouleversement (Fr.),* abolition, reduction, dissolution, disorganization, overturn, inversion.

OVERTHROW, *v.* 1. Cast down *(as from a position of power),* vanquish, defeat, overcome, overpower, overwhelm, put an end to by force, confound, crush, subjugate, suppress, ravage, put down, bear down, prostrate, rout, beat, discomfit, master, worst, conquer, destroy, demolish, ruin, subvert, disorganize, annihilate, exterminate, do away with, refute, level, invalidate, reverse, confute, obviate, quash, break up, disrupt, shatter, smash, nullify, fell, wreck, reduce, fling *or* dash down, raze, tear down, extirpate, abolish, obliterate, quell, subdue, get the upper hand of, break, overmaster, thrash, be victorious over, whip, surmount.

2. Throw over, overturn, upset, overset, invert, subvert, tip over, capsize, spill, turn topsy-turvy, tumble, upend, reverse, precipitate, disarrange.

OVERTONE, *n.* 1. *(Acoustics)* Frequency higher than the fundamental, harmonic, harmonic tone *(Mus.),* upper partial tone *(Mus. and Acoustics).*

2. *(Usually pl.)* Additional meaning, implication, intimation, connotation, coloring, effect, force, insinuation, inference, innuendo, indication, signification, scent, hint, suggestion, allusion, tenor, drift, hidden meaning.

OVERTOP, *v.* 1. Rise above *or* over the top of, surpass in height, tower above, surmount, dominate, top, command, crown, beetle over, jut over, cap, look over, overlook, overshadow.

2. Rise above in authority, override, prevail over, exceed, overbear, have the advantage *or* ascendancy over, be superior to, take precedence over, preponderate, transcend, lead, control, override, subjugate, dominate, be master of, have the upper hand, excel, outshine, outdo, outluster, overshadow, surpass.

OVERTURE, *n.* 1. Formal offer, proposal, opening of negotiations, preliminary, proposition, tender, motion, invitation, advance, prelude, submission, suggestion, postulate, premise, presupposition, proffer, presentation, exordium.

2. Introductory part *(as in music, poetry, etc.),* prelude, prologue, foreword, preface, preamble, voluntary, prolegomenon, exordium, descant, introduction, proem, heading, beginning, ritornel *(Mus.),* protasis *(Ancient Drama).*

OVERTURN, *v.* 1. Destroy the power of, vanquish, defeat, overthrow, destroy, undo, ruin, topple, beat down, overcome, cast down, overpower, overwhelm, crush, confound, put an end to, subjugate, suppress, put down, prostrate, rout, beat, discomfit, worst, master, demolish, subvert, disorganize, annihilate, exterminate, refute, do away with, level, invalidate, confute, reverse, obviate, quash, break up, disrupt, shatter, smash, nullify, fell, wreck, reduce, fling *or* dash down, raze, tear down, extirpate, abolish, obliterate, quell, subdue, get the upper hand of, break, overmaster, be victorious over, whip, surmount.

2. Turn over on its side, face, *or* back, upset, capsize, invert, overset, overthrow, upturn, upend, disarrange, precipitate, reverse, tumble, topple, turn topsy-turvy, spill, tip over, subvert.

OVERVALUE, *v.* Value too highly, put too high a value on, overprize, overrate, overestimate, make too much of, exaggerate, overpraise, stretch, magnify, enhance, puff, attach too much importance to, overesteem, amplify, overlaud, dilate, flatter, embroider, color.

OVERWEENING, *adj.* Conceited, overconfident, presumptuous, haughty, proud, arrogant, egotistical, supercilious, vain, puffed up, vainglorious, overbearing, cavalier, lordly, assuming, opinionated, stiff-necked, disdainful, contumelious, boastful, high and mighty, swelled-headed, hoity-toity, patronizing, uppish *(coll.),* bloated with pride, pompous, high-handed, snotty *(sl.),* self-important, magisterial, peacockish, strutting, know-it-all, fanfaronading, swollen, gasconading, affected, contemptuous, consequential, condescending, arbitrary, domineering, commanding, dictatorial, insolent, prideful, inflated, belittling, slighting, withering, braggart, flaunting, self-complacent, imperious.

OVERWEIGH, *v.* 1. Exceed in weight, outweigh, overbalance, preponderate, outbalance, be heavier than.

2. Weigh down, oppress, overtax, overload, overburden, overtask, strain, overwork, prostrate, exhaust, flag, jade, fag, encumber, overwhelm, crush, saddle, stagger, bow down, overpower.

OVERWHELM, *v.* 1. Come, rest, *or* weigh upon overpoweringly, crush, weigh down, oppress, overtax, encumber, overweigh, burden, hamper, saddle, daze, awe-strike, stagger, confound, bewilder, stun, bowl over, bow down, swallow, engulf, astonish, prostrate, impose on.

2. Overcome, overbear, overpower, overthrow, overmatch, worst, ruin, grind, master, defeat, sup-

press, vanquish, subjugate, override, whelm, triumph over, destroy, conquer, crush, rout, beat, discomfit, confound, quell, subdue, extirpate, break down, worst, overmaster, quash, shatter, get the upper hand of, surmount, annihilate.

3. Load, heap, *etc.*, with an excessive *or* overpowering amount of anything, cover *or* bury beneath a mass of something, overflow, spread over, whelm, swamp, drown, swallow, submerge, deluge, immerse, bury, overlay, hide, plunge into, engulf, flood, inundate, glut, choke, suffocate, obstruct, overrun, overspread, infest.

OVERWHELMING, *adj.* That overwhelms, so great as to render opposition useless, overpowering, oppressive, crushing, prodigious, engulfing, inordinate, irresistible, profuse, cataclysmic, awful, stupendous, irrefutable, damning, monstrous, more than flesh and blood can bear, weighty, harrowing, unbearable, pernicious, wasting, severe, hurtful, harmful, grievous, afflictive, operose, formidable, unyielding, irksome, devouring, arduous, onerous, exhausting, unendurable, grinding, galling, inevitable, inescapable, uncontrollable, inexorable.

OVERWORK, *v.* 1. Cause to work too hard *or* too long, weary, exhaust, overdo, overtax, tire, strain, drive too hard, fag, overlabor, overburden, oppress, overtask, fatigue, bleed white, jade, wear out, prostrate.

2. Work up excessively, stir up, overstimulate, overexcite, incite, inflame, arouse, irritate, foment, infuriate, madden, intoxicate, goad, spur, prick, whip, lash, urge on, fan into flame, raise to fever heat, kindle, exacerbate, exasperate, impassion, quicken.

OVERWROUGHT, *adj.* 1. Wearied by overwork, exhausted, worn out, tired out, spent, played out, enfeebled, pegged out *(sl.)*, fagged out, all in, weary, drooping, on one's last legs, fatigued, ready to drop, bushed *(coll.)*, pooped *(sl.)*, winded, prostrate, overfatigued, haggard.

2. Overexcited, excessively stirred, high-strung, fiery, frenzied, delirious, carried away, distracted, wild-eyed, inflamed, agitated, flustered, ruffled, affected, perturbed, disturbed, hysterical, ebullient, wild, frantic, tempest-tossed, emotional, impassioned, over-sensitive, neurotic, nervous, touchy, irritable.

3. Elaborated excessively, overdone, overworked, lavish, profuse, high-flown, grandiloquent, pompous, showy, ostentatious, highly colored, extreme, rococo, florid, ornate, pretentious, flashy, flamboyant, sumptuous, rich, bedecked, fancy, elegant, festooned, garish, meretricious, gaudy, conspicuous, bespangled, orotund *(of style)*, rhetorical, baroque, ornamented, embellished, frilly.

OVOID, *adj.* Having the general form, shape *or* outline of an egg, egg-shaped, egg-like, oval, oviform, elliptical, elliptic, ellipsoidal, obovate, ovate, obovoid.

OWE, *v.* Be indebted, be under obligation, be in debt, have a loan from, be beholden to, be bound in gratitude.

OWING, *adj.* 1. Due to be paid, due, owed.

2. Due, ascribable, attributable, imputable, traceable, chargeable, deriving from, resulting from.

OWN, *v.* 1. Be in possession of, have, possess, have hold of, be in receipt of, be possessed of, retain, maintain, keep.

2. Concede, allow, acknowledge, yield, grant, acquiesce, consent, own the validity of, admit, disclose, avow, concur, tell, assent, recognize, profess.

OWNER, *n.* Possessor, holder, proprietor, landlord, proprietress *(Fem.)*, proprietrix *(Fem.)*, master, mistress, householder.

OX, *n.* Bovine quadruped, longhorn, shorthorn, steer, bull, bullock, zebu, buffalo, gelding, castrate.

P

PABULUM, *n.* Food, diet, nutrition, nutriment, nourishment, sustenance, sustentation, meat, bread, daily bread, meat and drink, alimentation, board, pap, support, foodstuff, eatables, eats *(sl.)*, supplies, provisions, provender, rations, mess, forage, fodder, fare, cheer *(coll.)*, grub, grubbery, chow, chuck, refection, keep, subsistence, table, groceries, feed, pasturage, fodder, pasture, grain, barley, oats, grass, corn, ensilage, silage, hay, straw, mash, swill.

PACE, *n.* 1. Step, stride, gait, walk, football, carriage, bearing, movement, motion, quick pace, quickstep, quick march, military march, hop, jump, goose step, striding, straddle, saunter, shuffle, shuffling, totter, stagger, mincing gait, amble, skip, jog, jogtrot, saunter, sauntering, strut, swagger, slouch, slink, skulk, prance, stalk, flounce, sashay *(coll.)*, hobble, limp, scuttle, roll, swing, tread.

2. Speed, velocity, rate of speed, celerity, swiftness, tread, hurry, dispatch, haste, rapidity, quickness, clip *(coll.)*, progress, lick *(coll.)*, lightning speed, expedition, rate.

3. Slow pace, snail's pace, slowness, slow motion, crawling, creep, crawl, slow time, dead march, dog trot, rack, amble, leisurely gait, tortoise's pace.

PACE, *v.* Travel, walk, stride, amble, pedestrianize, hoof it *(coll.)*, beat one's feet *(coll.)*, peg along, jog along, shuffle along, trot, trot along, amble, ambulate, track, pad, foot it, leg it, step, tread, go on foot, go afoot, travel afoot, stir one's stumps, march, mush *(coll.)*, stroll, saunter, traipse, shuffle, shamble, toddle, lunge, barge, hobble, totter, dodder, limp, claudicate, bowl along, bundle along, piaffe, piaffer, stalk, strut, swagger, trip, skip, trot, mince, sashay, creep, crawl, stump, stomp, stamp, pussyfoot *(sl.)*, tiptoe, promenade, take a walk, take a promenade, stretch one's legs, perambulate, circumambulate, hit the road, pound the pavement, jolt, swing, roll, roll along.

PACER, *n.* 1. Horse, racehorse, equine, steed, mount, hoss *(dial.)*, prad, garran, nag, dobbin, neigher, charger, courser.

2. Pacemaker, standard-bearer, standard, leader, criterion, measure, measuring stick.

PACHYDERMATOUS, *adj.* Thick-skinned, callous, hardened, insensate, unfeeling, numb, insentient, insensible, senseless, insensitive, unsensitive, imperceptient, imperceptive, proof, impervious, dull, inured, steeled against, tough, hard-boiled *(coll.)*, obdurate, seared.

PACIFIABLE, *adj.* Placable, appeasable, forgiving, peaceable, conciliable, pacificatory, propitiable, propitiatory.

PACIFIC, *adj.* Peaceful, calm, placid, tranquil, soothing, gentle, smooth, unruffled, quiet, still, temperate, untroubled, halcyon, meek, mild, restful, composed, easygoing, unwarlike, meek, irenical, pacificatory, propitiative, placating, peacemaking, peace-loving, peaceable, peaceful, mollifying, appeasing, conciliatine, conciliatory, tame, soft, bland, equable, cool, slow, sober, reasonable, lenient, not violent, peace-like, unpugnacious, unbelligerent, unbellicose, uncontentious, noncombative, noncombatant, pacifistic, neutral, at peace, bloodless, congenial, agreeable, concordant, compatible, fraternal, like-minded, of the same mind, accommodative, propitial, placative, placatory, mediatory, enduring, tolerant, unresistant, forbearant, longanimous, long-suffering, undisturbed, composed, unimpassioned, subdued, gentle, clement, mild, soft.

PACIFICATION, n. Tranquilization, accommodation, adjustment, peace, peacefulness, rest, tranquility, conciliation, propitiation, atonement, assuagement, reconcilement, modulation, abatement, mitigation, alleviation, quieting, mollification, mollifying, subduement, reduction, remission, relaxation, diminution, allaying, reunion, reunition, settlement, arbitration, compromise, terms, mediation, placation, truce, armistice, suspension of hostilities, treaty, convention, appeasement.

PACIFICATORY, adj. Peaceable, peaceful, peacemaking, pacifying, pacific, conciliatory, accommodative, propitiatory, propitiating, propitiative, placatory, placative, mediative, concordant, mediatorial, intermediatory, intercessory, interventional, intervening, negotiable, interlocutory, accordant, agreeable, congenial, compatible, reconcilable, harmonious, en rapport (Fr.), like-minded, of the same mind, amicable, friendly, amiable.

PACIFY, v. Reconcile, bring to terms, make peace, restore to friendship, restore harmony, bring peace, appease, placate, mollify, mitigate, assuage, propitiate, conciliate, reunite, heal the breach, settle differences, tranquilize, moderate, accord, mediate, pour oil on troubled waters, bridge over, bridge the gap, settle, mend, patch, repair the breach, adjust, accommodate, wave the white flag, declare an armistice, negotiate peace, temper, soften, attemper, lull, soothe, compose, quiet, alleviate, smother, appease, smooth over, reconcile, harmonize, render concordant, arrange, intercede, mediate, intervene, negotiate, straighten out, adjust differences, patch up, bring to terms, bring to an understanding, arbitrate, pour balm onto, alleviate, relieve, lessen, calm down, soften.

PACK, n. 1. Quantity, number, group, bunch, mass, plenty, multitude, large number, a number, cluster, clump, set, batch, lot, parcel, package, kit, accumulation, conglomeration, agglomeration, glomeration, aggregation, congeries, congregation, acervation, coacervation, amassment, accumulation, lump, gob (sl.), heap, collection, miscellany, assortment, variety.

2. Crowd, throng, multitude, covey, flock, herd, mob, rabble, shoal, school, rout, flight, swarm, pride, gaggle, nest, tribe, herd, drive, drove, kennel, array, bevy, galaxy.

3. Pack, deck (of cards.)

4. Knapsack, rucksack, bindle (sl.), luggage, impedimenta, equipment, kit, burden, load, trunk, grip, truss, valise, handbag, kit bag, suitcase, swag (coll.), bag.

PACK, v. 1. Cram, fill, stow, load, charge, lade, freight, weight, pile, stuff, wad, assemble, gather, bring together, cram, truss, tie up, tie together, bind, ship, pad.

2. Carry, transport, bear, haul, shoulder, tote,

convey, lug (coll.), back (sl.), hump (coll.), carry off, convoy, conduct, carry away, asport, vehiculate, vehicle, cart, sled, wagon, boat, ferry, whisk, waft.

3. Depart, depart with haste, leave, get away, break away, dash off, dash, hasten off, make off, convoy, conduct, carry away, asport, vehicuone's flight, take off (coll.), whip off, whip away, scamper off, scamper away, tear off, go off like a shot, go like a shot out of a gun, take to one's heels, beat a retreat, run for one's life, fly away, flit away, speed, move quickly, scoot, scour, haste, post, spank, make time, shoot, get out, get, git (coll.), step along, step on it (coll.).

PACKAGE, n. Kit, bundle, parcel, budget, pack, packet, fascine, bindle (sl.), wrap, wrapping, bale, seroon, fagot, truss, tuft.

PACKED, adj. Wrapped, done up, tied, tied up, bound, crowded, jammed, compact, solid, solidified, swarming, dense, close, tight, stuffed, full, ample, to capacity, replete, brimming, brimful, plenary, chuck-full, chock-full, bursting, busting (coll.), ready to burst, filled to capacity, oozing, overloaded, overfull, overcharged, drenched, saturated, supercharged, plethoric, gorged, engorged, stuffed, full to overflowing.

PACKET, n. 1. Package, parcel, bundle, bindle (coll.), wrap, wrapping, pack, packet, kit, bale, seroon, fagot, truss, tuft, budget.

2. Boat, vessel, steamer, steamship, steamboat, ferry, passenger vessel, transport, transport ship, ship, craft, watercraft, packet boat, packet ship, packet steamer, ocean packet, Channel packet, mailer, mail boat, post boat.

PACKHORSE, n. Beast of burden, pack animal, draft horse, draft animal, sumpter, sumpter horse, horse, equine, garran, nag, dobbin.

PACKING, n. 1. Stowage, lading, dunnage, filling, ballast, contents, stuffing, padding, wadding, cargo, freight, bale, burden, load, lug (coll.), burthen (coll.).

2. Stopper, stopping, padding, stuffing, filling, wadding.

PACKSADDLE, n. Basto, kyack (U.S.), aparejo, saddle.

PACT, n. Compact, treaty, contract, agreement, dicker, bargain, understanding, paction, protocol, covenant, deed, bond, alliance, convention, concordat, concordance, security, paper, instrument, articles.

PACTION, n. Pact, compact, treaty, contract, agreement, dicker, bargain, understanding, protocol, covenant, deed, bond, alliance, convention, concordat, concordance, security, paper, instrument, article, articles.

PAD, n. 1. Horse, padnag, nag, hoss (dial.), equine, dobbin, steed.

2. Cushion, bolster, pillow, bed, bedding, mattress, feather bed, padding, wadding, cushioning, upholstery.

3. Pocketbook, notebook, memorandum book, desk pad, memo pad, tablet, blankbook, blotter, album.

4. Print, track, footprint, spoor, footstep, footmark, step, trail, mark, scent, trace, ichnite.

5. Leaf, foliage, dendron, leafage, foliation, frondescence.

6. Foot, paw, extremity, hoof, pedal extremity, trotter, pud (coll.), forefoot, hindfoot.

PADDING, n. 1. Filling, packing, ballast, contents,

stuffing, cargo, burden, load, burthen (coll.), lading, stoping, stuffing, wadding.

2. Diffuseness, verbosity, verbiage, tautology, prolixity, tautophony, tautologism, pleonasm, perissology, macrology, wordiness, exuberance, extravagance, circumlocution, dilogy, superfluousness, superfluity, battology, redundancy, redundance, superabundance, exorbitancy, exorbitance, surplusage, surplus, surfeit, glut, glut of words, surfeit of words.

PADDLE, v. 1. Ply the oar, row, scull, pull, punt, propel, drive.

2. Splash, plash, dabble, stir, slop.

3. Chastise, beat, whip, punish, flog, tan (coll.).

PADDLE, n. Oar, sweep, scull, pole.

PADDOCK, n. Enclosure, yard, stockyard, corral, pen, fold, confine, barnyard, pound, curtilage.

PADLOCK, n. Lock, fastening, closure, fastener, holdfast, latch.

PADRE, n. Priest, man of God, chaplain, clergyman, father, man of prayer, divine, minister, parson, monk, gospel-monger, sky pilot (sl.), cleric, churchman, preacher, ecclesiastic, revivalist, black-coat, reverend (coll.), clerk, cleric, clerk in holy orders, hierophant, presbyter, abuna, father in Christ.

PADRONE, n. 1. Master, host, innkeeper, hotelier, operator, proprietor, owner, landlord, proprietary, innholder, restaurateur.

2. Master, authority, seigneur, signior, headman, head, governor, overlord, ruler, superior, dean, lord, lord and master, captain, chief, big chief, sachem.

PAEAN, n. Hymn, praise, hymn of joy, hymn of praise, hymn of triumph, exultation, rejoicing, jubilation, celebration, ovation, salute, Te Deum, halleluiah, alleluia, hosanna, laud, glorification, doxology, psalm, motet, anthem, glory, laudation, magnification.

PAGAN, n. Heathen, non-believer, paynim, non-Christian, non-Jew, giaour (Turk.), infidel, atheist, disbeliever, idolator, skeptic, doubter, doubting Thomas, antichrist, antichristian, heretic, freethinker, agnostic, pantheist, animist, scoffer, irreligionist, misbeliever, dubitant, nihilist, gentile, worldling, earthling, Pyrrhonist, latitudinarian, minimifidian, sinner, wrongdoer, malefactor, idolizer, fetishist, idol worshiper, zoolater, animal worshiper, pyrolater, fire worshiper, sun worshiper, heliolater, star worshiper, heterodox, idolatrizer, demon worshiper, devil worshiper.

PAGAN, adj. Heterodox, unorthodox, heathen, heathenish, unchristian, antichristian, unenlightened, gentile, paynim, pantheist, pantheistic, animist, animistic, polytheist, polytheistic, idolatrous, paganistic, paganish, fetishist, idolatric, idolatrical, demonolatrous.

PAGANISM, n. Paganry, heathenism, pagandom, mythology, mythicism, animism, henotheism, ditheism, dualism, pantheism, theopantism, cosmotheism, idolatry, non-belief, disbelief, non-Christianity, infidelity, infidelism, skepticism, doubt, antichristianity, heresy, freethinking, agnosticism, dubitantism, nihilism, gentilism, worldliness, Pyrrhonism, latitudinarianism, minimifidianism, idol worship, demonism, demon worship, devil worship, zoolatry, animal worship, sun worship, heliolatry, fire worship, pyrolatry, heterodoxy, heathenry, animatism, sinning, sin, fetishism.

PAGE, n. 1. Boy, boy-servant, attendant, bellboy, bellhop (coll.), henchman, footboy, lackey, call boy, servant, servant boy, serving boy, usher, cup-bearer, squire, trainbearer, retainer, follower, ghillie (Scot.), employee, employe, buttons (coll.), tiger (sl.), valet, valet de chambre (Fr.), messenger, runner, flunky, garçon (Fr.), slavey (coll.), menial, servitor, hireling, waiter, office boy, chokra (Ind.), caddie, bootlick, boots (coll.).

2. Printed page, copy, type page, typescript, leaf, folio, sheet, fly leaf, recto, verso, title page, endpaper, paper.

PAGE, v. 1. Call, summon, find, locate, call out,

2. Paginate, leaf, leaf over, turn over, foliate, affix numbers to, number, number the pages of, mark the pages of.

PAGEANT, n. Pageantry, spectacle, view, scene, display, exposition, exhibition, exhibit, panorama, diorama, ostentation, ostentatious display, extravaganza, procession, show, gala, parade, float, ceremony, ritual, rite, pomp, sight.

PAGEANTRY, n. Spectacle, display, ostentation, ostentatiousness, pomp, ritual, extravagance, show, showiness, fuss, magnificence, flair, flourish, revel, revelry, glitter, festivity, array, splash (sl.), splurge, showing off (coll.), state, splendor, grandeur, grand array, grand display, dignity.

PAH!, interjection Bah!, faugh!, pfui!, fooey!, foh!, ugh!, ah!, ach!

PAID, adj. Bribed, suborned, mercenary, greased (coll.), anointed (coll.), hired, subsidized, bought, bought off, tampered with, corrupt, crooked, dishonest, approached.

PAIL, n. Container, receptacle, bucket, bail, bowie, piggin, tub, dipper, utensil, tool, implement.

PAIN, n. 1. Physical pain, bodily pain, suffering, hurt, ache, smart, twinge, pinch, gripe, nip, squeeze, gripes, colic, seizure, cramps, paroxysm, throe, convulsion, eclampsia (Med.), shooting, crick, stitch, laryngismus (Med.), throb, palpitation, throbbing, childbirth, labor pangs, pangs, parturition, labor, childbed, travail, discomfort, distress, sharp pain, piercing pain, stabbing pain, gnawing pain, sore, burning pain, grinding, grinding pain, aching, headache, cephalalgy, cephalalgia, migraine, hemicrania, megrim, earache, otalgia, backache, lumbago, smarting, tingle, tingling, stomach ache, bellyache, bends, caisson disease (Med.), neuralgia, ischialgia, rheumatism, tic douloureux (Fr.), arthritis, gout, podagra, torture, torment, lancination, anguish, cruciation, rack, martyrdom, hell on earth, agony.

2. Mental suffering, suffering, aggravation (coll.), annoyance, passion, ache, trial, pang, dolor, bale, grief, woe, agony, anguish, care, anxiety, worry, cark (arch.), ordeal, trouble, blow, fret, burden, shock, load, cross, affliction, bitterness, heartache, broken-heartedness, heavy heart, bleeding heart, misery, infelicity, unhappiness, despondency, slough of despond, wretchedness, tribulation, desolation, extremity, depths of despair, nightmare, ephialtes, incubus, prostration, uneasiness, disquiet, disquietude, sorrow, chagrin, vexation, ordeal, fiery ordeal, disquiet, discomposure, mortification, bother, botherment, pother, cruciation, crucifixion, purgatory, hell, hell on earth, worriment, visitation, curse, cross, thorn in one's side, crown of thorns, bitter cup, trials and tribulations, gall, gall and wormwood, nuisance, pest, grievance.

PAIN, v. 1. Wound, lacerate, hurt, gall, cut, sting, stab, grate, torture, rack, corrode, bite, agonize, wring, convulse, torture, torment, harrow, flog, abuse, maltreat, smite, assail, afflict, distress, lancinate, cut up, excruciate, martyr, martyrize, gripe, gnaw, bite, chafe, fret, gall, burn, injure, harm, scathe, cripple, disable, impair.

2. Vex, annoy, worry, fret, gall, disquiet, trouble, afflict, aggrieve, grieve, sadden, displease, bore, harass, tease, incommode, distress, torture, torment, cruciate, crucify, vivisect, distress, displease, discommode, faze, cut to the quick, cut to the heart, bite, snap at, assail, pierce, cut, stab, pester, plague, molest, tantalize, bullyrag, pother, bother, trouble, disturb, agitate, grate, grate on the feelings, jar on the feelings, harry, heckle, bait, martyr, martyrize, exasperate, try one's patience, pique, rile, roil, affront, harrow, agonize.

PAINED, adj. 1. Afflicted, seized, tweaked, pierced, chafed, raw, pricked, stabbed, excruciated, crucified, tortured, tormented, burning, burnt, stung, wounded, wrung, convulsed, martyred, martyrized, agonized, in a state of pain, hurt, in pain, hurting, on the rack, torminal, torminous, suffering.

2. Disquieted, ill-at-ease, suffering, excoriated, chafed, galled, nettled, on the rack, uneasy, uncomfortable, discontented, weary, disturbed, perturbed, uneasy, aroused, agitated, excited, unhappy, infelicitous, poor, miserable, wretched, woebegone, unfortunate, cheerless, heartsick, comfortless, heavy-hearted, heavy-laden, doomed, dejected, careworn, lost, stranded, crushed, ill-used, victimized, accursed, sorrowful, aggrieved, grieving, sad, morose, melancholy, mournful, horrorstruck, horror-stricken, chagrined, horrified, heartbroken, stricken, broken-hearted, dismal, sorry, gloomy, displeased, angered, disappointed.

PAINFUL, adj. 1. Aching, afflictive, hurtful, pained, sore, severe, raw, throbbing, palpitating, biting, oppressive, pestiferous, pestering, harassing, sharp, poignant, racking, distressing, distressful, hurtful, dolorous, consuming, corroding, biting, pungent, piercing, sharp, caustic, burning, tormentive, dolorific, dolorifical, smarting, stinging, tingling, grievous.

2. Unpleasant, grievous, irritating, insufferable, shocking, odious, disastrous, piteous, distressing, deplorable, pitiful, lamentable, dismal, disheartening, rueful, sad, affecting, moving, touching, pathetic, dreary, melancholy, unpleasing, disagreeable, unpalatable, displeasing, unwelcome, bitter, distasteful, uninviting, undesirable, unacceptable, unsatisfactory, annoying, aggravating (coll.), disquieting, disturbing, perturbing, tiresome, irksome, onerous, heavy, ponderous, weighty, vexatious, vexing, troublesome, troublous, galling, exasperating, oppressive, pestiferous, pestering, harassing, worrying, worrisome, tormenting, burdensome, cumbrous, intolerable, insupportable, unbearable, unendurable, ruinous, calamitous, disastrous, tragic, tragical, desolating, withering, unfortunate, hapless, unhappy, unfelicitous, infelicitous, destructive, ill-starred, inauspicious, unpropitious, untoward, disgusting, hateful, revolting, nauseating, execrable, repellent, repulsive, nasty, loathsome, vile, horrid, horrible, hideous.

3. Toilsome, hard, difficult, arduous, wearisome, severe, burdensome, onerous, heavy, hefty (coll.), tough (coll.), troublesome, troublous, uphill, hard-earned, hard-fought, hard-won, operose, strenuous, irksome, demanding, formidable, beset with difficulties, thorny, spiny, knotty, knotted, easier said than done (coll.), sooner said than done (coll.), delicate, ticklish, risky, critical, nice, exacting.

PAINS, n. Trouble, difficulty, labor, toil, effort,

diligence, care, laboriousness, troublesomeness, toilsome effort, special care, special consideration, special attention, deep study, close study, thought, labored attention, labored study, observant care, diligent care, carefulness, serious attention, exertion, struggle, effort, strain, stress, stress and strain.

PAINSTAKING, adj. Careful, heedful, diligent, earnest, attentive, sedulous, assiduous, laborious, hard-working, persevering, sparing no pains, strenuous, zealous, precise, scrupulous, thorough, thoroughgoing, plodding, regardful, energetic, never-tiring, untiring, operose, elaborate, industrious, particular.

PAINT, n. 1. Coloring, oil paint, oils, water paint, water colors, dry water colors, moist water color, coat, coating, coat of paint, calcimine, primer, priming, priming coat, undercoat, first coat, lacquer, lac, shellac, clear lacquer, orange shellac, white shellac, varnish, megilph, japan, ground, ground coat, flat coat, copaline, copalite, enamel, glaze, flat wash, fresco.

2. Cosmetics, lip rouge, lipstick, rouge, powder, makeup, facial makeup, greasepaint, liner (theatrical), base, mascara, eyeshadow, eye-makeup, pancake makeup (cant).

PAINT, v. 1. Color, daub, coat, veneer, cover, face, bedaub, besmear, gloss, glaze, enamel, varnish, shellac, lacquer, flat, prime, undercoat, decorate, colorize, apply color, hue, parget, gild, apply gilt, shade, shadow.

2. Apply cosmetics, apply makeup, makeup, rouge.

3. Represent, represent by paints, represent by colors, limn, delineate, draw, depict, describe, picture, picturize, portray, set forth, register, make a portrait, illustrate, elucidate, draw a picture, paint a picture, convey in oils, convey in paint, hit a likeness, catch a likeness.

PAINTABLE, adj. Colorable, describable, fait à peindre (Fr.), picturesque, pictorial, pictury, limnable.

PAINTER, n. Artist, portrait artist, landscape artist, portrayer, picturist, picturer, limner, delineator, oil colorist, water colorist, oil painter, impressionist, neoimpressionist, copyist, modernist, futurist, Dadaist, surrealist, cubist, expressionist, Fauvist, vorticist, academician, classicist, neoclassicist, dilettante, dabbler, dauber, miniaturist, caricaturist, landscapist, portraitist, miniature, painter, cartoonist, satirist, scene painter, marine painter, nature painter, flower painter, historical painter, still-life painter, trompe-l'oeil painter, naturalist, realist, romanticist, genre painter, pleinarist, enameler, enamelist, master, old master, muralist, frescoist, fresco painter, mural painter, wall painter.

PAINTING, n. 1. Scene, oil painting, water color, aquarelle, still-life painting, marine painting, portrait, interior painting, fresco, mural, wall painting, scene painting, landscape painting, encaustic, encaustic painting, grisaille, picture, canvas, delineation, pictorialization, depiction, representation, gouache, tempera, pastiche, miniature, silhouette, mosaic, stained glass painting, tomb painting, funerary painting, caricature, batik, tapestry, study, sketch, oil sketch, still life, trompe l'oeil (Fr.), head, bust, heroic painting, cartoon, image, likeness, scene, view, prospect, landscape, waterscape, seascape, seapiece, cloudscape, panorama, diorama, cyclorama, exterior, interior, riverscape, perspective view, likeness, copy, imitation, fake, graphic art, design, limnery, iconography, iconograph, icon (ikon), decoration, ornament, composition, conception, treatment, arrangement, work of art, piece, work, study, masterpiece, masterwork, brainchild, production, creation, tableau, perspective.

2. *(Styles)* Classicism, neoclassicism, romanticism, academism, impressionism, neoimpressionism, cubism, Fauvism, surrealism, superrealism, naturalism, genre, ornamentalism, idealism, pointillism, symbolism, expressionism Dadaism, vorticism, futurism, modernism, post-impressionism, eclecticism, naturalism.

3. Coloring, coloration, pigmentation, tinction.

PAIR, *n.* Couple, brace, span, yoke, team, duo, twosome, combination, collaboration, two, couplet, match, dyad, duad, twins, pair of twins, conjugation, tandem, married couple, wedded couple, wedded pair.

PAIR, *v.* 1. Unite in pairs, combine, unite, coalesce, pair off, bracket, couple, couple up, copulate, mate, match, conduplicate, league, confederate, associate, fraternize, ally, form an alliance, join, join with, hook up with *(coll.)*, partner, go into partnership, enter into partnership, team with, team, team up with *(coll.)*, cooperate, join with, join forces.

2. Marry, be married, get married, marry with, wed, nuptialize, conjoin, conjugate, wive, take to wife, be made one, pair off, intermarry, interwed, get hitched *(sl.)*, be spliced *(coll.)*.

PAL, *n.* Friend, associate, confederate, intimate, confidant, chum *(coll.)*, playmate, buddy *(coll.)*, crony, mate, companion, partner, brother, accomplice, fellow, consociate, connate, comrade, consort, compeer, copartner, side-partner, sidekick *(sl.)*, bedfellow, roommate, classmate, schoolmate, schoolfellow, bunkmate, bunkie *(sl.)*, fellow worker, playfellow, colleague, collaborator, best man, workfellow, benchmate, yokefellow, boon companion.

PAL, *v. Colloq.* Consort with, associate with, buddy up with *(sl.)*, socialize, ingratiate, be sociable, consociate with, sort with, mix with, mingle with, travel with, club together, keep company with, be seen with, fraternize, intercommunicate, be friendly with, move hand in hand with, have the friendship of, be acquainted with, have the ear of, take up with *(coll.)*, get in the good graces of, be chummy with *(coll.)*, be intimate with, be close with, be close to, hold the confidence of, fraternalize.

PALACE, *n.* Mansion, castle, palatial house, palatial residence, kingly house, kingly residence, great house, royal residence, royal house, stately house, stately mansion, dwelling, house, structure, building, edifice, *château (Fr.)*.

PALADIN, *n.* Advocate, defender, champion, knight-errant, vindicator, hero, fighter, combatant, contestant, disputant, contender, jouster, knight, brave, chevalier, *chevalier sans peur et sans reproche (Fr.)*, demigod, Don Quixote, Lancelot, Galahad, daredevil, brave man.

PALATABLE, *adj.* Agreeable, tasty, delicious, delectable, good, good-tasting, edible, potable, eatable, digestible, succulent, tasteful, sweet-tasting, flavorful, good-flavored, drinkable, relishable, tangy, zestful, piquant, flavorsome, pleasant, nice *(coll.)*, nectarean, gustful, savory, ambrosial, appetizing, pleasing, luscious, toothsome, delectable, exquisite, well-prepared, well-cooked, fit for a king, delicate, dainty, saporous, saporific, mouth-

watering, tempting, tantalizing, rich, rich-flavored, lickerish, liquorish, spicy, tender.

PALATE, *n.* 1. Roof of the mouth, soft palate, hard palate, pharynx, epiglottis, glottal region.

2. Taste, savor, sapidity, tongue, tooth, stomach, gusto, zest, appetite, appetency, gustation.

PALATIAL, *adj.* Stately, magnificent, grand, large, commodious, capacious, roomy, elegant, ornate, massive, splendid, imposing, pretentious, showy, ostentatious, ritzy *(coll.)*, high-toned *(coll.)*, lofty, tall, stylish, modish, fashionable, luxurious, majestic, sumptuous.

PALATINATE, *n.* Country, state, region, realm, domain, territory, province, county palatine, palatine state.

PALATINE, *n.* Officer, royal official, chamberlain, mayor of the palace, minister, royal minister, chief minister, lord, count palatine, earl palatine.

PALAVER, *n.* 1. Gabble, jargon, hash, nonsense, babble, twaddle, balderdash, stuff, stuff and nonsense, tripe, claptrap, hogwash, eyewash, wishwash, flummery, gibberish, rigmarole, prating, senselessness, senseless talk, idle talk, cajolery, blarney, gassing *(sl.)*, babblement, babbling, stultiloquence, voluble nonsense, jabber, jabberwocky, gibberish, patter, amphigory, fustian, rodomontade, drivel, drool, slaver, bombast, rant, blab *(sl.)*, poppycock, rubbish, trash, rot, fudge, bosh, fiddle-faddle, truck, flummadiddle, froth, air, mere air, wind, foolishness, absurdity, buncombe, gibble-gabble, flummery, trumpery, flapdoodle, loquaciousness, loquacity, garrulity.

2. Speech, talk, utterance, chin music *(coll.)*, verbal discourse, verbal communication, verbal intercourse, oral communication, word of mouth, words, conversation, collocution, colloquy, conference, communion, communication, chatting, verbal commerce, parley, confabulation, discussion, council, consultation, exchange of views, powwow *(U.S.)*, audience, audition, interview, meeting, gathering, hearing, session.

PALAVER, *v.* 1. Talk nonsense, babble, gabble, twaddle, twaddleize, gibble-gabble, gab, bibble-babble, prate, patter, prattle, rattle, run at the mouth, gush, flow, clack, gas *(sl.)*, rant, rodomontade, slaver, utter, drivel, mean nothing, speak without meaning, chatter, shoot off one's mouth *(sl.)*, spout, pour forth, talk another to death, talk another deaf and dumb, maunder, ramble, rant, expatiate.

2. Converse, confer, meet, talk, exchange views, discourse with, speak with, parley, chat, hold conversation, carry on a conversation, commune with, bandy words, have a talk with, chew the rag *(coll.)*, chew the fat *(coll.)*, dialogue, hold conference, consult, put heads together, counsel, advise, powwow, go into a huddle, discuss with, take up with, commerce with.

PALE, *n.* 1. Post, upright, paling, palisade.

2. Enclosure, fence, barrier, closure, close, pen, fold, confine, boundary, limit, palisade, palisado, outline, contour, delineation, lines, bounds, lineaments, circumference, border line, border land, edge, brink, verge, brow, brim, rim, bordure, confines, confine, hedge, skirt, frontier, outpost.

3. Region, area, realm, compass, quarter, part, territory, circuit, ambit, ground, soil, land, vicinity, vicinage, dominion, division, compartment, hemisphere, sphere, range, orb, orbit, precinct, province, premises, confines, field, quarter, section, demesne, purlieus.

4. Limit, uttermost, bourne, bound, bounds,

termination, terminal, end, terminus, marches, boundary line, landmark, line of demarcation, period, mark, march.

PALE, *v.* 1. Blanch, fade, grow dim, dim, dusken, darken, flicker, glimmer, lose color, become colorless, turn pale, decolor, dull, whiten, wan, vanish, fly, go, fade out, fade away, tone down, wash out, bleach, discolor, discolorate, etiolate, achramatize, change color.

2. Fear, grow pale, be afraid, have qualms, dread, stand aghast, start, apprehend, shy, fight shy, grow pale, turn pale, take alarm, flinch, wince, falter, hesitate, hang back.

PALE, *adj.* 1. Ashen, ashy, ash-colored, leaden, pallid, dull, wan, bloodless, bleached, etiolated, drained of blood, drained, blanched, colorless, dun-colored, whey-faced, sickly, sickly-looking, sick-looking, light, wannish, lurid, sallow, cadaverous, deathly pale, peaked, faded, ghastly, ghostlike, tallow-faced, death-like, unhealthy, unwholesome, anemic, colorless, hueless, achromatic, haggard, drab, lifeless, glassy, lackluster, greenish, chlorotic, white.

2. Dim, faint, obscure, indistinct, faded, washed out, uncertain, hazy, foggy, nebulous, nubilose, vague, dimmish, dimmed, indefinite, unclear, invisible, undefined, ill-defined, shadowy, blurred, blurry, mysterious.

PALEFACE, *n.* White man, Caucasian, Xanthochroid.

PALENESS, *n.* Achromatism, colorlessness, dimness, obscureness, obscurity, pallor, pallidness, etiolation, anemia, indistinctness, fulginosity.

PALEOLOGIST, *n.* Archaeologist, antiquary, antiquarian, historian, scholar, student, medievalist, classicist, expert, archist, archivist.

PALEOLOGY, *n.* Archaism, medievalism, antiquarianism, archaeology, paleontology, fossilology, paleography, paleotypography, palesophy, paleanthropography, paleanthropology, paleobiology, paleobotany, paleochorology, paleocosmology, paleoclimatology, paleodendrology, paleogeography, paleoherpetology, paleohistology, paleohydrography, paleolatry, paleolimnology, paleolithy, paleometeorology, paleopathology, paleophysiography, paleophysiology, paleophytology, paleopotamology, paleopsychology, paleozoology, paleoecology.

PALESTRA, PALAESTRA, *n.* 1. Athletics, calisthenics, athleticism, gymnastics, acrobatics, agonistics, exercise.

2. Gymnasium, stadium, sports arena, athletic field, field, football field, bowl.

PALESTRAL, *adj.* Athletic, gymnastic, acrobatic, calisthenic, agonistical, agonistic, schoolish, scholastic, scholastical, academic, institutional, gymnasial, palestrian.

PALETOT, *n.* Garment, outer garment, coat, outercoat, surcoat, topcoat, overcoat, greatcoat, surtout.

PALFREY, *n.* Horse, equine, steed, mount, padnag, doddin, neigher *(coll.)*, riding horse, saddle horse, saddler, remount.

PALIMPSEST, *n.* *Codex rescriptus (Lat.),* writing, rewriting, manuscript, written matter, inscription, re-inscription, piece, scroll, paper, document, script, scrip, scription, rewrite, overwriting.

PALINDROME, *n.* Word play, play upon words, reversible term, conceit, trick, play.

PALING, *n.* Enclosure, fence, pale, barrier, clo-

sure, close, pen, fold, confine, boundary, limit, palisade, palisado, outline, contour, delineation, lines, bounds, lineaments, circumference, border line, border, borderland, edge, brink, verge, brow, brim, rim, bordure, confines, hedge, skirt, frontier, outpost.

PALINODE, *n.* Tergiversation, recantation, retraction, withdrawal, contradiction, change of mind, recreancy, repudiation, forswearing, disavowal, renunciation, backsliding, recidivism, rejection, retractation, renouncement, revokement, abjuration, palinody, abjurement, disclaimer, disclamation, relinquishment.

PALISADE, *n.* 1. Fence, enclosure, barrier, closure, close, confine, limit, frontier, outpost, confines, defense, stockade, barricade, defense, fortification, bulwark, rampart.

2. Cliff, precipice, steep cliff, escarpment, scarp, bluff, wall, vertical drop.

PALL, *n.* Shroud, graveclothes, cerements, cerecloth, winding sheet, covering, concealment.

PALL, *v.* Weary, cloy, sicken, satiate, glut, surfeit, sate, gorge, fill to repletion, accloy, jade, satisfy, overdose, overgorge, overfeed, spoil, saturate, fill, bore.

PALLADIUM, *n.* Safeguard, refuge, safety device, safety appliance, bulwark, security, cloak, defense, fence, wall, guard, shield, protection, protector.

PALLET, *n.* Bed, couch, cot, litter, berth, bunk, doss, day bed, trundle bed, feather bed, duster bed, stretcher, mattress, paillasse, under-bed, underbedding.

PALLIATE, *v.* Soften, extenuate, varnish, gloss, smooth over, allay, ease, assuage, moderate, alleviate, relieve, lessen, quell, still, quiet, remedy, exonerate, veneer, glaze, mince, whitewash, abate, dull, mitigate, soothe, blunt, exculpate, gild, color, diminish, temper, make light of, justify, dulcify, lenify, sheathe, tranquilize, lull, appease, compose, cool, hush, slake, smother, slacken, still, subdue, chasten, obtund, take the edge off, tame, lay, damp, dampen, salve, pour balm on, lessen, excuse.

PALLIATION, *n.* Deliverance, relief, mitigation, alleviation, softening, easement, allayment, subduement, moderation, extenuation, apology, varnish, excuse, gloss, gloss over, extenuation, whitewashing, allowance, extenuating circumstances, glossing over, vindication, exculpation, exoneration, abatement, diminution, assuagement, relaxation, tranquilization, pacification, sedative, sedation, tempering.

PALLIATIVE, *n.* Alleviative, abirritant, sedative, lenitive, anodyne, calmative, emollient, demulcent, balm, assuasive, unguent, oil, liniment, anointment, drug, opiate, narcotic, dope *(sl.),* softener, softening agent, relief, relieving agent, analgesic, pain-killer, temperer, modulator, assuager, anaesthetic, hypnotic, anaesthetic agent.

PALLID, *adj.* Wan, pale, ashen, deathy, deathlike, colorless, white, gray, dim, sallow, pale as death, pale as ashes, pale as a ghost, white as a sheet, white as a ghost, ghostlike, ghastly, lurid, haggard, sickly, greenish, green, leaden, drab, cold, pale as a corpse, of a sickly hue.

PALLIUM, *n.* Pall, covering, cover, cloak, mantle, vestment, altar cloth, canonicals, robe.

PALLOR, *n.* Wanness, paleness, sickliness, bloodlessness, ghastliness, pallidity, etiolation, colorlessness, deathliness, whiteness, grayness, ashenness.

PALM, *n.* 1. Victor's token, laurels, trophy, prize, token of honor, token of victory, crown, laurel crown, laurel wreath, bays, bay-leaf crown, garland, chaplet, badge, mark of honor, feather in one's cap, decoration, ornament, award, reward.

2. Hand, paw, fist, fingers, digits.

3. Tree, timber, plant, spermatophyta, spermatophyte, seed plant, endogene, wood.

PALM, *v.* 1. Conceal, seize, take surreptitiously, hide (in the hand), steal, thieve, purloin, snatch, make off with, cabbage, pilfer, pinch, mooch *(sl.),* burgle, abstract, take, take away, snitch *(sl.),* filch, snare, cop *(sl.).*

2. Bribe, suborn, reach *(sl.),* grease the palm, oil the palm, tickle the palm, square *(sl.),* sugar *(sl.),* buy, buy off, purchase, corrupt, tamper with.

PALMATE, *adj.* Toothed, dentate, scalloped, lobed, hand-shaped, notched, nicked, serrated, serriform, escalloped, jagged, jaggy.

PALMIST, *n.* Chiromancer, chiromant, fortune-teller, palmister, forecaster, prophet, soothsayer, divinator, diviner, clairvoyant, foreseer, foreteller.

PALMISTRY, *n.* Chiromancy, pythonism, divining, divination, foretelling, forecasting, prophecy, prophesying, forecast, prediction, presagement, presage, foreknowledge, prognostication, hariolation, soothsaying, fortunetelling, omen.

PALMY, *adj.* Peaceful, sunny, calm, auspicious, prosperous, fortunate, bright, happy, enjoyable, halcyon, golden, pleasurable, pleasant, mirthful, bewitching, joyous, hilarious, lucky, cheering, cheerful, exhilarating, entrancing, delightful, propitious, of good omen, rosy, promising, halcyonic, thriving, carefree, Saturnian, blithe, blithesome, cheerly, cheery, jaunty, debonair, riant, buoyant, bright, easy, airy, optimistic, spirited, lively, animated, merry, laughing, joyful, breezy, free and easy, spry, sunny.

PALP, *n.* Feeler, antenna, tactile organ, organ of touch, palpus.

PALPABLE, *adj.* 1. Real, material, concrete, substantial, tactile, touchable, corporeal, sensible, corporal, materiate, fleshly, bodily, ponderable, hylic, tangible, parenchymatous, parenchymatic, parenchymal, bodily, somatic, somatical, incarnate, embodied, tactual, actual, factual.

2. Plain, manifest, obvious, apparent, clear, visible, patent, glaring, intelligible, easily seen, gross, unmistakable, self-evident, prominent, salient, open, striking, conspicuous, perceptible, discernible, perceivable, explicit, distinct, barefaced, unequivocal, unequivocable, indubitable, axiomatic, flagrant, undoubtable, definite, recognizable, autoptical, autoptic, plain as day, plain as a pikestaff, in bold relief, bold, in plain sight, pronounced, avowed, ostensible, seeable, observable, express, expressed, noticeable, naked, overt, open-and-shut, distinct, definite, revealed, unhidden, unobscured, unhid, unshaded, uncovered, unscreened, unveiled, unshrouded, uncurtained, manifestive, demonstrative, flagrant, arrant, flaming, flaunting, showy.

PALPATE, *v.* Handle, touch, feel, finger, paw, palm, thumb, caress, massage, rub, stroke, knead, manipulate, contact.

PALPATION, *n.* Feeling, handling, massage, rubbing, touch, contact, tangency, tangence, impact, feel, caress, rub, kneading, taction, sensation, stereognosis, stroke, stroking.

PALPITANT, *adj.* Pulsating, pulsing, beating, throbbing, agitated, agitnat, fluttering, twittering,

flickering, unquiet, disquieted, discomposed, disconcerted, turbulent, excited, shaking, tremulous, pulsative, pulsatory, pitapat, vibrant, vibrative, vibratory.

PALPITATE, *v.* Beat, throb, pulsate, pant, pulse, go pitapat, drum, flutter, tick, tremble, shake, vibrate, quiver, quaver, pound, beat, patter, thrum, shiver, quake.

PALPITATION, *n.* Throbbing, fluttering, beating, pulsation, pulsating, pulsing, throb, pitapat, drumming, flitter, flicker, flutter, pitter-patter, beat, fluster, trepidation, perturbation, disturbance, agitation, trembling, tremble, turbulency, turbulence, disquietude, disquiet, tremor, twitter, twittering, ferment, fermentation, commotion, pother, bother, stew, unrest, restlessness, nervousness, throbbing heart, heart quaking.

PALPUS, *n.* Feeler, antenna, organ of touch, tactile organ, palp.

PALSIED, *adj.* 1. Quaking, shaking, trembling, uncontrolled, disabled, impotent, paralyzed, weak, debilitated, atonic, paralytic, enfeebled, helpless, defenseless, palsy-stricken, diseased, vitiated.

2. Undecisive, irresolute, vacillating, tergiversating, shilly-shallying, unresolved, infirm of purpose, purposeless, hesitant, hesitating, vacillant, vacillatory, of two minds, undecided, fickle, unstable, variable, tremulous, doubtful, dubitant, doubting, irresolved, undependable.

PALSY, *n.* Paralysis, disability, numbness, helplessness, spastic paralysis, impotence, impotency, unsoundness, insensibility, physical insensibility, motor paralysis, sensory paralysis, general paralysis, incomplete paralysis, general paresis, incomplete paresis, shaking palsy, cerebral palsy, paralysis agitans.

PALTER, *v.* Trifle, prevaricate, quibble, equivocate, parry, fence, shy, evade, dodge, shift, elude, refine, pettifog *(coll.),* beat about the bush *(coll.),* shuffle, stickle, trifle with the truth, mince words, bluff, vary, vacillate, trim, waver, alternate, fluctuate, dillydally, oscillate, pendulate, shuffle, go around in circles, seesaw, wobble, back and fill, flounder, boggle, stumble, go back on one's word.

PALTRINESS, *n.* Insignificancy, unimportance, immateriality, immaterialness, insignificance, nugacity, nullity, ineffectuality, nothingness, inconsequentiality, triviality, trivialism, irrelevance, sorriness, pitiableness, poverty, meanness.

PALTRY, *adj.* 1. Little, small, insignificant, miserable, wretched, sorry, inconsiderable, slight, feeble, slender, petty, trifling, trivial, inconsequential, piddling, inferior, shallow, slim, mean, measly, meager, meagre, poor, shabby, beneath contempt, cheap, niggardly, catchpenny, worthless, vile, weedy, trumpery, beggarly, unimportant, nonessential, no great shakes, immaterial, irrelevant, unappreciable, small, minute, idle, petty, trifling, frivolous, inane, flimsy, airy, frothy, ridiculous, nugatory, indifferent, mediocre, passable, fair, so-so, common, ordinary, commonplace, worthless, rubbishy, scrubby, scurvy, fribbling, finical, not worth mentioning, not worth a rap, not worth a straw, not worth a dime, average, just-so, fair-to-middling, unobjectionable, unexceptional, secondary, second-best, second-rate, third-rate, fourth-rate, nothing to brag about.

2. Abject, base, vile, low, mean, worthless, shabby, scurfy, scurvy, contemptible, pitiable, trashy, groveling, beggarly, shifty, sordid, ignoble, rascally, dirty, foolish, unworthy, despicable, little,

scabby, wretched, deplorable, foul, odious, obnoxious, rank, execrable, peccant, nefarious, gross, atrocious, heinous, scandalous, shocking, opprobrious, unmentionable.

PAMPAS, *n.* Plains, grasslands, prairie, steppe, tundra, savanna, campo, level land, wide open spaces, campagna, champaign, pampa, veldt, veld, wold, sebkha, moor, moorland, common.

PAMPER, *v.* Coddle, indulge, gratify, spoil, fondle, overindulge, flatter, cosset, treat with affection, satisfy, please, caress, cherish, foster, cater to, make a pet of, feed, satiate, gorge, please, delight, charm, titillate, suit, tickle the palate of, humor.

PAMPHLET, *n.* Booklet, leaflet, brochure, book, folder, literature *(cant)*, writing, printed matter, printing, reading matter, throwaway, publication, circular, chapbook.

PAMPHLETEER, *n.* Writer, author, scribbler, essayist, journalist, publicist, discourser, descanter, descantist, commentator, satirist, polemicist, discusser, critic, reviewer.

PAN, *n.* Receptacle, container, cooking utensil, utensil, heater, ramikin, pot, kettle, dish, skillet, frying pan, tache, chafer, chafing dish, pattypan, bread pan, cake pan, saucepan, stewpan, spider.

PANACEA, *n.* Cure, cure all, universal remedy, universal cure, panace, solace, relief, remedy, polychrest, mepenthe, panchreston, panpharmacon, heal-all, catholicon, *elixir vitae (Lat.),* philosopher's stone, elixir of life.

PANACHE, *n.* Tuft, feather, plume, crest, topknot, egret, aigrette, ornament, decoration, embellishment, garnishment, garnish, frippery, gaudery, finery.

PANCRATIAST, *n.* Athlete, fighter, victor, contestant, combatant, pancratist, strong man, man of muscle, man mountain *(coll.),* acrobat, gymnast, wrestler, bruiser *(sl.),* winner, conqueror, subjugator, subduer, master, champion.

PANDECT, *n.* Code, code of laws, legal code, digest of laws, excursus, treatise, dissertation, thesis, monograph, essay, study, homily, sermon, disquisition, theme, paper, compendium, compendious abstract, compend, review, recapitulation, abbreviature, digest, condensation, epitome, brief, precis, corpus juris, capitulary, body of laws.

PANDEMIC, *adj.* Epizoötic, epidemic, contagious, infectious, communicable, catching, zymotic, pestilent, pestilential, pestiferous, universal.

PANDEMONIUM, *n.* Noise, confusion, hubbub, turbulance, disturbance, disorder, bedlam, wild confusion, riot, hue and cry, brouhaha, uproar, hell broken loose *(coll.),* turmoil, bear garden, donnybrook, stir *(coll.),* row, rowdydow, pother, fuss, bother, racket, melee, scramble, ruction, rumpus, rough-and-tumble, tumult, loud noise, din, clamor, hullabaloo, clang, clangor, charivari, shivaree *(coll.),* vociferation, roar, babel, belle, confusion worse confounded.

PANDER, *n.* Procurer, pimp, male bawd, go-between, reprobate, runner *(sl.),* procuress, white slaver, madam *(coll.),* mackerel, *maquereau (Fr.).*

PANDER TO, *v.* Cater to, be subservient to, subserve, officiate, minister, tend, promote, serve, be instrumental, assist, help, lend a hand, give a helping hand, administer to, tender to, work in the service of, attend, wait on, wait upon, fasten oneself on, be servile, lickspittle, toady, fawn, truckle to, do service, do the dirty work of, ingratiate one-

self, creep, cower, crawl, make a doormat of oneself, lick the dust of one's shoes, kiss one's boots, work oneself into the good graces of, curry favor, court favor, dance attendance on, follow at the heels of, pin oneself on.

PANDICULATION, *n.* Yawning, ascitancy, stretching, ascitation, stiffening, gaping, hiation, oscitance, oscitancy, dehiscence, drooping, nodding, dozing, lassitude, lethargy, sleepiness, drowsiness, stupor, languor, lassitude, hebetude, hebetation, torpor, torpidity, somnolence, somnolency.

PANE, *n.* Panel, glass, light, sheet, window pane, window glass, sheet glass, plate glass, shock glass.

PANEGYRIC, *n.* Praise, laudation, commendation, compliment, flattery, eulogy, oration, tribute, encomium, eulogium, glorification, glory, bepraisement, good word, honor, homage.

PANEGYRIC, PANEGYRICAL, *adj.* Encomiastic, eulogistic, laudatory, commendatory, eulogistical, flattering, complimentary, oratorical, approbatory, approbative, benedictory, encomiastical, acclamatory, uncensorious, uncritical, lavish in praise, unreproachful.

PANEGYRIST, *n.* Eulogist, eulogizer, commender, praiser, extoller, claquer, encomiast, applauder, lauder, laudator, *prôneur (Fr.),* adulator, cajoler, flatterer, tout, touter, booster, fawner, toady, bootlicker, sycophant, slaverer, courtier, backslapper, back-scratcher, wheedler, soft-soaper.

PANEGYRIZE, *v.* Extol, praise, applaud, laud, commend, pay tribute, eulogize, belaud, panegyricize, puff, glorify, swell, magnify, praise to the skies, compliment, pay a compliment, acclaim, exalt, congratulate, boost *(coll.).*

PANEL, *n.* 1. Draft, prospectus, schedule, calendar, program, lineup, agenda, protocol, bill, card, order of the day, docket, roster, register, cadre, muster, poll, parties in litigation, parties, litigants, jury, jurymen, country, coroners's jury, grand jury, jury of inquest, inquest, petty jury.

2. Part, partition, sheet, lamina, lamination, wainscoting, board, wood, insertion, saddle, table, tablet, compartment, pane, plank, wall, divider, bulkhead.

PANG, *n.* Pain, physical suffering, sharp pain, distress, dolor, nip, twinge, malaise, discomfort, pinch, twitch, shooting pain, piercing pain, stabbing pain, smart, kink, stitch, crick, displeasure, mental suffering, passion, ache, bale, affliction, woe, trials and tribulations, ordeal.

PANHANDLER, *n.* Mendicant, beggar, vagrant, outcast, parasite, petitioner, mumper, cadger *(sl.),* fakir, bum, bummer *(sl., U.S.),* idler, sponger, loafer, pauper.

PANIC, *n.* Fear, anxiety, fright, consternation, sudden fear, jitters *(coll.),* dismay, apprehension, agitation, flutter, perturbation, dread, great fear, confusion, turmoil, mental turmoil, emotional turmoil, trembling, trepidation, nervousness, awe, tremor, quivering, horror, alarm, funk *(coll.),* blue funk *(coll.),* stampede, abject fear, terror, phobia, unreasoning fear, irrational terror, cold sweat, inquietude, perturbancy, perturbation, palpitation, throbbing heart, pounding heart, shaking, hysteria.

PANIC-STRICKEN, *adj.* Fearful, terrified, horrified, terror-stricken, horror-stricken, terror-struck, horror-struck, alarmed, stampeded, overcome with fear, nervous, aghast, livid, quaking, appalled, frightened, haunted with fear, apprehensive, scary, shaky, shaking, skittish, panicky, terror-ridden, fear-ridden, horror-ridden, astounded, dismayed, hysterical, senseless with fear, petrified, stupefied, stunned, pale as a ghost, white as a sheet, startled, disquieted.

PANNIER, *n.* 1. Basket, wicker, wicker basket, carrier, container, wisket, whisket, dosser.

2. Underskirt, underwear, undergarment, clothing, clothing device.

3. *(Arch.)* Corbeil, abacus, ornament, decoration, decorative device, architectural device.

PANOPLIED, *adj.* Armed, armored, in arms, armor-clad, mailed, mail-clad, accoutred, harnessed, armed to the teeth *(coll.)*, armed cap-a-pie, ironclad, well-armed, heavily armed, bristling with arms, armed at all points, fully armed.

PANOPLY, *n.* Covering, protection, envelopment, environment, armor, full armor, shield, safeguard, protector, armory, stand of arms, weapons, deadly weapons, munitions, armature, armament, arsenal, display, display of arms, warlike display.

PANORAMA, *n.* View, perspective, bird's eye view, cyclorama, picture, general view, perspective view, conspectus, cosmorama, diorama, georama, scenic view, scenery, spectacle, scene, outlook, lookout, landscape, airscape, seascape, waterscape, cityscape, tableau, picture, representation, prospect, scenograph.

PANORAMIC, *adj.* Scenic, bird's-eye, general, collective, all-encompassing, all-inclusive, all-embracing, universal, wide, pictorial, representative.

PANSOPHIC, *adj.* Learned, all-knowing, omniscient, wise, sagacious, scientific, universally learned, solid, profound, abstruse, savant, erudite, deeply learned, well-posted, well-informed, deeply read, well-read, well-educated.

PANSOPHY, *n.* Learning, knowledge, profound knowledge, deep learning, universal knowledge, omniscience, pansophism, acroatic knowledge, acroamatic knowledge, encyclopedic knowledge, pantology, all-knowingness, universal wisdom, omnisciency, wide knowledge, vast knowledge, universal knowledge.

PANSY, *n.* 1. Flower, bloom, blossom, bud.

2. Homosexual, pervert, sodomite, hermaphrodite, epicene, gynandroid, bisexual, androgyne, sodomist, queer, homo, nancy, nance, fruit, fairy, queen, fag, fagot, painted Willy, Betty, Molly *(all slang).*

PANT, *v.* 1. Breathe hard, gasp, breathe shallowly, wheeze, puff, blow, gasp for breath.

2. Pulsate, throb, beat, palpitate, pulse, flutter, beat pitapat, go pitapat, flitter, splutter.

3. Desire, desiderate, long for, languish, thirst after, hunger for, gasp for, gape for, cry for, itch after, hanker after, lust after, burn for, aspire after, do for, run mad after, yearn for, hope for, have a yen for, be hungry for, lick one's chops for, have at heart, take into one's head, set one's cap for, set one's heart on, cast sheep's eyes upon, be desirous of, wish for, want, would fain have, sigh for.

4. Be hot, burn, roast, gasp, suffer with the heat, suffer from the heat, boil *(coll.)*, bile *(dial.)*, flush, glow.

5. Weary, tire, fatigue, exhaust, jade, fag out *(coll.)*, frazzle, use up, droop, flag, sink, decline, wear out, succumb, become sleepy.

PANTALOON, *n.* Comedian, comic, clown, harlequin, farceur, entertainer, polichinelle, punchinello, fool, motley fool, wearer of motley, columbine, mountebank, buffoon, funnyman, mime, pantomimist, pantomimer, actor, farcist, farcer,

jester, zany, merry-andrew, mummer, mimologist, mimic, guiser, Scaramouch.

PANTALOONS, *n.* Trousers, pants, knickers *(coll.)*, knickerbockers, knee breeches, breeches. bloomers, jeans *(coll.)*, britches *(coll.)*.

PANTHEISM, *n.* Theopantism, cosmotheism, paganism, paganry, pagan belief, heathenism, polytheism.

PANTHER, *n.* Beast, animal, wild animal, wild cat, feline, jungle cat, jaguar, bobcat, cheetah, puma, cat.

PANTING, *n.* 1. Gasp, gasping, heavy breathing, labored breathing, breathiness, anhelation, dyspnea, heaving.

2. Desire, desideration, want, wanting, hunger, thirst, lust, libido.

3. Excitement, agitation, turbulence, disturbance, perturbation, bother, pother, flutter, fluttering, palpitation, fidgets, unrest, restlessness, throb, throbbing, disquiet, disquietude, stir, whirl, flurry, fuss, ruffle, stew, ferment, ebullition.

PANTOMIME, *n.* Mime, mimology, acting, representation, drama, dramatic portrayal, gesture, mimicry, expression, gesticulation, dumb show, chironomy, play, play-acting, stage play, stage performance, dramatic art, art, theater *(coll.)*, theatrical performing, theatrical art.

PANTOMIMIST, *n.* Mime, actor, portrayer, player, performer, mimic, play-actor, masquer, masker, pantomimic, mute, artist, artiste, clown, harlequin, buffoon, comedian, mimologist, mimer, mimester.

PANTRY, *n.* Room, storeroom, larder, spence, buttery, food room, cold room, cuddy, cannery, stillroom.

PANTS, *n.* Breeches, trousers, pantaloons, knickers, knickerbockers, plus-fours, smallclothes, chaparejos, knee breeches, overalls, jeans, blue jeans, levis *(coll.)*, trews, britches *(coll.)*, pair of trousers, corduroy trousers, corduroys, peg-top trousers, peg-top pants, bell-bottomed trousers, tweeds, tweed trousers, bags, sacks, sponge-bag trousers, flannel bags, slacks, trouserettes, pantalets, shorts, Bermuda shorts, walking shorts, rompers, drawers, underpants, underdrawers, underwear pants, ducks.

PAP, *n.* 1. Nipple, tit, teat, dug, mamilla, papilla, breast, udder, mammillation, titty.

2. Paste, gluten, gum, mucilage, goo *(sl.)*, clot, coagulation, grume, semiliquid, semifluid.

3. Pulp, paste, dough, mash, crush, squash, smash.

PAPA, *n.* 1. Father, dad *(coll.)*, paternal ancestor, sire, male parent, pater *(coll.)*, the old man *(coll.)*, Abba, governor, pap, pappy, pop, pops, daddy, daddie, da, daddums.

2. The Pope, pontiff, Holy Father, Vicar of Christ, servant of God, Holiness, His Holiness.

PAPACY, *n,.* Papality, pontificate, popedom, the Vatican, the Holy See, See of Rome, Apostolic See, papal jurisdiction, papal line.

PAPAL, *adj.* Popish, pontifical, apostolic, papistic, Catholic, Roman, papish, papist, papistical, pontific.

PAPER, *n.* 1. Writing, written matter, scroll, piece, matter, piece of writing, document, composition, work, opus, inscription, instrument, penscript, script, typescript, manuscript, original, draft, original draft, holograph, autograph, MS., Ms., ms., palimpsest, certificate, deed, voucher, diploma, chronicle, annals, record, recording, register, docket, credential, warrant, memoir, memorial, memorandum, archives, public records, state paper, white paper.

2. Foolscap, vellum, parchment, parchment paper, onionskin, India paper, papyrus, tissue, tissue paper, filter paper, kraft paper, wrapping paper, paper board, cardboard, *papier mache (Fr.)*, blotting paper, drawing paper, watercolor paper, construction paper, tracing paper, wallpaper, writing paper, notepaper, stationery, letter paper, letterhead.

3. Newspaper, journal, tabloid, chronicle, gazette, periodical, publication, serial, daily, weekly, monthly, trade paper, house organ, news, newssheet, sheet.

4. Treatise, dissertation, thesis, paper, monograph, essay, study, disquisition, discourse, homily, descant, tractation, discussion, consideration, publication, lecture, sermon, digest, pandect, theme, composition, writing.

5. Notes, banknotes, bank draft, letter of credit, bill, commercial paper, negotiable instrument, legal tender, currency, money, bill of exchange, cash, pass, security, parchment, deed, title deed, debenture, bond, debenture bond, floating debenture, mortgage debenture, bill of sale, covenant, covenant of indemnity, deed of indemnity, note, docket, voucher, muniments, deed poll, deed of arrangements, deed of assumption.

PAPER MONEY, *n.* Cash, currency, legal tender, banknote, silver certificate, gold certificate, scrip, greenback, bill, Federal reserve note, Treasury note, folding money, the long green *(sl.)*, shinplaster, yellowback.

PAPERY, *adj.* Thin, flimsy, insubstantial, makeshift, transparent, translucent, chartaceous, papyraceous, sleazy, pasteboardy, cheap, frail, slight, delicate, breakable, fragile, paper-thin, gossamery.

PAPISM, *n.* Romanism, Roman Catholicism, Catholicity, the Catholic Church, popery, popism, Mariology, Mariolatry, popeism.

PAPIST, *n.* Roman Catholic, Catholic, Roman, Romist, Romanist, ultramontane, pape *(sl.)*, mick *(sl.)*, mackerel snatcher *(sl.)*.

PAPISTRY, *n.* Catholicity, Catholicism, Roman Catholicism, the Roman Church, the Roman Catholic Church, popery, popeism, papism, ultramontanism.

PAPOOSE, *n.* Infant, baby, babe, child, Indian child, Indian babe, youngling, young Indian, babe in arms, baby bunting, babykins, bouncing baby, young one, nursling, suckling, toddler, tot, little Indian.

PAPPOSE, PAPPOUS, *adj.* Hairy, downy, fuzzy, furry, pilose, pileous, hirsute, ciliate, ciliated, pilous.

PAPPUS, *n.* Seta, bristle, setule, setula, barb, striga, feeler, pile, brush, beard, arista, awn.

PAPPY, *n.* *(Colloq.)* Father, pater *(Lat. and coll.)*, sire, male parent, parent, governor *(coll.)*, papa, pa, paw, pap, poppa, paterfamilias, stepfather, aged parent *(sl.)*, aged P *(Lit.)*, daddy, dad, da, daddykins, foster father, father-in-law, paps, pops.

PAPULE, *n.* Bulge, convexity, protuberance, prominence, projection, swelling, bump, lump, rising, pimple, boil, pustule, gumboil, carbuncle, wen, growth, pock, whelk, bleb, blob, extosis, sore, fester, inflammation, polyp, furuncule, furuncle.

PAR, *n.* Equivalency, equivalence, equality, equalness, equiponderance, balance, equal footing, level, equilibrium, equipose, evenness, parity, quits, equipollence, coequality, owelty *(Legal)*, parallelism, isotropy, sameness, identity, identicalness, unity, oneness, synonymity, coalescence, coincidence, homoöusia, selfsameness, uniformity, stability, continuity, constancy, monotony, sameliness, invariability, even tenor.

PARABLE, *n.* Fable, story, tale, homily, similitude, comparison, narrative, biblical story, lesson, analogy, likeness, anecdote, lecture, talk, discourse, apologue, sermon, moral lesson, teaching.

PARABOLA, *n.* Curve, conic section, hyperbola, intersection.

PARABOLIC, PARABOLICAL, *adj.* 1. Allegorical, figurative, representative, symbolic, symbolical, metaphoric, metaphorical, expressed by parable, similitudinous.

2. Parabola-shaped, curved, hyperbolic, hyperbola-like.

PAR, ABOVE *adj., adv.* More, over, beyond the mark, above the mark, eminently, surpassingly, pre-eminently, prominently, principally, particularly, especially, specially, in the main, superlatively, supremely, nice, remarkable, above all, fine, good, excellent, estimable, pleasing, dandy *(coll.)*, swell *(sl.)*, keen *(coll.)*, neat *(coll.)*.

PARACLETE, *n.* Holy Ghost, Holy Spirit, comforter, consoler, God the Holy Ghost, the Spirit, Spirit of God, Spirit of Truth, the Dove, the Intercessor.

PARADE, *n.* 1. Flourish, glitter, fanfaronade, fuss, ostentatiousness, ostentation, show, display, pomp, magnificence, circumstance, pretentiousness, ceremony, flaunting, vainglory, airs, showing-off, figure, impressive effect, splash *(coll.)*, splurge *(coll.)*, strutting, vain pretensions, swagger, bounce, vanity, pride, exaggeration, affected manner, artificial manner, front *(sl.)*, veneer, pomposity, inflation, dog *(sl.)*, side *(sl.)*, swank *(coll.)*, peacockishness.

2. Procession, pageant, spectacle, pomp, splendor, march, demonstration, exposition, show, review, turnout, march past, promenade, gala, field day, doings *(coll.)*, grand doings, pageantry, fete, line, column, string, cavalcade, caravan, train, concatenation, progression, succession, flow, rank and file.

3. Walk, passageway, footpath, esplanade, promenade, public walk, sea walk, sidewalk, pathway, board walk, alameda, ambulatory.

PARADE, *v.* 1. March, hike, march in procession, file off, defile, go in a column, go on parade.

2. Be ostentatious, show off, display, vaunt, flaunt, make a show, make a display, cut a dash, cut a figure, make a splash, strut one's stuff *(coll.)*, come forward, put oneself forward, put on airs, give oneself airs, blow one's own horn, blow one's trumpet, play to the gallery, strut, peacock, grandstand *(sl.)*, mince, mince it, swell, attitudinize, strike an attitude, promenade, put on the dog, put on the ritz *(coll.)*, have no false modesty, put on a show.

PARADIGM, *n.* Example, model, pattern, exemplar, copy, specimen, prototype, archetype, sample, original, criterion, rule, module, scantling, antitype, protoplasm, proplasm, imitatee, standard.

PARADISE, *n.* 1. Heaven, Eden, Garden of Eden, Elysium, elysian fields, place of bliss, abode of the angels, city of God, our Father's house, the abode of the saints, Valhalla, the Holy City, Beatific Vision, the sight of God, Garden of Hesperides, God's dwelling place, heavenly kingdom, the Happy Land, kingdom come *(sl.)*, happy hunting ground, the world above, abode of the blessed, eternal home, nirvana, God's kingdom, presence of God, God's presence, glory, celestial glory, Abraham's bosom, Heavenly City, City of Light, Celestial City, Celestial Kingdom, Zion, New Jerusalem, God's throne, heaven of heavens, eternal bliss, unending bliss, incessant bliss, eternity, Beulah, Beulah Land, Land of Beulah, My Father's House, Olympus, Isles of the Blessed, Fortunate Isles, Arcadia, land of the Gods, afterlife, hereafter, life after death.

2. Bliss, ecstasy, delight, pleasure, gratification, joy, felicity, blessedness, ravishment, transport, third heaven, seventh heaven, beatitude, beatification, cheer, sunshine, gladness, gladsomeness.

PARADISAICAL, *adj.* 1. Empyrean, elysian, heavenly, paradisaic, supernal, celestial, Edenic, Arcadian, from on high, unearthly, beatific, beatifical, divine.

2. Felicitous, delightful, captivating, enchanting, entrancing, ecstatic, beatific, beatifical, ravishing, enravishing, thrilling, heartthrobbing, rapturous, seraphic, pleasurable, pleasure-giving, delectable.

PARADOX, *n.* Contradiction, inconsistency, logical contradiction, self-contradiction, incongruity, ridiculous incongruity, puzzle, sophism, enigma, ambiguity, antilogy, maze, confusion, perplexity, riddle, muddle, nonsense, absurdity, epigram, humor, jest, dilemma, horns of a dilemma, poser, problem, intricacy.

PARADOXICAL, *adj* Puzzling, opposite, contradictory, self-contradictory, humorous, ambiguous, enigmatic, bewildering, perplexing, paradoxal, problematic, problematical, self-annulling, odd, grotesque, unreasonable, trifling, irrational, extravagant, equivocal, equivocable, doubtful, unintelligible, inscrutable, impenetrable, incomprehensible, insolvable, unsolvable, beyond understanding, past understanding, incognizable, inapprehensible, inconceivable, past comprehension, unfathomable, obscure, inexplicable.

PARAGON, *n.* Pattern, model, nonpareil, masterpiece, superior, the best, good example, *beau idéal (Fr.)*, prototype, mirror, standard, criterion, original, archetype, precedent, paradigm, exemplar, one in a thousand, one in ten thousand, one in a million, pearl without price, flower, cream, *crème de la crème (Fr.)*, nonesuch, queen, the finest, supereminence, phoenix, chef-d'oeuvre, emblem of immortality.

PARAGRAPH, *n.* Division, part, section, clause, passage, column, writing, discourse, text, article, piece.

PARAGRAPHER, PARAGRAPHIST, *n.* Newsman, newswriter, newspaperman, journalist, reporter, gentleman of the press, interviewer, correspondent, foreign correspondent, leg man, publicist, rewrite man, writer, hack, Grub Streeter, inkslinger, penman, penwoman, penny-a-liner, scribbler, potboiler, editorialist, editorial writer, columnist, bookman, bookwright, hack writer, author.

PARALLEL, *adj.* 1. Equidistant, coextensive, collateral, aligned, even, equal, parallelistic, parallelotropic, parallelogrammic, parallelogrammical, parallelogrammatical, parallelinervate, parallelodrome, parallelodromous, parallelinerved, parallelinervous, parallelepipedonal, parallelepipedal, parallelipipedous, parallelipipedic, abreast, alongside.

2. Symmetrical, coextensive, even, equal, pro-

portioned, well proportioned, well-set-up, uniform, regular, coordinate, coequal, balanced.

3. Like, similar, analogous, allied, resembling, akin, correspondent, corresponding, uniform, analogical, homoöusian, correlative, connatural, congeneric, congenerous, twin, equivalent.

PARALLEL, *n.* 1. Match, equal, ditto, compeer, peer, equivalent, same, coequal, mate, fellow, analogue, synonym, homonym, correlate, congener, correlative, double, brother, sister, twin, complement, counterpart, companion, correspondent.

2. Parallel line, parallelogram, parallelepiped, parallelepipedon, parallelograph, parallelometer.

PARALLEL, *v.* Be parallel, coextend, run parallel to, equal, be equivalent to, compare, compare with, be comparable to, match, associate, relate, connect, correspond to, span, follow, take after, copy, double, imitate, repeat, duplicate, facsimile, echo, re-echo, balance, be equal with, amount to the same thing, tie, even off, ditto, run abreast of, keep pace with.

PARALLELISM, *n.* Comparison, affinity, equality, similitude, similarity, correspondence, sameness, owelty *(Law)*, equation, equalization, par, quits, coequality, isonomy, likeness, resemblance, consimilarity, approximation, analogy, homoöusia, semblance, alikeness, congruency, congruence, compatibility, accord, agreement, consonance, consonancy, concert, consistency, coherence, unison, coincidence, parallelization, concentricity, collimation, collineation, harmony, symmetry, coextension.

PARALLELIZE, *v.* Connect, relate, associate, parallel, draw a parallel, compare, contrast, collate, liken to, relate to, match, place in juxtaposition, place alongside, oppose, similitudinize, similarize, balance, weigh, juxtapose, juxtaposit.

PARALOGICAL, *adj.* Illogical, irrational, invalid, unsound, unsubstantial, insubstantial, inconsistent, incongruous, groundless, faulty, unscientific, untenable, undefendable, indefeasible, unwarranted, unproved, unproven, *non sequitur (Lat.)*, fallacious, specious, unreasoned, ill-thought-out, ill-judged, controvertible, questionable, dubious, doubtful, incorrect, wrong, false, untrue, unsound, debatable, contestable, disputable, weak, feeble, poor, loose, loosely thought, absurd, nonsensical, self-contradictory, self-annulling, unsustained, paralogistic.

PARALOGISM, PARALOGY, *n.* Sophistic syllogism, pseudosyllogism, illogicality, illogicalness, false reasoning, specious reasoning, sophistical argument, casuistry, jesuitism, special pleading, sophisticism, sophistry, sophism, speciosity, speciousness, fallacy, error, solecism, philosophism, elench, inconsistency, aberration, error, mistake, aberrancy, misconstruction.

PARALOGISTIC, *adj.* Unreasonable, fallacious, illogical, wrong, incorrect, ill-reasoned, faulty, invalid, irrational, unsound, insubstantial, unsubstantial, inconsistent, incongruous, groundless, unscientific, untenable, undefendable, indefeasible, unwarranted, unproved, unprovable, improbable, unproven, *non sequitur (Lat.)*, specious, ill-judged, ill-thought-out, controvertible, questionable, dubious, doubtful, incorrect, false, untrue, unsound, debatable, disputable, contestable, weak, feeble, poor, loose, loosely reasoned, absurd, nonsensical, self-contradictory, paradoxical, self-annulling, unsustained, paralogistical, paralogical.

PARALYSIS, *n.* Impotence, powerlessness, inactivity, diplegia, paraplegia, disability, sideration, hemiplegia, palsification, paresis, numbness, stroke, immobility, deterioration, physical disability, neural disability, neural degeneration, motor paralysis, narcosis, insentience, insusceptibility, unfeeling, insensibility, insensibleness, stroke of paralysis, paralytic stroke, general paralysis, general paresis, shaking palsy, paralysis agitans, Parkinson's disease, St. Vitus' dance, infantile paralysis, poliomyelitis, neuroparalysis.

PARALYTIC, *n.* Paralysis victim, cripple, palsy victim, paralyzed person, diseased person, paretic.

PARALYTIC, *adj.* Impotent, powerless, immobile, immobilized, inactive, diplegic, paraplegic, disabled, siderated, hemiplegic, palsified, paretic, numb, deteriorated, physically disabled, insentient, insusceptible, unfeeling, anaesthetic, anaesthetized, insensible, shaking, paralyzed, crippled, halt, ill, sick, laid up (*coll.*), lame.

PARALYZE, *v.* 1. Disable, deprive of power, immobilize, cripple, lame, becripple, incapacitate, unfit, make powerless, prostrate, deaden, numb, benumb, palsy, obtund, stupefy, render insensible, impalsy, weaken, debilitate.

2. Surprise, stagger, stupefy, take by surprise, startle, start, throw off one's guard, take away one's breath, joly (*sl.*), jar (*coll.*), stun, petrify, upset, strike all of a heap, unsettle, catch unaware, catch unprepared, amaze, astound, astonish, confound, flabbergast (*coll.*), overwhelm, shock, electrify, make the head swim, strike with wonder, strike with awe.

PARAMOUNT, *adj.* Supreme, chief, superior, dominant, principal, preëminent, unexcelled, unsurpassed, royal, unapproachable, unparalleled, matchless, peerless, important, significant, essential, outstanding, inimitable, main, predominant, imposing, above all, greatest, sovereign, unequaled, transcendental, supereminent, vital, on top, on top of the heap, highest, topmost, uppermost, foremost, maximal, maximum, utmost, topnotch, top-hole, top-drawer, of the first water, leading, capital, cardinal, hegemonic, hegemonical, prime, primary, ruling, overruling, superceding, unrivaled, unmatched, unapproached, unapproachable, beyond compare, incomparable, champion, superlative, beyond reproach, model, paragon, unparagoned, *facile princeps* (*Lat.*), apical, summital, vertical, acmic, acmatic, polaric, polar, in the front rank, at the top of the tree, very best, first-rate, choice, tiptop, bang-up, gilt-edge, gilt-edged, prevalent, preponderant, governing, supreme, in ascendancy, mighty, puissant, powerful.

PARAMOUNTCY, *n.* Distinction, importance, significance, moment, weight, mark, import, primacy, supremacy, pre-eminence, notability, salience, superiority, precedence, dominion, control, power, rule, sovereignty, leadership, headship, captaincy, ascendancy, prepotency, preponderance, predominance, predomination, domination, suzerainty, supremacy, unsurpassability, royalty, unapproachability, matchlessness, peerlessness, essentialness, inimitability, imposingness, greatness, supereminence, hegemony, unrivaledness, incomparability, incomparableness, superlativeness, irreproachability.

PARAMOUR, *n.* 1. Illicit lover, lover, gallant, boy friend (*coll.*), courtesan, reprobate, admirer, sweetheart, infatuate, amorist, inamorato, suitor, wooer, swain, courter, sparker (*coll.*), man, beau, follower, young man, flame (*coll.*), spark (*coll.*), Casanova, Lothario, Romeo, cavalier, gallant squire, rake, rakehell, libertine, profligate, immor-

alist, debauchee, rip (*coll.*), wolf, woman chaser, lady's man.

2. Mistress, concubine, woman, girl, lover, kept woman, doxy, spiritual wife, common-law wife, *petite amie* (*Fr.*), coutesan, ladylove, girl friend (*coll.*).

PARANOIA, *n.* Insanity, craziness, mania, idiocy, mental derangement, mental illness, aberration, mental aberration, dementia, psychopathia, psychopathic condition, lunacy, mental alienation, mental disorder, mental disease, unsoundness of mind, paranomia, amentia, frenzy, psychosis, psychotic condition, disordered reason, monomania.

PARANOIAC, *n.* Crazy person, mental defective, psychotic, victim of mental illness, madman, crazy man, psychopathic case, case (*coll.*), candidate for the asylum, candidate for bedlam, crackwit, crack-brain, Tom o' bedlam, phrenetic, loon (*sl.*), goof (*sl.*), nut (*sl.*), crackpot (*sl.*), bat (*sl.*), phobic, phobe, lunatic, dement, demoniac, psychopath, raving maniac, raving lunatic.

PARAPET, *n.* Elevation, rampart, defense, fortification, bulwark, vallation, countervallation, circumvallation, contravallation, embankment, bank, defilade, mound, earthwork, mole, dike, scarp, escarp, escarpment, ravelin, entrenchment, intrenchment, ditch, trench, barrier, barricade, dugout, stronghold, fasthold, battlement, glacis, casemate, buttress, abutment, banquette, redoubt, barbican, lines, machicolation, wall.

PARAPHERNALIA, *n.* Apparatus, equipment, tools, supplies, gear, rigging, furniture, appointments, machinery, properties, things, trappings, accoutrements, appurtenances, harness, tackle, tackling, implements, utensils, fittings, equipage, belongings, effects, personal effects, provisions, instruments, furnishment, caparison, traps (*coll.*), impedimenta, materials, matériel.

PARAPHRASE, *n.* Rendering, rewording, rendition, version, reddition, reading, translation, free translation, rehash (*coll.*), amplification, metaphrase, gloss, interlinear, interlinear gloss, interlinear translation, interpretation, restatement, elucidation, repetition, repeat, indirect quotation, borrowing.

PARAPHRASTIC, PARAPHRASTICAL, *adj.* Paraphrasing, paraphrased, amplifying, amplificatory, exegetical, interpretive, interpretative, elucidative, explicatory, explicative, illustrative, translational, translatory, exemplificative, exemplicatory, annotative, commentatorial.

PARASITE, *n.* 1. Sycophant, toady, flatterer, toadeater, timeserver, fawner, truckler, wheedler, hanger-on, bloodsucker, leech, pickthank, flunky, spaniel, lapdog, whiner, votary, admirer, dependent, loafer, dupe, henchman, jackal, panhandler, sniveler, mendicant, cadger, doormat, tool, cat's paw, doughface, adulator, craven, placehunter, devotee, hireling, sponger, leaner, deadbeat, minion, partisan, coat-tail rider, lickspittle, bootlicker, creature, guest, apple-polisher.

2. Creature, entozoon, zooparasite, bloodsucker, leech, slug.

PARASITICAL, *adj.* Predatory, taking, grasping, wolfish, predacious, all-devouring, ravening, ravenous, prehensive, prehensile, prehensory, lupine, despoiling, draining, exhausting, absorbing, sucking, drying, desiccating, sycophantish, servile, unctuous, subject, abject, obsequious, toadyish, flattering, timeserving, fawning, truckling, wheedling, blood-sucking, leech-like, spaniel-like, flunkyish, whining, dependent, loafing, jackal-like, sniveling, cadging, adulating, craven, sponging, leaning, deadbeat, menial, hireling, partisan, lickspittle, bootlicking.

PARASITISM, *n.* Flattery, sycophancy, obsequiousness, adulation, vernility, truckling, fawning, bootlicking, predatoriness, predaciousness, ravenousness, prehensiveness, prehensility, prehensoriness, exhaustingness, desiccation, servility, unctuousness, abjectness, toadyism, toadyishness, timeserving, fawningness, wheeding, bloodsucking, whining, dependency, dependence, loafing, sponging, sniveling, cadging, cravenness, leaning, partisanship.

PARASOL, *n.* Sunshade, umbrella, beach umbrella, parpluie, canopy, bumbershoot *(sl.),* en-tout-cas *(Fr.),* gamp, bumbersoll *(sl.),* mushroom *(sl.),* 'brella *(coll.).*

PAR, BELOW *adj.* Marked down, discounted, at a discount, under par, not up to scratch *(coll.),* below the mark, below standard, substandard, inferior, unsuitable, wanting, lacking, deficient, found wanting, imperfect, below strength, weak, faulty, at fault, found at fault, faulted, short, short of, below the full complement, not up to specification, not up to the sample, at a low ebb, at the bottom of the heap, below scale, at the bottom of the scale, below, scant, scanty, meager, paltry, brief, slight, sparse, passable, tolerable, middling, fair, fairish, indifferent, no better than it ought to be, at low water mark.

PARBOIL, *v.* Boil, cook, steep, simmer, prepare, tenderize, stew, ebulliate, brew, seethe, ebullate.

PARCAE, *n., pl.* The Fates, the Three Sisters, fate, kismet, the Weird Sisters, *Moirai (Greek),* Norns *(Ger. myth),* Roman Fates: Nona, Decuma, Morta, Norse Fates: Urth, Verthandi, Skuld, Greek Fates: Clotho, Lachesis, Atropos.

PARCEL, *n.* 1. Package, bundle, packet, bindle, bale, seroon, kit, pack, budget, fascine, wisp, fagot, wrap.

2. Lot, set, portion, fragment, division, dole, sector, ward, moiety, section, cantle, cantlet, fraction, frustum, segment, share, piece, part, cut *(sl.),* lot, allotment, allowance, end *(coll.),* tract, plot, patch, piece of land, field.

PARCEL, *v.* Divide, distribute, share, deal out, allot, apportion, partition, dispense, disperse, allocate, divvy *(sl.),* split, demarcate, deal, assign, billet, appropriate, detail, appoint, mete, cast, carve, split up.

PARCELMENT, *n.* Division, distribution, share, sharing, deal, dealing, allotment, apportioning, apportionment, partition, partitioning, dispensing, dispersal, allocation, divvying *(sl.),* divvying up *(sl.),* split, splitting, demarcation, deal, assigning, assignment, assigns, billeting, appropriation, detail, detailing, appointment, meting, casting, carving, splitting up.

PARCH, *v.* Roast, burn, dry, desiccate, shrivel, char, torrefy, scorch, singe, blister, sear, bake, cremate, combure, brand, shrivel up, dehydrate, dry up, dry out, exsiccate, anhydrate, mummify, vaporate, evaporate, sun, sun-dry, torrify, insolate, wither.

PARCHED, *adj.* Dry, dried, seared, burned, burnt, shriveled, thirsty, desiccated, dried out, dried up, burning up, withered, arid, drained, roasted, roasting *(coll.),* charred, torrified, scorched, singed, blistered, baked, cremated, combured, branded, dehydrated, anhydrated, mummified, vaporated, evaporated, sunned, sun-dried, torrefied, insolated,

sere, sear, siccate, adust, rainless, droughty, drouthy.

PARCHING, *adj.* Fiery, hot, drying, desiccating, searing, scorching, simmering, seething, sweltering, torrid, torrifying, torrefying, tropical, toasting, roasting, red-hot, sizzling, sizzling-hot, hot as fire, smoking-hot, scorching-hot, thermogenic, thermogenetic, burning, shriveling, withering, arid, singeing, evaporating, dehydrating, anhydrating, mummifying, insolating, dusty, rainless, droughty, drouthy.

PARCHMENT, *n.* 1. Sheepskin, skin, hide, pell, writing material, stationery, binding material.

2. Scroll, document, certificate, diploma, paper, instrument, palimpsest, security, bond, deed, muniment.

PARDON, *v.* Acquit, remit, exonerate, exculpate, remit the penalty of, reprieve, respite, clear, absolve, vindicate, whitewash, grant amnesty to, excuse, discharge, release, condone, wipe the slate clean, bury the hatchet, forgive, overlook, pass over, liberate, quash, set free, discharge, release, blink at, disregard, wink at, let pass, pass over, connive at, endure, bear an affront, give absolution, forgive and forget, let bygones be bygones.

PARDON, *n.* Forgiveness, amnesty, exoneration, vindication, freeing, remission, grace, absolution, mercy, deliverance, exculpation, acquittal, respite, reprieve, clearance, immunity, immunization, forbearance, excuse, condoning, condonation, indulgence, remission of sin, long-suffering, quittance, quietus, release, discharge.

PARDONABLE, *adj.* Excusable, venial, allowable, remissible, justifiable, forgivable, vindicable, expiable, reasonable, warrantable, legitimate, unobjectionable, inoffensive, inculpable, unblamable, right, correct, irreproachable, irreprehensible, irreprovable, unexceptionable, uncensurable, unimpeachable, above suspicion.

PARE, *v.* 1. Peel, decorticate, skin, excoriate, strip, bark, husk, shell, shuck, trim, cut away, cut, lay bare.

2. Prune, crop, cut away, reduce, trim, clip, lop, dock, retrench, shave, skive, shear, mow, shave off.

3. Lessen, reduce, diminish, decrease, minify, minish, bate, abate, lower, curtail, shorten, abbreviate, deduct, deduce, take away, take from, subtract, discount, withdraw, abstract, detract, slash, trim, cut, shave.

PARENT, *n.* Father, mother, progenitor, genitor, begetter, procreator, ancestor, paternal ancestor, maternal ancestor, sire, dam, progenitress, progenitrix, matriarch, patriarch, paterfamilias, father-in-law, foster-father, stepfather, stepmother, mother-in-law, materfamilias, male parent, female parent.

PARENTAGE, *n.* Ancestry, line, lineage, extraction, birth, race, pedigree, stock, origin, family, parenthood, descent, progenitors, antecedents, forefathers, foreparents, consanguinity, grandfathers, primogenitors, bloodline, derivation, line of ancestors, strain, sept, generation, genealogy, family tree, genealogical tree, affiliation, stem, filiation, house, stock, breed.

PARENTAL, *adj.* Ancestral, paternal, maternal, patrimonial, fatherly, motherly, fatherlike, motherlike, phylogenetic, phyletic, hereditary, familiar, family, racial, original.

PARENTHESIS, *n.* Punctuation, punctuation marks, crotchets, brackets.

PARENTHETIC, PARENTHETICAL, *adj.* Incidental, episodic, *obiter dictum (Lat.)*, inserted, interjacent, interposed, intervening, intermediate, intermedial, insinuated, interfering, interfered.

PARIAH, *n.* Outcast, outcast of society, leper, outlaw, castaway, derelict, relict, evictee, expelee, man without a country, evacuee, expatriate, exile, *déclassé (Fr.)*, stray, waif, Arab, vagabond, wanderer, roamer, rover, Ahasuerus, Wandering Jew, Flying Dutchman, Ancient Mariner, fugitive, runaway, refugee, nomad, bird of passage.

PARING, *n.* Chip, shaving, peel, skin, cut, slice, skive, small quantity, sliver, piece, snip, snippet, morsel, remains, remanence, refuse, garbage, remainders, scrap, trash, cutting, bit, clipping, shred, tatter, crumb, debris, detritus.

PARISH, *n.* 1. Society, diocese, archdiocese, congregation, flock, fold, class, laity, laymen, assembly, brethren, pastorate, glebe, church demesne, church.

2. Section, district, compartment, division, county, department, canton, shire, province, precinct, *arondissement (Fr.)*, diocese, township, riding, hundred, wapentake, lathe, soke, bailiwick, tithe, state.

PARITY, *n.* Equality, equivalence, correspondence, resemblance, similarity, alikeness, likeness, similitude, homogeneity, consimilarity, parallelism, approximation, comparison, affinity, sameness, owelty *(Law)*, equation, equalization, par, quits, coequality, isonomy, analogy, homoöusia, semblance, congruence, congruency, compatability, accord, agreement, consonance, consonancy, concert, consistency, coherence, unison, coincidence, parallelization, concentricity, collimation, colineation, harmony, symmetry, coextension, evenness, level, levelness, monotony, sameness.

PARK, *n.* Garden, pleasure garden, formal garden, grounds, plaisance, pleasance, common, commons, vivarium, paradise, woods, woodland, chase, valley, enclosure, inclosure, vale, dale, forest, grove, village green, lawn, greenyard, greensward.

PARKWAY, *n.* Road, highway, turnpike, way, thoroughfare, roadway, highroad, main road, state highway, state road, main highway, toll road, toll highway, first-class road, three-lane highway, four-lane highway, six-lane highway.

PARLANCE, *n.* Discourse, speech, talk, manner of speaking, phrasing, language, diction, cant, discussion, dialect, patois, lingua franca, tongue, idiom, lingo, patter, phraseology, jargon, argot, slang, colloquialism, regionalism, billingsgate, provincialism, localism, pronunciation, plain English, twang, accent, brogue, wording, vocabulary, verbiage, locution, expression, articulation, rhetoric, grammar, mode of expression, style, idiologism, enunciation, command of words, use of words, turn of speech, common parlance.

PARLEY, *n.* Meeting, conference, confab *(sl.)*, trate, consult, discuss, negotiate, temporize, discourse, treat, hold conference, address, speak up to, commune with, hold commerce with, confer with, exchange words with, colloquize, have a chat with, be closeted with, palaver, chin *(sl.)*, go into a huddle, put heads together, counsel, advise, take up with, reason with, talk over, debate, dispute, mediate.

PARLEY, *n.* Meeting, conference, confab *(sl.)*, huddle, talk, negotiation, oral treaty, words, address, discussion, discourse, palaver, confabulation, colloquy, interchange, exchange, exchange

of views, council, conclave, congress, argument, debate, controversy, hearing, reception, consultation, convention, mediation, arbitration, arbitrament, diplomatic consultation.

PARLIAMENT, *n.* Legislature, House of Commons, House of Lords, Congress, Senate, House of Representatives, State Legislature, assembly, state senate, convocation, convocation of notables, legislative body, council of state, General Assembly, *chambre des députés (Fr.)*, chamber of deputies, national assembly, bundestag, Reichstag, national council, Estates General, Bundesversammlung, Cortes, Oirechtas, soviet, Duma, Rigsdag, Riksdag, Cortes Geraes, witan, witangemot, First Chamber, upper house, upper chamber, legislative council, law-making body, governing body, government, House of Peers, Bundesrat, Landsting, Reichsrat, Eduskunta, Felsöház, Seanad Eirann, Forsta Kammaren, Ständerat, Camara de Senadores, The House, lower house, second house, Camara dos Deputados, Nationalrat, Folketing, Odelsting, Andra Kammaren, Képviselöház.

PARLIAMENTARY, *adj.* Senatorial, congressional, governmental.

PARLOR, *n.* Living room, drawing room, sitting room, front room *(coll.)*, room, apartment, living apartment, reception room, visiting room, best room *(coll.)*, cabin *(naut.)*, stateroom.

PARLOUS, *adj.* Clever, shrewd, cunning, dangerous, shocking, surprising, risky, perilous, hazardous, unsafe, uncertain, unhealthy, unwholesome, critical, slippery, ticklish, doubtful, insecure, infirm, unsound, untrustworthy, slippy, full of risk, full of hazard, shaky, tottering, tottery, rash, chancy *(coll.)*.

PAROCHIAL, *adj.* 1. Regional, local, regionalistic, topical, sectional, provincial, insular, parish, of the parish.

2. Petty, narrow, narrow-minded, bigoted, insular, opinionated, confined, provincial, intransigent, stiff-backed, stiff, opinioned, immovable, hidebound, set, set in one's ways, self-opinioned, egotistical, intolerant, illiberal, mean-spirited, prejudiced, deaf, purblind, small, little, strait-laced.

PARODIST, *n.* Author, writer, scribbler, hack, humorist, lampooner, satirist, comic, caricaturist, burlesquer, poet, poetaster, versifier, critic, ridiculer, pastiche-artist.

PARODY, *n.* Imitation, mimicry, ludicrous imitation, burlesque, caricature, farce, take-off, extravaganza, absurdity, macaronic, foolishness, nonsense, comicality, comedy, exaggeration, tomfoolery, buffoonery.

PAROL, *adj.* Spoken, verbal, unwritten, vocal, acroamatic, acroamatical, muncupative, phonic, phonical, not written, outspoken, conversational, glottal, colloquial, collocutory.

PAROLE, *n.* 1. Speech, talk, chatter, chin-music, verbalization, talking, discourse, utterance, oral communication, verbal utterance, word of mouth, prolation, palaver, prattle, gab *(coll.)*, spoken language, conversation, lip *(sl.)*, guff *(sl.)*, blarney *(coll.)*, locution, elocution.

2. Promise, word of honor, word, pledge, plight, undertaking, troth, guarantee, assurance, vow, avowal, affidavit, solemn promise, solemn word, solemn declaration, oath, profession, obligation, stipulation, warrant, warranty, avowance, avouchment, covenant, compact, gentleman's agreement, bond, pignoration, vadium, oral contract, security, personal security, recognizance.

PAR, ON A *adj.* Equal, equivalent, level, tantamount, equalized, drawn, in a draw, tied, homologous, equiparant, symmetrical, much at one, the same as, convertible into, on even terms, coordinate, on a level with, on equal footing with, much the same as, as broad as it is long, the same thing as, as good as, isochronous, isochronal, equiponderous, equiponderant, identical, square, neither more nor less than, all one, one and the same, one, homoösious, undistinguishable, synonymous, homonymous, analogous, coincidental, coincident, indistinguishable, consignificant.

PARONOMASIA, *n.* Pun, punning, word-play, play on words, *double-entendre (Fr.)*, equivocation, ambiguity, quibble, amphibology, amphibologism, equivocality, paragram, rime, rhyme, assonance.

PARONYMOUS, *adj.* Conjugate, similarly derived, common, related, connected, connatural, affinitive, collateral, connate, allied, affiliated, associated, equiparant, congenerous, congeneric, etymological, etymologically related.

PAROXYSM, *n.* Convulsion, seizure, fit, attack, spasm, throe, jactation, frenzy, excitation, excitement, storm, emotion, upheaval, raving, hysterics, anger, outbreak, outburst, delirium, explosion, whirling, fuming, sudden attack, tremor, violence, furor, tarantism, madness, twitching, fury, flare-up, agony, anguish, breaking-out, pain, morbid excitement, perturbation, visitation, catastrophe, high dudgeon, violent seizure, pang tantrum, eruption, subsultus, rage, raging, passion, agitation, disturbance, epitasis, eclampsia, grip, stroke, ictus, tonic spasm, entasia, colonic spasm, laryngismus, orgasm, tetanus, holotony, phrenitis, brain storm, calenture, vertigo, dizziness, light-headedness, swimming, giddiness, delirium tremens, epilepsy, epileptic fit, epileptic seizure, cramp, charley horse, tempestuousness, turbulence, boisterousness, violent emotion, emotional upheaval, emotional disturbance, towering rage, fume, conniption *(coll.)*, cat fit *(coll.)*, pique, huff, dudgeon.

PARQUET, *n.* 1. Floor, flooring, deck, ground floor, ground part, pavement.

2. Flooring, marquetry, parquetry, tessellation, mosaic, tessera, inlay, patterned inlay, tile, tile floor, checkerwork, checkerboard, checkerboarding.

3. Orchestra, orchestra pit, pit, orchestra seats.

PARQUETRY, *n.* Inlaid work, inlay, tessellation, tessera, mosaic, mosaic work, ornamentation, decoration, ornamental patterning, checkering, marquetry, patterned inlay, tile, tiling, tile flooring, checkerboard, checkerboard pattern, checkerwork.

PARRICIDE, *n.* 1. Patricide, father-killer, killer, homicide, murderer, slaughterer, criminal, sinner, offender, traitor, mother-killer, matricide, regicide.

2. Patricide, killing, murder, matricide, regicide, homicide, offense, crime, sin.

PARROT, *n.* 1. Bird, tropical bird, talking bird, fowl.

2. Chatterbox, chatterer, magpie, popinjay, windbag, chatterbag, gasbag *(sl.)*, blatherskite, talker, talkative person, idle gossip, gossipmonger, scandalmonger, hot-air artist *(sl.)*, jay.

3. Mimic, imitator, copyist, copy cat *(coll.)*, mimer, mimester, polly, poll-parrot, cuckoo, mockingbird, mocker, counterfeiter, plagiarizer, forger, ape, monkey.

PARROTRY, *n.* Apery, imitation, mimicry, mockery, parrotism, copying.

PARRY, *v.* 1. Avoid, dodge, shun, keep at a distance, repulse, repel, fend off, ward off, resist, keep off, beat off, hold off, stand off, put off, elude, evade, shift off, get around, circumvent, fight shy of, keep at a distance, keep away.

2. Fence, shuffle, equivocate, quibble, resort to quibbling, dodge, shy, shift, elude, evade, beat about the bush, beg the question, blow hot and cold, cavil, trifle, prevaricate.

3. Refute, thwart, confute, invalidate, answer, answer conclusively, rebut, negative, negate, disprove, explode, counter, contradict, overwhelm, defeat, silence, crush, smash the opposition of, show up, dismiss, down, overturn, overthrow, turn, settle, finish, dispose of.

PARSIMONIOUS, *adj.* Frugal, stingy, tight-fisted, grudging, ungenerous, close, niggardly, miserly, avaricious, sordid, shabby, mercenary, saving, hard-fisted, sparing, scrimping, skimping *(coll.)*, mean, penurious, grasping, covetous, skinflint, hard-hearted, unyielding, greedy, griping, bargaining, narrow, tight *(coll.)*, niggard, self-seeking, economical, illiberal, cheese-paring, save-all, money-grubbing, near, close-handed, stinting, chary, churlish, hidebound, grasping, venal, usurious, extortionate, rapacious, careful, thrifty, misanthropic.

PARSIMONY, *n.* Stinginess, ungenerosity, ungenerousness, niggardliness, penury, penuriousness, meanness, closeness, economy, frugality, illiberality, savingness, nearness, close-handedness, close-fistedness, hard-heartedness, avarice, avariciousness, covetousness, cupidity, miserliness, grudgingness, sordidness, shabbiness, mercenariness, scrimpingness, sparingness, skimpiness, unyieldingness, gripingness, venality, chariness, churlishness, usuriousness, usury, extortion, rapacity, rapaciousness, misanthropy, self-seeking, saving, thrift, thriftiness, tenacity, avidity, malversation, selfishness.

PARSON, *n.* Minister, minister of the Gospel, clergyman, cleric, priest, rector, sermonizer, ecclesiastic, churchman, divine, pastor, padre, curate, preacher, clerk, clerk in holy orders, theologian, angel, pulpiteer, pulpiter, blackcoat *(coll.)*, sky pilot *(cant)*, chaplain, hierophant, cassock, presbyter, father, father in Chirst, curé, confessor, spiritual father, the Reverend, the Right Reverend, the Very Reverend, shepherd, servant of God.

PARSONAGE, *n.* Parson's house, rectory, parish house, church house, manse, vicarage, presbytery, glebe, pastorate, pastorium, home, dwelling, house, homestead, clergyman's residence.

PART, *n.* 1. Portion, division, fraction, fragment, segment, section, piece, parcel, cantlet, cantle, ward, particular, item, detail, subdivision, detachment, installment, dividend, sector, particle, remnant, moiety, crumb, scrap, bit, shred, scale, cut, cutting, snip, snippet, chip, collop, slice, shaving, rasher, whack, snack, sliver, shiver *(coll.)*, lump, gob, smithereen *(coll.)*, hunch, hunk *(coll.)*, hank, stump, morsel, butt.

2. Stanza, verse, chapter, paragraph, section, phrase, clause, sentence, article, passage, number, book, volume, fascicle, serial.

3. Limb, member, arm, leg, extremity, bough, twig, spray, tendril, scion, ramification, horn, switch, runner, lobule, lobe, component, spur, offshoot, sarmentum, wing, link, joint.

4. Component, constituent, ingredient, factor, integral part, integrant, portion, part and parcel, element, appurtenance, leaven.

5. Contingent, share, portion, dose, allotment, allowance, measure, quota, proportion, dividend, commission, assignment, dole, pittance, meed, snack, lot, snip, whack, rake-off, cut (sl.).

6. Fractional part: half, third, quarter, fifth, sixth, seventh, eighth, ninth, tenth, etc.

7. (Music) Score, vocal score, instrumental score, copy, music, draft, transcript, transcription, arrangement, short score, compressed score, miniature score, opera score, passage, phrase, air, movement, section, verse, stanza, division, measure, overture, prelude, introduction, Vorspiel (Ger.), vamp, descant, coda, end, finale, tailpiece, interlude, intermezzo, melody, voice part, real part, auxiliary part, additional part.

8. Role, cue, lines, side (cant), piece, cast, character, lead, leading role, walk-on, subsidiary role, feeder, straight part, character part, ingenue, ingenue role, juvenile, juvenile role, comic-relief, heavy (cant).

9. Function, role, cue, capacity, province, department, compass, orb, sphere, realm, life, career, life course, field, walk, walk of life, beat, routine.

PART, v. 1. Divide, sever, separate, dismember, subdivide, dissever, break, piece, break into pieces, tear asunder, sunder, split, slit, slice, burst, bust (coll.), cut, divorce, break, break apart, disconnect, disjoin, dispart, disengage, disunite, abscind, decompose, disintegrate, analyze, dissect, anatomize, comminute, divide into elements, divellicate, unyoke, winnow, flail, cleave.

2. Isolate, separate, segregate, set apart, lay apart, lay aside, sort out, winnow, pick out, space, set at intervals, hiate, keep apart, remove, hold apart, stand between, intervene, divaricate.

3. Aberrate, diverge, radiate, go off on a tangent, file off, fly off, branch, branch out, ramify, ramificate, fork, bifurcate, recede, deviate, sink, divagate, stray, go astray, drift, rove, ramble, wander, meander, get away, drift away, recede, retrocede, fall back, retreat, retire, withdraw, go away, move away, swerve off, shrink away, ebb, decline, sheer off, stand off.

4. (Part With) Discard, throw away, jettison, throw to the dogs, cast to the dogs, remove, relegate, reject, sweep away, brush away, scatter, throw to the winds, rid oneself of, discard as useless, get rid of, be rid of, heave overboard, eliminate, give away, release, yield, surrender, give up, forgo, resign, have done with, abandon, renounce, lay aside, disuse, dismiss, let slip, spare, drop, waive, have done with, expropriate, sacrifice, spare, cede.

5. Depart, take one's leave, take one's departure, go one's way, start out, set forth, set out, go away, sally forth, hit the trail (coll.), take one's farewell, get up and go, make an exit, go off (Theatrical), quit, evacuate, vacate, part from, retire, withdraw, mosey, mosey along (sl.), saunter along, break away, break oneself away, tear oneself away, be gone, push off.

PARTAKE, v. Share, participate, go halves with, go halfers (coll.), share in, divide, apportion, go shares, come in for a share, divvy up (coll.).

PARTAKER, n. Sharer, communicant, participant, party, partner, copartner, companion, participator, shareholder, coparcener, coheir, cotenant, tenant in common, joint tenant.

PARTAKING, n. Sharing, participating, participation, possession, occupancy, common tenancy, tenancy in common, coparcenry, coheirship, joint ownership, joint tenancy, jointure, communion,

community of property, communization, collectivism, socialism, communalism.

PARTERRE, n. Floor, ground floor, parterre boxes, parquet circle, boxes, seats, balcony, balcony seats, orchestra circle.

PARTHENOGENESIS, n. Generation, birth, geniture, procreation, progeneration, reproduction, begetting, fecundation, fructification, multiplication, progeneration, germination, gemination, impregnation, spontaneous generation, virgin birth, archigenesis, abiogenesis.

PARTIAL, adj. 1. Uneven, unbalanced, irregular, inadequate, fragmentary, fractionary, multifid, sectional, divided, divisible, portional, disjunctive, unattached, unconnected, apart, asunder, isolated, cleft, split, withdrawn, deficient, incomplete, defective, in default, immature, wanting, scarce, slight, meager, hollow, jejune, sketchy, scanty, uncompleted, unfinished, crude, unprepared, fragmentary, inconsiderable, too little, insufficient, uneven.

2. Prejudiced, biased, prepossessed, interested, unfair, inequitable, influenced, bigoted, warped, unjust, one-sided, intolerant, narrow-minded, infatuated, besotted, unreasonable, iniquitous, wrong, wrongful, unbalanced, jaundiced, short-sighted, unjustified.

PARTIALITY, n. 1. State of being partial, bias, prejudice, one-sidedness, predilection, partisanship, injustice, inequity, leaning, inclination, favoritism, predisposition, warp, prepossession, sympathy, preference, nepotism.

2. Preference, pleasure, fancy, taste, inclination, disposition, relish, penchant, bent, attraction, weakness, leaning, liking, attachment, favor, proclivity, predilection, mind, propensity, sympathy, humor, affinity.

PARTIBLE, adj. Divisible, separable, severable, dividual, discerptible, scissile, dividuous.

PARTICIPANT, n. Participator, sharer, partner, copartner, shareholder, co-operator, partaker.

PARTICIPATE, v. Take part, join in, share, pull an oar, enter into, form a part of, engage in, be a participant, partake, bear a hand, have a finger in (coll.), pitch in (coll.), divide with, play a part.

PARTICIPATOR, n. Sharer, partner, copartner, shareholder, co-operator, partaker, participant.

PARTICLE, n. 1. Scrap, bit, trace, speck, doit, scratch, snippet, morsel, snip, spot, iota, grain, atom, mite, mote, micron, modicum, ion, whit, tittle, minim, hair, speckle, scintilla, freckle, pin, flyspeck, insignificancy, corpuscle, trifle, point, microbe, molecule, minutia, straw, cent, farthing.

2. (Gramm.) Wordlike element (which can only be used in combination), derivational affix, prefix, suffix.

PARTI-COLORED, PARTY-COLORED, adj. Variegated, many-tinted, polychromatic, polychrome, many-hued, rainbow-like, divers-colored, versicolored, multicolored, multicolor, rainbow-hued, daedal (Poet.), kaleidoscopic, checkered, colorful.

PARTICULAR, adj. 1. Specific, especial, special, exact, individual, concrete, express, fixed, definite, explicit, individualized, well-defined, respective, determinate, single, defined.

2. Single, sole, unique, solitary, peculiar, individual, separate, definite, lone.

3. Noteworthy, signal, momentous, considerable, consequential, special, important, salient,

marked, notable, remarkable, extraordinary, impressive, substantial, outstanding, prominent.

4. Hard to please, fussy, fastidious, scrupulous, hairsplitting, squeamish, punctilious, difficult, finical, finicky, overcritical, hypercritical, choosy, meticulous, picky, queasy, querulous, picking.

PARTICULARISM, *n.* Devotion to a particular cause, interest, *etc.,* partisanship, secularism, cultism, denominationalism, nationalism.

PARTICULARIZE, *v.* List in detail, itemize, account for, differentiate *(between various items, etc.),* give particulars, specify, give full account, give a detailed account.

PARTICULARLY, *adv.* 1. In a particular *or* exceptional degree, especially, supremely, mainly, principally, eminently, prominently, surprisingly, unusually, singularly, curiously, excessively, strikingly, strangely, extraordinarily, peculiarly, uncommonly, oddly, markedly, inordinately, above all.

2. In a particular manner, in particular, severally, explicitly, one by one, respectively, solely, alone, expressly, exclusively, individually, specially, singly, apart.

PARTING, *adj.* 1. Dying, final, departing, concluding, last, deathbed.

2. Acting as a division, dividing, splitting, rending, cutting, halving, cleaving, segregating, bisecting, separating, sundering, severing, isolating, insulating, partitioning.

3. Given, taken, done, *etc.,* on parting, farewell, leave-taking, final, last, embarking, entraining, departing, valedictory, send-off *(coll.).*

PARTING, *n.* 1. Breaking, rupture, fission, scission, segmentation, discerption, luxation, severance, tearing asunder, disengagement, divergence, partition, bifurcation, divarication, disruption, separation, division, disunion, disassociation, divorce, divorcement, deviation, section, disconnection, disjunction, segregation, detachment, bisection, dimidiation, resection *(Surg.),* ramification.

2. Leave-taking, death, departure, going, removal, withdrawal, embarkation, valediction, farewell, retreat, release, passing away, final summons, cessation, quietus, Godspeed, good-bye, decession, adieu, congé, diremption.

3. Place of division *or* separation, cleft, cut, gash, hiatus, interspace, breach, interstice, break, gulf, caesura, interval, fork, lacuna, crevice, crack, rent, chink, chasm, incision, rift, chap, part *(of the hair),* crotch, gap, space.

PARTISAN, *n.* Adherent, supporter, champion, party man, patron, upholder, sympathizer, devotee, hanger-on, henchman, seconder, attendant, satellite, well-wisher, sectary, sectarian, favorer, friend at court, advocate, abettor, Maecenas, heeler *(sl.),* sycophant, clansman, ally, puppet, zealot, votary, disciple, follower, appendage, believer, enthusiast.

PARTITION, *n.* 1. Distribution into shares, separation, division into portions, allotment, apportionment, segregation, deal, demarcation, assignment, allocation, severance, partitionment, septation.

2. Something that separates, dividing wall, barrier, diaphragm, dividing line, wall, brattice, phragma, dissepiment, party line, panel, screen, fence, *cloison (Fr.),* septum *(Biol.),* septulum, septation, bulkhead *(Naut.),* mediastinum *(Anat.).*

3. Division, section, part, portion, compartment, sector, apartment, stall, cell, booth, pigeon-

hole, niche, cubbyhole, panel, cabin, closet, enclosure, bin, segment, subdivision, box, drawer, locker, room, recess, pew, cage, kennel, manger, crib, bunker, nook, pen, chest, caddy, rack, case, cabinet, district.

PARTITION, *v.* Separate *(by a partition),* divide into parts *or* portions, apportion, distribute, parcel out, allocate, mete, share, dole, deal, disperse, split up, dispense, demarcate, allot, subdivide, part, sever, cleave, disconnect, dissect.

PARTLY, *adv.* In part, in some measure, to a degree, not wholly, somewhat, comparatively, relatively, within bounds, to a limited extent, after a fashion, incompletely, in a manner of speaking, partially.

PARTNER, *n.* 1. Associate, sharer, partaker, helper, accomplice, colleague, friend, participant, coadjutor, confederate, accessory, companion, fellow-worker, mate, adjunct, cohelper, copartner, consociate, confrere, cooperator, collaborator, teammate, aider, adjuvant, fellow, consort, comrade, ally, aid, familiar.

2. Spouse, husband, wife, consort, helpmeet, helpmate, yokefellow, better half *(joc.),* mate.

PARTNERSHIP, *n.* State *or* condition of being a partner, association, participation, interest, connection, cooperation, community, joint interest, alliance, union, company, society, fellowship, companionship, collusion, sharing, complicity, friendship, consociation, camaraderie, collaboration, amity, colleagueship, brotherliness, fraternization, cordial understanding, mutual trust, comradeship, connivance, conspiracy, abetment, concurrence, cabal, complot, intrigue, combination.

PARTY, *n.* 1. Group gathered for some purpose *(as amusement or entertainment),* company, assembly, conclave, levee, soiree, reception, dance, function, social assemblage, festivity, fete, meeting of friends, reunion, at home, get-together *(coll.),* housewarming, fraternity, sorority, club, blowout *(sl.),* revels, festive occasion, spree, jamboree *(sl.),* picnic, junket, bee, sociable *(coll.),* social.

2. Body, detachment of troops, company, unit, wing, squad, division, garrison, brigade, section, gang, crew, detail, troop.

3. Number *or* body of persons united in purpose *or* opinion *(in opposition to others),* combination, league, circle, faction, clique, coterie, confederacy, alliance, ring, set, junto, cabal, plot, cell, clan, side, interest, knot, caucus, camarilla, lodge, conclave, sect, outfit *(coll.),* caste, coalition, body of partisans, machine, federation, denomination.

4. Devotion *or* attachment to a side *or* faction, partisanship, practice *or* system of forming sides on public questions, adherence, sectarianism, partiality, preference, favoritism, allegiance, fealty, faithfulness, fidelity.

5. One of the persons *(or a body of persons)* who compose one side in an action *or* affair *(as in a lawsuit),* plaintiff, defendant, accused, accusant, suitor, contender, combatant, belligerent, complainant, claimant, libelant *(Law),* litigant, disputant, assailant, opponent, libelee *(Law),* respondent *(Law),* controversialist, competitor, petitioner *(Law),* contestant, appellant *(Law).*

PAR, UP TO *adj.* Good, good enough, tolerable, decent, acceptable, pretty good, better than nothing, pretty fair, not bad, not amiss, satisfactory, unexceptional, passable, admissible, unobjectionable, middling, so-so, mediocre, bearable, presentable.

PARVENU, *adj.* Upstart, forward, brash, risen from the ranks, common, plebeian, brazen, precocious, presumptuous, impudent, arrogant, bluff, obtrusive, self-assertive, insolent, impertinent, cheeky *(coll)*, cocky *(coll.),* brassy *(coll.),* baseborn, earthborn, mushroom, pretentious, audacious, newly rich.

PARVENU, *n.* One who has risen above his class to a position above his qualifications, upstart, impostor, intruder, newly rich, *nouveau riche (Fr.),* pretender, snob, mushroom, would-be, adventurer, nobody, codfish aristocrat.

PASS, *n.* 1. Way affording passage *(as through an obstructed region or any barrier),* navigable channel, narrow passage, gorge, defile, gap, course, lane, aisle, passageway, conduit, avenue, trail, opening, isthmus, neck, duct, path, strait, ravine, cut, canyon, cove, notch, gulch, gully, narrows, canal, tunnel, ford, ferry, bridge, inlet, outlet.

2. Permission to pass (go, come, *or* enter), license, ticket, passport, password, privilege, authorization to leave, safe-conduct, permit, furlough, credentials, release, countersign *(Mil.),* vacation *(from army camp, etc.),* warrant, Open sesame.

3. Thrust, lunge, tilt, push, transference *(of a ball, etc.),* swing, toss, chuck, shy, cast, hurl, heave, pitch, throw, butt, shove, poke, sling, fling, transfer, stab, cut, coup, jab, jugglery, trick, sleight of hand, blow, dint, stroke.

4. Free ticket, courtesy card, press card, free admission.

5. Stage in procedure *or* experience, state of things *or* affairs, predicament, difficulty, condition, situation, state, case, turn, complication, impasse, stand, pinch, push, extremity, quandary, emergency, exigency, crisis, plight, conjuncture, juncture, pickle *(coll.),* fix *(coll.),* hole *(coll.),* nonplus, hornet's nest, standstill, blind alley, cul-de-sac, perplexity, strait *(often pl.).*

PASS, *v.* 1. Go by, make one's *or* its way, go *or* move onward, proceed, move past, make a transit, flow, roll, run, travel, slide, glide, sweep, stream, journey, skirt, speed, hie, hasten, course, advance, direct *or* pursue one's way, work one's way, drift, progress.

2. Go by without acting upon *or* noticing, leave unmentioned, omit, disregard, neglect, refrain, skip, slight, snub, overlook, spare, abstain, hold, dismiss, condone, think little of, not interfere, not heed, ignore, miss, exclude, respond passively to, discharge *or* discard from one's thoughts *or* mind, pay no attention to, turn away from, let lie, shun, close *or* shut one's eyes to, turn a deaf ear to, blink *or* wink at, not trouble oneself about, have no hand *or* part in, let go, let slip, gloss over, take no notice of, excuse, forget, forgive, avoid, be blind to, drop, put (set, cast, lay) aside, jump dodge, laugh off *or* away, make light of, skim over, slur over, forbear, abandon, shelve, let be *or* alone, hold aloof from, pretermit, fight shy of, keep clear of, evade, elude, hang fire, leave undone.

3. Go over *or* across, go *or* get through, ford, cross, traverse, overleap, overjump, penetrate, make *or* force a passage, pervade, permeate, cut across, navigate, sail, find an opening in, overpass.

4. Undergo successfully *(as an examination),* qualify, live through, endure, get by, satisfy, stand up, stand the test, meet the requirements of, conform to, come up to scratch *or* the standard, accomplish, finish, achieve, get through.

5. Go beyond *(a point, degree, stage, etc.),* exceed, surpass, overstep, outstrip, extend farther than, outgo, override, transcend, excel, surmount, distance, overtake, outdistance, lead, get ahead of, forespeed, forereach, precede, overtop, take precedence, get the start of, leave behind, encroach, overrun, infringe, impinge, obtrude.

6. Cause to go, allow to proceed, project, insert, thrust, press, push, force, move, prompt, guide, give an impulse to, set going, forward, propel, introduce, shove, direct, place, put, slip.

7. Spend *(as time),* live through, while away, beguile, fill, occupy, employ, consume, use, take-up, put in, fritter *or* fool away, expend, dissipate, kill, squander, wait through.

8. Cause to go about *or* circulate, give currency to, cause to be accepted *or* received, report, promote, advance, make known *or* public, circulate, set afloat, broadcast, publicize, spread, tell, proclaim, voice, herald, air, vent, propagate, promulgate, raise a report, blazon, divulge, rumor, hawk about, noise about, disseminate, bruit, divulgate, bring into the open, put forth *or* forward.

9. Be current, circulate, have a run, be the rage, gain currency, be received, find credence, go down, be fashionable, be accepted, go about, be published, be *or* become public, fly (buzz, blow) about, get afloat, spread, run *or* spread like wildfire, go from mouth to mouth, go the rounds, issue, come out, be swallowed *(coll.).*

10. Convey, transmit, transfer, deliver, devolve, be transferred, reach, put in the hands of, render, make over, turn over, consign, forward, give, let have, grant, present, confer, fall.

11. Pledge *(as one's word),* promise, vow, swear, vouch, covenant, contract, plight, assure, guarantee, certify, warrant, engage, give.

12. Void, *(as excrement),* discharge, defecate, eject, excrete, evacuate, emit, expel, eliminate.

13. Approve, legalize, legitimize, be passed, sanction, enact, be enacted, ratify, legislate, ordain, put in force, fix, set, formulate, authorize, order, decree, prescribe, clear, institute, negotiate, establish by law, constitute.

14. Express *(as an opinion or judgment),* offer, impart, make known, pronounce, utter, deliver, state, speak, voice, phrase, declare, communicate, present, put *or* set forth, announce, deliver, enunciate, articulate, phrase.

15. Go away, depart, come to an end, leave, become extinct, vanish, cease to be, fade away, be lost, recede, sink, go, dissolve, evaporate, elapse, lapse, run its course, go out, exit, wear off, leave no trace, be no more, be gone, be all over, become void, end, draw to a close, disappear, die, expire, blow over, melt, perish, run out, run its course, peter out *(coll.).*

16. Elapse *(as time),* be spent, fly, crawl, run out, flow, drag, wear, continue, melt, dissolve, evaporate, vanish, linger, glide, flit, slip, pass away, lapse.

17. Occur, go on, happen, take place, transpire, befall, betide, come to pass, take effect, come off, fall out, supervene, bechance, rise, prevail, crop up, take its course, come around, spring up, ensue, result, eventuate, arise, issue, appear, come about, go wrong, miscarry, present itself.

18. *(Fol. by* FOR *or* AS) Be accepted *or* received, double, do, answer, imitate, do well enough, personate, substitute, serve, suffice, avail, be of use, replace, represent, be mistaken for, appear authentic, simulate closely, be thought, be taken for, fill the bill *(coll.),* meet the requirements, satisfy, be sufficient.

19. Be interchanged *(as between two persons)*, alternate, be bandied, be exchanged, go to and fro, go back and forth, come and go, pass and repass, reciprocate.

20. Undergo transition *or* conversion, change, convert, alter, transmute, assume a new phase, resolve, revert, be reduced, oxidize, lapse, disintegrate, decompose, merge, be transformed, metamorphose, grow, mellow, ripen, become, blend, melt, open, run, turn.

21. Go unheeded (uncensured, unchallenged), slip by, be unnoticed, be unregarded, escape notice *or* attention, not enter one's head, be overlooked, not fall *or* come under one's notice, be forgotten, circumvent, sneak, elude, evade, give the slip, get around *(coll.)*.

PASSABLE, *adj.* 1. That may be proceeded through *or* over *or* crossed, fit for travel, traversable, penetrable, navigable, clear, open, fordable, unobstructed, free, unimpeded, crossable.

2. Tolerable, moderate, fair, presentable, common, lightweight, ordinary, allowable, admissible, pretty good, middling, insignificant, inconsiderable, scant, bearable, trivial, paltry, just adequate, barely, sufficient, meager, no great shakes *(coll.)*, not bad, betwixt and between, average, innocuous, harmless, imperfect, secondary, second-rate, better than nothing, unobjectionable, unexceptionable, of sorts, mere, nothing to brag about, not much to boast of, indifferent, so-so, unimportant, decent, slender, slight, mediocre, commonplace.

3. That may be circulated, that has valid currency, current, acceptable, authoritative, standard, sound, uniform, prevailing, right, correct, proper, authentic, established, acknowledged, recognized, received, orthodox, approved, admitted, receivable.

PASSAGE, *n.* 1. Indefinite portion *(of a writing, speech, etc.)*, clause, paragraph, piece, bit, excerpt, extract, section, column, selection, analects *(pl.)*, quotation, sentence, verse, chapter.

2. *(Music)* Division of a piece, phrase, scalelike *or* arpeggio-like series of tones serving to embellish, run, roulade, theme, flourish, ornament, bar, melody, air, coda, portion of a tune, trill, flight, cadenza, measure.

3. Act of passing, transit, transition, movement, progression, progress, career, flow, transmigration, transportation, flux, drive, motoring, riding, run, motion, going, course, tour, trip, excursion, expedition, pilgrimage, issuance, onrush, emergence, outcoming, issue, sail, circuit, ambulation, rush, drift, flight, stream, locomotion, voyage, migration, journey, itinerancy, caravan, parade, ingress, egress, cruise, trek, roving, navigation, transudation, infiltration, evacuation, discharge, transilience, emanation, pervasion, peregrination, procession, penetration, permeation.

4. Liberty, leave, *or* right to pass, reception, entry, access, privilege of conveyance, unconstraint, vouchsafement, immunity, independence, safe-conduct, freedom to come and go, entree, admission, admittance, fare, invitation.

5. That by which a person *or* thing passes, means of passing, way, avenue, channel, route, opening, path, road, aperture, hole, orifice, entrance, exit, approach, access, adit, mouth, eyelet, pore, porthole, track, trail, street, course, thoroughfare, cut, conduit, duct, ditch, chute, airway, seaway, passageway, parkway, highroad, boulevard, gutter, highway, race, door, drain, entryway, artery, pass, portal, outlet, inlet, vent, aisle, tunnel, narrows, ford, ferry, bridge.

6. Lapse *(as of time)*, passing, departure, expiration, course, continuation, continuity, flow, sweep, current, extension, process, flight, duration, step, march, stream, flux, tide, wings, period, tract, career, drift, prolongation, progress, progression.

7. Course *(as of events)*, progress, chain, thread, string, round, parade, cycle, march, following, tide, flow, stream, order, rush, series, sequence, succession, consecution, consecutiveness, continuance, continuation, catenation, concatenation, progression, development.

8. Enactment, passing into law *(of a legislative measure)*, legalization, constitutionalization, legislation, approval, election, ordainment, codification, establishment, fixing, enforcement, authorization, endorsement, affirmation, confirmation, ratification, majority acceptance, approbation, sanction.

9. Interchange *(of communications, confidences, etc.)*, exchange, trading, reciprocation, communication, give-and-take, interlocution, converse, conversation, commerce, confabulation, colloquy, collocation, interchange of views, dialogue, negotiation, transaction, discussion, verbal intercourse, conference, consultation.

10. Exchange of blows, dispute, altercation, pass, encounter, combat, skirmish, tilt, affair, imbroglio, contest, brush, collision, conflict, contest, battle, strife, struggle, set-to, affray, fray, tournament, contention, duel, wrangle, engagement, fight, rencounter, action, concussion, tourney, clash, scuffle, fracas, jostle, fisticuffs, assault, charge, impingement, controversy, confrontation, tussle, impact, match, embroilment, scrimmage, melee, arms, game, feud.

11. Causing of something to pass, transference, transmission, transfer, transmittal, deportation, traction, infection, contagion, transplantation, transposition, translocation, conveyance, conduction, portage, haulage, delivery, change, transportation, carriage, shift, transition, interchange, metathesis, metastasis *(Physiol.)*, dispersion, dislocation, replacement, removal, shipment.

PASSAGEWAY, *n.* Way for passage *(as in a building or among buildings)*, passage, gallery, gate, port, portal, hall, corridor, aisle, doorway, exit, entrance, entryway, alley, lane, boardwalk, arcade, cloister, colonnade, stairwell, stairs, steps, thoroughfare, threshold, mall, sidewalk, walk, footpath, access, way, path, companionway *(Naut.)*, gangway *(Naut.)*.

PASSE, *adj.* Antiquated, past, faded, past the prime, out of date, obsolete, stale, on the shelf, worn-out, out of fashion, old-fashioned, fallen into disuse, ancient, antique, disused, gone to seed, retired, lapsed, extinct, archaic, hoary, dead, outworn, timeworn, discarded, expired, bygone, exploded, effete, forgotten, desuete, outdated, discredited, rejected, dismissed, former, refuted, neglected, superannuated.

PASSENGER, *n.* 1. One who travels by some form of conveyance, journeyer, traveler, voyager, itinerant, tourist, trekker, sightseer, commuter, rider, equestrian, horseman, fare, cruiser, globetrotter *(coll.)*, excursionist, straphanger *(coll.)*.

2. Wayfarer, traveler on foot, wanderer, hiker, roamer, rover, peregrinator, itinerant, drifter, courier, runner, walker, passer-by, nomad, vagabond, bird of passage, pedestrian, hitchhiker *(coll.)*, peripatetic *(chiefly hum.)*.

PASSER-BY, *n.* One who passes by, traveler afoot, bystander, witness, spectator, vagrant, vagabond, Wandering Jew, pedestrian, observer, on-looker, wayfarer, itinerant, looker-on, watcher.

PASSING, *adj.* 1. Elapsing, transient, fleeting, transitory, going by, momentary, mortal, preterient, volatile, evanescent, reducible, unstable, vanishing, transitive, diurnal, fugacious, provisional, intermediate, progressive, moving, impermanent, ephemeral, proceeding, temporal, temporary, precarious, shifting, short-lived, perishable, caducous, inconstant, forward-looking, progressing, fluent, fugitive.

2. Now happening, current, moving before one's eyes, occurring, present, existent, extant, taking place, of the moment, prevalent, rife, afloat, on foot, instant, doing, living, latest, in the wind, progressing.

3. Done *(given, etc.)* in passing, cursory, brief, quick, glancing, casual, shallow, impulsive, abrupt, brusque, hasty, short, fleeting, summary, fleet, brisk, slight, momentary, superficial, unthinking, sudden, rapid, impatient, extemporaneous, extempore.

PASSION, *n.* 1. Feeling *or* emotion of compelling force, ardor, zeal, impulse, glow, pain, vehemence, agony, violence, shock, strong feeling, excitement, transport, rapture, fervor, heat, enthusiasm, unction *(of speech)*, suffering, heart, impetuosity, eagerness, verve, ravishment, fire, furor, desperation, distraction, ecstasy, intensity, thrill, fervency, intoxication, agitation, earnestness, fever, enchantment, furor, gusto, pervading spirit, sensation, exigency, fullness of heart, avidity, longing, coveting, hunger, aspiration, ambition, itch, ache, pang, warmth, thirst, irresistible urge, urgency, need, flush, idolatry, idolization, insanity, compulsion, cacoëthes, mania, lust, distress, woe, intensity.

2. Strong amorous feeling *or* desire, sexual appetite *or* desire, vehement desire, appetite, craving, lust, appetence, animalism, carnality, concupiscence, yearning, amorousness, heat, infatuation, heart, flame, hankering, impatience, aphrodisia, crush *(sl.)*.

3. Object of strong feeling *(esp. love, desire, etc.)*, loved one, beloved, mania, craze, idol, desired, charm, spell, favorite, obsession, all-important thing, height of one's ambition.

4. Strong *or* extravagant fondness, great enthusiasm, like, love, mania, affection, attachment, warmth, devotion, adoration, liking, fancy, infatuation, warm regard, partiality, relish, veneration, fanaticism, obsession, reverence, avidity, ardor, zeal, zealotry, enthusiasm, intentness, bewitchment, delirament, enchantment, hunger, longing, thirst, ambition, aspiration, entrancement, captivation, weakness, worship.

5. Passionate outburst, violent anger, rampage, fire, ire, spleen, wrath, fury, vehemence, madness, fit, craze, bile, choler, temper, violence, fume, storm, flare-up, frenzy, paroxysm, excitement, rage, indignation, resentment, huff, furor, eruption, bluster, fierceness, hot blood, hatred, hot words, explosion, blind rage, seething, ranting, scene.

6. *(Often cap.)* The sufferings of Christ subsequent to the Last Supper *(esp. on the cross)*, Gospel narrative of Christ's sufferings, anguish, crucifixion, torture, torment, rack, martyrdom, agony.

PASSIONATE, *adj.* 1. Affected with or dominated by passion *or* vehement emotion, vehement, impassioned, intense, furious, violent, burning, ardent, warm, animated, impetuous, impulsive, fer-vid, flaming, amorous, aroused, zealous, earnest, excited, fiery, fervent, glowing, enthusiastic, transported, fierce, agitated, desperate, feverish, intoxicated, frenzied, stormy, inflamed, emotional, wrought-up, foaming, disturbed, boiling, unquiet, perturbed, kindled, delirious, raging, tempestuous, ebullient.

2. Easily moved to anger, irascible, quick- tempered, hot, touchy, peppery, excitable, hasty, choleric, angry, fiery, violent, irate, boisterous, susceptible, wrathful, quick, hot-headed, irritable, hot-blooded, stormy, tumultuous, hot-tempered, impatient, fractious, petulant, volcanic, explosive, mad, rampant, raging, pugnacious, unrestrained, fuming, uncontrollable, bellicose, ungovernable, waspish, quarrelsome, touchy, testy, spleenful, acerbic, bristling, headstrong, cross, captious, high-strung, churlish, huffy, bearish, cross-grained, snappish, mettlesome, bilious, iracund, splenetic, hostile, contentious, boorish, inflammable, nervous, like a barrel of gunpowder, like touchwood *or* tinder, vindictive, resentful.

PASSIONLESS, *adj.* Cold, without passion *or* feeling, stoical, phlegmatic, apathetic, impassive, unimpassioned, unemotional, cold-blooded, unimpressible, heartless, unsympathetic, unresponsive, distant, unfeeling, aloof, hard, frigid, without heart, torpid, sluggish, lukewarm, untroubled, unruffled, unconcerned, supercilious, unkindled, chill, icy, unapproachable, stiff, forbidding, nonchalant, remote, listless, insensible, half-hearted, callous, comatose, adamantine, unexcitable, numb, languid, supine, inert, unsolicitous, obdurate, stony, soulless, insensitive, unmoved, unstirred, indifferent, indurated, pococurante, inanimate, stolid, uncaring, impervious, untouched, calm, insentient, incurious.

PASSIVE, *adj.* 1. Not acting, not manifested in open *or* positive action, quiescent, inactive, inert, indifferent, dormant, latent, languid, undemonstrative, peaceful, sluggish, stagnant, feeble, weak, unperturbed, languorous, torpid, apathetic, unaffected, quiet, drowsy, heavy, tranquil, still, calm, motionless, static, abeyant, recessive, suspended, fixed, sleeping, careless, uninterested, slow, torpescent, dull, leaden, lazy, dronish, indolent, torporific, listless, bovine, lethargic, idle, lymphatic, otiose, phlegmatic, lifeless, recumbent, cool, soporific, faint, heedless, insipid, slack, zestless.

2. Being the object of action, suffering *or* submitting without resistance, acted upon, receiving impressions from without, nonresistant, submissive, enduring, unresisting, neutral, unprovoked, obedient, yielding, receptive, docile, subject, tractable, conformable, unassertive, acquiescent, meek, unopposing, compliant, pliant, servile, irresolute, patient, resigned, obsequious, restrained, bound, in harness, lamblike, under control, chastened, humble, forbearant, subdued, content, gentle, tame, in subjection, stoical, long-suffering, philosophic.

PASSIVENESS, PASSIVITY, *n.* Inactivity, resignation, apathy, inertia, inertness, inaction, dormancy, idleness, nonresistance, submissiveness, suspense, non interference, latency, *laissez faire,* abeyance, languor, torpor, stagnation, vegetation, obedience, immobility, indifference, sufferance, quiescence, calm, stupor, anesthesia, patience, rest, hebetude, lentitude, endurance, fixity, submission, compliance, lassitude, stoicism, forbearance, acquiescence, complaisance, tolerance, lethargy, impassiveness, suppression of feeling, subjection, watchful waiting, neglect, repose, ductility, humility, yielding, supineness, suspended animation, faineancy.

PASSPORT, *n.* Official document granting rights of travel and protection, authorization to pass *or* go, anything that gives admission *or* acceptance, certificate securing admission, permit, pass, license, warrant, safeguard, password, safekeeping, custody, auspices, protection, safe-conduct, sea letter *(Naut.),* credentials, dustuck *(India).*

PASSWORD, *n.* Secret word *(known only to authorized persons),* watchword, countersign, shibboleth, sign, pass, Open sesame.

PAST, *adj.* 1. Belonging to the past, gone by, passed away, dead and gone, historical, quondam, sometime, prior, elapsed, expired, by-past, departed, bygone, previous, former, ancient, gone, old, of yore *(Poet.),* olden *(Poet.),* ago.
2. *(Gramm.)* Preterit, aorist, pluperfect, perfect.
3. No longer functioning, ex- *(combining form),* retired, previous, late.
4. Extinct, obsolete, old-fashioned, ancient, archaic, antiquated, forgotten, lost, unremembered, passé, outdated, out-of-date, out-of-fashion, unfashionable, dead, gone by, disused, unrecollected, bygone.

PAST, *adv.* By, near, alongside, parallel, at hand, beside, abreast, neck and neck, by the side.

PAST, *n.* Previous time, former time, heretofore, ancient times, olden times *(Poet.),* yesterday, yesteryear, long ago, history, days gone by, antiquity.

PAST, *prep.* Beyond, near, nearby, through, by way of, by, via.

PASTE, *n.* 1. Dough, pulp, gluten, batter, mix, magma.
2. Glue, adhesive, gum, cement, agglutinant, size, mucilage, mastic, isinglass.

PASTEBOARD, *n.* Cardboard, millboard, strawboard, paperboard, binder's board, card.

PASTEBOARD, *adj.* 1. Unsubstantial, thin, paltry, trashy, meretricious, shoddy, gimcrack, flimsy, jerry-built, tinsel, tawdry.
2. Sham, false, fake, counterfeit, synthetic, brummagem *(sl.),* mock, artificial, pseudo, catchpenny, spurious, bogus, hollow, feigned, make-believe, pretended, simulated, imitation.

PASTEL, *n.* 1. Crayon, pencil, chalk, marking chalk, coloring pencil, lead, charcoal.
2. *(Lit.)* Light literary sketch, familiar essay, vignette, sketch, picturization, depiction, word painting, word picture, delineation.

PASTILLE, *n.* 1. Deodorizer.
2. Small, flavored cake *or* confection, electuary, drop, jujube, troche *(Pharm.),* bonbon, comfit, pill, bolus, tablet, sweet, sugarplum, sweetmeat, lozenge.

PASTIME, *n.* Pleasure, diversion, fun, distraction, avocation, recreation, amusement, entertainment, sport, play, relaxation, hobby, game, divertissement.

PASTOR, *n.* Clergyman *(with reference to his flock),* parson, priest, divine, minister, dominie, chaplain, father, one having spiritual care of a number of persons, ecclesiastic, chairman, padre, rector, curate, shepherd, curé, vicar.

PASTORAL, *adj.* 1. Of shepherds, rustic, rural, countrified, georgic, agrarian, agricultural, simple, Arcadian, provincial.
2. Portraying the life of shepherds *or* of the country, bucolic, idyllic, georgic, Arcadian.

3. Ministerial, of a pastor, ecclesiastical, priestly, sacerdotal, episcopal, clerical.

PASTORAL, *n.* Poem, play, *etc.,* dealing with the life of shepherds *or* rural life, bucolic, eclogue, georgic, idyl, pastorale *(Mus.).*

PASTORATE, *n.* Office *or* term of office of a pastor, pastorship, parish, living, curacy, presbyterate, bishopric, vicarship, church, charge, see, benefice, canonry, incumbency, diocese, episcopate, rectorship, ministry, priesthood, deaconry, abbacy, sacerdotalism, chaplaincy, prelacy.

PASTRY, *n.* Food made of paste, pie, pie crust, tart, French pastry, Danish pastry, patty, pâté *(Fr.),* puff, patisserie, turnover.

PASTURAGE, *n.* Growing grass for cattle, *etc.,* grazing land *or* ground, grassland, pasture, food for cattle, herbage, forage grass, field, meadow land, mead *(Poetic),* lea *(Poetic),* vegetation of the fields, range.

PASTURE, *v.* Supply with pasturage, feed *(cattle, etc.)* by putting them to graze on pasture, turn out to pasture, graze, forage.

PASTY, *adj.* Of *or* like paste *(in consistency, appearance, etc.),* doughy, sticky, chalky, clayey, loamy, adhesive, glutinous, gluey, mucous, gummy, stringy, flabby, ropy, lutose, gumbo, muddy, uliginose, miry, oozy, gooey *(sl.),* squashy, gelatinous, pulpy, white, cretaceous, succulent, pithy, spongy, amylaceous, starchy, soft, gummy.

PAT, *adj.* Exactly to the point *or* purpose, apt, fit, convenient, suitable, ready, opportune, in point, timely, adapted, felicitous, germane, happy, apposite, expedient, meet, seasonable, relevant, applicable, appropriate, pertinent, fitting, favorable, fortunate, advantageous, right, apropos, becoming, well-chosen, politic, well-timed, proper, seemly, befitting, desirable, auspicious.

PAT, *n.* 1. Light blow *or* stroke, caress, rap, tap, dab, gentle blow, sound of a light stroke *or* a light footstep, slap, flap, pad, patter, plump, thud, thump, small spank, drumming, tread, pitter-patter, rat-tat, tattoo, thwack, hit.
2. Small lump *or* mass *(as shaped by patting),* cake, piece, biscuit, patty, morsel, particle, mouthful, bite, bit, chunk, hunk *(coll.),* dab.

PAT, *v.* Strike lightly *or* gently, hit, caress, pet, patter, flap, slap, clap, rap, tap, dab.

PATCH, *n.* 1. Piece *(sewn on for repairs, etc.),* reinforcement, repair, mend, replacement.
2. Plot *(of land, grass, etc.),* lot, piece of ground, division, field, property, clearing, tract, part.
3. Excerpt *(from a piece of prose, poetry, etc.),* passage, quotation, bit, section, extract, selection, analects *(pl.),* paragraph, piece.
4. Small part, modicum, scrap, scratch, spot, iota, speckle, scintilla, ion, snip, cut, cutting, chip, fragment, sliver, chunk, whittling, paring, discard, tag, slice, morsel, particle, splint, speck, shred, piece, flake, splinter, remnant, snick, lamina, snicking, snippet, chipping, shaving, clipping, gobbet, cantle, cantlet, snatch, collop, snack, rasher, check, scantling, leaf, dib, peel, slug, wafer, scrip, shive, scale.

PATCH, *v.* Patch up, repair, mend, sew up, reinforce, replace, put a piece in, fix, tinker, retouch, vamp, revamp, splice, darn, clout.

PATCH UP, *v.* Act as mediator *(in a quarrel, etc.),* bring peace, adjust, pour oil on troubled waters, pour balm on, resolve differences, settle, appease, restore harmony, bring to terms, conciliate, propitiate, negotiate a peace, placate, pacify, heal the breach, settle differences, mediate, intervene, moderate, intercede, interpose, arbitrate.

PATENT, *adj.* 1. Public, available, accessible, open, free, published, unrestricted, free to all, unenclosed.

2. Plain, distinct, conspicuous, unscreened, unmasked, undoubted, decided, pronounced, explicit, revealed, undiguised, open, uncamouflaged, unhidden, disclosed, plain as a pikestaff, plain as the nose on one's face, prominent, recognizable, glaring, undeniable, perspicuous, overt, visible, lucid, obvious, unequivocal, unmistakable, ostensible, unquestionable, notable, bald, discernible, unconcealed, apparent, palpable, manifest.

3. Copyrighted, copyright, trademarked, with all rights reserved.

PATENT, *n.* Government grant *(to an inventor, etc.)* safeguarding his product's exclusiveness, copyright, license, certificate of invention, privilege of monopoly of ownership, right to profits accruing *(from an invention)*, permit, registry.

PATENT, *v.* Take out a patent on, obtain the exclusive rights to *(an invention)*, originate and establish as one's own, register, license, grant ownership *(to an inventor, of his product)*.

PATERNAL, *adj.* 1. Characteristic of *or* befitting a father, fatherly, kind, careful, tender, parental, benevolent, fond, mindful, benign, indulgent, loving, watchful, interested, concerned, solicitous, thoughtful, regardful, vigilant, anxious, well-disposed, considerate, well-meaning, well-intentioned, affectionate, fatherlike, good.

2. Derived *or* inherited from a father, related on the father's side, hereditary, lineal, family, patrimonial, patriarchal, ancestral.

PATERNALISM, *n.* Regulation of the affairs *(of a country, community, or of individuals)* in the manner of a father dealing with his children, socialism, welfare state, communism, nationalism, collectivism *(Pol. Sci.)*, universal benevolence, concern for the common *or* general welfare, control, oversight, patronage, protection, supervision, surveillance, jurisdiction, utilitarianism, totalitarianism, Fourierism.

PATERNITY, *n.* 1. State of being a father, fathership, fatherhood, sireship, paternal headship *or* rule, paternal parentage, procreation, progeniture, progenitorship.

2. Derivation from a father, descent, ancestry, parentage, line, lineage, family.

3. Authorship, origin, origination, creation, composition, fabrication, formation, shaping, innovation, invention, production, inditement, designing, writing, depiction, fashioning, forming, synthesis, portrayal, representation.

PATH, *n.* 1. Track, footway, trail, way *(beaten or trodden by the feet of men or beasts)*, walk, avenue, passage, passageway, channel, pathway, pavement, aisle, alley, route, by-path, byway, by-road, canal, conduit, crosscut, short cut, runway, access, road, *trottoir (Fr.)*, mall, lane, sidewalk, berm *(Fort.)*, approach, towpath.

2. Course in which something moves, route, track, run, orbit, rut, groove, loop, round, lap, journey, routine, rails, trajectory, itinerary, tour, turn, cycle, circuit, beat, walk, ambit, sphere, circle, traversal, compass, bounds, area, peregrination, circumference.

3. Course of action, conduct, *or* procedure, way, method, manner, mode, form, fashion, practice, project, behavior, life, career, scheme, plan,

policy, device, walk, role, line of conduct, system, means.

PATHETIC, *adj.* Exciting pity *or* sympathetic sadness, full of pathos, moving, affecting, distressing, plaintive, emotional, touching, grievous, woeful, lamentable, pitiful, tender, melting, heartrending, affective, piteous, dolorous, doleful, sad, mournful, to be pitied, sorrowful, exciting compassion, pitiable, deplorable, rueful.

PATHFINDER, *n.* One who finds a path *or* way *(as through a wilderness)*, pioneer, trail blazer, paver of the way, forerunner, scout.

PATHLESS, *adj.* Without paths, trackless, wayless, untracked, unexplored, dense, jungle, overgrown, waste, wilderness, unopened, closed, impervious, impassable, untrodden, impenetrable, unpathed, unpenetrated.

PATHOLOGICAL, *adj.* Of *or* pertaining to pathology, due to *or* involving disease, morbid, ill, sick, ailing, unwell, unhealthy, unbalanced, affected, tainted, diseased, disordered, abnormal, psychotic, psychoneurotic.

PATHOLOGY, *n.* The science of the origin, nature, and course of diseases, the conditions and processes of a disease, pathogeny, semiology, nosology, symptomatology, diagnostics, etiology, protozoology, parasitology, bacteriology, pathogenesis.

PATHOS, *n.* Quality *or* power of evoking pity *or* sympathetic sadness, touching *or* pathetic character *or* effect, sentiment, feeling, moving expression, affection, depression, heaviness, weight, desolation, agony, misery, heartache, anguish, grief, woe, pitiableness, tenderness, sadness, emotion, prostration, affliction, sentimentalism, sentimentality.

PATIENCE, *n.* 1. Calm and uncomplaining endurance *(as under pain, provocation, etc.)*, fortitude, submission, bearing, sufferance, longsuffering, serenity, ease *or* peace of mind, humility, yielding, poise, calm, inperturbability, meekness, lowliness, composure, quietness, nonresistance, longanimity, self-control, obedience, equanimity, passivity, passiveness, resignation, stoicism.

2. Calmness in waiting, forbearance, indulgence, tacit allowance, temperance, self-possession, content, equanimity, composure, understanding, sufferance, longanimity, leniency, forbearing, comfort, level head, coolness, imperturbation, lack of nervousness, cheerfulness, peace of mind, ease, tolerance, optimism, poise, good humor *or* temper, moderation, hope, long-suffering, self-control, serenity, even temper, placidity, tranquility, inirritability, unexcitability, forgiveness, self-command, *sang-froid (Fr.)*.

3. Quiet perseverance, persistence, plodding, industry, grit, stamina, resolution, endurance, sedulity, diligence, constancy, indefatigableness, singleness *or* tenacity of purpose, pluck, mettle, staying power, pertinacity, steadiness, application, doggedness, indefatigibility, firmness, courage, zeal, devotion, drudgery, devotedness, determination, stability, assiduousness.

PATIENT, *adj.* 1. Quietly persevering, persistent, pertinacious, dogged, tenacious, constant, assiduous, enduring, untiring, unfaltering, resolute, resolved, not to be shaken *or* put down, determined, unwavering, unflagging, steadfast, relentless, indomitable, strong-willed, plucky, mettlesome, businesslike, unsleeping, hard-working, game to the last *or* end, sedulous, industrious, stable, stern, stanch, inexorable, uncompromising, fixed, firm, unchangeable, diligent, indefatigable, unyielding, unswerving, unflinching, gritty, undeviating, unremitting, steady, unwearied, undaunted, plodding.

2. Enduring pain (trouble, affliction, hardship, etc.) with fortitude, submissive, calm, quietly enduring strain, annoyance, etc., serene, lamblike, yielding, humble, stoical, chastened, content, unprovoked, forbearing, longanimous, long-suffering, unrepining, uncomplaining, resigned, self-restrained, unresisting, obedient, docile, dutiful, subdued, armed with patience, unmurmuring, self-controlled, passive, subject, gentle, placid, meek, mild, imperturbable, restrained, acquiescent, compliant.

3. Enduring delay with calmness or equanimity, indulgent, lenient, calm, composed, content, placid, mild, cool, unruffled, serene, considerate, easygoing, unprovoked, long-suffering, untroubled, forgiving, philosophical, longanimous, unperturbed, unvexed, pacific, clement, undisturbed, peaceful, collected, cheerful, at ease, imperturbable, forbearing, tolerant, temperate, level-headed, not restless or nervous, self-controlled, satisfied, nonchalant, tranquil, poised.

PATIENT, n. 1. One who is under medical or surgical care, case, invalid, sufferer, sick person, outpatient, victim, valetudinarian.

2. Person or thing that undergoes action (opposed to AGENT), object, subject, victim, testee, recipient, receiver, experimentee.

PATIO, n. Court (esp. enclosed and open to the sky), courtyard, square, yard, compound, open porch, piazza.

PATOIS, n. Peasant or provincial form of speech, jargon, lingo, idiom, localism, provincialism, regionalism, accent, dialect, argot, brogue, twang, cant, vernacular, colloquialism, flash (coll.).

PATRIARCH, n. 1. (Eccles.) Earlier Biblical personage (regarded as a founder of the human race or of the Israelites), bishop of highest rank (Gk. Orthodox and Eastern non- Orthodox churches), Pope or highest bishop (Rom. Cath. Ch.), highest dignitary (Mormon Ch.), Evangelist (Mormon Ch.), hierarch, prelate, papas, papa, pontiff, reverence, Eminence, high or chief priest.

2. Elder, leading older member (of a community), male head of a family or tribal line, founder or father (of an order, class, etc.), venerable old man, ancestor, paterfamilias, master, oldster (coll.), forefather, grandfather, reverend sir, progenitor, sire (Poetic), primogenitor, forebear.

PATRICIAN, adj. 1. Of high social rank or noble family, of rank, noble, high, royal, exalted, wellborn, distinguished, highborn, aristocratic, of gentle blood, upper-class, pure-blooded, titled, reputable, genteel, lordly, imposing, estimable, blue-blooded, baronial, highly respectable, silk-stocking.

2. Befitting an aristocrat, high-principled, exemplary, princely, creditable, stately, manly, grand, majestic, imposing, just, meritorious, gentlemanly, princelike, high-minded, aristocratic, kingly, queenly, of sterling character, well-bred, worthy, honorable, upright, ladylike, proud, lordly, virtuous, courteous, courtly, genteel, dignified, cultured, formal, reputable, jealous of honor, impressive, moral, respectable, noble.

PATRICIAN, n. Aristocrat, noble, nobleman, peer, blue blood (coll.), silk-stocking, grandee, magnifico, thoroughbred, lord, gentleman, ruler, gentlewoman, peeress, seignior, signor (It.), señor (Sp.), don (Sp.).

PATRICIATE, n. The patrician class, nobility, aristocracy, gentry, royalty, cream of society, high society, elite, upper classes, landed proprietors, gentlefolk, peerage, baronage, lords, first families, knighthood, silk-stockings.

PATRIMONY, n. 1. Estate inherited from one's father or ancestors, heritage, paternal or hereditary estate, inheritance, legacy, bequest, dowry, dotation, endowment, fee (Law), jointure (Law), birthright.

2. Aggregate of one's property, holdings, possessions, goods, belongings, effects, estate, chattels, hereditament (Law).

PATRIOT, n. Lover of one's country, zealous supporter and defender of one's country and its interests, nationalist, citizen, loyalist, jingo, chauvinist.

PATRIOTIC, adj. Of or like a patriot, inspired by patriotism, jingo, chauvinistic, allegiant, nationalistic, public-spirited, loyal (to one's country and its interests), spread-eagle (coll.).

PATRIOTISM, n. Spirit or action of a patriot, love of country, devotion to one's country, nationalism, nationality, citizenship, civism, national spirit, public spirit, over patriotism, jingoism, chauvinism, patriolatry, spread-eagleism (coll.).

PATROL, n. 1. Person or body of persons charged with patrolling, guard, ranger, lifeguard, safeguard, bodyguard, guardian, sentry, detail, watchman, warden, warder, watch, keeper, lookout, convoy, escort, watchdog, policeman, constable, garrison, patrolman, vedette, picket, militia.

2. Act of patrolling, watch, guard, lookout, care, protection, safekeeping, defense, vigilance, vigil, safe-conduct, sentry duty.

PATROL, v. Go the rounds (as a guard), traverse a particular district (as a policeman), go on one's beat, watch, perform sentry duty, man the garrison, defend, protect, render safe, safeguard, keep vigil or guard.

PATROLMAN, n. Member of a police force patrolling a certain district, man who patrols, etc. See PATROL, n. above.

PATRON, n. 1. One who supports with his patronage, defender, protector, supporter, backer, giver, patroness, partisan, upholder, philanthropist, favorer, advocate, employer, promoter, encourager, friend, succorer, befriender, benefactress, benefactor, helper, well-wisher, sympathizer, Maecenas, friend in or at court, champion, good genius, tutelary saint, angel (sl.), guardian, subscriber, one whose support or protection is solicited (by the dedication of a book or other work).

2. Buyer, customer, attender, habitué, shopper, client, purchaser, frequenter, patronizer, marketer, vendee (chiefly Legal).

PATRONAGE, n. 1. Financial support afforded by customers (to a shop, business, etc.), custom, buying, dealing, habitual purchasing, trade, business, commerce.

2. Support (of a patron), encouragement, favor, countenance, assistance, influence, ministration, championship, backing, cultivation, fosterage, power, guidance, protection, aid, friendship, interest, advocacy, keeping, charge, wardship, preservation, auspices, approval.

3. Control of appointments to public service (or of other political favors), offices (or other favors) so controlled, favor, interest, advantage, auspices, instrumentality, bias, inside track (coll.), in (sl.), influence, backing, pull (sl.), drag (sl.).

4. Condescending favor, condescension, condescendence, patronizing, indulgence, toleration, insolence, audacity, stooping, disparagement, airs, detraction, impudence, insolence, contumely, impertinence, procacity, sauciness, underestimation, flippancy, abuse, disrespect, brazenness, assurance. effrontery, overbearingness, sufferance, deigning, gall (*sl.*).

PATRONIZE, *v.* 1. Favor with one's patronage, trade with, deal with, do *or* transact business with, frequent (*as a customer*).

2. Treat in a condescending way, indulge, suffer, arrogate, make free *or* bold, assume a lofty bearing, overbear, detract, derogate, presume, discredit, disparage, disrespect, underestimate, cast aspersions, slur, insult, dishonor, offend, be contemptuous, disdain, despise, look down one's nose at, esteem slightly, contemn, set down, humiliate, scorn, affront.

3. Act as patron toward, favor, countenance, support, aid, look after, minister to, stand by, second, stand behind *or* back of, endorse, defend, maintain, befriend, help, assist, protect, take the part of, espouse the cause of, lend one's name to, promote, foster, subscribe to, abet, encourage, smile upon, cultivate, approve, back.

PATRONYMIC, *n.* Surname, family name, cognomen, ancestral name.

PATTER, *n.* Pattering sound, act of pattering, spatter, drumming, pitter-patter, palpitation, beat, rap, tap, dab, gentle blow, slap, flap, pad, plump, thud, pat, rat-tat, tattoo.

PATTER, *v.* Strike *or* move with a succession of slight tapping sounds, tap, pat, palpitate, thrum, go pitter-patter, beat, rap, dab, clap, slap, flap, sprinkle, spatter.

PATTERN, *n.* 1. Decorative design, ornament, figure, stripe, plaid, check, decoration, limnery, engraving, chasing, etching, chiseling, motif, stipple, burr, adornment, garnishment, illumination, beautification, embellishment, embroidery, ornation, ornamentation.

2. Style, type, figure, form, shape, formation, figuration, conformation, configuration, structure, format, composition, turn, mold, cast, impression, make, build, make-up, construction, stamp, cut, frame.

3. Model proposed for *or* deserving of imitation, original, exemplar, archetype, criterion, norm, ideal, mirror, prototype, plan, template, nonesuch, guide, mold, rule, antitype, gauge, fugler, fugleman, yardstick, scale, test, check, canon, design, draft, layout, principle, arrangement, specifications, protocol, form, image, precedent, instance, sample, specimen, paragon, example, representative, illustration, quotation, case, protractor (*Math., etc.*), outline, idea, historic warrant, keynote, standard, last, paradigm.

PATTERN, *v.* 1. Model (*one's conduct, etc.;* foll. *by* **BY** *or* **AFTER**), copy, imitate, make after a pattern, shape, fashion, figure, govern, be guided, mold, form, make resemble, carve, double, echo, feign, match, assume, simulate, describe, trace, delineate, represent, emulate, mimic, follow closely, tread upon, reflect, repeat, parody, caricature, burlesque, hit *or* take off on, take after, travesty, personate, ape, parallel, do like, duplicate.

2. Cover *or* mark with a pattern, design, etch, trim, figure, chase, character, chisel, engrave, stipple, tool, print, carve, cut, inscribe, emboss, stamp.

PAUCITY, *n.* Fewness, smallness of quantity,

scantiness, scarcity, sparseness, sparsity, rarity, stint, scantness, poverty, exiguity, want, lack, dearth, famine, drought, need, deficiency, restriction, limitation, shortage, starvation, destitution, deprivation, thinness, small number, insufficiency.

PAUNCH, *n.* 1. Abdomen, belly, stomach, craw, crop (*of birds*), maw, tummy (*hum.*), ingluvies (*Zool.*), gizzard (*of birds*), breadbasket (*sl.*), pouch, first stomach (*of a ruminant*).

2. Large prominent belly, tun, potbelly, corporation (*sl.*), bay window (*hum.*).

PAUPER, *n.* Very poor person, one without means of support (*a charge on the community*), beggar, poorling, insolvent, mendicant, down-and-out, down-and-outer, bankrupt, sponger, moocher, bum, panhandler (*coll.*), have-not (*coll.*).

PAUPERISM, *n.* Utter *or* extreme poverty, indigence, penury, poverty, necessity, need, want, beggary, destitution, mendicity, impecuniosity, distress, difficulties, straits, lack, privation, slender *or* narrow means, hand-to-mouth existence, light purse, empty pocket *or* purse, loss of fortune, embarrassed (reduced, straitened) circumstances, wolf at the door, bankruptcy, mendicancy.

PAUPERIZE, *v.* Make a pauper of, impoverish, render poor, reduce to poverty, bankrupt, ruin, break, fleece.

PAUSE, *n.* 1. Temporary stop, lull, suspension, rest, cessation, break, ceasing, recess, respite, lapse, stay, time out, drop, parenthesis, breathing spell, intermittence, letup (*coll.*), discontinuity, disconnection, intermission, interval, stoppage, remission, halt, interruption, discontinuance, deadlock, standstill, interlude, vacation, holiday, abeyance, idling, spell, stopping, deferment, stillness.

2. Cessation proceeding from doubt *or* uncertainty, suspense, hesitation, stall, hesitancy, lag, waiting, pendency, protraction, prolongation, procrastination, play for time, suspension, moration.

3. (*In music, speech, reading, writing, or printing*) Break, breath, paragraph, parenthesis, rest (*Mus.*), whole rest, half rest, quarter rest, caesura (*Pros.*), colon, semicolon, period, stop, comma, point, dieresis (*Pros.*).

PAUSE, *v.* Make a pause, stop, wait, hesitate, demur, linger, dwell, interrupt, hold back, deliberate, waver, delay, desist, rest, stay, falter, suspend, stall, hold, stick, hang fire, tarry, hang back, be irresolute, be uncertain, hover, be at a standstill, mark time, relax, stay one's hand, take breath, slacken, stand, discontinue, intermit, forbear, loiter, fluctuate, breathe, break off.

PAVE, *v.* 1. Cover *or* lay (*a road, walk, etc.*) with some substance so as to make a firm, level surface, slab, cobble, face, tar, asphalt, macadamize, concrete, smooth, floor, flag, brick, pitch.

2. Prepare (*the way*) for, facilitate, make ready *or* easy, make preparations *or* arrangements, grease *or* soap the way, arrange for, ease, ready, break the ice, make way for, open the way *or* door, clear the way, smooth the path *or* road.

PAVEMENT, *n.* 1. Paved road, sidewalk, flagging, paving floor, walk, curbstone, pavé (*Fr.*).

2. Material used for paving, cobblestone, cobbles, flag, flagstones, tar, stone, concrete, cement, brick, asphalt, macadam, pavestones.

PAVILION, *n.* Light open structure (*for shelter, pleasure, etc.*), tent, canopy, shed, booth, hut, stall, lean-to, tabernacle, kiosk, covering, canvas, marquee, marquise, shade, awning, shelter, tarpaulin, shack (*coll.*).

PAW, *n.* Foot on an animal *(with nails or claws),* pad, forefoot, hind foot.

PAW, *v.* Strike *(with the feet or paws),* scrape, rub, skim, brush, graze, chafe, hit, rasp, stamp, comb, rake, scratch, grind, smite, kick, beat.

PAWL, *n.* Click, clasp, detent, ratchet, lever, stop, catch.

PAWN, *n.* 1. Something given *or* pledged as security, pledge, gage, thing *or* person serving as security, guaranty, guarantee, surety, stake, bail, bond, credit, loan, deposit, mortgage, pignoration, warrant, assurance, act of pawning, bottomry *(Marine Law).*
2. Unimportant person used as the tool of another, puppet, tool, dupe, automaton, hireling, henchman, menial, gull, gudgeon, expendable, piece, nonentity, nullity, obscurity, creature, servant, follower, jackal, hand, underling, instrument, satellite, little fellow, cat's-paw, toady, lackey, flunky, mercenary, dummy, pushover, *(coll.),* jay *(sl.),* sucker *(sl.),* pigeon *(sl.).*

PAWN, *v.* 1. Deposit as security *(as for money borrowed),* borrow on, mortgage, impignorate, raise, give security, bottomry, hypothecate, offer *or* give as security, pledge, hock *(sl.).*
2. Pledge, stake, lay, wager, bet, risk, hazard, chance, back, expose, compromise, ante *(Poker),* plunge *(sl.),* offer, endanger, plight, gamble, jeopardize, venture, imperil, speculate.

PAWNBROKER, *n.* One who lends money at interest on pledged personal property, lender, usurer, Shylock, moneylender, moneymonger, broker, pawn *(coll.),* lumberer *(sl.),* uncle *(sl.).*

PAWNSHOP, *n.* Shop of a pawnbroker, pawnbrokery, mont-de-piété, sign of the three balls, popshop *(sl.),* my uncle's *(sl.),* spout *(sl.),* pawn *(coll.),* hock shop *(sl.).*

PAY, *n.* 1. Payment *(as of wages),* wages, salary, stipend, income, fee, consideration, compensation, recompense, allowance, honorarium, disbursement, toll, earnings, annuity, bonus, sop, brokerage, percentage, tontine, receipts, pension, alimony, pittance, subsidy, bribe, remittance, tip, indemnity, perquisite, reimbursement, reward, settlement, freight, acknowledgment, remuneration, requital, hire, commission, emolument.
2. Paid employ, service, hire, use, engagement, employment.
3. Requital, reward, punishment, retaliation, compensation, payment, repayment, penalty, deserts, retribution, reprisal, avengement, retributive justice, recompense, dues, merits, price, solatium, remuneration, revenge, reparation, guerdon *(Poetic),* redress, satisfaction, reckoning, quittance, atonement, amends, prize, award, return, *quid pro quo (Lat.),* like for like, measure for measure, an eye for an eye, blood for blood.

PAY, *v.* 1. Discharge *(a debt, obligation, etc.),* defray *(cost or expense),* liquidate, settle, satisfy the claims of *(a person, as by giving money due),* refund, redeem, hand over *or* out, acknowledge, discount, honor, meet, foot, give, lay down, contribute, ante *(Poker),* chip in *(coll.),* spend, expend, clear off *(a debt, etc.),* prepay, pay in full, put one's money on the line *(sl.),* donate, present, confer, bestow, bribe, invest, disburse, fork over *(sl.),* shell out *(sl.),* cough up *(sl.),* come across *(coll.),* square *or* settle accounts.
2. Give compensation for, make amends, reward, recompense, compensate, requite, make pay to, discharge one's obligation to, cover, redeem, atone for, offset, indemnify, satisfy, coun-

terbalance, counteract, square up, equalize, make good, make up for, reimburse, remunerate.
3. Yield a recompense *or* return to, be profitable, produce, be remunerative, be a good investment, give a good interest, profit, avail, benefit, be advantageous *or* worth while, bear fruit, answer, forward, enhance, cause improvement *or* betterment, enrich, help, be of use, be useful, serve, contribute, be to good account, reap benefits, stand one in good stead, subserve, be instrumental.
4. *(Often fol. by* OFF *or* OUT*)* Requite *(as for good, harm, offense, etc.),* punish, retaliate upon, repay, settle accounts, take revenge upon, retort upon, have a reckoning with, get even with *(coll.),* guerdon *(Poetic),* reward, award, pay back, return, return the compliment, return like for like, reciprocate, match, give one his deserts, square accounts, recriminate, reckon with, discharge, get back at *(sl.),* settle the score *(coll.).*
5. Give *(attention, regard, court, compliments, etc.),* offer, render, proffer, extend, wait on *or* upon, be attentive, woo, court, curry favor, dance attendance on, worm oneself, ingratiate oneself, fawn upon, attend, address, sue, press one's suit.
6. Make *(a call, visit, etc.),* drop in, look in, call on *or* upon, look one up, pay one's respects, leave one's card, present oneself, wait on *or* upon.
7. Suffer, be punished, make amends, take the consequences, take one's punishment, take one's medicine, pay the piper, compensate, atone, be rightly served, take the rap *(sl.),* face the music *(coll.),* get one's deserts, reap the fruits of one's actions, reap where one has sown.

PAYABLE, *adj.* 1. Due, that may be *or* is to be paid, outstanding, mature, unpaid, owing, uncollected, unsettled, in arrears, owed.
2. Profitable, worth-while, productive, fruitful, fertile, useful, lucrative, paying, remunerative, valuable, beneficial, gainful.

PAYER, *n.* One who pays, defrayer, paymaster, cashier, teller, almoner, debtor, treasurer, liquidator.

PAYMASTER, *n.* Officer *or* official responsible for the payment of wages *or* salaries, purser, treasurer, teller, cashier.

PAYMENT, *n.* 1. Act of paying, discharge of a debt, remittance, defrayal, settlement, discount, outlay, spending, purchase, expenditure, disbursement, subvention, quittance, liquidation, outlay, reckoning, clearance.
2. That which is paid, installment, recompense, compensation, premium, fee, remuneration, satisfaction, requital, stake, earnest, expense, solatium, pay, emolument, remittance, consideration, handsel, money, charge, tontine, rebate, reimbursement, reward, subsidy, tribute, alimony, pittance, dole, alms, bonus, stipend, expenditure, allowance, quota, commission, discount, rent, wages, hire, bribe, salary, hush money, honorarium, contribution, pension, subscription, annuity.
3. Requital, redress, revenge, repayment, reparation, retaliation, desert, amends, quittance, atonement, compensation, satisfaction, acknowledgment, merits, dues, indemnification, reckoning, return, reward, penalty, retribution.

PAY-OFF, *n.* Payment of a salary, pay and discharge *(as of hired men),* time of payment, settlement, shutdown, conclusion, *(of a job),* end, culmination, close, completion, windup, stoppage, termination.

PEA, *n.* 1. Round vegetable seed, dicotyledon, chickpea.

2. Something small as a pea, spherule, drop, pellet, pill, marble, orblet, globule.

PEACE, *n.* 1. Freedom from civil commotion, public order and security, freedom from war *or* hostilities, truce, lull, hush, silence, stillness, public tranquillity, good order, quiet, quiescence, neutrality, the storm blown over, interlude, respite, abeyance, reconciliation, conciliation, pacifism, letup *(coll.)*.

2. Agreement between contending parties to abstain from further hostilities, truce, armistice, dove of peace, treaty, breathing spell *or* time, convention, terms, white flag, cartel, settlement, adjustment of differences, olive branch, pipe of peace, compromise, pacification, calumet, arbitration, *modus vivendi (Lat.)*.

3. Freedom from strife *or* dissension, peacefulness, amity, friendliness, harmony, congenialty concordance, accord, concord, brotherhood, friendship, cordiality, good will, symphony, rapport, agreement, fellowship, compatibility, love, union, unity, fraternalism, agreement, like-mindedness, understanding, cooperation, *entente cordiale (Fr.)*, joint assent, consensus, compliance, consentaneity, consentaneousness, one voice, affinity, oneness, conformity, adaptability, accordance, reconciliation.

4. Freedom from mental disturbance, tranquillity, calmness, placidity, imperturbability, quiescence, contentment, equanimity, composure, repose, serenity, comfort, rest, indisturbance, wellbeing, unruffled calm, sufferance, forbearance, patience, resignation, nonresistance, complacence, contentedness, quietude, imperturbation.

PEACEABLE, *adj.* 1. Inclined to avoid strife *or* dissension, slow to take offense, peace-loving, pacific, gentle, amicable, mild, equable, meek, unexcitable, restrained, clement, sober, lenient, even, calm, unruffled, sympathetic, friendly, kindly, inoffensive, disposed to peace, moderate, civil, good-tempered, amiable, noncombative, neutral, tolerant, long-suffering, unresisting, lamblike, tranquil, pacifist, forbearant, forgiving, bland, unbelicose, unpugnacious, uncontentious, longanimous, unimpassioned, bloodless, friendly, temperate, well-disposed, patient.

2. Peaceful. *See* PEACEFUL *below.*

PEACEFUL, *adj.* 1. Characterized by peace, free from strife *or* commotion, tranquil, quiet, undisturbed, unruffled, quiescent, placid, calm, still, composed, inactive, passive, pacific, at ease, amicable, untroubled, harmonious, concordant, easeful, comfortable, conciliatory, restful, orderly, halcyon, unwarlike, amiable, reposeful, serene.

2. Pertaining to *or* characteristic of a state of peace, peacetime, quiescent, pacific, untroubled, free from war, neutral, free from hostilities, silent, still.

3. Peaceable. *See* PEACEABLE *above.*

PEACEMAKER, *n.* One who makes peace *(as by reconciling parties at variance)*, mediator, makepeace, intercessor, pacifier, interceder, intervener, go-between, arbiter, arbitrator, pacificator, dove, umpire, referee, negotiator, ambassador of peace, propitiator, reconciler, intermediary, peacemonger *(contempt.)*.

PEACE OFFERING, *n.* 1. Offering of thanksgiving to God *(prescribed by Levitical law)*, atonement, amends, sacrifice, penance, incense, expiation, oblation, placation, propitiation, libation,

drink offering, holocaust, burnt offering, immolation, reparation, satisfaction, sin *or* piacular offering, sacramental offering, offertory *(Rom. Cath. Ch.)*.

2. Offering made to procure peace, proffer of peace, peace pipe, overture, terms, olive branch, calumet, placation.

PEACETIME, *adj.* See PEACEFUL, *adj.* 2, *above.*

PEACOCK, *n.* 1. Vain person, egotist, egoist, strutter, swaggerer, prig, self-seeker, boaster, one with a swelled head, braggart, brag, proudling *(contempt.)*, poser, *poseur (Fr.)*.

2. Dude, dandy, popinjay, man milliner, clotheshorse, fop, exquisite, macaroni, swell, fine gentleman, silk-stocking, silk-sock Sam, spark, coxcomb, beau, toff, buck, blade, man about town, jack-a-dandy.

PEAK, *n.* 1. Pointed top *(as of a mountain)*, point, spire, cone, cap, height, steeple, tower, turret, belfrey, cupola, dome, cusp, minaret, tiptop, summit, crown, crest, pinnacle.

2. Mountain with a pointed summit, eminence, alp, tor.

3. Projecting point, horn, end, tip, prominence, point, edge, extremity, crag, headland, protuberance, promontory, nib.

4. Maximum point *or* degree, flood tide, utmost height, crest, crown, summit, primacy, zenith, climax, top, pinnacle, tiptop *(coll.)*, highest point, apex, acme, maximum, supremacy, turning point, meridian, perfection, culminating point, head, *ne plus ultra (Lat.)*, vertex, crowning point.

PEAK, *v.* 1. Project in a peak, culminate, overtop, jut, cap, crest, beetle, protrude, tip, bulge, crown, protuberate, rise above, top, stand up, surmount, stand out, stick out.

2. Become weak *or* sickly, grow thin *or* lean, become emaciated, waste away, dwindle, weaken, sicken, fail, droop, languish, pine, wilt, flag, ail.

PEAKED, *adj.* 1. Having a peak, pointed, sharp, acute, needle-like, spiculate, thin, cusped, spiny, aciform, acicular, spiked, spiky, tapered, spinous, barbed, awl-shaped, subulate, mucronate *(Bot.)*.

2. Thin, lean, pinched, wizened, haggard, skinny, fleshless, shriveled, scraggy, skin and bones, scrawny, starved, skeletal, bony, gaunt, hungry-looking, emaciated, sickly, ailing, poor, pale.

PEAL, *n.* 1. Loud prolonged sound *(of bells, cannon, thunder, applause, laughter, etc.)*, blast, burst, shriek, shout, boom, cannonade, roll, roar, thundering, chorus, clap, crash, paean, acclamation, resounding, reverberation, outbreak, clang, blare, tintinnabulation, ring.

2. Set of bells tuned to one another, carillon, chimes, glockenspiel, tintinnabula.

PEAL, *v.* Give forth loudly and sonorously, resound, echo, bombilate, bombinate, rumble, resonate, quaver, throb, bong, toll, reverberate, roll, ring, roar, re-echo, sound, knell, blow, bugle, pipe, wind, chime, thunder, boom, tintinnabulate.

PEARL, *n.* 1. Something resembling a pearl *(in form, luster, etc.)*, capsule, dewdrop, tear, drop, nacre, tooth, pellet, mother-of-pearl, orblet, globule, spherule, droplet, mica, margarite *(Mineral)*.

2. Something precious *or* choice, finest example of anything, jewel, treasure, gem, pearl of great price, bijou, prize, flower, paragon, cream, one in a thousand *or* ten thousand, apple of one's eye, idol, find, trump *(coll.)*, pip *(sl.)*, pippin *(sl.)*, wonder, ace, masterpiece.

PEARLY, *adj.* 1. Adorned with pearls *or* pearl, abounding in pearls, pearl-studded, perlaceous, margaritiferous, pearl-producing.

2. Like a pearl, nacry, irisated, opaline, milky, mellow, opaloid, iridescent, nacreous, limpid, pure, clear, pellucid, translucent.

PEASANT, *n.* Rustic, farmer, churl, laborer, clown, swain, hind, countryman, bucolic, bumpkin, hobnail, hick *(sl.),* clodhopper, yokel, plowman, son of the soil, hayseed *(sl.),* hodge *(coll.),* chuff, kern, clod, lumpkin, joskin *(sl.),* jake *(coll.),* looby, gaffer, tiller of the soil, rube *(coll.),* agriculturalist, drone, boor, lubber, commoner.

PEASANTRY, *n.* 1. Laboring class, peasants *(collectively),* lower *or* humbler classes *or* orders, rank and file, herd of common people, horde, mob, rabble, proletariat, the million, hoi polloi *(Gk.),* the multitude *or* masses, great unwashed *or* unnumbered, commonalty, common people, salt of the earth, vulgar *or* common herd, rout, ruck, canaille.

2. Status *or* character of a peasant, coarseness, rusticity, lowness, meanness, indelicacy, incivility, vulgarity, unrefinement, boorishness, barbarism, inurbanity, inelegance, impropriety, clumsiness, gaucherie, tactlessness, awkwardness, doltishness.

PEBBLE, *n.* Small rounded stone *(esp. one worn by the action of water),* pebblestone, fingerstone, drakestone, jackstone, pellet, grain, gravel *(pl.).*

PECCABLE, *adj.* Liable to sin *or* err, evil, iniquitous, recreant, imperfect, weak, frail, sinning, faulty, sinful, unsaintly, wayward, arrant, wanton, slack, lax, unstable, infirm, reprobate, defective, ungodly, unholy, unrighteous, unvirtuous, erring, prodigal.

PECCADILLO, *n.* Petty sin, slight offense, trifling fault, misdeed, slight crime, petty trespass, infraction, fault, misdoing, misdemeanor, lapse, slip, trip, failure, indiscretion, breach, dereliction, delinquency, blunder, infringement, transgression, wrong, violation, nonfeasance *(Law),* omission.

PECCANT, *adj.* 1. Offending, sinning, erring, bad, foul, wicked, filthy, guilty, criminal, transgressing, sinful, villainous, arrant, defiled, untoward, flagrant, rank, scurvy, heinous, corrupt, rotten, nefarious, infamous, degraded, damned, damnable, depraved, debauched, degenerate, accursed, dissolute, felonious, base, abandoned, profligate, blameworthy, noisome, fulsome, sinister, dirty, repellent, loathsome, chargeable, culpable, obnoxious, noxious, odious, beastly.

2. Faulty, violating a principle *or* rule *(as of taste or propriety),* erroneous, inexpedient, unsuitable, unfit, wrong, incorrect, undue, distorted, indiscreet, improper, inadvisable, untoward, unbecoming, unseemly, unwise, inappropriate, unbefitting, indecorous, unmeet, out of place, undignified, discreditable, injudicious, dishonorable, ungentlemanly, inadmissible, objectionable, imprudent.

PECK, *n.* 1. Considerable quantity, abundance, profusion, host, volume, world *or* worlds, flock, ocean, mint, mass, sea, plenty, galore, sight, quite a few, good *or* great deal, multitude, deal, considerable *(coll.),* lot *or* lots *(coll.),* array, numbers, quantities, scores, bevy, army, legion, galaxy, a thousand and one, fund, tons *(coll.),* no end of, bunch, collection, store, stacks *(coll.),* hoard, stock, stack *(coll.),* batch, raft *or* rafts *(coll.),* pot *(sl.),* slew *or* slews *(coll.),* heap *or* heaps *(coll.),* pile *or* piles *(coll.),* wad *or* wads *(sl.),* accumula-

tion, scad *or* scads *(sl.),* oodle *or* oodles *(sl.),* gob *or* gobs, supply.

2. Pecking stroke, light blow, knock, poke, dig, jab, rap, tap, scratch, score, cut, dint, dent, hit.

3. Hole, mark *(made by or as by pecking),* pock, cavity, impression, concavity, depression, indentation, dint, dent, scar, score, scratch, speckle, spot, point, speck, flaw, fault, freckle, break, rent, rift, chap, dimple, chink, crack, crevice.

PECK, *v.* 1. Indent, impress, pick, tap, strike *(with the beak as a bird does, or with a pointed instrument),* dot, dab, make *(a hole, etc.)* by quick repeated strokes, rap, pat, kiss, stroke.

2. *(Fol. by* AT) Carp at, nag, twit, badger, importune, tease, faultfind, criticize, torment, rap, slur, reproach, harass, pull *or* pick to pieces, impugn, animadvert upon, reflect upon, knock *(sl.),* weary, exhaust, wear down, disturb persistently, plague, worry, vex, harry, heckle, bullyrag, chafe, grate, haunt, provoke, sting, nettle, bait, prick, hound, persecute, harrow, fret, hector, goad, egg, irritate, gibe, irk, banter, afflict, taunt, jeer, bully.

PECTINATE, *adj.* Formed into *or* with teeth *(like a comb),* comblike, toothed, serrate *(chiefly Biol.).*

PECTORAL, *adj.* 1. Of *or* pertaining to the breast *or* chest, thoracic, worn on the breast *or* chest.

2. Proceeding from the heart *or* inner consciousness, deep-rooted, deep-seated, inmost, innermost, intimate, interior, inner, inward, penetrating, pervading, indelible, deep, heartfelt, deeply felt, profound.

PECULATE, *v.* Embezzle *(public money),* appropriate dishonestly, purloin, filch, abstract, steal, rob, thieve, pilfer, mooch *(sl.),* pinch *(sl.),* hook *(sl.),* lift *(coll.),* defraud.

PECULIAR, *adj.* 1. Different from the usual *or* normal, distinguished in character *or* nature from others, singular, unusual, uncommon, rare, exceptional, special, particular, original, unique, abnormal, erratic, especial, striking, extraordinary, exotic, unconventional, out of the way, out of the ordinary, unnatural, unaccustomed, aberrant, unfamiliar, unparalleled, dissimilar, discordant, discrepant, curious, contrary, distinct, deviative, signal, notable, outstanding, conspicuous, quaint, remarkable, unprecedented, disagreeing, sole, solitary, individual, select, lone, irregular, outré.

2. *(Coll.)* Strange, odd, queer, grotesque, outlandish, bizarre, nondescript, fanciful, fantastic, eccentric, freakish, ridiculous, incredible, inconceivable, unnatural, curious, weird, monstrous, comical, wild, abnormal, preposterous, bohemian, capricious, erratic, maggoty, idiosyncratic, notional, crotchety, whimsical, quirked, outré.

3. *(Fol. by* TO) Characteristic of one only, that belongs characteristically, that specially pertains, proper, specific, exclusive, innate, unique, original, endemic, discriminative, indicative, representative, typical, distinctive, differential, diagnostic, diacritical, *sui generis (Lat.),* distinguishing, characteristic, idiomatic, idiosyncratic, individual, appropriate, marked, indigenous.

4. Belonging exclusively, privately owned, not common, personal, one's own, special, limited, esoteric, intimate, individual, exclusive, private.

PECULIARITY, *n.* 1. Odd trait *or* characteristic, individuality, oddity, freakishness, unusualness, uniqueness, singularity, strangeness, rarity, aberration, deviation, anomaly, quip, quirk, twist, idiosyncrasy, exceptionality, kink, crotchet, erraticism, eccentricity, queerness, unnaturalness, outlandishness, bizarreness, caprice, whim, capriciousness, idiocrasy, mannerism, trick, abnormality, flight of fancy.

2. Distinguishing quality or characteristic, distinction, specialty, distinctiveness, earmark, mark, character, indication, quality, lineament, trick, trait, badge, idiom, predisposition, attitude, habit, style, form, expression, stamp, mode, individuality, cast, idiasm, animus, propensity, bent, turn, warp, leaning, twist, inclination, tendency, idiocrasy, idiosyncrasy, manner, affection, disposition, temper, temperament, mannerism, feature, eccentricity, particularity, singularity.

PECUNIARY, adj. Consisting of or given or exacted in money, of or pertaining to money, monetary, nummary, financial, fiscal, numismatic, nummular, nummulary.

PEDAGOGIC, PEDAGOGICAL, adj. Of or pertaining to a pedagogue or pedagogy, educational, professorial, preceptorial, scholastic, tutorial, schoolish, academic, instructional, teaching, teacherlike, tuitional, instructive, disciplinal, disciplinary, schoolmasterly, schoolmasterish, schoolteacherish.

PEDAGOGY, n. Function, work, or art of a teacher, instruction, education, tutelage, guidance, edification, enlightenment, tuition, training, didactics, discipline, cultivation, preparation, interpretation, indoctrination, direction, teaching.

PEDAGOGUE, n. 1. Schoolteacher, teacher of children, schoolmaster, educator, master, preceptor, professor, tutor, schoolman, methodologist, docent, Gamaliel, instructor.

2. Person of pedantry, dogmatism, and formality, pedant, attitudinarian, attitudinizer, bigot, philosoph, sophist, precisionist, formalist, doctrinaire, vain scholar, conformist, conventionalist, dogmatist, casuist, precisian, Philistine, philosophist (contempt.), bromide (sl.), philosophaster, paralogist (Log.), bluestocking (coll.).

PEDAL, n. Lever worked by the foot, treadle.

PEDANT, n. One who makes a tedious or excessive show of learning or learned precision, one who possesses mere booklearning (without practical wisdom), precisian, bluestocking (coll.), ostentatious man of learning, pedagogue, etc. See PEDAGOGUE above.

PEDANTIC, PEDANTICAL, adj. Unduly emphasizing minutiae, formal, precise, ostentatious of learning, vain of knowledge, pompous, stilted, priggish, pedagogic, pragmatic, conceited, didactic, scholastic, affected, academic, grandiose, narrow, hidebound, unadaptable, unrealistic, stiff, bigoted, punctilious, wise in one's own conceit, overcritical, hypercritical, overscrupulous, meticulous, finical, overparticular, hairsplitting, overconscientious, puffed up, haughty, inflated, bookish, showy, sonorous, rhetorical, exact, Johnsonian, dogmatic, euphuistic.

PEDANTRY, n. Undue display of learning, slavish attention to rules, details, etc., minuteness, pedantism, exactness, exactitude, preciseness, nicety, precision, bookishness, sophistry, Philistinism, affectation of knowledge, narrow-mindedness, one-sidedness, meticulousness, bigotry, particularity, circumstantiality, pretension, dogmatism, finicality, finicalness, positivism.

PEDDLE, v. Carry about for sale at retail, hawk, deal out in small quantities, vend, sell, retail, dispose of, market, regrate, dispense.

PEDDLER, n. (Also **PEDLAR, PEDLER**) One who peddles, itinerant salesman, tinker, vender,

hawker, huckster, colporteur, packman, sutler, duffer (sl.), haggler, higgler, shopman, seller, faker (coll.), cheap-jack (coll.).

PEDDLING, adj. Trifling, paltry, piddling, trivial, niggling, mincing, idle, petty, puny, flimsy, superficial, inane. ridiculous, nonsensical, absurd, foolish, light, shallow, frothy, slight, nugacious, frivolous, airy, insignificant, silly, senseless, unworthy of serious consideration, fatuous, meaningless, picayune, fribbling, finicking, finicky, nugatory.

PEDESTAL, n. Architectural support (for a column, statue, vase, etc.), supporting structure or piece, base, foundation, rest, ground, platform, substructure, foot, bottom, stand, standard, underpinning, understructure.

PEDESTRIAN, adj. 1. Going or performed on foot, walking, afoot, ambulatory, perambulating, perambulatory, peripatetic (chiefly hum.).

2. Commonplace, prosaic, unimaginative, dull, trite, inferior, stale, mediocre, unimpressive, hackneyed, everyday, trivial, unimportant, ordinary, threadbare, banal, monotonous, prosy, matter-of-fact, general, stock, tedious, humdrum, platitudinous, homely, stereotyped, oft-repeated, slow, dry, uninteresting, sober, unvaried.

PEDESTRIAN, n. One who travels or goes on foot, foot-traveller, walker, hiker, tramper, itinerant, peregrinator, hitchhiker (coll.), hoofer (coll.), peripatetic (chiefly hum.).

PEDIGREE, n. 1. Ancestral line of descent (esp. recorded), geneological table, family tree, list of ancestors from which a man or animal descends.

2. Line, family, derivation, race, lineage, strain, birth, sept, stirps, bloodline, house, stock, breed, parentage, extraction, ancestry, descent, geneology, kindred, tribe, root, stem, clan, people, nation.

PEEK, n. Peeking look, peep, shy glance or look, glimpse, glance, cast, quick cast of the eyes, eyeshot, espial, spy, half an eye, quick or cursory look, flicker or twinkle of the eye.

PEEK, v. Peer, peep, play at bopeep or peekaboo, give a quick or cursory look, pass the eyes over, skim, glint, pry, squint, glance shyly.

PEEL, n. Rind, skin (of a fruit), coat, coating, pellicle, membrane, cover, epicarp, outer layer, hide, hull, bark, peeling.

PEEL, v. 1. Pare, decorticate, strip off the skin, rind, bark, etc., skin, hull, exfoliate, excoriate (Physiol.), denude, lay bare, shell, pod, excorticate, flay, bark, shave, scive, husk.

2. Come off (as skin or rind), loosen and fall off, shed, flake, scale, desquamate (Pathol.), exfoliate, cast, slough, molt, delaminate, exuviate.

PEEP, n. 1. Peeping look or glance, etc. See PEEK above.

2. First appearance, dawning, emergence, rise, breaking forth, prime, beginning, revelation, springing, opening, manifestation, materializing, rising, issuance, evidence, disclosure, unfolding, presentation, exposure.

3. Peeping cry or sound, chirp, chirrup, chitter, cheep, whimper, chatter, pipe, tweet, twitter, crick, creak, squeak.

PEEP, v. 1. Look through or as through a small aperture, look slyly or furtively, peer, peek, glance, glimpse, scan, survey, witness, regard, watch, view, pry, skim, squint.

2. Come partially into view, begin to appear, show or protrude slightly, come forth, issue, emerge, rise, show itself, show its face, become

visible, rear its head, peer out, pop up, see the light, reveal itself, become manifest, break through, spring up, look forth.

3. Utter a shrill little cry *(as a young bird, a mouse, etc.)*, chirp, cheep, squeak, pip, cry, twitter, pule.

PEEPHOLE, *n.* Hole through which to peep, aperture, slot, slit, gap, chink, crack, crevice, orifice, porthole, keyhole, loophole, sight, sighthole.

PEER, *n.* 1. Equal *(before the law)*, person of the same civil rank *or* standing, mate, match, like, compeer, fellow, coequal, equivalent, equipollent, parallel.

2. Nobleman, patrician, gentleman, aristocrat, noble, lord, blueblood *(coll.)*, silk-stocking, grandee, magnifico, thoroughbred, ruler, seignior, peeress, gentlewoman.

PEER, *v.* 1. Look closely *or* narrowly, gaze, gape, eye, ogle, pry, peep, peek, mouse, scrutinize, examine, squint, inspect, take stock of, look obliquely, look hard *or* intently, fix or rivet the eyes upon, fasten the eyes upon, stare, strain the eyes, give a sidelong look, snoop *(coll.)*.

2. Peep out *or* appear slightly, come into view, begin to appear, issue, emerge, rise, arise, show itself, show its face, become visible, rear its head, pop up, see the light, reveal itself, become manifest, look forth, spring up, break through.

PEERAGE, *n.* Rank *or* dignity of a peer, body of peers, nobility, aristocracy, patriciate, gentry, royalty, cream of society, elite, upper classes, gentlefolk, baronage, first families, knighthood.

PEERLESS, *adj.* Matchless, without an equal *or* peer, unequaled, unmatched, superlative, unique, highest, incomparable, superexcellent, unexcelled, ideal, quintessential, chief, capital, exalted, paramount, faultless, unparalleled, unapproached, rare, maximum, choice, select, first-rate, sublime, noble, supreme, transcendent, superior, nonpariel, inimitable, unrivaled, best, excelling, first-class, preëminent, of the first water, consummate, sovereign, second to none, foremost, first, uppermost, flawless, *ne plus ultra (Lat.)*, beyond compare *or* comparison, A one *(also A-1; coll.)*, prime, perfect, priceless, culminating, transcendental, unsurpassed.

PEEVE, *n.* Annoyance, aggravation, vexation, irritation, fret, bother, trouble, worry, care, thorn in the flesh, curse, scourge, plague, sore subject, offense, affront, infliction, affliction, torment, torture, provocation, molestation, canker, bitter pill, gall, pest, nuisance, grievance, pestilence.

PEEVISH, *adj.* Fretful *(as from vexation or discontent)*, querulous, cross, irascible, irritable, petulant, pettish, crusty, captious, snappish, ungracious, fidgety, moody, fractious, thin-skinned, sulky, grouchy *(coll.)*, censorious, perverse, faultfinding, morose, snarling, testy, ill-natured, illtempered, complaining, gruff, uncivil, quarrelsome, cantankerous, tetchy, sour, growling, sullen, nagging, angry, crabbed, churlish, out of humor *or* temper, cross as a bear with a sore head *(coll.)*, cross as two sticks *(coll.)*, cross-grained, huffy, bearish, bristling, peppery, currish, iracund, acerbic, choleric, jaundiced, bilious, inflammable, oversensitive, resentful, touchy, shrewish, uneasy, surly, vaporish, out of sorts, like touchwood *or* tinder, grumbling, waspish, spleeny, splenetic, discontented, acrimonious.

PEG, *n.* 1. Support, pin, spike, nail, dowel, fastener, skewer, toggle, plug, thole *or* tholepin, kevel *(Naut.)*, bollard *(Naut.)*, stake, post, spill, spile,

spigot, ratchet, sprocket, brace, cleat, tap, cog, tooth, staple, rivet, treenail.

2. Pretext, reason, occasion, excuse, motive, rationale, explanation, ground, basis, call, provocation, plea, handle, defense, claim, scapegoat, apology, argument, vindication, subterfuge, feint, alibi *(coll.)*, put-off, justification, rationalization.

PEG, *v.* 1. Drive *or* insert a peg into, fasten with *or* as with pegs, mark with pegs, strike *or* pierce with *or* as with a peg, harpoon, stick, spoke, plug, dowel, punch, smack, thwack, ram in, imbed, inset, infix, poke, smite.

2. *(Fol. by* AWAY, ALONG, ON, *etc.)* Work persistently, keep on energetically, persevere, persist, hang on, hold fast, carry on, endure, stick *or* stay with it, never say die, keep at, bear up, hold up, continue, plod, grind, drudge, grub, hammer, repeat, drive, keep doggedly at, be resolute, see it through *(coll.)*, not give up, be steadfast *or* constant.

PEIGNOIR, *n.* Dressing gown, loose robe *(woman's)*, undress, negligee, dishabille, wrapper.

PEJORATIVE, *adj.* Depreciative, disparaging, derisive, derisory, insolent, disrespectful, disapprobatory, bantering, ironical, contumelious, backhand, scornful, withering, censorious, critical, blameful, left-handed, disdainful, mocking, sarcastic, irreverent, cynical, caricatural, scurrilous, contemptuous, condemnatory, damnatory, insulting, objurgatory, abusive, faultfinding, carping, caviling, captious, detracting, derogatory, libelous, vilipenditory, slandering, hard upon, defamatory, vituperative, maledictory, calumnious, denunciatory.

PELAGE, *n.* Soft covering of a mammal, fur, wool, hair, pelt, hide, fell, fleece, coat, skin, jacket.

PELAGIAN, PELAGIC, *adj.* Of the ocean *or* sea, living at *or* near the surface of the sea *(far from land)*, marine, oceanic, maritime, oceanographic.

PELF, *n. (Usually contemptuous)* Money, riches, mammon, gain, lucre, spoils, profit, filthy lucre *(coll.)*, plunder, almighty dollar, booty, loot, take, greed, steal *(coll.)*, pillage, grab, haul *(coll.)*, wealth, muck, swag *(sl.)*.

PELLET, *n.* Round *or* spherical body *(esp. one of small size)*, ball, pill, stone, drop, bulb, pea, marble, orblet, spherule, globule, bullet, bead, pebble, grain.

PELLICLE, *n.* Thin skin *or* membrane, film, scum, crust, thin coating, lamina, layer, foil, sheet, flake, scale, peel, coating, veneer, cuticle, enamel, facing, sheath, varnish, integument, epithelium *(Biol.)*.

PELL-MELL, *adj.* Disorderly, tumultuous, indiscriminate, headlong, rash, impetuous, precipitate, reckless, helter-skelter, incautious, brash, eager, careless, unmeditated, abrupt, unchecked, furious, scrambling, impulsive, snap, madcap, thoughtless, subitaneous, harum-scarum, regardless, injudicious, breakneck, turbulent, premature, passionate, foolhardy, hotspur, frantic, boisterous, unbridled, indiscreet, mad-brained, ungoverned, precipitous, impassioned, feverish, uncontrolled, precipitant, giddy, dashing, desperate, uncircumspect, hot-headed, hare-brained, wanton, wild, flighty, volatile, distracted, rampant, irresponsible, rantipole, imprudent, devil-may-care.

PELL-MELL, *adv.* In an indiscriminate medley, in a confused mass *or* crowd, in confused haste, excitedly, irregularly, in disorder, in confusion, helter-skelter, headlong, hurry-scurry, higgledy-piggledy, hurriedly, posthaste, breathlessly, with great *or* all haste, straightway, like a shot, like mad *(coll.)*, hotfoot, full tilt, head over heels, head-foremost, for all one is worth *(coll.)*, at full blast, all out *(sl.)*, full pelt, heels over head, all at once, double quick, rashly, precipitately, without deliberation, thoughtlessly, abruptly, slapdash, recklessly, impatiently, feverishly, incautiously, unwarily, immaturely, impulsively, without due caution, impetuously, passionately, foolishly, injudiciously, slap-bang, incontinently, at half cock, summarily, confusedly, hastily.

PELLUCID, *adj.* 1. Allowing the passage of light, clear, limpid, translucent, transparent, bright, lucid, diaphanous, glassy, serene, pearly, transpicuous, crystalline, pure, hyaline, pervious, vitreous, crystal-clear.
    2. Clear in meaning, self-evident, comprehensible, graphic, straightforward, understandable, apparent, express, well-marked, unquestionable, vivid, manifest, undisguised, downright, decisive, articulate, positive, perspicuous, clear-cut, certain, salient, prominent, plain, pronounced, palpable, visible, unmistakable, intelligible, unhidden, revealed, disclosed, unconcealed, patent, distinct, obvious, rational, luculent, transparent, explicit, to the point, direct, specific, striking, open, determinate, sharply outlined, overt, bare, naked, pointed, unequivocal, bald, unambiguous, luminous, transpicuous, translucent.

PELT, *n.* 1. Vigorous stroke, blow *(with something thrown)*, knock, buffet, hit, slam, fillip, rap, box, cuff, whack *(coll.)*, smack, thwack, punch, poke, clip, thump, dig *(coll.)*, sock *(sl.)*, cut, jab, swat, plug *(sl.)*, clout *(coll.)*, belt *(coll.)*.
    2. Skin *(of a beast, with or without hair)*, hide, fell, fleece, coat, jacket.

PELT, *v.* 1. Strike *(with something thrown)*, assail with missiles *or* repeated blows, batter, beat, hit, smite, whip, attack, hurl against, thrash, riddle, shower, lapidate, punish, bombard, pepper, belabor, wallop *(coll.)*, distress, afflict, stone, thump, buffet.
    2. Throw *(missiles)*, hurl, cast, drive, fling, sling, teem, toss, heave, pitch, shoot, put, let fly, dash, jerk, lance, dart, bowl, fillip, cant, tilt, fire, discharge, catapult, launch, propel, shy, chuck.

PEN, *n.* 1. Enclosure for animals, *etc.*, pound, crib, sty, stall, coop, stockyard, manger, columbary *(for doves, pigeons, etc.)*, hutch, pinfold, confine, compound, booth, cote, stockade, fold, corral, paddock, cage.
    2. Instrument for writing with ink, writing instrument, feather, quill, stylus, fountain pen, ballpoint pen, stylograph.
    3. Writer, scribe, penman, composer, literateur, epistolographer, compiler, commentator, reviewer, annotator, correspondent, critic, reporter, journalist, librettist, poet, pamphleteer, essayist, fictioneer, novelist, historian, dramatist, playwright, newspaperman, romancer, lexicographer, hack *(derog.)*, quill-driver *(derog.)*, potboiler *(derog.)*, pen-pusher *(derog.)*.

PEN, *v.* 1. Write, draft, compose, draw up, inscribe, make up, indite, scrawl, engross, transcribe, copy, pencil, scribble, scratch.
    2. *(Often with* UP*)* Intern, jail, restrain, confine, cloister, hem in, coop, lock up, mew up, trap, immure, restrict, encage, impound, corral, imprison, incarcerate, cage, shut up *or* in, wall in, prison, inclose, incase.

PENAL, *adj.* Of *or* pertaining to punishment *or* penalties *(as for offenses or crimes)*, punitive, corrective, inflicting, punishing, punitory, retributive, castigatory, disciplinary, penalizing, inflictive.

PENALIZE, *v.* Subject to penalty, punish, lay under a disadvantage, deprive *(of property, advantage, etc.)*, fine, amerce, impose a fine upon, mulct, inflict a penalty upon, chasten, chastise, sconce, distrain, levy a distress upon, sentence, pass sentence upon, proscribe, nonsuit *(Law)*.

PENALTY, *n.* Punishment *(imposed or incurred for a violation of law or rule)*, penal retribution, fine, punition, handicap, disadvantage, loss, forfeiture, unfortunate consequence, chastening, correction, suffering, price, sconce, distress, distraint, confiscation, damages, sequestration, reward, infliction, condemnation, penance, forfeit, amercement, mulct, chastisement, castigation, payment, discipline, penalization, retribution.

PENANCE, *n.* Punishment undergone in token of penitence for sin, penitential discipline, mortification, sacrament, propitiation, lustration, flagellation, purification, atonement, placation, contrition, purgation, purgatory, humiliation, sackcloth and ashes.

PENCHANT, *n.* Strong inclination, propensity, proclivity, turn, bent, leaning, liking, taste, bias, fancy, attachment, fondness, predilection, predisposition, tendency, proneness, preference, pleasure, favor, mind, temper, relish, humor, weakness, partiality, attraction, affinity, disposition.

PENCIL, *n.* 1. Strip of writing material encased in wood, metal, *etc.*, marker, chalk, lead, pastel, crayon, charcoal, automatic pencil.
    2. Pencil-shaped piece of a substance, ray, finger, stream, shaft, stem, bar, rod, stick, narrow beam.

PENCIL, *v.* 1. Sketch, draw, depict, trace, outline, delineate, chalk, diagram, fashion, mark out, portray, limn.
    2. Write, draw up, inscribe, make up, indite, scrawl, engross, transcribe, copy, pen, scribble, scratch, draft, compose.

PEND, *v.* Be undecided, be unsettled, wait, await, hang in the balance, hang, dangle, hinge, turn upon, revolve around.

PENDANT, *n.* 1. Ornament, pendule, lavaliere, tassel, pendicle, tippet, necklace, eardrop, earring, necklet.
    2. Hanging appendage, flap, tag, tassel, tail, train, appendix, penduline *(Zool.)*, hanging, drop, tippet.
    3. Suspender, support, supporter, hanger.
    4. Companion piece, twin, parallel, congener, match, mate, counterpart, analogue, correspondent, complement, correlative, equivalent.

PENDENT, PENDANT, *adj.* 1. Suspended, hanging, swinging, pensile, dangling, pendulous, pendulant, penduline *(Zool. of birds' nests)*.
    2. Overhanging, projecting, overlying, impending, imminent, jutting, sticking out, protruding, beetling, protuberant, salient.
    3. Undetermined, in suspense, in the air, undecided, waiting, contingent, under consideration, unsettled, in the offing, imminent, pendente lite *(L. Leg.)*.

PENDING, *adj.* 1. Pendente lite *(L. Leg.)*, undetermined, undecided, *etc.* (See PENDENT, *adj.* 3)
    2. Overhanging, projecting, jutting, *etc.* (See PENDENT, *adj.* 2)

PENDULOUS, *adj.* 1. Suspended, hanging, swinging, pensile, dangling, pendent, pendulant, penduline (Zool. of birds' nests).

2. Swinging, hanging, dangling, swaying, vibrating, oscillating, rocking, nutant, wig-wagging, fluctuating, undulating, pulsating.

PENDULUM, *n.* Body suspended so as to swing, oscillator, pendant.

PENETRABLE, *adj.* Capable of being penetrated, permeable, pervious, passable, open, porous, impressible, susceptible, accessible, receptive, absorbent, spongy.

PENETRALIA, *n., pl.* Secret places, inner recesses, innermost parts, insides, bowels, center, heart, pith, depths, middle, substance, caverns, labyrinth, kernel, core, marrow, interior, nucleus.

PENETRATE, *v.* 1. Pierce into *or* through, enter the interior of, cut into, reach, run through, pass through, bore, gore, gouge, fathom, insert, invade, perforate, burrow, sink into, puncture, prick, punch, stab, bite into, transfix, dive, stick, traverse, spit, honeycomb, mine, tunnel, spike, spear, ream, lance, pink, drill, riddle, impale.

2. Enter and diffuse itself through, pervade, transude, permeate, soak into *or* through, be diffused through, compenetrate, filter through, percolate, seep in, fill, saturate, impregnate, interosculate, be disseminated, overspread, diffuse, inflow, overrun, pass through, absorb, infiltrate, interpenetrate.

3. Impress deeply, make sensible, touch, affect, thrill, arrest the thoughts, sink in *(coll.),* arouse, pervade, chafe, hit, wound, go to one's heart, pierce, disturb, irritate, stir, prey on, stimulate, provoke, excite, imbue, strike, get through to, come home to.

4. Arrive at the meaning of, see into, understand, discern, see, unfold, fathom, apprehend, conceive, get to the bottom of, realize, comprehend, perceive, catch the idea of, make out, cognize, recognize, assimilate, gain insight into, seize, absorb, digest, distinguish, see in its true colors, get the hang of *(coll.),* solve, resolve, unravel, unriddle, decode, decipher, crack, clear up, work out, interpret, figure out, find the solution to, savvy *(sl.).*

PENETRATING, *adj.* 1. That penetrates, piercing, sharp, biting, stinging, barbed, caustic, deepfelt, pervading, strong, redolent, heady, poignant, permeating, penetrative, reeking, severe, harsh, impressive, blaring, high, ear-splitting, acute, acrid, acrimonious, exciting, stirring, incisive, pungent, boring, bleak, cutting, shrill, pointed, searching, acerbic, keen.

2. Discerning, keen, intelligent, sharp-witted, acute, quick, knowing, prudent, clever, farseeing, discriminating, clear-headed, perspicacious, sagacious, thoughtful, artful, astute, wide-awake, shrewd, keen-sighted, wise, perceptive, percipient, cognitive, comprehending, long-headed, luminous, oracular, subtle, argute, judicious, alive, alert, aware, piercing, undeceived, gimlet-eyed, ferret-eyed.

PENETRATION, *n.* 1. Act *or* power of penetrating, incision, imbuement, permeation, impalement, terebration, influx, inflow, boring, passage, insinuation, access, interjection, intermixture, mixture, pervasion, transudation, fusion, diffusion, infusion, infiltration, impregnation, interpenetration, perforation, ingress, transforation *(Surg.).*

2. Extension *(usually peaceful)* of one country's influence over another, invasion, ingress, infiltration, intervention, implantation, infusion, impor-

tation, infixion, interjection, intrusion, permeation, encroachment, interspersion, imposition, introduction, insinuation.

3. Mental acuteness, understanding, keenness, judgment, sagacity, discernment, sagaciousness, insight, sharpness, discrimination, acumen, perspicacity, long-headedness, perception, prudence, subtlety, cleverness, genius, quickness, grasp, tact, capacity, cunning, intelligence, percipience, gumption *(coll.),* astuteness, shrewdness, apperception, perception.

PENINSULA, *n.* Piece of land almost surrounded by water, point, cape, headland, tongue, neck, foreland, promontory, spit, chersonese.

PENITENCE, *n.* State of being penitent, contrition, repentance, regret, remorse, sorrow, compunction, self-reproach, self-condemnation, expiation, confession, stings of conscience, atonement, penance, self-humiliation, submission, resipiscence, conviction, qualms, shame, attrition *(Theol.),* sackcloth and ashes, pangs of conscience, self-reproof.

PENITENT, *adj.* Disposed to atonement and amendment, repentant, sorry for sin *or* fault, conscience-stricken, regretful, remorseful, brocalligraphist, engrosser, copyist, transcriber, compunctious, sorrowful, self-reproaching, self-condemning, self-humiliating, self-convicting, touched, repining, rueful, affected.

PENITENT, *n.* Penitent person, repentant, penitential, prodigal, penance-doer, magdalene, pilgrim.

PENITENTIARY, *adj.* Punishable by imprisonment, pertaining to *or* intended for penal confinement and discipline, punitive, penal.

PENITENTIARY, *n.* Place for imprisonment and reformatory discipline, jail, prison, house of correction, state prison, bridewell *(coll.),* workhouse, penal institution, reformatory, pen *(sl.).*

PENMAN, *n.* 1. One who uses a pen, writer, scribe, copyist, recorder, scribbler, chirographer, quill-driver *(derog.),* secretary, amuensis, cacographer, inkslinger *(sl.).*

2. One skilled in penmanship, calligrapher, calligraphist, engrosser, copyist, transcriber, commercial artist.

3. Author, writer, composer, pen, scribbler, literateur, epistolographer, compiler, commentator, reviewer, annotator, correspondent, critic, reporter, journalist, librettist, poet, pamphleteer, essayist, fictioneer, novelist, historian, dramatist, playwright, newspaperman, romancer, lexicographer, hack *(derog.),* quill-driver *(derog.),* potboiler *(derog.),* pen-pusher *(derog.).*

PENMANSHIP, *n.* Style of writing, calligraphy, engrossment, scrivening, longhand, chirography, handwriting, holograph, scrivenery, style, griffonage, pencraft, scription, script, manuscript, signature.

PEN NAME, *n.* Pseudonym, nom de plume, anonym.

PENNANT, *n.* Flag, ensign, streamer, standard, bannerol, banneret, ancient, pendant, bunting, burgee, vexillum, banner, pennon, oriflamme, labarum, colors, jack, eagle, gonfalon.

PENNILESS, *adj.* Poor, needy, impecunious, beggared, bankrupt, wiped out, insolvent, depleted, on the rocks, strapped, moneyless, reduced, destitute, distressed, poverty-stricken, impoverished, ruined, unmoneyed, indigent, pauperized, bereft, necessitous, drained, broke *(sl.),* embarrassed, gazetted, stony (sl.), out of pocket, straitened, on the rocks (coll.).

PENNON, n. Flag, ensign, vexillum, banner, streamer, pennant, oriflamme, labarum, colors, jack, eagle, gonfalon, bunting, burgee, pendant, ancient, bannerol, banneret.

PENNY, n (Loosely) Cent, sou, copper, mill, red cent (sl.).

PENNY-A-LINE, adj. Gimcrack, trashy, paltry, beggarly, mean, sorry, gaudy, tawdry, meretricious, cheap, inferior, worthless, poor, base, second-rate, commonplace, scrubby, measly (sl.), shabby, shoddy, meager, contemptible, vulgar, trivial.

PENSILE, adj. Pendulous, swinging, hanging, suspended, pendulant, dangling, pendent, pendant, penduline (Zool. of birds' nests).

PENSION, n. Allowance, annuity, tontine, subsidy, gratuity, grant, subvention, pittance.

PENSIONER, n. Pensionary, dependent, beneficiary, grantee, accipient.

PENSIVE, adj. 1. Musing, dreamy, dreaming, thoughtful, in a reverie, contemplative, meditative, ruminating, cogitative, deliberating, weighing, concentrating, communing, thinking, reflective, introspective, wistful, engrossed, in a brown study, absorbed, philosophizing.

2. In despair, wistful, sad, discouraged, sorry, woeful, despondent, doleful, sorrowful, lamenting, bemoaning, dampened, sad, dispirited, downhearted, unhappy, mourning, melancholy, dejected, desolate, rueful, comfortless, crushed, bowed-down, cheerless, downcast, miserable, disconsolate, wretched, weighted, burdened, depressed, heartbroken, forlorn, woebegone, grieving, inconsolable, heavy-hearted, heartsick, joyless, prostrated.

PENT, adj. Penned up, confined, bottled up, corked up, enthralled, immured, restricted, impounded, imprisoned, mewed up, circumscribed, boxed up, restrained, encaged, caged, walled in, constrained, cloistered, incarcerated, shut up, locked up, hemmed in, buried, sealed, limited, curbed, interned, entombed, cooped.

PENTECOST, n. Whitsunday, seventh Sunday after Easter, the descent of the Holy Spirit on the Apostles.

PENULT, n. (Usually Gram. and Pros.) Penultimate, next to the last, last but one, penultima.

PENURIOUS, adj. Miserly, stingy, close, mean, tight (coll.), close-fisted, pinching, chary, mercenary, sparing, frugal, niggardly, parsimonious, illiberal, moneygrubbing, grasping, cheeseparing.

PENURY, n. Poverty, financial ruin, want, dire necessity, destitution, ruin, insolvency, impoverishment, privation, impecuniosity, mendicancy, mendicity, need, liquidation, pauperism, indigence, straitened circumstances, beggary, bankruptcy.

PEOPLE, n. 1. Persons, folk, individuals, public, men and women, citizenry, populace.

2. Political or national group, race, tribe, nation, clan, country, state, inhabitants, population, citizenry.

3. Humanity, men and women, human beings, mankind, human kind, mortals, homo sapiens, Homo.

4. Kinsmen, clan, family, folks (coll.), ancestors, relations, kin, strain, stock, house, relatives, line, dynasty.

5. The common people, the mob, the rabble, the masses, the many, the rank and file, bourgeoisie, hoi polloi, the crowd, the populace, subjects, canaille, rout, commonalty, multitude, proletariate, common run (coll.), salt of the earth, general public, society, citizenry, the million, the herd, peasantry.

PEOPLE, v. Inhabit, colonize, live in, settle, populate, reside, habitate.

PEPPER, v. 1. Season with or as with pepper, heighten the taste of, render pungent, savor, spice, flavor.

2. Sprinkle, spot, dot, stud, fleck, speck, speckle, mottle, stipple, dapple, maculate.

3. Pelt (with shot or missiles), shower, bombard, fire upon or at, shoot at, blitz, lapidate, stone, hurl at, shell, barrage, cannonade, fusillade, strafe.

PEPPERY, adj. 1. Pungent, hot, high-seasoned, piquant, stimulating, spicy, racy, nippy, keen, sharp, biting, high-flavored.

2. Sharp (as speech), stinging, biting, incisive, trenchant, harsh, cutting, astringent, mordant, mordacious, piercing, acrimonious, acerbic, caustic, severe, keen, corroding.

3. Irritable, irascible, churlish, waspish, passionate, testy, hot-tempered, choleric, petulant, excitable, hasty, quick, like tinder, like touchwood, sharp, acrimonious, acerbic, snappish, touchy, fiery, irate, hot-headed, hot-blooded, fractious, volcanic, impatient, explosive, quarrelsome, spleenful, bristling, cross, captious, huffy, bearish, cross-grained, hostile, contentious, inflammable, iracund, boorish, bilious, resentful.

PEPTIC, adj. Pertaining to or concerned in digestion, digestive, promoting digestion, enzymic, dietetic, gastric.

PERADVENTURE, n. Chance, question, uncertainty, doubt, hazard, lot, insecurity, fortune, luck, fortuitous or casual event, accident, fortuity, fluke, inadvertence, suspense, gamble, destiny, stroke, dubiousness, incertitude, unsureness, indetermination, precariousness, cast of the dice, flip of the coin, swing of fortune's wheel.

PERAMBULATE, v. 1. Walk through (about, over), tour, range, traverse, travel through or about, ramble, stroll, saunter, peregrinate, pace, go one's rounds, pedestrianize, circumambulate.

2. Traverse and examine or inspect, survey, overlook, scan, keep watch, patrol, reconnoiter, case (sl.).

PERCEIVABLE, adj. Capable of being perceived, perceptible, discernible, manifest, open, overt, knowable, appreciable, sensible, cognizable, distinguishable, visual, beholdable, seeable, observable, visible, palpable, in view, in sight, avowed, ostensible, distinct, obvious, perspicuous, understandable, express, glaring, autoptic, exoteric, disclosed, bold, conspicuous, exposed to view, noticeable, apparent, patent, plain, discoverable, evident, revealed, unhidden, unconcealed, unmistakable, clear, well-marked, well-defined, prominent, salient, notable, in bold (strong, high) relief, detectable, tangible, apprehensible, definable, ascertainable, intelligible, intuitional.

PERCEIVE, v. 1. Gain knowledge of (through one of the senses), discover (by seeing, hearing, etc.), sense, feel, intuit, hear, make out, see, note, recognize, spot, remark, descry, distinguish, behold, observe, discern, discriminate, detect, notice, become concious of, mark, sight, taste, smell, catch sight of, catch, glimpse, witness, identify, apprehend, trace, scan, be aware of, find.

2. Comprehend with the mind, understand, appreciate, know, cognize, ascertain, grasp, penetrate, conceive, realize, be aware of, determine, conclude, gather, deduce, derive, infer, collect, be cognizant of, savvy (sl.), read, find, deem, esteem, get (coll.), gain insight into, judge, fathom, discern, see, apprehend, recognize, make out.

PERCENTAGE, n. Rate per hundred, ratio, percent, proportion, duty, allotment, dividend, quota, rake-off (sl.), factorage, royalty, duty, cut (coll.), commission, part, share, portion, deduction, discount, rebate.

PERCEPT, n. Mental result or product of perceiving, that which is perceived, object of perception, meaning, perception, conception, concept, idea, theorem, thought, illusion, impression, notion, observation, image, apprehension.

PERCEPTIBLE, adj. Capable of being perceived, etc., from PERCEIVABLE above.

PERCEPTION, n. 1. Act or faculty of perceiving, taking cognizance, discernment, seeing, cognition, recognition, apprehension, sensation, sense, feeling, hearing, perceptivity, apperception, conception, cognizance, notice, descrial, sight, quick parts, common sense, sapience, eagle eye, perspicacity, ken, clear sight, vision, insight, cognizance, gumption (coll.), acumen, perceptivity, understanding, intellect, grasp, reason, consciousness, comprehension, sensibility, light, imagination, detection, discrimination, knowledge, penetration, sagaciousness, sagacity, wisdom, judgment, grasp, observation, astuteness, instinct, intuition, susceptibility.

2. Result or product of perceiving, concept, etc., from PERCEPT above.

PERCEPTIVE, adj. Having the power or faculty of perceiving, of or pertaining to perception, of ready or quick perception, sensitive, sensible, impressible, responsive, sentient, cognizant, aware, conscious, tactful, discreet, knowing, alive, responding, answering, quick of apprehension, of keen penetration, penetrating, discerning, piercing, intelligent, percipient, apperceptive, understanding, wise, shrewd, appercipient, selective, clear-headed, quick-witted, of acute mental vision, alert, alive, thoughtful, judicious, quick, sharp, subtle, cunning, acute, keen, astute, perspicacious, discriminating, discretional, critical.

PERCH, n. Pole or bar (for roosting, etc.), roost, rest, seat, cross bar, roosting place.

PERCH, v. Settle, alight, rest, land, sit, roost.

PERCIPIENCE, n. Mental acuteness, discernment, long-headedness, keenness, insight, smartness, quick sense, ingenuity, intuition, comprehension, astuteness, judgment, shrewdness, perception, acumen, penetration, perspicacity, sagacity, cleverness, mother wit, sharpness, quick, intelligence, foresightedness, wisdom, subtlety, assimilation, cognition, apperception, ability to grasp ideas, cognizance, sense.

PERCIPIENT, adj. Comprehending, bright, healthy, open-eyed, discretional, shrewd, wide-awake, acute, prudent, sharp, sharp-sighted, far-sighted, far-seeing, straightforward, honest, sagacious, keen, critical, discriminating, sensible, penetrating, alive, alert, aware, piercing, subtle, argute, quick-witted, provident, undeceived, quick, clear-headed, clear-eyed, lynx-eyed, sage, discerning, sapient, imaginative, level-headed, cool-headed, clear-witted, ferret-eyed, perspicacious, rational, eagle-eyed, Argus-eyed, judicious, keen-sighted, quick of apprehension, smart, wise.

PERCOLATE, v. 1. Filter, filtrate, strain.

2. Permeate, transude, exude, ooze through, penetrate, imbue (only of blood, gore, etc.), drench, impregnate, seep through, spread through, trickle through, soak, infiltrate, saturate.

PERCUSS, v. Bang sharply, tap, strike, hit, whop (coll.), jab, clout (coll.), bang, batter, tamp, clip, wallop (coll.), slap, punch, knock, cudgel, smite, thump, slug, pound, beat, pummel.

PERCUSSION, n. Impact, blow, collision, buffet, thump, slam, smack, bang, stroke, clash, cuff, shock, bump, crack, crash, appulse, whop (coll.), slam, rap.

PERDITION, n. 1. Destruction, ruin, debacle, extermination, eradication, disruption, breaking up, abolition, loss, bane, end, annihilation, extirpation, undoing, dissolution, doom, deathblow, extinction, cataclysm, ravage, holocaust, depredation, spoilation, wreckage, rack and ruin, smash, crash, havoc, downfall, ruination.

2. Damnation (of the soul, etc.), everlasting fire, bottomless pit, lake of fire, outer darkness, obliteration, Cocytus, Styx, limbus, purgatory, underworld, Phlegethon, netherworld, Lethe, pandemonium, inferno, Hades, abyss, lake of fire and brimstone, place of the lost, Gehenna (Jewish Hist.), Sheol (Hebr.), Avernus, Naraka (Hind. and Buddh.), Abaddon, Malebolge, Erebus (Gr. Myth.), Avichi (Buddh.), Acheron (Class Myth.), Tartarus (Myth.), Tophet (Lit.), Satan's kingdom.

PERDURABLE, adj. Very durable, lasting, permanent, long-lasting, everlasting, abiding, undying, imperishable, eternal, diuturnal, long-lived, perennial, perpetual, stable, endless, unchanging, undecaying, immutable, hardy, timeless, steadfast.

PEREGRINATE, v. Travel (from place to place), be itinerant, roam, wander, tour, trek, perambulate, go sightseeing, travel widely, globe-trot (coll.), rove, ramble, range, peragrate, nomadize.

PEREGRINE, adj. Introduced from a foreign country, strange, exotic, foreign, alien, not native, extraneous, outlandish, exceptional, unusual, peculiar, not indigenous, extrinsic.

PEREMPTORY, adj. 1. Decisive, categorical, incontrovertible, absolute, positive, flat, unavoidable, binding, cast-iron, irrevocable, unreserved, explicit, irreversible, incumbent, authoritative, obligatory, imperative, unequivocal, commanding, implicit, certain, imperious.

2. Magisterial, self-assertive, arrogant, overbearing, overweening, dogmatic, oracular, bigoted, dictatorial, opinonated, assertive, arbitrary, domineering, fanatical, warped, biased, intolerant, imperious, self-important, vainglorious, high and mighty, uppish, lordly, contumelious, swaggering, blustering, egotistical, despotic, authoritative, presumptuous, toplofty, pompous, magisterial, supercilious, self-assured, high-handed, disdainful.

PERENNIAL, adj. Lasting, everlasting, enduring, perpetual, unceasing, continual, constant, continuous, permanent, immortal, incorruptible, undying, uninterrupted, ceaseless, unfailing, imperishable, endless, amaranthine, immarcescible, fadeless, persistent, stable, immovable, chronic, fixed, durable, revolving, unchanging, undecaying, sempiternal (Lit.), evergreen, diuturnal, long-lived, long-lasting, longevous, undeviating, immutable, intransmutable, perdurable, hardy, timeless, interminable, infinite, indestructible, ever-flowing, sempervirent, macrobiotic.

PERFECT, adj. 1. In a state proper to a thing

when completed, having all essential elements, finished, completed, concluded, complete, absolute, entire, full, whole, unbroken, plenary, intact, undivided, integral, mellow, mature, ripe, lacking in no respect, ended, terminated, sound, uninjured, fully realized, regular, solid, consummate, radical, total, top, thorough, sped, wrought, all-sided, comprehensive, unqualified, unmitigated, utter, outright, sweeping, thoroughgoing, out-and-out, uppermost, utmost, replete, topmost, undefaced, undefiled, unscathed, unimpaired, undamaged.

2. In a state of complete excellence, without blemish or defect, faultless, ideal, excellent, consummate, pure, unqualified, exquisite, capital, superlative, good, spheral, august, paragon, crowning, holy, blameless, immaculate, spotless, unblemished, laudable, dignified, sublime, supreme, infallible, matchless, orient, unexceptionable, irreproachable, unsurpassed, paramount, *ne plus ultra (Lat.)*, unequalled, unrivaled, preëminent, maximal, tiptop, sinless, stainless, infinite, undefiled, inviolate, impeccable, peerless, best, highest, champion, unexcelled, incomparable, transcendent, second to none, inimitable, inestimable, priceless, superfine, superb, superexcellent, unmarred, untainted.

3. Skilled, disciplined, finished, polished, sure, capable, masterful, thoroughly trained, fully informed, expert, accomplished, skillful, accurate, seasoned, experienced, well-grounded, dextrous, adroit, adept, deft, wise, proficient.

4. Completely corresponding to a type or description, exact, admirable, thorough, pronounced, unerring, rigorous, correct, entire, precise, mirror, essential, accurate, religious, meticulous, mathematical, clear-cut, pure, unmixed, unmingled, correct in every detail, exhaustive, close, true, lifelike, strict, fastidious, finicking, scrupulous, particular, faithful, nice, conscientious, literal, regular, scientific, out-and-out.

5. Thorough, unqualified, complete, full, whole, utter, entire, downright, positive, dead, sheer, veritable, absolute, plenary, out-and-out.

PERFECT, v. 1. Bring to completion, finish, complete, accomplish, end, close, realize, fulfil, consummate, achieve, make, develop, perfectionate, conclude, enact, discharge, effect, perfectionize, terminate, carry through or out, perform, bring about, effectuate, follow or prosecute to a conclusion, set the seal on, bring to an end, make good, clinch, cap, crown, mature, ripen, round out, culminate, realize, compass, conclude.

2. Make perfect or faultless, bring to or nearer to perfection, improve, refine, mature, elaborate, correct, retouch, polish, reclaim, reform, purge, clarify, cleanse, rectify, emend, mellow, cultivate, purify, restore, correct, filter, enrich, enhance, develop.

3. Make fully skilled, make expert, train, nurture, prepare, drill, exercise, acclimatize, discipline, practice, teach, cultivate, prime, fit, inure, habituate, form, rear, foster, breed, develop, ground, season, adapt.

PERFECTION, n. 1. State or quality of being perfect, perfectness, fulfillment, completion, maturity, consummation, finish, correctness, goodness, fullness, holiness, superiority, infinity, ripeness, utterness, entireness, completeness, Utopia, virtue, transcendence, accomplishment, supereminence, faultlessness, wholeness, attainment, elaboration, culmination, achievement, realization, effectuation.

2. Highest degree of proficiency (or of a quality, trait, etc.), excellence, worth, prime, height, beauty, summit, merit, faultlessness, finish, lead, polish, superiority, priority, crowning point, peak, pinnacle, impeccability, precedence, preëminence, quality, utmost skill.

3. Perfect embodiment of something, acme, quintessence, height, paragon, standard, mirror, pattern, ideal, idealization, ultimate, bloom, pink, crown, essence, beau idéal, orient.

PERFECTLY, adv. In a perfect manner or degree, consummately, exquisitely, to the utmost, to the full, fully, entirely, totally, throughout, supremely, thoroughly, altogether, completely, quite, wholly, clean as a whistle, utterly, plenarily, infinitely, superlatively, preëminently, positively, absolutely, to the limit, to the nth degree, to perfection, purely, downright.

PERFERVID, adj. Violent, intense, heated, high-spirited, enthusiastic, active, excited, keen, ardent, sharp, assiduous, animated, flaming, fiery, impassioned, vehement, gushing, excitable, zealous, devoted, earnest, burning, fervent, glowing, intoxicated, wrought-up, delirious, ebullient, simmering, seething, inflamed, warm, feverish.

PERFIDIOUS, adj. Faithless, false, conniving, dishonest, traitorous, guileful, sham, Janus-faced, hollow-hearted, shifty, treacherous, insidious, deceitful, double-dealing, two-faced (coll.), knavish, betraying, treasonable, hollow, dishonorable, without honor, unscrupulous, sneaking, undependable, untrustworthy, disloyal, untruthful, corrupt, designing, scheming, unconscienced, fraudulent, dissembling, false-hearted.

PERFIDY, n. Breach of faith, disloyalty, Judas kiss, falseness, perfidiousness, prodition, desertion of the cause, treacherousness, faithlessness, Iscariotism, foul play, defection, betrayal, baseness, treason, duplicity, double-dealing, sedition, corruption, dissembling, guile, deceit, unscrupulousness.

PERFORATE, v. Bore, drill, transfix, prick, aperture, notch, crack, cut, scission, slot, slit, nick, punch, puncture, pink, stab, impale, spit.

PERFORATION, n. Hole, eyelet, opening, orifice, aperture, notch, crack, cut, scission, slot, slit, nick, puncture, prick, break, space, interstice.

PERFORM, v. 1. Carry out, do, execute, go through, compass, achieve, consummate, transact, complete, finish, perpetrate, bring to pass, bring about, accomplish, work, manage, engineer, pursue, prosecute, enact, attain, realize, commit, culminate, pull off (sl.), render a service, operate, knock off (coll.), dispose of, polish off, clinch, perfect, make good, adhere to an obligation, exercise, help, effect, work out, function, take in hand, practice, effectuate, make a reality, clench.

2. Carry into effect, fulfill, follow the ritual of, keep, observe, complete, be faithful to, comply with, adhere to, discharge, meet, satisfy, minister, do duty, celebrate, solemnize, ceremonialize, go through, redeem, serve, execute in due form, obey, officiate, administer.

3. Act (a play, part, etc.), render (music, etc.), play, sustain (a part), execute, produce, concertize, strut the boards, troupe, tread the stage or boards, support, personate, barnstorm (Theat.), take a part, mimic, act out, enact, ham (Theat. sl.), represent.

PERFORMANCE, n. 1. Entertainment (musical, dramatic, etc.), acting, exhibition, representation, review, act, production, play, show (coll.), presentation, work, product, composition, handiwork, offspring, creation, musical, musicale, opus, origination, invention, ceremony, stunt, trick, vaudeville, matinee, concert, spectacle, opera, drama, recital, audition, hearing, battle, première, pageant, extravaganza, variety, appearance, engagement, stand.

2. Performing, execution, doing, consummation, creation, production, skill, labor, practice, exercise, acquittal, completion, discharge, accomplishment, observance, perpetration, transaction, enterprise, endeavor, attempt, fulfillment, achievement, operation, compliance, employment, manipulation, perfection, elaboration, concurrence, functioning, redemption, conduct, dispatch, effectuation, workmanship, composition, invention, origination, construction.

3. Action, deed, proceeding, affair, function, procedure, act, exploit, work, office, enterprise, thing done, move, stroke, gest, step, transaction, business, touch, maneuver, make-believe, dissembling, pretense, dealings, doings, measure, handiwork, stunt (coll.), craftsmanship, musicianship, effort, adventure, effect, function, operation, endeavor, achievement, feat, attempt.

PERFUME, n. Sweet-smelling substance, fragrance, flavor, spice, savor, essence, aroma, pleasing scent, grateful odor, bouquet, attar, pastille, pungency, sachet, incense, balminess, redolence, musk, civet.

PERFUME, v. Impart fragrance to, scent, impregnate with a sweet odor, sweeten, incense, aromatize, cense, fumigate, imbue with odor, spray.

PERFUNCTORY, adj. Performed merely as an uninteresting or routine duty, indifferent, careless, mechanical, formal, passive, without enthusiasm, passionless, apathetic, lukewarm, unwilling, superficial, lackadaisical, unanimated, uncaring, dull, half-hearted, nonchalant, cursory, blasé, thoughtless, unmindful, languid, pococurante, stolid, spiritless, slack, neglectful, regardless, lame, scanty, poor, jejune, hollow, meager, indolent, immature, wanting, incomplete, inattentive, offhand, lax, loose, void, cold, cool, uninspired, routine, stereotyped, inadequate, deficient, listless, unconcerned, unsolicitous, slight, negligent, heedless, slovenly, reckless.

PERFUSE, v. Overspread with moisture, color, etc., diffuse (a liquid, etc.) through or over something, spread, cover, film, wrap, enwrap, overlay, immantle, envelop, encase, coat, sheathe, cloak, shroud, mantle, pervade, overcast, imbue, overlie, bespread, fill, penetrate, permeate, radiate through, overflow.

PERGOLA, n. Horizontal trellis, arbor, bower, kiosk.

PERHAPS, adv. Maybe, possibly, for all or aught one knows, perchance, it may be, peradventure, probably, as luck may have it.

PERIAPT, n. Amulet, charm, talisman, phylactery, lucky piece, rabbit's foot, good-luck piece, good-luck charm, voodoo, fetish, obeah (coll.).

PERICARP, n. Capsule, seed pod, pod, husk, shell, hull, shuck, episperm, seed vessel, seed capsule, shale, testa, boll, periderm, peridium, rind, skin, peel, cortex, bark, bran, chaff, theca.

PERICRANIUM, n. 1. Cranium, skull, headbone, braincase, brainpan, epicranium, brain box, periosteum.

2. Head, poll, think tank (coll.), noodle, dome, knob, topknot, bean (sl.), pate, belfry, etc. See HEAD.

PERIDERM, n. Epicarp, ectoderm, peel, rind, skin, cortex, hull, husk, bark, peridium, cortical tissue, integument, peeling, dermatogen.

PERIDOT, n. Chrysoprase, chrysolite, stone, mineral, green stone, olivine, gem, gem stone, jewel, precious stone.

PERIL, n. Danger, hazard, risk, jeopardy, apprehension, unsafety, pitfall, insecurity, chance, adventure, defenseless, openness to attack, vulnerability, exposure, instability, endangerment, imperilment, precariousness, cause for alarm, susceptivity, susceptibility, exposure to danger, threat.

PERIL, v. Risk, endanger, imperil, jeopardize, hazard, put in danger, expose to danger, expose, jeopard, put in jeopardy, compromise, venture, lay a trap for, trap, snare, ensnare, adventure, threaten, bring into peril, bring into danger, menace, lower.

PERILOUS, adj. Dangerous, imperiled, hazardous, risky, fraught with danger, beset with danger, fraught with peril, beset with peril, alarming, unsafe, imminent, headlong, full of danger, full of risk, precarious, insecure, slippery, ticklish, herculean, adventurous, adventuresome, pernicious, frightening, fearful, intimidating, chastening, terrible, terror-giving, awe-inspiring, startling, appalling, scary, scaring, dismaying, awful, dire, dreadful, unhealthy (coll.), slippy, ominous, threatening, unsure, uncertain, infirm, shaky, chancy.

PERIMETER, n. Outline, border, circumference, periphery, circle, delineation, contour, bounds, pale, edge, brink, margin, limit, curb, borderline, fringe, frontier, hem, skirt, outskirt, confine.

PERIOD, n. 1. Cycle, space, time stretch, time, interval, span, spell, duration, stage, quarter, term, semester, half, third, era, age, epoch, century, aeon, eon, epact, season, month, day, week, lunation, phase of the moon, octave, novena, triduum, quinquennial, luster, lustre, lustrum, decennial, decade, decennium, pilgrimage, generation, date, millennium, duration, continuance, circuit, space of time, time interval, round of years, revolution of time, year, twelvemonth, lunar year, solar year, calendar year, fiscal year, Marian Year, Holy Year, indiction, era of indiction, spring, summer, autumn, winter, fall, kalpa (Hindu), eternity.

2. Limit, bound, end, termination, conclusion, close, expiration, terminus, terminal, apodosis, stoppage, windup, determination (Arch.), goal, destination, stop, discontinuance, thirty (sl.), final curtain, denouement.

3. Sentence, clause, periodic sentence, proposition, writing, grammatical form, syntactical form.

4. Full stop, full point, dot, punctuation mark.

PERIODIC, PERIODICAL, adj. Recurring, recurrent, serial, seasonal, isochronous, epochal, pulsative, rhythmic, rhythmal, intermittent, remittent, cyclic, cyclical, regular, at regular intervals, at fixed times, at fixed intervals, weekly, monthly, seasonally, daily, diurnal, nightly, quotidian, hebdomadal, hebdomadary, menstrual, monthly, annual, triennial, biennial, biannual, centennial, decennial, frequent, sesquicentennial, bicentennial, tricentennial, bicentenary, tricentenary, centenary, alternating, alternate, every other, following, ensuing, succeeding, successive, consequent, sequential, subsequent, consecutive, proximate, proximal, fitful, spasmodic, skipping, epochal, punctual, secular, quarterly, semiannual, regular, occasional, hourly, by the minute, minute-by-minute, systematic, often, repeated.

PERIODICAL, *n.* Publication, magazine, newspaper, paper, review, monthly, weekly, quarterly, annual, serial, bulletin, gazette, rag *(sl.),* sheet, journal, tabloid, tab *(cant),* yearbook, daybook.

PERIODICALLY, *adv.* Recurringly, recurrently, serially, seasonally, isochronously, epochally, pulsatingly, pulsingly, pulsatively, rhythmally, rhythmically, intermittently, remittently, cyclically, regularly, weekly, monthly, daily, diurnally, nightly, nocturnally, quotidianly, hebdomadally, annually, biennially, triennially, biannually, centennially, tricentennially, alternately, alternatingly, ensuingly, successively, consequently, subsequently, sequentially, consecutively, proximately, proximally, fitfully, spasmodically, skippingly, often, frequently, punctually, secularly, quarterly, semiannually, regularly, occasionally, hourly, by the minute, minute-by-minute, systematically, repeatedly, repetitiously.

PERIPATETIC, *adj.* Itinerant, walking, perambulating, ambulating, ambulatory, ambulant, ambling, traveling, pedestrian, foot-borne, itinerary, ambulative, perambulatory, touristic, touristical, moving, wandering, errant, restless, unquiet, roaming, roving.

PERIPHERAL, *adj.* Outer, on the edge, perimetric, perimetrical, defined, outlined, clearly outlined, external, eccentric, outlinear,

PERIPHERY, *n.* Outside, perimeter, outline, edge, boundary, circumference, circumscription, line, outer boundary, extreme edge, eccentricity, borderlands, outpost, outlands, suburbs, precincts, purlieus, circumambiency, circumjacence, contour, fringe, hem, outskirt, border, confine, confines, bounds, border.

PERIPHRASE, PERIPHRASIS, *n.* Circumlocution, circumambages, ambages, digression, discursiveness, roundabout speech, excurses, quibbling, ambiguity, ambiguousness, indirect speaking, cavil, caviling, hairsplitting, evasion, tergiversation, redundancy, prolixity.

PERIPHRASTIC, PERIPHRASTICAL, *adj.* Circumlocutory, equivocating, equivocal, roundabout, wordy, prolix, verbose, ambiguous, vague, redundant, indirect, ambagiatory, ambagious, circuitous, evasive, discursive, excursive, circumfluent, devious, backhanded, backhand, sinuous.

PERISH, *v.* 1. Wither, sear, dry up, fade away, grow faint, expire, decline, ebb, wane, sink, go down, lapse, degenerate, retrograde, retrogress, fall off, wizen, decay, waste, go to waste, waste away, fall, rot, crumble, moulder, mold, break up, pass away, cease to exist, deteriorate, droop, totter, cave in, break down, dry rot, wither, shrink, collapse, come to ruin, come to naught, expire, breathe one's last, come to an end, fall dead, meet death, miscarry, abort, fail.

2. Go to ruin, be destroyed, be overwhelmed, be subdued, fall, fall to the ground, break up, crumble, go to smash, tumble, topple, fall to pieces, disappear, evaporate, melt, fade away, dissolve, vanish, die out, peter out *(coll.),* pass out of the picture, go, be gone, become extinct, be extinguished, be eradicated, succumb.

3. Die, expire, meet death, go to glory, end one's life, quit the world, make an exit, come to an end, bite the dust, *etc. See* DIE.

PERISHABLE, *adj.* Mortal, destructible, decomposable, transient, fleeting, transitory, frail, slight, weak, impermanent, temporary, volatile, evanes-

cent, flying, transeunt, transitional, transitive, preterient, ephemeral, ephemerous, fugacious, provisory, temporary, temporal, diurnal, short-lived, cursory, inconstant, unreliable, unstable, mercurial, changeful, uncertain, wavering, fluctuating, provisional.

PERISTALSIS, *n.* Vermiculation, movement, muscular movement, spiral movement, intestinal movement, visceral motion.

PERISTALTIC, *adj.* Vermicular, vermiculate, intestinal, spiral, visceral, digestive, enteric, muscular, wormlike.

PERISTYLE, *n.* Arcade, court, colonnade, column, portico, plaza, courtyard, place, square, cloister, close, piazza, forum, yard, enclosure.

PERIWIG, *n.* Wig, peruke, toupee, Georgian wig, powdered wig, Ramillie wig, scratch, scratch-wig, hairpiece.

PERIWINKLE, *n.* 1. Shellfish, crustacean, snail, shell, univalve.

2. Flower, blossom, wild flower, evergreen, plant.

PERJURE, *v.* Forswear, falsify testimony, bear false witness, be untruthful, lie, be a liar, utter a falsehood, deviate from the truth, manswear, break one's oath, prevaricate, stretch the truth, lie flatly.

PERJURER, *n.* Liar, Judas, criminal, falsifier, prevaricator, rascal, knave, equivocator, Ananias, false witness, fabricator, pseudologue, legal liar, romancer, storyteller.

PERJURY, *n.* False swearing, forswearing, perfidy, mendacity, dishonesty, crime, oath-breaking, falsehood, untruthfulness, untruth, perversion, misstatement, lie, lying, perversion of the truth, distortion of the truth, prevarication.

PERK, *v.* 1. Be proud, deign, act proudly, condescend, put on airs, give oneself airs, be arrogant, be insolent, hold one's head high, hold up one's head, act big, look big, act the grand seigneur, get on one's high horse, swagger, peacock, strut, stalk, show off, be vain, display vanity, boast, brag, cock, cut a figure, cut a dash, strut one's stuff *(sl.),* blow one's own horn, toot one's trumpet, puff, puff oneself up.

2. Jerk, twitch, tug, tweak, flick, pluck, twang, jet, jiggle, joggle, shake, jostle, yank, pull, wrench, snatch.

PERK UP, *v.* Take heart, be encouraged, take courage, cheer up, brighten up, bear up, raise one's spirits, be refreshed, come back, rally, revive, come to, regain one's strength, chase away care, recuperate, recover, keep a stiff upper lip, keep up one's spirits, light up, cheer up, become cheerful.

PERKY, *adj.* 1. Proud, haughty, uppish, toplofty, proudful, swollen with pride, puffed up, elevated, stuck up, perked up, proud as a peacock, highflown, highfalutin, condescending, **high and** mighty, boastful, vain.

2. Jaunty, spruce, natty, well-dressed, well turned out, trim, chic, trig, tidy, smartly dressed, smartly attired, smartly apparelled, well-tailored, well-clothed, sleek, glossy, classy *(coll.),* dapper, finical, finicky, foppish, dandified, silk-stocking.

3. Brisk, quick, alert, quick-stepping, lightsome, sportive, good-natured, lively, animated, vivacious, cheerful, of good cheer, lighthearted, light, smiling, free and easy, high-spirited, sprightly, full of spirit, spirited, sunny.

PERMANENCE, PERMANENCY, *n.* Duration,

durability, continuity, stability, immovability, impermeability, immutability, unchangeableness, imperishability, constancy, changelessness, durableness, steadiness, dependability, fixity, fixedness, continuance, lastingness, endurance, durability, inactivity, inaction, unactivity, inanimateness, inanimation, stagnation, standstillism, idleness, preservation, preservedness, keeping, serenity, placidity, calm, composure, peace, repose, rest, stillness, imperturbation, tranquillity, immobility, dormancy, stabilization, fixation, solidity, soundness equilibrium, prolongation, perpetuation, abidingness, sustentation, maintenance, conservation, survival, survivance, longevity, long-livedness, persistence, persistency.

PERMANENT, *adj.* Durable, continual, continuous, continued, stable, immovable, impermeable, immutable, unchangeable, imperishable, constant, changeless, steady, dependable, fixed, stationary, lasting, enduring, inactive, inanimate, stagnant, still, idle, preserved, kept, keeping, fast, serene, placid, calm, composed, peaceable, peaceful, in repose, at rest, restful, tranquil, dormant, stable, stabilized, fixated, solid, sound, equilibrated, balanced, prolonged, protracted, perpetual, perpetuated, abiding, sustained, maintained, preserved, conserved, surviving, survived, longevous, long-lived, persistent, eternal, endless, forever, sempiternal, forever and a day, everliving, immortal, undying, unintermitting, uninterrupted, evergreen, infinite, unending, dateless, never-ending, everflowing, ever-living, ineradicable, unerasable, steadfast, unfading, unyielding, adamant, invariable, stable, perdurable, everyday, unalterable, indestructible, unfailing, stock, standing, indelible, usual, general, ordinary, live, living, enduring, settled, irremovable, ceaseless, incessant, unceasing, never-stopping, never-ceasing, perennial, deathless, undying, immortal, perdurant, intact, inviolate, unchecked, established, unaltered, unalterable, undestroyed, unsuppressed, unrepealed, unrepudiated, inveterate, confirmed, strong, rooted, radicated, deep-rooted, entrenched, ingrained, ingrafted, engrafted.

PERMEABLE, *adj.* Pervious, porous, penetrable, openable, accessible, perforable, pierceable.

PERMEATE, *v.* Penetrate, pervade, run through, soak, fill, saturate, interpenetrate, overrun, overspread, diffuse, interfuse, infiltrate, intersperse, infuse, imbue, pass through.

PERMEATION, *n.* Diffusion, penetration, spreading, interpenetration, running through, filling, soaking, saturation, overrunning, interfusing, interfusion, infiltration, interspersing, interspersion, imbuing, passing through, imbuement, impregnation, suffusion, transfusion, mixture, mixing.

PERMISSIBLE, *adj.* Allowable, legal, tolerated, allowed, permitted, sanctioned, legitimate, lawful, unprohibited, unforbidden, unproscribed, proper, fitting, open, warrantable, excusable, free, sufferable, bearable, admissible, licit, patent, faculative, authorized, warranted, granted, empowered, franchised, enfranchised, licensed, chartered, constitutional, ordained, prescribed, privileged.

PERMISSION, *n.* Leave, license, grant, franchise, charter, consent, warrant, allowance, toleration, privilege, warranty, approval, approbation, *carte blanche (Fr.),* sufferance, dispensation, ordinance, ordination, permit, authorization, authority, power, pass, grace, favor, liberty, right, access, connivance, endurance, *congé (Fr.),* vouchsafement, indulgence, indulgency, exemption, release, special

favor, admission, accordance, concordance, brevet, imprimatur, passport, safeconduct, visa, enfranchisement, immunity, concession, acquiescence compliance, agreement, assent, prerogative, affranchisement.

PERMISSIVE, *adj.* Permitting, allowing, dispensatory, granting, legitimate, dispensative, facultative, assenting, consenting, consentant, consentive, consentful, acquiescent, agreeable, admissory, tolerable, legal, licit, legitimate, forbearing, tolerant, indulgent, unprohibited, unproscriptive, unproscripted, patent, authorized, warranted, granted, empowered, franchised, enfranchised, licensed, chartered, constitutional, ordained, prescribed, privileged.

PERMIT, *v.* Leave, license, allow, tolerate, ordain, authorize, legalize, let, suffer, endure, put up with, bear with, bear, accede to, indulge, favor, sanction, concede, empower, warrant, give permission, give leave, give *carte blanche* to *(Fr.),* admit, enfranchise, franchise, consent to, approve, privilege, vouchsafe, legalize, defend, authorize, give leave to, facultate, humor, gratify, accord, concur, assent, give assent, award assent, commission, give dispensation.

PERMIT, *n.* License, authorization, warrant, permission, card, passport, visa, patent, charter, franchise, firman, liberty, courtesy, brevet, grant, authority, sanction, imprimatur, safe-conduct, furlough, ticket of leave, copyright.

PERMITTED, *adj.* Allowable, legal, licensed, licensable, allowed, sanctionable, sanctioned, legitimate, licit, lawful, unprohibited, unproscribed, proper, fitting, open, warrantable, excusable, free, sufferable, bearable, admissible, patent, facultative, authorized, innocent, welcome, approved, approvable, warranted, granted, empowered, franchised, enfranchised, chartered, constitutional, ordained, prescribed, privileged.

PERMUTABILITY, *n.* Interchangeability, interchangeableness, commutability, mutability, changeableness, alterability, variability, versatility, modifiability, fluctuation, flux, instability, deviability, plasticity.

PERMUTABLE, *adj.* Changeable, modifiable, plastic, pliable, alterable, interchangeable, commutable, mutable, variable, versatile, fluctuating, unstable, deviable, eversible, checkered, everchanging, protean, kaleidoscopic, movable, mobile, alterative, metagenetic *(Biol.).*

PERMUTATION, *n.* Change, alteration, interchange, mutation, difference, variation, modification, shift, turnabout, deviation, diversion, transformation, transfiguration, transubstantiation, transmogrification *(coll.),* metamorphosis, metastasis, transmutation, commutation, counterchange, transposition, transposal, alternation, intermutation, exchange.

PERMUTE, *v.* Change, interchange, exchange, shuffle, switch, swap *(coll.),* trade, substitute, counterchange, reciprocate, bargain, barter, change hands, transfer, transmit, convey, hand over, pass over, turn over, deliver, negotiate, make over, consign, assign.

PERNICIOUS, *adj.* Harmful, hurtful, dangerous, injurious, deleterious, detrimental, mischievous, baleful, baneful, disadvantageous, damaging, prejudicial, destructive, ruinous, fatal, mortal, deadly, toxic, perversive, toxiferous, nocuous, malign, malignant, noxious, noisome, malicious, wicked, evil, malevolent, felonious, foul, bad, wrongful, unwholesome, nocent, adverse, immoral, unsanitary, unwholesome, insalubrious, malefical, male-fic, disserviceable, wasting, disastrous, corrupting, sinister, vicious, perverting, nyphitic, poisonous, unhealthy, pestilential, pestiferous, venomous, obnoxious, damnable, dire, grievous, morbific, virulent, septic, morbiferous, toxicant, putrefacient, putrefactive.

PERNICKETY, *adj.* *(Coll.)* Demanding, fastidious, particular, fussy, finical, overscrupulous, meticulous, hard to please, difficult to please, subtle, delicate, choosy, punctilious, punctual, thin-skinned, hypercritical, overcritical, censorious, squeamish, mincing, nice, affectedly nice, affected, priggish, prim, puritanical, Quakerish, stiff-necked, discriminating, discriminative, sensitive, impressionable, impressible, perceptive, elective, choosy, choicy, discretional, critical, differentiative, acute, dioristic, dioristical.

PERORATE, *v.* 1. Speak, make a speech, harangue, speak at length, rant, spout *(coll.)*, orate, make an oration, deliver an oration, lecture, give a talk, bombasticate, rodomontade, drool, run at the mouth, twaddle, drivel, protract a speech, tell at length, draw out a speech, relate at length, expatiate, descant, divagate, enlarge upon a theme, spin out, go on and on, flourish, elocutionize, mouth a speech, mouth words, declaim, speechify, spiel *(sl.)*, discourse, hold forth *(coll.)*, climb on the soapbox, get on the stump, take the stump, elocute, recite, take to the hustings.
2. End a speech, conclude, sum up, summarize, close.

PERORATION, *n.* 1. Speech, talk, elocution, address, lecture, speeching, discourse, harangue, declamation, diatribe, exhortation, jeremiad, sermon, preaching, preachment, formal address, public address, public talk, oration, rhetorical discourse, disquisition, dissertation, monologue, valedictory, valediction, valedictory address.
2. Summation, end, closing, conclusion, closing remarks, closing words, concluding remarks, concluding words, summary, termination.

PEROXIDE, *n.* Compound, substance, chemical substance, chemical compound, hydrogen peroxide, bleach, oxidizing agent, blanching agent.

PERPEND, *v.* Consider, ponder, attend, concentrate, weigh, ruminate, balance, think of, think carefully, cerebrate, mentalize, deliberate, think over, bethink, reflect, digest, reason, cogitate, contemplate, meditate, study, muse, revolve in one's mind, think over, apply the mind, turn over in one's mind, bend one's thoughts to, turn one's thoughts to, brood over, con over, reflect upon, muse over, use one's head, rationalize, intellectualize.

PERPENDICULAR, *adj.* Vertical, upright, at right angles, erect, on end, plumb, bolt-upright, straight, standing upright, precipitous, orthogonal, normal, sheer, straight-up-and-down, up-and-down, rectangular, right-angular.

PERPENDICULAR, *n.* Upright, vertical, normal, plumb, plumb line, right angle, orthogon.

PERPETRATE, *v.* Do, commit, perform, enact, actuate, execute, practice, transact, effect, act, carry into effect, carry out, bring about, get through, inflict, dispatch, despatch, prosecute, pursue, exercise, produce, pull off *(coll.)*, achieve, make, work out.

PERPETRATION, *n.* Deed, doing, commission, performance, enactment, actuation, execution, practice, practicing, transaction, effecting, action, act, carrying out, infliction, inflicting, dispatch,

prosecution, pursuit, exercise, exercising, production, achievement, making, working out, evil act.

PERPETUAL, *adj.* Permanent, durable, continual, continued, stable, immovable, immutable, unchangeable, imperishable, constant, changeless, steady, dependable, fixed, stationary, lasting, enduring, preserved, fast, fixated, stabilized, solid, sound, prolonged, protracted, perpetuated, abiding, sustained, maintained, everlasting, preserved, conserved, surviving, survived, longevous, long-lived, eternal, sempiternal, endless, forever, forever and a day, everliving, immortal, undying, unintermitting, uninterrupted, evergreen, infinite, unending, dateless, never-ending, everflowing, ineradicable, unerasable, steadfast, unfading, unyielding, invariable, perdurable, everyday, unalterable, indestructible, unfailing, stock, standing, indelible, usual, general, living, live, irremovable, ceaseless, incessant, unceasing, never-stopping, never-ceasing, perennial, deathless, immortal, perdurant, intact, inviolable, inviolate, unchecked, unstopped, unhindered, unimpeded, established, unalterable, unaltered, inveterate, ageless, confirmed, chronic, strong, rooted, deep-rooted, radicated, entrenched, ingrained, ingrafted, engrafted, long, habitual, gradual, sustained, persistent, unstopped, unshifting, sempervirent, termless, boundless, inexhaustible.

PERPETUALLY, *adv.* Ceaselessly, incessantly, unceasingly, perennially, deathlessly, undyingly, immortally, perdurantly, inviolably, inviolately, unstoppingly, unhinderably, without hindrance, unimpededly, unalterably, unfailingly, inveterately, agelessly, confirmedly, chronically, strongly, deep-rootedly, habitually, gradually, persistently, perseveringly, unshiftingly, lastingly, boundlessly, termlessly, inexhaustibly, permanently, durably, continually, stably, immovably, immutably, unchangeably, imperishably, constantly, changelessly, steadily, dependably, fixedly, stationary, lastingly, enduringly, fast, fastly, solidly, soundly, prolongedly, protractedly, abidingly, sustainedly, everlastingly, preservedly, eternally, sempiternally, endlessly, immortally, unendingly, datelessly, never-endingly, ineradicably, unerasably, steadfastly, unfadingly, unyieldingly, invariably, perdurably, unalterably, indestructibly, indelibly, usually, irremovably.

PERPETUATE, *v.* Perennialize, preserve from oblivion, eternize, immortalize, eternalize, memorialize, make everlasting, render deathless, make perpetual, make last, cause to endure, extend, protract, prolong, preserve, save, conserve, maintain, sustain, continue.

PERPETUATION, *n.* Continuation, perseverance, continuance, maintenance, sustenance, prolongation, protraction, extension, permanence, perpetuity, sempiternity, everlastingness, eternity, perdurability.

PERPETUITY, *n.* Continuousness, succession, continuity, everlastingness, eternity, forever, endlessness, constancy, endurance, perennity, sempiternity, durability, endless existence, ceaselessness, constant progression, infinity, perdurability, coeternity, timelessness, continued existence, uninterrupted existence, aye, endless time.

PERPLEX, *v.* Involve, complicate, confuse, mix up, muddle, confound, bother, pother, distract, bewilder, get *(coll.)*, embarrass, puzzle, pose, fog, nonplus, set, corner, beset, mystify, afflict, fluster, flurry, stump, mock, bepuzzle, stagger, astonish, put to it, amaze, abash, dazzle, flabbergast, disconcert, discompose, disquiet, rattle *(coll.)*, upset, unsettle, make one's head swim, make one's head spin, throw into confusion, perturb, flummox *(sl.)*, flustrate *(coll.)*, moider *(coll.)*, becloud, befuddle, addle one's wits, bamboozle, dismay, stick *(coll.)*, beat one *(coll.)*, get one down *(coll.)*, keep one guessing, daze, befog.

PERPLEXED, *adj.* Lost, confused, baffled, bewildered, bothered, pothered, bewitched, doubtful, doubting, dubious, uncertain, straitened, nonplussed, distracted, dismayed, disquieted, disconcerted, disordered, mystified, put to it *(coll.)*, at a loss *(coll.)*, involved, muddled, confounded, mixed up, distracted, got *(sl.)*, embarrassed, posed, befogged, puzzled, beset, afflicted, flustered, flustrated, flurried, stumped *(coll.)*, mocked, bepuzzled, bedazzled, dazzled, staggered, discomposed, rattled *(coll.)*, upset, unsettled, perturbed, flummoxed, moidered *(sl.)*, addled, bamboozled, stuck *(coll.)*, kept guessing, dazed, foggy.

PERPLEXING, *adj.* Enigmatic, puzzling, knotty, spiny, troublesome, embarrassing, intricate, complicated, complex, bewildering, confusing, confounding, vexatious, vexing, distracting, amazing, carking, trying, taxing, bothersome, annoying, aggravating *(coll.)*, mystifying, ambiguous, equivocal, equivocable, hard, difficult, tangled, thorny, entangled, mazy, obscure, disturbing, disquieting, paradoxal, paradoxical, labyrinthian, involved, labyrinthine, Gordian, crabbed, knotted, raveled, meandering, meandrous, irreducible, insoluble, unsolvable, problematic, problematical, arcane, inscrutable, inexplicable, riddling, awkward, plaguy *(coll.)*.

PERPLEXITY, *n.* Complexity, intricacy, involvement, implication, enigma, puzzle, bafflement, bewilderment, maze, meander, web, webwork, complexus, Gordian knot, befuddlement, daze, confusion, distraction, bewilderment, frustration, fluster, flustration *(coll.)*, disquietude, discomposure, muddle, flurry, disturbance, perturbation, dazzlement, bother, botheration *(coll.)*, pother, stew, puzzlement, quandary, straits, exigency, nonplussation, dilemma, confounding, disconcertion, hardness, obscurity, entanglement, meandering, coil, nonplus, tangle, disorder, care, anxiety, concern, solicitude, doubt, dubiety, uncertainty, hesitation, doubtfulness, amazement, worry, incomprehension, inexperience, suspense, nescience, hobble, difficulty, pickle *(coll.)*, pass, pinch, scrape, knot, riddle, paradox, critical situation, contingency, mist, haze, pucker *(coll.)*, ferment, excitement, ignorance, wonder, cobweb, conglomeration, sticky business *(coll.)*, inexplicable difficulty, emergency, astonishment.

PERQUISITE, *n.* Profit, pelf *(coll.)*, gain, emolument, reward, income, earnings, winnings, pickings *(coll.)*, receipts, proceeds, take, returns, innings, revenue, fees, tips, graft *(cant)*, boodle *(sl.)*, pork barrel *(Pol. cant)*, prize, loot, booty, recompense, guerdon, pay, payment, salary, wages, money, dole, solatium, honorarium, hire, financial reward, stipend, allowance, tribute, financial remuneration.

PERQUISITION, *n.* Examination, scrutiny, close examination, investigation, inquiry, perscrutation, scrutinizing, rigorous examination, strict investigation, strict inquiry, research, inquest, thorough search, careful search, deep study, concentration, application, study.

PERRON, *n.* Stoop, platform, steps, stairs, emplacement, landing, stage, flight of steps, stairway, staircase.

PERSCRUTATE, *v.* Study, search, investigate, examine, make a close study, scrutinize, pore over, try in every phase, pervestigate, study absorbedly, lose oneself in, take stock of, examinate, scan, peruse, overlook, look over, analyze, think over, think about, consider, contemplate, probe, fathom, sound, examine point by point, make a close study of, take the measure of, go into deeply, research, pursue for study.

PERSCRUTATION, *n.* Examination, perquisition, scrutiny, close examination, investigation, inquiry, scrutinizing, rigorous examination, strict investigation, strict inquiry, research, inquest, thorough search, careful search, deep study, concentration, application, study.

PER SE, *(Latin)* By itself, for itself, taken alone, apart from anything else, substantially, intrinsically, at bottom, in the main, in effect, practically, solely, simply, in the abstract, of itself.

PERSECUTE, *v.* Oppress, harry, harass, afflict, molest, worry, distress, tantalize, hunt down, pursue, punish, pursue malignantly, drive from pillar to post, annoy, tease, beset, pester, hector, aggrieve, enrage, dragoon, dragoonade, grind, harrow, rack, chastise, plague, maltreat, crush, transport, expel, badger, vex, torment, bully, bullyrag, rile, provoke, scourge, imprison, torture, strike, abuse, flog, beat, crucify, outrage, hound, tyrannize, castigate, bear hard on, bear down upon, trample, get into trouble, wound, injure, scathe, disserve, do a mischief, overburden, weigh down, faze, fash, trouble, sting, gall, chafe, nettle, bait, exasperate, roil, rile *(coll.)*.

PERSECUTION, *n.* Molestation, outrage, punishment, harassment, harassing, torment, torture, affliction, infliction, tyranny, heavy hand, oppression, wrong, hunting, cruelty, savagery, savageness, ruffianism, truculence, vindictiveness, inhumanity, ferocity, ferociousness, brutality, maltreatment, abuse, misusage, atrocity, ravaging, ill service, ill turn, disservice, chastisement.

PERSEUS, *n.* 1. Demigod, hero, brave man, paladin, man of mettle, man of courage, daredevil, intrepid hero, dreadnought, fearless man.

2. Constellation, asterism, configuration, group of stars.

PERSEVERANCE, *n.* Steadfastness, steadiness, persistence, tenacity, continuance, constancy, resolution, indefatigableness, go *(coll.)*, application, zeal, devotion, patience, determination, pursuance, grit *(coll.)*, stamina, sand *(coll.)*, backbone, pluck *(coll.)*, stick-to-itiveness *(coll.)*, inflexibility, resoluteness, diligence, endurance, unswerving determination, resolve, decision, decisiveness, firmness of mind, hardiness of spirit, intransigence, intransigency, purposefulness, purposiveness, courage, doggedness, stubbornness, obstinatenes, firmness of purpose, strength of purpose, sedulousness, sedulity, pertinacity, obduracy, selfwill, toughness of will, toughness of mind, cussedness *(coll.)*, obduration, ambition.

PERSEVERE, *v.* Be steadfast, continue, persist, endure, keep on, keep going, strive, go forward, work unflaggingly, maintain one's efforts, go on, keep on, be steady, go all the way, maintain one's ground, hold one's ground, not give up, stand fast, stand firm, be unyielding, not yield, stick to it, stick to the job, hang on, abide, follow up, pursue relentlessly, run on, jog on, hang on for dear life, stick to one's guns, do to a frazzle, never say die, stick to the ship, not give up the ship, adhere, hold fast, cling, cling to, be tenacious, cling tenaciously, plug along, keep at it, plug away, hammer away, leave no stone unturned, die in harness, die with one's boots on, die trying, go to any lengths, go the limit, see it through, go whole hog (coll.), move heaven and earth, plod, insist, act, do to a turn, chase, hold out, repeat, do nothing but, be determined, be resolute, have a mind of one's own, mean business, stick at nothing, stop at nothing, not stick at trifles, not take 'no' for an answer, die-hard, go down fighting, be obstinate, take no denial, brook no denial, have one's own way, labor, struggle, toil, work, moil, grub, grind, drudge, work day and night, toil unceasingly, work unceasingly, do thoroughly, not do by halves, do it up brown (coll.).

PERSEVERING, adj. Assiduous, constant, persistent, tenacious, unrelenting, unremitting, attentive, careful, painstaking, diligent, stalwart, steadfast, industrious, indomitable, indefatigable, unwearying, unflagging, sturdy, patient, pertinacious, untiring, unwearied, resolute, inflexible, unswerving, undeviating, continuing, zealous, stubborn, intractable, dogged, mulish, obstinate, adamant, obdurate, unfaltering, undistracted, undismayed, unaffected, undrooping, sedulous, plodding, resolute, unsleeping, never-sleeping, neverwearying, never-tiring, determined, unshrinking, grim, stern, fixed, immovable, relentless, unrelenting, not to be shaken, unshakable, intransigent, uncompromising, irrevocable, decided, decisive, firm, unflinching, game to the last, energetic, businesslike.

PERSIFLAGE, n. Banter, raillery, small talk, chatter, badinage, repartee, badinerie (Fr.), joke, joking, jesting, wit, flash of wit, facetiousness, comeback, snappy comeback, quid pro quo (Lat.), frivolous talk, frivolity, irony, ranting, quizzing, mockery, pleasantry, jocularity, jocosity, irrision, mockery, ridicule, chaff, chaffing, twit, twitting.

PERSIST, v. 1. Remain, endure, continue, survive, hold out, stand out, hold on, go on, be constant, abide, subsist, last, perdure, perennate, stay, run, run on, carry on, linger, prolong, not change, remain unchanged, live, keep, hold good, remain valid.

2. Persevere, be steadfast, continue, endure, keep going, strive, go forward, work unflaggingly, maintain one's efforts, go on, keep on, be steady, continue, maintain one's ground, hold one's ground, not give up, stand fast, stand firm, be unyielding, not yield, stick to it, stick to the job, hang on, abide, follow up, pursue, pursue relentlessly, run on, jog on, hang on for dear life, stick to one's guns, do to a turn, never say die, stick to the ship, not give up the ship, adhere, hold fast, cling, cling to, be tenacious, cling tenaciously, plug along, keep at it, plug away, hammer away, leave no stone unturned, die in harness, die with one's boots on, die trying, go to any lengths, go the limit, see it through, go whole hog (coll.), move heaven and earth, plod, insist, act, go all the way, chase, hold out, repeat, do nothing but, be determined, be resolute, have a mind of one's own, mean business, stick at nothing, stop at nothing, not stick at trifles, not take 'no' for an answer, die-hard, go down fighting, be obstinate, brook no denial, take no denial, have one's own way, labor, struggle, toil, work, strive, moil, grub, grind, drudge, work day and night, toil unceasingly, work unceasingly, do thoroughly, not do by halves, do it up brown (coll.), do to a frazzle.

PERSISTENCE, n. Steadfastness, steadiness, perseverance, tenacity, continuance, constancy, resoluteness, indefatigableness, indefatigability, go (coll.), application, zeal, ambition, devotion, patience, determination, pursuance, grit (coll.), stamina, backbone, pluck (coll.), stick-to-itiveness (coll.), inflexibility, diligence, endurance, unswerving determination, resolve, decision, decisiveness, firmness of mind, hardiness of spirit, intransigence, intransigency, purposefulness, purposiveness, inflexibility, courage, doggedness, stubbornness, obstinateness, obstinacy, firmness of purpose, strength of purpose, sedulousness, sedulity, stamina, pertinacity, obduracy, obdurateness, selfwill, toughness of will, toughness of mind, cussedness (coll.), obduration, insistence, insistency, contumacy, contumaciousness, resolution.

PERSISTENT, adj. Persevering, assiduous, constant, tenacious, unrelenting, unremitting, attentive, careful, painstaking, diligent, stalwart, steadfast, industrious, indomitable, indefatigable, unwearying, unflagging, sturdy, patient, pertinacious, untiring, unwearied, resolute, inflexible, unswervable, unswerving, undeviating, continuous, zealous, continuing, stubborn, intractable, intransigent, dogged, mulish, obstinate, adamant, obdurate, unfaltering, undistracted undismayed, unaffected, undrooping, sedulous, plodding, unsleeping, never-sleeping, never-wearying, never-tiring, determined, unshrinking, grim, stern, fixed, immovable, relentless, not to be shaken, unshakable, uncompromising, irrevocable, decided, decisive, firm, unflinching, game to the last, energetic, businesslike, permanent, unstopping, unceasing, incessant, continual, interminable, limitless, chronic, repetitious, frequent.

PERSNICKETY, adj. Hypercritical, captious, finicky, fussy, demanding, exacting, querulous, fastidious, hard to please, finicking, difficult to please, choosy (coll.), hairsplitting, discriminating, discriminative.

PERSON, n. Thing, something, an existence, body, flesh and blood, object, matter, substance, creature, personage, human, human being, individual, member of the human race, homo sapiens (Lat.), party, soul, living soul, mortal, fellow creature, earthling, worldling, hand, scout (coll.), customer (sl.), member, somebody, someone, one, wight (arch), duck (sl.), anthropos, humanity, substantiality, entity, being, spirit, chap, animal.

PERSONABLE, adj. Good-looking, handsome, comely, seemly, beautiful, attractive, pretty, well-favored, pleasing, agreeable, goodly, bonny (dial.), likely, sightly, fair, shapely, well-made, well-proportioned.

PERSONAGE, n. 1. Individual, being, creature, body, someone, one, somebody, flesh and blood, person, human, human being, member of the human race, homo sapiens (Lat.), party, soul, living soul, mortal, fellow creature, fellow man, fellow, chap, chappie (coll.), worldling, earthling, scout (coll.), customer (sl.), member, duck (sl.), anthropos, humanity, entity, man, woman.

2. Great man, man of mark, distinguished person, great personage, man of distinction, man of consequence, notability, notable, mogul, nabob, panjandrum, magnate, sachem, chieftain, chief, big gun (sl.), very important person, V.I.P., somebody, something, magnifico, pillar of society, big shot (coll.), heavyweight, big man, his nibs (coll.), worthy, figure, figure of importance, illustrious person.

PERSONA GRATA, adj. (Latin) Sympathizer,

friend, confidante, faithful friend, trusted friend, intimate, favorite, fondling, pet, cosset, minion, apple of one's eye *(coll.)*, confidant.

PERSONAL, *adj.* 1. Private, individual, special, subjective, own, peculiar, privy, intimate, not public, exclusive, nonobjective, intrinsic, inherent, internal, inward, inwardly felt, esoteric.

2. Physical, bodily, substantial, corporal, corporeal, exterior, material, essential, hypostatic, hypostatical.

PERSONALITY, *n.* 1. Self, ego, entire self, selfness, selfhood, I, me, oneself, egohood, yourself, itself, himself, herself, distinction, distinct identity, distinctiveness, character, individual characteristic, individuality.

2. Discourtesy, criticism, personal remark, personal criticism, rudeness. impoliteness, incivility, misconduct, reflection, aspersion, animadversion, censure, critical remark, stricture, exception, disparagement, detraction, libel, slander, defamation, indignity, insult, gibe, malediction, calumny, calumniation, opprobrium, scurrility, vilification, vituperation, affront, indignity, blame.

3. Character, make-up, nature, traits, quality, disposition, affection, temperament, humor, stripe, spirit, peculiarities, constitution.

PERSONATE, *v.* Play, act, impersonate, represent, masquerade, take the part of, take-off, mock, copy, make believe, mimic, hit off, assume the character of, imitate, personify, mask, assume a disguise, assume the guise of, pose as, appear as, characterize, act out.

PERSONATION, *n.* Representation, acting, act, miming, pantomime, take-off, simulation, personification, impersonation, embodiment, playing, play, play-acting, masquerade, part, role, mocking, mockery, copying, copy, make-believe, mimicry, characterization, disguise, pose, posing, acting out, imitation.

PERSONATOR, *n.* Impersonator, mime, mimic, actor, character actor, mimist, simulator, personifier, masquerader, mocker, copier, poser, *poseur (Fr.),* imitator.

PERSONIFICATION, *n.* 1. Figure of speech, rhetorical device, prosopopoeia, turn of expression, turn of phrase, image, imagery, figure.

2. Impersonation, personation, representation, acting, mime, pantomime, mimicry, imitation, simulation, play-acting, take-off, embodiment, playing, play, drama, masquerade, part, role, mockery, mocking, copying, copy, make-believe, characterization, disguise, pose, posing, acting out.

PERSONIFY, *v.* 1. Pose as, act, act out, impersonate, personate, represent, masquerade, take the part of, mock, copy, make-believe, mimic, hit off, assume the role of, assume the character of, assume the part of, imitate, assume a disguise, assume the identity of, appear as, characterize.

2. Embody, materialize, incorporate, substantify, substantiate, externalize, corporealize, make corporeal, substantialize, corporify, body, incarnate.

3. Figure, exemplify, symbolize, represent by metaphor, express, express by metaphor.

PERSONNEL, *n.* Staff, members, workers, employees, help, gang, force, office force, office staff, working people, associates, clerical staff, servantry, man power, labor, laborer, laboring force, labor supply.

PERSPECTIVE, *n.* Vista, view, proportion, sense of proportion, sense of values, picture, panorama,

outlook, aspect, distance, prospect, horizon, bird's-eye-view.

PERSPICACIOUS, *adj.* Acute, discerning, clearsighted, keen-sighted, quick, keen, shrewd, penetrating, eagle-eyed, sharp-sighted, thoughtful, clear-headed, lucid, sagacious, prudent, knowing, far-seeing, far-sighted, alert, canny, sharp, astute, argute, nimble-witted, alive, awake, alert, clearheaded, sharp-witted, piercing, alive to, apperceptive, appercipient, percipient, observant, seeing, discriminating, discretionary.

PERSPICACITY, *n.* Perspicaciousness, acuteness, shrewdness, astuteness, sharpness, discernment, discerningness, discriminatingness, discrimination, penetration, sagacity, far-sightedness, insight, acumen, capacity, sense, common sense, understanding, comprehension, tact, wisdom, prudence, clear-headedness, clear vision, clear-sightedness, subtleness, flair, judgment, meticulousness, refinement of perception, perceptiveness, perceptivity, apperceptiveness, apperception, refinement, delicacy, tact, sensitivity, acute discernment, sharpness of mind, sharpness of vision, percipience, appercipience, subtlety.

PERSPICUITY, *n.* Lucidity, lucidness, clearness, clarity, transparency, intelligibleness, intelligibility, distinctness, explicitness, comprehensibility, understandability, unambiguousness, definiteness, definition, translucency, transpicuity, limpidity, limpidness, clearness, conceivability, knowability, apprehensibility, explicability, penetrability, palpableness, exactness, plainness, perspicuousness, truthfulness, accuracy, factuality, reality, conspicuousness, prominence, saliency, salience, manifestness, apparentness, plain-spokenness.

PERSPICUOUS, *adj.* Lucid, clear, transparent, intelligible, distinct, understandable, comprehensible, unambiguous, definite, translucent, transpicuous, limpid, conceivable, knowable, apprehensible, explicable, penetrable, palpable, exact, plain, truthful, accurate, factual, real, genuine, conspicuous, prominent, salient, manifest, apparent, plainspoken, outspoken, express, defined, ostensible, shown, revealed, exhibited, exoteric, visible, patent, autoptical, autoptic, avowed, seeable, discernible, open, open-and-shut, overt, bare, naked, barefaced, admitted, unmistakable, manifestative, demonstrational, demonstrated, demonstrative, noticeable, notable, pronounced, noteworthy, plain as day, unhidden, unshrouded, unconcealed, undraped, unobscured, disclosed, discovered, undisguised.

PERSPIRATION, *n.* Sweat, exudation, sweating, diaphoresis, cutaneous excretion, exhalation, vapor, water vapor, water, sudation, sudoresis, profuse perspiration, emanation, transudation, efflorescence, excretion, secretion, waste matter.

PERSPIRE, *v.* Sweat, excrete, secrete, exude. exhale, respire, exudate, transude, swelter, be moist, reek, drip, pour sweat, be drenched with sweat.

PERSUADABLE, *adj.* Persuasible, undogmatic, unbigoted, disinterested, unjaundiced, unprejudiced, unaffected, unswayed, dispassionate, impartial, unimpassioned, objective, open, available to reason, open-minded, broad-minded, accessible, responsive, amenable, forbearing, unpositive, unprovincial, unopinionative, unopinionated, agreeable, reachable, available to argument, tractable, docile, susceptible, impressionable, soft, receptive, flexible, pliable, submissive, receptive, sensitive, supple, pliant, yielding, moldable, ductile, bendable, suasible, easygoing, manageable, complaisant, obeisant, acquiescent, passive, unresistant, nonresistant, unresisting, deferential.

PERSUADE, v. 1. Influence, induce, incite, impel, motivate, move, actuate, allure, entice, prevail upon, win, win over, bring 'round, get, bend, move, prevail with, carry, overcome, lead, bring to reason, make one see reason, turn, move by persuasion, draw over, talk into, lead one to, sell, sell one on (coll.), tempt, enlist, engage, procure, wheedle, cajole, coax, determine, turn the scale, inveigle, inspirit, vamp, entreat, inspire, obtain, bring, attract, decoy, urge, exhort, invite, importune, seduce, bribe, suborn, gain by a bribe, gain, sway, lure, prompt, arouse, dispose, rouse, occasion, magnetize, incline, bias, guide.

2. Convert, convince, wean, assure, gain the confidence of, have the ear of, make one feel sure of, make up one's mind, advise, counsel, enlighten, guide, rule.

PERSUASION, n. 1. Suasion, persuasiveness, exhortation, hortation, influence, incitement, bringing over, pressure, entreaty, homiletic, dissuasion, deterrent, proselytism, proselyting, conversion, propaganda, propagandizing, power, potency, pull (coll.), advice, recommendation, counsel, insistence, motivation, inducement, actuation, allurement, allure, enticement, prevailing, lead, talk, admonition, warning, wheedling, coaxing, cajolery, entreaty, inveigling, seduction, bribery, bribe, lure, prompting, subornation, guide, example, argument.

2. Belief, opinion, conviction, plerophory, convincement.

3. Sect, denomination, clan, ism, order, kind, school of thought, school, church, communion, creed, belief, tenet, dogma, way of thinking, manner of thinking, line of thought, religion, faction, sectarism, religious order, community, group, fellowship, body, organization, society, cult, faith, credo, position, view, articles of belief.

PERSUASIVE, adj. Cogent, convincing, compelling, logical, valid, inducive, suasive, moving, sound, weighty, conciliatory, eloquent, strong, powerful, forceful, rhetorical, coaxing, homiletic, winning, inviting, tempting, seductive, persuasory, tenable, believable, credible, satisfying, satisfactory, dependable, reliable, plausible, impressive, possible, suasory, hortative, hortatory, influential, provocative, inductional, alluring, attractive, engaging, prepossessing, winning, authoritative, effective, efficacious, telling, important, significant, urgent.

PERSUASIVENESS, n. Eloquence, rhetoric, cogency, logicality, logicalness, conviction, convincingness, compellingness, validity, induciveness, suasion, suasiveness, soundness, weightiness, strength, power, forcefulness, winningness, invitingness, temptingness, temptation, seduction, seductiveness, persuasoriness, tenableness, tenability, believability, credibility, satisfactoriness, dependability, reliability, plausibility, impressiveness, hortativeness, hortatoriness, influence, provocativeness, inductiveness, allure, alluringness, attractiveness, attraction, engagingness, prepossessingness, prepossession, winningness, authority, authoritativeness, effectiveness, efficacy, tellingness, importance, significance, urgency.

PERSUASORY, adj. Cogent, convincing, compelling, logical, valid, inducive, suasive, moving, sound, weighty, conciliatory, eloquent, strong, powerful, forceful, rhetorical, coaxing, homiletic, winning, inviting, tempting, seductive, persuasive,

tenable, believable, credible, satisfying, satisfactory, dependable, reliable, plausible, impressive, possible, suasory, hortative, hortatory, influential, exhorting, provocative, inductional, alluring, attractive, engaging, prepossessing, winning, authoritative, effective, efficacious, telling, important, significant, urgent.

PERT, adj. 1. Saucy, brisk, forward, bold, impudent, impertinent, flippant, free, presuming, presumptuous, malapert, indecorous, impolite, indiscreet, unmaidenly, unladylike, cocky, brassy, brazen, overbold, brazen-faced, insolent, brash, fresh (coll.), shameless, pushing, audacious, insulting, procacious, crusty, nervy (sl.), bodacious, obtrusive, precocious, smart, discourteous, smart-alecky (coll.), unabashed, unblushing, aweless, barefaced, conceited, stuck-up, egotistical, self-centered, vainglorious, vain, arrogant.

2. Brisk, smart, lively, quick, nimble, sprightly, chipper.

PERTAIN, v. Appertain to, connect with, relate to, have to do with, answer to, correspond to, tie in with, belong to, concern, regard, connect, bear upon, have reference to, adhere, be included, come under, fall under, enter into.

PERTINACIOUS, adj. Dogged, assiduous, constant, persistent, persevering, tenacious, unrelenting, unremitting, attentive, careful, painstaking, diligent, stalwart, steadfast, industrious, indomitable, indefatigable, unwearying, unflagging, sturdy, patient, pertinacious, untiring, unwearied, resolute, unwearying, inflexible, unswerving, undeviating, continuing, continuous, zealous, stubborn, intractable, mulish, stubborn, obstinate, adamant, obdurate, unfaltering, undistracted, undismayed, unaffected, undrooping, sedulous, plodding, unsleeping, never-sleeping, never-wearying, never-tiring, determined, unshrinking, grim, stern, fixed, immovable, relentless, unrelenting, not to be shaken, unshakable, intransigent, uncompromising, irrevocable, decided, decisive, firm, unflinching, game to the last, energetic, businesslike, headstrong, pervicacious, stanch, stiff, wilful, persisting.

PERTINACITY, n. Steadfastness, steadiness, persistence, perseverance, tenacity, continuance, constancy, resolution, resoluteness, indefatigability, indefatigableness, go (coll.), application, ambition, zeal, devotion, patience, determination, pursuance, grit, determination, stamina, sand (coll.), backbone, pluck (coll.), stick-to-itiveness (coll.), inflexibility, diligence, endurance, unswerving devotion, unswerving determination, resolve, decision, decisiveness, firmness of mind, hardiness of spirit, intransigence, intransigency, purposefulness, purposiveness, courage, doggedness, stubbornness, obstinateness, obstinacy, strength of purpose, sedulousness, sedulity, pertinacity, obduracy, obdurateness, self-will, tough-mindedness, cussedness (coll.), obduration, mulishness, insistence, stiffness, contumacy, contumacy, impersuadability, impersuasibility, intractability, incorrigibility.

PERTINENCE, PERTINENCY, n. Appropriateness, fitness, relation, relatedness, propriety, patness, relevance, aptness, smartness, suitability, applicability, relevancy, coaptation, admissibility, commensurability, cognation, agreement, agreeability, harmony, consistency, correspondence, compatibility, congruency, congruence, consentience, accordance, proportionateness, congeniality, consensuality, apposition, consonance, suitableness.

PERTINENT, *adj.* Appropriate, fit, apt, congruent, relating, relevant, apposite, applicable, suitable, congeneric, proper, pat, smart, applicable, coapt, admissible, commensurate, cognate, agreeing, agreeable, harmonious, consistent, corresponding, compatible, felicitous, consentient, according, accordant, proportionate, congenial, consensual, apposite, consonant, to the point, meet, smart, connected with, relative, adapted, germane, pertaining, appurtenant, concerning, regarding, in point, happy.

PERTNESS, *n.* 1. Forwardness, sauciness, impertinence, impudence, brashness, briskness, boldness, flippancy, freedom, presumption, presumptuousness, malapertness, indecorum, indecorousness, impoliteness, indiscretion, unmaidenliness, unladylikeness, cockiness, brass, brassiness, brazenness, overboldness, insolence, freshness *(coll.)*, shamelessness, audacity, insultingness, procacity, crust, crustiness, nerve *(sl.)*, bodacity, bodaciousness, obtrusiveness, precocity, smartness, discourtesy, unblushingness, awelessness, barefacedness, conceit, egotism, self-centeredness, vainglory, vanity, arrogance, bumptiousness, swagger, pretension, pride, conceit.

2. Nimbleness, briskness, sprightliness, quickness, smartness, chipperness, affability, affableness.

PERTURB, *v.* 1. Trouble, disquiet, disturb, ruffle, annoy, discompose, vex, harry, worry, agitate, distress, convulse, affect, unsettle, provoke, pique, stir, fluster, flurry, flutter, jolt, shock, jar, shatter, dumbfound, irritate, sting, excite, rouse, arouse, nettle, gall, chafe, vex, madden, infuriate, wound, foment, perturbate, churn, disconcert, broil, toss.

2. Confuse, disorder, flurry, upset, derange, bewilder, confound, rattle, perplex, put out, muddle, befuddle, addle the wits, faze *(coll.)*, distract, throw into confusion, flummox *(sl.)*, becloud, dizzy, make one's head swim.

PERTURBANCY, *n.* 1. Derangement, agitation, disturbance, fear, trepidation, disquietude, disquiet, restlessness, nervousness, anxiety, cold feet *(sl.)*, inquietude, trepidity, sweating, cold sweat *(coll.)*.

2. Confusion, disorder, muddle, flurry, flurrying, fluster, flustration, upset, derangement, bewilderment, perplexity, befuddlement, distraction, dizziness.

PERTURBATE, *v.* 1. Trouble, disquiet, disturb, ruffle, annoy, discompose, vex, harry, worry, agitate, distress, convulse, affect, unsettle, provoke, pique, stir, fluster, flurry, flutter, jolt, shock, jar, shatter, dumbfound, irritate, sting, excite, rouse, arouse, nettle, gall, chafe, vex, madden, infuriate, wound, foment, perturb, churn, disconcert, broil, toss.

2 Confuse, disorder, muddle, flurry, upset, derange, bewilder, confound, rattle, perplex, put out, befuddle, addle the wits, faze *(coll.)*, distract, throw into confusion, flummox *(sl.)*, becloud, make one's head swim.

PERTURBATION, *n.* Agitation, disquiet, confusion, trepidation, fear, anxiety, uneasiness, restlessness, discomposure, worry, ebullition, consternation, frenzy, shock, disorganization, flurry, fluster, turmoil, madness, hubbub, effervescence, mental conflict, furor, derangement, hysterics, hysteria, paroxysm, quiver, horror, distress, fear, resentment, timidity, excitation, delirium, storm,

frustration, violence, ferment, rage emotion, alarm, disconcertion, dread, ruffle, tremor, trembling, choler, jitters *(sl.)*, shakes *(sl.)*, fear and trembling, inquietude, disquietude, stage fright, buck fever *(coll.)*, ado, stir, turmoil, shaking, quaking, quivering, quavering, fuss, bother, pother, tumult, whirl, scurrying, excitement, stimulation, provocation, sensationalism, rout, fomentation, trepidity, unrest, hurlyburly, hustle, bustle, confoundment, bewilderment, flusteration, flustration, fidgets, fidgeting, disorganization, derangement, razzle-dazzle *(sl.)*, disorder, racket, riot, pandemonium, brouhaha, hugger-mugger.

PERTURBATORY, *adj.* Disturbing, troubling, disquieting, ruffling, annoying, discomposing, vexing, worrying, distressing, harrying, convulsing, affecting, unsettling, provoking, piquing, stirring, flustering, flurrying, fluttering, jolting, shocking, jarring, shattering, dumbfounding, irritating, stinging, exciting, maddening, infuriating, rousing, arousing, nettling, galling, chafing, wounding, hurtful, fomenting, perturbing, churning, disconcerting, broiling, tossing.

PERTURBED, *adj.* Agitated, uneasy, fretful, anxious, disquieted, confused, fearful, restless, discomposed, worried, ebullient, consternated, frenzied, shocked, disorganized, flurried, flustered mad, maddened, effervescent, deranged, hysterical, quivering, shaking, trembling, horrified, horror-struck, horror-stricken, resentful, timid, excited, delirious, frustrated, violent, fermented, in ferment, enraged, raging, emotional, alarmed, disconcerted, dreading, in dread, ruffled, choleric jittery *(sl.)*, in fear and trembling, inquiet, unquiet, bustling, stirred, in turmoil, quaking, scurrying, stimulated, provoked, fomented, fussing bothered, in a pother, in a stew, stewing *(coll.)* tumultuous, whirling, in a whirl, scurrying, routed in a state of unrest, hustling, confounded, bewildered, flusterated, flustrated, fidgety, fidgeting, disordered, rioting, in a riot, in pandemonium distressed, overwrought, wrought up, unsettled troubled, troublous, aflutter, displeased, offended nauseated, sickened, repelled, repulsed, uncomfortable, ill at ease, queasy, abhorrent, fazed *(coll.)*.

PERTUSION, *n.* 1. Perforation, hole, punched hole, orifice, puncture, wound, cut, terebration acupuncture, acupunctuation, acupuncturation pinhole.

2. Piercing, puncture, puncturing, perforation penetration, impalement, terebration, acupuncture, acupunctuation, acupuncturation.

PERUKE, *n.* Wig, false hair, hairpiece, scratch wig, periwig, perruque, toupee, rug *(sl.)*, top doilie *(sl.)*, Ramillies wig, Georgian wig, powdered wig

PERUSAL, *n.* Reading, scrutiny, examination scanning, inspection, study, learning, survey, review, investigation, indagation, conning.

PERUSE, *v.* 1. Read, scan, pore over, examine regard studiously, con, glance at, glance over, read carefully, dip into, turn the leaves of, thumb over spell, spell out, run through, wade through, run the eye over.

2. Survey, inspect, investigate, examine, scrutinize, observe, watch, look over, look at, turn one's gaze upon, subject to scrutiny, give a close examination to, examine carefully, overlook, look over, contemplate, consider, mull over, search research, seek out, search through, devote oneself to, pervestigate, overhaul, scan, inlook, in

spect, fathom, peer into, peer at, go over, go through, examinate, give the mind to, explore.

PERVADE, *v.* Permeate, penetrate, pass through, overspread, saturate, soak, fill, run into, run through, extend through, affect, animate, diffuse, infuse, leaven, traverse, make full, infiltrate, imbue, impregnate, be diffused through, be disseminated through, overrun, interpenetrate, tinge, entincture, tincture, interfuse.

PERVASION, *n.* Permeation, penetration, passing through, passage, overspreading, saturation, soaking, animation, diffusion, infusion, leavening, traversal, filling, infiltration, imbuement, imbuing, impregnation, dissemination, overrunning, interpenetration, tingeing, tincture, tincturing, entincturing, interfusion, inflowing, transudation, osmosis.

PERVERSE, *adj.* 1. Ungovernable, uncontrollable, hard to deal with, intractable, unyielding, unruly, untoward, refractory, wild, difficult, hard to manage, unbending, awkward, bulky, clumsy, troublesome, vexatious, wayward, wilful, factious, wanton, querulous, inconvenient.

2. Rude, impolite, discourteous, thoughtless, uncivil, unmannerly, unpolitic, unladylike, ungentlemanly, crude, ill-bred, ill-mannered, rough-hewn, rough, uncourtly, ungenteel, uncivilized, untrained, wild, barbaric, barbarian, unfeminine, unmasculine, abusive, insulting, uncomplaisant, unaccommodating, ungracious, bumptious, truculent, bellicose, belligerent, pugnacious, unceremonious, ungallant, inaffable, unfriendly, inimical, unbred, unpolished, ill-behaved, ill-conditioned, unneighborly, unmanly, inhuman.

3. Obstinate, wilful, dogged, mulish, headstrong, unyielding, untractable, pertinacious, assiduous, constant, persistent, persevering, tenacious, unrelenting, unremitting, indomitable, indefatigable, untiring, unwearying, unflagging, unwearying, unwearied, resolute, inflexible, unswerving, undeviating, zealous, stubborn, adamant, obdurate, unfaltering, sedulous, plodding, wrong-headed, hard-headed, pervicacious, opinionated, restive, bigoted, self-willed, contumacious, seditious, contrary, contradictory, headstrong, wayward, balky, stiff, pigheaded, unsubmissive, hard, contrarious, unflinching, froward, tough, case-hardened, tough-grained, obstreperous, hard-mouthed, hard-bitten.

4. Crabbed, testy, grouchy *(coll.)*, ill-tempered, sullen, out of humor, ill-humored, irascible, bad-tempered, cursed, cussed *(coll.)*, crabby *(coll.)*, snappish, waspish, snappy, cross, petulant, peevish, captious, cantankerous, cross-grained, wrong-headed, touchy, froward, morose, surly, snarling, spiteful, mean, wicked, splenetic, spleeny *(coll.)*, fractious, contentious, censorious, indocile, sour, moody, difficult, churlish, bearish, crusty, iracund, pettish, huffy, querulous, malignant, malevolent, evil-natured, atrabilious, bilious, humorsome, acerbic, acerb, shrewish, vixenish, vixenlike, hot-tempered, warm, hot-headed, quick, sudden, hasty, grim, grumpy, moping, mopey, mopish, growling, glaring, black-browed, glowering, frowning, mumpish, grum, fretful, fretting, piqued, in a dudgeon.

PERVERSION, *n.* 1. Declension, hardening of the heart, backsliding, reversion, regression, apostasy, recreancy, defection, desertion.

2. Misuse, abuse, misdirection, misapplication, misappropriation, misemployment, damage, impairment, harm, hurt, labefaction, scathe, hurting, loss, detriment, devastation, ravage, misrepresen-

tation, distortion, corruption, twisting, misstatment, lying, untruth, falsification, falsifying, mendacity, pseudology, subreption, deception, misinstruction, heresy, misrepresentation, sophistry, fallacy, invalidity, misinformation, misintelligence, misconception, misunderstanding, miscomprehension, mistranslation, misrendering, misconstruction, false construction, eisegesis, mistake, error, casuistry, illogicality, philophastry, sophisticism, speciousness, speciosity, illogicalness, special pleading, false argument, paralogism, paralogy, Jesuitism, chicanery.

3. Corruption, vitiation, injury, impairment, deterioration, degradation, depredation, debasement, prostitution, degeneration, depravity, wickedness.

PERVERSIVE, *adj.* Corrupting, harmful, hurtful, scathing, dangerous, hazardous, corruptive, pernicious, deleterious, detrimental, nocent, noxious, damaging, virulent, insalubrious, unsafe, twisting, injurious, impairing, deteriorating, degrading, debasing, degenerating, depraved, wicked, malignant, malefic, malefical, prejudicial, disadvantageous, disserviceable, corroding, corrosive, ruinous, destructive, mortal, deadly, crippling, defiling, contaminating, vitiating, polluting, demoralizing, brutalizing, adulterating, alloying, diluting, weakening, diminishing, enervating

PERVERT, *v.* 1. Stretch, distort, wrest, falsify, misuse, warp, torture, wrench, strain, misapply, mutilate, garble, misrepresent, misinterpret, misconstrue, misconstruct, skew, turn, wring, abuse, color, misconceive, misdeem, misread, misexplain, give a false color to, put a false interpretation on, misunderstand, misspell, misinstruct, misteach, miseducate, misguide, mislead, miscorrect, misstate, misquote, misrepresent, lie, prevaricate

2. Corrupt, lead away, tempt, deprave, degrade, debase, desecrate, subvert, defile, deflower, taint, infect, sophisticate, tamper with, warp, prostitute, demoralize, brutalize.

PERVERT, *n.* 1. Epicene, homosexual, bisexual, the third sex, lesbian, sodomite, sodomist, fairy, queer *(sl.)*, homo *(coll.)*, nance, queen *(sl.)*, Molly, Miss Molly, fag, dike *(sl.)*, gynandroid, hermaphrodite, androgyne, fagot, flute *(sl.)*.

2. Apostate, backslider, recidivist, renegade, recreant, turncoat, secessionist, schismatist, schismatic, reversioner, reversionist, turntail, deserter, seditionist, traitor.

PERVERTED, *adj.* 1. Hermaphrodite, androgynous, androgynal, gynandral, gynandrous, homosexual, epicene, monoclinous, amorphous, queer *(sl.)*, gynandrian, heteroclite, effeminate, lesbian, adelomorphic, adelomorphous, hermaphroditic.

2. Defective, fallacious, untrue, twisted, false, falsified, deceptive, unauthentic, untrustworthy, unreliable, baseless, unfounded, unsupported, unsound, erroneous, in error, aberrant, devoid of truth, heretical, unorthodox, invalid, sophistical, sophistic, preposterous, at fault, faulty, wrong, peccant, heterodox, imperfect, abortive, unsupportable.

3. Iniquitous, corrupt, corrupted, sinful, tainted, debased, debauched, vice-ridden, low, vile, base, foul, demoralized, dissolute, degenerate, degenerated, warped, peccant, infected, rotten, contaminated, vitiated, weakened, debilitated, abandoned, gone to the dogs, shameful, profligate.

PERVICACIOUS, *adj.* Obstinate, wilful, refractory, perverse, stubborn, hard-headed, pigheaded, strong-minded, dogged, mulish, headstrong, unyielding, intractable, untractable, pertinacious, assiduous, constant, persistent, persevering, tenacious, unrelenting, unremitting, indomitable, indefatigable, untiring, unwearying, unflagging, unwearied, resolute, resolved, inflexible, unswerving, undeviating, zealous, adamant, obdurate, unfaltering, sedulous, plodding, wrong-headed, opinionated, restive, bigoted, self-willed, strong-willed, contumacious, seditious, contrary, contradictory, wayward, balky, stiff, unsubmissive, hard, contrarious, unflinching, froward, tough, casehardened, toughgrained, obstreperous, hardmouthed, hardbitten.

PERVIOUS, *adj.* Penetrable, permeable, porous, transparent, passable, openable, accessible, transudatory, transudative, percolative, leaky, effusive, transpicuous, sheer, thin, gossamer, diaphanous, diaphane.

PESKY, *adj.* Vexatious, pestiferous, bothersome, annoying, aggravating *(coll.),* troublesome, worrisome, provoking, stinging, galling, wearisome, troublesome, irksome, mortifying, plaguing, awkward, importunate, boring, harassing, teasing, tormenting, exasperating, invidious, unaccommodating.

PESO, *n.* Money, coin, legal tender, hard money, cash, specie, hard cash, cold cash, circulating medium, medium of exchange, ready money, money in hand, lucre, coinage, mintage, coin of the realm.

PESSIMISM, *n.* Underestimation, undervaluing, underestimating, underrating, gloom, gloomy outlook, depression, unhappiness, low spirits, glumness, gloominess, despondency, despondence, despair, heaviness of heart, melancholy, dismals *(coll.),* doldrums, the dumps *(sl.),* blues *(sl.),* cynicism, hopelessness, lack of enthusiasm, dashed hopes, blighted hope, lack of expectation, faint hope, wretchedness.

PESSIMIST, *n.* Alarmist, cynic, gloomy Gus *(coll.),* growler, complainer, decrier, prophet of doom, Cassandra, sour-expert, calamity howler, naysayer, defeatist, croaker, misery-lover, malist, prophet of gloom, Job's comforter, crapehanger *(sl.),* faultfinder, detractor, sourpuss *(sl.),* sad person, sorrow-seeker, sourbelly *(sl.),* moper, pouter, wet blanket *(sl.),* killjoy *(sl.),* spoilsport, damper, malcontent, grumbler.

PESSIMISTIC, *adj.* Cynical, hopeless, gloomy, glum, peevish, foreboding, beyond hope, given up, beyond help, despairing, despite, incorrigible, irreversible, beyond recall, unpromising, irreparable, incurable, mortal, fatal, beyond remedy, remediless, irremediable.

PEST, *n.* 1. Plague, pestilence, infection, sickness, epidemic, fatal epidemic, ruin, poison, abomination, disease, malady, pandemia.
2. Nuisance, annoyance, blight, trouble, curse, bane, scourge, infliction, thorn in the flesh, thorn in the side, cross, burden, plague, infestation, affliction, evil, bugbear, *bête noir (Fr.),* burden, mischief, woe, gall, vexation, nettle, prick, trial, provocation, molestation, visitation, tribulation, bore, buttonholer, twaddler, dryasdust *(coll.),* wet blanket *(coll.),* pain in the neck *(sl.).*

PEST-BEARING, *adj.* Pestiferous, pest-ridden, infested, infected, pestilential, diseased, disease-ridden, epidemic, epizoötic, endemic, endemical, pandemic.

PESTER, *v.* Annoy, harass, provoke, nettle, gall, chafe, badger, vex, molest, plague, trouble, disturb, perturb, hector, bother, disquiet, unsettle,

fret, incommode, infest, torment, irritate, bore, tease, anger, bait, egg on *(coll.),* inflame, displease, perplex, pique, try the patience, exasperate, get one's goat, ruffle, sour, aggrieve, mortify, harry, tantalize, bait, persecute, bullyrag, bully, beset, faze, agitate, irk, get on one's nerves, grate on one's feelings, pain.

PESTHOUSE, *n.* Infirmary, hospital, lazaret, lazar-house, isolation hospital, isolation ward, lazaretto.

PESTIFEROUS, *adj.* 1. Pest-ridden, pest-bearing, infested, infected, pestilential, diseased, disease-ridden, epidemic, epizoötic, endemic, endemical, pandemic, malignant, morbid, morbiferous, unhealthy, unhealthful, catching, contagious, communicable, catchable *(coll.).*
2. Noxious, venomous, pernicious, harmful, hurtful, dangerous, injurious, deleterious, detrimental, mischievous, baleful, baneful, disadvantageous, damaging, prejudicial, destructive, ruinous, fatal, mortal, deadly, toxic, perversive, toxiferous, poisonous, nocent, nocuous, malign, malignant, noisome, malicious, wicked, evil, foul, malevolent, felonious, bad, wrongful, adverse, immoral, unsanitary, unwholesome, insalubrious, malefic, disserviceable, wasting, disastrous, corrupting, sinister, vicious, perverting, nyphitic, unhealthy, pestilential, obnoxious, damnable, dire, grievous, morbific, virulent, septic, morbiferous, toxicant, putrefacient, putrefactive, malefical.

PESTILENCE, *n.* Sickness, illness, disease, infection, contagion, plague, pest, scourge, fatal epidemic, contamination, pollution, pandemia, bubonic plague, Black plague, Black Death, visitation, curse, bane, affliction, afflictive evil, infestation, infestment, nuisance, vexation.

PESTILENT, *adj.* 1. Pestiferous, pest-bearing, pest-ridden, infested, infected, pestilential, diseased, disease-ridden, epidemic, epizoötic, endemic, endemical, pandemic, malignant, morbid, morbiferous, unhealthy, unhealthful, catching, contagious, communicable, catchable *(coll.).*
2. Noxious, venomous, pernicious, harmful, hurtful, dangerous, injurious, deleterious, detrimental, mischievous, baleful, baneful, disadvantageous, damaging, prejudicial, destructive, ruinous, fatal, mortal, deadly, toxic, perversive, toxiferous, poisonous, nocent, nocuous, malign, malignant, noisome, malicious, wicked, evil, foul, malevolent, felonious, bad, wrongful, unwholesome, adverse, immoral, unsanitary, insalubrious, malefical, malefic, disserviceable, wasting, disastrous, corrupting, sinister, vicious, perverting, nyphitic, unhealthy, pestilential, obnoxious, damnable, dire, grievous, morbific, virulent, septic, morbiferous, toxicant, putrefacient, putrefactive.

PESTLE, *n.* Grinder, pounder, pulverizer, brayer, muller, muddler, reducer, masher, implement, tool.

PET, *n.* 1. Favorite, darling, cosset, fondling, dear, 'duck,' baby, idol, apple of one's eye, spoiled darling, spoiled child, matinee idol, loved one, teacher's pet, general favorite, the people's favorite, idol of the people.
2. Peevishness, pique, dudgeon, fit of anger, sudden anger, miff *(coll.),* resentment, petulance, fit of temper, conniption *(coll.),* cat fit *(sl.),* tantrum, huff, high dudgeon, deep dudgeon, stew, ferment, gnashing of the teeth, sulk, sulking, tizzy *(coll.).*

PET, *adj.* Favorite, especially favored, favored, petted, cherished, fond, darling, dear, dearest, loved, beloved, cosseted, precious, dear to one's heart, favorite, popular, idolized, after one's own heart.

PET, *v.* Fondle, caress, indulge, coddle, cosset, gratify, dandle, pamper, humor, cocker, make a fuss over *(coll.),* make much of, pat, kiss, cuddle, clasp, hug, nuzzle, snuggle, take to one's arms, enfold in one's arms.

PETARD, *n.* Squib, fireworks, firecracker, explosive, detonator.

PETERMAN, *n.* Angler, fisher, fisherman, piscatorialist, piscator, troller, dibbler, Waltonian, trawler.

PETER OUT, *v.* *(Slang)* Fail, languish, dwindle, come to nothing, fade, evaporate, vanish, disappear, cease to exist, become nonexistent, dissolve, melt, melt away, pass away, fade out of the picture, cease, stop, sink, be no more, leave no trace, go, peg out *(sl.),* fail, flag, decline, weaken, become weak, go downhill, poop out *(sl.),* play out, fizzle out, wither on the vine, miscarry, go up in smoke, fall down, fall down on the job, not get to first base, go astray, abort, founder, slip, slip up, make a slip, do in vain, dash one's hopes, fall short, come a cropper.

PETIOLE, *n.* Petiolule, stalk, leafstalk, stem, caulis, petiolus.

PETITION, *n.* Request, address, prayer, invocation, supplication, solicitation, appeal, application, entreaty, suit, proposal, plea, requisition, importuning, importunity, rogation, imprecation, obsecration, adjuration, impetration, imploring, imploration, mendication, canvass, obtestation, appeal, intercession, orison, beseechment.

PETITION, *v.* Supplicate, invoke, pray, entreat, beseech, beg, ask, seek, sue, call, petition for, apply, solicit, desire, crave, apply to, make application to, plead, invite, put to, call to, call upon, appeal, appeal to, make an appeal, adjure, urge, dun, press, tax, imprecate, clamor, cry, cry aloud, beg for help, mendicate, seek, implore pity, request, address, propose, requisition, obsecrate, obtestate, intercede.

PETITIONARY, *adj.* Invitatory, imploring, beseeching, asking, supplicatory, imploratory, solicitous, rogatory, petitional, supplicative, suppliant, postulant, mendicant, begging, invoking, invocatory, obsecrationary, importunate.

PETITIONER, *n.* Solicitor, suppliant, suitor, complainant, applicant, asker, pleader, candidate, postulant, claimant, begger, mendicant, aspirant, questioner, bidder, beseecher, supplicant.

PETRESCENCE, PETRIFACTION, *n.* Hardening, durity, induration, petrescency, lapidification, lapidescence, lapidity, lithification, fossilization, fossilification, fossilation, stoniness.

PETRIFIED, *adj.* 1. Hard hardened, stony, indurated, indurate, lapidific, hard as a rock, hard as stone, lapidary, rock-like, rocky, lithoidal, lithoid, concrete, solidified, solid, dense.

2. Stupefied, paralyzed, confounded, terrified, frightened, astounded, astonished, flabbergasted, breathless, awe-struck, awe-stricken, frozen with fear, chilled, frozen, upset, taken unaware, startled, amazed, surprised, staggered, insensitized, seared, dumbfounded, struck dumb, struck all of a heap, shocked, electrified, dazed, bedazzled, scared, affrighted, horrified, fearful, terror-stricken, terror-struck, scared out of one's wits, creeping, alarmed, daunted, numb, benumbed, obtund,

obtuse, numbed, hebetudinous, jarred, jolted, shaken, stirred, galvanized.

PETRIFY, *v.* 1. Lapidify, indurate, harden, make hard, become hard, lithify, fossilize, fossilify, calcify, turn to stone, enmarble, inlapidate, solidify, mineralize.

2. Numb, freeze, chill, refrigerate, chill to the bone, make one's teeth chatter, glaciate, glacify, ice, congeal.

3. Stupefy, paralyze, confound, terrify, frighten, astound, astonish, flabbergast, take one's breath away, awe-strike, strike dumb, shock, electrify, strike all of a heap, daze, bedazzle, fright, scare, affright, horrify, startle, put in fear, make fearful, strike terror into, scare out of one's wits, make one's flesh creep, alarm, daunt, benumb, obtund, render numb, hebetate, insensitize, sear, stagger, take one's breath away, surprise, amaze, jar, start, startle, take unawares, upset, freeze, chill, freeze with fear.

PETROL, *n.* Gasoline, petroleum, petroleum product, petroleum derivative, fuel, combustible fluid, organic compound, gas *(coll.).*

PETROLEUM, *n.* Rock oil, oil, lubricant, stone oil, mineral oil, fossil oil, natural petroleum, crude oil, fuel, lubricating oil.

PETRONEL, *n.* Gun, firearm, handgun, pistol, weapon, carbine, shooter *(coll.),* shooting iron *(coll.),* small arms, piece *(sl.).*

PETTICOAT, *n.* 1. Undergarment, slip, skirt, underskirt, crinoline, farthingale, underwear, undies *(sl.),* lingerie, shift, camisole.

2. Woman, female, girl, dame *(sl.),* hen *(sl.),* chicken *(sl.),* skirt *(sl.).*

PETTIFOG, *v.* Argue, debate, contend, argufy, contest, dispute, equivocate, quibble, cavil, trifle, prevaricate, palter, beg the question, split hairs, refine.

PETTIFOGGER, *n.* *(Coll.)* Lawyer, attorney, counselor, attorney-at-law, solicitor, barrister, pleader, advocate, legal adviser, ambulance chaser *(coll.),* green-bag *(coll.),* mouthpiece *(sl.),* shyster *(coll.).*

PETTIFOGGERY, *n.* Chicanery, deceit, sharp practice, cheating, dodgery, jobbery, fishy transaction *(coll.),* underhand practice, corruption, guile, knavery, cunning, craftiness, craft, subtlety, fraudulent skill, intrigue, cleverness, treachery, stealth, humbug, fraudulency, fraudulence, bluff, imposture, cozenage, chicane, bamboozlement, collusion, underhand dealing, dishonesty.

PETTIFOGGING, *adj.* Prevaricating, hairsplitting, caviling, subtle, deceitful, captious, frivolous, finespun, over-refined, fencing, circumlocutory, equivocating, trifling, paltry, shifty, shifting, dodging, evasive, evading, elusive, sophistical, sophistic, Jesuitical, casuistic, casuistical, questionable, dubious, sneaking, crafty, venal, corrupt, recreant, unscrupulous, knavish, roguish, unprincipled, unconscionable, unconscientious, intriguing, conniving.

PETTISH, *adj.* Peevish, fretful, querulous, testy, irascible, moody, changeable, sour, surly, waspish, splenetic, fractious, huffy, huffish, irritable, snappish, hasty, crusty, grouchy, grumpy, cynical, cross, bearish, grumbling, choleric, atrabilious, touchy, bad-tempered, ill-humored, cross-grained, petulant, malignant, captious, carping, bristling, crabby, crabbed, jaundiced, cussed, sullen, sulky, glum, gloomy, moping, mopish, mopey, glowering, scowling, moodish, moody, spleeny.

PETTY, *adj.* 1. Small, trifling, mean, insignificant, unimportant, trivial, inconsiderable, frivolous, little, slight, diminutive, of small importance, of small account, pitiful, tawdry, imponderable, dinky, puny, paltry, meager, contemptible, piddling, piffing, minor, inferior, worthless, trumpery, miserable, beggarly, trashy, puny, wishy-washy, namby-pamby, nugatory, slight, minute, limited, skimpy, scant, scanty, sparse, brief, short, niggling, fribbling, picayunish, picayune, pokey, inane, filmsy, nugacious, mincing, inspid.

2. Base, low, mean, shabby, disreputable, little, scrubby, scabby, deplorable, obnoxious, foul, regrettable, discreditable, ignominious, inglorious, ignoble, wretched, infamous, shameful, disgraceful, small-minded, grudging, opprobrious, weak, cheap.

PETULANCE, *n.* Peevishness, pettishness, querulousness, irascibility, testiness, moodiness, changeableness, sourness, acidness, acidulousness, acidity, surliness, waspishness, spleen, spleenishness, fractiousness, huffiness, huffishness, irritability, snappishness, hastiness, crustiness, grouchiness grumpiness, grumpishness, cynicalness, cynicality, cynicism, crossness, bearishness, grumbling, choler, atrabiliousness, touchiness, bad temper, ill-humoredness, ill humor, malignance, malevolence, captiousness, carpingness, crabbiness, crabbedness, jaundice, cussedness, sullenness, sulkiness, glumness, gloominess, mopingness, mopiness, mopishness, moodishness, perversity, perverseness, procacity, insolence, doldrums, mumps, dolefulness.

PETULANT, *adj.* Crabbed, testy, grouchy, ill-tempered, sullen, out of humor, ill-humored, irascible, bad-tempered, cursed, cussed *(coll.)*, crabby, snappish, waspish, snappy, cross, peevish, captious, cantankerous, cross-grained, wrong-headed, touchy, froward, morose, surly, snarling, spiteful, mean, wicked, splenetic, spleeny *(coll.)*, fractious, contentious, censorious, indocile, sour, moody, difficult, churlish, bearish, crusty, iracund, pettish, peevish, huffy, huffish, querulous, malignant, malevolent, evil-natured, atrabilious, bilious, humorsome, acerbic, acerb, vixenish, shrewish, vixenlike, hot-tempered, warm, hot-headed, quick, sudden, hasty, grim, grumpy, moping, mopey, mopish, growling, glaring, black-browed, glowering, frowning, mumpish, grum, fretful, fretting, pettish, piqued, short, passionate, impassioned, excitable, tart, peppery, contentious, argumentative, disputatious, quarrelsome, short-tempered, crusty, choleric, snarling, censorious, acrimonious, perverse, out of sorts, out of humor, cavilling.

PEW, *n.* Box, bench, seat, compartment, stall.

PHAETON, *n.* Carriage, coach, *voiture (Fr.)*, four-wheeler, buggy, car, automobile, motor, motorcar, vehicle, transportation.

PHALANX, *n.* Body, group, formation, military formation, army formation, corps, corps of troops, troops, soldiers, fighting force, armed force, fighting machine, soldiery, military, rank and file.

PHANTASM, *n.* Apparition, shade, shadow, specter, ghost, spiritual apparition, vision, wraith, spook *(coll.)*, phantom, appearance, presence, shape, incorporeity, immateriality, eidolon, disembodied spirit, incorporeal being, revenant, vagary, imagining, illusion, hallucination, delusion, figment of the imagination, image, mental image, creation of the mind, fiction, fictive creation, chimera, vapor, fancy, phantasmagoria, fantasy, fantasia, pipe dream, idle fancy, gest, shadow,

optical illusion, creation of the imagination, misconception, bubble, fantod *(sl.)*, fantastic vision, snakes *(coll.)*, nightmares, pink elephants *(coll.)*, bad dream, incubus, trick of eyesight, phasm, mirage, looming, aftermirage, ghostly form.

PHANTASMAL, *adj.* Spectral, illusory, dreamy, fantastic, ghostly, imagined, imaginary, apparitional, fancy-bred, fanciful, fancied, figmentary, figmental, imaginational, imagerial, visionary, phantom, phantasmical, phantasmic, fictitious, legendary, chimerical, unsubstantial, unreal, delusory, delusive, illusive, hallucinational, hallucinative, hallucinatory, immaterial, incorporeal, bodiless, groundless, unsubstantial, ethereal, vaporish, vapory, airy, imponderable, tenuous, dreamlike, dreamy, gossamer, gossamery, fabulous, nonexistent, gaseous, nebulous, cloudlike, phantomic.

PHANTOM, *n.* Apparition, shade, shadow, specter, ghost, spiritual apparition, vision, wraith, spook *(coll.)*, phantasm, appearance, presence, manifestation, spiritual manifestation, shape, incorporeity, immateriality, eidolon, disembodied spirit, incorporeal being, revenant, vagary, imagining, illusion, hallucination, delusion, figment, figment of the imagination, image, mental image, creation of the mind, fiction, fictive creation, chimera, vapor, fancy, phantasmagoria, fantasy, fantasia, pipe dream, idle fancy, gest, optical illusion, creation of the imagination, misconception, bubble, fantod *(sl.)*, fantastic vision, snakes *(coll.)*, nightmares, pink elephants *(coll.)*, delirium tremens, bad dream, incubus, nightmare, trick of eyesight, phasm, mirage, aftermirage, looming, ghostly form.

PHANTOM, *adj.* Phantasmal, illusory, dreamy, fantastic, ghostly, imagined, imaginary, apparitional, fancy-bred, fanciful, fancied, figmentary, figmental, imaginational, imagerial, visionary, phantomic, phantasmical, phantasmic, fictitious, legendary, chimerical, unsubstantial, unreal, delusory, delusive, illusive, hallucinational, hallucinative, hallucinatory, immaterial, incorporeal, bodiless, groundless, ethereal, vaporish, vapory, airy, imponderable, tenuous, dreamlike, dreamy, gossamer, fabulous, nonexistent, gaseous, nebulous, cloudy, cloudlike.

PHARISAIC, PHARISAICAL, *adj.* Sanctimonious, hypocritical, self-righteous, formal, canting, over-righteous, tartuffian, pietistic, over-pious, insincere, dissembling, hypocrite, mealy-mouthed, smooth-tongued, two-faced, double-dealing, Machiavellian, Machiavellic, double-handed, bland, oily, unsincere, Janus-faced.

PHARISAISM, *n.* Hypocrisy, double-dealing, two-timing *(coll.)*, cant, insincerity, formalism, phariseeism, false piety, self-righteousness, sanctimony, sanctimoniousness, pietism, over-piety, excessive piety, dissembling, dissimulation, pretense, false pretense, bluff, hypocrisis, unsincerity, Machiavellism, Machiavellianism, mealy-mouthedness, mummery, misdevotion, tartuffism, lip service, mockery, solemn mockery, mere show, lip reverence, affectation.

PHARISEE, *n.* Canter, hypocrite, religious hypocrite, lip worshiper, Tartuffe, tartufe, dissimulator, dissembler, lip server, cant, ranter, pious fraud, pietist, formalist, bigot, attitudinarian, Pecksniff.

PHARMACIST, *n.* Druggist, drug dispenser, chemist, pharmaceutist, apothecary, pharmacologist, pharmaceutical chemist, posologist, dispenser of prescriptions, prescription filler, pharmacopolist.

PHARMACY, *n.* Pharmacology, posology, pharmaceutics, dosology, chemistry, pharmaceutical chemistry.

PHAROS, *n.* Beacon, lighthouse, tower, lookout, watchtower, guide-tower.

PHASE, *n.* Phasis, circumstance, condition, aspect, position, situation, standing, status, place, attitude, point, juncture, occasion, stage, look, appearance, side, slant, angle, twist (*sl.*), posture, stature, demeanor, bearing, carriage, favor, guise, ostent, feature.

PHENOMENAL, *adj.* Curious, prodigious, exceptional, unusual, freakish, extraordinary, marvelous, wonderful, amazing, miraculous, sensational, nonesuch, unmatched, peerless, nonpareil, rare, infrequent, unprecedented, spectacular, teratogenous, unnatural, unexampled, unaccountable, unexpected, incredible, uncommon, unwonted, uncustomary, unaccustomed, unheard-of, singular, unique, peculiar, strange, passing strange, queer, *outré* (*Fr.*), bizarre, remarkable, noteworthy, preternatural, supernormal, undescribable, undescribed, unchronicled, unparalleled, striking, monstrous, fearful, overwhelming, stupendous, surprising, astonishing, wondrous.

PHENOMENON, *n.* 1. Fact, doing, occurrence, event, episode, occasion, particular, transaction, affair, job, proceeding, happening, contingency, happenstance, contingence, spectacle, sight, view, scene, incident.
2. Marvel, wonder, prodigy, amazement, miracle, sensation, nonesuch, nonpareil, rarity, prodigiosity, wonderment, curiosity, exception, spectacle, sight, freak, freak occurrence, teratism, teratogeny.

PHIAL, *n.* Container, receptacle, holder, vessel, package, bottle, flask, cylinder, vial, flasket.

PHILANDER, *v.* Flirt, wander, coquet, gallivant, court, make love, trifle with one's affections, err, stray, go astray, play at dalliance, dally, play at lovemaking, play at courtship, spark, deceive, play fast and loose, two-time (*coll.*), toy, toy with one's affections, wanton, play wanton.

PHILANDERER, *n.* Gallant, lover, flirt, coquet, coquette, philander, male flirt, ladykiller (*coll.*), adulterer, wanton, trifler, two-timer (*coll.*), deceiver, dallier, lover, ladies' man, wanderer, gallivanter, sparker, profligate, immoralist, debauchee, lecher, satyr, satyriast, rake, rakehell, sensualist.

PHILANTHROPIC, PHILANTHROPICAL, PHILANTHROPISTIC, *adj.* Charitable, good-hearted, good-natured, humane, kind, kindly, altruistic, humanitarian, eleemosynary, almsgiving, beneficent, benign, benignant, benevolent, warm-hearted, sympathetic, well-meaning, large-hearted, big-hearted, generous, magnanimous, unselfish, selfless, bounteous, bountiful, gracious, high-minded, loving, amiable, compassionate, helpful, feeling, pitiful, pitying, friendly, chivalrous, well-disposed, public-spirited, munificent, good, devoted to others, righteous, considerate, praiseworthy, laudable, free-handed, paternal, maternal, fraternal, motherly, fatherly, sisterly, brotherly, affectionate, soft, soft-hearted, ruthful, touched, liberal, free, unsparing, unstinting, ungrudging, lavish, sumptuary, princely, hospitable, aidful, ministrant.

PHILANTHROPIST, *n.* Humanitarian, altruist, giver, donor, bestower, contributor, benefactor, presenter, benevolist, well-wisher, do-gooder (*coll.*), friend to man, patriot, eudaemonist, almsgiver, public servant, good Samaritan, sympathizer, favorer, good fellow, salt of the earth, Robin Hood, philanthrope.

PHILANTHROPY, PHILANTHROPISM, *n.* Charity, charitableness, good-heartedness, good-nature, humanity, humaneness, kindness, kindliness, altruism, humanitarianism, almsgiving, alms, beneficence, benignity, benignancy, benevolence, warm-heartedness, sympathy, large-heartedness, big-heartedness, cordiality, generosity, magnanimity, unselfishness, selflessness, bounty, bounteousness, bountifulness, graciousness, high-mindedness, loftiness of spirit, lovingness, love for mankind, amiability, compassion, compassionateness, helpfulness, feeling, pity, friendliness, friendship, chivalrousness, chivalry, public spirit, public spiritedness, munificence, good, goodness, devotion to others, righteousness, consideration, considerateness, praiseworthiness, free-handedness, paternalness, maternal feeling, fatherliness, sisterliness, motherliness, brotherliness, brotherly love, affection, affectionateness, softness, soft-heartedness, ruth, ruthfulness, liberality, liberalness, unsparingness, ungrudgingness, lavishness, princeliness, hospitality, hospitableness, helpfulness, ministrations, grace, amiability, good nature, kindly nature, bonhommie, toleration, clemency, commiseration, fellow feeling, mercy, forbearance, long-suffering, tenderness, quarter, self-sacrifice, disinterestedness, disinterest, self-devotion, self-denial, self-abnegation, brotherhood, confraternity.

PHILIPPIC, *n.* Tirade, inveighing, diatribe, denunciation, jeremiad, speech, acrimony, invective, malediction, commination, execration, calumny, calumniation, disparagement, vituperation, vilification, abuse, verbal abuse, obloquy, opprobrium, defamation, detraction, reproof, reproach, reprimand, scolding, berating, reprobation, chastisement, castigation, remonstrance, revilement, contumely, knocking (*coll.*), tongue-lashing, aspersion, aspersement.

PHILISTINE, *adj.* Uncultivated, uncultured, commonplace, ignorant, unlearned, uneducated, rude, unrefined, low-browed (*coll.*), lowbrow (*coll.*), Philistinic, Philistinian, Philistinish, unguided, unlettered, unread, untutored, untaught, unenlightened, bookless, illiterate, plain, everyday, prosaic, unsympathetic, hostile (*to Art and Letters*).

PHILISTINE, *n.* Conformist, formalist, conventionalist, pedant, precisian, vandal, barbarian, Hun, Yahoo, savage, Boeotian, Goth, foe, enemy, opponent, boor.

PHILISTINISM, *n.* Formalism, pedantry, conformism, conformance, conformancy, conventionalism, pedantism, precisianism, Philistinishness, barbarianism, vandalism, Hunnishness, Yahooism, savagery, hostility to culture, hostility to Art or Letters, uncomprehendingness, obtuseness, incomprehension, boorishness.

PHILOLOGIST, *n.* Philologian, grammarian, scholar, phonologist, etymologist, linguistic historian, linguistician, philologer, philologue, grammatist, etymologer, orthoëpist, lexicographist, lexicographer, glossologist, glossographer, dialectologist, dialectician, eponymist, lexiconist, glossarian, vocabularian, vocabulist, semanticist, semasiologist, linguistic scholar.

PHILOLOGY, *n.* Linguistic study, phonology, linguistics, glossology, linguistic science, etymology, paleography, glottology, science of language, linguistic history, semantics, semasiology, lexicology, grammar, phoneticism, lexigraphy, glottogony, terminology, orismology.

PHILOMEL, *n.* Nightingale, bird, night bird, song bird, warbler, feathered songster, singing bird.

PHILOSOPHER, *n.* 1. Reasoner, thinker, rationalist, logician, logicalist, philosophizer, philosoph, philosophist, philomath, logistician, arguer, dialectician, speculator, theorist, theorizer, wise man, savant, searcher for the truth, seeker of wisdom, sapient, pundit, scholar, student.

2. Cosmologist, Mystic, Agnostic, Dualist, Pluralist, Pantheist, Unitarian, Monist, Pyrrhonist, Zetetic, Skeptic, Skepticist, Berkeleianist, Transcendentalist, Immaterialist, Absolute Idealist, Subjective Idealist, Objective Idealist, Epistemological Idealist, Critical Idealist, Metaphysical Idealist, Vicoist, Sensist, Empiricist, Ontologist, Idealist, Associated Psychologist, Utilitarian, Spencerian, Neo-Hegelian, Kantian, Hegelian, Fichtean, Critical Philosopher, Herbartian, Schellingist, Schopenhauerist, Neocritic, Relativist, Traditionalist, Positivist, Logical Positivist, Comtist, Bergsonian, Hedonist, Psychological Hedonist, Leibnitzian, Panphenomenalist, Political Philosopher, Egoistic Hedonist, Spinozist, Cartesian, Voluntarist, Moralist, Rationalist, Empiricist, Sensationalist, Averroist, Neo-Scholasticist, Humanist, Sensationalist, Scholasticist, Scholastic, Thomist, Scotist, Nominalist, Realist, Manichaean, Augustinian, Alexandrian, Eclectic, Peripatetic, Epicurean, Platonist, Aristotelian, Neo-Platonist, Academicist, Academist, Eudaemonist, Stoicist, Stoic, Patristicist, Gnostic, Hedonist, Cyrenaic, Metaphysician, Epistemologist, Pragmatist, Cynic, Eretrianist, Elianist, Elian, Socratist, Experimentalist, Instrumentalist, Aesthetician, Aesthetic Philosopher, Social Philosopher, Sociologist, Ethicist, Deist, Theist, Pantheist, Sophist, Ionian, Ionicist, Heraclitean, Eleatic, Eleaticist, Atomist, Pythagorean, Neo-Pythagorean, Sophist, Pre-Socratic, Pythagorist, Pyrrhonian, Pyrrhonicist, Socratic, Socraticist, Megarian, Eristic, Megarianist, Universalistic.

PHILOSOPHIC, PHILOSOPHICAL, *adj.* 1. Philosophistic, philosophistical, rational, wise, thoughtful, sagacious, learned, informed, intelligent, knowing, sensible, reasonable, logical, understanding, keen, acute, cute *(coll.)*, clear-headed, perceptive, appercipient, perspicacious, perspicuous, percipient, piercing, penetrating, aware, judicious, judicial, reflecting, thoughtful, sound, discriminating, discriminative, profound, abstruse, deep, enlightened, erudite, acroamatic, educated, omniscient, well-read, deeply read, well-posted, oracular, dependable, authoritative, reflective, prudent, scientific, solid, serious, sober, earnest, speculative, cogitative, pensive, strong-minded, careful, cautious, staid, precise, pragmatic, unprejudiced, unbiased, unaffected, grave.

2. Calm, tranquil, stoic, stoical, imperturbable, unruffled, unexcitable, unexcited, cool, collected, composed, sedate, serene, patient, temperate, resigned, accustomed, unmoved, inured, unimpassioned, dispassionate, passive, content, contented, complacent, inexcitable, peaceful, quiet, poised, undemonstrative, self-contained, self-restrained, self-possessed, cool-headed, steady, nerveless, demure, easygoing, restrained, nonchalant, tolerant, unresisting, yielding, gentle, subdued.

PHILOSOPHY, *n.* 1. Calmness, calm, stoicism, serenity, tranquility, poise, aplomb, equanimity,

imperturbability, unexcitableness, unexcitability, coolness, collectedness, composure, sedateness, patience, forbearance, temperateness, moderation, resignation, resignedness, accustomedness, unimpassionedness, dispassion, dispassionateness, passiveness, passivity, content, contentedness, complacence, complacency, inexcitability, peace, peacefulness, quiet, quietness, poise, equipoise, undemonstrativeness, self-possession, self-restraint, cool-headedness, steadiness, nervelessness, demureness, easygoingness, restraint, nonchalance, tolerance, toleration, yieldingness, gentleness, imperturbation, quietism, quietude, *sang-froid (Fr.),* gravity, command of temper, philosophicalness.

2. Love of knowledge, love of learning, love of wisdom, pursuit of knowledge, pursuit of learning, pursuit of wisdom, science, ideas, theory of knowledge, epistemology, theory of values, aesthetics, aesthetic philosophy, logic, symbolic logic, mathematical logic, Aristotelian logic, experimental logic, instrumental logic, pragmatic logic, psychologism, ethics, social philosophy, sociology, metaphysics, doctrine of terms, doctrine of inference, doctrine of judgment, moral philosophy, mental philosophy, natural philosophy, natural science, philosophical system, philosophical school, school of philosophy, school of thought, science of ideas.

3. Cosmology, Mysticism, Agnosticism, Dualism, Pluralism, Pantheism, Unitarianism, Monism, Pyrrhonism, Zeteticism, Skepticism, Berkeleianism, Transcendentalism, Immaterialism, Absolute Idealism, Subjective Idealism, Objective Idealism, Epistemological Idealism, Critical Idealism, Metaphysical Idealism, Vicoism, Sensism, Empiricism, Ontology, Idealism, Associated Psychology, Utilitarianism, Spencerianism, Neo-Hegelism, Kantism, Hegelism, Fichteanism, Critical Philosophy, Herbartianism, Schellingism, Schopenhauerism, Neocriticism, Relativism, Traditionalism, Positivism, Logical Positivism, Comteism, Bergsonism, Hedonism, Psychological Hedonism, Universalistic Hedonism, Leibnitzism, Panphenomenalism, Political Philosophy, Egoistic Hedonism, Spinozism, Cartesianism, Voluntarism, Moralism, Rationalism, Empiricism, Sensationalism, Averroism, Neo-Scholasticism, Humanism, Scholasticism, Thomism, Scotism, Nominalism, Realism, Manichaeanism, Augustinism, Alexandrianism, Eclecticism, Peripatetic School, Epicureanism, Platonism, Aristotelianism, Neo-Platonism, Academicism, Academism, Eudaemonism, Stoicism, Patristicism, Gnosticism, Cyrenaicism, Metaphysics, Epistemology, Traditionalism, Pragmatism, Cynicism, Eretrianism, Elianism, Socratism, Experimentalism, Instrumentalism, Aesthetics, Aestheticism, Sociology, Ethics, Deism, Theism, Pantheism, Sophism, Ionianism, Ionicism, Heracliteanism, Eleaticism, Atomism, Pythagoreanism, Neo-Pythagoreanism, Pre-Socratism, Pyrrhonism, Pyrrhonianism, Megarianism, Eristicism.

PHILTER, *n.* Potion, cantharis, love-potion, stimulant, aphrodisiac, activator, drug, charm, magic potion, excitant, energizer, stimulator, stimulus.

PHLEBOTOMY, *n.* Venesection, bleeding, lancing, bloodletting, leeching, leeches, cupping, sanguisuge, incision, draining, drainage, tapping, transfusion, blood transfusion, extravasation.

PHLEGM, *n.* 1. Mucus, mucous secretion, secretion, excremental humor, humor, excretion, bodily secretion, semiliquid, mucosal fluid.

2. Apathy, lethargy, indifference, nonchalance, dullness, hebetude, hebetation, obtuseness, insensibility, sluggishness, lassitude, equanimity, coolness, insensitiveness, passiveness, passivity, torpor, torpidity, torpidness, unconcern, coldness, callousness, callosity, obduracy, stupefaction, obtundity, deadness, stupor, impassivity, impassiveness, inappetency, inappetence, calm, calmness, supineness, languor, lentor, lentitude, statuvolence, pandiculation, oscitancy, slowness.

PHLEGMATIC, *adj.* Apathetic, stoical, dull, sluggish, calm, cold, inert, tame, frigid, unfeeling, unsusceptible, impassive, indifferent, insensible, saturnine, spiritless, insouciant, nonchalant, dispassionate, unimpassioned, slack, lymphatic, morose, moody, careless, listless, hebetudinous, stupid, lackadaisical, unambitious, undemonstrative, obdurate, unimpressionable, weary, wearisome, unemotional, unexcitable, half-hearted, languid, imperturbable, stolid, staid, insentient, lethargic, lethargical, dull, obtuse, insensitive, torpid, lazy, impassive, passive, unconcerned, callous, unfeeling, cool, stupid, stupefied, stultified, statuvolent, obtund, dead, inappetent, calm, languid, lentitudinous, pandiculating, pandiculate, slow.

PHOBIA, *n.* 1. Fear, hatred, dislike, aversion, craze, obsession, neurosis, psychosis, neurotic symptom, neurotic manifestation, mania, monomania, paranoia, distaste, loathing, repugnance, abomination, disgust, terror, horror, abhorrence, detestation, antipathy, odium, execration, aversation.

2. Agoraphobia, claustrophobia, hypsophobia, acrophobia, doraphobia, demonophobia, phobophobia, bacteriophobia, dysmorphophobia, heresyphobia, batophobia, toxicophobia, sitiophobia, syphilophobia, lyssophobia, pharmacophobia, dermatophobia, zoöphobia, neophobia, airphobia, photophobia, pyrophobia, thanatophobia, herpetophobia, ichthyophobia, ornithophobia.

PHOEBUS, *n.* Apollo, Phoebus Apollo, Phaëton, Phaëthon, Titan, Sol, sun, Sun-god, god of day, Helios, Apollon, Hyperion.

PHOENIX, *n.* Mythical monster, emblem of immortality, paragon, *beau idéal (Fr.),* perfection, good example, standard, philosopher's stone, mirror, pattern.

PHONE, *n.* *(Coll.)* Wireless telephone, radiotelegraph, radiophone, telephone, instrument, means of communication, headphone, earphone, receiver, speaking apparatus, magnetotelephone, monotelephone, microtelephone, pantelephone, radiotelephone, thermotelephone, dial telephone, dictophone, geophone, magnetophone, techniphone, vitaphone, tracheophone, lithophone, kinetophone, radiophone, motophone, hydrophone, dyophone, detectaphone, osteophone, electrophone, topophone, motophone, photophone, optophone, odophone, megaphone, stethophone, microphone, mike *(sl.),* Dictograph (trade name), phonograph, graphophone, gramophone, record player, speaker, loudspeaker, audio transducer.

PHONE, *v.* Telephone, communicate, get in touch with *(coll.),* sound, call, call up, make a call, put in a call.

PHONETIC, *adj.* Spoken, oral, vocal, parol, phonic, enunciated, articulate, enunciate, tonic, tonal, enunciative, accented, accentuated, accentual, pretonic, post-tonic, phthongal, sounded, dental, dentalingual, linguadental, guttural, velar, cerebral, labial, fricative, uvular, close, rounded,

open, wide, tense, narrow, liquid, sibilant, aspirant, aspirate, hard, strong, soft, weak, flat, long, short.

PHONETICS, *n.* Phonics, phonology, acoustics, phonography, diacoustics, diaphonics, phonetism, ideophonics, linguistics, science of speech, science of languages, linguistic science, speechcraft, glottology, semasiology, semantics, philology.

PHONOGRAPH, *n.* Gramophone, graphophone, reproducing instrument, Victrola (trade name), record player, recording machine, recording instrument, record reproducer, transducer, electronic transducer, high-fidelity installation, high-fidelity instrument, hi-fi *(sl.),* hi-fi rig *(coll.).*

PHONOGRAPHY, *n.* Phonetics, sound transcription, sound-writing, shorthand, phonics, phonology, phonetic spelling, short writing, speed writing, stenography, brachygraphy, tachygraphy, stenotypy, pasigraphy.

PHONOLOGY, *n.* Phonetics, philology, lexicography, lexicology, lexigraphy, glossology, etymology, origin, study of word-sounds, linguistics, science of languages, linguistic science, phonics, acoustics.

PHONY, *adj.* *(Coll.)* Spurious, fake, ungenuine, unauthentic, imitation, unreal, artificial, sham, make-believe, bastard, forged, counterfeit, empty, mockery, hollow, unsubstantial, deceptive, beguiling, brummagem, jerry-built, fraudulent, fraud, trick, pretentious, untrue, insincere, pretended, mock, play.

PHOSPHORESCENCE, *n.* Tribophosphorescence, glow, glowing, luminescence, chemoluminescence, light, cold light.

PHOSPHORESCENT, *adj.* Phosphoric, phosphorical, luminous, luminescent, cold, light, glowing, radiating, radiant, bright, shining, luminiferous, nitid, lucent, luculent, lustrous, fulgid, fulgurant, rutilant, rutilous, nitidous, lambent, irradiate, irradiant.

PHOTOGRAPH, *n.* Picture, portrait, delineation, camera portrait, daguerreotype, collotype, wet-plate photograph, tintype, carte-de-visite, photo, Kodak (trade name), print, facsimile, photostat, photographic reproduction, image, minette, snapshot, snap *(coll.),* calotype, talbotype, ferrotype, heliochrome, heliochromatype, still photograph, close-up, still, still life, figure study, nude, rotograph, rotogravure, negative, positive, contact print, enlargement, transparency, color print, Kodacolor, Kodachrome (trade names), exposure, frame, motion picture, motion photography, cinematograph.

PHOTOGRAPHIC, *adj.* Exact, detailed, lifelike, graphic, pictorial, minute, full, in all particulars.

PHRASE, *n.* 1. Word-group, expression, section, part, passage, locution, portion, period, turn of phrase, turn of expression, utterance, peculiar expression.

2. Phraseogram, phraseograph, euphemism, figure of speech, set phrase, anglicism, colloquialism, Americanism, regionalism, idiom, patois, argot, slang, slang term, epithet, saying, motto, tag, tagline, saying, saw, maxim, proverb, paraphrase, paraphrasis, aphorism, apothegm, adage, dictum, epigram, gnome, gnomic, byword, mot, *bon mot (Fr.),* sentence, witticism, oracle, wise saying, platitude, trite expression, bromide *(coll.),* prescript, prescription, rule, law, formula, proposition, precept, truism, banality, cliché, chestnut *(sl.),* commonplace, triviality, trivialism, stereotyped

saying, hackneyed phrase, old hat *(sl.),* old saw, prosaism, prosaicism.

PHRASE, *v.* Express, give expression to, style, term, articulate, verbalize, clothe in words, put into words, put into language, vocalize, voice, find words to express, designate, call, christen, dub, entitle, put, present, speak, talk, say, word, sound, give voice to, utter, emit, deliver, pronounce, enunciate, accentuate, accent, breathe, say, present, come out with, mouth, prolate, parley, give tongue to, give utterance, recite, relate, convey, communicate, assert, asseverate, state, declare, tell, comment, remark, observe, aver, allege, have on one's lips, break the silence with, impart, make known.

PHRASEOLOGY, *n.* Phrasing, diction, style, expression, manner of expression, choice of words, mode of expression, locution, words, language, speech, utterance, wording, phrase, vocabulary, vocabulation, parlance, verbiage, vein, manner, mode, mode of speech, style of speech, peculiarity of phrasing, idiom, idiologism, use of words, selection of words, expression of ideas.

PHRENETIC, *adj.* 1. Raving, mad, delirious, maniac, maniacal, lunatic, insane, incoherent, flighty, wild, ranting, furious, frenzied, beside oneself, frantic, rabid, amuck, amok, foaming at the mouth, running wild, fitful, Corybantic, violent, enfuried, infuriated, wild-eyed, wild-looking, possessed, psychopathic, psychopathical.

2. Enthusiastic, fanatic, fanatical, monomaniac, monomaniacal, obsessed, infatuated, overzealous, excessively enthusiastic, zealotic, zealotical, extravagant, inordinate, feverish, flushed, febrile, heated, eager, earnest, zealous, keen, avid, ardent, impassioned.

PHRENOLOGIST, *n.* Craniologist, metoposcopist, physiognomist, prognosticator, predictor, student of character.

PHRENOLOGY, *n.* Craniology, physiognomy, craniognomy, metoposcopy, cranioscopy, craniometry, physiognomics.

PHTHISIS, *n.* Consumption, galloping consumption, tuberculosis, T. B. *(coll.),* disease, fever, wasting fever, white plague, pulmonary tuberculosis, wasting disease, marasmus.

PHYLACTERY, *n.* Charm, amulet, talisman, fetish, periapt, obeah *(coll.),* voodoo, lucky piece, good-luck-charm.

PHYLUM, *n.* Division, class, order, branch, species, subspecies, variety, family, kingdom, genus, strain, breed, kind, sort, tribe, caste, subgenus, subgroup, suborder.

PHYSIC, *n.* Drug, medicament, medicine, potion, pharmacon, medicinal, draft (draught), pill, bolus, powder, solution, mixture, preparation, laxative, cathartic, purgative, purge, purgation, dose, deobstruent, aperient, salts, Epsom salts, mineral salts, vegetable salts, fruit salts, mineral water, mineral oil, castor oil, carminative.

PHYSIC, *v.* Purge, purgate, dose, drench with physic, remedy, open, treat, medicate, cure, care for, minister to, give medicine to, drug, dope, relieve.

PHYSICAL, *adj.* Bodily, corporeal, corporal, real, actual, substantial, substantive, solid, tangible, existent, subsistent, subsistential, living, essential, materiate, unspiritual, hylic, incarnate, palpable, ponderable, sensible, parenchymatous, parenchymal, materialistic, somatic, fleshly, corporeous,

carnal, human, concrete, vital, animal, external, visible.

PHYSICIAN, *n.* Doctor, doctor of medicine, medical doctor, M.D., practitioner, medical practitioner, specialist, healer, Hippocratic, medical consultant, curer, professional man, doc *(coll.),* medic *(sl.),* medico *(coll.),* sawbones *(coll.),* croaker *(sl.),* medicine man, man of medicine, man in white, general practitioner, G.P., gynecologist, internist, chiropodist, orthopedist, homeopathist, homeopath, allopath, anaesthesiologist, anaesthetist, otologist, ophthalmologist, dermatologist, orthodontist, dentist, dental physician, osteopath, osteopathic physician, neurologist, psychiatrist, psychoanalyst, chiropractor.

PHYSICIST, *n.* Scientist, natural philosopher, theoretical physicist, nuclear physicist, atomic physicist, physical scientist, astronomical physicist, research scientist, research physicist, *(See* PHYSICS, *n.).*

PHYSICS, *n.* Knowledge, science, natural science, science of heat, science of light, science of sound, science of motion, dynamics, science of electricity, kinetics, system of knowledge, kinematics, mechanics, dynometry, astrography, astrophysics, phonics, acoustics, catacoustics, cataphonics, otology, thermodynamics, thermology, electrics, electromechanics, electrometrics, magnetology, trochilics, gyrostatics, tectology, geomorphology, morphology, statics, electrothermics, electrometallurgy, electrophysics, hydrology, hydrostatics, hydrodynamics, hydrometry, hydrokinetics, hydraulics, pegology, fluviology, pneumatology, pneumatostatics, pneumatonomy, aerology, hygrology, aerophysics, aerometry, aerotechnics, aerodynamics, aeromechanics, aerostatics, meteorology, atmospherology, pneumatics, hygrometry, hygrostatics, spectrology, spectrum analysis.

PHYSIOGNOMY, *n.* Face, visage, countenance, configuration, cast of countenance, phiz *(coll.),* lineaments, features, favor, traits, outline, contour, profile, silhouette, cut of one's jib *(coll.),* appearance, front, façade, mazard, pan, mush, mug, kisser, map, puss, lug, index *(all slang),* brow.

PHYSIQUE, *n.* Body, build, structure, configuration, organization, constitution, animality, flesh and blood, corporeality, corporeal nature, materiality, strength, vigor, power, ability, physical nature, bodily character.

PHYTIVOROUS, *adj.* Plant-eating, herbivorous, graminiverous, phytophagous, phytophagic, phytophagan, grass-eating, vegetarian, grain-eating, granivorous, vegetable-eating, lactovegetarian.

PIANIST, *n.* Musician, musical artist, artist, performer, instrumentalist, piano-player, soloist, virtuoso, piano virtuoso, jazz pianist, classical pianist, keyboard artist, boogie-woogie player, accompanist, pianofortist, ivory-tickler *(sl.),* harpsichordist, clavecinist, clavichordist.

PIANO, *n.* Pianoforte, musical instrument, pianola, spinet piano, clavier, *Hammerklavier (Ger.),* pianino, pianette, grand piano, baby grand piano, concert grand piano, upright piano, square piano.

PIAZZA, *n.* Veranda, porch, portico, stoop, close, yard, square, place, market place, court, courtyard, agora, quad, quadrangle, wynd.

PICARESQUE, *adj.* Roguish, rascally, swashbuckling, adventurous, adventuresome, roistering.

roisterous, sportive, waggish, romping, prankish, robust, venturesome, enterprising, bold.

PICAROON, *n.* 1. Rogue, rascal, thief, brigand, adventurer, scoundrel, villain, knave, rapscallion, recreant, miscreant, wrongdoer, caitiff, mean wretch, scalawag *(coll.),* blackguard, reprobate, varlet *(arch.),* good-for-nothing, devil, mischief-maker, ruffian, delinquent, defaulter, criminal, rip *(coll.).*

2. Pirate, corsair, freebooter, privateer, buccaneer, marauder, sea robber, sea rover, sea pirate, plunderer, robber, thief, bandit, viking, sea king, Captain Kidd, Long John Silver, Blackbeard, Teach.

PICAYUNISH, *adj.* Trifling, piddling, niggling, insignificant, inconsiderable, worthless, meaningless, skimpy, skimping, slight, moderate, modest, indifferent, fair, fairish, trivial, idle, petty, fribbling, mincing, pokey, poking, nugatory, nugacious, finicking, flimsy, frothy, light, poor, mean, fair, fairish, trivial, idle, petty, fribbling, mincing, measly, shallow, small-scale, beggarly, small.

PICCOLO, *n.* Flute, *piccolo flauto (Ital.),* octave flute, musical instrument, pipe, woodwind, woodwind instrument, wind instrument, transverse flute, Boehm piccolo.

PICK, *v.* 1. Pluck, clean, weed, pick off, detach, pull off, cut, plume, crop, cleanse, dress, pull out.

2. Choose, select, elect, fix upon, make one's choice, optate, opt, pick out, single out, cull, glean, winnow, separate, segregate, find occasion for, prefer, call, adopt, accept, decide between, settle upon, decide upon, make a selection, choose out, excerpt, draw the line, distinguish, set apart, separate the sheep from the goats, weed out, exclude, shut out, eliminate, eject, repel, expel, discard, bilge, get rid of, rid oneself of, abstract, isolate, lay aside, put aside, put apart, sort, sort out, weed, sift, lay apart, draw out, take out.

3. Harvest, gather, reap, mow, cut, pluck, garner, collect, gain, pick up, secure, obtain, get, procure, win, get together, scrape up, dig up, rake together, crop, reap and carry, net, bag, sack, find, gather in.

4. Peck, eat like a bird, nibble, lick, snack, piece, eat lightly.

PICK, *n.* 1. Pickaxe, mattock, bill, implement, tool, cutting tool, chopping tool, entrenching tool.

2. Plectrum, plectron.

3. Elect, choice, the best, the very best, champion, prize, cream, *crème de la crème (Fr.),* prime, flower, nonesuch, nonpareil, wonder, good thing, best ever, humdinger *(coll.),* winner, jim-dandy, honey *(coll.),* dazzler *(coll.),* knockout *(coll.),* pick of the crop.

4. Choice, choosing, selection, election, option, extract, excerpt, excerption, alternative, extraction.

PICKANINNY, *n.* Child, youth, Negro child, tot, little one, bantling, shaver, youngling, brat, elf, bratling, moppet, cherub, toddler, squirt, lamb, bud, chip off the old block, pullet, scrap of a child, chick, chickabiddy.

PICKAXE, *n.* Pick, mattock, bill, implement, tool, cutting tool, chopping tool, chopper, entrenching tool, digger.

PICKET, *n.* 1. Pale, palisade, stake, post, paling, tether, stanchion, upright, restraint.

2. Sentinel, outpost, vedette, guard, sentry,

warder, watch, watchkeeper, watchman, lookout, patrol, patrolman, patroller, night watchman, outlying picket, inlying picket.

PICKET, *v.* 1. Stake out, moor, tie, tether, peg out, tie-up, string, secure, fasten, make fast, leash, pinion, attach.

2. Strike, walkout, go out, lock out, do picket duty, go on picket duty, bar, bar out, boycott, blockade.

3. Corral, fence, fence in, hedge in, wall in, surround, enclose, inclose, circumscribe, bound, restrain, restrict, pen in, shut in, hem in, rail in, fence 'round.

PICKINGS, *n.* Winnings, innings, earnings, profits, gain, return, returns, avail, take, receipt, receipts, proceeds, outcome, harvest, gleanings, crop, fruit, income, prize, emolument, remuneration, reward, booty, residue, residuum, spoil, grab, swag *(sl.),* plunder, seizure, lcot, stealage, steal, stealings, perquisite, boodle *(cant),* pork barrel, scraps, leavings, leftovers, pilferings.

PICKLE, *n.* 1. Souring, vinegar, sweet pickle, cucumber pickle, dill pickle, bread-and-butter pickle, gherkin, sour pickle, pickled onions, pickled beets, piccalilli, relish, chutney, chow-chow, mustard pickle, pickled pears.

2. Plight, trouble, predicament, sorry condition, dilemma, tight spot, quandary, fix, crisis, hobble, mess, kettle of fish, pretty kettle of fish, how-de-do, pass, go, to-do, corner, emergency, exigency, position of difficulty, pretty pass, strait, troublesome circumstance, scrape, jam, trial, pretty pickle.

PICKLE, *v.* 1. Spice, marinate, season, salt, steep, soak, corn, make pungent, flavor, brine, devil, curry, preserve, conserve, marinade, kipper, cure.

2. Intoxicate, make drunk, inebriate, addle, befuddle, tipsify, give too much to drink, steep in drink, besot, souse, swill, tipple, pollute, stew, crock, bemuse.

PICK-ME-UP, *n.* Stimulant, energizer, activator, excitant, excitator, stimulus, bracer, stimulator, tonic, roborant, smelling salts, alcohol, coffee, tea, spirits of ammonia, aromatic spirits of ammonia, drink, nip, shot, tipple, dram, draft (draught), sip, hair of the dog that bit you, swig, peg, poticn, libation, cheering drink, the cup that cheers.

PICKPOCKET, *n.* Thief, purloiner, cutpurse, felon, miscreant, wrongdoer, criminal, evildoer, dip *(sl.),* rascal, rogue, bandit, lifter, crook, larcenist, larcener, fingersmith, ganif, purse snatcher.

PICKUP, *n.* 1. Acceleration, speed-up.

2. Woman of easy virtue, whore, trull, slut, baggage, streetwalker, prostitute, call-girl, loose woman, fornicatress, strumpet, wanton, harridan, jade, minx, drab, bitch, immoral woman.

PICNIC, *n.* Festivity, party, celebration, luncheon, feast, dinner, merrymaking, lark, festive occasion, junket, clambake, fish fry, steak fry, rural festival, highjinks, excursion, refection, repast, meal, feed *(sl.),* collation, mess, picnic supper, lunch, luncheon, breakfast, supper.

PICTORIAL, *adj.* 1. Illustrated, demonstrative, representational, illustrative, revealing, exemplary, pictured, ornamented, decorated, delineating, delineatory, depicting, depicted, graphically described.

2. Graphic, vivid, picturable, picturesque, artistic, artistical, attractive, imaginative.

PICTURE, *n.* 1. Image, portrait, likeness, similitude, resemblance, representation, living picture (*coll.*), dead image, spit and image, the very picture, close likeness, striking resemblance, startling likeness, ringer, dead ringer, spit, spitting image, copy, counterpart, duplicate, duplication, reproduction, double, facsimile, carbon copy, effigy.

2. Delineation, picturization, depiction, limning, portrayal, representation, cartoon, contour, mirror, study, minette, sketch, silhouette, figure, figurehead, bust, symbol, miniature, miniature painting, painting, oil painting, oil sketch, gesso painting, gouache, water color, aquarelle, wash drawing, drawing, pencil sketch, pencil drawing, engraving, steel engraving, wood engraving, woodcut, panorama, landscape, seascape, waterscape, townscape, spectacle, sciagraph, monochrome, polychrome, chromo, icon, ikon, iconograph, chromograph, zincograph, aquatint, collotype, etching, drypoint, silverpoint, carte-de-visite, daguerreotype, tintype, photograph, wet-plate photograph, dry-plate photograph, diorama, cyclorama, negative print, positive print, contact print, enlargement, offset, lithograph, illustration, perspective drawing, tracing, lithotint, primitive painting, pastiche, collage, montage, photogravure, photoengraving, mezzotint, rotogravure, pastel drawing, crayon drawing, chalk drawing, cosmorama, tableau, *tableau vivant (Fr.),* marine drawing, marine painting, fresco, mural, mosaic, radiograph, X-ray, skyscape, oleograph, zylograph, stereogram, half-tone, engraving, chrysotype, thermotype, chromolithograph, ambrotype, oristotype, diaphanotype, piece, heliograph, pyrograph, photo, snapshot, outline, tracing, tracery, cut, map, chart, prospect, cabinet photograph, sight, spectacle, view, scene, scenery, exhibit, exhibition, exposition, display, portraiture, design, art, fine art, graphic art, draft, draught, rough sketch, shadow-figure, stained-glass painting, tapestry, batik, profile, full-length portrait, three-quarters portrait, heroic portrait, life-sketch, nude, figure study, cartoon, caricature, comic drawing, exterior, interior, talbotype, calotype, ferrotype, heliochrome, heliochromatype, rotograph, sculptograph, work of art, composition, masterwork, masterpiece, *objet d'art (Fr.),* canvas.

PICTURE, *v.* 1. Portray, delineate, limn, represent, depict, picturize, set forth, paint, paint a picture, paint a portrait, hit off, catch a likeness, stroke a likeness, draw a picture, sketch, make a sketch, make an impression of, caricature, cartoon, illustrate, elucidate, exemplify, design.

2. Imagine, conjure up, envision, see, foresee, conceive, fancy, exercise the fancy, exercise the imagination, call to mind, summon up, let one's imagination run wild, indulge in fantasy, romanticize, romance, idealize, give one's imagination free rein.

3. Describe, set forth, narrate, verbalize, tell, recount, relate, say, paint a word-picture.

PICTURESQUE, *adj.* Pictury, graphic, pictorial, picture-like, scenic, suggesting a picture, pretty as a picture, beautiful, charming, alluring, exciting, stimulating, odd, unique, bizarre, exotic, quaint, artistic, realistic, attractive, romantic, compelling, clear, seemly, pleasing, striking, elegant, comely, graceful, vivid, well-proportioned, inviting, aesthetic, aesthetically pleasing, arty (*coll.*), paintable, well-composed, well-arranged, well-grouped, well-disposed.

PIDDLE, *v.* Idle, do nothing, be inactive, loaf,

dawdle, putter, fritter, fritter away one's time, lie idle, temporize, delay, oscitate, yawn, dillydally, dally, linger, loiter, lounge, lie about, lie down on the job, fidget, potter, swim with the stream, drift with the current, procrastinate, cool one's heels, play the grasshopper, lie fallow, lie around, laze, fall asleep at the switch, go to sleep over, nod, blink, wink, malinger, shirk one's duty, rest on one's laurels, lose time, waste time, let the grass grow under one's feet, not lift a finger, twiddle one's thumbs, kill time, while the time away, beguile the time, poke, take one's time, loll, lollop, dabble, lag, slouch, lead an easy life, live in the lap of luxury, lead the life of Riley, ride at anchor, not carry one's weight, lie on one's record, bum, bum around, sleep at one's job.

PIDDLING, *adj.* Picayunish, trifling, niggling, insignificant, inconsiderable, worthless, meaningless, skimpy, skimping, slight, moderate, modest, indifferent, fair, fairish, trivial, idle, petty, little, small, mincing, fribbling, pokey, poking, nugatory, nugacious, finicking, flimsy, frothy, light, poor, mean, measly, shallow, small-scale, beggarly, paltry, immaterial, piffling, shabby, shallow, inconsequential, of no moment, of no consequence, unimportant, imponderable, valueless, frivolous, cheap, catchpenny, trashy, weedy, seedy, contemptible, beneath contempt, wretched, miserable, vile, junky (*coll.*), tinhorn, small-fry, small potatoes, second-rate, third-rate, fourth-rate, unworthy.

PIE, *n.* Pastry, *pâtisserie (Fr.),* dessert, *pâté (Fr.),* sweets, fruit pie, vegetable pie, tarts, sweet stuff, meat pie.

PIEBALD, *adj.* 1. Mottled, parti-colored, dappled, spotted, motley, variegated, pied, divers-colored, flecked, multi-colored, many-colored, many-hued, colorful, polychrome, versicolor, versicolored.

2. Diversified, mixed, mongrel, heterogeneous, irregular, crossed, cross-bred, hybrid, amphibious, half-blooded.

PIECE, *n.* 1. Fragment, portion, part, bit, shard, scrap, hunk, chunk, shred, shaving, paring, gobbet, blob, cut, slice, amount, quantity, circle, blot, chuck, lump, pat, blank, division, parcel, moiety, cantlet, subdivision, slug, any, section, segment, cut, sector, crumb, snatch, collop, dollop, snitch, cutting, clipping, sliver, smithereen, hunk, hunch, scale, stitch, tatter, iota, splinter, rasher, particle, morsel, fritter, block, cutlet, chop, chip, bite, swatch.

2. Portion, apportionment, allottment, share, lot, allowance, contingent, pittance, stipend, measure, dole, portion, proportion, half, lion's share, percentage, dividend, commission, pay, quota, mess, modicum, *quantum (Lat.).*

3. Play, stage play, drama, tragedy, comedy, farce, legitimate drama, acting piece, one-acter, one-act play, sketch, monologue, dialogue, mystery, morality play, pantomime, miming, dumb-show, melodrama, mystery drama, detective drama, tragedietta, pageant, spectacle, extravaganza, vaudeville, opera, comic opera, opera buffo, grand opera, closet drama, review, musical review, *revue (Fr.),* lyric drama, music drama, vehicle, production, presentation, masque, mask, ballet, charade, proverb.

4. Work of art, masterwork, masterpiece, *objet d'art (Fr.),* study, sketch, article of virtue, conversation piece, bric-a-brac, picture, statue, drawing, painting, carving, piece of music, com-

position, creation, production, song, poem, writing, symphony, quartet, trio, duo, duet, quintet, solo piece, aria, opera, motet, cantata, oratorio, sonata, rhapsody, theme and variations, air, *Lied (Ger.)*, art song, study, *étude (Fr.)*, novel, ballad, story, narrative, short story, tale, rhyme, rime, sonnet, ode, lyric, epic, saga, edda, fantasy, allegory.

PIECE, *v.* 1. Patch, repair, fix, revamp, restore, mend, put in repair, put into shape, service, patch up, make do, tinker, cobble, retouch, vamp up, vamp, get into condition.

2. Join, unite, piece together, connect, attach, affix, conjoin.

PIECEMEAL, *adv.* Part by part, piece by piece, by degrees, inch by inch, drop by drop, little by little, in small quantities, in installments, foot by foot, in compartments, in small lots, by degrees, by snatches, gradually, partially, in pieces, by little bits, bit by bit, in fragments, in lumps, in chunks.

(IN) PIECES, *adj.* Gone to pieces, in smithereens, in small pieces, gone to dust, smashed, broken, fractured, reduced to ashes, ground to dust, reduced to powder, pulverized, powdery, granulated, disintegrated, detrited, detrital, crumbling, crumbled, fallen to pieces, broken up, comminute, ground, mashed, crushed, crunched, scrunched, levigated, in crumbs.

PIED, *adj.* Mottled, piebald, parti-colored, dappled, spotted, motley, variegated, diversified, divers-colored, flecked, multi-colored, multi-hued, many-colored, many-hued, colorful, polychrome, polychromed, versicolor, versicolored.

PIER, *n.* 1. Anchorage, jetty, dock, landing, quay, key, wharf, breakwater, embankment, landing place, jutty.

2. Buttress, hanging buttress, flying buttress, pier buttress, buttress pier, abutment, pillar, post, support, foundation, shoulder, pile, piling, upright, standard, perch, brace, column, pilaster, upright bar.

PIERCE, *v.* 1. Perforate, empierce, stick, prick, puncture, stab, punch, lancinate, spear, spike, lance, impale, spit, penetrate, drill, bore, auger, transfix, transpierce, inject, infix, inoculate, enter, insinuate, interject, intrude, stick in, thrust in, put in, interpenetrate, cut through, pass through.

2. Stab, run through, cut down, hew down, put to the sword, knife, bayonet, saber, prick, lancinate, wound, injure, harm, hurt, stab.

3. Nip, bite, freeze, benumb, numb, refrigerate, frigorify, chill, ice, glaciate, glacify, congeal, freeze to death, make one's teeth chatter, penetrate with cold.

4. Pierce the air, rend the air, pierce one's head, pierce one's ears, resound, be loud, fill the air, clatter, make a din, make a racket, deafen, stun, boom, thunder, crack one's ears, brawl, uproar, blare, honk, toot, rattle, blast, shake the earth, shake one's windows, split the head, split the ears, grate on the ear.

5. Damage, impair, hurt, harm, scathe, spoil, mar, cut, wound, lancinate, penetrate, stab, mangle, lacerate, mutilate, disfigure, scar, blemish.

6. Hurt one to the quick, cut, cut to the quick, hurt one's feelings, sting, wound, turn the knife in the wound, stir the blood, provoke, chafe, madden, irritate, annoy, touch the heart, touch a chord, touch the soul, go through one, afflict, give pain, distress, dismay, cut to the heart, cleave the heart in two, bite the hand that feeds one, hurt the feelings, wound the feelings, sadden, cast down, make unhappy, make wretched, aggrieve, grieve, make one's heart bleed, prey on one's mind, haunt the spirits, dispirit, dull, lower one's spirits, cast one down, dash one's hopes, discourage, dishearten, deject, lower, plunge into grief, cut up.

PIERCER, *n.* Needle, awl, gimlet, bodkin, punch, drill, stiletto, poignard, dagger, knife, perforator, puncturer, puncheon, auger, borer, punch pliers, chisel, bradawl, trocar, probe, scoop, gouge, corkscrew, dibble, pin, broach, spike, bit, lancet, lance, spear, javelin, assegai, sword, rapier, épée, foil, fencing foil, stylet, trephine, trepan, punch, die, reamer, cutter, blade, knife, bowie knife, pigsticker, eelspear, harpoon, gaff, pike, spontoon, jereed, shaft, arrow, bolt, reed, weet-weet, womera, missile, vire, chested arrow, quarrel, cloth-yard arrow, bobtail arrow, self arrow.

PIERCING, *adj.* 1. Cutting, keen, incisive, caustic, severe, furious, sharp, extreme, intense, fierce, acute, cruel, painful, hurtful, poignant, agonizing, torturous, excruciating, hard, biting.

2. Cold, freezing, nipping, nippy, sharp, bitter, frigid, keen, biting, wintry, numbing, raw, bleak.

3. Sharp, pungent, keen, poignant, biting, acrid, acid, acidulous, acerb, stinging, with a kick, mordant, mordacious, acerbate, snappy *(coll.)*, piquant, hot, peppery, seasoned, spicy, caustic.

4. Smelly, odoriferous, penetrating, smellsome, stenchy, reeking, foul-smelling, strong-smelling, pungent, acrid, noisome, smellful, heady, wiffy *(sl.)*, strong, strong-scented, sharp, keen, malodorous, odorific.

5. Shrill, loud, high-pitched, noisy, deafening, ear-splitting, ear-bursting, ear-shattering, enough to wake the dead, trumpet-voiced, ear-piercing, acute, sharp, high-toned, strident, grating, cacophonous, screeching, squeaking, squealing, high.

6. Shrewd, acute, cute *(coll.)*, perceptive, quick, alert, responsive, mordant, penetrating, informed, argute, astute, canny *(dial.)*, subtle, keen-witted, quick-witted, nimble, nimble-witted, clear-headed, far-seeing, foresighted, percipient, apperceptive, perspicuous, smart, brainy, discerning, alive to, aware, perspicacious.

7. Lively, quick, smart, cutting, strong, incisive, trenchant, keen, racy, piquant, pungent, poignant, profound, deep, far-reaching, soul-stirring, moving, impressive, harsh, astringent, severe.

8. Bitter, virulent, gruff, rough, harsh, stern, acrid, acrimonious, venomous, churlish, keen, brusque, austere, cavalier, cruel, grim, vituperative, short, trenchant, crabbed, crusty, biting, stinging, surly, tart, sour, astringent, stringent, sarcastic, mordant, acerb, acerbic, acerbate, bearish.

PIETISM, *n.* Pharisaism, double-dealing, two-timing *(coll.)*, cant, insincerity, formalism, phariseeism, false piety, self-righteousness, sanctimony, sanctimoniousness, over-piety, excessive piety, dissembling, dissimulation, pretense, false pretense, bluff, hypocrisy, hypocrisis, unsincerity, Machiavellism, Machiavellianism, mealy-mouthedness, mummery, misdevotion, tartuffism, lip service, mockery, solemn mockery, travesty, mere show, lip reverence, affectation.

PIETIST, *n.* 1. Believer, true believer, accepter, devotionalist, religionist, religious, theist, saint, churchman, proselyte, missionary, Christian, one of the faithful, pillar of the church, Nazarene, Nazarite, communicant.

2. Fraud, deceiver, pious fraud, hypocrite, Tartuffe, Holy Willy, canter, ranter, lip servicer, lip worshiper, dissimulator, dissembler, religionist, pharisee, bigot, fanatic, humbug, imposter, pretender, charlatan, sham, adventurer, opportunist, jackdaw, wolf in sheep's clothing, mountebank, fourflusher, bluff, bluffer, Pecksniff, falsifier, equivocator, prevaricator, perjurer.

PIETY, *n.* Religiousness, devotion, religiosity, devoutness, sanctity, spirituality, saintliness, sainthood, sanctitude, theopathy, religionism, odor of sanctity, zeal, religious zeal, reverence, worshipfulness, worship, godliness, fear of god, purity, purity of spirit, right-mindedness, respect, justice, holiness, goodness, grace, holy-mindedness, belief, virtue, sacredness, dedication, consecration, unworldliness, Christianity, unearthliness, humility, theodicy, faith, faithfulness, respectfulness, veneration, regard, duty, dutifulness, righteousness, rectitude, morality, reliance, trustfulness, credence, conviction, integrity, obedience.

PIG, *n.* 1. Swine, porker, hog, hoggerel, shoat, piglet, piggy, farrow, sow, suckling pig, boar, razorback, wart hog, peccary, Chester White, gilt, Hampshire, Poland China, Tamworth, Yorkshire, Cheshire, babirusa, wild boar.

2. Pork, swine flesh, pork flesh, ham, pork loin, pork chops, bacon, roast pork, pig's feet, pig's knuckles, meat.

3. Glutton, gourmand, large eater, hog (*coll.*), husky eater (*coll.*), ravenous eater, big eater, greedyguts (*coll.*), gorger, gormandizer, cormorant, gastronome, epicure, epicurean, gourmet, pantophage, vulgarian, boor, sloven, frump, slattern, barbarian, slut, drab, trollop.

4. Casting, metal casting, ingot, pouring, pig iron, cast iron, sow, mine pig.

PIGEON, *n.* Dove, squab, bird, fowl, gamebird, homing pigeon, wood dove, mourning dove, passenger pigeon, carrier pigeon.

PIGEONHOLE, *n.* Compartment, recess, hole, nook, cranny, niche, cubbyhole, cell, alcove, cove, loophole, storage space, slot.

PIGEON-HOUSE, *n.* Dovecote, columbary, pigeon roost, cote, columbarium, pigeon cote, aviary, bird cage, bird house, pigeon coop, coop, pen, enclosure.

PIGGERY, *n.* Pigsty, hogsty, pigpen, hogpen, pig farm, hog farm, pork farm, swineyard, swinery, pen, fold, confine, compound, stockyard.

PIGGISH, *adj.* Swinish, hoggish, piglike, hoglike, greedy, gluttonous, selfish, dirty, filthy, unclean, untidy, coarse, boorish, animal, animalistic, beastly, voracious, rapacious, ravening, ravenous, omnivorous, all-devouring, insatiable, insatiate, edacious, Apician, pantophagous, pantophagic, overindulgent, stuffed, overfed, messy, unkempt, begrimed, besmirched, unhygienic.

PIGHEADED, *adj.* 1. Obstinate, willful, stubborn, adamant, obdurate, insistent, dogged, persistent, persevering, bigoted, wrong-headed, contumacious, short-sighted, intractable, unpersuadable, self-willed, stupid, contrary, perverse, tenacious, pertinacious, bullheaded, thick-headed, stubborn as a mule, hard-set, casehardened, firm, immovable, unswayed, unyielding, incorrigible, obstreperous, uncontrollable, inflexible, uninfluenced, tough, hard-bitten, mulish, determined,

resistant, impervious, froward, wayward, hardmouthed, recalcitrant, refractory, irrepressible, indocile, balky, sullen, hidebound, stiff-backed, rooted, set in one's ways, opinionated, opinioned, self-opinioned, deaf to advice, blind to reason, unreasonable, purblind, intolerant, illiberal, small, petty, little, narrow-minded, insular, provincial, obsessed, infatuated, possessed, positive, positivistic.

2. Stupid, dull, doltish, slow-witted, dense, numskulled, cloddish, clodpated, addlepated, slow-minded, thick-skulled, blunt, crass, clodlike, undiscerning, uncomprehending, moronic, idiotic, imbecilic, mindless, unintelligent, witless, unreasoning, brainless, unteachable, retarded, lack-witted, lack-brained, insensate, unendowed.

PIGMENT, *n.* Color, coloring agent, coloring, coloring matter, coloration, tincture, tint, tinction, dye, dyestuff, colorant, coloring material.

PIGTAIL, *n.* Queue, tailpiece, pendant, appendage, hanging appendage, rat's tail, braid, plait, switch.

PIKE, *n.* 1. Spear, lance, assegai, javelin, bill, halberd, poleaxe, dart, shaft, harpoon, reed, bolt, weapon, arm, implement, tool.

2. Turnpike, road, highway, roadway, thoroughfare, throughway, speedway, drive, parkway, main road, state highway, King's highway, Queen's highway, first-class highway, first-class road.

3. Stile, turnstile, gate, barrier, blockade, obstacle, hindrance, bar.

PILASTER, *n.* Column, pillar, post, support, upright, standard, colonnette, columella, pier, brace, caryatid, atlas, telamon.

PILE, *v.* 1. Amass, heap, heap up, accumulate, hoard, stock, stockpile, garner, store, store up, lay away, collect, lay up, salt away, save up, save, agglomerate, cumulate, heap together, stack, stack up, treasure up, throw in a heap, rake together, gather into a pile, scrape together.

2. Load, charge, fill, burden, lade, freight, stuff, pack, wad, weight, weigh down, make heavy, press down, press hard upon.

PILE, *n.* 1. Mass, heap, accumulation, agglomeration, conglomeration, aggregation, aggregate, glomeration, amassment, collection, stack, batch, conglobation, pyramid, drift, snowdrift, congestion, concentration, hoard, store, treasure, treasury, assortment, miscellany, variety, mob, hodgepodge, medley, rick, hummock, mound, hill, knob, quantity, load, mess, lump, gob, carload, cartload, wagonload, abundance, plenty, profusion, bulk, lot (*coll.*), lots (*coll.*), slew (*coll.*), bushel, peck.

2. Tower, construction, structure, erection, edifice, building, fabric.

3. Money, wealth, fortune, large sum of money, vast fortune, modest competence, a cool million (*coll.*), good sum, goodly sum, stipend, goodly stipend, pots of money (*coll.*), money to burn, load, barrel of money, raft of money, wad, barrel, sackful, sockful.

4. Shag, tooth, warp, texture, fiber, fibrousness, grain, roughness, arista (*Bot.*), awn (*Bot.*), nap, bristle, seta, fleece, plush, fluff.

5. Piling, caisson, support, foundation, post.

PILFER, *v.* Steal, thieve, purloin, make away with, burglarize, spoil, despoil, filch, pick, pinch (*coll.*), take, grab, peculate, rob, plunder, commit larceny, larcenize, abduct, embezzle, abscond with, poach, practice theft, appropriate, convert, borrow (*joc.*), snaffle, snag (*sl.*), snatch, palm, bag, cabbage, mooch, hold up (*coll.*), stick up (*sl.*), plagiarize, pirate, spoliate, loot, ransack, hijack.

PILFERING, *n.* Theft, thievery, stealing, burglary, peculation, absconding, embezzlement, petty theft, petty larceny, pilfery, abstraction, abduction, thievishness, filching, grabbing, pinching, sneak thievery, plagiarism, piracy, appropriation, conversion, autoplagiarism, taking, dispossession.

PILGRIM, *n.* 1. Wanderer, traveler, wayfarer, journeyer, sojourner, tripper (*coll.*), tourist, roamer, rover, peregrinator, itinerant, drifter, floater, peripatetic, straggler, rambler, nomad, bird-of-passage, passerby, migrant, immigrant, emigrant, refugee, displaced person, *émigré* (*Fr.*), evacuee.

2. Crusader, palmer, devotee, worshiper, penitent, mendicant.

PILGRIM, *v.* Travel, wander, stray, roam, ramble, tour, peregrinate, wayfare, trek, go on a journey, make a journey, make a tour, make a pilgrimage, traverse, wander over, wend one's way, bend one's steps, sightsee, visit, pay a visit to, take the road, stump, course, scour the country, globetrot, travel extensively.

PILGRIMAGE, *n.* Journey, excursion, tour, travel, traveling, visit, sojourn, wandering, expedition, discursion, ramble, rambling, peregrination, campaign, trip, turn, voyage, passage, *Wanderjahr* (*Ger.*), grand tour, extended trip, extended journey, trek, hadj (*Arabic*), circuit.

PILL, *n.* Pellet, globule, spheroid, ball, bolus, tablet, capsule, remedy, cure, medicament, medicine, pharmaceutical, drug, patent medicine, nostrum, panacea, placebo, physic, pharmacon.

PILLAGE, *n.* 1. Spoliation, despoiling, plunder, plundering, destruction, rapine, looting, devastation, laying waste, deprivation, barbarity, atrocity, vandalism, larceny, robbery, theft, stealing, rape, havoc, desecration, thievery, piracy, confiscation, sack, sackage, latrocinium (*Roman*), brigandage, ravishment, foray, raid, raiding, visitation, piratism, buccaneering, filibustering.

2. Booty, spoils, loot, plunder, gains, ill-gotten gains, haul, take, seizure, stolen goods, prey, stealings, pickings, prize, filchings.

PILLAGE, *v.* Spoil, plunder, despoil, desecrate, steal, outrage, rape, sack, loot, raid, strip, rifle, harry, filibuster, pirate, lay waste, devastate, destroy, burn, level, hurt, waste, hold up, ruin, ruinate, damage, wreck, prey upon, buccaneer, rob, burglarize, depredate, seize, spoliate, sweep, gut, forage, maraud, privateer.

PILLAR, *n.* 1. Column, pile, columella, colonnette, upright, standard, post, stanchion, door post, door jamb, gatepost, crown post, king post, caryatid, atlas, telamon, pilaster, obelisk, monument, memorial, cenotaph.

2. Tower of strength, pillar of strength, rock, pillar of the church, pillar of society, pillar of the community, grandee, magnifico, sachem, chief, very important person, V.I.P. (*sl.*), personage, ranking personage, bigwig, nabob, great man, magnate, celebrity, man of mark, man of distinction, lion, social lion, cynosure, somebody (*coll.*).

3. Monolith, monument, shaft, column, memorial, memento, marker, grave marker, obelisk, shrine.

PILLARIST, *n.* Pillar saint, stylite, hermit, anchorite, saint, holy man, recluse, monk, hiero-

monach, solitudinarian, solitary, eremite, anchoret.

PILLOW, *n.* Cushion, bolster, rest, headrest, support, supporting cushion, bedcushion, feather cushion, down cushion, resting place.

PILOT, *n.* 1. Steersman, coxswain, helmsman, wheelman.

2. Airman, flyer, aeronaut, aviator, airplanist, birdman (*coll.*), avigator, aerialist.

3. Guide, guider, director, cicerone, conductor, leader, dragoman, courier.

PILOT, *v.* Steer, direct, manage, guide, show the way, take the lead, take the reins, handle the tiller, hold the reins, lead on, be at the helm, run, operate, handle, control, coxswain, fly, navigate, hold to one's bearings, avigate, navigate the air, fly blind, fly by instruments, convoy, take direction of, have direction of.

PIMP, *n.* Procurer, pander, panderer, white slaver, male bawd, whoremonger, *maquereau* (*Fr.*), runner, flesh-peddler.

PIMPLE, *n.* Eruption, skin eruption, pustule, wheal, carbuncle, boil, papule, blister, bleb, exostosis, excrescence, growth, wen, whelk, sore, infection, pock, mole, corn, chancre, scab, blain, swelling, tumescence, intumescence, polypus, polyp, furuncle, caruncle, verruca.

PIN, *n.* 1. Peg, bolt, dowel, thole, skewer, skittle, fibula, tenpin, ninepin, linchpin, tongue, nog, tang, duckpin, fin, candlepin, toggle, needle, plug, treenail, bodkin, point, key, spike, nail, tack, thumbtack, straight pin, safety pin, map pin, dressmaker's pin, common pin, cotter pin, pushpin, drawing pin, screw, rivet, spine, spikelet, tine, prong, punch, puncturer, probe, fastener.

2. Arbor, axle, axis, swivel, pole, trunion, pivot, gudgeon.

3. Jewel, brooch, breast pin, clip, jewelled pin, jewelled clip, medal, decoration, ornament.

PIN, *v.* 1. Fasten, secure, pin down, attach, affix, fix, nail, rivet, bolt, screw, hammer, clamp, bind, staple, transfix.

2. Pin down, hold down, press down, bear down, pinion.

PINAFORE, *n.* Garment, dress, outer garment, apron, frock, smock, gabardine.

PINCE-NEZ, *n.* Nose-glasses, eyeglasses, glasses, spectacles, specs (*coll.*), nippers (*sl.*), eyepieces, oculars.

PINCERS, *n.* 1. Pliers, forceps, tweezers, haemostat, nippers, clippers, tongs.

2. Claws, talons, chelae, paws, hands.

PINCH, *v.* 1. Squeeze, compress, crimp, nip, crush, tighten, tweak, rub, twist, grasp, grab, hold, contract, wring, extort.

2. Skimp, gripe, be stingy, be parsimonious, screw, skin a flint, hold back, hoard, be miserly, begrudge, grasp, grab, straiten, oppress, be greedy, extort, be tight-fisted, play the tightwad, scrimp.

3. Bite, tweak, nip, sting, pain, stab, prick, pierce, torment, torture, gripe, gall, fret, worry, harass, excruciate, wring, martyr, convulse, lacerate, rasp, chafe.

4. (*Coll.*), Arrest, make an arrest, apprehend, catch, catch up with, find, find out, take into custody, remand, give over, make a prisoner of, take captive, nab, lay by the heels, collar, snag (*sl.*), grab, restrain, capture, run in (*sl.*).

5. Steal, rob, purloin, appropriate, convert, snatch, abduct, embezzle, abscond, make off with,

bag, filch, pilfer, plagiarize, pirate, buccaneer, annex, snitch *(coll.)*, peculate, burgle, burglarize.

PINCH, *n.* 1. Theft, pilfering, annexation, appropriation, abduction, stealing, shakedown *(sl.)*, burglary, embezzlement, absconding, purloining, conversion, snatching, filching, piracy, buccaneering, peculation, plagiarism, burglary, robbery.

2. Pain, physical pain, torment, grief, anguish, suffering, dolor, pang, twinge, nip, stab, twitch, stitch, kink, throe, convulsion, spasm, seizure, attack, torture, trial, rack, excruciation, martyrdom, discomfort, distress, misery, hurt, hurting, soreness, malaise.

3. Emergency, exigency, need, requirement, crisis, strait, difficulty, predicament, pressure, push, necessity, critical need, extremity, squeeze, contingency, pass, rub, demand, call, call for, urgency, stress, matter of need, matter of life and death, lack, want, gravity, solemnity, seriousness, insistency, insistence, pickle, puzzle, puzzlement, pretty pass, trouble, matter, ticklish situation, scrape, jam, embarrassment, state of things, complication, dilemma, perplexity, paradox, delicate situation, adversity, hardship, adverse circumstances, affliction, misery, vicissitude, ordeal, trial.

4. Small quantity, bit, piece, morsel, scrap, smidgin, soupçon *(Fr.)*, trifle, suggestion, shade, trace.

PINCHBECK, *n.* Tinsel, frills, frippery, trappings, trickery, gaudery, frilliness, spangles, gingerbread, ornament, ornamentation, clinquant, superfluity, superfluousness, tawdriness, cheap display, ostentation, paste.

PINCHBECK, *adj.* Sham, imitation, unreal, alloy, brummagem, tinselly, glittery, glittering, shining, deceptive, unauthentic, synthetic, counterfeit, fake, spurious, trumpery, superficial, deceiving, paste.

PINCH-HIT, *v.* *(Slang)* Substitute, replace, supply, take the place of, play for, serve as a substitute, step into one's shoes, stand in for, fill one's shoes, act for, double for, succeed, supplant, supersede.

PINCHPENNY, *n.* Niggard, miser, churl, curmudgeon, skinflint, Scrooge, screw, tightwad *(coll.)*, skin *(sl.)*, muckworm, scrimp *(coll.)*, pinchfist, pinchgut, harpy, save-all, codger, moneygrubber, pincher, nipper, lickpenny, hunks *(coll.)*, mean man, mean fellow, meanie *(coll.)*, sordid fellow.

PINE, *v.* 1. Flag, droop, decline, go into a decline, give way, faint, fail, drop, break down, despair, decrease, wane, ebb, abate, waste away, diminish, sicken, languish, wither, let up, dwindle, die away, fall off, drop off, erode, waste, fizzle out *(coll.)*, take sick, become ill, decay, die, wilt.

2. Desire, be desirous of, covet, yearn for, languish for, hunger for, hunger after, thirst for, thirst after, run madly after, raven for, long for, sigh for, gasp for, pant for, die for, have a yen for *(coll.)*.

3. Languish, grieve, mourn, pine for, repine, lament, sorrow, despond, lose heart, droop, sink, brood over, brood, fret, fuss *(coll.)*, take on *(coll.)*, mope, ache, hurt, bemoan, bewail.

PINE, *n.* 1. Tree, evergreen, fir, timber.

2. Lumber, wood, soft wood.

PINGUID, *adj.* Fat, greasy, unctuous, lardy, oily, slick, smooth, adipose, oleaginous, fatty, oleic *(Chem.)*, sebaceous, lardaceous, lardiform, pin-

guidinous, unguinous, unguinaceous, unguentary, unguentiferous.

PINION, *n.* 1. Shackle, fetter, bond, tie, fastening, chain, restraining device, manacle, gyve, hobble, irons, check, curb, trammel, yoke, strait jacket, halter.

2. Plume, feather, plumule, quill, filoplume, remex, crest, tuft, scapular.

PINION, *v.* 1. Bind, fasten, tie, hold down, tie down, pin down, make fast, peg down, moor, tether, lash, leash, string, strap, make fast, trammel, chain, enchain, entrammel, shackle, place in irons, handcuff, tie hand and foot, hobble, manacle.

2. Tie, string, strap, hook, attach, affix, fix, truss, bandage, screw, nail, rivet, latch, lash, sew, lace, buckle, bolt, clamp, wedge, dovetail, graft, mortise, rabbet, couple.

PINK, *n.* Red-tint, rose-tint, rosiness, rose-color, light red, opera pink, cameo pink, mallow pink, flesh pink, livid pink, carnation rose, rose madder, tea rose, chrome primrose, madder lake, madder pink, flesh color, Italian pink, salmon pink, peach, apricot, English pink, Dutch pink, flesh red, flesh color.

PINK, *v.* 1. Scallop, cut, serrate, notch, indent, indentate, nick, score, tooth, mill, crimp.

2. Pierce, penetrate, stab, puncture, run through, cut, transfix, prick, punch, impale, drill, spit, riddle.

PINNACE, *n.* Boat, vessel, sailboat, sailing boat, sailing vessel, craft, watercraft, bark.

PINNACLE, *n.* 1. Spire, steeple, tower, bell tower, belfry, campanile.

2. Apex, crest, peak, top, summit, zenith, highest point, culmination, culminating point, tiptop, topmost point, height, headland, crown, tor, extremity, upper extremity, cap, tip, nib, acme, climax, meridian, maximum, loftiest point.

PIONEER, *n.* 1. Settler, leader, advocate, forerunner, vanguard, way-paver, pathfinder, dewbeater, road-leveler, colonist, immigrant, frontiersman, herald, precursor, trail-blazer, apostle, missionary, explorer, adventurer, scout, avantgarde *(Fr.)*, harbinger, outrider, bellwether, founder, establisher, founding father.

2. Soldier, sapper, engineer.

PIOUS, *adj.* Devout, pietistic, pietistical, reverent, god-fearing, godly, spiritual, spiritual-minded, right-minded, pure in heart, pure in spirit, purehearted, just, holy, saintly, sainted, good, full of grace, holy-minded, saintlike, seraphic, angelic, unworldly, unearthly, faithful, solemn, believing, worshipful, virtuous, hallowed, sanctified, sacred, sacrosanct, consecrated, dedicated, undoubting, uncorrupted, undemoralized, undebauched, undegenerate, innocent, clean of mind, clean of spirit, venerative, reverential, worshiping, adoring, adorant, prone, prostrate.

PIPE, *n.* 1. Wind instrument, flute, piccolo, fife, whistle, syrinx, flageolet, recorder, reed, bass flute, alto flute, soprano flute, G-major flute, tabor pipe, slide whistle, pitch pipe, tuning pipe, organ pipe, organ stop, organ reed, Dudelsack, bagpipe, willow whistle, penny whistle, pipes of Pan.

2. Tube, conduit, canal, conductor, tunnel, aqueduct, duct, funnel, stove pipe, conveyor, chimney, flue, channel, hollow cylinder, roll, fistula, pipette, tubule, capillary, tubulus, main, water pipe, gas pipe, oil pipe, gas line, water line,

oil line, fuel pipe, fuel line, standpipe, flume, pipe line, hose, rubber hose, fire hose, garden hose, smokestack.

3. Tobacco pipe, briar, bruyere, corncob pipe, cobeen, clay pipe, meerschaum pipe, hookah, narghile, peace pipe, calumet, Indian pipe, chibouque, water pipe.

4. Windpipe, trachea, breathing tube, throttle (*coll.*), bronchus, bronchial tube, weasand.

5. Bird call, whistle, bird song, song, piping.

PIPE, *v.* Sound, whistle, flute, fife, cheep, chant, chanter, shrill, sound shrill, sing, make music, voice, squeak, utter, peep, scream, roar, sough, moan, murmur, sigh, toot, tweet, tweetle, tootle, blow, wind, peal, shriek, squall, warble, trill, twitter, roulade, vocalize, chirp, chirrup, twit.

PIPE OF PEACE, *n.* Calumet, Indian pipe, ceremonial pipe, peace offering, propitiation, propitiatory gift.

PIPER, *n.* Player, musician, Pan, shepherd, Arcadian, wind musician, flutist, flautist (*Fr.*), piccolo-player, fifer, fife-player, piccoloist, satyr.

PIQUANCY, *n.* Spice, spiciness, zest, pepper, spirit, vigor, strength, salt, saltiness, seasoning, sharpness, poignancy, raciness, liveliness, sprightliness, tartness, sharpness, acuteness, acuity, wit, taste, tastefulness, tastiness, tang, twang (*coll.*), race, zip, acidity, acridity, acridness, sourness, high flavor, high relish, pungency, pungence, smack, punch, ginger (*coll.*), provocativeness, stimulation, excitement, animation, fascination, appeal.

PIQUANT, *adj.* 1. Pungent, poignant, zestful, zesty, tangy, savory, biting, acrid, acid, tart, peppery, well-seasoned, bitter, acidulous, spicy, hot, pricking, piercing, stinging, severe, gamy, high-flavored, high, strong-flavored, nutty, with a kick (*sl.*), salty, saline, high-seasoned, astringent, mordant, mordacious, acerb, acerbate, sharp, racy.

2. Pithy, terse, epigrammatical, aphoristic, proverbial, phylacteric, sententious, gnomic, gnomical, apothegmatic.

3. Spirited, lively, scintillating, sparkling, peppy, full of pep, full of oats (*coll.*), pointed, bright, impressive, zesty, animated, vigorous, strong, interesting, stimulating, smart, clever, chic (*Fr.*), provocative, telling, exciting, rousing, arousing, sensational, tantalizing, alluring, electric.

PIQUE, *n.* Resentment, umbrage, grudge, offense, wounded pride, hurt, hurt feelings, ill feeling, displeasure, irritation, annoyance, spite, vexation, malice, sourness, disaffection, bitterness, crossness, animosity, animus, mortification, humiliation, enmity, exasperation, indignation, prejudice, ire, irateness, dudgeon, spleen, aggravation (*coll.*), anger, wrath, warmth, hot temper, heat, vindictiveness, choler, soreness, chafing, huff, miff, fume, high dudgeon, cat fit, duck fit (*both slang*), dissatisfaction, discomfort, bitterness, despondency.

PIQUE, *v.* 1. Arouse, excite, incite, rouse, stimulate, stir up, kindle, enkindle, ignite, set fire to, goad, spur, put the spur to, agitate, stir up, incur, provoke, set in motion, fire.

2. Offend, displease, vex, annoy, irritate, aggravate (*coll.*), sting, wound, give offense to, perturb, miff, rile, exasperate, affront, insult, incense, infuriate, enrage, chafe, nettle, gall, sting, fret, wound, give umbrage to, pain, provoke, perturb, dismay, disquiet, anger, trouble, plague, roil,

pester, taunt, irk, ruffle, heckle, harass, badger, embitter, bother, get one's goat (*coll.*), disgust, mock, torture, torment, gall, fool, make wrathful, rouse one's ire, cut to the quick, madden, stir the blood, make one's blood boil, bullyrag, bully, tantalize, beset, tweak, tease, grate, grate on one's feelings, jar on one's feelings, try one's patience, sour one's temper, enflame, hurt one's feelings, give umbrage, put one's back up, make one's gorge rise, put out of countenance, put one's nose out of joint, huff, discompose, envenom, disturb.

PIQUED, *adj.* Maddened, vexed, irritated, annoyed, pestered, displeased, offended, aggravated (*coll.*), stung, wounded, perturbed, disturbed, miffed, riled, exasperated, affronted, insulted, incensed, infuriated, enraged, chafed, nettled, galled, fretful, wounded, hurt, pained, provoked, dismayed, disquieted, angered, troubled, plagued, harassed, pestered, taunted, irked, teased, beset, ruffled, heckled, badgered, embittered, bitter, bothered, disgusted, mocked, tortured, tormented, galled, wrathful, wrathy, irate, roused, aroused, excited, cut to the quick, maddened, stirred, stirred up, with one's blood in a boil, boiling, boiling mad, hopping mad (*coll.*), bullied, tweaked, teased, grated, jarred, tried, impatient, sour, inflamed, hurt, discomposed, put out of countenance, envenomed.

PIRACY, *n.* 1. Stealing, theft, robbery, hijacking, buccaneering, privateering, sea robbery, robbery on the high seas, piracy, waylaying, pillage, freebooting, larceny, grand larcency, felony.

2. Plagiarism, literary theft, literary piracy, copying, lifting, pinching, autoplagiarism.

PIRATE, *n.* 1. Corsair, buccanneer, sea rover, marauder, privateer, picaroon, freebooter, sea dog, sea wolf, plunderer, marooner, bandit, thief, desperado, robber, felon, criminal, plunderer, ranger, viking, Captain Kidd, Paul Jones, Blackbeard, Long John Silver, seafarer, seaman, sailor, navigator, mariner, seafaring man, sea rat.

2. Literary pirate, thief, purloiner, plagiarist, plagiarizer, copier, infringer.

PIRATE, *v.* 1. Steal, plunder, waylay, rob, maraud, depredate, appropriate, seize, lay hold of, thieve, commit robbery, commit piracy, take, rifle, pillage, spoil, despoil, strip, filibuster, forage, sweep, buccaneer, privateer.

2. Steal, copy, infringe a copyright, plagiarize, lift, borrow.

PIRATICAL, *adj.* Thievish, buccaneering, privateering, robbing, predatory, predacious, rapacious, lawless, criminal, felonious, marauding, plundering, spoliative, pirate-like, raptorial.

PIROUETTE, *n.* Whirling about (*on one foot or the points of the toes*), spin, twirl, whirl, gyre (*Poetic*).

PIROUETTE, *v.* Perform a pirouette, spin, twirl, revolve, swirl, gyrate, pivot.

PISCATORIAL, *adj.* 1. Pertaining to fishing, of rod and reel, angling, fishing, piscatory, piscatorian, piscatorious.

2. Of *or* pertaining to fish, piscine, pisciform, finny, ichthyoid, fishy, fish-like.

PISTOL, *n.* Revolver, automatic, repeater, derringer, petronel (*Hist.*), six-shooter (*coll.*), rod (*Crimin. sl.*), gat (*Crimin. sl.*).

PISTON, *n.* Movable disk *or* cylinder, plunger, sucker, ram, bucket.

PIT, *n.* 1. Hole in the ground, excavation, mine, well, hollow, cavity, trough, gully, gulch, grave, deep, dip, cleft, gulf, quarry, shaft *(Coal mining),* abyss, depression, furrow, burrow, cave, tunnel, cavern, crater, cistern.

2. Concealed excavation serving as a trap, snare, pitfall, trap, gin, trapdoor, meshes, false bottom, toils, springe, trapfall, deadfall.

3. *(With* THE*)* Abode of evil spirits and lost souls, hell, Hades *(Class. Myth.),* infernal regions, the lower world, the grave, purgatory, perdition, inferno, underworld, realms of Pluto, everlasting fire, bottomless pit, place of torment, abyss, limbo, nether world, hell-fire, Gehenna *(Jew. Hist.),* Tartarus *(Myth.),* Sheol *(Heb.),* Pandemonium, Tophet *(Lit.),* Avernus, Satan's Kingdom, Maraka, *(Hind. and Buddh.),* Styx, Abaddon, Erebus *(Gr. Myth.),* Acheron *(Class. Myth.).*

4. Hollow in a surface, indentation, small depressed scar, cavity, dip, sink, dimple, depression, dint, dent, pock, pockmark, puncture, spot, mark, furrow, trough, socket, honeycomb, imprint, alveolus *(Biol.),* lacuna *(Anat.),* sinus *(Anat.),* antrum *(Anat.),* cup, cell.

5. Enclosure for combats, arena, bowl, bear garden, ring, cockpit.

6. Main floor of a theater behind the musicians, parquet, orchestra, auditorium.

7. Stone of a fruit, seed, nut, kernel.

PIT, *v.* 1. Mark with pits *or* depressions, render concave, depress, hollow out, excavate, gouge, scoop, dig, honeycomb, dent, dint, pock, indent, notch, nick.

2. Place *or* bury in a pit, inter, tomb, entomb, inhume, sepulture, hearse, inearth *(chiefly Poet.).*

3. Set in active opposition, oppose, set at odds, match, set to fight, compare, juxtapose, place alongside, contrast, set over against, confront, sic on *or* at, incite, disunite, sow dissension, stir up dissension.

PITAPAT, *adv.* With a quick succession of beats *or* taps, in a flutter, in a twitter, convulsively, pitter-patter, in convulsions, atremble, aflutter, tremulously, agitatedly, with throbs, with palpitations, hop, skip and jump, flutteringly.

PITAPAT, *n.* Movement *or* sound of something going pitapat, pulsation, flutter, patter, rat-tat, rat-a-tat, tattoo, pound, throb, pulse, beat, palpitation, dance, shake, quiver, pitter-patter, shiver, drumming, rapping, tapping.

PITCH, *n.* 1. Degree of elevation, point *(as in a scale),* position, level, grade, step, round, rung, stair, mark, peg, measure, extent, range, rate, scope, caliber, remove, reach, compass, rank, status, stage, footing, place, standing, greatness, graduation, cut, notch *(coll.),* gradation, station.

2. Height, loftiness, highest point, peak, altitude, top, crown, utmost, summit, zenith, elevation, exaltation, meridian, apex, crest, greatest rise, eminence.

3. *(Music, speech, etc., referring to rapidity of vibrations.)* Acuteness, gravity, depth, tonality, note, height, voice, timbre, inflection, color, key, tone, modulation, intensity.

4. Throw, toss, cast, hurl, heave, lance, dart, serve, chuck, shy, sling, flirt, projection, jaculation, shot, peg *(coll.),* fling, launch.

5. Pitching movement, forward plunge, jerk, tumble, roll, rear, rock, reel, lurch, headlong fall, sway.

6. Downward inclination, slope, downgrade, descent, downhill, dip, drop, ramp, decline, declivity, hill, slant downward, fall.

7. Spot where a thing *or* person is placed *or* stationed, location, position, situation, spot, site, stand, point, ground, seat, post, whereabouts, station, place, plant, establishment.

8. Dark-colored viscous *or* tenacious substance used for sealing seams, *etc,* bitumen, rosin, resin, sap, asphalt, colophony.

PITCH, *v.* 1. Set up, erect *(tent, camp, etc.),* encamp, put in a fixed place, plant, fix firmly, establish, set, rear, raise, station, place, locate.

2. Throw, hurl, toss, cast, heave, launch, lance, dart, serve, chuck, shy, flirt, pelt, jaculate, fling, dash, fillip, let fly, sling, bowl, peg *(coll.),* shoot, fire, put.

3. Set at a certain point, degree, level, *etc.,* fix *(as price),* stabilize, determine, settle, localize, assign, consign, decide upon, adjust, arrange, put, place, situate, locate, establish.

4. Fall forward *or* headlong, plunge, lurch, topple, keel, tumble, stumble, reel, dip, dive, totter, swag, sway, cant, list, wallow, welter, flounder.

5. Slope downward, dip, descend, decline, fall, slope, slant, tilt, go downhill, drop, cant.

6. *(Fol. by* ON *or* UPON*)* Settle, light, fix, decide *(often casually),* like, select, chance, happen, hit, favor, choose, lean, tend, resolve, slide into, gravitate to *or* toward, desire, wish, fancy, commit oneself to, prefer, rest, elect, incline to, make up one's mind, determine.

7. Smear *or* cover with *or* as with pitch, tar, daub, bedaub, besmear, dab.

PITCHER, *n.* 1. Container usually having handle and spout *or* lip, jug, jar, ewer, cruse, stein, tankard, samovar, urn, pot, crock, toby, urceus *(Rom. Antiq.),* aiguière *(Fr.).*

2. One who pitches, thrower, hurler, flinger, chucker, jaculator, shot-putter, discobolus.

PITCHY, *adj.* 1. Tarry, resinous, gummy, tacky, sticky, mastic, bituminous.

2. Black, dark, nigrine, murky, caliginous, pitch-dark, pitch-black, nigrescent, lightless, ebony, jet, jetty, sloe-black, livid, nigritudinous, atramentous, sable, nigrous, nigricant, rayless, Cimmerian, funereal, ebon *(Poet.),* stygian, obscure, tenebrous, inky, unilluminated, unlighted.

PITEOUS, *adj.* Exciting compassion, full of pathos, wretched, miserable, poor, unhappy, dolorous, mournful, pitiable, rueful, distressing, affecting, heart-rending, plaintive, grievous, doleful, deplorable, sad, lamentable, touching, woeful, affective, pitiful.

PITFALL, *n.* Snare, trap, gin, trapdoor, deadfall, trapfall, springe, toils, false bottom, meshes, concealed excavation.

PITH, *n.* Marrow, gist, nucleus, radical, foundation, center, kernel, vital principle, fundamentals, midst, elixir, hypostasis *(Philos.),* principle, heart, quintessence, base, quiddity, essentials, elements, root, essence, substance, rudiments, inmost nature, core, spirit.

PITHY, *adj.* To the point, terse, pregnant with meaning, pointed, trenchant, summary, synoptic, direct, crisp, succinct, epigrammatic, straightforward, piquant, condensed, brief, concise, meaningful, short, compact, aphoristic, comprehensive, gnomic, forceful, sententious, substantial, compressed, packed, apothegmatic.

PITIABLE, PITIFUL, *adj.* 1. Exciting compassion, touching, lamentable, woeful, affective, piteous, grievous, doleful, deplorable, sad, distressing, affecting, heart-rending, plaintive, rueful, mournful, dolorous, unhappy, poor, miserable, full of pathos, wretched.

2. Worthy of contempt, contemptible, poor, sorry, cheap, worthless, scurvy, niggardly, despicable, base, mean, shabby, wretched, meager, unworthy, beggarly, dismal.

PITILESS, *adj.* Without pity, unfeeling, cruel, callous, unstirred, soulless, unmoved, impervious, relentless, inexorable, unmerciful, implacable, insentient, marble-hearted, inhuman, stony, ruthless, unpitying, heartless, hard-hearted, unsympathetic, unkind, obstinate, stern, obdurate, cold, unsparing, brutal, adamantine, frigid, aloof, distant, unresponsive, apathetic, barbarous, cold-blooded, passionless, indifferent, unconcerned, stiff, uninterested, disdainful, hostile, adverse, unimpressible, flinty, Laodicean, indurated, supine, stony, uncaring, untouched, hardened, sharp, insensible, iron-hearted, thick-skinned.

PITMAN, *n.* One who works in a pit, *etc.,* miner, excavator, sapper, digger, sandhog, tunneler, driller.

PITTANCE, *n.* Allowance, trifle, allotment, modicum, short allowance, insufficiency, mite, alms, gratuity.

PITTED, *adj.* Lacunose, pock-marked, punctate *(Bot., Zool. and Med.),* marked by pits, varioloid, variolic *(Med.),* variolate, foveate, foveated, foveolarious, scarred, foveolate.

PITTER-PATTER, *n.* Pattering sound, beating, gentle blows, tattoo, rap, tap, dab, rat-tat, thud, pat, plump, pad, slap, flap, beat, palpitation, patter, spatter, drumming.

PITY, *n.* Sympathy, ruth, lenity, indulgence, quarter, forbearance, humanity, forgivingness, liberality, magnanimity, placability, compassion, tenderness, condolence, kindliness, commiseration, heart, mercy, benevolence, soft-heartedness, grace, charity, lenience, clemency.

PITY, *v.* Have compassion for, be merciful, commiserate, feel grief for, express sympathy, lament with, compassionate, sympathize, feel for, weep for, give quarter, melt, condole, bleed for, relent, forbear, thaw.

PITYING, *adj.* Ruthful, sympathetic, magnanimous, exorable, liberal, tolerant, kind, charitable, ready to spare, pardoning, gentle, humane, benignant, mild, forgiving, placable, indulgent, lenient, soft, clement, gracious, merciful, compassionate, kindhearted, tender.

PIVOT, *n.* 1. Pin *or* shaft about which something turns, rotates *or* oscillates, axis, axle *(Mach.),* arbor, spindle, pin, hub, fulcrum, rowlock, oarlock, elbow, knee, swivel, joint, hinge, center, pole, gudgeon *(Mach.),* nave, reel, spool, bobbin, gimbals, radiant, stem, mandrel *(Mach.).*

2. That on which something turns, hinges *or* depends, focal point, critical point (factor, event, person, *etc.),* basis, base, bottom, cause, foundation, determinant, groundwork, substructure, turning point.

PIVOT, *v.* Turn, hinge, oscillate, wheel, whirl, swivel, swing around, pirouette.

PIVOTAL, *adj.* 1. Of, pertaining to *or* serving as a pivot, central, axial, focal.

2. Of critical importance, central, crucial, essential, primary, urgent, decisive, supreme, chief,

axial, radical, underlying, principal, main, paramount, prime, vital, basal, basic, original.

PIXILATED, *adj.* Amusingly eccentric, capricious, crotchety, giddy, frivolous, fanciful, fantastic, fitful, skittish, unpredictable, irresponsible, whimsical, wacky *(sl.),* screwy *(sl.).*

PIXY, PIXIE, *n.* Fairy, elf, sprite, imp, fay, peri, nisse, kobold, banshee, cluricaune, leprechaun, hobgoblin, puck, devilkin, ouphe, brownie, demon.

PLACABLE, *adj.* Capable of being placated *or* appeased, forgiving, reconcilable, appeasable, clement, unresentful, forbearant, benevolent, gracious, indulgent, ruthful, mild, equable, softhearted, tender, understanding, compassionate, touched, forbearing, lenient, tame, unrevengeful, long-suffering, longanimous, reasonable, charitable, satisfiable, pacifiable, merciful.

PLACARD, *n.* Written *or* printed notice *(to be posted in a public place),* poster, bill, broadside, bulletin, advertisement, flier, circular, handbill, notice.

PLACARD, *v.* Post, give notice of *(by means of placards),* announce, publish, proclaim, publicize, herald, circularize, disseminate, spotlight, broadcast, blaze abroad, blazon, make known, spread abroad, advertise.

PLACATE, *v.* Appease, pacify, conciliate, calm, quiet, temper, moderate, bring to terms, soothe, attemper, allay, assuage, tame, mollify, satisfy, silence, lull, hush, compose, tranquilize, still, gratify, propitiate, humor, win over, reconcile, arbitrate.

PLACATORY, *adj.* Conciliatory, reconciliatory, accommodative, pacific, placative, appeasing, mediatory, peace-making, pacifying, pacificatory, propitiatory.

PLACE, *n.* 1. Particular portion of space, space occupied by anything, spot set apart *or* used for a particular purpose, area, district, tract, scene, site, premises, locus, locality, situation, seat, position, location, quarter, region, locale, bounds, latitude and longitude, neighborhood, station, part, division, territory, bearings, habitat, venue *(Law),* zone.

2. Passage *(in a book or writing),* portion, part, section, paragraph, bit, piece, excerpt, extract, selection, chapter, verse, clause, sentence.

3. Position, situation, circumstances, predicament, plight, condition, state, shoes, standing, footing.

4. Office, job, position, employment, post, calling, occupation, station, appointment, function, work, job, charge, livelihood, billet, berth, role, capacity, pursuit, sinecure, trade, craft, career, commission, incumbency.

5. Function, duty, part, obligation, expectation, job, stint, charge, cue, role, care, province, assignment, business, onus, responsibility, compass, realm, orb, sphere, scope, capacity.

6. Position in the social scale *or* in order of merit *or* estimation, *etc.,* rank, standing, high position, mark, step, station, sphere, grade, precedence, dignity, class, prestige, consequence, order of importance, condition, degree, caste, gradation, importance, eminence, superiority, sublimity, notability, distinction, elevation, prominence.

7. Short street, court, lane, alley, close, square, plaza, piazza, mews, quadrangle, dead end, byway,

8. Portion of space used for habitation, town,

village, city, hamlet, country, territory, ground, kingdom, borough, resort, retreat, haunt, site, habitat, shire, colony, settlement, crossroads, suburb, township, municipality, precinct, province, metropolis, headquarters, rendezvous, encampment.

9. House, residence, dwelling, building, domicile, lodging, edifice, habitation, seat, mansion, abode, quarters, castle, hall, palace, bungalow, chalet, lodge, cottage, villa, messuage, structure, erection, homestead.

10. Stead, lieu, exchange.

11. Step in proceeding, point in order, consideration, instance, measure, move, act, action.

12. Fitting opportunity, room, occasion, reasonable ground, time, season, reason, golden opportunity, foundation, excuse, well-timed occasion, clear stage, favorable time, base, basis, rationale, call, instance, urge, inspiration, impulse, explanation, provocation, fair field, instigation, prompting, inducement, good cause, motivation.

PLACE, *v.* 1. Put in proper position *or* order, determine *or* indicate the place of, dispose, arrange, set, station, assign a certain position *or* rank to, seat, allot, array, post, marshal, sift, fix, group, rank, catalogue, tabulate, organize, index, consign, house, shelter, harbor, billet, ensconce, reposit, space, codify, grade, graduate, cradle, assort, line up, bestow, orient, orientate, classify, locate, class, establish, commit, deposit, settle, lay, lodge, plant, install, stand, rest, situate.

2. Put in a certain *or* suitable place, invest, put in particular *or* proper hands, give, grant, delegate, repose, put, relegate, consign, assign, commission, confer, commit, entrust, charge, farm out, contract.

3. Appoint to a post *or* office, find a place, situation, *etc.,* for, fill a vacancy, induct, establish in office, assign, nominate, commission, install, invest, hire, get a job for, employ, choose, engage the services of, take into service, take into one's employ, elect.

4. Identify, remember, recognize, recall, recollect, call *or* recall to mind, localize, spot *(coll.),* recover *or* recall knowledge of.

PLACEMENT, *n.* 1. Act of filling a job *or* position, employment, hiring, engaging, installation, investiture, election, induction, assignment, nomination, commission.

2. Location, arrangement, localization, collocation, allocation, deposition, insertion, disposition, fixation, lodgment, installation, establishment, emplacement, situation.

PLACID, *adj.* Quiet, tranquil, calm, unruffled, serene, peaceful, equable, unexcitable, collected, untroubled, meek, smooth, still, quiescent, halcyon, mild, peaceable, undemonstrative, philosophical, self-possessed, gentle, unexcited, cool, composed, unmoved, undisturbed, imperturbable, level-headed, steady, inirritable, pacific, restful, orderly, reposeful, harmonious, concordant.

PLACKET, *n.* Opening, slit, pocket, vent, hole.

PLAGIARISM, *n.* 1. Copying *or* imitating and presenting as one's own, literary theft, falsification, thievery, robbery, stealing, counterfeiting, forgery, imposture, deception, piracy, appropriation, taking, fraud, sham, dishonest borrowing, steal *(coll.),* crib *(coll.).*

2. Something appropriated and put forth as one's own, stolen idea, thought, expression *or* passage, copy, counterfeit, forgery, sham, fraud,

reproduction, unacknowledged quotation, crib *(coll.),* steal *(coll.).*

PLAGIARIST, *n.* Literary vandal *or* thief, plagiarizer, cribber, imitator, forger, pirate, counterfeiter, copier, borrower, stealer, lifter *(coll.).*

PLAGIARIZE, *v.* Appropriate by plagiarism, quote without acknowledgment, copy, crib *(coll.),* lift *(coll.),* forge, counterfeit, falsify, misrepresent, assume, imitate, pirate, make use of, help oneself to, borrow, take, purloin, usurp, thieve, arrogate, abstract, rob, steal, adopt and pass off as one's own.

PLAGUE, *n.* 1. Epidemic disease, pestilence, pest, infection, pendemia, contagious disease, death.

2. Affliction, evil, calamity, vexation, trouble, pest, bane, infliction, scourge, nettle, nuisance, curse, torment, thorn in the flesh, thorn in one's side, gall, woe, mischief, skeleton in the closet, cross, visitation, bugbear, oppression, trial, bitter pill, fret, worry, infestation, burden, annoyance, canker, grievance, abomination, pestilence, *bête noire (Fr.).*

PLAGUE, *v.* Annoy, smite, infect, trouble, torment, bother, pester, afflict, perplex, tantalize, distress, irritate, badger, incommode, chafe, fret, harry, molest, worry, tease, vex, infest, roil, scourge, bait, heckle, ruffle, mortify, harass, disturb, gall, bore into, hector, disquiet, embarrass, twit, gibe, pique, discompose, nag, grind, pain, persecute, bullyrag, exasperate, aggrieve, haunt, rack, weigh *or* prey on the mind, go against the grain, gripe, grate, irk, beset, provoke, get on one's nerves, try the patience.

PLAIN, *adj.* 1. Clear, distinct, prominent, manifest, obvious, palpable, conspicuous, glaring, open, patent, well-defined, comprehensible, pronounced, legible, luminous, discernible, evident, notable, apparent, visible, striking, exposed, standing out, staring, perceptible, self-evident, understandable, express, well-marked, vivid, unquestionable, undisguised, articulate, perspicuous, clear-cut, salient, prominent, pronounced, unmistakable, disclosed, revealed, unconcealed, distinguishable, public, avowed, naked, bare, frank, overt.

2. Conveying the meaning clearly *or* simply, easily understood, unequivocal, unambiguous, tangible, lucid, clear, terse, undisguised, explicit, literal, perspicuous, intelligible, distinct, self-evident, point-blank, luminous, legible, comprehensible, understandable, vivid, articulate, clear-cut, frank, bare, naked, barefaced, arrant, express, patent, direct.

3. Downright, sheer, mere, absolute, stark, utter, complete, positive, unqualified, flagrant, glaring, outright, veritable, total, unmitigated, rank, out-and-out, thorough, perfect, consummate.

4. Free from ambiguity *or* evasion, outspoken, candid, frank, sincere, honest, plain-dealing, unflattering, unaffected, direct, open, ingenuous, straightforward, blunt, crude, unreserved, undisguised, unconcealed, aboveboard, unsophisticated, open-hearted, undissembling, artless, guileless, plain-spoken, naïve, unfeigning, bona fide, upright, veracious, truthful.

5. Without special pretensions, superiority, elegance, *etc.,* artless, simple, unaffected, unsophisticated, innocent, modest, naïve, native, untutored, unsuspicious, trustful, unassuming, matter-of-fact, workday, garden, informal, household, plebeian, everyday, commonplace, common, homespun, homely, natural, unlearned, prosy,

prosaic, ordinary, insignificant, lesser, obscure, bourgeois, characterless, undistinguished, mediocre, unheard of, minor, subordinate, unnoticed, nameless, inferior, inglorious, renownless, unexalted, humble, of the street, average.

6. Not beautiful, homely, uncomely, unhandsome, unlovely, of plain features, without charm, unattractive, ill-favored, unbeautiful, beautiless, unpretty, ordinary, unprepossessing, graceless, ungraceful, displeasing to the eye.

7. With little *or* no embellishment, decoration *or* enhancing elaboration, without pattern, device *or* coloring, unornamental, unfigured, modest, unvaried, bare, untrimmed, unembellished, ungarnished, inelegant, unadorned, unvariegated, severe, frugal, unfurbished, blank, pure, simple, restrained, unmixed, inornate, clear, Attic, flat, spare, undecked, unarrayed, undecorated, chaste, economical.

8. Level, flat, even, flush, complanate, campestral, champaign, horizontal, plane, smooth, homaloidal *(Math.)*.

9. Without intricacies *or* difficulties, uncomplicated, unmixed, unencumbered, primary, elementary, simple, easy, basic, basal, incomplex, essential, rock-bottom, fundamental.

PLAIN, *n.* Relatively flat area of land *(usually low)*, level, plateau, champaign, grassland, pasturage, meadow, flat, moor, heath, tundra, savanna, campagna, prairie, lowland, tableland, veld *or* veldt, steppe, downs, pampas, field, open country, basin *(Phys. Geog.)*, peneplain *(Geol.)*.

PLAINLY, *adv.* Clearly, distinctly, openly, obviously, visibly, overtly, candidly, aloud, unmistakably, bluntly, noticeably, in full view, decidedly, beyond question, unequivocally, transparently, admittedly, palpably, patently, irrefutably, beyond doubt, starkly, prominently, pronouncedly, undoubtedly, undeniably, unquestionably, certainly, positively, discernibly, recognizably, markedly, surely, manifestly, evidently, perceptibly, apparently, conspicuously, irrefragably.

PLAINSONG, *n.* Unisonous vocal music, modal liturgical music, theme chosen for contrapuntal development, melody, canto, cantilena, *cantus firmus (Med. Lat.)*, *cantus planus (Med. Lat.)*, Gregorian chant.

PLAIN-SPOKEN, *adj.* Candid, frank, blunt, open, outspoken, bluff, unreserved, direct, straightforward, unflattering, unsparing, truthful, forthright, unconcealed, downright, unfeigning, honest, undissembling, free, bold, guileless, undisguising, unpretending, undissimulating, unvarnished, untrimmed, artless, ingenuous, sincere, aboveboard, inartificial, forward, straight from the shoulder, uncomplimentary.

PLAINT, *n.* Complaint, lament, lamentation, moan, jeremiad, cry, wail, expression of grief, pain *or* resentment, murmur, objection, charge, carping, blame, animadversion, censure, reproof, reproach, remonstrance, aspersion, accusation, scolding, dolorous tirade, grumble, mutter, whine, whimper, sob, ululation, sigh, regret, discontent.

PLAINTIVE, *adj.* Expressing sorrow *or* melancholy, discontent, mournful, full of pathos, sorrowful, sad, piteous, rueful, woeful, heart-rending, miserable, dolorous, wretched, unhappy, lamentable, affecting, moving, distressing, melancholy, dirgelike, wailing, touching, pathetic, querulous, elegiac, crying, complaining, whining, moaning, grievous, ululant, clamorous, weeping, pitiful.

PLAIT, *n.* 1. Braid, cue, pigtail, twist, wreath, plat, queue, band.

2. Fold, pleat, gather, double, flute, tuck, fluting, ruck, pucker, cockle, crinkle, goffer, plicature, plication, ruffle, corrugation, kilting.

PLAIT, *v.* 1. Braid, plat, intertwine, interweave, interlace, wreathe, entwine, interknit, weave, pleach, plash.

2. Pleat, fold, crease, plicate, ruck, shirr, gather, tuck, wrinkle, ruffle, flute, cockle, corrugate, pucker, crimp, double.

PLAN, *n.* 1. Scheme, project, purpose, method, design, program, policy, agenda, roster, mode of procedure, tactics, means, way, itinerary, schedule, bill, game, prospect, ambition, motion, intention, suggestion, syllabus, prospectus, stratagem, course, order, process, custom, line of action, conception, contrivance, proposal, proposition, idea, device, system, hope, arrangement.

2. Design *or* scheme of arrangement, layout, organization, disposition, distribution, system, order, array, outline, classification, catalogue, codification, ordination, grouping, apportionment, allocation.

3. Representation of a thing drawn on a plane, drawing to scale, sketch, map, diagram, chart, copy, ground plan, pattern, model, picture, draft, specifications, description, figure, projection, skeleton, elevation, cast, layout, plot, delineation.

PLAN, *v.* 1. Arrange a plan *or* scheme for, form a plan, project, provide for, contrive, scheme, devise, design, digest, block out, lay out, prepare, shape, outline, form, schedule, line up, build, book, erect, conceive, fabricate, frame, purpose, construct, think out, have in view, intend, engineer, invent, plot, project, map out, organize, calculate, systematize, concoct, measure.

2. Draw *or* make a plan of, represent, outline, sketch out, strike out, map out, draft, trace, depict, draw, chart, project, diagram, figure, delineate, measure.

3. Make plans, look ahead, conspire, hatch a plan, arrange, shape *or* mark out a course, draw up a plan, forecast, prearrange, premeditate, machinate, contemplate, think, foreordain, precontrive, predesign, predetermine, prepare, make arrangements *or* preparations, invent.

PLANE, *adj.* Level, flat, plain, horizontal, complanate, tabular, flush, smooth, even, homaloidal *(Math.)*, champaign.

PLANE, *n.* 1. Even surface, flat *or* level surface, horizontal projection, table, horizon, stratum, level, homaloid *(Math.)*, flat.

2. Level *(of dignity, character, existence, development, etc.)*, degree, status, position, station, rank, place, order, condition, standing, precedence, caste, elevation, class, height, sphere, footing.

3. Airplane, hydroplane, aircraft, air liner, seaplane.

4. Paring tool, planer, jointer, smoother, trowel.

PLANE, *v.* 1. Soar, glide, float, lift partly out of water at high speed *(as a racing boat)*, drift, be wafted, take wing, hover, wing, rise, be buoyed up.

2. Remove with a plane, shave, pare, smooth, dress, face, level, flatten, finish, planish, mill, even.

PLANETARIUM, *n.* Model *or* representation of

the planetary system, room *or* building containing a planetarium, orrery, eidouranion.

PLANETARY, *adj.* 1. Of the nature of planets, wandering, erratic, vagrant, errant, rambling, roving, nomadic, discursive, vagabond, deviative, circuitous, migratory, uneasy, restless, mundivagant, roundabout, undirected.

2. Terrestrial, mundane, worldly, earthly, subastral, sublunary, temporal, terrene.

PLANGENT, *adj.* 1. Beating *(as waves)*, dashing, pounding, breaking, hitting, pulsating, battering, buffeting, hurtling, smashing, butting, crashing, striking, throbbing.

2. Resounding loudly, echoing, sonorous, tonant, roaring, fulminating, thundering, rumbling, rolling, booming, reverberating, vibrant, blaring, drumming, pealing.

PLANK, *n.* Long flat piece of timber, board, flooring, planking *(coll.),* lumber *(coll.).*

PLANT, *n.* 1. Vegetable, herb, seedling, flower, wort, vine, weed, slip, legume, herblet, exotic, seaweed, annual, perennial, vegetation *(coll.),* herbage *(coll.),* flora *(coll.),* plantlet.

2. Equipment and buildings of an industrial business, property, factory, apparatus, workshop, mill, yard, foundry, laboratory, shop, works, establishment, manufactory.

PLANT, *v.* 1. Put in the ground *(as seed),* set in, sow, set out, scatter, implant, transplant, reset, seed.

2. Furnish with plants, grow plants on *or* in, seed, sow, stock, farm.

3. Implant *(ideas, sentiments, etc.),* establish *(principles, doctrines, etc.),* introduce, inculcate, infix, breed, lodge, innovate, infuse, infiltrate, engender, imbue, instill, interfuse, interject, inject, infect, insinuate, induct, bring in, import, teach, foster, cultivate, propagate, impress, disseminate, sow the seeds of, contaminate, tincture.

4. Insert in a surface, set firmly on a surface, put, place, fix, establish, lodge, infix, implant, bury, inlay, settle, embed, graft, engraft, inject, wedge, slap down, plump down, inset.

5. Post, station, pitch, set, seat, park, consign, put, place, house, billet, install, lodge, quarter, assign, locate, situate.

6. *(Of a colony, etc.)* Establish, set up, found, furnish inhabitants to, settle, build, people, populate, rear, raise, stock, erect, colonize, fix, institute, promote.

PLANTATION, *n.* Farm *(esp. tropical or semitropical),* estate, grange, demesne, grove, ranch, hacienda *(Sp. Amer.).*

PLANTER, *n.* One who plants, owner *or* occupant of a plantation, landowner, grower, raiser, farmer, husbandman, agriculturist, agronomist, granger.

PLAQUE, *n.* Flat plate of metal *or* porcelain, *etc.,* medal, badge of an honorary order, medallion, ornamental plate, brooch, plaquette, tablet, slab, cameo.

PLASH, *n.* 1. Sound of running water, splash, dash, rush, gush, drop, drip, trickle, eavesdrop, stillicide.

2. Puddle, pool, collection of standing water, water pocket, pond, pondlet, wallow, muddy place, water hole.

PLASH, *v.* 1. Splash, spatter, trickle, ripple,

gurgle, burble, dribble, murmur, purl, trill, lap, drip, drop, swash, wash, slosh, babble.

2. Plait, interweave, braid, interwine, interlace, interknit, weave, entwine, wreathe.

PLASTER, *n.* 1. Pasty composition for covering surfaces, calcined gypsum, stucco, mortar, parget, staff, grout, plaster of Paris, powdered gypsum, scagliola, roughcast.

2. Preparation applied to the body for remedial purposes, poultice, compress, pack, bandage, court plaster, stupe *(Med.),* diachylon *(Pharm.),* cataplasm *(Med.),* sinapism, epithem *(Med.).*

PLASTER, *v.* 1. Cover with plaster, mortar, cement, stucco, parget, roughcast, daub, bedaub, smear, coat, lay on roughly.

2. Apply a plaster to *(the body, etc.),* bandage, dress, medicate, poultice.

3. Overspread *(esp. thickly or to excess),* load, cover, burden, post, overlay, mantle, envelop, shroud, immantle, deck, bedeck.

PLASTIC, *adj.* Capable of being molded *or* of receiving form, soft, pliable, impressionable, flexible, formable, supple, fictile, pliant, easily molded, ductile, waxy, yielding, tractable, susceptible, malleable, tractile, extensile, elastic, receptive, sensitive, responsive, mobile, moldable, extensible.

PLASTICITY, *n.* Quality of being plastic, capability of being molded *or* receiving shape, malleability, modifiability, mobility, variability, pliancy, tractility, elasticity, tractability, extensibility, changeableness, versatility, softness, pliability, flexibility, ductility.

PLAT, *n.* 1. Plot of ground *(usually small),* piece of ground, lot, tract, patch, enclosure, close, yard, garden, court, parcel of land, clearing, field.

2. Plan *(as of land),* map, diagram, figure, chart, outline, delineation.

PLATE, *n.* 1. Shallow dish, platter, saucer, trencher *(Hist.).*

2. Contents of a plate, service of food for one person, portion, course, platter, dish, serving, helping.

3. Thin sheet of metal *or* other material, overlay, sheath, plaque, slab, coating, foil, leaf, layer, lamina, paten, disk, panel.

4. Printed impression from a prepared plate, cut, full page, inserted illustration, frontispiece, impression, imprint, lithograph, print, engraving, etching, intaglio.

PLATE, *v.* Coat with a thin film of metal, overlay, gild, silver, nickel, platinize, enamel, encrust, face.

PLATEAU, *n.* Elevated plain, highland, tableland, mesa, upland, savanna, table, down.

PLATFORM, *n.* 1. Raised flooring *or* structure in a hall *or* meeting place, stand, estrade, pulpit, predella, dais, rostrum, catafalque, deck, scaffold, proscenium, stage, boards, perron *(Archit.),* turntable, landing, soapbox, stump, emplacement *(Fort.),* roundtop *(Naut.),* tribune *(Archit.),* suggestum *(Rom. Antiq.).*

2. Body of principles of a political party, policy, plank, plans, campaign promises.

PLATITUDE, *n.* 1. Flat, dull *or* trite remark *(esp. one offered as if fresh and profound),* cliché, commonplace, truism, chestnut, prosaicism, prosaism, stereotyped expression, hackneyed saying, banality, bromide *(sl.),* fadaise *(Fr.),* drug-store philosophy *(coll.).*

2. Triteness, dullness, flatness, commonplaceness, banality, insipidity, mawkishness, aridity, jejuneness, vapidity, monotony, dreariness, prosaicness, uninventiveness.

PLATITUDINOUS, *adj.* Characterized by *or* given to platitudes, of the nature of a platitude, banal, trite, commonplace, stereotyped, stock, set, common, warmed-over, hackneyed, stupid, insulse, dreary, stale, moth-eaten, threadbare, familiar, bromidic *(sl.)*, prosaic, prosy, vapid, arid, dull, tasteless, uninteresting, insipid, flat, dry, pointless, jejune, unimaginative.

PLATONIC, *adj.* 1. *(Cap.)* Pertaining to love which extends beyond individual feeling to an ideal *or* pattern, transcendent, immaterial, philosophic, theoretical, animistic, unearthly, bodiless, hyperphysical, extramundane, supernatural, universal, insubstantial, ecstatic, ideal, spiritual, unworldly, unfleshly, incorporeal, platonistic, speculative, contemplative.
2. *(Cap. or l.c.)* Purely spiritual, free from sensuous desire, impassible, passionless, chaste, of the soul, inexcitable, tranquil, unruffled, placid, saintly, saintlike, intellectual, serene, calm, cool, angelic, pure, virtuous, rational, objective, hyperphysical, unfleshly, unearthly, bodiless, transcendent, disembodied, virginal, innocent, celibate, religious, heavenly-minded, unpassionate.

PLATOON, *n.* Military unit, set of persons, company, police force unit, detachment, wing.

PLATTER, *n.* Large shallow dish *(commonly oval)*, plate, charger, tray, salver, trencher *(Hist.)*.

PLAUDIT, *n.* Demonstration, round of applause, enthusiastic expression of approval, clapping of hands, clap, handclap, loud commendation, exultation, shouting, encomium, shout of approbation, acclamation, acclaim, cheering, paean, hosanna, hurrah, huzza, cheer, thunder of applause, peal of applause, chorus of praise, hallelujah, adulation.

PLAUSIBLE, *adj.* 1. Having an appearance of truth, seemingly worthy of approval *or* acceptance, probable, colorable, ostensible, tenable, conceivable, believable, glossy, credible, likely, reasonable, not impossible, admissible, apparently right, Jesuitical, fair-seeming, impressive, justifiable, feasible, sound, sane, sensible, illusive, inferable, logical, persuasive, satisfactory, casuistic, deceptive, illusory, misleading, hollow, sophistical.
2. Fair-spoken, apparently worthy of confidence, glib, insincere, using specious arguments, suave, bland, unctuous, oily, smooth-tongued, smooth-spoken, mealy-mouthed, Janus-faced, honeyed, fulsome, double-faced, hypocritical, dissembling, flattering, specious, fluent, smooth, persuasive, adulatory.

PLAY, *n.* 1. Dramatic composition *or* piece, drama, piece of stagecraft, entertainment, dramatic performance, spectacle, pageant, extravaganza, pantomime, legitimate drama, piece, vehicle, revue, theatricals, show *(coll.)*, representation, exhibition, comedy, tragedy, melodrama, farce, burlesque.
2. Exercise for amusement, game, recreation, contest, sport, diversion, frolic, romp, gambol, fun, frisk, caper, revel, treat, pleasure, pastime, festivity, dalliance, merriment, merrymaking, hobby, avocation, athletics, disport, festival, regalement, skylarking, lark *(coll.)*, jamboree *(sl.)*.
3. Jest, fun, trifling, make-believe, sham, pretense, prank, sport, pun, feigning, simulation of

seriousness, banter, farce, witticism, toying, fooling, joke, lark *(coll.)*.
4. The playing *or* carrying on of a game, manner *or* style of playing, use, practice, conduct, behavior, fashion, method, mien, bearing, demeanor, address, usage, custom, transaction, deportment, comportment.
5. State of being in use *(as of a ball)*, action, use, agency, employment, operation, operancy, work, force, exercise, maintenance, function, movement, motion, activity.
6. Playing for stakes, gaming, gambling, wager, betting, hazards, sporting, lots, speculation, cardsharping.
7. Action, activity, lambency, elusive change *(as of light or color)*, variegation, motion, movement, taction, stir, multicolor, iridescence, mobility, glance, liveliness, animation, motley, touch, hovering, rippling.
8. Freedom of movement, liberty of action, scope for activity, rein, swing, range, sweep, opportunity, room, latitude, elbowroom, free course *or* vent, free play, full swing, reach, margin, berth, leeway *(coll.)*.

PLAY, *v.* 1. Act on the stage, perform, sustain a part, personate a character, represent, act the part of, impersonate, mimic, take part in, enact, strut the boards, troupe, tread the stage *or* boards, support, barnstorm *(Theat.)*, ham *(Theat. sl.)*.
2. Give performances in, tour, visit, stop over at, have a run in, barnstorm *(Theat.)*.
3. Engage in *(a game, pastime, etc.)*, contend against in a game, compete, take part, be on a team, participate, join in, vie with, race.
4. Do something only in sport, amuse oneself, toy, trifle, idle, fool, befool, jest, banter, pun, joke, mock, chaff, twit, poke fun at, flirt, dally, wanton, josh, rally, gibe, tease, gag, sally, jig.
5. Represent *or* imitate in sport, exercise *or* employ oneself in diversion, amusement *or* recreation, waste *or* fritter away time, romp, gambol, frisk, revel, frolic, sport, disport, make fun, make merry, junket, carouse, spree, skip, trip, dance, make *or* keep holiday, cavort *(coll.)*, curvet, while away the time, beguile the time, antic, caper.
6. Lay a wager *or* wagers on, stake, punt, bet, sport, gamble, venture, speculate, game, practise gambling.
7. Use for one's own advantage, put to use, manipulate, profit by, employ, turn to account, make the most of, exploit, ply, avail oneself of, pit, foil, show up, oppose, set over against, incite, disunite, compare, contrast, juxtapose, confront.
8. Perform on a musical instrument, execute, render, produce, concertize, make music.
9. Move about *or* change quickly *or* lightly, hover, wave, vary, flutter, quiver, ripple, glance, touch, stir, fluctuate, flicker, flit, shift, waver, vacillate.
10. Operate *or* cause to operate continually *or* with repeated action, stream, be trained, flow, propel, shoot, fire, project, keep in motion, course, spout, spurt, gush, pour, issue, surge, well, drive.
11. *(With* OUT*)* Bring to an end, use up, exhaust, wear out, fag, run through, spend, drain, consume, deplete, impoverish, fatigue, expend, dissipate, flag, kill, weary, fatigue, tire, scatter to the winds, burn the candle at both ends.
12. Conduct oneself in a specified way, act, behave, do, function, operate, work, proceed,

transact, enact, pursue, serve, effect, practice, carry on, execute, exercise, perform, take action, take steps.

13. Move freely (as within a space), act, operate, have leeway, be unimpeded, have free play, have scope, swing, sway, roll, have elbowroom, go at large, have latitude.

PLAYBILL, n. Program, announcement of a play, notice, advertisement, placard, poster, flier.

PLAYER, n. 1. One who takes parts on the stage, actor, performer, actress, hero, heroine, mummer, trouper, supporter, leading man or lady, mimic, mime, imitator, character, walk-on, understudy, supernumerary, Thespian, comedian, tragedian, pantomimist, super (coll.), extra (coll.), bit player (coll.), ham (sl.).

2. Performer on a musical instrument, instrumentalist, musician, artist, virtuoso, recitalist, accompanist, soloist, member of an orchestra, chamber group, band, etc.

3. Participant, opponent, adversary, antagonist, gamester, sportsman, combatant, disputant, litigant, contender, contestant, competitor, tussler, fighter, assailant.

PLAYFUL, adj. Sportive, frolicsome, full of play, pleasant, humorous, frisky, blithesome, waggish, kittenish, mirthful, merry, fun-loving, laughing, wanton, playsome, half-serious, sprightly, convivial, amusing, lively, roguish, arch, mirth-loving, breezy, genial, sunny, light-hearted, vivacious, mischievous, tricksome, buoyant, gay, spry, racy, jocund, coltish, jocular, jolly, facetious, rollicking, gamesome, gleeful, prankish, rompish, tricksy.

PLAYGROUND, n. Ground used for open-air recreation, park, ball field, athletic field, recreation center, diamond, sand lot.

PLAYHOUSE, n. 1. Theater, opera house, music hall, odeum, concert hall, little theater, circus.

2. Toy house, doll house.

PLAYMATE, n. Playfellow, comrade, companion in play, chum, friend, buddy (coll.), pal (coll.), intimate, shadow, brother.

PLAYTHING, n. Thing to play with, toy, bauble, amusement, sport, gimcrack, gewgaw, kite, puzzle, trinket, knick-knack, game, pet, doll, bagatelle, whimwham, whirligig, top, popgun, air gun or rifle, water pistol, trifle.

PLAYTIME, n. Time for play or recreation, holiday, vacation, leisure, recess, jubilee, festival, carnival, junket, celebration, time off or out, spree, fete, heyday.

PLAYWRIGHT, n. Maker or writer of plays, dramatic author or writer, dramatist, dramatizer, librettist, playcraftsman, dramaturge, dramaturgist, mimographer, monodramatist, melodramatist, scenarist, scenario writer, farcer, farceur (Fr.), tragedian, tragedist, comedian, comedist.

PLAZA, n. Public square, market place, town square, rialto, piazza (mostly Ital.), forum (Rom. Antiq.), agora (Gr. Antiq.).

PLEA, n. 1. Excuse, justification, vindication, palliation, defense, apology, explanation, exculpation, extenuation, argument.

2. Pleading, supplication, imploration, solicitation, earnest request, adjuration, appeal, invocation, prayer, petition, entreaty, suit, application.

3. (Law) Defendant's answer to charges, demurrer, defense, allegation, pleading.

PLEAD, v. 1. Argue at the bar, defend a case, carry on suit in court, sue.

2. Petition, importune, appeal, solicit, entreat, beg, implore, pray, supplicate, beseech, obsecrate, enjoin, adjure, obtest, conjure.

PLEADER, n. Lawyer, attorney, attorney-at-law, counselor, counselor-at-law, barrister, juris-consult, advocate, solicitor.

PLEASANT, adj. 1. Pleasing, pleasure-giving, dulcet, heavenly, attractive, agreeable, inviting, pleasurable, nice, delectable, taking, winning, delicious, exquisite, felicitous, lovely, captivating, likable, gratifying, palatable, welcome, refreshing, sweet, harmonious, alluring, delightful, enjoyable, charming.

2. (Of persons) Well-mannered, civilized, conciliatory, mild, gentle, obliging, politic, mannerly, respectful, cordial, deferential, polished, genial, good-humored, winsome, polite, agreeable, affable, suave, well-behaved, well-bred, genteel, cultivated, urbane, gallant, courtly, chivalrous, diplomatic, decorous, compliant, gentlemanlike, gracious, complaisant, tactful, bland, cheerful, complacent, friendly, warm, amicable, amiable, neighborly, sympathetic, well-affected, well-disposed.

PLEASANTRY, n. 1. Banter, repartee, good-humored raillery, chaff, burletta, revel, levity, good humor, merriment, hilarity, tomfoolery, facetiousness, jocularity, clowning, nonsense, antics, teasing, word-play, mocking, twitting, quizzing, quipping, joking, waggery, laughing, joshing, wisecracking, scoffing, horseplay, parody, persiflage, badinage, ridicule, fun, derision.

2. Humorous story or deed, joke, quip, bon mot, prank, trick, farce, mot, crank, quirk, game, witticism, jest, quiz, sally, carriwitchet, jape, crack, gag, wisecrack, jeu d' esprit (Fr.), pun, paronomasia.

PLEASE, v. 1. Afford pleasure, satisfy, gratify, make happy, enravish, treat, regale, thrill, divert, amuse, humor, entrance, gladden, elate, delight, enrapture, interest, enamor, entertain, fascinate, enthrall, charm.

2. Be willing, choose, want, desire, prefer, opt, elect, incline towards.

PLEASED, adj. Jubilant, buoyant, carried away, glad, delighted, light-hearted, ecstatic, joyful, in paradise, in seventh heaven, carefree, joyous, cheerful, elated, enchanted, content, overjoyed, rapturous, rejoicing, in heaven, sunny, gladsome.

PLEASING, adj. 1. Pleasure-giving, dulcet, heavenly, attractive, agreeable, inviting, pleasurable, nice, delectable, taking, winning, delicious, exquisite, felicitous, lovely, captivating, likable, gratifying, palatable, welcome, refreshing, sweet, harmonious, alluring, delightful, enjoyable, charming.

2. (Of persons) Well-mannered, civilized, conciliatory, mild, gentle, obliging, politic, mannerly, respectful, cordial, amiable, deferential, polished, genial, good-humored, winsome, polite, agreeable, affable, suave, well-behaved, well-bred, genteel, cultivated, urbane, gallant, courtly, chivalrous, diplomatic, decorous, compliant, gentlemanlike, gracious, complaisant, tactful, bland, cheerful, complacent.

3. Handsome, good-looking, engaging, alluring, appealing, fascinating, becoming, likable, aesthetic, lovely, shapely, winning, seductive, attractive, pretty, charming, captivating, fetching, tasteful, picturesque, beautiful, delightful, preposses-

sing, tempting, enchanting, enticing, winsome, bewitching, fair, elegant.

PLEASURE, *n.* 1. An emotion of joy *or* pleasure, entrancement, enchantment, felicity, delectation, serenity, light-heartedness, comfort, sweetness, well-being, peace, kick *(sl.)*, contentment, exultant satisfaction, delight, great gladness, exultation, ecstasy, triumph, mirth, gaiety, cheerfulness, happiness, relish, content, elation, gratification, cheer, thrill, rapture, glee, enjoyment, exhilaration, excitement, oblectation, hedonism, jubilance, joy.

2. Source *or* cause of pleasure, charm, jewel, treat, gem, delight, thing of beauty, sight for sore eyes, pleasurableness, delectability, wonder, treasure, joy, precious possession, prize, find, flower, thing *or* person of great worth, one in a thousand *or* ten thousand.

3. Outward manifestation of pleasure, outward rejoicing, jubilation, festive gaiety, exultation, mirth, enthusiasm, cheer, glee, merriment, festivity, hilarity, cheerfulness, high spirits, light heart, jocundity, jocularity, jocoseness, laughter, rejoicing, merrymaking, levity, jollity, high glee, zest, sunshine, blitheness, celebration, glorification, triumph, jubilee.

4. Will, desire, propensity, bias, inclination, prepossession, partiality, predisposition, decision, extract, predilection, want, choice, bias, wish, preference, elect, pick, option, excerption.

PLEAT, *n.* Pucker, cockle, crinkle, goffer, plicature, plication, ruffle, corrugation, kilting, ruck, fluting, tuck, flute, double, gather, fold, plait.

PLEAT, *v.* 1. Pleach, weave, interknit, entwine, interlace, plait, braid, intertwine, interweave, wreathe, plash.

2. Pleat, fold, crease, ruck, wrinkle, double, crimp, ruffle, pucker, corrugate, shirr, gather, tuck, flute, cockle.

PLEBEIAN, *adj.* Belonging *or* pertaining to the common people, common, vulgar, commonplace, popular, lowborn, obscure, low, mean, ignoble, mob, baseborn, proletarian, base, rankless, bourgeois, mediocre, lesser, subordinate, nameless, inferior, average, inglorious, undistinguished, humble, lowly, of the street, of the citizenry.

PLEBISCITE, *n.* Vote, election, poll, ballot, referendum.

PLEDGE, *n.* 1. Solemn promise, vow, swearing, avowal, adjuration, solemn declaration, guarantee, obligation, seal, warranty, warrant, assurance, oath, word, adjuration, undertaking, plight, troth, indemnity, contract, covenant, compact, stipulation, parole, profession, pignoration, affidavit *(Law)*.

2. Anything delivered as security, surety, deposit, collateral, token, gage, pawn, bail, promissory note, commitment, stake, earnest, handsel, bond, vadium *(Law)*, replevin *(Law)*.

3. Person accepted for membership but not yet formally approved, probationer, tentative member, initiate, neophyte, newcomer, beginner, catechumen.

4. Health *(in drinking)*, toast, greeting, salute, token, cheer, recognition, acknowledgment.

PLEDGE, *v.* 1. Engage, bind by *or* as by a pledge, adjure, plight, compel, draft, press, require, oblige, restrain, pin down, enjoin, exact, coerce, assign, conscript, contract, affiance.

2. Engage to give, maintain, *etc.*, promise solemnly, plight, stake, assert solemnly, compact,

commit oneself, contract, vow, take oath, undertake, enter into, be answerable for, give one's word, avow, indent, swear, warrant, vouch, covenant, guarantee, certify, assure.

3. Give as a pledge, pawn, deposit as security, give as guarantee, deliver, plight, impawn, hypothecate, put in pledge, give as surety, handsel, go bail, bottomry, impignorate, mortgage.

4. Toast, drink to, drink the health of, salute, raise the cup to, drink in honor of.

PLENARY, *adj.* 1. Full, complete, unqualified, absolute, thorough, replete, ample, strong, unbounded, arbitrary, unconditional, unrestricted, unquestioned, perfect, whole, entire, abundant, limitless, unlimited, unstinted.

2. Attended by all qualified members, fully constituted, full, complete, whole, entire.

PLENIPOTENTIARY, *adj.* 1. Invested with full power *or* authority, potent, powerful, plenipotent, deputized, delegated, commissioned, qualified, authorized, consular, representative.

2. Absolute *(as power)*, full, *etc.* (See PLENARY, *adj.*, 1, *above*.)

PLENIPOTENTIARY, *n.* Person invested with full power *or* authority to transact business, diplomatic agent, ambassador, spokesman, agent, minister, envoy, emissary, diplomat, diplomatist, legate, consul, chargé d'affaires *(Govt.)*.

PLENITUDE, *n.* Abundance, condition of being full, fullness in quantity, measure *or* degree, completeness, repletion, amplitude, plethora, plenteousness, prolixity, satiety, mine, wealth, galore, exuberance, copiousness, enough, prodigality, enough and to spare, cornucopia, fat of the land, horn of plenty, full measure, overflow, opulence, plentifulness, plenty, completion, affluence, superabundance, lavishness.

PLENTEOUS, PLENTIFUL, *adj.* 1. Existing in great plenty, abundant, bountiful, profuse, copious, ample, lavish, bounteous, teeming, rife, swarming, countless, endless, many, overflowing, plethoric, replete, adequate, abounding, generous, liberal, galore, numerous, inexhaustible, myriad, diffuse, multifold, manifold, considerable, prevalent, rampant, widespread, multiple, multitudinous, innumerable, infinite, prevailing, prodigal, multifarious, affluent, complete, unsparing, unmeasured, unstinted, redundant, sufficient, enough.

2. Yielding abundantly, fruitful, plentiful, exuberant, productive, profitable, luxuriant, bountiful, rich, fertile, profuse, rife, prolific, teeming, bounteous, lavish, resourceful, overflowing.

PLENTY, *n.* 1. Full *or* abundant supply, abundance, great quantity, luxuriance, copiousness, overflow, store, richness, plethora, satiety, full measure, much, wealth, riches, numerousness, plenteousness, prodigality, lavishment, sufficiency, galaxy, bevy, array, legion, redundance, good *or* great deal, considerable *(coll.)*, lot or lots *(coll.)*, ocean *or* oceans, sea, world *or* worlds, volume, pack, mint, nimiety, flood, multitude, hoard, host, good supply, numbers, scores, multiplicity, plenitude, exuberance, fullness, opulence, superfluity, horn of plenty, cornucopia, enough and to spare, profusion, fertility, affluence, fund, luxury.

2. A time of abundance, prosperity, good times, clover, affluence, well-being, comfortable circumstances, ease, luxury, blessing, success, thriving condition, independence, high tide.

PLEONASM, *n.* Use of more words than necessary to express an idea, redundancy, tautology, prolixity, battology, verbiage, superfluity, repetition, ambages, padding, expletive, macrology, digression, periphrasis, reiteration, iteration, wordiness, circumlocution, diffuseness, verbosity, dilogy *(Rhet.).*

PLENOASTIC, *adj.* Redundant, tautological, battological, repetitious, superfluous, circumlocutory, bombastic, fustian, wordy, circuitous, roundabout, ambagious, periphrastic, reiterative, iterative, voluble, inflated, expletive, grandiloquent, flatulent, pompous, swelling, diffuse, verbose, windy.

PLETHORA, *n.* Superabundance, overfullness, superfluity, excess, redundance, exorbitance, nimiety, surplus, overplus, oversupply, overmeasure, repletion, enough and to spare, more than enough, surfeit, glut, overload, overburden, overdose, overflow, deluge, flood, drug on the market, supererogation, premium, bonus, luxury, extravagance, satiety, profusion, prodigality, affluence, lavishment, satiation, opulence, exuberance, supersaturation, congestion, engorgement, surcharge, fatness.

PLETHORIC, *adj.* Inflated, turgid, plump, full, redundant, overrun, distended, dilated, puffy, tumid, bloated, swollen, pregnant, bulging, bulbous, tumorous, gorged, tumescent, saturated, dropsical, satiated, jaded, sated, cloyed, packed, overflowing, stuffed, overcharged, supersaturated, obese, replete, fat, stout, surcharged, fraught *(Poetic), de trop (Fr.),* edematous.

PLEXUS, *n.* Network, webwork, meshwork, reticulation, reticulum, net, mesh, web, screen, lacing, lattice, reticle, interlacing, interweaving, reticule *(Physics),* anastomosis *(Anat.).*

PLIABILITY, PLIANCY, *n.* 1. Ability to be easily bent, flexibility, suppleness, facility, softness, plasticity, tractility, ductility, limberness, extensibility, elasticity, flaccidity, modifiability, mobility.
2. Yieldingness, readiness to be influenced, docility, adaptability, tractability, amenability, submissiveness, susceptibility, persuasibility, persuadability, passiveness, indifference, compliance, gentleness, obedience, sequacity, flexibility, acquiescence, conformability, assent, resignation, respect, bowing, deference, meekness, dutifulness, nonresistance, complaisance, passivity, homage.

PLIABLE, PLIANT, *adj.* 1. Flexible, plastic, flexile, supple, easily bent, extensible, malleable, ductile, tractable, tractile, sequacious, elastic, receptive, responsive, formable, flaccid, bendable, waxy, soft, lithe, limber, yielding, impressible, impressionable.
2. Yielding, adaptable, easily persuaded *or* influenced, manageable, tractable, submissive, obedient, passive, susceptible, willing, flexile, lamblike, sensitive, relaxed, impressionable, impressible, bending, receptive, sequacious, responsive, docile, obsequious, compliant, irresolute, respectful, assenting, conformable, acquiescent, resigned, inclined, accommodating, deferential, dutiful, relenting, nonresisting, meek, unassertive, biddable.

PLICATE, *adj.* Folded like a fan, pleated, puckered, corrugated, doubled, wrinkled, plicated, plicatulate, accordion pleated, pliciform.

PLICATION, PLICATURE, *n.* Folding, fold, gather, double, pucker, cockle, goffer, plait,

ruffle, corrugation, kilting, ruck, fluting, flute, tuck.

PLIERS, *n., pl.* Small pincers with long jaws *(for bending, holding, etc.),* nippers, forceps, pinchers, tweezers, tongs, extractor.

PLIGHT, *n.* Condition *(usually bad),* state, situation, case, predicament, turn, complication, dilemma, scrape, lot, mess, pass, exigency, embarrassment, extremity, crisis, push, pinch, stand, impasse, juncture, conjuncture, circumstance, position, contingency, difficulty, perplexity, shape, pickle *(coll.),* fix *(coll.),* strait *(often pl.),* cul-de-sac, standstill, hornet's nest, nonplus, hole *(coll.),* estate, trouble, kettle of fish, muddle, mishap, quandary.

PLIGHT, *v.* 1. Pledge *(one's troth)* in engagement to marry, vow, betroth, espouse, engage, affiance, affy, promise to marry.
2. Pledge, give in pledge, pawn, hypothecate, put in pledge, risk, swear, covenant, answer for, give as security, promise, give, offer, vouch, avow, certify, guarantee, hazard, wager, jeopard, venture, stake, gamble, engage, become bound to.

PLOD, *v.* 1. Trudge, move laboriously, walk heavily, tramp, lag, travel slowly, lumber, jog on, lump, stump, drag, stamp, peg along, poke along, waddle, flounder, inch, trail, stumble, shuffle, shamble, hobble, clump, barge, drag one's freight *(sl.).*
2. Work with dull perseverance, drudge, toil, moil, work steadily *or* doggedly, peg away *or* along, grind, grub, hammer, drive, stick *or* stay with it, never say die, endure, bear up, continue, not give up, struggle, be steadfast *or* constant, be resolute, ply one's trade, see it through *(coll.),* persevere, hold on, keep on, persist, plug *(coll.).*

PLOP, *n.* Plopping sound *or* fall, plump, blob, thump, bump, slap, drop, light thud.

PLOP, *v.* Fall with little sound *or* splash, thud, plump, tumble, drop, blob, thump, slap, bump.

PLOT, *n.* 1. Secret scheme *(especially for a hostile, unlawful or evil purpose),* conspiracy, stratagem, cabal, ruse, shift, maneuver, machination, intrigue, plan, project, junto, confederacy, party, league, clique, coalition, racket, complot, counterplot, device, collusion, frame-up.
2. Plan *(scheme, main story)* of a piece of literature, story, action, outline, pattern, summary, skeleton, design, abstract, précis.

PLOT, *v.* 1. Plan secretly *(something hostile or evil),* conspire, lay a plan, be in collusion, cooperate, premeditate, scheme, hatch, brew, concoct, organize, complot, cabal, intrigue, counterplot, deal secretly, contrive, machinate, maneuver, prepare, predesign.
2. Mark on a plan, map *or* chart, calculate, measure, represent, block in, draw to scale, compute, determine, chart.
3. Make a plot, plan *or* map of, survey, delineate, diagram, chart, lay out, measure, mark the bounds *or* limits of, represent, make an elevation of, design, depict, draw to scale, pace off.

PLOW, *v.* 1. Turn up *(soil),* work *(with a plow),* harrow, dig, spade, prepare, cleave, dress, furrow, make furrows in, break, ridge, rib, cultivate.
2. Move through anything in the manner of a plow, hack, score, cut, plunge, dive, lunge, drive, push, press, shove, ride roughshod, scratch, furrow, groove, elbow, hurtle, scoop, bulldoze *(sl.).*

PLOWMAN, *n.* Man who plows, plower, husbandman, farm laborer, cultivator, tiller, farmer, son of the soil, peasant, churl, plowboy, rustic, countryman, swain.

PLUCK, *n.* Spirit, courage in the face of difficulties, resolution, determination, manhood, daring, manliness, gameness, doggedness, endurance, resolve, fight, decision, firmness, perseverance, spunk *(coll.),* persistence, stamina, pluckiness, dauntlessness, singleness *or* tenacity of purpose, intransigence, devotion, boldness, stout heart, fortitude, stability, constancy, mettle, nerve, backbone, indomitableness, hardihood, grit, valor, self-reliance.

PLUCK, *v.* 1. Pull quickly, jerk, draw, pick, snatch, twitch, cull, gather, flick, flip, collect, tweak, twang, vellicate, tear, tug, grab, plunk, catch, strum, crop, snag, nip, thrum, cut, yank *(coll.).*
2. Pull the feathers, hair, *etc.,* from, pick, crop, fleece, strip, denude, deplume, displume, sheer.
3. *(With* UP) Uproot, pull up, exterminate, eradicate, demolish, weed out, ruin, tear out, extirpate, blast, scuttle, do *or* make away with, annihilate, abolish, root out, obliterate, wipe out, erase, cancel, nip, fell, raze, level, mow down, overthrow, overturn, strike at the root of, pull up by the roots, put out of existence, deal a death-blow to, put an end to, remove, destroy, sweep away, extinguish, sink, dissolve, dissipate, dispel, prostrate, blow up.
4. *(With* UP) Rouse *(courage, spirit, etc.),* muster, get up, summon, screw up, cheer, reassure, buoy up, embolden, rally, hearten, inspire.

PLUCKY, *adj.* Having *or* showing pluck *or* courage, brave, spirited, stanch, mettlesome, manly, undaunted, gritty, game, bold, stout, hardy, stouthearted, unflinching, resolute, gallant, heroic, strong, courageous, strong-willed, self-possessed, high-mettled, high-spirited, lion-hearted, spunky *(coll.),* intrepid, indomitable, valiant, doughty *(humorous).*

PLUG, *n.* 1. Piece of wood, *etc,* used to stop a hole *or* fill a gap, stopper, stopple, cork, wedge, valve, spill, spile, packing, stuffing, peg, wad, tap, block, obstruction, spigot, bung, dowel, pledget, tampon *(Surg.),* tampion, wadding, dossil *(Surg.),* tent *(Surg.).*
2. Piece of tobacco for chewing, chew, quid, cake, twist, pigtail, cud *(sl.).*

PLUG, *v.* Stop *or* fill with *or* as with a plug, insert *or* drive a plug into, close, occlude, block, dam, cork, bung, stanch, choke off, stuff, cover, shut.

PLUMAGE, *n.* Feathery covering of a bird, feathers, down, mantle, hackle, feathering, plumosity, mirror, mail *(of a hawk),* speculum *(Zool.).*

PLUMB, *adj.* True according to a plumb line, perpendicular, vertical, upright, straight, level, erect, sheer, straight up and down.

PLUMB, *n.* 1. Small piece of lead, plummet, plumb bob, lead, bob, plumb line, sinker, dipsey *(Naut.).* log *(Naut.).*
2. Position of a plumb line when freely suspended, perpendicular, vertical, upright.

PLUMB, *v.* 1. Test *or* adjust by a plumb line, make vertical, erect, level, plumb line, square, true, set, fix, regulate.
2. Sound *(the ocean, etc.),* measure *(depth),* penetrate to the bottom of, fathom, take soundings, plumb line, gauge, probe, heave (cast, sling) the lead.

PLUME, *n.* 1. Feather, plumage, topknot, ai-

grette, pinion, egret, hackle, panache, tuft, crest, quill, remex *(Ornith.),* covert *(Ornith.),* scapular *(Ornith.).*
2. Ornament, token of honor *or* distinction, badge, feather, rosette, star, epaulet, bow, knot, aglet, aiguillette, panache.

PLUME, *v.* *(With* ON *or* UPON) Feel satisfaction with *or* pride in *(oneself),* display, congratulate, boast, pride *(oneself),* be proud, flourish, exult, triumph, delight, brag, vaunt, rejoice, gloat, joy, crow, puff, hug oneself, glory, pat oneself on the back.

PLUMOSE, *adj.* Having feathers *or* plumes, feathery, feathered, plumelike, plumy, plumate, downy, soft, fluffy, furry.

PLUMP, *adj.* 1. Well filled out, rounded in form, somewhat fleshy *or* fat, chubby, rotund, corpulent, full-figured, obese, fleshy, round, buxom, pudgy, rotundate, full, ample, stocky, stubby, squabby, strapping, lusty, podgy, moonfaced, punchy *(coll.),* well-fed, puffy, sleek, portly, stout, fat, pursy, tubby *(coll.),* gibbous, chumpy *(coll.),* bouncing.
2. Direct, downright, blunt, abrupt, forthright, straight, straightforward, undeviating, unswerving.

PLUMP, *adv.* 1. With a heavy *or* sudden fall *or* drop, with sudden encounter, with direct impact, directly, heavily, suddenly, in an instant, abruptly, all at once, at a stroke, at one swoop, smack, ᵖlop, quickly, unexpectedly, plop, slap, plunk, to the mark, in a beeline, in a twinkling.
2. Directly *(as in speaking),* bluntly, straight, abruptly, forthright, straightforward, to the point, point-blank.

PLUMP, *n.* Heavy *or* sudden fall, plop, thump, thud, bump, drop, plunge, dip, dive, swoop, pounce, plunk *(coll.).*

PLUMP, *v.* 1. Fall heavily *or* suddenly and directly, drop, dip, plunge, tumble, swoop, pounce, dive, pitch, plop, spill, sprawl, flop *(coll.),* plunk *(coll.).*
2. Drop *or* throw suddenly *or* heavily, plop, slap, deposit, set down, plank down *(coll.),* plunk *(coll.).*
3. *(Often fol. by* OUT) Utter *or* say bluntly, emit, come out with, rap out, divulge, publish, let fall, pour forth, voice, announce, proclaim, spill, declare, give away, blurt out, speak out.

PLUNDER, *n.* 1. Plundering, spoliation, pillage, rapine, robbery, brigandage, depredation, raid, ravishment, foray, piracy, privateering, buccaneering, larceny, theft, desolation, deprivation, prey, marauding, devastation, harrying, freebooting, sack, pilfering, plunderage.
2. That which is taken in plunder, loot, booty, prey, stolen goods, pilferings, perquisites, prize, gain, spoil *or* spoils, pillage, seizure, take, grab, pickings, steal *(coll.),* swag *(sl.),* haul *(coll.).*

PLUNDER, *v.* Rob of goods *or* valuables, pillage, despoil, foray, fleece, lay waste, strip, sack, forage, spoliate, ravage, raid, ransack, pilfer, pirate, depredate, freeboot, seize, capture, steal from, gut, maraud, loot, desolate, harry, devastate, rifle, buccaneer, privateer, filibuster, prey on *or* upon.

PLUNGE, *n.* Leap, dive, dip, drop, headlong *or* impetuous rush *or* dash, sudden violent pitching movement, immersion, submergence, submersion, burst, engulfment, swoop, pounce, pitch, inundation, dead run, fall, header *(coll.).*

PLUNGE, *v.* 1. Immerse, submerge, thrust, cast

into, bring into *(some condition, situation, etc.),* sink, souse, dip, douse, lead, enmesh, drive, entangle, bury, inundate, involve, submerse, engulf, duck, drown, throw, put under.

2. Cast oneself, fall headlong, pitch, dash, rush, leap, dive, swoop, tumble, sprawl, sink, settle, wallow, welter, jump, descend, pounce, throw oneself, descend abruptly *or* precipitously, flounder, go down, go to the bottom, take a header *(coll.).*

PLURAL, *adj.* Consisting of, containing *or* pertaining to more than one, involving a plurality, upwards of, some, several, many, numerous.

PLURALITY, *n.* More than half of the whole, multitude, majority, greater number than unity, large number, excess, several, superiority of numbers, lion's share, preponderance.

PLUS, *adj.* Involving *or* denoting addition, positive, additional, added, annexed, supplemental, supplementary, extra, further, more, new, other, spare, surplus, auxiliary, additive.

PLUS, *n.* A plus quantity, something additional, surplus, gain, excess, leftover, surplusage, overplus, bonus, premium, survival, carry-over, overage *(Com.).*

PLUS, *prep.* More by the addition of, increased by, with the addition of, with, in addition, including, inclusive of, together with, and, also, added *or* linked to, coupled with, in conjunction with, with the increment of, as well as.

PLUTOCRAT, *n.* Rich man, man of great wealth (means, substance), capitalist, millionaire, billionaire, moneybags, nabob, richling, Croesus, Midas, Dives, Plutus *(Gk. Myth.),* silk-stocking.

PLUTONIAN, PLUTONIC *(Cap. or l. c.), adj.* Of *or* pertaining to Pluto, infernal, hellish, satanic, Tartarean, dark, stygian, Hadean, demoniac, fiendish, devilish, chthonian *(chiefly Gk. Myth.).*

PLUVIAL, PLUVIOUS, *adj.* Of *or* pertaining to rain, showery, rainy, drizzly, damp, wet, moist, misty, humid, vaporous.

PLY, *n.* 1. Fold, thickness, unit *(of yarn),* lamina, lamella, leaf, sheet, plate, sheath, foil, cut, slice, panel, wafer, scale, flake, pleat, stratum, layer, twist, plait.

2. Bent, inclination, bias, proclivity, predilection, grain, humor, disposition, proneness, propensity, direction, turn, aptitude, warp, leaning, tenor, set, vein, cast, drift, trend, twist, penchant, partiality, prejudice, prepossession, readiness, predisposition, tendency.

PLY, *v.* 1. Employ busily, utilize, use, make use of, apply, work at *or* with, wield, manipulate, exploit, press *or* enlist into service, handle, bend, put to use.

2. Carry on, pursue, practice, exercise, devote oneself to, exert oneself in, set to, buckle to, fall to, lay one's hand to, bend one's efforts to, prosecute, follow, undertake, persist, persevere at, hold to, be about, follow, lay *or* put one's shoulder to the wheel, put one's hand to the plow, occupy oneself with, labor, drive, attend to, busy oneself with, engage in, be absorbed in.

3. Treat with something repeatedly applied, provide, furnish, supply, feed, stuff, surfeit, glut, load, heap, stock, store, replenish, arm, equip, fit out, thrust, pour, fund, shower, lavish, sustain, nurture, nourish, provision.

4. Assail briskly *or* persistently, besiege, press hard, beset, overwhelm, tax, flog, thrash, scourge, lace, whip, beat, batter, storm, bombard, pommel, attack, drive, give no escape, beleaguer, bastinado, lash, box, hit, strike, smite, flagellate, flail, buffet, spank, baste, trounce, drub, rack, torture, torment.

5. Supply with something pressingly offered, offer repeatedly, present urgently, insist, force, compel, advance, induce, persuade, press upon, urge upon, take no denial, move, coax, prevail upon, coerce, beset, tax, dun, constrain, besiege, importune, thrust upon.

6. Address persistently *or* importunately, solicit, urge, coax, wheedle, entreat, supplicate, beg, clamor, cry, sue, appeal, invoke, implore, importune, beseech, plead, press, tax, dun, court, cajole, obsecrate, adjure, imprecate, impetrate.

7. Traverse on regular trips, travel regularly, pursue *or* direct the course, sail, navigate, run, beat, pass, go back and forth.

PNEUMATIC, *adj.* Of *or* pertaining to air *or* other gasses, operated by air, containing air, aeriform, ethereal, ethereous, filled with compressed air, pressure, aerostatic, airy, aerodynamic, aeromechanic, aerographic, aerial, aeriferous, atmospheric.

POACH, *v.* 1. Take game *or* fish illegally, steal, filch, thieve, purloin, pilfer, pirate, abstract, snare, smuggle, plunder, lift *(coll.),* pinch *(sl.),* mooch *(sl.),* hunt *or* fish out of season.

2. Become broken up *or* slushy *(of land),* trample, mix with water and reduce to uniform consistency, crush, squash, amalgamate, macerate, glutinize, chew, beat up, churn, emulsify, alloy, blend, stir, mash, pulp, fuse, knead, levigate, grind, pound, commix, immix, mingle, viscidize, masticate.

POCK, *n.* Mark, spot, pustule, scar, mole, blemish, fleck, speck, blister, patch, maculation, macula, scab, freckle, disfigurement, defacement, pockmark, flyspeck.

POCKET, *adj.* Suitable for carrying in the pocket, portable, miniature, bantam, compact, diminutive, compendious.

POCKET, *n.* 1. Pouch, cavity, receptacle, hollow, bag, bin, sac, sack, fob, burse, cul-de-sac, vesicle, cyst, bladder, pocketbook, bursa *(Anat., Zool.),* sabretache, placket, purse.

2. Money, means, financial resources, pocketbook, funds, treasury, finances, moneys, revenue, income, assets, excheqer, substance, stock, capital, riches, wealth, treasure, purse, budget.

3. Cavity in the earth *(esp. one containing ore),* small ore body, isolated mass of ore, pit, hole, streak, strain, strip, vein, lode.

POCKET, *v.* 1. Put into one's pocket, take possession of *(often dishonestly),* gain, obtain, come by, be in receipt of, receive, take in, usurp, appropriate, assume, arrogate, steal, lift *(coll.),* help oneself to.

2. Submit to without protest *or* open resentment, yield to, endure, bear, put up with, tolerate, defer to, comply with, sustain, support, accede to, acquiesce, suffer, resign oneself to, bow before *or* under, be subject to, stoop, bend, swallow, stomach, take, abide, brook, brave, make the best of, stand, make light of, grin and bear it, submit with a good grace, shrug the shoulders, forgive, ignore, turn the other cheek, condone, let pass, disregard, pass over, overlook, dismiss from one's thoughts, regard with indulgence.

3. Conceal, suppress, cover, swallow, hide, seal up, lock up, bottle up, bury, prevent from showing, disguise, withhold, keep to oneself, re-

serve, stifle, smother, muffle, keep back, not speak of, shroud, screen, cloak, veil, mask, dissemble, camouflage, put *or* keep out of sight.

POCKETBOOK, *n.* 1. Small bag *or* case, purse, wallet, pocket, moneybag, satchel, handbag, bag, porte-monnaie *(Fr.).*

2. Financial resources, *etc.* (See POCKET, *n.,* 2, *above.)*

POCKETKNIFE, *n.* Jackknife, clasp knife, blade, folding knife, penknife.

POCOCURANTE, *adj.* Caring little, indifferent, nonchalant, half-hearted, lethargic, languid, lukewarm, cold, cool, heartless, phlegmatic, heedless, careless, neutral, unfeeling, insensible, passive, passionless, apathetic, unstirred, perfunctory, uninterested, unconcerned, unsolicitous, unmoved, incurious, inappetent, disregarding, impassive, dispassionate, stolid, impartial, blasé, insouciant, untouched, unmindful, unaffected, spiritless, bloodless, unresponsive, sluggish, unkindled, supercilious, soulless, impervious, hardened, indurated.

POCOCURANTE, *n.* Careless *or* indifferent person, man of iron, stoic, Indian, Spartan.

POD, *n.* Dehiscent fruit, seed vessel, legume, capsule, jacket, husk, bur, silique, shuck, hull, boll, pericarp, shell, testa, follicle, theca, cocoon.

POEM, *n.* Verse composition, rhyme, song, lay, verselet, rhapsody, idyl, epic, bucolic, georgic, rondeau, eclogue, limerick, Anacreontic, dithyramb, lyric, sonnet, rondel, ode, palinode, epode, pastoral, elegy, macaronics, jingle *(derog.),* doggerel *(derog.).*

POET, *n.* Poetess *(fem.),* versifier, musician, versemaker, scop *(Hist.),* scald *(Hist.),* lyricist, bard, muse, imagist, symbolist, rhymer, dithyrambic, vers librist, poetaster *(derog.),* laureate, sonneteer, idylist, rhapsodist, elegiast, bucoliast.

POETIC, *adj.* Rhythmic, metrical, lyrical, rhapsodical, idyllic, tuneful, musical.

POETIZE, *v.* Write poetry, verse, *etc.,* compose, create, shape, indite, fashion, poeticize, rhyme, versify, sing.

POETRY, *n.* Metrical composition, rhyme, verse, versification, meter, song, poetization, numbers, poesy *(Poetic.),* poetcraft, versecraft, doggerel *(derog.).*

POGROM, *n.* Slaughter *(of innocent people),* massacre, mass murder, internecion, blood bath, mass homicide, carnage, wholesale killing, butchery, trucidation, effusion of blood, saturnalia of blood, slaying.

POIGNANCY, *n.* 1. Sharpness, pungency, causticity, fierceness, acuteness, intensity, severity, incisiveness, acidity, piquancy, trenchancy, acrimony, acridity, tartness, acetosity, astringency.

2. Quality *or* power of evoking sadness, sadness, agony, anguish, grief, emotion, woe, affliction, pathos, pitiableness, tenderness, misery, affection, feeling, sentimentality, sentiment.

POIGNANT, *adj.* 1. Pungent, pricking, acrid, sharp, sour, bitter, biting, stinging, tangy, caustic, acute, mordant, burning, tart, keen, hot.

2. Moving, touching, emotional, mournful, to be pitied, sorrowful, exciting compassion, pitiable, deplorable, grievous, woeful, lamentable, pitiful, piteous, dolorous, sad, plaintive, distressing, affecting, tender, rueful, melting, heart-rending, affective, doleful.

POINT, *n.* 1. Sharp extremity of an object, tapered end, tip, spit, prong, tooth, cap, vertex, spike, angle, head, capstone, apex, end, cusp, crown, peak, top, crest, pinnacle, nib.

2. Promontory of land, cape, foreland, bluff, tongue, reach, projection, spur, peninsula, breakwater, naze, ness, headland, isthmus, bill, strip, head, palisade, spit, reef, escarpment, eminence, chersonese.

3. Item, particular, detail, consideration, feature, issue.

4. Unit of scoring, *etc.,* mark, score, credit, notch.

5. Minute spot, period, dot, round mark, speck, point, particle, mite, mote, jot, iota, dab, tittle, atom, pinprick.

6. Feature, central idea, essential matter, essential, main thing, sum and substance, gravamen, substance, gist, kernel, keynote, heart, focus, marrow, core, essence, quiddity, quid.

7. Condition attained, step, stage, place, degree, position, mark, limit.

8. Thing *or* person to which attention *or* action is directed, mark, butt, target, spectacle, cynosure, sight, recipient, testee, victim, subject, fair game, gazing stock, dupe, monkey, object, joke, game, prey, quarry, bull's-eye, quintain *(Mediev.).*

9. End towards which effort is directed, motive, desire, objective, reason, jist, cause, substance, essence, design, use, ambition, marrow, meat, pith, object, aim, intent, intention, view, project, proposal, prospect, purpose, drift, goal, final cause, significance, heart, core, meaningfulness, plan, eye, purport, import, connotation, denotation, implication, will, scheme, resolution, spirit, tenor, bearing, force, effect, ground, occasion, mainspring, keystone, principle, root, prime mover, thing wanted, desideration.

POINT, *v.* 1. Indicate position *or* direction, direct attention, take aim, bend, turn, level, direct, aim.

2. Direct the mind *or* thought, be indicative of, suggest, allude, lead one to believe, think, *etc.,* indicate, designate, account for, betoken, refer, attribute, assign, ascribe, fix, trace, promise, imply, forebode, foretoken, foreshadow, foreshow, augur, signify, stand fair, divine, predict, portend, give probability to, put *or* set down to, lay down to, bode, presage, omen, bid fair, threaten, attest, bespeak, argue, testify, breathe, intimate, preindicate, presignify, connote, denote, mean, prove, evince, declare, manifest, demonstrate.

3. *(With* OUT) Indicate the presence *or* position of, call *or* direct attention to, bring under *or* to one's notice, inform of, specify, signify, designate, divulge, mark, note, show, notify, let one know, make manifest, mention, display, demonstrate, make plain, earmark, speak of, disclose, set forth, reveal, explain, report, make known.

4. Face, gravitate, verge, tend, lean, incline, dip, tip, trend, bend, be attracted, lead, head, front, go toward, be directed toward.

5. Furnish with a point, edge, sharpen, make pointed, acuminate, cuspidate, whet, strop, file, grind, taper, barb, set, spiculate.

POINT-BLANK, *adj.* Aimed *or* fired straight at the mark, direct, true, right, unbending, undeviating, unswerving, unavoidable, undisguised, tactless, straightforward, open, frank, abrupt, candid, forthright, outspoken, blunt, downright, plain, explicit, obvious, artless.

POINT-BLANK, *adv.* With a direct aim, directly, straight, straight as an arrow, at close range, direct, in a beeline, plainly, in plain words, to the point.

POINTED, *adj.* 1. Having a point *or* points, peaked, sharp, edged, keen, jagged, serrate, notched, spiculate, fine, tapering, conical, xiphoid, bearded, cusped, piked, spear-shaped, sagittate, setaceous, echinate, subulate, cuspidate, angular, acuminate *(Biol.),* acicular *(Biol.),* aciculate *(Biol.),* ensate *(Biol.),* ensiform *(Biol.),* mucronate *or* mucronated *(Bot.),* gladiate *(Bot.),* hastate *(Bot.).*

2. Sharp, piercing, having point *or* force, marked, emphasized, emphatic, pungent, poignant, keen, epigrammatic, acute, spicy, clear, curt, curtate, round, broad, flat, piquant, full of point, telling, effective, witty, vigorous, pregnant, crisp, succinct, trenchant, laconic, pithy, barbed, severe, penetrating, attic, neat, condensed, sententious, compact, elliptic, incisive, to the point, summary, direct, concise.

3. Directed particularly *(as at a person),* personal, marked, barbed, explicit, aimed, leveled, intended, salient, striking, prominent, bold, flagrant, arrant, glaring, in strong *or* high relief, noticeable, conspicuous, pertinent, distinct.

POINTER, *n.* One who *or* that which points (sharpens, points out, indicates, directs *or* aims), index, director, guide, indicator, polestar, lodestar, finger, hand, tip, blaze, needle, compass, landmark, cynosure, tongue, arm.

POINTLESS, *adj.* 1. Without a point, dull, blunt, unsharpened, unedged, rounded, worn down, obtuse, unpointed, bluff *(Naut.).*

2. Without force, meaning *or* relevance, devoid of interest, dull, vapid, aimless, flat, arid, insipid, dry, jejune, dreary, prosy, prosaic, wearisome, stale, slow, bald, wishy-washy, vague, stupid, inept, uninteresting, driftless, incongruous, unreasonable, illogical, immaterial, insignificant, invalid, irrational, unentertaining, inappropriate, beside the mark (point, purpose, question), inconsequent, inapplicable, irrelevant, purposeless, inapposite, impertinent, haphazard, ridiculous, groundless, unconnected, tasteless, inconsequential.

POISE, *n.* 1. Balance *(as from equality or equal distribution of weight),* equilibrium, equipoise, evenness, levelness, equivalence, par, parity, parallelism, correspondence, equipollence, symmetry, steadiness, equalization, equiponderance.

2. Self-possession, stability, composure, sanity, balance, equanimity, steadiness, calm, coolness, patience, self-restraint, self-control, self-command, presence of mind, inexcitability, mental calmness, assurance, aplomb, reason, perspective, prudence, common sense, discretion, rationality, dispassion, level-headedness, judgment, sense, ballast, sobriety, sophistication, *savoir-vivre (Fr.),* *sang-froid (Fr.).*

3. Suspense, indecision, irresolution, incertitude, uncertainty, doubt, indetermination, infirmity of purpose, fearfulness, misgiving, demur, vacillation, fluctuation, hesitation, hesitancy, wavering, unsettlement, precariousness, variability, alternation, pendulation, oscillation.

4. The way of being poised, held *or* carried, set, position, carriage, balance, state *or* position of hovering, bearing, port, situation, aspect, posture, pose, attitude, *tournure (Fr.).*

POISE, *v.* 1. Balance evenly, adjust, hold *or* carry in equilibrium, hold supported *or* raised

(ready to be cast, used, etc.), render equal, level, strike a balance, trim, weigh, equalize, equate, square, symmetrize, suspend, aim, hold aloft, elevate, raise.

2. Be balanced, rest in equilibrium, hang supported *or* suspended, hover, strike a balance, float, parallel, wait, crouch, be ready.

POISON, *n.* Substance which destroys life *or* impairs health, venom, pestilence, taint, bane, virus, noxious influence, contagion, toxin, virulence, pollution, miasma, plague, septicity, infection, harmful drug, toxicant, malignity, malignancy, contamination, corruption.

POISON, *v.* 1. Administer poison to, kill *or* injure with poison, disease, infect, contaminate, adulterate, taint, corrupt, canker, envenom, intoxicate, pollute, venenate, vitriolize.

2. Ruin, corrupt, embitter, infect, impair, mar, stain, vitiate, pollute, taint, deprave, inquinate, degrade, defile, canker, ulcerate, empoison, demoralize, eat away at, corrode, disease, debase, envenom, contaminate.

POISONOUS, *adj.* Full of *or* containing poison, having the properties *or* effects of a poison, venomous, baneful, pestilential, noxious, destructive, morbid, fatal, infective, noisome, leprous, contagious, malignant, lethal, viperous, toxic, mortal, deadly, putrefactive, virulent, contaminative, mephitic, septic, virose, morbific, pernicious, venenate, venenose, dangerous, unhealthy, bad, vicious, deleterious, pestilent.

POKE, *n.* Thrust, push, jab, nudge, shove, punch, thump, butt, jostle, jolt, dig, jog.

POKE, *v.* 1. Push, thrust against *or* into, drive, force, impel, butt, bunt, goad, jolt, shoulder, elbow, jostle, jog, gore, bore, jab, prod, nudge, punch, pole, dig, stab, stir up.

2. Direct *(fun)* at a person *or* thing, jeer, ridicule, flout, scoff at, sneer at, make a butt of, jape, twit, gibe, jest, hoot, grin at, banter, fleer, tease, haze, make a goat of *(sl.),* make a fool of, rag *(sl.),* laugh at, mock, taunt, deride, make game *or* sport of, rally, chaff, snicker, smile at, satire, caricature, lampoon, travesty, parody, burlesque, make merry with, fool, roast *(sl.),* guy *(sl.),* jolly *(coll.),* rail at.

3. Thrust obstrusively, intrude, search curiously, pry, worm in, push, press, snoop, nose, peer, interpose, insinuate, trespass, interfere, obtrude, meddle, busybody, concern oneself, officiously, butt in *(coll.),* mind other's business, horn in *(sl.).*

4. *(Fol. by* OUT) Thrust itself, excurve, protuberate, protrude, project, stand, bag, belly, bulge, bilge, jut, stick.

5. Go *or* proceed in a slow *or* aimless way, linger, idle, dawdle, delay, trifle, lag, drag, trail, potter, inch, stroll, saunter, slouch, shuffle, hobble, falter, dally, drift, dillydally, flag, limp, hang back, mince, shamble, mosey *(sl.),* loiter.

POLAR, *adj.* 1. Opposite in character *or* action, diametrically opposed, extreme, antithetic, counter, antipodal, contrasted, contrary, converse, reverse, inverse, antagonistic, repugnant, hostile, different, negative, at cross purposes, clashing, opposing, contradictory, conflicting, inimical, inconsistent.

2. Central, middlemost, midmost, pivotal, focal, medial, mesial, axial, nuclear, convergent.

POLARITY, *n.* Possession *or* exhibition of two opposite *or* contrasted principles *or* tendencies, duality, duplexity, dualism, counteraction, contraposition, antagonism, collision, conflict, opposition, contrariety, antipathy, biformity, repugnance, duplicity, contradiction.

POLE, *n.* Long slender piece of wood *or* other material, staff, rod, post, mast, shaft, thill, tongue, beam, bar, crosier, standard, upright, leg, stave, alpenstock, stick, cane, crook, sprit *(Naut.),* boom *(Naut.),* light spar *(Naut.),* reach.

POLEMIC, POLEMICAL, *adj.* Of *or* pertaining to disputation *or* controversy, argumentative, disputative, controversial, logomachic, eristic, dialectic, pilpulistic, litigious, discursive, contentious, disputatious.

POLEMICS, *n., sl.* Art *or* practice of disputation, controversy *(esp. on theological subjects),* controversial argument, debate, argumentation, dispute, argument, logomachy, litigation, disceptation, pilpul, contention, war of words, passage of words, wrangling, tonguefence, verbal engagement *or* contest.

POLEMIST, *n.* Controversialist *(esp. in theology),* one who argues in opposition to another, polemicist, polemic, mooter, reasoner, ratiocinator, logician, arguer, debater, wrangler, desceptator, disputant, logomachist, pilpulist, controverter, dialectician, tonguefencer.

POLESTAR, *n.* 1. North Star, polar star, Polaris, lodestar, loadstar.
2. Guide, cynosure, guiding star, guiding principle, ideal, lodestar, loadstar, rule, tenet, law, pilot, pointer, precept, sign, axiom, maxim, dictate, blaze, signpost, guidepost, light, signal, beacon, criterion, standard, governing principle.

POLICE, *v.* Regulate, control, keep in order, guard, keep watch, patrol, secure, protect, be on guard, be vigilant, go on one's beat, render safe, safeguard.

POLICEMAN, *n.* Member of a body *or* force of police, constable, gendarme, patrolman, officer, sheriff, bluecoat, sleuthhound, marshal, arm of the law, law enforcement agent, inspector, detective, commissioner, roundsman, sergeant, cop *(coll.),* dick *(sl.),* beagle *(fig.),* flatfoot *(sl.),* gumshoe *(sl.),* constabulary *(pl.).*

POLICY, *n.* 1. Course *or* line of action, mode of management, strategy, rule, platform, behavior, tactics, path, program, schedule, protocol, scheme, custom, organization, manner, means, ways and means, line of conduct, system, rule of action, procedure, principle, game, polity, design, project, habit, way, plan, role.
2. Prudence, practical wisdom, expediency, shrewdness, discretion, skill, cunning, acumen, sagacity, wile, maneuver, astuteness, stratagem, device, game, artifice, subterfuge, evasion, sageness, address, art, forethought, sharpness of wit *or* intelligence, perception, clear thinking, percipience, perspicacity, cleverness, keeness, quickness, acuteness, discernment, caution, care, blind, ruse, feint, juggle, dodge, trick, machination, circumspection, calculation, vigilance, heed, carefulness, precaution.

POLISH, *n.* 1. Substance used to give smoothness *or* gloss, wax, oil, rouge, abrasive, cleanser, lotion, rosin.
2. State of being polished, luster, brightness, smoothness, glaze, shine, sleekness, glint, shimmer, finish, gloss, sheen, splendor, brilliance, brilliancy, radiance, lubricity, slipperiness, burnish.

3. Refinement, elegance, smoothness, superior finish, culture, cultivation, grace, accomplishment, taste, good breeding, classicism, gentility, politeness, nobility, courtesy, propriety, finish, delicacy, distinction, gloss, tact, finesse, veneer, suavity, urbanity, good manners, Atticism, fine feeling, fastidiousness, *savoir-faire* (Fr.).

POLISH, *v.* 1. Make smooth *(esp. by friction),* make glossy, furbish, burnish, scour, wax, slick, rouge, varnish, add luster to, luster, sleek, abrade, emery, sand, rosin, make glisten, brighten, gloss, buff, smooth, shine, rub up, glaze, file, pumice, planish.
2. Render finished, refined *or* elegant, civilize, refine, rub off the corners *or* rough edges, groom, perfect, improve one's manners, humanize, cultivate, better, lift, meliorate, promote, advance, render civil, forward.

POLISHED, *adj.* 1. Smooth, glossy, lustrous, burnished, made bright *or* glossy, oily, glacé, shined, sheeny, slippery, glassy, slick, sleek, finished, glistening, shiny, bright, shining.
2. Refined, cultured, elegant, cultivated, polite, gentle, tasteful, proper, correct, civil, civilized, mannerly, courteous, well-spoken, finished, educated, fine, urbane, genteel, accomplished, courtly, well-bred, well-behaved, social, lettered, graceful, erudite.
3. Flawless, perfect, pure, classic, refined, chaste, Attic, aesthetic, classical, concinnate, excellent, academic, faultless, supreme, peerless, matchless, superlative, transcendent, exquisite, unblemished, unmarred, impeccable, consummate.

POLITE, *adj.* 1. Showing good manners toward others, genteel, suave, civil, courteous, agreeable, ingratiating, social, sociable, gallant, gentlemanly, gentle, well-behaved, well-mannered, well-bred, mannerly, obliging, attentive, respectful, gracious, urbane, courtly, complaisant, polished, refined, civilized, gently bred, tactful, ceremonious, cordial, unctuous, ladylike, affable, chivalrous, cultivated, genial, amiable.
2. Refined, cultured, urbane, gentle, social, polished, received, approved, decorous, established, proper, chic, modish, stylish, ceremonious, patrician, admitted, recognized, fashionable, civilized, delicate, elegant, genteel.

POLITIC, *adj.* 1. Characterized by *or* in keeping with policy, prudent, wise, sagacious, wary, cautious, subtle, safe, sage, sapient, knowing, reasonable, rational, sensible, sound, judicious, discreet, long-headed, provident, astute, sharp, acute, thoughtful, perspicacious, hard-headed, clear-headed, gingerly, watchful, prudential, informed, enlightened, argute, shrewd, keen, level-headed, cool-headed, clever, discerning, percipient, perceptive, diplomatic, careful, on guard, precautious, cagey *(coll.),* chary, vigilant, sober, reflecting, calculating, long-sighted, circumspect, discriminating, expedient, guarded.
2. Artful, shrewd, sly, cunning, contriving, conniving, clever, evasive, deceptive, designing, tricky, rascally, treacherous, temporizing, scheming, underhand, stealthy, shifty, insidious, slippery, slick *(sl.),* foxy, subtle, timeserving, intriguing, expedient, Machiavellian, unscrupulous, crafty.
3. In keeping with policy, well-devised, well-adapted, expedient, judicious, advantageous, convenient, advisable, seemly, commendable, meet, fit, fitting, appropriate, acceptable, sortable, suitable, seasonable, opportune, profitable, decorous,

worth-while, wise, practical, ethical, strategic, diplomatic, practicable, timely.

POLITICAL, *adj.* Of *or* pertaining to politics, a political party, the state *or* the government, civil, civic, public, politic, temporal, secular, party, partisan, state, government, governmental, national.

POLITICIAN, *n.* One active in party politics, one who holds political office, statesman, one skilled in political government *or* administration, legislator, politico, lawgiver, officer of state, public servant, boss, congressman, wirepuller, strategist, king maker, power behind the throne, statist, state monger, partisan.

POLITICS, *n.* Political science, political economy, science *or* art of government, political affairs, political methods *or* maneuvers, party leadership, public service, statesmanship, manipulation, Machiavellianism.

POLITY, *n.* Form of government, state, nation, commonwealth, country, republic, land, realm, body politic.

POLL, *n.* 1. Enumeration, demography, evaluation, nose count, count, tally, tabulation, statistics, figures, statement, census returns, listing.

2. Upper *or* anterior part of human body, head, cephalon, skull, sensorium *(Physiol. and Psychol.),* sensory *(Physiol. and Psychol.),* sconce *(coll.),* pate, brain, nob *(sl.),* noodle *(sl.),* bean *(sl.),* upper story *(sl.),* noddle *(joc.),* cap, costard *(contempt. or humor.),* mazard.

POLL, *v.* 1. Count, tabulate, register, enumerate, count noses, compute, sum up, total.

2. Solicit votes, bespeak, canvass, electioneer, ballot, request, elicit votes, endeavor to obtain, press, urge, petition, appeal for, sue for, entreat.

3. Vote, ballot, cast a vote, vote by ballot, show hands.

4. Shear, cut off, lop off, clip, pollard, prune, bob, crop, pare, trim, mow, dock, fleece, snip.

5. Record a name, register, list, enlist, catalogue, impanel, affix, assign, mark, sign up, enroll, engross, enter, inscribe.

POLLINATE, *v.* *(Bot.)* Pollinize, cross-fertilize, pollen, fertilize with pollen, cross-pollinate.

POLLUTE, *v.* Render filthy, defile, contaminate, desecrate, profane, vitiate, befoul, corrupt, soil, poison, adulterate, taint, canker, infect, dirty, sully, maculate.

POLTROON, *n.* Coward, craven, sneak, recreant, dastard, deserter, scaramouch, apostate, betrayer, snake in the grass, skulk, mean wretch, caitiff *(Poetic),* shirker, white feather, white liver, bolter, Judas, turncoat, traitor, weakling, renegade, malingerer, dodger, jellyfish, milksop, mollycoddle, sissy *(coll.),* quitter *(coll.),* funk *(coll.),* funker *(coll.),* welsher *(sl.),* doormat, namby-pamby, piker *(sl.).*

POLTROONERY, *n.* Cowardice, baseness, cowardliness, dastardliness, sneakiness, shirking, pusillanimity, timidity, meanness, desertion, betrayal, treachery, faint heart, abject fear, white feather, white liver, funk *(coll.),* yellow streak *(sl.).*

POLYCHROMATIC, *adj.* Having many colors, exhibiting a variety of colors, variegated, polychrome, nacreous, opalescent, many-colored, divers-colored, versicolor, colorful, iridescent, shot, prismatic, diversified, pavonine, kaleidoscopic, parti-colored, multicolored, decorated *or* executed in many colors.

POLYCHROMY, *n.* Polychromatic coloring, decoration *or* execution in many colors, variegation, play of colors, rainbow, motley, multicolor, parti-color, iridescence, spectrum, Joseph's coat, kaleidoscope.

POLYGAMY, *n.* Practice *or* condition of having many *or* several spouses at one time, plurality of wives *or* husbands, polyandry, polygyny, trigamy, bigamy.

POLYGLOT, *adj.* Knowing many *or* several languages *(as a person),* containing (made up of, in) many languages, languaged, bilingual, hexaglot, diglot, diglottic, polyglottal, polyglottic, polyglottous, polylingual, learned in languages.

POLYGLOT, *n.* 1. Mixture *or* confusion of languages, babel, gibberish, uproar, racket, discord, babble, hubbub, pandemonium, confusion worse confounded, Dutch concert, cat's concert.

2. Person who is master of a number of languages, linguist, polyglottist.

3. Book *or* writing *(esp. a Bible)* containing the same text in several languages, diglot, hexaglot, parallel edition.

POLYMORPHISM, *n.* State *or* condition of assuming *or* passing through many *or* various forms, multiformity, variability, changefulness, changeableness, mutability, metamorphosis.

POLYMORPHOUS, *adj.* Having, assuming *or* passing through many *or* various forms, stages, *etc.,* multiform, changeful, changeable, protean, proteiform, mutable, variable, polymorphic, metamorphic, multiphase.

POLYPHONIC, *adj.* Consisting of many voices *or* sounds, contrapuntal, with independent but harmonizing parts, orchestral, choral, harmonious, part *(Music).*

POLYTECHNIC, *n.* School in which instruction in various technical subjects is given, vocational school, polytechnic institute, technological school *or* institute, occupational *or* trade school.

POLYTHEISM, *n.* Doctrine *or* belief in many gods *or* more gods than one, henotheism, tritheism, ditheism.

POMACE, *n.* Pulpy residue *(as from crushed fruit),* refuse, pulp, mash, mush, squash, paste, dregs, sediment, waste.

POMADE, *n.* Scented ointment *(used for scalp and hair),* fragrant oil, balm, salve, pomatum.

POMADE, *v.* Dress with pomade, anoint, grease, oil, scent.

POMMEL, *n.* Knob *(as on the hilt of a sword),* ball, protuberant part *(at front and top of a saddle),* horn, handle.

POMMEL, *v.* Strike, beat, whip, bruise, flog, thump, pound, drub, trounce, belabor, thwack, bang, thrash, maul, club, cudgel, cuff, baste, lambaste *(sl.),* buffet, thresh, scourge, bastinado, flagellate, lace *(coll.),* wipe *(sl.),* wallop *(coll.),* box, beat up *(sl.),* lay on, lash, strap, fustigate, belt *(coll.).*

POMP, *n.* 1. Stately *or* splendid display, splendor, magnificence, state, solemnity, grandeur, grandiosity, array, brilliance, ceremony, gorgeousness, glory, heraldry, style, flourish, pageant, pageantry, display, show, parade.

2. Ostentatious *or* vain display *(esp. of dignity or importance),* vanity, pretension, pretentiousness, boasting, inflation, affectation, pompousness, mere show, front *(coll.),* ostentation, vainglory,

pride, fanfaronade, foppery, dandyism, bravado, veneer, gloss, swaggering, self-advertising, attitudinizing, peacockery, splash, splurge, glitter, bluster, grandiosity, coxcombery, orotundity, airs, self-applause, gaudery, strutting, arrogance, pose, the dog (coll.).

POMPON, n. Ornamental tuft or ball (of feathers, wool, etc.), topknot, plume, knob, crest, rosette, cockade, tassel.

POMPOSITY, n. 1. Quality of being pompous, pompous parade of dignity or importance, boastfulness, pomp, pompousness, pretension, pretentiousness, inflation, affectation, vanity, ostentation, vainglory, pride, fanfaronade, foppery, dandyism, bravado, swaggering, attitudinizing, peacockery, bluster, grandiosity, coxcombery, orotundity, airs, strutting, arrogance, posing, self-applause.

2. Ostentatious loftiness of language or style, bombast, tumidity, affectation, magniloquence, altiloquence, turgidity, rodomontade, pretension, inflation, rant, fustian, orotundity.

POMPOUS, adj. 1. Characterized by an ostentatious parade of dignity or importance, ostentatious, showy, self-important, vainglorious, arrogant, haughty, proud, flashy, vain, swaggering, blustering, affected, conceited, consequential, gaudy, theatrical, mannered, artificial, unnatural, overacted, overdone, flaunting, glittering, swank (sl.), swanky (sl.), grandiose, dandified, foppish, coxcombical, insincere, egotistic, specious, pretentious, patronizing, garish, stagey, imperious, overweening, overbearing, toplofty (coll.), uppish (coll.), magisterial, lordly, stilted, stiff-necked, high and mighty, contemptuous, snobbish, presumptuous, high-handed, disdainful, supercilious, high-hat (sl.).

2. (Of language, style, etc.) Ostentatiously lofty, swelling, inflated, bombastic, altisonant, specious, blustering, fustian, orotund, flatulent, stilted, sententious, showy, theatrical, affected, pedantic, declamatory, high-sounding, high-flown, ostentatious, turgid, pretentious, grandiloquent, puffy, flaunting, grandisonant, rhetorical, sonorous, lexiphanic, tumid, grandiose.

3. Characterized by pomp, stately splendor or magnificence, stately, dignified, princely, grand, majestic, glorious, magnificent, superb, splendid, august, gorgeous, sumptuous, spectacular, lofty, lordly, impressive, imposing, radiant, brilliant, sublime, eminent, lustrous, noble, exalted, magisterial, ceremonial, illustrious, worshipful.

POND, n. Body of water smaller than a lake, lagoon, lakelet, water hole, pool, aquarium, plash, reservoir, cistern, tarn (Lit.).

PONDER, v. 1. Consider deeply, brood, meditate, cogitate, reflect, muse, study, excogitate, cerebrate, intellectualize, dream, reason, rationalize, contemplate, speculate, ruminate, wonder, deliberate, chew the cud (coll.), rack or ransack the brains, beat or cudgel the brains, commune with oneself, put on one's thinking cap.

2. Consider carefully, weigh carefully in the mind, brood over, muse, study, revolve in the mind, deliberate upon, consider, value, con over, review, sleep upon, digest, reflect upon, think on or over, meditate upon, view from all sides, mull over (coll.), entertain an idea of, concentrate upon, discuss, wonder about, trouble one's head about, give thought to, put one's mind to, apply the mind to, occupy the mind or thoughts with, examine.

PONDERABLE, adj. Capable of being weighed, having appreciable weight, heavy, substantial, palpable, sensible, corporeal, physical, bodily, fleshly, real, embodied, incarnate, tangible, material, considerable.

PONDEROUS, adj. 1. Of great weight, ponderable, gross, heavy, massive, weighty, bulky, enormous, massy, onerous, oppressive, burdensome, hefty (coll.), elephantine, big, large, portly, unwieldy, substantial.

2. Without graceful lightness or ease, dull, bulky, lumpish, clumsy, hulking, lubberly, unlively, cumbersome, cumbrous, inert, labored, unwieldy, lugubrious, lumbering, slow-moving, repetitious, fatiguing, prolix, burdensome, corpulent, graceless, ungraceful, cramped, dry, halting, stiff, forced, heavy, gross, awkward, hippopotamic, arid, dreary, monotonous, wearying, wearisome, drearisome, boring, prosaic, droning, tedious, long-winded, corpulent, sluggish, lifeless, leaden, snail-like, lusterless, exanimate, stolid, bovine, supine, lymphatic, otiose.

PONIARD, n. Dagger, dirk, blade, creese, kris, skean, baselard, stiletto, stylet, steel, knife, katar (India).

PONIARD, v. Stab, dirk, pink, prick, stick, puncture, pierce, wound, scratch.

PONTIFF, n. Chief priest, high priest, pontifex (Ancient Rome), pope, bishop of Rome, archbishop, prelate, suffragan, dean, subdean, diocesan.

PONTIFICAL, adj. Of, pertaining to or characteristic of a pontiff, papal, pertaining to the Pope, clerical, ecclesiastical, episcopal, priestly, sacerdotal, apostolic, prelatic, papistical (disparaging).

PONTIFICAL, n. 1. Book of forms for rites and ceremonies performed by bishops, formulary, manual, ordinal, church book, service book, breviary, rubric, missal, mass book, lectionary.

2. (Plural) Vestments (of a pontiff), insignia, canonicals, vesture, cloth, robes, episcopal vestments, liturgical garments, sacramental attire, clericals (coll.).

PONTIFICATE, n. Office or term of office of a pontiff, papacy, prelacy, prelature, prelateship, episcopate, see, diocese, bishopric, episcopacy, priesthood, popedom.

PONTIFICATE, v. Speak in a pompous manner, orate, pronounce, perorate, harangue, mouth, preach, flourish, assume authority, presume, talk down, talk big (coll.), sermonize, lecture, declaim.

PONTOON, n. Boat or other floating structure (supporting a bridge); (Mil.), temporary dock (Nav.), floating bridge, raft, watertight box or cylinder used for its buoyancy, float (as of a seaplane).

PONY, n. 1. Small horse, shelty or sheltie, Shetland pony, Welsh pony, polo pony, cow pony (Western U. S.), tattoo (India).

2. Something small of its kind, midget, minikin, bantam, miniature, diminutive, dwarf, pygmy, shrimp, runt, homunculus, peewee, minnow, mite, elf, hop-o'-my-thumb, Tom Thumb, Lilliputian.

POOH, interj. Exclamation of disdain or contempt, pshaw, pah, pish, pooh-pooh, bah, nonsense, bosh, poppycock (coll.), phoo, phooey (coll.), tut, balderdash, rubbish, humbug, baloney *(sl.),* a fig for, fiddle-faddle *(coll.),* fiddle-de-dee, fiddlesticks, applesauce *(sl.),* fudge *(sl.).*

POOH-POOH, *v.* Express disdain *or* contempt for, deride, make light of, dismiss as unworthy of consideration, make game *or* fun of, ridicule, gibe, scoff, banter, disparage, sneer, scorn, grin at, poke fun at, laugh at, hoot, belittle, hiss, gird at, scout, mock, revile, jeer, point the finger of scorn, point at, hold up to scorn, twit, taunt.

POOL, *n.* 1. Small pond, small body of standing water, still, deep place in a stream, puddle, pondlet, plash, bath, swimming hole, swimming pool, natatorium, balneary, reservoir, tarn *(Lit.).*

2. Combination of interests, funds, *etc.,* for common advantage, trust, alliance, league, cooperation, merger, confederacy, combination, union, coalition, consolidation, incorporation, monopoly, syndicate, cartel, joint concern, joint stock, confederation.

3. Stakes *(as of a game),* pot, jack pot, bank, kitty.

POOL, *v.* Make a common interest, combine, merge, consolidate, unite, federate, unify, ally, lump together, amalgamate, league, associate, co-ordinate, collaborate, band together.

POOP, *n. (Naut.)* Stern deck, rear deck, deck above poop cabin, aft deck.

POOR, *adj.* 1. Straitened, out of pocket, embarrassed, penniless, impecunious, moneyless, reduced, destitute, poverty-stricken, unmoneyed, indigent, drained, necessitous, on the rocks *(coll.),* broke *(sl.),* needy, stony *(sl.),* depleted, strapped, distressed, impoverished, ruined, pauperized, bereft, empty-handed, in want, in need, badly off *(coll.),* pinched, stinted, hard up *(coll.).*

2. Inferior, mean, paltry, indifferent, trivial, scurvy, meager, meretricious, inadequate, scant, deficient, gimcrack, sorry, beggarly, shabby, contemptible, scrubby, shoddy, defective, unworthy, worthless, scamped, tawdry, trashy, cheap, vulgar, base, measly *(sl.),* second-rate.

3. *(Of land, etc.)* Severe, empty, worn, arid, bald, unproductive, waste, desolate, effete, meager, uncultivatable, forlorn, impoverished, austere, lean, dead, unfertile, naked, bare, miserable, scamp, exhausted, depleted.

4. Of uninspired quality, not rich in thought, ideas, *etc.,* vapid, inadequate, puerile, unsatisfying, fruitless, otiose, vacant, lean, hollow, wanting, colorless, prosaic, flat, devoid, uninteresting, addle, inefficacious, tame, poor, insipid, deficient, insulse, worthless, meager, jejune, barren, unfertile, uninspiring, unprofitable, inept, lame, stale, unfruitful, weak.

5. *(Coll.)* Wretched, miserable, grieving, sad, sorry, contemptible, abject, plaintive, woeful, rueful, pathetic, unhappy, distressed, mournful, dismal, doleful, pitiable.

POORHOUSE, *n.* Eleemosynary institution, home for the aged, poor, *etc.,* house for paupers, almshouse, asylum, shelter, retreat, townhouse *(euphem.).*

POORNESS, *n.* Financial ruin, financial straits, destitution, penury, impecuniosity, impoverishment, need, liquidation, indigence, straitened circumstances, beggary, poverty, ruin, want, dire necessity, mendicancy, mendicity, bankruptcy, pauperism.

POOR-SPIRITED, *adj.* Recreant, ignominious, low-minded, dastardly, contemptible, sorry, ungenerous, parasitical, despicable, pitiful, degener-ate, menial, mean-spirited, hangdog, unworthy, abject, sycophantic, dirty, mealy-mouthed, low, ignoble, degraded, venal, miserable, wretched, petty, mean, ungentlemanly, base, vulgar, sneaking, groveling, unmanly, cowardly, slavish, servile, scurvy, sordid, pettifogging, inglorious, cringing, churlish, sniveling, scabby, shabby, paltry, worthless, fawning, subservient, pusillanimous, discreditable, scrubby, craven, beggarly, obsequious, abased, common.

POP, *n.* 1. Small explosion, clap, crack, detonation, report, discharge, fulmination, burst, blast, bang, plump.

2. Soda, carbonated drink, soda pop, soft drink, limeade, lemonade, orangeade, ginger ale, *etc.*

POP, *v.* 1. Explode, crack, bang, burst, discharge, detonate, clap, boom, resound, snap, plump.

2. *(Usually with prep.* OUT, FORTH, *(etc.)* Issue forth suddenly, dart, leap, come out, jump out, run out, rush out, emanate, spring out, dash out, burst out, break out, tear out *(coll.),* thrust out.

POPE, *n.* Pontiff, bishop of Rome, pontifex, Holy Father, his Holiness, papa.

POPEDOM, *n.* The Vatican, Apostolic See, papacy, pontificate, See of Rome, papality.

POPINJAY, *n.* Coxcomb, jack-a-dandy, exquisite, buck, fine gentleman, ladies' man, Beau Brummell, dandy, fop, macaroni, dude, jackanapes, man about town, blade, swell *(sl.),* silk-sock Sam, silk-stocking.

POPPYCOCK, *n. (Colloq.)* Wish-wash, balderdash, flummery, jabberwocky, gob, twaddle, moonshine *(coll.),* blather, absurdity, gobbledegook *(sl.),* bosh, prating, nonsense, stuff, stuff and nonsense, rubbish, blabber, fiddle-faddle, clack, abracadabra, drivel, prattle, jargon, rigamarole, hocus-pocus, inanity, gibberish, flapdoodle, trash, bunk, froth, tommyrot, hogwash, bibble-babble, patter, rattle, *bavardage (Fr.),* prate, hooey *(sl.),* fudge *(coll.),* kibosh *(sl.),* piffle *(sl.),* jive *(sl.).*

POPULACE, *n.* Common people of a community, the people, the crowd, the multitude, the masses, the million, the herd, the vulgar, public, mob, rabble, commonality, community, the lower classes, commoners, the commons, proletariat, rank and file, bourgeoisie, yeomen, ruck, varletry, rout, canaille, commonage, common run *(coll.),* salt of the earth, horde, peasantry, citizenry, folks, dregs, riffraff, body politic, population, hoi polloi, great unwashed, great unnumbered.

POPULAR, *adj.* 1. Regarded with favor *or* approval, pleasing, in demand, in favor, in vogue, sought after, preferred, in high esteem *or* estimation, well-loved, well-liked, received, approved, praised, favorite, to *or* after one's mind (taste, fancy), estimable, fashionable, celebrated, accredited, admired, accepted, acceptable.

2. Pertaining to *or* representing the people, public, lay, common, secular, laic, laical, vulgar, democratic, plebeian, of the people, community, national, state, bourgeois, plebeian, social, societal, communal, general, civic, civil, joint, united, collective.

3. Prevailing among the people generally, current, common, familiar, well-known, general, prevalent, talked-of, celebrated, renowned, famed, stock, widespread, conventional, famous, known by every schoolboy, folk, household, proverbial,

universal, catholic, ecumenical, noted, notorious, rampant, rife, traditional, usual, habitual, daily, accustomed, everyday, often met with, commonplace, vernacular, garden-variety, pat *(coll.)*, homespun, standard, orthodox, well-trodden, regular, in the beaten path, routine, cut-and-dried, understood, workday, Philistine, settled, established.

4. Suited to *or* intended for ordinary people, familiar, plain, easy, adapted to the ordinary intelligence *or* taste, abridged, simple, simplified, accessible, open to all, for the million, popularized, geared down, comprehensible, cheap, inexpensive, intelligible to the meanest capacity, approachable, watered down.

POPULARITY, *n.* Quality *or* fact of being popular, popular regard *or* acceptance, repute, fame, favor of the people, note, notability, notoriety, acceptance, reputation, name, mark, distinction, renown, approval, sanction, kudos, glory, acclamation, approbation, vogue, celebrity, esteem, good odor, good report, regard, good *or* fair name, éclat, reputability, admiration, appreciation.

POPULARIZE, *v.* Make popular, render inintelligible, vulgarize, generalize, cheapen, adapt for popular consumption, make palatable, gild the pill, simplify, interpret, gear down, water down, produce in quantity, universalize, broadcast, spread, give currency to, familiarize.

POPULATE, *v.* Inhabit, people, furnish with inhabitants, dwell in, settle, crowd, live in, occupy, colonize, reside, fill, establish.

POPULATION, *n.* Number of people inhabiting an area, inhabitants, public, inhabitancy, habitancy, citizenry, citizens, folk, people, populace, body politic, commonalty.

POPULOUS, *adj.* Full of people *or* inhabitants, well populated, close, serried, peopled, alive with people, dense, thronged, thick, swarming, crowded, packed, teeming, studded, crawling with people.

PORCELAIN, *n.* China, ceramic ware, earthenware, clay ware, vitreous china, faïence, jasper ware, spode, Wedgwood ware, Dresden *or* Royal Dresden china, Berlin ware, Meissen ware, Derby *or* Crown Derby china, Rockingham ware, queen's ware, Worcester *or* Royal Worcester ware, Sèvres ware, Limoges ware.

PORCH, *n.* Exterior appendage to a building, portico, vestibule, entrance, piazza, veranda, galilee, stoop, gallery *(Southern U. S.)*, solarium, sun room, sun porch *or* parlor, sleeping porch, portecochere.

PORCINE, *adj.* Pertaining to swine, of the nature of *or* resembling swine, suggesting *or* characteristic of a swine, swinish, piggish, hoggish, hoglike, porky, fat, voracious, greedy, gluttonous.

PORE, *n.* Orifice, minute interstice, small opening, hole, outlet, aperture, spiracle, foraminule.

PORE, *v.* 1. *(Foll. by OVER, ON or UPON)* Meditate, ponder intently, read *or* study with steady attention *or* application, fix the attention, give one's mind, brood, dwell, study, peruse, examine diligently, consider, search, explore, go deep into, probe, indagate, delve into, wade through, inquire into, fathom, con, investigate, perscrutate, contemplate.

2. Gaze earnestly *or* steadily, look steadily *or* closely, inspect, study, scan, review, view, gape,

goggle, peer, survey, perlustrate, scrutinize, examine, eye, ogle, run the eye over, fix *or* rivet the eyes on, glare, glower.

PORKER, *n.* Swine *(fatted for killing)*, hog, sow, pig, piggy, shoat *or* shote, boar, razorback, porkling.

PORNOGRAPHIC, *adj.* Lewd, obscene, licentious, prurient, foul, smutty, filthy, dirty, impure, ruttish, lascivious, bawdy, ribald, lubricious, incestuous, concupiscent, Cyprian, dissolute, lurid, unclean, coarse, gross, vile, offensive, fulsome, Fescennine, indecent, lustful, bestial, beastly, swinish, animalistic, theroid, lickerish, lecherous, suggestive, salacious, erotic, sensual, brutish, risqué.

PORNOGRAPHY, *n.* Obscene literature *or* art, obscenity, grossness, vulgarity, scurrility, smut, dirt, filth, bawdry, ribaldry, Fescenninity, indecency, indelicacy, impurity, prurience.

POROUS, *adj.* Full of pores, permeable *(by water, air, etc.)*, open, honeycombed, perforated, loose, light, leaky, leachy, riddled, penetrable, pervious, holey, percolable, spongy, cellular, absorbent, bibulous, friable, cribriform, sieve-like, sandy, easily crumbled, lacy.

PORRINGER, *n.* Deep dish, cup, bowl, soup dish, porridge dish.

PORT, *n.* 1. Town *or* place where ships load *or* unload, place of refuge from storms, haven, harbor, dock, seaport, inlet, roadstead, anchorage, destination, shelter, basin, lagoon, moorings, breakwater, pier, mole, wharf, landing, quay, harborage, goal, bourn.

2. Manner of bearing oneself, bearing, demeanor, carriage, posture, set, aspect, guise, favor, look, attitude, appearance, mien, presence, air, behavior, ostent, turn, seeming, expression, impression, semblance, front, figure, deportment.

PORTABLE, *adj.* Capable of being carried in the hand *or* on the person, easily carried *or* conveyed, movable, portative, manageable, pocket, folding, small, pocket-sized, bantam, conveyable, compact, easily transported, convenient, handy, light.

PORTAGE, *n.* Act of carrying, carriage, conveyance, transportation, transport, cartage, ferriage, porterage, haulage, truckage, transportance, transportal, shipment, transference, transvection, waftage, freightage.

PORTAL, *n.* Gate, entrance *(esp. one of imposing appearance)*, gateway, entry, door, doorway, portico, vestibule, approach, threshold, portcullis, arch.

PORTATIVE, *adj.* Having *or* pertaining to the power *or* function of carrying, portable, easily conveyed *or* transported, movable, manageable, folding, small, conveyable, compact, convenient, light, handy, pocket.

PORTEND, *v.* Indicate beforehand, presage, forecast, forebode, herald, auspicate, preshow, augur, foreshadow, foreshow, betoken, foretoken, bode, signify, divine, vaticinate, prophesy, typify, point to, omen, be an omen of, be ominous, show promise of, foretell, denote, predict, prefigure, shadow forth, forewarn, warn of, menace, give token of, presignify, preindicate.

PORTENT, *n.* 1. Omen *(of something, esp. momentous, about to happen)*, augury, prefigurement, presentiment, premonishment, prognostic, presage, warning, sign, boding, prognostication, auspice, prophecy, premonitor, premonitory sign, prewarning, foreboding, token, threat, premonition, portention, preapprehension, symptom, gathering clouds, Mother Carey's chickens, handwriting on the wall, forewarning, foretelling.

2. Ominous significance, awful meaning, dire prospect, threat, ill, evil, omen, consequence, import, concern, portendance, prophecy, implication, connotation, urgency, ominousness, fearfulness, gravity, solemnity.

3. Prodigy, marvel, wonder, miracle, sensation, surprise, phenomenon.

PORTENTOUS, *adj.* 1. Of the nature of a portent, ominously indicative, ominous, premonitory, augural, menacing, foreboding, significant, inauspicious, unpropitious, predictive, presageful, bodeful, prophetic, fatidic, prognostic, oracular, alarming, foretelling, fell, solemn, dire, ill-boding, fatiloquent, divinatory, haruspical, vaticinal, premonitive, forewarning, minacious, lowering, minatory, precursive, pythonic, sibylline, prognosticatory, extispicious, monitory, dreadful, fateful, augurous, frightful, boding, intimidating, frightening, prophetical, dread, fearful.

2. Prodigious, marvelous, extraordinary, wonderful, monstrous, tremendous, stupendous, exceptional, rare, singular, incredible, noteworthy, notable, remarkable, memorable, superlative, great, significant, eventful, momentous, superb, wondrous, fearful, astonishing, inconceivable, amazing, awful, breath-taking, miraculous, surprising, stirring, striking.

PORTER, *n.* 1. Doorkeeper, gatekeeper, doorman, sentry, concierge.

2. Bearer, carrier, redcap, coolie, bus boy, transporter, conductor, conveyor, sustainer, supporter, holder.

PORTFOLIO, *n.* 1. Portable case for documents, *etc.,* brief case, folio.

2. Office and functions *(of cabinet minister, etc.),* position, bureau, department, secretariat.

PORTHOLE, *n.* Aperture *(as in the side of a ship),* opening *(in a wall, door, etc.),* slit, orifice, outlet, hole, slot, peephole, port *(Naut.),* gap, window, casement, fenestra *(Archit.),* vent, embrasure.

PORTICO, *n.* Structure consisting of columns and a roof, colonnade *(Archit.),* arcade, gallery, peristyle, cloisters, columniation, peripteros, piazza, corridor, columnar building, covered way, ambulatory, veranda *(U. S. and Canada).*

PORTION, *n.* 1. Part of a whole, piece, section, parcel, handful, cupful, quantity, tract, batch, lot, deal, amount, measure, sum, fragment, fraction, cantle, moiety, half, corner, dose, ward, sector, installment, segment, division, point, bit, slice, scrap, some, cutting, sample, specimen, contingent, percentage, district, eighth, quarter, third, percentile.

2. Part alloted to *or* belonging to a person *or* group, share, helping, serving, division, quantity, inheritance, interest, heritage, endowment, dotation, quota, quotum, percentage, commission, consignment, allowance, ration, dole, stint, assignment, pittance, dividend, dot *(mod. Civil Law),* cut *(coll.),* dowry, allotment, whack *(sl.),* rake-off *(sl.).*

3. That which is alloted one by God *or* fate, kismet, fortune, doom, lot, cup, dispensation, destiny, luck, fate, God's will, will of Heaven.

PORTION, *v.* 1. *(Foll. by* OUT) Divide into portions, partition, apportion, allot, deal out, dis-

tribute in shares, parcel, allocate, dole, split, carve, separate, disperse, demarcate, chapter, district, canton, break up, cut up, slice, sever, segment.

2. Supply with a portion, inheritance *or* dowry, dower, endow, bless, bequeath, bequest, settle upon, dotate, dot *(Civil Law),* leave, will to, devise *(Law).*

PORTLY, *adj.* 1. Large in person, stout, sturdy, rotund, full, round, corpulent, plump, in good case, stocky, fat, obese, heavy, big, lusty, tubby, stalwart, brawny, well-built, substantial, strapping *(coll.),* burly, fleshy.

2. Stately, dignified, majestic *or* majestical, grand, imposing, commanding, lordly, princely, regal, noble, lofty, important-looking, distinguished, august.

PORTRAIT, *n.* 1. Representation, likeness *(esp. of a face, usually made from life),* portraiture, facsimile, picture, image, study, photograph, semblance, portrayal, sketch, drawing, profile, head, effigy, miniature, silhouette, canvas.

2. Verbal picture *(usually of a person),* description, portrayal, word painting *or* picture, picturization, thumbnail sketch, depiction, vignette, representation, graphic account.

PORTRAITURE, *n.* 1. Art of portraying, portrait sculpture, description, representation, depiction, portrayal, painting, drawing, photography, picturization.

2. Pictorial representation, portrait (See PORTRAIT above.)

3. Verbal picture (See PORTRAIT above.)

PORTRAY, *v.* 1. Represent *(by a drawing, painting, carving, etc.),* take *or* catch a likeness of, picture, limn, depict, draw, sketch, paint, delineate, photograph, set forth, carve, model, sculpture.

2. Represent dramatically, impersonate, personate, mimic, ape, hit off, imitate, pose as, personify, enact, take off *(coll.),* act the part of, characterize, reproduce, simulate, take, sustain, register *(emotion, etc.),* assume.

3. Describe, set forth, reproduce, relive, recreate, hit off, characterize, revivify, analyze, represent, delineate, narrate, detail, picture, convey an impression of, shadow forth *or* out, body forth, figure, depict.

PORTRAYAL, *n.* 1. Act of portraying, delineation, illustration, painting, recital, reproduction, depiction, sculpture, drawing, personation, personification, impersonation, playing, imitation, mimicry, picturization, representation.

2. Representation portraying something, account, picture, description, portrait, sketch, delineation, narrative, painting, photograph, figure, cast, engraving, study, canvas, mural, impression, likeness, image, facsimile.

POSE, *n.* 1. Attitude *or* posture of body, position, bearing, stance, set, carriage, air, cast, mien, stand, poise, port, aspect, presence.

2. Studied attitude, affectation, semblance, seeming, ostentation, artificial behavior, hypocrisy, strut, swagger, crocodile tears, sanctimony, ostentation, pomposity, airs, pretension, falsification, exaggeration, pomp, fanfaronade, parade, display, pretense, front *(coll.),* chauvinism, dog *(coll.).*

POSE, *v.* 1. Affect a particular character *(with a view to impressing others),* present oneself before others, attitudinize, pretend, act, enact, simulate, assume, mimic, imitate, sham, fake (coll.), feign, parade, posture, give oneself airs, make-believe, make a show of, profess, put on.

2. Place in a suitable position or attitude (as for a picture, tableau, etc.), arrange, set, group, set out, allocate, compose, line-up, distribute, assign, posture, seat, situate, locate, align, space, range, dispose, order.

3. Assert, state, propound, propose, allege, aver, submit, broach, advance, declare, present, start, put or bring forward, put or set forth, offer, posit, affirm, predicate, postulate, open, throw out.

4. Embarrass by a difficult question or problem, nonplus, puzzle, confound, dumfound, put out, confuse, dismay, disconcert, perplex, mystify, bewilder, baffle, stagger, bamboozle, bother, muddle, addle the wits, render at a loss, try one, stump, fog, disturb, flummox (sl.), tree (coll.), floor (coll.).

POSER, n. 1. One who poses, model, poseur, posturist, attitudinarian, posture-maker, mannerist, actor, performer, impostor, humbug, posturer, show-off, affecter, hypocrite, grandstander (sl.), fraud (coll.), pretender, empiric, quack, charlatan, bluffer, mountebank, no modest violet, malinger, masquerader, jackdaw in peacock's feathers, wolf in sheep's clothing, ass in lion's skin, fake (coll.), faker (coll.).

2. Question or problem that poses, riddle, enigma, dilemma, mystery, knotty point, vexed question, stickler, staggerer, knot, conundrum, hard nut to crack, tough proposition (coll.), stumper (coll.), puzzle.

POSIT, v. 1. Set firmly, put, place, fix, set, station, arrange, deposit, settle, establish, reposit, make stable, install, secure.

2. Put forward (as a fact, etc.), postulate, aver, avow, state, asseverate, express, propound, maintain, pronounce, lay down, predicate, say, avouch.

POSITION, n. 1. Location, arrangement, deposition, disposition, fixation, establishment, situation, collocation, allocation, insertion, lodgment, installation, emplacement, placement.

2. Circumstances, standing, footing, predicament, plight, condition, state, place.

3. Job, post, work, commission, billet, capacity, berth, pursuit, occupation, office, livelihood, calling, function, appointment, charge, career, role, sinecure, trade, incumbency, duty, role, care, place, province, assignment, business, responsibility.

4. Opening, vacancy, job, place, opportunity, chance, work available.

5. Position in the social scale, estimation, order of merit, etc., order of importance, step, station, prominence, elevation, distinction, superiority, notability, caste, gradation, importance, eminence, condition, degree, class, prestige, consequence, place, precedence, grade, sphere.

6. Place of settlement or whereabouts, district, locale, locality, situation, quarter, patch, location, place, bailiwick, site, ground, demesne, bearings, province, whereabouts, zone, area, purlieu, range, neighborhood.

7. Superior location (in sports, contests, etc.), domination position, opportunity, purchase, leverage, play, odds, edge, hold, upperhand, precedence, vantage ground, whiphand, power, mastery, supremacy.

8. Physical position, position of the body, build, posture, stance, stand, pose, port, carriage, bearing, set, mien, air, cast, presence.

9. Mental attitude, mood, mind, point of view, disposition, inclination, bias, frame of mind, bent, leaning, propensity, direction, tendency, predilection, proclivity, affection.

POSITIVE, adj. 1. Allowing no doubt, definitely laid down, explicit, peremptory, decisive, certain, genuine, true, past dispute, conclusive, sure, plain, inescapable, unconfuted, evident, sound, trustworthy, absolute, inappealable, unanswerable, undisputed, unquestioned, reliable, irrefutable, irrefragable, unerring, cogent, incontestable, undeniable, infallible, incontrovertible, indisputable, unqualified, indubitable, unmistakable, unambiguous, authoritative, definite.

2. Sure, assured, believing, questionless, satisfied, convinced, certain, sold (sl.), confident, decided, credulous, undoubting, secure.

3. Dogmatic, self-assured, dictatorial, cocksure (coll.), domineering, obdurate, imperious, arrogant, bigoted, opinionated, immovable, assertive, overbearing, unchangeable.

4. Not relative, real, actual, absolute, factual.

5. Affirmative, not negative, affirmatory, assenting, assertory, declaratory.

POSITIVELY, adv. 1. Decidedly, emphatically, absolutely, categorically, unmistakably, clearly, certainly, affirmatively, ex-cathedra, with emphasis, without fear of contradiction, peremptorily, unqualifiedly, assuredly, indubitably, unquestionably, confidently, surely, dogmatically, arbitrarily.

2. Precisely, exactly, literally, directly, explicitly, expressly, definitely.

3. Truly, in truth, really, in reality, actually, in fact, verily.

POSSE, n. Body of men empowered to assist in preserving the peace and making arrests, posse comitatus, force armed with legal authority, detachment of police, armed band, crowd, throng, multitude, company, phalanx, horde, crew, faction, reserve forces, auxiliaries, corps, brigade, regiment, squadron, squad, platoon, cohort, vox populi (Lat.), group of deputies, police force, constabulary.

POSSESS, v. 1. Have as property, have belonging to one, have a title to, be possessed of, hold, inherit, own, command, maintain, occupy, take up, enjoy, receive, acquire, obtain, come in for, come into possession of, devolve upon, succeed, be heir to.

2. Seize, commandeer, expropriate, appropriate, win, take, gain, bag, grab, monopolize, forestall, corner, hog, impound, confiscate, help oneself to, make free with, intercept.

3. Engross, engage, occupy, immerse, absorb, fill, enwrap, rivet the attention, prey on the mind, arrest, fix, employ, busy, involve.

4. Control, dominate, obsess, influence, bedevil, actuate, entrance, fascinate, ensorcel, enchant, witch, charm, bewitch, cast a spell, hypnotize, mesmerize, voodoo, hoodoo, affect, diabolize, bespirit, inspirit, quicken.

5. Acquaint, make known, familiarize, impart, inform, advise, apprise, notify, instruct, enlighten, tip, send word to, make aware, mention to, signify to, advertise of, communicate to.

POSSESSED, adj. 1. Affected by supernatural influence, exalted, elevated, inspirited, animated, inbued, quickened, experiencing the divine afflatus, endowed with insight, breathed into, instilled, infused, stirred, aroused, filled with genius, inspired.

2. Demon-ridden, frenzied, phrenetic, beside oneself, maddened, moonstruck, incoherent, wandering, corybantic, dithyrambic, rabid, fanatical, lunatic, mad, crazed, *aliéné (Fr.)*, daft, demented, maniacal, delirious, rambling, lightheaded, doting, wandering, raving, frantic, distraught, distracted, bewildered.

POSSESSION, *n.* 1. Proprietorship, ownership, occupation, possessorship, occupancy, tenure, holding, hold, tenancy, seizin, possessing, *métayage (Fr.)*, sharecropping, shareholding, retention, control, feodality, villenage, title, vested interest, freehold, fief, seigniority, legal estate.

2. Monopoly, corner, exclusive possession, impropriation *(Law)*, preoccupancy, monopolism, economic pressure, protection, restriction, limitation.

3. *(Future)* Inheritance, heritage, birthright, patrimony, reversion, heirship, dowry, dower, dot, marriage portion, jointure, appanage, legacy, alimony.

4. Territorial dominion of a state, province, colony, territory, protectorate, state, dependency, margravate, mandate, sphere of influence.

5. State of being possession, obsession, monomania, fixed idea, *idée fixe (Fr.)*, prepossession, infatuation, blind side, partiality, craze, fixed conviction, bedevilment, fascination, ensorcelment, enchantment, hypnotism, mesmerism, bewitchment.

6. Self-control, presence of mind, self-possession, poise, equilibrium, inexcitability, dispassion, tranquil mind, even temper, composure, calmness, coolness, sang-froid, placidity, equanimity.

POSSESSIONS, *n., pl.* Belongings, holdings, property, effects, estate, assets, wealth, real estate, realty, real property, personalty *(Law)*, personal property, chattels, goods, shares, bonds, stocks, capital, heritage, inheritance, patrimony, appanage, marriage portion, dower, dot, dowry, legacy, means, circumstances, resources, what one is worth, lands, hereditaments, messuage, fixtures, furniture, things, traps, paraphernalia, equipage, appurtenances, movables, stock in trade, impedimenta, baggage, luggage, pelf, accouterments, income, revenue, proceeds, returns, gross receipts, earnings, annuity, pension, insurance, bird in hand, *utipossidetis (Lat.)*, *suum cuique (Lat.)*, freehold, treasure, funds, supplies, wherewithal, cash, fortune, domains, demesne.

POSSIBILITY, *n.* 1. Workability, practicability, feasibility, potentiality, potency, workableness, doableness.

2. Chance, contingency, hazard, probability, likelihood, likeliness, run of luck, odds, even chance, tossup, throw of the dice, wheel of fortune, heads or tails, hazard, risk, gamble, game of chance, drawing lots, pool, lottery, random shot, fluke, leap in the dark, blind bargain, accident, liability.

POSSIBLE, *adj.* 1. That may be, that may be the case, that can exist, conceivable, imaginable, cogitable, thinkable, credible, likely, compatible, in posse, potential, reasonable, probable, not improbable, admissible.

2. Workable, practicable, doable, feasible, actable, performable, achievable, manageable, attainable, surmountable, superable, accessible, within reach, obtainable.

3. Contingent, accidental, casual, incidental, fortuitous, chance, in the cards, at the mercy of,

within range of, subject, liable, exposed to, open to, apt to.

POSSIBLY, *adv.* Perhaps, maybe, *peut-être (Fr.)*, *forse (It.)*, *quizá (Sp.)*, *vielleicht (Ger.)*, perchance, mayhap, peradventure, haply, as luck may have it, it may be, as it may happen, *Deo volente (Lat.)*, God willing, if possible.

POST, *n.* 1. Upright piece of timber *or* stone, picket, stake, stock, newel, upright, baluster, banister, bollard, stanchion, puncheon, pale, stump, bole, pier, support, pillar, pilaster, column, prop, pedestal, shaft, pole, leg, shank, colonnette, mullion, columella, standard, pediment, caryatid, atlantes *(pl.)*, telamones *(pl.)*, stay, mainstay, shore, strut, brace, guy, buttress, splint, rib, truss, skid, abutment, pile, palisade, jamb, stile, crutch.

2. Position, incumbency, office, station, place, seat, employment, situation, living, job, billet, berth, appointment, assignment, mission, duty, charge, chore, work, task, stint, errand, capacity, part, function, role, enterprise, undertaking, calling, vocation, profession, line, métier, trade.

3. Quarter, round, beat, walk, range, routine, circle, arena, orb, field, compass, scope, department, sphere, whereabouts, locality, location.

4. Mail, post office, air mail, mail boat, post boat, mail train, mailer, registered mail, insured mail, parcel post.

5. Messenger, courier, express, runner, estafette, intelligencer, dispatch rider, commissionaire, mercury, hermes, postman, mailman, mail-carrier, letter-carrier, *facteur (Fr.)*, postboy, errand boy, bell hop, bell boy.

6. Trading post, settlement, exchange, post exchange, bazaar, fair, mart, marketplace, forum, staple.

POST, *v.* 1. Station at a post for some purpose, quarter, billet on, place, locate, lodge, house, install, localize, camp, stow, settle, establish, situate, bivouac, put, set, fix.

2. Register, enter, slate, record, book, post up, put upon record, calendar, chronicle, note, inscribe, set down, list, insert, enroll, catalogue, file, inscroll, put in a ledger, make requisite entries in.

3. Place in a letter box for transmission, put in the post office, drop in a mailbox, mail, put in the mail, dispatch, send by mail, express, transmit, ship, freight.

4. Speed, hasten, hurry, hie, go rapidly, travel with speed, spurt, scud, sprint, run, trip, dart, whiz, fly, tear, dash, rush, bolt, swoop, shoot, race, whisk, scorch, tear, skim, scurry, sweep, skedaddle, scamper, haste, scuttle, burn up the road, accelerate, make forced marches, outstrip the wind, crowd sail, wing one's way, ride hard, run like the wind, make haste, press on, flutter, bustle, scramble, bestir oneself, plunge, hustle.

5. Bring to public notice, publish, advertise, announce, make known, broadcast, placard, spread abroad, blaze abroad, bruit about, inform, supply with up-to-date information, propagate, promulgate, circulate, divulgate, disseminate, diffuse, rumor, trumpet, report, herald, proclaim, blazon, press agent, voice, give to the world.

6. Stigmatize by public notice, defame, vilify, vilipend, denigrate, blacken, brand, slur, hold up to shame, heap dirt upon, drag through the mire, impute shame to, reprehend, disgrace, dishonor.

POST-BELLUM, *adj.* Occurring after the war, postwar.

POSTDATE, *v.* 1. Date with a date later than

the current one, give a later date to than the true date, date after, misdate, overdate, anticipate.

2. Follow in time, come after, succeed, ensue, supervene.

POSTER, *n.* Placard, advertisement, handbill, broadside, flier, bill, affiche, notice, sticker, bulletin, circular.

POSTERIOR, *adj.* 1. Coming after in order *or* time, following, subsequent, ensuing, supervenient, succeeding, after, later, more recent, latter, successive, second-mentioned, posthumous, after-dinner, postprandial, future, consecutive, next after, sequential, sequent, next, proximate.

2. Situated behind, hind, hinder, hindmost, after, rear, postjacent, posticous (*Bot.*), caudal, dorsal.

POSTERIOR, *n.* Hinder parts of the body, posteriors, buttocks, backside, rear, *derrière (Fr.),* seat, rump, behind *(slang),* haunches, beam, hind quarters, tail *(slang),* croup, bottom, breech.

POSTERITY, *n.* 1. Rising generation, succeeding generations, progeny, issue, offspring, seed *(Biblical),* spawn, breed, descendants, children, family, heirs, brood, flesh and blood.

2. Scion, offshoot, chip of the old block, olive branch, heir, heiress, child, bantling, infant, bairn, son, daughter, *fils (Fr.), fille (Fr.),* papoose, baby, chit, cherub, pickaninny, kid, imp, urchin, innocent tot, tiny tot, brat.

3. Lineage, descent, succession, filiation, heredity, sonship, line, extraction, pedigree, birth, origin.

POSTERN, *n.* Back door, rear gate, posticum, rear portal, private entrance, lesser doorway, gateway, secret entry, wicket, hatchway, lich gate, *porte-cochere (Fr.),* ostiary.

POSTFIX, *v.* Affix at the end of, suffix, append, subjoin, tack to, postscript, add a P.S. to, attach after, tag, attach to the end, adjoin, add.

POSTHASTE, *adv.* With the haste of a post, with all possible speed, swiftly, rapidly, hastily, speedily, expeditiously, with expedition, apace, fast, quickly, at full speed, in double-quick time, full gallop, tantivy, whip and spur, with rapid strides, *ventre à terre (Fr.),* in seven-league boots, *à pas de géant (Fr.),* by leaps and bounds, under press of sail, in full sail, *remis velisque (Lat.),* hurriedly, hotfoot, full tilt, precipitately, headlong, headforemost, headfirst, breakneck, pellmell, heels over head, full drive, hurry-skurry, helter-skelter, slap-bang, slapdash, in haste, amain, with speed, with haste, with might and main, rashly, *tête baissée (Fr.),* recklessly.

POSTHUMOUS, *adj.* Born after the death of the father, published after the death of the author, continuing after one's death, arising after one's death, post-obit, after-death, future, more recent, ensuing, succeeding, subsequent, following, later, latter.

POSTLUDE, *n.* A voluntary at the end of a church service, afterpiece, concluding strains, final movement, finale, closing part, epilogue, *Nachspiel (Ger.).*

POSTMAN, *n.* Postal employee, mailman, letter-carrier, post, courier, mail carrier, *facteur (Fr.), Briefträger (Ger.), portalettere (It.), cartero (Sp.).*

POSTMERIDIAN, *adj.* Occurring after noon, pertaining to the afternoon, P.M., post meridiem.

POST-MORTEM, *adj.* Subsequent to death, after death, posthumous, postmortuary, post-obit.

POST-MORTEM, *n.* 1. Examination of the body after death, autopsy, necropsy, post-obit.

2. Any ex post facto analysis, interpretive explanation, review, critique, commentary, critical notice, reconsideration, survey, retrospect.

POSTPONE. *v.* 1. Procrastinate, delay, put off to a later time, retard, remand, protract, draw out, spin out, temporize, filibuster, stall, reserve, dally, prolong, suspend, lay over, stave off, adjourn, continue *(Law),* prorogue, lay on the table, let lie over, table, shelve, pigeonhole, throw into the background, push aside, skip over, let the grass grow under one's feet, slur over, *laisser aller (Fr.),* connive at, gloss over, pass by, skip, waive, keep for future action, respite, keep back, tide over, let the matter stand over, sleep upon it, consult one's pillow, defer.

2. Place after in order of importance *or* estimation, subordinate, subject, make secondary, keep under.

POSTPONEMENT, *n.* Procrastination, deferment, deferral, delay, putting off, adjournment, respite, suspension, prorogation, tabling, filibuster, cunctation, deferring, retardation, stay, reprieve, prolongation, protraction, moratorium, demurrage, Fabian policy, remand, leeway.

POSTSCRIPT, *n.* Supplement added to a letter, P.S., afterthought, second thought, reconsideration, change of mind, addition, appendix, suffix, pendant, postfix, appendage, subscript, attachment, tag, tab, codicil, rider, addendum, continuation, sequel, succeeding part.

POSTULANT, *n.* 1. One who asks *or* applies for something, petitioner, suitor, plaintiff, suer, appealer, apostrophizer, rogator, imprecator, asker, mendicant, panhandler, solicitor, entreater, importuner, supplicator, impetrator, obsecrator, implorer, obtestator, interpellator, supplicant, suppliant, cadger, claimant, aspirant, solicitant, seeker.

2. Candidate for admission into a religious order, conventual, neophyte, novice, catechumen, proselyte, beginner, novitiate, probationer, initiate, *religieuse (Fr.), béguine (Fr.),* sister, nun.

POSTULATE, *v.* 1. Assume as self-evident, take for granted, take as an axiom, presuppose, premise, conjecture, surmise, guess, divine, theorize, speculate, presurmise, presume, hypothesize, moot, propose, submit, hazard, brocard.

2. Entreat, beseech, implore, obsecrate, impetrate, solicit, supplicate, request, ask, crave, beg, sue, petition. pray, call upon, apply to, address, make application, plead, apostrophize, adjure, obtest, invoke, appeal to, cry to, ply, imprecate, importune, beset, press, cadge, mendicate, panhandle.

POSTULATE, *n.* 1. Something assumed without proof as a basis for reasoning, self-evident assumption, theory, hypothesis, supposition, speculation, conjecture, postulatum, proposition, assumed truth, axiom, principle, thesis, doctrine, premise, theorem, scholium, truism, protasis, precept, starting point, terms, data, lemma, presumption, surmise, rough guess, guesswork, shot.

2. A necessary condition, prerequisite, requirement, desideratum, necessity, presupposition.

POSTURE, *n.* 1. Position of the body and limbs as a whole, pose, stance, attitude, decubitus, decumbence, set, shape, structure, contour, gesture.

2. State of affairs, condition at a given time, frame of mind, attitude, aspect, situation, phase, relative disposition of the various parts of any-

thing, state, mood, pass, case, predicament, circumstance.

3. Relative position, arrangement, location, station, place, post, bearings, direction, status, footing, standing.

POSTURE, *v.* Assume a particular posture, pose, assume affected postures, attitudinize, posturize, contort the body in various ways, act in an artificial way, show off, take a conscious position, put through one's paces, expose to view, demonstrate, display, bring into notice, put oneself forward, attract attention, star it, cut a figure, make a show, strut.

POSTWAR, *adj.* After the war, post-bellum, peacetime, after the armistice.

POSY, *n.* 1. Bouquet, bunch of flowers, nosegay, corsage, boutonniere, lei, chaplet, garland.

2. Motto, inscription, legend, verse, epigraph.

POT, *n.* Round deep container, vessel, jug, mug, kettle, stoop, tankard, can, cup, porringer, jar, crock, pan, saucepan, skillet, canister, amphora, receptacle, epergne, decanter, cruse, ewer, carafe, flagon, canteen, demijohn, noggin, flask, cruet, phial, urn, percolator, samovar, pitcher, jorum, bowl, patella, beaker, goblet, cylix, chalice, tumbler.

POTABLE, *adj.* Fit for drinking, that may be drunk, drinkable, potulent.

POTATION, *n.* 1. Act of drinking, swilling, guzzling, tippling, quaffing, sipping, swigging, washing down, wetting one's whistle, gulping.

2. Draft of alcoholic liquor, potion, drink, dram, libation, beverage, drench, nip, spirits.

3. Drinking-bout, symposium, carouse, debauch, perpotation, compotation, wassail, carousal, jollification, spree, saturnalia, revelry, orgy, bacchanalia, booze party, winebibbing, bibacity.

POTBELLIED, *adj.* Having a protuberant belly, great-bellied, large-bellied, tun-bellied, big-bellied, abdominous, paunchy, swag-bellied, distended, patulous, bloated, obese, bay-windowed *(humorous)*.

POTENCY, *n.* 1. Strength, power, might, force, puissance, vigor, energy, brute force, stamina, lustihood, muscle, brawn, thews, sinews, virility, physique, grit, solidity.

2. Powerfulness, potentiality, efficacy, cogency, validity, authority, influence, weight, predominance, control, sway, command, almightiness, omnipotence, capability, efficiency, ability, capacity, effectiveness.

POTENT, *adj.* 1. Strong, powerful, puissant, mighty, able-bodied, lusty, robustious, robust, husky, sturdy, muscular, sinewy, brawny, stalwart, strapping, athletic, herculean, doughty, cyclopean, titanic, Atlantean, Briarean, indomitable, invincible, irresistible, impregnable, overpowering, formidable, indefatigable, virile, manly, stout, solid, stanch, tough.

2. Capable, able, forceful, forcible, efficacious, cogent, effective, energetic. dynamic, active, vigorous, valid, effectual, efficient, influential, almighty, omnipotent, vehement, brisk, lively, intense, deep, masterful, telling, impressive, convincing.

POTENTATE, *n.* One who possesses great power, sovereign, ruler, monarch, king, emperor, czar, kaiser, caesar, prince, Augustus, lord, suzerain, liege, overlord, imperator, crowned head, majesty, caliph, sultan, shah, mikado, imaum, khan,

mogul, rajah, maharajah, padishah, shereef, inca, doge, nawab, ameer, rao, thakur, gaekwar, mirza, pasha, viceroy, tetrarch, bey, khedive, satrap, mandarin, regent, despot, autocrat, tyrant, oligarch, sheik, sirdar, aga, dictator, margrave, nabob, king pin *(coll.)*, big shot *(slang)*, commander, chieftain, tycoon.

POTENTIAL, *adj.* Possible as opposed to actual, capable of being *or* becoming, in posse, latent, hidden, dormant, quiescent, abeyant, inactive, undisclosed, lurking, implicit, unexpressed, covert, concealed, unapparent, dynamic, magnetic, mighty, influential, pregnant, in the egg, contingent, conceivable, imaginable, likely, accessible, in the palm of one's hand, unexerted, slumbering, smoldering, passive, stagnant, unrealized.

POTENTIALLY, *n.* Latent power, unexpressed capacity, powerfulness, potency, puissance, strength, dormant energy, dynamic energy, force, vigor, might, efficacy, cogency, motive power, ability, capability, aptitude, competence, talent, faculty, endowment, quality, attribute, property, gift, virtue, qualification, possibility, what may be.

POTENTIALITY, *adv.* Not actually but possibly, virtually, in posse, conceivably, within the bounds of possibility, imaginably, by possibility, dynamically, in the egg, in the palm of one's hand.

POTHER, *n.* Turmoil, confusion, tumult, bustle, disturbance, fuss, to-do, flutter, turbulence, rumpus, hurly-burly, uproar, commotion, disorder, ferment, convulsion, trouble, row, melee, pandemonium, fracas, riot, flurry, fluster, trepidation, perturbation, stew, ruffle, whirl, state of excitement, fever.

POTHER, *v.* Worry, bother, embarrass, harass, beset, perplex, confound, confuse, pose, puzzle, bewilder, vex, fuss, pester, plague, disturb, persecute, infest, badger, importune, harry, irk, tease, rag, mortify, cross, thwart, trouble, discompose, annoy, harrow, ruffle, pique, nettle, provoke, irritate, rile, fret, gall, chafe.

POTHOUSE, *n.* Tavern, alehouse, public house, mug house, gin mill, café, saloon, speakeasy, bistro, bar, cocktail lounge.

POTION, *n.* Draft, dose, drink, beverage, dram, nip, cordial, pick-me-up, eye opener, bracer, stimulant, tonic, elixir, restorative, philter.

POTPOURRI, *n.* Medley, miscellany, confused mass, hodgepodge, mixture, mishmash, farrago, salmagundi, olio, gallimaufry, mélange, stew, goulash, hash, chow-chow, pasticcio, pastiche, omnium-gatherum, olla-podrida, mess, jumble, mingle-mangle, motley, Noah's ark, patchwork, mosaic.

POTTERY, *n.* Ware fashioned from clay and hardened by heat, earthenware, clay ware, ceramics, crockery, porcelain, china, ceramic ware, Sèvres ware, Wedgwood, majolica, gombroon, Satsuma ware, delft, faience, crown Derby, Staffordshire, spode, Limoges ware, Dresden china, eggshell porcelain, bisque, willowware, terracotta, Lowestoft ware, Worcester ware, Leeds pottery, jasper ware, Toft ware, crouch ware, Rockingham ware, Meissen ware, crackle, Palissy ware, luster ware, biscuit, Allervale pottery.

POUCH, *n.* Receptacle, container, sack, small bag, poke *(coll.)*, marsupium, wallet, pocket, purse, sheath, fob, scabbard, saccule, baggy fold of flesh, sac, cyst, vesicle, bladder, utricle, udder, paunch, ventricle, abdomen, potbelly, satchel, budget, rucksack, reticule, dittybag, kit.

POULTICE, *n.* Soft moist mass applied as a medicament, cataplasm, plaster, collyrium, embrocation, epithem, lenitive, liniment, sinapism, pepastic, traumatic, vulnerary, pledget, compress, ointment, cerate, lotion, salve.

POULTRY, *n.* Domestic fowls, chickens, turkeys, guinea fowls, geese, ducks, hens, roosters, broilers, chicks, partlets, barnyard fowls.

POUNCE UPON Seize with claws, clutch with the talons, swoop down suddenly and lay hold upon, drop from the clouds, take unawares, surprise, bear down upon, strike at, dash at, hawk at, fly at, attack tooth and nail, spring upon, snatch, snap at, jump at, make a grab at, come suddenly upon, fall upon.

POUND, *v.* 1. Strike repeatedly and with great force, deliver heavy blows, thump, beat, pommel, maul, bang, batter, lambaste, drub, thwack, belabor, clout, cuff, clobber *(coll.)*, rain blows on, slap, smack, spank, buffet, lay on, thrash, trounce, wallop, fustigate, larrup, dust one's jacket, rub down with an oaken towel, beat to a jelly, beat black and blue, pitch into, sandbag, hit on the head, give a dressing down, swinge, strap.

2. Pulverize, bruise, bray, triturate, levigate, comminute, crush, grind to powder, granulate, rub down, file, scrape, grate, grind, rasp, crunch, contuse, craunch, contund, cranch, scranch, muller, crumble, attenuate, disintegrate, abrade, reduce to dust.

3. Throb violently, palpitate, flutter, tremble, pulsate, go pitapat, flicker, jump about, toss, shake, agitate, convulse, heave, pant, quiver, be agitated, shudder, quake, quaver.

4. Move along with force or vigor, walk with heavy steps, traipse *(coll.)*, trudge, plod, stump, tramp, march, bowl along, stalk, jog on, tread, pace, straddle, foot it, bundle.

5. Shut up in, confine in a pound, impound, enclose, coop up, imprison, immure, incarcerate, corral, pen in, paddock, mew up, rail in, cage.

POUND, *n.* 1. Enclosure for confining stray animals, pen, shelter, keep, confine, fold, penfold, corral, kraal, sty, croft, paddock, compound, yard.

2. Unit of weight, pound avoirdupois *(7000 grains divided into 16 ounces),* pound troy *(5760 grains divided into 12 ounces),* lb. *(abbr.),* pound sterling *(Money, 20 shillings),* sovereign *(gold coin, British).*

POUR, *v.* 1. Send falling from a container into something, decant, pour out, effuse, spirt, squirt, slop, spill, draw off, tap, lade out, libate, tilt the bottle, fill the cup, turn on the tap.

2. Emit, let out, discharge, send forth, give vent to, despatch, secrete, excrete, disembogue, excern, secern, void, extravasate, shed, egest, evacuate, open the sluices, detrude, extrude, exude, transude, run out, leak, souse.

3. Issue in great quantity, flow forth, flow out of, emerge, seep, percolate, ooze, drain, perspire, sweat, filtrate, filter, gush, debouch, dribble, spout, find vent, cascade, cataract, well, jet, drip, drop, plash, spirtle, overflow, stream, deluge, inundate, splash.

4. Rain, shower, flood, rain in torrents, rain hard, rain cats and dogs, come down in sheets, rain pitchforks, pour with rain, sprinkle, mizzle, drizzle, drench.

5. Lavish, squander, pour forth like water, waste, exhaust, dissipate, fritter away, fool away,

pour water into a sieve, fling around, spend profusely, expend.

POURBOIRE, *n.* Tip, gratuity, *Trinkgeld (Ger.),* drink money, largess, bounty, donative, honorarium, present, pin money, baksheesh, donation, gift, *cadeau (Fr.),* benefaction, oblation, offering, grant, favor, boon, bonanza, bonus, premium, reward, tribute, allowance, subvention, contribution, sportule, douceur, fee, alms, bait, bribe, peace offering, hush money, handsel, consideration.

POURPARLER, *n.* Informal preliminary conference, consultation, palaver, powwow, colloquy, collocution, interlocution, confabulation, converse, verbal intercourse, talk, commerce, oral communication, communion, chat, causerie, parley, tête-à-tête, *conversazione (It.),* audience, interview, reception, session, séance, meeting, hearing.

POUT, *v.* 1. Protrude, project, bulge, bouge, bunch, bag, make prominent, stick out, jut out, poke out.

2. Thrust out the lips in displeasure, look sullen, show ill-temper, look black, sulk, be out of humor, glower, glout, scowl, frown, lower, grouse, crab, grouch, gloam, have a hangdog look, be irascible, knit the brow, look daggers, champ the bit, chafe, fume, stamp the foot, look downcast, hang down the head, make a long face, brood over, mope, fret.

POVERTY, *n.* 1. Indigence, neediness, penury, impecuniosity, destitution, pennilessness, privation, want, need, lack, necessity, difficulties, distress, straits, straitened circumstances, wolf at the door, narrow circumstances, *res angusta domi (Lat.),* broken fortune, insolvency, pauperism, bankruptcy, low water, impecuniousness, necessitude, beggary, mendicancy, begging, mendicity, mendication, needy circumstances, reduced circumstances, embarrassed circumstances, slender means, hand-to-mouth existence, empty pocket, empty purse, light circumstances, money pinch.

2. Scanty amount, deficiency, scantiness, sparingness, dearth, lack, meagerness, jejuneness, scarcity, insufficiency, inadequacy, poorness, inferiority, exiguity, paucity, shortage, inadequateness, shortcoming, stint, bare subsistence, starvation, famine, drought, exhaustion, depletion, reduction, vacancy, emptiness, ebb tide, indebtedness, liability, debt, debit, arrears, deficit, inanition, none to spare, half rations, short allowance.

3. Barrenness, sterility, infecundity, unfruitfulness, unproductiveness, aridity, infertility, effeteness.

POVERTY-STRICKEN, *adj.* Feeling the pinch of poverty, living from hand-to-mouth, penniless, indigent, impecunious, needy, poor, necessitous, moneyless, badly off, *sans un sou (Fr.),* short of money, hard up, poor as Job's turkey, poor as a church mouse, beggared, beggarly, destitute, straitened, distressed, involved, reduced, embarrassed, pinched, insolvent, in difficulties, in debt, short of, ill-provided, empty-handed, unfed, barefooted, shoeless, *descalzado (Sp.),* shirtless, *descamisado (Sp.),* ragged, famine-stricken, emaciated, starved, famished, at the end of one's tether, in want, without resources, broken, ruined, bankrupt, squalid, shabby, down-at-the-heels, flat, broke, out of cash, out at the elbows, seedy, strapped, bereft, put to one's last shifts, unable to keep the wolf from the door, unable to make both ends meet.

POWDER, *n.* 1. Solid substance in the state of fine loose particles, pulverized matter, dust, grit, sand, shingle, meal, farina, sporule, bran, spore, flour, rice, efflorescence, particle, grain, crumb, pounce, seed.

2. Face powder, cosmetic, toilet powder.

3. Gunpowder, explosive, powder and shot, ammunition, cordite, lyddite, melinite, dynamite, trinitrotoluene, T.N.T.

POWDER, *v.* 1. Reduce to powder, pulverize, triturate, comminute, levigate, granulate, grind, file, bray, scrape, grate, abrade, pound, rasp, bruise, disintegrate, craunch, crush, crumble, crunch, beat, mill.

2. Cover with powder, bepowder, dust, sprinkle, besprinkle, strew, flour, scatter, pounce.

POWDERY, *adj.* Pulverulent, mealy, farinaceous, pulveraceous, floury, granular, gritty, branny, furfuraceous, lentiginous, sandy, dusty, scurfy, arenose, arenaceous, crumbly, friable, crumbling, loose, shivery.

POWER, *n.* 1. Strength, might, force, puissance, potency, powerfulness, energy, vigor, potentiality, pressure, arm, dynamic energy, vim, forcefulness, stamina, drive, lustihood, muscle, brawn, nerve, thews, sinews, grit, physique, vitality, virility, firmness, solidity, spring, iron grip, heart of oak, intensity, mettle, punch, pep, animation, go *(coll.)*, dash, spirit, fire, verve, *vis viva (Lat.),* human dynamo.

2. Ableness to act, ability to do, efficacy, capability, competency, efficiency, competence, capableness, aptitude, talent, skill, faculty, attribute, virtue, affection, endowment, enablement, quality, property, gift, qualification.

3. Authority, warrant, carte blanche, control, prerogative, ascendancy, predominance, omnipotence, dominion, domination, sovereignty, rule, command, sway, supremacy, influence, authoritativeness, proxy, government, empire, weight, almightiness, dictation, bidding, grasp, hold, grip, prestige, divine right, primacy, suzerainty, prevalence, influentiality, jurisdiction, mastery.

4. Potentate, sovereign, monarch, ruler, lord, liege, suzerain, despot, autocrat, overlord, tyrant, emperor, crowned head, king, imperator, majesty, kaiser, caesar, czar, sultan, mikado, shah, imaum, caliph, padishah, grand Turk, mogul, khan, inca, tycoon, lama, emir, rajah, maharajah, nawab, nizam, negus, viceroy, regent, palatine, hospodar, khedive, bashaw, pasha, dey, bey, scherif, satrap, tetrarch, mandarin, doge, duke, prince, seignior, margrave.

POWERFUL, *adj.* 1. Physically strong, vigorous, robust, able-bodied, sturdy, mighty, hardy, potent, puissant, brawny, muscular, husky, sinewy, strapping, broad-shouldered, stalwart, well-knit, wiry, manly, manful, virile, in the prime of manhood, stout, adamantine, invincible, irresistible, unconquerable, impregnable, proof against, indomitable, more than a match for, made of iron, athletic, herculean, Atlantean, cyclopean, leonine, valiant, valorous, omnipotent, armipotent, bellipotent, multipotent.

2. Forcible, energetic, active, forceful, incisive, trenchant, live, brisk, strenuous, mettlesome, intense, keen, acute, sharp, vivid, rousing, virulent, mordant, caustic, corrosive, poignant, double-edged, drastic, racy, enterprising, severe.

3. Effective, influential, efficacious, efficient, operative, effectual, valid, cogent, convincing, telling, thorough, emphatic, conclusive.

POWERLESS, *adj.* 1. Weak, impotent, helpless, asthenic, debilitated, feeble, prostrate, adynamic, incapacitated, strengthless, disabled, crippled, paralytic, paralyzed, mightless, forceless, impuissant, nerveless, infirm, senile, superannuated, decrepit, emasculate, laid on one's back, sapless, debile.

2. Defenseless, resourceless, weaponless, unarmed, harmless, *hors de combat (Fr.), sine ictu (Lat.),* pregnable, vincible.

3. Unable, ineffective, incompetent, unqualified, unfit, inefficient, disqualified, unfitted, inefficacious, ineffectual, futile, vain, unavailing, inept, good for nothing, inadequate, inoperative, nugatory, null and void, dud.

POWWOW, *n.* Conference, council, meeting, consultation, parley, confabulation, colloquy, interlocution, converse, collocution, conversation, verbal, intercourse, talk, communion, causerie, chat, interview, *pourparler (Fr.), conversazione (It.),* palaver, hearing, audience, reception, sitting, session, séance, conventicle, conclave, assembly, caucus, durbar.

POX, *n.* Disease characterized by multiple skin pustules, smallpox, variola, chickenpox, varicella, great pox, syphilis, French pox, Italian sickness.

PRACTICABILITY, *n.* 1. Ability to be done, possibility, feasibility, feasibleness, practicableness, achievability, workability, workableness, potentiality, potency.

2. Openness to entrance, being open to travel, passableness, passability, fitness for use, usability.

PRACTICABLE, *adj.* 1. Capable of being put into practice, able to be done, doable, performable, achievable, effectible, feasible, attainable, possible, workable, potential, actable, obtainable, conceivable, thinkable, credible, likely, cogitable, imaginable.

2. Capable of being traversed, admitting of passage, passable, usable, capable of use, penetrable, capable of entrance, accessible, surmountable, within reach, superable.

PRACTICAL, *adj.* 1. Able to adopt means to an end, hard-headed, businesslike, sensible, judicious, using good judgment, mindful of the results of an action, free from fanciful views, able to turn what is at hand to account, unsentimental, unromantic, unimaginative, efficient.

2. Adapted for actual use, pragmatical, adapted to practice, not theoretical, not speculative, not visionary, prosaic, matter-of-fact, adjusted to facts.

3. Fitted for actual work, proficient, qualified, skilled, able, versed, practiced, *au fait (Fr.),* trained, experienced, accomplished, expert, thoroughbred, instructed, skillful.

4. Being such in practice *or* effect, virtual, effective, useful, workable, operative, serviceable, potential, effectual, exertive, efficacious, conative, operant.

PRACTICALLY, *adv.* In effect, virtually, substantially, intrinsically, essentially, inherently, in the main, at bottom, *au fond (Fr.),* in reality, fundamentally, actually, in fact, as a matter of fact, so far as results are concerned.

PRACTICE, *n.* 1. Method, procedure, habit, manner, customary course, usage, wont, custom, observance, consuetude, fashion, habitude, ways, process, conduct, line of action.

2. Application, exercise, exercitation, operation, performance, play, occupation, praxis, perpetration, labor, execution.

3. Business of a professional man, clientele, following, customers, clients, trade.

4. Systematic exercise for the purpose of acquiring skill, drill, training, discipline, constant use, warm-up, rehearsal, preparation.

5. Action, deed, exploit, achievement, feat, coup, gest, doing, accomplishment, stunt, work, act, stroke, move, job, doings, transaction, passage, bout, blow, tour de force.

6. Skilful management, dexterity, featness, art, skill, adroitness, facility, expertness, address, aptitude, ability, knack, aptness, cleverness, callidity, skilfulness, dexterousness, competence, proficiency, felicity, flair, readiness, turn, endowment, capacity, ingenuity.

7. Artifice, maneuver, trickery, scheming, stratagem, chicane, jugglery, device, plot, machination, wile, dodge, trick, ruse, subterfuge, shift, sharp practice, knavery, guile, duplicity, frame-up, intrigue, cabal, complot, conspiracy.

PRACTICE, v. 1. Perform, act, do, prosecute, perpetrate, carry out, put into action, put into practice, make a practice of, achieve, execute, exercise, transact, commit, work, labor, ply one's task, employ oneself.

2. Apply, pursue, carry on, use, utilize, employ, make use of, turn to use, put in action, set to work, bring into play, adhibit, wield, exert, exploit, avail oneself of, have recourse to, resort to, profit by.

3. Drill, train, discipline, warm up, perform repeatedly in order to acquire skill, prepare, familiarize with, qualify, ground, inure.

PRACTICED, adj. Experienced, versed, proficient, trained, instructed, expert, accomplished, skilled, thoroughbred, seasoned, qualified, able, practical, au fait (Fr.), adept, adroit, dexterous, up in, efficient, competent, capable, fit for, fitted, initiated, up to the mark, primed, prepared, finished, neat-handed, skilful, apt, slick, deft, smart, good at, master of, at home in, good hand at, crack, masterly, felicitous, ingenious, talented, gifted, endowed, veteran, inveterate, inured.

PRAENOMEN, n. First man of a person, personal name, Christian name, baptismal name, given name.

PRAGMATIC, adj. 1. Concerned with practical values, very matter-of-fact, fond of the material, absorbed in realism, realistic, stolid, earthy, obtuse to ideas, utilitarian, unromantic, unsentimental, businesslike, philistine.

2. Opinionated, dogmatic, conceited, self-satisfied, entêté (Fr.), wise in one's own conceit, pretentious, overwise, priggish, egotistic, puffed up, vainglorious, assured, overweening, inflated, pedantic, affected, canting, big-sounding, smug, prim.

3. Officiously busy, overbusy, meddlesome, officious, meddling, obtrusive, interfering, intermeddling, intrusive, impertinent, overactive, pushing.

PRAIRIE, n. Extensive level treeless tract of fertile land, savanna, open country, meadow, grassland, steppe, moor, sea of grass, plain, llano, heath, down, wold, champaign, moorland, pampas, tundra, playa, mesa, upland, campagna, veld.

PRAISE, v. 1. Commend, extol, laud, eulogize, panegyrize, preconize, celebrate, acclaim, approve, applaud, express admiration of, approbate, congratulate, compliment, cry up, puff, flatter,

crack up, boost, sing the charms, say a good word about, back, indorse, cheer, clap, encore, root for, recommend, sanction, stand up for, stick up for, uphold, think highly of, admire, look up to, set great store by, hold in esteem.

2. Offer grateful homage to, glorify, magnify, exalt, worship, bless, adore, do honor to, doxologize, pay tribute to, celebrate in song, give glory to, hymn, chant, give thanks, hallow, say grace, return thanks, idolize, idolatrize, adore, venerate, revere, reverence, offer one's vows, attend with worship, bow down and worship, burn candles to, burn incense before, bow the knee to, salaam.

PRAISE, n. 1. Eulogy, encomium, panegyric, eulogium, laud, acclaim, commendation, tribute of praise, plaudit, compliment, applause, blurb (slang), laudation, congratulation, good word, acclamation, hand clapping, hurrah, cheer, paean, peal of applause, recommendation, reference, testimonial, approbation, approval, collaudation, flattery, admiration, appreciation, adulation, honeyed words, glowing terms.

2. Glory, honor, renown, fame, distinction, celebrity, good opinion, credit, popularity, repute, kudos, éclat, regard, esteem, name, note, reputation, notability, vogue, report, aura popularis (Lat.), popular favor, prestige, respect, account.

3. Glorification, worship, homage, tribute of gratitude, exaltation, benediction, grace, thanksgiving, blessing, benison, Te Deum, Gloria in Excelsis, hosanna, alleluia, Gloria, Laus Deo, paean, doxology, magnification, magnificat, non nobis Domine (Lat.), Ave, Hail.

PRAISEWORTHY, adj. Deserving of approbation, meritorious, laudable, commendable, deserving of approval, estimable, admirable, worthy of admiration, to be commended, worthy, good, exemplary, excellent, creditable, unimpeachable, desertful, sterling.

PRANCE, v. Move in an elated manner, caper, dance, skip, leap, cavort, gambol, strut, swagger, spring, curvet, caracole, frisk, rear, jump, bound, vault, ramp, gambado, frolic, cut a dido, bounce, bob, buck jump.

PRANK, n. Trick of a frolicsome nature, escapade, gambol, antic, frolic, caper, vagary, capriccio (It.), romp, lark, rig, spree, monkeyshine, skylarking, espièglerie (Fr.), practical joke, tomfoolery, whimsey, quirk, crotchet, boutade (Fr.), flimflam, pleasantry, play, annoying conduct, devil's own trick, sport, horseplay, buffoonery.

PRANK, v. Deck showily, dress ostentatiously, bedizen, trick out, begaud, adorn, bedeck, prink, trim, fig out, dight, bedight, preen, spruce up, array, spangle, emblazon, bespangle, gild, embellish.

PRANKED OUT, adj. Ostentatious, bedizened, bedight, garish, flashy, showy, jaunty, airy, finical, tricked out, meretricious, gaudy, spangled, glittering, ornate, natty, dapper, spruce, trig, foppish, dandified, coxcombical, obtrusive, flaunting, loud, gingerbread, tawdry, bejeweled, tinsel.

PRANKISH, adj. Full of fun, mischievous, playful, full of play, sportive, gamesome, antic, frolicsome, rompish, roguish, ludibrious, elfish, waggish, capricious, humorsome, wayward, wanton, folâtre (Fr.), playsome, tricksy, mirth-loving, rollicking, mirthful, gleeful, allegro, cock-a-hoop, frisky, jocose, lively.

PRATTLE, v. Talk in a simple-minded way, chatter foolishly, babble, blather, blether, prate, gabble, tattle, jabber, palaver, be garrulous, be voluble, be loquacious, be stultiloquent, stultiloquize, talk hapazardly, clack, blab, cackle, rattle, confabulate idly, gab, gush, jaw *(slang)*, spout.

PRATTLE, *n.* Foolish talk, trifling discourse, childish garrulity, prate, gabble, twattle, twaddle, chatter, blather, babble, tittle-tattle, palaver, tattle, jabber, gab, chitchat, drivel, senseless talk, stultiloquence, stultiloquy, nonsense, gibble-gabble, *bavardage (Fr.)*, cackle, rattle, *caqueterie (Fr.)*, clack, jaw *(slang)*, talkee-talkee, hot air *(slang)*, gush, slush, blabber, bibble-babble, small talk, prittle-prattle, *tripotage (Fr.)*.

PRATTLER, *n.* Chatterer, chatterbox, blatherskite, babbler, prater, gabbler, tattler, rattlehead, blabbermouth, palaverer, rattlepate, windbag, hot-air artist *(slang)*, driveler, magpie, parrot, jay, gossip, patterer, tub-thumper, ranter, *moulin à paroles (Fr.)*, tell-tale, tale-bearer, popinjay.

PRAY, *v.* 1. Ask earnestly, make earnest petition to, solicit, entreat, beseech, beg, call upon, supplicate, petition, importune, adjure, make entreaty for, implore, invoke, request, conjure, imprecate, obtest, plead, cry to, apostrophize, urge, press, besiege, apply to, beg a boon, sue, crave, bid, appeal to, impetrate, throw oneself at the feet of.
2. Make devout petition to God, offer a prayer, commune with God, approach the mercy seat, seek the throne of grace, address the Supreme Being, invocate, say one's prayers, recite the rosary, tell one's beads, fall on bended knee.

PRAY AGAINST, *v.* Solicit to prevent, desire to avert, deprecate, urge against, pray for deliverance from.

PRAYER, *n.* 1. Supplication, imploration, solicitation, suit, entreaty, request, imprecation, obsecration, beseechment, obtestation, impetration, importunity, requisition, appeal, address, invocation, application, petition.
2. Spiritual communion with God, orison, litany, rogation, collect, suffrage, praise, adoration, thanksgiving, intercession, miserere, paternoster, Lord's prayer, Ave Maria, compline, Te Deum, benediction, grace, glorification, magnification, Magnificat, doxology, *non nobis domine (Lat.)*, eleison, Kyrie eleison.

PRAYER BOOK, *n.* Book of Common Prayer, breviary, missal, service book, euchology, pietas, liturgy, lectionary, litany, mass book, beadroll.

PRAYERFUL, *adj.* Given to prayer, devout, of much converse with God, religious, devotional, reverent, pious, solemn, lowly-minded, fervent, heavenly-minded, holy, spiritual-minded, reverential, godly, humble.

PREACH, *v.* Make known by sermon, proclaim in a religious discourse, sermonize, lecture, moralize, inculcate, advocate, press urgently, urge, give earnest advice, deliver a homily, homilize, evangelize, address the congregation, hold forth, expound, indoctrinate, propagate, disseminate, imbue, impregnate, instill, enlighten, profess, pronounce, declare, exhort, preachify, promulgate, pulpit.

PREACHER, *n.* Clergyman, pastor, minister, parson, evangelist, pulpiteer, catechist, liturgist, liturgiolist, ritualist, sermoneer, predicant, predicator, homilist, pulpitarian, sermonizer, divine, minister of the gospel, sky pilot *(coll.)*, revivalist, exhorter, missionary, discourser, Devil-dodger *(coll.)*, lecturer, ecclesiastic, churchman, clerk in holy orders, shepherd, abbé, reverend, Bible reader, rector, dean, canon, prebendary, vicar, curate, chaplain.

PREACHING, *n.* Sermon, preachment, discourse, religious harangue, exhortation, pastoral, homily, lecture, evangelization, homiletics, predicatory discourse, pulpitry, predication, prelection, lesson, explanation, disquisition, interpretation, edification, indoctrination, inculcation, sanctimonious moralizing, advocacy, propagation of the faith.

PREAMBLE, *n.* Introductory statement, introduction, prologue, prelude, preface, prolegomena, exordium, proem, foreword, prelusion, prolepsis, overture, voluntary.

PRECARIOUS, *adj.* Dependent on circumstances beyond one's control, not to be depended upon, undependable, unreliable, uncertain, insecure, involving danger, dangerous, perilous, hazardous, risky, critical, unsafe, exposed, vulnerable, under fire, at stake, problematical, dubious, ticklish, tottery, shaky, slippery, top-heavy, trembling in the balance, ramshackle, tumbledown, between Scylla and Charybdis, between two fires, between the frying pan and the fire, between the devil and the deep blue sea, ominous, minatory, ill-omened, sinister, dark, menacing, lowering, alarming, threatening, unassured, riskful, doubtful, equivocal, unsettled, unstable, unsteady, perishable, mortal, provisional, elusive, fugitive, evanescent, infirm, hanging by a thread, from hand-to-mouth, touch-and-go, chancy, fallible, questionable, debatable, disputable, untrustworthy, dependent on, contingent on, on the horns of a dilemma, fraught with danger, parlous, periculous, built upon sand, aleatory, between the hammer and the anvil, on the brink of a precipice, on the verge of a volcano, in the lion's den, on slippery ground, not out of the wood.

PRECATORY, *adj.* Expressing entreaty, supplicative, supplicatory, suppliant, precative, imprecatory, rogatory, entreating, begging, imploring, beseeching, praying, asking, postulant, importunate, mendicant, solicitous, urgent, cap in hand, on bended knee, adjuratory, obtestatory, invocatory.

PRECAUTION, *n.* 1. Measure taken beforehand to ward off possible evil, safeguard, caution, warning, vigil, watch, surveillance, watch and ward, lookout, reconnoitering, deep-laid plan, coast clear, safety-valve, means of escape, palladium, sheet anchor.
2. Forethought, providence, provision, prudence, prudent foresight, timely care, circumspection, wariness, carefulness, anticipation, premonition, vigilance, heed, heedfulness, watchfulness, attention, pains, alertness, guardedness, stitch in time, preparation, eyes of Argus, *l'oeil du maître (Fr.)*, solicitude.

PRECAUTIONARY, *adj.* Provident, prudent, careful, cautious, heedful, discreet, circumspect, judicious, alert, guarded, wary, chary, awake, on one's guard, observant, watchful, vigilant, Argus-eyed, forehanded, preventive, preservative, on the qui vive, regardful, strategic, tutelary, guardian, prophylactic, on the safe side, on sure ground.

PRECEDE, *v.* Go before, forerun, go ahead of, head, usher in, lead, take the lead of, herald, introduce, lead the way, come first, come before, antecede, be anterior to, antedate, take precedence of, outrank, outstrip, prevene, forestall, anticipate, preface, preamble, premise, prelude.

PRECEDENCE, *n.* 1. Priority in time, antecedence, anteriority, precedency, precession, anteposition, *le pas (Fr.),* the lead, preëxistence.

2. Preference, advantage, preëminence, supremacy, consequence, advantage, importance, right to precede others in social formalities, superiority, supereminence, transcendency, prevalence, predomination, ascendancy, vantage ground, supremeness, primacy, paramountcy, standing, rank, status, elevation, exaltation, seniority.

PRECEDENT, *n.* Preceding instance serving as an example for subsequent cases, authoritative rule for future similar cases, authority in past practice, historic warrant, prior instance, authoritative example, practice, usage, custom, original, standard, prototype, model, pattern, antecedent, standing order, convention, routine, consuetude, criterion, exemplar, archetype, paradigm, norm, decided case, decision, historical justification.

PRECEDING, *adj.* Antecedent, previous, precedent, prior, anterior, precursory, foregoing, preliminary, earlier, precursive, prodromal *(Med.),* before, superior, prefatory, introductory, prolegomenous, preludial, prelusive, prelusory, proemial, inauguratory, inaugural, former, aforementioned, preëxistent, aforesaid, said, abovementioned, above, above-stated, above-named, earlier, aforestated, prevenient, first-named.

PRECENTOR, *n.* Choir leader, corypheus, cantor.

PRECEPT, *n.* 1. Commandment given as a rule of action, direction, injunction, order, command, charge, instruction, mandate, ordinance, behest, decree, prescript, fiat, dictate, bidding, edict, regulation, law, ordination, canon, prescription, golden rule, lesson, requirement, regulation, *lex scripta (Lat.),* unwritten law, code, common law, convention, *corpus juris (Lat.),* rubric, act, statute, formulary, form, model, formula, ultimatum, caveat, rescript, writ.

2. Maxim, adage, apothegm, aphorism, saw, axiom, proverb, byword, apologue, dictum, saying, motto, sentence, epigram, mot, cliché, commonplace, truism, moral, self-evident truth, gnome.

PRECEPTIVE, *adj.* Expressing a precept, gnomic, aphoristic, phylacteric, proverbial, instructive, mandatory, didactic, moralizing, jussive, imperative, decretive, moralistic, epigrammatic, axiomatic.

PRECEPTOR, *n.* Instructor, teacher, tutor, adviser, counselor, mentor, trainer, master, director, disciplinarian, pedagogue, monitor, proctor, dominie, expositor, guide, pedant, schoolmaster.

PRECINCT, *n.* 1. Space of definite limits, confine, inclosing boundary, bound, enclosure, limit, terminus, term, border, march, frontier, regions immediately about any place, environs, purlieu, neighborhood, periphery, outskirt, ambit, close, circumjacencies, suburbs, vicinity, vicinage, entourage, milieu, surroundings, walled space within which a building is situated, ground immediately surrounding a temple.

2. District for administrative purposes, territorial division, small electoral area, zone, department, province, *arrondissement (Fr.),* canton, county, shire, commune, parish, ward, township, diocese, bailiwick, wapentake, *enceinte (Fr.).*

PRECIOSITY, *n.* Carefully affected refinement, fastidiousness, finicalness, preciousness, finicality, meticulosity, meticulousness, nicety, fussiness, squeamishness, daintiness, effeminacy, primness, prudishness, prudery, coyness, affectation, affectedness, airs, mannerism, foppery, conceit, dandyism, coxcombry, demureness, artificiality, pretension, quackery, charlatanism.

PRECIOUS, *adj.* 1. Of high price, of great worth, of great value, costly, expensive, dear, priceless, valuable, high-priced, high, sumptuous, beyond price, at a premium, dearly bought, not to be had for love or money, *à grande frais (Fr.),* inestimable, rare, choice.

2. Beloved, highly esteemed, darling, idolized, cherished, adored, prized, treasured, pet, favorite, well beloved, loved, dearly beloved, honey, sweet, lovable, adorable.

3. Affectedly delicate, excessively nice, fastidious, overnice, overrefined, precisian, finical, fussy, squeamish, particular, pernickety, meticulous, scrupulous, difficult, hard to please, dainty, niminy-piminy, effeminate, dandified, coxcombical, foppish, namby-pamby, simpering, mincing, *maniéré (Fr.),* artificial, demure, coy.

4. Egregious, arrant, gross, sheer, complete, perfect, utter, downright, consummate, pure, unqualified, clear.

PRECIOUS METAL, *n.* Nobel metal, gold, aurum, bullion, ingot, nugget, bar, silver, argentum, platinum.

PRECIOUS STONE, *n.* Jewel, gem, *bijou (Fr.),* stone, diamond, ice *(slang),* ruby, sapphire, emerald, cat's-eye, alexandrite, pearl, brilliant, beryl, aquamarine, chalcedony, chrysoprase, carnelian, bloodstone, jasper, agate, opal, girasol, heliotrope, onyx, sardonyx, sard, lapis lazuli, garnet, peridot, chrysolite, topaz, turquoise, spinel, amethyst, zircon, jacinth, moonstone, carbuncle, coral.

PRECIPICE, *n.* Cliff with a vertical or overhanging face, bluff, crag, abrupt declivity, steep, clift, scar, rock wall, palisade, krantz *(South Africa),* eminence, tor, scarp, escarpment.

PRECIPITANCY, *n.* 1. Haste, hurry, urgency, precipitation, flurry, rush, dispatch, acceleration, forced march, spurt, velocity, precipitousness, scurry, drive, scuttle, push, scramble, bustle, hustle, flutter, splutter, dash, helter-skelter.

2. Recklessness, rashness, heedlessness, temerity, thoughtlessness, inconsiderateness, impetuosity, indiscretion, imprudence, overconfidence, audacity, presumption, foolhardiness, levity, foolhardihood, desperation, carelessness, fire-eating, knight-errantry, quixotism.

PRECIPITATE, *adj.* 1. Hurried, hasty, rushing rapidly onward, proceeding rapidly, headlong, precipitous, quick, expeditious, speedy, swift, rapid, pushing, pressing, urgent.

2. Rash, reckless, impetuous, overhasty, indiscreet, imprudent, hot-headed, excitable, fiery, boisterous, furious, feverish, incautious, heedless, adventurous, foolhardy, fire-eating, harum-scarum, overconfident, heady, thoughtless, injudicious, impulsive, uncalculating, overweening, madcap, wild, breakneck, harebrained, headstrong, devil-may-care, intrepid.

PRECIPITATE, *v.* 1. Hasten the occurrence of, bring about suddenly, expedite, accelerate, hurry on, speed up, urge forward, bring on sooner, dispatch, quicken, advance, forward, further, spur, whip, flog, press, goad.

2. Throw, hurl headlong, fling, cast headlong, heave, catapult, project, propel, chuck, pitch, shy, jaculate, discharge, shoot, launch, let fly, send forth.

3. (*Meteorol.*) Condense from a state of vapor in the form of moisture, rain, drizzle, mist, fog up, sleet, hail, snow.

PRECIPITATELY, *adv.* Hurriedly, hastily, expeditiously, slapdash, hotfoot, full tilt, quickly, posthaste, slap-bang, hurry-skurry, helter-skelter, heels over head, pell-mell, headlong, apace, in haste, amain, at full speed, in double-quick time, full gallop, whip and spur, with rapid strides, *ventre à terre (Fr.)*, by leaps and bounds, in seven-league boots, under press of sail, *remis velisque (Lat.)*, headforemost, *tête baissée (Fr.)*, *à pas de geant (Fr.)*.

PRECIPITATION, *n.* 1. Impetuosity, rush, rashness, recklessness, heedlessness, thoughtlessness, temerity, inconsiderateness, indiscreetness, impulsiveness, imprudence, indiscretion, incautiousness, overconfidence, audacity, foolhardiness, hastiness, foolhardihood, desperation, carelessness, presumption.
2. (*Meteorol.*) Falling products of condensation in the atmosphere, condensation, rainfall, dewfall, hail, snow, sleet, shower, drizzle, fog, mist, mizzle, downpour, cloudburst, deluge, ice storm, blizzard.

PRECIPITOUS, *adj.* Perpendicular, steep, sheer, cliffy, abrupt, craggy, uphill, acclivous, rising, ascending, declivous, declivitous, downhill, shelving, descending, declining, falling away.

PRECIS, *n.* Brief summary of essential points, abstract, digest, epitome, abridgment, compendium, analysis, pandect, brief, sum and substance, aperçu, synopsis, outline, conspectus, syllabus, résumé.

PRECISE, *adj.* 1. Exact, strictly defined, definite, correct, express, strict, explicit, distinct, well-defined, pointed, accurate, severe, nice, unequivocal, clean-cut, specific, to the point, logical, mathematical, obvious, literal, concrete, clear-cut, scientific, unerring.
2. Being exactly that, neither more nor less, scrupulous, meticulous, punctilious, strict, careful, painstaking, right, just, rigidly particular, faithful, fastidious, true, truthful, punctual, methodical.
3. Prim, strait-laced, rigorous, puritanical, formal, stiff, starched, ceremonious, rigid, unbending, finical, triflingly nice, close, prudish, austere, buckram, inflexible, Procrustean, uncompromising, intransigent.

PRECISIAN, *n.* One who adheres punctiliously to the observance of rules or forms, formalist, stickler, prig, pedant, martinet, bluestocking, puritan, dogmatist, disciplinarian, pundit, academician, *bas-bleu (Fr.)*, bigwig, highbrow, doctrinaire.

PRECISION, *n.* 1. Exactness, exactitude, severe correctness, accuracy, preciseness, mechanical nicety, distinctness, regularity, literalism, textualism, fidelity, authenticity, truthfulness, factualness, actuality, the very words, *ipsissima verba (Lat.)*.
2. Formality, stiffness, ceremony, punctilio, etiquette, ceremonial, ritual, conventionality, rite, propriety, scrupulosity, punctiliousness, niceness, particularity, prudery, formalness.

PRECLUDE, *v.* Make impossible, check, prevent, inhibit, debar, hinder, prohibit, restrain, obviate, exclude, shut out, bar, stop, restrict, detain, retard, slacken, delay, avert, keep off, ward off, stave off, turn aside, forestall, draw off, nip in the bud, remove, arrest, obstruct, clog, block, choke, dam up, stay, put a stop to, intercept,

interrupt, interfere, oppose, frustrate, thwart, foil, balk, contravene, circumvent, counter, defeat, override, nonplus, tree, forbid, impede, anticipate, reject, foreclose, omit.

PRECOCIOUS, *adj.* Premature in development, advanced, over-forward, too forward, mentally premature, bright, smart, quick, prevenient, anticipatory.

PRECOGNITION, *n.* Foreknowledge, prescience, foresight, prospicience, prevision, long-sightedness, perception, forethought, omniscience.

PRECONCEPTION, *n.* Opinion formed beforehand, anticipatory notion, preconceived idea, conception previous to the fact, anticipation, prejudgment, prejudiced view, prejudice, bias, predilection, foregone conclusion, presumption, prepossession, prenotion, preapprehension, fixed idea, *idée fixe (Fr.)*.

PRECONCERT, *v.* Agree to beforehand, prearrange, prepare, concoct, consider in advance, predetermine, premeditate, predestine, preresolve, resolve beforehand, foreordain, project, forecast, map out, lay down a plan, preëstablish.

PRECONIZE, *v.* Proclaim, herald, commend publicly, blazon, noise abroad, blaze abroad, trumpet forth, announce with flourish of trumpets, give tongue, declare, raise a report, set news afloat, advertise, promulgate, evulgate, spread abroad, bruit, voice.

PRECURSOR, *n.* 1. One who precedes, predecessor, forerunner, antecedent, precedent, cause.
2. Harbinger, messenger, herald, usher, advance guard, vanguard, van-courier, avant-courier, pioneer, outrider, foreloper, bellwether, leader.
3. Omen, sign, presage, token, prognostic, augury, foreboding, portent, auspice, prefigurement, gathering clouds, warning.
4. Preface, foreword, prologue, introduction, prolegomena, exordium, proem, preamble, prelusion, prelude, prolepsis, voluntary, overture, groundwork, preparation, frontispiece, heading.

PRECURSORY, *adj.* 1. Preceding, prevenient, precursive, precedent, antecedent, forerunning, prior, anterior, previous.
2. Prefatory, introductory, preliminary, proemial, prelusory, prelusive, preludial, preparatory, inaugural, inauguratory, prodromel (*Med.*), prognostic, premonitory, initiatory, prognosticative.

PREDATE, *v.* 1. Antedate, occur earlier, precede in date, happen earlier in time.
2. Date before the actual time, anachronize, misdate, mistime.

PREDATORY, *adj.* 1. Living by prey, predacious, habitually preying upon other animals, raptorial, voracious, ravening, ravenous, wolfish, rapacious, greedy, bloodthirsty, hungry.
2. Addicted to robbery, plundering, robbing, plunderous, pillaging, pilfering, thievish, piratical, marauding, light-fingered, larcenous.

PREDECESSOR, *n.* 1. Precursor in any office, antecedent, forerunner, foregoer, former incumbent, antecessor, precedent.
2. Forefather, ancestor, elder, progenitor, forebear, procreator.

PREDESTINATE, *v.* Destine beforehand, appoint in advance, foreordain, predetermine, predestine, foredoom, preordain, preresolve, premeditate, resolve beforehand, preelect, project, propose, forecast, shape out a course, map out.

PREDESTINATION, *n.* 1. Preordination, foreordination, foreordainment, predetermination, foredoom, predeliberation, premeditation, *parti pris (Fr.)*, intention, project, forecast, foregone conclusion, preelection.

2. Fate, destiny, kismet, necessity, force of circumstances, necessarianism, necessitation, compulsion, inexorable fate, what must be, fatality, election, doom, fortune, lot, fatalism, inevitableness, determinism, astral influence, Fates, Parcae, Moirae, Norns, Sisters Three, Gods will, book of fate, will of Heaven, Ides of March, wheel of Fortune, matter of necessity, action of God in foreordaining from eternity whatever comes to pass, decree of God by which men are foreordained to everlasting happiness or misery.

PREDETERMINED, *adj.* Already settled, cut-and-dried, foregone, decided, appointed, destined, predestined, put-up, fated, premeditated, prepense, predesigned, aforethought, studied, calculated, deliberate, prearranged, intentional, planned, set apart.

PREDICABLE, *adj.* That may be predicated, affirmable, assertable, holding true, holding good, attributable, maintainable.

PREDICAMENT, *n.* Trying situation, dangerous condition, unpleasant state, sad plight, crisis, emergency, extremity, conjuncture, exigency, dilemma, quandary, pinch, fix, pass, corner, mess, scrape, push, hole, impasse, hot water, pickle, stew, deadlock, difficulty, imbroglio, trouble, embarrassment, intricacy, perplexity, knot, entanglement, puzzle, poser, maze, paradox, knotty point, strait, rub, crux, trial, hornet's nest, botch, muddle, quagmire, slough, uphill work, Augean task, herculean task, Sisyphean labor, tough job, hard nut to crack, vexed question, obstacle, stumbling block, impediment, cul-de-sac, bar, barrier, obstruction, hitch, tightrope walking .

PREDICANT, *n.* Preacher, minister, pastor, pulpiteer, sky pilot, prolocutor, prelector, lay reader, lecturer, capitular, missionary, propagandist, revivalist, Jesuit, Blackfriar, Jacobin, Dominican.

PREDICATE, *v.* 1. Assert, affirm, proclaim, declare, say, state, aver, maintain, allege, asseverate, have one's say, represent, protest, profess, put forth, propose, enunciate, advance, propound, set forth, broach, contend, pronounce, depose, avow, avouch, warrant, vouch, certify, attest.

2. Preach, sermonize, moralize, lecture.

PREDICT, *v.* Foretell the future, forecast, forebode, foresee, prognosticate, prophesy, forespeak, indicate beforehand, soothsay, omen, hariolate, augur, presage, premonish, vaticinate, divine, portend, haruspicate, prognose, herald, foredoom, bode, shadow forth, foreshadow, foretoken, betoken, point to, harbinger, herald, auspicate, read the signs, forewarn, signify.

PREDICTION, *n.* 1. Prognostication, vaticination, prophecy, divination, augury, foreboding, foretelling, soothsaying, presage, premonition, forecast, fortunetelling, horoscopy, necromancy, haruspication, haruspicy, extispicy, mantology, manticism, chiromancy, palmistry, pedomancy, sortilege, prognosis, premonstration, premonition, auguration, hariolation, bodement, omination, auspices, crystal gazing, oracle, sorcery, astrology, handwriting on the wall, *tekel upharsin*, portent, revelation, premonishment, warning, forewarning, token, sign, foretoken, symptom, astromancy, geomancy.

2. Delphic oracle, Pythia, sibyl, sibylline

books, Tiresias, oak of Dodona, Cumaean Sibyl, Cassandra, Sphinx, Witch of Endor, haruspex, haruspice, extispex, mantologist, mantic, vates, seer, augur, prophet, soothsayer, clairvoyant, medium, geomancer.

3. Announcement, declaration, intimation, notification, proclamation, enunciation, notice, advice, counsel, program, bulletin.

PREDICTIVE, *adj.* 1. Prophetic, vaticinal, fatidic, haruspical, fatidical, extispicious, hariolative, fatiloquent, oracular, Sibylline, mantic, soothsaying, Delphic, Dodonean, pythonic, orphic.

2. Premonitory, ominous, augural, portentous, prescient, monitory, significant, pregnant with, foretelling, presaging, betokening, portending, foreshadowing, propitious, auspicious.

PREDICTOR, *n.* Seer, soothsayer, haruspex, haruspice, extispex, mantic, mantologist, diviner, prophet, vaticinator, augur, forecaster, foreteller, weird, sibyl, witch, clairvoyant, medium, palmist, fortuneteller, crystalgazer, Pythia, Delphic-oracle, Tiresias, Cassandra, Cumaean Sibyl, Sphinx, itch of Endor, bird of ill omen, necromancer, astrologer, astrologist.

PREDILECTION, *n.* 1. Mental prepossession in favor of, preference, partiality, predisposition, fondness, liking, desire, love, taste, relish, proneness, propensity, penchant, proclivity, diathesis, inclination, fancy, bent, leaning, tendency, animus, appetite, appetency, hunger.

2. Bias, prejudice, one-sidedness, favor, partisanship, class consciousness, provincialism, infatuation, mote in the eye, narrow mind, bigotry, blind side, warped judgment, foregone conclusion, prepossession, prenotion, fixed idea, *idée fixe (Fr.)*.

PREDISPOSE, *v.* 1. Give a previous inclination to, dispose, incline, sway, bias, influence, render subject, weigh with, magnetize, prevail upon, induce, draw on, prompt, put up to, inspire, stimulate, rouse, incite, instigate, actuate, set on, encourage, work upon, persuade, bring 'round, talk over, win over, seduce, entice, tempt, suborn, bribe, grease the palm, gild the pill, bait the hook, throw a sop to, urge, exhort, goad, prick, spur, egg.

2. Prepare, make ready, sow the seed, plough the ground, cultivate the soil, make preparations, put in order, lay the groundwork, dig the foundations, lay the first stone, rough-hew.

PREDISPOSED, *adj.* Minded, fain, willing, inclined, favorably minded, favorable, favorably disposed, not loath, in the mood, in the vein, in the humor, ready, eager, enthusiastic, forward, bent upon, propense, partial to, desirous, appetitive, orectic, avid, keen, ardent, fervent, impatient, agog, set upon, mad after, intent upon.

PREDISPOSITION, *n.* 1. Natural tendency, proneness, propensity, proclivity, penchant, aptitude, bent, leaning, inclination, turn, bias, tone, set, warp, susceptibility, vein, cast, grain, idiosyncrasy, temperament, nature, quality, mood, humor, drift, diathesis, mettle, mind, animus.

2. Prepossession, preference, partiality, liking, love, fondness, desire, taste, relish, fancy, wish, hankering, longing, yearning, ardor, zeal, appetency, appetite, keenness, hunger.

PREDOMINANCE, *n.* Controlling influence, preponderance, prevalence, prepollence, prepotency, weight, sway, pull, predominancy, ascendancy, control, mastery, reign, supremacy, dominance, domination, dominion, rule, sovereignty, authority, superiority, leadership, hegemony, power, potency, puissance, warrant, command, omnipotence, almightiness, *carte blanche (Fr.)*, prerogative, prestige.

PREDOMINANT, *adj.* Having ascendancy over others, supreme, ruling, regnant, dominant, ascendant, sovereign, overruling, controlling, hegemonical, in the ascendant, authoritative, influential, paramount, at the head, gubernatorial, imperious, executive, administrative, official, bureaucratic, ministerial, peremptory, imperative, absolute, regal, royal, kingly, monarchical, imperial, princely, autocratic, mighty, almighty, omnipotent, puissant, powerful, potent, forceful, strong, vigorous, cogent, important, weighty, prevalent, prevailing, rampant, rife, telling, recognized.

PREDOMINATE, *v.* Exert controlling power, surpass others in authority, dominate over, prevail, tower over, be supreme, rule, be in the ascendant, be sovereign, preponderate, overrule, overshadow, exceed, subject, outweigh, override, gain head, be rife, spread like wildfire, gain the upper hand, make one's voice heard, play a leading part in, control, master, get the mastery over, make one's influence felt, pull the strings, take the lead, have influence, carry weight, sway, actuate, take root, take hold.

PREEMINENCE, *n.* 1. Commanding position, superiority, supremacy, paramountcy, priority of place, precedence, predomination, lead, supereminence, transcendency, preponderancy, ascendancy, predominance, prevalence, vantage ground, advantage, primacy, sovereignty, headship, chieftaincy, leadership.

2. Renown, repute, distinction, conspicuousness, prominence, eminence, greatness, celebrity, importance, prestige, respect, regard, honor, glory, public esteem, favor, report, fame, *aura popularis (Lat.)*, vogue, notability, éclat, popularity, note, mark, reputation, figure, name, solemnity, splendor, luster, grandeur, impressiveness, dignity, nobility, stateliness, nobleness, majesty, excellence, sublimity.

PREEMINENT, *adj.* 1. Superior to others, surpassing others, dominant, controlling, ascendant, prevailing, prevalent, regnant, ruling, overruling, sovereign, supreme, paramount, foremost, utmost, highest, maximal, greatest, maximum, principal, chief, second to none, transcendent, unequaled, unsurpassed, unapproached, unrivaled, matchless, peerless, crowning, incomparable, cardinal, superlative, capital.

2. Distinguished above others, conspicuous, renowned, dignified, lordly, stately, magnificent, grand, princely, august, imposing, majestic, heroic, sublime, noble, honorable, eminent, noted, notable, celebrated, remarkable, popular, honored, famed, famous, far-famed, glorious, *distingué (Fr.)*, illustrious.

PREEMINENTLY, *adv.* Supremely, inimitably, superlatively, incomparably, eminently, remarkably, conspicuously, prominently, emphatically, stupendously, notably, signally, unusually, extraordinarily, particularly, uncommonly, singularly, strikingly, mainly, pointedly, chiefly, incredibly, surprisingly, amazingly, mightily, powerfully, exceedingly, extremely, infinitely, intensely, largely, greatly, richly, in great measure, very much, surpassingly.

PREEMPT, *v.* Occupy in order to establish a prior right to, appropriate for use, acquire beforehand, establish squatter's rights.

PREEN, *v.* 1. Dress as a bird does its feathers, array carefully, plume, spruce, prink, prank, trim, trick out, deck, dress up, bedeck, bedizen.

2. Pride oneself in, take pride in, glory in, plume oneself, be proud of, swagger, strut, mount on one's high horse, look big, stalk abroad, perk oneself up, give oneself airs, set one's back up, spread one's plumage.

PREFACE, *n.* Preliminary statement setting forth the purpose and scope of, introductory part, introduction, foreword, prolegomena, preamble, prologue, proem, exordium, preliminary, premise, prelude, prolusion, prelusion, frontispiece, heading, protasis, prolepsis.

PREFACE, *v.* Introduce, premise, preamble, prelude, lead the way, usher in, herald, head, put first, say in advance.

PREFATORY, *adj.* Introductory, preliminary, prolegomenous, exordial, proemial, prelusory, prelusive, preambular, prevenient, preambulary, precursory, initiative, precursive, preparatory, prodromal, inaugural, inauguratory.

PREFECT, *n.* Chief magistrate, high administrative official, chancellor, provost, consul, archon, proconsul, warden, viceroy, commissioner, plenipotentiary, vizier, vice-regent, regent, governor, exarch, pasha, khedive, bashaw, scherif, bey, satrap, tetrarch, alcalde, syndic, seneschal, corregidor, sheriff, lord mayor.

PREFECTURE, *n.* 1. Administrative office, administration, consulship, proconsulship, magistracy, magistrature, seneschalship, raj, presidency, caliphate, protectorship, directorship, dictatorship, pashalic.

2. Jurisdiction of a prefect, prefectural territory, satrapy, official residence of a prefect, consulate, embassy.

PREFER, *v.* 1. Set above others in estimation, like better, choose rather, single out, count more desirable, fix upon, pick, pitch upon, adopt, elect, select, pick out, take to, think better, fancy, have rather, would as lief, had liefer, make one's choice, make choice of, set before, take up, embrace, espouse, coöpt, pick and choose, indulge one's fancy, take a fancy to, cling to, look sweet upon, would fain have.

2. Put forward for consideration, present for sanction, proffer, set forth, tender, bring forward, offer, address, file a claim, address a petition, ask for, make application, sue, bring an action.

3. Raise in office, advance in rank, promote, elevate, exalt, aggrandize, dignify, graduate, ennoble.

PREFERABLE, *adj.* Worthy to be preferred, deserving of preference, to be preferred, more desirable, worthier of choice, better, more eligible, preferential, more popular, choicer, more select, more pleasing, more in demand, more advantageous, superior, surpassing, excelling, more favored, favorite.

PREFERABLY, *adv.* By preference, rather, by choice, liefer, sooner than, rather than, in lieu of, first, before.

PREFERENCE, *n.* First choice, prior favor, precedence, estimation of one thing above another, predilection, partiality, liking, fancy, selection, election, option, discretion, discrimination, volition, decision, adoption, pick, alternative, coöptation, inclination, bias, predisposition, proclivity, propensity, proneness, prepossession, prejudice, coöption.

PREFERMENT, *n.* 1. Advancement, elevation, promotion, exaltation, aggrandizement, furtherance, betterment, improvement, melioration.

2. Priority, seniority, superiority, precedence, preëminence, antecedence, superior rank.

3. Position giving pecuniary advancement, office bestowing social advancement, appointment of honor, post of dignity, benefice, incumbency, living, advowson.

PREFIGURE, *v.* Represent beforehand, foretoken, foreshow, foreshadow, adumbrate, presignify, portend, betoken, indicate, forebode, herald, bode, shadow forth, preshow, ominate, typify, symbolize, prefigurate, precurse, point to, premise, announce, forecast, presage, augur.

PREFIX, *n.* 1. Affix, adjunct, addition, prefixture, preflection, preflex.

2. Title, compellation, denomination, designation, appellation, epithet, name, application, cognomen, praenomen.

PREGNANCY, *n.* Gestation, ingravidation, family way, gravidity, fecundity, pullulation, propagation, fructification, multiplication, procreation, superfetation, parturiency, maturation, conception, germination, genesis, generation, fertilization, epigenesis, fecundation, impregnation, productivity, productiveness, fertility, fruitfulness.

PREGNANT, *adj.* 1. Being with young, great with child, parturient, *enceinte (Fr.),* gravid, with child, gestant, expecting *(coll.),* big, heavy, in a family way *(coll.),* brought to bed of, confined, puerperal.

2. Replete, full, fraught, teeming, filled, abounding, rich, plenteous, plethoric.

3. Fertile, fruitful, fecund, prolific, procreant, productive, fructiferous, proliferous, uberous, fructuous, copious, generative, creative, lifegiving, genetic, formative.

4. Important, momentous, weighty, significant, highly meaningful, full of possibilities, potential, forceful, emphatic, telling, impressive.

PREHISTORIC, *adj.* Belonging to a period prior to that of recorded history, prehistorical, immemorial, primeval, ancient, antediluvian, primordial, primordinate, primitive, patriarchal, preadamite, paleozoic, paleocrystic, archaic, preglacial, fossil.

PREJUDGE, *v.* Pass judgment on in advance of due investigation, judge beforehand, prejudicate, forejudge, presume, presuppose, jump to a conclusion, run away with the notion, have a bias, entertain a prejudice, have a prepossession.

PREJUDICE, *n.* 1. Unfavorable opinion formed beforehand, feeling held without thought *or* reason, preconceived notion, prepossession, predilection, bias, preconscious opinion, partiality, preconception, prejudgment, unfairness, intolerance, warped judgment, preconceived idea, one-sidedness, favor, twist, warp, partisanship, clannishness, class consciousness, provincialism, blind side, infatuation, mote in the eye, crotchet, quirk, narrow-mindedness, bigotry, fixed idea, *idée fixe (Fr.),* fixation, anticipatory notion.

2. Impairment, detriment, inquination, injury, scathe, damage, dilaceration, loss, outrage, inroad, havoc, ravage, hurt, harm, mischief, disadvantage, ill.

3. Animosity, contemptuousness, enmity, spleen, spite, umbrage, aversion, revulsion, repugnance, displeasure, antipathy, disgust.

PREJUDICE, *v.* 1. Affect with a prejudice, bias, prepossess unfavorably, give previous inclination to, partialize, preëngage, influence against, turn, twist, incline, warp.

2. Affect detrimentally, damage, impair, hurt, harm, injure, labefy, scathe, mar, spoil, despoil, ravage, tamper with.

3. Poison, empoison, taint, infect, contaminate, canker, envenom, embitter, vitiate, inquinate, aggravate, exacerbate.

PREJUDICED, *adj.* Wedded to an opinion, bigoted, biased, intolerant, one-sided, partial, unfair, partisan, fanatical, narrow-minded, jaundiced, wrong-headed, purblind, short-sighted, illiberal, insular, parochial, provincial, infatuated, besotted, warped, cracked, *entêté (Fr.),* dogmatic, opinionated, opinionative, *opiniâtre (Fr.),* unreasoning, unreasonable.

PREJUDICIAL, *adj.* Detrimental, hurtful, injurious, noxious, deleterious, damaging, iniquitous, pernicious, harmful, baleful, malefic, mischievous, disadvantageous, disserviceable, irremediable, unfavorable, hostile, inimical, unlucky, untoward.

PRELACY, *n.* 1. System of church government by prelates, prelatism, hierachy, hierocracy, hierarchism, episcopacy, clericalism.

2. Office of prelate, episcopal office, prelature, prelateship, bishopric, pontificate, archbishopric, archiepiscopacy, episcopate.

PRELATE, *n.* Churchman of a higher order, church dignitary, bishop, archbishop, primate, cardinal, pontiff, ecclesiastic in authority, pope, patriarch, divine, hierarch, eminence, reverence, metropolitan, diocesan, dean, suffragan, archdeacon, canon, prebendary, rector, vicar, hierophant, presbyter, ecclesiarch, archimandrite, curate in charge, incumbent, residentiary.

PRELIBATION, *n.* Foretaste, taste beforehand, partial enjoyment in advance, brief experience beforehand, anticipation, antepast, presentiment, preconception, prior realization.

PRELIMINARY, *adj.* Preceding the main business, coming before the principal subject of consideration, leading up to the main matter, introductory, prefatory, initiatory, preparatory, prelusory, prelusive, precursive, proemial, precursory, antecedent, precedent, prior, previous, foregoing, precedaneous, prevenient, anterior, preparative.

PRELIMINARY, *n.* Introductory step, preparatory measure, anterior act, prefatory measure, opening, introduction, beginning, preface, precaution, rehearsal, note of preparation, tuning up, arrangement, adjustment, groundwork, steppingstone, cornerstone, foundation, scaffolding, training, novitiate.

PRELUDE, *n.* 1. Preface, preamble, exordium, proem, preliminary to a work of broader scope and higher importance, preliminary remarks, opening, introduction, prelusion, preparation, prologue, premise, prolegomena, foreword, frontispiece, heading, groundwork.

2. *(Music)* Piece which precedes a more important movement, introductory movement, relatively short instrumental composition free in form and of an improvised character, impro-

visation, overture, orchestral introduction to an opera, *Vorspiel (Ger.)*, voluntary.

PRELUSIVE, *adj.* Introductory, prelusory, preliminary, prefatory, proemial, precursory, precursive, prevenient, anterior, preparatory, preparative, precedaneous, initiatory, preludial, prodromal, inaugural, inauguratory.

PREMATURE, *adj.* 1. Occurring too soon, too early, untimely, unseasonable, forward, precipitate, overhasty, sooner than due, inopportune, anticipatory, ill-timed, advanced.

2. Mature before the proper time, precocious, too soon ripe.

3. Immature, unripe, green, raw, unprepared, incomplete, crude, callow, inchoate, undeveloped, embryonic, imperfect, unhatched, unfledged, vestigial, rudimental, rudimentary.

PREMATURELY, *adv.* Too early, too soon, untimely, inopportunely, unseasonably, beforehand, precipitately, too hastily, precociously, before its time, in anticipation, improvidently.

PREMEDITATE, *v.* Prearrange, precontrive, preconcert, predetermine, predesign, plan beforehand, deliberately intend, plot, deliberate, do on purpose, resolve, predeliberate, preordain, preresolve, foreordain, design, mean, purpose, propose to oneself, harbor an intention, have in contemplation, have an eye to, aim at, set before oneself, take into one's head, take upon oneself, contemplate, calculate, destinate, propose, project.

PREMEDITATED, *adj.* Intentional, intended, advised, prepense, predesigned, studied, calculated, aforethought, foregone, well-weighted, well-laid, cut-and-dried, maturely considered, cunning, in cold blood, wilful, deliberate, bent upon, prearranged, predeterminate, planned, predevised, purposive, purposed, voluntary, inclined, disposed.

PREMEDITATION, *n.* Predeliberation, predetermination, predestination, preordination, *parti pris (Fr.)*, forethought, previous reflection, distinct purpose, deliberate intention, preconsideration, project, resolve, intrigue, plot, machination, conspiracy, intentionally, intent, proposal, fixed purpose, sufficient forethought to impute deliberation and intent to commit the act *(Law).*

PREMIER, *n.* First minister of state, prime minister, chief officer, vizier, grand vizier, administrator, statemonger, statist, statesman, strategist, power behind the throne, prefect, chancellor, plenipotentiary.

PREMIERE, *n.* First public performance, opening night, preview, debut.

PREMISE, *v.* 1. Offer previously to aid in understanding what follows, state at the outset by way of explanation, lay down beforehand, preface, set forth at the beginning by way of introduction, explain previously, introduce, prelude, herald, announce, enter upon a subject, begin.

2. Assume a proposition as a premise for some conclusion, imply as preëxistent, postulate as a condition precedent, presuppose.

PREMISE, *n.* Proposition from which a conclusion is drawn, basis on which reasoning proceeds, basis of argument, either of the first two propositions of a syllogism, presupposition, argument, ground, antecedent, support, postulate, assumption, terms, something taken for granted, lemma, principle, starting point, inference, plea, case.

PREMISES, *n., pl.* 1. Statement of facts, testimony, data, evidence, facts rehearsed, circum-

stances, relations, conditions, attestation, deposition, *praecognita (Lat.),* grounds.

2. Property conveyed in a deed, property forming the subject of a conveyance, tract of land, real estate, piece of land, grounds, place, house with the grounds belonging to it, buildings.

PREMIUM, *n.* 1. Prize to be won in a competition, reward, guerdon, meed, remuneration, recompense, encouragement, bounty, payment, douceur, fee, gift, sum additional to wages, bonus, incentive, subsidy, benefit, drawings, gain, commission, handout, share, indemnity, indemnification, sop, consideration, *quid pro quo (Lat.),* return, requital, reparation, compensation, quittance.

2. *(Econ.)* Excess value of one form of money over another of the same nominal value, sum above the par value of a thing, amount over par, rate above par, appreciation, increased value, agio.

3. Annual rate of insurance, amount paid periodically as the consideration for a contract of insurance, yearly payment.

PREMONISH, *v.* Forewarn, prewarn, caution, warn, admonish, give warning, give notice, put on one's guard, sound the alarm, croak, forebode, notify, make aware, advise, inform, apprise.

PREMONITION, *n.* 1. Presentiment, foreboding, forewarning, omen, portent, presage, sign, auspice, augury, token, indication, caution, foreshadowing, misgiving, evil adumbration, notice, hunch, foretoken, symptom, prevision, prediction, handwriting on the wall, *tekel, upharsin (Bibl.).*

2. Admonition, caveat, warning, monition, intimation, notification, summons, premonishment, warning voice.

PREMONITORY, *adj.* Warning, forewarning, cautionary, threatening, ominous, portentous, minatory, foretokening, betokening, indicative, indicating, symptomatic, prodromal *(Med.),* presageful, augural, auspicial, prescious, precursory, pregnant with, significant of, predictive, fatidical, prophetic, vaticinal, haruspical, oracular, sibylline, threatening, lowering, admonitory, admonitive, monitory.

PREOCCUPATION, *n.* Engrossment, absorption, prepossession, distraction, inattentiveness, abstraction, inadvertence, inattention, inadvertency, absence of mind, woolgathering, daydreaming, castle-building, musing, reverie, brown study, absent-mindedness, heedlessness, detachment.

PREOCCUPIED, *adj.* Completely engrossed in thought, abstracted, inattentive, absorbed, musing, dreaming, in a brown study, inadvertent, unobservant, absent-minded, lost, absent, woolgathering, daydreaming, rapt, thoughtful, *distrait (Fr.),* dreamy, dazed, faraway, lost in thought, in a reverie, in the clouds, blind, deaf, unheeding, heedless, listless, distracted, removed, engrossed, brooding, abrood.

PREOCCUPY, *v.* Engross to the exclusion of other things, absorb, prepossess, rivet, arrest, fix, engage the attention, make uppermost in the mind, take up.

PREORDAIN, *v.* Preëstablish, predestinate, appoint beforehand, predestine, foreordain, predetermine, foredoom, resolve beforehand, preresolve, have in store for, devote, doom, destine, fix beforehand.

PREPARATION, *n.* 1. Proceeding by which one prepares for something, arrangement, development, formation, plan, evolution, maturation, manufacture, elaboration, adaptation.

2. Groundwork, foundation, base, substructure, basis, scaffolding, *échafaudage (Fr.)*, scaffold, outline, stetch, plot, draft, rough draft, layout, makeup, diagram, *ébauche (Fr.)*, drawing, chart, map, representation.

3. Teaching, education, edification, indoctrination, inculcation, initiation, guidance, direction, pedagogy, tutorship, tutelage, tuition, instruction, inurement, equipment, novitiate, apprenticeship, probation, tyronism, neophytism, training, qualification, fitting, experience.

4. Precaution, provision, anticipation, rehearsal, forecast, premunition, prior measure, provision, forethought, providence, foresight, prudence, circumspection, timely care, safeguard.

5. Preparedness, readiness, fitness, maturity, ripeness, mellowness.

6. Confection, composition, tincture, elixir, mixture, dressing, concoction, cooking, culinary art, cookery.

7. Plowing, tilling, sowing, semination, cultivation, horticulture, agriculture.

PREPARATORY, *adj.* Serving to make ready, preliminary, introductory, preparative, prefatory, forehanded, antecedent, inchoate, provident, provisional, precautionary, hatching, brewing, forthcoming, in embryo, rudimentary, elementary, embryonic, initial, elementary, primary, prelusive, preludial, precursory, afoot, in hand, afloat, in train, prospective, long-sighted, far-sighted, anticipatory, foreseeing, prescient, expectant, foresighted, provident, careful, watchful, under consideration, on the carpet, *sur le tapis (Fr.)*, in course of preparation.

PREPARE, *v.* 1. Make ready, make preparations, get ready, arrange, prime, get up, settle preliminaries, prepare the ground, do the groundwork, lay the foundations, erect the scaffolding, block out, rough-hew, devise, fix, fabricate, concoct, brew, dress, cook, contrive, manufacture, compose, compound, make.

2. Mature, season, mellow, nurture, bring to maturity, ripen, perfect, elaborate, develop, complete, hatch.

3. Equip, array, arm, accouter, man, fit up, fit out, rig out, dress, outfit, gird, provide, appoint, furnish.

4. Forearm, prepare for, guard against, provide against, make provision for, clear decks, make all snug, clear for action, set one's house in order, set aside for a rainy day, be prepared, watch and pray, hold oneself in readiness, be ready, lie in wait for, keep one's powder dry, foresee, anticipate, take steps, put things in order.

PREPAREDNESS, *n.* 1. State of being prepared, readiness, fitness, fit state, qualification.

2. Possession of an adequate military machine, militarism, state of military and naval preparation for adequate defense in case of hostilities, readiness for war, national mobilization, stockpiling of munitions.

PREPENSE, *adj.* Intended, intentional, deliberate, premeditated, predesigned, studied, calculated, advised, aforethought, well-weighed, maturely considered, cut-and-dried, cold-blooded, cunning-minded, spontaneous, wilful, volitional, volitive, predeterminate, designed, prearranged, well-considered, planned, purposed, purposive, contemplated, voluntary, express, willing, determinate.

PREPONDERANCE, *n.* Outweighing, superiority

of weight, predominance, preponderancy, supremacy, ascendancy, control, hegemony, rule, influence, preëminence, supereminence, lead, transcendency, prevalence, advantage, authority, paramountcy, sovereignty, primacy, leadership, lion's share, summit, highest position, maximum, upper hand, mastery, domination, influentiality, importance, sway.

PREPONDERANT, *adj.* Outweighing, preponderating, overbalancing, predominant, prevalent, prevailing, superior, controlling, dominant, supreme, paramount, in the ascendant, influential, rampant, rife, most general, extensively, existing, influential, potent, substantial, recognized, weighty, powerful, important, strong, authoritative, sweeping, current, widespread, comprehensive, universal, overruling, second to none, *nulli secundus (Lat.)*, transcendent, sovereign, foremost, principal, chief, leading.

PREPONDERATE, *v.* Prevail in force, be superior in number or amount, exceed in influence or power, predominate, have the superiority, excel, transcend, overbalance, outbalance, outdo, outrival, outweigh, outrank, surpass, overmatch, overtop, eclipse, outstrip, beat hollow *(coll.)*, have the upper hand, throw into the shade, have the advantage, take the cake *(slang)*, break the record, come first, take precedence, rank first, overpower, override, gain the upper hand, take the lead, get control of, turn the scale, dominate, sway, control.

PREPOSSESS, *v.* Bias, prejudice, color, warp, twist, incline, bigot, influence, affect, give a bias to, jaundice, turn.

PREPOSSESSED, *adj.* Prejudiced, biased, warped, twisted, intolerant, narrow-minded, bigoted, influenced, jaundiced, colored, unreasonable, irrational, unthinking, dogmatic, opinionated, opinionative, categorical, arbitrary, doctrinary, overzealous, besotted, overenthusiastic, peremptory, definite, decided, uncompromising, intransigent, unalterable, unswerving, obstinate, unyielding, stubborn, unfair, unjust, inequitable, one-sided, unbalanced, partial, interested, uncandid.

PREPOSSESSING, *adj.* Alluring, attractive, comely, handsome, pretty, good-looking, winning, fascinating, captivating, bewitching, charming, well-favored, pleasant, nice *(coll.)*, taking, engaging, inviting, enchanting, winsome, tantalizing, ravishing, entrancing, beautiful, heavenly, Elysian.

PREPOSSESSION, *n.* 1. Preoccupation, predisposition, prior possession, preoccupancy.

2. Bias, prejudice, prejudgment, predisposition, partiality, preconception, predilection, infatuation, absorption, inclination, bent, one-sidedness, bigotry, forejudgment, presumption, preapprehension, foregone conclusion, twist, warp, obsession, short-sightedness, blind spot, partialness, partisanship, partisan feeling, partisan preference, preference, preoption, preferability, liking, prelation, unfairness, inequity, inequitableness.

PREPOSTEROUS, *adj.* Unthinkable, out of the question, impossible, unwarranted, unjustified, overdone, exaggerated, hyperbolized, extreme, immoderate, outrageous, egregious, undue, excessive, fabulous, intemperate, overlarge, extravagant, high-flown, flighty, gross, flagrant, *outré (Fr.)*, absurd, imbecile, stupid, asinine, nonsensical, inane, fantastic, monstrous, inflated, bizarre, grotesque, bombastic, fatuous, fatuitous, foolish, unreasonable, ridiculous, irrational, exorbitant, perverted, improper, unfit, wrong, wrongful, queer, imaginary, unconscionable, amazing, unspeakable, dreamy, Utopian, chimerical, mythological, visionary, astonishing, flighty, incredible, unbelievable.

PREPOSTEROUSNESS, *n.* Absurdity, unreasonableness, irrationality, folly, foolishness, extravagance, inconsistency with reason, unthinkableness, impossibility, hyperbole, immoderateness, outrageousness, egregiousness, excess, excessiveness, fabulousness, intemperateness, flightiness, grossness, flagrance, flagrancy, imbecility, stupidity, asininity, nonsense, nonsensicality, nonsensicalness, inanity, fantasy, fantasticality, monstrousness, bizarreness, grotesquerie, grotesqueness, bombast, fatuousness, fatuity, ridiculousness, exorbitance, exorbitancy, perverseness, pervertedness, perversion, impropriety, unfitness, wrongness, wrongfulness, queerness, unconscionability, amazingness, unspeakableness, dreaminess, chimera, incredibility, unbelievability.

PREPOTENCY, *n.* Predominance, control, prepollency, prepollence, prestige, predomination, superiority, lead, priority, ascendancy, transcendence, transcendency, preponderation, force, power, vigor, potency, puissance.

PREPOTENT, *adj.* Potent, powerful, forceful, vigorous, puissant, dynamic, forcible, influential, weighty, prevalent, effective, authoritative, telling, prepollent, predominant, effectual, efficacious, hegemonical, hegemonic, supreme, chief, paramount.

PREPUCE, *n.* Foreskin, integument, covering, organ.

PREREQUISITE, *n.* Requisite, requirement, need, stipulation, qualification, want, essential, necessity, demand, prerequirement, essentiality, desideratum, necessary, necessaries, condition.

PREREQUISITE, *adj.* Imperative, needful, necessary, required, essential, indispensable, necessitous, demanded, in demand.

PREROGATIVE, *n.* Right, privilege, claim, birthright, advantage, liberty, franchise, due, grant, prescription, droit *(Law),* interest, title, demand, claim, pretension, immunity, freedom, license, exemption, authorization, potency, legal power, rightful power.

PRESAGE, *n.* 1. Prediction, forecast, prophecy, prognosis, pronostication, presagement, vaticination, foretelling, divination, divining, soothsaying, augury, auspice, bode, prefigurement, prefiguration, foreshowing, adumbration, heralding, pythonism, hariolation.

2. Foreboding, prediction, augury, foreknowledge, forewisdom, presentiment, preapprehension, prenotion, premonishment, omination, portention, portent, bode, abode, premonition.

PRESAGE, *v.* Divine, forebode, premonstrate, bode, foresee, foretell, predict, prophesy, soothsay, signify, foreshow, betoken, foretoken, prognosticate, augur, forecast, threaten, announce, vaticinate, augurate, portend, judge the future, hariolate, haruspice, omen, ominate, auspicate, preindicate, presignify, prefigurate.

PRESBYOPIA, *n.* Far-sightedness, long sight, long-sightedness, faulty eyesight, defective vision, imperfect vision, bad eyes, anopsia, anopsy *(Med.),* anopia *(Med.).*

PRESBYOPIC, *adj.* Far-sighted, long-sighted, poor-sighted, weak-eyed.

PRESBYTER, *n.* Priest, elder, minister, clergyman, preacher, bishop, church official, prelate, hierophant, sermoner, sermonizer, father, confessor, clerk, clerk in holy orders, pastor, parson, chaplain, churchman, theologian.

PRESBYTERY, *n.* 1. Vicarage, rectory, parish house, parsonage, pastorate, pastorium, deanery, prebendary, manse, church house, glebe.

2. Sanctuary, altar.

3. Ministry, clergy, priesthood, the cloth, the pulpit, holy orders, clericals, clerical order.

4. Council, court, parochial council, parochial court, convocation, synod, vestry, conclave, consistory, ecumenical council, diet, directory, chapter, church, conventicle, conference, session, classis.

PRESCIENCE, *n.* Precognition, foreknowledge, forewisdom, preapprehension, preconception, preconceived notion, premonition, presentiment, suspicion, prediction, wisdom, anticipation, expectation, forethought, sense, foreboding, prevision, forecast, prospicience, foresightedness, far-sightedness, far-seeingness.

PRESCIENT, *adj.* Foresighted, precognitive, far-sighted, far-seeing, anticipatory, precognizant, presciental, sagacious, forward-looking, provident, oracular, presageful, divinatory, vaticinal, vaticinatory, shrewd, quick-witted, perceptive, perspicacious, apperceptient, apperceptive, perceptive, discerning, penetrating, precautionary, cautious, precautious, provident.

PRESCRIBE, *v.* Direct, order, dictate, enjoin, decree, ordain, command, advocate, institute, establish, appoint, impose, spare, require, set, recommend, fix, legislate, codify, oblige, assign, mark out, appoint, requisition, require, demand, exact, tax, urge.

PRESCRIPT, *n.* Decree, mandate, directive, direction, law, precept, enactment, edict, ukase, prescription, instruction, order, charge, injunction, dictate, dictum, principle, recipe, receipt, set principle, dogmatic principle, dogma, canon, rule, code, rule of conduct, convention, maxim, regulation, formulary, formula, scholium, theorem, truism, axiom, ordinance, commandment, call, exaction, statute, rubric, institution, act.

PRESCRIPT, *adj.* Imperative, commanded, obligatory, mandatory, preceptive, decreed, decretory, decretive, jussive, instructive, didactic, according to rule, habitual, customary.

PRESCRIPTION, *n.* 1. Recipe, receipt, direction, bidding, dictate, rule, instruction, precept, formula, formulary, law, appointment, doctrine, authority, maxim, theorem, axiom, principle, principium, dictum, order, command, request, instruction, ruling, regulation.

2. Usage, custom, practice, institution, observance, wont, convention, conventional usage.

3. Privilege, prerogative, power, grant, due, pretension, interest, claim, title.

4. Recipe, nostrum, remedy, medicine, receipt.

PRESENCE, *n.* 1. Presentness, existence, substantiality, entity, being, subsistence, life, habitation, occupancy, ubiquitousness, ubiquity, attendance, company, neighborhood, residence, residency, inhabitancy, cohabitation, omnipresence.

2. Appearance, aspect, visage, look, looks, sight, features, bearing, mien, demeanor, carriage, expression, air, manner, ostent, favor, guise, image, cast, complexion, lineaments, favor, face, vis-

age, behavior, conduct, deportment, comportment, address, observance, manners.

3. Elegance, *savoir-faire (Fr.)*, gentility, good manners, politeness, courtliness, culture, gentility, urbanity, polish, refinement, culture, cultivation, mansuetude, amenity, compliance, complacency, good temper, good humor, comity.

4. Spirit, ghost, spiritual presence, manifestation, spiritual manifestation, incorporeality, shade, phantasm, phasm, spook, specter, wraith, revenant, shadow, apparition, eidolon, vision, haunt *(coll.)*.

PRESENCE OF MIND, *n.* Self-possession, *sangfroid (Fr.)*, balance, aplomb, mental poise, ballast, level-headedness, sobriety, level-head *(coll.)*, quick thinking, alertness, alertness of mind, alacrity, self-control, quickness, equanimity.

PRESENT, *adj.* To hand, at hand, on hand *(coll.)*, in the company of, in the presence of, nigh, near, in the room, vicinal, nearby, about, now, existent, extant, unremoved, embedded, rooted, implanted, ensconced, current, prevalent, subsistent, subsistential, under the sun, afloat, instant, actual, immediate, at the moment.

PRESENT, *n.* 1. Gift, giving, donation, offering, donative, benefaction, gratuity, largess, boon, grant, *douceur (Fr.)*, compound, compliment, tip, liberality, alms, bounty, endowment, vouchsafement, sportula, fee, oblation, legacy, bequest.

2. Now, today, the present time, the moment, this moment, this day and age, the times, the existing times, the nonce, the occasion, the present juncture, day, hour, crisis, the time being.

PRESENT, *v.* 1. Set forth, produce, offer, exhibit, show, draw forth, materialize, display, make a display of, put on display, bring to notice, visibilize, show forth, make visible, uncover, disclose, unscreen, uncurtain, unveil, expose to view, bring to light, register, read, furnish, hand in, submit.

2. Advance, produce, adduce, tender, instance, assign, allege, contribute, yield, afford, give, supply, provide.

3. Proffer, overture, offer, submit, propose, tender, hold out, put forward, invite, place at one's disposal, place at one's feet, donate, give, award, accord, vouchsafe, confer, bestow, give out, give away, dispose of, contribute, chip in *(coll.)*, make a present of, render, dole out, mete out.

4. Inform, tell, give by way of information, impart, communicate, mention, make known, apprise of, notify, give notice of, assert, asseverate, allege, state, profess, propose, advance, put forth, offer, broach, pronounce, expound, prelect, lecture, discourse, hold forth, harangue, express, put into words, phrase, express in words, couch in terms, term, put, deliver, emit, talk, utter, come up with *(coll.)*, give utterance, aver, declare, recite, relate, recount, narrate.

PRESENTABLE, *adj.* 1. Good enough, moderately good, tolerable, passable, acceptable, tidy, respectable, decent, better than nothing, not bad, unobjectionable, up to the mark, satisfactory, pretty good, pretty well, unexceptionable, so-so, fair-to-middling, up to par *(coll.)*.

2. Fashionable, being done, stylish, modish, in the mode, admissible, admissible in society, up-to-date, the newest thing, all the rage, decent.

PRESENTANEOUS, *adj.* Instantaneous, straightaway, immediate, instant, forthwith, momentary,

quick as lightening, without pause, unhesitating, sudden, prompt, summary, ready.

PRESENTATION, *n.* 1. Introduction, civility, politeness, act of courtesy, amenity, courteous act.

2. Representation, show, exhibit, exhibition, manifestation, appearance, production, exposition, display, demonstration, unenfoldment, materialization, revelation, disclosure, exposure, unfolding.

3. Offer, proffer, proffering, offering, overture, submission, proposal, proposition, advance, gift, bestowal, present, vouchsafement, giving, donative, benefaction, gratuity, largess, boon, grant, favor, *douceur (Fr.)*, compound, compliment, tip, fee, liberality, alms, bounty, endowment, sportula, oblation, legacy, bequest.

PRESENTIENT, *adj.* 1. Anticipatory, haruspical, predictive, prophetic, predictional, prognosticatory, prognostic, vaticinal, vaticinative, foreboding, boding, augurial, augural, monitorial, monitory, precursive, sibyllic, sibylline, precursal, ominous.

2. Prescient, precognitive, far-sighted, far-seeing, anticipatory, precognizant, presciental, sagacious, forward-looking, provident, oracular, presageful, divinatory, vaticinal, vaticinatory, shrewd, quick-witted, perceptive, perspicacious, appercipient, apperceptive, perceptive, discerning, penetrating, precautionary, cautious, precautious, provident.

PRESENTIMENT, *n.* Foreboding, foretaste, forethought, anticipation, expectation, apprehension, presage, premonition, description, intuition, forecast, inspiration, preapprehension, omination, premonishment, presagement.

PRESENTLY, *adv.* Directly, soon, in no time now, pretty soon, in a while, after a time, after a while, briefly, shortly, in a short time, in a short while, before long, ere long, by and by, anon, in due time, at the first opportunity, forthwith, speedily, without delay, instantaneously, instantly, straightaway, without delay.

PRESENTMENT, *n.* 1. Representation, presentation, offer, giving, bestowal.

2. Arraignment, impeachment, indictment.

PRESERVATION, *n.* 1. Salvation, saving, conservation, support, guard, defense, maintenance, protection, safekeeping, keeping, storage, safeguarding, ward, watch, watch and ward, self-protection, self-preservation, self-defense, security, custody.

2. Storage, drying, curing, tanning, embalming, mummification, desiccation, cold storage, refrigeration, freezing, deep-freezing, quick-freezing, sun-drying, painting, varnishing, shellacking, waxing, coating, covering, sugaring, candying, canning, pickling, ensilage, evaporation.

PRESERVATIVE, *n.* Preserving agent, preserver, prophylaxis, hygiene, hygienics.

PRESERVATIVE, *adj.* Prophylactic, conservative, preservatory, protective, conservatory, precautionary, saving.

PRESERVE, *v.* 1. Keep safe, keep, maintain, guard, watch over, nurse, protect, support, hold, sustain, keep sound, keep intact, shield, save, shelter, defend, secure, cherish, screen, safeguard, ward, uphold, cloak, harbor, foster, cover, shroud, spare, put away, conceal.

2. Cure, salt, corn, mummify, embalm, preservatize, kipper, marinate, season, dry, sun-dry, smoke, smoke-cure, pickle, refrigerate, freeze,

put in the deep freeze, dehydrate, keep from decaying, preserve from decay.

PRESERVE, *n.* 1. Jam, jelly, comfit, confiture *(Fr.),* marmalade, sweet, sweetmeat, compote, confection.

2. Enclosure, warren, domain, closure, fold, pen.

PRESERVER, *n.* 1. Preservative, preserving agent, prophylaxis, conserver.

2. Rescuer, freer, savior, deliverer, manumitter, redeemer, emancipator, liberator.

PRESHOW, *v.* Foreshow, auspicate, betoken, foreshadow, premonstrate, prefigurate, divine, presage, forebode, portend, ominate, omen, presignify, pretoken, preindicate, pretypify, shadow forth, prefigure, prognosticate, point to, signify, augur.

PRESIDE, *v.* Direct, govern, control, watch, supervise, superintend, manage, administrate, overlook, administer, oversee, keep order, keep in order, hold the chair, be in the chair, be in authority, hold a position of authority, have the portfolio, preside at the board, be the chairman, preside at a meeting, command, rule, regulate, boss *(coll.),* be at the head of, wield authority, hold authority.

PRESIDENCY, *n.* Presidentship, high office, chief executiveship, first executiveship, public office.

PRESIDENT, *n.* 1. Chief executive, first citizen, presider, official, chief official, public official, public servant, elected official, executive officer, executive, head of the nation, commander-in-chief, head of government, chief magistrate.

2. Ruler, chairman, toastmaster, speaker, provost, speaker of the house, President of the Senate, praeses, prefect, dean, deacon, marshal, moderator, functionary.

PRESIGNIFY, *v.* Foreshow, preshow, auspicate, betoken, foreshadow, premonstrate, prefigurate, divine, presage, forebode, portend, ominate, omen, presignify, pretoken, preindicate, pretypify, shadow forth, prefigure, prognosticate, point to, signify, augur, foretell, predict, prophesy.

PRESS, *n.* 1. Printing press, printing machine, hand press, flatbed press, rotary press, cylinder press, Linotype press, web press, electrotype press, platen press, proof press, letter press, perfecting press, roller press.

2. The Press, the Fourth Estate, journalism, newspaperdom, Fleet Street *(England),* the public press, public print.

3. Throng, crowd, multitude, mob, pack, rush, crush, swarm, body, legion, rabble, host, heap, squeeze *(coll.),* bunch, drove.

4. Pressure, urgency, hurry, dictate, need, motivation, inducement, provocation, instigation, incitation, incitement, impulse, actuation, prompting, stimulation, instance, insistence, advocacy, encouragement.

5. Business, press of business, great hurry, hum of business, the madding crowd, great affairs, the world of affairs, much going on *(coll.),* goings on, plenty to do, no sinecure, bustle, hustle, flurry, ferment, stew, bother, pother, fluster, ado, to-do *(coll.),* hurry.

6. Pressure, compulsion, duress, obligation, stress, constraint, coercion, coaction, enforcement, draft, conscription.

7. Closet, armoire, wardrobe, chiffonier, cupboard, bureau, repository, storage closet, cabinet,

chest, commode, cellarette, chest of drawers, clothespress, bunker.

PRESS, *v.* 1. Lower, take down, press down, depress, let down, force down, compress, condense, take down a peg *(coll.),* push down, detrude, thrust down, reduce, bear down, bear downward, cram, force, strain, jam, wrinkle, crowd, squeeze, crush, stuff.

2. Hot-press, iron, mangle, calender, smooth, flatten, roll, press hard, compress, make smooth, smoothen, steam, remove the wrinkles from.

3. Hug, embrace, enfold, clasp, clasp to one's bosom, take into one's arms, fondle, pet, pat, caress, snuggle, take to one's heart, clasp to one's heart, fold in one's arms, nuzzle.

4. Enjoin, force, enforce, urge, supplicate, entreat, exhort, impel, plead, invite, beg, drive, compel, insist, instigate, inculcate, constrain, beseech, implore, adjure, conjure, appeal, invoke, impetrate, importune, tax, dun, imprecate, beset, bid, bid for.

5. Compel, constrain, force, necessitate, make necessary, require, bear upon, bear down upon, take no denial, insist upon, make, drive, bring pressure to bear on, put pressure on, oblige, exact, twist from, extort, wring, wrench from, conscript, bind, impress, pin down, tie down, force from, put the screws on, make a point of.

6. Propel, impel, motivate, move, incite, urge, animate, prick, goad, spur, provoke, evoke, actuate, activate, call up, prompt, urge on, urge forward, hound, push, hurry, rush, instigate, arouse, exhort, excite, prod, whip, lash, set on, egg on *(coll.),* bear down upon, bring pressure to bear upon, hound on.

7. Hurry, rush, speed, accelerate, hurry up *(coll.),* hustle, fidget, make haste, scramble, scuttle, scurry, scamper, run, dash, cut along, press forward, lose no time, stir oneself, dash about, rush to and fro, move along, fuss, bustle, splutter, be in a hurry, be in haste, work under pressure, work against time, be precipitate, plunge ahead, plunge headlong, jump.

8. Crowd, throng, force a way, press in upon, crush, mill, congregate, assemble, come together, flock together, gather, forgather, collect, muster, gang up *(coll.),* bunch up, cluster, flock, surge, swarm, herd, herd together, conglomerate, concentrate, center around, huddle together, huddle, gather 'round, press in, rendezvous.

PRESS AGENT, *n.* Publicity agent, publicist, propagandist, public relations man, publicizer, ballyhooer *(sl.),* ballyhoo artist *(sl.),* blurb writer *(sl.),* blurbist *(sl.),* publicity man.

PRESSER, *n.* Calender, mangle, press, iron, steam iron, sadiron, hand iron, electric iron.

PRESSING, *adj.* Urgent, necessary, needed, critical, vital, important, constraining, distressing, imperative, cogent, grave, hard, incumbent, laborious, exigent, emergent, pushing, forceful, clamoring, crying, crucial, instant, insistent, importunate, requisite, required, indispensable, essential, necessitous, needful, demanded, called for, in demand, prerequisite.

PRESSMAN, *n.* 1. Printer, printer's devil, typesetter, compositor, stereotyper, stereotypist, linotyper, linotypist, book printer, job printer, journeyman printer, printer's apprentice.

2. Newsman, newspaperman, journalist, reporter, news writer, correspondent, foreign correspondent, gentleman of the press, leg man *(sl.),* interviewer, writer for the papers, writer for the

press, press representative, special correspondent, war correspondent, columnist, paragraphist, feature writer, editorialist, editorial writer, sports writer, editor, copy reader, copy editor, leader writer *(English)*, Grubb Street writer.

PRESSURE, *n.* 1. Influence, sway, power, force, weight, potency, potence, importance, consequence, moment, prestige, pull, drag *(sl.)*, influentiality, interest, bias, constraint, constraining force.

2. Insistence, urgency, stress, pinch, exigency, insistency, compulsion, coercion, coation, persuasion, stress, hurry, necessity, need, necessitude, want.

3. Weight, heaviness, gravity, density, relative density, relative weight, gravitation.

4. Affliction, grievance, adversity, pinch, rub, oppression, straits, difficulty, embarrassment, emergency, jam *(coll.)*, need, distress, anxiety, trouble, bother, botherment, scourge, visitation, trial, ups and downs, care, load, cross.

PRESSWORK, *n.* Typography, type printing, publishing, engraving, printing, print, imprint, letterpress, printed matter, the printed page, type matter, material, paleotypography, stereotypy, phototypy, gravure, rotogravure, chromotypography, chromoxylography, composition, composing, typesetting, autotypography.

PRESTIDIGITATION, *n.* Sleight-of-hand, legerdemain, magic, conjuring, conjuration, juggling, palming, thaumaturgics, thaumaturgy, deluding, hocus-pocus, jugglery, sorcery, trickery.

PRESTIDIGITATOR, *n.* Magician, conjurer, trickster, hoaxer, sleight of hand artist, legerdemainist, juggler, performer of tricks, sorcerer.

PRESTIGE, *n.* Authority, power, rank, influence, renown, sway, potency, potence, reputation, repute, rule, pre-eminence, superiority, ascendance, prepotency, prepotence, prepollence, prepollency, predominance, predomination, importance, pressure, moment, weight, consequence, influentiality, prominence, eminency, eminence, mark, import, notability, significance, distinction, nobility, dignity, grandeur, majesty, primacy, paramountcy, precedence, fame, high repute, esteem, high honor, regard, account, report, ascendancy.

PRESTO, *adv.* Quickly, in haste, promptly, fast, swiftly, speedily, rapidly, suddenly, at once, instantaneously, instanter, instantly, prestissimo, allegro *(Mus.)*, allegretto *(Mus.)*, veloce *(It.)*, vivace *(Mus.)*, con brio *(Mus.)*, subito *(It.)*, in a jiffy, at the same moment, no sooner said than done, at one swoop, in one fell swoop, slapdash, precipitately, unexpectedly, on the spot, at the instant, in nothing flat, in a trice, in no time, in no time at all, in the twinkling of an eye, like a shot out of hell *(coll.)*, right away.

PRESUMABLE, *adj.* Probable, reasonable, thinkable, credible, believable, apparent, doubtless, undoubted, undoubtable, indubitable, not to be doubted, likely, promising, presumptive, apt, liable, hopeful, supposable, imaginable, conjecturable, fanciable.

PRESUMABLY, *adv.* Apparently, probably, reasonably, conceivably, credibly, believably, thinkably, doubtlessly, undoubtedly, indubitably, promisingly, presumptively, hopefully, supposably, imaginably, conjecturably, fanciably, in all likelihood, in all probability, most likely, as like as not, to all appearances, all things considered, everything being equal.

PRESUME, *v.* 1. Take a liberty, make free with, venture, dare, take leave, arrogate, make free, make bold, patronize.

2. Assume, surmise, opine, be inclined to think, conclude, gather, expect *(coll.)*, imagine, divine, believe, dare say, say, deem, understand, consider, deduce, judge, calculate *(coll.)*, conceive, dream, allow *(coll.)*, fancy, suppose, presurmise, take, take for granted, be afraid *(coll.)*, venture a guess, hazard a guess, apprehend, have it, look upon as, hold, hold as, suspect, realize, derive, collect, infer, imply *(erron.)*, make up one's mind, advance, think likely, count upon.

3. Jump to conclusions, forejudge, prejudge, presuppose, preconceive, be prejudiced, come to a hasty conclusion, go off half-cocked.

PRESUMING, *adj.* Arrogant, proud, presumptuous, conceited, assuming, bold, confident, presumptive, arbitrary, audacious, impudent, pert, malapert, bumptious, forward, flippant, flip, nervy *(coll.)*, overconfident, brash, cheeky *(coll.)*, crusty *(sl.)*, procacious.

PRESUMPTION, *n.* 1. Prejudgment, preapprehension, assumption, preconceived opinion, preconception, predilection, predisposition, foregone conclusion, prenotice, prenotion, prejudication, persuasion, belief, conviction, mind, conception, thought, view, attitude, turn of mind, surmise, inference, deduction, supposition, conjecture, guess, anticipation, hypothesis, understanding, theory, supposal, speculation, guesswork, proposition, postulate, position, hope, expectation, trust, confidence, faith, reliance, affiance.

2. Rashness, arrogance, forwardness, audacity, effrontery, boldness, brass, gall, cheek *(coll.)*, daring, presumptuousness, pride, egotism, impudence, impertinence, insolence, hardihood, rudeness, pertness, nerve *(coll.)*, haughtiness, indiscretion, precipitancy, precipitance, folly, impetuousness, impetuosity, thoughtlessness, heedlessness, contumely, procacity, flippancy, assurance, hardened front, crust *(sl.)*, sauce, lip, malapertness.

3. Probability, grounds for believing, prospect, chance, favorable chance, confidence, firm expectation, great expectation, reliance, trust, conviction, presumptive evidence, circumstantial evidence, likelihood, likeliness, fair chance, reasonable chance, fair prospect, good chance, plausibility.

PRESUMPTIVE, *adj.* Constructive, hearsay, circumstantial, documentary, nuncupative, evidential, likely, probable, possible, plausible, promising, fair, hopeful, apt, liable, presumable, suppositional, suppositionary, conjectural, speculative, speculatory, postulative, postulatory, supposititious, suppository, hypothetical, academical, theoretical, assumptive.

PRESUMPTUOUS, *adj.* 1. Haughty, disdainful, proud, prideful, contumelious, cavalier, overbearing, snobbish, lordly, lofty, imperious, assuming, pompous, consequential, contemptuous, patronizing, arbitrary, dictatorial, magisterial, domineering.

2. Audacious, daring, insulting, impertinent, impudent, shameless, brazen, flippant, flip *(coll.)*, saucy, brash, bold, smart *(coll.)*, smarty *(coll.)*, smartalecky *(coll.)*, forward, fresh *(sl.)*, precocious, malapert, procacious, familiar, obtrusive, overfamiliar, cocky *(sl.)*, discourteous, impolite, disrespectful, rude, ungentlemanly, unladylike,

ill-bred, ill-mannered, unceremonious, uncourtly, ungenteel.

PRESUPPOSE, *v.* Assume, presume, infer, surmise, take for granted, suppose, prejudice, postulate, conjecture, imagine, divine, expect *(coll.)*, suspicion *(coll.)*, reckon, trow, deem, be inclined to think, opine, take it into one's head, give a guess, gather, conclude, conceive, dream, fancy, believe, think, guess, speculate, rush to a conclusion, jump to a conclusion.

PRESUPPOSITION, *n.* Presupposal, assumption, presumption, postulate, prolepsis, premise, proposition, position, thesis, hypothesis, basis, foundation, ground, assumed position, postulation, preapprehension, prejudgment, forejudgment, preconception, foregone conclusion, fixed conclusion, preconceived notion, preconceived opinion, preconceived judgment, prejudice, prenotion, prepossession, prenotice, surmise, putation, conjecture, guess, speculation.

PRETEND, *v.* 1. Sham, counterfeit, dissemble, dissimulate, feign, simulate, seem, play false, give a false appearance, disguise, affect, mask, bemask, make a show of, pass off for, gammon *(coll.)*, sail under false colors, put on, assume, four-flush *(coll.)*, play a double game, put on a false front, hide under a mask, act, portray, perform, take a part, fill a role, mimic, imitate, represent, impersonate, personify, make a pretext of, lie, prevaricate, deceive, twist the truth, make believe, fake.

2. Put forward, broach, claim, make a claim.

PRETENDED, *adj.* Feigned, affected, spurious, ostensible, purported, assumed, counterfeit, artificial, unauthentic, false, sophisticated, sham, fabulous, self-styled, *soi-disant (Fr.)*, nominal, surreptitious, fictitious, faked, fake, illegitimate, would-be, simulated, imitated, mimicked, imitation, shoddy, pastiche, mock, colorable, colored, phony *(coll.)*, dissimulated, dissembled, feinted, pretensive, bogus, supposititious, dummy, acted, specious, make-believe, trumped-up, scamped, forged, tricky, fraudulent, factitious, deceptive, bastard, pseudo, plated, tawdry, tinsel, flash, cheap, adulterated, unsound, not genuine, ungenuine.

PRETENDER, *n.* Humbug, impostor, charlatan, quack, cheat, knave, deceiver, rascal, mountebank, hypocrite, fake, fraud, deluder, dissimulator, dissembler, pharisee, sophist, cheater, sharper, trickster, rogue, swindler, perjurer, cozener, faker, fourflusher, liar, prevaricator, equivocator, romancer, fibber, storyteller *(coll.)*, fibster, poseur, malingerer, adventurer, adventuress, huckster, duffer, gouger, shyster, necromancer, chameleon, coxcomb, dandy, puppy, snob, upstart, parvenu, puffer, flatterer, sycophant, adulator, trumpeter, empiric, bluffer, bluff, wolf in sheep's clothing, jackdaw, attitudinarian, braggart, boaster, gasbag *(sl.)*, blowhard *(coll.)*, windbag *(sl.)*, poser, posturer, simulator, feigner, sciolist, actor, would-be, counterfeiter.

PRETENSE, *n.* 1. Show, false appearance, semblance, mask, deception, cloak, color, coloration, window dressing, surface, affectation, simulation, imitation, mimicry, veiling, tinsel, mummery, varnish, veneer, feint, subterfuge, gloss, cover, empty show, dust in the eyes.

2. Ostentation, showing-off, display, pretension, fanfaronade, parade, ostentatiousness, inflation, pomp, pomposity, affectation, solemnity,

glitter, show, dash, fuss, splendor, false show, splurge *(coll.)*, splash *(coll.)*, shine *(coll.)*, impressive effect.

3. Humbug, quackery, mummery, hypocrisy, charlatanism, charlatanry, cant, fraudulence, fraud, trumpery, bosh *(sl.)*, spoofery, humbuggery, humbuggism, bamboozling, trickery, pettifoggery, dishonesty, pretension, pretentiousness, hocus-pocus, equivocation, quackism, quackishness, four-flushing, bluffery, bluffing, affectation, affectedness, putting on airs *(coll.)*, fanfaronade, pomposity, veneer, surface, Pharisaism, mendacity, untruth, untruthfulness, fib, fibbing, lie, lying, falsehood, falsifying, falsification, perjury, puffing, flattery, trumpeting, absurdity, babble, babbling, nonsense, blather, folderol, chatter, chit-chat, wind, windiness, flatulence, rabble, rattle, claptrap, stuff, tergiversation.

4. Hoax, imposture, humbug, imposition, fraud, deceit, trickery, deception, trick, cheat, gammon, dodge, gouge, blind, feint, chouse, gull, sham, stuff, spoof, bunk, buncombe, hokum *(sl.)*, bamboozlement, misrepresentation, counterfeit, cheating, wile, cog, shift, blind, swindle, gyp *(sl.)*, fake, make-believe, guise, disguise, disguisement, false colors, camouflage, mockery, forgery, flimflam, fabrication, invention, pretension, pretentiousness.

5. Boasting, braggadocio, gas *(sl.)*, bragging, exaggeration, bravado, bounce, braggardism, braggartry, vaunt, vaunting, gasconade, bombast, rant, hot air *(sl.)*, swagger, self-advertising, overcommendation, highfalutin *(coll.)*, bluster, jactitation, overlaudation.

PRETENTIOUS, *adj.* Affected, presuming, conspicuous, showy, flashy, assuming, ostentatious, conceited, tawdry, flimsy, hollow, insubstantial, vain, priggish, inflated, bombastic, fatuous, brassy, smart, high-sounding, Tartuffian, exaggerated, snobbish, pedantic, didactic, sententious, theatrical, flatulent, over-inflated, stuffy, lofty, toplofty *(coll.)*, pompous, specious, swelling, swollen, vainglorious, hoity-toity *(coll.)*, grandiloquent, airy, thrasonical, immodest, high-flown, hypocritical, stilted, egotistic, egotistical, namby-pamby, charlatanic, pert, cocky, overweening, peacockish, foppish, dandified, puffed-up, swell-headed, arrogant, boastful, braggardly, bragging, self-glorifying, self-esteeming, self-important, over-confident, over-laudatory, self-approving, self-praising, self-opinionated, self-content, complacent, smug, self-admiring, conceited, stuck-up *(sl.)*, self-flattering, high-toned, flaunting, swelling, flashing, jazzy *(sl.)*, flamboyant, florid, flowery, ornate, gaudy, over-ornate, overdecorated, elaborate, magnificent, splendid, swank *(sl.)*, swanky *(sl.)*, grandiloquent, high-sounding, proudful, prideful, puffed up, blown up, swollen with pride, stagy, coxcomical, simpering, insincere, unnatural, gasconading, fanfaronading, imposing, overdone, extravagant, tall *(coll.)*, vainglorious, overbearing, high and mighty *(coll.)*, dictatorial, loud *(coll.)*, garish, glaring, flaming, screaming *(coll.)*, orotund, mouthy, sonorous, lexiphanic, Johnsonian, grandisonous, grandisonant.

PRETERHUMAN, *adj.* Superhuman, hypernormal, supernatural, preternatural, supernormal, hyperphysical, superphysical, unworldly, supramundane, preternormal, extramundane, unearthly.

PRETERIT, *adj.* 1. Past, pluperfect, perfect, past perfect, past absolute, imperfect *(all grammatical)*.

2. Past, bygone, former, late, preterlapsed,

lapsed, agone, gone, ago, elapsed, run out, expired, no more, irrecoverable, forgotten, obsolete, extinct, non-existent, non-extant.

PRETERITION, *n.* Times past, time gone past, times gone by, retrospection, past time, priority, former times, yesteryear, yesterday, long ago, the good old days, olden days, olden times, old times, things long gone, days of yore, auld lang syne *(Scot.),* antiquity, ancient history, ancientness, oldness, age, old age, remote past, distant past, remote times, things past, ancient times.

PRETERMISSION, *n.* Pretermitting, omission, disregardance, disregard, abandonment, neglect, negligence, default, slight, oversight, inadvertence, nonobservance, inattention, the go-by *(sl.),* paralepsis, remissness, laxity, laches, failure, nonchalance, dereliction.

PRETERMIT, *v.* Pass, ignore, overlook, disregard, neglect, leave out, pass over, omit, lose, fail to perform, leave undone, forbear, skip, bypass, abandon, leave alone, leave loose ends, miss, jump, gloss over, skim over, perform superficially, delay, shelve, suspend, intermit, interrupt, procrastinate, postpone, touch lightly, lay aside, table, let stand, put off, stave off, prorogate, respite, waive, defer, shunt, lay aside, cast aside, put aside, put off, put on the shelf, pigeonhole.

PRETERNATURAL, *adj.* Supernatural, unearthly, unnatural, marvelous, miraculous, extraordinary, anomalous, monstrous, abnormal, irregular, aberrant, supernormal, extranormal, hypernatural, preterhuman, hypernormal, hyperphysical, superphysical, unworldly, supermundane, extramundane, spiritual, odd, unwonted, uncommon, indescribable, unaccustomed, uncustomary, incredible, inconceivable, off the beaten track, prodigious, noteworthy, strange, supersensible, supersensuous, spectral.

PRETEXT, *n.* 1. Pretense, pretension, professed purpose, ostensible purpose, ostensible reason, motive, reason, ground, basis, allegation, claim, profession, false pretense, false pretension, alleged reason, alleged purpose, claim to notice.

2. Excuse, cover, semblance, peg, apology, vindication, justification, plea, warrant, license.

PRETTY, *adj.* 1. Pleasing, attractive, fair, comely, bonny *(dial.),* delicate, graceful, handsome, pulchritudinous, lovely, seemly, tasteful, good-looking, dainty, proportioned, well-proportioned, wellset, well-favored, charming, fetching, engaging, alluring, captivating, goodly, personable, sightly, shapely, well-made, pretty as a picture, fine, beauteous, symmetrical.

2. Foppish, elegant, exquisite, dandified, affected, affectedly nice, nice, flashy, coxcombical, swell *(sl.).*

PRETYPIFY, *v.* Foreshow, prefigure, presymbolize, prefigurate, forebode, omen, ominate, foretoken, betoken, foreshadow, predict, prophesy, divine, prognosticate, premonstrate, shadow forth, presage, foretell, foresee, soothsay, augur, threaten, announce, portend, vaticinate, augurate, hariolate, haruspicate, preindicate, premonstrate.

PREVAIL, *v.* 1. Triumph, win, be victorious, be the victor, lead, conquer, overcome, gain a victory, obtain a victory, carry the day, win out, gain the palm, take the laurels, win the laurels, bring home the bacon *(coll.),* tide over, weather the storm, keep one's head above water, have the game in one's own hands, make a killing *(coll.).*

have the field to oneself, win one's spurs, succeed, be successful, make a go of it *(coll.),* be a winner, be the victor, click *(sl.),* be a success, ring the bell.

2. Preponderate, predominate, succeed, reign, rule, exist, be, subsist, hold sway, have sway, be prevalent, abound, move, have force, be in force, stand, obtain, have being, abide, endure, go about, move about.

PREVAILING, *adj.* 1. Prevalent, common, widespread, usual, general, rife, sweeping, universal, world-wide, global, popular, catholic, current, besetting, epidemic, customary, habitual, going on, in the wind, afloat, accustomed, accustomary, wonted, frequent, stock, everyday, commonplace, set, conventional, normal, vernacular, established, household, settled, fixed, definite, definitive.

2. Plentiful, plenteous, bountiful, copious, flush, replete, rampant, prolix, numerous, lavish, besetting, luxuriant, luxurious, charged, richly charged, exuberant, profuse, unsparing, inexhaustible, abounding, abundant.

3. Forceful, moving, powerful, strong, effective, effectual, efficacious, preponderating, predominating, predominant, preponderant, overruling, influential, persuasive, ascendant, affecting, dominant, dominating, comprehensive, principal, potent, puissant, mighty, vigorous.

PREVAIL ON, PREVAIL UPON, *v.* Induce, persuade, convince, win over, prevail with, move, move by persuasion, bring over, bring 'round, lead, impel, propel, overcome, carry, weigh with, have weight with, carry weight with, procure, turn one's head, cajole, coax, influence, engage, enlist, wheedle, bring to one's senses, advise, tempt, seduce, conduce, affect, make *(sl.).*

PREVALENCE, *n.* 1. Prevalency, existence, being, currency, run, frequence, commonness, oftenness, continuance, rifeness, naturalness, usualness, generality, universality, popularity, catholicity, habituality, habitualness, customariness, commonplaceness, definition, definiteness, fixedness.

2. Lead, transcendence, superiority, preëminence, prepollence, predominance, predominancy, predomination, preponderance, preponderancy, ascendancy, prestige, prepotence, excellence, preponderation.

3. Force, forcefulness, power, strength, effectiveness, effectualness, effectuality, efficaciousness, persuasiveness, affectingness, effect, potency, puissance, might, mightiness, vigor, efficacity.

PREVALENT, *adj.* 1. Ruling, authoritative, in command, commanding, dominant, preponderant, predominating, predominant, ascendant, in the ascendancy, having the upper hand, in control, determining, at the head, governing, executive, influential, powerful, mighty, puissant, forceful, vigorous, supreme, paramount, chief, hegemonic, hegemonical, prepollent, regnant, overruling, peremptory, victorious, successful, swaying, overswaying, telling, weighty, authoritative, in authority, in ascendancy, preponderating.

2. Extant, existing, current, living, on foot, afloat, rampant, besetting, rife, world-wide, universal, catholic, extensive, far-reaching, widespread, far-going, far-embracing, all-embracing, wide, far-flung, happening, prevailing, usual, general, sweeping, global, popular, epidemic, customary, habitual, in the wind, accustomed, accustomary, commonplace, everyday, set, fixed, established, conventional, normal, definitive, definite, settled, stock, wonted, frequent, vernacular.

PREVARICATE, *v.* Lie, falsify, tell a falsehood, fib, equivocate, evade the truth, be evasive, hoodwink, dodge, gammon, cavil, shuffle, fence, hedge, ergotize, sophisticate, elude, stickle, defraud, tergiversate, shift, pettifog, palter, trifle, quibble, parry, shy, beat about the bush, beg the question, split hairs, be a liar, speak falsely, forswear, perjure, bear false witness, tell a story *(coll.),* lie in one's teeth, lie flatly, draw the longbow, stretch the truth, dissemble, put on, dissimulate, conceal the truth, pretend, sham, make-believe, counterfeit, be untruthful, deviate from the truth, misinform, exaggerate, hyperbolize, perjure oneself, weasel, embroider, gloss over, embroider the truth, distort, twist the truth, construe falsely, put a false construction on, give a false color to.

PREVARICATION, *n.* Equivocation, quibble, quibbling, cavil, caviling, lie, lying, casuistry, shuffling, evasiveness, evasion, deception, deceptiveness, mendacity, dishonesty, untruthfulness, chicanery, pretense, pettifoggery, pettifogging, elusiveness, untruth, falsehood, distortion of the truth, perversion of the truth, twisting of the truth, fabrication, fiction, factitiousness, counterfeiting, perjury, forswearing, false swearing, falsification, falsifying, false coloring, improbity, artfulness, guile, subterfuge, hairsplitting, overrefinement, fable, myth, romance, flimflammery, fibbing, fib, tarradiddle *(coll.),* falseness, claptrap, concoction, trumped-up story.

PREVARICATOR, *n.* Deceiver, liar, falsifier, false witness, perjurer, wrongdoer, malefactor, sophist, dodger, sophister, dissembler, dissimulator, equivocator, humbug, humbugger, cheat, cozener, deluder, beguiler, seducer, hoaxer, fooler *(coll.),* shuffler, evader, twister, casuist, quibbler, double-dealer, cockatrice, serpent, confidence agent, con man *(sl.),* impostor, bluffer, bluff, hypocrite, canter, pharisee, spinner of yarns, romancer, fabulist, fictioneer, pathological liar, consummate liar, fibber, fibster, fabricator.

PREVENIENT, *adj.* 1. Prefatory, preceding, introductory, going before, preliminary, antecedent, precursory, anticipatory, prior, anterior, prelusive, prelusory, preparatory, proemial, inaugural, foregoing, former, previous, prodromal.

2. Prophylactic, preventive, preventative, counteractive, reactionary, forestalling, oppositional, opposing, opposite, reactive, counteracting.

PREVENT, *v.* Stop, hinder, forestall, obstruct, inhibit, prohibit, impede, halt, deter, save, thwart, check, restrain, intercept, interrupt, obviate, debar, counteract, ward off, foreclose, neutralize, block, shield, shield off, forfend, hold back, stave off, nip in the bud, override, contradict, circumvent, contest, oppose, forbid, balk, constrain, foil, frustrate, baffle, retard, delay, check, checkmate, overrule, fend off, parry, turn away, deflect, turn aside, muzzle, anticipate, defend against, tie, detain, control, cut off, veto, avert, avoid, stay, corner, draw off, sidetrack.

PREVENTATIVE, *n.* Deterrent, hindrance, counteragent, counteractive, remedy, safeguard, protection, antidote, vaccine, serum, medicine, opposition, cross current, counterblast, obstructive, obstruction, offset, neutralizer, prophylactic, inhibitory, inhibitive, impediment, impedient, obstacle, stay, hitch, stop, bar, encumbrance, check, checkrein, arrest, hampering, determent, detention, interference, interception, setback, inhibition, preclusion, foreclosure, retardation, prevention,

blockade, block, blockage, stoppage, coarctation, barrier, impediment, difficulty, curb.

PREVENTION, *n.* Impediment, hindrance, obstruction, stoppage, interference, preclusion, deterrent, determent, restriction, constriction, interception, interruption, inhibition, obviation, elimination, arrest, arresting, contravention, opposition, anticipation, obstacle, restraint, thwarting, frustration, forestalling, exclusion, retardation, retardment, deadlock, counteraction, reaction, obtrusion, defeat, checkmate, foreclosure, embarrassment, infarction.

PREVENTIVE, *adj.* Preventative, hindering, obstructionist, obstructive, impedimental, onerous, burdensome, interfering, deterrent, preclusive, prophylactic, intrusive, cumbersome, cumbrous, encumbering, impeding, impedient, impeditive, inhibitive, inhibitory, restrictive.

PREVIEW, *n.* Preliminary study, preliminary view, pre-examination, presearch, presurvey, prior study, prior examination, early view, preliminary viewing.

PREVIOUS, *adj.* Precedent, prior, former, antecedent, anterior, foregoing, early, foregone, antedated, before, front, in front, at the front of, prefatory, preliminary, forerunning, precursory, initial, initiatory, preparatory, aforesaid, forementioned, predated, fore, untimely, introductory.

PREVIOUSLY, *adv.* Earlier, before, erstwhile, ere, theretofore, heretofore, before now, until now, before this time, on the eve of, then, once, once upon a time, fore, afore, hitherto, thitherto, ere this, ere now, beforetime, aforetime, formerly, in days of yore, in days of old, above, antecedently, at that time, at that instant, some other time, erst, a long time ago, ages ago, years ago, in years gone by, in times past, in times gone by, one fine day, ago, agone, whilom, erewhile, no longer.

PREVISION, *n.* Foreglimpse, prospicience, foresight, prospect, far-sightedness, prospection, anticipation, far-seeingness, forecast, presage, presagement, prediction, prophecy, vaticination, prognostication, preview, foretelling, prefiguration, foreknowledge.

PREY, *n.* 1. Plunder, booty, loot, prize, spoils, seizure, swag, pillage, steal, stolen goods, pilferage, grab, pickings, haul, filch, boodle, spoil, gain, pork barrel.

2. Game, quarry, victim, kill, raven, food.

3. Victim, sufferer, wretch, object of sympathy.

PREY ON, PREY UPON, *v.* 1. Plunder, pillage, ravage, loot, rapine, sack, destroy, despoil, depredate, ransack, gut, forage, sweep, maraud, filibuster, pirate, privateer, strip, fleece, seize, grab.

2. Feed upon, fatten upon, batten upon, feast upon, gorge oneself upon, devour, eat, consume, fasten upon, infest, fasten oneself to, suck the blood of, parasitize.

PRICE, *n.* 1. Cost, value, outlay, amount, expense, expenditure, worth, desert, credit, charge, prime cost, figuration, demand, quotation, damage *(sl.),* fare, hire, toll, score *(sl.),* current price, market price, selling price, retail price, wholesale price, par value, rate, estimate, estimation, list price, face value, outlay, demand, premium, interest, exchange value, consideration, purchase money, appraisement, market value.

2. Duty, toll, tax, levy, excise, impost, tariff, poll tax, property tax, personal property tax, income tax, assessment, poll, pollage, custom,

per capita tax, taxation, brokerage, towage, salvage, wharfage, freightage, exaction, exactment, tonnage, poundage, state tax, federal tax, commission, salt tax, tithe.

3. Reward, compensation, guerdon, recompense, remuneration, indemnification, indemnity, solatium, meed, redress, requital, reparation, atonement, retribution, satisfaction, award, prize, *quid pro quo (Lat.)*, return, punishment, comeuppance *(coll.)*, consequence, result, penalty.

PRICE, *v.* Set a price on, evaluate, determine the value of, appraise, valuate, value, ask the price of, rate, place the value of, place a value on.

PRICELESS, *adj.* Inestimable, valuable, invaluable, without price, precious, peerless, incomparable, irreplaceable, costly, high-priced, high, dear, expensive, beyond price, incalculable, exquisite, worth a king's ransom, worth its weight in gold, rare, extraordinary.

PRICK, *n.* 1. Prickle, spur, needle, spine, spicule, point, tang, spike, prong, tine, spiculum, nail, pin, tack, barb, rowel, quill, cusp, spit, snaggle, barbule, barblet, sticker.

2. Spur, incentive, goad, urging, lash, fillip, provocation, provocative, whet, inducement, motivation, actuation, impulse, compulsion, incitement, press.

PRICK, *v.* 1. Perforate, empierce, stick, pierce, puncture, stab, punch, lancinate, spear, spike, lance, impale, spit, penetrate, drill, bore, auger, transfix, transpierce, inject, infix, inoculate, enter, insinuate, interject, intrude, stick in, thrust in, put in, interpenetrate, cut through, pass through.

2. Motivate, spur, impel, propel, actuate, goad, rouse, incite, lash, urge, drive, quicken, stimulate, force, whip, set on, egg on *(coll.)*, prompt, call up, give an urge to, animate, forward, instigate, foment, hound on, encourage, give a slap on the back, give an impulse to, enforce, excite, push, hurry, hurry on, bring pressure to bear upon, put the pressure on, whip, flog, expedite, prod, hasten, speed, quicken, accelerate.

3. Sting, wound, pain, hurt, ache, smart, prickle, cut, damage, impair, harm, scathe, spoil, mar, cut, lancinate, stab, mangle, lacerate, mutilate, disfigure, scar, blemish.

4. Cut, cut to the quick, hurt, hurt to the quick, hurt one's feelings, gall, chafe, rub, sting, wound, turn the knife in the wound, stir the blood, provoke, madden, irritate, annoy, vex, harass, touch, touch the heart, touch a chord, touch the soul, go through one, afflict, give pain, distress, dismay, cut to the heart, cleave the heart in two, bite the hand that feeds one, hurt the feelings, wound the feelings, sadden, cast down, make unhappy, make wretched, nettle, aggrieve, make one's heart bleed, prey on one's mind, haunt the spirits, dispirit, dull, lower one's spirits, cast one down, dash one's hopes, discourage, dishearten, plunge into grief, deject, cut up.

PRICKLE, *n.* 1. Prick, spur, needle, spine, spicule, point, tang, spike, prong, tine, spiculum, nail, pin, tack, barb, rowel, quill, cusp, spit, snaggle, barblet, sticker, sting, nettle, bristle, thorn, jagger, acicule, briar, bramble, bur, cocklebur, barbule.

2. Tingling, the creeps *(coll.)*, chill, pricking sensation, formication, ants in the pants *(vulg.)*, paresthesia.

PRICKLE, *v.* Itch, tingle, tickle, thrill, sting, prick, have the itch, vellicate, titillate.

PRICKLY, *adj.* Echinate, echinated, brambly,
aculeate, briery, thorny, aciculate, aciculated, spiculated, spiculate, thistly, echinulate, echinulated, spiny, acute, spinulous, spinulose, spinous, spinulescent, spinuliferous, apiculate, hairy, pectinate, comb-like, muricated, muriculate, muriculated, brush-like, barbed, barbate, barbellate, barbulose, hispid, hispidulate, setigerous, setiform, setiferous, setose, strigal, strigose, strigillose, strigate, hirsute, bristle-like.

PRICK UP ONE'S EARS, *v.* Attend, give attention, lend attention to, listen, hearken, take interest in, take sudden interest, become interested in, give heed, heed, mind, observe, watch, notice, animadvert, give notice, bend the mind to, turn the attention to, devote oneself to, take note of, mark, be all ears, hark, list, give ear to, be curious, stare, gape, strain one's ears, listen with both ears, listen hard *(coll.)*, keep one's ears open.

PRIDE, *n.* Proudness, self-esteem, self-importance, self-exaltation, toploftiness, swagger, egotism, egoism, self-glorification, glory, conceit, ambition, self-complacency, self-satisfaction, smugness, haughtiness, loftiness, disdain, disdainfulness, hauteur, lordliness, superciliousness, assumption, insolence, vainglory, arrogance, pomposity, presumption, presumptuousness, contumacy, priggishness, imperiousness, contemptuousness, high-hat *(sl.)*, audacity, dignity, self-notions, condescension, boasting, boastfulness, ostentation, display, self-content, self-praise, self-laudation, self-glorification, self-gratulation, self-love, self-endearment, self-worship, self-exaltation, self-approval, self-approbation, self-applause, overweening pride, coxcombry, priggishness, priggery, foppishness, vain pretensions, airs, overestimation, braggadocio, peacockishness, cockiness, immodesty, show, ostentatious display, fanfaronade, parade, pomp, magnificence, overbearance, domineering, bumptiousness.

PRIEST, *n.* Divine, clergyman, minister, minister of the gospel, man of the cloth, man of God, cleric, pastor, hierophant, parson, vicar, ecclesiastic, churchman, worthy, presbyter, corybant, father, confessor, pope, druid, high priest, Brahmin, liturge, Brahman, lama, flamen, padre, hierarch, pontiff, *pontifex maximus (Lat.)*, seminarist, clerk, clerk in holy orders, pulpiteer, curate, servant of God, sermoneer, preacher, chaplain, cassock, father in Christ, abuna, curé, parish priest, spiritual father, prophet, rabbi, Levite, scribe, hierodule, religious, religionist, monk, friar, caloyer, cenobite, celibate, conventual, monastic, pilgrim, beadsman, prior, abbot, vicar general, Benedictine, Franciscan, Jesuit, Minorite, Capuchin, Carthusian, Carmelite, Dominican, Augustinian, Loyolite, Trappist, Cistercian, Cluniac, Bernardine, Maturine, Lorettine.

PRIESTCRAFT, *n.* Sacerdotalism, priesthood, clericalism, churchcraft, ecclesiology, the Church, monasticism, monkhood, monachism, episcopalianism, ultramontanism.

PRIESTESS, *n.* Vestal, clergywoman, ministress, preacheress, parsoness, pastoress.

PRIESTHOOD, *n.* Ministry, churchdom, Christendom, pale of the church, Christianity, hierarchy, apostleship, hierocracy, episcopacy, prelacy, sacerdotalism, clericalism, churchcraft, ecclesiasticism, monkhood, monachism, episcopalianism, ultramontanism, sectarianism, religious sects, the clergy, presbytery, the pulpit, Holy Orders, the cloth, the desk, clericals, monasticism.

PRIESTLY, *adj.* Ministerial, sacerdotal, pastoral, hierophantic, hierarchical, ecclesiastic, ecclesiastical, churchly, divine, levitical, hieratic, prelatical, prelatic, monkish, monastic, monasterial, conventual, ultramontane, episcopal, episcopalian, archiepiscopal, canonical, monachal, abbatical, abbatic, papal, pontifical, popish, papish, apostolic.

PRIG, *n.* 1. Thief, pilferer, stealer, purloiner, burglar, cutpurse, footpad, robber, prigger, lifter, larcenist, rifler, filcher, larcener, plunderer, marauder.
2. Prude, pedant, attitudinarian, precisionist, purist, precisian, puritan, bluestocking, formalist, affecter, mannerist, pretender, grimacer, bigot, hypocrite.
3. Dandy, fop, coxcomb, gentleman, dude (*coll.*), exquisite, blade, buck, popinjay, macaroni, swell (*coll.*), masher, affecter, man about town, knight, carpet knight, spark, blood, beau, ladies' man, jack-a-dandy, jackanapes, puppy, swaggerer, strutter, peacock, silk-stocking.

PRIG, *v.* Steal, rob, thieve, take, snitch, cop (*sl.*), purloin, pilfer, burglarize, lift, commit robbery, snatch, palm, make off with, baggage, pinch (*coll.*), mooch (*sl.*), burgle (*coll.*), commit burglary, cabbage (*sl.*), crib, nip.

PRIGGISH, *adj.* 1. Proud, overproud, overweening, conceited, self-esteeming, dandified, peacocky, vain as a peacock, swell-headed, puffed up, high-flown, egoistical, egotistical, affected, ostentatious, showy, selfish, self-praising, self-flattering, smug, complacent, self-satisfied, self-admiring, self-worshiping, self-endeared, stuck on oneself (*coll.*).
2. Pedantic, overnice, squeamish, punctilious, fastidious, trim, precious, prudish, prim, stiff-necked, hidebound, stiff, formal, formalistic, stilted, smug, demure, affectedly nice, mincing, starched, starchy (*coll.*), bigoted, hypocritical, canting, pompous.

PRIGGISHNESS, *n.* Prudery, prudishness, pedantry, false modesty, fastidiousness, bigotry, hypocrisy, cant, precisianism, purism, puritanism, formalism, affectation, mannerism, pretension, pretense.

PRIM, *adj.* Precise, starched, strait-laced, haughty, frigid, cold, unbending, puritanical, tidy, ceremonious, particular, demanding, exacting, pedantic, overnice, squeamish, punctilious, fastidious, precious, prudish, stiff-necked, hidebound, formalistic, formal, stilted, smug, demure, mincing, bigoted, hypocritical, canting, pompous.

PRIMACY, *n.* 1. Supremacy, headship, leadership, paramountcy, the highest degree, sovereignty, climax, summit, crest, maximum, consequence, importance, eminence, superiority, preëminence, supereminence, domination, authority, dominion, rule, control, regality, royalty, command, sway, majesty, imperiality, jurisdiction, judicature, influence, weight, predomination, predominancy, ascendancy, the whip hand, controlment, moment, regime, hold, grasp, clutches, kingship, dictation, dictature, preponderance, prepollency, prepollence, prestige.
2. Primateship, cardinalcy, cardinalate, archbishopric, archiepiscopate, prelateship, prelature, prelacy, prelatehood, bishopdom, bishopric, episcopate, episcopacy, deanery, deanship, papacy, popedom, pontificate, the Vatican, abbacy, abbotcy.

PRIMA DONNA, *n.* 1. Expert, star, proficient, master, past master, skilled hand, principal, chief, actress, singer, prima ballerina, *diva (It.),* play actress, lead, principal role, performer, star attraction, *prima buffa (It.).*
2. Singer, vocalist, vocalizer, soprano, mezzo soprano, alto, contralto, songstress, songster, melodizer, melodist, warbler, caroler.

PRIMA FACIE (*Latin*) On first sight, at first glance, on the face of the matter, on the face of it, superficial, superficially, as seen, seen at a glance, at first view, at a blush, on presentation, apparently, seemingly, to all appearances.

PRIMARILY, *adv.* At first, foremost, in the first place, first off, right off the bat, right away, first, principally, fundamentally, in the main, on the whole, ultimately, firstly, *imprimis (Lat.),* before anything else, before everything, first and foremost, at the beginning, in the beginning, in the bud, from infancy, from birth, at birth, congenitally, from the word go.

PRIMARY, *adj.* 1. Primitive, aboriginal, initial, primordial, primeval, primal, original, first, prime, pristine, earliest, oldest, generative, protogenic, immediate, elementary, authentic, formative, embryonic, rudimentary, archetypal, genitive, beginning, primigenial, embryonal, inchoate, incipient, initiative, initiatory, germinal, essential, rudimental, constitutive, determining, causal, basic, underlying, radical, native, normal, natural, intrinsic, immanent, innate, inherent, indwelling, infixed, implanted, ingrained, congenital, indigenous, genetic, incarnate, connate, rock-bottom, bedrock, bottommost, lowest, lowermost, nethermost, etiological, causative, basal, elemental, seminal, originative, formative, constitutive, institutive.
2. Chief, principal, main, important, head, capital, prominent, leading, star, greatest, supreme, maximal, highest, utmost, uppermost, predominant, tiptop (*coll.*), topmost, dominant, at the head of, hegemonic, hegemonical, cardinal, crowning, preëminent, supereminent, overruling, ruling, sovereign, matchless, peerless, incomparable, without peer, unapproachable, unapproached, unmatched, excellent, excelling, unsurpassed, transcendent, urgent, compelling, second to none, nonpareil, best, essential, paramount, radical, vital, necessary.
3. Preparatory, elementary, introductory, proemial, initial, premier, first, beginning, nascent, rudimental, rudimentary, inaugural, initiative, incipient, inchoate, primigenial, original, aboriginal.

PRIMATE, *n.* Church official, cardinal, archbishop, bishop, pope, pontiff, *pontifex (Lat.),* chief, prelate, metropolitan, hierarch, ecclesiarch, patriarch, high priest, church dignitary, Holy Father, Vicar of Christ on earth, reverence, eminence, cardinal bishop, exarch, cardinal priest.

PRIME, *adj.* 1. Primeval, primordial, archaic, diluvian, antediluvian, antediluvial, Noachian, Noachical, prehistoric, preadamite, protohistoric, dateless, antepatriarchal, fossil, ancestral, preglacial, primitive, aboriginal, oldest, first, primary, pristine, earliest, generative, protogenic, elementary, authentic, formative, embryonic, rudimentary, archetypal, genitive, beginning, primigenial, embryonal, inchoate, incipient, initiative, initiatory, germinal, essential, rudimental, constitutive, determining, causal, basic, underlying, radical, native, intrinsic, immanent, innate, inherent, indwelling, infixed, implanted, ingrained, congenital, indigenous, genetic, incarnate, connate, rock-bottom, bedrock, bottommost, lowest, lowermost, nethermost, etiological, causative, basal, elemental, seminal, originative, formative, institutive.

2. Main, chief, principal, important, head, capital, prominent, leading, star, greatest, supreme, maximal, highest, utmost, uppermost, predominant, hegemonic, overruling, ruling, sovereign, matchless, peerless, without peer, unapproachable, best, superlative, unapproached, unmatched, excelling, unsurpassed, transcendent, urgent, compelling, second to none, nonpareil, paramount, radical, vital, necessary, at the head of, hegemonical, cardinal, crowning, preëminent, supereminent.

3. Early, in good season, bright and early, timely, fit, expedient, in good time, seasonable, opportune, well-timed, seemly, provident, lucky, auspicious, suitable, fitting, befitting, propitious, happy, felicitous, convenient.

4. Very best, the best, grade-A, select, elect, choice, first-class, picked, specially selected, tophole (sl.), top-drawer (sl.), peerless, quality, of the best quality.

PRIME, n. 1. Start, beginning, opening, the first, commencement, initial, incipience, incipiency, installation, inauguration, alpha, onset, embarkment, embarkation, first move, first blush, inchoation, outset, outstart, setout.

2. Youth, infancy, prime condition, vigor of youth, dawn, morning, early days, early hours, prime of life, youthfulness, juvenility, juvenescence, youthhood, childhood, heyday of youth, salad days, glad season, the happy time, carefree youth, tender years, tender age, nonage, immaturity, juniority, boyhood, girlhood, babyhood.

3. Flower, bloom, perfection, zenith, best days, heyday, height, excellence, the height of one's power, greatest strength, full flowering, full beauty, full strength, maturity, blossoming.

PRIME, v. 1. Prepare, make ready, ready, put into readiness, fit, adjust, adapt, smooth a way, break the ice, get ready, prepare the ground, plow the ground, dress the stage, set the stage, settle the preliminaries.

2. Instruct, teach, give instructions, school, coach, tutor, educate, train, edify, guide, direct, pupilize, set right, put in the right mind for, put in the way of, beat into, drill, show, cram, get up on, bring up to date on.

PRIMED, adj. 1. Prepared, skilled, talented, able, capable, drilled, crammed, initiated, gifted, endowed, conversant, well-versed, well versed in, familiar with, up on, educated, taught, instructed, practiced, well-grounded.

2. Ready, alerted, loaded for bear (coll.), on the alert, set for anything, ready for anything, well-primed, in readiness, prepared, in a state of readiness, vigilant, watchful, expectant.

PRIME MINISTER, n. Premier, first minister, head of state, chief executive, chief official, public servant, public official, civil servant, functionary, executive, leader of the government.

PRIME MOVER, n. 1. Primum mobile (Lat.), motive, rationale, reason, the reason why, motivation.

2. Creator, generator, begetter, author, maker, constructor, introducer, founder, artificer, mover, first cause, primary cause, primordium, Great First Cause.

PRIMER, n. 1. Priming, prime coat, flat coat, primer coat, undercoat, first coat, ground, ground coat, undercoating, flat color, dead color.

2. Schoolbook, reader, reading book, textbook, text, manual, book of instruction, first reader.

PRIMEVAL, adj. Autochthonic, primitive, aboriginal, initial, primordial, primary, primal, original, first, prime, pristine, earliest, oldest, generative, protogenic, immediate, elementary, authentic, formative, embryonic, rudimentary, archetypal, genitive, beginning, primigenial, embryonal, inchoate, incipient, initiative, initiatory, germinal, essential, rudimental, constitutive, determining, causal, basic, underlying, radical, native, intrinsic, immanent, innate, inherent, indwelling, infixed, implanted, ingrained, congenital, indigenous, genetic, incarnate, connate, rock-bottom, bedrock, bottommost, nethermost, lowermost, lowest, etiological, causative, elemental, seminal, originative, formative, institutive, long-gone, remote, venerable, aged, prehistoric, fossil, antique, ancient, immemorial, antediluvial, antediluvian.

PRIMITIVE, adj. 1. Primeval, primordial, aboriginal, etc.

2. Autochthonal, indigenous, vernacular, native, natal, endemic, endemial.

3. Rude, crude, undeveloped, uncultured, uncultivated, unsophisticated, unlearned, unskilled, early, antique, simple, quaint, old-fashioned, aged, obsolete, obsolescent, uncomplicated, underdeveloped.

PRIMORDIUM, n. Prime mover, beginning, commencement, start, origin, origination, source, cause, inception, rise, base, basis, principle, element, incubation, generation, birth, genesis.

PRIMP, v. Embellish, dress, ornament, set off, prink, dress fastidiously, bedeck, bedizen, dress up, prank, array, smarten, smarten up, garnish, set out, deck out, spruce up (coll.), furbish, make up, dizen, dandify, trim, adorn, beautify.

PRINCE, n. Ruler, sovereign, atheling, lord, khan, satrap, potentate, monarch, feudatory, mirza, Fürst (Ger.), Prinz (Ger.), emir, shah, sheik, princeling, royal heir, princelet, crowned head, liege, overlord, nobleman, son of the king, son of the royal house, royal person, royal personage, crown prince, dauphin (Fr.), royal duke.

PRINCELY, adj. 1. Princelike, regal, royal, imperial, dynastic, dynastical, majestic, kingly, monarchical, monarchial.

2. Lordly, majestic, noble, mighty, eminent, prominent, stately, proud, dignified, august, noble, imposing, peerless, preëminent, grand, egregious, stately, patrician, of noble rank, aristocratic, genteel, of noble blood, of royal blood, highborn, nobly born, blue-blooded, wellborn, splendid, superb, supreme, patrician, rich, sumptuous.

3. Generous, kind, free-handed, liberal, magnanimous, munificent, benevolent, kindly, large-hearted, big-hearted, open-handed, forbearing, patient, benign, benignant, good, amiable, lenient, indulgent, considerate, humane, humanitarian, charitable, warm-hearted, tender-hearted, gracious, mild, compassionate, pitying, good-humored, good-natured, sympathetic, well-disposed, chivalrous, chivalric, courteous, polite, urbane, civil, courtly, gallant, brave, courageous, well-mannered, mannerly, bounteous, clement, philanthropic, temperate.

PRINCESS, n. Princesse (Fr.), infanta (Sp. and

Port.), *tzarevna (Russ.)*, shahzadi, begum, rani, maharani, empress, queen, sovereign, ruler, lady, duchess, marchioness, marquise, dauphinesse, sultana.

PRINCIPAL, *adj.* Chief, leading, main, prime, primary, first, highest, preëminent, cardinal, most important, most considerable, capital, essential, foremost, dominant, greatest, most powerful, basic, fundamental, ultimate, supreme, topmost, utmost, uttermost, uppermost, sovereign, superior, supereminent, imposing, prominent, prevailing, controlling, predominant, predominating, outstanding, arch, paramount, maximum, maximal, exceeding, surpassing, hegemonical, crowning, overruling, terminal, final, determinative, definitive, conclusive.

PRINCIPAL, *n.* 1. Master, headmaster, dean, superior, chief authority, person in authority.

2. Chief, paramount, chief party actor, star, featured player, participant, first fiddle *(coll.)*.

3. Capital sum, main body, invested sum, substance, fund, original sum.

PRINCIPALITY, *n.* 1. State, nation, country, monarchy, land, realm, archduchy, duchy, grand duchy, palatinate.

2. Angel, heavenly being, divine messenger, God's messenger, ministering spirit, invisible helper, guardian angel.

PRINCIPALLY, *adv.* Chiefly, mainly, mostly, essentially, in the main, in the first place, generally, most of all, particularly, especially, above all, eminently, egregiously, peculiarly, beyond everything else, still more, even, yea, indeed, all the more, of all things, the most, remarkably, surpassingly.

PRINCIPLE, *n.* 1. Beginning, prime, base, element, origin, source, fountain, prime mover, genesis, derivation, incubation, birth, incunabulum, primordium, ultimate cause, first cause, causative cause, causative agent, spring, fountainhead.

2. Fundamental, essence, inward element, element, substance, constituent, germ, rudiment, component, material, hypostasis, groundwork, substratum, materiality, brute matter, stuff, hyle, physical basis.

3. Scholium, axiom, theorem, precept, direction, injunction, dogma, dogmatic principle, rule, code, convention, canon, maxim, regulation, golden rule, dictum, dictate, formula, formulary, form, body of laws, legal code, receipt, recipe, settled principle, prescript, proposition, protasis, law, element, rudiment, fundamental, elementary proposition, truth, essential rule.

4. Doctrine, belief, tenet, article of faith, teaching, view, position, way of thinking, theory, system of belief, ism, credo, creed, morality, ethics, standards.

5. Reason, ground, motive, rationale, impulse, motivation, the reason why, the wherefore *(coll.)*, the whys and wherefores *(coll.)*, occasion, base, call.

6. Honor, honorableness, uprightness, righteousness, honesty, equity, justice, probity, rectitude, morality, integrity, virtue, goodness, incorruptibility, trustworthiness, trustiness, worth, character, spirit, right, morals, manly virtue, sense of honor, constancy, trustfulness, temperament, attitude, dependability, respectability, conscientiousness, scruples, scrupulosity, punctuality, inviolability, truth, faithfulness, fidelity.

PRINK, *v.* 1. Dress, embellish, ornament, deco-

rate, set off, primp, dress fastidiously, bedeck, bedizen, dress up, prank, array, smarten, smarten up, garnish, set out, deck out, spruce up *(coll.)*, furbish, make up, dizen, dandify, trim, adorn, beautify, titivate, spangle, bespangle.

2. Mince, assume airs, put on airs, put on, assume, affect, be affected, simulate, feign, sham, make believe, play-act, play a part, profess, make a show of, flaunt, attitudinize, pose, strut, swagger, put on a front, play to the gallery, parade, strut one's stuff, swell it *(coll.)*, put on the dog *(sl.)*, blow one's own horn.

PRINT, *v.* Impress, imprint, engrave, enstamp, emboss, lithograph, stereograph, stereotype, electrotype, reprint, pull a proof, engrave, strike off, set, set in print, put to bed *(cant)*, put to press, reissue, issue, offset, make up, run off, stamp.

PRINT, *n.* 1. Impress, imprint, impression, track, spoor, trace, trail, stamp, indentation, dent, dip, depression, concavity, mark, path, scent, wake, footstep, pad, step, footmark, thumbprint, fingerprint, handprint, finger mark, smudge, thumb mark, dactylogram, dactylograph, blaze, seal, stamp, cachet.

2. Newsprint, letterpress, impress, type, impression, typescript, type page, printed page, matter, offset, printed matter, page, column, reprint, reissue, issue, bookplate, colophon, text, context, dummy, type matter, reading matter, live matter, signature, folio, quarto, octavo, crown octavo, duodecimo, macule, letter.

3. Snapshot, photograph, lithograph, seriograph, silk screen print, oleograph, daguerreotype, tintype, negative print, negative, positive print, positive, proof, talbotype, skiagraph, callotype, ferrotype, heliograph, heliotype, heliochromotype, gravure, rotogravure, still, still photograph, photo, steel engraving, etching, gelatin print, imprint, impress, cerograph, wax engraving, encaustic, zinc plate, zincograph, stone engraving, photointaglio, intaglio, copperplate, copperplate engraving, aquatint, mezzotint, lithotint, chalk print, chalk engraving, graphotype, wood engraving, lignograph, xylograph, linoleum block, linoleum print, cut, woodcut.

PRINTER, *n.* Compositor, pressman, typographer, printer's devil, stereotypist, stereotyper, book printer, journeyman printer, master printer, job printer, linotyper, typesetter.

PRIOR, *adj.* Previous, earlier, former, preceding, precedent, anterior, foregoing, antecedent, forementioned, precursory, superior, going before, pre-existent, pre-existing, late, precursive, prodromal, prevenient, prelusive, preludial, proemial, prefatory, inaugural, preparatory, aforesaid, aforenamed, named, cited, introductory, above-mentioned, prelusory, sometime, quondam, whilom, ancient, old, ancestral.

PRIOR, *adv.* Previously, earlier, formerly, anteriorly, antecedently, precursorily, pre-existently, lately, precursively, prodromally, preveniently, prelusively, preludially, proemially, prefatorily, inaugurally, preparatorily, introductorily, prelusorily, sometime, anciently, ancestrally, heretofore, theretofore, erstwhile, erewhile, beforetime, aforetime, ere now, ere this, ere then, before then, yet, already, on the eve of, then, B. C., before Christ, ago, whilom, in the past, in days past, in olden times, in ancient times, in days of yore, long ago, a long time ago, once upon a time, no longer, a way back, some time ago, some time since, one fine morning, one day.

PRIOR, *n.* Monk, ecclesiastic, priest, hierophant, superior, holy man, monastic, grand prior, general prior, vicar general, conventual prior, claustral prior, abbot.

PRIORITY, *n.* Antecedence, pre-existence, precedence, anteriority, preference, precedency, seniority, previousness, precession, preterition, foreground, front, earliness, precursiveness, lateness, prelusiveness, preludialness, prelude, preludiousness, proemiality, preface, prefatoriness, prodromality, inauguration, preparation, anteposition, the lead, going before, van, front, superiority, pre-eminence.

PRIORY, *n.* Convent, cloister, monastery, nunnery, friary, abbey.

PRISM, *n.* Optical instrument, solid, crystal, spectroscope, spectrometer, kaleidoscope, geometrical body, geometrical figure.

PRISMATIC, *adj.* 1. Prismoidal, prismed, prismatoidal, prismal.

2. Kaleidoscopic, variegated, many-hued, multicolored, multicolorous, daedal, of all colors, all the colors of the rainbow, versicolored, versicolor, colorful, versicolorate, versicolorous, particolored, chromatic, polychromatic, polychromed.

PRISON, *n.* Jail, gaol, penitentiary, reformatory, workhouse, dungeon, cage, keep, lockup *(coll.)*, pen *(sl.)*, jug *(sl.)*, stir *(sl.)*, prison house, bastille, penal colony, prison colony, calaboose *(coll.)*, police station, station house, precinct station, tank *(coll.)*, state prison, federal prison, watchhouse, guardhouse, stockade, bridewell *(coll.)*, house of correction, house of reform, brig *(naut)*, den, cell, coop, house of detention, debtor's prison, quarantine station, detention station, cooler *(sl.)*, big house *(sl.)*, pokey *(sl.)*, black hole, donjon, can *(sl.)*, kitty *(sl.)*, crib, concentration camp, prison camp, the hulks, penal institution, Newgate, Sing Sing, Alcatraz, Devil's Island, King's Bench, gullpen, *conciergerie (Fr.)*.

PRISONER, *n.* Convict, jailbird, captive, culprit, cageling, *détenu (Fr.)*, criminal, malefactor, felon, lawbreaker, wrongdoer, gaolbird, stir bird *(sl.)*, accused, defendant.

PRISTINE, *adj.* Primitive, primeval, autochthonic, aboriginal, initial, primordial, primary, primal, original, first, prime, earliest, oldest, generative, protogenic, elementary, authentic, formative, embryonic, embryonal, foetal, rudimentary, archetypal, genitive, primigenial, inchoate, incipient, initiative, initiatory, germinal, rudimental, constitutive, determining, causal, basic, underlying, radical, intrinsic, immanent, innate, inherent, indwelling, infixed, implanted, ingrained, congenital, indigenous, genetic, connate, rock-bottom, bedrock, bottommost, nethermost, lowermost, lowest, etiological, causative, antediluvial, antediluvian, remote, aged, prehistoric, fossil, ancient, antique, preadamite, antepatriarchal, paleocystic, antemundane, primordiate, primordial.

PRIVACY, *n.* 1. Secrecy, hugger-mugger, closeness, secretiveness, suppression, subterfuge, evasion, evasiveness, silence, underhanded dealing, underhandedness, privity, reticence, repression, taciturnity, profound secret, private matter, personal matter, deep dark secret, deep secrecy, secret, confidence, reservation.

2. Retirement, seclusion, retreat, withdrawal, solitude, isolation, loneliness, aloofness, estrangement, hermitism, hermitship, recess, privateness, obscurity, intimacy, lonesomeness, solitariness, rustication, ruralism, unsociability, self-sufficiency, dissociation.

PRIVATE, *adj.* 1. Personal, individual, special, especial, peculiar, unofficial, non-public, own, close, non-official, singular, express, particular, specific, esoteric, intimate, respective, confined, limited, fixed, restricted, exclusive, determinate, definite, partial.

2. Confidential, privy, esoteric, underhand, underhanded, furtive, sly, stealthy, auricular, underground, undercover, hugger-mugger, surreptitious, covert, clandestine, inviolate, inviolable, arcane, mysterious, recondite, unrevealable, buried, concealed, hidden, cryptical, cryptic, obscure, murky, cabalistic, abstruse, dark, eclipsed, under a cloud, invisible, indistinct, undisclosed, unrevealed, disguised.

3. Secluded, seclusive, reclusive, privy, unfrequented, sequestered, isolated, backwater, out-of-the-way, solitudinous, deserted, lonely, alone, lonesome, unvisited, abandoned, desolate, forgotten, derelict.

PRIVATE, *n.* Foot soldier, common soldier, private soldier, warrior, man-at-arms, military man, enlisted soldier, enlisted man, buck private, Tommy, Tommy Atkins *(Brit.)*, poilu *(Fr.)*, doughboy, G.I., doughface, doughfoot *(sl.)*, foot slogger *(sl.)*, trooper, rifleman, infantryman.

PRIVATEER, *n.* 1. Pirate, buccaneer, viking, sea rover, corsair, sea king, Captain Kidd, Paul Jones.

2. Ship, pirate ship, pirate vessel.

PRIVATELY, *adv.* Quietly, modestly, privily, underhandedly, surreptitiously, secretly, on the sly, confidentially, between you and me, *sub rosa (Lat.)*, covertly, sneakingly, personally, individually, esoterically, specially, especially, peculiarly, unofficially, unpublicly, closely, intimately, respectively, in confinement, fixedly, restrictively, restrictedly, exclusively, partially, furtively, stealthily, underground, undercover, clandestinely, in concealment, cryptically, obscurely, under a cloud, invisibly, indistinctly, undisclosedly, in disguise, seclusively, in seclusion, reclusively, in solitude.

PRIVATION, *n.* 1. Loss, bereavement, deprivation, dispossession, consumption, exhaustion, dissipation, lapse, forfeiture, divestment, distress, attachment, deprivement, sequestration, confiscation, disinheritance, disentitlement, disfranchisement, disqualification.

2. Want, need, poverty, destitution, indigence, necessity, distress, beggary, misery, hardship, penury, necessitude, impecuniousness, impecuniosity, pauperism, neediness, lack, straits, financial straits, bad luck, bad fortune, narrow means, straitened means, mendicity, loss of fortune, bankruptcy, empty purse, light purse, hand-to-mouth existence, reduced circumstances.

PRIVILEGE, *n.* Right, prerogative, license, charter, franchise, enfranchisement, immunity, exemption, absolution, advantage, claim, favor, indemnity, patent, frank, monopoly, permission, grant, authority, authorization, indulgence, dispensation, sanction, benefit, concession, tolerance, title, prize, honor, faculty, freedom, liberty, warrant, warranty, accommodation, unconstraint, prescription, birthright, affranchisement, due, entitlement, sufferance, vouchsafement, allowance, grace, accordance, admission, consent.

PRIVILEGE, *v.* 1. Grant, enpower, entitle, enfranchise, franchise, warrant, admit, permit, allow, ordain, prescribe, authorize, confer a privilege, patent, commission, charter, license, allot, charge, entrust, convey, accredit, inaugurate, invest, facultate.

2. Immunize, excuse, free, liberate, give the franchise to, affranchise, dispense with, give dispensation to, absolve, exonerate, acquit, discharge, release, give one leeway, give enough rope to, give one free rein, allow full swing, leave the door open to, spare, exculpate, vindicate, clear, whitewash, pardon, remit a penalty, grant amnesty to, forgive.

PRIVILEGED, *adj.* Exempt, exempted, allowed, enfranchised, affranchised, licensed, warranted, granted, empowered, free, liberated, entitled, sanctioned, admitted, permitted, ordained, prescribed, authorized, patented, commissioned, chartered, allotted, charged, entrusted, conveyed, accredited, invested, vested, facultated, immune, excused, granted dispensation, remitted, absolved, exonerated, acquitted, discharged, released, vindicated, exculpated, cleared, pardoned, spared, released, unanswerable, unaccountable, unresponsible, not responsible, unliable, not liable, unsubject, not subject.

PRIVY, *adj.* 1. Personal, private, individual, special, especial, peculiar, unofficial, non-public, own, close, non-official, singular, express, particular, specific, esoteric, intimate, respective, confined, reserved, limited, fixed, restricted, exclusive, determinate, definite, partial.

2. Confidential, underhand, underhanded, furtive, sly, stealthy, auricular, underground, undercover, hugger-mugger, covert, surreptitious, clandestine, inviolate, inviolable, arcane, mysterious, recondite, unrevealable, buried, concealed, hidden, cryptical, cryptic, obscure, murky, cabalistic, abstruse, dark, eclipsed, invisible, indistinct, undisclosed, unrevealed, disguised.

PRIVY TO, *adj.* Apprised of, undeceived, no stranger to, aware of, in the know *(coll.)*, conscious of, cognizant of, made acquainted with, let into, allowed behind the scenes, in the secret, wise to *(coll.)*, awake to, in on the secret.

PRIVY, *n.* Water closet, outhouse, backhouse, latrine, toilet, necessary, jakes, john, johnny *(sl.)*, w.c., cloaca, can *(sl.)*, head *(Naut.)*, rest room, comfort station.

PRIZE, *n.* 1. Reward, premium, meed, trophy, palm, decoration, ribbon, guerdon, laurels, honors, medal, cup, stake, feather in one's cap, plate, blue ribbon, award, bays, crown, wreath, garland, chaplet, ornament, mark of honor, badge of honor, distinction, cordon, grand cordon, eulogy, citation, loving cup, garter, star, gold star, token, knot, favor, first prize, second prize, booby prize, consolation prize, recompense, remuneration, solatium, return, just deserts, take, profit, gain, receipts, winnings, earnings, emolument.

2. Booty, loot, capture, spoils, plunder, seizure, prey, windfall, swag, pickings, grab *(sl.)*, stealings, pillage, stolen goods, haul, take, boodle *(sl.)*.

3. *(Dial.)* Leverage, pry, purchase, fulcrumage, hold, foothold, vantage ground.

4. Pry, lever, crowbar, dog, jimmy, gavelock, crow, iron crow, iron, jemmy, marlinspike, handspike, arm, limb.

5. A good thing, jewel, gem, choice bit, pearl, diamond, diamond in the rough, pure gold, all wool and a yard wide, cream of the crop, cream, *crème de la crème (Fr.)*, salt of the earth, wonder,

prodigy, champion, best ever, first-rater, topnotcher, peach, lulu *(sl.)*, dandy *(sl.)*, daisy *(sl.)*, honey *(sl.)*, masterpiece, cock of the walk, treasure, find, elect, select, pick of the crop.

PRIZE, *v.* 1. Value, set a value on, valuate, appraise, meter, gauge, form an estimate, measure out, size up, take the measure of, assess, rate, appreciate, rank, count, account, size up *(coll.)*.

2. Esteem, value highly, cherish, hold dear, appreciate, approve, regard, respect, admire, set a high value on, set store by *(coll.)*, rate highly, value highly, give importance to, attach importance to, treasure, make much of, make a fuss about *(coll.)*, hold in affection, like, care for, bear an interest in, hold dear, revere, regard, approve, think good, endorse, look up to, hold in esteem, hail with satisfaction, hail.

3. Pry open, break open, open forcibly, break, burst, break into, wrench open, tear open.

PRIZE FIGHT, *n.* Boxing, boxing match, pugilistic contest, fisticuffs, pugilism, spar, sparring match, bout, round, set-to *(coll.)*, fight, the fights *(coll.)*.

PRIZE FIGHTER, *n.* Boxer, pugilist, fighter, athlete, pug *(sl.)*, sparrer, sparring partner, fighting man, bruiser, miller *(sl.)*, slugger *(sl.)*, artist of the squared circle *(cant)*, denizen of the prize ring, ringster *(sl.)*.

PRIZE RING, *n.* Arena, boxing arena, pugilistic arena, the squared circle, scene of action, scene, stadium, gymnasium, the canvas, the ring.

PROBABILITY, *n.* Likelihood, chance, liability, liableness, possibility, aptitude, contingency, susceptibility, tendency, exposure, likeliness, appearance of truth, verisimilitude, presumption, reasonable chance, fair chance, probabilism, curve of probability, even chance, good chance, ostensibility, plausibility, well-grounded possibility, good prospect, good expectation, believability, credibility, conceivability, reasonability, logicality, reasonableness, main chance, favorable prospect.

PROBABLE, *adj.* Presumable, credible, likely, liable, reasonable, believable, apparent, admissible, verisimilar, verisimilous, plausible, presumptive, possible, ostensible, supposed, in the cards *(coll.)*, inspiriting, logical, apt, in a fair way promising, rational, sensible, sound, well-grounded, well-founded, conceivable, tenable, reliable, dependable, to be depended upon, persuasive, fiduciary, unquestionable, indubitable, promising, auspicious, favorable, full of promise, looking up, within sight of land, assuring, encouraging, bright, cheering.

PROBABLY, *adv.* Apparently, logically, in all probability, in all likelihood, presumably, most likely, *prima facie (Lat.)*, perhaps, to be expected, seemingly, credibly, believably, reasonably, admissibly, verisimilarly, verisimilously, plausibly, presumptively, possibly, ostensibly, supposedly, promisingly, rationally, sensibly, soundly, conceivably, tenably, reliably, as like as not, to all appearances, all things considered, on the face of it, according to all expectations, indubitably, unquestionably.

PROBATION, *n.* Test, evidence, confirmation, verification, corroboration, substantiation, demonstration, authentication, conclusive evidence, rigorous demonstration, apodixis, conclusiveness, medium of proof.

PROBATIONER, *n.* Candidate, novice, tyro, beginner, novitiate, pupil, learner, newcomer, entrant, neophyte, initiate, catechumen, debutant, recruit, probationist, apprentice, tenderfoot, greenhorn, abecedarian.

PROBE, *n.* Search, investigation, examination, inspection, test, trial, exam (*sl.*), examen, survey, scrutiny, review, indagation, probation, exploration, exploratory examination, analysis, critical examination, close enquiry, searching examination, exhaustive study, careful search, prevestigation, perscrutation, rigorous search, strict examination, deep study.

PROBE, *v.* Prove, test, investigate, scrutinize, examine, perscrutate, search, sound, explore, sift, measure, fathom, look into, verify, study, pry into, hunt, inquire, question, poke into, sound out, question, interrogate, query, quiz, catechize, pump, pump for information, feel out, pursue, follow up, cross-examine, ask questions, ask about, make examination respecting, make inquiries respecting, put questions, put queries, demand to know, inquisite, inquisition, propound a question, cross-question, cross-interrogate, peer, go in search of, seek out, look for, seek after, pursue, think of, contemplate, scan, peruse, scrutinize, inspect, delve into, introspect, anatomize, dissect, break down, go over step by step, subject to close scrutiny, go into deeply, probe to the bottom, probe to the quick.

PROBITY, *n.* Honesty, integrity, uprightness, faith, faithfulness, fidelity, worth, rectitude, righteousness, loyalty, morality, goodness, honorableness, venerability, venerableness, trustiness, trustworthiness, fairness, equity, equitableness, equitability, principle, sincerity, truthfulness, truth, candor, veracity, honor, conscience, conscientiousness, justice, incorruptibility, soundness, singleness of heart, steadfastness, sobriety, moral excellence, impartiality, frankness, fair play, high principles, scrupulousness, punctilio, punctiliousness, nicety, delicacy, refinement, subtlety, dependability, inviolability, constancy, devotion, attachment, adherence, virtue, merit, deservingness, credit, desert, fortitude, courage, prudence, purity, reputability, rightfulness, seemliness, veraciousness, plain speaking.

PROBLEM, *n.* Subject of dispute, question, puzzle, riddle, conundrum, enigma, moot point, point in dispute, exercise, proposition, question at issue, point to be settled, query, leading question, catch (*coll.*), disputed point, puzzling question, bafflement, poser, mystery, crossword puzzle, arcanum, enigmatic question, stumper, floorer, theorem, tough nut to crack, charade, rebus, acrostic, riddle of the sphinx, riddle of the ages, inexplicability, labyrinth, intricacy, involvement, knotty problem, anagram, complexity, complication.

PROBLEMATIC, *adj.* Enigmatic, puzzling, enigmatical, riddling, mysterious, arcane, arcanal, inexplicable, inscrutable, unintelligible, insoluble, labyrinthine, labyrinthian, involved, complicated, complex, uncertain, doubtful, dubious, disputable, unsettled, unreliable, indefinite, contingent, indeterminate, vague, equivocal, undetermined, debatable, suspicious, ambiguous, apocryphal, shrouded in mystery, cryptic, cryptical, logogrammatic, anagrammatic, perplexing, worrisome, troublesome, untenable, implausible, controvertible, disputable, undemonstrable, fallible, improbable, hypothetical, paradoxical, tangled, knotty, raveled, snarled, knotted, daedal, difficult, tortuous, imperspicious.

PROBOSCIS, *n.* Olfactory organ, olfactory appendage, snout, snoot (*coll.*), nose, neb, muzzle, nozzle (*sl.*), trunk, antlia, beak, bill, pecker, nib, breather, nose holes, nares, smeller, olfactories.

PROCACIOUS, *adj.* Insolent, impudent, insulting, saucy, brash, fresh (*sl.*), audacious, malapert, brazen, flip, flippant, pert, bumptious, nervy (*sl.*), precocious, forward, smartalecky (*coll.*), bold as brass, bold, brazen-faced, cheeky (*coll.*), contemptuous, disrespectful, unabashed, unblushing, shameless, overfamiliar, obtrusive, presumptuous, daring, discourteous, uncourtly, unchivalrous, impolite, ill-bred, ill-mannered, boorish, rude, crude, common (*coll.*), low.

PROCACITY, *n.* Lowness, bad manners, want of breeding, ill-manneredness, commonness, insolence, crudity, rudeness, boorishness, unchivalrousness, pugnacity, impudence, shamelessness, insultingness, sauciness, brazenness, flippancy, malapertness, pertness, bumptiousness, audacity, audaciousness, forwardness, nerve (*coll.*), nerviness (*coll.*), gall (*coll.*), brass (*coll.*), cheek (*coll.*), contemptuousness, disrespect, disrespectfulness, unabashedness, unblushingness, temerity, boldness, brassiness (*coll.*), presumptuousness, presumption, daring, crustiness (*coll.*), crust (*coll.*), discourtesy, uncourtliness, contumely, impertinence, petulance, assurance, front, sauce, perversity, bad temper, ill humor, bad humor, querulousness, crabbedness, quarrelsomeness, contentiousness, choler.

PROCEDURE, *n.* 1. Function, usage, mode of use, method of treatment, wont, custom, practice, method of practice, manner of working, manner of operation, mode of operation, *modus operandi* (*Lat.*), line of action, conduct, means, way, form, tone, system, wise, guise, ways and means, process, proceeding, praxis.
2. Course of action, step, measure, plan, policy, stroke of policy, project, plan, scheme, device, trump, bold stroke.

PROCEED, *v.* 1. Move ahead, advance, progress, move on, move forward, go forward, move up, go on, pass on, make progress, push on, press on, get ahead, forge ahead, make headway, get forward, get along, hold to one's course, jog along, make one's way, force one's way, elbow one's way, shoulder one's way, carve one's way, shoot ahead, make rapid strides, get over the ground, gain ground, make up for lost time, run along, edge one's way, go with the stream, follow a course, stream, flow, run, glide, drift, flit, sweep along, keep moving, keep on the go, wend one's way, hie, make haste, hurry along, rush headlong, start forward, set oneself in motion, be on the go, be moving, be in motion.
2. Issue, arise, spring, come, emanate, originate, start, flow, follow, result, accrue, ensue, come forth, come out, be derived, be caused, take rise, be produced, descend, come of, take its rise, germinate, grow, bud, shoot, stem, hinge, turn.
3. Function, act, operate, undertake, move, play, work, put in motion, put into action, lift a finger, take action, execute, stretch forth one's hand, set forth, begin, start.

PROCEEDINGS, *n., pl.* 1. Actions, doings, goings on, transactions, series of events, affairs, concerns, matters, affairs in general, things, the world, state of affairs, stream of events, stream of things, incidents.
2. Records, archives, minutes, memoranda,

account, description, government records, Congressional Records, report, returns.

3. Lawsuit, suit, legal action, trial, litigation, suit at law, legal process, cause, dispute, action at law.

PROCEEDS, *n., pl.* Produce, product, end result, consequence, profit, reward, gain, remuneration, receipts, returns, yield, income, avails, issue, earnings, outcome, assets, revenue, rent, harvest, crop, pelf, lucre, winnings, pickings, take, output, fruit, aftermath, net profit, gross profit, gross receipts, value received.

PROCESS, *n.* 1. Course of action, step, measure, plan, policy, stroke of policy, project, scheme, function, usage, method of treatment, wont, custom, practice, method of practice, manner of working, manner of operation, *modus operandi* (*Lat.*), mode of operation, procedure, proceeding, praxis, line of action, conduct, manner, means, way, form, tone, system, wise, guise, cut, ways and means.

2. Projection, protuberance, outgrowth, appendage, condyle, condyloma, wattle, barbule, barbel, apophysis, caruncle, prominence, barb, node, boss, convexity, bulge, swelling, rise, hump, spur, nodulation, nodosity, growth, excrescence, abnormal protrusion, morbid development.

PROCESSION, *n.* Train, retinue, parade, cavalcade, march, progress, file, cortege, military display, military parade, triumph, ovation, caravan, succession, progression, rank, series, line, column, string, file, course, catenation, concatenation, skimmington, array, following, attendance, suite, train of followers, rout, spectacle, demonstration, pageant, turnout, review, march-past, promenade, gala, doings, fete, field day.

PROCLAIM, *v.* Publish, announce, herald, advertise, promulgate, declare, cry, circulate, broadcast, make known, blazon, trumpet, blaze abroad, spread abroad, bruit, noise abroad, report, assert, asseverate, affirm, diffuse, disseminate, annunciate, divulge, release, sing out, call out, enunciate, enounce, knell, blare, narrate, set forth, name, avow, state, bespeak, profess, gazette, communicate, give out, sound forth, preach, manifest, make manifest, tell, show, certify, utter, usher in, ventilate, air, propagate, promulgate, hawk about, whisper about, make public, declare, thunder forth, publicize.

PROCLAIMER, *n.* Announcer, publisher, herald, promulgator, disseminator, propagator, proclamator, proclaimant, enunciator, annunciator, nunciate, reporter, messenger, intelligencer, nuncio, dispatch bearer, dispatch rider, courier, runner, express rider, postrider, postilion, crier, trumpeter, evangel, harbinger, forerunner, bearer of glad tidings, message bearer, carrier, bellman, town crier, informant.

PROCLAMATION, *n.* 1. Publication, announcement, message, ventilation, pronouncement, pronunciamento, annunciation, report, declaration, edict, public announcement, public notice, blazon, promulgation, advertisement, ad (*coll.*), public avowal, cry, bull, sounding, trumpeting, heralding, tidings, news, notification, declaration.

2. Edict, decree, ordinance, rescript, fiat, manifesto, decreement, decretal, dictate, act, mandate, pronouncement, pronunciamento, warrant, order of the day, command, instruction, bid, caveat, writ, mittimus, indiction, declaration, imperative rule.

PROCLIVITY, *n.* Proneness, propensity, tendency, leaning, bias, inclination, predisposition, direction, predilection, disposition, bearing, drift, determination, predetermination, turn of mind, readiness, aptitude, talent, ability, yen, penchant, affection, appetite, liking, impulse, aim, appetency, desire, facility, gift, mood, instinct, natural sense, innate sense, innate disposition, inherent ability, propensitude, turn, bent, twist, warp, gravitation, vein, cast, humor, conduciveness, animus, frame of mind, idiosyncrasy, temper, temperament, idiocrasis, crasis, diathesis, peculiarities, traits.

PROCONSUL, *n.* Consul, representative, emissary, envoy, minister, ambassador, plenipotentiary, minister plenipotentiary, diplomat, diplomatist, diplomatic agent, agent, legate, nuncio, internuncio, embassy.

PROCRASTINATE, *v.* 1. Delay, stave off, put off, defer, table, place on the table, adjourn, retard, omit, neglect, prorogate, prorogue, respite, waive, suspend, let the matter stand, put on ice (*coll.*), hang up (*coll.*), shunt, push aside, shelve, pigeonhole, slacken, slow down, hold back, block, stop, hinder, put on the rack (*coll.*), put off until tomorrow.

2. Vacillate, hesitate, be vacillating, dally, dilly-dally, stall, temporize, play for time, stall around (*coll.*), talk against time, tarry, dawdle, linger, loaf, be idle, do nothing, wait till tomorrow, hang fire, hang back, filibuster, keep one waiting, kill time, tarry, idle, tide over, waste time, march in slow time, inch along, lag, drag one's feet, slow down, let up, decelerate, slacken speed, ease up, back water, twiddle one's thumbs, beguile the time, lie on one's oars, be dilatory, be inert, go to sleep, slumber, sleep on the job.

PROCRASTINATION, *n.* Dilatoriness, delay, postponement, protraction, putting off, tardiness, slowness, laziness, cunctation, neglect, dalliance, deferment, put off, deferral, prorogation, prolongation, adjournment, play for time, standoff, holdoff, suspension, neglectfulness, laches, laxity, indolence, laziness, disregardance, default, omission, faineancy, do-nothingness, idleness, inoccupation, indiligence, inertia, otosity, ergophobia, sloth, slothfulness.

PROCRASTINATOR, *n.* Delayer, neglector, negligent person, ignorer, wastrel, bum (*coll.*), drifter (*coll.*), trifler, idler, disregarder, waiter on Providence, Micawber, shirker, do-nothing, fainéant, good-for-nothing, dodger, quitter, welsher, funker, malingerer, timeserver.

PROCREATE, *v.* Beget, bear, fecundate, generate, progenerate, breed, engender, multiply, propagate, reproduce, proliferate, give life to, give rise to, give being to, hatch, impregnate, father, create, sire, produce, copulate, have coition, couple, mate, have sexual intercourse, come together, have sexual congress, fertilize, impregnate, make pregnant, make fertile, fructify, fecundize, pollinate, cross-pollinate.

PROCREATION, *n.* Generation, begetting, production, reproduction, breeding, creation, birth, childbirth, propagation, multiplication, fertilization, germination, pollination, geniture, genesis, progeneration, gemination, fecundation, impregnation, fructification, cross-fertilization, xenogamy, proliferation, reproduction, palingenesis, pullulation, proliferation, prolification, copulation, sexual intercourse, sexual union, coming together, sexual congress (carnal relations, marital relations, cohabitation, sleeping together, physical love, coition, coitus, sexual connection.

PROCREATIVE, *adj.* Procreant, reproductive, propagative, fertilizing, germinating, originating, genetic, pregnant, fecundative, fecund, life-giving, generative, progenerative, spermatic, multiparous, viviparous, oviparous, omnific, propagable, generant.

PROCREATOR, *n.* Begetter, father, sire, dam, generator, paternal ancestor, progenitor, genitor, parent, mother.

PROCTOR, *n.* Procurator, factor, steward, bailiff, curator, caretaker, seneschal, attorney, solicitor, reeve, agent, clerk, secretary, broker, functionary, placeman, servant, proxy, deputy, secondary, representative, surrogate, delegate, minister, vicar, lieutenant, second, instrument.

PROCUMBENT, *adj.* Lying down, supine, recumbent, discumbent, accumbent, couchant, jacent, prostrate, resupinate, resupine, recubant, recubate, on one's back.

PROCURABLE, *adj.* Obtainable, securable, acquirable, attainable, purchasable, annexable, apprehendable, apprehensible.

PROCURATION, *n.* 1. Procurement, agency, operation, office, function, play, interaction, management, instrumentality, causation, action, influence, medium, means.
2. Proxy, agency, commission, deputation, legation, mission, authority, authorization, brevet, thrust, warrant, charge, mandate, exequatur, diploma, errand, job task, assignment, agentship, office.
3. Obtaining, acquisition, procurement, accumulation, cumulation, money-making, attainment, getting, securing, obtainment, purchase, buying, appropriation, annexation, apprehension, capture.

PROCURATOR, *n.* 1. Proctor, steward, curator, factor, bailiff, agent, proxy, deputy, seneschal, major-domo, representative.
2. Jurist, proctor, counselor, attorney, lawyer, jurisconsult, jurisprudent, counsel, advocate, adviser, barrister, solicitor, pleader.

PROCURE, *v.* 1. Get, obtain, acquire, gather, come by, have, pick up, take possession of, glean, pick, earn, win, gain, secure, attain, achieve, receive, enlist, reap, win over, find, take, buy, draw, light upon *(coll.),* get into one's hands, get one's hands on, get together, gather in, dig up, scare up *(coll.),* rake together, bag, sack, come in for, lay hands on, crop, reap, gather in with the harvest, accumulate, treasure, appropriate, purchase, buy up, invest in, put one's money in, buy out, pay for, hire, rent, pay rent for, lease, make a purchase, buy into, buy off, help oneself to, commandeer, lift.
2. Bring, get, obtain, induce, effect, contrive, draw down upon, elicit, evoke, superinduce, open to, open the door to, incite, kindle, suscitate, motivate, achieve, accomplish, bring about, compass, negotiate, furnish.

PROCUREMENT, *n.* Attainment, obtainment, acquisition, getting, procuration, cumulation, accumulation, amassment, acquirement, appropriation, agency, operation, office, maintenance, exercise, force, interaction, causation, quickening power, sustaining power, operancy, working.

PROCURER, *n.* Pander, panderer, bawd, pimp, purveyor, go-between, reprobate, runner, white-slaver, procuress.

PROCURESS, *n.* Reprobate, whore, whoremonger, harlot, courtesan, Mrs. Warren, madam, white slaver.

PROCURVATION, *n.* Curvature, curvation, turn, forward curve, bend, sweep, flexure, flexion, excurvature, bow, bowing, excurvation, convolution, sinuosity, recurvature, recurvation.

PROD, *v.* Push, shove, impel, actuate, poke, stir, stir up, incite, prick, needle, goad, urge, boost, jolt, jostle, jog, elbow, shoulder, spur, animate, move, set in motion, prompt, instigate, throw, hustle, hurry, drive, propel, motivate, speed, quicken, accelerate, lash, whip, flog, press, forward, expedite, hasten, egg on, hound on, railroad *(coll.),* speed up, provoke, set on, bear upon, bring pressure upon, bear down upon, stimulate, give impulse to, encourage, give encouragement to, operate on, work on, call upon, exhort, excite.

PRODIGAL, *adj.* 1. Lavish, generous, profuse, abundant, abounding, numerous, teeming, countless, innumerable, numberless, in profusion, swarming, plentiful, myriad, copious, bounteous, multitudinous, multiple, sundry, divers, ever so many, studded, infinite, indeterminate, limitless, illimitable, incalculable, immeasurable, boundless, endless, interminable, measureless, unnumbered, without end, without bound, without limit, illimited, inexhaustible, ample, affluent, rich, replete, prolix, extravagant, profusive, unstinting, without stint, prevailing, rife, flush, luxuriant, enough and to spare, besetting, lavish, unmeasured, unsparing, unexhausted, exhaustless.
2. Wasteful, improvident, overliberal, spendthrift, unthrifty, profuse, lavish, dissipative, intemperate, reckless, extravagant, unnecessary, needless, surplus, overplus, inordinate, overmuch, overweening, immoderate, exorbitant, fancy, excessive, supernumerary, beyond all bounds, unwarranted, unmitigated, too many, too much, overblown, overgrown, crapulent, crapulous, gluttonous, uncurbed, unbridled, wanton, precipitate, headlong, impetuous, feverish, breakneck.
3. Wanton, wayward, arrant, errant, vicious, unmoral, immoral, vice-ridden, bad, naughty, evil, wrong, recreant, unrighteous, wicked, reprobate.

PRODIGAL, *n.* Spender, spendthrift, wastrel, squanderer, wastethrift, spend-all, scattergood, trifler, ignorer, drifter, procrastinator, negligent person, waiter on Providence.

PRODIGALISM, *n.* Prodigality, wastefulness, extravagance, waste, profusion, squandering, penny-wisdom, pound-foolishness, dissipation, use, using up, misspending, overindulgence, intemperance, wasting, useless consumption, decrement, expenditure, inabstinence, crapulence, indulgence, inordinancy, immoderation, unrestraint, luxuriousness, voluptuousness, sensuality, incontinence, sybaritism, intemperateness, excess, epicurism, licentiousness, wantoness, libertinism, debauchery, unchastity.

PRODIGALITY, *n.* 1. Lavishness, profusion, plenitude, plenteousness, plenty, amplitude, prolixity, exuberance, exorbitance, opulence, richness, affluence, copiousness, abundance, ample supply, sufficiency, fullness, plethora, repletion, great plenty, lavish supply, enough and to spare, superfluity, superabundance, nimiety, surplusage, surplus, overmeasure, overset, pleonasm, surfeit, congestion, glut, engorgement, redundancy, overfullness, too much, too many, unnecessariness, needlessness, inordinancy, inordinateness.

2. Prodigalism, wastefulness, extravagance, waste, profusion, squandering, consumption, dissipation, use, using up, misspending, overrindulgence, wastage, wasting, useless expenditure, useless consumption, decrement, inabstinence, crapulence, indulgence, inordinancy, immoderation, unrestraint, lack of restraint, luxuriousness, voluptuousness, sensuality, incontinence, sybaritism, intemperateness, excess, excessiveness, epicurism, licentiousness, wantonness, libertinism, debauchery, unchastity, intemperance.

PRODIGIOUS, *adj.* 1. Wonderful, stupendous, marvelous, noteworthy, remarkable, weird, fantastic, monstrous, outlandish, freakish, grotesque, preternatural, supernatural, abnormal, supernormal, strange, queer, passing strange, funny *(coll.)*, fanciful, teratogenic, rare, exceptional, singular, anomalous, bizarre, baroque, rococo, inconceivable, incredible, extraordinary, out of the ordinary, unimaginable, uncommon, out of the common run, unique, *sui generis (Lat.)*, unnatural, unwonted, uncustomary, unexampled, unprecedented, unheard-of, unfamiliar, startling, portentous, amazing, surprising, wondrous, miraculous, astonishing, astounding, dumfounding, indescribable, renowned, impressive, unthinkable, unconscionable, overwhelming, unaccountable, unaccustomed, unimaginable, curious, peculiar, *recherché (Fr.)*, striking, fearful, wonder-working.

2. Huge, vast, giant-like, gigantic, enormous, bulky, towering, immense, gargantuan, titanic, leviathan, great, grand, mammoth, monster, monstrous, monumental, colossal, cyclopean, stupendous, vasty, Brobdingnagian, herculean, jumbo *(coll.)*, elephantine, whacking, thumping, bumping, thundering, lolloping *(coll.)*, dinotherian, megatherian, dinosaurian, magnitudinous, large, big, mighty, howling, whaling, rousing *(coll.)*, dreadful, frightful, fearful, terrific, terrible, inexpressible, unutterable, ineffable, unspeakable, indescribable, unnamable, tall.

PRODIGY, *n.* 1. Wonder, champion, marvel, portent, miracle, phenomenon, sign, occurrence, rare occurrence, prodigiosity, sensation, astonishment, nonesuch, stunner, amazement, curiosity, spectacle, sight, wonderment, *rara avis (Lat.)*, exception.

2. Monstrosity, freak, prodigiosity, monster, anomaly, mooncalf, abortion, teratism, teratology, teratogeny, freak of nature, cacogenesis, miscreation.

3. Intellectual prodigy, genius, colossus of learning, giant of learning, wizard, savant, man of genius, mental giant, mastermind, masterhead, pantologist, walking encyclopedia, master, expert, past master, sage, sapient.

PRODITION, *n.* Treason, treachery, sedition, faithlessness, betrayal, perfidy, insidiousness, treacherousness, duplicity, petty treason, Judas kiss, Iscariotism, misprision of treason, lese majesty, high treason, revolt, insurrection, insurgence, insurgency, mutiny, mutineering, outbreak.

PRODUCE, *v.* 1. Set forth, manifest, display, exhibit, bring out, bring forward, bring into view, put on display, put on view, delate, show, present, materialize, bring to light, hold forth, bring to the fore, hold up to view, make visible, show forth, uncover, uncloak, unscreen, disclose, discover, unveil, unmask, unroll, unfurl, make plain, make no mystery of, visibilize, set before, place before, divulge, reveal, lay before one's eyes, stage, present, put on *(coll.)*, mount, put on a

show *(coll.)*, put on the stage, dramatize, film, screen, make a movie of, release for viewing.

2. Write, compose, author, indite, formulate, originate, draft, dash off, draw up, ghost, ghostwrite, knock off, put on paper, pen, pencil, scribble, spill ink, sling ink, scratch, scriven, engross, put in writing.

3. Effect, put into effect, do, transact, carry on, dispatch, perform, execute, enact, put into practice, carry out, bring about, work out, pull off *(coll.)*, bring off *(coll.)*, achieve, make, render, practice, pursue, prosecute, compass, effectuate, complete, consummate, make, put through, get through, hammer out, work out, discharge, fulfill, bring to pass, bring to a conclusion, bring to a head, attain, realize, make short work of, dispose of, finish, elaborate, perfect, bring to perfection, mature, maturate, put in force, carry through, carry into execution.

4. Cause, originate, effect, beget, create, occasion, give rise to, bring about, accomplish, achieve, institute, constitute, invent, give birth to, sow the seeds of, set up, set afloat, bring to pass, found, install, lay the foundations of, furnish, engender, conceive, procreate, hatch, give life to, bring into being, bring into existence, bear, yield, breed, fructify, cause to appear, spawn, turn out, mint, bring out, develop, make, give origin to, construct, compose, fashion, energize, devise, frame, fabricate, evolve, manufacture, compound, rear, grow, raise, get up, form, concoct, organize, carve, chisel, hew, weave, knock out *(coll.)* knock together, slap together *(coll.)*, build, erect, edify, make alive, quicken, animate, vivify, bring into being.

5. Yield, bear, render, give, afford, impart, result, result in, supply, furnish, bloom, flower, burgeon, sprout, bear fruit, fructify, proliferate, bring into the world, bear young, bring forth young, cub, whelp, drop, spring, throw, calve, fawn, lamb, spawn, kitten, foal, produce abundantly, multiply, teem, pullulate, be productive.

6. Make longer, lengthen, protract, extend, draw out, prolong, prolongate, stretch, stretch out, attenuate, drawl, spin out.

PRODUCE, *n.* 1. Product, yield, proceeds, return, crop, harvest, outcome, production, fruits, profit, revenue, amount, sum, emolument, increase, issue, take, gettings, booty, plunder, rakein *(coll.)*, superlucration, performance, result, consequence, blossom, flower, creature, handiwork, work, creation, outgrowth, output, coinage, origination, invention, composition, concoction, offspring, *oeuvre (Fr.)*, opus, writing, book, publication, effect, perquisite, aftermath, benefit.

2. Commodities, stock, goods, merchandise, agricultural products, vegetables, greengrocery, good for sale, vendibles, staple commodities, staples, foodstuffs, food.

PRODUCER, *n.* 1. Cause, causative agent, agency, origin, genesis, derivation, author, creator, generator, determining agent, determining factor, maker, originator, genitor, progenitor, prime mover, first cause, primary cause, occasion, inducement, impulse, provocation, impulsion.

2. Creator, begetter, manufacturer, builder, constructor, formulator, artificer, artifact, artifex, architect, author, founder, inventor, executor, originator, deviser, generator, prime mover, parent, father, mother, laborer, craftsman, worker.

3. Entrepreneur, impresario, theatrician, actor-manager, stage manager, theatrical producer, acting manager, backer, angel *(sl.)*.

PRODUCTION, *n.* 1. Origination, construction, manufacture, making, formation, fabrication, coinage, producing, establishment, constitution, building, architecture, execution, workmanship, manufacturing, effectuation, preparation, authorship, performance, concoction, invention, composition, conformation, organization, achievement, fulfillment, accomplishment, attainment, realization, discharge, consummation, dispatch, finish, conclusion, culmination, preparation, readying, gestation, incubation, maturation, perfection, causation.

2. Composition, compilation, authorship, invention, compilement, inditement, work, study, masterwork, masterpiece, work of art, art, piece, opus, *oeuvre (Fr.),* creation, handicraft, book, brainchild, writing, volume, tome, publication.

3. Protraction, lengthening, prolongation, attenuation, extension, elongation, stretching.

4. Showing, manifestation, exposition, exhibit, exhibition, display, unfoldment, materialization, presentation, show, demonstration, indication.

5. Theatrical performance, show, play, drama, musical show, musical production, dramatic production, musical comedy, musical extravaganza, stage performance, stage show, motion picture, cinema, film, the films, moving picture, cinematograph, movies, movie, entertainment, stage exhibit, dramatic exhibition, repertory performance, benefit performance, benefit, minstrel show, legshow, hootchy-kootchy, circus, carnival, the big top, photoplay, screenplay, movie show, photodrama, talking picture, sound motion picture, sound movie, talkie.

PRODUCTIVE, *adj.* 1. Fertile, prolific, fecund, rank, fruitful, fructiferous, proliferous, proliferative, teeming, uberous, rich, luxuriant, plenteous, plentiful, copious, creative, pregnant, fructuous, yielding, gainful, remunerative, profitable, potent, forceful, powerful, puissant, vigorous, dynamic, valuable, useful, worth-while, invaluable.

2. Imaginative, inventive, ingenious, original, prolific, creative, visionary.

PRODUCTIVITY, *n.* Fecundity, fruitfulness, creativeness, prolificacy, proliferateness, multiparity, pullulation, multiplication, uberty, luxuriance, prolificality, fertility, ingenuity, imagination, imaginativeness, creativity, inventiveness, orginality, fructiferousness, richness, copiousness, gainfulness, remunerativeness, profitability, profitableness, potency, forcefulness, power, dynamism, puissance, valuableness, value, potence.

PROEM, *n.* Preface, prelude, preamble, introduction, prolegomena, foreword, preliminary remarks, prologue, beginning, exordium, protasis, proemium, frontispiece, prefix, overture, voluntary, descant.

PROEMIAL, *adj.* Introductory, anterior, preceding, prodromal, antecedent, prelusive, prelusory, prevenient, prefactory, inaugural, preparatory, foregoing, prior, precursive, precursory, preludial, initial, initiative, incipient, inauguratory.

PROFANATION, *n.* 1. Abuse, misuse, pollution, misemployment, misapplication, perversion, misdirection, misusage, misappropriation, prostitution, outrage, atrocity, ill-usage, desecration, maltreatment, waste, molestation, ravage, ill turn, ill service, oppression, violation.

2. Impiety, sacrilege, profanity, blasphemy, irreverence, irreligion, mockery, desecration, impiousness, profaneness, vice, wickedness, badness, evil, ungodliness, unholiness, sinfulness, sin, vice, wrong, wrongdoing, peccancy, transgression, reprobacy, iniquity, obliquity, demerit.

PROFANE, *adj.* 1. Irreverent, irreligious, wicked, sinful, impious, evil, bad, peccant, ungodly, unholy, godless, derelict, delinquent, vicious, vice-ridden, unsaintly, virtueless, unvirtuous, shameless, heartless, conscienceless, defective, faulty, wrongful, wrong-minded, peccable, guilty, errant, wayward, defective, culpable, reprehensible, incontinent, unchaste, unregenerate, unhallowed, reprobate, perverted, undevout, unreligious, graceless, faithless, miscreant, unfaithful, infidelistic, impure, unconsecrated, unsanctified.

2. Worldly, temporal, secular, lay.

3. Maledictory, maledictive, foul-mouthed, foul-spoken, foul-tongued, evil-tongued, contumelious, vituperative, damnatory, imprecative, abusive, calumniatory, evil-spoken, swearing, cursing, cussing *(coll.),* obscene, bawdy, common, coarse, vulgar, low, dirty, indelicate, indecorous, unblushing, smutty, lurid, fulsome, vile, not fit for decent ears, unspeakable, unprintable, improper, unseemly, gross, broad, ribald, Fescennine, nasty.

PROFANE, *v.* 1. Desecrate, commit sacrilege, revile, blaspheme, be impious, sin, be profane, be irreverent, be irreligious, mock, scorn, be vicious, indulge in vice, be bad, be evil, be wicked, be ungodly, be unholy, do wrong, be peccant, be iniquitous, be a reprobate, offend, commit sin, transgress.

2. Abuse, misuse, pollute, misemploy, misapply, pervert, misdirect, misappropriate, prostitute, outrage, commit an atrocity against, ill-use, desecrate, maltreat, waste, molest, ravage, oppress, violate, pervert.

PROFANITY, *n.* Abuse, malediction, cursing, cussing *(coll.),* swearing, denunciation, vituperation, execration, anathema, imprecation, proscription, disparagement, vilification, opprobrium, calumniation, contumely, obloquy, invective, philippic, diatribe, jeremiad, scurrility, scurrilousness, impiousness, impiety, profanation, profaneness, irreverence, dirty talk, foul language, foul talk, blasphemy, billingsgate.

PROFESS, *v.* 1. Avow, acknowledge, confess, declare, affirm, own, allege, state, say, tell, admit, vouch, vouchsafe, teach, proclaim, announce, aver, asseverate, assert, protest, predicate, annunciate, enunciate, propound, offer, put forward, broach, advance, contend, hold out, hold forth, maintain, confirm, assent, depose, warrant, certify.

2. Pretend, dissemble, dissimulate, put on, assume, make out as if *(coll.),* sham, counterfeit, purport, feign, simulate, act, play-act, four-flush *(coll.),* sail under false colors, gammon *(coll.),* fake *(coll.),* malinger, allege, claim, make a pretense of, plead, lay claim to, varnish, whitewash, take a stand upon, put on, pass off.

PROFESSEDLY, *adv.* Purportedly, by report, ostensibly, under the pretext of, as an excuse, falsely, slyly, deceptively, under false pretense, with a double tongue, deceitfully, untruthfully, uncandidly, disingenuously, unveraciously, cunningly, on the sly.

PROFESSION, *n.* 1. Declaration, avowal, claim, assertion, statement, acknowledgement, testimony, deposition, billet, promise, confession, belief, confession of faith, declaration of faith, precept, dogma, principle, article of faith, affirmation, averment, word, say, dictum, announcement, enunciation, protest, protestation, attestation, allegation, pronouncement, pronunciation, saying, remark, observation, confirmation, swearing, vow, evidence, guarantee, assurance, parole, word of honor, pledge, plight, troth, insurance.

2. Pretext, pretense, pretension, representation, evasion, affectation, claim, purported purpose, professed purpose, ostensible ground, ostensible reason, ostensible motive, false plea, excuse, undertaking, word, promise.

3. Employment, vocation, calling, job, occupation, work, career, business, office, learned profession, line, undertaking, endeavor, post, walk of life, berth, line of work, field, pursuit, situation, position, craft, art, service, sphere, engagement, faculty, following, avocation, concern, trade, association, line of achievement, affairs, ministry, capacity, métier, cloth, industry, practice.

4. *(Professions)* Medicine, law, the clergy, the church, holy orders, advocacy, teaching, the military, the army, the navy, public service.

PROFESSIONAL, *adj.* Practical, businesslike, vocational, occupational, learned, skilled, trained, expert, adept, proficient, official, functional, trade, thorough, prompt, systematic.

PROFESSOR, *n.* 1. Assenter, sayer, teller, consenter, confirmist, professant, endorser, covenantor, claimant, subscriber.

2. Teacher, tutor, savant, learned man, professional, instructor, scholar, man of erudition, pundit, schoolman, school teacher, fellow, don, academician, doctor, intellectual, scholiast, commentator, preceptor, educator, master, schoolmaster, abecedarian, pedant, adviser, professor emeritus.

PROFESSORIAL, *adj.* Preceptorial, pedagogical, instructional, academic, pedagogic, tutorial, teacherish, schoolteacherish, schoolmasterish, tuitionary, scholarly, scholastic, collegiate, cultural, hortatory, doctrinal, humane, edifying, didactic, homiletic, disciplinary.

PROFFER, *n.* Tender, offer, offering, proposal, proposition, volunteering, presentation, submission, invitation, candidacy, candidature, overture, advance, gift, donation, vouchsafement, grant, boon, present, donative, bounty, largess, handsel.

PROFFER, *v.* Tender, offer, volunteer, advance, propose, set forth, give, donate, prefer, bid, invite, make an offer, make a bid, make an overture, submit, hold out, put forward, move, make a motion, bid for, offer for sale, advertise, place in one's way, make possible, put in one's power.

PROFICIENCY, *n.* 1. Learning, knowledge, enlightenment, apprehension, comprehension, understanding, awareness, information, savvy, knowhow, useful knowledge, accomplishments, attainments, acquired knowledge, experience, practical knowledge, experimental knowledge, professional knowledge, technical knowledge.

2. Skill, mastery, know-how, adroitness, dexterity, capability, knack, competency, deftness, capacity, cleverness, expertness, address, finesse, facility, ease, sufficiency, adequacy, dexterousness, efficiency, versatility, talent, natural endowment, qualification, faculty, genius, forte, turn, bent, aptitude, aptness, habilitude, the stuff *(sl.),* the goods *(sl.),* parts, craft, ability, ableness.

PROFICIENT, *adj.* Skillful, adroit, dexterous, capable, competent, deft, clever, expert, facile, easy, sufficient, adequate, efficient, versatile, talented, naturally endowed, qualified, facultative, apt, habilitated, able, skilled, adept, conversant, trained, well-versed, well-qualified, practised,

masterly, accomplished, finished, good, *au fait (Fr.),* experienced, artistic, advanced, professional, knowing, ingenious, quick, ready, handy, masterful, resourceful, fine-fingered, smart, sharp, sure, equal to, up to, effective, efficacious.

PROFICIENT, *n.* Master, expert, crackerjack *(coll.),* whiz *(sl.),* adept, old hand, a good hand, veteran, dexterous person, graduate, no slouch *(sl.),* past master, clean hand, wizard, genius, man of genius, mastermind, topnotcher *(coll.),* first fiddle *(sl.),* crack *(coll.),* prodigy.

PROFILE, *n.* 1. Portrait, picture, silhouette, side view, half face.

2. Contour, lineaments, outline, delineation, configuration, features, lines, traits, face, visage, countenance, physiognomy, side, shape, form, figure.

3. Vignette, drawing, sketch, character sketch, biography.

PROFIT, *n.* 1. Produce, take, takings, gain, earnings, yield, rake-off *(sl.),* return, emolument, clearance, net profit, gross profit, clear profit, fruit, lucre, avails, premium, remuneration, accruance, aggrandizement, money, accumulation, income, harvest, dividend, proceeds, realization, receipts, profit margin, marginal profit, revenue, issue, windfall, benefit, perquisite, winnings, pickings, output, outcome, financial reward, meed, compensation, pay, consideration, solatium, prize.

2. Interest, advantage, good, benefit, service, weal, utility, perquisite, improvement, advancement, use, value, expediency, increment, augmentation, acquisition, boon, benefaction, blessing, boot, avail, godsend, harvest, windfall.

PROFIT, *v.* 1. Serve, help, be a benefit, avail, contribute, boot, do good for, produce a good effect, produce a good result, confer a benefit on, produce good, conduce to good, make improvement, stand in good stead, reach fruition, yield returns.

2. Turn to account, make money by, gain an advantage, make money, coin money, make capital out of, draw profit from, make profit from, turn an honest penny, recover a profit from, seize an opportunity, avail oneself of, improve the opportunity, take time by the forelock, be improved by, be better for, make good use of, turn to the right account, make the most of, reap the benefit of, learn a lesson from, make use of, use, utilize, put to use, lay one's hand to.

PROFITABLE, *adj.* Of value, valuable, estimable, worth-while, gainful, remunerative, rewarding, invaluable, beyond price, priceless, fruitful, productive, commendable, expedient, advisable, desirable, meet, fit, suitable, proper, right, apt, opportune, seasonable, due, recommendable, salutary, beneficial, favorable, serviceable, lucrative, paying, emolumentary, moneymaking, well-paying.

PROFITLESS, *adj.* Vain, to no avail, unavailing, fruitless, useless, bootless, worthless, valueless, unprofitable, of no use, void of profit, gainless, futile, unpaying, thankless, unsuccessful, unserviceable, inefficacious, inutile, unsalable, good-for-nothing, unremunerative, empty, inane, idle, not worth the money, not worth the powder to blow it up *(coll.),* barren, sterile, unproductive, unrewarding, impracticable, unhelpful, disadvantageous, unbeneficial, ineffectual, ineffective.

PROFLIGACY, *n.* Dissoluteness, depravity, shamelessness, vice, sinfulness, viciousness, reprobation, profligateness, immorality, lewdness, dissipation, badness, evil, wrongfulness, wrong, turpitude, corruption, corruptness, abomination, pollution, degeneracy, decadence, abjectivity, abjectness, degeneration, degradation, looseness, laxity, immorality, delinquency, moral failure, moral laxity, weakness of the flesh, defection, abandon, abandonment, carnality.

PROFLIGATE, *adj.* Vitiated, sinful, loose, wanton, depraved, corrupt, immoral, dissolute, dissipated, wicked, graceless, vice-ridden, vicious, shameless, lost to virtue, abandoned, flagrant, iniquitous, casehardened, worthless, unrepentant, rascally, heinous, wasteful, flagitious, shameful, scandalous, foul, licentious, offensive, nefarious, degenerate, atrocious, demoralized, evil-minded, obscene, notorious, unrestrained, indelicate, peccant, dirty, carnal, disgraceful, disreputable, vile, erotic, unchaste, unprincipled, unbridled, lascivious, incestuous, indecent, lax, debauched, infamous, voluptuous, pornographic, lecherous, unregenerate, lewd, unredeemable, lost, irreclaimable, rotten, tainted, contaminated, perverted, degraded, steeped in inquity, lost to virtue, wild, fast, light, gay, rakehell, fallen, meretricious, whorish, Paphian of easy virtue, of easy morals, intemperate, nonabstemious.

PROFLIGATE, *n.* Rake, rakehell, debauchee, reprobate, *roué (Fr.),* sinner, degenerate, pervert, dissipater, libertine, wrongdoer, bounder, rip *(coll.),* satyr, satyriast, lecher, intrigant, whoremonger, fornicator, adulterer, violator, sodomite, defiler, ravisher, seducer, raper, rapist, voluptuary, adulteress, fornicatress, woman of easy virtue, woman of loose morals, sensualist, hedonist, tragalist, high liver, gay dog *(coll.),* glutton, sodomist.

PROFOUND, *adj.* 1. Deep, abysmal, fathomless, unfathomable, sunken, sunk, deep-rooted, downreaching, low, depressed, low-lying, deep-seated.

2. Penetrating, sagacious, learned, abstruse, complex, complicated, erudite, wise, intellectually deep, intellectual, acroamatic, comprehensive, scholarly, serious, well-informed, recondite, sage, knowing, knowledgeable, enlightened, accomplished, philosophical, able, solid, deep, well-read, well-posted, deeply read, book-learned, educated, informed, omniscient, all-knowing, gnostic, judicial, prudent, reflective, reflecting, thoughtful, staid, calculating, considerate, well-advised, well-judged, sober-minded, sober, authoritative, oracular.

3. Lively, deep-felt, deeply felt, strongly felt, vivid, far-reaching, intense, heartfelt, keen, keenly felt, acute, touching, fast, sincere, abject, hearty, cordial, deep-seated, deep-reaching, homefelt, indelible, soul-stirring, impressive, piercing, penetrating, exciting, thrilling, electric, stimulating, galvanic, overpowering, overcoming, moving, overmastering, heart-swelling, heart-stirring, cutting, biting, stinging, astringent, caustic.

4. Obscure, indeterminate, ambiguous, indistinct, unclear, tough *(coll.),* steep *(coll.),* heavy *(coll.),* recondite, abstruse, occult, esoteric, special, crabbed, perplexing, dark, dim, shrouded, mysterious, subtle, evasive, elusive, inexpressible.

5. Thorough, utter, complete, abject, pronounced, positive, consummate, essential, extreme, flagrant, thorough-going, out-and-out, stark, perfect, finished, desperate, pronounced, decided.

PROFUNDITY, *n.* 1. Deepness, depth, depression, lowness, subjacency.

2. Penetration, sagacity, learnedness, abstruseness, complexity, complicatedness, complication, erudition, wisdom, intellectuality, acroamaticism, comprehensiveness, scholarliness, scholarship, seriousness, reconditeness, knowingness, knowledgeability, enlightenment, accomplishment, philosophy, ability, solidity, depth, omniscience, gnosticism, judicialness, judiciousness, prudence, reflectiveness, thoughtfulness, staidness, calculation, considerateness, consideration, sobriety, authority, authoritativeness.

3. Liveliness, deep feeling, strong feeling, vividness, keen feeling, acuteness, acuity, sincerity, objectivity, heartiness, cordiality, indelibility, indelibleness, impressiveness, piercingness, penetratingness, penetration, excitement, thrillingness, thrill, galvanism, causticity, intensity, keenness.

4. Obscurity, indeterminateness, ambiguity, indistinction, indistinctness, murkiness, unclarity, abstruseness, occultism, esoterism, specialness, speciality, crabbednes, perplexingness, perplexity, darkness, dimness, mystery, subtleness, subtlety, evasiveness, elusiveness, inexpressibility.

5. Thoroughness, completeness, pronouncedness, positiveness, consummateness, essence, extremity, flagrancy, starkness, perfection, finesse.

PROFUSE, *adj.* 1. Lavish, prodigal, generous, abundant, abounding, numerous, teeming, countless, innumerable, numberless, in profusion, swarming, plentiful, myriad, copious, bounteous, multitudinous, multiple, multitudinary, ever so many, infinite, endless, limitless, illimitable, incalculable, immeasurable, boundless, interminable, measureless, unnumbered, without end, without bound, without limit, inexhaustible, ample, affluent, rich, replete, prolix, extravagant, profusive, unstinting, without stint, rife, flush, luxuriant, enough and to spare, unsparing.

2. Wasteful, improvident, unthrifty, overliberal, spendthrift, lavish, prodigal, dissipative, intemperate, reckless, extravagant, unnecessary, needless, surplus, overplus, inordinate, overmuch, immoderate, exorbitant, excessive, supernumerary, beyond all bounds, unwarranted, unmitigated, too many, too much, overblown, overgrown, uncurbed, unbridled, wanton.

3. Prolix, verbose, wordy, long-winded, discursive, diffuse, diffusive, copious, exuberant, longiloquent, protracted, maundering, long-drawn-out, long-winded, digressive, padded, rambling, desultory, bombastic, loquacious, garrulous, tautological, redundant.

PROFUSENESS, *n.* 1. Lavishness, prodigality, plenitude, plenteousness, plenty, amplitude, abundance, prolixity, exuberance, exorbitancy, opulence, richness, affluence, copiousness, sufficiency, fullness, plethora, repletion, lavish supply, enough and to spare, superfluity, superabundance, nimiety, surplusage, overmeasure, pleonasm, surfeit, congestion, glut, engorgement, redundance, overfullness, too much, too many, unnecessariness, needlessness, inordinacy, profusion.

2. Prolixity, diffuseness, wordiness, verbosity, discursiveness, verbiage, longiloquence, tautology, redundany, flow of words, logorrhea, grandiloquence, maundering, protractedness, discursiveness, desultoriness, long-windedness, rambling, garrulity.

PROGENERATE, *v.* Beget, generate, reproduce, give birth to, proliferate, procreate, multiply, propagate, give being to, give rise to, originate, start, give a start to, hatch, breed, bring into the world.

PROGENITOR, *n.* Ancestor, parent, father, mother, sire, dam, forebear, genitor, forerunner, predecessor, primogenitor, begetter, procreator.

PROGENY, *n.* Offspring, issue, children, race, breed, stock, line, lineage, young, sons, heirs, descendants, scion, offshoot, posterity, family, tribe, sept, succeeding generations, increase, kindred, kin, stem, blood, bloodline, birth, child, progeniture, progenity, clan.

PROGNOSIS, *n.* Forecast, prediction, diagnosis, prophasis, prophecy, premonstration, presagement, prefiguration, foretelling, vaticination, foreknowledge, prescience, prewisdom, forewisdom, prognostication.

PROGNOSTIC, *adj.* Foreshowing, foretokening, prophetic, diagnostic, predictive, fatidical, fatidic, prognosticatory, vaticinal, vaticinative, vaticinatory, pythonic, oracular, presageful, divinatory, sibylline, sibylic, precurrent, precursory, precursive, haruspical.

PROGNOSTIC, *n.* 1. Sign, token, omen, presage, augury, portent, boding, presentiment, foreboding, bodement, foretoken, forerunner, precursor, prognostication, indication, symptom, premonitory sign, auspice, divination, prefiguration, prefigurement, harbinger, indication.
2. Prophecy, prediction, prognostication, foretelling, forecast, portent, warning, premonition, diagnosis, prophasis, premonstration, foretelling, vaticination, foreknowledge, prescience, prewisdom, forewisdom.

PROGNOSTICATE, *v.* Predict, foretell, foreshadow, foresee, forecast, prophesy, indicate, portend, foretoken, augur, auspicate, hariolate, foreshadow, forebode, vaticinate, premonish, preadmonish, signify, ominate, prognose *(Med.),* divine, presage, augurate, haruspicate, soothsay, tell fortunes, fortunetell, foresee the future, predict the future, croak, presignify, premonstrate, betoken, pretypify, shadow forth, preannounce, herald, look forward to, look ahead to.

PROGNOSTICATION, *n.* 1. Sign, token, omen, presage, presagement, augury, portent, boding, presentiment, foreboding, bodement, foretoken, foretokening, forerunner, precursor, prognostic, indication, symptom, premonitory sign, auspice, soothsay, divination, prefiguration, prefigurement, harbinger, indication.
2. Prediction, prophecy, prognosis, diagnosis, foretelling, forecast, portent, warning, premonition, prophasis, premonstration, hariolation, haruspication, presagement, presage, foretelling, vaticination, foreknowledge, prescience, prewisdom, forewisdom.

PROGNOSTICATOR, *n.* Prophet, foreteller, soothsayer, herald, harbinger, forecaster, predictor, seer, diviner, wizard, magician, sorcerer, astrologer, conjuror, oracle, sibyl, oraculum, *vates (Lat.),* augur, druid, divine, divinator, extispex, crystal-gazer, star-gazer, palmist, fortuneteller, haruspex, haruspice, geomancer, psychic, weather man, weather prophet, python, pythoness, prophetess.

PROGRAM, *n.* Schedule, prospectus, card, bill, order of the day, order of business, agenda, things to be done, bill of fare, menu, *carte du jour (Fr.),* list of agenda, protocol, roster, panel, poll, cadre, outline, sketch, calendar, docket, book, slate, dramatis personae, list of players, playbill, syllabus,

notice, advertisement, list of selections, system, plan, plot, official bulletin, curriculum, line-up.

PROGRAM, *v.* Book, schedule, arrange, slate, calendar, poll, register, docket, list, draft, empanel, line up *(coll.),* bill.

PROGRESS, *n.* 1. Progressiveness, progression, advancement, advance, ongoing, furtherance, onward-going, headway, way, onward course, growth, change, alteration, betterment, amelioration, melioration, improvement, emendation, perfection, promotion, enhancement, enrichment, development, rise, preferment, revival, recovery, restoration, repair, purification, readjustment, rehabilitation, reconstitution, reclamation, reorganization, redemption, salvage, salvation, reinvestment, retrieval, replacement, prosperity, success, prosperous outcome, achievement, gain, accomplishment, profit.
2. Velocity, speed, celerity, swiftness, quickness, rapidity, haste, step, stride, pace, clip *(coll.),* gait, flight, movement, forward motion, pickup, acceleration, speed-up, quickening, dispatch, hurry, progressive motion, locomotion, passage, course, rate, proficiency, career.

PROGRESS, *v.* 1. Proceed, go forward, move ahead, move forward, make headway, work one's way forward, continue ahead, get ahead, get on, gain, forge ahead, push on, press on, roll on, jog on, step ahead, carve one's way, edge one's way, go with the stream, ride the current, shoot ahead, rush ahead, make rapid strides, hold the course, keep to one's course, lose no time, hurry, make haste, rush, hustle, bustle, make a fuss, stir one's stumps, flutter, scramble, kick up a fuss, keep the ball rolling, go full steam ahead, make headway, work ahead, gain ground, lose no ground, not let the grass grow under one's feet, develop, shoulder one's way.
2. Improve, become better, grow, increase, ameliorate, get better, grow better, advance, make progress, make rapid strides, lose no time, run up, spring up, mature, maturate, rally, round, come 'round, make a turn for the better, recuperate, convalesce, climb, rise, ascend, mount, turn the corner, ripen, fructify, pick up, grow up.

PROGRESSION, *n.* 1. Progressiveness, progress, advance, advancement, ongoing, furtherance, onward-going, forward motion, forward movement, headway, onward course, profluency, profluence, march, proceeding.
2. Continuance, continuation, consecutiveness, course, succession, unbroken line, catenation, concatenation, gradation, ceaselessness, perpetuity, sequence, constant flow, unbrokenness, continuousness, consecution, following after, run, pursuance, prolongation, persistence, repetition.
3. Order, gradation, shade, graduation, succession, series, rank, place.
4. Progress, advancement, amelioration, melioration, improvement, emendation, mending, perfection, promotion, enhancement, enrichment, development, lift, rise, preferment, achievement, success, attainment, prosperous outcome, successful outcome, headway, revival, recovery, restoration, profit, gain, salvation, salvage, retrieval, replacement, prosperity, reclamation, reconstitution, repair, recovery, redemption, reconstruction.

PROGRESSIVE, *adj.* 1. Advancing, forward-going, forward-moving, ongoing, profluent, forward-looking, dynamic, going ahead, transitional, traveling, restless, advanced, forward, gradual, onward.

2. Reformative, reformational, reformatory, reformationary, cultural, accultural, corrective, remedial, emendational, restorative, reparatory, restitutory, recuperative, reparative, revivatory.

PROHIBIT, v. Prevent, hinder, reject, delay, debar, preclude, omit, deny, inhibit, forbid, disallow, revoke, restrict, interdict, enjoin, refuse, veto, taboo, block, check, repress, suppress, proscribe, exclude, disqualify, withhold, restrain, shut, banish, ban, bar, stop, stay, forfend, embargo, shut out, shut off, cohibit, limit, circumscribe, deny, say no to, negative, negate, oppose, traverse, gainsay, impugn, join issue with, disown, disaffirm, disavow, controvert, abnegate, forswear, repudiate, interfere, impede, clog, obstruct, hamper, constrain, foreclose, discommode, incommode, suppress, smother, quell, quash.

PROHIBITION, n. Forbiddance, forbiddal, veto, disavowal, ban, taboo, embargo, interdiction, interdict, prevention, hindrance, rejection, disallowal, preclusion, omission, denial, inhibition, revocation, restriction, suppression, quelling, quashing, foreclosure, foreclosing, closure, shutting, constraint, hampering, obstruction, abnegation, forswearing, repudiation, interference, controversion, disaffirmation, disowning, impugning, gainsaying, traversal, negation, enjoining, injunction, refusal, veto, proscription, block, check, repression, debarment, disqualification, exclusion, restraint, banishment, stopping, estoppal, stay, cohibition, limit, limitation, circumscription, impediment, prevention, barrier, obstacle, elimination, eradication, exception, nonadmission, noninclusion, abstinence, temperance, teetotalism, outlawry, unconstitutionality, unlawfulness, illegality, illegitimacy.

PROHIBITIONIST, n. Temperance worker, teetotaler, abstainer, abstinent, teetotalist, hydropot, nephalist, Rechabite, water-drinker, W.C.T.U., Women's Christian Temperance Union.

PROHIBITIVE, adj Preventive, hindering, preclusive, inhibitive, forbidding, disallowing, revocative, restrictive, interdictive, impossible, exclusive, restraining, disqualifying, forfensive, forfending, cohibitive, limitative, limiting, circumscriptive, negative, traversive, disaffirmative, controvertive, abnegative, impeding, interfering, obstructive, inadmissible, exclusory, injunctive, taboo, repressive, suppressive, proscriptive.

PROJECT, v. 1. Excurve, protrude, excurvate, bulge, stick out, protuberate, belly out, swell, round out, bag, bouge, jut out, stand out, arch, concamerate, vault, embow, bow, start up, bristle, jut over, bend over, pout, bunch, be convex, overhang, perpend, beetle, rise above.

2. Throw, cast, throw out, eject, emit, ejaculate, fling, expel, propel, shoot, deliver, bolt, hurtle, fire, bowl, traject, jaculate, extrude, send, launch, discharge, vault.

3. Devise, scheme, plan, frame, intend, contrive, design, plot, concoct, brew, invent, propose, conspire, arrange, concert, hatch, plan ahead, forecast, lay down a plan, draw up a plan, map out, draft, delineate, outline, chalk out, cut out, take measures, take steps, predetermine, predesign, preconcert, prearrange, arrange beforehand, predestine, predestinate, foreordain, foreordinate, preorder.

PROJECT, n. Intention, plan, design, ambition, scheme, device, proposal, purpose, projected scheme, projected campaign, undertaking, job, task, game, enterprise, intent, intentionality, prospect, mind, contemplation, set purpose, fixed intention, resolution, resolve, decision, determination, predetermination, aim, end, goal, objective, projection, schema, presentation, suggestion, motion, resolution, game, venture, engagement, activity, occupation, work, employment, assignment, object.

PROJECTILE, n. Missile, bullet, shell, cannon ball, musket ball, trajectile, bolt, shot, cannon shot, shrapnel, explosive shot, canister shot, solid shot, chain shot, bar shot, slung shot, dumdum bullet, soft-nose bullet, expanding bullet, explosive bullet, torpedo, hand grenade, bomb, infernal machine, gas bomb, tear-gas bomb, smoke bomb, demolition bomb, incendiary bomb, rifle grenade, petard, grapeshot, fire bomb, depth bomb, rocket, congreve rocket, stone, slug, brickbat, BB shot.

PROJECTING, adj. Pendulous, overhanging, sticking out, prominent, eminent, protruding, salient, pendent, standing out, jutting, underhung, underslung, excurrent, outstanding, exsurgent, protrusive, swelling, projective, beetling, superincumbent, overlying, overlapping, pendular, suspended, loose, hanging, convex, excurvate, bulbous, excurved, bulging, bowed, bellied, belled, gibbous, gibbose, bumped, humped, swayed, in relief, *repoussé (Fr.)*, raised, bossed, embossed, chased, bossy, imbricate, imbricated, superimposed, supernatant.

PROJECTION, n. 1. Propulsion, throwing, emission, ejaculation, hurling, kick, shot, delivery, firing, ejection, sending out, cast, casting, jaculation, trajection, discharge, ejectment, detrusion, extrusion, dispatch, expedition, exudation.

2. Plan, device, scheme, schema, design, contrivance, proposition, proposal, suggestion, game, presentation, undertaking, enterprise, intention, purpose, resolution, resolve, motion, venture.

3. Extension, prominence, extrusion, protuberance, eminence, jutty, outshoot, outgrowth, spur, salience, prominence, extension, tooth, burr, cam, cog, eaves, ledge, elbow, convexness, convexity, excurvature, excurvation, swelling, gibbosity, protrusion, camber, swell, swollenness, excrescence, excrescency, nodosity, nodulation, bulge, bow, bell, tumescence, intumescence, hump, bump, hunch, knob, knurl, clump, lump, rising, flange, lip, process, apophysis, snag, peg, pin, tang, stud, button, node.

4. Sketch, outline, plan, delineation, pattern, rough draft, copy, protocol, agenda, diagram, skeleton, skeleton outline, layout, map, ground plan, outline map, relief map, summary, conspectus, prospectus, elevation.

PROLEGOMENON, n. Introduction, prelude, preface, foreword, preamble, proem, preliminary remarks, preliminary statement, beginning, start, opening, prologue, protasis, proemium, preliminaries, exordium, prolusion, prefix, frontispiece, preliminary, descant, ritornello, overture, heading, opening, start, starting point, outset, first, outstart, setout.

PROLEPSIS, n. 1. Anachronism, parachronism, misdate, misdating, anticipation, prochronism, antichronism, disregard of time, error in time, error in dating, mistiming, metachronism, false estimate of time.

2. Postulate, presupposition, premise, assumption, lemma, presumed lemma, position, term,

supposal, thesis, hypothesis, starting point, basis, postulatum, postulation, apriorism, principle, foundation, ground.

PROLETARIAN, *adj.* Common, low, mean, vulgar, plebeian, vile, of low birth, of low parentage, of lowly origin, humble, lowborn, lowbred, baseborn, parvenu, homely, homespun, of the lower classes, of the laboring classes, wage-earning, poor, impecunious, pauperish, pauperized.

PROLETARIAT, *n.* Laboring classes, the common people, the people, the masses, *hoi polloi (Gr.),* laborers, wage-earners, workers, employees, rank and file, the crowd, the mob, commoners, the common herd, commonalty, commonage, the common run *(coll.),* lower orders, common orders, humble class, lower classes, the vulgar herd, the common run of humanity, the multitude, the four million, the horde, the crowd, common ruck, *canaille (Fr.),* rabble, rout, Tom, Dick and Harry, ragtag and bobtail, everyman, the great unwashed, *profanum vulgus (Lat.).*

PROLIFERATE, *v.* Progenerate, generate, reproduce, give birth to, procreate, multiply, propagate, give being to, give rise to, originate, start, give a start to, hatch, breed, bring into the world, fecundate, fertilize, impregnate, make fertile, fructify, fecundify, fecundize, pollinate, cross-pollinate, make productive, pullulate.

PROLIFERATION, *n.* Progeneration, procreation, multiplication, reproduction, fertilization, begetting, birth, propagation, fructification, fecundization, pollination, germination, gemination, impregnation, parturition, origination, starting, hatching, breeding, fertilization, fecundification, cross-pollination, prolification, luxuriance, uberty, multiparity, pregnancy, fruitfulness, geniture, genesis, pullulation.

PROLIFIC, *adj.* Proliferous, procreative, teeming, plentiful, plenteous, copious, philoprogenitive, philoprogenitous, fructiparous, uberous, proliferative, multiplying, genital, ectogenous, fruitful, originative, progenitive, xenogenetic, digenetic, ontogenetic, gamic, digenetic, fabricative, constructive, formative, creative, germinative, recreative, reproductive, generating, fertile, fecund, generant.

PROLIX, *adj.* 1. Verbose, redundant, tautological, diffuse, circumlocutory, loose, long, overextended, full of detail, crowded, lengthy, prosaic, wordy, full of verbiage, prolongated, prolonged, protracted, long-drawn-out, long-spun, spun out, long-winded, discursive, rambling, wandering, errant, dilatory, maundering, attenuated, roundabout, extended, declamatory, padded, bombastic, roving, desultory, perfunctory, copious, extravagant, exuberant, longiloquent, flatulent, windy *(sl.),* gassy *(sl.),* battological, pleonastical, ambagious, circuitous, uneconomical, profuse, profusive, inexhaustible.

2. Boring, tedious, tiresome, tiring, wearisome, boresome, irksome, humdrum, monotonous, prosaic, harping, dry, dry as dust, dreary, drear, drearisome, prosy.

PROLOCUTOR, *n.* 1. Reader, lector, lecturer, prelector, speaker, talker, spokesman, speechmaker, orator, public speaker, rhetorician, reciter, preacher, expositor, expounder.

2. Presiding officer, chairman, deputy, agent, spokesman, second, go-between, intermediary, interlocutor, delegate, emissary, missionary, ambassador, legate, lieutenant, vicar, surrogate, representative, minister, secondary, negotiator, tool, factor, proctor, instrument, commissionary, commissionaire, mouthpiece, spokester.

PROLOGUE, *n.* Introduction, induction, prelude, preface, foreword, preamble, proem, proemium, preliminary statement, beginning, opening, prolegomenon, protasis, exordium, prelusion, prefix, frontispiece, preliminary, preliminaries, overture, descant, ritornello, heading, opening, curtain-raiser, starting point, outset, set out, expository scene, first scene, preliminary scene.

PROLONG, *v.* Make longer, lengthen, render long, extend, attenuate, extend out, reach out, protract, stretch, spin out, draw out, elongate, sustain, maintain, continue, perpetuate, prosecute to a conclusion, go on to the end, keep the ball rolling, stay with it, stick it out *(coll.),* hold one's course, maintain the course, endure, be steadfast, persevere, prorogue, linger, retard, slow down, delay, hold, carry, drag on, drag out, remain, delay, tarry, hold back, demur, postpone, put off.

PROLONGATION, *n.* 1. Extension, continuation, continuity, succession, continuance, subsequence, run, maintenance, pursuance, perpetuation, persistence, perseverance, lengthening, elongation, attenuation, stretching, tension, protraction.

2. Delay, tardiness, procrastination, putting off, retardation, retard, prorogation, protraction, deferment, deferral, dilatoriness, adjournment, cunctation, hold up, stay, hold off, stop, suspension.

PROMENADE, *n.* 1. Walk, stroll, airing, circuit, whirl *(coll.),* outing, junket, drive, ride, peregrination, saunter, constitutional, turn, stretch, exercise, perambulation, ambulation, hike, ramble, march, tramp.

2. Path, sidewalk, walk, course, run, road, footway, footpath, lane, avenue, passage, pathway, pavement, public walk, boardwalk, esplanade, parade, alameda, ambulatory, ambulatorium, colonnade, arcade, covered path, covered way.

3. Dance, prom *(coll.),* ball, shindig *(sl.),* hop *(coll.),* party, *levée, soirée,* reception, masked ball, *bal masqué (Fr.),* dancing, cotillion, debutantes' ball, costume ball.

PROMENADE, *v.* Walk, stroll, saunter, wander, peregrinate, take a walk, take a stroll, take a turn in the air, go for an airing, make a promenade, take a run, ambulate, pedestrianize, stir one's stumps, take the air, pad, foot it *(coll.),* hoof it *(coll.),* shag along, shuffle along, tramp, hike, march, slog along, stump it *(coll.),* circumambulate, navigate, take a stretch, stretch the legs, hit the road, hit the trail, amble, take a constitutional.

PROMINENCE, *n.* 1. Projection, extension, extrusion, protuberance, jutty, outshoot, outgrowth, spur, salience, tooth, burr, cam, cog, elbow, bulge, process, convexity, convexness, excurvature, excurvation, swelling, boldness, gibbosity, protrusion, camber, swell, swollenness, excrescence, excrescency, nodosity, bow, bell, tumescence, hump, bump, hunch, knurl, knob, clump, lump, rising, flange, lip, apophysis, snag, pen, pin, tang, stud, button, node, nodule, caruncula-tion, tumefaction, tumidity, intumescence.

2. High point, high place, knoll, hill, rise, mount, mountain, precipice, peak, height, elevation, hillock, alp, monticule, rising ground, loftiness, elevation, altitude, mound, barrow, dune, spine, comb, promontory, point, pinnacle, crag,

crest, tor, highlands, cliff, steep, summit, utmost heights, range, mountain range.

3. Eminence, fame, celebrity, conspicuousness, distinction, brilliancy, mark, influence, weight, figure, pre-eminence, greatness, high-and-mightiness, might, elevation, exaltation, prestige, significance, notability, nobility, grandeur, majesty, consequence, reputation, honor, credit, respectability, notoriety, popularity, illustriousness, splendor, highness, exaltedness, sublimity, dignity, importance, consideration, import, name, paramountcy, primacy, superiority, exaltation, precedence.

PROMINENT, *adj.* 1. Projected, projecting, extended, extruded, extrusive, protuberant, jutting, shooting out, salient, toothed, burred, ledged, elbowed, bulging, convex, excurvated, excurvate, swelling, swollen, gibbose, gibbous, protrusive, excrescent, nodose, bowed, belled, tumescent, intumescent, tumid, humped, hunched, bumped, knurled, knobbed, knobby, clumped, lumped, rising, flanged, lipped, snagged, pegged, pinned, tanged, studded, noded, nodulate, carunculated.

2. Eminent, famous, celebrated, conspicuous, distinctive, distinguished, paramount, primate, superior, exalted, precedent, dignified, important, considerable, substantial, named, known, renowned, illustrious, splendid, high, exalted, popular, notorious, respected, credited, honored, noble, grand, majestic, consequential, of consequence, of high reputation, brilliant, bold, of mark, influential, weighty, pre-eminent, great, high-and-mighty, powerful, significant, of high prestige, notable.

3. Glaring, arrant, staring, flagrant, showy, showing, flaunting, conspicuous, noticeable, unavoidable, obvious, discernible, palpable, striking, ostentatious, daring, gaudy, garish, loud, definite, plain, well-marked, evident, apparent, open, revealed, definite, recognizable, pronounced, staring, in high relief, remarkable, main, principal, primary, first, salient.

PROMISCUITY, *n.* Promiscuousness, indiscriminateness, indiscrimination, confusion, mixture, want of discrimination, lack of discrimination, lack of distinction, uncriticalness, lack of judgment, indistinction, looseness, laxity, laches, wantonness, licentiousness, debauchery, unchastity, incontinence, venery, fornication, libertinage, libertinism, immorality.

PROMISCUOUS, *adj.* 1. Indiscriminate, mingled, mixed, helter-skelter, composite, medley, miscellaneous, heterogeneous, commingled, intermixed, amalgamated, alloyed, mixed up with, mixed together, crossbred, crossed, intermarried, interlarded, interwoven, blended, fused, joined, conjoined, kneaded together, brewed, scrambled, jumbled, bemingled, variegated, diverse, disordered, disorderly, disorganized, out of gear, dislocated, misplaced, unsystematic, unmethodical, haphazard, straggling, aimless, undirected, desultory, chaotic, confused, perplexed, deranged, disarranged, indiscriminative, indistinguishable, uncritical, undiscriminating, unselected, unselective.

2. Loose, wanton, immoral, lax, debauched, unchaste, incontinent, unvirtuous, carnal, licentious, profligate, impure, immodest, dissolute, dissipated, free, wild, rampant, easy, of easy virtue, morally loose, intemperate.

PROMISE, *n.* 1. Vow, word, undertaking, assurance, agreement, parole, oath, pledge, contract, profession, betrothal, troth, plight, word of honor,

solemn word, solemn declaration, obligation, stipulation, warranty, covenant, avowal, guarantee, insurance, marriage vow, marriage contract, affidavit, compact, understanding, bicker, bargain, pact, paction, treaty, affidation, security, pignoration, bond, vadium, tie, earnest, handsel, agreement, concession, compliance.

2. Good omen, good auspices, well-grounded hope, reliance, conviction, faith, assumption, presumption, bright promise, clear sky, cheerful prospects.

PROMISE, *v.* 1. Pledge, engage, covenant, vow, make an avowal, plight, swear, take an oath, underwrite, subscribe, undertake, dedicate oneself to, aver, vouch, enter into an engagement, answer for, be bound for, sponsor, give one's word of honor, assure, guarantee, warrant, testify, attest, bear witness, vouch for, avow, plight one's honor, agree for, indent, certify, assure, indorse, take upon oneself, devote oneself to, venture upon, take one's oath, swear an oath, call heaven to witness, assert under oath, testify under oath, depose.

2. Give hope, be probable, hold a probability, indicate, imply, make one expect, make fair promise, hold the expectation of, stand fair, bid fair, lead one to expect, raise hope, inspirit, cheer, encourage, augur well, look up, be in a fair way.

3. Threaten, hold over one's head, menace, hold out by way of warning, utter threats against, show threatening signs, forewarn, warn of evil, admonish, intimidate, endanger.

PROMISING, *adj.* 1. Favorable, auspicious, propitious, full of promise, looking up *(coll.)*, encouraging, hopeful, inspiriting, bright, rosy, cheering, cheerful, of good omen, of good portent, roseate, within sight of land, on the road to, assuring, reassuring, optimistic, suitable, fair, inviting, flattering, happy, fortunate, lucky, prosperous, halcyon.

2. Probable, likely, in a fair way to, liable, apt, hopeful, possible, presumable, in the cards.

3. Votive, promissory.

PROMONTORY, *n.* Headland, height, cliff, precipice, embankment, projection, foreland, jutty, cape, ness, point of land, head, bill, tongue, spur, peak, neck of land, peninsula.

PROMOTE, *v.* 1. Advance, forward, push, railroad *(coll.)*, further, cultivate, help, aid, assist, encourage, foster, ameliorate, subserve, prefer, nourish, sustain, carry on, help forward, prosecute, organize, nurse, urge forward, urge on, advocate, speak for, patronize, abet, build up, sanction, support, hold up, maintain, develop, refine, fatten, enrich, enhance, mellow, refine upon, improve upon, succor, come to the aid of, come to the assistance of, give a leg up, lend a hand, do a good turn, minister to, speed, expedite, rush, hurry, hasten, render a service to, facilitate, make easy for, clear the way for, disencumber, disburden, unclog, deobstruct, disentangle, disengage.

2. Raise, elevate, prefer, dignify, pass, graduate, upgrade.

PROMOTION, *n.* Advancement, advance, furtherance, encouragement, cultivation, development, help, assistance, aid, succor, abetting, betterment, advertising, publicity, augmentation, melioration, amelioration, emendation, progress, headway, boosting, lifting, perpetuation, fostering, favor, aidance, service, accommodation, upkeep, maintenance, ministration, ministry, provision, conducement, hand *(coll.)*, uplift, lift *(coll.)*, benefit.

PROMPT, *adj.* 1. Done (performed, delivered, *etc.*) at once or without delay, timely, punctual, instant, quick, immediate, early, seasonable, summary, in good time, by return mail, instantaneous, unhesitating.

2. Ready in action, quick to act as occasion demands, apt, alert, active, businesslike, sharp, on the alert, on one's toes, acute, agile, speedy, animate, lively, on guard, observant, efficient, wide-awake, on the job *(coll.),* intent, bright, alive, spry, sprightly, nimble, mercurial, vigilant, attentive, agog, open-eared, open-eyed, on the *qui vive (Fr.),* all there *(coll.).*

3. Ready and willing, zealous, anxious, eager, favorable, forward, prone, apt, inclined, disposed, agreeable, compliant, enthusiastic, fervent, predisposed, minded, willed, fain, nothing loath, unasked, unforced, earnest, avid, keen, unsought, gratuitous, voluntary, spontaneous, game *(coll.),* Johnny on the spot *(coll.).*

PROMPT, *v.* 1. Move, incite to action, set on, spur on, goad, hustle, thrust, push, impel, stimulate, induce, set on, draw on, actuate, instigate, admonish, exhort, prick, force, determine, advise, inspire, press, hound, put up to, dispose, incline, urge, tempt, stir, persuade, influence, excite, alert, inspirit, rouse, arouse, encourage, prevail with (on, upon), bring pressure to bear upon.

2. Induce *(action, etc.),* suggest, dictate, inspire, foment, occasion, instigate, hunt, set going, actuate, activate, motivate, propel, impel, drive, forward, stimulate, animate, provoke, evoke, prescribe, advocate, recommend, put or set in motion, urge.

3. Supply with a cue from offstage *(Theat.),* assist *(a speaker),* put in mind or remembrance, remind, jog the memory, suggest, hint, set back on the track, renew or refresh the memory, put words in one's mouth.

PROMPTER, *n.* One who or that which prompts, reminder, jogger, instigator, abettor, provoker, suggester, firebrand, incendiary, agitator, memorandum, mnemonic device, memo *(coll.),* sponsor, forwarder, initiator.

PROMPTITUDE, *n.* Promptness, readiness, expedition, punctuality, dispatch, precipitance, precipitation, impetuosity, urgency, velocity, zeal, haste, celerity, quickness, swiftness, alacrity, alertness, smartness, nimbleness, activity, agility, speed, earliness.

PROMULGATE, *v.* 1. Make known by open declaration, proclaim formally, publish, make public, bring into the open, noise abroad, spread abroad, advertise, announce, disseminate, report, promote, give to the world, circulate, propagate, broadcast, divulge, herald, notify of, pronounce, annunciate, break the news of, give tidings of, issue, emit, give publicity to, publicize, declare, bruit, trumpet, blaze, air, vent, hawk about, blazon, enounce.

2. Set forth, teach publicly, foster, sponsor, promote, propagandize, exposit, expound, elucidate, interpret, explain, present, communicate, enunciate, instruct, preach.

PRONE, *adj.* 1. Having a natural inclination or tendency to something, disposed, liable, predisposed, favorable, partial, ready, willing, tending, inclined, subject, minded, leaning, likely, eager, easily persuaded, consenting, well-disposed, idiocratic, apt, bent.

2. Lying face downward, having the front or ventral part downward, prostrate, recumbent, ac-

cumbent, decumbent, flat, procumbent, horizontal, couchant, reclining, level, recubate, crouching, jacent.

3. Having a downward direction or slope, sloping, inclining, aslope, slant, aslant, leaning, tilted, slanting, pitching, oblique, declivous, inclined.

PRONG, *n.* Pointed division *(of a fork),* pointed projecting part *(as of an antler),* tine, spike, cusp, barb, fluke, spur, hook, nib, neb, spit, spine, horn, branch, point.

PRONOUNCE, *v.* 1. Utter in a particular manner, enunciate *(words, etc.),* give forth, express, emit, say, speak, frame, stress, emphasize, accent, burr, form, sound, enounce, accentuate, garble, clip.

2. Declare to be *(as specified),* affirm, assert, allege, state, aver, adjudicate, condemn, express, judge, announce, proclaim, pass judgment, pass sentence upon, sit in judgment.

3. Utter formally, deliver formally, announce authoritatively or officially, give an opinion or decision, make a statement or assertion, declaim, voice, give tongue to, communicate, predicate, annunciate, enunciate, enounce, preach, aver, orate.

PRONOUNCED, *adj.* Strongly marked, clearly indicated, decided, salient, striking, clear, broad, plain, bold, noticeable, stark, gross, crass, pointed, distinct, rank, glaring, staring, unmistakable, notable, palpable, obvious, definite, well-defined, patent, prominent, conspicuous, evident, recognizable, in bold (strong, high) relief, graphic, well-outlined, certain, clear-cut, positive, perspicuous, undisguised, vivid, unquestionable, manifest, visible, unhidden, very.

PRONOUNCEMENT, *n.* Formal or authoritative statement, opinion, decision, report, utterance, notice, notification, imperative, declaration, enunciation, announcement, saying, dictum, proclamation, indiction, fiat, edict, manifesto, pronunciamento, affirmation, annunciation, assertion, remark, observation, comment, sentence, law, expression, word, order, profession, position, allegation, asseveration, averment, *ipse dixit (Lat.).*

PRONUNCIATION, *n.* Act or result of producing the sounds of speech, utterance, articulation, expression, enunciation, word formation, voice, accent, elocution, diction, dialect; phonation, delivery, speaking, mode of speech, vocalization, manner of speaking, intonation.

PROOF, *adj.* Impervious, invulnerable, of tested or proved strength or quality, impenetrable, firm, stable, fixed, settled, stanch, steeled, sound, resistant, armed, armored, tough, unyielding, cast-iron, sure, steadfast, proven, protected, inured, hardened, callous, repellent, tight, defensible, unassailable, inexpugnable.

PROOF, *n.* 1. Evidence sufficient to establish a thing as true, clear indication, certainty, conviction, satisfaction, facts, substantiation, certification, show, sign, telltale manifestation, verification, corroboration, probation, ratification, confirmation, testimony, grounds, assurance, apodixis, conclusiveness.

2. Act of testing or making trial of anything, test, trial, demonstration, assay, examination, probation, check, ordeal.

3. Establishment of the truth of anything, confirmation, demonstration, attestation, substantiation, probation, manifestation, certification, deduction, verification, ratification, corroboration.

4. Proved strength, invulnerability, might, vig-

or, puissance, potency, solidity, stamina, toughness, stoutness, power, inviolability, resistance, imperviousness, impenetrability, invincibility, indomitableness.

5. Trial impression *(Print.)*, trial print *(Photog.)*, revise *(Print.)*, proof sheet, copy, rough copy, artist's proof.

PROOFREAD, *v.* Read to detect and mark errors for correction, read, proof-correct, read *or* correct copy.

PROP, *n.* Support, stay, upholder, sustainer, mainstay, arm, stick, pole, rod, rigid support, supporter, block, brace, rib, rest, stand, standard, base, splint, strengthener, reinforcement, pediment, stanchion, pillar, underpin, underset, leg, staff, stud, fulcrum, shore, buttress, strut, cane,, crutch, pin, foundation, cornerstone, bracer, coin *(Archit.)*, raker *(Building)*.

PROP, *v.* 1. Support, prevent from falling, hold up, shore up, shoulder, back up, uphold, carry, bear, stand by, truss, brace, base, found, bottom, ground, underpin, underset, underbrace, assist, help, maintain, scotch, bolster.

2. Rest *(a thing)* against support, lean, set, lay, stand, support.

PROPAGANDA, *n.* 1. Doctrines *or* principles propagated by an organization, dogma, theology, system of belief *or* opinions, cult, ism, creed, view, school, teaching, gospel, position, religion.

2. Organization propagating doctrines, concerted movement for dissemination, radical sect, fanatical group, order, religion, mission, persuasion, faction, proselytizing group, congregation.

PROPAGANDISM, *n.* Zealous propagation of particular doctrines *or* principles, persuasion, proselytism, publication, promotion, conversion, promulgation, dissemination, circulation, diffusion, spreading, missions, broadcast, fanaticism, evangelism, psychological warfare.

PROPAGANDIST, *n.* One devoted to the propagation of particular doctrines *or* principles, proselytizer, evangelist, missionary, indoctrinator, apostle, teacher, revivalist, colporteur, disseminator, salesman, hawker, zealot, devotee.

PROPAGANDIZE, *v.* Propagate *or* spread *(principles, etc.)* by a propaganda, indoctrinate, teach, instruct, spread, disseminate, broadcast, infuse, instill, implant, sow the seeds, inoculate, inculcate, diffuse, circulate, publish, promulgate.

PROPAGATE, *v.* 1. Multiply, increase, breed, reproduce, develop, progenerate, bring forth, give birth, proliferate, procreate, engender, generate, beget, bear, hatch, spawn, drop *(of animals.)*.

2. Cause to spread, extend, spread, promulgate, multiply, increase, disseminate, transmit, diffuse, broadcast.

3. Spread from person to person, publish, broadcast, scatter, bestrew, noise abroad, disseminate, report, whisper about, divulge *(rare in this sense)*, rumor, issue, give currency to, notify, proclaim, circumfuse, make known, hint abroad, repeat, intersperse, disperse, hawk about, trumpet, air, blaze, promulgate, blow, bring into the open, give out, put forth, emit, tell, proclaim from the housetops, enunciate, blazon, herald, vent, ventilate, give to the world, sow, strew, irrigate, spray, sprinkle, publicize, evulgate, make public.

PROPAGATION, *n.* 1. Act of producing young, giving birth, breeding, procreation, parturience, reproduction, gestation, conception, yielding,

pregnancy, delivery, delivering, germination, spawning, casting, hatching, laying, bearing, dropping *(of animals)*.

2. Act of publishing *or* spreading abroad, publication, manifesto, circuiteering, emanation, dispersion, circuiting, evulgation, irrigation, publishing, circuity, diffusion, spreading, transmission, dissemination, making public, notification, issuance, circulation, distribution, reporting, bruiting, printing, advertisement, circumfusion, divulgation, ventilation, broadcast, broadcasting, compassing, announcement, proclamation.

PROPEL, *v.* Push forward, drive, set in motion, start, launch, discharge, toss, sling, shy, chuck, impel, thrust, force, shoot, push, shove, cast, punt, trundle, hurl, heave, pitch, prod, poke, goad, send, catapult, precipitate, emit, eject, project.

PROPELLANT, *n.* Propelling agent for projectiles, shells, *etc.*, explosive, charge, cordite, gunpowder, *etc.*

PROPELLENT, *n.* Something which drives forward, propelling agent, propeller, pulsive, propulsor, driver, propulsive, impellent, impeller.

PROPELLER, *n.* *(Aeronaut.)* Screw, airscrew, screw propeller, prop *(coll.)*.

PROPENSITY, *n.* 1. Natural inclination, natural capacity, leaning, innate ability, turn, adeptness, adroitness, competence, dexterity, felicity, sharpness, proclivity, deftness, gift, qualification, aptitude, bent, disposition, talent, forte, bias, knack, genius, art, skill, facility, mastery.

2. Liking, preference, partiality, attraction, affinity, leaning, disposition, humor, weakness, like, bent, bias, sympathy, penchant, relish, temper, mind, proclivity, predilection, inclination, favor, fancy, taste, pleasure.

PROPER, *adj.* 1. Peculiar, distinctive, indigenous, specific, representative, particular, characteristic, marked, appropriate, individual, discriminative, differential, typical, diagnostic, distinguishing.

2. Belonging to the essential constitution, exact, specific, particular, express, concrete, determinate, defined, single, correct, precise, fixed, true, definite, explicit, well-defined.

3. Correct, right, fit, fitting, exact, precise, accurate, applicable, appropriate, congruous, expedient, timely, apt, suited, meet, pertinent, conformable, consonant, condign, harmonious, germane, apropos, apposite, relevant.

4. In good taste, decent, decorous, tasteful, seemly, fitting, befitting, fit, becoming, modest, delicate, acceptable, suitable, nice, orthodox, right.

PROPERTY, *n.* 1. Quality, peculiarity, singularity, idiosyncrasy, cast, diagnostic, essential, aspect, particularity, individuality, feature, trait, attribute, characteristic, point, badge, mark, earmark.

2. Belongings, wealth, chattels, holdings, seizin *(Leg.)*, effects, investments, means, possessions, assets, appointments, appurtenances, goods, tenements, resources, commands, substance, funds, stock, capital, treasure, moneys.

3. Real estate, lands, estates, acres, realty, demesne, stake, holding, grounds, messuage, acquest *(Law.)*, allodium, dominions, claim, hereditaments, territory, freehold property.

4. Right of possession, possession, ownership, tenure, lordship, proprietorship, hold, holding, monopoly, lease, leasehold.

PROPHECY, *n.* 1. Prediction of what is to come, forecast, prognostication, forecasting, foretelling, augury, divination, prognosis, mantology, hariolation, soothsaying, vaticination, presage.

2. That which is declared by a prophet, prediction, divinely inspired utterance *or* revelation, preaching, exhortation, warning, instruction, handwriting on the wall, portent, augury, forecast, vaticination, presage, presagement, prognostication, prognosis.

PROPHESY, *v.* Predict, indicate beforehand, foretell, prognosticate, omen, soothsay, hariolate, foresee, premonish, augur, vaticinate, forebode, forecast, presage, divine, haruspicate, herald, prognose *(Med.)*.

PROPHET, *n.* 1. One who speaks for God *or* a deity *or* by divine inspiration, inspired leader *or* teacher, mediator, medium, spokesman of some doctrine, cause, *etc.,* proclaimer, oracle, disciple, apostle, guide, saint, evangelist, Mohammed, interpreter, intercessor, voice crying in the wilderness, preacher.

2. One who foretells *or* predicts what is to come, predictor, foreteller, prophesier, prophetess *(Fem.),* fortuneteller, palmist, forecaster, astrologer, sibyl, oracle, seer, soothsayer, prognosticator, herald, mantologist, augur, divinator, vaticinator, python, Merlin, crystal-gazer, extispex, haruspice, haruspex, geomancer, geomant, *vates (Lat.).*

PROPHETIC, *adj.* 1. Of *or* pertaining to a prophet, of the nature of *or* containing prophecy, prophetical, predictive, fatidic, prescient, having the function *or* powers of a prophet, prognostic, vaticinal, sibylic, pythonic, haruspical, presageful, predictory, vaticinatory, divinatory, oracular, apocalyptic, revelatory, instructive, druidic, sibylline, vatic, fatiloquent, precursive, augural, symptomatic, revelational, presentient, indicative, foreseeing, extispicious.

2. Predictive, presageful, ominous, monitory, premonitory, dire, fell, menacing, foreboding, inauspicious, unpropitious, bodeful, alarming, solemn, ill-boding, forewarning, minacious, lowering, dreadful, fateful, fearful, frightful, intimidating, frightening, dread.

PROPHYLACTIC, *adj.* Defending *or* protecting from disease, preventive, protective, preservative, healthful, beneficial to health, hygienal, hygienic, salutory, health-giving, benign, strengthening, roborant, good, tonic, conservatory, conservative, bracing, wholesome, salubrious, invigorating, sanitary, nutritious, nutritive.

PROPHYLACTIC, *n.* Prophylactic medicine *or* measure, preventative, counteractant, counteragent, vaccine, serum, preventive, offset, antidote, neutralizer, injection, shot *(sl.),* germicide, antiseptic, bactericide, disinfectant, protective substance *or* measure.

PROPHYLAXIS, *n.* Preventing of disease, prophylactic treatment, elimination of disease-producing conditions, arrest, control *(of disease),* hygiene, prevention, hygienics, avoidance, caution, preservation of health, precaution.

PROPINQUITY, *n.* 1. Nearness in place, closeness, proximity, vicinity, appropinquity, vicinage, apposition, presence, juxtaposition, adjacence, neighborhood, convergence, conflux, close quarters *or* range, concourse, confluence, approximation, contiguity.

2. Nearness of relation, kinship, close association, nearness of blood, consanguinity, kindred, ties of blood, cognation, agnation, common ancestry, connection, relationship, filiation.

3. Affinity of nature, similarity, rapport, congeniality, likeness, analogy, oneness, unity, accord, coincidence, pertinence, relevance, commensurability, identity, aptness, fitness, resemblance, agreement, concert, concinnity, concord, harmony, parallelism, connaturalness, Homoiousian, homogeneity, comparison, correspondence, conformation, compatability, semblance, similitude, alikeness, synonymity, equivalance.

4. Nearness in time, close sequence, simultaneity, simultaneousness, coincidence, concurrence, opportuneness, synchronization, timeliness, correspondence, concurrency, coexistency, coetaneity, conjuncture, contemporaneity, concomitance, coevality, synchronism, contemporaneousness, coexistence, juncture, consonance, concomitancy, coextension, synchronousness.

PROPITIATE, *v.* Make favorably inclined, concilate, appease, gain the favor of, mediate, intercede, atone, bring to terms, please, mollify, compose, satisfy, reconcile, soothe, content, tame, placate, assuage, moderate, allay, soften, beguile, disarm, speak peace, ingratiate, still, make peace, tranquilize, arbitrate, humor, gratify, win over, settle, adjust, accommodate, heal the breach, restore harmony, touch, melt, appeal to, hold out the olive branch to, make a peace offering, pour balm into, quell *or* stem the anger *or* wrath of, attemper, temper, mitigate, prevail with, beg pardon, recompense, make amends, compensate, expiate.

PROPITIATION, *n.* 1. Act of propitiating, conciliation, reconciliation, atonement, satisfaction, expiation, peacemaking, sacrifice, placation, mollification, arbitration, appeasement, pacification, reparation, atoning, redress, reclamation, redemption, quittance, adjustment, settlement, composition, intercession, reconcilement, mediation.

2. That which propitiates, satisfaction, sacrifice, penance, peace offering, apology, incense, immolation, libation, oblation, atonement, calumet, peace pipe, olive branch.

PROPITIATOR, *n.* Intercessor, mediator, arbiter, arbitrator, referee, moderator, interceder, go-between, negotiator, peacemaker, pacificator, intermediary, intermediate, intermediator, justice, umpire, reconciler.

PROPITIATORY, *adj.* Serving *or* intended to propitiate, conciliatory, making propitiation, peacemaking, pacifying, irenic, mediatorial, atoning, reconciling, prostrate, obeisant, placatory, pacific, persuasive, sacrificial, piacular, winning, atoning, intermediatory, intermedial, intercessory, apologetic, satisfactional, mediatory, pacificatory, reconciliatory, expiatory.

PROPITIOUS, *adj.* 1. Indicative of favor, presenting favorable conditions, favorable, encouraging, fortunate, auspicious, sunny, good, seasonable, of good omen, smiling, fair, roseate, promising, bright, hopeful, advantageous, providential, prosperous, well-disposed, timely, lucky, happy, opportune, cheering, pleasing, rose-colored, heartening, reassuring, satisfactory, golden, full of promise, salubrious, salutary, conducive, looking up, halcyon, expedient.

2. Favorably inclined, disposed to bestow favors *or* forgive, well-disposed, well-affected, benevolent, clement, kindly, felicitous, merciful, benign, gracious, well-meaning, obliging, ruthful, amicable, unhostile, approving, amiable, accommodating, good, indulgent, kind, favorable,

friendly, pitying, benignant, helping, helpful, inspiriting, salutary, beneficial, compassionate, cordial, considerate, sympathetic, complacent, kindhearted, good-natured, good-hearted.

PROPONENT, n. On who puts forward a proposition or proposal, one who supports a cause or doctrine, advocate, defendant, enthusiast, justifier, vindicator, apologist, defender, spokesman, apologizer, upholder, abettor, backer, champion, representative, votary, sectary, partisan, patron, wellwisher, sympathizer, friend, angel (coll.).

PROPORTION, n. 1. Comparative relationship between things, ratio, relative estimate, arrangement, adaptation of parts, contrast, balance, opposition, weight, correlation, distribution, comparative size, adjustment, perspective, likenesses and differences, relative importance or significance, correspondence.
2. Proper relation between things or parts, adjustment, agreement, symmetry, eurhythmy, concinnity, ideal distribution, analogy, commensuration, harmony, balance, correspondence, commensurateness, perspective, Atticism, classicism, shapeliness, regularity, conformity, congruity, keeping, consistency, proportionality, beauty, evenness, uniformity, poise, euphony, propriety, grace, parallelism.
3. (Plural) Relative size or extent, dimensions, bulk, measurements, expanse, scope, range, spread, span, width, area, breadth, magnitude, amplitude, volume, mass, greatness, capacity.
4. Part, portion, quota, measure, share, lot, just degree, division, quantity allotted, quotum, endowment, percentage, consignment, commission, allowance, ration, dole, stint, dividend, cut (coll.), allotment, whack (sl.), rake-off (sl.).
5. Relation, comparison, analogy, contrast, reference, bearing, apposition, oppositeness, likening, perspective, confrontment, confrontation, juxtaposition, opposition, balance.

PROPORTION, v. Adjust (in proper proportion or relation), adjust the proportions of, regulate, modulate, equalize, order, equate, fit, poise, balance, conform, grade, correct, rectify, space, form, shape, match, square, true, similarize, homologize, harmonize, accommodate, graduate, put in proportion.

PROPORTIONAL, adj. 1. Having due proportion, corresponding, proportionable, consistent, compatible, being in or characterized by due proportion, approximative, symmetrical, agreeing, synchronized, proportionate, suiting, consonant, concinnous, in accordance with, accordant, comparable, like, analogous, akin, equivalent, parallel, twin, similar, metaphorical, harmonious, commensurable, shaped, uniform, commensurate, matching, even, on a proper scale, well-proportioned.
2. Of or pertaining to proportion, relative, distributional, related, parallelistic, contrastive, according, comparative, collative, connective.

PROPOSAL, n. 1. Offer, proposition, overture, tender, recommendation, proffer, terms proposed, suggestion, motion, bid, thesis, nomination, condition, position, presentation, resolution, hypothesis, plan, program, measure, appeal, ultimatum, conjecture, guess, assumption, theorem, theory, postulate, draft, outline, delineation, sketch, pattern, layout, diagram, suit, request, invitation, arrangement, bill.
2. Plan, scheme, prospectus, intention, intent, ambition, prospect, resolution, design, program,

plot, project, purpose, goal, end, aim, object, objective, hope, idea, conception, line of action, course, stratagem, aspiration.

PROPOSE, v. 1. Put forward for consideration, acceptance or action, offer, proffer, advocate, introduce, make a motion, submit, put, pose, present, recommend, move, invite, suggest, tender, overture, moot, maintain, come up with, comment, project, bid, contend, advance, put forth or forward, bring forward, hold out, nominate.
2. Put before oneself as something to be done, design, mean, purpose, intend, plan, expect, aim, aspire, determine, hope, drive, tackle, pursue, undertake, set about, talk of, dream of, have in mind, have a mind to, have in view, contemplate, take in hand, venture upon.
3. Present to the mind or attention, state, propound, affirm, set forth, voice, submit, broach, assert, pose, put, enunciate, advance, put or set forth, maintain, contend, bring to one's attention, open, suggest, throw out, aver, allege, say, declare, posit, predicate, postulate, bring forward.
4. Make a proposal (esp. of marriage), make one's suit, ask for one's hand, make an offer, plight one's troth, affiance, pop the question (coll.).

PROPOSITION, n. 1. Act of proposing, offer, plan, scheme, proposal, suggestion, bid, thesis, condition, presentation, motion, tender, recommendation, plan, measure, theorem, postulate, request, arrangement, invitation, resolution, project, idea, premise, undertaking.
2. Offer of terms for a transaction (as in business), negotiation, bargain, engagement, compact, agreement, barter, contract, assurance, stipulation, guarantee, dicker (coll.).
3. Anything stated or affirmed for discussion or illustration, subject of argument or discourse (Rhet.), conviction, position, thesis, axiom, postulate, predication, theorem, tenet, assertion, doctrine, topic, proposal, maxim, hypothesis, argument, concept, conception, thought, reflection, observation, supposition, issue, premise, point, idea, surmise, opinion, view, belief, question, principle, problem, dictum, declaration, statement.

PROPOUND, v. Put forward for consideration, acceptance or adoption, offer, proffer, advocate, introduce, make a motion, submit, put, pose, present, recommend, move, tender, overture, moot, maintain, project, contend, advance, put forth, bring forward, state, affirm, voice, enunciate, open, throw out, aver, declare, posit, predicate, postulate.

PROPRIETARY, adj. 1. Being a proprietor or proprietors, landed, holding property, praedial, propertied, established, manorial.
2. Pertaining to property or ownership, property, praedial, freehold (Law), hereditary, real (Law), entailed, personal, undisputed, exclusive, restrictive.

PROPRIETOR, n. Owner, manager (of a business, etc.), possessor, lord, one with exclusive right or title, master, mistress, proprietress, host, hostess, landlord, landlady, keeper, householder, landowner, innkeeper, hotelkeeper, impropriator, restaurateur.

PROPRIETY, n. 1. Sense of what is proper or fitting, observation of the proprieties, decorum, decency, good behavior, modesty, proper formality, decorousness, delicacy, taste, grace, good manners, good breeding, gentlemanly or ladylike conduct, prudery, polish, conformity, sophistication, refinement, morality, discrimination, *savoir-faire (Fr.)*.

2. Appropriateness to the purpose *or* circumstances, suitability, suitableness, fitness, rightness, seemliness, correctness, accuracy, adaptation, reasonableness, expediency, felicity, pertinence, advisability, conventionality, relevance, aptitude, applicability, admissibility, conformity, commensurability, consonance, becomingness, aptness, justness.

3. *(Plural with* THE*)* Standards, code, rules, conventionally correct, behavior, duties, formalities, customs, manners, the thing, decorum, ethics, morality, morals, principles, punctilio, etiquette, dictates of society, prevailing form, usual practice, good form, form, *bienséance (Fr.)*.

PROPULSION, *n.* Act of propelling *or* driving forward, state of being propelled, propulsive force, impulse, push, thrust, projection, drive, impetus, impulsion, propulsity, momentum, putting, dash, propelment, pulsion, advancement, prompting, motivation, throw, shove, discharge, instigation.

PRORATE, *v.* Distribute proportionately, make an arrangement on a basis of proportional distribution, apportion, portion, parcel out, allocate, appropriate, deal, allot, partition, divide, share, dole, mete out, split up, carve.

PROSAIC, *adj.* 1. Having the character *or* spirit of prose *(as opposed to poetry)*, prosy, unpoetical, unpoetic, prose, rhymeless, unrhymed.

2. Commonplace, unimaginative, matter-of-fact, dull, flat, uninteresting, unentertaining, tiresome, tedious, vapid, tame, humdrum, pedestrian, spiritless, jejune, dry, usual, trite, stale, hackneyed, mediocre, common, everyday, stock, platitudinous, homely, sober, unvaried, ordinary.

PROSAISM, *n.* 1. Prosaic character, prosaicism, dullness, flatness, heaviness, monotony, triteness, jejunity, jejuneness, commonplaceness, wearisomeness, tediousness, tedium, insipidity, platitudinousness, banality, sameness.

2. Prosaic expression, commonplace, prosaicism, old maxim, axiom, platitude, truism, banality, triviality, twaddle, trite *or* uninteresting saying, trite remark, stale saying, cliché, hackneyed expression, *fadaise (Fr.)*, common sentiment, familiar tune.

PROSCRIBE, *v.* 1. Denounce as dangerous, condemn, prohibit, censure, execrate, circumscribe, enjoin, repudiate, disallow, convict, deny, veto, damn, discriminate against, curse, reject utterly, eliminate, exclude, disapprove.

2. Put out of the protection of the law, banish, exile, outlaw, interdict, exclude, forbid, restrict, doom, excommunicate, expatriate, ostracize, expel, ban, bar, debar, taboo, sentence, boycott, blackball, transport, deport, relegate.

PROSCRIPTION, *n.* Act of proscribing, state of being proscribed, interdiction, denunciation, censure, outlawry, exile, banishment, ban, expulsion, ostracism, relegation, curse, condemnation, excommunication, exilement, deportation, transportation, conviction, veto, eviction, forbiddance, disallowance, attainder, sentence, elimination, expatriation, expelling, exclusion, prohibition, injunction, embargo, interdiction, malediction, execration, commination, anathema.

PROSECUTE, *v.* 1. *(Law)* Institute legal proceedings against, seek to enforce *or* obtain by legal

process, indict, arraign, transact, implead, sue, bring before a court, prefer charges, accuse, charge, go to law, seek in law, take to court, prefer *or* file a claim, bring action against, impeach, put on trial, bring to trial, bring to justice, go into litigation, bring suit, litigate.

2. Go on with *(something undertaken or begun)*, follow out *or* up, persevere, continue, pursue, sustain, maintain, endure, prolong, perpetuate, protract, conclude, extend, be resolute in, complete, see it through, stick to, accomplish, effect, effectuate, work out, achieve, bring about, bring to pass, dispose of, make short work of, finish, put into effect *or* practice, attain, enact, execute, consummate, compass, keep at *or* on, perform, persist, push, realize, make good, mature, perfect, elaborate, culminate.

3. Carry on, practice, conduct, exercise, occupy oneself with, busy oneself about, perform, execute, pursue, transact, discharge, direct, pilot, steer, effect, devote oneself to, engage in, labor at, work at, deal with, handle, ply, undertake, be employed in, advance, forward, administer, proceed with, manage.

PROSECUTOR, *n. (Law)* One who institutes and carries on legal proceedings in a court of justice, accuser, plaintiff, prosecuting attorney, suitor, petitioner, public prosecutor, accusant, complainant, claimant, delator, libelant.

PROSELYTE, *n.* One who has come over *or* changed from one opinion (religious sect, *etc.*) to another, convert, neophyte, disciple, catechumen, accepter, receiver.

PROSELYTE, *v.* Make a proselyte of, convert, make proselytes, proselytize, reclaim, redeem, regenerate, persuade, win over, bring round, wean.

PROSODY, *n.* Science *or* study of poetic meters and versification, system of metrics and versification, poetry, poetization, numbers, metrical rules.

PROSPECT, *n.* 1. Outlook for the future, expectation, anticipation, probability, likelihood, promise, foresight, hope, trust, reliance, speculation, certainty, chance, trust, confidence, faith, assurance, reasonable *or* fair chance, well-grounded hope.

2. View presented to the eye, outlook, scene, scenery, field, landscape, show, display, survey, aspect, perspective, vista, vision, spectacle, picture, ken, exhibition, pageant, setting, exhibit, scope, range, exposure, eyeshot, eyereach, panorama.

3. A mental looking forward, a mental view *or* survey *(as of a subject or situation)*, perspective, forecast, foreglance, forethought, presurmise, predeliberation, foresight, expectancy, anticipation, contemplation, expectation, calculation, resolution, determination, decision, mind, ambition, purpose, presumption, assumption, intention, proposal, design, plan, prospicience, prevision.

PROSPECT, *v.* Work *(a mine, claim, etc.)* experimentally, explore, search, survey, examine, sample, try, scan, inspect, investigate, study, scrutinize, probe, test, analyze, indagate.

PROSPECTIVE, *adj.* Future, expected, in prospect *or* expectation, looked for, hoped for, in view, coming, approaching, impending, foreseen, objective, future, near, ulterior, at hand, in store, in the wind, to come, on the horizon, close at hand, about to be, instant, destined, to be, immediate, subsequent, forthcoming, eventual, hereafter, imminent, threatening, looming, brewing, preparing, intended.

PROSPECTUS, *n.* Printed statement regarding a forthcoming literary work, project, *etc.*, plan, syllabus, outline, design, sketch, advertisement, synopsis, digest, brief, layout, diagram, compendium, agenda, schedule, flier, draft, handbill, announcement, notice, program, scheme, description, bulletin, catalogue.

PROSPER, *v.* 1. Be prosperous *or* successful, thrive, flourish, rise, gain, fare well, run smoothly, succeed, get on *or* ahead, advance, boom, make headway, look up, triumph, make one's fortune, make good, grow rich, live in clover, come off well, live on the fat of the land, sail before the wind, flower, bask, increase, batten, feather one's nest, bear fruit, progress, live on velvet *(sl.)*, live a life of ease *or* luxury.

2. Make prosperous *or* successful, befriend, aid, help, forward, abet, favor, support, nurture, endorse, speed, promote, advance, further, sustain, cherish, nourish, foster.

PROSPERITY, *n.* Flourishing *or* thriving condition, success, good fortune, felicity, welfare, run of luck, time of ease, profit, advance, gain, good luck, happiness, palmy days, affluence, heyday, boom, smiles of fortune, halcyon days, progress, advance, ease, high tide, flood, clover, blessings, prosperousness, bed of roses, well-being, advantage, wealth, fair wind, opulence, golden age *or* time, milk and honey, life of ease, fleshpots of Egypt, favorable conditions, fat of the land, long *or* full purse, advancement, plenty, abundance, well-lined purse, velvet *(sl.)*.

PROSPEROUS, *adj.* 1. Having *or* characterized by continued good fortune, thriving, successful, flourishing, well-off, well-to-do, rich, palmy, golden, in easy circumstances, opulent, lucky, fortunate, happy, blooming, victorious, triumphant, in full swing, in good case, booming, in a fair way, ascendant, undefeated, unbeaten, in comfortable circumstances, comfortable, swimming, at one's ease, moneyed, flush, fat, abounding in riches, on a bed of roses, in full *or* high feather, born under a lucky star, born with a silver spoon in one's mouth, on velvet *(sl.)*.

2. Propitious, favorable, halcyon, bright, providential, promising, rosy, fortunate, golden, sunny, good, auspicious, seasonable, of good omen, smiling, fair, roseate, well-disposed, timely, lucky, happy, opportune, heartening, cheering, pleasing, reassuring, salubrious, salutary, conducive, expedient.

PROSTITUTE, *n.* 1. Harlot, whore, streetwalker, strumpet, lewd woman, bawd, jade, trull, wanton, drab, procuress, doxy, lewd, reprobate, Cyprian, demirep *(sl.)*, trollop, loose woman, grisette, harridan, adventuress, bitch *(vulgar)*, Paphian, temptress, woman of easy virtue *or* morals, tart *(sl.)*, fornicatress, adulteress, hussy, pander, quean, slut, fallen woman, daughter of joy, courtesan, cocotte, stew, bat *(sl.)*, woman of the profession *(euphemistic)*, Lais, madam *(coll.)*, conciliatrix *(Fr.)*, Mrs. Warren, Delilah, harlotry, unfortunate woman, white slave, woman of the town, erring sister, baggage, frail sister, Sadie Thompson, Jezebel, abandoned woman, chippy *(sl.)*, pickup, demimondaine, broad *(sl.)*, scarlet woman, meretrix, cat *(sl.)*, Messalina, painted woman, hetaera *(Gk. Antiq.)*, Thaïs.

2. Base hireling, hack, mercenary, tool, venal henchman, flunky, instrument, myrmidon, corrupt person, Judas, turncoat, traitor, deceiver, rogue, knave, rascal, villain, reprobate, black sheep, recreant, wretch, caitiff *(Poet.)*, rotter *(sl.)*.

PROSTITUTE, *v.* Put to any base *or* unworthy use, misuse, abuse, mar, spoil, corrupt, deprave, pervert, profane, debase, misapply, impair, defile, debauch, misemploy, desecrate, ill-use, misdirect, contaminate, misappropriate, waste, pollute.

PROSTITUTION, *n.* 1. Act *or* practice of prostituting, harlotry, whoredom, bordel, whoremastery, fornication, adultery, illicit relations, meretricious traffic, streetwalking, Mrs. Warren's profession, whoremongering, free love, cuckoldom, criminal conversation *(Law)*, cuckoldry.

2. Devotion to any base *or* unworthy use, misuse, abuse, contamination, misapplication, profanation, desecration, perversion, misemployment, corruption, pollution, misappropriation, debauchery, defilement, vitiation, degradation, ill-usage, ill-use, misdirection.

PROSTRATE, *adj.* 1. Lying flat *or* full length, prone, recumbent, supine, recubate, resupine, flat, stretched, prostrated, laid out, accumbent, decumbent, horizontal, couchant, reclining, jacent, crouching, procumbent.

2. Overthrown, overcome, prostrated, physically weak *or* exhausted, helpless, defenseless, impotent, downthrown, paralyzed, worn out, abject, down, downtrodden, cast down, with one's hands tied, despondent, despairing, played out, shattered, abased, out of the fight, on one's last legs, *hors de combat (Fr.)*, crippled, disabled, incapacitated, crushed, exhausted, spent, powerless, oppressed, downcast, overpowered, collapsed, upset, fallen, laid up, on one's back, on one's beam ends, finished, worn out, at the end of one's resources.

3. Humble, submissive, bowed low *(as in adoration or worship)*, worshiping, groveling, cringing, servile, fawning, obsequious, obedient, toadying, supplicant, supplicating, unresisting, passive, resigned, yielding, sycophantic, subservient, worshipful, adorant, devout, devotional, at the feet of, lowly, meek, abased, on one's knees, knuckling, on bended knee, crouching, adulatory, prone before, in the dust before.

PROSTRATE, *v.* 1. Cast *(oneself)* down in humility *or* adoration, bow down, yield, be servile, make obeisance, submit, resign oneself, bend, bow and scrape, truckle, cringe, kowtow, demean oneself, debase oneself, throw oneself at the feet of, fall at one's feet, fall on one's knees, kneel, crouch, knuckle, idolatrize, lick the dust, obey, be subject, fawn, toady, cower, stoop, kiss the hem of one's garment.

2. Overthrow, drop, throw down level with the ground, lay flat, cast down, raze, floor, bring down, supinate, fell, overturn, destroy, ruin, demolish, cut down, hew down, cast down, level, flatten, knock down, mow down, render horizontal, upset, overset, tumble, capsize, tip over, upend, precipitate, whack down.

3. Reduce to helplessness, overthrow, overcome, reduce to physical weakness *or* exhaustion, disable, destroy, demolish, tire, weary, jade, depress, bring low, overpower, overwhelm, defeat, vanquish, confound, crush, put down, bear down, ravage, suppress, subjugate, rout, beat, discomfit, master, worst, conquer, ruin, subvert, annihilate, exterminate, do away with, invalidate, render impotent, confute, obviate, quash, nullify, smash, shatter, disrupt, wreck, extirpate, abolish, quell, subdue, get the upper hand of, break, overmaster, whip, surmount, be victorious over, thrash, exhaust.

PROSTRATION, *n.* 1. State of being prostrated, overthrow, demolition, destruction, submission, ruin, loss of power, wreck, overturn, wrack, bow, reverence, lowliness, fall, defeat, downfall, desolation, discomfiture, undoing, subversion, inversion, collapse, beating, drubbing, ravage, waste, cataclysm, extinction, breakdown, upset, overset, crack-up, vanquishment, ruination, reduction, dissolution, disorganization, rout, obeisance, genuflection, kneeling, subjection, abasement.

2. Extreme physical weakness, exhaustion, enervation, consumption, emaciation, weariness, collapse, lassitude, feebleness, breakdown, helplessness, sickness, illness, impotence, debility, stupor, coma, swoon, faint, decay, decrepitude, paralysis, suffering, extreme pain, fall.

3. Extreme mental depression, dejection, distress, woe, wretchedness, sorrow, anguish, desolation, nervous debility *or* exhaustion, neurasthenia, ordeal, the iron entering the soul, mental suffering *or* pain, grief, despair, passion, pang, ache, desperation, despondency, misery, depth of misery, extremity, heartache, agony.

PROSY, *adj.* 1. Of the nature of *or* resembling prose, prosaic, unpoetical, unpoetic, prosaical, rhymeless, unrhymed, prose.

2. Prosaic, commonplace, dull, flat, unimaginative, matter-of-fact, uninteresting, unentertaining, tedious, tiresome, prolix, spiritless, humdrum, vapid, wearisome, insipid, tame, dry, jejune, pedestrian, usual, trite, stale, hackneyed, mediocre, common, everyday, stock, platitudinous, homely, unvaried, ordinary, monotonous.

PROTAGONIST, *n.* 1. Leading character in a play, principle character, lead, principal, leading man, hero, male actor.

2. Leading character *or* figure, personage, leader, spokesman, agent, prime mover, principal, exponent, champion, prolocutor, mouthpiece, helmsman, pilot, defender, advocate, director, steersman.

PROTEAN, *adj.* Readily assuming different forms *or* characters, variable, changeable, proteiform, multiform, mutable, changeful, polymorphic, polymorphous, versatile, permutable, ever-changing, alterable, omniform, multiphase, metamorphic, metamorphotic, kaleidoscopic.

PROTECT, *v.* Defend *(from attack, invasion, annoyance, insult, etc.)*, guard, cover, shield from injury *or* danger, watch over, keep, safeguard, flank, ensconce, shadow, attend, fortify, shelter, preserve, save, harbor, secure, house, screen, look after, tend, hedge round, bulwark, cherish, hide, foster, champion, patronize, nurse, conserve, overshadow, befriend, arm, garrison, lodge, cushion, shroud, armor, escort, chaperon, care for, take care of, conduct, convey, sustain, maintain.

PROTECTION, *n.* 1. Act of protecting, preservation from injury *or* harm, aid, support, safeguard, preserval, safekeeping, care, defense, saving, guidance, patronage, championship, ministry, custody, tutelage, ministration, keep, charge, ward, guardianship, escort, convoy, auspices, assistance, oversight, supervision, superintendence, surveillance.

2. State of being protected, safety, custody, care, security, freedom from danger, intrenchment, immunity, safekeeping, defense, preservation.

3. Something that protects, safeguard, sanctuary, asylum, shade, cover, rock, screen, anchor, fence, retreat, wall, bulwark, buckler, shield,

aegis, palladium, hedge, amulet, charm, fender, cage, fortification, armor, safety zone, shadow, coverture, shelter, safety device, hiding place, haven, buffer, weapon, preserver, preservative, sanctum, convoy, bodyguard, strong arm, good hands.

4. Writing which secures from molestation, treaty, pass, passport, safe-conduct, permit for safe passage, warrant of security, safeguard.

PROTECTIVE, *adj.* Having the quality of protecting, tending to protect, designed to protect, shielding, sheltering, defensive, guarding, guardian, preservative, protectory, remedial, fatherly, motherly, preventive, prophylactic, tutelary, tutelar, conservative, conservatory, armed, fortifying, ironclad, armored, jealous, smothering, solicitous, heedful, vigilant, watchful, defensive, ministering.

PROTECTOR, *n.* One who *or* that which protects, guardian, defender, champion, shepherd, watchman, warden, custodian, safeguard, caretaker, curator, bodyguard, advocate, vindicator, sentinel, patrol, watch, benefactor, sentry, lookout, paladin, familiar spirit, chaperon, conservator, patron, warder, preserver, defense, protection, keeper, shelter, shield, buckler, pastor, ruler, savior, guardian angel, attendant spirit, promachos *(Gk. Antiq.)*.

PROTECTORATE, *n.* 1. Relation of a strong state toward a weaker which it protects, authority, hegemony, protection, guardianship, superintendence, government, rule, sway, defense, regulation, empire, guidance, government, governance, sovereignty, suzerainty, jurisdiction, administration, control, reign.

2. State *or* territory under protectorship, colony, toparchy, province, possession, dependency, dominion.

PROTEGE, *n.* One who is under the protection *or* friendly patronage of another, client, dependent, ward, pupil, student, charge.

PROTEST, *n.* Formal expression of disapproval, objection, complaint, dispute, scruple, exception, rejection, challenge, demur, protestation, remonstrance, expostulation, kick *(sl.)*, disagreement, dissentience, dissidence, deprecation, dissuasion, recusancy, opposition, difference of opinion, dissent, boggle, negation, denial, contradiction, agreement, renunciation, disclamation, disclaimer, dehortation, disapprobation, discountenance, non-agreement, renunciation, disclamation, disclaimer.

PROTEST, *v.* 1. Give formal expression to objection *or* disapproval, remonstrate, expostulate, demur, object, refuse, counteract, reprehend, dehort, scruple, boggle, dissent, differ in opinion, challenge, disagree, disapprove, contravene, controvert, negate, deny, contradict, beg to differ, carp, cavil, stick at, censure, denounce, inveigh, veto, gainsay, obtest, exclaim against, oppose, take exception, rail at, vote against, disaffirm, belie, traverse, scold at, cry out against, deprecate, disavow, disclaim, negative, discountenance, impugn.

2. Make solemn declaration, declare formally, assert, testify, predicate, pronounce, announce, annunciate, enounce, enunciate, state, allege, assure, insist, aver, asseverate, affirm, profess, attest, offer, contend, promise, broach, propound, maintain, hold out, put forward, put *or* set forth, speak.

PROTESTATION, *n.* 1. Act of protesting *or* affirming, solemn declaration, pronouncement, affirmation, asseveration, avowal, assurance, profession, position, protest, saying, dictum, confirmation, announcement, annunciation, enunciation, predication, affirmance, statement, attestation, assertion, averment, utterance, notification, notice, proclamation, allegation, *ipse dixit (Lat.).*

2. Formal expression of objection *or* disapproval, protest, objection, remonstrance, declaration of dissent, complaint, scruple, exception, rejection, challenge, demur, expostulation, deprecation, dissuasion, opposition, difference of opinion, dissent, boggle, negation, denial, contradiction, recantation, retraction, disavowal, dehortation, disapprobation, discountenance, renunciation, disclamation, disclaimer.

PROTOCOL, *n.* 1. Agreement *(between states or nations),* contract, minute, draft, record, treaty, charter, compact, concordat.

2. Customs and regulations governing court *or* diplomatic etiquette, conventions, conventional usage *or* practice, prevailing form, proprieties, dictates of society, decorum, formality, punctilio, observance, *bienséance (Fr.),* code of behavior, manners, customs, good form, standards.

PROTOTYPE, *n.* Original after which anything is formed, model, pattern, paradigm, ideal, example, exemplar, type, precedent, archetype, mirror, criterion, norm, plan, mold, historic warrant, sample, primary form *or* type, first copy, standard, rule, measure, ancestor, module, beau idéal, source, protoplast, first, foreshadowing.

PROTRACT, *v.* Prolong, extend the duration of, lengthen in time, continue, stretch out, elongate, maintain, sustain, perpetuate ,keep going, pad, fill out, perorate, repeat, tell in detail, enlarge, expand, amplify, draw out, prorogue, drag out, eke out, delay, keep on foot, preserve, perendinate, spin out, iterate, ramble, maunder, shelve, table, pigeonhole, be circumlocutory, dwell on *or* upon, keep up, keep alive, tautologize, battologize.

PROTRUDE, *v.* Project, thrust forward, jut, bulge, extend, shoot out, be convex, hang out, swell, belly, peep out, stick out, round out, arch over, concamerate, protuberate, overhang, hang over, beetle, push forth, stand out, nodulate, dilate, bouge, bilge, pout, impend.

PROTUBERANCE, *n.* Protuberant part, projection, prominence, knob, hump, bump, elevation, bunch, knot, nub, convexity, bulge, process, roundness, lump, ridge, wale, pimple, dilation, fungosity, bow, excurvature, camber, salient, protuberosity, tuberosity, node, nodule, dilatation, tubercle, growth, gnarl, rising, bouge, caruncle *(Biol.),* intumescence, swelling, excrescence, protuberancy, whelk, weal, head, hunch, bilge, bud, boss *(Biol.).*

PROTUBERANT, *adj.* Bulging out beyond the surrounding surface, swelling, gibbous, excurvate, protruding, rounded, warped, bulbous, swelled, prominent, projecting, gnarly, bold, salient, protrusive, excurved, bowed, bellied, arched, humpy, hummocky, bulgy, convex, knotty, bulging, lumpy, tumid, noded, nodular, noduled, tuberous, tumorous, lenticular, excrescential, odontoid, caruncular, raised, in relief, goggle, bossy.

PROUD, *adj.* 1. *(Often fol. by OF, an infinitive, or a clause)* Feeling pleasure *or* satisfaction over something, pleased, delighted, satisfied, honored, contented, gratified, happy, repaid, rewarded, well satisfied, well pleased, compensated.

2. Having *or* cherishing an inordinately high opinion of oneself, haughty, lordly, boastful, assuming, insolent, egotistical, uppish *(coll.),* orgulous *(humorous),* arrogant, disdainful, supercilious, big, stiff, swelled-headed, contemptuous, aloof, hoity-toity, overbearing, fatuous, pompous, puffed up, high and mighty, consequential, conceited, condescending, bloated, distended with self-esteem, self-sufficient, high-hat *(sl.),* overweening, imperious, swollen, affected, patronizing, high-headed *(sl.),* stiff-necked, vain, snotty *(sl.),* sniffy *(coll.),* toplofty *(coll.),* uppity *(coll.),* snooty *(coll.),* stuck-up *(coll.),* self-important, vainglorious, prideful, peacockish, chesty *(sl.),* wise in one's own conceits, self-glorious, inflated, gasconading, fanfaronading, braggart, bragging, flaunting, thrasonical, self-complacent, self-applauding, self-lauding, self-flattering, self-praising, intolerant, cocky *(coll.),* self-opinionated, know-it-all.

3. Highly honorable *or* creditable, stately, majestic, noble, exalted, of lofty dignity *or* distinction, magnificent, distinguished, laudable, important, illustrious, sublime, glorious, excellent, stately, worthy, high, reputable, elevated, righteous, upright, square, significant, trustworthy, equitable, high-minded, praiseworthy, admirable, principled, great, estimable, aboveboard, faithful, open, good, sound, white *(coll.),* sans peur et sans *reproche (Fr.).*

PROVE, *v.* 1. Establish the truth *or* genuineness of, demonstrate, confirm, evince, substantiate, affirm, bear out, support, attest, uphold, back up, corroborate, certify, testify, verify, justify, sustain, make good, ascertain, document, validate, show clearly, manifest, evidence, probate *(Law.),* authenticate, witness.

2. Put to the test, try, test, analyze, check, examine, assay, experiment upon, submit to the test *or* proof, make trial of, give a test run, give demonstration of by action, give a tryout *(coll.),* show, tempt, probe, put in operation, subject to trial, assay, probate *(Law.),* look into.

3. Turn out, be found *(by trial or experience)* to be, come about, eventuate, come off, happen, occur, fall, befall, chance, ensue, issue, result, betide, bechance, come to pass, supervene, fall out.

PROVENANCE, *n.* Place of orgin *(as of a work of art, etc.),* source, birthplace, native land, home, provenience, fountain, fountainhead, spring, root, cradle, nest, nursery, derivation.

PROVENDER, *n.* Dry food for beasts, fodder, forage, feed, grain, pasturage, provisions, grass, ensilage, hay, straw, meal, barley, oats, corn.

PROVERB, *n.* 1. Short popular saying embodying a familiar truth *or* useful thought, wise saying, maxim, precept, adage, dictum, saw, apothegm, general *or* universal truth, gnome, byword, mot, truism, moral, axiom, motto, accepted truth, aphorism, epigram.

2. Person *or* thing that has become proverbial, familiar *or* famous figure, byword, legend, myth, hero, fiction, example, type, tradition, idealization *(of a quality, etc.).*

PROVERBIAL, *adj.* 1. Having been made the subject of a proverb, having become an object of common mention *or* reference, legendary, idealized, heroic, familiar, notorious, traditional, common, current, acknowledged, oft-repeated, well-known, general, circulating, noted, recognized, universal, prevalent, received, popular, axiomatic, unquestioned, expressed in a proverb *or* proverbs, representative.

2. Of the nature of *or* resembling a proverb, pithy, succinct, aphoristic, terse, epigrammatic, piquant, gnomic, sententious.

PROVIDE, *v.* 1. Supply, furnish, yield, afford, produce, confer, grant, offer, give, present, donate, bestow, allow, contribute, pay, accord, award, put *or* place at one's disposal, tender, submit, deliver, impart, render, dispense, dispose of, vouchsafe.

2. Prepare, get ready, ensure *or* procure beforehand, make ready, make provision, arrange, lay in, lay up, anticipate needs, take measures, plan, store, get, acquire, stock, furnish supplies, replenish, stow away, put *or* lay away, recruit, pave the way, provision, collect for use, gather, supply, amass, fund, cache, stash *(sl.)*, reserve, accumulate, garner up, treasure up, save up, hoard up, put up, salt down *or* away *(coll.)*, smooth the path *or* road, ready, outfit, gear, appoint, munition, man, arm.

3. Make arrangements for supplying *(means of support, money, etc; fol. by* FOR*)*, support, equip, nourish, provision, feed, accommodate, fit out, victual, care for, look after, accouter, pension, keep, serve, purvey to *or* for, cater to, supply the wants of, provender, make provision for, shower down upon, lavish, secure, uphold, conserve, sustain, preserve, maintain.

PROVIDED, *conj.* It being stipulated *or* understood *(that)*, on the condition *or* supposition *(that)*, if, on condition, granted, on these terms, in case, in the event, if it be so, conditionally, provisionally, with this proviso, assuming that, by stipulation, supposing, with the understanding, subject to, if it so happen *or* turn out, in such a case (contingency, event), according as, admitting, allowing.

PROVIDENCE, *n.* 1. Foreseeing care and guardianship of God over His creatures, manifestation of divine care *or* direction, divine government, divine aid *or* assistance, the hand of God, fortune, fate, kismet, destiny, lot, heaven, ministry, guardian angel, divine intervention.

2. Provident *or* prudent management of resources, economy, frugality, thriftiness, prevention of waste, saving, care, preparation, husbandry, parsimony, reduction of expenses, retrenchment, anticipation, forethought, precaution, foresight, prudence.

PROVIDENT, *adj.* 1. Having *or* showing foresight, careful *(in providing for the future)*, prudent, cautious, prepared, ready, foreseeing, farseeing, politic, wary, forehanded, discreet, precautious, judicious, anticipating, prescient, discerning, equipped, in practice, foresighted, far-sighted, thoughtful, with one's lamps trimmed, precautionary.

2. Frugal, economical, careful, thrifty, sparing, saving, managing, chary, parsimonious, prudent.

PROVIDENTIAL, *adj.* Of, pertaining to *or* proceeding from divine providence, fortunate, lucky, opportune, propitious, advantageous, favorable, appropriate, fitting, suitable, timely, seasonable, auspicious, sunny, smiling, promising, bright, hopeful, prosperous, happy, cheering, heartening, reassuring, golden, salubrious, salutary, in the nick of time, felicitous, kind, kindly.

PROVINCE, *n.* 1. Territory, region, country, administrative division *or* unit of a country, area, zone, section, field, land, tract, quarter, part, pre-

cinct, county, parish, settlement, borough, township, kingdom, state, city, town, village, colony, dependency, dominion, realm, domain.

2. Branch of learning *or* activity, jurisdiction, department, division, subdivision, office, branch, discipline, school, plant, authority, mission, commission, post, assignment, field, specialty, category, appointment, study, persuasion, doctrine, denomination, cause, art, science, teaching.

3. Field of action of a person, *etc.*, business, office, employment, charge, sphere, circle, compass, walk, status, function, capacity, part, post, calling, duty, domain, order, estate, range, course, career, life, path, role, line, service, occupation, trade, place, billet, situation, station, berth, incumbency, job, assigned task, round, orbit, circuit, orb, scope, realm, latitude, ambit, span.

PROVINCIAL, *adj.* 1. Belonging *or* peculiar to some particular province, regional, of a province, colonial, sectional, topical, territorial, divisional, topographic, topographical, local, independent, home.

2. Having *or* showing the manners characteristic of inhabitants of a province, rustic, countrified, inurbane, rude, unrefined, unpolished, bucolic, rural, upcountry, uncourtly, clownish, oafish, gauche, ill-mannered, awkward, yokelish, unsophisticated, small town, country, backwood *or* backwoods, boorish, loutish, clodhopping, cloddish, churlish, hayseed, hinterland, hick *(sl.)*, hobnailed, rough, ungraceful, gawky.

3. Narrow, illiberal, bigoted, parochial, insular, hidebound, creed-bound, rigid, inflexible, dogmatic, fanatical, purblind, deaf to advice *or* reason, intolerant, unbroadened, untraveled, ingrown, set in one's own ways, closed-minded, uncompromising, opinionated, near-sighted, stiff-necked, confined, small, little, puritanical, prudish, unreasonable, narrow-minded, strait-laced, impervious to reason, unpersuadable, prepossessed, prejudiced, partial, one-sided, positive, *ex parte (Lat.)*.

PROVINCIALISM, *n.* 1. Provincial character *or* peculiarity, characteristic of a province *or* the provinces, localism, trait, idiosyncrasy, idiom, provinciality, dialect, patois, regionalism, distinctive feature, earmark, giveaway *(coll.)*.

2. Devotion to one's own province *(before the large unit)*, localism, bias, warp, partiality, narrowness, narrow-mindedness, blind spot, bigotry, one-sidedness, patriolatry, patriotism, jingoism, prejudice, illiberality, intolerance, cliquishness, chauvinism, parochialism.

PROVISION, *n.* 1. Proviso, stipulation, clause *(in legal instrument, law, etc.)*, condition, qualification, limitation, restriction, requisite, exemption, exception, modification, obligation, term, prerequisite, previous arrangement, reservation, circumstance, article of agreement.

2. Supplying *(as of necessaries or food)*, furnishing, providing, accommodation, endowment, purveyance, charity, donation, maintenance, nourishment, nurture, sustentation, armament, accouterment, ministry, ministration, construction, benevolence, upkeep, keep, arrayal, reinforcement, replenishment.

3. Preparation, something provided, means *(for meeting a need)*, arrangement beforehand, provident care, readiness, anticipation, forethought, forehandedness, agency, provident measures *or* steps, equipment, precaution, prior measure, aid, wherewithal, resources, resourcefulness, expedient, shift, prearrangement, establishment, adjustment,

adaptation, far-sightedness, long-sightedness, organization, calculation, deliberation, providence, intervention, accommodation, invention, concoction, composition.

4. Stock (of something provided), store, supply, hoard, wealth, mass, staples, garner, harvest, supplies, cumulation, fund, resources, equipment, pile, stockpile, means, repository, budget, goods, abundance, cache, effects, subsistence, gleaning, reserve, livelihood, savings, sustenance, capital, collection, amassment, nest egg, sustentation, fittings, equipage, apparatus, furniture, paraphernalia, plant, upholstery, armament, reservoir, mine, munitions, accouterments, trappings, appointments, impedimenta.

5. (Plural) Supplies of food, stores, victuals, provender, viands, board, table, fare, eatables, commons, feed, edibles, forage, fodder, ration, sustenance, diet, comestibles, staff of life, daily bread, groceries, bread (fig.), meat (fig.).

PROVISIONAL, adj. Provided for the time being, temporary, passing, transient, tentative, makeshift, transitory, fleeting, substitute, alternate, pro tempore (Lat.), pro tem (Lat.), temporal, substitutive, substitutional, substitutionary, impermanent, transitional.

PROVISO, n. Clause (In a statute, contract, etc.) by which a condition is introduced, provision, condition, term, stipulation, qualification, reservation, limitation, requisite, prerequisite, exemption, exception, modification, obligation, circumstance, article of agreement.

PROVISORY, adj. 1. Temporary, provisional, provisionary, provided for the time being, passing, transient, tentative, makeshift, transitory, fleeting, substitute, alternative, pro tempore (Lat.), pro tem (Lat.), substitutive, substitutional, substitutionary, impermanent, transitional.

2. Containing a proviso or condition, conditional, subject, dependent, qualifying, contingent, circumstantial, limitative, experimental, hypothetical, pending, limiting, incidental, probative, probatory, qualificatory, stipulatory, qualified, speculative, probationary.

PROVOCATION, n. 1. Action of provoking, vexation, angering, incitement, prodding, motivation, inducement, prompting, urge, defiance, actuation, irritation, exasperation, aggravation (coll.), allurement, excitation, inspiration, agitation, stimulation, instigation, impulsion, seduction, fascination, perturbation, invitation, intoxication, galvanism, electrification, animation, excitement.

2. Something that incites, instigates, angers or irritates, affront, indignity, insult, aggression, dare, incentive, twit, spur, taunt, contumely, wound, annoyance, slap, gibe, hurt, injury, defiance, offense, abuse, disrespect, pressure, urge, rub, inspiration, fascination, passion, prick, stimulant, stimulus, whip, goad, outrage, atrocity, humiliation, embarrassment, slight, stroke, shock, blow, gall, thorn, sting, cut, grievance, red rag, last straw, sore subject, invitation, ill turn, exasperation.

PROVOCATIVE, adj. 1. Alluring, seductive, exciting, stimulating, attractive, enchanting, entrancing, ravishing, intriguing, captivating, desirable, tantalizing, inviting, tempting, persuasive, electrifying, thrilling, galvanic, inciting, irresistible.

2. Aggravating, provoking, irritating, vexing, annoying, exasperating, stinging, mortifying, cutting, galling, caustic, shocking, irksome, vexatious, bitter, grating, invidious, cruel, biting, harsh.

PROVOKE, v. 1. Exasperate, enrage, vex, anger, incense, chafe, gall, insult, irk, hector, distress, fret, move to anger, taunt, enkindle, defy, fire, madden, envenom, egg on, aggravate (coll.), irritate, nettle, annoy, sting, agitate, perturb, gibe, drive, challenge, torment, get one's goat (sl.), exacerbate, infuriate, affront, pique, offend, beset, huff, lash into a fury, wound, disquiet, mortify, roil, grate, gripe, outrage, bait, tease, heckle, bullyrag, try one's patience, badger, plague, molest, discompose, displease, put out, raise one's ire, make one's blood boil, alarm, startle, disturb, pester, persecute, harass, give offense or umbrage to, put out of humor, work into a passion.

2. Stir up, arouse, induce, give rise to, bring about, call forth, summon up, awaken, cause, promote, instigate, occasion, elicit, produce, kindle, fan, fire, evoke, spur, initiate, foster, foment, revive, feed the fire, stir the embers, blow the coals, lie at the root of, put in motion, heighten, effect, contrive, open the door to, establish, create, institute, generate, sow the seeds of, give origin or rise to, inspire, forward, prompt, propel, motivate, actuate, exacerbate.

3. Excite (a person, etc.), stimulate to action, incite, kindle, inspire, rouse, arouse, stir, tempt, fan, fire, lure, seduce, warm, shake, affect, wake up, tantalize, inflame, thrill, pierce, impel, intoxicate, animate, awaken, move, instigate, quicken, sharpen, revive, spur, lash, whip, drive, heat one's blood, foment, compel, electrify, strike, penetrate, touch to the quick, disturb, induce, work up, stir up, egg on, force, infect, impassion, push, hound, inspirit, motivate, put up to (sl.), goad.

PROVOST, n. One appointed to superintend or preside, officer, executive, president, overseer, head, superintendent, administrator, assistant director (as in American universities).

PROW, n. Fore part (of a boat or ship), nose, rostrum, bow, beak, stem, prore (Poetic).

PROWESS, n. Bravery, intrepidity, daring, martial skill, valorous achievement, valor, courageous deeds, courage, heroism, hardihood, boldness, manliness, grit, might, nerve, fearlessness, gallantry, spirit, contempt or defiance of danger, stout heart, pluck, backbone, knight-errantry, dauntlessness, fortitude, endurance, mettle, game, resoluteness, firmness, hardiness, stamina, bottom, chivalry, strength, stability, constancy, vigor, temerity, sand (sl.), perseverance, vitality, pith, doughtiness, moral fiber, doggedness, intransigency, élan (Fr.), heart of oak, guts (sl.), spunk (coll.), sinew, sturdiness, virility, lustiness, derring-do.

PROWL, v. Go about stealthily (in search of prey, plunder, etc.), rove, sneak, slink, skulk, scavenge, stray, lurk, ramble, raven, saunter, range, meander, couch, steal, roam, wander, mouse, gumshoe (sl.).

PROXIMAL, adj. Situated toward the point of origin or attachment (opposite to DISTAL), near, nearest, inner, upper, inside, inward, innermost.

PROXIMATE, adj. 1. Next, nearest, closely, adjacent, next in a chain of relation, immediate, succeeding, adjoining, vicinal, neighboring, propinquant, propinquous, subsequent, contiguous, direct, closest, at hand, neighbor, impending, imminent, close by, close at hand, sequent, consequent, consecutive, sequential, ensuing, following, successive, juxtapositional, juxtapositive, nigh, approaching, inevitable.

2. Fairly accurate, approximate, approximative, relative, comparative, reasonable, similar, parallel, resembling, not far off, solid, substantial, roughly true, nearly exact, well-grounded, of a piece, analogous, near the point, in the right direction, comparable, approaching, equivalent.

PROXIMITY, *n.* Nearness *(in place, time or relation)*, closeness, propinquity, contiguity, vicinage, vicinity, adjacency, presence, juxtaposition, contiguousness, appropinquity, apposition, adjacence, neighborhood, convergence, conflux, close quarters *or* range, concourse, confluence, meeting, approximation, kinship, association, kindred, cognation, connection, filiation, relationship, affinity, similarity, likeness, relevance, pertinence, coincidence, accord, unity, analogy, oneness, resemblance, agreement, concert, identity, commensurability, concord, parallelism, compatibility, semblance, conformation, correspondence, synonymity, equivalence, sequence, simultaneity, concurrence, conjuncture, juncture, consonance, concomitancy, coextension, coexistence.

PROXY, *n.* 1. Agency of a person deputed to act for another, business, mediation, substitute service, instrumentality, intervention, good offices, intermediation, subservience, mediatorialism, appointment, power, intercession, negotiation, intermediacy.

2. Substitute, agent, delegate, attorney, double, alternate, supplanter, succedaneum, commissioner, lieutenant, secondary, mediator, messenger, steward, deputation, surrogate, representative, deputy, fill-in, dummy, minister, instrument, procurator *(Law)*, negotiator, emissary.

3. Written authorization empowering another to act for the signer, commission, warrant, charge, power of attorney, assignment, procuration, deputation, authority, mandate *(Roman and Civil Law)*.

PRUDE, *n.* Person who affects extreme modesty, prig, affecter, mannerist, pretender, pietist, puritan, posturer, prudist, precisian, formalist.

PRUDENCE, *n.* 1. Cautious practical wisdom, discretion, good judgment, presence of mind, care, providence, sense, caution, judiciousness, policy, tact, deliberation, attention, consideration, forethought, calculation, discrimination, perspicacity, penetration, vigilance, subtlety, counsel, carefulness, circumspection, common sense, foresight, watchfulness, heed, skill, shrewdness, acumen, sagacity, solicitude, preparedness, precaution.

2. Regard for one's own interests, provident care in management, providence, economy, frugality, thrift, thriftiness, saving, careful budgeting, husbandry, parsimony, precaution, anticipation, oversight, supervision, surveillance, jurisdiction, administration, superintendence, close watch, foresight, forethought, calculation, good stewardship.

PRUDENT, *adj.* 1. Discreet, sagacious, cautious, circumspect, wise in practical affairs, prudential, sage, shrewd, wary, solicitous, sensible, guarded, prepared, heedful, careful, canny, politic, provident, foreseeing, chary, safe, forearmed, sapient, thoughtful, level-headed, considerate, vigilant, worldly-wise, far-sighted, wide-awake, well-advised, reasonable, advisable, rational, reflecting, precautious, precautionary, advertent, calculating, sober, discerning, discriminating, sound, wise as

a serpent, judicious, self-possessed, penetrating, cool.

2. Careful of one's own interests, provident, thrifty, frugal, saving, sparing, managing, chary, economical, parsimonious.

PRUDERY, *n.* Extreme modesty *or* propriety, coyness, stuffiness, priggishness, primness, prudishness, demureness, preciousness, strictness, preciseness, precision, affected reserve, stiffness, false *or* mock modesty, fastidiousness, punctiliousness, punctilio, pedantry, oversubtlety, false shame, squeamishness, delicacy, excessive nicety, overrefinement, overscrupulousness, meticulousness.

PRUDISH, *adj.* Extremely modest *or* proper, priggish, coy, over-modest, sanctimonious, smug, mincing, fastidious, puritanical, precise, affectedly nice, prim, demure, stilted, in buckram, self-righteous, starched, proper, particular, stiff, precious, squeamish, queasy, scrupulous, finical, finicking, skittish, shy, unctuous, pharisaic, pharisaical, canting, timid, punctilious, precise, strait-laced, formal, pedantic.

PRUNE, *v.* 1. Lop, cut off, crop, nip, chop, curtail, dock, clip, snub, amputate, detach, poll, dissever, sever, shear, mow, trim, thin.

2. Cut *or* lop superfluous *or* undesired twigs (branches, roots) from, rid *or* clear of anything undesirable *or* superfluous, make orderly, trim, shorten, crop, mow, top, cut down, cut short, mutilate, truncate, detruncate, obtruncate, pollard, thin out, clip, dress.

PRURIENT, *adj.* 1. Inclined to *or* characterized by lascivious thought, lewd, course, incestuous, concupiscent, impure, ruttish, bawdy, lascivious, ribald, lubricious, obscene, pornographic, Cyprian, light, loose, whorish, scarlet, dissolute, dissipated, debauched, adulterous, lurid, smutty, unclean, dirty, gross, foul, filthy, unchaste, unvirtuous, incontinent, wanton, vile, offensive, fulsome, Fescennine, indecent, immodest, lustful, beastly, bestial, swinish, animalistic, theroid, lickerish, lecherous, libidinous, licentious, suggestive, fleshly, carnal, salacious, shameless, abandoned, scurrilous, profligate, satyric, goatish, erotic, sensual, brutish.

2. Morbidly uneasy *(as desire or longing)*, itching, raging, craving, gnawing, ravening, bestial, disturbing, frenzied, rampageous, orgiastic, primitive, ravenous, devouring, agitated, unquiet, furious, mad, tumultuous, turbulent, incestuous, burning, covetous, longing, rampant.

PRY, *v.* 1. Look curiously, peer, peep, look closely *or* narrowly, inspect, look hard *or* intently at, scan, survey, watch, squint, peek, ogle, eye, gape, gaze, spy, mouse, examine, scrutinize, stare, rubber, rubberneck *(sl.)*, crane, goggle, gawk *(coll.)*, view, witness, follow with the eye, search.

2. Search *or* inquire curiously *or* inquisitively, meddle, explore, busybody, poke *or* stick one's nose in, ferret, spy, investigate, mouse, hunt out, interfere, intrude, mind others' business, tamper with, reconnoiter, question, go over, dive *or* delve into, probe, fathom, study, sound, indagate, snoop *(coll.)*, rake, scour, rummage, ransack, pursue, scout, quest, analyze, trail, follow a scent *or* clue, follow up, smell *or* sniff out, nose.

3. Open by force of leverage, force, move, raise, lift, prize, lever, hoist, pull open, work up from underneath, dig up.

4. Get *or* obtain with difficulty, wrench, extract, dig up, root up, worm out, fish for, angle

for, ferret out, smoke out, drag out, tear out, pull out, grub up *or* out, force, squeeze, dredge, uproot, excavate, wrest, wring.

PRYING, *adj.* Looking *or* searching curiously, unduly curious, inquisitive, peeping, peering, meddlesome, quizzical, scrutinizing, impertinent, prowling, meddling, agog, agape, all agog, intrusive, obtrusive, busy, busybody, officious, nosy *(coll.),* snoopy *(coll.),* rubberneck *(sl.),* forward.

PSALM, *n.* Sacred *or* solemn song, hymn, metric version *or* paraphrase of a Psalm, song of praise *or* jubilation, response, report, answer, anthem, antiphon *(Eccles.),* spiritual song, paean, exaltation, alleluia, hallelujah, hosanna, chant, triumph, carol, laud, canticle, glorification, marching song *(Ancient Hebrew Hist.).*

PSALMODY, *n.* Arrangement of psalms for singing, psalms *or* hymns collectively, art, practice *or* act of singing psalms *or* hymns, hymnody, hymnology, psalter, adaptation, psalmistry, harmonization, metrification.

PSALTER, *n.* Book containing the Psalms for liturgical *or* devotional use, the Book of Psalms, Psalm Book, the Psalms, hymnbook, Book of Common Order, the Psaltery.

PSEUDO, *adj.* False, spurious, sham, counterfeit, pretended, imitation, bogus, feigned, would-be, supposititious, make-believe, quasi, near-, fraudulent, plausible, forged, mimic, mock, phony *(sl.),* imitative, trumped up, colorable, fictitious, bastard, artificial, deceptive, simulated, fake *(coll.).*

PSEUDONYM, *n.* False name, assumed name *(to conceal identity),* professional name, pen name, stage name, anonym, allonym, sobriquet, fictitious name, nickname, alias, *nom de plume (Fr.), nom de guerre (Fr.).*

PSYCHE, *n.* Human spirit, soul, mind, self, heart, vital spirit *or* principal, personality, reason, intellect, divine soul, life force *or* energy, *anima humana (Lat.),* seat of consciousness, understanding, intelligence, divine spark, ego, subconscious, psychical *or* spiritual principal, true being, inner man, inmost *or* essential nature, *nous (Gk. Philos.),* pneuma *(Gk. Philos.).*

PSYCHIATRIST, *n.* One who is versed in *or* practices psychiatry, psychopathologist, psychopathist, psychoanalyst, psychotherapist, psychoanalyzer, psychiater *(Med.),* alienist.

PSYCHIATRY, *n.* Practice *or* science of treating mental diseases, psychotherapy, psychopathology, psychotherapeutics, psychosomatic, medicine, psychophysics, psychobiology, alienism, psychoanalysis, psychognosis.

PSYCHIC, *adj.* 1. Of *or* pertaining to the human soul *or* mind, mental, spiritual, intellectual, psychological, cognitive, cerebral, subjective, nooscopic, noological, perceptive, percipient, appercipient, sensory.

2. Pertaining to *or* proceeding from some nonphysical agency, immaterial, spiritualist, otherworldy, unearthly, disembodied, insubstantial, spiritist, psychal, supernatural, occult, preternatural, ghostly, spectral, hallucinatory, supersensible, supersensory, incorporeal, intangible, telepathic, clairsentient, telekinetic *(Psychical Research),* mediumistic, clairvoyant, clairaudient, psychomantic, extramundane, supersensual, superhuman, superphysical, hyperphysical.

PSYCHOLOGICAL, *adj.* Pertaining to the mind

or to mental phenomena, of *or* pertaining to psychology, mental, intellectual, behavioristic, spiritual, psychic, psychical, percipient, appercipient, perceptive, sensory, cognitive, cerebral, noological, emotional, irrational, subjective, personal, personality, psychometric.

PSYCHOLOGIST, *n.* One trained in psychology, psychologer, psychographer, psychologue, psychotechnician.

PSYCHOLOGY, *n.* Science of mind *or* of mental states and processes, psychonomics, psychologics, psychography, psychopathology, psychophysics, psychodynamics, psychobiology, psychometry.

PUBERTY, *n.* Sexual maturity, pubescence, adolescence, youth, young manhood *or* womanhood, teens, ripeness, virility.

PUBESCENT, *adj.* Arriving *or* arrived at puberty, adolescent, newly mature, budding, new-fledged, youthful, teen-age, virile, callow, hebetic *(Physiol.).*

PUBLIC, *adj.* 1. Of, pertaining to *or* affecting the people as a whole, national, state, civil, political, general, common, nationwide, statewide, countrywide, united, joint, popular, proletarian, plebeian, bourgeois, civic, social, societal, communal, widespread, universal, world-wide, commutual, collective, extensive, sweeping, ecumenical, comprehensive, encyclopedic, catholic.

2. Open to all the people, community, municipal, used by all, not private *or* exclusive, maintained at public expense and under public control, unrestricted, not enclosed *(as by barriers),* shared, available, accessible, unenclosed, elective, unbarred, unfenced, passable, unbounded, not circumscribed, volitional, voluntary, unconditional, without prohibition, free to all, unobstructed, that may be used *or* entered by all.

3. Open to the view *or* knowledge of all, existing, done, *etc.,* in public, published, known, outward, overt, popular, evident, general, notorious, unconcealed, unashamed, unabashed, recognized, acknowledged, received, widely-known, pat *(coll.),* well-kenned, noted, established, familiar, exposed, plain, apparent, naked, frank, undisguised, revealed, discernible, observable, in sight *or* view, aboveboard, barefaced, investigable, in broad daylight, in circulation, avowed, perspicuous, manifest, in evidence, perceivable, conspicuous, visible, patent, obvious.

PUBLIC, *n.* 1. The people constituting a state, community *or* nation, society, populace, population, community, men, commonalty, commonwealth, multitude, laymen, hoi polloi, rabble, citizenry, body politic, the many, proletariat, bourgeoisie, commonality, mob, social state, habitancy, folk, the million, rank and file.

2. Particular section of the people, group, individuals, buyers, persons, clientele, patronage *(coll.),* trade. custom, patrons *(coll.),* those interested, following, followers, attendance, purchasers,

PUBLICATION, *n.* 1. Publishing *(of a book, etc.),* printing, writing, editing, issuance, production, marketing, creation, impression, composition, formation, preparation for press, compilation, authorship, origination, manufacture, presentation to the public.

2. That which is published, literary production, printing, edition, work, article, composition, creation, opus, book, writing, offering, journal, periodical, paper, monograph, treatise, monthly, quarterly, annual, daily, weekly, sheet, number,

serial, printed matter, news items, bulletin, review, press (coll.), oeuvre (Fr.), opuscule, issue, newspaper.

3. Act of publishing, promulgation, propagation, proclamation, advertisement, circulation, diffusion, broadcasting, dissemination, divulgation, disclosure, declaration, report, announcement, issue, issuance, production, notification, evulgation, pervulgation, reportage, annunciation, pronouncement, enunciation, exposition, publicity, exposure, revelation, revealing, expression, exhibition, publishment, emblazonment, ventilation, manifestation, utterance.

PUBLICIST, n. 1. One who is expert in or writes on current public or political affairs, commentator, news analyst, journalist, columnist, editorialist, editorial writer, pressman, columner, reviewer, critic, essayist, expositor, pamphleteer, political economist, correspondent, political scientist.

2. Press agent, public relations man, advertiser, publicizer, publicity man or agent, copy writer, plugger (sl.), blurbist (coll.), ballyhooer (sl.), ad writer (coll.), adman.

PUBLICITY, n. Public notice (brought about by advertising or other means), currency, spotlight, limelight, outlet, light, build up, circulation, presentation, familiarity, report, broadcast, publication, common knowledge, flagrancy, glare of public observation, puff, airing, ballyhoo (sl.), blurb, plug (sl.), press notice, write-up (coll.), publicness, notoriety, ventilation.

PUBLICIZE, v. Give publicity to, bring to public notice, advertise, spread word of, make public, make known, placard, blurb, publish, announce, blazon, herald, report, post, promulgate, propagate, broadcast, circularize, promote, disseminate, plug (sl.), ballyhoo (sl.), throw the spotlight on, bring into the limelight, offer for sale.

PUBLIC-SPIRITED, adj. Having or showing an unselfish desire for the public good, loving mankind, charitable, beneficent, altruistic, philanthropic, humane, humanitarian, large-hearted, big-hearted, princely, liberal, high-minded, munificent, handsome, almsgiving, magnanimous, eleemosynary, civic-minded, generous, bounteous, unstinting, ungrudging.

PUBLISH, v. 1. Issue for public sale or distribution (as a book), print, compile, edit, bring out, strike off, get out, put to press, collect, write, author, put to bed (cant).

2. Announce formally, make publicly or generally known, proclaim, promulgate, declare, post, placard, circulate, trumpet, divulgate, communicate, advertise, disclose, ventilate, make public, give out, diffuse, air, tell, disseminate, spread, blaze abroad, impart, bruit, reveal, propagate, utter, noise, abroad, promote, give to the world, broadcast, herald, give publicity to, publicize, enounce.

PUBLISHER, n. One whose business is publishing, business head of a newspaper organization, journalist, printer, newspaperman, newsman, editor, bookmaker.

PUCK, n. Mischievous or malicious demon or spirit, goblin, imp, bad fairy, elf, deviling, devilkin, öuphe, pixy, sprite, bad peri, hobgoblin, Robin Goodfellow.

PUCKER, n. Wrinkle, irregular fold, gather, pleat, plication, rimple, crumple, fold, tuck, pinch, crinkle, crease, cockle, ruck, ruffle, corrugation, rumple.

PUCKER, v. Draw together, gather into wrinkles or folds, purse, shirr, pinch, compress, shrink, wither, contract, furrow, squeeze, tighten, knit, crinkle, cockle, corrugate, shrivel, wrinkle, crease.

PUCKERY, adj. 1. Puckering, puckered, wrinkly, crabbed, plicate, gathered, pinched, corrugated, corrugate, pliciferous, plicatulate, creased, shirred, rumpled, ruffled, contracted, wizened, shriveled, crumpled, wrinkled.

2. Tending to pucker, astringent, acerbic, sour, tart, contractive, acerb, bitter, acetic, acidulous, vinegary, unripe, green, acid, acetous, constringent.

PUCKISH, adj. Impish, mischievous, roguish, sportive, playful, tricksome, coltish, gamesome, rompish, tricksy, prankish, wanton, waggish, capricious, jocular, facetious, arch.

PUDDING, n. Soft food made of various ingredients usually with a thickening agent, custard, flummery, rennet custard, junket, soufflé.

PUDDLE, n. Small pool of liquid, plashet, plash, pond, pondlet, mudhole, wallow, water pocket, muddy place, slop.

PUDDLE, v. Wet with dirty water, etc., fill with puddles, make muddy or dirty, soil, spot, bespot, speck, bespeck, foul, drabble, dabble, daggle, bemire, besmear, sully, besplash, besplatter, bespatter, splatter, spatter, splash, blur, blotch, daub, besmudge, besmirch, smear, smudge.

PUDGY, adj. Short and fat or thick, plump, squat, stubby, squabby, stout, pursy, buxom, chunky, stocky, squatty, dumpy, squattish, stodgy, rotund, chubby, stubbed, thick-set, punchy (coll.), tubby (coll.), chumpy (coll.).

PUERILE, adj. 1. Of or pertaining to a child or boy, boyish, childlike, childish, youthful, juvenile, youthlike, young, girlish, tender, unfledged, new-fledged, juvenescent, immature, infantile, unripe, callow, underage, green, raw, beardless, kiddish (sl.).

2. Childishly foolish, irrational, trivial, silly, idle, weak, petty, wandering, rambling, slight, childish, ineffectual, infantile, immature, imbecile, inane, senseless, nonsensical, simple, trifling, frivolous, jejune, inept, asinine, inadequate, fruitless, lame, flimsy, unworthy of serious consideration, ridiculous, nugatory, meager, insignificant, inefficacious, dotard, unwise, unthinkable, worthless, poor, fatuous, fribbling, injudicious, meaningless, piddling, vacant, vapid, feeble, hare-brained, shallow.

PUERILITY, n. Childish foolishness or triviality, folly, nonsense, inanity, insipidity, senility, second childhood, dotage, ineptitude, fatuity, asininity, imbecility, farce, drivel, twaddle, bathos, irrationality, ludicrousness, absurdity, nugacity, sophism, futility, frivolity, silliness, weakness, illogicality, blunder, imprudence, indiscretion, infatuation, want of good sense, unreasonableness.

PUFF, n. 1. Whiff, short quick blast (as of wind or breath), breath, sudden gust, abrupt emission (of air, vapor, etc.), small cloud, whiffet, flurry, flaw.

2. Inflated or distended part, swelling, protuberance, balloon, bulb, ball, bubble, extension, rising, boil, blister, growth, protrusion, excrescence bilge, bouge, intumescence, protuberancy, tumescence, turgidity, bulla, distention, inflammation, nodule, node, tuberosity, convexity, knob, hump, bunch, bulge, elevation, lump, bow, dilation, globule, excurvation, blain (Pathol.), polyp

(*Pathol.*), bladder (*Pathol.*), vesicle (*Pathol.*), cyst (*Pathol.*).

3. Commendation (*esp. exaggerated*), inflated *or* exaggerated praise (*esp. uttered or written from interested motives*), seller's talk, publicity, blurb, puffery, flattery, euphemism, overlaudation, overcommendation, overpraise, overrating, overvaluation, much cry and little wool, much ado about nothing, panegyric, jingoism, overestimation, misrepresentation, flummery, encomium, plug (*sl.*), ballyhoo (*sl.*), bombast, bluster.

PUFF, *v.* 1. Blow with short quick blasts (*as the wind*), blow in puffs, whiff, float, freshen, breeze, emit, draw, pull, smoke, drag, flaw, squall.

2. Breathe quick and hard, pant, wheeze, be out of breath *or* wind, exhale, heave, gasp, steam.

3. (*Usually foll. by* UP) Become inflated *or* distended, blow up, swell, inflate, distend, stretch, bloat, sufflate, pump up, expand, dilate, extend, amplify, increase, belly out, enlarge.

4. Inflate with pride, *etc.*, praise extravagantly, flatter, laud, boast about, brag about, extol, exaggerate, enhance, magnify, compliment, eulogize, make much of, enlarge, overestimate, amplify, vaunt, trumpet, flourish, cry up, applaud, vapor, gasconade, acclaim, talk big, celebrate, exalt, swell, slaver, humor, fawn, adulate, soft-soap, lay it on thick (*coll.*), lay the flattering unction to one's soul, commend lavishly, butter up (*coll.*), hyperbolize.

5. Advertise with exaggerated commendation, boost, plug (*sl.*), ballyhoo (*sl.*), promote, advance, magnify, overestimate, overesteem, overrate, enhance, exaggerate the worth of, give publicity to, publicize, color, embroider, hyperbolize, press-agent (*coll.*).

PUFFERY, *n.* Act of praising unduly, exaggerated commendation, publicity, blurb, seller's talk, flattery, puff, euphemism, overlaudation, overcommendation, overpraise, overrating, overvaluation, overestimation, misrepresentation, jingoism, panegyric, flummery, encomium, bluster, bombast, ballyhoo (*sl.*), plug (*sl.*).

PUFFY, *adj.* 1. Gusty, windy, blasty, breezy, blustery, airy, squally, flawy.

2. Short-winded, out of breath, breathless, winded, windless, blown, short-breathed, panting, blowing, anhelose, anhelous, broken-winded, puffing.

3. Inflated, distended, swollen, swelled, round, fleshy, inflamed, sleek, stout, turgid, tumid, puffed out, expanded, full, fat, plump, obese, pursy, blown, bulging, bouncing, tubby (*coll.*), ample, bellied out, bowed out, bulbous, plethoric, well-fed, dropsical, edematous, punchy (*coll.*), large, buxom, chubby, rotund, corpulent, gibbous.

4. Conceited, puffed up, self-important, opinionated, egotistical, peacockish, haughty, contemptuous, proud, pompous, self-esteeming, blown, swell-headed, supercilious, disdainful, snobbish, swollen, overbearing, inflated, overproud, lofty, vain, overweening, lordly, affected, consequential, insincere, egotistic, toplofty (*coll.*), uppish (*coll.*), stilted, arrogant.

5. Bombastic, inflated, extravagant, bloated, puffed up, flatulent, tumid, turgid, pompous, boasting, bragging, gasconading, strutting, fanfaronading, showy, ostentatious, blustering, swaggering, flashy, gaudy, consequential, affected, mannered, overacted, overdone, flaunting, glittering, grandiose, dandified, foppish, coxcombical,

specious, pretentious, patronizing, garish, stagey, imperious, overweening, overbearing, magisterial, lordly, high and mighty, presumptuous, high-handed, disdainful, supercilious, cock-a-hoop, altisonant, fustian, orotund, sententious, theatrical, high-sounding, high-flown, grandiloquent, grandisonant, rhetorical, sonorous.

PUGILISM, *n.* Boxing, fighting with the fists, sparring, fisticuffs, prize fighting, mill (*sl.*).

PUGILIST, *n.* One who fights with the fists, boxer, sparrer, prize fighter, pug (*sl.*), miller (*sl.*).

PUGNACIOUS, *adj.* Given to fighting, quarrelsome, aggressive, unpeaceful, belligerent, contentious, bellicose, combative, warlike, with fists doubled, unpacific, defiant, hostile, antagonistic, fractious, litigious, disputatious, militaristic, militant, passionate, threatening, unfriendly, inimical, with teeth bared, argumentative, fighting.

PUISSANCE, *n.* (*Poetic*) Power, might, force, strength, potence, vigor, vitality, robustness, stamina, dint, brawn, energy, strength, stoutness, lustiness, dynamic firmness, pith, nerve, grit, strong arm, sinew *or* sinews, robust *or* rugged physique, guts (*sl.*), steam (*coll.*), beef (*coll.*).

PUISSANT, *adj.* Powerful, potent, mighty, forceful, strong, great, vigorous, dynamic, herculean, forcible, sinewy, lusty, adamantine, hardy, hard, high-powered, high-geared, muscular, rugged, hale, stout, sturdy, able-bodied, brawny, strapping, stalwart, armipotent, hefty (*coll.*), doughty (*humorous*), beefy (*coll.*), Atlantean.

PUKE, *v.* Vomit, throw up (*coll.*), egurgitate, disgorge, spew, bring *or* cast up, heave, retch, cast *or* heave the gorge.

PULCHRITUDE, *n.* Beauty, comeliness, loveliness, grace, gracefulness, elegance, beautifulness, charm, concinnity, harmony of features, good looks, bloom, refinement, glow, prettiness.

PULCHRITUDINOUS, *adj.* Beautiful, beauteous, lovely, graceful, fair, pretty, exquisite, good-looking, well-favored, endowed with beauty, handsome, attractive, captivating, bewitching, entrancing, enravishing, fetching, charming, pleasing, goodly, comely, easy on the eyes (*sl.*), not hard to look at (*sl.*), elegant.

PULE, *v.* Whine, whimper, cry in a thin voice, wail, weep, pipe, snivel, mew, meow, peep.

PULL, *n.* 1. Act of pulling *or* drawing, strain, draw, jerk, pluck, stroke (*of an oar*), tug, tweak, snatch, lug, draft, twang, twitch, shake, yank (*coll.*), adduction (*Physiol.*), wrench.

2. Force used in pulling, pulling power, magnetism, gravity, lure, exertion, effort, energy, attraction, drawing power, attractiveness, fascination, enticement, allurement, gravitation, strain, work, drag, draw, loadstone, seduction, decoy, captivation.

3. Part of a thing to be pulled, handle, hold, grasp, bail, trigger, lever, crank, knob, tiller (*Naut.*), rounce (*Print.*).

PULL, *v.* 1. Draw, haul, tow, take in tow, jerk, snake, rake, transport, ferry, draggle, troll, trail, trawl, draft, puff, inhale, sip, decoy, lure, attract, magnetize, drink, suck, lug, row, tug, drag, adduct (*Physiol.*), yank (*coll.*).

2. Pluck away (*from a place of growth, attachment, etc.*), draw out, detach, rend, tear, disjoint, remove, cull, crop, collect, withdraw, extract, pick, gather, grab, snatch, unroot, uproot, root up

or out, weed out, dig out, wring, exact, extort, wrest, dismember.

3. Pluck, strip *(of feathers, hair, etc.)*, pick, crop, shear, denude, deplume, displume, fleece.

PULLULATE, *v.* 1. Come forth in growth, sprout, send forth sprouts, spring up abundantly, bud, germinate, vegetate, generate, develop, increase, wax, put forth, burst forth, open, burgeon, outgrow, flower, flourish, blossom, shoot forth, bloom.

2. Breed, multiply, grow rank *or* lush, teem, luxuriate, be productive, be produced *(as offspring)*, increase, flourish, proliferate, generate, crowd, swarm, prolify, hatch, rise, bring forth *or* produce.

PULMONARY, *adj.* Of *or* pertaining to the lungs, affecting the lungs, of the nature of a lung, pulmonic, consumptive, lobar.

PULP, *n.* 1. Soft part, succulent part, fleshy part, marrow, flesh, pith.

2. Soft moist and slightly cohering mass, mash, mush, dough, magma, gluten, pomace, gel, gelatin, starch, paste, jelly, curd, pap, batter, emulsion, smash, poultice, butter, squash, crush, sauce, grume, coagulum *(Physiol.)*.

PULPIT, *n.* 1. Raised structure in a church *(from which service is conducted)*, rostrum, desk, platform, lectern, dais, estrade, ambo *(early Christian Church)*.

2. *(With* THE*)* Preachers collectively, clergy, priesthood, ministry, preaching, body of ecclesiastics, clergymen, clericals, pastorate, holy orders, cassock, clerical *or* priestly office, the Fathers, prelacy, hierachy, church, the cloth, episcopacy, presbytery.

PULPY, *adj.* Of the nature of *or* resembling pulp, soft, fleshy, semiliquid, pulpous, mushy, pappy, squashy, macerated, pulpal, pulpaceous, pulplike, flabby, pithy, thick, starchy, loamy, clayey, spongy, mucid, gelatinous, viscous, viscid, semifluid, succulent, grumous, doughy, pultaceous.

PULSATE, *v.* Expand and contract rhythmically, beat, throb, vibrate, quiver, pulse, drum, tick, wave, flutter, come and go, thump, pant, palpitate, waver, shake, dance, shiver, twitter, quaver, reverberate, pitapat, alternate, undulate, shudder, tremble, ebb and flow, thrum, pound.

PULSATION, *n.* Beating, beat, throb, throbbing, drumming, accent, vibration, undulation, dance, flicker, flutter, tick-tock, shudder, stroke, rhythm, pant, quiver, palpitation, pitapat, shake, shiver, twitter, reverberation, quaver, tremor, pulse, tremble.

PULSATIVE, *adj.* Pulsating, pulsatile, periodic, rhythmic, beating, throbbing, recurrent, alternate, intermittent, pulsatory, metrical, recurring, cadent, vibrating, panting, thumping, quavering, thrumming, wavering, quivering, undulating, fluttery, trembling, pitapat, shuddering, dancing, shaking, drumming.

PULSE, *n.* Beating *or* throbbing, pulsation, throb, beat, undulation, rhythmic recurrence *(of strokes, vibrations or undulations)*, stroke, accent, accentuation, stress, emphasis, ictus *(Pros.)*, oscillation, vibration, measured *or* regular beat.

PULVERABLE, *adj.* Pulverizable, pulverulent, friable, breakable, brittle, chalky, crumbly, shivery, crisp, short, splintery, shatterable, crushable.

PULVERIZE, *v.* 1. Reduce to powder *or* dust, disintegrate, triturate, comminute, grind, levigate,

pulverate, granulate, crush, splinter, crunch, mince, hash, crumble, mill, make small, pound, powder, beat, shiver, mince, grate, wear away, crumb, erode, bruise, bray.

2. Demolish, decimate, crush, shatter, mutilate, destroy, grind under heel, batter, ruin, wreck, devastate, break *or* cut up, smash, desolate, ravage, make mincemeat of, dismantle, undo, tread under foot, mow down, break down, overthrow, overwhelm, overturn, stamp out, dispel, dissolve, blow up, prostrate, trample in the dust, exterminate, annihilate, raze, crumble, tear down.

PULVERULENT, *adj.* Consisting of dust *or* fine powder, dusty, covered with dust *or* powder, crumbling to dust, powdery, pulverous, pulveraceous, pulverant, comminute, triturate, fine, mealy, chalky, floury, distintegrated, granulated, farinaceous, detrital, crumbled, reduced to powder, shivery, friable, short, brittle, crisp.

PUMICE, *n.* Porous *or* spongy form of volcanic grass *(used as an abrasive, etc.)*, pumice stone, lava.

PUMICE, *v.* Rub with pumice, clean, scour, abrade, scrub, smooth, burnish, furbish, polish, glaze, gloss, sand, emery, buff, luster.

PUMP, *n.* Apparatus for raising, driving, exhausting *or* compressing fluids, plunger, piston, forcer, lift, air chamber, bellows, blower.

PUMP, *v.* 1. Raise *(with or as with a pump)*, inflate, pump up, blow up, force, lift, extend, distend, heave, expand and contract, enlarge, puff up, sufflate, swell, bloat, dilate.

2. Free from water, *etc. (by means of a pump)*, extract, draw out, bail out, empty, evacuate, void, exhaust, siphon, clear out, clean, force out, withdraw, tap, purge, flush, drain.

3. Cross-examine, cross-question, interrogate, extract, extort, elicit, quiz, inquire, sound, probe, worm out of, draw out, catechize, pick *or* suck the brains of, put the pressure on, put the screws on, third degree *(sl.)*, question, examine, grill *(coll.)*.

PUN, *n.* Word twisting for humorous effect, play on words, equivocality, conceit, witticism, equivoque, double-entendre, riddle, ambiguity, homonym, carriwitchet, paragram, witty saying, bon mot, *jeu de mots (Fr.)*, *calembour (Fr.)*.

PUNCH, *n.* 1. Blow, thrust *(esp. with the fist)*, hit, stroke, box, cuff, buffet, pelt, thump, jab, poke, push, dig, swat *(coll.)*, soak *(sl.)*, sock *(sl.)*.

2. Tool *or* apparatus for punching, perforating, stamping, *etc.*, perforator, die, puncheon, borer, intaglio, stamp, gouge, bodkin, drill, trepan, awl, wimble, lancet, needle, stiletto, seal, stylet, pin, lance, bradawl *(Carp.)*.

PUNCH, *v.* 1. Give a sharp thrust *or* blow to *(esp. with the fist,)*, poke, prod, push, smite, box, drive, strike, thwack, beat, dig, jab, buffet, pommel, pelt, soak *(sl.)*, sock *(sl.)*, paste *(sl.)*, plug *(sl.)*, clout *(coll.)*, wallop *(coll.)*, thump, clip *(coll.)*, swat *(coll.)*.

2. Pierce, puncture, perforate, cut, stamp, drive, form, penetrate, bore, spike, lance, gore, spear, trepan, spit, riddle, honeycomb, prick, pink, stab.

PUNCHINELLO, *n.* Grotesque *or* absurd person *or* thing, Scaramouch, harlequin, droll, zany, clown, buffoon, fool, motley fool, pantaloon, Columbine, slapstick comedian, jester, comic, Punch, wearer of the cap and bells, jack pudding, low comedian, merry-andrew, Hanswurst, Pickle-hering *(Ger.)*, idiot, wearer of the motley.

PUNCTATE, *adj.* Marked with points *or* dots, having minute spots *or* depressions, spotted, pitted, dotted, specked, speckled, pocked, spotty, freckled, maculate, speckly, flecked, fleckled, perforated, polka-dotted.

PUNCTILIO, *n.* 1. Fine point *(as of conduct, ceremony or procedure)*, particular, nicety, detail, convention, rule, duty, code, standard, usage, form, formality, etiquette, moral, manner, the thing, ethic, decorum, usual practice, dictate, delicacy, observance, subtlety, refinement.

2. Strictness in observance of forms, exactness, care, propriety, particularity, rigid adherence, rigor, severity, discharge of duty, fulfillment, circumstantiality, finicalness, finickiness, finicality, scrupulousness, exactitude, delicacy, nicety, refinement, respectability, inflexibility, punctiliousness, preciseness, precision, conscientiousness, meticulousness, squeamishness, fastidiousness, decorum, conformity, subtlety.

PUNCTILIOUS, *adj.* Attentive to punctilios, strict *or* exact in observance of forms, minutely correct, particular, exact, nice, formal, scrupulous, conscientious, ceremonious, hyperprecise, starched, stiff, rigid, observant of decorum, fastidious, punctual, overscrupulous, precise, careful, meticulous, accurate, severe, rigorous in adherence, religious, squeamish, dutiful, obdurate, firm, finicky, finicking, refined, literal, uncompromising.

PUNCTUAL, *adj.* Prompt, strictly observant of an appointed *or* regular time, not late, seasonable, early, on time, regular, constant, when expected, instantaneous, well-timed, summary, expeditious, immediate, regular as clock work, quick, instant, systematic, Johnny on the spot *(coll.)*, in good time, ready, timely, cyclic, steady.

PUNCTUALITY, *n.* Quality *or* state of being punctual, strict observance in keeping engagements, *etc.,* promptness, alertness, regularity, dispatch, promptitude, punctualness, alacrity, quickness, readiness, expedition.

PUNCTUATE, *v.* 1. Point, mark with punctuation marks *(to make the meaning clear)*, break, separate, grammaticize.

2. Interrupt at intervals *(as a speech by cheers)*, break in, intervene, stop, halt, arrest, obtrude, interlope, burst in, press in, cut in, thrust in, interfuse, intersperse, permeate, interpose, interfere, barge in *(coll.)*, hinder, put in, butt in *(coll.)*, pepper, scatter, sprinkle, encumber.

3. Give point *or* emphasis to, accentuate, emphasize, lay emphasis *or* stress on, accent, underline, make much of, underscore, feature, stress, point out, point up, put in italics *or* capitals, write in letters of gold.

PUNCTURE, *n.* Act of pricking *or* perforating, mark made with a pointed instrument *or* object, hole, eyelet, orifice, wound, pit, opening, aperture, notch, crack, cut, stab, slot, slit, scission, nick, prick, interstice, break, terebration.

PUNCTURE, *v.* Prick, pierce, perforate, make a hole, bore, drill, foraminate, terebrate, punch, riddle, pink, stab, spit, honeycomb, impale, transpierce, gore, spit, trepan, lance, spike, spear, transfix, stick, penetrate.

PUNDIT, *n.* Learned man, sage, savant, scholastic, man of letters *or* learning, scholar, wise man, mentor, philosopher, intellectual, thinker, genius, mastermind, Solomon, master, luminary, giant of learning, prodigy, Plato, Socrates, pantologist, colossus of knowledge, walking encyclopedia, illuminati *(pl.)*, literati *(pl.)*, wizard *(coll.)*, sapient.

PUNGENT, *adj.* 1. Sharply affecting the organs of taste, biting, penetrating, acrid, burning, mordant, sour, acid, stinging, smarting, odorous, tart, nippy, strong, highly flavored, astringent, savory, piquant, flavorous, flavorsome, palatable, saporous, sapid, tasty, pricking, stimulating, racy, salty, peppery, hot, acetous, mordacious, bitter, caustic, highly seasoned, sharp, salt, tangy.

2. Acutely distressing to the feelings *or* mind, poignant, severe, trenchant, acute, keen, caustic, biting, smart, intensely felt, mordant, harrowing, harsh, hurtful, corroding, wounding, consuming, cruel, inimical, hostile, shocking, piercing, piquant, satirical, pointed, cutting, acrimonious, tart, distressing, waspish, irritating, painful, sarcastic, gnawing, bitter, excruciating, crushing, racking, incisive, torturous, agonizing, affecting, touching, galling, afflicting, afflictive, heartbreaking, heartrending, mortifying, invidious, stinging, vexatious.

3. Mentally stimulating *or* appealing, exciting, sparkling, clever, brilliant, keen-witted, quick-witted, pithy, full of point, spirited, lively, witty, pointed, provocative, electric, galvanic, sententious, tantalizing, stirring, sensational, thrilling, spicy, piquant, Attic, sprightly, nimble-witted, scintillating.

PUNISH, *v.* Subject to a penalty (pain, loss, confinement, death, *etc.*) for some offense, inflict a penalty upon, chastise, lash, correct, whip, torture, trounce, decimate, rebuke, admonish, reprove, sentence, sconce, mulct, distrain, proscribe, castigate, chasten, scourge, flog, warm one's hide *(coll.)*, keelhaul *(naut.)*, afflict, cudgel, lambaste *(sl.)*, dust one's jacket *(coll.)*, dress down *(coll.)*, tan one's hide *(coll.)*, lesson, discipline, penalize, take vengeance on, bring to retribution, bring *or* call to account *or* order, take to task, get even with, take revenge, retaliate, requite, pay, repay, reward, pay off, make requital, imprison, fine, persecute, amerce, give one his deserts, settle *or* square accounts with, revenge, take disciplinary action.

PUNISHABLE, *adj.* Liable to punishment, deserving of punishment, guilty, chargeable, faulty, to blame, at fault, impeachable, peccant, culpable, criminal, blameworthy, blamable, answerable, reprehensible, in the wrong, reprovable, accusable, censurable.

PUNISHMENT, *n.* 1. Act of punishing, fact of being punished, chastisement, retribution, trial, correction, requital, condemnation, penalization, judgment, nemesis, amercement, infliction, castigation, chastening, lesson, scourging, discipline, imprisonment, payment, rod, impalement, retaliation, punition, whipping, avengement, vengeance, cyphonism.

2. That which is inflicted as a penalty in punishing, penal retribution, persecution, pain, price, fine, penalty, judgment, visitation, reward, punition, distress, distraint, sconce, damages, infliction, confiscation, reparation, redress, hard labor, loss, forfeiture, wages of sin, payment, deserts, capital punishment, retribution, reckoning, comeuppance *(coll.)*, scourge, vengeance, suffering, talion, mulct.

PUNITIVE, *adj.* Serving for, concerned with *or* inflicting punishment, penal, penalizing, avenging, retaliatory, retaliative, inflictive, revengeful, vindictive, castigatory, retributive, disciplinary, corrective, vengeful, talionic, recriminatory, punitory, castigating, vindicatory.

PUNY, *adj.* 1. Of less than normal size and strength, weakly, weak, little, small, feeble, inferior, delicate, fragile, tender, immature, scanty, sickly, poor, bantam, half-pint, pint-sized, thin, starved, underfed, emaciated, undernourished, runty, nanoid, minikin, miniature, scrubby, dwarfish, Lilliputian, tiny, undersized, underdeveloped, stunted, dinky *(coll.)*, diminutive, frail, minute, atrophied, pygmy.

2. Petty, insignificant, unworthy of serious consideration, frivolous, trivial, idle, slight, weak, silly, childish, puerile, vapid, feeble, impotent, infantile, unimportant, immature, inept, poor, worthless, jejune, inadequate, trifling, inane, senseless, simple, flimsy, fruitless, paltry, ineffectual, fatuous, piddling, meaningless, inefficacious, meager, nugatory, fribbling, inconsiderable, insufficient, indifferent, shallow, superficial, airy, frothy, light, niggling, harebrained.

PUP, *n.* Young dog *or* seal, whelp, puppy, cub, youngling *(Poetic)*.

PUPA, *n.* Insect in nonfeeding stage between larva and imago, cocoon, chrysalis, aurelia *(Zool.)*, nymph *(Entomol.)*.

PUPIL, *n.* One under an instructor *or* teacher, student, learner, beginner, scholar, disciple, educatee, schoolgirl *or* schoolboy, tyro, novice, catechumen, neophyte, collegian, undergraduate, initiate, matriculant, apprentice, ward, probationer, coed *(coll.)*.

PUPILAGE, *n.* State *or* period of being a pupil, youth, school days, education, learning, novitiate, apprenticeship, tutorage, indoctrination, initiation, instruction, schooling, childhood, tutelage, wardship, minority, nonage.

PUPILLARY, *adj.* Pertaining to a pupil *or* student, apprentice, scholarly, scholastic, collegiate, monitorial, probational, probationary, academic, educational, student.

PUPPET, *n.* 1. Artificial figure moved by wires *(as on a miniature stage)*, lay figure, marionette, manikin, image, toy, doll, Punch, Judy, Polichinelle, fantoccini *(pl.)*.

2. Person whose actions are prompted and controlled by another, tool, pawn, dupe, gull, sycophant, figurehead, lay figure, man of straw, creature, instrument, menial, jackstraw, mercenary, hireling, easy mark, gudgeon, cat's paw, toady, toadeater, appendage, flunky, servant, carpet knight, hanger-on, jackal, spaniel, courtier, heeler, henchman, yes man *(coll.)*, sucker *(sl.)*, dummy.

PUPPETRY, *n.* 1. The art of making puppets perform, puppet show, marionettes, Punch and Judy show, fantoccini *(pl.)*.

2. Mummery, mere show, ostentation, pretense, affectation, display, parade, flourish, flaunting, pomposity, pompousness, vanity, flashiness, gaudery, gaudiness, superfluity, tinsel, gilt, strutting, glitter, peacockery, spectacle, exhibition, speciousness, veneer, splash, coxcombery, foppery, inflation, pose, swagger, orotundity, showiness, pageantry, vaunting, pretension, pomp, airs, front *(coll.)*, swank *(sl.)*.

PUPPY, *n.* 1. Young dog *or* seal, pup, whelp, cub, youngling *(Poetic)*.

2. Presuming, conceited *or* empty-headed young man, fine gentleman, fop, prig, dandy, coxcomb, dude, beau, ladies' man, jackanapes, whippersnapper, jack-a-dandy, popinjay, spark, blood, buck, blade, macaroni, exquisite.

PURBLIND, *adj.* 1. Nearly *or* partially blind, with impaired vision, dim-sighted, near-sighted, partially sighted, dim-eyed, weak-eyed, half-blind, blear-eyed, snow-blind, star-blind, mope-eyed, myopic, short-sighted, hemeralopic, nyctalopic, night-blind, day-blind.

2. Dull in discernment *or* understanding, undiscerning, stupid, obtuse, doltish, gauche, stolid, thick-headed, witless, dumb *(coll.)*, cloddish, ignorant, lumpish, oafish, foggy, mope-eyed, dense, uncomprehending, bovine, blunt, sluggish, slow, slow-witted, dull-pated, insulse, dull-witted, imbecile, idiotic, moronic, thick *(coll.)*, weak-minded, shallow-witted, muddle-brained, mutton-headed *(coll.)*, simple-minded, simple, dronish, numskulled *(colloq.)* clodpated, addlepated, addleheaded.

PURCHASABLE, *adj.* 1. Capable of being bought, on the market, available, salable, vendible, marketable, in stock, for sale, offered, commercial, wholesale, retail, staple.

2. That may be won over by bribing, dishonorable, venal, unprincipled, two-faced, Janus-faced, unreliable, not to be trusted, fickle, of bad faith, perfidious, slippery, treacherous, corrupt, double-dealing, treasonous, untrustworthy, unscrupulous, bribable, unconscienced.

PURCHASE, *n.* 1. Acquisition *(by the payment of money or its equivalent)*, buying, barter, gaining, acquirement, obtainment, custom, trade, patronage, attainment, procurement, procuration, coemption, bribery, subornation, graft *(coll.)*.

2. Something purchased *or* bought, bargain, buy, property, possession, acquisition.

3. Means of increasing power, hold, advantage, pry, leverage, tackle, capstan, windlass, pulley, lever to multiply power, vantage ground, support, foothold, fulcrum, fulcrumage, power, force, play, edge.

PURCHASE, *v.* 1. Acquire *(by payment of money or its equivalent)*, buy, bargain for, barter for, put one's money in, procure, invest in, get, gain, obtain, shop for, rent, hire, pay for, give a price for, pick up, collect.

2. Win over by a bribe, buy, buy off, hire, throw a sop to, angle for, corrupt, oil, tip *(coll.)*, suborn, square *(sl.)*, grease *(sl.)*, fix.

3. Haul *(by aid of a mechanical power)*, draw, pry, get a leverage *or* purchase on, apply a purchase to, raise by use of mechanical advantage, force, lift, hoist, boost.

PURE, *adj.* 1. Free from extraneous matter, unmodified by admixture, unadulterated, uncontaminated, unmixed, real, true, valid, fair, clear, genuine, single, simple, homogeneous, faultless, sterling, flawless, undefiled, clarified, unpolluted, expurgate, clean, unalloyed, perfect, unmingled, fresh, authentic, straight, untainted, stainless, undistorted, unstained, undisguised, unblemished, untarnished, uncorrupted, orient, unmarred, unsophisticated, unqualified, uncolored, tempered *(Mus.)*, eighteen-carat, all wool and a yard wide *(coll.)*, in its true colors, clarion *(of sound)*, silvery *(of sound)*, sweet *(of sound)*, uninfected.

2. Of unmixed descent, purebred, pure-blooded, blue-blooded, full-blooded, thoroughbred, aristocratic, pedigreed.

3. *(Of literary style)* Straightforward, unaffected, classic, classical, attic, restrained, simple, plain, chaste, unornamented, inornate, severe, unadorned, strict, precise, formal, refined, proper,

natural, flawless, faultless, undecked, tasteful, idiomatic (of language), bare, polished.

4. Abstract (opposed to APPLIED), theoretical, independent of sense or experience, hypothetical, conjectural, academical, postulational, speculative.

5. Unqualified, being that and nothing else, utter, absolute, mere, sheer, thorough, complete, full, plenary, perfect, entire, whole, downright, dead, positive, out-and-out, veritable, stark.

6. Clean, germ-free, antiseptic, fit to drink or eat, sterilized, harmless, drinkable, eatable, edible, fresh, uninfected, unpolluted, unadulterated, uncontaminated, healthful, untainted, wholesome, innocuous, uninjurious, sterile, disinfected, sanitary, aseptic.

7. Untainted with evil, innocent, chaste, guiltless, guileless, sinless, blameless, snowy, undefiled, unsullied, virtuous, true, virgin, modest, holy, incorrupt, candid, unsoiled, virginal, spotless, immaculate, vestal, untarnished, unstained, unblemished, clean-minded, wholesome, above suspicion, uncorrupted, angelic, divine, inviolable, moral, sincere, clean, white, continent, upright, righteous, inculpable, with clean hands, inviolate, impeccable, unimpeachable, faultless, stainless, heavenly, godlike, incontaminate.

PUREBRED, adj. Having all ancestors of the same standard breed (of animals), of unmixed descent, pure-blooded, full-blooded, thoroughbred, blue-blooded, aristocratic, pedigreed.

PURELY, adv. 1. In a pure manner, without admixture, exclusively, singly, solely, simply, alone, apart, only, truly, directly, genuinely, sincerely, severally, respectively, individually, in the abstract, intrinsically, per se (Lat.).

2. Merely, entirely, totally, utterly, truly, verily, indeed, altogether, completely, absolutely, wholly, all, fully, thoroughly, certainly, assuredly, downright, throughout, in all respects, essentially, in truth, really, totally, unequivocally, in all conscience, seriously, unconditionally.

3. Cleanly, innocently, incorruptibly, virtuously, guilelessly, chastely, holily, piously, devoutly, morally, justly, fairly, worthily, admirably, uprightly, in all honor, bona fide, in or with good faith.

PURGATION, n. Act of purging, clearing, purification, acquittal, atonement, riddance, washing, epuration, expurgation, detersion, clarification, cleansing, evacuation, exoneration, aspersion, purge, cleaning, elutriation, defecation, lustration, lavation, lavage, edulcoration, ablution, catharsis (Med.), expulsion, ejection, ventilation, irrigation, disinfection, fumigation, abstersion (Med.).

PURGATIVE, adj. Purging, cleansing, purifying, abstersive, abstergent, cathartic, detergent, detersive, cleaning, balneal, depurative, expurgative, expurgatory, emetic, vomitive, vomitory, lavational, diarrheal, diarrhetic, evacuant, aperient (Med.), deobstruent (Med.).

PURGATIVE, n. Purgative medicine or agent, purge, physic, cathartic, laxative, detersive, detergent, emetic, vomitive, depurative, purifier, aperient (Med.), deobstruent (Med.).

PURGATORIAL, adj. Removing sin, of, pertaining to or suggestive of purgatory, purifying, exonerating, acquitting, conciliatory, sacrificial, cleansing, piacular, atoning, purgatory, propitiatory, expiatory.

PURGATORY, n. Condition or place of tempo-

rary suffering or expiation, etc., limbo, hell, Tartarus, Sheol, Hades, ordeal, torture, torment, penance, inferno, misery, distress, sackcloth and ashes, penitence, repentance, contrition, sorrow for sin, shades below, infernal regions, lower world, underworld, Gehenna, punishment.

PURGE, v. 1. Rid of whatever is impure or undesirable, cleanse, clear, purify, free from impurity, deterge, empty, evacuate, defecate, wash, physic, clarify, bathe, scrub, scour, epurate, elutriate, lave, void, drain, edulcorate, absterge, decrassify, depurate, expurge, expurgate.

2. Clear away or wipe out legally (an offense, accusation, etc.) by atonement, etc., clear (a person, etc.) of imputed guilt, absolve, acquit, clear, pardon, expiate, redress, redeem, free, excuse, exempt, ransom, give satisfaction, reclaim, make good, grant absolution, forgive, propitiate, release, amnesty, condone, remit, recompense, compensate, exculpate, exonerate, make compensation, vindicate, let off (coll.), shrive, grant remission, wipe off old scores, wipe the slate clean, cleanse from sin.

3. (Often fol. by AWAY, OFF or OUT) Remove by cleansing or purifying, clear, empty, cleanse, scour, deterge, clean out, evacuate, wash, rout out, wash away, sweep out, ejaculate, extrude, expel, deracinate, extirpate, do away with, get rid of, exterminate, root up or out, eradicate, discharge, eliminate.

PURIFICATION, n. 1. Cleansing, purifying, catharsis, expurgation, clarification, aspersion, defecation, clearing, purgation, acquittal, atonement, washing, epuration, detersion, evacuation, purge, cleaning, elutriation, lustration, lavation, lavage, edulcoration, ablution, expulsion, ventilation, irrigation, disinfection, fumigation, abstersion (Med.).

2. Removal of evil or base elements, sanctification, refinement, consecration, canonization, subtilization, rarefaction, justification, beatification, exaltation, edification, distillation, eugenics, euthenics, sublimation, lustration, rectification (Chem.).

PURIFY, v. 1. Free from extraneous matter, free from foreign or objectionable elements, free from impurity (pollution, contamination, etc.), filter, strain, filtrate, separate, sublimate, rectify (Chem.), make pure, rarefy, clarify, defecate, fumigate, sweeten, deodorize, extract, sift, sieve, bolt, winnow, deterge, cleanse, clear, purge, expurgate, expurge, depurate, decrassify, absterge, edulcorate, elutriate, epurate, disinfect.

2. Free from whatever is evil or base, sanctify, hallow, bless, better, correct, uplift, restore, beatify, edify, shrive, absolve, canonize, consecrate, exalt, glorify, inspire, make or pronounce holy, baptize, anoint, purge, lay hands on, administer absolution.

PURISM, n. Scrupulous or excessive observance of or insistence on purity in language, style, etc., nicety, fastidiousness, squeamishness, correctness, particularity, stiffness, formality, punctilio, pretension, affectation, elegance, euphuism, pedantry, precisianism, minuteness, subtlety, meticulousness, finicality, exactitude, refinement, preciseness, finicalness.

PURITAN, n. One who affects great purity or strictness of life and religious principles, moralist, prude, bigot, pietist, formalist, precisian, dogmatist, zealot, pharisee, fanatic, religionist, Tartuffe.

PURITANIC, PURITANICAL, *adj.* Excessively strict, austere, puritan, narrow, rigid, prim, ascetic, overscrupulous, arbitrary, prudish, sanctimonious, canting, pietistic, formal, hidebound, stiffnecked, bigoted, dogmatic, hyperorthodox, anchoritic, fanatical, tartuffian, unctuous, pharisaical, uncompromising, precise in religious matters, severe, strait-laced, stiff, stilted.

PURITANISM, *n.* Strictness in matters of conduct *or* religion, puritanical austerity, asceticism, anchoritism, sobriety, mortification, abstinence, bigotry, dogmatism, precisianism, hyperorthodoxy, eschewal, abstemiousness, narrow-mindedness, zealotry, sternness, intolerance.

PURITY, *n.* 1. Pureness, freedom from contamination *or* extraneous matter, clearness, lucidity, clarity, limpidity, asepsis, cleanness, cleanliness, immaculacy, immaculateness, salubrity, salubriousness, healthfulness, wholesomeness, brilliance, chroma *(of color)*, saturation *(of color)*, fineness.

2. Freedom from admixture *or* modifying addition, simpleness, simplicity, plainness, chasteness, homogeneity, genuineness, excellence, directness, conformity to an ideal, integrity, absoluteness, homozygosis *(Biol.)*.

3. *(Of literary or artistic style, etc.)* Freedom from foreign *or* inappropriate elements, careful correctness, truth to an ideal *or* model, fidelity, propriety, polish, finish, distinction, elegance, felicity, clarity, taste, clearness, incorruptness, restraint, classicism, perfection, euphony, severity, refinement, Atticism, concinnity, beauty, excellence, impeccability, faultlessness, gracefulness.

4. Freedom from evil *or* guilt, chastity, modesty, virtue, holiness, piety, uprightness, integrity, virginity, continence, chasteness, saintliness, pudicity, morality, decency, rectitude, immaculacy, temperance, sanctity, probity, pucelage, clean hands, clear conscience, spotlessness, honesty, guiltlessness, innocence, guilelessness, righteousness, incorruptibility, incorruptness, virtuousness, immaculateness, impeccability, honor, excellence.

PURL, *v.* Flow with curling *or* rippling motions *(as a shallow stream over stones)*, flow with a murmuring sound, murmur, ripple, burble, gurgle, surge, whirl, swirl, plash, trill, trickle, lap, reel, spin, babble, flow gently, twist, bubble, meander, wind, turn, eddy, dribble, splash.

PURLIEU, *n.* 1. Bordering, neighboring *or* outlying district *or* region, outskirt, border, suburb, bound, precinct, edge, frontier, rim, confine, perimeter, surrounding, periphery, borderland, boundary, circumambiency, circumjacency, circumference, neighborhood, environ, vicinage, outpost, fringe, verge.

2. *(Plural)* Neighborhood, place where one may range at large, haunt, resort, haven, usual vicinity, frequented place, abode, realm, asylum, locality, habitat, locale, whereabouts, environs, sanctuary, demesne, territory, stamping ground *(coll.)*, hangout *(sl.)*, range, pale, compass, area, province, beat, sphere, orbit, orb, precinct, bailiwick, zone, district.

PURLOIN, *v.* Take dishonestly, steal, thieve, abstract, rob, filch, snatch, make off with, spirit away, appropriate dishonestly, pirate, plagiarize, peculate, embezzle, seize, poach, kidnap, cabbage, abduct, take feloniously, swipe *(sl.)*, crib *(coll.)*, snitch *(sl.)*, lift *(coll.)*, cop *(sl.)*, hook *(sl.)*, mooch *(sl.)*, pinch *(sl.)*.

PURPLE, *adj.* 1. Of purple color, livid, lilac, violet, magenta, puce, mulberry, mauve, hyacin-

thine, amethyst, plum-colored, purplish, damson, raisin-colored, fuchsia, scarlet, solferino, violaceous, purpuric *(Her.)*, orchid, lavender.

2. Imperial, royal, kingly, majestic, princely, regal, sovereign.

3. Brilliant, richly wrought, elaborate, resplendent, gorgeous, sumptuous, elegant, glittering, rich, fine, bright, radiant, glorious, beaming, splendrous, magnificent, ravishing, glowing, illustrious, lustrous, shining, bespangled, bejeweled, adorned, sublime, bedecked, flashing, gilt, begilt, dazzling, highly wrought, scintillating, splendid.

4. Full of literary devices and effects, ornate, orotund, euphuistic, colorful, lurid, florid, vivid, flowery, rhetorical, elaborate, embellished, frilly, figured, pompous, resounding, baroque, rococo, figurative, affected, bombastic, overdrawn, highflown, extravagant, strained, pretentious, rhapsodical, flamboyant, extreme, hyperbolic.

PURPLE, *n.* 1. Color having components of red and blue, lavender, magenta, orchid, mulberry, crimson, fuchsia, plum, purpure *(Her.)*, mauve, damson, violet, hyacinth, murrey, solferino, porphyrous, heliotrope.

2. Robe of state, regalia, vestments, insignia, ermine, trappings, canonicals.

3. Imperial *or* lofty rank *or* position, majesty, imperiality, eminence, high degree, regality, royalty, the throne, kingship, aristocracy, nobility, blood, prestige, notability, consequence, superiority, noblesse, rule, sovereignty, suzerainty, the crown, empire, sway, dignity, distinction, high descent, noble birth, prominence, predominance, place, precedence, elevation, bishopric, command, primacy, dominion, quality, sphere, gentility, blue blood, optimacy.

PURPORT, *n.* Meaning, tenor, bearing, import, significance, design, expression, implication, force, effect, spirit, aim, intention, intent, tendency, sense, scope, gist, signification, significancy, reason, rationale, kernel, heart, burden, object, essence, substance, ground, pith, point, marrow, meat, core, end in view, coloring, purpose, current, drift, connotation, denotation.

PURPORT, *v.* Profess, claim, convey to the mind *(as the meaning or thing intended)*, imply, express, say, insinuate, import, show, signify, mean, intend, denote, connote, indicate, contend, maintain, pass for, affect, declare, aim, infer, intimate, implicate, suggest, have in mind, assert, plead, pretend, allege, betoken, breathe, bespeak, argue, pose as, point to, design.

PURPOSE, *n.* 1. Object for which anything exists *or* is done (made, used, *etc.*), purport, sense, meaning, cause, reason, pith, point, root, essential matter, explanation, principle, central idea, end, intention, tenor, import, significance, design, implication, force, effect, spirit, aim, intention, intent, tendency, scope, gist, rationale, kernel, heart, burden, object, essence, substance, gronud, marrow, meat, core, end in view, coloring, current, drift, connotation, denotation, signification, significancy.

2. Intended *or* desired result, objective, goal, that which one holds as something to be accomplished, destination, fate, destiny, disposition, plan, project, errand, aim, intent, intention, end, object, design, expectation, ambition, occasion, desire, scheme, proposal, prospect, consummation, resolution, teleology, mainspring, keystone, motivating idea, guiding principle, desideration, wish,

motive, call, basis, hope, search, decision, thing wanted, contemplation.

3. Intention, determination, resolve, resolution, drive, mind, pleasure, desire, perseverance, zeal, doggedness, adherance, decision, strong motivation, ambition, volition, aspiration, will, deliberation, intransigence, constancy, obstinacy, devotion, devotedness, ardor, avidity, intentness, earnestness, inflexibility, diligence, assiduity, assiduousness, industry, singleness, eagerness, application, tenacity, firmness, resolution, persistence.

4. Subject in hand, point at issue, heart, gist, core, kernel, object, essential or essentials, issue, thesis, central idea, topic, problem, affair, theme, argument, business, matter, text, case, question.

5. Practical result, advantage, use, issue, product, destination, effect, end, consequence, outcome, outgrowth, conclusion, culmination, eventuality, sequel, success, utility, gain, avail, return, service, profit, benefit, good, utility, blessing, best interest.

PURPOSE, *v.* 1. Put before oneself as something to be done or accomplished, determine on the performance of, intend, design, harbor a design, mean, think of, meditate, plan, expect, aspire, aim, hope, undertake, set about, talk of, dream of, wish, have in view, have in mind, have a mind to, take in hand, venture upon, contemplate, propose, resolve upon, engage in, take upon oneself, direct, destine, think to, endeavor.

2. Be resolved, determine, drive at, resolve, push on, make up one's mind, conclude, steel oneself, grit one's teeth, persist, pursue, persevere, fix, seal, take the bit in one's mouth or teeth, stick at nothing, mean business, buckle to, stand firm, commit oneself, set one's jaw, settle, set one's back against the wall, burn one's bridges, nail one's colors to the mast, decide, will, choose, elect.

PURPOSEFUL, *adj.* 1. Full of purpose or determination, guided by a definite aim, having a purpose, enduring, resolved, resolute, determined, earnest, patient, decided, peremptory, unswerving, relentless, inexorable, sedulous, unflagging, zealous, fixed, firm, obstinate, intent, settled, unhesitating, intransigent, uncompromising, strongminded, strong-willed, tenacious, persevering, persisting, dogged, pertinacious, indomitable, grim, stern, stanch, steadfast, unshrinking, not to be shaken or put down, undeviating, unwavering, unflinching, unfaltering.

2. Serving or indicating the existence of a purpose, not aimless, meaningful, useful, utilitarian, significant, advantageous, worth-while, valuable, fruitful, fertile, creative, helpful, profitable, beneficial, practical, serviceable, productive, contributory.

PURPOSELY, *adv.* Intentionally, with a particular purpose specified, with intent, expressly, voluntarily, studiously, with one's eyes open, with malice aforethought, advisedly, on purpose, by design, designedly, deliberately, volitionally, by choice, at will, optionally, willingly, wittingly, consciously, of one's own accord or free will, of one's own initiative, on one's own account or responsibility, knowingly.

PURR, *v.* Utter a low continuous sound expressive of satisfaction, express by or as if by purring, hum, coo, thrum, whir.

PURSE, *n.* 1. Small bag or case, pocketbook, receptacle for money, wallet, pocket, pouch,

burse, handbag, moneybag, satchel, bag, *portemonnaie (Fr.),* gipser *(Hist.).*

2. Money, resources, wealth, sum of money collected as a present, *etc.,* sum offered as a prize, funds, finances, treasure, budget, exchequer, treasury, pocket, principal, reserves, riches, means, assets, substance, ways and means.

PURSE, *v.* Contract into folds or wrinkles, pucker, pinch, gather, shirr, compress, wither, furrow, squeeze, tighten, crinkle, knit, corrugate, wrinkle, crease, shrink, cockle, shrivel.

PURSER, *n.* Officer *(esp. on board ship)* charged with keeping accounts, *etc.,* steward, treasurer, cashier, bursar, maniple, trustee, cash keeper, paymaster, teller, banker, almoner, purse bearer, depositary.

PURSUANCE, *n.* Carrying out *(of some plan, course, injunction, etc.),* following, pursuit, prosecution, perseverance, maintenance, endeavor, quest, execution, essay, continuation, perpetuation, continuance, extension, prolongation, dispatch, aquittal, realization, satisfaction, attainment, completion, repetition, fulfilment, discharge, persistence, conclusion, effectuation, achievement, accomplishment, follow-up, performance.

PURSUANT, *adj.* 1. *(Fol. by* TO) Proceeding conformably, according, agreeing, agreeable, conformable, in accordance with, acting or done in consequence of, in harmony with, in prosecution of, in step, in accord, consonant, harmonious, correspondent, commensurate, relevant, apropos, adaptable, consentaneous, of a piece, consistent with, congenial, compatible, consentient, of one mind, at one with, pertinent, following.

2. Pursuing, in pursuit, in hot pursuit, chasing, hunting, searching, tracking down, following, on the scent of, in quest of, on the lookout for, in full cry, on the track or trail of.

PURSUANTLY, *adv.* *(Fol. by* TO) In a manner conformable, according, in consequence of, in prosecution of, in accordance with, conformably, agreeably, pertinently, relatively, suitably, adhering to, in respect of, bound by, acknowledging, in the spirit of, in the terms of, in keeping with, following, uniformly with, consistently with, after.

PURSUE, *v.* 1. Follow *(with the view of overtaking, capturing, killing, etc.),* seek, chase, track, hound, give chase to, hunt, dog, shadow, gun for, mouse, search out, prowl after, follow the trail or scent of, nose out, sniff or smell out, ferret out, stalk, run down, trace, course, run after, quest, fish for, start *(game).*

2. Attend, go with, follow close upon, cling to, hound, shadow, accompany, heel to, follow on the heels of, follow in the steps of, trail, follow in the trail of, follow in the wake of, hang on the skirts of, wait or hang upon, dog, stick to, tail *(coll.),* seek out, persecute, go hand in hand with, be unavoidable, be inescapable, follow in one's train, be inevitable, be relentless, be inexorable.

3. Seek to attain or accomplish *(an end, object, purpose, etc.),* set as one's goal, push toward, set before oneself, desire, aspire to, covet, contrive to gain, determine upon, endeavor to gain, be bent upon, try to obtain, strive for, struggle for, labor for, exert oneself for, be determined to get, solicit, resolve on, be intent upon, beg for, contend for, try one's best or utmost, do all in one's power for, have in mind, aim for or at,

bespeak, crave, petition, undertake, push, make a bold push, move heaven and earth for, spare no effort *or* pains for, set one's cap for, set one's heart *or* mind on, coax for, wangle *(coll.)*, gun for, not leave a stone unturned.

4. Proceed in accordance with *(a method, plan, etc.)*, continue, go on with, carry on *(a course of action, train of thought, etc.)*, execute, carry out, go after, follow up, persist in, keep up, prosecute, conduct, push, practice, hold to, forward, sustain, complete, persevere in, cultivate, maintain, exercise, perpetuate, be resolute in, protract, prolong, endure, proceed with, discharge, advance, adhere faithfully to, see through, accomplish, perform, enact, put into effect *or* practice, make short work of, bring to pass, achieve, bring about, dispose of, work out, effect, effectuate, culminate, perfect, mature, make good, elaborate, realize, compass, consummate, adopt *(a course)*, take *(a course)*, stick to, follow out.

5. Practice *(an occupation, pastime, etc.)*, engage in, work at, be occupied in, occupy oneself with, perform, conduct, carry on, busy oneself about, execute, discharge, transact, devote oneself to, labor at, handle, ply, be employed in, undertake, deal with, advance, proceed with, prosecute, cultivate, forward, take in hand, venture upon, take part in, participate in, go in for, exercise.

PURSUIT, *n.* 1. Act of pursuing, effort to secure, quest, search, course, following, inquiry, inquest, probe, survey, investigation, research, exploration, race, chase, hunt, hue and cry *(Law)*, shikar *(India)*.

2. Following with a view to reach, accomplish *or* obtain, endeavor to attain to, gain *or* achieve, objective, plan, prosecution, execution, essay, continuation, perpetuation, continuance, extension, prolongation, completion, fulfilment, discharge, effectuation, conclusion, follow-up, performance, maintenance, dispatch.

3. Occupation, pastime, undertaking, business, living, employment, walk of life, trade, craft, concern, province, work, line, calling, lifework, vocation, profession, job, career, enterprise, activity, specialty, specialization, racket *(sl.)*, hobby, amusement, engagement, project, venture, adventure, mission, avocation, exercise, diversion, sport, game, relaxation.

PURSUIVANT, *n.* Attendant, valet, adjunct, auxiliary, herald, aid, consort, menial, man, boy, girl, maid, hand, train bearer, adjuvant, assistant, helper, usher, waiter, domestic, squire, helping hand, messenger, errand boy, footman, orderly, servant, page, factotum, follower, retainer, lackey, man Friday, right-hand man, handy man.

PURSY, *adj.* 1. Short-breathed *(esp. from corpulence)*, short-winded, out of breath, breathless, thick-winded *(Veter.)*, winded, windless, blown, blowing, panting, puffy, puffing, anhelose, anhelous, puffing and blowing, broken-winded, dispneal *(Pathol.)*, dispneic *(Pathol.)*.

2. Plump, fleshy, corpulent, pudgy, podgy, fat, well filled out, rounded in form, chubby, rotund, full-figured, obese, fleshy, round, buxom, ample, stocky, lusty, punchy *(coll.)*, well-fed, puffy, sleek, portly, stout, tubby *(coll.)*, chumpy *(coll.)*, bouncing.

PURULENCE, *n.* 1. Condition of containing *or* forming pus, inflammation, discharge, pimple, pustule, blister, ulcer, bleb, boil, rising, swelling, fester, papule, abscess, ulceration, gathering, blain

(Pathol.), enanthema *(Med.)*, exanthema *(Med.)*, purulency.

2. Pus, matter, fluid, grume, mucus, suppuration, discharge, humor *(Biol.)*, ichor *(Pathol.)*, rheum *(Med.)*, sanies *(Pathol.)*.

PURULENT, *adj.* Full of, containing, forming *or* discharging pus, attended with suppuration, of the nature of *or* like pus, suppurating, suppurative, feculent, festering, putrid, unclean, mattery, sanious, mucid, slimy, pussy *(Med.)*, impetiginous *(Pathol.)*.

PURVEY, *v.* Supply *(equipment or provisions)*, provision, provide, cater, procure, furnish, victual, provender, feed, stock, store, equip, fit out.

PURVEYANCE, *n.* 1. Act of purveying, providing, preparation, furnishing, provision, reinforcement, replenishment, endowment, armament, upkeep, ministering, accommodation, keep, maintenance, commissariat.

2. That which is purveyed, replenishment, victuals, provisions, stock, commons, rations, larder, stores, groceries, food, supplies, reinforcements, provender, commissary.

PURVEYOR, *n.* One who provides *or* procures, victualer, caterer, supplier, grocer, landlord, host, purveyancer, steward, provider, commissary *(Mil.)*, quartermaster *(Mil.)*.

PURVIEW, *n.* Range of operation, activity, concern, *etc.*, view, range of vision, extent, reach, compass, sphere, scope, limit, span, measure, area, swing, stretch, expanse, breadth, width, circuit, term, latitude, field, territory, gamut *(Mus.)*, bounds, boundary, zone, belt, orbit, ambit, round, ring.

PUS, *n.* Purulence, purulent matter, grume, fluid, mucus, suppuration, discharge, humor *(Biol.)*, matter, sanies *(Pathol.)*, ichor, *(Pathol.)*, rheum *(Med.)*.

PUSH, *n.* 1. Act of pushing, thrust, impulsion, shove, impulse, pulsion, propulsion, jog, jolt, bunt, butt, jostle, boost, detrusion, throw, acceleration, pressure, impetus.

2. Vigorous effort, determined pushing forward, onset, assault, charge, attack, endeavor, thrust, onslaught, invasion, offense, raid, foray, storm, storming, cannonade, bombardment, inroad, irruption, incursion, strong effort, aggression.

3. Pressure of circumstances, emergency, contingency, critical situation, juncture, conjuncture, pass, strait, pinch, exigency, trial, test, crisis, trouble, adversity, compulsion, urgency, predicament, burden, weight, load, rub, impediment, obstacle, difficulty, seriousness, gravity, stress, severity, solemnity, encumberance, tight place *(coll.)*, squeeze *(coll.)*, affliction, scourge, infliction, scrape, jam *(coll.)*, plight, pickle *(coll.)*.

PUSH, *v.* 1. Move by exerting force, exert force upon *or* against, thrust, shove, impel, drive, press, trundle, give impetus to, shuffle, crowd, elbow, jolt, jog, prod, goad, knock against, cant, jerk, start, propel, bump against, put *or* set in motion, butt, bunt, nudge, pole, jostle, justle, hustle, poke, boost, stick.

2. Make *(one's way)* by thrusting obstacles aside, elbow, butt, ram, fight, ride roughshod, wedge, squeeze, shove, shoulder, jostle, hustle, force a way.

3. Urge *(a person, etc.)* to some action *or* course, press with solicitation, importune, urge, whip, animate, encourage, motivate, incite, goad,

prod, impel, propel, move, spur, prompt, lash, prick, stimulate, tease, instigate, inspire, inspirit, sway, exhort, rouse, nag, persuade, induce, hound, prevail upon, arouse, provoke, embolden, egg.

4. Press *(an action, etc.)* with energy and insistence, carry further *or* too far, carry to a conclusion *or* extreme, urge, advance, drive on, press forward, expedite, insist on, direct, promote, subserve, aid, assist, instigate, quicken, support, lend wings to, speed, get behind, endorse, hasten, back, facilitate, advocate, foster, abet, cherish, cultivate, uphold, take up the cudgels for, take up *or* espouse the cause of, stand behind, nurture, go to bat for, motivate, boost, forward, maintain, second, rush, hurry, work for, follow up *or* out, further, pursue, proceed with, go ahead *or* on with, advertise, prosecute to a conclusion, see it through, railroad *(coll.)*.

5. Press the adoption, use, sale, advancement, *etc.* of, promote, make known, advocate, recommend, propagandize, advance, boost, publicize, advertise, plug *(sl.)*, ballyhoo *(sl.)*.

6. Press *(a person, etc.)* as in dealings, bear hard upon, embarrass, put out, constrain, pain, wring, mortify, harass, compel, dragoon, gripe, oppress, squeeze, put the screws on, coerce, drive to the wall, tree *(coll.)*, put on the spot *(sl.)*, pin down, strong-arm *(coll.)*, put one in a difficult position, grind, browbeat, disarm, prostrate, cow, hound, trouble, beset, discompose, pursue, confuse, afflict, agitate, exasperate, exacerbate, disconcert, worry, distress, vex, abuse, plague, heckle, chafe, bleed, fatigue, exhaust, badger, wear down *or* out, harry, persecute, intimidate, buffalo *(sl.)*.

7. *(Foll. by* FOR*)* Put in straits, cause to lack, make one be at a loss for, stint, pinch, deny, grudge, begrudge, hold back, scrimp, refuse, withhold, gripe.

8. Make one's way with effort *or* persistence *(as against difficulty or opposition)*, endeavor, exert oneself, drive on, endure, persevere, put forth vigorous *or* persistent efforts, persist, strive, try, continue, struggle on, forge ahead, advance, gain a foothold, gain ground, grub, hammer, plod, lay about one, climb, redouble one's efforts, lay one's shoulder to the wheel, go all lengths, keep on, keep the ball rolling, not give up, edge along, inch along, fight one's way, labor, drudge, grind, plug away *(coll.)*, peg away *(along, on)*, never say die, be resolute, hold up, bear up, not stick at trifles, mean business, be undaunted, be undeterred, stick at nothing, carry on, work one's way, carve one's way, force one's way, press on.

9. *(With* OFF*)* Move from the shore, *etc.*, depart, leave, shove off, launch out, farewell *(Naut.)*, put off *or* out.

PUSHCART, *n.* Light cart to be pushed by hand, handcart, barrow, trolley, push car, handcar, handbarrow, go-devil *(Railway sl.)*.

PUSHER, *n.* One who *or* that which pushes, ambitious person, enthusiast, zealot, busy bee, man of action, crasher, interloper, intruder, busybody, intermeddler, meddler, hard worker, new broom, human dynamo *(coll.)*, go-getter *(coll.)*, go-ahead *(coll.)*, hustler *(coll.)*, hummer *(sl.)*, live wire *(sl.)*, rustler *(sl.)*.

PUSHING, *adj.* 1. Enterprising, energetic, ambitious, adventurous, pressing, forward, eager, avid, strong-willed, ardent, zealous, mettlesome, keen, aggressive, venturesome, dogged, pertinacious,

resolute, enduring, game, plucky, serious, tenacious, persisting, perseverant, hard-working, unwearied, strenuous, unflagging, persevering, sedulous, diligent, up-and-coming *(coll.)*, industrious, assiduous, go-ahead *(coll.)*, indefatigable.

2. Aggressive, presuming, intrusive, officious, prying, curious, busy, busybody, meddling, meddlesome, forward, bold, pressing, shoving, obtrusive, offensive, self-assertive, bumptious.

PUSILLANIMITY, *n.* Cowardice, timidity, faintheartedness, fear, panic, irresolution, trepidity, fearfulness, poltroonery, recreancy, dastardliness, cowardliness, mean-spiritedness, effeminacy, pusillanimousness, apprehension, cravenness, weakmindedness, baseness, anxiety, trepidation, weakness, sneaking, cold feet *(sl.)*, Dutch courage, yellow streak *(sl.)*.

PUSILLANIMOUS, *adj.* Lacking strength of mind *or* courage, cowardly, faint-hearted, lily-livered, timid, feeble, spiritless, weak, afraid, fearful, vacillating, irresolute, white-livered, chickenhearted, uncourageous, poor-spirited, shy, soft, cowering, sneaking, effeminate, recreant, dastardly, caitiff *(Poetic)*, wavering, hesitant, skulking, base, craven, poltroon, infirm of purpose, anxious, apprehensive, terrified, without a will of one's own, with a yellow streak *(sl.)*, yellow *(sl.)*, mean-spirited, timorous, indecisive.

PUSS, *n.* 1. Cat, pussy, feline, tabby, tabby-cat, domestic cat, house cat, pussycat, catling, kitty, kitten, mouser, grimalkin.

2. Girl, woman, lass, lassie, wench, maid, maiden, demoiselle, damsel, miss, missy, gal *(sl.)*, filly *(coll.)*, cutie *(sl.)*, dame *(sl.)*, flapper *(coll.)*, baby *(sl.)*, babe *(sl.)*, colleen *(Irish)*, chicken *(coll.)*, heifer *(sl.)*.

PUSSYFOOT, *v.* Go with a soft stealthy tread *(like that of a cat)*, creep, steal, tiptoe, pick one's steps, move warily, slink, lurk, prowl, skulk, feel the ground *or* way, gumshoe *(sl.)*, sneak *(coll.)*.

PUSTULE, *n.* Blister, pimple, swelling, elevation, imposthume, ulcer, protuberance, gumboil, carbuncle, pock, abscess, sore, gathering *(Med.)*, blain *(Pathol.)*, aposteme *(Med.)*, welk, boil, canker *(Pathol.)*, fester.

PUT, *v.* 1. Move into *or* out of some position, bring into some relation, state, *etc.*, place, deposit, fasten, seat, situate, station, park, affix, plump, reposit, replace, bring, set, lay, plant, mount, post, fix, stand, add, store, quarter, lodge localize, slap, tuck, imbed, implant, install, instill, inject, infuse, rest, plunk *(coll.)*, assign, collocate, locate, repose, stick, pack.

2. Place in the charge *or* power of a person, *etc.*, rest, settle, commit, invest, entrust, repose, venture, sink, lease, give, risk, embark, consign, confide, assign, relegate, charge, delegate, place, implant, station, lodge.

3. Subject to the endurance of, cause to suffer, reduce, lead, send, convict, doom, sentence, consign, dispatch, relegate, commit, condemn.

4. Set to a duty, task, action, *etc.*, assign, impel, compel, start, move, forward, drive, cause, actuate, animate, stimulate, incite, force, shove, instigate, push, thrust, prompt, urge, motivate, whip, press, lash, levy, enjoin, inflict, impose, oblige.

5. Drive to some course *or* action, force, propel, compel, oblige, hasten, enforce, press, push, require, coerce, dispatch, send, dragoon, leave no alternative, constrain, necessitate.

6. Render, translate, interpret, turn, transcribe.

7. Assign, attribute, imply, infer, construe, understand, place, find, impute, ascribe, fix, lay, derive, discover, receive, gather, interpret.

8. Set in place in a scale of estimates, guess, judge, think, consider, hazard, place, assess, rate, value, appraise, size up, regard, deem, set, esteem, rank, account, count, prize, gauge, measure, evaluate, estimate, figure (coll.), calculate (coll.), conclude.

9. Express, state in language, phrase, utter, word, voice, vocalize, find words for, style, present, give expression or words to, give utterance or voice to, articulate, sound, enunciate, pronounce, couch in terms.

10. Apply (as to a use or purpose), turn, use, adopt, set, employ, appropriate, convert, exploit, press, call, draw, enlist, exert, exercise.

11. Make (an end to, etc.), set, give, bring about, achieve, accomplish, finish, terminate, complete, create, cause, effect, conclude, execute, enact, compass, perform, dispel, discharge, culminate, prosecute, round out.

12. Submit (for answer, consideration, deliberation, etc.), propose, offer, present, bring forward, propound, pose, throw out, set forth, state, affirm, voice, advance, enunciate, open, suggest, aver, allege, posit, predicate, postulate, bid, move, extend, make a motion.

13. (Foll. by ON, TO, etc.) Lay (the blame of), charge, assign, fix, place, affix, ascribe, attribute, impute, pin, attach, bring home, set down, father upon, point to, saddle, tax, accuse.

14. Throw, cast, heave, sling, pitch, let fly, shy, hurl, toss, fling, dash, chuck.

15. Go, move, proceed, put off or out, advance, ply, sail, direct one's way or course, pass, travel, depart, push, press, progress, betake oneself.

16. (With ABOUT, Naut.) Change direction, tack, change or alter course, turn, yaw, bear off or away, change bearings, veer, sheer, deviate, swerve, shift, cast, haul, wear, jib, bring or go about, bring or heave round, starboard, port.

17. (With ASIDE, AWAY, BY) Lay away, save up, store up, set aside, hoard, lay up, reserve, retain, stow away, treasure up, heap up, garner, amass, accumulate, stash (sl.), cache, bank, deposit, assemble, collect, keep in reserve, keep by one, keep or hold back, secure, protect, guard, nurse, preserve, husband, feather one's nest, salt down or away (coll.).

18. (With DOWN) Write, record, put or place on record, list, register, inscribe, enroll, catalogue, chronicle, docket, set down, enter, insert, note down, jot down, mark down, put in black and white, commit or reduce to writing, calendar.

19. (With DOWN) Repress, crush, confute, suppress, destroy, conquer, silence, abash, overthrow, subdue, reduce, quell, restrain, vanquish, humble, extinguish, quash, disconcert, defeat, overcome, overpower, overwhelm, put an end to, confound, subjugate, ravage, prostrate, rout, beat, discomfit, master, worst, demolish, ruin, subvert, annihilate, exterminate, do away with, level, invalidate, obviate, disrupt, shatter, smash, nullify, fell, wreck, extirpate, abolish, break, overmaster, surmount.

20. (With IN, Naut.) Enter a port or harbor, land, sail for, approach anchorage, close with the land, come to land, arrive at port or land, lay or make for port.

21. (With OFF) Postpone, delay, defer, waive, shunt, shirk, avoid, ignore, push or cast aside, table, shelve, pigeonhole, neglect, dodge, vacil-

late, suspend, procrastinate, dally over, be dilatory, hinder, omit, overlook, pretermit, slacken, slow down, hang up, linger over, filibuster, block, protract, dawdle over.

22. (With OFF) Get rid of (a person, demand, etc.) by delay or evasive shifts, dispose of, evade, baffle, frustrate, sidetrack, shift, turn aside from, avoid, dodge, shun, parry, keep one's distance, keep at arm's length, stall off (sl.), play for time, mark time, temporize, throw off the scent, circumvent, elude, slight, shy, fence, beg the question, beat about the bush, keep clear of, hold off, equivocate, quibble, keep a respectful distance.

23. (With OFF) Lay aside, divest oneself of, rid oneself of, divorce, reject, discard, disuse, doff, cast off, relinquish, shake off, abandon, disavow, disown, strip off, take off, renounce, abjure, abnegate, drop, resign, surrender, give up, leave behind, throw over, wash one's hands of, dispose of, spurn, relegate, dispense with, forswear, disclaim, jettison, eliminate, throw out, repudiate.

24. (With OFF, Naut.) Start out (as on a voyage), leave shore, push from land, put forth, board, take ship, launch, embark, get under way, unmoor, shove off, bear off from shore, hoist the blue peter, unfurl or spread sail, set sail, hoist sail, weigh anchor.

25. (With ON) Assume, take on, counterfeit, play, pretend, sham, simulate, dissimulate, dissemble, make believe, act, affect, profess, make a show of, give oneself airs, fake (coll.).

26. (With OUT) Extinguish (fire, etc.), snuff, choke, smother, stamp out, blow out, quench, stifle, annihilate, douse (sl.), turn or switch off.

27. (With OUT) Confuse, interrupt, distract, disturb, disconcert, discompose, perturb, trouble, bait, molest, render at a loss, unsettle, upset, mix up, muddle, confound, heckle, fluster, perplex, bewilder, put in a difficult position, frustrate, balk, thwart, foil, persecute, pose, nonplus, stump, harry, harrass, rattle (coll.), befuddle, faze (coll.), tree (coll.), dismay, flummox (sl.), discomfit, badger, embarrass.

28. (With OUT) Subject to inconvenience, retard, hinder, send out of one's way, cause extra work, discommode, incommode, give one trouble, obstruct, hamper, be a nuisance to, trouble, bother, make things awkward for, be a drag on, be an encumbrance to, hold back.

29. (With OUT) Annoy, vex, irritate, provoke, cross, anger, offend, sting, sadden, grieve, affront, displease, stab, prick, pierce, mortify, afflict, wound, pain, hurt, exasperate, try the patience, roil, enrage, disgruntle, kindle wrath, pique, incense, inflame, envenom, grate, go against the grain, get on one's nerves, get one's goat (sl.), fret, gall, chafe, outrage, make one hot under the collar, nettle, burn up, make one's blood boil, infuriate, give umbrage, foil, embitter.

PUTATIVE, adj. Reputed, supposed, commonly regarded or esteemed as such, believed, undisputed, accepted, uncontested, presumptive, presumed, assumed, postulational, putationary, reported, deemed, reckoned, undoubted, unquestioned, popular, standard, conventional, orthodox, recognized, accredited, acknowledged, current, in vogue, time-honored, settled, established, fashionable.

PUTREFY, v. Rot, render putrid, become putrid, cause to rot or decay, become gangrenous, become rotten, decay, decompose, smell to high heaven, addle, stink, reek, go bad, spoil, taint, defile, contaminate, fester, corrupt, pollute, putresce, stagnate, beslime, suppurate, mortify *(Pathol.)*, gangrene *(Pathol.)*, sphacelate *(Pathol.)*.

PUTRID, *adj.* 1. In a state of foul decay *or* decomposition, having the odor of decaying flesh, rotten, decomposed, stinking, corrupt, decayed, purulent, strong, addled, moribund, unclean, dungy, foul, offensive, rancid, carious, odorous, tainted, noisome, diseased, putrefied, saprogenic, rank, maggoty, bad, corrupted, polluted, mephitic, nasty, odious, flyblown, ulcerous, feculent, fecal, contaminated, excrementitious, stercoraceous *(Physiol.)*, stagnant, putrescent, noxious, sphaculate *(Pathol.)*, necrotic *(Pathol.)*.

2. Thoroughly corrupt, offensively *or* disgustingly objectionable *or* bad, depraved, foul, disgusting, vile, evil, base, offensive, loathsome, filthy, pernicious, execrable, detestable, scurvy, rank, sickening, malefic, virulent, nauseating, revolting, repulsive, defiled, obscene, peccant, rotten, odious, noisome, low, mean, hideous, abominable, malignant.

PUTTER, *v.* Busy *or* occupy oneself in an ineffectual manner, move *or* go aimlessly, loiter, dilly-dally, idle, loaf, dawdle, fiddle, fritter away time, dally, trifle, fuss, loll, lounge, let the grass grow under one's feet, fool away time, potter *(Lit.)*, piddle, peddle, dabble, squander time, laze away, burn daylight, kill time, while away time, consume *or* waste time, drift, lag, fribble.

PUTTY, *n.* 1. Cement *(of doughlike consistency, used for filling holes, etc.)*, lute, solder.

2. *(Fig.)* Person *or* thing easily molded, clay, wax, dough, butter, pushover *(sl.)*, dupe, weakling, weathercock, doormat, easy mark, milksop, mollycoddle, jellyfish, weak sister *(sl.)*, namby-pamby, invertebrate, extremely pliable person, impressionable person.

PUZZLE, *v.* 1. Mystify, outwit, nonplus, confound, stump *(coll.)*, perplex, foil, baffle, confuse, distract, flabbergast, hoodwink, bluff, bewilder, bamboozle *(coll.)*, daze, dumfound, hoax, trick, surprise, astonish, amaze, fog.

2. Solve, untangle, unravel, decode, figure out, resolve, crack, fathom, unriddle, decipher, work out, find the key, unlock, clear up.

PUZZLE, *n.* 1. Enigma, riddle, conundrum, problem, maze, arcanum, knotty point, quodlibet, brain teaser, poser, secret, jumble, labyrinth, Asian mystery, intricacy, anagram, Hercynian wood, *terra incognita (Lat.)*, *crux criticorum (Lat.)*.

2. Perplexity, mystery, enigma, riddle, problem, difficulty, quandary, bafflement, bewilderment, confoundment, muddle, poser *(sl.)*, dilemma, stickler *(sl.)*, uncertainty, predicament, puzzlement.

PUZZLED, *adj.* Perplexed, confounded, mystified, confused, lost, at a loss, bewildered, uncertain, in a bother, fogged, stuck, muddled, baffled, befogged, dumfounded.

PUZZLING, *adj.* Mystifying, inscrutable, baffling, bewildering, labyrinthine, perplexing, intricate, complicated, knotty, problematical, brain-teasing, enigmatic, paradoxical, arcane, riddling, hard to fathom, strange, curious, difficult.

PYGMEAN, *adj.* Dwarfish, diminutive, tiny, Lilliputian, puny, stunted, shrunk, nanoid, wee, midget, bantam, pigmy.

PYGMY, *n.* Dwarf, midget, mite, dapperling, elf,

Tom Thumb, Lilliputian, manikin, runt, hop-o'-my-thumb, atomy, bantam, shrimp, homunculus.

PYLON, *n.* 1. Gateway, arch, entrance, portal.

2. Tower, pillar, pilaster, standard, upright, monolith, column, post, shaft, support, pier, pagoda.

PYRAMID, *n.* Monument, mound, shrine, tomb, cairn, cromlech, dolmen, megalith, cyclolith, tope *(Buddhist)*, stupa *(Buddhist)*.

PYRE, *n.* A heap to be burnt *(for a funeral)*, pile, funeral pile, combustibles *(of a funeral fire)*.

PYROMANIA, *n.* Irresistible impulse to set fires, incendiarism, arson.

PYROTECHNICS, *n.* 1. Fireworks, pyrotechny.

PYROMANIAC, *n.* Incendiary, firebug *(coll.)*, arsonist, conflagrator, firer.

2. Spectacular display of talent, ability, *etc.*, brilliance, virtuosity, ostentatious performance.

PYXIS, *n.* Jewel case, casket, box, chest.

Q

QUACK, *n.* Fraudulent pretender to specialized skill, charlatan, mountebank, impostor, saltimbanco, empiric, humbug, dissembler, swindler, hypocrite, deceiver, confidence man, carpetbagger, quacksalver, dissimulator, deluder, sharper, cheater, trickster, cheat, fraud, knave, rogue, cozener, fourflusher, faker, medicine man, witch doctor, shaman, adventurer, medicaster, bunco steerer, shuffler, sophist, circumforaneous doctor, nostrum-peddler, hot-air artist, *soi-disant (Fr.)*, Cagliostro, spieler.

QUACK, *v.* Utter the cry of a duck, gaggle, guggle, cackle, gobble, cluck, clack, squeak, screech.

QUACKERY, *n.* Charlatanism, saltimbankery, charlatanry, empiricism, imposture, quackism, mountebankery, humbug, pretension, pretense, nostrum-peddling, buncombe, gammon, flimflam, misrepresentation, fraudulence, false coloring, simulation, dissimulation, pretending, sham, duplicity, shallow profundity.

QUADRANGLE, *n.* 1. Plane figure having four angles and four sides, four-sided figure, tetragon, quad, trapezium, quadrilateral, parallelogram, rhombus.

2. Quadrangular space surrounded by buildings, area, court, courtyard, yard, precinct, confine, compound, square, close, enclosure, wynd.

QUADRANGULAR, *adj.* Four-cornered, four-angled, quadrilateral, square, rectangular, four-square, multilateral, polygonal, rhomboidal, tetragonal, four-sided.

QUADROON, *n.* Person who is one-fourth Negro, offspring of a mulatto and a white, octoroon (one-eighth Negro), mongrel, crossbreed, hybrid.

QUADRUPED, *n.* Four-footed animal, dumb animal, beast of the field, livestock, domestic animal, beast of burden, pack animal.

QUADRUPLE, *adj.* Consisting of four parts, quadruplicate, quadruplex, biquadratic, quadrigeminal, fourfold, four-cycle, quadripartite, four-way, four times as great.

QUAFF, *v.* Drink copiously, swallow in large drafts, slake one's thirst with hearty enjoyment, swig, tipple, guzzle, swill, take a pull at, drain, wet one's whistle, toss off, carouse, drink up,

Q
R

drink one's fill, empty one's glass, suck up, sip, lap, drain the cup, wash down, bend one's elbow, pass the bottle, take a whet.

QUAGGY, *adj.* Marshy, boggy, queachy, swampy, fenny, poachy, plashy, muddy, soft, paludal, moory, squashy, spongy, slimy, sodden, sloppy.

QUAGMIRE, *n.* 1. Piece of miry ground whose surface yields under the tread, bog, marsh, mire, morass, fen, slough, swamp, wash, quag, marish, sump, sludge.

2. Situation from which extrication is difficult, pickle, jam, dilemma, involvement, perplexity, entanglement, intricacy, Gordian knot, deadlock, stalemate, meshes, quandary, nonplus, pass, strait, pinch, crisis, critical situation, scrape, hot water, imbroglio, muddle, mess, cul-de-sac, hitch.

QUAIL, *v.* Shrink with fear, cower, quake, blench, flinch, faint, droop, lose courage, lose heart, give way, lose spirit, be cast down, be quelled, tremble, falter, recoil, wince, funk, be cowardly, fight shy, shy, run away, show the white feather, hesitate, crouch, take fright, start, shake, shudder, shiver in one's shoes, quaver, quiver, have cold feet, show a yellow streak.

QUAINT, *adj.* Odd, strange, queer, curious, unusual, singular, uncommon, unique, oddly picturesque, extraordinary, fanciful, original, *sui generis (Lat.)*, in a class by itself, eccentric, bizarre, grotesque, outlandish, unfamiliar, unwonted, rare, uncustomary, unconventional, unorthodox, fantastic, whimsical, out of the way, old-fashioned, antiquated, antique, archaic, primitive, anomalous, droll, freakish, baroque, rococo, peculiar, rummy, preposterous.

QUAKE, *v.* Shake, quiver, shiver, tremble, shudder, vibrate, flutter, quaver, writhe, throb, pulsate, palpitate, sway, rock, reel, vacillate, fluctuate, falter, hesitate, waver, stagger, oscillate, nutate, librate, wobble, pendulate, flounder, toss, pitch, totter, twitch, vellicate, squirm, chill, turn cold, quail, blench, stand aghast.

QUAKE, *n.* 1. Earthquake, eruption, upheaval, cataclysm, tremor, temblor, shock, blast, displosion, dissilence, seismic disturbance.

2. Tremulous agitation, shake, vibration, trembling, shudder, shiver, oscillation, nutation, pulsation, throb, wave, swing, beat, lurch, ripple, stir, jolt, jog, succussion, jerk, jar, jactation, throe, spasm, convulsion, palpitation, paroxysm.

QUALIFICATION, *n.* 1. Accomplishment which qualifies for some function, competency, fitness, capacity, capability, requisite, required circumstance for exercising a power, legal right, ability, suitableness, eligibility, endowment, capacitation, enablement, efficiency, efficacy, talent, skill, aptitude, faculty, property, virtue, gift.

2. Restriction, limitation, stipulation, proviso, exception, modification, condition, arrangement, provision, saving clause, exemption, coloring.

3. Extenuating circumstances, allowance, consideration, abatement, mitigation, diminution, grains of allowance.

4. Adaptation, preparation, fitting, modulation, mood, inflection, innovation, shift, deviation.

QUALIFIED, *adj.* 1. Possessed of qualities which fit one for some function, having qualifications required by law, fit, competent, eligible, fitted, adapted, capable, able, accomplished, suitable, suited, apt, ingenious, adept, expert, talented, proficient, efficacious, equal to, experienced, knowing, skilful, meet, versed, equipped, practiced, trained, efficient.

2. Limited, restricted, modified, circumscribed, bounded, narrowed, limitative, restrictive, provisory, conditional, provisional, qualificatory, modificatory, exceptional, contingent, hypothetical.

3. Extenuatory, extenuating, palliative, lenitive, emollient, mitigative, mitigatory, alleviative.

QUALIFY, *v.* 1. Invest with necessary qualities, fit, capacitate, make fit, make competent, prepare, equip, make suitable, make capable, empower, adapt, entitle, enable, give power, authorize, commission, sanction, license, permit, delegate, endue, endow.

2. Limit, modify, restrict, narrow, restrain, circumscribe, moderate, temper, reduce, soften, mitigate, assuage, abate, diminish, ease, regulate, allow for, vary, modulate, affect, give a color to, take into account.

QUALITY, *n.* 1. Characteristic, attribute, property, trait, feature, character, nature, kind, grade, essential, singularity, peculiarity, qualification, mark, virtue, affection, timbre, tone, color, tinge, flavor, savor, essence, constitution, structure, inner nature, type, disposition, humor, spirit, temperament, tenor, aspect, vein, grain, endowment, idiosyncrasy, individuality, distinctiveness, temper, mood, faculty, genius, caliber, capacity, stamp, strain.

2. High rank, high descent, distinction, preëminence, eminence, blood, blue blood, *pur sang (Fr.)*, high social position, standing, high station, social status, dignity, grandeur, importance, fame, notability, superiority, precedence, caste.

3. *(With* THE *prefixed)* Gentry, aristocracy, nobility, persons of rank, fashionable world, silkstockings, smart set, *monde (Fr.)*, high life, bon ton, *beau monde (Fr.)*, elite, upper ten-thousand, four hundred, F.F.V.'s, Vanity Fair, Mayfair, Park Avenue, Fifth Avenue, Madison Avenue, noblesse, patriciate, *haut monde (Fr.)*.

QUALM, *n.* 1. Uneasy scruple, pang of compunction, twinge of conscience, feeling of apprehensive uneasiness, sudden misgiving, remorse, demur, distrust, misdoubt, suspicion, anxiety, apprehension, solicitude, hesitation, recoil, shrinking, indisposition, unwillingness, disinclinaton, reluctance, selfreproof, repentance, penitence, contrition, regret, self-condemnation, inner voice.

2. Sensation of illness, sickness of the stomach, queasiness, nausea, repugnance, disgust, turn, loathing.

QUALMISH, *adj.* Queasy, nauseated, sick at the stomach, squeamish, ill, inclined to vomit.

QUANDARY, *n.* 1. State of embarrassing uncertainty, indecision, incertitude, dubiousness, uncertainness, doubtfulness, doubt, perplexity, suspense, hesitation, embarrassment, bewilderment, confusedness, Morton's fork, indetermination, vacillation, wavering, insecurity, precariousness, dilemma, puzzle, riddle, conundrum, enigma.

2. Plight, predicament, difficulty, strait, nonplus, state, pass, pinch, impasse, fix, corner, crisis, exigency, deadlock, mess, imbroglio, stew, pickle, pretty kettle of fish, hot water, trouble, maze, entanglement, Gordian knot, juncture, tangle, emergency, jam, involvement, stalemate, scrape, muddle, cul-de-sac, crossroads.

QUANTITY, *n.* 1. Amount, volume, extent, mass, bulk, abundance, substance, extension, measurement, strength, measure, magnitude, weight, sum, content, aggregate, duration, length, size, number, greatness. area, amplitude, heap, multitude, vastness, expanse, capacity.

2. Share, portion, quantum, quota, proportion, driblet, dole. pittance, spoonful, mouthful, armful, handful, dose, batch, lot, stock, dosage, allotment, apportionment, pinch.

QUARANTINE, *n.* Strict isolation to prevent the spread of disease. medical segregation, *cordon sanitaire (Fr.),* enforced sequestration of persons infected with contagious disease, confinement, restraint of movement, inhibition of intercourse, forced stoppage of communication, forty days of detention imposed upon ships on arrival at a port.

QUARREL, *n.* 1. Angry dispute, disagreement marked by a break in friendly relations, altercation, controversy, strife, wrangle, squabble, brawl, fray, feud, vendetta, affray, dissension, tumult, open variance, contention, breach of concord, contest, misunderstanding, spat, broil, tiff, miff, row, rupture, difference, jar, clash, discord, embroilment, bickering, falling out, imbroglio, rumpus, branglement, racket, commotion, hubbub, Donnybrook, dissidence, contradiction, fracas, personal conflict, huff, words, high words, polemics, litigation, friction, declaration of war, outbreak, breach of the peace, scrimmage, riot, squall, disturbance, pandemonium, schism, faction.

2. Subject of dispute, battle ground, ground of quarrel, bone of contention, question at issue, disputed point, vexed question, apple of discord, *casus belli (Lat.),* cause of complaint, objection, ill will.

QUARREL, *v.* Dispute, altercate, wrangle, disagree angrily, litigate, cavil, clash, fall out, bicker, squabble, brawl, have words, raise one's voice, spar, scold, spat, be at variance, jangle, have an altercation, be at each other's throats, broil, be at loggerheads, brangle. break a straw, be at odds, fall to loggerheads, bicker, jar, carp, find fault, raise a complaint, differ, contend, feud with, carry on a vendetta, fight, scuffle, break a lance with, argue, dissent, conflict, misunderstand, talk back to, have words with, pick a crow with, controvert, row, nag, break with, pick a quarrel, join issue, go on the warpath.

QUARRELSOME, *adj.* Contentious, disputatious, exceptious, dissentious, wranglesome, petulant, choleric, waspish, snappish, cantankerous, irascible, cross, irritable, pugnacious, combative, discordant, bellicose, belligerent, litigious, polemical, controversial, fiery, peppery, argumentative, cat-and-dog, brawling, antagonistic, inharmonious, hostile, fractious, quick-tempered, unamiable, unpacific, heated, inimical, at loggerheads, at strife, at cross-purposes, at sixes and sevens, at daggers drawn, at issue, embroiled, at variance, up in arms, dissentient, dissident, discordant, incompatible, contradictory, disagreeing, contrary, adverse, bad-tempered, thin-skinned, ugly, huffy, cross-grained, churlish, splenetic, hot-tempered, querulous, fretful, captious, peevish, testy, touchy, ill-humored, grouchy, turbulent, hasty, currish, unpeaceful, hot, boisterous, clamorous, rampant, tumultuous, uproarious, tempestuous, squally, furious, impetuous, violent, vixenish, shrewish, termagant, turbulent, scolding, vehement, bickering, excitable, rash, unruly, impassioned, rebellious, recalcitrant, jarring, cacophonous, loud-mouthed,

rough, snappy, passionate, discrepant.

QUARRY, *n.* 1. Open excavation from which building stone is obtained by blasting, stone bed, stone pit, vein, mine, lode.

2. Object of the chase, prey, game, victim, beast hunted, bird pursued, kill, ravin, raven, food.

QUART, *n.* Measure of capacity, one-fourth of a gallon, two pints, one-eighth of a peck *(dry measure),* one thirty-second of a bushel.

QUARTAN, *n.* Intermittent fever which returns every fourth day, chills and fever, estivo-autumnal fever, malaria, ague, calenture, littoral fever.

QUARTER, *n.* 1. One of four equal parts, one fourth, guarten, fourth part, fourth, three months, half a semester, quarter dollar, 25 cents, silver coin.

2. Mercy, mildness shown by a combatant, clemency, pity, compassion, sympathy, humanity, considerateness, consideration, gentleness, temperateness, lenity, moderation, tenderness, tolerance, indulgence, toleration, forbearance, favor.

3. Direction, district, region, locality, place, point of compass, specific place, position, station, ground, tract, zone, province, territory, sphere, soil, area, space, domain, arena, realm, scene, hemisphere, locale, spot, terrain, situation, part, clime, meridian, latitude, climate, bailiwick, precinct, ward, location.

QUARTER, *v.* 1. Station in a particular place, assign to a position for living purposes, billet, lodge, furnish with quarters, locate, settle, post, place, situate, park, stow, localize, install, house.

2. Have lodgings, take up one's quarters, abide, lodge, be stationed, tarry, dig in, stay, squat, take abode, take residence, take root, settle down, locate oneself, bivouac, encamp, pitch one's tent, burrow, keep house.

3. Divide, cut up, carve, separate into parts, cut to pieces, cut into quarters, quadrisect.

QUARTERS, *n., pl.* Lodgings, shelter, abode, lodgement, lodge, dwelling, habitation, temporary residence, barracks, chambers, diggings, rooms, home, billet, bivouac, domicile, inhabitance, seat, cantonment, encampment, camp, berth, housing, headquarters, address, habitat.

QUARTZ, *n.* Silicon, dioxide, mineral, rock crystal, silex, silica, stone, chert, citrine, amethyst, agate, bloodstone, chalcedony, jasper, false topaz, onyx.

QUASH, *v.* 1. Suppress completely, quell, subdue, crush. repress, extinguish, stop, put down, squelch, obliterate, blot out, strike out, delete, expunge, cancel, efface, erase, dissolve, dispel, squash, overturn, subvert, put an end to, overwhelm, undo, eradicate, exterminate, annihilate, quench, extirpate, devastate, smash, overthrow.

2. Nullify, annul, invalidate, set aside, make void, abolish, abrogate, disannul, rescind, retract, revoke, repudiate, overrule, vacate, repeal, reverse, recall, withdraw, override, declare null and void, nol-pros *(Law),* counterorder, disestablish, countermand, deny, disclaim, break off, recant, discard, dismiss.

QUASI, *adv.* Seemingly but not actually, as it were, as though, as if, to a certain extent, in a certain sense, in a manner, so to speak, apparently.

QUATERNARY, *adj.* Consisting of four, fourfold,

four, quadruplicate, quadruple, quadruplex, biquadratic, quadrigeminal, quadrifoliate, quadripartite, quartered, quadriphyllous, arranged in fours.

QUATERNION, *n.* Group of four, tetrad, quartet, quatre, quadruplicature.

QUAVER, *v.* Shake tremulously, tremble, trill, quiver, vibrato, vibrate, oscillate, wave, librate, wobble, pendulate, throb, pulsate, beat, wriggle, shake, flicker, flutter, shudder, falter, writhe, quake, waver.

QUAVER, *n.* 1. Quavering tone, tremulous shake in the voice, vibrato, vibration, trill, tremor, quiver, trembling.
2. *(Music)* Eighth note, half of a crotchet, quarter of a minim, eighth of a semibreve, breve.

QUAY, *n.* Landing, landing-place, wharf, dock, levee, pier, artificial bank, mole, bund.

QUEAN, *n.* Impudent woman, minx, baggage, harridan, slut, mopsy, jade, drab, trull, hussy, bitch, trollop, piece, wench, punk, chippy, cocotte, grisette, lorette, demirep, demimondaine, *petite dame (Fr.),* wanton, streetwalker, *fille de joie (Fr.),* broad, whore, prostitute, harlot, hustler, tart, courtesan, strumpet, fancy woman, doxy, kept woman, *bona roba (It.),* mistress, concubine.

QUEASY, *adj.* 1. Sick at the stomach, nauseated, inclined to nausea, qualmish, disposed to vomit, uneasy, uncomfortable.
2. Squeamish, sensitive, hard to please, overparticular, overnice, difficult, fastidious, delicate, scrupulous, exacting, meticulous, finical, thinskinned, finicky, dainty, prudish, querulous, discriminating, hypercritical, censorious.

QUEEN, *n.* 1. Female monarch, wife of a king, royal consort, female sovereign, empress, queen consort, czarina, sultana, begum, Kaiserin, princess, rani, maharani, majesty, grace, worship, infanta.
2. Inamorata, lady love, belle, sweetheart, darling, beloved, idol, goddess, angel, favorite, mistress, dulcinea, truelove, flame, jewel, honey.
3. Woman preëminent in any respect, paragon, pink of perfection, nonesuch, nonpareil, flower, ideal, phoenix, model, mirror, pattern, *beau idéal (Fr.),* standard, *ne plus ultra (Lat.).*

QUEENLY, *adj.* Befitting a queen, proper to a queen, royal, regal, sovereign, imperial, autocratic, reginal, exalted, highborn, patrician, aristocratic, courtly, blue-blooded, well-born, stately, majestic, grand, imposing, lofty, eminent, supreme, glorious, noble, illustrious, august, grand, sublime, dignified, haughty, imperious, condescending, domineering, commanding, authoritative, gracious.

QUEER, *adj.* 1. Strange from a conventional point of view, odd, singular, unusual, peculiar, curious, extraordinary, uncommon, unique, fantastic, quaint, unprecedented, unparalleled, freakish, eccentric, anomalous, unconventional, bizarre, outlandish, exceptional, irregular, unexampled, unfamiliar, erratic, abnormal, grotesque, ridiculous, ludicrous, comical, preposterous, rum, fanciful, nondescript, capricious, egregious, astonishing, uncomfortable, unnatural, out of the common run, out of the beaten track, uncustomary, rare, unwonted, remarkable, original, *sui generis (Lat.),* bohemian, unorthodox, *outré (Fr.),* preternatural, exotic, *tombé des nues (Fr.),* droll, waggish, out of the way, extravagant, absurd.
2. Out of the normal state of physical feeling,

faint, giddy, vertiginous, light-headed, qualmish, reeling, dizzy.
3. Mentally unbalanced, deranged, unhinged, irrational, *aliéné (Fr.),* not right, unsettled in mind, crazy, non compos mentis, touched, cracked, bereft of reason, beside oneself, insensate, daft, frenzied, phrenetic, barmy, crack-brained, bughouse, off one's head, delirious, loco, rambling, incoherent, wandering, raving, frantic, rabid, Corybantic, wild, distracted, flighty, bewildered, distraught, *distrait (Fr.),* of unsound mind, mad, out of one's mind, off one's rocker *(slang).*

QUELL, *v.* 1. Vanquish, subdue, conquer, crush, overcome, subjugate, overpower, overwhelm, put down, suppress, defeat, worst, overthrow, beat down, rout, reduce, do for, stamp out, squelch, disperse, scatter.
2. Quiet, silence, still, calm, hush, lull, pacify, compose, reduce to peace, tranquilize, becalm, stay.
3. Allay, assuage, alleviate, soothe, mitigate, moderate, appease, mollify, dull, deaden, soften, blunt, palliate, abate, stem.

QUENCH, *v.* 1. Sate, satiate, slake, extinguish, satisfy, glut, pall, gorge, surfeit, cloy, saturate, have one's fill, appease.
2. Cool suddenly, damp, dampen, douse *(sl.),* smother, stifle, annihilate, slack, put out, stamp out, blow out.

QUENCHLESS, *adj.* Inextinguishable, unquenchable, ever-burning, insatiate, insatiable, unsatisfied, unslaked, unsated, irrepressible, unsmotherable, rabid, omnivorous, greedy, voracious, ravenous, keen, avid, dry, droughty, famished, pinched with hunger, parched with thirst, athirst, thirsty, ravening, with an empty stomach, craving.

QUERIST, *n.* Interrogator, inquirer, questioner, catechizer, investigator, inquisitor, questionist, catechist, examiner, inspector, quizzer, quiz master, cross-examiner.

QUERULOUS, *adj.* Complaining, fault-finding, fretful, plaintive, whining, murmuring, querimonious, discontented, dissatisfied, peevish, petulant, cross, irritable, touchy, crabbed, disputatious, censorious, grumbling, contentious, perverse, finicky, hypercritical, testy, overparticular, fastidious, scrupulous, squeamish, pernickety, fussy, overnice, meticulous, difficult, exacting, finical, punctilious, thin-skinned, captious, irascible, choleric, splenetic, nettlesome, spleeny, grouchy, impatient, cross-grained, shrewish, pettish, disagreeable, resentful, obstinate, sour, repining, oversensitive, mourning, lamenting, bewailing, clamorous, lachrymose, tearful, mournful, long-faced, in tears.

QUERY, *n.* Inquiry, question, interrogatory, issue, problem, poser, matter in dispute, desideratum, demand, request, percontation, inquisition, prosecution, scrutiny, investigation, quest, search, inquest, interrogation, quiz, questioning, examination, third degree, cross-examination, catechism, grilling, pumping, knotty point, question at issue, topic, subject.

QUERY, *v.* 1. Inquire, question, ask, make inquiry, put a query to, ask questions, seek by asking, examine, sound out, pump, grill, put through the third degree, interrogate, demand, interpellate, catechize, cross-examine, cross-question, survey, ferret out, fish out, nose out, probe, fathom, thresh out, analyze, look into, investigate, scrutinize, subject to examination, inspect, quiz, put to the proof.

2. Question as doubtful, dispute, doubt, consider questionable, challenge, controvert, hesitate to believe, discredit, disbelieve, dissent, misbelieve, mistrust, distrust, have one's doubts, deny, wrangle, cavil, split hairs, harbor suspicions, smell a rat, suspect, take exception, object, demur, stick at, protest, shy at, raise objections, waver.

QUEST, *n.* 1. Expedition undertaken to achieve something, journey, crusade, search, hunt, pursuit, reconnaissance, reconnoitering, exploration, seeking, inspection, survey.

2. Inquiry, investigation, inquisition, scrutiny, prosecution, inquest, percontation, examination, trial, analysis, inspection, consideration, ventilation, quiz, interrogation, third degree, Socratic method, catechism, cross-examination, interpellation, debate, discussion.

3. Demand, request, solicitation, prayer, invitation, petition, entreaty, supplication, suing, appeal, suit.

QUESTION, *n.* Query, puzzle, enigma, conundrum, issue, problem, interrogation, interrogatory, poser, point in dispute, desideratum, moot point, topic, question at issue, subject, knotty point, bone of contention, quodlibet, riddle, mystery, subject of investigation, theme of inquiry, thesis, motion, proposition.

QUESTION, *v.* 1. Interrogate, inquire, ask, interpellate, catechize, put questions to, examine, quiz, grill, pump, put through the third degree, sound out, seek out, cross-examine, cross-question, probe, make inquiry about, demand, roast *(colloq.),* heckle, rummage, fish for, ferret out, seek a clue, leave no stone unturned, dip into, fathom, test, thresh out, look into, investigate, subject to examination, discuss, put to the proof, bombard with questions, pry into.

2. Consider questionable, hesitate to believe, be uncertain of, doubt, impugn, challenge, take exception to, contest, mistrust, distrust, discredit, disbelieve, lift an eyebrow, lack confidence in, demur, dispute, call in question, controvert, contradict, assail, oppose, attack by arguments, gainsay, contend against, refuse to believe, dissent, have one's doubts, deny, smell a rat, suspect, harbor suspicions.

QUESTIONABLE, *adj.* Disputable, debatable, doubtful, ambiguous, liable to question, equivocal, controversial, controvertible, problematical, puzzling, enigmatical, undecided, suspicious, fishy *(sl.),* inconceivable, uncertain, dubious, shady (sl.), arguable, moot, tentative, undetermined, in dispute, in question, at issue, fallible, untrustworthy, unauthentic, unreliable, unsure, unsettled, experimental, indefinite, vague, perplexing, confusing, paradoxical, mysterious, apocryphal, cryptic, oracular, veiled, obscure, false, unsound, contingent, indeterminate, provisional, impeachable, queer, occult, untrue, unbelievable, incredible, open to question, hypothetical, hard to believe, open to discussion.

QUESTIONER, *n.* 1. Interrogator, inquirer, querist, inquisitor, quizzer, asker, examiner, investigator, inspector, questionist, catechist, analyst, scrutinizer, scrutator, interlocutor, companion in conversation.

2. Disbeliever, skeptic, cynic, nullifidian, agnostic, atheist, unbeliever, infidel, aporetic, misbeliever, pyrrhonist, heretic, protestant, recusant, heathen, pagan, doubting Thomas, giaour, back-

slider, apostate, iconoclast, freethinker, *esprit fort (Fr.),* rationalist, latitudinarian, nihilist.

QUEUE, *n.* 1. Braid of hair worn hanging down behind, pigtail, horse's tail, pony tail, Martha Washington, cue.

2. Line of persons, file, row of people ranged one behind another, rank, string, series, range, tier, train, chain, sequence, succession, order, concatenation, progression, cordon.

QUIBBLE, *n.* 1. Ambiguous *or* prevaricating language used to evade a point at issue, cavil, quirk, subterfuge, shift, evasion, equivocation, shuffle, sophism, prevarication, subtlety, pretense, dodge, paralogism, paltering, double-dealing, ambiguity, artifice, amphiboly, amphibology, casuistry, white lie, duplicity, sophistry, mental reservation, *arrière-penseé (Fr.),* hairsplitting.

2. Pun, *calembour (Fr.),* play upon words, double-entendre, *jeu de mots (Fr.),* word play, Delphic oracle, riddle, conundrum, puzzle, enigma.

QUIBBLER, *n.* Captious reasoner, sophist, casuist, amphibolist, amphibologist, paralogist, caviler, equivocator, prevaricator, shuffler, trimmer, palterer, double-dealer, hairsplitter, sphinx, Delphic oracle.

QUIBBLING, *adj.* Caviling, prevaricative, pettifogging, sophistical, elusive, evasive, deceptive, casuistic, amphibological, paralogistic, equivocative, equivocal, ambiguous, misleading, amphibolous, amphibolic, enigmatical, double-tongued.

QUICK, *adj.* 1. Moving with speed, rapid, speedy, swift, fast, fleet, expeditious, flying, hurried, hasty, light-footed, nimble-footed, winged, precipitate, headlong, express.

2. Brief, fleeting, fugacious, transient, transitory, fugitive, evanescent, passing, caducous, elusive, temporary, impermanent, short-lived, ephemeral, diurnal, perishable, deciduous, volatile, meteoric, cursory, summary, momentary, pressed for time, instantaneous, sudden, spasmodic, mercurial.

3. Ready, alert, prompt, brisk, immediate, smart, sprightly, lively, agile, animated, nimble, active, vigorous, energetic, spry, instant, sharp, snappy, up-and-coming, wide-awake, go-ahead, vivacious, spirited, frisky, vigilant, watchful, aggressive, pushing.

4. Adroit, dexterous, deft, facile, skilful, apt, expert, able, handy, adept, nimble-fingered, clever, neat-handed.

5. Of ready intelligence, prompt to perceive, acute, sagacious, keen, shrewd, discerning, intelligent, perspicacious, brainy, hard-headed, astute, long-headed, far-sighted, penetrative, thoughtful, sharp-witted, inventive.

6. Irascible, irritable, choleric, waspish, splenetic, spleeny, petulant, snappish, peppery, fiery, hot-blooded, touchy, testy, passionate, temperamental, hot-tempered, impetuous, impatient, excitable, high-strung, high-mettled, high-spirited, impulsive.

7. Endowed with life, living, alive, animate, live, not dead, viable, existing, alive and kicking, breathing.

QUICKEN, *v.* 1. Make more rapid, accelerate, hasten, expedite, hurry, speed, dispatch, hurry on, precipitate, press, spur, goad, whip, flog, express, rush, drive, race, wing, hustle, bestir, dash off, make short work of, work against time, propel, advance, impel, further, egg on, lash, urge.

2. Stimulate, incite, kindle, fire, rouse, actuate, refresh, sharpen, excite, whet, enkindle, arouse, animate, inspire, affect, move, inspirit, instigate.

3. Infuse new life into, restore vigor to, introduce new blood, warm, fan, foment, revive, vivify, resuscitate, restore life to, make alive, energize, animate, give life to, awaken, vitalize, reanimate, reinvigorate, enliven, strengthen.

4. Become more active, come alive, take effect, work, go, strike, operate, function, act.

QUICKLY, *adv.* 1. Swiftly, speedily, nimbly, rapidly, fast, readily, with haste, quickly, post-haste, with celerity, apace, under press of canvas, by forced marches, in seven-league boots, hastily, briskly, at full speed, in double-quick time, full gallop, whip and spur, tantivy, by leaps and bounds, *a pas de géant (Fr.),* with rapid strides, in full sail, *remis velisque (Lat.),* under press of sail, hurriedly, hotfoot, expeditiously, precipitately, full-tilt, helter-skelter, slapdash, hurry-skurry, headlong, heels over head, pell-mell, amain.

2. Without delay, very soon, immediately, in a short time, forthwith, presently, instantly, in a flash, shortly, directly, anon, ere long, plump, instantaneously, at once, on the spur of the moment, on the instant, on the spot, offhand, at sight, straightway, by and by, at short notice, extempore.

QUICKNESS, *n.* Haste, dispatch, speed, rapidity, expedition, swiftness, celerity, fleetness, velocity, speediness, fastness, hurry, bustle, movement, hastiness, agility, alertness, liveliness, promptness, briskness, promptitude, nimbleness, spryness, activity, alacrity, punctuality, dash, animation, snap, go *(colloq.),* energy, vim.

QUICKNESS OF INTELLECT Sagacity, acuteness, acumen, sharpness, shrewdness, penetration, keenness, perspicacity, quick perception, intelligence, capacity, apperception, brains, understanding, mother wit, hard-headedness, mentality, smartness, gumption, subtlety, good judgment, discernment, discrimination, insight.

QUICKSAND, *n.* 1. Soft loose wet sand apt to engulf whatever comes upon it, syrtis, Goodwin sands, sandy foundation.

2. Trap, ambush, pitfall, snare, toils, meshes, involvement, entanglement, strait, pinch, pass, slough, quagmire.

QUICK-SIGHTED, *adj.* Clear-sighted, sharp-sighted, Argus-eyed, eager-eyed, hawk-eyed, eagle-eyed, lynx-eyed, perspicacious, discerning, keen-sighted, acute, penetrating, sharp-witted.

QUICKSILVER, *n.* 1. The metallic element mercury, hydrargyrum, Hg *(Chem.).*

2. Changeabless, inconstancy, mutability, mobility, instability, vicissitude, fluctuation, alternation, agitation, unrest, shifting sands.

QUICK-TEMPERED, *adj.* Irascible, choleric, irritable, excitable, temperamental, passionate, touchy, testy, fiery, brash, like tinder, like touch-wood, petulant, pettish, snappy, waspish, shrewish, peppery, susceptible, bad-tempered, fretful, thin-skinned, hot, warm, captious, quarrelsome, cantankerous, pugnacious, churlish, restive.

QUICK-WITTED, *adj.* Nimble-witted, smart, sharp, clever, attic, witty, salty, keen, sprightly, brilliant, sparkling, jocose, jocular, facetious, waggish, humorous, *spirituel (Fr.),* epigrammatic.

QUID, *n.* 1. Portion for chewing, cud, plug, chew.

2. Chewing tobacco, nicotine, snuff.

QUIDDITY, *n.* 1. Essential nature, that which makes a thing what it is, essence, constitution, quintessence, hyparxis, hypostasis, elixir, substance, pith, gist, marrow, core, heart, essentialness.

2. Trifling nicety of subtle distinction, subtlety, cavil, quibble, sophism, equivocation, subterfuge, evasion, prevarication, quirk, hairsplitting, chicane, casuistry, paralogism, sophistry, Jesuitry, mental reservation, *arrière-pensée (Fr.),* speciousness.

QUIDNUNC, *n.* One who is curious to know everything that passes, busybody, officious person, meddler, intermeddler, talebearer, gossip, tattler, know-all, newsmonger, stickybeak *(sl.),* Paul Pry, gadabout, babbler, chatterer, telltale.

QUID PRO QUO *(Lat.)* One thing in return for another, tit for tat, compensation, alternative, reciprocation, barter, battledore and shuttlecock, cross fire, retaliation, reprisal, counterstroke, retribution, *lex talionis (Lat.),* eye for an eye, tooth for a tooth, desert, requital, blow for blow, give and take, a Roland for an Oliver, diamond cut diamond, measure for measure, game at which two can play, the biter bit, boomerang, revenge, retort, repartee, persiflage, badinage, banter, return, redress, quittance, remuneration, reward, recompense, indemnity, reckoning, amends.

QUIESCENCE, *n.* Rest, quiet, repose, stillness, tranquility, calmness, quietude, peacefulness, peace, calm, motionlessness, immobility, stagnation, catalepsy, dead calm, sleep, dormancy, abeyance, remission, suspense, intermission, latency, not a mouse stirring, not a breath of air, inactivity, lull, pause, standstill, deadstop, inertness, inertia, somnolence, drowsiness, lethargy, hibernation, waiting, silence, noiselessness, soundlessness, hush.

QUIESCENT, *adj.* Motionless, still, stationary, at rest, at a standstill, stock-still, immobile, becalmed, quiet, stagnant, unruffled, restful, calm, serene, immovable, cataleptic, sleeping, lethargic, inactive, asleep, comatose, dormant, latent, resting, placid, unagitated, undisturbed, tranquil, untroubled, inert, at a stand, pacific, peaceful, passive, unmoved, in abeyance, suspended, silent, noiseless, soundless, hushed.

QUIET, *adj.* 1. Calm, still, hushed, quiescent, making no sound, noiseless, silent, saying little, reticent, taciturn, soundless, hushful, uncommunicative, reserved, mum, inarticulate, speechless, mute, voiceless.

2. Motionless, unmoved, stationary, fixed, immovable, immobile, stable, stagnant, becalmed, stock-still, at a standstill, at rest, moveless, undisturbed, unagitated, dormant, latent, sleeping, slumbering, comatose, lethargic, dozing, resting, passive.

3. Peaceful, pacific, halcyon, peaceable, untroubled, tranquil, serene, unruffled, mild.

4. Gentle, unobtrusive, meek, modest, undemonstrative, restrained, moderate, making no disturbance, not turbulent, free from tumult, contented, demure, sedate, grave, sober, composed, temperate, unimpassioned, inexcitable, cool-headed, stoical, imperturbable, dispassionate, philosophical, level-headed, steady, well-balanced, collected, unperturbed, easy-going, mild, unassuming, patient, long-suffering, forbearing, clement, diffident, retiring, unpretentious, humble, unpresumptuous, unassuming, unostentatious.

QUIET, *n.* 1. Silence, hush, stillness, still, quietude, quietness, noiselessness, soundlessness, lull, muteness, uncommunicativeness, reticence, reserve, close-mouthedness, mumness, tight-lippedness.

2. Repose, rest, relaxation, quiescence, calmness, calm, gentleness, ease, serenity, tranquility, security, peacefulness, peace, freedom from disturbance, freedom from tumult, composure, patience.

3. Stagnation, stagnancy, immobility, motionlessness, catalepsy, dormancy, latency, standstill, stand, full stop, let-up, intermission, stop, pause, cessation.

QUIET, *v.* 1. Silence, make quiet, hush, still, muffle, stifle, muzzle, gag, choke, throttle, mute, strangle, put a padlock on the lips, bridle one's tongue, smother.

2. Allay, soften, moderate, mitigate, alleviate, assuage, palliate, mollify, blunt, dull, relieve, comfort, set at ease, appease, temper, soothe, compose, lull, still, calm, tranquilize, pacify, sober, quell, smooth, lessen, deaden, slacken, decrease, weaken, curb, subdue, chasten, restrain, tame, check, settle.

3. Stop, stay, arrest, suspend, intermit, put a stop to, interrupt, discontinue, remit, interfere with, bring to a standstill, cut short, bring to an end, terminate, finish, conclude, close, wind up.

QUIETISM, *n.* Religious mysticism, passive meditation on divine things, withdrawal from worldly interests, ethical antinomianism, passive absorption in the contemplation of God, extinction of the will, self-annihilation, indifference of the soul to the calls of the world, annihilation of disturbing desires, nirvana, ataraxia.

QUIETLY, *adv.* 1. Silently, noiselessly, soundlessly, *sub silentio (Lat.),* softly, inaudibly, in perfect silence, mutely, inarticulately, speechlessly, reservedly, taciturnly, uncommunicatively.

2. Modestly, diffidently, humbly, bashfully, coyly, unobtrusively, unostentatiously, unboastfully, unpretentiously, unassumingly, demurely, constrainedly, without beat of drum, without ceremony, *sans façon (Fr.).*

3. Calmly, patiently, placidly, serenely, tranquilly, undemonstratively, temperately, moderately, collectedly, composedly, unexcitedly, unperturbedly, meekly, tamely, contentedly, mildly, peacefully, pacifically, philosophically, stoically, dispassionately, staidly, cold-bloodedly, soberly, sedately, level-headedly.

QUIETUDE, *n.* Composure, mental calmness, placidity, tranquility, sang-froid, indisturbance, serenity, imperturbation, peace of mind, inexcitability, passiveness, apathy, dispassion, coolness, philosophicalness, staidness, sobriety, equanimity, self-possession, stoicism, self-restraint, command of temper, presence of mind, forbearance, fortitude, longanimity, endurance, sufferance, submission, long-sufferance, resignation, patience of Job.

QUIETUS, *n.* 1. Anything that effectively ends *or* settles, finishing stroke, death blow, *coup de grâce.*

2. Death, decease, demise, dissolution, obit, rest, release, cessation, end, extinction of life, death warrant, deathbed.

3. Rout, defeat, rebuff, repulse, overthrow, beating, discomfiture, subjugation, nonsuit, checkmate, perdition, downfall, ruin, losing game.

4. Acquittal, clearance, acquitment, exoneration, exculpation, release, discharge, reprieve, absolution, pardon, compurgation, respite.

QUILL, *n.* 1. Hollow spine, shaft, plume, feather, pinion.

2. Pen, goose-quill, reed, stylus.

QUILT, *n.* 1. Wadded bedspread, comforter, bedquilt, counterpane, coverlet, bedcover, eiderdown.

2. Patchwork, crazy quilt, variegation, mosaic, tesselation, checkers, chess board, patches of color, Joseph's coat, plaid, check, tartan.

QUINTESSENCE, *n.* Pure and concentrated essence of a substance, essential part, extract, most perfect embodiment of something, pith, cream, spirit, elixir, marrow, core, kernel, soul, heart, flower, lifeblood, essentialness, quiddity, hyparxis, hypostasis, gist.

QUINTET, *n.* Group of five persons or things, set of five, pentad, musical composition for five voices or instruments, quintette, quincunx, quintuplets, cinque, fivesome, Pentateuch, pentagon, pentameter, pentathlon.

QUINTUPLE, *adj.* Consisting of five parts, fivefold, quincunical, pentavalent, pentad, pentagonal, pentangular, five times as great.

QUIP, *n.* 1. Cutting remark, mordant jest, gibe, taunt, scoff, jeer, flout, sneer, mock, sarcasm, sharp saying, mordant retort, satire, fling, squib, take-off, caricature, farce, travesty, burlesque, parody, mockery, raillery, snigger, irrision, derision, ridicule, scoffing.

2. Witticism, witty saying, *jeu d'esprit (Fr.),* banter, persiflage, badinage, repartee, riposte, atticism, *quid pro quo,* conceit, quirk, quiddity, crank, *plaisanterie (Fr.),* pleasantry, *concetto (It.),* sally of wit, bright thought, *mot pour rire (Fr.),* bon mot, epigram, word play, *jeu de mots (Fr.),* pun, play upon words, double-entendre, conundrum, quibble, riddle.

QUIRK, *n.* 1. Peculiarity, idiosyncrasy, eccentricity, crotchet, odd fancy, whimsical notion, caprice, maggot, vagary, fad, kink, freak, whimsy, mannerism, whim, monomania, obsession, blind devotion, fetishism, abnormity, aberration, oddity, bohemianism, cult, craze, warp, hobby, *idée fixe (Fr.),* infatuation, partiality, blind side, fixation.

2. Sophistry, quibble, shift, subtlety, subterfuge, equivocation, pretext, loophole, pretense, excuse, evasion, prevarication, artifice, dodge, shuffle, makeshift, casuistry, Jesuitry, paralogy, chicane, quiddity, word fence, antilogy, elenchus, hairsplitting, amphibology, ambiguity.

3. Clever retort, riposte, repartee, sally, quip, conceit, *quid pro quo,* pleasantry, persiflage, badinage, airy nothings, chaff, raillery, banter, witticism, wise crack, smart saying, gag, flash of wit, *mot pour rire (Fr.), jeu d'esprit (Fr.),* bon mot, epigram, play upon words, *jeu de mots (Fr.),* pun, double-entendre, *calembour (Fr.),* equivoque, paranomasia, conundrum, riddle, carriwitchet, jest, joke, flash of wit.

4. Sudden twist, curve, sharp turn, acute angle, flourish, twirl, contortion, flexure, winding, ambages, convolution, coil, spiral.

QUISLING, *n.* Person who undermines his own country from within, fifth columnist, collaborationist, traitor, subversive, betrayer, renegade, perfidious person, Judas, turncoat, conspirator, deserter, insurgent, mutineer, blackguard, mischiefmaker, recreant, truant, rat, timeserver, trimmer, ambidexter, recidivist.

QUIT, *v.* 1. Leave, depart, withdraw, go away from, get away from, retire from, cut and run, take French leave, decamp, skip, flit, vamoose, abscond, evacuate, remove, shut up shop, cut stick, flee the coop, take wing, take flight, fly, strike tents, vacate, emigrate, remove, weigh anchor, put to sea, sail, set sail, take ship, embark, entrain, enplane, harness up, hitch up, bridle, saddle, wing one's flight, whip off, take off, hop off, get under way, make tracks, disappear, evaporate, evanesce, vanish, recede from view, pass out of sight, be lost to view, bid a long farewell.

2. Resign, relinquish, abandon, give up, forsake, desert, leave in the lurch, renounce, go back on, waive, forgo, drop, have done with, nol-pros, cast off, jettison, maroon, fling away, discard, set aside, lay aside, reject, recall, revoke, disavow, disclaim, repudiate, disown, deny, recant, backslide, part with, dismiss, give away, dispose of, lay down, abdicate, forbear, let go, cease from, yield, surrender, demit, table the motion, give up, secede from, back out of, go back on one's word, write off, wash one's hands of, lose interest in, jilt, break off, desist, give over, throw up the game, forswear, make an end of, knock off, cry quits, break off.

3. Discharge, settle, liquidate, acquit oneself of, account for, be even, be quits with, square accounts with, wipe off old scores, pay in full, satisfy, clear, pay up, reimburse, make compensation, refund, disgorge, come across, cough up (sl.), shell out, fork over, expend, tickle the palm, put down, lay down, make payment, pay on the nail, acknowledge, honor a bill, redeem, pay in kind, requite, repay.

QUIT, adj. Released from obligation, absolved, clear, rid of, free of, discharged, acquitted, quits, exonerated, exculpated, exempt, all straight, immune, owing nothing, clear of debt, clear of encumbrance.

QUITE, adv. 1. Completely, totally, wholly, entirely, in toto (Lat.), fully, altogether, utterly, at all points, outright.

2. Positively, out and out, perfectly, precisely, exactly, throughout, in all respects, effectually, in every respect, from head to foot, cap-a-pie, from first to last, from top to toe, every inch, every whit, root and branch.

3. Really, truly, actually, absolutely, verily, certainly, in reality, indeed, in truth, in fact, veritably, forsooth, assuredly.

4. Considerably, to a considerable extent, in a great degree, very, exceedingly, highly, hugely, vastly, enormously, extremely, surpassingly, to a high degree, excessively, remarkably.

QUITTANCE, n. 1. Payment, discharge, defrayment, acquittance, defrayal, clearance, settlement, arrangement, liquidation, satisfaction, remittance.

2. Acknowledgment of payment, receipt, voucher, release.

3. Reward, recompense, requital, repayment, return, reimbursement, guerdon, remuneration, indemnification, compensation, redress, reparation, amends, atonement, retribution, quid pro quo (Lat.), redemption, expiation, propitiation.

QUITTER, n. One who gives up easily, shirker, slacker, deserter, welsher, craven, turncoat, truant, shirk, gold brick (sl.), skulker, runaway, fugitive, refugee, renegade, backslider, recidivist.

QUIVER, v. Shake with a slight rapid motion, tremble, quake, be agitated, twitch, shudder, twitter, quaver, shiver, vibrate tremulously, palpitate, oscillate, flicker, flutter, wobble, pulsate, throb, beat, waggle, wag, reel, fluctuate, wriggle, totter, flounder, toss, writhe, squirm, vellicate, pitapat,

undulate, hitch, ripple, jolt, jog, jerk, convulse, jactitate, jump, floccillate, nutate.

QUIVER, n. Tremulous motion, tremble, tremor, shudder, shiver, shake, quaver, flutter, hitch, throb, tic, ripple, stir, agitation, jolt, jog, jar, twitter, jerk, pitapat, flutter, pulsation, flicker, palpitation, throe, convulsion, spasm, paroxysm, seizure, cramp, jactitation, vellication, subsultus, jumps, floccillation, twitching, vibration, oscillation, undulation, nutation, libration.

QUIVERING, adj. Trembling, tremulous, shaking, quaking, shuddering, quivery, convulsive, agitated, nervous, jerky, saltatorial, saltant, saltatory, vellicative, restless, unquiet, vibrative, vibratory, oscillatory, undulatory, vibratile, pulsatory, seismic.

QUIXOTIC, adj. Extravagantly chivalrous, absurdly romantic, fantastic, fanciful, imaginary, mad, wild, chimerical, utopian, preposterous, impracticable, impulsive, enthusiastic, precipitate, hot-headed, madcap, reckless, rash, headlong, brash, absurd, high-flown, adventurous, ridiculous, whimsical, devil-may-care, harebrained, flighty, idealistic, dreamy, imaginative, foolhardy, fanatical, rhapsodical, in the clouds, notional, vaporous, entranced, venturesome, overconfident, fire-eating, cavalier, breakneck, wanton, giddy, heedless, temerarious, visionary.

QUIXOTISM, n. 1. Fanaticism, infatuation, fascination, quixotry, tête montée (Fr.), madness, delirium, hallucination, brain storm, distraction, frenzy, raging passion, intoxication, furor, raving, flurry, fuss, fluster, ferment, transport, precipitancy, impetuosity, foolhardihood, knight-errantry, fire-eating, indiscretion, rashness, temerity, caprice, whim, maggot, crotchet, fancy, freak, humor, vagary, quirk, whimsy.

2. Imagination, invention, originality, empathy, heated imagination, mind's eye, romanticism, castle-building, utopianism, reverie, dreaming, trance, cloudland, afflatus, flight of fancy, vision, chimera, fantasy, rhapsody, romance, extravaganza, castle in the air, illusion, vapor, stretch of the imagination.

QUIZ, v. 1. Examine, question, query, investigate, sound out, interrogate, ask, interpellate, pump, catechize, cross-examine, cross-question, grill, put through the third degree, roast (colloq.), subject to examination, put to the proof, probe, test, make inquiry, inquire.

2. Make fun of, ridicule, make sport of, mock, deride, laugh at, snigger, rally, banter, twit, chaff, jolly, poke fun at, rag, fleer, play tricks on, show up, parody, satirize, burlesque, caricature, travesty, make merry with, make a fool of, turn into ridicule, make a laughingstock of, scoff.

QUIZ, n. 1. Examination, test, interrogation, third degree, questioning, catechism, cross-interrogation, cross-examination, inquisition, inquest, prosecution, percontation, investigation, inquiry, quest, trial, inspection, review.

2. Mockery, banter, irony, persiflage, irrision, snigger, scoffing, chaff, raillery, badinage, ridicule, derision, jest, joke, hoax, humbug.

QUIZZICAL, adj. 1. Given to mocking inquisitiveness, chaffing, quizzing, bantering, ridiculing, teasing.

2. Being a fit subject for quizzing, queer, odd, eccentric, rum, waggish, amusing, comical, bizarre, quaint, outlandish, strange, absurd, ludi-

crous, ridiculous, droll, laughable, funny, *pour rire (Fr.)*, farcical, grotesque, fantastic.

QUOIT, *n.* Flattish ring thrown in play to encircle a peg stuck in the ground, discus, disk, horseshoe.

QUONDAM, *adj.* That formerly was or existed, former, old-time, pristine, past, in former times, *ci-devant (Fr.)*, sometime, has-been, over, gone by, bygone, foregone, elapsed, expired, no more, whilom, run out, extinct, ancestral, recent, preterite, late.

QUOTA, *n.* Proportional part of a total, proportion, share, apportionment, allotment, portion, contingent, quantity, quantum, driblet, dole, assignment, appropriation, distribution, dispensation, allocation, dividend, lot, dose, measure, ration, ratio, modicum, tribute.

QUOTATION, *n.* 1. Citation, reference, allusion, excerption, epigraph, excerpt, extract, selection, clipping, cutting, passage, analect, illustration, data, reproduction, copy, duplication, repetition.

2. *(Com.)* Market price of a commodity *or* security, current price, rate, price current, charge, cost, expense, valuation, appraisement, worth, value, amount, estimate, estimation, figure, outlay, face value, par.

QUOTE, *v.* 1. Cite a passage, adduce, illustrate, instance, excerpt, repeat, extract, document, evidence, refer to, bring forward, exemplify, reproduce, reflect, echo, attest, mention, allege, detail, explain, bear witness, circumstantiate, establish, substantiate, note, confirm, corroborate, paraphrase, plagiarize, appropriate, imitate.

2. *(Com.)* State the current price of, set the price of, fix a price, appraise, estimate, demand, charge, exact.

QUOTIDIAN, *adj.* Occurring every day, daily, diurnal, day-by-day, ordinary, of an everyday character, commonplace, trivial, run-of-the-mill, customary, wonted, regular, habitual, periodic, cyclic, intermittent.

QUOTIENT, *n.* *(Math.)* Result of division, the number of times one quantity is contained in another, computation, difference quotient, differential quotient, quotient hypothesis, quotient limen.

R

RABBI, *n.* *(Jewish Relig.)* Hebrew doctor, master, rabbin, teacher, graduate of a rabbinical school, preacher, religious functionary, expounder of the law.

RABBIT, *n.* Lagomorph mammal of the genus *Sylvilagus*, hare, *Lepus cuniculus*, bunny, cottontail, cony, jack rabbit, Easter bunny.

RABBITRY, *n.* Place where rabbits are kept, warren, hutch.

RABBLE, *n.* Tumultuous crowd of vulgar noisy people, disorderly crowd, mob, horde, rabble-rout, riffraff, trash, canaille, hoi polloi, vulgar herd, *profanum vulgus (Lat.)*, dregs of the people, *faex populi (Lat.)*, scum of society, lower classes, proletariat, the masses, commonalty, populace, ragabash, ragtag and bobtail, ignoble multitude, lowest class of people, the great unwashed, chaff, rank and file, king Mob, outcasts of society.

RABID, *adj.* Unreasonably excited, violently intense, irrationally extreme, raging, furious, fran-

tic, mad, berserk, daft, frenzied, maniacal, amuck, frenetic, raving, feverish, hysterical, fanatical, overzealous, rampant, corybantic, possessed, mad after, *enragé (Fr.)*, foaming at the mouth, fuming, infuriate, savage, fiery, rageful, wild, moonstruck, dithyrambic, *aliéné (Fr.)*, *non compos mentis (Lat.)*, insensate, unhinged, hipped, lunatic, deranged, insane.

RABIES, *n.* Canine madness, cynomania, hydrophobia, lyssa, acute infectious animal disease communicable to man by inoculation, brain disease due to virus occurring in saliva and transmitted by the bite of an afflicted animal.

RACE, *n.* 1. Population connected by common descent, ethnic stock, nation, people, folk, human race, mankind, group of persons connected by blood or heredity, main division of the human species, tribe, phylum, sept, caste, nationality, subspecies, variety, group, class, kind, coterie, clique, genus, species.

2. Lineage, pedigree, extraction, family stock, strain, breed, family, house, line, kindred, paternity, ancestry, generation, genealogy, birth, family tree, parentage, descent, stirps.

3. Descendants, progeny, issue, stock, breed, children, offspring, flesh and blood, seed, brood.

4. Competitive trial of speed, contest, competitive action, run, sprint, dash, heat, pursuit, chase, spurt, rush, round pace, clip, scurry, gallop, trot, canter, steeplechase, derby, sweepstakes, handicap, match, regatta, turf, *concours (Fr.)*, competition. marathon, lampadephoria, lampadedromy.

5. Career, course, province, walk, campaign, life, line of conduct.

6. Strong rapid current of water, mill race, head race, tail race, tide race, sluice, channel, flume, stream, creek, passage, rapids, torrent, flood, flux, flow.

RACE, *v.* 1. Engage in a contest of speed, contend in running, run a race, try to beat in a contest of speed.

2. Run swiftly, hasten, hurry, hie, move at an accelerated rate of speed, spurt, speed, trip, sprint, dart, whiz, scud, post, tear, fly, swoop, skim, whisk, shoot, scorch, dash, rush, skedaddle, scamper, bolt, scuttle, scurry, ride hard, run like mad, haste, burn up the road, outstrip the wind, wing one's way, crowd sail, plunge ahead, dash on, press on, bustle, scramble, hustle, bestir oneself, hotfoot it.

3. Cause to move rapidly, drive swiftly, spur, goad, whip, urge, press, flog, precipitate, dispatch, expedite, accelerate, quicken.

RACECOURSE, *n.* Race track, racing ground, course, hippodrome, turf, track, circus, *corso (It.)*, Epsom Downs, Ascot, Churchill Downs, Hialeah, Pimlico, Auteuil.

RACER, *n.* 1. Race horse, courser, charger, thoroughbred, Arab, blood-horse.

2. Racing car, stock car.

3. Runner, sprinter, pacer, entrant, competitor, marathoner, lampadephore.

RACHIS, *n.* Backbone, spinal column, spine, vertebral column, chine *(of an animal)*, vertebrae.

RACHITIS, *n.* Rickets, deficiency disease due to lack of vitamin D *or* insufficient ingestion of calcium, deficiency of earthy matter in the bones, constitutional disease of infancy.

RACIAL, *adj.* Pertaining to race *or* extraction, phyletic, genetic, phylogenetic, ethnic, ethnologic, lineal, ancestral, patriarchal, paternal, parental.

RACINESS, *n.* 1. Pungency, spiciness, piquancy, sharpness, gaminess, acridity, tartness, *haut goût (Fr.)*, tanginess, saltiness, mordancy.

2. Liveliness, sprightliness, vivacity, spirit, vigor, verve, enthusiasm, fire, warmth, mettle.

3. Suggestiveness, lewdness, pornography, indelicacy, impropriety, smuttiness, indecency, obscenity, ribaldry, impudicity, bawdiness, pruriency, carnality, salacity, lubricity, lecherousness, grossness, coarseness, broadness, eroticism, lasciviousness, licentiousness.

RACK, *n.* 1. Instrument of torture that stretches the body, wheel, thumbscrew, boot, iron maiden, wooden horse, iron heel.

2. Torture, torment, castigation, crucifixion, impalement, martyrdom, auto-da-fé.

3. Intense suffering, pain, pang, agony, anguish, distress, violent affliction, ache, throe, twinge, stab, hell upon earth, cruciation.

4. Wreck, perdition, destruction, adversity, evil, plight, infliction, visitation, downfall, extremity, undoing, ruination, havoc, crash, smash, debacle, crackup, wreck, wrack, shipwreck, cataclysm, annihilation, demolition.

5. Mass of broken clouds driven by the wind, scud, floating vapor, moisture, flying clouds, spray, low drifting clouds.

6. Gait of a horse in which the legs move in lateral pairs, single-foot.

7. Framework on which articles are arranged *or* deposited, frame, stand, shelf, ledge, bracket, whatnot, hat rack, clothes rack, trevet, trivet, counter, trestle, arbor, perch.

RACK, *v.* 1. Torment, torture, distress acutely, put to torture, agonize, pain intensely, excruciate, harass, rend, stretch, strain, wrest, force, wrench, disjoint, shake violently, tear, wring, lacerate, crucify, harrow, convulse, wound, hurt.

2. Obtain in excess by extortion, treat unfairly in money-matters, oppress, grind, exact, exhaust.

3. Rack one's brains, ransack, cudgel, beat, crack, set one's wits to work, strain one's invention, excogitate.

RACKET, *n.* 1. Loud noise of a confusing kind, hubbub, hullabaloo, fracas, din, tumult, commotion, noisy fuss, uproar, clatter, disturbance, blare, charivari, stir, turmoil, turbulence, hurly-burly, brawl, caterwauling, Donnybrook, vociferation, clamor, outcry, babel, babble, shouting, bear garden, rumpus, riot, row, squall, clangor, roar, pandemonium.

2. Social excitement, hilarity, carouse, carousal, spree, frolic, gaiety, dissipation, revel, revelry, jollification, debauch, orgy, hot time, saturnalia, drinking bout.

3. Organized illegal activity, illicit scheme, illegitimate undertaking, trick, dishonest game, occupation by which money is made illegitimately, extortion, graft, hush money, protection money, bootlegging, blackguardism, conspiracy, cabal, imbroglio, plot, intrigue, rascality, lawlessness, machination.

RACKETEER, *n.* One who terrorizes legitimate business by threat of violence, terrorist, gangster, gunman, apache, one who engages in illegal operations, miscreant, contrabandist, bootlegger, rumrunner, graft collector, extorter of protection money, desperado, bludgeon man, roughneck, bully, hooligan, ugly customer.

RACKETY, *adj.* 1. Noisy, uproarious, clamorous, loud, vociferous, stentorian, loud-voiced, obstrep-

erous, turbulent, blustering, ear-splitting, shrill, deafening, piercing, blatant, thundering, sonorous, turbulent, clangorous.

2. Fond of dissipation, roistering, rowdy, raffish, dissipated, drunken, orgiastic, crapulent, winebibbing, inebrious, alcoholic, spirituous, hilarious, exhilarated, carousing, reveling, saturnalian.

RACKING, *adj.* Acutely painful, excruciating, acute, grave, harsh, sharp, cruel, severe, consuming, torturous, agonizing, cutting, sore, raw, poignant, afflictive, hurtful, aching, dreadful, appalling, dire, grim, terrific, crushing, fearful, rending, unendurable, insupportable, insufferable, intolerable, oppressive, burdensome, worrisome, aggravating, disquieting, annoying, irritating, galling, vexatious, wearing, harrowing.

RACONTEUR, *n.* Skilled storyteller, person adept at relating anecdotes, habitual narrator, fabulist, teller of tales, spinner of yarns, romancer, anecdotist, relator, Scheherazade.

RACY, *adj.* 1. Having a characteristic flavor indicative of origin, of a peculiar savor, tasting of the soil *(as wine)*, flavorous, pungent, piquant, strong, fresh, sharp, smart, rich, fragrant, spicy, gamy, odorous, savory, tasty, fine-flavored, appetizing, palatable, high, tart, full-flavored, high-seasoned, tangy.

2. Vigorous, spirited, exciting, exhilarating, forcible, stimulating, lively, sprightly, vivacious, buoyant, sparkling, ready-witted, sportive, playful, animated, entertaining, interesting, cogent, irresistible, energetic, mettlesome, glowing, forceful, trenchant, bold, pointed, vivid, graphic, picturesque, emphatic, striking.

3. Suggestive, risqué, off-color, immodest, indecent, improper, indelicate, of doubtful propriety, Fescennine, indecorous, shameless, loose, gross, coarse, smutty, broad, ribald, bawdy, obscene, pornographic, salacious, lecherous, lewd, licentious, libidinous, lascivious, lickerish, prurient, carnal-minded, erotic.

RADDLE, *v.* Twist together, weave together, interweave, intertwine, wattle, interlace, entwine, inweave, plait, mat, braid, plat, twill, ravel, tangle, knot, net, dishevel, interdigitate, interlink.

RADIAL, *adj.* Radiating from a central point, extending out from a center, having bars arranged like radii, emitted in rays, radiated, arranged like rays, outspread, branched, branching, ramiform, spreading apart, divergent, divaricative, radiative, fanlike, separate, centrifugal, flying off.

RADIANCE, *n.* Brilliancy, brightness, radiancy, brilliance, splendor, luster, luminosity, light, effulgence, resplendence, sparkle, refulgence, glister, glitter, glare, radiation, emission of light, emanation, luminousness, iridescence, coruscation, glint, gleam, scintillation, shimmer, scintilla, glisten, glance, fulguration, gloss, sheen, shimmer, glowing, shining, nimbus, halo, aureole, glory, aura, corona, illumination, phosphorescence, lucency, aurora borealis.

RADIANT, *adj.* 1. Emitting rays of light, brilliant, shining, beaming, sparkling, glittering, luminous, resplendent, effulgent, refulgent, splendid, lustrous, gleaming, scintillating, coruscating, lucent, transplendent, fulgent, beamy, sunny, illuminated, nitid, vivid, lambent, lucid, fulgurant, phosphorescent, flashing, scintillant, glossy, sheeny, burnished, ablaze, aglow, sunshiny, splendrous, dazzling, gorgeous, rich, superb, magnificent.

2. Bright with joy, ecstatic, blissful, pleased, happy, overjoyed, joyous, rapturous, transported, beatific, enraptured, ravished, enchanted, jocund, blithe, elated, delighted, blithesome, buoyant, merry, gladsome.

RADIATE, *v.* 1. Emit in straight lines, diffuse, shed, spread, pour out, transmit, give out, scatter, disseminate from a center, disperse, broadcast, circulate, dispel, sprinkle, strew, send out in rays from a point.

2. Shine, light up, illuminate, brighten, illumine, irradiate, glitter, glow, glisten, gleam, glimmer, glare, flare, flicker, blaze, sparkle, beam, flash, scintillate, fulgurate, coruscate, bedazzle, dazzle, reflect, shimmer.

3. Branch out from a center, diverge, spread like radii from a center, divaricate, ramify, fly off at a tangent, deviate, part.

RADIATION, *n.* 1. Diffusion in all directions possible from a common center, dissemination, emission, divergence, ramification, distribution, dispersal, broadcast, disjunction, spread, propagation, dissipation, scattering, furcation, divarication, deviation, dispersion, refraction, diffraction, polarization.

2. Giving off of rays by a radioactive substance, radioactivity.

3. Radiant heat, radiant energy, infrared rays, ultraviolet rays, actinic rays, actinism, visible radiation, Roentgen rays, X-rays.

RADICAL, *adj.* 1. Forming part of the essential nature, fundamental, constitutional, natural, original, native, existing inherently, innate, inherent, intrinsic, ingrained, organic, deep-seated, essential, not accidental, indigenous, immanent, incarnate, indwelling, implanted, inbred, inborn, congenital, inherited, ingenerate, inner, hereditary, connate.

2. Forming the basis, underived, basic, uncompounded, primitive, simple, essential, vital, cardinal, primary.

3. Complete, carried to the farthest limit, entire, total, thorough, thoroughgoing, perfect, positive, sweeping, comprehensive, exhaustive, absolute, plenary, full, unabridged, intact, all, universal, whole, consummate.

4. Fanatical, favoring drastic reforms, extreme, ultra, insurgent, rebellious, leftist, iconoclastic, liberal, immoderate, freethinking, revolutionary, intransigent, advanced, Red, Bolshevistic, Communistic, insurrectionary, mutinous, seditious, riotous, lawless, anarchistic, nihilistic, unruly, insubordinate, refractory, restive, recusant, recalcitrant.

RADICAL, *n.* 1. One who holds extreme principles, one who advocates drastic political reforms by direct and uncompromising methods, repudiator of established usages, one who holds the most advanced *or* progressive views, avant-garde, liberal, advocate of liberal principles, freethinker, radical reformer, extremist, sansculotte, red republican, iconoclast, rioter, Communist, Red, Bolshevik, nihilist, *carbonaro (It.),* rebel, insurgent, fifth-columnist, traitor, revolter, revolutionary, mutineer, anarchist, firebrand.

2. Underived part of a word to which inflections are added, root, etymon, radix, primitive word, stem.

RADICALLY, *adv.* Fundamentally, essentially, thoroughly, in a complete manner, basically,

vitally, primarily, mainly, chiefly, principally, intrinsically, inherently, indigenously, inseparably, subjectively.

RADIO, *n.* 1. Wireless, wireless telegraphy, radiotelephony, radiotelegraphy.

2. Receiving set for anything transmitted by the energy of sound waves without the agency of wires, apparatus for receiving radio broadcasts.

RADIOACTIVITY, *n.* 1. Dynamic property in bodies of high atomic weight of spontaneously emitting invisible but penetrative rays, property of emitting radiation from an atomic nucleus, radiation, radiant heat, radiant energy, actinism, actinic rays, infrared rays, ultraviolet rays, X-rays.

2. Uranium, uranite, pitchblende, thorium, polonium, radium, actinium.

RADIOGRAM, *n.* Message transmitted by radiotelegraphy, radiotelegram, cable, wireless telegram, cablegram, marconigram, skiagram.

RADIOGRAPH, *n.* X-ray photograph, picture produced by the action of X-ray on a photographic plate, skiagraph, roentgenogram, roentgenograph, photogram made with Roentgen rays, actinograph, radiograph, negative.

RADIUS, *n.* 1. Straight line extending from the center of a circle *or* sphere to the circumference *or* surface, semidiameter, spoke.

2. Field of influence, range of operation, scope, compass, sweep, margin, extent of possible travel.

RAFFISH, *adj.* Disreputable, vulgar, questionable, ignominious, notorious, egregious, shady, opprobrious, abject, low, disgraceful, infamous, unmentionable, ribald, ignoble, vile, base, common, scrubby, beggarly, lowbred, churlish, brutish, boorish, loutish, uncouth, crude, rude, vulgarian, unkempt, frowsy, garish, flashy, gaudy, meretricious, worthless.

RAFFLE, *n.* Disposition of a prize among shareholders by lot, lottery, tombola, sweepstake, drawing lots, sweep, pool, wagering, betting, game of chance, pari mutuel, throw of the dice, tossup, even chance, wheel of fortune, stake, wager, speculation, bet, flyer, gambling, gaming, fluke, random shot, whirligig of chance, long odds, run of luck.

RAFT, *n.* 1. Rigid floating platform made of buoyant materials, collection of planks fastened together for floating on water in an emergency, catamaran, pirogue, dugout, kayak, coracle, umiak, radeau, float, surfboat, jangar, jangada, kelek, crib, boom of logs, floating mass, pontoon.

2. *(Colloq.)* Large motley collection of things, assortment, heap, lot, multitude, great number, legion, host, throng, swarm, drove, pack, pile, conglomeration, batch, great amount, stack.

RAFTER, *n.* Beam giving form to a roof, sloping member sustaining a roof covering, timber, girder, lintel, cantilever, joist, trave, crossbeam, roof timber, angle rafter, auxiliary rafter, cushion rafter, binding rafter, curb rafter, valley rafter, arched rafter, kneeling rafter, chief rafter, principal rafter, common rafter.

RAG, *v.* Tease, taunt, badger, mock, annoy, abuse, irritate, bullyrag, play rough jokes on, molest, pester, harass, harry, heckle, bait, importune, persecute, beset, worry, wherret, vex, irk, discommode, discompose, disturb, incommode, displease, rally, scoff, twit, poke fun at, chaff, deride, jolly, roast, make a fool of, gibe, niggle, flout, fleer, guy, lead one a dance, have a fling at, ridicule, plague, bother.

RAGAMUFFIN, *n.* 1. Ragged disreputable person, tatterdemalion, ragabash, scarecrow, ragged robin, beggar, wretch, vagrant, vagabond, hobo, knight of the road, tramp, beachcomber, panhandler, mudlark, sans-culotte, bum, weary Willie, ragpicker, *chiffonier (Fr.)*.
2. Ragged child, street Arab, gamin, guttersnipe.

RAG BABY, *n.* Doll made of rags, rag doll, moppet, mopsey, Raggedy Anne.

RAGE, *n.* 1. Violent anger, extreme agitation, fury, wrath, passion, furor, madness, rampage, raving, indignation, excitement, storm, violence, vehemence, explosion, huff, hysterics, exasperation, heat, resentment, tiff, ferocity, dudgeon, temper, tantrum, choler, ire, perturbation, bile, spleen, *acharnement (Fr.)*, paroxysm, outburst, vials of wrath, hot blood, high words, umbrage, pique, ferment, asperity, virulence, bitterness, acerbity, gall, acrimony, ebullition, irascibility, irritation, animosity, displeasure, resentment, fit, berserk, throe, blow up, squall, fever heat, fume, frenzy.
2. Inextinguishable desire, extreme eagerness, ardor, fervor, absorbing enthusiasm, engrossing propensity, estrus, rut, heat.
3. Object of widespread enthusiasm, fad, craze, mania, fashion, style, mode, vogue, monomania, the thing, the go, the last word, *le dernier cri (Fr.)*, prevailing taste, the latest thing, *ton (Fr.)*, high fashion.

RAGE, *v.* Show violent anger, act with fury, be violently agitated with passion, act with unrestrained violence, storm, bluster, rave, be furious, fret, fume, chafe, boil over, foam, seethe, flare up, fulminate, fly into a passion, blow one's top, froth at the mouth, splutter, explode, lose one's temper, bristle up, fire up, vent one's spleen, raise Cain, stamp with rage, look daggers, look black, snap at, gnash, snarl, scowl, lower, take umbrage, take offense, flash up, simmer, redden, run amuck, go berserk, work oneself up, run mad, fly off the handle, rant, go into hysterics, go on the rampage, make a riot, raise a storm, wreak, ride roughshod, blow up.

RAGGED, *adj.* 1. Worn to rags, tattered, rent, torn, frayed, frazzled, threadbare, worn-out, shoddy, patched, out at the seams, shredded, the worse for wear, battered, worn to a thread, having loose-hanging shreds.
2. Clothed in tattered garments, dressed in rags, shabby, seedy, wearing worn clothes, ill-dressed.
3. Full of rough sharp projections, jagged, craggy, rocky, broken, irregular, uneven.
4. Shaggy, hirsute, rugged, rough.
5. In a wild state, neglected, desolate, abandoned, dilapidated.
6. Harsh, unmusical, cacophonous, dissonant, discordant, inharmonious, rasping, grating, raucous, hoarse.

RAGING, *adj.* Extremely angry, enraged, furious, infuriated, incensed, infuriate, rabid, irate, wrathful, wroth, ireful, fierce, violent, impassioned, burning, foaming, seething, storming, raving, frenzied, rampant, berserk, amuck, wrought up, blazing, black in the face, boiling over, flaming, fuming, wild, carried away by passion, frantic, mad, beside oneself, demoniacal, ready to burst,

feverish, hysterical, vehement, hot-headed, fiery, turbulent, tempestuous, simmering, volcanic, blustering, towering, ebullient, savage, explosive, *acharné (Fr.)*.

RAGOUT, *n.* Highly seasoned stew, stewed meat and vegetables, hash, gallimaufry, mulligatawny, goulash, réchauffé, salmagundi, olla-podrida, olio.

RAGPICKER, *n.* One who picks up waste material from the streets, ragman, dumpman, *chiffonnier (Fr.)*.

RAGS, *n., pl.* 1. Worthless fragments of cloth, frayed bits of garment, tatters, scraps, shreds, patches, remnants, frazzles, castoff clothes, orts, trash, sweepings, waste, rubbish, litter, odds and ends, shoddies, refuse.
2. Mean attire, tattered clothing, shabby clothes, old clothes, duds.
3. Glad rags, best clothes, Sunday clothes, holiday attire, best bib and tucker, finery, frills and furbelows, foppery, frippery.

RAGTIME, *n.* Syncopated time in dance music, rhythm marked by frequent syncopation, characteristic syncopation of negro melodies, Dixieland jazz, boogie-woogie, blues, rock-and-roll, barrel-house jive, swing, swing music, jitterbug.

RAID, *n.* 1. Plundering expedition, sudden and rapid military operation, sudden onset upon something to be seized, hostile cavalry incursion, predatory invasion, irruption, illapse, inroad, attack, foray, descent, *razzia (It.)*, *coup de main (Fr.)*, onslaught, charge, outbreak, sortie, sally, forced entrance, surprisal, storming.
2. Plunder, pillage, loot, spoliation, rapine, sack, highway robbery, brigandage, holdup, piracy, hijacking, privateering, filibustering, cattle rustling, poaching, direption.

RAID, *v.* Launch a hostile incursion against, assault, fall upon, invade, pillage, plunder, loot, forage, set upon, pounce upon, assail, rush, strike at, march upon, thrust at, harry, storm, make forced entrance, swoop down upon, make a descent on, attack, devastate, trespass on another in order to steal, rustle, poach, hijack, filibuster, sack, rifle, ransack, despoil, gut, strip, maraud, burgle, holdup, lift, make off with, pirate, board.

RAIDER, *n.* Invader, marauder, pillager, depredator, spoiler, brigand, bandit, freebooter, bushranger, land shark, Bedouin, pirate, buccaneer, viking, corsair, privateer, rapparee, filibuster, wrecker, poacher, picaroon, plunderer, racketeer, highwayman, hijacker, pilferer, filcher, rifler, robber, thief, sharper, rustler, cattle lifter, looter, predator, assailant, desperado, holdup man, assaulter.

RAIL, *n.* Bar fixed horizontally for support, fence, railing, paling, barrier, banister, pale, wall, weir.

RAIL, *v.* Utter bitter complaint, denounce vehemently, scold, censure, upbraid, reproach, inveigh, exprobrate, vituperate, abuse, objurgate, rate, bark at, anathematize, vilify, vilipend, revile, backbite, fulminate against, declaim against, exclaim against, protest against, raise one's voice against, decry, scoff at, sneer at, animadvert upon, find fault with, depreciate, criticize, pick to pieces, take exception, cavil at, carp at, peck at, execrate, reprimand, castigate, blow up, lash, chastise, trounce, call to account, reprove, take to task, rebuke, recriminate, remonstrate, blame, impugn, reprobate, condemn, slate, disparage, discommend, speak ill of, lambaste, indulge in a tirade, harangue, jaw, rattle, spout, rant, mouth, bluster.

RAILER, *n.* Calumniator, reviler, detractor, reprover, censurer, censor, carper, caviler, critic, word catcher, cynic, slanderer, defamer, lampooner, backbiter, traducer, knocker, libeler, satirist, daw plucker, vituperator, disapprover, castigator, impugner, disparager, scold, shrew.

RAILING, *n.* 1. Barrier made of rails, banister, balustrade, baluster, rail, paling, fence, parapet, bar.

2. Abuse, vituperation, reproach, censure, invective, contumely, aspersion, reviling, scolding, upbraiding, obloquy, blame, disparagement, denunciation, condemnation, stricture, animadversion, objection, reflection, criticism, censoriousness, carping, faultfinding, increpation, reprobation, reprimand, jobation, fireworks (coll.), castigation, curtain lecture, dressing down, blow up, berating, jeremiad, diatribe, philippic, tirade, execration, exprobration, objurgation.

RAILLERY, *n.* Jesting language, banter, chaff, persiflage, badinage, slight ridicule, genteel irony, polite and ingenious derision, good-humored satire, satirical merriment, asteism, witty talk, pleasantry, joke, quip, squib, sarcasm, mockery, disparagement.

RAILROAD, *n.* Tracks for locomotive and cars, tramway, railway, line, artery for trains, switchback, funicular, third rail, El, rolling stock, chemin de fer (Fr.), ferrocarril (Sp.), ferrovia (It.), strada ferrata (It.), Eisenbahn (Ger.).

RAILROAD, *v.* 1. Push forward with great speed, accelerate, expedite, rush, hurry, hasten, quicken, make haste, make forced marches, speed up, whisk along, precipitate, urge on, goad ahead, spur on, dash off, put through with undue speed.

2. Imprison on a false charge, frame.

RAIMENT, *n.* Wearing apparel, attire, clothing, clothes, garments, vestments, habiliments, dress, vesture, garb, array, habit, costume, wardrobe, togs, duds (sl.), glad rags, toilette, robes, finery, trousseau, outfit, turnout, accouterment, rigging, livery, guise, drapery, palliament, things, garniture, tailoring, millinery, best bib and tucker, caparison, suit, trappings, traps, toggery.

RAIN, *n.* 1. Water condensed from the aqueous vapor in the atmosphere, rainfall, shower, cloudburst, downpour, rainstorm, precipitation, serein, drizzle, mizzle, sprinkle, mist, condensation, scud, plash, drencher, deluge, flood, waterspout, monsoon, bursat, driving rain, pouring rain, drenching rain.

2. Large quantity of anything falling thickly, outpouring, repletion, satiety, amplitude, lots, galore, abundance, fulness, fill, plenitude, plenty, copiousness, profusion, full measure.

RAIN, *v.* 1. Shower, pour, drizzle, mizzle, sprinkle, set in, spit (coll.), come down in buckets, rain pitchforks, rain cats and dogs, come down in sheets, rain in torrents, rain hard.

2. Abound, flow, teem, shower down, stream, exuberate, bristle with, swarm, pour in.

3. Give abundantly, bestow plenteously, offer freely, lavish, pour out, spend lavishly.

RAINBOW, *n.* Arc of prismatic colors appearing in the heavens opposite the sun and due to the refraction and reflection of the sun's rays in drops of rain, iris, bow of colors, weather gall, weather gaw, sundog, spectrum.

RAINBOW-LIKE, *adj.* Of all the colors in the rainbow, of all manner of colors, iridescent, kaleidoscopic, variegated, many-hued, multi-colored, parti-colored, versicolor, polychromatic, prismatic, opalescent, irisated, gorge de pigeon (Fr.), chatoyant (Fr.), varicolored, divers-colored, pleochroic, daedal, pavonine, cymophanous.

RAINCOAT, *n.* Waterproof coat worn for protection against rain, mackintosh, slicker, oilskin, waterproof, trench coat, rubber coat, Burberry, Aquascutum.

RAIN GAUGE, *n.* Instrument for measuring rainfall, pluviometer, pluviograph, hyetometer, hyetometrograph, udometer, ombrometer, ombrograph, udomograph.

RAINPROOF, *adj.* Waterproof, watertight, impervious to rain, proof against rain, dry, impermeable, impenetrable.

RAINY, *adj.* Showery, drizzly, mizzly, hyetal, pluvial, pluvious, drizzling, wet, moist, dripping, drippy, juicy (coll.), dirty (coll.), stormy, pluviose, stillicidous.

RAISE, *v.* 1. Move to a higher position, lift, elevate, heave, hoist, boost, uplift, make upright, upraise, raise up, set upright, upheave, lift aloft, jack up, pull up, haul up, pry up, tilt up, set up, prize, lever.

2. Set up the framework of, erect, build, rear, construct, fabricate, put together, establish, fashion, model.

3. Heighten, increase, enlarge, augment, enhance, ameliorate, aggravate, make higher, intensify, add to, greaten, magnify, double, reinforce, extend, exaggerate, inflate.

4. Promote in dignity, dignify, exalt, advance in rank, ennoble, aggrandize, honor.

5. Produce, grow, breed, beget, propagate, generate, cause to grow, bring up, nurture, nurse, cultivate, hatch, develop, foster.

6. Gather together, collect, muster, bring together, assemble, congregate, levy, rally, mobilize, convene.

7. Cause to rise by expansion, leaven, ferment, work, effervesce, pepsinate.

8. Excite, arouse, rouse, stir up, animate, incite, awake, wake, kindle, inspirit, stimulate, brew, goad, whet, sharpen, urge, fillip, instigate, spur, foster, foment, revive, resuscitate, bring back to life, raise from the dead, restore to life, summon up.

9. Cause to appear, give rise to, cause to arise, originate, bring about, effect, cause, produce, occasion, set going, start, put in action, put in motion.

RAJAH, *n.* Indian prince, king, monarch, ruler, chief, emir, nawab, nizam, negus, maharajah, nabob, dignitary, honorary title conferred on Hindus.

RAKE, *n.* 1. Man of pleasure, libertine, roué, debauchee, lecher, profligate, dissolute man, voluptuary, sensualist, hard liver, rip, loose fish, rakehell, fast man, fornicator, seducer, whoremonger, goat, satyr, adulterer, paillard (Fr.), Lothario, Don Juan, Casanova, prodigal, black sheep, vaurien (Fr.), wolf (colloq.).

2. Tined instrument for gathering together, broom, sweep, besom, whisk, wisp, brush, scraper, strigil.

3. Long sweep, strong pull, traction, draught, haul, towage.

RAKE, *v.* 1. Draw together, heap together, collect, gather, heap up, gather together, amass, lump together, mass, pile, round up, dredge, bunch, cram, pack, bundle, accumulate, agglomerate, group.

2. Comb, scrape, scratch, rasp, card, hackle, brush up, sweep, whisk, trim, tidy, pick, weed.

3. Scour industriously, search closely, ransack, rummage, explore, pry, peer, reconnoiter, scan, look round, spy, sound, seek, look for, survey, overhaul, unearth, ferret out, pursue, trace, leave no stone unturned.

4. Fire guns lengthwise on, enfilade, sweep.

RAKE-OFF, *n.* Unearned share of profits, illegitimate portion of profits, share of a sum involved, amount received illicitly, kickback, rebate, commission, fee, compensation.

RAKISH, *adj.* 1. Lewd, licentious, libidinous, debauched, dissipated, dissolute, depraved, lascivious, prurient, loose, fast, wanton, adulterous, immoral, lustful, lickerish, lip-licking, voluptuous, sensual, libertine, concupiscent, carnal, erotic, salacious, bawdy, pornographic, smutty, ribald, shameless, obscene, risqué, lecherous.

2. Smart, jaunty, dashing, dapper, spruce, trim, trig, debonair, chic, showy, gay, gallant, breezy, nonchalant, pococurante, airy, sprightly, natty, foppish, dandyish, coxcombical, silk-stocking, dandified.

RALE, *n.* Abnormal sound heard on auscultation of the chest indicative of the nature or stage of a disease, rhonchus, whistling sound, rattle, wheeze, bubbling sound indicating accumulation of fluid in the bronchial tubes, mucous râle, crepitant râle, râle redux, sonorous râle, subscrepitant râle, sibilant râle, cavernous râle, consonating râle, tracheal râle, death rattle.

RALLY, *v.* 1. Bring together again, reassemble, collect, reunite, gather, assemble, unite, draw together for common action.

2. Inspire courage, encourage, hearten, embolden, reassure, inspirit, stimulate, nerve, cheer, rouse, revive, brighten.

3. Be courageous, make bold, venture, dare, confront danger, brave danger, face danger, beard, meet, defy, take heart, pluck up courage, nerve oneself, present a bold front, face the music, show fight.

4. Recover strength, get better, acquire fresh strength, gain ground, recuperate, convalesce, pick up, improve, take a favorable turn, take a turn for the better, come round, pull through, weather the storm, get well.

5. Ridicule good-humoredly, satirize, treat with raillery, quiz, mock, taunt, deride, banter, chaff, twit, joke, poke fun at, jolly, rag, roast, fleer, parody, burlesque, caricature, travesty, make merry with, turn into ridicule, make game of.

RALLY, *n.* 1. Recovery from disorder, renewal of strength, resuscitation, revivification, reorganization, renaissance, renascence, rejuvenation, rebirth, rejuvenescence, regeneration, palingenesis, reconversion, resurgence, resurrection, recovery, convalescence, redintegration, rehabilitation, restoration, renovation, renewal, revivescence, revival.

2. Coming together of persons for common action, mass meeting, concourse, conflux, assemblage, mobilization, convergence, meet, muster, congregation, forgathering, reunion, caucus, convocation, convention, levee.

RALLYING CRY, *n.* Gathering word (*of a Highland clan in Scotland*), war cry, battle cry, alarum, trumpet signal, trumpet call, slogan.

RALLYING POINT, *n.* Gathering place, headquarters, rendezvous, haunt, resort, tryst, place of meeting, trysting place, *point de réunion (Fr.),* clubhouse, retreat.

RAM, *v.* 1. Strike with great force, dash violently against, run into, butt, batter, collide with, bump, crash, clash, hurtle, telescope, jostle, buffet, smash, twack, clip, wham, whack, thump, slam, jog, jolt, run against and sink.

2. Stuff, cram, compress, force in, crowd, stop, dam, drive, tamp, choke, throttle, plug, fill up, stuff up, barricade, blockade, constipate, squeeze.

3. Drive down by heavy blows, push firmly, force down, beat, thrust, poke, hammer, belabor, cudgel, strike, slap, hit.

RAM, *n.* 1. Male sheep, tup, Aries (*Zodiac*).

2. Device for battering *or* forcing, battering ram, rammer, pile driver, monkey, punch, tamping iron, tamper, bat, sledge-hammer, maul, mall, piston.

3. Man-of-war equipped with a heavy beak on its bow, iron-clad, turret-ship, floating battery, Monitor, Merrimac, "Old Ironsides," Constitution.

RAMBLE, *v.* 1. Stroll without definite aim *or* direction, wander about in a leisurely manner, take a course with many turns *or* windings, meander, straggle, range, rove, saunter, prowl, zigzag, roam, stray, drift, perambulate, deviate, detour, go round about, gad, jaunt, nomadize, gad about, peregrinate, divagate, hike, flit.

2. Talk discursively, write without sequence of ideas, digress, maunder, expatiate, be diffuse, rant, prose, pad, protract, beat about the bush, descant, dwell on, harp upon, amplify, enlarge, talk nonsense, blather, rave, talk at random, drivel, dote.

RAMBLE, *n.* A walk without a definite route, stroll, perambulation, round, turn about, wandering, roving, rambling, trip, excursion, tour, divagation, drift, jaunt, peregrination, circuit, outing, constitutional (*colloq.*), saunter, promenade, tramp, hike, wayfaring, vagabondage, gadding, flitting, flit.

RAMBLER, *n.* Straggler, vagrant, rover, wanderer, excursionist, stroller, roamer, gadabout, wayfarer, traveler, journeyer, tripper, tourist, migrant, hiker, leisurely walker, trekker, itinerant, peregrinator, landlouper, hobo, tramp, nomad, arab, gypsy, vagabond, bird of passage, scatterling, globetrotter, gadling, stray, beachcomber, peripatetic, noctambulist, somnambulist.

RAMBLING, *adj.* 1. Wandering about aimlessly, straggling, meandering, taking an irregular course, zigzagging, roving, itinerant, peripatetic, ambulatory, gadding, migratory, vagrant, circumforaneous, nomadic, wayfaring, perambulatory.

2. Irregular, uneven, erratic, capricious, fitful, unsystematic, aberrant, circuitous, indirect.

3. Straying from one subject to another, discursive, digressive, desultory, rhapsodical, disconnected, disjointed, incoherent, excursive, diffuse, prolix, maundering, periphrastic, circumlocutory, roundabout, ambagious, episodic.

RAMBUNCTIOUS, *adj.* 1. Noisy, boisterous, clamorous, obstreperous, stentorian, stentorophonic, rackety, uproarious, ear-splitting, enough to wake the dead, deafening, thundering, blustering, blatant, clangorous, turbulent, shrill, vociferant, vociferous, loud-mouthed.

2. Perverse, unruly, recalcitrant, restive, wayward, pervicacious, refractory, headstrong, con-

tumacious, *entêté (Fr.)*, unsubmissive, disobedient, insubordinate, ungovernable, impatient of control, self-willed, arbitrary, unyielding, unpersuadable, incorrigible, intractable, impervious to reason.

RAMIFICATION, *n.* 1. Configuration of branching parts, arborescence, divarication, radiation, forking, branching, arborization, divergency.

2. Branch, bough, offshoot, scion, twig, sprig, tendril, withe, switch, spray, sarmentum, runner, spur, link, joint, sprout, shoot.

RAMIFORM, *adj.* Having the form of a branch, branch-like, branched, dendriform, ramose, tree-shaped, arboriform, arborescent, dendroid, dendritic, dendroidal.

RAMIFY, *v.* 1. Cause to branch, separate into branches, spread out in branch-like parts, disbranch, divide, subdivide, detach, bisect, interpose between, dissociate.

2. Send forth shoots, extend by means of branches, shoot into branches, branch, divaricate, branch out, sprout, radiate, diverge, branch off, splay apart, spread like a network, be interlaced.

RAMMER, *n.* Stopper, plug, stopple, bung, cork, stopcock, spill, tap, spike, piston, ramrod, wadding, padding, stuffing, stopping, pledget, tampion, wad.

RAMOSE, *adj.* Having many branches, branching, ramous, branchy, arborescent, arboriform, dendriform, dendroid, dendroidal, tree-shaped, dendritic.

RAMP, *n.* Sloping surface connecting two different levels, inclined plane, sloping passageway between levels, incline, short slope, acclivity, grade, gradient, rise, ascent, declivity, devexity, dip, downhill, gentle slope, easy approach.

RAMP, *v.* 1. Stand on the hind legs, stand with forelegs raised, rear as if to spring, rear up.

2. Spring violently, act furiously, dash with fury, rage, storm, rampage, act violently, run amuck, run berserk.

3. Rush about excitedly, bound, spring, leap, gambol, romp, frolic, prance, sport, play, hop, cut capers, vault, skip, trip, caper, caracole, curvet, bob, flounce, foot it, bounce, frisk, jump about, buck.

RAMPAGE, *n.* Violent behavior, riotous action, boisterous excitement, wild agitation, dashing about with violence, ebullition, vehemence, bluster, turbulence, amok, rage, ferocity, berserk, fury, ferment, tempest, storm, turmoil, uproar.

RAMPAGEOUS, *adj.* Given to displays of recklessness, rampaging, noisily rampant, violent, unruly, wild, boisterous, uncontrollable, unrestrained, stormy, destructively frenzied, berserk, amuck, infuriate, ravening, fierce, savage, ferocious, excited, unbridled, vicious, turbulent, vehement, raging.

RAMPANCY, *n.* Exuberance, luxuriance, rankness, excessiveness, excess, wild unrestraint, extravagance, prevalence, predominance, preponderance.

RAMPANT, *adj.* 1. Growing without check, rank, luxuriant, exuberant, profuse, wanton, excessive, exceeding all bounds, unrestrained, wild, overabundant, lavish, extravagant.

2. Widespread, prevalent, predominant, rife, regnant, dominant, in the ascendant.

3. Standing on the hind legs, rearing the fore-

legs, ramping, *effrayé (Fr.)*, vertical, bolt upright, erect, standing up, perpendicular, attolent.

4. Licentious, lewd, lustful, libidinous, lickerish, prurient, lecherous, carnal, ruttish, concupiscent, lascivious, impassioned, erotic, salacious, voluptuous, debauched, adulterous, dissolute, rakish, incontinent, meretricious, gross, coarse, obscene, ribald, pornographic, bawdy.

5. Vehement, violent, vicious, wild, impetuous, turbulent, blustering, disorderly, raging, tumultuous, ravening, frenzied, infuriate, desperate, towering, frantic, outrageous, fierce, savage, ferocious, excited, unruly, unbridled, ungovernable, unmitigable, unappeasable, uncontrollable.

RAMPART, *n.* 1. Mound of earth raised as a fortification, embankment around a place on which the parapet is raised, protected elevation, acropolis, arx.

2. Protective barrier, barricade, barbican, redan, outwork, parapet, breastwork, circumvallation, protective wall, mole, defense, bulwark, fortification, security, fence, guard, vallum, muniment, parados, fieldwork, earthwork, gabions, contravallation, scarp, glacis.

RAMSHACKLE, *adj.* About to go to pieces from age and neglect, dilapidated, rickety, shaky, tumble-down, falling to pieces, unsteady, loose, loosely held together, loose-jointed, disjointed, out of repair, decrepit, infirm, tottering, crumbling, top-heavy, nodding to its fall.

RAMULOSE, *adj.* Having many small branches, composed of small branchlets, branchy, ramulous, minutely branched, ramose, ramous.

RANCH, *n.* Establishment for the grazing and rearing of livestock, horse and cattle farm, messuage, plantation, hacienda, dude ranch, stock-raising grange, *estancia (S. Amer.)*, stock farm.

RANCHMAN, *n.* Rancher, herdsman, ranchero, herder, cowboy, *vaquero (S. Amer.)*, cowpuncher, broncobuster, horse trainer, stock breeder, granger, neathered, cowherd, shepherd, drover, grazier, cowkeeper.

RANCID, *adj.* Strong-smelling, unpleasant to the taste, rank, sour, musty, stale-smelling, fusty, fetid, tainted, foul, reeky, noisome, putrid, malodorous, evil-smelling, contaminated, gamy, impure, fulsome, putrescent, stinking, noxious, decaying, mephitic, feculent, cloacal, rotten, saprogenous, reasty, frowsty, stercoraceous, ordurous, nasty, disgusting, disagreeable, offensive, bad, turned, graveolent, high, strong, sharp, moldy, carious, putrefactive.

RANCOR, *n.* Rankling resentment, bitter ill will, animosity, deep-seated hate, hatred, venom, spite, virulence, bile, spleen, gall, spitefulness, vindictiveness, revengefulness, enmity, malice, grudge, pique, umbrage, dudgeon, antipathy, hostility, ill-feeling, unfriendliness, malevolence, malignity, aversion, antagonism, hardness of heart, uncharitableness, harshness, ill-blood, acrimony, mordacity, acerbity, vengeance, retaliation, implacability, vengefulness, ruthlessness, vendetta, feud to the death, day of reckoning, eye for an eye, tooth for a tooth, full retribution, blood for blood.

RANCOROUS, *adj.* Spiteful, vindictive, vengeful, resentful, revengeful, malicious, implacable, retaliative, ruthless, remorseless, stony-hearted, relentless, malignant, malign, virulent, malevolent, bitter, acrimonious, unforgiving, deadly, invidious, hateful, caustic, mordacious, maleficent, envenomed, venomous, surly, sullen, cold-blooded, hard-hearted, feral, ferine, fell, truculent.

RANDOM, *adj.* Occurring without definite purpose, done without reason, chance, fortuitous, haphazard, casual, accidental, unexpected, stray, irregular, unintentional, aimless, unforeseen, unpremeditated, undesigned, contingent, adventitious, incidental, occasional, offhand, without definite method, indeterminate, provisional, chancy, adventive, causeless, unintended, not meant, unpurposed, promiscuous, indiscriminate, undirected, never thought of.

RANGE, *n.* 1. Series, tier, row, line, rank, file, chain, queue, string.

2. Extent, scope, compass, limit, sweep, reach, latitude, breadth, extension, prolongation, distance, bound, register, view, diversity, amplitude, command, ken, play, field, sphere, circuit, comprehension, room, stretch, area, margin, swing, elbowroom, headway, leeway, spread.

3. Cooking stove, kitchener, cookstove, oven, cooker, stove, brick oven, coal stove, gas stove, oil stove, electric stove, kitchen range.

RANGE, *v.* 1. Move through a region in all directions, stray, wander, ramble, stroll, cruise, course, roam, rove at large, straggle, traverse, pass over, explore, search, reconnoiter, scour.

2. Class in a particular group, classify systematically, rank, dispose in order, arrange, draw up in a line, set in a row, align, array, form into ranks.

3. Vary within certain limits, have range of operation, go in a certain direction, extend, run, bend, lie, correspond in direction.

RANGER, *n.* 1. Keeper, custodian, warden, *custos (Lat.),* jailer, warder, gaoler, castellan, turnkey, guard, watchdog, sentry, watch and ward, gamekeeper, concierge, coast guard, *guarda costa (It.).*

2. Rover, privateer, rapparee, picaroon, plunderer, buccaneer, freebooter, bandit, brigand, corsair, pirate, viking, dacoit, bushranger, marauder, depredator, pillager, spoiler, highwayman, footpad, knight of the road, poacher, smuggler, filibuster.

RANGY, *adj.* Slender and long-limbed, lanky, gangling, lank, spindling, spindly, scraggy, skinny, gaunt, attenuated, slim, weedy, scrawny, lean, macilent, rawboned, bareboned, extenuated, lean as a rake.

RANK, *adj.* 1. Growing with excessive luxuriance, exuberant, tall of growth, luxuriant, lush, overgrown, tropical, jungly, dense with vegetation, wild, high-growing, overabundant, strong in growth, vigorous, fertile, productive, rich, prolific, fructiferous.

2. Extreme, utter, sheer, gross, unmitigated, very great, flagrant, rampant, excessive, inordinate, extravagant, absolute, egregious, crass, arrant, downright, glaring, outrageous, preposterous, undue.

3. Rancid, strong-smelling, frowzy, musty, gamy, fetid, strong, malodorous, noxious, noisome, fusty, graveolent, putrid, sour, stale, tainted, reeky, foul, putrescent, stinking, rotten, reasty, turned, moldy, high, ill-smelling.

RANK, *n.* 1. Grade, class, order, degree, gradation, step, mark, point, rate, stage, standard, plane, pitch, height, caliber, strength, intensity, shade.

2. Row, line, file, tier, series, range, order, division, group, string, chain, queue.

4. Position, status, standing, station, condition, precedence, caste, *pas (Fr.),* place, grade, order, footing, situation, circumstances.

5. Blood, birth, quality, eminence, nobility, distinction, high degree, dignity, pre-eminence, *pur sang (Fr.),* high descent, aristocracy, peerage, optimates, prestige, front rank, birthright.

RANK, *v.* 1. Classify, arrange, class, dispose in suitable order, range, draw up in ranks, assign to a particular position, array, sort, assort, marshal, locate, station, distribute, categorize, group, place, assign places to, organize, allocate.

2. Have place, have rank, be ranked, take rank, be classed, be included, be counted in.

3. Take precedence of, precede, outrank, take the lead, have supremacy, have the advantage, be pre-eminent, go before, go ahead of, antecede, be anterior to, come first, forerun, head.

RANK AND FILE, *n.* 1. Body of an army exclusive of its officers, common soldiers, privates, private soldiers, troopers, cannon fodder, standing army, the line, militia, troops of the line, trainband, yeomanry, auxiliaries, volunteers, reserves, the expendables.

2. Commonalty, common people, low society, bourgeoisie, lower orders, masses, common herd, *profanum vulgus (Lat.),* the many, *hoc genus omne (Lat.),* proletariat, king Mob, man in the street, great unwashed, small fry, tagrag and bobtail, canaille, horde, rabblerout, chaff, *ignobile vulgus (Lat.),* commoners, plebeians.

RANKLE, *v.* 1. Fester, be inflamed, ulcerate, suppurate, reek, gather, putresce, putrefy.

2. Irritate, inflame, gall, chafe, fret, mortify, infest, pique, nettle, roil, rile.

RANKLING, *n.* 1. Festering, inflammation, putrefaction, putrescence, suppuration, decay, matter, pus, peccant humor.

2. Cancer, canker, ulcer, mortification.

3. Animosity, malevolence, hatred, resentment, heartburning, gall, spleen, bitterness, virulence, acerbity, acrimony, umbrage, pique, dudgeon, miff, huff, soreness, anger, displeasure, indignation, wrath, exasperation, vexation, irascibility, ill humor, irritation, bile, ferment, ire, choler, tiff, pet, dander, angry mood, pucker, *acharnement (Fr.),* rancor, venom, vindictiveness, vengeance, revenge, implacability.

RANSACK, *v.* 1. Pillage, plunder, rifle, sack, strip, loot, despoil, ravage, filibuster, spoil, burgle, forage, gut, poach, maraud, hijack, hold up, rustle, lift, thieve, pilfer, purloin, filch, crib *(colloq.),* pirate, steal, rob, bag, pinch *(sl.).*

2. Rummage through, explore vigorously, search thoroughly, seek everywhere, scour, rake through, pry, look round, scan, look for, reconnoiter, peer, sound, spy, look behind the scenes, overhaul, ferret out, nose out, hunt out, track down, leave no stone unturned, look into, investigate, scrutinize, probe.

RANSOM, *n.* 1. Deliverance, redemption, release, salvation, liberation, rescue, extrication, respite, reprieval, acquittance, manumission, emancipation, discharge, disenthralment, exemption, restoration.

2. Reparation, redress, indemnification, amends, restitution, atonement, compensation, requital, recompense, satisfaction, liquidation, expiation, propitiation, peace offering, atoning sacrifice.

RANSOM, *v.* 1. Redeem by paying a price demanded, buy off, extricate, rescue, save, make reparation for, pay for.

2. Set free, release on receipt of a ransom, liberate, free, deliver, emancipate, manumit, unchain, unfetter, unmanacle.

RANT, *v.* Vociferate, spout, rave in high-sounding phrases, declaim rhetorically, harangue, mouth, gabble, twaddle, exaggerate, hyperbolize, descant, speechify, flourish, boast, vaunt, brag, trumpet, vapor, crow over, exult, gloat, jubilate, talk big, rave, fume, foam, fly off at a tangent, strut and fret one's hour upon a stage.

RANT, *n.* Extravagant declamation, bombast, fustian, rodomontade, prose run mad, flowers of speech, flourish, rhetoric, turgescence, altiloquence, hyperbole, high coloring, exaggeration, balderdash, flummery, jabber, mere words, verbiage, twaddle, moonshine, fiddle-faddle, verbosity, wordiness, harangue, tirade, grandiloquence, multiloquence, histrionics, raving, brain storm, hysterics, heroics, vaporing, puffery, fanfaronade, gasconade, braggardism, braggadocio, bravado, jactitation, highfalutin, bluster, venditation, teratology, hot air *(sl.),* vox et praeterea nihil *(Lat.),* vociferation.

RAP, *n.* 1. Smart blow, quick knock, light stroke, thump, pat, whack, thwack, cuff, slap, fillip, tap, smack, dab, flap, clip, swat, poke, bat, jab, buffet, bang, slam, clout, hit, swipe, swap whop punch, pelt, lunge, thrust.

2. The least bit, a trifle, straw, fig, pin, bulrush, continental, button, halfpenny, feather, jot, pinch of snuff, fiddlestick, snap of the fingers, mite, sou, doit, cent, hoot, iota.

RAP, *v.* 1. Knock lightly, strike suddenly, buffet, clip, tap, slap, cuff, whack, thwack, wham, wallop, hit, thump, beat, bang, slam, punch, bat, hammer, ram, dash, batter, cudgel, belabor, flap, pat, dab.

2. Utter sharply, affirm vigorously, rap out, raise one's voice, lay down the law, assert roundly, lay stress on, emphasize, ejaculate, blurt out, vociferate.

RAPACIOUS, *adj.* 1. Preying, predatory, predacious, raptorial, ravening, ravenous, wolfish, lupine, marauding, plundering, pillaging, piratical, vulturine, cormorant.

2. Given to seizing for the satisfaction of greed, greedy, avaricious, grasping, extortionate, voracious, insatiable, covetous, insatiate, sordid, exacting, omnivorous, venal, mercenary, usurious.

RAPACITY, *n.* 1. Rapaciousness, voracity, voraciousness, ravenousness, omnivorousness, appetitiveness, appetite, bloodsucking, vampirism.

2. Greediness of grain, greed, avarice, avariciousness, avidity, graspingness, covetousness, cupidity, tenacity, venality, itching palm, *auri sacra fames (Lat.).*

3. Thievishness, exercise of plunder, depredation, direption, spoliation, marauding, plunder, pillage, sack, rapine, thievery, robbery, extortion, pilfering.

RAPE, *v.* 1. Ravish, defile, violate, debauch, force, ruin, deflower, seduce, attack, assault, abuse, ill-use, ill-treat, maltreat, stuprate, constuprate, molest, devirginate, corrupt, rob of virginity.

2. Seize and carry off by force, kidnap, abduct, impress, shanghai, crimp, spirit away, convey off, run away with, make off with, lay violent hands on, snatch.

RAPE, *n.* 1. Forcible violation of a woman, criminal ravishment, stupration, constupration, defilement, devirgination, defloration, seduction, abuse, molestation, ill-usage, maltreatment, enforced sexual intercourse.

2. Abduction, kidnapping, depredation, abstraction.

RAPID, *adj.* Quick, swift, fleet, fast, speedy, hasty, winged, hurried, posthaste, expeditious, brisk, lively, smart, spanking, light-footed, nimble, express, agile, active, eagle-winged, precipitate, cursory, impetuous, headlong, feverish, urgent, pushing, instant, prompt, spry, snappy, go-ahead, bustling, rushing, agitated, flying, galloping, electric, mercurial, telegraphic, light of heel, light-legged, quick as lightning, swift as an arrow, accelerated, volant.

RAPIDITY, *n.* 1. Swiftness, celerity, velocity, speed, agility, haste, quickness, rapidness, expeditiousness, expedition, fleetness, dispatch, promptitude, pernicity, fastness, nimbleness, activity, precipitancy, precipitation, acceleration, alertness, drive, bustle, flurry, scamper, scurry, scuttle, hustle, scramble, hurry, urgency, rush, clip, sprint, spurt, dash, flight, flying, race, canter, tantivy, gallop, run, sprint, swoop.

2. *(Metaphors)* Electricity, light, greased lightning, arrow, canon ball, dart, rocket, express train, telegraph, quicksilver, wind, hurricane, cyclone, torrent, flash, split second, thought, radio, race horse, courser, eagle, gazelle, antelope, doe, hare, grayhound, ostrich, swallow, squirrel, speed maniac, scorcher *(sl.),* Mercury, Hermes, Iris, Camilla, Ariel, Puck.

RAPIDLY, *adv.* Swiftly, expeditiously, fast, quickly, posthaste, briskly, by leaps and bounds, like a house afire, like blazes, apace, on eagle's wings, at full speed, in double-quick time, full gallop, tantivy, whip and spur, with rapid strides, *à pas de géant (Fr.), ventre à terre (Fr.),* in seven-league boots, under press of sail, *remis velisque (Lat.),* hastily, hurriedly, hotfoot, precipitately, hurry-skurry, helter-skelter, pell-mell, slap-dash, full-tilt, slap-bang, headlong, heels over head, amain, at a great rate, like a shot, as fast as one's legs will carry one, at the top of one's speed, in high gear, in full swing.

RAPIDS, *n.* Torrent, chute, shoot, dalles, current, tide race, undertow, vortex, whirlpool, maelstrom, eddy, gulf, reflux, indraught, undercurrent, gurge.

RAPIER, *n.* Sword with long pointed blade used only for thrusting, small sword, glaive, tuck, bilbo, skean, falchion, cutlass, claymore, creese, kris, Ferrara, Toledo, whinyard, brand, scimitar, cutlass, foil, halberd, yataghan.

RAPINE, *n.* Violent seizure and carrying off of the property of others, spoliation, pillage, plunder, depredation, direption, robbery, latrociny, abstraction, thievery, theft, sackage, sack, brigandage, razzia, foray, highway robbery, privateering, piracy, buccaneering, cattle-rustling, filibustering, shoplifting.

RAPPAREE, *n.* Armed freebooter, plunderer, robber, desperado, bandit, thief, marauder, depredator, brigand, pillager, corsair, dacoit, viking, pirate, buccaneer, filibuster, privateer, thug, picaroon, wrecker, poacher, smuggler, highwayman, racketeer, footpad.

RAPPORT, *n.* Harmonious relation, sympathetic connection, intimate accord, close understanding, mutual dependence, affinity, conformity, harmony, agreement, correspondence, accordance, compatibility, sympathy.

RAPPROCHEMENT, *n.* Act of being drawn together, state of cordial relations, state of reconciliation, restoration of cordial relations, mutual friendliness, *réunion (Fr.),* reciprocity, amity, *entente cordiale (Fr.),* alliance, good understanding, league, unanimity, bonds of harmony, happy family, unison, unity, fraternization, fellow-feeling, *camaraderie (Fr.),* goodwill.

RAPSCALLION, *n.* One outside of social recognition, outcast, pariah, miscreant, scapegrace, mean wretch, scamp, good-for-nothing, *vaurien (Fr.), Taugenichts (Ger.),* scalawag, ne'er-do-well, black sheep, vagabond, caitiff, reprobate, rascal, scoundrel, rogue, blackguard, villain, knave, roué, rip, rake, fallen angel, *âme damnée (Fr.),* recreant, castaway, prodigal, misdemeanant, delinquent, malefactor, outlaw, varlet.

RAPT, *adj.* Deeply engrossed, absorbed, entranced, enraptured, transported with emotion, fascinated, enchanted, spellbound, ecstatic, inspired, ravished, struck all of a heap, delighted, in a quiver, charmed, rapturous, dreamy, bemused, preoccupied, intent on, dreaming, abstracted, wistful, contemplative, pensive, in a reverie, thoughtful, meditative, daydreaming, moonraking, enrapt, moonstruck, bewitched.

RAPTORIAL, *adj.* Preying upon other animals, predatory, predacious, rapacious, predal, predatorial, furtive, furacious, ravenous, ravening, prehensile, adapted for seizing prey.

RAPTURE, *n.* Great happiness, heavenly joy, transport, joyful ecstasy, bliss, enchantment, ravishment, transport, beatification, beatitude, exaltation, rhapsody, delight, enthusiasm, fervor, infatuation, gratification, felicity, elysium, paradise, *summum bonum (Lat.),* seventh heaven, halcyon days, extreme pleasure, oblectation, devotion, passion, adoration, idolatry.

RAPTUROUS, *adj.* Filled with delight, blessed, happy, blissful, beatified, thrice happy, *ter quaterque beatus (Lat.),* in paradise, in a blissful state, entranced, in a transport of delight, in ecstasies, ecstatic, enchanted, overjoyed, enraptured, transported, enravished, captivated, fascinated, ensorceled, radiant, with sparkling eyes, enamored, smitten, charmed, over head and ears in love, amorous, ardent, fervent, passionate, devoted, perfervid, joyful, blest.

RARA AVIS *(Lat.),* Rare bird, rarity, one in a thousand, rare thing, curiosity, tidbit, a wonder, phenomenon, prodigy, unusual thing, great card, gem of the first water, masterpiece, chef d'oeuvre, nonesuch, nonpareil, cynosure, paragon, article of virtu, curio, bibelot, *bizarrerie (Fr.),* oddity, *lusus naturae (Lat.),* freak, marvel, miracle.

RARE, *adj.* 1. Having the component parts not closely compacted together, thin, tenuous, subtile, attenuated, rarefied, fine, compressible, light, flimsy, slight, unsubstantial, uncompressed, uncompact, airy, porous.

2. Meagerly distributed over an area, few and widely separated, thinly scattered, sparse, hard to find, existing in small quantities, scarce, dispersed, sparing, unabundant, sporadic, spread here and there, infrequent, scant, few, occasional.

3. Seldom to be met with, out of the way, often sought after, recherché, exceptional, unwonted, thousand-to-one, uncommon, singular, extraordinary, unusual, strange, unique, uncustomary,

unaccustomed, odd, curious, noteworthy, remarkable, unfamiliar, out of the beaten track, out of the common run.

4. Excellent, choice, incomparable, fine, inimitable, exquisite, admirable, peerless, unexampled, select, matchless, unparalleled, unprecedented, *sui generis (Lat.),* original, capital, estimable, golden, precious, priceless, gilt-edged, invaluable, of the first water, top-hole, unequaled.

5. Nearly raw, *saignant (Fr.),* not thoroughly cooked, underdone, moderately done, imperfectly cooked, red.

RAREFY, *v.* Make rarer, make less gross, make less dense, attenuate, thin, make thin, subtilize, dilute, refine, purify, make porous, clear, clarify, depurate, spiritualize, cleanse, adulterate, water, volatilize, vaporize, aerify, aerate.

RARELY, *adv.* 1. On rare occasions, not often, infrequently, seldom, hardly, scarcely, unoften, scarcely ever, hardly ever, uncommonly, only occasionally, sporadically, once in a blue moon, once in a great long while.

2. Remarkably well, exceptionally, in an unusual degree, excellently, finely.

RARITY, *n.* 1. Rareness, thinness, tenuousness, attenuation, rarefaction, ethereality, subtility, etherealness, subtlety, tenuity.

2. Rare occurrence, infrequency, uncommoness, seldomness, fewness, sparseness, sporadicalness, unwontedness, singularity, scarcity, paucity.

3. Scarce thing, uncommon thing, rara avis *(Lat.),* rare bird, unusual object, phenomenon, wonder, sight, marvel, curiosity, curio, spectacle, article of virtu, knickknack, bric-a-brac, bibelot, object of art, *objet d'art (Fr.).*

RASCAL, *n.* Rapscallion, miscreant, misdoer, malfeasor, felon, recreant, bounder *(coll.),* rakehell, delinquent, scamp, reprobate, villain, knave, rogue, vagrant, scalawag, blackguard, varlet, scoundrel. *(See also* CROOK, n.)

RASCALITY, *n.* Profligacy, chicanery, knavery, trickery, treachery, baseness, wickedness, dishonesty, culpability, guile, villainy, blackguardism, varletry, improbity, disreputability, roguery, knavishness.

RASH, *adj.* Acting too hastily *or* without consideration, characterized by *or* showing too great haste, madcap, heady, careless, reckless, headlong, headstrong, heedless, thoughtless, imprudent, precipitate, unadvised, injudicious, imprudent, indiscreet, impulsive, incautious, devil-may-care, irresponsible, premature, harum-scarum, impetuous, sudden, adventurous, harebrained, hot-brained, hot-headed, foolhardy, unwary, precipitous, foolish, unthinking, indiscreet, brash, unbridled, unchecked, abrupt, frantic, hotspur, passionate, immature, hurried, aimless, breakneck, excited, impulsive, impetuous, subitaneous, uncontrolled, ungoverned, feverish.

RASH, *n.* Eruption, efflorescence on the skin, breaking-out, exanthema *(Pathol.),* pox, hives, nettle rash, tetter, eczema *(Pathol.),* dartre *(Med.),* herpes *(Med.),* lichen *(Pathol.),* impetigo *(Pathol.),* urticaria *(Pathol.),* psoriasis *(Pathol.).*

RASHER, *n.* Slice *(of pork or bacon),* cut, thin piece, chip, shaving.

RASP, *n.* 1. Rasping sound, squeak, screak, crick, scratch, squawk, cronk, croak, creak, stridulation.

2. Coarse file, toothed *or* threaded tool for initial smoothing, grater, grinder.

RASP, *v.* 1. Scrape with a rough instrument, abrade, rub down, scratch, grind, rub roughly, file coarsely.

2. Grate harshly upon, rub the wrong way, offend, vex, irritate *(the nerves, feelings, etc.)*, try the patience, jar, jangle, set one's teeth on edge, sting, burn, cut, gall, nettle, rack, chafe, fret, stab, agonize, wring, prick, harrow, excruciate, kill by inches, afflict, affront.

3. Utter with a grating sound, scrape, scratch, grind, crunch, talk hoarsely, creak, grate, croak, cronk, sound harshly, caw, bray, jar, clash, buzz, jangle, snore, saw, squeak, squawk, crick, stridulate.

RASPING, *adj.* Harsh, grating, creaking, stertorous, jarring, twanging, grinding, clashing, dissonant, strident, hoarse, cacophonous, scratching, husky, croaking, gruff, raucous, absonant, squawking, jangling, grum, guttural.

RATABLE, *adj.* 1. Capable of being rated *or* appraised, estimable, to be rated, assessable, appraisable, measurable, mensurable, gaugeable, determinable, evaluable, appreciable, computable.

2. Proportional, proportionable, proportionate, *pro rata (Lat.)*, correspondent, comparable, akin, like, parallel, relative, similar, fair, to scale, equivalent, analogous, commensurable, commensurate, compatible, similar.

RATCHET, *n.* Toothed bar with which a pawl engages, mechanism consisting of ratchet and pawl, click, detent, pawl, ratch, sprocket wheel, catch, quoin *(Print.)*, cogwheel.

RATE, *n.* 1. Amount of a charge *or* payment, fare, hire, cost, price, expense, quotation, figure, assessment, fee, quotation, commission, dues, freightage, truckage, duty, wharfage, brokerage, towage, expenditure, capitation, custom, obligation, outlay, payment, toll, tollage, tax, poll.

2. Degree *(of speed, progress, etc.)*, comparative extent of action *or* procedure, proportion, ratio, relative speed, *etc.*, pace, flow, gradient, scale, scope, intensity, swiftness, quickness, acceleration, length, distance, quota, gait, rapidity, celerity, movement, velocity, motion, tread, range, stretch, span, mileage, footage, yardage, clip *(coll.)*.

3. Assigned position in a series of graded classes, rating, classification, standing, gradation, station, class, estimate, rank, value, valuation, worth, pitch, allowance, esteem, degree of precedence, order of importance.

RATE, *v.* 1. Estimate the value *or* worth of; fix at a certain rate *(as of charge or payment)*, class, reckon, compute, price, weigh, rank, count, gauge, meter, account, size up *(coll.)*, quantify, set a value on, appraise, value, evaluate, measure, prize, calculate, assess, appreciate.

2. Have value *or* standing, *etc.*, have position in a certain class, count, figure, glow, glitter, shine, have prestige, be distinguished, make a mark, flourish, be important, deserve *or* merit notice *or* regard, tell, weigh, carry weight, cut a figure, signify, import, be indispensable, be invaluable, be valuable, make a splash *(coll.)*.

3. Scold, asperse, reprimand, chide, censure, blame, berate, reprove, find fault with, abuse, vilify, traduce, upbraid, lash, lecture, contemn, remonstrate, carp at, charge, declaim against, attack, denounce, animadvert, condemn, fulminate against, arraign, decry, inveigh against, reprehend, incriminate, proscribe, disparage, deprecate, inculpate.

RATHER, *adv.* 1. In a measure, to a certain extent, in some measure, somewhat, slightly, fairly, moderately, a bit, after a fashion, in reason, within bounds, quite, pretty, very, more or less, tolerably, kind of *(coll.)*, sort of *(coll.)*, in some degree.

2. More properly *or* justly, with better reason, the sooner, the more so, to be exact, accurately, exactly, precisely, instead, especially, strictly speaking, more correctly speaking.

3. Preferably, more readily, more willingly, sooner, in preference, by choice, first.

RATIFY, *v.* Confirm *(by expressing consent, approval or formal sanction)*, consent to, make valid, agree to, approve, indorse, seal, substantiate, establish, bear out, insure, guarantee, underwrite, corroborate, make good, bear witness to, sustain, warrant, settle firmly, certify, quote, testify to, accede, acknowledge, acquiesce, uphold, second, OK., subscribe to, bind, sanction, affirm, vouch for, pass.

RATING, *n.* 1. Classification according to grade *or* rank, assignment, designation, relegation, consignment, rank, disposition, grade, sort, status, denomination, sphere, degree, station, class, standing, footing, state, remove, position, place, mark, valuation, evaluation, estimation, assessment, appraisal, accounting, weight.

2. Angry reprimand *or* rebuke, reproval, lashing, scolding, objurgation, upbraiding, remonstrance, reprehension, exprobration, nagging, castigation, lecture, setdown, reproof, chiding, diatribe, philippic, jeremiad, tongue-lashing, piece *or* bit of one's mind, expostulation, dressing-down *(coll.)*, bawling out *(sl.)*, roasting *(coll.)*, abuse, calling down *(sl.)*, going-over *(coll.)*, contumely, invective, jobation *(coll.)*.

RATIO, *n.* Proportional relation, quotient, proportion, rate, fixed relation, percentage, quota, degree, share, adaptation of parts, balance, weight, correlation, distribution, adjustment, correspondence, arrangement, relative estimate, perspective, contrast, opposition.

RATIOCINATE, *v.* Reason, rationalize, intellectualize, logicize, infer, derive, speak logically, deduce, examine, think, excogitate, cerebrate, cogitate, syllogize, philosophize.

RATIOCINATION, *n.* Reasoning, science of inference, induction, thought, deduction, argumentation, logic, thinking, syllogization, dialectics, epistemology, epagoge, analysis, rationalization, synthesis.

RATION, *n.* Portion *(of food or drink)*, fixed allowance, share, meed, dole, measure, allotment, provision, mess, quota, part, piece, pittance, ratio, proportion, modicum.

RATION, *v.* 1. Distribute proportionally, apportion, deal out, dole out, partition, allocate, disperse, appoint, mete, deal, dole, split, detail, share, carve, allot, assign, divide, appropriate, parcel, dispense.

2. Put on rations, restrict to rations, supply, stock, provide for, circumscribe, feed, limit, victual, furnish, provender, distribute to, put on a diet.

RATIONAL, *adj.* 1. Reasonable, sensible, of sound judgment *or* good sense, exercising reason, just, right, intelligent, sapient, fair, moderate, agreeable to reason, wise, humane, cool, discreet, prudent, circumspect, politic, level-headed, impartial, bright, knowing, understanding, subtle, sage, thoughtful, analytical, reflective, philosophic, discerning, perspicacious, far-sighted, enlightened, well-advised, discriminating, judicious, logical, ratiocinative, objective, intellectual.

2. Endowed with the faculty of reason, intelligent, percipient, ratiocinative, perceiving, cerebral, cognitive, reasoning, thinking, mental, conscious.

3. Sane, lucid, in one's right mind, sound, sober, in possession of one's faculties *or* senses, conscious, responsible, reasonable, normal, clear-headed, right-minded, compos mentis *(Law)*, all there *(sl.)*.

4. Proceeding *or* derived from reason, based on reasoning, judicious, enlightened, discreet, intelligent, sage, wise, advisable, logical, fit, proper, right, just, reasonable, humane, normal, equitable, thoughtful, far-sighted, deductive, subtle, possible, plausible, justifiable, probable, credible, understandable, sensible, sagacious, philosophic, philosophical, well-grounded, well-founded, inferential, inferable, legitimate, wholesome, admissible, discerning.

RATIONALE, *n.* Statement of reasons, exposition, reason, cause, solution, ascription, ground, account, basis, theory, hypothesis, attribution, interpretation, motivation, explication, motive, definition, the why and the wherefore, key, exegesis, elucidation.

RATIONALISM, *n.* Principle *or* habit of accepting reason as supreme authority *(in matters of opinion, belief or conduct)*, humanism, dialecticism, logic, skepticism, materialism, nullifidianism, analysis, induction, deduction.

RATIONALIZE, *v.* 1. Employ reason, think in a rational *or* rationalistic manner, think logically, reason, cogitate, cerebrate, excogitate, mentalize, intelligize, intellectualize, reflect, deliberate, speculate, logicize, syllogize, philosophize, try conclusions, ratiocinate, contemplate.

2. Make rational *or* conformable to reason, treat *or* explain in a rational *or* rationalistic manner, remove unreasonable elements from, reconcile, make acceptable, account for, explain away, logicize, logicalize, attribute, assume, vindicate, justify, make allowance for, put a gloss upon, give good reason for, make excuses for, excuse, construe, whitewash, color, put a good face upon.

RATTLE, *n.* 1. Rapid succession of sharp clattering sounds, noise, racket, clatter, chatter, rattling, din, clack, clamor, clutter.

2. Instrument with which a rattling sound is made, noisemaker, clapper, ticktack, clack, clacker, bones, rattlebox, castanets, whizzer, bullroarer, razzle-dazzle.

RATTLE, *v.* 1. Make a rapid succession of short sharp noises, clack, chatter, clutter, clatter, clank, clink, jar, roll loosely.

2. Move *or* proceed with a clatter, racket, clang, clangor, blunder, bluster, brawl, clack, clank, bang.

RATTLE-BRAINED, *adj.* Harebrained, flighty, giddy, rattle-headed, foolish, unthinking, scatter-brained, empty-headed, rattlepated, forgetful, puerile, unsteady, wild, reckless, headlong, rash, careless, volatile, harum-scarum *(coll.)*, changeable, vagrant, capricious, foolhardy, flustered, unsettled, changeful, quixotic, heedless, silly, unstable, frivolous, inconstant, variable, crazy *(coll.)*, slap-happy *(sl.)*, undependable, addlepated, erratic, unreliable, scatterbrained, bird-witted, light-minded, barmy-brained, fickle, feverish, fire-eat-

ing, bemused, woolgathering, befuddled, mercurial, irresponsible, rantipole, featherbrained, barmy, hasty, punch-drunk, incautious, improvident, imprudent, indiscreet, wanton, madcap, devil-may-care, hot-headed, impetuous, precipitate, absent-minded, confused, muddle-headed, bewildered, impulsive, preoccupied.

RATTLETRAP, *n.* Rickety rattling vehicle, jalopy, wreck, heap *(sl.)*, hot rod *(sl.)*.

RAUCOUS, *adj.* Hoarse, harsh, strident, discordant, husky, rough, cacophonous, piercing, grating, jarring, twanging, atonal *(Mus.)*, grinding, sour, rasping, dissonant, scratching, shrill, croaking, unharmonious, creaking, unmusical, gruff, absonant, stridulatory, squawking, jangling, ear-piercing, grum, guttural, blatant, ear-splitting, loud, sharp, acute, blaring, braying, dry, cracked, stertorous.

RAVAGE, *n.* 1. Violently destructive action, ill-treatment, pillage, rapine, robbery, spoliation, foray, ravishment, raid, depredation, brigandage, piracy, larceny, theft, devastation, marauding, prey, deprivation, desolation, privateering, buccaneering, harrying, freebooting, sack, pilfering, plunderage, ravin.

2. Damage, ruin, devastation, havoc, waste, desolation, destruction, wreck, impairment, loss, injury, harm, hurt, detriment, outrage, inroad, violation, collapse, breakdown, privation, bereavement.

RAVAGE, *v.* Lay waste, plunder, lay in ruins, impair, spoil, ruin, waste, destroy, despoil, sack, pillage, harry, overrun, consume, strip, desolate, ransack, devastate, maraud, smash, overthrow, demolish, crush, raze, shatter, wrest, foray, prey, rob, forage, spoliate, raid, pirate, depredate, seize, capture, gut, loot.

RAVE, *v.* 1. Talk irrationally *(as in delirium)*, be delirious, wander, utter, ramble, babble, drivel, be mad, rage, rant, have a demon *or* devil, dote, fume, foam *or* froth at the mouth.

2. Utter in madness *or* frenzy, rage, storm, sputter, burn, simmer, thunder, fulminate, fume, be furious, be angry, be mad, be wild, tear, foam, seethe, boil, bluster, explode, run *or* go amuck, be hysterical, become excited, lose one's temper, flare up, flame up, fire up, burst into flame, break out, work oneself up, fly into a passion, fly off the handle *(sl.)*, quiver *or* swell with rage, blow one's top *(sl.)*.

3. Talk with excessive enthusiasm, praise excessively, speak glowingly, thrill, romanticize, let one's imagination run wild, idealize, rhapsodize, rant, be loquacious, glow, gush, be vehement *or* ardent, enlarge, harangue, amplify, dilate, expand, expatiate.

RAVEL, *v.* 1. Become untwisted (unwoven, unwound), untwist, unravel, unweave, unwind, undo, fray, unroll, take apart, comb, card, separate, unbind, loose, unloose, divide, loosen, disconnect, disjoin, disengage, untie.

2. Disentangle, make plain, solve, straighten out, unriddle, resolve, decipher, disembroil, simplify, systematize, classify, elucidate, sift, winnow, decode, explain, get to the bottom of, figure out, unravel, work out, fathom, puzzle out, organize, disinvolve, clear up.

RAVEN, *adj.* Black, ebony, sable, pitch-black, pitchy, coaly, nigrine, nigrous, inky, jet-black.

RAVEN, *v.* Devour eagerly, prey with rapacity, feed greedily, gulp, plunder, glut, eat with voracity, be *or* become ravenous, hunger, covet, crave, lust after, itch for, pant for, grasp at, catch at, be gluttonous, indulge one's appetite, gluttonize, gormandize, gorge gobble, bolt, wolf, hanker after, run mad after, long for, gasp for.

RAVENOUS, *adj.* 1. Voracious, rapacious, violent, mad, ravening, furious, predatory, insatiable, taking, grasping, looting, privative, wolfish, keen, fierce, devouring, insatiate, lupine, plundering, predacious, thieving, all-devouring, parasitic, exacting, furtive, furacious, extortionate, piratical, spoliative, raptorial *(Zool.)*, ferocious.

2. Eager for food (satisfaction, gratification), greedy, gluttonous, open-mouthed, hungry, craving, omnivorous, insatiable, devouring, covetous, grasping, hoggish, piggish, swinish, Apician, edacious, crapulent, crapulous, insatiate, gormandizing, unquenchable.

RAVIN, *n.* 1. Rapine, rapacity, rapaciousness, plunder, destruction, pillage, ravage, spoliation, ravishment, foray, raid, depredation, brigandage, piracy, larceny, theft, devastation, marauding, prey, desolation, deprivation, harrying, freebooting, plunderage, pilfering, sack, buccaneering, privateering, robbery.

2. Plunder, prey, goods obtained by violence, loot, booty, pilferings, perquisites, prize, gain, spoil *or* spoils, pillage, seizure, take, grab, pickings, steal *(coll.)*, swag *(sl.)*, haul *(coll.)*.

RAVINE, *n.* Depression worn out by running water, chasm, gorge, flume, notch, cut, gap, channel, trench, clough, cleft, defile, gulch, gully, pass, dell, arroyo *(Sp.)*, barranca *(Sp.)*.

RAVING, *adj.* Talking wildly *or* irrationally, delirious, frenzied, beside oneself, frenetic, violent, stormy, raging, rabid, impassioned, wild, frantic, distracted, fiery, fuming, seething, distraught, overwrought, amuck, maniacal, mad, hysterical, wandering, angry, deranged, boisterous, irrational, foaming *or* frothing at the mouth, off one's head, fitful, haggard, wild-eyed, out of one's head *or* mind, tempestuous, furious, fierce, feverish, harrowed, ranting, demoniac, agitated, carried away, rambling, incoherent, flighty, doting.

RAVING, *n.* Irrational, wild *or* extravagant utterance, furor, frenzy, fury, vehemence, passion, rage, hysterics, paroxysm, ranting, fit, delirium, turbulence, madness, incoherence, outburst, anger, brain fever, distraction, wandering, towering rage *or* passion, tempestuousness, phrenitis *(Med.)*, raging violence, fever.

RAVISH, *v.* 1. Seize and carry away by violence, snatch, kidnap, abduct, wrest, hook, grab, catch, capture, apprehend, take by assault *or* storm, make *or* run off with, crimp, impress, shanghai, spirit away, lay *or* clap hands on, bear away, collar *(coll.)*, nab *(sl.)*, nip.

2. Transport with emotion *(esp. joy or delight)*, enchant, captivate, enrapture, delight, enravish, tickle, titillate, rapture, allure, bewitch, gladden, enamor, charm, enthrall, attract, fascinate, rejoice, cheer, warm the cockles of one's heart, do one's heart good, overjoy, entrance, electrify.

3. Abduct *(a woman)*, seduce, rape, commit rape upon, dishonor, outrage, defile, deflower, violate, ruin, prostitute, take by force, debauch, abuse, force, stuprate.

RAW, *adj.* 1. In *or* nearly in the natural state, uncooked, little changed by art, unwrought, crude, rough, unrefined, unpolished, green, unripe, fal-

low, undressed, undigested, rare, underdone, unbaked.

2. Untrained, unfinished, not prepared for use *or* enjoyment, inexperienced, unseasoned, untried, fresh, new, crude, green, immature, young, tender, youthful, unrefined, uninured, unhabituated, callow, unripe, unpracticed, unfledged, uncivilized, undisciplined, rookie *(sl.)*, inept, unskilled, unaccustomed, artless, unconversant, amateurish, ignorant, uninitiated, undeveloped, half-baked *(coll.)*, half-cooked *(coll.)*, not dry behind the ears *(joc.)*.

3. Deprived of skin, galled, bare, sore, skinned, open, exposed, excoriated, sensitive, chafed, rubbed, irritated, painful.

4. Cold, bleak, damp, chilly, piercing, inclement, cutting, biting, bitter, pinching, numbing, keen, freezing, squally, blustery, nipping, exposed, windswept.

5. Indelicate, coarse, crude, uncouth, graceless, boorish, crass, uncivil, barbaric, barbarous, unpolished, rough, brutish, gaudy, garish, flashy, churlish, loutish, rough-hewn, roughcast, uncultured, uncultivated.

RAWBONED, *adj.* Having little flesh, gaunt, spare, lank, lanky, lean, scrawny, haggard, attenuated, macilent, spindling, spindly, scraggy, bony, wizened, thin, poor, starveling, gangling, spindle-shanked, spindle-legged, emaciated, withered, pinched, starved, shriveled, meager.

RAY, *n.* 1. Line of light which appears to radiate from a bright object, gleam, shaft, beam, radiance, radiation, pencil, stream, glimmer, streak, patch, glitter, blink, sparkle, scintilla, glint, blaze, twinkle, flicker, flame, flash, streamer, luster, spark, emanation, irradiation.

2. Perception, sight, vision, glance, glimpse, flash, peep, cast, look, eyeshot, apprehension, notice, glimmer, flicker *or* twinkle of an eye, peek, view, inspection, squint, survey, ogle, stare, observance, gaze, espial, half an eye, ken, discernment, descrial, detection.

3. Small amount, particle, iota, scintilla, bit, scrap, trace, speck, doit, morsel, grain, atom, mite, modicum, whit, tittle, straw, snip, spot, snippet, ounce.

RAYLESS, *adj.* Destitute of rays, dark, blind, sunless, dismal, dull, somber, obscure, uniluminated, Cimmerian, darksome, lightless, overcast, nubilous, umbrageous, turbid, gloomy, murky, shadowy, cloudy, funereal, dusky, black, moonless, starless, tenebrous, caliginous, overshadowed, unlighted, shrouded, nebulous.

RAZE, *v.* 1. Scrape, graze, wound slightly, rub, skim, skin, glance, grate, brush, rub, abrade, abrase, gall, chafe, grind, scratch, file, rasp, friction, affricate.

2. Erase, scrape off, cut off, shave off, wipe out, sponge off, obliterate, remove, efface, cancel, rub out, blot, expunge, dele *(Print.)*.

3. Overthrow, destroy, level, ruin, break down, wreck, scatter, fell, demolish, subvert, tumble, annihilate, exterminate, capsize, spill, precipitate, topple, flatten, pull down, tear down, batter down, knock *or* cast down, dismantle, smash, reduce.

REACH, *n.* 1. Act of reaching, stretch, clutch, effort, strain, aspiration, hold, grasp.

2. Extent, stretch, distance, spread, span, space, range, compass, expanse, degree, scope, limit, bounds, jurisdiction, precinct, purview, capacity, orbit, circuit, orb, vicinage, purlieu, function, circumscription, latitude, field, zone, scale, ter-

ritory, stint, height, sphere, area, round, sweep, amplitude, measure, swing, margin, demesne, premises, realm, part, width, breadth, length, room, gamut *(Music)*.

3. Promontory, tongue of land, level stretch, plain, champaign, open country, flat, point of land, spit, foreland, spur, headland, isthmus, strip, head, peninsula, plateau, moor, heath, tundra, savanna, prairie, field, lowland, tableland, veld *or* veldt, steppe, down.

4. Arm of the sea *(extending up into the land)*, inlet, cove, mouth, creek, estuary, bayou, lagoon, strait, narrow *or* narrows, firth, fiord.

5. Extent *or* range of force, capacity, *etc.*, earshot, authority, carrying distance, jurisdiction, influence, penetration, dominion, dominance, sound, command, sway, rule, power, grasp, control, clutches, grip, sovereignty, talons, mastery, administration, government.

REACH, *v.* 1. Extend, stretch out, thrust out, strain after something, make an effort, outstretch, outreach, grab at, elongate, catch at, snatch at, clutch at.

2. Strike, hit, touch, grasp, seize, attain, extend to, go as far as, go to, be level with, spread to, range, equal, approach, parallel, lead to, neighbor, impinge upon, abut on *or* upon, be contiguous to, adjoin, contact, conjoin, border on, come to, match.

3. Arrive at, come to, get to, make, overtake, attain, gain, set foot in *or* on, land at *or* on, enter, put in *or* into *(Naut.)*.

4. Influence, impress, excite, arouse, touch, affect, move, interest, stimulate, strike, hit the mark, kindle, stir, quicken, waken, whet, fire, awake, awaken, warm, penetrate to, come home to, animate, impassion, inspirit.

5. Communicate with, get through to, meet, get in touch with, commune, hold intercourse *or* converse, correspond with, transfer ideas to, commerce with, convey thought to, contact *(coll.)*.

REACT, *v.* 1. Act *(on or upon)* in turn *or* in return, act reciprocally, exert a return (reciprocal, counteracting) influence, counteract, counterwork, counterbalance, offset, conflict, reciprocate, retaliate, match, cap, top, give in exchange, repay, requite, have play, return, act in response *(as to a stimulus, influence, reagent)*, respond, be affected, reply, get back at, hit back at, come back at.

2. Show a reaction *or* reverse trend, turn back to a prior condition, revert, return, rebound, recede, recoil, retrovert, retrocede, retrograde, regress, retrogress, retreat, back out *or* down, relapse, retire, withdraw, back up, back, draw back, ebb, backslide, slip *or* sink back, shy, right-about-face, renege *(coll.)*, draw *or* pull in one's horns.

3. *(Loosely)* Act *(esp. under particular circumstances)*, behave, operate, function, move, work, play, respond, proceed, comport oneself *or* itself, conduct oneself *or* itself, take *or* adopt a course.

REACTION, *n.* 1. Reciprocal *or* return action *or* influence, reverse action, counter tendency, opposition, compensation, antagonism, resistance, retroaction, contradiction, counterpoise, counterbalance, neutralization, offset, boomerang, renitence, reprisal, exchange, like for like, measure for measure, recalcitration, tit for tat, a Roland for an Oliver, an eye for an eye, give-and-take, blow for blow.

2. Movement toward a former *(political or social)* policy, return, recoil, retroversion, reversion, revulsion, retreat, recession, reversal, relapse, res-

toration, retrocession, retrogradation, throwback, regression, regress, recedence, retirement, atavism *(Biol.)*, rebound, withdrawal, ricochet.

3. Retaliatory *or* responsive effect of stimulation, response, reflex, reply, backlash, repercussion, reflection, effect, retort, reciprocation, answer, rebound, retaliation, retribution, echo.

REACTIONARY, *adj.* Of, pertaining to, marked by *or* favoring reaction *(as in politics)*, conservative, ultra-conservative, radically conservative, reversionary, regressive, retrogressive, revulsionary, tory, counteractive, Bourbon *(derog.)*, die-hard, opposed to change, preservative, unprogressive, uncompromising, rigid, hard-shell *(coll.)*, standpat *(coll.)*, reactionist.

READ, *adj.* Having knowledge gained by reading, versed, learned, conversant, at home, forward, strong, proficient, familiar, master of, up in, grounded, acquainted, skilled.

READ, *v.* 1. Observe and apprehend the meaning of *(something written, printed, etc.)*, peruse, study, con, pore over, go over, thumb over, wade through, run over *or* through, glance *or* run the eye over *or* through, dip into, consume, scan, skim over, devour, plunge into, bury oneself in.

2. Utter aloud *(something written, printed, etc.)*, render in speech, deliver, recite, present, give a public reading *or* recital, elocutionize.

3. Understand, comprehend, make out the significance of *(by scrutiny or observation)*, make out the character of *(as by the interpretation of outward signs)*, interpret, decipher, spell out, construe, discern, perceive, deduce, analyze, gather, define, express, explain, take to mean, translate, discover.

4. Foretell, foresee, predict, forecast, prognosticate, prophesy, indicate beforehand, omen, soothsay, hariolate, premonish, vaticinate, divine, haruspicate, prognose *(Med.)*.

5. Introduce *(something not expressed or directly indicated)* into what is read *or* considered, construe, interpolate, assume, interject, insert, insinuate, place in, add, import, intrude, drag in, draw in, foist in.

6. Register, indicate, show, have a certain wording, exhibit, point to, specify, represent, designate.

READABLE, *adj.* 1. Easy *or* interesting to read, rewarding, pleasing, pleasant, pleasurable, worth reading, worth-while, entertaining, fit to be read, engaging, inviting, likable, worthy, gratifying.

2. Capable of being read, legible, clear, fair, decipherable, fluent, flowing, distinct, regular, precise, uniform, careful, tidy, orderly, neat, painstaking, clear-cut, comprehensible, graphic, intelligible.

READER, *n.* 1. One who reads, bookworm, student, scholar, book lover, literary person, bookman, bibliosoph, classicist, grind *(coll.)*, man of letters.

2. Schoolbook *(for instruction and practice in reading)*, primer, manual, text, textbook.

3. One employed to read critically manuscripts, *etc.*, assistant who grades examinations, *etc.*, proofreader, copyholder, copyreader *(Journ.)*, editor, proof corrector.

4. One who reads *or* recites before audiences, lector, elocutionist, reciter, prelector, monologist, speaker, lecturer.

READILY, *adv.* 1. Quickly, promptly, easily, immediately, without difficulty, in no time, effortlessly, with no effort, apace, without delay, at once, instantly, smoothly, swimmingly, with one hand tied behind one's back, on easy terms, on the spur of the moment, offhand, extempore, speedily, straightforth, straightway, pronto *(sl.)*, hands down *(coll.)*, at short notice, aptly, at the drop of a hat *(coll.)*.

2. In a ready manner, willingly, with pleasure, freely, gladly, cheerfully, with good will *or* right good will, with a will, with all one's heart, with good grace, graciously, nothing loath, joyously, without reluctance *or* demur, lief, fain, happily, ungrudgingly, heart and soul, with open arms, zealously.

READINESS, *n.* 1. Condition of being ready, preparedness, preparation, maturity, punctuality, promptness, promptitude, fitness, fit state, ripeness, provision, mellowness, cultivation, adjustment, adaptation, maturation, perfection, accouterment.

2. Ready action *or* movement, quickness, promptness, tendency, propensity, predilection, dexterity, expertness, facility, knack, skill, ease, bias, turn, bent, warp, leaning, agility, haste, rapidity, nimbleness, ingenuity, faculty, ability, versatility, cleverness, finesse, address, aptness, aptitude, adroitness, proficiency, efficiency, alacrity, alertness.

3. Willingness, inclination, cheerful consent, disposition, cheerfulness, alacrity, gladness, promptness, ardor, fervor, devotion, acceptance, enthusiasm, cordiality, good will, geniality, intentness, desire, assent, spontaneity, consent, will, compliance, pleasure, eagerness, mind, wish, acquiescence, avidity, approval, concurrence, agreement, affirmation.

READING, *n.* 1. Action *or* practice of one who reads, perusal, inquiry, education, examination, research, search, quest, scrutiny, skimming, scanning, exploration, grind *(coll.)*, scholarship, study.

2. Rendering, recitation, recital, delineation, speech, address, elocution, representation, prelection, talk, monologue, disquisition, discourse, declamation.

3. Extent to which one has read, literary knowledge, acquirements, enlightenment, attainments, learning, body *or* store of knowledge, scholarship, erudition, lore, accomplishments, pedantry, education, proficiency, bookishness, treasury of information, edification.

4. Matter read *or* for reading, printed matter, print, literature, belles-lettres, text, pericope *(Eccles.)*, journalism.

5. Interpretation, version, construction, lection, analysis, view, opinion, metaphrase, paraphrase, translation, conception, impression, conclusion, consideration, apprehension, observation.

READJUST, *v.* Adjust again *or* anew, rearrange, accord, assimilate, harmonize, reconcile, agree, reset, restore, equalize, dovetail, readapt, square, balance, poise, redintegrate, adapt, suit, fit, accommodate, regulate, fix, set, put back, replace, reorganize, re-establish, return to a former status.

READY, *adj.* 1. Completely prepared, in due condition for immediate action *or* use, duly equipped (completed, adjusted, arranged) as for the occasion *or* purpose, punctual, mature, in readiness, ripe, fit, primed, loaded, set, armed, all set, alacritous, equipped, expeditious, speedy, alert, prompt, on the *qui vive (Fr.)*, *semper paratus (Lat.)*, booted and spurred, in the saddle, in harness, snug, in practice, well-stocked, well-pro-

vided, furnished, fitted out, up to, equal to, in working order, in gear.

2. Willing, happy, agreeable, eager, cheerful, avid, keen, glad, minded, willed, inclined, favorably minded, prone, predisposed, concurrent, well-disposed, content, nothing loath, acquiescent, compliant, delighted, fervent, assenting, cordial, content, genial, gracious, consenting, enthusiastic, forward, prompt, game *(coll.)*, fain.

3. Prompt *or* quick in perceiving (comprehending, speaking, writing, *etc.*), proceeding from *or* showing quickness, dexterous, agile, apt, deft, nimble-witted, attentive, adroit, facile, alert, skilful, sharp, argute, knowing, acute, piercing, arch, artful, quick-witted, wide-awake, fleet, nimble, sprightly, cunning, sagacious, clever, active, swift, brisk, ingenious, expectant, masterly, resourceful, shrewd, versatile, energetic, animated, lively, percipient, perceptive, alive, subtle, bright, penetrating, discerning, apperceptive, astute, keen, expert.

4. Inclined, disposed, apt, likely, given, prone, free, forward, predisposed, minded.

5. In such condition as to be about, likely at any moment *(to do something)*, tending, expectant, waiting, liable, on the verge of, prone, subject, on the brink of, exposed, in a fair way, open, endangered, in danger of, disposed, predisposed.

6. Immediately available *(for use)*, present, convenient to hand, at hand, at one's finger tips, accessible, commodious, handy, opportune, facile, pat, fluent, spontaneous, glib, usable, on hand, adaptable, on tap, applicable.

READY-MADE, *adj.* 1. Made for sale to any purchaser *(rather than to order)*, prefabricated, standard, bulk, quantity, ready-to-wear *(of clothing)*, ready-prepared, preformed, ready-cooked, ready-mixed.

2. Unoriginal, conventional, hackneyed, prosaic, trite, standard, commonplace, unimaginative, matter-of-fact, stale, tame, dull, pedestrian, jejune, usual, stock, tedious, mediocre, common, everyday, platitudinous, homely, ordinary, uninspired.

REAL, *adj.* 1. In existence, actual, tangible, existent, corporeal, sensible, physical, embodied, substantial, *de facto (Lat.)*, bodily, solid, material, palpable, perceptible.

2. Genuine, true, authentic, rightful, actual, well-grounded, factual, veritable, unimagined, unquestionable, legitimate, veracious, essential, positive, valid, categorical, certain, bona fide *(Lat.)*, absolute, demonstrable, truthful.

REAL ESTATE, *n.* Land and whatever *(by nature or artificial annexation)* pertains to it, property, realty, lands, holdings, acres, tenements, grounds, messuage.

REALISM, *n.* Interest in *or* concern for the actual *or* real *(as distinguished from the abstract, speculative, etc.)*, tendency to view *or* represent things as they really are, fidelity to nature *or* real life *(as opposed to idealism; Lit.)*, authenticity, naturalism, actuality, reality, verisimilitude, graphicalness, naturalness, pragmatism.

REALIST, *n.* One who tends to represent things as they really are *(esp. a writer or artist)*, pragmatist, delineator, illustrator, naturalist, photographer.

REALISTIC, *adj.* Interested in *or* concerned with what is real *or* practical, representing things as they really are, graphic, down to earth, natural, true to facts *or* nature, scientific, mathematical, authentic, real, pragmatic, genuine, illustrative, imitative, sterling, veracious, truthful, constant, faithful, exact, precise, correct, delineatory, representative, depictive, lifelike, straightforward, undisguised, undistorted, descriptive.

REALITY, *n.* 1. State of being real, actual existence, corporeality, perceptibility, substantiality, true being, tangibility, palpability, absoluteness, solidity, materiality, actuality, sensibility.

2. A thing which is actual, tangible thing, existing thing, fact, entity, truth, matter of fact, verity, realness.

3. Realism, graphicalness, verisimilitude, naturalism, actuality, fidelity to nature, life, *etc.,* truth to nature, naturalness, authenticity.

REALIZE, *v.* 1. Attain, fulfil, carry into effect, compass, engineer, bring about, bring to pass, work out, operate, get, act, effectuate, produce, do, turn, carry out, dispatch, discharge, complete, perform, achieve, carry through, consummate, perfect, effect, accomplish.

2. Cause to seem real, picture, feel strongly, see into, be cognizant of, apprehend, conceive, make out, penetrate, see, imagine, recognize, understand, discern, appreciate, fathom, perceive, comprehend, grasp, cognize.

3. Make a profit, gain, make money, profit, obtain a return, make capital of, capitalize, clear.

REALLY, *adv.* Certainly, in fact, actually, positively, absolutely, surely, truthfully, veritably, indeed, truly, literally, unquestionably, undoubtedly, categorically, genuinely.

REALM, *n.* 1. Kingdom, dominion, country, demesne, monarchy, empire, domain, land, principality, state, nation.

2. Sphere of work, influence, *etc.,* domain, empery, bailiwick, field, ground, province, sway, orbit, jurisdiction, beat, department, circuit, authority, estate, region, ward, territory.

REALTY; *n.* Land owned, property, acres, real estate, lands, holdings, grounds, tenements, messuage.

REANIMATE, *v.* Give new life to, revive, resuscitate, invigorate, refresh, enliven, cheer, revivify, rekindle, restore, renovate, encourage, quicken, renew, regenerate, remake, brace, stimulate.

REAP, *v.* 1. Cut *(with a scythe, sickle, etc.),* crop, mow, glean, pick, strip the fields, pluck, cull, take the yield, harvest, gather the fruits.

2. Gain, obtain, glean, make capital of, acquire, get, procure, secure, realize, pick up, receive, come to have.

REAR, *n.* 1. Hind part, hinder part, end, back, stern, heel, reverse, wake, posterior, tail end, reverse side, behind, occiput *(of the skull),* nape *or* scruff *(of the neck).*

2. Rump, backside, fundaments, loins, buttocks, hindquarters, croup *(of animals).*

REAR, *v.* 1. Raise upright, set up, put up, erect, straighten, tilt up, render vertical, hoist, lift, stand up, boost, cock, stick up.

2. Build, construct, edify, run up, put up, fabricate, put together, set in place.

3. Move to a higher position, erect, stand up, pick up, mount, buoy, direct upward, elevate, raise, lift, uplift, uprear, sublevate, hoist, heave, upraise, set up, take up.

4. Bring up, foster, nurture, train, develop, cultivate, nurse, raise, breed.

REASON, *n.* 1. Clarifying statement, explanation, clarification, elucidation, exegesis, unfoldment, interpretation, exposition, enucleation, explication, rationale.

2. Cause, root, occasion, prime mover, source, spring, origin, incentive, excitation, inspiration, stimulation, motive, actuation, inducement, fomentation, incitation, instigation, provocation, incitement, agent, fountainhead, mainspring, genesis, primary cause, derivation, beginning, ultimate cause, primordium, generator, author, producer.

3. Rationalization, reasoning, synthesis, argumentation, logic, thinking, analysis, epistemology, epagoge, dialectics, syllogization.

4. Capacity to understand, comprehension, power to grasp ideas, intelligence, mental capacity, understanding, capability, insight, mind, mental grasp, ability to know, cognition, conception, discernment, realization, assimilation, apprehension, perception, recognition, awareness, knowledge, liberality, command of thought, penetration, enlightenment, apperception, perspicacity, cognizance, imagination, intuition, wisdom, sense, intellect.

5. Soundness of mind, sanity, sense, balance, clear-headedness, lucidity, coherence, normality, sobriety, rationality.

REASON, *v.* 1. Think *or* argue in a logical manner, think out *(a problem, etc.)* logically, justly *or* properly, draw conclusions *or* inferences from facts *or* premises, conclude, infer, make deductions, cogitate, cerebrate, turn over in the mind, weigh, consider, take counsel, ratiocinate, intellectualize, syllogize, deliberate, philosophize, study, logicize, excogitate, rationalize, concentrate upon, mull over *(coll.),* revolve, contemplate, speculate, reflect, examine, meditate, ponder, judge, deduce, induce, confer, advise, talk over.

2. Urge reasons which should determine belief *or* action, persuade by reasoning, point out, explain, expound, plead, expostulate, speak logically, remonstrate, bring to reason, join issue, discuss, debate, try conclusions, maintain, argue, convince, contend, ventilate a question, convict, induce, assure, prevail with, on *or* upon, move, coax, dispute, win over, conciliate, be convincing, dissuade, set forth, put it to one, constrain by reason, restrain, advise.

REASONABLE, *adj.* 1. Agreeable to reason *or* sound judgment, logical, sane, intelligent, justifiable, plausible, credible, wise, equitable, sensible, right, enlightened, tolerable, sound, sagacious, well-founded, well-grounded, judicious, likely, suitable, rational, vindicable, discreet, advisable, fit, proper, just, far-sighted, deductive, subtle, possible, probable, understandable, philosophic, inferential, inferable, legitimate, wholesome, admissible, discerning.

2. Of sound judgment *or* good sense, exercising reason, just, right, intelligent, rational, sensible, sapient, fair, moderate, agreeable to reason, humane, wise, cool-headed, level-headed, prudent, discreet, politic, circumspect, impartial, knowing, understanding, sage, thoughtful, thinking, analytical, reflective, philosophic, discerning, perspicacious, enlightened, well-advised, discriminating, judicious, logical, ratiocinative, objective, intellectual.

3. Not exceeding the limit prescribed by reason, not excessive, moderate, sober, sane, sensible, just, fair, conscionable, tolerable, not extreme, lenient, restrained, limited, tempered, temperate.

proper, fit, fitting, equitable, constrained, nominal, worth the money, low-priced.

4. Endowed with reason, rational, intelligent, thinking, capable of reason, percipient, ratiocinative, perceiving, cerebral. cognitive, reasoning. mental, conscious.

REASONING, *n.* 1. Process of drawing conclusions *or* inferences from facts *or* premises, ratiocination, argumentation, induction, inference, thinking, reason, discussion, debate, logic, dialectics. syllogization, epistemology, epagoge. thought, analysis, rationalization, synthesis.

2. Reasons, arguments, proofs, rationale. exposition, cause, solution, ascription, ground, account, basis, theory, hypothesis, attribution, interpretation, motivation, explication, motive, definition, the why and the wherefore. key, exegesis, elucidation.

REASONLESS, *adj.* Not according to reason, irrational, unreasoning, unwise, ignorant, lackbrained, insensate, witless, brainless, unintelligent, mindless, senseless, insane, mad, crazy, lunatic, unsound, lean-witted, bereft of reason, emptyheaded, void of reason, thoughtless, unbalanced, unhinged, demented, deranged, obtuse, undiscerning, stupid, unenlightened, uncomprehending, dull, slow-witted, addlepated, addleheaded.

REASSURE, *v.* Restore (*a person, etc.*) to assurance *or* confidence, hearten, encourage, inspirit, nerve, rally, infuse courage, give hope, set one's mind at rest, enhearten, strengthen, comfort, buoy up, augur well, promise well, satisfy one's mind, remove *or* dismiss doubt, keep in countenance, pat on the back, raise expectations, bid fair, inspire (raise, hold out) hope, embolden, cheer, uplift, revitalize, quicken.

REBATE, *n .* Return of part of an original amount paid, repayment, discount, decrease, abatement, cut, tare, offtake, agio, deduction, allowance, reduction, percentage, drawback (*Com.*), concession (*Com.*).

REBATE, *v.* Allow as a discount, deduct, subtract, reduce, cut, abate, discount, strike off, mark down, take off, make allowance, allow.

REBEL, *n.* One who refuses allegiance to, resists *or* rises in arms against the established order, one who *or* that which resists authority *or* control, insurgent, revolter, mutineer, rioter, agitator, separatist, recreant, deserter, demagogue, revolutionist, malcontent, noncontent, apostate, dissenter, schismatic, sectarian, irreconcilable, heretic, nonconformist, dissentient, revolutionary, protestant, recusant, secessionist, anarchist, nonjuror, seceder, turncoat, traitor.

REBEL, *v.* 1. Rise in arms *or* active resistance against the established order, resist lawful authority, riot, defy authority, strike, revolt, kick over the traces, secede, boycott, walk out, refuse to support, fly in the face of, mutiny, break with, revolutionize, overthrow, overturn, upset, bolt (*Pol.*) insurrect (*coll.*).

2. Manifest *or* feel utter repugnance, turn away, shrink, recoil, shy, recede, be unwilling, pull *or* draw back, react, rebound, flinch, quail, avoid, demur, stick at, scruple, flee, fly from, be repelled by, despise, retire, hate, wince.

REBELLION, *n.* Open, organized and armed resistance to government, *etc.*, resistance against *or* defiance of authority *or* control, insurrection, rising, defiance, revolt, disobedience, insubordination, insurgency, upheaval, convulsion, revolution,

opposition, subversion, anarchy, upset, overturn, strike, tie-up, lockout, lese majesty, *coup-de-état* (*Fr.*), disturbance, treason, sedition, riot, contumacy, flare-up, mutiny, outbreak, walkout (*coll.*), *émeute* (*Fr.*).

REBELLIOUS, *adj.* Defying lawful authority, insubordinate, refractory, mutinous, contumacious, seditious, anarchic, insurgent, insurrectionary, revolutionary, insolent, renitent, contrary, oppositional, unresigned, unsubmissive, up in arms, unruly, unwilling, ungoverned, ungovernable, with teeth bared, with fists doubled, daring, recalcitrant, uncontrollable, unmanageable, pugnacious, radical, fractious, factious, intractable, disobedient, defiant, disorderly, turbulent, quarrelsome, restive, resistant.

REBIRTH, *n.* Being born again, second birth, regeneration, revival, new activity *or* growth, revivement, renaissance, renascence, resurrection, reviviscence, rejuvenation, rejuvenescence, regenesis, revivification, reanimation, reformation, resumption, renewal, restoration, resuscitation, palingenesis.

REBOUND, *v.* Bound *or* spring back (*from force of impact*), recoil, reverberate, kick, fly back, spring back, react, resile, repercuss, reflect, surrebound, resonate, resound, echo, reflect, return, ricochet.

REBUFF, *n.* Blunt *or* abrupt check, peremptory refusal, snub, repulse, resistance, repulsion, reaction, opposition, discouragement, defiance, defeat, refusal, repugnance, rejection, repudiation, chiding, rebuke, damper, rout, checkmate, hindrance, reproach, cold shoulder, denial, slight, spurn, renouncement, renunciation, go-by (*coll.*), cut (*coll.*), slap in the face, dash of cold water, undoing, beating, drubbing, vanquishment, overthrow, overturn, disapproval, flat *or* point-blank refusal, discomfiture, setback, counteraction.

REBUFF, *v.* Give a rebuff to, repel, refuse, oppose, check, snub, reprove, rebuke, chide, rock *or* set back on one's heels, reject, resist, ignore, slight, disregard, spurn, cold shoulder, put in one's place, repulse, resist, cross, set one's face against, keep at a distance, keep at arm's length, give the go-by (*coll.*), slam the door in one's face, cut (*coll.*), turn down (*sl.*), decline, deny, disallow, give the cold shoulder.

REBUKE, *n.* Reprimand, reproof, censure, expostulation, rating, berating, blame, admonition, scolding, reproach, reprehension, chiding, punishment, exprobration, objurgation, upbraiding, correction, castigation, setdown, admonishment, tongue-lashing (*coll.*), affliction, remonstrance, reproval.

REBUKE, *v.* Censure, reprove, reprimand, upbraid, scold, blame, exprobrate, berate, rate, call down, punish, check, rebuff, reproach, remonstrate with, find fault with, lecture, admonish, chide, reprehend, objurgate, silence, take to task, take one down a peg.

REBUS, *n.* Enigmatical representation of a word *or* phrase by pictures, symbols, *etc.*, device, cipher, charade, anagram, riddle, puzzle, symbol, monogram.

REBUT, *v.* Oppose (*by contrary proof*), refute (*by evidence or argument*), disprove, retort, confute, respond, crush, riposte, respond conclusively, retaliate, answer back, parry, expose one's weak point, explode, dismiss, defeat, negate, show the fallacy of, answer, rejoin, overthrow, belie, contradict, overturn, floor, down, silence, show up, negative, invalidate, reduce to silence, have the better of, squelch *(coll.)*.

RECALCITRANT, *adj.* Resisting authority *or* control, not obedient *or* compliant, refractory, disobedient, obstinate, opposing, defiant, mutinous, stubborn, intractable, immovable, willful, renitent, repugnant, oppugnant, contrary, perverse, headstrong, bullheaded, mulish, pigheaded, pervicacious, resistant, rebellious, antagonistic, contumacious, unyielding, sulky, sullen, unsubmissive, insubordinate, unmanageable, unruly, uncontrollable, reactionary, factious, fractious, balky, unwilling, restive.

RECALCITRATE, *v.* Make resistance *or* opposition, show strong objection *or* repugnance, oppose, run counter, conflict, traverse, oppugn, be refractory, kick against, contradict, resist, contravene, cross, play at cross purposes, balk, repel, reluct, withstand, make a stand against, repudiate, reluctate, set oneself against, fly in the face of, be antagonistic to, check, hinder, impede, obstruct, interfere with.

RECALL, *v.* 1. Recollect, recognize, remember, revive, review, recover knowledge of, call to remembrance, think back to, pass in review, evoke, remind, bring back, commemorate, retrace, place, reminisce, keep in memory, call to mind.

2. Call back, summon to return, revive, revivify, encore, resuscitate, reanimate, applaud.

3. Take back, revoke, retract, disavow, disclaim, withdraw, repeal, recant, deny, abjure, annul, cancel, countermand, renounce, call back, reject, set aside, nullify, rescind, overrule, repudiate, abnegate, swallow, reverse, override, invalidate, void, make void, disannul, abolish, forswear, unsay.

RECANT, *v.* Withdraw or disavow *(a statement, etc.)* *esp.* formally, retract, forswear, objure, repudiate, disown, disavow, recall, annul, abnegate, countermand, unsay, renounce, rescind, void, deny, nullify, disclaim, disannul, abjure, repeal.

RECAPITULATE, *v.* Review *(by way of an orderly summary)*, sum up, run over, restate, reiterate, repeat, relate, name *or* call over, reword, enumerate, narrate, recount, recite, rehearse, summarize, give a summary of.

RECAPTURE, *v.* Recover by capture, capture again, retake, redeem, regain, retrieve, revendicate, ransom, resume, get back, replevy, replevin, repossess.

RECEDE, *v.* 1. Move toward a more distant point, go *or* move back, become more distant, fall *or* stand back, abate, wane, fade, depart, desist, return, ebb, subside, regress, retreat, withdraw, retrograde, retire, sink, decline.

2. Slope backward, incline, fall inward, fall away, slant.

3. Draw back, withdraw *(from a position taken, from an undertaking, promise, etc.)*, recoil, react, fall, give in, lapse, slip *or* sink back, recidive, fall from grace, back down, subside, quail, return, shrink back, retrovert, revert, relapse, turn tail, beat a retreat, change one's mind, yield, regress, retrogress.

RECEIPT, *n.* 1. Written acknowledgment of payment, acquittance, quittance, voucher, discharge, release, cancellation.

2. *(Pl.)* Amount *or* quantity received, income, revenue, returns, avails, wages, pay, payment, re-

imbursement, gain, assets, proceeds, earnings, remuneration, take *(sl.)*, profits.

3. Act of receiving, state of being received, reception, acceptance, receival, susception, acquisition, assumption, recipience, admittance, admission, possession.

4. Recipe, prescription, directions, method, formula, ways and means, device, nostrum.

RECEIPT, *v.* Acknowledge in writing the payment of *(a bill)*, give a receipt for, cancel, nullify, wipe off the records *or* books, make null and void, invalidate, make void, mark off, release, clear, acquit, discharge.

RECEIVE, *v.* 1. Take into one's hand *or* one's possession, have *(something)* bestowed, conferred, *etc.*, have delivered *or* brought to oneself, take, accept, come by, acquire, get, inherit, procure, gain, obtain, take possession, take in, assume, arrogate, appropriate, earn, draw, pocket, admit, win, secure, collect, derive, be in receipt of, come by.

2. Get, learn, discover, be informed of, hear, be told, absorb, drink in, pick up, be notified of, take in, take into the mind, apprehend mentally, understand, awaken to, acquire knowledge of, open one's eyes to, see, discern, find out.

3. Hold, contain, accommodate, retain, include, carry, admit, enclose, have capacity for, be composed of, incorporate, comprise, embody, embrace, cover, encompass, involve, take in, reckon among, number among, take into account *or* consideration, subsume.

4. Meet with, encounter, submit to, taste, feel, endure, sustain, bear, suffer, undergo, experience, have inflicted on one, go *or* pass through, have as one's lot.

5. Be at home to *(visitors)*, greet upon arriving, welcome, admit *(a person)* to a place, harbor, entertain, meet, shelter, take in, give entrance to, bid welcome, keep an open house, open the door to, give entrée, let in, give a warm reception to, have the latchstring out.

6. Accept as authoritative (valid, true, approved), believe, assent, embrace, approve, credit, adopt, follow, accredit, agree with, swear by *(coll.)*, acquiesce, place reliance in *or* on, allow *or* attach weight to, place weight on, trust, have faith in, give credence to, take on trust, take for granted, hold with, subscribe to, accede to.

RECEIVER, *n.* 1. One who receives, recipient, accepter, beneficiary, teller, treasurer, creditor, believer, accipient, trustee, legatee, collector *(Com.)*, donee *(Law)*, grantee *(Law)*, devisee *(Law)*, assignee *(Law)*, depository, depositary, liquidator.

2. That which receives, receptacle, device *or* apparatus for receiving something, container, utensil, vessel, recipient, receptor *(Physol.)*, hamper, hopper, envelope, wrapper, depository, repository, jacket, hole, compartment, sheath, capsule.

RECENSION, *n.* Revision *(of an early work by critical study)*, edition, version of a text, redaction, rescript, rectification, examination, review, reexamination, emendation, reconsideration.

RECENT, *adj.* Of late occurrence (appearance, origin), lately happening (done, made, *etc.)*, late, new, novel, fresh, newly come, of yesterday, not long past *(as a period)*, not remote *or* primitive, foregoing, preceding, up-to-the-minute, newfangled, neoteric, young, modern, latter, untried, unknown, unfamiliar, up-to-date, last.

RECEPTACLE, *n.* That which serves to receive *or* hold something, holder, container, repository, depository, vessel, receiver, reservoir, box, well, bin, hamper, envelope, compartment, sheath, capsule, jacket, hold, wrapper, hamper, hopper, utensil.

RECEPTION, *n.* 1. Act of receiving, fact of being received, admission, access, manner of being received, recognition, welcome, entertainment, greeting, acceptance, entrée, receipt, annexation, embrace, hug, arrival, comprisal, entry, hospitality, inclusion, incorporation, recipience, receival, ingress, interjection, injection, immission, intromission, entrance.

2. Function *or* occasion when persons are formally received, party, levee, soiree, audience, hearing, interview, social gathering, at-home, wedding breakfast.

RECEPTIVE, *adj.* 1. Having the quality of receiving, taking in, admitting, able *or* quick to receive ideas, *etc.,* open-eyed, introceptive, admissive, absorbent, recipient, capable, sensitive, clear-thinking, discerning, clear-sighted, lucid, cognitive, understanding, comprehending, penetrating, perspicacious, sagacious, luminous, of sound judgment, sharp, astute, sensible, prudent, undeceived, perceptive, discriminating, critical, keen, wide-awake, alert, aware, piercing, undeceived, quick-witted.

2. Having a disposition to receive *(a suggestion, offer, etc.),* with favor, flexible, hospitable, pliant, pliable, responsive, open-minded, sensible, accessible, susceptible, tractable, impressible, impressionable, amenable, unprejudiced, tolerant, unbiased, broad-minded, undogmatic, impartial, persuadable, reasonable, liberal, unjaundiced, unwarped, unswayed, open to suggestion, acquiescent.

RECESS, *n.* 1. Withdrawl or cessation for a time from usual occupation (work, activity), intermission, break, respite, pause, rest, vacation, holiday, interim, interlude, interval, remission, suspension of business, intermittence, spell, breathing spell, time out, lull, truce, letup *(coll.).*

2. Receding part *or* space, bay, indentation *(in a line or extent of hills, coast, forest, etc.),* nook, alcove, niche, corner, hollow, cave, cove, inlet, cavern, pass, wing, gulf, harbor, gap, break, fold, notch, gorge, hook, bend, arm *(of the sea),* cleft.

3. *(Pl.)* Secluded *or* inner place *or* part, interior, depths, retreat, place of retirement, innermost part, halls, cover, corner, closet, crypt, vault, refuge, concealment, middle, center, heart, haven, isolation, solitude, loneliness, cell, adytum, sanctum, sanctuary, safehold, sanctum sanctorum.

RECESS, *v.* 1. Place *or* set in a recess, set *or* form as *or* like a recess, inset, niche, inlay.

2. Take a recess, interlude, intervene, vacation, shut up shop, interval, intermit, take time out, let up *(coll.).*

RECESSION, *n.* 1. Act of receding *or* withdrawing, outward-moving procession, withdrawal, retrocession, retrogression, recoil, return, regress, reaction, reversal, retrocedence, exit, exodus, egress, leaving, going, decampment, departure, recedence, recidivism, reversion, regression, falling back, backing out, retirement, retreat, flight, leave-taking, removal, remigration, retrogradation, decession, going back.

2. Receding part of a wall, *etc.,* slope, slant, inset, obliquity, deflection, deviation, cranny, nook, hole, inclination, curvature, curve, pitch,

tilt, declination, bay, alcove, niche, hollow, cove, cavern, wing, break.

3. Temporary decline in business, depression, slump, falling off, reaction, retrocession, relapse.

RECESSIVE, *adj.* Tending to recede, receding, regressive, relapsing, reactionary, dormant, latent, suspended, not aggressive, ebbing, refluent, submissive, quiescent, idle, slack, abeyant, unassertive, inactive, retrograde, retrogressive, passive.

RECHERCHE, *adj.* 1. Sought out with care, unusual, choice, rare, select, singular, out of the ordinary, extraordinary, unique, prized, strange, odd, exceptional, remarkable, fanciful, uncommon, fine, exquisite, curious, wonderful, peculiar.

2. Of studied refinement *or* elegance, fashionable, fine, nice, subtle, stylish, chic, smart, tasteful, delicate, cultivated, finical, dainty, precise, à la mode, *comme il faut (Fr.),* discriminative, fastidious, elegant.

RECIDIVISM, *n.* Repeated *or* habitual relapse into crime, backsliding, degeneration, regression, perversion, diversion, devolution, declension, reversion, falling back, lapse, deterioration, retrogression, retrogradation, recrudesce

RECIPE, *n.* 1. Prescription, formula *(esp. for preparing a dish in cookery),* receipt, directions, method.

2. Method to attain a desired end, means, way, manner, policy, scheme, plan, device, system, expedient, resources, resort, plot, game, design.

RECIPIENCE, *n.* 1. Act of receiving, reception, consent, assent, approval, admission, recognition, welcome, entertainment, greeting, acceptance, entrée, receipt, entry, hospitality, inclusion, incorporation, receival, entrance.

2. State *or* quality of being receptive, receptiveness, willingness, acceptance, acquiescence, compliance, consent, friendliness, sympathy, partiality, yieldingness, inclination, disposition, turn, bent, bias, proneness, tendency, propensity, openness, eagerness, assent, geniality, proclivity, promptness, readiness, alacrity, cordiality, concession, agreement, approval.

RECIPIENT, *n.* One who *or* that which receives, receiver, beneficiary, donee, grantee, assignee, pensioner, creditor, trustee, legatee, depository, depositary, liquidator, receptacle, container, repository.

RECIPROCAL, *adj.* Given, felt, *etc.,* by each to *or* toward each, given (performed, felt, *etc.*) in return, mutual, correspondent, commutual, correlative, interrelated, retaliatory, exchanged, requited, complementary, common, equivalent, corresponding, complemental, retributive, retaliative, give-and-take, returned, interchanged, to-and-fro, reciprocative.

RECIPROCATE, *v.* 1. Give, feel, *etc.,* in return, give and receive reciprocally, make return *(as for something given),* interchange, give and take, return the compliment, retaliate, retort, bandy, requite, exchange, barter, swap, agree, echo, pull together, respond, accord, harmonize, enter into the feelings of each other, understand one another, transfer, sympathize with.

2. Move alternately backward and forward, seesaw, come and go, oscillate, alternate, vary, ebb and flow, wigwag, teeter, shuttle, back and fill, fluctuate, swing, pendulate, undulate.

RECIPROCATION, *n.* Making return for something, state of being reciprocal *or* corresponding, mutual giving and receiving, requital, interchange, mutuality, exchange, give-and-take, paying, ebb and flow, correlation, return, alternation, dicker, retort, tit for tat, measure for measure, transfer, an eye for an eye, reciprocity, correspondence, shuffling, swapping *(coll.)*, counterchange, reprisal, retribution, commutation, permutation, transposition, switch, trade, reprisal, retaliation, barter, *quid pro quo (Lat.)*.

RECIPROCITY, *n.* Reciprocal state *or* relation, mutual rights and privileges, exchange, mutuality, reciprocation, giving and taking, commerce, return, alternation, reciprocalness, interchange, ebb and flow, transfer, swapping *(coll.)*, counterchange, transposition, trade, switch, barter, agreement.

RECITAL, *n.* 1. Musical entertainment, concert, musical.
   2. Act of reciting, recitation, portrayal, report, rehearsal, repetition, relation, oral exercise, description, explanation, narration, telling, talk, rendition, elocution.
   3. Detailed statement, sketch, word painting *or* picture, narrative, history, story, tale, graphic account, particulars, specifications, dissertation, monograph, summary, review, saga, yarn, interpretation, depiction, delineation, exposition, picturization, rendition, representation, discourse, explanation, relation, narration, description, report, portrayal, retelling, recapitulation.

RECITATION, *n.* Reciting *or* repeating of memorized *or* prepared material before an audience, elocutionary delivery, recital, rehearsal, repetition, disquisition, prelection, talk, address, valediction, valedictory, allocution, soliloquy, elocution, oration, monologue, discourse, rendition, intonement, cantillation, narration, lesson, reading, account, declamation, speech.

RECITE, *v.* 1. Repeat from memory, rehearse, repeat by rote, say by heart, present, utter, emit, hold forth, make a speech, declaim, deliver, address, mouth, elocutionize, lecture, prelect, preach, relate, convey, perform, render, pronounce.
   2. Give an account of, report, chant, quote, utter, relate, narrate, tell, describe, recount, mention, give words to, give *or* render an account of, characterize, set forth, draw up a statement, articulate, state, communicate, convey, impart, make a report of, picture, unfold, recapitulate, retell, render, rehearse, portray, represent, give utterance *or* expression to, divulge, elucidate, limn, depict, delineate, voice, put *or* set forth, deliver, let fall.
   3. Enumerate, numerate, tell over, name *or* call over, figure, compute, run over, detail, recapitulate, count, calculate, reckon, sum up, cast up, recount, total, score up, add up, census, poll, muster, specify, particularize, itemize, number.

RECK, *v.* *(Often foll. by* OF*)* Have care (concern, regard), take heed, mind, heed, notice, consider, feel solicitude, have *or* feel interest, look to *or* after, attend to, watch over, exercise oversight, preserve, minister to, protect, defend, nurse, foster, harbor, guard, safeguard.

RECKLESS, *adj.* Without caution *or* prudence, utterly careless of consequences, rash, thoughtless, heedless, unmindful, regardless, headlong, precipitate, inattentive, unobservant, negligent, neglectful, inconsiderate, unwatchful, forgetful, mindless, slovenly, loose, oblivious, unobserving, unsolicitous, slack, remiss, shiftless, happy-go-lucky, indolent, unconcerned, hasty, unwary, wild,

harebrained, uncircumspect, unthinking, improvident, insouciant, unaware, imprudent, impulsive, indifferent, scatterbrained, insensible, unheeding, lax, nonchalant, indiscreet, unheeding, giddy, foolish, fickle, witless, irresponsible, preoccupied, volatile, flighty, unsteady, giddy-brained, harumscarum, distracted, incautious, breakneck, wanton, devil-may-care, dare-devil, foolhardy, heady, hotheaded, quixotic, madcap, temerarious.

RECKON, *v.* 1. Count, total, compute, calculate, cipher, place, arrange, number, cast, enumerate, add, figure, balance, foot up.
   2. Esteem, consider, judge, estimate, regard, account, class, value, appreciate, adjudge, guess, figure *(coll.)*, come to *or* arrive at a conclusion regarding, determine, count, find, decide, surmise, presume, imagine, rate, fancy, deem, rank, appraise, assess, gauge, prize, discern, perceive, ascertain.
   3. Count on *(as in expectation)*, depend on, rely on, have faith in, pin one's faith on, put trust in, trust, plan on, bank on *or* upon *(coll.)*, bargain for, lay one's account for, contemplate, anticipate, look for, foresee, assume.
   4. Deal *(with)*, face, handle, include, refer to, encompass, make allowance for, take into account *or* consideration, be involved in, comprehend, cover, embrace, hold, heed, mind, observe, notice, attend to, give thought to, receive, incorporate, note, have regard for, allow for, recognize, take cognizance of, consider, acknowledge, concede, grant, hold in view, be attentive to.

RECKONING, *n.* 1. Count, computation, calculation, footing, adding, consideration, estimation, estimate, gross, aggregate, score, summation, total, cast, sum, tally, product.
   2. Settlement of accounts *(as between parties)*, accounting *(as for things received or done)*, adjustment, redress, amends, pay, payment, acquittance, quittance, repayment, reimbursement, atonement, valuation, squaring, appraisal, assessment, evaluation, measurement, summation, estimate, estimation, balancing, satisfaction, liquidation, clearance, arrangement, numeration, enumeration, reparation, crediting, return, requital, recompense, compensation.
   3. Statement of an amount due, fee, figure, debt, charge, bill, toll, poll, quotation, assessment, obligation, price, register, score, account, tab.

RECLAIM, *v.* Bring into usable condition, recover from refuse, *etc.*, bring back to right courses (living, principles, *etc.*), recondition, reform, amend, retrieve, right, rescue, remodel, rectify, reinstate, repossess, convert, enhance, develop, replevin, replevy, revendicate, rehabilitate, reëstablish, correct, redeem, get back, regenerate, restore, regain, recall, revive, ransom, civilize, tame, domesticate, make gentle.

RECLAMATION, *n.* Reclaiming *(of waste material, land, etc.)*, for use, restoration, restitution, reinstatement, reform, recovery, regeneracy, reformation, rehabilitation, retrieval, redemption, repair, salvage, enhancement, development, betterment, improvement, compensation, revendication, rectification, cultivation, civilization.

RECLINE, *v.* Lean, lie back, rest in a recumbent position, be supported, cause to lean back, place in a recumbent position, prop, take one's ease, couch, repose, loll, lounge, sprawl.

RECLUSE, *adj.* Shut off *or* apart from the world, living in seclusion, reclusive, retired, private, sequestered, secluded, out-of-the-world, isolated, hermitic, immured, shut up, eremitical, solitary, monastic, estranged, alone, lonely, in solitude, anchoritic, ascetic, austere.

RECLUSE, *n.* One who lives in seclusion *or* apart from society, hermit, solitudinarian, solitary, anchorite, eremite, troglodyte, stylite *(Eccles. Hist.),* santon, ascetic, monastic.

RECLUSION, *n.* Condition *or* life of a recluse, shutting *or* being shut up in seclusion, retreat, withdrawal, alienation, estrangement, hermitism, privacy, loneliness, aloneness, solitude, eremitism, retirement, isolation, seclusion.

RECOGNITION, *n.* 1. Perception of something as identical with something previously known *or* in the mind, recollection, recall, recognizance, memory, remembrance, mental reproduction *or* recurrence, reidentification, identification, cognizance.

2. Perception of something as existing *or* true, realization, acknowledgment of something as valid *or* entitled to consideration, recognizance, apprehension, avowal, confession, comprehension, knowledge, notice, insight, intuition, enlightenment, intelligence, apperception, discovery, detection, diagnosis, divination, sensibility, appreciation.

3. Acknowledgment of kindness (service, merit, *etc.*), expression of acknowledgment by a token of thanks, appreciation, memorial, celebration, commemoration, courtesy, presentation, compliments, reparation, compensation, solatium, meed, guerdon, amends, reckoning, satisfaction, quittance, requital, consideration, reward, thanks, notice, citation.

4. Acknowledgment of the right to be heard *or* given attention, hearing, courtesy, the nod, the floor, audition, audience, preference, priority, introduction, consideration, notice.

RECOGNIZE, *v.* 1. Know again, perceive to be identical *(with something previously known),* identify *(from knowledge of),* call (summon up, conjure up) to mind, remember, recall, verify, recollect, be familiar with, diagnose, place, establish the identity of, sight, descry, make out, distinguish, recover knowledge of, retain the impression of, spot *(coll.),* reidentify.

2. Perceive as existing *or* true, acknowledge as entitled to consideration, treat as valid, accept, vouchsafe, permit, notice, accord, realize, verify, own, confess, concede, allow, grant, discover, detect, ascertain, determine, diagnose, know, apprehend, avow, respect, expose, reveal, fathom, understand, see in its true colors, discern, distinguish, sense, acquiesce in, see, admit, solve, see through, penetrate, make out, observe, sight, descry, mark, note, hit upon, fix upon, abide by, submit to, corroborate, confirm, certify, endorse, be convinced of, appreciate, conceive.

3. Acknowledge as the person entitled to speak, respect, defer to, concede to, yield *or* submit to, give the floor to, give the nod to.

4. Acknowledge acquaintance with *(a person, etc.),* greet, salute, hail, accost, beckon, nod to, signal to, give the high sign *(sl.),* extend the hand, uncover, doff the cap, touch the hat *or* cap, smile upon, make a sign.

5. Show appreciation of *(kindness, service, merit, etc.)* by some reward *or* tribute, cite, honor, thank, pay, repay, requite, compensate, reverence, venerate, memorialize, show gratitude, commemorate, observe, pay homage to, celebrate,

solemnize, signalize, toast, drink to, exalt, pledge, distinguish, hallow, keep, dignify, elevate, glorify, reimburse, recompense, pay respect to.

RECOIL, *n.* Act of recoiling, length through which a weapon moves back after its discharge, rebound, reaction, elasticity, backstroke, reverberation, revulsion, refluence, reflux, withdrawal, ebb, reflection, retreat, regress, recession, reversal, counteraction, backlash, retroaction, return, reflex, reversion, shrinking, ricochet, kick, boomerang, repercussion, resilience.

RECOIL, *v.* 1. Draw back, start *or* shrink back *(as in alarm, horror or disgust),* flinch, falter, wince, dodge, demur, revolt, scruple, blink, swerve, hang back, shirk, stick at, duck, fail, quail, blench.

2. Rebound, react, spring *or* fly back *(as from force of impact),* return, resile, kick, bound back, reverberate, ricochet, repercuss, reflect, surrebound, resonate.

3. *(Foll. by* ON *or* UPON*)* Spring *or* come back, react, act in turn *or* return, act reciprocally, exert a return (reciprocal, counteracting) influence, counteract, counterwork, counterbalance, offset, conflict, reciprocate, retaliate, match, cap, top, give in exchange, repay, requite, respond, reply, get back at.

RECOLLECT, *v.* Recall to mind, remember, call to mind *or* remembrance, recover knowledge of, recognize, revive, evoke, call up, pass in review, think back to, keep in memory, commemorate, retrace, place, summon up, think of.

RECOLLECTION, *n.* 1. Act *or* power of recalling to mind, mental reproduction *or* recurrence, memory, remembrance, recalling, remembering, reminiscence, review, retrospection, reidentification, reconsideration, reflection, contemplation of the past.

2. That which is recollected, memory, memoir, remembrance, thought, impression, mental picture *or* image.

RECOMMEND, *v.* 1. Present as worthy *(of confidence, acceptance, use, etc.),* commend by favorable representation, compliment, acclaim, laud, praise, approve, sanction, applaud, endorse, sing the praises of, speak well *or* highly of, celebrate, eulogize, panegyrize, cry up, advocate, guarantee, second, confirm, stand by, favor, undersign, underwrite, accept, O.K. *(coll.),* back, vouch for, warrant, set one's hand and seal to, support, uphold, ratify, confirm, sustain, favor, approbate, countenance, root for *(sl.).*

2. Urge as advisable *or* expedient, advise, proscribe, suggest, counsel, forward, advance, force, offer, propose, warn, direct, remonstrate, persuade.

3. Make acceptable *or* pleasing, make desirable, improve, enhance, sweeten, promote, popularize, favor, make preferable.

RECOMMENDATION, *n.* 1. Advice, advocacy, counsel, suggestion, proposal, tip, word to the wise, admonition, steer, hint, flea in the ear, guidance, charge, direction, instruction, remonstrance, order, precept, exhortation, injunction.

2. Representation in favor of a person *or* thing, praise, commendation, sanction, nod of approval, esteem, good opinion, approval, approbation, testimonial, boost, credential, tribute, encomium, good word, blessing, blurb, laudation, celebration, panegyric.

RECOMPENSE, *n.* 1. Reward, remuneration,

compensation *(as for service, loss)*, commutation, satisfaction, indemnification, indemnity, payment, atonement, gratuity, amends, return, consideration, wages, fee, propitiation, redress, redemption, expiation, measure for measure, quittance, reparation, conciliation, composition, acknowledgment, substitution, salary.

2. Requital, repayment, retribution, deserts, retaliation, revenge, punishment, nemesis, judgment, penalty, talion, retort, recrimination.

RECOMPENSE, *v.* Make compensation, reward, repay, requite, compense, make good, refund, atone, cover, equalize, remit, replace, expiate, propitiate, guerdon, restitute, make restitution, offset, neutralize, redeem, pay for, make amends for, redress, reimburse, indemnify, satisfy, remunerate, make up for.

RECONCILE, *v.* 1. *(Foll. by TO)* Render no longer opposed, bring in acquiescence, content, resign, appease, lull, soothe, compose, make contented *or* resigned, put *or* set at ease, enable to submit (bear, endure, *etc.)*, win over, disarm, propitiate, pacify, tranquilize, conciliate, satisfy, comfort.

2. Win over to friendliness, make peace with *or* between, appease, placate, bring together, propitiate, pacify, conciliate, bring to terms, restore to friendship, reunite, agree, make up, meet halfway, heal the breach, put in tune *or* accord.

3. Settle *(a quarrel, difference, etc.)*, compose, adjust, heal, accommodate, set straight, fix up, negotiate, harmonize, accord, bridge over, arbitrate, patch up, mediate, moderate, mollify, make up, render concordant, square, homologize, regulate, adapt, bring into agreement *or* harmony, make compatible *or* consistent, assimilate, similarize, suit, fit, readjust.

RECONCILIATION, *n.* 1. Act of reconciling, process of making consistent *or* compatible, adaptation, pacification, reconcilement, accommodation, reunion, adjustment, compromise, restoration of harmony, settlement, assimilation, atonement, propitiation, appeasement, expiation, conciliation, mollification, amnesty, mediation, arbitration, understanding, rapprochement.

2. State of being reconciled, harmony, concordance, consistency, accord, congruity, agreement, correspondence, accordance, concord, congruency, concinnity, rapport, concert, coherence, terms, unison, union, congruence, congeniality, compatibility, apposition, affinity, coincidence, keeping, line, assent, similarity, amity, peace, sympathy, cooperation, unanimity, parallelism, concurrence, uniformity, symphony, understanding, conformance, conformity.

RECONDITE, *adj.* 1. Dealing with abstruse *or* profound matters, deep, learned, mysterious, esoteric, abstract, enigmatic, ambiguous, occult, profound, abstruse, subtle, crabbed, intricate, involved, tangled, knotty, complex, perplexed, difficult.

2. Removed from ordinary knowledge *or* understanding, little known, abstruse, profound, occult, hidden, dark, obscure, concealed, mystic, mystical, transcendental, mysterious, shrouded in mystery, perdu, cryptic, arcane, enigmatic, secret, imperspicuous, impenetrable, nebulous, equivocal.

RECONDITION, *v.* Restore to a good *or* satisfactory condition, repair, regenerate, mend, fix, remedy, renew, rejuvenate, revamp, recreate, re-

form, rebuild, reconstruct, renovate, make over, overhaul, service, patch, doctor *(coll.)*, cobble.

RECONNAISSANCE, *n.* Preliminary survey, scrutiny, preview, view, examination, observation, reconnoitering, inspection, exploration, exploitation, espial, study, investigation, espionage, once-over *(sl.)*.

RECONNOITER, *v.* Inspect, survey, examine, observe, make a reconnaissance, inquire, view, search, spy out, investigate, study, size up, take stock, inspect, scout, probe, look the ground over, scan, case *(sl.)*.

RECONSIDER, *v.* Consider again *(esp. with a view to a change of decision or action),* re-examine, think over, revise, recheck, retrace, reinquire, review, sleep upon, take under advisement, view in a new light, think better of, correct, emend, amend.

RECONSTRUCT, *v.* Construct again, recompose, reconstitute, re-establish, rebuild, make over, restore, reproduce, remodel, revamp, remake, refashion, reform, recreate, regenerate, rehabilitate, reinstate, repair, renovate, recondition.

RECORD, *n.* 1. Information *or* knowledge preserved in writing, *etc.*, account, register, chronicle, annals, diary, note, report, list, item, roll, minute, score, file, docket, proceedings, registry, memoir, roster, catalouge, chartulary, testimony, deed, contract, covenant, book, jotting, certificate, inventory, journal, ledger, inscription, chronology, census, document, scroll, logbook, muniment *(Law)*, memorandum.

2. Report *(list, aggregate)* of actions *or* achievements, career, account, history, life, transcript, memoirs, biography, autobiography, experiences, confessions, adventures, summary, fortunes, description, enumeration, sketch, obituary, necrology, relation, recital, vignette, résumé, journal, review, specifications, particulars.

3. Device which reproduces sound, disk, platter, tape, cylinder, wax *(Motion pictures)*.

4. Notable degree of achievement, best rate *(amount, etc.)* attained, top performance, perfection, acme, height, summit, superior attainment, ultimate, paragon, unbeaten mark, par *(Golf)*.

RECORD, *v.* Set down *(in writing, etc.),* register, fix, take down, chronicle, enter, note, enroll, journalize, catalogue, list, log, put *or* place on record, calendar, book, insert, take a minute, copy, post, enumerate, document, make an entry of, make a memorandum, score, jot down, file, tally, narrate.

RECORDER, *n.* 1. One who records *(esp. as an official duty)*, registrar, chronicler, clerk, scribe, stenographer, bookkeeper, copyist, amanuensis, annalist, historian, biographer, accountant, prothonotary, secretary, marker, scorer, score-keeper.

2. Recording *or* registering apparatus *or* device, phonograph, reproducer, dictaphone, wax *(Motion pictures)*.

RECOUNT, *v.* 1. Give the facts *or* particulars of, relate, narrate, tell in detail, describe, detail, enumerate, recite, rehearse, report, mention, portray, particularize, repeat, state, retell, recapitulate, give an account of, utter, characterize, set forth, articulate, communicate, convey, impart, picture, unfold, render, represent, divulge, elucidate, depict, delineate, voice, deliver.

2. Narrate in order, tell one by one, enumerate, recapitulate, name *or* call over, detail, count, sum up, particularize, itemize, specify, recite.

RECOUP, *v.* Provide *or* be an equivalent for, return an amount equal to, redeem, reimburse, reindemnify, compensate for, pay, recover, retrieve, reward, requite, repay, compense, refund, make good, atone, remit, replace, expiate, fee, guerdon, restitute, make restitution, make amends for, redress, indemnify, satisfy, remunerate, make up for.

RECOURSE, *n.* 1. Resort *(to a peson or thing for help or protection),* appplication, escape, flight, petition, prayer, suit, beseaching, turning, request, solicitation, appeal, entreaty, supplication.

2. Person *or* thing resorted to for help *or* protection, refuge, heaven, safehold, place of security, retreat, resort, resource, rock, pillar, anchor, tower, escape, stronghold, cloister, hiding place, asylum, sanctum, sanctuary.

RECOVER, *v.* 1. Regain, get back, recapture, repossess, make good, make up for, recruit, retrieve, resume, recall, rally, recoup, replevin, replevy, renew, find, reconquer, win back, re-establish, ransom, restore, reinstate.

2. Rally, regain strength *(composure, balance, etc.),* regain a former and better state *or* condition, mend, heal, come around, be restored to health, recuperate, get well, convalesce, pull throught, recruit, improve, return to health, revive, be oneself again, survive, perk up, take a turn for the better, take a favorable turn, live again, rise again.

3. Reclaim *(from a bad state, practice, etc.),* regain *(a substance)* in usable form, save, rescue, salvage, redeem, recondition, reform, amend, retrieve, right, rescue, remodel, rectify, reinstate, repossess, convert, replevin, replevy, revendicate, rehabilitate, regenerate, re-establish, correct, recall, revive, restore.

RECREANT, *adj.* 1. Cowardly, craven, base, dastardly, poltroon, fearful, pusillanimous, spiritless, timid, yielding, mean-spirited, faint-hearted, unrepentant, erring, nefarious, incorrigible, irreclaimable, lacking strength of mind *or* courage, lily-livered, feeble, afraid, white-livered, chicken-hearted, effeminate, vacillating, irresolute, caitiff *(Poetic),* skulking, without a will of one's own, with a yellow streak *(sl.),* yellow *(sl.),* timorous, wavering, hesitant, uncourageous, soft, cowering, sneaking.

2. Unfaithful, disloyal, false, untrue, traitorous, faithless, renegade, apostate, apostatic, treacherous, backsliding, relapsing, recidivistic, unreliable, undependable, perfidious, dishonest, conniving, guileful, sham, hollow-hearted, shifty, insidious, deceitful, double-dealing, two-faced, knavish, betraying, treasonable, hollow, dishonorable, without honor, unscrupulous, untrustworthy, corrupt, scheming, designing, unconscienced, dissembling, false-hearted.

RECREANT, *n.* 1. Coward, craven, dastard, poltroon, sneak, scaramouch, skulk, mean wretch, weakling, malingerer, dodger, jellyfish, milksop, caitiff *(Poetic),* shirker, white feather, white liver, mollycoddle, sissy *(coll.),* quitter *(coll.),* funk *(coll.),* funker *(coll.),* doormat, namby-pamby, piker *(sl.).*

2. Apostate, traitor, renegade, runagate, runaway, bolter, deserter, backslider, turntail, turncoat, recidivist, reactionary, rat *(sl.),* heretic, betrayer, quisling, Brutus, informer, double-dealer, snake in the grass, dissembler, dissimulator, Benedict Arnold, deceiver, Judas Iscariot, welsher *(sl.).*

RECREATE, *v.* 1. Refresh *(by means of relaxation and enjoyment),* restore, gladden, divert, entertain, enliven, relax, interest, rejuvenate, rehabilitate, regenerate, inspirit, mend, heal, invigorate, exhilarate, refocillate, relieve, revive, reanimate, renew, amuse, cheer.

2. Take recreation, unbend, relax, be refreshed, be restored, rest, play, sport, drown care, be amused *or* diverted, unbend, beguile the time, make *or* keep holiday.

3. Create anew, reproduce, refashion, make over, re-establish, renovate, remake, reconstruct, reform, regenerate, duplicate, match, echo, double, reorganize, remodel, rebuild, facsimile.

RECREATION, *n.* 1. Refreshment *(by means of pastime, agreeable exercise, etc.),* amusement, diversion, rest, restoration, relaxation, cheer, invigoration, strengthening, stimulation, revivification, refocillation, reviviscence, rejuvenation, easement, exhilaration, renewal, revival, regalement, relief, entertainment.

2. Form *or* means of refreshment, pastime, diversion, exercise, play, sport, resource affording relaxation and enjoyment, festivity, frolic, game, fun, treat, pleasantry, hobby, labor of love, regalement, pleasure, divertissement, skylarking, avocation, holiday, vacation.

3. Act of creating anew, reconstruction, reformation, reduplication, reproduction, remaking, re-establishment, regeneration.

RECRIMINATE, *v.* Bring a countercharge against an accuser, accuse in return, hit back, turn on *or* upon, have revenge, strike back, lash back, pay back, requite, retaliate, countercharge, retort, return an accusation, give one a dose of his own medicine *(coll.),* return the compliment, cap, match, give in kind, come back at, turn the tables on, even the score, get even with, exchange blows, reciprocate, pass the buck *(coll.),* shift the blame *or* responsibility.

RECRUDESCE, *v.* Break out afresh *(as a sore, disease, etc., which has been quiescent),* reappear, recur, return, resume, flare up, revivify, resurge, renew activity, erupt, reactivate, revive, strike again.

RECRUDESCENCE, *n.* Breaking out afresh *or* into renewed activity, return, renewal, revival, reappearance in active existence, reanimation, reviviscence, revivification, resumption, resurgence, recurrence, eruption, reactivation.

RECRUIT, *n.* Newly acquired *or* drafted soldier *or* newly secured member, supporter, conscript, tyro, initiate, novice, helper, auxiliary, rookie *(sl.),* beginner, draftee, fledgling, newcomer, aid, tenderfoot, apprentice, reinforcement, probationer, greenhorn, neophyte, contingent (pl.).

RECRUIT, *v.* 1. Enlist *(men)* for military *or* naval service, raise *(a force)* by enlistment, strengthen with new men, call to arms, mobilize, reinforce, supply with new men, rally.

2. Furnish with a fresh supply, replenish, add to stock, store, fill up, supply a lack, repair, swell the ranks of, fortify, replace, recoup, provide, buttress, enlarge, augment, increase, renovate, restore, refresh, revive, reinvigorate, strengthen, equip, arm, fit out.

3. Renew *(health, strength, etc.),* return to health, recover, revive, regain health, take a new lease on life, convalesce, get well, be restored to health, mend, heal, come around, recuperate, pull through, improve, be oneself again, survive, perk

up, take a turn for the better, take a favorable turn, rise again.

RECTANGULAR, *adj.* Right-angled, square, oblong, angular, quadrate, foursquare, oblongitudinal, quadrangular, quadrilateral, orthogonal *(Math.).*

RECTIFY, *v.* Make (put, set) right, correct, redress, mend, amend, meliorate, right, perfect, refine, emend, reform, adjust, cure, restore, revise, remedy, renovate, put *or* set to rights, make all square, ameliorate, unravel, regulate, straighten, purify, untangle, align, cure, better, improve, repair.

RECTILINEAR, *adj.* Forming (formed by, characterized by *or* moving in) a straight line, right-lined, straight, straight-lined, undeviating, unswerving, unturning, in a line, lineal, even, true, direct, virgate, undistorted, perpendicular, rectilineal.

RECTITUDE, *n.* 1. Rightness *(of principle or practice),* integrity, equity, justice, honesty, righteousness, virtue, goodness, purity, veracity, morality, conscientiousness, probity, right, uprightness, honor, fidelity, fairness, truthfulness, scrupulousness, reputability, merit, principle, veridity, veraciousness, impeccability, uncorruptibility, faithfulness, straightforwardness, trustworthiness, faith, truth-loving, respectability, honorableness, responsibility, impartiality, loyalty to the good.
2. Correctness, accuracy, freedom from error, conformity to truth, exactitude, exactness, precision, justness, fidelity, regularity, truth, nicety, strictness, minuteness, severity, closeness, accordance, perfection, veracity, truthfulness, verity, probity, faultlessness, soundness, propriety, validity, equity, integrity, accurateness.

RECTOR, *n.* Clergyman, minister, priest, curate, parson, pastor, ecclesiastic, divine, churchman, preacher, vicar, chaplain, cleric, theologian, clerical, father, pulpiter, servant of God, canonist, confessor, spiritual director, dignitary, penitentiary, evangelist, bishop, dean, padre, curé, presbyter, deacon, dominie *(coll.),* reverend *(coll.).*

RECTORY, *n.* Parsonage, rector's house, pastorate, manse, presbytery, vicarage, deanery, church house, clergy house.

RECUMBENT, *adj.* 1. Reclining, leaning, lying down, prostrate, prone, supine, resting, at full length, recubate, resupine, flat, stretched out, prostrated, laid out, accumbent, decumbent, procumbent, horizontal, couchant, jacent, lounging, lolling, sprawling.
2. Inactive, listless, idle, reposing, passive, indifferent, laggard, lacking zest, torpid, indolent, slack, languid, sluggish, supine, drowsy, comatose, heavy, inanimate, dull, phlegmatic, soporific, lethargic, faineant, dormant, lifeless, stupefied, inert, lazy, leaden, slow, ponderous, weary, without vivacity or vitality, lifeless, dronish, torpescent, torporific, lentitudinous, stolid, lumpish, hebetate, quiescent, apathetic, static, hebetudinous, drowsy, soporose.

RECUPERATE, *v.* Recover from sickness *or* exhaustion, regain health *or* strength, get back, rally, recruit, convalesce, mend, heal, come around, be restored to health, get well, pull through, improve, return to health, revive, be oneself again, survive, perk up, take a turn for the better, take a favorable turn, live again, rise again, take a new *or* fresh lease on life.

RECUPERATIVE, *adj.* Having the power of re-

cuperating, pertaining to recuperating, healing, restorative, restoring, restitutive, revivatory, reviviscent, reparative, sanative, curative, improving, remedial, corrective, therapeutic, medicinal, alterative *(Med.),* analeptic *(Med.).*

RECUR, *v.* 1. Occur again, re-occur, come back *or* again, return, repeat, resume, revert, revolve, repullulate, persist, reappear, alternate, come and go, come 'round, persevere, continue, intermit, come in turn.
2. Return to the mind, be remembered, flash on the mind, flash across the memory, live *or* dwell in the memory, haunt one's thoughts, badger one, nag, harass, trouble, run in the head, rankle, intrude itself on one's thoughts.

RECURRENT, *adj.* That recurs, occurring *or* appearing again *(esp. periodically or repeatedly),* returning at intervals, intermittent, renewed, cyclic, reappearing, fluctuating, reiterated, reiterative, reduplicated, repetitional, periodic, periodical, systematic, continual, haunting, chronic, iterated, iterative, remittent, alternate, repetitious, regular, frequent, atavistic, isochronal, habitual, incessant, thick-coming, re-echoing, epochal, seasonal, serial, rhythmic, pulsative, pulsating, throbbing, repeated, repetitive.

RECUSANCY, *n.* Obstinate refusal *or* opposition, nonconformity, dissent, disobedience, heterodoxy, heresy, disagreement, infraction, recreancy, perversion, secession, defection, sectarianism, unorthodoxy, violation, abnegation, denial, disavowal, irrepentance, impenitence, abjuration, recantation, apostasy, infringement of custom *or* usage, unconventionality, noncompliance, nonobservance, disconformity, nonconformance, induration, obduracy, uncontriteness, declination, discord, discordance, schism, dissentience, dissidence, unwillingness of assent.

RECUSANT, *adj.* Refusing to submit *or* comply, etc., obstinate in refusal, dissenting, dissentient, abnegative, abjuratory, apostate, deserting, heretic, nonconforming, counteractive, opposed, contrary, unwilling, refusing, unconsenting, discordant, schismatic, resistant, at odds, inimical, hostile, antagonistic, negative, protestant, nonjuring, unconverted, repugnant, oppugnant, recalcitrant, rebellious, unresigned, oppositional, dissident.

RECUSANT, *n.* One who is recusant, dissenter, dissentient, nonjurer, sectary, noncontent, nonconformist, malcontent, rebel, heretic, insurgent, seceder, apostate, separatist, protestant, reactionary, pervert, skeptic, iconoclast, irreconcilable.

RED, *adj.* 1. Ruddy, scarlet, blood-colored, sanguine, bloody, flaming, cherry-colored, carmine, rubicund, reddish, vinaceous, rubric, auburn, claret-colored, rufous, erubescent, gridelin, wine-colored, salmon, coral, rosy, pink, cerise, chaudron, terra cotta, cochineal, miniate, puniceous, miniaceous, Castilian red, cardinal.
2. Blushing, flushing, glowing, florid, burning, rosy, inflamed, aglow, rubescent, sanguine, bloodshot, blooming, flushed, reddened.
3. Radical, pink, socialist, Marxian, Soviet, communistic, communist, Russian, Fourieristic, Saint-Simonian.

REDACT, *v.* 1. Bring into presentable literary form, revise, edit, amend, emendate, improve, correct, review, emend.
2. Draw up *(a statement, etc.),* form, compose, fabricate, devise, frame, compile, make up, constitute, draft, weave, produce, chisel, hew, ham

mer out, evolve, construct, erect, carve, fashion, contrive, formulate, set up.

REDEEM, *v.* 1. Recover *(something pledged or mortgaged)*, reclaim, retrieve, buy back, repurchase, buy *or* pay off, repay, ransom, regain, recapture, repossess, make good, recoup, replevin, replevy, find, win back, restore, reinstate.

2. Fulfill *(a pledge, promise, etc.)*, discharge, keep, perform, make good, carry out, complete, dispatch, consummate, accomplish, realize, see through, execute, enact, be as good as one's word, be faithful to, obey, adhere to, keep faith with, acquit, satisfy, meet, act up to, abide by.

3. Compensate, recompense, make restitution, recoup, reclaim, redress, expiate, atone for, make amends for, propitiate, absolve, purge, satisfy, settle, defray, reward, requite, compense, cover, restitute.

4. Obtain the release *or* restoration of *(as from captivity)*, free, ransom, liberate, retrieve, recover, reclaim, release, rescue, save, set free, emancipate, extricate.

5. Deliver from sin and its consequences, regenerate, save, recover, rescue, reclaim, reform, purge, shrive, absolve, intercede for, mediate on behalf of, set straight again, turn from sin, convert, reform, reinstate.

REDEEMABLE, *adj.* Capable of being redeemed, retrievable, deliverable, exchangeable, good, curable, corrigible, improvable, amendable, correctable, restorable, rescuable, extricable, worth something, salvageable.

REDEEMER, *n.* Ransomer, savior, freer, emancipator, manumitter, liberator, rescuer, deliverer.

REDEMPTION, *n.* Act of redeeming, state of being redeemed, repurchase, recovery by payment, paying off *(as of a mortgage, bond or note)*, compensation, retrieval, restoration, restitution, buying, rehabilitation, reinstatement, re-establishment, regeneration, conciliation propitiation, reconstitution, reformation, redintegration, return, conversion, salvage, comeback *(coll.)*, saving, freeing, expiation, ransom, reclamation, liberation, deliverance, rescue, release, salvation, reprieve, escape, emancipation, atonement, repossession, reparation, rebirth, repentance, amends.

RED-HANDED, *adj.* In the very act of a crime, in the act, while one is at it, while one's hand is in, flagrante delicto *(Law)*.

RED-HOT, *adj.* 1. Very hot, red with heat, fiery, calorific, torrid, sizzling, scorching, white-hot, molten, glowing, recalescent, decalescent, burning.

2. Very excited *or* enthusiastic, fervent, fervid, ardent, passionate, hot-blooded, warm, hot, hearty, devout, zealous, glowing impassioned, vehement, flushed, quivering, wrought up, agitated, fanatical, rabid, gushing *(coll.)*, delirious, avid, eager, earnest, keen, flushed, febrile, feverish, boiling over.

3. Violent, furious, raving, raging, frenzied, wild, overwrought, hot-headed, inflamed, fuming, seething, delirious, flaming, rabid, mad, carried away, beside oneself, out of one's wits, turbulent, rampant, tempest-tossed, distracted, vehement, foaming at the mouth, ranting, tumultuary, boisterous, tempestuous, frantic, demoniac, fierce, ferocious.

4. Fresh, new, most recent, latest, up-to-the-minute, just off the press, brand new, novel, modern, neoteric, untried, up-to-date, current, instant, fashionable, startling.

REDINTEGRATE, *v.* Make whole again, restore to a perfect state, recreate, reconstitute, re-establish, rehabilitate, renovate, reconstruct, remake, regenerate, mend, heal, repair, renew, recover.

REDIVIVUS, *adj.* Having new life, revived, restored, renewed, renascent, reanimated.

REDOLENCE, *n.* Scent, perfume, odor, balm, incense, fragrance, essence, flavor, breath, exhalation, effluvium, pungence, savor, spice, emanation, aroma, bouquet, smell.

REDOLENT, *adj.* Fragrant, perfumed, spicy, scented, odorous, balmy, ambrosial, savory, sweet, pungent, odoriferous.

REDOUBT, *n.* Fortification, rampart, entrenchment, breastwork, fortress, buttress, bulwark, stronghold, bastion, citadel, redan, battlement.

REDOUBTABLE, *adj.* Formidable, dread, dire, terrifying, alarming, disquieting, dismaying, startling, fearful, terrible, frightening, terror-giving, dreadful, awful, astounding, awe-inspiring.

REDOUND, *v.* Occur as a result of, be a consequence, result, follow, yield, flow from, rebound, come from, accrue, ensue, issue, proceed, be derived from.

REDRESS, *n.* 1. Reparation, amends, correction, satisfaction, atonement, quittance, retribution, conciliation, adjustment, rectification, remedy, restoration, compensation, requital, propitiation, repair.

2. Relief, improvement, amelioration, help, alleviation, rescue, aid, deliverance, mitigation, pacification, appeasement, easement.

REDRESS, *v.* 1. Set right, make amends, correct, adjust, rectify, right, readjust, regulate, amend, fix, repair, put right, make square, remedy, restore.

2. Atone, help, appease, allay, aid, mollify, compensate, ease, improve, relieve, alleviate, subdue, expiate, propitiate, recompense, mitigate, soften, pacify.

RED TAPE, *n.* Excessive attention to formality in business *or* official matters, officialdom, bureaucracy, delay, procrastination, stickling for detail, red-tapism, pettiness, pomposity, routine, bumbledom, beadledom

REDUCE, *v.* 1. Bring down *(to a smaller extent, size, amount, number)*, decrease, shorten, contract, render less, lessen, pare, deduct, discount, concentrate, detract from, abstract, constrict, confine, curtail, narrow, stunt, stub, nip, cheapen, shave, cut, slash, truncate, clip, check the growth of, reef *(Naut.)*, shrink, shrivel, abridge, mark down, boil down, epitomize, depreciate, take away from, condense, dwarf, slim down, slenderize, deliquesce.

2. Lower *(in degree, intensity, etc.)*, slacken, ease, remit, attenuate, extenuate, abate, dilute, weaken, retard, relax, let up, curb, check, rarefy, enfeeble, moderate, mitigate, exhaust, blunt the edge of, bate, rein in, dull, temper, incapacitate, devitalize, cut, lenify, water, assuage, inactivate, tone *or* tune down, modulate, slow down, soften, throttle down, break, brake.

3. Lower *(in rank, dignity, etc.)*, humble, humiliate, take power *or* authority from, detract from, belittle, break, minimize, overthrow, subdue, quell, embarrass, ruin, shame, quash, put in one's place, lay by the heels, confound, checkmate, crush, put out, put to shame, degrade, bring low, lower, disgrace, squelch *(coll.)*, abash, abase, degrade, mortify, enfeeble, bankrupt, extenuate, de-

vitalize, invalidate, debilitate, incapacitate, enfeeble, weaken.

4. Bring to a certain state (condition, arrangement), alter, transform, resolve, mutate, modify, convert, change, transmute, transfigure, metamorphose.

REDUCTION, *n.* 1. Act of reducing, state of beng reduced, decrease, subtraction, discount, diminution, contraction, shortening, depression, shrinkage, loss, abatement, concision, constriction, curtailment, subduction, abbreviation, retrenchment, condensation, syncope, ellipsis, elison, assuagement, mitigation, remission, decrement, relaxation, decline, moderation, modulation, abridgement, lessening, decrescence.

2. Amount by which something is reduced *or* diminished, discount, cut, rebate, agio, abatement, deduction, concession, depreciation.

3. Form produced by reducing, miniature, copy on a smaller scale, model, abridgement, condensation, digest, summary, abstract, draft, sketch, pandect, brief, epitome, recapitulation, review, résumé, précis.

REDUNDANCY, *n.* State of being redundant, redundant thing (part, amount), superfluity, surcharge, saturation, overexpansion, overdose, verbosity, excess, excessiveness, superabundance, immoderation, amplification, battology, tautology, pleonasm, opulence, overflow, enlargement, affluence, repletion, exorbitance, surplus, oversupply, surfeit, congestion, engorgement, glut, plethora, overplus, inordinacy, nimiety, prodigality, padding, expletive, overgrowth, extravagance, overfullness, inflation, profusion, prolixity, diffuseness, exuberance, lavishment, orotundity, pretension, grandiosity, turgescence, turgidity, coloring, stretch, embroidery, hyperbole, magnification, exaggeration, rodomontade, macrology, redundance.

REDUNDANT, *adj.* 1. Being in excess, exceeding what is usual *or* natural, prodigal, surplus, undue, superfluous, intemperate, needless, exaggerated, superabundant, overmuch, inordinate, exorbitant, extravagant, immoderate, unwarranted, overdone, uncalled-for, unnecessary, out of bounds *or* all bounds, lavish, profuse, expletive, excessive, excess, supernumerary, hyperbolic, outrageous, egregious, prolix, rampant, copious.

2. Characterized by *or* using too many words to express an idea, tautological, declamatory, pleonastic, verbose, diffuse, hyperbolic, repetitious, circumlocutory, loquacious, grandiloquent, superfluous, battological, fustian, mouthy, pedantic, altiloquent, periphrastic, ambagious, inflated, sonorous, circuitous, windy, showy, magniloquent, roundabout, bombastic, lexiphanic, tumid, turgid, pompous, flatulent, flaunting, swelling.

REDUPLICATE, *v.* Double, repeat, imitate, reproduce, duplicate, redouble, ditto, echo, recapitulate, geminate, retell, copy, mimeograph, remake, recreate, reform, match, parallel, mimic, mirror, facsimile, refashion.

REECHO, *v.* Echo back *(as a sound)*, give back an echo, resound, reiterate, repeat, resonate, rebound, answer, harp upon, iterate, dwell on, insist on, toll, din, beat, drum, throb, quaver, reverberate, hammer, roll, rumble.

REED, *n.* Straight stalk of tall grass *(or anything made from it or a similar substance)*, twig, stem, shaft, arrow, cane, spire, blade, spear.

RE-EDUCATE, *v.* Educate again, educate for re-

sumption of normal activities *(as a cripple)*, retrain, rehabilitate, return to its function, reclaim, redeem, recover, refit, readjust.

REEDY, *adj.* 1. Consisting *or* made of reeds, like reed, cane-like, cane, reed-like, arundinaceous *(Bot.),* calamiform.

2. Noting *or* having a tone like that of a reed instrument, piping, warbling, shrill, high-pitched, high-toned, piercing, dulcet, bird-like, sweet, clear, silvery, sharp, acute, mellifluous.

REEF, *n.* Narrow ridge of rocks *or* sand at *or* near the surface of the water, bar, shoal, shallow, bank, flat.

REEK, *n.* 1. Strong unpleasant smell, effluvium, mephitis, stench, stink, fetidness, malodor, miasma, fetor, nidorosity, graveolence, frowst, empyreuma.

2. Vapor, steam, effluvium, cloud, exhaust, ether, fume, gas, volatile essence.

REEK, *v.* 1. Smell strongly and unpleasantly, be strongly pervaded with something unpleasant *or* offensive, stink, smell, smell to high heaven, be malodorous, offend the nostrils, effluviate.

2. Give off steam, *etc.,* be wet with sweat, blood, *etc.,* expose to *or* treat with smoke, emit *(smoke, fumes, etc.),* vaporize, be watery *or* moist, be hot, evaporate, gasify, atomize, aerify, exhale, volatilize, smoke, steam, fume, perspire, drip, leak, ooze, exhaust, etherify *(Chem.),* sublime *(Chem.).*

REEL, *n.* Cylinder (frame *or* other device) on which to wind something, rotary device, spool, roll, boom, bobbin, wheel, pin, axis, pivot, spindle, arbor, axle.

REEL, *v.* 1. Sway *(under a blow, shock, etc.),* move uncertainly *(as from dizziness, intoxication, etc.),* stagger, waver, fall back, rock, swing, lurch, wallow, toss, totter, roll, pitch, flounder, stumble.

2. Turn round and round, whirl, swirl, rotate, revolve, spin, surge, eddy, wheel, gyrate, gyre, twirl, circle, pirouette, circumrotate, circumvolve, circumvolute, circumgyrate, swivel, whirligig, vertiginate.

REFECTION, *n.* Refreshment *(esp. with food or drink),* portion of food *or* drink, repast, stimulation, invigoration, nourishment, restoration, regalement, relief, nurture, bite, snack, feast, meal, cheer, spread *(coll.).*

REFECTORY, *n.* Dining hall *(in a religious house, college, etc.),* commons, mess hall, eating quarters, eating club.

REFER, *v.* 1. Direct attention *or* thoughts of *(as for information),* point, indicate, intend, mean, bend, turn, send, denote, signify, conduct, suggest, have to do with, connote.

2. Hand over *(for information, consideration, decision, etc.),* advise with, take up with, confer with, discuss with, consult, commit, talk over with, call in, ask help of, place *or* leave in the hands of, deliver over, relegate, give in charge, consign, resign, deliver, entrust, deposit, submit, render, bestow, transfer, discharge, invest, surrender, yield, commend.

3. Assign *(to a class, period, etc.),* regard as belonging *or* related, attribute, ascribe, lay to, put *or* set down to, impute, trace, assume to be of *or* from, father upon, blame on, accredit to, credit with, arrogate.

4. Have relation, apply, connect, answer to, correspond with, relate, belong, pertain, concern, have reference, appertain, touch, point, have to

do with, bear upon, comprise, tie in with, include, take into account *or* consideration, take in, cover, hold, embrace, encompass, involve, incorporate, deal with.

5. Turn *(as for aid or information)*, have recourse, appeal, have resort, invoke, defer, advise *or* confer with, ask help of, talk over with, ask, supplicate, entreat, plead, address, apply, consult, take up with, call in.

6. Direct a remark *or* mention, make reference or allusion, advert, allude, direct attention, quote, cite, hint at, mention, indicate, notice, suggest, touch upon, adduce, extract, exemplify, give as example, instance, excerpt, use as illustration.

REFEREE, *n.* One to whom something is referred *(esp. for decision or settlement)*, arbitrator, judge, umpire, arbiter, mediator, intermediator, moderator, reconciler, peacemaker, go-between, intervener, intermediary, referendary.

REFEREE, *v.* Preside over as referee, judge, act as referee, mediate, decide between, intercede, harmonize, adjust differences, intervene, negotiate, straighten out.

REFERENCE, *n.* 1. Mention, allusion, direction of the attention, attribution, hint, ascription, citation, intimation, assignment, imputation, relegation, quotation, parallel, accounting for, arrogation, enumeration, quoting, substantiation, illustration, instance, extract, evidence, excerpt, witness, adduction, bringing forward, innuendo.

2. Note indicating direction *(as to a book, passage, etc.)*, reference mark, symbol, figure, indicator, indicant, key, pointer, sign.

3. Written testimonial as to character, abilities, *etc.*, witness, attestation, warrant, voucher, declaration, affirmation, statement, authority, allegation, deposition *(Law)*.

4. Respect, regard, relation, bearing, affinity, concern, connection, applicability, alliance, relevance, aptness, pertinence, correlation.

REFERENDUM, *n.* Submission of measures to public approval *or* rejection, vote, election, suffrage, poll, plebiscite, *vox populi (Lat.)*.

REFINE, *v.* 1. Bring to a fine *or* pure state, free from impurities, rarefy, sublime, purge, subtilize, purify, clarify, fine, clear, cleanse, defecate, filter, strain, sift, separate, rectify *(Chem.)*, elutriate, develop, cultivate, winnow, mellow, clean, expurgate, absterge, epurate, depurate, wash, lave, edulcorate.

2. Purify from what is coarse (vulgar, debasing), make elegant *or* cultured, better, meliorate, cultivate, correct, uplift, sublime, restore, advance, forward, perfect, expurgate, devulgarize, decrassify, subtilize, rarefy, humanize, spiritualize, improve, liberalize, civilize, soften, temper, elevate, season, sensitize, sublimate.

3. Make more fine (nice, subtle, minutely precise), elaborate, perfect, complete, detail, be meticulous about, regulate, render true, make accurate, adjust, square, strive for accuracy, consummate.

4. Become pure, become more fine (elegant, polished), be clarified, ripen, rise, improve, soften, develop, fine, mellow.

5. Make fine distinctions in thought *or* language, be overnice, split hairs, mince, cavil, quibble, make useless distinctions, affect, be pedantic, be fastidious, prevaricate, equivocate, wiredraw, beg the question, subtilize.

REFINED, *adj.* 1. Imbued with *or* showing nice

feeling, taste, *etc.*, free from coarseness, vulgarity, *etc.*, cultivated, cultured, polished, elegant, genteel, polite, courtly, finished, fine, well-bred, civilized, spiritual, gentlemanly, ladylike, urbane, noble, gentle, pure, mannerly, high-minded, aesthetic, tasteful, graceful, in good taste, dainty, chaste, attic, classic, correct, restrained, sublimated, aristocratic, civil, gently bred, discriminating, exquisite, elevated, delicate.

2. Freed from impurities, clarified, purified, clean, pure, rarefied, subtilized, expurgate, cleaned, sublimed *(Chem.)*, sublimated *(Chem.)*.

3. Subtle, exact, minutely precise, meticulous, formal, proper, equivocal, discriminating, punctilious, strict, fastidious, squeamish, finicking, finical, overnice, dainty, overscrupulous, hypercritical, prudish, oversensitive, overconscientious, hairsplitting, overcritical.

REFINEMENT, *n.* 1. Fineness of feeling, taste, *etc.*, elegance, polish, politeness, breeding, grace, tact, gentleness, purity, cultivation, civilization, civility, delicacy, culture, graciousness, beauty, tastefulness, fine feeling, finish, gentility, elevation, courteousness, subtlety, nicety, discretion, finesse, discrimination, fastidiousness, propriety, chivalry, good manners, urbanity, courtesy, savoir-faire, mildness.

2. Subtilization, clarification, purification, defecation, cleaning, cleansing, purgation, epuration, abstersion, sublimation, filtration, lixiviation, edulcoration, elutriation, lustration, detersion, expurgation.

3. Improvement, betterment, reform, reformation, melioration, rectification, revision, emendation, amendment, advancement, progress, mending, enrichment, enhancement, elevation, development, lift, perfection, progression, rise, ascent, advance, amelioration.

4. Subtle point *or* distinction, subtle reasoning, discrimination, exactness, sophistry, nicety, subtility, delicacy, fineness, nuance, differentiation, hairsplitting, oversubtlety, fastidiousness, overpreciseness, meticulousness, scruple, punctilio, punctiliousness, critical niceness, finicality, finicalness, precision, hypercriticism, differentia *(pl.)*.

REFLECT, *v.* 1. Cast back, give back *or* show an image of, cause to return *or* rebound, mirror, throw back, copy, resonate, be resonant, repercuss, resound, surrebound, rebound, reproduce, ditto, send back, reply, reverberate, re-echo, echo, return, image, flash, revert, imitate.

2. Reproduce, show, exhibit, manifest, demonstrate, evince, display, disclose, reveal, indicate, evidence, set forth, betoken, denote, imply, connote, expose, show up, register, present, lay bare, uncover, breathe, represent, express, bring to light, give token of.

3. Think carefully, cogitate, meditate, ponder, study, consider, contemplate, dwell upon, muse, deliberate, ruminate, turn over, concentrate, weigh, revolve in the mind, view, reason, excogitate, be in a brown study, brood, cerebrate, dream, speculate, wonder, commune with oneself.

4. Serve to cast *or* bring credit, discredit, *etc.*, blame, condemn, rebound, recriminate, impugn, animadvert, cast *or* bring reproach.

REFLECTION, *n.* 1. Act of reflecting, recoil, reaction, retroaction, ricochet, backlash, repercussion, revulsion, return, reflex, reflux, echo, dispersion.

2. Reflected image, echo, shadow, representa-

tion, counterpart, duplicate, likeness, picture, image, copy, reproduction, specter.

3. Fixing of the thoughts on something, exercise of the intellect, thought, meditation, rumination, consideration, cogitation, contemplation, deliberation, thinking, musing, study, imagination, observation, speculation, ponderation, cerebration, intellection, excogitation, self-communing, self-counsel, lucubration, mentation, reverie, concentration, abstraction, absorption, scrutiny, pensiveness, attention.

4. Thought (occurring in consideration or meditation), idea, remark, opinion, notion, speculation, imagining, comment, image in the mind, consideration, sentiment, theory, fancy, view, conviction, perception, impression, apprehension, train of thought.

5. Unfavorable remark or observation, casting of imputation or reproach, criticism, censure, reproach, reprehension, animadversion, denouncement, obloquy, imputation, stricture, lampoon, insinuation, slur, reproof, accusation, condemnation, hit, reprobation, knock (sl.), slam (sl.), innuendo, blame, disparagement.

REFLECTIVE, adj. Given to or concerned with meditation, thoughtful, musing, cogitating, pondering, contemplative, museful, dreamy, meditative, sober, absorbed, rapt, wrapped in thought, lost in thought, considerate, thinking, studious, philosophical, cogitative, intellectual, wistful, preoccupied, abstracted, in a reverie, deliberative, pensive, reasoning, deliberating, excogitative, engrossed, speculative.

REFLECTOR, n. One who or that which reflects, looking glass, mirror, glass, speculum, reverberator, pier glass, resonator, sounding board.

REFLEX, adj. 1. Occurring in reaction, responsive, reflective, reactive, recidivous, repercussive, refluent, reactionary, retroactive, automatic (Physiol.), involuntary (Physiol.).

2. Cast back (as light, etc.), reflected, mirrored, copied, resounding, repercussive, resonant, imitated, resilient, returned, rebounding, re-echoed, echoed, reverberative.

3. Turned back, crooked, hooked, flexed, bent back, reflected, reflexed, curved, adunc, hamate (Anat.), aduncous, uncate, uncinate.

REFLUENT, adj. Ebbing, flowing back, recoiling, receding, recessive, subsiding, regressive, rebounding, returning, waning, declining, outgoing, neap, reversing, retreating, retiring, withdrawing.

REFLUX, n. Flowing back, ebb, refluence, recoil, return, rebound, revulsion, recession, lapse, decline, subsidence, wane, regress, outgo, regurgitation, regression, neap tide, reversal, reversion, retreat, retirement, withdrawal, reflow.

REFORM, n. Improvement of what is wrong, corrupt, etc., amendment, rectification, correction, reformation, recovery, reclamation, amelioration, reconstitution, regeneration, progress, recreation, repair, remaking, renewal, conversion, renovation, new leaf, revolution, radicalism.

REFORM, v. 1. Restore to a former and better state, improve (by alteration, substitution, abolition, etc.), convert, mend, amend, emend, cure, remedy, correct, remodel, redeem, rehabilitate, reorganize, repair, rectify, better, meliorate, ameliorate, restore, regenerate, refashion, remake, rebuild, set straight again, restore, reclaim, reconstruct, reconstitute, revolutionize.

2. Abandon evil conduct or error, progress, repent, recant, be converted, amend, mend one's ways, turn over a new leaf, put on the new man, atone, make amends, set one's house in order, perform or do penance.

REFORMATORY, adj. Serving or designed to reform, reforming, progressive, corrective, reformational, restorative, forward-looking, restoring, curative, sanative, sanatory, recuperatory, medicinal, therapeutic, alterative, healing, analeptic (Med.), emendatory, recuperative, restitutive, restitutory, reviviscent, revivatory, reviviscible, reformative.

REFORMATORY, n. Reform school, penal institution for reformation of young offenders, house of correction, farm school.

REFRACTION, n. (Physics) Change of direction of a ray of light, heat etc., deflection (of rays), deviation, turning, distortion, divergence, flection, deflexure, obliquation, refringence, refractivity.

REFRACTORY, adj. 1. Stubborn, unmanageable, intractable, headstrong, mulish, perverse, obstinate, dogged, cross-grained, unyielding, contumacious, self-willed, disobedient, unruly, ungovernable, recalcitrant, cantankerous, incoercible, fractious, factious, obstreperous, balky, defiant, mutinous, untoward, unsubmissive, insubordinate, lawless, restive, naughty, resistant, opposing, willful, renitent, repugnant, oppugnant, contrary, pigheaded, bullheaded, pervicacious, rebellious, antagonistic.

2. Resisting ordinary methods of treatment, difficult to fuse (reduce, work, as ore or metal), unmalleable, unyielding, hard, impliable, infusible, unworkable, tough, inflexible, unmeltable.

REFRAIN, n. Phrase or verse recurring at intervals (in a song or poem), chorus, burden, repeated part, falderal, response, strophe, antistrophe, repetend (Mus.), bourdon (Mus.), envoy (Pros.), ritornel, overword.

REFRAIN, v. Keep oneself from, withhold, abstain, forbear, discontinue, cease, stay, stop, halt, quit, hold or stay one's hand, desist, refuse, govern oneself, not do or act, contain oneself, keep in check, curb oneself, check oneself, avoid, stop, eschew, spare, hang fire, deny oneself, exercise self-control (self-denial, self-restraint), swear off, renounce, take no part in, let well enough alone, have no hand in, stand or hold aloof, let be, be temperate.

REFRESH, v. 1. Make fresh again, reinvigorate, cheer, reanimate, comfort, vivify, cool, quicken, rejoice, strengthen, fortify, feast, buttress, sustain, animate, revive, brace, air, regale, slake, give fresh vigor to, freshen, enliven, recreate, recruit, brisk, exhilarate, invigorate, sharpen, stimulate, energize, relieve, reinforce, rest, rejuvenate, resuscitate, put or infuse new blood into, key up, whet.

2. Stimulate (the memory), jog, arouse, revive, reimpress, animate, quicken, set in motion, stir up, motivate, give impetus to, prod, cause to recall or remember, fire, kindle, enkindle, prompt, awaken, rouse, sharpen, excite, activate.

3. Freshen (in appearance, color, etc.), clean, refurbish, repair, restore, retouch, renovate, recondition, brush up, vamp up, rub up, polish, brighten, remodel, recreate, regenerate, rejuvenate, mend, treat, renew, revamp, put in repair.

REFRESHMENT, n. 1. That which refreshes (esp. food and drink), repast, nourishment, refection, entertainment, regalement, collation, snack, bite, treat, feast, viands, victuals, provisions.

2. Act of refreshing, state of being refreshed, entertainment, invigoration, relief, restoration, revival, renewal, renovation, refection, reinvigoration, diversion, recreance, recreation, pleasure, reanimation, resuscitation, reviviscence, revivification, easement, soothing, rejuvenation, regeneration, enlivenment, bracing, palingenesis, relaxation, stimulation, vivification, exhilaration, strengthening, refocillation, regenesis.

REFRIGERATE, *v.* Make *or* keep cool *or* cold, cool, chill, freeze *or* near freeze *(food, etc.)* for preservation, reduce the heat of, congeal, frigorify, glaciate, infrigidate, regelate *(Physics).*

REFRIGERATION, *n.* Production of low temperatures, cooling, preservation by cold, glacification, freezing, infrigidation, regelation, glaciation,

REFRIGERATOR, *n.* Box (room, cabinet) in which food and drink, *etc.*, are kept cool, refrigeratory, cooler, freezer, refrigerated room *or* box, icebox, ice chest, cold storage, refrigerator car, frigidarium, frigidaire *(coll.).*

REFUGE, *n.* 1. Shelter *(from danger, trouble, etc.)*, protection, safety, safekeeping, security, anchorage, resort, oversight, surveillance, auspices, asylum, retreat, retirement, hiding, resource, seclusion, privacy, care, aid, defense, preservation, support, custody, concealment, patronage, escort, convoy, ward, keep, charge, guardianship, sanctum.

2. Place of shelter, protection *or* safety, asylum, haven, covert, sanctuary, stronghold, place of safety, harbor, hiding place, ark, home, fastness, retreat, cover, safehold, lodging, resort, journey's end, fortress, mew, keep, ward, citadel, tower, rock, pillar, cloister, hermitage, port in a storm, hide-out, den, lair, nest, subterfuge, cell, bourn, safety zone, harborage, shade, fortification.

3. Anything to which one has recourse *(for aid, relief or escape)*, resort, expedient, tactic, shift, device, loophole, cover, subterfuge, artifice, stratagem, blind, feint, stopgap, contrivance, provision, evasion, dodge *(coll.)*, sleight, juggle, art, wile, machination, game, ruse, trick, maneuver, circumvention.

REFUGEE, *n.* One who flees for refuge *or* safety, fugitive, escaper, escapee, deserter, runaway, exile, displaced person, D.P.

REFULGENT, *adj.* Shining, glowing, radiant, lustrous, resplendent, bright, effulgent, argent, sunny, brilliant, luminous, illuminated, incandescent, aglow, ablaze, luminiferous, phosphorescent, relucent, sparkling, lucid, orient *(Poetic)*, shiny, lambent, lit, irradiated, lucent, alight, luminescent, blazing, radiative, nitidous, fulgent.

REFUND, *n.* Repayment, reimbursement, abatement, reduction, return, rebate, allowance, offtake, cut, discount, percentage, concession *(Com.)*, drawback *(Com.).*

REFUND, *v.* Give back *(esp. money)*, make repayment to, repay, reimburse, return, reward, restore, pay back, recompense, compensate, remunerate, redeem, make amends, redress, make good, make restitution, settle, fee, balance, square with, cover, indemnify, make compensation, remit, recoup, replace, requite, adjust, satisfy.

REFURBISH, *v.* Renovate, polish up, brighten, repair, renew, retouch, refresh, revamp, put in repair, cobble, overhaul, service, freshen, mend,

clean, recondition, restore, rub up, vamp up, remodel, rejuvenate, treat.

REFUSAL, *n.* 1. Act of refusing, denial, negation, disclaimer, nonconsent, unwillingness, disapproval, veto, dissent, disavowal, regrets, noncompliance, nonacceptance, repudiation, rejection, rebuff, disfavor, declinature, renouncement, renunciation, forswearing, abjuration, abnegation, withholding, repulse, nay, dissallowance, declension, declination.

2. Priority in refusing *or* taking something, emption, election, pre-emption, option, choice of accepting *or* declining, privilege.

REFUSE *v.* Reject, disallow, forswear, not allow, not permit, decline consent for, withhold consent, negate, abnegate, withhold one's assent, grudge, begrudge, negative, say no to, protest, disclaim, turn down, deny, refuse point blank, put one's foot down, be unwilling, not budge an inch, not yield an inch, dissent, disapprove, frown upon, view with disfavor, not countenance, discountenance, veto, not hear of, shake the head at, boggle, demur, scruple, look askance at, think ill of, take exception to, renounce, disclaim, debar, bar, prohibit, balk, keep back, protest, disavow, rebuff, repel, repudiate, exclude, revoke, send back, abstain from, spurn, forbid, oppose, discredit, cast aside, throw aside, throw out, not comply with, dismiss, repulse, contradict, stand off, disown, abjure, refuse to have anything to do with, except, set at naught, scout, scorn to receive, reject with contempt, reject with scorn, withdraw, renege, hold out, be obstinate, stick at, stickle, blink, dodge *(coll.)*, shirk, avoid, controvert, contravene, dispute, gainsay, traverse, contradict, rebut, refute, retract, recant, view with disfavor, object to, raise objections to, raise the voice against, cavil, revolt from the idea of, slam the door in one's face, turn one's back on, have nothing to do with, cast behind one, not hear of, stand aloof from, set one's face against, wash one's hands of, resist, cross.

REFUSE, *n.* Sediment, dregs, scum, dross, castoffs, leavings, litter, garbage, scraps, remainders, lees, sweepings, chaff, offal, waste, scoria, offscourings, excrement, trash, rubbish, offscum, junk, slag, culls, residuum, fragments, remnants, debris, fag-ends, shoddy, relicts, rags, rubble, rejectamenta, feculence, cheese parings, sewage, clinker, odds and ends, flotsam, jetsam, orts, stuff, lumber, dust, truck, stubble, tares, weeds, bones, rags, wastepaper, carrion, slough, swill, hogwash, bilge, scourings, rinsings, scurf, furfur, tartar, detritus, oddments, grounds, sordes, sprue, bottoms, settlings, residue.

REFUTATION, *n.* Confutation, contradiction, rebuttal, disproval, disprovement, disproof, rebutment, answer, retort, contradiction, conclusive argument, unanswerable argument, squelcher, finisher, invalidation, negation, denial, final argument, disclaimer, disavowal, disaffirmation, abjurement, controversion, contravention, gainsaying, forswearing, recusancy, disownment, counter-argument, counter-statement, conviction, formal denial, formal disclaimer, formal disproof.

REFUTE, *v.* Disprove, confute, repudiate, contradict, contravene, rebut, deny, overthrow, give the lie to, belie, impugn, convict of error, controvert, negate, negative, knock into a cocked hat, knock the bottom out of, parry, invalidate, explode, show up, expose, convict, confound, oppugn, answer, argue against, falsify, reply to, make retort, show one's weak point, dismiss, overwhelm, overthrow, down, floor, dispose of, quash, squash, squelch, shut up, reduce to silence, get the better of, dispute, contend, argue, debate, crush, put to rout, put to flight, oppose, gainsay, traverse, disown, disclaim, abnegate, forswear, abjure.

REGAIN, v. Recover, get back, win back, reobtain, repossess, retrieve, recapture, gain anew, redeem, revendicate, reoccupy, resume, replevin, retake, replevy, reclaim.

REGAL, adj. Royal, kingly, sovereign, imperial, imposing, noble, august, princely, monarchical, monarchal, majestic, magnificent, sceptred, dynastic, suzerain, royalistic, kinglike, princelike, imperialistic, autocratic, feudal, lordly, proud, stately, splendid, grand.

REGALE, v. 1. Gratify, slake, satiate, sate, quench, please, refresh, treat, recreate, nurture, feed, nourish, sustain, foster, strengthen, delight, comfort, appease the appetite of, victual, provision, purvey, provender, forage, pasture, refect, freshen, brace, reanimate, revivify, cheer, give refreshment, restore.
2. Entertain, please, gratify, amuse, divert, delight, interest, treat, entrance, bewitch, indulge, enliven, transport, enchant, humor, comfort, enrapture, titillate, put in humor, gladden, flatter, captivate, fascinate, take, becharm, warm the heart of, ravish, charm.

REGALIA, n. 1. Right, privilege, power, prerogative, dominion, ascendancy, domination, sovereignty, suzerainty, primacy, supremacy, royalty, regality, dynasty, imperiality, majesty, kingship, the throne, the crown, kinghood, rule, sway, command, reign, empery, control, prepollency, influence.
2. Badge, emblem, symbol, insigne (pl. insignia), toga, mantle, uniform, robe of office, emblem of office, mace, scepter, orb, crown, baton, wand, staff, truncheon, ensign, coronet, diadem, tiara, miter, keys of office, crook, red hat, cardinal's hat, shovel hat, crosier, triple crown, fillet.

REGARD, v. 1. Observe, look at, mark, notice, view, see, watch, gaze at, behold, set eyes on, take cognizance of, look upon, turn one's eyes toward, survey, scan, peruse, hold in view, cast the eyes on, take a gander at (sl.), keep in sight, keep in view, perceive, realize, remark, heed, be aware of, be conscious of.
2. Consider, respect, be of the opinion, opine, surmise, fancy, suspect, deem, esteem, allow, reckon (coll.), be afraid (coll.), conceive, realize, see, apprehend, set down as, set down for, mark down as, view as, account as, take for, estimate, guess, suppose, daresay.
3. Esteem, hold in regard, hold in affection, have affection for, value, admire, respect, revere, reverence, honor, prize, hold in high esteem, exalt, cherish, care for, treasure, hold dear, adore, idolize, love, like, harbor affection for, have eyes for, have a liking for, be fond of, have regard for, dote upon, venerate, think well of, think highly of, hold a high opinion of, look up to.
4. Concern, bear upon, have connection with, have relation to, relate to, refer to, affect, touch, have to do with, tie in with, answer to, correspond to, pertain to, appertain to, belong to, be associated with, be linked to, compare with, be apposite with, be in rapport with, have an affinity with.

REGARD, n. 1. View, look, gaze, sight, seeing, espial, aspect, glance, observation, observance, stare, survey, inspection, examination, scrutiny, perlustration, contemplation, watch, lookout, once-over (sl.).
2. Heed, heedfulness, attention, attentiveness, mindfulness, consideration, thought, ear, mind, notice, observation, note, respect, care, concern, devotion, diligence, assiduity, assiduousness, circumspection, scrutiny, study, contemplation, reflection, meditation, respect, consideration, veneration, reverence, honor, homage, awe, admiration, esteem.
3. Affection, liking, love, esteem, admiration, attachment, sympathy, interest, deference, honor, value, estimation, fondness, opinion, repute, approbation, approval, fancy, shine (sl.), devotion, tender feeling, passion, ardor, fervor, adoration, idolization, infatuation, crush, fellow feeling, friendship.
4. Repute, reputation, esteem, account, note, eminence, fame, importance, reputability, honor, credit, good name, celebrity, famousness, distinction, notoriety, report, glory, kudos, popularity, éclat (Fr.), figure, popular favor, popular repute, luster, illustriousness, eminency, elevation, prestige, dignity, grandeur, nobility, majesty, notability, nobility, pre-eminence, sublimity, exaltation.

REGARDFUL, adj. Mindful, heedful, cautious, careful, attentive, watchful, observant, thoughtful, considerate, deferential, obedient, circumspect, advertent, vigilant, on the watch, on the lookout, intent, all ears, all eyes, open-eyed, with one's eyes open, with one's ears open, awake, wakeful, alert, quick, perceptive, percipient, solicitous, painstaking, prudent, conscientious, scrupulous, exact, meticulous, accurate, punctilious, particular, fastidious, precise, faithful, loyal, correct.

REGARDLESS, adj. Unobservant, inattentive, heedless, nonobservant, disregardful, thoughtless, inconsiderate, unheeding, inadvertent, blind, deaf, offhand, neglectful, unreflecting, imprudent, unwise, reckless, foolhardy, insensible, unaware, mindless, listless, incurious, cursory, unsolicitous, remiss, perfunctory, loose, lax, slack, slovenly, sloppy, improvident, inert, otiose, slothful, nonchalant, shiftless fainéant, apathetic, lethargic, lentitudinous, lifeless, inanimate, neutral, unconcerned, blasé, insouciant, pococurantish, uninterested, easygoing, dispassionate, unambitious, incautious, respectless, spiritless, passionless, insentient, numb.

REGARDS, n., pl. Respects, compliments, commendations, remembrances, good wishes, greetings, best regards, best wishes, kind regards, token of esteem, devoirs (Fr.).

REGATTA, n. Boat race, sculling race, course competition, contest, rowing race, rowing competition, yacht race, yachting competition.

REGENCY, n. Regentship, rule, authority, government, dominion, royalty, right, power, privilege, prerogative, ascendancy, sway, sovereignty, suzerainty, primacy, supremacy, prepollency, dynasty, imperiality, majesty, throne, kinghood, kingship, rulership, command, empery, control, influence, might, monarchy, nobility.

REGENERATE, v. 1. Recreate, reproduce, renovate, make new, make over, repair, restore, reclaim, resuscitate, reform, re-establish, resurrect generate anew, refashion, remake, revivify reanimate, recall to life, recondition, rewarm remodel, remedy, overhaul, put in shape, mend, fix, service, retouch, reinstate, reinvest, patch up, retrieve, rehabilitate, reconstitute.

2. Reorganize, remodel, refound, revolutionize, produce anew, change radically, strike out something new, convert, change, amend, save, set straight, reclaim, redeem, make a new man of, give salvation to.

REGENERATION, *n.* 1. Remaking, reconstruction, reproduction, reformation, reëstablishment, regenesis, palingenesis, renovation, reconditioning, overhauling, repairing, remodeling, mending, fixing up, patching up, repairing, restoration, reclamation, resuscitation, resurrection, refashioning, rehabilitation, reinvestment, reinstatement, reconstitution, readjustment, recuperation, retrieval, salvage, recovery, salvation, redintegration, restitution, reconversion, rejuvenation, renascence, rebirth.

2. Sanctification, grace, conversion, salvation, redemption, reclamation, adoption, rebirth, new birth.

REGENT, *n.* Governor, ruler, vice-regent, commander, director, palatine, exarch, khedive, satrap, mandarin, tetrarch, nabob, deputy, representative, agent, minister, commissioner, sheriff, margrave, burgrave, pasha, bey, viceroy, viceking, vice-ruler, vice-emperor, vice-gerent, vicar, vice-sultan, vice-caliph.

REGIME, *n.* Rule, management, government, governmental system, political system, administration, governmental administration, form of government, reign, sway, dominion, kinghood, kingship, regality, regulation, guidance, conduct, oligarchy, monarchy, power, royalty, sovereignty, suzerainty, supremacy, primacy, the throne, the crown, command, empery, might.

REGIMEN, *n.* Diet, dietary, regime, treatment, course of treatment, therapy, medical treatment, medication.

REGIMENT, *n.* Military organization, body of troops, body of soldiers, army, military unit, outfit *(sl.),* corps, force, troop, troupe, combat force.

REGIMENT, *v.* Methodize, systematize, regulate, arrange, co-ordinate, harmonize, adjust, dispose, group, classify, rank, grade, graduate, divide, class, order, standardize, normalize, control, regulate, rule, master, have control of, hold authority, wield authority.

REGIMENTALS, *n., pl.* Uniform, khaki, olivedrab, military clothes, garments, military dress, dress uniform, equipment, fittings, kit, gear.

REGIMENTATION, *n.* Standardization, organization, methodization, regulation, arrangement, harmonization, adjustment, disposition, grouping, classification, gradation, graduation, division, ordering, normalization, control, rule, mastery, authority, method, system, discipline, routine, ordination, grouping, distribution, preparation, policy.

REGION, *n.* Territory, place, locale, location, district, community, scene, province, quarter, locality, tract, latitude, clime, climate, domain, circle, area, pale, province, zone, realm, kingdom, dominion, land, country, part, portion, space, neighborhood, vicinity, terrain, spot, sphere, walk, section, confines, whereabouts, field, ground, earth, environs, department, compartment, purlieus, vicinage, demesne, compass, circuit, precinct, premises, orbit, ambit, colony, settlement, com-

mune, ward, diocese, wapentake, close, plot, plat, tract, arena, enclave, yard, court, enclosure, site, position, situation, point, hole, stand, venue, seat, environment.

REGIONAL, *adj.* Regionary, regionalistic, local, parochial, topical, provincial, insular, topographic, locationary, locational, sectional, territorial, geographical, positional, environmental.

REGISTER, *n.,* 1. Registry, day book, accounts, account book, journal, ledger, record book, cashbook, petty cash record, cash register, logbook, log, balance sheet, docket, schedule, calendar, agenda, protocol, program, panel, poll, roster, list, muster, cadre, slate, ticket, bill, order of the day, card, written record, paper, document, parchment, manuscript, chronicle, annals, recording, credential, warrant, certificate, minutes, notes, jottings, score card, score sheet, archives, public records, proceedings, memorandum book, memorandum, notebook, scrapbook, memory book, catalogue, diary, yearbook, annual, ephemeris, almanac, chronology, file, tablet, scroll, rota.

2. Recorder, recordist, registrar, registrary, keeper of the records, archivist, record clerk, bookkeeper, record maker, secretary, prothonotary, chronicler, annalist, chronologist, chronographer.

3. Range, compass, scale, diapason, stop.

4. Radiator, heater, heat outlet, heat vent, hotair vent, hot-air duct, heat duct.

REGISTER, *v.* 1. Record, make a record of, list, make an entry, inscribe, note, annotate, enlist, post, enroll, matriculate, catalogue, tally, inscribe, indite, book, docket, chronicle, invoice, bill, file, index, poll, slate, schedule, line up, keep score, empanel, put in writing, take a minute, note down, jot down, write down, put on the record, make a note of, program, draft.

2. Portray, represent, delineate, limn, picture, set forth, shadow forth, convey a likeness of, illustrate, convey an impression of, picture, draw, paint, adumbrate, copy, trace.

3. Show, indicate, denote, signify, betoken, represent, disclose, set forth, evince, bespeak, give token of, exhibit, present, demonstrate, stand for, typify, attest, testify, denote.

REGISTRAR, *n.* Record-maker, record-keeper, register, registry, registrary, archivist, record clerk, bookkeeper, accountant, secretary, prothonotary, chronicler, annalist, chronographer, chronographist, chronologist, actuary, calculator, auditor, CPA, Certified Public Accountant, chartered account.

REGISTRATION, *n.* Enrollment, enlistment, matriculation, registry, entry, bookkeeping, tabulation, tally, score, insertion.

REGNANT, *adj.* Reigning, ruling, potent, puissant, powerful, weighty, authoritative, predominant, prepollent, ascendant, prevalent, dominant, preponderant, controlling, in the ascendant, important, influential, effective, telling, efficacious, paramount, supreme, chief, hegemonic, imperious, overruling, absolute, positive, governing,

REGRESS, *n.* Regression, recidivism, backwardness, retrogression, retrocession, retroaction, retrogradation, reversion, reversal, withdrawal, retirement, flight, retreat, backward movement, recidivation, motion from, recession, relapse, reflux, ebb flow, passage back, retrocedence, recedence, recoil, revulsion, ricochet, rebound, kick, backlash, repercussion, reflex, recalcitration, springing back, drawing back, backsliding, fall from grace, recrudescence.

REGRESS, *v.* Backslide, apostasize, relapse, fall back, have a relapse, fall again into, recidivate, be overtaken, yield again to, regress, retrogress, move backward, retrocede, retroact, revert, reverse, withdraw, retire, retreat, fly, flee, move away from, ebb, pass back, recoil, revolt, be repulsed, ricochet, rebound, recalcitrate, spring back, fall from grace, recrudesce, stand off, sheer off, swerve off, decline, wane, sink, back up, unmake, undo.

REGRESSIVE, *adj.* Retrogressive, reversionary, reactionary, atavistic, reversional, reflex, receding, recidivous, retrograde, crab-like, recessive, recedent, retrocedent, recalcitrant, revulsive, repercussive, refluent, ebb, backward, reverse, recrudescent, backsliding, lapsing, relapsing.

REGRET, *n.* Regretfulness, nostalgia, bitterness, remorse, penitence, grief, sorrow, longing, concern, lamentation, rue, disappointment, compunction, heartburn, discontent, ruth, qualm, dissatisfaction, anxiety, worry, worriment, pain, anxiousness, vexation, hardship, repining, self-condemnation, self-reproach, contrition, penitency, sting of conscience, deprecation, frustration, buffet, blow, bafflement, dashed hopes, blighted hopes, mortification, cold comfort, inquietude, disquietude, resipiscence.

REGRET, *v.* Lament, grieve at, deplore, bewail, bemoan, moan, deprecate, be sorry for, sorrow for, repine, complain, fret, feel sorrow, be remorseful, be stung with remorse, be stung by conscience, mourn for, rue, be rueful, be penitent, repent, be full of grief, lament, weep over, keen, express sorrow, rue the day, cast a longing look behind.

REGRETFUL, *adj.* Rueful, contrite, penitent, remorseful, sorry, sorrowful, mournful, compunctious, conscience-stricken, penitential, homesick, nostalgic, lamenting, disappointed, discontented, bitter, frustrated, thwarted, balked, disgruntled, dissatisfied, malcontent, glum, sad, doleful, dolorous, displeased, in bad temper, in bad humor, out of humor, touched, self-accusing, self-reproachful, self-condemning, self-convicting.

REGRETTABLE, *adj.* Lamentable, woeful, grievous, deplorable, unfortunate, terrible, dire, dreadful, frightening, horrible, horrid, villainous, scandalous, flagitious, infamous, nefarious, sinful, wicked, evil, pitiful, pitiable, shocking, flagrant, gross, despicable, hateful, detestable, fulsome, noisome, odious, base, obnoxious, foul, atrocious, fearful, sad, grave, dismal, lamentable, heinous, reprehensible, blameworthy, culpable, malevolent, malefic, adverse, calamitous, ruinous, disastrous, catastrophic, untoward, unhappy, unlucky, unblest, hapless, out of luck, inauspicious, ill-starred, ill-omened, unsuccessful, troublous, reprovable, faulty, exceptionable, uncommendable, censurable, unjustifiable.

REGULAR, *adj.* Customary, normal, formal, conventional, usual, habitual, classic, natural, typical, ordinary, according to rule, wonted, prescriptive, accustomary, commonplace, frequent, cyclic, periodical, fixed, established, recurring, recurrent, seasonal, rhythmic, correct, proper, canonical, daily, legitimate, allotted, graded, controlled, certain, predictable, foreseeable, vernacular, household, popular, current, set, stock, besetting, everyday, matter-of-fact, consuetudinal, prevalent,

universal, well-regulated, uniform, even, constant, steady, level, unvarying, unchanging, unchanged, invariable, homologous, of a piece, harmonious, in harmony with, consonant, undeviating, monotonous, humdrum, connatural, stable, orderly, methodical, in good shape, in normal condition, tidy, neat, shipshape, unvaried.

REGULARITY, *n.* Symmetry, uniformity, order, orderliness, harmony evenness, constancy, sameness undeviatingness, monotony, invariabililty, tedium, routine, habit, periodicity, steadiness, regularness, recurrence, regular return, rhythm, cadence, meter, self-sameness, similarity, method, order, rule, system, even tenor, regular course, regular arrangement, homogeneity, homologousness, exactness, precision, shapeliness, routine, punctuality, fixed procedure, fixed practice, exactitude.

REGULARLY, *adv.* Constantly, at stated times, repeatedly, continuously, continually, periodically, frequently, perpetually, at stated periods, at fixed times, duly, in due order, like clockwork, statedly, at fixed intervals, at established intervals, from day to day, from hour to hour, from time to time, minute by minute, invariably, generally, commonly.

REGULATE, *v.* 1. Agree, bring into agreement, harmonize, bring into accord, homologate, adjust, fix, arrange, fit, suit, accommodate, equalize, equate, level, dress, balance, square, restore equilibrium, make equal, compensate, systematize, methodize, standardize, normalize, time, set, coordinate, readjust, make true, correct, remedy, make right, dispose, reduce to method, put in order, allocate, shape, classify, counterbalance, counterpoise, balance, graduate, moderate, adapt, compose, alter, change, readjust, establish, reconcile, conditionate, qualify, rectify, trim, strike a balance.

2. Direct, order, govern, manage, control, conduct, administrate, administer, rule, guide, look after, have charge of, overlook, superintend, discipline, police, organize, handle, run, carry on, steer, pilot, codify, decree, constitute, constitutionalize, legitimatize, make legal, legalize, sanction, prescribe, fix, establish, ordain, set, formalize, formulate, decree, order, authorize.

REGULATION, *n.* 1. Law, rule, order, canon, rubric, precept, command, edict, ukase, ordinance, protocol, decree, statute, institution, prescription, prescript, dictate, decision, formula, formulation, formulary, form, act, enactment, standing order, bylaw, legislation, direction, instruction, injunction, charge, dogma, principle, code, convention, maxim, standard, commandment, appointment, criterion, method, system, norm.

2. Discipline, course, system, arrangement, array, routine, subordination, management, direction, conduct, government, steerage, guidance, handling, control, disposition, disposal, shaping, economy.

REGULATIVE, *adj.* Controlling, directive, administrative, supervisory, gubernative, governmental, hegemonic, jurisdictional, ruling, predominant, authoritative, regnant, dictatorial, ascendant, paramount, supreme, executive, imperious, peremptory, overruling, powerful, mighty, puissant, sovereign, suzerain, commanding, prepollent, predominant.

REGURGITATE, *v.* Disgorge, regorge, render up,

bring up, bring back, vomit, spew up, throw up, reissue, rush out, rush up,

REHABILITATE, *v.* Restore, re-establish, reconstitute, renew, reinvigorate, reinstate, reconstruct, redintegrate, renovate, revamp, make over, fix, regenerate, reinstall, readjust, make whole, refit, replace, put into shape, restore to operation, return, recoup, reconvert, bring back, remake, revert, salvage, save, redeem, improve, relieve, mend, amend, ameliorate, meliorate, promote, perfect, make sound, develop, enhance, deliver, free, liberate, alleviate, ease, mitigate, palliate, revivify, refresh.

REHABILITATION, *n.* Restoration, reinstatement, reinvestiture, repair, reparation, reëstablishment, reconstruction, rebuilding, renovation, renewal, reconstitution, revivification, reinvigoration, restitution, return, recuperation, reinvestment, atonement, rendition, replacement, reorganization, retrieval, reclamation, salvage, salvation, saving, redemption, improvement, relief, mending, amendment, melioration, amelioration, promotion, perfection, development, enhancement, deliverance, alleviation, easement, mitigation, palliation.

REHASH, *v.* Reword, repeat, paraphrase, state differently, restate, rephrase, reiterate, duplicate, re-echo, ditto *(coll.)*, say the same thing, go over the same ground, recount, recapitulate, retell, tell over, repeat oneself, reproduce, reduplicate, rehearse, tautologize, battologize, hammer, din, drum, beat, chew one's cabbage twice *(sl.)*.

REHEARSAL, *n.* 1. Repetition, recounting, refrain, encore, paraphrase, restatement, résumé, recurrence, reiteration, the same old story, retold story, twice-told tale, drumming, hammering, din, the same all over again, tautology, battology, reduplication, reproduction, recital, recapitulation, retelling, re-echoing.

2. Recital, description, narration, telling, relation, detailed account, minute account, full particulars, recital of the facts, mention, story, history, statement, narrative, recounting, graphic account.

3. Practice, preparation, drill, repetition, making ready, dress rehearsal, preliminary performance, tryout, reading, first reading.

REHEARSE, *v.* 1. Perform, tryout, practice, prepare, act, go through a part, read one's lines, recite to oneself, speak to an imaginary audience, get ready, prepare oneself, study one's lines, walk through a part, block the action, prepare a performance.

2. Rehash, paraphrase, repeat, reiterate, state differently, restate, chew one's cabbage twice *(sl.)*, hammer, beat, drum, din, tell over, tell again, repeat oneself, go over the same ground, recount, recapitulate, retell, say the same thing, ditto *(coll.)*, re-echo, reduplicate, reproduce, rephrase, recite, recount, encore, tautologize, battologize, go twice round.

3. Relate, narrate, say, tell, recite, recount, describe, paint a word picture, portray, delineate, enumerate, set forth, depict, detail, give a full account of, particularize, deliver, expound, sum up, summarize, go over, make a report, make a statement, render an account of, review.

REHEAT, *v.* Warm over, rewarm, heat again, heat over, calefy, recalefy, recook, tepefy, make hot.

REIGN, *v.* Rule, prevail, be predominant, dominate, hold authority, wear the crown, sit on the throne, wield the scepter, exercise authority, govern, regulate, hold sway, command, occupy the throne, have ascendancy, have mastery, have superiority, master, exercise sovereignty, administer.

REIGN, *n.* 1. Regnancy, rule, authority, power, right, privilege, prerogative, monarchy, oligarchy, kinghood, kingship, ascendancy, sovereignty, suzerainty, royal power, imperial sway, imperial power, supremacy, control, might, influence, dynasty, supreme power, the throne, the crown, dominion, dominance, domination, pre-pollency, regality, royalty, administration, government.

2. Reigning years, kingship, kinghood, royalty, years in power, time on the throne, time of authority.

REIGNING, *adj.* Regnant, ruling, potent, puissant, powerful, weighty, authoritative, predominant, prepollent, ascendant, prevalent, dominating, dominant, preponderant, controlling, in the ascendant, important, influential, paramount, supreme, chief, hegemonic, imperious, imperial, imperative, overruling, absolute, governing, positive.

REIMBURSE, *v.* 1. Repay, refund, pay back, return, make good, make up, make repayment, compensate, pay in kind, make up for, recompense, square up, defray the the expenses of, remunerate, put in pocket.

2. Recoup, require, compensate, satisfy, remunerate, indemnify, make restitution, remit.

REIMBURSEMENT, *n.* Paying back, compensation, recompense, indemnity, indemnification, payment, remuneration, satisfaction, requital, restitution, return, repayment, restoration, redress, amends, solatium, allowance, wages, financial return, financial reward, damages.

REINCARNATION, *n.* Incarnation, reëmbodiment, corporealization, materialization, substantialization, rebirth, regeneration, new birth, renascence, renaissance, reanimation, regenesis, new arrival, second coming.

REINFORCE, *v.* Replenish, fill up, recruit, provide for, provender, provision, make up, make good, replace, restore, rehabilitate, reinstate, reinstall, readjust, reorganize, reconstitute, reconvert, make whole, make fit, strengthen, make stronger, re-establish, put back into shape, put in working order, recondition, refurbish, return to strength, return to service, augment, increase, enlarge, make larger, aggrandize, intensify, amplify, expand, double, redouble, triple, quadruple, deepen, thicken, heighten, raise, lengthen, widen, broaden, magnify, boost, inflate, exalt, distend, buttress, restrengthen, reinvigorate, brace up, screw up, harden, gird up, revivify, reanimate, quicken, stimulate, exhilarate, help, aid, assist, succor, promote, further, contribute to, set on one's legs, get going, expedite, speed up, give impulse to, hasten.

REINFORCEMENT, *n.* Assistance, help, succor, aid, accommodation, service, provision, sustenance, promotion, ministry, ministration, furtherance, helping hand, lift, boost, support, upkeep, advancement, conducement, care, guidance, protection, fosterage, backing, interest, favor, maintenance, auxiliaries, relief, contingents, replenishment, purveyance, supplies, subvention, shore, strut, retaining wall, retainer, buttress, flying buttress, strengthener, block, suspender, maintainer, upholder, augmentation, additive, addition, adjunct, increment, accessory, appurtenance, extension, supplement, continuation, complement, annexation, increase, enlargement, extension, accumulation, aggrandizement, redoubling, magnification, intensification, accretion, increment, replenishment, filling, restoration, rehabilitation, reinstatement.

REINS, *n., pl.* Confinement, captivity, restraint, thrall, enthrallment, detention, constraint, strings, leads, ties, harness, gear, equipment, paraphernalia, traps, direction, government, management, guidance, steerage, helm, rudder, reins of government, pilotage, regime, supervision, ministration, check, grasp, hold, conduct, regulation, strap.

REINSTATE, *v.* Restore, put back into service, restore to office, restore to power, re-establish, reinaugurate, make perfect, mend, amend, remodel, salvage, redeem, improve, save, remake, bring back, reconvert, recover, make effective again, make forceful again, restore to operation, restore to effectiveness, put back into shape, make fit, make suitable, readjust, regenerate, make sound again, make over, repair, fix, renovate, renew, revamp, redintegrate.

REINVIGORATE, *v.* Reanimate, refresh, revivify, quicken, restore, recuperate, recover, fortify, stimulate, revive, refect, reënliven, brace up, uplift, exhilarate, put new life into, quicken the blood, stir up, renew, cheer, regale, enliven, infuse new life into, inspirit, rehabilitate, re-establish, reconstitute, renovate, revamp, fix, repair, readjust, make fit, restore to health, restore to vigor, bring back, save, salvage, redeem, meliorate, ameliorate, relieve, cure, remedy, make sound, give a lift to, ease, make new, resuscitate, rejuvenate, regenerate, rewarm, rekindle, fortify, strengthen, make strong, screw up, give strength to, rejuvenesce.

REITERATE, *v.* Repeat, reword, paraphrase, state again, restate, state differently, rephrase, iterate, rehash, echo, re-echo, duplicate, reduplicate, reproduce, ditto *(coll.),* say the same thing again, say over, go over the same ground, recount, recapitulate, retell, repeat oneself, rehearse, tautologize, battologize, hammer, din, drum, redouble.

REITERATION, *n.* Repeating, repetition, tautology, battology, iteration, recounting, rehearsal, refrain, encore, paraphrase, duplication, reproduction, echo, re-echoing, recapitulation, retelling, recital, reduplication, the same all over again, twice round, restatement, hammering, drumming, din, noise, twice-told tale, retold story, the same old story, rehash, recurrence, résumé, doubling, redoubling.

REITERATIVE, *adj.* Repetitious, tautologistic, redundant, verbose, wordy, prolix, battologistic, talkative, loquacious, garrulous, duplicative, monotonous, singsong, repetitive, repetitional, reiterant, reduplicative, reduplicatory, endless, unceasing, never-ending, twice-told, retold, warmed up, warmed over, chattering, longiloquent, profuse, discursive, wandering, maundering, voluble, prattling, prating, chattering, talkative, talky, multiloquent.

REJECT, *v.* 1. Expel, eject, ejaculate, throw out, remove, exclude, discard, cast away, cast off, turn out, cast aside, throw overboard, jettison, preclude, leave out, leave behind, abandon, maroon, dismiss, cashier, pluck out, throw aside, renounce,

give up, forswear, forbear, ignore, abnegate, turn down, oust, dislodge, boycott, cut out, close the door on, eliminate, prohibit, forbid, proscribe, give the go-by *(coll.),* set aside, forsake, drive out, cast down, banish, put away, brush aside, take exception to, pass over, overrule, relegate, throw to the dogs, send packing, send about one's business, show the door to, give the bounce, give the bum's rush *(sl.),* give the air, rid oneself of, wash one's hands of, throw into the wastebasket, part with, excise, extirpate, cut out, cast behind, whisk away, throw overboard, throw to the winds, tear out, extract, weed out, uproot, eradicate, exterminate, pull up by the roots.

2. Decline, refuse, discredit, disallow, repudiate, scout, disbelieve, repel, rebuff, deny, veto, forbid, interdict, slight, despise, detest, spurn, disapprove, renounce, proscribe, explode, abjure, disdain, disbar, bar, negate, negative, discountenance, dismiss, shrug off, disown, disinherit, refuse to recognize, repel, repulse, banish, disclaim, forswear, scorn, abhor, ostracize, disavow, waive, exempt, place no value on, contravene, contradict, controvert, oppose, gainsay, say no to, traverse, impugn, dispute, belie, give the lie to, disaffirm, turn a deaf ear to, refuse to listen to, ignore, challenge, hold in question, skepticize, disagree with, dissent from, revolt at, turn from, not countenance, demur to, scruple at, boggle at, object to, cavil with, wrangle with, quibble with, protest against.

3. Disdain, despise, hold in contempt, contemn, have no regard for, have no use for, place no value on, set no store by, set at naught, disprize, misprize, treat with disdain, scorn to accept, hold cheap, make light of, make nothing of, snap one's fingers at, tread upon, trample underfoot, flout, revile, snub, hold in derision, mock, jeer at, gibe, sneer at, laugh at, poke fun at, make fun of, spit upon, scout, rebuff, cold shoulder, pass by, disregard, neglect, dodge, shun, pay no notice to, give no notice to, cut dead *(sl.),* keep at arm's length, keep at a distance, leave out in the cold, leave out.

REJECTION, *n.* 1. Banishment, relegation, excommunication, expatriation, ostracism, exile, deportation, exilement, ostracization, extradition, transportation, rustication, dismissal, walking papers, ticket of leave, the sack, discharge, firing, ouster, dispossession, eviction, dislodgement, deposition, deposal, exclusion, rejectment, ejectment, extrusion, removal, displacement, elimination, repulsion, discard, disownment, disinheritance, riddance, shutting out, omission, noninclusion, preclusion, lockout, disbarment, debarment, eradication, erasure, expulsion, throwing out, throwing away, jettison, abandonment, marooning, cashiering, screening, renunciation, ignoring, abnegation, ousting, excision, proscription, the go-by *(coll.),* exception, overruling, extirpation, uprooting, unrooting.

2. Repudiation, repulse, repulsion, spurning, scorning, abnegation, denial, reprobation, disownment, disallowance, veto, disbelief, disapproval, disapprobation, refusal, declination, declension, abjuration, renunciation, intoleration, discrediting, scouting, rebuff, interdiction, slight, banning, negation, discountenancing, dismissal, disinheritance, nonrecognition, disclaimer, disavowal, waiver, exemption, contravention, contradiction, controversion, opposition, gainsaying, traversion, impugning, disaffirmation, doubting, dubiety, dubiousness, refusal, distrust, mistrust, question-

ing, disagreement, dissent, revolt, objection, scruple.

3. Hatred, despising, loathing, abhorrence, scorn, detestation, dislike, abomination, execration, unpopularity, disfavor, unfashionableness, disdain, contempt, disregardance, neglect, abandonment, disprizement, misprizement, spurning, revilement, flouting, sneering, rebuff, shunning, slight, cutting (coll.), exclusion.

REJOICE, v. Exult, be glad, be happy, celebrate, exhilarate, be pleased, be delighted, be transported with joy, be overjoyed, be tickled (coll.), be elated, make merry, sport, luxuriate, felicitate, fill with joy, fill with pleasure, become glad, be enraptured, jubilate, delight, congratulate oneself, skip, frolic, dance, hop, shout, yell, triumph, make jubilee, give a cheer, applaud, crow, sing, chirp, chirrup, carol, cry out with joy, sing for joy, be animated, be invigorated, be enlivened, be inspired, be inspirited, be in good humor, blow the trumpet, beat the drum, kill the fatted calf, hold a feast, hold a celebration, glory, gloat over, crow over, luxuriate in, riot, bask, glow, revel.

REJOICING, n. Festivity, celebration, exultation, gladness, happiness, gaiety, elation, triumph, jubilee, jubilation, delight, exultancy, reveling, revelry, merrymaking, thanksgiving, paean, cheering, jubilance, merriment, mirth, pleasure, joyfulness, liveliness, ecstasy, jollity, jocundity, levity, hilarity, joviality, exhilaration, amusement, good cheer, festivity, conviviality, sportiveness, revelment, gambol, frisk, romp, caper, carrying-on, goings on, high time, lark, holiday, ovation, laudation, fanfaronade.

REJOIN, v. 1. Answer, retort, make retort, reply, respond, return an answer, riposte, come back with, come back at, flash back, rebut, refute, make rebuttal, parry, answer back, talk back, confute.

2. Muster, assemble, collect, reunite, reassemble, congregate, bunch together, cluster, crowd, concentrate, regroup, convoke, convocate, reamass, draw together, scrape together, tie together, reassociate, reconcentrate.

3. Return to, meet with, rendezvous with, come across, arrive at, join again, come upon.

REJOINDER, n. Answer, response, reply, retort, repartee, replication, riposte, return, comeback, rebuttal, surrebuttal, refutation, contradiction, plea, surrejoinder, counterstatement, countercharge, counterblast, counterclaim, counterargument.

REJUVENATE, v. Reinvigorate, make young, juvenate, reanimate, refresh, revive, revivify, quicken, restore, fortify, strengthen, stimulate, refect, reënliven, brace up, exhilarate, put new life into, stir the blood, renew, renovate, restore to health, restore to youth, remove the years, restore to vigor, resuscitate, regenerate, make strong, rejuvenesce, uplift, give a lift to.

REJUVENATION, n. Reinvigoration, restoration, renewal, rejuvenescence, juvenation, reanimation, refreshment, revival, quickening, restoration, fortifying, strengthening, stimulation, reënlivening, exhilaration, resuscitation, regeneration, second youth, second childhood, second wind, rebirth, new birth, renascence, renaissance.

RELAPSE, v. Turn back, fall back, lapse, backslide, apostatize, revert, weaken, recidivate, slide, retrogress, regress, be overcome, suffer a relapse,

fall again into, be overtaken, yield again to, move backward, retrocede, retroact, reverse, withdraw, retire, retreat, fly, flee, move away from, reflow, ebb, pass back, rebound, recalcitrate, spring back, fall from grace, recrudesce, decline, wane, sink, avoid, back up, unmake, undo, avert, deteriorate, degenerate, retrovert.

RELAPSE, n. Reversion, retrogression, retrocession, apostasy, backsliding, falling back, recidivism, recidivation, recrudescence, retrogradation, throwback, lapse, laxity, slackness, fall, deterioration, degeneration, weakening, regression, withdrawal, retreat, retirement, flight, reflow, ebb flow, rebound, recalcitration, fall from grace, declination, decline, sinking, retroversion.

RELATE, v. 1. Tell, narrate, recount, give an account of, recite, report, mention, say, speak, utter, detail, describe, repeat, allude, inform, particularize, set forth, rehearse, enunciate, announce, tell about, divulge, enumerate, retail, give words to, recapitulate, make a statement, tell a story, specify, emit, pour forth, give expression to, give words to, give voice to, articulate, pronounce, convey, impart, communicate, remark, observe, present, spiel (sl.), breathe, proclaim, disseminate, phrase, express, put into words, verbalize, couch in terms, vocalize, make known, vent, ventilate, air, broadcast, diffuse, declare, report, give news of, acquaint, convey knowledge of, represent, apprise, let fall.

2. Relate to, refer to, be connected with, have a relation to, touch, affect, concern, pertain to, appertain to, have a bearing on, tie in with (sl.), bear upon, be linked with, be associated to, be joined with, be united with.

RELATED, adj. 1. Associated, implicated, connected, allied, relevant, appropriate, comparable, applicable, common, affinitive, connatural, apposite, germane, equiparant, collateral, connate, congeneric, congenerous, akin, in common with, referable to, en rapport, conjugate, conjoined, pertinent, correlated, appurtenant to, interconnected, interdependent, reciprocal, interactive, mutual, commutual, equivalent, equal, complementary, interrelative, interrelated.

2. Kindred, akin, consanguineous, consanguine, of the same family, propinquitous, of one blood, affinal, intimate, allied, cognate, agnate, fraternal, affiliated, german, germane.

RELATION, n. 1. Account, story, narrative, description, telling, recital, rehearsal, statement, history, chronicle, narration, tale, detailing of the facts, factual account, report, mention, explanation, repetition, communication, memoir, summary of the facts, full particulars, facts, biography, autobiography, retelling, recapitulation, depiction, delineation, recital, written account, recitation, version, representation.

2. Relationship, connecton, apposition, appositeness, tie-in, communality, applicability, interest, concern, bearing, dependency, relevance, correlation, affinity, application, bearing, relevancy, pertinency, correspondence, contingency, contiguousness, alliance, association, union, propinquity, rapport, commerce, interconnection, interrelationship, cognation, connation, mutuality, collation, comparableness, indentification, likeness, resemblance, similarity, similitude.

3. Relationship, kinship, consanguinity, family tie, blood tie, blood relationship, family relationship, affinity, cousinship, fraternity, paternity, agnation, filiation, affiliation, sibness, ancestry,

descent, connaturalness, brotherhood, sisterhood, parentage, lineage, line, blood stock, stock, paternality, maternality, maternity.

RELATIVE, *adj.* Referring, comparable, relational, referable to, pertinent to, appurtenant to, correlative, in common with, common to, belonging to, interrelative, correlated, interdependent, interconnected, common, communal, commutual, mutual, equivalent, correspondent, complementary, collateral, affine, referential, with reference to, touching, respecting, concerning, connective, agnate, cognate, kindred, germane, apposite, appositional.

RELATIVE, *n.* Relation, kinsman, brother, sister, sibling, twin, father, mother, male parent, female parent, child, son, daughter, male child, female child, offspring, issue, progenitor, ancestor, forebear, sire, dam, begetter, procreator, cousin, uncle, aunt, grandfather, grandmother, kinfolk, kith, kin, connection, flesh and blood, blood relative, consanguinean, next of kin, heir, nephew, niece, father-in-law, mother-in-law, near relation, close relative, distant relative, testatee, legatee, legal heir, legitimate child, natural child, bastard.

RELATIVELY, *adv.* Proportionally, proportionately, respectively, with reference to, comparatively, in respect to, in a relative manner, in a like manner, not absolutely, pertinently, appositely, apropos of, in part, only, merely, moderately, purely, partially, partly, to a certain extent, ever so little, to a degree, to a certain degree, in a manner of speaking.

RELAX, *v.* 1. Loosen, slacken, loose, unbrace, unrestrain, unconstrain, unbind, liberate, free.

2. Decelerate, retard, delay, slow down, check, curb, moderate, temper, allay, put on the brakes, brake, slacken one's pace, reduce speed, rein in, throttle, make leisurely, make gradual.

3. Soften, mollify, dulcify, demulcify, laxate, make soft, dissolve, melt, lenify, mellow, assuage.

4. Show pity, have mercy, be lenient, be compassionate, commiserate, show clemency, melt, thaw, weep for, relent, forbear, take pity upon, sympathize, feel for, enter into the feelings of, condole, share sorrow, share grief.

5. Abstain, refrain, hold back, delay, linger, tarry, be idle, mark time, rest on one's oars, lie dormant, be inert, be motionless, be lazy, idle, lie around *(coll.),* loaf, loiter, take one's time, unbend, rest, repose, enjoy oneself, take recreation, vacation, holiday, catch one's breath, enjoy idleness.

RELAXATION, *n.* 1. Loosening, slackening, unbending, mitigation, relief, untautening, untightening, laxity, remission, mollification, assuagement, diminution, abatement, moderation, falling off, alleviation, tranquilization, pacification, quieting, quietus, decrement, reduction, lowering, lassitude, sluggishness.

2. Ease, repose, rest, sleep, quiet, recreation, fun, enjoyment, diversion, amusement, refreshment, inactivity, quiescence, respite, vacation, holiday, breather, breathing spell, lull, halt, stay, intermission, pause, entertainment, pleasurable diversion, sport, games, regalement, hobby, avocation, pastime.

3. Laxity, remissness, negligence, dereliction of duty, nonfulfillment, noncooperation, looseness, laxness, idleness, nonchalance, shirking, indolence.

RELEASE, *v.* 1. Liberate, set free, rescue, save, loose, deliver, manumit, exempt, disengage, untie, set loose, extricate, set at liberty, ransom, disenthrall, clear, let out, redeem, emancipate, let off, acquit, vindicate, exonerate, absolve, excuse, pardon, forgive, grant amnesty to, remit the penalty of, exculpate, disculpate, compurgate, give clearance, reprieve, set at large, let out, demobilize, disband, unchain, untie, unharness, unfetter, unshackle, unhook, unpin, unpinion, unmanacle, unbridle, unbind, uncage, unmuzzle, unhandcuff, untruss, untether, unhobble, unstrap, unyoke, enfranchise, affranchise, unloose.

2. Cede, surrender, yield, relinquish, give up one's hold on, spare, drop, waive, forgo, have done with, abandon, throw over, renounce, dispose of, discard, lay aside, cast away, resign, dismiss, let slip, remit, make restitution, give back, render up.

RELEASE, *n.* 1. Liberation, rescue, saving, unloosing, deliverance, manumission, exemption, discharge, disengagement, untying, setting loose, extrication, ransom, disenthrallment, dismissal, clearance, redemption, emancipation, letting off, acquittal, vindication, exoneration, absolution, excusal, pardon, pardonment, forgiveness, amnesty, remission, exculpation, disculpation, compurgation, quietus, reprieve, demobilization, disbanding, unchaining, untying, unharnessing, unfettering, unshackling, unhooking, unpinning, unpinioning, unmanacling, unbridling, unbinding, disentanglement, uncaging, unmuzzling, unhandcuffing, untrussing, untethering, unhobbling, unstrapping, unyoking, enfranchisement, affranchisement, salvation, redemption, immunity, respite, indemnity.

2. Renunciation, relinquishment, cession, dereliction, surrender, capitulation, yielding, sparing, waiver, forgoing abandonment, disposal, dispossession, discarding, laying aside, casting away, resignation, dismissal.

3. Death, decease, demise, dissolution, obit, passing of the spirit, going beyond, end of life, last breath, the end, cessation of life, passing away, extinction, extermination, termination of living, eternal rest, lasting peace, final rest, final sleep.

RELEGATE, *v.* 1. Assign, entrust, intrust, confide, commit, consign, invest, delegate, depute, dispatch, commission, ship, transport, convey, carry, transfer.

2. Eliminate, eradicate, remove, exclude, bar, bar out, omit, repudiate, strike off, strike out, shut out, separate, isolate, segregate, elide, set apart, reject, oust, ejaculate, throw out, extrude, expel, cast out, turn out, remove, exile, dispossess, dislodge, ostracize, banish, drum out, expatriate, excommunicate, extradite, outlaw, ban, proscribe, fling out, throw to the winds, cast off, jettison, get rid of, wash one's hands of, cast behind, give away, throw overboard.

RELEGATION, *n.* Elimination, eradication, removal, barring, omission, repudiation, separation, segregation, elision, excision, exclusion, rejectment, rejection, ouster, ejaculation, throwing out, discard, extrusion, expulsion, casting out, turning out, removal, exile, banishment, expatriation, extradition, exportation, deportation, excommunication, outlawing, proscription, jettisoning, noninclusion, nonadmission, preclusion, lockout, debarment, withdrawal, isolation, dispatch, disposal, deposition, dislodgement, dispossession, eviction, ostracization, rustication, dismissal, discharge.

RELENT, *v.* Soften, be mollified, be assuaged, be placated, relax, comply, unbend, grow lenient, be forgiving, forbear, yield, be tolerant, grow less severe, have pity, be merciful, be compassionate, commiserate, condole, give quarter, sympathize, feel for, accede, acquiesce, give way, succumb, be submissive, give in to, be compliant, remit, be moderate, sober down.

RELENTLESS, *adj.* Ruthless, unfeeling, uncompassionate, unyielding, intransigent, inexorable, unforgiving, unpitying, obdurate, adamant, adamantine, vindictive, cruel, remorseless, unmerciful, unkind, unappeasable, rancorous, pitiless, hard, austere, ferocious, hard-hearted, unforgiving, intolerant, unsympathetic, fell, savage, tyrannical, unsparing, stern, unrelenting, cold-blooded, stony-hearted, marble-hearted, peremptory, arbitrary, truculent, brutish, heedless, grim, purposeful, indomitable, iron, uncompromising, unflinching, unswerving, unshrinking, steadfast, persevering, dogged, pertinacious, unremitting, unintermitting, undeviating, unflagging, unsleeping, indefatigable, undaunted, sedulous, stringent, rigid, stiff, rigorous, dour, exigent, ironhanded, unsparing, domineering, high-handed, dictatorial, Procrustean, pressing, imperious, autocratic, vengeful, revengeful, grudging, punitive, unmitigable, inflexible, retaliatory, hard of heart, fierce, inhumane, inhuman, merciless, inclement, unsympathizing.

RELEVANCE, *n.* Pertinence, aptness, fitness, appropriateness, suitability, suitableness, applicability, compatibility, accord, harmoniousness, congruence, correspondence, cognation, consonance, consentaneousness, consentience, congruity, agreement, consistency, conformance, reference, concern, bearing, relationship, relation, appurtenance, appositeness, tie-in, affinity, cognation, harmony, connection, homogeneity, correlation, association, rapport, application.

RELEVANT, *adj.* Pertinent, apt, fit, appropriate, suitable, conformant, conforming, applicable, compatible, accordant, harmonious, congruent, correspondent, cognate, consonant, consentaneous, consentient, consistent, referring, concerning, bearing upon, related, correlated, allied, appurtenant, apposite, tied in with, connected, homogeneous, correlevant, associated, *en rapport (Fr.),* felicitous, pat, happy, in point, seasonable, suited to, apropos, germane.

RELIABLE, *adj.* Trustworthy, authoritative, dependable, reputable, conscientious, honest, upright, faithful, truthful, punctual, punctilious, strict, credible, believable, scrupulous, careful, sound, responsible, methodical, finicky, painstaking, meticulous, certain, assured, unquestionable, undeniable, indisputable, incontrovertible, incontestable, indubitable, infallible, factual, irrefutable, convincing, unfailing, inerrant, unerring, authentic, standard, tenable, plausible, conceivable, genuine, real, legitimate, accurate, exact, true, valid, veracious, veridical, trusty, well-grounded, well-founded.

RELICS, *n., pl.* 1. Remnants, remains, scraps, fragments, leavings, remainder, reliquiae, orts, traces, vestiges, antiques, archaisms, remains of the past, ancient ruins, fossils, petrifications, organic remains, reminders, records, antiquities, signs, evidence, keepsakes, souvenirs, mementos, memorabilia, remembrances, trophies, heirlooms, inheritances, residuum, residue, scraps, oddments, debris, detritus, skeleton, bones.

2. Corpse, dead body, carcass, cadaver, skeleton, the deceased, the dead, stiff *(sl.),* the dear departed, food for worms, dry bones, carrion, mummy, earth, mortal clay, ashes.

RELIEF, *n.* Remedy, redress, help, aid, assistance, reinforcement, deliverance, support, alleviation, redress, indemnification, assuagement, palliation, mitigation, easement, softening, rest, respite, comfort, exemption, freeing, liberation, strengthening, abatement, extrication, deliverance, corrective, cure, analeptic, restorative, sedation, calming, anodyne, palliative, narcotic, sedative, balm, emollient, calmative, demulcent, liniment, salve, embrocation, ointment, unguent, opiate, drug, medicine, therapy, tonic, bracer, stimulation, stimulant, roborant, alleviative, panacea, remission, consolation, release, solace, comfort, refreshment, riddance.

RELIEVE, *v.* Cure, remedy, redress, help, aid, assist, deliver, alleviate, palliate, indemnify, assuage, mitigate, ease, soften, rest, comfort, exempt, free, liberate, strengthen, abate, extricate, correct, restore, calm, demulcify, abirritate, mollify, salve, embrocate, drug, medicate, treat, brace, tone, stimulate, roborify, remit, console, release, solace, rid, relax, allay, soothe, subdue, rehabilitate, regenerate, revivify, reinvigorate, exhilarate, freshen, reanimate, quicken, cheer, minister to, attend, pacify, appease, slacken, slake, quench, disburden, set loose.

RELIGION, *n.* 1. Theologics, theology, monotheism, theism, polytheism, divinity, doctrinalism, dogmatic theology, revealed religion, theosophy, divine wisdom, deism, dogmatics, hagiology, hagiography, canonics, dogma, canon, creed, belief, religious faith, hierology, hierography, pantheism.

2. Piety, devotion, devoutness, holiness, sanctity, reverence, faith, faithfulness, virtue, godliness, goodness, grace, religiosity, religiousness, sainthood, saintship, spirituality, belief, veneration, worship, adoration, homage, profession of faith, pietism, righteousness.

3. System of faith, system of religion, system of worship, sect, denomination, persuasion, affiliation, fellowship.

RELIGIOUS, *adj.* 1. Godly, holy, devout, pious, spiritual, spiritual-minded, devotional, solemn, celibate, cenobite, good, faithful, righteous, worthy, pietistic, celestial, heavenly, divine, hallowed, sacrosanct, blessed, sanctified, glorifying, religious-minded, saintly, saintlike, pure, zealous, just, unworldly, seraphic, angelic, reverential, reverent, believing.

2. Conscientious, scrupulous, nice, exact, strict, rigid, faithful, accurate, right, constant, unerring, unswerving, undeviating, unfailing, meticulous, particular, finicking, stern, severe, rigorous, definite, positive, punctilious, fastidious.

3. Divine, theological, doctrinal, canonical, doctrinary, dogmatic, doctrinarian, sectarian, orthodox, schismatic, denominational.

RELINQUISH, *v.* 1. Quit, leave, abandon, forsake, evacuate, vacate, withdraw from, leave behind, turn one's back on, pull out, secede from, desert, bolt from.

2. Forbear, renounce, forgo, give up, cede, yield, resign, repudiate, abdicate, abjure, deliver up, waive, give up claim to, renounce claim to, deny, drop all idea of, disclaim, hand over, sign away, break off, demit, demise, release, do without, go without, spare, dismiss, wash one's hands of, jettison, throw overboard, lay aside, cast off, rid oneself of, relegate, reject, eliminate, throw into the discard, extirpate.

RELIQUARY, *n.* Shrine, tabernacle, monstrance, casket, case, box, container, memorial, monument, vessel, sepulcher, holder, respository.

RELISH, *n.* 1. Zest, savor, gusto, taste, flavor, sapor, sapidity, liking, fondness, desire, want, wish, hankering, longing, love, fancy, partiality, desideration.

2. Pleasure, enjoyment, gratification, satisfaction, animal delight, carnal pleasure, titillation, sensuality, sensuousness, delight.

3. Condiment, preserve, flavoring, sauce, spice, seasoning, chutney, chili-sauce, pickle relish, sweet relish, tomato relish, piccalilli.

RELISH, *v.* 1. Like, enjoy, taste, smack one's lips over, have a liking for, eat with pleasure, eat with savor, delight in, appreciate, find something delicious, sip, sup, sample, roll on the tongue.

2. Feel pleasure, feel gratification, enjoy, love, like, prefer, appreciate, delight in, feast on, gloat over, luxuriate in, indulge in, revel in, wallow in, bask in, rejoice in, be pleased with, derive pleasure from, get a kick from *(coll.)*.

RELUCTANCE, *n.* Indisposition, unwillingness, disinclination, renitency, aversion, indocility, scruple, demur, recoil, shrinking, hesitancy, hesitation, fastidiousness, delicacy, qualm, recoiling, nolition, disaffection, distaste, disfavor, disapproval, fear, phobia, disrelish, disgust, repugnance, horror, loathing, hatred, antipathy, abhorrence, backwardness, holding back, detestation, squeamishness, diffidence, shyness.

RELUCTANT, *adj.* Averse, unwilling, loath, backward, disinclined, hesitant, hesitating, indisposed, demurring, hanging back, diffident, shy, uncertain, squeamish, remiss, laggard, opposed, in opposition, renitent, shrinking, shy of, fastidious, irreconcilable, involuntary, protestant, dissentious, dissenting, intolerant, discontented, inacquiescent, refusing, uncomplaisant, uncomplying, rejective, declinatory, querulous, particular, choosy *(coll.)*, discriminating, discriminative.

RELY, *v.* Depend, confide, rest, hope, hang, calculate on, turn on, be dependent on, count on, place one's trust in, credit, believe, trust, be trustful, accept, repose confidence in, trust to, attach weight to, give credence, give credit, swear by, bet on, gamble on, take for granted, accept on trust, lean on, feel sure, cling to hope, be confident.

REMAIN, *v.* 1. Last, endure, continue, abide, stay, bide, hold, prevail, hang on, draw out, subsist, persist, tarry, linger, run on, perdure, go on, keep a hold on life, stay put *(coll.)*, stand pat *(coll.)*, survive, outlive, drag on, be protracted, persevere, remain alive, be left behind, be protracted, carry on, hold up, outlast.

2. Stay, tarry, dwell, abide, sojourn, reside, attend, lodge, linger, inhabit, bide, exist in space, occur in a place, stay at home, keep indoors, vegetate, be established at, not stir, not move, be motionless, be immobile, be immobilized, be dormant, rest, settle down, locate oneself, park, put up at, make one's abode, domesticate, take up one's quarters, get a footing.

REMAINDER, *n.* 1. Deposit, residue, sediment, dregs, scum, dross, discard, castoffs, leavings, litter, garbage, scraps, refuse, lees, sweepings, chaff, offal, waste, waste matter, offscourings, excrement, trash, rubbish, offscum, junk, slag, culls, residuum, discard, fragments, remnants, debris, fag ends, shoddy, relics, rags, rubble, rejectamenta, feculence, cheese parings, sewage, clinker, throwaway, pickings, odds and ends, flotsam, jetsam, orts, stuff, lumber, dust, truck, stubble, tares, weeds, bones, carrion, slough, swill, bilge, hogwash, bilge water, scourings, rinsings, scurf, froth, foam, smoke, detritus, oddments, grounds, sordes, sprue, bottoms, settlings, scoriae, heeltaps, deposit, precipitate, alluvium, ember, ashes, cinder, silt, precipitation, sublimate, sinter, lava, smut, dirt, soot, condensation, settlement, candle ends, straw, fossil, ruins, skeleton, butt, stump, peels, flings, sawdust, raspings.

2. Reversion, futurity, subsequence, posteriority, sequence, sequel, consequence, aftermath, wake, trail, train, aftergrowth, afterpiece, afterpart, suffix, postfix, afterglow, outgrowth, appendix, postscript, conclusion, postface, subscript, postlude, epilogue.

3. Estate, property, inheritance, bequest, right, entail, claim, title.

REMAKE, *v.* Transform, recreate, transmute, transfigure, mutate, re-form, refashion, make anew, revive, revivify, reconstruct, reconstitute, reinvigorate, reanimate, reinstitute, transmogrify, rebuild, revamp, revise, reshape, reconvert, vary, alter, modify, qualify, convert, renovate, restore, renew, make over, change.

REMAND, *v.* 1. Recommit, send back, return, revert, restore, replace, render up.

2. Commit, consign, send, relegate, entrust, assign, confide, dispatch, depute, delegate, commission, convey, carry, transport, transfer.

3. Order, command, instruct, bid, enjoin, charge, decree, act, enact, direct, dictate.

REMARK, *n.* 1. Word, saying, utterance, talk, allegation, expression, assertion, comment, mention, declaration, statement, observation, sentence, phrase, pronouncement, dictum, vocalization, prolation, enunciation, articulation.

2. Notice, heed, attention, regard, consideration, perception, reflection, thought, animadversion, respect, ear, observance.

REMARK, *v.* 1. Utter, say, speak, express, verbalize, articulate, assert, state, asseverate, comment upon, mention, deliver, emit, come out with, let fall, voice, give utterance, allege, declare, aver, recite, convey, communicate, present, pour forth.

2. Note, take notice, attend, pay heed, observe, regard, look at, give heed to, pay attention to, find, see, mind, mark, view, make note of, take note of, animadvert, fix the mind on, fix the attention on, experience, feel, receive an impression of, respond to.

REMARKABLE, *adj.* Noticeable, noteworthy, worthy of note, notable, signal, observable, memorable, singular, unique, unusual, wonderful, marked, distinct, distinctive, peculiar, striking, apparent, prominent, conspicuous, eminent, famous, celebrated, distinguished, rare, strange, uncommon, extraordinary, surprising, astonishing, amazing, astounding, dumfounding, notorious, firstrate, classic, renowned, well-known, salient, outstanding, egregious, noted, illustrious, eventful, exceptional, impressive, significant, prodigious, wondrous, marvelous, stupendous, miraculous, inconceivable, incredible, unbelievable, unheardof, overwhelming, unimaginable, inexpressible, indescribable, unspeakable, unutterable, ineffable, august, lofty, imposing, exalted, unforgettable, momentous, consequential, exceptional, rare, special.

REMEDIABLE, *adj.* Curable, reparable, rectifiable, adjustable, medicable, corrigible, correctable, improvable, sanable, recoverable, restorable, retrievable.

REMEDIAL, *adj.* Curative, healing, corrective, recuperative, tonic, sanative, health-giving, sanatory, restorative, prophylactic, therapeutic, antidotal, alterative, analeptic, medicinal, medical, therial, bactericidal, antiseptic, germicidal, antibiotic, disinfectant, detergent, cleansing, purifying, allopathic, homeopathic, hydropathic, salubrious, salutary, beneficial, benign, wholesome, healthy (*coll.*), bracing, roborant, stimulating, hygienic, invigorating, sanitary, reformative, reparatory, restitutive, revivifying, lenitive, alleviative, palliative, soothing, easing, assuasive, calmative, balmy, emollient, anodyne, analgesic.

REMEDY, *n.* 1. Antidote, cure, counteragent, counteractive, panacea, nostrum, medicine, preventive, preventative, neutralizer, prophylactic, serum, injection, inoculation, antitoxin, vaccine, vaccination, shot (*sl.*), help, aid, relief, corrective, restorative, specific, therapy, analeptic, alterant, alterative, nostrum, physic, drug, medicament, potion, elixir, physic, laxative, cordial, balm, balsam, tincture, bracer, tonic, stimulant, alleviative, palliative, assuasive, anodyne, analgesic, demulcent, sedative, calmative, abirritant, embrocation, salve, ointment, unguent, lotion, pill, bolus, purgative, cathartic, vermifuge, antibiotic, disinfectant, bactericide, germicide, antiseptic, aperient, deobstruent, carminative, theriac, electuary, vulnerary, alterant, dose, sanative, cure-all, materia medica, pharmaceutical, prescription.

2. Relief, mitigation, palliation, assuagement, comfort, easement, rescue, aid, help, assistance, succor, restoration, correction, emendation, alteration, analepsis, allopathy, homeopathy, medicine, stimulation, hygiene, invigoration, reconstitution, reformation, reparation, restitution, analgesis, antisepsis.

REMEDY, *v.* 1. Redress, correct, rectify, make sound, restore, revive, mend, repair, cure, help, relieve, satisfy, palliate, alleviate, assuage, overhaul, put into condition, put into shape, restore to health, bring round, save from death, work a cure, effect a remedy, revive, reanimate, resuscitate, revivify, reinvigorate, improve, ameliorate, make better, mend, soothe, ease, make easy, calm, mollify, mitigate.

2. Redress, restore, right a wrong, make right, rectify, regulate, fix, make better, adjust, make square, put to rights.

REMEMBER, *v.* Think back, recall, reminisce, recollect, call to mind, look back, recall to mind, recall to the memory, carry one's thoughts back, review, review in retrospect, renew old memories, indulge in reminiscing, recover knowledge of, recall knowledge of, memorialize, commemorate, place, spot, reidentify, think upon, bethink oneself, have at one's finger tips, keep in mind, return to the thoughts of, dwell upon the past, retain in one's memory, retain the thought of, bear in mind, bear in memory, treasure a memory of, tax the memory with, memorize, have by heart, keep in one's heart, treasure, store up memories.

REMEMBRANCE, *n.* 1. Memento, memorial, remembrancer, reminder, prompter, mnemonic, mnemonicon, souvenir, keepsake, token, relic, mnemonic device, testimonial, monumental record, shrine, reliquary.

2. Memory, memoria, recognition, total recall, recollection, reidentification, recognizance, inward eye, commemoration, the mind's eye, mental reproduction, retrospection, reminiscence, rememoration, recordation, retention in the mind, retention in the memory.

3. Immortality, lasting fame, celebrity, notoriety, posthumous fame, immortal name, celebration, place in the hall of fame, place in the memory, glorification, exaltation, elevation, enshrinement, immortalization, apotheosis, deification, consecration, dignification.

REMIND, *v.* Cause to remember, put in memory, put in mind (*coll.*), bring back to the memory, cause to recollect, awake memories of, jog the memory, suggest to, give a cue to, prompt, refresh the memory of, renew memories of, bring to recollection, give an inkling of, give a clue to, hint at, make an allusion to, throw out a hint, drop a hint.

REMINDER, *n.* Memento, memorial, remembrance, remembrancer, prompter, mnemonicon, mnemonic device, keepsake, relic, souvenir, token of remembrance, testimonial, monumental record, shrine, reliquary, intimation, hint, suggestion, allusion, reference, inkling, suspicion, glimmer, clue, innuendo, insinuation, implication, subaudition.

REMINISCE, *v.* Recollect, remember, call to mind, bring to mind, reflect, muse, cogitate, mull over, be mindful, summon to mind, call to mind, recall to remembrance, conjure up, summon up, carry one's thoughts back, look back upon, be retrospective, rescue from oblivion, give oneself up to reminiscence, indulge in remembrances, indulge in reminiscence, bethink oneself, think upon, pass in review, review in retrospect, recall knowledge of, recover knowledge of, ponder, muse over.

REMINISCENCE, *n.* Recalling, remembering, contemplation, thinking back upon, retrospection, retrospect, review, reviewing the past, thinking back upon, reflection, reconsideration, afterthought, remembrance of things past, memory, recognition, reidentification, recognizance, commemoration.

REMINISCENT, *adj.* Recollective, mindful, remindful, suggestive, mnemonic, recollecting, retentive, remembering, commemorative.

REMISS, *adj.* Slack, neglectful, indifferent, careless, heedless, sloppy, dilatory, perfunctory, cursory, negligent, unheeding, unthinking, unmindful, unsolicitous, lax, inconsiderate, thoughtless, disregardful, disregardant, offhand, imprudent, procrastinative, cunctatory, indolent, lazy, slothful, inattentive, unobservant, oblivious, unmindful, shiftless, improvident, inadvertent, happy-go-lucky, insouciant, careless, devil-may-care, unguarded, unthinking, do-nothing, fainéant, laggard, lackadaisical, unfaithful, indiscreet, injudicious, temerarious, loose, slipshod, unwatchful, inactive, torpid, dronish, idle, lukewarm, tepid, sluggish, hebetudinous, lentitudinous, supine, languid, loafing, inactive, torpescent, phlegmatic, otiose, lymphatic, forgetful.

REMISSION, *n.* 1. Allayment, assuagement, modulation, abatement, relief, relieving, alleviation, mitigation, relaxation, respite, rest, release, tranquilization, diminution, lessening, decrease, reduction.

2. Suspension, intermission, pause, letup, delay, recess, hesitation, interruption, hitch (*coll.*), abeyance, truce, lull, break, caesura, lapse, interval,

halt, stay, stand, standstill, check, discontinuance, suspense, stoppage, cessation, subsidence, stop.

3. Absolution, forgiveness, indulgence, pardon, discharge, acquittal, exoneration, exculpation, excuse, grace, condonation, oblivion, amnesty, reprieve, forbearance, expurgation, vindication, acquittance, quittance, compurgation, release, discharge, liberation, disculpation, clearance.

REMIT, *v.* 1. Return, replevin, restore, send back, reinstate, replace, make restitution, bring back, disgorge, render up, release, let go, reimburse, recoup, indemnify, compensate, reinvest, readjust, redeem, rectify, repair, ransom, remedy, redress, make good, put to rights, make square.

2. Lessen, diminish, minimize, decrease, reduce, abate, ease, lenify, mitigate, weaken, extenuate, lower, take away, arrest, stop, interrupt, relax, break, intermit, suspend, hold up, put a stop to, halt, stall, check, brake, stem the tide, obtund, sheathe, dull, deaden, soften, moderate, attemper, temper, appease, soothe, calm, assuage, quell, sober, tame, tranquilize, quiet, hush, alleviate, palliate, slacken, slake, chasten, subdue, lull, still, pacify, sober, smother.

3. Give amnesty, grant amnesty, forgive, allow, excuse, pardon, absolve, overlook, condone, pass over, acquit, waive, forgo, spare, exonerate, exculpate, drop the charges against, forgive and forget, grant remission, clear, wipe the slate clean, shut one's eyes to, bury the hatchet *(coll.),* let bygones be bygones, not give the matter a second thought, not be hard upon, vindicate, whitewash, liberate, release, let out.

REMNANT, *n.* Relic, reminder, remains, scraps, fragment, leavings, reliquiae, orts, traces, vestiges, archaism, relic of the past, fossils, petrification, reminder, record, antiquity, sign, evidence, keepsake, souvenir, memento, memorabilia, token of remembrance, trophy, heirloom, inheritance, leftover, residuum, residue, oddment, debris, detritus, skeleton, bone, ashes, the rest, refuse, waste, piece, bit, little bit, stump, paring, butt, peel, odds and ends, surplus, surplusage, chip, strip, precipitate, residue, scum, dross, dregs, discard, castoffs, chaff, litter, leavings, garbage, lees, sweepings, offal, waste matter, scoriae, offscourings, excrement, trash, rubbish, culls, offscum, junk, slag, fag ends, shoddy, relicts, rags, rubble, dross, feculence, feces, cheese parings, sewage, clinker, pickings, flotsam, jetsam, stuff, lumber, dust, truck, stubble, tares, weeds, wastepaper, carrion, swill, hogwash, bilge water, rinsings, grounds, sordes, dregs, sprue, bottoms, settlings, heeltaps, deposit, alluvium, ember, cinder, silt, sublimate, sinter, lava, smut, dirt, soot, condensation, settlement, straw, plugs, filings, raspings, sawdust, peels.

REMONSTRANCE, *n.* Expostulation, protest, protestation, dissuasion, reproof, invective, representation, objection, reproach, rebuke, argument, admonition, warning, admonishment, censure, blame, criticism, reprimand, reproval, reprehension, scolding, berating, opprobrium, exprobration, objurgation, upbraiding, chastisement, castigation, nagging, revilement, bawling out *(coll.),* berating, lecture, abuse, roasting *(coll.),* talking-to *(coll.),* speaking-to *(coll.),* dressing-down *(coll.),* tongue-lashing *(coll.),* calling-down *(coll.),* going over *(coll.),* correction, dehortation, deprecation, advisement, counsel, suggestion, instruction, injunction, guidance, recommendation, determent, discouragement, demur, scruple.

REMONSTRATE, *v.* Make objections to, take ex-

ception to, decry, frown upon, knock, disparage, find fault, pick flaws, disapprove, animadvert, reprimand, object to, recriminate, complain, contend, dispute, argue, altercate, expostulate, protest, dissuade, reprove, make representations, reproach, rebuke, reprove, admonish, warn, censure, blame, criticize, reprove, reprehend, scold, berate, exprobrate, objurgate, upbraid, chastise, castigate, nag, revile, bawl out *(coll.),* lecture, abuse, roast *(coll.),* talk to *(coll.),* dress down *(coll.),* give a talking-to *(coll.),* give a tongue-lashing *(coll.),* correct, dehortate, deprecate, advise, counsel, suggest, instruct, enjoin, guide, recommend, deter, discourage, object, demur, protest.

REMONSTRATIVE, *adj.* Remonstrant, expostulative, expostulatory, protestant, discouraging, objecting, demurring, scrupling, injunctive, enjoining, guiding, recommending, instructive, suggestive, counseling, advising, deprecative, deprecatory, dehortatory, dehortative, corrective, abusive, castigative, nagging, reviling, chastising, objurgative, exprobrative, opprobrious, critical, reprimanding, censorious, blaming, admonitory, warning, argumentative, disputatious, contentious, invective, objecting, reproachful, rebuking, dissuasive, reproving, reprobatory.

REMORSE, *n.* Sorrow, contrition, compunction, regret, penitence, repentance, contriteness, self-reproach, self-accusation, self-condemnation, self-conviction, voice of conscience, stings of remorse, sting of conscience, sorrow for sin, pangs of conscience, prick of conscience, self-reproof, self-criticism, grief, anguish, resipiscence, lamentation, regretfulness, repining, rue, bitterness, heartburn, discontent, lamentation.

REMORSEFUL, *adj.* Repentant, contrite, sorry, sorrowful, regretful, compunctious, penitent, self-reproachful, self-accusatory, conscience-stricken, lamenting, repining, penitential, touched, smitten with conscience, self-condemning, self-accusing, self-convicting, self-humiliating, self-reproaching.

REMOTE, *adj.* 1. Far, distant, far off, far removed, away from, out of the way, back, ultimate, uttermost, outermost, aloof, a long way off, far from, distal, faraway, yonder, ulterior, transpontine, transalpine, transatlantic, ultramundane, hyperboreal, hyperborean, out-of-sight, antipodean, inaccessible, unobtainable, unapproachable, unattainable, unreachable.

2. Foreign, alien, disconnected, unconnected, unrelated, unassociated, dissociated, disaffiliated, unallied, strange, extraneous, outlandish, rare, exotic, detached, separate, apart, segregated, distinct, heterogeneous, isolated, solitary, sequestrated, sequestered, obscure, alone, lonely.

REMOVAL, *n.* Dislodgment, dislocation, displacement, deposition, unplacement, transplacement, translocation, transplantation, transshipment, transfer, transference, shift, relegation, change of place, sequestration, segregation, isolation, abolition, elimination, purge, deportation, sublation, conversion, translation, transportation, exclusion, noninclusion, omission, exception, rejection, ejection, debarment, repudiation, prohibition, separation, abandonment, withdrawal, eradication, extraction, taking away, excision, expulsion, obliteration, erasure.

REMOVE, *v.* 1. Deduct, subtract, abstract, sublate, curtail, amputate, resect, mutilate, cut away, detruncate, truncate, obtruncate, dismiss, discharge, ejaculate, emit, banish, excommunicate, proscribe, exile, ostracize, dispossess, extradite, disembogue, disgorge, evacuate, erupt, defecate, eructate, vomit, effuse, drain, extravasate, secern, secrete, exude, clear, extirpate, extricate, export, exterminate, kill, liquidate, execute, dislodge, dislocate, elocate, displace, depose, transplace, translocate, transplant, transship, transfer, shift, change, relegate, abstract, sequestrate, sequester, segregate, isolate, abolish, eliminate, purge, deport, eloign, translate, transport, exclude, omit, except, reject, bar, debar, eject, repudiate, separate, eradicate, extract, erase, rub out (coll.), take away, excise, dispel, expel, obliterate, deterge.

2. Disjoin, dissociate, disconnect, detach, part, divide, set apart, insulate, loose, unbind, undo, unfasten, untie, unattach, unchain, uproot, pluck out, pull up, pull out, excavate, dig out, dig up, exhume, raise, disburden, disturb, obviate, take out, take away, cut off, lop off, chop off, withdraw from circulation, strip, tear off, dismantle, jettison, cast off, throw overboard, discard, destroy, ruin, desolate, lay waste, wreck, ravage, annihilate, delete, expunge, blot out, cancel.

3. Depart, withdraw, go forth, go out, go away, set forth, set out, take leave, get along, go one's way, sally forth, vacate, evacuate, quit, leave, decamp, retreat, retire, debouch, make an exit.

REMOVE, n. Distance, interval, separation, stage, degree, measure, amplitude, reach, pitch, standard, height, scale, scope, caliber, amount, ratio, mark, stand, status, station, rank, sphere, footing, interval, term, rung, cut, notch, peg, position, step, extent, graduation, gradation, grade.

REMUNERATE, v. Repay, reward, compensate, recompense, satisfy, return, pay for, yield profit to, profit, bear fruit, benefit, do a good service, reimburse, indemnify, redress, fee, guerdon, atone, make amends, make payment, discharge a debt, settle, balance the accounts, liquidate a debt, strike a balance, make payment.

REMUNERATION, n. Requital, reward, recompense, compensation, repayment, liquidation, satisfaction, fee, hire, meed, salary, wages, premium, lucre, guerdon, amends, reparation, restitution, indemnity, indemnification, atonement, profit, gain, yield, income, dividends, defrayment, discharge, settlement, clearance, quittance, acquittance, payoff, tribute, subsidy, support, maintenance, subsistence, retribution, reimbursement, redress, return, solatium, honorarium, price, requital, remittance, emolument, stipend, damages, earnings, net income, gross income, receipts, winnings, innings, pelf, avails, pickings, take, proceeds.

REMUNERATIVE, adj. Profitable, rewarding, paying, lucrative, gainful, compensatory, fruitful, useful, fat, remuneratory, requiting, recompensing, liquidating, satisfying, reparative, indemnifying, atoning, settling, clearing, subsidizing, supporting, maintaining, sustaining, retributive, reimbursing, redressive, gainful, productive, well-paying, advantageous, utilitarian, practical, helpful, beneficial, salutary, pragmatical, practicable.

RENAISSANCE, n. Regeneration, rebirth, renascence, remaking, reconstruction, reconstitution, reformation, reproduction, reëstablishment, regenesis, palingenesis, renovation, reconditioning, overhauling, repairing, remodeling, mending, fixing up, patching up, reparation, restoration, reclamation, resuscitation, resurrection, refashioning, reanimation, rehabilitation, retrieval, salvage, redintegration, restitution, reconversion, rejuvenation, revivification, awakening.

RENASCENT, adj. Resurgent, reappearing, rejuvenated, revivified, restored, renewed, redivivus, reborn, remade, reconstituted, re-formed, reproduced, re-established, renovated, reconditioned, overhauled, repaired, reclaimed, resuscitated, resurrected, refashioned, recreated, regenerated, reanimated, revived, rehabilitated, salvaged, redintegrated, awakened.

RENCOUNTER, n. 1. Touch, meeting, contiguity, contiguousness, apposition, juxtaposition, connection, tangency, appulsion, appulse, junction, conjunction, conjugation, jointure, joining, coexistence, proximity, nearness, closeness, abutment, abuttal.

2. Rencontre, fray, affray, contest, conflict, fight, combat, scrap (coll.), action, collision, meeting, clash, encounter, tussle, skirmish, scramble, melee, joust, scuffle, struggle, embroilment.

REND, v. 1. Splinter, tear, rip, break, sever, dissever, sunder, rive, rupture, shiver, cleave, cut, hew, split, crack, snap, dismember, disrupt, divide, destroy, burst, fracture, lacerate, dilacerate, tear asunder, break asunder, break into pieces, break in two, splinter, break up, mince, chop, hack, dissect, harrow, shatter, lancinate, cut off, amputate, mangle, chew, dispiece, disunite, decorticate, slice, slash, slit, saw, snip, carve, whittle, decompose, disintegrate, tear to pieces, smash to smithereens, reduce to fragments, anatomize, hash, decimate, dislimb, debranch.

2. Rupture, come apart, break, burst, shatter, crack, snap, rive, tear, crash, crumble, splinter, fracture, fly apart, fall to pieces, come apart, fall apart, be brittle, give way.

RENDER, v. 1. Impart, communicate, present, give, donate, grant, vouchsafe, accord, dispense, dole out, deal out, deliver, put into the hands of, hand over, pass out, hand out, assign, apportion, distribute, allot, come across with (coll.), surrender, shell out (coll.).

2. Yield up, give up, give back, restore, disgorge, regurgitate, release, let go, make restitution of, reimburse, remit, pay back, reindemnify, indemnify, requite, make requital, make quittance, make payment, give payment, give tribute.

3. Play, execute, perform, sing, instrumentalize, make music, make melody, play tunes, produce music, sing a song, play a piece, symphonize, interpret, give a reading of, recite.

4. Translate, rephrase, paraphrase, restate, define, expound, enunciate, construe, commentate, comment upon, exemplify, expand upon, discourse upon, elucidate, make intelligible, reword, rehash, explicate.

5. Make, do, achieve, perform, work, execute, pursue, prosecute, follow, carry on, transact, enact, carry out, carry through, put into practice, put into effect, bring about, make, practice, engage in, have a hand in, participate in, take part in, have to do with, accomplish.

RENDEZVOUS, n. 1. Meeting, tryst, resort, encounter, assemblage, assembly, gathering, forgathering, congregation, collection, aggregation, confluence, concourse, muster, levy, colligation, collocation, ingathering.

2 Meeting place, gathering place, trysting place, resort, rallying place, retreat, habitat, haunt, stamping ground, hangout (sl.), headquarters, place of meeting, place of assignation, lovenest (coll.), hideout.

RENDITION, n. 1. Reddition, return, restitution,

compensation, atonement, reinvestment, restoration, repayment, indemnification, reparation, rehabilitation, replevin, replevy, reversion, remittance.

2. Version, rendering, reading, lection, translation, construction, explanation, interpretation, rewording, paraphrase, amplification, gloss, key, glossary, interlinear translation, interlinear, delineation, reproduction, representation, definition, commentary, comment, explication, redaction, metaphrase.

RENEGADE, *n.* 1. Recreant, apostate, backslider, tergiversant, tergiversator, double-dealer, trimmer, equivocator, bolter, mugwump, runaway, runagate, schismatist, recidivist, reversioner, secessionist, dissenter, traitor, rebel, heretic, timeserver, turncoat, revolutionist, revolter, reactionary, insurgent, mutineer, separatist, betrayer, treasonist, arch-traitor, rascal, rat, deserter, outcast.

2. Fugitive, runaway, eloper, absconder, refugee, deserter, vagabond, vagrant, wanderer.

RENEGADE, *adj.* Apostate, apostatic, unfaithful, false, reactionary, recidivist, recidivistic, reactionary, backsliding, revulsionary, recreant, unfaithful, relapsing, recrudescent, regressive, retrograde, recidivous, refluent, recessive.

RENEGE, *v.* Quit, leave, abandon, forsake, evacuate, vacate, withdraw, leave behind, turn one's back, pull out, secede, bolt, desert, cast off, demur, decline, retreat, funk, back out, revoke, abrogate, rescind, retract, reverse, recall, repeal, countermand, contradict, counterorder, annul, abolish, nullify, quash, invalidate, make null and void, dissolve.

RENEW, *v.* Restore, rehabilitate, re-establish, reconstitute, reinvigorate, reinstate, reconstruct, redintegrate, renovate, revamp, make over, fix, regenerate, reinstall, readjust, make whole, refit, replace, put back, put into shape, restore to operation, return, reconvert, bring back, remake, salvage, save, redeem, improve, relieve, mend, amend, ameliorate, meliorate, promote, perfect, make sound, develop, enhance, revive, revivify, resuscitate, replenish, refresh, rejuvenate, resurrect, modernize, recoup, make new, make perfect.

RENEWAL, *n.* Restoration, rehabilitation, reëstablishment, reconstitution, reinvigoration, reinstatement, reconstruction, redintegration, renovation, revamping, making over, fixing, regeneration, reinstallation, readjustment, restoration, recoupment, salvage, improvement, mending, amendment, emendation, amelioration, melioration, promotion, perfection, development, refitting, enhancement, revivification, resuscitation, replenishment, resurrection, modernization, rebirth, renaissance, renascence, regeneration, reproduction.

RENITENT, *adj.* Resistent, opposed, reactionary, recalcitrant, repugnant, reluctant, indisposed, antagonistic, unwilling, disinclined, aversionary, indocile, demurring, recoiling, shrinking, hesitant, hesitating, fastidious, squeamish, qualmish, disaffected, repelled, disapproving, disgusted, loath, antipathetic, abhorrent, detesting, intractable, intransigent.

RENOUNCE, *v.* 1. Refuse, decline, discredit, disallow, repudiate, scout, repel, rebuff, deny, veto, forbid, interdict, slight, despise, detest, spurn, disapprove, reject, proscribe, abjure, disdain, disbar, bar, negate, negative, discountenance, dismiss, shrug off, disown, disclaim, repel, repulse, banish, forswear, scorn, abhor, ostracize, disavow, waive,

exempt, set at naught, place no value on, contravene, contradict, controvert, oppose, gainsay, say no to, traverse, impugn, dispute, belie, disaffirm, turn a deaf ear to, ignore, challenge, hold in question, bring into question, skepticize, disagree with, dissent, revolt at, turn from, not countenance, demur to, scruple at, boggle at, raise objections to, cavil with, quibble, protest at, protest against.

2. Abandon, forsake, relinquish, forbear, forgo, give up, give back, cede, yield, resign, repudiate, abdicate, abjure, deliver up, part with, lay down, waive, give up claim to, deny, yield up, disclaim, hand over, sign away, demit, demise, dismiss, wash one's hands of, jettison, throw overboard, lay aside, cast aside, cast off, rid oneself of, relegate, throw aside, reject, eliminate, discard, throw into the discard.

RENOVATE, *v.* Restore, rehabilitate, re-establish, reconstitute, reinvigorate, reinstate, reconstruct, renew, redintegrate, revamp, make over, fix, regenerate, reinstall, readjust, make whole, refit, recoup, reconvert, remake, salvage, redeem, improve, relieve, mend, amend, ameliorate, meliorate, perfect, promote, make sound, develop, revive, revivify, resuscitate, rejuvenate, resurrect, modernize, make new.

RENOVATION, *n.* Restoration, rehabilitation, reëstablishment, reconstitution, reinvigoration, reinstatement, reconstruction, redintegration, saving, renewal, revamping, making over, fixing, reparation, repairs, regeneration, reproduction, reinstallation, readjustment, refitting, refurbishment, restoral, recoupment, recovery, salvage, redemption, improvement, mending, amendment, emendation, amelioration, melioration, perfection, development, enhancement.

RENOWN, *n.* Importance, eminence, consequence, distinction, fame, celebrity, paramountcy, primacy, pre-eminence, repute, laurels, praise, reputation, nobility, superiority, supereminence, significance, import, mark, momentousness, value, weight, note, sublimity, grandeur, majesty, dignity, prestige, splendor, popularity, credit, respect, report, glory, éclat, high repute, reputability, esteem, regard, account, exaltation, eminency, greatness, illustriousness, brilliance, elevation, posthumous fame, immortality, glorification, canonization, consecration, aggrandizement, deification, mark of honor, feather in one's cap, notoriety, luster, credit, bays.

RENOWNED, *adj.* Notable, majestic, reputable, notorious, celebrated, famed, famous, well-known, eminent, of mark, remarkable, noteworthy, extraordinary, unusual, august, distinguished, sublime, out of the ordinary, unparalled, singular, unique, indescribable, rare, unexampled, unprecedented, great, popular, conspicuous, brilliant, glorious, much-touted, acclaimed, outstanding, egregious, consequential, imposing, impressive, stately, of the first water, matchless, pre-eminent, momentous, noteworthy, signal, honored, farfamed, noble, powerful, peerless, exalted.

RENT, *n.* 1. Chasm, rift, cleft, split, rupture, interval, chap, chink, fissure, gash, cut, incision, rime, fracture, break, cranny, gap, breach, hole, flaw, leak, cavity, crack, scissure, slit, dilaceration, tear, crevasse, lacuna, gulf, aperture, perforation, puncture, acupuncture, slot, orifice, foramen, laceration.

2. Rental, hire, dues, fee, assessment, toll, tariff, cost, price, land revenue, proceeds, profit,

income, return, payment, remuneration, income from real estate.

RENT, v. Lease, let, grant a lease, demise, let for hire, rent out, sublet, sublease, subrent, underlet.

RENUNCIATION, n. 1. Rejection, banishment, relegation, excommunication, expatriation, ostracism, exile, deportation, ostracization, extradition, dismissal, walking papers, ticket of leave, the sack (coll.), discharge, firing, ouster, dispossession, eviction, dislodgment, deposition, deposal, exclusion, ejectment, rejectment, emission, extrusion, removal, displacement, elimination, repulsion, discard, disownment, disinheritance, riddance, shutting out, omission, noninclusion, preclusion, lockout, disbarment, eradication, expulsion, throwing out, jettison, abandonment, marooning, cashiering, abnegation, boycott, exsection, excision, proscription, the go-by (coll.), extirpation, uprooting.

2. Relinquishment, forbearance, forgoing, cession, yielding, resignation, repudiation, abdication, abjuration, waiver, disclaimer, surrender, remission, demission, demise, expropriation, jettisoning, recantation, apostasy, revocation, retraction, recantation, capitulation, abstention, spurning, repulsion, scorn, denial, reprobation, disownment, disallowance, veto, disapproval, disapprobation, declination, rebuff, interdiction, slight, ban, negation, contradiction, contravention, controversion, opposition, gainsaying, traversion, impugning, disaffirmation, refusal, distrust, mistrust, disagreement.

REORGANIZE, v. Refound, regenerate, remodel, revolutionize, reclaim, improve, make better, ameliorate, meliorate, correct, emend, emendate, refurbish, touch up, brush up, elaborate, develop, enhance, rectify, revive, restore, rehabilitate, readjust, reconstruct, rebuild, revamp, renovate, salvage, redeem, overhaul, mend, fix, resuscitate, reconstruct, make over, revise, edit.

REPAIR, v. Make improvement upon, improve, ameliorate, meliorate, correct, emend, emendate, make better, refurbish, touch up, brush up, rehabilitate, readjust, salvage, reconstruct, rebuild, restore, revamp, recondition, service, cobble, tinker, overhaul, fix.

2. Hie to, resort to, betake oneself to, bend one's steps toward, visit, direct one's course to, move in the direction of, move toward, hasten to, hurry to.

REPARABLE, adj. Retrievable, restorable, reclaimable, redeemable, curable, improvable, recoverable, remediable, reformable, correctable, corrigible, emendable, amendable, rectifiable.

REPARATION, n. 1. Redress, repayment, indemnification, requital, quittance, satisfaction, retribution, atonement, amends, solatium, compensation, return, indemnity, peace offering, reimbursement, repayment, restitution, reddition, restoration, instauration, remuneration, expiation, reward.

2. Reconstruction, rebuilding, revamping, renovation, replacement, readjustment, salvage, rehabilitation, restoration, restoral, rectification, brushing up, reconditioning, servicing, tinkering, cobbling, rejuvenation, making over, refurbishment.

REPARTEE, n. Retort, response, rejoinder, answer, riposte, return, comeback, replication, clever reply, witty reply, give-and-take, witty conversation, word-play, banter, chaff, bon mot,

bandying of words, lively exchange, quip, crank, jest, witticism, mot (Fr.), happy thought, persiflage, badinage, quiddity, joke, wisecrack (sl.), gag (sl.), quirk, jeu d' esprit (Fr.), clever sally.

REPAST, n. Meal, victuals, food, diet, viands, nourishment, refection, eats (sl.), refreshment, collation, table, feast, banquet, feed (sl.), spread (coll.), board, regalement, breakfast, lunch, luncheon, brunch (coll.), high tea, dinner, supper, snack, picnic, junket, bite to eat (sl.), full-course-dinner, man-sized meal.

REPATRIATE, v. Restore, readmit, reinstate, rehabilitate, take back, restore citizenship to, restore nationality to.

REPAY, v. 1. Refund, reimburse, compensate, pay back, make restitution, return, requite, render, recompense, make amends, pay in kind, reward, indemnify.

2. Retaliate, hit back at, get back at, make requital, pay off an old score, return the compliment, pay back in kind, make reprisal, make retribution, give as good as one takes, settle the score, square accounts with, reciprocate, match, give in exchange, pay one in his own coin, make quits, even the score, give one a dose of one's own medicine, pay in the same coin, give one his just deserts, give one his comeuppance.

REPAYMENT, n. Retaliation, retribution, recompense, compensation, remuneration, indemnity, indemnification, reimbursement, restitution, return, revenge, vengeance, quittance, requital, comeuppance, just deserts, restitution, reciprocation, reprisal, recrimination, redress, reparation, atonement, amends, emolument, measure for measure.

REPEAL, v. Rescind, abrogate, revoke, recall, reverse, annul, cancel, abolish, remit, set aside, quash, nullify, overrule, dissolve, retract, renege, countermand, counterorder, override, void, invalidate, set aside, throw overboard, put an end to, terminate, declare null and void.

REPEAL, n. Rescission, abrogation, revocation, recall, reversal, annulment, cancellation, abolition, remission, quashing, disannulment, nullification, overruling, dissolution, revocation, countermandent, overriding, voiding, invalidation, termination, abjuration, repudiation, revokement, abolishment, recantation, retraction.

REPEAT, v. Reiterate, reword, restate, rephrase, paraphrase, state again, iterate, rehash, echo, re-echo, duplicate, reduplicate, reproduce, ditto (coll.), say over, go over the same ground, recount, recapitulate, retell, tell over, tautologize battologize, hammer, din, drum.

REPEATED, adj. Repetitious, reptitive, reiterated, duplicated, reduplicated, re-echoed, successive, recurrent, monotonous, singsong, habitual, incessant, ever-recurring, frequent, common, customary, wonted, regular, commonplace, stock, everyday, consuetudinary.

REPEL, v. 1. Push back, thrust back, repulse, dispel, chase away, drive away, put to flight, send packing (coll.), hold off, fend off, ward off, forfend, keep at arm's length, beat back, force back, resist, scatter, disperse, rebuff, repercuss, oppose, check, withstand, parry, make a stand against, throw off, stave off, obviate, deflect, sidetrack, avert, foil, checkmate, frustrate, scotch, balk, traverse, contravene, confound, nonplus, recalcitrate, withstand, keep at bay, divert.

2. Disclaim, repudiate, reject, disown, exclude, refuse to deal with, have nothing to do with, dis-

allow, scout, rebuff, veto, deny, forbid, interdict, slight, spurn, disapprove, renounce, proscribe, abjure, disbar, shrug off, forswear, waive, oppose, gainsay, dispute, belie, disaffirm, turn a deaf ear to, challenge, dissent from, revolt at, not countenance, object to, protest against, cut *(coll.)*, give the cold shoulder to, contemn, have no use for, set no store by, snub.

3. Revolt, offend, disgust, nauseate, sicken, turn one's stomach, set one's teeth on edge, stick in one's throat, go against the grain, grate on one's nerves, make one's flesh crawl, give one goose pimples, make one shudder, make one's hair stand on end, displease, vex, irritate, set one against, alienate, be hateful.

REPELLENT, *adj.* 1. Repelling, repulsive, offensive, foul, filthy, dirty, smudged, bespotted, tainted, corrupt, contaminated, putrid, putrescent, rank, foul-smelling, bad-smelling, nauseous, nauseating, sickening, abominable, beastly, vile, obnoxious, noisome, fulsome, loathsome, odious, revolting, disgusting, distasteful, slimy, feculent, rotten, lentiginous, scurfy, maggoty, decaying, saprogenic, putrefactive, reeking, sloppy, unsightly, unbearable, hateful, detestable, obscene, gross, abhorrent, forbidding, repulsing, frightful, despicable, abominable, unclean, impure.

2. Resistant, oppugnative, recalcitrant, renitent, unsubmissive, unresigned, rebellious, unyielding.

REPENT, *v.* Regret, be sorry for, have contrition for, be penitent for, be grieved for, lament, be regretful for, show regret for, own up to *(coll.)*, make a clean breast of, repine, deplore, rue, bewail, bemoan, weep over, humble oneself, own oneself in the wrong, plead guilty, do penance, atone for, expiate, redress, make amends, make up for, pay the penalty, pay the forfeit.

REPENTANCE, *n.* Contrition, penitence, remorse, regret, compunction, sorrow, contriteness, self-reproach, self-condemnation, self-accusation, self-conviction, resipiscence, pangs of conscience, pangs of remorse, sorrow for sin, confession of error, self-humiliation, self-abasement, self-denunciation, propitiation, admission, shift, renunciation of sin, lamentation, reformation, sacrament of Penance, the Confessional.

REPENTANT, *adj.* Contrite, penitent, remorseful, regretful, sorrowful, self-reproving, self-condemnatory, self-accusatory, resipiscent, conscience-stricken, self-humiliating, self-abasing, self-denouncing, self-denunciative, propitiative, redressive, placatory, lamenting, weeping, keening, bewailing, suspirant, sighing, reformative, penitential.

REPERCUSSION, *n.* Reverberation, rebound, recoil, echo, report, noise, sound, resilience, backlash, ricochet, reflex, reflux, springing back, boomerang, explosion, fulmination, discharge, detonation, bang, blowup, blast.

REPERTORY, *n.* Stock, storeroom, storehouse, stockroom, repository, depot, reservoir, magazine, warehouse, treasury, cache, depository, repertorium, closet, cupboard, coffer.

REPETITION, *n.* Iteration, reiteration, refrain, encore, echo, recapitulation, same old thing, restatement, rehash, tautology, battology, pleonasm, macrology, superfluity, redundance, periphrasis, recounting, rehearsal, retelling, restatement, drumming, hammering, twice-told tale, sameness, diffuseness, verbosity, largiloquence, longiloquence, logorrhea, ding-dong, monotony, profuseness,

prolixity, wordiness, magniloquence, verbiage, exuberance, excess, surplusage, surfeit, glut, plethora.

REPETITIVE, *adj.* Repetitious, reiterant, reduplicative, tautological, reiterative, repeated, re-echoed, successive, recurrent, monotonous, sing-song, habitual.

REPINE, *v.* Be discontented, be disconsolate, look glum, be disheartened, be discouraged, be malcontent, be dissatisfied, pull a long face, knit one's brows, rue the day, be sorry for, be penitent, feel contrite, grieve, lament, be regretful, be sad, be downcast, despair, be despondent, droop, languish, pine away, lose heart, give way to despair, fret, brood, mope, pout, look blue, carry a broken heart, beweep, cry one's eyes out, bemoan, deplore, decry.

REPLENISH, *v.* 1. Refill, supply again, eke out, piece out, recharge, reload, make complete, make full, supply deficiencies, make up a lack, fill to the brim.

2. Furnish, supply, yield, contribute, present, give, make provision for, provide for, cater, purvey, provender, store, deposit, provision.

REPLETE, *adj.* Rife, plethoric, abundant, full, abounding, fraught, pregnant, redundant, gorged, filled to repletion, well-stocked, well-provided, fully supplied, crammed, flush, brimming, chock-full, laden, full-to-bursting, saturated, crammed full, jam-packed, crammed solid, closely packed, loaded, affluent, bounteous, lavish, teeming, profuse.

REPLETION, *n.* Surfeit, satiety, glut, plethora, plenty, bounty, exuberance, profusion, fullness, satiation, fatness, plenitude, saturation, superabundance, superfluousness, oversupply, engorgement, more than enough, rifeness, amplitude, redundancy, copiousness, lavishness, prodigality, opulence, inordinacy, excessiveness, surpulsage, surplus, overmeasure, pleonasm, overload.

REPLICA, *n.* Imitation, model, copy, duplicate, reproduction, facsimile, likeness, image, double, counterpart, transcript, mimeograph copy, reflection, tracing, carbon copy, cast, ditto *(coll.)*, faithful copy.

REPLY, *v.* Respond, answer, rejoin, make rejoinder, retort, riposte, come back with, rebut, refute, come back at, parry, answer back, talk back *(coll.)*, confute, plead, negate, negative, acknowledge, contradict, controvert, squelch, down, floor *(coll.)*, reduce to silence.

REPLY, *n.* 1. Letter, epistle, note, writing, missive, message, billet, communication, line, chit, answer, correspondence.

2. Replication, response, return, comeback, riposte, rebuttal, refutation, confutation, rejoinder, retort, answer, surrejoinder *(Law)*, surrebuttal *(Law)*, acknowledgment, remonstrance, plea, explanation, defense, justification, alibi, excuse.

REPORT, *v.* 1. Inform, apprise, advise, tell, make known, impart, acquaint, divulge, divulgate, proclaim, communicate, enlighten, express, mention, announce, set forth, expound, give an account of, specify, declare, describe, set forth, narrate, recapitulate, rehearse, characterize, recount, relate, detail.

2. Broadcast, spread, disseminate, publish, advertise, promulgate, herald, circulate, rumor, allege, notify, bruit about, noise abroad, declare, voice, speak out, blazon, make public, publicize, give out to the world, annunciate, enunciate.

3. Record, put down, write down, put in writing, inscribe, make a note of, docket, make a memorandum of, take minutes of, chronicle, place on the record, jot down, enter into the minutes, calendar.

REPORT, *n.* 1. Announcement, statement, declaration, communication, account, description, pronouncement, enunciation, proclamation, advertisement, relation, recounting, recital, rehearsal, narration, broadcast, communiqué, tidings, news story, article, intelligence, information, commentary, review, writeup (*coll.*), discussion, criticism, recapitulation, summary, exposition, chronicle, history, record, annals, saga, manifesto, notification, reportage, disclosure, revelation, press release, publicity, dissemination, propagation, diffusion, circulation, ventilation, issuance.

2. Explosion, sound, noise, detonation, bang, fulmination, discharge, blowout, crack, shot, backfire, crash, thunderclap, boom, bombination, cannonade, rumble, bombilation, eruption, gunfire, salvo, volley, repercussion, echo, reverberation.

3. Reputation, fame, celebrity, esteem, regard, credit, good odor, fair name, mark, distinction, figure, notability, note, notoriety, famousness, glory, éclat, popular favor, praise, laurels, kudos, luster, honors, glorification, immortality, import, moment, importance, eminence, paramountcy, prestige, respect.

4. Judgement, verdict, judication, finding, upshot, result, decision, sentence, decree, opinion, award.

REPORTER, *n.* Newsman, newsmonger, journalist, newspaperman, columnist, leg man, publicist gentleman of the press, representative of the press, member of the fourth estate, writer, news writer, ink-slinger, pressman, foreign correspondent, editor, copy man, rewrite man, science reporter, sports columnist, theatrical reporter, book reviewer, news analyst, newcaster, news commentator, newshawk, scribbler, scribe, sob-sister (*cant*), typewriter jockey, member of the writing fraternity, knight of the quill, pad-and-pencil boy, newshound.

REPOSE, *v.* 1. Recline, lie prostrate, couch, lean on, rest on, lie on, be supported by.

2. Rest, relax, take ones ease, loll, sprawl, take it easy (*coll.*), recline, lie down, go to bed, sleep, lie still, be dormant, be quiet, be quiescent, be motionless, be inert, loaf, loiter, slumber, snooze (*coll.*), rest in the arms of Morpheus, doze, nap, drowse, settle oneself, close one's eyes, go off to sleep, compose oneself to rest.

REPOSE, *n.* Ease, relaxation, rest, sleep, quiet, quietude, quiescence, slumber, inactivity, dormancy, somnolence, drowsiness, sopor, lethargy, hebetude, stillness, respite, breathing space, breathing spell, passivity, inertness, immobility, composure, coma, inaction, languor, supineness, proneness, torpor, tranquility, motionlessness, immobility.

REPOSITORY, *n.* Depository, conservatory, storehouse, warehouse, treasury, vault, safe, magazine, repertory, receptacle, container, storeroom, thesaurus, chrestomathy, depot, armoire, wardrobe, chest, box, trunk, closet, cache, stash (*sl.*), armory, arsenal, coffer, cupboard, granary, pantry, larder, buttery, reliquary, shrine, cabinet, commode, chiffonier, locker, bin, bureau, crypt, bursary, strongbox, hold.

REPREHEND, *v.* Find fault with, take exception

to, call to account, chide sharply, reprove, upbraid, rebuke, charge with a fault, reprimand, reproach, censure, accuse, blame, animadvert, increpate, objurgate, chastise, check, scold, reprobate, denounce, object to forcibly, impeach, take to task, lecture, bring to book, castigate, overhaul, hold up to reprobation, remonstrate, recriminate, expostulate, impugn, condemn, slate, disapprove, protest against, raise one's voice against, decry, exprobrate, berate, rate, call down, rebuff, admonish, take down a peg.

REPREHENSIBLE, *adj.* Deserving censure, blameworthy, censurable, culpable, blamable, rebukable, condemnable, reprovable, uncommendable, exceptionable, not to be thought of, peccable, illaudable, guilty, weighed in the balance and found wanting, objectionable, delinquent, redhanded, disgraceful, discreditable, unworthy, disreputable, base, shameful, ignoble, infamous, foul, nefarious, opprobrious, flagitious, villainous, flagrant, heinous, incorrigible, reprobate, immoral, iniquitous, recreant, unrighteous, evil, wicked, unprincipled, sinful, bad, wrong, naughty, criminal, unpardonable, inexpiable, indefensible, unjustifiable, inexcusable.

REPREHENSION, *n.* Expression of blame, reprimand, reproof, rebuke, reproach, admonition, censure, finding fault, animadversion, reproval, scolding, objurgation, disapproval, upbraiding, expostulation, remonstrance, reprobation, increpation, castigation, dressing down, curtain lecture, blow up, rating, set down, rebuff, rap on the knuckles, *coup de bec (Fr.)*, hit, home thrust, jeremiad, diatribe, philippic, tirade, chiding, exprobration, cutting words, invective, vituperation, contumely.

REPREHENSIVE, *adj.* Intended as reproof, reprehensory, condemnatory, censorious, scolding, objurgatory, disapproving, denunciatory, damnatory, disparaging, vituperative, reproachful, abusive, clamorous, scandalized, defamatory, derogatory, sarcastic, cynical, sardonic, trenchant, cutting, sharp, virulent, acrimonious, withering, biting, severe, captious, critical, carping.

REPRESENT, *v.* 1. Present in words, describe, depict, delineate, set forth, picture, sketch, give an account of, relate, report, narrate, express, state, portray, exhibit, show, shadow forth, adumbrate, outline, define, relate as true, designate, denote.

2. Picture, present the likeness of, figure, draw, sketch, paint, shape, sculpt, figure, sculpture, engrave, mold, copy, trace, reproduce, film, photograph, illustrate.

3. Bring a mental image before the mind, present to knowledge, picture to the mind, place clearly before the mind, envision, envisage, contemplate, conjure, imagine, form an image of, conceive, fancy, idealize, dream of, strain one's invention, give reins to the imagination, indulge in reverie, empathize, conjure up a vision, figure to oneself.

4. Assume a character, personate, impersonate, act the part of, appear in the character of, pose as, personify, portray by action, imitate, mimic, perform, enact, sustain the role of.

5. Speak and act by delegated authority, hold legal rights conferred by another, act vicariously, act as authorized agent for, act as a substitute for, be proxy for, replace, stand in the place of, stand for, be in the position of, be the equivalent of, correspond to, be deputy for.

6. Serve as an example *or* specimen of, appear as an instance of, typify, symbolize, exemplify, be typical of, prefigure, characterize.

REPRESENTATION, *n.* 1. Depiction, illustration, portraiture, delineation, designing, imagery, drawing, sketch, picture, draught, copy, painting, canvas, tableau, outline, study.

2. Image, reproduction, figure, model, likeness, semblance, resemblance, portrait, icon, effigy, facsimile, waxwork, marionette, manikin, bust, puppet, fantoccini, figurehead, replica, appearance, impression, counterpart, silhouette, profile, head, torso, statuette, figurine, cast, statue.

3. Personification, impersonation, personation, simulation, portrayal, dramatic performance, acting, rendition, stagecraft, stage business.

4. Production of a play, performance, public exhibition, show, spectacle, sight, *mise en scène (Fr.)*, stage setting.

5. Assertion of facts, critical assertion, narration, account, description, relation, statement, narrative, recitative, expression, report, record, recital, explanation, rehearsal, asseveration, declaration.

6. Chart, map, diagram, plan, outline, bird's-eye-view, ground plan, photograph, photo, print, snapshot, telephoto, daguerreotype, X-ray, radiograph, skiagraph, radiogram.

7. Argument against something, remonstrance, expostulation, protest, appeal, challenge, kick *(coll.)*, protestation, objection, reproof.

8. Right of acting for others by virtue of some lawful authority, authorized acting in the place and stead of another, supplying of another's place, vicarship, delegation, deputization, deputation, proxy, commission, warrant, instruction, authorization, charge, mandate, brevet, trust.

9. Number of representatives of a constituency, members collectively as representing a constituency, body of delegates, body of deputies.

REPRESENTATIVE, *adj.* 1. Exemplifying a class, typical, illustrative, figurative, typifying, descriptive, symbolical, exemplary, representing, being the best instance procurable, most suitable to represent, having power to represent vividly to the mind, imitative, similar, like, faithful.

2. Acting for others, deputed, delegated, procuratory, delegatory, agential, accredited, officiating, vicegerent, substituting, official, operative, consular, ambassadorial.

REPRESENTATIVE, *n.* 1. Diplomatist, diplomat, plenipotentiary, diplomatic, agent, legate, consul, ambassador, resident, attaché, envoy, emissary, commissioner, delegate, messenger, nuncio, deputy, substitute, proxy, lieutenant, locum tenens, vicegerent, surrogate, vicar, spokesman, mouthpiece *(coll.)*, trustee, nominee, steward, factor, clerk, bailiff, attorney, solicitor, proctor, broker, middleman, go-between, negotiator, traveling, salesman, commercial traveler, drummer *(U. S.)*.

2. One who represents a constituency in a legislative body, member of the lower house of congress, congressman, congresswoman, assemblyman, councilor, senator, member of parliament, M.P.

3. Typical instance, example, specimen, type, sample, typical embodiment, exponent, exemplar, instance, exemplification, illustration.

REPRESS, *v.* 1. Keep under control, press back, hold back, restrain, control, rein in, bridle, check, curb, constrain, restrict, stay, muzzle, inhibit,

bottle up, pen up, stifle, hold in, strangle, smother, damp, coerce, harness, gag, leash, withhold, pull in, suppress, prohibit, limit, fetter, fasten, trammel, shackle, enchain, hobble, picket, impound, hem in, seal up, cork up, box up, shut up, keep a tight hand on, hold in leading strings, keep in check.

2. Reduce to subjection, keep down, quell, put down, overpower, subdue, vanquish, conquer, domineer over, bring under, crush, silence, choke, overcome, defeat, subjugate, overbear, master, put down, get the better of, overturn, overwhelm, overmaster, prostrate.

3. Master one's feelings, quiet, calm, compose, propitiate, allay, still, hush, appease, make one's mind easy, cool down.

REPRESSION, *n.* 1. Suppression, restriction, restraint, constraint, mortification, withholding, keeping back, coercion, quelling, control, curb, check, stay, inhibition, strangulation, suffocation, smothering, stifling, prohibition, limitation, impoundment, subjection, domination, defeat, subjugation.

2. *(Psychoanal.)* Rejection from consciousness of painful *or* disagreeable memories, unconscious exclusion from conscious admission of a desire *or* impulse unacceptable to one's ego.

REPRIEVE, *n.* 1. Respite from impending punishment, suspension of punishment, amnesty, grace, pardon, remission, absolution, exculpation, exoneration, acquittal, release, clearance, discharge, dispensation, quittance, truce, stay, stop, prorogation, suspension, deferment, moratorium, remand, compurgation, armistice, exemption.

2. Temporary relief, quietus, cessation, breathing spell, interval of rest, day of grace.

REPRIEVE, *v.* 1. Grant a stay of punishment to, delay the punishment of, give a respite to, grant a delay of execution, respite from impending punishment, suspend temporarily the execution of a sentence, pardon, absolve, extenuate, exonerate, exculpate, wipe the slate clean, give absolution, make allowances for, put off, stave off, remand, prorogue, shelve, temporize, let off, overlook, condone, forgive.

2. Relieve temporarily, free from, remit, slacken up on, grant a breathing spell, abate, relax, mitigate, allay, palliate, lessen, assuage, ease, alleviate.

REPRIMAND, *v.* Find fault with, rebuke for a fault, reprove severely, reprehend, blame, censure, admonish, reproach, upbraid, chide, castigate, lecture, berate, haul over the coals, take to task, scold, trim, chastise, denounce, impeach, overhaul, blow up, correct, dress down, trounce, give a tongue lashing, abuse, rail at, revile, execrate, deprecate, recriminate, accuse, run down, asperse, disparage, speak ill of, knock, condemn, call to account, bring to book, take exception to, object to, view with disfavor, frown upon, look black upon, dispraise, discommend, slate, *fronder (Fr.)*, reprobate, impugn, bring to order, give it one, gibbet, accuse, stigmatize, cry 'shame' upon, raise a hue and cry against, exprobrate, vituperate, rate, objurgate, jaw at, bark at, anathematize, call by hard names, vilify, vilipend, fulminate against, thunder against, load with reproaches, protest against, inveigh against, exclaim against, raise one's voice against, criticize, cut up, pick to pieces, cavil, lampoon, satirize, taunt, carp at, peck at, have words with, give a rap on the knuckles, pluck a crow with, take down, make a fuss about.

REPRIMAND, *n.* Severe formal reproof by one in

authority, condemnation, sharp censure, reproach, reprehension, reproval, rebuke, reprobation, blame, disapprobation, lecture, admonition, chiding, upbraiding, dressing down, jobation, rebuff, rating, correction, trimming, castigation, scolding, objurgation, remonstrance, expostulation, abuse, invective, tirade, diatribe, philippic, sharp words, execration, taunt, insinuation, sarcasm, innuendo, criticism, exception, objection, stricture, denunciation, derogation, dispraise, depreciation, disapproval, displeasure, improbation, obloquy, detraction, animadversion, disparagement, reflection, left-handed compliment, increpation, rap on the knuckles, slap on the face, *coup de bec (Fr.)*, home thrust, hue and cry, clamor, outcry, vituperation, personal remarks, contumely.

REPRINT, *n.* Reproduction in print of matter already printed, new unaltered impression of any printed work, new edition, republication, reimpression, replica, second edition.

REPRISAL, *n.* Infliction of retaliatory injury on another, using force to secure redress of a grievance, retaliation, paying back, retribution, vengeance, revenge, injury inflicted in return for one received, tit for a tat, *quid pro quo (Lat.)*, Roland for an Oliver, tooth for a tooth, eye for an eye, requital, *lex talionis (Lat.)*, counterblast, counterstroke, recrimination, *revanche (Fr.)*, retortion, compensation, desert, measure for measure, give and take, diamond cut diamond, blow for blow, the biter bit, boomerang, blood for blood, death feud, vendetta, game at which two can play, reciprocation, forcible seizure of anything by way of indemnification, recaption.

REPROACH, *v.* Charge with something wrong, find fault with, censure, criticize, scold, rebuke, upbraid with opprobrium, reprimand, reprove, reprehend, chide, castigate, call to account for, blame, accuse, exprobrate, denounce, speak ill of, condemn, bring imputations upon, asperse, disparage, discredit, defame, vilify, vilipend, revile, abuse, denounce, depreciate, malign, cast reproach upon, detract, brand, blot, calumniate, slander, vituperate, stigmatize, impute, tax, taunt, twit, slur, criminate, inculpate, incriminate, implicate, indict, arraign, impeach, saddle with, rail at, frown upon, shake the head at, slate, reprobate, increpate, impugn, take to task, bring to book, hold up to reprobation, expose, gibbet, rate, objurgate, load with reproaches, thunder against, fulminate against, lash with the tongue, inveigh against, protest against, cry out against, hoot, hiss, blackball, lay to one's door, bring home to, throw in one's teeth, have a crow to pluck with, keep a rod in pickle for, take down a peg.

REPROACH, *n.* 1. Censure, disapproval, sharp criticism, reprehension, reprimand, reproof, rebuke, reprobation, disapprobation, expostulation, remonstrance, upbraiding, railing, invective, vituperation, contumely, condemnation, increpation, reviling, vilification, contempt, abuse, scurrility, scorn, blame with anger, revilement, disparagement, imputation, insinuation, innuendo, objurgation, castigation, chastisement, scowl, frown, tirade, philippic, lecture, hard words, ribaldry, billingsgate, execration, catcall, hue and cry, outcry, clamor, jobation, dressing down, rebuff, rating, obloquy, depreciation, denunciation, reflection, animadversion, stricture, exception, objection, sneer, taunt, carping, cavil, set down, admonition, rebuff, rap on the knuckles, home thrust, jeremiad, charge, accusation, inculpation, incrimina-

tion, recrimination, challenge, impeachment, diatribe.

2. Opprobrium, disgrace, odium, disrepute, dishonor, turpitude, shame, ignominy, obloquy, discredit, scandal, stigma, stain, blemish, blot, slur, brand, spot, taint, blur, tarnish, badge of infamy, insult, indignity, ill-repute, ill-favor, humiliation, vileness, baseness, ingloriousness, abasement, debasement, derogation, degradation, scorn, offense.

REPROACHFUL, *adj.* Expressing censure, censorious, condemnatory, scolding, abusive, upbraiding, opprobrious, railing, invective, reproving, calumnious, scurrilous, damnatory, vituperative, sarcastic, trenchant, cutting, critical, virulent, caustic, acrimonious, contumelious, contemptuous, insulting, offensive, insolent, gruff, blunt, brusque, brutal, harsh, scornful, derogatory, detractory, defamatory, calumniatory, slanderous, cynical, sardonic, satirical.

REPROBATE, *adj.* 1. Morally depraved, unprincipled, abandoned, lost to all sense of duty, wicked, base, vile, bad, corrupt, vicious, profligate, graceless, hardened, irredeemable, shameless, vitiated, cast-away, incorrigible, degenerate, iniquitous, irreclaimable, sinful, dissolute, recreant, unrighteous, criminal, wrong, facinorous, felonious, infamous, nefarious, flagitious, heinous, flagrant, evil-minded, unconscionable, steeped in iniquity, obdurate, recidivistic, past praying for, immoral.

2. Rejected by God, excluded from the number of the elect, impious, unholy, unsanctified, unregenerate, accursed, ungodly, unhallowed, profane, irreligious, irreverent.

REPROBATE, *n.* One lost to all sense of decency or duty, abandoned person, unprincipled fellow, miscreant, sinner, vile wretch, outcast, pariah, castaway, knave, rogue, malefactor, blackguard, scroundrel, rascal, villain, caitiff, scamp, ne'er-do well, blacksheep, *âme damnée (Fr.)*, good-for-nothing, *vaurien (Fr.)*, outlaw, bad man, hellhound, ruffian, wastrel, profligate, debauchee, roué, rake, libertine, prodigal, seducer, whoremonger, scalawag, rakehell, rounder, immoralist, rapist, voluptuary, sensualist, rip, loose fish, fast man, fornicator, lecher, satyr, goat, pander, pimp, white slaver, worker of iniquity, wrongdoer, evil-doer, scapegrace, fallen angel, *mauvais sujet (Fr.)*, recreant, delinquent, misdemeanant, criminal, culprit, felon, rapscallion, varlet, cur, *âme de boue (Fr.)*, hound, scum of the earth, renegade, truant, recidivist, rotter, spendthrift, waster, betrayer, wanton, loose liver, transgressor, bad example, viper, reptile, trickster, shyster, sneak, sharper, swindler, crook, thief, hellion, devil, monster, demon, devil incarnate, mischief-maker, brute, desperado, ruffian, tough, hooligan, hoodlum, gangster, gunman, hijacker, racketeer, cutthroat, traitor, wolf in sheep's clothing, turncoat, jailbird, lawbreaker.

REPRODUCE, *v.* 1. Produce by generation *or* propagation, propagate, generate, beget, breed, spawn, multiply, fructify, give birth to, bring forth, engender, proliferate, fecundate, procreate, create, progenerate, impregnate, sire, father, form in the womb, fertilize, pollinate, spermatize, conceive, foal, calve, farrow, drop, throw, whelp, fawn, kitten, cub.

2. Make a duplicate of, copy, duplicate, imitate, represent, repeat, reflect, mirror, forge, match, counterfeit, parallel, re-echo, follow, approximate.

3. Renovate, regenerate, restore, revive, renew,

resuscitate, revivify, refashion, reanimate, refresh, reinvigorate, redintegrate, recondition, rebuild, reconstruct, rehabilitate, rejuvenate.

REPRODUCTION, *n.* 1. Natural process by which new individuals are generated and the species perpetuated, propagation, generation, procreation, multiplication, proliferation, fecundation, progeneration, impregnation, breeding.

2. That which is made by reproducing, copy, duplicate, facsimile, imitation, representation, replica, likeness, counterpart, semblance, tracing, cast, transcript, reprint, transfer, forgery, counterfeit, simulation.

3. Renovation, renewal, palingenesis, revival, revivification, regeneration, restoration, resuscitation, resurrection, reanimation, rejuvenation, resurgence, rejuvenescence, renaissance, renascence, rebirth, regenesis, *rifacimento (It.)*, rehabilitation, reconstruction, redintegration, reparation, repair, reclamation.

REPRODUCTIVE, *adj.* Serving to reproduce, generative, progenitive, germinative, sexual, gametal, conceptive, proliferous, life-giving, prolific, fructiferous, formative, creative, procreative, generant.

REPROOF, *n.* Expression of disapproval, censure, rebuke, reprimand, reproach, reproval, reprehension, admonition, monition, correction, castigation, condemnation, criticism, objurgation, increpation, upbraiding, dressing down, lecture, chiding, rating, berating, scolding, exprobration, animadversion, objection, insinuation, reflection, remonstrance, expostulation, jobation, tirade, philippic, diatribe, invective, contumely, vituperation, disparagement, trimming, wigging, rebuff, reprobation, hue and cry, clamor, outcry, catcall, hiss, hoot, execration, stricture, exception, obloquy, dispraise, depreciation, derogation, detraction.

REPROVE, *v.* Censure openly and directly, criticize, correct, find fault with, rebuke, express disapproval of, blame, condemn, reprehend, castigate, chasten, reprimand, take to task, call to account, bring to book, scold, upbraid, rate, berate, lecture, chide, remonstrate with, objurgate, inculpate, criminate, reproach, expostulate with, admonish, mispraise, dispraise, disparage, frown upon, dress down, rap on the knuckles, trim, animadvert, increpate, denounce, impugn, reprobate, accuse, impeach, brand, show up, overhaul, trounce, lash, execrate, rail at, revile, vilipend, vilify, cry down, run down, depreciate, asperse, malign, belittle, discredit, knock, underrate, speak ill of, lampoon, satirize, sneer at, scoff at, boycott, blackball, blacklist, object to, take exception to, view with disfavor, reject, negative, veto, disallow, refuse.

REPTILE, *adj.* 1. Creeping, reptant, reptilian, repent, reptatorial, saurian, lacertilian, lacertine, lacertoid, snake-like, lizard-like, crocodilian, crawling, serpentine, ophidian.

2. Morally abject, mean, base, vile, low, groveling, cringing, servile, obsequious, treacherous, sneaking, malignant, venomous, vulgar.

REPTILE, *n.* 1. Cold-blooded air-breathing vertebrate, creeping animal, reptilian, saurian, ophidian, lacertilian, lacertian, lizard, Gila monster, gecko, chameleon, eft, iguana, newt, dragon, dinosaur, pterosaur, ichthyosaur, pterodactyl, alligator, crocodile, gavial, cayman, yacare, magar, viper, adder, cobra, asp, rattlesnake, rattler, python, boa constrictor.

2. Groveling abject person, morally contempti-

ble person, knave, scoundrel, rascal, rogue, miscreant, villain, caitiff, traitor, serpent, snake in the grass, sneak, telltale, tattletale, squealer, recreant, mischief-maker, renegade, shyster, cheat, trickster, jackal, wretch, viper.

REPUBLIC, *n.* State in which supreme power rests in body of citizens, state in which head of government is an elected president, presidency, commonwealth, commonweal, representative government, democracy, popular government, constitutional government, popular sovereignty, self-determination, self-government, realm, federalism, body politic.

REPUBLICAN, *adj.* Democratic, representative, electoral, elective, popular, autonomous, Jeffersonian *(U.S.)*, national.

REPUBLICAN, *n. (U.S.)* Member of the Republican party, member of the GOP, the old guard, Conservative, isolationist, supporter of the party of special privileges.

REPUDIATE, *v.* 1. Disclaim, disavow, abjure, nullify, rescind, annul, void, quash, reverse, abrogate, contravene, cancel, revoke, recant, retract, change sides, apostatize, recidivate, deny, countermand, contradict, gainsay, forswear, recall, unsay, disannul, dissolve, abolish, declare null and void, abandon, protest, reject, cast off, lay aside, discard, ignore, set aside, disregard, bolt, set at naught, scout, override, trample under foot, toss to the dogs, fling to the winds, repeal, overrule, dismiss, demur, wash one's hands of, fail, refuse assent, raise one's voice against, disagree, change one's mind, decline, bar, transgress, infringe, violate, neglect, slight, evade, dishonor, spurn.

2. Renounce, abdicate, put away, oust, unseat, dethrone, depose, uncrown, cashier, drum out, strike off the roll, disbar, disbench, unfrock, unsaddle, disown, divorce, banish, proscribe, ostracize, relegate.

REPUDIATION, *n.* Rejection, renouncement, renunciation, abjuration, denial, declination, disclaimer, disavowal, disowning, disclaiming, divorce, putting away, setting aside, annulment, nullification, voidance, declension, veto, refusal, repellence, dismissal, discard, disapproval, disallowance, disproof, refutation, disproval, disaffirmation, contradiction, protest, recantation, revocation, retractation, confutation, dissent, negation, tergiversation, change of mind, defection, retraction, reversal, cancellation, repeal, rescission, defeasance, deposition, deposal, dethronement, ouster, sack, abolition, dissolution, counterorder, default, defalcation.

REPUGNANCE, *n.* 1. Unwillingness, aversion, reluctance, detestation, distaste, antipathy, dislike, hatred, hostility, antagonism, repulsion, abhorrence, animosity, disinclination, distaste, disrelish, disapprobation, displeasure, disgust, loathing, nausea, horror, abomination, execration, disfavor, grudge, umbrage, pique, queasiness, coolness, alienation, estrangement, *bête noire (Fr.)*, bitter pill.

2. Opposition, resistance, contest, struggle, renitency, whitstanding, oppugnancy, recalcitrance, reaction, refusal, snub, rejection, rebuff, repulse, oppugnation, reluctation, recalcitration.

3. Contradictoriness, contrariness, contrariety, irreconcilableness, incompatibility, unsuitableness, inconsistency, disagreement, clashing, oppositeness, discrepancy, antithesis.

REPUGNANT, *adj.* 1. Offensive, distasteful, repulsive, repellent, disagreeable, disgusting, objectionable, obnoxious, abominable, hateful, odious, loathsome, abhorrent, nauseating, revolting, fulsome, insufferable, unsavory, unpalatable, unappetizing, inedible, disliked, unacceptable, unpopular, undesirable, unpleasant.

2. Hostile, antagonistic, inimical, unfriendly, opposed, averse, adverse, reluctant, contrary, at variance, refractory, unwilling, counter, objecting, disinclined, indisposed, loath.

3. Inconsistent, incongruous, irreconcilable, conflicting, unconformable, oppugnant, contradictory, antipathetic, incompatible, inharmonious, discordant, clashing, inaccordant.

REPULSE, *v.* 1. Repel, drive back, beat back, chase, dispel, rout, resist, oppose, defeat, overthrow, contest, withstand, obstruct, frustrate, thwart, dispute, gainsay, defend, make a stand, stem, counteract, countervail, impede, hinder, check, grapple with, confront, oppugn.

2. Reject, discard, repudiate, snub, refuse, rebuff, deny, turn one's back upon, keep at arm's length, give the cold shoulder, be deaf to, stand aloof, turn up the nose at, look askance at, avoid, eschew, shun, recoil from, shrink from, spurn.

REPULSE, *n.* 1. Driving back, repelling, successful opposition, oppugnation, reluctation, renitence, *contrecoup (Fr.),* boomerang.

2. Refusal, rejection, rebuff, denial, incompliance, declension, negation, discountenance, recusancy, disclaimer, protest, dissent, noncompliance.

3. Nonsuccess, failure, nonfulfilment, miscarriage, disappointment, labor in vain, inefficaciousness, no-go, ineffectual effort, frustration, flash in the pan, botchery, fiasco, setback, rout, defeat, discomfiture, overthrow, perdition, losing game, checkmate, breakdown, foozle, blighted hope, balk, vain expectation, much cry and little wool, miscalculation.

REPULSION, *n.* 1. Driving away, driving back, repulse, rebuff, repellence, rejection, discarding, spurning, repercussion, refusal, snub, discountenance, retroaction.

2. Antipathy, distaste, aversion, dislike, disrelish, disgust, loathing, repugnance, hatred, abhorrence, abomination, detestation, nausea, horror, disinclination, renitency, unwillingness, indisposition, nolition, reluctance, revulsion.

3. Hostility, antagonism, inimicalness, unfriendliness, polarity, enmity, animosity, alienation, discord, estrangement.

REPULSIVE, *adj.* 1. Distasteful, unsavory, nauseous, unpalatable, sickening, ill-flavored, obnoxious, nasty, loathsome, revolting, disgusting, disagreeable, uninviting, unpleasant, objectionable, bitter, offensive, displeasing, sourish, rancid, turned, curdled, vinegary, unripe, tart, inedible, uneatable, unappetizing, fulsome.

2. Frigid, cold, icy, stern, harsh, unsympathetic, reserved, forbidding, aloof, distant, offish, unsociable, stony, stiff, cool, uncordial, unfriendly, uncomplaisant, inaffable, unaccommodating, austere, brusque, gruff, churlish.

3. Hateful, odious, abhorrent, repellent, abominable, execrable, unpopular, insufferable, squalid, haggard, grisly, foul, hideous, ugly, frightful, shocking, horrid, ill-favored, unprepossessing, monstrous, misshapen, unsightly, ghastly, ill-looking, grim, appalling, fearful, dreadful, dire, vile, detestable, gross, brutish, gruesome.

REPUTABLE, *adj.* Held in good repute, estimable, respectable, in good odor, honorable, creditable, worthy, in high favor, unimpeachable, high-principled, upright, trustworthy, fair and square, aboveboard, virtuous, scrupulous, righteous, conscientious, straightforward, reliable, dependable, honest, good, faithful, candid, noble, uncorrupt, honored, renowned, celebrated, prominent, eminent, high-minded, frank, open-hearted, incorruptible, true-hearted, constant, stanch, loyal.

REPUTATION, *n.* Estimation in which a person is held, standing one occupies in the opinion of others, publicly recognized standing, repute, notoriety, name, character, note, mark, notability, éclat, celebrity, vogue, famousness, fame, popularity, renown, distinction, esteem, *aura popularis (Lat.),* prestige, credit, respect, regard, report, influence, eminence, glory, honor, account, approbation, approval, *succès d'estime (Fr.),* name to conjure with, talk of the town, illustriousness, luster, respectability, rank, status, precedence, station, position in society, caste, *locus standi (Lat.),* importance, pre-eminence, feather in one's cap, blushing honors, blaze of glory, laurels, niche in the temple of fame, *magni nominis umbra (Lat.),* celebration, glorification, deification, apotheosis, exaltation, dignification, top of the ladder, primacy, name in lights, star billing, consideration, popular favor, figure, excellence, conspicuousness, prominence, halo, nimbus, aureole, commemoration, immortal name, caliber, consequence, blue ribbon, bays, palm, trophy, civic crown, admiration, kudos, applause, acclaim, plaudit, personality, individuality.

REPUTE, *v.* Consider to be as specified, regard, account, esteem, estimate, reckon, judge, deem, hold, think, call, believe, opine, look upon, suppose, count, imagine, believe, take for, rate, view, gauge, appraise, value, set a price on, compute, measure, decide.

REQUEST, *n.* 1. Entreaty, supplication, solicitation, beseechment, petition, suit, prayer, importunity, appeal, invocation, impetration, obsecration, imploration, obtestation, call, invitation, interpellation, demand, claim, requisition, order, application, behest, requirement, plea, postulation, inquiry, instance, orison, intercession, rogation, ultimatum, direction, testament, round robin, apostrophe, imprecation, mendicancy, panhandling, begging, exaction, call for, run upon, want, desideratum.

2. Proposal, suggestion, proposition, overture, motion, offer, advancement, canvass, submission, address.

REQUEST, *v.* Ask, entreat, solicit, plead, beseech, implore, supplicate, adjure, conjure, seek, appeal to, cry to, apostrophize, invoke, press, importune, besiege, clamor for, dun, cry for, make application, demand, claim, sue, petition, pray, canvass, beg, crave, apply to, order, call for, requisition, bid, invite, summon, call to, desire, counterclaim, reclaim, summon, cite, send for, beckon, subpoena, want, wish for, incline to, enjoin, command, make bold to ask, pop the question, address, trouble one for, whistle for, obtest, kneel to, impetrate, ply, beset, urge, tax, fall on one's knees, send the hat around, cadge, mendicate, panhandle, knock at the door, court, bespeak, tout, bid for, exact.

REQUIEM, *n.* Mass celebrated for the repose of the souls of the dead, *missa solemnis (Lat.),* elegy, threnody, death song, coronach, dirge, nenia, epicedium, funeral song.

REQUIESCAT IN PACE *(Lat.)* Prayer for the repose of the dead, rest in peace, *sit tibi terra levis (Lat.)*, may the earth rest light on thee, *hic iacet (Lat.)*, *ci-gît (Fr.)*, here lies, *R.I.P. (abbr.)*.

REQUIRE, *v.* 1. Ask for imperatively, demand, importune, beseech, implore, request, sue, beg, pray, crave, dun, requisition, claim, exact, bid, call for, summon, invite, petition, canvass, solicit, entreat, plead, seek, supplicate, conjure, adjure, appeal to, apostrophize, urge, press, besiege, clamor for.

2. Stand in need of, want, have need of, desire, lack, must needs have, miss, pine for, hanker after, long for, covet, be bent upon, care for, wish for, have an eye to, have at heart, have a fancy for, set one's heart upon, sigh for, yearn for, hope for, desiderate, have a mind to.

3. Call on authoritatively, direct, prescribe, order, enjoin, dictate, insist upon, exact, oblige, enforce, tax, command, decree, ordain, enact, charge, appoint, lay out, give orders, set a task, issue a command, set to work, inflict, impose, wrest, wring from, commandeer, draft, impress, conscript, take by force, put in force, force upon, pin down, wring from, squeeze, extort, screw, dragoon, constrain, coerce, necessitate, enforce, oblige, make necessary, impose occasion for, make indispensable.

REQUIREMENT, *n.* 1. Essential desideratum, requisite, demand, want, need, pinch, market, request, call for, sale, needfulness, urgency, necessity, essentiality, indispensability, exigency, compulsion, sine qua non, case of need, extremity, stress, claim, requisition, constraint, coercion, pressure, *force majeure (Fr.)*, obligation, necessitation, conscription, enforcement, liability, accountability, responsibility, onus, trust, task, part, commission, business, charge, function, service, fulfillment, observance, acquittal, discharge, redemption, satisfaction, performance, attention.

2. Bidding, order, command, injunction, behest, mandate, exaction, precept, decree, ultimatum, imposition, dictate, caveat, prescript, ordination, writ, rescript, edict, bull, ukase, firman, prescription, enactment, act, subpoena, summons, citation, order of the day, *l'ordre du jour (Fr.)*, dispensation, decretal, word of command, warrant, commandment, precept, regulation, fiat, ordinance, call, word, beck, nod, beck and call, direction, ruling, dictation, instructions.

REQUISITE, *adj.* Required by the nature of things, essential to circumstances, indispensable, needed, needful, necessary, called for, imperative, in demand, expedient, requisitory, in request, exigent, urgent, instant, insistent, pressing, crying, stringent, peremptory, impelling, necessitative, compulsive, compelling, inexorable, coercive, obligatory, compulsory, inevasible, inevitable, ineluctable, binding, vital, irrevocable, mandatory, imperious, incumbent on.

REQUISITE, *n.* Essential desideratum, prerequisite, necessity, essential, vital part, sine qua non, indispensable element, matter of necessity.

REQUISITION, *n.* Demand, order, claim, request, behest, bidding, injunction, command, mandate, direction, ultimatum, draft, enforcement, conscription, levy, main force, obligation, necessitation, pressure, compulsion, no choice, constraint, coercion, necessity.

REQUITAL, *n.* 1. Repayment, recompense, return, reward, compensation, payment, satisfaction,

amends, remuneration, reparation, restitution, quittance, guerdon, meed, indemnification, indemnity, redress, acknowledgment, sop, consideration, emolument.

2. Revenge, retribution, punishment, retaliation, reprisal, return, boomerang, desert, *lex talionis (Lat.)*, counterstroke, measure for measure, a Roland for an Oliver, eye for an eye, tooth for a tooth, blow for blow, tit for tat, diamond cut diamond, give and take, *quid pro quo (Lat.)*, the biter bit, death feud, vendetta, blood for blood, day of reckoning, *dies irae (Lat.)*, retributive justice, castigation, chastisement, punition, correction, infliction, penalty, nemesis, thunderbolt.

REQUITE, *v.* 1. Repay, recompense, compensate, make repayment for, make return to, reward, remunerate, pay, satisfy, reciprocate, pay off, make amends, make good, settle with, pay back, indemnify, reimburse, acknowledge, exchange, tip, indemnify, fee, redress, remember, atone.

2. Avenge, give in return, revenge, retaliate, punish, turn the tables upon, return like for like, pay off old scores, be even with, be quits, pay back, reciprocate, take revenge, vindicate, wreak one's vengeance, give no quarter, give a Roland for an Oliver, wipe the slate clean, get even with, settle with, castigate, deal retributive justice, visit upon, make an example of, serve one right, strafe, make short work of, do for.

RESCIND, *v.* Invalidate by a later action, abrogate, void, countermand, annul, repeal, revoke, reverse, abolish, vacate, declare null and void, set aside, cancel, quash, recall, overrule, disclaim, discharge, dissolve, discard, disannul, retract, recant, take back, nullify, override, repudiate, counterorder, sweep aside, throw overboard, scatter to the winds, get rid of.

RESCISSION, *n.* Abrogation, annulment, rescindment, revocation, repeal, retraction, abolition, cancellation, recall, overruling, nullification, revokement, defeasance, dissolution, abolishment, counterorder, retractation, recantation, abnegation, renunciation, recusancy, disclaimer, negation, tergiversation, change of mind, abjuration, apostasy, disavowal, reversal, countermand, repudiation.

RESCRIPT, *n.* 1. Authoritative order, decree, edict, ukase, firman, decretal, mandate, proclamation, law, ordinance, command, fiat, dictum, behest, injunction, dispatch, charge, direction, instructions, requisition, ultimatum, caveat, prescript, bull, writ, ordination, dispensation, brevet, prescription, placet, warrant, citation, subpoena, summons, mandamus, enactment, act, ruling, statute, rule, institution, regulation.

2. Transcript, copy, draft, fair copy, holograph, duplicate.

3. Answer, acknowledgment, rescription, repartee, retort, rejoinder, riposte, reply, response, replication, rebutter, countercharge, plea, defense, antiphon, contradiction.

RESCUE, *v.* Liberate, set free, deliver, free, save, extricate, release, ransom, redeem, emancipate, manumit, reprieve, disenthral, come to the rescue, disimprison, let loose, let out, acquit, absolve, unfetter, unchain, clear, form a life line, snatch from danger, recover, preserve, come to the aid, hold out a hand, take in tow, bring through, *tirer d'affaire (Fr.)*, salvage, keep clear, reclaim.

RESCUE, *n.* Liberation, deliverance, release, extrication, emancipation, manumission, salvation, redemption, ransom, reprieve, acquittal, freeing, disenthrallment, disimprisonment, absolution, discharge, escape, feedom, liberty, salvation, close call, exemption, relief, help at a dead lift, *deus ex machina (Lat.)*, aid, assistance, opitulation, succor, subvention, subministration.

RESEARCH, *n.* Systematic investigation in order to discover facts *or* principles, diligent inquiry into a subject, exploration, examination, scrutiny, careful search, study, analysis, factfinding, indagation, quest, prosecution, pursuit, inquest, percontation, inquisition, consideration, reconnaisance, survey, inspection.

RESEARCH, *v.* Investigate carefully, make researches, inquire into, scrutinize, study systematically, examine thoroughly, indagate, probe into, dip into, analyze, dissect, look into, subject to examination, inspect, explore, scan, make an experiment, essay, prosecute, be absorbed in search, reconnoiter, trace up, unearth, leave no stone unturned, pursue an inquiry, delve into, go deep into.

RESEMBLANCE, *n.* 1. Likeness in appearance, similarity, affinity, semblance, similitude, agreement, analogy, approximation, correspondence, parallelism, uniformity, identity, repetition, sameness, simulation, parity, identicalness, selfsameness, homogeneity, duplication, iteration, accord, congruity, conformity.
2. Counterpart, image, facsimile, representation, duplicate, replica, effigy, mold, pattern, imitation, type, cast, archetype, matrix, portrait, parallel, prototype, double, model, match, congener, fellow, mate, pair, twin, brother, sister, birds of a feather, chip off the old block, reprint, reproduction, ditto, copy, sample, specimen, illustration.

RESEMBLE, *v.* Be similar to, be like, bear resemblance to, appear like, bear likeness to, look like, favor, have the earmarks of, seem to the view, simulate, duplicate, savor of, agree with, parallel, match, counterfeit, imitate, copy, echo, mimic, approximate, take after, follow, reproduce, smack of, tally, dovetail, follow the fashion, swim with the stream.

RESENT, *v.* Feel displeasure at, show indignation at, take amiss, be provoked at, be offended at, take offense at, take ill, take umbrage at, be piqued at, be in a dudgeon over, be indignant at, take in bad part, take exception, dislike, view with dissatisfaction, be angry, bristle over, bridle at, flare up, fly into a rage, chafe, boil with indignation, fume, foam, lose one's temper, frown, pout, snarl, gnash, growl, lower, scowl, look black, look daggers, bluster, be irascible, glower, grouch, sulk, keep the wound open, harbor revenge, bear malice, have rankle in the breast, harbor a grudge, kick up a row, show one's teeth, bite one's thumb, champ the bit, be in a huff about.

RESENTFUL, *adj.* In high dudgeon, in a huff, miffed, huffy, touchy, indignant, offended, sore, bitter, hurt, on one's high horse, up in arms, acrimonious, irascible, irritable, angry, revengeful, choleric, malignant, irate, wroth, wrathful, raging, fuming, hot under the collar, infuriate, *acharné (Fr.)*, convulsed with rage, foaming at the mouth, rabid, restive, envious, jealous, green-eyed, distrustful, mistrustful, suspicious, grudging, invidious, bad-tempered, tart, crusty, sour, crabbed, virulent, sarcastic, venomous, surly, sullen, grim, grouchy, sulky, splenetic, bristling, contumelious,

caustic, morose, moody, churlish, not on speaking terms, on bad terms, at loggerheads, at daggers drawn, spiteful, malicious, waspish, peppery, fretful, petulant, captious, querulous, fractious, peevish, peeved, testy, vindictive, vengeful, rancorous, unforgiving, implacable, inexorable, cantankerous, grumpy, glum, gruff, ill-disposed, refractory, cynical, intractable, passionate, outraged, frantic, scorching, inflamed, red-hot, abrupt, rude, brusque, sharp-tongued, vehement, disturbed, furious, smoldering, volcanic, explosive.

RESENTMENT, *n.* Indignation, high dudgeon, pique, umbrage, soreness, bitterness, displeasure, exasperation, animosity, exacerbation, vexation, irritation, annoyance, irascibility, choler, ire, anger, wrath, ferment, acrimony, asperity, virulence, spleen, gall, bile, spite, huff, sulks, dander, fury, rage, acerbity, tiff, pet, tantrum, fit, vengefulness, malignity, jealousy, envy, invidiousness, suspiciousness, vehemence, passion, *acharnement (Fr.)*, vials of wrath, paroxysm, explosion, high words, hot blood, hatred, venom, rankling, disgust, grievance, suspicion of injury, ill will, asperity, wounded pride, mortification, malice, perturbation, heartburning, offense, outraged spirit, *casus belli (Lat.)*, ill turn, indignity, affront, sore subject, last straw, surliness, peevishness, gruffness, bad temper, crabbedness, grouchiness, moroseness, tartness, sullenness, sourness, black looks, scowl, frown, rancor, disaffection, estrangement, alienation, coolness, iciness, aloofness, irritability, crossness, petulance, huffishness, vindictiveness, churlishness, perversity, moodiness, glumness, doldrums, dumps.

RESERVATION, *n.* 1. Tract of public land set aside for a special purpose, settlement, plantation, encampment, colony, cantonment, situation, location, habitation, installation, lodgment, establishment, bivouac, retreat, haunt, habitat, resort, castrametation, accommodation.
2. Suppression, concealment, reserve, hiding, secrecy, reticence, mental reservation, aside, *arrière pensée (Fr.)*, qualification, restriction, exception, evasion, white lie, secretiveness, closeness, misprision, silence, equivocation, tonguefence, mystification, speciousness, ambiguity, pretext, pretense, false plea, shift, subterfuge, shuffle, profession, hypocrisy, dissimulation, fraud, prevarication, false coloring, distortion, perversion, misrepresentation.

RESERVE, *v.* 1. Keep back, save for future use, retain, withhold, preserve, husband, hold, set by, lay up, lay by, store up, amass, spare, treasure, garner, appropriate, stow away, put by, hoard up, conserve, deposit, bank, hide, cache, bury, salt away, put by for a rainy day.
2. Make an exception of, except, stipulate, dispense with, do without, not use, forbear, not touch, spare, abstain, neglect, waive, keep back, shelve.

RESERVE, *n.* 1. Avoidance of familiarity in social relationships, self-restraint in action *or* speech, aloofness, distance, standoffishness, constraint, coldness, iciness, uncommunicativeness, taciturnity, reticence, close-mouthedness, closeness, unresponsiveness, unsociability, secretiveness, secrecy, silence, reservedness, restraint, cautious behavior, guardedness, backwardness, suppression, concealment, delicacy, prudery, shyness, coyness, demureness, modesty, self-control, offishness, frigidity, obmutescence, muteness, pauciloquy, curtness, diffidence, timidity, timorousness, bashfulness, unobtrusiveness, verecundity, retiring disposition.

2. Savings, provision, supply, treasure, capital, resources, backlog, stock, margin, store, fund, cache, safe-deposit, larder, nest egg, something for a rainy day.

RESERVED, adj. 1. Set apart, withheld, kept in reserve, held, taken, retained, booked, bespoken, excepted, set aside, engaged, in reserve, provided for, waiting, in prospect, appointed, destined, in store, ready, choice.

2. Distant, offish, aloof, uncommunicative, reticent, taciturn, unsocial, unsociable, restrained, disposed to keep one's feelings to oneself, of few words, quiet, frigid, cold, icy, close-mouthed, secretive, guarded, cautious, backward, silent, self-contained, standoff, retiring, diffident, verecund, shy, modest, coy, demure, unassuming, unobtrusive, bashful, undemonstrative, tight-lipped, unresponsive, unneighborly, high-hat, condescending, sparing of words, mum, laconic, inconversable, curt, evasive, noncommittal, buttoned up, constrained, timorous.

RESERVOIR, n. 1. Place where water is collected and stored for use, cistern, basin, tank, standpipe, pond, fount, well, spring, water back, forebay, millpond, sump.

2. Receptacle, receiver, chamber, catch basin, container, depository, repository, vessel, safe, bin, basket, box, reservatory, enclosure, barrel, vase, caldron, vat, cask, keg, tun, firkin, hogshead, carboy, demijohn.

3. Reserve supply, great supply of something, store, stock, reserve, magazine, cache, accumulation, hoard, vein, mine, fund, lode, bed, treasure, depository.

RESIDE, v. 1. Inhabit for a considerable time, dwell permanently, have one's abode for a time, domicile, abide, live, domiciliate, sojourn, remain, room, stay, lodge, roost, bunk, bide, settle, occupy, tenant, take up one's abode, nestle, perch, strike root, come to an anchor, establish oneself, squat, hive, bivouac, se nicher (Fr.), have a footing, burrow, pitch one's tent, put up at, keep house.

2. Be present habitually, rest in, exist, be inherent, be vested in, inhere, lie within, exist as a part, belong, be immanent, pertain, be fixed, be ingrained, be innate, be intrinsic.

RESIDENCE, n. 1. Time during which one resides in a place, sojourn, stay, habitancy, domiciliation, sojournment, commorancy, legal settlement, inhabitancy, tarrying, stop, habitation.

2. House, domicile, lodging, abode, dwelling-place, seat, dwelling, address, quarters, resort, retreat, haunt, refuge, nest, perch, roost, sanctum sanctorum, place, diggings, where one's lot is cast, berth, homestead, chimney corner, fireside, hearth, household goods, Lares and Penates, housing, household, roof, dulce domum (Lat.), building, rooms, apartments, maisonette, flat, lodging, house, bungalow, manor, villa, lodge, cottage, hermitage, castle, chateau, manor house, palace, mansion, town house, country seat, hacienda, farmhouse, grange, chalet, cabin, cot, hut, shack, croft, tenement, messuage, chamber, shanty, igloo, tepee, hovel, stall, wigwam, sty, kennel, cote, hutch, coop, byre, barn, stable, cowshed, nidus, bower, arbor, covert, bivouac, barracks, camp, pavilion, crib, pen, fold, inn, hotel, hostelry, hostel, caravansary, hospice.

RESIDENT, n. Resider, dweller, inhabitant, so-journer, inhabiter, residentiary, denizen, occupant, tenant, occupier, inmate, indweller, householder, incumbent, addressee, squatter, settler, habitant, colonist, citizen, burgher, burgess, townsman, cotter, villager, cottager, lodger, boarder, roomer, islander, aborigine, native, autochthon, aboriginal, indigene, renter, paying guest, locum tenens (Lat.), commorant, oppidan, compatriot.

RESIDUAL, adj. Constituting a residuum, remaining, left over, surplus, excessive, superfluous, expletive, useless, spare, de trop (Fr.), unnecessary, superabundant, residuary, remanent, surviving, odd, over, supplementary, over and above, net, left, outlying, outstanding, formed by the subtraction of one quantity from another (Math.).

RESIDUE, n. 1. Remainder, residuum, rest, remains, remnant, leavings, relic, odds and ends, caput mortuum (Lat.), result, educt, draff, dregs, heeltap, lees, ruins, stubble, skeleton, wreck, stump, fossil, butt, rump, relics, corpse, organic remains, reliquiae, scattered parts, disiecta membra (Lat.), ashes, bones, dead body, empty husks, refuse, trash, detritus, rubble, rubbish, debris, litter, garbage, junk, shoddy, rags, orts, scum, dross, sweepings, waste, offscourings, chaff.

2. Surplus, excess, overplus, balance, surplusage, redundance, superfluity, survival, glut, plethora, supersaturation, surfeit.

RESIGN, v. 1. Lay down, give up, relinquish, hand over, surrender, throw up, vacate, make vacant, abdicate, tender one's resignation, give up office, yield, abandon, forsake, leave, quit, give back, assign back, commit to another, withdraw from, part with, send in one's papers, demit, cede, relegate, retire, give notice to quit, step down, drop, lay aside, discard, divest oneself of, jettison.

2. Renounce, abjure, disclaim, forgo, disavow, retract, recant, disown, reject, deny, repudiate, wash one's hands of, desert, abrogate.

3. Yield to, submit, concede, reconcile, make the best of, let well enough alone, put up with, take in good part, acquiesce in, deign, vouchsafe, condescend, stoop, humble oneself, bear with, brook, tolerate, stand, bide, support, carry on, give in, grin and bear it.

RESIGNATION, n. 1. Abdication, retirement, abandonment, relinquishment, disclaimer, abjuration, renunciation, surrender, cession, vacation, forsaking, retractation, recantation, retraction, disclamation.

2. Submission, patience, compliance, acquiescence, forbearance, endurance, sufferance, long-suffering, fortitude, submissiveness, passiveness, resignedness, toleration, tolerance, longanimity, repression of feeling, meekness, self-abasement, obedience, yielding, non-resistance, deference, capitulation, perseverance, reconciliation, conciliation.

RESIGNED, adj. Unresisting, reconciled, complying, submissive, yielding, acquiescent, patient, passive, obedient, meek, uncomplaining, philosophical, disciplined, compliant, unrepining, cheerful, chin-up, stoical, enduring, composed, unperturbed, unruffled, forbearing, tolerant, long-suffering, nonresistant, law-abiding, docile, humble, deferential, subservient, imperturbable, dispassionate, collected, composed, subdued, chastened, bearing with, forbearant, clement, henpecked, pliant, weak-kneed.

RESILIENCE, n. 1. Elasticity, resilient action, resilient power, spring, springiness, rebound, recoil, snap, renitency, buoyancy, reflexion, reaction, rebound, ricochet, *contrecoup (Fr.),* recalcitration, repercussion, kick, springing back, boomerang.

2. Rubber, gutta-percha, caoutchouc, gum elastic, whalebone, latex.

RESILIENT, *adj.* Springing back, returning to the original position, recoiling, rebounding, elastic, springy, tensile, renitent, ductile, yielding, rubbery, buoyant, rapidly recovering.

RESIN, *n.* Nonvolatile vegetable substance obtained from plant exudations, rosin, copal, mastic, amber, dammar, lac, guaiacum, sandarac, acouchi, bdellium, asafetida, gamboge, myrrh, jalap, scammony, colophonium, shellac, gum, elemi, varnish, oleoresin, anime, japan, megilp, sealing wax, lacquer, ambergris, pitch, asphaltum, bitumen, tar, turpentine.

RESINOUS, *adj.* Rosiny, gummy, resiny, gummed, gummous, pitchy, tarry, asphaltic, pitched, bituminous, lacquered, waxed.

RESIST, *v.* 1. Oppose, confront, face, grapple with, oppugn, antagonize, breast, front, withstand attack, show a bold front, make a stand, encounter, defend, repulse, repel, stem the tide, breast the current, stand at bay, sell one's life dearly, fight, attack, rise up in arms, revolt, strike, rebel, mutineer, mutinize, fly in the face of, die hard, take the bit between one's teeth, *prendre le mors aux dents (Fr.),* assail, impugn, strike back, bear up against, retaliate, stand up to, combat, weather, beat back, kick against, recalcitrate, reluctate, wrestle with, hold out against, hold the line against, overcome, overpower, .defeat, not yield an inch, put to flight, stand siege, show fight, parry, fend.

2. Withstand, stop, stand firm, stand against, stand one's ground, stand fast, obstruct, hinder, impede, stem, check, thwart, counteract, frustrate, boycott, countervail, neutralize, strive against, defy, block, rebuff, baffle, disappoint, refrain from, abstain from, militate against, contradict, react, work against, counterwork, contravene, run counter to, countermine, disobey, refuse, infringe, interfere with, cross, clash, slack, shirk, set at naught, violate, transgress, disregard, take the law into one's own hands, rise, kick over the traces, bolt, gainsay, cope with, protest, object, vie with, contend, emulate, rival, compete, force out, dispute.

RESISTANCE, *n.* Opposition, renitency, withstanding, front, stand, oppugnance, impeding, hindrance, blocking, repugnance, recalcitrance, repulsion, repulse, rejection, rebuff, repercussion, revolt, insurgence, revolution, uprising, rebellion, insurrection, mutiny, secession, riot, Jacquerie, *levée en masse (Fr.),* disorder, sabotage, strike, *émeute (Fr.),* lockout, turnout, sit-down, passive resistance, interdiction, boycott, embargo, isolation, reaction, refusal, counteraction, antagonism, contradiction, collision, clashing, frustration, interference, friction, neutralization, counterblast, check, nullification, hindrance, preventive, antidote, counteragent, corrective, outbreak, tumult, sedition, insubordination, disobedience, noncompliance, recalcitrance, contumacy, obstinacy, infringement, infraction, violation, transgression, treason, *lèse-majesté (Fr.),* defiance, defection, contravention, counterinfluence, restraint, obstruction, crossing, struggle, encounter, combat, fight, battle, strife, clash, contention, emulation, com-

petition, contest, tug of war, stumbling block, impediment, obstacle, refusal, disclaimer, repudiation, protest, recusancy, self-defense, protective part, *tutamen (Lat.),* self-preservation, security means, protection.

RESISTANT, *adj.* Resistive, resisting, refractory, recalcitrant, renitent, unruly, unwilling, fractious, defiant, restive, turbulent, oppositional, repellent, opposing, repugnant, up in arms, mutinous, seditious, rebellious, insurgent, anarchic, revolutionary, antagonistic, counteractive, reactionary, combative, contrary, disobedient, intractable, insubordinate, unmanageable, ungovernable, contumacious, unresigned, unsubmissive, stubborn, recusant, unyielding, dissentient, riotous, lawless, inflexible, opinionated, stiff-necked, self-willed, headstrong, wilful, perverse, unruly, untoward, forward, immovable, inexorable, obdurate, mulish, determined, opposed, oppugnant, oppositive, unfavorable, at cross-purposes, at daggers drawn, in rivalry with, competitive, noncompliant, uncomplying, defensive, ironclad, bulletproof, protective, armored, asbestine, stain-proof, hard, iron, firm, indomitable, invincible, unsubduable, unconquerable, uncompromising, intransigent, tenacious.

RESOLUTE, *adj.* Set in purpose, firm in opinion, resolved, earnest, unflinching, tenacious, inflexible, relentless, determined, decided, strong-willed, bold, sturdy, hardy, stanch, steady, steadfast, stouthearted, stout, game, plucky, gritty, serious, grim, persevering, unalterable, unyielding, undaunted, unshaken, constant, pertinacious, unbending, unwavering, unfaltering, strong-minded, peremptory, self-possessed, fixed, iron, adamantine, inexorable, indomitable, relentless, *tenax propositi (Lat.),* unbending, obstinate, stubborn, bulldog, stern, intentional, deliberate, prepense, premeditated, cold-blooded, manful, manly, virile, mettlesome, dogged, irrevocable, doughty, self-reliant, confident, intrepid, spirited, valiant, courageous, brave, gallant, stalwart, lion-hearted, audacious, daring, undismayed, unafraid, adventurous, enterprising, chivalrous, dashing, heroic, soldierly, impetuous, impulsive, purposive, unswerving, undeviating, mulish, opinionative, plodding, persistent, industrious, indefatigable, strenuous, untiring, unflagging, faithful, loyal. obdurate, imperturbable, vigorous, indomitable, stable, fast, zealous, bigoted, partisan, militant, uncompromising, intransigent.

RESOLUTION, *n.* 1. Determination, resolvedness, fortitude, perseverance, steadfastness, constancy, stamina, backbone, grit, pluck, iron will, sand, strength of will, manliness, courage, tenacity, boldness, aplomb, self-assurance, zeal, self-possession, self-reliance, self-mastery, *retenue (Fr.),* moral courage, self-restraint, self-command, self-denial, vigor, energy, devotedness, devotion, persistence, spirit, nerve, valor, intrepidity, pertinacity, bravery, hardihood, steadiness, inflexibility, relentlessness, decision, earnestness, fidelity, fixed purpose, heart, derring-do, daring, dash, gallantry, élan, prowess, heroism, audacity, virtue, spunk, bulldog courage, push, persistence, aggressiveness, indefatigability, patience, application, industry, effort, endurance, bottom, staying power, doggedness, obduracy, zealotry, faith, stability, obstinacy, virility, vitality, firmness of purpose, resolve, resoluteness.

2. Intention, intent, intentionality, plan, purpose, view, design, ambition, proposal, undertak-

ing, project, contemplation, aim, object, end, bent, set, objective, destination, inclination, be-all and end-all, goal, bull's-eye, target, mark, butt, point.

3. Formal expression of opinion, finding, official determination, decree, judgment, declaration, conclusion, verdict.

4. Decomposition, dissolution, conversion, disintegration, separation, solution, analysis, explication, disentanglement, unraveling, explanation, transformation, transmutation, metamorphosis, assimilation, deoxidization, naturalization.

5. (Med.) Disappearance, removal, breaking up, termination, dispersion, reduction.

RESOLVE, v. 1. Come to a determination, make up one's mind, settle on by deliberate will, decide, determine, fix in purpose, will, purpose, take a decisive stand, form a resolution, conclude, take upon oneself, fix upon, bring to a crisis, stand firm, insist upon, devote oneself to, set one's heart upon, make a point of, not stick at trifles, stick at nothing, persist, persevere, make short work of, go all lengths, go the limit, go through fire and water, go the whole hog, take a decisive step, cross the Rubicon, nail one's colors to the mast, nerve oneself, summon up courage, stand to one's guns, take heart, hold out, bear up, show fight, present a bold front, run the gantlet, face the music, be courageous, venture, dare, make bold, brave, confront, face, defy, meet, beard, not yield an inch, die hard, take no denial, hold on, keep to one's course, maintain one's ground, go all lengths, die in harness, die at one's post, stick fast, be firm, stand pat, weather the storm, build one's house on a rock.

2. Intend, mean, design, calculate, project, propose, premeditate, plan, destine, meditate, dream of, think of, contemplate, aim at, bid for, aspire to, pursue, labor for, have in view, desire, long for, desiderate, feel a desire for.

3. Solve, elucidate, explain, explicate, answer, clear up, settle, decipher, interpret, disentangle, unravel, unfold, find the solution to, find a clue to, see through, unriddle, disclose, catch, smell out, detect, scent, trace, confirm, verify, clinch, prove, establish, substantiate, identify, realize, recognize, make certain of, discover, make out, find out, ascertain, unearth, uncover, root out, manifest, bring to light, reveal, fathom, plumb.

4. State formally, settle by vote, declare, express, pass on, determine on, ordain, rule, decree, adjudge, enact, decide, order, appoint, enjoin, command, write out, conclude, pass upon, vote on.

5. Break up, reduce, separate, convert, disintegrate, split up, decompose, analyze, dissolve, change, transform, transmute, metamorphose, alter, vary, metabolize, exchange, reorganize, reform, absorb, assimilate, digest, scatter, disperse, dispel.

RESONANCE, n. Prolongation of sound by reflection, amplification of vocal tone, increase of intensity of sound by sympathetic vibration, vibrato, twang, timbre, reverberation, vibration, tintinnabulation, ringing, chime, clang, ring, clangor, roll, boom, thunder, roar, rumble, sonorescence, sonification, audibility, polyphony, echoing, bombilation, booming, quaver, ding-dong, bell-note, peal of bells, plangency, sonorousness.

RESONANT, adj. Resounding, sonorous, sonorescent, reverberating, reverberant, vibrant, deep-toned, singing, canorous, deep-mouthed, clangorous, plangent, ringing, re-echoing, remugi-

ent, booming, roaring, thunderous, thundering, hollow, sepulchral, soniferous, sonoric, melodious, mellifluous, clear, distinct, audible, tinnient, tintinnabulary.

RESORT, v. 1. Go frequently, frequent, repair, haunt, visit, revisit, overrun, infest, hie, betake oneself to, attend regularly, hover about.

2. Convene, meet, congregate, assemble, flock, muster, collect, come together, unite, cluster, swarm, surge, stream, rush, crowd, herd, huddle, mass, throng, forgather, concentrate, converge, pour in, rally, enter in, focalize.

3. Have recourse to, apply, use, make use of, adhibit, administer, take up, try, recur to, avail oneself of, exercise, practice, exert, play, bring into play, utilize, employ.

RESORT, n. 1. Refuge, retreat, haunt, place frequented, rendezvous, vacation place, sanctuary, asylum, den, dive, joint (sl.), spa, sanctum sanctorum, hiding place, roost, nest, habitat, covert, perch.

2. Recourse, use, application, employment, appliance, adhibition, utilization, service, usage, avail.

RESOUND, v. 1. Ring in the ear, echo, re-echo, reverberate, tintinnabulate, ring with sound, make an echoing, sound, give forth loudly, peel, vibrate, chime, chink, tinkle, clink, jingle, plash, murmur, roll, roar, boom, rumble, thunder, ding, tink, gurgle, guggle, rend the skies, bellow, fulminate, swell, clang, fill the air, din in the ear.

2. Extol, praise, sound, celebrate, proclaim loudly, magnify, exalt, glorify, acclaim, cheer, applaud, bepraise, pay tribute, laud, commend, acclamate, encore.

RESOURCE, n. 1. Capability in dealing with a situation, capacity for meeting difficulties, source of supply or aid, wherewithal, de quoi (Fr.), contributing force, card to play, strings to one's bow, sheet anchor.

2. Measure to which one may have recourse in an emergency, resort, expedient, means, instrumentality, appliance, contrivance, device, agency, factor, instrument, medium, vehicle, tool, materials, elements, substances, essentials, matériel (Fr.), stuff.

RESOURCEFUL, adj. Full of resource, fertile in expedients, ingenious, sharp, skilful, adroit, dexterous, handy, apt, deft, smart, ready, slick, proficient, accomplished, practiced, experienced, capable, competent, trained, able, clever, felicitous, talented, gifted, inventive, shrewd, cunning, artistic, scientific, technical, workmanlike, productive, creative, original, sagacious, bright, artful.

RESOURCES, n. pl. Collective wealth, property which can be converted into money, pecuniary means, capital, assets, funds, money, income, reserve, available means, finances, ways and means, wherewithal, de quoi (Fr.), revenue, estate, stock in trade, possessions, vested interests, trust fund, dowry, dower, dot, marriage portion, jointure, inheritance, appanage, patrimony, heritage, alimony, legacy, belongings, circumstances, what one is worth, effects, realty, hereditaments, messuage, personal property, personalty, goods, chattels, movables, things, paraphernalia, traps, appurtenances, competence, substance.

RESPECT, v. 1. Hold in honor, revere, think highly of, worship, reverence, admire, esteem, venerate, honor, look up to, regard, have a high opinion of, prize, value, entertain respect for, do honor to, pay respect to, defer to, pay attention to, pay homage to, hallow, hail, show courtesy, do the honors, stand upon ceremony, observe due decorum, make room for, keep one's distance, drop the knee before, genuflect, bow before, kowtow, curtsy, kneel before, make obeisance, prostrate oneself, salaam, bow the head, bow down, salute, make way for, pay tribute to, glorify, magnify, laud, pay deference to, have a reverential regard for, approve, appreciate, commend, praise, speak well of, set great store by, present arms, doff the cap, raise the hat, exalt, lionize, celebrate, solemnize.

2. Treat with consideration, spare, refrain from interfering with, let alone, forbear, treat with forbearance.

3. Observe, notice, comply with, be obedient to mind, heed, do the will of, consider, acknowledge, abide by, follow, act up to, carry out, meet, keep one's word, perform, execute, fulfill, discharge, redeem, keep faith with, be faithful to, adhere to, obey, serve faithfully.

4. Relate to, have reference to, refer to, pertain to, bear upon, be concerned with, appertain to, have regard to.

RESPECT, *n.* 1. Veneration, reverence, esteem, deferential regard, deference, homage, honor, obeisance, prostration, fealty, genuflection, salaam, kowtow, proskynesis, kneeling, hat-tipping, cap-doffing, admiration, approbation, approval, estimation, courtesy, civility, attention, kind consideration, good will, favor, recognition, notice, politeness, urbanity, etiquette, *bienséance (Fr.),* polish, gentility, refinement, breeding, amenity, elegance, suavity, chivalry, gallantry, good manners, courtliness, good breeding, courteousness, pink of politeness, curtsy, bow, bowing and scraping, nod, shaking hands, salute, affection, love, appreciation, laudation, praise, commendation, hero worship, eulogy, encomium, panegyric, awe, prestige, credit.

2. Reference, relation, connection, regard, relationship, bearing, aspect.

3. Detail, particular, point, circumstance, point of view, matter, feature.

RESPECTABILITY, *n.* Respectableness, respectable social standing, decorum, decency, probity, rectitude, integrity, honor, honesty, faith, uprightness, *bona fides (Lat.),* good faith, virtue, clean hands, fidelity, morality, faithfulness, constancy, loyalty, candor, trustworthiness, veracity, truthfulness, principle, equity, rank, standing, caste, status, station.

RESPECTABLE, *adj.* 1. Worthy of esteem, estimable, upright, honorable, worthy, proper, decorous, decent, becoming, honest, truthful, veracious, noble, virtuous, aboveboard, open-hearted, candid, frank, straightforward, constant, loyal, stanch, faithful, incorruptible, trustworthy, high-principled, conscientious, punctilious, high-minded, religious, correct, pure, innocent, inviolate, stainless, unsullied, untainted, unstained, jealous of honor, chivalrous, generous, valorous, chivalric, knightly, in good odor, creditable, presentable, *comme il faut (Fr.),* well-bred, genteel, gentlemanly, ladylike, polite, polished, urbane, suave, civil, courtly, thoroughbred, refined, reputable.

2. Of moderate excellence, fairly good, fair, moderate, considerable, mediocre, passing, tolerable, so-so, average, ordinary, normal, medium, indifferent, middling, commonplace, everyday, admissible, second-rate.

RESPECTFUL, *adj.* Polite, decorous, deferential, ceremonious, attentive, reverential, courteous, gentlemanly, polished, urbane, civil, suave, obliging, complaisant, formal, mannerly, gentle, well-mannered, well-bred, refined, chivalrous, knightly, gallant, chivalric, gracious, cordial, amiable, bland, obsequious, accommodating, ingratiatory, winning, cap in hand, bareheaded, prostrate, genuflecting, kneeling, curtsying, salaaming, kowtowing, on one's good behavior, genial.

RESPECTIVE, *adj.* Pertaining individually to each of a number, individual, particular, several, own, proportionate, commensurate, proportional.

RESPECTIVELY, *adv.* Each to each, separately, individually, severally, in equal shares, by lot.

RESPECTS, *n., pl.* Deferential compliments, greetings, salutations, regards, commendations, devoirs, *égards (Fr.),* duty, remembrances, flattering remarks, honeyed phrases, best love, considerations, attentions, honor, reverence, homage, approbation, salute, handshake, hug, embrace, genuflection, kneeling, bowing and scraping, kowtow, salaam, curtsy, bow, obeisance, ceremonial presentation, reception, introduction, recognition, *accueil (Fr.),* welcome, amenities.

RESPIRATION, *n.* Inhalation and exhalation of air for the purpose of maintaining life, breathing, inspiration, expiration, eupnoea *(easy),* dyspnoea *(labored),* inflation, huffing, puffing, panting, gasping, wheezing.

RESPIRE, *v.* Inhale and exhale air, breathe, live, inspire, expire, pant, puff, wheeze, blow, gasp.

RESPITE, *n.* 1. Temporary suspension of punishment, stay of execution, reprieve, acquittal, quietus, pardon, absolution, exoneration, exculpation, clearance, release, discharge, dispensation, quittance, remission, deliverance, commutation.

2. Postponement, delay, adjournment, prorogation, procrastination, retardation, deferment, truce, moratorium, suspension, mora, remand, continuance, default, protraction.

3. Interval, pause, intermission, temporary stoppage, stop, recess, break, cessation, breathing spell, letup, interruption, interregnum, hitch, attest, check, block, impediment, halt, lull, abeyance.

RESPITE, *v.* 1. Suspend the punishment of, stay the execution of, reprieve, pardon, remit, release, extenuate, clear, exculpate, exonerate, acquit, forgive, absolve, whitewash, discharge, free, liberate, rescue, deliver, extricate, let off, excuse, spare, pass over, dispense with.

2. Grant delay, postpone, delay, defer, procrastinate, put off, lay over, retard, continue *(Law),* remand, prorogue, adjourn, protract, shelve, table, stall, temporize, filibuster, reserve, draw out, prolong, stave off.

3. Interrupt, intermit, suspend, interfere with, check, cut short, stop, arrest, put an end to, bring to a standstill, punctuate, obstruct, halt, discontinue.

RESPLENDENT, *adj.* Shining brilliantly, brilliant, radiant, luminous, gleaming, refulgent, effulgent, glittering, beaming, lustrous, lucent, lucid, transplendent, relucent, fulgent, argent, bright, splendid, gorgeous, glorious, glaring, dazzling, sunny, solar, luminiferous, luculent, lucific, luciferous, light, illuminating, nitid, splendent, vivid, shiny, beamy, scintillant, sheeny, lambent, glossy, meridian, burnished, garish, blazing, rutilant, ablaze, aglow, phosphorescent, sparkling, splendorous, splendrous, glowing.

RESPOND, v. 1. Give a reply in words, rejoin, reply, answer, retort, rebut, say, give answer, surrejoin, counterclaim, surrebut, pronounce, utter, give utterance, break silence, open one's lips, talk, raise one's voice, put in a word, hold forth, discourse, declaim, have one's say, speak one's mind, expatiate, recite, tell, pour forth, prate, palaver, parley, confabulate, advise, apprise, let fall, mention, communicate, make known, let one know, instruct, point out, report, announce, send word, render an account, state, disclose, hint, insinuate, make allusion to, tip off, prompt, whisper in the ear, speak volumes, open the eyes of, correct, set right, enunciate, contend, maintain, protest, profess, represent, assert, affirm, declare, broach, avow, aver, asseverate, warrant, vouch, assure, emphasize, attest, expound, describe, set forth, particularize, relate, narrate, recount, recite, run over, sum up, rehearse, recapitulate, unfold, enter into details, make a clean breast, indicate, express, reveal, divulge, evince, come out with, give vent, blurt out, admit, confess, unburden one's mind, unbosom oneself, voice, proclaim, testify, argue.

2. Make a return by some action, acknowledge, react, exhibit some action as if in answer, make a sign, signalize, beckon, gesture, gesticulate, nod, nudge, shrug, wink, leer, glance, raise the hand, tip the wink, saw the air, suit the action to the word.

3. Receive an impression, feel, enter into the spirit of, catch the flame, be fired by, be stimulated by, be impressed with, be touched by, be moved by, be affected by, swell, flush, glow, blush, mantle, change color, crimson, blench, tingle, heave, thrill, throb, pant, palpitate, go pitapat, quiver, tremble, be agitated, flutter, be excited, draw a deep breath.

4. Be agreeable to, accord, suit, correspond, tally, harmonize, be concordant, meet, fall in with, acquiesce, consent, concur, coincide, conform, fit.

RESPONSE, n. 1. Reply, rejoinder, retort, answer, riposte, repartee, echo, respondence, acknowledgment, return, rebuttal, replication, surrejoinder, countercharge, contradiction, counterblast, counterstatement.

2. Password, shibboleth, *mot d'ordre, mot de jour (Fr.),* watchword, secret parole, countersign.

3. Bonds of harmony, sympathy, empathy, concord, harmony, accord, agreement, symphony, unity, union, unanimity, assent, amity, rapprochement, reciprocity, entente cordiale, alliance, good understanding, fellow-feeling, camaraderie, fraternization.

4. Impression, sensation, deep sense, emotion, affection, pathos, inspiration, experience, feeling, fervency, ardor, passion, zeal, enthusiasm, excitation of feeling, verve, ecstasy, suffusion, blush, warmth, fire, glow, gusto, vehemence, flush, thrill, kick, tingling, agitation, heaving, quiver, flutter, tremor, twitter, throb, palpitation, pulsation, panting, trepidation, perturbation, ferment.

5. Verse sung in reply, antiphony, antistrophe, responsory, chant.

RESPONSIBILITY, n. Bounden duty, burden of obligation, accountability, accountableness, trustworthiness, responsibleness, liability, answerability, answerableness, onus, fealty, allegiance, tie, charge, trust, debt, part, function, task, service,

office, conscience, still small voice, inward monitor, sense of duty, the right thing to do, discharge, acquittal, observance, fulfilment, performance.

RESPONSIBLE, adj. 1. Having a capacity for moral decisions, capable of rational thought *or* action, answerable, accountable, liable, amenable, trustworthy, reliable, sane, moral, ethical, conscientious, creditable, seemly, decorous, sound.

2. Subject, open to, dependent on, under obligation, beholden to, bound by, incumbent on, able to discharge obligations, solvent.

REST, v. 1. Repose, slumber, sleep, doze, snooze, nap, catnap, catch forty winks, drowse, drop asleep, hibernate, estivate, fall asleep, lie in the arms of Morpheus, be still, be quiet, lie still, lie motionless, lounge, recline, pillow, couch, relax, vegetate, take one's ease, unbend, take rest, be inactive, be tranquil, close the eyes, lie down, retire, go to bed.

2. Stop, cease, desist, halt, come to a stand, come to a standstill, stand still, pause, hold, stop short, let up, abstain, discontinue, wait, remain, tarry, stay, pull up, mark time, draw up, heave to, cast anchor, bring to, lay to, ride at anchor, come to anchor, anchor, take breath, rest on one's oars, rest on one's laurels, dismount, alight, settle down, arrive, roost, perch, abide, await, wait, sojourn, dwell.

3. Idle, laze, loaf, potter, fritter away time, fool away time, putter, dillydally, dabble, slouch, hang back, gold-brick (sl.), do nothing, lag, dawdle, loll, drawl, loiter, take it easy, sleep at one's post, sleep at the switch, languish, flag, droop.

4. Calm, becalm, tranquilize, quell, hush, pacify, allay, appease, lull, still, soften, mollify, mellow, dulcify, assuage, palliate, mitigate, extenuate, alleviate, lessen, abate, subdue, tone down, temper, moderate, relieve, refresh, lay at rest, quiet, give rest to.

5. Depend, rely, lean upon, trust, repose in, confide, pin one's hopes on.

REST, n. 1. Sleep, repose, slumber, siesta, resting, doze, snooze, nap, catnap, forty winks, somnolence, Morpheus, Somnus, the Sandman, Land of Nod, dreamland, coma, catalepsy, sopor, trance, stupor, drowsiness, hibernation, estivation, relaxation.

2. Tranquility, calm, quiet, quiescence, peace, stillness, dead calm, hush, silence, serenity, calmness, motionlessness, immobility, peacefulness, fixity, stagnation, stagnancy, quietism, quietness, quietude, peaceableness, security.

3. Pause, cessation, lull, stop, letup, intermission, remission, recess, standstill, breathing spell, full stop, stay, caesura, interval, interruption, discontinuance, deadlock, stand, dead stand, stalemate, respite.

4. The grave, long last sleep, death, demise, decease, mortality, requiem, departure, dissolution, obit, quietus, release, cessation, end, the great adventure, crossing the bar, stygian shore, rigor mortis.

5. Inactivity, relaxation, leisure, otiosity, breathing time, day of rest, holiday, vacation, vacant hour, ease, idleness, convenience, time to spare, loafing, *dolce far niente (It.),* unemployment, vegetation, indolence.

6. Resting place, refuge, shelter, retreat, haven, lodging place, bivouac, encampment, camp, abode, home, destination, goal, bourn.

7. Support, pillar, stay, prop, buttress, shore, trestle, foundation, seat, mainstay, strut, brace,

abutment, guy, truss, splint, skid, rib, underpinning, supporting device, base, substruction, stereobate, socle, bedding, tie, sleeper, sill, cornerstone, grillage, substratum, purchase, footing, flooring, scaffold, platform, bracket, shelf, ledge, console, sawhorse, sawbuck, trivet, platform, stand, emplacement.

8. That which remains, that which is left, remainder, remnant, residue, residuum, balance, result, survival, redundance, superfluity, surplusage, overplus, excess, surplus.

RESTAURANT, n. Dining establishment, public dining room, eating place, café, cafeteria, automat, tearoom, chophouse, coffee house, lunch room, diner, grillroom, seafood house, steak house, hash house, *rôtisserie (Fr.),* beanery *(sl.),* hamburger palace, eatery *(sl.),* delicatessen, one-arm joint *(sl.),* canteen, refectory, buffet, public house, tavern, inn, night club, bistro, taproom, *estaminet (Fr.),* bar, *posada (Sp.),* snack bar, sandwich shop, drugstore counter, ice cream parlor, confectionery, *pâtisserie,* hot dog stand, greasy spoon *(sl.),* oyster bar, short-order counter.

RESTFUL, adj. Being at rest, reposeful, pacific, peaceful, tranquil, quiet, comfortable, calm, still, hushed, silent, quiescent, sleeping, resting, slumbering, motionless, undisturbed, unagitated, at rest, sedentary, relaxed, composed, soft, yielding, gentle, genial, mild.

RESTITUTION, n. 1. Restoration of property previously taken away, return of rights surrendered, repossession, retrieval, recovery, replevin *(Law),* reversion, redemption, recapture, reinvestment, reinstatement, repatriation.

2. Reparation, atonement, rehabilitation, remuneration, indemnification, compensation, reimbursement, amends, recompense, requital, repayment, satisfaction, redress, paying back, reddition.

RESTIVE, adj. Impatient of control, recalcitrant, refractory, stubborn, unwilling, disobedient, rebellious, mutinous, seditious, unruly, unsubmissive, ungovernable, insubordinate, contumacious, recusant, insurgent, lawless, revolutionary, riotous, fractious, intractable, balky, fidgety, resentful, averse, loath, disinclined, reluctant, renitent, irreconcilable, intransigent, demurring, obstinate, mulish, headstrong, inflexible, obdurate, pervicacious, heady, wayward, *entêté (Fr.),* incorrigible, crotchety, skittish, fretful, perverse, splenetic, moody, cantankerous, restless, uneasy, ill at ease, unquiet, sulky, sullen, humorsome, exceptious, deaf to reason, unaccommodating, glum, grumpy, morose, grim, frumpish, peevish, out of sorts, uncomplaisant.

RESTLESS, adj. 1. Changeable, transient, unstable, inconstant, unsettled, variable, wandering, roving, astatic, on the move, on the go, in motion, mutable, protean, kaleidoscopic, vagrant, nomadic, itinerant, peripatetic, roaming, migratory, unsteady.

2. Fitful, mercurial, fickle, vacillating, irresolute, undecided, shilly-shally, unsteadfast, unreliable, irresponsible, unstable, capricious, frothy, volatile, light-minded, giddy, pliant, erratic, capricious, eccentric, whimsical, maggoty, inconsistent, skittish, humorsome, crotchety, wayward, wanton, frivolous, touch-and-go.

3. Disturbed, uneasy, fidgety, agitated, disquieted, restive, fretful, ill at ease, unquiet, unresting, sleepless, wakeful, uncomfortable, awake, insomnious, insomnolent, nervous, anxious, worried, apprehensive, fretful, turbulent, twitching,

shaking, skittish, discontented, dissatisfied, rattled, flurried, excited, excitable, high-strung, neurotic, irritable, peevish, impatient, feverish, delirious, hysterical, vehement, rampant, volcanic.

RESTLESSNESS, n. 1. Agitation, unrest, perturbation, disquiet, animation, excitement, commotion, bustle, disturbance, to-do, ado, fluster, stir, flutter, flurry, turmoil, fuss, ferment, stew, flush, fever, tumult, trepidation, whirl, nervousness, impatience, frenzy.

2. Fidgets, fidgetiness, anxiety, inquietude, disquietude, uneasiness, dysphoria, itchy feet, splutter, scuttle.

RESTORATION, n. 1. Reëstablishment, replacement, rehabilitation, reinstatement, reconstruction, *rifacimento (It.),* renovation, remodeling, repair, reparation, redintegration, reproduction, revival, renewal, revivification, resuscitation, reorganization, reanimation, restitution, redemption, rectification, return, resumption, relief, retrieval, reclamation, redress, regainment, recovery, reddition, recall, reconversion, instauration, repristination, regeneration.

2. Rebirth, renascence, renaissance, new birth, palingenesis, rejuvenescence, regeneration, regenesis, regeneracy, resurgence, resurrection, reappearance, second youth, rejuvenation.

3. Convalescence, cure, recovery, recruitment, recuperation, recruital, reinvigoration, refreshment, relief, clean bill of health, eupepsia, euphoria.

RESTORATIVE, adj. Capable of renewing health, strength-promoting, invigorating, stimulating, curative, recuperative, remedial, restoring, analeptic, sanative, recuperatory, sanatory, healing, refreshing, refreshful, therapeutic, medicinal, medical, tonic, dietetical, alimentary, nutritive, digestive, peptic, corrective, amendatory, restitutory, restitutive, salubrious, salutiferous, wholesome, salutary, healthful, bracing, hygienic, good for, palliative, prophylactic, corroborant, assuasive, relieving, soothing, balsamic, lenitive.

RESTORATIVE, n. Restorative agent, stimulant, curative, corrective, reparative, analeptic, corroborant, remedy, cure, medicine, help, prophylactic, pick-me-up, bracer, tonic, palliative, alterative, specific, medicament, catholicon, nostrum, elixir, panacea, balm, cordial, ptisan, theriac, antidote, electuary, alexipharmic, antitoxin, counterpoison, emetic, carminative, physic, purgative, lenitive, eye opener.

RESTORE, v. 1. Make restitution of, put back, return, give back, render up, repay, refund, remit, compensate, make amends for, pay back, make good, make up for, reimburse, recompense, indemnify, remunerate, requite, satisfy, redress, reinstate, reseat, reinstall, re-establish, place in status quo, recoup, redeem, recover, reclaim, retrieve, rescue, repatriate, redeliver, release, disgorge.

2. Reconstruct, rehabilitate, rebuild, rearrange, reorganize, recondition, renovate, renew, make whole, redintegrate, convert, rejuvenate, regenerate, put in repair, mend, tinker, repair, retouch, darn, patch up, cobble, splice, calk, repristinate, put in order, fix, refit, touch up, remodel, emend, reproduce, represent in the original state, recreate, refashion.

3. Cure, bring round, doctor up, remedy, set on one's legs, heal, recruit, refresh, reinvigorate, resuscitate, reanimate, revive, revivify, quicken, bring to life again, freshen up, stimulate,

strengthen, brace, brisken, exhilarate, relieve, palliate, minister to, treat, nurse, attend, physic, dose, medicate, fortify, sustain, buttress, steel, harden, set on one's feet, energize, nerve, remain.

4. Recover, come to, rally, come 'round, pull through, be oneself again, come to oneself, weather the storm, survive, come to life again, get well, convalesce, recuperate, improve in health, regain one's strength, get on one's legs again.

RESTRAIN, *v.* 1. Keep under control, check, restrict, constrain, rein in, curb, hinder, coerce, debar, harness, muzzle, bridle, hold in leash, gag, pull in, hold back, snub, stop short, govern, control, compel, trammel, shackle, picket, hobble, tie, enchain, fasten, fetter, pinion, handcuff, tether, manacle, bind, inhibit, repress, withhold, suppress, strangle, smother, prohibit, hold, limit, control, rule, handicap, curtail, deter, detain, subdue, quell, still, contain, stifle, temper, prevent, bar, interdict, stop, forbid, discountenance, rebuff, keep from, preclude, exclude, put the brakes on, call a halt, chasten, discourage, chill, oppose, obstruct, cohibit, coarct, circumscribe, narrow, abridge, retard, disallow, taboo, enjoin, proscribe, divert from, overpower, subjugate, subdue, vanquish, dragoon, impel, force, oblige, necessitate, enforce, pin down.

2. Arrest, take into custody, apprehend, nab *(colloq.),* pinch *(colloq.),* take prisoner, commit, send to prison, take in charge, lead captive, take charge of, captivate.

3. Deprive of liberty, imprison, incarcerate, jail, lock up, pen up, confine, entomb, immure, cage, inclose, coop up, impound, wall in, bolt in, rail in, hem in, seal up, bottle up, box up, cork up, blockade, invest, hold in custody, detain, put in irons, cast into prison, clap under hatches, put into bilboes, cloister, close the door upon, mew up, button up, clap up, shut up.

RESTRAINT, *n.* 1. Control, compulsion, discipline, coercion, curb, check, restriction, hindrance, determent, deterrence, deterrent, stop, prohibition, limitation, inhibition, repression, constraint, bridle, stay, prevention, suppression, arrest, rein, barrier, bar, obstruction, impediment, retardation, discouragement, holdback, drawback, circumscription, pressure, necessity, blockade, embargo, ban, proscription, veto, taboo, damper, dissuasion, wet blanket, forbiddance, disallowance, interdict, injunction, interdiction, contraband, obstacle, hitch, knot, snag, brake, encumbrance, onus, burden, tether, clog, snaffle, bit, load, drag, disadvantage, interference, disapproval, obtrusion, disapprobation, opposition, censure, hampering, interruption, interception, counteraction, stoppage, delay, stumbling block, setback, interposition.

2. Imprisonment, detention, confinement, incarceration, durance vile, bondage, duress, thralldom, servitude, slavery, limbo, captivity, coarctation, mancipation, entombment, arrestation, keep, custody, care, ward, charge, restringency, safekeeping, guardianship, deprivation of liberty, penal servitude, chain gang, hard labor, rock pile, galleys.

3. Jail, prison, jug *(sl.),* clink *(sl.),* hoosegow *(sl.),* cell, cage, coop, dungeon, keep, oubliette, stir *(sl.),* bastille, penitentiary, lockup, pen, stationhouse, workhouse, reformatory, death house, bridewell, can *(sl.),* black hole.

4. Bonds, shackles, manacles, fetters, trammels, gyves, pinions, handcuffs, stocks, irons, bilboes,

wristlets, bracelets, gag, muzzle, bit, tether, bolts, bars, padlock, hatches, chains, ball and chain, wall, fence, rail, palisade, paling, stockade, barred windows, barbed-wire entanglement, barricade, pillory.

5. Constrained manner, constraint, stiffness, formality, aloofness, reserve, unnaturalness, embarrassment, containment, self-control, modesty, moderation, even temper, inexcitability, imperturbability, dispassion, calmness, coolness, composure, indisturbance, placidity, sang-froid, tranquillity, sobriety, gravity, equanimity, stoicism, philosophy, presence of mind, longanimity, fortitude, forbearance.

RESTRICT, *v.* Keep within limits, circumscribe, demarcate, confine, limit, hedge in, restrain, bound, hem in, curb, check, hamper, narrow, restringe, prohibit, obstruct, inhibit, prevent, proscribe, bar, repress, cramp, frustrate, muzzle, gag, stifle, constrain, stint, abridge, straiten, qualify, modify, rein in, harness, hold in leash, govern, rule, lay down the law, control, bridle, command, sway, exercise authority, regulate, supervise, direct, order, manage, conduct, guide, have charge of, dominate, superintend, hold, suppress, stop short, pull in, hold back, debar, veto, taboo, forbid, disallow, forfend, cohibit, clip the wings of, interdict, censor, exclude, shut out, handicap, encumber, trammel, tie one's hands, choke off, foil, balk, circumvent, override, put on the brake, put a stop to, interrupt, intercept, interclude, cut off, nip in the bud, counteract, preclude, foreclose, hold in leading strings, keep a tight hand on, handcuff, pinion, manacle, enchain, fetter, entrammel, shackle, hobble, bind hand and foot, swaddle, tether, peg down, picket, pin down, secure, bottle up, button up, box up, wall in, pen, coop, cage, cloister, immure, thwart.

RESTRICTION, *n.* 1. Control, limitation, coercion, discipline, regulation, government, determent, deterrence, compulsion, curb, check, protection, stop, constraint, economic pressure, hindrance, inhibition, disallowance, circumscription, repression, coarctation, oppilation, impedition, retardation, confinement, demarcation, distinction, contraction, construction, compression.

2. Provision, reservation, proviso, qualification, stipulation, modification, condition, coloring, exception, prerequisite, previous agreement, obligation, covenant, contract, concordat, consideration, postulate, clause.

3. Prohibition, veto, interdiction, interdict, injunction, embargo, ban, taboo, proscription, *verboten (Ger.),* picketing, blockade, closure, forbidden fruit, stricture.

4. Impediment, handicap, strait, embarrassment, obstacle, knot, hitch, barrier, impasse, dead end, cul-de-sac, preventive, drag, brake, stay, interclusion, stoppage, obstruction, preclusion, prevention.

RESTRICTIVE, *adj.* 1. Prohibitory, prohibitive, proscriptive, exclusive, inhibitive, inhibitory, interdictory, interdictive, prohibitionary, repressive, suppressive, strait-laced, inflexible, obdurate, narrow, preclusive, preventive, preventative, deterrent, opposing, oppositional, opposed, oppugnant, contrary, restringent, stiff, cohibitive, coactive, hindering, impeditive, impedient, burdensome, onerous, cumbrous, obtrusive, unfavorable.

2. Limitative, qualificatory, qualifying, limiting, conditional, provisory, provisional, contingent, modificatory, exceptional, hypothetical.

RESULT, *v.* 1. Proceed as a consequence from, be the outcome, be the effect, follow, issue, come, flow, happen, come forth, emerge, evolve, redound, spring, arise, rise, emanate, accrue, turn out, ensue, be derived, originate, depend upon, hinge upon, succeed, supervene, germinate from, be due to, be owing to, sprout from, derive its origin.

2. End in a specified manner, eventuate, terminate, finish, culminate, come to a head, run its course, reach the goal, wind up.

RESULT, *n.* 1. Effect, issue, consequence, outcome, denouement, conclusion, end, upshot, event, aftermath, aftergrowth, afterclap, catastrophe, outgrowth, development, derivative, product, harvest, fruit, yield, crop, output, turnout, handiwork, work, offshoot, offspring, first fruits, *primeur (Fr.),* eventuality, proceeds, termination, sequel, corollary, inference, deduction, reaction, sequela, superconsequence, wake, train, trail, consummation, solution, aftereffect.

2. Decision, resolution, resolve, verdict, finding, determination, judgment, award, opinion, decree, sentence, adjudication, arbitrament, arbitration, appraisement, appraisal, estimate, estimation, appreciation, assessment, report, notice, critique, criticism, review.

RESUME, *v.* Continue, renew, recommence, go on with after interruption, begin again, take up again, get a fresh start on, try again, summarize, recapitulate, return to, retell, reword, paraphrase, duplicate, reiterate, repeat, iterate, reproduce, reecho, harp upon, revert, recur, go back, return, tell over, begin at the beginning, start afresh, begin de novo, restate, review.

RESUME, *n.* Condensed statement, synopsis, recapitulation, abstract, epitome, summary, précis, syllabus, summing up, compendium, *multum in parvo (Lat.),* digest, pandect, sum and substance, analysis, brief, apercu, abridgment, minute, draft, conspectus, prospectus, outline, note, review.

RESURRECTION, *n.* Rising again from the dead, resuscitation, revivification, revival, renewal, resurgence, revivescence, reanimation, phoenix, renascence, renaissance, rebirth, rejuvenescence, new birth, regeneration, palingenesis, renovation, restoration, reappearance, atavism, reincarnation, metempsychosis, judgment day, *dies irae (Lat.),* apotheosis, deification, translation, eternal home, life after death, eternal life, future state, eternity, heavenly kingdom, heaven, inheritance of the saints in light, abode of the blessed, paradise, celestial bliss, New Jerusalem, Elysian fields, bowers of bliss, happy hunting ground, seventh heaven, Nirvana, Valhalla, Islands of the Blessed.

RESUSCITATE, *v.* Revive from death *or* unconsciousness, restore to life, reanimate, bring back to life, revivify, recall to life, quicken, raise from the dead, reinvigorate, renew, renovate, revivificate, requicken, bring to, refresh, restore, refocillate, recreate, regenerate, stir the embers, refashion.

RETAIL, *v.* 1. Sell directly to the consumer, sell in small quantities, peddle, hawk, vend, dispense, distribute, dispose of, market, deal in.

2. Repeat in detail to others, relate, mention one by one, enumerate, recount, narrate, specify, signify, describe, confide to, explain, give the lowdown, purvey inside information, communicate, apprise, tip, impart, advise.

RETAIN, *v.* 1. Keep possession of, continue to hold, keep, secure, reserve, hold, preserve, withhold, keep in possession, detain, save, husband, cling to, clinch, grasp, keep close, clutch, hold back, keep back, hug, hold in, hold fast, maintain, clench, grip, embrace, gripe, restrain.

2. Keep in mind, remember, recollect, recall, bear in mind, memorize, cause to be remembered, dwell upon, brood over, hold in remembrance, treasure, call up, bethink oneself, conjure up, summon up, retrace, call to mind, look back upon, review, rake up the past, call to remembrance, redeem from oblivion, commit to memory, learn by heart, con over, fix in the mind, impress upon the memory, memorialize, have at one's fingers' tips, know by rote, master.

3. Engage by paying a fee, maintain, employ, hire, keep in pay.

RETAINER, *n.* 1. One owing service to a noble household, dependent, attendant, servant, vassal, adherent, henchman, liegeman, servitor, follower, squire, page, footman, trainbearer, cupbearer, livery servant, flunky, lackey, groom, equerry, hostler, orderly, chamberlain, bailiff, seneschal, major-domo, castellan, serf, helot, bondsman, client, hanger-on, satellite, janissary, myrmidon, hireling, mercenary.

2. Fee paid to secure services, preliminary fee, retaining fee.

RETALIATE, *v.* Return like for like, make return for, return evil for evil, get back, get even, requite, pay back, repay, retort, revenge, avenge, match, take revenge, give quid pro quo, give a Roland for an Oliver, give tit for tat, turn the tables, take vengeance, pay off a few scores, strike back, serve the same sauce, reciprocate, take retribution, turn upon, pay off, return the compliment, exchange blows, give as good as was sent, give and take, vindicate, wreak one's vengeance, give no quarter, keep the wound open, bear malice, have no mercy, harass, dragoon, persecute, give measure for measure, exact one's pound of flesh, take an eye for an eye, pay in the same coin, get quits.

RETALIATION, *n.* Requital of evil, return of like for like, retribution, nemesis, vengeance, revenge, avengement, reprisal, punishment, condign desert, *lex talionis (Lat.),* counterblast, counterstroke, retortion, accusation, recrimination, compensation, measure for measure, a Roland for an Oliver, eye for an eye, tit for tat, *quid pro quo (Lat.),* diamond cut diamond, give and take, the biter bit, blow for blow, boomerang, repayment, vindictiveness, death feud, vendetta, blood for blood, Eumenides, Furies, Erinyes, cross fire.

RETARD, *v.* 1. Slacken speed, slow up, decelerate, slow down, check, put on the brake, brake, move slowly, drag, inch along, jog on, falter, flag, take one's time, crawl, creep, lag, trail, worm one's way, hitch, dawdle, loiter, linger, hobble.

2. Put off, delay, postpone, defer, procrastinate, prorogue, adjourn, suspend, lay over, remand, continue *(Law),* shelve, table, temporize, stall, filibuster, protract, prolong, spin out, dally, draw out, pigeonhole.

3. Obstruct, impede, hamper, hinder, check, detain, slacken, clog, restrain, prevent, inhibit, preclude, debar, arrest, dam up, block, intercept, interrupt, interpose, interfere, encumber, cramp, handicap, cumber, saddle with, burden, entrammel, overload.

RETARDATION, *n.* Deceleration, delaying, retardment, hindrance, negative acceleration

(Mech.), obstacle, obstruction, delay, mincing steps, slowdown, hitch, hobble, limp, dogtrot, jogtrot, sluggishness, dilatoriness, tardiness, slowness, loitering, lingering, lagging, prolongation, protraction, procrastination, suspension, moratorium, remand, mora, stay, stop.

RETCH, *v.* Make efforts to vomit, heave, keck, strain, gag, feel nausea, puke, spew, disgorge, bring up, hawk.

RETENTION, *n.* 1. Capacity for retaining, maintenance, custody, hold, keeping, safekeeping, grasp, tenacity, grip, gripe, retentivity, retentiveness, retaining, holding, detention, reservation, keep, firm hold, clutch, hug, embrace, clasp, clench.

2. Tentacle, manus, vise, forceps, tweezers, pincers, monkey wrench, pliers, fist, hook, talon, claw, teeth, fangs, tongs, paw, finger, digit.

3. Remembrance, power of remembering things, retentiveness, memory, recollection, retrospection, reminiscence, reminder, memorandum, memo, memento, keepsake, souvenir, relic, token, remembrancer, hint, suggestion, monument, testimonial, memorial, commemorative record, mnemonics, mnemotechny, mnemotechnics, mnemonization.

RETENTIVE, *adj.* Having power to remember, having a good memory, unforgetting, tenacious, retaining, reliable, apt to retain, grasping, unforgetful, trustworthy, remindful, reminiscential, recollective, reminiscent, mindful, enduring, green, fresh, vivid, indelible, never to be forgotten, memorable, commemorative, mnemosynic, mnemotechnic.

RETICENCE, *n.* Uncommunicativeness, taciturnity, laconicism, reserve, untalkativeness, secretiveness, silence, closeness, concealment, pauciloquy, curtness, terseness, aposiopesis, muteness.

RETICENT, *adj.* Disposed to be silent, not inclined to speak freely, pauciloquent, taciturn, laconic, tight-lipped, close-mouthed, terse, curt, secretive, uncommunicative, mum, reserved, dumb, silent, self-contained, sparing of words, impenetrable, mute, costive, inconversable, concise, short, brief, pithy, succinct, compendious, sententious, crisp, furtive, surreptitious, evasive, sly, clandestine, inviolate, confidential, undercover, covert, recondite, cryptic.

RETICULAR, *adj.* Having the form of a net, retiform, meshlike, netted, netlike, meshy, reticulated, cancellated, areolar, latticed, interfretted, secant, textile, plexal, twisted, convoluted, tortile, intricate, involved, complicated, entangled.

RETICULATION, *n.* Network, mesh, reticulated work, decussated work, cancellation, reticulated arrangement, interlacement, intersection, intertwinement, decussation, convolution, transversion, meshwork, intertexture, plexus, net, web, plait, wattle, trellis, lattice, grille, grating, tracery, gridiron, fretwork, reticle, tissue, netting, filigree, entanglement.

RETICULE, *n.* Small purse, handbag, vanity bag, sac, sack, saccule, net, ditty bag, kit, poke, satchel, budget.

RETINUE, *n.* Body of retainers, corps of attendants, train, entourage, suite, tail, queue, bodyguard, escort, convoy, menage, procession, following, cavalcade, equipage, royal household, court, followers, hangers-on, satellites, staff, personnel, force, partisans, company, cortege.

RETIRE, *v.* 1. Go to bed, hit the hay *(colloq.)*, hit the sack *(colloq.)*, consult one's pillow, turn in, call it a day, lie down to rest.

2. Go away, go apart, withdraw, depart, retreat, leave, remove, recede, retrocede, fall back, beat a retreat, evacuate, secede, back out, draw back, abandon, quit, abscond, lose ground, give way, shut up shop, ebb, regress, take a back seat, rusticate, hibernate, estivate, debouch, take flight, flit, take wing, disappear, decamp, vacate, separate oneself, keep apart, take the veil.

3. Resign, abdicate, give up one's business, be pensioned, be superannuated, be shelved, give up office, tender one's resignation, hand over, relinquish, lay down, give up.

RETIRED, *adj.* 1. Withdrawn, removed, secret, private, solitary, secluded, sequestered, sequestrated, apart, unfrequented, hidden, covert, remote, outlying, aloof, in the backwoods, out of the world, lonely, inhospitable, *sauvage (Fr.)*, bye, out of the way, in a backwater, unvisited.

2. No longer occupied with one's business, withdrawn from one's profession, pensioned, superannuated, overage, leisured.

RETIREMENT, *n.* 1. Retreat, departure, withdrawal, regression, evacuation, retrocession, recession, retrogression, flight, retrogradation, countermarch, countermovement, reversion, countermotion, relapse, quitting.

2. Removal from service, abdication, abandonment, resignation, relinquishment, forsaking, renunciation, disclamation, abjuration, leave.

3. Solitude, privacy, isolation, sequestration, concealment, obscurity, seclusion, loneliness, rustication, *villeggiatura (It.)*, background, reclusion, aloofness, anchoretism, cenobitism, unsociability, insociableness, self-sufficiency.

RETIRING, *adj.* Withdrawing from contact with others, reserved, modest, diffident, demure, shy, coy, bashful, unassuming, quiet, shrinking, unsociable, meek, unobtrusive, unofficious, unpretentious, evasive, elusive, distant, aloof, inconversable, uncommunicative, eremitic, cenobitic, anchoritic, solitary, ascetic, humble, timorous, timid, skittish, offish, reticent, unsocial, quiet, self-contained, stand-off, verecund.

RETORT, *v.* Reply in retaliation, reply in kind to, rejoin, answer, respond, rebut, say, return, acknowledge, give answer, surrejoin, surrebut, counterclaim, answer an argument by another to the contrary, counter, say in defense, vindicate, contend for, clear, exculpate, justify, defend, give the devil his due, exonerate, speak for.

RETORT, *n.* 1. Incisive counter to a previous statement, witty reply, smart response, rejoinder, pointed answer, repartee, riposte, flash of wit, quip, sharp return, acknowledgment, sally, rebuttal, counterblast, counterstatement, replication, surrejoinder, surrebutter, clincher, knock-down argument, *reductio ad absurdum (Lat.)*, recrimination, retaliation, *quid pro quo (Lat.)*, attic wit, *esprit (Fr.)*, salt, drollery, ready wit, banter, persiflage, badinage, bright thought, *mot pour rire (Fr.)*, bon mot, witticism, word-play, *jeu d'esprit (Fr.)*, *jeu de mots (Fr.)*, epigram.

2. Vessel used for distilling *or* decomposing substances by heat, crucible, alembic, sublimatory, vaporizer, boiler, melting pot, still, atomizer, seething caldron.

RETOUCH, *v.* Improve by new touches, touch up, brighten, furbish, restore to freshness of appearance, rub to brightness, polish up, burnish, refresh, renovate, smooth, recondition, rejuvenate, repair, mend, put in repair, vamp, doctor, tinker, patch up, revamp, correct, amend, emend.

RETRACT, *v.* 1. Draw in, pull back, withdraw, draw back, abduce, draw away, retrude, purse up, pack, stow, stive, put in compactly, wedge in.

2. Recall, recant, take back, disavow, rescind, unsay, abjure, disown, revoke, cancel, annul, nullify, declare null and void, disclaim, forswear, renounce, repeal, abolish, reverse, override, overrule, set aside, disannul, quash, dissolve, repudiate, do away with, countermand, counterorder, wash one's hands of, demit, relinquish, abandon, forgo, change one's mind, go to the right about, shift one's ground, tergiversate, apostatize, draw in one's horns, eat one's words, eat humble pie, back out of, repent, turn over a new leaf, deny, gainsay, swallow, abnegate, abrogate.

RETRACTION, *n.* Withdrawal of a statement *or* opinion, recantation, revocation, abjuration, rescission, disavowal, unsaying, taking back, disowning, cancellation, annulment, nullification, voidance, disclaimer, renunciation, repeal, abolishment, reversal, disannulment, dissolution, repudiation, demission, relinquishment, abandonment, tergiversation, apostasy, repentance, denial, abnegation, abrogation, palinode, abjurement, retractation, disclaimer.

RETREAT, *v.* Withdraw, give way, recede, retire, draw back, recoil, back away, depart, fall back, steal off, give place, turn tail, run away, show one's heels, move back, back out, lose ground, retrocede, go off in haste, regress, abscond, flee, fall to the rear, take to one's heels, cut and run, take flight, fly, make off, part company, decamp, make oneself scarce, levant *(sl.),* bolt, desert, abandon, decamp, break camp, evacuate, vacate, escape, get clear of, make off, skedaddle, give one the slip, make a get-away.

RETREAT, *n.* 1. Resort, haunt, refuge, habitat, asylum, place of refuge, den, lair, lurking place, sanctuary, sanctum sanctorum, hibernaculum, haven, covert, aerie, rookery, nest, nidus, roost, perch, dugout, cavern, cave, grotto, hiding place, hole, cell, hermitage, convent, monastery, abbey, priory, friary, nunnery, cloister, study, library, snuggery, cache, bivouac, cabin, cot, shack, croft, hut, shanty, wigwam, tepee, villa, lodge, *rus in urbe (Lat.),* cottage, bungalow, fastness, stronghold, last resort, keep, ark, shelter, adytum, creephole, ambuscade, alcove, niche, recess.

2. Strategic retirement of an armed force before an enemy, withdrawal from action, recession, departure, recoil, flight, evacuation, backing out, falling back, katabasis, retrogression, retrogradation, relapse, reversion, countermarch, *volte-face (Fr.),* rout, hegira, exodus, stampede, pell-mell running, escape, avolation, getaway, *reculade (Fr.),* remigration.

3. Seclusion, retirement, solitude, *villeggiatura (It.),* rustication, privacy, isolation, concealment, obscurity, separation, background, aloofness, loneliness, distance, anchoritism, voluntary exile, recess, reclusion.

RETRENCH, *v.* 1. Cut off, lop, prune, lop off, clip, dock, pare, cut down, cut short, curtail, defalcate, amputate, subtract, subduct, cut back, mutilate, obtruncate, delete, hack, hew, snip, crop, shear, stunt, pollard, nip, foreshorten, take in, abbreviate, abridge, shorten, compress, diminish, decrease, lessen, reduce, remove, deduct, take from, bereave, deprive of.

2. Reduce expenses, economize, cut corners *(colloq.),* save, manage frugally, scrimp, meet one's expenses, make both ends meet, husband, keep one's head above water, save for a rainy day, lay by, conserve, reserve.

RETRENCHMENT, *n.* 1. Curtailment, diminution, abridgment, reduction, decrease, cutting down, lessening, obtruncation, subduction, subtraction, amputation, docking, paring, clipping, lopping off, pruning, mutilation, deletion, cropping, snipping, stunting, shearing, foreshortening, taking in, nipping, shortening, lessening, removal, deduction,.

2. Economy, frugality, thriftiness, husbandry, prudence, repayment, savingness, good housewifery, care, thrift, prevention of waste, parsimony, parsimoniousness, stint.

RETRIBUTION, *n.* Requital according to deserts, condign judgment, penalty, desert, retaliation, recompense, repayment, compensation, reward, return, *quid pro quo (Lat.),* revenge, vengeance, nemesis, tit for tat, eye for an eye, tooth for tooth, the biter bit, boomerang, avengement, reparation, paying back, liquidation, amends, atonement, sackcloth and ashes, satisfaction, propitiation, reprisal, *lex talionis (Lat.),* counterstroke, recrimination, accusation, a Roland for an Oliver, measure for measure, give and take, diamond cut diamond, blow for blow, vengefulness, vindictiveness, death feud, vendetta, blood for blood, day of reckoning, *dies irae (Lat.),* judgment day, reciprocation, thunderbolt, turning the tables, punishment, justice, indemnification, reimbursement.

RETRIEVE, *v.* Recover, regain, bring back, get again, find and fetch, recoup, redeem, come by one's own, revendicate, replevy, recruit, re-establish, repair, rescue, save, restore, recall, make good, make amends for, reclaim, revive, rally, come to oneself, come 'round, pull through.

RETROACTION, *n.* Counteraction, opposition, polarity, antagonism, contrariety, reaction, resistance, collision, clashing, renitency, repercussion, counterblast, neutralization, check, recoil, rebound, ricochet, revulsion, *contrecoup (Fr.),* reflux, reflex, elasticity, kick, recalcitration, reverberation, repulse, rebuff, return, boomerang, spring, regression, retrocession, retrogradation, retrogression, *reculade (Fr.),* recession, refluence. resilience, *volte-face (Fr.),* countermotion, impingement of a later agreement *(Law).*

RETROACTIVE, *adj.* 1. Antagonistic, renitent, counteracting, conflicting, contrary, reactionary, repercussive, recalcitrant, recoiling, refluent, counterclockwise, crablike, resilient, reflex, regressive, retrogressive, retrograde.

2. That affects the past, operative with respect to past occurrences, backtracking, retrospective, ex post facto, looking back.

RETROCEDE, *v.* Give place, regress, recede, retire, retrograde, go back, withdraw, retreat, yield, fall back, turn back, hark back, draw back, lose ground, fall astern, put about, backwater, veer round, double, countermarch, wheel, ebb, turn tail, beat a retreat, retrace one's steps, turn upon one's heel, rebound, revert, return, shrink, sheer off, depart, run away.

RETROCESSION, *n.* Going back, retrogradation, retrogression, regression, recession, regress, retroaction, withdrawal, *reculade (Fr.),* retreat, retirement, recess, remigration, reflux, refluence, return, ebb, backwater, resilience, *volte-face (Fr.),* recoil, departure, flight.

RETROGRADE, *v.* 1. Move backward, go back, retreat, retire, recede, retrocede, retrogress, regress, backslide, ebb, reverse, retrace one's steps, revert, back down, withdraw, fall back, turn back, drop astern, countermarch, beat a retreat, lose ground.

2. Decline to a worse condition, worsen, degenerate, deteriorate, decay, wane, fall off, droop, go downhill, fade, wither, fall into decay, crumble, relapse, recidivate, fail.

RETROGRADE, *adj.* 1. Moving backward, having a backward direction, inverse, retrogressive, regressive, boustrophedon, recessive, refluent, returning, resilient, counterclockwise, reflex, recidivous, crablike.

2. Exhibiting degeneration, pejorative, deteriorated, altered for the worse, on the decline, on the wane, degenerate, tabid, shaken, far-gone, decayed, moldering, crumbling, tottering to its fall, blighted, decrepit, broken down, done for, in a bad way, at a low ebb, on one's last legs, underminded, deciduous, on the downgrade.

RETROGRESSION, *n.* 1. Backward movement, retrogradation, retrocession, regression, recession, regress, retroaction, *reculade (Fr.),* retirement, retreat, withdrawal, refluence, ebb, reflux, return, *volte-face (Fr.).*

2. Decline, deterioration, degeneration, retrograde, metamorphosis, degeneracy, declination, growing worse, pejoration, decadence, failure, relapse, impairment, vitiation, demoralization, depravity, depravation, degradation, declension, caducity, dilapidation, atrophy, collapse, disorganization, *délabrement (Fr.).*

RETROSPECT, *n.* Contemplation of the past, survey of time past, review, reminiscence, recollection, retrospection, looking backward, remembrances of things past, mental reproduction, retentive memory, retention, retentiveness, tenacity, *veteris vestigia flammae (Lat.),* tablets of the memory, recurrence, recognition, rememoration, afterthought, reconsideration, second thought.

RETROSPECTIVE, *adj.* 1. Directed to the past, looking backward, retroactive, that affects the past, directed back.

2. Looking back, contemplative of past events, pensive, thoughtful, meditative, cogitative, reflective, speculative, wistful, museful, deliberative, introspective, absorbed in thought, deep-musing, mindful, reminiscential, taken up with, engrossed in, rapt, absorbed, preoccupied.

RETURN, *v.* 1. Come back, revert, turn back, reverse, retreat, go back, relapse, recur, recidivate, recoil, regress, recede, ebb, wane.

2. Reappear, rebound, revolve, retrograde, recrudesce, reoccur, come round again, intermit, alternate.

3. Reply, retort, answer, respond, rejoin, rebut, say in return, give answer, acknowledge, surrejoin, surrebut, recriminate, announce officially, communicate, render a verdict, report, tell, pass sentence, sentence, condemn, doom, pass judgment upon, adjudicate, adjudge.

4. Give back, restore, put back, bring back, send back, restitute, render, release, give up, let go, disgorge, replace, reinstate, reseat, reinstall, rehabilitate, re-establish.

5. Reflect, echo, reverberate, resound, reëcho, ring, repeat, cast back.

6. Give in recompense, repay, recompense, compensate, remunerate, refund, recoup, indem-

nify, reimburse, give a good interest, yield a revenue, be profitable.

7. Requite, reciprocate, retaliate, redress, revenge, avenge, vindicate, wreak one's vengeance, give no quarter.

RETURN, *n.* 1. Response, reply, answer, rejoinder, respondence, acknowledgment, rebuttal, retort, respondency, repartee, riposte, counterstatement, echo, reverberation, antiphony, antiphon, counterblast, countercharge, plea, defense, rebutter, surrebutter, surrejoinder, report, statement.

2. Recurrence, repetition, reappearance, iteration, renewal, rehearsal, recapitulation, reiteration, duplication, monotone, harping, ding-dong.

3. Restoration, restitution, recovery, reinstatement, rehabilitation, reinvestment, retrieval, atavism, recrudescence, reincarnation, metempsychosis.

4. Home-coming, coming back, advent, arrival, reëntry, junction, encounter, meeting, passage back repatriation.

5. Reversion, regression, regress, retrogression, retrogradation, recession.

6. Repayment, reimbursement, remittance, reparation, recompense, requital, reward, compensation, rendition, reciprocation, retaliation, quittance, redress, retribution, amends, atonement, meed, guerdon, indemnification, indemnity, consideration, *quid pro quo (Lat.).*

7. Profit, gain, advantage, yield, benefit, rent, revenue, income, interest, avails, account, increase, proceeds, results, *rente (Fr.),* receipts, earnings, rental, premium, bounty, harvest, crop, bonus, reward, gain.

REUNION, *n.* Festive gathering, forgathering, meeting, assembly, convention, levee, convocation, congress, conflux, levy, concourse, mobilization, convergence, meet, congregation, muster, concentration, ingathering, association, caucus, brotherhood, fraternity, league, tribe, sept, family, caste, clan, phyle, reconciliation, correspondence, concordance, agreement.

REVAMP, *v.* Touch up again, vamp afresh, reconstruct, mend, patch up, make over, rehabilitate, renovate, repair, renew, rebuild, recondition, make whole, redintegrate, put in repair, retouch, darn, cobble, tinker, doctor up, regenerate, refashion, transform, work a change, convert, revolutionize, reshape, modify, diversify, alter, change, tamper with, innovate.

REVEAL, *v.* Lay open to view, display, show, exhibit, betray, make known, divulge, disclose, communicate, expose, uncover, unveil, unmask, unseal, open, tell, publish, announce, impart, confess, declare, inform, notify, let slip, blab, let out, take the secrecy lid from, unearth, lay bare, unfold, bring to light, confide to, utter, breathe, let into the secret, squeal, peach, squeak *(slang),* vent, bruit, blurt out, break the news, whisper about, let fall, broadcast, acknowledge, concede, admit, grant, avow, own, spill *(sl.),* make a clean breast, come clean, unbosom oneself, confirm, verify, report, proclaim, promulgate, disseminate, acquaint, apprise, advise, enlighten, instruct, mention, affirm, intimate, specify, signify, describe, retail, explain, give inside information, give the low-down, hint, indicate, allude to, insinuate, imply, give a pointer to, tip off, give the cue, prompt, open the eyes of, make public, circulate, spread abroad, rumor, evulgate, diffuse, give out, voice, blazon, herald, noise abroad, evince, evidence, manifest, tell tales out of school, come out with,

REVEILLE, *n.* Bugle call, signal by drum to awaken soldiers for the day's duties, morning signal, trumpet call, alarum, taps.

blow the gaff, throw off all disguise, unburden one-self, disburden one's heart, tell a piece of one's mind, drop the mask, debunk, undeceive, disabuse, set right, *désillusionner (Fr.),* give an inkling of, point out, speak volumes.

REVEL, *v.* 1. Indulge in festivities, carouse, make merry, sport, disport, roister, feast, tipple, junket, banquet, have one's fling, gambol, frolic, romp, caper, live high, riot, run riot, sow one's wild oats, paint the town red, plunge into dissipation, hit the booze, go on a spree, drown care, take one's pleasure, keep holiday, swill, slake one's thirst, rake.

2. Take great pleasure, indulge, luxuriate, delight, wanton, rejoice, relish, enjoy, bask in, wallow in, gloat over, smack the lips, derive pleasure from.

REVEL, *n.* Boisterous merrymaking, intemperate festivity, orgy, spree, carousal, saturnalia, revelry, drinking bout, debauch, revels, jollification, racket, hot time, inebriety, dissoluteness, dissipation, high living, crapulence, debauchery, epicureanism, sybaritism, winebibbing, bacchanalia, libations, bacchanal, whoopee, merriment, junket, frolic, jollity, party, *fête (Fr.),* fiesta, festival, gala, carnival, brawl, high jinks, banquet, feast, symposium, wassail, jamboree, round of pleasures, celebration, holiday, red letter day.

REVELATION, *n.* 1. Divulgence, exposure, unveiling, *exposé (Fr.),* disclosure, discovery, detection, find, divulgement, betrayal, vent, expression, utterance, publication, exposition, declaration, admission, confession, acknowledgment, confessional, avowal, unfolding, showing, ascertainment, espial, unearthing, enlightenment, acquaintance, appraisal, recital, mention, telling, particularization, specification, publicity, intimation, representation, communication, insinuation, proclamation, announcement, tidings, information, news, hearsay, rumor, bruit, story, report, newsmongery, tittle-tattle.

2. Divine communication of truth, gospel, apocalypse, oracle, inspiration, Bible, scriptures, afflatus, theopneusty, the Word of God, sacred writings.

REVELER, *n.* Merrymaker, roisterer, carouser, bacchanalian, maenad, satyr, winebibber, boozer, tippler, toper, sot, inebriate, drunkard, dipsomaniac, alcoholic, lush *(slang),* tosspot, lovepot, thirsty soul, devotee to Bacchus, *bon vivant (Fr.),* cormorant, glutton, belly-god, gormandizer, epicure, debauchee, rake roué, rakehell, lecher, goat, fast man, voluptuary, libertine, loose fish, rip, gay deceiver, sensualist, sybarite, man of pleasure, hedonist, hard liver.

REVELRY, *n.* Boisterous festivity, reveling, roistering, carousal, merrymaking, jollification, riot, revel, carouse, rout, jamboree, high jinks, jollity, wassail, conviviality, orgy, bacchanal, saturnalia, drinking bout, debauch, hot time, license, crapulence, debauchery, inebriety, drunkenness, dissoluteness, dissipation, high living, winebibbing, libations, carnival, festival, whoopee, bat *(slang),* spree, junket.

REVENANT, *n.* One who returns as a spirit after death, ghost, shade, specter, visible incorporeal spirit, phantom, apparition, shadow, vision, materialization, wraith, spook, banshee, genie, *manes (Lat.),* sprite, appearance, phantasm, *lemures (Rom. Relig.).*

REVENGE, *v.* Exact expiation on behalf of, wreak one's vengeance, retaliate, in a vindictive spirit, requite with resentment, have one's revenge, take vengeance for, avenge, vindicate by punishment, repay, make reprisal for, take revenge, breathe vengeance, give no quarter, take an eye for an eye, turn the tables upon, reciprocate, pay back, return like for like, give as good as was sent, be quits, pay off old scores, be even with, demand one's pound of flesh, undertake a vendetta, call for blood, set the day of reckoning, cut up rough, pour out the vials of one's wrath, vent one's rage, breathe fire and fury, have a fling at, bring a hornet's nest about one's ears, have no mercy, grind into the dust, hound, persecute, oppress, harbor a grudge, bear malice, shut the gates of mercy.

REVENGE, *n* Retaliation for wrongs, injury inflicted in return for one received, retaliatory punishment, reprisal, retribution, nemesis, requital, vengeance, avengement, repayment, revengefulness, vindictiveness, vengefulness, rancor, implacability, malevolence, ruthlessness, death feud, vendetta, satisfaction, eye for an eye, *quid pro quo (Lat.),* quits, even score, blood for blood, tooth for a tooth, day of reckoning, judgment day, *dies irae (Lat.), lex talionis (Lat.),* counterstroke, counterblast, compensation, a Roland for an Oliver, measure for measure, tit for tat. the biter bit, boomerang, venom, virulence, tender mercies, bad blood, animosity, malignancy, malice aforethought, malice prepense, pique, grudge, resentment, umbrage, acerbity, bitterness, spleen, gall, rankling, *acharnement (Fr.),* violence, vials of wrath, hot blood, fire and fury, *casus belli (Lat.),* red rag to a bull, crow to pluck, sore subject, Eumenides, Furies, Erinys, Tisiphone, Alecto, Megaera.

REVENGEFUL, *adj.* Vindictive, vengeful, spiteful, implacable, rancorous, resentful, malevolent, malicious, out to get even, ruthless, pitiless, retaliative, planning reprisal, avenging, rigorous, unforgiving, inexorable, unrelenting, remorseless, stony-hearted, retributive, requiting, reciprocal, recriminatory, ill-intentioned, ill-disposed, venomous, virulent, malign, maleficent, vicious, envenomed, bitter, grinding, cold-blooded, grim, unfeeling, bloodthirsty, ferocious, feral, fell, merciless, draconian, harsh, inflexible, indignant, sore, peeved, hurt, waxy, *acharné (Fr.),* offended, infuriate, flushed with anger, up in arms, in a fume, on one's high ropes, in high dudgeon, in the heat of passion, malignant, relentless.

REVENUE, *n.* Amount of money regularly coming in, income, incomings, proceeds, return, gross receipts, net profit, earnings, gain, resources, means, wherewithal, capital, ways and means, finances, money matters, accounts, funds, assets, cash, wealth, sum total, circumstances, competence, provision, substance, maintenance, alimony, livelihood, dowry, rental, rentage, annuity, pension, emolument, salary, wages, stipend, pay, hire, remuneration, recompense, compensation, payment, reward, yield.

REVERBERATE, *v.* 1. Resound, echo, reëcho, echo back, boom, bombinate, rumble, roar, thunder, bound back, ring, peal, sound, ring in the ear, tintinnabulate, vibrate, chime, jingle, tinkle, mutter, gurgle, roll.

2. Rebound, recoil, be deflected, reflect, cast back, send back, ricochet, repercuss.

REVERBERATION, *n.* Multiple reflection of sound, echoing, reëchoing, echo, peal, resonance, ringing, repercussion, vibration, tintinnabulation, boom, chime, roar, clangor, roll, thunder, rumble, reply, return, polyphony, audibility, sonorescence, sonority, report, noise, sound, bombilation, *berloque (Fr.),* bombination, tattoo.

REVERE, *v.* Regard with respect tinged with awe, hallow, worship, venerate, esteem, reverence, honor, adore, admire, look up to, think much of, do honor to, entertain respect for, defer to, pay homage to, treat with consideration, stand upon ceremony, observe due decorum before, kowtow to, salaam before, do obeisance to, beatify, sanctify, enshrine, consecrate, hail, have a high opinion of, pay tribute to, salute, kneel to, bend the knee to, bow to, prostrate oneself, fall down before, kiss the hem of one's garment, humble oneself before, do service to, bless, glorify, laud, praise, magnify, sing the praises of, offer sacrifice to, burn candles to, send up incense before, make much of, treasure, prize, hold dear, cling to, hug, cherish, idolize, feast one's eyes on, dote on.

REVERENCE, *n.* 1. Attitude of deep respect tinged with awe, worship, esteem, deference, adoration, veneration, awe, honor, admiration, regard, homage, fealty, estimation, devotion, humility, prostration, consecration, glorification, magnification, hosanna, benediction, allelujah, sacrifice, oblation, libation, incense, votive offering.

2. Gesture indicative of deep respect, curtsy, bow, kowtow, salaam, obeisance, proskynesis, genuflection, kneeling, bowing and scraping, salute, devoirs, respects, ceremonial.

REVEREND, *adj.* Worthy to be revered, entitled to reverence, venerable, worshipful, sacred, divine, emeritus, time-honored, estimable, esteemed, ordained, in holy orders, called to the ministry, sacerdotal, clerical, pastoral, priestly, ministerial.

REVERENTIAL, *adj.* Reverent, devotional, deferential, prostrate, bareheaded, cap in hand, ceremonious, respectful, decorous, obsequious, abject, abased, religious, pious, sanctimonious, devout, humble, heavenly-minded, spiritual, pure in heart, pietistic, godly, solemn, faithful, believing, sanctified, converted, inspired, consecrated, dutiful, submissive.

REVERIE, *n.* Dreamy meditation, fanciful musing, daydream, brown study, preoccupation, woolgathering, castle-building, abstraction, travels in the blue, dreamland, waking dream, absorption, absence of mind, engrossment, detachment, distraction, flight of fancy, divine afflatus, fertile imagination, mind's eye, trance, golden dream, contemplation, workings of the mind, depth of thought, inmost thoughts, self-communing, self-consultation, current of thought, invention, thoughtfulness.

REVERSAL, *n.* Revocation, repeal, annulment, nullification, voidance, abrogation, recantation, palinode, abjuration, renunciation, retraction, retractation, going over, defection, apostasy, disavowal, withdrawal, revokement, cancellation, repeal, rescission, dissolution, abolition, abolishment, repudiation, counterorder.

REVERSE, *v.* 1. Turn in an opposite direction, transpose, turn inside out, invert, turn upside down, turn topsy-turvy, turn end for end, subvert,

upset, overturn, upturn, capsize, overbalance, topple, *culbuter (Fr.),* overthrow, *bouleverser (Fr.),* introvert, invaginate, put the cart before the horse, turn the tables, turn turtle, tilt over.

2. Revoke, repeal, rescind, retract, recant, annul, nullify, vacate, cancel, withdraw, recall, abrogate, override, overrule, countermand, counterorder, set aside, disannul, invalidate, nol-pros *(Law),* quash, abolish, declare null and void, repudiate, disclaim, deny, contradict, controvert, contravene, disaffirm, gainsay, refute, negate, abjure, disavow, renounce, forswear, unmake, undo.

REVERSE, *n.* 1. Other side, converse, back, verso, rear, tail, opposite, contrary, counterpart, inverse, antithesis, antipodes, pole, *vis-à-vis (Fr.),* extremity, terminal point, turn of the tide.

2. Adverse change of fortune, calamity, misfortune, setback, adversity, mishap, mischance, misadventure, trial, infliction, ordeal, affliction, hardship, reversal, blow, defeat, check, upset, downfall, catastrophe, undoing, frowns of fortune, disaster, casualty, accident, visitation, sorrow, comedown, scourge, contretemps, failure, fiasco, crash, wreck, ruin, ruination, overthrow, losing game, gathering clouds, rainy day, hard times, ill wind, trouble, blight, curse, harm, evil, humiliation, collapse, deathblow, tragedy, rebuff, repulse, rout, beating, fizzle, frustration, nonsuccess, labor in vain, no go *(coll.),* vain attempt, washout, disappointment, buffet, fatal mischief.

REVERSE, *adj.* Turned backward, with the rear part toward one, verso, converse, inverse, opposite, antipodal, transposed, palindromical, hyperbatic, reversed, inverted, contrary, backward, counter, antithetic, polar, oppositive.

REVERSION, *n.* 1. Return, reverting, returning, revulsion, alternation, recurrence, rotation, recoil, inversion, reaction, reconversion, retrospection, restoration, relapse, repercussion, rebound, *contrecoup (Fr.),* boomerang, ricochet, backlash, turn of the tide, reverberation, reflux, repulse, reflex, retroaction, ebb, *volte-face (Fr.),* regress, retrogression, retrogradation, falling back.

2. Reapearance of ancestral characters, return to a primitive type, throwback, atavism, recidivism, resurgence, renaissance, renascence, regeneracy, revival, revivification, resuscitation, renewal.

3. Inheritance, succession, escheat, devisal, bequeathal, legacy, bequest, devise, assignment, conveyance.

REVERT, *v.* 1. Go back, turn back, return, reverse, hark back, recur, come back, recidivate, relapse, regress, retreat, recoil, backslide, retrograde, ebb.

2. Turn the scale, turn the tide, undo, unmake, turn back, put back.

REVIEW, *v.* Comment upon, notice critically, criticize, discuss in a critical review, analyze, write a critical report of, edit, revise, correct, inspect formally, retrace mentally, pass in review, look over again, reconsider, re-examine, go over again, survey officially, look back upon, view retrospectively, investigate, dissect, treat of a subject, interpret, explain, con over, study, digest, brood over, mull over, appreciate, weigh, sum up, recapitulate, summarize, restate briefly, reiterate, run over, skim, abstract, epitomize, note down.

REVIEW, *n.* 1. Critical article, critique, commentary, criticism, reviewal, appreciation, editorial, animadversion, discussion, dissertation, exposition, study, disquisition, investigation, discourse, tract, treatise, essay, theme, thesis.

2. Synopsis, résumé, analysis, digest, pandect, compendium, epitome, abstract, compend, précis, bulletin, brief, abridgment, condensation, reapitulation, abbreviation, summary, substance, extract, excerpt, syllabus, outline, contents, prospectus, heads, conspectus, aperçu, sketch, general survey, report, account.

3. Contemplation of past events, second view of, going over a subject again in order to fix it in the memory, revision, retrospection, re-examination, survey, retrospect, reconsideration, reflection, cogitation, rumination, speculation, meditation, lucubration, study, mentation, cerebration.

4. Formal examination, official, inspection, parade, pageant, spectacle, exhibition, demonstration, procession, turnout, field day, march past, promenade, gala day, fête, exposition, show, array, military display, cavalcade, file, caravan, cortège, column.

REVIEWER, *n.* Critic, commentator, essayist, student, publicist, editor, leader writer, scrutinizer, analyst, examiner, inquisitor, inspector, investigator, interpreter, expositor, expounder, explainer, demonstrator, exponent, annotator, scholiast, censor, arbiter, assessor, connoisseur, pamphleteer.

REVILE, *v.* Assail with contemptuous language, address abusively, speak ill of, vilify, vilipend, slander, defame, denigrate, disparage, anathematize, calumniate, vituperate, belittle, depreciate, condemn, blacken, decry, malign, asperse, execrate, reproach, traduce, backbite, abuse, upbraid, inveigh against, cry down, reflect upon, detract, rail at, lampoon, taunt, desecrate, censure, scoff at, sneer at, scandalize, contemn, despise, curse, swear at, libel, run down, blaspheme, profane, dispraise, discredit, knock (*colloq.*), satirize, call names, denounce, criticize, impugn, impeach, accuse, gibbet, brand, stigmatize, reprobate, reprehend, reprove, reprimand, chastise, castigate, flay, excoriate, lash, speak daggers, rate, objurgate, bespatter, clapperclaw, fulminate against, load with reproaches, lash with the tongue, thunder against.

REVILEMENT, *n.* Aspersion, vilification, calumniation, traducement, abuse, reproach, discommendation, obloquy, censure, detraction, depreciation, disparagement, condemnation, denunciation, animadversion, stricture, reflection, criticism, insinuation, innuendo, satire, reprehension, reprobation, reproof, increpation, castigation, diatribe, tirade, philippic, hue and cry, outcry, execration, upbraiding, exprobration, vituperation, objurgation, invective, contumely, bitter words, bad language, billingsgate, evil-speaking, desecration, profanity, blasphemy, sacrilege, sarcasm.

REVISE, *v.* Look over to correct errors, edit, retouch, improve, overhaul, make an up-to-date version of, bring up to date, emend, amend, alter, review, polish, re-examine, correct, doctor, make corrections, rectify, touch up, make improvements, improve upon.

REVISION, *n.* Correction, editing, amendment, emendation, recension, re-examination, revise, revisal, improvement, revised edition, new edition, renovation, *limae labor (Lat.),* overhauling, retouching, alternation, rectification, radical reform.

REVIVAL, *n.* 1. Revivification, rebirth, renascence, palingenesis, quickening, reawakening, resuscitation, reanimation, renewal, regeneration, restoration, resurrection, recovery, resurgence, recreation, rejuvenescence, regenesis, regeneracy, recruitment, recuperation, reclamation, convalescence, redintegration, *rifacimento (It.),* reviviscence, reëstablishment, reincarnation, phoenix, atavism, reappearance, renaissance.

2. Service to effect a religious awakening, camp meeting, revival meeting, prayer meeting.

3. Reproduction of an old play, restaging, new version.

REVIVALIST, *n.* One who holds religious revivals, evangelist, itinerant preacher, sky pilot, black coat, parson, clergyman, shepherd, pastor, minister, missioner, missionary, field preacher, propagandist.

REVIVE, *v.* 1. Restore to life *or* consciousness, bring back to life again, resuscitate, regenerate, revivify, reanimate, resurrect, rejuvenesce, recreate, reinspirit, reinvigorate, revitalize, rejuvenate, redintegrate, return to the original state, recall to life, reincarnate.

2. Refresh, rouse, animate, strengthen, invigorate, renew, quicken, recruit, recreate, renovate, awaken, inspire, animate, freshen, repair, encourage, comfort, cheer, stimulate, inspirit, stir up, infuse new life into, introduce new blood, give new life to, whet, sharpen, fan the flame, summon up, call up, impassion, perk up, recover from depression, rally.

3. Set going again, set in activity again, bring back into use, make operative again, reproduce, repeat, restage, remount.

REVOCATION, *n.* Annulment, nullification, repeal, retraction, recall, repudiation, abrogation, recantation, abjuration, reversal, abolition, rescission, withdrawal, taking back, cancellation, vacatur, defeasance, *nolle prosequi (Law),* counterorder, countermand, retractation, abolishment, invalidation, disavowal, revokement, dissolution, defection, negation, apostasy, palinode, renunciation, tergiversation, backsliding, recidivation, abnegation, denial, disclaimer, contravention, contradiction, recusation, recusancy.

REVOKE, *v.* 1. Recall what has been said, take back, retract, rescind, reverse, abrogate, abjure, recant, disenact, nullify, annul, vacate, cancel, declare null and void, repeal, withdraw, call back, renounce, repudiate, overrule, counterorder, countermand, negate, quash, abolish, override, overrule, set aside, disannul, dissolve, disclaim, do away with, sweep away, discard, dismiss, relinquish, back down, change sides, apostatize, forswear, unsay, eat one's words, back out of, think better of, own oneself in the wrong, be sorry for, repent, regret, rue, turn over a new leaf, go back on one's word.

2. (*Cards*) Fail to follow suit when one can, renege, break a rule of play.

REVOLT, *v.* 1. Renounce allegiance to, break away from constituted authority, rise up against, cast off subjection, to those in authority, rebel, mutiny, secede, desert, fall off, defect, violate, infringe, disobey, shirk, set at naught, defy, transgress, ignore, take the law into one's own hands, disregard, kick over the traces, run riot, bolt, refuse to support, strike, resist, rise in arms, hurl defiance at, throw down the gantlet, fly in the face of, *prendre le mors aux dents (Fr.),* not submit, repugn, reluctate, withstand, confront, grapple with, kick against, recalcitrate, oppose, lift the hand against, run restive, champ the bit, demur, dissent, differ in opinion, say no, disagree, protest, raise one's voice against, contradict, make bold to differ.

2. Affect with disgust, sicken, nauseate, repel, disgust, offend, go against, turn the stomach, set the teeth on edge, make one sick, stick in one's throat, go against the grain, appal, horrify, shock, make the flesh creep, make the blood curdle, distress, afflict, gripe, excite disapprobation, scandalize, do violence to.

3. Turn away in abhorrence, abominate, abhor, feel horror, detest, loathe, shrink from, recoil at, shudder at, execrate, view with horror, disrelish.

REVOLT, *n.* 1. Active resistance against civil authority, casting off of allegiance, vigorous outbreak, insurrection, rebellion, mutiny, secession, defection, sedition, desertion, change of sides, faithlessness, apostasy, tergiversation, disobedience, uprising, revolution, insurgency, insubordination, *bouleversement (Fr.)*, subversion, political upheaval, *coup d'état (Fr.)*, noncompliance, recalcitrance, infraction, violation, rising, tumult, riot, strike, sabotage, *émeute (Fr.)*, sit-down, lockout, defiance, *lèse-majesté (Fr.)*, war cry, *levée en masse (Fr.)*, *Jacquerie (Fr. Hist.)*, disorder, turnout, interdiction, boycott, antagonism, opposition, counteraction, counterplot, hostility, collision, strife, clash, discord, conflict, combat, noncompliance.

2. Aversion, disgust, disrelish, distaste, loathing, repugnance, repulsion, antipathy, dislike, abhorrence, detestation, execration, abomination, disinclination, reluctance, hatred, horror.

REVOLTING, *adj.* 1. Offensive, abhorrent, obnoxious, sickening, disgusting, objectionable, nauseous, nauseating, odious, abominable, execrable, loathsome, nasty, repulsive, repellent, vile, horrid, hateful, unpleasant, disagreeable, bitter, unpalatable, distasteful, shocking, grim, grisly, appalling, dreadful, frightful, fearful, dire, harrowing, horrific, fulsome, horrible, noisome, malodorous, stinking, mephitic, fetid, smelling, graveolent, rank, foul, rotten, putrid, strong-smelling, rancid, tainted, moldy, musty, gamy, noxious, filthy, unclean, dirty, grimy, slimy, reeky, beastly, gone bad, maggoty, putrescent, feculent, stercoraceous, excrementitious, rotting, peccant.

2. Mutinous, rebellious, seditious, insurgent, insurrectional, revolutionary, bolshevistic, riotous, lawless, anarchical, nihilistic, anarchistic, Red, dissentient, recusant, ungovernable, refractory, disobedient, unruly, insubordinate, restive, defiant.

REVOLUTION, *n.* 1. Rotation, circular motion, gyration, whirling, turning, single turn, circumvolution, revolving, course in circuit back to a starting point, whirl, round, cycle, twirl, roll, circulation, circuit, wheel, gyre, cyclic recurrence, circumgyration, circumrotation, turbination, convolution, whirligig, pirouette, reel, spin.

2. Overturn, overthrow, reversal, marked change, upset, upheaval, earthquake, cataclysm, eruption, explosion, throe, revulsion, convulsion, spasm, *bouleversement (Fr.)*.

3. Rebellion, uprising, revolt, insurgence, insurrection, mutiny, secession, defection, *coup d'état (Fr.)*, sedition, disorder, riot, outbreak, *émeute (Fr.)*, anarchy, nihilism, bolshevism, lawlessness, insubordination, tumult, turbulence, march away from the past, fundamental reconstruction, subversion, debacle, breakup, destruction, violation, infringement, sabotage, defiance, disruption, demolition, dissolution, disorganization, incendiarism.

REVOLUTIONARY, *adj.* 1. Subversive to established principles, rebellious, insurrectionary, mutinous, seditious, bolshevistic, Red, insurgent, riotous, lawless, anarchistic, nihilistic, restive, defiant, ungovernable, disobedient, unmanageable, insubordinate, refractory, recalcitrant, dissentient, subversionary, incendiary, annihilative, intransigent.

2. Extreme, advanced, ultra, progressive, forward, new-fangled, thoroughgoing, drastic, sweeping.

3. Revolving, rotary, rotatory, rotational, gyral, whirling, gyratory, circumvolutory.

REVOLUTIONIST, *n.* One who advocates revolution, participator in rebellion, rebel, mutineer, insurgent, insurrectionary, seditionist, secessionist, revolutionary, *frondeur (Fr.)*, traitor, subversive, fifth-columnist, Communist, Bolshevist, Bolshevik, malcontent, anarchist, nihilist, renegade, apostate, Sinn Feiner, rioter, *sans-culotte (Fr.)*, *carbonaro (It.)*, brawler, incendiary, dynamiter, firebrand, iconoclast, radical, attacker of cherished beliefs, reformer, progressive, *agent provocateur (Fr.)*, instigator.

REVOLUTIONIZE, *v.* Bring about a revolution in, effect a radical change in, charge fundamentally, break with the past, reform, recast, change the face of, reconstruct, refashion, remodel, reorganize, subvert, model anew, transform, alter, tamper with, work a change, innovate, turn over a new leaf, revamp, chop and change, change drastically.

REVOLVE, *v.* 1. Rotate, whirl, turn, gyrate, move in an orbit, turn round on an axis, move round a center, circulate, wheel, circumvolve, circle, swing, roll, spin, move in a curving course about a central point, encircle, swirl, trundle, twiddle, twist.

2. Come round in the process of time, return, devolve, recur, reoccur, occur again, intermit, alternate, reappear.

3. Think about, ruminate over, meditate, cerebrate, mentate, reflect upon, brood over, consider, study, ponder, speculate, con over, weigh, advise with one's pillow, run over in the mind, bethink oneself.

REVOLVING, *adj.* Moving round, circumrotary, rotatory, rotary, gyratory, gyrating, gyral, turning, whirling, rolling, revolutionary, trochilic, vortical, circumvolutory, Ixionian, cyclical, recurrent, periodical, cyclic, rhythmic, intermittent, alternate.

REVULSION, *n.* 1. Act of drawing something back or away, withdrawal, abstraction, shrinking, recoil, violent separation, retroaction, ricochet, rebound, recalcitration, repercussion, springing back, *contrecoup (Fr.)*, reflex, reverberation, repulse.

2. Sudden change of feeling, violent reaction in sentiment, antipathy, dislike, detestation, contempt, disgust, abhorrence, abomination, execration, distaste, disrelish, reluctance, repugnance, turn, queasiness, loathing, nausea, horror, animosity, aversion, *bête noire (Fr.)*.

REWARD, *v.* Compensate for achievement, requite for service, remunerate, recompense for merit, pay, indemnify, remember, gratify, repay, tip, fee, bribe, make amends, atone, redress, acknowledge, satisfy, square *(colloq.)*, grease the palm, suborn, shell out, hand out, contribute.

REWARD, *n.* 1. Compensation, recompense, remuneration, indemnification, guerdon, meed, indemnity, bonus, bounty, prize, reparation, quittance, acknowledgment, redress, amends, requital, consideration, *quid pro quo (Lat.)*, sop, return, recoupment, grant, windfall, remembrance.

2. Salary, wages, emolument, pay, stipend, payment, allowance, tribute, hire, fee, honorarium, premium, solatium, mileage, overtime, extra pay, time-and-a-half.

3. Gratuity, perquisite, tip, *Trinkgeld (Ger.)*, *pourboire (Fr.)*, douceur, baksheesh, donation, hush money, rake-off, bribe, graft, boodle, velvet *(slang)*, palm-grease *(slang)*, blackmail, largess, handout, peace offerings.

4. Condign desert, punishment, retribution, atonement, nemesis, vengeance, revenge, retaliation, penalty, pound of flesh, reprisal, counterstroke, counterblast, Roland for an Oliver, give and take, measure for measure, due, what's coming to one *(colloq.)*.

RHAPSODICAL, *adj.* Like a rhapsody, unconnected, irregular, disconnected, broken, rambling, confused, uneven, erratic, capricious, fitful, desultory, spasmodic, imaginary, romantic, fanciful, fantastic, whimsical, vaporous, dreamy, notional, visionary, illusory, extravagantly enthusiastic, ecstatic, effusive, flighty, quixotic, preposterous.

RHAPSODIST, *n.* 1. Reciter of epic poetry, bard, laureate, lyrist, troubadour, skald, minstrel, *improvisatore (It.)*, ballad monger, Meistersinger, minnesinger, jongleur.

2. Fanatic, enthusiast, visionary, seer, dreamer, crank, high-flier, *exalté (Fr.)*, eccentric, Don Quixote, knight errant, romanticist, idealist, romancer.

RHAPSODY, *n.* Composition irregular in form and suggestive of improvisation, exalted expression of feeling, rambling opus, fantasia, dithyramb, vagary, *romanza (It.)*, extravaganza, capricious composition, rapture, effusion, ecstasy.

RHETORIC, *n.* 1. Sience of literary uses of language, art of prose, compositional skill, art of using the figures of speech, figurativeness.

2. Art of influencing the thought and conduct of one's hearers, elocution, oratory, eloquence, diction, expression, allocution, delivery, recitation, discourse, harangue, exhortation, address, appeal, invocation, vocalization, enunciation, articulation, modulation, intonation.

3. Artificial eloquence, use of display, declamation, grandiloquence, multiloquence, oration, verbosity, polylogy, fluency, *flux de paroles (Fr.)*, *copia verborum (Lat.)*, gift of gab, altiloquence, orotundity, well-rounded periods, flowers of speech, flourish, euphuism, euphemism, macrology, *sesquipedalia verba (Lat.)*, sesquipedalianism.

RHETORICAL, *adj.* Concerned with oratorical style *or* effect, oratorical, elocutionary, eloquent, lingual, oral, declamatory, grandiloquent, acroamatic, Tullian, Ciceronian, Demosthenean, euphonious, sonorous, orotund, mellifluous, melodious, fluent, glib, silver-tongued, golden-voiced, polyloquent, multiloquent, episodic, periphrastic, exuberant, copious, verbose, florid, ornate, flowery, euphuistic, euphemistic, high-sounding, turgescent, pompous, high-flown, sententious, grandiose, magniloquent, altiloquent, sesquipedalian, fustian, bombastic, figurative, antithetical, alliterative, metaphorical, catachrestical, tralatitious, forensic, persuasive, highly wrought, canorous, deep-toned, mellisonant, ringing, resonant.

RHETORICIAN, *n.* 1. One versed in the art of rhetoric, proficient in rhetoric, adept in rhetoric, one given to display in language, elocutionist, Demosthenes, Cicero, Tullius, Hermes, spellbinder, prolocutor, speechmaker, public speaker, reciter, soliloquist, phrasemonger, euphuist, euphemist.

2. Public speaker, orator, declaimer, tubthumper, *improvisatore (It.)*, ranter, speechifier, spouter, gasbag *(slang)*, blatherskite.

RHYME, *n.* 1. Agreement in the terminal sounds of words, rime, jingle, doggerel.

2. Poesy, poetry, minstrelsy, song, verse, poetics, versification, Calliope, Muse, Parnassus, Pierian spring, Helicon, tuneful Nine, Pierides, afflatus, rune.

RHYMESTER, *n.* Maker of inferior verse, poetaster, versifier, versemonger, rhymist, rhymer, poeticule, poetling, poetizer, doggerel-writer, jingler, limerick-penner, troubadour, satirist, minstrel, jongleur, bard.

RHYTHM, *n.* Pattern of regular pulses caused by the recurrence of beats, movement with uniform recurrence of a beat, measured movement, periodical emphasis, regular movement, pulsation, cadence, harmonious flow, swing, lilt, measure, meter, numbers, orthometry, scansion, scanning, prosody, harmonious correlation, periodicity, numerosity, euphony, concinnity, well-rounded periods, the right word in the right place, symmetry, proportion, balance, strain, foot, accentuation, iambus, dactyl, spondee, trochee, anapest, pentameter, hexameter, Alexandrine.

RHYTHMIC, *adj.* Characterized by intermittent regularlity in movement, periodic in motion, rhythmical, measured, melodious, having a flowing rhythm, regular, pulsatile, pulsating, elegiac, iambic, dactylic, trochaic, spondaic, anapestic, Sapphic, Pindaric, Alcaic, Ionic, balanced, symmetrical, tripping, fluent.

RIB, *n.* 1. Long slender curved bone occurring in pairs and enclosing the thoracic cavity, supporting part, brace, arch, stay, shore, truss, skid, splint, arched member forming a support of a vault, structural member supporting the shape of something, curved members, primary vein *(Bot.)*, ridge, camber, stud, button, peg, jutty, trunnion, dome, cupola, beehive.

2. Wife squaw, helpmeet, helpmate, better half, alter ego, gray mare, good wife, old woman, battle axe *(humorous)*, wife of one's bosom.

RIBALD, *adj.* Offensive in language, scurrilous in speech, coarsely abusive, wantonly low, smutty, pornographic, obscene, crude, vile, base, lewd, filthy, gross, indecent, foul-mouthed, vulgar, raffish, lascivious, indecorous, licentious, indelicate, dirty, shameless, outrageous, insulting, scurrile, unseemly, opprobrious, uncouth, bestial, brutish, loose, obnoxious, rude, nasty, depraved, ungentlemanly, unladylike, sluttish, ignoble, contemptible, disreputable, impure, blackguardly, gutter, unrefined, disgraceful, discreditable, questionable, despicable, unbecoming, degrading, dedecorous, scandalous, unmentionable, infamous, shocking, unchaste, debauched, adulterous, Fescennine, dissolute, prurient, concupiscent, lickerish, lustful, carnal-minded, lecherous, salacious, erotic, libidinous, ruttish, voluptuous, immodest, risqué, suggestive, broad, bawdy, equivocal, fulsome, sensual, rakish, fast.

RIBALDRY, *n.* Obscenity, smuttiness, pornography, coarseness, smut, vile language, scurrility, billingsgate, lewdness, grossness, indecency, immodesty, impudicity, indelicacy, bawdry, *double-entendre (Fr.)*, Aretinism, carnality, sensuality, sexiness, filthiness, crudeness, vulgarity, raffishness, indecorum, license, shamelessness, unseemliness, opprobrium, uncouthness, bestiality, looseness, nasty-mindedness, depravity, impurity, infamy, unchastity, dissoluteness, pruriency, concupiscence, lustfulness, lechery, salacity, eroticism, libidinousness, suggestiveness, broadness, bawdiness, turpitude, blackguardism, rowdyism.

RIBBON, *n.* 1. Woven strip, band of fine material finished off at the edges, riband, filament, tie, fillet, fascia, band, tape, string.

2. Badge of an order of knighthood, sash, cordon, blue ribbon.

3. *(Pl.)* Tatters, shreds, ragged strips, cast-off clothes, odds and ends, shoddy, rags, orts, refuse, trash.

RICH, *adj.* 1. Abundantly supplied with funds, having great possessions, wealthy, pecunious, well-off, affluent, opulent, well-to-do, moneyed, flush, prosperous, dollared, well-heeled, rolling in riches, on easy street, independent, capitalistic, thriving, propertied, landed, flourishing, *nouveau riche (Fr.)*, purse-proud, swanky.

2. Plenteous, plentiful, copious, bountiful, ample, abundant, rife, profuse, lavish, prodigal, teeming, full, well-supplied, sufficient, chock-full, well-provided, replete, luxuriant, inexhaustible, unstinted, exhaustless, enough, to spare, bounteous, up to the mark, adequate, satisfactory, commensurate.

3. Fruitful, fertile, fecund, productive, prolific, exuberant, frugiferous, fructiferous, fruit-bearing, uberous, pregnant, multiparous, propagable.

4. Beautiful, elegant, gorgeous, superb, princely, embellished, ornate, florid, bejeweled, bedizened, splendid, precious, luxurious, sumptuous, costly, expensive, fine, valuable, highly valued, estimable, brilliant, sparkling, resplendent, dazzling, showy, magnificent, sublime, grand, imposing, majestic, aesthetic, artistic, ornamental, tesselated, inlaid, enameled, gilt, topiary, festooned, flowery, spangled, bedight, pranked out, well-groomed, flashy, gaudy, meretricious, garish, decorative, flamboyant.

5. Containing nutritious ingredients, finely flavored, fragrant, savory, luscious, delectable, delicious, mellow, spicy, fruity, toothsome, racy, gamy, pungent, piquant, highly seasoned, full-bodied, nutritive, odorous, aromatic, palatable, tasty, appetizing, ambrosial, nectareous.

6. Vivid, gay, bright, chromatic, polychromatic, intense, deep, dark, fresh, unfaded, glaring.

7. Melodious, canorous, sonorous, resonant, harmonious, symphonic, mellow, sweet, dulcet, orotund, soft, deep-toned, mellifluous, mellisonant, euphuistic, flowery, musical, tuneful, silvery, euphonious, euphonic.

8. Highly amusing, ridiculous, absurd, preposterous, derisible, diverting, entertaining, laughable, funny, comical, humorous, salty, waggish, witty, jocose, jocular, facetious, whimsical, ludicrous, droll, farcical, ironical.

RICHES, *n., pl.* Abundant possessions, wealth, fortune, affluence, opulence, money, treasure, property, means, gold, easy circumstances, independence, capital, mint of money, bonanza, Golconda, El Dorado, windfall, Pactolian sands, purse of Fortunatus, mammon, pelf, lucre, com-

mand of money, substance, resources, income, revenue, bank account, gilt-edged securities, assets, almighty dollars, money to burn, dough, spondulics, mazuma, jack, clinkers, wad, bucks, shekels, velvet, wampum, patrimony, heritage, inheritance, jointure, dowry, dot, legacy, bequest, endowment, belongings, estate, personal property, chattels, effects, goods, exchequer, bank, fiscus, strongbox, safe, coffer, money-box, till, cash register, purse, moneybag, wallet, pocketbook, securities, stocks and bonds, shares, abundance, plenitude, amplitude, profusion, full measure, cornucopia, surfeit, horn of Amalthaea, fat of the land, repletion, fill, profit, benefit, reward, prize, gain.

RICH MAN Plutocrat, millionaire, capitalist, moneyed man, Dives, Croesus, moneybags, man of substance, multimillionaire, billionaire, nabob, silk-stocking, banker, Plutus, Midas, profiteer, mogul, captain of industry, tycoon, bigshot *(slang)*, magnate, baron, self-made man, *nouveau riche (Fr.)*, bigwig, czar, grandee, lord, don, hidalgo, nobleman, patrician, great gun *(colloq.)*, kingpin, his nibs *(jocose)*, proprietor, owner, landlord, boss, autocrat, financier, man of means.

RICHNESS, *n.* 1. Copiousness, abundance, fulness, opulence, affluence, luxuriance, profusion, lavishness, repleteness, repletion, prodigality, sumptuousness, exuberance, plenty, horn of plenty, cornucopia, plenitude, plentifulness, bounty, bountifulness, amplitude, full measure, surfeit, fat of the land, satiety, fill, sufficiency, redundance.

2. Fertility, productiveness, fruitfulness, fecundity, uberty, prolificness, frugiferousness, fructiferousness.

3. Brightness, brilliancy, resplendence, splendor, showiness, magnificence, garishness, flamboyancy, gorgeousness, elegance, ornateness, floridness.

4. Melodiousness, sweetness, harmoniousness, sonority, resonance, orotundity, mellifluence, mellisonance, tunefulness.

RICK, *n.* Thatched stack, pile covered for protection, haystack, heap, hoard, crib, granary, garner, silo, bunker.

RICKETS, *n.* Childhood disease marked by softening of the bones, rachitis, inflammation of the spine, disease due to lack of vitamin D and insufficient ingestion of calcium, chronic changes in the osseous system.

RICKETY, *adj.* 1. Affected with the rickets, rachitic.

2. Liable to fall or collapse, feeble in the joints, infirm, tottering, decrepit, dilapidated, frail, tumbledown, ramshackle, shaky, approaching ruin, broken, shattered, insecure, weak, debilitated, enfeebled, unstrung, weakly, unsteady, helpless, fragile, lame, crazy, on its last legs, the worse for wear, deteriorated, unsound, sleazy, unsubstantial, gimcrack, jerry-built, brittle, frangible, wasted, withered, shattery, laid low, impotent, groggy.

RICOCHET, *v.* Rebound, recoil, bounce, bound, glance, skip, resile, react, reverberate, recalcitrate, repercuss.

RID, *v.* 1. Free of something objectionable, disencumber, disburden, unload, relieve of, disembarrass, get off one's hands, become free from, get rid of, clear, sweep out, scour, weed out, eject, drive away, abolish, dispose of, dispatch, remove by violence, make away with, destroy, extirpate, annihilate, deracinate, uproot, redeem, liberate, exterminate, eliminate, shake off, do away with, evacuate, purge, void, tap, draw off, drain, cast up, spew, vomit, disgorge.

2. Cut off, divorce, sever, dissever, disunite, sunder, separate, dissolve, repudiate, disinherit, desert, extricate.

RIDDANCE, *n.* Clearing away of anything undesirable, deliverance, relieving from, disencumberment, disembarrassment, extrication, relief, freedom, release, escape, freeing, liberation, rescue, redemption, emancipation, ransom, salvation, respite, reprieve, ejection, ejaculation, rejection, expulsion, dislodgment, removal, ouster, expedition, discharge, eruption, evacuation, drainage, eructation.

RIDDLE, *v.* 1. Propound riddles, speak enigmatically, oraculate, oracle, puzzle, perplex, pose, confuse, mystify, bewilder, nonplus, *spargere voces in vulgum ambiguas (Lat.).*

2. Pierce with many holes, perforate, empierce, bore, transpierce, puncture, pink, punch, stave in.

3. Separate fine matter from coarse with a riddle, sift, sieve, screen, winnow, pick, comb, weed, rack, refine, filter, strain.

RIDDLE, *n.* Dark saying, enigma, oracle, conundrum, puzzle, problem, poser, mystery, secret, arcanum, logograph, rebus, charade, *crux criticorum (Lat.),* puzzling question, inexplicable thing, sealed book, *le dessous des cartes (Fr.),* hard nut to crack, acrostic, crossword, labyrinth, maze, *terra incognita (Lat.),* paradox, ambiguity, obscurity, unintelligibility, doubtful meaning, spinosity, mystification, *dignus vindice nodus (Lat.),* steganography, unfathomableness, impenetrability, inscrutability, incomprehensibility, tangle, intricacy, cipher, cryptogram, code, cryptograph, dilemma, quandary, perplexity, entanglement, knotty point, hidden meaning, occult meaning, symbolism, anagoge.

RIDE, *v.* 1. Sit on and manage in motion, mount, bestride, perch, be carried on the back of, be borne along on, be supported by, rest on.

2. Move along, drive, vehiculate, go driving, take horse, trot, canter, amble, prance, gallop, scour the plain, race, bound, flit, scorch the ground, outstrip the wind, clap spurs to one's horse, dash off, bowl along, whiz, whisk, shoot, race, scurry, fly, spurt, post, scuttle, spank, sprint, hasten, hie, speed, traverse, motor, automobile, taxi, tour, travel, journey, take an airing.

3. Ride roughshod over, tyrannize over, dominate, control, hector, domineer, bulldoze, lord it over, beat down, browbeat, trample under foot, intimidate, terrorize, dragoon, harass, torment, vex, tease, badger, heckle, bully, annoy, persecute, molest, rag, irk, mortify, bother, plague, pester, harry, bait.

RIDE, *n.* 1. Drive, outing, airing, spin, excursion, journey, trip, tour, circuit, peregrination, trek, course, turn, wayfaring, expedition, gadding.

2. Horsemanship, equitation, *manège (Fr.),* riding.

RIDER, *n.* 1. Equestrian, horseman, horsewoman, equestrienne, jockey, roughrider, bareback rider, Cossack, cavalryman, breaker, whip, postilion.

2. Coachman, driver, reinsman, cabman, charioteer, Jehu, *cocher (Fr.), voiturier (Fr.),* cabby, hackman, wagoner, teamster, mahout, trainer, cameleer, muleteer, chauffeur, automobilist, motorist, traveler, excursionist, journeyer,

courier, Arab, nomad, postrider, dispatch rider, estafette.

3. Additional clause, codicil, corollary, amendment, addition, appendix, supplement, suffix, adjunct, affix, attachment, appendage, addendum, sequel.

RIDGE, *n.* 1. Rib, rim, seam, ripple, corrugation, crinkle, wrinkle, weal, ledge, whelk, welt, wale, streak, crimp, burr, bar, fret, stripe, carination, bulge, swell, protuberance, protrusion, projection, excrescency, gibbosity, outgrowth, tumor, intumescence, pimple, pustule, papule, wen, wart, blister, boil, hump, bunch, knob, boss, fillet, inion, ridgelet, hummock, keel, carina.

2. Narrow elevation of land, chine, hogback, saddle, esker, *arête (Fr.),* watershed, range, chain of hills, long crest, summit, back, upland, land bridge, reef, bank, hill, barrow, mound, knoll, butte, mount, highland, kopje, alp, bluff, cliff, peak, foreland, headland, promontory, rise, dune, brae, down, hillock.

RIDGED, *adj.* Furrowed, corded, ribbed, twilled, wrinkled, corrugated, ridgy, seamed, ripply, crinkled, welted, streaked, burred, crimped, barred, striped, fretted, carinated, protuberant, protrusive, excrescent, gibbous, intumescent, blistered, bunched, humped, bossed, knobbed, filleted, apical, cristate, crested, porcate, rangy, hilly, mountainous, Alpine.

RIDICULE, *v.* Assail with scornful laughter, deride, taunt, laugh at, make fun of, mock, make a monkey of, imitate insultingly, caricature, satirize, burlesque, parody, lampoon, make a butt of, make sport of, make game of, scoff at, sneer at, disparage, laugh to scorn, bemock, rally, jeer, scout, twit, gibe at, josh, guy, rag, roast, chaff, mimic, travesty, banter, hoot, hiss, vilify, vilipend, contemn, despise, harass, harry, belittle, depreciate, grin at, snicker, make merry with, haze, skit, cartoon, humiliate, cheapen, undervalue, treat with disrespect, detract from, call names, abuse, traduce, laugh in one's sleeve, poke fun at, joke, jolly, fleer, play tricks upon, fool to the top of one's bent, show up, have a fling at, tar and feather, toss in a blanket, snigger.

RIDICULE, *n.* Words *or* actions intended to excite contemptuous laughter, derision, burlesque, sneering mimicry, scornful imitation, mockery, gambol, travesty, parody, caricature, take-off, farce, ludicrous representation, satire, raillery, roasting, guying, irony, quip, squib, game, taunt, lampoon, sarcasm, chaff, banter, badinage, persiflage, skit, wit, jeer, gibe, poke, sneer, scorn, disparagement, snicker, grin, leer, horseplay, foolery, buffoonery, laughingstock, butt, monkey, sport, byword, joke, April fool, flout, disrespect, amusement, prank, antic, practical joke.

RIDICULOUS, *adj.* Such as to excite derision, ludicrous, derisible, risible, farcical, preposterous, laughable, comical, droll, waggish, funny, asinine, foolish, irrational, absurd, nonsensical, burlesque, amusing, extravagant, *outré (Fr.),* quixotic, chimerical, fabulous, fantastic, eccentric, outlandish, odd, queer, astonishing, destitute of reason, unreasonable, grotesque, satirical, sarcastic, ironical, mock, quizzical, bizarre, quaint, out-of-the-way, senseless, inconsistent, paradoxical, incongruous, incredible, without rime *or* reason, fatuous, idiotic, imbecile, inane, frivolous, diverting, entertaining, sidesplitting, jocose, festal, sportive, arch, roguish.

RIDOTTO, *n.* Social gathering in masquerade, bal masqué, *bal costumé (Fr.),* fancy dress ball, masquerade, Beaux Arts prom, fete, gala, festival, revel, carnival, Mardi Gras, *fête champêtre (Fr.)*, *fête galante (Fr.)*, saturnalia.

RIFE, *adj.* 1. Prevalent, current, prevailing, of frequent occurrence, common, general, widespread, universal, regular, pandemic, catholic, ecumenical, worldwide, wonted, ordinary, customary, accustomed, habitual, usual, dominant, rampant, regnant, predominant, far-reaching, cosmopolitan, extensive.

2. Abundant, plentiful, replete, abounding in, numerous, well supplied, rich, plenteous, teeming, multitudinous, alive with, outnumbering, thick, crowded, populous, profuse, studded, galore, many, divers, sundry, various, several, thick-set, serried, solid, swarming, close, dense, manifold.

RIFFRAFF, *n.* Disreputable element of society, dregs of the people, *faex populi (Lat.)*, lower classes, *profanum vulgus (Lat.)*, common herd, scum of society, *canaille (Fr.)*, rabble, roughscuff, the great unwashed, swinish multitude, the masses, trash, king mob, ragtag and bobtail, ruck, rank and file, proletariat, rout, chaff, horde, low persons.

RIFLE, *v.* Search and rob, strip bare of, plunder, ransack, pillage, despoil, rob, fleece, loot, sack, spoliate, forage, gut, pirate, maraud, poach, rustle, filch, appropriate, abstract, spirit away, run away with, make off with, shanghai, kidnap, abduct, carry off, pilfer, purloin, lift, thieve, bag, steal, pluck, skin.

RIFLE, *n.* Shoulder firearm, musket, carbine, blunderbuss, gun, shooting iron, flintlock, firelock, fowling-piece, *fusil (Fr.)*, shotgun, matchlock, caliver, musketoon, harquebus, breechloader, petronel, muzzle-loader, repeating rifle, magazine rifle.

RIFLEMAN, *n.* Musketeer, sharpshooter, marksman, *Freischütz (Ger.)*, carabineer, jaeger, fusileer, skirmisher, trooper, dragoon, chasseur, fowler, huntsman.

RIFT, *n.* Opening made by riving, crack, fissure, breach, cleft, slit, rent, break, fracture, gap, crevice, chink, aperture, interstice, cranny, split, flaw, hiatus, lacuna, chimney, puncture, hole, fault, cut, gash, cleavage, crevasse, chasm, abyss, canyon, pass, ravine, abysm, defile, *couloir (Fr.)*, gorge, notch, gully, gulf, gulch, clough.

RIG, *v.* 1. Dress in a fanciful manner, deck with clothes, accouter, clothe, attire, set out, bedizen, dight, bedight, invest, array, drape, enrobe, habilitate, garb, apparel, fit out, perk, dress up, trick out, prank, adorn, bedeck, spruce up, titivate, preen, dress up, bespangle, prink, garnish, trim, fig out, smarten, embellish, ornament, decorate, enrich.

2. Provide with equipment, furnish with gear, fit with tackling, harness, equip, caparison, fit out, fit up.

3. Manipulate fraudulently, speculate, deceive, fleece, swindle, peculate, embezzle, chouse, defraud, jockey, cheat, cozen, do, bilk, diddle, gyp, cully, double-cross, pluck, victimize, cog the dice, play with marked cards, live by one's wits, obtain money under false pretenses, juggle, rook, pigeon, skin.

RIG, *n.* 1. Oddly fanciful dress, peculiar costume, conspicuous garb, getup, raiment, attire, apparel, drapery, clothing, guise, toilette, habiliment, trim, vesture, palliament, garment, livery, wardrobe, array, best bib and tucker, finery, garniture, trous-

seau, outfit, uniform, harness, gear, caparison, accouterment, turnout, trappings, togs.

2. Frolic, sportive trick, gambol, prank, romp, lark, antic, skylarking, spree, monkeyshine, vagary, escapade, *espièglerie (Fr.)*, practical joke, *gambade (Fr.)*.

RIGGING, *n.* Ropes of a ship, gear, tackle, equipment, paraphernalia, apparatus, tackling, trice, appliances, trappings, fittings, harness, accouterments, equipage, appointments.

RIGHT, *v.* 1. Set upright, restore to the proper position, make straight, straighten, rectify, put straight, plumb, put in order, set right, rule, regulate, adjust, correct, square, true, make true, set, fix.

2. Do right, make restitution, vindicate, recompense, do justice to, see righted, relieve from wrong, see justice done, see fair play, give every one his due, hold the scales even, *audire alteram partem (Lat.)*, redress, keep one's promise, redeem one's pledge, discharge an obligation, do one's duty.

RIGHT, *adj.* 1. Rectilinear, direct, not crooked, straight, right-lined, lineal, linear.

2. *(Not left)* Dextrous, dextral, dexter, dextrorse, right-hand.

3. Having the axis perpendicular to the base, erect, upright, plumb, not oblique, perpendicular.

4. Not wrong, correct, unerring, accurate, perfect, inerrable, infallible, strict, unmistaken, regular, inerrant, valid, admissible, allowable, warrantable, definite, truthful, regular, relevant, pertinent, veracious, not erroneous, exact, free from error, factual, sound, sane, normal, rational, satisfactory, well, rigorous, literal, textual, scientific, mathematical, rigid, severe, well-defined, concrete.

5. Righteous, just, equitable, square, honest, reasonable, true, upright, good, equable, equal, fair, genuine, even-handed, legitimate, rightful, legal, lawful, justifiable, in accordance with duty, unswerving, punctilious, honorable, scrupulous, meticulous, ethical, aboveboard, fair and square, moral, religious, sacrosanct, inviolable, prescriptive, orthodox, virtuous, morally excellent, right-minded, whole-souled, duteous, exemplary.

6. Suitable, fit, becoming, meet, proper, seemly, *comme il faut (Fr.)*, decorous, appropriate, fitting, as it should be, orderly, well-performed, well-regulated, well-done, in good order, due, creditable.

7. Favorable, auspicious, propitious, advantageous, desirable, fortunate, convenient, preferable, well-advised.

8. Actual, real, authentic, unquestionable, sterling, irrefutable, undisputed, clear-cut, precise, axiomatic, incontestable, irrefragable, Simon-pure, undisguised, unvarnished, true-blue, pure, unimpeachable, realistic, certain.

RIGHT, *adv.* 1. Toward the right hand, to the right, dextrally, dextrously.

2. Directly, in a direct line, in a straight line, straightforwardly, straightly, lineally, in a beeline, point-blank, in a direct course, as the crow flies, straight as an arrow, full tilt at.

3. Immediately, forthwith, presto, at once, pronto, straightaway, straightway, now, instantly, forthright, in less than no time, subito, at a stroke, in a trice, eftsoons, plump, slap, at one fell swoop, on the spot, slap dash, on the spur of the moment, at sight, summarily, apace, presently, in no time.

4. Truly, actually, exactly, really, precisely,

unquestionably, irrefutably, incontestably, irrefragably, unimpeachably, to a nicety, to a T, to a turn, *ad unguem (Lat.),* accurately, verbatim, word for word, *mot à mot (Fr.), totidem verbis (Lat.).*

5. Righteously, uprightly, rightfully, rightly, fairly, equitably, lawfully, legitimately, justly, in justice, *à bon droit (Fr.),* upon even terms, in reason, without distinction of persons, by right, *de jure (Lat.),* on the level, on the square, on the up-and-up, in good faith, in all honor, by fair means, with clean hands.

6. Fitly, properly, fittingly, suitably, correctly, appropriately, decorously, dutifully, meetly, seemly, duly.

7. Extremely, very, in great degree, completely, quite, totally, entirely.

RIGHT, *n.* 1. What should be, what ought to be, integrity, uprightness, rectitude, probity, morality, propriety, fitness, goodness, virtue, straight course, honor, morals, moral excellence, nobleness, goodness, good behavior, welldoing, good actions, duty, merit, worth, desert, worthiness, faith, accountability, allegiance, loyalty, fealty, principle, trustworthiness.

2. Justice, equity, fairness, legality, lawfulness, square deal, fair play, justness, impartiality, equitableness, fair treatment, *summum jus (Lat.),* scales of justice, strict law, *suum cuique (Lat.),* to each his own, even-handed justice, fair field and no favor, Rhadamanthus, Themis, Nemesis, Astraea, Dike.

3. Prerogative, privilege, license, exemption, immunity, advantage, power, grant, liberty, legal power, authority, due, legal title, just claim, deed, ownership, droit *(Law),* justification, birthright, inheritance, interest, heritage, franchise, property, jointure, tenure, domain, proprietorship, patent, charter, faculty, liberty, jurisdiction, authorization, sanction, permission, warrant.

4. Right side, starboard, decanal side, recto, right-hand-division, offside, dexter.

5. *(Polit.)* Conservatives, reactionaries, diehards, Tories.

RIGHTEOUS, *adj.* 1. Pious, godly, God-fearing, devout, religious, reverent, holy, heavenly-minded, spiritual, pietistic, saintly, solemn, seraphic, converted, consecrated, pure in heart, sacred, believing, sanctified, regenerated, angelic, noble, virtuous, incorrupt, good, moral, honest, innocent, whole-souled, sterling, chaste, unsullied.

2. Just, equitable, upright, rightful, fair, right, lawful, justifiable, charitable, philanthropic, well-intentioned, trustworthy, exemplary, meritorious, laudable, deserving, commendable, praiseworthy, dutiful, worthy, reputable, honorable, right-living, goody-goody *(coll.).*

RIGHTEOUSNESS, *n.* 1. Piety, sanctity, godliness, saintliness, holiness, religion, theism, faith, religiousness, sanctimony, reverence, veneration, devotion, grace, consecration, devoutness, inspiration, purity, innocence.

2. Rectitude of conduct, morality, virtuousness, virtue, purity, goodness, acting from principle, uprightness, honesty, rightfulness, integrity, practice of right, equity, justice, faithfulness, duty, justness, cardinal virtues, well-spent life, good faith, *bona fides (Lat.),* incorruptibility, probity, nobleness, honor.

RIGHTFUL, *adj.* Having a just claim, having a right, legal, legitimate, licit, lawful, equitable, due, fair, true, honest, proper, merited, deserved, right,

correct, reasonable, meet, suitable, appropriate, fitting, square, creditable, befitting, seemly, becoming, allowable, legalized, allowed, warranted, sanctioned, authorized, constitutional, prescriptive, privileged, ordained, enfranchised, chartered, sacrosanct, inviolable, inalienable, presumptive, authoritative, sound, valid, according to law, statutory, vested.

RIGID, *adj.* 1. Stiff, hard, unpliant, inflexible, firm, unyielding, unbending, stiffened, implastic, taut, tense, stony, adamantine, flinty, rocky, sclerotic, bony, horny, indurate, stark, brassy, steely, callous, cartilaginous, tough, resistant, inelastic.

2. Conventional, hidebound, strait-laced, puritanical, Procrustean, orthodox, formal, cut-and-dried, uncompromising, academic, canonical, Draconian, starched, ascetic, Spartan, grim, set, stringent, fixed, dour, relentless, inexorable, obdurate, arbitrary, exacting, wooden, peremptory, sharp, stern, austere, harsh, unmitigated, unrelenting, stubborn, dictatorial.

3. Exact, precise, definite, well-defined, severe, strict, clear-cut, rigorous, scientific, mathematical, meticulous, punctilious, literal.

RIGMAROLE, *n.* Succession of confused *or* foolish statements, incoherent discourse, rambling talk, jargon, balderdash, gibberish, verbiage, palaver, twaddle, trash, flummery, nonsense, bosh, amphigory, jabber, hocus-pocus, rant, fustian, patter, babble, *baragouin (Fr.),* inanity, *bavardage (Fr.), niaiserie (Fr.),* rodomontade, fudge, stuff and nonsense, drivel, rubbish, tommyrot, flapdoodle, moonshine, fiddle-faddle, verbosity.

RIGOR, *n.* 1. Chilliness, horripilation, gooseflesh, chattering of teeth, chilblain, frostbite, shivering, algidity, algor, inclemency, gelidity, frigidity, cold.

2. Hardness, rigidity, stiffness, rigidness, inflexibility, renitence, durity, callosity, induration, petrifaction, cornification, ossification, vitrification, lapidification, lapidescence.

3. Severity, harshness, asperity, austerity, sternness, stringency, strictness, tyranny, despotism, absolutism, dictatorship, domineering, autocracy, oppression, coercion, hard measure.

4. Mathematical precision, punctilio, exactitude, accuracy, exactness, meticulousness, nicety, scrupulousness, carefulness, care, conscientiousness.

RIGOROUS, *adj.* 1. Inclement, bitter, biting, chilly, frigid, gelid, algid, cold, bleak, keen, raw, cutting, niveous, piercing, nipping, pinching, shivering, frostbitten, frostbound, glacial, icy, freezing, frosty, brumal, wintry, boreal, hibernal, polar, arctic, antarctic, hyemal, Siberian, hyperboreal, icebound.

2. Rigid, firm, stiff, hard, stark, unyielding, unbending, implastic, inelastic, inflexible, tense, taut, indurate, adamantine, adamantean, stony, concrete, lithic, vitreous, rocky, granitic, corneous, horny, osseous, bony, cartilaginous.

3. Austere, severe, stringent, strict, stern, harsh, ascetic, puritanic, Spartan, Draconian, strait-laced, prudish, relentless, obdurate, inexorable, *exigeant (Fr.),* exacting, uncompromising, intransigent, dour, iron-handed, unsparing, peremptory, hardheaded, despotic, tyrannical, grinding, oppressive, cruel.

4. Revengeful, vindictive, vengeful, resentful, revenging, rancorous, ruthless, pitiless, retaliative, avenging, unforgiving, unrelenting, implacable, inexorable, remorseless, stony-hearted.

5. Severely exact, rigidly accurate, scrupulously nice, meticulous, punctilious, precise, definite, well-defined, close, correct, literal, scrupulous, scientific, mathematical, unerring, particular, curious, careful, delicate, fine.

RILE, *v.* Disturb the temper of, annoy, anger, vex, irritate, offend, pique, nettle, exacerbate, exasperate, disquiet, discompose, displease, incommode, discommode, plague, cross, thwart, harry, harass, beset, badger, infest, importune, persecute, harrow, sting, provoke, try the patience, fret, gall, chafe, wound, affront, aggrieve, ruffle, enrage, sour the temper, give umbrage, affront, huff, stir up bile, incense, inflame, aggravate, embitter, envenom, infuriate, put out of humor, raise one's dander, madden, throw into a ferment.

RILL, *n.* Small brook, rillet, rivulet, runnel, streamlet, stream, brooklet, creek, run, burn (*Scot.*), gill, sike, beck, reach.

RIM, *n.* Outer edge, circular part of a wheel furthest from the axle, boundary of a circular *or* curved area, border, margin, brim, brink, verge, flange, ring, curb, girdle, confine, skirt, hem, brow, frame, side, ledge, lip, mouth, sill threshold, shore, coast, strand, foreshore, waterside, bank, fringe, fimbriation, selvage, welt, beach.

RIME, *n.* 1. Rough icy covering formed from fog *or* vapor-bearing air, hoarfrost, congealed dew, frost icicle, sleet, ice, snow.

2. Crack, chink, interstice, cleft, crevice, cranny, chap, fissure, flaw, slit, rift, scissure, slot, gash, breach, fracture, rent, leak, cut, lacuna.

RIND, *n.* Thick outer coat firm covering, integument, coating, skin, husk, bark, shell, peel, hull, crust, incrustation, incrustment, efflorescence, cortex, casing, involucrum, sheath, pod, capsule, ocrea, slough.

RING, *v.* 1. Surround with a ring, encircle, circle, enclose, girdle, environ, encompass, ensphere, loop, gird, engrid, hem in, circumscribe, beset, beleaguer, blockade, invest, besiege, circumvent, embrace.

2. Give forth a clear resonant sound when set in sudden vibration, sound loudly, resound, keep sounding, tingle, jingle, clang, peal, tintinnabulate, chime, knell, toil, reverberate, tinkle, re-echo, vibrate, clink, chink, fill the air, sing, ding, ding-dong, jangle, twang.

3. Announce, proclaim, make known, hymn, sing, call, cry, herald, broadcast, honor, celebrate, commemorate, signalize, usher in.

RING, *n.* 1. Circular band, circle, circlet, hoop, annulet, whorl, round, girdle, annulus, annulation, eyelet, loop, grommet, ringlet, orb, crown, halo, aureole, nimbus, disc, circuit, zonule, cordon, baldric, cincture, cestus, garland, wreath, coronet, crown, chaplet, collar, necklace, armlet, bracelet, anklet, noose, coil, ferrule, torque.

2. Arena, prize ring, lists, enclosed area in which some sport takes place, racecourse, racing-ground, hippodrome, circus, amphitheater, gymnasium, mat, field, platform, scene of action, track, corso, stadium, turf, cockpit, bear garden, palestra, tilting ground, rodeo, gridiron.

3. Group of persons, co-operating for illicit purposes, clique, cabal, gang, faction, set, machine, coterie, junto, combine, combination, confederacy, league, party, camarilla, knot, push, syndicate, coalition, alliance, federation, confederation, *Bund* (*Ger.*), *Verein* (*Ger.*), tong (*Chinese*), merger, trust, fraternity, fraternal order, sodality,

brotherhood, community, crew, team, side, clan.

4. Chime, bell-note, clang, clangor, tintinnabulation, peal of bells, ringing, tinkle, resonance, reverberation, echo, re-echo, din, vibration.

RINGLEADER, *n.* 1. Director, chief, leader, conductor, precentor, fugleman, bellwether, corypheus, guiding star, adviser, guide, helmsman, pilot, steersman, man at the wheel, wirepuller, headman, speaker, principal, spokesman, agitator, demagogue, mouthpiece, shepherd, governor, manager, supervisor, superintendent, overseer, foreman, master.

2. Rebel, insurgent, revolter, mutineer, rioter, *carbonaro* (*It.*), *sans-culotte* (*Fr.*), brawler, seceder, anarchist, bolshevist, bolshevik, insurrectionist, secessionist, traitor, apostate, recidivist, protestor, protestant, separatist, schismatic, sectarian, recreant, heretic, turncoat, tergiversator, bolter, rat, mugwump, turntail, runagate, renegade, reactionary, striker, scab (*sl.*), factionist, recusant, cultist, disaffectionist, repudiator, abjurant, deviationist, diversionist.

RINGLET, *n.* 1. Small ring, circlet, annulet, annulus, clasp, areola, hoop, roundlet, eyelet, loop.

2. Curled lock of hair, curl, lovelock, tuft, tussock, fringe, plume, tress.

RINSE, *v.* Put through clean water, wash lightly, lave, cleanse, wring, mundify, sponge, swab, scrub, flush, full, wipe, shampoo, launder, absterge, deterge, purify, clear, depurate, remove impurities, lixiviate, elutriate, edulcorate, filter, filtrate, strain.

RIOT, *v.* 1. Take part in a disorderly public outbreak, raise an uproar, be seditious, run riot, run amuck, rebel, revolt, kick over the traces, take the law into one's own hands, transgress, set at defiance, defy, violate, disobey, rise up against, resist, strike, rise in arms, mutiny, secede, fling down th gantlet, die hard, stand at bay, pit against, protest against, object, obstruct, oppugn, gainsay, resist, withstand, counteract, oppose, rampage, run high, be violent, break the peace, kick up a row, storm, rage, ride roughshod, bear down, clash, jostle, jar, pull different ways, conflict, declare war, join issue, sow dissension, recalcitrate, present a front, grapple with, reluctate, repugn, fly in the face of, bolt.

2. Live in a loose *or* wanton manner, indulge in unrestrained revelry, carouse, revel, luxuriate, sow one's wild oats, paint the town red, be intemperate, be excessive, live high, wallow in, plunge into dissipation, rake, live hard, slake one's thirst, swill.

RIOT, *n.* 1. Rebellion, revolt, mutiny, secession, sedition, insurrection, strike, sit-down (*coll.*), lockout (*coll.*), outbreak, uprising, sabotage, high treason, *lèse-majesté* (*Fr.*), revolution, defection, insurgence.

2. Violent disorder, breach of the peace, public disturbance, tumult, strife, uproar, commotion, brawl, row, broil, Donnybrook, rumpus, hubbub, turbulence, pandemonium, melee, affray, fray, scrimmage, rampage, squabble, altercation, quarrel, shindy, imbroglio, outburst, lawlessness, din, noise, racket, wild confusion, turmoil, violence, ferment, bustle, trouble, convulsion, fracas, bear garden, bedlam, babel, brute force, excitement, ebullition, boisterousness, bluster, tumultuousness.

3. Merrymaking, wild festivity, excess, revel, orgy, bacchanal, saturnalia, debauchery, unrestrained revelry, wanton living, dissipation, licentiousness, crapulence, carousal, jollification,

debauch, wassail, drinking bout, spree, high living, indulgence.

4. Brilliant display, *étalage (Fr.)*, show, exhibition, flourish, parade, array, splash, glitter, splendor, magnificence, spectacle, pageantry.

RIOTER, *n.* 1. Brawler, rebel, *frondeur (Fr.)*, insurgent, mutineer, revolter, *sans-culotte (Fr.)*, *carbonaro (It.)*, demagogue, firebrand, anarchist, instigator, ringleader, incendiary, *agent provocateur (Fr.)*, bolshevik, bolshevist, communist, traitor.

2. Reveler, roisterer, carouser, dissipator, fornicator, lecher, satyr, rake, roué, reprobate, *vaurien (Fr.)*, ne'er-do-well, *âme damnée (Fr.)*, loose fish, prodigal, libertine, sensualist, hedonist, hard liver, belly-god, drunkard, toper, sot, tippler, winebibber, soak, lovepot, tosspot, devotee of Bacchus, debauchee, rip, rakehell, wastrel, spendthrift, squanderer, playboy, losel.

RIOTOUS, *adj.* 1. Turbulent, tumultuous, tumultuary, violent, disorderly, unruly, ungovernable, refractory, restive, recalcitrant, recusant, lawless, insubordinate, disobedient, mutinous, seditious, rebellious, insurgent, insurrectionary, revolutionary, rampant, troublous, uproarious, boisterous, obstreperous, unquiet, noisy, agitated, rowdy, unmanageable, defiant, contumacious, dissentient, anarchical, anarchistic, nihilistic, Bolshevistic, Red.

2. Given to unrestrained revelry, wanton, reveling, loose, fast, gay, wild, licentious, dissolute, dissipated, crapulent, bacchic, saturnalian, orgiastic, self-indulgent, sensual, luxurious, voluptuous, rakish, debauched, bestial, piggish, swinish, porcine, inebrious, temulent, elevated, merry, boozy, flushed, plastered, sozzled, potvaliant, potulent, primed, lushy, bibacious, drunken, sottish, bibulous, hedonistic, libertine, rampant, lascivious.

RIP, *v.* Tear apart roughly, tear open, split, rend, cut vigorously, slash, slit, rive, lacerate, burst, sever, rupture, wrench, gash, hack, gore, stave in, lay open, riddle, puncture, stab, split, spear, spike, impale, transpierce, punch, prick, trepan, lance.

RIP, *n.* 1. Rent made by ripping, tear, laceration, slash, slit, split, fracture, severance, cleavage, rupture, fissure, rift, breach, cut, cleft, incision.

2. Dissolute fellow, rake, roué, libertine, debauchee, dissipater, voluptuary, loose fish, fast man, rakehell, fornicator, seducer, satyr, lecher, whoremonger, goat, Lothario, adulterer, *paillard (Fr.)*, reprobate, ne'er-do-well, *vaurien (Fr.)*, *âme damnée (Fr.)*, blacksheep, *mauvais sujet (Fr.)*, prodigal, wastrel.

RIPE, *adj.* 1. Complete in natural growth, mature, grown, mellow, full-blown, golden, ruddy, soft, edible, advanced, seasoned, ready for reaping, pucka *(East Indian)*, adult, full-grown, fully developed, arrived at the stage most fit for use.

2. Fully prepared, ready to do something, fit, primed, experienced, practiced.

3. Finished, consummate, perfected, perfect, complete, accomplished, ideal, elaborate, highly wrought.

RIPEN, *v.* Mature, fructify, mellow, bear fruit, enrich, fatten, become full-blown, maturate, come to perfection, improve, season, culminate, come to a head, consummate, elaborate, complete, perfect, finish, crown, accomplish, perfectionate.

RIPOSTE, *n.* 1. *(Fencing)* Quick thrust given after parrying a lunge, counterattack, swift retaliation, sharp return.

2. Incisive retort, quick reply, response, answer, replication, rejoinder, rebutter, surrejoinder, surrebutter, repartee.

RIPPLE, *v.* 1. Form small waves on the surface, flow with a slight ruffling of the surface, be lightly agitated, lap, play, ruffle, quiver, quaver, shake, toss about, purl, gurgle, babble, murmur, bubble, guggle, spurt, spirtle, trill, swash, splash, meander, surge, swirl, plash.

2. Give a wavy form to, crisp, undulate, dimple, fret, curl, crumple, crinkle, rumple, crimp.

RIPPLE, *n.* 1. Little wave, wavelet, undulation, rimple, ruffling of water, ripplet, fretting, surge, billow, comber, riffle, heave, breaker, whitecap, surf.

2. Purl, gurgle, murmur, lap of waves, babble, plash, wash, swash, splash.

RISE, *v.* 1. Arise, mount, ascend, levitate, go up, take off, climb, clamber, move upward, scale, scan, work one's way up, swarm, shin *(coll.)*, scrabble, scramble, escalade, surmount, go aloft, transcend.

2. Soar, tower, spire, surge, overtop, spring up, protuberate, extend directly upward, slope upward, rear, uprise, stand.

3. Start, begin, originate, have source, proceed, issue, spring up, grow, flow from, emanate, head, appear, come forth, come into existence, exsurge, occur, happen, come up, commence, set in, dawn, enter upon, take rise, crop up, initiate, inaugurate, open, institute, usher in, forerun, take the lead.

4. Increase, enlarge, swell, become greater, thrive, prosper, improve, flourish, heighten, excel, succeed, be successful, rise in the world, turn out well, flower, blossom, bear fruit, bloom, get on.

5. Become active in opposition, become hostile, go to war, take up arms, rebel, insurrectionize, revolt, mutiny, secede, resist, break forth, strike, upheave, defy, run riot, take the law into one's own hands, kick over the traces, bolt, refuse to support, fly in the face of, disobey.

RISE, *n.* 1. Ascension, ascent, grade, slope, hill, acclivity, rising ground, elevation, hillock, elevated place, knoll, ramp, upgrade, gradient, climb, pitch, inclined plane, bank, glacis, eminence.

2. Advance, increase, expansion, gain, addition, augmentation, progression, advancement, progress, onward motion, ongoing, headway, development, improvement, growth, march, enlargement, extension, accession, spread, increment, accumulation, accretion, intensification, aggrandizement, inflation, enhancement, multiplication, propagation, proliferation, production, begetting, reproduction, breeding.

3. Source, origin, cause, spring, fountainhead, commencement, beginning, starting point, start, incipience, outset, inception, opening, dawn, prelude, introduction, overture, *Vorspiel (Ger.)*, prologue, prolegomena, preface, preamble, foreword, inauguration, debut, coming out *(coll.)*, exordium, onset, outbreak, first move, new departure, germ, bud, embryo, egg, genesis, rudiment, nativity, birth.

RISIBLE, *adj.* Capable of exciting laughter, droll, laughable, farcical, ludicrous, ridiculous, funny, amusing, comical, salty, waggish, comic, grotesque, *pour rire (Fr.)*, burlesque, absurd, extravagant, fanciful, whimsical, preposterous, mock heroic, derisive, derisory.

RISING, *n.* 1. Height, ascent, slope, acclivity,

eminence, elevation, hill, monticle, butte, slant, obliquity, inclination, incline, ramp, tilt, rise, gradient, grade, bank, glacis, knoll, hillock, hummock, mound, bluff, vantage ground, tor, levee, clough, craig, peak, pike, escarpment, brae, dune, hog's back, moor, down, upland, foreland, headland, promontory, cape.

2. Stairs, staircase, stair, stairway, flight of stairs, flight of steps, elevator, escalator, lift, companionway, ladder.

3. Progress, advancement, advance, progression, ongoing, headway, flood tide, onward march, promotion, increase, elevation.

4. Rebellion, mutiny, revolt, insurgence, insurrection, uprising, sedition, secession, outbreak, *Putsch (Ger.), émeute (Fr.),* tumult, riot, strike, lockout, sitdown, barring out, defiance, resistance, renitence, reluctation.

RISK, *v.* Expose to the chance of injury *or* loss, endanger, hazard, peril, jeopardize, put to hazard, put in jeopardy, put in peril, imperil, venture, adventure, dare, stake, wager, bet, run one's chance, walk a tightrope, take one's chance, try one's luck, speculate, gamble, take a flyer, tempt providence, fly in the face of fate, chance, leap in the dark, dance on the edge of a precipice, try, have a fling at, undertake, run the gantlet, sail too near the wind, compromise, toss up, draw for, go it blind, plunge, invest, sink, intrust, put into a lottery, raffle, buy a pig in a poke, shuffle the cards, stand the hazard of the die, put one's head in the lion's mouth.

RISK, *n.* Dangerous chance, venture, hazard, danger, peril, jeopardy, imperilment, insecurity, instability, endangerment, precariousness, vulnerability, exposure, Achilles' heel, breakers ahead, hairbreadth escape, clouds gathering, storm brewing, clouds on the horizon, uncertainty, gamble, tossup, throw of the dice, even chance, heads or tails, stake, wager, wheel of fortune, speculation, bet, *pari mutuel (Fr.),* flyer, plunge, gambling, gaming, game of chance, lottery, sweepstakes, drawing lots, pool, fluke, random, shot, blind bargain, leap in the dark, pig in a poke.

RISKY, *adj.* Involving risk, dangerous, hazardous, precarious, perilous, fraught with danger, venturesome, unsafe, insecure, jeopardous, daring, daredevil, parlous, exposed, vulnerable, dubious, uncertain, at stake, under fire, critical, slippery, ticklish, shaky, top-heavy, helpless, nodding to its fall, trembling in the balance, between two fires, between the devil and the deep blue sea, between the frying pan and the fire, between Scylla and Charybdis, ominous, threatening, menacing, alarming, black, dire, dark, sinister, lowering illomened, minatory.

RISQUE, *adj.* Daringly close to impropriety, suggestive, indelicate, off-color, lascivious, shameless, improper, vulgar, smutty, pornographic, Fescennine, dirty, lewd, immodest, obscene, coarse, indecent, ribald gross, filthy, vile, immoral, licentious, lustful, libidinous, lecherous, salacious, concupiscent, sensual, Paphian, dissolute, incontinent, offensive, indecorous, nastyminded, broad, equivocal, free, fulsome, bawdy, erotic.

RITE, *n.* 1. Formal act prescribed in religious use, ceremonial procedure, observance, solemnity, ceremony, sacrament, form, function, duty, ritual, ordinance, ceremonial formulary, usage, rubric, service, office, ministration, worship, liturgy,

ministry, hieurgy, devotion, adoration, invocation, prayer, orison, confessional, remission of sins, absolution, bead-telling, rosary, asperges, aspersion, incense, thurification, supplication, petition, homage, cult, vow, rogation, collect, litany, miserere, compline, oblation, sacrifice, libation, collect, offertory.

2. Christening, baptism, chrism, immersion, font, baptismal, regeneration, laying on of hands, confirmation, Lord's Supper, Eucharist, Holy Communion, Mass, celebration, the sacrament, bread and wine, consecrated elements, impanation, intinction, transubstantiation, penitential acts, penance, fasting, flagellation, hair shirt, castigation, sackcloth and ashes, maceration, last rites, extreme unction, viaticum, holy orders, consecration, ordination, marriage, matrimony, wedlock.

RITUAL, *n.* Observance of set forms in public worship, formulary of worship, liturgy, rubric, manual, ordinal, breviary, canon, missal, Mass book, litany, beadroll, Book of Common Prayer, psalm book, psalter, hymnal, hierurgy.

RITUALISTIC, *adj.* 1. Ceremonial, ritual, formal, hierurgical, liturgical, solemn, Anglican, High Church, religious, holy, reverent, fervent, prayerful, spiritual-minded, pious, devout.

2. Prostrate before, worshiping, idolatrous, idolistic, fetishistic, chthonian.

RIVAL, *n.* One who is in pursuit of the same object as another, one in a position to dispute pre-eminence *or* superiority, competitor, emulator, opponent, antagonist, contestant, adversary, disputant, controversialist, oppositionist, obstructionist, aspirant, candidate, entrant, contender, the field *(collective).*

RIVAL, *v.* 1. Compete with in rivalry, contend with, vie with, challenge, emulate, oppose, try to excel, strive to outdo, contest, dispute, run a race, cope with, measure swords, join issue, enter the lists, take up the gantlet, tilt, fence, grapple, wrestle, scramble, antagonize, contend, do battle with, pit against, confront, counteract, thwart, cross, oppugn, defy, clash with, collide with.

2. Prove to be a worthy rival of, equal, match, outrival, surpass, eclipse, cast in the shade, outdo, outstrip, excel, overshadow, outvie outshine.

RIVAL, *adj.* Standing in rivalry, emulous, opposing, emulative, competitive, contending, competing, emulating competitory, cutthroat, contentious, antagonistic, counteractive, adverse.

RIVALRY, *n.* Contest, competition, race, rivalship, emulation, contention, strife, handicap, tug of war, opposition, antagonism, oppugnancy, collision, clashing, conflict, two of a trade, war to the knife, struggle, corrivalry, agonism, match, hostile meeting.

RIVE, *v.* Tear apart, rend asunder, cleave, split, rift, burst, slit, lacerate, sever, wrench, rip, break, rupture.

RIVER, *n.* Considerable natural stream of water flowing in a definite course, tributary, reach, current, affluent, watercourse, fluvial, wadi, anabranch, stream, feeder, torrent, body of water, rapids, flood, spate, gorge, vortex, whirlpool, maelstrom, eddy, effluence, profluence, flux, flow, race, cataract, cascade, chute, force, estuary.

RIVET, *v.* 1. Fasten with a rivet, spread out the end of in order to form a head and secure something, clinch, fix firmly, make firm, fasten securely, unite, join, pinion, attach, tie, gird, splice, yoke, link, pin, clamp, clasp, lock, hasp, bolt, screw, nail, fuse, weld, solder.

2. Focus the attention on, devote the attention to, take stock of, pore over, scrutinize, scan, examine closely, occupy oneself with, look at closely, contemplate, bend the mind to, keep in sight, take notice, regard, observe, watch, keep the eyes upon, absorb, prey on the mind, fascinate, galvanize, electrify.

RIVULET, *n.* Brook, creek, small stream, streamlet, riverlet, riverling, riverain, riveret, burn, rill, runnel, run, runlet, brooklet, gill, branch, beck, rillet.

ROAD, *n.* 1. Open way for passage, roadway, highway, highroad, superhighway, speedway, thoroughfare, turnpike, throughway, parkway, boulevard, crossroad, *carrefour (Fr.)*, crossway, underpass, viaduct, fairway, avenue, path, street, route, lane, pathway, pike, byroad, artery, public way, drive, esplanade, trail, track, lane, channel, course, passage, beat, footpath, shortcut, alley.

2. Protected place near shore where ships may ride at anchor, roadstead, anchorage, basin, port, mooring.

3. Traveling, tour, peregrination, excursion, journey, round, circuit, course, pilgrimage, perambulation, trek, expedition, trip, itinerary, wayfaring.

ROAM, *v.* Travel about without a fixed direction, wander over, stray, ramble, jaunt, meander, prowl, stroll, gad, rove, gypsy, nomadize, peregrinate, trek, walk with no specific purpose, range over, straggle, saunter, perambulate, shuffle along, jog on, paddle, toddle, flit, traipse, pad, tramp, wend, bowl along, stalk.

ROAMER, *n.* Vagrant, itinerant, peripatetic, arab, wanderer, stroller, rover, ranger, gypsy, rambler, voyager, trekker, traveler, journeyer, migrant, wayfarer, knight of the road, vagabond, beachcomber, loafer, landloper, tramp, hobo, globetrotter, adventurer, peregrinator, straggler, gadabout, bird of passage, estray, scatterling.

ROAR, *v.* 1. Bellow, bray, howl, bay, wail, cry, ululate, yelp, bark, yap, snarl, growl, whine, snort, grunt, neigh, latrate, trumpet, squeak, caterwaul, bleat, moo, low, blat.

2. Shout, bawl, yell, vociferate, bluster, rage, storm, explode, fulminate, detonate, rampage, fume, run amuck, cry aloud.

3. Thunder, boom, clash, clang, peal, resound, rend the air, stun, deafen, din, clamor, rattle.

ROAR, *n.* 1. Bellow, howl, ululation, latration, bark, yap, wail, bowwow, yelp, growl, snort, grunt, trumpet, hoot, screech, squawk, squeak.

2. Thunder, boom, detonation, clangor, roll, rumble, outburst, discharge, explosion, volley, blowup, blast, crash, squall, din, uproar, blare, charivari, noise, racket, clatter, fracas, pandemonium.

3. Outcry, yell, bawl, vociferation, shout, exclamation, clamor, ejaculation, shriek, call, scream, hullabaloo, hubbub, hue and cry, boohoo.

4. Guffaw, cachinnation, horselaugh, chuckle, crow, laughter, shout, cheer, snigger.

ROAST, *v.* 1. Bake by dry heat, embed in hot coals to cook, heat violently, brown, char, grill, cook, parch, broil, dry, griddle, pan, braise, fricassee, fry.

2. *(Coll.)* Ridicule, guy, criticize mercilessly, pan *(sl.)*, chaff, travesty, burlesque, satirize, caricature, make fun of, rag, haze, josh, banter, gibe,

deride, taunt, mock, disparage, vilify, belittle, derogate from, traduce, flay, excoriate, run down, pull to pieces, asperse, lampoon, decry.

ROB, *v.* Take possession of by unlawful violence, seize possessions which belong to others, despoil, pillage, rifle, pilfer, strip, plunder, sack, rook, pirate, steal, loot, forage, take by theft, thieve, purloin, filch, spoliate, appropriate, embezzle, peculate, defraud, deprive of, plagiarize, forge, fleece, cheat, bilk, bamboozle, skin, prey upon, stick up, hold up, strong-arm, pinch, bag, crib, abstract, finger, shoplift, misappropriate, run off with, make away with, carry off, rustle, lift, burgle, ransack, maraud, hijack, poach, victimize, pluck, swindle, housebreak, help oneself to, make free with.

ROBBER, *n.* Burglar, bandit, stick-up man, thief, highwayman, desperado, brigand, footpad, pickpocket, cutpurse, pillager, rifler, marauder, poacher, despoiler, plunderer, depredator, freebooter, forager, raider, spoliator, crook, gangster, ladrone, dacoit, blackleg, dip, thug, housebreaker, yegg, safecracker, yeggman, pirate, rustler, cattle thief, picaroon, buccaneer, outlaw, ruffian, corsair, swindler, embezzler, peculator, sharper, forger, counterfeiter, rogue, shoplifter, rifler, filcher, privateer, hijacker, strong-arm man, nighthawk, fleecer, diddler, cracksman, sneak-thief, second-story man, magsman.

ROBBERY, *n.* Felonious taking of the property of another, larceny, theft, despoliation, spoliation, despoilment, depredation, thievery, stick-up, burglary, holdup, hijacking, plunder, direption, abstraction, appropriation, pilfering, pillage, rapine, sack, brigandage, highway robbery, privateering, piracy, buccaneering, housebreaking, shoplifting, cattle rustling, embezzlement, plagiarism, swindle, peculation, forgery, seizure, dispossession, freebooting, safecracking, looting, filching, marauding, ransacking.

ROBE, *v.* Invest, clothe, array, apparel, dress, deck, attire, costume, rig out, fit out, drape, gown, enrobe, garb, enclothe, dight, accouter, swathe, wrap, muffle, cover, swaddle, shroud, slip on.

ROBE, *n.* 1. Loose flowing gown, garment, dress, costume, vestment, habit, apparel, attire, raiment, covering, toilette, habiliment, vesture, garb, array, finery, frock, toga, sarong, sari, chiton, tunic, peplum, praetexta.

2. Dressing gown, dishabille, negligee, wrapper, kimono, housecoat, hostess gown, tea gown, *peignoir (Fr.)*, smock, bathrobe.

3. Mantle, burnoose, cloak, cope, capote, pelerine, cape, cardinal, cassock, caftan, dolman, surcoat.

4. Canonicals, surplice, cassock, pontificals, scapular, alb, dalmatic, stole, maniple, pallium, mantelletta, chasuble.

ROBORANT, *n.* Strengthening medicine, tonic, cordial, elixir, panacea, cure-all, catholicon, theriac, balm, ptisan, specific, stimulant, restorative, pick-me-up, palliative, remedy, physic, portion, draught, demulcent, syrup.

ROBOT, *n.* Machine-made person, mechanical being, manufactured man, automaton, Frankenstein.

ROBUST, *adj.* Strong, powerful, able-bodied, stalwart, brawny, muscular, athletic, sinewy, hardy, tough, iron, sturdy, lusty, husky, virile, manly, strapping, sound, rugged, stout, masculine, healthful, hearty, seasoned, mighty, potent, puissant, forceful, vigorous, energetic, firm, self-assertive, enduring, inured, hardened, active, persevering, herculean, mighty, forcible, hard, adamantine, indomitable, irresistible, invincible, overwhelming, all-powerful, broad-shouldered, gigantic, gymnastic, wiry, well-knit, fit, stanch, brave, bursting with health, in fine fettle, hale.

ROCK, *v.* Sway to and fro, move backward and forward, wobble, oscillate, shake, roll, vacillate, vibrate, swing, totter, teeter, jiggle, reel, librate, wave, nutate, dangle, pendulate, waggle, wag, bob, nod, curtsy, falter, quake, waver, quaver, tremble, quiver, pitch, toss, flounder, stagger, seesaw, curvet, wriggle, waddle, shuttle.

ROCK, *n.* 1. Boulder, crag, stone, cliff, fossil, marble, granite, flint, quartz, adamant, lava, pumice, mineral matter, reef, shelf, shoal, snag, pebble.

2. Protection, defense, safeguard, refuge, strength, support, firm foundation, anchor, mainstay, sanctuary, fastness, retreat, stronghold, castle, fortress, keep, *sanctum sanctorum (Lat.),* ark, bulwark, capitol, citadel, tower, fortification, security.

ROCK-BOTTOM, *adj.* At the lowest limit, at the lowest level, low-water, ebb-tide, nether, level with the ground, insufficient, too little, not enough, wanting, deficient, ill-furnished, ill-provided, ill-stored, unreplenished, scrimp, meager, sparing, stinted, skimpy, scarce, scant, poverty-stricken, penniless, indigent, flat, broke, destitute, bereft, reduced, straitened.

ROCKY, *adj.* 1. Stony, craggy, boulder-strewn, rugged, hard, rough, flinty, adamantine, broken, uneven, lithic, granitic, concrete, bumpy, unlevel, irregular, jagged, gnarled, cragged, pebbly.

2. Unfeeling, obdurate, inexorable, stubborn, callous, unyielding, inconsiderate, harsh, severe, insensate, cruel, drastic, inflexible, relentless, exacting.

3. *(Coll.)* Weak, shaky, tottering, dizzy, light-headed, giddy, vertiginous, unsteady.

ROCOCO, *adj.* Tastelessly florid, highly ornamented, flamboyant, baroque, fantastic, extravagant, *outré (Fr.),* gimcrack, bizarre, outlandish, fanciful, ornate, gorgeous, right-wrought, bedecked, highly embellished, gaudy, ostentatious, garish, tawdry, brummagem, glittering, showy, flashy, gilt, gilded, begilt, gingerbread, bedizened.

ROD, *n.* 1. Switch, cane, birch, rattan, stick, birch rod, cudgel, ferrule, truncheon, scourge, bullwhack, whip, cat-o'-nine-tails, lash, cowhide, thong, cat, knout, rawhide, quirt.

2. Staff, wand, shaft, scepter, baton, bar, pole, cane, alpenstock, crosier, stump, crutch, crook, thyrsus, caduceus, kerykeion, lituus, fasces, post, stake, picket, pale, pile, palisade, jamb, stanchion.

3. Stem, stalk, pedicel, caulis, peduncle, caudex, haulm, culm, cauliculus, caulicle, petiole, stipe, spear, stipes, twig, shoot, branch, scion, offshoot.

4. *(Coll.)* Revolver, firearm, automatic, pistol, shooting iron, repeater, gun, six-shooter.

5. Tyrannical rule, authority, sway, dominion, suzerainty, sovereignty, command, domination, supremacy, ascendancy, mastery, domain, control, hegemony, jurisdiction, supreme power, mastership, lordship, regency, regnancy, reign, empire, government, direction, omnipotence, predominance.

RODENT, *adj.* Gnawing, nibbling, corroding,

consuming, erosive, eating away, mordant, mordacious, biting, mumbling, chewing, crunching, munching, champing, masticating.

RODOMONTADE, *n.* Pretentious talk, vainglorious boasting, blustering rant, bragging, gasconade, vainglory, braggadocio, bluster, hot air *(sl.),* wind *(sl.),* fanfaronade, bravado, ostentation, swashbuckling, bombast, exaggeration, pretensions, puffery, bunkum, flourish, jactitation, vaporing, venditation, fine talking, magniloquence, gas *(sl.),* heroics, highfalutin, *vox et praeterea nihil (Lat.),* much cry and little wool, glorification, egotism, elation, hyperbole, extravagance, high coloring, embroidery, turgescence, orotundity, altiloquence, declamation, flowers of speech, rhetoric, euphuism, macrology, fustian, inflation, balderdash, gush.

RODOMONTADE, *v.* Talk big, brag, boast, swagger, bluster, gasconade, rant, cry up, flaunt, show off, blazon forth, blow one's trumpet, strut, cut a figure, make a splash, be ostentatious, vapor, give oneself airs, roister, kick up a dust, lord it over, assume a lofty bearing, act the grand seigneur, put on big looks, ride the high horse, toss the head, make mountains of, exaggerate, magnify, extol to the skies, panegyrize, eulogize, puff, gush, hyperbolize, overstate, stretch a point, overcolor, embroider, spin a long yarn, deal in the marvelous, draw a long bow, out-Herod Herod, make the most of, swashbuckle.

ROGATION, *n.* Solemn supplication, earnest entreaty, petition, request, prayer, suit, imprecation, apostrophe, appeal, orison, impetration, obsecration, obtestation, imploration, invocation, importunity, solicitation, postulation, intercession, litany.

ROGUE, *n.* Dishonest person, villain, scoundrel, rascal, knave, scamp, scapegrace, blackguard, blacksheep, *âme damnée (Fr.),* miscreant, trickster, sharper, cheat, caitiff, shyster, recreant, renegade, varlet, bad man, snake in the grass, wolf in sheep's clothing, truant, evildoer, wretch, ne'er-do-well, reprobate, *vaurien (Fr.),* ruffian, rough, malefactor, misdemeanant, felon, criminal, delinquent, culprit, outlaw, jailbird, *polisson (Fr.),* rapscallion, sneak, *âme de boue (Fr.),* dog, cur, scum of the earth, outcast, riffraff, swindler, thief, crook, forger, hellion, rotter, good-for-nothing, dissembler, deceiver, liar, storyteller, *menteur (Fr.),* perjurer, fraud, imposter, humbug, adventurer, mountebank, charlatan, quack, scalawag, picaroon, mischief-maker, urchin, sly fellow, mischievous fellow, wag.

ROGUERY, *n.* Roguish conduct, knavery, villainy, rascality, knavish tricks, dishonest practices, sharp practices, trickery, fraud, fraudulency, swindling, cheating, improbity, dishonesty, deception, bad faith, lying, infidelity, betrayal, Judas kiss, faithlessness, breach of trust, baseness, turpitude, shuffling, trimming, perfidiousness, perfidy, Punic faith, double-dealing, jobbery, foul play, fishy transaction, venality, graft, corruption, falsification, misrepresentation, guile, perjury, mendacity, subreption, forgery, evasion, prevarication, dissimulation, hypocrisy, duplicity, Machiavellianism, charlatanism, quackery, flimflam, criminality, deviation from rectitude, misconduct, malpractice, dereliction, delinquency, misdemeanor, malefaction, imposture, imposition, cozenage, circumvention, chicanery, hocus-pocus, ingannation, cunning, craftiness, maneuvering, jugglery, machination, artifice, artful dodge, stratagem, wiliness, wile, thin end of the wedge.

shift, subterfuge, practical joke, waggery, mischievousness, *espièglerie (Fr.)*, prank, ruse.

ROGUISH, *adj.* 1. Rascally, knavish, scoundrelly, tricky, fraudulent, dishonest, unscrupulous, disingenuous, false-hearted, crooked, slippery, insidious, perfidious, fishy, blackguard, sneaking, pettifogging, venal, corrupt, faithless, untrustworthy, false, deceitful, covinous, cunning, artful, crafty, Machiavellian, sly, wily, foxy, stealthy, subdolous, underhand, shifty, iniquitous, criminal, scampish, recreant, sinister, facinorous, nefarious, felonious, infamous, villainous, flagitious, unconscionable, incorrigible, reprobate, irreclaimable, culpable, reprehensible.

2. Sportive, mischievous, arch, waggish, puckish, playful, wanton, witty, festive, jocund, rompish, jolly, jovial, ludibrious, drollish, frolicsome, mirthful, merry, happy, cheerful, blithe, in high spirits, in fine feather, debonair, buoyant, *allegro (It.)*, jaunty, spirited, vivacious, breezy, animated, sparkling, hilarious, gleeful, *folâtre (Fr.)*, frisky, tricksy, gamesome, jocose, rollicking, roistering, laughter-loving, rejoicing, jubilant, cock-a-hoop.

ROIL, *v.* 1. Make turbid by stirring up sediment, muddy, blur, stain, bemire, smudge, smutch, befoul, beslime, stain, begrime, contaminate, obfuscate, defile.

2. Irritate, vex, annoy, harass, harry, bother, plague, rile, disturb, disquiet, discommode, worry, anger, pique, heckle, persecute, displease, thwart, perplex, cross, tease, molest, irk, rag, mortify, pester, wherret, badger, beset, bait, importune, infest, harrow, nettle, try the patience, fret, gall, chafe, sour the temper, ruffle, huff, sting, incense, wound, enrage, inflame, aggravate, embitter, envenom, infuriate, exasperate, exacerbate, kindle wrath, put out of humor.

ROILY, *adj.* Muddy, turbid, discolored, opaque, obfuscated, cloudy, fuliginous, murky, dirty, dun, lurid, sodden, unclean, grimy, filthy, dreggy, thick, slimy, foul.

ROISTER, *v.* Act in a boisterous manner, revel noisily, swagger, vapor, kick up a dust, bluster, snap one's fingers, carouse, junket, make merry, feast, drown care, gambol, drive dull care away, frisk, frolic, caper, romp, sow one's wild oats, paint the town red, have one's fling, take one's pleasure, make holiday, disport, wanton, run riot.

ROISTERER, *n.* Blustering fellow, reveler, carouser, Bacchante, brawler, swaggerer, vaporer, rioter, swashbuckler, mohock, rowdy, braggadocio, *fanfaron (Fr.)*, trumpeter, jack-pudding, blowhard, fourflusher, windbag.

ROLE, *n.* 1. Part which an actor presents in a play, character, impersonation, personification, representation, leading man, juvenile, heavy lead, villain, character man, comedian, harlequin, pantaloon, pantomimist, farceur, buffoon, first tragedian, ingenue, soubrette, leading lady, supernumerary, extra, headliner, star.

2. Function, task, chore, duty, assignment, undertaking, matter, concern, affair, work, job, mission, care, charge, cue, lookout, capacity, department, orb, sphere, line, field, round, career, place, office, post, billet, service, engagement, calling, vocation, métier, profession, craft, trade, policy, business, course, demeanor, guise, observance, procedure.

ROLL, *v.* 1. Rotate, revolve, gyrate, turn, trundle, turn over, wheel, bowl, incline, sway, lurch, gybe,

welter, reel, swing, yaw, lean, wallow, undulate, swell, wave, billow, spin, toss, tumble, go round, perform a periodical revolution in an orbit, turn over and over, circumgyrate, rock from side to side, stagger, be tossed about, vibrate, surge, fluctuate, move tumultuously, titubate, tumble about, spin, rev, swirl, circulate, twiddle, whirl.

2. Enfold, envelop, wrap, muffle, inclose, involve, swathe, inwrap, lap, wind, whip, fold, bind, curl, enroll, coil, furl, twist, entwine, wreathe, twirl, convolve, loop, scallop, indent.

3. Smooth, spread out, flatten, press, level, compact, even, smoothen, grade, iron, mangle, plane, dress, lay, horizontalize, ground, floor, squash, mow down, symmetrize.

4. Reverberate, resound, echo, re-echo, thunder, rumble, bombinate, boom, drum, roar, fulminate, quaver, shake, patter, clatter, clack, rattle, hum, whir, trill, peal, chime, tootle, beat, tick, ring in the ear, tintinnabulate, jingle, tinkle, clink, chink, blare.

ROLL, *n.* 1. Scroll, bundle, volume, document, rota, record, chronicle, register, list, inventory, file, catalogue, dossier, schedule, roster, docket, bulletin, muster roll, beadroll, class roll, panel, ballot, poll, slate, ticket, calendar, census, statistics, cadaster, *cadre (Fr.)*, directory, atlas, index, gazetteer, table, ledger, book.

2. Reverberation, rumble, resonance, bombination, bombilation, echo, re-echo, boom, *berloque (Fr.)*, thunder, fulmination, drumming, cannonade, barrage, tattoo, ratatat, pitapat, rubadub, pitterpatter, quaver, rattle, racket, charivari, clatter, drone, dingdong, clangor, clutter, howl, whir, peal, ringing, vibration, tintinnabulation, chime, clang, roar, drumbeat.

3. Loaf of bread rolled up while in the dough, biscuit, twist, small cake, loaflet, scone.

4. Convolution, involution, undulation, circuit, twirl, twist, contortion, ambages, meander, sinuosity, curl, coil, helix, spiral, corkscrew, volute, worm, tendril, scroll, kink, scallop, labyrinth, maze, snake, serpent, eel, spire, buckle, whorl, wave, tortuosity.

5. Currency, money, hard cash, dollar, purse, money in hand, ready money, spending money, shekels, lucre, jack, rhino, brass, dough, spondulics, wad, pile, bankroll, loose cash, wampum, paper money, treasury notes, greenbacks, long green.

ROLLER, *n.* 1. Wheel upon which something is rolled along, cylinder, cylindrical body revolving on a fixed axis, drum, barrel, treadle, trolley, rundle, trundle, truck, caster, pulley, sheave, cogwheel, gyrostat, gyroscope, gearwheel, flywheel.

2. Long swelling wave, breaker, whitecap, billow, swell, surge, ground swell, surf, white horse, comber, choppy sea.

ROLLICK, *v.* Act carelessly, move in a frolicsome manner, behave in a jovial way, frisk, gambol, romp, give a loose to mirth, sport, disport, revel, frolic, caper, have one's fling, run a rig, paint the town red, sow one's wild oats, take one's pleasure, hold one's sides, be mirthful, play the fool, chirp, cast away care, perk up, rejoice, chirrup, lilt, carol.

ROLLICKING, *adj.* Frolicsome, sportive, jovial, jocund, jolly, playful, frisky, lively, sprightly, merry, blithe, happy, cheerful, in high spirits, in fine feather, gay, allegro, debonair, jaunty, buoyant, free and easy, airy, spry, bright, spirited, vivacious, animated, breezy, pococurante, nonchalant, insouciant, sparkling, full of play, sunny, joyous, gleeful, hilarious, exhilarated, blithesome, rattling, hearty, playsome, tricksy, *folâtre (Fr.)*, gamesome, jocular, waggish, jocose, laughter-loving, mirthful, exultant, elated, jubilant, flushed, cock-a-hoop, rejoicing.

ROMANCE, *n.* 1. Love affair, romantic, experience, liaison, love suit, intrigue, amour, *affaire d'amour (Fr.)*, *affaire de coeur (Fr.)*, idolization, tender passion, flame, infatuation, romantic attachment, gallantry, fascination, affinity, dalliance, billing and cooing, courtship, wooing, addresses, court.

2. Work of fiction, novel, story, tale, narrative, fable, yarn, anecdote, myth, fairy tale, legend, allegory, parable, epic, novelette, penny dreadful, ballad, apologue, fantasy, extravaganza.

3. Imaginativeness, imagination, fumes of fancy, afflatus, flight of fancy, originality, creative thought, invention, mind's eye, word painting, idealism, castle building, dreaming, imagery, rhapsody, reverie, daydream, figment, illusion, phantasm, castle in the air, *château en Espagne (Fr.)*, man in the moon, Arabian nights, dream of Alnaschar.

4. Falsehood, lie, fabrication, whopper, tall story, exaggeration, cock-and-bull story, fish story, traveler's tale, untruth, falsity, fib, misrepresentation, false coloring, bouncer *(coll.)*, concoction, bosh, moonshine, hoax, canard, sell *(coll.)*, equivocation, shift, evasion, white lie, half truth.

ROMANTIC, *adj.* 1. Imaginative, fictitious, imaginary, visionary, extravagant, fanciful, chimerical, fantastic, fabulous, mythical, legendary, idealistic, poetic, ideal, utopian, high-flown, quixotic, flighty, preposterous, unsubstantial, unreal, notional, whimsical, figmental, fairy, dreamy, improbable, impractical, rhapsodical, in the clouds, *in nubibus (Lat.)*, hypothetical, theoretical, vaporous, starry-eyed.

2. Sentimental, amorous, fervent, erotic, ardent, enamored, fond, passionate, tender, amatory, impassioned, anacreontic, overemotional, maudlin, lackadaisical, devoted, zealous, sensitive, impressible, susceptible, impressionable, warm-hearted.

ROMANTICIST, *n.* Idealist, visionary, *exalté (Fr.)*, dreamer, castle-builder, daydreamer, romancer, enthusiast, rhapsodist, Don Quixote, fanatic, seer, knight errant, stargazer, zealot, devotee, partisan, utopian, optimist.

ROMP, *v.* Play in a lively manner, frisk, caper, frolic, sport, gambol, bound, raise Cain, disport, have one's fling, dance, leap, run a rig, paint the town red, take one's pleasure, keep up the ball, curvet, caracole, vault, spring, hop, cut capers, skip, trip, foot it, bounce, jump about, trip it on the light fantastic toe.

ROOF, *n.* 1. External upper covering of a building, cover of a house, roofing, ceiling, thatch, shingles, slates, leads, tiles, clapboard, weatherboard.

2. Arch, dome, cupola, vault, mansard, canopy, awning, marquee, canvas, tent, *tente d'abri (Fr.)*, top, tester, hood, tepee, wigwam, capote, cowl, gambrel, deck, curb roof, sunshade, parasol, baldachin, tilt, shield, pavilion, rotunda, kiosk.

3. Dwelling, shelter, house, home, habitation, lodging, abode, place, domicile, housing, quarters, diggings, berth, headquarters, refuge, retreat, haunt, bower, arbor, hut, shack, shanty, crib, cabin, igloo, booth, stall, pen, shed, kennel, cote,

hutch, coop, sty, cottage, chalet, lodge, villa, hermitage, mansion, flat, apartment, room, suite, tenement, croft, chateau, bungalow, penthouse, duplex, three-decker, hall, grange, hacienda, cache, tabernacle, ark, seat.

ROOK, *n.* 1. Trickish fellow, cheat, sharper, swindler, crook, blackleg, thimblerigger, defaulter, welsher, trickster, artful dodger, peculator, skittle-sharper, cardsharper, shark, adventurer, decoy, deceiver, inveigler, rascal, charlatan, pretender, fraud, bilk, confidence man, twister, mountebank, rogue, pettifogger, knave, gyp, gypper.

2. Castle in chess.

3. Black crow, *Corvus frugilegus.*

ROOK, *v.* Cheat, fleece, defraud, swindle, peculate, pluck, ruck, rob, diddle, mulct, sponge, pigeon, bilk, skin, obtain under false pretenses, embezzle, live by one's wits, impose upon, gull, hoax, bamboozle, dupe, jockey, cozen, do, nab, gyp, chouse, cully, bite, victimize, double-cross, hoodwink, hook in, trick, hocus, gammon, humbug, play with marked cards, cog the dice, palm off, fob off.

ROOKERY, *n.* Breeding place of animals, colony of animals, nest, aerie, nidus.

ROOM, *n.* 1. Lodging place, lodging, chamber, apartment, dormitory, berth, boudoir, closet, cell, salon, den, sanctuary, hall, cubbyhole, cabin, flat, parlor, saloon, drawing room, waiting room, anteroom, vestibule, foyer, cubicle, bedroom, ward, dining room, refectory, breakfast nook, nursery, study, library, rumpus room, playroom, studio, atelier, sanctum, adytum, loft, attic, vault, kitchen, scullery, pantry, storeroom, laundry, shed, outhouse, lean-to, penthouse, lobby, gallery, arcade, arbor, bower, pergola, stoa, kiosk, sun parlor, solarium, loggia, smoking room, rotunda, compartment.

2. Scope, range, compass, leeway, expanse, field, latitude, swing, extent, play, capacity, accommodation, space, margin, elbowroom, *Lebensraum (Ger.)*, *lieu (Fr.)*, stead, place, opportunity, sweep, area, arena, sphere, longitude, whereabouts, locus, site, situation, location, spot, region, locale, tract, point, scene, locality, ground, realm, territory, quarter, part.

ROOMMATE, *n.* Comrade, chum, buddy, close friend, associate, companion, mate, *confrère (Fr.)*, partner, colleague, fellow, consort, pal, side kick *(sl.)*, playmate, bunkie, bedfellow, tentmate, messmate, classmate, commensal, shipmate, confidant, intimate, other self, alter ego, trusty, bosom friend, fidus Achates.

ROOMY, *adj.* Spacious, affording ample room, large, wide, broad, extensive, capacious, ample, expansive, commodious, comfortable, comprehensive, vast, airy, big, immense, huge, wide-open, long, outstretched, lengthy, interminable, boundless, unlimited.

ROOST, *v.* Perch, stay for the night, put up, settle, lodge, take up one's abode, squat, *se nicher (Fr.)*, bivouac, plant oneself, locate oneself, hive, get a footing, burrow, nestle, sojourn, stay, occupy, tenant, haunt, resort to, frequent, bunk, abide, room, live, reside, inhabit, dwell, people, colonize.

ROOST, *n.* Perch, rookery, aerie, retreat, covert, resort, habitat, haunt, nest, nidus, snuggery, hiding place, cache.

ROOT, *n.* 1. Part of plant growing downward into the soil and fixing it there, radicle, underground part, lower part, basal portion, embedded part, basic element, basic part, radical, bottom, radix, stem, tubes, bulb, rootlet, nucleus, germ, rootstock, taproot, tap, fundamental, foundation, base, rhizoid *(Bot.)*.

2. Reason, rationale, motive, cause, occasion, source, origin, rise, commencement, spring, fountainhead, leaven, mainspring, causality, determining condition, variable, moment, well, wellspring, font, *fons et origo (Lat.)*, ground, wherefore, support.

3. Primitive word, etymon, morpheme, derivation.

4. *(Math.)* Power, exponent, logarithm, index, modulus.

ROOT, *v.* 1. Uproot, unearth, eradicate, tear out, extirpate, deracinate, tear up by the roots, rootle, dig out, weed out, exterminate, remove utterly, destroy utterly, eliminate, do away with, abolish.

2. Implant, embed, plant, place, fix, fasten, set, situate, lay, put, station, deposit, graft, insert, sink deep, establish deeply.

3. Send out roots, begin to grow, take root, strike, settle, get a footing, strike root.

4. *(Sl.)* Give encouragement, applaud, shout for, boost, acclaim, stick up for, cheer, clap, praise, encore, cry up, eulogize, laud, commend, uphold, look up to.

ROOTED, *adj.* Fixed, firm, implanted, fast, confirmed, ingrained, radicated, immovable, riveted, firmly established, ineradicable, deep-rooted, stable, durable, perennial, inveterate, radical, chronic, fundamental, traditional, ensconced, embedded, inherent, inbred, inborn, congenital, ineffaceable, ingrafted, permanent, habituated, accustomed, wonted, set.

ROPE, *n.* Strong thick cord, line of twisted strands, cable, line, hawser, halyard, halter, painter, stay, foretack, lanyard, ratlin, cordage, guy, cablet, tackle, bowline, buntline, gasket, tether, gut, braid, funiculus, funicle, twist, sennit, rigging, leash, thong, strap, lasso, lariat, cabestro, loop, noose, slipknot, hitch.

ROPE, *v.* 1. Draw by a rope, fasten, tether, picket, secure, fetter, shackle, tie, bind, lasso, tow, pull, restrain, curb in, hold in leash, stop short, pull in, hold back, rein in, check, coerce, harness, attach, hitch, moor, lash, catch with a lariat.

2. Inveigle into, entice, lure, beguile, allure, tempt, intrigue, take in, deceive, victimize, set a snare for, lay a trap for, bait the hook, spread the toils, forelay, waylay, decoy, delude, entrap, hook in, ensnare, sniggle, illaqueate, entangle.

ROPEDANCER, *n.* Ropewalker, funambulist, equilibrist, high-wire performer, acrobat, tightrope balancer.

ROPY, *adj.* Viscid, viscous, stringy, mucilaginous, glutinous, gelatinous, albuminous, amylaceous, mastic, tacky, tenacious, adhesive, mucous, thick, muculent, mucid, pituitous, lentous, tough, filamentous, filamentary, filar, threadlike, fibrous, filiform, fibrillose, wiry, thready, sticky.

ROSARY, *n.* 1. String of beads for counting prayers, series of prayers, Ave Maria, paternoster, telling of beads.

2. Rose garden, rosarium, rosery, bed of roses.

3. Chaplet, garland, wreath, crown, corona, coronal, festoon.

ROSEATE, *adj.* Rose-colored, tinged with rose, rosy, erubescent, primrose-colored, pink, magenta, carnation, rubric, damask, cerise, cherry, cram-

oisy, crimson, carmine, vermilion, scarlet, *sang de boeuf (Fr.)*, red, cardinal, coral, ruby, claret, vinaceous, rufous, purplish-red.

ROSTER, *n.* List, roll, register, scroll, inventory, catalogue, rota, schedule, beadroll, panel, muster, ballot, poll, ticket, slate, census, docket, statistics, index, canon, *cadre (Fr.)*, directory, bulletin, table, gazetteer, calendar, cadaster, tally, ledger, row, score, file.

ROSTRUM, *n.* 1. Beak, neb, prow, nib, bow, bill, bowsprit, prore, stem, jib.

2. Stage for public speaking, platform, tribune, stand, pulpit, dais, desk, hustings, forum, reading desk, lectern, ambo.

ROSY, *adj.* 1. Blushing, blooming, flushed, ruddy, florid, rubicund, high-colored, hectic, glowing, erubescent, inflamed, blowzy.

2. Bright, promising, favorable, auspicious, prosperous, full of promise, of good omen, *de bon augure (Fr.)*, encouraging, reassuring, inspiriting, cheering, *couleur de rose (Fr.)*, looking up, fortunate, in luck, lucky, providential, propitious, halcyon, palmy, felicitous.

3. Cheerful, optimistic, sanguine, buoyant, hopeful, confident, in good heart, secure, buoyed up, exultant, elated, enthusiastic, ardent, fervent, zealous, self-reliant, in high feather.

ROT, *v.* 1. Decay, putrefy, decompose, putresce, spoil, addle, mold, canker, fester, molder, rust, fall into decay, go to pieces, disintegrate, degenerate, deteriorate, retrograde, break down, rankle, go bad, decline, fall off, gather, suppurate, reek, smell strong, be fetid.

2. Defile, taint, corrupt, pollute, debase, pervert, contaminate, stain, sully, befoul, smirch, dirty, soil, tarnish, infect, envenom, poison, deprave, vitiate, degrade, tamper with, brutalize, demoralize, impair, mar, damage, injure, despoil, harm, hurt, waste, mutilate, disfigure, deface, blemish, warp, mangle.

ROT, *n.* 1. Putrefaction, putrescence, putridity, cariousness, cariosity, caries, decay, decomposition, corruption, canker, contamination, discoloration, decadence, disintegration, atrophy, blight, mildew, rottenness, deterioration, vitiation, mold, mucor, must, taint, rust, suppuration, purulence, empyema, gangrene, mortification, slime, muck, ooze, sludge.

2. *(Sl.)* Nonsense, absurdity, gibberish, jargon, jabber, tommyrot, balderdash, flummery, inanity, *niaiserie (Fr.)*, fudge, twaddle, trash, stuff and nonsense, rubbish, bosh, drivel, fiddle-faddle, flapdoodle, moonshine.

ROTARY, *adj.* Turning round on an axis, trochilic, peristrephic, rotating, rotatory, rotative, rotational, revolutionary, circular, moving round, circumrotatory, revolving, whirling, gyratory, gyral, gyrational, vortical, circumvolutory, circumgyratory, vorticose, vertiginous, cyclic, periodic, cyclical, recurrent, recurring, rhythmic, intermittent, serial, pulsatory.

ROTATE, *v.* 1. Turn round on an axis, revolve, spin, whirl, twirl, turn, rev, circulate, encircle, gyre, gyrate, twist, swirl, trundle, twiddle, wheel, roll, move about a center, circumrotate.

2. Proceed in a fixed routine of succession, go through a round of changes, alternate, act interchangeably, recur, intermit, occur again, reappear, return, come round again.

ROTATION, *n.* 1. Turn on an axis, revolution, gyration, circumrotation, circumgyration, circumvolution, turbination, roll, wheel, circulation, spinning, twirl, spin, twist, whirl, whirligig, reel, pirouette, swirl, gyre, gyrostatics, trochilics.

2. Turbine, whirlabout, screw, propeller, top, windmill, teetotum, treadmill, gearwheel, flywheel, turnspit, cogwheel, gyroscope, merry-go-round, carrousel, gyrostat, caster, puller, roller, sheave, axle, pivot, pin, spool, mandrel, whorl, bobbin, quill, wharve, cop, gimbals, hinge, gudgeon, axis, swivel.

3. Maelstrom, whirlpool, eddy, vortex, Charybdis, surge.

4. Tornado, twister, cyclone, whirlwind, tempest, hurricane, samiel, typhoon, gale, squall.

5. Alternation, succession, order, sequence, series, round, procession, run, course, cycle, period, periodicity, regular recurrence, intermittence, reoccurrence, rhythm, return, pulsation, beat, pulse, ictus, oscillation, rota, vibration, bout.

ROTE, *n.* Fixed course of procedure, routine, mechanical repetition, memorization through reiteration, use of the memory with little intelligence, art of artificial memory, *memoria technica (Lat.),* mnemonics, mnemotechnics, retentive memory, learning by heart, rememoration, perfunctory performance.

ROTTEN, *adj.* 1. Decayed, putrid, putrescent, carious, putrefied, overripe, decaying, decomposed, tainted, mildewed, moldy, moldering, blighted, cankered, worm-eaten, maggoty, putrefactive, purulent, touched, rancid, bad, musty, fetid, foul, reeky, malodorous, ill-smelling, strong, rank, noisome, noxious, discolored, spotted, soft, crumbling, fly-blown, lentiginous, fusty, mucid, high, reasty, peccant.

2. Unsound, brittle, friable, yielding, crumbly, soft, pulverable, frangible, fragile, frail, fissile, shivery, splitting.

3. Immoral, corrupt, indecent, immodest, gross, obscene, vile, lewd, smutty, pornographic, off-color, risqué, salacious, lickerish, libidinous, lustful, lecherous, licentious, unchaste, coarse, shameless, ribald, filthy, incontinent, dissolute, lascivious, sensual.

4. Treacherous, deceitful, untrustworthy, hollow, forsworn, insincere, Janus-faced, mealy-mouthed, two-faced, double-dealing, pharisaical, hypocritical, evasive, unfair, faithless, dishonest, dishonorable, slippery, crooked, venal, mercenary, fraudulent, mendacious, bogus, spurious, questionable, unscrupulous, knavish, perfidious, arrant, base, contemptible, scurvy, dirty, criminal, vicious, iniquitous, disgraceful, felonious, facinorous, flagitious, flagrant, nefarious, villainous, unconscionable, incorrigible, irreclaimable.

ROTUND, *adj.* 1. Spherical, round, globular, orbicular, circular, rotundate, globate, spheroidal, globoid, bulbous, globous, cylindrical, bell-shaped, campaniform, campanulous, campaniliform, pear-shaped, pyriform, egg-shaped, oviform, ovoid, elliptical, obovate, bead-shaped, moniliform, annular, discoid, rotundate, ring-like, rounded, curved, curvate, lunar, moon-shaped, luniform, fan-shaped, flabelliform.

2. Plump, chubby, stout, obese, corpulent, buxom, pudgy, fat, full-fleshed, well-fed, portly, fleshy, lumpish, puffy, expansive, distended, dropsical, bloated, tumid, pot-bellied, pursy, puffy, patulous.

3. Sonorous, full-toned, orotund, grandiloquent, altiloquent, magniloquent, rhetorical, mellifluous,

golden-tongued, fluent, mouth-filling, resonant, ringing, vibrant.

ROTUNDA, *n.* Round building with a dome, tholos, high circular hall, vault, arcade, cupola, beehive.

ROTUNDITY, *n.* 1. Roundness, rotundness, sphericity, globosity, spheroidicity, cylindricity, cylindricalness, sphericality, orbicularity, circularity.

2. Ball, sphere, globe, globoid, ellipsoid, spheroid, globule, geoid, spherule, drop, pea, bulb, pellet, knob, pill, bullet, marble, cylinder, drum, barrel, cylindroid, column, rundle, rolling pin, circlet, circle, annulus, ring, oval, ellipse, ovum, ellipsoid, egg.

3. Plumpness, corpulence, obesity, stoutness, buxomness, embonpoint, chubbiness, pursiness, pudginess, fatness, intumescence, tumefaction, distension, pandiculation.

4. Sonority, resonance, sonorousness, magniloquence, grandiloquence, fluency.

ROUE, *n.* Dissolute man, libertine, debauchee, rake, profligate, reprobate, satyr, goat, lecher, voluptuary, sensualist, rip, loose-fish, rakehell, fast man, fornicator, seducer, adulterer, *paillard (Fr.),* whoremonger, Don Juan, Lothario, hedonist, man about town, playboy, gallant, *intrigant (Fr.),* Sybarite, man of pleasure, hard-liver, carouser, reveler, dissipator, scapegrace, ne'er-do-well, *vaurien (Fr.),* black sheep, prodigal, spendthrift, losel.

ROUGH, *adj.* 1. Irregular, uneven, not smooth, rugged, bumpy, jagged, stony, rocky, cragged, craggy, scraggy, stubbly, stubbled, scratchy, broken, unlevel, knotted, gnarled, nodulose, nodular, wrinkly, crinkly, corrugated, rugulose, rugose, coarse, scaly, scabrous, cross-grained.

2. Shaggy, hairy, hirsute, bristly, unkempt, hispid, bristling, bushy, stubby, disheveled, unshorn, disordered, setaceous, setose, setulose, prickly, setigerous, setiferous, strigate, strigose, tufted, bearded, pileous, pilose, unshaven, ciliated, villous, crinite, crinose, trichoid, nappy, ulotrichous, wooly-haired, kinky, filamentous, downy, pubescent, fluffy, flocculent, lanate, lanuginous, plumate, plumous, tomentose.

3. Rough-hewn, crude, unwrought, uncut, unfashioned, shapeless, formless, amorphous, incomplete, not elaborated, not perfected, unfinished, imperfect, sketchy, vague, approximate, inexact, cursory, superficial, rudimentary, preliminary, general.

4. Violently disturbed, turbulent, tempestuous, tumultuous, choppy, stormy, agitated, vehement, boiling, inclement, boisterous, wild, untamed, savage, riotous, berserk, amuck, disorderly, noisy, uproarious, rowdy, rowdyish, raging, blustery, wintry, rampant, frenzied, infuriate, ferocious.

5. Tart, crabbed, sour, astringent, acrid, acidulous, sharp, biting, pungent, bitter, mordant, spicy, peppery.

5. Discordant, inharmonious, cacophonous, harsh, raucous, jarring, grating, strident, stridulous, unmusical, gruff, hoarse, husky.

6. Hard, cruel, austere, unfeeling, insensate, inconsiderate, unpleasant, severe, brutal, ungentle, drastic, extreme.

7. Discourteous, impolite, uncivil, ungentlemanly, unrefined, unpolished, inurbane, ungracious, rude, blunt, brusque, bluff, surly, churlish, boorish, bearish, gruff, burly, clownish, loutish, uncouth, uncourtly, awkward, gauche, clumsy, in-

elegant, ungenteel, unceremonious, vulgar, coarse, indelicate, abrupt, ill-mannered, ill-bred.

ROUGH, *n.* Coarse fellow, rowdy, roughneck, ruffian, barbarian, savage, brute, desperado, thug, hooligan, hoodlum, larrikin, ugly customer, bludgeon man, apache, gunman, racketeer, gangster, terrorist, cutthroat, assassin, felon, criminal, scoundrel, rascal, miscreant, villain, caitiff, thief, pickpocket, burglar, footpad, blackguard, rogue, malefactor, jailbird, garroter, butcher, mobster.

ROUGH DRAFT Preliminary outline, sketch, *ébauche (Fr.),* rough cast, *brouillon (Fr.),* design in outline, blueprint, crude delineation, first drawing, initial plan, skeleton, rough picture, rudimentary drawing, tracing, specifications, summary of facts, prospectus.

ROUGHHOUSE, *n.* Rowdy conduct, rough behavior, manhandling, disorderly play, rowdyism, ruffianism, blackguardism, brutality, ferocity, brutishness, inhumanity, barbarity, violence, impetuosity, brute force, severity, outrage, *coup de main (Fr.).*

ROUGHNESS, *n.* 1. Irregularity, unevenness, corrugation, rugosity, nodulation, nodosity, villosity, hairiness, pilosity, hispidity, hirsuteness, scratchiness, stubble, ruggedness. (See *Adjectives.*)

2. Hair, pubescence, down, thatch, shock, mat, coat, wool, villus, fimbriae, filament, fringe, shag, tangle, mane, whiskers, beard, burnsides, sideburns, Vandyke, mutton chops, goatee, imperial, mustache, bristle, awn, setula, feeler, vibrissae, strigae, arista, plume, feather, plumule, quill, crest, tuft, panache, feathering, plumage, hackle, pile, nap, fur, fluff, wool, fleece, locks, tresses, ringlets, curls, waviness.

3. Tempestuousness, turbulence, storminess, violence, inclemency, severity, vehemence, fury, boisterousness. (See *Adjectives.*)

4. Harshness, rudeness, incivility, inelegance, impoliteness, gruffness, bluntness, coarseness, grossness, crudeness. (See *Adjectives.*)

5. Unsavoriness, tartness, bitterness, sourness, acerbity, astringency, acridity, acidulousness, pungency, mordancy.

ROUND, *v.* 1. Make circular, curve, make round, make cylindrical, make spherical, orbiculate, coil, wreathe, curl, twine, wind, reel, roll, sphere incurvate, bend, arcuate, arch, concamerate.

2. Encircle, surround, circuit, encompass, ring, compass, circle, inclose, girdle, environ.

3. Make the complete circuit of, go the round, move about, traverse, go round, circulate.

ROUND, *adj.* 1. Circular, ring-shaped, orbicular, globular, spherical, orbed, cylindrical, globose, conglobulatory, rotund, spheroidal, globoid, globate, ringlike, annular, discoid, rotundate, oval, ovoid, elliptical, egg-shaped, ovate, bell-shaped, campanulate, campaniform, campaniliform, pear-shaped, pyriform, rounded, bulbous.

2. Full-fleshed, plump, stout, chubby, portly, obese, corpulent, bulging, protuberant, potbellied, pudgy, buxom, full-formed.

3. Entire, whole, full, complete, unbroken, integral, undivided, intact, plenary, perfect, thorough, total, comprehensive, exhaustive, detailed.

4. Harmonious, sonorous, orotund, resonant, fluent, flowing, smooth, mellifluous, magniloquent, grandiloquent, altiloquent.

5. Candid, frank, outspoken, straightforward, blunt, direct, plain, open, honest, fair, upright,

ingenuous, artless, free, sincere, honorable, guileless, naive, aboveboard, open-hearted.

ROUND, *n.* 1. Complete course, series, group, chain, suite, sequence, succession, continuity, train, progression, catena, gradation, string, queue, row, file, retinue, procession.

2. Revolution, circumrevolution, gryation, circumgyration, cycle, rotation, circumrotation, succession, turn, bout, lap, spell, volley, ring, circle, rota.

3. Circuit, circumference, periphery, compass, bound, perimeter, outline, zone, orbit, complete path, wheel, ambit, circulation, perambulation, tour, routine, watch, beat, jurisdiction.

ROUND, *adv.* 1. Around, about, on all sides, encircling.

2. Circularly, in a rounded course, in a circuit, in a circle, in circumference, peripherally, in girth.

3. From first to last, throughout, from beginning to end, from alpha to omega, everywhere, in every part, from head to foot, from top to toe, cap à pie, from end to end.

ROUND, *prep.* 1. Around, about, circularly, all over, in all parts of, in various directions from, throughout, here and there in.

2. In the vicinity of, near, environing, close to, nigh, not far from, close by.

ROUNDABOUT, *adj.* 1. Indirect, circuitous, tortuous, ambagious, anfractuous, sinuous, meandering, mazy, labyrinthine, devious, winding, zigzag, discursive, desultory, circumlocutory, periphrastic, stray, vagrant, erratic, excursive, aberrant, rambling, loose.

2. Encircling, encompassing, surrounding, ambient, circumambient, circumjacent, circumfluent, circumferential, peripheral.

ROUNDER, *n.* 1. Idle frequenter of disreputable resorts, habitué, denizen, vagrant, miscreant, knave, habitual drunkard, carouser, tippler, petty criminal, felon, malefactor, blacksheep.

2. Playboy, carouser, sport, dissolute, spendthrift, prodigal, wastrel, profligate, reprobate, roue, dissipator, libertine.

ROUNDNESS, *n.* 1. Circularity, rotundity, sphericity, globosity, rotundness, globularness, globularity, orbicularity, orbicularness, cylindricity, cylindricalness, spheroidicity, spheroidity, orbiculation, annularity, convexity.

2. Fullness, sonorousness, resonance, sonority, smoothness of flow, fluency, mellifluousness, grandiloquence, magniloquence.

3. Entirety, completeness, wholeness, integrity, entireness, ensemble, totality, total, aggregate, gross, sum total.

ROUNDUP, *n.* 1. Exhibition of cowboys' skills, rodeo, horse-breaking, broncobusting, lariat-throwing, lasso-twirling, driving together of cattle for inspection.

2. Gathering in *(as of criminals),* dragnet, ingathering.

ROUSE, *v.* 1. Bring out of a state of sleep, awaken, waken, wake up, raise, shake, arouse, call, summon, get awake, get up.

2. Incite, stimulate, excite, inspire, whet, egg, goad, agitate, move, fire, touch, animate, kindle, enkindle, provoke, stir up, bestir, brace, rally, put in action, influence, persuade, fan, perk up, affect, strike, impress, penetrate, interest, infect, imbue, evoke, illumine, pique, sting, irritate, inflame, touch to the quick, inspirit, quicken, sharpen,

fillip, urge, instigate, infuse new life into, foster, introduce new blood, foment, heat, magnetize, galvanize, electrify, revive, rivet the attention, prompt, induce, dispose, prevail on, bring round, persuade, motivate, encourage, actuate, entice, tempt, wheedle, allure, lure, coax, inveigle, propel, drive, prick, lash, hound on, compel, constrain, enforce, impel, make, drive, thrill.

3. Drive from cover, surprise, startle, flush, cause to start up, cause to fly off.

ROUSTABOUT, *n.* Unskilled laborer who lives by odd jobs, stevedore, dock-worker, deck hand, wharf laborer, cargo-loader, ·vagrant who does chance jobs, general handyman, doer of odd jobs, factotum, circus tentman.

ROUT, *v.* Vanquish, put to flight, drive off, repel, subdue, defeat, quell, overthrow, overpower, subjugate, worst, overmaster, overcome, overwhelm, discomfit, repulse, conquer, drub, lambaste, beat, lick *(coll.)*, swamp, throw into confusion, disperse in disorderly flight, outmaneuver, outgeneral, checkmate, thrash, floor, trim *(coll.)*, do for, settle, crush, reduce, suppress, put down, drive to the wall, panic, be triumphant over, carry by storm, gain the day, outflank, upset, trample under foot, roll in the dust, chase away, scatter, drive away, make a clean sweep of.

ROUT, *n.* 1. Disorderly flight, total repulse, complete dispersal, disorganization, discomfiture, defeat, utter overthrow, wild debacle, vanquishment, ruin, ruination, headlong panic, scattered rebuff, drubbing, beating, quietus, deathblow, subdual, conquest, subjugation.

2. Disturbance of the peace, brawl, tumult, uproar, clamor, tumultuous noise, din, fracas, turmoil, turbulence, perturbation, tumulation, hubbub, racket.

3. Disorderly mob, rabble, lawless concourse, clamorous multitude, herd, horde, *canaille (Fr.)*, chaff, dregs of the people, *faex populi (Lat.)*, profanum vulgus, riffraff, ragtag and bobtail.

4. Fashionable assembly, soirée, large evening party, drum, ridotto, ball, festival.

ROUTE, *n.* Way for passage, road for travel, path, course, passage, circuit, itinerary, direction, track, journey, tour, trip, plan, beat, tack, lane, channel, artery, highway, postroad, thoroughfare, throughway, turnpike, roadway, state road, boulevard, parkway, speedway, transit, trajectory, orbit.

ROUTINE, *n.* 1. Regular course of procedure, method, ordinary way, practice, system, order, disposition, arrangement, systematization, established usage, perfunctory, operation, customary duty, custom.

2. Red tape, groove, rut, treadmill, convention, wont, path, conformity, cut-and-dried rule, rota, mere form, protocol, habitude, consuetude, prescription, beaten path, matter of course, second nature, observance, formality.

3. Round, beat, walk, race, career, range, arena, field, scope, sphere.

ROVE, *v.* Wander about without definite destination, move hither and thither at random, roam, straggle, range, ramble, stray, stroll, prowl, meander, perambulate, peregrinate, trek, traverse, gad about, flit, nomadize, gypsy, bum, jaunt, saunter, wend.

ROVER, *n.* Wanderer, peripatetic, gadabout, gadling, bird of passage, straggler, rambler, traveler, journeyer, tripper, migrant, gypsy, nomad, arab, Bedouin, wayfarer, pilgrim, trekker, globetrotter,

sightseer, voyager, adventurer, itinerant, roamer, peregrinator, vagrant, landlouper, hobo, tramp, vagabond, fugitive, runaway, runagate.

ROVING, *n.* Vagrancy, wandering, *Wanderlust (Ger.)*, emigration, vagabondage, nomadism, vagabondism, gadding, hoboism, peripateticism, wayfaring, peregrination, perambulation, trekking, globetrotting, sightseeing, rambling, landlouping, flitting.

ROW, *n.* 1. Rank, series, file, line, string, range, queue, tier, column, chain, catena, concatenation, cordon, sequence, succession, continuity, round, progression, suite, train, retinue, cavalcade, cortege, procession, parade.

2. Street, alley, court, road, place, lane, quadrangle, yard, close, passage, esplanade, terrace.

3. Noisy dispute, squabble, quarrel, fracas, brawl, melee, altercation, rumpus, scrimmage, feud, *brouillerie (Fr.)*, embroilment, imbroglio, tiff, spat, words, *tracasserie (Fr.)*, wrangling, jangle, broil, hubbub, racket, rixation, embranglement, breach of the peace, squall, riot, disturbance, commotion, Donnybrook, tumult, uproar, outbreak, affray, fisticuffs, fistfight, scrape, stir, disorder, tumultuousness.

ROWDY, *n.* Disorderly person, ruffian, rough, roughneck, hoodlum, hooligan, tough, larrikin, miscreant, desperado, gangster, terrorist, apache, thug, gunman, criminal, malefactor, outlaw, felon, rapscallion, blackguard, knave, scoundrel, villain, brawler, bully, roisterer, vandal.

ROWDY, *adj.* Disorderly, blackguard, disreputable, rough, unruly, tumultuous, raffish, barbarous, brutish, savage, gross, coarse, rowdyish, vicious, evil, unprincipled, lawless, recreant, criminal, corrupt, abandoned, sunk in iniquity, iniquitous, sinister, felonious, nefarious, flagitious, villainous, heinous, flagrant, demoniacal, hellborn, atrocious, scurvy, shameful, opprobrious, incorrigible, recidivous, reprobate, unruly, refractory, irreformable, discreditable, culpable, malignant, malicious, ill-disposed, inimical, mischievous.

ROWDYISM, *n.* Ruffianism, hooliganism, hoodlumism, blackguardism, vandalism, brutality, grossness, low life, barbarism, viciousness, malevolence, mischief-making, mischievousness, atrociousness, knavery, recidivism, villainy, wrongdoing, flagrancy, infamy.

ROYAL, *adj.* 1. Kingly, princely, queenly, regal, kinglike, lordly, sovereign, imperial, monarchical, courtly, majestic, august, imposing, authoritative, stately, impressive, imperious, commanding, absolute, autocratic, sceptered, aristocratic, regnant, basilic, noble, highborn, patrician, grand, magnificent, lofty, elevated, sublime, exalted, paramount, dynastic, despotic, dominant, gubernatorial, peremptory, overruling, hegemonic.

2. *(Coll.),* First-rate, excellent, fine, superior, prime, of the highest order, first-class, of the best sort, tiptop, eminent, crack, choice, extremely good.

ROYALTY, *n.* 1. Kingship, sovereignty, monarchy, royal status or power, nobility, regality, regalness, majesty, kingliness, princeliness, autocracy, imperialism, absolutism, Caesarism, czarism, kaiserism, lordship, mastership, primacy, supremacy, suzerainty, rod of empire, iron sway, divine right, prerogative, prestige, dominion, authority, domination, command, bidding, reign, sway, dynasty authoritativeness, hegemony, regime, regnancy, monocracy, aristarchy.

2. Fixed portion of the proceeds from, per-

centage on coypright, share, payment, compensation, return, commission, remuneration, recoupment, reimbursement, recompense, reward, brokerage, demurrage, salvage, subsidy, installment.

RUB, *v.* 1. Subject to friction in order to clean or smooth, furbish, scour, polish, burnish, clean, wipe, smooth, scrub, curry, scrape, abrade, rasp, fray, graze, grind, file, chafe, fret, grate, embrocate, triturate, levigate, groom.

2. Knead, stroke, massage, pet, touch, fondle, finger, manipulate, palm, palpate, handle, twiddle, pass the fingers over, brush, grope, feel, thumb, paw, fumble, pinch.

3. Irritate, hurt, annoy, ruffle, wound, gall, pique, inflame.

RUB, *n.* 1. Friction, abrasion, embrocation, rubbing, massage, attrition, confrication, arrosion, affriction, limature, frication, contrition, elbow-grease, anatripsis, erasure, palpation, manipulation, handling, stereognosis, kneading, contrectation, stroking, stroke, glance, brush, graze.

2. Annoying circumstance, difficulty, obstacle, pinch, impediment, hardship, tough job, embarrassment, dilemma, perplexity, quandary, nonplus, strait, pass, trial, emergency, exigency, scrape, pickle, mess, stew, hitch, adversity, mishap, frowns of fortune, ups and downs, jinx, trouble, plight, setback, check, reverse, casualty, accident, catastrophe.

3. Something irritating to the feelings, gibe, reproof, jeer, taunt, sarcasm, stinging rebuke, stricture, reflection, animadversion, criticism, innuendo, insinuation, sneer, left-handed compliment, remonstrance, increpation, reprimand, jobation, castigation, lecture, dressing down, scolding, rating, rap on the knuckles, diatribe, tirade.

RUBBER, *n.* 1. Elastic material derived from latex, caoutchouc, gum elastic, India rubber, gutta-percha.

2. Overshoe, galosh, sandal.

RUBBISH, *n.* 1. Refuse, waste matter, debris, trash, litter, junk, detritus, fragments, fag ends, orts, sweepings, scoria, lumber, dregs, scum, dross, shoddy, odds and ends, leavings, rags, garbage, offscourings, rubble, stubble, chaff, trumpery, *fatras (Fr.),* froth, offal, recrement, feculence, ordure, frippery.

2. Nonsense, moonshine, bosh, twaddle, jargon, jabber, gibberish, balderdash, babble, inanity, rigmarole, fudge, stuff and nonsense, drivel, rot, flapdoodle.

RUBICUND, *adj.* Reddish, erubescent, ruddy, rufescent, rufous, red, florid, flushed, incarnadine, sanguine, roseate, rosy, blowzy, russet, reddish-brown, murrey, carroty.

RUB OUT, *v.* Erase, expunge, efface, obliterate, wipe out, cancel, blot out, strike out, sponge out, wipe off, render illegible, delete.

RUCK, *n.* 1. Ruffle, rumple, dog's-ear, crinkle, crumple, wrinkle, rimple, pleat, fold, plicature, crease, plait, tuck, gather, corrugation, flounce, pucker.

2. Heap of inferior things, great mass of undistinguished persons, common sort, run of the mill, throng, multitude, crowd, mob, large number, horde, herd, riffraff, canaille, rabble, vulgus, small fry, ragtag and bobtail.

RUDDY, *adj.* Of a red color, reddish, rufus, rufescent, rosy, rubicund, incarnadine, roseate, sanguine, murrey, russet, erubescent, florid, rosy-

cheeked, having a fresh healthy color, blowzy, flushed, burnt, blushing, cherry-cheeked.

RUDE, *adj.* 1. Uncouth, coarse, boorish, vulgar, uncultured, unpolished, uncivilized, unrefined, loutish, churlish, clownish, barbarous, untutored, unlearned, ignorant, undisciplined, illiterate, untaught, untrained, ungraceful, unskilled, unskilful, savage, gross, clumsy, gauche, uncultivated, primitive, wild, brutish, countrified, uneducated, provincial, ungainly, unfashionable, homespun, homebred, inartistic, homely, imperfect, outlandish, crude, rustic, inelegant, raw, artless.

2. Uncourteous, discourteous, impudent, impertinent, uncivil, impolite, insulting, ill-bred, blunt, brusque, unmannerly, insolent, surly, saucy, currish, bluff, gruff, bad-mannered, disrespectful, ungentlemanly, misbehaved, flippant, bold, inurbane, ungracious, unaccommodating, arrogant, sullen, unladylike, hoydenish, crusty, scornful, abusive, bullying, bearish, acrimonious, crabbed, unceremonious, contumelious, indelicate, scurrilous, profane, uncourtly, indecorous, undignified, ungallant, unneighborly, fresh, pert, malapert, obtrusive, forward, ill-humored, ill-tempered, sour, tart, trenchant, sharp, caustic, sarcastic, bitter, virulent, snarling, venomous, morose, perverse, grouchy, sulky, splenetic, peevish, thorny, cross, short, harsh, stern, austere, raffish, low, offensive, plebeian, caddish, snobbish, *contra bonos mores (Lat.),* ribald, foul-mouthed, smutty, indecent, obscene, base, vile, blackguardly, disdainful, abrupt, derisive, supercilious, disparaging, contemptuous, opprobrious.

3. Rough, uneven, ill-formed, unwrought, unfashioned, amorphous, shapeless, unformed, rugged, roughly wrought, unfinished, formless, unshapely, asymmetric, misshapen, unhewn, malformed, unshapen, scraggy.

4. Violent, tempestuous, turbulent, tumultuous, inclement, fierce, boisterous, ungentle, impetuous, severe, discordant, blustering, forcible, vehement, riotous, raging, vigorous, robust, obstreperous, tumultuary, uproarious, tameless, ravening, frenzied, frantic, furious, infuriate, ferocious, savage, stormy.

RUDENESS, *n.* 1. Coarseness, uncouthness, boorishness, vulgarity, loutishness, churlishness, barbarity, illiteracy, ignorance, grossness, clumsiness, gaucherie, brutishness, ungainliness, homeliness, outlandishness, crudeness, rusticity.

2. Discourteousness, incivility, impoliteness, impertinence, impudence, brusqueness, bluntness, unmannerliness, insolence, surliness, sauciness, currishness, gruffness, bluffness, disrespectfulness, ungentlemanliness, misbehavior, flippancy, boldness, inurbanity, ungraciousness, arrogance, sullenness, hoydenism, crustiness, scornfulness, acrimoniousness, crabbedness, indelicacy, scurrility, profanity, uncourtliness, indecorum, pertness, freshness, malapertness, obtrusiveness, tartness, sourness, acerbity, ill-breeding, effrontery, overassurance, face, brass, cheek, lip, presumption, sharpness, causticity, sarcasm, bitterness, virulence, moroseness, perversity, grouchiness, sulkiness, spleen, peevishness, shortness, harshness, austerity, sternness, raffishness, caddishness, snobbishness, ribaldry, smuttiness, obscenity, abruptness, derision, contemptuousness, opprobriousness.

3. Roughness, inelegance, imperfection, shapelessness, formlessness, amorphism, amorphousness, asymmetry, unshapeliness, misshapenness, malformity.

4. Storminess, violence, vehemence, inclemency, boisterousness, tempestuousness, tumultuousness, turbulence, fierceness, severity, ungentleness, impetuosity, riotousness, obstreperousness, uproariousness, frenzy, franticness, furiousness, fury, ferocity, savageness.

RUDIMENT, *n.* Undeveloped form, first slight appearance, mere beginning, rude state, embryo, germ, seed, root, nucleus, radical, radix, egg, ovum, sperm, semen, spawn, milt, roe, stirps, starting point, foundation, principia, commencement, first principle, elements, essential point, ultimate cause, prime mover, determinant, generator, leaven, mainspring, fountainhead, source, spring, font, remote cause, *fons et origo (Lat.).*

RUDIMENTARY, *adj.* 1. Embryonic, fetal, germinal, *in ovo (Lat.),* natal, rudimental, elementary, initial, primal, primary, original, elemental, initiatory, primordial, germinative, originative, formative.

2. Undeveloped, premature, immature, simple, incomplete, vestigial, inchoate, imperfect, unhatched, unfledged.

RUE, *v.* Feel sorrow over, regret bitterly, repent of, wish undone, lament, deplore, be sorry for, mourn, bewail, sorrow over, grieve for, repine, bemoan, fret, think better of, brood over, mope about, prey on the mind, cast a lingering look behind, *infandum renovare dolorem (Lat.),* own oneself in the wrong, plead guilty, sing *miserere,* cry *peccavi,* don sackcloth and ashes, turn over a new leaf, learn by experience, be contrite, be conscience-stricken, accuse oneself.

RUEFUL, *adj.* 1. Regretful, penitent, repentant, penitential, sorry, remorseful, compunctious, conscience-stricken, apologetic, repining, sorrowful, ruesome, homesick, nostalgic, contrite, self-accusing, touched, softened, affected, tearful, lachrymose, compassionate, querulous, plaintive.

2. Mournful, sorrowful, lugubrious, melancholy, pitiful, doleful, dolorous, woeful, regretful, depressed, cheerless, funereal, woebegone, heartsick, hypochondriac, despondent.

RUFF, *n.* Wheel-shaped stiff collar arranged in rows of radiating folds trimmed with lace, lace neckpiece, ruffle, ruche, stock, dicky, boa.

RUFFIAN, *n.* Tough lawless person, desperado, thug, apache, brutal fellow, cutthroat, hoodlum, hooligan, rough, roughneck, rowdy, blackguard, barbarian, brute, bully, robber, assassin, highwayman, gunman, gangster, murderer, felon, bandit, footpad, killer, miscreant, scoundrel, villain, rogue, knave, caitiff, monster, wretch, ugly customer, criminal, malefactor, outlaw, jailbird, marauder, brigand, racketeer, terrorist, savage, bludgeon man, larrikin, roisterer, bully, yahoo, reprobate.

RUFFLE, *v.* 1. Draw up into pleats, gather into folds, plait, pucker, overlap, fold, cockle, flounce, wrinkle, ruff, crinkle, corrugate, smock, plicate, pleat, crease, twill, rimple.

2. Destroy the smoothness of, disorder, roughen, muss, disarrange, rumple, derange, dishevel, entangle, jumble, ripple.

3. Disturb, discompose, torment, harass, vex, agitate, upset, unsettle, disquiet, annoy, plague, molest, badger, heckle, worry, trouble, confuse, excite, perturb, fret, irritate, nettle, pique, aggravate, chafe, fluster, disconcert, inflame, infuriate.

4. Turn over rapidly, pass through the fingers deftly, shuffle, riffle, mix up.

RUFFLE, *n.* 1. Strip of cloth drawn up by gathering along one edge, frill, lace neckpiece, ruche, ruff, edging, ruck, flounce, frounce.

2. Disturbance, fluster, pother, to-do, flurry, hurry-skurry, bustle, ado, confusion, commotion, flutter, agitation, excitement, stew, restlessness, trepidation, fuss, hurry, whirl, ferment, fever of excitement, tumult, annoyance, vexation, disturbing experience, perturbation, irritation, trial of temper.

RUG, *n.* Floor covering, piece of carpeting, floorcloth, mat, carpet, scatter rug, drugget, Oriental carpet, Persian rug, linoleum, oilcloth, runner.

RUGGED, *adj.* 1. Rough, uneven, craggy, cragged, jagged, scraggy, seamed, wrinkled, furrowed, corrugated, irregular, roughly broken, rocky, boulderstrewn, bumpy, unlevel, gnarled, knotted, invious, pathless, trackless, scabrous.

2. Unkempt, bristly, shaggy, hirsute, ragged, hairy, tufted, crinose, bushy, villous, hispid, bearded, pappose, pilous, shagged, fringed, setose, setaceous, woolly, prickly, kinky, setigerous.

3. Of coarse features, hard-featured, weathered, weather-beaten, hard in outline, heavy, homely, plain, ugly, rude, misshapen, unsightly, unseemly, gaunt, unprepossessing, graceless, uncouth, gross, awkward, gawky, lumpish.

4. Difficult, severe, hard, trying, thorny, tough, onerous, arduous, laborious, operose, formidable, herculean, stubborn, unmanageable, plaguy, labyrinthine, impracticable, complicated, intricate, ticklish, perplexing.

5. Stormy, tempestuous, turbulent, inclement, boisterous, wild, violent, raging.

6. Discordant, inharmonious, harsh, strident, stridulous, unmusical, grating, raucous, hoarse, jarring, gruff.

7. Hardy, robust, hale, robustious, vigorous, sturdy, able-bodied, husky, brawny, wiry, sinewy, well-knit, stalwart, sound, fit, hearty, stanch, weatherproof, in fine fettle.

8. Stern, harsh, dour, severe, austere, drastic, unfeeling, inconsiderate, churlish, blunt, brusque, unrefined, barbarous.

RUGOSE, *adj.* Wrinkled, rugous, seamed, furrowed, gnarled, knurled, crinkly, rugulose, corrugated, wrinkly, ridged, crow's-foot marked.

RUIN, *v.* 1. Reduce to wreckage, destroy, devastate, demolish, overthrow, fell, floor, raze, overturn, subvert, overwhelm, wreck, smash, shatter, crush, desolate, prostrate, lay waste, spoliate, despoil, pillage, sack, ravage, blast, annihilate, exterminate, extirpate, nullify, blot out, obliterate, dissolve, disintegrate, dismantle, bring tottering down, ruinate, rout, defeat, damn, undo, shipwreck, scuttle, wreck, swamp, level, gut, eradicate, pull to pieces, batter, squash, efface, quash, quell, pull down, cut down, put an end to, upset, injure irretrievably, spoil, mar, harm, impair, maim.

2. Seduce, debauch, ravish, deflower, devirginate, violate, rape, stuprate, defile, betray, pollute.

3. Reduce to poverty, impoverish, beggar, bankrupt, bring to want, pauperize, fleece.

RUIN, *n.* 1. Destruction, downfall, overthrow, devastation, demolition, wreck, ruination, perdition, subversion, prostration, undoing, fall, wrack, desolation, havoc, loss, shipwreck, disintegration, discomfiture, failure, defeat, damnation, decay, dilapidation, wreckage, calamity, disaster, adversity, waste, breakdown, misfortune, dissolution, doom, rack and ruin, labefaction, fiasco, catastrophe, disruption, abolition, ravage, crack-up, cataclysm, debacle, extermination, annihilation, extirpation, casualty, blow, scourge, reverse, infliction, setback, extremity, disorganization.

2. Loss of purity, seduction, devirgination, violation, ravishment, rape, stupration, defilement, pollution, betrayal.

3. Impoverishment, bankruptcy, beggary, pauperization, insolvency, mendicity, mendicancy, impecuniosity, pauperism, straits, wolf at the door, low water, destitution, difficulties, distress, neediness, pennilessness, penury, indigence, poverty, want, necessity, privation.

RUINOUS, *adj.* 1. Fallen into ruin, dilapidated, run-down, demolished, decayed, battered, weather-beaten, time-worn, crumbling, moldering, broken-down, decrepit, worn-out, rotten, blighted, mildewed, moth-eaten, threadbare, shabby, frayed, seedy, faded, rusty, antiquated, gone by, tumbledown.

2. Destructive, deleterious, disastrous, pernicious, calamitous, baneful, baleful, lethal, deadly, pestilential, harmful, injurious, noxious, pestiferous, noisome, damnatory, adverse, subversive, mischievous, wasteful, mortal, fatal, annihilative, extirpatory, exterminative, demolitionary, incendiary, subversionary, cataclysmic, catastrophic, tragic, lethiferous, internecine, suicidal, homicidal, murderous, sanguinary, slaughterous.

RUINS, *n., pl.* Remains, relics, debris, scattered parts, *disiecta membra (Lat.)*, reliquiae, wreckage, rubbish, remnants, husks, chaff, waste, shreds, refuse, detritus, disintegrated material, spilth.

RULE, *v.* 1. Exercise dominating power over, exercise dominion over, dominate, control, command, direct, govern, administer, lead, manage, regulate, reign over, head, master, sway, discipline, restrain, bridle, conduct, run, predominate, have the upper hand, boss, preponderate, lord it over, tyrannize, domineer, be at the head of, preside over, bend to one's will, be master of the situation, rule the roost, lay down the law, have it all one's own way, give orders, superintend, supervise, influence, persuade, prevail on, advise, guide.

2. Adjudicate, decide, decree, settle, establish, determine, fix, judge, conclude, hold, pass upon, declare authoritatively, arbitrate, adjudge, pronounce, sentence, award, find, opine, consider.

RULE, *n.* 1. Domination, sovereignty, dominion, mastership, lordship, command, mastery, control, reign, regency, regnancy, direction, jurisdiction, administration, hegemony, sway, authority, empire, government, governance, supremacy, influence, predominance, preponderance, masterdom, ascendancy, regime, dynasty, suzerainty, primacy, magistracy, consulship, dictatorship, despotism, tyranny, kingship, leadership, bidding, grasp, hold, grip, prestige, prerogative, dictation, absolutism, Czarism, Caesarism, kaiserism, imperialism, autocracy, divine right, bureaucracy, officialdom.

2. Guide, precept, formula, criterion, standard, canon, convention, model, maxim, law, ruling, regulation, decision, prescription, precedent, measure, system, test, even tenor, routine, rut, custom, order, *règlement (Fr.)*, habit, normality, method, nature, normal state, principle, normalcy, order of things, hard and fast rule, touchstone, Procrustean law, standing order, law of the Medes and Persians, regularity, exactness, uniformity, clockwork

precision, consistency, punctuality, constancy, policy, code, form, doctrine, adage, axiom, aphorism, formulary, norm, theorem.

RULER, *n.* 1. King, sovereign, potentate, monarch, emperor, lord, dynast, czar, Caesar, kaiser, liege, prince, suzerain, crowned head, overlord, imperator, majesty, caliph, sultan, shah, imam, khan, mogul, mikado, padishah, shereef, doge, inca, rajah, maharajah, nawab, ameer, nizam, mirza, khedive, satrap, pasha, bey, viceroy, regent, viceregent, tetrarch, pasha, mandarin, hierarch, pharoah, autocrat, tyrant, despot, oligarch, dictator, sachem, sirdar, sheik, aga, sahib, emir.

2. Chief, head, governor, commandant, commander, president, protector, kingpin *(coll.)*, big shot *(slang)*, chieftain, boss, master mind, prefect, archon, chancellor, magistrate, provost, mayor, corregidor, syndic, seneschal, alcalde, functionary, official, generalissimo, marshal, commander-in-chief, dominator, subjugator, victor, vanquisher, controller, director, master, patriarch, manager, *Führer (Ger.)*, *duce (It.)*.

3. Straightedge, yardstick, folding rule, tape measure, slide rule, parallel ruler.

RULING, *adj.* 1. Sovereign, paramount, commanding, supreme, regnant, reigning, regent, controlling, chief, governing, gubernatorial, regulating, autocratic, despotic, tyrannical, imperious, imperial, majestic, imperialistic, princely, regal, royal, lordly, high-handed, authoritative, magisterial, dictatorial, domineering, monarchical, kingly, dynastic, administrative.

2. Predominant, prevalent, current, rife, predominating, preponderant, habitual, prevailing, natural, normal, typical, customary, regular, usual.

RUMBLE, *n.* Thunder, reverberation, booming, rumbling, grumble, growl, boom, din, roll, bombilation, cannonade, barrage, drumming, resonance, tattoo.

RUMINATE, *v.* 1. Chew the cud, chew over again, chew again what has been chewed slightly and swallowed, regurgitate.

2. Bring up again and again for mental consideration, meditate, speculate, muse, cogitate, mull, brood over, ponder, reflect, think, consider, deliberate, excogitate, reason, bestow consideration upon, contemplate, con over, study, animadvert, apply the mind, weigh, take counsel, commune with oneself, turn over in one's mind, revolve in the mind, sleep upon, advise with one's pillow, collect one's thoughts, bethink oneself.

RUMINATION, *n.* 1. Chewing the cud, merycism, regurgitation.

2. Meditation, cogitation, musing, reflection, consideration, pondering, brown study, reverie, contemplation, abstraction, self-communing, self-consultation, excogitation, lucubration, study, deliberation, speculation, exercitation of the intellect, brainwork, headwork, mentation, cerebration, mental application, close study.

RUMMAGE, *v.* Search thoroughly through by turning things over, bring to light by a thorough search, ransack, look through, turn over, explore, examine, disarrange, poke around in, snoop through *(coll.)*, frisk, look about for, ferret out, leave no stone unturned, pry into, peer into, delve into, probe to the bottom, scrutinize, winnow, sift through, hunt out.

RUMMAGE, *n.* 1. Careful search by turning things over, exploration, scrutinization, examination, quest, research, investigation, indagation, perscrutation, inquest, sifting, winnowing, reconnaissance, reconnoitering, prying.

2. Upheaval, turmoil, derangement, confusion, miscellaneous articles, odds and ends, litter, rubbish, confused mass, mishmash, jumble, hodgepodge, disorder, disorderly mixture.

RUMOR, n. Statement in general circulation without certainty as to facts, bruit, flying report, talk, hearsay, gossip, common voice, town talk, scandal, *on dit (Fr.),* tittle-tattle, current tale, common fame, grapevine, scuttlebutt, supposition, newscast, dispatch, repute, reputation, tidings, information, *oui-dire (Fr.),* scoop *(newspaper),* cry, canard, communiqué, hint, innuendo, insinuation, whisper, whispering campaign, word to the wise, *verbum sapienti (Lat.),* subaudition, intimation, representation, monition, divulgence, revelation, exposé, utterance, publicity, notoriety, *vox populi (Lat.),* currency, circulation, eavesdropping, topic of the day, idea afloat.

RUMOR, v. Assert by a rumor, report, circulate, bruit, noise abroad, tell, spread abroad, broadcast, put into circulation, bandy about, whisper, murmur, tattle, utter, gossip, newsmonger, make known, publish, broach, diffuse, put forward, disseminate, divulgate, divulge, give out, buzz about, hawk about, voice, blazon, herald, blaze abroad, set news afloat, apprise, tip, represent, intimate, communicate, give the low-down, give inside information, announce, make known, promulgate, insinuate, hint, suggest, breathe, let fall, put a bee in one's bonnet, tip the wink.

RUMP, n. Hinder part of an animal's body, croup, podex, pygidium, buttocks, hind quarters, posterior, rear, rear end, *derrière (Fr.),* bottom, backside, fag end, seat, breech, scut, loin, dorsum, tail.

RUMPLE, v. Draw into wrinkles, crumple, wrinkle, crush, dishevel, disarrange, ruffle, muss, pucker, crease, corrugate, tousle, disorder, derange, crisp, engrail, crinkle, cockle up, crankle, rimple, ruck, flounce, twill, pucker, crimple.

RUMPLE, n. Irregular fold, rimple, pucker, crease, muss, wrinkle, corrugation, gather, plait, pleat, plicature, ply, tuck, crinkle, crankle, crumple, ruck, dog's-ear, ruffle, crow's-feet, frounce, flounce, flexure, undulation, ripple, wave, fluctuation.

RUMPUS, n. Disturbing noise, uproar, tumult, noisy disturbance, violent commotion, fracas, outbreak, confusion, riot, affray, Donnybrook, melee, altercation, brawl, squabble, row, feud, quarrel, discord, disagreement, tiff, spat, *tracasserie (Fr.),* wrangling, racket, hubbub, embranglement, embroilment, scrimmage, breach of the peace, imbroglio, squall, contention, perturbation, disquiet, turbulence, turmoil, rout, hurly-burly, vortex, tempest, boisterousness, obstreperousness, bluster, outburst, blow up, explosion, eruption, detonation, ferment, storm, broil.

RUN, v. 1. Make off rapidly, move swiftly, step quickly, race, hasten, hustle, dart, fly, scud, hurry, hie, scamper, sprint, scorch, scurry, take flight, scuttle, lope, bolt, course, gallop, scour, speed, post, trip, trot, take to one's heels, skip, flee, spread one's legs, show a light pair of heels, spurt, whiz, swoop, shoot, whisk, tear along, gain ground, sweep past, skim along, dash, rush, skedaddle, ride hard, haste, accelerate, burn up the road, outstrip the wind, wing one's way, plunge, scram-

ble, bestir oneself, flit, cut and run, bowl along, bound, spring, stir one's stumps, set off at a score, go off like a shot.

2. Flow, glide, stream, roll on, move on, proceed, go, pour, spill, gush, trickle, surge, swirl, swash, meander, lapse, elapse, issue, traverse, pass, go by, advance, continue, circulate, migrate, trail, climb, creep, budge, stir, slide, shift, drift, sweep along, wander.

3. Vanish, evanesce, steal away, abscond, depart privately, flee, escape, beat a retreat, disappear, dissolve, melt away, evaporate, be lost, sink, vamoose, decamp.

4. Become fluid, melt, fuse, be fusible, liquefy, deliquesce, mold, cast, smelt, liquate, lixiviate.

5. Drive, propel, turn, operate, impel, actuate, mobilize, thrust, push, force, manage, direct, maintain, cause to ply.

6. Smuggle, bootleg, rustle, poach, convey, transport, shanghai.

7. Incur, be liable to, fall into, encounter, be exposed to, bring on, invite, court, meet with.

8. Stand for election, compete, vie, strive to attain, take the stump, contend, be a candidate, enter the lists, bid for, canvass, solicit votes.

RUN, n. 1. Brook, stream, streamlet, flow, runnel, runlet, rill, rivulet, burn, watercourse, current, brooklet, kill, creek, rillet, course, race.

2. Pace, canter, trot, gallop, jog, single foot, amble, gait, sprint, spurt, stride, step, burst, rush, dash, clip, scamper, scurry, scuttle, swoop, steeplechase, race, expedition, velocity, speed, celerity, rapidity, swiftness, haste, acceleration.

3. *(Music)* Roulade, cadenza, *fioritura (It.),* bravura, shake, trill, arpeggio, turn, variation.

4. Course, onward movement, current, flow, progress, passage, motion, migration, tide, march, sweep, flight, duration, drift, driftage, flux, stir, tendency, direction, journey, excursion, trip, travel, locomotion, expedition, pilgrimage, voyage, cruise, sail, circuit, tour, peregrination, drive, outing, jaunt, trek, perambulation, turn, tramp, stalk, hike, ramble, stroll, promenade, saunter, walk, constitutional *(coll.),* campaigning, wayfaring, automobiling, motoring, equitation, riding, manège, horsemanship, sightseeing, globetrotting, vagrancy, nomadism, roving, vagabondage, emigration, flitting, gadding, route, itinerary, procession, cavalcade, caravan, parade, cortege, train, column, file, succession.

5. Way, wont, habit, habitude, addiction, usage, custom, consuetude, use, practice, procedure, vogue, fashion, mode, observance, prescription, conventionality, beaten path, matter of course, second nature, aptitude, tendency, routine, groove, rut, convention, precedent.

6. Rule, average, mean, golden mean, middle, balance, mean proportion, norm, medium, medial estimate, trend, generality.

7. Continued course, continuance, spell, period, currency, popularity, time, duration, term, space, span, season, while, continuation, extension, prolongation, perpetuation, maintenance, persistence, repetition, perseverance.

RUN AFTER, v. Pursue, follow, chase, prosecute, prowl after, make after, shadow, trail, follow the trail, press on, give chase, course, hunt, dog, stalk, hound, tread on the heels of, run down, try to find, search for, track down.

RUN AWAY, v. Flee, elope, escape, fly, desert, abscond, beat a retreat, turn tail, take to one's heels, show a light pair of heels, cut and run, be off like a shot, take to flight, scamper off, shuffle off, steal away from, part company, play truant, sneak out of, give leg bail, give one the go-by, take French leave, decamp, bolt, flit, skedaddle, levant, make oneself scarce, lead one a chase, dodge, shirk, elude, evade, retire, shy away from, shun, avoid, steer clear of.

RUNAWAY,. *n.* Deserter, fugitive, renegade, runagate, absconder, refugee, truant, eloper, decamper, slacker, shirker, seceder, caitiff, poltroon, coward, recreant, defaulter, ticket-of-leave man, outlaw, jailbird, dastard.

RUN DOWN, *v.* Chase to weariness, catch by chasing, pursue and nab, hunt down, snatch, ensnare, entrap, tackle, seize, embrace, net, bag, claw, hook, capture, collar, catch, grapple with, pocket, secure, apprehend, arrest, take prisoner, overthrow, overwhelm, conquer, lay by the heels, pounce upon.

2. Bear down upon, run against and sink, collide with, dash against, deal a blow at, pitch into, close with, ride full tilt against, dash at, fly at, have at, be hard upon.

3. Depreciate, belittle, underestimate, disparage, misprize, ridicule, minimize, think nothing of, set at naught, decry, traduce, cry down, condemn, detract, think ill of, disvalue, discommend, dispraise, not speak well of, impugn, pass censure upon, denounce, impeach, stigmatize, blackball, blacklist, animadvert upon, reflect upon, defame, criticize, find fault with, pick to pieces, carp at, sneer at, asperse, blow upon, vilify, malign, brand.

RUNG, *n.* Rounded crosspiece of a ladder, round, spoke, rundle, stave, step, shaped horizontal piece for strengthening, bar, stout stick.

RUNLET, *n.* Small stream, streamlet, brook, brooklet, runnel, rivulet, run, little channel of water, race, flow, rill, burn, rillet, gill.

RUNNER, *n.* 1. Messenger, courier, post, postrider, express, estafette, dispatch bearer, Mercury, Hermes, Iris, Ariel, emissary, dak, commissionaire.

2. Hotel runner, touter, tout, steerer, barker, canvasser, drummer, solicitor, agent.

3. Smuggler, bootlegger, poacher, racketeer, privateer.

4. Branch, tendril, sarmentum, creeper, withe, sprig, twig, switch, offshoot, spray, ramification, bough, scion.

RUN-OF-THE-MILL, *adj.* Average, ordinary, mediocre, middling, tolerable, passable, commonplace, everyday, fair, indifferent, so-so, decent, moderate, not bad, bearable, admissible, secondrate.

RUN OUT, *v.* 1. Expend, exhaust, waste, run through, misspend, be prodigal, lavish, squander, dissipate, spill, overdraw, fritter away, sow, broadcast.

2. Expire, be at an end, terminate, close, finish, conclude, discontinue, stop, wind up, cease, come to a close, stop short.

RUNT, *n.* Undersized person, stunted creature, dwarf, pygmy, Lilliputian, chit, midget, pigwidgeon, elf, urchin, hop-o'-my-thumb, manikin, homunculus, fingerling, dapperling, dandiprat, cock sparrow, Tom Thumb, Humpty Dumpty, peewee.

RUPTURE, *v.* Burst, break, cause a breach of, disunite, rend, separate, crack, lacerate, wrench, disjoin, dissociate, part, sunder, divide, dissever, unfasten, disrupt, dismember, break up, dislocate, tear, snap.

RUPTURE, *n.* 1. Burst, break, fracture, split, hernia (*Med.*), breach, disruption, disjunction, separation, disunion, disengagement, dissociation, discontinuity, cleavage, severance, fissure, rent, crack, rift, slit, cleft.

2. Schism, faction, feud, quarrel, vendetta, embroilment, disagreement, discord, dissension, dissidence, variance, contention, clash, misunderstanding, disunion, dispute, altercation, squabble, strife, controversy, friction, litigation, outbreak, polemics, brawl, broil.

RURAL, *adj.* Agricultural, rustic, country, agrarian, bucolic, pastoral, countrified, provincial, agrestic, georgic, praedial, Arcadian, sylvan, geoponic, agronomical.

RUSE, *n.* Artifice, trick, stratagem, dodge, wile, subterfuge, hoax, maneuver, deception, sham, fetch, crafty device, machination, blind, scheme, feint, sharp practice, contrivance, deceit, fraud, chouse, imposture, shift, trickery, chicane, finesse, evasion, flimflam, swindle, bunco, trap, net, sell, plot, art, chicanery, circumvention, strategy, jugglery, duplicity, guile, cheat, hanky-panky, knavery, double-dealing, plant, fake, pitfall, snare, gin, bait, decoy, toils, meshes, ambuscade, false colors, disguise, masquerade, mask, camouflage, veil, cloak, borrowed plumes, mummery, make-believe, forgery, illusion, delusion, fallacy, chimera, mirage, myth, phantasm, deceptive appearance.

RUSH, *v.* 1. Move with speed, go with impetuosity, plunge with headlong haste, press on, push on, sweep, charge, hurry, dash forward, hurtle, drive, career, tear, precipitate, surge, gush, speed, whisk, scud, bolt, dart, whiz, scuttle, scurry, fly, hasten, swoop, hustle, bustle, flounce, streak, hie, sprint, post, trip, shoot, scorch, skim, skedaddle, haste, flutter, scramble, bestir oneself, work against time, work under pressure, make short work of, lose no time, spur, quicken, accelerate, expedite, goad, urge, whip, dispatch, run, lunge.

2. Attack, assault, assail, storm, beleaguer, beset, pounce upon, set upon, fall upon, thrust at, strike at, come to close quarters, cut and thrust, close with, go over the top, scale the walls, board.

3. Swarm, congregate, flock, converge, assemble, concentrate, come together, collect, cluster, surge, herd, stream, throng, mass, huddle, forgather.

RUSH, *n.* 1. Drive, dash, headlong, rapid onward movement, onset, onrush, plunge, precipitancy, precipitation, charge, sudden advance, rampage, rout, stampede, onslaught, assault, attack, sudden access, hurried activity, busy haste, bustle, flurry, scramble, scurry, scuttle, scamper, spurt, acceleration, hurry, urgency, press of work, impetuosity, velocity, expeditiousness, dispatch, quickness, celerity, speed, haste, nimbleness, swiftness, promptitude, burst, sprint, race, descent, swoop, gallop, trot, canter, scrimmage, whirlwind, hurry-scurry, helter-skelter, intensity, gust.

2. Throng, crowd, multitude, assemblage, concourse, confluence, influx, conflux, gathering, concentration, congregation, muster, convergence, convocation, flood, deluge, mob, host, crush, horde, troop, gang, shoal, swarm, covey, drove, flock, bevy, galaxy, bunch, drive, array, batch, pack, lot, bunch, bundle, bale, shock, stack, sheaf, shower, volley, flight, conglomeration, aggregation, congestion, pile, heap.

RUSSET, *adj.* Reddish-brown, yellowish-brown, light brown, brownish, auburn, adust, cinnamon, chestnut, hazel, nutbrown, puce, ecru, fawn, fuscoùs, tawny, maroon, foxy, rust-colored, copperly, henna, sorrel, roan, rufous, rubicund, murrey, brickdust-colored.

RUST, *v.* 1. Gather rust, grow rusty, corrode, oxidize, patinate, be oxidized, erode, discolor, deteriorate, crumble, flake off.

2. Become impaired, degenerate, decay, go to seed, fade, wither, shrivel, rot, molder, go bad, rankle, fall into decay, ebb, retrograde, wane, fall off, have seen better days, go downhill, decline.

3. Blight, eat away, gnaw at, wear away, sap, undermine, break up, disorganize, destroy, injure, harm, damage, scathe, mar, spoil, dilapidate, ravage.

RUST, *n.* 1. Ferric oxide coating on the surface of iron, film on metal due to oxidation, patina, verdigris, aerugo, corrosion, stain resembling iron rust, discoloration.

2. Plant disease caused by fungi, mildew, must, blight, mold, moldiness, mustiness, cankerworm.

RUSTIC, *n.* Peasant, countryman, swain, bumpkin, hind, hayseed, clodhopper, clodpole, yokel, boor, chawbacon, churl, landman, gaffer, clout, lout, farmer, ruralist, unsophisticated country person, Corydon, serf, clown, hawbuck, oaf, plowman, rube, Tony Lumpkin.

RUSTIC, *adj.* 1. Rural, agrarian, agrestic, geoponic, georgic, bucolic, pastoral, agricultural, country, countrified, provincial, backwoods, sylvan, agronomical, Arcadian.

2. Rude, simple, crude, awkward, plain, homespun, uncouth, unpolished, clownish, rough, loutish, boorish, clodhopping, outlandish, untaught, churlish, carlish, cloddish, gawky, gauche, inelegant, unrefined, uncourtly, unmannerly, coarse, homely, artless, unsophisticated, naive, honest, unaffected.

RUSTICATE, *v.* Sojourn in the country, ruralize, rusticize, seclude oneself, retire to the country, estivate, stagnate.

RUSTICITY, *n.* Rudeness, boorishness, churlishness, clownishness, coarseness, crudeness, inurbanity, inelegance, unmannerliness, simplicity, artlessness, naiveté, ingenuousness, ungainly manners, insuavity, provincialism.

RUSTLE, *v.* 1. Swish, susurrate, whisper, sibilate, froufrou, murmur.

2. Steal, purloin, filch, poach, thieve, pilfer, take, bag, pinch, convey away, abduct, make off with, run away with, spirit away, lift, seize, pillage, plunder, filibuster, despoil, maraud, forage, hijack.

3. Hustle, push, keep moving, bustle, stir about, fuss, bestir oneself, moil, toil, plod, drudge, persevere, make haste, lose no time.

RUSTLE, *n.* Succession of slight soft sounds, rustling, susurrus, sibilation, sibilance, froufrou, murmur, susurration, bustle, whisper, faint sound.

RUSTLING, *adj.* Whispering, susurrant, susurrous, softly murmuring, rustly, swishing, crackling, muffled, silken, sibilant, sibilous.

RUSTY, *adj.* 1. Affected with rust, covered with rust, corroded, rusted, patinated, patinous, patinized, incrusted, aeruginous, ferruginous, discolored, oxidized, stained.

2. Mildewed, fusty, musty, rubiginous, blighted, moldy, cankered, rotten, tainted, lentiginous, worm-eaten.

3. Time-worn, antiquated, inactive, decrepit, fallen into disuse, impaired by wear, dull, faded, shabby, moth-eaten, decayed, moldering, crumbling, broken-down, dilapidated, worn-out, ruinous, used up, useless, sluggish, out of practice, having lost agility, stiff, dormant, idle, inactive, stagnant, inert, effortless.

RUT, *n.* 1. Track of a wheel, groove, channel, furrow, sulcation, hollow, cut, crack, score, seam, flute, stria, ditch, trench, fosse, dike, gutter, trough, depression, moat, cutting.

2. Habit, custom, practice, course, fixed mode of procedure, established way of life, even tenor, system, routine, *règlement (Fr.),* standing order, normalcy, Procrustean law.

3. Periodic sexual excitement of animals, heat, erotic desire, estrus.

RUTHFUL, *adj.* Compassionate, merciful, clement, forgiving, tender, sorrowful, touched, moved, sympathetic, humane, humanitarian, philanthropic, soft-hearted, lenient, forbearing, exorable, gentle, mild, indulgent, tolerant, long-suffering, complaisant, pitiful.

RUTHLESS, *adj.* Merciless, uncompassionate, hard-hearted, pitiless, unmerciful, unpitying, unsparing, relentless, cruel, dire, fell, savage, inhuman, unrelenting, stony-hearted, ferocious, barbarous, inexorable, obdurate, truculent, remorseless, harsh, revengeful, vindictive, brutal, vengeful, implacable, brutish, ferine, malevolent, cutthroat, murderous, lethal, deadly, cold-blooded, marble-hearted, rancorous, bloodthirsty, sanguinary, grim, feral, heartless, unfeeling, atrocious, fiendish, demoniac, diabolical, hellish, devilish, vicious, malign, venomous, poisonous, virulent, maleficent, malignant, treacherous, retaliative, unforgiving, inclement, inflexible.

S

SABBATH, *n.* Seventh day of the week *(as observed by Jews),* first day of the week *(as observed by Christians),* Sunday, Saturday, Lord's day, day of rest, holy day, day of religious observance, First day *(Quaker).*

SABBATICAL, *adj.* Bringing a period of rest, vacational, ferial, festal, holiday.

SABLE, *adj.* Black, ebon *(Poetic),* ebony, dark, dusky, jet, pitchy, raven, jetty, inky, nigrine, nigrous, atramentous, pitch-dark, coal-black, sooty.

SABOTAGE, *n.* Malicious injury *(to work, tools, machinery, etc.),* underhand interference, undermining of a cause, subversion, destruction, treason, retardation, blockage, opposition, disablement, impairment, stoppage, corrosion, inroad, obstruction, hampering, hindrance, erosion, corruption, eating away, deterioration.

SABOTAGE, *v.* Injure by sabotage, attack, destroy, undermine, subvert, hinder, hamper, obstruct, clog, retard, impede, delay, stop, deteriorate, conspire against, hamstring, cripple, eat away at, waste, sap the foundations of, shackle, disable, weaken, scotch, balk, thwart, slacken, paralyze, render powerless, enervate, exhaust, incapacitate, devitalize, debilitate, enfeeble, act as a drag.

SABULOUS, *adj.* Sandy, gritty, sabuline, arenoid, granular, arenose, arenaceous, tophaceous, calculous, sabulose.

SAC, *n.* Baglike structure *(in plant or animal),* pocket, cyst, vesicle, vesica, blister, bleb, pod, cell, pouch, bladder, saccule, utricle, sacculus, legume, venter, ventricle, follicle *(Anat.),* theca *(Bot.),* bursa *(Biol.),* silique *(Bot.),* calyx *(Biol.),* loculus *(Biol.),* pericarp *(Bot.),* capsule *(Biol.).*

SACCHARINE, *adj.* Sweet, sugary, honeyed, candied, nectareous, sugared, cloying, rich, luscious, sweetened, sacchariferous, sugar-coated, granular, saccharoid.

SACERDOTAL, *adj.* Priestly, of *or* pertaining to priests *or* the priesthood, ministerial, clerical, ecclesiastical, churchly, pastoral, papal, prelatic, episcopal, canonical, pontifical, apostolic, monastic, hierarchic, theocratical.

SACERDOTALISM, *n.* System (spirit, methods) of the priesthood, prelacy, episcopacy, papalism, churchcraft, theocrasy, papacy, hierarchy, priestcraft *(derog.),* clericalism.

SACHET, *n.* Small bag (case, pad) containing perfuming powder, perfumer, scent bag, pomander, potpourri.

SACK, *v.* Plunder, pillage after capture, ravage, pouch, satchel, pocket, gunny bag *or* sack, haversack, duffel bag, rucksack, knapsack, saddlebag, wallet.

2. Plundering of a captured place, pillage, ravage, waste, desolation, destruction, robbery, despoliation, spoliation, devastation, havoc, rapine, brigandage, depredation, ravishment, raid, piracy, larceny, theft, marauding, harrying, pilfering, plunderage.

3. Loose-fitting coat, jacket, coatee, kimono, sackcoat, dressing gown, smock, bed jacket, mandarin jacket, mantua *(Hist.).*

SACK, *v.* Plunder, pillage after capture, ravage, spoil, despoil, waste, loot, devastate, desolate, ransack, lay waste, rifle, rapine, strip, rob, destroy, fleece, raid, pilfer, pirate, depredate, freeboot, steal from, gut, maraud, harry, prey on *or* upon.

SACKCLOTH, *n.* Coarse cloth, stout woven material *(of hemp, jute, etc.),* gunny, homespun, fustian, linsey-woolsey, net, netting, canvas, tarpaulin, burlap, ticking, hopsacking, haircloth.

SACRAMENT, *n.* 1. Something regarded as possessing a sacred character *or* mysterious, significance, sign, token, symbol, ritual, rite, ceremony, observance, mystery, formula, relic, form, formulary, solemnity, ceremonial, liturgy, incantation, laying on of hands, invocation, sacramental, ministry, ministration.

2. *(Often cap.)* Eucharist, Lord's Supper, consecrated elements, communion, Holy Communion, transubstantiation, consubstantiation, altar, reception of the Eucharist, celebration of the Lord's Supper.

3. Oath, solemn pledge, word, promise, vow, swearing, avowal, adjuration, solemn declaration, seal, warrant, warranty, obligation, guarantee, assurance, adjuration, undertaking, plight, troth, indemnity, contract, covenant, compact, profession, pignoration, affidavit *(Law),* affirmation.

SACRAMENTAL, *adj.* Of, pertaining to *or* of the nature of a sacrament, symbolic, formal, peculiarly sacred, hallowed, set apart, inviolable, ritual, mysterious, consecrated, solemn, devoted, devotional, baptismal, Eucharistic, sacrosanct, sanctified, sacramentarian, religious, blessed, formular, ceremonious, ceremonial, ritualistic.

SACRED, *adj.* 1. Appropriated *or* dedicated to a deity *or* some religious purpose, holy, consecrated, dedicated, devoted, divine, set apart, hallowed, sanctified, blessed, sacrosanct, solemn, religious, devotional, ceremonial, ceremonious, spiritual, clean, purified.

2. Regarded with reverence, entitled to veneration *or* religious respect, holy, divine, sublime, blessed, godly, saintly, saintlike, reverend, pious, celestial, righteous, just, moral, heavenly-minded, profoundly good, perfect, sinless, angelic, immaculate, virtuous, unstained, guileless, upright, unworldly, otherworldly, uncorrupted, pure in heart, pietistic, sanctified, heaven-sent, seraphic, right-minded, unspotted, clean, blameless, sainted, revered, heavenly, heaven-born, venerable.

3. Pertaining to *or* connected with religion *(as opposed to profane and secular),* religious, hallowed, heavenly, ecclesiastical, church, hieratic, priestly, righteous, celestial, godly, Biblical, scriptural, divine, divinely inspired, theopneustic.

4. Secured against violation, infringement, *etc.,* properly immune *(from violence, interference, etc.,),* inviolate, inviolable, exempt, hidden, safe, out of harm's way *or* reach, respected, protected, impregnable, unassailable, inexpugnable, invulnerable, defended, sheltered, unthreatened, unmolested.

SACRIFICE, *n.* 1. Offering, oblation, lustration, immolation, corban, chiliomb, piaculum, idolothyte, incense, drink offering, holocaust, burnt offering, hecatomb, mactation, sacramental slaughter.

2. Surrender, loss, relinquishment, resignation, release, cession, dispensation, renunciation, abandonment, capitulation, destruction, yielding, giving up.

SACRIFICE, *v.* 1. Make a sacrifice *or* offering of, offer up, burn, pour out, crucify, libate, immolate, Molochize, oblate *(Eccles.).*

2. Dispose of regardless of profit, surrender, give up, let go, part with, spare, yield, cede, concede, resign, waive, relinquish, renounce, give away, abandon, release, lay down, forgo.

SACRIFICIAL, *adj.* Pertaining to *or* concerned with sacrifice, atoning, satisfactional, piacular, propitiatory, expiatory, conciliatory.

SACRILEGE, *n.* Profanation of anything held sacred, violation, impiety, impiousness, desecration, blasphemy, curse, obliquity, reprobacy, profanity, misuse, mockery, irreverence, irreligion, atrocity, scoffing, outrage, perversion, iniquity, sinfulness, wickedness, sin, profaneness.

SACRILEGIOUS, *adj.* Guilty of sacrilege, irreverent, perverted, reprobate, unregenerate, desecrating, profane, profaning, impious, irreligious, blasphemous, hardened, sinful, malefactory, recreant, misbelieving, ungodly, undevout, disobedient.

SACRISTY, *n.* Repository for sacred vessels, vestments, *etc.,* vestry, vestry-room, robing room, diaconicon *(Eccles.).*

SACROSANCT, *adj.* Especially *or* superlatively sacred, inviolable, divine, hallowed, heavenly, religious, holy, godly, celestial, consecrated, sanctified, indefeasible, unimpeachable, inalienable, unchallengeable, imprescriptible *(Law),* solemn, devoted, spiritual, ceremonial, purified, set apart.

SAD, *adj.* 1. Sorrowful, mournful, melancholy, downcast, heavy, disconsolate, depressed, unhappy, dejected, cheerless, cast down, crestfallen, wretched, pathetic, dispirited, broken-hearted, joyless, desolate, funereal, elegiac, lamentable, touching, woebegone, atrabilious, plaintive, dirge-like, somber, afflicted, despondent, deplorable, heavy-hearted, long-faced, long-visaged, lugubrious, blue, miserable, subdued, grave, sober, staid, saturnine, pensive, doleful, dismal, gloomy, dreary, wan, rueful, tearful, grief-stricken, pained, burdened, encumbered, bowed down, full of care, troubled, stricken, crushed, woeful, heavy-laden, pessimistic, distressed, hurt, grieved, infelicitous, lamenting, despairing, forlorn, inconsolable, unmanned, prostrated, chapfallen, down in the mouth *(coll.).*

2. Causing sorrow, grievous, afflictive, lamentable, grave, serious, trying, distressing, unfortunate, calamitous, disastrous, deplorable, heart-rending, dire, troublesome, vexatious, burdensome, harsh, onerous, cruel, severe, hard, difficult, wearying, trying, oppressive, noxious, laborious, arduous, toilsome, tiring, wearing, painful, wearisome, overbearing, irksome, troublesome, taxing, evil, crushing, exhausting, perverse, awkward, untoward, weighty, solemn, rueful, tragic, dismal, woeful, adverse, sinister, black, regrettable, disagreeable, bitter, melancholy, dolorous, mournful, grim, ponderous, overwhelming.

3. *(Of color)* Dark, dull, gray, somber, drab, dismal, depressing, dun, ashen, cinereous, leaden, flat, dead, dreary, favillous, lifeless, deadened, muted, grave, sober, gloomy, subdued, autumnal, mouse-colored, iron-gray, deep, lugubrious, toneless.

SADDEN, *v.* Make *or* become sad, weigh heavily upon, deject, depress, grieve, discourage, dash, cast a gloom *or* shade on, sink, lower, dispirit, dishearten, tone down, lay to heart, darken, subdue, despond, droop, languish, prostrate, unman, prey on the mind, damp, make the heart bleed, sorrow, pine, crush, burden, disconcert, frown upon, plunge into sorrow, cut up *(coll.),* dash *or* wither one's hopes, wring (pierce, rend) the heart.

SADDLE, *n.* Seat for a rider on the back of an animal (bicycle, machine, *etc.*), pad, panel, packsaddle, pillion, *recado (South Amer.), aparejo (Span.),* demipique *(18th Cent.).*

SADDLE, *v.* 1. Put a saddle on, prepare for riding, harness, cinch, yoke, hitch, bridle.

2. Load *(as with a burden),* charge, impose *(as a burden or responsibility),* burden, encumber, weight, freight, weigh down, hamper, handicap, tax, overload, overwhelm, obstruct, shackle, restrain, cramp, fix, place, clog, enjoin, prescribe, assign, bind, exact, oblige, require, lay to one's charge, impede, embarrass.

SADNESS, *n.* Quality *or* state of being sad, unhappiness, sorrow, despondency, depression, dejection, distress, pathos, desolation, calamity, melancholy, despondence, sinking heart, infestivity, doldrums, weariness, lamentation, regret, discontent, despair, megrims, remorse, dolefulness, grief, heaviness, gloominess, melancholia, lachrymals, mopes, blue devils, blues, infelicity, misery, disappointment, mournfulness, soberness, hardship, gloom, sorrowfulness, hypochondria.

SAFE, *adj.* 1. Protected, secure from liability to harm (injury, danger, risk), guarded, unexposed, safe and sound, in shelter, snug, under lock and key, out of reach of danger, high and dry, on terra firma, immune, impregnable, defended, inviolable, invulnerable, inexpugnable, unassailable, proof, unattackable, under the wing *or* shadow, armed, in harbor *or* port, on sure ground, guaranteed.

2. Free from hurt (injury, danger, risk), unharmed, intact, preserved, kept, safe and sound, unhurt, unscathed, undamaged, harmless, alive, with a whole skin, scatheless, unscratched, unimpaired, unbroken, in perfect condition, well, hale.

3. Involving no risk of mishap (error, *etc.)* cautious, modest, conservative, timid, wary, prudent, gingerly, circumspect, incontrovertible, on the safe side, on sure ground, orthodox, discreet, noncommittal, precautious, precautionary, chary, leery *(sl.),* suspicious, on guard, politic.

4. Trustworthy, harmless, dependable, sure, faithful, steady, sound, fixed, solid, established, bona fide, legitimate, honest, unerring, valid, infallible, firm, stable, certain, trusty, reliable, rooted, to be trusted, not to be moved, unfailing, unchangeable, authoritative, substantial, tried and true, incorruptible, inviolable, upright, rightful, scrupulous, honorable, on the level *(coll.),* authentic, steadfast, constant.

SAFE, *n.* Steel *or* iron box *or* repository for valuables, coffer, chest, strongbox, treasury, locker, strongroom, vault, crypt, abditory, cashbox, moneybox, depository, bank, treasure house, safe deposit *or* safety-deposit box *or* vault.

SAFE-CONDUCT, *n.* 1. Document securing safe passage through a region *(esp. in time of war)* pass, passport, permit, safeguard, warrant of security, license, password, countersign *(Mil.),* credentials, furlough, ticket, authorization, auspices, sea letter *(Naut.).*

2. A conducting in safety, privilege of safe passage, escort, convoy, protection, safeguard, entry, passage, admission, freedom, immunity, vouchsafement, unconstraint, access, privilege of conveyance.

SAFEGUARD, *n.* 1. Something serving as a protection *or* defense, something ensuring safety, protection, security, defense, armor, bulwark, shield, preserver, sanctuary, asylum, cover, screen, wall, buckler, aegis, palladium, amulet, charm, fender, fortification, coverture, shelter, safety device, bodyguard, convoy, strong arm, good hands, sanctum, preservative.

2. Permit for safe passage, passport, pass, convoy, guard, safe-conduct, escort, warrant of security, password, license, countersign *(Mil.),* credentials, authorization, sea letter *(Naut.).*

SAFEGUARD, *v.* Guard, protect, watch, secure, cover, shield, keep, flank, ensconce, attend, fortify, shelter, preserve, harbor, house, screen, look after, tend, hedge 'round, bulwark, cherish, hide, buckler, foster, champion, nurse, conserve, overshadow, arm, garrison, cushion, shroud, armor, escort, chaperon, care for, take care of, conduct, convoy, sustain, maintain.

SAFEKEEPING, *n.* Protection, guardianship, preservation, care, ward, charge, custody, safeguard, preserval, defense, guidance, patronage, championship, ministry, tutelage, ministration, keep, escort, convoy, auspices, assistance, oversight, supervision, superintendence, surveillance.

SAFETY, *n.* Freedom from injury *or* danger, state of being safe, security, safeness, preservation, refuge, surety, sureness, storm blown over, exemption, sanctuary, harbor, anchorage, shelter, custody, immunity, protection, salvation, covert, concealment, danger past *or* over, safekeeping, guard, cover, escape, impunity.

SAG, *v.* 1. Bend downward by weight *or* pressure *(esp. in the middle),* sink, hang down unevenly, hang loosely, list, keel, sway, plunge, lapse, subside, dip, fall, drop, droop, lean, give way, settle, swag, descend, pitch, tilt, slump.

2. Yield (through weakness, lack of effort, etc.), give in, surrender, back down or out, recant, collapse, fail, relinquish, flag, weary, bend, tire, give ground, let go, succumb, capitulate, be impotent or helpless, break down, faint, fizzle out (coll.), submit, cave in (coll.).

3. Decline (as in price), depreciate, slump, drop, lower, reduce, cheapen.

SAGA, n. Narrative of heroic exploits, legend, geste, history, tale, epic, adventure, fortunes, tradition, romance, chronicle, yarn, lay.

SAGACIOUS, adj. Having acute mental discernment and keen practical sense, shrewd, discerning, intelligent, judicious, sage, wise, enlightened, sapient, prudent, far-sighted, hard-headed, deep, discreet, tactful, discriminating, quick-witted, calculating, diplomatic, foxy, knowing, circumspect, apt, acute, astute, rational, perspicacious, penetrating, able, sharp-witted, keen-sighted, clear-sighted, clear-headed, nimble-witted, ingenious, long-headed, percipient, perceptive, smart, sharp, brainy, alert, argute, clever, cunning, sound, sensible.

SAGACITY, n. Acuteness of mental discernment and soundness of judgment, quickness of intellect, sagaciousness, sageness, shrewdness, acumen, cleverness, good sense, judiciousness, percipience, experience, poise, intelligence, sharpness, penetration, discernment, insight, wisdom, readiness, profundity, mother wit, perspicacity, ingenuity, astuteness, acuteness, brightness, cunning, keenness, discretion, far-sightedness, genius, subtlety, sapience, judgment, discrimination.

SAGE, n. Profoundly wise man, man venerated for wisdom, judgment and experience, savant, wise man, philosopher, pundit, scholar, scholastic, learned man, oracle, authority, prophet, luminary, pantologist, colossus of knowledge, giant of learning, mastermind, rishi (Hinduism), Nestor (Gk. Legend).

SAIL, n. 1. Expanse of fabric spread to the wind to propel a vessel, apparatus for catching wind (as on a windmill), canvas, wing, rag (contempt. or joc.), muslin (Naut. sl.; pl.), cloth (pl.).

2. Voyage (esp. in a sailing vessel), excursion, cruise, journey, course, passage.

SAIL, v. 1. Travel in a vessel, be conveyed by wind, steam, etc., pass by water, navigate, cruise, range, manage a sailboat (esp. for sport), traverse, plow through the deep (main, ocean), boat, steam, plow the waves, seafare, steer, guide, pilot, helm, yacht, ride the sea or waves.

2. Set out on a voyage, put to sea, get under way, set sail, begin a voyage, make sail (Naut.), put out or off, push from land, launch, embark, unmoor, shove off, hoist sail, weigh anchor, unfurl or spread sail, hoist the blue peter, bear off from shore, put forth, take ship.

3. Move along in a manner suggestive of sailing, fly, scud, roll, flow, stream, course, drift, flit, sweep, float, coast, wing, run, glide, skate, skim, glissade.

SAILOR, n. One whose occupation is sailing or navigation, seaman, mariner, seafaring man, seafarer, shipman (Poetic), captain, mate, boatman, navigator, shellback, tar (coll.), bluejacket, gob (sl.), limey (coll.), lobscouser (Naut. sl.), windjammer (coll.), lascar (East Indies), privateer, midshipman, middy (coll.), tarpaulin, lubber, hand,

voyager, Jack Tar or jack tar, Jacky or jacky, salt (coll.), water dog (coll.).

SAINT, n. Holy person, canonized person, worthy, martyr, model, believer, pietist, religious, exemplar, confessor, guardian, devotee, rishi (Hinduism), pir (Moham.), saint-errant (sometimes iron.).

SAINTLY, adj. Holy, devout, pious, religious, sainted, righteous, spotless, good, heavenly, angelic, immaculate, heavenly-minded, godly, right-minded, dedicated, unspotted, sanctified, pietistic, upright, unworldly, uncorrupted, pure in heart, guileless, unstained, virtuous, chaste, sinless, saint-like, perfect, profoundly good, innocent, otherworldly, spiritual, unearthly, clean, blameless.

SAKE, n. 1. Account, interest, cause, consideration, regard, respect, wish, care, need, concern, desire, good, gain, behalf, welfare, advantage, benefaction, favor, blessing, well-being, avail, service, profit, use, behoof, benefit.

2. Purpose, end, reason, intention, intent, aim, goal, plan, design, prospect, score, object, objective, basis, rationale, destination, view, eye, motive, inducement, occasion, ground, call, prompting, principle.

SALABLE, adj. Subject to or suitable for sale, readily sold, vendible, marketable, merchantable, desirable, in demand, staple, of ready sale, popular, exchangeable, commercial, commerciable.

SALACIOUS, adj. Lustful, lecherous, lewd, carnal, lascivious, lickerish, libidinous, indecent, incontinent, unchaste, loose, prurient, concupiscent, wanton, goatish, licentious, ruttish, bestial, voluptuous, obscene, incestuous, impure, bawdy, ribald, lubricious, pornographic, light, Cyprian, whorish, scarlet, dissolute, dissipated, debauched, lurid, smutty, unclean, dirty, coarse, gross, foul, filthy, vile, offensive, fulsome, Fescennine, swinish, animalistic, theroid, suggestive, fleshly, shameless, abandoned, scurrilous, profligate, erotic, sensual, brutish.

SALARY, n. Fixed periodical compensation for regular work or services, pay, hire, payment, wages, stipend, income, remuneration, recompense, emolument, allowance, earnings, honorarium.

SALE, n. 1. Act of selling, transfer of goods for money or credit, vendition, selling, vent, custom, truck, wholesale, retail, business, commerce, mercantilism, merchantry, transaction, exchange, auction, vendue, deal (coll.), dicker, speculation, bargaining, traffic, disposition, negotiation, jobbing, agiotage, trade, barter.

2. Opportunity to sell, demand, market, vent, buyers, customers, purchasing public, purchasers, outlet (com.), consumers.

3. Special disposal of goods (as at reduced prices), reduction, cut, discount, rebate, markdown, fire sale, closing-out sale, disposal, bargain sale.

SALESPERSON, n. One engaged in selling, salesman, salesclerk, saleswoman, saleslady, salesgirl, seller, clerk, shopman, counterjumper (sl.), middleman, mercantile, drummer, agent, barker (coll.), commercial traveler, traveling salesman, solicitor, vendor, canvasser.

SALIENCE, n. Projection, salient or projecting object (part, feature), saliency, convexity, protuberance, bow, knob, hump, angle, prominence, elevation, bump, bulge, process, excurvature, protuberosity, tuberosity, rising, protuberancy, intumescence, tumescence, extension.

SALIENT, *adj.* 1. Conspicuous, prominent, marked, signal, outstanding, remarkable, striking, important, consequential, noteworthy, notable, pronounced, momentous, noticeable, urgent, palpable, in bold (strong, high) relief, staring, stark, glaring, arrant, flagrant, memorable, imposing, eminent, unforgettable, substantial, considerable, commanding, manifest, egregious.

2. Pointing outward, jutting, projecting, bulging, bowed, swelling, protrusive, protuberant, bold, protrusile, protuberous, arched, bellied, standing out, prominent, in relief.

3. Leaping, springing, jumping, bounding, flying, vaulting, hopping, fulgurating, darting, dashing, capering, shooting, saltatory, saltatorial, saltatoric (*Med.*).

SALINE, *adj.* Containing *or* tasting like salt, salty, saltlike, salted, salt, briny, brackish.

SALIVA, *n.* Glandular secretion into the mouth, spittle, spit, slobber, sputum, slaver, water, froth, salivation, drool (*coll.*).

SALLOW, *adj.* Of a pale, sickly color *or* complexion, yellowish, muddy, colorless, wan, pale, anemic, pallid, ashen, lackluster, xanthic, washed-out, tallow-faced.

SALLY, *n.* 1. Sortie (*of troops from a beseiged place*), sudden rushing forth *or* activity, raid, foray, attack, dash, eruption, thrust, ejection, charge, egress, egression, bursting forth, issuance, emergence, exodus, outburst, outbreak, efflux, effluence, outflow, outpouring, outpour, proruption.

2. Expedition, excursion, peregrination, ramble, passage, trip, journey, turn, tour, trek, walk, drive, run, circuit, voyage, course, airing, junket, outing.

3. Outburst (*of passion, fancy, etc.*), flight, upheaval, outbreak, convulsion, frolic, escapade, eruption, leap, sudden excursion, cataclysm, paroxysm, stream, fit, frenzy, throe, blowup, blowout, explosion, spasm, effusion, effluence, overflowing, turbulence, flare, rush, torrent, flash, fountain, spurt, turmoil, outpouring, jet, gush, orgasm, fulguration.

4. Sprightly *or* brilliant utterance *or* remark, jest, joke, mot, conceit, pleasantry, flash of wit, quirk, quip, witticism, fancy, bon mot, repartee, banter, badinage, persiflage, retort, scintillation, ready reply, wit, wisecrack (*sl.*), jeu d'esprit (*Fr.*), prank, crank, quiz, carriwitchet, gag, pun, paronomasia.

SALLY, *v.* 1. Rush out, issue suddenly, erupt, explode, gush, break out, surge, well, escape, pour, flow, dash, leap, spring, outgo, attack, debouch.

2. Set out (*on an excursion or expedition*), fare forth, make off, push off, start out, embark, take leave, go, depart, leave, be off, be gone, undertake, get off *or* away, be on one's way, go *or* get along.

SALMAGUNDI, *n.* Medley, miscellany, mixture, hodgepodge, gallimaufry, compound, potpourri, hotchpotch, jumble, farrago, olio, tumble, salad, ollapodrida, confusion, puzzle, mélange, huddle, stew, commixture, concoction, intermixture, conglomeration, composite, accumulation, muddle, mix, patchwork, omnium-gatherum, chow-chow, hash.

SALON, *n.* 1. Drawing room, reception room, hall, gallery, assembly room, ballroom, state room *or* chamber, presence chamber, meeting place, club room, lounge.

2. Assembly of guests (*esp. leaders of fashion, art, politics, etc.*), party, company, reception,

soirée, at home, social gathering, entertainment, levee, function, assemblage, festivity, fete.

SALOON, *n.* Place for sale and consumption of intoxicating liquors, barroom, bar, inn, roadhouse, taproom, alehouse, mughouse, wine shop, cocktail lounge, café, night club, beer parlor, rum shop, cabaret, sample room, dramshop, grogshop (*contempt.*), groggery (*sl.*), barrel house (*sl.*), bistro (*coll. Fr.*), tavern.

SALT, *n.* 1. Crystalline compound used for seasoning, preserving, *etc.*, condiment, flavoring.

2. That which gives liveliness, relish, seasoning, zest, flavor, savor, tang, piquancy, pungency, poignancy, humor, sarcasm, wit, Attic wit, Attic salt, Atticism, vigor, punch (*sl.*), force, humor, pleasantry, drollery.

SALT, *v.* 1. Season with salt, flavor, savor, make pungent.

2. Preserve with salt, brine, corn, cure, pickle, marinate, kipper, souse.

SALTATION, *n.* 1. Leaping, dancing, vaulting, bounding, springing, hopping, salience, fulguration, darting, dashing, flying, jumping, shooting, capering, dart, shot, caper, flight, dash, bound, spring, leap.

2. Abrupt movement *or* transition, rift, break, hiatus, chasm, breach, rupture, disruption, cleft, split, caesura, gulf, fissure, scissure, interval, jerk, hitch, lurch, yank (*coll.*), pull, wrench, jolt.

SALTY, *adj.* Saline, salt, briny, brackish, saltlike, salted.

SALUBRIOUS, *adj.* Favorable to health, promoting health, healthful, healthy, wholesome, tonic, bracing, invigorating, healing, salutary, benign, sanatory, corrective, curative, nuritive, nutritious, roborant, corroborant, medicinal, alterative, therapeutic, preventive, protective, therial, advantageous, beneficial, remedial, restorative, analeptic, reparative, reparatory, recuperative, reviviscent, revivatory, prophylactic, sanitary, hygienic, nourishing, salutiferous, sanative, life-giving, good for one, sustentative, sustaining, regenerative.

SALUTARY, *adj.* 1. See SALUBRIOUS *above*.

2. Promoting *or* conducive to some beneficial purpose, wholesome, advantageous, good, useful, profitable, favorable, valuable, subservient, helpful, edifying, serviceable, beneficial, practical, utilitarian, beneficent, instrumental.

SALUTATION, *n.* Salute, greeting, hail, address, appeal, invocation, apostrophe, salaam, salutatory, appellation, bow, welcome, kiss, acclamation, obeisance, expression of good will, compliment, compellation, presenting arms, curtsy, homage, reverence, hello, mark *or* sign of recognition.

SALUTATORY, *n.* Greeting, address of welcome, speech, recitation, salutation, allocution.

SALUTE, *n.* Act of saluting, address, greeting, honor, salvo, ovation, jubilee, triumph, presentation, celebration, commemoration, laudation, fanfare, fanfaronade, flourish of trumpets, kiss, salaam, notice, salutation, welcome, bow, acclamation, compellation, expression of good will, compliment, curtsy, homage, hello, mark *or* sign of recognition, reverence.

SALUTE, *v.* Make a bow, gesture, *etc.*, in greeting, address with expressions of good will, respect, *etc.*, greet, welcome, cheer, signal, nod to, wave to, speak to, curtsy, bow, accost, hail, recognize, drink to, send greeting to, embrace, salaam, touch the hat *or* cap, approach, call to, invoke, apostrophize, halloo, bid *or* say hello, shake hands, extend the right hand of friendship, present arms, doff the cap, do *or* pay homage to, raise *or* lift the hat, pay respect *or* tribute to, uncover.

SALVAGE, *n.* 1. Saving of anything (*from fire, shipwreck, danger, etc.*), recovery, reclamation, restoration, retrieval, rescue, salvation, restitution, deliverance, liberation, extrication, repossession, redemption.

2. Property saved, value *or* proceeds from salvaged goods, reclaimed materials, junk, scrap, remains.

SALVAGE, *v.* Save (*from shipwreck, fire, etc.*), rescue, snatch out, deliver, extricate, liberate, restore, rehabilitate, retrieve, ransom, redeem, release, recover.

SALVATION, *n.* Act of saving *or* delivering, state of being saved *or* delivered, redemption, deliverance, preservation, rescue, saving, extrication, release, exemption, restoration, restitution, reprieve, ransom, salvage, recuperation, retrieval, reclamation, justification, regeneration, liberation, absolution, sanctification, acquittance, acquittal, emancipation, reinstatement, rehabilitation, reprieve, conversion, rebirth, new birth, reformation, respite.

SALVE, *n.* 1. Healing ointment, lotion, lenitive, liniment, oil, balm, unguent, embrocation, demulcent, abirritant, emollient (*Med.*), cerate (*Pharm.*).

2. Anything that soothes *or* mollifies, palliative, remedy, help, unction, lenitive, balm, opiate, oil, drug, narcotic, comforter, assuager, assuasive, demulcent, anodyne, calmative, sedative, alleviative, antidote, corrective, paregoric (*Pharm.*).

SALVE, *v.* Soothe as if with salve, assuage, mend, gloss over, calm, relieve, palliate, relax, moderate, compose, still, ease, extenuate, varnish, slake, slacken, abate, smooth, alleviate, quell, quiet, gloze, whitewash, pacify, hush, mollify, mitigate, modulate, soften, temper, help, remedy, dulcify, deaden, dull, lenify, take off the edge, blunt, allay, appease, tranquilize, make allowance for, put a good face upon, justify, vindicate, pour balm *or* oil into.

SALVER, *n.* Waiter, tray, platter, plate.

SALVO, *n.* 1. Proviso, quibbling excuse, means of saving one's name *or* feelings, *etc.*, exception, reservation, argument, article, saving clause, condition, plea, alibi, justification, defense, pleading, pretext, apology, feint, subterfuge, mask, cover, varnish, color, evasion, loophole, qualification.

2. Simultaneous discharge of shots, volley, burst (*as of shouts or cheers*), salute, explosion, fusillade, broadside, eruption, blowup, blowout, bombardment, fireworks, cannonade, blast, peal, roar, spray, thunder.

SAME, *adj.* Being one, identical, like, similar, of like kind (sort, degree), one, cognate, no other, equal, all one, equivalent, analogous, selfsame, synonymic, homologous, homoöusian, one and the same, of a piece, parallel, analogical, homological, uniform, twin, alike, synonymous, on a footing with, on even terms, equalized, on a par, as broad as long, very, as good as, tantamount, consistent, homogeneous, invariable, corresponding, isonomic, isomeric (*Phys. and Chem.*).

SAMENESS, *n.* 1. State of being the same, identity, identicalness, oneness, coincidence, synonymity, regularity, similarity, analogy, resemblance, repetition, alikeness, homogeneity, correspondence, likeness, equivalence, evenness, precision,

parity, constancy, uniformity, consimilarity, semblance, unity, isonomy, connaturality, unison, community, connaturalness, isomerism (*Phys. and Chem.*), selfsameness, homoöusia, parallelism.

2. Want of variety, tedious monotony, tautology, routine, undeviation, fixed practice, habit, tedium, humdrum, tediousness, dullness, flatness, triteness, prosaicism, repetition, round, track, beat, banality, dearth of ideas, beaten path, groove, rut, grind, run, wearisomeness.

SAMPLE, *n.* Part presented for inspection, specimen, instance, illustration, trial, taster, foretaste, type, bite, sup, sip, test, warning, prospect, exemplification, exemplar, example, model, pattern, scrap, dummy, representative, cross section, swatch.

SANATORIUM, *n.* Health resort, establishment for treatment of the sick, sanitarium, retreat, hospital, springs, baths, home, asylum, mineral spring, hot *or* warm springs, watering place, spa, nursing home, convalescent home.

SANATORY, *adj.* Healing, sanative, curative, remedial, salutary, sanitary, medicinal, restorative, wholesome, therapeutic, curing, beneficial, healthful, assuasive, assuaging, lenitive, comforting, soothing, therial, theriacal, corrective, emollient, salutiferous, mollifying, salubrious, anodyne, paregoric, palliative, mitigative, demulcent, balsamic, restitutive, abirritant, alexipharmic, alexiteric (*Med.*), vulnerary, reparative, reparatory, revivatory, recuperatory, roborant, recuperative, corroborant, febrifugal, purifying, antidotal, invigorating, bracing, tonic, sedative, reviviscent, benign, prophylactic, easing, unctuous, regenerative, regeneratory, restoring, restitutory.

SANCTIFIED, *adj.* Free of sin, set apart to sacred duty *or* use, hallowed, consecrated, divine, pious, holy, blessed, clean, cleansed, purified, spiritual, ceremonious, ceremonial, devotional, religious, solemn, sacrosanct, dedicated, sainted, celestial, just, righteous, perfect, sinless, spotless, godly, saintly, immaculate, unstained, unworldly, otherworldly, sacred.

SANCTIFY, *v.* 1. Make holy *or* sacred, set apart, hallow, consecrate, canonize, glorify, dedicate, anoint, enshrine, beatify, bless, devote, exalt.

2. Make free from sin, cleanse, absolve, purify, excuse, redeem, exonerate, exculpate, clear, propitiate, expiate, save, redeem, atone for, justify, shrive, restore, uplift, correct, better, make *or* pronounce holy, baptize, anoint, purge, lay hands on, administer absolution to.

3. Impart *or* impute sacredness *or* inviolability to, sanction, ratify, justify, give sanction to, license, warrant, ordain, authorize, legalize, legitimate, vindicate, support, defend.

SANCTIMONIOUS, *adj.* Making a show of sanctity, hypocritically devout *or* pious, affectedly holy, pietistic, canting, insincere, dissembling, overrighteous, unctuous, self-righteous, pharisaic, pharisaical, bigoted, false, affected, tartuffian.

SANCTIMONY, *n.* Outward *or* artificial saintliness, cant, pietism, formalism, hypocritical devoutness, affected holiness, hypocrisy, sanctimoniousness, pretense of holiness, dissembling, dissimulation, simulation, pharisaism, purblindness, mote in the eye, duplicity, piety, falseness, piousness, tartuffism, pretension, affectation, mummery, religiosity, religionism, front *or* false front, appearance, empty *or* mere show, hollowness, mockery, empty ceremony.

SANCTION, *n.* Confirmation, ratification, approbation, approval, endorsement, allowance, countenance, authority, warranty, authorization, support, vouchsafement, leave, grant, liberty, accession, assent, nod, license, seal, advocacy, appreciation, commendation, permission, passage, indulgence, privilege, acquiescence, consent, law, warrant, *carte blanche (Fr.),* encouragement.

SANCTION, *v.* Give sanction to, confirm, be pleased with, accept, validate, underwrite, undersign, legalize, warrant, allow, endorse, support, authorize, countenance, pass, recommend, boost, praise, applaud, acclaim, admire, uphold, approbate, ordain, entitle, enfranchise, subscribe to, commend, co-operate with, approve, esteem, foster, encourage, corroborate, abet, protect, empower, enforce, defend, favor, promote, permit, agree to, sustain.

SANCTITY, *n.* 1. Purity, holiness, saintliness, godliness, piety, goodness, devotion, piousness, religiosity, virtue, righteousness, unworldliness.
2. Sacredness, inviolability.

SANCTUARY, *n.* 1. House of worship, church, holy place, sanctum, oratory, conventicle, basilica, sacellum, sanctum sanctorum, chapel, cathedral, synagogue, shrine, chantry, bethel, pantheon, mosque, house of God, house of prayer.
2. Place of security, refuge, asylum, cover, hiding-place, shelter, safehold, adytum, haven, sanctum, seclusion.

SAND, *n.* 1. Shingle, grit, gravel, attritus.
2. *(Often pl.)* Beach, seabeach, shore, seaboard, strand.

SAND, *v.* 1. Cover with sand, spread sand, lay down sand, sprinkle, overlay, cover, spread.
2. Sandpaper, smooth, abrade, polish, burnish, buff, scour, rub, file.

SANDAL, *n.* Slipper, lounging shoe, open shoe, loafer, slip-on, openwork pump, moccasin.

SANDBANK, *n.* Ridge of sand built up by currents, tides, *etc.,* spit, shoal, sandbar, reef, shallow, bar.

SANDGLASS, *n.* Hourglass, half-hour glass, half-minute glass, egg glass, three-minute glass.

SANDWICH, *v.* Insert, interpose, throw in, work in, dovetail, interlard, interjaculate, edge in, wedge in, introduce, interpolate, interject.

SANDY, *adj.* 1. Consisting of *or* containing sand, granular, gritty, gravelly, calculous, earthy, sabulous, arenose, arenaceous, arenoid, sabuline, sabulose.
2. Unstable, shifting, infirm, uncertain, unsubstantial, vicissitudinous, changeable, changeful, unsound, shaky, slippery, untrustworthy, unreliable, insecure.
3. Sand-colored, yellowish-red, auburn, tawny, ocherous, reddish, muddy.

SANE, *adj.* 1. Sound in mind, rational, right, normal, underanged, sober, lucid, right-minded, self-possessed, reasonable, sensible, of sound judgment, exercising reason, intelligent, sapient, level-headed, understanding, discerning, judicious, logical, ratiocinative, perceiving, in possession of one's faculties *or* senses, responsible, compos mentis *(Law),* all there *(sl.),* sound-minded.
2. Proceeding from a sound mind, sensible, reasonable, derived from reason, judicious, enlightened, discreet, intelligent, sage, wise, advisable, logical, fit, proper, right, just, humane, equitable, thoughtful, far-sighted, deductive, plausible,

possible, justifiable, probable, credible, understandable, sagacious, well-grounded, well-founded, inferential, inferable, admissible, discerning, wholesome.

SANGUINARY, *adj.* 1. Attended with *or* concerning much bloodshed, bloody, slaughterous, murderous, gory, sanguine, sanguinolent, sanguineous, cruel, ensanguined, homicidal, bloodstained.
2. Harsh, pitiless, ruthless, inhuman, barbarous, cruel, bloodthirsty, savage, ferocious, ensanguined, fell, truculent, remorseless, unfeeling, callous, relentless, inexorable, unmerciful, implacable, stony, unpitying, heartless, hard-hearted, stern, unsparing, brutal, cold-blooded, hostile, flinty, stony, uncaring, untouched, hardened, iron-hearted, sharp, soulless, savage.

SANGUINE, *adj.* 1. Red, crimson, bloodlike, scarlet, gory, florid, flushed, sanguinolent, sanguineous, ruddy, rosy, rubicund, blood-red, inflamed, blooming, glowing.
2. Warm, ardent, fervent, enthusiastic, forward, avid, zealous, cheerful, lively, inspirited, buoyant, heated, animated, expectant, keyed up, anticipative, elated, devout, burning, on tiptoe, fervid, passionate, hearty, vehement, eager, feverish, sincere, bent, intent, cordial, agog, resolute, keen, earnest, flushed, zestful, hot, vigorous, fiery, red-hot, impassioned, whole-hearted.
3. Anticipating the best, hopeful, confident, buoyant, optimistic, trusting, reassured, trustful, assured, buoyed up, sanguineous, in good heart, in good *or* high spirits, exultant, bright, sunny, cheerful, happy, content, light-hearted, undoubting, assured.
4. Sanguinary, bloodthirsty, *etc. (See* SANGUINARY *above.)*

SANITARY, *adj.* Of *or* pertaining to health *or* the preservation of health, hygienic, free from agencies, injurious to health, salubrious, healthful, healthy, sanitarian, sanative, wholesome, health-promoting, clean, cleanly, disinfected, hygienal, germ-free, sterile, disease-free, aseptic, uninjurious, innoxious, harmless.

SANITATION, *n.* A rendering sanitary, use of sanitary measures *or* provisions, cleansing, hygiene, hygienics, hygiastics, hygiology, hygienization, regimen *(Med.),* public health, cleanliness, hygiantics.

SANITY, *n.* Soundness *or* health of mind, mental balance, saneness, rationality, reason, sense, clear-headedness, lucidity, coherence, normality, sobriety.

SAP, *n.* Juice *(of a plant),* vital circulating fluid, blood, lifeblood, milk, latex *(Bot.).*

SAP, *v.* Undermine, destroy, weaken insidiously, bleed, ruin, mine, tax, enfeeble, drain, enervate, affect by degrees, exhaust, subvert, supplant, impoverish, wear, rob, devitalize, debilitate, impair, reduce, shatter, afflict, attack, oppress, cripple, blight, shake, devastate, despoil, break down, make inroads on, harry.

SAPID, *adj.* Having taste *or* flavor, palatable, tasteful, savory, pungent, gustatory, saporous, agreeable, to one's taste *or* liking, delicious, delectable, tempting, racy, poignant, seasoned, piquant, spiced, saporific, mouth-watering, appetizing, toothsome, tasty *(coll.),* flavorful, flavorsome, gustative, gustful, gustable, relishing, flavorous.

SAPIENCE, *n.* Sagacity, wisdom, sageness, sense, enlightenment, intelligence, shrewdness, knowledge, acuteness of mental discernment, soundness of judgment, quickness of intellect, sagaciousness, acumen, cleverness, judiciousness, percipience, sharpness, penetration, discernment, insight, profundity, mother wit, perspicacity, astuteness, brightness, cunning, keenness, far-sightedness, genius, subtlety, discrimination.

SAPIENT, *adj.* Wise, sage, sagacious, sensible, knowing, rational, judicious, discreet, oracular, philosophical, acute, keen, shrewd, discerning, intelligent, enlightened, prudent, far-sighted, hardheaded, deep, discriminating, quick-witted, calculating, foxy, knowing, circumspect, apt, astute, perspicacious, penetrating, able, sharp-witted, keen-sighted, clear-sighted, clear-headed, nimble-witted, long-headed, percipient, perceptive, smart, sharp, brainy, argute, clever, cunning, sound.

SAPLESS, *adj.* 1. Without sap, destitute of sap, dry, shriveled, shrunk, wizened, withered, juiceless, decayed.

2. Lacking vitality, insipid, weak, jejune, debilitated, pithless, nerveless, sinewless, lustless, weakly, effete, colorless, powerless, impotent, faint, flaccid, ineffectual, ineffective, tame, meager, arid, empty, wanting, prosaic, insulse, deficient, lean, hollow, flat, barren, devoid, inefficacious, vacant, vapid, inadequate, puerile, poor, unsatisfying, fruitless, otiose, unfertile, uninspiring, unprofitable, inept, stale, lame, unfruitful.

SAPLING, *n.* 1. Young tree, seedling, youngling.

2. Young person, youth, sprig, slip, young hopeful, stripling, fledgling, urchin, tot, tad, juvenile, offspring, scion, shaver (*coll.*), young fry (*coll.*), chicken (*coll.*), kid (*sl.*), cub (*humor. or contempt.*), whelp (*contempt.*).

SAPONACEOUS, *adj.* Soaplike, soapy, slippery, saponified.

SAPOR, *n.* Flavor, quality in a substance which affects the sense of taste, savor, taste, smack, sapidity, tang, pungency, relish, piquancy, poignancy.

SAPPY, *adj.* 1. Abounding in sap, succulent, watery, juicy, lush, lymphatic, hydrous, seepy, oozy.

2. Full of vitality and energy, potent, vigorous, strong, forceful, active, vivacious, spirited, animated, unflagging, intense, brisk, strenuous, dynamic, peppy (*sl.*), snappy (*coll.*), stirring.

SAPROGENIC, *adj.* Producing putrefaction or decay, formed by putrefaction, putrefactive, rancid, putrid, foul, filthy, carious, decayed, polluting, fetid, putrescent, rank, rotten, flyblown, gangrened, mortified, bad, decomposed, saprogenous, saprophytic (*Bot.*), saprophilous (*Bacteriol.*).

SARCASM, *n.* Harsh or bitter derision or irony, sneering or cutting remark, gibe, taunt, fleer, satire, irony, ridicule, flout, sneer, cutting jest, fling, jeer, quip, censure, lampoon, contempt, scoffing, cynicism, mockery, hit, aspersion, wipe (*coll.*), causticity, abuse, disparagement, flouting, rub, nip, acrimony, superciliousness, slur, contumely.

SARCASTIC, *adj.* Characterized by, of the nature of or pertaining to sarcasm, sharp, mordant, mordacious, sardonic, taunting, cutting, biting, severe, given to the use of sarcasm, derisive, scornful, astringent, stringent, stinging, acerbic, poignant, cynical, trenchant, keen, ironical, piercing, abusive, slashing, sneering, scurrilous, chaffing, mocking, supercilious, withering, venomous, contemptuous, disparaging, Rabelaisian, tart, Hudibrastic, quizzical, pert, hostile, captious, pungent, harsh, contumelious, bitter, caustic.

SARDONIC, *adj.* Sneering, bitterly ironical, malignant, grim, scornful, cynical, *etc.* (*See* SARCASTIC *above.*)

SASH, *n.* 1. Band, scarf, tie, girdle, belt, waistband, cestus, cincture, girth, cummerbund.

2. Part of a window which moves, frame, casement.

SATAN, *n.* Devil, the Evil One, the Arch-Fiend, Belial, the Tempter, the Prince of Darkness, the Old Serpent, the Foul Fiend, Asmodeus, the Archenemy, the Prince of the Power of the Air, Abaddon, the Author of Evil, Lucifer, Beelzebub, Mephistopheles, Apollyon, Ahriman, Eblis, Azazel, Moloch, Mammon, Diabolus, the Adversary, the Serpent, Old Nick, Old Harry, Old Scratch, Old Bogy, god of this world.

SATANIC, *adj.* Characteristic of *or* befitting Satan, diabolical, devilish, wicked, demoniacal, hellborn, malignant, malicious, malevolent, infernal, hellish, evil, false, fiendish, blasphemous, vile, bad, vicious, fiendlike, impious, slanderous, irreverent, infamous, corrupt, sinful, Mephistophelian, inhuman, heinous, iniquitous, accursed.

SATCHEL, *n.* Small bag, little sack, purse, reticule, grip, handbag, valise, case, brief case *or* bag.

SATE, *v.* 1. Satiate, satisfy to the full, saturate, fill, suffice, charge, lade, pack, quench, stuff, complete.

2. Glut, surfeit, overfeed, jade, stuff, overfill, gorge, cloy, pall, weary, overload, overburden, supersaturate, surcharge, choke, suffocate, engulf, drug, inundate, overweigh, flood, deluge, drench.

SATELLITE, *n.* 1. Attendant, retainer, dependent, follower, servant, disciple, partisan, aider, vassal, sectarian, mate, companion, shadow, partner, accompanier, assistant, henchman, proselyte, apostle, adherent, apprentice, auxiliary, menial, acolyte, sectary.

2. Subservient *or* obsequious follower, henchman, hanger-on, puppet, stooge (*sl.*), parasite, dependent, vassal, minion, tagtail, fawner, toady, votary, toadeater, sponger, sycophant, tufthunter, groveler, spaniel, truckler, appendant, handshaker (*sl.*), apple-polisher (*sl.*), sidekick (*sl.*), yes man (*sl.*), appendage, bootlicker, footlicker, lackey, shadow, flunky, sectary, dangler, courtier, carpet knight, wheedler, bur, heeler (*sl.*), lickspittle, barnacle.

3. Country under the dominion *or* influence of another, protectorate, colony, daughter country, dependency, possession, dominion, mandate, territory.

SATIATE, *v.* Supply to excess, satisfy, sate, suffice, fill, give one's fill, surfeit, indulge, glut, overfeed, pall, cloy, slake, gorge, regale, gratify, flood, deluge, drench, overweigh, inundate, drug, engulf, overwhelm, suffocate, choke, surcharge, supersaturate, weary, overload, overburden, jade, stuff, overfill.

SATIETY, *n.* State of being satisfied, fullness, surfeit, satiation, cloyedness, redundance, repletion, glut, pleasure, plethora, satisfaction, prodigality, lavishment, exuberance, prolixity, profusion, amplitude, abundance, saturation, weariness, engorgement, overfullness, plenty, fill, superfluity, superabundance, excess, surplus, overplus, congestion, nimiety, opulence, affluence, overflow.

SATINY, *adj.* Smooth, silken, silklike, silky, sericeous, lustrous, shiny, sheeny.

SATIRE, *n.* 1. Burlesque, diatribe, lampoon, take-off, parody, travesty, macaronic, pasquinade, squib.

2. Acrimony, superciliousness, harsh *or* bitter irony, ridicule, slur, contumely, fleer, censure, cynicism, criticism, scoffing, aspersion, contempt, mockery, cut, gibe, jeer, taunt.

SATIRICAL, *adj.* Tart, Rabelaisian, disparaging, Hudibrastic, pungent, bitter, contumelious, caustic, sardonic, severe, derisive, biting, stinging, cutting, astringent, mordant, ironical, mordacious, sharp, sarcastic, acerbic, captious, hostile, sneering, abusive, mocking, chaffing, stinging, cynical, trenchant, keen, scornful, scurrilous.

SATIRIST, *n.* One who satirizes, burlesquer, Pantagruelist, sillograph, lampooner, caricaturist, pasquinader.

SATIRIZE, *v.* Burlesque, laugh at, ape, ridicule, take off, caricature, render absurd, pasquinade, lampoon, mimic, travesty, mock, buffoon, make ludicrous, stultify.

SATISFACTION, *n.* 1. Pleasure, delight, contentment, content, gratification, comfort, felicity, happiness.

2. Right return for wrong *or* suffering, recompense, answering, redemption, measure for measure, gratification, requital, remuneration, redress, atonement, acknowledgment, expiation, reimbursement, justice, commutation, restoration, settlement, remission, compromise, substitution, counteraction, reckoning, adjustment, amends, equalization, compensation, retaliation, reciprocation, recoupment, correction, neutralization, nullification, rectification, restitution, *quid pro quo (Lat.),* bloodwite *(Law),* solatium, penalty, price, wergild *(Law).*

3. Payment, reimbursement, remittance, repayment, remuneration, price, defrayal, coverage, settlement, remittal, quittance, reckoning, damages, deserts.

SATISFACTORY, *adj.* Meeting requirements, adequate, acceptable, up to standard, up to scratch *(coll.),* sufficing, sufficient, suitable, up to the mark, enough.

SATISFY, *v.* 1. Make content, gratify, please, content, delight, satiate, sate.

2. Pay, pay off, settle, remit, settle accounts, recoup, indemnify, reimburse, repay, adjust, discharge, square up, recompense, replace, compensate, atone, clear, requite, annul.

3. Meet the requirements, stand the test, suffice, do, serve, be adequate, answer.

4. Convince, assure, reassure, deliver from uncertainty, persuade, confirm, ensure, make one sure.

SATURATE, *v.* Soak, impregnate, drench, imbrue, imbue, supersaturate, steep, sate, fill, infiltrate, charge, surcharge, infuse, instill.

SATURATED, *adj.* Filled to repletion, full to capacity, sated, filled, satiated, drenched, charged, soggy, sodden, impregnated, imbrued, imbued, steeped, dripping, soaked, infused, surcharged, irriguous.

SATURNALIA, *n.* Reckless revelry, orgy, debauch, spree, bacchanal, potation, carousal, drunken bout, libation, binge *(sl.).*

SATURNINE, *adj.* Pensive, lumpish, heavy, gloomy, dull, morose, supine, lentitudinous, moody, bovine, phlegmatic, glum, elephantine, torpid, serious, lymphatic, lethargic, sluggish, lifeless, without vitality, languid, doleful, stolid, cumbersome, passive, static, obtuse, sottish, crass.

SATYR, *n.* Lecher, seducer, rake, libertine, ravisher, roué, profligate, Bluebeard, voluptuary, fornicator, debauchee, goat, rapist.

SATYRIASIS, *n.* Uncontrolled sexual desire *(in the male),* carnality, passion, sensuality, lust, lubricity, bodily appetite, salacity, lewdness, lechery, lasciviousness, pruriency, aphrodisia.

SAUCE, *n.* Seasoning, condiment, dressing, relish, flavoring, gravy, catchup, catsup.

SAUCEPAN, *n.* Cooking utensil, pot, pan.

SAUCER, *n.* Dish, patera *(Rom. Antiq.),* trencher *(Hist.).*

SAUCY, *adj.* Impertinent, unabashed, smart-alecky *(coll.),* bumptious, bold, rude, barefaced, malapert, flippant, cocky *(coll.),* fresh *(coll.),* brazen, brash, brazen-faced, pert, overbearing, cheeky, audacious, insolent, self-assertive, discourteous, impolite, disrespectful.

SAUNTER, *v.* Walk casually, stroll, ramble, straggle, roam, promenade, amble, wander, meander, loiter, dawdle along, stretch one's legs.

SAURIAN, *n.* Lizard, dragon, eft, newt, chameleon, salamander, Gila monster, iguana.

SAUSAGE, *n.* Minced *or* spiced meat, meat pudding, sausage meat, salami, bologna, blood pudding, boloney, liverwurst, frank *(coll.),* hot dog *(sl.),* weiner, frankfurter.

SAVAGE, *adj.* 1. In nature, wild, untamed, undomesticated, uncultivated, uncivilized.

2. Uncivilized, rude, crude, crass, uncouth, raw, troglodytic, uncultured, unpolished, barbarous, brutish, rough, Gothic, untamed, outlandish, untutored, loutish, ill-bred, barbaric, boorish, churlish, unlettered, vulgar, uncivil, heathenish.

3. Inhuman, slaughterous, bloodthirsty, hellish, fell, pitiless, unkind, hard-hearted, bloody, ferocious, brutish, sanguinary, feral, devilish, unfeeling, remorseless, barbarian, barbaric, cannibalistic, heathenish, unmerciful, relentless, merciless, ferine, ruthless, homicidal, murderous, marble-hearted, wild, cruel, sadistic, diabolic, brutal.

SAVAGE, *n.* 1. Vandal, Goth, cannibal, brute, yahoo, troglodyte, barbarian, Hottentot.

2. Hooligan, tough, rowdy, larrikin, lout, ruffian, ugly customer, bully, hoodlum, roughneck.

3. Opponent of culture, obscurantist, anti-intellectual, proletarian, Philistine, plebeian, bourgeois, peasant.

SAVANT, *n.* Man of learning, sage, master, wise man, doctor, scholar, pundit, erudite person, man venerated for his wisdom, philosopher, scholastic, oracle, authority, prophet, luminary, pantologist, colossus of knowledge, giant of learning, mastermind, rishi *(Hinduism),* Nestor *(Gk. Legend).*

SAVE, *prep., conj.,* Except, but, saving, exclusive of, omitting, less, minus, short of, bar, barring, without, lacking, with exception of, besides, but for, deducting, not including, leaving out, excepting, unless.

SAVE, *v.* 1. Preserve from harm (injury, loss), rescue from danger, redeem, deliver, free, help, salvage, recover, intercede for, atone for, ransom, mediate in behalf of, snatch.

2. Keep safe (intact, unhurt), safeguard, preserve, shield, protect, defend, secure, sustain, maintain, cover, take care of, watch over, look after, guard, nurse, uphold, support, stay, upbear.

3. Avoid spending (consumption, waste of), reserve, lay by, set apart, store, hoard, keep, hold, conserve, amass, curtail expenses, treasure, retrench, heap up, scrape, retain, economize, husband, lay up, put away, stock, garner, set aside, feather one's nest, accumulate, provide for a rainy day.

4. Treat carefully *(to reduce wear, fatigue, etc.)*, spare, conserve, preserve, take care of, withhold, guard, protect, value, be conservative of, refrain from using *or* overusing.

5. Prevent the occurrence (use, necessity) of, obviate, hinder, avert, spare, fend off, keep off, ward off, stave off, insure against.

SAVE-ALL, *n.* Means *or* contrivance for preventing loss *or* waste, receptacle, retainer, hamper, container, vessel, catch-all.

SAVING, *adj.* 1. Rescuing, that saves, redeeming, reclaiming, sparing, redemptory, preserving, restorative, reparative, restoring, reparatory, restitutive, restitutory, delivering.

2. Economical, sparing, thrifty, provident, stingy, near, close, conservative, miserly, chary, save-all, pennywise, moneygrubbing, frugal, careful, prudent, tight *(coll.)*, hardfisted, stinting, preserving, scrimping, closehanded, closefisted, cheeseparing, penurious, parsimonious, niggardly.

3. Making a reservation, provisional, conditional, qualifying, stipulatory, extenuating, extenuatory, palliative, palliatory, mitigatory, mitigative, contingent, provisory, modificatory, qualificative.

SAVING, *n.* 1. Economy *(in expenditure, outlay, use, etc.),* thrift, lessening of expenditure *or* outlay, reduction, care, conservation, preserval, preservation, safekeeping, thriftiness, parsimony, retrenchment, parsimoniousness, cheeseparing, pinching, stinginess, savingness, husbandry, frugality, maintenance, scrimping.

2. That which is saved, profit, bonus, return, dividend, gain, produce, earning, receipt, premium, income, remainder, proceeds, increase, surplus, overplus.

3. *(Pl.)* Sums of money saved and laid away, nest egg, capital, reserve fund, assets, reserves, resources, reservoir, backlog.

SAVIOR, *n.* 1. One who saves (rescues, delivers), rescuer, redeemer, emancipator, liberator, deliverer, freer, champion, protector, defender, guard, guardian, manumitter, lifeguard, preserver, benefactor, vindicator, knight-errant.

2. *(Cap.)* Title of God, *esp.* of Christ, Redeemer, the Messiah, the Anointed, the Mediator, the Intercessor, Lord, Prince of Peace, Son of Man, the Only-Begotten Son of God, the Good Shepherd, the Advocate, the Lamb of God.

SAVOIR-FAIRE, *n.* Knowledge of just what to do in any situation, civility, manners, tact, gentility, polish, culture, amenity, courtesy, poise, suavity, breeding, complaisance, chivalry, urbanity, refinement, presence, cultivation, comity, self-possession, composure, assurance, aplomb, discretion, social grace, graciousness, finesse.

SAVOR, *n.* 1. Quality in a substance which affects the sense of taste *or* smell, aroma, flavor, taste, relish, smack, odor, smell, scent, fragrance, sapor, zest, spice, tang, sapidity, piquancy, poignancy, pungency, essence.

2. Characteristic property, distinctive feature, nature, character, essence, quintessence, quiddity, temper, trait, trick, vital principle, gist, pith, core, soul, spirit, elixir, substance, constitution, quality,

singularity, particularity, peculiarity, individuality, kernel, nucleus.

3. Power to excite *or* interest, relish, piquancy, zest, tang, smack, attraction, delectability, taste, palatability, enticement, inducement, allurement, fascination, lure, charm, magnetism, bewitchment, hypnotism, seduction, draw, enchantment, excitement, ravishment, stimulation.

SAVOR, *v.* 1. Have savor (taste, odor), taste, smell, be savory, tickle the palate, tempt the appetite, be appealing to the senses of taste and smell.

2. *(Fol. by* OF*)* Exhibit the peculiar characteristic, show traces of the presence *or* influence of, smack, betoken, partake of, have a touch of, resemble, have all the earmarks of, be comparable to, match, suggest, approximate, approach.

3. Give a savor to, season, flavor, render pungent, devil, pickle, salt, spice.

4. Perceive by taste *or* smell *(esp. with relish),* give oneself to the enjoyment of, appreciate, enjoy, relish, like, fancy, roll on the tongue, degust, rejoice in, riot in, take a fancy to, take to, revel in, feast on, luxuriate in, bask in, swim in, delight in, gloat over *or* on, wallow in.

SAVORY, *adj.* Having savor, agreeable in taste *or* smell, giving a relish, pleasing, piquant, to one's taste, well-tasted, gustatory, gustative, aromatic, fragrant, tempting, racy, luscious, palatable, tasteful, tasty *(coll.),* nectareous, ambrosial, fullflavored, gustable, exquisite, gratifying, heady, balmy, odorous, delicious, good, appetizing, pungent, delectable, dainty, rich, sapid, delicate, toothsome, tangy.

SAW, *n.* Sententious saying, proverb, maxim, apothegm, dictum, byword, precept, axiom, aphorism, adage, gnome, mot, moral, motto, epigram, truism.

SAW, *v.* Cut as if using a saw, flail, gesticulate, gesture, wave.

SAW-TOOTHED, *adj.* Serrate, serrated, notched, nicked, toothed, crenate, crenated, serrulate, serratile, serratic, dentelated, dentate *(Biol.),* dentated *(Biol.),* denticulate *(Biol.).*

SAY, *n.* What a person says *or* has to say, assertion, averment, pronouncement, word, allegation, advice, opinion, speech, declaration, affirmation, remark, observation, announcement, utterance, protestation, profession, attestation, comment, discourse, recital, diatribe, declamation, tirade, harangue, preachment, sermon, prolection, monologue, recitation, spiel *(sl.),* annunciation, pronunciation.

SAY, *v.* 1. Express in words, speak, declare, pronounce, tell, utter, mention, mouth, word, answer, add, respond, reply, announce, phrase, rejoin, retort, reveal, divulge, come out with, breathe, make known, cite, whisper, communicate, articulate, remark, state, convey, aver, disclose, impart, put, cry, vocalize, betray, let out, give utterance to, present, couch in terms.

2. State as an opinion *or* with assurance, voice, declare, assert, tell, asseverate, enunciate, pronounce, allege, announce, be sure *or* certain, know, predicate, feel convinced, asseverate, affirm, determine, stress, emphasize, lay down, propose, dogmatize.

3. Repeat, recite, declaim, relate, present, orate, speak, deliver, rehearse, mouth, perform, render, pronounce.

4. Assume as a hypothesis *or* an estimate,

presume, assume, suppose, guess, argue, reason, imagine, expect, surmise, hazard a guess, judge, conjecture, dare say.

5. Report, allege, maintain, hold, believe, announce, take for granted, presume, suppose, conjecture, assume, implicate, hint, intimate, contend, imply, suggest, spread, insinuate, affirm, infer, circulate, promulgate, propagate, expect, suspect, take it, disseminate, rumor, put forth *or* forward, gather, judge, imagine, dare say, understand, deduce.

SAYING, *n.* Proverb, maxim, dictum, apothegm, saw, aphorism, adage, mot, byword, sententious saying, sentiment, quotation, gnome, moral, motto, truism, epigram, precept.

SCAB, *n.* Incrustation which forms over a sore during healing, scale, scurf, crust, slough *(Pathol.),* eschar *(Pathol.).*

SCABBARD, *n.* Cover for the blade of a sword *or* dagger, *etc.,* sheath, case, casing, socket.

SCABBY, *adj.* Covered with scabs, blotchy, scabious, scurvy, coarse, flaky, broken, rough, scabbed, sloughy, mangy, furfuraceous, psoriatic *(Pathol.).*

SCABROUS, *adj.* 1. Rough with minute points *or* projections, scaly, coarse, gnarled, scurfy, flaky, craggy, furrowed, notched, rugose, ridged, jagged, cragged, scraggy, uneven, rugged.

2. Full of difficulties, harsh, rough, risky, tortured, treacherous, precarious, exacting, ticklish, difficult, ominous, perilous, dangerous, rigorous, hazardous, chancy *(coll.),* threatening, alarming, sinister, slippery, arduous, dire, critical, insecure.

3. Somewhat indelicate, risqué, questionable, dubious, doubtful, ungenteel, in poor taste, indecorous, loose, unbecoming, unseemly, immodest, improper, ungentlemanly, unladylike, bohemian, unconventional.

SCAFFOLD, *n.* 1. Raised framework, scaffolding, stage, skeleton, frame, platform.

2. Elevated platform for executing criminals, gallows, block, drop, gibbet.

SCALAWAG, *n.* Rogue, knave, scoundrel, vagrant, rapscallion, felon, bounder *(coll.),* rakehell, delinquent, scamp, villain, malfeasor, miscreant, misdoer, recreant, rascal, reprobate, blackguard.

SCALD, *v.* Burn, boil, broil, steam.

SCALE, *n.* 1. Lamina, flake, lamella, squama, palea *(Bot.).*

2. Thin covering, coating, veneer, film, skin, incrustation, layer, membrane, shell, crust.

3. Graduation, measure, check, gradation, gauge, rule.

4. Order of importance, order of merit *or* rank, degree, place, sphere, grade, prominence, caste, range, gradation, status, station, distinction, eminence, condition, position, step, precedence.

5. Complete range, gamut, length, scope, extent, field, expanse, reach, spread, expansion.

6. Relative dimensions *(of a map, chart, etc.).*

7. *(Often pl.)* Device for weighing, weighing machine, beam, weigh scale, steelyard, measure, balance, scale beam, weighbeam, weighbridge.

8. *(Music)* Register, range, diapason, sol-fa, gamut.

SCALE, *v.* 1. Peel, shell, husk, delaminate, desquamate, flake, exfoliate, chip off, rub off, clean *(of fish),* scour, abrade, shave.

2. Climb, mount, ascend, clamber, rise, work

upwards, surmount, swarm up, progress upwards go up, escalade.

3. Grade, rate, weigh, judge, rank, graduate mark, group, classify.

SCALP, *n.* Top of the head, crown of the head epicranium.

SCALPEL, *n.* Surgical knife, dissecting instrument, lancet, bistoury.

SCALY, *adj.* Covered with scales, squamous squamose, squamosal, scutate *(Zool.),* lamellate lamellar, spathic.

SCAMP, *n.* Rapscallion, villain, delinquent, rake hell, bounder *(coll.),* felon, rogue, knave, vagrant scoundrel, scalawag, malfeasor, miscreant, blackguard, reprobate, rascal, recreant, misdoer.

SCAMPER, *v.* Move with haste, hurry, proceed with haste, tear, fly, shoot, ride hard, make time rush, sprint, race, scurry, flee, hasten, lose no time, scour, scoot *(coll.),* bolt, dart, skedaddle *(sl.),* fly on the wings of the wind, bowl along cut along *(coll.),* clap spurs to one's horse, wing one's way, crowd sail *(Naut.),* mend one's pace spank, post, hie *(often reflex.),* scuttle, trip, flit, be on the run, hustle, pace, swoop, career, bestir oneself, move quickly, haste *(Lit.),* rip *(coll.),* whiz, sweep, cover ground, get over the ground, dash off *or* on, go on the double *(coll.),* beat a retreat, not lose a moment, stir one's stumps, work against time, spin, leap, go like lightning *or* greased lightning *(coll.),* go like a shot *(coll.),* go hell-bent *(coll.),* clip, bound, boom, spring, bustle, burn up the road *(coll.),* press on, zip, skim, brush, whip off *or* away, jump, bundle, hump it *(sl.),* step, crack on, speed up, put on more speed, hurry up, quicken, take wing, go all out, canter, trot, gallop, lope, make strides, step lively *(coll.),* run wide open, pack off, pack away.

SCAN, *v.* 1. *(Of poetry)* Analyze, recite metrically, divide into feet.

2. Look at carefully, examine, explore, review, peruse, indagate, break down, anatomize, scrutinize, study, inspect, sift, consider, size up, take stock of, investigate, search, probe, winnow, overhaul, check, dip into, plunge into, pry into, delve into, sound, fathom.

SCANDAL, *n.* 1. Malicious gossip, defamatory talk, abuse, disparagement, accusation, obloquy, scandalmongering, slander, backbiting, calumny, imputation, aspersion, libel, detraction, revilement, traducement, vituperation, evil-speaking, railing.

2. Disgrace, dishonor, disfavor, degradation, disesteem, attaint, smirch, infamy, ignominy, opprobrium, ill-repute, defilement, stain, debasement, shame, discredit, blot, stigma, odium.

SCANDALIZE, *v.* Shock the moral sense of, horrify, shame, revolt, offend, disgust, sicken, nauseate, repel, cause to raise the eyebrows.

SCANDALOUS, *adj.* 1. Disgraceful, shameful, shocking, inglorious, horrifying, unmentionable, profligate, disreputable, ignominious, atrocious, felonious, fulsome, heinous, illaudable, flagrant, low, reprehensible, outrageous, nefarious, base, unworthy, indecent, dastardly, immoral, sinister, corrupt, execrable, sneaking, diabolic, despicable, mean, facinorous, flagitious, uncommendable, iniquitous, odious, opprobrious, black, deplorable, infernal, arrant, despicable.

2. Damnatory, derogatory, complaining, rude, defamatory, abusive, querulous, vitriolic, reproachful, crabbed, carping, thersitical, vilificatory, invective, blackguard, hurtful, denunciatory,

objurgatory, fulminating, acrimonious, injurious, satirical, insulting, scolding, uncharitable, chiding, upbraiding, faultfinding, contumelious, censorious, calumniatory, calumnious, vituperative, condemnatory, petulant, opprobrious, critical, scurrilous, gossiping, muckraking, disparaging, scathing.

SCANTY, adj. Meager, slender, scrimpy, modest, sparse, small, lean, few and far between, insufficient, thinly scattered, inadequate, light, stunted, short, thin, scant.

SCAPEGOAT, n. Fall guy (sl.), victim, substitute (in bearing blame), dummy.

SCAPEGRACE, n. Knave, incorrigible miscreant, scoundrel, scamp, rapscallion, rogue, reprobate, blackguard, rascal, recreant, misdoer, malfeasor, villain, delinquent, rakehell, bounder (coll.), felon.

SCAR, n. Mark (of a wound), gash, cicatrix (Zool.), cicatrice (Bot.), disfigurement, stripe, indentation, deformity, pock, brand, blemish.

SCAR, v. Wound, gash, cut, mark, brand, mutilate, scarify, mangle, scratch, lacerate, deface, bruise.

SCARAMOUCH, n. Rascal, scamp, zany, buffoon, clown, harlequin, punch, punchinello, merry-andrew, jester, droll, antic, fool, comedian, funnyman, farceur, pantaloon, grimacer, mountebank, comic, wearer of the cap and bells, joker, mummer, mime, pantomimist, mimic, mimer, wit, wag, Jack Pudding, Pickelhering (Ger.), wearer of the motley, farcist, pickle-herring, Hanswurst (Ger.).

SCARCE, adj. 1. Insufficient for need or demand, incomplete, deficient, wanting, inadequate, sparing, little, sparse, slender, insignificant, inconsiderable, low, skimpy, meager, short, slim, slack, lame, poor, failing, defective, scant, partial, paltry, unplentiful, thin, tight, lean, not plentiful, not abundant, exiguous, trivial, sketchy, fractional, perfunctory.

2. Seldom met with, uncommon, sparse, singular, out of the way, unique, dear, infrequent, thinly scattered, few and far between, exceptional, choice, unrepeated, almost unheard of, to be counted on the fingers of one hand, spasmodic, not to be had, occasional, rare, unusual, unprecedented.

SCARCELY, adv. 1. Hardly, barely, scantly, with difficulty, ill, rarely, scarce (Lit.), no more than, not easily, but just, merely, uncommonly, infrequently, sparsely, not often, seldom, little, only arduously, only against the grain, faintly, miserably, slightly, by the skin of one's teeth, imperceptibly, once in a blue moon, once in a coon's age (coll.), only laboriously.

2. Definitely not, probably not, hardly, certainly not, by no means, in no way, not at all, nowise, noway, never, not in the least, on no account, on no occasion, not a bit (whit, jot, shadow, etc.), in no manner, not by great deal.

SCARCITY, n. 1. Smallness of supply, scarceness, dearth, want, lack, insufficiency, deficiency, shortage, stint, deprivation, exiguity, scantiness, scantness, destitution, need, famine, indigence, paucity, poverty, bankruptcy, depletion, exhaustion, necessity, privation, drought, thinness, penury.

2. Rarity, rareness, infrequency, uncommonness, exiguity, sparseness, sparsity, seldomness, fewness, scarceness.

SCARE, n. Fright, alarm, start, shock, dismay, panic, sudden terror, horror, shaking, quaking, shiver, shake, consternation, palpitation, nervousness, jitters (sl.), funk (sl.).

SCARE, v. 1. Strike with sudden fear or terror, become frightened, frighten, intimidate, appall, terrify, daunt, disquiet, awe, strike terror into, unman, horrify, abash, bully, disconcert, threaten, make afraid, put in fear, quail, browbeat, faze (coll.), make one's flesh creep, make one's hair stand on end, make one's blood run cold, give a turn, dishearten, cow, startle, deter, overawe, terrorize, harrow.

2. (With UP) Raise, get, recruit, acquire, obtain, gain, secure, collect, glean, gather, pilfer, sack, bag, net, take, dig up, rake up, appropriate, scrounge (sl.), hunt up, procure, scrape up or together.

SCARECROW, n. 1. Person in ragged clothes, tramp, eyesore, fright, pauper, jade, wreck, beggar, bum (coll.), down-and-out, down-and-outer, tacky (Southern U. S.), ragamuffin, tatterdemalion.

2. Anything terrifying but not really dangerous, bogy, bugbear, hobgoblin, apparition, fright, demon, sprite, specter, imp, ghost, ghoul, troll, spook, bugaboo, puck, banshee, bête noire, boggart, ogre, gorgon, mumbo jumbo, fee-faw-fum, bad fairy, gnome, poker.

SCARF, n. 1. Long broad strip of fabric worn about the neck (shoulders, head), muffler, necktie, cravat, neckerchief, ruff, boa, tippet, girdle, sash, neckcloth, neckband, fichu, cornet, kerchief, lambrequin, tallith, throw, veil, choker (coll.), rebozo (chiefly rural Span. and Mexican), yashmak (Moslem), purdah (India, etc.).

2. Long cover of cloth (for bureau, table, etc.), runner, cloth, doily.

SCARFSKIN, n. Outermost layer of skin, cuticle, epidermis, rind, ectoderm (Embryol.), ecderon (Anat.).

SCARLET, adj. Bright red, flaming red, vermilion, flamingo, Babylonian, flame-red, carmine, flame-colored.

SCATHING, adj. Envenomed, harsh, brutal, abrupt, acrimonious, blunt, rude, tart, gruff, brash, curt, short, austere, stern, vitriolic, cruel, unkind, hurtful, biting, sharp, sarcastic, keen, cutting, stinging, brusque, virulent, discourteous, bearish, churlish, ungentle, bitter, malevolent, venomous, malignant, crabbed, mordacious, derisive, excoriating, crusty, derisory, insulting, lashing, galling, ill-natured, malicious, maleficent, spiteful, rancorous, invidious, uncordial, uncharitable, unamiable, unbenevolent.

SCATTER, v. 1. Dissipate, dispel, disperse, rout, dismember, disband, dismiss, cause to vanish, dissolve, banish, separate.

2. Strew, broadcast, sow, cast, shed, sprinkle, spread, bespread, circulate, spatter, disperse.

SCATTERBRAINED, adj. Harebrained, flighty, giddy, bewildered, muddle-headed, devil-may-care, hot-headed, impetuous, precipitate, absent-minded, wanton, madcap, confused, improvident, indiscreet, imprudent, featherbrained, punch-drunk, befuddled, mercurial, irresponsible, ranti-pole, woolgathering, light-minded, bird-witted, shatterbrained, rattlebrained, slap-happy (sl.), crazy (coll.), silly, unstable, quixotic, foolhardy, flustered, harum-scarum (coll.), volatile, careless, rash, headlong, wild, reckless, unsteady, forgetful, rattlepated, empty-headed, unthinking, foolish.

SCAVENGER, n. Cleaner, trash man, garbage collector, street sweeper.

SCENARIO, *n.* Outline, plot, synopsis, sketch, plan, résumé, screenplay *(Movies)*, brief.

SCENE, *n.* 1. Place where any action occurs, location, site, spot, region, setting, milieu, arena, surroundings, theater, background, environment, sphere, locale, locality, whereabouts, bearings, position, situation, *mise en scène (Fr.).*

2. View, picture, vista, landscape, tableau, prospect, seascape, panorama, show, spectacle, display, vision, pageant, lookout, survey, aspect, sight, representation, scenery, ken, field, range, scope, eyeshot, exposure, outlook, perspective, eyereach.

3. Outbreak of excited *or* violent feelings, outburst, spectacle, exhibition, display, eruption, explosion, upheaval, disturbance, altercation, furor, storm, rage, passion, violence, high words, tantrum *(coll.),* flare-up *(coll.).*

4. Division of a play, unit of dramatic action, episode, act, turn, number, situation.

SCENERY, *n.* 1. General appearance of a place, aggregate of landscape features, atmosphere, prospect, terrain, physical characteristics, aspect, contour, layout, countenance, lineaments, traits, adornment.

2. Stage decorations, background, properties, props, set, stage setting, *mise en scène (Fr.).*

SCENIC, *adj.* 1. Of *or* pertaining to natural scenery, having fine scenery, picturesque, grand, awe-inspiring, breathtaking, beautiful, pleasing to the eye.

2. Of *or* pertaining to the stage *or* stage scenery, theatrical, dramatic, stagy, stagelike, dramaturgic, histrionic, Thespian, make-believe, spectacular.

SCENT, *n.* 1. Distinctive odor *(esp. agreeable),* aroma, smell, incense, essence, perfume, fragrance, fume, savor, whiff, breath, bouquet, pungency, balm, balminess, redolence.

2. Odor left in passing *(by which an animal or person may be traced),* trail, spoor, wind, path, pursuit, wake, course, track.

SCENT, *v.* 1. Perceive *(by or as by the sense of smell),* recognize, smell, detect, get wind of, spoor, breathe, inhale, nose, trace, track, distinguish, discern, suspect, sniff, snuff, trail.

2. Fill with an odor, perfume, odorize, give odor to, aromatize, incense, cense, essence, thurify, breathe, exhale.

SCEPTER, *n.* 1. Rod borne in the hand *(as emblem of regal or imperial power),* wand, staff, baton, insignia, ensign, truncheon, fasces *(Roman).*

2. Royal *or* imperial power, authority, sovereignty, divine right, potency, supremacy, primacy, dominion, prerogative, majesty, imperiality, kingship, crown, regalia, throne, suzerainty, regality, royalty, empire, sway, rule, command, empery *(Poetic).*

SCHEDULE, *n.* Statement of details *(often in classified or tabular form),* record, list, inventory, register, appendix, explanatory addition, itemized bill, synopsis, agenda, summary, program, brief, digest, prospectus, outline, catalogue, roll, table, calendar, invoice, timetable.

SCHEMATIC, *adj.* Pertaining to *or* of the nature of a scheme *or* diagram, representational, illustrative, diagrammatic, depictive, descriptive, delineatory, figurative, graphic.

SCHEMATIZE, *v.* Reduce *or* arrange according to a scheme, classify, tabulate, lay out, dispose, range, distribute, organize, categorize, catalogue, allocate, docket, assort, grade, rank, methodize,
codify, collocate, group, segregate, pigeonhole divide, file.

SCHEME, *n.* 1. Design to be followed, project program of action, plan, objective, system, prospectus, outline, purpose, schema, suggestion course of action, proposal, method, strategy, way procedure, enterprise, *modus operandi (Lat.)* policy, roster, tactics, schedule, syllabus, process order.

2. Underhand plot, contrivance, intrigue, conspiracy, stratagem, cabal, machination, connivance, ruse, shift, maneuver, junto, confederacy league, coalition, racket, complot, counterplot collusion, frame-up.

3. Visionary *or* impractical project, flight of fancy, dream, daydream, reverie, caprice, whim vision, castle in the air, air castle, castle in Spain vagary, pipe dream *(sl.).*

4. Body of related doctrines *or* theories, *etc.* system, school, discipline, belief, thought, persuasion, doctrine, dogma, teaching, view, position method.

5. System of correlated things *or* parts, arrangement, classification, schematism, grouping, codification, systematization, allocation, distribution methodizing, categorization, apportionment, organization, division, graduation, tabulation, gradation, taxonomy, biotaxy *(Biol.),* disposition.

6. Analytical *or* tabular statement, schedule register, agenda, synopsis, summary, itemization digest, brief, catalogue, roll, calendar, table, invoice.

7. Diagram, map, sketch, delineation, layout, outline, draught, drawing, design, chart, model projection, figure, elevation.

SCHEME, *v.* Plan, plot, devise, contrive, frame imagine, design, project, intend, hatch, machinate maneuver, connive, meditate, build, conspire, lay a plan, premeditate, brew, concoct, organize, complot, cabal, intrigue, prepare, predesign.

SCHEMING, *adj.* Given to forming plots *(esp. underhand ones),* artful, sly, cunning, insidious, wily, crafty, Machiavellian, tricky, conniving, shrewd, arch, slippery, contriving, designing, calculating, subtle, intriguing.

SCHISM, *n.* 1. Division *(esp. into mutually opposed parties),* discord, disunion, dissent, heresy, heterodoxy, rupture, rent, breach, split, dissension, falling out, difference, separation, faction, secession, desertion, reactionism, apostasy, sectarianism, nonconformity.

2. Party formed by division, faction, sect, division, persuasion, communion, ism, cult, denomination, sectarism.

SCHISMATIC, *adj.* Of, pertaining to *or* of the nature of schism, guilty of schism, nonconforming, reactionary, apostate, dissenting, protestant, sectarian, heretical, heterodox, denominational, dissentient, discordant, schismatical.

SCHISMATIC, *n.* One who promotes schism, adherent of a schismatic body, recreant, seceder, secessionist, factionist, recusant, cultist, protestant, rebel, sectarian, denominationalist, separatist, nonconformist, sectary, heretic, apostate, dissenter, dissentient.

SCHOLAR, *n.* 1. Pupil, student, disciple, learner, youth, schoolboy, schoolgirl, beginner, educatee, tyro, novice, catechumen, neophyte, collegian, undergraduate, initiate, matriculant, apprentice, ward, probationer, coed *(coll.).*

2. Learned man, erudite person, savant, pundit, man of letters, sage, master, wise man, doctor,

philosopher, scholastic, oracle, authority, luminary, pantologist, colossus of knowledge, giant of learning, mastermind.

SCHOLARLY, *adj.* Scholar-like, befitting a scholar, intellectual, bookish, literary, lettered, educated, wise, academic, scholastic, cultured, cognitive, cerebral, brainy, rational, mental, erudite, learned, studious, profound.

SCHOLARSHIP, *n.* 1. Academic attainments, learning, knowledge acquired by study, enlightenment, accomplishments, erudition, body of knowledge, reading, booklore, pansophy, letters, education, culture, lore, polymathy.

2. Money *or* other aid granted a student of merit, maintenance for a student, endowment, foundation for support of worthy students, grant, teaching assistantship, research assistantship.

SCHOLASTIC, *adj.* 1. Of *or* pertaining to schools, scholars *or* education, academic, educational, instructional, cultural, tutorial, tuitional, pedagogic, scholarly, literary, learned, collegiate, professorial, preceptorial, lettered.

2. Pedantic, formal, precise, ostentatious of learning, stilted, pompous, emphasizing minutiae, pedagogic, pragmatic, priggish, didactic, affected, academic, hidebound, narrow, stiff, grandiose, bigoted, exact, punctilious, overcritical, hypercritical, meticulous, overscrupulous, finical, hairsplitting, bookish, dogmatic, sonorous, rhetorical, euphuistic.

SCHOLASTIC, *n.* 1. *(Sometimes cap.)* Schoolman, disciple of the schoolmen, adherent of scholasticism, scholar, savant, canonist, theologian, academician, intellectual, classicist, classicalist.

2. Pedantic person, pedant, precisionist, precisian, bluestocking *(coll.),* attitudinarian, attitudinizer, bigot, philosoph, sophist, formalist, doctrinaire, vain scholar, conformist, conventionalist, dogmatist, casuist, philosophist *(contempt.),* paralogist *(Log.),* philosophaster, bromide *(sl.).*

SCHOLIAST, *n.* Commentator upon the classics, one who writes scholia upon an author, annotator, expositor, discourser, dissertator, critic, editor, glossarist.

SCHOLIUM, *n.* Explanatory note, annotation, commentary, scholion, observation, comment, remark, gloss, elucidation, glossary, criticism, critique, exegesis.

SCHOOL, *n.* 1. Place *or* establishment where instruction is given, conservatory, academy, seminary, gymnasium, institute, phrontistery, kindergarten, university, college, lyceum.

2. Body of pupils *or* followers of a master (system, method, *etc.),* order, way of thinking, belief, style, thought, method, sect, denomination, art, persuasion, faith, faction, ism, party, class, doctrine, dogma, creed, credo, teaching, profession, view, position, communion, fellowship, disciples, system.

3. Large number *(of fish, porpoises, whales, etc.),* horde, group, shoal, throng, multitude, community, pack.

SCHOOL, *v.* Instruct, teach, train, educate, tutor, govern, nurture, exercise, foster, develop, coach, direct, breed, practice, inform, inculcate, enlighten, rear, cultivate, ready, break in, prepare, bring up, edify, drill, indoctrinate, discipline, guide.

SCHOOLBOOK, *n.* Book for study in school, textbook, text, primer, manual, copybook, grammar, hornbook.

SCHOOLING, *n.* Process of being taught in a school, education, instruction, nurture, discipline, edification, enlightenment, teaching, tuition, exercise, breeding, tutelage, tutorage, indoctrination, inculcation, cultivation, preparation, informing, pedagogy, initiation, drill, practice, development, direction, guidance, tutorship, training.

SCHOOLMATE, *n.* Companion *or* associate at school, classmate, classfellow, schoolfellow, school companion, fellow student *or* pupil, roommate, friend, buddy, chum *(coll.).*

SCHOOLTEACHER, *n.* Teacher in a school, instructor, preceptor, tutor, master, pedagogue, schoolmaster, schoolmistress, educator, professor, schoolman, docent, Gamaliel, methodologist.

SCHOONER, *n.* Sailing vessel with two *or* more masts and fore-and-aft rig, sailboat, three-master, four-master, shallop, fore-and-after *(Naut.),* windjammer *(coll.),* bark *(Naut.),* ketch *(Naut.).*

SCIENCE, *n.* 1. Systematized knowledge, learning, doctrine, theory, ology *(coll.),* erudition, cognition, enlightenment, apprehension, comprehension, scholarship, philosophy.

2. Branch of knowledge, discipline, doctrine, theory, subject, study.

3. Skill, proficiency, craftsmanship, skillfulness, technique, art, expertness, adroitness, address, finesse, aptitude, aptness, genius, capacity, competence, efficiency, technology, finished execution, acquirement, facility, dexterity.

SCIENTIFIC, *adj.* 1. Of *or* pertaining to science *or* the sciences, physical, etiological, technological, philosophical, pantologic, pantological, technical.

2. Regulated by *or* conforming to the principles of exact science, systematic, accurate, verifiable, verified, exact, precise, valid, literal, tangible, physical, material, mathematical, unerring, proven.

SCIENTIST, *n.* One versed in *or* devoted to science, investigator, scientician, physicist, research worker, technician, man of science, scholar, scient.

SCINTILLA, *n.* Particle, jot, iota, spark, modicum, glimmer, trace, shadow, whit, grain, scrap, speck, tittle, mite, atom, ace, bit, mote, corpuscle, point, trifle, minim, hair, minutia, speckle, pin, straw, cent, farthing, doit, micron, snip, spot, rap, ion, insignificancy.

SCINTILLANT, *adj.* Scintillating, sparkling, vivid, light, sharp, twinkling, bright, brilliant, nitid, nitidous, shining, scintillescent, scintillose, glittering, lucent, luminous, blinking, beamy, orient, transplendent, radiant, lambent, shimmery, resplendent, effulgent, fulgent, bespangled, spangled.

SCINTILLATE, *v.* Sparkle, twinkle, flash, glimmer, shimmer, spark, emit sparks, radiate, dazzle, effulge, bedazzle, fulgurate, blaze, glow, glisten, glint, waver, dance, blink, flicker, coruscate, glance, shine, glitter, beam, gleam, glare.

SCIOLISM, *n.* Superficial knowledge, slight *or* imperfect knowledge, superficiality, smattering, shallowness, superficialness, ignorance, pretense, pretension, dilettantism, half-learning, vague notion, simulation, dissembling, quackery, charlatanry.

SCION, *n.* 1. Shoot, twig, cutting, sprig, switch, cion, graft, slip, sprout, spray, stem, branch.

2. Descendant, heir, offspring, offshoot, son, progeny, youth, offset, child, successor, issue.

SCISSION, *n.* Division, splitting, separation, dividing, cutting, fission, sunderance, disseverance, discerption, cleavage, diremption, abstriction, abscission, disruption, cataclasm, dissection, fracture, elision, laceration, dilaceration, dismemberment, abjunction *(Bot.),* severance, divulsion, avulsion, abruption.

SCLEROUS, *adj.* Hard, firm, bony, hardened, solidified, rigid, sclerosed, inflexible, implastic, fossilized, ossified.

SCOFF, *n.* 1. Expression of mockery, derision *or* scorn, reproach, ridicule, mock, jeer, sneer, gibe, flout, taunt, biting jest, derision, scorn, hoot, sarcasm, aspersion, disparagement, fleer, defamation, obloquy, slur, invective, pasquinade, pasquil, roorback, malediction, cut, scurrility, insult, indignity, thrust, brickbat *(coll.),* caustic remark, contempt, abuse, offense, affront, quirk, banter, fling, rub, slander, assault, rap *(sl.),* knock *(sl.),* dig *(coll.),* slap in the face, quip, burlesque, wipe *(coll.),* parody, twit, lampoon, raillery, chaff, persiflage, wisecrack *(sl.),* derogation, slam *(sl.).*

2. Object of mockery *or* derision, laughingstock, jestingstock, joke, gazingstock, butt, jest, game, derision, fair game, dupe, victim, monkey, buffoon, byword, fool, gull, gudgeon, jay *(sl.),* goat *(sl.),* sucker *(sl.).*

SCOFF, *v.* *(Often fol. by* AT) Mock, speak derisively, jeer, deride, rail at, ridicule, quip, make sport of, twit, make light of, revile, scout, contemn, laugh at, poke fun at, flout, taunt, fleer, jape, hiss, banter, scorn, catcall, whistle at, knock *(sl.),* have a fling at, rebuff, slander, backbite, satirize, lampoon, run down, traduce, malign, defame, vilify, cast aspersions, curl up one's lip, derogate, decry, be contemptuous, disparage, point the finger of scorn, hold up to scorn, gibe, jest, hoot, razz *(sl.),* slur, chaff, gird at, make game of, harass, spurn.

SCOLD, *n.* Person *(esp. a woman)* addicted to abusive speech, shrew, termagant, she-wolf, tigress, common scold, rebuker, chider, vituperator, reviler, castigator, Xanthippe, virago, vixen, hag, harridan, fury, old cat *(coll.),* hellhag, hellcat, grandmother, fishwife, battle-ax *(sl.),* crone, beldam, old witch, ogress.

SCOLD, *v.* Chide, find fault with, lash out at, objurgate, trounce, correct, bring to book, upbraid, score, dress down, blame, reprimand, reprove, berate, rate, reprehend, castigate, take to task, deliver a lecture to, exprobrate, vituperate, rebuke, censure, brawl, storm at, remonstrate, rail at, blow up *(coll.),* denounce, tongue, lecture, nag, declaim against, set down, give a piece of one's mind, rake *or* haul over the coals, trim *(coll.),* jaw *(sl.),* huff, thunder *or* fulminate against, tongue-lash *(coll.),* roast *(sl.),* put on the carpet.

SCONCE, *n.* 1. Sense, wit, judgment, discretion, shrewdness, wisdom, sagacity, brain, acumen, perception, apperception, penetration, intuition, reasoning, percipience, level-headedness, common sense, discernment, keenness, judiciousness, understanding, insight, discrimination, acuteness.

2. Wall bracket for holding candles *or* lights, candleholder, candelabrum, torch staff, light socket, lamp holder, lamp stand, girandole.

SCOOP, *n.* 1. Ladle, small deep shovel with a short handle, bail, dipper, bucket *(of a steam shovel, dredge, etc.),* spoon, cyathus *(Gk. Antiq.).*

2. Hollow, place scooped out, hole, ditch, crater, sink, excavation, bowl, concavity, cavity, impression, pit, dip, well, gulf, burrow, grave, gully, trough, quarry.

SCOOP, *v.* 1. Take up *or* out with *or* as with scoop, empty with a scoop, ladle, lade out, bail, lift out, shovel, spade, bucket, dish up *or* out, dip.

2. Form a hollow *or* hollows in, form with *or* as with a scoop, hollow out, excavate, render concave, pit, indent, dent, depress, dig, gouge, mine, sweep, burrow, dig out.

SCOPE, *n.* 1. Extent *or* range of view (outlook, application, operation, effectiveness, *etc.),* object, purpose, aim, mark, drift, intent, intention, tendency, view, end, plan, tenor, purview, destination, application, design, direction, scheme, trend, policy, influence, circuit, orbit, compass, reach, stretch, area, spread, span, sweep, limit, amplitude, swing, expanse, margin, ambit, realm, territory, region, zone, play, distance, field, sphere, bound, boundary, motive, goal, bearing, force, effect, prospect, ambition, determination, grasp.

2. Space for movement *or* activity, opportunity for operation, room, field, range, latitude, sphere, play, freedom, vent, margin, liberty, free course, blacken, slur, defame, blast, excoriate, calumny, zone, length, width, territory, area, berth, swing, sweep, rein, leeway *(coll.).*

3. Extent in space, length, tract, area, compass, bounds, boundary, span, stretch, sweep, spread, limit, extension, line, margin, circuit, acreage, realm, orbit, distance, mileage, breadth, width, confines, field, division, territory, region, quarter, section, zone, premises, demesne, reach.

SCORCH, *v.* 1. Burn superficially, parch, shrivel with heat, char, roast, singe, blast, blight, brown, blacken, brand, wither, dry, blister, dehydrate, cauterize, scar, torrefy, sear.

2. Criticize severely, scorn, backbite, flay, censure, castigate, roast *(sl.),* stigmatize, scathe, blacken, slur, defame, blast, excoriate, calumniate, libel, slander, reprehend, blame, impugn, detract, upbraid, gibbet, muckrake *(coll.),* slam *(sl.),* rap *(sl.),* cut up, pick to pieces, reproach, inveigh against, accuse, black-list, blackball, decry, cry down, denunciate, denounce, damn, condemn, malign, vilify, anathematize, dishonor, insult, traduce, vilipend, asperse, find fault with, lash, charge, attack, disparage.

SCORCHING, *adj.* 1. Very hot, burning, searing, withering, fiery, roasting, parching, red-hot, white-hot, torrid, sweltering, broiling, calorific.

2. Caustic, sarcastic, scathing, harsh, envenomed, abrupt, brutal, acrimonious, blunt, rude, tart, gruff, brash, curt, short, austere, stern, keen, cruel, cutting, unkind, vitriolic, hurtful, sharp, biting, stinging, virulent, brusque, bearish, churlish, bitter, malevolent, venomous, malignant, crabbed, mordacious, derisive, excoriating, insulting, lashing, galling, ill-natured, malicious, maleficent, spiteful, rancorous, invidious, uncharitable, severe.

SCORE, *n.* 1. Record of points made by competitors *(in a game or match),* reckoning, sum, account, count, computation, summation, total, cast, tally, aggregate.

2. Mark, notch, scratch, stroke, groove, line, incision, stripe, streak, gash, cut, nick, scotch, slash, slit, jag.

3. Account *(showing indebtedness),* amount due, bill, charge, reckoning, debt, credit, fee, figure, toll, poll, quotation, assessment, obligation, price, tab, register.

4. *(Plural)* A great many, host, multitude, band,

troop, cavalcade, mob, lot, legion, confluence, conflux, levy, muster, tribe, drove, brood, mess, swarm, array, conclave, convocation, throng, congregation, company, concourse, gathering, meeting, convention.

5. Reason, ground, account, consideration, motive, sake, cause, interest, regard, respect, concern, behalf, welfare, behoof, use, profit, service, benefit, occasion, inducement, incitation, instigation, actuation, provocation, incentive, stimulation, inspiration.

6. Successful move (remark, *etc.*), stroke, good hit, coup, master stroke, great idea, bright thought *or* idea, blow, feat, maneuver, trump, fluke, triumph, victory, achievement, conquest, piece of good luck *or* fortune, feather in one's cap, knockout, ten-strike *(coll.)*, win *(coll.)*, killing *(coll.)*.

SCORE, *v.* 1. Gain for addition to one's score *(in a game)*, make a score of, make a point *or* points, tally, keep score, register, enter.

2. Make notches, cuts *or* lines in *or* on, notch, cut, scratch, rule, engrave, furrow, abrade, inscribe, etch, incise, chisel, carve, flute, groove, chase, gash, crack, slit, channel, hatch, tool.

3. *(Often fol. by UP)* Reckon, write down *(as a debt)*, charge, count, total, compute, calculate, cipher, cast, enumerate, add, figure, balance, foot up.

4. Gain advantage, win, achieve success, register, succeed, meet with success, strike, triumph, win *or* carry the day, come off with flying colors, carry by storm, make a killing *(coll.)*, click *(sl.)*.

SCORIFY, *v.* Burn, oxidize, reduce to slag, torrefy, bake, sear, carbonize, char, oxidate, smelt, incinerate, cremate, burn off, burn to a cinder, burn to a crisp.

SCORN, *v.* Spurn, contemn, despise, disdain, disregard, slight, hold in contempt, snarl at, scout, repulse, set at naught, refuse to deal with, have nothing to do with, disown, rebuff, slight, disapprove, explode, refuse to recognize, ostracize, disavow, turn a deaf ear to, refuse to listen to, ignore, hold oneself aloof from, skepticize, dissent from, turn from, not countenance, shun, cut *(coll.)*, cut dead *(coll.)*, give a cold shoulder to, have no use for, place no value on, deride, laugh at, hold up to ridicule, treat with disdain, revile, flout, snub, hold in derision, mock, jeer at, sneer at, gibe at, laugh at, spit upon, look down upon, abuse, hoot at, reproach, taunt, be contemptuous of, hold cheap, esteem lightly, care nothing for, twit, point the finger of scorn at, poke fun at, fleer, curl one's lip at, wipe one's feet upon, pooh-pooh, hiss, catcall, give the Bronx cheer *(sl.)*, give the raspberry *(sl.)*, upstage, highhat, hold oneself superior to.

SCORN, *n.* Opprobrium, contempt, contumely, derision, laughter, mockery, scoffing, contemptuousness, insolence, arrogance, disregard, heedlessness, haughtiness, ridicule, sarcasm, hissing, booing, catcall, taunting, flouting, gibe, scornfulness, snubbing, disregard, rebuff, disrespect.

SCORNFUL, *adj.* Arrogant, haughty, prideful, contemptuous, insolent, disrespectful, defiant, disdainful, derisive, mocking, gibing, cynical, cavalier, rude, impolite, discourteous, contumelious, withering, ironical, sardonic, supercilious, insulting, scurrilous, disparaging, derisory, quizzical, patronizing, domineering, presumptuous, highhanded, overweening, impudent, audacious, malapert, flippant, flip *(coll.)*, pert, fresh *(sl.)*.

SCOTCH, *v.* 1. Cut, indent, notch, scar, scarify, dent, nick, damage, mark, mar, deface, gash, score, blaze, scratch, lacerate, mill, tooth, crenelate, hurt, scathe, impair, spoil, disfigure, mutilate, mangle.

2. Balk, frustrate, thwart, foil, checkmate, counteract, traverse, contravene, circumvent, upset, override, overthwart, stop, confound, flummox *(coll.)*, overwhelm, encumber, inconvenience, handicap, hamper, burden, weigh down, faze *(coll.)*, damp, throw cold water on, discomfit, floor *(coll.)*, suppress, crush, overpower, overcome, trim *(coll.)*, lick *(coll.)*, ruin, ruinate.

SCOT-FREE, *adj.* 1. Independent, footloose, free, disengaged, at liberty, at large, free-coming, freegoing, unconstrained, unhampered, unimpeded, untrammeled, uncurbed, unmuzzled, uncontrolled, reinless, unshackled, unbound, unobstructed, unbridled, unfettered, unrestricted, ungoverned, unbounded.

2. Free, gratuitous, for nothing, for love, gratis, untaxed, without cost, without charge, free of expense, rent-free, unpaid-for, unbought, expenseless, honorary, complimentary, freely given, donated, contributed, contributory.

SCOUNDREL, *n.* Rogue, knave, villain, wretch, malefactor, rascal, scamp, cheat, trickster, humbug, sharper, swindler, caitiff, miscreant, reprobate, varlet, scalawag, bezonian, libertine, base fellow, ruffian, rapscallion, bad one, blackguard, black sheep, scapegrace, rotter *(sl.)*, cad *(sl.)*, bounder *(sl.)*, recreant, rakehell, dog, whelp, hound, mongrel, cur, snake in the grass, serpent, mischiefmaker, evildoer, sinner, transgressor, wrongdoer, malfeasor, offender, criminal, crook *(sl.)*, felon, jailbird, convict, outlaw, ticket-of-leave-man, impostor, liar, cheat, renegade, apostate, backslider, prodigal, traitor, betrayer, Judas, good-for-nothing, ne'er-do-well, charlatan, quack, deceiver, mountebank, hypocrite, fake, fraud, perjurer, prevaricator, equivocator, confidence man, shyster, thief, robber, bandit, brigand, footpad, holdup man, turncoat, runagate, recidivist, tergiversator.

SCOUR, *v.* 1. Polish, rub, buff, shine, scrub, cleanse, brighten, make clean, affricate, abrade, frictionize, burnish, rub up, scrub down, sponge, soap, swab, deterge, launder, lave, tub, wash out, elute, bathe.

2. Overrun, roam, wander, hurry, chase, traverse, cross, move fast, move quickly, tear along, course, zip, whiz, skip along, bound, sprint, scurry, scamper, scuttle, trip, hie, skedaddle *(sl.)*, bolt, bowl along, dart, fly, outstrip the wind, go like the wind, dash along, cover ground, chase, bundle along, go like a bat out of hell *(coll.)*, go like a shot, put the spurs to one's horse, stir one's stumps, lope, trot, gallop, canter, scorch the ground, burn up the track.

SCOURGE, *n.* 1. Whip, flail, lash, cat-o'-nine-tails, flagellum, thong, cowhide, cord, knout, rod, switch, bastinado, strap, rawhide, blacksnake whip, quirt, bullwhack, rattan, cane, stick, birch rod, cudgel, truncheon, billy, blackjack, nightstick, club.

2. Plague, pest, pestilence, visitation, affliction, punishment, infestation, vexation, bane, curse, annoyance, nuisance, misfortune, calamity, disaster, tragedy, woe, sorrow, anguish, unpleasantness, molestation, stroke, blow, cut, troublement, grievance, worry, fret, gall, mortification, bother, botherment, oppression, load, cross, thorn in one's side, sting, bitter cup, trials and tribulations, pain,

wound, injury, hurt, hardship, adversity, care, misery, bitter pill, ordeal, distress, bad luck, ill fortune, misfortune, hard luck, unhappiness, hard lot, evil destiny, mishap, mischance, accident, casualty, catastrophe, hard times.

SCOURGE, *v.* 1. Lash, whip, flagellate, flog, lace, give a hiding, thrash, spank, cane, birch, pommel, flail, smite, buffet, thump, baste, trounce, bastinado, horsewhip, belt, strap, switch, cudgel, club, fustigate, give the stick.

2. Punish, chastise, beat, afflict, persecute, chasten, castigate, smite, administer punishment, penalize, take to task, bring to book, give one his deserts.

SCOUT, *v.* 1. Scorn, spurn, contemn, despise, disdain, hold in contempt, reject, have nothing to do with, refuse, abhor, ignore, hold oneself aloof from, revolt at, turn from, not countenance, object to, protest against, shun, give a cold shoulder to, have no regard for, have no use for.

2. Reconnoiter, make reconnaissance, spy, spy out, engage in espionage, investigate, search, examine, scrutinate, scrutinize, survey, case *(sl.)*, examine, inquire, question, be on the lookout, be on watch, stand watch.

SCOUT, *n.* 1. Precursor, forerunner, pioneer, herald, outrider, vanguard, leader, harbinger, avant-courier, advance guard, guide, watch, watchman, emissary, envoy.

2. *(Sl.)* Man, person, human being, fellow, chap, guy, personage, creature, individual, soul, mortal, party, geezer *(sl.)*, wight, hand, chappie *(coll.)*, mister.

SCOW, *n.* Boat, barge, vessel, carrier, conveyance, flatboat, lighter, canal boat, catamaran, skiff, wherry, punt, coracle.

SCOWL, *v.* Frown, look angry, look mad *(coll.)*, sulk, look stern, lower, glower, look sullen, mope, pout, fret, grumble, look black, knit the brow, be angry, be morose, be ill-tempered.

SCOWL, *n.* Frown, black looks, long face, angry look, morose appearance, reproving look, dirty look, nasty look.

SCRAMBLE, *v.* 1. Struggle, contest, fight, combat, contend, scrap, battle, scuffle, tussle, jostle, joust, strive, reluctate, come to blows, grapple with, scrimmage, clash, run up against, collide, conflict, run headlong against, join issue with, tilt, lock horns, have a struggle with, have a tussle with, spar, fence, duel, engage, compete, vie with, rival, outvie, come into rivalry with.

2. Mix, intermix, mingle, jumble, mix up, commingle, intermingle, stir together, confuse, shuffle, disarrange, disorder, bring into disorder, muddle, disorganize, tumble, mess up, make a hash of, dishevel, ruffle, rumple, turn topsy-turvy, disjoint, unsettle, upset, disturb, discompose, throw into confusion, agitate, toss, raddle, mat, ravel, entangle, scatter.

SCRAMBLE, *n.* 1. Turmoil, contest, confusion, perturbation, disturbance, row *(coll.)*, fuss, riot, uprising, stir, turbulence, squall, storm, tumult, commotion, uproar, racket, ruckus, rumpus, bluster, fracas, ruction, pandemonium, Donnybrook, embroilment, melee, free-for-all, huff, dispute, quarrel, contention, litigation, strife, struggle, broil, brawl, imbroglio, scrap, fray, feud, run-in, snarl, tangle, bickering, wrangling, encounter, conflict, affray, battle, fight, action, engagement, scrimmage, tournament.

2. Mix-up, confusion, mixture, commingling,

intermingling, jumble, shuffling, disarrangement, disorder, unruliness, mess, muddle, hash, stew, dishevelment, rumpling, disjointure, agitation, tossing, matting, raveling, entanglement.

SCRAP, *n.* 1. Small quantity, morsel, particle, atom, speck, jot, iota, molecule, corpuscle, dab, whit, tittle, scintilla, touch, glimmer, modicum, minimum, minim, grain, granule, drop, crumb, bite, sprinkling, smattering, inch, patch, spice, droplet, taste, lick, smell, smack, tincture, dole, pittance, little bit, dose, snippet, smithereen, sliver, chip, splinter, fraction, thimbleful, spoonful, hair, shaving, paring, shred, fritter, seed, nutshell, fragment, drop in the bucket, hint, suggestion, soupçon, sample, specimen, trace.

2. *(Sl.)* Fight, turmoil, contest, confusion, perturbation, scramble, disturbance, row *(coll.)*, fuss, mess, riot, uprising, insurgency, stir, turbulence, roil, bother, pother, squall, storm, tumult, brouhaha, commotion, uproar, racket, ruckus, rumpus, bluster, fracas, ruction, eruption, pandemonium, Donnybrook, embroilment, melee, free-for-all.

SCRAPBOOK, *n.* Memory book, commonplace book, album, birthday book, photograph album, clipping book, cutting book.

SCRAPE, *v.* 1. Graze, rub, brush, skim, grind, rasp, abrade, file, sand, sandpaper, rub down, grate, scuff, bark, scour, scrub, affricate, frictionize, polish, shine, burnish, smooth, buff, rub hard, clean, cleanse, brighten, make clean, rub up, rub down.

2. Get, acquire, procure, obtain, amass, collect, gather, glean, pick up, secure, gather in, aggregate, hoard, assemble, lump together, take in, rake up, pile up, agglomerate, compile, accumulate, concentrate, garner, lay up, stack, stash, cache.

3. Rasp, sound harshly, scratch, grind, grate, crunch, buzz, saw, whiz, scrunch, burr.

4. Engrave, grave, etch, carve, chisel, inscribe, chase, enchase, tool, incise, cut, emboss.

5. Bow, make obeisance, salaam, bend the knee, genuflect, bow the head, make one's bow, curtsy, fall on one's knees, grovel, kiss the hem of one's garment, kiss one's feet, nod.

SCRAPE, *n.* 1. Predicament, trouble, tight spot, pretty pickle, plight, dilemma, difficulty, perplexity, embarrassment, entanglement, straits, sea of trouble, complication, pretty kettle of fish, pass, troublesome situation, tough spot, imbroglio, embroilment, tight squeeze.

2. Bow, obeisance, genuflection, kowtow, homage, reverence, curtsy, bob, nod, salaam, salute, salutation.

SCRATCH, *n.* Cut, incision, abrasion, laceration, hurt, injury, wound, opening, striation, scar, gash, puncture, stab, scuff, groove, furrow, streak, crack, chink, scoring, slit, mark.

SCRATCH, *v.* 1. Gash, graze, mar, mark, cut, lacerate, score, scarify, incise, crack, streak, furrow, slit, affricate, abrade, fray, rasp, file, grind, grate, disfigure, mutilate, blemish, mangle.

2. Scribble, scrawl, scrabble, pen, indite, inscribe, scriven, trace, take down, copy down, write down.

3. Eliminate, exclude, expunge, erase, rub out, blot out, cancel, omit, cross out, strike out, rule out, draw the pen through, sponge out.

4. Rasp, scrape, sound harshly, scrunch, grind, grate, crunch.

SCRAWL, *n.* Handwriting, penmanship, scribble,

pothooks, hen-scratchings, illegible writing, bad penmanship.

SCRAWNY, *adj.* Thin, tabid, tabescent, puny, skeletal, skinny, emaciated, wasted, sickly, drawn, lean, sinewy, spare, fleshless, gaunt, lank, lanky, scraggy, rawboned, spindle-shanked, bony, under-fed, undernourished, spindly, starveling, attenu-ated, peaked, poor, poorly *(coll.),* marasmic, runty, dwarfed, pygmy, nanoid, stunted, under-sized, scrubby.

SCREAM, *v.* Howl, wail, roar, pipe, shriek, strid-ulate, cry out, screech, squawk, shrill, whine, cat-erwaul, hoot, yell, shout, yowl, roar, bellow, yelp, squall, blare, ululate, bay.

SCREAM, *n.* Shriek, yell, holler, outcry, shrill cry, ululation, screech, squeal, squall, squawk, shout, roar, bellow, yelp, wail, whine, lamentation.

SCREEN, *n.* 1. Veil, cover, mask, shelter, blind, curtain, partition, lattice, grate, grating, purdah, sash, sash curtain, window blind, Venetian blind, shutter, reredos, iconostasis, screen door, portiere, jalousie *(Fr.).*

2. Safeguard, buffer, defense, shield, fender, ward, guard, safety device, refuge, palladium, camouflage, false colors, incognito, dissemblance, shelter, covert, shroud, coat, mantle, cloak, in-vestment, coverage.

3. Sieve, sifter, network, mesh, web, webwork, riddle, grate, reticulum, colander, strainer, crib-ble. filter, honeycomb.

SCREEN, *v.* 1. Separate, refine, select, filter, strain, rack, winnow, sift, riddle, eliminate, weed out, filtrate, percolate, sort, assort, order, arrange, size, group, array, rank, rate, evaluate, range, class, classify, group, graduate, grade, tabulate, file, index, get rid of, eject, discard, throw away, throw out.

2. Protect, guard, safeguard, shelter, shield, watch over, cloak, panoply, shroud, cover, defend, secure, keep, preserve, maintain.

3. Shade, veil, darken, obscure, hide, cloak, cover up, shroud, curtain, cloud, keep hidden, keep in the background, eclipse, occult, secrete, conceal, put into concealment, hide from sight, disguise, mask, dissemble, camouflage, counterfeit, keep secret, keep dark, reserve, withhold, muffle, suppress, stifle, smother, hush up, draw a curtain over, throw a veil over, dim, cast a shadow on.

SCREW, *n.* 1. Spiral, helix, pin, hardware, iron-mongery, flat-headed screw, oval-headed screw, round-headed screw, worm, bolt, screw-bolt.

2. Churl, niggard, miser, pinchpenny, skinflint, muckworm, moneygrubber, curmudgeon, lick-penny, codger, tightwad, scrimp *(coll.).*

3. Propeller, driver, twin screws, ship's screw.

SCREW, *v.* 1. Contort, twist, turn awry, gnarl, buckle, distort, writhe, warp, knot, wrench, wring, misshape, deform, wrest, torture, pervert, garble, convolve, twine, twirl, wind, twist and turn, curl, kink, crisp, twill, worm, serpentine, entwine, in-dent, crimp.

2. Attach, fix, affix, join, bind, fasten, clamp, hasp, bolt, rivet, pin, tighten, link, hook.

3. Exact, wring, wrest, put the screws on, wrench, extort, force from, wring from, force, compel, drive, press, constrain, bear down upon, require, necessitate, use violence upon, coerce, shake down *(sl.),* levy, blackmail, sponge, squeeze,

SCRIBBLE, *v.* Scrawl, scratch, scrabble, pen, jot down, scriven, trace, take down, write in long-

hand, copy down, write down, make scratchings, make chicken-tracks *(coll.).*

SCRIBE, *n.* Scrivener, writer, pen-pusher, ink-slinger, pencil-pusher, scribbler, amanuensis, sec-retary, stenographer, transcriber, copier, copyist, chirographer, calligraphist, recorder, clerk, author, essayist, poet, dramatist, playwright, novelist, pamphleteer, short-story writer, hack *(coll.),* com-piler, penny-a-liner, journalist, newsman, newspa-perman, editorialist, ghost writer, reporter, cor-respondent, reviewer, critic, registrar, bookkeeper, prothonotary, notary.

SCRIMMAGE, *n.* Scramble, turmoil, contest, con-fusion, perturbation, disturbance, row *(coll.),* fuss, riot, uprising, stir, turbulence, bother, pother, squall, storm, tumult, brouhaha, commotion, up-roar, racket, ruckus, rumpus, bluster, fracas, ruc-tion, pandemonium, Donnybrook, embroilment, melee, free-for-all, predicament, huff, dispute, quarrel, contention, litigation, strife, struggle, broil, brawl, imbroglio, scrap, fray, feud, fight, run-in, snarl, tangle, bickering, wrangling, con-flict, affray, battle, match, game, bout, event, affair, encounter, rencounter, action, engagement, tournament, tourney, mix-up, disorder, unruliness, muddle, stew.

SCRIMP, *v.* Stint, pinch, be parsimonious, be pe-nurious, be stingy, grudge, begrudge, skimp *(coll.),* pinch a penny till it squeaks, economize, cut cor-ners, be sparing, dole out sparingly, reduce, straiten, curtail, limit.

SCRIPT, *n.* 1. Writing, handwriting, manuscript, autograph, holograph, chirography, scripture, written matter, inscription, paper, document, opus, work, composition, jottings, typescript, manu-script, MS., penscript, calligraphy, cacography, scribble, scrawl, pencraft, penmanship, scrivening, author's copy, original copy, codex, palimpsest, Italian script, Chancery script, Roman hand, Gothic script, German script, Spencerian script, Palmer method, round hand, slanting hand, copy-book hand, longhand, cursive hand, cuneiform, ideograph, ideogram, hieroglyphic, hieratic script, demotic, script, character, symbol.

2. Playbook, book, scenario, shooting script *(cant),* promptbook, libretto, score, dialogue, side *(cant),* text, lines, scene.

SCRIPTURAL, *adj.* Orthodox, evangelical, divine, canonical, sound, firm, catholic, textual, literal, authentic, accepted, authoritative, approved, re-ceived, standard, inspired, apocalyptic, revela-tional, theopneustic, prophetic, ecclesiastical, bib-lical.

SCRIPTURE, *n.* Holy Writ, the Bible, the Good Book, the Gospels, New Testament, Old Testa-ment, the Word of God, the Scriptures, the Book of Books, inspired writings, sacred writings, the Vulgate, Authorized Version, Douay Version, King James Bible, the Law, Mosaic Law, the Prophets, Pentateuch, Hexateuch, Octateuch, Sep-tuagint, Hagiographa, Apocrypha, Evangelists, Epistles, Pauline Epistles, Acts of the Apostles, Synoptic Gospels, Masorah, Talmud, Gemara.

SCRIVENER, *n.* Writer, scribe, copyist, amanuen-sis, ink-slinger, pen-pusher, pencil-pusher, penman, pen-driver, scribbler, secretary, stenographer, transcriber, copier, chirographer, calligrapher, cal-ligraphist, recorder, clerk, recording secretary, compiler, registrar, bookkeeper, prothonotary, no-tary public, engrosser.

SCROLL, *n.* 1. Register, inventory, catalogue, file,

list, tally, roll, account, chronicle, paper, writing, document, inscription, piece of writing, manuscript, MS., parchment, vellum, sheepskin, diploma, papyrus, annals, certificate, voucher.

2. Spiral, flourish, paraph, ornament, decoration, embellishment, wave, guilloche, running scroll, zigzag.

SCRUMPTIOUS, *adj.* Palatable, agreeable, tasty, delicious, delectable, good, edible, potable, eatable, digestible, succulent, tasteful, sweet, sweet-tasting, flavorful, relishable, enjoyable, tangy, zestful, piquant, flavorsome, pleasant, nectarean, gustful, savory, ambrosial, appetizing, pleasing, luscious, toothsome, exquisite, well-prepared, well-cooked, fit for a king, delicate, dainty, saporous, saporific, mouth-watering, tempting, tantalizing, rich, rich-flavored, spicy, tender, juicy.

SCRUPLE, *n.* 1. Unit of weight, one-third dram, twenty grains.

2. Hesitation, hesitancy, qualm, perplexity, puzzlement, dilemma, conscientiousness, moral faculty, objection, question, scrupulousness, scrupulosity, misgiving, demur, recoil, shrinking, punctilio, concern, fearfulness, apprehensiveness, apprehension, anxiety, care, solicitude, anxious concern, suspension, boggle, demurral, fastidiousness, squeamishness, finickiness, meticulousness, meticulosity, overparticularity, finicality, protestation, remonstrance, expostulation, rejection, drawback, dubiety, dubiousness, doubtfulness, diffidence, mistrust, distrust, uncertainty.

SCRUPLE, *v.* Hesitate, doubt, waver, have a qualm, puzzle, oscillate, fluctuate, halt, be timorous, demur, boggle, falter, pause, stick at, be in suspense, hang back, object, take exception, cavil, carp, wrangle, shy at, protest, disagree, differ, dissent, kick *(coll.)*, raise objections, raise one's voice against, look askance at, dodge, fight shy of, duck *(coll.)*, shrink, blench, hang back, not have the heart, not have the stomach, be loath, blink, frown upon, make a face at, discountenance, turn up the nose at, make a mouth at *(coll.)*, make a wry face.

SCRUPULOUS, *adj.* Diffident, hesitant, cautious, careful, apprehensive, fearful, mistrustful, distrustful, dubious, expostulative, protesting, protestant, remonstrating, remonstrative, precise, overparticular, finical, finicking, finicky, meticulous, squeamish, on guard, qualmish, perplexed, puzzled, conscientious, demurring, punctilious, concerned, anxious, solicitous, boggling, fastidious, religious, exacting, demanding, overnice, choosy *(sl.)*, hypercritical, censorious, discriminating, discriminative, selective, observant, obedient, literal, adverse, unwilling, disinclined, loath, reluctant.

SCRUTINIZE, *v.* Investigate, examine, search, canvass, pry into, search into, probe, dissect, inquire into, study, sift, explore, overhaul, look into, look at closely, research, survey, keep under surveillance, look beneath the surface, peer into, scan, look over, inspect, regard carefully, anatomize, analyze, observe, perlustrate, speculate, give the once-over *(sl.)*, review, peruse, indagate, give one's minute attention, fix the eye on, rivet the gaze on, contemplate, sound, delve into, fathom, winnow, sift, check, audit, prove, take stock of.

SCRUTINY, *n.* Careful examination, research, search, inspection, observation, perlustration, scrutation, contemplation, observance, surveillance, the once-over *(sl.)*, review, perusal, examen, indagation, exploration, inquisition, inquest, inquiry,

study, analysis, minute attention, sifting, probe, search, close investigation, viewing, close view, close look, prying.

SCUFF, *n.* Mark, damage, hurt, injury, scrape, abrasion, rub, contusion.

SCUFFLE, *v.* Tussle, jostle, reluct, come to blows, fight, contend, contest, exchange blows, grapple with, scrimmage, clash, run up against, collide with, conflict, run headlong against, join issue with, tilt, lock horns, spar, duel, fence, compete, vie with, rival, outvie, wrestle with, struggle, combat, put up a fight, scrap, battle.

SCUFFLE, *n.* Conflict, battle, contest, contention, run-in, snarl, tangle, bickering, wrangling, feud, fight, scrap, imbroglio, brawl, broil, struggle, dispute, quarrel, litigation, strife, free-for-all, ruction, fracas, Donnybrook, embroilment, melee, uproar, racket, rumpus, ruckus, bluster, commotion, tourney, fray, affray, engagement, action, match, game, bout, row *(coll.)*, riot, uprising, squall, racket, tumult, brouhaha.

SCULLERY, *n.* Kitchen, cookroom, cookery, galley, cookhouse, bakery, bakehouse.

SCULPTOR, *n.* Artist, modeler, sculptress, chiseler, carver, stonecarver, woodcarver, molder, worker in clay, worker in marble, worker in stone, worker in bronze, designer, fashioner.

SCULPTURE, *n.* Carving, modeling, sculpturation, sculpturing, statue, figure, heroic statue, heroic sculpture, monumental figure, monumental statuary, life-size figure, life-size statue, decorative sculpture, architectural sculpture, portrait sculpture, portrait modeling, garden sculpture, classical sculpture, statuary, xylography, anaglyptics, cast, ceramic sculpture, cameo, intaglio, relief, high relief, half-relief, low relief, bas-relief.

SCULPTURE, *v.* Fashion, cast, mold, model, sculpt, chisel, carve, cut, shape, form, figure, knead, hew, rough-hew, block out.

SCUM, *n.* 1. Riffraff, rubbish, trash, chaff, vermin, common people, offscourings of society, dregs of society, offscum of society, swinish multitude, scum of the earth, the lowest of the low, sons of Belial, children of the devil, outcasts, pariahs.

2. Film, spume, foam, froth, dross, offscourings, residuum, refuse, leavings, orts, remains, detritus, waste, deposit, precipitate, dregs, chaff, lees, offal, waste matter, scoriae, offscum, slag, feculence, sewage, flotsam, slough, swill, bilge, grounds, sordes, settlings, silt, loess, alluvium, alluvion.

SCURRILITY, *n.* Slander, libel, abuse, derogation, contumely, disparagement, detraction, backbiting, vilipendity, malediction, sarcasm, traducing, condemnation, defamation, disdain, irreverence, disrespect, discourtesy, contemptuousness, opprobrium, grossness, lowness, lewdness, vulgarity, uncouthness, ribaldry, imprecation, foulness, vituperation, calumny, denunciation, execration, obloquy, invective, blackguardism, indignity, insult, aspersion, gibe, obscenity, impudicity, indelicacy, impropriety, smut, dirt, filth.

SCURRILOUS, *adj.* Indecent, shameless, indelicate, Fescennine, smutty, ribald, coarse, low, gross, dirty, immodest, obscene, uncomplimentary, insulting, offensive, slanderous, abusive, derogatory, contumelious, disparaging, detracting, vilipenditory, maledictory, derisive, sarcastic, libelous, defamatory, rude, insolent, irreverent, disrespectful, discourteous, contemptuous, opprobrious, lewd, maledictive, imprecatory, foul-mouthed, vituperative, calumnious, reviling, satirical, outrageous, sardonic.

SCURRY, v. Hurry, scramble, speed, move fast, move swiftly, move double-quick, hie, hasten, bolt, dart, bowl along, sprint, post, charge along, scuttle, scud, scoot, scamper, scour, fly, flit, wing one's way, outstrip the wind, breeze along, whiz, whisk, whip along, clip, burn up the highway, make tracks, race, shoot, tear along, bundle along, stir one's stumps (sl.), step on it (sl.), step on the gas, go like lightning, go like a bat out of hell, go like a shot, trot, gallop, canter, hustle, bustle, plunge ahead, dash along, rush, push on, press on, be in haste, be in a hurry, plunge headlong, spurt, mend one's pace, gather speed, lose no time, rush headlong, rush pellmell, make time.

SCUTCHEON, n. Escutcheon, shield, badge, ensign, insigne, crest, heraldic symbol, heraldic badge, heraldry, arms, bearings, armorial bearings, coat of arms, emblem, hatchment.

SCUTTLE, v. 1. Ruin, destroy, wreck, ship-wreck, submerge, sink, swamp, overturn, overset, capsize, upset, heel over, keel over, send to the bottom, send to Davy Jones's locker, upset the boat.

2. Hurry, speed, scramble, move quickly, move fast, move swiftly, trip, hie, make haste, hasten, bolt, dart, sprint, run, post, charge, scurry, scud, scoot, scamper, scour, fly, flit, whiz, whisk, whip, clip, dash, shoot, tear, race, bundle, lope, trot, gallop, canter, hustle, plunge, rush, push on, spurt, bustle.

SCYTHE, n. Knife, blade, cutlery, tool, imple-ment, cutter, sickle, edged tool, snath, falchion.

SEA, n. 1. Ocean, main, deep, the briny deep, the deep sea, the deep blue sea, Davy Jones's locker (coll.), salt water, the big drink (sl.), high seas, seaway, ocean lane, sea lane, waterway, ship route, steamer track.

2. Great quantity, lots (coll.), peck, pack, par-cel, multitude, abundance, quantity, mass, volume, profusion, oceans, great deal, big amount, galore, slew, batch, heaps, load, carload, wagonload, flood, bunch, aggregation, oodles (sl.), piles, stacks, wad, gob, scads, host, army, legion, scores, tons, flock, covey, brood, litter, swarm, shoal.

SEACOAST, n. Coast, beach, seaboard, shore, sea-shore, littoral, foreshore, strand, sea marge, seaside, coastland, coastal region, edge of the sea, waterside, rock-bound coast.

SEAFARING, adj. Nautical, maritime, naval, marine, ocean-going, seagoing, oceanic, at sea, afloat, on the sea.

SEAL, n. 1. Stamp, intaglio, die, brand, sigillum, cachet, impression, mark, impress, signet, label, imprint, imprimatur, paraph, countersign, counter-mark, counterstamp, counterfoil, privy seal, great seal, bull.

2. Signature, identification, warrant, authority, authorization, visa, endorsement, ratification, ap-proval, confirmation, authentication, validation, OK (sl.), affirmation, stamp of approval, corrobo-ration, assurance, pledge.

3. Mammal, fur-seal, walrus, sea lion, sea cow, elephant seal, sea elephant.

SEAL, v. 1. Close, fasten, secure, lock, shut, occlude, seal up, clasp, snap, cork, plug, stop, shut up, stop up, bar, bolt, dam, bung, blockade, button up, zip (coll.), choke, throttle, shut the door, close the door.

2. Approve, ratify, endorse, sanction, affirm, confirm, validate, certify, accept, verify, O.K. (sl.), warrant, sign, countersign, underwrite, under-sign, subscribe to, guarantee, set one's seal to, set one's signature to, stamp, close, set the seal on, execute.

SEAM, n. 1. Closure, suture, stitch, joint, weld, commissure, line of juncture, junction, raphe, ridge, miter, connection, articulation, joining, gusset, gore, dart, bond, meeting, conjunction, ligation.

2. Crevice, furrow, fissure, cleft, chasm, break, chink, cranny, crack, gap, incision, scissure, cut, rupture, flaw, hole, leak, opening, aperture, breach, rime, gorge, canyon, gulch, crevasse, clough, abyss, gulf, chimney.

3. Scar, cicatrix, cicatrice, cut.

SEAMAN, n. Sailor, mariner, navigator, seafarer, tar, Jack Tar, old salt, sailorman, seafaring man, sea dog, shipman, matelot (Fr.), limey, lime-juicer (sl.), man-o'-war's-man, marine, leatherneck (sl.), ordinary seaman, able seaman, common seaman, foremast hand, shellback (sl.), barnacle back (sl.), coxswain, midshipman, fresh-water sailor, deep-sea man, Jonah, Ancient Mariner, Flying Dutch-man.

SEAMSTRESS, n. Sempstress, sewing woman, modiste, dressmaker, needleworker, couturière (Fr.), tailoress, dress designer.

SEANCE, n. 1. Session, assembly, meeting, gather-ing, get-together, turnout (coll.), congress, levee, conventicle, assemblage, forgathering, congrega-tion, meet, concourse, sitting, convocation, con-clave, consultation, audience, palaver, caucus.

2. Mediumism, spiritualism, psychomancy, spiritism, mediumistic communication, divination, spirit communication.

SEAR, v. 1. Wither, fade, shrivel, dry, blight, kill, parch, scorch, burn, singe, cauterize, brand, ensear, char, carbonify, incinerate, combust, burn up, consume, cremate, scorify, desiccate, exsiccate, siccate, sun-dry, torrefy, bake.

2. Blunt, dull, make callous, steel, harden, hebetate, stupefy, caseharden, brutalize, deaden, paralyze, numb, benumb, make insensible, make numb, anaesthetize.

SEARCH, v. Nose out, ferret out, peep, hunt, ex-plore, ransack, examine, investigate, scrutinize, sift, inspect, look into, look for, pry into, peer into, scour, seek, probe into, look up, fish for, track down, follow the trail of, seek a clue, rum-mage, leave no stone unturned, scout out, study, scan, give the once-over (sl.), peruse, indagate.

SEARCH, n. Examination, hunt, quest, research, inspection, observation, perlustration, scrutiny, scrutinization, pursuit, chase, surveillance, the once-over (sl.), perusal, examen, indagation, ex-ploration, inquest, inquisition, inquiry, study, analysis, sifting, probe, query, questioning, close look into, scan, give the once-over (sl.), peruse, terrogation, reconnaissance, reconnoitering, patrol.

SEASICK, adj. Sick, ill, nauseated, bilious, mo-tion-sick, travel-sick, airsick, unwell, sickish, queasy, qualmish, squeamish, laid low, prostrate, vomiting, carsick.

SEASIDE, n. Beach, seabeach, seaboard, coast, strand, seacoast, seashore, littoral, foreshore, sea margin, sea bank, seaside, coastland, coastal region, edge of the sea, waterside, rock-bound coast, iron-bound coast.

SEASON, *n.* Period, time, stage, interval, term, duration, tenure, spell, Spring, Summer, Autumn, Fall, Winter, division of the year, recurrent period, vernal equinox, dog days, canicular days, autumnal equinox, Indian summer, semester, quarter, lunation.

SEASON, *v.* 1. Naturalize, acclimatize, habituate, accustom, wont, familiarize, adapt, domesticate, acclimate, inure, train, get used to, break in, familiarize with, tame, drill, exercise, practice, discipline, form, rear, take in hand, nurture, cultivate.

2. Spice, give relish to, make palatable, salt, tincture, corn, preserve, kipper, cure, brine, marinate, dry, pickle, prepare, mix, blend.

SEASONABLE, *adj.* Opportune, timely, fit, apt, appropriate, convenient, suitable, welcome, apropos, early, forehanded, prompt, punctual, on time, apposite, acceptable, well-timed, becoming, due, fitting, befitting, proper, seemly, politic, expedient, auspicious, propitious, providential, fortunate, lucky, timeful.

SEASONED, *adj.* 1. Pungent, savory, salty, peppery, zestful, spicy, tangy, high-flavored, piquant, snappy, keen, full-flavored, strong, sharp, high, nippy, salted, hot, saline, astringent, gamy, high-tasting, spiced.

2. Adapted, hardened, casehardened, inured, used to, veteran, wonted, habituated, in the habit of, conversant with, familiar with, inveterate, confirmed, steeped in, adapted, naturalized, experienced, at home in, addicted to, given to, imbued with, wedded to, established, ingrained, deep-rooted, trained, hard-boiled, hardened, toughened, proficient, skilled, well-versed, well-grounded.

SEASONING, *n.* 1. Sprinkling, tinge, tincture, dash, spice, suffusion, soupçon, smack, infusion, admixture, condiment, relish, herb, flavoring, sauce, mace, allspice, nutmeg, cinnamon, thyme, marjoram, clove, potherbs, ginger, parsley, shallot, *fines herbes (Fr.),* peppermint, dill, mint, dillseed, salt, pepper, white pepper, black pepper, red pepper, paprika, Cayenne pepper, tabasco sauce, mustard, ketchup, catsup, chili pepper, chili sauce, radish, cubeb, horse radish, onion, wild onion, garlic, vinegar, pickle, chutney.

2. Hardening, habituation, inurement, familiarization, domestication, training, preparation, acclimation, acclimatization, orientation.

SEAT, *n.* 1. Site, stead, place, position, situation, whereabouts, habitat, locale, locality, stand, station, status, post, footing, standpoint, ground, venue, bearings, latitude and longitude, region.

2. Dwelling, abode, house, habitation, residence, lodging place, dwelling place, diggings *(sl.),* digs *(sl.),* domicile, housing, quarters, address, headquarters, berth, roost, nest, perch, stopping place, family seat, homestead, home, home roof, ancestral hall, household, hearth, fireside, chimney corner.

3. Rump, buttocks, croup, rear end, posterior, anal region, gluteal region, hindquarters, haunches, loin, tail, bottom, fundament, rear *(vulg.),* crupper, podex, ass *(vulg.),* arse *(vulg.),* backside *(vulg.),* stern *(coll.),* behind *(vulg.),* fanny *(sl.),* bum *(vulg.), derrière (Fr.).*

4. Bench, chair, sofa, davenport, chaise longue *(Fr.),* long chair, armchair, rocking chair, Morris chair, wheelchair, stool, footstool, wing chair, easy chair, milking stool, folding stool, camp stool, school bench, divan, ottoman, couch, studio couch, day bed, love seat, rumble seat, throne,

seat of state, saddle, cushion, bleacher, grandstand, settee.

SEAT, *v.* 1. Situate, place, locate, put, deposit, settle, set down, park, station, post, install, establish, localize, assign to a place, lodge, quarter, house, shelter.

2. Seat oneself, sit down, take a seat, sit, perch, roost, accommodate, cause to seat, usher, enthrone.

SEAWORTHY, *adj.* Watertight, sound, navigable, A-1 at Lloyd's, unsinkable, navigable, sailable, fit for sea duty, maneuverable, safe, secure, reliable, trusty, dependable, well-built, well-designed, soundly constructed.

SEBACEOUS, *adj.* Greasy, oily, sweaty, unctuous, fatty, adipose, oleaginous, pinguid, unguentous, unguentary, oleic, slick, sleek, slippery, wet, damp, moist, lardaceous, lardy.

SECEDE, *v.* Forsake, abandon, withdraw, pull out, desert, rat *(sl.),* leave, quit, relinquish, evacuate, vacate, bolt, leave in the lurch *(coll.),* go back on *(coll.),* turn one's back on, have done with, wash one's hands of, apostatize, retire, resign, renounce, repudiate, back out, change sides, disaffiliate, join the opposition, join the enemy, recant, tergiversate, shift one's ground, change one's mind, deviate, rebel, mutiny, revolt, insurrect, riot, rise up, revolutionize, kick over the traces, dissent, differ, revolt at, say no to.

SECESSION, *n.* Apostasy, withdrawal, rebellion, insurrection, insurgence, mutiny, revolution, repudiation, backsliding, recidivism, sedition, schism, dissidence, recusancy, abandonment, sectarianism, recantation, retraction, desertion, defection, quittance, tergiversation, abrogation, rightabout, change of heart, recreancy, reaction, disavowal, rejection, renunciation, renouncement, resignation, relinquishment, forswearing, disavowal, retractation, abjuration, disclamation, mutineering, outbreak, riot, upset, overthrow, overturn, anarchy.

SECESSIONIST, *n.* Seceder, rebel, backslider, insurrectionist, insurgent, mutineer, apostate, recidivist, deserter, dissenter, nonconformist, protestant, separatist, schismatist, schismatic, sectarian, heretic, recreant, tergiversator, turncoat, bolter, mugwump, rat *(sl.),* turntail, renegade, reactionary, scab *(sl.),* factionist, denominationalist, recusant, disaffectionist, repudiator, deviationist, anarchist.

SECLUDE, *v.* 1. Separate, sequester, exclude, blackball, embargo, ostracize, outlaw, exile, send to Coventry, isolate, maroon, evict, expatriate, keep out, shut out, banish, relegate, extradite, excommunicate, drum out, deport, proscribe, ban.

2. Retire from sight, seclude oneself, hide, hide out *(coll.),* lie low *(coll.),* keep aloof, hibernate, retire from the world, hermitize, rusticate, hole up *(coll.),* dissociate, go into retreat, retire.

SECLUDED, *adj.* Withdrawn, remote, covert, closed, shut in, shut away, hidden, sequestered, sequestrated, isolated, private, curtained, screened, monastic, out-of-the-way, monastical, reclusive, cloistered, confined, anchoritic, solitary, backwoods, out-of-the-world, solitudinous, lonesome, lonely, unfrequented, unvisited, deserted, forsaken.

SECLUSION, *n.* Hiding, concealment, ambush, retreat, retirement, solitude, secrecy, withdrawal, loneliness, solitariness, isolation, sequestration, hangout *(sl.),* lair, den, cave, covert, cloister, aerie, hermitage, asylum, sanctuary, hideaway, hiding place, vault, crypt, rustication, anchoritism, eremitism, desolation, desertion, exilement, exile, hermitism.

SECOND, *adj.* Secondary, next after the first, duplicate, sequential, subsequent.

SECOND, *n.* 1. Subordinate, inferior, underling, subaltern, second fiddle *(coll.)*, sub *(coll.)*, second-stringer, understrapper, helper, auxiliary, supporter, henchman, fill-in, supplanter, surrogate, stand-in, alternate, double, substitute, stopgap, pinch hitter, understudy, proxy, succedaneum, representative, agent, deputy, minister, delegate, tool, lieutenant, vicar, champion, patron, advocate, twin, aide, assistant, backer.

2. Moment, instant, trice, jiffy, twinkling, minute, wink, bat of an eye, breath, flash, burst, stroke of time, crack, shake of a lamb's tail.

SECOND, *v.* Help, aid, assist, forward, promote, back, encourage, abet, further, sustain, advance, stand by, side with, take the part of, back up, bolster, support, uphold, defend, stick by, get behind, stand back of, endorse, work for, take up the cudgels for, advocate, espouse the cause of, countenance, give moral support to, subscribe to, patronize, smile upon, favor, befriend, lend one's support to, hold a brief for *(coll.)*, go to bat for *(sl.)*, fight for, join in with, rally round, make common cause with, unite with, join hands with, swing in with *(coll.)*, be in cahoots with *(coll.)*, enlist under the banner of.

SECONDARY, *adj.* 1. Second, another, other, next after the first, next, alternate, sequential, subsequent, consequent, following, resultant.

2. Lesser, smaller, inferior, lower, minor, junior, subordinate, second-rate, subaltern, humble, mediocre, middling, fair to middling, tolerable, second-best, medium, average, so-so *(coll.)*, ancillary, auxiliary, subsidiary.

SECOND-HAND, *adj.* Used, hand-me-down, old, antique, shopworn, worn, impaired, damaged, deteriorated, the worse for wear, altered for the worse, worn to a shadow, passé, shabby, seedy, timeworn, ragged, frayed, washed-out, faded, out of kilter *(coll.)*, out of whack *(coll.)*, sprung, decrepit, fit for the wastebasket, ramshackle, dilapidated, fit for the trash barrel, aged, venerable, out of fashion, out of style, antiquated, superannuated, archaic, rusty, mildewed, hoary, old-fashioned, old-style, unfashionable.

SECRECY, *n.* Stealth, concealment, furtiveness, stealthiness, surreptitiousness, clandestineness, hugger-mugger, seclusion, retirement, privacy, hiding, solitude, reticence, covertness, confidence, isolation, mystery, private, reservation, secretiveness, subterfuge, evasion, underhandedness, dark dealing, taciturnity, shade, recess, sequestration, coverture, muteness, silence, uncommunicativeness, laconicism.

SECRET, *n.* Confidential matter, private affairs, privacy, privity, secrecy, secret communication, dark secret, skeleton in the closet, mystery, enigma, riddle, puzzle, arcanum, cabal, intrigue, hugger-mugger, conundrum, mystery of mysteries, occult meaning, obscure factor, secretiveness, closeness, reticence, subterfuge, evasion, concealment, furtiveness, stealthiness, surreptitiousness, clandestineness, covertness, confidence, obscurity, private.

SECRET, *adj.* Unrevealed, hidden, covered, covert, concealed, private, privy, veiled, unknown, mysterious, cryptic, arcane, recondite, cabalistic, clandestine, underhand, furtive, surreptitious,

stealthy, hugger-mugger, undercover, confidential, inviolable, unrevealable, undisclosed, unpublished, undemonstrable, esoteric, occult, perdu, buried, dark, abstruse, arcanal, mystic, unrevealed, unseen, invisible, incognito, disguised, camouflaged, cryptogrammic, cryptographic, riddling, enigmatic, puzzling, logogriphic, sealed, labyrinthine, symbolic, acroamatic.

SECRETARIAT, *n.* Bureau, office, department, portfolio, cutcherry *(Ind.)*, administrative body, administrative group, recording body, recording group.

SECRETARY, *n.* 1. Clerk, scribe, stenographer, amanuensis, quilldriver, scrivener, deputy, agent, factor, assistant, aide, helper, typist, transcriber, shorthand writer, stenotypist, bookkeeper, registrar, notary, chronicler, annalist, retainer, employee.

2. Desk, escritoire, writing desk, writing table, cabinet.

SECRETE, *v.* 1. Conceal, shroud, hide, bury, disguise, cover, entomb, harbor, seclude, withdraw, occultate, cache, ensconce, cloak, screen, curtain, veil, make invisible, keep secret, blind, camouflage, dissemble, draw the curtain over, mask, eclipse, keep to oneself, keep back, suppress, stifle, smother, seal up, befog, becloud, screen from sight, withhold from view.

2. Emit, discharge, disgorge, egest, give out, give off, excrete, secern, debouch, perspire, sweat, leak.

SECRETION, *n.* Secernment, excretion, evacuation, clearance, egestion, ejaculation, elimination, disgorgement, drainage, effusion, disemboguement, eruption, emesis, extravasation, emission, discharge, extrusion, sweat, perspiration, leakage, voiding, emptying, micturition, urination, wetting, drooling, driveling, salivation, ptyalization, slavering, slobbering, squirting, spurting, emanation, exudation, transudation, flux, effusion, suppuration, ecchymosis.

SECRETIVE, *adj.* 1. Reticent, reserved, evasive, uncommunicative, close-mouthed, taciturn, laconic, stealthy, sly, furtive, feline, cunning, cautious, careful, surreptitious, underground, undercover, covert, obreptitious, underhanded, skulking, privy, private, camouflaged, incognito, cryptic, cryptogrammatic, mysterious, arcane, unrevealing, undisclosing, unconversable, word-bound, pauciloquent, curt, brief, concise, mute, mum, dumb, silent, sparing of words, speechless, wary.

2. Excretive, excretory, secretory, eliminative, ejective, excretionary, exudative, secretionary.

SECT, *n.* Set, clique, coterie, group, classification, division, persuasion, denomination, order, school of thought, ism, interest, side, party, caste, circle, ring, knot, club, camarilla, cabal, faction, religious order, affiliation, community, fellowship, organization, cult, belief, faith, schism, creed, canon, dogma, doctrine, tenet, principle, position, view, credo, cathechism.

SECTARIAN, *n.* Schismatist, heretic, rebel, apostate, bolter, dissenter, dissentient, nonconformist, nonjuror, protestant, separatist, secessionist, reactionary, iconoclast, misbeliever, factionist, denominationalist, recusant, cultist, partisan, fanatic, eccentric.

SECTION, *n.* 1. Part, division, segment, piece, portion, compartment, subdivision, district, plot, territory, divide, land, ground, zone, region, ward, sector, moiety, detachment, detail, particular, item, installment, dividend, share, allotment, dose, cut (*coll.*), allowance, measure, modicum, proportion, ratio, ration, lion's share (*coll.*), mess, quota, percentage, department, domain, province, estate, range, sphere, terrain, realm, hemisphere, compass, orb, circuit, ambit, circle, precinct, premises, pale, field, vicinage, purlieus, vicinity, neighborhood, country, soil, county, shire, parish, ward, canton, township, diocese, bailiwick, wapentake, commune, settlement, colony, continent, land mass, enclosure, arena, area, close, enclave, tract, patch.

2. Stanza, verse, passage, phrase, part, movement, measure, musical phrase, chorus, burden, refrain, bourdon, introduction, prelude, overture, voluntary, descant, coda, tutti.

3. Book, number, issue, division, part, passage, chapter, verse, stanza, clause, phrase, column, page, leaf, folio.

SECULAR, *adj.* 1. Nonreligious, worldly, temporal, lay, laical, popular, civil, nonclerical, nonecclesiastic, secularistic, profane, nonministerial, nonpastoral, material, nonspiritual, mundane, carnal, terrestrial, earthy, earthly, worldly-minded, earthly-minded, carnal-minded.

2. Periodic, periodical, recurrent, centenary.

SECULARISM, *n.* Worldliness, carnality, worldly-mindedness, irreligion, irreligiousness, anticlericalism, profanity, unspirituality, mundaneness, earthiness, nonbelief, agnosticism, atheism, heresy, apostasy, unbelief, skepticism, freethinking, latitudinarianism, theophobia, nihilism, paganism, irreligionism, hylotheism, substantialism.

SECURE, *adj.* 1. Safe, free from danger, unperilous, dependable, reliable, sure, steady, firm, sturdy, out of danger, in safety, in security, at anchor, in port, in harbor, on the safe side, unhazarded, unmolested, unthreatened, trusty, trustworthy, high and dry, above water, not dangerous, unimperiled, substantial, protected, impregnable, stable, sheltered, defended, invulnerable, inexpugnable, unassailable, unattackable, fixed, set, taut, tight, close, immovable.

2. Confident, assured, convinced, settled, determined, in the bag (*sl.*), established, solid, firm, conclusive, convincing, incontestable, irrefutable, incontrovertible, well-founded, well-grounded, proved, demonstrated, indubitable, undoubtable, undeniable, decisive, irrefragable, undoubted, uncontested, unquestioned, absolute, definite, surefire (*sl.*), positive, categorical, unmistakable, evident, clear, apparent, authentic, authoritative, definitive, canonical, infallible, unerring, reliable, sound, trustworthy, dogmatic, axiomatic, standard, catholic, doctrinal, unimpeachable.

SECURE, *v.* 1. Make safe, protect, guard, shelter, fortify, strengthen, ensconce, preserve, shield, defend, anchor, harbor, ensure, guarantee, make certain, make sure, establish, confirm, save, uphold, sustain, support, conservate, conserve, take care of, keep sound, ward, forfend, safeguard, shelter, barricade, entrench, fortify, garrison, man, arm, blockade, accouter, house, keep watch over, mind, attend, chaperon, look after, look out for, keep an eye on.

2. Fix, immobilize, attach, affix, make fast, tie, bind, hitch, screw, nail, lash, hook, bind, seal, tighten, make tight, brace, pin, anchor, moor, tie up, belay, stitch, sew, baste, clinch, leash, truss, swathe, swaddle, gird, tether, picket, tack, knit, lace, buckle, button, bend, splice, couple, lock, latch, chain, fetter, clamp, rivet, clasp, inosculate,

wedge, miter, join, fuse together, weld, glue, paste, solder, cement, agglutinate, conglutinate, gum, dam, occlude, block, shut up, lock up, seal up, staple, manacle, handcuff, tie one's hands, hobble, bridle, entomb, incarcerate, imprison, jail, cage, immure, impound, intern, coop, throw into prison, throw into jail, throw into irons, lock in, wall in, capture, catch, put under arrest, take into custody, make a prisoner of.

3. Get, acquire, obtain, procure, get possession of, gain, attain, keep, buy, purchase, win, reap, land (*coll.*), seize, come by, receive.

SECURITY, *n.* 1. Safety, safeness, secureness, freedom from danger, surety, steadiness, firmness, trustiness, trustworthiness, protection, impregnability, shelter, defense, invulnerability, inexpugnability, unassailability, unattackability, health, firmness, tautness, tightness, closeness, immovability, safeguard, bulwark, shelter, guard, palladium, anchor, strength, refuge, rampart, bastion, protectorship, safekeeping, care, heed, keep (*coll.*), ward, watch, custody, auspices, guardianship, safeconduct, preservation, salvation, conservation, support, maintenance, stability.

2. Secureness, assurance, reliance, trust, faith, hope, confidence, conviction, affiance, reassurance, promise, assumption, presumption, conclusiveness, irrefutability, incontestability, incontrovertibility, indubitability, decisiveness, undeniability, irrefragability, definiteness, absoluteness, positiveness, authenticity, authority, unimpeachability.

3. Pledge, pawn, deposit, collateral, surety, bail, stake, gage, guarantee, warranty, bond, debenture, stipulation, stock, covenant.

SEDAN, *n.* Car, coach, automobile, carriage, sedan chair, conveyance, vehicle, carrier, autocar, motorcar, gas buggy (*coll.*), motor, machine, sedan limousine, convertible sedan, touring car, cabriolet,

SEDATE, *adj.* Calm, quiet, dignified, composed, collected, placid, serene, tranquil, still, unruffled, severe, matronly, thoughtful, contemplative, reserved, grave, sober, philosophical, cool, staid, serious, imperturbable, settled, earnest, unimpassioned, decorous, undemonstrative, self-possessed, poised, temperate, inexcitable, undisturbable, *dégagé* (*Fr.*), nonchalant, self-controlled, coolheaded, level-headed, steady, unnervous, soberminded, unexcited, unimpassioned, subdued, mild, solemn.

SEDATIVE, *n.* Allleviative, palliative, remedy, calmative, lenitive, anodyne, analgesic, paregoric, emollient, demulcent, balm, assuasive, salve, lotion, embrocation, ointment, liniment, unguent, narcotic, opiate, drug, dope (*sl.*), hypnotic, anesthetic, calmant, medicament, medication, specific, pharmaceutical, mitigator, moderator, modifier, soporific, sleep-inducer.

SEDATIVE, *adj.* Soothing, tranquilizing, allaying, composing, anodyne, analgesic, alleviative, calmative, calming, assuasive, lenitive, demulcent, balmy, stupefacient, palliative, anesthetic, soporific, somnifacient, sleep-inducing, somnific, hypnotic, calmant, anodyne, narcotic, paregoric, easing, relieving, comforting, consolatory, restorative.

SEDENTARY, *adj.* Inactive, immobile, sluggish, torpid, motionless, unmoving, fixed, seated, sitting, resting, stationary, still, quiescent, unstirring, immotile, moveless, standing still, sitting still, cataleptic, inert.

SEDIMENT, *n.* Remains, traces, remainders, leavings, orts, reliquiae, vestiges, organic remains, residue, residuum, offscourings, oddments, debris, detritus, ashes, refuse, waste, bits and pieces, deposit, precipitation, precipitate, scum, dross, dregs, discard, litter, lees, trash, rubbish, offscum, draff, junk, slag, feculence, pomace, sewage, slough, swill, bilge, grounds, sordes, dregs, mother, bottoms, settlings.

SEDITION, *n.* Withdrawal, apostasy, rebellion, insurrection, insurgence, mutiny, revolt, revolution, backsliding, recidivism, separation, secession, schism, dissidence, dissentience, difference, disagreement, recusancy, nonassent, disaffection, abandonment, sectarianism, recantation, retraction, desertion, defection, quittance, tergiversation, abrogation, turnabout, change of mind, disloyalty, infidelity, recreancy, deviationism, disavowal, rejection, renunciation, relinquishment, forswearing, retractation, abjuration, disclaimer, mutineering, outbreak, riot, treason, treachery, upset, overthrow, anarchy, uproar, sans-culottism, *émeute (Fr.),* disturbance.

SEDITIONIST, *n.* Secessionist, seceder, rebel, insurgent, insurrectionist, backslider, mutineer, traitor, apostate, recidivist, deserter, dissenter, nonconformist, nonjuror, protestant, separatist, schismatist, schismatic, sectary, sectarian, heretic, recreant, tergiversator, turncoat, bolter, mugwump, turntail, runagate, renegade, secessioner, reversionist, factionist, separatist, archtraitor, snake in the grass, disaffectionist, deviationist, anarchist, sansculotte.

SEDITIOUS, *adj.* Rebellious, mutinous, refractory, insurgent, tumultuous, factious, riotous, turbulent, insubordinate, unruly, traitorous, treacherous, insurrectionary, lawless, revolutionary, disobedient, secessionist, apostate, recidivistic, dissenting, nonconformist, protestant, separatist, schismatic, sectarian, recreant, tergiversating, turncoat, mugwump, renegade, runagate, reactionary, denominationalist, separatist, cultist, disaffected, forswearing, deviationary.

SEDUCE, *v.* Lead astray, allure, entice, entrap, attract, tempt, inveigle, ensnare, corrupt, defile, debauch, vamp, violate, prostitute, deprave, abuse, disgrace, dishonor, lure, charm, captivate, ruin, pervert, deflower, ravish, force, compel, stuprate, rape, inflame with love, turn one's head, enrapture, offer allurement, hold out temptation.

SEDUCER, *n.* Gallant, tempter, Lothario, reprobate, debaucher, betrayer, charmer, libertine, dissolute man, rake, wanton, profligate, cad, womanchaser, wolf *(sl.),* lecher, fast man, fornicator, adulterer, ravisher, defiler, debauchee, rapist, raper, Don Juan, Bluebeard, voluptuary, goat, violator, siren, enchanter, enchantress, temptress, vampire, vamp *(sl.).*

SEDUCTION, *n.* Seducement, temptation, allurement, allure, fascination, bewitchment, enchantment, tantalizing, coaxing, cajolery, soft words, honeyed words, blandishment, golden apple, debauchery, debauchment, violation, ravishing, ravishment, abuse, defilement, defloration, enticement, betrayal, ruination.

SEDUCTIVE, *adj.* Enchanting, tempting, alluring, attractive, entrancing, engaging, prepossessing, enravishing, taking, winsome, exciting, tantalizing, inviting, appetizing, provocative, heart-robbing, deceptive, deceitful, cajoling, coaxing, wheedling, winning, baiting, bewitching.

SEDULOUS, *adj.* Persevering, assiduous, constant, persistent, tenacious, unrelenting, unremitting, attentive, careful, painstaking, diligent, stalwart, steadfast, industrious, indomitable, indefatigable, unwearying, unflagging, patient, pertinacious, untiring, unwearied, resolute, resolved, inflexible, undeviating, unswerving, determined, zealous, dogged, unfaltering, undrooping, plodding, relentless, unrelenting, unyielding, uncompromising, decisive, firm, unflinching, game to the last, energetic, businesslike.

SEE, *n.* Authority, office, seat, jurisdiction, episcopate, bishopric, diocese, episcopacy, cardinalship, cardinalcy, Holy See, archbishopric, prelature, prelateship, prelacy, bishopdom, papacy, pontificate. See of Rome, the Vatican, Apostolic See.

SEE, *v..* 1. Behold, descry, observe, make out, spot, sight, hold in view, discern, perceive, view, have in sight, catch sight of, take in, regard, look at, glimpse, recognize, distinguish, notice, witness, set one's eyes on, stare at, gaze at, get a load of *(sl.),* lay eyes on, cast the eye upon, lamp *(sl.),* scan, survey, pipe *(sl.),* ogle, keep the eyes riveted on, eye, gape at, peek, peep, glare, glower at, spy out, reconnoiter, get an eyeful, keep the eyes peeled, give the eye *(coll.),* take a gander at *(sl.).*

2. Notice, espy, perceive, discern, observe, distinguish, know, remark, comprehend, understand, witness, take notice of, be cognizant of, mark, realize, observe, be aware of, heed, appreciate, be conscious of, identify, make out, be familiar with, be acquainted with, cognize, understand, fathom, realize, conceive, ken, get the drift *(sl.),* apprehend, grasp, penetrate, see daylight, take in, visualize.

3. Be attentive, attend, pay attention, observe, pay heed, mind, advert to, animadvert, devote the attention to, give thought to, contemplate, consider, ruminate, meditate, inspect, scrutinize, direct the mind to, occupy oneself with, have in mind, have an eye to, bear in mind, sit up and take notice, keep an eye on the ball.

4. Oversee, boss, superintend, supervise, overlook, watch, see to, look after, control, administer, administrate, direct, guide, hold authority over, be in the seat of authority, keep in order, manage, govern, conduct, regulate, pilot, steer.

SEED, *n.* 1. Germinal matter, germ, spore, sperm, spermatozoon, embryo, germ cell, egg, ovum, egg cell, milt, roe, semen, biogen, biophore, zygote, gametophyte, gametophore, zooid, zoon, spermatocyte, microgamete, macrogamete, nucleus, spawn, spat, fetus, seedling, seedlet, ovule.

2. Progeny, offspring, descendants, children, issue, posterity, progeniture, breed, family, generation, descent, sons, heirs, brood, litter, young, spawn, offshoot.

3. Minute quantity, morsel, scrap, particle, speck, jot, iota, molecule, corpuscle, dab, whit, tittle, scintilla, touch, cast, glimmer, shade, point, minim, grain, granule, drop, tatter, crumb, bite, sprinkling, smattering, inch, patch, droplet, globule, scruple, pittance, little bit, dose, snippet, smithereen, cutting, sliver, chip, splinter, fraction, shaving, paring, shred, nutshell, fragment, drop in the bucket, hint, suggestion, soupçon, sample, specimen, trace.

SEEDLING, *n.* Sprout, young tree, young plant, sapling, plantlet, seed plant, sproutling.

SEEK, *v.* 1. Search, nose out, spy, ferret out, peep, hunt, probe for, explore, ransack, examine, investigate, scrutinize, overhaul, sift, inspect, look into, pry into, peer into, inquire, question, scour, make inquiry, look up, look into, dig for, delve, fish for, track down, follow the trail of, seek a clue, sniff out, rummage, leave no stone unturned, follow the trace of, scout out, dissect, study, scan, anatomize, analyze.

2. Solicit, ask for, beg, beseech, petition for, angle for, bid for, be a candidate, offer oneself, volunteer for, present oneself, crave, petition, entreat, beg leave, make application for, canvass, make petition, court.

3. Try, essay, attempt, endeavor, struggle, strive for, try one's hand, venture upon, hazard, take a chance, undertake, take up, set about, go about, launch into, go in for, embark upon, try hard, file a strong bid for, give it a whirl (sl.), have a go at it (coll.), do the best one can, do one's utmost.

SEEM, v. Look, appear, present the appearance, strike one as being, evidence, exhibit, show, have the semblance of, beseem, wear the appearance of, look like, look as if, manifest, leap to the eye, stare in the face, loom large.

SEEMLY, adj. 1. Fit, proper, suitable, decorous, seasonable, timely, apt, appropriate, convenient, apropos, felicitous, happy, apposite, acceptable, meet, well-timed, becoming, due, fitting, befitting, right, politic, expedient, opportune, auspicious, propitious, providential, fortunate, lucky, acceptable, eligible, correct.

2. Comely, fair, good-looking, handsome, pretty, beautiful, beauteous, well-favored, graceful, personable, tidy, neat, tasteful, proper, elegant, refined, polished, pure, chaste, artistic, pleasing, agreeable, goodly, bonny, decent, well-made, well-proportioned, trim, trig, attractive, charming, engaging, enchanting, ravishing, alluring.

SEEP, v. Ooze, percolate, trickle, infiltrate, water, dribble, drop, drip, distill, spurtle, babble, gurgle, guggle, exudate, exude, extravasate, disembogue, filter, drain, effuse, debouch, discharge, emit, sweat, perspire, lixiviate, leach.

SEEPAGE, n. Drainage, exudation, effusion, trickling, percolation, oozing, infiltration, dropping, distillation, spurting, gurgling, extravasation, disemboguement, filtration, debouchment, discharge, emission, sweating, perspiration, leakage, lixiviation, leaching.

SEER, n. Predictor, foreteller, prophet, soothsayer, vaticinator, diviner, crystal-gazer, wise man, clairvoyant, fortuneteller, palmist, phrenologist, palmreader, stargazer, thaumaturgist, conjurer, wizard, magician, Merlin, sorcerer, necromancer, mantologist, medium, spiritualist, witch doctor, magus, warlock, dowser, theurgist, druid, sibyl, augur, divinator, geomancer, extispex, haruspicator, oracle, prophetess, astrologer.

SEETHE, v. 1. Be angry, rage, storm, boil, be indignant, chafe, fret, smolder, foam at the mouth, breathe fire, stamp one's foot, bluster, carry on, take on (coll.), stew (coll.), rave, rant, raise a rumpus, raise Cain, raise a shindy (coll.), kick up the dust.

2. Stew, simmer, singe, swelter, burn, be hot, grow hot, roast, toast, scald, parch, scorch, ebulliate, cook, brew, parboil, prepare, steam.

3. Macerate, steep, soak, drench, douse, saturate, sodden, wet.

SEGMENT, n. Section, portion, division, sector, part, fragment, piece, fraction, dole, moiety, subdivision, share, allotment, bit, cutting, clipping,

partition, half, quarter, eighth, sixteenth, fourth, fifth, sixth, etc., measure, lot, allowance, snack, snip (coll.).

SEGREGATE, v. Isolate, insulate, separate, set apart, set aside, detach, divorce, divide, disengage, disconnect, dispart, part, disunite, keep apart, classify, graduate, rank, sort, grade, group, severalize, separate the sheep from the goats, separate the wheat from the chaff, weed out, detach, ostracize, dissociate, single out, select, discriminate, pick and choose, differentiate, draw the line at, seclude, sequester, sequestrate, occultate, cache, ensconce.

SEGREGATION, n. Isolation, insulation, separation, partition, parting, divorcement, division, disengagement, disconnection, disunification, classification, graduation, grading, ranking, grouping, severalization, severance, weeding out, ostracization, ostracism, detachment, dissociation, selection, discrimination, distinction, differentiation, sequestration, withholding, seclusion, withdrawal, occultation, caching, ensconcing.

SEIGNOR, n. 1. Mister, master, Mr., monsieur (Fr.), M. (Fr.), signor (It.), Herr (Ger.), sir, sire, señor (Sp.), senhor (Port.), Don.

2. Seigneur, master, overlord, lord and master, ruler, rector, governor, chief, superior, head man, commander, captain, dictator, paramount, commandant, controller, overman, supervisor, sachem, big chief, grand sachem, kingpin (coll.), first fiddle, top sawyer (coll.), boss.

3. Nobleman, aristocrat, baronet, baron, viscount, count, earl, duke, peer, magnifico, grandee, hidalgo (Sp.), daimio (Jap.), blue-blood, don, patrician, thoroughbred, lord, upper-cruster (coll.), aristocrat, laird (Scot.), squire, lordling, gentleman, notable, silk-stocking, archduke, grand duke, marquis, count, knight, cavalier, chevalier, boyar, thane, knight banneret, palgrave, armiger, margrave, atheling, khan, sheik, princeling, rajah, man of distinction, great man, man of merit, big man, V.I.P. (coll.), maharajah.

SEIZE, v. Confiscate, impress, impound, sequestrate, preëmpt, levy, sequester, intercept, usurp, filibuster, ravish, embrace, grip, lay hands upon, take hold of, fasten upon, capture, apprehend, catch, take into custody, clutch, snatch, shanghai, grasp, grab, grip, distrain, take possession of, prey upon, possess, nab, bag (coll.), loot, plunder, carry away, fleece, pillage, appropriate, maraud, take hold of, swipe (coll.), sack, stick up (sl.), steal, kidnap, abduct, strip, rustle (coll.), pounce upon, snap up, carry off, rifle, crib, purloin, rape, fasten upon, commandeer, take captive, lay by the heels, pinch (sl.), collar, pocket, bag, disseize, dispossess, adopt, annex, pirate, lift, plagiarize, arrogate.

SEIZURE, n. 1. Taking, grasping, capture, appropriation, apprehension, snatching, abstraction, pillage, confiscation, usurpation, rape, attachment, retention, possession, hold, appropriating, annexing, impropriation, ablation, abduction, ademption, acquisition, disseizin, dispossession, bereavement, divestment, deprivation, sequestration, impressment, interception, filibustering, ravishment, preying, looting, plundering, marauding, stealing, kidnaping, holdup, rustling, rifling, purloining, cribbing, plagiarism, piracy, commandeering.

2. Stroke, spasm, shock, fit, paroxysm, throe, epitasis, convulsion, eclampsia, ictus, attack, grip, visitation.

SELDOM, adv. Rarely, infrequently, occasionally, now and then, sparingly, not often, hardly ever, not frequently, scarcely, uncommonly, unoften, sparsely, once in a great while.

SELECT, *v.* Pick, choose, elect, fix upon, make one's choice, pick out, single out, cull, glean, winnow, separate, segregate, prefer, decide between, settle upon, draw the line, distinguish, set apart, separate the sheep from the goats, weed out, exclude, shut out, eliminate, reject, isolate, lay aside, put aside, sort out, sift, take out, abstract.

SELECTIVE, *adj.* Choosy, discriminating, eclectic, elective, picky *(sl.),* finical, fastidious, discretional, critical, perspicacious, scrupulous, squeamish, particular, punctilious, hard-to-please, finicking, querulous, refined, delicate, dainty, overcritical, overnice, subtle, overparticular, censorious, exacting, meticulous, careful, cautious.

SELF, *n.* Ego, the I, spirit, soul, person, psyche, animus, mind, heart, the inner man, essential nature, true self, true being, selfhood, selfness.

SELF-ABNEGATION, *n.* Asceticism, stoicism, unselfishness, disinterestedness, acquiescence, submissiveness, submission, yielding, self-degradation, servility, obsequiousness, subservience, prostration, obeisance, servitude, subjection, slavery, deference, compliance, passiveness, passivity, nonresistance, self-subjugation, self-denial, self-renunciation, self-control, self-immolation, self-forgetfulness, self-subordination.

SELF-ABUSE, *n.* Masturbation, self-pollution, onanism, secret vice, manustupration, secret sin, carnality, carnal vice, carnal enjoyment.

SELF-ACTING, *adj.* Self-propelling, automatic, self-moving, self-propellent, automatical, automotive, autokinetic.

SELF-ADMIRATION, *n.* Vanity, conceit, conceitedness, self-approbation, self-approval, self-conceit, egoism, egotism, self-worship, self-esteem, self-endearment, self-praise, self-flattery, self-applause, self-love, self-satisfaction, complacency, smugness, self-content, self-glorification, self-importance, self-opinion, swell-headedness, self-centeredness, egocentricity, selfishness, self-laudation, self-gratulation, self-endearment, *amour propre (Fr.),* self-exaltation, foppery, coxcombry, priggishness, ostentation, overestimation, boasting, braggadocio, airs.

SELF-ASSURANCE, *n.* Assurance, confidence, cockiness, brashness, courage, fearlessness, intrepidity, cocksureness, resoluteness, boldness, spirit, dash, derring-do, bravery, gallantry, prowess, self-reliance, self-confidence, manliness, pluck, grit, backbone, mettle, stamina, guts *(sl.),* fortitude, hardihood, gameness, bottom *(coll.).*

SELF-CENTERED, *adj.* Egocentric, self-absorbed, egoistic, egotistic, self-seeking, selfish, self-concerned, self-indulgent, self-advancing, self-efficient, wrapped in oneself, self-aware, self-conscious, self-interested, self-blind, vain, conceited, proud, vainglorious, pretentious, foppish, dandified, puffed-up, peacockish, swell-headed, self-important, self-opinionated, self-glorious, self-content, smug, complacent, self-satisfied, self-esteeming.

SELF-CONFIDENCE, *n.* Self-assurance, assurance, confidence, cockiness, brashness, fearlessness, intrepidity, courage, cocksureness, resolution, resoluteness, boldness, spirit, dash, derring-do, bravery, gallantry, prowess, self-reliance, manliness, pluck, grit, backbone, mettle, mettlesomeness, stamina, guts *(sl.),* fortitude, hardihood, gameness, bottom *(coll.).*

SELF-CONSCIOUS, *adj.* Self-aware, self-concerned, awkward, timorous, fearful, hesitant, diffident, shy, reserved, constrained, sheepish, blushing, flushing, bashful, shrinking, reticent, coy, modest, skittish, irresolute, clumsy, faltering, unsure, uncertain.

SELF-CONTAINED, *adj.* Reticent, reserved, constrained, taciturn, laconic, impassive, uncommunicative, untalkative, close-mouthed, mum, dumb, mute, silent, word-bound, pauciloquent, undemonstrative, dignified, not given to talking, unconversable, concise, brief, curt.

SELF-CONTROL, *n.* Patience, self-abnegation, temperance, abstinence, coolness, self-command, self-discipline, self-conquest, self-mastery, self-government, strength of will, will power, strength of character, gravity, soberness, sobriety, continence, stoicism, aplomb, savoir-faire, equanimity, equilibrium, firmness, stability, constancy, soundness, poise, mental balance, sang-froid, presence of mind, self-possession, level-headedness, coolheadedness, imperturbability, inexcitability.

SELF-DENIAL, *n.* Self-abnegation, self-renunciation, self-forgetfulness, unselfishness, selflessness, self-mortification, self-giving, asceticism, abstemiousness, temperance, continence, self-sacrifice, will power, strength of mind, strength of character, self-command, self-control, self-restraint, self-government, self-mastery, self-conquest, self-abasement, martyrdom, stoicism, magnanimity, bigness of spirit, generosity, humaneness, humanity, nobility, largeness of heart, philanthropy.

SELF-DESTRUCTION, *n.* Suicide, self-murder, self-extermination, felo-de-se, hara-kiri, disembowelment, sutteeism, suttee.

SELF-DETERMINATION, *n.* Spontaneity, self-activity, spontaneousness, volition, self-will, voluntarism, voluntariness, conation, conative power, velleity, conatus, originality, determination, will power, mind, pleasure, wish, desire, free will, political freedom, political independence, liberty, unconstraint, license, initiative, prerogative, privilege, right, franchise, enfranchisement, autonomy.

SELF-ESTEEM, *n.* Vanity, egocentricity, selfishness, egotism, egoism, self-concern, self-indulgence, self-sufficiency, self-awareness, self-consideration, self-interest, self-blindness, vainness, conceitedness, conceit, pride, vainglory, vaingloriousness, cockiness, pretentiousness, foppery, foppishness, dandyism, swell-headedness, arrogance, haughtiness, hauteur, self-importance, airs, self-opinion, self-glorification, self-complacency, self-contentedness, smugness, self-praise, self-satisfaction, self-commendation, self-laudation, self-applause, self-flattery, self-love, *amour propre (Fr.),* self-worship, self-endearment.

SELF-EVIDENT, *adj.* Apparent, plain, perceptible, visible, manifest, axiomatic, obvious, unavoidable, inescapable, undeniable, incontrovertible, palpable, tangible, perspicuous, definite, clear, explicit, express, noticeable, observable, self-evidencing, ostensible, patent, distinct, unmistakable, manifestative, demonstrative, plain as day.

SELF-GOVERNMENT, *n.* 1. Autonomy, home rule, self-rule, democracy, republic, constitutional government, representative government, republicanism, self-determination, political independence.

2. Self-control, temperance, abstinence, continence, chastity, self-command, self-discipline, self-conquest, self-mastery, strength of will, will power, character, sobriety, stoicism, equanimity, balance,

equilibrium, firmness, stability, constancy, soundness, inflexibility, poise, sang-froid, presence of mind, self-possession, level-headedness, coolheadedness, imperturbability, inexcitability.

SELF-IMPORTANT, *adj.* Presumptuous, presumptive, proud, vain, conceited, self-esteeming, self-endeared, self-infatuated, self-loving, pompous, arrogant, consequential, puffed-up, swollen, inflated, egotistic, vainglorious, cocky, swell-headed, egocentric, selfish, self-absorbed, self-concerned, self-interested, self-assuming, pretentious, haughty, toplofty, having a high opinion of oneself, self-commendatory, self-lauding, self-applauding, self-flattering, prideful, insolent, contemptuous, immodest, bragging, boastful, self-advertising, self-advancing, self-seeking, condescending.

SELF-INDULGENCE, *n.* Sensuality, sensualness, carnal pleasure, physical gratification, bodily enjoyment, carnality, sensual pleasure, relish, titillation, immoderation, intemperance, incontinence, unchastity, excess, crapulence, unrestraint, voluptuousness, sensualism, overindulgence, dissipation, licentiousness, debauchment, debauchery, prodigality, onanism, masturbation, self-pollution, self-defilement, secret vice, manustupration.

SELFISH, *adj.* Illiberal, ungenerous, grudging, mean, parsimonious, stingy, close-fisted, acquisitive, narrow-minded, self-seeking, egotistic, calculating, conniving, grasping, covetous, self-interested, uncharitable, self-indulgent, self-centered, egocentric, hoggish, piggish, miserly, greedy, mercenary, worldly, sordid, self-regardant, self-advancing, churlish, tight-fisted, pinching, close, near, sparing, venal, avaricious, usurious, extortionate, rapacious, self-concerned.

SELF-LOVE, *n.* Self-esteem, self-endearment, self-concern, self-centeredness, egocentricity, egotism, self-absorption, self-seeking, self-consideration, self-interest, self-blindness, vanity, conceit, pride, vaingloriousness, cockiness, pretentiousness, foppery, foppishness, dandyism, swell-headedness, arrogance, hauteur, haughtiness, self-importance, airs, self-opinion, self-glorification, self-satisfaction, smugness, self-complacency, self-praise, self-commendation, self-laudation, self-applause, self-flattery, self-worship, *amour propre (Fr.).*

SELF-POSSESSED, *adj.* Placid, calm, poised, cool-headed, level-headed, collected, pacific, unruffled, unexcited, unaroused, imperturbable, undisturbed, dignified, sedate, quiet, serene, tranquil, reserved, grave, sober, staid, serious, earnest, unimpassioned, undemonstrative, proper, courteous, unexcitable, *dégagé (Fr.),* nonchalant, unembarrassed, self-controlled, self-disciplined, untroubled, unimpassioned.

SELF-REGULATING, *adj.* Self-adjusting, self-directing, mechanical, automatic, autokinetic.

SELF-RELIANCE, *n.* Confidence in one's own capacities, self-confidence, assurance, aplomb, self-possession, self-poise, collectedness, coolness, firmness, resolution, intrepidity, courage, pluck, grit, sand, mastery over self, self-mastery, self-command, self-control, self-possession, moral courage, moral fiber, perseverance, decision, backbone, determination, will, strength of will, resolve, manliness, energy, vigor, boldness, daring, spirit, mettle, gameness, hardihood, spunk, fortitude.

SELF-RELIANT, *adj.* Mettlesome, valiant, resolute, resolved, self-confident, cool, collected, poised, assured, independent, intrepid, indomitable, manly, virile, bold, strong-minded, willful,

doughty, hardy, firm, determined, enterprising, spirited, dauntless, undaunted, unflinching, stouthearted, game, plucky, *dégagé (Fr.),* quite at home, free and easy, autonomous, uncontrolled, strongwilled, self-possessed, earnest.

SELF-RENUNCIATION, *n.* Self-abnegation, self-denial, self-effacement, self-sacrifice, altruism, loftiness of purpose, magnanimity, chivalrous spirit, sublimity, elevation, nobleness of mind, heroism, self-immolation, martyrdom, devotion, stoicism, labor of love, exaltation.

SELF-REPROACH, *n.* Censure by one's own conscience, remorse, seared conscience, uneasy conscience, repentance, self-blame, self-accusation, regret, compunction, contrition, penitence, self-reproof, self-condemnation, twinge of conscience, qualms of conscience, pangs of conscience, voice of conscience, apology, confession.

SELF-RESPECT, *n.* Proper regard for the dignity of one's character, *amour-propre (Fr.),* self-esteem, pride, *mens sibi conscia recti (Lat.),* self-approbation, self-complacency.

SELF-RESTRAINT, *n.* Self-control, self-command, self-mastery, self-government, equanimity, self-possession, poise, aplomb, stoicism, temperance, abstinence, forbearance, soberness, sobriety, abnegation, frugality, asceticism, imperturbability, inexcitability, even temper, tranquil mind, tolerance, dispassion, patience, calmness, coolness, composure, staidness, gravity, presence of mind, endurance, resignation, longanimity, fortitude, subjugation of feeling, self-discipline, self-conquest, moral fiber.

SELF-RIGHTEOUS, *adj.* Righteous in one's own esteem, sanctimonious, pharisaic, smug, pharisaical, canting, hypocritical, pietistical, unctuous, puritanical, tartufian, insincere, hollow, jesuitical, Janus-faced, smooth-tongued, mealy-mouthed.

SELF-SACRIFICE, *n.* Sacrifice of one's own interests for the good of another, self-denial, self-abnegation, unselfishness, selflessness, disinterestedness, devotion, altruism, liberalism, generosity, benevolence, magnanimity, self-effacement, self-immolation, martyrdom, suttee, self-mactation.

SELFSAME, *adj.* The very same, identical, exactly the same, similar, same, equal, like, ditto, one, equivalent, indistinguishable, exact, comparable, analogous, synonymous, correspondent, all kindred, cognate, akin to, congenerous, cast in the same mold, of a feather.

SELF-SATISFACTION, *n.* Satisfaction with one's own accomplishments, self-approval, self-content, complacency, smugness, self-conceit, self-approbation, self-gratulation, self-applause, self-admiration, vanity, pride, elation, vainglory, heart's ease, exultation, flush of success, egotism, jubilation, self-exhilaration, self-pleasure, high spirits, toploftiness, bumptiousness, boastfulness, braggadocio.

SELF-SATISFIED, *adj.* Self-approving, self-content, self-conceited, smug, complacent, conceited, proud, vain, overweening, elated, exultant, jubilant, triumphant, rejoicing, flushed with success, exhilarated, puffed up, egotistic, self-pleased, in high spirits. self-admiring, self-applauding, vainglorious, inflated, cock-a-hoop, toplofty, high and mighty, swollen, blown, bumptious, consequential, *en grand seigneur (Fr.),* boastful, braggart, gasconading, supercilious, precocious.

SELF-SEEKER, *n.* One who seeks his own selfish

ends, egoist, monopolist, timeserver, opportunist, adventurer, nepotist, tufthunter, dog in the manger, hog, toady, fortune-hunter, gold-digger, sycophant, moneygrubber, harpy, profiteer, worldling, trimmer, temporizer.

SELF-SEEKING, *adj.* Opportunistic, timeserving, monopolistic, egoistic, adventurous, nepotistic, hoggish, dog-in-the-manger, gold-digging, fortune-hunting, sycophantic, profiteering, worldly, selfish, mean, illiberal, unprincipled, self-indulgent, self-interested, wrapped up in self, egocentric, venal, mercenary, covetous, *alieni appetens (Lat.),* interested, avaricious, usurious, rapacious, greedy, extortionate, hireling, sordid, piggish, grasping.

SELF-STYLED, *adj.* Would-be, self-dubbed, self-named, pretended, *sogenannt (Ger.),* soi-disant *(Fr.),* self-called, self-christened, so-called, bluff, assuming, bumptious, pretentious, big-sounding, *ad captandum (Lat.).*

SELF-SUFFICIENCY, *n.* Contentedness, contentment, self-complacency, smugness, self-esteem, self-conceit, self-confidence, inflation, aplomb, assurance, conceit, self-admiration, narcissism, egoism, selfism, pride, self-content, self-glorification, toploftiness, overweeningness, arrogance, superciliousness, self-love, vaingloriousness, exclusiveness, self-indulgence, egocentrism.

SELF-SUFFICIENT, *adj.* 1. Self-content, smug, egoistic, egocentric, self-complacent, conceited, narcissistic, self-centered, self-loving, self-indulgent, selfish, self-interested, wrapped up in oneself.

2. Haughty, overbearing, proud, overweening, lordly, magisterial, consequential, arrogant, vainglorious, inflated, puffed up, blustering, toplofty, cock-a-hoop, cocky, pretentious, affected, boastful, egotistic, self-satisfied.

3. Able to supply one's own needs, resourceful, ingenious, inventive, competent, efficient, self-confident, self-assured.

4. Secluded, private, exclusive, retired, snug, stay-at-home, unsociable, inhospitable, eremitic, isolated, solitary.

SELF-WILL, *n.* Willfulness, obstinacy, obstinateness, tenacity, doggedness, mulishness, perversity, obduracy, obdurateness, dogged resolution, inflexibility, immovability, perseverance, blind side, contumacy, indocility, pervicacity, opinionativeness, bigotry, fanaticism, headstrongness, unruliness, waywardness, pigheadedness, arbitrariness, incorrigibility, intractableness, intractability, crotchetiness.

SELF-WILLED, *adj.* Perversely insistent on one's own will, willful, headstrong, intractable, obstinate, contumacious, stubborn, pigheaded, arbitrary, cross-grained, unyielding, uncompliant, refractory, mulish, obdurate, high-handed, perverse, capricious, maggoty, peevish, wayward, dogged, resolved, bent, set, autocratic, despotic, absolute, bossy, dictatorial, tyrannical, domineering, inflexible, immovable, inexorable, pervicacious, restive, heady, *entêté (Fr.),* opinionated, dogmatic, positive, stiff-backed, deaf to advice, impervious to reason, full of whims, eccentric, whimsical, crotchety, contrary, humorsome, undisciplined.

SELL, *v.* 1. Make over to another for a consideration, dispose of for a price, put up for sale, market, vend, peddle, deal in, hawk, traffic, trade, exchange, barter, retail, wholesale, offer for sale, put on sale, handle, auction, keep for sale, nego-

tiate, turn into money, effect the sale of, dispense, furnish, offer, bargain, realize, unload, dump, bring under the hammer, undersell, truck, nundinate, ply a trade, be in business, keep a shop, transact, do business with, drive a trade, haggle, dicker, higgle, huckster, charge, ask, put on account, bill.

2. Cause acceptance, persuade of, convince, satisfy by proof, win over, prevail upon, influence, induce, sway, bias, dispose, predispose, incline, talk over.

3. Take a bribe for, betray, sell out, deliver up, knife *(sl.),* play false.

4. Cheat, humbug, hoax, deceive, gull, dupe, impose upon, trick, take in, string *(sl.),* defraud, do, diddle, jockey, cozen, gyp, double-cross, chouse, bilk, pluck, cully, victimize, swindle, spoof, hoodwink, foist upon, palm off upon, set a snare for, lay a trap for, decoy, bait the hook, delude, beguile, inveigle, practice upon, befool, bamboozle, stuff up, gammon, juggle, conjure, practice chicanery.

SELLER, *n.* Merchant, vender, trader, tradesman, shopkeeper, storekeeper, retailer, wholesaler, hawker, peddler, huckster, auctioneer, jobber, salesman, saleswoman, salesclerk, dealer, chandler, monger.

SELVAGE, *n.* Edge of woven fabric finished to prevent raveling, strip of cloth forming an edge, list, listing, edging, skirting, hem, welt.

SEMBLANCE, *n.* 1. Resemblance, similarity, affinity, similitude, approximation, agreement, parallelism, correspondence, analogy, uniformity, identity, sameness, verisimilitude.

2. Counterpart, facsimile, copy, model, cast, duplicate, analogue, likeness, effigy, tracing, representation, imitation, portrait, presentment, transcript, transcription, replica, reprint, reproduction, counterfeit, forgery, fake, paste, example, pattern, archetype, prototype, make-believe, brummagem, plagiarism, tinsel, fraud, simulacrum.

3. Outward aspect, show, seeming, appearance, mien, air, form, figure, exterior, bearing, visage, outside, guise, look.

SEMICIRCLE, *n.* Half of a circle, hemicycle, arc, arch, curve, crescent, meniscus, half moon, lunule, horseshoe, crane-neck.

SEMICIRCULAR, *adj.* Hemicyclic, curved, curvilineal, curviform, curvilinear, bowed, falciform, crescentic, lunate, semilunar, meniscal.

SEMILIQUID, *adj.* Semifluid, half-melted, semifluidic, half-frozen, clotted, gelatinous, tremelloid, gelatinoid, jellied, gelatiniform, colloidal, viscid, glutinous, albuminous, mucilaginous, pasty, gummous, gummy, slimy, pituitous, mucous, mucid, muculent, thick, curdled, uliginous, crass, emulsive, lacteous, milky, lactescent.

SEMILIQUIDITY, *n.* 1. Semifluidity, semifluidness, colloidality, coagulation, jellification, thickening, incrassation, gummosity, spissitude, inspissation, mucosity, viscosity, gumminess, glutinosity.

2. Mud, mire, sludge, slush, ooze, muck, slime, dirt.

3. Aspic, jelly, gelatin, colloid, gluten, starch, albumen, protein, treacle, syrup, cream, emulsion, jam, pudding, grume, mush, pap, curd, paste, pulp, dough, soup.

SEMINAL, *adj.* Having possibilities of future development, rudimental, germinal, generant, generative, procreant, germinating, radical, original, primordial, primary, embryonic, inceptive, embryotic, productive, formative.

SEMINAR, *n.* Group of scholars engaged in research, class.

SEMINARY, *n.* Preparatory school, secondary school, day school, boarding school, Latin school, private school, academy, grammar school, institute.

SEMPITERNAL, *adj.* Going on continually, everlasting, forever abiding, without beginning *or* end, illimitable, incessant, eonian, perpetual, eternal, timeless, constant, ceaseless, ever-enduring, interminable, perennial, endless, unending, unceasing.

SENATE, *n.* Governing body *(of a state, university, etc.),* upper branch of the legislature *(U. S. Gov.),* state council, legislative body, caucus, conclave, assembly.

SEND, *v.* 1. Transmit, broadcast, convey, televise, telegraph, telecast, radio.

2. Direct, guide, head, point the way, show the way, put upon the track, indicate the course, lead, conduct to.

3. Dispatch, send off, consign to, dismiss.

4. Discharge, send forth, empty, emit, eject, project, throw off, exude, ooze, disembogue, void, excrete, leak, give forth, gush.

5. Send forth *(as a missile),* shoot, deliver a charge, detonate, let fly, explode, burst, pour forth, deliver.

SENESCENT, *adj.* Growing old, aging, senile, ancient, veteran, patriarchal, antiquated, declining, mellow, superannuated, aged, elderly, hoary, old, gray-headed, time-honored, venerable, old as Methuselah, waning.

SENILITY, *n.* Infirmity, old age, dotage, declining years, senescence, superannuation, decrepitude, second childhood, dotardism, caducity.

SENIOR, *adj.* 1. Elder, older, first-born, primogenitary.

2. Higher in rank, superior, over, above.

3. Highest, chief, top, paramount, uppermost, pre-eminent, supreme, main, principal, leading, commanding, controlling, supervisory.

SENIOR, *n.* 1. Elder, first-born, primogenitor.

2. One of higher rank, more experience, *etc.,* superior, master.

SENSATION, *n.* 1. Physical knowledge *(i. e., through the senses),* feeling, experience, perceptivity, impression, discernment, consciousness, comprehension, awareness, cognizance, perception, sensibility, detection.

2. Emotion, intensified feeling, sentiment, passion, excitement, mental agitation, inward fermentation.

SENSATIONAL, *adj.* Moving the feelings, exciting, dramatic, melodramatic, stirring, emotional, thrilling, galvanic, electrical, heart-throbbing, heart-expanding, soul-stirring.

SENSATIONALISM, *n.* Emotionalism, sentimentality, yellow journalism, melodrama, mawkishness, morbid excitement, maudlinness.

SENSE, *n.* 1. Sharpness of mind, discernment, keenness, grasp, common sense, sapience, judiciousness, understanding, acuteness, discrimination, insight, percipience, skill, level-headedness, acumen, power, reasoning power, reasoning, shrewdness, penetration, perceptiveness, ability, taste, intuition, perception, apperception, diagnosis, brain, mental faculty, perspicacity, wisdom, sagacity, judgment.

2. Meaning *(of a word, etc.),* signification, value, force, connotation, denotation, effect.

3. Direction, trend, drift, significance, meaning, scope, purpose, scheme, import, expression, design, purport, implication, intent, aim.

SENSE, *v.* Become aware of, feel, apprehend, realize, discover, discern, take in, perceive, see, regard, note, recognize.

SENSELESS, *adj.* 1. Unconscious, insensible, numb, deadened, in a coma, comatose, asleep, sleeping.

2. Foolish, stupid, inane, witless, brainless, reckless, giddy, wild, flighty, harum-scarum *(coll.),* thoughtless, foolhardy, heedless, unwary, silly, unstable, frivolous, inconstant, crazy *(coll.),* rattle-brained, rattleheaded, giddy-brained, giddy-pated, addlepated, erratic, bird-witted, harebrained, light-minded, empty-headed, brainless, bemused, wool-gathering, befuddled, frothy, mercurial, irresponsible, rantipole, empty-skulled, featherbrained, madcap, muddle-headed, bewildered, absent-minded.

3. Without reason, meaning, relevance, *etc.,* haphazard, ridiculous, pointless, groundless, inconsequential, purposeless, aimless, irrelevant, inapplicable, inconsequent, inappropriate, beside the point, irrational, immaterial, illogical, unreasonable, incongruous, vague, stupid, inept.

SENSIBILITY, *n.* 1. Ability to receive physical impressions, perceptivity, susceptibility, responsiveness, response, sensitivity, impressibility, feeling, sensitiveness.

2. Acuteness of feeling, tenderness, sensitiveness, sensitivity, sore spot, soft spot, thin skin.

3. Delicacy *(of an instrument, etc.),* sensitiveness, fineness, fidelity, nicety, precision, discrimination, accuracy, exactness.

SENSIBLE, *adj.* 1. Capable of being sensed *or* perceived, tangible, knowable, ascertainable, intelligible, apprehensible, detectable, notable, discoverable, evident, apparent, plain, noticeable, perspicuous, ostensible, palpable, visible, observable, seeable, beholdable, distinguishable, cognizable, manifest.

2. Perceiving, cognizant, knowing, perceptive, discerning, enlightened, cognitive, intelligent, aware, informed, alive, conscious, apprised, understanding, apperceptive, knowledgeable.

3. Having good sense, thoughtful, rational, discerning, wise, cool-headed, level-headed, circumspect, enlightened, analytical, reasonable, sage, reflective, sapient, prudent, ratiocinative, discreet, politic, well-advised, logical, judicious, discriminating, thinking, philosophic, understanding, perspicacious.

4. Conforming to reason *or* sound judgment, plausible, logical, sane, credible, equitable, seasonable, right, enlightened, well-grounded, well-founded, sagacious, sound, tolerable, judicious, likely, suitable, rational, vindicable, discreet, advisable, fit, proper, just, far-sighted, deductive, subtle, possible, probable, understandable, philosophic, inferential, inferable, legitimate, wholesome, admissible, discerning, justifiable, wise.

SENSITIVE, *adj.* 1. Conveying impulses, *etc. (as nerves),* sensory, sensorial, sensuous *(rare in this sense).*

2. Delicate *(as an instrument),* precise, fine, faithful, discriminating, exact, accurate.

3. Susceptible, thin-skinned, impressible, perceptive, susceptive, responsive, feeling.

SENSITIVITY, *n.* 1. Ability to receive impressions, perceptivity, feeling, sensitiveness, susceptivity, responsiveness, sensibility, response.

2. Delicacy *(of an instrument, etc.)*, sensitiveness, nicety, exactness, fidelity, faithfulness, fineness, sensibility, precision, discrimination, accuracy.

SENSITIZE, *v.* Render sensitive to *(certain actions, etc.)*, sharpen, refine, stimulate, cultivate a sensitivity, make sensitive, perceptive, *etc.*

SENSUAL, *adj.* Inclined to, characterized by *or* inciting lust, incestuous, gross, dissipated, debauched, bawdy, lascivious, ruttish, impure, ribald, obscene, lubricious, pornographic, Cyprian, concupiscent, dissolute, scarlet, whorish, loose, fast, adulterous, lurid, smutty, unclean, dirty, coarse, foul, filthy, unchaste, unvirtuous, incontinent, wanton, vile, offensive, fulsome, Fescennine, indecent, immodest, lustful, beastly, bestial, swinish, animalistic, theroid, prurient, lickerish, lecherous, libidinous, licentious, suggestive, fleshly, carnal, salacious, shameless, satyric, goatish, lewd, erotic, free, Paphian, brutish.

SENSUALISM, *n.* Sensual appetite, inordinate desire, sensuality, carnality, sexuality, bodily appetite, salaciousness, longing, satyrism, venery, concupiscence, salacity, impurity, lechery, lasciviousness, libidinousness, bestiality, animal appetite, pruriency, lewdness, lust, ruttishness, animalism, grossness, desire, aphrodisia, lubricity, crudeness.

SENSUALIST, *n.* Man of pleasure, voluptuary, sybarite, libertine, rake, roué, Heliogabalus, softling, debauchee, Sardanapalus, silk-stocking, lecher, goat, satyr, whoremonger, fornicator, seducer, gallant, fast man, hedonist, Lothario, Don Juan, Casanova, epicure, carpet knight, votary of Epicurus, gourmet, glutton, gourmand, free liver.

SENSUOUS, *adj.* Gratifying *(through the senses)*, sensual, luxurious, voluptuous, hedonistic, bodily, physical, epicurean, fleshly, carnal.

SENTENCE, *n.* 1. Unit of speech, writing *or* thought, subject and predicate, expression, utterance, word group, declaration, pronouncement, statement.

2. Verdict, judgment, order, resolution, determination, opinion, ruling, adjudication, declaration, finding, doom, award, decree, view.

SENTENCE, *v.* Pass sentence, pronounce sentence, condemn, doom, impose penalty, decree, order, convict, ordain, rule.

SENTENTIOUS, *adj.* 1. Full of maxims, pregnant with meaning, terse and meaningful, concise, crisp, piquant, synoptic, pithy, aphoristic, forceful, epigrammatic, packed with meaning, meaningful, apothegmatic, compact, terse, succinct, gnomic.

2. Declamatory, ostentatious in speech, expression, *etc.*, sonorous, lexiphanic, turgid, high-flown, theatrical, orotund, bombastic, puffy, stilted, pretentious, grandisonant, tumid, grandiose, inflated, rhetorical, affected, altisonant, showy, flatulent.

SENTIENT, *adj.* Capable of feeling, conscious, cognitive, discerning, sensible, cognizant, perceiving, aware, apperceptive.

SENTIMENT, *n.* Mental attitude *(colored by thought, feeling, etc.)*, affection, feeling, thoughts, way of looking at, point of view, ideas, emotional nature, sentimentality, passion, response.

SENTIMENTAL, *adj.* 1. Characterized by emotion *or* feeling, feeling, sympathetic, soft-hearted,

susceptive, impressionable, responsive, tender, tender-hearted, impassioned, warm-hearted.

2. *(Often derog.)* Having an excess of emotion, overindulging in sentiment, emotional, maudlin, overdone, tear-jerking *(coll.)*, affected, over-romantic, emotive, mushy, insipid.

SENTIMENTALIZE, *v.* Imbue with sentiment, emotionalize, emote *(jocose)*, express feeling.

SENTINEL, *n.* Guard, watch, lookout, vedette *(Mil. and Nav.)*, watchman, picket, patrol, sentry.

SEPARABLE, *adj.* Capable of being separated, breakable, divisible, scissile, partible, severable, discerptible, dividual, dividuous.

SEPARATE, *adj.* 1. Single, solitary, distinct, diverse, individual, disjunct, disconnected, unassociated, disparate, different, disjoined, dissimilar, disunited, unconnected.

2. Disjoined, subdivided, quartered, divorced, divided, detached, unattached, isolated, disconnected, multipartite, multisegmental, cut, halved, reft, sundered, split, bisected, parted.

SEPARATE, *v.* 1. Disunite, part, disconnect, sever, divide, sunder, divorce, dimidiate, comminute, intersect, cleave, disjoin, subdivide, dispart, quarter, halve, rive, rend, split, detach, bisect, disengage.

2. Keep apart, come between, intervene, divide, space, hiate, split, partition.

3. Come apart, be sundered *or* severed, rend, gape, tear, crack, split, uncover, cleave, gap, yawn, unclench, part, give.

4. Isolate, single out, segregate, cull, set apart, glean, winnow, sift, select, pick out.

5. Secure *or* eliminate by separating process, refine, drain, percolate, sift, screen, eliminate, exclude, eject, filter, sieve, abstract, weed out, discard, expel.

6. Set at variance, come between, cause to quarrel, *etc.*, cause dissension, make hostile, disunite, part, cause to fall out, antagonize, split, alienate, estrange, disaffect.

7. Distinguish between, distribute, classify, group, name, allot, file, tabulate, tag, analyze, index, type, collocate, codify, segregate, ticket, grade, rank, dispose, allocate, docket, size, rate, sort.

8. Branch out *(as a road, river, etc.)*, go separate *or* different ways, divaricate, split, fork, bifurcate, open, ramify, spread, radiate.

SEPARATION, *n.* 1. Act of separation, state of being separated, disjunction, segregation, bifurcation, cleavage, disunion, divergence, disassociation, divorce, severance, fracture, detachment, isolation, disengagement, disconnection, partition, division, disintegration, decomposition, dissolution, breach, rupture, difference, interruption, withdrawal, split, segmentation, sunderance, dismemberment, bifidity, dichotomy, discerption, abscission, dilaceration, rent, break, disjointure, branching, fission, scission, divarication, dimidiation, divulsion, dissection, diremption, ramification, mitosis *(Biol.)*, abstriction *(Bot.)*, furculum *(Anat. and Zool.)*.

2. Place (line, point) of parting, interval, crack, split, gulf, breach, rupture, fracture, bifurcation, hiatus, opening, rift, chasm, scissure, aperture, fissure, interspace, interstice, slot, foramen, crevice, chink, chap, incision, trench, hole, gash, cut, rent, rime, slit, caesura, synapse *(Physiol.)*, furrow, lacuna, break, disruption, cleft, channel, orifice, gap, space, cranny, cavity, score, fork, ramification, crotch.

SEPARATIST, *n.* One who separates (withdraws,

secedes), advocate of separation (as from established church, political organization, etc.), insurgent, revolutionary, mutineer, revolutionist, dissenter, seceder, sectary, schismatist, malcontent, nonconformist, recreant, secessionist, factionist, recusant, protestant, rebel, sectarian, dissentient, heretic, denominationalist.

SEPTIC, *adj.* Infective, infected, pus-forming, putrefactive, morbid, diseased, contaminated, vitiated, corrupt, peccant, noxious, poisoned, carious, pestilential, infectious, contagious, tainted.

SEPULCHER, *n.* Tomb, grave, burial place, vault, crypt, ossuary, pit, resting place, cinerarium, mound, tumulus, catacombs, mausoleum, barrow (*Anthropol.*), mastaba (*Ancient Egypt*), monument, necropolis, cenotaph.

SEPULCHRAL, *adj.* 1. Of *or* pertaining to *or* serving as a tomb, of *or* pertaining to burial, mortuary, funereal, funeral, funerary, burial, cinerary, obsequial, exequial.

2. Proper to *or* suggestive of a tomb, funereal, dismal, gloomy, depressing, dreadful, doleful, dreary, dim, uncheerful, lowering, somber, murky, sad, black, dark, dusky, melancholy, shadowy, stygian, lugubrious, mournful, woeful, sorrowful, clouded, lightless, cheerless, joyless.

3. Hollow, deep, resonant, echoing, cavernous, ghostly, resounding, vacant, empty, weird, spooky (*coll.*), phantom, spectral, uncanny, unearthly, eerie, grave.

SEQUEL, *n.* Event *or* circumstance following something, subsequent course of affairs, epilogue, conclusion, result, consequence, inference, deduction, end, sequent, outcome, consecution, afterglow, aftertaste, aftermath, extension, supplement, continuation, catastrophe, development, offshoot, effect, outgrowth, aftereffect, product, yield, train, trail, wake, postlude, postscript, corollary, correlative, implication, culmination, denouement, finale, finish, finishing stroke *or* blow, death stroke, fruit, issue, upshot, eventuation, indication, coup de grâce, pay-off (*coll.*).

SEQUENCE, *n.* 1. Following (*of one thing after another*), succession, order, consecution, pursuit, continuity, posteriority, perpetuity, unbrokenness, continuousness, concatenation, catenation, prolongation, supervention, subsequence, gradation, course, flow, ceaselessness, continuance, successiveness, progression, gradation, run, repetition, arrangement, rotation, pursuance, consecutiveness.

2. Continuous *or* connected series, chain, procession, train, string, succession, cycle, continuity, cavalcade, course, progression, line, rank, file, thread, queue, column, tier, range, row, set, round, suite, catena, parade, array, catenation, concatenation.

3. Something that follows, subsequent event, sequel, *etc.* (*See* SEQUEL, *n.,* above.)

SEQUENTIAL, *adj.* 1. Following, successive, subsequent, succeeding, ensuing, sequacious, next, proximate, immediate, later, future, after, posterior, linear, sequent.

2. Following logically *or* naturally, resultant, inevitable, consequent, resultative, eventual, secondary, derived, derivative, owing to, due to, illative, deductive, inferential, inferable, deducible, attributable, resulting, contingent.

3. Characterized by continuous succession, consecutive, having regular succession of parts, sustained, serial, continued, uninterrupted, progressive, continuous, incessant, unceasing, regular, everyday, permanent, perpetual, continual, unin-

termitting, unbroken, chronic, persistent, monotonous, endless, ceaseless, constant, unremitting.

SEQUESTER, *v.* Remove *or* withdraw into solitude *or* retirement, seclude, isolate, separate, put *or* set aside, remove, keep aloof, retire, conceal, confine, hide, hibernate, dissocialize, cover, secrete, closet, stow away, suppress, couch, keep under a bushel, ensconce, hoard, entomb, eclipse, bury, shroud, shadow, hood, curtain, obscure, cloud, mask, disguise, screen, veil, shelter, adumbrate, wrap, envelop, camouflage.

SEQUESTERED, *adj.* Secluded, out of the way, withdrawn, clandestine, covert, hidden, cloistered, secreted, secret, private, secured, camouflaged, lurking, obscure, buried, in ambush, unseen, snug, eclipsed, retired, perdu, under cover, solitary, in solitude, unvisited, unfrequented, alone, lonely, isolated, concealed, withdrawn, clouded, cloaked, veiled, close, sealed, unobserved, screened, indiscernible, hermitic, unexposed, invisible, undetected.

SEQUESTRATION, *n.* 1. Removal, separation, banishment, exile, ejection, exclusion, debarment, rejection, transference, extraction, elimination, eradication, expulsion, ousting, dispatch, expatriation, ostracism, ostracization, deportation, dismissal, transportation, discharge, excommunication, expedition, relegation, eviction, dispossession, dislodgment, displacement.

2. Withdrawal, retirement, seclusion, retreat, hiding, cloistering, privacy, avoidance, rustication, aloneness, loneliness, solitude, isolation, departure, recess, concealment, hermitism.

SERE, *adj.* Dry, withered, shrunk, dried, parched, burnt, desiccated, shrunken, shriveled, wizened, sear (*chiefly poetical*).

SERENADE, *n.* Complimentary performance of music, evening song, love song, ballad, barcarole, aubade (*Fr.*), morning serenade *or* music.

SERENADE, *v.* Entertain with *or* perform a serenade, sing to, ballad, minstrel, woo with song.

SERENE, *adj.* Calm, peaceful, clear, fair, tranquil, unperturbable, cool, poised, composed, inexcitable, untroubled, quiet, unperturbed, undisturbed, smooth, halcyon, placid, unruffled, reconciled, meek, still, sedate, nonchalant, platonic, level-headed, unimpassioned, pellucid, unobscured, limpid.

SERENITY, *n.* Calmness, tranquillity, clearness, quiescence, content, contentment, nonchalance, coolness, quietude, quiet, sang-froid (*Fr.*), collectedness, peacefulness, placidity, peace of mind, composure, complacence, equanimity, rest, repose, ease.

SERF, *n.* One in servitude owing services to a lord *or* landowner, tiller of the soil, countryman, thrall, bondman, slave, vassal, son of the soil, peasant, clod, helot, villein, menial, churl (*Hist.*).

SERIAL, *adj.* 1. Published in installments *or* successive parts, continuous, continued, periodic, consecutive, successive, recurring, regular.

2. Of, pertaining to *or* arranged in a series, sequential, consecutive, successive, sustained, uninterrupted, continuous, progressive, incessant, regular, perpetual, constant, periodic.

SERIAL, *n.* Anything published (broadcast, *etc.*) in installments at regular intervals, journal *or* report issued in successive numbers, periodical, quarterly, monthly, weekly, annual, yearbook, gazette, magazine.

SERIES, *n.* Number of things *or* events, *etc.*, ranged *or* occurring in *(spatial, temporal, etc.)* succession, sequence, set, progression, procession, continuity, succession, train, range, tier, chain, suite, suit, list, scale, cycle, round, file, rank, string, cavalcade, parade, catenation, concatenation, ordering, array, catena, row, column.

SERIOUS, *adj.* 1. Of grave *or* solemn disposition *or* character, thoughtful, of grave aspect, sedate, earnest, demure, sad, staid, sober, rueful, grim, pensive, saturnine, long-faced.

2. Being in earnest, not trifling, resolute, decided, sincere, purposeful, determined, resolved, unfaltering, unswerving, unflinching, settled, steadfast, fixed, firm, stern, solid, not to be shaken *or* moved, relentless, inexorable, indomitable, stanch, tenacious, unyielding, obstinate, dogged, uncompromising, strong-willed, iron.

3. Demanding earnest thought *or* application, weighty, important, solemn, intense, mighty, great, high, of great consequence, large, deep, considerable, heavy, ponderous, urgent, critical, principal, chief, crucial, primary, decisive, vital, radical, essential, paramount, profound, momentous, earnest.

4. Giving cause for apprehension, critical, grave, fatal, dire, dreadful, mortal, fearful, severe, sore, acute, dangerous, bad, formidable, awful.

SERMON, *n.* 1. Discourse of religious instruction *or* exhortation, preachment, preaching, homily, talk, lecture, prelection.

2. Long tedious speech, tirade, harangue, oration, lecture, prelection, peroration, diatribe, screed, invective, bombast, dilation, philippic, ranting, effusion, declamation, spouting, long-windedness, rodomontade, verbosity, expatiation, prolixity, longiloquence, rigmarole, amplification, loquacity, verbiage, diffuseness, profuseness, wordiness, flow of words.

SERMONIZE, *v.* Deliver *or* compose a sermon, give serious exhortation to, preach, lecture, prelect, moralize, give *or* read a lesson, expound, exposit, discourse.

SEROUS, *adj.* Of a watery nature, liquid, containing *or* secreting serum, thin, juicy, sappy, sanious, watery, aqueous, hydrous, lymphatic, rheumy *(Med.)*, ichorous *(Pathol.)*.

SERPENT, *n.* 1. Snake, viper, dragon, ophidian.

2. Wily (treacherous, malicious) person, deceiver, devil, beguiler, evildoer, snake, trickster, tempter, Janus, Judas, cheat, humbug, reptile, traitor, rogue, dissembler, dissimulator, double-dealer, snake in the grass, Satan, Machiavel, cockatrice.

SERPENTINE, *adj.* 1. Moving in a winding course, having a winding form, tortuous, sinuous, winding, anguine, colubrine, twisting, convoluted, sinuose, sinuate, flexuous, meandering, meanderous, circuitous, anfractuous, wormlike, vermicular, vermiform, anguiform, mazy, devious, zigzag, crooked, spiral, serpentile, ambagious, roundabout, labyrinthine.

2. Having the qualities of a serpent, subtle, wily, snakelike, sneaky, viperish, viperine, viperous, cunning, reptilian.

SERVANT, *n.* Person employed in domestic duties, person in the service of another, agent, deputy, minister, retainer, inferior, attendant, subordinate, factotum, help, domestic, assistant, man, girl, slave, employee, menial, flunky *(contempt.)*, lackey, maid, hand, valet, do-all, boy, girl, servitor, hired man, orderly.

SERVE, *v.* 1. Act as a servant, attend, minister to, wait on, be in the service of, work for, be subservient to, accommodate, be at one's beck and call, dance attendance on, take care of.

2. Render assistance, help, contribute to, oblige, advance, forward, benefit, conduce to, advantage, aid, assist, promote, succor, attend, do good, profit, better, improve, bestead, lend wings to, facilitate, hasten, expedite, speed, coöperate, be instrumental, accommodate, give a lift, prosper, uphold, smooth *or* pave the way, ease, endorse, avail, favor, stand by, bolster, enhance, disburden, disencumber, set up, give a shove *or* impulse to, go to bat for *(sl.)*, stick up for *(coll.)*, take up the cudgels for, take the part of.

3. Go through a term of service, do duty, perform the duties of, carry out, officiate, dispatch, exercise, take part in, enlist, enroll, join, prosecute, transact, work at, practice, act, hold *or* fill an office.

4. Have definite use, suit, be of use, be adequate, answer the purpose, be favorable (suitable, convenient), suffice, answer the requirements of, be instrumental, satisfy, content, profit, avail, subserve, do, do no harm, fill the bill *(coll.)*.

5. Render obedience *or* homage, be faithful *or* loyal, follow, revere, venerate, bow down to, adore, reverence, honor, worship, be dutiful, obey.

6. Wait at table, set food on a table, supply with food, carve, help one to.

7. Treat in a specified manner, pay, repay, be fair, requite, be one's deserts, do justice to, settle, even the score, balance the scales, compensate, be equitable, recompense, be one's due.

SERVICE, *n.* 1. Act of helpful activity, supplying of articles (commodities, activities, *etc.*) in demand, aid, help, labor, office, favor, ministry, benefit, kindness, good turn, promotion, helping hand, support, furtherance, utility, ministration, usefulness, serviceability, welfare, good, advantage, interest, assistance, applicability, avail, advancement, accommodation, profit, subservience, instrumentality, benefaction.

2. System for providing accommodations, organization giving service, office, department, force, corps, agency, commission, bureau, body *(of public servants)*.

3. Performance of duties as a servant, occupation *or* employment as a servant, office, duty, berth, place, capacity, position, situation, employment, employ, incumbency, appointment, station, billet, attendance, engagement.

4. Public religious worship *(by prescribed form and order)*, ritual, form, office, devotions, liturgy, meeting, ceremony, sacrament, rite, celebration, observance, ordinance, solemnity, duty, formality, function, ceremonial.

5. Set *(of dishes, utensils, etc.)* for a particular use, unit, assemblage, gear, outfit, appointments, appurtenances, fixtures, furnishings, equipment.

SERVICEABLE, *adj.* 1. Being of service, useful, instrumental, helpful, conducive, utilitarian, profitable, convenient, operative, beneficial, advantageous, handy, favorable, effective, valuable, accessory, coöperative, contributory, attendant, functional, practical, salutary, subservient.

2. Wearing well, durable, utilitarian, substantial, practical, strong, rugged, tough, lasting, resistant.

SERVILE, *adj.* 1. Slavishly submissive *or* obsequious, abject, fawning, mean, low, beggarly, cowering, base, unctuous, oily, sycophantic, groveling, cringing, truckling, subservient, whining, toadying, scraping, menial, ingratiating, bootlicking *(sl.)*, prostrate, vernile, footlicking *(sl.)*, mealy-mouthed, docile, honey-mouthed.

2. Of *or* befitting a slave, abject, humble, dependent, menial, subject, slavish, compliant, enslaved, lowborn, submissive, downtrodden, subservient, ignoble, unresisting, passive, docile, lowly, subdued, obeisant, unassertive, deferential, resigned, poor, meek, in bonds, in harness, obedient, henpecked, tractable, prostrate, restrained.

3. Slavishly exact, without originality, conscientious, undeviating, direct, unimaginative, inflexible, straightforward, prosaic, strict, close, faithful.

SERVITUDE, *n.* Slavery, bondage, subjugation, submission, bonds, thralldom, enslavement, vassalage, drudgery, confinement, suppression, constraint, subordination, yoke, subjection, serfdom, service, enthralment, compulsion, restraint, villeinage, obedience, dependence, coercion, fetters, harness, bridle, shackles, chains, oppression.

SESSION, *n.* Sitting *(of a court, council, legislature, etc.)*, meeting, assembly, séance, assize, council, court, consultation, conference, hearing, audience, synod, congress, conclave, caucus, convention, powwow *(coll.)*.

SET, *adj.* 1. Fixed beforehand, predetermined, prescribed beforehand, prearranged, agreed upon, established, formal, regular, ordained, settled, appointed, anticipated.

2. Deliberately composed, customary, trite, established, accustomed, habitual, familiar, repeated, prescriptive, wonted, regular, universal, prevalent, everyday, banal, routine, normal, stock, usual, hackneyed, stale, threadbare, commonplace, ordinary, popular, vernacular, household, conventional.

3. Fixed, rigid, congealed, stiff, taut, tight, firm, stern, close, austere, severe, forced, artificial, frozen.

4. Resolved, determined, habitually *or* stubbornly fixed, inflexible, rigid, bigoted, intolerant, hidebound, hardened, steadfast, obstinate, immovable.

5. *(As in compounds:* THICK-SET, *etc.)* Made as specified, formed, built, composed, delineated, constructed, contoured, arranged, cast, fashioned, constituted, figured, shaped, hewn, chiseled, molded.

SET, *n.* 1. Number of things customarily used together, complete assortment, outfit, collection, kit, gear, unit, series, suite, suit, packet, assemblage, service, library, works *(of books)*, equipment, compilation, rig, scale, range, array, continuity, furnishings, fixtures, appointments, appurtenances.

2. Number of persons associated *or* classed together, party, group, circle, clique, coterie, company, crowd, sect, knot, faction, cabal, club, gang, interest, society, fraternity, association, ring, bunch *(coll.)*, junto.

3. Fit *(as of clothing)*, fixed direction, bent *(of mind)*, inclination, propensity, attitude, form, turn, trend, trait, tone, tenor, cast, drift, penchant, hang, mold, tendency, proclivity, aptitude, idiocrasy, bias, warp, shape, humor, idiosyncrasy, twist, figure, predisposition, proneness, grain, vein, formation, leaning, predilection, conformation, configuration, figuration, structure, texture, constitution, format, flow.

4. Bearing, carriage, pose, port, aspect, air, poise, posture, position, turn, demeanor, cast, attitude, *tournure (Fr.)*.

5. Assumption of a fixed, rigid *or* hard state, solidification, coherence, cohesion, adherence, adhesion, jellification, conglutination, agglutination, cementation, congelation, conglomeration, consolidation, coagulation.

SET, *v.* 1. Move into position, repose, place, deposit, fasten, seat, situate, station, park, affix, reposit, plump, replace, bring, lay, plant, mount, post, fix, stand, add, store, quarter, lodge, localize, slap, tuck, imbed, put, implant, install, instill, inject, infuse, rest, plunk *(coll.)*, assign, collocate, locate, stick, pack.

2. Place in the charge *or* power of a person, rest, settle, station, lodge, relegate, charge, delegate, confide, assign, embark, risk, give, lease, sink, put, venture, repose, entrust, invest, commit.

3. Cause to become *(as set afire)*, make, be the cause of, bring about, effect, bring to pass, induce, give occasion, create, originate, begin, give rise to, generate, instigate.

4. Adjust *(to a desired position, as an instrument)*, orient, arrange, alter, time, regulate, collimate, line up, balance, right, focus, square, gauge, make exact, fix, align.

5. Congeal, gel, solidify, gelatinize, jellify, gelatinate, jell *(coll.)*, thicken.

6. Set to a duty, task, *etc.*, oblige, press, impose, inflict, enjoin, levy, lash, whip, motivate, urge, prompt, thrust, push, instigate, shove, force, incite, stimulate, animate, actuate, cause, drive, forward, move, start, compel, impel, put, assign.

7. Drive to some course, *etc.*, necessitate, constrain, coerce, require, dispatch, dragoon, send, press, push, enforce, hasten, oblige, compel, propel, force.

8. Express in language, music, *etc.*, utter, word, voice, vocalize, find words for, style, present, give expression, give words to, give utterance *or* voice to, put to, articulate, sound, enunciate, pronounce, couch in terms.

9. Apply *(as to use or purpose)*, turn, use, adopt, exercise, exert, enlist, draw, call, press, put, exploit, convert, appropriate, employ.

10. Make an end to, *etc.*, write, finish, put, give, bring about, achieve, accomplish, terminate, complete, create, cause, effect, conclude, enact, execute, compass, perform, dispel, discharge, culminate, prosecute, round out.

11. Submit *(a plan, etc.)*, propose, offer, present, bring forward, propound, pose, throw out, put, state, affirm, voice, advance, enunciate, open, suggest, aver, allege, posit, predicate, postulate, bid, move, extend, make a motion.

12. *(With* DOWN) Lay the blame on, charge, assign, fix, place, ascribe, attribute, impute, pin, attach, bring home, lay at the door of, put down to, father upon, point to, saddle, accuse.

13. *(With* OUT) Begin, leave *(on a journey, etc.)*, launch, embark, make off, get going *(coll.)*, take off *(coll.)*, hit the trail, be off, venture out *or* forth, set forward, depart, go, sally forth, push off *(coll.)*, march off, take oneself off, set sail.

14. *(With* ON) Attempt violence to, begin hostilities against, attack, assail, beset, assault, invade, storm, charge, make an onset against, tackle, engage, oppugn, fall upon, have at, run at, fly at, rush upon, bear down upon, spring upon, have a cut at, make aggression on, push, beleaguer, besiege, bombard, combat, strike, sally against, waylay, pitch into, pelt, stone, fire upon, shoot at, snipe at, open fire on, pepper, rake, fusillade, close with.

15. (With ABOUT) Begin, start, commence, open, engage upon, undertake, enter upon, make a beginning, take the first step, get to, embark on, go ahead, lay the first stone, put one's hand to the plow, set the ball in motion, pitch in (coll.), plunge into, take up, turn one's hand to, put one's shoulder to the wheel, put in execution, launch, break ground, break the ice, set on foot, fall to, buckle down (coll.), set forward.

16. (With ASIDE, BY) Lay away, save up, store up, put away, put aside, lay up, reserve, retain, stow away, treasure up, heap up, garner, amass, accumulate, stash (sl.), cache, bank, deposit, assemble, collect, keep on reserve, keep by one, keep or hold back, secure, protect, guard, nurse, preserve, husband, feather one's nest, salt away or down (coll.).

17. (With DOWN) Write, record, put or place on record, list, register, inscribe, enroll, catalogue, chronicle, docket, put down, enter, insert, note down, jot down, mark down, put in black and white, commit or reduce to writing, calendar.

18. (With ASIDE) Lay aside, rid oneself of, divest, divorce, reject, discard, disuse, throw off, doff, cast off, put off, relinquish, shake off, abandon, disavow, disown, strip off, take off, renounce, abjure, abnegate, drop, resign, surrender, give up, leave behind, throw over, wash one's hands of, dispose of, spurn, relegate, dispense with, forswear, disclaim, jettison, eliminate, throw out, repudiate.

19. Wane (as the sun, etc.), pass away, sink, dip below the horizon, decline, descend, diminish, die away, disappear.

SETBACK, n. Reversal, disappointment, backset, mishap, deadlock, repulse, rebuff, stalemate, opposition, hindrance, stumbling block, foil, checkmate, bafflement, check, relapse, falling back, balk, upset, drawback, rejection, recession, impediment, obstruction, arrest, detention, interruption, determent.

SET SAIL, v. Start out (as a voyage), leave shore, push from land, put forth, board, take ship, embark, launch, get under way, unmoor, shove off, hoist the sail, unfurl or spread sail, bear off from shore, put off, put out to sea, weigh anchor.

SETTEE, n. Couch, sofa, settle, lounge, squab, chaise longue, divan, davenport, ottoman.

SETTING, n. Background, environment, scheme, milieu, local color, scene, fabric, circumstances, framework.

SETTLE, v. 1. Appoint, fix definitely, decide, arrange, agree upon, make stable, place on a permanent basis, stabilize, make certain, choose, rule, resolve, organize, define, ground, elect, set, confirm, conclude, seal, straighten out, set at rest, make up one's mind, ascertain, confirm, will, purpose, come to a conclusion, adjudge, adjudicate, coördinate, systematize, pass upon, ordain, determine, methodize, establish.

2. Place in a desired position or in order, arrange, compose, order, reduce or bring to order, put or set to rights, set out, array, align, line up, group, segregate, assort, sieve, screen, classify, pack, space, range, class, distribute, parcel out, apportion, allot, marshal, allocate, collocate, rally.

3. Pay (a bill, etc.), close (an account) by payment, dispose of finally (as an estate), make a financial arrangement, disburse, adjust, balance, discharge, defray, square, liquidate, satisfy, wipe off, clear, acquit oneself of.

4. Take up residence, make a home, inhabit, dwell, abide, reside, remain, move in, carve a home, establish oneself, put down roots, encamp, lodge, locate, squat, pitch tent, take or strike root, moor, anchor, hang up one's shingle (coll.), live, nest, get a footing, set up housekeeping, set up in business.

5. Furnish (a place) with inhabitants or settlers colonize, people, populate, plant, found, inhabit, occupy, establish, fill.

6. (Sometimes fol. by DOWN) Bring or come to rest, quiet, subside, recede, become quiescent, become stable, soothe, allay, quell, calm, still, lull, compose, pacify.

7. Cause to deposit dregs, sink down gradually, collect at the bottom, become clear (by the sinking of particles), precipitate, purify, clarify, clear, filter, gravitate.

8. Become firm or compact (as the ground), sink or cause to sink gradually, gravitate, incline, drop, sag, swag, cave in, subside, plunge, droop, descend.

9. Come to rest (as from flight), light, alight, land, repose, perch, lodge, sit down.

10. Arrange matters in dispute, come to an agreement, compose, reconcile, prove, conclude, dispose, resolve, rectify, clinch, arbitrate, compromise, show, demonstrate, commute, compound, pacify, make peace, bring to terms, heal, accommodate, mend, patch, disembroil, unravel, disentangle, harmonize, clear up, make clear, free from doubt, solve, adjust, simplify, regulate, straighten out, negotiate, accord, mediate, bridge over, come to terms, pour oil on troubled waters.

SETTLEMENT, n. 1. Act of making stable, adjustment, putting on a permanent basis, establishment, installation, fixture, ordination, appointment, execution, decision, completion, conclusion, confirmation, foundation, ratification, resolution, stabilization, fixation, placement, arrangement.

2. Settling of persons in a new country or place, colony, colonization, small village, denization, denizenation, naturalization, post, encampment, clearing, founding, peopling, plantation, forging, dependency, protectorate, mandate, group migration, satellite, possession.

3. Satisfying of a claim or demand, coming to terms, payment, reconciliation, disposition, liquidation, pacification, arbitration, agreement, satisfaction, reckoning, covenant, contract, compromise, release, acquittance, quittance, defrayment, clearance, terms, reciprocal concession or abatement, rapprochement, conciliation, discharge, reconcilement, composition, mollification, negotiation, accommodation, placation, reunion, propitiation, appeasement, defrayal.

SETTLER, n. Colonist, pioneer, immigrant, squatter, alien, frontiersman, colonial, colonizer, Pilgrim, outlander, pioneer, planter, redemptioner, emigree, homesteader, founder, nester (West. U.S.).

SETUP, n. Organization, composition, form, arrangement, formula, constitution, make-up, structure, character, embodiment, comprisal, layout, nature, compaction, combination, confirmation, array, lay, plan, sketch, draft, foundation, getup (coll.), crasis, inclusion, outline, make, framework, texture, formation.

SEVER, v. 1. Part, break off, separate, cut, cleave, sunder, saw, split, splinter, shatter, dissect, slit, rive, segment, slice, exscind, dislimb, disband, amputate, divorce, tear, rend, divide, disjoin, disunite, detach, dismember, dissever, disengage, lop off, lancinate, disconnect, dimidiate, comminute, dispart, partition.

2. Separate, part from one another, break off or apart, dissolve, disband, disperse, segregate, severalize, distinguish, differentiate, split up, part, disjoin, disunite, alienate, estrange, unclench, yawn, gap, go separate ways, diverge, fork.

SEVERAL, *adj.* 1. More than two *or* three *(but not many)*, some, few, certain, plural, not a few, no few.

2. Respective, individual, single, particular, separate, different, chosen, exclusive, singular, personal, private, divers, diverse, independent, special, local, express, own, specific, distinct, marked, distinctive, representative, peculiar, proper, unique, appropriate, assorted, fixed, definite, distinguishable, certain, sundry.

SEVERALLY, *adv.* Singly, separately, individually, respectively, distinctly, one by one, apart, each to each, alone, apiece, each, of *or* by itself *or* themselves, particularly.

SEVERANCE, *n.* Separation, partition, breaking off, parting, disunion, distinction, interruption, disjunction, cleavage, bifurcation, divergence, disassociation, divorce, fracture, detachment, isolation, disengagement, disconnection, partition, division, disintegration, dissolution, breach, rupture, difference, withdrawal, split, segmentation, sunderance, dismemberment, bifidity, dichotomy, discerption, abscission, scission, fission, divarication, dimidiation, rent, disjointure, dilaceration, divulsion, dissection, diremption, mitosis *(Biol.)*, abstriction *(Bot.)*, furculum *(Anat. and Zool.).*

SEVERE, *adj.* 1. Harsh, harshly extreme, hard, sharp, bitter, rigorous, grinding, drastic, cruel, rough, acute, unsparing, stinging, galling, inclement, intense, relentless, violent, vigorous, bad, piercing, cutting, biting, incisive, raging, heavy, tempestuous, fuming, fierce, furious, persistent, unremitting, tumultuous, turbulent, penetrating, pitiless, ruthless, demoniac, rampant, overpowering, overwhelming, rampaging, boisterous, ravening, wild, unruly, frenzied, trenchant, savage, rude.

2. Serious, stern, austere, hard, stiff, rigid, forbidding, unsympathetic, sharp, granite, straitlaced, bitter, cold, autocratic, arrogant, tyrannical, obdurate, pitiless, uncompromising, sober, sedate, somber, grave, implacable, grim, saturnine, flinty, iron-clad.

3. Grave, serious, critical, mortal, fatal, dire, dreadful, fearful, sore, acute, dangerous, bad, formidable, awful, causing apprehension.

4. Rigidly restrained in style *or* taste, simple, plain, unadorned, chaste, attic, unembellished, puritanical, ascetic, unornamental, unfigured, modest, bare, untrimmed, ungarnished, frugal, unfurnished, pure, blank, inornate, clear, unmixed, flat, spare, undecked, undecorated, economical.

5. Hard to endure (perform, fulfill, *etc.)*, exacting, trying, drastic, critical, stern, cruel, rigorous, difficult, puritanical, stringent, toilsome, racking, afflictive, distressing, excruciating, supreme, agonizing, painful, grievous, sore, sharp, intense, harsh, ruthless, pitiless, unsparing, inexorable, uncompromising, merciless, heavy, bitter, exigent, unreasonable, inhuman, strict, unpleasant, stiff, stark, austere, distressing, Spartan, caustic, insufferable, baleful, despotic, inquisitorial, iron-handed, iron-fisted, uncharitable, obdurate, insupportable, tyrannical, unbearable, extortionate, sore, noxious, grinding, abusive, overbearing, inflexible, Draconian, coercive, torturous, distressful, tormenting, brutal, punitive, cold-blooded, vindictive,

vengeful, oppressive, peremptory, poignant, intolerable, corroding.

6. Rigidly exact (accurate, methodical), servile, strict, close, faithful, prosaic, inflexible, straightforward, direct, undeviating, slavish, punctilious, precise, scrupulous, minute, rigorous, absolute, scientific, meticulous.

SEVERITY, *n.* 1. Rigor, harshness, violence *(as of cold, pain, etc.)*, grievousness, hard *or* trying character *or* effect, sharpness, acrimony, rudeness, keenness, cruelty, inclemency, intensity, stringency, venom, savagery, ferocity, ferity, asperity, spinosity, rage, frenzy, malignity, malevolence, tumult, rigor, turbulence, causticity, hardness, relentlessness, virulence, fierceness, ferociousness, furiousness, force, might, vehemence, acerbity, acridness, fury, poignancy, acuteness, bitterness, edge, point, inhumanity, pitilessness, mercilessness, ruthlessness, inexorability, extremity, affliction, pungency, trial, sting, hardship, afflictiveness, peremptoriness, inquisition.

2. Austere simplicity *(as of style or taste)*, plainness, austerity, purity, rigor, chastity, restraint, chasteness, unornamentation, unadornment, asceticism, unembellishment, refinement, clarity, puritanism.

3. Gravity, austerity, solemnity, discipline, sternness, sobriety, seriousness, stiffness, strictness, urgency, staidness, hardness, formality, rigidity, stringency, self-restraint, exigency, hard lines, paramountcy, primacy, insistence, supremacy, grimness.

4. Rigid exactness, accuracy, strictness, niceness, rigor, precision, preciseness, faithfulness, care, exactitude, rigidity, conformity, constancy, fidelity, conscientiousness, carefulness, scrupulousness, meticulousness.

SEW, *v.* Join by a thread, *etc.,* stitch, make, repair, attach, tack, hem, embroider, seam, baste, secure, fasten with stitches, bind.

SEWAGE, *n.* Waste matter which passes through sewers, filth, refuse, sewerage, drainage.

SEWER, *n.* Artificial conduit for carrying off waste water and refuse, cloaca, drain, ditch, trough, outlet, culvert, gutter, subterranean canal, trench, sink, channel, watercourse, headchute *(Naut.).*

SEX, *n.* 1. Character of being either male *or* female, men *or* women collectively, gender *(coll.),* sexuality, masculinity, femininity.

2. Instinct drawing one sex toward another, sex appeal, pulling power, pull, seduction, attraction, allure, allurement, magnetism, seducement, tantalization, fascination.

SEXTON, *n.* Church official who cares for the edifice and its contents, sacristan, janitor, warden, bell-ringer.

SEXUALITY, *n.* 1. Sexual character, possession of sex, manhood, womanhood, masculinity, femininity, gender *(coll.).*

2. Recognition *or* emphasizing of sexual matters, carnality, prurience, lasciviousness, sensuality, fleshliness, physical nature, earthly nature, desire, concupiscence, lust, passion, lewdness, satyrism, venery, lechery, libidinousness, bestiality, salaciousness, wantonness, grossness, crudeness, impurity, ruttishness, bodily appetite.

SHABBY, *adj.* 1. Having the appearance impaired by wear, use, *etc.,* seedy, wearing worn clothes, ragged, faded, worn, making a poor appearance, disreputable, threadbare, mangy, sorry, scrubby, impoverished, dowdy, frumpy, down and out, shopworn, ill-dressed, ramshackle, scrubby, broken-down, tumble-down, slovenly, dirty, down at the heels, deteriorated, tacky (coll.), frayed, the worse for wear, out at the elbows, dilapidated.

2. Mean, meanly ungenerous or unfair, stingy, penurious, beggarly, contemptible, scurvy, miserly, paltry, petty, sordid, low, meager, cheap, poor, unworthy, inferior, unhandsome, ungentlemanly, beneath contempt, illiberal, parsimonious, tight (coll.), tight-fisted, wretched, miserable, vile, abject, despicable, ignoble, base, dishonorable, sorry, inglorious, unbecoming, coarse, depraved, uncouth, vulgar, discreditable, lamentable, common, opprobrious, heinous, rascally, abominable, degenerate, mean-spirited, yellow, ignominious.

SHACKLE, *n.* 1. Fastening for securing wrist, ankle, *etc.,* fetter, hobble, clinch, clamp, trammel, check, curb, stocks, pinion, holdfast, bar, cuffs, handcuff, manacle, chain, gyves, irons, band, coupling, bilboes, gag, muzzle, ropes, picket, strait jacket, bonds.

2. Anything that serves to prevent freedom of procedure, thought, *etc.,* stay, duress, stop, knot, prison, clog, brake, obstacle, drag, obstruction, impediment, stoppage, hitch, frustration, lumber, embarrassment, check, hamper, checkmate, restraint, dead weight, encumbrance, cross, onus, snag, difficulty, hindrance, barrier, prohibition, retardation, opposition, handicap, blockage, determent, preclusion, interception, interference, catch, imprisonment, stumbling block, spoke in the wheel, millstone 'round one's neck.

SHACKLE, *v.* 1. Put a shackle or shackles on, confine, restrain, fetter, chain, manacle, gyve, hamper, lash, pinion, secure, leash, strap, string, couple, incatenate, enfetter, enchain, bolt, tie, hobble, hopple, handcuff, immure, entomb, pen, cage, clinch, coop, intern, entrammel, trammel, tether, imprison, jail, incarcerate.

2. Restrain *(in action, thought, etc.),* trammel, embarrass, impede, confine, hinder, cripple, disable, deter, hamstring, bind, cumber, clog, obstruct, prevent, retard, thwart, check, debar, bar, arrest, encumber, deadlock, hold from or back, inhibit, frustrate, counterwork, clog or scotch the wheels, cross, oppose, counteract, curb, foil, block, incommode, choke, stem, stall, traverse, bring to a stand or standstill, be or play at cross purposes, discommode, limit, circumscribe, go against, forestall, cramp, prohibit, baffle, balk, stop, forbid, smother, rein in, tie one's hands, bind or tie hand and foot, restringe, trap, pinion, spike, silence, annul, cancel, invalidate, offset, vitiate, constrict, fetter, clip one's wings, stalemate, obviate, stay, contravene.

SHADE, *n.* 1. Comparative darkness, shadow, twilight, duskiness, dusk, umbrage, gloom, semidark, dimness, crepuscule, haze, film, adumbration, tenebrity, tenebrosity, cloud, vapor, lightlessness, eclipse, fuliginosity, indistinctness, penumbra (*Astron.*).

2. Comparative obscurity, shadow, covert, latency, dimness, seclusion, dormancy, vagueness, insignificance, quiescence, abeyance, inactivity, imperceptibility, concealment, equivocalness, ambiguity, imperspicuity.

3. Specter, ghost, spirit, apparition, illusion, phantom, revenant, presence, appearance, incorporeal being, vision, eidolon, phantasm, wraith, sprite, shadow, spook (coll.).

4. Slight variation, amount, degree, grain, iota, particle, shadow, nuance, tone, hint, complexion, tint, nicety, cast, tinge, suggestion, delicacy, distinction, scintilla, atom, touch, subtlety, minimum, jot, modicum, glimmer, spark, trace, whit, grain, scrap, speck, tittle, mite, ace, mote, bit, corpuscle, point, minim, trifle, hair, minutia, speckle, pin, straw, cent, farthing, doit, micron, snip, spot, rap, ion, insignificancy.

5. Something used for protection against excessive light, heat, *etc.,* blind, hood, screen, awning, concealment, shutter, canopy, veil, mask, curtain, shield, umbrella, parasol, roof, shroud, mantle, arbor, cover, pavilion, tent, shelter.

SHADE, *v.* 1. Produce shade in or on, obscure, darken, dim, cloud, render the values of light and dark *(in a painting or drawing),* dusk, shadow, eclipse, obfuscate, overcast, overshadow, darkle, becloud, fog, haze, adumbrate, befog, gloom, frost, cloak, blur, blacken, dull, mist, tint, dye, stipple, nubilate, gradate, crosshatch, obtenebrate.

2. Screen, cover, protect, hide from view, cloud, conceal, shroud, mask, beshade, shelter, shadow, overshadow, ensconce, eclipse, blind, render invisible, becloud, befog, occultate, blur, cloak, occult, veil, curtain, disguise, secure, shield, harbor, guard, safeguard, defend.

3. Change by imperceptible degrees into something else, pass by slight gradations, slide, slip, advance, glide, roll, graduate, progress, run, flow, sink, lapse.

SHADOW, *n.* 1. Dark figure cast by a body intercepting light, image, outline, copy, double, reflection, counterpart, duplicate, silhouette.

2. Comparative darkness, shade, *etc. (See* SHADE, *n.* 1, *above.)*

3. Shelter, protection, shade, safeguard, sanctuary, asylum, cover, rock, screen, anchor, fence, retreat, wall, bulwark, shield, aegis, palladium, hedge, cage, fortification, safety zone, coverture, hiding place, haven, sanctum, patronage, preserval, preservation, custody, oversight, supervision, keep, charge, tutelage, care, safekeeping, defense, support, buckler.

4. Slight suggestion, trace, degree, shade, *etc. (See* SHADE, *n.* 4, *above.)*

5. Specter, ghost, shade, *etc. (See* SHADE, *n.* 3, *above.)*

6. Faint image, foretaste, ghost, remains, imagining, hint, suggestion, skeleton, prefiguration, prelibation, presentiment, conception, representation, foreshadowing, premonition.

7. Mere semblance, fantasy, chimera, vapor, figment, will-o'-the-wisp, illusion, bubble, vision, trance, reverie, imagination, thin air, phantom, hallucination, mockery, trick, seeming, delusion, mirage, *ignis fatuus* (Lat.).

8. Cloud *(as on a friendship or reputation),* blot, blight, defect, flaw, taint, smear, defacement, blemish, smudge, smirch, stigma, spot, scar, stain, tarnish, imputation, slur, reproach, brand.

9. Inseparable companion, crony, pal, chum, mate, fellow, comrade, close friend, satellite, hanger-on, buddy (coll.), side-kick (sl.), attendant, confidant, intimate, other self, double, bosom friend.

10. One who follows a person to keep watch on him, spy, detective, follower, investigator, reconnoiterer, secret agent, dick (sl.), gumshoe (sl.), hawkshaw, plain-clothes man, sleuth (coll.), sleuthhound (coll.).

SHADOW, *v.* 1. Overspread with shadow, shade,

cloud, cast gloom over, etc. (See SHADE, v. 1, above.)

2. Screen, protect, hide, shroud, cover, etc. (See SHADE, v. 2, above.)

3. Follow (a person) secretly, watch, trail, track, trace, hound, dog the footsteps of, pursue, heel, tag after (coll.), tail (sl.).

4. (Often fol. by FORTH) Represent faintly or prophetically, typify, foreshadow, adumbrate, prefigure, predict, be indicative of, foretell, forecast, indicate, betoken, body forth, intimate, denote, presage, omen, preindicate, give token, index, forerun, herald, point to, signify, presignify, preshow, auspicate, prognosticate, augur, portend, forebode, symbolize.

SHADOWY, adj. 1. Resembling a shadow (in faintness, slightness, etc.), indistinct, opaque, faint, vague, pale, filmy, misty, smoky, glimmering, twilight, bleary, bleared, blurry, foggy, nubilous, blurred, nebulous, clouded, cloudy, obscure, dim, hazy, unclear, indefinite, ill-defined, indistinguishable, shrouded, fuzzy, out of focus, smeared, crepuscular, overshadowed, flickering, overcast.

2. Unsubstantial, unreal, illusory, impalpable, intangible, visionary, imaginary, false, ghostly, spectral, chimerical, deceptive, hallucinatory, maggoty, figmental, fictitious, immaterial, incorporeal, castle-built, air-built, phantom, phantasmagorial, fabulous, idealistic, dreamy, cloudbuilt, imponderable, vaporous, airy, vain, romantic, delusive, mysterious, phantasmic, fancybred, dreamlike, gossamer, tenuous, ethereal, uncertain, gaseous.

3. Abounding in shadow, shady, umbrageous, caliginous, cloudy, tenebrous, obscured, dark, gloomy, bosky, sylvan, bowery, screened, sheltered, overshadowed, overcast, murky, bushy, unlighted, unilluminated, lightless, sunless, moonless, hidden, somber, stygian, dim, crepuscular, twilight.

SHADY, adj. 1. Abounding in shade, shaded, etc. (See SHADOWY, adj. 3, above.)

2. Shadowy, indistinct, spectral, etc. (See SHADOWY, adj. 1, above.)

SHAFT, n. 1. Long slender rod, pole, long handle, helve, tongue, thill, mast, spear, arrow, lance, axis, arbor, stem, stalk, trunk, quill, stick, post, stave, staff, axle, spindle, support, bar, bolt, dart, pile, hold, shank, spile, diaphysis (Anat.), beam.

2. Something directed as in sharp attack, barb, bolt, slap, shot, flout, blow, cut, jeer, taunt, gibe, aspersion, personality, provocation, brickbat (coll.), atrocity, affront, insult, offense, indignity, retort, contumely, thrust, buffet, reproach, scurrility, outrage, malediction.

3. Ray, beam, patch, stream, gleam, streak, glade, pencil, finger.

4. Column, tower, trunk, memorial, monument, pillar, monolith, pylon, minaret, pilaster, spire, obelisk, pinnacle, needle, guglia, peristyle, totem, pier, martello, campanile, steeple.

5. Well, enclosed vertical space, cavity, depth, flue, chimney, funnel, chasm, gulf, excavation, colliery, mine, vent, spiracle, duct, pipe, tube, abysm, abyss, pit, hole.

SHAG, n. Rough matted hair or wool, etc., fleece, pelt, coat, nap, shock, mop, mane, tuft, knot, mat, crop, crine, fur, wool, fell, thatch.

SHAG, v. Make rough or shaggy (esp. with vegetation), make sharp, roughen, coarsen, knurl, corrugate, rumple, crinkle, ruffle, overrun, crum-

ple, overgrow, rough-hew, roughcast, mantle, bristle, run riot, overwhelm, fungate, grow rank or lush.

SHAGGY, adj. Covered with or having long rough hair, forming a bushy mass, shagged, unkempt, matted, rough, rugged, having a rough nap, tufted, crested, bristly, setaceous, leonine, hairy, nappy, hispid, hirsute, pily, downy, lanate, setose, spiked, prickly, barbed, flocculent, woolly, unshaven, unshorn, bewhiskered, whiskered, bearded, pileous, pappose (Bot.), barbellate (Bot., Zool.), strigose (Bot.), bushy, bristling, ragged.

SHAKE, n. 1. Act of shaking, tremulous motion, quiver, quaver, shuffle, joggle, jog, jig, twitch, jiggle, bounce, jounce, sway, lurch, rock, twitter, shiver, tremble, tremor, agitation, flutter, shivering, quaking, trembling, vibration, motion, dance, sputter, flicker, splutter, jerk, palpitation, ripple, pulsation, throb, bump.

2. Disturbing blow, shock, start, knock, stroke, dint, hit, jerk, slam, fillip, rap, jolt, jar, concussion, sting, thorn, swat, buffet, thwack, bang, whack, smack, cuff, box, belt (coll.), clout (coll.).

3. Crack, fissure, scissure, break, fracture, rupture, hiatus, split, slit, gash, cut, cleft, crevice, chasm, chink, gap, chap, cranny, breach, rent, rift, groove, furrow, hole, score, opening, cavity.

SHAKE, v. 1. Move or sway with short quick irregular vibrations, vibrate, tremble, jerk, quiver, shudder, shiver, flutter, jiggle, upheave, convulse, quake, quaver, oscillate, trill, tremolo, toss, rock, fluctuate, jog, joggle, squirm, dance, flicker, twitch, fidget, wriggle, wiggle, thrill, vellicate, splutter, sputter, twitter.

2. (Fol. by DOWN, OFF, etc.) Fall by shaking motion, brush, drop, remove, settle, sweep, slough, whisk, rid oneself of, throw off.

3. Totter, become unsteady, waver, vary, reel, wobble, sway, be cold, be afraid, stumble, flounder, shift, roll, shuffle, alternate, fluctuate, vacillate, rock, lurch, stagger, be excited, be weak, tremble.

4. Brandish, flourish, wave, flap, oscillate, flaunt, swing, wield, wag, display, dangle, exhibit, put forth or forward.

5. Rouse (bring, throw, force, etc.) by vigorous movement to and fro, cause to quiver or tremble, jostle, hustle, bounce, buffet, bump, twang, flip, wrench, flick, jiggle, joggle, jounce, pluck, tweak, twitch, jerk, jog.

6. Cause to totter or waver, weaken, unsettle, threaten, dissuade, disorder, endanger, make less firm, devitalize, enfeeble, impair, poison, envenom, injure, wound, contaminate, taint, infect, hurt, harm, disease, deviate, damp, render averse, disincline, discourage, perplex, stagger, enervate, cripple, unstring, impoverish, sap, mine, undermine, damage, disenchant, disaffect, extenuate, debilitate, chill, blunt, cool, wean, fill with doubt, reduce, exhaust, incapacitate, invalidate.

7. Agitate, disturb profoundly in feeling, frighten, move, stagger, startle, affect, touch, intimidate, daunt, unnerve, confuse, ruffle, stir, trouble, rouse, excite, foment, flurry, incite, convulse, infuriate, madden, whet, lash, urge, quicken, discompose, perturb, stimulate, strike, disquiet, perturbate, rattle, jar, jolt, inflame, enkindle, kindle, fire, arouse, smite, hit, galvanize, electrify, astound, stun, impress, animate, impassion, awaken.

8. (With DOWN) Condition, try, test, prove, put to the test, subject to trial, give a tryout (coll.).

9. (With UP) Mix, loosen, churn, whip, whisk, beat, emulsify, free, agitate, stir.

SHAKY, adj. 1. Shaking, trembling, tremulous, agitated, fearful, quaky, uneasy, jiggly, skittish, startled, jumpy, nervous, jolting, convulsive, vellicative, unquiet, fidgety, jerky, giddy, apprehensive, restless, saltatory, jittery (sl.), successatory, successive, quassative.

2. Liable to break down or give way, insecure, not to be depended upon, teetery, unsteady, unsafe, rickety, vulnerable, tottering, unsound, flimsy, infirm, frail, slight, unsubstantial, decrepit, unreliable, dangerous, hazardous, precarious.

3. Wavering (as in allegiance), irresolute, hesitant, desultory, lacking confidence, dubious, infirm of purpose, inconstant, half-hearted, tremulous, undecided, vacillating, quibbling, unresolved, fickle, uncertain, timid, unsure, fluctuating, dallying, unsettled, faltering, demurring, debating, pausing, shilly-shallying, sitting on or straddling the fence, hanging back, hovering, wobbling, considering, seesawing, variable, alternating, halting, oscillating, oscillatory, equivocating, hesitative.

SHALLOW, adj. 1. Not deep, shoal, depthless.

2. Not profound, superficial, unintellectual, slight, cursory, trivial, empty, without substance, skin-deep, light, narrow, frivolous, trashy, frothy, inane, airy, flimsy, puerile.

SHALLOW, n. Shallow stretch of water, flat, bar, sand bank, tongue, bank, spit, ridge, reef, shelf.

SHAM, adj. Not genuine, fake, feigned, simulated, fraudulent, forged, artificial, unauthentic, pretended, counterfeit, imitation, bogus, bastard, false, spurious, make-believe, mock, affected.

SHAM, n. Counterfeit, copy, imitation, substitute, fraud, forgery, bastard, fake, spurious article, make-believe.

SHAM, v. Pretend, counterfeit, make believe, simulate, imitate, play, sail under false colors, feign, affect, assume, fake, dissemble, be deceptive, put on, falsify, act, pose.

SHAMBLE, v. Shuffle, hop, drag along, walk clumsily, claudicate, lag, stagger, hobble, limp, lumber, jog, falter, hitch, jolt, flounce, toddle.

SHAME, n. 1. Modesty, decorum, pudicity, delicacy.

2. Disgrace, dishonor, opprobrium, ignominy, infamy, smirch, attaint, stigma, blot, disfavor, degradation, disesteem, debasement, odium, scandal, ill-repute, defilement, stain.

3. Guilt, feeling of shame, grievance, shamefacedness, self-abomination, abasement, horror, mortification, remorse, wrong, humiliation, self-disgust, feeling of unfitness or unworthiness.

SHAME, v. 1. Bring shame upon, disgrace, dishonor, disparage, stigmatize, vilify, slur, derogate, drag in the mire or mud, heap dirt upon, taint, smirch, blot, pollute, brand, attaint.

2. Dismiss with discredit, abase, strip of honors, humiliate, dismiss from favor, mortify, humble, degrade, defame.

SHAMEFACED, adj. 1. Modest, shy, coy, diffident, retiring, demure, blushing, shrinking, constrained, skittish, reserved, bashful.

2. Abashed, crestfallen, humiliated, confused, confounded, disconcerted, embarrassed, bewildered, conscience-stricken, mortified, chagrined, ashamed, hangdog, chapfallen.

SHAMEFUL, adj. Reprehensible, outrageous, nefarious, flagrant, low, base, unworthy, indecent,

shocking, inglorious, horrifying, felonious, fulsome, heinous, illaudable, dastardly, disgraceful, unmentionable, profligate, disreputable, ignominious, atrocious, immoral, sinister, execrable, scandalous, diabolic, despicable, black, deplorable, infernal, arrant, mean, corrupt, sneaking, facinorous, flagitious, uncommendable, iniquitous, odious, opprobrious.

SHAMELESS, adj. Saucy, brazen, flippant, boldfaced, unabashed, immodest, fresh, forward, barefaced, frank, candid, audacious, bluff, daring, unblushing, unreserved, cheeky, presumptuous, insolent, indecorous, malapert, pert, impudent, unseemly, brash.

SHANK, n. 1. Lower part of the leg, shin.

2. Shaft, hilt, haft, helve.

SHANTY, n. Small mean dwelling, cabin, den, cot, cottage, hutch, dump (sl.), lean-to, chalet, hovel, dugout, shack (coll.), ramshackle building.

SHAPE, n. 1. Form, outline, contour, structure, features, profile, silhouette, impression, pattern, cut, lineaments.

2. Guise, likeness, color, pretense, appearance, show, fashion, phase, image, look, mien, air, complexion, cast, semblance, seeming.

3. Figure, physique, form, build.

4. Phantom, ghost, wraith, specter, apparition, ghoul, spook, shee, banshee, image.

SHAPE, v. 1. Create, make, form, mold, manufacture, design, devise, pattern, put together, compound, produce, erect, frame, coin, fashion, weave, build, model, construct, fabricate, edify.

2. Sculpture, engrave, incise, stipple, enchase, etch, cut, form, fashion, trim, roughcast, carve, grave, scrape, hew, model, chisel, mold, insculp, pattern, rough-hew, block out, tool.

SHAPELESS, adj. Without shape, formless, grotesque, disfigured, deformed, unshapely, unsymmetrical, misshapen, ill-proportioned, amorphous, unformed, sloppy, crude, untidy, irregular, unshapen.

SHAPELY, adj. Well-formed, symmetrical, trim, well-proportioned, well-made, neat, comely.

SHARD, n. Fragment, piece, splinter, chip, sliver, particle, snippet, flint, snip, shred, point, scintilla, chunk, cantle, scrap, bit, grain, micron, cut, cutting, paring, tag, scantling, wafer, scrip, scale, flake, snicking, shaving, clipping, gobbet, lamina.

SHARE, n. Part allotted to a person or group, part belonging to a person or group, pittance, helping, allotment, dividend, quota, quotum, quantity, division, dotation, endowment, heritage, inheritance, portion, serving, percentage, cut (coll.), commission, consignment, allowance, ration, dole, stint, assignment, whack (sl.), rake-off (sl.).

SHARE, v. 1. Divide into shares, partition, deal out, demarcate, disperse, cut up, slice, allot, apportion, measure out, distribute, allocate, parcel, split, separate, segment, dole, carve, award, mete out, appropriate, subdivide.

2. Partake of a thing, engage in, participate, join in, divvy up with (sl.), divide with, be a participant, play a part in, chip in (coll.).

SHARK, n. Knave, chiseler, trickster, swindler, humbug, adventurer, hypocrite, jockey, deceiver, decoy, inveigler, rascal, rogue, pretender, enticer, charlatan, crook, quack, scaramouch, fraud, allurer, blackleg, bilk, impostor, confidence man, mountebank, dissembler, cheat, twister, sharper, empiric, medicaster, quacksalver, picaroon, masquerader, pettifogger, bluff, dodger, wolf in sheep's clothing.

SHARP, *adj.* 1. Thin-edged, razor-edged, knife-like, keen, acute, pointed, needle-sharp, edged, cutting, thin, sharp as a bayonet, sharp as a butcher knife.

2. Pointed, toothed, acute, peaked, spiculate, barbed, crotched, apiculate, cuspidate, acuminate, bristly, echinate, spinous, needle-sharp, prickly, pectinated, tapering, thorny, craggy, dentiform, jagged, angular, serrate, fine, xiphoid, cusped, piked, spear-shaped, setaceous, sagittate, subulate.

3. Bitter, cutting, trenchant, hurtful, stinging, brutal, acrimonious, mean, brusque, tart, drastic, curt, brash, gruff, rude, blunt, abrupt, churlish, bearish, discourteous, virulent, stern, austere, unmannerly, scathing, mocking, satirical, malevolent, venomous, malignant, ungracious, ungentle, uncivil, ill-bred, inaffable, impolite, crabbed, mordacious, insulting, derisory, crusty, excoriating, ill-natured, maleficent, malicious, lashing, galling, rancorous, spiteful, unbenevolent, envenomed, invidious, unamiable, uncharitable, uncordial, unkind, cruel, acrid, severe.

4. Shrewd, intelligent, smart, quick-witted, bright, acute, knowing, calculating, hawk-eyed, politic, diplomatic, artful, wily, foxy, crafty, sly, cunning, astute, sagacious, subtle, wise, clever, discriminating, wide-awake, long-headed, clear-headed, ingenious, far-sighted, lynx-eyed, hard-headed, open-eyed, aware, penetrating, keen, argute, gimlet-eyed, ferret-eyed, sapient, imaginative, quick of apprehension, judicious, comprehending, prudent, provident, Argus-eyed, forehanded, prepared, discretional.

5. Eager, persevering, zealous, ardent, diligent, perfervid, feverish, vehement, spirited, earnest, ambitious, avid, high-mettled, unfaltering, assiduous, animated, enterprising, aspiring, active, sedulous.

6. (*Of noise, etc.*) Shrill, piercing, high-pitched, ear-splitting, strident, acute, high-toned.

7. (*Medical, etc.*) Sudden, violent, crucial, severe, cutting, acute, intense, piercing, critical, fierce, extreme.

8. Steep, abrupt, sudden, rapid, sheer, vertical, straight-up, extreme, precipitous, stiff, arduous.

SHARPEN, *v.* Make sharper, put an edge on, make keen, point, tip, hone, strop, whet, file, acuminate, cuspidate, spiculate, grind, taper, set.

SHARPER, *n.* Trickster, swindler, adventurer, crook, deceiver, decoy, inveigler, rascal, enticer, pretender, charlatan, scaramouch, fraud, shark, blackleg, confidence-man, twister, cheat, bluff, dissembler, mountebank, pettifogger, rogue, knave, humbug.

SHARPSHOOTER, *n.* Good shot, dead shot, crack shot, marksman.

SHARP-SIGHTED, *adj.* All-observant, vigilant, watchful, wary, wide-awake, broad-awake, alert, on the lookout, on the qui vive, lynx-eyed, all-seeing, eagle-eyed, hawk-eyed, keen-sighted, quick-sighted, on the watch, circumspect, prudent, wakeful, alert, Argus-eyed.

SHARP-WITTED, *adj.* Bright, far-seeing, discriminating, critical, discerning, clever, sagacious, wide-awake, shrewd, discretional, prudent, forehanded, astute, penetrating, alive, alert, aware, piercing, smart, wise, sensible, comprehending, judicious, keen-sighted, rational, ferret-eyed, nobody's fool, level-headed, perspicacious, sapient, perceptive, gimlet-eyed, lynx-eyed, subtle, argute,

quick, quick-witted, cool-headed, imaginative, clear-witted.

SHATTER, *v.* 1. Break into pieces, split, crack, detonate, shiver, break open, disintegrate, deflagrate (*Chem.*), blow up, blow out, explode, tear asunder, fulminate, blast, burst, pop open, part, rupture.

2. Cause the ruin of, damage, overwhelm, spoil, squash, crush, smash, destroy, demolish, raze, subvert, scuttle, overturn, waste, overthrow, devastate, swallow up, batter, consume, upset, wreck, blast, gut, ravage, devour, topple.

SHAVE, *v.* 1. Pare off, cut, clip, crop, lop, dock, prune, nip, shear, mow, whittle, trim, pollard, retrench, check the growth of, fleece, crop, snip, poll.

2. Touch lightly, graze, glance, brush, flick, rub, skim, caress, kiss, sweep.

SHAWL, *n.* Wrap, kerchief, mantle, stole.

SHEAF, *n.* Bundle, gathering, stack, wisp, fagot, packet, batch, shock, fascicle, tussock, knot, cluster, truss, bale, tuft.

SHEAR, *v.* Cut with shears *or* other sharp instrument, crop, clip, trim, fleece, strip, shave, poll.

SHEARS, *n., pl.* Large scissors, cutting implement *or* machine, clippers.

SHEATH, *n.* Case (*as for a sword*), casing, covering, envelope, scabbard, coat, coating, sheathing, wrapper, skin, capsule, jacket, cuticle, involucre, membrane, protection, wrapping, boot, socket, quiver, incasement, integument (*Bot., Zool.*), lorica (*Zool.*), fascia (*Anat., Zool.*), theca (*Anat., Zool.*), ocrea (*Bot., Zool.*).

SHEATHE, *v.* Put into a sheath, enclose in a sheath, enclose in *or* as in a casing *or* covering, incase, case, enwrap, incrust, line, swaddle, shroud, swathe, envelop, tie up, bind, protect, surround, plate, sheet, face, cloak, coat, clothe, veneer, wrap.

SHED, *n.* Slight *or* rude structure (*for shelter, storage, etc.*), large strongly built structure (*often open at sides or end*), hut, cabin, cote, cover, box, hutch, shanty, lean-to, hangar, shelter, roundhouse, outhouse, cot, hovel, shack (*coll.*), stall, booth, fold, stable, barn, warehouse.

SHED, *v.* 1. Pour forth, emit and let fall, let flow *or* cause to flow, drop, stream, discharge, effuse, spill, give vent to, exude, shower, lavish.

2. Give *or* send forth, cast, emanate, emit, radiate, dispel, diffuse, strew, bestrew, distribute, disperse, disseminate, scatter, broadcast.

3. Throw off readily, resist, fail to absorb, repel, repulse, withstand, slough.

4. Cast off *or* let fall by natural process, doff, drop, exfoliate, slough, peel, exuviate, discard, flake, molt, abandon, lose, relinquish, desquamate (*Pathol.*).

SHEEN, *n.* Brightness, radiance, luster, brilliancy, gleam, light, shine, splendor, polish, glimmer, burnish, luminosity, dazzle, opalescence, gloss, glow, glint, nitency, lucidity, lambency, incandescence.

SHEEPISH, *adj.* 1. Awkwardly bashful *or* embarrassed, timid, shy, diffident, overmodest, coy, demure, skittish, foolish, shrinking, timorous, shamefaced, meek, abashed, crestfallen, ashamed, chapfallen, dashed, chastened, out of countenance, humble, blushing, hangdog, subdued.

2. Like sheep (*as in meekness, timidity, etc.*), timid, tractable, docile, submissive, servile, pliant,

easily led, obedient, subject, compliant, ignoble, under one's thumb, obsequious, in one's power, used as a doormat, subservient, passive, unassertive, abased, prostrate, obeisant, lamblike, plastic, yielding, in leading strings, led by the nose, unresisting, subdued, henpecked.

SHEER, *adj.* 1. Transparently thin, diaphanous, translucent, naked, filmy, flimsy, gossamer, glassy, clear, crystal, hyaline.

2. Unmixed with anything else, unqualified, bare, stark, clear, simple, mere, utter, unadulterated, plain, complete, total, dead, absolute, unconditional, single, out-and-out, unmitigated, homogeneous, uniform, veritable, unrestricted, perfect, outright, elementary, elemental, consummate, unalloyed, downright, unmingled.

3. Extending down *or* up very steeply, headlong, steep, precipitous, perpendicular, upright, plumb, bluff, abrupt, vertical, sharp, bold, breakneck, stiff, arduous, straight up and down.

SHEER, *n.* 1. Thin diaphanous material, gauze, netting, cloud, mist, veil, film.

2. Deviation, divergence, swerve, diversion, declination, obliquity, angle, tilt, pitch, cant, turn, bend, warp, bias, slope, slant, inclination, digression, sway, swag, sag, lurch, excursion, drift, divagation, divarication, refraction, skew, twist, bent, list.

SHEER, *v.* Deviate from a course, swerve, move aside, decline, oblique, bear off, skew, slue, turn, twist, veer, angle, slant, diverge, deflect, be distorted, yaw, curve, shift, depart from, alter one's course, digress, vary, sag, swag, bow, stray, drift, shelve, slope, list, keel, pitch, tilt, careen, bias, bend, wear *(Naut.),* haul *(coll.),* tack *(Naut.).*

SHEET, *n.* 1. Broad thin mass, layer, covering, lamina, sheath, plate, blanket, foil, leaf, membrane, film, pane, panel, peel, veneer, skin, pellicle, integument, stratum, coating, overlay, fold, flap, slab, ply, coat.

2. Piece of paper *or* parchment, page, folio, leaf *(of a book),* foolscap *(pl.).*

3. Newspaper, leaflet, folder, broadside, broadsheet, flyer, journal, magazine, paper, news, circular, publication, daily, weekly, monthly, quarterly.

4. Extent, stretch, sweep, expanse, length, reach, scope, swing, span, range, field, spread, width, area, breadth.

SHELF, *n.* 1. Slab of wood *or* other material fixed horizontally for supporting objects, bracket, hob, cupboard, mantel, mantelpiece, banquette, shoulder, bookrack, bookcase *(often pl.),* stack *(often pl.),* corbel *(Archit.).*

2. Contents of a shelf, set, row, array, display, line, file, procession, collection, tier, string, range.

3. Shelflike surface *or* projection, ledge, overhang, height, sill, shelve, protrusion.

4. Submerged extent of rock in sea *or* river, sandbank, sandbar, bar, reef, shoal, ridge, flat.

SHELL, *n.* 1. Hard outer covering, hard case, crust, rind, husk, pod, hull, shuck, pericarp, carapace, shard, capsule, coating, bur *(Bot.),* theca *(Bot.),* chaff, bran, exuviae *(pl.),* testa *(Bot.),* spermoderm *(Bot.),* episperm *(Bot.),* incrustation, epicarp *(Bot.).*

2. Object resembling a shell *(in being concave or hollow),* framework, cavity, crater, scull, cup, bowl, crust *(Cookery).*

3. Hollow projectile, missile, grenade, ball *(Hist.),* artillery shot *or* ammunition, bomb *(Mil.).*

SHELL, *v.* 1. Take out of the shell *or* pod, strip the shell from, husk, hull, skin, peel, bark, shuck.

2. Throw shells *or* explosive projectiles into (upon, among), bombard, fire upon, cannonade, pound, besiege, attack, bomb, torpedo, fusillade, pepper, strafe, barrage.

3. Come away, fall off *(as a shell or outer coat),* exfoliate, shed, peel off, drop, doff, flake, scale, slough, exuviate, discard.

SHELTER, *n.* 1. Something which affords protection *or* refuge, place of refuge *or* safety, asylum, haven, covert, sanctuary, stronghold, harbor, hiding place, ark, house, home, fastness, retreat, cover, safehold, lodging, resort, journey's end, fortress, mew, keep, ward, citadel, tower, rock, pillar, cloister, hermitage, port in a storm, hideout, den, lair, nest, subterfuge, cell, safety zone, shade, harborage, fortification, shield, screen.

2. Protection afforded, refuge, safety, safekeeping, security, anchorage, resort, oversight, surveillance, auspices, asylum, retirement, hiding, retreat, sanctum, seclusion, privacy, care, aid, defense, preservation, support, custody, concealment, patronage, escort, convoy, ward, keep, charge, guardianship.

SHELTER, *v.* 1. Protect, take under one's protection, shield, screen, hover over, harbor, preserve, overshadow, watch over, cherish, safeguard, take care of, guard, house, ensconce, defend, hide, keep, flank, shadow, attend, fortify, look after, tend, hedge round, bulwark, buckler, foster, champion, patronize, nurse, take in, befriend, arm, garrison, lodge, cushion, shroud, escort, chaperon, care for, maintain, sustain, convey, conduct.

2. Be a shelter for, afford shelter to, place under cover, provide with a shelter, cover, screen, shield, enclose, house, wrap, dike, veil, curtain, surround, shroud, sheathe, ensconce, conceal, hide.

3. Take shelter, lodge, hide; find refuge, billet, quarter, hole up, retire, lie hid, shut oneself up, lurk, couch, skulk, steal, seclude oneself, lie perdu, lie snug *or* close, lie low *(coll.).*

SHELVE, *v.* 1. Place on a shelf *or* shelves, arrange, fix, set out, line up, space, range, align, group.

2. Lay *or* put aside from consideration, remove from active service, delay, put on the shelf, dismiss, postpone, defer, put aside, lay *or* set by, retire, stay, reserve, put off, prorogue, put on ice, table, suspend, waive, hang up, pigeonhole, shunt, sleep on.

3. Slope gradually, incline, fall away, drop, slant, list, pitch, cant, keel, descend, decline, sheer, tilt.

SHEPHERD, *n.* 1. Man who herds, tends and guards sheep, herder, herdsman, sheepherder *(Western U. S.).*

2. One who cares for a group of people, clergyman, pastor, minister, priest, parson, divine, dominie, chaplain, father, ecclesiastic, churchman, padre, rector, curate, curé, vicar.

SHEPHERD, *v.* Tend, guard, watch over carefully, shelter, protect, guide, hover over, overshadow, shield, screen, preserve, cherish, safeguard, take care of, care for, defend, keep, flank, shadow, attend, look after, foster, sustain, maintain, escort, chaperon, convey, pilot, direct, conduct, lead, supervise, oversee.

SHIBBOLETH, *n.* 1. Peculiarity of pronunciation *or* habit, mode of dress, *etc. (distinguishing a class of persons),* mark, symbol, stamp, badge, brand, label, hallmark, identification, trademark, earmark, singularity, lineament, idiom, trait, differentia, mannerism, characteristic, trick, feature, idiosyncrasy.

2. Pet phrase (of a party, sect, etc.), test word, password, sign, watchword, countersign, catchword, party cry.

SHIELD, n. 1. Piece of defensive armor carried on the arm, buckler, pavis, aegis (Gk. Myth.), ancile (Rom. Antiq.), pelta (Gk. Antiq.).

2. Anything used or serving to protect, screen, cover, guard, shade, mantle, aegis, buckler, fender, buffer, safeguard, protection, hood, blind, umbrella, parasol, tent, pavilion, arbor, mantle, canopy, roof.

SHIELD, v. Fortify, secure, screen, house, hedge round, defend, protect, guard, keep, cover, shelter, safeguard, watch over, preserve, harbor, armor, cushion, bulwark, hide.

SHIFT, n. 1. Alteration, aberration, metamorphosis, swerving, evolution, transposition, metathesis, inflection, difference, diversion, deviation, metastasis, move, trade, exchange, reorganization, permutation, interchange, change, reformation, vacillating, switch, restyling, turning, substitution, tempering, commutation, reconstruction, shuffling, transubstantiation, remodeling, revolution, transshaping, conversion, transmutation, transfiguration, veering, shifting, transformation, metamorphism, modification, modulation, variation, fluctuation, wavering, alternating.

2. Spell of work, stint, tour of duty, assignment.

SHIFT, v. 1. Alter, vary, transpose, re-form, vacillate, reorganize, reconstruct, denature, re-style, reduce, translate, change, deflect, remodel, revolutionize, transshape, transmogrify (hum.), swerve, convert into, metamorphose, modulate, mutate, modify, fluctuate, diversify.

2. Exchange, move, budge, interchange, reverse, change, alter, substitute, switch, swap (coll.), permute, give and take.

3. Get along, make do, scrape along, paddle one's own canoe, be independent, stand on one's own legs, struggle along, take care of oneself.

SHIFTLESS, adj. Lazy, lax, good-for-nothing, inefficient, slack, loose, do-nothing, idle, slothful, inactive, slow, ne'er-do-well, remiss, careless, fainéant, happy-go-lucky, lackadaisical.

SHIFTY, adj. Tricky, insidious, wily, contriving, treacherous, artful, maneuvering, deceitful, scheming, foxy, crafty, canny, cunning, snaky, machinative, intriguing, subdolous.

SHILLY-SHALLY, v. Be irresolute, hesitate, falter, dilly-dally, vacillate, alternate, hem, dally, waver, fluctuate, blow hot and cold, seesaw, straddle the fence, tergiversate, balance, oscillate, hang back, linger, hover, debate.

SHIMMER, v. Gleam, glimmer, glisten, beam, sparkle, phosphoresce, shine, scintillate, glow, coruscate, flash, dance, flicker, flutter, twinkle, blink.

SHIN, n. Lower part of the leg, shank, shinbone, tibia.

SHIN, v. (Usually with UP) Clamber, scale, scramble, surmount, climb, swarm up, go up, shinny (coll.).

SHINE, n. Brightness, radiation, illumination, burnish, effulgence, nitency, glint, luminousness, lambency, radiance, irradiance, resplendence, incandescence, luminosity, dazzle, opalescence, glim-

mer, luster, lucidity, refulgence, glitter, brilliance, glare, glow, gloss, sheen, blare.

SHINE, v. 1. Shed luster, emit light, be bright, flare, blaze, dazzle, flash, glitter, be illuminated, beacon, glow, glint, gleam, beam, glisten, irradiate, light up, scintillate, fulgurate, radiate, shimmer, coruscate, sparkle, luminesce.

2. Make glossy, burnish, furbish, glaze, varnish, gloss, buff, smooth, polish, rub up, luster, abrade, emery, sand, rosin, brighten, sleek, slick, file, planish, pumice.

SHINGLE, v. Cut the hair closely, bob, clip, trim, shave the head, shorten, shear, prune, lop, dock, give a crew cut to.

SHINY, adj. Polished, irradiant, radiant, beamy, glittering, brilliant, gaudy, bright, flaming, effulgent, scintillating, twinkling, glistening, beaming, lustrous, gleaming, resplendent, lambent, luminous, shimmering, coruscating, sparkling, flashing, refulgent, glossy, nitid, spangled, incandescent, illuminated, silvery, argent, burnished, sheeny, fulgid, fulgurant, fulgent, sunny, orient, rutilant.

SHIP, n. Vessel, craft, bark, boat, hulk, liner, steamer, merchantman, freighter, packet. (See BOAT, n. and BATTLESHIP, n.)

SHIP, v. 1. Go on board ship, embark, board ship, sail, go on shipboard, go aboard, set sail, take ship, put to sea.

2. Transport, send, convey, carry, send off, dispatch, consign, convoy, cart, transplant, haul, transmit, move, bear.

SHIPMENT, n. Shipload, wagonload, burden, goods, freight, load, charge, haul, cargo, carload, lading, bale.

SHIPWRECK, n. 1. Wreckage, wreck, hull, sunken ship derelict.

2. Accident, crash, running aground, collision, disaster, smash-up, foundering.

SHIRK, v. Evade (as a work, duty, danger, etc.), close one's eyes to, avoid, run from, duck (coll.), escape, steer clear of, dodge, shun, funk, ignore, shrink from, blench at, blink at, elude, omit, malinger, neglect, eschew, leave undone, gold-brick (U. S. Army sl.).

SHIVER, v. 1. Break into pieces, rupture, blast, burst open, fulminate, tear asunder, explode, blow out, disintegrate, break open, break, shatter, detonate, crack, split.

2. Tremble, quiver, palpitate, shudder, jerk, convulse, oscillate, sputter, splutter, flutter, quaver, vibrate, chatter (of the teeth).

SHIVERY, adj. 1. Brittle, friable, breakable, shattery, frangible, fragile, crushable, frail, delicate, splintery, brash (of timber).

2. Tremulous, shaking, teeth-chattering, quivering, palpitating, shuddering, jerking, quavering, vibrating, spluttering, sputtering, oscillating, convulsive, fluttering.

SHOAL, n. 1. Shallow stretch of water, flat, bar, tongue, sandbank, bank, spit, ridge, shelf, shallow, reef.

2. School (of fish, etc.), crowd, throng, swarm, horde, multitude, community, pack.

SHOCK, n. 1. Sudden and violent blow, impact, collision, crash, concussion, stroke, percussion, bump, onset, assault, brunt, attack, encounter, jar, jolt, shake, quake, jostle, jounce, jerk, lurch, sway, start, rock, clash, smash, smash-up, crackup, appulse.

2. Sudden disturbance, commotion, agitation,

conflict, outburst, uproar, imbroglio, racket, explosion, clash, fray, affray, brush, impingement, sharp contest, joust, tilt, duel, passage at arms, dogfight, clash of arms, tussle, riot, scuffle, combat, battle, engagement, action, strife, fight, struggle, disruption, rupture, brawl, squabble, melee, fisticuffs, litigation, skirmish, fracas, rencounter, wrangle.

3. Something that shocks mentally, emotionally, *etc.*, surprise, violent disturbance, start, trauma, cut, blow, stroke, turn, jar, wound, perturbation, dismay, prostration, breakdown, injury, hurt, nociassociation *(Med.)*, offense, collapse.

4. Group of sheaves of grain on end, stack, cock, shook, rick, sheaf, mow, stook *(New Eng.)*.

5. Thick bushy mass *(as of hair)*, mat, crop, crine, knot, mop, shag, mane, tuft, thatch.

SHOCK, *v.* 1. Strike with intense surprise, horror, disgust, *etc.*, astonish, electrify, galvanize, disturb, astound, upset, perturb, stir, ruffle, disquiet, discompose, agitate, unsettle, catch unprepared, disconcert, bowl over, spring upon, pounce upon, jar, jolt, throw off one's guard, take away one's breath, give a turn, stagger, petrify, paralyze, stupefy, stun, startle, repel, scandalize, shake, offend, revolt, horrify, strike dumb, appall, overwhelm, dumfound, bewilder, confound, make the hair stand on end, make the blood curdle *or* run cold, freeze the blood, flabbergast *(coll.)*.

2. Strike against violently, jar, collide, hit, brunt, buffet, jerk, joggle, bump, jounce, agitate, shake, knock, clash, beat against, hurtle against, dash, smash, impinge, jostle, slap, smite, thump, slug, shatter, pound, beat, whop, whack, cuff, box, bang, batter, pelt, larrup, pommel, sock *(sl.)*, soak *(sl.)*.

SHOCKING, *adj.* Causing intense surprise, disgust, horror, *etc.*, offensive, detestable, obnoxious, disgusting, repugnant, loathsome, abominable, terrible, horrible, frightful, appalling, monstrous, awful, outrageous, lamentable, astounding, startling, ugly, ignominious, intolerable, infamous, scandalous, portentous, insufferable, grisly, abhorrent, tragic, direful, formidable, repulsive, hateful, execrable, odious, revolting, disgraceful, foul, dreadful, horrid, fearful, dire, horrific, hideous, ghastly, vulgar, painful, villainous, horrifying, reprehensible, wretched. opprobrious, grievous, shameless.

SHODDY, *adj.* Pretending to a superiority not possessed, sham, mock, spurious, bogus, false, specious, counterfeit, trumped-up, imitation, tricky, fictitious, forged, artificial, brummagem, bastard, feigned, fraudulent, colorable, simulated, illegitimate, quasi, pseudo, flashy, tawdry, tinsel, meretricious, catchpenny, pinchbeck, sophisticated, adulterated, phony *(sl.)*, fake *(coll.)*.

SHODDY, *n.* 1. Anything inferior made to resemble what is of superior quality, sham, brummagem, deception, hoax, cheat, forgery, bastard, swindle, fraud, mockery, mock, whited *or* painted sepulcher, make-believe, tinsel, paste, counterfeit, spurious article, phony *(sl.)*, gyp *(sl.)*, sell *(sl.)*, fake *(coll.)*, flam *(coll.)*, flimflam *(coll.)*.

2. Pretense *(as in art, manufacture, etc.)*, trick, simulation, stratagem, claptrap, dishonesty, artifice, dissimulation, pretension, dissembling, disguise, deceit, deception, make-believe. humbug. humbuggery, charlatanry, bluff, hypocrisy, insincerity, cant, fraudulence, mere show, buncombe, quackery, false front *(coll.)*, front *(coll.)*, fake

(coll.), fakery *(coll.)*, four-flushing *(sl.)*, flimflam *(coll.)*, flam *(coll.)*.

SHOE, *n.* 1. External covering for the foot, footwear, sandal, loafer, boot, slipper, patten, moccasin, cothurnus, oxford, blucher, bottine, chopine, bootee, balmoral, brogue, brogan, clog, pump, creedmore, clodhoppers, sabot, stogy, leathers, buskin *(Hist.)*, chaussure *(Fr.)*.

2. Thing *or* part resembling a shoe in form, position *or* use, ferrule, plate, drag, skid, cap, metal rim, boot, brake, iron band *(on sleigh runner)*.

SHOEMAKER, *n.* One who makes *or* mends shoes, bootmaker, cobbler, Crispin.

SHOO, *interj.* Exclamation used to scare *or* drive away poultry, birds, *etc.*, begone!, along with you!, get *or* go away!, get you gone!, skedaddle! *(sl.)*, get *or* git! *(sl.)*, off with you!, away!, scram! *(sl.)*, beat it! *(sl.)*.

SHOOT, *n.* 1. Match, contest at shooting, act of shooting, bout, game, trial of shooting skill.

2. New *or* young growth, twig, branch, sprout, switch, tendril, stem, sprig, scion, offshoot, sucker *(Bot.)*, burgeon, sarmentum *(Bot.)*, graft *(Hort.)*.

SHOOT, *v.* 1. Hit with a missile discharged from a weapon, wound, kill, put to death, drop, plug, execute, riddle, pelt, fire on *or* at, open fire, shell, snipe at, cannonade, pepper, pick off, strike, spray, fell, bring down, fusillade, blitz, barrage, draw a bead on, blow one's brains out, pump full of lead *(sl.)*.

2. Send forth *(arrows, bullets, etc.)* from a bow *or* firearm, *etc.*, discharge *(a weapon)*, fire, expel, propel, let fly, eject, hurl, go off, bark, explode, let off, detonate, hurl, catapult.

3. Send forth like an arrow *or* bullet, fire, let fly, toss, shy, hurl, heave, pitch, put, pelt, cast, sling, chuck, fling, throw, launch, propel, send, lance, dart, dash, peg.

4. Move *or* pass suddenly *or* swiftly, dart, speed, rush, spring, hasten, sprint, post, spank, gallop, cut along, scoot, slide, skim, scud, run, bowl along, bolt, outstrip the wind, wing, stride, whisk, sweep, brush, bundle, whip, zip, tear, race, fly, flit, cover ground, make strides, go full steam ahead, get over the ground, barrel *(coll.)*.

5. *(Sometimes fol. by* UP*)* Put forth buds *or* shoots, burgeon, bud, germinate, grow *(esp. rapidly)*, come forth, increase, multiply, prolificate, sprout, spread, develop, wax, outgrow, burst forth, leap up, bloom, blossom, flower, vegetate, pullulate, flourish, luxuriate, spring up.

6. Variegate by threads, streaks, *etc.*, of another color, stripe, diversify, streak, striate, iris, make iridescent, iridesce, speck, fleck, speckle, interweave, mix, spot, dapple, stipple, mottle.

7. Take a picture of, photograph, snap.

8. Jut, project, extend, stretch, push, protuberate, bulge, stick out, stand out, put forth, protrude, thrust forth.

9. Engage in *or* follow the sport of killing game, hunt, chase, give chase, stalk, course, sport, pursue, hound, dog, go hunting.

10. Take the altitude of a heavenly body, take bearings from, take a sight on.

SHOP, *n.* 1. Place for selling goods, market, mart, store, *boutique (Fr.)*, emporium, stall, booth, counter, establishment, *magasin (Fr.)*, Laden *(Ger.)*, tienda *(Sp.)*, bottega *(It.)*, bazaar.

2. Place for doing certain work, workshop, plant, mill, factory, works, yard, studio.

SHOP, *v.* Visit shops for purchasing *or* examining goods, market, buy, procure, search, hunt, be in the market for.

SHOPKEEPER, *n.* Merchant, tradesman, storekeeper, dealer, trader, businessman, retailer.

SHORE, *n.* 1. Edge of the land, waterside, seaside, beach, strand, margin of the sea, brink, brim, seashore, seacoast, foreshore, littoral, seaboard, loom of the land.

2. Stay, prop, underpin, pillar, underset, leg, staff, stud, upholder, support, stand, standard, base, splint, strengthener, foundation, pin, mainstay, brace, rib, rest, reinforcement, pediment, stanchion, bracer, crutch, cane, strut, buttress.

SHORT, *adj.* 1. Not long, little, small, not of great length.

2. Not tall, stunted, wizened, scrubby, atomic, elfin, bantam, dwarfish, cramped, scraggy, pygmy, runty, dumpy, light, slight, puny, Lilliputian, petite, little, squat, stubby, minikin, diminutive, breviped, pint-sized, pocket-sized, truncated, Tom Thumb, amoebic, pug, pollard.

3. Of brief duration, momentary, temporary, fugacious, short-lived, fleet, perishable, mortal, transitory, fleeting, hasty, brief, volatile, quick, cursory, precarious, ephemeral, evanescent, transient, unenduring.

4. Gruff, curt, acetose, grouchy, irascible, unmannerly, bearish, petulant, abrupt, brash, peevish, ungraceful, froward, harsh, sharp, trenchant, stern, austere, choleric, brusque, tart, acrimonious, caustic, virulent, currish, crusty, splenetic, sour, snappish, growling, mordant, discourteous, blunt, waspish, impolite, sarcastic, thorny, surly, touchy, testy, rude, peppery, snarling, crabbed, sullen.

5. Concise, curtailed, abridged, abbreviated, compressed, pointed, curt, terse, succinct, comprehensive, laconic, summary, pithy, compact, close, neat, condensed, epigrammatic, crisp, trenchant, curtate, elliptical, sententious, pauciloquent, gnomic, straightforward, emphatic, to the point, reticent, sparing of words, synoptic, contracted, direct, sharp.

6. Defective, deficient, missing, wanting, lacking, insufficient, shy (*sl.*), tight, lean, scanty, unplentiful, thin, in arrears, not abundant, failing, skimpy, sparse, slender, low, meager, slim, scarce.

SHORTAGE, *n.* Deficiency, deficit, insufficiency, scarcity, sparsity, ullage (*of liquors, grains, etc.*), want, inadequacy, lack, failure, famine, need, scantiness, dearth, short (*coll.*).

SHORTCOMING, *n.* Weak point, fault, failing, weakness, frailty, deficiency, defect, flaw, imperfection, infirmity, drawback, foible.

SHORTEN, *v.* Cut short, cut down, trim, pare down, prune, curtail, abridge, reduce, abbreviate, retrench, contract, condense, abstract, compress, shrink, brief, epitomize, digest, summarize, synopsize, contract, dock, clip, lop, pollard (*of trees, shrubs, etc.*).

SHORTHAND, *n.* System of writing with ciphers or symbols, stenography, polygraphy (*Hist.*), pasigraphy, tachygraphy, cryptography, phonography, brachygraphy.

SHORT-LIVED, *adj.* Of brief duration, unenduring, cursory, fleet, fleeting, precarious, ephemeral, hasty, perishable, momentary, temporary, mortal, transitory, brief, volatile, short, fugacious, quick, evanescent, transient.

SHORTLY, *adv.* Soon, before long, presently, directly, in a short while, by and by, anon.

SHORT-SIGHTED, *adj.* 1. Near-sighted, myopic,

mope-eyed, purblind, weak-eyed, dim-eyed, dim-sighted, partially sighted, half-blind, unable to see distances.

2. Stupid, insulse, dense, dull-pated, thick (*coll.*), mutton-headed (*coll.*), numskull (*coll.*), dull, stolid, bovine, dull-witted, weak-minded, simple-minded, clodpated, thick-headed, oafish, slow, idiotic, simple, addlepated, addleheaded, dronish, muddle-brained, moronic, purblind, slow-witted, uncomprehending, witless.

SHORT-TEMPERED, *adj.* Touchy, snarling, crabbed, rude, peppery, gruff, unmannerly, irascible, grouchy, acetose, sullen, blunt, sour, caustic, stern, peevish, bearish, petulant, brash, abrupt, trenchant, sharp, harsh, short, froward, ungraceful, choleric, brusque, tart, acrimonious, splenetic, virulent, currish, discourteous, snappish, mordant, growling, crusty, waspish, testy, impolite, sarcastic.

SHOT, *n.* 1. Discharge (*of a firearm, etc.*), fusillade, blast, explosion, salvo, report, rafale (*Mil.*), volley, detonation, pop, crash.

2. Missile, projectile, trajectile, shell, ball, bullet, arrow, *etc.*

3. Guess, attempt, suggestion, notion, idea, hint, intimation, surmise, conjecture.

4. Distance of a missile's flight, range, span, extent, reach, stretch, space, sweep, swing.

5. Marksman, rifleman, shooter, archer, bowman.

6. (*Games*) Stroke, play, move.

SHOULDER, *n.* Protrusion (*from a building, wall, rock, etc.*), projection, protuberance, shelf, shelve, prominence, salient, excurvature, mantel, hob, predella, abutment, ledge, corbel (*Archit.*), sill.

SHOULDER, *v.* 1. Push roughly *or* rudely against, jostle, push aside, strike against, bounce, jounce, lunge against, hustle, elbow, batter, joggle, collide with, butt against, press against, bump, agitate.

2. Assume responsibility, carry, take over, undertake, support, bear, maintain, keep up, back up, sustain, hold.

SHOULDER BLADE, *n.* Shoulder-bone, omoplate, scapula.

SHOUT, *n.* Cry, hue and cry, shouting, racket, hullabaloo, blast, outcry, bray, clamor, clangor, wild chorus, loud protest, caterwauling, call, hubbub, agitation, jangle, vociferation, yell, yelling, rumpus, uproar, disturbance, commotion, tumult, catcall.

SHOUT, *v.* Cry out, give full voice, roar, vociferate, yell, scream, halloo, hollo, hail, bellow, bawl, exclaim, clamor, thunder, whoop, cheer.

SHOVE, *n.* 1. Act of shoving, thrust, impulsion, impetus, boost, pressure, acceleration, jostle, butt, bunt, jolt, jog, propulsion, pulsion.

2. Vigorous effort, onset, assault, charge, attack, endeavor, invasion, storm, storming, foray, raid, offense, inroad, irruption, incursion, strong effort, aggression.

SHOVE, *v.* 1. Push roughly *or* rudely aside, butt against, bump, press against, elbow aside, batter, joggle, collide with, agitate, hustle, lunge against, jounce, bounce, strike against, shoulder.

2. Move by exerting force, impel, drive, press, trundle, prod, goad, knock against, propel, push, thrust, bump against, butt, bunt, nudge, poke.

3. Make one's way (*by forcing obstacles aside, etc.*), elbow, wedge, squeeze, shoulder, push, jostle, hustle, force a way, fight one's way, ram, butt.

4. Press *(an action, etc.)*, carry further, drive on, advance, press forward, expedite, direct, promote, subserve, abet, aid, facilitate, assist, advocate, endorse, foster, hasten, insist on, instigate, quicken, get behind, speed, support, lend wings to, hurry, pursue, go ahead, prosecute to a conclusion, see it through, rush, proceed, work for, go on with, railroad *(coll.)*.

5. Press *(a person in dealings, etc.)*, bear hard upon, persecute, badger, wear down, harry, intimidate, put on, constrain, pain, wring, mortify, harass, compel, dragoon, oppress, squeeze, put the screws on *(sl.)*, coerce, drive to the wall, tree *(coll.)*, put on the spot *(sl.)*, pin down, strong-arm *(coll.)*, grind, browbeat, cow, hound, trouble, beset, discompose, push, confuse, afflict, agitate, worry, plague, heckle, chafe, bleed, buffalo *(sl.)*.

6. *(Often with ON)* Keep going, grind away, make one's way with effort *or* persistence, endeavor, exert oneself, drive on, endure, persevere, put forth vigorous *or* persistent efforts, force one's way, press on, work one's way, carve one's way, stick at nothing, be undeterred, be undaunted, bear up, hold up, be resolute, never say die, peg away, labor, drudge, plug away *(coll.)*, edge along, inch along, keep the ball rolling, keep on, go all lengths, redouble one's efforts, hammer, plod, climb, advance, forge ahead, struggle, persist, strive, try, continue.

7. *(With OFF)* Move from the shore, *etc.*, depart, launch out, farewell *(Naut.)*, leave, push off, put off *or* out.

SHOVEL, *n.* Instrument for digging, *etc.*, scoop, spade, trowel.

SHOVEL, *v.* 1. Spade, scoop out, bail, bucket, dip, lade, ladle.

2. Break up and turn over earth, *etc.*, work with a spade, dig, unearth, quarry, exhume, bring to the surface, plow, harrow.

SHOW, *n.* 1. Display, demonstration, sight, array, representation, showing, revelation, exhibit, exposition, spectacle, unfoldment, divulgence, materialization, production, ceremony, performance.

2. Ostentatious display, ostentation, parade, pretentiousness, pretense, flourish, flaunting, pomposity, pompousness, vanity, flashiness, gaudery, gaudiness, superfluity, frills, tinsel, gilt, gilding, effect, figure, strut, glitter, peacockery, spectacle, exhibitionism, foppery, speciousness, veneer, splash, affectation, coxcombry, inflation, pose, swagger, orotundity, dog *(coll.)*, showiness, pageantry, vaunting, pomp, dash, front *(coll.)*, trappings, airs, swank *(sl.)*.

3. Appearance, sight, spectacle, representation, view, scene, performance, showing, look, aspect, image, formation, vision, impression, lineaments, form, figure, presence, apparition.

4. Unreal *or* deceptive appearance, delusion, trick, pretense, air, pretext, distortion, sham, pose, semblance, plausibility, speciousness, simulation, illusion, impression, effect, profession, allegation, moonshine, claptrap, empty words, seeming, apparent character, likeness, mask, color, front *(coll.)*.

5. Indication, trace, evidence, intimation, suspicion, inkling, glimmer, expression, evincement, hint, suggestion, implication, cue, clue, scent, sign, mark, idea, notion, tinge, gleam, token, whisper, taste, touch, manifestation.

SHOW, *v.* 1. Display, evince, manifest, disclose, evidence, betoken, reveal, inform, tell, argue,

attest, denote, testify, exhibit, demonstrate, set forth, expose, imply, put in plain sight, represent.

2. Bestow, confer, favor, endow, shower down upon, dispense, impart, lavish, distribute, deal out.

3. Make known, reveal, disclose, bare, unmask, bring to light, uncloak, unscreen, unveil, uncover, lay bare, undrape.

4. Explain to, demonstrate, instruct, teach, guide, tutor, inform, indoctrinate, direct, school, coach, give an idea of, prime, inaugurate.

5. Verify, certify, document, confirm, demonstrate, corroborate, validate, bear out, manifest, substantiate, show clearly, sustain, ascertain, prove, uphold, establish, authenticate, witness, support, settle.

6. Indicate *(as an instrument)*, record, read, register, signify, point to.

7. Be visible, appear, be within view, seem, present oneself, come in sight, dawn, break forth, peep forth, heave in sight, loom up, arrive, come forth, burst forth, come into view, crop up, arise.

8. *(With OFF)* Exhibit ostentatiously, display, flaunt, make a parade of, wave, brandish, hold up, strut, swagger, be vain, be ostentatious, put forth *or* forward, brag, vaunt, peacock, boast, swell, look *or* talk big, put on airs, give oneself airs, pose, attitudinize, parade, gasconade, trumpet, puff, put on the dog *(coll.)*, put up a front *(coll.)*.

9. *(With UP)* Expose, refute, reveal, lay bare, open, rebut, confute, disprove, negative, invalidate, dismiss, betray, explode, bring to light, unfold, uncover, disclose, unmask, evince, evidence, stultify, make ridiculous, make a goat of *(sl.)*.

SHOWDOWN, *n.* Forced disclosure *(of actual resources, power, etc.)*, manifestation, revelation, revealment, exposure, exposé, disenchantment, debunkment *(coll.)*, disillusionment, undeception, publication, crisis, head, climax, ventilation, disabusal, divulgation.

SHOWER, *n.* 1. Brief fall *(of rain, hail, etc.)*, sprinkle, downpour, pour, drizzle, precipitation, cloudburst.

2. Fall *(as of tears, sparks, bullets, questions, etc.)*, large quantity *or* supply, barrage, deluge, rain, volley, salvo, flood, bombardment, profusion, stream, wealth, overflow, lavishment, gush, surge, rush, torrent, opulence, excess, nimiety, superfluity, superabundance, surplus, prodigality, copiousness.

SHOWER, *v.* 1. Pour down in a shower, precipitate, fall, teem, sprinkle, drizzle, spit.

2. Bestow liberally *or* lavishly, sparge, furnish *or* supply in abundance, open the purse, loose *or* untie the purse strings, thrust, pour, lavish, indulge, give freely, dissipate, squander, be prodigal.

SHOW-OFF, *n.* 1. Pretentious display, ostentation, parade, pretentiousness, pretense, flourish, flaunting, pomposity, pompousness, vanity, flashiness, gaudery, gaudiness, superfluity, frills, tinsel, gilt, gilding, effect, figure, strut, glitter, peacockery, spectacle, exhibitionism, foppery, speciousness, veneer, splash, affectation, coxcombry, inflation, pose, swagger, orotundity, dog *(coll.)*, showiness, pageantry, vaunting, pomp, dash, front *(coll.)*, trappings, airs, swank *(sl.)*.

2. One given to pretentious display, boaster, braggart, braggadocio, blusterer, fanfaron, flaunter, egotist, strutter, swaggerer, vaporer, trumpeter, exhibitionist, windbag *(sl.)*, gasbag *(sl.)*.

SHOWY, *adj.* 1. Making an imposing display, grand, stately, bright, magnificent, gorgeous, sumptuous, brilliant, glowing, conspicuous, striking, flaunting, ornate, daring, bold, elegant, glorious, spectacular, elaborate, decorative, ornamental, rich, fine, flowery, jeweled, embroidered, grandiloquent, bespangled, radiant, pompous, dashing, splendid.

2. Ostentatious, pretentious, gaudy, affected, orotund, crude, raw, florid, garish, loud, daring, conspicuous, overdone, intended to attract notice, dandified, turgid, theatrical, extreme, fancy, ornate, overwrought, glittering, meretricious, foppish, coxcombish, tawdry-mannered, artificial, sententious, magisterial, high-flown, swelling, grandiose, obtrusive, specious, vain, lofty, fustian, bombastic, thrasonical.

SHRED, n. 1. Strip, slip, band, fascia, ribbon, shiver, sliver, shaving, filament, list, fillet, spill, splinter, rag, tatter, scrap, bit, fragment.

2. Scrap, bit, fragment, tatter, rag, piece, particle, snip, atom, trace, speck, doit, scratch, snippet, morsel, spot, iota, grain, mite, mote, micron, modicum, ion, whit, tittle, minim, hair, speckle, scintilla, freckle, pin, flyspeck, insignificancy, corpuscle, trifle, point, microbe, molecule, minutia, straw, cent, farthing.

SHRED, v. Cut or tear into small pieces, reduce to shreds, strip, grate, decimate, pulverize, rip, filament, atomize, splinter, demolish.

SHREW, n. Woman of violent temper and speech, scold, fury, virago, hag, Xanthippe, vixen, spitfire, termagant, brawler, she-wolf, tigress, common scold, rebuker, chider, vituperator, reviler, castigator, harridan, old cat (coll.), hellhag, hellcat, grandmother, fishwife, battle-ax (sl.), crone, beldam, old witch, ogress.

SHREWD, adj. Sharp in practical matters, astute, sagacious, sly, cunning, artful, crafty, wary, foxy, Machiavellian, acute, canny, keen, penetrating, discriminating, sharp-witted, sharp-sighted, clearheaded, arch, subtle, wily, long-headed, circumspect, quick, politic, clever, watchful, careful, far-seeing, sapient, guarded, prudent, cautious, deliberate, knowing, ingenious, discerning, perspicacious, calculating, mindful, wide-awake, intelligent, judicious, hard-headed, discreet, tactful, diplomatic, percipient, perceptive, smart, alert.

SHREWISH, adj. Having the disposition of a shrew, ill-humored, quarrelsome, contentious, brawling, clamorous, petulant, peevish, vixenish, termagant, nagging, peppery, hot-tempered, discordant, overhasty, blatant, scolding, froward, ill-tempered, fractious, polemical, unpeaceful, troublesome, blustering, trouble-making, pugnacious, argumentative, loud-mouthed, volcanic, litigious, disputatious, exceptious, vociferous, obstreperous, refractory, contrary, turbulent, violent, perverse, bawling, noisy.

SHRIEK, n. 1. Loud, sharp, shrill cry or sound, scream, screech, yell, wail, squawk, trumpet, caterwaul, yelp, shrill, screak, ululation, bawl, outcry.

2. Loud, high sound of laughter, shout, burst, roar, peal, outburst, scream, cachinnation.

SHRIEK, v. Utter a loud, sharp, shrill sound, howl, shrill, scream, screech, squeal, yell, cry out, screak, bellow, roar, brawl, squawk, stridulate, vociferate, clamor, squall, bawl, yowl, hoot, trumpet, peal, yelp, shout.

SHRILL, adj. High-pitched, piercing, ear-splitting, ear-rending, ear-piercing, strident, acute, sharp, high, piping, thin, treble, stridulous, thrilling,

screeching, loud, vibratory, penetrating, penetrative, clamorous, blaring, clarion-voiced, stirring.

SHRINE, n. 1. Receptacle for sacred relics, reliquary, sacred tomb, coffer, casket, catafalque, mausoleum, cenotaph, monument, pyx (Eccles.), monstrance (Rom. Cath. Ch.), ciborium, sepulcher, memoria (Eccles.).

2. Structure or place consecrated to a saint or deity, place hallowed by its history or associations, sacred place, altar, sanctuary, martyry, church, chapel, cradle, adytum, tabernacle, holy ground, holy of holies, consecrated spot, monument, fane (Poetic), sacrarium (Eccles.), stupa (Buddhist), tope (Buddhist), birthplace (of a man, woman, nation, etc.).

SHRINK, v. 1. Become reduced in extent or compass, contract, wither, diminish, decrease, dwindle, shrivel, purse, pucker, collapse, shorten, lessen, draw together, waste, melt away, wear away, compress, cramp, consume, narrow, concentrate, crumble, constringe, tabefy, dry up, sear, constrict, ebb, decline, wane, sink, wizen.

2. Draw back (as in retreat or avoidance), recoil, demur, blench, quail, balk, retire, flee, fly, swerve, withdraw, wince, flinch, cringe, falter, boggle, hesitate, shun, startle, abominate, abhor, start back, scruple, funk (coll.), pull or hang back, feel disgust, react, hang fire, shirk, duck, shudder at, have an aversion to, disrelish, stick at, stickle, shy, blink, be unwilling, slink, skulk, cower, rebound, revolt, dodge.

SHRINKAGE, n. Act or fact of shrinking, amount or degree of shrinking, reduction, contraction, depreciation, diminution, decrease, diminishment, lessening, curtailment, abatement, attenuation, waste, loss, decrement, declension, consumption, erosion, wear and tear, decline, abridgment, astringency, constriction, condensation, compression, reflux, ebb, wane, defalcation, compaction, concentration, tabefaction, abbreviation, retrenchment, atrophy, emaciation, marasmus (Pathol.).

SHRIVE, v. 1. Impose penance on for sin, grant absolution to, hear the confession of, administer absolution, redeem, absolve, purge, penalize.

2. Confess to a priest to obtain absolution, go to or make confession, make amends, repent, atone, do or perform penance, confess, receive penance.

SHRIVEL, v. Contract and wrinkle, shrink, make or become impotent, wither, purse up, buckle, dry up, parch, scorch, burn, decrease, dwindle, decay, pucker, corrugate, desiccate, fade, waste, corrode, crumble, degenerate, deteriorate, dehydrate, sear, consume.

SHROUD, n. 1. Something which covers or conceals like a garment, cloak, mantle, pall, veil, blanket, covering, garment, disguise, cape, robe, screen, shield, mask, cloud, covert, guard, shade, hood, blind, canopy, wrap.

2. White cloth or sheet in which a corpse is wrapped for burial, cerecloth, cerement, pall, graveclothes, winding sheet.

SHROUD, v. Cover, wrap, clothe, cloak, protect, mask, veil, muffle, shelter, conceal, hide, shadow, envelop, overshadow, bury, screen, secrete, suppress, hush, overlay, couch, closet, dissemble, harbor, seclude, withhold, obstruct, eclipse, hush up, curtain, hood, disguise, camouflage, render invisible, keep in the shade, latentize, adumbrate, hugger-mugger.

SHRUB, n. Woody perennial plant (smaller than

a tree), bush, low tree, dwarf tree, scrub, coppet, fern, broom, furze.

SHRUBBERY, *n.* Thicket, boscage, brake, bracken, undergrowth, brushwood, underbrush, coppice, copse, brush.

SHRUG, *v.* Raise and contract the shoulders *(expressing indifference, disdain, etc.),* submit, succumb, yield, accede, resign, bear, endure, make the best of, forbear, suffer, acquiesce, not countenance, view with disfavor, shake the head, snap one's fingers, put up with, tolerate, abide, bear with, turn up the nose at, look askance at, disdain, contemn, scorn, be contemptuous, toss the head.

SHUCK, *n.* Husk, pod, outer covering *(as of corn, nuts, etc.),* shell, hull, coating, capsule, shard, bur *(Bot.),* case, casing, testa *(Bot.).*

SHUDDER, *n.* Convulsive movement of the body *(as from horror, fear or cold),* tremor, shake, quake, quaver, quiver, jerk, throb, shiver, didder, disquietude, agitation, flutter, fluster, pulsation, shaking, trembling, shuddering, twitch, throe, spasm, pang, paroxysm.

SHUDDER, *v.* Tremble with a sudden convulsive movement *(as from horror, fear or cold),* shake, shiver, quiver, quake, pulsate, chill, didder, trepidate, twitter, vibrate, vellicate, jerk, flutter, twitch, be agitated.

SHUFFLE, *n.* 1. Scraping movement, dragging gait, limp, hobble, scuttle, hitch, faltering, staggering, halt, pull, toddle.

2. Evasive trick, blind, guise, quibble, artifice, subterfuge, ambiguity, dodge, shift, quirk, cavil, cloak, feint, put-off, mask, ambages, elusion, sham, shunning, evasion, side step, pretext, retreat, subtlety, circumlocution, hairsplitting, begging the question, malingering, shirking, quiddity, jesuitism, quibbling, prevarication, circumvention.

SHUFFLE, *v.* 1. Walk without lifting the feet, walk with clumsy steps and a shambling gait, scrape, halt, lumber, lunge, shamble, scuff, drag, falter, flag, inch, lag, linger, hobble, limp, hitch, plod, scuttle, slouch, claudicate.

2. Get *(into, etc.)* in a clumsy manner, scramble, jerk, hitch, struggle, hustle, tumble.

3. Act in a shifting *or* evasive manner, employ deceitful pretenses, equivocate, defraud, cheat, quibble, prevaricate, palter, evade, get *(in, out of, etc.)* in an underhand *or* evasive manner, sophisticate, dodge, cavil, pettifog, fence, lie, shift, parry, trifle, elude, beg the question, shy, beat about the bush, throw off the scent, mislead, distort, pervert, draw a red herring across the path *or* trail, mince the truth, varnish, mystify, color, gloss over, split hairs, refine, subtilize.

4. Jumble together, confuse, mix in a disorderly heap, throw into disorder, derange, intermix, shift, tangle, muddle, mess, discompose, complicate, huddle, muss, clutter, botch, entangle, disarrange, displace, litter, strew about, upset, dishevel, scatter, lumber, turn topsy-turvy, heap, bunch, cram, disorganize, toss at random.

SHUN, *v.* Avoid, keep away from *(through dislike, caution, etc.),* keep clear of, elude, escape, evade, keep one's distance, circumvent, dodge, steer clear of *(coll.),* fight shy of, shy away from, put off, parry, shirk, shrink from, boycott, abhor, neglect, eschew, let alone, spurn, rebuff, snub, have no hand in, have no part of, have nothing to do with, double, disregard, turn away from, get around *(coll.),* cold-shoulder, keep (stand, hold) aloof.

SHUNT, *v.* Shove *or* turn aside *or* out of the way, shift, get rid of, transfer, sidetrack, by-pass, shelve, postpone, translocate, transpose, dislocate, displace, table, waive, suspend, defer, reserve, stand *or* lay over, divert, deviate, deflect, dislodge, pigeonhole, remove, switch.

SHUT, *v.* 1. Put *(a door, cover, etc.)* in position to close *or* obstruct, close, slam, snap, clasp, secure, fasten, latch, seal, clap.

2. *(Often fol. by* UP) Close the doors of, close up, put the lid on, lock *or* lock up, fold, cover, seal, button, zip, stanch, stop, occlude, block off, obstruct, bolt, dam, plug, bung, cork.

3. Confine, enclose, imprison, incarcerate, impound, immure, cage, lock up, coop up, incase, rope in, circumscribe, mew, choke off, curb, check, throttle, cloister, blockade, hinder, restrict, impede, hamper, surround, environ, retard, bound, encompass, encincture, fence in, delineate, picket, ensphere, gird, invest, circumpose, enwrap, envelop, embrace, belt, beleaguer, corral, hem in, intern, constrain, occlude, barricade, trap.

4. Bar, exclude, prohibit, preclude, close out, debar, hold back, choke off, reject, eliminate, relegate, remove, forbid, disallow, deny, interdict, embargo, ban, warn off, repel, decline, except, eject, expel, oust, ostracize, banish, dismiss, deport, exile.

5. *(With* DOWN) Close for a time *(as a factory),* stop, cease, discontinue, terminate, interrupt, quit, break off, suspend, silence, halt, leave off, knock off *(coll.).*

SHUT-IN, *adj.* Confined to the house, hospital, *etc.,* ailing, ill, convalescent, sick, indisposed, hospitalized, bedridden, invalided, laid up.

SHUTTER, *n.* Folding cover for a window, blind, shade, jalousie, Venetian blind.

SHUTTLE, *v.* Move quickly to and fro like a shuttle, alternate, pass and repass, come and go, seesaw, back and fill, shuttlecock, wigwag, zigzag.

SHY, *adj.* 1. Timid, easily frightened away, bashful, retiring, coy, diffident, reserved, strange, skittish, humble, shrinking, backward, timorous, afraid, scared, fearful, anxious, nervous, apprehensive, distant, sheepish, modest, unsocial, tremulous, constrained, cowardly, alarmed, startled, meek, verecund, shamefaced, demure, blushing, uncourageous.

2. Cautious, wary, chary, heedful, reluctant, loath, averse, adverse, evasive, careful, elusive, crafty, suspicious, demurring, grudging, renitent, unwilling, indisposed, opposed, disinclined, dissenting, slack, slow to, shrinking, cunning, shifty, gingerly, safe, distrustful, circumspect, guarded, on guard, stealthy, leery *(sl.),* precautious, politic, discreet, noncommittal, prudent.

3. Not bearing *or* breeding freely *(as plants or animals),* impotent, unfruitful, meager, barren, infertile, scant, scanty, skimpy, scarce, unplentiful, not abundant, infecund, issueless, unproductive, arid, unprolific, jejune, exhausted, spent, acarpous *(Bot.),* teemless *(Poetic).*

SHY, *n.* 1. Sudden start aside *(as in fear),* shock, rebound, flinch, wince, dodge, recoil, reaction, blink, springing *or* drawing back, blench, duck.

2. Quick sudden throw, fling, sling, cast, hurl, chuck, heave, pitch, shot.

SHY, *v.* 1. Start back *or* aside *(as in fear),* draw back, recoil, react, rebound, blink, blench, flinch, dodge, duck, wince, waver, falter, shrink, spring back, stickle, take alarm, boggle, retreat, demur, shift, evade, avoid, swerve, hesitate, cower, pale, scruple, stick at, get cold feet *(sl.)*.

2. Throw with a swift sudden movement, fling, jerk, cast, hurl, chuck, sling, pitch, flirt, toss, thrust, pelt, peg *(coll.)*, heave, let fly, cant, dart, fillip, bat, bowl, chunk, shoot, drive, project, propel, put *(a shot)*.

SIBILANT, *adj.* Hissing, sibilous, sibilatory, buzzing, wheezy.

SIBILATE, *v.* Hiss, utter *or* pronounce a hissing sound, buzz, wheeze, aspirate, lisp, fizz, whiz.

SIBYL, *n.* Prophetess, witch, fortuneteller, sorceress, crystal-gazer, divineress, pythoness, palmist, medium, Pythia *(Gk. Myth.)*, Cassandra *(Class. Legend)*.

SIBYLLINE, *adj.* Oracular, prophetic, predictive, sage, wise, sapient, vaticinal, knowing, magisterial, arbitrary, foretelling, Delphian, Delphic, foreknowing, fatidic, prognostic, pythonic, Dodonaean, vatic, presaging, significant, predictory, sibyllic, augural, divinatory, fatiloquent, haruspical, boding, suggestive, revelatory, apocalyptic, druidic, extispicious.

SICCATIVE, *adj.* Causing *or* promoting absorption of moisture, drying, desiccant, desiccative, desiccatory, exsiccative, exsiccant, evaporative, siccant, absorbent, withering, searing, parching.

SICK, *adj.* 1. Affected with any disorder of health, unwell, ill, ailing, indisposed, laid up, bedridden, confined, under the weather *(coll.)*, delicate, infirm, hurt, afflicted, injured, qualmish, valetudinary, suffering, valetudinarian, invalid, queasy, nauseated, poorly *(coll.)*, sickly *(coll.)*, seedy *(coll.)*.

2. Deeply affected with some feeling comparable to physical disorder *(as sorrow, longing, repugnance, weariness, etc.)*, surfeited, shocked, squeamish, repelled, sorrowful, heavy, satiated, fed up, uneasy, pining, languishing, weary, tired, offended, disturbed, discomposed, perturbed, heartbroken, heavy-laden, troubled, disquieted, crushed, stricken, woeful, miserable, wretched, nauseated, heavy, queasy, cut up *(coll.)*.

3. Not in proper condition, impaired, pale, wan, diseased, disordered, distempered, feeble, weak, unsound, unhealthy, morbid, on the wane *or* decline, waning, languid, crippled, hurt, injured, imperfect, useless, deteriorated, reduced, corrupt, flagging, drooping, lame, disabled, decrepit, vitiated, worn, broken, altered for the worse, contaminated, tainted, unsteady, infected, withered, wilted, wasted, marcescent *(Bot.)*, out of whack *(sl.)*, out of commission *(coll.)*.

SICKEN, *v.* 1. Become sick, fall sick *or* ill, ail, droop, pine, languish, weaken, decay, fall victim to disease, waste away, be stricken, wilt, fail, flag, lose strength.

2. Make sick, disease, vitiate, derange, infect, taint, contaminate, weaken, nauseate, decay, disorder, afflict, make qualmish, turn one's stomach, poison, impair, injure, enfeeble, wound, cripple, incapacitate, devitalize, debilitate.

3. Disgust, weary, revolt, offend, nauseate, spoil, satiate, surfeit, shock, repel, gnaw, corrode, jade, horrify, pall, gall, appall, tire, be unsavory, overdose, wring, rankle, convulse, turn the stomach, gorge, cloy, glut, upset, disturb.

SICKENING, *adj.* 1. Making sick, causing nausea, nauseous, nauseating, palling, sickish, poisonous,

qualmish, infectious, tainted, contaminated, sickly, unwholesome.

2. Causing disgust *or* loathing, distressing, disgusting, repulsive, revolting, distasteful, loathsome, fulsome, horrible, unsavory, hateful, execrable, obnoxious, noxious, nasty, noisome, abhorrent, mawkish, vile, bad, detestable, offensive, foul, nauseating, nauseous, contemptible, repugnant, repellent.

SICKLY, *adj.* 1. Of, connected with *or* arising from ill health, not strong, ailing, unhealthy, in poor health, feeble, languid, squeamish, drooping, flagging, anemic, chlorotic, diseased, weakly, morbid, infirm, languishing, faint, peaked, pale, sick, wan, unsound, invalid, miserable, delicate, puny, unwell, haggard, valetudinary, lackluster, cadaverous, decrepit, reduced to a skeleton, ashen, dull, lifeless, leaden, glassy, poorly *(coll.)*.

2. Causing sickness, nauseating, qualmish, *etc.* *(See* SICKENING, *adj.* 1, above.)

3. Weak, mawkish, faint, feeble, lifeless, dull, dead, bloodless, colorless, pale, silly, emotional, simpering, maudlin, anemic, namby-pamby, pallid, without distinction, wishy-washy, prosaic, indifferent, characterless, cold, apathetic, torpid, sluggish, nerveless, stolid, sinewless, undistinctive, uninspired, ineffective, unmoving, tepid, spiritless, ineffectual, flat, insipid, vapid, tame, dilute, thin, lacking in fervor, vague, drab, jejune, pithless.

SICKNESS, *n.* 1. Disease, illness, malady, nausea, disorder, ailment, infirmity, complaint, affliction, queasiness, qualmishness, pain, qualm, affection *(Pathol.)*, disability, infection, indisposition, morbidity.

2. State of being sick, ill health, illness, indisposition, weariness, pain, suffering, delicacy, decline, invalidism, impairment, attack, weakness, collapse, breakdown, infirmity, delicate health, loss of health, visitation, seizure, affection *(Pathol.)*, disability, prostration.

SIDE, *adj.* 1. Being at *or* on one side, collateral, flanking, lateral, skirting, fringe, marginal, border.

2. Coming from one side, directed toward one side, oblique, indirect, lateral, sideward, sideway, sideways, slant, sidelong, askance, askant, asquint, vagrant, stray, deviative.

3. Subordinate, resultant, lesser, lower, secondary, incidental, insignificant, less considerable, minor, second-rate, indirect, contingent, less important, by-, dependent, subsidiary, casual, related, allied, collateral, accessory, parenthetical.

SIDE, *n.* 1. One of the surfaces *or* lines bounding a thing, edge, border, flank, front, back, shore, top, hem, frame, bottom, exterior, verge, margin, bound, pale, curb, wall, limit, boundary, brow, brim, rim, brink, extremity, lip, perimeter, fringe, skirt, confine.

2. Lateral part of a thing, half, segment, quarter, section, region, position, direction, territory, sector, flitch *(of bacon)*, hand, division.

3. Aspect, phase, either of two surfaces *(of paper, cloth, etc.)*, view, slant, face, angle, direction, standpoint, light, hand, point of view, viewpoint.

4. Slope *(as of a hill)*, hillside, gradient, bank, ramp, climb, pitch, tilt, grade, incline, upgrade, downgrade, acclivity, declivity, rise, uprise, decline, glacis, fall, drop, dip, descent.

5. One of two *or* more parties concerned in a case, contest, *etc.*, part, position, faction, sect, cause, interest, affiliation, class, division, order, school, caste, body of partisans, coalition, set,

circle, clique, coterie, confederacy, alliance, league.

6. Line of descent, extraction, derivation, lineage, bloodline, genealogy, family tree, house, family, progeny, generation, stock, stirps, sept, strain, breed, filiation.

SIDEBOARD, *n.* Piece of furniture for holding articles of table service, cupboard, buffet, dresser, commode.

SIDE LIGHT, *n.* 1. Light coming from the side, aperture for light *(in the side of a building, ship, etc.)*, porthole, fanlight, transom, embrasure, afterglow, sunset glow, indirect illumination.

2. Incidental information, embellishment, aside, elaboration, enlightenment, episode, deviation, digression, dilation, expansion, appendix, discursus, expatiation, enlargement, amplification.

SIDELONG, *adv.* Sideling, laterally, edgeways, obliquely, sloping, sidewards, sidewise, on a slant, askant, indirectly, at an angle, askew.

SIDEREAL, *adj.* Of *or* pertaining to stars, astral, starry, stellar.

SIDESPLITTING, *adj.* Extremely funny, causing laughter, very comical, uproarious, very humorous, screamingly funny, killing *(coll.)*, too funny for words *(sl.)*, risible, laughable, farcical, ludicrous.

SIDE-STEP, *v.* Evade *(an issue, etc.)*, equivocate, avoid, dodge, shun, funk, ignore, steer clear of, close one's eyes to, duck *(coll.)*, run from, elude, shrink from, omit, leave undone.

SIDEWALK, *n.* Part of a road *or* street for pedestrians, *etc.*, boardwalk, footpath, promenade, mall, esplanade, almeda.

SIDEWAYS, *adv.* Laterally, sidewise, indirectly, at an angle, obliquely, sloping, on a slant, askant, askew, sidelong, sideling, edgeways, sideward, sidewards.

SIDLE, *v.* Move *or* walk sideways, sidelong, etc., walk crab-fashion, edge along, veer, skew *(coll.)*.

SIEGE, *n.* Act of besieging, besiegement, encompassment, surrounding, investment *(Mil.)*, blockade, beleaguerment, storm, storming, offense, onslaught, attack, cannonade, bombardment.

SIEGE, *v.* Lay siege to, beleaguer, try to take by storm, try to starve into submission, blockade, besiege, invest *(Mil.)*, surround, encompass, storm, attack, assault, bombard.

SIESTA, *n.* Rest or sleep *(usually during midday heat)*, snooze, nap, doze, midday rest, cat nap.

SIEVE, *n.* Strainer, sifter, bolter, screen, filter, riddle, colander, grate, grating, cribble.

SIEVE, *v.* Strain, sift, screen, refine, separate, bolt, riddle, search, winnow, filter, pan, rack.

SIFT, *v.* 1. Strain, bolt, filter, *etc. (See* SIEVE, *v. above.)*

2. Examine *(as evidence, facts, etc.)*, scrutinize, study, investigate, explore, analyze, winnow, test, probe, search, inspect, thresh, sound, put under the microscope, ransack, review, survey thoroughly, overhaul, weigh, fathom, rummage.

SIGH, *n.* Deep and audible breath, suspiration, sough, wail, moan, sob, whine, hiss.

SIGH, *v.* 1. Sough, wail, moan, suspire, breathe loudly, hiss, sob, whine.

2. *(With* FOR*)* Lament for, grieve for, weep for, bewail, fret over, sorrow for, mourn for, deplore, bemoan.

3. *(As the wind)* Moan, pine, rustle, pipe, wail, roar, sing, whistle, scream, shriek.

SIGHT, *n.* 1. View, spectacle, prospect, display, show, aspect, vision, scene, field, perspective, outlook, scope, exposure, vista, panorama, pageant.

2. Ability *or* power to see, vision, eyesight, perception, eye *or* eyes.

3. *(As within sight of)* Range of vision, field of vision, eyeshot, eyereach, gaze, scrutiny, inspection, glimpse, stare, look, survey, view, ken, glance.

4. Way of looking *or* appearing, appearance, aspect, mien, favor, guise, turn, expression, demeanor, condition, presence, air, countenance, revelation, ostent, complexion, cast, color, fashion, figure, shape, show, impression, front, effect, semblance, seeming, phase.

5. Device for aiming a rifle, *etc.*, sighthole, peep sight, open sight, telescopic sight, aiming pattern, bead.

6. Line of fire, bead, aim.

SIGHT, *v.* 1. Gain a glimpse of, see, glimpse, catch sight of, spy, perceive, spot, have one's eye fall upon.

2. Stare, see, watch, cock the eye, contemplate, spy, gaze, scrutinize, gape, study, peek, look, squint, scan, peer, survey, ogle, regard, peep, behold, observe, take stock, attend.

3. Take aim, align a rifle, aim a rifle, *etc.*, draw a bead on, aim at.

SIGHTLESS, *adj.* 1. Without power to see, without sight, blind, eyeless, unseeing, visionless, amaurotic *(Med.)*, stone-blind, blind as a bat.

2. Invisible, hidden to view, unseeable, nonapparent, unseen, imperceptible, unperceptible, indiscernible, unbeholdable, unapparent, unbeheld.

SIGHTSEEING, *n.* Act of seeing objects *or* places of interest, ramble, excursion, guided tour, peregrination, circuit, expedition, rubbernecking *(sl.)*, globetrotting *(coll.)*.

SIGHTSEER, *n.* One who visits places of interest, tourist, traveler, excursionist, spectator, bystander, observer, looker, rubberneck *(sl.)*, globetrotter *(coll.)*.

SIGN, *n.* 1. Token, indication, identification, signature, proof, mark, beacon, diagnostic, trait, feature, earmark, badge, denotation, characteristic, designation, index, signification, symptom, ensign, note, device, signal, semaphore, watchword, trademark, pointer, shibboleth, password, indicant, indicator, landmark, seamark, scepter, clue, cue, impress, stamp, brand, quality, blaze, key, lineament, peculiarity.

2. Conventional mark *or* figure, symbol, abbreviation, notation, emblem, cipher, figure, letter, initial, mark, character, ideograph, phonogram.

3. Motion intended to convey *or* express an idea, nod, shrug, beckon, touch, signal, gesticulation, gesture, glance, action, leer, wink, nudge, pantomime, dactylology, dactylography, countersign, grip, chironomy.

4. Inscribed board, space, *etc.*, for advertisement, information, *etc.*, post, signboard, nameplate, billboard, milestone, guidepost, shingle *(coll.)*.

5. Trace, vestige, evidence, trail, track, footprint, footstep, spoor, manifestation, path, hint, mark, wake, scent, print, telltale, suggestion, inference, cicatrix, scar, mark left behind, remains, relic, ichnite *(Paleontol.)*, clue, tinge, reminder, indication, token, whisper, reference, taste, touch.

6. Omen, portent, prodigy, wonder, auspice, foreboding, miracle, warning, presage, augury, foretoken, premonition, prognostic, presentiment, divination, boding, soothsay, foreshadowing, hand-

writing on the wall, forecast, foreknowledge, herald, vaticination, prophecy, prelude, hint, symptom, promise, prefigurement, prefiguration, implication, bodement.

SIGN, *v.* 1. Affix a signature to, endorse, ratify, subscribe to, countersign, pledge, put one's name to, initial, mark, stamp, character, letter, inscribe, acknowledge, confirm, accept, guarantee, corroborate, seal, approve, validate, verify, certify, accept, sanction, underwrite, undersign, set one's hand and seal to, visa, visé, O.K. *(coll.),* okay *(coll.).*

2. *(Fol. by* AWAY, *etc.)* Dispose of by affixing one's signature to, relinquish, release, bestow, sacrifice, yield, waive, renounce, wash one's hands of, forgo, cede, let go, quit one's hold on, sell off, turn over, make over, deliver over, give away, part with, abandon, surrender, give up.

3. Engage by written agreement, hire, employ, contract, enlist, contract with, take into one's employ, take into service, covenant.

4. Direct by a sign, indicate, betoken, signify, signalize, mean, convey, portend, infer, intimate, indicate, imply, symbolize, stand for, typify, purport, suggest, hint, argue, bespeak, augur, represent, forebode, omen, foretell, herald, presage, point to, forerun, shadow forth, promise, prefigure, preindicate, foreshadow, foreshow, predict, prognosticate, import.

5. Communicate by a sign, signal, gesture, gesticulate, nod, beckon, wink, nudge, shrug, motion, raise *or* hold up the finger *or* hand, wave, break out a flag, show one's colors, hail, salute, dip, unfurl (hoist, hang out) a banner, *etc.*

SIGNAL, *adj.* 1. Serving as a sign, beacon, indicative, directing, indicatory, pointing, directive, pilot, guiding.

2. Notable, conspicuous, great, grand, considerable, eminent, extraordinary, memorable, remarkable, unforgettable, substantial, outstanding, momentous, noted, splendid, eventful, distinguished, important, noticeable, brilliant, unmistakable, salient, noteworthy, intense, strong, stirring, commanding, rare, imposing, exceptional, significant, impressive, noble, august, worthy of notice *or* remark, prominent, marked, consequential.

SIGNAL, *n.* 1. Anything serving to warn, direct, command, *etc.,* token, mark, indication, sign, light, flag, guide, beacon, motion, cue, cry, catchword, ensign, alarm, countersign, call, gesture, semaphore, watchword, whistle, flare, balefire, landmark, omen, warning, monitor, pilot light *or* lamp, lighthouse, skyrocket, rocket, bell, horn, symptom, wigwag *(Naval, etc.),* seamark.

2. Thing agreed upon *or* understood as the occasion for concerted action, exciting cause, cue, nod, sign, device, motion, gesture, mark of readiness, high sign *(coll.).*

SIGNAL, *v.* Make a signal to, make known by a signal, make communication by signals, speak, hail, gesture, dip, salute, wave, unfurl an ensign, hoist *or* hang out a banner, *etc.,* break out a flag, show one's colors, give the cue, raise *or* hold up the finger *or* hand, motion, beckon, wigwag *(Naval, etc.).*

SIGNALIZE, *v.* Make notable, point out, indicate particularly, honor, consecrate, commemorate, mark out, celebrate, distinguish, exalt, dignify, solemnize, immortalize, preserve in memory, mark, perpetuate, hallow, memorialize, salute, keep, observe, be mindful of, recognize, laud, sing

the praises of, make public notice of, make honorable mention of, grant a testimonial to, praise, commend, glorify, bestow honor upon, ennoble, aggrandize, extol, lionize, elevate, acclaim, pay tribute to, deify, eulogize, applaud, panegyrize, enthrone, revere.

SIGNATURE, *n.* 1. Person's name, stamp, mark representing a name, sign, identification, autograph, hand, cross, frank, John Hancock *(coll.),* sign manual.

2. Act of signing a document, endorsement, signation, acknowledgment, ratification, confirmation, approval, authority, authentication, verification, validation, affirmation, subscription, acceptance, certification, O.K. *(coll.).*

SIGNER, *n.* One who signs his name indicating agreement, endorser, participant, participator, joiner, cosigner, sponsor, cosponsor, signatory, cosignatory.

SIGNET, *n.* Small seal *(as in a finger ring),* official seal, stamp, privy seal, sigil, cachet.

SIGNIFICANCE, *n.* 1. Importance, consequence, force, emphasis, impressiveness, salience, eminence, exaltation, elevation, portent, moment, weight, value, figure, name, mark, interest, notability, nobility, note, grandeur, dignity, majesty, sublimity, concern, materiality, distinction, consideration, gravity, greatness, solemnity, urgency, seriousness, insistence, prestige, pre-eminence, paramountcy, primacy, superiority, worth, virtue, merit, excellence, prominence.

2. Meaning, import, matter, tenor, drift, moral, sense, allusion, purport, implication, import, coloring, bearing, expression, signification, force, effect, intent, intention, aim, explanation, definition, suggestion, purpose, object, acceptation.

SIGNIFICANT, *adj.* 1. Important, of consequence, striking, vital, grave, weighty, momentous, remarkable, material, prominent, notable, outstanding, forcible, portentous, emphatic, telling, celebrated, famous, considerable, substantial, distinguished, principal, foremost, chief, critical, memorable, meaningful, exceptional, renowned, noteworthy, consequential, salient, glaring, paramount, eventful, grand, august, stirring, primary, eminent, signal, essential, impressive, great.

2. Expressing a meaning, denoting, indicative of, betokening, connoting, implying, meaningful, signifying, significative, allusive, suggestive, expressive, exhibitive, demonstrative, representative, symbolic, characteristic, distinguishing, diacritical, distinctive, emblematic, symptomatic, inferential, implicative, significatory.

3. Having a special *or* covert meaning, significative, suggestive, expressive, bodeful, threatening, secret, hidden, understood, insinuating, insinuative, oracular, fraught with meaning, lowering, minacious, minatory, sly, canny, sinister, knowing, pregnant, teeming with meaning, subtle, presageful, boding, ominous, prognostic, artful, wily, clandestine, surreptitious, furtive, fateful, fearful, menacing, premonitive, premonitory, prophetic, fatidic, warning, private, foreboding.

SIGNIFICATION, *n.* 1. Meaning, sense, import, *etc.* (*See* SIGNIFICANCE, *n.* 2, *above.*)

2. Act *or* fact of signifying, indication, conveyance of meaning, denotation, suggestion, manifestation, inference, designation, demonstration, implication, connotation, symbolization, evincement, exposition, presentation, showing, materialization, prediction.

SIGNIFICATIVE, *adj.* Serving to signify, having a signification, significant, suggestive, *etc.* (*See* SIGNIFICANT, *adj.* 2, *above.*)

SIGNIFY, *v.* 1. Make known by signs, speech *or* action, express, communicate, declare, proclaim, impart, display, evidence, evince, manifest, designate, specify, indicate, point out, attest, inform, tell, reveal, disclose, utter, give notice of, announce, nod, gesticulate, show, state, testify, exhibit, represent, set forth, demonstrate, mark, expose.
2. Be a sign of, mean, portend, denote, imply, purport, argue, hint, bespeak, import, augur, suggest, omen, forebode, represent, presage, foretell, herald, point to, forerun, shadow forth, prefigure, promise, preindicate, foreshadow, foreshow, predict, prognosticate, typify, stand for, symbolize, betoken, indicate, intimate.
3. Import, be of importance *or* consequence, matter, weigh heavily, carry weight, deserve *or* merit notice *or* regard, cut a figure, count, tell, make *or* cut a figure, make a splash, shine, figure, excel, predominate, preponderate, prevail, warrant consideration, leave one's *or* its mark.

SILENCE, *interj.* Hush!, quiet!, sh!, hist!, be still!, be silent!, soft!, whist!, hold your tongue!, mum!, shut up! (*coll.*), not another word!, pipe down! (*coll.*), be quiet!

SILENCE, *n.* 1. Absence of sound *or* noise, stillness, soundlessness, noiselessness, hush, quiet, lull, peace, calm, quietude, quiescence, quietness, repose, inaudibility, inactivity, placidity, serenity, tranquillity, dead, q.t. (*sl.*), rest (*Mus.*).
2. State *or* fact of being silent, muteness, speechlessness, dumbness, reticence, taciturnity, mutescence, mutism, dysphonia, reservation, reserve, absence *or* want of voice, pauciloquy, laconism, laconicism, uncommunicativeness, aphonia (*Pathol.*).
3. Omission of mention, oblivion, secrecy, secretiveness, reserve, reservation, suppression, privacy, stealth, repression, furtiveness, evasion, obscurity, dormancy, latency, delitescence, concealment, darkness, adumbration, closeness, inexpression, passivity, inactivity, abeyance.

SILENCE, *v.* 1. Still, put *or* bring to silence, hush, quiet, deaden, stifle, soft-pedal, muffle, soothe, render mute, stop one's mouth, drown the voice, cut one short, deafen, choke off, throttle, mute, stop, suppress, muzzle, gag.
2. Restrain from the exercise *or* function of instruction (*esp. preaching*), suppress, check, throttle, choke off, crush, extinguish, put down, depose, excommunicate, ostracize, make ineffectual, tie the hands of, tie hand and foot, handcuff, hamstring, vanquish, overcome, quell, subdue, inhibit, repress, cripple, muzzle, paralyze, prostrate, invalidate, disqualify, incapacitate, render powerless, deprive of power, disarm, disable.
3. Put to rest (*doubts, etc.*), quiet, allay, calm, appease, reconcile, quell, still, pacify, settle, soothe, lull, put an end to, relieve, curb, check, lessen, slacken, slake, palliate, smooth, abate, assuage, temper, moderate, soften, compose, tranquilize, dulcify, mitigate, modulate, stay, bring under control, blunt, obtund, ease, alleviate, dull, lighten, deaden.
4. Put to rest *or* into abeyance, confute, refute, expose, show up, show *or* prove the fallacy of, explode, dismiss, defeat, overthrow, overwhelm, confound, overcome, vanquish, rebut, negative, disprove, invalidate, crush, quash, put down, bring

to a standstill, worst, master, rout, dumfound, strike dumb, get the upper hand of, finish, settle, conquer, shatter, nullify, quell, subdue, override, upset, nonplus, trump, checkmate, not leave a leg to stand on, cut the ground from under, parry, squash (*coll.*), squelch (*coll.*).

SILENT, *adj.* 1. Making no sound, inaudible, still, quiet, calm, noiseless, soundless, hushed, toneless, echoless, deathlike, solemn, muffled, stifled, muted, dampened, stilly (*Poetic*).
2. Taciturn, reticent, uncommunicative, inarticulate, indisposed to talk, unconversable, close, curt, laconic, close-mouthed, pauciloquent, sparing of words, sententious, not given to conversation, brief, concise.
3. Refraining from speech, speechless, voiceless, wordless, tongueless, unvocal, mum, tongue-tied, inarticulate, nonvocal, dumb, mute.
4. Tacit, implied, unspoken, meant, inferred, understood, implicit, indirect, unexpressed, unsaid, unpronounced, untalked-of, unwritten, unrevealed, unmentioned, hidden, concealed, buried, obscure, clouded, veiled, screened, latent, disguised, undeclared, unuttered, unarticulated, intimated, insinuated, hinted, suggested, unworded, unbreathed, untold, unsung, unpublished.
5. Omitting mention of something, uninformative, secretive, reserved, uncommunicative, elusive, evasive, reticent, hugger-mugger, cryptic, arcane, underhand, underground, mysterious, obreptitious, furtive.
6. Inactive, quiescent, peaceful, at rest, reposing, reposeful, resting, sleeping, static, passive, abeyant, suspended, slumbering, smoldering, idle, dead, lifeless, stagnant, inert, sedentary, becalmed, unstirring, unmoved, calm, placid, tranquil, dormant, undisturbed.
7. Not sounded *or* pronounced, mutescent, mute, voiceless, unvocalized, nonintoned, inaudible, unpronounced, surd (*Phonet.*), aphonic (*Phonet.*), aphonous (*Phonet.*).

SILHOUETTE, *n.* Outline, dark image outlined against a lighter background, contour, form, shadowgram, shadowgraph, profile, shadow figure, skiagram, skiagraph.

SILKEN, *adj.* Soft, velvety, velvetlike, satiny, velutinous, silky, smooth, silklike, sericeous, lustrous, shiny, sheeny.

SILK-STOCKING, *n.* Aristocrat, patrician, blueblood, noble, nobleman, optimate, lord, peer, gentleman, magnate, grandee, dignitary, squire, swell, coxcomb, exquisite, beau, dude, buck, spark, blade, fashion plate.

SILL, *n.* 1. Lower part of a frame (*esp. of windows*), ledge.
2. Threshold, horizontal support, beam, door sill, socle.

SILLY, *adj.* 1. Stupid, weak-minded, foolheaded, simple, green, unwise, ill-advised, inane, foolish, undiscriminating, indiscreet, tactless, ill-judged, childish, witless, brainless, absent-minded, muddleheaded, rantipole, empty-skulled, featherbrained, irresponsible, mercurial, woolgathering, frothy, bemused, empty-headed, bird-witted, harebrained, light-minded, simple-minded, giddy-brained, giddy-pated, erratic, rattleheaded, rattlebrained, crazy (*coll.*), unstable, frivolous, unwary, heedless, foolhardy, thoughtless, reckless, giddy, harum-scarum (*coll.*).
2. Without reason, sense, *etc.* (*as an action*), foolish, farcical, aimless, vapid, pointless, unwise, ill-judged, absurd, ridiculous, unreasonable, pre-

posterous, nonsensical, senseless, ludicrous, meaningless, mad, crazy *(coll.)*, purposeless, irrelevant, inappropriate, haphazard, driftless, inconsequential, unconnected, groundless, incongruous.

SILT, *n.* Sediment, deposit, alluvium, mud, gravel, detritus, sand, wash, slime, sludge, ooze, drift, precipitation, loess, diluvium, dregs, settlement, moraine *(of a glacier)*.

SILVER, *n.* Money, hard money, specie, change, piece, coin, hard cash, chinker *(sl.)*, jingler *(sl.)*, buttons *(sl.)*.

SILVER-TONGUED, *adj.* Golden- *or* silver-mouthed, mellifluous, Demosthenean, fluent, forceful, graceful, inspired, Ciceronian, Tullian, sublime, grandiloquent, ringing, eloquent, altiloquent, impassioned, declamatory, oratorical, rhetorical.

SILVERY, *adj.* 1. Of the color of silver, glittering, brilliant, shining, polished, bright, glistening, gleaming, sheeny, lustrous, lambent, shimmering, coruscating, glossy, flashing, sparkling, refulgent, nitid, argent, burnished, fulgid, fulgurant, fulgent, rutilant, orient.

2. *(Of music, sound, etc.)* Mellifluous, euphonious, dulcet, soft, melodious, musical, sweet, rich, full, resonant, sonorous.

SIMIAN, *adj.* Of *or* pertaining to apes *or* monkeys, apelike, monkeylike, simious, quadrumanous.

SIMIAN, *n.* Ape, monkey, anthropoid, quadrumane, gorilla, mandrill, primate, baboon, chimpanzee, orang-utan, lemur, marmoset.

SIMILAR, *adj.* Nearly alike, alike, connatural, resembling, much the same, correspondent, corresponding, comparable, conformable, analogous, parallel, cognate, equivalent, like, kindred, allied, akin, agreeing, congeneric, consanguineous.

SIMILARITY, *n.* Resemblance, similitude, consimilarity, agreement, comparability, parallelism, equivalence, conformability, correspondence, comparison, likeness, semblance, connaturalness, approximation, accordance, congruity, analogy, homogeneity, homoiousia, concordance.

SIMILE, *n.* Similitude, comparison, analogy, parallel, figure of speech.

SIMILITUDE, *n.* 1. Resemblance, likeness, *etc.* *(See* SIMILARITY, *n. above.)*

2. Simile, parallel, *etc.* *(See* SIMILE, *n. above.)*

3. Figurative treatment of a story, allegory, parable, fable, apologue, myth.

4. Representation, image, counterpart, depiction, copy, picture, icon, effigy, drawing, reproduction, adumbration, reflection, reflex, echo, shadow, statue, tableau, snapshot, likeness, photograph, fair copy, faithful copy, model, replica, tracing, delineation, portrayal, profile, illustration, facsimile, transfer, print, duplicate, sketch, portrait, cast, study, simulacrum.

SIMMER, *v.* 1. Be on the point of boiling, boil gently, seethe, stew, bubble, burble *(coll.)*, ebullate, gurgle.

2. Be agitated, be angry, boil inwardly, chafe, fume, languish, burst with anger, seethe, fret, burn, sizzle, foam, boil.

SIMON-PURE, *adj.* Genuine, real, authentic, bona fide, unadulterated, not spurious *or* false, unalloyed, pure, faithful, true, veritable, actual, true to claims, untainted, undiluted, valid, full, sterling, unvarnished, undefiled.

SIMPER, *v.* Smile, grin *or* laugh affectedly, smirk, titter, snigger, snicker, giggle, tee-hee *(coll.)*.

SIMPLE, *adj.* 1. Single, elementary, uncombined, uncompounded, unmixed, pure, unalloyed, bare, sole, alone, unblended, simplex.

2. Rudimentary, basic, elemental, incipient, elementary, fundamental, introductory, first, primary, embryonic, inaugural, inchoate, beginning.

3. Not difficult, not elaborate, uninvolved, uncomplicated, wieldy, submissive, easy, soft *(coll.)*, manageable, facile, unexacting, smooth, pliant, ductile.

4. Free of duplicity, straightforward, reliable, sound, straight, dependable, square, uncorrupted, true, honest, true to one's word, undissembling, decent, fair, upright, unperjured, unbought, uninfluenced, true-dealing, righteous, equitable.

5. Open, ingenuous, sincere, artless, innocent, guileless, unaffected, direct, incapable of deceit, childlike, wholesome, simple-hearted, aboveboard, undisguised, unsophisticated, blunt, downright, straightforward, plain-spoken, trustful, undissimulating, undissembling, rustic, plain.

6. Unadorned, unarrayed, chaste, Attic, artless, unaffected, plain, natural, unsophisticated, untrimmed, severe, undecked, pure, undecorated, unembellished, inornate, restrained.

7. Without special pretensions, modest, workday, household, plebeian, prosaic, homely, informal, everyday, prosy, ordinary, garden, commonplace, common, insignificant, lesser, characterless, mediocre, humble, unassuming, obscure, bourgeois, undistinguished, minor, subordinate, matter-of-fact.

8. Simple-minded, witless, green, unwise, rattleheaded, foolheaded, ill-advised, childish, brainless, muddle-headed, indiscreet, tactless, absent-minded, rantipole, empty-skulled, silly, featherbrained, irresponsible, mercurial, woolgathering, bemused, light-minded, harebrained, crazy *(coll.)*, frivolous, dumb *(coll.)*, numskull, stupid, insulse, sluggish, sottish, crass, hebetate, thick-skulled, purblind, simpletonian, wanting, lunk-headed *(coll.)*, boneheaded, chowder-headed *(coll.)*, pigheaded, thick-witted, weak-minded, feeble-minded, fatheaded *(coll.)*, beef-headed, addlebrained, dopey *(sl.)*, imbecile, idiotic, moronic, lacking, weak in the upper story, vacant, vacuous, doltish, obtuse, dense, dullard, bovine.

SIMPLETON, *n.* Dolt, blockhead, clod, clodpoll, dunderhead, dunce, ignoramus, dullard, numskull, blunderhead, jackass, oaf, clodpate, ninny, fool, nincompoop, dunce, ninnyhammer, jay, booby, beetlehead, babbler, witling, moron, idiot, imbecile, addlebrain, scatterbrain, giddybrain, dotard *(of the aged)*, zany, half-wit, clown, coot *(coll.)*, mooncalf, thickskull, woodenhead, loon, pigsconce, loggerhead, ass, goose, donkey, clown, jerk *(sl.)*, cabbagehead *(coll.)*, shallowbrain, simkin.

SIMPLICITY, *n.* 1. Clearness, lucidity, cognizability, plainness, limpidity, accuracy, straightforwardness, openness, intelligibility, legibility, distinctness, prominence, explicability, clarity, penetrability, manifestness, obviousness, directness, conspicuousness, perceptibility, overtness, decipherability, palpability, unmistakability, evincement, perspicuity, transpicuity, precision, transparency, explicitness, salience, luminosity.

2. Purity of line, cleanliness of design, classic simplicity, lucidity, clarity, plainness, lack of embellishment, chasteness, Atticism, severity, restraint, unadornment.

SIMPLIFY, *v.* Make easier *or* more simple, uncomplicate, unravel, clarify, disentangle, unfold, clear up, disintegrate, untwist.

SIMULACRE, *n.* Image, representation, copy, depiction, sketch, portrait, facsimile, portrayal, delineation, replica, model, likeness, reproduction, drawing, effigy, icon, picture, counterpart, adumbration, similitude, echo, shadow, statue, tableau, snapshot, photograph, cast, study.

SIMULATE, *v.* Feign, be deceptive, affect, assume, put on, fake, act, pose, represent, pretend, imitate, counterfeit, ape, make believe, fabricate, play, falsify.

SIMULTANEOUS, *adj.* Occurring at the same time, concomitant, concurrent, accompanying, coincident, contemporaneous, cotemporary, cotemporaneous, coinstantaneous, contemporary, synchronous, synchronal, synchronic, synchronical.

SIN, *n.* 1. Act of transgression, offense, evil deed, infraction, sacrilege, transgression, misdemeanor, misdeed, impiety, contravention, blasphemy, infringement, profanity, vice, crime, delinquency, violation, desecration, felony, malfeasance, wickedness, breach, wrong, peccancy.

2. Condition of sinfulness, crime, vice, debauchery, wrong, wrongdoing, reprobacy, guilt, corruption, evil, peccancy, degradation, badness, profligacy, turpitude, villainy, delinquency, immorality, sinfulness, iniquity, misconduct.

SINCE, *adv.* 1. (*Often preceded by* EVER) From then till now, between a particular past time and the present, subsequently, after, from, henceforth from, later, henceforward from, whereupon, upon which, whereat, thereupon, afterwards, thereafter, hereon, hereupon.

2. Ago, before this, formerly, earlier, previously, back, hitherto, heretofore, in the past, ere now, once, aforetime.

SINCE, *conj.* 1. In the period following the time when, continuously from *or* counting from the time when, subsequently, after, from, henceforth from, later than, henceforward, upon, subsequent to, following upon.

2. Because, inasmuch as, by reason of, as, considering, in that, in *or* under the circumstances *or* conditions, on account of, accordingly, seeing that, forasmuch as, for this reason, such being the case, as matters stand, owing to, thanks to, therefore, whereas, consequently, hence, taking into account that, in consideration of, in view of the fact that, as the wind blows, as times go, as things go, that being so.

SINCE, *prep.* Continuously from, counting from, between a past time (event, *etc.*) and the present, after, subsequently to, from the time of, from, henceforth from, later than, henceforward from, hereupon, hereon, thereafter, thereupon, therefrom, afterwards, whereat, whereupon, dating from.

SINCERE, *adj.* Free from any element of deceit, dissimulation *or* duplicity, genuine, true, real, unvarnished, honest, natural, deceitless, undeceitful, straightforward, unaffected, inartificial, candid, ingenuous, open, frank, artless, wholehearted, aboveboard, heartfelt, veracious, cordial, innocent, just, serious, fervent, earnest, blunt, trustworthy, stanch, single-hearted, conscientious, direct, simple, straight, plain, guileless, truthful, single, outspoken, undissembling, unreserved, unsophisticated, undisguised, uncorrupted, unclouded, unfeigning, forthright, pure, simple-hearted,

childlike, bona fide, clean-cut, open-hearted, unflattering, plain-spoken.

SINCERITY, *n.* Freedom from deceit, dissimulation *or* duplicity, honesty, ingenuousness, candor, probity, frankness, truthfulness, genuineness, simplicity, directness, honor, veracity, uprightness, fidelity, artlessness, guilelessness, unaffectedness, earnestness, straightforwardness, integrity, plaindealing, cordiality, innocence, plain speaking, unreserve, openness, purity, bonhomie, inartificiality, unsophistication, forthrightness.

SINECURE, *n.* Office requiring little *or* no work (*esp. one yielding profitable returns*), snap (*sl.*), soft spot (*coll.*), child's play, cinch (*sl.*), gravy (*sl.*), picnic (*sl.*).

SINEW, *n.* That which supplies strength, vigor, power, might, force, thews, vitality, lustiness, dynamic, energy, stoutness, stamina, robustness, potence, grit, pith, brawn, dint, nerve, strong arm, firmness, guts (*sl.*), steam (*coll.*), beef (*coll.*), puissance (*Poetic*), brawniness, muscle, pithiness.

SINEWY, *adj.* 1. Having strong sinews, strong, wiry, energetic, robust, powerful, brawny, muscular, herculean, sturdy, able-bodied, stalwart, strapping, athletic, firm, vigorous, mighty, potent, forceful, lusty, hardy, hard, rugged, hale, stout, armipotent, hefty (*coll.*), doughty (*humorous*), beefy (*coll.*), Atlantean, adamantine.

2. Vigorous (*as language, style, etc.*), forcible, biting, mordant, trenchant, stringent, strenuous, emphatic, powerful, forceful, strong, incisive, vivid, keen, intense, acute, pointed, marked, dynamic.

3. Like a sinew, tough, stringy, fibrous, fibroid, filamentous, filamentary, tensile, membranous, resilient, springy, elastic, thready, threadlike, ropy, wiry.

SINFUL, *adj.* Evil, wicked, iniquitous, depraved, transgressive, peccant, immoral, wrong, bad, unrighteous, guilty, ungodly, vile, unchristian, infamous, sinister, devious, despicable, blamable, culpable, profligate, villainous, unclean, errant, corrupt, profane, unholy, criminal, mischievous, impious, nefarious, abandoned, accursed, reprobate, dissolute, degenerate, erring, recreant, wayward, wanton, defiled, damned, transgressing, peccable, heinous, vicious, flagitious, shameless.

SING, *v.* 1. Utter words with musical modulations of the voice, execute a song, produce melodious sounds, carol, chant, troll, warble, lilt, croon, pipe, descant, intone, quaver, hum, hymn, singsong, solmizate, sol-fa, serenade, ballad, minstrel, lullaby, flute, trill, melodize, choir, chirp, yodel, vocalize, cantillate, tremolo, chirrup, psalmodize, roulade (*Mus.*).

2. Compose verse, tell of something in verse, poetize, versify, rhyme, rhapsodize, poeticize, poesy.

3. Give out a continuous ringing, whistling, murmuring, *etc.*, babble, whistle, hum, whisper, ripple, pipe, trill, howl, wail, breathe, scream, sough, sigh, murmur.

4. Proclaim enthusiastically, praise, make immortal, jubilate, rejoice, celebrate, paean, honor, glorify, dignify, glory, speak highly of, sound the praises of, laud, acclaim, signalize, exult, carol, bless, triumph, rhapsodize, idealize, cry for joy, cheer, blazon, lilt, commend, extol, panegyrize, aggrandize, exalt, toast, raise, lionize, elevate, salute, eulogize, cheer, immortalize, belaud, ennoble.

SINGE, *v.* Burn superficially, subject to flame in order to remove hair, blister, brand, torrefy, grill, sear, scorch, parch, cauterize.

SINGER, *n.* 1. One who sings, songster, melodist, vocalist, diva, musician, warbler, crooner, precentor, cantor, caroler, chorister, soloist, descanter, hymner, songbird, chantress, chanteuse, cantatrice, prima donna, psalmodist, lyrist, rhapsodist, orpheonist, wren, thrush, nightingale, philomel, lark.

2. Poet, bard, minstrel *(Poetic)*, jongleur *(Hist.)*, troubadour *(Hist.)*, gleeman *(Hist.)*, Meistersinger *(Hist.)*, minnesinger *(Hist.)*.

SINGLE, *adj.* 1. One only, separate, individual, singular, sole, azygous *(Bot.)*, whole, entire, complete, independent.

2. Alone, solitary, only, unique, lone, singular, isolated, secluded, exclusive, lonely, select, detached, separate, unaccompanied, unrepeated, odd, apart, disjoined, disconnected, distinct, unsimilar, disparate, unconnected.

3. Unmarried, bachelor, unwedded, celibate, virgin, spouseless, wifeless, husbandless, maidenly, old maid, spinster, virginal, mateless, companionless.

4. Of one against one *(as combat or fight)*, single-handed, unaided, by oneself, acting *or* working alone, unaccompanied, lone, unsupported, unassisted.

5. Sincere, honest, single-hearted, single-minded, loyal, stanch, firm, unfailing, resolute, true, constant, devoted, faithful, simple, frank, steady, artless, ingenuous, true-hearted, true-blue, steadfast, unbiased, undeviating, unswerving, straight, straightforward, aboveboard, wholehearted, unaffected, inartificial, candid, open, deceitless, genuine, direct, simple, open-hearted, unflattering, plain-spoken, clean-cut, bona fide, unfeigning, forthright, pure, unclouded, simple-hearted, unsophisticated, undisguised, uncorrupted, undissembling, unreserved, truthful, guileless, plain, conscientious, trustworthy, undeceitful.

6. Consisting of one part, element *or* member, simple, uncomplicated, uncomplex, uncombined, uncompounded, unmixed, plain, pure, uniform, homogeneous, of a part, elementary, unalloyed, bare, unblended, simplex.

SINGLE, *v.* *(Usually fol. by* OUT) Choose, pick out from others, select, make choice of, decide on, draw, like, will, take, fancy, prefer, assign, fix upon, appoint, opt, accept, embrace, elect, cull, co-opt, co-optate, adopt, set apart, excerpt, extract, settle on, segregate, glean, winnow, separate out, favor, incline toward.

SINGLY, *adv.* 1. Apart from others, separately, of *or* by itself, alone, simply, solely, purely, only, exclusively, particularly, specially, apart, individually.

2. One at a time, in succession, one by one, in order, successively, severally.

3. Single-handed, alone, easily, *etc.* *(See* SINGLE, *adj.* 4, *above.)*

SINGSONG, *adj.* Monotonous in rhythm, uniform in tone, ding-dong, even, regular, tiresome, humdrum, jogtrot, unvaried, unvarying, measured, repetitious, wearisome, tedious, rhythmical, metrical.

SINGULAR, *adj.* 1. Extraordinary, remarkable, unprecedented, particular, rare, exceptional, unexampled, eminent, unparalleled, rarely equaled, noteworthy, wonderful, marvelous, peerless, su-

perior, matchless, prodigious, preternatural, supreme, supernatural, inestimable, choice, select, invaluable.

2. Unusual, uncommon, curious, odd, strange, queer, bizarre, surprising, fanciful, freakish, unconventional, unheard-of, quaint, out-of-the-way, peculiar, unwonted, inusitate, whimsical, aberrant, abnormal, out-of-the-ordinary, anomalous, unnatural, out of *or* off the beaten track, unaccountable, unfamiliar, uncustomary, outré.

3. Being the only one of the kind, unique, single, alone, special, lone, select, lonely, detached, unparalleled, unconnected, several, respective, specific, exclusive, isolated, solitary, separate, individual, sole, particular, odd, distinct, apart, unrepeated, unsimilar, disparate.

SINGULARITY, *n.* 1. State, fact *or* quality of being singular, uncommonness, rarity, oddness, rareness, freakishness, anomaly, irregularity, abnormality, strangeness, aberration, curiosity, deviation, eccentricity, queerness, oddity, outlandishness, exceptionalness, unnaturalness, erraticism, individuality, capriciousness, uniqueness, unusualness.

2. Something singular, peculiarity, individuality, trait, characteristic, oddity, idiosyncrasy, idiocrasy, animus, propensity, stamp, badge, idiom, style, warp, aberration, anomaly, mode, deviation, cast, quip, quirk, abnormality, rarity, twist, trick, kink, eccentricity, crotchet, feature, property, differentia, lineament, earmark, quality, mannerism, whim, caprice, flight of fancy.

SINISTER, *adj.* 1. Threatening *or* portending evil, ominous, sinistrous, portentous, inauspicious, unpropitious, menacing, ill-starred, dangerous, minatory, perilous, fell, direful, evil-starred, doomed, ill-fated, impending, minacious, premonitory, unpromising, disastrous, unlucky, hopeless, bad, fearful, unblest, luckless, clouded, hapless, unprosperous, planet-struck, dire, alarming, fateful, ill-boding, jinxed *(coll.)*, Jonahed, lowering, frightening, fear-inspiring, disquieting, disturbing, hoodooed *(coll.)*, comminatory, dismaying.

2. Bad, evil, base, sinful, dishonest, disingenuous, reprehensible, horrible, wicked, heinous, nefarious, infamous, villainous, peccant, rank, criminal, foul, despicable, cursed, damnable, infernal, devilish, diabolical, accursed, detestable, vile, abominable, odious, hellish, malignant, rascally, corrupt, lawless, perfidious, crooked, venal, felonious, treacherous, dark, crafty, insidious, Machiavellian, malign, ill-contrived, evil-affected, evil-favored, evil-fashioned, evil-eyed, malevolent, maleficent.

3. *(Fol. by* TO) Unfortunate, unfavorable, disastrous, adverse, deleterious, hurtful, harmful, ill, baleful, injurious, untoward, pestilential, unlucky, contrary, baneful, dire, noxious, conflicting, poisonous, deadly, pernicious, mischievous, unpropitious, detrimental, malignant, malign, fatal, lethal, corrupting, damaging, ruinous, destructive, calamitous, prejudicial.

4. Of *or* on the left side, left, sinistral, sinistrous, left-hand, left-handed, sinistrorse, sinistrogyrate, sinistromanual, sinistrodextral, sinistrocular, sinistrocerebral, port *(Naut.)*, larboard *(Naut.)*.

SINK, *n.* 1. Basin, receptacle for water, washbowl, washbasin, bowl, tub, washtub, piscina *(Eccles.)*.

2. Low-lying area where waters collect *or* disappear by sinking into the ground, dip, hole, hollow, cavity, depression, sinkhole, pothole,

crater, pit, fen, bog, wash, marsh, swamp, chuckhole, pitchhole, cahot (chiefly Can.).

3. Place of vice or corruption, den of iniquity, hellhole, Alsatia, Domdaniel, dive (coll.), joint (sl.).

4. Sewer, drain, cloaca, ditch, conduit, trough, outlet, culvert, gutter, subterranean canal, trench, channel, watercourse, headchute (Naut.).

SINK, v. 1. Descend gradually to a lower level, settle or fall gradually (as a heavy structure), subside, drop, wane, lapse, droop, sag, swag, recede, dip, slump, precipitate, gravitate, ebb, bury, mire, decline, wallow, fall.

2. Slope downward (as ground), dip, descend, decline, fall, slant, tilt, go downhill, drop, cant.

3. Go under or to the bottom, become submerged, capsize, submerge, plunge, drown, disappear, engulf, immerse, vanish from sight, scuttle, founder, go to Davy Jones's locker, bury, submerse, inundate.

4. Fall slowly (from weakness, fatigue, etc.), despond, flag, ebb, droop, collapse, relapse, pine, lose strength, drop, decay, wane, dwindle, languish, tire, succumb, degenerate, decline, sag, slump, give way, be subdued, be overcome, be overwhelmed, pine away, repine, faint, wilt, jade, yield, slip, retrogress, retrograde, lapse.

5. Pass or fall into a lower state, deteriorate, decline, degenerate, decrease in amount, extent, degree, etc., go down, go downhill, devaluate, depreciate, lower, reduce, debase, lessen, diminish, ruin, bring or let down, relapse, retrovert, revert, recede, backslide, retrogress, retrograde, abase, depress, run to seed, go to the dogs, go to pot, go from bad to worse, recidive, degrade, regress.

6. (Fol. by IN, INTO, etc.) Enter, penetrate, permeate, pierce, reach, fathom, impress, make sensible, touch, affect, arrest the thoughts, hit, arouse, disturb, stir, provoke, excite, stimulate, strike, come home to, get through to.

7. Fall in, become hollow, cave in, collapse, become depressed or concave.

8. Put down (a pipe, post, etc.) as into the ground, make (a hole, shaft, well, etc.) by excavating or boring downward, hollow out, scoop out, drive, lower, set in, gougé, bury, excavate, dig, drill.

9. Suppress, ignore, omit, dismiss, slight, drop, nullify, annul, abrogate, treat with indifference, laugh off, conceal, hide, cover up, occultate, occult, eclipse, render invisible, bury, mask, veil, camouflage, disguise, turn a deaf ear to, close or shut the eyes to, refuse to notice, sneeze at, give the go-by (coll.), keep in or throw into the shade, put or cast aside, think no more of, throw into the background, turn one's back upon, not trouble oneself with.

10. Invest (money, now esp. unprofitably), lose (money) in an unfortunate investment, place or put out, risk, venture, fund, entrust, embark, commit.

SINKER, n. Weight of lead, etc., lead, plumb, plummet, bob.

SINLESS, adj. Free from or without sin, pure, blameless, spotless, guileless, innocent, unspotted, impeccable, good, guiltless, holy, godly, righteous, perfect, undefiled, untarnished, unblemished, immaculate, faultless, untainted, chaste, snowy, unsullied, virtuous, incorrupt, vestal, above suspicion, uncorrupted, inviolable, moral, angelic, divine, clean, wholesome, upright, inculpable,

with clean hands, inviolate, unimpeachable, incontaminate, heavenly.

SINNER, n. One who sins, transgressor, misdemeanant, felon, trespasser, lawbreaker, wrongdoer, criminal, offender, delinquent, reprobate, evildoer, wicked person, malfeasant, miscreant, rascal, culprit, recidivist, backslider, apostate, malefactor.

SINUOSITY, n. Sinuous turn or character, curve, turn, bend, winding, sinuation, flexuosity, undulation, tortuosity, sinus, crook, maze, turning, crinkle, spiral, incurvature, incurvation, excurvation, corkscrew, coil, curlicue, curl, zigzag, excursion, digression, helix, anfractuosity, ambages, ambagiousness, circuit, whorl, recurvature, recurvation, inflection, meandering, labyrinth, circuity, torsion, intorsion, circumvolution, volute, convolution, circularity, involution, flexure, curvature, crookedness, excurvature.

SINUOUS, adj. 1. Having many bends, curves or turns, winding, curved, crooked, curvilinear, sinuate, serpentine, flexuous, tortuous, tortile, coiled, volute, convoluted, twisted, perplexed, meandrous, complex, tangled, circumvolant, intricate, circumfluent, circumambient, labyrinthine, circuitous, zigzag, daedalian, bending, wavy, undulating, ambagious, anfractuous, vermiculate, meandering, sinuated, mazy, curly, rivose, sigmoid, kinky.

2. Indirect, devious, discursive, excursive, rambling, desultory, circuitous, roundabout, backhanded, ambagious, circumlocutory, vagrant, loose, wandering, erratic, undirected, periphrastic, aberrant, deviative.

SINUS, n. 1. Curve, bend, sinuosity, etc. (See SINUOSITY, n. above.)

2. Curving part, recess, opening, hollow, groove, cavity, pocket, lacuna, honeycomb, antrum (Anat.).

SIP, n. Small quantity taken by sipping, taste, drink, dram, swallow, nip, thimbleful, mouthful, sup, suck, lap, toothful, soupçon, lick, drop, swig, gobbet, bite, sample, taster, small draught.

SIP, v. Drink a little at a time, sup, suck, lap, taste, take a nip, take a thimbleful, sample, savor, relish, absorb, take in.

SIRE, n. Male parent of a quadruped, stud animal, father, procreator, progenitor.

SIREN, adj. Dangerously alluring, seducing, seductive, luring, fascinating, tempting, bewitching, enticing, drawing, captivating, intriguing, attractive, irresistible, inviting, tantalizing, enravishing, exciting, provocative, entrancing, enchanting, charming, sweet.

SIREN, n. 1. Alluring or dangerous woman, bewitching or fascinating woman, tempter, seducer, seductress, charmer, seamaid, sprite, vampire, enchantress, Circe (Gk. Legend), Lorelei (Ger. Legend), vamp (sl.), Parthenope (Gk. Legend).

2. Whistle, fog signal, alarm, horn, steam whistle, calliope, foghorn.

SISTER, n. 1. Daughter of the same parent or parents, sibling, female friend, sister-german, blood sister, sis (coll.), sissy (coll.).

2. Thing regarded as feminine and associated as if by kinship (as a ship), twin, counterpart, companion, match, pendant, parallel, double, fellow, complement, correspondent, correlative, analogue, congener, equivalent, correlate.

3. Female fellow member (as of a church, re-

ligious community, etc.), nun, novice, deaconess, conventual, clergywoman, *religieuse (Fr.).*

SIT, *v.* 1. Rest on the lower part of the body, be seated, perch, roost, bestride, bestraddle, be supported, squat, have a seat, repose, recline, loll, sprawl, settle, establish, seat oneself.

2. Be situated, rest, dwell, abut, be based, bear, lean, recline, occupy, lodge, stay, reside, sojourn, remain, settle, inhabit, be built, be supported.

3. Place oneself in position *(for an artist, photographer, etc.),* pose, act as a model, model.

4. Remain quiet *or* inactive, stay, be, rest, abide, repose, be quiescent, mark time, tarry, be at a standstill, stick, stand, stop, not stir, pause, refrain, abstain, fold one's arms, hold, spare, cease, neglect, lie fallow, idle, smolder, slumber, vegetate, sleep, be inert, stagnate, be latent, lie dormant, bide one's time, while away the time, hang fire, forbear.

5. Cover eggs to hatch them, brood, incubate, cover, nest, hatch.

6. Fit, be adjusted *(as a garment),* suit, become, hang, drape, conform to, be suited, shape, follow the lines of, correspond, harmonize, befit, accord, agree.

7. Occupy a seat in an official capacity, hold office, reign, fill an office, officiate, preside, take *or* occupy the chair, fill *or* occupy a post, superintend, supervise, govern, direct, rule, manage, administer, have direction, have the portfolio, have *or* possess authority, exercise *or* wield authority, be resident *or* established in, be in, retain, hold down *(sl.).*

8. Be convened *or* in session *(as an assembly),* meet, gather, convocate, join, unite, assemble, hold a hearing, conduct business.

9. *(Often with* DOWN*)* Cause to sit, seat, locate, put, situate, establish, assign a seat, place.

SITE, *n.* 1. Position *(of a town, building, etc.)* esp. as to its environment, surroundings, purlieus, neighborhood, vicinity, locale, environs, territory, district, circumjacencies, circumambiencies, circumstances, milieu, vicinage, precincts, atmosphere, setting, background, scene, area.

2. Position. location, placement, area, deposition, disposition, establishment, situation, collocation, allocation, lodgment, emplacement, locale, locality, place, ground, bearings, demesne, whereabouts, quarter, station, region, province, zone, latitude and longitude.

SITTING, *n.* 1. Session *(as of a court or legislature),* period of remaining seated *(as for a portrait),* council, séance, meeting, assembly, assize, court, conference, hearing, consultation, audience, synod, congress, conclave, caucus, convention, powwow *(coll.).*

2. Brooding *(as of a hen upon eggs),* incubation, number of eggs to be hatched, hatching.

SITTING ROOM, *n.* Front room, lounge, drawing room, living room, reception room, parlor, salon.

SITUATE, *v.* Place *(in a certain position),* put, post, dispose, settle, orient, install, lay, reposit, lodge, plant, stand, line up, ensconce, consign, house, billet.

SITUATION, *n.* 1. Location, demesne, quarter, territory, spot, environment, locality, station, vicinage, zone, purlieus, place, site, position, district, region, province, neighborhood, terrain, area.

2. Arrangement, disposition, fixation, insertion, placement, location, collocation, establishment, allocation, lodgment, emplacement, installation.

3. Circumstances, standing, footing, predicament, condition, state, position, place, plight.

4. Job, post, work, commission, pursuit, livelihood, career, role, duty, responsibility, berth, calling, appointment, sinecure, business, capacity, function, trade, care, position, assignment, province, incumbency, charge, billet.

SIZE, *n.* Physical magnitude, dimensions, largeness, volume, amplitude, bulk, scope, mass, capacity, measurement, proportions, quantity, extent.

SIZZLE, *v.* 1. Fry, broil, roast, grill, bake, toast, cook, seethe.

2. Hiss, sibilate, frizzle, fizz, sputter.

SKATE, *v.* Glide *(on skates),* sweep along, skim along, glissade.

SKEIN, *n.* Complexity, involution, tangle, coil, knot, perplexity, intricacy, gnarl, maze, web.

SKELETON, *n.* 1. Bony framework of the body, bones.

2. Rough sketch *or* outline *(of a plan, etc.),* diagram, outline, sketch, draft, plan, blocking in, layout, lines, tracing, suggestion.

3. Underlying *or* supporting structure, framework, scaffold, scaffolding, platform.

4. General sketch indicating only the main features, *etc.,* synopsis, syllabus, review, abridgment, argument, prospectus, program, summary, plot, basis, recapitulation, compendium, condensation, abstract, idea, plan, digest, thumbnail sketch, protocol, epitome, conspectus, résumé, analysis, pattern, scheme, brief, agenda, roster.

SKEPTIC, *n.* 1. Doubter, doubting Thomas, questioner, scoffer, iconoclast, pyrrhonist, misbeliever.

2. *(Of religious belief, etc.)* Atheist, agnostic, unbeliever, disbeliever, infidel, nullifidian.

SKEPTICISM, *n.* Uncertainty, doubt, dubiety, dubiosity, mistrust, incredulity, suspicion, agnosticism, pyrrhonism, disbelief, unbelief, demur, scruple, compunction, scoffing.

SKETCH, *n.* 1. Simply *or* hastily executed drawing *or* painting, preliminary drawing, study, rough outline, draft, depiction of essential features *(with details omitted),* representation, tracing, delineation, configuration, diagram, *ébauche (Fr. Art).*

2. Rough design, plan *(as of literary work),* draft, outline, compendium, abstract, brief *or* hasty statement *(of facts, occurrences, etc.),* summary, idea, representation, delineation, plot, brief, skeleton plan, rough account, synopsis, syllabus, prospectus, abridgment, review, condensation, pattern, analysis, résumé, conspectus, epitome, digest.

3. Short play, slight dramatic performance, skit, act, charade, scene, depiction, interlude, pantomime, characterization, lampoon, take-off.

SKETCH, *v.* 1. Make a sketch of, draw in outline, make a rough draft of, design, outline, contour, draft, trace, block out, rough in, portray, depict, limn, scratch, stencil, represent, delineate, dash off, chalk out, mark out, pencil, demarcate.

2. Set forth in a brief *or* general account, frame, devise, project, dash off, plot, plan, report, mark out, envision, describe, picture, delineate, depict, portray, represent, chart, map out, work up, determine, draw up, cast, form, define, invent, fashion, figure, pattern, shape, hammer *or* knock out, contrive, outline.

SKETCHY, *adj.* 1. Like a sketch, giving only outlines, unfinished, rough, preliminary, unexecuted, preparatory, crude, provisional, initial, unrefined, coarse, rough-hewn, incomplete, unpolished.

2. Slight, imperfect, superficial, incomplete, feeble, deficient, defective, short, brief, low, lame, poor, skimpy, depthless, cursory, shallow, skin-deep, few, half-baked, wanting, immature, weak, crude, childish, slipshod, careless, puerile, inexact, skimp, scrimp, scrimpy, meager, insufficient, light, modest, inconsiderable, insignificant, slender, inadequate, shy (sl.).

SKEW, adj. Having an oblique direction or position, askew, slanting, twisted, aslant, wry, awry, bias, sidelong, sidewise, crosswise, asymmetrical, asquint, oblique, aside, askant, distorted, out of line, diagonal, slant, tilted, inclined, sloping, transverse, indirect.

SKEW, n. Oblique movement, direction or position, turn, crookedness, deviation, declination, excursion, deflection, deflexure, digression, divergence, diagonal, swerve, bias, distortion, curvature, angle, bent, bend, warp, twist, slope, tilt, slant, list, pitch, incline.

SKEW, v. 1. Turn aside, swerve, oblique, take an oblique course, deviate, angle off, edge, diverge, deflect, bend, bear off, bias, curve, crook, turn, twist, slue, sheer, veer, lateralize, shift, distort.

2. Look obliquely, squint, look askance, give a sidelong look, look asquint, cock the eye.

3. Distort, depict unfairly, twist, warp, misrepresent, wrest, wring, torture, pervert, garble, misteach, misinterpret, misrepresent, belie, falsify, misapprehend, give a false coloring, put a false construction on, abuse, exaggerate, embroider, varnish, sophisticate, disguise, misquote, misapply, misuse, misconstrue, misrender, stretch or strain the meaning or sense.

SKID, n. 1. Plank (bar, log, etc.) on which something heavy may be slid or rolled, support, supporter, prop, brace, rib, splint, drag, dray, runner, sled, sledge, runway.

2. Shoe, etc., which prevents rotation, brake, clog, drag.

3. Act of skidding, twirl, glissade, slide, slip, loss of control.

SKID, v. 1. Place on or slide along a skid or skids, slide, shoot, ease, glide, skate, skim, ski, sled, coast, glissade, toboggan.

2. Check with a skid (as a wheel), brake, slacken the pace of, put a drag on, apply the brake, halt, arrest, slow down or up, delay, retard, decelerate, hold back.

3. Slide along without rotating, slip sideways, not hold the course or track, move by inertia or centrifugal force (without mechanical aid), veer, sheer, sideslip, be out of control.

SKIFF, n. Small boat (manageable by one person), rowing boat, rowboat, canoe, jolly boat, catboat, cat, shell, kayak, sampan, piragua, pirogue, dugout, cockle, caïque.

SKILL, n. Ability (coming from knowledge, practice, aptitude, etc.) to do something well, competent excellence in performance, skillfulness, dexterity, expertness, adroitness, talent, mastery, address, ingenuity, subtlety, finesse, callidity, knack, adeptness, capacity, inventiveness, sharpness, deftness, efficiency, acumen, sagacity, artistry, faculty, parts, gift, cunning, ingeniousness, aptness, readiness, quickness, craft, facility, power, panurgy, felicity, endowment, competence,

proficiency, art, prowess, handiness, technique, cleverness.

SKILLFUL, adj. 1. Having skill, experienced, trained, clever, able, gifted, talented, quick, adroit, expert, capable, competent, keen, sharp, endowed, conversant, apt, cunning, qualified, accomplished, inventive, fit, fitted, well-versed, proficient, efficient, deft, ingenious, practiced, dexterous, masterly, masterful, ready, handy, facile, neat, clean, felicitous, veteran, professional, studied, politic, strategic, subtle, sly, foxy.

2. Showing, involving or requiring skill (as work), requiring apprenticeship or training, exacting, difficult, intricate, delicate, critical, precision.

SKIM, v. 1. Take up (floating matter) from a liquid, remove, clear (liquid) by skimming, top, collect, cream, despumate.

2. Move lightly over or along the surface, glide, cause (a thing) to fly over or near a surface, flit, pass lightly or superficially, skate, graze, shave, brush, scrape, fly, scud, shoot, coast, glissade, skid, spank, spring, scoot, trip, speed, sweep, bound, skip, slip.

3. Go over (in reading, treatment, etc.) in a superficial manner, pass quickly, dip into, glance, examine cursorily, run or pass the eyes over, run over, skip over or through, scan, trifle with, toy with, scamp, skimp, play with, slur, slight, flip through the pages, hit the high spots (coll.), give a lick and a promise (coll.), touch upon lightly.

4. Cover (liquid, etc.) with a thin layer, coat, form a surface on, freeze, overlay, film, mask, coagulate on the surface.

SKIMP, v. 1. Be sparing of or in, use severe economy, scrimp, save, economize, be parsimonious, pinch, gripe, grudge, begrudge, screw, stint, dole out, keep on short allowance, hold back, withhold, make both ends meet, keep within one's means or budget, cut down expenses, retrench.

2. Scamp, perform in a hasty or careless manner, be negligent, slight, do perfunctorily, neglect, overlook, forget, do carelessly or superficially, do by halves, trifle, fribble, do in a slipshod fashion, do anyhow, pass over, play with, toy with, touch lightly, slip or skip over, toss off or out, withhold one's best efforts from.

SKIMPY, adj. 1. Lacking in size, fullness, etc., scanty, sketchy, slight, imperfect, superficial, incomplete, feeble, deficient, defective, short, brief, low, lame, poor, depthless, cursory, shallow, skin-deep, few, half-baked, wanting, immature, weak, crude, childish, slipshod, careless, puerile, inexact, skimp, scrimp, scrimpy, meager, insufficient, light, modest, inconsiderable, insignificant, slender, inadequate, shy (sl.).

2. Too thrifty, stingy, penurious, parsimonious, niggardly, close, close-handed, close-fisted, pinching, miserly, stinting, scrimping, tight-fisted, save-all, mean, tight (coll.), chary, sparing, frugal, mercenary, illiberal, moneygrubbing, grasping, cheeseparing, churlish, narrow, sordid, pennywise, usurious, shabby, beggarly, venal, grudging.

SKIN, n. 1. External covering of an animal body, integument, cuticle, epidermis, coat, fell, jacket, fur, scarfskin, cutis (Lat.), hide (sl.), corium (Anat.), derma (Anat., Zool.), the raw, birthday suit (jocose).

2. Integument stripped from an animal body, pelt, hide, fell, cast, coat, slough, desquamation, exuviae (pl.), fleece, vellum, shagreen, fur.

3. Integumentary covering, outer coating, surface layer, investing membrane, rind, peel, husk,

crust, pod, jacket, film (on liquid), coat, cover, pellicle, sheath, case, epicarp, bark, hull, integument, scale, overlay, veneer, shell, foil, sheet, lamina, incrustation, casing, involucre, lorica (Zool.), aponeurosis (Anat.), coleorhiza (Bot.), theca (Anat., Zool.), corea (Bot. Zool.), fascia (Anat., Zool.), capsule, envelope.

4. Container made of animal skin (used for holding liquids), pouch, bottle.

SKIN, v. 1. Strip or deprive of skin, peel, flay, bark, shave, excoriate, bare, excorticate, decorticate, hull, lay bare, scalp, pod, shell, expose, husk, uncover, unwrap, divest, denude, exfoliate.

2. Strip off (as or like skin), loosen and fall off, shed, flake, molt, scale, delaminate, exuviate, peel, slough, cast, exfoliate, desquamate (Pathol.).

3. Cover with or as with skin, film, coat, invest, heal, cicatrize, laminate, plate, face, loricate, veneer, overlay, skim, clothe.

SKIN-DEEP, adj. Superficial, shallow, slight, cursory, trivial, without substance, empty, frivolous, trashy, frothy, insignificant, inadequate, slender, meager, insufficient, slipshod, careless, skimpy, scrimpy, half-baked, wanting, immature, depthless, inane, airy, flimsy, puerile, not profound, sketchy.

SKINFLINT, n. Mean, niggardly person, miser, churl, niggard, screw, moneygrubber, tightwad (sl.), pinchfist, Silas Marner, curmudgeon, skin (sl.), Euclio, Daniel Dancer, save-all, lickpenny, codger, Harpagon, muckworm, scrimp (coll.), pinchpenny, hunks, harpy.

SKINNY, adj. 1. Lean, emaciated, gaunt, fleshless, scrawny, gawky, weedy, thin, lank, poor, shrunk, rawboned, shriveled, scraggy, attenuated, extenuated, wizened, pinched, withered, slender, spare, meager, gangling, skeletal, starved, spindly, spindling, rattleboned (coll.).

2. Of or like skin, cutaneous, membranous, dermoid, dermatoid, dermal, dermic, epidermoid, epidermic, epidermal, cuticular.

SKIP, n. 1. Skipping movement, light jump, skipping gait, bound, hop, spring, leap, caper, gambol, frisk, saltation, prance, flounce.

2. Passing from one point or thing to another with disregard of what intervenes, omission, gap, miss, interval, exclusion, preclusion, exception, slip, break, rift, lacuna, separation, hiatus, interspace, gulf, hole, caesura, blank, rupture, neglect, oversight, breach, elision.

SKIP, v. 1. Leap lightly, jump, spring, gambol, caper, hop, dane, skim, sport, bound, bounce, buck, buckjump, prance, leapfrog, romp, saltate, curvet, bob, vault, upleap, upspring, trip.

2. Pass from one point (thing, subject, etc.) to another disregarding or omitting what intervenes, pass over without reading (notice, mention, action, etc.), omit, overlook, miss, neglect, disregard, dodge, ignore, skim, evade, not heed, forget, elude, shun, not trouble oneself with, avert.

3. Ricochet, rebound along a surface, hop, skim, move lightly, glide, flit, fly, skate, graze, shave, brush, scrape, scud, shoot, coast, skid, spank, glissade, scoot, spring, trip, sweep, bound, slip, kick.

SKIPPER, n. Master (of a small vessel), captain, leader, seaman, sea captain, commander, sailing master, master mariner, old man (coll.).

SKIRMISH, n. Fight, encounter, combat, scrimmage, battle, brush, conflict, fray, duel, engagement, tilt, rencounter, action, concussion, joust, meeting, imbroglio, run-in (sl.), ruction, bout, mêlée (Fr.), appulse, fracas, tussle, clash, dogfight, scrap (coll.), struggle, fisticuffs, set-to (coll.).

SKIRT, n. 1. Petticoat, crinoline, farthingale, hoop skirt, gown.

2. (Usually pl.) Surroundings, outpost, environs, outlying districts, perimeter, bounds, borderland, rim, edge, periphery, fringe, suburb, border, verge, circumjacencies.

3. Margin, rim, border, edge, boundary, fringe, circumference, periphery, perimeter, compass, limit, contour, confine, purlieus, frame, ambit, circuit, girth, extremity, circumspection, tire, hem, pale, zone, girdle.

SKIRT, v. 1. Surround, border, circuit, beset, hem, in, endue, lie around, round, envelop, loop, belt, gird, enclose, circumscribe, hedge in, girdle, ring, compass, encircle, ensphere, encompass, circle, marginate.

2. Go around, elude, shun, keep away from, make a detour, circumambulate, circle, circuit, fight shy of, avoid, evade.

SKIT, n. Short humorous play, story, etc., sketch, burlesque, travesty, mock tragedy, parody, burletta, take-off, farce, paratragoedia.

SKITTISH, adj. 1. Erratic, impulsive, flighty, changeable, mercurial, uncertain, inconstant, whimsical, fitful, fickle, variable, wayward, volatile, unsteady, vacillating, indecisive, irresolute, capricious, deviative, heteroclite, uneven, crotchety, undecided, faddish, fanciful, moody, wanton, spasmodic, changeful, shilly-shallying, infirm of purpose, unstable, irregular, irresponsible, stray, wavering.

2. (Esp. of horses) Easily frightened, startled, etc., jumpy, restless, nervous, restive, timid, fearful, excitable, fidgety.

3. Shy, demurring, suspicious, crafty, elusive, careful, evasive, coy, renitent, cautious, reluctant, loath, wary, chary, unwilling, averse, noncommittal, prudent, precautious, stealthy, opposed, disinclined, slack, distrustful, circumspect, leery (sl.), dissenting, slow to, gingerly, guarded, on guard, politic, discreet, indisposed, shrinking safe.

SKULK, v. 1. Lurk, sneak about, slink, lie in hiding, lie concealed, lie low (coll.), crouch, prowl, go furtively, lie in ambush, gumshoe (sl.).

2. Evade (a duty, etc.), blench at, blink at, neglect, eschew, duck (coll.), shirk, escape, dodge, shun, shrink from, leave undone, malinger, sidestep, avoid, run from, steer clear of, gold-brick (U. S. Army sl.), funk, ignore.

SKULL, n. 1. Cranium.

2. Pate, crown, top of the head.

SKY, n. The blue, the heavens, vault of heaven, arch of heaven, firmament, hyaline (Poet.), empyrean, azure, either, cerulean.

SKY-BLUE, adj. Cerulean, smalt, cobalt blue, azure, ultramarine, sky-colored, peacock blue.

SKYLIGHT, n. Casement, fanlight, bull's-eye, porthole, port.

SKY LINE, n. Horizon, outline (of a city, etc., against the sky), silhouette, profile.

SLAB, n. Thick slice (of anything), board, hunk, plank, puncheon (Carpent.), thick fragment, piece, wad, chunk.

SLACK, adj. 1. Not exercising care, remiss, neglectful, unthinking, lax, insouciant, loose, injurious, imprudent, thoughtless, inattentive, indifferent, unconcerned, inconsiderate, heedless, reckless, forgetful, unwary, disgraceful, absent-minded, unguarded, uncircumspect, unmindful.

2. Moving at slow speed (*as wind, water, etc.*), having little movement, gentle, easy, crawling, creeping, slow, slow-moving, slow-paced, imperceptible.

3. Lax, unexacting, undemanding, easy, easygoing, offhand, perfunctory, cursory, heedless, negligent, neglectful, weak, careless, undemanding.

4. Not taut, not tight, loose, free, unfastened, flexible, untied, lax, pliant, limp, flaccid, relaxed.

5. Not busy, quiet, easy, peaceful, slow, limited.

6. Untidy, slapdash, sluttish, untrustworthy, nonchalant, apathetic, messy, slipshod, remiss, loose, indifferent, perfunctory, slovenly, casual, lax, inexact, disorderly, incorrect, offhand, listless, lackadaisical, slatternly, forgetful.

7. Without firmness, energy, will power, *etc.*, insipid, weak, bloodless, spineless, characterless, wishy-washy, flabby, unsteady, powerless, nerveless, sinewless, pithless, lethargic, weak-kneed, irresolute, easily influenced, infirm, frail, shaky, limp, sapless, formative, effete, impressionable, impressible.

SLACKEN, *v.* 1. Moderate, mitigate, ease, extenuate, loosen, ameliorate, diminish, soften, reduce, weaken, relax, attenuate, lessen, step down (*coll.*), slack.

2. Retard, slow down, choke off, delay, detain, arrest, check, keep back, stem, hinder, stay, stall, curb, limit, cramp, stanch.

3. Cause to become loose, limp, *etc.*, untie, relax, free, let go, release.

SLACKER, *n.* One who evades his duty, one who evades military service, shirker, dodger, malingerer, indolent, drone, loafer, quitter (*coll.*), fainéant, do-little, dallier, dawdler, sluggard, laggard, truant, idler, absentee, fugitive, runaway, clock-watcher, sleeping partner, procrastinator, renegade, runagate, bum (*coll.*), funker (*coll.*), welsher (*sl.*), gold-brick (*Army*).

SLAG, *n.* Vitrified matter from the refinement of metal ore, waste, refuse, scoria (*from a volcano*), draff, residue, cinder, dregs, clinker, dross, ash, sediment, lava, deposit, precipitate.

SLAKE, *v.* 1. Allay (*thirst, desire, wrath, etc.*) by satisfying, quench, sate, slacken, satiate, abate, appease, relieve, mollify, assuage, take off the edge, lenify, moderate, decrease, extinguish, mitigate, temper, ease, gratify, satisfy, salve, palliate, check, smooth, alleviate, curb, dulcify, pacify, tame, soothe, quell, hush, quiet, calm, cool, still, compose, obtund, subdue, tranquilize.

2. Cool, refresh, chill, revive, brace, cheer, air, freshen, restore, regale, ventilate, revivify.

3. Make less active, vigorous, intense, *etc.* (*See* SLACKEN, *v.* 1, *above*).

SLAM, *v.* 1. Shut with noise and force, bang, clap, dash, slap, snap, bump, smack, crash.

2. Strike with violent and noisy impact, dash, hurl, hit, knock, punch, collide, heave, bang, thwack, whack, slap, swat (*coll.*), crack (*coll.*).

SLANDER, *n.* Defamation, calumny, malicious report, libel, obloquy, detraction, aspersion, backbiting, abuse, vilification, injury, odium, traducement, vituperation, scandal, commination, falsehood, invective, disparagement, slur, denunciation, revilement, depreciation, execration, anathema, reproach, imprecation, censure, malison, stricture, scurrility, castigation, exprobration, denigration.

SLANDER, *v.* Utter slander concerning, defame,

calumniate, decry, malign, asperse, libel, anathematize, insult, belie, backbite, blacken, traduce, reproach, vilify, scandalize, disparage, detract from, falsify, stab, injure, cry down, assail, belittle, accuse falsely, misrepresent, sneer at, derogate, criticize, speak ill of, run down, denigrate, vituperate, depreciate, detract, hold up to scorn, discredit, muckrake, gibbet, expose, blemish, revile, blacken, besmirch, stigmatize, give a bad name, engage in personalities, smear (soil, sully) one's reputation, slur, abuse, maledict, defile, curse, damn, imprecate, denounce, exprobrate, brand.

SLANG, *n.* Markedly colloquial language (*below standard of cultivated speech*), special vocabulary (*as of thieves, vagabonds, etc.*), jargon, cant, lingo, back slang, barbarism, caconym, rhyming slang, flash (*coll.*), low language, argot, vulgarism, thieves' Latin.

SLANT, *n.* 1. Slanting *or* oblique direction, slope, tilt, bend, pitch, list, cant, bias, diagonal, descent, bent, obliqueness, obliquity, inclination, downgrade, fall, dip, drop, ramp, declivity, hill, turn, deviation, declination, deflection, deflexure, digression, divergence, swerve, incline, sheer.

2. Mental leaning *or* tendency, bias, viewpoint, propensity, light, angle, aspect, twist, approach, point of view, standpoint, inclination, turn, proclivity, gift, bent, disposition, talent, genius, knack.

SLANT, *v.* Slope, lean, incline, tilt, pitch, descend, list, lie obliquely, cant, shelve, keel, careen, ascend, be crosswise, deviate, deflect, diverge, swerve, bear off, angle off, decline, skew, bend, bias, curve, crook, turn, sheer, slue, veer, shift, lateralize.

SLANTING, *adj.* At an angle, sideways, sidelong, inclined, askew, biased, bearing at an angle, sloping, oblique, tilted, tilting, inclining.

SLAP, *n.* 1. Whack, stroke, stripe, buffet, thwack, bang, lick, rap, lash, blow, pommel, beating, hit, smack, knock, jab, dab, swipe, wallop, cuff.

2. Blunt *or* abrupt check, peremptory refusal, snub, counteraction, setback, discomfiture, pointblank refusal, beating, drubbing, overthrow, vanquishment, undoing, cut (*coll.*), spurn, renouncement, renunciation, go-by (*coll.*), cold shoulder (*coll.*), checkmate, reproach, denial, rout, damper, rebuke, chiding, rebuff, rejection, repudiation, repugnance, refusal, defeat, defiance, discouragement, opposition, reaction, repulsion, resistance, repulse.

SLAP, *v.* 1. Whack, box, knock, cuff, punch, wallop, belabor, thwack, beat, thump, lash, pat, bump, swipe, clap, strike, pat, bang, slug, cudgel, strike, clip, pommel, thrash, tap, bat, dab, hit, jab, pound.

2. Give a rebuff to, snub, check, rebuke, reprove, give the cold shoulder (*coll.*), deny, decline, slam the door in one's face, give the go-by (*coll.*), cross, resist, spurn, put in one's place, repulse, resist, reject, ignore, slight, chide, rebuff, set back on one's heels.

SLAPDASH, *adj.* Lax, disorderly, inexact, offhand, lackadaisical, remiss, heedless, thoughtless, slatternly, casual, untrustworthy, apathetic, nonchalant, listless, lazy, sluttish, messy, untidy, slack, loose, slipshod, slovenly.

SLAPSTICK, *adj.* Broadly comical, farcical, boisterous, burlesque, low comedy, clowning, buffoonish, absurd.

SLASH, *n.* Gash, cut, hack, nick, snip, cleft,

trench, rift, cleave, chop, rupture, crevice, fissure, tear, slit, jag, incision, split, blaze, serration.

SLASH, *v.* 1. Gash, cut, rend, disjoint, butcher, snip, tear, sunder, slit, chop, abscind, dismember, slice, rip, hack, incise, lop, rive, prune, cleave, knife, bayonet, saber, pierce, chisel, lacerate, hew, quarter, cut to pieces, mangle, disfigure, scar, haggle, mutilate.

2. *(Of prices, etc.)* Lower, diminish, drop, curtail, pare down, decrease, ease, retrench, cut, relax, lenify.

SLASHING, *adj.* Merciless, unkind, ruthless, unsparing, unfavorable, heavy, cruel, cutting, brutal, unfeeling, bitter, severe, vindictive, vengeful, remorseless, punitive, exigent, stringent, unreasonable, hard, rough, devastating, biting, overbearing, unbending, inhuman, harsh, relentless, uncompassionate, unrelenting, hard-boiled *(coll.)*, cold-blooded, caustic, insufferable, pressing, agonizing.

SLAT, *n.* Thin bar *(for support, strength, etc.)*, strut, support, brace, lath.

SLATTERN, *n.* Dowdy, frump, drab, slut, sloven, drabbletail, draggletail, trollop.

SLATTERNLY, *adj.* Untidy, sluttish, slack, slipshod, messy, loose, slovenly, lax, slapdash, sloppy, disorderly, dowdy.

SLAUGHTER, *n.* 1. Act of killing *(as of cattle, etc.)*, butchery, destruction, destroying, slaying.

2. Massacre, slaying, wholesale killing, effusion of blood, blood-bath, trucidation, destruction, mass homicide, internecion, havoc, saturnalia of blood, butchery, mass-murder, pogrom, genocide, decimation.

SLAUGHTER, *v.* 1. Butcher *(as animals)*, destroy, slay, kill, put to sleep, do away with.

2. Slay, destroy, do to death, massacre, assassinate, cut down, butcher, immolate, dispatch, exterminate, put to death, put to the sword, annihilate, shed the blood of, execute, decimate, cut to pieces.

SLAUGHTERHOUSE, *n.* Butchery, abattoir, shambles, slaughter pen.

SLAVE, *n.* 1. Serf, mameluke *(Mohamm.)*, hierodule *(Gr. Antiq.)*, odalisque *(esp. Turk.)*, helot.

2. Drudge, work-horse *(coll.)*, menial, worker, toiler, hack, plodder, fag, moiler.

SLAVE, *v.* Grind, drudge, fag, sweat, plod, moil, toil, hammer away, work one's fingers to the bone, overlabor, burn the candle at both ends, burn the midnight oil, grub, slog.

SLAVER, *v.* Slobber, dribble, drivel, slabber, drool, salivate.

SLAVERY, *n.* Bondage, shackles, chains, reins, trammels, subjection, subjugation, serfdom, enslavement, vassalage, thralldom, villeinage, bonds, manacles, yoke, durance, helotry, duress, servility, servitude.

SLAVISH, *adj.* 1. Of *or* befitting a slave, abject, humble, restrained, obedient, henpecked, tractable, prostrate, in harness, deferential, resigned, poor, meek, unassertive, passive, docile, lowly, subdued, obeisant, unresisting, ignoble, subservient, downtrodden, submissive, lowborn, enslaved, compliant, servile, subject, menial, in bonds.

2. Slavishly submissive *or* obsequious, abject, fawning, honey-mouthed, footlicking *(sl.)*, mealy-mouthed, bootlicking *(sl.)*, ingratiating, subservient, servile, toadying, sycophantic, scraping, menial, truckling, cringing, whining, groveling,

oily, unctuous, base, cowering, beggarly, low, mean.

3. *(As a law, ruler, etc.)* Tyrannical, stiff, rigid, stringent, unbending, unforgiving, harsh, inexorable, inquisitorial, strict, severe, ironclad, autocratic, pitiless, cruel, stern, punitive, brutal, oppressive.

4. Slavishly exact *(as a translation, etc.)*, close, strict, faithful, literal, prosaic, straightforward, undeviating, direct, unimaginative, inflexible, conscientious, without originality.

SLAY, *v.* Do to death, kill, dispatch, destroy, murder, massacre, execute, exterminate, put to death, immolate, put to the sword, butcher, annihilate, assassinate, slaughter, cut down, cut to pieces.

SLEAZY, *adj.* Wanting firmness, substance, *etc.*, flimsy, thin, poor, unsubstantial, weak, flabby, slender, slight, jerry-built, gimcrack, pasteboard.

SLED, *n.* Sleigh, pung, cutter, bobsled, toboggan, jumper, cariole *(Canad.)*, runner, sledge.

SLEEK, *adj.* 1. Polished, shiny, glazed, glossy, burnished, silken, lustrous, waxed, varnished, smooth, satin, silky.

2. Bland, smooth, honeyed, ingratiating, unctuous, smug, oily, blandiloquous, adulatory, suaviloquent, buttery *(coll.)*, suave, specious, honey-tongued.

SLEEK, *v.* Make glossy, smooth, polish, varnish, wax, slick, make lustrous, sleeken, burnish, planish, glaze, furbish, scour, beautify, brighten, plane, buff.

SLEEP, *n.* Slumber, repose, rest, hibernation, siesta, the arms of Morpheus, dormancy, doze, snooze *(coll.)*, shut-eye *(sl.)*, nap, forty winks *(coll.)*, trance, coma, swoon.

SLEEP, *v.* Repose, slumber, rest, hibernate, rest in the arms of Morpheus, estivate *(Zool.)*, take forty winks *(coll.)*, nod off *(coll.)*, drop off *(coll.)*, lie dormant, snooze *(coll.)*, hit the sack *(sl.)*, nap, turn in *(coll.)*, doze, retire.

SLEEPINESS, *n.* Torpidness, torpidity, kef, torpor, lassitude, comatoseness, comatosity, hypnesthesis, drowsiness, somnolence, languor, doziness, lethargy, oscitancy.

SLEEPING, *adj.* Dozing, napping, dead to the world, somnolent, dormant, sound asleep, asleep, comatose, inactive, quiescent, snoozing *(coll.)*, dreaming, hibernating, resting, reposing, soporous.

SLEEPLESSNESS, *n.* Inability to sleep, wakefulness, insomnia, insomnolence, restlessness, pervigilium.

SLEEPWALK, *v.* Somnambulate, walk in one's sleep.

SLEEPY, *adj.* Weary, drowsy, faint, nodding, somnolent, oscitant, tired, fatigued, yawning, exhausted, half asleep, heavy, torpid, dozy *(coll.)*.

SLEET, *n.* Frozen rain, glaze, snow pellets, graupel, hail.

SLEIGH, *n.* Pung, cutter, bobsled, runner, cariole *(Canad.)*, jumper, sled, sledge.

SLEIGHT, *n.* 1. Stratagem, trick, sly artifice, flummery, deceit, hocus-pocus, trumpery, delusion, wile, device, hoax.

2. Expertness, dexterity, artistry, adroitness, sharpness, facility, faculty, skill, deftness, knack, cunning, adeptness, efficiency.

SLEIGHT OF HAND, *n.* Legerdemain, feint,

jugglery, juggler's trick, thaumaturgy, conjuring, conjuration, deception of the eyes, prestidigitation.

SLENDER, *adj.* 1. Thin, slim, lean, puny, emaciated, stunted, fleshless, narrow, spare, petite, gracile, delicate, slight.

2. Of small amount, degree, *etc.,* inconsiderable, little, tiny, restricted, diminutive, teeny *(coll.),* minute, slight, imperceptible, wee, impalpable, inappreciable, evanescent, infinitesimal, limited, pocket-sized, dinky *(coll.),* bantam, modest, moderate, minikin, miniature.

3. Frail, flimsy, feeble, perishable, light, fragile, fine, delicate, weak, faint, gentle, tenuous, ethereal, will-o'-the-wisp, dainty, frangible, jerry-built, breakable, sleazy, gossamery, unsteady, gimcrack, unstable, rickety, teetery, tottering, tottery.

SLENDERIZE, *v.* Make *or* become thinner, reduce, diet, slim, lose weight, Bantingize.

SLICE, *n.* Piece, wedge, hunk, slab, rasher, collop, cut, serving *(of food, etc.),* chunk *(coll.).*

SLICE, *v.* 1. Cut, carve, pare, separate, divide, shave, dismember, haggle, skive, sever, whittle, segment.

2. *(Often with* UP) Parcel out, mete, dispense, dissect, apportion, share, allocate, allot, partition, subdivide, sever, dole, deal, split up, part.

SLICK, *adj.* 1. Clever, astute, dexterous, quick-witted, deft, keen, nimble, adroit, capable, artful, skillful, wily, proficient, sharp, cunning, masterful, canny, facile, adept.

2. Sleeked over with oil, *etc.,* smooth, glassy, slippery, unroughened, slithery *(sl.).*

SLICK, *v.* Make glossy, make lustrous, plane, buff, shine, smooth, wax, sleek, sleeken, glaze, scour, beautify, polish, varnish, burnish, planish, furbish, brighten.

SLIDE, *n.* 1. Act of sliding, glide, skid, slip, glissade, twirl.

2. Smooth surface for sliding on, chute, trough, tube, spout, ramp, flume, canal, duct, funnel.

SLIDE, *v.* 1. Glide, glissade, skate, coast, toboggan, shoot, ease, slither, skid, sled, ski.

2. Lose one's balance, fall, skid, slither, slip, veer, sideslip.

3. *(Often preceded by* LET) Become a matter of indifference, pass, elapse, lapse, sink into oblivion, slip.

SLIGHT, *adj.* 1. Small in amount, degree, *etc.,* minute, intangible, diminutive, little, tiny, restricted, finite, wee, fine, limited, evanescent, impalpable, imperceptible, teeny *(coll.),* infinitesimal, inappreciable, pocket-sized, minikin, miniature, bounded, circumscribed, petite, bantam, dinky *(coll.),* conditioned, modest, moderate, subtle.

2. Of little weight *or* importance, trifling, unimportant, petty, paltry, idle, worthless, meager, frivolous, fair, tolerable, frothy, trivial, inane, foolish, insignificant, of no consequence, unworthy of notice, inconsiderable, negligible, moderate, modest, airy, nugatory, childish, enervated, puerile, passable, indifferent, ridiculous, small.

3. Slender, thin, slim, spare, puny, petite, poor, dapper, emaciated, gracile, delicate, skinny, filamentous, filiform, narrow, fleshless, stunted, lean.

4. Frail, flimsy, feeble, perishable, fragile, weak, delicate, light, fine, faint, attenuated, gentle, tenuous, ethereal, dainty, jerry-built, sleazy, teetery, tottery, tottering, rickety, unstable, un-

steady, gimcrack, gossamery, will-o'-the-wisp, frangible, breakable.

5. Lacking in substantial qualities, undependable, cursory, superficial, careless, scanty, negligent, hasty, desultory, shallow, sketchy, vacuous, frothy, fatuitous, deficient, insufficient, skin-deep, depthless, lame, hollow, void, poor, precarious, unsubstantial, insubstantial, volatile, indifferent, perfunctory, skimpy, below *or* under the mark, below *or* under par, ephemeral, jejune, defective, imponderable, cursory.

SLIGHT, *n.* Slighting indifference *or* treatment, pointed and contemptuous ignoring, affront, inattention, neglect, discourtesy, disregard, contempt, disfavor, slur, nonobservance, omission, insult, laxness, rebuff, evasion, snub, oversight, nonfulfillment, default, noncompliance, spurn, indifference, cold shoulder, disrespect, indignity, irreverence, incivility, cut *(coll.),* the go-by *(coll.),* laches *(Law).*

SLIGHT, *v.* 1. Treat as of slight importance, treat with indifference, disregard, neglect, disparage, slur, contemn, forget, snub, ignore, scorn, leave out of consideration, spurn, set aside, omit, skip *or* skim over, overlook, discountenance, misprize, gloss over, pass over *or* by, let pass, cut *(coll.),* turn up one's nose at, sneeze at, blink *or* wink at, take no thought *or* account of, make light of, not trouble oneself about, dismiss from one's thoughts, cold shoulder, disdain, disregard, reject, rebuff, high-hat *(sl.),* give the go-by *(coll.).*

2. Do negligently, scamp, slur over, be negligent, do perfunctorily, neglect, overlook, forget, trifle, do carelessly *or* superficially, do by halves, fribble, do in a slipshod manner, do anyhow, pass over, play with, toy with, touch lightly, slip *or* skip over, toss off *or* out, withhold one's best efforts from.

SLIGHTING, *adj.* Derogatory, disparaging, degrading, humiliating, scornful, disrespectful, backhand, insolent, contemptuous, detracting, detractive, defamatory, backhanded, left-handed, discourteous, scurrilous, depreciative, contumelious, withering, disdainful, insulting, derisive, abusive, damnatory, supercilious, haughty.

SLIM, *adj.* 1. Slender *(as in girth or form),* slight *(in build or structure),* lank, narrow, spare, thin, skinny, lean, destitute of fat, filiform, gaunt, gracile, delicate, svelte.

2. Small, inconsiderable, scanty, inadequate, meager, deficient, insufficient, slender, modest, sparse, short, light, lean, moderate, limited, restricted.

3. Poor, slight, weak, flimsy, paltry, unsubstantial, inconsiderable, insubstantial, trivial, trifling, petty, worthless, meager, inane, foolish, airy, puerile, nugatory, indifferent, ridiculous.

SLIM, *v.* Make slim, become slim, slenderize, reduce, lose flesh, taper, contract, narrow, thin down, attenuate, Bantingize *(Med.).*

SLIME, *n.* 1. Thin glutinous mud, ooze, muck, clay, mire, silt, seepage, leakage, sludge, gumbo, slop, alluvium, transudate, transudation.

2. Ropy *or* viscous liquid matter *(esp. of a foul or offensive kind),* mucus, glair, pus, phlegm, grume, pituate, albumen, gleet *(Pathol.).*

SLIMY, *adj.* 1. Of *or* like slime, abounding in *or* covered with slime, miry, oozy, muddy, purulent, suppurating, dauby, fishy, glutinous, ropy, clammy, viscid, viscous, mucid, smeary, pasty, seepy, wet, watery, weepy, quaggy, sloshy, mucky, slushy, gumbo, clayey, glutinous, gummy, paludial, marshy, sticky, limous, slippery, muculent, slabby, mucous, lubricous, gelatinous, mucilaginous, puslike, pussy *(Med.)*, feculent, fecal, excremental, slobbery, impetiginous *(Pathol.)*.

2. Vile, foul, bad, tainted, filthy, odorous, offensive, obnoxious, sickening, nauseating, fetid, stagnant, nauseous, unpalatable, rank, decayed, rotten, nasty, defiled, evil, repulsive, putrid, stinking, polluted, loathsome, high, putrefactive, putrescent, saprogenic, saprogenous, flyblown.

SLING, *n.* 1. Instrument for hurling missiles, *etc.,* slingshot, mortar, trebuchet, ballistra, arbalest, catapult.

2. Rope *or* chain for hoisting *(as cargo, etc.),* strap, band, loop, suspending apparatus, bandage for supporting an injured part, belt, girdle, brace, harness.

3. Act of slinging, shot, throw, fling, hurl, cast, shy, chuck, pitch, heave, discharge, lance, dart, flirt, projection, jaculation, peg *(coll.)*.

SLING, *v.* 1. Throw, cast, hurl, fling, shy, catapult, pitch, chuck, toss, peg *(coll.),* launch, let fly, shoot, precipitate, expel, send, discharge, propel.

2. Place in *or* secure with a sling, raise by means of a sling, lower, suspend, hoist, sway, weigh, crane, jack, winch, windlass.

SLINK, *v.* Go in a furtive, abject manner, slip, steal, prowl, skulk, lurk, gumshoe *(sl.)*.

SLIP, *n.* 1. Act of slipping, slipping of the feet *(as on slippery ground),* slide, glide, skid, glissade.

2. Mishap, accident, failure, misfortune, misadventure, mischance, grief, casualty, calamity, disaster, catastrophe, contretemps, crackup, smash-up, reverse, adversity, setback, check.

3. Mistake *(often inadvertent)* as in speaking *or* writing, error in conduct, indiscretion, blunder, bungle, misdeed, fault, oversight, misstep, peccadillo, shortcoming, miss, solecism, bevue, stumble, folly, imprudence, malapropism, slip of the pen *or* tongue, lapse, fumble, howler *(coll.),* lapsus linguae *(Lat.),* boner *(coll.),* bloomer *(sl.),* slip-up *(coll.),* faux pas *(Fr.)*.

4. Slipping away from a pursuer, evasion, dodge, escape, desertion, flight, elusion, side step, truancy, elopement, run-around *(sl.),* go-by *(coll.),* decampment.

5. Woman's underdress, petticoat, camisole, underskirt, chemise, shimmy *(coll.)*.

6. Pillowcase, pillowslip, case, bolstercase.

7. Inclined plane sloping to the water *(for building or repairing vessels),* landing place for boats, space between wharves *or* in a dock *(for vessels to lie in),* harbor, basin, runway, roadway, roads, moorings, anchorage, jetty, quay, dock, wharf.

8. Place suitable for propagation *(cut from a plant),* scion, cutting, graft, sprig, offshoot, shoot, sarmentum *(Bot.),* switch, sprout.

9. Long narrow piece, strip, shred, list, spill, ribbon, splinter, slat, sliver, shiver, tape, fillet, taenia, fascia, band.

10. Young person *(esp. of slender form),* wisp, waif, stripling, sapling, bantam, shrimp, diminutive, runt, fledgling, youth, sprig *(humorous)*.

11. Small paper *(on which information is noted),* form, card, jotting, notation, note, voucher, memo, memorandum, certificate.

SLIP, *v.* 1. Pass *or* go smoothly *or* easily, glide, slide, put *or* draw quickly *or* stealthily, creep, flow, pour, worm, wiggle, wriggle, penetrate, insinuate, filter.

2. Slide suddenly and involuntarily *(as on a*

smooth surface), skid, slither, lose one's foothold, glissade, veer, sheer, sideslip, be out of control.

3. Move (slide, start) from place *(position,* fastenings, the hold, *etc.),* get away, be lost, release, fly, flee, untie, undo, unfasten, escape, displace, quit, depart, leave, withdraw, drop, desert, abandon, make a break for it, dislocate, evacuate, vacate, break away, get clear of, become free.

4. Go quietly, steal, slink, sneak, skulk, lurk, prowl, gumshoe *(sl.)*.

5. Let pass unheeded, omit, miss, neglect, pass over, overlook, slight, bypass, slur over, disregard, drop, forfeit, ignore, skim, not think of, be careless of, let ride, leave undone, dodge, pay no attention to, shirk, shun, avoid, steer clear of, elude, eschew, avert, malinger, not heed, except, pretermit, leave out, skip.

6. *(Fol. by* AWAY, BY, *etc.)* Pass insensibly *(as from mind or memory),* pass quickly *or* imperceptibly, elapse, escape, flit, fly, flow, slide, glide, drift.

7. Pass superficially (carelessly, without attention) over a matter, skim, glance, pass *or* run the eyes over, run over, scan, trifle with, toy with, play with, skip over *or* through, scamp, skimp, slur, slight, flip through, touch lightly, dip into.

8. *(Often fol. by* UP*)* Make a mistake *or* error, blunder, trip, stumble, botch, boggle, muff, fumble, flounder, mar, fail, spoil, put one's foot in it *(coll.),* make sad work of, fall, do amiss, deviate, offend, transgress, misbehave, trespass, lapse, relapse, go astray, retrovert, regress, backslide, fall from grace, make a faux pas, make a mess of *(coll.),* mess up *(coll.),* hash up *(coll.)*.

SLIPPAGE, *n.* Amount *or* extent of slipping, play, give, slip, sideslip, scope, range, deviation, berth, latitude, swing, margin, leeway, liberty, rope.

SLIPPER, *n.* Light shoe easily slipped on *(usually for indoor use),* pump, mule, sandal, moccasin, house shoe, loafer, slip-on.

SLIPPERY, *adj.* 1. Tending to cause slipping *or* sliding, smooth, glossy, glassy, waxy, soapy, polished, sleek, slick, oily, greasy, unroughened, unwrinkled, lubricated, lubricous, mucous, synovial.

2. Tending to slip from the hold *or* grasp *or* from position, likely to slip away *or* escape, transient, passing, transitory, transitive, temporal, fleeting, elapsing, momentary, preterient, volatile, evanescent, unstable, vanishing, diurnal, fugacious, provisional, intermediate, moving, impermanent, ephemeral, temporary, precarious, shifting, shortlived, perishable, caducous, inconstant, fluent, fugitive.

3. Not to be depended on, fickle, shifty, changeful, irresolute, capricious, fitful, skittish, unctuous, timeserving, tergiversating, unreliable, frivolous, giddy, light-minded, mercurial, changeable, erratic, inconstant, variable, undependable, irresponsible, wayward, unstable, unsteady, unsteadfast, treacherous, Janus-faced, two-faced, double-dealing, perfidious, false, deceptive, glib, faithless, dishonest, tricky, insidious, wily, contriving, maneuvering, deceitful, foxy, crafty, cunning, snaky, machinative.

4. Unstable *(as conditions, etc.),* insecure, precarious, dangerous, risky, hazardous, perilous, ticklish, insubstantial, speculative, unsafe, unsure, uncertain, built upon sand, tottery, shaky, critical, infirm, untrustworthy, dubious, doubtful, unsound, hanging by a thread, trembling in the balance, rash, chancy *(coll.)*.

SLIPSHOD, *adj.* Loose, slack, untidy, sloppy

(*coll.*), messy, sluttish, casual, lazy, nonchalant, apathetic, listless, untrustworthy, slovenly, slatternly, thoughtless, heedless, remiss, lax, disorderly, offhand, lackadaisical.

SLIT, *n.* Trench, rift, incision, fissure, gash, jag, tear, blaze, cut, hack, split, cleave, nick, crevice, rupture, cleft, snip, slash, chop.

SLIT, *v.* Snip, mutilate, haggle, cut, tear, abscind, hack, incise, scar, gash, chop, slash, pierce, lacerate, hew, rip.

SLITHER, *v.* Glide, glissade, skate, ski, sled, skid, ease along, shoot, coast, slide, toboggan.

SLIVER, *n.* Chipping, shaving, modicum, splinter, scantling, scrip, shive, chip, fragment, tag, flake, snicking, scrap, whittling, splint, shred, snippet.

SLOBBER, *v.* Dribble, drool, salivate, drivel, slabber, slaver.

SLOG, *v.* 1. Beat aimlessly, rain blows upon, thrash, bastinado, flail, flagellate, buffet, pound, thump, bump, lambaste (*coll.*), cuff, cudgel, scourge, baste.

2. Toil, hammer away, moil, grind, drudge, fag, sweat, plod, slave, work one's fingers to the bone, burn the candle at both ends, overlabor, burn the midnight oil, grub.

SLOGAN, *n.* Watchword, catchword, party cry, shibboleth, sign, password, countersign, pet phrase, test word.

SLOP, *n.* 1. Clay, mire, silt, slush, ooze, muck, alluvium, transudate, transudation, sludge, seepage, leakage, gumbo.

2. (*Often plur.*) Refuse (*fed to pigs, etc.*), swill, garbage, waste, bilge, bilge water, hogwash (*coll.*), rinsings, scourings.

SLOP, *v.* Slop over, wash around, spatter, spill, splatter, splash, swash, slosh over.

SLOPE, *n.* Incline, divergence, declination, deviation, deflexure, turn, hill, declivity, ramp, drop, dip, fall, obliqueness, downgrade, inclination, obliquity, pitch, bent, descent, cant, bias, list, slant, diagonal.

SLOPE, *v.* Incline, lean, slue, veer, shift, turn, crook, lateralize, bear off, bias, bend, diverge, swerve, angle off, decline, deflect, deviate, be crosswise, careen, ascend, slant, descend, keel, cant, list, pitch.

SLOPING, *adj.* Bearing at an angle, inclined, askew, oblique, tilted, inclining, slanting, biased, sidelong, sideways, tilting.

SLOPPY, *adj.* Sodden, soggy, marshy, squashy, swampy, sloshy, quaggy, watery, oozy, boggy, plashy, splashy, sludgy, muddy, slushy, wet.

SLOT, *n.* Place for key, coin, *etc.*, aperture, crack, orifice, opening.

SLOTH, *n.* Indolence, laziness, torpidity, sluggishness, lethargy, supineness, dilatoriness, languor, do-nothingness, phlegm, lentitude, lassitude, faineance.

SLOTHFUL, *adj.* Lazy, lumpish, indolent, sluggish, dilatory, fainéant, heavy, lentitudinous, donothing, lifeless, supine, listless, phlegmatic, inert, lethargic, torpid.

SLOUCH, *n.* 1. Sluggard, lazybones, ne'er-do-well, wastrel, gold brick (*sl.*), laggard, shirker, drugstore cowboy (*sl.*), lounge lizard (*sl.*), fainéant, drone, lazy person, good-for-nothing, malingerer, idler, loafer, lounger, lingerer, bum (*sl.*), dead beat (*sl.*), slug.

2. Stoop, stooping, crouch, hunchback, ungainly posture.

SLOUCH, *v.* Stand, move, *etc.*, with a slouch, droop, slump, lumber, stoop.

SLOUCHY, *adj.* Slouching, drooping, stooping, lumbering, ponderous, clumsy.

SLOUGH, *n.* Bog, mire, marsh, quagmire, quicksand, morass, swamp, swampland.

SLOUGH, *v.* 1. Cast the skin, shed, molt, exuviate (*Zool.*), discard, drop, doff.

2. Discard, get rid of, cast off, dismiss from use, throw away, shelve, dispense with, abjure, reject, relinquish, forsake, jettison, abandon, have done with, get rid of, drop, shed.

SLOUGHY, *adj.* Marshy, miry, swampy, quaggy, oozy, boggy, squashy.

SLOVEN, *n.* Drabbletail, draggletail, trollop, slut, slattern, drab, frump, dowdy.

SLOVENLY, *adj.* Disorderly, lax, slapdash, sloppy (*coll.*), dowdy, loose, messy, slipshod, slack, sluttish, untidy.

SLOW, *adj.* 1. Stupid, retarded, insulse, dull, dull-pated, thick (*coll.*), mutton-headed (*coll.*), numskull (*coll.*), stolid, bovine, dull-witted, dumb (*coll*), blunt, sluggish, weak-minded, simple-minded, clod-pated, thick-headed, oafish, idiotic, shallow-witted, simple, addlepated, addle-headed, dronish, muddle-brained, moronic, slow-witted, uncomprehending, witless, imbecile, undeveloped, inept, feeble, feeble-minded, unintelligent, doltish, asinine, childlike, fatuous, blockish, unteachable, Boeotian, foolish, silly, senseless, irrational, puerile, green.

2. Taking a long time, gradual, protracted, lingering, lengthened, spun-out, leisurely, gentle, unhurried, moderate, prolonged, deliberate, long-continued, imperceptible, easy, drawn-out.

3. Moving at slow speed, not rapid, crawling, snail-like, dawdling, sluggish, faltering, plodding, tortoise-like, lagging, hesitant, pausing, hanging back, shuffling, going at a snail's pace.

4. Lacking confidence, reserved, recalcitrant, constrained, equivocating, oscillatory, oscillating, halting, alternating, seesawing, variable, hovering, wobbling, straddling the fence, hanging back, debating, pausing, shilly-shallying, demurring, faltering, unsettled, dallying, fluctuating, doubtful, timid, uncertain, unresolved, undecided, fickle, tremulous, vacillating, wavering, quibbling, half-hearted, irresolute, inconstant, fidgety, infirm of purpose, hesitative.

5. Not on time, late, tardy, behind, backward, lagging, belated, loitering, laggard, unpunctual, remiss, behindhand, overdue, slack, delayed, detained, in arrears.

SLOW, *v.* 1. Delay, retard, control, rein, inhibit, check, brake, arrest, hold, restrain, gag, muzzle, withhold, keep back, bridle, handicap.

2. (*Often with* DOWN *or* UP) Put the brakes on, throttle down, slacken speed, reduce speed, check speed, take it easy (*coll.*), relax, curb or moderate speed.

SLUDGE, *n.* 1. Mire, muck, seepage, clay, excretion, squash, secretion, leakage, silt, transudation, transudate, alluvium, gumbo, slime, ooze, slush, slosh, slop.

2. Refuse, filth, drainage, sewage, sewerage.

SLUG, *n.* Lazy fellow, lazybones, idler, loafer, lounger, lingerer, drone, fainéant, good-for-nothing, lounge lizard (*sl.*), drugstore cowboy (*sl.*), slouch, shirker, laggard, sluggard, gold brick *(sl.)*, wastrel, ne'er-do-well.

SLUGGISH, *adj.* 1. Lazy, torpid, lethargic, inert, phlegmatic, listless, supine, lifeless, heavy, lentitudinous, do-nothing, fainéant, dilatory, indolent, lumpish.

2. Not rapid, moving at slow speed, crawling, snail-like, dawdling, slow, going at a snail's pace, shuffling, hanging back, pausing, hesitant, lagging, tortoise-like, plodding, faltering.

SLUGGISHNESS, *n.* Indolence, laziness, faineance, lassitude, phlegm, dilatoriness, languor, supineness, do-nothingness, sloth, torpidity, lethargy, lentitude.

SLUICE, *n.* 1. Tide gate, flood gate, dock gate, sluice gate, head gate, lock gate, lock.

2. Conduit, channel, flume, trough, dike, watercourse, trench, moat.

SLUM, *n.* Group of ramshackle buildings, depressed area, dwelling, *etc.,* tenement, rookery, shanty town *(coll.).*

SLUMBER, *n.* Repose, rest, hibernation, siesta, the arms of Morpheus, nap, forty winks *(coll.),* shut-eye *(sl.),* snooze *(coll.),* sleep, doze, dormancy.

SLUMBER, *v.* Repose, retire, doze, turn in *(coll.),* nap, hit the sack *(sl.),* snooze, lie dormant, sleep, drop off *(coll.),* nod off *(coll.),* take forty winks *(coll.),* estivate *(Zool.),* rest in the arms of Morpheus, hibernate.

SLUMBEROUS, *adj.* Weary, drowsy, faint, nodding, somnolent, oscitant, dozy *(coll.),* torpid, heavy, half-asleep, exhausted, fatigued, tired, sleepy, yawning.

SLUMP, *n.* Decline, falling off, subsidence, lapse, wane, ebb, reaction, comedown, downfall, sink, dip, drop, droop, plunge, swag, sag, failure, tumble, reflex.

SLUMP, *v.* 1. Sink, fall through, fall gradually, lag, settle, subside, wane, lapse, droop, dip, recede, sag, drop, ebb, mire, decline, wallow, gravitate, give way, succumb, faint, wilt, jade, repine, slip, decay.

2. Fall suddenly and markedly *(as prices, the market, etc.),* have a decided falling off in progress, dip, decline, depreciate, lose ground, recede, plunge, ruin, relapse, devaluate, deteriorate, degenerate, diminish, retrogress, retrograde, go to the dogs, go to pot, go from bad to worse, collapse, cave in.

SLUR, *n.* 1. Disparaging remark, slight, reproach, derision, contempt, censure, reflection, innuendo, affront, discourtesy, insult, rebuff, snub, spurn, disrespect, indignity, irreverence, incivility, cut *(coll.),* imputation, reprehension, animadversion, criticism, denouncement, obloquy, stricture, lampoon, insinuation, reproof, hit, condemnation, reprobation, knock *(sl.),* slam *(sl.),* disparagement, denigration.

2. Blot *(as upon reputation),* stain, mark, spot, speck, blemish, bad name, disrepute, smudge, smutch, badge of infamy, tarnish, flaw, stigma, brand, disgrace, bar sinister, taint, smirch, imputation, reproach.

SLUR, *v.* 1. *(Often fol. by* OVER*)* Pass over lightly, slight, disregard, gloss over, neglect, treat with indifference, contemn, forget, ignore, scorn, snub, leave out of consideration, spurn, set aside, omit, skip *or* skim over, overlook, discountenance, misprize, pass by, let pass, cut *(coll.),* turn up one's nose at, sneeze at, blink *or* wink at, take no

thought *or* account of, make light of, dismiss from one's thoughts, cold shoulder, disdain, reject, rebuff, high-hat *(sl.),* give the go-by *(coll.),* do negligently, scamp, fribble, do by halves, play with, toy with.

2. Pronounce indistinctly, utter hurriedly *or* carelessly, mumble, mutter, elide, drag, drawl, mouth, speak thickly, be inarticulate, slide.

3. Reproach, disparage, calumniate, depreciate, stigmatize, taint, give a bad name, stain, brand, tarnish, sully, bespatter, blacken, defile, speak of slightingly *or* disrespectly, asperse, traduce, taunt, twit, defame, censure, belittle, libel, slander, debase, degrade, ridicule, insult, dishonor, malign, soil, denigrate, vilify, deride, drag through the mire, tread *or* trample under foot, discredit, detract, vilipend, condemn, denounce, cast a stone at, cry down, derogate, decry.

SLUSH, *n.* 1. Partly melted snow, lolly, slosh, mush.

2. Liquid mud, slime, watery mire, slosh, sludge, ooze, muck, clay, silt, seepage, leakage, gumbo, slop, alluvium, transudate, transudation.

3. Refuse, greasy mixture, sludge, muck, scum, waste, smut, grime, soot, smudge, garbage, rubbish.

4. Silly *or* weakly emotional talk *or* writing, *etc.,* fudge, mush *(coll.),* gush *(coll.),* trumpery, effusion, twaddle, volubility, verbosity, bosh, babble, nonsense, patter, slaver, doting, drivel, sentimentality, insipidity, drool *(coll.).*

SLUT, *n.* Dirty slovenly woman, hag, wench, alley cat, dowdy, frump, drab, sloven, drabbletail, draggletail, trollop, slattern.

SLY, *adj.* 1. Cunning, wily, artful, crafty, shifty, treacherous, slippery, evasive, tricky, disingenuous, dishonest, perfidious, guileful, misleading, contriving, intriguing, conniving, scheming, cagey *(coll.),* timeserving, dark, sneaking, untrustworthy, false, deceitful, deceptive, shrewd, cautious, foxy, politic, designing, snaky, subtle, insidious, satanic, Machiavellian, sneaky.

2. Insidious, secret, surreptitious, stealthy, covert, underhand, clandestine, furtive, hugger-mugger, hidden, screened, unrevealed, masked, dissembled, obscured, buried, delitescent, disguised, camouflaged, unseen, secreted, private, secluded, feigned, evasive, dark, arcane, sneaking, ensconced, veiled, with secret design, collusive, underground, cunning, confidential, skulking, undercover, privy.

3. Playfully artful, mischievous, roguish, arch, knowing, crafty, skillful, sagacious, wise, clever, sapient, cunning, shrewd, appealing, perceptive, percipient, winning, saucy, sportive, frolicsome, playful, waggish, merry, mirthful, jocose, subtle, designing, intriguing, tricksy.

SMACK, *n.* 1. Taste, flavor *(esp. distinctive or suggestive of something),* savor, tang, tincture, pungency, aroma, relish, odor, sapor, sapidity, zest, piquancy, poignancy, essence.

2. Trace, touch, suggestion, tinge, tincture, dash, spice, modicum, little, particle, point, scintilla, smell, scantling, soupçon, infusion, sprinkling, scrap, bit, doit, speck, snippet, morsel, snip, spot, iota, atom, mite, mote, grain, micron, ion, whit, tittle, minim, trifle, minutia, straw.

3. Taste, mouthful, bite, small quantity, sip, lick, gobbet, crumb, morsel, nip, nibble, taster, sup, spoonful, sample, dram, swallow, thimbleful, suck, lap, toothful, soupçon, lick, drop, swig, drink.

4. Resounding kiss, osculation, loud kiss, buss (*coll.*).

5. Smart *or* resounding blow, crack, slap, snap, rap, hit, buffet, fillip, thwack, cuff, box, plump, plunk, whack, stroke, stripe, bang, knock, swipe, wallop, pommel, blow, lash.

SMACK, *v.* 1. (*Often fol. by* OF) Have a taste *or* flavor, taste, savor, resemble, have a trace *or* suggestion, have a savor *or* tincture, show traces of the presence *or* influence of, betoken, partake of, have a touch of, be comparable to, match, suggest, approximate, approach, have all the earmarks of.

2. Bring (put, throw, send, *etc.*) with a sharp resounding blow *or* smart stroke, snap, crash, pitch, plunk, plump, plop, crack, slash, plank (*coll.*), heave, slam.

3. Strike smartly, make a sharp sound, slap, crack, spank, whack, box, knock, cuff, punch, wallop, belabor, thwack, beat, thump, pound, lash, clap, swipe, bang, slug, cudgel, clip, pommel, tap, bat, hit, jab.

SMACKING, *adj.* Smart, brisk, strong (*as a breeze*), spanking, fresh, forceful, animated, quick, lively, vigorous, stirring, crisp, spirited, snappy (*coll.*).

SMALL, *adj.* 1. Of limited size, of comparatively restricted dimensions, not big, little, minute, microscopic, short, stunted, fine, infinitesimal, scrubby, elfin, Lilliputian, tiny, wee, diminutive, dwarfed, cramped, breviped, scraggy, shrunken, undersized, puny, imperceptible, inappreciable, pygmy, runty, squat, pint-sized, pocket-sized, shriveled, miniature, vestigial, stocky, pug, pugged, truncated, snub, half-pint, molecular, microbic, toy, child's, minikin, Tom Thumb, pollard.

2. Slender, thin, narrow, slight, spare, puny, dapper, petite, emaciated, gracile, delicate, skinny, filamentous, filiform, fleshless, stunted, lean.

3. Not great in amount (degree, extent, duration, value, *etc.*), short, brief, compact, curt, elliptical, terse, ephemeral, succinct, laconic, clipped, decurtate, curtate, momentary, compendious, passing, temporary, fugacious, fugitive, summary, circumscribed, concise, short-lived, perishable, mortal, transitory, hasty, abbreviatory, fleet, volatile, quick, brisk, cursory, compact, condensed, precarious, scant, impalpable, imperceptible, evanescent, meager, fleeting, inappreciable, intangible, infinitesimal.

4. Not great numerically, denoted by a low number, few, thinly scattered, to be counted on one's fingers, slender, thin, scrimpy, few and far between, sparse, scant, skimpy, deficient.

5. Having but little land (capital, *etc.*), carrying on business on a limited scale, individual, private, independent, chain (*of a store*).

6. Of minor importance (moment, weight *or* consequence), meager, paltry, petty, inconsequential, shallow, impalpable, insignificant, unimportant, tenuous, evanescent, modest, moderate, slender, scanty, inappreciable, superficial, inconsiderable, trivial, trifling, feeble, exiguous, of no account, lightweight, middling, mediocre, ordinary, common, not vital, immaterial, piddling, mincing, nugatory, mean, niggling, one-horse (*coll.*), poor, indifferent, picayune, no great shakes (*coll.*), unworthy of serious consideration, scanty, trifling, flimsy, inferior, tin-horn (*sl.*), nameless, renownless, unnoticed, unknown, obscure, lowly, secondrate, third-rate, foolish, pitiful, two-by-four (*sl.*), ignoble, tin-pot (*sl.*), worthless, negligible.

7. Humble, lowly, modest, unpretentious, inferior, junior, secondary, second-rate, meek, sheepish, low, minor, beggarly, poor, lesser, subordinate, subaltern, unassuming, unostentatious, unobtrusive, unknown, obscure, common, submissive, plebeian, ignoble, servile, meek, prostrate, tractable, docile, subject, obeisant, subservient, simple, plain, vulgar, inglorious, lowborn, menial, baseborn, wretched, nameless, renownless, abject.

8. Characterized by *or* indicative of littleness of mind *or* character, mean-spirited, ungenerous, bigoted, mean, narrow, illiberal, miserly, close, chary, sordid, penurious, superficial, stinting, meager, paltry, stingy, pinching, churlish, inflexible, limited, provincial, insular, intolerant, prejudiced, purblind, unreasonable, narrow-minded, stiff, stiffnecked, near-sighted, short-sighted, immovable, uncompromising, opinionated, parsimonious, beggarly, shabby, tight (*coll.*), niggardly, near.

9. Ashamed, mortified, embarrassed, regretful, discomposed, humiliated, chagrined, bowed-down, abashed, out of countenance, confounded, dashed, crestfallen, chapfallen, humbled, uneasy, uncomfortable.

10. Of little strength *or* force, feeble, faint, slight, puny, delicate, frail, flimsy, fragile, weak, inefficient, strengthless, tenuous, ethereal, attenuated, dainty, gossamery, frangible, unsteady, teetery, tottery, tottering, rickety, unstable, insubstantial, jejune.

11. (*Of sound or the voice*) Gentle, soft, low, light, faint, whispering, quiet, delicate, hushed, unclear, colorless, baby, indistinct, murmuring, subdued, muted, stifled, inaudible, muffled, scarcely *or* barely audible.

12. Weak, diluted, watery, reduced, thinned, rarefied, attenuated, insipid, wishy-washy.

SMART, *adj.* 1. Sharp, keen, severe, painful, poignant, pricking, stinging, intense, pungent, bitter, cutting, trenchant, hurtful, acrimonious, tart, rude, abrupt, drastic, curt, scathing, satirical, malevolent, venomous, crabbed, mordacious, crusty, derisory, insulting, excoriating, maleficent, malicious, lashing, galling, rancorous, spiteful, envenomed, invidious, uncharitable, unkind, cruel, acrid, bearish, mean, brusque, blunt, gruff.

2. Sharply severe (*as blows*), hard, resounding, rude, rough, vigorous, brisk, stinging, fast, sudden, swift, precipitate, painful, sore, stiff, harsh, abrupt.

3. Prompt in action, quick, ready, jaunty, perky, lively, fresh, nimble, active, spirited, sprightly, agile, alert, vivacious, enterprising, spry, alive, zealous, mettlesome, earnest, breezy, hearty, fervent, ardent, buoyant, airy, full of life, full of spirit, full of action, jocund, sportive, animated, bright, vivid, heated, eager, violent, enthusiastic, excited.

4. Having *or* showing quick intelligence *or* ready capability, clever, sharp, shrewd, quick, bright, apt, expert, adroit, alert, prudent, dexterous, talented, gifted, versatile, brilliant, astute, hardheaded, common-sense, intelligent, quick-witted, acute, knowing, calculating, hawk-eyed, politic, diplomatic, artful, wily, foxy, crafty, sly, cunning, sagacious, subtle, wise, discriminating, wide-awake, long-headed, clear-headed, ingenious, far-sighted, open-eyed, sapient, imaginative, quick of apprehension, judicious, comprehending, provident, forehanded, discretional, efficient, capable, resourceful, competent, able, witty, skilled, skillful,

endowed, precocious, fertile, argute, inventive, perspicacious, discerning.

5. Cleverly ready *or* effective, witty, acute, apt, ingenious, masterly, deft, forcible, adroit, sharp, vigorous, pertinent, piquant, trenchant, stirring, caustic, saucy, racy, keen, humorous, funny, whimsical, droll, to the point, brilliant, jocose, jocular, scintillating, sparkling, pungent, quick-witted, nimble-witted, pointed, barbed.

6. Spruce, trim, neat, elegant, fashionable, trig, chic, natty, showy, fine, dandy, dashing, dapper, stylish, jaunty, well-groomed, up-to-the-minute, modish, handsome, rakish, classy *(sl.),* soigné *(Fr.).*

SMART, *n.* 1. Sharp local pain *(usually superficial),* sting, bite, nip, pinch, ache, burn, sore, tingle, pang, twinge.

2. Keen mental suffering *(as from wounded feelings, affliction, loss, etc.),* pain, infliction, injury, woe, cut, blow, canker, offense, sting, gall, torment, torture, agony, grievance, fret, thorn, shock, stroke, curse, infestation, the iron entering the soul, aggravation, vexation, oppression, bitterness, bitter dose *or* pill, trial, bitter cup, blight, load, burden, cross, worry, mortification, sorrow.

SMART, *v.* 1. Be a source of sharp local pain, cause a sharp pain, irritate, prick, bite, tingle, nettle, burn, chafe, fret, prickle, gall, pierce, rasp, itch, pinch, nip, gripe, sting.

2. Wound the feelings, sting, hurt, stab, vex, annoy, irritate, injure, gall, trouble, aggrieve, grate, offend, affront, plague, pester, provoke, nettle, go against the grain, mortify, gripe, agitate, disturb, harass, worry, torment, rile, inflame, rankle, distress, madden, pique, roil, irk, incense, chagrin, aggravate.

3. Suffer keenly from wounded feelings, suffer in punishment *or* in return for something, hurt, ache, writhe, undergo trial, pass through deep waters, agonize, endure (undergo, sustain, *etc.)* pain, wince, flinch, bleed, be troubled in mind, come to grief, bear the cross, droop, despond, sink, despair, grieve, sorrow, languish, stagger under a load, drain the cup of misery, fall sacrifice to, labor under, sit on thorns, be on pins and needles, be victim of.

SMARTEN, *v.* 1. Make more trim *or* spruce, improve in appearance, order, groom, arrange, shine, polish, adjust, tidy, beautify, primp, dress, brush, organize, tone up, set off, deck out, slick up *(coll.),* prink.

2. Make brisker *(as a pace),* quicken, hasten, liven, step up, accelerate, stimulate, vivify, animate, rouse, urge on, push forward, goad, whip, spur, precipitate, speed, press on, promote, prick, hurry, lend wings to, advance, whisk, impel, propel, drive, hustle, kindle, lash, force, inflame, thrust, boost, jog, prompt, move, motivate, bestir, excite, inspirit, zip up *(coll.).*

SMASH, *n.* 1. Smashing, shattering, collision, smack, impact, thwack, encounter, shock, shog, crash, concussion, brunt, appulse, jolt, blow, percussion, jostle.

2. Ruin, destruction, overthrow, crash, collapse, wreck, crackup, smash-up, breakdown, breakup, cataclysm, accident, knockout, defeat, rout, demolition, desolation, undoing, prostration, subversion, overturn, debacle, perdition, reversal, beating, drubbing, consumption, havoc, ravage, waste, extinction, mutiny, reverse, revolt, upset, overset, deathblow, catastrophe, convulsion, vanquishment, ruination, reduction, dissolution.

3. Financial failure, ruin, bankruptcy, adversity,

insolvency, misfortune, crash, collapse, fall, downfall, ill success, evil times, poverty, hard times, flop *(coll.).*

SMASH, *v.* 1. Break to pieces violently, crush, shatter, dash, wreck, crumple, shiver, batter, splinter, mash, disintegrate, pulverize, crack, deflagrate, *(Chem.),* comminute, triturate, reduce to powder *or* dust, grind, levigate, pulverate, granulate, crunch, mince, hash, crumble, grate, crumb, erode.

2. Overthrow, defeat utterly, destroy, devastate, raze, ravage, vanquish, overcome, overpower, overwhelm, put an end to, confound, crush, subjugate, suppress, put down, prostrate, rout, beat, discomfit, master, worst, conquer, demolish, ruin, subvert, level, invalidate, confute, obviate, quash, break up, disrupt, shatter, nullify, fell, wreck, reduce, fling *or* dash down, extirpate, abolish, obliterate, quell, subdue, break, overmaster, thrash, whip, surmount, be victorious over.

3. *(Fol. by* AGAINST, INTO, THROUGH, *etc.)* Dash with great violence *or* shattering force, collide, batter, break, strike, plunge, jar, jolt, hurtle, beat, crack, crash.

4. Ruin financially, become financially ruined, bankrupt, fail, collapse, reduce to poverty, pauperize, go into debt, break, impoverish, become insolvent, crash, go on the rocks, go broke *(sl.).*

SMATTERING, *n.* Slight *or* superficial knowledge, smatter, dabbling, sciolism, least bit, drop, smack, superficiality, shallowness, superficialness, ignorance, pretense, pretension, dilettantism, half-learning, vague notion, simulation, dissembling, trace, suggestion, scantling, sprinkling, scrap, bit, trifle, minimum.

SMEAR, *n.* Mark made by *or* as by smearing, stain, blotch, blot, daub, soil, dirt, grime, smutch, splotch, blur, spot, smudge, smirch, patch.

SMEAR, *v.* 1. Rub with grease (oil, paint, dirt, *etc.),* daub, spread, bedaub, besmear, splotch, spatter, coat, blur, besmudge, ruddle, ensanguine, overspread, inunct, cover, film, plaster, lubricate, paint, begrime, lay on, oil, grease, anoint, dress, tar, dab, lard.

2. Soil *(as one's reputation),* sully, smirch, stain, tarnish, spoil, contaminate, smudge, smutch, impair, pollute, stigmatize, deface, mar, spot, corrupt, foul, blacken, damage, bespatter, besmirch, denigrate, drag in the mud, blemish, degrade, bring down, dishonor, detract from, debase, belittle, reduce, depreciate, subvert, cheapen, defile, malign, undermine, brand, vilipend, vilify, discredit, decry, derogate, disparage, reflect upon, slight, slander, libel, cast aspersions at.

SMEARY, *adj.* 1. Showing smears, smeared, bedaubed, splotchy, smirchy, smudgy, cloudy, filmy, foggy, hazy, sooty, smoky, muddy, dirty, besmirched, smirched, bleared, bleary, fuliginous, grimy, blurry, nubilous.

2. Tending to smear *or* soil, dauby, sticky, messy, gummy, viscid, viscous, gelatinous, doughy, pasty, slushy, sloppy, clammy, oozy, mucky, muddy, squashy, gooey *(sl.).*

SMELL, *n.* 1. Faculty *or* sense of smelling, scent, olfaction.

2. Quality of a thing which is *or* may be smelled, scent, odor, perfume, aroma, redolence, stink, stench, fetor, exhalation, emanation, pollution, fetidness, reek, malodor, graveolence, fume, bouquet, effluvium, fragrance, pungency, incense, essence, nidor, aura, savor.

3. Trace, suggestion, whiff, smack, touch, tinge,

tincture, dash, modicum, spice, particle, scintilla, scantling, soupçon, infusion, sprinkling, scrap, bit, doit, speck, snippet, morsel, snip, spot, iota, atom, mite, grain, micron, ion, whit, tittle, minim, trifle, minutia, straw, mote.

SMELL, *v.* 1. Perceive through the nose *or* olfactory sense, scent, get scent of, breathe, inhale, sniff, snuff, get wind of, spoor.

2. Give out an odor (*esp. as specified*), reek, have a scent, emit an odor, breathe, exhale, effluviate, stink, be fragrant, emanate, yield an odor, have a perfume, be malodorous, offend the nostrils.

3. (*Fol. by* OUT, ABOUT) Search, find, investigate, nose, trail, track, trace, follow, seek, look, pry, peer, mouse, hunt, pursue, quest, scout, ferret out, sniff out, follow the trail *or* scent of.

4. Perceive (*by shrewdness or sagacity*), detect, discover, suspect, discern, be near the truth, be aware of, be on the right path, be hot *or* warm (*coll.*), spot, descry, remark, recognize, see, note, make out, intuit, feel, sense, distinguish, observe, discriminate, notice, mark, catch, apprehend, trace.

SMELLY, *adj.* Emitting a strong *or* offensive smell, odorous, rank, fetid, strong, malodorous, odoriferous, effluvious, redolent, heady, pungent, penetrating, reeking, sharp, rancid, putrid, off, tainted, high, stinking, nidorous, stenchy, graveolent, olid, nosy (*coll.*), olent, nidorulent.

SMELT, *v.* Fuse (*ore*), refine, reduce, melt, separate out (*metal from ore*), scorify.

SMILE, *n.* 1. Act of smiling, smiling expression, grin, smirk, simper, fleer.

2. Favoring look *or* regard, propitiousness, favor, good graces, blessing, tolerance, indulgence, benediction, hope, promise, mercy, clemency, support, aid, help, furtherance, countenance, care, auspices, fosterage, patronage, backing, nurture, encouragement.

SMILE, *v.* 1. Assume an expression of pleasure (favor, kindliness, amusement, derision, scorn, *etc.*), smirk, grin, simper, nod, snicker, fleer.

2. Look favorably upon, countenance, patronize, favor, advocate, support, cherish, foster, take up, aid, befriend, further, promote, be benevolent toward, advance, forward, humor, cheer, shine upon, encourage, embrace, salute.

SMIRCH, *n.* 1. Dirty mark *or* smear, stain, blotch, blot, daub, soil, dirt, grime, smutch, blur, spot, smudge, patch, splotch.

2. Stain (*as on a reputation*), blot, blemish, stigma, discredit, mark, spot, speck, bad name, dishonor, detract from, belittle, reduce, debase, tarnish, flaw, brand, disgrace, taint, imputation, reproach.

SMIRCH, *v.* 1. Discolor, soil, smear, daub, splotch, spatter, blur, besmudge, begrime, dab, smudge, smutch.

2. Sully (*as with disgrace*), tarnish, slur, smear, soil, stain, spoil, contaminate, smudge, smutch, impair, pollute, stigmatize, deface, mar, spot, corrupt, foul, blacken, damage, bespatter, besmirch, drag in the mud, blemish, degrade, bring down, dishonor, detract from, belittle, reduce, debase, depreciate, subvert, cheapen, defile, malign, denigrate, undermine, brand, vilipend, vilify, discredit, decry, derogate, disparage, reflect upon, slight, slander, libel, cast aspersions at.

SMIRK, *n.* Affected smile, simper, offensively familiar look sneer, leer, fleer, grin, ogle, grimace.

SMITE, *v.* 1. Deal a blow *or* stroke, strike, knock,

come against, wallop (*coll.*), clip, punch, dash, fustigate, hurt, switch, flagellate, slog, drub, bastinado, trounce, swing at, flail, beat, tamp, baste, pommel, tan (*coll.*), sock (*sl.*), flog, thresh, batter, pelt, larrup, lambaste (*sl.*), paste (*sl.*), scourge, strap, whale (*coll.*), lash, lace, spank, whip, thrash, bat, belt (*sl.*), jab, whop (*coll.*), douse (*sl.*), plug (*sl.*), clout (*coll.*), box, bang, cuff, club, slam, whack, poke, clap, buffet, pat, cudgel, hit, cane, birch, strike together, collide with, slug, thump, bump, smash, shatter, devastate, pound.

2. Vex, trouble, wear down, disturb, bully, bulldoze (*sl.*), taunt, agitate, excite, anger, incommode, deride, traduce, exacerbate, discommode, dragoon, dispirit, ridicule, incense, afflict, reproach, fleer, twit, vilify, calumniate, infuriate, arouse, exorcise, scourge, banter, confuse, delude, upbraid, overrun, plague, worry, distress, assault, annoy, harass, harry, tease, gall, badger, molest, heckle, bullyrag, abuse, chafe, grate, haunt, huff, baffle, provoke, sting, pique, aggrieve, ruffle, weigh upon, grip, get (*coll.*), jade, fag, tire out, wear out, nettle, gnaw, roil, bait, prick, prostrate, buffalo (*sl.*), intimidate, cow, browbeat, terrorize, tantalize, infest, enrage, hound, embarrass, persecute, harrow, nag, fret, pester, toss, hector, haggle, rack, pother, macerate, disquiet, goad, distract, wring, perplex, grind, pain, squeeze, bother, mortify, egg, revile, grieve, irritate, injure, oppress, beset, irk.

3. Destroy, demolish, crush, smash, batter, despoil, overwhelm, break, ravage, lay waste, desolate, devour, swallow, subvert, blast, gut, waste, ruin, wreck, overthrow, upset, throw down, pull down, annihilate, extinguish, abolish, wipe out, unbuild, undo, quell, blight, finish, end, quash, extirpate, eradicate, root out, eliminate, efface.

SMITH, *n.* Forger, metalworker, blacksmith.

SMITHEREEN, *n.* (*Usually plur.*) Piece, atom, shred, particle, bit, scrap, flinder, tatter, sliver, splinter, shiver.

SMITHY, *n.* Smith's workshop, forge, smithery, stithy.

SMITTEN, *adj.* 1. Afflicted, distressed, grieved, troubled, burdened, vexed, harassed, overburdened, haunted, crushed, beset, squeezed, irked, harrowed, roiled, galled, abused, embarrassed, hounded, chafed, worried, wounded, plagued, overcharged, bowed down.

2. (*Colloq.*) In love, entranced, enchanted, under a spell, spellbound, attracted, captivated, charmed, attached, fascinated, allured, bewitched, engrossed, enthralled, enraptured, enslaved, carried away, hypnotized, inflamed.

SMOCK, *n.* Chemise, frock, mantle, apron, shift, slip, pelisse.

SMOG, *n.* Heavy, dirty fog, brume, soup (*sl.*), mist, drisk, haze.

SMOKE, *n.* 1. Exhalation from burning *or* smoldering substance, sooty vapor, smudge, reek, fume, mist, dust, smut, smutch, cloud, puff, effluvium, smog (*coll.*), steam.

2. Something unsubstantial *or* evanescent, something without results, chimera, dream, imagining, fancy, ephemera, bubble, froth, foam, vision, illusion, vapor, phantasy, castle in Spain, castle in the air, pipe dream, myth, fiction, shadow, cobweb, chaff.

3. Obscuring conditions, screen, curtain, camouflage, feint, blind, shroud, veil, blanket, shield, mask, covert, disguise, pall.

4. Act *or* spell of smoking tobacco, *etc.*, puff, drag *(sl.)*.

5. That which is smoked, pipe, pipeful, cigar, cigarette, butt, stub, stogy, cheroot, fag *(sl.)*, weed *(coll.)*, toby *(sl.)*.

SMOKE, *v.* 1. Give off *or* emit smoke, cloud, billow, exhale, steam, reek, exhaust, fume, smolder, funk *(sl.)*.

2. Draw in and puff out smoke *(of tobacco, etc.)*, inhale, puff, draw, pull, drag *(coll.)*, funk *(sl.)*.

3. Ride *or* travel along with great speed, hurry, race, scurry, flee, skip, spurt, push on, whisk, run, sprint, rush, ride hard, shoot, tear, fly, scour, scoot *(coll.)*, bolt, dart, skedaddle *(sl.)*, outstrip the wind, bowl along, cut along *(coll.)*, spank, wing one's way, post, hie, scuttle, flit, scamper, hustle, pace, swoop, career, rip *(coll.)*, whiz, sweep, spin, go like lightning *or* greased lightning *(coll.)*, go like a shot *(coll.)*, go hell-bent *(coll.)*, clip, bound, bustle, bundle, hump it *(sl.)*, make strides, step on it *(coll.)*, step lively *(coll.)*.

4. Fumigate, expose to smoke, cure by exposure to smoke, disinfect, infumate, smudge, smoke-cure, smoke-dry.

5. Color *or* darken by smoke, cloud, becloud, fog, befog, mist, muddy, smear, haze, nigrify, soot, smirch, smudge, smutch, nubilate, smut, dim, sully, tarnish, grime, blacken, black, blot, blotch, darken.

6. *(Fol. by* OUT, *etc.)* Drive out by means of smoke, force into public view *or* knowledge, root out, ferret out, expose, dig up, hunt out, pry out, spy out, uncover, unearth, disinter, make manifest, disclose, bring to light, lay open, bare, elicit, educe.

SMOKESTACK, *n.* Pipe for the escape of smoke *or* gases, funnel, tube, chimney, flue, stovepipe, smokeshaft.

SMOKY, *adj.* 1. Emitting smoke *or* much smoke, smoldering, reeky, fumy, vaporous, fuming, reeking, fumacious.

2. Darkened with smoke, blurred, dingy, grimy, dirty, besmirched, fumed, smudgy, fuliginous, discolored, opaque, unclean, dim, sooty, begrimed, blackened, obfuscated, murky, black, dark, foggy, obscure, misty, smutty, smutchy, dusty, dusky, lackluster, clouded, nubilated, nebulous, infumate *(Zool.)*.

3. Having the character *or* appearance of smoke, pertaining to *or* suggestive of smoke, dense, foggy, cloudy, thick, muddy, turbid, murky, misty, fuliginous, volatile, vaporous, nubilous.

SMOLDER, *v.* 1. Smoke, burn without flame, fume, steam, reek, emit smoke, funk *(sl.)*.

2. Continue in a suppressed state, exist without outward demonstration, be inert, stagnate, fester, rankle, lie dormant, hang fire, kindle, sizzle, smoke, burn, fret, slumber, sleep, rage, be quiescent, foam, boil, swell, chafe, fume, lurk, lie hid, simmer, seethe, underlie.

3. Display repressed feelings *(esp. of indignation)*, flash, fulgurate, radiate, flicker, glitter, waver, lance, spark, glow, beam, blaze, glint, gleam, spill over *or* out, flare, burst, flame, fire, shoot, look daggers.

SMOOTH, *adj.* 1. Free from projections *or* irregularities of surface, free from hairs *or* hairy growth, free from irregularities of surface (hollows, ridges, obstructions, *etc.*), calm, level, flat, plane, horizontal, glabrous *(Zool.)*, polished, lubricous, glassy, greasy, slick, slippery, un-

wrinkled, unruffled, fine-grained, burnished, velvet, soft, flush, oily, regular, uniform, sleek, silky, satiny, glossy.

2. Free from *or* proceeding without breaks *or* abrupt bends, *etc.*, free from unevenness *or* roughness, easy, uniform, free from hindrance *or* difficulties, facile, regular, steady, stable, accustomed, methodical, orderly, uneventful, harmonious, businesslike, rhythmical, well-ordered, well-regulated, unvaried, unchanging, constant, monotonous, systematic.

3. Undisturbed *(as the feelings, temper, etc.)*, calm, tranquil, serene, placid, even, equable, quiet, pacific, untroubled, moderate, mild, complacent, unruffled, peaceful, unperturbed, composed, cool, poised, inexcitable, reconciled, philosophic, meek, sedate, nonchalant, level-headed, unimpassioned, collected, self-possessed, unmoved, inirritable, reposeful.

4. Easy, flowing *(as speech, a speaker, etc.)*, mellifluous, elegant, fluent, voluble, measured, glib, facile, polished, deliberate, proper, correct, tasteful, seemly, neat, tripping, refined, comely, happy, felicitous, graceful, concinnate.

5. Pleasant *(as manners, persons, etc.)*, agreeable, ingratiatingly polite, soft-spoken, suave, bland, insinuating, fawning, flattering, unctuous, adulatory, soothing, disarming, well-mannered, polite, civil, urbane, mannerly, obsequious, obliging, conciliatory, gracious, good-natured, cultivated, polished, complaisant, genteel, civilized, mild-mannered.

6. Bland, free from harshness *or* sharpness of taste, mild, mellow, gentle, moderate, soft, ripened, delicate, tempered, aged.

7. Not harsh to the ear, mellifluous, euphonious, liquid, flowing, metrical, rhythmical, sweet, soothing, dulcet, mellifluent, musical, lyric, tuneful, silvery, mellisonant.

SMOOTH, *v.* 1. Make smooth of surface *(as by scraping, planing, pressing, stroking, etc.)*, remove projections from, lubricate, press, level, flatten, mangle, iron, smoothen, dress, burnish, levigate, polish, file, align, abrade, roll, plane, scrape, rub, pumice, even, equalize, sandpaper, emery, grease, oil, sand, wax, sleek, buff.

2. Make more polished (elegant, plausible, agreeable, *etc.)*, refine, polish, correct, cultivate, perfect, temper, soften, improve, devulgarize, declassify, subtilize, develop, elaborate, civilize, meliorate.

3. Tranquilize *(as the feelings)*, calm, soothe, allay, mollify, mitigate, alleviate, moderate, assuage, compose, modulate, temper, attemper, dulcify, lenify, quell, sober, soften, appease, lull, hush, still, pour oil on troubled waters, pour balm into.

4. *(Usually fol. by* OVER) Gloss over *(as something unpleasant or wrong)*, palliate, extenuate, soften, whitewash, gloze over, explain away, cover up, make allowance for, color, varnish, disguise, vindicate, dress up, pretext, slur, cloak, cover, mince, conceal, embroider, justify, put a good face upon, find a loophole, crawl *or* creep out of, allow for, excuse.

5. Prepare *(the way)*, facilitate, ready, pave, soap, grease, make easier, ease, open, clear, provide, help, promote, disembarrass, disencumber, disburden, free, lighten, lubricate.

SMOOTH-FACED, *adj.* 1. Beardless, clean-shaven, whiskerless, hairless, depilous, glabrous.

2. Having a smooth surface *(as cloth)*, napless,

silky, sleek, glossy, slippery, polished, lustrous, shiny, sheeny.

3. Deceitfully ingratiating, dissembling, plausible, flattering, canting, insincere, cozening, adulatory, unctuous, tartuffian, hypocritical, fair-spoken, two-faced, bland, Janus-faced, false, mealy-mouthed, pharisaic, sanctimonious, faithless, deceptive, cunning, artful, perfidious, treacherous.

MOTHER, *n.* 1. Dense stifling smoke, smoldering fire, smoking *or* smoldering state, soot, smolder, smut.

2. Dust *(in a dense or enveloping cloud)*, fog, spray, vapor, mist, cloud, haze, spread, film, storm, blanket, pea soup *(coll.)*, screen.

MOTHER, *v.* 1. Stifle, deprive of air, suffocate, extinguish, deaden *(a fire, etc.)*, strangle, burke, garrote, throttle, asphyxiate, damp, snuff, quench, choke.

2. *(Often fol. by* UP*)* Cover closely *or* thickly, envelop in, obscure, adumbrate, surround, wrap, blanket, shower, compass, beset, hem in, invest, besiege, shroud, conceal, infold, eclipse.

3. Suppress, repress, conceal, hide, restrain, keep secret, quell, mask, silence, moderate, keep down *or* back, keep to oneself, secrete, cloak, stifle, gloss over, gloze over, soften, subdue, tone down, reserve, stop, veil, muffle, disguise, quiet, soft-pedal *(coll.)*, choke back, hush, cover, shroud, camouflage, withhold, dissemble, keep under a bushel, squash, squelch *(coll.)*.

MUDGE, *n.* 1. Stain, smirch, grime, spot, smutch, soil, smear, splotch, blur, dirt, daub, blot.

2. Sooty vapor, smut, smutch, cloud, puff, effluvium, reek, fume, smoke, mist, dust.

MUDGE, *v.* 1. Smoke *(as an orchard)*, fumigate, treat against insects, pests, *etc.*

2. Stain, smirch, sully, blacken, blemish, bedaub, spot, besmirch, splotch, begrime, daub, smutch, mar, bespatter, spatter, besmudge.

MUG, *adj.* 1. Neat, trim, spruce, dapper, correct, chic, natty, jaunty, stylish, well-groomed, tidy, elegant, showy, dashing, modish, rakish, trig, fine, dandy, handsome, classy *(sl.)*.

2. Self-satisfied, pleased, serene, placid, imperturbable, gratified, prim, complacent.

MUGGLE, *v.* Convey in a clandestine manner, run, bring *or* take secretly, rustle *(of cattle)*, bootleg, traffic in contraband.

MUGGLER, *n.* Pirate, runner, rustler, contrabandist, bootlegger.

MUT, *n.* 1. Filth, dirt, dust, soot, muck, smutch, grime.

2. Lasciviousness, lewdness, bawdiness, obscenity, dirt, ribaldry, impurity, immodesty, indecency, coarseness, grossness, lubricity, wantonness, scurrility, vileness, debauchery, profligacy, salaciousness, lechery, suggestiveness, foulness, prurience.

MUTCH, *n.* Stain, blot, daub, blur, dirt, spot, smudge, soil, smear, splotch, grime, smirch.

MUTCH, *v.* Blacken, blemish, bespatter, spatter, besmirch, splotch, begrime, daub, mar, smudge, spot, bedaub, stain, smirch, sully.

MUTTY, *adj.* Ribald, lubricious, obscene, pornographic, erotic, free, scurrilous, shameless, salacious, carnal, suggestive, fleshly, licentious, lickerish, lecherous, libidinous, prurient, indecent, immodest, filthy, vile, gross, coarse, dirty, unclean, lurid, lewd, bawdy, lascivious, offensive.

SNACK, *n.* Light *or* brief meal, taste, bite *(coll.)*, light repast, light lunch.

SNAG, *n.* 1. Concealed log, branch, *etc.*, projecting tooth, projection, prominence, gnarl, hidden obstruction.

2. Knotty point, oppilation, hindrance, hitch, check, stop, stumbling-block, balk, obstacle, impediment, block, retardment, enigma, barrier, clog, obstruction, impedition, snarl, rub, restriction, Gordian knot, problem, difficulty, holdback, dilemma, halt, curb, stay, handicap, involvement, hamper, drag, catch, complication, intricacy, brake, catch.

SNAG, *v.* Get caught *or* catch (by an obstruction, *etc.*), become entangled, clutch, catch, arrest, hook, ensnare, fasten upon.

SNAIL, *n.* Lazy fellow, slow-moving person, lazybones, idler, loafer, ne'er-do-well, laggard, shirker, slouch, drone, fainéant, good-for-nothing, gold brick *(sl.)*, lounge lizard *(sl.)*, lingerer, slug, sluggard.

SNAIL-PACED, *adj.* Crawling, lagging, tortoise-like, hesitant, snail-like, dawdling, faltering, hanging back, pausing, sluggish, plodding, slow, shuffling.

SNAKE, *n.* 1. Serpent, viper, ophidian.

2. Rascal, scoundrel, blackguard, evildoer, treacherous person, serpent, miscreant, misdoer, malfeasor, rogue, knave, reprobate, humbug, trickster, snake in the grass, Janus, Judas, traitor, beguiler, rat *(sl.)*, seducer, delinquent, rakehell, villain, wolf in sheep's clothing, cockatrice, double-dealer, reptile.

SNAKY, *adj.* 1. Moving in a winding course, winding, twisting, tortuous, serpentine, anfractuous, convoluted, anguine, meandering, wriggly, snake-like, turning, sinuous, colubrine, devious, zigzag, ambagious, serpentile, spiral, roundabout, sinuate, flexuous, meanderous, circuitous, mazy, wormlike, vermicular, vermiform, anguiform, labyrinthine.

2. Having the qualities of a snake, artful, subtle, wily, reptilian, viperous, cunning, crafty, treacherous, snakelike, sneaky, viperish, viperine, untrustworthy, false, guileful, foxy, insidious, satanic, Machiavellian, serpentine, designing, contriving, misleading, scheming, conniving, dark, sneaking, deceitful.

SNAP, *n.* 1. Hook, catch, buckle, bolt, link, holdfast, lock, clasp, bar, brace, bond, latch, coupler, copula, clamp, fastener, grip, clinch.

2. Bite, seizure, nip, gnashing, champ, crunch, nibble.

3. Duration of time *(esp. of cold weather)*, spell, period, wave, interval.

4. Sharp, slight noise, tick, clack, click, clap, tink, tap, beat, clink.

5. Picture, photograph, snapshot, shot *(sl.)*.

SNAP, *v.* 1. Bite, gnash, nip, lunge at.

2. *(With* UP*)* Swoop on, take, clutch, hook, grasp, nab, seize, fasten upon, snare, clench, pluck, grab, pounce on, pick, grip, snag, claw.

3. Break in two, break, crack, part, separate, sever, sunder.

4. Fasten with a snap, snap closed, catch, hook, lock, link, clamp, secure, clinch, clip, latch, hasp, bar, couple, bolt, clasp, pin, buckle.

SNAPPISH, *adj.* Cross, irascible, irritable, petulant, crusty, acrimonious, discontented, grumbling, waspish, surly, vaporish, out of sorts, touchy, resentful, peevish, bilious, inflammable, oversensitive, peppery, currish, iracund, acerbic, choleric, jaundiced, bearish, huffy, cross-grained, churlish, crabbed, angry, sullen, growling, sour, tetchy, cantankerous, ill-tempered, ill-natured, quarrelsome, gruff, complaining, snarling, morose, faultfinding, censorious, perverse, grouchy (coll.), sulky, thin-skinned, ungracious, moody, fractious, captious.

SNARE, n. Trap, gin, noose, trapdoor, net, deadfall, pitfall, meshes, trepan, concealed excavation, springe, trapfall, toils, false bottom.

SNARE, v. Ensnare, catch, capture, bag, trap, take captive, seize, lay hold of, waylay, hook, entoil, entrap, trepan.

SNARL, n. 1. Snarling sound or utterance, growl, deep throaty sound, murmur, threat, gnarl.

2. Tangle, knot, twist, kink, raveling, coil, jungle, network, wilderness, sleave, mat.

3. Complicated or confused condition or matter, complexity, entanglement, embroilment, labyrinth, complexus, involution, poser, jungle, maze, dilemma, perplexity, complication, intricacy, hitch, paradox, vexed question, problem, circuity, tortuosity, ambages, inscrutability, obscurity, sinuosity involvement, wheels within wheels, tangled skein, arcanum, difficulty, predicament, enigma, sleave, Gordian knot, kink, twist, puzzle, imbroglio, stew (coll.), bafflement, riddle, knotty point, quandary, disorder, confusion, hornets' nest, embarrassment, intrigue.

SNARL, v. 1. Growl angrily or viciously, threaten, menace, sound from the throat.

2. Speak in a savagely sharp (angry or quarrelsome) manner, snap, be rude, growl, threaten, lash out, fire up, flare up, menace, bark, gnarl, bite one's head off (coll.).

3. Bring into a tangled condition, tangle, become tangled, interlace, gnarl, ravel, knot, twist, entangle, mat, derange, interweave, shuffle, tumble, tousle, dishevel, jumble, muddle, disorder, scramble, mix up.

4. Render complicated, make confused, complicate, confuse, involve, entangle, vex, perplex, obscure, embarrass, encumber, confound, muddle, bedevil, mix up, render unintelligible, implicate, hinder, hobble, clog, handicap, impede, hamper, spike one's guns, jumble, embroil, darken, conceal.

SNATCH, n. Part or sample of a thing, piece, section, specimen, cutting, scrap, slice, bit, point, dose, installment, segment, division, portion, corner, moiety, cantle, fraction, fragment, sum, measure, small amount, deal, handful, some.

SNATCH v. 1. (Usually fol. by AT) Make a sudden effort to seize something, catch at, grope for, try to grasp, grapple for, pursue, clutch at, reach desperately for, make a grab at, tug, scramble for, jump at, make a leap at, spring upon, pounce on, swoop down upon, claw at.

2. (Often fol. by UP, FROM, OUT OF, AWAY, etc.) Take (get, secure, etc.) suddenly or hastily, seize suddenly, grip, grasp, clutch, jerk, nip, capture, cleave, hug, clench, hang on to, lay hold of, fasten upon, snag, embrace, hook (coll.), twitch, tweak, gripe, pick, clinch, prehend, snap up, apprehend, tear away, steal, pull, wring, wrest, catch, pluck, grab, nab (coll.), yank (coll.).

SNATCHY, adj. Consisting of (occurring in or characterized by) snatches, spasmodic, irregular, sporadic, periodic, brief, recurrent, patchy, infrequent, discontinuous, disconnected, capricious, flickering, erratic, fitful, desultory, disjointed, broken, occasional, intermittent, inconstant.

SNEAK, v. 1. Go in a stealthy or furtive manner, act in a furtive, underhand or mean way, advance stealthily, prowl, slink, steal, lurk, skulk, slip, gumshoe (sl.), ambush, ambuscade, keep snug or close, seclude oneself, couch, lie in ambush, lie low (coll.), hide, keep in the background, snoop.

2. Move (put, pass, etc.) in a stealthy or furtive way, slip, slide, drop, cast unobtrusively, steal, grab.

SNEAK, n. One who sneaks, underhand, sneaking or contemptible person, lurker, craven, knave, poltroon, slinker, thief, snake in the grass, traitor, skulker, mean fellow, dastard, coward, miscreant, rascal, caitiff, renegade, shirker, white feather, white liver, rat (sl.).

SNEAKING, adj. 1. Acting in a furtive or underhand way, deceitfully underhand, contemptible, skulking, slinking, furtive, sinister, insidious, dishonest, dishonorable, unscrupulous, disingenuous, pettifogging, recreant, dark, crafty, cunning, artful, sly, wily, thieving, stealthy, false, shifty, slippery, poltroon, caitiff, cowering, cowardly, cringing, slavish, obsequious, hangdog, mean, crouching, groveling, thievish, lurking, abject, servile, truckling.

2. Secret, not generally avowed (as a feeling, notion, suspicion, etc.), unconfessed, private, hidden, intuitive, unmentioned, unexpressed, undivulged, unrevealed, undisclosed, impulsive, instinctive, nagging, inherent, innate, divinatory, spontaneous.

SNEER, n. 1. Look or expression suggestive of derision, scorn or contempt, smirk, scoff, insinuating glance, sardonic grin, leer, fleer, mock, ogle, wink, evil eye, blighting glance.

2. Derisive or scornful utterance or remark (esp. when covert or insinuative), jeer, scoff, gibe, disparagement, slight, intimation, derision, insult, irony, quip, scorn, sarcasm, abuse, taunt, ridicule, fling, hoot, flout, aspersion, fleer, defamation, derogation, obloquy, invective, slur, pasquinade, malediction, cut, indignity, thrust, caustic remark, insolence, jest, banter, rub, slander, rap (sl.), slam (sl.), knock (sl.), dig (sl.), provocation, slap, wipe (coll.), brickbat (coll.), depreciation, vilification, rude reproach, mockery, travesty, parody, lampoon, raillery, twit, quiz, chaff, wisecrack (sl.), persiflage.

SNEER, v. 1. Smile or curl the lip (showing scorn, contempt, etc.), leer, mock, smirk, fleer, laugh, look askance, ogle, gloat, grin, give the evil eye, squint, cut one's eye (sl.).

2. Speak or write so as to show derision (scorn, contempt), scoff, jeer, disparage, mock, rail, fleer, turn up the nose at, gibe, flout, sneeze at (coll.), hiss, banter, scorn, scout, twit, revile, throw mud at, taunt, ridicule, catcall, knock (sl.), have a fling at, spurn, rebuff, slander, backbite, satirize, lampoon, run down, traduce, malign, defame, vilify, cast aspersions, derogate, decry, calumniate, point the finger of scorn, hold up to scorn, jest, hoot, slur, chaff, deride, contemn, gird at, treat with insolence.

SNEEZE, n. Involuntary forcible emission of breath, sternutation.

SNICKER, v. Laugh (in a half-suppressed and indecorous or disrespectful manner), giggle, snigger, titter, ridicule, te-hee, mock, laugh in one's sleeve, chuckle, cackle.

SNIFF, n. 1. Short audible inhalation, snuff, sniffle, snuffle, snivel.

2. Scent perceived, odor, smell, snuff, aroma, essence, incense, fragrance, savor, whiff, breath, bouquet, redolence, pungency.

SNIFF, v. 1. Draw air in audibly, sniffle, inhale, breathe in, snuffle, snuff.

2. Smell by short inhalations, scent, inhale, nose, snuff, detect, breathe in, trace, track, trail.

3. (Often fol. by AT) Show disdain, contempt, etc., by a sniff, spurn, scorn, disdain, scoff, slight, brush aside, disregard, disparage, slur, contemn, snub, ignore, discountenance, misprize, turn up one's nose at, sneeze at, blink or wink at, make light of, reject, rebuff, high-hat (sl.), give the go-by (coll.), loathe, look down upon, despise, scout, laugh at, treat with contempt, flout, mock, consider beneath oneself, deem unbecoming, abhor.

SNIP, n. 1. Small cut made by snipping, clip, nip, gash, rift, rent, incision, slash, split, cleft, notch, slit, nick, blaze, score, scotch, break, scissure, fissure.

2. Small piece snipped off, small bit or amount of anything, modicum, bit, share, snippet, shred, scrap, tatter, splinter, tag, particle, fragment, swatch, shaving, sliver, slip, chip, clipping, slice, trifle, collop, paring, morsel, speck, mite.

SNIP, v. Cut with small quick stroke or strokes, clip, nip, crop, dock, lop, slash, hew, split, slit, chop, gash, hackle, hack, whittle.

SNIPE, v. Shoot (individually) from a concealed position, take a potshot, pelt, riddle, pot (Hunting).

SNIVEL, n. 1. Weak or pretended weeping, hypocritical show of feeling, crocodile tears, semblance of sorrow.

2. Light sniff, snuff, sniffle, snuffle.

SNIVEL, v. Weep or cry with sniffling, affect a tearful state, blubber, whine, pule, sob, lament, grovel, sniffle, whimper, fret, cry crocodile tears.

SNOB, n. One who admires (imitates or cultivates) those with social rank or wealth, etc., condescending or overbearing person, one who affects social importance and exclusiveness, climber, toady, flunky, pretender, truckler, spaniel, fawner, parvenu, upstart, apple-polisher, high-hat (sl.), pretentious person.

SNOBBERY, n. Snobbish character (conduct, trait, act), haughtiness, procacity, audacity, arrogance, loftiness, pomposity, presumption, overbearance, airs, disdain, condescension, pretension, pretentiousness.

SNOBBISH, adj. Of, pertaining to or characteristic of a snob, haughty, lofty, lordly, overbearing, pretentious, uppish (coll.), uppity (coll.), high-hat (sl.), parvenu, presumptuous, disdainful, stuck-up (coll.), high-nosed (coll.), high-headed, patronizing, supercilious, contemptuous, assuming, consequential, would-be, overweening, self-assertive, snooty (coll.), sniffy (coll.).

SNORE, v. Breathe harshly or hoarsely during sleep, snort, wheeze, buzz, saw wood (coll.).

SNORT, v. 1. Force the breath violently through the nostrils, snuff, sputter, grunt, honk, bark, hiss, bellow, wheeze, chortle.

2. Express contempt (indignation, etc.), utter a snort, hoot, grunt, contemn, deride, be angry, be outraged, hiss, spurn, scout, scoff, gibe, jeer, flout, scorn, hold cheap, look down upon, esteem slightly, revile, despise, set at naught, ridicule, spit upon, snap one's fingers at, snicker at, laugh to scorn, sneer, curl one's lip.

SNOUT, n. 1. Forward projecting part of an animal's head (containing mouth and nose), muzzle, beak, bill, nib, neb, jaws, trunk, proboscis, snoot (sl.).

2. Nozzle, spout, sprinkler, spray, sprayer, rose, rosehead, sparge, sparger, mouth.

SNOW, v. 1. Fall as snow, flurry, flutter, drift.

2. (Fol. by OVER, UNDER, UP, etc.) Cover, bury, obstruct, blanket, overwhelm, swamp, obscure, hide, obfuscate, shroud, disguise, curtain, adumbrate, screen, veil, obtenebrate, cloak, frost, occult, eclipse, overlay, immerse, heap, load, overflow, spread over, drown, swallow, submerge, deluge, engulf, flood, inundate, choke, suffocate, overspread.

SNOW, n. 1. Frozen aqueous vapor falling in flakes, slush, sleet, firn, névé.

2. Precipitation of snow, snowfall, snowstorm, flurry, blizzard.

SNOWY, adj. Snow-white, stainless, shining, pure, spotless, immaculate, unsullied, unstained, niveous, unblemished, clean, bright, speckless, unsoiled.

SNUB, n. Slight, disdainful affront, rebuff, check, rebuke, reproof, reprimand, peremptory refusal, repulse, defiance, repugnance, rejection, repudiation, chiding, reproach, cold shoulder, denial, spurn, renouncement, renunciation, go-by (coll.), refusal to recognize, cut (coll.), slap in the face, dash of cold water, counteraction, overturn, overthrow.

SNUB, v. 1. Check (with a cutting retort, etc.), cut, squelch, put in one's place, be unkind, spurn, slap in the face, repel, reprove, cross, rebuff, chide, rebuke.

2. Treat with indifference, contemn, forget, turn up one's nose at, not trouble oneself about, cold shoulder, high-hat (sl.), slur, ignore, disdain, give the go-by, reject, disparage, neglect, slight, scorn, disregard, overlook, omit, set aside, discountenance.

SNUFF, v. 1. Draw in air audibly, sniffle, inhale, breathe in noisily, snuffle, sniff.

2. (Often of dogs, animals, etc.) Perceive through the nose, sniff, get wind of, spoor, breathe, inhale, smell, scent, get scent of.

SNUG, adj. 1. (of ships) Well-made, well-built, seaworthy, trim, waterproof, shipshape, sturdy.

2. Cozy, enjoyable, homelike, comfortable, habitable, peaceful, cheery, easeful, wind-proof, tranquil.

3. Sufficient, desirable, adequate, satisfactory, comfortable, ample, commensurate, satisfying, acceptable.

4. Screened, secret, unseen, sheltered, obscured, buried, unapparent, invisible, concealed, hidden, secreted, disguised, camouflaged, imperceptible, clandestine.

5. Close or tight-fitting, tight, skin-tight.

SNUGGLE, v. Be cozy, curl up, hug, coddle, cuddle, nestle, nuzzle, cuddle up.

SO, adv. 1. In the way or manner indicated (described, implied), thus, in such wise, thus and thus, thus and so, in this or that way or fashion.

2. As stated or reported, true, unerroneous, veritable, reliable, faithful, factual, truthful, sure, correct, accurate, actual, real, verifiable.

3. To that extent, in that degree, as, this, that.

4. For a given reason, hence, therefore, because of, consequently, accordingly, on account of this, whence, logically, that being the case, under the circumstances or conditions, wherefore, in consequence, inevitably, naturally, on that

ground, on that account, thus, then, that being so.

5. Likewise, correspondingly, also, too, moreover, to boot, into the bargain, in like manner, in addition, similarly, as well, further, besides, and also, additionally.

SOAK, *v.* 1. Lie in and become saturated with liquid, be permeated, be thoroughly wet, keep in liquid, steep, wet thoroughly, drench, immerse, macerate, marinate, seethe, souse, sop, sodden, impregnate, flood, inundate, immerge, absorb, imbrue.

2. *(Usually fol. by* IN, THROUGH, OUT, *etc.)* Pass through pores *or* interstices, seep, permeate, penetrate, infiltrate, impregnate, irrigate, enter, diffuse, pervade, transude, compenetrate, filter, percolate, fill, saturate, interosculate, interpenetrate, be disseminated, inflow.

3. *(Followed by* IN*)* Become known slowly to, sink in, penetrate, get through to, pervade, pierce, come home to, be perceived, reach the consciousness, unfold, be revealed, absorb, assimilate, recognize, break in upon, become clear, strike, arouse, arrest the thoughts, affect, touch.

SOAPY, *adj.* Containing *or* impregnated with soap, of the nature of *or* resembling soap, lathery, bubbling, sudsy, foamy, frothy, saponaceous.

SOAR, *v.* 1. Fly *or* extend upward, tower, rise, mount, rear, loom, spring up, leap up, uprise, upshoot, spire, aspire, climb, wing, ascend, bulk.

2. Glide at a height, be high, float, wing, hover, plane, be wafted, drift, be buoyed up, volitate.

3. Rise *or* aspire to a higher *or* more exalted level, transcend, mount, look up *or* ahead, aim, hope, be ambitious, improve, desire, long, crave, yearn, pant for, labor for, drive at, endeavor, grasp at, hunger after, covet, set one's cap for *(coll.),* set one's mind *or* heart upon, set one's eyes on.

SOB, *v.* Sigh, cry, wail, moan, weep, lament, gasp, blubber, snivel, whimper.

SOBER, *adj.* 1. Unintoxicated, temperate, abstinent, abstemious, teetotal, sworn off, on the wagon *(sl.),* able to walk the chalk mark *or* line *(coll.).*

2. Grave, solemn, sedate, serious, quiet in demeanor, demure, severe, sad, grim, rueful, subdued, somber, pensive, thoughtful, long-visaged, long-faced, earnest, musing, contemplative, wistful, sorrowful, saturnine, reflective, meditative, staid.

3. Subdued in tone *(as color),* not gay *or* showy, dull, soft, mellow, drab, dark, quiet, somber, heavy, grayed, leaden, softened, sad, mousy, dun, dreary.

4. Free from excess (extravagance *or* exaggeration), hard, harsh, realistic, cold, substantial, sound, solid, real, material, tangible, severe, chaste, pure, unembroidered, unvarnished, unadorned, prosaic.

5. Showing self-control, composed, calm, moderate, cool, deliberate, undemonstrative, unimpassioned, dispassionate, steady, rational, temperate, reasonable, well-regulated, philosophical, self-possessed, regular, unruffled, collected, matter-of-fact, serene, imperturbable, undisturbed, unemotional, peaceful, cool-headed, even-tempered, inexcitable, inirritable, level-headed, tranquil, poised, balanced, sane, controlled, quiet, discreet, agreeable to reason, impartial, prudent, circumspect, thoughtful, analytical, discerning,

enlightened, judicious, discriminating, objective, intellectual.

SOBRIETY, *n.* 1. Temperance, abstemiousness, moderation, abstinence, soberness, self-denial, renunciation, abstention, teetotalism, nephalism.

2. Seriousness, gravity, solemnity, equanimity, sober-mindedness, thoughtfulness, calmness, coolness, self-control, placidity, level-headedness, balance, soundness of mind, staidness, demureness, self-restraint, self-possession, composure, tranquillity, serenity, modesty, sanity, sedateness.

SOBRIQUET, *n.* Fanciful name, nickname, cognomen, byname, moniker *(sl.),* alias, assumed name *or* title, fictitious name, pseudonym, *nom de guerre (Fr.), nom de plume (Fr.),* pet name, little name.

SOCIABILITY, *n.* Familiarity, agreeableness, coöperation, mutual trust, friendship, society, company, mutual confidence, intimacy, consociation, camaraderie, fellowship, association as companions, partnership, colleagueship, community of interests, amity, social intercourse, fraternization, collaboration, close acquaintance, cordial understanding, party spirit, *esprit de corps (Fr.),* comradeship, brotherliness, friendly relations, rapport, sociableness, companionableness, good-fellowship, affability, conviviality.

SOCIABLE, *adj.* Fitted to be a companion, gregarious, brotherly, neighborly, communicative, warm, warm-hearted, genial, gracious, lovable, cordial, well-affected, familiar, intimate, well-disposed, conversable, amicable, friendly, jovial, jolly, affable, social, convivial, accessible, clubbish, hearty, ingratiating, affectionate, harmonious, cosmopolitan, chummy *(coll.),* hail-fellow-well-met, approachable, agreeable, kindly, pleasant, hospitable.

SOCIAL, *adj.* 1. Pertaining to a community, common, cosmopolitan, mutual, used by all, popular, collective, widespread, proletarian, bourgeois, plebeian, national, communal, civic, civil, united, joint. societal.

2. *See* SOCIABLE, *adj. Above.*

SOCIALISM, *n.* Collectivism, nationalization, communization, social democracy, Saint-Simonianism, Fourierism, Fabianism, managed economy.

SOCIETY, *n.* 1. Fellowship, group, circle, association, body, congregation, tribe, club, fraternity, sorority, affiliation, alliance, league, incorporation, combination, federation, consociation, camaraderie, colleagueship, amity, guild, union.

2. The public, the general public, mankind, the world, the commonwealth, the body politic, humanity, people, the folk, the community, the human race.

3. The upper classes, the nobility, the blue-bloods, the aristocracy, patriciate, peerage, high society, the elite, gentility, the upper ten, *haut monde (Fr.),* the fashionable world, the upper crust *(sl.),* the higher classes, the rich, the privileged classes.

SOCK, *n.* 1. Stockings, hose, hosiery.

2. Wind gauge *or* indicator, wind vane, wind cone.

SOD, *n.* Clod, divot, lawn, piece of soil, grassland, turf, sward, greensward, glebe *(Poet.),* ground.

SODDEN, *adj.* 1. Soaked with liquid *or* moisture, steeped, soggy, drenched, saturated, bloated, plashy, soppy, dripping, squashy, quaggy, marshy, thoroughly wet, spongy, muddy, swampy, soft, paludial, lutose, clammy, uliginous, miry, oozy.

2. Heavy *(as food)*, doughy, soggy, thick, pulpy, solid, concentrated, compact, lumpy, indigestible, starchy, glutinous, stodgy, sticky, tacky, gummy.

3. Expressionless, dull, stupid, phlegmatic, stolid, gross, inert, insensible, languid, unemotional, lethargic, listless, lifeless, exanimate, stupefied, doltish, insulse, blockish, sottish, comatose, indolent, indifferent, dumb *(coll.)*, passive, static, lifeless, dead, obtuse, numb, unfeeling, insentient, insensate, apathetic, torpid, flat, fixed, motionless, undiscerning, hebetudinous, slow, bovine, supine, lymphatic, foggy.

SODOMY, *n.* Unnatural sexual intercourse, buggery, pederasty, homosexuality.

SOFA, *n.* Long upholstered seat *(with back and arms)*, couch, lounge, love seat, divan, ottoman, settee, squab, tête-à-tête, causeuse *(Fr.)*

SOFT, *adj.* 1. Yielding readily to touch *or* pressure, easily penetrated (divided, altered) in shape, not hard *or* stiff, plastic, limp, flimsy, pliable, malleable, pulpy, easily molded, flaccid, supple, tractable, lithe, flexible, fictile, ductile, limber, creamy, spongy, doughy, ripe, crumbly, soggy, sodden, flabby, pasty, mushy, squashy, loamy, clayey, lax, extensile, relaxed.

2. Smooth, agreeable to the touch, not rough *or* coarse, downy, silky, satiny, fleecy, furry, velvety.

3. Producing agreeable sensations, pleasant, easeful, comfortable, luxurious, inviting, attractive, dulcet, heavenly, gratifying, welcome, refreshing, sweet, enjoyable, delightful, alluring, delectable, exquisite, felicitous, pleasurable, easy, commodious, cozy, genial, grateful, amiable, restful, tranquil.

4. Low *(in sound)*, subdued, gentle, melodious, soothing, mellifluous, dulcet, sweet, faint, mellow, quiet, hushed, feeble, muted, murmured, small, weak, stifled, euphonious, musical, melic, lyrical, whispered, mellifluent.

5. Not harsh *or* unpleasant to the eye, not glaring, dim, subdued, harmonious, delicate, of low intensity, grayed, semi-dark, clouded, pale, shaded, twilight, shadowy, shadowed, low, mellow, faint, gentle, pastel, diffused, indirect.

6. Not hard *or* sharp *(as outlines)*, blurred, blurry, fuzzy, indistinct, ill-defined, hazy, misty, indefinite, blended, vague, ill-marked, unclear, bleared, diffused.

7. Gentle *(as wind, rain, etc.)*, mild, genial *(as climate, air, etc.)*, balmy, moderate, sunny, summery, calid, tepid, temperate, halcyon, calm, agreeable, estival, tranquil, pacific, still, quiet, peaceful, equable.

8. Gentle, mild, lenient, compassionate, soothing, lax, forgiving, pitying, yielding, persuasive, affecting, touching, bland, kind, tolerant, indulgent, reasonable, merciful, clement, forbearant, long-suffering, tender-hearted, peaceful, pacific, easygoing, affectionate, loving, equable, tame, sweet, amorous, even-tempered, ruthful, humane, charitable, restrained.

9. Smooth, soothing, ingratiating, conciliatory, bland, flattering, unctuous, oily, winning, tactful, polite, persuasive, urbane, placable, decorous, disarming, amiable, gracious, placative, obliging, deferential, conciliative, pacifying, propitiatory, reconciliatory.

10. Yielding readily to the tender emotions, impressionable, malleable, tractable, pliable, flexible, affectionate, docile, sentimental, forgiving, compliant, submissive, amenable, subject, meek, kind, sensitive, affected, acquiescent, formable, receptive, responsive, susceptible, deferential, complaisant, romantic, maudlin, plastic.

11. Not strong *or* robust, delicate, incapable of great endurance *or* exertion, feminine, weak, faint, tender, unhardened, flaccid, strengthless, nerveless, effeminate, frail, dainty, weakly, feeble, out of practice, out of condition, rusty, womanish, puerile, muliebrous, unmanly, debilitated, pithless, sinewless, female, petticoat, womanlike, sissyish *(coll.)*.

SOFTEN, *v.* 1. Make soft, mellow, incite sympathy, make tender, touch, melt, disarm.

2. Moderate, assuage, tame, compose, tranquilize, win over, reconcile, appease, quiet, lull, mollify, hush, still, humor, arbitrate, conciliate, calm, satisfy, silence, gratify, propitiate.

3. Ameliorate, relieve, palliate, ease, assuage, abate, lessen, blunt, temper, dulcify, allay, relax, tone down, lenify, mitigate, tranquilize, mollify, extenuate, mince, cushion.

4. Make *or* grow soft *or* weak, weaken, enervate, emasculate, debilitate, unstrengthen, enfeeble, exhaust, sap, unman, impair, unnerve.

5. *(Of noise, etc.)* Deaden, muffle, tone down, silence, subdue, damp down, throttle down, mute, dull, repress, quiet, soft-pedal.

6. Relent, give in, weaken, acquiesce, thaw, melt, bend, relax, yield, succumb, forbear, accede, unbend, submit.

SOGGY, *adj.* Saturated with moisture, heavy with moisture, mushy, spongy, drenched, soppy, doughy, plashy, loamy, pasty, sodden, dripping, heavy.

SOIL, *n.* 1. Earth, ground, turf, marl, loam, humus, compost.

2. Dirt, filth, muck, grime, dust, soot, smut, smutch.

SOIL, *v.* 1. Stain, smear, tarnish, sully, smirch, pollute, smudge, begrime, blur, spot, smutch, grease, grime, splotch, defile, contaminate, taint, deface, blacken, muddy, impair, blur.

2. Damage *(as one's reputation, etc.)*, contaminate, foul, besmirch, drag in the mud, degrade, smudge, blacken, smutch, impair, blemish, sully, smirch, stain, tarnish, spoil, bring down, ruin, cast aspersions at, dishonor, belittle, subvert, brand, vilipend, disparage, reflect upon, detract from, reduce, cheapen, undermine, vilify, derogate, slight, debase, depreciate, defile, malign, discredit, slander, libel, denigrate.

SOJOURN, *n.* Visit, vacation, relaxation, residence, temporary dwelling, halt, pause, holiday, repose, respite, stopover.

SOJOURN, *v.* Stay in a place *(temporarily)*, live *(temporarily)*, abide, tarry, rest, reside, vacation, stop over, dwell, visit, repose, take the air.

SOLACE, *v.* Grant respite, calm, sustain, help, hearten, palliate, assuage, compose, support, nourish, relieve, revive, reanimate, revivify, aid, lighten one's burdens, console, cheer, soothe, encourage, gladden, restore, allay, quiet one's fears, regale, provide easement, warm, salve, disburden, invigorate, mitigate, soften, enhearten, inspirit, assist, bolster up, reassure, alleviate, ameliorate, bear up, refresh, rejuvenate.

SOLACE, *n.* Relief in affliction, mitigation, easement, alleviation, deliverance, tranquillity, quietism, lenitive, allayment, consolation, help in trouble *or* need, comfort, amelioration, reassurance, restorative, encouragement.

SOLDER, *v.* Seal, weld, congeal, coalesce, bind, set, glue, paste, braze, indurate, amalgamate, cleave, agglutinate.

SOLDIER, *n.* Warrior, fighting-man, serviceman, militarist, man-at-arms, swordsman, combatant, fighter, belligerent, battler, gladiator, jouster, tussler, military man, legionnaire, doughboy, infantryman, paratrooper, private, guardsman, sharpshooter, skirmisher, rifleman, gunner. artilleryman, cavalryman, trooper, rookie *(sl.)*, recruit, conscript.

SOLDIERLY, *adj.* 1. Of, like *or* befitting a soldier, warlike, combative, contentious, military, martial, fighting, fierce, savage, belligerent, bellicose, pugnacious.

2. Brave, valiant, intrepid, heroic, chivalrous, gallant, valorous, chivalric, courageous, daring, fearless, dauntless, doughty, manful, stout-hearted, hardy, mettlesome, unflinching, unblenching, unshrinking, virile, resolute, spirited, undaunted, Spartan, game, firm, bold, lion-hearted, determinded, unappalled, undismayed.

SOLE, *adj.* 1. Being the only one *or* ones, only, single, alone, individual, exclusive, particular, isolated, one, solitary, lonely, separate, detached, unaccompanied, lone.

2. Being the only one of the kind, unique, individual, odd, lone, singled out, singular, select, strange, curious, unusual, distinguished, outlandish, uncommon, unrepeated, bizarre, freakish, peculiar, unparalleled, unequaled, unmatched, unfamiliar, *outré (Fr.)*.

3. Belonging *or* pertaining to one individual *or* group *(to the exclusion of all others)*, exclusive, private, granted *or* attributed to but one person *or* group, entire, whole, select, distinct, special, specific, express, complete, undisputed, proper, personal, unquestioned, respective, restricted, determined, fixed, unique, limited.

4. Functioning automatically *or* with independent power, independent, complete unto itself, free, clear, sovereign, self-sufficient, disengaged, autonomous, self-determined, self-reliant, self-governing, self-acting, self-propellent.

SOLE, *n.* Bottom *or* under surface of the foot (shoe, boot, *etc.*), lower surface of anything, foot, base, foundation, ball *(of the foot)*, pad *(of an animal's foot)*.

SOLECISM, *n.* 1. Substandard intrusion into standard speech, grammatical error, impropriety in language, blunder, slip, vulgarism, corruption, inelegance, cacology, slang, misuse, incorrectness, barbarism, mistake, incongruity, ungrammaticism, gothicism, inconsistency.

2. Breach of good manners *or* etiquette, mistake, social blunder, slip, impropriety, error, indiscretion, bevue, bad taste, infraction, indelicacy, barbarism, grossness, infelicity, indecorum, rusticism, inurbanity, ill breeding, discourtesy, misconduct, *faux pas (Fr.)*.

SOLEMN, *adj.* 1. Grave, somber, mirthless, pensive, gloomy, staid, funereal, sober, earnest, mournful, sad, sedate, quiet in demeanor, demure, severe, grim, rueful, subdued, thoughtful, long-visaged, long-faced, musing, contemplative, wistful, sorrowful, saturnine, reflective, meditative.

2. Gravely *or* somberly impressive, such as to cause serious thoughts *or* a grave mood, dread, ominous, alarming, thought-provoking, direful, weighty, imposing, profound, venerable, august, terrible, awful, grim, portentous, important, intense, mighty, great, high, of great consequence, deep, considerable, heavy, ponderous, urgent, critical, crucial, decisive, vital, momentous, earnest, dreadful, dire, fearful, sore, formidable, significant.

3. Serious, earnest, sincere, fixed, faithful, steadfast, well-meant, determined, purposeful, unswerving, unflinching, clear, certain, marked, confident, firm, secure, trustworthy, express, unfailing, sound, reliable, dependable, sure, unqualified, explicit, emphatic, absolute, positive.

4. Characterized by dignified *or* serious formality, of a formal *or* ceremonious character, made in due legal *or* other express form, formal, stately, ritual, distinguished, ceremonial, dignified, state, awe-inspiring, majestic, significant, memorial, ceremonious, commemorative, notable, correct, proper, fitting.

5. Marked *or* observed with religious rites, sacred, holy, having a religious character, reverential, liturgical, worshipful, devotional, devout, pious, sacramental, divine, hallowed, sanctified, set apart, spiritual.

SOLEMNITY, *n.* 1. State *or* character of being solemn, earnestness, gravity, impressiveness, seriousness, urgency, insistence, importance, consequence, significance, weight, moment, mark, dignity, majesty, primacy, greatness, notability, paramountcy, supremacy, grandeur.

2. *(Often pl.)* Solemn observance, ceremonial, formality, celebration, office, ritual, form, ceremony, rite, obsequies, exequies, function, invocation, practice, ordinance, service, sacrament, custom, incantation.

SOLEMNIZE, *v.* Celebrate with rites *or* ceremonies, observe, honor, commemorate, keep, sanctify, hallow, signalize, minister, ceremonialize, remember, memorialize, consecrate.

SOLICIT, *v.* 1. Seek for *(by entreaty, earnest or respectful request, formal application, etc.)*, endeavor to obtain, appeal for, invite, approach one for, sell, petition, drum up, canvass.

2. Ask, entreat, importune, petition, urge, appeal to, apply to, plead, invoke, beseech, implore, crave, request, pray, beg, supplicate, conjure, press, obsecrate, impetrate, cry, clamor, ply, fish for, demand, claim, beg leave, bid for, sue, bespeak, agitate, obtest, adjure, postulate.

3. Seek to influence to *(esp. unlawful or wrong)* action, incite, beguile, lure, woo, awaken, arouse, court, invite, allure, tempt, sway, bring influence *or* pressure to bear, bias, dispose, prejudice, draw on, lead on.

SOLICITOR, *n.* 1. One who solicits, asker, petitioner, salesman, canvasser, solicitant, lobbyist, agent, suitor, supplicant, applicant, drummer, runner, barker *(coll.)*, touter *(coll.)*.

2. Officer having charge of the legal business of a city *or* town, *etc.,* attorney, legal agent, legal representative.

SOLICITOUS, *adj.* 1. *(Fol. by ABOUT, FOR, etc., or a clause)* Anxious over something, concerned, troubled, uneasy, disturbed, agitated, perturbed, alarmed, nervous, disquieted, aroused, upset, apprehensive, fearful, uncomfortable.

2. *(Sometimes fol. by the infinitive)* Anxiously desirous, eager, earnest, zealous, begging, hopeful, wistful, importunate, cap in hand, supplicatory, supplicant, longing, itching, sedulous, ardent,

aspiring, intent, breathless, avid, keen, ambitious, burning, on one's knees, petitionary, pleading, imploring, beseeching.

3. Careful, particular, scrupulous, prudent, cautious, wary, advertent, thoughtful, fastidious, punctilious, mindful, heedful, regardful, strict, circumspect, conscientious, watchful, guarded, discreet, politic, vigilant, considerate.

SOLICITUDE, *n.* 1. State of being solicitous, anxiety, concern, care, carefulness, heedfulness, vigilance, fearfulness, watchfulness, pains, prudence, heed, circumspection, perplexity, alarm, fear, trouble, worry, caution, precaution, forethought, zeal, ardor, thought, tenderness, thoughtfulness, apprehensiveness, uneasiness, eagerness, affection, conscientiousness, regard, qualm, consideration.

2. Anxiety *or* assistance greater than required *or* proper, effusion, unrestraint, excessive indulgence, fluttering, showering of attention, importunity, impatience, smothering, over-anxiety, gush *(coll.).*

SOLID, *adj.* 1. Having three dimensions, having the interior completely filled up, free from cavities, not hollow, cubic.

2. Without openings *or* breaks, unbroken, continuous, uninterrupted, impenetrable, serial, successive, undivided, consecutive, constant, ceaseless, linear, in a row, block, unremitting, unintermitting, sequential.

3. Firm, hard, compact, congealed, frozen, imporous, impenetrable, impermeable, incompressible, clotted, solidified, lumpish, heavy in nature *or* appearance, grumose, costive, undissolved, unmelted, unthawed, coherent, cohesive, crystallized, crystalline, indissoluble, soggy, sodden, inseparable, indivisible, rocky.

4. Dense, thick, close, close-textured, teeming, serried, packed, crowded, massed, swarming, impermeable, compact, compressed, concentrated, tight, full, close-knit, clustered, conjunct, inseparable, united, stuffed, conjoined, corporate, bunched, populous.

5. Substantial, not flimsy (slight *or* light), stout, firm, heavy, strong, well-built, well-constructed, rugged, hard, lasting, resistant, tough, durable, sturdy.

6. Of a substantial character, not superficial (trifling *or* frivolous), true, real, philosophical, learned, profound, thorough, thoroughgoing, consummate, full, deep, ample, trustworthy, reliable, authoritative, genuine, meaningful.

7. Whole, entire, complete, total, intact, undivided, unrelieved, uninterrupted.

8. Forming the whole, being the only substance *or* material, genuine, pure, unalloyed, unmodified by admixture, free from extraneous matter, valid, clear, simple, homogeneous, unmixed, unadulterated, uncontaminated, sterling, unmingled, authentic, straight, unsophisticated, perfect.

9. Sound, sober, stable, good, sensible, soberminded, well-founded, wise, just, valid, wellestablished, unerring, reliable, dependable, convincing, decisive, conclusive, rational, level-headed, incontrovertible, well-advised, well-grounded, sage, sagacious, knowing, sapient, demonstrable, trustworthy, proven, discriminative, accurate, reasonable.

10. Financially strong *or* sound, stable, solvent, good, reliable, responsible, unindebted, with good credit *or* rating, in good standing.

11. *(Emphatic, often after* GOOD*)* Thorough, vigorous, big, memorable, strong, energetic, great, powerful, potent, forceful, forcible, effective, competent, mighty, efficacious, dynamic, strenuous, stout, heavy, hefty *(coll.).*

12. Firmly united, consolidated, unanimous, consentient, in agreement, resolute, accordant, harmonious, strong, settled, firm, fixed, relentless, iron, adamantine, inexorable, indomitable, stanch, cohesive, determined, resolved, undivided, concordant.

SOLID, *n.* Body having three dimensions, solid substance *or* body, substance exhibiting rigidity, block, cake, lump, mass, cube, rock, knot, crystal, conglomerate, conglomeration.

SOLIDARITY, *n.* Solidary character *or* relation, consolidation of interests and responsibilities, close fellowship, joint interest, union, unity, strength, stability, community of interests (feelings, purposes, actions, *etc.),* mutual responsibility, concurrence, coöperation, participation, cotenancy, communion, agreement, harmony, amity, affinity, accord, unanimity, consentaneity, homogeneity, like-mindedness, compatibility, rapport, concord, comradeship, good understanding, unison, assent, meeting of minds, parallelism.

SOLIDIFY, *v.* 1. Make into a hard *or* compact mass, form into crystals, make *or* become solid, compact, densify, harden, set, thicken, cake, strengthen, petrify, congeal, fix, candy, curdle, cement, coagulate, conglomerate, inspissate, curd, indurate, stiffen, fossilize, granulate, concrete, incrassate, compress, lapidify, vitrify, hornify, ossify, deposit, crystallize.

2. Unite firmly, consolidate, combine, league, associate, join, link, establish, incorporate, unify, syndicate, confederate, amalgamate, merge, ally, pool efforts, meet, consolidate, coördinate, synergize, hold together.

SOLILOQUIZE, *v.* Utter a soliloquy, talk to oneself, monologize, monologue, think out loud *or* aloud, address the four walls, say aside, apostrophize *(Rhet.).*

SOLILOQUY, *n.* Act of talking when alone *or* as if alone, discourse *or* utterance by one talking to oneself, monologue, monology, apostrophe.

SOLITARY, *adj.* 1. Quite alone, without companions, unattended, apart, separate, lonely, lonesome, companionless, deserted, in solitude.

2. Avoiding the society of others, living alone, reclusive, unsociable, hermitical, retiring, eremitical, eremitish, friendless, outcast, derelict, solitudinous, monastic, anchoritic, stylitic *(Eccles. Hist.).*

3. Being the only one *or* ones, alone by itself, sole, lone, isolated, singular, individual, one, only, exclusive, particular, lonely, odd, unique, unrepeated, freakish, peculiar, unparalleled, unequaled, unmatched, unfamiliar.

4. Characterized by solitude, unfrequented, lonely, secluded, retired, deserted, desert, sequestered, abandoned, forlorn, private, cloistered, forsaken, untraveled, uninhabited, out-of-the-way, remote, desolate, apart, wilderness, hidden, hid, buried, in a backwater, unvisited, concealed, cut off, withdrawn, privy.

SOLITUDE, *n.* 1. Loneliness, seclusion, isolation, solitariness, remoteness, privacy, reclusion, desolation, reclusiveness, aloneness, retirement.

2. The wilderness, the wide open spaces, desert, the wild, wasteland, waste.

SOLUBLE, *adj.* 1. Capable of being dissolved, dissolvable, dissoluble, solvable.

2. Capable of being solved, solvable, explainable, resolvable, decipherable, ascertainable, penetrable, discernible.

SOLUTION, *n.* 1. Clearing up, solvent, denouement, penetration, revealing, discovery, hitting upon, exposition, resolution, riddling, deciphering, ascertainment, discernment, falling upon, finding out.

2. Answer, elucidation, explication, key, exegesis, enucleation, clue, disclosure, exposition, interpretation, *éclaircissement (Fr.).*

3. Emulsion, suspension, mixture, infusion.

SOLVABLE, *adj.* 1. Capable of being dissolved, dissolvable, soluble, dissoluble.

2. Capable of being solved, explainable, resolvable, decipherable, ascertainable, penetrable, discernible.

SOLVE, *v.* Find a solution to, resolve, find the answer, decipher, interpret, crack, enucleate, elucidate, disentangle, clear up, explain, unravel, fathom, unriddle, work out, make plain, translate, untangle, decode, unlock, find the key, penetrate, get at the truth.

SOLVENT, *adj.* 1. Able to pay debts, responsible, in good financial condition, reliable, sound, solid.

2. Dissolvent, diluent, alkahestic, resolvent, resolutive.

SOLVENT, *n.* 1. That which dissolves *(as a liquid),* dissolving agent, resolvent, dissolvent, menstruum, diluent, flux, alkahest.

2. Clearing up, denouement, solution, deciphering, falling upon, finding out, ascertainment, discernment, riddling, resolution, exposition, hitting upon, discovery, revealing, penetration.

SOMBER, *adj.* 1. Rayless, black, umbrageous, blurred, cloudy, nebulous, moonless, gloomy, overcast, murky, turbid, misty, dim, foggy, dusty, lightless, dark, shadowy, lowering, funereal, gray, leaden, grim, stygian, sable, cheerless, dreary, unlighted, dirty, dingy, unilluminated, muggy, obscure, overshadowed, soupy *(sl.),* sepulchral, smoky, shady, starless, sunless, tenebrous, caliginous, viscid.

2. Grave, melancholy, depressing, trying, wearying, onerous, mournful, dolorous, bitter, rueful, woeful, lamentable, dismal, tragic, solemn, crushing, irksome, troublesome, oppressive, severe, burdensome, heart-rending, deplorable, disastrous.

3. *(Of color)* Dark, dull, gray, toneless, lugubrious, deep, autumnal, mouse-colored, iron-gray, subdued, gloomy, dreary, favillous, lifeless, deadened, muted, grave, dead, flat, leaden, cinereous, ashen, dun, depressing, dismal, drab.

SOME, *adj.* 1. A certain *or* specified quantity *or* amount, a few, any.

2. Certain, a few, specified ones.

3. More or less, about, approximately, not far from, well-nigh, almost, near, towards.

SOMEBODY, *n.* 1. Someone, some person, one.

2. Person of importance, big shot *(coll.),* figure, prominent person, worthy, name, personage, something, man of note, bigwig *(sl.).*

SOMEHOW, *adv.* By some means or other, by hook or by crook, in one way or another, by fair means or foul, someway *(coll.),* in somewise.

SOMEONE, *n.* 1. Somebody, some person, one.

2. Person of importance, bigwig *(sl.),* figure, something, personage, prominent person, name, worthy, man of note, big shot *(coll.).*

SOMERSAULT, *n.* A leap *(turning head over heels),* handspring, somerset, cartwheel.

SOMERSAULT, *v.* Turn head over heels, somerset, turn topsy-turvy, turn over.

SOMETHING, *n.* 1. Thing, object, device, article, contrivance, gadget.

2. Matter, affair, subject, concern, item, particular, phenomenon, issue.

SOMETIME, *adj.* Former, late, quondam, erstwhile.

SOMETIME, *adv.* At some unspecified future time, one day, some day, in due time, in the long run, one of these days, eventually, ultimately, in time, by and by.

SOMETIMES, *adv.* From time to time, now and then, at times, occasionally, once in a while, on different occasions, every so often, at various times.

SOMEWHAT, *adv.* To some extent, partly, more or less, to a degree, moderately, in some measure, in part, a little, rather, reasonably, in a limited degree, passably, tolerably.

SOMEWHERE, *adv.* In some place or another, someplace, here and there.

SOMNAMBULISM, *n.* Sleepwalking, noctivagation, somnambulation, nightwalking, noctambulation, noctambulism.

SOMNAMBULIST, *n.* Noctambule, somnambule, somnambulator, sleepwalker, nightwalker, noctambulist.

SOMNIFEROUS, *adj.* Causing *or* tending to cause sleep, somnific, sleep-inducing, somnifacient, opiate, narcotic, hypnotic, soporiferous, mesmeric, somnolent, sedative, soothing, balmy, slumberous, dormitive, soporific.

SOMNOLENCE, *n.* Languor, oscitancy, comatoseness, lassitude, doziness, sleepiness, comatosity, torpor, lethargy, drowsiness, torpidity, kef, torpidness, hypnesthesis.

SOMNOLENT, *adj.* Half-asleep, asleep, oscitant, tired, fatigued, heavy, torpid, drowsy, weary, faint, sleepy, yawning, exhausted, dozy *(coll.).*

SON, *n.* Male descendant, male child, heir, offspring, scion, heir apparent, heir presumptive, boy, successor, chip off the old block *(coll.),* progeny, youth, offset, issue, cadet, lineal descendant, junior.

SONG, *n.* 1. Short musical composition intended *or* adapted for singing, lyric, ballad, melody, canticle, lay, aria, lullaby, air, paean, chantey, chorus, carol, ditty, tune, canzone, madrigal, anthem, psalm, hymn, strain, descant, serenade, dirge, round, spiritual, chant, rhapsody, pastoral, barcarole, *Lied (Ger.).*

2. Poetical composition, poetry, canzone, rhyme, verse, versification, meter, poetization, numbers, poesy *(Poetic),* poetcraft, versecraft.

3. Musical *or* tuneful sounds *(produced by birds, insects, etc.),* chorus, carol, chirping, note, clamor, stridulation, warble, pipe, whistle, roll, trill, wood note.

SONGFUL, *adj.* Abounding in song, melodious, musical, melodic, tuneful, melic, sweet, dulcet, mellifluent, lyric, tunable, mellifluous, mellisonant, mellow, ariose, canorous, euphonious.

SONGSTER, *n.* 1. One who sings, singer, warbler, vocalist, vocalizer, chorister, soloist, melodist, diva, musician, crooner, precentor, cantor, caroler, descanter, hymner, songbird, chantress, chanteuse, cantatrice, prima donna, psalmodist, lyrist, rhapsodist, orpheonist.

2. Writer of songs *or* poems, poet, versifier, versemaker, scald *(Hist.)*, lyricist, bard, muse, rhymer, dithyrambic, laureate, sonneteer, idylist, rhapsodist, elegiast, bucoliast, poetaster *(derog.)*, minstrel *(Poetic)*, jongleur *(Hist.)*, troubadour *(Hist.)*, gleeman *(Hist.)*, Meistersinger *(Hist.)*, minnesinger *(Hist.)*.

SONORITY, *n.* Condition *or* quality of being resonant *or* sonorous, loudness, sonorousness, surge of sound, swell, tone, vibration, clamor, resonancy, sonance, timbre, resonance.

SONOROUS, *adj.* 1. Capable of deep resonant sound, rich, full, resonant, full-toned, ringing, orotund, deep, resounding, sounding, vibrant, rolling, round, booming, big, vibrating, mellifluous, reverberating, reverberant, musical, strong, powerful, loud, heavy.

2. Pompous, bombastic, high-flown, overdrawn, extravagant, strained, pretentious, high-colored, inflated, hyperbolic, extreme, rhapsodical, magniloquent, fustian, showy, orotund, tumid, altisonant, ornate, mouthy, flatulent, florid, affected, turgid, lofty, glittering, grandiloquent, sententious, declamatory, grandiose, rhetorical, grandisonant, Johnsonian, flamboyant, lexiphanic, sesquipedalian *(hum.)*, high-falutin *(coll.)*.

SOON, *adv.* 1. Within a short period, in the near future, at an early date, before long, shortly, presently, anon, in a short time, in no time, by and by, directly, early, ere long, betimes, quickly, after awhile, speedily, in due time, at the first opportunity, promptly, forthwith, without delay, straightway.

2. Readily, willingly, with a will, with pleasure, gladly, heartily, nothing loath, volitionally, from choice, of one's own accord, optionally, graciously, with delight, voluntarily, lief, fain, freely, by preference, preferably.

SOOT, *n.* Black carbonaceous substance produced in combustion, crock, black, smut, residue, smoke, smudge, deposit, carbon, lamp black, sediment, charcoal.

SOOTHE, *v.* 1. Tranquilize, comfort, refresh, relieve, pacify, quiet, assuage, appease, sober, still, compose, lull, hush, console, balm, mollify, ease, put to rest, heal, solace, calm, subdue, cause to relax, ease one's mind, settle, dulcify, becalm, placate, smooth, lenify, tame, soften, conciliate, reconcile, propitiate, cheer, gladden, restore, hearten, salve, enhearten, disburden, reassure.

2. Mitigate, assuage, allay, moderate, mollify, soften, check, deaden, temper, quell, stay, blunt, take the edge off, relieve, repress, lessen, lenify, palliate, alleviate, pour oil on the troubled waters, qualify, ease, dull, extenuate, remit, reduce, slake, render less, minimize, relax, abate, cushion.

SOOTHSAY, *v.* Foretell events, prophesy, predict, forecast, prognosticate, indicate beforehand, omen, hariolate, foresee, premonish, augur, vaticinate, forebode, presage, divine, haruspicate, herald.

SOOTHSAYER, *n.* One who professes to foretell events, prophet, seer, foreteller, diviner, augur, sorcerer, vaticinator, predictor, herald, medium, prophesier, fortuneteller, palmist, forecaster, astrologer, sibyl, oracle, prognosticator, mantologist, divinator, python, Merlin, crystal-gazer, extispex, haruspex, geomancer, geomant, *vates (Lat.)*.

SOOTY, *adj.* 1. Covered with soot, dingy, grimy,

blurry, blurred, bleary, bleared, smutty, dirty, smeared, smutchy, smirched, murky, besmeared, besmirched, fuliginous.

2. Of a black *or* dusky color, dark, murky, sable, somber, fuliginous, dusky, lackluster, leaden, dun, dull, lacklustrous, ebon, ebony, jet, pitchy, raven, jetty, inky, nigrine, nigrous, atramentous, pitch-dark, coal-black.

SOPHISM, *n.* Specious but fallacious argument *(to display ingenuity in reasoning or to deceive)*, fallacy, false logic, quibble, paralogy, paralogism *(Logic)*, subterfuge, blind, dodge, feint, chicanery, antilogy, paradox, delusion, stratagem, untruth, misrepresentation, illogicalness, speciousness, misinterpretation, irrationality, absurdity, elenchus, pseudosyllogism, philosophism, philosophastering, quackery, error, misjudgment.

SOPHIST, *n.* 1. One who reasons adroitly and speciously rather than soundly, captious *or* fallacious reasoner, casuist, caviler, shuffler, equivocator, quack, charlatan, quibbler, artful logician, affecter, deceiver, sophister, paralogist, paralogician, philosophist, Jesuit, philosophaster *(contempt.)*.

2. Man of learning, savant, sage, philosopher, master, wise man, doctor, scholar, pundit, erudite person, scholastic, oracle, authority, prophet, luminary, pantologist, colossus of knowledge, giant of learning, mastermind, rishi *(Hinduism)*, Nestor *(Gk. Legend)*.

SOPHISTIC, *adj.* Of the nature of sophistry, given to the use of sophistry, fallacious, philosophistic, illogical, quibbling, casuistical, unsound, tricky, deceptive, subtle, false, captious, misleading, Jesuitic, plausible, incongruous, paradoxical, irrational, unreasonable, specious, hollow.

SOPHISTICATE, *v.* 1. Make less natural (simple, ingenuous), make worldly-wise, disenchant, disillusion, destroy one's idealism, burst one's bubble, unblindfold, disabuse, puncture one's balloon, expose to harsh *or* stark reality, open one's eyes.

2. Mislead, pervert, corrupt, misguide, misdirect, lead astray, falsify, adulterate, misstate, misinform, misinterpret, deceive, play one false, doctor *(coll.)*, strain, stretch, give a false coloring, dupe, gull, fool, anamorphose, infect, taint, twist, garble, distort, take in, blind, impose on, betray, defile, contaminate, debase, warp, tamper with.

3. Use sophistry, quibble, reason in a circle, paralogize, reason ill, reason illogically, cavil, equivocate, trifle, palter, fence, parry, elenchize, varnish, prevaricate, evade, shy, dodge, pervert *or* distort the meaning, prove that black is white, beg the question, refine, be circumlocutory, split hairs, subtilize.

SOPHISTICATED, *adj.* 1. Altered by education (worldly experience, *etc.*), changed from the natural character *or* simplicity, artificial, seasoned, veteran, experienced, feigned, broad, unprovincial, socially adept, blasé, hard-boiled *(coll.)*, not born yesterday *(coll.)*, knowing, worldly-wise.

2. Deceptive, misleading, impure, cunning, spurious, corrupting, fraudulent, sham, adulterated, flam, flimflam, meretricious, delusive, pretended, guileful, simulated, counterfeit, insidious, tricky, deceiving, treacherous, perfidious, illusory, illusive, conniving, false, dishonest, delusory, feigned, factitious, colorable, shoddy, fake *(coll.)*, phony *(sl.)*.

SOPHISTICATION, *n.* 1. Sophisticated character (ideas, tastes, ways) as a result of education *or* worldly experience, *etc.*, artificiality, change from the natural character *or* simplicity, experience, worldly-wisdom, knowledge of the world, savoir-faire, *savoir-vivre (Fr.)*, tact, address, social proficiency *or* adroitness, discretion, poise, sagacity, diplomacy, tactfulness.

2. Impairment *(as of purity or genuineness)*, debasement, adulteration, corruption, pollution, poisoning, vitiation, alteration, mixture, contamination, coloring, misrepresentation, misconstruction, prostitution, perversion, alloy, defilement.

3. Use of sophistry, false reasoning, sophism, quibble, fallacious argument, deception, paralogy, shift, evasion, cavil, equivocation, chicanery, casuistry, perversion, philosophism, prevarication, Jesuitism, distortion, mystification, dissembling, dissimulation, subtlety, pretense, misleading argumentation, philosophastry, philosophastering, false teaching.

SOPHISTRY, *n.* 1. Subtle (tricky, beguiling) method of reasoning *(generally fallacious)*, chicanery, casuistry, quibble, chicane, sophisticism, misleading argumentation, special pleading, cavil, evasion, shift, equivocation, deception, philosophism, prevarication, Jesuitism, perversion, distortion, false teaching, quackery, philosophastry, philosophastering, subtlety, pretense, dissimulation, dissembling, mystification.

2. False argument, sophism, fallacy, false logic, quibble, paralogism *(Logic)*, subterfuge, blind, dodge, feint, chicanery, antilogy, paradox, delusion, stratagem, untruth, misrepresentation, illogicalness, speciousness, misinterpretation, irrationality, absurdity, elenchus, pseudosyllogism, philosophism, philosophastering, quackery, error, misjudgment.

SOPHOMORIC, *adj.* Suggestive of *or* resembling the traditional sophomore, intellectually pretentious, self-assured, foolish, foolhardy, rash, overconfident, overweening, brash, indiscreet, cocksure, temerarious, giddy, self-important, pert, arrogant, know-it-all, cocky *(coll.)*.

SOPORIFIC, *adj.* 1. Causing *or* tending to cause sleep, somniferous, somnific, sleep-inducing, dormitive, slumberous, soothing, balmy, sedative, mesmeric, somnolent, opiate, narcotic, hypnotic, soporiferous, somnifacient.

2. Pertaining to *or* characterized by sleep *or* sleepiness, sleepy, drowsy, soporose, somnolent, sluggish, slumberous, heavy, lethargic, yawning, oscitant, comatose, dozy, sleep-filled, somnific, somniferous, somnolescent.

SOPORIFIC, *n.* Something causing sleep *(esp. a medicine)*, hypnotic, anesthetic, narcotic, gas, somnifacient, sedative, sleep-inducer, sleeping potion.

SOPPY, *adj.* 1. Soaked, drenched, very wet, saturated, sloppy, sodden, dripping, soggy, soft, seepy, oozy, madid, liquid, juicy, sweaty, watery, wringing-wet, mushy, spongy, plashy, pasty.

2. Rainy *(as weather)*, dripping, pluvial, pluvious, drizzly, drippy, wet, cat-and-dog, muggy, moist, misty, sticky, dank, damp, vaporous, humid.

SOPRANO, *n.* Uppermost part *or* voice, treble, air, descant, melody, falsetto, canto *(Music)*, cantus *(Music)*.

SORCERER, *n.* One supposed to exercise supernatural powers through evil spirits, magician, enchanter, witch, medicine man, necromancer, shaman, wizard, diviner, soothsayer, seer, exorcist,

charmer, thaumaturgist, diabolist, demonist, demoniast, demonologist, warlock, theurgist, witch doctor, obi doctor, voodooist, wangateur *(Southern U.S.)*.

SORCERY, *n.* Art (practice, spells) of a sorcerer, magic, enchantment, witchery, conjuration, incantation, wizardry, alchemy, theurgy, black art, voodoo, charm, thaumaturgy, necromancy, psychomancy, rune, invocation, glamour, witchcraft, exorcism, hoodoo, voodooism, shamanism, obeah, betwitchment, fetishism, sortilege, satanism, demonianism, devilry, vampirism, demonry, demonology, diabolism, exsufflation *(Eccles. Hist.)*.

SORDID, *adj.* 1. Dirty, filthy, soiled, grimy, smutty, foul, unclean, impure, offensive, squalid, slovenly, rank, putrid, noxious, putrefied, rotten, fulsome, mucky, defiled, unwashed, sooty, slatternly.

2. Morally mean, ignoble, low, degraded, base, vile, ill-gotten, gross, poor, abject, low-minded, inferior, groveling, scurvy, corrupt, sunken, wicked, scoundrelly, blackguardly, profligate, abandoned, debauched, demoralized, sorry, sneaking, dishonorable, disgraceful, depraved, coarse, vulgar, discreditable, dastardly, cowardly, common, raffish, disreputable, ignominious, cheap, yellow, rascally, beggarly, odious, execrable, degenerate, opprobrious, arrant, tainted, petty, abominable, rattish, dirty, fallen, reprobate, reptilian, inglorious.

3. Meanly selfish, self-seeking, churlish, close, mercenary, covetous, avaricious, miserly, stingy, illiberal, penurious, small, grasping, paltry, parsimonious, greedy, ungenerous, niggardly, usurious, chary, shabby, stingy, stinting, scrimping, rapacious, grudging, extortionate, pinching, meager, cheeseparing *(coll.)*, tight *(coll.)*, near, close-handed, close-fisted.

SORE, *adj.* 1. Physically painful *or* sensitive, tender, raw, inflamed, irritated, smarting, ailing, hurt, afflicted, affected, touchy, aching, with exposed nerves, ulcerated, burning, stinging.

2. Suffering bodily pain, bruised, buffeted, in pain, hurting, ailing, unwell, ill, sick, queasy, nauseated, beaten, qualmish, injured, wounded, hurt, prostrate.

3. Suffering mental pain, grieved, distressed, sorrowful, galled, troubled, agonized, hurt, racked, pained, offended, unhappy, stung, in limbo, wounded, on the rack, under the harrow, harrowed, tortured, convulsed, crucified, lancinated, in agony, grieved.

4. Causing great mental pain *or* sorrow, causing very great suffering (misery, hardship, *etc.*), racking, painful, sharp, harsh, agonizing, distressing, grievous, heavy, burdensome, unbearable, severe, violent, acute, poignant, tormenting, torturous, oppressive, afflictive, excruciating, troublesome, insufferable, intolerable, harrowing, grinding, searing, consuming, cruel, caustic, corroding, cutting.

5. Being an occasion of irritation, painful, vexing, irritating, provocative, ticklish, critical, touchy, upsetting, unmentionable, risky, precarious, knotty, exacting, entangled, offensive, embarrassing, perplexing, awkward, disconcerting, troubled, spiny, thorny, irksome, difficult, delicate, uneasy.

SORE, *n.* 1. Sore spot *or* place on the body, wound, inflammation, hurt, swelling, pang, twinge, ulcer, imposthume, abscess, fester, ulceration, exulceration, crick, kink, stitch, gripe, burn, smart, abrasion, bruise, scuff, laceration, ache, pimple, boil, pustule (*Pathol.*), blain (*Pathol.*), carbuncle, canker (*Pathol.*), spasm, throe, convulsion.

2. Source *or* cause of grief (distress, irritation, *etc.*), tribulation, annoyance, vexation, grief, wound, sorrow, blight, care, burden, injury, load, pain, trauma, sting, thorn, oppression, canker, trial, mortification, gall, cross, fret, nuisance, grievance, cut, trouble, exasperation, worry, displeasure, disagreeableness, stroke, blow, shock, offense, provocation, smart, ordeal, visitation, infliction, molestation, infestation, pestilence, scourge, woe, curse, plague, unpleasantness, bitter cup *or* draft, aggravation (*coll.*).

SORROW, *n.* 1. Grief, sadness, regret, distress, heaviness of heart, anguish, woe, heartache, dolor, affliction, ruth, vexation, repentance, remorse, contrition, penitence, disconsolateness, agony, unhappiness, misery, bereavement, lamentation, woefulness, trouble, mourning, compunction, wretchedness, infelicity, dole, desolation, oppression, depression, suffering, heartbreak, bitterness.

2. Cause *or* occasion of grief *or* regret, affliction, misfortune, trial, tribulation, sore, disaster, evil, grief, bale, grievance, undoing, discomfort, calamity, catastrophe, hardship, vexation, visitation, trouble, oppression, privation, adversity, purgatory, cloud, curse, travail, ordeal, rub, stress, austerity, bitter draft, difficulty, pinch, plight, frown of fortune, strait, cancer, bitterness, canker, worry, hard luck, ill luck, peck *or* sea of troubles, bad fortune *or* luck, bewilderment, extremity, burden, cross, load, care, scourge, infliction, disaster, mischance, injustice, reverse, stroke, pestilence, torment, blight, onus, incubus, millstone round one's neck, handicap, hindrance, impediment.

SORROW, *v.* Feel sorrow, grieve, mourn, pine, despair, fret, lose heart, repine, droop, bemoan, lament, bewail, be in pain of mind, rue, regret, lay to heart, take to heart, be sad, weep, despond, deplore, brood, languish, sink.

SORROWFUL, *adj.* 1. Full of *or* feeling sorrow, grieved, sad, downcast, melancholy, heavy, disconsolate, depressed, unhappy, dejected, cheerless, cast down, crestfallen, wretched, pathetic, dispirited, broken-hearted, joyless, desolate, funereal, elegiac, lamentable, touching, woebegone, atrabilious, plaintive, somber, afflicted, despondent, heavy-hearted, long-faced, long-visaged, lugubrious, blue, miserable, subdued, grave, sober, staid, saturnine, pensive, doleful, dismal, gloomy, dreary, wan, rueful, tearful, grief-stricken, pained, burdened, encumbered, bowed down, full of care, troubled, stricken, crushed, woeful, heavy-laden, pessimistic, distressed, hurt, infelicitous, tristful, lamenting, despairing, forlorn, inconsolable, unmanned, prostrated, chapfallen, down in the mouth (*coll.*).

2. Indicative of *or* expressive of sorrow, mournful, plaintive, wailing, sad, wistful, full of pathos, pathetic, piteous, rueful, woeful, heart-rending, dolorous, unhappy, wretched, miserable, lamentable, affecting, moving, distressing, melancholy, dirgelike, touching, querulous, elegiac, crying, complaining, whining, moaning, grievous, ululant, clamorous, weeping, pitiful.

3. Involving *or* causing sorrow, distressing, grievous, inflictive, afflictive, lamentable, grave, serious, distressing, unfortunate, calamitous, disastrous, deplorable, dire, troublesome, vexatious, burdensome, harsh, onerous, cruel, severe, hard, difficult, wearying, trying, oppressive, noxious, laborious, arduous, toilsome, tiring, wearing, painful, wearisome, overbearing, irksome, troublesome, taxing, evil, crushing, exhausting, perverse, awkward, untoward, weighty, solemn, rueful, tragic, dismal, adverse, sinister, black, regrettable, disagreeable, bitter, melancholy, dolorous, mournful, grim, ponderous, overwhelming.

SORRY, *adj.* 1. Feeling regret (compunction, sympathy, pity, *etc.*), regretful, remorseful, repentant, penitent, regretting, lamenting, touched, contrite, disappointed, penitential, penitentiary, softened, melted, self-condemning, self-accusing, self-reproachful, conscience-stricken, conscience-smitten.

2. Of a deplorable kind, pitiable, miserable, poor, mean, wretched, pitiful, paltry, low, inferior, indifferent, scurvy, meager, meretricious, inadequate, scant, deficient, gimcrack, beggarly, shabby, contemptible, scrubby, shoddy, defective, unworthy, worthless, scamped, tawdry, trashy, cheap, vulgar, base, second-rate, measly (*sl.*).

3. Sorrowful, grieved, sad, downcast, melancholy, heavy, disconsolate, depressed, unhappy, dejected, cheerless, cast down, crestfallen, wretched, pathetic, dispirited, broken-hearted, joyless, desolate, woebegone, atrabilious, somber, afflicted, despondent, heavy-hearted, long-faced, long-visaged, lugubrious, blue, miserable, subdued, grave, sober, staid, saturnine, pensive, doleful, dismal, gloomy, dreary, wan, rueful, tearful, grief-stricken, pained, burdened, encumbered, bowed down, full of care, troubled, stricken, crushed, woeful, heavy-laden, pessimistic, distressed, hurt, infelicitous, tristful, lamenting, despairing, forlorn, inconsolable, unmanned, prostrated, chapfallen, down in the mouth (*coll.*).

4. Associated with sorrow, suggestive of grief *or* suffering, melancholy, dismal, dirgelike, elegiac, funereal, mournful, plaintive, wailing, sad, wistful, pathetic, piteous, rueful, woeful, heart-rending, dolorous, unhappy, wretched, miserable, lamentable, affecting, moving, distressing, touching, querulous, crying, complaining, whining, moaning, grievous, ululant, clamorous, weeping, pitiful, lugubrious, doleful, dismal, gloomy, sober, solemn, pensive, grave.

SORT, *n.* 1. Kind, species, class, description, order, variety, strain, stripe, genus, rank, race, quality, nature, type, character, denomination, stamp, color, breed, kidney, category, brand, distinction, like (*coll.*), selection, grade, genre, constitution, aspect, temper, disposition, school, form, set, classification, feather, grain, make, cast, mold, suit, sect.

2. Example (*more or less adequate*), kind, type, degree, semblance, appearance, pretext, substitute, simulation, representation, seeming, figure, shape, effect, show, impression, illustration, delineation.

3. Manner, fashion, method, way, style, means, form, system, guise, plan, device, line of conduct, tone, cut, procedure, design, scheme, policy, strategy.

SORT, *v.* Organize, put in order, type, index, name, allot, group, brand, analyze, co-ordinate, ticket, digest, collocate, list, alphabetize, tag, methodize, distinguish, divide, order, size, pigeonhole, docket, label, rate, tabulate, systematize, file, assort, number, dispose, rank, grade, catalogue, segregate, place in a category, classify, categorize, class, range, distribute.

SORTIE, *n.* Foray *(of troops)*, sudden rushing forth, dash, issuance, emergence, exodus, outburst, attack, egression, bursting forth, egress, outbreak, ejection, thrust, raid, eruption, charge, efflux, effluence, outflow, outpouring, proruption, sally, outpour.

SORTILEGE, *n.* Divination by magic, art of a sorcerer, exercising supernatural powers through evil spirits, enchantment, wizardry, charm, invocation, voodoo, fetishism, devilry, exsufflation *(Eccles. Hist.)*, witchery, alchemy, thaumaturgy, glamour, voodooism, sorcery, vampirism, conjuration, theurgy, necromancy, witchcraft, shamanism, satanism, demonry, incantation, black art, psychomancy, exorcism, obeah, demonianism, demonology, diabolism, bewitchment, hoodoo, rune.

SO-SO, *adj.* *(Colloq.)* Moderate, average, indifferent, bearable, ordinary, fair, passable, commonplace, mediocre, second-rate, tolerable, allowable, better than nothing, middling, betwixt and between.

SOT, *n.* Inebriate, oenophilist, lush, dram-drinker, hard-drinker, alcoholic, drunkard, swill, souse *(sl.)*, boozer, winebibber, love-pot, dipsomaniac, tippler, soak, toper, guzzler.

SOTTISH, *adj.* Muddled, stupefied, drunk, drunken, intoxicated, inebriated, under the influence of alcohol, addicted to strong drink *or* the bottle, befuddled, dulled, intemperate, senseless, bibulous. *Slang Terms:* out, potted, high, blotto, soaked, tight, plastered, cockeyed, out cold, fried, pickled, glowing, blind, boiled, pie-eyed, lit up, loaded, tanked, looped, under the table, canned, heeled, well-oiled, three sheets to the wind.

SOUGH, *n.* Sighing *(as the wind)*, sigh, whistle, whistling, moan, moaning, sob, sobbing, whine, whining, pipe, piping, roar, roaring, wail, wailing, hiss, hissing, shriek, shrieking.

SOUGH, *v.* Sing, scream, whistle, shriek, wail, roar, sigh, moan, pine, rustle.

SOUL, *n.* 1. Essence *or* animating principle of human life, spirit, immortal part, psyche, heart, personality, reason, intellect, anima humana, divine soul, seat of consciousness, understanding, intelligence, ego, subconscious, true being, inner man, inmost nature, nous *(Gr. Philos.)*, pneuma *(Gr. Philos.)*.

2. Central nature, embodiment, principle, entity, actuality, essence, quintessence, essentials, elements, reality, root, inmost substance, main features, hypostasis, being, center, fundamentals, sum and substance, keynote, foundation, flower, truth, quiddity, verity, tenor, sense, significance, heart, pith, marrow, spirit, essentialness, drift, core, gist, purport, backbone, kernel, import, life, lifeblood.

3. Inner feelings, deep sense, sensibility, passion, emotion, mood, humor, temperament, heart, spirit, disposition, response, life, sentiment, feeling, nature.

4. Liveliness, animation, vigor, mettle, dynamic, vim, briskness, intensity, vitality, pep, verve, alacrity, activeness, snap *(coll.)*, drive, fire, energy, vivacity, spirit, sprightliness, kick, go *(coll.)*.

5. That which makes *or* keeps alive, world spirit, vivifying principle, universal life force, impelling force, breath, animus, urge, vital impulse, oversoul, God, Nature, archeus, logos, the Absolute, life principle, life breath, divine spark, *vis*

vitae (Lat.), heart, psyche, Promethean spark, animating principle.

6. Member of the human race, a living being, individual, human, folk *(pl.)*, person, creature, child, woman, anthropos, personage, man, mortal.

7. Valor, doughtiness, mettle, stanchness, awelessness, bravery, fearlessness, spirit, heroism, audacity, braveness, pluck, courage, lion-heartedness, manfulness, dauntlessness, stoutness, stalwartness, sand *(coll.)*, unappalledness, guts *(sl.)*, grit *(coll.)*, stout-heartedness, boldness, firmness, resoluteness, daring, gameness, gallantry, backbone *(coll.)*, fortitude, spunk *(coll.)*, audaciousness, resolution.

SOULFUL, *adj.* Full of feeling, expressive, fraught with meaning, meaningful, sensitive, pregnant, eloquent, alive, delicate.

SOULLESS, *adj.* Pitiless, uncompromising, unreasonable, hard, tough, stiff, iron-handed, obdurate, extortionate, brutal, remorseless, unbending, vindictive, vengeful, hard-boiled *(coll.)*, cold-blooded, heartless, implacable, unconcerned, insensitive, unfeeling, uncompassionate, inflexible, mean, unbearable, tyrannical, despotic, inquisitorial, stern, inhuman, strict, stringent, merciless, unremitting, unsparing, ruthless.

SOUND, *adj.* 1. Free from defect, unmarred, unblemished, unscathed, unimpaired, undamaged, entire, perfect, unspoiled, unhurt, intact, whole, undefaced.

2. In good physical condition, sound as a bell, sturdy, tough, burly, robust, robustious *(humor.)*, full of life and vigor, well, in trim, in good health, strong, salubrious, unimpaired, undecayed, good, cured, fit, buxom, hardy, firm, stout, flourishing, ruddy, fresh, whole, of a sound constitution, vigorous, lusty, florid, flush, staminal, sound of wind and limb, healthy, in fine fettle, blooming, lively, rosy-cheeked, fit as a fiddle, virile, plump, hearty, in fine whack *(sl.)*, fine *(sl.)*, in the pink, in the pink of condition, spirited, chipper *(coll.)*, bobbish *(sl.)*.

3. Substantial, not flimsy, well-built, well-constructed, lasting, stout, strong, rugged, resistant, solid, sturdy, firm, heavy, hard, tough, durable.

4. Not superficial *(in thought, reasoning, etc.)*, philosophical, thorough, meaningful, deep, ample, valid, full, real, profound, trustworthy, solid, consummate, true, learned, authoritative, reliable, thoroughgoing.

5. Of sound mind, wise, knowing, rational, discriminative, reasonable, incontrovertible, sage, sagacious, conclusive, reliable, level-headed, just, sober-minded, stable, accurate, well-advised, well-grounded, sapient, decisive, solid, convincing, dependable, trustworthy, sensible, good, sober.

6. Financially strong, solvent, solid, good, unindebted, of good credit *or* rating, stable, reliable, responsible, in good standing.

7. *(Emphatic, often after* GOOD) Effective, competent, mighty, efficacious, dynamic, stout, great, powerful, potent, forceful, forcible, strenuous, thorough, vigorous, big, hefty, memorable, heavy, strong, energetic.

SOUND, *n.* 1. That which is heard, tone, noise, sonance, pitch, sound vibrations.

2. Sense *or* perception of sound, act of perceiving sound, audibility, auscultation, hearing, ear.

3. Noise, disturbance, clangor, clang, vociferation, outcry, hubbub, jangle, din, agitation, clamor, racket, blast, hullabaloo, tumult.

4. Range *(as within range or sound of)*, earshot,

hearing distance, hearing, earreach, carrying distance.

5. Import (as in the sound of a document, idea, letter, etc.), importance, force, suggestion, significance, consequence, purpose, object, meaning, effect, drift, bearing, intent, intention, allusion, coloring, aim, emphasis, tone, value, matter, moment, weight, tenor, color.

6. (Of the sea) Arm of the sea, cove, creek, bay, gut, firth (Scot.), euripus, bight, narrows, fiord, strait, belt (Geog.).

SOUND, v. 1. Utter a noise, make a noise, produce sound, produce noise, enunciate, pronounce, resound, articulate, phonate, vocalize, voice.

2. Reverberate, resonate, repercuss, rebound, resound, re-echo, echo.

3. Test for depth (with a sounding line), fathom, plumb the depths, sling the lead, plumb.

4. Dive (as a hooked fish), go to the bottom, run for the bottom, plunge, descend suddenly and rapidly.

5. Extol (as praises, etc.), laud, belaud, cry, cheer, acclaim, magnify, commend, voice, utter, shout, hail, noise abroad, declare, encore, sing, celebrate, call out.

SOUNDING, adj. Vibrant, rolling, ringing, deep, booming, vibrating, orotund, resounding, full, loud, reverberant, sonorous, resonant, full-toned, rich.

SOUNDLESS, adj. Not sounding, inaudible, muffled, stilled, stifled, muted, still, quiet, silent, noiseless, toneless, echoless, deathlike, calm, hushed.

SOUP, n. Pottage, julienne, chowder, bisque, broth, consommé, stock, purée, bouillon, okra, gumbo, mulligatawny.

SOUR, adj. 1. Having an acid taste, tart, sharp, acetous, vinegary, acidulous, astringent, subacid, acetic, acerbic, acrid.

2. Fermented, rendered acid by fermentation, rancid, bad, spoiled, curdled, turned, acidulated, clabbered (of milk).

3. Distasteful, disagreeable, unpleasant, bitter, unsavory, offensive, odious, nasty, undesirable, unwelcome, repulsive, repugnant, insufferable, dislikable, thankless, unacceptable, uncared-for.

4. Harsh (in spirit or temper), austere, morose, peevish, sullen, moody, surly, crusty, choleric, bilious, jaundiced, acrimonious, bitter, embittered, cross, churlish, crabbed, crabby, irritable, caustic, dour, grouchy, virulent, unamiable, acerbate, acidulous, disagreeable, splenetic, sore (coll.), bad-tempered, petulant, currish, ill-tempered, uncivil, ill-humored, stinging, biting, stern, brusque, bluff, tart, venomous, astringent, rude, mordacious, ill-natured, grumpy, snappish, waspish, perverse, cynical, huffy, touchy, testy, spleenful, gruff, atrabilious.

SOUR, v. Become or make sour, become acid, acidify, acerbate, ferment, curdle, spoil, acidulate, acetify, tartarize, clabber.

SOURCE, n. 1. Thing or place from which something arises or is obtained, origin, root, well, taproot, cause, original, germ, egg, seed, nucleus, fountainhead, foundation, wellhead, spring, head, beginning, rise, issue, outlet, vent, dawn, womb, stem, stock, rudiment, element, agent, impulse, matrix, cradle, basis, base, wellspring, commencement, reason, occasion, derivation, mainspring, headspring, genesis, instigation, provocation, motivation, principle, generator, ground, primogenitor.

2. Spring of water from the earth or place of issue, fountain, beginning of a stream or river, well, fount, fountainhead, jet, spout, seep, headspring, wellspring, wellhead.

3. Book (statement, person, etc.) supplying information, authority, reference, source material, manuscript, informant, oracle, witness, horse's mouth (coll.).

SOUSE, v. 1. Plunge into water or other liquid, soak, seep, sink, dip, immerse, submerge, duck, douse, splash, dive, immerge, deluge, drench, submerge, sop, flood, inundate, engulf, drown, wallow, mire, wet thoroughly.

2. Dash (as water), pour, splash, stream, well, gush, spatter, bespatter, splatter, swash, squirt, spurt, slop, spill, heave, throw, fling, spout, jet, surge.

3. Steep in pickle, brine, pickle, preserve, seethe, marinate, marinade.

SOUVENIR, n. Something given or kept for remembrance, memento, keepsake, reminder, remembrancer, token, memorial, emblem, trophy, relic.

SOVEREIGN, adj. 1. Belonging to or characteristic of a sovereign or sovereignty, princely, royal, imperial, kingly, queenly, crown, monarchal, reigning, potent, powerful, monarchical, regal, ruling, kinglike, majestic, dynastic, independent, autonomous, self-governing, self-directing.

2. Supreme, greatest in degree, utmost, extreme, above all others, commanding, highest, chief, predominant, principal, paramount, invincible, maximal, maximum, excellent, superior, controlling, unexcelled, unapproached, superlative, major, prime, main, dominant, predominant, preëminent, leading, uppermost, top, topmost, peerless, incomparable, unmatched, matchless.

3. Efficacious (as a remedy), effectual, efficient, potent, effective, useful, applicable, adequate, competent, capable, sufficient.

SOVEREIGN, n. Monarch, autocrat, potentate, supreme ruler, suzerain, queen, king, prince, lord, ruler, emperor, overlord, crowned head, his majesty, royalty, chief, chieftain, sultan (Moham.).

SOVEREIGNTY, n. 1. Quality or state of being sovereign, dominion, supreme power, absolute authority, empire, majesty, sway, supremacy, supreme rule, reign, lordship, kingship, command, regality, throne, crown, headship, predominance, paramountcy, primacy, scepter, dynasty, royalty, imperialism, domain, monarchy, despotism, empery (Poetic).

2. Supreme and independent power or authority in government, autocracy, autonomy, self-rule, self-government, home rule, freedom, self-determination, independence.

SOW, v. 1. Scatter (seed) over land for growth, strew, plant, implant, set in, seed, spread, cast, shed, sprinkle.

2. Introduce for development, seek to propagate or extend, disseminate, disperse, broadcast, diffuse, cultivate, foster, sponsor, spread, inculcate, infix, establish, breed, lodge, innovate, infiltrate, instill, interfuse, interject, inject, infect, induct, import, teach, circulate, shed, extend, transmit, diffuse, publish, report, noise abroad, whisper about, rumor, give out, tell, publicize.

SPA, n Mineral spring or locality of such springs, sanatorium, health resort, watering place, springs, baths, warm or hot springs, thermae, pump room.

SPACE, n. 1. Unlimited or indefinitely great expanse containing all things, universe, infinity, the heavens, abyss, vacuum, sky, ether, plenum, air, creation, firmament, the void, boundlessness, illimitability, immensity.

2. Extent, room, area, portion, containing power, place, proportions, sweep, capacity, amplitude, acreage, span, breadth, width, stretch, scope, swing, expanse, expansion, extension, extensiveness, spread, dimensions, reach, range, arena, sphere, latitude.

3. Room, seat (berth, *etc.*) on a public vehicle, place, reservation, accommodation.

4. Linear distance, particular distance, interval, interstice, intersection, chasm, gulf, caesura, hiatus, openness, gap, span, hole, cavity, break, hollow, interspace, separation, lacuna, spandrel (*Archit.*).

5. Extent of time, interval, while, period, term, age, epoch, era, cycle, stage, tenure, season, stretch, spell, span, duration.

SPACE, *v.* 1. Fix the space *or* spaces of, divide into spaces, place, group, align, rank, order, array, range, arrange, interval, set some distance apart, line up, distribute, interspace, mark out, graduate, measure, separate, set out.

2. Extend by inserting more space, expand, elongate, lengthen, stretch, distend, pad out, enlarge, spread out, fill out, prolong, protract, draw out, let out, spin out.

SPACIOUS, *adj.* 1. Containing much space, amply large, broad in scope (range, inclusiveness, *etc.*), commodious, capacious, expansive, accommodating, immense, ample, roomy, voluminous, comprehensive.

2. Occupying much space, of a great extent *or* area, wide, vast, extensive, broad, large, great, extended, widespread, far-flung, sizable, massive, bulky.

SPADE, *n.* Tool for digging (*with an iron blade and long handle*), spud, shovel, dibble.

SPADE, *v.* Dig (cut, remove) with a spade, turn over, shovel, dibble.

SPAN, *n.* 1. Limit to which anything reaches, proportions, stretch, length, borders, dimensions, reach, bounds, limitations, continuance, duration, term, period, extent, measure, distance, circuit, gauge, confines, gamut, desmesne, territory, width, breadth, sweep, scope, region, area, range.

2. Pair of animals (*yoked together for work, etc.*), yoke, pair, team.

3. Spell (*of time*), time, period, while, interval, term, stage, stretch.

4. Viaduct, bridge, arch, vault, overpass, ogive, archway.

SPAN, *v.* Connect, bridge, bridge over, cover, catenate, yoke, join, concatenate, cross, link.

SPANGLE, *v.* 1. Glisten, shine, glow, fulgurate, radiate, dazzle, glint, flash, gleam, scintillate, shimmer, coruscate, sparkle, luminesce.

2. Decorate (*with spangles*), besprinkle, ornament, embellish, enhance.

SPANGLED, *adj.* Bright, garish, twinkling, coruscating, argent, gleaming, shiny, radiant, scintillating, flashing, sheeny, shining, gaudy, irradiant, sparkling, shimmering, refulgent, silvery, lustrous.

SPANK, *v.* 1. Punish by striking, strike, slap, cane, whop (*coll.*), flagellate, wallop, trounce, birch, whale, belt, whip, beat, switch, lick (*coll*)., hit, cudgel, strap, lambaste (*sl.*), bastinado.

2. Move with haste, hurry, proceed, tear, fly, shoot, ride hard, make time, rush, sprint, race,

scurry, flee, hasten, lose no time, scour, scoot (*coll.*), bolt, dart, skedaddle (*sl.*), outstrip the wind, fly on the wings of the wind, bowl along, clap one's spurs to one's horse, wing one's way, crowd sail (*Naut.*), post, hie, scamper, career, bestir, move quickly, haste, rip (*coll.*), whiz, sweep, cover ground, get over the ground, dash off *or* on, go on the double (*coll.*), beat a retreat, not lose a moment, stir one's stumps, work against time, spin, leap, go like lightning, go hell-bent (*coll.*), go like a shot (*coll.*), clip, bound, boom, spring, bustle, burn up the road, press on, zip, skim, brush, whip along, jump, bundle, hump it (*sl.*), step, crack on, speed up, put on more speed, quicken, take wing, trot, gallop, make strides, step lively, pack off, pack away.

SPAR, *v.* Fight (*in a scientific manner*), box, play at fisticuffs, square off with, scrap (*sl.*), exchange *or* bandy blows.

SPAR, *n.* Timber, beam, boom, mast, spit, bowsprit, yard.

SPARE, *adj.* 1. Kept in reserve (*as for possible use*), stored, on hand, in stock, emergency, substitute, auxiliary, supplemental, supplementary, subsidiary.

2. Being in excess of present need, free from other use, extra, additional, remaining, unnecessary, leisure (*of time*), not engaged, unoccupied, superfluous, surplus, supernumerary, supplemental, auxiliary, extraneous, further, accessory, new, more, fresh, adscititious, remnant, odd, over, left, unused, unconsumed, exceeding, supplementary.

3. Frugally restricted (*as living, diet, etc.*), meager, scanty, scant, small, lean, short, barely adequate, modest, scrimpy, stinted, frugal, slender, insufficient, restricted, limited, light, inconsiderable, deficient, inadequate.

4. Lean, thin, raw-boned, emaciated, skinny, slim, puny, starved, stunted, fleshless, gaunt, scraggy, slender, lank, extenuated, attenuated, wizened, withered, spindling, rattleboned (*coll.*), starveling, undernourished, skeletal, gangling, pinched, gawky, poor, haggard, lanky, weedy, shriveled, scrawny.

5. Sparing, economical, temperate, chary, frugal, parsimonious, careful, thrifty, saving, penurious, niggardly, miserly, tight (*coll.*), save-all, close-fisted, mean, illiberal, narrow, avaricious, sordid, ungenerous, close-handed, close, stingy, churlish, stinting, penny-wise, shabby, near, tight-fisted, beggarly, venal, grasping, mercenary, grudging, scrimping, cheeseparing (*coll.*), greedy.

SPARE, *v.* 1. Refrain from harming *or* destroying, leave uninjured, forbear to punish, deal gently *or* leniently with, show consideration for, be lenient, be merciful, forgive, bear with, exonerate, acquit, liberate, give quarter, respite, reprieve, free, deliver, redeem, rescue, let off, discharge, excuse, release, tolerate, secure.

2. Save (*from strain, discomfort, annoyance, etc.*), preserve, exempt, conserve, safeguard, guard, shield, defend, shelter, protect.

3. Refrain from (*as action or speech*), forbear, omit, withhold, stand *or* hold aloof, abstain, not use, wait, hang fire, not stir, hold back, neglect, waive, have no hand in, take no part in, eschew, let *or* leave well enough alone, let be, let pass *or* slip, discontinue, cease, stay, stop, halt, desist, refuse, govern oneself, give over, contain oneself, check *or* curb oneself, avoid, renounce, swear off.

4. Part with (*esp. without inconvenience or loss*), let go, relinquish, afford, concede, cede, give,

grant, allow, do without, dispense with, not miss, forgo, yield, surrender.

5. Use economically *or* frugally, refrain from using up *or* wasting, economize, pinch, be parsimonious, conserve, hold, treasure, amass, lay up, keep, store, hoard, reserve, avoid using (consuming, spending, *etc.*), accumulate, put away, set aside, husband, retain, retrench.

SPARING, *adj.* 1. Economical, chary, parsimonious, penurious, stingy, miserly, careful, thrifty, frugal, saving, save-all, economical, temperate, spare, niggardly, tight *(coll.)*, close-fisted, mean, illiberal, narrow, avaricious, sordid, ungenerous, close-handed, close, churlish, stinting, penny-wise, shabby, near, tight-fisted, beggarly, venal, grasping, mercenary, grudging, scrimping, cheeseparing *(coll.)*, abstemious.

2. Lenient, merciful, compassionate, forgiving, touched, mild, easy, moderate, tolerant, humane, ruthful, clement, long-suffering, indulgent, benevolent, charitable, soft-hearted, tender-hearted, soft, kind-hearted, placable, exorable, sympathetic, patient, considerate, magnanimous, longanimous, pardoning, forbearing, chivalric.

3. Frugally restricted, scanty, limited, scant, scarce, meager, spare, thin, poor, puny, lean, slender, stinted, slight, slim, frugal, little.

SPARK, *n.* 1. Ignited *or* fiery particle, flash, sparkle, blink, twinkle, flicker, scintillation, shimmer, glimmer.

2. Small amount *or* trace of something, particle, scintilla, jot, iota, modicum, glimmer, shadow, mite, atom, ace, bit, mote, corpuscle, point, trifle, minim, hair, minutia, speckle, pin, straw, cent, farthing, doit, micron, snip, spot, rap, ion, insignificancy.

3. Trace of life *or* vitality, germ, seed, active principle, element, flutter, fire, blood, breath, essence of life, impulse of life, life force, vital flame, anima, psyche, lifeblood, soul, Promethean spark, spirit, heart.

4. Elegant and showy man, fop, buck, dandy, coxcomb, macaroni, dude, silk-sock Sam, jackanapes, jack-a-dandy, silk-stocking, popinjay, blade, gallant, man about town, swell *(sl.)*, ladies' man, blood, carpet knight, sheik.

5. Beau, lover, suitor, sweetheart, courter, squire, swain *(chiefly Poetic)*, gallant, Romeo, Casanova, Lothario, Strephon, wooer, young man, cavalier, fellow *(coll.)*, boy friend *(coll.)*.

SPARKLE, *n.* 1. Little spark, light, glitter, glimmer, fiery particle, flicker, glint, blink, flash, scintillation, twinkle, shimmer.

2. Sparkling appearance, play of light, luster, gleam, glow, glitter, glare, brilliance, radiance, refulgence, irradiance, illumination, radiation, incandescence, luminosity, dazzle, burnish, effulgence, glare, gloss, sheen, shine, glimmer, glint, nitency, lucidity, resplendence, lambency, luminousness.

3. Brilliance, liveliness, vivacity, animation, life, spirit, verve, quickness, alertness, dash, vitality, briskness, readiness, cheerfulness, cheer, gaiety, geniality, jollity, mirth, exhilaration, pep *(sl.)*, ginger *(sl.)*, vim *(coll.)*, snap *(coll.)*.

SPARKLE, *v.* 1. Issue in *or* as in little sparks, shine, emit little sparks *(as burning matter)*, twinkle, flash, gleam, coruscate, glow, radiate, scintillate, glisten, glitter, blink, dance, shimmer, flicker, dazzle.

2. Effervesce *(as wine)*, bubble, foam, froth, fizz, fizzle, pop, snap, burble.

3. Be brilliant (lively, vivacious), glow, be cheerful, scintillate, rejoice, laugh, caper, drown care, be witty, be gay, frolic, make merry, be the life of the party.

SPARSE, *adj.* Thinly distributed, scattered, thin, meager, scanty, dispersed, sporadic, spread here and there, few, rare, innumerous, disseminated, widespread, strewn, few and far between, broadcast, stray, infrequent.

SPARTAN, *adj.* 1. Suggestive of *or* befitting the ancient Spartans, rigorously simple, frugal, austere, sternly disciplined, severe, plain, hard, stiff, restricted, restrained, exacting, ascetic, stark, exigent, inexorable, inflexible, stern, stringent, puritanical, Draconian.

2. Brave, hardy, daring, dauntless, bold, valorous, chivalric, lion-hearted, heroic, doughty, valiant, fearless, intrepid, undaunted, courageous, stout, resolute, manly, virile, game, stout-hearted, aweless, indomitable, enduring, unyielding, spirited, potent, soldierly, mettlesome, plucky, gallant, enterprising, adventurous, venturesome, high-spirited, tenacious, resisting, confident, mighty, defiant, hard, unshrinking, unalarmed, unappalled, undismayed, unflinching, stalwart, invincible, unabashed, gritty, formidable, dynamic, spunky *(coll.)*.

SPASM, *n.* 1. Sudden involuntary contraction, twitch, cramp, crick, fit, seizure, convulsion, paroxysm, jerk, pain, grip, throe, holotonia *(Med.)*, entasia *(Med.)*, tetanus *(Pathol.)*, laryngismus *(Med.)*, eclampsia *(Pathol.)*, caisson disease *(Pathol.)*, the bends *(coll.)*, ictus *(Pathol.)*, epitasis *(Med.)*, spell *(coll.)*.

2. Sudden brief spell *(of unusual energy, activity, strong feeling, etc.)*, spurt, fit, start, pang, throe, fury, furor, passion, frenzy, tempest, storm, rage, turbulence, convulsion, raptus, seizure, flash, explosion, eruption, upheaval, impulse, hysterics, madness, delirium, paroxysm.

SPASMODIC, *adj.* 1. Pertaining to *or* of the nature of a spasm, jerky, twitchy, convulsive, spastic *(Pathol.)*, paroxysmal, spasmodical, vellicative, saltant, saltatoric, saltatorial.

2. Resembling a spasm *or* spasms, sudden *or* violent and brief, intermittent, fleeting, fitful, uncertain, irregular, sporadic, capricious, erratic, discontinuous, unsystematic, variable, broken, eccentric, periodic, recurrent, fickle, flighty, transient, mercurial, changeable, unsteady, desultory, unequal, uneven, inconstant, wavering.

SPAT, *n.* 1. Petty quarrel, tiff, bicker, huff, words, odds, disagreement, misunderstanding, disparity, difference, dispute, scrap *(sl.)*, dissent, litigation, dissension, contention, strife, fight, cross-purposes, run-in *(sl.)*.

2. Light blow, slap, smack, whack, stroke, stripe, buffet, thwack, lick, rap, lash, hit, knock, jab, dab, swipe, cuff.

SPAT, *v.* Strike lightly, slap, whack, knock, cuff, box, punch, thwack, thump, lash, pat, bump, swipe, clap, strike, clip, tap, bat, dab, jab, hit.

SPATTER, *v.* Sprinkle, splash, spot, scatter, spray, strike as in a shower, dash in small particles *or* drops, shower, smear, daub, splutter, bespatter, besprinkle, plash, strew, bestrew, swash, sparge, asperge, moisten, radiate, spread, diffuse, splatter, besmear.

SPAWN, *n. (Usually disparaging)* 1. Swarming brood, numerous progeny, farrow, seed, spat, young, litter.

2. Offspring *(of a stock idea, etc.)*, product

fruit, effect, by-product, result, consequence, sequence, creation, upshot, outcome, issue, derivative, corollary, side issue, episode, supplement, outgrowth, aftermath, wake, train, trail, after-effect, eventuality.

SPAWN, *v.* 1. Give birth to, give rise to, produce, generate, bring forth, beget, engender, give origin to, procreate, progenerate, propagate, yield, sprout, furnish, bear, give being to, create, evolve, fructify, compose, bear fruit, construct, form, formulate.

2. *(Usually disparaging)* Produce in large numbers, show excessive fecundity, reproduce prolifically, teem, hatch, breed, multiply, proliferate.

SPEAK, *v.* 1. Utter words *or* articulate sounds, pronounce, voice, articulate, mutter, whisper, murmur, mumble, sputter, enunciate, bark, vocalize, talk, intone, express, give utterance (tongue, voice, expression), break silence, lift *or* raise one's voice, sound, emit.

2. Make oral communication *or* mention, converse, commune, treat, express, inform, consider, discuss, hold intercourse, exclaim, soliloquize, let fall, say, chatter, chat, come out with, give utterance (tongue, voice, expression), talk, state, assert, convey, phrase, breathe, take up with, remark, comment, relate, recite, observe, counsel, consult, confer, tell, declare, allege, aver, confabulate, parley, palaver, chin *(coll.).*

3. Deliver a discourse, address, lecture, perorate, declaim, harangue, preach, sermonize, expatiate, expand, expound, exposit, hold forth, prelect, spiel, pronounce, dwell on, spellbind, rant, soapbox, tirade, stump *(coll.),* rodomontade, dilate, spout *(coll.).*

4. *(Fol. by* FOR*)* Make a plea *or* recommendation in behalf of, plead, present, propose, propound, back, favor, sponsor, offer, broach, put forward, justify, make a defense, uphold, support, argue for, sustain, contend for, maintain, put in a good word for, stick up for *(coll.),* defend.

5. Make known, indicate, reveal, disclose, make communication *or* disclosure, convey significance, bespeak, imply, infer, suggest, say, tell, announce, express, advise, signify, inform, acquaint, apprise, enlighten, represent, impart, divulge, proclaim, declare, exhibit, publicize, circulate, promulgate, vocalize, put into words, couch in terms, cry about *or* abroad, hawk about, rumor, publish, enunciate, annunciate, give voice (utterance, tongue, expression), air, divulgate, ventilate, spread, bruit, report, present, notify.

6. Emit a sound, make a noise *or* report, bark, voice, resound, phonate, resonate, echo, re-echo, repercuss, reverberate.

7. Communicate *(as by voice or signal),* accost, greet, hail, address, signal, salute, gesture, gesticulate, nod, beckon, motion, wave, wigwag *(Naval, etc.),* acknowledge.

SPEAKER, *n.* One who speaks formally before an audience, orator, discourser, lecturer, talker, prolocutor, spokesman, elocutionist, demagogue, interlocutor, voice, mouthpiece, advocate, Boanerges, rhetorician, valedictorian, spouter *(coll.),* prelector, expounder, expositor, preacher, sermonizer, reader, reciter, declaimer, stump orator, soapbox orator, speechmaker.

SPEAKING, *adj.* 1. That speaks, giving information as if by speech, living, graphic, talking, oral, vocal, verbal, communicative.

2. Highly expressive, eloquent, meaningful,

clear, pregnant, forceful, graphic, dynamic, pithy, vivid, telling, impressive, significant, indicative.

3. Lifelike, like, true, real, realistic, faithful, strict, servile, the very picture *or* image of, close, literal, exact, conscientious, similar.

SPEAR, *n.* 1. Long sharp-pointed weapon *(for thrusting or throwing),* lance, bolt, shaft, dart, pike, javelin, gaff, harpoon, jereed, assegai, trident.

2. Shoot *(of a plant),* spire, sprout, stem, stalk, blade, tuft, stipe *(Bot.),* acrospire *(of grain).*

SPEAR, *v.* 1. Pierce, penetrate, puncture, impale, stick, stab, transfix, gore, spit, spike, lance, pike, thrust through, run through, gouge, bore, pass through, perforate, prick, pink.

2. Shoot, sprout, send up, rise, burgeon, break through, germinate, bud, grow, burst forth, leap up, vegetate, spring up.

SPEARHEAD, *v.* Act as spearhead for, pioneer, scout, begin, lead, originate, initiate, create, undertake, lay the foundation of, start, conceive, give birth to, launch, institute, form, occasion, produce, construct, inaugurate, found, establish, set on foot, beget, fashion, usher in, introduce, inchoate, broach, fabricate, evolve, bring about, sow the seeds of, develop, generate, engender, draft, hew, carve, forge, open.

SPECIAL, *adj.* 1. Of a distinct *or* particular kind *or* character, being a particular one, peculiar, individual, certain, having a particular function (purpose, application, *etc.*), specific, unique, private, proper, exclusive, personal, typical, especial, characteristic, determinate, distinguishing, limited, defined, express, appropriate, restricted, set aside, fixed, reserved, respective, endemic, representative, several, specialized.

2. Distinguished from what is ordinary *or* usual, different, outstanding, original, uncommon, unique, distinct, esoteric, unusual, private, separate, select, dissimilar, discrepant, idiocratic, idiosyncratic, distinctive, inconformable, novel, new, fresh, untried, underived, unconventional, odd, rare, unorthodox, out of the ordinary, curious, singular, extraordinary.

3. Extraordinary, exceptional, especial, signal, memorable, distinguished, outstanding, noteworthy, significant, gala, momentous, noble, remarkable, important, august, eminent, imposing, striking, stirring, rare, eventful, urgent, critical, unparalleled, primary, crucial, pressing, commanding, distinguished, prominent, conspicuous, impressive, substantial.

4. Great, in exceptional degree, intimate *(of friends, etc.),* particular, near, good, close, warm, fast, devoted, ardent, stanch, tried and true, hand and glove, hand in hand, thick *(coll.).*

SPECIALIST, *n.* One who devotes himself to one subject *or* branch of a subject *or* pursuit, expert, adept, proficient, past master, connoisseur, skilled *or* practiced hand, master.

SPECIALIZE, *v.* 1. Pursue a special line of study *or* work, *etc.,* make a specialty, focus one's attention, do advanced study, concentrate one's efforts.

2. Render special *or* specific, invest with special character *or* function, adapt to special conditions, restrict to specific limits, single out, differentiate, particularize, severalize, modify, separate, mutate, designate, set apart, distinguish, segregate, individualize.

SPECIALTY, *n.* 1. Special subject of study *or* line of work, object of special attention, hobby, forte, talent, genius, faculty, aptitude, endowment, bent, turn, technique, acquirement, propensity, accomplishment.

2. Article particularly dealt with *or* manufactured, particularity, mark, badge, distinctive product, stamp, identification, earmark, feature.

3. Special *or* particular point (item, matter, characteristic *or* peculiarity), particularity, peculiarity, idiosyncrasy, individuality, oddity, singularity, rarity, quip, quirk, twist, idiocrasy, kink, crotchet, erraticism, eccentricity, caprice, whim, mannerism, trick, flight of fancy, distinction, earmark, character, quality, badge, idiom, habit, style, stamp, mode, animus, propensity, bent, turn, warp, leaning, inclination, tendency, affection, temper, feature.

SPECIE, *n.* Coined money, coin, cash, silver, change, copper, coinage, mintage, rouleau, hard cash, hard money.

SPECIES, *n.* Class of individuals having common characteristics, basic category of biological classification, group, genre, type, feather, make, cast, form, color, mold, description, designation, kind, sort, variety.

SPECIFIC, *adj.* 1. Having special application (bearing, reference), specifying, explicit, definite, direct, relevant, pointed, respective, apt, pertinent, applicable, detailed, precise, minute, to the point, apposite, in point, bearing upon.

2. Particular, precise, specified, definite, limited, special, express, concrete, clearly stated, fixed, clear-cut, restricted, confined, bounded, stated, certain, determinate, exact, circumscribed, unequivocal.

3. Peculiar *(as characteristics, qualities, effects, etc.)*, especial, characteristic, appropriate, marked, typical, special, endemic, distinctive, idiosyncratic, idiocratic, individual, intrinsic, particular, unique, diagnostic, intimate, esoteric, private, singular, personal.

SPECIFY, *v.* 1. Name specifically *or* definitely, state in detail, particularize, define, detail, indicate, enumerate, note, mark, point to, name, mention, show clearly, designate, assign, determine, denote, allot, set apart, point out, cite, stipulate, label, tag, ticket, differentiate, select, denominate, itemize.

2. Give a specific character to, limit, define, christen, baptize, term, style, determine, describe, call, set forth, individualize, characterize, distinguish, demarcate, outline, restrict, delimit, represent, circumscribe, qualify, fix, differentiate, analyze, set forth.

3. Name *or* state as a condition, offer, outline, cite, present, make terms, condition, stipulate, make a condition, stickle for, make a point of, insist upon, bargain, compact.

SPECIMEN, *n.* Part *or* individual exemplifying a mass *or* number, typical individual, pattern, sample, type, exemplar, representative, example, copy, model, paradigm, exponent, exemplification, taste, taster, instance, case in point, illustration, bite, sip, test, trail, cross section.

SPECIOSITY, *n.* Something pleasing but deceptive, fallacy, quibble, ambiguity, paralogism, claptrap, moonshine, sophism, quiddity, sophisticism, elench, solecism, philosophism, sophistry, quackery, chicanery, perversion, special pleading, casuistry, Jesuitism, distortion.

SPECIOUS, *adj.* Apparently good *or* right without real merit, deceptive, plausible, superficially pleasing, tenable, conceivable, casuistic, illusory, persuasive, misleading, hollow, sophistical, glossy,

credible, Jesuitical, suave, bland, smooth-tongued, smooth-spoken, mealy-mouthed, honeyed, smooth, double-faced, Janus-faced, fulsome, dissembling, flattering, hypocritical, unctuous, oily, fair-seeming, probable, colorable, ostensible.

SPECK, *n.* 1. Stain, spot, flaw, blot, blur, dot, mark, freckle, speckle, blemish, defect, nick, patch, flyspeck, smudge, smutch, smirch, maculation, macule, macula, daub, taint, blotch, scratch.

2. Bit, particle, scintilla, corpuscle, pinpoint, pinprick, vanishing point, tittle, atom, mote, mite, jot, iota, spark, modicum, glimmer, trace, shadow, whit, grain, scrap, ace, point, trifle, minim, hair, minutia, pin, straw, cent, farthing, doit, micron, snip, rap, spot, ion, insignificancy.

SPECTACLE, *n.* 1. Anything striking presented to the sight *or* view, wonder, curiosity, phenomenon, picture, vision, revelation, manifestation, marvel, sight, scene, prodigy, panorama, materialization, miracle, freak, sign, sensation, phantasmagoria, rarity, prodigiosity, gazingstock.

2. Public show, exhibition, display, presentation, pageant, review, parade, representation, scene, sight, exhibit, production, extravaganza, panorama, exposition, demonstration.

3. *(Pl.)* Device to aid vision *or* protect the eyes, glasses, eyeglasses, blinkers, goggles, specs *(coll.)*, sunglasses, glims *(sl.)*, gig lamps *(sl.)*.

SPECTACULAR, *adj.* Pertaining to *or* of the nature of a spectacle, marked by *or* given to great display, dramatic, thrilling, ostentatious, theatrical, stagy, vivid, striking, dramaturgical, melodramatic, operatic, magnificent, scenic, histrionic, impressive, showy, grand, stately, gorgeous, sumptuous, brilliant, elegant, glorious, elaborate, decorative, flowery, grandiloquent, radiant, splendid, pompous, bespangled, embroidered, jeweled, ornamental, rich.

SPECTATOR, *n.* One who looks on, observer, looker-on, beholder, witness, gazer, bystander, viewer, inspector, eyewitness, watcher, sightseer, attendant, theatergoer, patron, attender, gallery *(pl.)*, house *(pl.)*, audience *(pl.)*, sidewalk superintendent *(joc.)*, rubberneck *(sl.)*.

SPECTER, *n.* Visible incorporeal spirit *(esp. terrifying)*, ghost, apparition, phantom, illusion, demon, spook, hobgoblin, shade, banshee, sprite, goblin, shadow, wraith, manes, bugbear, ghoul, imp, bad fairy, bugaboo, bête noire, fetish, boggart, ogre, gorgon, Puck, Robin Goodfellow, mumbo jumbo, fee-faw-fum, bad peri *(Persian)*, kobold *(Ger. folklore)*, leprechaun *(Irish folklore)*, revenant, presence, appearance, eidolon.

SPECTRAL, *adj.* Ghostly, phantomlike, ethereal, spiritual, phantom, supernatural, incorporeal, ghostlike, eerie, uncanny, specterlike, pale, weird, unreal, unsubstantial, gossamery, airy, vaporous, spooky *(coll.)*, wraithlike, unearthly, disembodied, bodiless, discarnate, illusory, imaginary, intangible, chimerical, immaterial, visionary, animistic, asomatous, shadowy.

SPECULATE, *v.* 1. *(Often fol. by* ON, UPON *or a clause)* Engage in thought *or* reflection, cogitate, ponder, reflect, meditate, muse, ruminate, think, consider, contemplate, brood, study, cerebrate, deliberate, wonder, chew the cud *(coll.)*, rack *or* ransack the brains, beat *or* cudgel the brains, commune with oneself, put on one's thinking cap.

2. Indulge in conjectural thought, guess, conjecture, experiment, surmise, wonder, theorize, suppose, conceive, imagine, judge, fancy, dare

say, hazard an opinion, have it, take it, assume, presume, infer, hypothesize, dream, conclude.

3. Buy and sell in expectation of profit, engage in a business transaction involving risk, trade hazardously, wager, venture, gamble, chance, game, sport, play, take a chance, plunge *(sl.)*, buy low and sell high, rig the market.

SPECULATION, *n.* 1. Contemplation of a subject, reflection, consideration, cogitation, intellection, rumination, meditation, study, thought, deliberation, lucubration, intellectual examination, self-counsel, self-communing, ponderation, a priori reasoning, mentation, absorption, abstraction, concentration, reverie, excogitation, imagination, observation, thinking, pensiveness.

2. Conclusion, opinion, hypothesis, theory, guess, plan, vision, thought, inkling, suspicion, intimation, notion, impression, proposition, observation, postulate, assumed position, venture, reflection, surmise, inference, presumption, scheme, supposition, conjecture, proposal.

3. Conjectural consideration, conjecture, surmise, experimentation, essay, assay, guesswork, inference, presumption, assumption, supposition.

4. Trading in hope of profit caused by market changes, engagement in risky business transactions, venture, hazard, gamble, risk, play, futures, agiotage, stockbrokerage, betting, sporting, gaming, plunge *(sl.)*, trading in futures.

SPECULATIVE, *adj.* 1. Contemplative, conjectural, abstract, theoretical, ideal, academic, notional, imaginary, philosophical, speculatory, presumptive, assumptive, putative, postulational, empirical, trial-and-error, analytic, projected, unreal, experimental, probative, tentative, impractical, suppositional, uncertain, dubious, doubtful, questionable, hypothetical, debatable, contestable, improbable, provisional, controvertible, unproven, vague, unreliable, indefinite, undemonstrated, unconfirmed.

2. Involving commercial *or* financial speculation, risky, hazardous, adventurous, chancy *(coll.)*.

3. Given to speculation, thoughtful, meditative, pensive, thinking, cogitative, excogitative, deliberative, experimental, contemplative, museful.

SPECULATOR, *n.* 1. One engaged in commercial *or* financial speculation, gambler, stockbroker, gamester, hazarder, better, stockjobber, venturer, plunger *(sl.)*, bull *(Stock Exchange sl.)*.

2. One devoted to mental speculation, theorist, philosopher, surmiser, speculatist, theorizer, theoretician, conjecturer, hypothesist, assayer, essayer, cogitator, doctrinaire, notionalist, experimenter, experimentalist, analyst, tester.

SPEECH, *n.* 1. Faculty *or* power of speaking, oral communication, expression of human thought and emotion by sound and gesture, conversation, parlance, colloquy, articulation, verbal intercourse, dialogue, talk, mention, tongue, voice, lip, prattle, confabulation, commerce, oratory, chat, vocalization, phonation, discussion, pronunciation, enunciation, converse, collocution, discourse, interlocution, accents, word of mouth.

2. That which is spoken, utterance, remark, declaration, statement, word, say, saying, dictum, talk, observation, allegation, expression, assertion, apostrophe, pronouncement, comment, mention.

3. Communication by a speaker to an audience, oration, declamation, palaver, harangue, discourse, lecture, address, allocution, philippic, tirade, eloquence, prelection, sermon, recitation, diatribe,

homily, appeal, salutation, exhortation, dissertation, disquisition, soliloquy.

4. Form of utterance characteristic of a particular region *or* people, locution, language, dialect, idiom, brogue, tongue, phraseology, jargon, vocabulary, lingo, cant, argot, patois, localism, regionalism, accent, isogloss, twang, idioticon, provincialism.

5. Manner of speaking *(as of a person)*, diction, style, attack, delivery, articulation, presentation, rhetoric, selection *or* choice of words, use of words, expression of ideas, literary power, composition, enunciation, utterance, elocution, command of words.

SPEECHLESS, *adj.* 1. Temporarily deprived of speech by strong emotion *or* physical weakness *or* exhaustion, wordless, breathless, astonished, agape, aghast, open-mouthed, unable to believe one's senses, thunderstruck, awe-struck, dumbstruck, amazed, lost in wonder (amazement, *etc.*), spellbound, tongue-tied, inarticulate.

2. Lacking the faculty of speech, dumb, mute, silent, gagged, taciturn, mum, voiceless, inarticulate, wordless, tongueless, unvocal, tongue-tied, non-vocal.

SPEED, *n.* Haste, celerity, swiftness, rapidity, fleetness, hurry, dispatch, velocity, quickness, pace, drive, agility, dash, rate, alacrity, acceleration, expedition, nimbleness, hastiness, briskness, fastness, rapidness, urgency, liveliness, instantaneity, flight, exertion, precipitation, smartness, readiness, instantaneousness, promptness, alertness, promptitude, career, bustle.

SPEED, *v.* 1. Promote the success of, further, forward, aid, assist, advance, expedite, succor, befriend, favor, take in tow, help, facilitate, nourish, foster, nurture, lend one's aid, boost, give a lift, contribute to, subscribe to, set, set agoing, second, stand by, back, bolster, sustain, maintain, support, take up the cudgels for, patronize, smooth, lend wings to, quicken, reinforce, give an impulse to, put *or* push forward, ease the way, disburden, pave the way, open the way, prepare *or* clear the way, disencumber.

2. Direct *(the steps, course, way, etc.)* with speed, move (go, pass, proceed) with speed *or* rapidity, hasten, make haste, run, hie, whisk, race, scud, scamper, gallop, post, scurry, hurry, rush, peg, be in a hurry, lose no time, flee, skip, spurt, push on, sprint, make time, ride hard, shoot, tear, fly, scour, scoot *(coll.)*, bolt, dart, skedaddle *(sl.)*, outstrip the wind, fly on the wings of the wind, bowl along, cut along *(coll.)*, clap spurs to one's horse, wing one's way, crowd sail *(Naut.)*, mend one's pace, spank, scuttle, flit, haste *(Lit.)*, rip *(coll.)*, whiz, sweep, cover ground, get over the ground, go on the double *(coll.)*, stir one's stumps, work against time, spin, leap, go like lightning *or* greased lightning *(coll.)*, go like a shot *(coll.)*, go hell-bent *(coll.)*, clip, bound, burn up the road *(sl.)*, zip *(coll.)*, bundle, hump it *(sl.)*, give her the gas *(coll.)*, make strides *or* rapid strides, do some tall stepping, step on it *(coll.)*, step lively *(coll.)*.

3. (Usually fol. by UP) Increase the rate of speed of, accelerate, quicken, hasten, step up, put on more speed, spurt ahead, crack on, mend one's pace, pick up speed, give her the gas *(coll.)*, put on a burst of speed, step on her tail, step on it *(coll.)*

4. Cause to move (go, proceed) with speed, expedite the going of, hasten, dispatch, hustle, bustle, move along, urge *or* press forward *or* on, precip-

itate, spur, push, bundle, ship, goad, lash, rush, prod, press, prick, drive, set on, egg on, hound on, stimulate, vivify, animate, rouse, festinate, promote, drive on, express, lend wings to, facilitate, pack off *or* away, impel, propel, post, incite, kindle, encourage, force, inflame, thrust, boost, jog, prompt, shove, move, bestir, flog.

5. Get on (*in a specified or particular manner*), advance, proceed, progress, contrive, come off, manage, get along.

SPEEDWAY, *n.* Course for fast driving, race track, road, turnpike, throughway, highway, main road, thoroughfare, fairway.

SPEEDY, *adj.* 1. Characterized by speed, swift, rapid, hasty, hurried, fast, agile, snappy, expeditious, electric, headlong, mercurial, light-footed, fleet, abrupt, winged, sudden, precipitate, quick, nimble, rushing, running, lively, snappy, bustling, light-legged, eagle-winged, spirited, light of heel.

2. Coming quickly *or* soon, prompt, not delayed, ready, expeditious, immediate, instant, instantaneous, without delay, punctual, quick, early, summary, in good time, unhesitating.

SPELL, *n.* 1. Form of words supposed to possess magic power, charm, incantation, exorcism, voodoo, hoodoo, jinx, witchery, sorcery, enchantment, bewitchment, magic, invocation, formula, trance, glamour, rapture, hypnotism, suggestion, open-sesame, mumbo jumbo, hocus-pocus, abracadabra.

2. Continuous course, fit, turn, bout, season, period, time, duration, stage, space, tenure, span, stretch, interim, interval, round, snap, term, interlude, respite, break, pause, lull, stay, spurt, recess, breathing spell, letup (*coll.*).

SPELL, *v.* 1. Name *or* write, *etc.*, the letters of, form words *or* syllables, represent by letters orthegraphize.

2. (*Often fol. by* OUT) Read letter by letter *or* with difficulty, study, pore over, trace, unfold, unriddle, unravel, interpret, decipher, con, disentangle, wade through, decode, solve, resolve, untangle, peruse, uncover gradually.

3. Discern, find, discover, make out, see, detect, descry, determine, fix upon, light upon, ascertain, distinguish, recognize, pitch upon, lay one's finger *or* hands upon, perceive, penetrate, grasp, apprehend, comprehend, read, infer, derive, deduce, fathom, gain insight into, get (*coll.*), savvy (*sl.*), realize, conceive, understand.

4. Signify, amount to, indicate, point to, mean, imply, foretell, forecast, portend, denote, purport, hint, bespeak, import, augur, omen, suggest, forebode, represent, presage, herald, shadow forth, prefigure, promise, stand for, typify, symbolize, betoken.

SPELLBIND, *v.* Render spellbound, cast a spell over, hold, bind as by a spell, hex, charm, glamour, entrance, enchant, enrapture, hypnotize, bewitch, fascinate, transport, magnetize, overpower, mesmerize.

SPELLBOUND, *adj.* Bound by *or* as by spell, enchanted, fascinated, entranced, astonished, possessed, haunted, amazed, speechless, under magic influence, under a spell, transported, charmed, bewitched, enraptured, rapt, agape, breathless, wordless, aghast, dumbstruck, awe-struck, lost in wonder (*amazement, etc.*), tongue-tied.

SPEND, *v.* 1. Pay out, disburse, expend, dispose of, open the purse, make expenditure, lay out money, incur expense, be liberal, fork *or* shell out (*sl.*), go (run, get) through, loose *or* untie the purse strings, be prodigal, dissipate, waste, lavish, squander, invest.

2. Employ (*labor, thought, words, time, etc.*) on some object *or* in some proceeding, give, use, devote, drain, take, put in, waste, lavish, consume, squander.

3. Pass (*time*), fritter away, fill, occupy, engage, busy, while away, squander, beguile, employ, use, consume, take up, put in, fool away, expend, kill, dissipate, wait through.

4. Use up, consume, burn out, dissipate, exhaust, wear out, deplete, destroy, drain, impoverish.

SPENDTHRIFT, *n.* One who spends his possessions *or* money extravagantly *or* wastefully, prodigal, waster, scattergood, spender, spend-all, wastrel, wastethrift, squanderer.

SPENT, *adj.* Used up, exhausted, consumed, effete, wearied, played out, impotent, disabled, prostrate, powerless, overwrought, tired out, done for, weak, weakened, done, debilitated, strengthless, faint, languid, with one foot in the grave, on one's last legs, drooping, ready to drop, fagged out, enfeebled, dead-beat (*coll.*), hors de combat (*Fr.*), worn out, fatigued, infirm, weary, laid low, feeble, bushed (*sl.*).

SPEW, *v.* Discharge the contents of the stomach through the mouth, vomit, cast up, eject, disgorge, puke, throw up (*coll.*), regurgitate, keck, heave, retch, cast *or* heave the gorge.

SPHERE, *n.* 1. Round body, globular mass, globe, orb, ball, globule, spheroid, globoid, globulet, orblet.

2. Heavenly body, planet, star, orb, luminary, celestial body, earth.

3. Place within which a person *or* thing exists, field of activity *or* operation, arena, environment, habitat, circuit, course, ambit, orbit, bounds, pale, compass, province, section, beat, jurisdiction, zone, district, domain, territory, bailiwick, realm, walk, range, precinct, demesne, quarter, routine, traversal, path, area, capacity, department, function, office, scope, occupation.

4. Particular social world, stratum of society, walk of life, rank, place, position, standing, estimation, order of importance, step, station, prominence, elevation, distinction, superiority, caste, notability, gradation, importance, eminence, condition, degree, class, prestige, consequence, precedence, grade.

SPHERICAL, *adj.* 1. Having the form of a sphere, globular, round, orbicular, orbic, spheroid, spheriform, spherular, spherelike, orblike, orbiculate, cycloidal, annular, globose, globous, globated, circular, rotund, orbed.

2. Pertaining to the heavenly bodies, uranic, planetary, celestial, heavenly, astral, stellar, starry, astronomical, empyrean.

SPICE, *n.* 1. Pungent *or* aromatic substance of vegetable origin, flavor, flavoring, relish, condiment, seasoning.

2. Something that gives zest, piquant element *or* quality, tang, savor, taste, interest, flavor, relish, smack, scent, fragrance, sapor, sapidity, piquancy, poignancy, pungency, essence.

SPICY, *adj.* 1. Aromatic, fragrant, seasoned with *or* containing spice, savory, racy, heady, pungent, piquant, keen, sharp, hot, peppery, nippy, strong, rich, balmy, redolent, scented, snappy (*coll.*), zippy (*coll.*).

2. Piquant, pungent, pointed, exciting, to the point, trenchant, sharp, piercing, emphatic, marked,

keen, poignant, acute, clear, curt, curtate, epigrammatic, telling, effective, witty, vigorous, pregnant, crisp, succinct, laconic, pithy, barbed, severe, penetrating, attic, neat, condensed, sententious, compact, incisive, summary, direct, concise, sparkling, clever, brilliant, spirited, lively, provocative, electric, galvanic, stirring, sprightly, scintillating, nimble-witted, tantalizing, thrilling.

3. Of a somewhat improper nature, untasteful, coarse, indecent, doubtful, questionable, dubious, risqué, indelicate, indecorous, unseemly, rude, ribald, ungenteel, unbecoming, of doubtful propriety, únrefined, racy, suggestive.

SPIDER, *n.* 1. Trivet, tripod.

2. Evil person who entraps others, one who lures others by his wiles, siren, sorceress, seducer, seductor, seductress, tempter, temptress, enchantress, shaman, Circe, Lorelei, witch, ghoul, Harpy,

SPIGOT, *n.* 1. Small peg for stopping the vent of a cask, *etc.,* plug, tap, bung, faucet, spill, stopper, spile, stopple, cork, wedge, valve, wad, packing, stuffing, block, obstruction, dowel, pledget, tampon *(Surg.),* tampion, dossil *(Surg.).*

2. Faucet, cock, tap, stopcock, valve.

SPIKE, *n.* 1. Large nail, rivet, pin, peg, skewer, stake, support, dowel, fastener, toggle, staple, treenail.

2. Sharp stiff part *or* projection, point, spine, horn, prong, hib, neb, tine, spikelet, prickle, rowel, spur, barb, barblet, cusp, spit, barbule, spicule, spiculum *(Zool.),* quill, thorn, beard, bramble, briar, comb, bristle, hair.

3. Ear *(of grain),* shoot, spear, cob, beard *(Bot.),* awn *(Bot.),* arista *(Bot.),* sprig, scion, stem, offshoot, burgeon, branch, sprout, twig, growth, switch, sarmentum *(Bot.).*

SPIKE, *v.* 1. Fasten *or* snare with spikes, pierce with *or* impale on a spike, nail, pin, perforate, pink, stab, spear, puncture, prick, spit,. stick, transfix, enfilade.

2. Make ineffective, frustrate the action *or* purpose of, checkmate, cripple, disable, pinion, stop, hinder, foil, trammel, hamper, prevent from acting, retard, check, thwart, bar, arrest, obstruct, encumber, deadlock, hold from *or* back, be an obstacle *or* impediment to, inhibit, clog *or* scotch the wheels, hamstring, cross, embarrass, oppose, counteract, curb, block, incommode, choke off, stem, stall, traverse, conflict with, shackle, bring to a stand *or* standstill, be *or* play at crosspurposes, discommode, limit, circumscribe, go against, hold up, forestall, cramp, deter, prohibit, baffle, balk, preclude, impede, forbid, handicap, restringe, occlude, countervail, disappoint, disallow, spoil, invalidate, annul, cancel out, neutralize, offset, vitiate, put a spoke in one's wheels, muzzle, hobble, fetter, constrict, clip one's wings, stalemate, interfere, detain.

SPILL, *v.* 1. Allow to run *or* fall from a container accidentally *or* wastefully, pour out, overflow, drip, fall, waste, drop, slop, effuse, scatter, drain, lavish, squander, slosh, flood, debouch, slabber, slobber.

2. Shed *(blood),* pour out, let flow, release.

SPIN, *v.* 1. Make *(yarn)* by drawing out, twisting and winding, form into a thread, twist.

2. Turn rapidly as on an axis, rotate, wheel, gyrate, twirl, eddy, reel, revolve, roll, whirl, whirligig, swivel, circle, circumvolute, circumrotate, swirl, pirouette.

3. Tell *(a yarn or story),* produce, invent, evolve, fabricate, narrate, relate, recount, concoct, give

words to, rehearse, render, run over, unfold, recapitulate.

4. *(Often fol. by* OUT) Draw out, prolong, protract, lengthen, extend, expatiate, continue, stretch out, elongate, sustain, perpetuate, keep going, pad, fill out, perorate, tell in detail, enlarge, expand, amplify, prorogue, drag out, eke out, iterate, ramble, maunder, be circumlocutory, dwell on *or* upon, keep up, tautologize, battologize.

5. Move (go, run, ride, travel) rapidly, bolt, speed, hasten, sprint, scud, scamper, post, scurry, go it, fly, flit, trundle, scour, bowl along, whisk, run, hie, race, gallop, hurry, rush, peg, make haste, flee, skip, spurt, make time, shoot, ride hard, tear, scoot *(coll.),* dart, skedaddle *(sl.),* outstrip the wind, cut along *(coll.),* spank, scuttle, haste *(Lit.),* rip *(coll.),* whiz, sweep, go on the double *(coll.),* leap, clip, bound, zip *(coll.),* bundle, hump it *(sl.),* make strides *or* rapid strides.

6. Be affected with a sensation of whirling *(as the head),* reel, be staggered, be confused, be dizzy, whirl, falter, startle.

SPINDLE, *n.* Pin, axis, axle, rod, arbor, shaft, mandrel, swivel, trunnion, pivot, pole, radiant, gudgeon.

SPINDLING, *adj.* Long *or* tall and slender *(disproportionately so),* lean, rawboned, thin, skinny, emaciated, slim, starved, gaunt, scraggy, lank, extenuated, attenuated, rattleboned *(coll.),* starveling, skeletal, weedy, pinched, gawky, lanky, gangling.

SPINE, *n.* 1. Vertebral column, spinal column, backbone, chine, vertebrae, rachis *(Anat.).*

2. Pointed process *or* projection, spike, ray *(of fish's fin),* prickle, barb, spur, quill, point, thorn, horn, prong, nib, neb, tine, spikelet, rowel, spit, spicule, barbule, cusp, barblet, spiculum *(Zool.),* briar, bristle, hair, comb, bramble, beard.

3. Ridge *(of ground, rock, etc.),* chine, horseback, hogback *(Geol.),* asker *(Geol.),* arête *(Phys. Geog.).*

SPINELESS, *adj.* 1. Having a weak spine, flaccid, limp, invertebrate, flexible, limber, slack, bending readily, lax, pliable, pliant, flexile, soft, supple, flimsy, yielding, flabby.

2. Without moral force (resolution, courage), feeble, infirm, slack, light, loose, weak, frail, soft *(coll.),* easily influenced *or* persuaded, faint-hearted, cowardly, pusillanimous, lily-livered, timid, spiritless, afraid, fearful, vacillating, irresolute, whitelivered, chicken-hearted, uncourageous, poorspirited, shy, cowering, sneaking, effeminate, dastardly, caitiff *(Poetic),* wavering, hesitant, anxious, apprehensive, without a will of one's own, yellow *(sl.),* mean-spirited, timorous, indecisive.

SPINSTER, *n.* Unmarried woman, old maid, spinstress, maiden, celebate, miss, virgin, bachelor girl, feme sole *(Law).*

SPINY, *adj.* Covered with *or* having spines, armed with *or* bearing sharp-pointed processes, spiniferous, thorny, briery, spinous *(chiefly Biol.),* prickly, spiked, spiky, spinelike, pointed, awned, awny, aristate, barbed, barbate, thistly, pectinate, studded, snaggy, brambly, spiculate, spinulous, spinulescent, setaceous, bearded, whiskered.

SPIRACLE, *n.* Opening in confined space for communication with outer air, breathing hole, air hole, outlet, inlet, slot, duct, shaft, vent, orifice, pore, blowhole, tube, pipe, mouth, perforation, cavity, cranny, fissure, eye, break, eyelet, pinhole, passage, puncture.

SPIRAL, *adj.* Pertaining to *or* of the nature of a spire *or* coil, spirelike, winding, curled, helical, screw-shaped, whorled, spiroid, helicoid, corkscrew, crooked, coiled, circumgyrated, turbinate, cochlear, cochleated.

SPIRAL, *n.* Single circle *or* ring of a spiral *or* helical curve *or* object, spiral *or* helical object, formation *or* form, helix, coil, curl, circle, circumgyration, screw, twist, whirl, worm, curlicue, whorl, roll, volute, tendril, corkscrew, twirl, ringlet.

SPIRAL, *v.* Take a spiral course *or* form, wind, convolve, twirl, turn, twist, serpentine, screw, curl, intort, worm, reel, incurvate, entwine, wreathe, sinuate, wheel, intervolve.

SPIRE, *n.* 1. Tall tapering structure *(on a tower, roof, etc.)*, steeple, tower, turret, belfry, cupola, dome, shaft, obelisk, bell tower, minaret, martello, campanile, *tourelle (Fr.)*, flèche *(Arch.)*.

2. Tapering pointed part of something, tall sharp-pointed summit, peak, cone, point, cap, aiguille, height, crown, crest, pinnacle.

3. Highest point, summit, apex, pinnacle, point, peak, top, height, zenith, climax, tiptop *(coll.)*, acme, meridian, vertex.

4. Sprout, shoot of a plant, acrospire *(of grain)*, blade, spear, growth, twig, branch, sprig, scion, offshoot, switch, tendril, burgeon, sucker *(Bot.)*, sarmentum *(Bot.)*.

5. Spiral, convolution *(in a coil or spiral)*, curl, wreath, coil, spring, twist, curlicue, helix, circle, circumgyration, screw, whirl, worm, whorl, roll, volute, tendril, corkscrew, twirl, ringlet.

SPIRIT, *n.* 1. Principle of conscious life, vital essence *or* principle, breath, incorporeal part of man, soul, divine essence, intellect, heart, mind, immortal part, psyche, personality, reason, *anima humana (Lat.)*, understanding, intelligence, ego, inner man, inmost nature, nous *(Gr. Philos.)*, pneuma *(Gr. Philos.)*.

2. Supernatural incorporeal being *(esp. inhabiting a place or thing or having a particular character)*, apparition, ghost, shade, specter, shadow, demon, angel, elf, fairy, sprite, phantom, goblin, illusion, spook, hobgoblin, banshee, wraith, manes, bugbear, ghoul, imp, bugaboo, bête noire, fetish, boggart, poker, ogre, gorgon, fee-faw-fum, revenant, presence, eidolon.

3. Inspiring *or* animating principle *(pervading and tempering thought, feeling, action, etc.)*, soul, heart, impulse, genius, mind, urge, breath, animus, Promethean spark, *vis vitae (Lat.)*, life.

4. *(Cap.)* The third person of the Trinity, Holy Spirit, Holy Ghost, God, the Comforter, Paraclete, the Spirit of God, the Dove, the Intercessor, the Spirit of Truth, the Sanctifier.

5. *(Pl.)* Feelings *(with respect to exaltation or depression)*, emotion, affection, passion, sentiment, temper, condition, humor, state, mood.

6. Fine *or* brave vigor, mettle, liveliness, vivacity, energy, animation, ardor, spice, piquancy, glow, warmth, cheerfulness, enterprise, valor, stanchness, bravery, fearlessness, doughtiness, heroism, audacity, pluck, dauntlessness, sand *(coll.)*, grit *(coll.)*, guts *(sl.)*, unappalledness, stoutheartedness, boldness, daring, gameness, backbone *(coll.)*, resoluteness, firmness, fortitude, audaciousness, resolution, spunk *(coll.)*, courage, lionheartedness, stoutness, manfulness.

7. Disposition, temper, grain, humor, frame of mind, turn of mind, temperament, constitution, mood, affection, vein, stripe, streak, tendency,

tone, character, cast, cue, heart, animus, propensity, proclivity, predisposition, idiocrasy, idiosyncrasy, twist, turn, bias, warp, inclination, natural capacity, competence, genius.

8. Person characterized according to character *(disposition, action, etc.)*, being, creature, individual, man, soul, mortal, body, character, embodiment, impersonation, characterization, figure.

9. Dominant tendency *or* character of anything, nature, complexion, quality, essence, quintessence, characteristic, principle, embodiment, entity, actuality, reality, root, inmost substance, elements, hypostasis, being, center, fundamentals, sum and substance, foundation, keynote, truth, quiddity, verity, tenor, sense, significance, foundation, heart, pith, marrow, core, gist, kernel, life, lifeblood.

10. Vigorous sense of membership in a group, loyalty, enthusiasm, bond, allegiance, devotion, attachment, ardor, fervor, adherence, eagerness, avidity, zest, verve, furor, warmth, glow, fire, passion, vehemence, singleness of heart.

11. General meaning *or* intent *(of a statement, etc.)*, meaning, significance, purport, gist, drift, tenor, tone, pith, essence, sense, substance, matter, moral implication, coloring, bearing, signification, force, effect, intention, aim, explanation, definition, suggestion, purpose, object, acceptation.

SPIRIT, *v.* 1. Encourage, animate with fresh ardor *or* courage, stir up, urge on, excite, inspirit, enliven, move, propel, motivate, arouse, provoke, stimulate, impel, prompt, actuate, instigate, spur, incite, hound on, hurry on, set on, call on, egg on, whip, lash, inspire, prick, goad, prod, push, press, exhort, rouse, kindle, infect, impassion.

2. Carry *(away, off, etc.)* mysteriously *or* secretly, secrete, abduct, kidnap, take (carry, bear) off, make *or* run off *or* away with, impress, crimp, carry *or* convey away, shanghai *(Naut.)*, seize.

SPIRITED, *adj.* Having *or* showing spirit (mettle, courage, vigor, liveliness, *etc.*), lively, high-spirited, hardy, vigorous, sparkling, energetic, mettlesome, resolute, fiery, daring, bold, valiant, game, courageous, plucky, gritty, lion-hearted, earnest, stout, heroic, ardent, passionate, vehement, hasty, quick, fervent, zealous, keen, eager, avid, venturesome, audacious, fearless, intrepid, adventurous, undaunted, tenacious, alive, glowing, hearty, buoyant, sprightly, airy, vivacious, brisk, full of life, full of spirit, animated, active, bright, vivid, heated, intense, violent, sharp, excited, enthusiastic, determined, stalwart, invincible, forceful, dynamic, spunky *(coll.)*, dashing, breezy.

SPIRITLESS, *adj.* Without spirit, without ardor (vigor, animation, *etc.*), dull, cold, apathetic, inert, feeble, soulless, languid, indifferent, listless, phlegmatic, sluggish, tame, timid, melancholy, lowspirited, depressing, discouraging, dispirited, weary, lifeless, bloodless, dead, torpid, unenterprising, heavy, prosaic, prosy, uninteresting, flat, watered down, insipid, weak, commonplace, unimaginative, matter-of-fact, tiresome, tedious, vapid, humdrum, pedestrian, jejune, dry, usual, trite, stale, hackneyed, mediocre, common, everyday, stock, platitudinous, ordinary, infelicitous, prolix, wearisome, gross, lumbering, dreary, laborious, monotonous, stagnant, static, tumid, turgid, stupefying, benumbing, stolid, crass, elephantine, soporific.

SPIRITUAL, *adj.* 1. Of, pertaining to *or* consisting of spirit *or* incorporeal being, immaterial, psychical, ghostly, supersensible, unsubstantial, transcendental, metaphysical, superphysical, unearthly, decarnate, bodiless, disembodied, ethereal, supernatural, spectral, specterlike, phantom, wraithlike, asomatous, impalpable, intangible, extramundane, supramundane, spooky *(coll.)*, incorporeal.

2. Of *or* pertaining to the spirit *or* soul *(as distinguished from physical nature)*, mental, intellectual, rational, reasoning, psychic, perceiving, apprehending, cerebral, intelligent, sensible, psychological, percipient, human, higher, appercipient, understanding, elevated, thinking, conscious.

3. Characterized by *or* suggesting predominance of the spirit, ethereal, delicately refined, graceful, light, dainty, frail, airy, elfin, slight, fine, breezy, debonair, sprightly, gay, fastidious, subtle, will-o'-the-wisp, sensitive, buoyant, volatile, feathery, gossamery, imponderable.

4. Of *or* pertaining to the spirit as the seat of the moral *or* religious nature, inner, innermost, ethical, moral, unworldly, devout, holy, solemn, pure, highest, reverent, pious, religious, worshipful, exalted, ideal, heavenly-minded, virtuous, believing, godlike.

5. Of *or* pertaining to sacred things, pertaining *or* belonging to the church, ecclesiastical, religious, devotional, sacred, holy, divine, pure, just, righteous, Christian, consecrated, dedicated, devoted, set apart, hallowed, sanctified, sacrosanct, solemn, ceremonial, blessed, church, hieratic, priestly, celestial, godly, Biblical, scriptural.

SPIRITUALISM, *n.* 1. Belief in *or* practice of communication with spirits of the dead, divination, spiritism, animism, occultism, pythonism, mantology, psychomancy, mediumism, sitting, séance, necromancy.

2. Spiritual quality *or* tendency, immaterialism, psychism, immateriality, incorporeality, idealism, Platonism, ghostliness, supernaturalism, transcendentalism, impalpability, insubstantiality, intangibility, spirituality.

3. Insistence on the spiritual side of things *(as in philosophy or religion)*, holiness, devoutness, piety, sanctity, sanctimoniousness, godliness, righteousness, purity, religiosity, saintliness, unction, sanctitude, goodness, spirituality, theopathy, virtue, virtuousness, spiritual-mindedness, charism *(Theol.)*, unworldliness.

SPIRITUALITY, *n.* 1. Incorporeal *or* immaterial nature, immateriality, *etc. (See* SPIRITUALISM, 2.)

2. Predominantly spiritual character as shown in thought *or* life, *etc.,* spiritual tendency *or* tone, *etc. (See* SPIRITUALISM, 3.)

SPIRITUALIZE, *v.* Make spiritual, invest with a spiritual meaning, idealize, purify, sanctify, spiritize, dematerialize, immaterialize, refine, elevate, etherealize, unsubstantialize, discarnate, disembody, hallow, consecrate, set apart, canonize, dedicate, anoint, saint, enshrine, glorify, beatify, exalt, bless, devote, purge, uplift, cleanse, better, edify.

SPIRITUEL, *adj.* 1. Showing a refined and graceful mind *or* wit, clever, subtle, witty, sagacious, sophisticated, tactful, perceptive, discreet, perspicacious, cultivated, cultured, fastidious, delicate, acute, nice, keen, fine, discriminating, nimble-witted, scrupulous, meticulous, apperceptive, appercipient, percipient, discerning.

2. Light and airy in movement, ethereal, spiritual, delicate, refined, graceful, light, dainty, frail, elfin, slight, fine, breezy, debonair, sprightly, gay, fastidious, will-o'-the-wisp, sensitive, buoyant, volatile, feathery, gossamery, imponderable.

SPIRY, *adj.* 1. Having the form of a spire (slender shoot *or* tapering body), pointed, tapering, pyramidal, peaked, sharp, conical, xiphoid, cusped, piked, spear-shaped, sagittate, setaceous, echinate, subulate, cuspidate, acuminate *(Biol.)*, acicular *(Biol.)*, aciculate *(Biol.)*, ensate *(Biol.)*, ensiform *(Biol.)*, mucronate *or* mucronated *(Bot.)*, gladiate *(Bot.)*, hastate *(Bot.)*.

2. Spiral, coiled, curling, spirelike, winding, helical, screw-shaped, whorled, spiroid, helicoid, corkscrew, crooked, circumgyrated, turbinate, cochlear, cochleated.

SPIT, *n.* 1. Spittle, saliva *(esp. when ejected)*, secretion of some insects, sputum, rheum.

2. Light fall of snow *or* rain, sprinkle, shower, flurry, drizzle, drip.

3. Bar *(for holding roasting meat)*, pin, rod, grill, turnspit.

4. Narrow point of land projecting into the water, long narrow shoal extending from the shore, bar, flat, tongue, sandbank, bank, ridge, shelf, reef, shallow, promontory, reach, spur, breakwater, naze, ness, headland, bill, strip, head, palisade, escarpment, isthmus, peninsula.

SPIT, *v.* 1. Eject saliva from the mouth, expectorate, spew, slobber, salivate, drivel, drool, dribble, froth, slabber, sputter, splutter.

2. Express hatred *or* contempt, *etc.,* jeer, hiss, be contemptuous, sneer, flout, fleer, jape, scout, revile, throw mud at, taunt, ridicule, slander, backbite, traduce, vilify, curl up one's lip, scoff, decry, disparage, calumniate, jest, rail, hoot, slur, deride, chaff, contemn, cavil at, razz *(sl.)*, snort, give the raspberry *or* Bronx cheer *(sl.)*, gibe, fling.

3. Sputter, splutter, stutter, stumble, fall over oneself, mouth, falter, halt, gibber, jabber, stammer, speak thickly.

4. Fall in scattered drops *or* flakes *(as rain or snow)*, spatter, shower, sprinkle, drizzle, precipitate.

5. Stab, pierce, perforate, penetrate, puncture, thrust through, impale, transfix, cut into, run through, pass through, bore, gore, gouge, sink into, prick, bite into, stick, traverse, spike, spear, lance, ream, pink.

SPITE, *n.* Keen ill-natured desire to humiliate (annoy, injure) another, venomous ill will, malice, rancor, gall, venom, grudge, rivalry, maliciousness, malignity, hate, hatred, enmity, spleen, bitterness, resentment, revengefulness, vengeance, acrimony, opposition, defiance, contempt, umbrage, malevolence, aversion, abhorrence, detestation, hostility, antipathy, animosity, odium, bad blood, loathing, dissension, vindictiveness, acerbity, mordacity, evil, rankling.

SPITE, *v.* Wreak spite *or* malice on, annoy out of spite, thwart, mortify, hurt, harm, wound, bear malice against, bear a grudge, hate, stab, pierce, do evil to, do an ill office to, disservice, wrong, aggrieve, grind, oppress, victimize, pain, molest, treat maliciously, injure, antagonize, ill-treat, illuse, misuse, abuse, slap in the face, fly in the face of, harrow, spike, confound, hinder, rack, torture, break on the wheel, gall, sting, nettle, batter, punish, bruise, buffet, defeat, crush, put out, oppose, disconcert, stand in the way of, cut the ground out from under, provoke, irritate, irk, vex, resist, maltreat, distress, torment, discommode, persecute, frustrate, foil, disappoint, cross, balk, scotch, counteract, checkmate, resist, counterwork.

SPITEFUL, *adj.* Full of spite *or* malice, showing spite, venomous, malicious, malevolent, malignant, revengeful, hateful, hostile, vindictive, ill-natured, evil-minded, ill-disposed, malign, rancorous, invidious, mean, ugly, inimical, cold, antipathetic, disdainful, bristling, belligerent, fractious, snappish, contrary, harsh, cranky, disputatious, cantankerous, splenetic, crabbed, huffy, froward, iracund, touchy, testy, bearish, crusty, bitter, virulent, treacherous, truculent, low, intolerable, intolerant.

SPITFIRE, *n.* Person (*esp. a woman*) of fiery temper, one easily provoked to outbursts, vixen, shrew, Xanthippe, scold, fury, virago, termagant, hag, brawler, she-wolf, tigress, common scold, rebuker, chider, vituperator, harridan, old cat (*coll.*), hellhag, hellcat, grandmother, fishwife, battle-ax (*sl.*), crone, beldam, old witch, ogress.

SPITTLE, *n.* Saliva, spit, frothy protective secretion (*exuded by certain insects*), sputum, rheum.

SPLANCHNIC, *adj.* Of *or* pertaining to the viscera *or* entrails, visceral, intestinal, abdominal.

SPLASH, *n.* 1. Act *or* sound of splashing, swash, rush, gush, spurt, jet, squirt, spray, spatter, splatter, flush.

2. Spot caused by something splashed, liquid *or* semiliquid substance splashed, splotch, blemish, mark, smear, smudge, blot, blotch, daub, stain, macule, maculation, discoloration, smutch, smirch.

3. Patch (*as of color or light*), dash, ray, beam, spot, plot, glade, streak, stream, pencil, stroke, touch, daub.

4. Striking show, ostentatious display, pageantry, ostentation, pretension, parade, flourish, flaunting, pomposity, pompousness, pretense, vanity, flashiness, gaudery, gaudiness, superfluity, frills, tinsel, gilt, gilding, effect, figure, strut, glitter, peacockery, spectacle, exhibition, speciousness, veneer, affectation, coxcombery, foppery, inflation, pose, swagger, orotundity, dog (*coll.*), showiness, vaunting, pomp, dash, front (*coll.*), trappings, airs, swank (*sl.*).

SPLASH, *v.* 1. Wet *or* soil by dashing water *or* mud, *or,* upon, fall upon in scattered masses *or* particles, smear, shower, smirch, sprinkle, spatter, splatter, splotch, plash, bespatter, besprinkle, daub, cover, film, begrime, blur.

2. Dash (*water, etc.*) about, scatter, shower, strew, dabble, spatter, splatter, swish, swash, play, plop, bestrew, spread, diffuse, shed, cast, disperse.

3. Dash with force, break, wash, surge, toss, throw itself, slosh, strike, batter, buffet, billow, heave, hurl, cast, fling, smack, hit, beat.

SPLAY, *adj.* 1. Wide and flat, spread out, turned outward, broad, outstretched, outspread, fan-shaped, fanned, fanlike, flabelliform (*Zool.*), rhipidate (*Bot. and Zool.*).

2. Oblique, awry, crooked, distorted, bent, askew, bias, wry, warped, contorted, irregular, unsymmetrical, skewgee (*sl.*), angular, tilted, slanted, sloping, skew, aslant, inflected, inclined, slanting, transverse, acclivous, diagonal.

SPLAY, *v.* 1. Spread out, expand, extend, widen, stretch, broaden, mantle.

2. Form with an oblique angle, make slanting, bevel, slope, slant, deviate, bend, turn, shift, diverge, deflect, bear off, curve, crook, oblique, veer, sheer, angle.

3. Disjoin, dislocate, disconnect, disengage, part, dispart, detach, remove, disunite, dissociate, separate, unhinge, divide, segment, throw out of joint, dislodge, luxate, sever, sunder, unattach, unbind, undo, loose, dissever, cut, cleave, break, snap, crack, split.

SPLEEN, *n.* Peevish temper, ill humor, spite, animosity, rancor, gall, malignity, malevolence, grudge, vexation, asperity, bile, moroseness, hatred, malice, peevishness, acerbity, bitterness, sullenness, touchiness, venom, enmity, resentment, revengefulness, vengeance, acrimony, hostility, antipathy, bad blood, vindictiveness, rankling, mordacity, evil, irritability, short temper.

SPLENDENT, *adj.* 1. Shining, radiant, lustrous, gleaming, polished, irradiant, beamy, glittering, brilliant, gaudy, bright, flaming, effulgent, scintillating, twinkling, glistening, beaming, resplendent, lambent, luminous, shimmering, coruscating, sparkling, flashing, refulgent, glossy, nitid, spangled, incandescent, illuminated, silvery, argent, burnished, sheeny, fulgid, fulgurant, fulgent, sunny, orient, rutilant.

2. Brilliant (*in appearance, color, etc.*), gorgeous, magnificent, splendid, *etc.* (See SPLENDID, 1.)

3. Very conspicuous, illustrious, brilliant, glorious, outstanding, distinguished, distinctive, notable, prominent, splendid, imposing, grand, noteworthy, consequential, significant, striking, commanding, impressive, special, big, august, great, important, remarkable, substantial, considerable, unforgettable, memorable, salient, signal, marked, momentous, eminent.

SPLENDID, *adj.* 1. Gorgeous, magnificent, sumptuous, superb, grand, showy, stately, majestic, palatial, ornate, rich, elegant, beautiful, adorned, pompous, costly, luxurious, regal, royal, splendent, resplendent, princely, flashing, glittering, gleaming, radiant, ravishing, splendorous, dazzling, orient, imposing.

2. Glorious (*as a name, reputation, victory, etc.*), illustrious, renowned, famous, exalted, eminent, prominent, lofty, high, elevated, sublime, august, proud, imposing, noble, worshipful, lordly, peerless, revered, preëminent, immortal, never-fading, deathless, time-honored, imperishable, conspicuous, splendent, brilliant, celebrated, distinguished.

3. Strikingly admirable *or* fine, outstanding, excellent, thoroughly satisfactory, noteworthy, remarkable, honorable, exceptional, estimable, creditable, noble, choice, select, worthy, laudable, praiseworthy, distinguished, unimpeachable, commendable, meritorious, rare, deserving, brilliant, virtuous, exemplary, prime, best, sterling.

SPLENDOR, *n.* 1. Brilliant *or* gorgeous appearance *or* clothing, *etc.*, magnificence, grandeur, pomp, radiance, luster, gorgeousness, show, shine, glow, dash, stateliness, pageantry, state, pomp, elegance, beauty, sublimity, impressive effect, display, parade.

2. Brilliant distinction, glory, importance, consequence, prominence, eminence, notability, illustriousness, luster, significance, report, mark, moment, majesty, esteem, honor, good report, respect, credit, renown, loftiness, nobleness, sublimity, supremacy, paramountcy, repute, fame, primacy, superiority, blaze of glory, halo, resplendence, greatness, name, dignity, preëminence, prestige, grandeur.

3. Great brightness, luster, brilliance, radiance, refulgence, dazzle, light, fire, gleam, glitter, sheen, effulgence, fulgency, luminosity, luminousness, resplendence, irradiance, burnish, nitency, opalescence, gloss, shine, lucidity, lambency.

SPLENETIC, *adj.* Spiteful, irritable, peevish, churlish, cross, choleric, petulant, waspish, pettish, bitter, perverse, sullen, sulky, sour, crabbed, surly, irascible, moody, quarrelsome, ill-tempered, acrimonious, testy, touchy, querulous, crusty, captious, snappish, morose, thin-skinned, grouchy *(coll.)*, snarling, gruff, uncivil, ill-natured, vaporish, shrewish, currish, bristling, peppery, cross-grained, huffy, bilious, jaundiced, over-sensitive, resentful, out of sorts, spleeny, discontented, acrimonious.

SPLICE, *v.* Braid together, join together, knit, connect, plait, interweave, intertwine, tie, interlace, interknit, intertwist, twine, lace, wedge, overlap, mortise, rabbet, dovetail, graft, miter, bend *(Naut.)*, unite.

SPLINT, *n.* 1. Thin rigid piece *(of wood, etc.)* used to support *or* immobilize, splinter, rib, reinforcement, prop, support, supporter, strengthener, brace.

2. Thin strip *(in woven chair seat, etc.)*, split, slat, sliver, shiver, reed, cane.

SPLINTER, *n.* Rough piece *(usually long, thin and sharp)* broken from a main body, flinder, chip, sliver, shiver, shaving, shred, paring, fragment.

SPLINTER, *v.* Split *(into thin pieces)*, break into splinters, rend, shiver, sliver, rupture, blast, be brittle, fly apart, chip, fall to pieces, smash, hash, disintegrate, crash, crumble, granulate, be pulverized, break up, mince, explode, burst open, shatter, crunch, atomize, break to flinders, break to smithers *or* smithereens, reduce to fragments.

SPLIT, *n.* 1. Crack, rent, separation, fracture, cleft, fissure, interval, gulf, breach, bifurcation, hiatus, rift, opening, aperture, chasm, scissure, interspace, interstice, slot, crevice, chap, chink, incision, hole, gash, cut, foramen, rime, furrow, lacuna, break, disruption, channel, gap, space, orifice, cranny, cavity, score, fork, ramification, crotch.

2. Breach, rupture, separation, dissension, rift, division, schism, quarrel, disunion, variance, scission, break, eruption, cleavage, divorce, segregation, disagreement, divergence, disassociation, severance, detachment, isolation, disengagement, disconnection, partition, division, disintegration, decomposition, dissolution, difference, interruption, withdrawal, segmentation, sunderance, dismemberment, bifidity, dichotomy, discerption, abscission, dilaceration, disjointure, divarication, dimidiation, divulsion, dissection, diremption, falling out.

3. Party formed by rupture *or* scission, faction, clique, coterie, confederacy, ring, alliance, set, cell, clan, knot, caucus, camarilla, conclave, sect, body of partisans, federation, denomination, rebels, revolutionaries.

SPLIT, *v.* 1. Rend lengthwise, cleave, divide, rive, bisect, halve, detach, rescind, dimidiate, dichotomize, slash, hew, hemisect, slice, carve, cut off.

2. Tear asunder, break, rend, open, burst, separate, part, hack, rip, disjoin, isolate, sever, segment, splinter, shatter, disconnect, divide, part, dissect, loose, unloose, loosen, dissever, sunder, undo, abscind, unbind, untie, disjoin.

3. Divide into distinct parts *or* portions, apportion, partition, distribute, parcel out, allocate, mete, dole, share, allot, demarcate, carve, subdivide, segregate, disperse, portion, dispense, assign, detail, appropriate, whack *(sl.)*, deal.

4. Divide *(persons)* into different groups *(factions, parties, etc.)* as by discord, disunite,

cause division *or* rupture, come between, set against, set at odds, set by the ears, sow dissension, part, alienate, provoke *or* excite hatred, incense, segregate, disperse.

5. Break *or* part lengthwise, part, separate, become separated off, rend, be split, be rent, be riven, tear, rive, fracture, give way, rupture, snap, crack, shatter, shiver, splinter, burst.

SPLITTING, *adj.* 1. Overpoweringly noisy, ear-splitting, loud, sonorous, stentorian, enough to wake the dead, tonant, fulminating, ear-rending, deafening, shrill, booming, piercing, thundering, high, acute, sharp.

2. Severe *(as a headache)*, violent, harsh, cruel, grinding, acute, intense, relentless, persistent, bad, unremitting, pitiless, ruthless, overpowering, prostrating, overwhelming, raging, penetrating.

SPLOTCH, *n.* Large irregular spot, stain, blot, smudge, smutch, smear, splash, daub, soil, smirch, patch, grime.

SPLUTTER, *n.* 1. Sputtering utterance *or* talk, dispute, noise, fuss, flutter, bluster, stutter, agitation, excitation, flurry, fluster, ferment, shake, perturbation, sputter, quiver, ado, hubbub, fidget, scramble, bustle, hustle *(coll.)*, stew *(coll.)*.

2. Sputtering *or* spattering of liquid, *etc.*, spray, splash, sprinkle, diffusion, spurt, spirt, spouting, squirt, scattering, dispersion.

SPLUTTER, *v.* 1. Talk hastily and confusedly *or* incoherently, sputter, stutter, stammer, falter, stumble, fidget, halt, jabber, gibber, gabble, shake, mouth, flutter, quiver.

2. Make a sputtering sound, emit particles of something explosively, spit, spew, expectorate, spray, burst, boil, seethe, bubble, froth, sputter.

3. Fly, fall in particles *or* drops, shower, spatter *(as a liquid)*, bespatter, sprinkle, splash, spray, dash, besprinkle, plash, strew, bestrew, diffuse, spread, sparge, asperge.

SPOIL, *n.* 1. *(Often pl.)* Booty *(taken in war or robbery)*, plunder, loot, prey, pillage, stolen goods, prize, taking, illegal gain, grab, take, filch, haul *(coll.)*, stealings, boodle *(sl.)*, stealage, swag *(sl.)*, steal *(coll.)*.

2. Treasures won *or* accumulated, hoard, gain, heap, batch, pile, store, cumulation, accumulation, collection, stock, amassment, aggregation, mass, savings, budget.

3. Waste materials *(as from mining, excavating, quarrying, etc.)*, slag, dregs, sordes, grounds, lees, settlings, sediment, residue, draff, sprue, dross, refuse, deposit, cinder, smut, soot, ash, ember, offscourings, scourings, sweepings, precipitate, charcoal, carbon, rubbish.

SPOIL, *v.* 1. Damage irreparably *(as to excellence, value, usefulness, etc.)*, impair, ruin, mar, disfigure, muddle, hurt, harm, injure, botch, deface, destroy, deform, corrupt, blemish, disable, blight, mangle, mutilate, scar, disorganize, crack, disrupt, break, mess up, hash up, bosh, make sad work of, bungle.

2. Impair in character *or* disposition *(by unwise treatment, esp. excessive indulgence)*, demoralize, gratify, vitiate, pamper, humor, coddle, defile, debase, indulge.

3. Become spoiled (bad, unfit for use), become tainted *or* putrid, decompose, decay, sour, turn, addle, rot, putrefy, putresce, go bad, mold, mildew, deteriorate.

4. Plunder, pillage, prey, sack, devastate, rob, pilfer, forage, raid, pirate, freeboot, maraud, loot, buccaneer, privateer.

SPOILAGE, *n.* Decomposition, deterioration, rot, waste, dissolution, disintegration, rotting, putrefaction, putrescence, moldiness.

SPOKE, *n.* Bar, rod, round, handle, pin, rung, radius.

SPOKEN, *adj.* Uttered by speaking, oral, verbal, expressed, vocal, conversational, nuncupative, acroamatic, unwritten, viva-voce, enunciated, articulated, parol *(Law).*

SPOKESMAN, *n.* 1. One who speaks for another *or* others, speaker, mouthpiece, advocate, representative, messenger, mediator, go-between, vicar, surrogate, secondary, proxy, agent, attorney, parliamentary, instrument, negotiator, minister, delegate, interpreter, chairman, deputy, informant, interlocutor, adviser, foreman *(of a jury).*
2. Public speaker, orator, discourser, talker, lecturer, prolocutor, elocutionist, demagogue, interlocutor, voice, mouthpiece, advocate, Boanerges, concionator, rhetorician, valedictorian, spouter *(coll.),* prelector, expounder, expositor, preacher, sermonizer, reader, reciter, declaimer, stump orator, soapbox orator, speechmaker.

SPOLIATION, *n.* Act of spoiling, despoliation, plundering, robbery, deprivation, pillage, rapine, devastation, depredation, theft, direption, destruction, brigandage, raid, ravishment, foray, piracy, privateering, buccaneering, larceny, desolation, prey, marauding, harrying, freebooting, sack, plunder, pilfering, plunderage.

SPONGE, *v.* 1. Wipe *or* rub with a wet sponge, wash, blot, cleanse, clean, moisten, swab, rinse, mop, flush, soap, polish.
2. *(Fol. by* OFF, AWAY, OUT) Remove, efface, expunge, rub out, erase, obliterate, cancel, strike out *or* off, scratch out (off, away), wipe off (out, away).
3. *(Often foll. by* UP) Take up, absorb, assimilate, soak up, take in, suck in *or* up, drink in *or* up, sop, become impregnated, be permeated, steep, be suffused.

SPONGER, *n.* Person who sponges on others, hanger-on, beggar, bloodsucker, parasite, trencher friend, trencherman, sycophant, wheedler, borrower, bum *(coll.),* panhandler *(coll.),* dead beat *(sl.),* deadhead *(coll.),* dependent, tagtail, fawner, toady, toadeater, votary, tufthunter, groveler, spaniel, truckler, lickspit, appendant, appendage, bootlicker, footlicker, courtier, carpet knight, bur, heeler *(sl.),* barnacle.

SPONGY, *adj.* 1. Resembling a sponge, yielding, light, porous, springy, spongiose, spongoid, spongious, readily compressible, sievelike, soft, pulpy, pithy, incompact, fleshy, succulent, doughy, pulplike, medullary *(Anat.).*
2. Absorbing and holding liquid *or* yielding it as when pressed, bibulous, absorbent, marshy, wet, soaked, saturated, miry, oozy, splashy, plashy, boggy, lutose, moory, fenny, swampy, quaggy, paludal, uliginose, squashy, edematous *(Pathol.).*

SPONSION, *n.* Engagement *(esp. one made on behalf of another),* promise, surety, gage, pledge, security, warranty, sponsorship, hostage, assurance, bail *(Law).*

SPONSOR, *n.* One who vouches *or* is responsible for a person *or* thing, surety, guarantor, patron, one who makes an engagement *or* promise on behalf of another, witness, warrantee, guarantee, backer, bail *(Law),* hostage, mainpernor *(Law),* attester, testifier, deponent *(Law),* compurgator,

supporter, upholder, partisan, defender, protector, favorer, advocate, promoter, friend, succorer, befriender, benefactor, well-wisher, sympathizer, angel *(sl.),* guardian, champion, friend in *or* at court.

SPONTANEITY, *n.* Spontaneousness, spontaneous activity, directness, impulse, conatus, urge, volition, will, volitiency, choice, pleasure, wish, desire, mind, voluntariness, self-determination, self-activity, instinct, native *or* natural tendency, natural *or* unreasoning prompting, independence, own initiative, involuntariness.

SPONTANEOUS, *adj.* 1. Proceeding from a natural personal impulse, without effort *or* premeditation, arising from internal forces *or* causes, independent of external agencies, natural, unconstrained, uncompelled, voluntary, instinctive, unwitting, unthinking, mechanical, compulsive, blind, uncontrollable, extemporaneous, unprompted, unguarded, self-directing, independent, self-determined, snap, rash, unpremeditated, unforced, irresistible, unstudied, inevitable, unintentional, unconscious, involuntary, automatic, self-moving, free, willing, unbidden, gratuitous, self-acting.
2. Growing naturally *or* without cultivation, wild, in a natural state, uncultivated, overrun, overgrown, rank, lush, flourishing, luxuriant, jungled, dense.

SPOOL, *n.* Cylindrical piece on which something is wound, reel, bobbin, pirn.

SPOON, *n.* Utensil for taking up *or* stirring liquid, *etc.,* scoop, ladle, bail, dipper, trowel, cochleare, lavis *(East. Ch.).*

SPOOR, *n.* Trail *(esp. that of wild game animal),* track, path, scent, mark, print, trace, footprint.

SPORADIC, *adj.* Appearing *or* happening at intervals in time, occasional, appearing in scattered *or* isolated instances, occurring singly *or* widely apart, irregular, isolated, spotty, rare, sparse, single, uncommon, here and there, now and then, dispersed, infrequent, scattered, separate, unexpected, chance, incidental, accidental, capricious, periodic, indefinite, seldom, fragmentary, spasmodic, uncertain, casual, few, scarce, unsystematic, fitful, intermittent, variable, thin, meager, spread out, strewn, few and far between, stray, widespread, solitary, disparate, disjunct, individual.

SPORT, *n.* 1. Pastime pursued in the open air, pastime of an athletic nature, athletic contest, exercise, game, play, walk, constitutional, contention, pugilism, tournament, athletics, gymnastics, palaestrics.
2. Diversion, pastime, recreation, frolic, gambol, game, amusement, play, fun, entertainment, regalement, distraction, hobby, avocation, relaxation, divertissement, distraction.
3. Playful trifling, mirth, jesting, prank, gaiety, fun, merriment, joviality, jollity, pleasantry, antics, hilarity, skylarking, mummery, revelry, festivity, waggery, waggishness, drollery, merrymaking.
4. Derisive jesting, ridicule, derision, mockery, insult, contemptuous mirth, irrision, scoffing, detraction, badinage, raillery, banter, persiflage, jest, joke, quiz, chaff, sarcasm, irony, asteism *(Rhet.),* slur, depreciation, satire, disparagement, grin, fleer, leer, snicker, smirk, traducement, twit.
5. Object of derision, laughingstock, jestingstock, gazingstock, butt, byword, quiz, derision,

victim, monkey, fair game, game, joke, buffoon, scapegoat, goat (sl.).

6. Something sported or tossed about like a plaything, victim, puppet, gudgeon, cat's-paw, gull, dupe, buffoon, easy mark (coll.), sucker (sl.), pigeon (sl.).

SPORT, v. 1. Amuse oneself with pleasant pastime or recreation, play, gambol, antic, caper, beguile the time, while away the time, make merry, carouse, spree, skip, trip, dance, make or keep holiday, cavort (coll.), curvet, junket, disport, make fun, frisk, revel, frolic, romp, jest, joke, lark, dally, skylark.

2. Deal lightly, trifle, slight, tease, torture, pain, underestimate, take advantage of, toss about, toy, slur, play cat and mouse, maltreat, ill-treat, ill-use, abuse, misuse, rack, kill by inches, torment, dupe, make a fool, play upon, gull, take in, practice on one's credulity, fool, befool.

3. Ridicule, mock, laugh at, grin at, make fun or game of, fleer, flout, point at, scout, gibe, rally, banter, chaff, jest, joke, twit, satirize, parody, burlesque, jibe, point the finger of scorn at, fool, disparage, travesty, caricature, show up (coll.), scoff, laugh to scorn, make merry with, make a goat of (sl.), stultify, taunt, deride, poke fun at, laugh at, grin at, roast (sl.).

SPORTING, adj. 1. Engaging in (given to, interested in) open-air or athletic sports, athletic, playing, participating.

2. Sportsmanlike, fair, honorable, courageous, self-controlled, unprejudiced, just, honest, equitable, square, square-shooting (coll.), square-dealing (coll.).

3. Interested in or connected with sports or pursuits involving betting or gambling, betting, chance, gambling, speculative, risky, uncertain, dangerous, hazardous, chancy (coll.).

SPORTIVE, adj. 1. Frolicsome, playful, merry, jesting, gay, lively, gamesome, jocose, jocular, riant, saturnalian, coltish, romping, cheerful, amusing, roguish, jaunty, debonair, jovial, spirited, mischievous, jolly, sparkling, buoyant, lighthearted, airy, blithe, frisky, tricksy, hilarious, wanton, prankish, sprightly, waggish, humorous, comic, facetious, funny, ludicrous, vivacious, mirthful, jocund, blithesome, kittenish, whimsical, rollicking, gleeful, sunny, racy, arch.

2. Pertaining to or of the nature of sports, athletic, agonistic, palaestral, gymnastic, acrobatic, exercising.

SPORTSMAN, n. 1. One who engages in sport (esp. open air), player, contestant, opponent, combatant, antagonist, adversary.

2. One exhibiting qualities esteemed in a participant in sports, man of honor, gentleman, square or straight shooter, sport (coll.), brick (coll.), regular fellow (coll.).

SPORTSMANSHIP, n. 1. Character or practice of a sportsman, skill, cunning, ability, skillfulness, adroitness, expertness, dexterousness, dexterity, proficiency, facility, mastery, mastership.

2. Sportsmanlike conduct, fairness, self-control, honor, conscientiousness, scrupulosity, good will, probity, honorableness, rectitude, integrity, principles, justice, inviolability, incorruptibility, reliability, trustworthiness, uprightness.

SPOT, n. 1. Mark made by foreign matter, speck, blot, stain, soil, fleck, freckle, speckle, mottle, dapple, patch, maculation, blemish, splotch, flaw, taint, pock, blotch, discoloration, blur, dot, mote,

measle, defect, nick, flyspeck, smudge, smutch, smirch, macula, daub, scratch, taint.

2. Moral stain (as on character or reputation), blemish, flaw, reproach, disgrace, stigma, defect, fault, brand, imputation, slur, taint, tarnish, smudge, smirch, smutch, blot, defect, soil.

3. Place, locality, site, locale, position, point, region, situation, space, area, district, tract, scene, locus, premises, seat, quarter, bounds, latitude and longitude, neighborhood, station, part, territory, zone, habitat.

SPOT, v. 1. Stain with spots, smear, smudge, smutch, sprinkle, speckle, spatter, splash, soil, sully, blemish, dapple, dot, stud, speck, blot, diversify, bespatter, mottle, maculate, daub, tarnish, grime, spray, shower, plash, strew, bestrew, sparge, asperge.

2. Place on a particular spot, set, locate, dispose, arrange, station, seat, allot, post, array, fix, group, rank, establish, deposit, settle, lay, plant, rest, stand, install, situate.

3. Become spotted, discolor, stain, speck, speckle, fade, show marks.

SPOTLESS, adj. Free from spot (stain, blemish, marks, etc.), pure, clean, clear, perfect, undefaced, unspotted, flawless, white, unsoiled, untarnished, unblemished, unstained, untainted, unsullied, immaculate, faultless, snowy, bright, speckless, shining, washed, uncorrupted, unmarred, unpolluted, expurgate, fair, virginal.

SPOTLIGHT, n. 1. Strong light thrown on a particular spot, limelight, floodlight, footlight, searchlight, arc light, flashlight, klieg light, spot (Motion Pictures).

2. Conspicuous public attention, publicity, limelight, currency, circulation, familiarity, publication, glare of public observation, notoriety, ventilation.

SPOTTED, adj. 1. Marked with or characterized by spots, speckled, bespeckled, punctate, maculate, ocellated, spotty, freckled, dotted, dappled, guttate, parti-colored, pinto, blotchy, splotchy, mottled, variegated, specky, macular, flea-bitten (of a horse, etc.), flecky, measly, pied, piebald, flecked.

2. Sullied, blemished, imperfect, soiled, maculate, dirty, smutched, smudged, smeared, discolored, stigmatic, blotchy, black-and-blue.

SPOTTY, adj. 1. Full of or having spots, occurring in spots, mottled, etc. (See SPOTTED, 1.)

2. Irregular, uneven in quality or character, sporadic, uncertain, undependable, unreliable, ununiform, disparate, intermittent, partial, capricious, erratic, spasmodic, fitful, unequal, variable, unsystematic, unsteady, desultory, inconstant, unmethodical, flickering, wavering.

SPOUSAL, adj. Matrimonial, nuptial, bridal, marital, connubial, conjugal, wedded, hymeneal, epithalamic, epithalamial.

SPOUSAL, n. Ceremony of marriage, nuptials, wedding, bridal, espousals, espousement, hymeneals, hymen, hymeneal rites.

SPOUSE, n. Either member of a married pair (in relation to the other), husband, wife, married person, mate, partner, helpmate, helpmeet, matron, groom, bride, bridegroom, newlywed, benedict, yokemate, better half (joc.), consort, companion, marital partner.

SPOUT, n. 1. Tubular or liplike projection (for discharging or pouring liquid), pipe, tube, shoot, trough, conduit, jet, nose, nozzle, beak, rose, rosehead, vent, sluice, waterspout, gargoyle, outlet, snout.

2. Continuous stream of liquid, *etc.*, jet, stream, spurt, sparge, shoot, squirt, rush, fountain, swash, spray, flush, gush.

SPOUT, *v.* Discharge *or* emit *(a liquid, etc.)* in a stream with some force, spurt, squirt, jet, pour out, flow, spurtle, discharge, debouch, disgorge, stream, spirt, issue, gush, vomit forth, exude, disembogue, effuse, extravasate, surge, shoot, spray, fountain, well.

SPRAIN, *v.* Strain, wrench, overstrain *(a joint of the body)*, twist.

SPRAWL, *v.* 1. Stretch out in irregular *or* ungraceful fashion, spread in straggling *or* irregular manner, extend out, reach out, prolong, elongate, wind, meander, straggle, branch.

2. Lie *or* sit with limbs stretched out in careless *or* ungraceful posture, outstretch, loll, recline, repose, lean, slouch, flop, loaf, languish, relax, slump.

3. Work one's way awkwardly along, scramble, hitch, hobble, limp, tumble, jerk, jog, jolt, drag, shuffle, scuttle, stagger, falter, flounce, shamble, linger, lag, halt, hop, totter, pause.

SPRAY, *n.* 1. Liquid broken up into small particles and blown *or* falling through the air, jet of fine particles, foam, froth, spume, mist, spindrift, surf, fume, fizz, squirt, splash, insecticide, fungicide, drizzle, spoondrift.

2. Appliance for discharging fine particles of liquid, atomizer, sprinkler, nozzle, syringe, evaporator, vaporizer, rosehead, rose, sprayer, sparge, sparger.

3. Quantity of small objects flying *or* discharged through the air, barrage, shower, shot, shrapnel, burst, discharge, explosion, volley, salvo, drumfire, fireworks, fusillade.

4. Single slender shoot (twig, branch) with leaves *or* flowers, *etc.*, sprig, bush, bough, switch, blossom, foliage, bouquet, wreath, garland, chaplet, corsage, posy, nosegay.

5. Ornament *(decorative figure, etc.)* with the form of a spray, wreath, festoon, garland, corsage, bay, boutonniere, chaplet.

SPRAY, *v.* Scatter in the form of fine particles, shower, sprinkle, atomize, drizzle, spit, fall, precipitate, wet lightly.

SPREAD, *n.* 1. Expansion, extension, diffusion, dilation, dilatation, increase, dispersion, dissemination, circulation, circumfusion, enlargement, augmentation, advance, distention, inflation, reinforcement, aggrandizement, amplification, increment, interfusion, interspersion, distribution, dissipation, aspersion, deployment *(Mil.)*, propagation.

2. Extent of spreading, capacity for spreading, expanse, stretch, scope, compass, reach, distance, breadth, elasticity, stretchability, length, tract, area, bound, bounds, boundary, span, sweep, limit, extension, margin, orbit, width, field, circuit.

3. Cloth covering *(for bed, table, etc.)*, cover, cloth, tablecloth, bedspread, bedcover, robe, blanket, coverlet, counterpane.

4. Food preparation for spreading on bread, conserve, preserves, jam, jelly, sauce, butter *(as designated: peanut-, apple-, etc.)*.

5. Advertising covering several columns *or* a full page, notice, public notice, sheet, program, poster, placard.

SPREAD, *v.* 1. *(Often fol. by* OUT*)* Draw *or* stretch out to full width, open, become stretched *or* extended, unfold, unroll, unfurl, expand, ex-

tend, dilate, diverge, branch, augment, inflate, blow up, untwine, untwist, uncoil, unwind, burst forth, lengthen, enlarge, broaden, increase, bud, develop, divaricate, unravel, mantle, stretch, deploy *(Mil.)*, overgrow, overrun, widen, deepen, heighten, grow, magnify, swell, fill out, bloat, aggrandize, amplify, incrassate.

2. Force apart under pressure, flatten out, expand, crush, open, squash, level, make flush, clamp, fold *or* bend back.

3. Display to the full extent, set forth in full, be *or* lie outspread *or* fully extended *or* displayed, be revealed, meet the eye, manifest, present, produce, flaunt, show conspicuously, lay open, exhibit, bare, uncover, unscreen, uncloak, hold up to view, reveal, bring to light, disclose, divulge, flaunt, unfold, unmask, unveil.

4. Distribute *or* dispose in a sheet *or* layer, apply in a thin layer *or* coating, overlay, coat, cover, overspread, lay on, veneer, cloak, mantle, face, spatter, diffuse, spray, besmear, smear, daub, bedaub, pave, plaster, parget, gild, plate, gloss, enamel, loricate.

5. Send out in various directions, shed, scatter abroad, diffuse, distribute, disperse, dispense, sow, radiate, sprinkle, strew, flair, diverge, divaricate, overspread, suffuse, cast forth, bestrew, cast.

6. Diffuse, publish, disseminate, broadcast, circulate, propagate, divulge, proclaim, rumor, bruit, go the rounds, herald, promulgate, make public, make known, air, announce, advertise, blazon, report, run, notify, circumfuse, distribute, whisper about, issue, repeat, give currency to, intersperse, vent, ventilate, noise abroad, put about, hawk about, give out, emit, trumpet, declare, tell, enunciate, publicize.

7. Prepare *(a table, etc.)* as for a meal, set, lay, make ready, put in order, arrange.

SPREE, *n.* 1. Lively frolic, gambol, romp, merriment, escapade, frisk, caper, revel, vagary, antic, prank, holiday, play, lark *(coll.)*, monkeyshine *(sl.)*.

2. Bout *or* spell of drinking to intoxication, revel, frolic, debauch, jollification, revelry, carousal, saturnalia, debauchery, fling, potation, compotation, bacchanals, orgy, wassail, dissipation, drinking bout, cups, carouse, jamboree *(sl.)*, high-go *(low)*, jag *(sl.)*, drunk *(sl.)*, guzzle *(vulgar)*, binge *(sl.)*, bat *(sl.)*, bender *(sl.)*, hellbender *(sl.)*, soak *(coll.)*, bust *(sl.)*, tear *(sl.)*, rantan *(sl.)*, skate *(sl.)*, souse *(sl.)*, bum *(sl.)*, toot *(sl.)*.

SPRIG, *n.* 1. Small spray of a plant *(with leaves, flowers, etc.)*, shoot, bush, bough, switch, blossom, foliage, bouquet, wreath, garland, chaplet, corsage, posy, nosegay, boutonniere.

2. Small branch, shoot, twig, slip, spray, sprout, switch, tendril, stem, scion, offshoot, sucker *(Bot.)*, burgeon, sarmentum *(Bot.)*, graft *(Hort.)*.

3. Decorative figure in the form of a spray, wreath, festoon, garland, corsage, bay, boutonniere, chaplet.

4. Youth, young fellow, boy, lad, offspring, descendant, heir, heir apparent *or* presumptive, offset, minor, offshoot, juvenile, colt, cub, cadet, chip off the old block, puppy, pup, scion.

SPRIGHTLINESS, *n.* Liveliness, life, vivacity, vigor, cheer, cheerfulness, lilt, glee, activity, pertness, briskness, alertness, jocundity, animation, nimbleness, gaiety, frolicsomeness, spark, ardor, warmth, brightness, energy, fire, dash, élan, zeal, speed, spirit, spiritedness, promptitude, airiness, swiftness, force, alacrity, eagerness, enthusiasm, buoyancy, celerity, jollity, merriment, high spirits, fun, sportiveness, blithesomeness, playfulness, mirth, joviality, jollification, sport, felicity, festivity, jubilee, merrymaking, pleasantry.

SPRIGHTLY, adj. Lively, animated, vivacious, gay, light-hearted, brisk, buoyant, blithe, blithesome, vigorous, mercurial, agile, sportive, playful, humorous, whimsical, jolly, light, cheery, smart, prompt, chipper, spry, genial, merry, witty, jovial, jocund, jaunty, happy, debonair, frolicsome, joyous, airy, cheerful, racy, active, glowing, spirited, zealous, alert, mettlesome, hearty, full of life, full of spirit, elated, bright, vivid, heated, keen, eager, intense, enthusiastic, breezy.

SPRING, n. 1. Leap, bound, jump, elastic or springy movement, vault, hop, saltation, skip, bounce, pounce, caper, upleap, upspring, gambol, frolic, prance, curvet, leapfrogging.

2. Elasticity, springiness, elastic force, resiliency, recoil, buoyancy (fig.), tensility, stretch, stretchability, ductility, flexibility, rebound, reflex, reflux, backlash, kick, ricochet, repercussion.

3. Split, crack, warp, bend, fissure, gap, cranny, crevice, rent, separation, cleft, slot, chap, chink, gash, rime, lacuna, furrow, break, space, score, channel.

4. Issue of water from the earth, well, spa, pool, fount, fountain, baths, thermae, water hole, wellhead, headspring, watering place, jet, spout, seep, wellspring.

5. Source of something, origin, root, well, taproot, cause, original, germ, egg, seed, nucleus, fountainhead, foundation, wellhead, head, beginning, rise, issue, outlet, vent, dawn, womb, stem, stock, rudiment, element, agent, impulse, matrix, cradle, basis, base, wellspring, commencement, reason, occasion, derivation, mainspring, headspring, genesis, instigation, provocation, motivation, principle, generator, ground, primogenitor.

6. First and freshest period, strength, vigor, force, youth, bloom, flower, power, glow, vitality, glory, full bloom, fine fettle.

7. Elastic contrivance or body which recovers shape after being bent, compressed, etc., coil, spiral, leaf spring, volute spring.

SPRING, v. 1. Rise or move suddenly and lightly, leap, jump, bound, start, rise from cover, vault, dart, rush, bounce, prance, dance, hop, saltate, buck, skip, bob, gambol, leapfrog, curvet, upspring, frisk, buckjump.

2. Fly back or away from a forced position (as by elastic force or action of a spring), rebound, recoil, kick, reverberate, resile, repercuss, reflect, surrebound, return, ricochet, flex.

3. (Often fol. by FORTH, OUT, UP) Issue suddenly, gush, pour, rush, jet, break or burst forth, stream, spurt, shoot, squirt, flow, surge, emanate, fountain, spray, well, spout, discharge, vomit forth, disembogue, exude, effuse, extravasate.

4. (Often fol. by UP) Come into being, rise, arise, grow, emerge, open, burst forth, thrive, wax, shoot up, appear, mushroom, develop, sprout up, start up, crop out, upshoot, break through, pop up, issue, loom, be disclosed.

5. Proceed (as from a source or cause), originate, flow, emanate, take its origin, start, rise, come forth, result, derive, begin, germinate, follow, come into existence, come into the world, become, stem, commence, burst forth, see the light, sprout, ensue, issue, descend, come, bud, grow, accrue, take birth.

6. Have one's birth, be descended, rise, derive,

arise, take rise, originate, take birth, follow after.

7. Rise or extend upward (as a spire), take an upward course or curve (as an arch), soar, upcurve, ascend, shoot up, tower, rear, uprise, mount, spire.

8. Split, crack, warp, bend, rime, rend, break, burst, fly open, part, loose, unloose, sunder, dissever, abscind, be riven, splinter, shiver, fracture, rupture, snap, rive.

9. Bring out or make, etc., suddenly, produce, disclose, reveal, expose, open, bare, pop, pounce, bring unexpectedly, surprise with.

SPRINGE, n. Snare (for small game), toils, net, trap, gin, noose, hook, trepan, pitfall, meshes, deadfall, trapfall.

SPRINGHEAD, n. 1. Spring from which a stream flows, fountainhead, well, spa, pool, issue of water, fount, fountain, water hole, wellhead, headspring, jet, spout, seep, wellspring.

2. Source, origin, root, well, taproot, cause, original, germ, egg, seed, nucleus, fountainhead, foundation, wellhead, head, beginning, rise, issue, outlet, vent, dawn, womb, stem, stock, rudiment, base, wellspring, commencement, reason, occasion, derivation, mainspring, headspring, genesis, instigation, provocation, motivation, principle, generator, ground, primogenitor, element, agent, impulse, matrix, cradle.

SPRINGY, adj. Characterized by spring or elasticity, elastic, resilient, buoyant, youthful, flexible, extensible, yielding, recoiling, spongy, rebounding, queachy, stretchable, extensile, wiry, light, fleshy, succulent, doughy.

SPRINKLE, v. 1. Scatter in drops or particles, distribute here and there, overspread (with drops or particles), strew, bestrew, disperse, asperge, spatter, dust, powder, bedew, besprinkle, dredge, dabble, rain, spread, wet, splash, spot, dash, shower, plash, swash, sparge, diffuse, splatter, shed.

2. Diversify, intersperse, dot, spot, vary, stripe, streak, fleck, speck, striate, variegate, speckle, bespeckle, bespot, stipple, dapple, maculate, mottle, besprinkle.

SPRINKLING, n. Small quantity or number scattered here and there, few, mixture, modicum, drop, droplet, dash, infusion, driblet, suspicion, soupçon, scantling, seasoning, smack, scattering, touch, handful, fistful, minimum.

SPRINT, n. Short race at full speed, brief spell of great activity, dash, rush, spurt, spirt, burst, exertion, scorch (coll.).

SPRINT, v. Race at full speed (esp. for a short distance), post, spank, scud, scoot, scour, tear, zip, race, whiz, whisk, bound, spring, dart, shoot, scamper, bundle, get over the ground, clip, dash, scorch (coll.), go like a shot or lightning, cut along, bowl along, go it.

SPRITE, n. Fairy, elf, goblin, specter, imp, ghost, ghoul, Puck, Robin Goodfellow, demon, peri (Persian), spirit, apparition, phantom, dryad, gremlin, gnome, banshee, kelpie, familiar, brownie, nymph, spook, illusion, wraith, manes, bugbear, bugaboo.

SPROUT, n. 1. New growth, shoot of a plant, twig, stem, sprig, switch, burgeon, offshoot, scion, tendril, branch, sucker (Bot.), sarmentum (Bot.), graft (Hort.), offset, branchlet, petiole, runner, limb, leafstalk, bine, ramification, outgrowth, tigella (Bot.).

2. Something resembling or suggesting a sprout as in growth, upstart, offspring, branch, shoot, spur, division, subdivision, adjunct, offset, limb, wing, annex, supplement, extension, ramification,

member, colony, dependency, descendant, young, colt, chick, lamb, kitten, puppy, pup, minor, offshoot.

SPROUT, *v.* Begin to grow, develop *or* grow quickly, shoot forth, put forth, bloom, bud, come up, ramify, burgeon, germinate, increase, multiply, prolificate, spread, wax, outgrow, leap up, blossom, flower, flourish, pullulate, luxuriate, spring up.

SPRUCE, *adj.* Neat, trim, smart in dress *or* appearance, trig, tidy, dapper, chic (*coll.*), sleek, spic and span, natty (*coll.*), shipshape, regular, in place.

SPRUCE, *v.* (*Often fol. by* UP) Make smart *or* spruce, clean up, trim, dress, arrange, deck, order, clear up, plume, preen, bedizen, tidy up, fix up, array, furbish, do up (*coll.*), fig out (*coll.*), primp, prink, trick up *or* out, titivate, neat, neaten.

SPRY, *adj.* Active, brisk, nimble, lively, alive, alert, mettlesome, vigorous, hearty, buoyant, airy, sprightly, vivacious, brisk, full of life, full of spirit, full of action, sportive, animated, bright, keen, excited, sharp, frisky, fast, chipper, debonair, blithe, jaunty, busy, gay, playful, lightfooted, stirring, smart, prompt, ready, agile, supple, quick, spirited.

SPUME, *n.* Foam, froth, scum, spray, mist, spindrift, spoondrift, surf, fume, fizz, squirt, splash.

SPUME, *v.* Send forth as *or* like foam *or* froth, froth, foam, boil, bubble, blow, fiz, fizzle, effervesce.

SPUR, *n.* 1. Pointed device on a horseman's boot heel, prick, point, rowel, goad.

2. Anything that goads (impels, urges) to action *or* speed, incitement, lash, whet, rowel, incentive, goad, whip, motive, provocation, instigation, impulse, stimulus, fillip, stimulant, impetus, bribe, inducement, prick, dare, taunt, gibe, sting.

3. Snag, projection, stunted branch *or* shoot, horny process (*on leg of fowl*), promontory, wing, offshoot, scion, ramification, leg, knob, knot, point, gnarl, horn, dead end, spike, prong, tooth, spit, tip, tongue, strip.

SPUR, *v.* 1. Prick with *or* as with the spur, urge on, whip, lash, goad, inflame, induce, impel, incite, rouse, arouse, stimulate, drive, animate, instigate, encourage, pique, excite, move, stir, lend wings, prompt, provoke, prod, egg on, forward, exhort, press, push, actuate, propel, motivate, motive, awaken, quicken, hound, start, set in motion, force, poke, precipitate, catapult, shoot, launch, hasten, speed, advance, expedite, assist, vivify, festinate, jog, jolt, boost, inspire, bestir, flog.

2. Prick one's horse with a spur, ride quickly, hasten, press forward, proceed hurriedly, press on, gallop, hurry, race, make haste, spurt, push on, sprint, whisk, outstrip the wind, fly on the wings of the wind, bolt, dart, scour, ride hard, fly, clap spurs to one's horse, cut along (*coll.*), bowl along, spank, mend one's pace, post, pace, cover ground, get over the ground, dash, clip, burn up the road (*sl.*), canter, trot, lope, make strides *or* rapid strides, go *or* run wide open.

SPURIOUS, *adj.* Not authentic, not genuine *or* true, sham, false, mock, counterfeit, meretricious, deceitful, supposititious, feigned, make-believe, bastard, bogus, imitation, pretended, unauthentic, artificial, forged, fraudulent, fake, simulated, hollow, phony, adscititious, unsound, illegitimate, fabricated, illusory, delusive, gaudy, paste, bad,

adulterate, fictitious, claptrap, pinchbeck, brummagem, adulterated, shoddy, misrepresented, sophisticated, apocryphal.

SPURN, *n.* 1. Disdainful rejection, contemptuous treatment, disrespect, slight, rebuff, indignity, offense, affront, derision, ridicule, cut (*coll.*), mockery, detraction, disparagement, raillery, flout, insult, contumely, slap, scurrility, snub, the go-by (*coll.*), the cold shoulder (*coll.*).

2. Kick, boot, calcitration.

SPURN, *v.* Reject with disdain, treat with contempt, scorn, despise, disdain, look down upon, hold in contempt, contemn, frown upon, cast aside, turn down, neglect, repudiate, decline, sneer at, laugh at, slight, censure, depreciate, disparage, repulse, mock, scout, disapprove, trample upon, ostracize, ignore, slur, sneeze at, blink *or* wink at, cold shoulder, disregard, rebuff, high-hat (*sl.*), give one the go-by (*coll.*), cut (*coll.*), set aside, snub, turn up one's nose at.

SPURT, *n.* 1. Forcible gush of water, spout, jet, sudden gushing, ejection, stream, sparge, shoot, squirt, rush, fountain, swash, spray, flush.

2. Sudden outburst (*as of feeling*), impulse, flash, inspiration, eruption, burst, discharge, outpouring, outbreak, dissilience, blowup, ebullition, cataclysm, explosion, proruption.

3. Marked increase of effort for a short period *or* distance, sprint, exertion, race, dash, rush, spirt, burst, scorch (*coll.*), brief spell of great activity.

SPURT, *v.* 1. Gush, jet, issue suddenly in a stream *or* jet, spurtle, spout, burst, emit, pour out, well, spring out, squirt, flow, discharge, disgorge, debouch, stream, spirt, vomit forth, disembogue, surge, shoot, spray, fountain.

2. Show marked activity *or* energy for a short period, dash, sprint, race, post, spank, scud, scoot, scour, tear, zip, whiz, whisk, spring, dart, bundle, clip, scorch (*coll.*).

SPUTTER, *v.* 1. Emit particles of anything explosively, spit, spew, splutter, froth, slobber, expectorate, shoot, spatter, sprinkle, shower.

2. Utter (*words or sounds*) in an explosive *or* incoherent manner, splutter, stutter, stumble, fall over oneself, mouth, falter, halt, gibber, jabber, stammer, speak thickly.

SPY, *n.* One who keeps secret watch on others, one employed to obtain secret information *or* intelligence, scout, informer, watcher, reconnoiterer, investigator, tout, undercover man *or* agent, *mouchard* (*Fr.*), *hircarra* (*India*), spotter (*coll.*), stool pigeon (*chiefly sl.*), mark (*sl.*).

SPY, *v.* 1. Make secret observations, watch secretly, play the spy, keep watch, reconnoiter, make a reconnaissance, scout, peep out, shadow, pry, tout, case (*sl.*).

2. Catch sight of, see, gain sight of, discover, observe, sight, view, perceive, make out, descry, distinguish, look at, glimpse, recognize, detect, espy, behold, discern, spot (*coll.*), catch, witness, identify, apprehend, trace, scan, find, remark, notice, note.

3. Discover by close search *or* examination, search narrowly *or* carefully, scrutinize, examine closely, explore, inspect, view, find out, search out, detect, be on the lookout, make out, observe, fix upon, hit upon, trace, smoke out, fall upon, unearth, expose, root out, hunt down, dig up, disinter, bring to light, uncover, reveal, scout out, worm out, ferret out, bring out, determine, ascertain, spot (*coll.*).

SQUAB, *adj.* Short and thick *or* broad, fat, plump, pudgy, chubby, chunky, dumpy, bulky, thick-set, squat, fleshy, heavy, stubby, squabby, squatty, stout, pursy, buxom, stocky, stodgy, rotund, stubbed, punchy *(coll.)*, tubby *(coll.)*, chumpy *(coll.)*.

SQUABBLE, *n.* Petty quarrel, dispute, disagreement, spat, jangle, litigation, snarl, huff, tiff, bicker, words, odds, misunderstanding, disparity, difference, scrap *(sl.)*, dissent, dissension, contention, strife, fight, cross-purposes, run-in *(sl.)*, argument.

SQUABBLE, *v.* Engage in a petty quarrel, wrangle, fight, brawl, scuffle, struggle, dispute, litigate, differ, conflict, clash, jostle, huff, tiff, altercate, spat *(coll.)*, scrap *(sl.)*, row *(coll.)*, nag, bicker, have words, set to, make the fur fly, broil, argue, lock horns, spar, bandy words, contest.

SQUAD, *n.* Small group *or* party of persons, company, set, knot, crew, gang, band, troop, pack, platoon, squadron, force, cohort, section, unit, outfit *(coll.)*, class, troupe, federation, partnership, league, alliance.

SQUALID, *adj.* 1. Dirty, foul and repulsive, filthy, unclean, evil, uncared-for, slovenly, mucky, unkempt, sloppy, dowdy, frowzy, grimy, impure, unwashed, careless, reeking, offensive, horrid, abominable, smutty, repellent, slimy, soiled, slatternly, frumpish, sluttish, draggletailed, drabbletailed, odious, nasty, decayed.
2. Wretched, degraded, miserable, depressed, slummy, neglected, poor, poverty-stricken, uncared-for, dingy, corrupt, rotten, undesirable, in disrepair, run-down, ruinous, tumble-down, dilapidated, shabby, deteriorated, debased, ramshackle, battered, broken-down.

SQUALL, *n.* 1. Storm, sudden and violent gust of wind, blast, flaw, flurry, brief gale, tempest, hurricane, flurry.
2. Cry, howl, yowl, bawl, scream, mewl, outcry, racket, wailing, weeping, ululation, yell.

SQUALL, *v.* 1. Blow in a squall, rage, storm, blow a gale, bluster, flaw, blow hard *or* furiously, blow great guns, blow a hurricane.
2. Cry out loudly, scream violently, utter in a screaming tone, howl, yowl, weep, wail, racket, mewl, ululate, rend the air, yell, bawl.

SQUALLY, *adj.* Characterized by squalls, windy, gusty, stormy, blustering, tempestuous, dirty, foul, blustery, flawy, blasty, raging, furious, wild, frenzied, rampageous, turbulent, tumultuous, typhoonish, cyclonic.

SQUALOR, *n.* Degraded condition, foulness, dirtiness, uncleanness, filth, disorder, ugliness, squalidness, dirt, uncleanliness, immundicity.

SQUAMOUS, *adj.* Covered with *or* formed of squamae *or* scales, scalelike, scaly, squamate, squamosal, squamose, squamulose, lamellate, lamellar, spathic, scutate *(Zool.)*.

SQUANDER, *v.* (Often fol. by AWAY) Spend extravagantly *or* wastefully, lavish, lose, throw away, be prodigal with, scatter, misspend, misuse, dissipate, spill, drain, cast before swine, spend like water, deplete, fritter away, spend recklessly, run through, consume, exhaust, blow *(sl.)*.

SQUARE, *adj.* 1 Of the form of a right angle, having some part *or* parts rectangular, having four sides and four right angles, cubical, quadratic, foursquare, rectangular, right-angled, quadrangular, right-angular, tetragonal *(Geom.)*.

2. At right angles, perpendicular, sheer, plumb, upright, bolt upright, vertical, straight-up-and-down, orthodiagonal *(Cryst.)*, orthogonal *(Math.)*.
3. Having a solid and sturdy form with rectilinear *or* angular outlines, foursquare, substantial, strong, stout, sound, stable, heavy, weighty, cubic, hefty *(coll.)*, rectangular.
4. Even, level, straight, accurate, true, right, equal, exact, settled, adjusted, balanced, rectilinear, rectilineal, direct, in a line, linear, symmetrical.
5. Leaving no balance of debt on either side, having all accounts settled, concluded, equal, even, on even terms, quits, ended, on *or* upon a par, balanced, equalized.
6. Just, fair, honest, upright, equitable, impartial, disinterested, honorable, aboveboard, reputable, estimable, scrupulous, worthy, unbiased, lawful, licit, right, even-handed, fair and square, open and aboveboard, foursquare, on the up-and-up *(coll.)*, on the level *(coll.)*, legitimate, according to agreement, faithful to contract, just as represented, free from tricks, creditable, reasonable, sound, faithful, reliable, trusty, ethical, conscientious, moral, straight, decent, veracious, truthful, rightful.
7. Straightforward, direct, unequivocal, clear, blunt, frank, foursquare, definite, true, indubitable, unambiguous, sure, unmistakable, unquestionable, unqualified, incontrovertible, unerring, incontestable, undeniable, irrefragable, certain, reliable, undisputed, inescapable, positive, irrefutable, unquestioned, evident, sound, cogent, unconfuted, plain, conclusive.

SQUARE, *n.* 1. Four-sided plane figure with equal sides and right angles (or a figure approximating this), quadrate, rectangle, quadrangle, quadrant, quadrilateral, tetragon *(Geom.)*.
2. Rectangular *or* quadrilateral area in a city *or* town (bound by intersecting streets), one side of such an area, block, city block.
3. Open area, plaza, park, quadrangle, quad *(coll.)*, market place, parade.
4. Instrument for determining *or* testing right angles, *etc.*, T square, try square, set square, carpenter's square, triangle.

SQUARE, *v.* 1. Reduce to square (rectangular, cubical) form, mark out in squares *or* rectangles, set at right angles, quadrate, block out.
2. Test with measuring device for deviation from right angle (straight line, plane surface), plumb, true, regulate, adjust, set, try, render true.
3. Set (the shoulders, arms, etc.) as to present a square *or* rectangular outline, straighten, stiffen, throw back, tense, make rigid.
4. Make straight (level, even), flatten, smooth, even out, roll, align, plane, horizontalize, planish, equalize, levigate.
5. Regulate (as by a standard), adapt, suit, mold, shape, balance, methodize, order, fit, meet, accommodate, render true, coordinate, adjust, tune, time, dress, conform, reconcile, poise, set, trim, normalize, systematize, standardize, equate, equalize, level, make uniform, organize.
6. Adjust harmoniously *or* satisfactorily, settle, balance, compensate, make even, close, compose, reach agreement, arrange matters, resolve, reconcile, rectify, compromise, arbitrate, dispose, prove, conclude, clinch, compound, pacify, make peace, bring *or* come to terms, patch up, mend, disembroil, unravel, disentangle, harmonize, clear

up, solve, accommodate, heal, regulate, straighten out, accord, negotiate, mediate, bridge over.

7. *(Often fol. by* OFF*)* Assume a posture of defense *or* offense, raise one's fists, be on guard, poise, threaten, take a stance.

8. *(Often fol. by* WITH*)* Accord, agree, suit, fit, tally, correspond, comport with, harmonize, fall in, chime in, be congruous, cohere, blend, sympathize, conform with, concur, match, sort, jibe, consist, accommodate, be in unison, tune, acquiesce, assent, hold with, comply, gee *(sl.),* consort, dovetail, accede, come to terms, consent, combine, team, symphonize, consonate.

SQUASH, *v.* 1. Press into a flat mass *or* pulp, crush, compress, mash, pulp, smash, pulpify, cram, crowd, compact, ram down, squeeze, masticate.

2. Suppress, put down, quash, quell, prostrate, squelch, subvert, upset, repress, shatter, crush, lay by the heels, lay *or* trample in the dust, flatten, fell, level, throw down *or* over, undermine, dispel, dissipate, engulf, submerge, sink, swamp, tread *or* trample under foot, overwhelm, overturn, overthrow.

3. Fall heavily *(of a soft, heavy body),* plump, plunk *(coll.),* plop, flop *(coll.),* thud, blob, thump, bump, sprawl.

4. Make a splashing sound, splash, wash, hit, slosh, smack, beat, cast, hurl, strike, toss.

SQUASHY, *adj.* Easily squashed, pulpy, soft and wet, sodden, viscid, marshy, fleshy, semiliquid, pulpous, mushy, pappy, macerated, pulpal, pulpaceous, pulplike, flabby, pithy, thick, starchy, loamy, clayey, spongy, mucid, gelatinous, viscous, semifluid, succulent, grumous, doughy, pultaceous.

SQUAT, *adj.* 1. Short and thick, thick-set, pudgy, stocky, dumpy, stubby, squatty, squab, stumpy, fat, plump, chubby, chunky, bulky, heavy, fleshy, squabby, stout, pursy, buxom, stodgy, rotund, stubbed, punchy *(coll.),* chumpy *(coll.),* tubby *(coll.).*

2. Seated *or* being in a squatting position, crouching, low, crouched, doubled over, lowlying, cowering, cringing, shrinking.

SQUAT, *v.* 1. Crouch, lie low, cower, sit close to the ground, bend down, slouch, cringe, double over, shrink.

2. Settle on land *(with or without title or right),* take up residence, make a home, inhabit, dwell, abide, reside, move in, carve a home, establish oneself, put down roots, encamp, locate, pitch tent, take *or* strike roots, get a footing, set up housekeeping.

SQUATTER, *n.* One who settles on land *(with or without title or right),* settler, colonist, pioneer, alien, frontiersman, colonizer, outlander, planter, redemptioner, homesteader, founder, nester *(West. U.S.).*

SQUAWK, *n.* Loud harsh sound, cry, stridulation, squeal, stridor, caterwaul, call, howl, ululation, stridence, scream, cacophony, raucity, raucousness, harshness, shriek, screech, screak.

SQUAWK, *v.* Utter a loud harsh cry, ululate, blare, bawl, bleat, cry, call, yowl, howl, stridulate, yap, yelp, bray, shriek, scream, squall, squeal, screech, shout, yell, hoot, screak.

SQUEAK, *n.* Short sharp shrill cry, sharp highpitched sound, acute note, squeal, screak, squawk, shriek, screech, pule, whine, peep, chirrup, chirp, tweet, yap, yelp, squall, shrill, twang, cheep.

SQUEAK, *v.* Cry, squeal, tweet, chirp, yap, yelp, whine, pule, peep, screech, shriek, squawk, screak, cheep, chirrup, twang, shrill, squall, chirp.

SQUEAL, *n.* Prolonged sharp shrill cry *(as of pain, fear, etc.),* howl, yell, blare, bleat, whinny, screak, shriek, screech, yelp, squall, shrill, ululation, caterwaul.

SQUEAL, *v.* Cry, yell, shriek, scream, howl, blare, bleat, whinny, screak, screech, squall, yelp, shrill, ululate, caterwaul, stridulate, bray, squawk, shout, hoot, bawl.

SQUEAMISH, *adj.* 1. Easily shocked by anything slightly immodest, excessively particular *or* scrupulous as to the moral aspect of things, prudish, modest, priggish, coy, smug, mincing, sanctimonious, puritanical, precise, affectedly nice, prim, demure, stilted, in buckram, pedantic, self-righteous, starched, proper, stiff, precious, queasy, scrupulous, finical, finicking, skittish, unctuous, pharisaic, pharisaical, canting, timid, punctilious, strait-laced, formal.

2. Fastidious, dainty, delicate, particular, meticulous, priggish, hard to please, overnice, hypercritical, difficult, hairsplitting, chary, querulous, critical, captious, fussy, carping, queasy, scrupulous, discriminating, finicky, finicking, exacting, finical, faultfinding, punctilious, choosy, picky, quibbling, oversubtle, equivocating, oversensitive, caviling, overrefined.

3. Easily nauseated, delicate, queasy, qualmy, qualmish, sick, sickish.

SQUEEZE, *n.* 1. Act of squeezing, fact of being squeezed, weight, pressure, burden, compression, constraint, constriction, oppression, strangulation, pinching, confining, ramming, cramming, crushing, constringing, shortening, densification, abbreviation, consolidation, thickening, narrowing, ellipsis, abridgment, stricture, shrinking, crowding, reduction, contraction, compaction.

2. Tight pressure of the hand *(as in friendliness),* clasp, grip, grasp, hold, handclasp, handshake.

3. Hug, close embrace, enfoldment, envelopment, snuggling, cuddling, clutch, nestling.

4. Small quantity *or* amount, pinch, bit, drop, droplet, particle, modicum, dripping, trace, scrap, morsel, spot, atom, mite, trifle, point, molecule, speck.

SQUEEZE, *v.* 1. Press forcibly together, compress, pinch, cram, nip, clutch, constrict, densify, consolidate, pack, abbreviate, force into smaller space, ram, crowd, concentrate, compact, tighten, cramp, reduce, shorten, contract, abridge, shrink, restrict in area, constringe, narrow, coarctate, curtail, reduce in volume, bind tightly, wrap closely, stuff, wedge, hug, embrace.

2. *(Usually fol. by* OUT *or* FROM*)* Force out, extract, procure by pressure, wrest, wring, withdraw, pry, wrench, draw out, weed out, pull out, tear out, express, distill, elicit, extricate, pluck out.

3. Harass *or* oppress *(a person, etc.)* by exactions, extort *(Law),* exact, wring, screw, prey on, put the screws on, swindle, blackmail *(Law),* sponge *(coll.),* shake down *(sl.).*

4. *(Fol. by* THROUGH, IN, OUT, *etc.)* Force a way, press, elbow, push, drive, crowd, make one's way, butt, ram, fight, wedge, shove, shoulder, jostle, hustle.

5. Obtain a facsimile impression of, take a likeness of, make a mold of.

SQUELCH, *v.* 1. Strike *or* press with crushing

force, squash, crush down, flatten, compress, mash, pulp, smash, cram, crowd, compact, ram down, pulpify, masticate.

2. Make a splashing sound, tread heavily and noisily in water (mud, wet shoes, *etc.*), suck, ooze, slosh, plash, splash, swash.

SQUIB, *n.* Short witty *or* sarcastic saying *or* writing, lampoon, satire, pasquinade, gibe, libel, personality, take-off, pasquil, burlesque, parody, travesty, diatribe, macaronics, fling, ridicule, byword.

SQUIB, *v.* Write squibs, assail in squibs *or* lampoons, satirize, ridicule, dip the pen in gall, burlesque, laugh at, ape, take off, caricature, render absurd, pasquinade, mimic, travesty, mock, buffoon, make ludicrous, stultify.

SQUINT, *n.* 1. Looking obliquely *or* askance, sidelong look, glance, wink, blink, glare, glower, scowl, leer, sly look *or* glance, half an eye, cast, slant *(coll.).*

2. Indirect reference, inclination, intimation, inkling, innuendo, insinuation, suggestion, indication, clue, scent, implication, inference, imputation, allusion, reflection, subaudition.

3. Oblique *or* perverse tendency, slant, bias, kink, crank, vagary, maggot, fit, digression, divergence, deflection, deviation, declination, bigotry, prejudice, idiosyncrasy, idiocrasy, excursion, twist, warp, sheer, illiberality, fanaticism, monomania, skew, distortion, obsession, quirk, waywardness, misuse, misapplication, misdirection, irregularity, perversion, caprice, whim, crotchet, blind spot, blind side, one-sidedness, prepossession, infatuation, mote in the eye.

SQUINT, *v.* 1. Look with the eyes partly closed, peer, peek, peep, strain the eyes, scrutinize, examine narrowly, screw up the eyes, blink, wink, nictate, nictitate.

2. Glance sidewise, look obliquely, give a sidelong look, look askance *or* askant, glint, skim, cock the eyes, pass the eyes over, skew, wink.

3. *(Fol. by* TOWARD, *etc.)* Make *or* have an indirect reference, tend, incline, suggest, concern, have an indirect bearing *or* implication, influence, belong to, answer to, have to do with, interest, appertain to, touch, affect, pertain to, refer to, regard, correspond to.

SQUINT-EYED, *adj.* 1. Affected with *or* characterized by strabismus, cross-eyed, strabismal, strabismic, walleyed, cockeyed, squinting, squinty, asquint.

2. Looking obliquely *or* askance, questioning, doubting, skeptical, suspicious, scrutinizing, distrustful, peering, leering, insinuating, indirect, malignant, oblique, sinister.

SQUIRE, *n.* 1. Personal attendant *(as of a person of rank),* man, servant, servitor, retainer, orderly, valet, right-hand man, page, assistant, secretary, factotum, underling, auxiliary, clerk, messenger, lackey, henchman, esquire *(Middle Ages),* armiger *(Hist.).*

2. Man who attends *or* escorts a lady in public, escort, conductor, cavalier, attendant, gallant.

SQUIRE, *v.* Attend *(in the manner of a squire),* escort, conduct, assist, aid, serve, oblige, accommodate, accompany, wait on *or* upon, tend, help, subserve, minister to, dance attendance upon.

SQUIRM, *v.* 1. Writhe, wriggle, wiggle, shift, shuffle, toss, pitch, tumble, jerk, twitch, twist.

2. Be sharply *or* painfully affected *(as by reproof or sarcasm),* suffer, shrink, smart, wince, be

pained *or* hurt, quaff the bitter cup, eat one's words, flinch, shy, recoil, writhe, quail, blench.

SQUIRT, *n.* 1. Jet *(as of water),* stream, fountain, swash, spray, spurt, sparge, shoot, spout, douche, gush, flush, rush.

2. Instrument for squirting, syringe, sparge, sparger, atomizer, needle bath, douche, sprayer, sprinkler, spray.

SQUIRT, *v.* 1. Eject liquid in a jet from a narrow orifice, spirt, issue in a jetlike stream, shoot, flow, stream, spout, spurt, surge, emanate, discharge, effuse, vomit forth, rush forth, well, gush, spray, fountain.

2. Wet with liquid forcefully ejected, shower, spray, spatter, bespatter, sprinkle, splash, scatter, dash, splutter, besprinkle, plash, swash, splatter.

STAB, *n.* 1. Thrust made with a pointed weapon, prick, jab, cut, dig, hit, coup, bayonet, stroke, lunge, home thrust, pass, punch, poke, blow, dagger-stroke.

2. Wound *(made by stabbing),* slash, injury, cut, trauma, incision, gash, laceration, puncture, scratch.

STAB, *v.* 1. Pierce *(with a pointed weapon),* spear, penetrate, perforate, strike, stick, jab, hit, impale, gore, transfix, transpierce, bayonet, prick, knife, run through, wound, spit, spike, lance, pike, thrust through, gouge, bore, pink, slash.

2. Thrust *(a knife, etc.)* into something, plunge, jab, stick, bury, drive, slash, poke.

STABILITY, *n.* 1. Firmness in position, fixedness, permanence, steadiness, rest, immobility, solidity, solidness, repose, static condition, inertia, soundness, suspense, dormancy, balance, fixation, fixture, fixity, immutability, equilibrium, establishment, inaction, inactivity, inertness, quiescence, stableness, durability, immovability.

2. Continuance without change, continuity, permanence, uniformity, persistence, unity, fixity, similarity, unchangeableness, pursuance, extension, prolongation, abidingness, changelessness, endurance, maintenance, durability, duration, perseverance, perpetuation.

3. Steadfastness *(as of character or purpose),* reliability, constancy, steadiness, resolution, determination, obstinacy, resoluteness, backbone, grit, mettle, indomitable spirit, endurance, resolve, poise, aplomb, decision, will, pluck, pertinacity, stubbornness, perseverance, tenacity, consistency, devotion, adherence, doggedness, intransigence, cussedness *(coll.).*

STABILIZE, *v.* 1. Make stable, steady, establish, define, set, settle, root, make fast, make good *or* sure, retain, hold in place, fix, attach, fasten, ground, secure, clinch, immobilize.

2. Maintain at a given *or* unfluctuating level *or* quantity, uphold, preserve, support, sustain, prolong, perpetuate, protract, keep up, keep on foot, carry on, extend.

STABLE, *adj.* 1. Not likely to fall *or* give way, firm, steady, fixed, sound, solid, immovable, established, riveted, moored, anchored, substantial, fast, still, stout, inert, quiescent, sturdy, stanch, statuelike, motionless, stationary, irremovable.

2. Able *or* likely to continue *or* last, enduring, permanent, fixed, constant, established, steady, firm, unchangeable, unalterable, invariable, rooted, grounded, immutable, riveted, deeprooted, deep-seated, indissoluble, lasting, uniform, confirmed, incontrovertible, reliable, sound, valid, abiding, inveterate, unchanging, durable, settled,

secure, proved, even, undeviating, ascertained, determined, predetermined, decided, long-lived, long-lasting, long-standing, lasting, well-grounded, well-founded, longevous, persistent, chronic, perdurable, endless, perpetual, everlasting, intact, inviolate, revolving, irrevocable, irreversible.

3. Steadfast, not wavering or changeable, constant, firm, uniform, steady, stanch, true, faithful, unshaken, resolute, unwavering, methodical, resolved, determined, serious, decided, unswerving, unflinching, not to be shaken, persevering, sedulous, industrious, untiring, plodding, unflagging, enduring, patient, indefatigable, undeviating, unwearied, indomitable, undaunted, inexorable, grim, settled, fixed, unshrinking, intransigent, game, plucky, gritty, persistent, relentless, solid, stern, unbending, pertinacious, unfaltering, unhesitating, strong-willed, uncompromising, unyielding, obstinate, tenacious, inflexible.

STABLE, n. Building for lodging and feeding livestock, barn, cowshed, fold, sty, stall, shed.

STABLEBOY, n. Stableman, equerry, groom, tiger (old sl.).

STACK, n. 1. Large pile of hay (straw, etc.), cock, pile, bank, heap, mass, shock, gathering, rick, sheaf, haycock, hayrick, mow.

2. Pile, heap, assemblage, mass, mound, load, huddle, fagot, packet, cluster, bale, bundle, gathering, deposit, jumble, accumulation, clump, hoard, bunch, stock, budget, barrow, cartload, carload, wagonload, congeries, pyramid, rouleau, batch, block, pyre, hill, aggregation, amassment, bank, collection, mountain.

3. Chimney, funnel (for smoke), smokestack, flue.

STACK, v. Arrange in orderly fashion, pile, bank, hoard, heap, pack, gather in one place, group, rake together, bunch, garner, deposit, lump, bundle, amass, truss, shock, mound, lump together, get in, load, ruck, collect, batch together.

STADIUM, n. Structure for athletic games, arena, coliseum, lists, bowl, circus, racecourse, turf, ring, palestra, amphitheater, gymnasium, hippodrome.

STAFF, n. 1. Stick (for use in walking, climbing, as a weapon, etc.), pole, rod, cane, crutch, wand, stave, shaft, cudgel, walking stick, bludgeon, bat, billy, club, quarterstaff, shillelagh (Ireland).

2. Rod (serving as ensign of office or authority), baton, crozier, truncheon, insignia, mace, wand, scepter, caduceus, fasces (Roman).

3. Something which serves to support or sustain, prop, stay, tent pole, pile, flagstaff, splint, supporter, upholder, brace, rib, block, rest, stand, standard, base, reinforcement, pediment, pillar, stanchion, underpin, underset, leg, stud, fulcrum, shore, buttress, strut, foundation, raker (Building), rod, pole, arm, mainstay.

4. Body of assistants to an executive head, personnel, retinue, train, faculty, force, officers, help, crew, gang, servantry, associates, cabinet, employees, council, committee.

STAGE, n. 1. Single step (in a process), degree, period (in a process of development), portion (of a journey, etc.), level, age, grade, time, space, spell, tenure, term, span, course, milestone, position, era, epoch, cycle, generation, interval, phase, transition, passage, stretch, point, achievement.

2. Raised platform or floor, rostrum, dais, the boards, scaffold, soapbox, stump, lectern, estrade, pulpit, staging, proscenium, tribune, hustings.

3. Theater, dramatic profession, the footlights,

drama, the play, show business, acting, the boards (Theat.), Thespian art, histrionic art, stageland, stage playing.

4. Scene of action or career, setting, arena, frame, place, location, site, spot, region, milieu, surroundings, theater, background, environment, sphere, locale, locality, whereabouts, bearings, position, situation, mise en scène (Fr.).

5. Stagecoach, diligence.

STAGE, v. Put (represent, exhibit) on or as on a stage, dramatize, convert or make into a drama, present, theatrize, theatricize, produce, put on (coll.), melodramatize, act, play, perform, scenarize (Motion Pictures).

STAGECRAFT, n. Skill in writing, adapting or staging plays, stagery, theatercraft, dramaturgy, theatrics, scenecraft, dramatization.

STAGEHAND, n. Person working behind the scenes in a dramatic production, sceneshifter (Theater), grip (Theat. and Motion Pictures), stageman, sceneman, carpenter, electrician, flyman (Theat.), scenist, scenewright, scene painter, prompter, pit man, costumer, callboy, make-up man or artist.

STAGGER, v. 1. Walk or stand unsteadily, sway, reel, waver, fall, totter, stumble, lurch, wobble, rock, swing, toss, wallow, lumber, barge, hobble, shamble, flounder, roll, pitch, drag, slouch, shuffle, vacillate, titubate.

2. Begin to give way, begin to doubt or waver, hesitate, falter, vacillate, startle, fall back, halt, flag, be uncertain or irresolute, demur, pause, not know what to do, shy, pull back, tergiversate, oscillate, hang back, hover, debate, shilly-shally, seesaw, alternate, recoil, swerve, shrink, fluctuate, scruple, think twice, dally, shift, equivocate, stickle, wait, balk, deliberate, dillydally, trim.

3. Cause to reel (totter, become unsteady), render helpless with amazement, etc., cause to waver or falter, throw off one's guard, shock, astonish, surprise, nonplus, shake, puzzle, bewilder, pose, amaze, astound, dumfound, confound, electrify, galvanize, disturb, upset, perturb, discompose, agitate, unsettle, catch unprepared, disconcert, bowl over, jar, jolt, take away one's breath, give a turn, petrify, paralyze, stupefy, stun, startle, strike dumb, appall, overwhelm, flabbergast (coll.), flummox (sl.).

4. Arrange in a zigzag order or manner, overlap, spread out, zigzag, take in turns, alternate.

STAGING, n. 1. Act or process of putting a play on the stage, presentation, production, exhibition, adaptation, rehearsal, preparation.

2. Temporary platform or structure for support, scaffolding, framework, stage, frame, skeleton.

STAGNANT, adj. 1. Not running (as water, air, etc.), motionless, close, quiet, still, standing, inert, quiescent, lifeless, dead, inactive, idle, calm, dormant, static, placid, reposing, at rest, undisturbed, stationary, unstirring, tranquil.

2. Foul from standing, filthy, putrid, putrefied, putrescent, rank, offensive, high, strong, slimy, polluted.

3. Sluggish, inactive, dull, dead, vegetative, lifeless, heavy, dormant, torpid, inert, lazy, supine, phlegmatic, listless, lethargic, lentitudinous, do-nothing, fainéant, dilatory, lumpish, indolent, slow, clumsy, ponderous, stupid, leaden, dronish, drony, torpescent, torporific, stolid, bovine, elephantine, loutish, sottish, crass, doltish, obtuse,

hebetate, apathetic, passive, static, lymphatic, languid, otiose, hebetudinous.

STAGNATE, *v.* 1. Cease to run *or* flow, repose, not stir, idle, remain motionless, lie *or* stand still, rest, stop, stand, be stagnant.

2. Become foul from standing, putresce, putrefy, rot, become stagnant, decay, decompose, smell to high heaven, stink, reek, contaminate, fester, corrupt, pollute, beslime, suppurate.

3. Become dull, become inactive *or* sluggish, vegetate, lie idle, loaf, slumber, fold one's arms, drift, while away the time, idle (trifle, fritter, fool) away one's time, let the grass grow under one's feet, bum, twiddle one's thumbs, kill time, go to seed, go to pot, deteriorate.

STAGY, *adj.* Of, pertaining to *or* suggestive of the stage, theatrical, Thespian, showy, histrionic, acted, artificial, unnatural, spectacular, make-believe, stagelike, theaterlike, dramatic, dramaturgic, ostentatious, hammy *(Theat. sl.).*

STAID, *adj.* Of settled *or* sedate character, not flighty *or* capricious, sober, steady, composed, solemn, settled, cool, undemonstrative, somber, severe, pensive, grim, thoughtful, subdued, quiet, sedate, calm, demure, serious, grave, wistful, discreet, tranquil, placid, serene, prudent, circumspect, contemplative, meditative, wistful, sorrowful, reflective, musing.

STAIN, *n.* 1. Discoloration produced by foreign matter, spot, blot, soil, blemish, tarnish, flaw, defect, imperfection, blur, speck, smutch, smudge, smear, patch, maculation, splotch, taint, pock, blotch, smirch, macule, macula, daub.

2. Blemish, cause of reproach, stigma, slur, taint, spot, shame, blot, infamy, disgrace, brand, flaw, defect, fault, imputation, tarnish, smudge, smirch, smutch, soil, defect.

3. Dye in solution, color, tint, tincture, pigment, coloring, dyestuff.

STAIN, *v.* 1. Discolor with spots *or* streaks of foreign matter, soil, spot, smear, tarnish, blot, blotch, smudge, splotch, smirch, blemish, sully, maculate, mar, injure, blacken, mark, blur, spoil, impair, sprinkle, speckle, spatter, splash, bespatter, daub, plash, grime.

2. Bring reproach upon, blemish, stigmatize, corrupt, disgrace, pollute, defile, debase, contaminate, taint, tarnish, sully with guilt *or* infamy, foul, attaint, befoul, blot, deprave, dishonor, damage, besmirch, drag in the mud, blacken, impair, spoil, bring down, ruin, subvert, brand, vilipend, disparage, reflect upon, detract from, reduce, cheapen, undermine, vilify, derogate, depreciate, malign, discredit, slander, libel, denigrate.

3. Color with something which penetrates the substance, dye, imbue, imbrue, impregnate with color, tint, pigment.

STAIRS, *n., pl.* Series *or* flight of steps, staircase, stairway, ladder, escalator, hatchway, fire escape, stepladder, companionway *(Naut.).*

STAKE, *n.* 1. Stick *(pointed for driving into the ground),* pale, post, rod, bar, pin, peg, pile, spike, palisade, picket, upright, column, pillar, standard.

2. *(With* THE) Death by burning, auto-da-fé.

3. That which is wagered, sum, bet, pot, jack pot, pool, play, hazard, kitty, bank, ante, tiger *(Faro),* cave *(Card Playing).*

4. Interest held in something, risk, right, title, venture, hazard, speculation, die, jeopardy, adventure.

5. *(Often pl.)* Prize *(in a race or contest),*

trophy, spoils, take, grab, haul, winnings, gain, reward, award, profit, pickings, receipts, returns, loot, plunder, booty.

STAKE, *v.* 1. *(Often fol. by* OFF *or* OUT) Mark with stakes, define, delineate, outline, limit, circumscribe, delimit, demarcate, contour, determine, mark off, bound.

2. Protect (separate, shut in *or* out, close) with a barrier of stakes, enclose, confine, shut in, hem in, circumscribe, bound, pen in, wall, surround, circle, cincture, compass about, corral, picket, fence in, hedge in, environ, embrace, engird, envelop, span, ring, girdle, comprehend, blockade, gird, encase, cloister, intern, immure, contain.

3. Support with a stake *(as a plant),* brace, prop, stay, hold up.

4. Tether to a stake *(as an animal),* secure, tie, fasten, lash, trammel, hitch, picket, moor, make fast, fetter, peg down *or* out.

5. Put at hazard, venture, risk, bet, chance, hazard, speculate, back, imperil, jeopardize, pawn, gamble, give as surety, punt, wager, sport, game, ante up *(Poker).*

STALE, *adj.* 1. Not fresh, vapid, flat, dry, hardened, musty, fusty, insipid, tasteless, savorless, weak, close *(of air),* indifferent, jejune.

2. Having lost novelty *or* interest, trite, hackneyed, common, commonplace, old, vapid, stereotyped, dull, banal, threadbare, usual, mediocre, worn out, prosaic, tame, ordinary, familiar, everyday, pedestrian, monotonous, prosy, stock, tedious, humdrum, platitudinous, homely, oft-repeated, dry, unimaginative, unvaried, uninteresting.

3. Having lost fresh vigor (quick intelligence, initiative, *etc.*), old, aged, effete, timeworn, worn out, vitiated, weary, past one's prime, shabby, seedy, passé, shopworn, faded, decayed, gone to seed, feeble, exhausted, withered, wasted, wilted, spent, tacky, dowdy, ancient, antiquated, superannuated, senectuous, no chicken *(coll.),* declining, waning, fading, rusty, decrepit, stricken with years, doddering, with one foot in the grave, on one's last legs, washed-out, broken-down, motheaten.

STALEMATE, *n.* Position in which no action can be taken, deadlock, standstill, stand, halt, check, checkmate, quietus, collapse, blockage, defeat, dilemma, vanquishment, embarrassment, rout, fall, downfall, overthrow, misfire, frustration, deathblow, extremity, nonplus, impasse, stoppage, stop, stay, full stop, fix, blind alley, corner, cul-de-sac, dead stop *or* stand, hole *(coll.).*

STALEMATE, *v.* Subject to a stalemate, bring to a standstill, check, checkmate, deadlock, nonplus, nonsuit, trump, stump, impede, incapacitate, undermine, prostrate, paralyze, obstruct, inhibit, embarrass, clog, cramp, trammel, preclude, block, bar, blockade, shackle, debar, disable, run *or* drive into a corner, drive to the wall, put hors de combat, tree *(coll.),* corner, confuse, bewilder, confound, flummox *(sl.),* thwart, interrupt, stop, spike, hinder, silence, put a spoke in one's wheels, render powerless, chase up a tree *(coll.),* put the kibosh on *(sl.).*

STALK, *n.* 1. Main axis of a plant *or* animal, stem, petiole *(Bot., Zool.),* peduncle *(Bot.),* pedicle *(Bot.),* culm, spire, caulicle *(Bot.),* spear, shaft, cane, trunk, caulis *(Bot.),* caudex *(Bot.),* tigella *(Bot.),* haulm *(Bot.),* funicle *(Bot.),* gynophore *(Bot.).*

2. Stem, shaft, slender supporting part, axis,

pin, rib, splint, peg, axle, shank, stud, spar, nail, spike, dowel, stake, swivel, spindle, pivot, skewer.

3. Act or course of stalking game, drive, hunt, chase, still hunt, coursing, shikar (India).

4. Slow stiff stride or gait, flounce, strut, swagger, stamp, goose step.

STALK, v. 1. Pursue or approach (game, etc.) stealthily, give chase, walk quietly, creep up on, sneak, still-hunt, hound.

2. Walk with slow stiff or haughty strides, strut, pace, swagger, march, goose-step, stamp, peacock, tramp.

STALL, n. 1. Compartment (as in a stable) for one animal, cell, pen, recess, pound, crib, sty, coop, manger, confine, booth.

2. Stable, barn, cowshed, fold, sty, shed.

3. Chairlike seat in a theater (separated from others by arms or rail), box, baignoire (Fr.).

4. Compartment, chamber, sheath, bandage, guard, shield, cover.

STALL, v. 1. Put or keep in a stall, confine to a stall, bed down.

2. Bring or come to a standstill, check the progress or motion of (esp. unintentionally), be brought to a stop, pull up or stop short, arrest, bog, stalemate, check, nonplus, impede, incapacitate, prostrate, paralyze, undermine, obstruct, inhibit, clog, cramp, trammel, block, bar, shackle, disable, confound, interrupt, hinder, render powerless.

3. Cause to stick fast (as in mire or snow), set fast, fix in a slough, suck in, grip, mire, stodge, sink, bog down, flounder.

STALLION, n. Male horse not castrated, stud horse, breeding horse, stud, entire horse.

STALWART, adj. 1. Strong, stout, well-developed, robust, powerful, vigorous, sturdy, lusty, muscular, sinewy, brawny, puissant, gigantic, herculean, able-bodied, strapping, athletic, mighty, forceful, great, hardy, hard, rugged, hale, hefty (coll.), doughty (humorous), beefy (coll.), Atlantean.

2. Brave, strong, valiant, valorous, plucky, hardy, high-spirited, bold, manly, gallant, daring, firm, resolute, redoubtable, courageous, indomitable, intrepid, mettlesome, gritty, game, stouthearted, unflinching, heroic, strong-willed, self-possessed, high-mettled, lion-hearted, spunky (coll.), stanch.

3. Firm, steadfast, uncompromising, stable, constant, unwavering, steady, stanch, true, faithful, unshaken, resolute, methodical, resolved, determined, serious, decided, unswerving, unflinching, not to be shaken, persevering, unflagging, enduring, patient, indefatigable, undeviating, unwearied, indomitable, undaunted, inexorable, settled, fixed, unshrinking, intransigent, game, plucky, gritty, persistent, relentless, stern, solid, unbending, pertinacious, unfaltering, unhesitating, uncompromising, unyielding, tenacious.

STAMINA, n. Power to endure (disease, fatigue, privation, etc.), strength of physical constitution, endurance, puissance, vigor, force, sturdiness, power, lustiness, stoutness, might, vitality, dynamic, pith, strong arm, sinew or sinews, robust or rugged physique, guts (sl.), steam (coll.), beef (coll.), brawn, dint, potence, energy.

STAMMER, n. Hesitant utterance, stutter, falter, drawl, mytacism, traulism.

STAMMER, v. Speak with involuntary breaks and pauses or with spasmodic repetitions, stutter,

speak hesitantly, halt, stumble, haw, sputter, splutter, fumble, falter, hum or hem and haw.

STAMP, n. 1. Mark, impression (design, characters, words, etc.) made with a stamp, indentation, indention, brand, print, impress, dent, imprint, seal, engraving, label, paraph, sigil, signet, identification, signature, hallmark.

2. Die, engraved block (for impressing marks), mold, signet, last, seal, mint, punch, intaglio, matrix (Print.), mat (Print.).

3. Official mark (indicating genuineness, validity, etc.) ratification, seal, voucher, signature, endorsement, emblem, certificate, authentication, validation, certification, attestation, sigil, signet, O.K. (coll.).

4. Peculiar or distinctive impress, mark, quality, ring, conviction, peculiarity, earmark, trait, individuality, oddity, uniqueness, singularity, aberration, deviation, quirk, twist, idiosyncrasy, kink, crotchet, eccentricity, caprice, idiocrasy, trick, mannerism, specialty, character, mode, cast, habit, form, idiom, badge, temper, feature, characteristic, style.

5. Character, kind, type, sort, species, class, description, order, variety, strain, stripe, genus, rank, nature, grade, genre, school, form, set, classification, make, cast, mold, suit, sect, denomination, color, breed, kidney, category, brand, distinction, like (coll.).

6. Small adhesive paper showing charges to have been paid, etc., trading stamp, postage stamp, ticket, postmark.

7. Instrument for stamping (crushing, pounding, etc.), weight, hammer, knocker, tamper, mallet, ram, rammer, sledge hammer, punch, puncher, pile driver.

STAMP, v. 1. Strike or beat with a forcible downward thrust of the foot, step smartly on the ground, trample, drive, force, crush, smash.

2. Crush, pound, demolish, ruin, smash, crumble, beat, mash, crunch, crumb, disintegrate, granulate, batter, devastate, pulverize, powder, triturate, disintegrate, comminute, grind, levigate, splinter, mince, hash, mill, shiver, grate, erode, bruise, bray.

3. Impress with mark or device (showing genuineness, approval, ownership, etc.), imprint, mark, brand, engrave, form, shape, mold, cast, letter, initial, inscribe, sign, set the seal on, seal, fix deeply.

4. Characterize, distinguish, reveal, describe, set forth, disclose, manifest, evince, evidence, show, differentiate, bespeak, personify, mark, betray, display, bare, exhibit, demonstrate, present, expose, show forth, bring out in bold (strong, high) relief.

5. Walk with forcible or heavy resounding steps, tramp, storm, flounce, goose-step, stalk, strut, prance, bluster, stride, trudge, lunge, barge, lumber.

STAMPEDE, n. Headlong flight, sudden scattering (from fright), rush, rout, dash, panic, race, debacle, chute (Western U.S.), lam (sl.).

STAMPEDE, v. Scatter, flee, make an unconcerted general rush, take flight, beat a retreat, make a break for it, take to one's heels, show the heels, skedaddle, issue forth, lam, pack off or away.

STANCH, adj. 1. Firm (in principle, adherence, loyalty, etc.), steady, constant, steadfast, stable, zealous, trusty, strong, unwavering, resolute, true, faithful, unshaken, resolved, determined, serious, decided, unswerving, unflinching, not to be shaken, persevering, sedulous, industrious, untiring, plodding, unflagging, enduring, patient, grim, unwearied, undeviating, indefatigable, indomitable, undaunted, inexorable, settled, fixed, plucky, unshrinking, intransigent, game, gritty, persistent, relentless, solid, stern, unbending, pertinacious, unfaltering, unhesitating, strong-willed, uncompromising, unyielding, obstinate, tenacious, inflexible.

2. Strong, sound, stout, substantial, hale, firm, rugged, lasting, well-constructed, well-built, not flimsy, solid, sturdy, heavy, tough, durable, hard.

3. Impervious to liquids, watertight, impermeable, impassable, imperforable.

STANCH, *v.* Stop the flow of, stop from running, dam, close, plug, stuff, fill, shut, occlude, cork, seal, choke, cicatrize, obstruct, cause to coagulate.

STANCHION, *n.* Upright bar, beam, support, post, brace, pillar, shore, stay, upholder, sustainer, mainstay, arm, rod, block, rib, rest, stand, bracer, standard, splint, reinforcement, pediment, underpin, underset, leg, staff, stud, strut, crutch, pin.

STAND, *n.* 1. Act of standing, assumption of an upright position, position, stance, posture, pose, port, bearing, carriage, set, mien.

2. Coming to a position of rest, halt, stop, standstill, cessation, lull, breathing-spell, spell, wait, lapse, letup (*coll.*), break, rest, desistance, respite, interlude, interval, pause, discontinuance.

3. Determined effort against *or* for something, opposition, resistance, defense, withstanding, drive, front, standing fast *or* firm, holding ground, maintenance, sustainment, safekeeping, support, upholding, sustenance, preservation, protection, vindication, boycott, strike, revolt, rebellion, recalcitrance, reluctance, contravention, defiance, obstruction, barricade, blockade.

4. Place where a person *or* thing stands, site, station, accustomed position, post, box, location, standing, footing, foothold, purchase, hold, vantage point *or* ground, placement, emplacement, installation, lodgment, collocation, allocation, establishment, disposition, deposition, fixation, whereabouts, quarter, ground, bearings, demesne, locale, toehold.

5. Place where a witness sits *or* stands to testify in court, witness box *or* stand, dock.

6. Raised platform *or* structure (*for spectators, etc.*), bleachers, reviewing stand, grandstand, gallery, stage, rostrum.

7. Framework on *or* in which articles are placed (*for exhibition, sale, etc.*), booth, stall, tent, enclosure, compartment, cell, counter, pavilion.

8. Small light table, base, console, easel, frame, tree, pulpit, whatnot, tripod, trivet, turntable, rack.

9. Growing trees, *etc.*, on a given area, crop, growth.

10. Halt of a theatrical company on tour, stopover, appearance, performance, engagement.

11. Position taken *or* maintained with respect to others *or* a question, mental attitude, mood, mind, point of view, disposition, viewpoint, bias, standpoint, inclination, frame of mind, leaning, bent, propensity, direction, tendency, predilection, proclivity, affection.

STAND, *v.* 1. Be erect, remain upright, remain motionless *or* steady on the feet, rise, rise to one's feet, continue erect, hold one's head up, draw oneself up to one's full height, spring up, get up, jump up, hold oneself up *or* erect.

2. Cease walking *or* moving, halt, stop, be quiescent, become still *or* stationary, rest, repose, stay, tarry, be at a stand *or* standstill, hold, draw up, wait, pause, linger, break, abide, stall, stick, pull up, mark time, stop short, come to a stop, brake, rein in, slacken.

3. Take a position *or* stand as indicated, step, move, turn, draw, edge, shy, sidle, dodge, shrink.

4. Remain firm *or* steadfast, stay, be resolute, hold out, bear up, be proof against, be fixed, be steady, maintain one's ground, keep one's position, stand one's ground, withstand, resist, not submit, make *or* take a stand, adopt a certain course, put one's foot down (*coll.*), insist, continue, persist, carry on, keep on, resolve, will, purpose, not fail, persevere, not give way, steel oneself, grit one's teeth, set one's jaw, determine, go ahead, stick to one's guns, stick at nothing, mean business, be obstinate, adhere resolutely, fight to the last ditch, die fighting, nail one's colors to the mast, take the bit in one's mouth *or* teeth, stand pat (*coll.*), commit oneself, not yield an inch, never say die, not give up, peg away *or* along, plod, plug (*coll.*), set one's back against the wall, die hard, put (lay, set) one's shoulder to the wheel, buckle to.

5. (*Of things*) Be in an upright position, be set on end, rest on *or* as on a support, be set (placed, fixed), stick *or* cock up, rise, tower, soar, extend upward.

6. Be located *or* situated, lie, have its seat (*in*), be placed, be built, be present, be permanent, exist, occur, rest, stay, tarry, continue, persist, remain, be.

7. Remain erect *or* entire, resist change (decay, destruction), endure, continue in force, remain valid, remain intact, be proven, prove good, be fixed, abide, hold, extend, sustain, stay, perdure, go *or* run on, persist, subsist, linger on, be the case, prevail, obtain, exist, be indestructible, be extant.

8. Be *or* become stagnant, stagnate, cease to run *or* flow, repose, not stir, idle, lie still, rest, stop, be calm, remain motionless.

9. Set upright, upend, cause to stand, build, put together *or* up, raise, rear, stick *or* cock up, elevate, pitch, uprear, upraise, uplift, set on its feet, raise on its legs, uphoist, hoist, heave, place *or* set on a pedestal, mount.

10. Face, encounter, brave, dare, confront, venture, await, anticipate, bear up under *or* against, endure, set one's face against, struggle (fight, strive) against, grapple with, defy, meet, parry, fend off, drive off, ward off, beat off, resist, counteract, breast, buffet, keep at bay, fight, repel, repulse, stem, despise, mock, look in the face, make a determined resistance.

11. Endure without hurt *or* injury, undergo, submit to, tolerate, abide, swallow, suffer, brook, sustain, weather, bear up under *or* against, bear, take, stomach.

12. Tolerate, endure, abide, stomach, swallow, be patient with, forgive, feel a liking for, admit, countenance, yield to, submit to, pardon, excuse, understand, be content with, take, pocket the affront, resign oneself to, condone, disregard, let pass, pass over, blink *or* wink at, be indulgent, close *or* shut the eyes to, overlook, ignore, grin and bear it, reconcile oneself to, resign oneself to, bear with, allow for, make allowances for, shake hands with, bury the hatchet, permit, be lenient toward, become reconciled to.

13. (*With* BY) Aid, uphold, second, back, stand up for, sustain, support, vindicate, justify,

maintain, stick by, endorse, side with, befriend, advocate, be near with aid, defend, patronize, favor, work for, stand behind *or* back of, abet, lend one's name to, subscribe to, go to bat for *(sl.)*, advocate, take up the cudgels for, take the part of, take up (adopt, espouse) the cause of, lend one's favor *or* support to.

14. *(With BY)* Adhere to, abide by, be faithful to, make good, own, admit, acknowledge, keep, observe, be true to, act up to, comply with, respect, meet, fulfill, obey, satisfy, perform, execute, carry out, discharge, cling to.

15. *(With ON)* Rest *or* depend on, rely on, act on the strength of, trust in, have faith in, pin one's faith to, hang upon, take for granted, take one's oath upon, swear by, build upon, count *or* calculate on, give credit *or* credence to, lean on, hope in, bank on *(coll.)*, set store by *(coll.)*, gamble on *(coll.)*, bet on *(coll.)*, bet one's bottom dollar on *(coll.)*.

16. *(With ON)* Be punctilious about *(ceremony, etc.)*, claim respect for *(one's rights, dignity, etc.)*, be strict about, be scrupulous *or* fastidious, act up to, practice faithfully, adhere to, observe closely, perform, fulfill, be faithful to, comply with, discharge, expect, demand, be rigid about.

17. *(With OUT)* Project, protrude, loom, jut, be prominent *or* conspicuous, be evident, glare, stick out, beetle, thrust forward, impend, excurve, protuberate, overhang, poke out, shoot out, be convex, bulge, bag, bow, appear, catch *or* strike the eye, burst upon the view *or* sight.

18. *(With OUT)* Hold aloof, persist in opposition *or* resistance, be obstinate, not comply, be noncommittal, withhold, forbear, eschew, refrain, dodge, fight shy, hold out, fly in the face of, be cautious, remain neutral, keep at a respectable distance, let well enough alone, move warily, refuse to join, keep out of harm's way, keep out of troubled waters, evade, side-step, hang back, abstain, have nothing to do with, dissent, disagree, hesitate, recoil, avoid the issue, pick one's steps, shrink.

19. *(With UP FOR)* Defend the cause of, seek to extenuate, support, justify, excuse, seek indulgence for, praise, laud, acclaim, commend, speak well *or* highly of, recommend, panegyrize, vindicate, sustain, uphold, maintain, sanction, honor, approbate, apologize for, make apology for, accredit, argue for, put in a good word for, plead for, speak up for, champion, advocate, endorse, OK *(coll.)*, countenance, be in favor of.

STANDARD, *adj.* 1. Serving as a basis of weight (measure, value, comparison, *etc.*), universal, accepted, common, normal, metric, linear, mean, average, avoirdupois.

2. Of recognized excellence *or* authority, final, definitive, authoritative, conclusive, reliable, preferred, classic, timeless, accepted, orthodox, staple, official, cathedral, doctrinal, ultimate, canonical, authentic.

STANDARD, *n.* 1. Approved model, basis of comparison *(by general consent)*, gauge, pattern, scale, measure, authorized exemplar, prototype, basis, original, archetype, criterion, norm, ideal, mirror, plan, template, nonesuch, guide, mold, rule, fugler, fugleman, yardstick, test, check, canon, design, draft, layout, principle, specifications, form, precedent, instance, sample, paragon, specimen, example, historic warrant, paradigm, last, keynote, touchstone, precept.

2. Grade *or* level of excellence *or* advance-

ment, degree, achievement, rank, grade, class, estate, station, status, sphere, situation, standing, manner, mode.

3. Flag (emblematic figure, *etc.*) raised on a pole, pennant, streamer, ensign, banner, colors, gonfalon, bannerol, banneret, ancient, pendant, bunting, burgee, vexillum, pennon, oriflamme, labarum, jack, eagle.

4. Support, upright, pillar, post, base, leg, foot, pier, column, stanchion, platform, foundation, rest.

STANDARD-BEARER, *n.* Conspicuous leader of a movement (political party, *etc.*), ringleader, agitator, commander, instigator, insurgent, boss, bellwether, demagogue, Draco, dictator, politico, politician, firebrand, chief, man behind the throne, strategist, wirepuller, kingmaker, incendiary, hero.

STANDARDIZE, *v.* Bring to *or* make of an established size (weight, quality, strength, *etc.*), trim, regulate, systemize, adjust, methodize, make alike, cut to size, similarize, organize, normalize, harmonize, order, approximate, uniform, smooth, dress, level, make uniform, make to conform, assimilate.

STAND-BY, *n.* Stanch supporter *or* adherent, one who can be relied upon, the faithful *(pl.)*, friend, partisan, upholder, follower, disciple, champion, sympathizer, fautor, votary, sectary, advocate, patron, favorer, well-wisher, backer, seconder, sustainer, abettor, angel *(coll.)*.

STAND-IN, *n.* Substitute, stunt man, understudy, proxy, double, dummy, alternate, supplanter, fill-in, secondary, ghost, ghost writer, pinch hitter, locum tenens, succedaneum, sub *(coll.)*.

STANDING, *adj.* 1. That stands erect *or* upright, vertical, perpendicular, stand-up, upright, erect, upended, rampant, ramping, straight-up-and-down.

2. Still, not flowing, motionless, quiet, inert, quiescent, stationary, stagnant, lifeless, dead, idle, inactive, calm, dormant, static, placid, at rest, undisturbed, unstirring, tranquil.

3. Continuing without cessation *or* change, settled, established, fixed, continuing in operation (force, use, *etc.*), stable, conventional, immovable, admitted, recognized, permanent, lasting, confirmed, ingrained, durable, firmly seated, deep-rooted, pat, stabilized, ingrafted, radicated, cut and dried, stipulated, prescriptive, wonted, stated, staple, valid, sound, unchecked, unrepealed, constant, inviolate, enduring intact, stationary, vested, current, acknowledged, received, approved, orthodox.

4. Out of use, idle, inactive, passive, dormant, abeyant, suspended.

STANDING, *n.* 1. Position, status, rank, condition, reputation, class, estimation, order of merit, order of importance, step, station, prominence, elevation, distinction, superiority, notability, condition, caste, gradation, importance, eminence, degree, prestige, consequence, place, precedence, grade, sphere.

2. Length of existence (continuance, residence, membership, experience, *etc.*), duration, survival, continuance, persistence, permanence, endurance, diuturnity, constancy, age, perpetuity, time, course, space, tenure, term, period, life, durability, lastingness.

3. Place where a person *or* thing stands, position, post, station, stand, ground, hold, footing, foothold, toehold, site, box, location, purchase, vantage point *or* ground, placement, emplacement, installation, lodgment, collocation, allocation,

establishment, disposition, deposition, quarter, whereabouts, bearings, locale, demesne.

STAND-OFF, *adj.* Standing off *or* apart, holding aloof, reserved, distant, unsociable, cold, modest, not cordial, cool, stand-offish, disinclined, dissenting, shifty, shrinking, gingerly, abstemious, wary, abstinent, renitent, careful, evasive, chary, cautious, reluctant, elusive, demurring, prudent, distrustful, guarded, leery *(sl.)*, politic, noncommittal, precautious, stealthy, circumspect, remote, passive, suspicious, inaccessible, unapproachable.

STAND-OFF, *n.* 1. A standing off *or* aloof, shyness, reserve, reluctance, taciturnity, modesty, closeness, coolness, caution, wariness, care, silence, reservation, reticence, uncommunicativeness, precaution, bashfulness, evasion, secretiveness, distrust, evasiveness, demurral, renitence, shrinking, circumspection, prudence, suspicion, passivity, unobtrusiveness, diffidence, timidity, constraint, unsociability.

2. Tie, draw, dead heat, even score, tied score, even Stephen *(sl.)*, neck and neck race *(Racing)*.

STANDPOINT, *n.* 1. Point at which one stands to view something, position, vantage point, seat, observation post, situation, location, post, point, spot, locale, locality, quarter, station, site, ground, bearings, observatory, lookout.

2. Mental position from which one views and judges things, point of view, viewpoint, position, angle, light, mood, mind, disposition, inclination, bias, frame of mind, bent, propensity, leaning, direction, tendency, predilection, proclivity, affection.

STANDSTILL, *n.* Halt, stand, cessation of movement *or* action, stop, pause, rest, deadlock, lull, interruption, breathing-spell, spell, wait, lapse, letup *(coll.)*, break, respite, desistance, interlude, interval, discontinuance of activity.

STANZA, *n.* Regularly repeated metrical division of a poem, strophe, stave *(Pros.)*, envoy *(Pros.)*, antistrophe, verse, response, refrain, chorus.

STAPLE, *adj.* Chief, principal, prominent *(among products exported, produced, dealt in, consumed, etc.)*, principally used, basic, vital, merchantable, established, marketable, foremost, main, leading, fundamental, essential, important, popular, in demand, salable, vendible.

STAPLE, *n.* 1. Principal commodity, goods in steady demand, goods of recognized *or* known quality, stock, salable items, stock in trade, vendible *or* marketable goods, resource, standard goods.

2. Principal item (thing, feature, element, part), bulk, substance, mass, body, base, basis, greater part, chief ingredient, major part, burden, gist, essentials, main part, tissue, basics, fundamentals, fabric, salient point, cardinal point, keynote, gross, skeleton, essential part, almost *or* nearly all, heft *(coll.)*.

3. Fiber *(of cotton, wool, etc.)*, pile, thread, filament, strand, threadlet.

4. Loop of wire *or* metal *(for holding, binding, clamping, etc.)*, pin.

STAR, *adj.* Brilliant, prominent, distinguished, chief, leading, first, supreme, principal, main, illustrious, topmost, lofty, great, famous, grand, in the zenith, elevated, exalted, august, eminent, uppermost, glorious, lustrous, preëminent.

STAR, *n.* 1. Heavenly body, luminary, orb, sphere, planet, comet, meteor, meteoroid, asteroid, planetoid, meteorite, candle of the night, burning tapers of the sky.

2. Fate, fortune, destiny, portion in life, condition, doom, lot, state, plight, estate, luck, walk, status, cup, planets, situation, case, kismet, predestination, predicament.

3. Asterisk, pentagram, pentacle, pentalpha, tick.

4. Preëminent *or* distinguished person *(in art, profession, etc.)*, one who plays a leading role, leading man *or* lady, principal, lead, protagonist, hero, heroine, diva, prima donna, headliner *(Theat. sl.)*, headline *or* feature attraction.

STAR, *v.* 1. Set with *or* as with stars, spangle, stud, brighten, bejewel, garnish, blazon, emblazon, burnish.

2. Present *(an actor, etc.)* as a star, feature, make much of, promote, advance, introduce, give prominence to.

3. Mark with a star *or* asterisk *(as for special notice)*, tick, check, indicate, note, dot.

4. Shine as a star, be brilliant *or* prominent, appear as a star *(of an actor, etc.)*, figure, cut a figure, be distinguished, make a figure, make a splash, have a run, be important, be lionized.

STARCH, *n.* Stiffness *or* formality *(as of manner)*, rigidity, punctiliousness, primness, preciseness, ceremony, fastidiousness, squeamishness, finicalness, etiquette, exactness, exactitude, prudery, punctilio, propriety, decorum, meticulousness, scrupulousness.

STARE, *n.* Staring gaze, fixed look with the eyes wide open, glare, glower, gaping, ogling, scrutiny, blank look, empty *or* vacant gaze.

STARE, *v.* 1. Gaze fixedly *(esp. with the eyes wide open)*, gape, look intently, fasten *or* rivet the eyes upon, eye, watch, ogle, goggle, gawk *(coll.)*, glare, glower, rubber *(sl.)*, rubberneck *(sl.)*.

2. Stand out boldly *or* obtrusively to view, be conspicuous, project, protrude, loom, jut, be prominent, stick out, glare, beetle, thrust forward, protuberate, poke out, shoot out, excurve, bulge, bag, bow, catch *or* strike the eye, burst upon the view *or* sight.

3. *(Of hair, feathers, etc.)* Stand on end, bristle, stick up.

STARK, *adj.* 1. Sheer, downright, utter, arrant, mere, simple, bare, bald, pure, plain, palpable, patent, evident, obvious, unmistakable, staring, glaring, flagrant, conspicuous, absolute, gross, entire, unqualified, complete, total, dead, single, out-and-out, unmitigated, veritable, perfect, outright, consummate, unalloyed, unmingled.

2. Absolutely naked, nude, divested, bare, bald, undressed, in a state of nature, in the raw, in the buff *(coll.)*, without a stitch, in one's birthday suit *(joc.)*.

3. Stiff *(in substance or muscles, etc.)*, rigid, hard, unpliant, unpliable, unbending, unyielding, unlimber, cold, inflexible, dead, congealed, ossified, petrified.

4. Harsh *(to the view)*, grim, desolate, barren, bare, ungraced, stricken, wasted, laid waste, desert, ravaged, void, vacant, abandoned, forsaken, empty, austere, lean, dead, unfertile, miserable, exhausted, depleted, meager, forlorn, uncultivated, severe, worn, arid, unproductive.

STARK, *adv.* Utterly, completely, entirely, wholly, vigorously, absolutely, fully, altogether, to the *n*th degree, quite, clearly, clean, downright, out and out, plain, plumb *(coll.)*, through and through.

STARLIGHT, *n.* 1. Light proceeding from the stars, gleam, glow, glitter, glimmer, twinkle, sparkle, shimmer, glint, afterglow, sunset glow, scintillation, flicker.

2. Time when the stars shine, night, evening, nighttime, half-light, semidark, dusk, crepuscule, darkness of night, semidarkness, twilight.

STARLIKE, *adj.* 1. Star-shaped, radiated, stellate, starry, stelliform, stellular, stellated.

2. Shining, lustrous, bright, radiant, luminous, nitid, irradiate, lucent, lucid, gleaming, orient, beaming, shiny, lambent, glittering, shimmering, sparkling, twinkling, spangled, star-studded, incandescent.

STARLIT, *adj.* Lighted by the stars, luminous, alit, dim, twilight, twinkling, lustrous, shining, nitid, irradiate, lucent, lucid, spangled.

STARRY, *adj.* 1. Abounding with *or* lighted by stars, full of stars, star-spangled, star-studded, bespangled, flashing, scintillating, sheeny, shining, twinkling, radiant, irradiant, sparkling, coruscating.

2. Of, pertaining to *or* proceeding from the stars, stellar, astral, sidereal, celestial, uranic, astronomical, empyrean, heavenly, empyreal, planetary, nebular, asteroidal.

3. Resembling a star, starlike, stellate, star-shaped, radiated, stelliform, stellular, stellated.

4. Shining like stars, brilliant, sparkling, twinkling, lustrous, bright, luminous, nitid, irradiate, lucent, gleaming, orient, lambent, shiny, beaming, glittering, shimmering, spangled, incandescent.

START, *n.* 1. Beginning to move (go, act), onset, setting in motion, departure, outset, inception, birth, threshold, origination, commencement, opening, genesis, initiation, outbreak, dawn, head, spring, inauguration, incipience, foundation, inchoation, incubation, first move, infancy, rise of the curtain, coming, take-off (*coll.*), embarkation, first step, origin, entrance, prelude, preface, overture, morning, installation, debut, kick-off (*coll.*).

2. Sudden springing motion, leap, bound, jump, elastic *or* springy movement, vault, hop, saltation, skip, bounce, pounce, upleap, upspring, gambol, prance, curvet, frolic, leapfrogging.

3. Sudden involuntary jerking movement of the body, startle, spasm, twitch, jump, jar, jolt, turn (*coll.*), fit, seizure, convulsion, paroxysm, throe.

4. Lead (*as over competitors or pursuers*), advance, advantage, priority, odds, superiority, precedence, precession, head start, antecedence, anteposition, vantage point *or* ground, jump (*coll.*), edge (*coll.*), drop (*coll.*), inside track (*coll.*).

5. Chance (*given one starting on a course or career*), opportunity, opening, support, backing, introduction, occasion, advantage, place, means, moment, possibility, encouragement, favor, assistance, aid, fosterage, guidance, protection, friendship, interest, advocacy, charge, auspices, influence, ministration, championship.

6. Spurt of activity, fit, spasm, pang, throe, fury, furor, passion, frenzy, tempest, storm, rage, turbulence, convulsion, flash, explosion, eruption, impulse, madness, paroxysm, burst, brief spell, scorch (*coll.*), sprint, exertion, race, dash, rush, spirt.

START, *v.* 1. (*Often fol. by* OUT) Begin to move (go, act), set out, set off, commence, leave, embark, make off, get going (*coll.*), take off (*coll.*), hit the trail, be off, venture out *or* forth, set forward, depart, sally forth, push off (*coll.*), set sail, enter upon, take the first step.

2. Come suddenly into activity (life, view, *etc.*), rise *or* issue suddenly, spring, move suddenly,

happen, jump, leap, bound, issue, gush, rush, jet, break *or* burst forth, stream, spurt, shoot, squirt, surge, fountain, spray, well, spout, emerge, mushroom, sprout, crop out, upshoot, pop up.

3. Move with an involuntary twitch *or* jerk, jump, be alarmed *or* startled, be taken by surprise, be given a start, blink, shy, draw back, recoil, quail, cower, startle, blench, flinch, wince, shrink, lurch, bounce, convulse, be shaken.

4. Burst out, pop, bulge, be wide open, stare, protrude, protuberate, dilate.

5. Spring, slip, work loose from place *or* fastenings, bend, warp, burst, fly open, part, loose, sunder, crack, be riven, dissever, abscind, fracture, rupture, snap, rive.

6. Set moving (going, acting), set in operation, establish, initiate, put in motion, break the ice, kindle, introduce, launch, set going, originate, touch off, send off, set on foot, institute, inaugurate, create, give origin *or* rise to, invent, devise, improvise, hatch, formulate, lay the foundation of, conceive, draw up, give birth to, breed, occasion, form, cause to be, construct, found, establish, beget, fashion, usher in, inchoate, coin, raise, begin, fabricate, design, contrive, evolve, bring about, sow the seeds of, lie at the root of, develop, generate, engender, draft, chisel, hew, carve, think out, organize, forge, block out, open, make, propagate.

7. Enter upon, begin, commence, undertake, open, engage upon, initiate, set about, make a beginning, take the first step, embark on, turn to, inchoate, lay the first stone, put one's hand to the plow, pitch in (*coll.*), venture on, take up, plunge into, turn one's hand to, put one's shoulder to the wheel, put in execution, launch, broach, break ground, break the ice, set on foot, fall to, buckle down (*coll.*).

8. Enable (*a person, etc.*) to set out (*on a journey, course, career, etc.*), impel, subsidize, underwrite, patronize, encourage, back, second, prompt, urge, set going, promote, prompt, aid, set up, befriend, abet, endorse.

9. Rouse (*game, etc.*), flush, move suddenly, alarm, startle, disturb, discompose, frighten, scare, disquiet, throw into confusion, disconcert, upset, agitate, confuse, fluster, oust, evict, displace, eject, dispossess, convulse, toss, perturb, trouble, wrest, wrench, unhouse, turn out, dislodge.

10. Cause parts, *etc.*, to start from place *or* fastenings, dislocate, displace, disengage, disconnect, disjoint, wrench, shake, jiggle, jerk, dislodge, luxate, unhinge, shift, unseat, unloose, loose, throw out of joint *or* gear, divide, separate, detach, slip, release, drop, free.

11. Draw (*liquid, etc.*) from a vessel *or* container, empty, evacuate, spill, extract, withdraw, drain, siphon, pour, void.

STARTLE, *n.* Sudden shock (*of surprise, alarm, etc.*), surprise, violent disturbance, trauma, cut, blow, stroke, turn (*coll.*), jar, wound, perturbation, breakdown, injury, nociassociation (*Med.*), offense, collapse, dismay, prostration.

STARTLE, *v.* 1. Disturb suddenly, agitate, cause to start, frighten, disquiet, take off one's guard, take aback, surprise, shock, scare, alarm, affright, terrify, electrify, intimidate, daunt, unman, abash, disconcert, threaten, quail, faze (*coll.*), make one's hair stand on end, cow, overawe, terrorize, harrow, make one's blood run cold, astonish, astound, perturb, unsettle, discompose, bowl over, spring upon, pounce upon, jar, jolt, take away one's breath, give a turn (coll.), stagger, paralyze, stupefy, stun, shake, bewilder, flabbergast (coll.), upset.

2. Start involuntarily (as from a shock of surprise or alarm), shrink, wince, flinch, jump, blink, blench, draw back, recoil, shy, quail, lurch, convulse, be shaken, be taken by surprise, be given a start.

STARVATION, *n.* Extreme hunger, inanition, famishment, famine, deprivation, emptiness, fasting, destitution, indigence, poverty, need, want, lack, exigency, punishment of Tantalus.

STARVE, *v.* 1. Suffer severely from hunger, die or perish with hunger, go hungry, famish, hunger, fast.

2. Suffer from extreme poverty and need, lack, want, be poor, be in need, be in dire circumstances, be indigent, live from hand to mouth, have little or nothing, have seen better days, find it hard going, not have a penny, be up against it (coll.), be broke (sl.), be bankrupt.

3. (Fol. by FOR) Pine, suffer for lack of something specified, hunger, be hungry, thirst, crave, covet, itch, yearn, desire earnestly, long, burn, aspire, run mad, sigh, grasp at, gasp, languish, raven, lust, have one's heart or mind set upon, yen (coll.).

4. Cause to starve, kill with hunger, weaken by lack of food, reduce, cut off from food.

5. Subdue, force to some condition or action (by hunger), besiege, reduce, subjugate, overcome, suppress, quell, put down.

6. Cause to suffer for lack of something needed or craved, deprive, disinherit, disown, decline, grudge, begrudge, deny, refuse, divest, bereave, rebuff, cut off, repulse, repel, withhold, shut or slam the door in one's face, cross, turn a deaf ear to.

STARVELING, *adj.* Starving, suffering from lack of nourishment, pining with want, poverty-stricken, poor in condition or quality, hungry, emaciated, meager, lean, lank, gaunt, scraggy, thin, ill-fed, ill-conditioned, attenuated, rawboned, skinny, inferior, scurvy, paltry, inadequate, scant, deficient, sorry, beggarly, shabby, contemptible, meretricious, scrubby, shoddy, defective, tawdry, secondrate, pitiable, pathetic, dismal, sad, puny, stunted, wizened, withered, spindling, rattle-boned (coll.), undernourished, skeletal, pinched, haggard, shriveled, scrawny.

STARVELING, *n.* Person (animal, plant) that is starving, weakling, pauper, mendicant, beggar, poorling, insolvent, down-and-outer, bankrupt, sponger, moocher, bum, panhandler (coll.), havenot (coll.), poor specimen.

STATE, *adj.* 1. Of or pertaining to government or the body politic, national, public, common, communal, social, federal, governmental, provincial.

2. Of or pertaining to ceremonial occasions, ceremonial, governmental, official.

STATE, *n.* 1. Form, estate, shape, guise, likeness, phase, appearance, look, semblance, seeming, condition, constitution.

2. Awkward, bewildered or unfortunate position, condition, position, case, difficulty, predicament, plight, circumstances, uncertainty, pass, strait, mess (coll.), perplexity, impasse, corner.

3. Rank, quality, condition, grade, place, degree, stage, station, mark, pitch.

4. Country, nation, commonwealth, commonweal, body politic, monarchy, people, republic, land, realm, dominion, kingdom, principality.

STATE, *v.* Avow, aver, express, give utterance, submit, articulate, propose, offer, present, assure, affirm, utter, assert, style, propound, sound, bring forward, say, name, put, word, postulate, predicate, enunciate, pronounce, couch in terms, maintain, claim, recite, avouch, report, premise, profess, specify, testify, recount, narrate, explain, declare, asseverate.

STATECRAFT, *n.* Diplomatic skill, statesmanship, premiership, senatorship, queencraft, diplomacy, kingcraft.

STATED, *adj.* Appointed, predetermined, set, prescribed, stabilized, ascertained, defined, established, fixed, regular, prearranged, agreed.

STATELY, *adj.* Majestic, dignified, exalted, elevated, lordly, eminent, distinguished, grand, noble, elegant, great, imposing, superior, sovereign, queenly, regal, kingly, impressive, princely.

STATEMENT, *n.* 1. Record, tale, narrative, memoir, recital, recitation, unfolding, account, chronicle, history, delineation, story, detail, commentary, exposition.

2. Assertion, utterance, articulation, speech, proposition, postulation, pronouncement, presentation, naming, affirmation, evidence, assurance, vocalization, claim, prediction, avowal, profession, specification, explanation, declaration, testimony, asseveration.

3. Statement of monetary transactions, bill, account, count, record, tally, charge, reckoning, valuation, check, tick, balance, sheet, entry, tab (coll.).

STATEROOM, *n.* Cabin (Naut.), quarters, drawing room, apartment.

STATESMAN, *n.* Man versed in the management of affairs of state, statist, official, public servant, congressman, politician, Solon, lawgiver, politico, legislator.

STATESMANSHIP, *n.* Skill in the management of public affairs, statecraft, governorship, kingcraft, queencraft, premiership, senatorship, legislation, diplomacy, diplomatic skill.

STATIC, *adj.* 1. Pertaining to or characterized by a fixed or stationary condition, immobile, inert, still, passive, abeyant, resting, dormant, inactive, suspended, latent, quiescent, fixed, motionless, torpid, stagnant, lifeless, dead, at rest, reposing, incumbent, sedentary, becalmed.

2. Denoting or pertaining to atmospheric electricity, electrostatic.

STATION, *n.* 1. Place, position, location, stand, seat, situation, deposition, disposition, fixation, establishment, collocation, allocation, lodgment, emplacement, placement, post.

2. Regular stopping place, place at which something stops, station house, stop-off, stop, terminal, terminus, depot, railway station, layover, destination.

3. Headquarters of a police force, station house, watchhouse, calaboose (coll.), guardhouse (Mil.), jail, prison.

4. Standing in a scale of estimation, position, rank, degree, dignity, status, condition, grade, prestige, quality, caliber, character, state, footing, step, importance, prominence, elevation, distinction, superiority, notability, caste, gradation, eminence, class, consequence, place, precedence, sphere.

5. Position, office, function, rank, calling, sphere, realm, employment, business, job, post, work, commission, billet, capacity, berth, pursuit,

occupation, livelihood, appointment, charge, career, role, sinecure, trade, incumbency, duty, care, province, assignment, responsibility.

STATION, v. Assign a station to, place, post, seat, lodge, establish, locate, appoint, induct, nominate, hire, commission, install, invest, employ, elect, choose, engage, house, billet, ensconce.

STATIONARY, adj. 1. Not moving, having a fixed position, not movable, standing still, immobile, statuelike, inert, firm, fast, rooted, riveted, moored, sedentary, stuck, transfixed, at anchor, stock-still, dead-still, motionless, quiescent, immovable, standing, fixed, stable, irremovable, steady, sound.

2. Established in one place, not itinerant or migratory, permanent, settled, home, constant, perpetual, continuing, enduring, central, base, grounded, abiding, steady, durable.

3. Remaining in the same condition or state, not changing, stable, continuing, lasting, enduring, permanent, fixed, constant, established, steady, firm, unchangeable, unalterable, invariable, rooted, grounded, immutable, deep-rooted, deep-seated, indissoluble, uniform, confirmed, incontrovertible, reliable, sound, valid, abiding, inveterate, unchanging, durable, settled, secure, proved, even, undeviating, ascertained, determined, predetermined, decided, long-lived, long-lasting, longstanding, well-grounded, well-founded, longevous, persistent, chronic, perdurable, endless, perpetual, everlasting, intact, inviolate, revolving, irrevocable, irreversible.

STATIONERY, n. Writing materials, writing paper, note paper, business paper, pens, ink, fasteners.

STATISTICAL, adj. Of or pertaining to statistics, based on or consisting of statistics, mathematical, arithmetical, analytical, numerical.

STATISTICS, n. 1. (Construed as singular) Science dealing with the collection and classification of numerical facts or data, statistiology.

2. (Construed as plural) Numerical facts or data, figures, returns, census, poll, recapitulation, score, account, count, tally.

STATUARY, adj. Of, pertaining to or suitable for statues, statuesque, monumental, monumentary, sculptural, sculptitory, sculpturesque, anaglyphic, glyphic (Fine Arts).

STATUARY, n. Statues (collectively), sculpture, carving, anaglyphy, waxworks.

STATUE, n. Representation (of person, animal, etc.) carved (molded, cast) in the round, image, figurine, statuette, monument, figure, idol, icon, effigy, colossus, acrolith, sculpture, figurehead, bust, wax figure, waxwork, caryatid (Archit.), xoanon (Gk. Antiq.).

STATUESQUE, adj. Like or suggesting a statue, dignified, graceful, beautiful, fixed, still, regal, queenly, kingly, tall, lithe, still, imposing, impressive, stately, lofty, grand, majestic, noble.

STATURE, n. 1. Height, size, tallness, altitude, loftiness, elevation, procerity.

2. Elevation or development attained, rank, position, prominence, eminence, significance, achievement, place, nobility, quality, loftiness, estimation, distinction, superiority, notability, importance, prestige, consequence, precedence.

STATUS, n. 1. State of affairs, condition, situation, character, circumstance, juncture, phase, con-

juncture, tone, tenor, turn, complexion, make-up, predicament, plight, course, pass, ups and downs, stream, tide, form, estate, shape, guise, appearance, semblance, seeming, look, constitution. ·

2. Standing socially or professionally, class, footing, station, condition, position, rank, caste, state, estimation, degree, dignity, grade, prestige, quality, importance, caliber, prominence, elevation, distinction, superiority, notability, gradation, eminence, consequence, place, precedence, sphere.

STATUTE, n. (Law) Enactment made by a legislature, act, law, ordinance, canon, dictate, rule, decree, edict, regulation, dictum, bylaw, ruling, institution, prescript.

STATUTORY, adj. 1. Of, pertaining to or of the nature of a statute, legal, legislative, jurisprudent, judicial, juridical, legislatorial, jurisprudential, nomothetic.

2. Prescribed or authorized by statute, legal, legislative, legitimate, lawful, legalized, constituted, constitutional, statutable, vested, rightful, licit, permitted, within the law, according to law.

3. (Of an offense) Legally punishable, capital, lawbreaking, prohibited, fraudulent, against the law, criminal, illicit, illegitimate, wrongful, actionable, unconstitutional, unlawful, nonlicit, illegal.

STAVE, n. 1. Stick, rod, pale, rib, prop, staff, crook, stay, shaft, cane, crutch, wand, cudgel, walking stick, bludgeon, bat, billy, club, quarterstaff, alpenstock, shillelagh (Ireland), post, standard, upright.

2. Rung (of a ladder, chair, etc.), round, footing, step.

STAVE, v. 1. (Often fol. by IN) Break a hole in, crush inward, burst, cave in, rip, tear, lance, lay open, split, throw open.

2. Beat with a stave or staff, flog, thrash, box, thump, bruise, thresh, spank, smite, thwack, whack, wallop, batter, pelt, whip, lace (coll.), larrup (coll.), lambaste (sl.), paste (sl.), flail, flagellate, lash, scourge, buffet, pommel, cudgel, baste, switch, lay on, belabor, drub, trounce, birch, cane, fustigate.

3. (Fol. by OFF) Put off (as by force or evasion), ward off, keep off, avoid, shun, keep at bay, defer, delay, postpone, procrastinate, impede, inhibit, hinder, intercept, hamper, obstruct, hold in leash, suspend, waive, block, blockade, cramp, detain, obviate, repel, fend off, deflect, avert, keep at arm's length, sidetrack, check, nip in the bud, prevent, turn aside, shelve, pigeonhole.

STAY, n. 1. Stop, halt, standstill, pause, stand, intermission, cessation, detention, desistance, reprieve, respite, suspension, lull, spell, breathingspell, wait, lapse, time out (coll.), letup (coll.), break, abeyance, rest, recess, leaving off, interval, interlude, stoppage, discontinuance.

2. Temporary residence, sojourn, rest, repose, halt, respite, visit, stopover, pause, vacation, holiday, residency, habitation.

3. Brace, support, prop, supporter, buttress, guy, upholder, sustainer, mainstay, arm, stick, pole, rod, block, rib, rest, stand, standard, base, splint, strengthener, reinforcement, stanchion, underpin, underset, leg, staff, stud, shore, strut, cane, crutch, pin, bracer, coin (Archit.), raker (Building).

STAY, v. 1. Remain (in a place, situation, company, etc.), sojourn, dwell, rest, take up quarters, reside, lodge, tarry, abide, inhabit, put up, cohabit, visit, haunt, frequent, hang around or about, live, occupy, room, bunk, tenant, settle, establish oneself.

2. Continue to be *(as specified)*, keep oneself, remain, maintain, sustain, be permanent, be stable, cling to, cleave to, hold to, endure, persist, not change, stand pat *(coll.)*.

3. Wait *(before proceeding)*, stop, halt, linger, pause, tarry, loiter, lag, mark time, dawdle, bide, take time, attend, delay, idle, trifle, potter, hang back, vacillate, loaf, hover, falter, let the grass grow under one's feet.

4. Stop, halt, hold back, detain, restrain, suspend, postpone, delay, arrest, withhold, check, curb, obstruct, adjourn, keep in, rein in, hinder, retard, interrupt, impede, prevent, bring to a stand *or* standstill, stem, balk, deter, thwart, suppress, scotch, undermine, deadlock, checkmate, intermit, intercept, embarrass, frustrate, foil, clog, hamper, block, constrain, shackle, counteract, contravene, prohibit, incommode, forbid.

5. Suppress, quell, crush, silence, destroy, put down, overpower, subdue, smash, abolish, stop, stifle, rout, upset, overcome, overturn, defeat, vanquish, check, discomfit, reduce, master, put an end to, deal a deathblow to, bring to naught, break the neck *or* back of, nip in the bud, make short work of, stamp *or* trample out, wipe out, prostrate, dissolve, dispel, dissipate, root up, disorganize, squelch *(coll.)*.

6. Appease the cravings of, satisfy temporarily, cause to subside, allay, reduce, still, hush, comfort, compose, soothe, alleviate, tranquilize, calm, quiet, remedy, pacify, lull, settle, stop, put at rest.

7. *(Fol. by* OUT*)* Remain through *or* during, remain to the end of *or* beyond, survive, endure, last out, stick to, stick it out *(coll.)*, persevere, see it through, die in the last ditch, be in at the death, die in harness, prosecute to a conclusion, outlive, weather, hold out, persist, carry on, run on, stand, extend.

8. *(Sometimes fol. by* UP*)* Support, sustain, prop, shore up, hold up, uphold, brace, buttress, guy, strengthen, prevent from falling, shoulder, back up, carry, bear, truss, base, found, ground, underpin, underset, underbrace, bolster. ·

9. Sustain, strengthen mentally *or* spiritually, uphold, encourage, bear up, inspirit, carry, inspire, renew the strength of, refresh, reinforce, preserve, invigorate, keep from falling, assist, help, aid.

STEAD, *n.* 1. Place *(as occupied by a successor or substitute)*, name, lieu, behalf, shoes, exchange.

2. Service, avail, advantage, good, use, help, worth, benefit, behalf, efficacy, profit, value, purpose, utility, adequacy, subservience, usefulness, helpfulness, instrumentality.

STEADFAST, *adj.* 1. Fixed in direction, steadily directed, steady, direct, unflinching, unwavering, undeviating, attentive, thoughtful, discerning, rapt, aware, undistracted, absorbed, engrossed, watchful, vigilant, intent, wakeful, piercing, open, candid, keen, searching, penetrating.

2. Firm in purpose (resolution, faith, attachment, *etc.*), resolute, stanch, determined, stable, unshaken, resolved, faithful, unreserved, unhesitating, unwavering, pertinacious, persevering, zealous, true, unfaltering, unyielding, undeviating, unmoved, stern, steady, inflexible, unswerving, constant, strong, serious, decided, not to be shaken, sedulous, untiring, industrious, unflagging, enduring, patient, grim, plodding, indomitable, undaunted, inexorable, settled, fixed, intransigent, gritty, persistent, relentless, strong-willed, uncompromising, obstinate, tenacious, dedicated, devoted.

3. Firmly established *(as an institution or a state of affairs)*, rooted, deep-rooted, deep-seated, enduring, durable, stable, firm, fixed, fast, permanent, grounded, indissoluble, lasting, sound, abiding, settled, secure, proved, long-lived, longlasting, longstanding, perpetual, inviolate, intact, unchangeable, unalterable.

4. Firmly fixed in place *or* position, steady, stable, fixed, firm, sound, solid, immovable, established, riveted, moored, anchored, substantial, fast, stout, sturdy, stanch, irremovable, stationary.

STEADY, *adj.* 1. Firmly placed *or* fixed, stable in position *or* equilibrium, even *or* regular in movement, fast, hard, level, solid, on firm footing, *etc.* *(See* STEADFAST, *adj.* 4 *above.)*

2. Free from change (variation, interruption), uniform, continuous, constant, even, unremitting, undeviating, measured, wearisome, persistent, unyielding, humdrum, monotonous, unvarying, tedious, consistent, ceaseless, undying, unintermitting, incessant, steadfast, unceasing, perpetual, unending, rhythmic.

3. Constant, regular, habitual, chronic, inveterate, frequent, periodical, recurrent, faithful, settled, perpetual, ingrained, repeated, methodical, continual, established, reiterative, punctual, iterative, customary, daily (weekly, monthly, *etc.*), rooted, seasoned, accustomed, addicted, consistent, given to.

4. Free from excitement *or* agitation, equable, calm, cool, even-tempered, constant, consistent, tranquil, easygoing, inexcitable, imperturbable, undisturbable, unirritable, dispassionate, composed, collected, quiet, poised, serene, unruffled, patient, stoical, tolerant, passive, unnervous, nerveless, coolheaded, self-controlled, self-possessed, placid, peaceful, peaceable, nonchalant, unconstrained, unemotional, sane, rational, level-headed.

5. Firm, unwavering, resolute, *etc.* *(See* STEADFAST, *adj.* 2 *above.)*

6. Settled, staid, sober, grave, composed, solemn, cool, thoughtful, sedate, calm, serious, discreet, tranquil, placid, serene, prudent, circumspect, contemplative, meditative, reflective, musing, sane, moderate, deliberate, unimpassioned, objective, judicious, analytical, discriminating, impartial, reasonable, rational, poised, balanced, controlled, level-headed, regular, philosophical, dispassionate.

STEADY, *v.* 1. Make steady, sober, stabilize, maintain, establish, take in hand, bring to one's senses, restore, settle, uphold, support, sustain, ground, preserve, secure, make fast, root, calm, soothe, quiet, ease, subdue, cause to relax, smooth, disburden, reassure.

2. Become steady, gain equilibrium, gain a footing *or* foothold, relax, remit, relent, sober, take oneself in hand, regain equanimity, come to one's senses, cool down *or* off, see things in proper perspective, get things in proportion, strike a balance, steer *or* preserve an even course, keep the golden mean, keep a happy medium, get on even keel.

STEAL, *v.* 1. Pilfer, peculate, purloin, thieve, take dishonestly *or* wrongfully, misappropriate, embezzle, filch, abstract, rob, mooch *(sl.)*, pinch *(sl.)*, hook *(sl.)*, lift *(coll.)*, defraud, cop *(sl.)*, swipe *(sl.)*, kidnap, cabbage, poach, pirate, make off with, come by unlawfully, swindle, usurp, extort, misappropriate, abscond with, loot, snatch, pocket.

2. Appropriate *(ideas, credit, words, etc.)* without right *or* acknowledgment, plagiarize, copy,

crib *(coll.)*, lift *(coll.)*, forge, counterfeit, falsify, misrepresent, assume, imitate, pirate, make use of, help oneself to, borrow, purloin, usurp, thieve, arrogate, abstract, adopt and pass off as one's own.

3. *(Fol. by* AWAY, FROM, IN, INTO, *etc.)* Make (bring, convey, put) secretly *or* quietly, sneak, slip, worm, slide, secrete, insinuate, extract, infuse, inject, conceal, insert.

4. Pass stealthily, move (go, come) secretly *or* quietly, slip, creep, sneak, pass unobserved, be concealed, prowl, lie in ambush, couch, slink, skulk, lurk, lie hidden, gumshoe *(sl.)*, pussyfoot.

5. Pass (come, spread, *etc.*) imperceptibly *or* gradually, slide, slip, flow, elapse, creep, glide, escape, filter, infuse, diffuse, insinuate, flit, fly, drift, infiltrate.

STEALING, *n.* 1. Act of stealing, plunder, theft, robbery, burglary, piracy, plagiarism, depredation, cribbing, larceny, thieving, peculation, shoplifting, housebreaking, safecracking, safebreaking, safeblowing, abduction, kidnapping, pillage, abstraction, looting, embezzlement, pilfering, pocket picking, holdup *(coll.)*, highway robbery, stick-up *(sl.)*, rustling *(West. U.S.)*, brigandage, freebooting, thievery, misappropriation.

2. *(Chiefly pl.)* Something stolen, plunder, loot, booty, prey, stolen goods, pilferings, perquisites, prize, gain, spoil *or* spoils, pillage, seizure, take, grab, pickings, steal *(coll.)*, swag *(sl.)*, haul *(coll.)*, counterfeit, forgery.

STEALTH, *n.* Secret (clandestine, surreptitious) procedure, secrecy, stealthiness, furtiveness, slyness, stalking, hiding, ambush, occultation, taciturnity, silence, darkness, concealment, closeness, privacy, reservation, secretiveness, evasion, repression, underhand dealing, suppression, subterfuge.

STEALTHY, *adj.* Done (characterized, acting) by stealth, furtive, underhand, clandestine, secret, private, sly, subtle, cautious, covert, thievish, surreptitious, skulking, sneaking, artful, undercover, crafty, obreptitious, elusive, dissembled, cloaked, unrevealed, unseen, underground, cunning, confidential, undisclosed, disguised, collusive, taciturn, shrouded, obscure, secretive, veiled, masked, evasive, sneaking, hugger-mugger, secluded, privy, arcane, conspiring.

STEAM, *n.* 1. Vapor *(esp. of water)*, gas, volatile.

2. Mist *(formed from condensation of gas or vapor)*, cloud, haze, film, miasma, fume, smoke, reek, fog, pea soup *(coll.)*, effluvium, exhalation, emanation.

STEAM, *v.* 1. Emit *or* give off vapor, rise in the form of steam, pass off, exhale, smoke, vaporize, volatilize, gasify, atomize, finestill, distill, reek, exhaust, sublime *(Chem.)*, sublimate *(Chem.)*.

2. Become covered with condensed steam, mist, fog, dim, blur, bemist, befog, cloud, smoke, frost, become opaque, be obscured.

3. Move by the agency of steam, travel, cruise, navigate, boat, yacht, go by ship.

4. Expose to *or* treat with steam, sterilize, stew, braise, simmer, subject to steam pressure, pressurecook, autoclave.

STEAMER, *n.* 1. Something propelled *or* operated by steam, liner, steamship, steamboat, ocean liner, freighter, packet, merchantman, excursion boat, stern-wheeler, side-wheeler, paddle boat.

2. Device *or* container in which something is steamed, pressure cooker, sterilizer, pot roaster, autoclave.

STEAMY, *adj.* 1. Consisting of *or* resembling steam, vaporous, volatile, gaseous, moist, evaporating, smoky, fumy.

2. Covered with *or* as if with condensed steam, fogged, opaque, hazy, befogged, coated, cloudy, clouded, filmy, bleary, blurred, moist, misty, smeared.

STEED, *n.* Horse *(esp. for riding)*, mount, saddle horse, saddler, rider, palfrey, hunter, polo pony, charger, courser *(chiefly Poetic)*.

STEEL, *adj.* 1. Like steel in color, gray-blue, iron-gray, steel-gray.

2. Like steel in hardness *or* strength, tough, flinty, rigid, unyielding, indurated, adamantine, inflexible, resistant, steely, dintless, intractile, inelastic, unbending, stiff, hardened, impregnable, dense, strong, rugged, proof, sound, impervious, solid, cast-iron.

STEEL, *n.* Sword, knife, saber, rapier, blade, dirk, dagger, cold steel, foil, machete, broadsword, bayonet, bolo, scimitar, cutlass, falchion, claymore, poniard, yataghan, pigsticker.

STEEL, *v.* 1. Fit with steel, edge *or* point with steel, reinforce, harden, strengthen, temper, caseharden *(Metall.)*.

2. Render insensible (inflexible, unyielding, determined, *etc.*), brace, harden, fortify, make firm, caseharden, nerve, temper, season, inure, accustom, discipline, train, anneal, key up, screw up, prime, equip, prepare, break in, develop, toughen, habituate, stiffen, braze, arm, endow, enable, reinforce, buttress, wind up, energize, gird, dynamize, vivify.

STEEP, *adj.* Having an almost perpendicular slope *or* pitch, having a relatively high gradient, precipitous, sheer, abrupt, sudden, sharp, bold, craggy, vertical, rigid, high, arduous, declivitous, headlong, upright, plumb, bluff, breakneck.

STEEP, *n.* 1. Steep place, declivity, height, elevation, alp, rise, precipice, crag, scarp, acclivity, bluff, cliff, hill, escarpment, pinnacle, sharp incline, crest, palisade.

2. Act *or* process of steeping, brewing, soaking, extraction.

3. Liquid in which something is steeped, brew, broth, stock, extract, liquor.

STEEP, *v.* 1. Soak in liquid *(to soften, cleanse or extract some constituent)*, immerse, macerate, marinate, seethe, souse, sop, impregnate, flood, inundate, immerge, imbrue, infuse, water, saturate, drench, brew.

2. Immerse in some pervading *or* absorbing influence *or* agency, stupefy, saturate, drench, imbrue, imbue, diffuse, suffuse, gorge, satiate, surfeit, pervade, fill, soak, sate, assimilate, infiltrate, indoctrinate, instill, plunge, infuse, surcharge, impregnate, lose, bury, engulf, submerge.

STEEPLE, *n.* Lofty tower, spire, turret, minaret, belfry, dome, cupola, shaft, obelisk, bell tower, martello, campanile, *tourelle (Fr.)*, flèche *(Arch.)*.

STEEPLECHASE, *n.* Race *(across country or over an obstacle course)*, course, career, chase, hunt, the turf, Derby, sweepstakes, handicap, hurdle race.

STEER, *n.* Castrated male bovine *(esp. raised for beef)*, ox, beef, castrate.

STEER, *v.* 1. Guide the course of *(by use of a rudder, helm, wheel, etc.)*, direct, helm, coxswain, run, operate, pilot, conduct, lead, navigate, control, manage, handle, regulate, shape *or* chart a course, drive, hold the reins, lay a course, conn, order, head, take the lead, preside over, govern, have *or* take the direction of.

2. *(Of a vessel, etc.)* Be directed, admit of being steered, be steered *or* guided, be manipulated, be governed, respond to the wheel.

3. Follow *or* pursue a course, direct one's course, go towards, point, make for, be bound, bend one's steps, run *or* stand for, bear up to, bear down upon, lay for, bear for, prosecute, make a beeline, follow, aim at, bend one's steps, align one's march, put in *or* into, lay *or* lie in, close with, take *or* adopt a course.

STEERSMAN, *n.* One who steers a ship *or* drives an automobile, *etc.,* helmsman, pilot, director, postilion, driver, wheelman, coxswain, guide, conductor, motorman, chauffeur.

STELLAR, *adj.* 1. Of *or* pertaining to the stars, consisting of stars, starry, sidereal, astral, celestial, uranic, astronomical, empyrean, heavenly, empyreal, planetary, nebular, asteroidal.

2. Starlike, stelliform, star-shaped, stellate, stellular, stellated, radiated.

3. Pertaining to a leading actor, *etc.,* principal, leading, chief, main, first, foremost, famous, prominent, eminent.

STEM, *n.* 1. Ascending axis of a plant, stalk, trunk, cane, caudex *(Bot.),* caulis *(Bot.),* stipe *(Bot.).*

2. Peduncle *(Bot.),* pedicel *(Bot.),* petiole *(Bot.),* spire, spear, blade, pedicle *(Bot.),* stalk, creeper, runner, caulicle *(Bot.),* culm, stipe *(Bot.),* leafstalk, bine, tendril, burgeon, switch, sprig, shoot, sarmentum.

3. Long slender part, leg, limb, shank, link, peg, prop, tube, branch, support, ramification, tongue, thill, axis, arbor, stalk, quill, axle, spindle.

4. Line of descent, stock, origin, ancestry, pedigree, family, lineage, generation, parentage, progeniture, heredity, clan, sept, people, genealogy, birth, house, extraction, strain, root, blood, race, breed, stirps, caste, gens *(Rom. Hist.).*

5. *(Naut.)* Forepart of a ship, prow, bow, cutwater, beak.

STEM, *v.* 1. Arise, originate, rise, spring, emanate, flow, begin, proceed, start, commence, derive, break out, burst forth, sprout, germinate, ensue, issue, descend, come, bud, grow, accrue, result, follow.

2. Stop, check, oppose, confront, obstruct, stay, quell, halt, hold back, arrest, detain, restrain, delay, withhold, curb, keep in, rein in, hinder, retard, interrupt, impede, prevent, bring to a stand *or* standstill, stall, balk, deter, thwart, suppress, scotch, deadlock, checkmate, intermit, intercept, frustrate, foil, clog, hamper, block, constrain, shackle, counteract, contravene, prohibit, incommode, forbid, resist, repulse, reluct, veto, proscribe, recalcitrate, contend.

3. Tamp, plug, dam up, make tight, stop, fill, close, occlude, block, cork, bung, stanch, choke, stuff, cover, shut.

4. Make headway *or* progress against, oppose successfully, resist, breast, surmount, rise above, repel, buffet, withstand, hold one's own against, bear up against, repulse, keep at bay, face, confront, hinder, thwart, stand, not submit, grapple with, hold out, hold one's ground, engage, attack, cope with, assail, grapple with, face, brave, dare, endure, defy, meet, fend off, ward off, make a determined resistance.

STENCH, *n.* Ill smell, offensive odor, stink,

malodor, effluvium, fetor, fetidness, miasma, redolence, graveolence, nidorosity, mephitis, empyreuma *(Chem.).*

STENOGRAPHER, *n.* Person who specializes in taking dictation *or* reporting by stenography, shorthand writer, secretary, stenotypist, scribe, stenographist, phonographer, brachygrapher *(Hist.),* tachygrapher, tachygraphist.

STENOGRAPHY, *n.* The art of writing shorthand, stenotypy, speed writing, phonography, shorthand, tachygraphy, brachygraphy *(Hist.).*

STENTORIAN, *adj.* Very loud, powerful, strong, thundering, loud-voiced, sonorous, trumpet-like, vociferous, rich, full, full-toned, ringing, orotund, deep, resounding, sounding, vibrant, rolling, round, booming, big, vibrating, mellifluous, reverberating, reverberant, heavy.

STEP, *n.* 1. Movement of the foot as in walking, *etc.,* space measured in stepping, pace, stride, tread, footstep.

2. Sound made by the foot in stepping, footfall, beat, tramp, pound, patter, tread, hoofbeat, pitter-patter.

3. Footprint, footstep, trail, vestige, track, trace, spoor, scent, mark, footmark, pad.

4. Manner of stepping, gait, pace, stride, clip, port, walk, bearing, carriage, footfall, movement, motion, rate of motion, strut, hitch, shuffle, shamble, hobble, stalk, saunter, swagger, prance, hop, jog, trot, jump.

5. *(Pl.)* Movements in stepping *or* walking, course, path, way, passage, trip, journey, circuit, beat, round, road, route.

6. Move, proceeding, motion, movement, deed, measure, means, expedient, act, action, transaction, procedure, feat, blow, coup, achievement, course, stroke, initiative, volition, maneuver, process.

7. Stage in progress, grade, gradation, level, interval, advance, advancement, degree, progression, attainment, period, portion, space, spell, span, course, milestone, cycle, phase, stretch, point, passage.

8. Support for the foot in ascending *or* descending, stair, tread, rung, round, footing, foothold, purchase.

9. Very short distance, stone's throw, close quarters, close range, bowshot, span, few inches, earreach, earshot, gunshot.

10. Repeated pattern of movement in a dance, unit, figure, figuration, design, form, shape, pas, structure, gesture.

STEP, *v.* 1. Move *or* go by using the feet, walk, tread, stride, ambulate, perambulate, pace, tramp, pedestrianize, trip, progress, peg, jog, foot it, hoof it *(coll.),* peripateticate, shuffle, shamble, strut, plod, leg, clump, stalk, pad, track.

2. Go briskly *or* fast *(as a horse),* pace, highstep, speed, canter, gallop, trot, run, race, post, scamper, scurry, peg, hurry, spurt, sprint, ride hard, scour, scoot *(coll.),* bolt, dart, outstrip the wind, fly on the wings of the wind, bowl along, cut along *(coll.),* leap, clip, bound, sweep, get over the ground, spank.

3. Come as if by a step, advance, pass, succeed, inherit, fall, progress, ascend, rise, climb, mount, be thrust, be promoted.

4. Press with the foot to operate a mechanism, tread, treadle, tap, kick *(as a potter's wheel).*

5. *(Sometimes fol. by OFF or OUT)* Measure *(distance, ground, etc.)* by steps, pace, estimate, span, gauge.

STEPPE, n. Extensive plain (esp. without trees), prairie, flat, level, champaign, savanna, tundra, mesa, pampas (pl.), wold, down, marsh, heath, moor, veld or veldt, weald (Poetic), campagna.

STEPPING STONE, n. 1. Stone (usually one of a line) used in crossing water, stepstone, block, mounting or ascending, etc., foothold, toehold.

2. Anything serving as a means of advancing or rising, foothold, bridge, connection, bond, link, tie, toehold, agent, agency, medium, means, hand, instrument, vehicle, device, resort, shift, measure, resource, key, way, aid, go-between, expedient.

STEREOTYPE, n. Set form, convention, habit, tradition, usage, custom, wont, mode, fashion, system, mannerism, pattern, groove, rut, regime, one's old way, institution, routine, beaten path, form, method, rule, proclivity, prescription, matter of course.

STEREOTYPE, v. Give fixed or settled form to, fix, ground, confirm, conventionalize, stabilize, define, establish, set, settle, make permanent, sustain, perpetuate, create, organize, methodize, systematize.

STEREOTYPED, adj. Fixed or settled in form, hackneyed, conventional, commonplace, trite, ordinary, unchangeable, stale, stock, banal, worn, worn-out, platitudinous, regular, set, threadbare, humdrum, old, matter-of-fact, common, bromidic (coll.), plodding, pedestrian.

STERILE, adj. 1. Free from living germs or microörganisms, pure, sterilized, harmless, uninfected, disinfected, sanitary, aseptic.

2. Incapable of producing offspring or vegetation, barren, unfruitful, childless, unproductive, teemless (Poetic), poor, dry, empty, bare, fallow, arid, desert, infecund, unprolific, acarpous (Bot.).

3. Unproductive of results, fruitless, useless, stillborn, abortive, futile, doomed, hopeless, in vain, jejune, otiose, unprofitable, ineffective, ineffectual, inefficacious, worthless, barren, bootless, profitless, unavailing, impotent, inoperative, unrewarding, unremunerative, lame, dead, inane, empty, nugatory, fatuous, effete, inadequate, null and void.

STERILIZE, v. 1. Destroy microörganisms, fumigate, depurate, disinfect, purify, autoclave.

2. Destroy the ability to reproduce, geld, spay, castrate, capon, evirate, unman, emasculate, eunuchize, alter (coll.).

STERLING, adj. Thoroughly excellent, genuine, pure, meritorious, exemplary, sound, unmingled, unalloyed, true, real, worthy, prime, superior, peerless, matchless, noble, creditable, superlative, unadulterated, good, superb, invaluable, of great price, priceless, precious, high-wrought, exquisite, spotless, faultless, perfect, exceptional, extraordinary, consummate.

STERN, adj. 1. Firm, strict, uncompromising, immovable, implacable, steadfast, unrelenting, inflexible, incorruptible, resolved, resolute, sore, unyielding, inexorable, rigid, stiff, puritanical, unfeeling, ascetic, strait-laced, unmerciful, hard, obdurate, relentless, determined, demanding, exacting, heavy, unremitting, exigent, unreasonable, severe, Spartan, despotic, stringent, drastic, austere, iron-handed, iron-fisted, cruel, ruthless, pitiless, tyrannical, extortionate, overbearing, grim, Draconian, pressing, coercive, inclement, cold-blooded, hard-boiled (coll.), sharp, extreme, unbending.

2. Hard, harsh, cruel, biting, trenchant, caustic,

scolding, severe, peremptory, arbitrary, acrid, blunt, curt, bluff, crusty, mordant, mordacious, stringent, short, keen, acerbic, brusque, cutting, piercing, virulent, bitter, brutal, acrimonious, venomous, churlish, brutal, ungentle, afflictive, unkind, unsparing, devastating, stinging.

3. Rigorous, austere, trying, hard, troublesome, of an unpleasantly serious character, bitter, toilsome, perplexing, hard, thorny, knotty, rugged, harsh, Spartan, formidable, burdensome, exacting, critical, Herculean, laborious, operose, painful, irksome, difficult, afflictive, unfavorable, stark, distressing.

4. Forbidding in aspect, grim, dour, gaunt, sharp, frowning, saturnine, jaundiced, acetose, acerbic, bristling, unkind, austere, fierce, granite, ferocious, crusty, severe, gruff, crabbed, sour, brusque, serious, rigid, stiff, unsympathetic, cold, autocratic, sober, sedate, somber, grave, flinty, implacable.

STERN, n. Hinder part (of a ship or boat), rear part (of anything), poop, backside, posterior, tail, behind, back, heel, rudder, counter, afterpart.

STEVEDORE, n. Firm or individual engaged in loading or unloading of vessels, dock laborer, longshoreman, roustabout, docker, lumper, loader, wharf or dock hand, dock walloper (sl.).

STEW, n. Preparation of meat, etc., cooked by stewing, salmagundi, ragout, stive, salmi, goulash, fricassee, bouillabaisse, mulligan (sl.).

STEW, v. Cook by simmering or slow boiling, seethe, simmer, fricassee.

STEWARD, n. 1. One who manages another's property or financial affairs, administrator of another's affairs, agent, trustee, retainer, treasurer, deputy, landlord, functionary, comptroller, controller, executor, attorney, representative, proctor (Law), procurator (Law).

2. One in charge of the household or personal affairs of another, chamberlain, seneschal, housekeeper, major-domo, maniple, butler, bailiff, castellan, valet, landreeve, matron, purveyor (Eng. Hist.), khansamah (India).

3. One in charge of table and servants, etc. (in a club, on shipboard, etc.), ship's attendant, purser, stewardess (fem.), caterer, waiter, provider, commissary, victualer, quartermaster, maître d'hôtel.

STICK, n. 1. Branch (cut or broken off), twig, shoot, long slender piece of wood, switch, birch, pole, bat, cudgel, bludgeon, spar, cue, bar, club, skewer, fagot, stake, stave, staff, shaft, cane, crook, alpenstock, baton, wand, rod.

2. Thrust with a pointed instrument, jab, poke, prick, puncture, cut, dig, lunge, stroke, bayonet, stab.

3. Stoppage, standstill, hitch, halt, obstruction, estoppal, quandary, interruption, check, stop, impediment, preclusion, limitation, disallowance, impedition, blockage, prohibition, constraint, proscription, repression, forbiddance, hindrance, retardation, embarrassment, disconcertion, puzzlement, dilemma, perplexity.

4. Something causing delay or difficulty, snag, obstacle, obstruction, hindrance, catch, impediment, mishap, mischance, contretemps, check, interruption, node, complication, curb, stay, stop, estoppal, intricacy, nodus, clog, paradox, barrier, hamper, drag, spoke, enigma, poser, problem, pinch, puzzle, nonplus, restraint, stumbling block or stone, grit in the oil, spoke in the wheel, halt, Gordian knot, holdback, difficulty, handicap,

restriction, embargo, trammel, constraint, oppilation, injunction.

5. Quality of adhering *or* causing things to adhere, stickiness, adherence, viscosity, adhesion, cohesion, spissitude, mucosity, mucidness, viscousness, tenaciousness, gumminess, glutinousness, viscidity, adhesiveness, cohesiveness.

STICK, *v.* 1. Furnish with a stick *or* sticks for support *(as a plant)*, prop, stake, brace, secure, truss, hold up, tie up, bolster, shore up.

2. Pierce with a pointed instrument, puncture, stab, perforate, transfix, gore, spear, impale, penetrate, bore, drill, foraminate, terebrate, pink, spit, transpierce, spike, punch.

3. Thrust *(something)* in (through *or* into a place *or* position indicated), jab, poke, set, infix, insert, lunge, fix, arrange, station, dispose, reposit, ensconce, locate, establish, deposit, situate, rest, stand, install, plant, lodge, lay, settle, commit.

4. Fasten in position by *or* as by something thrust through, pin, nail, tack, fix, impale, screw, affix, attach.

5. Fasten by causing to adhere, attach, affix, join, bind, fuse, weld, paste, glue, cement, seal.

6. Bring to a stand, render unable to proceed *or* go back, inhibit, hold, hinder, obstruct, check, checkmate, curb, detain, restrain, counteract, impede, bar, bind, imprison, constrain, hobble, trammel, shackle, thwart, frustrate, scotch, balk, enthrall, pen, immure, impound, block, stop, incommode, discommode, hamper, hogtie.

7. Become fastened (hindered, checked, *etc.*) by an obstruction, be at a standstill, cease, stall, stop, vegetate, stagnate, swim against the current *or* stream, be tangled *or* snarled, hit a snag, struggle, beat about, flounder, grope, lose one's way, not know which way to turn.

8. Remain attached, hold, cleave, cling, cohere, adhere, remain persistently *or* permanently, clasp, grip, grasp, fuse, congeal, amalgamate, harden.

9. *(Fol. by* TO *or* AT) Remain firm, hold faithfully, continue, persevere, keep steadily *or* unremittingly at, be faithful, be true, be firm, be constant, abide, persist, endure, carry on, last, peg away (along, on, *etc.*), plug *(coll.)*, bear up, plod, grind, drudge, hammer, drive, keep doggedly at, not give up, see it through *(coll.)*, repeat, grub.

10. *(Usually fol. by* AT) Be embarrassed *or* puzzled, hesitate, scruple, demur, question, pause, be reluctant, waver, stickle, doubt, falter, hang back, shy at, be confused, boggle, debate, shilly-shally, tergiversate, alternate, ponder, recoil, shrink, vacillate, fluctuate, shift, equivocate, balk, deliberate, dillydally, think twice, straddle the fence.

11. *(Fol. by* THROUGH, FROM, OUT, UP, *etc.)* Be thrust, extend, project, protrude, stand, jut, bulge, shoot, peep, nodulate, bilge, bouge, pout, swell, arch, push, impend, beetle, hang, overhang, protuberate, concamerate.

STICKER, *n.* 1. One who *or* that which sticks, persistent *or* diligent person, adherer, adherent, follower, leech, bulldog, plodder, toiler, ant, bee, slave, hack, drudge, plugger *(coll)*.

2. Adhesive label, tag, seal, plaster.

3. Bur, thorn, bramble, prickle, cocklebur, brier.

STICKLE, *v.* 1. Argue insistently *(esp. on trivial matters)*, haggle, higgle, dispute, quibble, bargain, altercate, hold out, stand out, make a point *or* an issue of, beat down, have the last word, insist,

not yield an inch, contend, contest, cavil, chaffer, prevaricate.

2. Raise objections, scruple, demur, stick, shift, waver, doubt, be skeptical, shrink, be afraid, hold back, be reluctant, boggle, be unwilling, not care to, rather not, grudge, begrudge, shy, fight shy of, refuse, duck, dissent, oppose, protest, resist, reluct, withstand, defy, contradict.

STICKLER, *n.* 1. *(Fol. by* FOR) Person who insists on something unyieldingly, contender, bigot, dogmatist, martinet, precisian, opinionist, higgler, haggler, zealot, disciplinarian, positivist, intransigent, energumen, monomaniac, devotee, fanatic, enthusiast, bug *(sl.)*, nut *(sl.)*, infatuate, crank *(coll.)*.

2. Puzzling *or* difficult problem, enigma, node, mystery, puzzle, arcanum, dilemma, hard nut to crack, knotty point, vexed question, poser, riddle, conundrum, paradox, nodus, Gordian knot, floorer *(coll.)*, sticker *(coll.)*, Asian mystery, riddle of the Sphinx, staggerer *(coll.)*, tough proposition *(sl.)*, stumper.

STICKY, *adj.* 1. Adhering, adhesive, gluey, ropy, viscid, viscous, gummy, adherent, juicy, watery, sweaty, viscose, viscoid, mucid, tenacious, tacky, glutinous, clinging, mucilaginous, clingy, pasty, clammy, smeary, cementitious, muculent, gelatinous, squashy, starchy, gooey *(sl.)*, doughy, dauby, cledgy, stringy, cohesive, agglutinative.

2. *(Of the weather)* Humid, dank, damp, wet, moist, madid, moisty, muggy, misty, vaporous, clammy, rainy.

STIFF, *adj.* 1. Firm in substance, rigid, inflexible, stark, set, fixed, unyielding, unbending, inelastic, unlimber, impliable, immobile, tense, crisp, brittle, inductile, unpliant, unpliable, congealed, ossified, petrified, hard.

2. Blowing strongly (violently *or* with steady force), fresh, spanking, vigorous, steady, pounding, keen, brisk, intense, persistent, gusty, raging, howling.

3. Firm in purpose *or* resolution, unyielding, stubborn, obstinate, pertinacious, strong, serious, tenacious, persevering, constant, earnest, decided, peremptory, unfaltering, unswerving, unflinching, unhesitating, steadfast, fixed, settled, stern, grim, stanch, inexorable, relentless, indomitable, iron, irrevocable, intransigent, uncompromising, game, steeled, strong-willed, strong-minded, mettlesome, persistent, dogged, steady, undaunted, sedulous.

4. Stubbornly maintained, brave, courageous, determined, resolute, dogged, valiant, ferocious, steadfast, unshrinking, unflinching, unfaltering, unshaken, resolved, against odds, strong, constant, fixed, settled, steady, durable, enduring, intense.

5. Rigidly formal, dignified, priggish, wooden, cold, distant, aloof, stilted, prim, ceremonious, constrained, chilling, frigid, haughty, prudish, unnatural, conventional, stately, starch, precise, punctilious, fastidious, overscrupulous, squeamish, strict, accurate, meticulous, rigorous in adherence, obdurate, finicky, finicking, cool.

6. Inelegant, lacking ease and grace, awkward, excessively regular, wooden, harsh, cramped, severe, graceless, abrupt, crude, austere, plain, bare, spare, stilted, pedantic, cold, homely, labored, forced, affected, mannered, artificial, halting, ungainly, clumsy.

7. Laborious *(as a task)*, difficult, severe, tough, hard, exacting, trying, stern, cruel, rigorous, stringent, toilsome, racking, afflictive, distressing, excruciating, agonizing, painful, sore, grievous,

sharp, harsh, ruthless, unsparing, heavy, inexorable, merciless, exigent, unreasonable, inhuman, strict, unpleasant, stark, Spartan, despotic, insupportable, tyrannical, grinding, noxious, unbearable, extortionate, abusive, cold-blooded, Draconian, coercive, torturous, brutal, punitive, oppressive, peremptory, poignant, intolerable.

8. Severe *(as a penalty)*, rigorous, strict, acute, stringent, positive, austere, uncompromising, hard, inexorable, harsh, absolute, extreme, drastic, unsparing, galling, violent, heavy, ruthless, pitiless, sharp, fearful, formidable, awful, sore, grievous, cruel, supreme, afflictive, bitter, merciless, baleful, despotic, brutal, punitive, mortal, extortionate.

9. Unusually high *or* great *(as a price, demand, etc.)*, exorbitant, excessive, unwarranted, heavy, immoderate, extravagant, undue, fancy, inordinate, unchristian *(coll.: hyperbolical)*, steep *(coll.)*.

10. Relatively firm in consistence, dense, thick, tenacious, compact, inspissated, close, compressed, solid, hard, heavy, grumous, clotted, viscid, viscous, viscose, solidified, gelatinous, jellied.

STIFFEN, *v.* Make *or* become stiff, harden, clot, callous, indurate, petrify, lapidify, temper, fossilize, vitrify, glacify, solidify, ossify, hornify, cornify, concrete, cement, set, fix, gell, gelatinize, inspissate, incrassate, coagulate, congeal, thicken, densify, compact.

STIFF-NECKED, *adj.* Stubborn, obstinate, perverse, refractory, mulish, dogged, obdurate, contumacious, unruly, bigoted, arbitrary, intractable, cross-grained, headstrong, unmanageable, unyielding, unreasonable, self-willed, disobedient, ungovernable, recalcitrant, cantankerous, incoercible, fractious, factious, obstreperous, balky, defiant, lawless, restive, insubordinate, opposing, willful, renitent, resistant, repugnant, oppugnant, contrary, pigheaded, bullheaded, rebellious, antagonistic, pervicacious.

STIFLE, *v.* 1. Kill by impeding respiration, smother, throttle, burke, garrote, choke, strangle, suffocate.

2. Keep back, repress, still, hush, silence, restrain, mask, subdue, drown, throttle, smother, conceal, gag, muffle, muzzle, withhold, keep to oneself, reserve, stop, choke off, deaden, mute, suppress, soften, soft-pedal.

3. Suppress, crush, stop, check, quell, put down, snuff out, restrain, annihilate, squelch, quench, destroy, extinguish, nip in the bud, hold, bar, arrest, inhibit, put a stop to, constrain, prevent, balk, circumscribe, obstruct, choke, control, block, frustrate, thwart, break up, confute.

4. Become stifled *or* suffocated, suffer from difficulty in breathing, smother, gag, gasp for air, be breathless, suffocate.

STIGMA, *n.* 1. Mark of disgrace *or* infamy, reproach *(as on one's reputation)*, stain, blot, dishonor, shame, slur, badge, blotch, flaw, taint, tarnish, blemish, brand, infamy, defect, imputation, smudge, smirch, smutch, soil, defect, fault.

2. Characteristic mark *or* sign of defect (degeneration, disease, *etc.*), discoloration, maculation, macula, macule, spot, blotch, taint, mole, blemish, freckle, bruise, lentigo *(Med.)*.

STIGMATIZE, *v.* 1. Mark with a stigma *or* brand, tattoo, blemish, mar, blot, blotch, deface, docket, tag, ticket, label, score.

2. Set a mark of disgrace *or* infamy upon, slur, post, hold up to shame, expose, reproach, disgrace, maledict, vilify, dishonor, brand, defame, dis-

credit, gibbet, boycott, black-list, **denounce,** curse, imprecate, damn, execrate, confound, blackball, disbar, unfrock, mark, abuse, exprobrate, implicate, accuse, slander, blacken, libel, calumniate, disparage, denigrate.

STILETTO, *n.* 1. Dagger having a narrow blade, dirk, stylet, poniard, blade, creese, kris, skean, baselard, steel, knife, *katar (India)*.

2. Bodkin, small sharp pointed instrument used in needlework, perforator, piercer, punch, puncher, stylet, needle, pin, eyeleteer, puncheon *(in goldsmith work)*.

STILL, *adj.* 1. Remaining at rest *or* in place, motionless, stationary, stable, static, at rest, quiescent, passive, stagnant, inactive, reposing, resting, abeyant, suspended, slumbering, idle, inert, sedentary, becalmed, unstirring, unmoving, dormant, undisturbed, immobile, fixed, dead, lifeless.

2. Free from sound *or* noise, silent, noiseless, mute, mum, toneless, deathlike, echoless, soundless, quiet, awful, solemn, hushed, nonvocal, dumb, voiceless, speechless, tongueless, muffled, stifled, calm, unvocal.

3. Subdued in sound, low, hushed, **gentle,** silent, inaudible, whispering, mild, muffled, stifled, muted, dampened, quiet, soft, dim, feeble, weak, noiseless, faint, dulcet, susurrant, whispered, barely audible, softened, murmured, stilly *(Poetic)*.

4. Free from commotion, quiet, tranquil, calm, peaceful, placid, stable, pacific, untroubled, undisturbed, serene, unruffled, quiescent, harmonious, easeful, halcyon, mild, peaceable, restful, orderly, reposeful.

5. Without waves *or* perceptible **current,** smooth, calm, quiet, quiescent, unruffled, untroubled, tranquil, peaceful, stagnant, halcyon, standing, unstirring.

STILL, *adv.* 1. At this *or* that time, up to this *or* that time, as previously, yet, to this *or* the present day, as yet, until now, even now.

2. In the future as in the past, subsequently, forever, evermore, even then, always, continuing on, everlastingly.

3. *(With comparatives or the like)* Yet, even, ever.

4. Even then, yet, nevertheless, despite all, notwithstanding, regardless, all the same.

STILL, *conj.* But yet, and yet, nevertheless, however, even so, notwithstanding, regardless, for all that, in any event *or* case, nonetheless.

STILL, *v.* 1. Silence, hush, lull, stifle, muffle, deaden, soft-pedal, render mute, stop one's mouth, drown the voice, cut one short, deafen, choke off, throttle, suppress, muzzle, gag.

2. Calm, appease, allay, soothe, silence, lull, quiet, compose, tranquilize, quell, mitigate, settle, palliate, propitiate, assuage, becalm, smooth over, put at rest, reconcile, pacify, relieve, curb, check, lessen, slacken, slake, abate, temper, moderate, soften, modulate, stay, control, blunt, ease, alleviate, lighten.

STILT, *n.* High post underneath structure *(above land or over water)*, support, supporter, brace, post, prop, shaft, shank, stalk, skeleton, scaffold *(pl.)*, framework *(pl.)*, foundation *(pl.)*, trestle *(pl.)*, pile, piling.

STILTED, *adj.* Stiffly dignified *or* formal, pedantic, pompous, inelegant, lacking ease and grace, awkward, wooden, excessively regular, harsh, cramped, severe, graceless, abrupt, crude, austere, plain, bare, spare, cold, forced, labored, affected, mannered, artificial, rigid, priggish, distant, aloof, prim, ceremonious, constrained, chilling, frigid, prudish, unnatural, stately, starched, precise, strict, fastidious, meticulous, rigorous.

STIMULANT, *n.* 1. *(Physiol., Med.)* Stimulating medicine, cordial, tonic, bracer *(coll.),* energizer, excitant *(Physiol.),* pickup *(sl.),* roborant *(Med.).*

2. Alcoholic liquor *or* beverage, intoxicant, spirits, inebriant, the bottle, the cup.

STIMULATE, *v.* Rouse to action *or* effort, prompt, spur on, move, incite, set on, goad, hustle, actuate, instigate, prick, force, inspire, press, hound, dispose, urge, tempt, stir, influence, excite, alert, inspirit, arouse, propel, impel, drive, forward, animate, provoke, electrify, sharpen, activate, egg on, nettle, invigorate, initiate, sting, vivify, jog, irritate, enkindle, hearten, wake, fan, inflame, foment, awaken, encourage.

STIMULUS, *n.* 1. Something that incites to action *or* exertion *or* quickens action (feeling, thought, *etc.),* incentive, provocation, fillip, spur, goad, incitement, motive, inducement, encouragement, excitement, lash, whet, whip, impulse, impetus, prick, sting, motivation.

2. *(Physiol.)* Something that excites an organism *or* part to functionable activity, stimulant, tonic, cordial, bracer *(coll.),* pickup *(sl.),* excitant *(Physiol.),* energizer, roborant *(Med.).*

STING, *n.* 1. Wound caused by stinging, hurt, smart, prickle, tingling, pain, tingle, sore, burn, bite, nip, pinch, paresthesia *(Med.).*

2. Anything *or* an element in anything that wounds (pains, irritates), capacity to wound *or* pain, barb, thorn, bane, bite, rub, irritation, gall, poison, venom, worm, canker, scourge, fang, grievance, nuisance, pest, vexation, blow, cut, offense, shock, fret, mortification, annoyance, woe, curse, affliction, stroke, blight, fly in the ointment, wormwood, bitter cup, bitter draft, tribulation, trial, bitterness, oppression, cross, load, burden, bitter pill.

3. Sharp stimulus *or* incitement, goad, prick, *etc. (See* STIMULUS, *n.* 1., *above.)*

STING, *v.* 1. Prick, affect painfully *or* irritatingly, wound with a sharp organ *or* part, stab, afflict, penetrate, nip, bite, burn, hurt, nettle, pierce, be pungent, chafe, irritate.

2. Pain sharply, wound, hurt, cut to the quick, rack, wring, affect with acute mental pain, rasp, grate, provoke, pique, agonize, harrow, kindle wrath, anger, incense, inflame, vex, roil, nettle, irritate, torture, torment, lash into a fury, gripe, grind, gnaw, fret, madden, infuriate, stir the blood, make one's blood boil, gall.

3. Drive *(as by sharp irritation),* provoke, goad, impel, nettle, prick, irritate, stir up, arouse, awaken, instigate, elicit, kindle, fan, fire, spur, foment, prompt, propel, motivate, actuate, exacerbate, excite, inflame, pierce, intoxicate, affect, shake, shock, move, quicken, sharpen, lash, whip, compel, electrify, work up, egg on, force, infect, impassion, disturb.

4. Feel a smarting pain, smart, burn, writhe, itch, prick, tingle, shoot, wince, twinge.

STINGY, *adj.* 1. Reluctant to give *or* spend, penurious, niggardly, parsimonious, close, mean, sordid, miserly, tight *(coll.),* close-fisted, pinching, chary, mercenary, sparing, frugal, illiberal, money-grubbing, grasping, cheeseparing, grudging, covetous, avaricious, greedy, beggarly, churlish, un-

generous, shabby, scrimping, selfish, small, paltry, usurious, stinting, rapacious, extortionate.

2. Scanty, meager, scant, slender, scrimpy, modest, sparse, small, lean, few and far between, insufficient, inadequate, thin, light.

STINK, *n.* Strong offensive smell, stench, fetor, bad smell, effluvium, unpleasant odor, funk *(sl.),* redolence, exhalation, emanation, pollution, fetidness, reek, malodor, graveolence, miasma, mephitis, nidorosity, empyreuma *(Chem.).*

STINK, *v.* 1. Emit a strong offensive smell, reek, smell to heaven *or* high heaven, effluviate, be malodorous, offend the nostrils, funk *(sl.).*

2. Be in extremely bad repute *or* disfavor, be in disrepute, have a bad name, lose caste, incur disgrace, seal one's infamy, forfeit one's good opinion, stoop, derogate.

STINT, *n.* 1. Limitation *(esp. as to amount),* restriction, scarity, dearth, restraint, bound, paucity, scantness, shortage, bar, heck, curb, limit, halt, stricture, stoppage, constriction, modification, control.

2. Limited *or* prescribed quantity (share, rate, *etc.),* quota, ration, proportion, portion, stock, lot, dose, measure, allowance, meed, allotment, provision, mess, part, piece, pittance, ratio, modicum, helping, dividend, division, dotation, endowment, percentage, cut *(coll.),* commission, consignment, whack *(sl.),* rake-off *(sl.).*

3. Quantity assigned, allotted portion *or* piece of work, job, quota, task, batch, proportion, assignment, allotment, share, part, division, consignment.

STINT, *v.* 1. Limit to a certain amount (number, share, allowance), bind, bound, set limits to, restrict, restrain, confine, delimit, delimitate, define, circumscribe, fix, check, bar, specify, proscribe, constrain, curb, prohibit, inhibit.

2. Deny oneself, get along on a scanty allowance, scrimp, save, gripe, pinch pennies, be parsimonious, hold back, withhold, economize, sacrifice, grub, live on nothing.

STIPEND, *n.* Fixed *or* regular pay, salary, periodic payment *(as a pension),* hire, wages, income, remuneration, recompense, emolument, allowance, earnings, honorarium.

STIPPLE, *v.* Paint *or* draw by means of dots *or* small touches, dapple, dot, dab, daub, spatter, engrave, fleck, speck, sprinkle, etch, mottle, spot, speckle, bespeckle, bespot, maculate.

STIPULATE, *v.* 1. Make express demand *or* arrangement for, specify in terms of agreement, require as an essential condition, condition, bargain, contend for, stickle for, insist upon, make a point of, petition, negotiate, settle, arrange, propose, name, state, offer, outline, cite, present, compact, designate.

2. Promise, provide, agree, contract, engage, covenant, accept as terms, afford, grant, accord, pledge, render, guarantee, undertake, offer, give, allow, certify, specify, insure, assure, vouch, become bound to, warrant, arrange, underwrite, concur, assent, indent.

STIPULATION, *n.* Condition in an agreement *or* contract, specification, obligation, indenture, pact, provision, term, proviso, arrangement, convention, concordat, covenant, engagement, agreement, contract, article, promise.

STIR, *n.* 1. Act of stirring *or* moving *(or the sound made),* shake, quiver, tremor, whisper, breath, rustle, murmur, sigh, undertone, susurration, shudder, shiver, tremble, quake, activity, motion, movement, flicker, flutter, throb, palpitation, pulsation, pinfall, twitching, quaver, hum, buzz.

2. Brisk *or* busy movement, hustle, bustle, hurry, ado, flurry, fuss, fidget, pother, agitation, to-do *(coll.)*, fluster, perturbation, ferment, whirl, flutter.

3. Occasion of general excitement, disorder, commotion, turmoil, tumult, bustle, agitation, confusion, flurry, ado, activity, to-do *(coll.)*, uproar, convulsion, storm, perturbation, fomentation, outbreak, burst, upheaval, eruption, outburst, squall, turbulence, furor, violence, ferment, heaving, ebullition, clash.

4. Mental impulse (feeling, sensation), stirring, awakening, response, emotion, inspiration, susceptibility, life, spirit, thrill, impression, stimulation, kindling, excitement, excitation, calling forth, upsurge, passion, coming to life *or* alive.

STIR, *v.* 1. Move *(as by passing an implement continuously through),* set in motion, combine, fuse, scramble, commix, mix, immix, intermix, blend, intermingle, mingle, merge, immingle, commingle.

2. Move in some slight way, disturb oneself, act, attempt, offer, make an effort, trouble oneself, budge, be bothered, exert oneself.

3. Set in tremulous (fluttering *or* irregular) motion, shake, rustle, agitate, cause to quiver *or* shiver, jiggle, make to quake *or* quaver, rock, jog, joggle, cause to dance (flicker, twitch), ruffle, rouse, convulse, disturb, animate, vibrate.

4. Be active, be in motion, move briskly, hustle, bustle, bestir, whirl, flutter, scramble, step lively *(coll.),* lay about one, keep moving, keep on, hasten, speed, rush, scurry, scamper, dart to and fro.

5. *(Often fol. by* UP) Rouse from inactivity (quiet, contentment, indifference, *etc.),* move, budge, goad, prod, jog, instigate, transfer, transport, awaken, propel, animate, drive, shove, stimulate, force, whip, boost, arouse, wake, waken, awake, actuate, forward, push, set in motion, motivate, jostle, hustle, prompt, start.

6. *(Often fol. by* UP) Instigate, incite, prompt, spur, set on, agitate, bestir, foment, stimulate, animate, provoke, rouse, arouse, excite, awaken, quicken, goad, pique, inspire, promote, kindle, fire, electrify, actuate, whip, lash, impel, inflame, drive, encourage, start, poke, precipitate, catapult, speed, jolt, vivify, energize.

7. Affect strongly, excite, touch, cause to respond, move, arouse, disturb, trouble, infect, impassion, set on fire, motivate, perturb, inspirit, impel, inspire, smite, strike, stimulate, impress, quicken, animate, interest, work up, provoke, act upon, set astir, upset, jar, jolt, shake, disquiet, agitate, foment, fan, play on the feelings, sharpen, whet, discompose, startle, stagger, galvanize, electrify, shock, kindle, enkindle, incite.

8. Be in circulation *or* current, be afoot, pass from mouth to mouth, come out, issue, have currency, be public, get about *or* abroad, spread, pass current, go (fly, buzz, blow) about, circulate, be published.

STIRRING, *adj.* 1. That stirs, moving, active, astir, bustling, lively, excited, alive, spirited, energetic, animated, quick, vivacious, brisk, alert, vigorous, nimble, sprightly, up and doing *(coll.),* busy, on the run, engaged, employed, occupied, peppy *(sl.),* snappy *(coll.),* on the move, on one's toes, on the hop *or* jump.

2. Rousing, exciting, thrilling, eventful, momentous, grand, great, august, noble, special, swelling, telling, conspicuous, signal, outstanding, commanding, impressive, provocative, extraordinary, imposing, sensational, electric, galvanic, stimulating.

STITCH, *n.* 1. Single loop *or* portion of thread *(as in sewing, knitting, crocheting, etc.),* link, suture *(Surg.).*

2. Thread *or* bit of fabric *or* of clothing, *etc.,* piece, article, particle, tatter, shred, scrap.

3. Sudden sharp pain *(esp. in the intercostal muscles),* pang, twitch, tingle, shoot, twinge, kink, crick.

STITCH, *v.* Join *or* fasten with stitches, ornament with stitches, embroider, staple *(as cartons),* lace, baste, tack, attach, seam, secure, bind.

STOCK, *adj.* 1. Kept regularly on hand *(as for use or sale),* standard, permanent, staple, basic, merchantable, salable, vendible, marketable, essential, in demand, popular.

2. Of the common *or* ordinary type, commonplace, in common use, trite, stale, usual, hackneyed, mediocre, worn-out, common, threadbare, prosaic, tame, familiar, banal, monotonous, prosy, pedestrian, matter-of-fact, general, tedious, humdrum, platitudinous, homely, stereotyped, oft-repeated, unimaginative, dry, sober, unvaried, uninteresting.

STOCK, *n.* 1. Aggregate of goods kept on hand *(as by a merchant, for sale),* quantity of goods, merchandise, store, wares, produce, assets, goods, inventory, effects, assortment, stock in trade, capital, staples, commodities, investment.

2. Quantity of something accumulated *(as for future use),* stock pile, hoard, fund, reserve, supply, store, provision, cache, accumulation, backlog, savings, nest egg, reservoir.

3. Livestock, animals kept for use on a farm *or* ranch, domestic animals, cattle, herd.

4. Trunk *(of a tree or other plant),* stalk, main stem, axis, petiole *(Bot.),* peduncle *(Bot.),* pedicle *(Bot.),* culm, spire, caulicle *(Bot.),* spear, shaft, cane, caulis *(Bot.),* caudex *(Bot.),* tigella *(Bot.),* haulm *(Bot.),* gynophore *(Bot.),* funicle *(Bot.).*

5. Race, lineage, line of descent, ethnic group, tribe, nationality, descent, house, parentage, pedigree, ancestry, strain, breed, progeniture, heredity, clan, sept, people, birth, genealogy, extraction, family tree, root, blood, trunk, dynasty, stirps, caste, stem, gens *(Rom. Hist.).*

6. Type from which animals *or* plants have been derived, person from whom a given line of descent is derived, progenitor, origin, prototype, original, ancestor, source, first, patriarch, founder, father, forefather, grandfather, forebear, primogenitor, elder.

7. Handle *(of an instrument),* haft, butt, hilt, lug, bail, hold, helve, shank, grasp, shaft, withe, pull.

8. Dull *or* stupid person, dolt, dullard, loggerhead, simpleton, idiot, clod, lunkhead *(coll.),* lackwit, woodenhead, dunce, chowderhead *(coll.),* knucklehead *(coll.),* imbecile, numskull, incompetent, pigsconce, lack-brain, fool, zany, loon, clodpoll, lout, tyke, bumpkin, oaf, thickskull, goon, goof *(coll.),* looby, clodpate, ninny, dunderhead, jackass, ignoramus, blunderhead.

9. Something lifeless *or* senseless, corpse, body, carcass, cadaver, stump, block, log, pole, remains, stiff *(sl.),* wood.

10. Main upright part of anything, pillar, post, stake, block, shaft, shank, pin, pile, rod, upright, column, standard.

11. Raw material from which anything is made, substance, newsprint, staple, stuff, fabric, broth, bouillon.

12. Collar fitting like a band about the neck, cravat, neckpiece, neckcloth, neckerchief, neckband, scarf, choker (coll.).

STOCK, v. 1. Furnish with a stock or supply, keep in stock, handle, sell, store, supply, provide, furnish, produce, offer, put or place at one's disposal, afford, fit out, equip, gear, appoint, accouter, provision.

2. Lay in a stock of, lay up in store (as for future use), accumulate, hoard, save, reserve, garner, reposit, lay by, treasure up, set apart, keep, hold, conserve, amass, heap up, retain, husband, put away, feather one's nest, provide for a rainy day, stow away, cache, stash (sl.), salt down or away (coll.).

STOCKADE, n. Enclosure of posts and stakes, pen, fortification, fence, defense, barrier, paling, rampart, bulwark, muniment, corral, palisade, compound, fold, barricade, vallation (Fort.).

STOCKADE, v. Protect or encompass with a stockade, fortify, defend, enclose, safeguard, shelter, secure, hedge round, bulwark, dike, garrison, ring, compass, circumscribe, encompass, environ, wall in.

STOCKING, n. Close-fitting covering for foot and leg (or something resembling this), hose, sock, hosiery (pl.).

STOCK-STILL, adj. Motionless, perfectly still, stone-still, static, stagnant, inactive, stationary, dormant, lifeless, immobile, fixed, dead, unmoving, unstirring, becalmed, slumbering, reposing, resting, suspended, abeyant, statuelike, still as a statue (post, mouse), still or calm as death.

STOCKY, adj. Of solid and sturdy form or build, squat, thick-set, stout, plump, stubby, dumpy, chubby, pudgy, squatty, squab, stumpy, heavy, chunky, bulky, fleshy, squabby, pursy, buxom, squattish, stodgy, rotund, stubbed, punchy (coll.), chumpy (coll.), tubby (coll.).

STODGY, adj. 1. Heavy, dull, uninteresting, tediously commonplace, dry, clumsy, infelicitous, prolix, humdrum, tiresome, dreary, tedious, wearisome, gross, lumbering, insipid, exanimate, soulless, without vivacity or interest, boring, laborious, monotonous, flat, torpid, dead, stagnant, prosy, prosaic, static, tumid, turgid, diffuse, pedantic, arid, tasteless, vapid, jejune, stupefying, benumbing, undiscerning, stolid, crass, elephantine, soporific.

2. Of a thick semisolid consistency, heavy (as food), dense, insufficiently raised or leavened, indigestible, solid, rich, flatulent, concentrated, compact, lumpy, fatty, greasy.

STOIC, n. One who maintains or affects the mental attitude required by the Stoics, man of iron, strong man, Indian, Spartan, pococurante.

STOICAL, adj. Characterized by calm or austere fortitude, impassive, repressing emotion, self-disciplined, enduring, meek, tolerant, unresisting, self-forgetful, self-abasing, disinterested, phlegmatic, unmoved, indifferent, patient, philosophic, unimpassioned, passionless, apathetic, imperturbable, placid, resigned, passive, forbearant, long-suffering, chastened, content, ascetical, dispassionate, undisturbed, unperturbed, untroubled, unstirred, unruffled, mild, clement, submissive.

STOICISM, n. Conduct conforming to the precepts of the Stoics, repression of emotion, self-disci-

pline, indifference to pleasure or pain, apathy, nonchalance, fortitude, sobriety, abstention, abstinence, abstemiousness.

STOKE, v. Tend (a fire or furnace), fuel, feed, coal, poke, stir up.

STOLID, adj. Not easily moved or stirred mentally, heavy, slow, impassive (as from dullness or stupidity), foolish, obtuse, oafish, half-witted, backward, doltish, lumpish, phlegmatic, sluggish, ponderous, leaden, dronish, lazy, drony, indolent, torpescent, torporific, bovine, elephantine, inert, lethargic, loutish, crass, sottish, dense, hebetate, hippopotamic, apathetic, supine, lymphatic, languid, otiose, hebetudinous, lumbering, undiscerning.

STOMACH, n. 1. Part of the body containing the stomach, abdomen, belly, crop, craw, maw, gizzard, paunch, tun, bay window (hum.), corporation (sl.), breadbasket (sl.), tummy (hum.), venter (Anat., Zool.), potbelly, rumen, ingluvies (Zool.), proventriculus (Zool.).

2. Appetite for food, hunger, keenness, relish, taste, edge of appetite or hunger, thirst, mouth-watering, torment of Tantalus.

3. Desire, inclination, liking, disposition, keenness, taste, lust, hunger, appetence, appetition, appetency, appetite, pleasure, fancy, proclivity, predilection, mind, temper, relish, propensity, bias, bent, like, humor, sympathy, weakness, leaning, affinity, attraction, partiality.

STOMACH, v. Endure, bear, tolerate, like, suffer, submit to, brook, abide, swallow, stand, put up with, be patient with, forgive, admit, countenance, excuse, pardon, understand, be content with, take, pocket the affront, resign oneself to, condone, disregard, let pass, pass over, blink or wink at, be indulgent, close or shut the eyes to, overlook, ignore, reconcile oneself to, allow for, make allowance for, bear with, permit, be lenient toward.

STOMACHIC, adj. 1. Of the stomach, gastric, abdominal, stomachal.

2. Beneficial to the stomach, exciting the action of the stomach, stimulating, sharpening the appetite, stomachal, cordial, tonic, salutary, bracing, roborant, corroborant, medicinal, wholesome, sanative, analeptic (Med.), alterative (Med.).

STONE, n. 1. Rock, pebble, cobble, cobblestone, gravel, flag, flagstone, crystal, flint, adamant, slab, curbstone, cornerstone, pavestone, coping stone, boulder, shale, concretion (Pathol.), whetstone, grindstone, monolith, megalith (Archeol.), calculus (Pathol.).

2. Precious stone, jewel, gem, brilliant, bijou, birthstone, ice (sl.), pivot (Watchmaking), bearing (Watchmaking).

3. Hard stonelike seed, pit, nut, kernel, endocarp (Bot.).

4. Gravestone, tombstone, monument, marker, shrine, memento, monolith, memorial, cenotaph, footstone, headstone, tablet, slab, shaft, obelisk.

STONE, v. 1 Throw stones at, pelt with stones, lapidate, hurl at or against, brickbat (coll.).

2. Face with stone, line with stone, provide or fit with stone, inlay, front, pave, floor.

3. Rub with or on a stone (as to sharpen, polish, smooth, etc.), whet, burnish, scour, smooth, emery, abrade, abrase, pumice, grind, grate.

4. Free from stones (as fruit), pit.

STONY, adj. 1. Full of or abounding in stones or rock, gravelly, pebbly, hard, uneven, coarse, rocky, craggy, rough, bumpy, jagged, rugged, broken.

2. Pertaining to or characteristic of stone, hard, impenetrable, inflexible, adamantine, flinty, rigid, unyielding, indurated, resistant, implastic, concrete, heavy, ossified, cement, impregnable, lapideous, stonelike, rocklike, lithoid, dense, marble, granite, petrified, fossilized, crystallized, rocky, osseous.

3. Unfeeling, merciless, obdurate, insensible, unkind, severe, exacting, untender, austere, unsympathetic, unyielding, callous, hard-hearted, reprobate, mean, close, harsh, remote, soulless, obtuse, untouched, unimpressible, unaccommodating, unstirred, cold, unemotional, passionless, unreasonable, implacable, unresponsive, cruel, frigid, indifferent, hostile, unkindled, inexorable, impervious, pitiless, insentient, chill, icy, unmoved, stern, forbidding, relentless, heartless, indurate, stoical, stolid, unconcerned, unsparing, flinty, steely, insensitive, deadened, inured, hardened, ruthless, bowelless, inclement, uncompassionate, brutal, unnatural, unaffected, uncaring, hardboiled (coll.), hard-shell (coll.), brazen, unbending, casehardened, bloodless, cold-blooded, cold-hearted, inhumane, inhuman.

4. Motionless or rigid, without expression (as the eyes or look), blank, wide, blind, empty, cold, cruel, vacant, vacuous, icy, unfeeling, heartless, emotionless, expressionless, frigid, unresponsive, hard, freezing, chilling, unkindled, disdainful, hateful, withering, unfriendly, scathing, chill, contemptuous, forbidding, flinty, adamantine, callous, hostile, untouched, unmoved, uncaring, antipathetic, unconcerned, indifferent, cold-blooded, cold-hearted.

5. Petrifying, unnerving, paralyzing, disabling, stunning, enervating, demoralizing, spellbinding, awful, deadening, stupefying, terrifying, frightful, frightening, freezing, blood-chilling, blood-curdling, fear-inspiring, disquieting, appalling, dismaying.

STOOL, n. 1. Seat for one (without arms or back), hassock, ottoman, taboret, footstool, cricket, camp stool, prie-dieu, faldstool.

2. Decoy duck or bird, stool pigeon, bait, lure.

3. Privy, commode, latrine, cloaca, water closet, toilet, outhouse, backhouse.

4. Mass of matter evacuated, dung, excrement, excreta, feces, ordure, movement, stercoration, feculence.

5. Window sill, window ledge.

STOOP, n. 1. Inclination, act of stooping, stooping position or carriage, bend, nod, bowing, droop, dip, tilt, sag, swag, curvature, prostration, curtsy, scrape, salaam, kneeling, lowering, genuflexion.

2. Descent from dignity or superiority, condescension, submission, debasement, self-abasement, deference, meekness, subservience, subjection, humility, forbearance, sufferance, obeisance, prostration, servility, resignation, lowliness, mortification.

3. Downward swoop, plunge, drop, dive, nose dive, dip, pounce.

4. Raised entrance platform with steps, porch, doorstep, steps, perron (Archit.).

STOOP, v. 1. Bend forward and downward, lean, bow, couch, crouch, droop, incline, nod, make obeisance, kneel, genuflect, prostrate oneself, scrape, salaam, curtsy, fall on one's knees, cower, cringe.

2. Carry the head and shoulders habitually bowed forward, slouch, be doubled up or over, lean forward, be round-shouldered.

3. Descend from one's level of dignity, condescend, deign, humble oneself, consent, concede, grant, bend, bow, bend the neck, succumb, prostrate oneself, resign, lower oneself, defer to, acquiesce, yield, submit, degrade oneself.

4. Swoop down, drop, fall, plunge, dip, dive, descend, bear down, pitch down, pounce.

STOP, n. 1. Cessation, arrest of movement, end, truce, halt, intermission, rest, stoppage, pause, suspension, discontinuation, interruption, stand, discontinuance, interlude, interval, respite, leaving off, recess, standstill, desistance, abeyance, break, letup (coll.), time out (coll.), lapse, wait, breathing-spell, spell, lull.

2. Stay, sojourn, temporary residence, rest, repose, visit, respite, stopover, residency, habitation, holiday, vacation, pause.

3. Place where vehicles halt, station, terminal, terminus, depot, layover, destination, stop-off, station house.

4. Blocking (as of a passage or way), obstruction, closing (as of a hole), filling up, check, closure, barricade, occlusion, blockage, stoppage, hindrance, constipation, infarction (Pathol.), embolism (Pathol.).

5. Plug, stopper, stopple, cork, wedge, valve, spill, spile, peg, tap, wad, spigot, bung, pledget, packing, stuffing, obstruction, dowel, tampon (Surg.), tampion, wadding, dossil (Surg.), tent (Surg.).

6. Hindrance, impediment, obstacle, barrier, bar, obstruction, ban, difficulty, curb, preclusion, block, disallowance, impedition, estoppal (Leg.), barricade, prohibition, dam, snag, catch, stoppage, balk, embargo, injunction, trammel, constraint, enjoining, barrage, retardment, cohibition, bridle, stopper, proscription, oppilation, restraint, restriction, repression, forbiddance, retardation, embarrassment, obstruent (chiefly Med.).

STOP, v. 1. Cease, desist, come to an end, conclude, leave off, discontinue, break off, forbear, pause, finish, terminate, close, expire, be all over, run its course, wind up (coll.), perfect, run out, quit, halt, stay, hold, drop, culminate, reach completion, come to a stand or standstill, crown, pass away, lapse, surcease, abandon, consummate, give over, shut up shop, call it a day (coll.), draw to a close, have done with, knock off (coll.), withdraw from, throw up, ring down the curtain.

2. Cause to cease, put an end to, silence, end, stay, quiet, quell, crush, destroy, put down, subdue, overpower, smash, abolish, stifle, rout, defeat, check, reduce, master, deal a deathblow to, discomfit, vanquish, overcome, overturn, upset, bring to naught, break the neck or back of, nip in the bud, make short work of, stamp or trample out, wipe out, prostrate, dissolve, dispel, dissipate, root up, disorganize, squelch (coll.), stanch, choke, stem.

3. Hinder, repress, restrain, interrupt, prevent, bar, stay, obstruct, suppress, scotch, nonplus, deter, check, arrest, preclude, stanch, block, stall, halt, hold, bring to a stand or standstill, stem, muzzle, cut short, hold back, detain, suspend, postpone, withhold, curb, rein in, keep in, retard, thwart, undermine, deadlock, checkmate, intermit, embarrass, frustrate, foil, clog, hamper, constrain, shackle, counteract, contravene, incommode, forbid.

4. Cut off, intercept, withhold, refuse, interrupt the flow of, put an end to, discontinue, suspend,

arrest, intermit, terminate, end, choke off, impede, prohibit, disallow, countermand, deny.

5. *(Often fol. by* UP) Close, obstruct, block, fill the hole *or* holes in, plug, cork, occlude, clog, render impassable, barricade, blockade, stanch, shut, caulk, stuff, dam, bung, cram, seal, ram, curb, throttle.

6. Halt, pause, come to a stand *or* standstill, rest, alight, stand, wait, linger, idle, falter, draw up, pull up, stall, cast anchor, become inactive, brake.

7. *(Fol. by* OFF), Halt for a brief stay, stop over, rest, dwell, remain, lodge, put up, tarry, linger, visit, abide, sojourn, take up quarters, repose, suspend one's journey.

STOPCOCK, *n.* Valve, cock, tap, spigot, turn valve, faucet, petcock.

STOPGAP, *n.* Temporary substitute, alternate, alternative, makeshift, temporary expedient, resort, resource, shift, apology, working proposition, *pis aller (Fr.),* jury mast *(Naut.).*

STOPOVER, *n.* Stopping in the course of a journey, stop-off, layover, encampment, halt, pause, respite, sojourn.

STOPPAGE, *n.* Cessation of activity, state of being stopped, blockage, hindrance, arrest, prevention, stay, shutdown, pause, suppression, delay, impediment, discontinuance, interruption, check, closure, intermission, suspension, leaving off, recess, stand, standstill, desistance, abeyance, break, lapse, lull, breathing-spell, wait, letup *(coll.),* time out *(coll.),* respite, end, truce.

STORAGE, *n.* 1. Capacity *or* space for storing, room, area, limit, content, accommodation, poundage, tonnage, roomage, stowage, tankage, roomstead.

2. Place where something is stored, storehouse, cache, depot *(Mil.),* warehouse, storeroom, store, cellar, depository, repository, reservoir, stock room, garner, granary, yard, vault, loft, silo, elevator, bank, coffer, closet, hold, magazine.

STORE, *n.* 1. Place where goods are kept for sale, shop, market, emporium, mart, establishment, booth, counter, stall, *magasin (Fr.), tienda (Sp.), bottega (It.), Laden (Ger.).*

2. Stock, supply, hoard, reserve, deposit, fund, wares, goods, assets, inventory, effects, assortment, stock in trade, capital, staples, commodities, stockpile, provision, cache, accumulation, backlog, savings, reservoir, nest egg.

3. State of being stored up *or* on hand, reserve, readiness, preparedness, preparation, inventory, service, use, stock, deposit, supply, availability.

4. Measure of esteem *or* regard, credence, value, estimation, credit, reliance, confidence, trust, faith, dependence.

5. Abundance, plenty, great quantity *or* number, overflow, luxuriance, copiousness, richness, plethora, satiety, full measure, much, riches, wealth, numerousness, plenteousness, prodigality, lavishness, array, legion, sufficiency, redundance, good *or* great deal, lot *or* lots *(coll.),* ocean *or* oceans, sea, world *or* worlds, volume, pack, mint, nimiety, flood, multitude, hoard, host, good supply, numbers, scores, multiplicity, plenitude, exuberance, fullness, opulence, superfluity, horn of plenty, cornucopia, enough and to spare, profusion, fertility, affluence, fund, luxury.

STORE, *v.* 1. Supply *(as for future use),* stock, furnish, provide, replenish, provision, accouter,

appoint, gear, equip, fit out, afford, produce, offer, put *or* place at one's disposal.

2. *(Often with* UP *or* AWAY) Save, garner, hoard, stow away, reserve, lay up *or* by, lay in, put away, lay aside, deposit, husband, treasure up, accumulate, amass, heap up, reposit, keep, hold, conserve, retain, feather one's nest, provide for a rainy day, cache, stash *(sl.),* salt down *or* away *(coll.).*

STOREHOUSE, *n.* Source of supply, repository, depot, depository, magazine, warehouse, cache, silo, arsenal, cellar, granary, garner, armory, stash *(sl.),* treasury, thesaurus, godown *(India and eastern Asia),* store, vault, bank, barn, coffer, locker, cyclopedia, encyclopedia.

STORIED, *adj.* 1. Recorded in history *or* story, celebrated, famed, famous, chronicled, renowned, well-known, honored, sung, epic, historic, Homeric, traditional, fabled, remembered, legendary, mythical.

2. Ornamented with designs representing historical (legendary, *etc.)* subjects, frescoed, pictured, depictive, illustrated.

3. Having stories *or* floors, leveled, layered, floored.

STORM, *n.* 1. Disturbance of normal atmospheric conditions, tempest, squall, gale, rough weather, violent wind, deluge, downpour, cloudburst, blow, flood, torrent, spout, whirlwind, blizzard, typhoon, tornado, hurricane.

2. Violent assault on a fortified place (strong position, *etc.),* attack, invasion, foray, sortie, raid, onset, onslaught, offense, charge, aggression, incursion, cannonade, bombardment, irruption, strafe, *Blitzkrieg (Ger.),* blitz *(coll.).*

3. Heavy discharge *or* descent of missiles *or* blows, *etc.,* rain, shower, deluge, barrage, salvo, broadside, explosion, volley, spray, cannonade, bombardment, fusillade.

4. Violent disturbance of affairs *(civil, political, domestic, etc.),* commotion, tumult, agitation, hubbub, turmoil, clamor, outbreak, outburst, insurrection, racket, turbulence, disorder, upheaval, pother, ado, to-do *(coll.),* altercation, ruckus, affray, violence, bustle, furor, fuss, uproar, stir, row, riot, quarrel, flurry, hullabaloo, fight, encounter, affair, contest, skirmish, fracas, conflict, tussle, scuffle, tilt, concussion, clash, brush, ruction, appulse, combat, bout, fray, set-to *(coll.),* jolt, imbroglio, struggle, passage of *or* at arms, scrap *(sl.),* fisticuffs, *mêlée (Fr.),* dogfight, embroilment.

5. Violent outburst *or* outbreak *(as of applause),* thunder, roar, passion, convulsion, tempest, peal, burst, eruption, explosion.

STORM, *v.* 1. Blow (rain, hail, snow, *etc)* violently, set in, squall, roar, bluster, blow great guns, rage, howl, wail, snarl, scream, whistle, sing in the shrouds, blow a gale.

2. Rage, complain with violence *or* fury, rave, rant, tear, riot, bluster, run riot *or* amuck, run wild, cut loose, go on a rampage, carry on, raise the roof, raise the devil, rampage, fume, raise Cain *or* Ned, lose one's temper, breathe fire and fury, foam at the mouth, boil, seethe, raise hell *or* Hail Columbia, flare up, become excited, burst into a passion, vent one's rage *or* spleen, thunder, fulminate, fly into a passion, fly off the handle *(sl.),* blow one's top *(sl.).*

3. Deliver a violent attack *or* fire, charge, assail, assault, attack heavily, bear down upon, rush, make an onslaught, invade, raid, make an

inroad, make an incursion, beset, strike, have at, fall upon, ride against, make a dash at, close upon, launch against, blitz *(coll.).*

4. Rush with violence, stamp, rush headlong, tear, tramp, strut, rage, stalk, flounce, stride, prance, bluster.

STORMY, *adj.* 1. Affected *or* characterized by *or* subject to storms, tempestuous, windy, turbulent, raging, blustering, gusty, squally, inclement, sleety, snowy, foul, rainy, rampaging, boisterous, dirty, howling, roaring, severe, rugged, wild, frenzied, bleak, exposed, raw, windswept, cyclonic.

2. Characterized by violent commotion (actions, speech, passions, *etc.*), raving, rampant, angry, frenzied, boisterous, mad, contentious, loud, fierce, disturbed, rampageous, violent, passionate, turbulent, riotous, wild, agitated, furious, blustering, vehement, intense, burning, impetuous, flaming, aroused, excited, fiery, desperate, feverish, inflamed, emotional, wrought up, foaming, disturbed, perturbed, kindled, boiling, raging, tempestuous, delirious, irascible, hot, excitable, choleric, irate, wrathful, quick, hot-headed, hot-blooded, hot-tempered, fractious, volcanic, explosive, inflammable, uncontrollable, ungovernable, quarrelsome.

STORY, *n.* 1. Narrative, tale, fiction, fable, account, plot, sketch, incident, legend, yarn, parable, allegory, anecdote, memoirs, biography, autobiography, recital, narration, recitation, rehearsal, epic, romance, novel, novelette, apologue, experiences, confessions, fortunes, adventures, life.

2. Report, account, statement, allegation, news article, news item, record, rumor, word, news, dispatch, aviso, information, intelligence, tidings, piece, copy, scoop *(Journalism sl.),* beat *(U.S. Journalism).*

3. Horizontal section of a building, layer, level, floor, tier.

STORYTELLER, *n.* One who tells stories, narrator, author, relator, raconteur, anecdotist, teller of tales, fabulist, fabler, spinner of yarns, word painter, littérateur, epic poet, writer, biographer, historian, sagaman, novelist, romancer, romancist.

STOUT, *adj.* 1. Large, corpulent, portly, bulky in figure, solidly built, thick-set, sturdy, rotund, round, full, plump, in good case, stocky, fat, obese, heavy, big, tubby, lusty, stalwart, brawny, well-built, substantial, fleshy, burly, strapping *(coll.).*

2. Bold, hardy, dauntless, intrepid, brave, daring, courageous, resolute, manly, virile, game, stout-hearted, austere, audacious, aweless, masculine, indomitable, enduring, unyielding, continuing, dogged, firm, spirited, unapprehensive, heroic, chivalric, soldierly, herolike, mettlesome, plucky, gallant, adventurous, enterprising, venturesome, doughty, lion-hearted, high-spirited, Spartan, fearless, resistant, confident, mighty, Roman, valorous, defiant, hard, unshrinking, unalarmed, unblenched, unappalled, high-mettled, undismayed, unflinching, stalwart, invincible, unabashed, dreadless, valiant, vigorous, gritty, formidable, powerful, spunky *(coll.),* potent, redoubtable *(usually in contempt or burlesque.).*

3. Stubborn, resolute, steadfast, undaunted, determined, earnest, firm, proud, obstinate, contumacious, stanch, stable, unshaken, resolved, faithful, unreserved, unhesitating, unwavering, pertinacious, persevering, zealous, true, unfaltering, unyielding, undeviating, stern, steady, inflexible, unswerving, constant, strong, serious, decided, not to be shaken, sedulous, untiring,

industrious, unflagging, enduring, grim, **patient,** plodding, indomitable, inexorable, settled, **fixed,** intransigent, gritty, persistent, relentless, strong-willed, uncompromising, tenacious, dedicated, devoted, unmoved.

4. Strong of body, hardy, sturdy, stalwart, strapping, sinewy, athletic, lusty, robust, vigorous, muscular, able-bodied, tough, powerful, brawny, enduring, rugged, inured, healthy, cast-iron, able, fresh, mighty, wiry, seasoned, in good case, burly, well, fit, leathery, in good condition, in fine fettle, capable of endurance, with bottom, stanch, flourishing, buxom, florid, youthful, staminal, puissant, beefy, resilient, husky *(coll.),* acclimatized, Herculean, Atlantean, solid, substantial, hefty *(coll.),* virile.

5. Strong in substance *or* construction, sound, firm, solid, hardy, sturdy, compact, durable, substantial, enduring, heavy, hard, tough, lasting.

STOVE, *n.* Apparatus for furnishing heat, heated chamber *or* box, range, heater, kiln, furnace, oven, forge, firebox, reverberatory.

STOW, *v.* 1. Put in a place *or* receptacle as for storage *or* reserve, hide, pack, store, load, stuff, crowd, tuck, wedge, hoard, secrete, closet, ensconce, conceal, cache, bury, reposit, deposit, garner, stash *(sl.),* salt down *or* away *(coll.).*

2. Afford room for, hold, contain, have capacity for, take in, bear, comprehend, enclose, include, carry, accommodate, compose, involve, incorporate, cover, encompass, retain, receive, admit.

STOWAGE, *n.* 1. Room *or* accommodation for stowing something, storage, capacity, room, area, limit, content, poundage, tonnage, roomage, tankage, roomstead.

2. Place in which something is *or* may be stowed, storage, storehouse, cache, depot *(Mil.),* warehouse, storeroom, store, cellar, depository, repository, reservoir, stockroom, garner, granary, yard, vault, loft, silo, elevator, bank, coffer, closet, hold, magazine.

3. That which is stowed *or* to be stowed, cargo, shipment, lading, haul, load, freight, baggage.

STRADDLE, *v.* Walk (stand, sit) with legs wide apart, stand *or* sit astride, ride, bestride, bestraddle.

STRAFE, *v.* Attack by airplanes with machine-gun fire, bombard heavily, assail with gunfire, mow down, spray, storm, open fire, snipe at, blitz, barrage, shell, cannonade, fusillade, pepper.

STRAGGLE, *v.* Stray from the road *or* course, wander about in scattered fashion, spread out, meander, rove, lag, ramble, range, roam, stroll, deviate, gad about, prowl, nomadize, digress, go astray, scatter, saunter, draggle, jaunt, peregrinate, drift, go adrift, vagabond.

STRAGGLY, *adj.* Straggling, unconnected, disorderly, rambling, roving, straying, wandering, strolling, zigzag, scattered, aimless, undirected, irregular, disorganized, loose, meandering, desultory, confused, careless, helter-skelter, scrambled, shapeless, casual, random, unmethodical, haphazard.

STRAIGHT, *adj.* 1. Without a bend (crook, curve), even, true, unbent, direct, the shortest possible, rectilinear, right, linear, undistorted, unturned, in a line, undeviating, unswerving, inflexible, plumb, vertical, straightaway, not curved, virgate.

2. Evenly formed *or* set, squared, square, rectangular, erect, upright, held high.

3. Without circumlocution, candid, direct, forth-

right, square, straightforward, definite, reliable, clear, blunt, frank, foursquare, true, indubitable, unambiguous, sure, unmistakable, unquestionable, unqualified, incontrovertible, incontestable, undeniable, unerring, irrefragable, certain, unequivocal, undisputed, inescapable, positive, irrefutable, unquestioned, evident, sound, unconfuted, plain, cogent, conclusive.

4. Honest, upright, honorable, straightforward, fair, just, equitable, impartial, disinterested, aboveboard, reputable, estimable, scrupulous, worthy, unbiased, lawful, licit, right, even-handed. fair and square, open and aboveboard, on the up-and-up (coll.), on the level (coll.), legitimate, according to agreement, faithful to contract, just as represented, free from tricks, creditable, reasonable, sound, faithful, reliable, trusty, ethical, conscientious, moral, decent, veracious, truthful, rightful.

5. Right (as reasoning, thinking, etc.), correct, sane, sound, accurate, true, veracious, knowing, rational, discriminative, sage, sagacious, reliable, level-headed, just, sober-minded, stable, well-advised, well-grounded, sapient, decisive, solid, convincing, dependable, trustworthy, sensible, good, sober.

6. In proper order or condition, orderly, neat, tidy, trim, disposed, classified, filed, regular, even, systematic, in sequence, spruce, uniform, formal, harmonious, shipshape, in place, consistent, proportioned, balanced, coördinate, in meaningful order, patterned, homogeneous, methodical, unconfused, symmetrical, cosmic, planned, designed, businesslike, tabular, arranged, constant.

7. Continuous, unbroken, successive, sequential, serial, uninterrupted, unintermitting, consecutive, sequent, succeeding, ensuing, incessant, ceaseless, unvarying, sustained, persistent.

8. Thoroughgoing, unreserved, outright, complete, total, entire, utter, downright, full, comprehensive, unqualified, unmitigated, absolute, consummate, out-and-out, sweeping, radical, thorough, sheer, veritable, dead, unconditional, undiminished, exhaustive, solid, undivided, perfect.

9. Unmodified, unaltered, undiluted, unmixed, pure, unadulterated, unrelieved, free from extraneous matter, uncontaminated, real, valid, clear, genuine, simple, homogeneous, sterling, undefiled, uninfected, unpolluted, expurgate, clean, unalloyed, unmingled, authentic, untainted, undisguised, uncorrupted, unsophisticated, unqualified.

STRAIGHT, adv. 1. In a straight line, in an even form or position, in alignment, evenly, straight as an arrow, straightaway, straightforwardly, to the mark, in a beeline, as the crow flies, directly.

2. Directly, immediately, right away, instantly, on the spot, forthwith, straightaway, at once, promptly, in no time, speedily, quickly, summarily, apace, before you can say "Jack Robinson," point-blank, without delay, pronto (sl.).

3. (Often fol. by OUT) Without circumlocution, directly, candidly, crudely, to the point, precisely, exactly, bluntly, square, abruptly, accurately.

4. Honestly, honorably, fairly, squarely (coll.), in all conscience, aboveboard, in or with good faith, bona fide, in earnest, on the level (coll.), on the square (coll.).

5. In a continuous course, consecutively, in unbroken succession, running, in turn, in a series, in file, at a stretch, step by step, gradually.

STRAIGHTEN, v. Make or become straight, unbend, rectify, align, adjust, correct, right, untangle, uncurl, unfold, square, regulate.

STRAIGHTFORWARD, adj. 1. Going or directed straight forward, open, artless, frank, steadfast, candid, honest, guileless, sincere, outspoken, steady, fixed, unflinching, direct, unwavering, undeviating, attentive, undistracted, intent, piercing, keen, searching, penetrating, clean-cut, plain-spoken, man-to-man, aboveboard.

2. Free from crookedness or deceit, honest, truthful, veracious, trustworthy, forthright, uncorrupt, honorable, fair, just, square, upright, straight, conscientious, even-handed, equitable, reputable, open, innocent, guileless, plain, candid, impartial, aboveboard, estimable, scrupulous, worthy, unbiased, lawful, licit, right, foursquare, ethical, moral, decent, rightful, on the level (coll.), legitimate, creditable, reasonable, on the up-and-up (coll.), sound, faithful, trusty.

3. Proceeding without roundaboutness, direct, straight, undeviating, even, true, unbent, rectilinear, right, linear, undistorted, unturned, in a line, unswerving, inflexible, plumb, vertical, straightaway, virgate.

STRAIGHTWAY, adv. At once, immediately, straight, forthwith, directly, promptly, instantly, without delay, on the spot, without further ado, in no time, speedily, quickly, summarily, apace, point-blank, pronto (sl.).

STRAIN, n. 1. Force tending to alter shape or cause fracture, etc., pressure, stress, tension, tensity, traction, pull, draw, haul, stretch, tautness, extension, distention, elongation, protraction.

2. Great effort, exertion, excessive striving, exaggeration, overstatement, stretch, hyperbole, magnification, excessiveness, immoderacy, inordinacy, embroidery, coloring, misrepresentation, absurdity, misstatement, distortion, falsification.

3. Injury to a muscle or tendon (due to excessive tension or use), sprain, injury to or deformation of any body or structure (caused by stress), wrench, twist.

4. Severe demand on resources (feelings, a person, etc.), extreme tension, stress, overexertion, burden, pressure, hardship, urgency, grind, pinch, exigency, insistence, obligation, affliction, trial, scourge, curse, rack, load, cross, care, infliction, agony, intensity, tenseness.

5. Flow of language or eloquence, etc., burst, deluge, torrent, stream, rush, outburst, passage, outpouring.

6. (Sing or pl.) Passage of music or poetry, lilt, song, air, melody, tune, measure, lay, descant, tone, phrase, period, verse, cadence, line, stanza.

7. Tone, style, spirit in expression, timbre, vein, nature, character, mood, cast, complexion, quality, essence, quintessence, characteristic, principle, embodiment, entity, reality, substance, elements, hypostasis, being, center, fundamentals, keynote, tenor, sense, significance, heart, pith, marrow, gist, kernel, core.

8. Body of descendants of a common ancestor, family, stock, offspring, children, young, lineage, progeny, issue, succession, successors, seed, posterity, tribe, progeniture, blood, race, people, nature, clan, line, dynasty, kindred, stirps.

9. Variety or group of a species (distinguished by some characteristic), kind, sort, type, race, breed, description.

10. Ancestry, descent, extraction, lineage, line, birth, derivation, parentage, progeniture, stock, heredity, clan, sept, people, genealogy, house, race, root, blood, trunk, family, breed, dynasty, stirps, caste, stem, gens (Rom. Hist.).

11. Hereditary *or* natural character, tendency, trait, characteristic, disposition, temper, grain, humor, frame, temperament, constitution, affection, vein, stripe, streak, tone, cast, animus, propensity, predisposition, turn, bias, warp, inclination, natural capacity, competence, genius.

12. Streak, trace, mark, sign, vestige, evidence, indication, manifestation.

STRAIN, *v.* 1. Stretch (*esp. to the utmost tension*), draw tight *or* taut, make tense *or* tight, tighten, put under tension, put in traction, extend, protract, distend, elongate.

2. Exert to the utmost, put to the utmost strength, rack (*the brain*), peel (*the eye*), cock (*the ear*), sharpen, whet, sensitize, intensify, key up, stir, refine, make sharp.

3. Impair by stretching *or* overexertion, weaken, injure, sprain, cause deformation in (*a body or structure*) by stress, wrench, overwork, overtax, overtask, overexert, tire, tax, task, fatigue, twist.

4. Stretch beyond the proper point *or* limit, push too far, pervert, overrate, overstep, exaggerate, overstate, overlay, overestimate, misrepresent, overesteem, think *or* make too much of, overdraw, overcharge, distort, falsify, hyperbolize, overprize, magnify, color, embroider.

5. Make excessive demands upon, force, tax, task, overtax, overburden, overstrain, overreach, burden, impose upon, push to the limit, make ineffectual, nullify, negate, run into the ground (*coll.*), overshoot, carry too far, overdraw.

6. Pass through a filter *or* sieve, filter, percolate, trickle, flow, ooze, screen, purify, drain, rack, pan, winnow, refine, sift, riddle, bolt, tammy, separate.

7. Clasp tightly (*in the arms, the hand, etc.*), squeeze, press, hug, embrace, fold closely, grasp, hold, enfold, envelop, lock, press, clutch, seize.

8. Pull forcibly, stretch (*muscles, nerves, etc.*) to the utmost, make violent physical efforts, try hard, tug, heave, struggle, ply, put forth one's strength, put forth a strong arm, huff and puff, trouble oneself, make a supreme effort.

9. Be subjected to tension *or* stress, suffer strain, overdo, struggle, overwork, overexert, grind, drudge, expend oneself prodigally, overfatigue, drive oneself, work day and night, burn the midnight oil, burn the candle at both ends, do double duty, work one's fingers to the bone, work like a dog, work like a horse *or* cart horse, work like a slave *or* galley slave.

STRAINED, *adj.* Affected, produced by effort, not natural *or* spontaneous, ponderous, forced, formal, stiff, high-sounding, pretentious, laborious, artificial, mannered, swelling, high-flown, grandiloquent, declamatory, pompous, big-sounding, bombastic, unctuous, canting, theatrical, insincere, ostentatious, flashy, pedantic, tartufian, extravagant, overdrawn, magniloquent, orotund, tumid, showy, rhapsodical, inflated, overwrought, high-colored, hyperbolic, flatulent, florid, magisterial, sententious, turgid, lofty, flamboyant, ornate.

STRAINER, *n.* Sieve, filter, sifter, bolter, screen, riddle, tamis, tammy, colander, searce, searcer, grate, grating, cribble.

STRAIT, *n.* 1. (*Often pl. with sing. sense*) Narrow passage of water (*connecting two large bodies of water*), narrows, gut, canal, inlet, channel, arm, sound.

2. (*Often pl.*) Position of difficulty *or* need, distress, pass, predicament, crisis, quandary, poverty, pinch, exigency, emergency, dilemma,

embarrassment, critical situation, plight, turn, complication, impasse, push, extremity, conjuncture, pickle (*coll.*), fix (*coll.*), hole (*coll.*), nonplus, hornet's nest, standstill, blind alley, cul-de-sac.

STRAITEN, *v.* 1. Put into difficulties (*esp. financial ones*), distress, perplex, put in a hole (*coll.*), involve, enmesh, entangle, pinch, embarrass, press, corner, drive to the wall, have on the ropes, reduce, fleece, pauperize, disconcert, impoverish, break, ruin, bankrupt.

2. Restrict in range (extent, amount, pecuniary means, *etc.*), circumscribe, limit, confine, constrain, constrict, proscribe, curb, trammel, lash, shackle, interdict, withhold, impede, repress, bridle, hobble, inhibit, deny, debar, prohibit, tie one's hands, check.

STRAITENED, *adj.* Restricted, difficult, badly *or* poorly off, needy, poor, limited, pinched, perplexed, distressed, poverty-stricken, indigent, reduced, stripped, penniless, impecunious, destitute, fleeced, impoverished, embarrassed, bankrupt, in debt, broke (*sl.*), hard up (*coll.*), under hatches, in want, in need, at the end of one's rope, put to one's shifts, on the edge *or* ragged edge, unable to keep the wolf from the door, unable to make both ends meet.

STRAIT-LACED, *adj.* Excessively strict in conduct *or* morality, puritanical, prudish, rigorous, formal, rigid, stiff, stern, austere, uncompromising, narrow, prim, ascetic, overscrupulous, arbitrary, sanctimonious, pietistic, hidebound, stiff-necked, bigoted, dogmatic, hyperorthodox, anchoritic, fanatical, tartufian, unctuous, pharisaical, precise, severe, stilted.

STRAND, *n.* 1. Number of yarns *or* threads forming part of a rope *or* cord, fiber, filament, rope, cord, string, line, inkle, cable, braid, twist, tress (*of hair*).

2. (*Poetic*) Land bordering the sea *or* ocean, shore, beach, bank, ground, coast, seashore, seacoast, littoral, margin of the sea, brink, brim, foreshore, loom of the land.

STRAND, *v.* 1. Run aground, be wrecked, be cast away, shipwreck, go aground, beach, ground, pile up (*coll.*).

2. Bring into a helpless position, desert, leave high and dry, abandon, reject, have done with, cast off, forsake, quit, turn one's back on, leave in the lurch, discard, drop, ostracize, forswear.

3. Form (*a rope, etc.*) by twisting strands, twist, interlace, intertwine, plait, braid, weave, intertwist, twine.

STRANGE, *adj.* 1. Unusual, extraordinary, curious, odd, queer, out of the ordinary, irregular, uncommon, outlandish, far-fetched, eccentric, singular, peculiar, anomalous, exceptional, rare, unaccountable, irrational, surprising, astonishing, erratic, startling, amazing, remarkable, wild, grotesque, unaccustomed, quaint, droll, bizarre, abnormal, unnatural, unique, out-of-the-way, unheard of, original, monstrous, fantastic, irrelevant, whimsical, insusitate, unwonted, aberrant, unconventional, fanciful, freakish.

2. Out of one's natural environment, ill-at-ease, uncomfortable, lost, overwhelmed, bewildered, baffled, mystified, nonplused, puzzled, confounded, uneasy, discomposed, confused, perplexed, disoriented.

3. Situated (belonging to *or* coming from) outside a particular locality, foreign, alien, new, exotic, remote, distant, external, outside, overseas,

outland, ulterior, barbarian, outlandish, exterior, tramontane, ultramontane.

4. Outside of one's previous experience, new, fresh, unfamiliar, hitherto unknown, novel, unique, foreign, unaccustomed, unexplored, extraneous, unheard-of, unperceived, undiscovered, different, unsuspected, dissimilar, unlike, divergent, varied, unique, unusual, never encountered, diverse.

5. Unacquainted, unaccustomed to, inexperienced at, untried, raw, green, unfamiliar with, a stranger to, a novice at, ignorant, amateurish, unskilled, naïve, unpracticed, unversed, unseasoned, unconversant, unused to, unenlightened, uninformed, uninitiated, new to, uninured, unwonted, ungiven to, unhabituated.

6. Distant, reserved, shy, detached, remote, withdrawn, bashful, distrustful, uncommunicative, retiring, diffident, shrinking, skittish, afraid, fearful, timid, sacred, nervous, modest, unsocial, constrained, cowardly, meek, startled, demure, shamefaced, uncourageous, wary, cautious, chary, reluctant, evasive, careful, elusive, suspicious, demurring, renitent, gingerly, circumspect, guarded, on guard, prudent, noncommittal, leery *(sl.)*, precautious, stealthy.

STRANGER, *n.* Newcomer, visitor, guest, alien, outsider, foreigner, immigrant, barbarian, interloper, obtruder, incomer, entrant, ultramontane, intruder, unknown person, crasher *(coll.)*.

STRANGLE, *v.* 1. Kill by stopping the breath, choke, stifle, garrote, suffocate, squeeze, smother, tighten the hold upon, throttle, burke.

2. Prevent the continuance (growth, rise, action) of, suppress, stifle, keep back, repress, hush, silence, restrain, mask, subdue, drown, throttle, smother, conceal, gag, muffle, muzzle, withhold, keep down, reserve, stop, choke off, deaden, soften, crush, check, quell, put down, snuff out, annihilate, squelch, quench, destroy, extinguish, nip in the bud, bar, arrest, inhibit, put a stop to, balk, circumscribe, obstruct, block, frustrate, thwart, break up, confute.

3. Be choked (stifled, suffocated), stifle, suffer, from difficulty in breathing, smother, gag, gasp for air, be breathless, suffocate.

STRAP, *n.* 1. Strip of flexible material *(for holding and fastening things)*, thong, leather string, cord, band, tie, lash, leash, lead, rawhide, crupper, knout, tendon, ligature, ligament, sinew, blacksnake, cat-o'-nine-tails.

2. Strop, razor strap, sharpener.

STRAP, *v.* 1. Fasten *or* secure with a strap, bind, tie, lash, leash, bandage, tether, shackle, fetter, pinion, truss.

2. Sharpen on a strap *or* strop, strop, whet, edge.

3. Beat *(with a strap)*, whip, flog, flail, lash, lace, thrash, scourge, flagellate, belt, cowhide, horsewhip.

STRATAGEM, *n.* Plan for deceiving *(the enemy, etc.)*, artifice, trick, plot, scheme, ruse, game, trap, trickery, dodge, device, intrigue, maneuver, machination, feint, deceit, policy, deception, delusion, blind, shift, wile.

STRATEGIC, *adj.* 1. Pertaining to, characterized by *or* of the nature of strategy, careful, calculated, clever, tricky, cunning, cautious, diplomatic, politic, wary, gingerly, well-thought-out, circumspect, prudent, guarded, safe, vigilant, stealthy, precautious, precautionary, discreet, chary.

2. Important in strategy, turning, critical, cru-

cial, decisive, vital, key, significant, momentous, cardinal, telling, solemn, salient, signal, consequential, pregnant, essential, radical, prime, primary, supreme, main, principal, grave.

STRATEGIST, *n.* One versed in strategy, tactician, schemer, politician, contriver, machinator, maneuverer, kingmaker, fox, wirepuller, statesman, politico, reynard, sly dog *(coll.)*, Machiavelli, Machiavellian.

STRATEGY, *n.* 1. Planning and directing *(military movements and operations)*, generalship, tactics, military evolutions, art of war, military science, strategetics, maneuvering.

2. Skillful management in getting the better of an adversary *or* attaining an end, policy, artfulness, craft, craftiness, artifice, diplomacy, maneuvering, wiles, tactics, devices, expedients, game, cunning.

STRATIFICATION, *n.* Lamination, lamellation, delamination, scaliness, exfoliation, foliation *(Petrog.)*, desquamation *(Pathol.)*, squamousness.

STRATIFY, *v.* Form in strata *or* layers, laminate, flake, scale, delaminate, desquamate.

STRATUM, *n.* Layer, bed, story, tier, level, ledge, seam, vein, streak, lode, plane.

STRAW, *n.* 1. Stalk, stem *or* culm of grain, mass of dried stalks used as fodder, hay, feed, provender, ensilage, stubble, chaff, spear, shaft.

2. Anything of trifling value *or* consequence, pin, snap, penny, farthing, button, fig, particle, scrap, bit, trace, speck, doit, scratch, snippet, morsel, spot, iota, grain, atom, mite, mote, micron, modicum, ion, whit, tittle, minim, hair, speckle, scintilla, freckle, flyspeck, insignificancy, corpuscle, trifle, point, microbe, molecule, minutia, cent.

3. Hollow tube used for drinking, *etc.,* pipette, tubulet, tubule.

STRAY, *adj.* 1. Straying *or* having strayed, lost, wandering, strayed, errant, loose, gone astray, adrift, rambling, roving, vagrant, homeless, off the beaten track, undirected.

2. Found *or* occurring apart from others, random, chance, scattered, unconformable, deviative, dispersed, strewn, disseminated, errant, erratic, accidental, divergent, aberrant, wanton, anomalous, abnormal, misplaced, egregious, irregular, capricious, unexpected, out of step, out of line, eccentric, exceptional, heteroclite.

STRAY, *n.* Homeless *or* friendless creature *or* person, domestic animal wandering at large, runaway, vagabond, rover, roamer, nomad, bird of passage, straggler, itinerant, waif, gypsy, Romany, foundling, Arab, street Arab, beachcomber, Flying Dutchman, Ancient Mariner.

STRAY, *v.* 1. Go from the proper course *or* place *or* beyond proper limits, roam, wander, ramble, digress, prowl, drift, nomadize, peregrinate, divagate, lose one's way, rove, range, meander, stroll, straggle, deviate, go astray, swerve.

2. Deviate from the set *or* right course, go astray, miss the truth, fall into error, lapse, fall from grace, sin, err, be deceived, transgress, misbelieve.

STREAK, *n.* 1. Long narrow mark, band, smear, vein, line, ridge, furrow, seam, striation, stain, blotch, blot, daub, dirt, smutch, splotch, blur, spot, smudge, smirch, mark, stripe.

2. Portion distinguished by color *or* nature, layer, vein, lode, stratum, seam, ledge, level, bed, plane.

3. Vein, strain, touch, admixture, tone, style, spirit, timbre, character, mood, cast, complexion, quality, essence, quintessence, substance, tenor.

STREAK, *v.* 1. Mark with a streak *or* streaks, striate, furrow, band, iridize, iridesce, variegate, stripe, smear, smudge, smutch, stain, soil, splotch, blur, daub, smirch.

2. Flash, go rapidly, scud, fly, dash, rush, tear, shoot, sprint, race, make time, scurry, flee, hasten, hurry, scour, scoot *(coll.),* bolt, dart, skedaddle *(sl.),* outstrip the wind, fly on the wings of the wind, bowl along, cut along *(coll.),* clap spurs to one's horse, wing one's way, spank, post, hie *(often reflex.),* hustle, pace, swoop, career, sweep, cover ground, trip, go like a shot *(coll.),* clip, bound, go like lightning *or* greased lightning *(coll.),* spring, zip, skim, brush, speed, take wing, spin, go hell-bent *(coll.).*

STREAKY, *adj.* Occurring in streaks, marked with *or* characterized by streaks, streaked, striate, barred, striped, striated, veined, watered, brindled.

STREAM, *n.* 1. Body of water in a channel *or* bed, river, tributary, rivulet, brook, creek, rill, run, confluent, affluent, streamlet, watercourse, runlet, trickle, race, flow, branch, feeder, freshet.

2. Steady current in water, course, flow, tide, rush, onrush, run, drift, surge, sluice, river, race, torrent, flight, flux, flood, undertow.

3. Flow of liquid (gas, light, *etc.*), jet, spout, flash, current, bolt, ray, gleam, rush, draft, trail, beam, streak, pencil.

4. Continuous flow, succession, gush, effusion, torrent, outbreak, outburst, eruption, discharge, cadence, burst, rush, storm, deluge, explosion, eloquence, fluency, volubility, wave, garrulity, loquacity.

5. Prevailing direction, drift, current, tendency, tide, trend, course, tenor, bent, inclination, set, impulse, bearing, tone, turn, leaning, cast, vein, humor, mood, pleasure, proclivity, propensity, grain.

STREAM, *v.* 1. Flow, pass in a stream, issue, run, spout, pour, spurt, rush, gush, drift, course, well, sweep, flood, surge, spurtle, burst, emit, squirt, discharge, disgorge, debouch, spirt, disembogue, shoot, spray, fountain, vomit forth.

2. Send forth, throw off in a stream, spill, pour out, shed, issue, emit, abound, let fall, let flow, drop, discharge, effuse, give vent to, exude, shower.

3. Float outward, hang in a loose flowing manner, wave, extend, stretch out, blow, flap, waft, emanate, radiate.

4. Move *or* proceed continuously like a flowing stream, flow, parade, file, abound, crowd, go on endlessly, teem, swarm.

STREAMER, *n.* 1. Narrow, ribbonlike flag, banner, banneret, pennant, pennon, gonfalon, ensign, colors, banderole, bannerol, bunting, standard.

2. Newspaper headline extending across entire page, banner head, banner line, flag, screamer, scarehead, spread, hanger, drophead, spreadhead.

STREAMLET, *n.* Watercourse, small stream, run, tributary, gill, creek, brook, brooklet, rill, rillet, burn, rivulet, trickle, runlet, runnel, feeder, race, freshet, branch, flow.

STREET, *n.* Thoroughfare, highway, road, roadway, highroad, parkway, boulevard, artery, way, public way, avenue.

STREETWALKER, *n.* Prostitute, whore, harlot,

fallen woman, scarlet woman, drab, strumpet, trull, courtesan, white slave, lady of the evening.

STRENGTH, *n.* 1. Bodily *or* muscular power, lustiness, vigor *(as in robust health),* stamina, dint, muscles, hardiness, sturdiness, endurance, force, power, stoutness, might, vitality, dynamic, pith, strong arm, sinew *or* sinews, beef *(coll.),* brawn, potence, energy, thews, robustness, grit, puissance *(Poetic).*

2. Mental power, vigor, force, energy, boldness, efficiency, potency, capacity, ability, faculty, competence, endowment, will power, intellect, iron will, dynamic.

3. Courage, firmness, moral power, fortitude, spirit, tenacity, resolution, determination, mettle, ardor, pluck, audacity, doughtiness, bravery, fearlessness, energy, animation, spice, piquancy, glow, warmth, cheerfulness, enterprise, valor, gameness, daring, boldness, spunk *(coll.),* backbone *(coll.),* resoluteness, stout-heartedness, unappalledness, grit *(coll.),* sand *(coll.),* stoutness, manfulness, gameness.

4. Power by reason of influence (authority, resources, numbers, *etc.*), greatness, sway, control, might, dominance, predominance, pre-eminence, superiority, prominence, consequence, distinction, eminence, precedence, transcendence, importance, prepotency, prestige, ascendancy, dignity, jurisdiction, excellence, significance, preponderance, reign, scepter, rule, command, sovereignty, prerogative, dominion, despotism, sublimity, majesty.

5. Number of men *or* ships *(in a force or body),* troops, numbers, forces, line, soldiery, fleet.

6. Effective force, cogency, potency, validity, conclusiveness, soundness, efficacy, vigor, energy, boldness, solidity, sobriety, stability, wisdom, justice, reliability, dependability, decisiveness, rationality, sageness, sagacity, sapience, accuracy, reasonableness, trustworthiness, demonstrability.

7. Power of resisting force (strain, wear, *etc.*), resistance, durability, toughness, hardness, proof, endurance, sturdiness, solidity, impregnability, firmness, stoutness, impenetrability, renitency, rigor, callosity, durity, steel, adamant, temper, imperviousness, immutability.

8. Vigor *(of language, action, feeling, etc.),* energy, vehemence, intensity, loudness, spirit, violence, impetuosity, point, piquancy, warmth, enthusiasm, verve, ardor, force, emphasis, nerve, glow, fire, vociferousness, punch *(coll.),* pep *(sl.).*

9. Large proportion of the effective *or* essential properties, pungency, spirit, virtue, potency, body, excellence, nature, quality, essence, quintessence, principle, embodiment, root, substance, keynote, quiddity, verity, sense, significance, pith, heart, marrow, core, kernel, gist, life, lifeblood.

10. Proportion of properties, intensity, brilliance, fullness, richness, amplitude, vitality, vividness, clarity, clearness, brightness.

11. Something that makes strong, support, stay, anchor, rock, help, aid, succor, security, mainstay, sustenance, buttress, brace, prop, upholder, sustainer, strong arm, splint, reinforcement, underpin, underset, staff, shore, strut, crutch, cane, pin, bracer.

STRENGTHEN, *v.* 1. Make strong *or* stronger, give strength to, renew, restore, sustain, reinforce, buttress, harden, brace, steel, indurate, nerve, energize, invigorate, freshen, vitalize, empower, nourish, fortify.

2. Gain strength, grow stronger, improve, return to health (a former state, *etc.*), recover, re-

vive, rally, mend, heal, come around, recuperate, get well, convalesce, perk up, rise again, take a favorable turn.

STRENUOUS, *adj.* 1. Zealously active, energetic, vigorous, ardent, intense, eager, resolute, earnest, animated, dynamic, busy, sedulous, diligent, assiduous, industrious, dogged, aggressive, unwearied, untiring, unsleeping, sleepless, on the run, on one's toes, hard-working, indefatigable, painstaking, pushing, enterprising.

2. Characterized by vigorous exertion, spirited, bold, strong, resolute, determined, uphill, urgent, vehement, stirring, rousing, laborious, difficult, doughty, intrepid, unflagging, hard-fought, hardearned, thorny, operose, trenchant, intense.

STRESS, *n.* 1. Importance, significance, weight, emphasis, pressure, pinch, urgency, necessity, force, consequence, salience, eminence, prominence, portent, moment, value, name, mark, figure, notability, note, dignity, grandeur, majesty, sublimity, concern, materiality, distinction, consideration, gravity, greatness, solemnity, urgency, seriousness, insistence, prestige, pre-eminence, paramountcy, primacy, superiority, virtue, worth, merit, excellence.

2. Emphasis, accent, accentuation, beat, pulse, throb, ictus *(Pros.)*, intonation, downbeat, pulsation.

3. Physical pressure, strain, pull, force, tension, tensity, traction, draw, haul, stretch, tautness, extension, distention, elongation, protraction.

STRESS, *v.* 1. Lay stress *or* emphasis on, emphasize, assert roundly *or* positively, insist upon, repeat, reassert, reaffirm, punctuate, accent, accentuate, promote, underline, mark, underscore, put in italics *or* capitals, feature *(coll.)*.

2. Subject to stress *or* strain, overstrain, bear heavily upon, fatigue, put under pressure, burden, tax, overtax, overwork, overtask, drive, lay a burden upon, bleed white, prostrate, exhaust, oppress, wear upon, weary, jade, tire, fag, harass.

STRETCH, *n.* 1. Period of time, duration, term, period, spell, tenure, stage, while, span.

2. *(Colloq.)* Period of time spent in jail, prison, *etc.,* term, sentence, spell, time, number of years.

3. Tension, strain, exaggeration, stress, effort, exertion, overexertion, intensity, tenseness.

STRETCH, *v.* 1. Reach out, extend, stretch forth, unfold, increase, aggrandize, incrassate, dilate, untwist, untwine, unwind, swell, amplify, expand, spread, deepen, widen, heighten, lengthen, sprawl, grow, magnify, uncoil, enlarge, overgrow, broaden, overrun.

2. Pull out, make longer, elongate, lengthen, strain, draw tight *or* taut, make tense *or* tight, tighten, distend, dilate, extend, wiredraw, finedraw, put under tension, protract.

3. Be elastic, bear extension, expand, be expandable, be extendible, be extensible.

4. Impair by stretching *or* overexertion, exert, tire, task, fatigue, twist, overtask, wrench, overwork, sprain, push too far, pervert, overdraw, overcharge, overtax, overburden, overstrain, burden, carry too far, push to the limit, run into the ground *(coll.)*.

STRETCHER, *n.* Bed for carrying sick, wounded, *etc.,* litter, portable couch.

STREW, *v.* 1. Scatter over, spread, bestrew, sprinkle, overspread, litter, coat, cover, spatter, diffuse, spray.

2. Spread abroad, disseminate, vent, distribute,

broadcast, issue, repeat, tell, ventilate, report, blazon, herald, announce, advertise, declare, trumpet, bruit, rumor, proclaim, propagate, circulate.

STRICKEN, *adj.* Smitten, wounded, injured, hurt, hit, spent, afflicted, struck, lame, done, down, exhausted, crippled.

STRICT, *adj.* 1. Rigorous, disciplining, severe, martinet-like, austere, tyrannical, dictatorial, despotic, stiff, puritanical, imperious, Spartan, Draconian, inflexible, stern, unyielding, exact, harsh, uncompromising, exigent, stringent, exacting, autocratic, Procrustean.

2. Absolute, exact, accurate, religious, meticulous, scrupulous, reliable, authoritative, unerring, literal, nice, perfect, close, correct, scientific, careful, unmistakable, conscientious, clean-cut, formal, positive, right, fastidious, precise, true, veracious, sure, proper, faithful.

STRICTURE, *n.* 1. Reproof, crimination, reproach, inculpation, calumny, animadversion, reprimand, incrimination, disapproval, disapprobation, charge, imputation, objurgation, upbraiding, diatribe, carping, philippic, blame, censure, tirade, vituperation, aspersion, castigation, obloquy, reprobation, criticism, reprehension, rebuke.

2. Binding, contract, contraction, limitation, curb, modification, qualification, condition, check, proscription, injunction, determent, confinement, control, constriction, restraint, bond, trammel, cohibition.

3. *(Med.),* Contraction *(of a blood vessel, etc.),* shrinking, diminution, compression, astriction, constriction.

STRIDE, *n.* 1. Long step, pace.

2. Good progress, advance, advancement, furtherance, headway, improvement, development.

STRIDE, *v.* Take long steps, step out, pace, swing, march, goose-step.

STRIDENT, *adj.* Harsh-sounding, grating, jarring, guttural, acute, jangling, ear-piercing, squawking, stridulatory, harsh, absonant, raucous, husky, discordant, untuneful, scratching, gruff, unmusical, unharmonious, croaking, shrill, cacophonous, hoarse, dissonant, rasping, sour, clashing, out of tune, grinding, atonal, twanging.

STRIDULATE, *v.* Make shrill sounds *(as insects, etc.),* creak, crick, chirp, screak, squeak, shriek, shrill.

STRIFE, *n.* 1. Rivalry, competition, fight, clash, conflict, debate, match, game, scramble, tilt, combat, engagement, tournament, contest, race, trial, struggle, pitting of strength, joust, counteraction, litigation, contention, handicap, opposition, athletic encounter, pitting of wits.

2. Trouble, turmoil, explosion, fuss, bother, rout, bluster, babel, cataclysm, scramble, commotion, upheaval, unrest, altercation, restlessness, warfare, disturbance, dissension, fomentation, rumpus, fray, disquiet, broil, hurly-burly, convulsion, fracas, melee, agitation, struggle, scuffle, stir, pother, dispute, storm, wrangle, row, bickering, embroilment, hubbub, imbroglio, tumult, flurry, bustle, violence, eruption, pandemonium, outbreak, outburst.

STRIKE, *n.* 1. Act of quitting work, labor strike, tie-up, walk-out, sit-down, lock-out, picket-line.

2. Sudden find *(as of oil, gold, etc.),* sudden success, discovery, windfall.

3. Clash, collision, bump, shock, blow, stroke, fillip, buffet, cuff, box, tap, carom, dint, slug,

thwack, rap, slam, thump, cut, chop, bang, hit, punch, pelt, jab, bat (coll.), clip (coll.), whack, smack, plunk (coll.), spank, paste (sl.), wallop (coll.), plug (sl.), lick (coll.), stab, swat (coll.), smash (coll.), clout (coll.), crack (coll.), crash, appulse, douse (sl.), poke, slap, dig, belt (sl.), whop (coll.), sock (sl.).

STRIKE, v. 1. Walk out, leave the job, quit work, picket.

2. Deal a blow or stroke, slap, smite, cane, birch, collide with, slug, thump, bump, bang, smash, shatter, poke, clap, buffet, pat, cudgel, beat, pound, devastate, clout (coll.), box, club, cuff, slam, whack, bat, belt (sl.), jab, plug (sl.), thrash, whip, spank, lace, lash, whale (coll.), strap, scourge, flog, thrash, batter, pelt, larrup, lambaste (sl.), soak (sl.), tan (coll.), pommel, baste, tamp, sock (sl.), bastinado, trounce, flail, drub, flagellate, punch, dash, switch, wallop (coll.), clip (coll.).

3. Succeed in hitting, reach (with missile, weapon, blow, etc.), shoot, stone, plug (sl.), fell, kill, sink, pepper, pelt, riddle, bring down, drop, pour a broadside, aim true, go straight, make a bull's-eye on, cut down.

4. Touch effectively, affect severely, abash, accuse, condemn, assail, overwhelm, attack, vilify, revile, put in one's place, deal a deathblow, baste, overcome, damn, strike at the root of, make an inroad into, rouse, blackball, arouse, kindle, provoke, hit, stir, shatter, fire, inflame, denounce, heat, foment, warm, quicken, pierce, prostrate, quash, upset, cripple, crush, reproach, impugn, undo, wound, knock (coll.), rap (sl.), criticize, black-list, incite, stimulate, move, touch, thrill, blame, bring to bay, strike home, censure, devastate, impress, foil, thwart, discomfit, frustrate, assault, assail, charge.

5. (Sometimes with UPON) Come or light upon, run into, meet with, find, discover, chance upon, stumble upon, encounter, learn, pitch upon, blunder upon, come into contact with, make out, espy, spy, descry, pick up, fall upon, detect, distinguish, recognize, spot (coll.), find out, come across, burst upon.

6. Meet head-on, run into (physically), come into collision, crack up, come together, collide, smash together, dash against, jostle, hit, beat against, hurtle against, knock into, run or fall foul of, buffet, jounce, jolt, jar.

STRIKING, adj. Remarkable, unusual, astounding, wondrous, incredible, singular, astonishing, extraordinary, surprising, stupendous, strange, marvelous, miraculous, fabulous, unexpected, wonderful, out-of-the-ordinary.

STRING, n. 1. Cord, braid, hemp rope, thong, cable, thread, twine, cordage, line, fiber, strap, filament, whipcord, strand.

2. Rank, row, file, procession, series, line, column, range, parade, cavalcade, queue, chain, tier.

3. (Of a musical instrument) Gut, chord, wire, piano wire, catgut, snare (of a drum).

STRING, v. 1. Furnish with strings, strengthen, brace, bind, reinforce, wind, tie up.

2. Tune (an instrument), attune, synchronize, chord, harmonize, tune up.

3. String together, thread, put on a string, put in line.

4. Form a line along, arrange a line along, fringe, spread, bound, dot, border, margin, hem, sprinkle along.

5. Tie, bind, lace, cinch, pinion, harness, leash, tie up, strap, truss, tether, hitch, bandage, moor.

STRINGENT, adj. 1. Disciplining, austere, strict, Procrustean, uncompromising, Draconian, dictatorial, rigorous, despotic, inflexible, exigent, stern, stiff, unyielding, exact, harsh, autocratic, Spartan, imperious, tyrannical, puritanical.

2. Persuasive, telling, forceful, unequivocal, definite, infallible, potent, powerful, inescapable, trustworthy, answerable, forcible, puissant, effectual, influential, weighty, valid, efficacious, suasive, suasory, inducive, incontrovertible, authoritative, certain, sound, evident, positive, sure, cogent, past dispute, conclusive, convincing, undeniable, plain.

STRINGY, adj. 1. Fibrous, wiry, ropy, threadlike, thready, filamentary, filamentous.

2. Viscous, viscid, gelatinous, pasty, gooey, sticky, tacky, gluey, gummy, doughy.

STRIP, n. 1. Act of stripping, plundering, etc., brigandage, marauding, depredation, privateering, buccaneering, desolation, devastation, harrying, freebooting, spoliation, pilfering, robbery, raid, piracy, larceny, deprivation, sack, pillage, rapine, ravishment, foray, plunderage, theft, prey.

2. Narrow or long piece of cloth, land, etc., ribbon, stripe, band, slip, shred, ribband, sliver.

3. Pencil-shaped piece of substance, shaft, stick, stream, rod, ray, bar, finger, stem, narrow beam.

STRIP, v. 1. Strip or deprive of skin, expose, lay bare, scalp, pod, shell, husk, uncover, unwrap, divest, denude, exfoliate, hull, decorticate, excorticate, bare, excoriate, shave, bark, skin, flay, peel.

2. Strip off (as or like skin), loosen and fall off, shed, flake, molt, scale, exfoliate, cast, slough, peel, skin, delaminate, exuviate, desquamate (Pathol.).

3. Rob of goods or valuables, despoil, prey upon, desolate, rifle, maraud, steal from, gut, loot, depredate, pirate, pilfer, ransack, raid, ravage, spoliate, forage, sack, plunder, lay waste, fleece, foray.

4. Undress, make or become naked, divest of clothing, lay bare, uncover, unclothe, peel, disrobe, cast off, undrape, expose, put off, unarray, doff, unwrap.

STRIPE, n. 1. Piece or band of material, band, fillet, strip, sash, belt, cestus, surcingle, girdle, binding, thong, ribbon, zone, withe, cincture, braid, baldric, frontlet, collar, maniple, ferrule, strap, ring, streak, cordon, tape.

2. Long narrow mark of color, shade, etc., band, striation, stain, smirch, seam, smear, vein, furrow, mark, line, ridge.

3. Wheal, welt, scar, wale, gash, disfigurement, brand, cicatrix (Zool.), cicatricle (Bot.), line, indentation, score, deformity.

4. Kind, sort, nature, description, variety, cast, quality, race, mold, make, grain, feather, disposition, school, form, set, classification, temper, aspect, grade, like (coll.), kidney, category, breed, color, stamp, denomination, character, type, strain, genus, order.

STRIPE, v. Make stripes upon, make variegated, streak, line, iridize, iridesce, furrow, brand, striate.

STRIPED, adj. Striate, barred, striated, veined, brindled, streaky, streaked.

STRIPLING, n. Youth, youngling, pubescent, sapling, juvenile, small fry (coll.), lad, boy, whippersnapper, youngster, slip, minor, brat, bratling.

STRIVE, *v.* (*Usually followed by* TO) Try hard, make efforts, struggle, leave no stone unturned, take pains, do one's best, do one's utmost, ply the oar, exert oneself, endeavor, labor, strain, attempt, do all one can, essay, strain every nerve, push, spare no pains, move heaven and earth, work like a Trojan, pull.

STROKE, *n.* 1. Impact, blow, dig, slap, poke, appulse, stab, cut, chop, bang, punch, pelt, jab, thump, slam, rap, thwack, fillip, buffet, hit, cuff, box, tap, carom, clip (*coll.*), bat (*coll.*), whack, smack, plunk (*coll.*), spank, paste (*sl.*), wallop (*coll.*), plug (*sl.*), lick, swat (*coll.*), sock (*coll.*), whop (*coll.*), crack (*coll.*), smash, clout (*coll.*), bump, collision, shock.

2. Lucky chance, stroke of fortune, successful stroke, boon, success, find, profit, gain, coincidence, prosperity, chance, windfall, felicity, piece of good luck, master stroke, trump card, feat, go, coup, blessing, golden opportunity, ten-strike (*coll.*), fluke (*sl.*), bold stroke, triumph, victory, smash (*sl.*).

3. Stroke of satire, touch (*in a work of art, etc.*), effective *or* telling expression, happy remark, home thrust, dig (*coll.*), adverse criticism, insult, reproach, rap (*sl.*), slam (*coll.*), cutting remark, knock (*sl.*), stricture, reprehension, insinuation, slap in the face, aspersion, caustic remark, animadversion, back answer, short answer, well-chosen words, hit, brickbat, quip, thrust, cut, slap, fling, verbal thrust, apt expression, sarcasm, comeback (*sl.*), gibe, coup.

4. Sudden attack of paralysis, convulsions, *etc.*, brain hemorrhage, spasm, convulsion, apoplectic fit, epileptic fit, paroxysm, seizure, eclampsia, ictus (*Med.*).

5. Accomplishment, piece of work, effort, exploit, procedure, job, transaction, action, deed, feat, coup, stunt, performance, move.

6. Sound of a clock, gong, *etc.*, striking, booming, tolling, clank, clanking, ding-dong, reverberation, clang, chime, knell, peal, vibration, ringing, clash, crash, bong, jangle, gong, tintinnabulation.

7. Beat (*as of a heart, etc.*), pumping, pounding, throb, pulse, pulsing, pulsation, palpitation, oscillation, diastole and systole (*both pert. to the heart*).

8. (*Of a pen, instrument, etc.*) Mark, line, delineation, underscoring, stripe, hyphen, dash, streak, marking, tick, score.

STROKE, *v.* 1. Sound (*as a clock, etc.*), ring, peal, clangor, ding, reverberate, sound, jingle, strike, gong, ding-dong, ting, clash, boom, toll, tinkle, chime, tintinnabulate, clang, knell, tink, vibrate.

2. Soothe by touching gently, touch gently, rub gently *or* softly, brush lightly, massage, caress, pass the fingers over.

STROLL, *v.* 1. Travel casually from place to place, wander, meander, traverse, range, vagabondize, peregrinate, rove, roam, spatiate, tour, jaunt, tramp.

2. Walk slowly, take the air, saunter, dawdle along, wander, meander, stretch one's legs, ramble, perambulate, straggle, promenade, amble, spatiate.

STROLL, *n.* Walk, ramble, promenade, tour, trip, excursion, spatiation, airing, turn.

STRONG, *adj.* 1. Having great strength, powerful, mighty, forceful, Herculean, muscular, able, stout, strapping, hardy, stalwart, athletic, sinewy, rigor-ous, Atlantean, tough, wiry, robust, virile, lusty, vigorous, seasoned, burly, brawny.

2. Well-made, not flimsy, sound, lasting, resisting, compact, tenacious, hard, tough, sturdy, rugged, well-constructed, well-built, solid, durable, heavy, substantial, well-founded.

3. Strong in belief, conviction, *etc.*, impassioned, perfervid, eager, keen, spirited, animated, ardent, zealous, confirmed, rabid, vehement, sharp, assiduous, fervent, fervid, fierce, earnest, heated, active, busy, sedulous, intense, violent, high-spirited, diligent, dogmatic, opinionated.

4. (*Of flavors, odors, etc.*) Sharp, highly-flavored, highly-spiced, stinging, acid, penetrating, savory, nippy, smarting, sour, acrid, burning, mordant, odorous, tart, astringent, biting, pungent, tangy, highly-seasoned, piquant, hot, acetous, flavorous, racy, salty, peppery, mordacious, bitter, caustic.

5. (*As a storm, etc.*) Violent, vivid, dreadful, intense, grave, serious, severe, acute, bad, dire, forceful, awful, formidable.

6. Acutely distressing to the feelings, *etc.*, acutely felt, mordant, cruel, inimical, distressing, biting, harrowing, smarting, hurtful, corroding, consuming, severe, trenchant, acute, harsh, keen, caustic, wounding, hostile, invidious, afflicting, satirical, pointed, stinging, waspish, bitter, excruciating, agonizing, afflictive, vexatious, cutting, vexing, gnawing, crushing, torturous, heartbreaking, shocking, heart-rending, piercing, piquant, acrimonious, tart, painful, sarcastic, racking, incisive, mortifying.

7. Potent (*as a beverage, etc.*), inflaming, exhilarating, stimulating, disquieting, provocative, maddening, quickening, intoxicating, fiery, heady, going to the head, powerful, highly-spirituous, discomposing, exciting.

STRONGBOX, *n.* Steel *or* iron box for valuables, *etc.*, safety deposit box *or* vault, depository, money box, treasury, safe, cash box, locker, vault, chest, crypt, coffer.

STRONGHOLD, *n.* Fortification, fort, fortress, rampart, donjon, battlement, keep, safehold, bastion, bulwark, castle, citadel, redoubt, chateau, tower, stockade, fastness, hold, rock.

STROP, *v.* Strap, sharpen, hone, put an edge on, acuminate.

STRUCTURAL, *adj.* 1. (*Pert. to architecture*) Architectural, tectonic, constructional, edificial, architectonic

2. Formal, organic, anatomical, textural, modal, geotectonic (*Geol.*).

STRUCTURE, *n.* 1. Something built *or* constructed, edifice, framework, building, erection, pile, superstructure, construction, scaffold.

2. Arrangement (*of component parts, etc.*), interrelation, mode, form, make-up, constitution, configuration, relationship, style of arrangement, organization, anatomy, physique, conformation, formation, texture, design.

STRUGGLE, *n.* 1. Labor, work, exertion, strain, striving, taking pains, pains, attempt, push, pull, endeavor, grind, stress, force, tension, draw, haul, trouble, trial.

2. Contention, fight, fighting, battle, encounter, combat, scrimmage, brush, scramble, scuffle, tussle, skirmish, conflict, engagement, joust, fisticuffs, fracas, appulse, meeting, fray, tilt, concussion, scrap (*coll.*), melee, affray, set-to (*coll.*), imbroglio, duel, rencounter, action, dogfight,

clash, bout, ruction, run-in (*sl.*), rivalry, competition, match, debate, fomentation, altercation, digladiation, pother, agitation, bother, disturbance, opposition, broil, hurly-burly.

STRUGGLE, *v.* 1. Leave no stone unturned, do all one can, attempt, strain, exert oneself, ply the oar, take pains, labor, strive, push, endeavor, do one's utmost, do one's best, spare no pains, move heaven and earth, work like a Trojan, pull.

2. Fight, combat, scuffle, scramble, tussle, skirmish, battle, contend, joust, litigate, engage with, match, meet, tilt, scrap (*coll.*), clash, join issue, brush, squabble, duel, broil, feud, quarrel, exchange blows, close with, grapple with, cross swords with, oppose, bicker with, argue, lock horns, spar, wrangle, brawl, differ, jostle, spat (*coll.*).

STRUM, *v.* Tweak (*the strings of a guitar, etc.*), thrum, play upon, finger, twang, plunk, pick, pluck, touch gently *or* idly.

STRUMPET, *n.* Whore, prostitute, harlot, streetwalker, bawd, jade, lewd, doxy, procuress, drab, wanton, trull, Cyprian, demirep (*sl.*), trollop, loose woman, Paphian, bitch (*vulgar*), adventuress, harridan, grisette, temptress, woman of easy virtues *or* morals, tart (*sl.*), fornicatress, slut, quean, hussy, adultress, stew, cocotte, courtesan, daughter of joy, fallen woman, bat (*sl.*), woman of the profession (*euphemistic*), Lais, madam (*coll.*), conciliatrix (*Fr.*), Mrs. Warren, Delilah, white slave, woman of the town, erring sister, baggage, frail sister, Sadie Thompson, Jezebel, abandoned woman, chippy (*sl.*), pickup, demimondaine, broad (*sl.*), scarlet woman, meretrix, cat (*sl.*), Messalina, painted woman, hetaera (*Gk. Antiq.*), Thais.

STRUT, *v.* 1. Walk pompously, prance, peacock, swagger, stalk, parade, promenade, bounce.

2. Act proudly *or* pompously, bluster, peacock, put on airs, be arrogant, flourish, throw out one's chest, talk big, vapor, vaunt, blow one's own trumpet, roister, brag, puff, boast, hug oneself, swagger.

STUB, *n.* Short blunt part of anything, stump, end, tail, butt, counterfoil (*of a check, etc.*), dock (*of a dog's tail*).

STUBBED, *adj.* Short and thick, squidgy, snub (*of the nose*), squab, chunky, dumpy, stocky, stubby, blunt, stumpy (*coll.*), squat.

STUBBLE, *n.* Rough stumps of anything, chaff, straw, bristle.

STUBBORN, *adj.* Unyielding, unmalleable, unmanageable, pervicacious, intractable, unimpressible, obdurate, obstinate, mulish, unbending, inflexible, uninfluenced, perverse, firm, unmovable, refractory, bullheaded, pigheaded, opinionated, self-willed, wilful, uncontrollable, bullet-headed (*coll.*), ungovernable, recalcitrant, bigoted, headstrong, uncompliant.

STUBBY, *adj.* Chubby, chumpy (*coll.*), pudgy, squatty, squab, buxom, squat, squattish, thick-set, stout, plump, stodgy, stubbed, dumpy, stocky, tubby (*coll.*), stumpy (*coll.*).

STUD, *n.* 1. Ornamental knob, boss, ornamental nail.

2. Buttonlike attachment, collar fastener.

3. Male animal for breeding, sire, stallion (*of horses*).

STUDENT, *n.* 1. Learner, pupil, schoolboy, schoolgirl, coed (*coll.*), probationer, apprentice, matriculant, initiate, neophyte, collegian, under-

graduate, novice, tyro, educatee, beginner, scholar, opsimath (*one who begins late in life*), catechumen.

2. Learned man, erudite person, giant of learning, mastermind, colossus of knowledge, scholastic, authority, luminary, pantologist, philosopher, doctor, wise man, master, sage, man of letters, pundit, savant, seer.

3. Observer (*of society, manners, morals, etc.*), commentator, critic, discourser, dissertator, reader, scholiast, interpreter, reviewer, examiner, spectator, analyst, exegete.

STUDIED, *adj.* 1. Scholar-like, befitting a scholar, intellectual, profound, scholarly, learned, erudite, mental, rational, scholastic, cultured, cognitive, cerebral, brainy, academic, wise, educated, lettered, literary, bookish.

2. Well-arranged, well thought-out, premeditated, well laid-out, plotted, advised, careful, well-planned, well-designed, labored, preconcerted, thoughtful, calculated.

STUDIO, *n.* 1. Artist's workshop, atelier.

2. Place where motion pictures are made, movie lot.

3. Broadcasting studio, broadcasting booth.

STUDIOUS, *adj.* 1. Scholarly, scholar-like, intellectual, scholastic, rational, profound, studied, learned, erudite, cultured, brainy, cognitive, cerebral, academic, bookish, wise, literary, educated, lettered.

2. Diligent, industrious, hard-working, plodding, assiduous, earnest, zealous, ardent, sedulous, slogging, grinding, painstaking, persevering, teachable, determined, alert, bustling, unsleeping, instructable, unflagging, apt, engrossed, busy, active, occupied, laborious, intent.

STUDY, *n.* 1. Act of noticing, perceiving, examining, observing, *etc.*, speculation, deliberation, concentration, watching, advertence, once-over (*sl.*), sightseeing, mindfulness, search, scrutiny, sight, attention, inspection, probe, attentiveness, consideration, reconnaissance, cognizance, eying, observation, perlustration, heed, absorption, note, espionage, lookout, intentness, interest, heedfulness, watchfulness, perception, dissection, thought, analysis, investigation, check, examination, survey, exploration, research, glance, ken, view, regard, vision, preoccupation.

2. Application (*to a task, reading, etc.*), addiction, sedulity, sedulousness, attention, hard work, effort, intentness, diligence, enterprise, intenseness, heed, care, industry, industriousness, labor, assiduity.

3. Knowledge, academic attainments, mental cultivation, pansophy, reading, letters, inquiry, polymathy, culture, erudition, lore, booklore, enlightenment, instruction, education, accomplishment.

4. Mental absorption, preoccupation, fascination, occupation, reverie, musing, intense thought, concentration, engrossment, close application, engagement, brown study, heed, rumination, fixed regard, close effort, deliberation, reflection, cognition, profound thought, meditation.

5. Room for study, reading, work, *etc.*, office, library, schoolroom, workroom, studio, study hall, den.

STUDY, *v.* 1. Cast the eye over, take note of, note, heed, scan, notice, overlook, size up, search through, observe, watch, ogle, eye, contemplate, explore, audit, glance over, examine, peruse, cognize, consider, investigate, dissect, reconnoiter, take stock of, scrutinize, attend, pore over, probe, inspect, inquire into, view, mind, survey, review.

2. Consider deeply, ruminate, wonder, brood, deliberate, commune, put on one's thinking cap, excogitate, cerebrate, intellectualize, speculate, meditate, cogitate, reflect, muse, ponder, dream, reason, rationalize, contemplate.

3. Acquire knowledge, apply the mind, school oneself, learn, educate oneself, cram (coll.), wade through, peruse, dip into, hit the books (coll.), grind (coll.), slog (coll.), memorize, con, plunge into, scan, bury oneself, pore over, read, burn the midnight oil.

STUFF, n. 1. Matter, material, substance, hyle (Philos.).

2. Material (of which something is made), raw material, substance, staple, stock.

3. Fabric, textile, cloth, felt, material, tissue, rag, dry goods.

4. Stuff and nonsense, nonsense, trash, humbug, trumpery, twaddle, flummery, absurdity, poppycock, stupidity, balderdash, fiddle-faddle (coll.), asininity, moonshine, blatherskite, tommyrot, bosh, inanity, fatuity, bunkum, rubbish, rot, piffle (coll.), baloney (sl.), tripe, patter, palaver, prate, gabble, blah (coll.), hogwash (coll.), blather, guff (sl.), bibble-babble, applesauce (coll.), babblement.

5. Inmost substance, hypostasis, inmost being, inwardness, quintessence, entity, pith, backbone, actuality, quiddity, kernel, gist, vital element, central nature, principal, essence, reality, main feature, heart, core, marrow, soul.

STUFF, v. 1. Feed gluttonously, eat with voracity, raven, stow it away (coll.), gulp, gluttonize, cram, gobble, batten, gormandize, bolt, wolf, overeat, overindulge, gorge, satiate oneself.

2. Fill, heap, pile, pad, stack, implete, charge, stow, burden, load, weight, lade, pack, lumber, wad.

3. Put in a receptacle, store, load, secrete, reposit, garner, pack, crowd, hoard, ensconce, bury, stash (sl.), hide, truck, wedge, conceal, cache, salt away (coll.).

4. Stuff or fill (as a hole), block, occlude, cover, dam, shut, plug, close, cork, bung, stanch, choke off.

STUFFING, n. 1. Anything used to fill an object (as a cushion, etc.), wadding, filling, packing, padding.

2. (Cookery) Dressing (for a fowl, etc.), farce, forcemeat, filling, seasoning.

STUFFY, adj. 1. Ill-ventilated, close, fusty, warm, unventilated, stifling, suffocating, sultry, heavy, sweltering, muggy, uncomfortable, motionless, stale-smelling, oppressive, stagnant, humid, musty.

2. Heavy, dull, uninteresting, stale, crass, dry, humdrum, tiresome, dreary, wearisome, insipid, exanimate, soulless, boring, laborious, stagnant, monotonous, flat, torpid, dead, jejune, turgid, prosy, prosaic, static, wooden, tumid, pedantic, stodgy, arid, tasteless, vapid, stolid, pedestrian, tedious.

STULTIFY, v. 1. Make or cause to appear silly or stupid, make foolish, make a laughingstock, get a laugh on, show up, ridicule, deride, befool, mock.

2. Make invalid (as a law, etc.), invalidate, frustrate, check, stop, neutralize, veto, repress, overbalance, annul, vitiate, nullify, negate, hinder, counteract, prevent, obstruct, choke, smother, suppress, muzzle, thwart, trammel, cohibit, balk,

impede, restrain, circumscribe, bridle, estop, hold, inhibit.

STUMBLE, v. 1. Fall, sprawl, topple, trip, take a spill, precipitate, come a cropper (coll.), measure one's length, pitch forward, lurch.

2. Walk unsteadily, sway, reel, waver, lumber, totter, shamble, hobble, stagger, flounder, roll, pitch, shuffle, slouch.

3. Make mistakes, blunder, fall into error, misjudge, miscalculate, hash up, bosh, misreckon, mess up, bungle, boggle, misestimate, botch, make a faux pas, slip up, be careless.

4. Do wrong, be wicked, fall, trip, leave the narrow path, wander, be in the wrong, sin, backslide, transgress, err, be delinquent, lapse, take a wrong course, go astray, deviate.

STUMBLING BLOCK, n. Impediment, embarrassment, retardation, limitation, barrier, obstacle, embargo, bar, snag, restraint, restriction, bridle, hindrance, forbiddance, proscription, oppilation, stopper, cohibition, barrage, stay, trammel, curb, constraint, obstruction, catch, block, impedition, preclusion, ban, difficulty.

STUMP, n. 1. Lopped trunk of a tree, bush, etc., remains.

2. Short blunt part of anything, end, tail, butt, stub, dock (of a dog's tail).

3. Heavy tramping sound, heavy footfall or footstep, stomping, lumbering, plunk, plump, plodding, clunk, bump, tramp, thud.

STUMP, v. 1. Cut off or reduce to a stump, truncate, trim, pollard, poll, cut short, lop, chop down, obtruncate, prune, clip, crop, amputate, dock.

2. Walk clumsily, hobble, plod, lumber, goose-step, peg, drag one's feet, stomp, shuffle, stamp, waddle, trudge, stride, clump.

3. Perplex, nonplus, hoodwink, distract, confuse, foil, hoax, trick, surprise, baffle, bluff, daze, bewilder, mystify, astonish, outwit, dumfound, confound, bamboozle (coll.), amaze, befog.

STUN, v. 1. Dumfound, startle, confound, dazzle, electrify, galvanize, astound, astonish, stagger, flabbergast, awe, daze, strike with amazement, petrify.

2. Deprive of sensibility, make torpid, render unconscious, knock out, stupefy, daze, shock, deaden, numb, paralyze, put to sleep (euphem.), obtund.

STUNNING, adj. 1. Unusual, remarkable, fabulous, miraculous, amazing, astounding, astonishing, out-of-the-ordinary, strange, unprecedented, wonderful, unexpected, marvelous, stupendous, surprising, extraordinary, incredible, preternatural, singular, inconceivable, striking, prodigious.

2. Engaging, rapturous, thrilling, entrancing, charming, fascinating, prepossessing, attractive, sweet, tempting, graceful, lovely, absorbing, winsome, fetching, beautiful, seductive, engrossing, winning, alluring, exquisite, transporting, pleasing, fair, delightful, magnetizing, diverting, inducing, catching, irresistible, handsome, tantalizing, enthralling, electrifying, likable, titillating, delectable, enamoring, intriguing.

STUNT, n. (Colloq.) Feat, trick, act, gag (coll.), turn, performance, number.

STUNT, v. Check or hinder the growth of, dwarf, curb, restrain, stint, restrict, confine, delimitate, delimit, cramp.

STUPEFACIENT, n. Stupefactive, calmative, narcotic, sleeping-draught, opiate, tranquilizer, paregoric, anesthetic, anodyne, alleviative, sedative.

STUPEFACTION, *n.* Insensibility, stupor, coma, languor, lassitude, torpor, torpescence, tiredness, oscitancy, inactivity, phlegm, drowsiness, inertia, torpidity, stupidity, latency, heaviness, doze, inertness, supineness, insouciance, somnolence.

STUPEFIED, *adj.* Comatose, somnolent, lifeless, inanimate, insensible, unconscious, supine, inert, impassive, drugged, fainéant, dormant, insouciant, soporific, slumbrous, obtuse, torpid, lackadaisical, heavy, stupid.

STUPEFY, *v.* 1. Deprive *or* render insensible, paralyze, make unconscious, deaden, put to sleep (*euphem.*), daze, shock, knock out, stun, numb, render torpid.

2. Dumfound, flabbergast, surprise, confound, dazzle, electrify, galvanize, startle, astound, awe, astonish, stagger, petrify, daze, strike with amazement, wonder, astonishment, *etc.*

STUPENDOUS, *adj.* 1. Mammoth, prodigious, enormous, excessive, gigantic, monstrous, grand, commanding, strapping (*coll.*), extravagant, vast, ponderous, incredible, monumental, spectacular, megatherine, megatherian, leviathan, Atlantean, magnitudinous, jumbo, dinosaurean, dinotherian, Gargantuan, lofty, massy, imposing, mountainous, big, tall, very large, Cyclopean, elephantine, tremendous, bulky, capacious, massive, ample, mighty, titanic, very great, giant, Herculean, colossal.

2. Unusual, remarkable, prodigious, stunning, unprecedented, astounding, wonderful, surprising, inconceivable, strange, singular, incredible, extraordinary, unexpected, marvelous, astonishing, out-of-the-ordinary, fabulous, amazing, preternatural.

STUPID, *adj.* 1. Insensible, senseless, somnolent, unconscious, supine, impassive, lackadaisical, inert, heavy, insouciant, soporific, slumbrous, obtuse, torpid, dormant, fainéant, drugged, lifeless, inanimate, comatose.

2. Weak-minded, brainless, indiscreet, witless, rantipole, reckless, frivolous, rattle-headed, inane, simple-minded, empty-headed, irresponsible, silly, muddle-headed, childish, undiscriminating, foolish, green, simple, unwise, fool-headed, tactless, ill-judged, ill-advised, absent-minded, heedless, crazy, foolhardy, thoughtless, reckless, harum-scarum, giddy, rattlebrained, giddy-pated, light-minded, light-witted, bemused, mercurial, featherbrained, short-witted, beef-witted, doltish, dunce-like, clod-pated, muddy-headed, dunderheaded, clownish, shallow-pated, stolid, obtuse, oafish, boorish, thick (*coll.*), dumb (*coll.*), unintelligent, moronic, idiotic, imbecilic, lumpish, half-witted, vacant.

3. Without reason, sense, intelligence, *etc.* (as an *action, book, thought, etc.*), senseless, nonsensical, preposterous, meaningless, ludicrous, vapid, aimless, pointless, unreasonable, farcical, ill-judged, ill-constructed, absurd, crazy (*coll.*), mad, purposeless, irrelevant, haphazard, driftless, inappropriate, unconnected, groundless, prosaic, incongruous, silly, tame, inept, fatuous, tedious, tiresome, humdrum, dull, crass, inconsequential, asinine, flat.

STUPIDITY, *n.* 1. Nonsense, twaddle, humbug, balderdash, trash, asininity, stuff, stuff and nonsense, absurdity, poppycock, moonshine, gabble, blather, patter, fatuity, inanity, flummery, bosh, bunkum, rot, rubbish, fiddle-faddle (*coll.*), piffle

(*coll.*), blah (*coll.*), guff (*sl.*), applesauce (*coll.*), babblement, blatherskite.

2. Idiocy, asininity, foolishness, nonsensicality, absurdity, folly, imbecility, silliness, nugacity, inanity, ineptitude.

STUPOR, *n.* Dullness, apathy, sleepiness, phlegm, weariness, slowness, somnolence, coma, oscitancy, inertness, heaviness, doze, indolence, insensibility, inertia, lassitude, latency, stupefaction, lethargy, laziness, sluggishness, drowsiness, torpor, obtuseness, insouciance, supineness, languor, torpidity, torpescence.

STURDY, *adj.* 1. Intrepid, brave, daring, manly, audacious, unyielding, lasting, chivalric, plucky, dashing, manful, resistant, hardy, high-mettled, invincible, forcible, virile, valiant, irresistible, undismayed, unshrinking, stubborn, spirited, soldierly, gallant, doughty, tenacious, confident, courageous, stout, resolute, masculine, stout-hearted, game, aweless, indomitable, enduring, undaunted, dogged, firm, heroic, determined, unapprehensive, mettlesome, hero-like, resisting, venturesome, enterprising, high-spirited, Spartan, fearless, dauntless, defiant, unalarmed, dreadless, unblenched, unappalled, gritty, spunky (*coll.*), unabashed.

2. Having great strength, powerful, mighty, seasoned, burly, Atlantean, tough, wiry, sinewy, rigorous, robust, virile, vigorous, stalwart, hardy, strapping, stout, able, muscular, strong, forceful.

3. Well-made, not flimsy, durable, heavy, substantial, lasting, solid, well-built, sound, tenacious, hard, tough, compact, resisting, rugged, strong, well-constructed.

STUTTER, *n.* Hesitant utterance, falter, drawl, stammer, stammering, mytacism, splutter, traulism.

STUTTER, *v.* Speak with involuntary pauses, breaks, hesitations, *etc.*, speak hesitantly, halt, haw, stumble, stammer, splutter, sputter, fumble, falter, drawl, hem and haw.

STY, *n.* 1. Pigsty, pigpen, hogpen, piggery.

2. Filthy place, den, hovel, dump (*sl.*), flop house (*sl.*), shanty, shack, hole (*sl.*), slum, sink, rookery, Augean stable, lair.

STYGIAN, *adj.* Black, dark, dim, funereal, dreary, muggy, smoky, viscid, caliginous, sunless, shady, tenebrous, starless, sepulchral, soupy (*sl.*), over-shadowed, obscure, unlighted, dirty, dingy, gray, unilluminated, cheerless, sable, grim, lowering, leaden, somber, shadowy, lightless, dusty, foggy, misty, turbid, murky, overcast, gloomy, nebulous, cloudy, blurred, umbrageous, rayless.

STYLE, *n.* 1. Mode of expression, choice of words, manner of presentation, manner, quality, form, language, way, phraseology, procedure, presentation, cut, texture, make-up, individual method, stamp, system, tone, guise.

2. Fashion, contemporary taste, vogue, rage, fashionableness, mode, bon ton, trend.

3. Writing instrument (*of the ancients*), any sharp instrument for marking, stylus, stylograph, etching-needle, graver, burin.

4. Form of address, appellative, denomination, title, appellation, designation.

STYLE, *v.* Name, call, designate, dub, term, christen, denominate, title, entitle.

STYLET, *n.* 1. Dagger with narrow blade, dirk, poniard, blade, kris, skean, baselard, steel, knife, stiletto, *katar (Ind.)*, creese.

2. Small sharp pointed instrument for needle-

work, *etc.,* perforator, puncheon *(Goldsmith.),* eyeleteer, pin, needle, stiletto, puncher, piercer.

3. *(Surg.)* Probe, specillum.

4. *(Zool.)* Wattle, appendage, spine, prickle, tuft, acumination, barblet.

STYLISH, *adj.* Modish, fashionable, up-to-date, in vogue, new, modern, chic *(colloq., in this sense),* latest, up-to-the-minute, dressy, *bien soigné (Fr.),* well-groomed, elegant, genteel, à la mode, voguish, smart, in fashion, silk-stocking.

STYLIST, *n.* Author, composer, *etc.,* who emphasizes style, purist, classicist, craftsman.

STYLITE, *n.* One living in seclusion usually on top of a pillar *(Eccl. Hist.),* pillarist, pillar saint, recluse, solitary, hermit, anchorite, eremite.

STYLIZE, *v.* Make formal *or* conventional, conventionalize, formalize, form according to fashion, represent according to set pattern.

STYLOGRAPH, *n.* Instrument for writing with ink, writing instrument, fountain pen, ball-point pen, stylus.

STYLOGRAPHY, *n.* Style of writing, calligraphy, scrivening, signature, script, manuscript, pencraft, scrivenery, style, griffonage, holograph, longhand, handwriting, chirography, engrossment.

STYLUS, *n.* 1. Writing instrument, any sharp instrument for marking, graver, burin, etching-needle, stylograph.

2. Phonograph needle, needle, diamond tip, osmium tip, *etc.*

SUAVE, *adj.* Pleasant, agreeable, polite, urbane, bland, diplomatic, soft, genteel, civilized, complaisant, gracious, conciliatory, obliging, civil, obsequious, mannerly, mild-mannered, soothing, disarming, flattering, ingratiating, insinuating, unctuous, fawning.

SUBALTERN, *adj.* Of lower rank, subordinate, inferior, secondary, subsidiary, lesser, underling.

SUBAQUEOUS, *adj.* Underwater, marine, submarine, undersea, submerged, submersed, subaquatic.

SUBAUDITION, *n.* 1. Act of understanding *or* mentally supplying something not expressed, inference, reading between the lines, deduction.

2. Something mentally supplied, understood *or* implied meaning, hint, inkling, glimmer, allusion, suspicion, intimation, indication, scent, inference, insinuation, implication, subauditor, suggestion, clue.

SUBCONSCIOUS, *adj.* Existing *or* operating beneath *or* beyond consciousness, imperfectly *or* not wholly conscious, subliminal *(Psychol.),* innermost, deep-rooted, inmost, extramarginal *(Psychol.),* deep.

SUBCONSCIOUS, *n.* Totality of mental processes of which the individual is unaware, unreportable mental activities, subliminal, soul, ego, psyche, inmost mind, inner man, inmost *or* essential nature.

SUBCUTANEOUS, *adj.* Situated (lying, introduced, *etc.*) under the skin, hypodermic, hypodermal, subsurface.

SUBDIVIDE, *v.* Divide into smaller parts, grade, redivide, separate into subdivisions, partition, graduate, categorize, classify, dissect, analyze, apportion.

SUBDIVISION, *n.* Part, portion, partition, class, section, subgroup, subclass, subcategory, subhead,

subspecies, suborder, subfamily, share, fraction, piece, compartment, sector.

SUBDUE, *v.* 1. Bring into subjection, overcome, overpower, conquer, subjugate, rout, discomfit, put to flight, overrun, oppress, triumph over, browbeat, humble, defeat, crush, vanquish, worst, master, surmount, quell, foil, get the better of, bend, break, down, put down, bow, get the upper hand of, still, compel, overwhelm, checkmate, thrash, trim, trample in the dust, subject, whip, drub, floor, reduce, smash.

2. Bring into moral subjection *(as by persuasion, inspiring fear, awe, etc.),* subject, tame, make submissive, control, discipline, break in, make docile, capture, charm, captivate, gentle, domesticate, domesticize, enthrall, master, oppress, dominate, trample under foot, hold *or* keep at one's beck and call, make a puppet (sport, plaything) of, use as a doormat.

3. Reduce, repress *(feelings, impulses, etc.),* curb, check, choke, soften, suppress, mellow, moderate, temper, restrain, harness, rein, control, hold back, bridle, withhold, inhibit, smother.

4. Reduce the intensity (force, vividness) of, tone down, soften, mellow, temper, moderate, muffle, ameliorate, deaden, silence, damp down, throttle down, mute, quiet, soft-pedal, repress, dull.

5. Allay *(inflammation, etc.),* relieve, mollify, ease, appease, salve, deaden, slake, slacken, abate, remedy, soothe, temper, mitigate, assuage, reduce, ameliorate, palliate, lenify, tranquilize, cushion, blunt, dulcify.

SUBJACENT, *adj.* Below, underlying, forming a basis, underneath, lower, under, beneath, nether, inferior, foundation, basic, supporting.

SUBJECT, *adj.* 1. *(Often fol. by TO)* Being under domination (control, influence), owing allegiance *or* obedience to, being under dominion (rule, authority), subordinate, subjected, subservient, enslaved, inferior, dependent, under the lash, at one's command, answerable, at one's mercy, at one's beck and call, servile, slavish, under one's thumb, humble, menial, lowborn, abject, submissive, downtrodden, ignoble, passive, lowly, subdued, obeisant, meek, poor, in bonds, in harness, obedient, henpecked, restrained, prostrate.

2. *(Fol. by TO)* Exposed to, being under the necessity of undergoing, open to, susceptive to, prone, disposed, liable, in danger of, amenable, at the mercy of, obnoxious to, victim of, unprotected from, vulnerable, susceptible, pregnable.

3. *(Fol. by TO)* Being dependent *or* conditional upon, contingent, provisional, provisory, incident to, qualificatory, following from, stipulatory.

SUBJECT, *n.* 1. Something that forms a matter of thought (discourse, investigation, *etc.*), substance, topic, theme, point, matter, subject matter, matter in hand, thesis, text, motif, affair, business, problem, food *or* material for thought, issue, field of inquiry, point at issue, case *or* point in question, gist, pith, nub *(coll.),* proposition *(Logic).*

2. Ground, motive, cause, reason, source, position, basis, provocation, occasion, factor, instance, inducement, call, impulse, determining condition.

3. Object *(chosen for representation in art),* model, scene, incident, prototype, original.

4. One who is under the dominion *or* rule of a sovereign, citizen, liege, people *(pl.),* inhabitant, civilian, taxpayer, voter, resident, commoner.

5. Person as an object of medical (surgical,

psychological) treatment *or* experiment, victim, medium, object, patient, case, recipient, experimentee, testee, guinea pig.

6. Dead body as used for dissection, cadaver, carcass, corpse, stiff *(sl.)*.

SUBJECT, *v.* 1. *(Usually fol. by* TO) Bring under rule, bring under domination (control, influence, dominion, authority), subdue, control, make submissive, make subordinate, subjugate, master, overcome, break in, tame, overthrow, conquer, vanquish, enslave, enthrall, lead captive, oppress, triumph over, browbeat, humble, crush, defeat, worst, quell, get the better of, get the upper hand of, compel, down, bend, break.

2. *(Fol. by* TO) Cause to undergo *or* experience, expose, make liable, lay open, endanger, put through, abandon, bare, surrender, submit, jeopardize, imperil, hazard.

SUBJECTION, *n.* Durance, servility, manacles, serfdom, yoke, enslavement, servitude, vassalage, helotry, thralldom, duress, slavery, subjugation, chains, shackles, allegiance, bondage, reins, trammels.

SUBJECTIVE, *adj.* 1. Colored by personal bias, not objective, colored by emotional *or* personal background, prejudiced, biased, personal, individual, inherent, preformed, preconceived.

2. *(Gramm.)* Of *or* pertaining to a subject *(of a sentence)*, nominative, substantive.

3. In the mind of the subject, conditioned by personal characteristics, intellectual, mental, psychological, emotional.

SUBJECT MATTER, *n.* Subject of thought, study, *etc.*, essentials, contents, material, essence, thesis, argument, topic, text, matter, substance, sum and substance.

SUBJOIN, *v.* Add as an accessory *or* appendix, postfix, add at end, suffix, tag, tack to, superadd, attach, join, adjoin, affix, append, add to.

SUBJUGATE, *v.* 1. Enthrall, hold captive, rule, enslave, master, subdue, command, hold in subjugation, sway, suppress, hold in bondage, subject, overrule, give the law to, be master of, dominate, have on the hip, overbear, manage, boss *(coll.)*, govern.

2. Beat, put down, overturn, upset, reduce, quash, outdo, crush, conquer, vanquish, rout, defeat, overcome, overwhelm, overpower, quell, put to flight, outflank, trample, subdue.

SUBJUNCTIVE, *adj.* *(Gramm.)* Pertaining to the mood of a verb denoting possibility, doubt, probability, *etc.*, optative.

SUBLIMATE, *v.* 1. Cause to make sublime *or* raise, aggrandize, elevate, uphold, exalt, heighten, uplift, magnify, lift, ennoble, promote, raise, advance, elate, boost.

2. Make gaseous, vaporize, cause to evaporate, distill, volatilize, gasify, sublime.

3. Direct into other channels, change the course of, divert, turn, bend, shunt, deflect, shift.

SUBLIME, *adj.* 1. Lofty *(in thought, language, etc.)*, elevated, high, noble, pure, excellent, dignified, exalted, beautiful, virtuous, high-minded, honorable, princely, upright, reputable, worthy, estimable, guileless, righteous, moral, principled, spiritual, high-toned, heroic, sterling, praiseworthy, meritorious, distinguished, admirable, good, creditable, stately, refined, magnanimous, *sans peur et sans reproche (Fr.)*.

2. Impressing the mind with a sense of grandeur *or* power, inspiring awe (veneration, *etc.*),

stately, dignified, magnificent, splendid, marvelous, impressive, solemn, majestic, august, glorious, awe-inspiring, towering, overpowering, transcendent, extraordinary, heavenly, radiant, dazzling, mighty, great, noble, grand, eminent, supreme, vast, immense, profound, imposing, lofty.

3. Supreme, perfect, peerless, unsurpassed, unexcelled, transcendent, faultless, ideal, excellent, consummate, pure, unqualified, exquisite, superlative, good, spheral, holy, blameless, immaculate, spotless, unblemished, laudable, orient, matchless, infallible, irreproachable, paramount, inviolate, impeccable, untainted.

SUBLIME, *n.* *(Fol. by* OF) Highest degree *or* example, paragon, model, that which is sublime, the noblest, the best, the ineffable, the highest, perfection, beau ideal, quintessence, spire, pinnacle, height, peak, summit, upper extremity, maximum, optimum, acme, climax, meridian, zenith, supremacy, culmination, crown, *ne plus ultra (Lat.)*.

SUBLIME, *v.* 1. Refine, free from extraneous matter *or* foreign matter, free from impurity, contamination, pollution, *etc.*, epurate, elutriate, disinfect, edulcorate, absterge, expurgate, expurge, depurate, decrassify, bolt, sieve, sift, purge, clarify, cleanse, clear, winnow, deodorize, extract, deterge, fumigate, sweeten, defecate, make pure, rectify, purify, separate, filter, strain, filtrate.

2. Free from evil *or* baseness, *etc.*, purge, anoint, baptize, sanctify, hallow, bless, purify, ennoble, beatify, exalt, consecrate, correct, uplift, elevate, uphold, magnify, lift, advance, elate, boost.

3. Pass directly from solid to gaseous state, vaporize, volatilize, gasify, sublimate.

SUBLIMINAL, *adj.* Existing *or* operating beyond *or* beneath consciousness, imperfectly conscious, subconscious, extramarginal.

SUBLIMITY, *n.* Grandeur, loftiness, eminence, exaltation, preëminence, rank, standing, esteem, greatness, notability, excellence, dignity, glory, supereminence, majesty, stateliness, preferment.

SUBLUNARY, *adj.* Beneath the moon, terrestrial, telluric, tellurian, on earth, earthly, mundane, under the stars, sun, *etc.*

SUBMARINE, *adj.* Underwater, submersed, submerged, subaqueous, subaquatic, marine, undersea.

SUBMARINE, *n.* Sub *(coll.)*, U-boat *(usually restr. to German vessels of World Wars I and II)*, submersible, underwater torpedo boat.

SUBMERGE, *v.* 1. Put under water, submerse, immerge, immerse, plunge, dunk *(coll.)*, dip, souse, sink, bathe, wash, douse *(coll.)*, wet, baptize, drown, rinse.

2. Flood, cover with water, *etc.*, stream over, pour over, inundate, bury, engulf, exundate, submerse, drown, deluge, cover completely, pour torrents upon.

3. Dive, crash dive *(of submarines)*, go under, sink, sound *(of a fish, whale, etc.)*, plunge, go down, duck.

SUBMERSED, *adj.* Underwater, subaquatic, subaqueous, submersible, marine, undersea, underwater, sunk, sunken, on the bottom, below the surface.

SUBMISSION, *n.* 1. Willingness to comply, yield, *etc.*, conformability, tractableness, malleability, dutifulness, capitulation, assent, resignation, docility, obedience, adaptability, respect, bowing, tractability, deference, pliancy, meekness, passiveness, passivity, biddableness, homage, complaisance, nonresistance, compliance.

2. Subservience, slavishness, bootlicking *(sl.)*, ingratiation, subjection, compliance, self-effacement, self-surrender, prostration, self-subdual, self-renunciation, obsequiousness, scraping, bending, bowing, toadying, truckling, abasement, cowering, fawning, cringing, obeisance, servility.

SUBMISSIVE, *adj.* 1. Willing to yield, assenting, acquiescent, respectful, malleable, biddable, meek, passive, nonresisting, unassertive, dutiful, manageable, willing, capitulating, deferential, deferring, relenting, pliant, ductile, compliable, bowing, tractable, adaptable, adapting, subdued, inclined, conforming, docile, obedient, resigned, disposed, yielding, compliant, conformable, accommodating.

2. Scraping, subservient, servile, obsequious, truckling, bowing, self-effacing, prostrate, abased, obeisant, ingratiating, bootlicking *(sl.)*, toadying, crawling, slavish, fawning, self-surrendering.

SUBMIT, *v.* 1. Refer *(to others for judgment, opinion, etc.)*, turn for aid, appeal, defer, call in, ask help of, have recourse to, have resort to, invoke, talk over with, take up with, address, apply, consult.

2. Yield, fall before, be conquered by, succumb, resign to, defer to, knuckle to, kneel to, acquiesce, accede, bend the neck, relent, surrender, bend, give way to, bow, comply, stoop, prostrate oneself before, cringe to, truckle to, humble oneself, capitulate, lay down *or* give up one's arms, hoist the white flag, cede, acknowledge defeat.

3. Offer *(as on opinion, assertion, etc.)*, propose, tender, move, bid, put forward, volunteer, hold out, suggest, put forth.

SUBNORMAL, *adj.* 1. Below normal, below average, of inferior quality, worth, *etc.*, inferior, below standard.

2. Weak-minded, witless, simple-minded, inane, foolish, idiot, imbecile, moronic, childish, unintelligent, half-witted, vacant, oafish, stupid, dumb *(coll.)*.

SUBORDINATE, *adj.* Of low rank, inferior, dependent, ancillary, auxiliary, junior, lower, subject, secondary, subsidiary, subaltern, lesser, underling.

SUBORDINATE, *n.* Thrall, vassal, servant, inferior, subject, underling, hireling, assistant, help, attendant, worker, menial, serf, domestic, valet, servitor, lackey, hand, flunky *(contempt.)*.

SUBORDINATION, *n.* Subjection, submission, subjugation, inferiority, servitude, subserviency, slavery, bondage, thralldom, enslavement, oppression, suppression, helotry, serfdom, deference, resignation, conformity, restraint, vassalage, dependence, second fiddle, obedience, subdual, constraint, repression, back seat *(coll.)*, subordinacy.

SUBORN, *v.* Bribe unlawfully, hire, procure, buy, oil, purchase, tamper with, corrupt, perjure, grease *(sl.)*, throw a sop to.

SUBPOENA, *n.* Writ process for the summoning of witnesses, summons, warrant, citation, writ of summons, order to appear.

SUBPOENA, *v.* Serve with a subpoena, cite, summons, serve with a writ, call, arraign *(Law)*.

SUBROGATE, *v.* Put into the place of another, substitute, supplant, succeed, supersede, change for, replace, ring in *(sl.)*, dub in *(Motion Pictures)*, suffect.

SUB ROSA, *adv.* Privately, confidentially, secretly,

in secret, in silence, under the breath, in the dark, between you and me, between ourselves, *entre nous (Fr.)*, behind *or* with closed doors, under the table, underground, covertly, under cover, underhand, on the sly *(coll.)*, nobody the wiser, in *or* up one's sleeve, hugger-mugger, like a thief in the night, behind the scenes, in private, off the record.

SUBSCRIBE, *v.* 1. Promise to give *or* pay, contribute, serve, help, aid, befriend, undertake, lend one's aid, open one's purse strings, chip in *(coll.)*, pledge.

2. Express assent *or* adhesion to something by signing, sign, attest, undersign, approve, accede, consent, second, endorse, sanction, set one's name to, affix one's signature to, acknowledge, ratify, countersign, initial, mark, stamp, character, inscribe, confirm, accept, corroborate, seal, validate, certify, verify, O.K. *(coll.)*.

SUBSCRIPT, *n.* Something written below, sequel, subscription, affix, addition, appendage, suffix, postscript, adjunct, colophon, epilogue, conclusion, extension, appendix, supplement, pendant, codicil, rider, addendum, additament.

SUBSCRIPTION, *n.* 1. Contribution, donation, largess, oblation, present, gift, subsidy, charity, gratuity, bounty, subvention, grant.

2. Fund raised through sums of money subscribed, charity, collection, offering, offertory.

3. Act of subscribing by signing, endorsement, assent, approval, agreement, ratification, confirmation, authentication, acceptance, affirmation, certification, signature, support, validation, verification, O.K. *(coll.)*.

4. Something subscribed *or* written beneath *or* at the end, subscript, signature, postscript, sequel, affix, addition, appendage, suffix, adjunct, colophon, epilogue, conclusion, extension, appendix, supplement, pendent, codicil, rider, addendum, additament.

SUBSEQUENT, *adj.* Coming later *or* after, following, succeeding, sequent, ensuing, posterior, sequacious, immediate, linear, proximate, future, successive, next, appended, subjoined, consequent, eventual, hereafter, ulterior, to come, to be, expected, prospective, attendant, secondary, subjoined, postliminary.

SUBSERVE, *v.* Be useful *or* instrumental in promoting *(a purpose, action, etc.)*, promote, further, assist, aid, serve, help, contribute, advance, conduce, encourage, minister to, benefit, advantage, attend, profit, better, improve, bestead, lend wings to, facilitate, hasten, expedite, speed, coöperate, accommodate, give a lift, prosper, smooth *or* pave the way, ease, uphold, endorse, favor, stand by, bolster, enhance, set up, take the part of, avail, abet, sustain, foster, forward, quicken.

SUBSERVIENT, *adj.* 1. Serving *or* acting in a subordinate capacity, subordinate, inferior, dependent, ancillary, auxiliary, junior, lower, subject, secondary, subsidiary, subaltern, lesser, underling.

2. Obsequious, servile, excessively submissive, obedient, oily, unctuous, fawning, sycophantic, slavish, whining, toadying, scraping, menial, truckling, ingratiating, bootlicking *(sl.)*, prostrate, vernile, footlicking *(sl.)*, cringing, unassertive, docile, tractable, mealy-mouthed, honeymouthed.

3. Of use as a means to promote a purpose *or* end, useful, helpful, conducive, auxiliary, subsidiary, instrumental, serviceable, contributory, aiding, accessory, ancillary, beneficial, advanta-

geous, constructive, adjunct, adjuvant, propitious, ministrant, effective, utilitarian, valuable, sympathetic, synergetic, handy, favorable, aidful, profitable, favoring, salutary, applicable.

SUBSIDE, *v.* 1. Sink to a low *or* lower level, settle, recede, drop, fall, precipitate, sag, swag, droop, cave in, dip, decline, ebb, slump, gravitate, wane, lapse, descend.

2. Become quiet (less violent *or* active), diminish, decrease, lessen, recede, calm, abate, intermit, ebb, wane, lull, lapse, mitigate, dwindle, let up, remit, shrink, fall off *or* away, moderate, melt *or* die away, languish.

SUBSIDIARY, *adj.* 1. Serving to assist *or* supplement, supplementary, tributary, assistant, auxiliary, ministerial, additional, supplemental, complementing, accessory, ancillary, conducive, instrumental, subservient, coöperating, corroborative, helping, aiding, adjuvant, helpful, serviceable, contributory, beneficial, advantageous, constructive, adjunct, propitious, ministrant, utilitarian, sympathetic, favorable, profitable, favoring.

2. Subordinate, secondary, subservient, inferior, dependent, ancillary, auxiliary, junior, lower, subject, subaltern, lesser, underling.

SUBSIDIZE, *v.* 1. Furnish *or* aid with a subsidy, finance, back, promote, befriend, patronize, subserve, keep, maintain, sustain, support, underwrite, uphold, foster, shoulder.

2. Purchase the assistance of, secure the coöperation of by bribery, buy over, tip, suborn, hire, procure, oil, grease *(sl.)*, throw a sop to, corrupt, tamper with.

SUBSIDY, *n.* 1. Pecuniary aid, contribution of money, pension, annuity, contribution, gratuity, grant, gift, bonus, backing, subvention, allowance, subsistence, maintenance, reward, help.

2. Sum paid by agreement for services *(as between governments)*, tribute, tax, duty, custom, impost.

SUBSIST, *v.* 1. Be, exist, breathe, draw breath, respire, live, continue in life, fare, endure, persist, survive, stand fast, hold on, maintain, remain, abide.

2. Feed, nourish, support, foster, sustain, provide sustenance for, nurture, victual, supply, ration, strengthen, provision, cater.

SUBSISTENCE, *n.* 1. Life, existence, being, entity, quiddity, vital principle, actuality, reality, continuance, endurance, persistence, preservation, maintenance, inherency, inherence.

2. Nourishment, nurture, upkeep, livelihood, support, maintenance, nutriment, provision, sustenance, aliment, meat, food, rations, pabulum, provender, fodder, corn, cheer, fare, diet, regimen, commissariat, board, bread, dietary, staff of life, victuals, eatables, comestibles, viands, grub *(sl.)*, edibles, foodstuff, manna, flesh, repast, refection, meal, chops, collation, potluck, feast, picnic, junket, banquet.

SUBSOIL, *n.* Stratum of earth directly below the surface soil, substratum, undersoil, pan, hardpan, mould, glebe, loam, clay, cledge, marl, gravel, clod.

SUBSTANCE, *n.* 1. Matter, body, stuff, element, essential nature, essence, texture, material, ingredient, constituent, principle, protoplasm, substratum, parenchyma, corpus, hyle *(Philos.)*, corporality, corporeity, physical nature, bodiliness, flesh and blood, incarnation, substantiality,

hypostasis, reality, actuality, groundwork, solid character, species, genus.

2. Solidity, content, weight, extent, quantity, bulk, mass, volume, measure, magnitude, sum, extension, measurement, abundance, amount, strength, size, aggregate.

3. Sense, significancy, burden, import, meaning, drift, core, gist, heart, soul, pith, gravamen, chief part, vital part, kernel, essential part, spirit, life, purport, purpose, intent, signification, bearing, force, tenor, implication, acceptation, allusion, denotation, connotation, suggestion, upshot, interpretation, reference, effect, sum and substance, value, subject, subject matter, argument, quintessence, quiddity, hypostasis, elixir, keynote, backbone, lifeblood, marrow, essentialness, flower.

4. Means, property, possessions, resources, wealth, estate, livelihood, money, income, command of money, revenue, capital, competence, gold, mint, treasure, bonanza, purse, Golconda, El Dorado, Pactolian sands, the golden touch, the Midas touch, purse of Fortunatus, lucre, pelf, patrimony, heritage, legacy, endowment, bequest, belongings, assets, circumstances, effects, chattels, wherewithal, stock, *de quoi (Fr.)*, ways and means, dough, jack, mazuma, velvet, shekels, spondulics, simoleons, kale, long green, chips, wad, bucks, specie, hard cash, circulating medium, currency, receipts, proceeds, wampum.

SUBSTANTIAL, *adj.* 1. Material, bodily, corporeal, somatic, hypostatic, concrete, tangible, physical, palpable, ponderable, corporal, incarnate, embodied, somatological, temporal, materialistic, hylozoistic, hylic.

2. Existent, real, subsistent, actual, virtual, essential, considerable, substantive, fixed, positive, true, absolute, factual, potential, veritable, genuine.

3. Important, indispensable, basic, fundamental, vital, consequential, necessary, valuable, weighty, valid, cogent, just, influential, efficient.

4. Strong, massive, solid, stout, sound, well-made, firm, sizable, stable, goodly, heavy, ample, large, considerable, bulky, durable, compact, lasting, notable, noteworthy, signal.

5. Prosperous, pecuniarily responsible, solvent, wealthy, well-to-do, rich, flourishing, thriving, commercially sound, propertied, moneyed, well-off, affluent, independent, opulent, flush, landed.

SUBSTANTIALITY, *n.* Materiality, corporeity, corporealness, substantialness, hypostatization, tangibility, realness, actuality, factuality, verity, trueness, reification, flesh and blood, hypostasis, entity, material existence, bodiliness.

SUBSTANTIATE, *v.* 1. Materialize, hypostasize, incarnate, embody, reify, actualize, substantialize, realize, incorporate, exteriorize, materiate, externalize.

2. Establish by proof, prove, verify by complete evidence, ratify, corroborate, make good, confirm, testify to, settle firmly, demonstrate, evidence, bear witness, vouch for, depose, attest, certify, support, bear out, endorse, countersign, uphold, vindicate, warrant, authenticate, circumstantiate, sanction.

SUBSTANTIATION, *n.* Confirmation, proof, ratification, attestation, endorsement, corroboration, verification, establishment, warranty, sanction, authorization, support, authentication, recognition, avowal, acknowledgment, acceptance, approval, vindication.

SUBSTANTIVE, *n.* Word having nominal function, noun, pronoun, common noun, proper noun.

SUBSTITUTE, *v.* 1. Put in the place of, change, exchange, interchange, suffect, depute, surrogate, subrogate, delegate, duplicate, redeem, commute, alternate, vary, deputize, ablegate, commission, accredit, empower, authorize.

2. Replace, supersede, supplant, take the rap for, pinch-hit, act for, cut out *(coll.),* be the goat *(sl.),* understudy, take the place of, stand for, represent, answer for, stand in the shoes of, make way for.

SUBSTITUTE, *n.* 1. Agent, representative, alternative, alternate, understudy, deputy, proxy, vicar, pinch hitter, locum tenens, lieutenant, succedaneum, surrogate, double, changeling, dummy, *quid pro quo (Lat.),* delegate, envoy, regent, viceroy, vice-president, vice-chairman, minister, ambassador, consul, plenipotentiary, emissary, commissioner, messenger, consignee, nominee, trustee, factor, middleman, go-between, mediary, steward, fall guy *(sl.),* goat, scapegoat.

2. Temporary expedient, makeshift, *pis aller (Fr.),* shift, stopgap, apology, equivalent, second-best, secondary.

SUBSTITUTION, *n.* 1. Replacement, commutation, exchange, supplanting, change, shift, supersedure, supersession, novation, interchange, mutuality, reciprocity, reciprocation, metonymy, synecdoche, enallage, metaphor, tralatition, allegory, parable, apologue, fable, spoonerism, malapropism, surrogation.

2. Equivalent, *quid pro quo (Lat.),* equipollence, consideration, equal, compensation, exchange value, price, purchase money, payment, permutation, intermutation, transmutation, transposition, swap, shuffle, commerce, barter, tit for tat, reprisal, retaliation, requital, give-and-take.

SUBSTITUTIVE, *adj.* Provisional, tentative, makeshift, temporary, imitational, experimental, counterfeit, pseudo, resembling, near, *ersatz (Ger.),* synthetic, supposititious, spurious, bogus, pretended, *soi-disant (Fr.), sogenannt (Ger.),* subdititious, foisted in.

SUBSTRATUM, *n.* Something underlying, that which is spread under something else, frame, groundwork, underlying substance, matter, element, principle, fundamentum, primordial substance, parenchyma, corpus, stuff, brute matter, protoplasm, hyle *(Philos.),* body, basis, foundation, interior, endocrine, marrow, pith, penetralia, innermost recesses, floor, bed, layer, stratification, subsoil.

SUBSTRUCTURE, *n.* Underbuilding, groundwork, basement, cellar, subcellar, hypogeum, foundation, base, earth, ground, paving, floor, pavement, carpet, flag, bottom, keel, sole, foot, root, nadir.

SUBTERFUGE, *n.* Expedient, stratagem, artifice, shuffle, dodge, sophistry, trick, shift, finesse, excuse, pretext, evasion, pretense, mask, quirk, smoke screen, camouflage, elusion, apology, deception, lie, prevarication, fib, falsehood, untruth, fabrication, forgery, counterfeit, fable, fiction, sell, myth, legend, make-believe, sham, casuistry, perversion, equivocation, Jesuitry, paralogy, chicane, quiddity, speciousness, tongue-fence, quibble, antilogy, mere words, subtlety, ostensible motive, guise, color, gloss, loophole, dust in the eyes, put-off, blind, white lie, maneuver, jugglery, duplicity, guile, ruse, diplomacy, jobbery, Machiavellism, machination, art, device, wile, *espièglerie (Fr.),* imposture.

SUBTERRANEAN, *adj.* 1. Below the surface of the earth, subterraneous, hypogean, underground, hypogeal, hypogeous, plutonic, buried, sunk, subterrane.

2. Operating out of sight, clandestine, underhand, sub rosa, privy, secret, furtive, stealthy, hidden, latent, occult, concealed, veiled, private, *in petto (It.),* undercover, undisclosed, covert, surreptitious.

SUBTILIZE, *v.* 1. Make thin, rarefy, attenuate, volatilize, etherealize, thin out, refine.

2. Make useless distinctions, split hairs, introduce subtleties into, quibble, evade, equivocate, cavil, beat about the bush, reason in a circle, beg the question, varnish, gloss over.

SUBTLE, *adj.* 1. Thin, tenuous, light, rare, superfine, rarefied, attenuated, fine, delicate, filmy, gossamery, diaphanous, transparent, silken, airy, ethereal, subtile, nice, slender, sublimated, volatile, refined, buoyant, slight, porous, unsubstantial, imponderous, floating.

2. Crafty, insidious, wily, cunning, sly, artful, foxy, tricky, designing, astute, intriguing, arch, politic, diplomatic, sophistical, Jesuitical, casuistic, Machiavellian, insinuating, crooked, shrewd, *rusé (Fr.),* feline, underhand, stealthy, deceptive, shifty, canny, strategic, sagacious, acute, profound, keen, penetrating, discerning, deep, discriminating, elusive.

3. Clever, ingenious, expert, skillful, adroit, dexterous, deft, feat, quick, apt, slick, crackajack, good at, proficient, smart, ready, *au fait (Fr.),* masterly, accomplished, finished, sophisticated, felicitous, resourceful, neat-handed, fine-fingered, artistic.

SUBTLETY, *n.* 1. Attenuation, rarefaction, subtileness, delicacy, fineness, subtility, refinement, rareness, nicety, filminess, airiness, etherealness, buoyancy, unsubstantiality.

2. Craftiness, artfulness, slyness, artifice, craft, guile, cunning, astuteness, Machiavellianism, intrigue, strategy, stratagem, deception, diplomacy, ruse, sleight, sophistication, casuistry, Jesuitism.

3. Sagacity, penetration of mind, discernment, keenness, sharpness, acumen, astuteness, cleverness, shrewdness, acuteness, discrimination, intelligence, ready wit, ingenuity, dexterity, adroitness, deftness, quickness, proficiency, resourcefulness.

SUBTRACT, *v.* Diminish in sum, take away from, deduct, withdraw, abstract, take from, reduce, remove, retrench, subduct, abridge.

SUBTRACTION, *n.* Deduction, diminution, withdrawal, abstraction, taking away from, subduction, reduction, retrenchment, ademption, ablation.

SUBURB, *n.* District lying immediately outside a city, residential section, outskirt, faubourg, purlieu, environs, entourage, milieu, circumjacencies, vicinage, neighborhood, vicinity, confines, environment, encompassment, surroundings, *alentours (Fr.),* banlieu.

SUBURBANITE, *n.* Suburban resident, exurbanite, commuter, *faubourien (Fr.).*

SUBVENTION, *n.* Grant of pecuniary aid, subsidy, bounty, largess, dole, aid, help, support, underwriting, furnishing of relief, assistance, sustentation, aidance, succor, lift, maintenance, alimentation, accommodation, sportula, alms, oblation, donative, offertory, charity, philanthropy, generosity, benefaction, boon.

SUBVERSION, *n.* Violent overturn, overthrow,

disestablishment, ruination, inversion, breakup, revolution, *bouleversement (Fr.)*, destruction, *coup d'état (Fr.)*, debacle, upheaval, revulsion, ruin, demolition, demoralization, abolition, disruption, perdition, havoc, *délabrement (Fr.)*, annihilation, extinction, devastation, suppression, *razzia (It.)*, espionage, sabotage, extirpation, incendiarism, overturn, fifth column, Trojan horse.

SUBVERSIVE, *adj.* Tending to overthrow, destructive, upsetting, ruinous, incendiary, deletory, undermining, demoralizing, revolutionary, seditious, traitorous, treasonous, riotous, insurgent, insurrectionary, disruptive.

SUBVERT, *v.* Cause the downfall of, ruin, overturn, overthrow, upset, turn upside down, invert, pull down, sap, undermine, topple, demolish, raze, destroy, level, dismantle, capsize, swamp, wreck, reduce, throw down, extinguish, abolish, demoralize, disrupt, disestablish, upheave, extirpate, annihilate, devastate, spy against, overwhelm, corrupt, pervert, injure, vitiate, undo, put an end to, scuttle, lay waste, ravage, despoil.

SUBWAY, *n.* 1. Underground thoroughfare, tunnel, subterranean passage, burrow, *souterrain (Fr.)*.

2. Electric railroad beneath the street surface, underground, tube, Metro *(Fr.)*.

SUCCEED, *v.* 1. Come next in order, supersede, ensue, follow, come subsequently, come afterward, result, be subsequent to, take the place of, replace, assume the office of, inherit, come into possession, take over, become heir, supervene, attend, accompany.

2. Turn out successfully, terminate according to desire, have the desired result, accomplish what is intended, attain a goal, bring off successfully, realize, achieve, surmount obstacles, triumph, gain, win, prevail, conquer, make a hit, go along well, turn up trumps, feather one's nest, click, come through, have a run of luck, hit, thrive, flourish, prosper, make hay, have the game in one's hands, hit the nail on the head, gain one's end, gain a victory, crown with success, manage to, effect, contrive to, strike oil, progress, turn to account, score a success, win the day, carry all before one, weather the storm, master, outmaneuver, benefit, avail, do well, bear fruit, make a hit.

SUCCEEDING, *adj.* Next in order, subsequent, following, ensuing, sequent, sequential, consecutive, consequent, proximate, later, posterior, successive, after, latter, future, oncoming, prospective, coming, imminent, impending, close at hand, near, immediate, eventual.

SUCCESS, *n.* Favorable termination, felicitous issue, attainment, achievement, accomplishment, prosperity, prosperous issue, progress, advance, good fortune, luck, godsend, windfall, blessing, profit, fat of the land, milk and honey, bed of roses, Easy Street, masterstroke, feat, *coup de maître (Fr.)*, go, hit, prize, ten-strike, triumph, victory, conquest, upper hand, killing *(sl.)*, feather in one's cap, trump card, advantage, whip hand, walkover, ascendancy, mastery, palm, laurels, crown, top of the world, grand slam, going concern, welfare, weal, affluence, well-being, happiness.

SUCCESSFUL, *adj.* Lucky, fortunate, auspicious, happy, felicitous, triumphant, favorable, flourishing, prosperous, crowned with success, victorious, booming, high-flying, winning, unbeaten, thriving,

halcyon, palmy, rich, affluent, well-off, propitious, providential, rosy, bright, promising, flushed with victory, in the ascendant, set up, in full swing.

SUCCESSION, *n.* 1. Sequence, order, course, progression, consecution, procession, concatenation, rotation, series, cycle, chain, suite, round, run, turn, alternation, following, train, gradation, continuity, prolongation, continuation, extension.

2. Line of descendants, lineage, dynasty, descent, filiation, heredity, sonship, extraction, derivation, birth, pedigree, family, race, offspring, progeny, posterity, issue, seed, rising generation.

SUCCESSIVE, *adj.* Following in uninterrupted course, ensuing, succeeding, subsequent, later, after, posterior, sequential, consecutive, sequent, progressive, seriatim.

SUCCESSOR, *n.* 1. Follower, disciple, sectary, partisan, adherent, attendant, proselyte, satellite, client, parasite, sycophant, dangler, hanger-on, dependent.

2. Inheritor, heir, beneficiary, grantee, devisee, legatee.

3. Progeny, issue, posterity, brood, offspring, seed, spawn, family, scion, descendant.

SUCCINCT, *adj.* Expressed in few words, characterized by verbal brevity, terse, laconic, curt, concise, brief, short, clipped, compendious, compact, pithy, condensed, summary, to the point, pointed, crisp, neat, trenchant, epigrammatic, sententious, synoptic, taciturn, close-mouthed, reticent, reserved, pauciloquent, sparing of words.

SUCCOR, *v.* Help, aid, abet, assist, befriend, adjuvate, relieve, support, sustain, rescue, deliver, minister, alleviate, comfort, nurse, foster, cherish, encourage, take care of, bolster up, further, favor, forward, grubstake, finance, feed, victual, reinforce, strengthen, brace, fortify, protect, champion, defend, patronize, uphold, back up, second, countenance, shield, lend a hand, lend one's aid, come to the aid of, render assistance, stretch out a helping hand, take in tow, give new life to, recruit, give a lift to, promote, nurture, tender to, wait on, accommodate, oblige, stand by, take up the cudgels for, espouse the cause of, advocate, side with.

SUCCOR, *n.* Aid, help, assistance, helping hand, support, relief, aidance, lift, promotion, furtherance, advance, coadjuvancy, championship, patronage, advocacy, countenance, auspices, subvention, sustentation, subsidy, bounty, maintenance, alimentation, manna in the wilderness, accommodation, rescue, reinforcement.

SUCCUBUS, *n.* 1. Demon fabled to have sexual intercourse with men in their sleep, incubus, vampire, fiend.

2. Lascivious person, whore, prostitute, strumpet, doxy, wench, hustler, chippy, tart, jade, harlot, broad, *fille de joie (Fr.)*, bitch, streetwalker, demirep, trollop, baggage, trull, hussy, drab, slut, cocotte, lorette, grisette, demimondaine.

SUCCULENT, *adj.* Juicy, having fleshy tissues *(plants)*, pulpy, sacculous, lush, sappy, not dry, spongy, nutritive, serous, nutritious, rich in desirable qualities.

SUCCUMB, *v.* 1. Submit, yield, capitulate, surrender, give way, give in, defer to, resign, accede, lay down one's arms, strike one's colors, hand over one's sword, come to terms, beat a retreat, draw in one's horns, cave in, give ground, bend to one's yoke, reel back, bite the dust, throw oneself at the feet of, lose the day, have the worst of it, fall a prey to, fall to the ground, fail, come to naught, falter, flounder, run aground, sink, break down, come to grief, ground.

2. Be fatigued, flag, droop, drop, faint, swoon, die, expire.

SUCH, *adj.* Like similar, of that particular character, suchlike, of the like, of that kind, being as stated, resembling, twin, analogous, alike, corresponding, congenerous, duplicate, consimilar, homologous, parallel, of a piece, cognate, akin to, connatural, kindred, close, approximate, representing, true to life, simulating.

SUCK, *v.* Draw into the mouth with the lips, apply the mouth to, draw upon by producing a partial vacuum, quaff, lap up, tipple, swig, sip, imbibe, engulf, swallow up, absorb by action of the tongue, drink, mouth, pull at with the mouth, extract, draw off.

SUCKER, *n.* 1. Person easily imposed upon, victim, dupe, gull, fall guy *(sl.)*, April fool, gudgeon, cully, pigeon, Simple Simon, puppet, greenhorn, parasite, tool, novice, pawn.

2. Mouth, aperture, nozzle, orifice, *embouchure (Fr.),* muzzle, gullet.

3. Sprout, shoot, branch, twig, offshoot, creeper, tendril, runner, sprig, branchlet, ramulus.

SUCKLE, *v.* Feed at the breast, give suck to, breast-feed, nurse, nurture, nourish.

SUCKLING, *n.* An infant that is not yet weaned, nursling, baby, babe, bantling, bambino, papoose, pickaninny, bairn, chit, chick, brat, little one, little child.

SUDATORIUM, *n.* Hot-air bath for inducing sweating, sweating-bath, sweating-room, vapor bath, Turkish bath, tepidarium, caldarium, thermae, bagnio, stew, warm bath, Russian bath, sudatory, Swedish bath.

SUDDEN, *adj.* 1. Unlooked for, unforeseen, unexpected, without warning, without gradual approach, unanticipated, instantaneous, prompt, instant, immediate, precipitate, subitaneous, precipitous.

2. Rapid, quick, swift, speedy, alacritous, abrupt, brief, short-lived, momentary, ephemeral, transient, hasty, meteoric, spasmodic, expeditious, express, hurried, headlong, pressing, feverish, urgent, brisk, fleet, summary, fugitive, fleeting.

SUDDENLY, *adv.* Immediately, instanter, forthwith, at once, all of a sudden, unexpectedly, plump *(coll.),* pop, abruptly, on the spur of the moment, unlooked for, presto, smack, slap, instantaneously, in an instant, without warning, all at once, apace, speedily, quickly, on the spot, at short notice, straightway, instantly, in no time, in a trice, in a jiffy, in the twinkling of an eye, in double-quick time, posthaste, hastily, with haste, pell-mell, amain, headlong, slap-bang, slapdash, helter-skelter, hotfoot, expeditiously, precipitately.

SUDORIFIC, *adj.* Causing sweat, perspirant, diaphoretic, sudoriparous, sweltering, sudoriferous.

SUDS, *n.* Soapy water, lather, foam, froth, spume, spray, bubbles, head, spindrift, barm, surf.

SUE, *v.* 1. Institute process in law against, prosecute, indict, bring a civil action against, impeach, litigate, serve with a writ, summons, subpoena, arraign, prefer a claim, accuse, bring to justice, put on trial, bring to the bar, go to law, contest, appeal to the law, cite.

2. Petition, beg, entreat, make appeal to, supplicate, obtest, beseech, obsecrate, implore, plead,

pray, seek by request, appeal, demand, apply for, solicit, claim, crave, ask, request, canvass, adjure, conjure, invoke, cry to, importune, besiege, urge, press, dun, clamor for.

3. Court, woo, seek after, spark, philander, serenade, address, set one's cap at, pay one's addresses to, pay court to, propose, pop the question, plight one's troth.

SUET, *n.* Hard fatty tissue, tallow with adhering membranes, mutton-fat, beef-fat, grease, lard, dripping, blubber.

SUFFER, *v.* 1. Endure, feel, undergo, meet with, go through, experience, be subjected to, bear up under, bear with, abide, brook, sustain, tolerate, support, stand, put up with, stomach, pocket, be affected by, receive, be acted upon.

2. Let, permit, recognize, vouchsafe, accord, concede, admit, allow, gratify, oblige, favor, humor, wink at, close the eyes to, stretch a point, indulge, connive at, grant, privilege, sanction, empower, license, give leave to, acquiesce.

3. Feel pain, ache, smart, groan, agonize, twinge, writhe, gasp, convulse, grieve, sweat, bear the cross, wince, bleed, droop, lament, languish, pine, despair, break down, give way.

SUFFERANCE, *n.* 1. Permission, tolerance, tacit allowance, toleration, connivance, leave, congé, license, accordance, favor, indulgence, grace, liberty, concession, authorization.

2. Long-suffering, patience, submission, capacity to endure, equanimity, command, stoicism, sobriety, gravity, staidness, self-control, self-possession, self-restraint, resignation, supportance, fortitude, placidity, imperturbation, quietude, sang-froid, tranquillity, indisturbance, composure, calmness, coolness.

SUFFERER, *n.* Victim, martyr, prey, quarry, game, shorn lamb, wretch, patient, *malade imaginaire (Fr.),* hypochondriac, valetudinarian, convalescent, invalid, case, cripple.

SUFFERING, *n.* 1. Discomfort, ache, pang, pain, distress, throe, misery, twinge, hurt, gripe, smart, nip, pinch, shooting, lancination, laceration, cut, soreness, seizure, spasm, paroxysm, convulsion, cramp, stitch, throbbing, anguish, affliction, rack, torment, torture, agony.

2. Endurance, sufferance, pathos, martyrdom, affection, susceptibility, feeling, distress, grief, woe, sorrow, dolor, heavy heart, heartache, misery, prostration.

3. Worry, care, concern, solicitude, anxiety, cark, ordeal, burden, trial, trouble, blow, shock, load, fret, tribulation.

SUFFICE, *v.* 1. Be enough, be adequate, be sufficient, do, pass muster, answer, serve, avail, satisfy, content, please, gratify, appease.

2. Abound, teem, be rife, superabound, exuberate, bristle with, swarm, pile up, redound, load, inundate, deluge, flood, drench, overflow, run over.

3. Satiate, sate, saturate, pall, cloy, gorge, glut, surfeit, slake, quench.

SUFFICIENCY, *n.* 1. Enough, sufficientness, adequacy, *quantum sufficit (Lat.),* wherewithal, *de quoi (Fr.),* satisfaction, competency, adequate resources, contentment.

2. Plenty, plenitude, ample stock, supply, abundance, amplitude, copiousness, cornucopia, horn of Amalthaea, horn of plenty, affluence, full measure, profusion, luxuriance, repletion, fill, satiety, surfeit, fullness, saturation, redundance,

exuberance, profuseness, plethora, glut, congestion, engorgement, satiation, accumulation, store, hoard, fund, vein, mine, lode, reservoir, quarry, well, fountain, spring, treasure, cache.

3. Qualification, competence, fitness, efficiency, ability, capacity, skill, skillfulness, capability.

SUFFICIENT, *adj.* 1. Enough, ample, adequate to meet a want, full, up to the mark, satisfactory, commensurate with need, sufficing, lavish, plenty, plenteous, plentiful, copious, replete, abundant, chock-full, well-provided, affluent, opulent, rich, luxuriant, bountiful, bounteous, rife, exuberant, proportionate, gratifying, satisfying, profuse.

2. Competent, qualified, efficient, fit, capable, able, responsible, equal to.

SUFFIX, *v.* Attach to the end of, append, affix, postfix, annex, add on to, tack to, subjoin, tag.

SUFFIX, *n.* Element added to a preceding one, affix, postfix, ending, termination, addition, rider, terminant, appendage, subscript, postscript, tag, adjunct, pendant, codicil, addendum, tab.

SUFFOCATE, *v.* Strangle, choke, kill by stopping respiration, impede the respiration of, mug *(sl.),* asphyxiate, smother, stifle, burke, garrote, throttle.

SUFFOCATION, *n.* Strangulation, asphyxiation, extinguishment, extinction, smothering, choking, throttling, garrote, thuggee, mugging.

SUFFRAGE, *n.* Vote, ballot, franchise, voice, say, election right, ticket, plebiscite, *vox populi (Lat.),* poll, referendum, option, choice, preferment, volition, discretion, decision, judgment, co-option, co-optation, pick, selection, determination, preference.

SUFFUSE, *v.* 1. Spread over, overspread, cover, fill, bathe, infuse, imbue, diffuse, infiltrate, mantle, transfuse.

2. Change color, redden, crimson, blush, flush, glow, warm.

SUGAR, *n.* Sweet crystalline substance, sucrose, saccharin, dulcin, glucose, crystallose, saccharose, dextrose, lactose, maltose, levulose, fructose, muscovado, cassonade, caramel, inositol.

SUGARY, *adj.* 1. Sweet, candied, saccharine, dulcet, cloying, saccharoid, honey-sweet, luscious, nectareous, sacchariferous, honied.

2. Deceitfully agreeable, flattering, sycophantic, complaisant, complimentary, adulatory, buttery, mealy-mouthed, smooth-tongued, blandiloquent, soapy, unctuous, specious, servile, fulsome.

SUGGEST, *v.* 1. Counsel, advise, recommend, propose, propound, present as possible, submit, move, put forward, advance, advocate, mention, urge, prompt, prescribe, exhort, guide, persuade, place before consideration.

2. Hint, give an inkling of, insinuate, intimate, allude to, refer to, indicate, imply, whisper, tip, breathe, give a pointer to, give the cue, let fall.

SUGGESTION, *n.* 1. Hint, presentation, representation, insinuation, intimation, allusion, reference, innuendo, reminder, prompting, exhortation, implication, prompture, cue, inkling, whisper, word to the wise, *verbum sapienti (Lat.),* pointer, tip, advice, counsel, recommendation, surmise, supposition, assumption, conjecture.

2. Slight trace, suspicion, soupçon, dash, tinge, sprinkling, grain, touch, smack, little, taste, dab, shade, aftertaste.

SUGGESTIVE, *adj.* 1. Indicative, stimulative, expressive, evocative, portentous, reminiscential, ominous, allusive, vivid, fresh, graphic, pictorial, remindful, referential, commemoratory, indelible, reminiscent, recollective, unforgettable, memorable.

2. Such as to suggest something indecent, risqué, off-color, lewd, coarse, gross, licentious, pornographic, smutty, lickerish, lascivious, lustful, libidinous, seductive, bawdy, impure, shameless, indecent, indelicate, loose, free, broad, ribald, sensual, inflammatory, erotic, obscene, carnal, lecherous, salacious, voluptuous, wanton, dissolute.

SUICIDAL, *adj.* Self-destructive, deadly, lethal, ruinous, slaughterous, murderous, sanguinary, bloodstained, sanguinolent, red-handed, bloody-minded, homicidal, sanguineous, gory, lethiferous, fatal, mortal, mortiferous, death-dealing.

SUICIDE, *n.* 1. Intentional taking of one's own life, self-murder, self-destruction, self-homicide, self-slaughter, hara-kiri, self-immolation, suttee, *seppuku (Jap.),* car of Juggernaut, felo-de-se.

2. Self-murderer, self-killer, self-executioner.

SUI GENERIS, *(Lat.)* Of its own kind, unique, extraordinary, exceptional, rare, uncommon, unusual, individual, peculiar, original, unparalleled, unmatched, unexampled, unwonted, inimitable, out-of-the-way, curious, singular, odd, bohemian, nondescript, strange, bizarre, *outré (Fr.),* exotic, unfamiliar, novel.

SUIT, *v.* 1. Fit, conform, agree, harmonize, meet, correspond, accord, comport, match, tally, serve, answer, coincide, concur, respond, fall in with, equal, parallel, dovetail, resemble.

2. Adapt, accommodate, adjust, make suitable, fashion, level, make appropriate, rectify, square, graduate, calibrate, correct, regulate, reconcile.

3. Befit, become, beseem, be fitted to, be appropriate for, be suitable for, be expedient, conduce.

4. Satisfy, gratify, please, prove satisfactory, make content, delight, be agreeable to, be acceptable to, take the fancy of, captivate, gladden, rejoice, elate, tickle one's fancy, make glad, oblige, seem good to.

SUIT, *n.* 1. Vestments intended to be worn together, set of garments, costume, clothing, habit, apparel, attire, clothes, dress, toilet, raiment, habiliment, vesture, garb, wearing apparel, wardrobe, array, outfit, livery, regimentals, rigging, gear, accouterment, turnout, trappings, caparison, togs, duds, uniform.

2. Entreaty, supplication, petition, appeal, request, prayer, solicitation, objuration, invocation, plea, application, call, beseechment, impetration, obsecration, obtestation, imploration, importunity, interpellation, requisition, canvass, proposal, overture, suggestion, submission, proposition.

3. Legal prosecution, action at law, trial, process, case, lawsuit, litigation, proceeding, suit in law, cause, judicial contest, replevin, assumpsit, arraignment, indictment, presentment, accusation, true bill, subpoena, summons, citation, writ.

4. Courtship, addresses, wooing, attention, court, love-making, amorous glances, serenading, sheep's eyes, flirtation, gallantry, coquetry, petting, spooning, necking, embrace, caressing, dalliance, fondling, billing and cooing, blandishment, endearment, osculation, kissing, bussing, smack, romance, *affaire de coeur (Fr.), affaire d'amour (Fr.),* love affair, amour, tryst, rendezvous, tender passion, date, devotion, passion, rapture, ecstasy, flame.

SUITABLE, *adj.* Appropriate, becoming, fitting, apt, agreeable, worthy, just, meet, fit, befitting, seemly, apposite, advisable, merited, useful, apropos, *comme il faut (Fr.),* feasible, practicable, reasonable, expedient, favorable, compatible, applicable, proper, relevant, pertinent, germane, rightful, congruent, congruous, opportune, seasonable, timely, conformable, congenial, right, decorous, qualified, decent, eligible, to the point, adequate, commodious, to the purpose, convenient, harmonious, consonant, accordant, consistent, graceful, commensurate, correspondent, admissible, likely, due, condign, deserved, cut out for, neat, capable, accommodating, coherent, reconcilable, proportionate, pat, felicitous, happy, *ad rem (Lat.),* desirable, acceptable, worthwhile, advantageous.

SUITABLENESS, *n.* Fitness, suitability, aptness, aptitude, appropriateness, agreeableness, agreement, congruity, congruousness, congruence, consistency, compatibility, consonance, harmoniousness, harmony, symmetry, unanimity, conformity, correspondence, compliance, pertinence, relevancy, appositeness, germaneness, decorum, decency, propriety, expedience, convenience, timeliness, opportuneness, seasonableness, seemliness, usefulness, advantageousness, feasibility, practicability, applicability, congeniality, adequacy, accordance, commensurateness, neatness, capability, coherency, desirability, acceptability.

SUITCASE, *n.* Flat oblong valise, traveling bag, grip, Gladstone, two-suiter, portmanteau, duffel bag, kitbag, carpetbag, overnight bag, bandbox, ditty bag, rucksack, knapsack, haversack, satchel, luggage, baggage, impedimenta.

SUITE, *n.* 1. Train of attendants, company of followers, retinue, cortege, staff, bodyguard, escort, court, convoy, following, force, entourage, parade, column, cavalcade.

2. Series, set, progression, sequence, chain, catena, round, continuity, succession, row, queue, line, tier, range.

3. Apartment, flat, connected number of rooms, penthouse, habitation, residence, domicile, lodging, diggings, abode, berth, quarters, housing, headquarters.

SUITOR, *n.* 1. Lover, sweetheart, flame, gallant, beau, boy friend, steady *(coll.),* admirer, wooer, swain, adorer, follower, fiancé, inamorato, young man *(coll.),* truelove, Lothario, cavalier, squire, escort, cicisbeo, aspirant, attendant.

2. Petitioner, applicant, solicitor, suppliant, supplicant, plaintiff, libelant, litigant, postulant, claimant, competitor, candidate, bidder, canvasser.

SULCATE, *adj.* Having long narrow channels, grooved, furrowed, channeled, fluted, scored, cleft, corrugated, ribbed, striated, canaliculated, bisulcate, trisulcate.

SULK, *v.* Hold aloof in a sullenly ill-humored mood, wear a long face, show ill temper, be sullen, be offended, take umbrage, show offense, be indignant, pout, be sulky, mope, scowl, fret, frown, be out of humor, glower, lower, have a hangdog look, grouch, be in a huff, be miffed, be in a pet, take amiss, resent, take exception, fume, chafe, be irascible, take ill, grumble, grouse, complain, growl, look glum, make a wry face, repine, be disgruntled, be put out, brood over.

SULKINESS, *n.* 1. Moroseness, churlishness, ill temper, ill humor, sullenness, moodiness, mump-

ishness, sulks, sourness, crabbedness, crabbiness, bad blood, spleen, gall, bile, resentment, resentfulness, long face, hangdog look, glumness, dourness, umbrage, indignation, pouting, mopishness, fretfulness, scowling, frowning, grouchiness, huffiness, miff, pet, irascibility, grousing, wryness, disgruntlement, unamiability, unsociableness, perverseness, grumpiness, dudgeon, doldrums.

2. Obstinacy, stubbornness, indocility, intractability, thorniness, spinosity, mulishness, recalcitrancy, cussedness, obduracy, contumacy, self-will.

3. Gloominess, dismalness, somberness, melancholy, dejection, despondency, depression, blues, hypochondria, pessimism.

SULKY, *adj.* Sullen, ill-humored, resentful, morose, ill-tempered, churlish, grouchy, out of humor, cross-grained, perverse, wayward, sour, crabbed, crabby, splenetic, spleenish, surly, mumpish, mopish, huffy, miffed, in a pet, out of tune, out of temper, peevish, cross, dogged, grouty, glum, fretful, petulant, captious, reticent, taciturn, aloof, reserved, obdurate, unsociable, unamiable, bitter, acerbous, grumpy, cantankerous, growling, glowering, frowning, scowling, gruff, ill-disposed, crusty, sore, cussed, restive, refractory, intractable, mulish, stubborn, thorny, recalcitrant, contumacious, self-willed, moody.

SULLEN, *adj.* 1. Showing ill humor by a gloomy silence, frowning, scowling, glowering, morose, grumpy, sour, glum, crusty, surly, grim, ill-tempered, out of humor, sore, grouchy, sulky, cross, crabbed, crabby, splenetic, waspish, snappish, churlish, acerbous, ill-natured, moody, mumpish, petulant, unsociable, unamiable, cantankerous, peevish, peeved, resentful, touchy, indignant, acrimonious, huffy, on one's high ropes *(coll.),* choleric, nettlesome, querulous, fractious, captious, temperamental, tart, sarcastic, virulent, trenchant, caustic, contumelious, blunt, gruff, boorish, harsh, brusque, in high dudgeon, irritable.

2. Dismal, gloomy, funereal, melancholy, hypochondriac, somber, foreboding, dark, cheerless, mournful, doleful, dolorous, depressing, dull, heavy, sluggish, down-in-the-mouth, in the doldrums, blue, pessimistic, dejected, despondent, low-spirited, weary, forlorn, disconsolate, desolate, dreary.

3. Obstinate, mulish, dogged, perverse, refractory, recalcitrant, restive, stubborn, intractable, balky, obdurate, inflexible, pigheaded, self-willed, headstrong.

SULLENNESS, *n.* 1. Moroseness, ill humor, ill temper, ill-disposedness, sulkiness, moodiness, sourness, crabbedness, sulks, dudgeon, pique, umbrage, resentment, spleen, gall, bile, virulence, churlishness, bad blood, glumness, grouchiness, mopishness, grumpiness, mumps, doldrums, long face, wry look, scowl, black look, frown, unsociableness, unamiability, morosity, irascibility, huff, miff, pet, displeasure, choler, indignation, vexation, bitterness, acrimony, soreness, acerbity, irritability, petulance, querulousness, tartness, crossness, gruffness, captiousness.

2. Somberness, dismalness, dreariness, gloominess, gloom, funerealness, pessimism, melancholia, hypochondria, despondency, cheerlessness, dolor, heaviness, dullness, sluggishness, apathy, weariness.

3. Obstinacy, mulishness, doggedness, perversity, refractoriness, recalcitrancy, stubbornness, restiveness, intractability, balkiness, pigheadedness, self-will.

SULLY, *v.* 1. Soil, blur, daub, blot, stain, tarnish, taint, spot, smirch, contaminate, dull, foul, defile, blemish, mar, bedim, spoil, attaint, injure, deface, mar the purity of, smear, smudge, smutch, spatter, drabble, besmear, bemire, splash, befoul, pollute, corrupt.

2. Defame, denigrate, blacken, asperse, slur, disgrace, dishonor, stigmatize, shame, put to shame, discredit, degrade, debase, vilify, brand, drag through the mire, run down, decry, insinuate, depreciate, dispraise, traduce, malign, belittle, disparage, knock, speak ill of, deprecate, condemn, ostracize, blackball, boycott, black-list, revile, denounce, impeach, impugn, gibbet, expose.

SULPHUR-COLORED, *adj.* Greenish-yellow, citrine, yellow, xanthic, luteous, citron-colored, lemon-colored, xanthous, saffron, fulvous, fulvescent, amber, tawny, ocherous.

SULTAN, *n.* Mohammedan sovereign, grand Turk, Ottoman ruler, grand-seignior, padishah, Turkish potentate, caliph, imaum, shah, sophi, pasha, dey, bey, scherif, khedive, bashaw.

SULTRINESS, *n.* 1. Moist heat, oppressiveness, mugginess, humidity, closeness, dog days, Canicula, Sirius, stifling weather, stuffiness, sweltering heat.

2. Lewdness, wantonness, sexiness *(coll.)*, eroticism, ardency, passion, lasciviousness, lechery, libidinousness, licentiousness, pruriency, sensuality, concupiscence, carnality, lustfulness, salacity, lubricity, incontinence, debauchery, obscenity.

3. Choler, irascibility, explosiveness, hotheadedness, anger, ire, animosity, pique, miff, huff, tantrum, dudgeon, soreness, vials of wrath, hot blood.

SULTRY, *adj.* 1. Muggy, warm and damp, sweltering, close, hot and moist, humid, oppressive, stuffy, reeking, suffocating, sudorific, sweaty, canicular, estival, stifling.

2. Passionate, erotic, sexy *(coll.)*, ardent, lascivious, wanton, lewd, lecherous, libidinous, licentious, lustful, lickerish, prurient, ruttish, obscene, bawdy, carnal, concupiscent, salacious, sensual, dissolute, incontinent, debauched, dissipated, bestial, adulterous, ribald.

3. Hot-headed, choleric, irascible, excitable, high-strung, temperamental, inflammable, wrathful, hasty, impatient, irritable, fidgety, fretful, testy, quick, touchy, peppery, petulant, huffy, waspish, fiery, snappy, moody, querulous, restive, peevish, fractious.

SUM, *n.* 1. Aggregate amount, totality, aggregate, total, all, sum total, entirety, the whole, gross amount, wholeness, omnitude, *ensemble (Fr.),* everything, Alpha and Omega, be-all and end-all, length and breadth.

2. Quantity of money, amount, balance, balance sheet, proceeds, receipts.

3. Arithmetical question, problem, example, product, summation, tally, tale, difference.

4. Summary, sum and substance, compendium, gist, digest, minute, draft, note, outline, synopsis, conspectus, résumé, *multum in parvo (Lat.),* condensation, abridgment, epitome, brief, abstract, précis, aperçu.

SUM, *v.* 1. Combine into an aggregate, total, ascertain the sum of by addition, sum up, reckon, calculate, add together, cast up, add, compute, account, figure up, foot, enumerate, numer-

ate, count, number up, tell off, estimate, tot up, take an account of, call over, score.

2. Bring into a small compass, put in a nutshell, state in brief, summarize, epitomize, condense, abstract, abridge, compress, digest, curtail, contract, abbreviate, shorten.

SUMMARILY, *adv.* 1. Without delay, forthwith, at short notice, readily, promptly, with dispatch, by a short method, arbitrarily, despotically, autocratically, precipitately, suddenly, extempore, on the spur of the moment, at once, on the spot, straightway, instanter, quickly, speedily, immediately, presently, apace, directly.

2. In a few words, concisely, tersely, laconically, compactly, compendiously, briefly, in short, in a nutshell, in a word, to come to the point, to make a long story short.

SUMMARIZE, *v.* Make a summary of, express in a concise form, abridge, epitomize, abstract, digest, recapitulate, sum up, skim over, review, abbreviate, condense, blue-pencil, edit, compile, curtail, shorten, take in, reduce, compress, cut short, retrench, prune down, cut back.

SUMMARY, *adj.* 1. Quickly performed, unceremoniously fast, conducted without delay, direct, expeditious, prompt, rapid, quick, brief, brisk, fleet, hasty, cursory, instantaneous, spasmodic, pressed for time, momentary, sudden, hurried, volatile, meteoric.

2. Concise, succinct, terse, laconic, short, curt, pithy, condensed, compendious, compact, synoptical, sparing of words, abridged, *abrégé (Fr.),* comprehensive.

SUMMARY, *n.* Brief and comprehensive presentation of facts, short version of a longer work, detailed outline, digest, résumé, abstract, syllabus, précis, epitome, compendium, compend, pandect, conspectus, breviary, brief, abridgment, synopsis, abbreviation, sketch, sum and substance, pith of the matter, capitulation, the short and the long, bird's-eye view, restatement of minor points, compressed statement, recapitulation, review, analysis, bulletin, condensation, *multum in parvo (Lat.),* minute, draft, note, prospectus, contents, aperçu, extracts, excerpts, compilation.

SUMMER, *n.* 1. Second and warmest season of the year, period from June through August, season of most direct sunshine, summer solstice, dog days, canicule, canicular days, midsummer, Bengal summer, broiling sun, baking heat, summertime, summertide, Indian summer.

2. Period of finest development *or* perfection, time of maturing powers, fruition, fulfillment, consummation, early middle age.

SUMMER, *v.* Spend the summer, estivate, vacation, holiday.

SUMMERHOUSE, *n.* Rustic structure in a garden for shade and coolness, gardenhouse, arbor, pergola, bower, kiosk, hermitage, grotto, alcove, vinery, greenhouse, conservatory.

SUMMIT, *n.* Highest point, top, peak, pinnacle, apex, crest, crown, acme, zenith, tiptop, culminating point, head, cap, vertex, ne plus ultra, brow, capsheaf, culmen, culmination, climax, maximum, pitch, spire, turning point, consummation, goal, utmost, height.

SUMMON, *v.* 1. Call together for some task, call upon to do something, bid to some duty, call for, muster, call forth for performance, rouse, gather, call out, send for, invite, ask, call into action, rouse, invoke, challenge, convocate, preconize, call with authority, beckon, order, command, give orders, direct, prescribe, instruct, bid, enjoin, charge, appoint, ordain, set, impose a task, issue a command, set to work, call to order, demand, require.

2. Subpoena, arraign, cite, call to witness, notify to appear at a specified place, call for the presence of, convoke, convene, give notice to, summons, command to appear, serve with a writ.

SUMMONS, *n.* 1. Authoritative command, official notice, notification, direction, injunction, behest, commandment, precept, dictation, ruling, charge, regulation, order, bidding, fiat, ordinance, nod, beck, word, call, instructions, exaction, demand, requisition, imposition, ultimatum, claim, requirement, request, dictate, decree, rescript, mandate, writ, edict, caveat, prescript, word of command, ukase, firman, solicitation, alarum, alarm, invitation, convocation, invocation.

2. Authoritative citation to appear before a court, subpoena, signal by which one is summoned, warrant, writ, *habeas corpus (Law),* arraignment, indictment, presentment, conjuration, roll call.

SUMMON UP, *v.* 1. Recall, recollect, remember, flash on the mind, bethink oneself, conjure up, call up, retrace, look back upon, bring to mind, review, rake up the past, remembrance, fan the embers, keep in mind, prompt, renew, refresh the memory, redeem from oblivion, commemorate, revive, rekindle.

2. Rouse, arouse, excite, drum up, muster, call into action, pluck up, call up, raise, work oneself up, impassion, inspire, set astir, awaken, call forth, evoke, provoke, get up, wake up, get up steam, nerve oneself, screw one's courage to the sticking point.

SUMMUM BONUM, *n. (Lat.)* Highest good, chief good, greatest good, best, common weal, paradise, heaven, elysium, unalloyed happiness, beatitude, felicity, bliss, golden age, Arcadia, Eden, *Saturnia regna (Lat.),* well-being, fruition, gratification, pleasure, contentment, satisfaction, comfort, ease, advantage, benefit, interest, improvement, behalf, behoof, service, gain, profit, boot, benison, blessing, boon, world of good.

SUMPTUOUS, *adj.* Entailing great expense, costly, dear, rich, expensive, luxurious, high-priced, de luxe, valuable, magnificent, splendid, superb, gorgeous, prodigal, lavish, munificent, showy, pompous, grand, stately, princely, regal, elegant, pretentious, ostentatious, spectacular, glittering, bespangled, bejeweled, palatial, majestic, ornate, florid, gilded, resplendent, refulgent, lordly, imposing.

SUN, *n.* 1. Orb of day, daystar, luminary, self-luminous heavenly body, central star of the solar system, light of heaven, parhelion *(mock sun),* source of light.

2. Sun god, Apollo, Helios, Phoebus, Hyperion, Phaëthon, Sol, Ra, Shamash.

SUNBURNT, *adj.* Bronzed, tanned, burned, brown as a berry, ruddy-faced, tan, blowzy, browned, coppery.

SUNDAY, *n.* Day of rest, first day of the week, Sabbath, Lord's day, *dies non (Lat.),* day of special worship.

SUNDER, *v.* Sever, separate, disjoin, part, divide, disunite, disconnect, dispart, dissever, dissociate, tear asunder, break, split, cut, rend, dissolve,

cleave, disengage, detach, slit apart, cut off, divorce, quarter, dissect, partition, dismember, rupture, lacerate, snap, rive.

SUNDRY, *adj.* More than one, various, several, many, divers, numerous, manifold, different, not a great many, abundant.

SUNLESS, *adj.* Lightless, rayless, unillumined, unilluminated, unlighted, beamless, darksome, darkling, shaded, shady, dark, dismal, somber, pitchy, black, Stygian, Cimmerian, tenebrous, obscure, caliginous, sombrous, dusky, gloomy, nocturnal, murky, umbrageous, overcast, cloudy, dark as Erebus, darkened, opaque, fuliginous, misty, nebulous, nubilous, hazy, foggy, vaporous, dirty.

SUNLIGHT, *n.* Light of day, daylight, sunshine, light of heaven, day, broad daylight, noontide light, morning sun, glare, refulgence, dazzlement, splendor, brilliancy, brightness, fulgor, luminousness, luminosity, radiance, irradiation, luminescence.

SUNNY, *adj.* 1. Abounding in sunshine, warmed by the direct rays of the sun, sunshiny, warm, hot, bright, brilliant, shining, unclouded, cloudless, sunlit, clear, fair, radiant, luminous, sunbright, glittering, effulgent, glowing, beaming, glorious, splendid, fine, mild, summery, pleasant, lucent, meridian, blazing, aglow, torrid, estival, tropical, canicular, sweltering.

2. Smiling, happy, cheery, joyous, cheerful, genial, joyful, jolly, optimistic, propitious, auspicious, blithe, light-hearted, debonair, buoyant, breezy, jaunty, lively, animated, vivacious, sparkling, sportive, hopeful, sanguine, palmy, merry, jocund, hearty, jovial, blithesome.

SUNRISE, *n.* 1. Ascent of the sun above the horizon, daybreak, dawn, break of day, dawning, sunup, first blush of the morning, cockcrow, aurora, rosy-fingered dawn, peep of day, morningtide, dayspring, Eos, matins, morn, morning, forenoon, ante meridiem, A.M.

2. East, Orient, Levant.

SUNSET, *n.* 1. Descent of the sun below the horizon, dusk, sundown, eventide, close of day, nightfall, curfew, eve, eveningtide, going down of the sun, evensong, twilight, decline of day, vespers, candlelight, cockshut, gloaming, crepuscule.

2. West, Occident.

SUNSHADE, *n.* Sun-umbrella, parasol, *tente d'abri (Fr.),* canopy, baldachin, awning, tilt, shutter, blind, shade, curtain, screen, shield, veil, jalousie, sunglasses, colored spectacles, smoked glasses.

SUNSHINE, *n.* 1. Sunlight, light of day, illumination, radiance, light of heaven, broad daylight, glare, brightness, blaze, splendor, brilliancy, fulgor, refulgence, dazzlement, resplendence, luminosity, luminousness, irradiation.

2. Cheerfulness, optimism, rose-colored glasses, sanguineness, buoyancy, happiness, geniality, gaiety, good spirits, vivacity, alacrity, animation, levity, jocundity, exhilaration, rejoicing.

3. Good auspices, good omen, promise, well-grounded hopes, bright prospect, clear sky, silver lining, fair weather, run of luck, halcyon days, high tide, golden age, bed of roses, milk and honey, fat of the land, well-being, prosperity, welfare, affluence, success.

SUNSTROKE, *n.* Sun prostration, insolation, siriasis, *coup de soleil (Fr.),* aprication, heatstroke.

SUP, *v.* 1. Eat the evening meal, take supper, feed, take tea, munch, pick, peck, tuck in, snack.
2. Quaff, sip, suck up, lap, swig, nip.

SUP, *n.* Small mouthful, tiny portion, taste,, sip, modicum, molecule, atom, particle, speck, tittle, minim, grain, sprinkling, drop, mite, dab, nip, dash, bit, snack, pinch, morsel, snatch, fragment, crumb, trifle, scrap, peeling, paring.

SUPERABLE, *adj.* Surmountable, that can be overcome, vincible, conquerable, accessible, attainable, obtainable, within reach, achievable, feasible, practicable.

SUPERABOUND, *v.* Overflow, overabound, swarm, teem, bristle with, overrun, run riot, suffocate, choke, pile up, inundate, drench, flood, deluge, overwhelm, engulf, overgrow, overspread, spread over, infest, be all over, exceed, know no bounds, meet one at every turn, creep with, well with, brim over, go abegging, remain on one's hands.

SUPERABUNDANCE, *n.* Overflow, superfluity, plethora, excess, redundance, surfeit, oversupply, swarming, repletion, teeming, exuberance, too many, too much, supersaturation, profuseness, profusion, glut, plenty, congestion, engorgement, inundation, deluge, flood, avalanche, mountains of, overdose, *embarras de richesses (Fr.),* diffuseness, luxuriance, surplus, surplusage, overplus, remainder, tautology, pleonasm, verbosity, prolixity.

SUPERABUNDANT, *adj.* Exceedingly abundant, more than sufficient, overabundant, excessive, superfluous, inordinate, unnecessary, redundant, tautological, lavish, prodigal, plethoric, profuse, exuberant, replete, overmuch, copious, plentiful, fulsome, exorbitant, immoderate, overflowing, extravagant, uncalled for, needless, *de trop (Fr.),* spare, supernumerary, supererogatory, pleonastic, over and above, wasteful.

SUPERANNUATED, *adj.* Too old for work, retired on account of infirmity, unfit for service, pensioned, aged, decrepit, let out to pasture, senile, anile, doting, disqualified, waning, timeworn, stricken in years, having one foot in the grave, patriarchal, antiquated, effete, *passé (Fr.),* imbecile, rusty, obsolete.

SUPERB, *adj.* 1. Grand, magnificent, gorgeous, rich, sumptuous, costly, expensive, luxurious, de luxe, splendid, stately, princely, regal, elegant, majestic, lordly, imposing, choice, select, rare, golden, priceless, inimitable, matchless, peerless, recherché, elect, picked, exquisite, rich-wrought, admirable, precious.
2. Admirably fine, excellent, A-1, crackajack, topnotch, tiptop, first-rate, first-class, top-hole, bully, superfine, of the first water.

SUPERCILIOUS, *adj.* Haughtily disdainful, cavalier, presumptuous, contemptuous, overbearing, overweening, haughty, arrogant, insolent, dictatorial, domineering, lordly, high and mighty, magisterial, consequential, stuck-up *(coll.),* proud, vainglorious, toplofty, arbitrary, imperious, intolerant, pompous, contumelious, scornful, withering, cynical, upstage, bumptious, with nose in air, derisive, prideful, uppish, egotistical, puffed up, swollen.

SUPEREMINENT, *adj.* Of superior rank *or* dignity, distinguished, conspicuous, noteworthy, above others, pre-eminent, transcendent, superexcellent, surpassing, paramount, peerless, superfine, above par, matchless, unequaled, capital,

choice, prime, first-rate, the best, tiptop, unusually good, second to none, *nulli secundus (Lat.),* supreme, foremost, crowning, unrivaled, unparalleled, unsurpassed, *facile princeps (Lat.),* overruling, unapproached, incomparable, inimitable, sovereign, *sans pareil (Fr.),* ineffable.

SUPEREXCELLENCE, *n.* Supereminence, superiority, pre-eminence, transcendence, extreme goodness, perfection, quintessence, *chef d'oeuvre (Fr.),* masterpiece, flower, prime, pick, élite, *crème de la crème (Fr.),* cream, gem of the first water, nonpareil, A number 1, treasure, salt of the earth, one in a thousand, jewel, prodigy, *rara avis (Lat.),* marvel, wonder, pearl, phoenix, paragon, beau ideal, ne plus ultra, ideal, pink of perfection, nonesuch.

SUPERFICIAL, *adj.* 1. Outer, external, exterior, on the surface, outside, outward, outermost, extraneous, outlying, frontal.
2. Shallow-brained, frivolous, concerned with only what is obvious, not profound, not thorough, skin-deep, shallow, empty-headed, ignorant, uneducated, unschooled, sciolistic, careless, desultory, summary, hurried, hasty, short-sighted, purblind, myopic, cursory, perfunctory, slight, flimsy, meretricious, untrustworthy, worthless, apparent rather than real, trivial, inane, silly, empty-headed, shallow-pated, trashy, showy, flashy, lowbrow, partial, one-sided, narrow-minded, insular, parochial, provincial, illiberal, besotted, nescient, uninformed, untaught, uninitiated, half-learned, green, unread.

SUPERFICIES, *n.* Surface, outer face, outward appearance, outside, exterior, façade, exteriority, superstratum, face, facet, veneer, skin, husk, shell, coat, sheath, casing, wrapper, envelope, involucrum, facing, varnish.

SUPERFLUITY, *n.* Excessive amount, superabundance, surfeit, plethora, more than enough, excess, enough and to spare, surplusage, redundance, surplus, too many, too much, supersaturation, profuseness, exuberance, profusion, glut, plenty, congestion, overdose, engorgement, repletion, deluge, flood, oversupply, avalanche, inundation, overplus, remainder, *embarras de richesses (Fr.),* lavishness, wastefulness, waste, extravagance, prodigality.

SUPERFLUOUS, *adj.* Over and above, more than enough, enough and to spare, too much, too many, *de trop (Fr.),* excessive, spare, superabundant, useless, unnecessary, inordinate, redundant, needless, uncalled for, wasteful, overmuch, extravagant, prodigal, profuse, lavish, luxuriant, exuberant, copious, exorbitant, inexhaustible, overflowing, overrunning, pleonastic, plethoric, excess, replete, plentiful, fulsome, immoderate, turgid, gorged, swollen, duplicate, supernumerary, supererogatory, residuary, surplus, remanent.

SUPERHUMAN, *adj.* 1. Having a higher nature than man, divine, heavenly, celestial, supernal, demiurgic, almighty, omnipotent, all-knowing, omniscient.
2. Exceeding ordinary human power, hyperphysical, preternatural, supernatural, preterhuman, miraculous, thaumaturgic, magical, Herculean, Atlantean.

SUPERIMPOSE, *v.* Place on something else, superpose, cover, lay on, overlay, face, pave, veneer, coat, case, incrust, plaster, stucco, plate, revet.

SUPERINDUCE, *v.* Bring on, cause, bring about,

generate, occasion, produce, suscitate, kindle, spark, entail, evoke, provoke, elicit, promote, open the door to, engender, work a change, modify, revamp, transform, metamorphose, transmute, transfigure, convert, revolutionize, resolve, ring the changes, reshape, recast, influence.

SUPERINTEND, *v.* Supervise, exercise supervision over, oversee, have charge of, direct, manage, have the direction of, administer, conduct, preside over, control, guide, boss, regulate, overlook, rule, govern, manipulate, instruct, command, handle, dispose, prescribe, lead, head, orientate, pilot, steer, be at the helm, see to, look after, hold the reins, order, cut out work for, keep in order.

SUPERINTENDENCE, *n.* Supervision, surveillance, oversight, inspection, overseeing, management, direction, guidance, control, care, charge, gubernation, government, regulation, conduct, eye of the master, auspices, administration, stewardship, command, helm, rudder, guiding star, agency, ministry, order, pilotage, steerage.

SUPERINTENDENT, *n.* Supervisor, surveyor, inspector, intendant, guardian, overseer, foreman, boss, controller, custodian, director, headman, manager, master, warden, curator, taskmaster, administrator, impresario, guide, pilot, helmsman, steerer, steersman, adviser, cicerone, chief, steward, factor, agent, major-domo, factotum, seneschal, proctor, official, functionary, bureaucrat, officer, captain, chairman, president, principal, leader, dean, conductor, coryphaeus, bellwether, precentor, fugleman, demagogue, ringleader, organizer, *entrepreneur (Fr.),* monitor, moderator, guiding star, man at the wheel, wirepuller, croupier, bailiff, shepherd, housekeeper.

SUPERIOR, *adj.* 1. Higher, upper, over, ultra, above, greater, major, exceeding, extreme, more elevated, finer, better.

2. Above the average in excellence, surpassing, pre-eminent, paramount, distinguished, unsurpassed, incomparable, inimitable, nonpareil, preferable, unexcelled, unrivaled, matchless, peerless, sovereign, topping, noble, transcendent, illustrious, choice, exceptional, superexcellent, first-rate, superfine, unequaled, de luxe, second to none, *nulli secundus (Lat.), facile princeps (Lat.),* foremost, crowning, principal, chief, maximal.

3. Showing a feeling of being above others, aloof, reserved, lordly, stand-offish, at a distance, distant, unsocial, offish, cold, domineering, proud, imperious, haughty, supercilious, overbearing, despotic, arrogant, insolent, upstage *(coll.),* overweening, high and mighty, consequential, vainglorious.

SUPERIOR, *n.* Leader, chief, chieftain, captain, head, dux, *duce (It.), Führer (Ger.),* ruler, suzerain, sovereign, liege lord, overman, superior being, superman, *Übermensch (Ger.),* prince, patrician, aristocrat, master, nobleman, don, peer, grandee, magnifico, magnate, hidalgo, big gun, nabob, big wig, bashaw, mogul, panjandrum, his nibs *(coll.),* first-fiddle, boss, prima donna, star, cock-of-the-walk, celebrity, hero, lion, somebody, notable, paragon, cynosure, authority, expert, proficient, specialist, crackajack, master hand, adept, director, governor, regent, commander, commandant, sultan, czar, caesar, kaiser, potentate, autocrat, tyrant, despot, dictator.

SUPERIORITY, *n.* Pre-eminence, ascendancy, predominance, preponderancy, lead, eminence,

excellence, greatness, prevalence, supereminence, advantage, authority, influence, rank, prestige, nobility, supremacy, primacy, paramountcy, supremeness, sovereignty, leadership, hardship, captaincy, chieftaincy, crest, peak, summit, apogee, apex, lion's share, plurality, bulk, seniority, mastery, notability, superexcellence, perfection, masterpiece, chef d'oeuvre, nonesuch, nonpareil, gem of the first water, one in a thousand, *rara avis (Lat.),* cream, *crème de la crème (Fr.),* élite, pick, flower.

SUPERLATIVE, *adj.* 1. Supreme, transcendent, pre-eminent, surpassing all others, most excellent, consummate, incomparable, peerless, matchless, unequaled, unrivaled, unapproached, unmatched, inimitable, best, highest, greatest, utmost, maximal, foremost, paramount, principal, chief, unparalleled, crowning, unsurpassed, second to none, *facile princeps (Lat.), nulli secundus (Lat.),* sovereign, nonpareil, *sans pareil (Fr.),* culminant, uppermost, topmost, unparagoned, superfine, superexcellent, cardinal, tiptop, first-rate, of the first water, prime, crack.

2. Being more than is normal, exaggerated in language, effusive, altiloquent, magniloquent, grandiloquent, ornate, flowery, euphuistic, pompous, sonorous, inflated, tumid, turgid, high-sounding, stilted, pedantic, declamatory, rhetorical, grandiose, sesquipedalian, fustian, bombastic, hyperbolical, extravagant.

SUPERNAL, *adj.* Of more than earthly excellence, divine, being on high, celestial, heavenly, godlike, angelic, seraphic, ethereal, lofty, supramundane, exalted, paradisaical, beatific, elysian, Olympian, sacred, hallowed, almighty, holy.

SUPERNATURAL, *adj.* Beyond the powers of nature, hyperphysical, preternatural, superhuman, metaphysical, otherworldly, unearthly, occult, mysterious, unknown, unintelligible, mystic, spectral, fabulous, ghostly, abnormal, transcendental, extraordinary, marvelous, miraculous, thaumaturgical, inscrutable, incomprehensible, unfathomable, hidden, spooky *(coll.),* haunted, spiritual, superphysical, supramundane, uncanny, weird, portentous, ominous, eerie.

SUPERNUMERARY, *adj.* Being in excess of the usual *or* prescribed number, excessive, superfluous, above the regular number, over and above, more than is necessary, dispensable, *de trop (Fr.),* extra, spare, additional, redundant, odd, surplus, superabundant, inordinate, overmuch, overcharged, plethoric, needless, supervacaneous, uncalled for, adscititious, duplicate, supererogatory.

SUPERPOSE, *v.* Place above something else, superimpose, lay upon, impose, overlay, face, veneer, coat, pave, paper, case, cap, tip, revet, bind, varnish, plate, electroplate, lacquer, japan, whitewash, enamel, gild, bedaub, besmear, wash, plaster, dab, cement, stucco, incrust.

SUPERSCRIPTION, *n.* Inscription, epigraph, endorsement, title, heading, rubric, paraph, direction, address on a letter.

SUPERSEDE, *v.* 1. Displace, supplant, replace, succeed to the office of, take the place of, take precedence of, cut out *(coll.),* pinch-hit *(coll.),* act for, stand in the stead of, stand in the shoes of, represent.

2. Suspend, override, overrule, obviate, preclude, set aside as void, annul, nullify, make void, neutralize, abolish, subvert, discard, dismiss, remove, oust, shelve, table, leave off, make away

with, throw aside, renounce, abjure, dispose of, abandon.

SUPERSTITION, *n.* 1. Belief entertained despite reason *or* knowledge, blindly accepted notion, blind belief, warped notion, notion, *idée fixe (Fr.),* fixed idea, *idée reçue (Fr.),* illusion, delusion, self-deceit, false impression, mists of error, hallucination, false light, fallacy, misapprehension, misrepresentation, perversion, mare's nest, myth, fable, moonshine, bigotry, bias, fanaticism, prejudice, *mentis gratissimus error (Lat.),* prepossession, mote in the eye, dogmatism, monomania.

2. Irrational fear of what is unknown *or* mysterious, belief in omens, credulity, gullibility, infatuation, blind reasoning, blind side, evil eye, *male occhio (It.),* hobgoblin, werewolf, banshee, zombie, *loup-garou (Fr.),* sorcery, occult art, black magic, necromancy, the black art, thaumaturgy, demonology, *diablerie (Fr.),* fetishism, witchcraft, voodoo, hoodoo, shamanism, vampirism, exorcism, conjuration, incantation, powwow, enchantment, mysticism, obsession, weird, exsufflation, abracadabra, hocus-pocus, open sesame, mumbo jumbo, amulet, talisman, periapt, phylactery, scarab, philter, wishbone, wand.

3. Collection of superstitious customs, irrational worship, false religion, idolatry, heathenism, mythology, animism, paganism.

SUPERSTITIOUS, *adj.* Fearful, apprehensive, credulous, gullible, bigoted, biased, prejudiced, fanatical, zealous, overcredulous, infatuated, simple, green, silly, fallacious, erroneous, apocryphal, untrue, false, ungrounded, unreal, groundless, unsubstantial, illusory, delusive, refuted, exploded, discarded, mythical, heathen, pagan, polytheistic, animistic, fetishistic, idolatrous, mystic, talismanic, cabalistic, phylacteric, incantatory, magical.

SUPERVENE, *v.* Come as something additional *or* extraneous, be added, come as an accessory, ensue, issue, follow upon, take place, happen, befall, occur, come off, come round, come about, come to pass, present itself, turn out, fall out, bechance, betide, eventuate, crop up, spring up, emanate, arrive, take its course, arise, result, succeed.

SUPERVISE, *v.* Oversee during execution, inspect during performance, have the oversight of, have the direction of, attend to, superintend, survey, regulate, overlook, guard, govern, exert surveillance over, manage, conduct, direct, keep in order, control, see to, look after, ministrate, administer, have charge of, have care of, pull the wires, take the direction, rule, preside over, be in the chair, hold the reins, pilot, steer, guide, show the way, lead, head, cut out work for, prescribe, order, boss, engineer, instruct, maneuver, handle, manipulate, dispose, command, orientate, orient, order, patronize, destine, address.

SUPERVISION, *n.* Superintendence, oversight, surveillance, command, control, charge over, stewardship, management, administration, guidance, government, direction, ministry, agency, order, regulation, conduct, eye of the master, orientation, steerage, reins, pilotage, managery, gubernation, controls, rudder, helm, compass, needle, guiding star, polestar, auspices, proctorship.

SUPERVISOR, *n.* Overseer, surveyor, superintendent, inspector, manager, director, administrator, controller, governor, impresario, entrepreneur, organizer, agent, taskmaster, master, leader, ringleader, coryphaeus, conductor, precentor, fugleman, bellwether, pilot, guide, helmsman, steersman, adviser, cicerone, mentor, counselor, instructor, monitor, head, principal, chief, boss, official, officer, minister, functionary, bureaucrat, chairman, president, superior, captain, wirepuller, strategist, power behind the throne, factor, steward, foreman, major-domo, factotum, seneschal, curator, proctor, master, big shot, kingpin, commander, captain, comptroller, rector, intendant, overlooker, moderator, guiding star, man at the wheel, procurator, shepherd.

SUPINE, *adj.* 1. Lying with face upward, flat on one's back, recumbent, prostrate, complanate, accumbent, decumbent, prone, couchant, jacent.

2. Leaning backward, inclined, oblate, flattened, horizontal, aslant, bias, aslope, slanting, tilted, sloping, oblique, inverted, clinal, skew.

3. Sluggish, indolent, otiose, slothful, languid, lazy, indifferent, apathetic, lethargic, inattentive, negligent, heedless, torpid, listless, drowsy, lumpish, dull, inert, idle, thoughtless, careless, vapid, inactive, comatose, spiritless, passive, spineless, torpescent, dozy, dormant, somnolent, napping, heavy, soporous, hypnotic, dreamy, laggard, leaden, remiss, slack, exanimate, dronish, motionless, impassive, unfeeling, phlegmatic, obtuse, flat, tame, numb, lukewarm, regardless, Laodicean, unconcerned, insouciant, nonchalant, pococurante, vegetative, impervious.

SUPPER, *n.* Last meal of the day, evening meal, tea, repast, snack, spread, collation, refection, dinner.

SUPPLANT, *v.* 1. Replace by something else, supersede, displace by stratagem, remove, usurp, take the place of, take over.

2. Uproot, extirpate, eradicate, deracinate, abolish, overthrow, undermine, subvert, upset, bring about the downfall of, bring low, overpower, drive away, drive out, expel, force away, degrade, depose, oust, dismiss, dethrone, displace, reduce, break, cashier, unseat, discharge, eject, fire, turn out, retire.

SUPPLE, *adj.* 1. Bending readily, pliant, flexible, pliable, flexile, elastic, resilient, tractable, malleable, limber, willowy, lithesome, lithe, bendable, ductile, extensible, plastic, tractile, flexuous.

2. Compliant, submissive, yielding, complaisant, docile, sequacious, acquiescent, concurring, amenable, tame, obedient, patient, passive.

3. Servile, slavish, sycophantic, parasitical, fawning, obsequious, groveling, cringing, bootlicking, sniveling, mealy-mouthed, beggarly, abject, prostrate, abased, crouching, sneaking, oily, adulatory, flattering, timeserving, truckling, subservient, honeyed, smooth-tongued, buttery, unctuous, fulsome.

SUPPLEMENT, *v.* Form an addition to, extend by supplement, supply, complete, fill up, add to, supplete, augment, reinforce, strengthen, meet a deficiency, supply a need, subvent, subsidize, buttress, fortify.

SUPPLEMENT, *n.* Addition in order to supply something wanting, complement, continuation, sequel, appendix, addendum, postscript, codicil, adjunct, affix, prefix, suffix, subscript, postfix, appendage, pendant, attachment, tab, rider, tag, interpolation, insertion, annex, wing, extension, ell, accession, increment, increase, reinforcement, augmentation, accompaniment, appurtenance, corollary, allonge, correlative, counterpart.

SUPPLEMENTARY, *adj.* Additional, extra, accessory, supplemental, suppletory, advenient, adscititious, auxiliary, ancillary, subsidiary, contributory, appurtenant, additive, adjunct, subordinate, adventitious, supervenant, spare, other, further, fresh, new, concomitant, attendant, intensitive, intensifying, augmentative, increscent.

SUPPLIANT, *adj.* Begging, supplicating, supplicatory, precatory, entreating, suing, beseeching, praying, imploring, supplicant, imprecatory, rogatory, mendicant, postulant, obsecratory, obtestative, solicitous, importunate, on bended knee, cap in hand.

SUPPLIANT, *n.* Humble petitioner, postulant, supplicant, solicitor, applicant, suitor, aspirant, candidate, claimant, mendicant, requisitioner, imprecator, obsecrator, obtestator, impetrator, importuner, invocator, interpellator, cadger, beggar, panhandler, canvasser.

SUPPLICATE, *v.* Pray humbly, implore, make earnest entreaty, beseech, entreat, petition, beg, importune, call upon, invoke, obsecrate, obtestate, apostrophize, solicit, appeal to, pray to, crave, prefer a request to, sue, plead, put up a prayer, adjure, conjure, ask, postulate, request, requisition, canvass, bid, beg a boon, call to, apply for, seek, kneel to, cry to, urge, press, besiege, clamor for, dun, bombard, make bold to ask, put to, trouble one for, impetrate, imprecate, ply, beset, tax, throw oneself at the feet of, fall on one's knees, mendicate, cadge, panhandle, send the hat round.

SUPPLICATION, *n.* Petition, entreaty, request, solicitation, importunity, requisition, suit, prayer, orison, invocation, impetration, obsecration, obtestation, appeal, apostrophe, overture, application, rogation, postulation, instance, imploration, interpellation, begging, asking, mendicancy, panhandling, address, imprecation.

SUPPLICATORY, *adj.* Petitionary, suppliant, precatory, imprecatory, invocatory, rogatory, postulant, obsecratory, imploratory, obtestative, importunate, solicitous, clamorous, urgent, on bended knee, cap in hand, mendicant, humble, abject.

SUPPLY, *v.* 1. Furnish with what is lacking, provide with what is requisite, outfit, equip, fit out, accouter, invest, stock, refill, replenish, endue, minister, store, fill up, endow, present, cater, administer, accommodate, deliver, render, grant, give, afford, bestow, lavish, contribute, yield, provision, victual, purvey, forage, feed, recruit, serve, deal out, distribute, oblige, avail.

2. Take the place of, make up for, serve instead of, stand in lieu of, occupy as a substitute, fill a vacancy, fill the place of.

SUPPLY, *n.* Quantity of something on hand, stock, reserve, store, provision, fund, reservoir, cache, hoard, accumulation, abundance, vein, mine, quarry, lode, bed, well, treasure, nest egg, savings, vintage, harvest, crop, gleaning, yield, resources, grist, equipment, *de quoi (Fr.)*, wherewithal, *matériel (Fr.)*, aggregation, amassment, conglomeration.

SUPPORT, *v.* 1. Hold up, uphold, bear up, prop, sustain, shore up, truss, brace, buttress, bolster up, gird, cradle, pillow, underpin, underprop, stay, upbear, underset, carry, bed, base, embed.

2. Tolerate, suffer, endure, brook, abide, stand, bear, undergo, put up with, withstand, go through, experience, submit to.

3. Provide for, nourish, maintain, keep, cherish, foster, feed, victual, provision, finance, nurture, board, pay for, subsidize.

4. Advocate, defend, champion, patronize, befriend, protect, back up, second, countenance, shield, vindicate, justify, forward, further, assist, aid, succor, help, favor, strengthen, reinforce, abet, encourage, promote, espouse, relieve, stand up for, side with, sanction, stick up for.

5. Confirm, substantiate, verify, corroborate, bear out, make good, accredit, vouch for, attest, warrant, guarantee, endorse, ratify, vote for, clinch, establish.

6. Take the part of, play, enact, perform, act, represent, assume, personate.

SUPPORT, *n.* 1. Prop, brace, stay, mainstay, buttress, shore, guy, underpinning, abutment, pier, trestle, underprop, post, pillar, stanchion, beam, substructure, groundwork, bolster, supporter, bracer, reinforcement, undersetter, truss, peg, fulcrum, cushion, pillow, cradle, purchase, foothold, hold, staff, frame, stilt, horse, stud, stirrup, tread, hanger, seat, strut, rib, skid, splint, *point d'appui (Fr.),* stave, rundle, spoke, rung, bar, step, emplacement, stand, platform, scaffold, bracket, ledge, shelf, console, buck, sawbuck, board, table, counter, trivet, underbuilding, socle, stereobate, foundation, base, basis, bed, sill, bedding, ground, substratum, flooring, deck, pavement, dais, rostrum, pole, post, shaft, leg, pale, stake, picket, pile, palisade, jamb, stile, pilaster, mullion, balustrade, baluster, banister, colonnette, column, pedestal, caryatid, telamon, atlas, rafter, girder, joist, lintel, balk, batten, timber, tie, traverse, transom, crossbeam, trave, cantilever, casement, skeleton, sash, crib, rack, yoke, backbone, rachis, spine, vertebra, chine, fornix, arch, vault, span, skewback, ogive, apse, keystone, saddle, chair, settle, bench, stool, hassock, couch, hammock, cot, pallet, shakedown, stretcher, litter, berth, bunk, roost, mattress, lap, stall, rod, staff, cane, stick, baton, alpenstock, upright, crosier, crutch, crook, thyrsus, caduceus, lituus.

2. Maintenance, subsistence, sustenance, sustentation, sustainment, upkeep, living, livelihood, keeping, nutriment, aliment, bread, food, manna, provisions, necessaries, victuals, stores, alimony, relief, dole, charity, nurture, nourishment, subsidy, alimentation, bounty, means.

3. Favor, aid, assistance, help, succor, subvention, backing, advocacy, championship, defense, patronage, encouragement, countenance, behalf, approval, espousal, comfort, strengthening, approbation, protection, vindication, influence, auspices, aegis, shield, surety, strength, consolation, advancement, lift, boost, furtherance, coadjuvancy, promotion, interest.

SUPPORTABLE, *adj.* 1. Tolerable, endurable, sufferable, bearable, abidable.

2. Tenable, defensible, maintainable, vindicable, justifiable, excusable.

SUPPORTER, *n.* Maintainer, sustainer, backer, advocate, adherent, upholder, partisan, defender, patron, champion, stand-by, seconder, assistant, follower, accomplice, aider, helper, friend-in-need, guardian angel, tutelar, patron saint, paraclete, comforter, benefactor, good genius, good fairy, fairy godmother, good Samaritan, adjuvant, auxiliary, adjunct, helping hand, coadjutor, confrere, coöperator, friend, ally, confederate, accessory, disciple, votary, sectary, sectarian, abettor, friend-at-court, mediator, deus ex machina, special providence, well-wisher, favorer, Maecenas, sympathizer, collaborator.

SUPPOSE, v. 1. Assume for the sake of argument, predicate, think with reference to mere opinion, opine, presuppose, presume, conjecture, take for granted, hypothesize, theorize, speculate, posit, judge, imagine, conceive, consider, deem, conclude, apprehend, deduce, infer, guess, be of the opinion, take it, receive as true, understand, surmise, view, regard, fancy, dream, suspect, feel, divine, doctrinize, believe in the absence of positive knowledge, ween, nurture an idea.

2. Put forth a suggestion, hazard a supposition, allude to, intimate, hint, suggest, imply, insinuate, submit, set forth, put a case, propose, propound.

SUPPOSITION, n. 1. Surmise, presumption, guesswork, conjecture, guess, suspicion, shot (coll.), association of ideas, belief, opinion, view, speculation, idea, fancy, notion, suggestion, hint, inkling, conception.

2. Assumed position, hypothesis, presumption, assumption, theory, doctrine, postulate, thesis, supposal, presupposition, data, theorem, possibility, probability, likelihood, *vraisemblance (Fr.)*, verisimilitude, potentiality.

SUPPOSITIONAL, adj. Suppositive, conjectural, presumptive, theoretical, hypothetical, speculative, academic, doctrinal, speculatory, reputed, assumed, putative, supposed, imagined, gratuitous, imaginary, allusive, referential, suggestive, fanciful, mythical, fantastic, chimerical, notional, figmental, fictitious, Utopian, visionary, unreal, unsubstantial, creamy, romantic, abstract, intellectual, idealistic, ideal, presumable, verisimilar.

SUPPOSITITIOUS, adj. Fraudulently substituted, counterfeit, not genuine, bogus, spurious, pseudo, sham, forged, pretended, feigned, mock, deceptive, suppositive, false, subdititious, foisted in, make-believe, fictitious, faked, so-called, *soi-disant (Fr.), sogenannt (Ger.),* trumped up, factitious, bastard, artificial, tricky, scamped, illegitimate, surreptitious, meretricious, adulterated, contraband, pinchbeck, tinsel, paste, brummagem, catchpenny, plated, simulated.

SUPPRESS, v. 1. Put an end to, do away with, abolish, overthrow, put down, overwhelm, overpower, destroy, annihilate, eradicate, extirpate, quash, quell, vanquish, overcome, subdue, subvert, crush, eliminate, trample down, nullify, obliterate, efface, demolish, annul, do for, upset, break down, undo, blot out, erase, cancel, delete, expunge, strike out, swamp, sink, shipwreck, wreck, scuttle, raze, level, ravage, lay waste, gut, devastate, blast, exterminate, quench, extinguish, shatter, squash.

2. Keep secret, conceal, hide, withhold, stifle, smother, choke, gag, tone down, muffle, still, muzzle, hush up, squelch, silence, mask, secrete, cloak, veil, screen, put under wraps, camouflage, shroud, disguise, dissemble, bury, keep in the background.

3. Repress, restrain, keep back, check, keep in, inhibit, arrest, stop, obstruct, restrict, curb, harness, hold in leash, confine, coerce.

SUPPRESSION, n. 1. Abolition, overthrow, destruction, annihilation, eradication, extirpation, vanquishment, subdual, subversion, elimination, nullification, effacement, obliteration, demolition, annulment, erasure, cancellation, deletion, extermination, extinguishment.

2. Secrecy, concealment, retention, censorship, camouflage, smoke screen, reticence, taciturnity, closeness, secretiveness, silence, reservation, reserve, evasion, white lie.

3. Repression, restraint, stoppage, check, detention, obstruction, inhibition, restriction, confinement, limitation, control, curb, coercion, determent, deterrence, hindrance, blockade, prohibition.

SUPPURATE, v. Produce pus, fester, gather, maturate, discharge, putrefy, ripen, rot, rankle, become unclean.

SUPPURATION, n. Generation of pus, maturation, festering, rankling, purulence, pyosis, diapyesis, gathering of virulent matter, putrescence, putrefaction, decay, corruption.

SUPREMACY, n. Sovereignty, domination, hegemony, ascendancy, upper hand, mastership, mastery, lordship, primacy, supreme authority, headship, predominancy, supremeness, preëminence, precedence, leadership, omnipotence, masterdom, superiority, dominion, influence, sway, rule, power, command, control, victory, triumph, predomination, lead, preponderancy, transcendency, paramountcy, chieftaincy, scepter, captaincy, highest position, summit, crest, peak.

SUPREME, adj. First, leading, greatest, highest, chief, paramount, sovereign, transcendent, predominant, preëminent, principal, dominant, foremost, uppermost, topmost, maximum, all-powerful, omnipotent, omniscient, consummate, finest, perfect, beyond all others, nonpareil, maximal, utmost, crowning, peerless, excellent, superlative, extreme, last, greatest possible, matchless, unsurpassed, unexcelled, unequaled, incomparable, inimitable, unrivaled, best, almighty, absolute, unapproached, unparalleled, *facile princeps (Lat.),* overruling, *nulli secundus (Lat.),* second to none, *sans pareil (Fr.),* unmatched, culminant, culminal, supernal, commanding, ruling, regnant, influential, preponderant, royal, regal, monarchical, princely, kingly, imperial, despotic, autocratic, unconditional, boundless, illimitable, infinite, unlimited, immeasurable, perfect, full, plenary, sheer, thorough, unqualified, prime, main, capital.

SURCEASE, v. Cease from some action, desist, stop, end, bring to an end, put an end to, intermit, refrain from, stay, leave off, drop work, take a respite, discontinue, have done with, break off, pull up, hold, check, pause, give over, give up, shut up shop, suspend, interrupt, remit, cut out, arrest, cut short, stem.

SURCEASE, n. Cessation, end, stop, respite, discontinuance, desinence, desistance, remission, intermission, interruption, suspension, stoppage, hitch, halt, pause, lull, rest, abeyance, dead stop.

SURCHARGED, adj. Overcharged, overburdened, overloaded, overfull, plethoric, surfeited, congested, drenched, supersaturated, overflowing, running over, superfluous, replete, overmuch, excessive, superabundant, inordinate, exuberant, redundant, too much, profuse, crammed, gorged, supervacaneous, over and above, turgid, stuffed.

SURCINGLE, n. Belt, band, girth, girdle, girt, cincture, clasp, zone, baldric, circlet, cordon.

SURE, adj. 1. Free from doubt, fully persuaded, positive, confident, convinced, assured, certain beyond question, undoubting, unhesitating.

2. Worthy of confidence, trustworthy, reliable, authoritative, accurate, dependable, never-failing, unmistakable, unerring, never-slipping, never

missing, unfailing, infallible, unquestionable, indisputable, secure, faithful, indubitable, apodictical, fixed, firm, safe, steady, stable, abiding, enduring, fast, permanent, strong, solid, well-founded, settled, absolute, true, categorical, unequivocal, actual, unqualified, incontrovertible, irrefutable, irrefragable, incontestable, indisputable, undisputed, decisive, authentic.

3. Inevitable, unavoidable, ineluctable, necessary, inescapable, that must be, destined, fated, foreordained, doomed, predestined.

SURELY, *adv.* 1. Certainly, assuredly, undoubtedly, indubitably, infallibly, without doubt, definitely, unquestionably, admittedly, positively, true, yes, of course, just so, certes, for certain, precisely, no doubt, *sans doute (Fr.),* doubtless, to be sure, truly, in truth, without fail, as a matter of course, *coûte que coûte (Fr.),* come what may, be it so, willingly, freely, nothing loath, by all means.

2. Securely, safely, steadily, stoutly, firmly, soundly, on the safe side.

SURETY, *n.* 1. Safety, security, invulnerability, impregnability, invulnerableness, coast clear, danger past, safety valve, storm blown over, sheet anchor, safeguard, rock, palladium, shield, aegis, precaution, refuge.

2. Confidence, certainty, certitude, assurance, sureness, indubitableness, reassurance, trust, reliance, certainness, infallibility, infallibleness, reliability, positiveness, dogmatism, arbitrariness.

3. Guaranty, pledge, bond, security, guarantee, warranty, gage, tie, debenture, lien, pignus, pignoration, vadium, bail, collateral, deposit, stake, handsel, earnest, promissory note, covenant.

4. Bondsman, bailsman, sponsor, guarantor, voucher, insurer, fiduciary.

SURF, *n.* Swell of the sea breaking upon a shore *or* shoals, breaking waves, breakers, line of foamy water, ground swell, white horses, combers, rollers, billows, choppiness, spume, spray, whitecap.

SURFACE, *n.* Outward appearance, outer face, superficies, outside, exterior, external part, area, top, veneer, crust, finish, covering, facet, façade, shell, complexion, skin, carapace, superstratum, coat, grain, tissue.

SURFEIT, *v.* 1. Supply to excess, glut, satiate, gorge, cram, sate, overfeed, fill full, stuff, fill to repletion, indulge to satiety, choke, suffocate, lay on thick, lavish, drench, load, inundate, flood, deluge, overwhelm, engulf, saturate.

2. Nauseate, cloy, pall, sicken, weary, bore, tire.

SURFEIT, *n.* 1. Excessive amount, excess, oversupply, surplus, repletion, plethora, fullness, glut, superabundance, overabundance, redundance, superfluity, nimiety, plenitude, waste, too much, supersaturation, profuseness, exuberance, profusion, plenty, engorgement, congestion, overdose, inundation, overflow, avalanche, deluge, pleonasm, diffuseness, tautology, overplus, surplusage.

2. Satiety, satiation, disorder of the system due to excess, general disgust caused by satiety, nausea.

SURGE, *v.* 1. Rise, tower, mount, cumulate, ascend, arise, lift, spring up, spire, soar, leap.

2. Flock, swarm, stream, mass, concentrate, forgather, resort.

3. Swell, swirl, rise high, billow, sweep, rush, roll along, wallow, heave, rise and fall, increase

suddenly, oscillate violently, overflow, deluge, inundate, flow over, plash, splash, swash, spout, jet, gush, well, spurt.

SURGE, *n.* 1. Surging movement, rush, sweep, swell, roll, jump, leap, rising, ascension, deluge, flood, swarm.

2. Billow, wave, whitecap, roller, white horse, breaker, comber, undulation, surf, heave.

SURLY, *adj.* Rude, discourteous, ill-tempered, ill-natured, ill-humored, sullen, abrupt, snarling, morose, crabbed, cross, touchy, testy, crusty, waspish, peevish, snappish, fretful, petulant, grouchy, uncivil, pettish, perverse, grumpy, froward, captious, gruff, sour, ungracious, churlish, harsh, rough, impolite, blunt, unamiable, unfriendly, doggish, sulky, splenetic, cantankerous, cynical, sarcastic, ironical, glum, unsociable, spleenish, glowering, scowling, mumpish, spiteful, retractable, malignant, bad-tempered, tart, acidulous, vinegary, ungentlemanly, impudent, trenchant, virulent, bristling, bearish, boorish, brusque.

SURMISE, *v.* Infer without certain evidence, conjecture, fancy, guess, imagine, think, opine, ween, trow, suppose, suspect, divine, believe, presume, presuppose, consider, theorize, hypothesize, speculate, posit, predicate, deem, judge, conclude, regard, view, dream, conceive, apprehend, feel, doctrinize.

SURMISE, *n.* Idea as to something's being possible, surmisal, conjecture, guess, opinion, theory, hypothesis, supposition, hazarded notion, vaguely formulated thought, suspicion, doubt, speculation, divination, view, belief, suggestion, inkling, guesswork, hint, shot *(coll.),* presumption, supposal, assumption.

SURMOUNT, *v.* 1. Climb, rise above, scale, ascend, top, overtop, crown, clear, vault, cap, tower above, clamber, scrabble, escalade, scramble up, shin *(coll.),* work one's way up, mount, crest, ride, leap over, go over the top, overlook, command.

2. Surpass, excel, exceed, overpass, go beyond, transcend, pass by, overshoot, rival, outshine, outvie, eclipse, throw into the shade, overshadow, outdo, outrival, overmatch, outstrip, precede.

3. Overcome, conquer, subdue, vanquish, subjugate, dominate, master, overpower, get the better of, prevail over, triumph over, defeat, rout, discomfit, overthrow, outmaneuver, checkmate, beat, worst, floor, lick *(coll.),* trim, drub, reduce, do for, put down, gain the day, take by storm, score a success, weather the storm, stem the torrent.

SURMOUNTABLE, *adj.* That may be surmounted, superable, conquerable, accessible, attainable, within reach, within measurable distance, achievable, performable, feasible, obtainable.

SURNAME, *n.* Family name, cognomen, patronymic, appellation added to original baptismal name, agnomen.

SURPASS, *v.* Go beyond, be greater than, be superior to, excel, exceed, transcend, surmount, overtop, cap, rise above, tower over, top, crest, best, worst, distance, outshine, overshadow, eclipse, throw into the shade, outstrip, outdo, override, outrun, beat, outclass, outvie, outmaneuver, outgeneral, leave behind, take precedence, carry the field, bear the palm, win laurels, gain the day, triumph over, outweigh, outrival, cut out *(coll.),* outplay, take the shine out of, have the upper hand, have the advantage, prevail, predominate, come first, rank first, take the cake *(coll.)*, break the record, overpass, overreach, overshoot the mark, leave in the rear, go one better.

SURPASSING, *adj.* Superior, greater, exceeding, overruling, dominant, transcendent, sovereign, second to none, *nulli secundus (Lat.)*, *sans pareil (Fr.)*, having no equal, nonpareil, incomparable, peerless, matchless, unsurpassed, unparalleled, unrivaled, unequaled, *facile princeps (Lat.)*, superlative, preëminent, supreme, excellent, supereminent, extraordinary, inimitable, superfine, paramount, crowning, foremost, principal, chief, conspicuous, towering, prominent.

SURPLUS, *n.* Amount in excess of what is requisite, that which remains above what is needed, superfluity, excess, overplus, oversupply, surplusage, superplus, residue, remainder, overflow, redundance, nimiety, residuum, balance, remnant, enough and to spare, leavings, dregs, lees, odds and ends, *caput mortuum (Lat.)*, draff, educt, result, refuse, stubble, *embarras de richesses (Fr.)*, overdose, surfeit, glut, plethora, repletion, profusion, exuberance, supersaturation, superabundance, too many, too much, *de trop (Fr.)*.

SURPRISE, *v.* 1. Come upon suddenly and unexpectedly, take by surprise, take unawares, take off one's guard, discover suddenly, catch in the act of, catch in flagrante delicto, nab, catch napping, burst upon one, turn up, pop in on, drop from the clouds, steal upon one, pounce upon, throw off one's guard, attack without warning, assail suddenly, spring a mine upon.
2. Astonish, dumfound, flabbergast, amaze, astound, stagger, stun, strike with wonder, strike dumb, confound, take aback, startle, electrify, take away one's breath, overwhelm, dazzle, dumfounder, daze, stupefy, bewilder, petrify, alarm, confuse, fascinate, strike with awe, leave spellbound, throw on one's beam ends, make one's hair stand on end, make one stare, baffle, beggar description, stagger belief, leave aghast, make all agog, leave open-mouthed, find thunderstruck, strike all of a heap, make unable to believe one's senses.

SURPRISE, *n.* Nonexpectation, the unforeseen, unforeseen contingency, blow, shock, bolt out of the blue, thunderclap, bombshell, astonishment, amazement, bewilderment, wonder, wonderment, consternation, dumfounderment, eye-opener, sudden burst, unpreparedness, awe, stupefaction, fascination, stupor, marvel, wonderwork, prodigy, miracle, phenomenon, portent, curiosity, rarity, *rara avis (Lat.)*, spectacle, *coup de théâtre (Fr.)*.

SURPRISING, *adj.* Marvelous, miraculous, prodigious, portentous, unheard of, unforeseen, unthought of, unaccountable, extraordinary, unexpected, astonishing, startling, astounding, electrifying, wonderful, remarkable, strange, striking, amazing, *mirabile dictu (Lat.)*, unlooked for, unanticipated, sudden, *foudroyant (Fr.)*, without notice, like a bolt from the blue, wondrous, striking, inconceivable, stupendous, incredible, unprecedented, signal, singular, unusual, unwonted.

SURRENDER, *v.* Yield to the possession of another, deliver up, cede, give over, give up, sacrifice, capitulate, submit, comply, succumb, fall, give in, strike one's colors, cry quits, cry quarter, back down, concede, lay down arms,

hand in the sword, pass under the yoke, eat crow, eat humble pie, forgo, abandon, relinquish, part with, forsake, waive, renounce, abdicate, resign, vacate, remit, let go, yield control of, render, acquiesce, defer to, accede, come to terms, give ground, knuckle down to, bend before the storm, grin and bear it, bow to, kneel to, lick the dust, fall at one's feet, throw oneself at the mercy of, kiss the rod, quit one's hold.

SURRENDER, *n.* Capitulation, yielding, relinquishment, cession, submission, abdication, abandonment, renunciation, delivery, resignation, abnegation, abjuration, subjection, quarter, backdown, recedence, recession, homage, prostration, nonresistance, compliance, white flag, acquiescence, obedience, yoke, subjugation.

SURREPTITIOUS, *adj.* Stealthy, underhanded, clandestine, furtive, secret, concealed, tricky, covert, insidious, secretive, hidden, feline, obreptitious, sly, evasive, dark, cryptic, veiled, privy, *in petto (It.)*, foxy, mysterious, skulking, sneaking, crafty, cunning, artful, vulpine, strategic, wily, subdolous, deceitful, deceptive, crooked, fraudulent, illegitimate, illegal, illicit, disguised, simulated, feigned, pretended, covinous, elusive, untrue, sham, mock, counterfeit, pseudo, faked, spurious, bogus, trumped up, snide, unauthorized, stolen, foisted in, palmed off, fraudulently introduced, done by stealth, *rusé (Fr.)*, supposititious, indirect, muffled, delitescent, unseen, unspied, impenetrable, unapparent, unknown, in the background, invisible, lurking, indiscoverable, unsuspected, unbreathed, untold, undisclosed, unexpressed.

SURREPTITIOUSLY, *adv.* By stealth, stealthily, underhandedly, fraudulently, secretly, on the sly, without authority, sub rosa, under cover, *in petto (It.)*, *sub silentio (Lat.)*, by a side wind, in the background, behind the scenes, behind one's back, under the surface, by mutual understanding, in private, in the dark, hugger-mugger, behind closed doors, *januis clausis (Lat.)*, *à huis clos (Fr.)*, under the table, *à la dérobée*, *en tapinois (Fr.)*, aside, *sotto voce (It.)*, *à la sourdine (Fr.)*, in a whisper, in strict confidence, under the seal of secrecy, like a thief in the night, *in camera (It.)*, under false colors, under the garb of, over the left.

SURROGATE, *n.* One appointed to act for another, deputy, representative, proxy, delegate, lieutenant, substitute, *locum tenens (Lat.)*, successor, vice, secondary, regent, vice-regent, viceroy, vizier, minister, proconsul, warden, plenipotentiary, commissioner.

SURROUND, *v.* Form an enclosure around, enclose on all sides, encompass, environ, compass, encircle, circumscribe, girdle, hem in, beset, invest, fence about, box off, loop, belt, engirdle, hedge, blockade, encincture, beleaguer, envelop, ring around, cut off retreat, pen in, ensphere, embrace, confine, engird, besiege.

SURROUNDING, *adj.* Enclosing, encompassing, encircling, engirding, circumambient, circumjacent, begirt, circumfluent, ambient, circumferential, peripheral, encincturing, embracing, environing, circumscribing, besetting, enveloping.

SURROUNDINGS, *n., pl.* External circumstances, environing conditions, environment, neighborhood, entourage, medium, outskirts, suburbs, faubourgs, purlieus, *banlieue (Fr.)*, vicinity, environs, precincts, circumjacencies, vicinage, setting, background, habitat, scene, confines, *alentours (Fr.)*.

SURVEILLANCE, *n.* Watch kept over, superintendence, supervision, inspection, charge, direction, care, oversight, management, control, surveyorship, custody, heed, vigilance, vigil, eyes of Argus, watchfulness, solicitude, *l'oeil du maître (Fr.),* lookout, watch and ward, circumspection, guidance, regulation, conduct, command, auspices, aegis, stewardship, ministration.

SURVEY, *v.* 1. Take a comprehensive view of, observe, view generally, overlook, reconnoiter, scan, scout, look the ground over, watch, keep an eye upon, review, contemplate, peruse, superintend, supervise, inspect, examine, oversee, scrutinize, eye, keep watch, watch for, pore over, rivet the eyes upon, attend, witness.

2. Measure and estimate lands *or* buildings, determine the extent of by linear and angular measurements, plot, delimit, block out, trace, graph, lay out, draw to scale, rule, gauge, plumb, fathom, caliper, calibrate, span.

SURVEY, *n.* 1. Comprehensive view, general prospect, bird's-eye view, air view, vista, panorama, reconnaissance, scrutiny, examination, inspection, investigation, prospectus, sight, *coup d'oeil (Fr.),* glimpse, ken, contemplation, regard, observation, lookout, watch, sightseeing, viewpoint, field of view, theater, arena, horizon, perspective.

2. Mensuration to determine areas, determining of extent by linear and angular measurements, metage, appraisement, assessment, estimate, gauging, cartography, topography, hypsography, triangulation, cadastration.

SURVEYOR, *n.* 1. Topographer, geodesist, cartographer, land-measurer.

2. Inspector, overseer, supervisor, superintendent.

SURVIVE, *v.* Succeed in keeping alive against odds, live longer than, outlive, outlast, outwear, weather the storm, continue to live, stay in existence, remain alive, live on, subsist, endure, last, persist, continue, abide, be extant, stand fast, bide, hold one's ground, hold one's footing.

SUSCEPTIBILITY, *n.* 1. Capability of being easily affected, capacity for receiving impressions, tendency to be emotionally affected, sensitive feelings, thin skin, susceptivity, excitability, susceptibleness, impressibility, sensitiveness, sensitivity, sensibility, sentimentality, delicacy of feeling, sympathy, empathy, affectibility, perceptivity, tenderness, emotionality, emotionalism, temperamentalism.

2. Propensity, proclivity, predisposition, penchant, bias, leaning, inclination, tendency, bent, affection, set, turn, warp, aptitude, liability, proneness, idiosyncrasy, temperament, heredity, matrocliny, patrocliny, Mendelianism.

SUSCEPTIBLE, *adj.* 1. Capable of being affected by, readily impressed, impressible, susceptive, sensitive, high-strung, emotional, temperamental, thin-skinned, excitable, receptive, retentive, impressionable, tender, vulnerable, sentient, sensible, sensuous, alive to impressions, perceptive, sympathetic, responsive, tender-hearted, warm-hearted, soft-hearted, sentimental, mobile, plastic.

2. Especially liable, accessible, open, unresistant, likely to, in a fair way to, conducive, tending, inclined, inclining, predisposed, disposed, prone, apt, bent on, hereditary, matroclinous, patroclinous.

SUSPECT, *v.* 1. Imagine to be the case, surmise, conjecture, fancy, guess, opine, theorize, hypoth-

esize, posit, believe, think, judge, suppose, conclude, presume, presuppose, predicate, take for granted, deem, regard, speculate, view, divine.

2. Doubt, have no confidence in, misdoubt, mistrust, distrust, scent, smell a rat *(coll.),* harbor suspicions, deny, question, have one's doubts, dispute, challenge, stick at, demur, shy at, hesitate, waver, be jealous.

3. Believe to be guilty, be suspicious of, lay to one's door, cast in one's teeth, arraign, impeach, indict, pull up for questioning, grill, pump, give the third degree, incriminate, inculpate, call to account, question, investigate, query, interrogate, look into, probe, catechize.

SUSPECT, *adj.* Suspected, accused, under suspicion, under surveillance, under a cloud, in custody, under detention, pulled up for questioning, under interrogation, questionable, shifty-eyed, crooked, fishy *(coll.),* shady *(coll.),* slippery *(coll.),* in bad odor, weighed in the balance and found wanting, in bad repute, disreputable, untrustworthy.

SUSPEND, *v.* 1. Attach so as to allow free movement, append, sling, swing, hang, hitch, hook up, fasten to, dangle, draggle.

2. Interrupt, arrest, intermit, stop, break off, leave off, give over, stay, hinder, discontinue, stave off, withhold, stall, put a stop to, cease, bring to a stop, interfere with, remit, check, obstruct, punctuate, cut short, bring to a standstill, put an end to, hang fire, stop short, quit, pull up.

3. Refrain from concluding definitely, keep undetermined, put off, delay, defer, adjourn, prorogue, procrastinate, table, shelve, postpone, retard, remand, protract, prolong, draw out, spin out, dally, continue *(Law),* temporize, reserve, filibuster.

4. Debar from office temporarily, dismiss, fire, sack, bounce *(coll.),* unseat, unfrock, discharge, cashier, turn out, send packing, eject, discard, expel, send to Coventry, bundle out.

5. Be unable to meet financial obligations, stop payment, go into bankruptcy, become bankrupt, go into the red, become insolvent.

SUSPENDED, *adj.* 1. Hanging, pensile, pendent, pendulous, decumbent, drooping, dangling, depending, nodding, cernuous, tail-like, caudal, caudated, lowering, imminent, overhanging.

2. Undecided, in suspense, unsettled, undetermined, unresolved, in continuance, in abeyance, delayed, belated, behindhand, postliminious, tardy, late, slow, backward, unpunctual, dilatory, overdue.

SUSPENDERS, *n., pl.* Straps worn over the shoulders for holding up the trousers, braces, galluses.

SUSPENSE, *n.* 1. State of mental indecision, doubtful condition of affairs, incertitude, indetermination, uncertainty, quandary, dilemma, dubiety, doubtfulness, doubt, dubitation, dubitancy, dubiousness, vagueness, diaporesis, bewilderment, Morton's fork, fog, haze, ambiguity, ambiguousness.

2. Hesitancy, hesitation, irresolution, misgiving, vacillation, scruple, wavering, perplexity, anxiety, solicitude, apprehension, demur, ambivalence.

3. Expectation, excited curiosity, anticipation, prospect, contemplation, horizon, destiny, waiting, eagerness, impatience, ardency, sanguineness, pins and needles, gooseflesh, breathlessness, tantalization.

4. Suspension, interruption, intermission, remission, cessation, respite, rest, stop, stay, stoppage,

discontinuance, quiescence, abeyance, deferment, delay, procrastination, prorogation, temporary abrogation, reprieve, truce, armistice, breathing spell, recess, postponement, adjournment, desinence, desistance, hitch, closure, halt, lull, interregnum.

SUSPICION, *n.* 1. Surmise, assumption, conjecture, guess, piece of guesswork, shot *(coll.)*, supposition, vague notion, presupposition, postulation, presumption, postulate, hypothesis, theory, opinion, view, belief, divination, speculation.

2. Suggestion, hint, *soupçon (Fr.),* trace, dash, touch, inkling, tinge, grain, little, smack, taste, sprinkling.

3. Anxiety, dread, apprehension, fear, diffidence, timorousness, timidity, fearfulness, apprehensiveness, solicitude, care, qualm, hesitation, consternation, dismay, panic, funk, cold feet, scare, trepidation, flutter, perturbation, fear and trembling, tremor, palpitation, restlessness, disquietude, nervousness.

4. Distrust, doubt, mistrust, misgiving, want of confidence, unbelief, imagination of the existence of guilt, feeling that appearances are not reliable, jealousy, green eyes, jaundiced eye, envy, resentment, grudging, heartburn.

SUSPICIOUS, *adj.* 1. Inclined to suspect, distrustful, mistrustful, given to suspicion, jealous, green-eyed, envious, wary, watchful, vigilant, uneasy, anxious, yellow-eyed, jaundiced, apprehensive, resentful, solicitous, concerned.

2. Questionable, doubtful, disputable, unworthy of belief, suspect, open to doubt, hard to believe, incredible, staggering, inconceivable, undemonstrable, fallible, controvertible, fallacious, apocryphal, groundless, unsubstantial, illogical, unsound, illusory, unauthenticated, untrustworthy, exploded, discarded, refuted, enigmatic, problematical, hypothetical, theoretical, precarious, ticklish, slippery, debatable, equivocal, ambiguous, oracular, cryptic.

SUSTAIN, *v.* 1. Reinforce, strengthen, fortify, support, bolster, prop, hold up from below, bear up, buttress, uphold, keep from giving way, brace, steel, harden, shore up, truss, underpin, underset.

2. Perpetuate, preserve, maintain, keep going, protract, prolong, stay, provide with necessaries, nourish, feed, supply with food and drink, keep alive, nurture, promote, tend, furnish sustenance to, nurse, contribute to, foster, cradle, cherish.

3. Relieve, aid, comfort, assist, help, succor, minister to, lend a hand, recruit, promote, further, forward, oblige, favor, second, back up, stand by, stick up for, espouse the cause of, advocate, countenance, patronize, champion, abet, buoy up, side with, befriend.

4. Confirm, sanction, approve, corroborate, validate, endorse, subscribe to, justify, prove, make evident, evidence, bear out, vindicate, warrant, establish, substantiate, authenticate, circumstantiate, vouch for, avouch, attest, certify, ratify.

5. Suffer, endure, undergo, experience, brave, bear, tolerate, weather, brook, stand, abide, carry on under, labor under.

SUSTENANCE, *n.* Nourishment, nutrition, nutriment, aliment, food, victuals, provisions, pabulum, fodder, bread and butter, provender, means of sustaining life, means of livelihood, maintenance, subsistence, manna, alimentation, subvention, bounty.

SUSURRUS, *n.* Soft murmuring sound, sibilation, susurration, sough, rustle, rush, whisper, murmur, hum, undertone, purr, buzz, moan, sigh.

SUTTEE, *n.* Self-immolation, self-killing through fire, suicide, self-cremation, pyricide, martyrdom, holocaust, felo-de-se, empyrosis, self-sacrifice, mactation.

SUTURE, *n.* 1. Sewing of the lips of a wound by stitching, fastening, stitch, seam, line of closure, line of junction, articulation, joint, chain stitch, cross-stitch.

2. Catgut, silk, thread, filament, fiber, fibril, string, packthread, cord.

SUZERAIN, *n.* Feudal lord, liege lord, overlord, lord paramount, sovereign, potentate, monarch, despot, autocrat, lord of the ascendant, crowned head, tyrant, anointed king, emperor, majesty, imperator, caesar, czar, kaiser, khan, mogul, mikado, padishah, shah, caliph, sultan, lama, inca, tycoon, rajah, doge, seignior, margrave, emir, nawab, nizam, negus, pasha, bey, dey, tetrarch, scherif, satrap, mandarin, nabob.

SUZERAINTY, *n.* Sovereignty, lordship, seigniory, divine right, absolutism, despotism, prerogative, jurisdiction, power, authority, command, sway, empire, rule, domination, dominion, supremacy, headship, chiefdom, hegemony, masterdom, control, dictation, tyranny, grip, hold, iron sway, rod of empire, regnancy, regime, reign, dictatorship, dynasty, autocracy, monocracy.

SVELTE, *adj.* Gracefully slim in figure, slender, lean, wasp-waisted, sylphlike, lithe, lissome, thin, lank.

SWAB, *v.* Clean, wipe up, mop, sponge up, swob, scour, scrub, brush up, cleanse, rinse, wring, mundify, wash, lave, absterge, disinfect, fumigate, sterilize, deodorize, ventilate.

SWADDLE, *v.* Bind with long narrow strips of cloth to prevent free movement, wrap round with bandages, wrap tightly with clothes, swathe, bandage, invest, envelop, involve, enwrap, muffle up, sheathe, roll up in, shroud, circumvest.

SWAG, *n.* Booty, plunder, loot, spoil, prize, pickings, boodle, graft, prey, spolia opima, stolen goods.

SWAGGER, *v.* Walk with a defiant air, strut insolently, swashbuckle, act with a high hand, feel one's oats, exult, crow, flourish, ruffle, swell, domineer, boast, be insolent, vapor, bluster, brag, bully, roister, vaunt, show off, puff, gasconade, blow one's own horn, draw the long bow, talk big, put on dog, put on side, give oneself airs.

SWAGGER, *n.* Swaggering gait, insolent air, arrogant show of affected superiority, swashbuckling, bluster, boastfulness, strut, ruffling, preening, airs, braggadocio, arrogance, side, front, highhorse, pretentiousness, bravado, bluster, gasconade, rodomontade, flourish, fanfaronade, boasting, bluff, hot air *(coll.),* vaunting, puff, highfaluting, dog *(sl.), blague (Fr.),* bounce, buncombe, bombast, toploftiness, grandiloquence, magniloquence, heroics, chauvinism, jingoism, spread-eagleism.

SWAGGERER, *n.* Braggadocio, boaster, braggart, Gascon, bully, blusterer, swashbuckler, fanfaron, roisterer, fire-eater, vaporer, pretender, blower, bluffer, ranter, brawler, jingoist, chauvinist, egotist, egomaniac, Thraso, Drawcansir, hot-air artist, spellbinder, fanatic, zealot, bigot, doctrinaire, dogmatist, windbag *(sl.).*

SWAIN, *n.* 1. Rustic, peasant, countryman, hind, country lad, bumpkin, clodhopper, hayseed, boor, farmer, churl, clown, hobnail, yokel, hick, chawbacon, cider squeezer, bogtrotter, looby, gaffer, lout, rube.

2. Lover, beau, spark, suitor, wooer, adorer, amoroso, inamorato, gallant, admirer, follower, amoret, sweetheart, truelove, flame, boy friend.

SWALLOW, *v.* 1. Take into the stomach through the throat, ingurgitate, ingest, bolt, gulp, gorge, gobble, englut, engorge, ingulf, consume, devour, absorb, eat, drink, imbibe, swill, quaff, suck, sip, sup, swig, toss off, guzzle, wet one's whistle, tipple, tuck in, dine, feed, feast, gluttonize, gormandize, dispatch, masticate, chew, crunch, peck, gnaw, nibble, graze, browse, crop, champ, bite, ruminate, munch.

2. Withdraw from sight, assimilate, submerge, overwhelm, swamp, engage completely, involve, engross, appropriate, employ, monopolize, corner, arrogate.

3. Accept without question, accept as true, receive implicitly, believe without scruple, credit, be gullible, be credulous, follow implicitly, take on faith, take for granted, give credence to, nibble at the bait.

4. Endure, submit to, bear, tolerate, suffer, stand, brook, abide, put up with, stomach, digest, pocket, undergo, acquiesce in, go through, support, brave, make the best of.

5. Retract, abjure, renounce, recant, recall, take back, disclaim, repudiate, reject, disavow, forswear, deny, abnegate, unsay.

6. Exhaust, consume, use up, waste, lavish, expend, squander, spend, dissipate, wear out, run through, fritter away.

SWALLOW, *n.* 1. Gulp, deglutition, ingurgitation, ingestion, immission, imbibition, absorption, introception, eating, drinking, epulation, manducation, mastication, rumination.

2. Mouthful, sip, little drink, draught, taste, dose, crumb, morsel, spoonful, driblet, sippet, sop, gobbet, bolus, nip.

SWAMP, *v.* 1. Swallow up, engulf, submerge, overwhelm, whelm, sink, drown, flood, drench.

2. Fell, scuttle, wreck, shipwreck, crash, overset, upset, capsize, founder, ruin, run aground, plunge into difficulties, embarrass.

SWAMP, *n.* Tract of wet spongy land, morass, fen, bog, marsh, quagmire, slough, marish, soft ground, moss, sump, squash, mud, slush, wash.

SWAMPY, *adj.* Marshy, boggy, sloughy, fenny, swampish, plashy, quaggy, poachy, muddy, soft, undrained, wet and spongy, queachy, moist, paludal, squashy, sloppy, miry, moory, moorish, soaking, sodden, irriguous.

SWAN, *n.* 1. Slender-necked swimming bird of the family *Cygninae,* cygnet, mute swan *(Cygnus olor),* black-necked swan *(Cygnus melanocoryphus),* black swan *(Chenopis atrata),* whooper swan, whistling swan, trumpeter swan.

2. Sweet singer, bard, poet, minstrel, minnesinger, troubadour, scald, lyrist, laureate.

SWANK, *n.* Dashing smartness, ostentatiousness in dress, style, stylishness, chic, swagger, pretentiousness, loudness, dog *(sl.),* ritz *(sl.),* showing off, splendor, gorgeousness, magnificence, display, parade, *étalage (Fr.),* flourish, array, splash, strut, glitter, side, fancy dress, foppery, frippery.

SWANKY, *adj.* Showy, dashing, smart, stylish, modish, chic, ostentatious, splashy, loud, ritzy, doggy, pretentiously grand, grandiose, magnificent, resplendent, pompous, jaunty, palatial, gorgeous, garish, gaudy, glittering, gay, flaunting, sumptuous, expensive, theatrical, foppish, dapper, spruce, natty, rich, swaggering, swashbuckling.

SWAN SONG, *n.* Fabled song of the dying swan, *chant du cygne (Fr.),* last artistic creation, deathsong, dirge, nenia, coronach, threnody, pavane, elegy, requiem, epicedium, threne.

SWAP, *v.* Exchange one thing for another, barter, trade, reciprocate, interchange, counterchange, shuffle, bandy, permute, transpose, give and take, commutate, truck, traffic, transact, drive a trade, bargain, negotiate, dicker, huckster, strike a bargain.

SWARD, *n.* Grassy surface of land, turf, sod, lawn, greensward, green, common, village green, grassland, grass, meadow, lea, pasture, park, mead, field, downs, prairie, wold, heath, moor, savanna, pampas, tundra.

SWARM, *v.* 1. Move about in great numbers, fly off together in a body, congregate, throng, crowd, gather, teem, overrun, abound, be abundant, occur in multitudes, flock, hive, assemble, collect, muster, cluster, surge, rush, stream, mass, herd, associate, huddle, forgather, concentrate, resort, group, amass, unite, bristle with, superabound.

2. Climb a tree by drawing oneself up with the arms and legs, shin, shinny up, clamber, scramble, ramp, escalade, surmount, scale.

SWARM, *n.* Multitude *(of winged insects),* great number, large body, group, aggregation, concourse, throng, flock, crowd, press, mass, shoal, horde, host, drove, colony, cloud, hive, brood, assemblage, galaxy, flight, bevy, covey, school, cluster, myriad, conflux, ingathering, convergence, forgathering, concentration, muster, meet, tribe, gang, squad, troupe.

SWARTHY, *adj.* Of a dark complexion, darkskinned, swart, tawny, dark-hued, dark, dusky, somber, sable, black, inky, atramentous, ebon, jet-black, coal-black, pitchy, fuliginous, sooty, Ethiopic, nigrescent, raven, Negroid, African.

SWASHBUCKLE, *v.* Saber-rattle, bluster, bully, boast, brag, vapor, swagger, vaunt, strut, flourish, show off, gasconade, blow one's own trumpet, bluff, talk big, give oneself airs, draw the long bow, put on side, posture, pose.

SWASHBUCKLER, *n.* Swaggering swordsman, saber-rattler, belligerent, mosstrooper, fire-eater, daredevil, duelist, bludgeon-man, gladiator, rough, bully, *sabreur (Fr.),* armigerent, blusterer, swaggerer, braggadocio, fanfaron, roisterer, boaster, Captain Bobadil, vaporer, brawler, braggart, terrorist, roughneck, hoodlum, hooligan, Drawcansir, Mohock, ruffian, larrikin, Thraso, Bombastes Furioso, Hector, Pistol, desperado, rowdy, jingoist, chauvinist.

SWASTIKA, *n.* 1. Cross with arms of equal length each having a continuation at right angles, figure with clockwise arms, triskele, gammadion, fylfot, triskelion, *Hakenkreuz (Ger.),* Nazi emblem, cross cramponnee.

2. Sign of good luck, charm, religious token, talisman, fetish, phylactery, amulet, periapt.

SWATCH, *n.* Owner's tag attached to cloth sent to a dyer, sample of fabric, characteristic specimen, piece, example, model, pattern, copy, scrap, bit, fragment, chunk, cut.

SWATHE, *v.* Bind fully, swaddle, clothe, bandage, wrap up closely, roll, enfold, envelop, encircle, confine, surround, invest, involve, muffle, circumvest, shroud, sheathe.

SWATHE, *n.* 1. Swaddling clothes, band of linen, wrapping, bandage, envelope, sheath.

2. Bond, fetter, gyve, shackle, trammel, chain, hamper, clog, encumbrance, handcuff, manacle.

SWAY, *v.* 1. Lean, incline, lurch, yaw, reel, roll, totter, rock, wave, swing, vibrate, wobble, oscillate, fluctuate, vacillate, waver, stagger, waddle, heel over, careen, sidle, sag, skid, cant, slant, slope, teeter, gybe, wallow, welter.

2. Move to and fro, brandish, flourish, wield, swing, balance, shake, poise, wag, flap, undulate, pendulate, dangle, librate, nutate, pulsate, flicker.

3. Bias, persuade, influence, urge, bend, turn toward, motivate, actuate, prompt, induce, move, inspire, rouse, stimulate, animate, win over, lead, prevail on, dispose, predispose, carry, bring round, talk over, enlist, incite, instigate, encourage, whet, prod, impel, spur, goad, egg on, prick, constrain.

4. Govern, dominate, rule, manage, control, guide, direct, overrule, master, subject, overpower, gain the upper hand.

SWAY, *n.* 1. Ascendancy, influence, control, omnipotence, dominion, domination, authority, government, reign, sovereignty, power, empire, command, rule, mastership, mastery, masterdom, predominance, hegemony, leadership, supreme power, lordship, domain, supremacy, jurisdiction, weight, direction, potency, autocracy, absolutism, regnancy, iron sway, rod of empire, iron hand, dictatorship, kingship, despotism, tyranny, dictation, grasp, grip, prerogative, suzerainty, primacy, hold.

2. Swing, oscillation, fluctuation, vibration, libration, nutation, wag, wave, undulation, pulsation, wavering.

SWEAR, *v.* 1. Make a solemn declaration in confirmation, make affirmation by some sacred being, take an oath, utter under oath, affirm earnestly, declare solemnly, depose, bear witness, attest, state on oath, testify, give evidence, depone, avow, aver, avouch, acknowledge, profess, asseverate, make an affidavit, warrant, vouch, vow, allege, assure, certify, promise, guarantee, take upon oneself, bind oneself by oath, pledge oneself, plight one's honor, be answerable for, adjure, engage in solemn manner.

2. Use profane language, blaspheme, curse, imprecate, revile, cuss (*sl.*), take the name of God in vain, commit sacrilege, accurse, damn, call down curses on the head of, devote to destruction, anathematize, execrate, excommunicate, thunder against, fulminate, proscribe, censure, denounce, rap out an oath.

3. Rely on as of highest authority, take as gospel, name as one's guarantee, believe implicitly, give credit to, pin one's faith upon, build upon, know for certain, doubt not, rest assured, confide in, put one's trust in.

SWEAT, *v.* 1. Excrete watery fluid through the pores of the skin, perspire profusely, exude moisture, emit by the pores, ooze, swelter.

2. Work hard, exert oneself strenuously, labor, drudge, toil, fag, bestir oneself, strain, moil, drag a lengthened chain, slave, strive, tug at the oar, buckle to, work like a horse, redouble one's efforts, overtask, tax oneself.

SWEAT, *n.* 1. Cutaneous excretion, exudation, perspiration, emanation, discharge, extravasation, sudation, ooze, reek.

2. Labor, drudgery, toil, exertion, strain, effort, stress, struggle, spurt, strong pull, dead lift, exercise, exercitation, uphill work, travail, moil, fagging, slavery, pains, trouble.

3. Perturbation, anxiety, dither, ado, to-do, impatience, disquietude, restlessness, fidgets, agitation, flurry, ruffle, skurry, flutter, fluster, stew, ferment, pother, whirl, trepidation, flurry.

SWEATER, *n.* Knitted jacket, heavy woolen garment, jersey, cardigan, blazer, surtout, spencer, coat-sweater, jumper, overblouse, vest, jerkin, waistcoat.

SWEATY, *adj.* 1. Moist with perspiration, perspiring, sweating, damp, sticky, sudorific, sweltering, sudorous, reeking, oozing, clammy, drenched, wringing wet, saturated, wet through, soaked, swashy, soggy, dripping, dank, sodden, odorous, malodorous, rank, odoriferous, effluvious, graveolent, smelly, salty, saline.

2. Toilsome, operose, arduous, laborious, burdensome, wearisome, troublesome, uphill, herculean, energetic, hard-working, painstaking, strenuous.

SWEEP, *v.* 1. Clean with a broom, whisk, brush, brush up, tidy, spruce up, comb, weed, riddle, pick, screen, winnow, sift, rake, rout out, wipe, mop, swab, scour, sponge, scrub.

2. Be curved, curve, bend, sag, turn, deviate, crook, round, hook, arch, bow, curl, arch over, coil, incurve, inflect.

3. Touch in passing, graze, rub over, rake, rub, scour, skim, scrape, shave, glance.

4. Speed, scurry, streak, hie, spurt, sprint, hasten, scud, post, dart, whiz, tear, shoot, swoop, whisk, scorch, scuttle, skedaddle, scamper, hurry, accelerate.

SWEEP, *n.* 1. Compass, range, reach, amplitude, scope, play, leeway, elbowroom, movement, latitude, continuous extent, unbroken stretch, expansion, spread, swing, accommodation, extension, space, room, margin, comprehension.

2. Curvature, curve, bend, flexure, deflexion, hook, crook, conflexure, curvation, curvity, incurvation, bending, arcuation, turn, devexity, deviation, detour, curl, aduncity.

3. Swift onward course, rush, onset, onrush, dash, stampede, tear, precipitancy, precipitation, rout, career, push, press, charge, drive, surge, hurtle, plunge.

SWEEPING, *adj.* Of wide range, of great scope, amplitudinous, latitudinous, extensive, broad, capacious, all-inclusive, all-embracing, universal, comprehensive, general, wholesale, unlimited, unqualified, indiscriminate, widespread, large-scale, radical, thoroughgoing, exhaustive, thorough, plenary, absolute, full, total, outright, complete, whole, entire, sheer, unconditional, panoramic, encyclopedic, bird's-eye, miscellaneous, pandemic, catholic, ecumenical, collective.

SWEEPINGS, *n., pl.* Matter swept up, litter, trash, waste, rubbish, dirt, offscourings, refuse, odds and ends, lumber, shoddy, orts, rubble, slag, dross, drast, debris, leavings, stubble, cinders, ashes, recrement, precipitate, settlement.

SWEEPSTAKES, *n.* 1. Total stakes at a horse-race, earnings, profit, winnings, clean-up, proceeds, prize, return, pool, premium, bonus, tontine, drawing.

2. Steeplechase, race, horse race, *concours (Fr.)*, heat, turf, Derby.

SWEET, *adj.* 1. Sugary, honeyed, candied, saccharine, saccharous, saccharoid, honey-sweet, cloying, nectareous, luscious, nectarean, ambrosial, nectared, Hyblaean.

2. Pleasing to the taste, sapid, flavorous, flavorsome, toothsome, delicious, savory, tasty, palatable, gustable, tastable, appetizing, relishable, saporous, saporific, gustative, delectable, wholesome, pure, fresh, refreshing, clean, free from sourness.

3. Pleasing to the smell, redolent, fragrant, sweet-smelling, perfumed, spicy, odorous, balmy, aromatic, scented, odoriferous.

4. Pleasing to the ear, melodious, musical, symphonious, harmonious, dulcet, mellifluous, euphonious, tuneful, canorous, silver-toned, mellow, soft, mellisonant, melic, lyric, clear, resonant, ringing, smooth, soothing.

5. Pleasing to the eye, fair, comely, beautiful, beauteous, bonny, handsome, good-looking, winsome, attractive, shapely, charming, captivating, lovely, alluring, exquisite, enchanting, graceful, pretty, personable, bewitching, dainty, entrancing, seductive, glamorous.

6. Pleasant, agreeable, delightful, pleasing, gratifying, pleasurable, enjoyable, delightsome, acceptable, welcome.

7. Amiable, good-natured, gentle, agreeable, bland, mild, kind, lovable, affectionate, beloved, dear, darling, precious, gracious, winning, engaging, tender, sympathetic, adorable, angelic, favorite, fond, devoted, ardent, amorous, amatory, erotic, impassioned, passionate, loving, benignant, serene.

SWEET, *n.* Saccharine, sucrose, dulcin, dextrose, glucose, crystallose, saccharose, dulcite, beet sugar, syrup, treacle, honey, molasses, manna, nectar, mead, hydromel, metheglin, cordial, liqueur, sweet wine, cane sugar, sugar.

SWEETEN, *v.* 1. Make sweet, dulcify, candy, sugar, saccharize, saccharify, syrup, mull, disembitter, edulcorate.

2. Cleanse, purify, deodorize, ventilate, aerate, air, fumigate, disinfect, freshen.

3. Soften, make tender, make mild, make kind, milden, mollify, mellow, alleviate, solace, relieve, soothe, pacify, temper, palliate, allay, assuage, mitigate, ease, moderate, abate.

4. Give zest to, give a relish to, renew, revive, renovate, reinvigorate.

SWEETHEART, *n.* 1. One of a pair of lovers, beloved person, lover, adorer, inamorato, love, swain, beau, spark, suitor, wooer, valentine, follower, admirer, flame, truelove, sweetie, betrothed, fiancé, cavalier, boy friend, gallant, knight, Lothario, amorist, honey boy, darling, duck, Cupid, sweetiepie.

2. Mistress, inamorata, cara sposa, fiancée, dulcinea, ladylove, idol, queen, angel, goddess, belle, Venus, Aphrodite.

SWEETMEAT, *n.* 1. Dainty prepared with sugar *or* honey, confection, confectionery, comfit, bonbon, candy, goody, sweet, sugarplum, tidbit, *bonne bouche (Fr.)*, taffy, carmel, butterscotch, chocolate, jujube, lollipop, confiture, preserve, jam, marmalade, jelly, licorice, marshmallow, jellybean, julep, toffee, mint.

2. Pastry, pie, cake, pâtisserie, tart, pudding, puff.

SWEETNESS, *n.* 1. Saccharinity, dulcitude, sugariness, nectareousness, cloyingness, ambrosialness.

2. Redolence, fragrance, spiciness, odorousness, balminess, sweet-scentedness, odoriferousness, perfume, bouquet.

3. Sapor, savoriness, flavorousness, toothsomeness, tastiness, palatability, gustability, pureness, freshness, cleanness.

4. Melodiousness, mellifluence, melody, harmony, musicality, dulcetness, euphoniousness, euphony, canorousness, tunefulness, softness, mellowness, mellisonance, lyricality, resonance.

5. Pleasantness, agreeableness, amiableness, amiability, mildness, gentleness, suavity, urbanity, agreeability, lovableness, kindliness, graciousness, tenderness.

6. Loveliness, fairness, comeliness, beauty, prettiness, handsomeness, personability, winsomeness, shapeliness, attractiveness, attraction.

SWEET-SCENTED, *adj.* Fragrant, sweet-smelling, aromatic, perfumed, redolent, odorous, incense-breathing, odoriferous, spicy, balmy, ambrosial.

SWEET-SOUNDING, *adj.* Musical, canorous, singing, resonant, melodious, symphonious, harmonious, dulcet, tuneful, lilting, euphonic, euphonious, mellifluent, mellifluous, mellow, soothing, soft, crooning, silver-toned, melodic, mellisonant, melic, lyric, songful, Orphean, sonorous, plangent, modulated, clear as a bell.

SWEET-TEMPERED, *adj.* Amiable, gentle, kind, equable, level-headed, calm, mild, serene, tranquil, pacific, irenic, benignant, benign, kindhearted, friendly, affectionate, fond, warm, sympathetic, tender, agreeable, pleasant, charming, winning, quiet, placid, unruffled, self-possessed, composed.

SWELL, *v.* 1. Expand, dilate, increase, grow, augment, distend, bulge, protuberate, fill out, tumefy, intumesce, inflate, billow, belly, project, extend, protrude, puff, grow larger by expansion, bloat, enlarge, amplify, magnify, lengthen, elongate, stretch, prolong, fatten, thicken, solidify, inspissate, widen, spread out, blow up, wax, sprout, shoot, bud, burst forth, germinate, gather, mantle, burgeon, pullulate, vegetate, flower, blow, aggrandize, develop, bag, bunch, round, stick out, jut out, heave, surge, rise high, tower.

2. Strut, swagger, ride a high horse, look big, swashbuckle, vapor, put on airs, behave pretentiously, be puffed up with pride, be arrogant, be insolent, bluster, give oneself airs, kick up a dust, presume, lord it over, snub, toss the head, carry with a high hand.

3. Be filled with emotion, glow, thrill, warm, throb, be elated, emote, heave, be impressed, respond, catch fire, catch the flame, flush, blush, pant, palpitate, quiver, go pitapat, flutter, feel one's heart mount to one's throat.

SWELL, *n.* 1. Protuberance, bulge, projection, excrescency, swelling, augmentation, convexity, prominence, protrusion, gibbosity, abnormal increase, intumescence, growth, tumor, increment, spread, development, dilatation, tumefaction, diastole, distention, inflation, puffiness, obesity, dropsy.

2. Elevation of land, hill, rise, ascent, barrow, mount, mound, butte, knoll, highland, hillside, brae, ridge, crest, spine, hogback, chine, *arête (Fr.)*, saddle, spur, bluff, peak, foreland, promontory, headland, cape, ness, tor, alp, down, dune, knob, hummock, cliff.

3. Volume of sound, crescendo, boom, loudness, resonance, sonorousness, sonority, noise, clang,

roar, din, clangor, charivari, racket, uproar, hubbub, clatter, hullabaloo, blast, blare, fanfare,
alarum, crash, detonation, thunder, roll, report,
rumbling, reverberation, bombilation, intensity,
force, power, peal.

4. Wave, undulation, billow, whitecap, roller,
breaker, surge, comber, surf, heave, ground swell.

5. Fashionably dressed man, fashion plate,
dude, fop, coxcomb, beau, dandy, buck, spark,
silk-stocking, blade, dandiprat, jack-a-dandy, silk-
sock Sam, jackanapes, exquisite, man milliner,
popinjay, Johnny, fine gentleman, fox, man of
dress, toff, dasher, man about town, playboy,
clotheshorse.

6. Patrician, aristocrat, silk-stocking, superior,
social leader, *arbiter elegantiae (Lat.)*, blue blood,
peer, optimate, gentleman, squire, lord, nobleman,
noble, magnate, grandee, dignitary, celebrity, notability, notable, social lion, great gun *(coll.)*.

SWELL, *adj.* 1. *(Of things)* Stylish, elegant, grand,
modish, à la mode, de luxe, fashionable, luxurious,
chic, smart, toney, high-toned, new-fangled,
recherché (Fr.), comme il faut (Fr.), soigné (Fr.).

2. *(Of persons)* Of high social standing, patrician, aristocratic, silk-stocking, highborn, titled,
princely, courtly, gentle, blue-blooded, wellborn,
genteel, *distingué (Fr.)*, poised, *dégagé (Fr.)*,
throughbred, refined, polished, gentlemanly,
urbane, refined.

3. First-rate, jim-dandy, excellent, top-flight,
superior, prime, first-class, of the highest grade.

SWELTER, *v.* Be oppressed with heat, perspire
profusely, be bathed with sweat, sweat, pant, be
hot, glow, be flushed with heat, be overcome by
heat, stew, scorch, bake, warm up, fry, cook,
simmer, reek, seethe, boil, scald, broil, languish
with the heat, be dripping wet.

SWELTERING, *adj.* Characterized by oppressive
heat and humidity, sultry, muggy, close, humid,
stuffy, stifling, suffocating, oppressive, torrid,
thermal, tropical, calorific, roasting, baking, dog-
day, canicular, broiling, hot, incalescent, sweaty,
smoldering, perspiring, sudorific, thermogenic.

SWERVE, *v.* Diverge, deviate, turn, deflect, incline, bend, turn aside, depart, change direction,
digress, veer, shy, warp, wind, alter one's course,
tack, sheer, vary, curve, bear off, heel, jibe, yaw,
sidle, go about, slew, twist, wheel, jib, dodge,
glance off, switch, shift, sidetrack, shunt, divaricate, fork, go astray, drift, ramble, meander,
straggle, stray, wander, rove, yield.

SWIFT, *adj.* 1. Moving with velocity, fleet, fast,
quick, speedy, rapid, flying, expeditious, agile,
spry, winged, nimble, lively, alert, express, brisk,
active, hasty.

2. Sudden, instant, instantaneous, momentary,
abrupt, unexpected, precipitate, immediate,
prompt, in a flash.

SWIFT-FOOTED, *adj.* Light-footed, nimble, agile,
fleet, speedy, brisk, lively, active, spry, sprightly,
tripping, light-heeled, alert, prompt, supple,
winged, light-legged, quick as lightning, swift as
an arrow, galloping, flying, expeditious.

SWIFTLY, *adv.* Speedily, quickly, expeditiously,
posthaste, at full speed, on eagle's wings, like
lightning, in a trice, in a flash, in a jiffy, in
double-quick time, with speed, apace, fleetly,
rapidly, trippingly, nimbly, agilely, spryly, spright-
lily, in seven-league boots, by forced marches,
under press of sail, at a great rate, full-gallop,
atilt, tantivy, instantaneously, like a shot, *velis et*

remis (Lat.), with giant strides, *à pas de géant (Fr.)*,
whip and spur, as fast as one's legs will carry
one, *ventre à terre (Fr.)*, at top speed, by leaps
and bounds, in high gear, hurriedly, hotfoot,
precipitately, slapdash, helter-skelter, hurry-
scurry, full-tilt, pell-mell, heels over head, headlong, amain, immediately, at short notice, instanter, in no time, presto, forthright, at once,
forthwith, in the twinkling of an eye, on the
spur of the moment, plump, in the same breath.

SWIFTNESS, *n.* Velocity, celerity, quickness,
speed, rapidity, fleetness, alacrity, expedition, dispatch, pernicity, fastness, promptitude, activity,
agility, haste, nimbleness, acceleration, hastiness,
spurt, sprint, race, dash, burst of speed, clip,
tantivy, scuttle, scamper, scurry, flight, gallop,
pace, run, canter, greased lightning, cannon ball,
arrow, split second, dart, rocket, hurricane, electricity, flash, impetuosity, rush, precipitancy, precipitation, hurry, urgency, instantaneity, instantaneousness, immediateness, abruptness, promptness,
suddenness, trice, jiffy, twinkling.

SWILL, *v.* Quaff excessively, drink greedily,
guzzle, swallow noisily, gulp down, tipple, tope,
soak up, drink up, sip, lap, suck up, swig, drain
the cup, wet one's whistle, wash down, slake
one's thirst, booze, sot, bib, drink deep, liquor up,
toss up.

SWILL, *n.* 1. Greedy draughts of liquor, potations, compotations, large drams, libations, bacchanals, winebibbing, bibacity, inebriety, temulency, insobriety, inebriosity, oenomania, dipsomania, drop too much, flowing bowl, booze,
alcoholic drinks, blue ruin, punch bowl, carousal,
debauch, jollification, wassail, drinking bout,
Saturnalia, excess, too much, dissipation, crapulence, drench, gulp, nip, sip.

2. Partly liquid food for animals, kitchen
refuse given to swine, hogwash, garbage, swill-
ings, slops, sweepings, rinsings, offscourings,
cheeseparings, filth, offal.

SWILLER, *n.* Tippler, toper, lush, drunkard, tosspot, sot, hard drinker, bibber, soak, lovepot,
sponge, thirsty soul, dipsomaniac, alcoholic,
devotee to Bacchus, inebriate, lushington, boozer,
carouser, reveler, bar fly, oenophilist.

SWIM, *v.* 1. Be borne up on a liquid, float, be
borne along on water, float with the current,
propel oneself through water, buffet the waves,
go smoothly over the surface, cut the water,
tread water, crawl, kick the feet, skim, glide,
dive, be buoyed up.

2. Be drenched in, be steeped in, be immersed,
be inundated, be flooded, be doused, be soaked.

3. Be dizzy in the head, be giddy, feel vertigo,
have a whirling sensation, be light-headed.

SWIMMING, *n.* 1. Floating, natation, super-
natation, acquatics, diving, water polo.

2. Dizziness, light-headedness, giddiness, vertigo, scotomy.

SWIMMINGLY, *adv.* Without difficulty, easily,
with great success, successfully, prosperously,
smoothly, readily, with flying colors, single-
handed, triumphantly, in full swing, felicitously,
effectively, victoriously, beyond all expectation,
beyond one's wildest dreams, as good luck would
have it, propitiously, auspiciously, providentially,
agreeably, palmily, luckily, fortunately, favorably.

SWIMMING POOL, *n.* Artificial tank for swimming, natatorium, public bath, public bathing

establishment, thermae, tepidarium *(warm)*, caldarium *(hot)*, frigidarium *(cold)*.

SWINDLE, *v.* Use unscrupulous artifice to defraud, put forward plausible schemes, cheat out of money, defraud, fleece, victimize, diddle, embezzle, peculate, steal, obtain under false pretenses, trick, deceive, hoax, dupe, cozen, gull, pluck, do, bunko, impose upon, chouse, overreach, practice upon, take in, mislead, pull the wool over one's eyes, bamboozle, ensnare, circumvent, outwit, outmaneuver, throw dust into the eyes, take advantage of, palm off upon, inveigle, delude, hoodwink, fool, befool, humbug, bluff, practice chicanery, sell, juggle, live by one's wits, foist off, bilk, pigeon, rook, misappropriate, gyp, welsh.

SWINDLE, *n.* Fraudulent transaction, piece of knavery, embezzlement, peculation, fraud, steal, misappropriation, abstraction, depredation, forgery, direption, thievery, theft, stealing, diddling, cardsharping, confidence game, fleecing, trickery, thimblerigging, bunko, juggle, chicane, blind, feint, wile, cheat, trick, plant, hoax, fake, hanky-panky, hocus-pocus, sharp practice, chicanery, piece of deception, duplicity, deceit, wiliness, ruse, imposition, imposture, guile, fraudulence, bluff, misrepresentation, double-dealing, treachery, counterfeit, make-believe, humbug, fake, gyp.

SWINDLER, *n.* Peculator, embezzler, defaulter, welsher, forger, counterfeiter, sharper, fleecer, trickster, hawk, *chevalier d'industrie (Fr.)*, bunkoman, rook, thimblerigger, diddler, card cheat, harpy, swagman, shark, land pirate, crook, robber, thief, depredator, pillager, faker, fraud, jockey, impostor, blackleg, charlatan, mountebank, deceiver, fourflusher, quack, pretender, scamp, scoundrel, knave, rogue, villain, rascal, ringer, con man, gyp, humbug, adventurer, empiric, juggler, prestidigitator, cozener.

SWINE, *n.* Pig, hog, sow, boar, razorback, porker, pigling, hogling, grunter, shoat.

SWING, *v.* Dangle, sway, wave, wag, vibrate, oscillate, fluctuate, rock, move to and fro, move backward and forward, nutate, librate, undulate, wobble, pendulate, dangle, hang, depend, be suspended, waggle, bob, waver, vacillate, teeter, alternate, seesaw, pass and repass, come and go, ebb and flow, swish, flap, flop, lope, careen, revolve, turn, trail, draggle, droop.

SWING, *n.* 1. Movement in alternate directions, curving course, oscillation, fluctuation, nutation, libration, vibration, pendulation, undulation, waving motion, variation, vibratility, pulsation, beat, throb, sway, rhythm, lilt, wag, shake, alternation, teeter, seesaw, to-and-fro, coming and going, flux and reflux, dependency, pendulousness, suspension, pendency, pendulosity, pensility, droop, hanging, inclination.
2. Freedom of action, scope, play, range, free play, margin, elbowroom, leeway, full play, free course, sweep, liberty, unrestraint.

SWINGE, *v.* Punish, chastise, castigate, lay on, buffet, bastinado, switch, whip, flog, beat, lash, scourge, flagellate, fustigate, cudgel, excoriate, belabor, baste, trounce, drub, thrash, pommel, cuff, smack, box the ears, smite, administer the lash, deal a blow to, strike, slap, thwack, spank, thump, strap, larrup, lick, wallop, birch, cane, horsewhip.

SWINISH, *adj.* Piggish, hoggish, porcine, suilline, voracious, devouring, crapulent, boarish, gluttonous, edacious, greedy, overfed, overgorged, bestial,

brutish, gross, beastly, coarse, sensual, licentious, animal, omnivorous.

SWIRL, *v.* Move along with a whirling motion, eddy, whirl, surge, turn, twist, roll along, rotate, churn, spin, revolve, turn around, circulate, circumvolve, gyrate, twirl, wheel, bowl, trundle, slew round, twirl.

SWIRL, *n.* 1. Whirl, eddy, gyration, twist, whirlpool, maelstrom, gurge, vortex, turbination, circination, volutation, convolution, pirouette, circumrotation, circumgyration, circumvolution, roll, circulation, rotation, revolution.
2. Cyclone, tornado, twister, hurricane, whirlwind, samiel, typhoon, whirligig, wheel, merry-go-round, carrousel, top, screw, wheel, windmill, teetotum, flywheel, dizzy round, vertigo.

SWISH, *v.* Make a sibilant sound, sibilate, rustle, whiz, buzz, hiss, fizz, sizzle, fizzle, whistle, wheeze, ripple, murmur, sough, whisper, purl, gurgle, hum, babble, steal on the ear, float on the air.

SWITCH, *v.* 1. Whip, lash, horsewhip, flagellate, cane, birch, fustigate, bastinado, scourge, swinge, beat, strike, flog, slash, cut, chastise, castigate, punish, chasten, strafe, smite, cuff, spank, thwack, buffet, wham, cowhide, pommel, thrash, trounce, lace, belabor, trim, lambaste, lay about one.
2. Sidetrack, shunt, shift, divert, turn, change course, deflect, jib, steer clear of, dodge, slew, diverge, veer, sidle, tack, yaw, sheer, go about, gybe, heel, swerve, bear off, curve, bend, alter one's course.
3. Swing, flourish, brandish, agitate, wield, convulse, shake, toss, flap, wave, whisk, swish, sweep, tumble, hitch, jerk, joggle.

SWITCH, *n.* 1. Slender flexible rod, twig, withe, branch, offshoot, spray, sprig, tendril, runner, sarmentum, ramification, bough, scion.
2. Whip, birch, cane, rattan, stick, scourge, lash, cowhide, strap, knout, cat-o'-nine-tails, cat, bullwhack, quirt, rawhide, thong, kurbash, ferule, cudgel.
3. By-pass, shunt, detour, shift, turn, change, deflection, swerve, divergence, deviation, digression, declination, sheer, warp, drift, divarication, ramification, forking, fork.
4. Whisking movement, flourish, agitation, hitch, shake, tremor, jolt, jerk.

SWIVEL, *n.* Pivoted support, caster, jack, roller, axle, axis, spindle, pivot, spool, pole, pin, gimbals, bobbin, shaft, mandrel, turning link in a chain.

SWOLLEN, *adj.* 1. Enlarged by swelling, swelled, puffed up, tumid, tumescent, dropsical, edematous, expanded, distended, bloated, hypertrophied, swagbellied, pursy, puffy, patulous, inflated.
2. Bombastic, fustian, high-sounding, sesquipedalian, altiloquent, grandiloquent, magniloquent, euphuistic, high-flown, florid, flowery, sonorous, turgid, pompous, pedantic, stilted, grandiose, declamatory, mouthy, Thrasonic, gasconading, boastful, braggart, vainglorious, hyperbolical, *outré (Fr.)*.

SWOON, *v.* Faint, lose consciousness, faint away, fall into a swoon, collapse, feel one's head spin, succumb, drop, black-out.

SWOON, *n.* Fainting fit, loss of consciousness, syncope, deliquium, lipothymy, faint, faintness, blackout, prostration, collapse, stupor, coma.

SWOOP, *v.* Sweep down upon prey, descend, plummet, pounce, bear upon, bear down on, come down in a sudden swift attack, drop down on, fall, gravitate, plunge, dive, precipitate oneself.

rush headlong, rampage, run amuck, catch while on the wing, take at one stroke, seize, clutch, hook, nab, ravish, spring upon, snatch, fasten upon, grapple, clasp, take by the throat, snatch at.

SWOOP, *n.* Sudden swift descent, dive, drop, hostile assault, rush, flight, pounce, clutch, seizure, prensation, prehension, abreption, ablation, predacity, rapacity, wrench, grip.

SWORD, *n.* 1. Sharp-bladed weapon with one end pointed and the other fixed in a hilt, broadsword, blade, rapier, saber, cutlass, claymore, falchion, steel, hanger, brand, bilbo, Toledo, creese, spadroon, glaive, diego, curtana, damascus, tuck, skean, scimitar, machete, bolo, kukri, dagger, foil, stiletto, poniard, bowie knife, dirk, cold steel, bayonet, whinyard, Ferrara, dudgeon, stylet, yataghan.

2. Symbol of military power, emblem of vengeance, sign of authority, emblem of punitive justice, arbitrary power, absolutism, brute force, *ultima ratio* (Lat.), *le droit du plus fort* (Fr.).

3. Destruction by the sword, combat, slaughter, carnage, war, strife, bloodshed, massacre, butchery, havoc, murder, warfare, hostilities, onslaught, fray.

SWORD-SHAPED, *adj.* Ensiform, ensate, gladiate, xiphoid.

SWORDSMAN, *n.* One who is skilled in the use of a sword, gladiator, fencer, *sabreur* (Fr.), dueler, duelist, blade, foilsman.

SYBARITE, *n.* One devoted to luxury and pleasure, effeminate voluptuary, epicure, man of pleasure, sensualist, silk-stocking, high-liver, Sardanapalus, votary of Epicurus, gourmet, hedonist, libertine, Heliogabalus, debauchee, wanton.

SYBARITIC, *adj.* Luxurious, voluptuous, silken, effeminate, sensual, wanton, licentious, Lydian, soft, epicurean, intemperate, self-indulgent, fleshly, carnal, dissolute, rakish, debauched, Paphian, pampered.

SYCOPHANCY, *n.* Self-seeking flattery, obsequiousness, servility, fawning, sycophantism, adulation, truckling, flunkyism, parasitism, vernility, soft soap, blandiloquence, blandishment, wheedling, captation, toadeating, cajolery, incense, flummery, honeyed words, blarney, buncombe, rose water, mouth honor, unctuousness, lip-homage, subserviency, slavishness, prostration, toadyism, abasement, bootlicking, groveling.

SYCOPHANT, *n.* Self-seeking flatterer, fawner, cringer, toady, parasite, bootlicker, wheedler, sponger, groveler, puppet, cat's-paw, tool, stooge, partisan, lapdog, spaniel, pickthank, hanger-on, truckler, sniveler, rubber-stamp, timeserver, toadeater, tufthunter, lickspittle, doormat, footstool, snob, flunky, lackey, dead beat, *cavaliere servente* (It.), sponge, yes-man, *Graeculus esuriens* (Lat.), courtier, slave, jackal, touter, *claqueur* (Fr.), booster, encomiast, laudator, adulator, eulogist.

SYCOPHANTIC, *adj.* Slavish, servile, obsequious, subservient, meanly submissive, abject, groveling, cringing, fawning, bootlicking, adulatory, parasitic, prostrate, flattering, oily, mealy-mouthed, honeyed, unctuous, soapy, smooth-tongued, blandiloquent, specious, fair-spoken, plausible, fulsome, courtierly, supple, pliant, sniveling, beggarly, abased, crouching, sneaking, mean, base, timeserving, buttery, candied, acquiescent, obedient.

SYLLABUS, *n.* Brief statement of the main parts of, digest, compendium, epitome, compend,

abstract, outline, précis, breviary, prospectus, synopsis, summary, brief, abridgment, sum and substance, gist, pith, *multum in parvo* (Lat.), pandect, aperçu, minute, draft, note, conspectus, contents, heads, résumé, review, recapitulation, compilation, analecta, abbreviature, abbreviation, compression, contraction, shortening.

SYLLOGISM, *n.* Argument with two premises and a conclusion, deductive reasoning, categorical syllogism, hypothetical syllogism, disjunctive syllogism, enthymeme, sorites, trilemma, elenchus, argumentation, ratiocination, dialectics, logic, art of reasoning, prologism, perilepsis, dilemma, *a priori* reasoning.

SYLPH, *n.* Slender, graceful, imaginary being supposed to inhabit the air, dainty girl, fairy, fay, peri, nymph, sylphid, undine, dryad, hamadryad, naiad, oread, nereid.

SYLVAN, *adj.* Forestlike, wooded, shady, woody, arborescent, arboreous, arborary, dendritic, rustic, bosky, moss-carpeted, umbrageous, bowery, scenic, mountainous, shaded, shadowy, woodsy, leafy, verdant, bushy, shrubby, timbered, forested, wild, uncultivated, luxuriant, dense, overgrown, rural, bucolic, thicket-grown, grove-clad, coppiced, copse-covered, forest-clad, piny, laurel-strewn, evergreen, woodland, backwoodsy.

SYLVAN, *n.* 1. Person dwelling in a woodland region, bushman, forest-dweller, forester, woodsman, rustic, backwoodsman, woodlander.

2. Fabled spirit of the woods, Silvanus, Pan, satyr, faun, dryad, hamadryad, oread, nymph.

SYMBOL, *n.* Material object standing for something immaterial, something regarded as representing something else, emblem, representation, token, sign, badge, figure, type, exponent, character, mark, representative, picture, pictograph, hieroglyph, cuneiform, ideograph, device, attribute, ensign, note, letter, initial, protogram, cipher, signum, indicium, star, asterisk, cue, key, clue, hint, pointer, indicant, trait, earmark, property, quality, signal, fiery cross, swastika, countermark, trademark, hallmark, monogram, signet, seal, caste mark, brand, cross, frank, flag, streamer, banner, pennant, colors, standard, pennon, oriflamme, eagle, jack, tricolor, Stars and Stripes, arms, crest, coat of arms, escutcheon, armorial bearings, epaulet, cockade, brassard, chevron, image, metaphor, effigy, likeness, diagram, icon.

SYMBOLICAL, *adj.* Serving as a symbol of, emblematic, emblematical, symbolic, representative, typical, figurative, significative, hieroglyphical, ideographic, pictographic, cuneiform, indicative, indicatory, significatory, characteristic, expressive, indicant, suggestive, denotative, connotative, symptomatic, descriptive, pictorial, allusive, allegoric, metaphorical, informatory, informational, monitory, advisory, monitorial, exegetical, communicatory, meaningful, prognostic, synonymous, equivalent, tantamount, virtual, inferred, involved, connoted, understood, tacit, implicit, implied, bodeful, mystical, mystic, cabalistic.

SYMBOLIZE, *v.* Indicate, stand for, be a symbol of, emblemize, typify, illustrate, symbolify, signify, prefigure, emblematize, represent, denote, depict, imply, express, mean, show, delineate, limn, image, personify, allegorize, metaphorize, adumbrate, foreshadow, fable, allude to, shadow forth, connote, betoken, evidence, manifest, present, reveal, evince, register, designate, note, mark, earmark, ticket, label, blaze, seal, signalize, notify, picture, portray, sketch, reproduce, exemplify, be a substitute for, stand in the place of.

SYMMETRICAL, *adj.* 1. Regular in arrangement of corresponding parts, well-proportioned, proportional in the several parts, shapely, congruent, parallel, corresponding, balanced, even, harmonious, eurythmic, well-formed, uniform, orderly, graceful, well-set, beautiful, well-balanced, peloric, equal, coextensive, commensurate, isolateral, finished, chaste, classic, severe, divisible into similar parts, actinomorphic, exhibiting a regular repeated pattern of the component parts.

2. Branched, branching, tree-shaped, dendriform, arboriform, arborescent, arborized, dendroid, dendritic, ramous, ramiform, ramose, actiniform, radiated, raylike, actinoid.

SYMMETRIZE, *v.* Make symmetrical, make eurythmic, balance, proportionate, regularize, even, make correspondent, proportion, harmonize, parallelize, form gracefully, equalize.

SYMMETRY, *n.* Correspondence of parts in form and arrangement, regular arrangement, proportionality, conformity, regularity, uniformity, parallelism, evenness, proportion, congruity, balance, order, harmony, shapeliness, agreement, keeping, peloria, formalism, form, eurythmics, beauty, finish, elegance, gracefulness, grace, comeliness, equality, accordance, unity, conformation, disposition, orderliness, system, systematization, equalization, poise, equilibrium.

SYMPATHETIC, *adj.* Compassionate, commiserative, sympathizing, condolatory, pitying, comforting, sharing another's sorrow, pitiful, tenderhearted, humanitarian, humane, touched, moved, emotional, susceptible, ruthful, soft-hearted, melting, warm-hearted, merciful, considerate, kindly, benevolent, philanthropic, charitable, altruistic, indulgent, forbearing, obliging, benignant, beneficent, large-hearted, fellow-feeling, affectionate, fond, loving, devoted, friendly, well-disposed, amicable, brotherly, fraternal, harmonious, hearty, cordial, fervent, zealous, ardent, congenial, allied, at one with, of one mind with, well-wishing, partisan, consonant, kindred, neighborly, anxious, with the heart in the right place, affected by a special natural affinity, looking with favor upon.

SYMPATHIZE, *v.* 1. Enter into the feelings of, share the sorrow of, feel for, feel sympathy for, commiserate, be compassionate, condole, have pity for, feel compassion for, console, soothe, solace, comfort, lament with, mourn with, compassionate, grieve with, pity, be sorry for, comprehend, understand, be impressed, be moved, be touched.

2. Be in agreement of feeling, share in a feeling, be in approving accord with, make common cause with, have a common feeling, fraternize with, harmonize with, agree, correspond, side with, be concordant, go hand in hand, pull together, fall in with, assent, acquiesce, reciprocate, swim with the stream, bear good will toward, have a leaning to, receive with open arms, have one's heart in the right place, regard with favor, take an interest in.

SYMPATHIZER, *n.* 1. Condoler, pitier, compassionator, commiserator, comforter, solacer, soother, consoler, fellow-feeler, sharer of misery, good Samaritan.

2. Well-wisher, patron, favorer, partisan, cham-

pion, defender, advocate, friend-at-court, benefactor, altruist, philanthropist, zealot, fan, fanatic, backer, Maecenas, good genius, tutelar, tutelary saint, ally, friend in need, helping hand, upholder, seconder, abettor, supporter, deus ex machina, guardian angel.

SYMPATHY, *n.* 1. Commiseration, condolence, compassion, pity, soft-heartedness, tenderness, fellow-feeling, kindliness, bowels of compassion, charity, clemency, mercifulness, mercy, humaneness, humanity, humanitarianism, consolation, solace, comfort, brotherly love, benevolence, melting mood, community of feeling, consideration, affection, love, tolerance, forbearance, yearning, lenity, ruth, long-suffering, sensibility, pathos, sentiment, emotion, concern, anxiety, response, responsiveness, susceptibilities, feelings, grace, quarter, lamentation, sob, tears, weeping, lachrymation, loving-kindness, benignity, bonhomie, milk of human kindness, charitableness, philanthropy, altruism, almsgiving, bounty, beneficence, good works, acts of kindness, camaraderie, warmheartedness.

2. Harmony, agreement, correspondence, accord, acquiescence, congeniality, affinity, communion, concord, reciprocity, consonance, union, correlation, concert, unanimity, spontaneous understanding, rapport, regard, alliance, assistance, insight, amity, favor, approval, backing, partisanship, advocacy, patronage, well-wishing, fellowship, intercourse, communication, *entente* (Fr.).

SYMPHONIOUS, *adj.* Harmonious, symphonic, musical, accordant, consonant, concordant, in tune, unisonant, concentual, isotonic, homophonous, assonant, euphonious.

SYMPHONY, *n.* 1. Harmony of sounds, euphony, concert, consonance, concord, unisonance, homophony, chime, minstrelsy, polyphony, music, accord, homology.

2. Elaborate instrumental composition for orchestra, symphonic poem, tone poem, concerto, sonata, fantasia, overture, concert piece, opus, orchestral score, program music.

SYMPOSIUM, *n.* 1. Convivial meeting for drinking and intellectual entertainment, drinking together, compotation, feast, banquet, revel, festival, regale, party, fete, saturnalia, jollification, wassail, carouse, gala, social intercourse, conviviality, consociation, camaraderie, loving cup.

2. Conference for discussion of some subject, round table, panel discussion, collection of opinions expressed, parley, colloquy, powwow, pourparler, *conversazione* (It.), collocution, confabulation, congress, synod, convocation, debate.

SYMPTOM, *n.* Phenomenon accompanying something, circumstance serving as evidence of, indication, danger signal, warning, diagnostic, prognostic, sign, token, mark, caveat, caution, notice, premonishment, monition, alarm, earmark, characteristic, trait, means of recognition, index, note, peculiarity, feature, denotation, demonstration, proof, portent, boding, omen, foretoken, augury, foreshowing, prognostication, presage, yellow flag, handwriting on the wall, monitor, warning voice, gathering clouds.

SYMPTOMATIC, *adj.* Indicative, suggestive, diagnostic, prognostic, indicatory, significatory, significative, significant, characteristic, emblematic, symptomatical, representative, indicant, typical, denotative, circumstantial, cautionary, premonitory, demonstrative, portentous, ominous, monitory.

SYNAGOGUE, *n.* Jewish house of worship, temple, Sanhedrin, tabernacle, bethel, religious assembly, congregation.

SYNCHRONISM, *n.* Coexistence, synchronization, coincidence, concomitancy, concurrence, simultaneity, coinstantaneity, contemporaneousness, coevality, contemporariness, coetaneousness, isochronism, simultaneousness, coinstantaneousness.

SYNCHRONOUS, *adj.* Occurring at the same time, simultaneous, synchronal, synchronical, contemporaneous, contemporary, coincident, synchronic, going on exactly together, recurring together, coeval, coinciding in time, coinstantaneous, coexistent, concomitant, concurrent, coetaneous.

SYNCOPATE, *v.* Contract by omitting from the middle, elide, slur, shorten, place the accent on beats which are normally unaccented.

SYNCOPE, *n.* 1. Fainting fit, faint, swoon, brief loss of consciousness, deliquium, lipothymy, stupor, faintness, fainting, prostration, blackout, collapse, coma.

2. *(Gram.)* Elision in the middle of a word, contraction of a word by omitting one *or* more sounds from the middle, slurring.

SYNDICATE, *n.* 1. Trust formed to regulate prices and output, cartel, combine, monopoly, combination of capitalists, company, association, alliance, league, union, coalition, federation, merger, holding company, partnership, guild, corporation, firm, house, machine, clique, coterie, gang, set, circle, ring.

2. Council, directorate, board, committee, plenum, cabinet, chamber, staff, bench.

SYNDROME, *n.* Pattern of symptoms in a disease, number of characteristic signs occurring together, set of phenomena occurring at the same time, simultaneous indications, prognostics, diagnostics.

SYNERGETIC, *adj.* Working together, coöperative, coöperating, synergistic, collaborative, socialistic, communal, communistic, profit-sharing, partaking, participant, share-and-share-alike.

SYNOD, *n.* 1. Assembly of church delegates duly convoked, council of ecclesiastics, college of cardinals, consistory, vestry, presbytery, chapter, consistorial court.

2. Deliberative assembly, formal consultative meeting, convention, advisory body, convocation, congress, conclave, comitia, board, bench, staff, diet, congregation, conventicle.

SYNONYM, *n.* Equivalent word, expression accepted as another name for something, interchangeable word of nearly the same meaning, poecilonym, analogue, polyonym, equivalent, convertible term, apposition.

SYNONYMOUS, *adj.* Expressing the same idea, equivalent in meaning, of similar interpretation, equipollent, interchangeable, tantamount, equal, poecilonymic, polyonymic, convertible, synonymic, like, same, correspondent, allied, alike, similar, cosignificative, metaphrastic, paraphrastic.

SYNOPSIS, *n.* Brief statement giving a general view of some subject, compendium, digest, epitome, summary, outline, abstract, précis, apercu, abridgment, condensation, syllabus, abbreviation, general view, sum and substance, pith, review, résumé, breviary, brief, compend, pandect, *multum in parvo (Lat.)*, minute, draft, note, conspectus, prospectus, contents.

SYNTHESIS, *n.* Putting together, combination of elements into a complex whole, composition, integration, blend, compound, union, incorporation, composite, coadunation, unification, conjuncture, consolidation, coalescence, amalgamation, fusion, mixture, admixture, alloy, resultant, amalgam.

SYNTHESIZE, *v.* Put together, make up by combining parts *or* elements, combine into a complex whole, integrate, incorporate, compose, unite, embody, alloy, compound, intermix, concentrate, merge, blend, amalgamate, fuse, agglutinate, consolidate, coalesce, lump together.

SYNTHETIC, *adj.* Pertaining to compounds formed by chemical reaction in a laboratory as opposed to those of natural origin *(Chem.)*, artificial, factitious, not natural, counterfeited, counterfeit, not genuine.

SYRINX, *n.* Shepherd's pipes, Panpipe, Pandean pipes, reed, flute, aulos, piccolo, fife, reed instrument, whistle, flageolet.

SYRTIS, *n.* 1. Quicksand, bog, fen, marsh, quagmire, slough, morass, swamp.

2. Trap, snare, pitfall, slippery ground, meshes, net, decoy, trap door, gin, springle, noose, cobweb, toils, ambush, false bottom, booby trap.

SYSTEM, *n.* 1. A whole with reference to interdependent parts, organism, combination of parts forming a whole, universe, cosmos, set of correlated members, body.

2. Method, uniformity, regularity, organization, order, rule, custom, routine, regimen, mode of management, mode of operation, *modus operandi (Lat.)*, course of action, policy, program, way, complex plan of procedure, orderly manner of arrangement, philosophy, regime, economy, government, procedure, usage, protocol, consistency, constancy, exactness, precision.

3. Design, scheme, plan, theory, hypothesis, connected view, systematization, disposition, outline, draft, sketch, layout, diagram, drawing, chart, map, agenda, prospectus, platform, slate, plank.

SYSTEMATIC, *adj.* Arranged in ordered system, orderly, methodical, according to rule, regular, well-organized, tidy, neat, precise, uniform, formal, stated, recognized, certain, steady, constant, customary, habitual, planned, blocked out, in order, in trim, *en règle (Fr.)*, shipshape, symmetrical, well-regulated, businesslike.

SYSTEMATIZE, *v.* Arrange in a system, regulate, methodize, make systematic, systemize, standardize, classify, categorize, organize, order, reduce to order, regiment, regimentate, put into a systematic form, sort out, dispose, adjust, array, control, map out, shape out a course, recast, block out, prepare, cast, devise, frame, conduct, direct, put first things first.

T

TAB, *n.* 1. Small appendage, flap, strap, loop, lappet, lap, noose, eyehole.

2. Tag, label, stub, ticket, criterion, badge, countermark, check, tally, duplicate, billet, counter, cachet, stamp, trademark, hallmark.

TABBY, *n.* 1. Old maid, spinster, bachelor girl, Amazon, unmarried woman, *femme sole (Fr.)*, virgin, nun.

2. Newsmonger, tattletale, tattler, gossip, talebearer, chatterer, magpie, chatterbox, quidnunc,

busybody, meddler, babbler, windbag, rattle, jay, poll parrot, Paul Pry, *moulin à paroles (Fr.)*.

TABERNACLE, *n.* 1. Temporary habitation, tent, hut, dwelling place, pavilion, baldachin, marquee, tilt, canopy, domicile, abode, lodging, residence, diggings, quarters, sojourn, awning.

2. Jewish temple, synagogue, sanctuary, sanctum sanctorum, sacred place, place of worship, meeting house, bethel.

3. Canopied niche for an image, recess, reliquary, pyx, shrine.

TABID, *adj.* Wasting away, phthisical, tuberculous, tubercular, consumptive, tabescent, tabetic, diseased, marasmic, emaciated, morbose, sickly, ailing, macilent, gaunt, marcid.

TABLE, *n.* 1. Flat surface, level area, tablet, slab, plate, plane, even superficies, stratum.

2. Stand, counter, desk, board, trivet, teapoy, taboret, mahogany, sideboard.

3. Menu, fare, cuisine, diet, food, provision, repast, victuals, bill of fare, table d'hôte, à la carte, refection, refreshment, collation.

4. Arrangement in parallel columns, record, list, file, tabulation, index, syllabus, schedule, catalogue, chart, synopsis, compendium, time-table, résumé, digest.

TABLEAU, *n.* Picturesque grouping, pageant, spectacle, striking scene, tableau vivant, picture, representation, painting, canvas, portrait.

TABLELAND, *n.* Level region of considerable extent, elevated plain, plateau, mesa, downs, open country, tundra, steppe, desert, savanna, pampas, prairie, heath, champaign, veld, wold, common, moor, bush, uplands, fell, campagna.

TABLET, *n.* 1. Pocket memorandum-book, writing pad, notebook, paper, stationery.

2. Small flat surface, slab, plaque, tablature, plaquette, panel, cartouche, tessera, diglyph, triglyph.

3. Flat cake, lozenge, wafer, troche, trochiscus, tabloid, capsule, bolus.

TABOO, *v.* Put under a taboo, put under an interdict, forbid, interdict, prohibit, forbid to be used, bar, ban, proscribe, veto, frown upon, exclude, ostracize, forfend, disallow, censor, imban, outlaw, maledict, anathematize, declare verboten.

TABOO, *n.* Forbiddance, interdiction, prohibition, proscription, disallowance, veto, injunction, interdict, *Verbot (Ger.)*, ban, Index Expurgatorius, repression, embargo, restriction, exclusion, ostracism, anathema, outlawry.

TABOO, *adj.* Set apart as sacred *or* unclean, forbidden to general use, placed under a ban, interdictive, prohibited, *verboten (Ger.)*, inviolable, sacrosanct, proscribed, not permitted, under a ban, not to be thought of, not allowed, unlawful, actionable, not permissible, untouchable.

TABORET, *n.* Low seat without back *or* arms, stool, bench, footstool, faldstool, hassock, tripod, prie-dieu.

TABULATE, *v.* Form into a table, put into tabular form, table, chart, tabularize, formulate into a scheme, catalogue, classify, index, file, class, register, list, alphabetize, range, graduate, grade, systematize, organize, methodize, coördinate, sort, assort, distribute, allocate, assign the parts, assign places to, group, rank, marshal, arrange, array, dispose, line up, make parallel, collimate.

TACIT, *adj.* Not openly expressed, understood, implicit, inferred, implied, unspoken, undeclared, unstated, unsaid, inferential, unmentioned.

TACITURN, *adj.* Not inclined to conversation, given to few words, sparing of words, reserved in speech, reticent, laconic, uncommunicative, self-contained, keeping one's own counsel, close-mouthed, tight-lipped, habitually silent, refraining from speech, close-tongued, unconversable, sententious, mum, secretive, unsociable, curt, still, mute, word-bound, pauciloquent, concise, inarticulate, tongue-tied.

TACITURNITY, *n.* Laconicism, uncommunicativeness, reticency, reticence, laconism, reserve, pauciloquy, habitual silence, closeness, obmutescence, speechlessness, secretiveness, clammishness *(coll.)*, muteness.

TACK, *v.* 1. Secure by some slight fastening, fasten lightly, sew, stitch, baste, bind, lace, fix, attach, tie, clinch, hitch, knit, splice, truss, nail, couple, yoke, bracket, tether.

2. Join together, combine, unite, tag, affix, add, append, annex, prefix, suffix, subjoin.

3. *(Naut.)* Change the course of a ship, proceed to windward, go about, yaw, gybe, point towards, steer for, be bound for, hold a course, heel, swerve, bear off, warp, veer, sheer, chop, deviate.

TACK, *n.* 1. Short sharp-pointed pin, nail, carpet tack, thumbtack, peg, brad, spike, treenail, trunnel, drawing pin, tholepin, toggle, dowel, holdfast.

2. Direction, course, run, way, road, path, route, beat, pathway, trail, track, cut, lane, channel, waterway, bearing, orbit, trajectory, drift, set, aim.

3. Zigzag, yaw, sidling, gybe, leeway, deviation, divagation, aberration, deflection, alternation, declination, wandering, divergence, sheer, swerve, warp, drift, shunt, by-pass, detour, switch, forking, divarication, bending, obliquation, flexion, sweep.

4. Food, fare, aliment, pabulum, nutriment, sustenance, provender, provision, fodder, ration, board, keep, feed, commons, regimen, dietary, diet.

TACKLE, *v.* 1. Lay hold upon, seize, grapple, come to grips with, grab, grasp, snatch, hold, clasp, embrace, collar, catch, overthrow, lay by the heels, spring upon, pounce upon, swoop down upon, scramble for, intercept.

2. Undertake to deal with, attempt, try, endeavor, set about, begin, enter upon, launch, resume, pursue, engage in, devote oneself to, embark upon, take on, take in hand, turn one's hand to, go about, broach, assume, put one's shoulder to the wheel, bend an oar, take the bull by the horns, take up.

TACKLE, *n.* Apparatus, equipment, gear, tools, implements, instruments, paraphernalia, weapons, harness, cordage, tackling, rigging, mechanism, lifting machine, crane, halyard, contrivance, appliances, accouterments, trappings, matériel, appointments, leverage, crowbar, gavelock, handspike, pulley, jemmy, pinion, winch, cramp, crank, capstan, derrick, windlass, lift, hoist.

TACT, *n.* 1. Knack of dealing with delicate situations, keen sense of savoir-faire in avoiding giving offense, adroitness in evaluating circumstances and acting accordingly, nice perception, discernment, quick judgment, insight, intuition, penetration, subtlety, skill in doing what is most decorous, discriminatory powers, discrimination, discretion, shrewd diagnosis, acumen, acuteness, sharpness, wisdom, comprehension, understanding, sagacity, wit, quick parts, esprit, grasp, perspicacity, clear thinking, prudence, foresight.

2. Address, dexterity, adroitness, cleverness, finesse, touch, diplomacy, expertness, faculty, delicacy, feeling, refinement, competence, proficiency, felicity, *curiosa felicitas (Lat.)*, qualification, capacity, efficiency, capability, deftness, finish, polish, featness, facility, adeptness, craft, sleight, technique, art, ingenuity, talent, endowment, parts, genius, turn, resourcefulness.

TACTFUL, *adj.* Diplomatic, smooth, conciliatory, politic, shrewd, sagacious, prudent, artful, suave, bland, complaisant, urbane, polished, chivalric, gallant, gracious, adept, gentlemanly, fine-spoken, obliging, genial, addressful, adroit, feat, dexterous, skillful, discerning, discriminating, penetrative, perspicacious, quick-witted, keen-sighted, astute, far-sighted, clear-headed, argute, judicious, considerate.

TACTICIAN, *n.* Military strategist, artful maneuverer, adroit manager, wirepuller, planner, expert, proficient, connoisseur, master hand, specialist, past master, old campaigner, veteran, nice hand, practiced eye, mastermind, sharp fellow, diplomat, politician, Machiavelli, fox, sly boots, Reynard, schemer, intriguer, trickster.

TACTICS, *n.* 1. Military science, strategy of disposing forces for battle, battle maneuver, art of war, generalship, planned campaign, castrametation, old soldiership, military evolutions.

2. Mode of procedure for gaining advantage *or* success, maneuvering, diplomacy, politics, policy, management, devices, dealing, conduct, game, polity, statesmanship, strategics, manipulation, behavior, line of action, *modus operandi (Lat.)*.

TACTILE, *adj.* Pertaining to the sense of touch, perceptible to the touch, palpable, tangible, tactual.

TACTLESS, *adj.* Blunt, brusque, obtrusive, malapropos, ill-behaved, ill-advised, forward, precocious, impudent, impertinent, pert, uncomplaisant, boorish, churlish, blundering, thoughtless, inconsiderate, gross, gauche, awkward, uncouth, bungling, inapt, maladroit, clumsy, untoward, imprudent, injudicious, outspoken, abrupt.

TAG, *v.* 1. Fit with a tag, label, attach a tag to, mark, ticket.

2. Attach, add to, affix, join to, append, tack on, fasten, annex.

3. Run after, dog, pursue, hound, follow close upon, tail, shadow, accompany, hang on the skirts of, trail, attend.

TAG, *n.* 1. Label, ticket, tab, stub, marker, card, slip, tally, hallmark, countermark.

2. Tail, pendant, tip, appendage, attachment, adjunct, affix, suffix, annex, postfix, prefix, appendix, queue.

3. Codicil, rider, addendum, supplement, postscript, afterpiece, sequel, continuation, epilogue, postlude, peroration.

4. Fag end, butt, remnant, fragment, scrap, remainder, stump, rump, shred, rag, sliver, snip.

5. Stock phrase, catchword, refrain, cue, bob, cliché, quotation, moral of a fable, *envoi (Fr.)*, burden, chorus, reprise, repetition.

TAIL, *n.* 1. Caudal appendage, cauda, dock, hinder part, hind end, rear, rump, fundament, podex, dorsum, tergum, breech, brush, flag, scut, seat, crupper, buttock, *derrière (Fr.)*, croup, rumble seat *(humorous)*, posterior, bottom.

2. Rudder, empennage, tail fin, flipper, tail unit, tail assembly, stabilizer.

3. Extremity, tag, stub, end, fag end, appendage, conclusion, tip, nib.

4. Train, queue, retinue, suite, entourage, trail, wake, following.

TAILOR, *n.* Clothier, garment maker, *couturier (Fr.)*, dressmaker, modiste, seamstress, sempstress, *costumier (Fr.)*, costumer, snipper, needlewoman.

TAINT, *v.* 1. Stain, dye, tinge, tint, color, tone, hue, ingrain, imbue, impregnate, discolor.

2. Pollute, infect, corrupt, contaminate, spoil, defile, make putrid, make noxious, poison, vitiate, mildew, touch, flyblow, debase, besmirch, blot, sully, tarnish, attaint, soil, canker, rot, blight, rust, corrode, oxidize, consume, erode, gnaw.

TAINT, *n.* 1. Infection, pollution, contagion, virus, plague, pestilence, epidemic, endemic, poison, malady, ailment, illness, sickness, disease, affection, disorder, complaint.

2. Stain, stigma, tinge, tincture, touch, defilement, blot, brand, contamination, depravation, vitiation, impurity, corruption, spot, tarnish, blur.

3. Blemish, fault, defect, flaw, imperfection, shortcoming, peccadillo, weakness, drawback, failing, foible, weak point, rift, frailty, deficiency, defectiveness.

TAKE, *v.* 1. Snatch, grab, lay hold of, seize, clasp, grip, grasp, hold, clutch, gripe, get hold of, lay hands on, nab, avail oneself of.

2. Receive, procure, obtain, get, accept, derive, pick from a number, select, gather, cull, reap, pluck, crop, draw, choose, elect.

3. Capture, ensnare, entrap, arrest, make prisoner of, bag, apprehend, collar, captivate, net, claw, secure, acquire, overthrow, lay by the heels, take prisoner, attain, hook, embrace, tackle, grapple, cause to surrender, conquer, subdue, subjugate, vanquish, swoop down upon, pounce upon, steal upon, take by assault.

4. Abstract, appropriate, intercept, confiscate, sequestrate, arrogate, pocket, usurp, exact, filch, steal, purloin, pilfer, despoil, sack, plunder, loot, help oneself to, impound, make free with, possess oneself of, commandeer, lay under contribution, dispossess, wrest from, extort, wrench from, tear from, take away from, bereave, deprive of, accroach, distrain, divest, levy, adeem, sequester, disinherit, strip, bleed *(coll.)*, fleece, pluck, diddle, swindle, rifle, pillage, embezzle, misappropriate.

5. Have capacity for, accommodate, hold, furnish room for, house, include, comprehend, comprise, admit, entertain, let in.

6. Purchase, rent, hire, lease, subscribe for, buy.

7. Require, demand, necessitate, call for, need, claim, use up, expend, occupy, employ, use, consume.

8. Understand, regard, interpret, hold, consider, suppose, opine, believe, comprehend, assume, derive, deduce, infer, detect, discover, conclude, look upon, deem, esteem, apprehend, grasp, see, discern, perceive, make out, know, find out, ascertain, decide, determine, settle, fix, feel, experience, conceive, be sensible of, be conscious of.

9. Bear, endure, suffer, tolerate, brook, stomach, put up with, stand, submit to, undergo, abide, bear with.

10. Surmount, leap over, clear, top, go over.

11. Move, convey, transport, conduct, carry, remove, escort, lead, usher, transfer.

12. Charm, allure, delight, captivate, fascinate, ensorcel, rivet, appeal, attract, lure, bewitch, engage, interest, please, hold, enchant, move, affect, win, prepossess, obsess, engross, absorb, inveigle.

13. Deceive, trick, impose upon, fool, cheat, hoax, defraud, gull, dupe, throw sand in the eyes, outwit, overreach, lead astray, mislead, circumvent, practice upon, bamboozle, victimize, cozen, chouse, betray.

TAKE ABACK, v. Take by surprise, astonish, astound, flabbergast, startle, surprise, stun, dumfound, overcome with bewilderment, amaze, dazzle, strike with wonder, electrify, stupefy, stagger, throw on one's beam ends, strike dumb, take away one's breath, throw off one's guard, catch napping.

TAKE ADVANTAGE OF, v. 1. Make use of, avail oneself of, profit by, turn to account, make the most of, make hay while the sun shines, take time by the forelock, strike while the iron is hot.

2. Impose upon, dupe, gull, cozen, chouse, cheat, deceive, beguile, fool, bamboozle, hoax, outwit, overreach, catch by surprise, trick, defraud.

TAKE AFTER, v. 1. Look like, resemble, be like, parallel, match, favor, reproduce, bear resemblance, be the image of, be a chip off the old block.

2. Follow the example of, copy, imitate, echo, parrot, mirror, repeat, reflect, follow suit, emulate, do like, model after, ape, mimic, mock, simulate.

TAKE AMISS, v. Be offended at, resent, take offense at, take ill, be indignant, take umbrage at, be provoked at, harbor resentment, be angry, bristle, bridle, be incensed, be exasperated, be wroth, fume, fret, chafe, flare up, look black as thunder, knit one's brows, make a wry face, pull a long face, grouse, grumble, repine, be put out, take in bad part.

TAKE BACK, v. Retract, rescind, abjure, disavow, recant, revoke, recall, retire, withdraw, change one's mind, renounce, go to the right about, back down, forswear, apostatize, unsay, eat one's words, draw in one's horns, swallow the leek, back out of, disclaim, forgo, relinquish, abandon, deny, repudiate, disaffirm.

TAKE CARE, v. Be cautious, be vigilant, take heed, reck, heed what one is about, be on one's guard, be on the qui vive, be canny, think twice, look before one leaps, feel one's way, wait to see how the cat jumps, see how the land lies, keep out of harm's way, let sleeping dogs lie, keep on the safe side, beware, be wary, watch out for, mind one's P's and Q's, keep one's eyes open.

TAKE CARE OF, v. Take charge of, keep an eye on, care for, superintend, oversee, look after, see to, pay attention to, watch over, protect, keep, chaperon, attend, accompany, escort.

TAKE DOWN, v. 1. Pull down, pull to pieces, dismantle, take apart, pull apart, disassemble, undo, demolish, break up, raze, level with the ground, efface.

2. Humble, humiliate, abash, mortify, show up, take down a peg, bring low, put one's nose out of joint, put to the blush, disconcert, discompose, throw off one's center, put out of countenance, depreciate, animadvert upon, run down, pick to pieces, give a rap on the knuckles, snub, have a fling at, pluck a crow with, give one a lick with the rough side of the tongue, expose.

3. Record, jot down, write down, make a note

of, make a memo of, note, place upon record, commit to writing, set down in black and white, put on paper, minute.

TAKE EXCEPTION, v. 1. Make objection, object, differ, dissent, demur, disagree, raise one's voice against, refuse assent, say no, make bold to differ, protest, expostulate, remonstrate, contradict, dispute, rebut, join issue upon, controvert, gainsay.

2. Disapprove, frown upon, shake the head at, look askance, knit the brows, make a wry face, condemn, censure, disapprove, lament, think ill of, view with disfavor, improbate, deprecate, not speak well of, impugn.

TAKE FLIGHT, v. Take to one's heels, abscond, decamp, vamoose, bolt, make off, scamper off, fly, flee, beat a retreat, turn tail, run off, be off like a shot, cut and run, sneak off, desert, steal away, take French leave, give leg bail, flit, skedaddle, levant, show a light pair of heels, escape, make oneself scarce.

TAKE FOR, v. Mistake for, confuse with, err, be mistaken, receive a false impression, fall into error, deceive oneself, misapprehend, misunderstand, take the wrong sow by the ear, put the saddle on the wrong horse, take the shadow for the substance, reckon without one's host, be credulous, be in the wrong box, fall into a trap, nibble at the bait, swallow the hook.

TAKE HEED, v. Beware, be wary, be careful, be cautious, guard against, think twice, have a care, mind what one is about, be on one's guard, keep one's weather eye open, count the cost, keep out of harm's way, keep at a respectful distance, keep on the safe side.

TAKE IN, v. 1. Admit, receive, accommodate, entertain, let in, acquire, get.

2. Embrace, include, comprise, comprehend, enclose, encompass, absorb, contain, cover, embody, subsume, involve, number among, reckon among, take into account.

3. Understand, grasp, discern, comprehend, apprehend, perceive, see, know, believe, make out, sense, learn.

4. Make smaller, contract, reduce, lessen, diminish, shorten, narrow, furl, curtail.

5. Deceive, impose upon, fool, hoax, bamboozle, gull, dupe, victimize, swindle, outwit, trick, cheat, defraud, cozen, chouse, hoodwink, inveigle, decoy, ensnare, mystify, delude, bluff, humbug, foist off, palm off, take advantage of, practice upon, steal a march on, outreach, throw dust into the eyes, overreach, circumvent, lead astray, mislead.

TAKE IN GOOD PART, v. Take without offense, receive kindly, make the best of, make light of, put a good face on, keep one's countenance, submit with good grace, acquiesce in, abide with, put up with, bear up under, stand, tolerate, bear the brunt, brave, take things as they come, take coolly, *aequam servare mentem (Lat.),* reconcile oneself to, brook, master one's feelings, assent, be reconciled to, get over it, make one's peace with.

TAKE IN HAND, v. 1. Familiarize with, discipline, train, bring up, ground, educate, teach, exercise, drill, habituate, practice, break in, initiate, inure, indoctrinate, rehearse.

2. Undertake, set the hand to, engage in, embark in, plunge into, launch, take upon oneself, take upon one's shoulders, tackle, take up, go about, set about, fall to, put one's shoulder to the

wheel, ply an oar, put in execution, put one's hand to, turn one's hand to, institute, broach, lay one's hand to the plow.

3. Befriend, be of use to, aid, subserve, render a service to, take up the cudgels for, stand by, second, back up, espouse the cause of, uphold, support, accommodate, reinforce, succor, help, assist, lend one's aid, hold out a hand, give one a lift.

TAKE INTO ACCOUNT, *v.* Allow for, make allowance for, weigh carefully, consider, take into consideration, bear in mind, remember, realize, appreciate, have in one's mind.

TAKE INTO CUSTODY, *v.* Arrest, apprehend, take prisoner, seize, take captive, commit to prison, imprison, incarcerate, clap under hatches, put into bilboes, put in irons, cloister, immure, coop up, pen, impound, confine, nab, pinch (*coll.*).

TAKE LEAVE, *v.* Take one's departure, take one's congé, bid farewell, bid adieu, say good-by, depart, retire, go away, leave, withdraw, remove, decamp, abscond, vamoose, disappear, take wing, go forth, take flight, march out, sally forth, take off, exit, make one's exit, leave a place, quit, vacate, evacuate, go off the stage, flit, cut and run, hop off, weigh anchor, whip away.

TAKE NOTICE, *v.* Pay attention, pay heed, observe, heed, remark, note, see, perceive, attend, be attentive, view, look, regard, mark, animadvert, contemplate, occupy oneself with, direct the eye to, give the mind to, keep in view, have regard to, take cognizance of, mind, examine, run over, scrutinize, scan, take stock of, inspect, revert to, watch.

TAKE OFF, *v.* 1. Divest oneself of, remove, doff, strip, denude, bare, unclothe, undress, disrobe, peel off, shed.

2. Mimic, imitate, personate, impersonate, reproduce, copy, mirror, reflect, do like, follow suit, emulate, follow the example of, model after, echo, simulate, ape, mock, represent, parody, caricature, travesty, burlesque, satirize, laugh at, ridicule, deride, poke fun at.

TAKE-OFF, *n.* Caricature, burlesque, travesty, parody, imitation, mimicry, copy, apery, mimicking, mockery, impersonation, simulation, masquerade, representation, satirization, satire, farce, buffoonery, mummery.

TAKE ONE'S CHANCE, *v.* Try one's luck, tempt fortune, venture, try one's fortune, stand a chance, draw lots, toss up, cast lots, chance it, incur the risk, speculate, stand the hazard of the die, shuffle the cards, buy a pig in a poke, risk, stake, hazard, wager, essay, try.

TAKE ONE'S CHOICE, *v.* Pick and choose, elect, prefer, coöpt, fix upon, cull, glean, pitch upon, select, single out, pick out, choose.

TAKE ONE'S FANCY, *v.* Please, delight, charm, afford pleasure, titillate, gladden, captivate, enrapture, enchant, amuse, warm the cockles of the heart, interest, stimulate, allure, attract, fascinate, enravish, transport, bewitch, ensorcel, entrance, whet the appetite, tempt, tantalize.

TAKE PLACE, *v.* Happen, come to pass, occur, eventuate, come into existence, come off, come about, present itself, fall out, betide, befall, bechance, crop up, spring up, turn up, supervene, ensue, issue, arrive, arise, emanate, take its course, start.

TAKE SIDES, *v.* Espouse the cause of one side, take up the cudgels for, favor one side, be partisan, befriend, be one-sided, be unilateral, be biased in favor of, be prejudiced for, stand by, second, back up, abet, stick up for, adopt the cause of, advocate, countenance, give moral support to, shine upon, smile upon, enlist under the banners of, side with, concur, stand shoulder to shoulder, act in concert, fraternize, join forces, be in league with, confederate, make common cause, go along with, join hands over, cast in one's lot with, rally round, lend oneself to, be a party to.

TAKE THE LEAD, *v.* Go in the van, precurse, precede, forerun, introduce, herald, usher, pioneer, go ahead of, antecede, head up, commence, begin, be the first to start, take up, initiate, inaugurate, institute, broach, set on foot, be the vanguard.

TAKE THE PLACE OF, *v.* Be a substitute for, supply the place of, stand in the shoes of, displace, supplant, supersede, cut out, replace, succeed, assume the authority of.

TAKE TO, *v.* 1. Be fond of, like, be kindly disposed to, derive pleasure from, delight in, rejoice in, relish, have a liking for, care for, fancy, be partial to, take an interest in, be in love with, harbor affection for, bear love to, regard, set one's affections on, make much of, treasure, prize, cling to, cherish, idolize, adore, dote on, worship, be stuck on, fall for, look sweet upon, become enamored of, lose one's heart over, set one's cap at, covet.

2. Addict oneself to, have recourse to, habituate, fall into a habit, accustom, get into the way of, resort to.

TAKE TO HEART, *v.* Lay to heart, feel keenly, be much affected by, be touched to the quick, be sensible to, be soft-hearted, take on, grieve over, mourn over, lament, brood over, mope, pine, repine, languish, pout, fret, frown, sulk, droop, despond, be dejected, look downcast, be disheartened, be discouraged.

TAKE TO TASK, *v.* Call to account, bring to book, reprove, reprehend, chide, criticize, reprimand, rebuke, remonstrate with, blame, object to, view with disfavor, shake the head at, make a wry face at, discommend, dispraise, deprecate, slate, reproach, pass censure on, impugn, recriminate, expostulate, admonish, rake over the coals, call to order, lecture, chastise, impeach, denounce, hold up to reprobation, exprobrate, scold, vituperate, upbraid, bark at, fulminate against, thunder against, give a tongue-lashing, inveigh against, have a fling at, pick to pieces, find fault with.

TAKING, *adj.* 1. Infectious, contagious, catching, epidemic, communicable, pandemic, pestilential, pestiferous, zymotic, epizoötic, virulent, toxic, noxious, morbific.

2. Predatory, predacious, raptorial, pillaging, plundering, looting, rapacious, ravening, wolfish, piratical, thievish, larcenous, light-fingered, pilfering, thieving, prehensile, privative, predal.

3. Captivating, winning, alluring, pleasing, attractive, winsome, charming, prepossessing, bewitching, enchanting, engaging, fascinating, delightful, irresistible, persuasive, overpowering, seductive, enticing, entrancing, ravishing.

TALE, *n.* 1. Factual narrative, oral relation, story, anecdote, recital, narration, yarn, account, fiction, fable, saga, romance, apologue, legend, conte, parable, allegory, myth, novel, rehearsal, communication, invention, description, thriller *(coll.)*, whodunit *(sl.)*, explanation, sketch, epic.

2. Piece of malicious gossip, rumor, canard, talk, scandal, hearsay, report, scuttlebutt *(sl.)*, bruit, tittle-tattle, scoop *(cant).*

3. Falsehood, fabrication, lie, fib, untruth, tall story, cock-and-bull story, misrepresentation, falsification, falsity.

4. Enumeration, tally, score, count, numbering, reckoning, calculation, computation.

TALEBEARER, *n.* Gossip, tattler, newsmonger, scandalmonger, mumblenews, telltale, busybody, quidnunc, informer, meddler, Paul Pry, snooper.

TALENT, *n.* Special natural ability, capacity for achievement, capability for success, gift, genius, faculty, turn, forte, endowment, aptitude, skill, cleverness, knack, ableness, aptness, power, parts, ingenuity, accomplishment, attainment, sharpness, resourcefulness, savoir-faire, mother wit, finesse, technique, know-how, proficiency, *curiosa felicitas (Lat.)*, dexterity, address, competence, efficiency, expertness, adroitness, mastery, deftness, facility, featliness, finish, polish, flair.

TALENTED, *adj.* Gifted, accomplished, of brilliant parts, able, qualified, competent, clever, learned, ingenious, feat, artistic, skillful, apt, dexterous, deft, adroit, expert, proficient, smart, good at, master of, crack *(coll.)*, masterly, *au fait (Fr.)*, crackajack, practiced, efficient, trained, finished, polished, felicitous, neat.

TALISMAN, *n.* Superstitious object supposed to possess occult powers, amulet, charm, phylactery, fetish, mascot, wishbone, rabbit's foot, swastika, scarab, triskelion, gammadion, fylfot, caduceus, wand, divining rod, magic ring, wishing cap, furcula, merrythought, Aladdin's lamp, periapt.

TALISMANIC, *adj.* Magical, phylacteric, charmed, necromantic, Circean, witching, cabalistic, incantatory, thaumaturgical, wonderworking, fetishistic.

TALK, *v.* 1. Speak, utter, declaim, say, tell, declare, mention, express, pronounce, proclaim, break silence, open one's lips, wag the tongue, raise one's voice, breathe, give utterance to, deliver, enunciate, state.

2. Converse, confabulate, comment, parley, palaver, chat, descant, expatiate, prattle, chatter, prate, communicate, commune, discourse, pour forth, harangue, monologize, soliloquize, discuss, babble, harp, chirp, chin, jaw, splutter, gab, gabble, rhapsodize, rant, banter, orate, blurt out, rap out, address, accost, spout, stump, speechify, sermonize, lecture, recite, consult, gossip, colloquize, blather, cackle, gush, blab, maunder, rave, effuse, bandy words, clack, twaddle, preach, inform, intimate, announce, apprise, hint, insinuate, advise, impart to, describe, narrate, relate, recount, rehearse.

TALK, *n.* 1. Converse, conversation, speech, parlance, utterance, colloquy, interlocution, confabulation, communication, oral intercourse, discourse, chat, chitchat, palaver, parley, dialogue, conference, gab, prattle, patter, causerie, pourparler, *conversazione (It.)*, consultation, lecture, address, locution, oration, recitation, declamation, allocution, harangue, tirade, sermon, exhortation, homily, commerce, babble, tittle-tattle, tête-à-tête, powwow, badinage, persiflage, raillery, banter, slack jaw *(sl.)*, twaddle, rhapsody, effusion, rant, jargon, chaff, blatherskite, blarney, buncombe.

2. Gossip, towntalk, scuttlebutt, rumor, bruit, report, hearsay, scandal, fame, *oui-dire (Fr.)*, scoop, beat, canard, tidings.

3. Language, dialect, lingo, brogue, patois, cant, lingua franca, gibberish, slang, argot.

4. Oratory, eloquence, elocution, rhetoric, grandiloquence, magniloquence, altiloquence, *copia verborum (Lat.)*, gift of gab, command of words.

TALKATIVE, *adj.* Communicative, loquacious, garrulous, verbose, voluble, wordy, fluent, glib, long-winded, prolix, chatty, windy, conversational, babbly, gossipy, multiloquent, eloquent, declamatory, grandiloquent, oratorical, facund, polyloquent, effusive, rhapsodical, diffuse, profuse, diffusive, exuberant, discursive, rambling, confabulatory, interlocutory.

TALKER, *n.* 1. Speaker, orator, rhetor, conversationalist, converser, lecturer, elocutionist, speechifier, interlocutor, spokesman, prolocutor, mouthpiece, speechmaker, prelector, preacher, reciter, reader, spellbinder.

2. Loquacious person, prattler, chatterer, chatterbox, magpie, windbag, babbler, *moulin à paroles (Fr.)*, blatherskite, gossip, newsmonger, scandalmonger, ranter, jay, parrot, braggart, boaster, gascon, spouter, gasbag, hot-air artist.

TALL, *adj.* 1. High, elevated, lofty, towering, soaring, gigantic, colossal, big, aerial, Alpine, cloud-capt, heaven-kissing, skyscraping, Patagonian, beetling.

2. Lank, lanky, gangling, long-limbed, rangy, stringy, weedy, gaunt.

3. Hard to believe, exaggerated, incredible, hyperbolical, preposterous.

4. Large in amount, exorbitant, excessive, *de trop (Fr.)*, padded, unreasonable.

5. High-flown, grandiloquent, altiloquent, altisonant, magniloquent, grandiose, bombastic, fustian, pompous, highfaluting, vainglorious, pretentious, turgid, inflated, thrasonic, plethoric, toplofty.

TALLOW, *n.* Fatty animal tissue, grease, fat, suet, lard, blubber, stearin, oleagine.

TALLY, *v.* 1. Enter on a tally, list, record, register, enroll, inscribe, docket, inventory, catalogue, post, tabulate, book, manifest, invoice.

2. Count, reckon up, total, score, compute, cast up, sum up, calculate.

3. Correspond, agree, accord, match, jibe *(coll.)*, square, coincide, conform, fit, suit, harmonize, concur, dovetail.

TALLY, *n.* 1. Label, tag, badge, stub, ticket, countermark, emblem, insignia, voucher, docket, slip, check, mate, duplicate, match, counterpart.

2. Notch, mark, scratch, score, stroke, dash, line, impression, streak, blaze.

3. Score, roll, file, muster, record, roll call, tale, enumeration, reckoning, calculation, computation, counting, census, poll, statistics.

TALON, *n.* 1. Claw of a bird of prey, nail, hook, toenail.

2. Slide-fastening device, zipper.

TAME, *v.* 1. Make tame, domesticate, break in, make docile, train, gentle, discipline, make tractable, meeken, soften, domesticize, reclaim, yoke, break to harness.

2. Subdue, subjugate, master, overcome, conquer, control, subject, vanquish, defeat, overthrow, reduce, repress, hold in leading strings, keep under.

TAME, *adj.* 1. Changed from the wild *or* savage state, domesticated, acclimatized, reclaimed, domestic, gentle, mild, docile, tractable, broken, mansuete.

2. Subdued, unresisting, meek, submissive, downtrodden, in leading strings, under control, in harness, henpecked, tied to one's apron strings, under one's thumb, on the hip, used as a doormat, at one's beck and call, at the mercy of, a slave to, dependent, subject, servile, slavish, enslaved, humble, forbearing, pusillanimous, shy.

3. Lacking in animation, spiritless, feeble, dull, vapid, insipid, languid, flat, jejune, prosy, prosaic, tedious, barren, lean, lifeless, watery, apathetic, phlegmatic, uninteresting, commonplace, poor.

TAMPER, *v.* 1. Meddle, interfere, have to do, tinker, trifle, "monkey," dabble, intermeddle, interpose, have a hand in, put in one's oar, have a finger in the pie, moil.

2. Obtrude, intrude, butt in, poke one's nose in, horn in, intrigue, deal secretly, act improperly, undertake underhand dealings, seduce, bribe, suborn, use bribery, bait with a silver hook, cross the palm with silver, grease the palm, prejudice, subvert, demoralize, pervert.

3. Alter, diversify, vary, variegate, change, commute, temper, qualify, modify, transform, transmute, metamorphose, revolutionize, convert, revamp, resolve.

4. Alloy, adulterate, doctor, debase, injure, damage, impair, spoil, mar, scathe, harm, degrade, vitiate.

TAN, *v.* 1. Impregnate with tannin, steep in oak *or* hemlock bark solution, convert into leather.

2. Imbrown, make tawny, make brown by exposure to the sun, imbrown by exposure, weather, bronze, brown.

3. Beat, thrash, drub, trounce, larrup, fustigate, lick, trim, cob, warm, comb, strap, give a dressing, belabor, baste, lambaste, leather, pommel, buffet, thump, spank, cuff, smack, thwack.

TAN, *adj.* Tan-colored, tawny, brownish, light yellowish brown, bronzed, sun-tanned, adust, chestnut, nutbrown, cinnamon, fuscous, fawn, foxy, brown as a berry, mahogany, khaki, sorrel, roan, sunburnt.

TANDEM, *adv.* One after the other, in single file, Indian-file, not abreast, lengthwise.

TANG, *n.* 1. Sharpness, nip, bite, tartness, keenness, sting, piquancy, pungency, acridness, mordancy, acridity, *haut goût (Fr.)*.

2. Strong flavor, distinctive taste, savor, smack, aftertaste, relish, sapidity, spice, twang.

TANGENT, *adj.* Passing through several points of a surface, touching, tangential, in contact, pertingent, contiguous, abutting, stereognostic, adjacent.

TANGIBLE, *adj.* 1. Discernible by the touch, touchable, tactile, corporeal, physical, material, hylozoistic, embodied, solid, stable, palpable, perceptible, sensible, tactual, bodily, incarnate, corporal, materialized, ponderable, sensuous, somatic, somatologic, hylic.

2. Real, evident, plain, obvious, certain, definite, not elusive, actual, open, not vague, positive, factual, veritable, well-founded, valid, concrete, well-defined, precise, clear-cut.

TANGLE, *v.* 1. Bring together into a confused mass, intertwine, twist, interweave, entangle, snarl, mat, plait, dishevel, jumble, disorder, tousle, rumple, ruffle, mix, involve, disarrange, ravel, muss, complicate, intertwist, interlace, raddle, knot, muddle.

2. Perplex, bewilder, embroil, confuse, confound, embarrass, puzzle, rattle, pose, nonplus, disconcert, daze.

TANGLE, *n.* 1. Disorder, snarl, jumble, knot, maze, labyrinth, imbroglio, tanglement, entanglement, confusion, intricacy, complication, complexity, disarrangement, discomposure, litter, mess, disarray, untidiness, hodgepodge, muddle, clutter, network, skein, Gordian knot, jungle, coil, wilderness, meshwork, reticulation, net, web, Hercynian wood.

2. Perplexity, bewilderment, embarrassment, quandary, dilemma, puzzle, confusedness, incertitude, strait, vexed question, poser, hard nut to crack, crux, riddle, enigma, conundrum, paradox, problem.

TANK, *n.* 1. Reservoir, cistern, boiler, vat, large receptacle, sump, pound, millpond, lake, aquarium, well, tarn, mere, loch, lough, pool.

2. Armored self-propelled combat vehicle moving on a caterpillar tread, armored car.

TANKARD, *n.* Large drinking cup with a handle and a hinged cover, mug, stein, beaker, pot, jug, toby, pipkin, pitcher, skeel, chalice, goblet.

TANTALIZE, *v.* 1. Lure with the sight of something desired but out of reach, tempt, allure, bait, attract, entice, intrigue, whet the appetite, make one's mouth water, take one's fancy, appetize, charm, excite desire, titillate, stimulate, beckon, fascinate, captivate, bewitch, ensorcel.

2. Tease by arousing and disappointing expectations, torment, balk, disappoint, frustrate, plague, irritate, vex, worry, aggravate, provoke, annoy, taunt, baffle, foil, dash one's hopes, disconcert, disillusionize, balk, jilt, dash the cup from the lip, disgruntle, dissatisfy.

TANTAMOUNT, *adj.* Equivalent, equal, identical, convertible, synonymous, alike, comparable with, similar, analogous, correlative, correspondent, all the same, selfsame, same, ditto, indistinguishable.

TANTRUM, *n.* Burst of ill-humor, outburst, fit of passion, paroxysm, fit, tiff, pet, towering rage, *acharnement (Fr.)*, ferment, fume, ire, pucker, choler, spleen, virulence, dudgeon, pique, miff, umbrage, huff, indignation, bitter resentment, animosity, displeasure, wrath, anger, exasperation, vexation, asperity, acrimony, fire and fury, explosion, hot blood, vials of wrath, high words, gnashing of teeth, temper, procacity, irritability, petulance, protervity, spinosity, moodiness, sulks, mumps, *bouderie (Fr.)*, black looks, doldrums, dander.

TAP, *v.* 1. Touch with slight blows, strike lightly, pat, rap, smack, dab, flap, peck, thump, slam, punch, slap, hit, knock, hammer, beat, bat, bang, dash, clip, plug, whack, thwack, ram, wham, batter, buffet, tamp, crack.

2. Draw off, broach, drain, run off, exhaust, deplete, sap.

3. Bore, pierce, perforate, drill, transpierce, spit, spear, gore, pink, stab, lance, puncture, prick, stick.

TAP, *n.* 1. Gentle but audible blow, light stroke, pat, touch, rap, smack, thump, thwack, knock, slap, dab, fillip, flap, hit, bang, jab, clip, poke, whack, bat, swat, punch, buffet, cuff, crack, slam.

2. Spigot, faucet, plug, stopcock, cock, petcock, stopple, stopper, spile, bung, cork, spill.

TAPE, *n.* Long narrow strip, ribbon, string, fillet, band, fascia, riband, roll.

TAPER, *v.* Become gradually slenderer toward one end, grow gradually lean, thin out, diminish, narrow, lessen, become conical, contract, point.

TAPERING, *adj.* Conical, pyramidal, narrowing, fusiform, diminishing, pointed, spiked, aculeated, mucronate, spindle-shaped, peaked, cusped, cuspidate, barbed.

TAPESTRY, *n.* Woven fabric with colored pictorial design, arras, wall hanging, drapery, furniture covering, Gobelin.

TAPROOM, *n.* Drinking establishment, tavern, barroom, bar, saloon, bistro, café, public house, pub, alehouse, pothouse, gin-mill, speak-easy *(sl.),* shebeen *(Irish),* wine shop, *bodega (Sp.), estaminet (Fr.),* mughouse, roadhouse, cocktail lounge, night club, beer parlor, rumshop, dramshop, cabaret, grogshop, barrel house.

TAR, *n.* 1. Seaman, sailor, mariner, seafaring man, seafarer, argonaut, navigator, jack tar, gob, salt, sea dog, shellback, able-bodied seaman, blue-jacket, middy, marine, mate, skipper, boatswain, coxswain, pilot, helmsman, *lascar (East Indian), matelot (Fr.), marinero (Sp.), marinaio (It.), Matrose (Ger.).*

2. Dark-colored viscid product obtained by distillation of organic substance like wood *or* coal, pitch, bitumen, asphalt, resin, gum, rosin, colophony, lac, shellac.

TARDINESS, *n.* Lateness, slowness, dilatoriness, sluggishness, sloth, lentitude, retardation, slackening, delay, procrastination, cunctation, prorogation, postponement, deferring, deferment, filibuster, prolongation, protraction, Fabian policy, remand, moratorium, leeway, high time, reprieve, stay, respite, suspension, temporization, slothfulness, backwardness, leisure, inaction, remissness, idleness, indolence, dawdling, otiosity, languor, pottering.

TARDY, *adj.* Slow, late, overdue, behindhand, backward, slow-paced, behindtime, dilatory, procrastinative, remiss, slack, reluctant, eleventh-hour, last-minute, unpunctual, sluggish, languid, snail-like, Fabian, delaying, belated, long-delayed, leisurely, phlegmatic, apathetic, tardigrade, creeping, slower than molasses in January.

TARGET, *n.* 1. Mark to be shot at, device marked with concentric circles to be aimed at, bull's-eye, butt, goal, quintain, objective, destination, point, aim.

2. Small round shield, buckler, targe, breast-plate, aegis, cuirass, carapace, plastron.

TARIFF, *n.* Official list of customs imposed by a government, schedule of duties on imports *or* exports, scale of prices, charge, toll, trade controls, table of charges, tax, duty, *douane (Fr.),* impost, levy, tallage, *octroi (Fr.),* assessment, excise.

TARN, *n.* Small steep-banked mountain lake, mere, pond, pool, loch, lough, lin, broad, plash.

TARNISH, *v.* 1. Grow dull, lose luster, oxidize, discolor, patinate, darken, dim, cloud, blur, fade, corrode, erode.

2. Destroy the purity of, stain, soil, sully, smudge, smirch, smear, pollute, contaminate, dirty, defile, befoul, corrupt, taint, spot, blot, blemish, deface, spatter, draggle, begrime, beslime, bemire, splash, maculate.

3. Disgrace, defame, slur, besmirch, stigmatize, blacken, denigrate, asperse, dishonor, brand,

vilify, drag through the mire, discredit, shame, degrade.

TARNISH, *n.* 1. Discoloration, alteration of luster, oxidation, oxidization, patination, corrosion, erosion.

2. Stain, blemish, soil, spot, blot, patina, disfigurement, defacement, flaw, taint, blur, speckle, blotch, macula, smudge, defilement, pollution.

3. Disgrace, blot on the escutcheon, disrepute, discredit, bad repute, ill repute, bad odor, bad name, odium, disfavor, disapprobation, dedecoration, debasement, degradation, obloquy, ignominy, opprobrium, reproach, slur, imputation, innuendo, insinuation, aspersion, turpitude, stigma, brand, scarlet letter, badge of infamy, scandal, dishonor, infamy, bar sinister.

TARPAULIN, *n.* Protective covering of waterproofed material, canvas, sailcloth, oilcloth.

TARRY, *v.* 1. Linger, loiter, dally, delay, be tardy, wait, hang back, stay behind, lag, pause, prolong, protract, procrastinate, bide, defer, put off, prorogue, stop, take time, dawdle, suspend, stave off, postpone, retard, draw out, spin out, table, shelve, temporize, stall, reserve, filibuster, cool one's heels, expect, await, abide, endure.

2. Abide temporarily, sojourn, take up one's quarters, pitch one's tent, rest, lodge, stay, have lodgings, reside, dwell, remain.

TART, *adj.* 1. Sour, acid, acrid, acidulous, astringent, acetic, sharp, acetous, piquant, pungent, bitter, acescent, sourish, unripe, green.

2. Crabbed, sarcastic, acrimonious, acerbous, caustic, cutting, trenchant, acerb, curt, ill-humored, ill-tempered, testy, harsh, snarling, waspish, snappish, petulant, austere, severe, crusty, virulent, surly, contumelious, venomous, splenetic, perverse, morose, sullen, bristling, grouchy, peevish, cross-tempered, churlish, gruff, brusque, boorish.

TART, *n.* 1. Woman of low character, prostitute, broad, wench, chippy, doxy, harlot, whore, demimondaine, demirep, strumpet, courtesan, hustler, *fille de joie (Fr.),* Cyprian, streetwalker, fallen woman, trollop, hussy, trull, baggage, drab, jade, bitch, slut, wanton, grisette, cocotte, lorette, fancy woman, kept woman, mistress, concubine.

2. Pastry shell filled with cooked fruit, pie, pasty, pâtisserie, puff.

TARTAR, *n.* Savage intractable person, barbarian, savage, fire-eater, spitfire, hellion, mischief-maker, demon, tiger, fury, vixen, virago, harridan, shrew, termagant, beldam.

TARTAREAN, *adj.* Hellish, infernal, stygian, demon-haunted, diabolic, satanic, Mephistophelian, devilish, fiendish, accursed, atrocious, evil, abominable, damnable, damned, Avernian, Acherontian, Cocytean, Lethean, Plutonian.

TARTARUS, *n.* Bottomless pit, sunless abyss, lower world, underworld, Hades, hell, place of torment, hell fire, limbo, purgatory, pandemonium, Erebus, infernal regions, Styx, Phlegethon, Cocytus, Avernus, Lethe, Acheron, realms of Pluto, shades below, Tophet, place of punishment for the wicked, Inferno.

TARTNESS, *n.* 1. Sourness, acidity, acidulousness, acridity, acridness, astringency, sharpness, pungency, piquancy, bitterness, greenness, unripeness.

2. Sarcasm, crabbedness, acrimony, acerbity, causticity, trenchancy, curtness, harshness, testiness, waspishness, snappishness, petulance, auster-

ity, crustiness, dourness, severity, virulence, surliness, contumely, spleen, moroseness, perverseness, sullenness, grouchiness, peevishness, churlishness, gruffness, boorishness, brusqueness, asperity, captiousness, cynicism, moodiness, bluntness.

TARTUFFE, *n.* Hypocritical pretender to piety, hypocrite, pharisee, dissembler, charlatan, mountebank, quack, saltimbanco, bigot, sabbatarian, puritan, pietist, fanatic, religionist, ranter.

TASK, *v.* 1. Subject to severe labor, impose excessive exertion, put a strain upon, overwork, strain, tax, oppress, burden, exert, fatigue, overtask, overtax, overdo, exploit, exhaust, expend, wear out, tire, harass, fag, prostrate.

2. Put to task, set to work, put into operation, put in action, utilize, employ, occupy, make use of, use, apply, work, ply, practice, exercise.

TASK, *n.* 1. Definite piece of work assigned, stint, chore, duty, job, labor, mission, undertaking, charge, enterprise, business, employment, toil, drudgery, occupation, pursuit, activity, venture, concern, errand, commission, role, beat, part, function, capacity, post, office, position, métier, craft, trade, line, industry.

2. Exercise, lesson, assignment, imposition, practice, drill, example.

TASKMASTER, *n.* 1. Monitor, overseer, supervisor, superintendent, inspector, director, manager, rector, proctor, comptroller, intendant, overlooker, boss, foreman, surveyor, moderator, master, precentor, fugleman, guide, adviser, steersman, whip, driver, headman, superior, major-domo, seneschal, tasker.

2. One whose task it is to assign burdensome tasks to others, oppressor, slave driver, Simon Legree, merciless master, tyrant, martinet, disciplinarian, Draco, despot, inquisitor, bashaw.

TASTE, *v.* 1. Try the flavor of, smack, savor, sip, degustate, degust, relish.

2. Experience, assay, meet, encounter, feel, have, perceive, undergo, participate in, partake of.

3. Distinguish, discern, discriminate, judge, differentiate, criticize, appreciate, enjoy, like.

TASTE, *n.* 1. Act of tasting, gustation, degustation, libation, prelibation.

2. Flavor, savor, piquancy, relish, sapor, sapidity, saporosity, relish, smack, zest, gusto, *goût (Fr.),* tang, subflavor, toothsomeness, aftertaste, tastiness, savoriness, palatability.

3. Touch, hint, dash, suggestion, suspicion, *soupçon (Fr.),* shade, streak, spice, strain, vein, thought, tinge, trace, admixture, infusion, sprinkling, grain.

4. Small quantity tasted, tincture, fragment, morsel, bit, bite, sip, mouthful, sample, nip.

5. Liking, appetite, appetency, predilection, fancy, propensity, penchant, leaning, partiality, bias, inclination, fondness, desire, mind, whim, bent, hankering, yearning, hunger, craving, longing, stomach, thirst.

6. Discernment of beauty, judgment of excellence, discrimination, nice perception, refinement, elegance, polish, culture, cultivation, delicacy, nicety, acumen, fine feeling, distinction, differentiation, penetration, aestheticism, finesse, tact, grace.

7. Style, mode, fashion, manner, *ton (Fr.),* bon *ton (Fr.),* correctness, the thing, good usage, form, custom, conventionality, felicity, finish, purity, clarity, euphony, propriety, restraint, symmetry, rhythm, balance, proportion.

TASTEFUL, *adj.* 1. Savory, tasty, toothsome, palatable, pleasing to the taste, appetizing, flavorsome, luscious, delicious, delectable, relishable, gustable, gustative, gustatory, saporous, sapid, saporific, mouth-watering, flavorous, spiced, seasoned, flavored, gustful, succulent, nectareous, ambrosial.

2. Showing good taste, elegant, aesthetic, attractive, artistic, cultivated, classical, fastidious, cultured, refined, discriminative, polished, charming, dainty, chaste, pure, Attic, *simplex munditiis (Lat.),* comely, graceful, shapely, symmetrical, well-proportioned, rhythmical, correct, restrained, finished, felicitous, neat, inspired, happy, appropriate, *comme il faut (Fr.),* decorous, becoming, pretty, choice, rare, delicate, exquisite, luxurious.

TASTELESS, *adj.* 1. Without savor, insipid, flavorless, flat, savorless, without relish, unpalatable, unflavored, watery, weak, stale, milk-and-water, aqueous.

2. Dull, uninteresting, vapid, spiritless, *fade (Fr.),* meager, jejune, barren, sterile, thin, monotonous, pointless, prosaic, heavy, dead, unanimated, lifeless, wishy-washy.

3. Coarse, gross, meretricious, loud *(coll.),* flashy, garish, tawdry, crude, gaudy, showy, vulgar, gimcrack, brummagem, cheap, tinsel, trumpery.

TATTERDEMALION, *n.* Person in tattered clothing, ragged fellow, scarecrow, ragamuffin, tramp, bum, hobo, vagrant, ragpicker, *chiffonier (Fr.),* vagabond, sans-culotte, mudlark, muckworm, panhandler, beggar.

TATTERS, *n., pl.* Ragged clothing, cast-off clothes, rags, patches, old clothes, shreds, pickings, scraps.

TATTLE, *v.* 1. Talk idly, speak at random, talk thoughtlessly, prate, chatter, prattle, jabber, chat, babble, palaver, patter, maunder, gush, jaw, gabble, cackle, chirp, clack, blather.

2. Tell tales, let out secrets, gossip, divulge, betray, peach, inform, blab, blat, rumor, buzz, squeal, reveal, vent, blurt out, let slip, whisper about, bruit, tip, advise, notify, repeat.

TATTLE, *n.* Idle talk, prattle, chatter, twaddle, small talk, chitchat, tittle-tattle, prate, gabble, gossip, scuttlebutt, rumor, bruit, babble, conversation, palaver, jabber, *bavardage (Fr.),* rattle, cackle, gibble-gabble, clack, *caqueterie (Fr.),* gab, talkee-talkee, blather, slack jaw *(sl.).*

TATTLER, *n.* 1. Chatterer, chatterbox, babbler, prattler, rattlehead, prater, idle talker, windbag *(coll.),* magpie, blatherskite, ranter, parrot, jay, driveler, *moulin à paroles (Fr.),* cackler, gabbler, gabber.

2. Talebearer, tattletale, blabbermouth, newsmonger, informer, gossip, scandalmonger, whisperer, gadabout, busybody, quidnunc, telltale, tabby, snoop, snooper, Paul Pry, eavesdropper.

TATTOO, *n.* 1. Beat of drum, drumming, roll, rub-a-dub, rat-a-tat, beating, pulsation, reverberation, thumping, rapping.

2. Signal, summons, taps, reveille.

3. Practice of marking the skin with indelible pictures, puncture and insertion of pigments into the skin, pattern, picture, design, legend, motto.

TAUNT, *v.* Mock, ridicule, deride, chaff, gibe, flout, tease, tantalize, rally, rail at, revile, poke fun at, make fun of, make game of, make a butt of, sneer at, scoff at, make merry with, twit, reproach, jeer, treat with scorn, censure, upbraid, cast in the teeth, fling at, slur, disparage, vilify, stigmatize, gibbet, run down, chide, rebuke, berate, insinuate, lampoon, satirize, burlesque, asperse, speak slightingly of, hold in disrespect, misprize, trifle with, laugh in one's sleeve, call names, vilipend, point at, bite the thumb, pluck by the beard, snigger, niggle, fleer, gleek, roast, guy, turn into ridicule, rag, insult, harass, vex, torment, provoke.

TAUNT, *n.* Insulting sarcasm, derision, ridicule, gibe, caustic remark, quip, biting jest, lampoon, pasquinade, insult, scoff, quirk, jeer, disparagement, detraction, insinuation, innuendo, oblique hint, indirect allusion, sly suggestion, remote intimation, affront, contumely, indignity, vilipendency, dishonor, outrage, scurrility, sibilation, irrision, mockery, irony, flout, hoot, gleek, sneer, wipe, fling, slap in the face, rebuff, home thrust, objurgation, invective, personal remarks, cutting words, abuse, exprobration, vituperation, snigger, persiflage, banter, badinage, raillery, chaff, squib, satire, parody, travesty, burlesque, caricature, slur, imputation.

TAUT, *adj.* 1. Tightly drawn, tight, not slack, stretched, tense, strained, stiff, rigid, firm, hard, unbending, inflexible.
2. In good condition, orderly, tidy, neat, trig, trim, spruce, shipshape, smart, snug.

TAUTOLOGICAL, *adj.* Repetitious, redundant, repetitional, pleonastic, iterative, reiterative, tautophonous, repetitionary, recurrent, harping, monotonous, battological, perissological, prolix, verbose, wordy, diffuse, circumlocutory, periphrastic, ambagious, roundabout, exuberant, copious, long-winded, diffusive, protracted, maundering, episodic, discursive, digressive, loose, turgid, rambling, frothy, multiloquent, polyloquent.

TAUTOLOGY, *n.* Needless repetition of the same thought in different words, pleonasm, redundancy, wordiness, verbosity, diffuseness, iteration, reiteration, circumlocution, periphrasis, recurrence, harping, battology, tautophony, monotony, amplification, verbiage, *copia verborum (Lat.),* perissology, exuberance, prolixity, ambages, expletive, padding, profuseness, flow of words, loquacity, roundaboutness, indirection, looseness.

TAVERN, *n.* 1. Public house, hostelry, hotel, inn, caravansary, *posada (Sp.),* hospice, hostel, khan.
2. Eating-house, restaurant, rotisserie, grillroom, buffet, coffee house, café, cafeteria, public dining room, canteen.
3. Saloon, taproom, bar, barroom, pub, alehouse, mughouse, barrel house, beer garden, grogshop, rumshop, dramshop, wine shop, bodega, estaminet, bistro, gin-mill, cocktail lounge, cabaret, roadhouse, night club, speak-easy, shebeen.

TAWDRY, *adj.* Showy without elegance, flashy, loud, gaudy, garish, meretricious, inelegant, brummagem, glittering, tinsel, gingerbread, in bad taste, cheap, pretentious, bedizened, flaunting, obtrusive, crass, gimcrack, trumpery, vulgar, ornate, florid, baroque, rococo, begilt, bespangled.

TAWNY, *adj.* Dark yellowish-brown, dull yellow, fulvous, tan-colored, fulvid, xanthous, flavous, sallow, dusky, dark-skinned, swarthy, olive, luteous, sandy, jaundiced, creamy, fuscous, fawn-colored.

TAX, *v.* 1. Impose a tax upon, assess tribute upon, rate, audit, appraise, levy, exact, charge, require, demand, ask, lay claim to, reclaim,

counterclaim, withhold, inflict, enact, assign one's share to.
2. Make demands upon, burden, task, load, strain, push too far, overtax, overwork, overtask, overburden, overdo, overstrain, wear out, exhaust.
3. Accuse, charge, censure, implicate, arraign, impeach, impute, ascribe, indict, saddle with, cite, challenge, prosecute.

TAX, *n.* 1. Payment of money to the government, duty, impost, excise, tithe, toll, rate, custom, assessment, levy, exaction, tariff, tribute, surtax, dues, capitation, contribution, scot, poll tax, taxation, pollage, *octroi (Fr.),* exactment, return, appraisement, valuation, estimation, amount.
2. Imposition, burdensome obligation, subsidy, requisition, charge, burden, demand, strain, fatiguing duties, exertion, drudgery, labor, toil.
3. Accusation, charge, censure, imputation, incrimination, arraignment, denunciation, inculpation, delation, citation, challenge, impeachment, indictment.

TAXABLE, *adj.* 1. Assessable, ratable, dutiable, tithable, compensative, reparative, compensatory, leviable, exactable.
2. Answerable, responsible, liable, reprovable, censurable, accountable.

TAXICAB, *n.* Public passenger vehicle equipped with a taximeter, cab, taxi, hack, coach for hire, fiacre, hackney, hansom, fly, droshky, *vettura (It.),* gig, trap, sulky, jinrikisha, jitney, *voiture (Fr.).*

TEACH, *v.* Guide the studies of, act as teacher, direct as an instructor, impart knowledge of, educate, instruct, give instruction to, give lessons in, tutor, indoctrinate, school, inform, enlighten, initiate, edify, drill, coach, catechize, imbue, qualify, prepare, ground, prime, discipline, train, exercise, beat into, cram, inculcate, implant, impart, communicate, preach, instill, propagate, disseminate, counsel, lecture, profess, explain, interpret, admonish, persuade, illustrate, expound, advise, show, indicate to, signify, tell, point out to, manage as preceptor, impregnate, hold forth, moralize, sermonize, enlarge the mind, sharpen the wits, open the eyes, familiarize with, rear, form, inure, graduate, acquaint, notify, apprise, retail, describe, enunciate, annunciate, make known, promulgate, broadcast, publish, define, spell out, clear up, elucidate, account for, shed light upon, comment upon, unfold, annotate, commentate, exemplify, popularize, infix, propagandize, bring up, practice, habituate, nurture, suggest to.

TEACHABLE, *adj.* Capable of being instructed, apt to learn, docile, tractable, amenable, manageable, bright, scholarly, studious, scholastic, industrious, disposed, ready, suasible, ardent, quick, alert, sharp, smart, zealous, assiduous, diligent, intent, able, clever, endowed, keen, astute, perceptive, rational, sensible, discerning.

TEACHER, *n.* 1. Instructor, educator, schoolmaster, master, dominie, pedagogue, tutor, professor, doctor, preceptor, paedotribe, trainer, lecturer, principal, coryphaeus, guru, maestro, mystagogue, crammer, coach, reader, don, educationist, licentiate, drill master, catechist, docent, scholar, rhetor, rabbi, sophist, inculcator, informant, interpreter, expounder, expositor, explainer, demonstrator, exponent, annotator, gownsman, savant, pundit, academician, classicist, graduate, pedant, philosopher, mastermind, specialist, logician, schoolteacher.

2. Guide, adviser, mentor, counselor, director, conductor, leader, pilot, cicerone, dragoman, apostle, propagandist, missionary, preacher, pastor, minister, pattern, example, model.

TEACHING, *n.* 1. Work of a teacher, instruction, education, pedagogy, pedagogics, grounding, tuition, tutelage, didactics, drill, indoctrination, inculcation, instillation, discipline, tutorship, edification, initiation, guidance, direction, qualification, preparation, schooling, training, practice, explanation, disquisition, prelection, interpretation, discourse, homily, recitation, harangue, lecture, lesson, sermonizing, sermon, example, exercise, assignment, task, imposition, course, curriculum, lyceum, lore, information, enlightenment, knowledge, acquaintance, communication, monition, monitorship, representation, elucidation, explication, exposition, definition, *éclaircissement (Fr.)*.
2. That which is taught, doctrine, dogma, precept, tenet, principle, rudiment, element, article of faith, rule, maxim, rubric, creed, credo, belief, opinion, persuasion, conception, way of thinking, canon, catechism.

TEAM, *n.* 1. Set of draft animals harnessed together, yoke, span, pair, couple, rig, tandem, four-in-hand, spike team, unicorn, equipage.
2. Number of persons associated in some joint action, one of the sides in a match, crew, side, group, band, body, nine *(Baseball),* eleven *(Football),* five *(Basketball),* gang, coterie, clique, partnership, pool, coalition, alliance, association, company, set, posse, club, guild, federation, faction, party, circle, knot.

TEAMWORK, *n.* Coördination of effort, collective efficiency, pulling together, party spirit, partisanship, joint operation, coöperation, esprit de corps, cliquism, collaboration, coadjuvancy, concert, complicity, collusion, connivance, conspiracy, confederacy, alliance, association, gentlemen's agreement, fellowship, comradeship, freemasonry, fraternity, fraternization, unanimity, accordance, consentaneity, harmony, concord, morale, clanship, entente cordiale, good understanding.

TEAR, *v.* 1. Pull apart by force, separate by pulling into ragged edges, rend, rip, burst, shred, rive, slit, split, divide, cleave, pull to pieces, part with violence, lacerate, dilacerate, lancinate, shatter, laniate, sunder, sever, hack, wrench, pluck, butcher, mangle, dismember, injure, wound, unravel, disentangle, undo, dissever, break, snap, rupture, dissect, quarter, anatomize, snip, splinter, nip, crack, chip, disrupt, disintegrate.
2. *(Coll.)* Move with violence, rush along, go with great haste, dash, gallop, make haste, race, fly, hasten, run, scoot, hie, speed, sprint, spurt, scud, post, whiz, dart, shoot, swoop, whisk, scorch, skim, bolt, sweep, scurry, scuttle, scamper, accelerate, skedaddle, burn up the road, outstrip the wind, plunge, bustle, scramble, wing one's way, bestir oneself, push.
3. Rage, fume, rave, run amuck, go berserk, rant, chafe, foam, champ the bit, break out, lose one's temper, fly off the handle, flare up, explode, raise Cain, go into hysterics.

TEAR, *n.* 1. Rent, rip, split, slit, laceration, fissure, rupture, break, opening, wrench, injury, wound, breach, rift, crack, cleft, incision, cut, fault, gap, flaw, fracture, broken thread, unravelment.
2. Violent flurry, outburst, rage, passion, raptus, paroxysm, fit, tumult, outbreak, explosion,

outburst, scene, fury, violence, furor, raving, distraction, hysterics, frenzy, convulsion, spasm, throe, agitation, orgasm, erethism, access, attack.
3. *(Slang)* Drunken festivity, wild revelry, orgy, spree, bacchanal, whoopee, lark, debauchery, dissipation, crapulence, carousal, wassail, drinking bout, Saturnalia, libations.
4. Drop of fluid secreted by lachrymal glands, weeping, lachrymation.

TEARFUL, *adj.* Shedding tears, weeping, lachrymose, teary, weepy, mournful, maudlin, sorrowful, plaintive, querulous, bathed in tears, swimming, moist, wet, damp, lamenting, in sackcloth and ashes, crying, dissolved in tears, elegiac, epicedial, threnodial, whimpering, sobbing, blubbering, sniveling.

TEASE, *v.* Annoy, irritate, vex, badger, harry, bother, molest, worry, plague, torment, hector, harass, provoke, pester, chafe, exacerbate, chagrin, importune, rag, trouble, irk, disturb, haze, nag, bullyrag, nettle, needle, distress, anger, mortify, distract, aggravate, thwart, frustrate, foil, balk, displease, embarrass, excite, inflame, tantalize, make fun of, mock, taunt, indulge in raillery, deride, defy, mimic, ape, take off, parody, caricature, burlesque, travesty, trifle with, scoff, ridicule, laugh at, gibe, twit, guy, roast, flout, discompose, cross, fret, heckle, bait, beset, persecute, rile, pique, ruffle, gall.

TEAT, *n.* Protuberance on the female breast, mammilla, nipple, dug, udder, pap, mamma, breast, tit, tittie.

TECHNICAL, *adj.* Pertaining to an art *or* science, scientific, specialized, artistic, daedalian, shipshape, workmanlike, skillful, experienced, practiced, skilled, qualified, competent, trained, fitted, capable, efficient, fine-fingered, neat-handed.

TECHNICIAN, *n.* One versed in the technicalities of a science, one skilled in the technique of an art, proficient, adept, connoisseur, virtuoso, master hand, whiz, top sawyer, past master, specialist, professional, old hand, veteran, genius, scientist, expert.

TECHNIQUE, *n.* Method of performance, technology, technical skill, artistry, virtuosity, bravura, art, touch, form, brilliant performance, display of technical mastery, know-how, execution, finish, technic, finesse, forte, flair, aptitude, aptness, genius for, felicity, *curiosa felicitas (Lat.),* callidity, proficiency, facility, knack, mastery, dexterity, deftness, skillfulness, adroitness, address, expertness, craft, competence, practiced hand, ingenuity, ability, parts, faculty, talents, capacity, turn, endowment, gift.

TEDIOUS, *adj.* Dull, uninteresting, operose, wearisome, irksome, dry, tiresome, jejune, trying, fatiguing, humdrum, laborious, soporific, monotonous, too long, long-winded, prolix, prosy, wordy, verbose, prosaic, poky, slow, long-drawn-out, tardy, dilatory, sluggish, lifeless, unprofitable, pointless, unfruitful, fruitless, barren, arid, sterile, insipid, vapid, ponderous, unimaginative, elephantine, heavy-footed, dismal, stagnant, dreary, listless, dead, meager, bald, commonplace, drab, matter-of-fact, platitudinous, tiring, wearing, boring, boresome.

TEDIOUSNESS, *n.* Dreariness, dullness, wearisomeness, dryness, aridity, lifelessness, flatness, heaviness, slowness, stupidity, stagnation, apathy, sluggishness, jejuneness, want of originality, commonplaceness, platitudinousness, bromidity, dearth of ideas.

TEDIUM, *n.* Boredom, boresomeness, ennui, sameness, monotony, tiresomeness, irksomeness, heavy hours, time on one's hands, dull work, routineness, rut, world-weariness, surfeit, indifference, satiety, languor, lassitude, twice-told tale.

TEEM, *v.* 1. Bring forth young, produce, generate, bear, engender, spawn, multiply, proliferate, beget, reproduce, propagate, fecundate, conceive, impregnate, progenerate, create, procreate.

2. Abound, be prolific, be full, be stocked, exuberate, swarm, overflow, superabound, bristle with, run riot, overrun.

TEEMING, *adj.* Replete, full to the utmost, chockfull, crammed, fraught, overflowing, abounding, swarming, pregnant, prolific, plentiful, plenteous, copious, abundant, fertile, rife, fruitful, exuberant, redundant, superabundant, lavish, profuse, prodigal, fulsome, gorged, swollen, stuffed, superfluous, *de trop (Fr.),* supererogatory, supernumerary, sufficient, ample, well-provided, affluent, luxuriant, rich, opulent, wealthy, bountiful, bounteous, thick, brimming, brimful, laden, saturated.

TEENAGE, *adj.* Juvenile, youthful, callow, green, unfledged, fledgling, under age, pubescent, adolescent, unripe, beardless, immature, juvenescent, tender, awkward, junior.

TEETER, *v.* Move unsteadily, seesaw, titter, totter, flounder, stagger, bob up and down, vibrate, oscillate, librate, undulate, rock, sway, waggle, wobble, wamble, shake, pitch.

TEETOTALER, *n.* Total abstainer from alcoholic beverages, nephalist, dry, prohibitionist, waterdrinker, teetotalist, prude, ascetic, Rechabite, abstinent, Encratite.

TEETOTALISM, *n.* Total abstinence from spirituous liquor, strict temperance, nephalism, prohibitionism, sobriety, water wagon, abstemiousness, asceticism, Rechabitism, Encratism.

TELEGRAM, *n.* Communication sent by telegraph, wire, day letter, night letter, telegraphic despatch, marconigram, radiogram, cable, cablegram, radiotelegram, wireless, flash.

TELEGRAPH, *v.* Transmit by telegraph, wire, radio, wireless, marconigraph, announce by telegraph, radiograph, cable, radiotelegraph.

TELEPATHY, *n.* Communication of one mind with another by preternatural means, thought transference, telepathic transmission, cryptesthesia, clairaudience, subconscious audition, premonition, presentiment, spirit communication, extrasensory perception.

TELEPHONE, *n.* Apparatus for transmission of sound to a distant point, phone, wireless telephone, radiotelephone, radiophone, *Fernsprecher (Ger.).*

TELESCOPE, *n.* Optical instrument for making distant objects appear nearer and larger, field glass, spyglass, binocular, opera glass, refracting glass, reflecting glass, tube, equatorial, lorgnette, polemoscope, helioscope, teinoscope, telespectroscope, view finder, hyposcope, altiscope, omniscope, periscope, polariscope.

TELL, *v.* 1. Relate, rehearse, give an account of, recount, describe, narrate, report, explain, recite, recapitulate, set forth, portray, picture, paint, depict, sketch, delineate, represent, romance, chronicle, record, detail, define, repeat, epitomize.

2. Utter, pronounce, enunciate, express, state, speak, communicate, mention, speak of, say, unfold, herald, rumor, bruit, assure, enlighten, blab, babble, prate, affirm, dictate, intimate, spread abroad, advise, impart, acquaint, inform, teach, apprise, instruct, make known to, declare, signify, retail, promulgate, disseminate, publish, insinuate, suggest, hint, breathe, let fall, disclose, reveal, confess, divulge, acknowledge, betray, own, spout, orate, harangue, rant, lecture, recite, discourse, sermonize, expatiate.

3. Discern so as to be able to identify, make out, distinguish, discover, perceive, espy, ascertain, recognize, identify, verify, apprehend.

4. Reckon, compute, count, enumerate, number, run over, sum up, calculate, estimate, cast, rate, cast up.

5. Be effective, take effect, weigh, have force, operate effectively, be potent, be influential, carry weight.

TELLING, *adj.* Effective, efficacious, cogent, significant, impressive, striking, important, influential, weighty, momentous, material, to the point, prominent, notable, signal, salient, remarkable, memorable, noteworthy, eventful, stirring, graphic, vivid, clear-cut, positive, definite, expressive, illustrative, exciting, pointed, conclusive, definitive, powerful, potent, puissant, sensational, overpowering, overwhelming, provocative.

TELL OFF, *v.* Rebuke severely, scold, chide, reprehend, admonish, rake over the coals, call to account, take to task, lecture, reprove, chastise, reprimand, denounce, castigate, exprobrate, execrate, vituperate, objurgate, rate, upbraid, berate, rail at, anathematize, slate, condemn, recriminate, vilipend, revile, fulminate against, inveigh against.

TELLTALE, *n.* 1. Talebearer, tattler, gossip, tattletale, newsmonger, blabbermouth, informer, whisperer, scandalmonger, gadabout, snoop, tabby, busybody, quidnunc, eavesdropper.

2. Means of recognition, trait, characteristic, feature, lineament, earmark, hallmark, birthmark, footfall, footprint, token, clue, track, scent.

3. Traitor, betrayer, conspirator, Judas, stool pigeon, snake in the grass, squealer, sneak, trimmer, mischief-maker, renegade, recreant, truant.

TELLURIC, *adj.* Pertaining to the earth, tellurian, earthly, terrestrial, chthonian, geodetic, cosmogonal, mundane.

TEMBLOR, *n.* Earthquake, quake, tremor, upheaval, eruption, cataclysm, seismic disturbance, detonation, blast, explosion, displosion, shock, convulsion, spasm, throe.

TEMERARIOUS, *adj.* Reckless, rash, venturesome, adventurous, incautious, injudicious, ill-advised, presumptuous, heedless, hasty, precipitate, headlong, devil-may-care, fire-eating, foolhardy, impetuous, impulsive, brash, audacious, daring, overbold, indiscreet, imprudent, cheeky, thoughtless, uncalculating, improvident, unwary, careless, quixotic, madcap, death-defying, wild, intrepid, desperate, hot-headed, breakneck, harebrained.

TEMERITY, *n.* Reckless boldness, foolhardiness, rashness, recklessness, incautiousness, injudiciousness, indiscretion, carelessness, heedlessness, imprudence, improvidence, overconfidence, impulsiveness, impetuosity, cheek, nerve, brass, daring, derring-do, audacity, hardihood, sauciness, procacity, swagger, bluster, bumptiousness, brashness, assurance, impudence, front, face, gall, effrontery, fire-eating, knight-errantry, Quixotism, precipitancy, precipitation, presumption, presumptuousness, hastiness, thoughtlessness, inconsiderateness, desperation, venturesomeness, adventurousness, leap in the dark.

TEMPER, v. 1. Bring to the right degree of hardness (as iron) by sudden cooling, work into proper consistency, harden, anneal, steel, firm, indurate, solidify, stiffen.

2. Soften, mollify, attemper, moderate, assuage, calm, abate, soothe, relax, palliate, tone down, subdue, allay, mitigate, appease, pacify, restrain, alleviate, compose, lull, still, tranquilize, quell, quiet, hush, lessen, sober, decrease, diminish, smother, deaden, weaken, mute, tame, check, blunt, curb, chasten.

3. Modify, qualify, fit, adapt, adjust, suit, accommodate, prepare, proportion, make conformable.

TEMPER, n. 1. Anger, heat of mind, ill temper, passion, spleen, irritability, irritation, irascibility, animus, animosity, huffishness, acrimony, asperity, acerbity, petulance, churlishness, resentment, displeasure, choler, ire, wrath, indignation, vexation, exasperation, annoyance, ferment, bitterness, bile, virulence, gall, pique, dudgeon, umbrage, tiff, sulks, pet, tantrum, high words, hot blood, black looks, surliness, peevishness.

2. Disposition, particular state of mind, frame, humor, spirits, mood, vein, tone, grain, character, nature, temperament, structure, quality, constitution, type, diathesis, tenor, idiosyncrasy, individuality.

3. Solidity, toughness, rigidity, hardness, firmness, inflexibility, callosity, induration.

TEMPERAMENT, n. Natural disposition, personal make-up, constitution, nature, temper, idiosyncrasy, organization, mettle, habit, spirit, mood, propensity, animus, character, humor, endowment, individuality, leaning, bent, inclination, tendency, affection, proclivity, penchant, set, bias, turn, warp, trend, tone, aptitude, liability, proneness, predisposition, susceptibility, quality, cast, grain, vein.

TEMPERAMENTAL, adj. 1. Having a strongly marked individual temperament, distinctive, idiosyncratic, peculiar, unique, sui generis (Lat.), singular, exceptional, striking, particular, especial, eccentric.

2. Constitutional, deep-rooted, inveterate, congenital, inherent, ingrained, inbred, innate, inborn.

3. Moody, high-strung, sensitive, irritable, impressionable, hasty, susceptible, excitable, thin-skinned, warm, hot-headed, hasty, touchy, fiery, peppery, passionate, choleric, impressible, impassioned, mettlesome, spirited, vivacious, expressive, mobile, hysterical.

TEMPERANCE, n. 1. Moderation, self-control, forbearance, self-restraint, frugality, soberness, abnegation, self-denial, abstention, temperateness.

2. Total abstinence from spirituous liquors, teetotalism, prohibition, abstemiousness, nephalism, Rechabitism, sobriety, Encratism, asceticism, blue-ribbonism.

3. Tolerance, toleration, patience, sedateness, calmness, clemency, lenity, compassion, tenderness, humanity, humanitarianism, mercy, quarter, indulgence.

TEMPERATE, adj. 1. Abstemious, teetotal, water-drinking, Rechabitic, ascetic, abstinent, nephalistic, prohibitionistic, dry, sober.

2. Frugal, moderate, self-restrained, self-con-

trolled, self-denying, chaste, austere, continent, sparing, puritanical.

3. Genial, balmy, warm, soft, calm, summery, pleasant, sunny, mild, clement, halcyon.

4. Dispassionate, cool-headed, unperturbed, sedate, composed, pacific, easygoing, unruffled, unexcited, tranquil, patient, quiet, reasonable, unimpassioned, collected, self-possessed, rational, sane.

TEMPEST, n. 1. Violent storm, hurricane, tornado, cyclone, twister, gale, squall, high wind, whirlwind, blizzard, thunderstorm, blow, typhoon, samiel, simoom, sirocco, mistral, northeaster.

2. Agitation, commotion, excitement, perturbation, disturbance, turmoil, tumult, violent outbreak, turbulence, hubbub, convulsion, spasm, ferment, ebullition, uproar.

TEMPESTUOUS, adj. 1. Stormy, squally, windy, cyclonic, blowy, breezy, blustery, gusty, blasty, blusterous, boisterous, raging, violent, turbulent, typhonic, furious, rough.

2. Tumultuous, impetuous, impulsive, passionate, hysterical, agitated, restless, wrought-up, overwrought, nervous, feverish, flushed, distracted, frantic, frenzied, berserk, amuck, beside oneself.

TEMPLE, n. 1. Place of worship, holy place, house of God, fane, tabernacle, sanctuary, church, hieron, delubrum, house of prayer, pagoda, joss house, pantheon, cella, naos, sacellum, shrine, stupa, tope, dagoba, mosque, synagogue, conventicle, basilica, cathedral, duomo, kirk, meeting house, chapel, oratory, chantry, holy of holies, sanctum sanctorum.

2. Cloister, monastery, monkery, convent, nunnery, friary, priory, cenoby, abbey, lamasery.

TEMPO, n. Rate of movement, time, relative rapidity, pattern of activity, rhythm, speed, beat, measure.

TEMPORAL, adj. 1. Secular, worldly, terrestrial, mundane, of this world, subastral, earthly, terraqueous, terrene, telluric, sublunar, sublunary.

2. Unspiritual, material, carnal, mortal, profane, lay, civil, political, laical, nonclerical.

3. Enduring for a time only, fugitive, transient, evanescent, fleeting, transitory, temporary, passing, brief, ephemeral, short-lived, monohemerous, diurnal, caducous, elusive, impermanent, deciduous, perishable, provisional, meteoric, instantaneous.

TEMPORARY, adj. Lasting for a time only, fleeting, momentary, impermanent, unenduring, transient, transitory, of short duration, short-lived, ephemeral, monohemerous, deciduous, caducous, perishable, passing, soon past, fugitive, evanescent, brief, fleet, for a time, provisional, tentative, interimistic, temporal, changeable, substitutional, provisory, stand-by, flash-in-the-pan, mushroom, stopgap, shifting, summary, instantaneous, elusive, precarious, mortal, quick, brisk, volatile, mercurial, meteoric, hurried, hasty, cursory, sudden, spasmodic, pressed for time, in passing, in transitu (Lat.), en passant (Fr.), pro tempore (Lat.), vagrant, hasty, swift, precipitate.

TEMPORIZE, v. Act evasively to gain time, hedge, stall, procrastinate, drag one's feet, act the timeserver, diplomatize, trim, yield to circumstances, comply with occasions, be an opportunist, sit on the fence, watch how the wind blows, wait to see which way the cat will jump, effect a compromise, fall in with current opinion, play a deep game, maneuver, gerrymander, intrigue, finesse, stoop to conquer, double, delay, protract, come to terms, prolong, postpone, lengthen out, talk against time, defer, prorogue, lay over, put off, stave off, waive, remand, dally, tide over, keep back, let the matter stand over, consult one's pillow, sleep upon a thing, hang fire, let hang in the balance, look after one's own interests, feather one's nest, consult one's own wishes, have an eye to the main chance, take care of number one, give an inch and take an ell, wangle, know on which side one's bread is buttered.

TEMPORIZER, *n.* One who adapts his conduct to conditions, timeserver, opportunist, hedger, trimmer, shuffler, self-seeker, fortune hunter, worldling, jobber, schemer, trickster, intriguer, fox, Fabianist, sly boots, profiteer, nepotist.

TEMPT, *v.* Entice seductively, lure, allure, captivate, attract, fascinate, ensorcel, charm, seduce, appeal strongly to, tantalize, endeavor to persuade, inveigle, draw on, prevail upon, bring over, dispose, incline, lead on, incite, provoke, instigate, prompt, render strongly disposed, invite, bait, pull, intrigue, whet the appetite, make one's mouth water, take one's fancy, appetize, solicit, stimulate, rouse, arouse, sway, win over, bewitch, magnetize, hypnotize, goad, prick, risk provoking, venture on, attempt, try, essay, put to the test, fly in the face of.

TEMPTATION, *n.* Seductive enticement, allurement, seduction, attraction, fascination, ensorcelment, bewitchment, bewitchery, captivation, charm, decoy, bait, lure, magnet, loadstone, bribe, golden apple, song of the sirens, inducement, incentive, stimulus, appetite, stomach, hunger, thirst, keenness, hankering, longing, aspiration, yearning, appetency, itch, concupiscence, libido, lust, biological urge, carnal passion, estrus, craving, ardor, fancy, propensity, predilection, relish, fondness, love, liking, inclination, desire, covetousness, avidity, voracity, cupidity, torment of Tantalus, mania, magnetism, witchery, glamor, spell, blandishment, cajolery, prompting, influence, instance, dictate, impulse, incitement, insistence, press, persuasion, instigation, exhortation, solicitation, spur, goad, fillip, provocative, impulsion, cacoëthes, predisposition, leaning, taste.

TEMPTER, *n.* 1. Seducer, charmer, inveigler, siren, prompter, coaxer, Circe, instigator, inciter, abettor, vampire, enchanter, enchantress, temptress, Lorelei, suggester, wheedler, solicitor, *agent provocateur (Fr.),* firebrand, incendiary, libertine, Lothario, rake, voluptuary, debauchee, rip, fast man, satyr, lecher, gay deceiver, Don Juan, pander, pimp, procurer, roué.
2. The Devil, Old Nick, Satan, Lucifer, the Evil One, the Foul Fiend, the Old Serpent, Prince of Darkness, Author of Evil, Apollyon, Beelzebub, Abaddon, Belial, the Archfiend, Mephistopheles, Mephisto, Asmodeus, Samael, Eblis, Ahriman, *le Diable (Fr.),* Diabolus, the Archenemy, Azazel, Moloch, Mammon, Loki, the Fallen Angel, Angel of the Bottomless Pit.

TEMPTING, *adj.* Alluring, enticing, seductive, fascinating, charming, bewitching, glamorous, sorcerous, Circean, attractive, irresistible, inviting, persuasive, desirable, pleasing, appetizing, agreeable, exciting, mouth-watering, provocative, sexy *(sl.),* hot *(sl.),* magnetic, galvanic, thrilling, stirring, sensational, overwhelming, overpowering, stimulating, piquant, tantalizing, electrifying, prepossessing, winsome, engaging, captivating,

taking, enchanting, enravishing, entrancing, ravishing, luscious, ambrosial, nectareous, toothsome, delicious, delectable.

TENABLE, *adj.* Capable of being held, defensible, maintainable, unattackable, unassailable, inexpugnable, impregnable, proof against, invulnerable, imperdible, trustworthy, on sure ground, on the safe side, on terra firma, veracious, equitable, incorruptible, to be depended on, dependable, correct, scrupulous, inviolable.

TENACIOUS, *adj.* 1. Holding fast, keeping a firm hold, adhesive, viscous, viscid, sticky, mucilaginous, glutinous, adherent, stringy, ropy, gummy, cohesive, clinging, smeary, fast, tough, dauby, resisting, strong, cartilaginous, gristly, coriaceous, leathery, tacky, sequacious.
2. Obstinate, dogged, stubborn, unwavering, unyielding, resolute, persistent, pertinacious, obdurate, uncompromising, intransigent, persevering, purposeful, mulish, bigoted, prejudiced, biased, stiff-necked, determined, indomitable, partisan, constant, perverse, inflexible, unbending, immovable, unchangeable, pigheaded, balky, hard-bitten, hard-set, refractory, contumacious, arbitrary, dogmatic, positive, cross-grained, incorrigible, steadfast, unfaltering, unswerving, undeviating, strong-minded, strong-willed, fixed, iron, adamantine, inexorable, relentless, *tenax propositi (Lat.),* grim, set, unalterable, unshaken.
3. Apt to retain, retentive, unforgetful, retaining, unforgetting, grasping, trustworthy, reliable, dependable, recollective, commemorative.

TENACITY, *n.* 1. Adhesiveness, stickiness, viscousness, viscidity, glutinousness, gumminess, stringiness, toughness, cohesiveness, strength, mucilaginousness, ropiness, smeariness, tackiness, tenaciousness, adhesion, cohesion.
2. Obstinacy, stubbornness, doggedness, mulishness, pigheadedness, perseverance, persistency, stick-to-itiveness, pertinacity, resolution, resoluteness, resolve, grit, mettle, pluck, sand, backbone, firmness, unyieldingness, noncompliance, recalcitrance, intransigence, perverseness, immovability, obduracy, inexorability, inflexibility, contumacy, self-will, perversity, intolerance, bigotry, opinionativeness, narrow-mindedness, prejudice, bias, partisanship, determination, constancy, steadfastness, stamina, iron will, bulldog courage, endurance.
3. Retentivity, retentiveness, retention, remembrance, recollection, readiness of memory, grasp, grip, memory, reminiscence, retrospection.

TENANCY, *n.* Holding by title, temporary possession, tenure, occupancy, *métayage (Fr.),* dependency, hold, occupation, proprietorship, possessorship, ownership, possessing, property, real estate, realty, personalty *(Law),* real property, householding, leasing, renting.

TENANT, *n.* One who holds a lodging for a period of time, occupant, occupier, householder, lessee, renter, dweller, resident, inhabitant, leaseholder, possessor, termor, *métayer (Fr.),* freeholder, lodger, proprietor, owner, landowner, landholder, residentiary, inhabiter, inmate, indweller, addressee, incumbent, denizen, cottager, cotter, boarder, roomer, paying guest, sojourner, commorant.

TEND, *v.* 1. Shepherd, graze, pasture, breed, break in, corral, train, round up, domesticate, tame, bridle, harness, drive, hitch, yoke, currycomb, groom, shear, incubate, hatch, milk.

2. Watch over, guard, keep, protect, take care of, care for, manage, look after, nurse, nurture, foster, wait on, minister to, serve, attend, be attentive to, mind, observe carefully, aid, succor, take in hand, help, assist, keep an eye upon, do for, squire, valet, be useful to, work for, oblige, service.

3. Tend towards, incline, verge, be directed, trend, aim at, dip, point to, bend, be bound for, steer toward, gravitate, aim, make for, lead, head, work towards, lean, be disposed, be inclined, conduce, contribute, bid fair to, predispose, influence, move towards, warp, affect, redound to.

TENDENCY, *n.* Natural disposition, temperament, temper, inclination, leaning, penchant, predisposition, proclivity, propensity, proneness, aptitude, turn, susceptibility, liability, gravitation, direction, drift, bent, twist, trend, bias, prejudice, warp, set, bearing, aim, course, aspiration, objective, determination, purpose, object, humor, habit, mood, goal, purport, tenor, appetency, scope, affection, tone, aptness, Mendelianism, heredity, matrocliny, patrocliny, quality, idiosyncrasy, nature, vein, cast, grain.

TENDER, *v.* Present formally for acceptance, make formal offer of, proffer, offer, volunteer, cede, propose, suggest, bid, make overture, express readiness, be a candidate, come forward, stand for, seek, submit, extend, hold out, advance, put forward, urge upon, lay before, press, propound, place at one's disposal, invite, make possible, sacrifice, undertake, endeavor, try, attempt, essay, strive, dare, venture, give.

TENDER, *n.* 1. Offer, proposal, proffer, advance, proposition, overture, offering, bid, presentation, submission, invitation, motion, nomination, ultimatum.

2. Legal tender, currency, money, circulating medium, specie, cash, paper money, bill, note, bank note, greenback, long green *(sl.).*

TENDER, *adj.* 1. Delicate, soft, subdued, muted, weak, fragile, feeble, gentle, mellow, subtle, softened, pure, not strong, not tough, mild.

2. Young, immature, callow, unfledged, fledgling, youthful, puerile, infantile, juvenile, juvenescent, impressible, plastic, underage, teen-age, budding, boyish, childish, inexperienced, uninitiated.

3. Effeminate, womanly, unmanly, feminine, weakly, dainty, timorous, yielding, meek, clement, lenient, mollescent.

4. Sensitive, easily pained, painful, sore, raw, red, aching, inflamed.

5. Affectionate, loving, amorous, erotic, sentimental, amatory, fond, ardent, lovesick, impassioned, passionate, hot *(sl.),* devoted, burning, desirous, uxorious, lustful, libidinous, lecherous.

6. Sympathetic, compassionate, soft-hearted, humane, kind, merciful, pitiful, charitable, ruthful, pitying, indulgent, benevolent, cordial, genial, accommodating, gracious, considerate, warmhearted, benign, forgiving, beneficent, altruistic, unselfish, philanthropic.

7. Maternal, motherly, parental, fatherly, paternal, brotherly, sisterly, fraternal, sororal.

8. Pathetic, moving, distressing, afflictive, dolorific, unpleasant, disagreeable, bitter, grievous, dolorous, piteous, lamentable, pitiable, touching, soul-stirring, sad, heartbreaking, harrowing, cruel, harsh, agonizing, racking, calamitous, desolating, oppressive, tragic.

TENDERFOOT, *n.* Inexperienced person, raw recruit, novice, tyro, fledgling, neophyte, beginner, greenhorn, pupil, catechumen, probationer, initiate, apprentice, learner, sciolist, dabbler, dilettante, amateur, abecedarian, alphabetarian, *débutant (Fr.),* inceptor, dupe, sucker, gull, pigeon, Simple Simon, blunderhead, bungler, fumbler, lubber, bad hand, slow coach, yokel, clod, hick, *blanc-bec (Fr.).*

TENDER-HEARTED, *adj.* Compassionate, sympathetic, merciful, ruthful, pitying, indulgent, clement, lenient, gentle, humane, humanitarian, kind-hearted, generous, amiable, soft-hearted, benevolent, benignant, gracious, mild, beneficent, affectionate, touched, moved, melting, forbearing, altruistic, philanthropic, unselfish, self-denying, tolerant.

TENDERNESS, *n.* 1. Delicacy, softness, weakness, fragility, feebleness, gentleness, mellowness, subtileness, mildness.

2. Youthfulness, youngness, youth, callowness, puerility, infantilism, juvenility, juvenescence, impressionableness, childishness, boyishness, inexperience.

3. Effeminacy, womanliness, womanishness, unmanliness, femininity, weakliness, daintiness, timorousness, meekness.

4. Sensitivity, painfulness, soreness, rawness, redness, aching, inflammation, smarting, hurt, twinge, pang, shooting.

5. Affectionateness, affection, love, amorousness, eroticism, sentimentality, sentimentalness, amatoriness, fondness, ardor, ardency, passionateness, devotion, desirousness, uxoriousness.

6. Sympathy, compassion, kindness, kindliness, pity, gentleness, benevolence, generosity, beneficence, leniency, clemency, benignity, lovingkindness, humanity, humanitarianism, charitableness, charity, philanthropicalness, philanthropy, indulgence, goodness, lenity, unselfishness.

7. Pathos, sadness, dolor, bitterness, heartbreak, tragedy, suffering, emotion, emotionalism, soulfulness, melancholy.

TENDON, *n.* Cord of tough white fibrous tissue connecting a muscle with a bone, ligament, sinew, cartilage, thew, gristle.

TENEBROUS, *adj.* Dark, gloomy, black, darkling, darksome, somber, dusky, stygian, Cimmerian, shadowy, caliginous, murky, shady, obscure, jet, ebon, swart, pitch dark, atramentous, sable, dingy, nigrescent, lurid, umbrageous, overcast, cloudy, sunless, dark as Erebus, nocturnal, sombrous.

TENEMENT, *n.* 1. Dwelling house, habitation, domicile, dwelling, abode, residence, court, hall, lodging, address, diggings, quarters, berth, seat, sojourn, habitat.

2. Apartment, flat, suite of rooms, maisonette, duplex, rooms, penthouse, cold-water flat, lodging house, den, hive, rookery, slum, lair.

TENET, *n.* Article of belief, dogma, doctrine, credo, creed, conviction, opinion, view, persuasion, belief, notion, faith, principle, conception, assumption, position, way of thinking, certainty, surmise, impression, judgment, conclusion, teaching, rule, maxim, theory, canon, gospel, confession, avowal, postulation, hypothesis, thesis, matter of fact, idea, supposition, catechism.

TENOR, *n.* 1. Continuous course, onward movement, progress, tendency, trend, scope, direction, bearing, aim, run, set, dip, tack, path, line, track, road, line of march, trajectory, orbit.

2. Sense, significance, signification, meaning, purport, spirit, drift, gist, pith, import, intent, effect, intention, purpose, scheme, design, object, force, essence, denotation, connotation, implication, thread, allusion, upshot, substance, sum and substance, burden, content, argument, subject matter, keynote, kernel, core, marrow, elixir.

3. Nature, character, cast, stamp, cut, fashion, tone, mood, form, manner, principle, type, constitution, disposition, quality, diathesis, temper, temperament, humor, aspect, grain, feature, idiocrasy, vein, endowment, idiosyncrasy, individuality, distinctiveness, peculiarity, structure.

4. High adult male voice, Irish tenor, Italian tenor, vocalist, singer, caroler, chanter, warbler, soloist, songbird, melodist, songster, crooner, chorister.

5. Tenor viol, viola, rebec, viola d'amore, viola da gamba, viola da braccio.

TENSE, *adj.* 1. Rigid, taut, drawn, stiff, stretched tight, strained, inflexible, unyielding, hard, strict, strung-up.

2. Nervous, in a state of mental strain, highstrung, excited, fearful, timorous, diffident, shaky, tremulous, apprehensive, fidgety, restless, restive, afraid of one's shadow, wrought-up, overwrought.

3. Intent, rapt, woolgathering, pensive, meditative, cogitative, reflective, musing, contemplative, wistful, deliberative, speculative, introspective, absorbed, engrossed in, lost in thought.

TENSILE, *adj.* Capable of being stretched, tensible, capable of being drawn out, ductile, elastic, springy, resilient, renitent.

TENSION, *n.* 1. Stiffness, tightness, rigor, tenseness, tensity, intensity, strain.

2. Severe effort, expansive force, elastic force, tone, traction, brace, spring, tonicity, exertion, tug, pull, pressure, struggle.

3. Intense suppressed excitement, anxiety, nervousness, stress, strain, apprehensiveness, apprehension, diffidence, fearfulness, solicitude, misgiving, care, mistrust, restlessness, disquietude, inquietude, trepidation, perturbation, trembling, tremor, flutter, shaking, mortal funk, panic, alarm, pavor, dread, dismay.

TENT, *n.* Portable shelter of skins *or* canvas supported by poles, portable lodge, wigwam, tepee, tabernacle, booth, praetorium, pavilion, marquee, canvas, awning, kibitka, *tente d'abri (Fr.),* encampment, marquise, lean-to tent, fly tent, bell tent, canoe tent, "A" tent, dog tent, pup tent, wall tent.

TENTACLE, *n.* Flexible appendage serving as organ of touch, tactile limb, prehensile process, tentaculum, feeler, tubular suctorial arm.

TENTATIVE, *adj.* Of the nature of a trial *or* experiment, empirical, provisional, temporary, probative, probationary, makeshift, essaying, trying, undecided, unsettled, trial, probatory, probational, experiential, speculative, analytic, investigative, under consideration, proposed, in question, in issue, on trial, docimastic, docimastical.

TENUITY, *n.* 1. Thinness of consistency, wateriness, gaseity, gaseousness, vaporousness, rarity, rarefaction, rareness, subtility, subtilization, refinement.

2. Slenderness, fineness, etherealness, attenuation, exiguity, smallness, parvitude.

3. Insignificance, unimportance, inconsiderableness, immateriality, nothingness, nullity, triviality, paltriness.

TENUOUS, *adj.* 1. Thin, rarefied, subtile, rare, unsubstantial, watery, aqueous, gaseous, aeriform, ethereal, airy, gasiform, etheric, vaporous, volatile, evanescent, diluted, attenuated.

2. Slender, minute, small, little, diminutive, tiny, wee, minikin, comminuted, fine, scant, slight, narrow, infinitesimal, microscopic, homeopathic, atomic, molecular, exiguous, miniature, microbial, animalcular, embryonic.

3. Unimportant, inconsequential, paltry, trifling, picayune, piddling, trivial, insignificant, petty, flimsy, shallow, frivolous, idle, niggling, fribbling, finical.

TENURE, *n.* Possession, occupancy, occupation, tenancy, tenement, use, holding, tenantship, lease, ownership, seizin, proprietorship, possessorship, *métayage (Fr.),* incumbency.

TEPID, *adj.* Lukewarm, moderately warm, warmish, mild, moderate, warmed, heated, genial, thermic, thermal, calorific.

TERGIVERSATE, *v.* Change one's opinion repeatedly, blow hot and cold, quibble, renege, equivocate, play fast and loose, shuffle, trim, straddle, hedge, change sides, apostatize, recant, retract, wheel round, go to the rightabout, shift one's ground, go upon another tack, back down, crawfish, crawl, abjure, unsay, forswear, eat one's words, turn over a new leaf, hold with the hare but run with the hounds, prevaricate, back out, evade, backslide, dodge, stall, go back on one's word, turn renegade.

TERGIVERSATION, *n.* Equivocation, apostasy, prevarication, chicanery, casuistry, evasion, recidivation, backsliding, relapse, change of mind, afterthought, recantation, renunciation, palinode, abjuration, defection, retraction, revocation, disavowal, reversal, vacillation, timeserving.

TERM, *n.* 1. Word with a definite meaning, technical word, expression, phrase, locution, designation, appellation, name, cognomen, denomination, nickname, vocable, patronymic, eponym, compellation, appellative, heading, title, praenomen, surname, moniker, agnomen, epithet, sobriquet, alias, handle to one's name, substantive, noun, technical term, cant, idiom.

2. Duration, season, period, span, space of time, spell, time, stage, interval, cycle, semester, lifetime, course, snap, year, hour, date, moment, glass of time, noiseless foot of Time, interim, while, recess, interlude, interregnum, pause, intermission, interruption, respite, epoch, era, eon, Kalpa, dynasty, age, reign, administration, incumbency.

3. End, terminus, termination, boundary, bound, post, bourn, confine, limit, mete, line of demarcation, verge, border, precinct, extreme, station, terminal, landmark, utmost extent, edge, ne plus ultra, pale, march, frontier, mark, turning point.

4. Proviso, condition, stipulation, article of agreement, item, provision, clause, covenant, *sine qua non (Lat.),* compromise, bargain, deal, agreement, contract, compact, transaction, pact, bond, settlement, convention, qualification.

5. *(Pl.)* Friendly relations, footing, standing, status, circumstance, state, situation, phase.

TERM, *v.* Apply a particular name to, designate, name, style, denominate, entitle, dub, call, phrase, christen, baptize, characterize, nickname, label, specify, coin, define, distinguish by name, mark.

TERMAGANT, *n.* Turbulent woman, brawling female, vixen, harridan, shrew, virago, scold,

Xanthippe, beldam, amazon, hag, dragon, spitfire, fury.

TERMINAL, *adj.* Situated at the end, forming the extremity, bounding, limiting, restraining, restrictive, confining, bordering, boundary, frontier, limitary, clear-cut, fixed, ultimate, final, terminating, determinate, definite.

TERMINAL, *n.* Boundary, terminus, term, limit, bound, termination, border, edge, ne plus ultra, utmost extent, verge, bourn, pale, confine, march, mete, extremity.

TERMINATE, *v.* 1. Bound spatially, form the extremity of, set bounds to, limit, confine, delimit, demarcate, circumscribe, encompass.

2. Put an end to, end, complete, conclude, bring to an end, finish, close, discontinue, cease, stop short, expire, run out, lapse, culminate, drop, wind up, accomplish, achieve, consummate.

TERMINATION, *n.* 1. Boundary, terminal, term, terminus, extremity, limit, bound, bourn, pale, verge, extreme, ne plus ultra, utmost extent, confine, frontier, march, mark, pillars of Hercules.

2. End, conclusion, close, completion, finale, finish, ending, finis, windup, denouement, final event, consummation, catastrophe, peroration, epilogue, fall of the curtain.

3. Consequence, result, issue, upshot, effect, outcome, sequel.

TERMINATIVE, *adj.* Definitive, absolute, determining, conclusive, crowning, finishing, ultimate, determinate, exhaustive, consummate, perfect, thorough, complete.

TERMINOLOGY, *n.* System of terms belonging to a subject, group of linguistic forms, glossology, nomenclature, technology, orismology, classification, technical expressions, toponomy, technical terms, particularization, specification.

TERNARY, *adj.* Involving three, threefold, triple, triplicate, triform, tertiary, triune, trinomial, treble, ternate, ternal, trinal, trinary, triplex, triadic, trilogistic, tripartite, trifid, trichotomous, trifurcate, trisulcate, tridental, triarch.

TERRACE, *n.* 1. Raised level rising above another, plateau, esplanade, platform, plain, parterre, estrade, ledge, bank, embankment, parade, promenade, step.

2. Open gallery, balcony, portico, stoa, colonnade, arcade, cloister, peristyle.

TERRA FIRMA, *n.* 1. Solid ground, dry land, firm earth, soil.

2. Support, foundation, basis, base, point d'appui, fulcrum, bearing, footing, purchase, *locus standi* (*Lat.*), resting place.

3. Safety, security, danger past, impregnability, coast clear, sheet anchor, tower of strength, rock, Gibraltar, palladium, safeguard.

TERRAIN, *n.* Tract of land with reference to its natural features, topography, region, area, zone, countryside, ground, territory, realm, district, domain, field of activity, environment, milieu, surroundings, external conditions, entourage, encompassment, scene, setting, circumjacencies, background, vicinage.

TERRA INCOGNITA, *n.* Unknown land, unexplored country, virgin soil, unfamiliar ground, sealed book, tabula rasa, unacquaintance.

TERRESTRIAL, *adj.* Pertaining to the earth, earthly, earthy, mundane, worldly, tellurian, terrene, sublunary, subastral, subcelestial, telluric, chthonian, sublunar, cosmical, temporal, mortal,

riparian, riparious, alluvial, growing on land (*Bot.*), living on the ground, chthonic.

TERRIBLE, *adj.* 1. Exciting great fear, fearful, formidable, frightful, terrifying, terrific, appalling, dreadful, alarming, dread, dire, fell, tremendous, shocking, horrible, redoubtable, awful, awe-inspiring, ghastly, horrid, horrendous, distressing, hideous, grisly, repulsive, revolting, monstrous, heinous, nefarious, horrific, grim, harrowing, rending.

2. Excessive, extreme, great, severe, intolerable, insufferable, unendurable, unreasonable, immoderate, inordinate, enormous, undue, unconscionable, outrageous, preposterous, monstrous, gross, crass, sheer, arrant, prodigious, stupendous.

3. Extremely unpleasant, bad, offensive, obnoxious, distasteful, displeasing, unbearable, odious, hateful, execrable, objectionable.

TERRIFY, *v.* Make greatly afraid, frighten, affright, strike with terror, dismay, shock, daunt, intimidate, cow, overawe, startle, petrify, appall, scare, fright, alarm, horrify, bulldoze, astound, unman, stampede, panic, abash, deter, haunt, prey on the mind, beset, obsess, disturb, arouse, excite, agitate, make one's hair stand on end, make one's flesh creep, make one's blood run cold, make one's teeth chatter, terrorize, disquiet.

TERRITORIAL, *adj.* Regional, topographical, sectional, continental, praedial, riparian, littoral, riparial, parochial, local, regionary, regionalistic, provincial, insular, frontier, boundary, border.

TERRITORY, *n.* 1. Realm, kingdom, empire, province, protectorate, mandate, state, dependency, principality, sphere of influence, colony, dominion, commonwealth, domain.

2. Tract of land, district, region, quarter, section, division, area, county, canton, shire, department, commune, arrondissement, parish, ward, diocese, precinct, township, wapentake, riding, hundred, bailiwick, beat, march, enclave, latitude, meridian field, close, garth, paddock, orb, pale, circuit, locale, spot, scene, terrain, hemisphere, arena, ambit, countryside, demesne, bourn, confine, zone, clime.

TERROR, *n.* Overpowering fear, consternation, alarm, fright, dismay, panic, extreme dread, horror, affright, trepidation, funk, scare, cold feet, stampede, fear and trembling, flutter, tremor, perturbation, disquietude, apprehension, palpitation, intimidation, terrorism, nightmare, *bête noire* (*Fr.*), hobgoblin, specter, bogy, qualm, misgiving, awe, apprehensiveness, timidity, solicitude, anxiety, cowardice, pusillanimity, cravenness, timorousness, faint-heartedness, white feather, yellow streak, diffidence, mistrust, cold sweat, pavor, goose flesh, spine-tingling, shock.

TERRORIST, *n.* 1. Evil-doer, ruffian, bludgeon man, hooligan, hoodlum, larrikin, ugly customer, rough, roughneck, tough, desperado, bully, brawler, brute, Mohock, apache, gunman, racketeer, gangster, cutthroat, highwayman, footpad, mugger.

2. Subversionary, nihilist, revolutionary, iconoclast, communist, Bolshevik, incendiary, arsonist, pyromaniac, firebug, firebrand, destroyer.

TERRORIZE, *v.* Overcome with terror, dominate by intimidation, coerce, cow, daunt, intimidate, bulldoze, bully, browbeat, ride roughshod over, dragoon, panic, stampede, scare, alarm, frighten, menace, threaten, hold in terror, thunder, fulminate, bluster.

TERSE, adj. Laconic, curt, pithy, sententious, epigrammatic, compendious, summary, succinct, condensed, compact, close to the point, concise, brief, short, neat and effective, pointed, trenchant, free from superfluity, expressive, forcible, cogent, smooth, polished, exact, crisp, commatic, comprehensive, compressed, pregnant, taciturn, reticent, close-tongued, close-mouthed, reserved, pauciloquent, sparing of words, word-bound, abrupt, *abrégé (Fr.).*

TESSELLATED, adj. Formed of small squares, mosaic, checkered, inlaid, variegated, plaid, versicolor, many-colored, parti-colored, polychromatic, kaleidoscopic, motley, pied, piebald, marbled, mottled, daedal, ornate, showy, rich, ornamental.

TEST, v. 1. Try, give a trial to, make experiment with, subject to trial, make trial of, experiment upon, put to the proof, examine, prove, try for size, probe, sound, fathom, plumb, essay, venture, verify, rehearse, put through paces, send up a pilot balloon, feel one's way, fumble, grope, throw out a feeler, tempt, speculate.

2. Assay, refine, make an analysis, analyze, titrate, reduce, resolve, sample.

TEST, n. 1. Trial, examination, essay, attempt, proof, probation, experiment, try, ordeal, venture, tryout, analysis, assay, verification, investigation, criterion, touchstone, standard, flyer, speculation, leap in the dark, *ballon d'essai (Fr.),* feeler, endeavor, crack (coll.).

2. Quiz, interrogation, questioning, third degree, catechism, review, questionnaire, inquiry, inquest, inquisition, percontation.

TESTAMENT, n. 1. Formal declaration of wishes for disposition of property after death, will, last will and testament, legacy, bequest, devise, dot, dower, codicil, settlement.

2. Covenant between God and man, Old Testament, New Testament, Scriptures, sacred writings, revelation, divine inspiration, the Bible, the Good Book, the Word of God, Holy Writ, Gospel, Septuagint, Vulgate, Pentateuch, Octateuch, the Law and the Prophets, Hagiographa, Hierographa, Apocrypha.

TESTATOR, n. Bequeather, devisor *(Law),* grantor, conferrer, donor, bestower, testatrix.

TESTIFY, v. State as fact *or* truth, affirm under oath, make solemn declaration, depose, bear witness, swear, attest, give evidence, certify, acknowledge openly, asseverate, vouch, aver, avow, declare, profess, evidence, depone, signify, witness, confirm, indicate, endorse, ratify, verify, support, adduce, document, prove, manifest, evince, corroborate, validate, vindicate, bear out, sustain, uphold, establish, warrant, authenticate, circumstantiate, substantiate, plead, allege.

TESTIMONIAL, n. 1. Writing certifying to a person's character, written reference, recommendation, credential, voucher, certificate, citation, data, facts, indorsement, deposition, affidavit, document.

2. Record, monument, memento, souvenir, remembrancer, memorial, trophy, escutcheon, medal, order, ribbon.

TESTIMONY, n. 1. Declaration of witness under oath, attestation, affirmation, deposition, corroboration, asseveration, certification, verification, authentication, circumstantiation, substantiation, indorsement, confirmation, profession, confession, admission, demonstration, exemplification, ratification, testification, averment, avowal.

2. Proof by a witness, affidavit, voucher, record, credentials, evidence in support of, ground of belief, witness, warranty, warrant, testamur, muniments, deed.

TESTINESS, n. Peevishness, fretfulness, captiousness, irascibility, touchiness, irritability, petulance, hastiness, restiveness, techiness, acerbity, crossness, temper, procacity, susceptibility, protervity, tartness, contentiousness, excitability, hot blood, bad temper, churlishness, asperity, acrimoniousness, sullenness, spinosity, moodiness, crabbedness, sulks, mumps, dudgeon, *bouderie (Fr.),* impatience.

TESTUDINATED, adj. Formed like the carapace of a tortoise, arched, vaulted, curved, roofed, bowed.

TESTY, adj. Irritable and impatient, snappish, fretful, peevish, waspish, splenetic, pettish, petulant, cross, irascible, choleric, touchy, techy, quick-tempered, hot-blooded, fiery-tempered, peppery, acrimonious, acerbous, crabby, sullen, morose, moody, captious, fractious, querulous, perverse, crusty, tart, sharp-tongued, snarling, grumpy, ill-humored, susceptible, thin-skinned, temperamental, hasty, huffy, passionate, shrewish, contentious, cantankerous, restive, exceptious, churlish.

TETE-A-TETE, adv. Face to face, for two persons together, together in private, *entre-nous (Fr.),* cheek by jowl, confidentially, privately, *vis-à-vis (Fr.),* familiarly, side by side, at close quarters, in presence of.

TETE-A-TETE, n. Private conversation, private interview, intimate conference, pourparler, *conversazione (It.),* audience, parley, powwow, confidential causerie, confabulation, colloquy, converse, duologue.

TETHER, v. Fasten, picket, stake, tie, chain, curb, control, restrict, restrain, enchain, trammel, hobble, secure, rein in, check, hold in leash, harness, bridle, moor.

TETHER, n. Rope for fastening so that range of movement is limited, picket, chain, tie, halter, stake, check, restriction, utmost length in action, utmost limit of ability.

TETRAD, n. Group of four, quaternion, quartet, quaternary, quadruplet, quaternity, foursome.

TEXT, n. 1. Print, imprint, impress, impression, letterpress, context, matter, typography, printing, typesetting, composition, presswork, type.

2. Main body of a literary work, true copy, original words of an author, *ipsissima verba (Lat.),* passage, verse, actual wording, sentence, quotation, scripture, clause, paragraph.

3. Subject matter, topic, thesis, theme, subject, motif, leitmotif, locus, matter in hand.

TEXTILE, n. Woven material, fabric, stuff, webbing, cloth, tissue, gossamer, web, homespun, frieze, fustian, linsey-woolsey, twill, tweed, drill, serge.

TEXTURE, n. 1. Characteristic disposition of interwoven threads, web, fabric, weft, intertexture, manner of weaving, arrangement, contexture, make, structure, character, organization, constitution, composition, make-up.

2. Fineness, coarseness, fiber, grain, grit, tissue, tooth, nap, warp and woof, surface, quality, substance.

THANK, v. Be grateful, express gratitude, return thanks to, bless, make acknowledgments to, tender thanks, requite, acknowledge, overflow with gratitude, lie under an obligation, be beholden, never forget, *remercier (Fr.), agradecer (Sp.), ringraziare (It.), danken (Ger.),* repay, reward, recompense, remember.

THANKFUL, *adj.* Appreciative, grateful, obliged, under obligation, beholden, indebted to, impressed, contented, mindful, gratified, pleased.

THANKFULNESS, *n.* Gratefulness, gratitude, sense of obligation, thanksgiving, requital, appreciation, recognition, acknowledgment, "a lively sense of favors to come," benediction, thanks, paean, beholdenness, indebtedness, mindfulness.

THANKLESS, *adj.* 1. Not appreciative, inappreciative, ingrate, unthankful, ungrateful, unmindful, ingrateful.

2. Not appreciated, fruitless, bootless, profitless, vain, useless, unrequited, unacknowledged, unrewarded, unreturned, unavowed, unremembered, forgotten.

3. Unpopular, unacceptable, undesirable, unpleasant, disagreeable, distasteful, obnoxious, unwelcome, undesired, uninviting, ungracious.

THANKS, *interj.* Thank you, gramercy, many thanks, much obliged, Heaven be praised, *merci (Fr.), grazie (It.), gracias (Sp.), danke schön (Ger.).*

THANKS, *n., pl.* Expressions of gratitude, acknowledgments for favors, blessing, benediction, grace, thankfulness, praise, Te Deum, paean.

THANKSGIVING, *n.* Giving thanks, benediction, allelujah, blessing, rejoicing, jubilation, eucharist, hosanna, magnificat, magnification, laudation, glorification, exaltation, paean, grace, Te Deum, oblation, homage, devotion.

THAUMATURGICS, *n.* Art of the magician, miraculous performances, wizardry, sleight of hand, prestidigitation, legerdemain, magic, trickery, conjuring, hanky-panky, hocus-pocus, thimblerig, illusion, conjuration, jugglery.

THAUMATURGIST, *n.* Wonderworker, thaumaturge, sorcerer, wizard, magician, seer, necromancer, conjurer, exorcist, charmer, voodoo, shaman, diviner, mage, medicine man, dowser, witch doctor, clairvoyant, astrologer, soothsayer, Cagliostro, Katerfelto, Merlin, demonologist, juggler, prestidigitator.

THAUMATURGY, *n.* Wonderworking, feats of magic, wizardry, sorcery, magic, witchcraft, theurgy, necromancy, occult art, the black art, voodoo, shamanism, voodooism, diablerie, demonology, witchery, fetishism, hoodoo, conjuration, exorcism, incantation, enchantment, mesmerism, clairvoyance, table-turning, spirit-rapping, ouija board, thought transference, telepathy, automatic writing, *planchette (Fr.),* divination, chiromancy, pedomancy, palmistry, oracle, sortilege, vaticination, mantology, augury, hariolation, auspices, soothsaying, horoscope, crystal gazing.

THAW, *v.* 1. Pass from a frozen to a liquid state, melt, liquefy, deliquesce, liquate, run, dissolve, soften, be freed from frost, become fluid, fuse, condense.

2. Become less formal, shed one's reserve, unbend, relax, break the ice, relent, bend, yield, calm down, give quarter, forbear, enter into the feelings of, commiserate, take pity on, sympathize, submit, acquiesce, *aequam servare mentem (Lat.),* take in good part, live and let live.

THEATER, *n.* 1. Building for dramatic presentations, playhouse, legitimate theater, movie palace, cinema palace, first-run house, second-run house, movies, cinematograph, vitascope, the silver screen, auditorium, amphitheater, arena, lyceum, odeum, colosseum.

2. Drama, theater piece, play, stage entertainment, tragedy, comedy, comedietta, farce, burlesque, harlequinade, spectacle, masque, pantomime, curtain raiser, divertissement, entr'acte, interlude, vaudeville, opera, operetta, ballet, extravaganza, melodrama, mystery, tableau, theatricals, dramaturgy, buskin, cothurnus, sock, histrionic art, Thespis.

3. Stage, scene, place of action, field of operations, spotlight, limelight, proscenium, orchestra, gallery.

THEATRICAL, *adj.* 1. Dramatic, histrionic, Thespian, dramaturgical, melodramatic, scenic, spectacular, tragic, buskined, comic, tragicomic, farcical, stagy, operatic, cinematographic.

2. Impressive, striking, vivid, graphic, imposing, ostentatious, vainglorious, ritualistic, stately, majestic, solemn, glittering, sumptuous, meretricious, spangled, tinsely, ambitious, pretentious, conspicuous, gaudy, garish, flaunting, gorgeous, pompous, showy, ceremonious, artificial, flashy, grandiose, extravagant.

3. Bombastic, fustian, affected, stilted, unnatural, self-important, presumptuous, consequential, boastful, turgid, grandiloquent, magniloquent, altiloquent, swaggering, *maniéré (Fr.),* mannered.

THEFT, *n.* Wrongful taking of another's personal goods, robbery, larceny, thievery, spoliation, depredation, pilfering, stealing, purloining, filching, burglary, brigandage, hijacking, piracy, freebooting, direption, abstraction, holdup, stick-up, swindling, fraud, embezzlement, misappropriation, expropriation, dispossession, peculation, cheating, plagiarism, shoplifting, safecracking, kleptomania, forgery, pillage, plunder, rapine, sack, looting, buccaneering, privateering, housebreaking, cattle rustling, abaction, abduction, booty, swag, graft, pickings, boodle.

THEME, *n.* 1. Subject, text, matter, subject matter, topic, motif, affair, matter in hand, problem, question, proposition, point, moot point, keynote, argument, focus of interest, general idea.

2. *(Mus.)* Tune, melody, air, strain, *Leitmotif (Ger.),* song, measure, lay, chanson.

3. Composition, essay, treatise, dissertation, thesis, report, narrative, discourse, tract, memoir, disquisition, homily, study, investigation, exposition, discussion, commentary, critique, appreciation, article, editorial.

THEN, *adv.* 1. At that time, immediately, soon afterward, afterwards, hereafter, next in order of time, later, on that occasion, hereupon, whereupon, thereupon, thenceforth.

2. Consequently, therefore, for this reason, wherefore, on that account, in those circumstances, since that is so, accordingly, hence, ergo, so, thus, whence, as a deduction, finally, in fine, in conclusion, *au bout du compte (Fr.),* in consideration of, whereas, seeing that.

3. In the next place, in addition, besides, also, further, furthermore, moreover.

THENCE, *adv.* 1. Caused by, from that source, therefore, for, hence, on account of, since, on that account, owing to, due to, forasmuch as, thanks to, *propter hoc (Lat.),* for that reason, inasmuch as, in consideration of, considering, consequently, ergo, accordingly, whereas, *ex concesso (Lat.).*

2. From that place, from there, therefrom, hence, henceforth, thenceforth, thenceforward.

THEOLOGIAN, *n.* One versed in theology, divinity student, divine, theologist, ecclesiastic, theologue, theologaster, clergyman, theist, monotheist, polytheist, pantheist, Christian philosopher, canonist, Church Father, patrist, textualist, Scholastic.

THEOLOGICAL, *adj.* Canonical, patristic, patristical, divine, religious, sectarian, ecclesiastical, orthodox, doctrinal, spiritual, holy, Christian, reverential, devout, pious, godly, consecrated, inspired, charismatic, sanctified, not of the earth, heavenly-minded, Biblical, scriptural, prophetic, sacred, evangelical, evangelistic, apostolic, theopneustic, apocalyptic, textuary, isagogical, hierologic, hagiological, theosophical, theistic, monotheistic, homiletic, dogmatic.

THEOLOGY, *n.* Science of God and His relations to man, scientific statement of religious facts, divine wisdom, theologics, hagiography, articles of faith, dogma, creed, credo, divinity, science of religious truth, dogmatics, homiletics, patrology, patristics, isagogics, theosophy, hierology, hagiology, theism, monotheism, religion, religious persuasion, tenet, doctrine, teaching, gospel.

THEOPNEUSTY, *n.* Divine inspiration, revelation, apocalypse, afflatus, word of God, oracle, inspired utterance.

THEOREM, *n.* Proposition to be demonstrated, statement embodying something to be proved, rule expressed by a formula, thesis, dictum, position, problem, question, postulation, assumption, hypothesis, postulate, moot point, scholium, axiom.

THEORETIC, *adj.* Consisting in theory, theoretical, speculative, hypothetical, conjectural, doctrinaire, pure, abstract, not practical, unapplied, ideal, ideological, academic, impractical, notional, mooted, given, postulatory, assumed, suppositive, supposititious, suppositional, putative, presumptive, speculatory.

THEORIST, *n.* One who is expert in the theoretical side of a subject, doctrinaire, doctrinarian, theorizer, theoretician, speculator, notionalist, ideologist, one who draws inferences from principles, dreamer, philosopher, speculatist, hypothesist, notionist, woolgatherer.

THEORIZE, *v.* Form theories, speculate, doctrinize, hypothesize, impute to, ascribe to, assign as cause, derive from, account for, conjecture, suppose, surmise, divine, guess, suspect, presurmise, presume, presuppose, fancy, take it, assume, propound, propose, put forth, moot, hazard a conjecture, predicate, posit.

THEORY, *n.* 1. Untested opinion, hypothesis, speculation, conjecture, surmise, postulate, assumption, presumption, rationale, principle, mental view, contemplation, thesis, supposition, presupposition, postulation, condition, data, theorem, association of ideas, divination, proposition, guesswork, shot, intuition, ascription, attribution, reference to, derivation from, imputation.

2. System of rules *or* principles, science, abstract principles, doctrine, philosophy, etiology, pandect, body of doctrine, school, dogma.

THERAPEUTIC, *adj.* Pertaining to the treating of disease, curative, sanatory, healing, remedial, sanative, medicinal, medical, salutiferous, prophylactic, hygienic, restorative, corrective, palliative, chirurgical, surgical, orthopedic.

THERAPY, *n.* Treatment of disease, remedial process, curative power, prophylaxis, remedy, regimen, dietary, *vis medicatrix (Lat.),* posology, pathology, therapeutics, pharmacopoeia, homeopathy, allopathy, dietetics, chirurgery, surgery, healing art, osteopathy, chiropractic, orthopraxy, massage, hydropathy.

THERE, *adv.* In that place, at that place, to that point, thither, yon, yonder, thereat, at a distance, in place, *in situ (Lat.), in loco (Lat.),* in presence of, at that point, in that matter.

THEREABOUTS, *adv.* 1. Near that place, thereat, therebesides, thereby, here and there, *passim (Lat.),* hereabouts, whereabouts, nigh, fast by, hard by, close to, at the point of, next door to, within reach, within range, but a step, not far from, in the environs of, on the verge of, at one's door, under one's nose, within a stone's throw, in sight of, at close quarters, alongside, at the threshold, on the confines of, bordering upon.

2. Almost, approximately, *circa (Lat.),* in round numbers, roughly, well-nigh, nearly, about, all but, generally, roundly.

THEREAFTER, *adv.* Afterward, after that, afterwards, subsequently, later, since, at a later period, close upon, next, thereupon, eftsoons, from that time, in process of time.

THEREBY, *adv.* By that means, in consequence of that, through, per, whereby, by the agency of, by dint of, by virtue of, through the medium of, with the aid of.

THEREFORE, *adv.* Consequently, by consequence, accordingly, as a result, wherefore, so, then, hence, thence, whence, for that reason, for that, on that account, ergo, inasmuch as, forasmuch as, seeing that, on account of, for which reason, from the nature of the case, because that, thus, owing to, due to, whereas, as a deduction.

THEREIN, *adv.* Wherein, herein, within, inly, withinside, *ab intra (Lat.),* inwards, internally.

THEREUPON, *adv.* Whereupon, then, upon this, upon that, thereon, thereafter, upon which, eftsoons, in process of time, following that, immediately, at once, without delay, pronto, subito, all at once, in a trice, in a moment, in the twinkling of an eye, at a stroke, suddenly, instanter, at one fell swoop, extempore, on the spur of the moment, on the spot, slapdash, at sight, straightway, apace, directly, forthwith.

THERMAE, *n., pl.* Public bathing establishment, hot baths, warm baths, natatorium, caldarium, tepidarium, sudatorium, sudatory, hammam, Turkish bath.

THERMAL, *adj.* Warm, thermic, hot, heated, lukewarm, tepid, calorific, sudorific, thermogenic, recalescent.

THERMOMETER, *n.* Instrument for measuring temperature, glass, mercury, thermopile, calorimeter, pyrometer, thermometrograph, thermoscope, thermoregulator, thermostat, telethermometer, Reaumur, Centigrade, Fahrenheit.

THESAURUS, *n.* 1. Treasury, tholos, depository, repository, storeroom, storehouse, cache, depot, pantechnicon, vault, reservatory, arsenal, armory.

2. Dictionary, lexicon, glossary, wordbook, encyclopedia, vocabulary, cyclopedia, concordance, index, gradus, delectus.

THESIS, *n.* 1. Proposition, doctrine, dictum, presupposition, argument, postulate, hypothesis, proposal, assumption, theory, dogma, tenet, theorem, data, postulation, condition, supposition, conjecture, conceit, surmise, speculation, allegation.

2. Theme, topic, subject, matter, subject matter, text, what it is about, affair, field of inquiry, moot point, question.

3. Dissertation, essay, tract, monograph, treatise, composition, digest, discourse, disquisition, excursus, tractate, lecture, memoir, pandect, homily, critique, commentary, review, article, editorial, study, investigation, discussion, exposition.

THESPIAN, *n.* Actor, stage player, strolling player, stage performer, comedian, tragedian, straight man, Roscius, star, mime, pantomimist, harlequin, farceur, mute, walk-on, supernumerary, extra, mummer, leading man, lead, leading woman, protagonist, juvenile lead, *jeune premier (Fr.),* heavy, character actor, soubrette, ingénue, hero, heroine, villain, villainess, actress.

THEURGIST, *n.* Wonderworker, thaumaturgist, sorcerer, prestidigitator, magician, necromancer, conjurer, juggler, wizard, exorcist, warlock, charmer, mage, dowser, voodoo, witch doctor, medicine man, shaman, witch, fairy, seer, lamia, figure finger.

THEURGY, *n.* System of magic professing aid from beneficent deities, working of some supernatural agency in human affairs, wonderworking, thaumaturgy, sorcery, necromancy, magic, the black art, witchcraft, shamanism, voodoo, hoodoo, superstition, occult art, black magic, demonology, *diablerie (Fr.),* witchery, bedevilment, fetishism, exorcism, conjuration, incantation, enchantment, possession, obsession, sortilege, divination, hocus-pocus, legerdemain, prestidigitation, sleight of hand, jugglery, hanky-panky, trickery.

THEWS, *n., pl.* 1. Sinews, muscles, ligaments, nerves.

2. Physical strength, brawn, musculature, lustihood, stoutness, brute force, power, puissance, vigor, energy, stamina, physique, virility, vitality, athleticism, feats of strength, gymnastics, grit, potency, firmness, solidity, calisthenics, agonistics, iron grip.

THEWY, *adj.* Muscular, brawny, sinewy, wiry, strong, adamantine, mighty, potent, powerful, puissant, vigorous, forcible, robust, stout, hardy, sturdy, able-bodied, athletic, gymnastic, husky, well-knit, herculean, strapping, broad-shouldered, gigantic, stalwart, virile, manly, masculine, healthy, hale, robustious, lusty, doughty.

THICK, *adj.* 1. Having great extent from one surface to its opposite, not thin in measure, compact, solid, dense, close, bulky.

2. Inspissate, inspissated, having great consistency, crass, gross, heavy, viscous, viscid, gelatinous, clotted, grumous, mucilaginous, ropy, coagulated, condensed, firm, feculent, sedimental, roiled, roily, muddy, turbid, colloidal, muculent, curdled, glutinous, pasty, tacky, gummous, albuminous.

3. Thick-set, squat, squab, dumpy, stubby, chunky, plump, roly-poly, stocky, stumpy, hefty, tubby, pursy.

4. Abundant, plentiful, plenteous, copious, plethoric, numerous, frequent, multitudinous, heaped, packed, crowded, populous, swarming, teeming.

5. Intense, deep, excessive, profound, extreme, very great, of high degree, acute, poignant, grievous, strong, keen, sharp, potent.

6. Indistinct, inarticulate, guttural, throaty, harsh, hoarse, husky, muffled, muted, not clear, confused, obscure, blurred.

7. Cloudy, misty, foggy, hazy, vaporous, murky, obnubilated, nebulous, nubilous, overcast, lowering.

8. Slow of mental apprehension, dull, dull-witted, obtuse, Boeotian, torpid, stultified, not quick-witted, doltish, stupid, unintelligent, wooden, stolid, dumb *(coll.),* thick-headed, inept, inert, fat-headed, addlepated.

9. Close in friendship, familiar, intimate, well-acquainted, hand-in-glove, friendly, neighborly, confidential, fraternal, cordial, chummy, inseparable, bosom, very dear, near and dear, personal, brotherly, sisterly, devoted, harmonious, sympathetic, on intimate terms with, hail-fellow well-met.

THICKEN, *v.* 1. Make dense, inspissate, stiffen, coagulate, congeal, condense, inviscate, curdle, turn, jelly, clot, cake, set, petrify, solidify, harden, compact, concrete, candy, incrassate, curd, clabber, jellify, gelatinize, jell, cohere.

2. Deepen, darken, intensify, roil, befoul, becloud, bemire.

THICKET, *n.* Dense growth of bushes, thick coppice, copse, canebrake, bosk, covert, bosket, brake, bocage, underbrush, boskage, undergrowth, jungle, shrubbery, wood, forest, grove, scrub, brushwood, hedge, clump, woodland, bush, veldt, chaparral, spinney.

THICKHEAD, *n.* Stupid fellow, blockhead, oaf, lout, moron, chump, dunderhead, bullhead, addle-head, giddyhead, thickskull, numskull, half-wit, fathead, dunderpate, dunce, sot, dullard, idiot, fool, tomfool, simpleton, nitwit, witling, jackass, donkey, ninnyhammer, booby, looby, noodle, goose, imbecile, nincompoop, ignoramus.

THICK-HEADED, *adj.* Stupid, dull-witted, dull, obtuse, doltish, asinine, ignorant, foolish, slow-witted, wanting, *borné (Fr.),* insulse, stolid, fatuous, imbecilic, idiotic, moronic, unintelligent, witless, brainless, not bright, muddleheaded, pig-headed, fatheaded, rattlebrained, addlepated, weak in the upper story, sottish, blockish, unteachable, Boeotian, inept, hebetudinous.

THICKNESS, *n.* 1. Denseness, density, heaviness, compactness, crassness, diameter, third dimension, bore, crassitude, spissitude, crowdedness, closeness, grossness, coarseness, body, bulk.

2. Stiffening, inspissation, solidification, coagulation, condensation, jellification, gelatinization, concentration, stiffness, viscosity, viscidity, clot, coagulum, semiliquidity, colloidality, gummosity, stickiness, glutinosity, adhesiveness, pastiness, mucosity, thickening, congelation, cohesion.

3. Blockheadedness, stupidity, stupidness, ignorance, thick-headedness, ineptitude, dullness, opacity, benightedness, nescience, incomprehension, imbecility, poverty of intellect, clouded perception, stolidity, hebetude, incapacity.

THICK-SET, *adj.* 1. Close-planted, dense, close, serried, compact, cohesive, solid, impenetrable, imporous, impervious, impermeable.

2. Of thick form *or* build, heavily built, solid, stocky, massive, stout, sturdy, squat, squab, short, scrimpy, stubby, stumpy, podgy, dumpy, roly-poly, tubby.

THICK-SKINNED, *adj.* Pachydermatous, insensitive, callous, insensible, unsusceptible, unimpressible, unfeeling, impercipient, hardened, proof, obtuse, dull, numb, impassive, dead to, sluggish, torpid, comatose, inert, supine, indifferent, regardless, Laodicean, inattentive, disregarding, unconcerned, pococurante, insouciant, nonchalant, unimpressed, unruffled, unmoved, vegetative, impervious, inured, casehardened, imperturbable.

THIEF, *n.* 1. One guilty of larceny, petty robber, stealer, pilferer, filcher, purloiner, depredator, lifter, snatcher, pickpocket, shoplifter, cutpurse, pickpurse, dip *(sl.),* light-fingered gentry, housebreaker, burglar, yeggman, Raffles, yegg, sneakthief, cracksman, second-story man, safecracker, crook, picklock.

2. Bandit, brigand, highwayman, freebooter, hijacker, filibuster, road agent, thug, footpad, holdup man, strong-arm man, nighthawk, bushranger, kidnaper, abductor, poacher, cattle rustler, contrabandist, smuggler, runner, rifler, kleptomaniac, plagiarist, marauder, pillager, spoiler, corsair, pirate, buccaneer, viking, privateer.

3. Swindler, sharper, embezzler, peculator, bunkoman, rook, thimblerigger, diddler, trickster, hawk, fleecer, defaulter, *chevalier d'industrie (Fr.),* welsher, cardsharper, spieler, counterfeiter, forger, coiner, defrauder, receiver of stolen goods, fence, swagman, shark, harpy, blackmailer, extortionist.

THIEVE, *v.* 1. Practice petty thievery, take by theft, pilfer, filch, steal, rob, purloin, lift, pinch, palm, crib, bag, prig, sneak, abstract, finger, carry off, misappropriate, pirate, impress, shanghai, abduct, kidnap, spirit away, make off with, hold for ransom, seize, rustle, hijack, sack, ransack, rifle, despoil, loot, spoil, burgle, filibuster, plunder, strip, pillage, forage, poach, smuggle, maraud, hold up, stick up, smuggle, appropriate, plagiarize, commandeer, make free with, intercept, dispossess, extort, blackmail, bleed, usurp, bone.

2. Swindle, embezzle, peculate, obtain under false pretenses, pigeon, live by one's wits, bilk, chouse, trick out of, bunko, fleece, defraud, cozen, cheat, victimize, pluck, diddle, forge, counterfeit, coin, shark, rook.

THIEVERY, *n.* 1. Petty robbery, thieving, larceny, theft, thievishness, stealing, filching, purloining, pilfering, lifting, shoplifting, palming, direption, spoliation, brigandage, hijacking, holdup, stick-up, highway robbery, pillage, plunder, rapine, sack, foray, raid, privateering, piracy, buccaneering, burglary, cattle rustling, abaction, housebreaking, safecracking, second-story work, kidnaping, abduction, rapacity, depredation, extortion, blackmail, hush money, *chantage (Fr.),* protection money, kleptomania, plagiarism.

2. Swindling, defrauding, cheating, embezzlement, misappropriation, peculation, swindle, fraud, cardsharping, thimblerigging, forgery, counterfeit, boodle, swag, pickings, booty, loot, spoil, prey, prize, graft, bribe, stolen goods.

THIEVISH, *adj.* 1. Inclined to theft, given to stealing, larcenous, burglarious, predatory, light-fingered, pilfering, rapacious, furacious, thieving, predacious, raptorial, piratical, plundering, plagiaristic, cribbing, pillaging.

Characteristic of a thief, stealthy, clandestine, furtive, underhand, sly, secretive, secret, sneaking, unprincipled, dishonest, unscrupulous, fraudulent, knavish, insidious, crooked, slippery, corrupt, venal, mercenary, feline, obreptitious, surreptitious, evasive.

THIEVISHNESS, *n.* Mania for stealing, kleptomania, propensity to steal, furaciousness, latrociny, thievery, direption, appropriation, depredation, spoliation, brigandage, privateering, piracy, buccaneering, filibustering, housebreaking, shoplifting, safecracking, burglary, larcenousness, pilfering, filching, purloining, rapacity, peculation, embezzlement, fraudulence.

THIGH, *n.* Part of the leg between the hip and the knee, femur, ham.

THIMBLE, *n.* Small metal cap worn on the finger to push the needle in sewing, ferrule, thumbstall, sleeve, ring, poucer.

THIMBLEFUL, *n.* Small quantity, modicum, moiety, little, trifle, whit, bit, dab, pinch, touch, tinge, suspicion, soupçon, dash, scintilla, particle, iota, morsel, scrap, speck, fragment, jot, mite, grain, crumb, mouthful, capful, spoonful, taste, swallow, drop, sip, sup, sprinkling, drop in the bucket, minimum, snack.

THIN, *adj.* 1. Having little extent from one surface to its opposite, not thick in measure, of small cross section in comparison with the length, fine, tenuous, small.

2. Threadlike, delicate, slender, slight, finespun, flimsy, gossamery, light, easily seen through, transparent, diaphanous, silken, silky, chiffon, sheer, clear, pellucid, translucent, gauzy, transpicuous, porous, open, limpid, vitreous, glassy, sleazy, cobweb.

3. Having slight consistency, rarefied, rare, subtile, attenuated, watery, fluid, dilute, serous, aqueous, waterish, gaseous, unsubstantial, imponderable.

4. Having little flesh, lean, spare, slim, slender, svelte, gaunt, spindly, lanky, bony, lank, scraggy, fleshless, scrawny, skinny, haggard, peaked, pinched, emaciated, wizened, starveling, shrunken, not well-grown, meager, macilent, fallen away, skeletal, cadaverous, rawboned, wasted, spindling, weedy, spindle-shanked, frail, unsound, fragile, frangible.

5. Having the constituent parts few and not close together, not dense, sparse, scattered, scanty, infrequent, scarce, insufficient, inadequate, spare, sporadic, few, exiguous, few and far between.

6. Lacking fullness *or* volume, weak and shrill, high-pitched, faint, feeble, supersonic, indistinct, reedy, acute, high, piercing.

THIN, *v.* Make thin, reduce, curtail, diminish, remove, thin out, prune, eliminate, rarefy, attenuate, dilute, adulterate, water, water down, weaken, extenuate, emaciate, wizen, weed out, lessen, decimate, exclude, condense, subtilize, clarify, clear, depurate, refine, purify.

THING, *n.* 1. Material object without life *or* consciousness, inanimate object, lifeless substance, lump of matter, article, something, gadget, thingumajig, thingumbob, doohickey, dingus *(sl).*

2. Being, entity, creature, monad, created being, substance, person, body, protoplasm, corpus, hyle, flesh and blood, matter, substantiality, materiality, corporeity, physical nature, corporality, material existence, incarnation, brute matter, stuff, protoplasm, parenchyma.

3. Event, deed, affair, feat, fact, occurrence, act, transaction, circumstance, action, concern, arrangement, performance, business, eventuality,

incident, proceeding, phenomenon, happening, adventure, accident, doing.

4. Particular, respect, instance, detail, particularity, item, feature, special point, regard, consideration, reference, bearing, connection, aspect.

5. (Pl.) Articles of dress, clothes, raiment, apparel, accessories, duds, clothing, garb, wardrobe, togs, toggery, wearing apparel, costume, guise, toilette, habiliments, vesture, garments, array, finery, accouterments, rigging, trappings.

6. (Pl.) Personal possessions, chattels, effects, appurtenances, goods, gear, luggage, baggage, impedimenta, oddments, paraphernalia, traps, movables, commodities, furnishings, suum cuique (Lat.), personalty, equipage, parcels.

THINK, v. 1. Form in the mind, use the mind actively, turn over in the mind, have a mental image of, exercise the mind, dwell intently upon, apply the mind, mull over, meditate, reason, speculate, reflect, understand, ponder, contemplate, muse, cogitate, ruminate, deliberate, conceive, excogitate, fancy, dream, brood over, con over, rack one's brains, cerebrate, mentalize, set one's wits to work, digest.

2. Hold as an opinion, opine, believe, reckon, deem, suppose, trow, judge, ween, surmise, imagine, presume, conclude, apprehend, take it, be of an opinion, determine, guess, count, nurture an idea, credit, give faith, accept, swallow.

3. Keep in mind, recollect, remember, reminisce, recall, call to mind, bethink.

4. Have in mind, purpose, design, intend, propose, mean, envision, envisage, picture, ideate, plan, plot, contrive, compass.

THINKABLE, adj. Conceivable, cogitable, imaginable, possible, presumable, believable, credible, probable, plausible, specious, likely, reasonable.

THINKER, n. Sage, pundit, wise man, master spirit, mastermind, longhead, philosopher, authority, esprit fort (Fr.), Solomon, Nestor, man of learning, wizard, wiseacre (coll.), scholar, savant, bookworm, bibliophile, highbrow, intelligentsia, pantologist.

THINKING, adj. Reasoning, reasonable, rational, reflective, cogitative, thoughtful, pensive, introspective, cogitant, contemplative, meditative, deliberative, wistful, studious, philosophical, museful, absorbed, engrossed, rapt, lost in thought, intent, attentive, heedful, conscientious, careful, considerate.

THINKING, n. 1. Brainwork, cerebration, mentation, ratiocination, cogitation, excogitation, intellection, contemplation, musing, meditation, reflection, thought, consideration, rumination, speculation, study, lucubration, deliberation, perception, consciousness, train of thought, mental process, association of ideas, application, close study, absorption, abstraction, engrossment, reverie, self-communing, brown study, depth of thought, retrospection, introversion, introspection, review.

2. Judgment, conclusion, opinion, deduction, inference, belief, thought, view, conception, conviction, persuasion, teaching, tenet, dogma, doctrine, credo, creed, position, impression, article of faith, surmise, surmisal, certainty.

THINNESS, n. 1. Slenderness, slimness, leanness, lankness, gauntness, emaciation, attenuation, weediness, spindliness, meagerness, boniness, lankiness, skinniness, scrawniness.

2. Tenuity, fineness, flimsiness, transparency, sheerness, transpicuousness, translucency, diaphanousness, diaphaneity, silkiness, gossameriness, delicacy, lightness, airiness, etherealness, rarefaction, rareness, subtilization, frailness, fragility.

3. Sparseness, scantiness, scarcity, fewness, paucity, spareness, exiguity, sparsity, rarity, infrequency.

4. Shaving, lath, rail, skeleton, cadaver, shadow, scrag, thread, wafer, strip, skin and bone.

THIN-SKINNED, adj. 1. Physically sensible, sensitive, sentient, impressionable, responsive, perceptive, sensuous, impressive, lively, susceptible, susceptive, excitable, ticklish, itchy, titillative.

2. Irascible, irritable, choleric, touchy, easily offended, querulous, peevish, ill-tempered, fidgety, fretful, overhasty, testy, huffy, petulant, pettish, fiery, waspish, captious, moody, contentious, quarrelsome, disputatious, exceptious, cantankerous, cross, churlish, fractious, sulky, sullen, resentful, crabbed, splenetic, cross-grained, humorsome, refractory, intractable, grumpy, morose.

3. Fastidious, exacting, meticulous, finical, nice, overnice, dainty, delicate, namby-pamby, squeamish, queasy, overparticular, prudish, prim, discriminating, hypercritical.

THIRD, adj. Next after the second, next but one, coming after two others, ranking next below the second.

THIRST, v. 1. Desire to drink, feel thirst, be thirsty, be parched, spit dust (sl.).

2. Hanker, desire, crave, long for, yearn, pant for, covet, hunger for.

THIRST, n. 1. Desire for drink, polydipsia, dipsomania, thirstiness, mouth-watering, winebibbing, alcoholism, oenomania.

2. Dryness, aridity, drought, aridness, parchedness, dehydration, desiccation.

3. Eager longing, strong desire, hankering, yearning, craving, hunger, appetite, stomach, keenness, ravenousness, greed, voracity, cupidity, pruriency, urge, lust, passion, appetency, itch, concupiscence, libido, ardor, fervor, relish.

THIRSTY, adj. 1. Craving drink, suffering from thirst, athirst, dipsetic, thirstful, dry, droughty, parched, without moisture, arid, desiccated, anhydrous, dehydrated.

2. Eagerly desirous, craving, longing, hankering, ravening, sharp-set, voracious, covetous, insatiate, insatiable, unsated, unsatisfied, appetitive, burning.

THISTLE, n. 1. Prickly plant, bramble, brier, Canada thistle, prickle, nettle, thorn.

2. Thistledown, pappus from the ripe flower head of a thistle, gossamer, down, cobweb, flue.

THITHER, adv. To that place, thitherward, thitherwards, toward that place, there, yon, yonder, towards, on the road to, hither, straight as an arrow, in a straight line to, point-blank, as the crow flies, full tilt at.

THONG, n. Narrow strip of hide, leathern strip, string of hide, latchet, lace, string, whip, lash, scourge, strap, cowhide, knout.

THORAX, n. 1. Trunk of the body, chest, thoracic cavity, breast, torso.

2. Breastplate, cuirass, corselet, aegis, hauberk, plastron, mail, brigandine, lorica.

THORN, n. 1. Sharp excrescence on a plant, sharp-pointed aborted branch, spine, prickle, brier, spike, spiculum, point, prick, spur, barb, bramble, nettle.

2. Annoyance, bane, nuisance, curse. plague, torment, evil, infliction, scourge, care, fang, sting, woe, harm, hurt, injury, bitter pill, gall and wormwood, vexation, trial, affliction, trouble, wound, sore subject.

THORNY, *adj.* 1. Spinose, prickly, spiny, spinous, briery, toothed, barbed, spurred, sharp, acuminated, pointed, tapering, spiked, spiky, thistly, bristling, pricking.

2. Annoying, trying, harassing, vexatious, painful, troublesome, difficult, dangerous, perplexing, rugged, irksome, formidable, plaguy, embarrassing, critical, ticklish, baneful, harmful, hurtful, pernicious, dire, injurious.

THOROUGH, *adj.* 1. Carried out through the whole, fully executed, complete, perfect, total, entire, out-and-out, finished, sweeping, exhaustive, all-inclusive, all-embracing, absolute, arrant, extreme, radical, unmitigated, unqualified, thoroughgoing, leaving nothing undone, drastic, full, plenary, utter, downright, top-to-bottom, consummate, regular *(coll.),* intact, unabridged, sheer, definitive, mature, determinate, downright, workmanlike.

2. Constant, consistent, homogeneous, uniform, of a piece, symmetrical, correspondent, equable, correct, accurate, reliable, trustworthy, ingrained,– uncompromising.

THOROUGHBRED, *adj.* 1. Of full blood, of pure breed, full-blooded, pedigreed, blooded, of unmixed stock.

2. Fashionable, polished, refined, courtly, *distingué (Fr.),* patrician, aristocratic, silk-stocking, genteel, *dégagé (Fr.),* poised, decorous, well-bred, gentlemanly, urbane, suave, well-mannered, cultured, cultivated, chivalrous, gallant, elegant, graceful.

3. Thoroughly trained, accomplished, skilled, instructed, practiced, finished, well-versed, proficient, adept, *au fait (Fr.),* well-educated, able, qualified, good at, master of, at home in, conversant with, crack, masterly, a good hand at, expert.

THOROUGHFARE, *n.* Main road, passage free from obstruction, street open at both ends, highway, boulevard, roadway, King's highway, turnpike, parkway, speedway, pike, avenue.

THORP, *n.* Small town, hamlet, village, dorp, kraal, ham, burgh, borough, wick, settlement, community, rancho *(Sp. Amer.),* pueblo.

THOUGH, *conj.* 1. Granting that, although, even if, admitting, in spite of the fact that, notwithstanding that, despite that, allowing that, for all that, albeit.

2. Yet, however, for all that, nevertheless, still, in the face of, in the teeth of, in defiance, *quand même (Fr.), per contra (Lat.).*

THOUGHT, *n.* 1. Mental exercitation, intellectual action, cogitation, rumination, cerebration, mentation, brainwork, ratiocination, intellection, lucubration, meditation, reflection, excogitation, speculation, deliberation, consideration, ponderment, contemplation, engrossment, thinking, musing, absorption, reverie, brown study, thoughtfulness, study, train of thought, application, association of ideas, stream of consciousness, abstraction, self-communing, depth of thought, self-consultation, perception, understanding, consciousness.

2. Concern, solicitude, anxiety, anxiousness, heed, care, worry, reck, attention, provision, re-

gard, caution, circumspection, wariness, vigilance, watchfulness, apprehension.

3. Idea, opinion, belief, view, conception, imagination, notion, fancy, concept, credo, creed, tenet, dogma, doctrine, conclusion, judgment, supposition, surmise, sentiment, conceit.

4. Intent, intention, expectation, purpose, design, aim, object, anticipation, end, objective, plan, scheme, resolution, resolve.

5. Retrospection, review, reconsideration, introversion, reëxamination, introspection, afterthought, recollection, reminiscence, remembrance, memory.

THOUGHTFUL, *adj.* 1. Given to thought, lost in thought, meditative, reflective, contemplative, speculative, absorbed, pensive, deliberative, engrossed, musing, introspective, cogitative, ruminative, ratiocinative, cerebrative, intellectual, sagacious, philosophical, judicious, wistful, studious, metaphysical, abstract, rapt, intent, regardful, mindful, careful, heedful, conscientious, watchful, attentive, circumspect, discreet, wary, prudent, provident, brainy, canny, wise, cunning, keen, far-sighted, clear-headed, discerning, shrewd, preoccupied.

2. Considerate, kindly, friendly, kind-hearted, kind, neighborly, amicable, anxious, concerned, solicitous, loving, charitable, altruistic, philanthropic.

THOUGHTLESS, *adj.* Not taking thought, unthinking, imprudent, improvident, indiscreet, scatterbrained, rattleheaded, rash, unreflecting, precipitate, headlong, inadvertent, remiss, reckless, flighty, harebrained, unmindful, unreflective, unobservant, negligent, careless, heedless, neglectful, regardless, inattentive, unwatchful, ill-advised, light-headed, inconsiderate, unreasoning, unintellectual, woolgathering, abstracted, distracted, absent-minded, distrait, unintelligent, stupid, insensate, dull, vacuous, vacant, blank, irrational, incogitant, musing, engrossed, rapt, preoccupied, far-away, dreamy, dazed, in the clouds, in a reverie, in a brown study, irresponsible, foolhardy, wild-eyed, blind.

THOUGHTLESSNESS, *n.* Inattention, absence of mind, absent-mindedness, lack of consideration, oversight, inadvertence, neglect, negligence, carelessness, heedlessness, rashness, temerity, unthinkingness, vacuousness, blankness, giddiness, light-headedness, precipitation, precipitancy, unconcern, disregard, want of thought, inconsideration, inconsiderateness, abstraction, engrossment, absorption, detachment, preoccupation, woolgathering, daydreaming, distraction, remissness, imprudence, improvidence, recklessness.

THOUSAND, *n.* Ten times one hundred, ten hundred, milliad, chiliad, millenary, millennium, myriad, multitude, great number.

THRALL, *n.* One who is in bondage, bondman, serf, slave, vassal, peon, servitor, helot, bondslave, creature, puppet, *âme damnée (Fr.),* peasant, ryot.

THRALLDOM, *n.* Servitude, slavery, enthrallment, thrall, serfdom, bondage, subjection, subjugation, vassalage, peonage, dependence, feudalism, villenage, oppression, yoke, submission, domination, tyranny, autocracy, despotism, brute force, iron hand, coercion.

THRASH, *v.* 1. Whip, beat, lash, flagellate, trounce, maul, drub, punish, pommel, flog, thwack, bruise, wallop, comb, strap, baste, lambaste, castigate, belt, bang, curry, whale, smite, strike, spank, cuff, bethwack, wham, buffet, thump, lace, belabor, cowhide, trim, scourge, horsewhip, cane, birch, switch, sandbag, beat black and blue, strafe, chastise, chasten.

2. Defeat, conquer, vanquish, overcome, overwhelm, overthrow, master, overpower, worst, rout, lick, beat hollow, do for, settle, trample, reduce, crush, subjugate.

THRASONICAL, *adj.* Boastful, braggart, bragging, vainglorious, pretentious, swashbuckling, swaggering, ostentatious, vaporing, highfaluting, pompous, bombastic, gasconading, strutting, magniloquent, grandiloquent, altiloquent, high-flown, toplofty, cockahoop, turgid, tumid, inflated, swollen, puffed up, grandiose, windy, self-praising, jingoistic, spread-eagle, chauvinistic, exultant.

THREAD, *n.* 1. Fine cord of spun-out fibrous material, thin string of several filaments twisted together, fiber, filament, yarn, staple, twist, strand, twine, pile, flax, cotton, linen, lisle, wool, silk, rayon, nylon, packthread.

2. Course, drift, tenor, motif, theme, subject, matter.

THREAD, *v.* 1. Pass through, string, draw out, twist, braid, wind, twine, reeve, enfilade.

2. Permeate, pervade, penetrate, go through, pass over, ford, force a passage, cut one's way through, traverse.

THREADBARE, *adj.* 1. Worn to a thread, napless, pileworn, frayed, worn-out, the worse for wear, shabby, worn to a rag, weather-beaten, ragged, faded, seedy, tacky.

2. Trite, stereotyped, cliché, bromidic, hackneyed, commonplace, dull, dry, uninteresting, tedious, monotonous, prosy, prosaic, humdrum, jejune, wonted, everyday, conventional, well-known, overfamiliar, vernacular, banal, stock, proverbial.

3. Meager, scanty, poor, paltry, sorry, wretched, scrubby, miserable, niggardly, scurvy, beggarly, niggling, piddling, trivial, trifling.

THREAD-SHAPED, *adj.* Threadlike, filamentous, filiform, filamentar, filar, fibrillose, fibrous, stringy, thready, hairlike.

THREAT, *n.* Indication of probable evil to come, portent, commination, omen, presage, foreboding, sign, auspice, augury, prognostic, warning, menace, gathering clouds, thunder, fulmination, thunderbolt, intimidation, defiance, denunciation, abuse, terrorism, alarm, scare, fright, caution, caveat, admonition, premonishment, premonition, handwriting on the wall, bird of ill omen, storm brewing, danger, peril, jeopardy, hazard, risk, vulnerability, challenge, dare, dismay, consternation, funk, panic, cold feet, stampede, curse, malediction, malison, imprecation, execration.

THREATEN, *v.* 1. Menace, intimidate, cow, overawe, frighten, alarm, denounce, fulminate, thunder, look daggers, comminate, shake the fist, bluster, bullyrag, terrorize, bulldoze, growl, snarl, mutter, look black, dare, challenge, beard, throw down the gauntlet, imprecate, curse, execrate, vituperate, anathematize, excommunicate, proscribe, deter, abash, daunt, browbeat, badger, hector, affright, appall, unman, startle, stampede, panic, scare.

2. Give an ominous indication of, forebode, portend, foreshadow, presage, prognosticate, augur, warn, indicate, bode, forewarn, admonish, caution, put on one's guard, forecast, foretoken, shadow forth, lower.

3. Be near at hand, impend, be imminent, overhang, stare one in the face, hang over, be in store, beetle, hover over, loom, come on, approach.

THREATENING, *adj.* Menacing, minacious, minatory, comminatory, cautionary, monitory, premonitory, comminative, admonitory, foreboding, ill-omened, ominous, unpropitious, unpromising, inauspicious, dark, forbidding, black, lowering, baneful, sinister, baleful, fulminating, denunciatory, defiant, direful, abusive, ill-boding, grim, dire, dangerous, perilous, alarming, symptomatic, clouded over, thundery, overhanging, imminent, impending, oncoming, drawing near, approaching, destined, in store, at hand, instant, near, brewing, in the wind, looming, precarious, critical, ticklish, trembling in the balance, insecure, tottering, unstable, shaky, tumble-down, crumbling, ramshackle, nodding to its fall, dismal, frowning, sullen, nigrescent, somber, lurid, murky, overcast.

THREE, *n.* Trio, triplet, ternary, ternion, trey, tierce, triangle, delta, cube, trigon, triskelion, trinity, trident, trireme, tripod, triumvirate, trilemma, trigraph, triad.

THREE, *adj.* 1. Triform, threefold, tripartite, triple, tertiary, triune, trinomial, treble, three-ply, ternary, triadic, triplicate.

2. Three-cornered, triquetrous, triangular, trigonous, trigonal, triquetral, cuboid, deltoid, three-sided, trilateral.

THREESCORE, *adj.* Three times twenty, thrice twenty, sixty.

THRENODIC, *adj.* Mournful, lamenting, sorrowful, querulous, tearful, lachrymose, plaintive, crying, unhappy, querimonious, epicedial, threnetic, elegiac, languishing, keening, dirgelike, heart-stricken, heartsick, woebegone, cheerless, broken-hearted, heartbroken.

THRENODY, *n.* Song of lamentation, dirge, requiem, elegy, funeral song, lament, lamentation, coronach, deathsong, nenia, keen, epicedium, threne, jeremiad, ululation, monody.

THRESH, *v.* 1. Beat with a flail, separate the seeds from, winnow.

2. Thrash, flog, beat, drub, trounce, pommel, maul, manhandle, thwack, wallop, bruise, lash, flagellate, whip, horsewhip, birch, cane, larrup, scourge, switch, bastinado, fustigate, sandbag, lick, comb, strap, bang, trim, leather, belabor, baste, swinge, spank, thump, smite.

THRESHOLD, *n.* 1. Doorsill, sill, limen, groundsel, entrance, door, gate, vestibule, porch, portal, portico, entry, wicket, postern, gateway, lobby.

2. Outset, beginning, start, commencement, inception, opening, dawn, incipience, debut, exordium, prelude, preamble, prologue, preface, overture, foreword, onset, outbreak, verge, edge, brink.

THRICE, *adv.* 1. Three times repeated, on three occasions, triply, threefold, trebly.

2. Very, extremely, greatly, abundantly, profusely, without stint, to one's heart's content, *ad libitum (Lat.)*, amply, gratifyingly, fully, exuberantly, copiously, plenteously, bountifully, lavishly.

THRIFT, *n.* 1. Economy, thriftiness, good husbandry, frugality, savingness, economical management, careful administration, Hooverism, economization, prudence, sparingness, providence, retrenchment, care, prevention of waste, parsimony, close-fistedness, parsimoniousness, stint, niggardliness, cheeseparing, good housewifery.

2. Acquisition, gain, moneymaking, money-grubbing, lucre, pelf, emolument, earnings, profit, winnings, cleanup, net profit, proceeds, welfare, prosperity, well-being, affluence, success, roaring trade.

3. Vigor, growth, flowerage, herbage, vegetation, vegetable growth, plant life.

THRIFTLESS, *adj.* Unthrifty, wasteful, extravagant, lavish, prodigal, profuse, overliberal, too free, imprudent, improvident, unfrugal, shiftless, heedless, careless, inefficient, negligent, lax, inconsiderate, thoughtless, remiss, slack, incautious, impulsive, impetuous, rash, capricious, dissipated, squandering, penny-wise and pound-foolish.

THRIFTY, *adj.* 1. Frugal, parsimonious, sparing, prudent, provident, saving, economical, careful, chary, penurious, stingy, penny-wise, close-fisted, tight-fisted, economizing.

2. Prosperous, thriving, well-off, set-up, fortunate, profitable, gainful, advantageous, remunerative, paying.

3. Growing vigorously, flourishing, vigorous, vegetative, blooming, exuberant, luxuriant, prolific, lush, rank, rife.

THRILL, *v.* 1. Affect with a sudden wave of keen emotion, inspire, stir, electrify, galvanize, penetrate, rouse, move, arouse, agitate, touch, pierce, strike, excite, stimulate, sensitize, tickle, titillate, finger, feel, paw, lick, kiss, rub, knead, massage, stroke, palpate, manipulate, impress, imbue, awaken, call forth, kindle, fire, rivet the attention, possess, sharpen, quicken, spur, urge, incite, instigate, foment, fan, magnetize, impassion, set astir, work up, go through one, intoxicate, overpower, enrapture, send *(sl.)*.

2. Be excited, tingle, throb, quiver, palpitate, flutter, tremble, twitter, flush, glow, pant, heave, soften, melt, go pitapat, itch, prickle, be gooseflesh, vibrate, get a kick out of.

THRILL, *n.* Tingling sensation passing through the body, excitement, titillation, pleasurable feeling, kick *(coll.)*, tremor, enravishment, electrification, galvanization, magnetism, agitation, vibration, quivering, goose flesh, flutter, twitter, inspiration, response, tingle, shock, flurry, throb, palpitation, pulsation, panting, excitation, stimulation, piquancy, perturbation, intoxication, entrancement, emotional appeal, sensationalism, contact, palpation.

THRILLING, *adj.* Pleasing, stirring, pleasurable, pleasant, agreeable, delicious, voluptuous, seductive, sensual, engaging, prepossessing, fascinating, enticing, alluring, ravishing, captivating, inviting, enchanting, absorbing, exquisite, delightful, ecstatic, enrapturing, rapturous, beatific, blissful, transporting, exciting, sensational, overpowering, piquant, provocative, tantalizing, teasing, tickling, itching, titillating, acute, sharp, deep-felt, electric, electrifying, galvanic, magnetic, penetrating, pervading, absorbing, feverish, breathless, overmastering, fervent, passionate, ardent, glowing, burning, lively, warm, emotional, sensuous, tingling, itchy, prickly.

THRIVE, *v.* 1. Grow, wax, develop vigorously, bloom, flower, bear fruit, increase, batten, boom, mushroom, improve, make improvement, flourish, advance, make headway, luxuriate, sprout, germinate, vegetate, shoot up, blossom, bud, blow, fatten.

2. Prosper, grow rich, become wealthy, succeed, be successful, get ahead, be fortunate, turn out well, rise in the world, get on, feather one's nest, have a run of luck, make one's pile, swim with the tide, drive a roaring trade, get along swimmingly, sail before the wind, run smoothly, light on one's feet, bear a charmed life, bask in the sun, live in clover, be well-off.

THRIVING, *adj.* 1. Flourishing, vigorous, growing, blooming, blossoming, luxuriant, rank, lush, prolific, flowering, waxing, battening, mushrooming, germinative, exuberant.

2. Prosperous, successful, well-to-do, well-off, rich, wealthy, fortunate, halcyon, palmy, at one's ease, in clover, on Easy Street, propitious, auspicious, favorable, promising, bright, fair, rosy, providential, buoyant, in a fair way, set-up, in full feather, in luck, lucky.

THROAT, *n.* Pharynx, gullet, fauces, larynx, trachea, windpipe, esophagus, maw, gorge, jugular region, jugulum, weasand *(archaic)*, mouth, orifice, sucker, nozzle, placket, bronchus, bronchia, spiracle.

THROB, *v.* Palpitate, vibrate, beat, pulsate, pitapat, heave, pant, quiver, flutter, tremble, twitter, shake, be agitated, convulse, jerk, hitch, vellicate, twitch, oscillate, quaver, jactitate, ripple.

THROB, *n.* Palpitation, beat, throbbing, pulsation, beating, vibration, agitation, oscillation, vellication, throe, spasm, convulsion, paroxysm, twitching, jerk, quaver, quiver, jactitation, flutter, twitter, tremor, ripple, heave, panting.

THROE, *n.* 1. Violent spasm of pain in childbirth, childbirth, parturition, delivery, confinement, travail, accouchement, labor, geniture, obstetrics.

2. Paroxysm of extreme physical pain, dolor, cramp, spasm, convulsion, agony, anguish, shooting pain, torture, torment, excruciation, ache, shooting, pang, fit, agitation, twinge, stab, ordeal, qualm, revulsion.

3. Sharp attack of emotion, raptus, seizure, passion, visitation, hysterics, orgasm, immoderate excitement, outburst, discharge, explosion, torrent, storm, squall, ferment, turmoil, transport, fever of excitement, tumult, frenzy.

THRONE, *n.* 1. Royal seat, chair of state, ceremonial dais, *musnud (Oriental), guddee (India),* divan, woolsack.

2. Symbol of sovereign office, crown, diadem, coronet, pall, orb, purple, ermine, robes of state, seal, signet, uraeus, miter, tiara, crook, crozier, staff, caduceus, staff of office, lituus, truncheon, wand, mace, fasces, rod of empire, baton, scepter, insignia, regalia.

3. Sovereign power, sovereignty, sway, rule, dominion, regality, royalty, reign, regnancy.

THRONG, *n.* Great number, crowd, pack, horde, jam, multitude, assemblage, convocation, congregation, cluster, press, collection, host, army, mob, aggregation, muster, concourse, conflux, agglomeration, conglomeration, mass, flock, herd, swarm, gathering, group, gang, band, crew, posse, company, body, myriad, shoal, clan, cloud, ingathering, levy, concentration, meet, mobilization, forgathering, convergence, congress, flood, deluge, rush, crush, rabble, tribe, knot, covey, troupe, corps, force, drove, bevy, bunch, galaxy, array, congestion.

THRONG, *v.* Go in large numbers, assemble, flock, congregate, press, crowd, swarm, collect, gather, meet, mobilize, muster, jam, infest, jostle, cluster, surge, rush, stream, herd, mass, huddle, associate, concentrate, forgather, resort, repair, cram, bunch, group, converge, focalize, pour in, rally, snowball, pack, mill.

THROTTLE, *v.* 1. Stop the breath of, compress the throat, strangle, choke, suffocate, garrote, stifle, asphyxiate, smother.

2. Check, silence, gag, mute, close, plug, occlude, obstruct, stop, seal, shut.

THROUGH, *prep.* 1. In at one end and out at the other, from one end of to the other, over the whole surface of, between the sides of, within.

2. By the agency of, by means of, by the aid of, by the instrumentality of, by reason of, because of, in consequence of, *per* (*Lat.*), by way of, by dint of, for, by virtue of.

3. Among, in the midst of, between, amid, amidst, amongst.

4. Having reached the end of, having finished successfully, from beginning to end, to the end, throughout.

5. During, until, pending, for the period of, over.

THROUGH, *adv.* 1. In at one surface and out at the other, from one side to the other, from beginning to end, from A to Z, from alpha to omega, all the way, along the whole distance.

2. To a favorable conclusion, successfully, favorably, swimmingly, with flying colors.

THROUGHOUT, *prep.* Completely through, to every part of, in all directions, *quaquaversum* (*Lat.*), through every part of, quite through, from one extremity to the other of, everywhere in, over.

THROUGHOUT, *adv.* From beginning to end, from A to Z, from alpha to omega, from first to last, from end to end, from top to toe, from head to foot, cap-a-pie, everywhere, *ubique* (*Lat.*), in every part, at every point, extensively, wherever, far and wide, all over, right and left, in every quarter, under the sun, from pole to pole, from Dan to Beersheba, on the face of the earth.

THROW, *v.* 1. Cast, fling, propel, sling, toss, hurl, let fly, jaculate, chuck, pitch, launch, heave, dart, pelt, lance, emit, jettison, flounce, impel, pitchfork, send, project, drop, shy, retroject, jerk, deliver, hurtle, plunge, precipitate, dash, put, tilt, bolt.

2. Bring to the ground, floor, fell, prostrate, throw down, overturn, lay flat, upset, vanquish, defeat, discomfit, overthrow, overcome, overpower, rout, drub, beat hollow, worst, subjugate, reduce, make bite the dust, trample under foot, roll in the dust.

THROW, *n.* 1. Propulsion, projection, impulsion, cast, fling, pitch, toss, chuck, heave, lob, delivery, push, jaculation, ejaculation, ejection, shot, shy, discharge, shove, thrust, sling, hurl, dart, pelt, flounce, jerk, hurtle, precipitation, bolt, tilt.

2. Venture, chance, fortune, hazard, haphazard, toss up, heads or tails, flutter, stake, flier, gamble, random shot, pitch and toss, chuck farthing, cuptossing, wager, risk, bet.

3. Scarf, shawl, stole, boa, mantle, pelisse, mantlet, mantua, yashmak, muffler, comforter, mantilla, chlamys, burnous, pall, cloak, chasuble, alb, cope, scapulary, dalmatic, cassock, surplice, hood, cowl, wrap.

4. Light blanket, afghan, cover, counterpane, coverlet, eiderdown, quilt.

THROW OFF, *v.* 1. Eject, expel, drive away, drive off, cast off, put off, lay aside, abandon,

oust, evict, dislodge, deport, relegate, banish, ostracize, show the door to, dismiss, strike off the roll, turn out, bundle out, sack, fire, boycott, discard, reject, renounce, repudiate, cut, send to Coventry, send packing, eliminate.

2. Misdirect, mislead, deceive, misrepresent, misinform, misguide, put on a false scent, draw a red herring across the trail, bewilder, mystify, flummox (*sl.*), confuse, confound, lead astray, beguile, delude, falsify, misstate, garble.

THROW UP, *v.* 1. Lay down, resign, abdicate, demit, give up, renounce, abjure, disclaim, forgo, relinquish, abandon, retract, desert, vacate, retire.

2. Disgorge, vomit, spew, retch, puke, eructate, belch out, keck, bring up, eruct, egest, ejaculate, excrete, void, emit, eject.

THRUM, *v.* Pluck the strings, play upon, strum, drum, twang, finger, thumb, tap idly with the fingers.

THRUST, *v.* 1. Push forcibly, drive with force, impel, propel, shove, poke, plunge, stick, jab, jam, clap, ram, dig, force, start, prod, butt, jog, jolt, elbow, shoulder, set going, boost, urge forward, batter, press.

2. Attack, lunge, pass, cut, stab, pierce, punch, carte and tierce (*Fencing*), bayonet, deal a blow at, pounce upon, bear down upon, close with, tilt at, assault, assail, set upon, charge, rush.

THRUST, *n.* 1. Forcible drive, propulsion, shove, push, impulsion, impetus, momentum, pressure, boost, boom, kick, send-off, start, impulse, jolt, jog, brunt, impact, occursion.

2. Blow, poke, dig, jab, lunge, plunge, stab, pass, tilt, riposte, punch, passado, dint, thump, swipe, pelt, kick, calcitration, ruade, arietation, knock, stroke, rap, tap, smack, slap, dab, pat, fillip, bang, slam, whack, clout, hit, thwack, cuff, dowse, swap, bump, clip, flap, bat, swat, buffet.

3. Assault, attack, onset, raid, charge, foray, encounter, onslaught, aggression, incursion, *coup de main* (*Fr.*), irruption, sortie, sally, outbreak.

THUD, *n.* Dull sound, thump, clump, knock, blow, stroke, nonresonance, snap, rap, crepitation, clap, smack, report.

THUG, *n.* 1. Cutthroat, murderer, assassin, garroter, mugger, bravo, slayer, butcher, Cain.

2. Professional robber, bandit, ruffian, footpad, highwayman, brigand, depredator, marauder, spoiler, pillager, bushranger, falcon, freebooter, hijacker, dacoit, racketeer, gunman, mobster, gangster, pickpocket, cutpurse, crook, blackleg, housebreaker, burglar, cracksman, safecracker, cat man, thief.

THUMB, *n.* Short thick inner digit of the human hand, pollex, *pouce* (*Fr.*).

THUMP, *v.* 1. Strike, knock, whack, thwack, beat, hit, pound, punch, belabor, buffet, batter, thrash, pommel, bounce, drub, bang, lambaste, slap, hammer, paste, slam, dash, bat, clip, plug, smash, wham, ram, cudgel, jab, cuff, spank, trounce, lace, trim, cowhide, horsewhip, flog, scourge, lash, cane, birch, switch, lay about one, sandbag, bash, rap, swat, take a poke at.

2. Make a dull sound, clump, knock, tap, click, snap, crack, slam, pop, clap, bang, plump, backfire.

THUMP, *n.* 1. Punch, swipe, dint, blow, knock, stroke, rap, tap, dab, pat, slam, smack, fillip, slap, bang, thwack, whack, hit, cuff, clout, buffet, dowse, swap, squash, jab, clip, bat, pommel, bastinado, flagellation, castigation, thrust, push, poke, swat.

2. Dull sound, thud, nonresonance, rap, snap, crepitation, report, clap, clump, plump.

THUMPING, *adj.* (*Coll.*) Big, fat, stout, overgrown, large, hulking, corpulent, plump, obese, upholstered, bouncing, strapping, lusty, portly, brawny, burly, fleshy, stalwart, chopping, chubby, lumpish, lubberly, spanking, unwieldy, whopping, whacking, thundering, enormous, huge, mighty, immense, amplitudinous, stupendous, gigantic, colossal, elephantine, monstrous, Gargantuan, Cyclopean, Titanic, Brobdingnagian, massive, towering, bulky.

THUNDER, *v.* 1. Make a loud resounding noise, resound, peal, roll, rumble, boom, roar, detonate, crack, crash, reverberate, explode, burst.

2. Utter threateningly, fulminate, denounce, menace, snarl, growl, bark, mutter, threaten, intimidate, bluster, curse, imprecate, swear at, damn, execrate, anathematize, proscribe, excommunicate.

THUNDER, *n.* Reverberating report of a discharge of electricity in the atmosphere, loud noise, rumbling, detonation, roar, boom, outburst, discharge, explosion, blast, crash, crack, roll.

THUNDERBOLT, *n.* 1. Thunderclap, thunderstroke, fulguration, sudden burst.

2. The unexpected, unforeseen contingency, surprise, shock, blow, bolt out of the blue, eye opener.

3. Denunciation, threat, fulmination, menace, intimidation, curse, imprecation, execration, anathema, proscription, excommunication.

THUNDERSTORM, *n.* Rainstorm accompanied by thunder and lightning, squall, tempest, thundershower, downpour, deluge, cloudburst.

THUNDERSTRUCK, *adj.* Overcome with consternation, astonished, confounded, astounded, flabbergasted, dumfounded, amazed, aghast, flummoxed (*sl.*), bewildered, confused, surprised, all agog, agape, breathless, open-mouthed, awestruck, moonstruck, spellbound, rapt, struck all of a heap.

THURIBLE, *n.* Portable swinging incense pot, censer, frankincense receptacle.

THUS, *adv.* 1. In the way just indicated, this way, in this wise, in such wise, in this manner, in the following manner, as follows, *sic* (*Lat.*), so, by this means, so far, to this degree.

2. Consequently, accordingly, in accordance with this, for this reason, therefore, this being the case, wherefore, hence, *ergo* (*Lat.*), all the more, *a fortiori* (*Lat.*).

THWACK, *v.* Beat vigorously, belabor, thrash, whack, lambaste, pommel, thump, bang, rap, strike, paste (*sl.*), slam, knock, bash, hit, slap, bat, punch, batter, swap, dab, pat, tap, flap, baste, dowse, pelt, buffet, poke at, butt, whip, punish, deal a blow to, smite, cuff, smack, swinge, spank, lay on, leather, drub, trounce, lace, trim, larrup, wallop, whop, lick, flog, cane, birch, scourge, horsewhip, flagellate, bastinado, switch, towel, fustigate, pitch into, sandbag.

THWACK, *n.* Sharp blow, whack, thump, rap, pat, tap, stroke, knock, dab, dint, slap, smack, fillip, bang, slam, clout, hit, cuff, swap, dowse, squash, punch, jab, swipe, jolt, thrust, push, shove, pile driver, bat, box on the ear, stick law, bastinado, estrapade, strappado, fustigation, flagellation, beating, stripe, buffet, pommel.

THWART, *v.* Frustrate, foil, balk, prevent from accomplishing a purpose, cross, contravene, counteract, obstruct, hinder, oppugn, oppose, baffle, disconcert, defeat, bar, retard, impede, outmaneuver, check, discommode, nip, bring to naught, hamper, withstand, blight, scotch, stymie, block, checkmate, circumvent, stop, contradict, undermine, override, contend against, victimize, delay, detain, check, restrict, restrain, debar, inhibit, preclude, obviate, stay, intercept, interrupt, interpose, interfere, stave off, avert, ward off, turn aside, forestall, discompose, embarrass, perplex, corner, nonplus, tree (*coll.*), clip the wings of, mar, spoil, damp, cripple, dishearten, cut the ground from under one, take the wind out of one's sails, take down a peg, pull off one's high horse, trouble, disturb, mortify, plague, badger, importune, persecute, spike the guns, act as a drag, cope with, set oneself against.

TIARA, *n.* Jeweled ornamental coronet, diadem, triple-crown (*of the Pope*), mitre.

TIC, *n.* Sudden muscular contraction in the face, vellication, twitching, twitch, spasm, tic douloureux (*Pathol.*).

TICK, *v.* 1. Click, beat, ticktock, clack, clatter, rattle, tap, rap.

2. Oscillate, librate, vibrate, undulate, alternate, rock, wave, swing, pulsate, waggle, wobble, dangle, swag, fluctuate, bob.

3. Tick off, record, put upon record, chronicle, calendar, set down, note, mark down, enter, book, list, register, docket.

TICK, *n.* 1. Click, ticktock, dickery-dickery-dock, tap, beat, oscillation, libration, motion of a pendulum, nutation, throb, pulse.

2. Mark, check, stroke, line, dash, stripe, score, streak, scratch, nick, notch, blaze, point, dot.

3. Trust, credit, tally, score, account, charge, charge account.

4. Moment, instant, jiffy, trice, twinkling, minute, second, breath, flash, crack, *coup* (*Fr.*).

TICKET, *n.* 1. Certificate, printed slip of paper, cardboard (*coll.*), Annie Oakley (*sl.*), pass, billet, voucher, coupon, label, tag, card, badge, notice, check, tally, stub, tessera, stamp, *carte de visite* (*Fr.*), *laissez-passer* (*Fr.*), credentials.

2. List of political candidates, slate, roster, plank, platform, ballot.

TICKLE, *v.* 1. Stroke lightly with the fingers, excite a tingling sensation in, touch, titillate, palpate, finger, feel, paw, thumb, grope, grabble, rub the fingers over, twiddle, knead, massage, manipulate, handle, palm, kiss, lick, tongue, graze, brush.

2. Please, amuse, delight, enliven, divert, gladden, make glad, gratify, rejoice, regale, give joy to, do one's heart good, take one's fancy, charm, pleasure, captivate, fascinate, enrapture, enchant, enthrall, transport, bewitch, ravish, entrance, laetificate, cheer, interest, thrill, stimulate, treat, refresh.

TICKLING, *n.* Titillation, palpation, stroking, caressing, fingering, feeling, kneading, twiddling, massage, manipulation.

TICKLISH, *adj.* 1. Sensitive to tickling, easily tickled, itchy, tickly, prickly, tingling, prurient.

2. Requiring careful action, critical, difficult, delicate, touchy, troublesome, arduous, tough, hard, awkward, gauche, thorny, rugged, knotty, intricate, complicated, impracticable, embarrassing, perplexing.

3. Uncertain, unstable, tottering, unsteady, unreliable, fallible, questionable, debatable, disput-

able, untrustworthy, dubious, doubtful, indecisive, ambiguous.

4. Dangerous, hazardous, perilous, parlous, risky, precarious, slippery, aleatory, at stake, hanging by a thread, between Scylla and Charybdis, between two fires, between the devil and the deep blue sea.

TIDBIT, *n.* Delicate morsel, choice morsel, delicious mouthful, *bonne-bouche (Fr.)*, nice bit, titbit, delicacy, dainty, nonpareil, *crème de la crème (Fr.)*.

TIDE, *n.* 1. Periodic rise and fall of the sea, ebb tide, flow tide, neap tide, flood tide, riptide, undertow, spring tide, high tide, full tide, reflux, refluence.

2. Current, flow, stream, inflow, outflow, flood, course, flux, race, torrent, sluice.

3. Tendency of events, movement, concurrence of influences, direction of happenings, state of affairs, order of the day, march of time, ups and downs of life, chapter of accidents.

4. Period of time, season, occasion, hour, anniversary, festival.

TIDINESS, *n.* Neatness, orderliness, trimness, regularity, apple-pie order, methodicalness, systematicalness, systematism, trigness, spruceness, uniformity, symmetry, immaculateness, spotlessness, immaculacy, cleanness, cleanliness.

TIDINGS, *n., pl.* News of special import, information, message, word, intelligence, report, rumor, bruit, dispatch, advice, hearsay, *oui-dire (Fr.)*, talk, newsmongery, gossip, tittle-tattle, scandal, canard, grapevine, scuttlebutt *(sl.)*, communication, broadcast, bulletin, flash, letter, wire, telegram, cable, radio, telephone call, hint, insinuation, innuendo, whisper, inkling, cue, suggestion, word to the wise, *verbum sapienti (Lat.)*, pointer, tip, intimation, representation, monition, announcement, communiqué, statement, revelation, utterance, exposé, confession, avowal, declaration, acknowledgment, admission.

TIDY, *adj.* 1. Neat, trig, orderly, shipshape, trim, spruce, methodical, systematic, well-ordered, presentable, regular, symmetrical, in apple-pie order, *en règle (Fr.)*, uniform, businesslike, well-regulated, disciplined, kempt, well-groomed, *soigné (Fr.)*, clean-cut, punctilious, meticulous, dapper, nice, exact, particular, precise, careful, prim, scrupulous, strict, ideal, faultless, impeccable, immaculate, intact, spotless.

2. Considerable, sizable, large, ample, sufficient, substantial, bulky, voluminous, comprehensive, capacious, immense, huge, enormous.

TIDY, *v.* 1. Arrange, dispose, order, systematize, methodize, set in order, array, marshal, group, rank, size, range, align, line up, sort, assort, sift, class, classify, list, file, catalogue, tabulate, alphabetize, index, grade, graduate, regulate, organize, coördinate.

2. Neaten, make neat, clean up, polish up, trim, spruce up, brush up.

TIE, *v.* 1. Draw together and knot, form by looping and interlacing, unite, join, bind, fasten, secure, connect, link, enlink, knit, yoke, lock, rope, engage, brace, moor, fix, attach, tether, make fast, trammel, manacle, fetter, shackle, confine, constrain, oblige, restrict, restrict, limit, hinder, hamper, pinion, tighten, clinch, strap, truss, lash, gird, interlock, entwine, interweave, interknit, plait, weave.

2. Marry, wed, hitch, couple, splice.

3. Make the same score as, equal in a contest, vie with, emulate, compete with, divide the honors, come out even, draw, match, keep pace with, run abreast, come up to, run neck-and-neck, equate, balance, parallel.

TIE, *n.* 1. Necktie, cravat, ascot, neckcloth, bowtie, neckerchief, stock, scarf, muffler.

2. Link, bond, connection, fastening, ligature, knot, vinculum, nexus, connective, copula, yoke, coupler, brace, hyphen, bracket, cord, string, funicle, twist, funiculus, rope, cable, line, hawser, catena, chain, lace, cordage, band, binder, fillet, strap, leash, thong, cincture, girth, girdle, cinch, surcingle, sash, belt, cummerbund, cestus, zone, zoster, noose, lariat, loop, lasso, hitch, slipknot, halter, beam, post, sleeper, splint, truss, rib, guy, shore, strut, stay, prop, rafter, girder, joist, timber, lintel, traverse, crossbeam.

3. Obligation, allegiance, duty, devoir, liability, responsibility, onus, fealty.

4. Kinship, relationship, liaison, consanguinity, blood, kindred, affinity, propinquity, affiliation.

5. Equal number, drawn game, dead heat, equality in points, neck-and-neck, parity.

TIER, *n.* Row, range, series, rank, bank, layer, line, file, string, chain, queue, catena, progression, sequence, succession, suite, slab, stage, escarpment, stratum, bed, course, zone, stratification, story.

TIFF, *n.* Petty quarrel, miff, pet, huff, spat, dispute, wrangle, altercation, imbroglio, disagreement, dissidence, disaccord, discord, difference, variance, dissension, misunderstanding, *brouillerie (Fr.)*, feud, breach, rippet, *tracasserie (Fr.)*, words, squabble, snip-snap, snit, brawl, broil, embranglement, embroilment, fracas, rumpus, scrimmage, squall, commotion, bone of contention, apple of discord, *casus belli (Lat.)*, cat-and-dog life, passion, rage, ire, choler, fume, angry mood, slight fit of anger, ill-humor, displeasure, resentment, umbrage, animosity, indignation, wrath, soreness, pique, dudgeon, spleen, bitterness, pucker, bile, dander, ferment, tantrums.

TIFFIN, *n.* Noon meal, lunch, luncheon, *déjeuner (Fr.)*, repast, collation, refection, spread, feed, tea, snack, refreshment.

TIGHT, *adj.* 1. Firmly held together, compact, firm, solid, indissoluble, inseparable, taut, close, constricted, confined, compacted, compressed.

2. Not easily moved, secure, firmly fixed in place, stable, immovable, fast, steadfast, constant.

3. Not open, impervious, impermeable, not leaky, airtight, watertight, impenetrable, impassable.

4. Close-fitting, not loose, form-fitting, skin-tight, snug.

5. *(Coll.)* Stingy, close-fisted, parsimonious, penurious, niggardly, miserly, illiberal, ungenerous, mean, close-handed, curmudgeonly, churlish, penny-wise, sparing, grudging, frugal.

6. *(Coll.)* Drunk, inebriated, intoxicated, temulent, in one's cups, tipsy, high, fuddled, befuddled, mellow, boozy, plastered, squiffy, sozzled, groggy, thick-tongued, pot-valiant, potulent, screwed, oiled, primed, sewed up, raddled, lushy, muddled, crapulous, maudlin, the worse for liquor, three sheets in the wind, under the table, sottish, bibulous, bibacious.

TIGHTEN, *v.* Make tight, straiten, take up the slack, tauten, draw, tense, make tense, brace, lace up, cramp, coarctate, narrow, contract, constringe, constrict, compress, condense, squeeze, purse up, pinch, strangle.

TIGHT-FISTED, *adj.* Stingy, penurious, niggardly, parsimonious, miserly, avaricious, mean, scrubby, shabby, penny-wise, frugal, near, strait-handed, grudging, chary, griping, ungenerous, illiberal, hidebound, churlish, mercenary, covetous, sordid, venal, extortionate, usurious, rapacious, greedy.

TIGHT-LIPPED, *adj.* Reluctant to speak, close-mouthed, taciturn, reticent, sparing of words, laconic, curt, reserved, inconversable, mum, silent, mute, secretive, uncommunicative, reserved, of few words.

TIGHTS, *n., pl.* Close-fitting pantaloons, trunk hose, breeches, opera stockings.

TIGHTWAD, *n.* Close-fisted person, stingy person, miser, churl, niggard, screw, skinflint, codger, crib, moneygrubber, scrimp, pinchfist, curmudgeon, lickpenny, harpy, Harpagon, usurer, extortioner.

TILL, *v.* Dress the ground, cultivate, labor upon land for the raising of crops, prepare for crops, plow, harrow, farm, hoe, sow, grow, garden, plant, manure, spade, dig, delve, rake, seed.

TILL, *prep.* Until, up to the time of, up to, (with a negative) before, as far as, to, down to.

TILL, *conj.* Up to the time when, until, whilst, as long as, while.

TILL, *n.* Money-drawer, coffer, cash register, cashbox, safe, strongbox, treasury, thesaurus, bursary, fisc, depository.

TILLABLE, *adj.* Cultivable, cultivatable, arable, plowable.

TILLAGE, *n.* Husbandry, cultivation of land, farming, agriculture, geoponics, agronomics, agronomy, gardening.

TILLER, *n.* 1. Husbandman, farmer, plowman, cultivator of land, plower, agriculturist, yeoman, agronomist, granger, gardener.
2. Rudder-bar, helm.
3. Shoot of a plant, sapling, sprout, sucker, branch.

TILT, *v.* 1. Slope, slant, incline, lean, tip, cant, dip, sheer, shelve, sink, decline, subside, settle, drop, fall.
2. Heel over, reel, careen, roll, lurch, sidle, sag, slouch, skid, toss, ride unsteadily, bob, plunge, pitch.
3. Tumble, sprawl, come a cropper, trip, founder, topple.
4. Come to blows, tussle, box, skirmish, fence, fight, battle, join issue, enter the lists, take up the gantlet, couch one's lance, contest, contend, oppose, spar, point for attack, thrust, rush at, charge, joust.

TILT, *n.* 1. Sloping position, slant, slope, inclination, acclivity, declivity, cant, incline, tip, dip, rake, diagonal, bias, list, curve, bend, rise, pitch, ascent, gradient, ramp, grade, inclined plane.
2. Trip, lurch, stumble, slip, tumble, debacle, comedown, downfall.
3. Encounter, joust, combat, practice of arms, contest, tournament, tourney, conflict, bout, skirmish, rencounter, collision, brush, scrimmage, melee, fracas, scuffle, tussle, broil, affray, thrust, lunge, pass.
4. Dispute, quarrel, tiff, altercation, strife, contention, litigation, feud, controversy, squabble, polemics, row, brawl, imbroglio, Donnybrook Fair.

5. Covering overhead, awning, canopy, tent, cover, baldachin, marquee.

TIMBER, *n.* 1. Wood for building, lumber, stumpage, raff, beam, squared stick, joist, piling, rafter, tiebeam, balk, crossbeam, truss, rib, scantling.
2. Timberland, woods, forests, wooded land, woodland, grove, coppice, copse, bosk, covert, spinney, plantation, canebrake, thicket, clump, bush.
3. Personal character, individual quality, stock, material, stuff, temperament, disposition, temper, grain, mettle, nature, spirit, cast, frame.

TIMBRE, *n.* *(Music)* Tone color, quality of sound, resonance, clang, *Klangfarbe (Ger.),* pitch, intonation, overtone.

TIME, *v.* Keep time, measure, regulate, adjust, note the rate of, record the duration of, adapt to the occasion, harmonize with, synchronize with.

TIME, *n.* 1. Indefinite continuous duration in which events succeed one another, chronology, method of reckoning, system of measuring, relative rapidity of movement, tempo.
2. Particular period, spell, season, tide, term, instar, space, stage, course, span, snap, sequence, while, date, moment, year, hour, glass of time, whirligig of time, occasion, instant, point, minute, second, day, week, fortnight, month, lifetime, generation, present life, existence.
3. Interval, interim, meanwhile, recess, interlude, pause, intermission, interruption, interregnum, respite, instance.
4. Era, age, epoch, cycle, eon, decade, chiliad, reign, dynasty, administration.
5. Vacant time, leisure, unoccupied time, spare time, ease, convenience, freedom, chance, liberty, opportunity, idleness, otiosity, holiday.
6. Proper time, fit season, due season, high time, suitable time, timeliness, opportuneness, seasonableness, nick of time, golden opportunity, fair field, clear stage.
7. Crisis, emergency, conjuncture, juncture, turning point, climax.
8. Period of childbirth, period of gestation, hour of travail, delivery, confinement, parturition, accouchement, birth-throe, labor, obstetrics.

TIME-HONORED, *adj.* 1. Revered because of antiquity, respected because of long continuance, worthy of honor by reason of antiquity, venerable, in high esteem, emeritus, illustrious, eminent, *aere perennius (Lat.),* immortal, imperishable.
2. Of long standing, immemorial, ancient, primeval, old, olden, antique, primordial, aboriginal, antediluvian, prehistoric, patriarchal, classic, archaic, ancestral, traditional, inveterate, old as the hills.

TIMELINESS, *n.* 1. Opportuneness, seasonableness, matureness, convenient time, proper time, high time, suitable time, suitability, nick of time, opening, opportunity, occasion, chance, place, room, scope, space, clear stage, golden opportunity, *mollissima fandi tempora (Lat.),* fair field.
2. Critical period, crisis, climax, climacteric, turning point, conjuncture, juncture, emergency, turn.

TIMELY, *adj.* Occurring at a suitable time, seasonable, well-timed, opportune, convenient, appropriate, punctual, early, timeous, suitable, prompt, welcome, proper, providential, propitious, auspicious, fortunate, favorable, happy, felicitous, expedient, advantageous, due, seemly.

TIMEPIECE, n. Apparatus for measuring the progress of time, clock, watch, timekeeper, hourglass, water glass, horologue, clepsydra, chronometer, chronoscope, isochronon, sundial, repeater, chronograph.

TIMESERVER, n. One who adapts his conduct to conditions, one who for selfish ends conforms with the opinions of persons in power, opportunist, apple-polisher (coll.), trimmer, weathercock, timepleaser, temporizer, double-dealer, turncoat, chameleon, Vicar of Bray, timist, ambidexter, Janus, sycophant, parasite, apostate.

TIMESERVING, adj. Self-seeking, opportunistic, temporizing, trimming, double-dealing, obsequious, unscrupulous, ambidexterous, crooked, tricky, slippery, sneaking, untrustworthy, fawning, bootlicking, truckling, cringing, crouching, servile, pliant, supple, selfish, expedient, morigerous, politic, Machiavellian, diplomatic, worldly-wise, mean, groveling, soapy, apple-polishing, mealymouthed, slavish, parasitical, sycophantic, disingenuous, false-hearted, double-tongued, tortuous, insidious, treacherous, perfidious, perjured, infamous, blackguard, venal, mercenary, crafty, cunning, artful, vulpine, subtle, designing, strategic, sly, wily, subdolous, stealthy, foxy, underhand, shifty.

TIMEWORN, adj. Showing the ravages of time, impaired by time, dilapidated, antiquated, decrepit, rusty, antique, ancient, obsolete, venerable, old, superannuated, antediluvian, prehistoric, preadamite, paleozoic, immemorial, moth-eaten, fusty, outworn, passé, crumbling, second-hand, doddering, wrinkled, patriarchal, gerontic, deteriorated, the worse for wear, out of repair, battered, weathered, frayed, faded, shabby, threadbare, moldy, seedy, moss-grown, broken-down, done for.

TIMID, adj. 1. Subject to fear, easily alarmed, fearful, timorous, terrified, apprehensive, pavid, frightened, alarmed, panic-stricken, panicky, afraid, scary, scared, nervous, tremulous, skittish, aghast, uneasy, shaky.
2. Bashful, diffident, retiring, shrinking, shy, coy, demure, shamefaced, blushing, sheepish, modest, humble, overmodest, unobtrusive, unassuming, poor in spirit, constrained, reserved, reticent.
3. Cowardly, craven, pusillanimous, irresolute, faint-hearted, spineless, soft, weak-kneed, skulking, spiritless, recreant, half-hearted, inadventurous, pliant, chicken-hearted, effeminate, unmanly, lily-livered, yellow, milksop, dastardly, poltroon.

TIMIDITY, n. 1. Fearfulness, timorousness, want of courage, timidness, alarm, dread, nervousness, apprehensiveness, cold feet, Dutch courage, anxiety, solicitude, misgiving, qualm, inquietude, disquietude, trepidation, flutter, perturbation, trembling, tremor, cold sweat, mortal funk, fright, affright, pavor, terror, panic, consternation, dismay, stampede, scare, bugaboo, bugbear, hobgoblin, scarecrow.
2. Bashfulness, diffidence, shyness, coyness, demureness, sheepishness, modesty, unobtrusiveness, humility, reserve, reticence, constraint, retiring disposition, blushing, mauvaise honte (Fr.), verecundity.
3. Cowardice, cowardliness, pusillanimity, pusillanimousness, irresolution, faint-heartedness, softness, recreancy, half-heartedness, pliancy, effeminacy, unmanliness, dastardliness, poltroonery, baseness, dastardy, white feather.

TINCTURE, n. 1. Solution of a medicinal substance in alcohol, grain, infusion.
2. Stain, tinge, tint, tone, nuance, shade, hue, color, chroma, dye, glow, flush, luminosity, coloration, pigmentation, cast.
3. Trace, smack, smattering, admixture, taste, flavor, spice, touch, suspicion, soupçon, dash, seasoning.

TINDER, n. Dry substance that readily takes fire, touchwood, amadou, spunk, punk.

TINE, n. Sharp projecting point, spike of a fork, prong, tooth, spine, spiculum, barb, spur, cusp, nib.

TINGE, v. 1. Impart a degree of color to, tint, stain, dye, color, tincture, paint, wash, hue, tone, ingrain.
2. Imbue, infuse, impregnate, impress, diffuse, suffuse, transfuse, infiltrate, instill, saturate, lace, entincture, fortify, dash, flavor, season.

TINGE, n. 1. Slight degree of coloration, stain, tint, tincture, cast, color, shade, nuance, hue, dye, tone, chroma, complexion, luminosity, glow, intensity, flush.
2. Slight admixture, smack, quality, suspicion, soupçon, flavor, taste, relish, trace, touch, taint, dash, spice, strain, vein, infusion, seasoning.

TINGLE, v. Have a pricking sensation, prickle, sting, thrill, itch, creep, prick, tickle, titillate, throb, heave, palpitate, quiver, tremble.

TINKER, v. Mend, put in repair, patch up, repair in a makeshift way, restore unskillfully, cobble, retouch, vamp, doctor, botch, bungle.

TINKER, n. Itinerant mender, repairer, cobbler, renewer, unskillful worker, jack-of-all-trades, factotum, one skilled in various minor kinds of mechanical work.

TINKLE, v. Make a succession of light ringing sounds, jingle, chink, clink, ting, ring, tingle, chime, ting-a-ling, peal, tintinnabulate, vibrate, echo, resound, reverberate, ding.

TINKLING, n. Jingle, tinkle, tintinnabulation, clinking, ringing, resonance, reverberation, vibration, bell-note, chime, clang, clangor, peal, ding-dong.

TINSEL, n. 1. Glittering metallic substance in thin sheets, metallic yarn, spangle, glitter, sequin.
2. Finery, frippery, tawdriness, gewgaw, pinchbeck, paste, worthless ornament, clinquant, curio, bric-a-brac, scrimshaw, decoration, flamboyance, trinketry, bangle, bauble, gimcrack, brummagem, knickknack, frills and furbelows, scagliola.
3. Showy pretense, sham, imitation, counterfeit, forgery, make-believe, gloss, masquerade, mummery, borrowed plumes, false colors, disguise, camouflage.

TINSEL, adj. Glittering, garish, flashy, gaudy, showy, worthless, specious, superficial, flaunting, meretricious, tawdry, gay, ornamental, fancy, decorative, spangled, ornate, florid, gilt, begilt, gilded, refulgent, flamboyant, rococo, baroque.

TINT, v. Color delicately, apply a tint to, stain, dye, tinge, hue, wash, tone, ingrain.

TINT, n. Variety of a color, color of less than maximum chroma or purity, tinge, tincture, shade, nuance, hue, grain, dye, stain, tone, cast, tinct, glow, luminosity, coloration.

TINTINNABULATION, n. Sound of bells, ringing, jingle, tinkle, clang, clangor, peal, tintamarre, din, tintamar, resonance, reverberation, ding-dong, chime.

TINY, *adj.* Very small, wee, miniature, minikin, dainty, diminutive, minute, minuscule, microscopic, little, puny, dwarfish, pygmean, Lilliputian, pygmy, stunted, midgety, exiguous, fine, elfin, undersized, runty, pocket-size, nanoid, molecular, atomic, imperceptible, homeopathic, infinitesimal, animalcular, microbic, scanty.

TIP, *v.* 1. Furnish with a tip, cap, top, put a point on, sharpen, crest, crown, head, point, whet, barb, spiculate, acuminate, cuspidate.

2. Cause to assume a slanting *or* sloping position, tilt, incline to one end, cant, slant, slope, bend.

3. Overthrow, overturn, upset, tumble, topple, subvert, capsize, dump, invert, upturn, turn topsyturvy, turn turtle.

4. Give a small present of money to, remunerate, reward, fee, pay, bribe, recompense, grease the palm, oil *(sl.),* donate, award, bestow, grant, compensate.

5. Tip off, inform, apprise, acquaint, tell, advise, enlighten, notify, communicate, intimate, insinuate, hint, suggest, give the low-down, confide to.

TIP, *n.* 1. Pointed extremity, top, summit, cap, crown, crest, head, point, end, peak, pinnacle, vertex, apex, zenith, nib, horn, brow, *ne plus ultra (Lat.),* tiptop, culmination, capsheaf, acme, culmen, climax, maximum, pitch, height, consummation.

2. Inclination, slant, slope, tilt, obliquity, incline, rake, bias, diagonal, list, zigzag, bevel, sag, lurch, cant, curve, bend, deviation, acclivity, ascent, rise, gradient, ramp, declivity, dip, fall.

3. Small present of money, donation, perquisite, douceur, reward, gratuity, fee, gift, bonus, pay, recompense, compensation, remuneration, bait, bribe, largess, bounty, *pourboire (Fr.), Trinkgeld (Ger.),* baksheesh, cumshaw, handout, palm grease *(sl.),* sop, pin money, benefaction, favor, boon, consideration.

4. Piece of private *or* secret information, tip-off, pointer, hint, suggestion, *verbum sapienti (Lat.),* intimation, insinuation, innuendo, whisper, inkling, cue, word to the wise, advice, warning, admonition.

TIPPLE, *v.* Be addicted to strong drink, drink hard, guzzle, swill, tope, booze, carouse, nip, quaff, sip, drain the cup, suck up, swig, toss off, wash down, wet one's whistle, soak, drink like a fish, take a hair of the dog that bit you.

TIPPLER, *n.* Hard drinker, toper, swiller, guzzler, dipsomaniac, alcoholic, drunkard, sot, drunk, winebibber, debauchee, compotator, carouser, nipper, sipper, wassailer, bibber, Borachio, sponge, soak, tosspot, thirsty soul, Bacchanalian, reveler, inebriate, lushington, lush, boozer, oenophilist.

TIPSY, *adj.* Drunk, drunken, inebriated, intoxicated, tight, in one's cups, temulent, mellow, primed, oiled *(sl.),* screwed *(sl.),* high, lush, maudlin, boozy, muzzy, in liquor, muddled, bemused, fuddled, inebrious, squiffy, pifflicated *(sl.),* potvaliant, sozzled, plastered *(sl.),* groggy, bleary-eyed, thick-tongued, potulent, raddled, crapulous, *inter pocula (Lat.),* three sheets in the wind, half seas over, under the table, bibulous, bibacious, sottish, staggering, reeling, unsteady, overcome, fuli *(sl.),* lit up *(sl.),* winebibbing, dipsomaniacal.

TIPTOP, *adj.* 1. Situated at the very top, highest, topmost, uppermost, supreme, polar, head, meridian, capital, supernal.

2. Of the highest quality, excellent, first-rate, perfect, choice, first-class, first-water, very best, superfine, picked, superior, above par, select, elect, eximious, recherché, superlative, prime, crack, gilt-edged, top-flight, cardinal.

TIRADE, *n.* Prolonged outburst of denunciation, long vehement speech, harangue, diatribe, invective, billingsgate, verbal rough-and-tumble, jeremiad, philippic, obloquy, censure, detraction, condemnation, criticism, reprehension, expostulation, increpation, reprobation, reproof, remonstrance, reproach, reprimand, jobation, castigation, lecture, blowup, rating, dressing-down, scolding, vituperation, exprobration, upbraiding, objurgation, contumely, execration, malediction, commination, anathema, curse, malison, imprecation, fulmination, vilification, aspersion, scurrility, abuse.

TIRE, *v.* Reduce the strength of, exhaust, weary, fatigue, fag, overtax, knock up, tucker, exert, prostrate, overwork, wear out, strain, jade, irk, bore, bother, harass, worry, overtask.

TIRED, *adj.* 1. Fatigued, wearied, weary, spent, fagged, exhausted, played out, knocked up, defatigated, worn-out, used up, *épuisé (Fr.),* toilworn, haggard, footsore, faint, prostrate, overtired, overstrained, all in *(sl.),* dog-tired, ready to drop.

2. Impatient, disgusted, fed up *(sl.),* blasé, *ennuyé (Fr.),* uninterested, bored, sick of, dispirited, life-weary, world-weary, jaded.

TIRESOME, *adj.* Wearisome, fatiguing, fagging, irksome, tedious, monotonous, dull, humdrum, arduous, laborious, toilsome, hard, troublesome, uphill, difficult, operose, vexatious, exhausting, uninteresting, long-winded, diffuse, prolix, annoying, trying, dry, prosy, heavy, prosaic, boring, borish, bald, arid, flat, soporific, somniferous, dismal, stupid, commonplace, drab, matter-of-fact, platitudinous.

TISSUE, *n.* 1. Substance of which an organism is composed, aggregate of cells forming structural material in an animal *or* plant, muscle, parenchyma, cartilage, ligament, membrane, prosenchyma, cinenchyma.

2. Texture, web, grain, fiber, grit, surface, tooth, warp and woof, nap, contexture, intertexture, interlacement.

3. Woven fabric of light *or* gauzy texture, woven stuff, cloth, net, lace, netting, mesh, textile, webbing, gossamer, chiffon, silk, film, gauze, muslin.

4. Tissue paper, onion skin, papyrus, parchment, *pelure (Fr.).*

5. Interwoven mass, interconnected series, combination, conglomeration, network, collection, chain, set, accumulation, assemblage, compilation, aggregation.

TITAN, *n.* Primordial deity of gigantic size and enormous strength, giant, Hercules, Atlas, Cyclops, Antaeus, Samson, Goliath, tower of strength, Gog and Magog, Brobdingnagian, Gargantua, mammoth, monster, colossus, behemoth, leviathan.

TITANIC, *adj.* Gigantic, huge, colossal, enormous, prodigious, monstrous, mighty, immense, towering, thumping, strapping, vast, stupendous, massive, amplitudinous, tall, elephantine, Brobdingnagian, Cyclopean, Gargantuan, Herculean, Atlantean, Patagonian, beetling.

TIT FOR TAT Equivalent given in retaliation, measure for measure, blow for blow, *quid pro quo (Lat.),* give and take, a Roland for an Oliver, counterstroke, reprisal, *lex talionis (Lat.)*, retribution, requital, an eye for an eye, the biter bit, diamond cut diamond, boomerang, a game at which two can play, revenge, punishment.

TITHE, *n.* Tenth part of annual produce *or* revenue, tax, impost, duty, dues, toll, tariff, custom, assessment, excise, taxation, exactment.

TITILLATE, *v.* 1. Excite an itching sensation in by touching, tickle, stroke lightly, finger, palpate, feel, touch, grabble, grope, pass the fingers over, twiddle, knead, massage, manipulate.

2. Provoke desire, whet the appetite, attract, allure, tempt, take one's fancy, seduce, captivate, fascinate, entrance, enchant, transport, enravish.

3. Please, amuse, entertain, enliven, divert, tickle the fancy, put in good humor, rejoice, interest, delight, charm.

TITILLATION, *n.* Tickling, palpation, stroking, fingering, massage, manipulation, itching, pleasurable sensation, handling, kneading, rubbing, sensation, formication, goose flesh.

TITLE, *n.* 1. Name, appellative, epithet, designation, appellation, denomination, compellation, proper name, style, praenomen, given name, cognomen, surname, patronymic, eponym, agnomen, moniker *(sl.)*, sobriquet, nickname, alias, handle to one's name, nom de plume, pen name.

2. King, emperor, czar, kaiser, caesar, leader, *Führer (Ger.)*, *Duce (It.)*, president, consul, baron, archon, prince, count, marquis, duke, lord, excellency, earl, grace, majesty, highness, lordship, reverence, worship, sir, master, esquire, Mr., monsieur, signor, señor, Herr, your honor, chevalier, knight, maharaja, rana, raja, sultan, amir, khan, pasha, sahib.

3. Inscription, heading, caption, legend, head, lemma.

4. Ground of claim, recognized right, prerogative, privilege, due, part, possession, ownership, immunity, license, power, grant, advantage, exemption, droit *(Law)*.

TITTER, *v.* Laugh with restraint, snigger, snicker, chuckle, giggle, smirk, simper, laugh in one's sleeve, crow, smicker, cackle.

TITTLE, *n.* Very small quantity, small mark in printing *or* writing, jot, particle, scrap, whit, mite, iota, ace, bit, corpuscle, atom, molecule, ion, scintilla, grain, speck, spark, dot, mote, fragment, crumb, magneton, monad, electron, trifle, dab, modicum, tinge, pinch, touch, dash, snick, minim, minimum, sprinkling, drop, snip.

TITTLE-TATTLE, *n.* Trifling conversation, prittle-prattle, prate, gossip, gabble, babble, prattle, cackle, idle talk, *on dit (Fr.)*, hearsay, rumor, bruit, buzz, table-talk, scandal, canard, chitchat, causerie, *tripotage (Fr.)*, scuttlebutt *(sl.)*, grapevine *(coll.)*.

TITULAR, *adj.* Of the nature of a title, titulary, nominal, verbal, in name only, cognominal, nuncupative, nuncupatory, yclept, hight, known as, *soi-disant (Fr.)*, *sogenannt (Ger.)*.

TOADY, *n.* Fawning flatterer, yes-man, obsequious sycophant, parasite, flunky, bootlicker, fawner, footlicker, hanger-on, wheedler, tufthunter, lickspittle, *Graeculus esuriens (Lat.)*, stooge, timeserver, pickthank, tool, courtier, truckler, sponge, cringer, puffer, adulator, toadeater, rubber stamp.

TO AND FRO, *adv.* Back and forth, seesaw, in and out, shuttlewise, zigzag, up and down, from side to side, wibble-wobble, *hin und zurück (Ger.)*, *hin und her (Ger.)*, *çà et là (Fr.)*.

TOAST, *v.* 1. Brown by exposure to heat, warm thoroughly, dry by heat, heat, torrefy, singe, scorch, parch.

2. Drink a health to, drink to, drink in honor of, pledge, propose, drink the health of, honor, clink glasses, bumper, name, compliment, signalize, celebrate, do honor to, extol, laud, magnify, solemnize, commemorate, glorify, lionize, applaud, dedicate to.

TOAST, *n.* 1. Bread in slices superficially browned by heat, toasted bread, *rôtie beurré (Fr.)*, *tostada (Sp.)*, *pane abbrustolito (It.)*, *geröstetes Brot (Ger.)*.

2. Proposal of health in drinking, *santé (Fr.)*, *salud (Sp.)*, *salute (It.)*, *Gesundheit (Ger.)*, *skoal (Scand.)*, pledge.

3. Sentiment uttered at a convivial meeting, *Trinkspruch (Ger.)*, *brindisi (It.)*, *brindis (Sp.)*, *brinde (Fr.)*.

TOBACCO, *n.* Nicotine, snuff, smoke, cigarette, cigar, pipe, briar, corncob, meerschaum, hookah, quid, fag, cheroot, weed, Havana, stogy, Lady Nicotine, narghila, calumet, peace pipe.

TOBOGGAN, *n.* Long, narrow flat-bottomed sled curved upward and backward at the front end, sledge, sleigh, bobsled, bobsleigh, luge.

TOCSIN, *n.* 1. Signal of alarm sounded on bells, alarm-bell, alarum, call-to-arms, *alerte (Fr.)*.

2. Any warning signal, sound of trumpet, beat of drum, signal of distress, S.O.S., hue and cry, note of alarm, red-light, blue-light, warning, war cry, foghorn, yellow flag, siren, danger signal, red flag, fire alarm, burglar alarm, stop-thief, police whistle.

TODAY, *adv.* The present day, this very day, present time, *heute (Ger.)*, *aujourd'hui (Fr.)*, *hoy (Sp.)*, *oggi (It.)*, now, on the present occasion.

TODDLE, *v.* Walk unsteadily, waddle, tottle, bundle, bowl along, stump, strut, foot it, trudge, wend, plod, tread, mince, stalk, paddle, wobble, traipse, shuffle, shamble, hobble.

TO-DO, *n.* Ado, commotion, disturbance, stir, bustle, flurry, confusion, fluster, pother, turmoil, fuss, tumult, noise, hustle, great doings, press of business, many irons in the fire, thick of things, scurry, scuttle, push, scramble, splutter, flutter, stew, perturbation, trepidation, hubbub, rout, hurly-burly, ferment, fermentation, pressure, exertion, spurt, spell, excitement, disquietude, restlessness, agitation, exercitation, ruffle, whirl.

TOE, *n.* Terminal member of the foot, foot digit, *orteil (Fr.)*, *doigt du pied (Fr.)*, *Zehe (Ger.)*, *dedo del pie (Sp.)*, *dito del piede (It.)*.

TOGETHER, *adv.* 1. In a body, collectively, en masse, unitedly, jointly, in one mass, conjointly, concertedly, in company, in union, reciprocally, mutually, side by side, in one gathering, in concert, hand in hand, arm in arm, cheek by jowl, hand in glove, *ensemble (Fr.)*, *zusammen (Ger.)*, *insieme (It.)*, *juntamente (Sp.)*.

2. Simultaneously, contemporaneously, at the same time, concurrently, *pari passu (Lat.)*, coinstantaneously, in the same breath, synchronously, concomitantly, coetaneously, *zugleich (Ger.)*, *en même temps (Fr.)*, *al mismo tiempo (Sp.)*, *nello stesso tiempo (It.)*.

TOIL, *n.* 1. Hard and continuous work, exhausting effort, fatiguing labor, travail, exertion, drudgery, grind, grinding pains, hardship, sweat of one's brow, elbow grease *(humorous)*, struggle, dead lift, industry, diligence, laborious task, exercise, exercitation, assiduity, laboriousness, sedulousness, application, perseverance, persistence, activity, aggressiveness, fatiguing duties, exhaustion, painstaking, busy hum of men, slavery, fagging, operoseness, hammering, *labor limae (Lat.).*

2. *(Pl.)* Snare, trap, gin, net, noose, springe, pitfall, decoy, springle, hook, meshes, baited trap, cobweb, birdlime, mousetrap, ambush.

TOIL, *v.* Engage in severe and continuous work, labor arduously, drudge, slave, sweat, plod, exert oneself, take pains, moil, strive, work hard, busy oneself in, stir one's stumps, peg away, kick up a dust, lay about one, persist, persevere, have one's hands full, not have a moment to spare, put in one's oar, put forth a strong arm, set one's shoulder to the wheel, bend the bow, work like a carthorse, hammer at, stick to, do one's level best, have one's whole soul in one's work, strain every nerve, put all one's strength into, ply the oar, grub.

TOILER, *n.* Hard worker, drudge, fag, laborer, workman, man of action, hack, plodder, grind, slave, helot, proletarian, busy bee, hustler, shaft horse, ant, factotum, artisan, handicraftsman, operative, mechanic, laboring man, hewer of wood and drawer of water, navvy, journeyman, hand, day laborer, beast of burden, stevedore, longshoreman, docker.

TOILET, *n.* 1. Water closet, bathroom, privy, outhouse, latrine, jakes, W.C., powder room, men's room, ladies' room.

2. Dress, toilette, attire, mode of dressing, costume, apparel, raiment, array, guise, habiliment, vesture, garb, wardrobe, palliament, wearing apparel.

TOILSOME, *adj.* Laborious, arduous, hard, wearisome, difficult, fatiguing, operose, onerous, tiring, tiresome, herculean, backbreaking, uphill, tedious, severe, painful, burdensome, strenuous, taxing, troublesome, tough, not easy, irksome, formidable, rugged, thorny, intricate, complicated, elaborate.

TOKEN, *n.* 1. Characteristic indication sign, mark, evidence, symbol, trace, trait, index, note, manifestation, badge, signal, expression, emblem, symptom, prognostic, vestige, signum, device, cipher, figure, indicium, hint, clue.

2. Souvenir, keepsake, memento, memorial, reminder, remembrance, relic, handsel, remembrancer, monument, testimonial.

TOLERABLE, *adj.* 1. Bearable, endurable, supportable, sufferable, permissible, allowable, abidable, experienceable, undergoable.

2. Middling, betwixt and between, mediocre, average, so-so, indifferent, ordinary, run-of-the-mill, pretty good, passable, not too bad, fair, innocuous, decent, good enough, second-rate, secondary, inferior, adequate, satisfactory, respectable, commonplace.

TOLERANCE, *n.* Disposition to be patient and fair toward those with different opinions, freedom from bigotry, lack of prejudice, liberal spirit, forbearance, charity, mercy, sufferance, endurance, receptivity, toleration, lenity, benevolence, democratic spirit, indulgence, clemency, compassion, quarter, patience, dispassion, good will, philanthropy, altruism, kindliness, brotherly love, benignity, humanity, fellow feeling, sympathy, *bonhomie (Fr.).*

TOLERANT, *adj.* Forbearing, lenient, indulgent, charitable, liberal, unprejudiced, unbigoted, magnanimous, broad-minded, latitudinarian, catholic,

patient, philosophical, moderate, uncomplaining, meek, altruistic, philanthropic, gentle, soft, easygoing, clement, complaisant, long-suffering, sympathetic, imperturbable, dispassionate, stoical, level-headed, submissive, resigned, bearing with, benevolent, considerate, humanitarian, humane, large-hearted, generous.

TOLERATE, *v.* 1. Permit, admit, allow, sanction, concede, indulge, recognize, accord, oblige, stretch a point, gratify, wink at, vouchsafe, favor, warrant, give quarter, show mercy, *parcere subjectis (Lat.),* spare the vanquished, be lax, give the reins to, hold a loose rein, be lenient, give carte blanche, *laissez-faire (Fr.).*

2. Suffer, undergo, submit to, stand, brook, abide, put up with, swallow, stomach, endure, bear with, take patiently, sustain, support, experience, brave, go through, pocket, digest, make the best of, keep one's countenance, carry on, put a good face on.

3. *(Med.)* Resist the action of, withstand.

TOLERATION, *n.* 1. Concession, laxity, sufferance, tolerance, freedom, laissez-faire, forbearance, endurance, independence, liberty, scope, play, range, latitude, free stage, full swing, rope, enfranchisement.

2. License for free opinion, franchise, permission, indulgence, clemency, lenity, allowance, recognition of the right of private judgment, lenience, favor, moderation, mercy, compassion, quarter, open-mindedness, magnanimity, largeness of mind, liberality, liberalism, catholicity, impartiality, absence of prejudice, freedom from bigotry, high-mindedness, candor, benevolence, charity, altruism, fellow feeling, philanthropy, humanitarianism, humaneness, humanity, good will, benignity, brotherly love, *bonhomie (Fr.),* milk of human kindness, generosity, consideration, considerateness.

TOLL, *v.* Cause to sound, sound a knell, ring, peal, knell, sound warningly, chime.

TOLL, *n.* Payment for some right *or* privilege, impost, duty, tax, levy, assessment, fee, exaction, contribution, rate, tribute, compensation, tariff, capitation, pollage, custom, *octroi (Fr.),* excise.

TOMB, *n.* Place for the reception of a dead body, sepulcher, burial place, house of death, grave, crypt, catacomb, vault, mausoleum, mastaba, tholos, ossuary, cenotaph, necropolis, cemetery, narrow house, charnel house, long home, sepulture, bier, mound, last home, cromlech, cairn, tumulus, barrow, graveyard, polyandrion, God's acre, mortuary, deadhouse.

TOMBOY, *n.* Boisterous girl, hoyden, bold girl, tomrig, romp, filly, *garçonnière (Fr.), Range (Ger.),* wench, baggage, flapper, *Backfisch (Ger.),* minx.

TOME, *n.* Ponderous volume, large book, opuscule, codex, album, portfolio, work, writing, treatise, manual, enchiridion, publication, folio, octavo, quarto.

TOMENTOUS, *adj.* Downy, fleecy, flocculent, tomentose, nappy, hairy, bristly, hirsute, villous, hispid, crinose, pilous, shaggy, lanate, woolly, lanuginous.

TOMFOOLERY, *n.* Foolish behavior, silly doing, monkeyshine, escapade, roguish trick, frolic, antic, skylarking, *espièglerie (Fr.),* buffoonery, mummery, nonsense, vagary, absurd trifling, sport, merriment, folly, harlequinade, fooling around, *boutade (Fr.),* practical joke, monkey trick, whoopee, merriment, fun, drollery, romp, gambol, rig, spree, lark, waggishness, waggery.

TOMORROW, *n.* The day after today, the next day, the morrow, *demain (Fr.), morgen (Ger.), mañana (Sp.), domani (It.).*

TOM-TOM, *n.* Native drum, tam-tam, tabor, taboret, taborine, kettledrum, tympani, tambourine, timbrel, tymbal.

TON, *n.* 1. Twenty hundredweight, twenty hundred gross, 2240 pounds *(long ton)*, 2000 pounds *(short ton)*.
2. Fashion, style, elegance, bon ton, distinction, manners, breeding, savoir-faire, air, decorum, gentility, *bienséance (Fr.),* etiquette, punctilio, vogue, mode, *dernier cri (Fr.).*

TONE, *n.* 1. Sound, pitch, harmonic, overtone, note, voice, vibration.
2. Tonality, intonation, cadence, lilt, accent, modulation, inflection, stress, emphasis, sonority, resonance, strain, key, tune, twang.
3. Character, quality, temper, spirit, mood, tenor, condition, state, mode, trim, kilter, fettle.
4. *(Physiol.)* Healthy sensitivity, tension, firmness, force, elasticity, health, strength, vigor, energy.
5. Prevailing color, variety of color, chroma, shade, hue, tint, tinge, complexion, dye, cast, luminosity.
6. General effect, style, manner, mode, guise, demeanor, appearance.

TONE DOWN, *v.* 1. Give a lower tone to, darken, shade, obscure, dim, lower, overshadow, overcast, obfuscate, cloud, bedim, achromatize, decolorize, etiolate, bleach, blanch.
2. Subdue, moderate, diminish, relax, soften, weaken, temper, chasten, smother, deaden, mute, hush, quiet, silence.

TONG, *n.* 1. Two-armed implement for seizing *or* lifting, fire-iron, pincer, forcep, tweezer, plier, nipper, vise.
2. *(China)* Association, secret society, political party, faction, side.

TONGUE, *n.* 1. Language, utterance, vernacular, dialect, speech, discourse, accent, patois, brogue, lingo, argot, phraseology, idiom, vocabulary, diction, verbal expression, use of words.
2. Protrusible, freely movable organ occupying the floor of the mouth in man, organ of taste, lingua, lingula.
3. Projection, pole, neap, post, shaft, nib, shank, pale, stake, palisade.
4. Nation, race, people, stock, tribe, lineage, breed, strain, stirps, clan.

TONGUE-TIED, *adj.* 1. Unable to speak, elinguid, mute, dumb, speechless, voiceless, aphasiac, aphonic, aphonous.
2. Inarticulate, reticent, taciturn, diffident, shy, timid, timorous, modest, bashful, skittish, nervous, coy, sheepish.

TONIC, *n.* 1. Strengthening medicine, bracer, roborant, invigorant, stimulant, pickup, analeptic, restorative, cordial, ptisan.
2. Musical note, keynote, key, fundamental note, first note of the scale, leading note.

TONIC, *adj.* 1. Invigorating, bracing, analeptic, invigorant, stimulating, remedial, strengthening, restorative, curative, corroborant, balsamic, peptic, eutrophic, eupeptic, benign.
2. Voiced, sonant, vocalized, sonantized, vocal, intonated, phonetic.

TONIGHT, *n.* The present night, this coming night, the night following the present day, *ce soir (Fr.), heute abend (Ger.), heute nacht (Ger.), esta noche (Sp.), stasera (It.), stanotte (It.).*

TONSILLITIS, *n.* Suppurative inflammation of the tonsils, quinsy, amygdalitis.

TONSURED, *adj.* Shaven, clipped, shorn, hairless, shaved, clean-shaven, baldheaded, acomous, beardless, smooth-shaven, bareheaded.

TOO, *adv.* 1. Moreover, also, furthermore, likewise, additionally, in addition, withal, as well as, *au reste (Fr.),* besides, to boot, further, conjointly, together with, as well as, in conjunction with, along with, *cum multis aliis (Lat.).*
2. To an excessive extent, beyond what is fitting *or* right, over and above, more than should be, extremely, overmuch, over, too much, out of measure, beyond the mark, extra.

TOOL, *n.* 1. Contrivance for doing work, implement, instrument, device, utensil, machine, appliance, apparatus, mechanism, engine, motor, turbine, equipment, weapon, gear, *matériel (Fr.),* lever, jimmy, crowbar, jack, pry, pedal, treadle, crank, pinion, cam, winch, capstan, flywheel, tackle, pulley, derrick, crane, wedge, key, screw, hilt, handle, haft, shank, shaft, tiller, lug.
2. Vehicle, medium, intermediary, agent, means, channel, wherewithal.
3. Person used by another for his own ends, cat's-paw, hireling, pawn, puppet, dupe, greenhorn, hayseed, stool pigeon, come-on, stooge, foil, straight man, victim, jay, creature, parasite, satellite, dependent, jackal, hanger-on, man of straw, jackstraw.

TOOT, *v.* Cause to sound by blowing, tootle, blow, sound.

TOOTH, *n.* 1. Fang, tusk, incisor, molar, grinder, canine, tang, snag, cusp, nib.
2. Projection, point, spike, tine, spine, spiculum, barb, spur, prickle, pin, needle, nail, tack, rowel, spit, antler, horn, bristle, thorn, cog, spoke, ratchet, calcar.
3. Taste, liking, relish, gusto, *goût (Fr.),* fondness, discrimination, savor, sapidity, piquancy, flavor, partiality, predilection, desire, appetite.

TOOTH AND NAIL Using every means of attack *or* defense, biting and scratching, with might and main, energetically, fiercely, with all one's might, strenuously, *pignis et calcibus (Lat.),* hammer and tongs, amain, violently, by force, *vi et armis (Lat.),* lustily, *totis viribus (Lat.), manibus pedibusque (Lat.), unguibus et rostro (Lat.),* on the offensive, *bec et ongle (Fr.), à belles dents (Fr.).*

TOOTH-SHAPED, *adj.* Toothlike, odontoid, dentiform, cuspidate, pointed, cuspate, tapering, spiked, dentoid.

TOOTHSOME, *adj.* Pleasant to the taste, agreeable, palatable, tasty, luscious, delicious, delectable, tasteful, gustable, sweet, dainty, nice, savory, ambrosial, nectareous, candied, melliferous, honeyed, sugary, saccharine, appetizing, relishable, gustatory, saporous, sapid, saporific, flavorous, flavorsome.

TOP, *v.* 1. Put a top on, tip, cap, head, crown, cover, crest, roof, overlay, revet.
2. Surmount, overtop, rise above, ride, clear, vault over.
3. Exceed, excel, surpass, outdo, overtop, transcend, eclipse, overshadow, outshine.

4. Take the top off, lop, prune, crop, clip, dock, snip, nip, cut down.

TOP, *n.* 1. Highest point, summit, pinnacle, vertex, acme, peak, apex, zenith, crest, meridian, culminating point, crown, head, culmination, climax, tip, cap, brow, capsheaf, culmen, epistyle, architrave, cornice, corona, coping, capital, capstone, headpiece, fastigium, pediment, entablature, ceiling, roof, lid.

2. Head, highest place, chief, big shot *(sl.)*, boss, headman, foreman, manager, director, rector, governor, supervisor, superintendent, overseer, inspector, surveyor, taskmaster, ringleader, coryphaeus, demagogue, fugleman, bellwether, precentor, guiding star, helmsman, pilot, guide, president, principal, chairman, captain, dean, superior, premier, dictator.

TOP, *adj.* 1. Uppermost, highest, topmost, upper, apical, culminating, culminant, culminal, head, polar, supernal, apicular, crowning.

2. Foremost, greatest, chief, principal, capital, superior, supreme, excellent, first-rate, top-drawer, first-water, first-grade, best, maximal, paramount, preëminent, peerless, unequaled, overruling, dominant, *sans pareil (Fr.)*, second to none, superlative, sovereign, transcendent, incomparable.

TOPCOAT, *n.* Lightweight overcoat, upper coat, outer coat, surcoat, greatcoat, surtout, mackintosh, trench coat, waterproof, ulster, pea jacket, monkey jacket, redingote.

TOPE, *v.* Be addicted to strong drink, drink hard, tipple, soak up, swill, guzzle, booze, sot, bib, carouse, lush, swig, drink like a fish, drain the cup, take a hair of the dog that bit you, wet one's whistle, liquor up, tank up, bend the elbow, toss off, pass the bottle, drink bottoms-up, quaff, lap up, wash down.

TOPER, *n.* Hard drinker, chronic drunkard, alcoholic, souse, dipsomaniac, tippler, winebibber, inebriate, guzzler, tosspot, lovepot, dram-drinker, sot, borachio, wassailer, swiller, debauchee, sponge, soak, thirsty soul, devotee to Bacchus, reveler, lush, lushington, boozer, oenophilist.

TOP-HEAVY, *adj.* Disproportionately heavy at the top, liable to fall from too great weight above, overburdened, unbalanced, inverted, unstable, precarious, tipsy, dangerous, tottering, unsteady, shaky, trembling in the balance, nodding to its fall, threatening.

TOPIC, *n.* 1. Subject of conversation *or* discussion, theme of a discourse, motiv, *Leitmotiv* (*Ger.*), matter, subject matter, text, thesis, business, matter in hand, affair, commonplace, problem, maxim, question, theorem, motion, resolution, proposition, point, moot point, case, point at issue, debatable point.

2. Field of inquiry, research field, subject of thought, food for the mind, matter for thought, mental pabulum.

TOPICAL, *adj.* 1. Subjective, limited, particular, restricted, especial, local, current, contemporary, moot, controversial, in issue.

2. Probable, likely, possible, presumable, inconclusive, presumptive, on the cards.

TOPLOFTY, *adj.* Arrogant, insolent, imperious, haughty, arbitrary, high-handed, magisterial, pompous, bombastic, fustian, pretentious, proud, baronial, lordly, stately, high-flown, high-toned, high-plumed, high and mighty, puffed up, swollen, vainglorious, disdainful, supercilious, bumptious, consequential, overweening, contemptuous, scorn-ful, contumelious, withering, snooty *(sl.)*, upstage, derisive, cavalier, dictatorial, intolerant, domineering, audacious, impudent, impertinent, vaporing, swaggering, thrasonic, blustering.

TOPMOST, *adj.* Uppermost, highest, supreme, chief, head, leading, preëminent, prominent, culminal, culminant, apical, tiptop, overmost, capital, polar, supernal.

TOPPLE, *v.* Fall top foremost, pitch forward, tumble down, topple down, topple over, tumble over, overturn, lurch, titubate, swag, sprawl, tilt, come a cropper, plump down, fall prostrate, fall to the ground, perish, go to pieces, crumble, break up, go to smash.

TOPSY-TURVY, *adj.* 1. With the top where the bottom should be, inverted, in a reversed position, upside down, wrong side up, bottom upward, keel upward, top side the other way, *sens dessus sens dessous (Fr.)*.

2. Disorderly, disordered, in complete disorder, upset, confused, disarranged, out of order, disorganized, out of place, disheveled, untidy, unsystematic, unmethodical, messy, slovenly, chaotic, hugger-mugger, deranged, knotted, entangled, inextricable.

TORCH, *n.* Source of illumination, flaming brand, flambeau, link, firebrand, light, mussal, cresset, beacon.

TOREADOR, *n.* Bullfighter, torero, matador, picador.

TORMENT, *v.* 1. Afflict with great suffering, torture, agonize, put to torture, rack, distress, excruciate, put to the rack, harass with anguish, pain extremely, harrow, lacerate, pierce, crucify, wring, convulse.

2. Annoy excessively, tease, plague, harry, tantalize, badger, harass, vex, worry, irritate, fret, chafe, provoke, nettle, trouble, persecute, hector, grill, molest, nag, taunt, pique, ruffle, displease, pester, treat maliciously, mistreat, abuse, bait, heckle, beset, infest, mortify, aggrieve, rile.

TORMENT, *n.* State of great suffering, agony, anguish, misery, extreme pain, acute distress, rack, torture, pang, excruciating pain, martyrdom, crucifixion, wretchedness, tribulation, extremity, despair, prostration, seizure, spasm, convulsion, paroxysm, throe, throb, lancination, laceration, shooting, soreness, twinge, bane, abomination, thorn, hell, curse, vexation, scourge.

TORNADO, *n.* Destructive rotary storm, whirlwind, hurricane, violent squall, cyclone, twister, whirling funnel, tempest, blizzard, samiel, typhoon, blast, gust, gale.

TORPEDO, *n.* Self-propelled explosive missile, underwater missile, shell, projectile, cartridge of gunpowder, detonating device, weapon, petard, rocket.

TORPID, *adj.* Passive, dormant, inactive, inert, sleepy, sluggish, dull, listless, apathetic, stupid, hebetudinous, indolent, otiose, slow, lethargic, comatose, motionless, numb, benumbed, insensate, drowsy, lifeless, insensible, heavy, stagnant, supine, languid, unfeeling, spiritless, unimpressible, cold, lazy, sedentary, latent, callous, inanimate, leaden, somnolent, phlegmatic, frigid, languorous, stupefied, indifferent, impervious, unconscious, insusceptible.

TORPOR, *n.* State of suspended physical activity, torpidity, torpescence, sluggishness, inactivity, inaction, inertness, dormancy, numbness, insensibil-

ity, coma, lethargy, stupor, inertia, dullness, stupefaction, drowsiness, lassitude, laziness, sloth, otiosity, heaviness, apathy, indifference, insensitiveness, impassibility, impassivity, insusceptibility, unimpressionableness, indifference, lukewarmness, unconcern, frigidity, coldness, callousness, hebetude, trance, catalepsy, suspended animation, daze, lull, languor, stagnation, somnolence.

TORREFY, v. Dry by fire, roast, parch with heat, scorch, simmer, seethe, singe, broil, grill, toast, fry, bake, char, sear, parboil, scald.

TORRENT, n. 1. Strong current, rapid stream, burn, brook, rivulet, rill, gill, rillet, gullet, brooklet, runnel, river, rapids, flush, spate, bore, freshet, vortex, eddy, maelstrom, whirlpool, gurge.

2. Rapid and copious flow, flood, inundation, deluge, downpour, shower, scud, cascade, fall, waterfall, waterspout, cataract, Niagara.

TORRID, adj. 1. Oppressively hot, tropical, sultry, broiling, parching, burning, arid, scorching, fiery, calorific, igneous, baking, roasting, close, stifling, sweltering, muggy, suffocating, stuffy.

2. Passionate, ardent, fervent, amorous, erotic, perfervid, amatory, impassioned, rapturous, affectionate, loving, sexual, desirous, lustful, appetitive.

TORSO, n. Trunk of the human body, butt, stock, body, main part, bole, axis, caudex.

TORT, n. (Law) Civil wrong, willful or negligent injury, wrongful act, trespass, breach, transgression, violation, delict, malpractice, misdeed, dereliction, delinquency, misconduct, misdoing, lapse, misdemeanor, malefaction, felony, offense.

TORTUOSITY, n. Twisted course, crooked form, sinuosity, sinuousness, tortuousness, crookedness, winding, ambagiousness, bend, curvature, crook, twist, convolution, circumvolution, involution, anfractuosity, sinuation, circuit, meandering, circumbendibus, twirl.

TORTUOUS, adj. 1. Full of twists, twisting, twisted, sinuous, meandering, mazy, labyrinthine, serpentine, winding, crooked, sinuate, curvilinear, curved, wreathed, anfractuous, ambagious, flexuous, bending in and out, zigzag, complicated, irregular, vermicular, convoluted, tortile, undulatory, sigmoidal, complicated, involved, daedalian.

2. Not straightforward, circuitous, indirect, roundabout, perverse, crooked, deceitful, ambiguous, dishonorable, dishonest, devious, corrupt, unscrupulous, knavish, fraudulent, disingenuous, false-hearted, two-faced, double-tongued, Machiavellian, insidious, conniving, perfidious, questionable, shady, slippery, perjured, treacherous, venal, mercenary, disloyal, faithless, untrustworthy.

TORTURE, v. 1. Afflict with severe pain, put to the rack, break on the wheel, agonize, torment, excruciate, rack, martyr, put to extreme distress, harrow, lacerate, harass, persecute, crucify, wound, hurt, pierce, stab, prick, wring, convulse, maltreat, flog, punish, abuse, assail, smite, chastise, strafe, castigate, gibbet, impale, martyrize.

2. Misrepresent, garble, twist unnaturally, pervert, wrest, distort, misapply, misinterpret, misrender, misuse, misconstrue, misdirect, falsify, misstate, travesty, caricature, burlesque.

TORTURE, n. 1. Persecution, cruelty, martyrdom, impalement, Inquisition, screws, rack, wheel, crucifixion, brutality, atrocity, outrage, fiendishness, inhumanity, barbarity, punishment, ordeal, trial, infliction, rough treatment, beating, lash,

galleys, flagellation, bastinado, stripe, blow, pillory, cyphonism, the stake.

2. Acute suffering, torment, agony, anguish, excruciation, intense distress, extreme pain, pang, dolor, ache, woe, affliction, hurt, twinge, shooting, lancination, laceration, soreness, discomfort, seizure, spasm, gripe, throe, paroxysm, convulsion, eclampsia, throbbing.

TORY, n. (English Politics) Supporter of royal authority, adherent of the crown, loyalist, one opposed to reform or radicalism, conservative, Silk-Stocking, Cavalier.

TOSS, v. 1. Throw by the hand, throw upward, pitch, fling, hurl, cast, propel, put, heave, shy, jerk, jaculate, dart, tilt, lance, pelt, sling, let fly.

2. Agitate, rock, sway, shake, disturb, flounce, move irregularly, convulse, wield, tumble, brandish, flap, wave, whisk, flourish, hitch, jerk, joggle, jolt, stir, churn, jostle.

3. Sway, tumble, flounder, roll, oscillate, undulate, vibrate, nutate, librate, wobble, pendulate, dangle, swing, waggle, vacillate, falter, waver, reel, fluctuate, quake, quiver, wriggle, quaver, tremble, stagger, totter, writhe, agonize, tumble about, be in violent commotion.

TOT, n. Infant, babe, baby, child, papoose, bambino, bairn, little one, mite, brat, chick, chit, kid, pickaninny, urchin, bratling, bantling, sprig, slip, cub, stripling, nestling.

TOTAL, adj. 1. Whole, full, complete, entire, integral, gross, integrate.

2. Absolute, unqualified, utter, thorough, concrete, universal, radical.

TOTAL, v. 1. Sum up, add, reckon, calculate, enumerate, compute, number, cast, numerate, cipher, figure.

2. Amount to, come to, involve, comprise, tot up to, mount up to.

TOTAL, n. Aggregate, sum, amount, totality, whole, gross, mass, lump, sum total, gross amount, all, accumulation, entirety, integer, integrality, completeness, everything.

TOTALITARIAN, adj. Pertaining to a centralized form of government intolerant of differing opinions, despotic, tyrannous, dictatorial, absolute, Fascist, Fascistic, Nazi, Communist, nationalistic.

TOTALITARIANISM, n. Highly centralized form of government allowing no representation to other political parties, Fascism, Nazism, Hitlerism, despotism, tyranny, dictatorship.

TOTE, v. Carry, transport, convey, bear, transfer, move, lead, forward, shift, remove, transplant, relegate, fetch, bring, conduct, transmit, dispatch

TOTEM, n. Object in nature assumed as the emblem of a clan or related group, distinctive mark, fetish, object of blind reverence, symbol, token, representation, sign, emblem, device, type, figure.

TOTTER, v. 1. Walk with faltering steps, reel, falter, stagger, wobble, sway, limp, hitch, vacillate, shake, oscillate, tremble, waddle, rock, waver, titubate, threaten to fall, lurch, flounder, dodder, claudicate, lumber, slug.

2. Flag, fail, fall, give way, crumble, droop, languish, decline, faint, fade.

TOUCH, v. 1. Perceive by the sense of feel, put the hand into contact with, finger, handle, paw, thumb, feel of, take in the hand, palm, grope, fumble, grabble, pass the fingers

palpate, stroke, twiddle, rub, massage, knead, manipulate, graze over, sweep, brush over, glance over, kiss, play with, fondle, caress, pet, cuddle, hug.

2. Meet, contact, be contiguous to, reach, abut on, attain to, arrive at, come to, join, border on, appertain to, be adjacent to, adjoin, impinge on, strike against, neighbor, hit.

3. Move, affect, thrill, inspire, possess, influence, penetrate, imbue, tinge, melt, soften, work upon, impress, act upon, go to one's heart, mollify, arouse, fire, stir, enkindle, interest, strike, excite, reach.

4. Irritate, annoy, sting, hurt, wound, nettle, ruffle, pique, abrade, scratch, cut, blemish, injure, impair, mar, spoil, damage, harm, infect, taint.

5. Refer to, treat of, allude to, make reference, hint at, speak of, make allusion to, bear upon, regard, pertain to, concern.

6. Call at, stop, tarry, stay, visit, halt, drop in, sojourn.

7. Touch up, doctor, amend, correct, improve, refine, emend, finish off, patch up, veneer, gloss.

TOUCH, *n.* 1. Feeling, tactility, taction, palpability, tangency, contact, impact, feel, sensation, tactile sense.

2. Manipulation, contrectation, palpation, handling, stereognosis, rubbing, massaging, fondling, fingering, kneading, stroking, massage, stroke, brush, grazing over, lambency.

3. Juncture, contiguity, juxtaposition, proximity, meeting, nearness, closeness, close union, propinquity, vicinity, adjacency, vicinage, connection, communication, reunion, concourse, intercommunication, harmony, accord, understanding, correspondence, agreement, intercourse, entente, comprehension, fellowship, sympathy.

4. Hand, finger, dukes (*sl.*), paw, feeler, thumb.

5. Power of exciting the affections, influence, impression, impressibility, pull, attraction, emotion, passion, sensibility, pathos, tenderness, concern, affection, response, inspiration, excitement, thrill, flutter, quiver, throb, palpitation, pulsation, tremor, flurry, agitation, warmth, ardor, ecstasy, zeal, *verve* (*Fr.*), *empressement* (*Fr.*).

6. Quality of touch, technique, performance, execution, virtuosity, interpretation, finish, polish, skill, rendition.

7. Trace, suggestion, dash, suspicion, soupçon, tinge, little, hint, intimation, smack, sprinkling, grain, taste, twinge, slight amount, pinch, bit, shade, cast, infusion, spice, savor.

8. Defect, flaw, imperfection, taint, blemish, fault, weakness, shortcoming, deficiency, error, failing, stain, spot, blot, speck, patch, blur, blotch, macula, smudge.

TOUCHABLE, *adj.* Tactile, tangible, palpable, tactual, substantial, material, real, corporeal, physical, bodily, somatic, sensible, ponderable, incarnate, fleshly.

TOUCH-AND-GO, *adj.* 1. Sketchy, superficial, desultory, hasty, perfunctory, facile, glib, mercurial, erratic, inconstant, unsteady, unstable, spasmodic, fitful, wayward, mobile, plastic, transient, fleeting, precipitate, premature, precocious, prevenient.

2. Risky, precarious, slippery, dangerous, perilous, hazardous, parlous, ticklish, aleatory, critical, hanging by a thread, at stake, in question, on slippery ground, shaky, threatening, explosive, ominous.

TOUCHED, *adj.* 1. Slightly crazy, unbalanced, unhinged, balmy (*sl.*), loco (*sl.*), eccentric, erratic, idiosyncratic, anomalous, abnormal, wayward, perverse, singular, odd, cranky, crotchety, whimsical, outlandish, screwball (*sl.*), crackpot (*sl.*), non compos mentis, cracked, deranged, moonstruck, crackbrained, hipped.

2. Compassionate, pitying, pitiful, sympathetic, tender-hearted, soft-hearted, commiserative, demonstrative, emotional, susceptible.

TOUCHINESS, *n.* Fretfulness, peevishness, irritability, petulance, testiness, pettishness, huffiness, irascibility, snappishness, waspishness, spleen, pepperiness, fieriness, temperamentalism, crabbedness, crustiness, surliness, fractiousness, contentiousness, refractoriness, perverseness, frowardness, grouchiness, sensitivity, excitability, tartness, impetuosity, nervousness, ferment.

TOUCHING, *adj.* 1. Soul-stirring, heartbreaking, heart-rending, pathetic, pitiable, moving, affecting, melting, impressive, tender, sad, plaintive, distressing, lamentable, sorrowful, mournful, rueful, doleful, deep-felt, indelible, poignant.

2. Inspiring, thrilling, electrifying, galvanic, magnetic, hypnotic, mesmeric, rapturous, ecstatic, telling, penetrating, pervading, absorbing, striking, exciting, sensational, overpowering, overwhelming, stimulating, provocative.

3. Adjacent, tangent, tangential, bordering, abutting, adjoining, contiguous, conterminous, close, near, neighboring.

TOUCHING, *prep.* Regarding, concerning, with regard to, relating to, apropos of, in reference to, respecting, in relation to, about, with respect to, anent, as regards, pertaining to, as to, as for, in connection with, in the matter of, re (*Law*).

TOUCHSTONE, *n.* 1. Black siliceous stone used to test the purity of gold and silver, basanite, Lydian stone, flint.

2. Criterion, standard, rule, proof, test, ordeal, touch, trial, assay, diagnostic, acid test, crucial test, tryout, probation, verification, canon, measure, formulary.

TOUCH UP, *v.* Improve by slight touches, repair, rework, rub up, mend, retouch, revamp, refurbish, modify, brush up, brighten up, polish up, doctor, tinker.

TOUCHY, *adj.* Apt to take offense on slight provocation, irritable, like touchwood, petulant, like tinder, huffy, resentful, exceptious, querulous, crabbed, crabby, crusty, quick-tempered, hot-tempered, fiery, temperamental, thin-skinned, captious, irascible, splenetic, snappish, peevish, testy, fractious, perverse, surly, froward, peppery, passionate, choleric, cross, fretful, waspish, contentious, quarrelsome, sour, edgy, excitable, nettlesome, hasty, impatient, moody, ill-natured, grouchy, churlish, cantankerous, dissentious, wrangling, disputatious, with a chip on the shoulder, indignant, offended, bitter, acrimonious, morose, sullen, unsociable, grumpy, sulky, gruff, mumpish, spiteful, cynical.

TOUGH, *adj.* 1. Adhesive, cohesive, tenacious, not tender, not brittle, chewy, leathery, coriaceous, viscous, viscid, stringy, cartilaginous, fibrous, ropy, sticky, clammy, clingy, glutinous, gristly, sinewy, gummy.

2. Not easily influenced, refractory, obdurate, incorrigible, unruly, unmanageable, stubborn, dogged, mulish, intractable, intransigent, rigid, stiff-necked, inflexible, unyielding, dour, callous.

3. Strong, sturdy, hardy, stout, firm, indomitable, invincible, muscular, athletic, hardened, lusty, robust, stalwart, brawny, powerful, vigorous, thick-set, well-set, forcible, strapping, puissant, Herculean, wiry.

4. Difficult, arduous, onerous, hard, trying, troublesome, laborious, grievous, formidable, uphill, irksome, thorny, labyrinthine, puzzling, knotty, perplexing, ticklish, critical, awkward, involved, intricate, exacting.

TOUPEE, *n.* Patch of false hair worn to cover a bald spot, wig, periwig, peruke, transformation, hairpiece.

TOUR, *n.* Traveling around from place to place, journey in a circuit, peregrination, periegesis, itinerary, pilgrimage, excursion, perambulation, circuit, round, course, expedition, trip, jaunt, ramble, outing, hadj, drive, trek, ride, turn, cruise, voyage, passage, sail, wayfaring, globetrotting, sightseeing, vagabondage, nomadism, roving, *Wanderlust (Ger.),* gadding, migration, emigration, pererration.

TOUR DE FORCE, *n.* Feat requiring unusual skill *or* strength, *coup de maître (Fr.), chef-d'oeuvre (Fr.),* masterpiece, good stroke, trick, sleight of hand, accomplishment, attainment, master stroke, stratagem, stroke of policy, *coup d'état (Fr.),* clever hit, bold move, bright thought, maneuver, juggle, *ruse de guerre (Fr.),* display, *coup de théâtre (Fr.),* demonstration, spectacle, exhibition.

TOURIST, *n.* Pilgrim, traveler, wayfarer, voyager, excursionist, tripper, sightseer, rubberneck *(sl.),* journeyer, wanderer, migrant, rambler, rover, hadji, trekker, motorist, globetrotter, adventurer, explorer, peregrinator, periegete, landlouper, itinerant, gadabout, roamer, gypsy, vagabond, nomad, palmer, peripatetic, tramper, hiker, passenger.

TOURNAMENT, *n.* Trial of skill in some game *or* contest, combat, tourney, joust, contest, match, martial sport, fight, battle, spear play, hastilude, skirmish, conflict, scrimmage, mêlée, clash of arms, scuffle, tussle, bout, engagement, action, passage of arms, agonism, concourse, set-to, fray, velitation, colluctation, tilt, tilting, list.

TOUSLED, *adj.* Disheveled, unkempt, disordered, slovenly, messy, untidy, knotted, entangled, tangled, frowzy, slatternly, draggletailed, uncombed, dowdy.

TOUT, *v.* 1. Solicit importunately, petition, supplicate, canvass, importune, dun, urge, press, appeal to, request urgently, ask earnestly, implore, entreat, beseech, endeavor to obtain, seek.

2. Describe in glowing terms, hail, praise highly and insistently, proclaim, eulogize, laud, extol, panegyrize, puff, praise to the skies, applaud, commend, acclaim, glorify, exalt, magnify, celebrate, sing praises, admire extravagantly, cry up, vaunt.

3. Spy on a race horse to obtain information for betting purposes, watch, espy, scrutinize, look into, investigate, pry into, inquire into.

TOW, *n.* 1. Fiber of flax prepared for spinning by scutching, jute, hemp, hards, oakum, yarn, cord, twist, whipcord.

2. Towage, pull, lift, drag, traction, drawing, draught, haul, haulage.

TOW, *v.* Draw along, drag, haul, take in tow, pull, tug, lug, draggle, trawl, yank, trail.

TOWARD, *prep.* 1. In the direction of, towards, on the road to, versus, to, in a line with, full tilt at, as the crow flies, point-blank.

2. Respecting, anent, apropos of, as regards, with regard to, with respect to, regarding, concerning, relating to, in reference to.

3. Nearly as late as, shortly before, near about, almost, nigh, near, about, not quite, close upon, at the point of, on the verge of, all but, approximately, thereabouts, roughly, well-nigh.

TOWARD, *adj.* 1. Promising, hopeful, apt, favorable, propitious, suitable, timely, seasonable, auspicious, encouraging, in a fair way, well-disposed.

2. Docile, compliant, tractable, manageable, towardly, ready, facile, easy, submissive, yielding, ductile, pliant, pliable.

3. That is to come, imminent, impending, oncoming, near at hand, destined, about to happen, in store, coming, brewing, forthcoming, on the cards, in the wind, in prospect, looming, in the future, on the horizon.

TOWER, *v.* Rise far upward, extend above, rise aloft, mount, soar, overtop, transcend, spire, loom, shoot up, surge, surmount, bulk large, uprise, rear, ascend, hover, impend, overhang, overlook, beetle, jut, culminate, cap, command.

TOWER, *n.* Steeple, spire, turret, skyscraper, column, campanile, citadel, fortress, arx, acropolis, castle, stronghold, pillar, refuge, rock, prison, dungeon, lookout, monument, pyramid, dome, cupola, bastille, belfry, minaret, fastness, capitol, asylum, obelisk, *flèche (Fr.),* tourelle, pagoda, keep.

TOWERING, *adj.* Very high, altitudinous, lofty, alpine, mountainous, tall, sublime, eminent, soaring, exalted, aerial, elevated, cloud-capt, heaven-kissing, snow-clad, rangy, beetling, overhanging, looming, crowning, apical, topmost, gigantic, colossal, big, sheer, climbing, ascending, scandent, mounting, mighty, stupendous, immense, huge, enormous, monstrous, supernal.

TOWN, *n.* 1. Relatively small collection of inhabited houses, borough, municipality, burg, village, thorp, hamlet, township, wick, settlement, kraal, pueblo, county seat, parish.

2. Large populous center, city, metropolis, cosmopolis, megalopolis.

TOWN HALL, *n.* 1. Building for transaction of a town's business, *hôtel de ville (Fr.), mairie (Fr.), Rathaus (Ger.), casa de ayuntamiento (Sp.), palazzo municipale (It.),* city hall.

2. Place of public assembly, meeting hall, meeting place, assembly room, auditorium.

TOWNSMAN, *n.* Inhabitant of a town, citizen, burgher, burgess, dweller, resident, habitant, residentiary, oppidan, villager.

TOWN-TALK, *n.* Hearsay, rumor, scuttlebutt *(sl.),* gossip, unauthenticated report, grapevine *(coll.), on dit (Fr.),* news stirring, bruit, buzz, scandal, *oui-dire (Fr.),* tittle-tattle, table-talk, idea afloat, topic of the day, canard, tidings, news, information, chitchat, idle talk, tattle, babble, cackle.

TOXIC, *adj.* Poisonous, virulent, noxious, toxicant, pernicious, venomous, unhealthy, pestilential, insalubrious, morbific, unwholesome, septic, azotic, pestiferous, deleterious, narcotic, deadly, lethal, fatal.

TOXIN, *n.* Poisonous disease-causing agent, pathogen, pathogene, infective agent, virus, venom.

TOY, *v.* 1. Bill and coo, fondle, caress, spoon, neck, cuddle, hug, pet, woo, philander, flirt, coquet, gallivant, wanton.

2. Dally, finger, fiddle, twiddle, play with, sport with, trifle, dandle, disport, revel, amuse oneself, carouse, make merry, caper, frisk, frolic, gambol, romp, sow one's wild oats.

TOY, *n.* 1. Plaything, doll, puppet, teddy bear, pull-toy, marionette, ball, top, whirligig, kewpie, popgun.

2. Bauble, gewgaw, knickknack, trinket, gimcrack, kickshaw, bagatelle, trifle, whimwham, teetotum, frippery.

TOY SHOP, *n.* Shop for the sale of children's toys, *boutique fantasque (Fr.)*, *Spielwarenladen (Ger.)*, *jugueteria (Sp.)*, *negozio di giocattoli (It.)*.

TRACE, *v.* 1. Follow footprints, trail, track, dog, hound, pursue, scent, nose out, hunt out, ferret out, mouse, shadow.

2. Ascertain by investigation, find out, discover, unearth, detect, probe, solve, sift, winnow out, search out, seek out, reconnoiter, look for, rummage, explore, sound, ransack, scour, peer, pry, survey, overhaul, examine, analyze, scrutinize, inspect, elicit, find, dig up, root out.

3. Draw, sketch, delineate, limn, mark out, copy, describe, make out the course of, follow the line of, represent, depict, portray, shape, figure, engrave.

4. Derive, etymologize, reduce, infer, draw from, conclude from.

TRACE, *n.* 1. Token of the former presence of, footprint, vestige, footmark, footstep, trail, track, spoor, scent, wake, remains, sign, mark, evidence, indication, impression, relic, imprint, pad, ichnite *(fossil)*, *piste (Fr.)*.

2. Very small amount, hint, suspicion, soupçon, tinge, touch, dash, bit, suggestion, flavor, streak, tincture, scintilla, iota, smack, trifle, shade.

TRACERY, *n.* Ornamental work of ramified ribs *or* bars, delicate interlacing work of lines, network, reticulation, fretwork, filigree, lattice, interlacement, gridiron, grille, grating, wattle, trellis, plait, plexus.

TRACK, *v.* 1. Follow by a track, trail, trace, chase, pursue, hunt, scent, tail, dog, hound, shadow.

2. Make one's way through, traverse, pererrate, wander over, pass through, range through.

TRACK, *n.* 1. Footmark, footprint, impress, imprint, impression, spoor, vestige, trace, footstep, mark left by anything that has passed along, wake, trail, scent, *piste (Fr.)*, pad.

2. Parallel lines of rails with cross ties, line of travel, course, road, path, way, pathway, beaten path, runway, rut, wheel rut, route, tack, beat, thoroughfare, line, railway.

TRACKLESS, *adj.* Pathless, untrodden, invious, impervious, impassable, impermeable.

TRACT, *n.* 1. Region, stretch, area, space, quarter, district, territory, sphere, place, soil, arena, ground, realm, domain, scene, hemisphere, terrain, locale, location, locality, part, spot, situation, orb, circle, circuit, pale, precinct, bailiwick, beat, march, piece of land, plot, lot, patch, field, real estate.

2. Thesis, treatise, essay, written discourse, tractate, disquisition, homily, sermon, dissertation, composition, pamphlet, booklet, monograph, brochure, theme, memoir, descant, lecture, exposition, study, investigation, research, critique,

commentary, criticism, review, leader, article, editorial.

TRACTABLE, *adj.* 1. *(Persons)* Docile, submissive, manageable, yielding, willing, governable, teachable, controllable, amenable, compliant, complaisant, obedient, dutiful, affable, guidable, leadable.

2. *(Things)* Readily wrought, plastic, malleable, ductile, tractile, adaptable, facile, pliable, pliant, flexible, flexile, supple, extensible, flexuous, argillaceous, clayey.

TRACTION, *n.* Hauling, drawing, haulage, transportation, draught, pulling, towage, yank, tug, drag, trawl, jerk.

TRACTIONAL, *adj.* Pulling, tractive, drawing, tractile, ductile, attractive.

TRADE, *v.* Exchange in commerce, buy and sell, carry on commerce, do business, merchandise, drive a trade, drive a bargain, interchange, bargain, swap, barter, chaffer, dicker, negotiate, speculate, deal in, traffic in, nundinate, keep a shop, ply a trade, transact, bid for, haggle, higgle, huckster.

TRADE, *n.* 1. Commerce, purchase and sale, buying and selling, merchandising, business, negotiation, truck, traffic, dealing, barter, bargaining, exchange of commodities, transaction, nundination, speculation, interchange, marketing, swap, business intercourse, commercial enterprise, mercantile business, merchantry, mercantilism, commercialism, jobbing, brokerage, stockjobbing.

2. Manual occupation, handicraft, craft, mechanical employment, industrial art.

3. Profession, occupation, business, employment, vocation, metier, craft, line of work, livelihood, pursuit, calling, avocation, office, situation, position, job, post, undertaking, concern, affair, line, function, duty, task, assignment, charge, incumbency, living, berth, billet, enterprise.

TRADEMARK, *n.* Name of a manufacturer used to designate a line of goods, hallmark, label, ticket, badge, countermark, countercheck, countersign, counterfoil, criterion, identification, tally, billet, cachet, voucher, witness, stamp, seal, monogram, sigil, signet, superscription, brand, insigne, token, symptom, symbol, letter.

TRADER, *n.* Merchant, merchandiser, dealer, retailer, shopkeeper, tradesman, businessman, monger, trafficker, hawker, vendor, seller, huckster, peddler, shopman, chandler, sutler, chapman, colporteur, moneychanger, broker, cambist, banker, financier, stockbroker, stockjobber, buyer, jobber.

TRADITION, *n.* 1. Handing down of beliefs from generation to generation, unwritten body of doctrines, usage, unwritten law, traduction, oral report, custom, folklore, lore, prescription, immemorial usage, assuetude, use, practice, observance, conventionality, old school, consuetude, standing order, precedent, routine, superstition.

2. Legend, myth, saga, annals, memorials, epos, epic, tale, story, fiction, narrative.

3. *(Law)* Legal transfer of possession, formal delivery.

TRADITIONAL, *adj.* Orally transmitted from generation to generation, traditive, traditionary, unwritten, prescriptive, immemorial, rooted, inveterate, customary, conventional, old, legendary, fabulous, mythical, ancestral, wonted, consuetudinous, established, acknowledged, fixed, ingrafted, ingrained, historic, epic, storied.

TRADUCE, *v.* Speak disparagingly of, run down, vilify, malign, revile, disparage, asperse, defame, calumniate, detract, decry, depreciate, derogate, denigrate, blacken, besmirch, slander, scandalize, brand, speak ill of, degrade, abuse, expose to contempt, blaspheme, willfully misrepresent, criticize, belittle, pull to pieces, lampoon, libel, anathematize, backbite, berate, impeach, impugn, accuse, denounce, stigmatize, gibbet, censure, reprobate, berate, rail at, execrate, dispraise, discredit, blackball, ostracize.

TRADUCER, *n.* Vilifier, calumniator, detractor, maligner, defamer, slanderer, censor, derogator, carper, critic, knocker, backbiter, satirist, lampooner, libeler, vituperator, reviler, denigrator, blackener, besmircher, censurer.

TRAFFIC, *v.* 1. Engage in commercial dealings, carry on commerce, buy and sell, deal, trade, chaffer, bargain, barter, swap, exchange, hawk, vend, huckster, merchandise, truck, market, ply a trade, haggle, higgle, dicker, negotiate.
2. Trade illicitly, sell improperly, bootleg, smuggle, run, poach, be a fence for, engage in white-slaving.

TRAFFIC, *n.* 1. Commercial dealings, trade, buying and selling, commerce, merchantry, merchandising, mercantilism, truck, exchange of commodities, barter, swap, chaffer, business, mongering, hawking, vending, transaction, interchange, marketing, nundination, business intercourse, commercial enterprise, mercantile business, stockjobbing, brokerage.
2. Illicit business, white-slaving, dope-peddling, bootlegging, rumrunning, smuggling.
3. Coming and going along a way of passage, transportation, movement, transport, conveyance, portage, freight, transit.

TRAGEDIAN, *n.* Tragic actor, actor of tragedy, Thespian, performer of tragedy, tragedienne, player.

TRAGEDY, *n.* 1. Dramatic composition of somber character with an unhappy ending, buskin, cothurnus, Melpomene, Thespis.
2. Dreadful event, shocking misfortune, fatal affair, catastrophe, calamity, disaster, cataclysm, blow, adversity, affliction, evil day, mishap, misadventure, accident, casualty, bale, woe.

TRAGIC, *adj.* 1. Dramatic, theatrical, buskined, histrionic.
2. Deadly, fatal, lethal, calamitous, disastrous, catastrophic, cataclysmic, dire, mortal, lethiferous, sanguinary, gory, bloodstained, slaughterous, mournful, dolorous, grievous, dismal, depressing, melancholy, dreary, cheerless, funereal, lugubrious, woeful, pitiable, lamentable, sad, pathetic, touching, appalling, grim, shocking, crushing, dreadful, heartbreaking, destructive, ruinous, hapless, ill-starred, ominous, inauspicious.

TRAIL, *v.* 1. Track, pursue, hound, hunt, follow, trace, tail, shadow, dog.
2. Drag along, haul, tug, draw, creep, crawl, steal, glide stealthily, grovel.
3. Hang down loosely from behind, float, flow, stream, be pendent, swing, droop, dangle, sag, flap, daggle.

TRAIL, *n.* 1. Trace, track, footmark, footprint, footstep, vestige, spoor, scent, *piste (Fr.)*.
2. Footpath, path, road, way, pathway, roadway, bridlepath, beaten track, byway.

3. Wake, trail, rear, queue, tail, appendage, afterpiece, tag.

TRAIN, *v.* Discipline, habituate, accustom, exercise, rehearse, familiarize, domesticate, housebreak, break in, inure, prepare, educate, instruct, school, tutor, drill, teach, bring up, qualify, nurture, equip, nurse, rear, prime, initiate, coach, guide, enlighten, inform, ground, indoctrinate, instill, implant, inculcate, brainwash, infuse, direct, tame, impregnate, imbue.

TRAIN, *n.* 1. Retinue, suite, cortege, entourage, staff, body of attendants, followers, following, cavalcade, escort, clientage, clientele, adherents, attendance.
2. Wake, rear, trail, tail, queue, tag, appendage, afterpart, extension, prolongation, continuation.
3. Series, succession, chain, sequence, consecution, sequel, line, row, set, gradation, progression.
4. Rolling stock, railroad cars, coaches, flatcars, boxcars, railroad train, express, limited, special, freight train, Pullmans, sleepers, day coaches.

TRAINED, *adj.* Disciplined, broken, tamed, domesticated, housebroken, reared, brought up, experienced, skilled, practiced, qualified, educated, fitted, thoroughpaced, competent, deft, versed, grounded, initiated, drilled, *au fait (Fr.)*, skillful, expert, dexterous, adroit, handy, quick, proficient, up to, good at, master of, crack, masterly, accomplished, efficient, capable.

TRAINING, *n.* Instruction, preparation, apprenticeship, schooling, practice, discipline, teaching, drilling, education, tuition, breeding, nurture, tutorship, tutelage, pedagogy, didactics, inculcation, edification, indoctrination, direction, guidance, initiation, qualification.

TRAIT, *n.* Characteristic, peculiarity, feature, particularity, mark, distinguishing quality, idiosyncrasy, lineament, diagnostic, mannerism, trick, differentia, singularity, detail, item, cast, property, earmark.

TRAITOR, *n.* Deceiver, betrayer, apostate, renegade, turncoat, perfidious person, snake in the grass, wolf in sheep's clothing, serpent, Judas, Iscariot, deserter, mutineer, insurgent, rebel, revolter, conspirator, reprobate, ingrate, hypocrite, false friend, recreant, knave, villain, rogue, scoundrel, rascal, caitiff, miscreant, cheat, archtraitor, complotter, colluder, accomplice, squealer, sneak, telltale, mischief-maker, varlet.

TRAITOROUS, *adj.* Perfidious, treacherous, Punic, Iscariotic, recreant, faithless, false-hearted, unfaithful, disloyal, insidious, seditious, treasonable, apostate, renegade, venal, mercenary, disingenuous, two-faced, double-tongued, perjured, corrupt, untrustworthy.

TRAMMEL, *v.* 1. Fetter, shackle, manacle, handcuff, pinion, hobble, enchain, put in irons, entrammel, muzzle, bridle, tie, gag, bind hand and foot, tie up.
2. Restrain, restrict, curb, hamper, cumber, cramp, confine, clog, hinder, thwart, retard, check, frustrate, obstruct, oppose, impede, circumvent, discommode, incommode, constrain, coerce, debar, control, hold back, suppress, repress, prohibit, handicap.

TRAMMEL, *n.* 1. Anything that impedes free action, impediment, shackle, fetter, bond, clog, pinion, handcuff, manacle, chain, gyve, irons, bracelets, darbies, halter, yoke, harness, gag, muzzle, bit, snaffle, bridle, lines, leading strings, tether, brake, drag.

2. Restraint, coercion, hindrance, constraint, cohibition, durance, confinement, duress, coarctation, imprisonment, thralldom, incarceration, detention, custody.

3. Prevention, preclusion, prohibition, interruption, interclusion, interception, impedition, retardation, oppilation, restriction, inhibition, obstruction.

TRAMONTANE, *adj.* 1. Beyond the mountains, pertaining to the other side of the mountains, ultramontane, transalpine.

2. Distant, remote, far away, ulterior, yonder, antipodean, hyperborean, out of the way, inaccessible, unapproachable, telescopic, distal, far off.

3. Foreign, alien, barbarous, exotic, heathenish, pagan, strange, outlandish, barbaric, barbarian.

TRAMP, *v.* 1. Tread with a heavy resounding step, trudge, march, plod, traipse, jog on, stamp, clatter, stump.

2. Travel on foot, itinerate, go on a walking journey, hike, peregrinate, pererrate, perambulate, wander, rove, roam, nomadize, trek, tour, pilgrim, migrate, flit, prowl, range, wend, patrol, straggle, meander, ramble, jaunt, stroll, stray, saunter, gad about.

TRAMP, *n.* 1. Journey on foot, stroll, hike, walking excursion, march, walk, saunter, ramble, trek, peregrination, perambulation, pererration, itineration, expedition, circuit, trip, tour, pilgrimage, hadj, jaunt, periegesis, vagabondage, gadding, flit.

2. Resounding footfall, heavy tread, stamp, firm walk.

3. Idle wanderer, tramper, stroller, vagrant, vagabond, nomad, gypsy, hobo, bum, knight of the road, landloper, beachcomber, derelict, outcast, flotsam and jetsam, loafer, rogue, beggar, itinerant, migrant, okie, wayfarer, hiker, hitchhiker, pilgrim, hadji, trekker, floater, sundowner, ragamuffin, panhandler, pariah.

TRAMPLE, *v.* 1. Tread heavily, step noisily, stamp, stump, traipse.

2. Trample in the dust, humiliate, knock down, fell, prostrate, subvert, upset, debase, lower, take down a peg, abase.

3. Subjugate, vanquish, grind under foot, conquer, defeat, rout, overcome, overpower.

4. Treat with scorn, defy, disregard, set at naught, fling to the winds, infringe, violate, transgress, break, do violence to, spurn, ride roughshod over, tempt Providence, carry with a high hand, domineer, hector, bully, bulldoze, beard, fly in the face of, intimidate, browbeat, dragoon.

TRANCE, *n.* 1. Half-conscious state between sleeping and waking, dazed and bewildered condition, catalepsy, coma, suspended animation, lethargy, stupor, stupefaction, daze, torpor.

2. Hypnosis, mesmerism, somnambulism, automatism, ecstasy.

3. Fit of complete mental absorption, preoccupation, prepossession, reverie, brown study, deep musing, woolgathering, castles in Spain, abstraction.

TRANQUIL, *adj.* Free from commotion *or* tumult, peaceful, halcyon, serene, irenic, undisturbed, unruffled, untroubled, unperturbed, placid, quiet, calm, still, smooth, even, pacific, composed, quiescent, sedate, hushed, unexcited, reposeful, restful, peaceable, dispassionate, equable, stoical, philosophical, unimpassioned, undemonstrative,

easygoing, agreeable, temperate, mild, moderate, gentle, soft, submissive, resigned, uncomplaining, passive, reasonable, sober, cool.

TRANQUILIZE, *v.* Calm, compose, soothe, quiet, pacify, hush, quell, allay, appease, assuage, moderate, ease, lay, lull, still, silence, alleviate, palliate, soften, mitigate, mollify, temper.

TRANQUILLITY, *n.* Quiet, composure, quietude, serenity, placidness, placidity, peacefulness, tranquilness, repose, calmness, peace, quietness, stillness, calm, equanimity, rest, concord, harmony, amity, pacifism, suspension of hostilities, truce, armistice, calumet, peace pipe, olive branch.

TRANSACT, *v.* 1. Carry through to a conclusion, perform, carry out, complete, accomplish, perpetrate, consummate, dispatch, execute, achieve, settle, do, work, enact, commit, prosecute, exercise, function, operate.

2. Negotiate, treat, conduct, manage, carry on, direct, regulate, administer, deal, discharge, supervise, superintend, govern, guide.

TRANSACTION, *n.* 1. Performance, completion, accomplishment, perpetration, consummation, dispatch, execution, achievement, enactment, commission, exercise, operation.

2. Negotiation, treatment, management, direction, regulation, administration, superintendence, supervision, procedure, method, proceeding.

3. Deed, act, business, affair, deal, dealing, matter, job, piece of business, doings, measure, maneuver, enterprise, move, *coup (Fr.),* feat, exploit, pursuit, task.

4. Incident, event, happening, occurrence, fact, episode, phenomenon, circumstance, experience, adventure, contingency, eventuality, pass.

TRANSCEND, *v.* Overstep, overpass, pass over, go beyond, transgress, trespass, overleap, exceed, rise above, surmount, excel, eclipse, overshadow, outdistance, outrival, overtop, outstrip, surpass, outvie, outdo, be superior, outrank, outweigh, throw into the shade, prevail, predominate, take precedence, take the cake *(sl.),* beat hollow, outshine.

TRANSCENDENCY, *n.* Superior excellence, pronounced superiority, supereminence, predominance, predomination, ascendancy, preëminence, preponderancy, prevalence, advantage, authority, influence, prestige, primacy, supremacy, paramountcy, sovereignty, record.

TRANSCENDENT, *adj.* 1. Going beyond ordinary limits, extraordinary, unparalleled, unrivaled, very superior, supereminent, supreme, consummate, peerless, preëminent, unique, unequaled, inimitable, nonpareil, unsurpassed, matchless, incomparable, paramount, sublime, magnificent, foremost, utmost, principal, crowning, unapproached, dominant, second to none, *sans pareil (Fr.),* sovereign.

2. Transcending the scope of knowledge, transcendental, supersensible, noumenal, metempirical, transcending the limits of possible experience, not realizable in human experience, outside consciousness, beyond direct apprehension, beyond the range of reason.

3. Vague, obscure, speculative, indefinite, occult, abstruse, indistinct, intangible, impalpable, recondite, abstract, mystical, dark, mystic, mysterious, fantastic, thin, rarefied, attenuated, unreal, unintelligible, puzzling, supernatural, preternatural, hidden, innate, intuitive, immanent.

TRANSCRIBE, *v.* Make a copy of in writing, write a copy of, reproduce, copy, imitate, set down in black and white, translate, write out in other characters, transliterate, decode, decipher, rewrite, reword.

TRANSCRIBER, *n.* Copyist, copier, scribe, scrivener, writer, amanuensis, clerk, secretary, penman, stenographer, shorthand writer, typist.

TRANSCRIPT, *n.* Written copy, transcription, duplicate, rescript, facsimile, engrossment, counterpart, tracing, revise, reprint, replica, reproduction, imitation.

TRANSFER, *n.* 1. Removal, change of place, displacement, dislodgment, translocation, shift, transference, relegation, transportation, transit, shipment, transmission, assignment, commitment, traduction, removal, translation, disposition, devolution, convection, transplantation, committal, conduction, transposition, transposal, transvection, movement, carriage, transshipment, truckage, cartage, portage, freightage, ferriage, telpherage, waftage, transition, passage.

2. Disposal, bequest, devisal, devise, conveyance, alienation, abalienation, release, legacy, bequeathal, demise, deed, lease, sale, quitclaim, exchange, barter, enfeoffment, gift, grant, cession.

3. Lading, cargo, freight, goods, load, luggage, baggage, traffic, mail.

TRANSFER, *v.* 1. Convey from one place to another, transport, dispatch, send, transmit, remit, translate, remove, remand, change residence, tote, waft, bear, forward, pass on, hand over, relegate, shift, transpose, dislodge, displace, fetch, bring, convoy, conduct, consign, delegate, deliver, embark, ship, mail, freight, express, post.

2. Assign, grant, devise, bequeath, will, donate, leave, mancipate, give, pass down, hand down, convey, alienate, enfeoff, sequester, cede, demise, lease, deed, sell, rent, let, exchange, negotiate, make over, transmit, dispossess, disinherit, disown, cut off, exheredate.

TRANSFERABLE, *adj.* 1. Assignable, conveyable, transmissible, transmittible, transmissive, alienable, abalienable, negotiable, bequeathable, reversional, devisable, communicable, contagious, infectious, catching.

2. Portable, movable, portative; conductible.

TRANSFIGURATION, *n.* Change in appearance, metamorphosis, change of form, transformation, transmutation, transmogrification, alteration, permutation, modification, metastasis, transubstantiation, metagenesis, metathesis, avatar.

TRANSFIGURE, *v.* 1. Change in outward form, alter in appearance, metamorphose, transform, transmogrify, convert, transmute, revamp, work a change, modify, revolutionize.

2. Change so as to glorify, idealize, dignify, exalt, immortalize, signalize, deify, apotheosize, enthrone, consecrate, enshrine, lionize, crown with laurel.

TRANSFIX, *v.* 1. Fix fast on something sharp, impale, spear, skewer, spit, stake, perforate, transpierce, pierce through, penetrate, broach, pin, run through, thrust through, empierce, bore, enfilade, spike, gore, pink, stab, puncture, trepan, lance, stick, riddle, prick, stave in, punch.

2. Make motionless with amazement, rivet, possess, ensorcel, fascinate, entrance, enchant, bewitch, electrify, galvanize, hypnotize, mesmerize, captivate, intrigue, absorb, intoxicate, overpower, astound, stun, petrify.

TRANSFORM, *v.* Change the form of, transfigure, transfigurate, metamorphose, transmute, trans-

mogrify, translate, convert, resolve, revolutionize, alter, transubstantiate, ring the changes, remold, recast, remodel, reconstruct, reform.

TRANSFORMATION, *n.* Transmutation, transfiguration, metamorphosis, avatar, change of form, transmogrification, transfigurement, transmorphism, translation, conversion, metastasis, regeneration, metempsychosis, alteration, permutation, modification, transubstantiation.

TRANSFUSE, *v.* Pour from one container into another, transfer by pouring, transmit, convey, instill, infuse, inject, imbue, diffuse through.

TRANSFUSION, *n.* Transfer, transference, transmission, convection, transplantation, conduction.

TRANSGRESS, *v.* 1. Overstep, intrude, overpass, pass over, encroach, go beyond, cross the line, transcend, exceed, trespass, invade.

2. Disobey, disregard, violate, infringe, contravene, break, set at naught, refuse submission to, defy, ignore, go counter to, take the law into one's own hands, run riot, kick over the traces, secede, rebel, mutiny.

3. Sin, err, offend, do amiss, slip, stray, fall, lapse, relapse, recidivate, misbehave, misconduct oneself, trip, go astray, deviate from the line of virtue, sow one's wild oats, do wrong.

TRANSGRESSION, *n.* 1. Encroachment, infringement, infraction, breach, violation, disobedience, nonobservance, transgressing, overstepping, transilience, inroad, contravention, invasion, disobedience, lawlessness, omission, noncompliance, lawbreaking.

2. Crime, sin, misdeed, misdemeanor, delinquency, dereliction, peccadillo, iniquity, offense, misdoing, trespass, error, wrong, evil deed, fault, slip, lapse, recidivism, wrongdoing, outrage, moral obliquity, the old Adam, knavery, infamy, debauchery, immorality, impurity, unchastity.

TRANSGRESSIVE, *adj.* Culpable, reprehensible, guilty, sinful, wrong, lawless, faulty, peccable, censurable, uncommendable, blameworthy, objectionable, *in flagrante delicto (Lat.),* in the act, red-handed, iniquitous, vicious, immoral, evil, corrupt, wicked, criminal, felonious, bad, abandoned, shameless, infamous, nefarious, flagitious, opprobrious, heinous, flagrant, incorrigible, recidivistic, reprobate.

TRANSGRESSOR, *n.* Trespasser, delinquent, malefactor, culprit, criminal, offender, sinner, wrongdoer, evildoer, misdemeanant, reprobate, violator, recidivist, malfeasant, felon, rotter *(sl.),* ne'er-do-well, black sheep, *âme damnée (Fr.),* villain, scoundrel, blackguard, miscreant, libertine, wanton, debauchee, profligate, rake, roué, thug, gunman, hoodlum, hooligan, gangster, ruffian.

TRANSIENCE, *n.* Impermanence, temporariness, evanescence, fugaciousness, fugacity, ephemerality, caducity, mortality, volatility, transitoriness, brevity, changeableness, span, swiftness, nine days wonder, bubble, kaleidoscope, shifting sands, wheel of fortune, vicissitude, uncertainty, twinkling, split second, flash, moment, breath, instant.

TRANSIENT, *adj.* 1. Passing with time, not lasting, not enduring, impermanent, transitory, fugitive, fugacious, evanescent, ephemeral, diurnal, short-lived, fleeting, here today and gone tomorrow, ephemerous, caducous, deciduous, volatile, meteoric, temporary, perishable, unenduring, mortal, soon past, vanishing, migratory, cursory, monohemerous, provisional, provisory, elusive, temporal, precarious, kaleidoscopic, changeful, inconstant, unstable.

2. Brief, hasty, fleet, quick, hurried, summary, brisk, momentary, instantaneous, sudden, abrupt, spasmodic, fitful, expeditious, speedy, precipitate, headlong, immediate, express.

TRANSIT, *n.* 1. Passing, change, movement, going, motion, migration, flight, wing, course, transition, journey, voyage, route, crossing, departure.

2. Conveyance, transportation, transfer, transport, translation, carriage, moving, transvection, shipment, transshipment, truckage, cartage, portage, ferriage, freightage.

TRANSITION, *n.* Passage from one state to another, change, passing, shifting, transit, gradation, graduation, variation, alteration, modification, modulation, flux, motion, saltation, break, jump, leap, shift, conversion, transmutation, transformation, progress, metastasis, metabasis, phase.

TRANSITIONAL, *adj.* Passing, changing, transitionary, alterative, modifiable, changeable, plastic, alterable, mobile, fluctuating, variable, mutable, kaleidoscopic, protean, versatile.

TRANSITORY, *adj.* Passing away, not permanent, transient, flitting, fleeting, evanescent, fugacious, temporary, momentary, short-lived, ephemeral, here today and gone tomorrow, brief, temporal, unenduring, fugitive, vanishing, flying, provisional, deciduous, cursory, mortal, meteoric, cometary.

TRANSLATE, *v.* 1. Change into another form, transmute, transform, transmogrify, alter, convert, transfigure, metamorphose, remold, recast, remodel, reconstruct.

2. Carry from one place to another, remove, transfer, transport, move, convey, tote, forward, bear, transpose, dislodge, displace, transplant, convoy, conduct.

3. Turn from one language into another, decode, decipher, interpret, construe, render, reword, rephrase, paraphrase, literalize, explain, spell out, elucidate.

TRANSLATION, *n.* 1. Removal, transference, conveyance, transportation, transvection, carry, transport, movement, carriage, shipment, transshipment, cartage, freightage.

2. Version, rendition, interpretation, rendering, key, decoding, deciphering, definition, paraphrase, rewording, elucidation, explanation, reddition, reading, construction, sense, metaphrase, interlinear, gloss, equivalent meaning.

TRANSLUCENCY, *n.* Semitransparency, translucence, diaphaneity, diaphanousness, limpidity, pellucidness, transparency, sheerness, semiopacity, pearliness, glassiness, gossameriness, milkiness, opalescence, gauziness, filminess, mistiness.

TRANSLUCENT, *adj.* Transmitting light diffusely, semitransparent, semiopaque, pellucid, translucid, semidiaphanous, pearly, opalescent, opaline, milky, misty, frosted, glassy, crystalline, tralucent.

TRANSMIGRATE, *v.* 1. Pass from one place to another, migrate, trek, emigrate, peragrate, roam, nomadize, peregrinate.

2. Be reborn at death into another body, transanimate, turn into, be converted into, become, assume the state of, undergo a change, assume a new phase, resolve into, metamorphose.

TRANSMIGRATION, *n.* 1. Seasonal migration, transhumance, trek, peregrination, pererration, pilgrimage, nomadism, emigration.

2. Passage of the soul at death into another body, transanimation, metempsychosis, reincarnation, rebirth, avatar, transfiguration, metamorphosis, transubstantiation, metagenesis, transmogrification.

TRANSMISSION, *n.* Transference, transfer, translocation, transmittal, conveyance, transmittance, circulation, radiation, traduction, transportation, forwarding, sending, dispatch, conduction, propagation, delivery, dispersion, passage, permeation, penetration, infiltration, transudation.

TRANSMIT, *v.* 1. Transfer, send, consign, dispatch, mail, forward, remit, deliver, express, post, ship, send on.

2. Bequeath, give by will, devise, leave to, hand down, cede, endow.

3. Radiate, emit, irradiate, relume, broadcast.

TRANSMUTABLE, *adj.* Changeable, commutable, convertible, modifiable, alterative, transitional, mutable, versatile, protean, proteiform, alterable.

TRANSMUTATION, *n.* 1. Change, conversion, reduction, resolution, alteration, mutation, permutation, variation, modification, development, transition.

2. Transformation, transfiguration, metamorphosis, transmogrification, transubstantiation, metagenesis, metathesis, catalysis.

TRANSMUTE, *v.* Change from one form *or* nature into another, transform, turn, convert, adapt, be converted into, become, turn into, merge into, assume the state of, assume a new phase, undergo a change, reorganize, come round to.

TRANSOM, *n.* Crosspiece separating a door from a window above it, ventilator, fanlight, lintel.

TRANSPARENCY, *n.* 1. Diaphaneity, translucency, transparence, diaphanousness, translucidity, clearness, glassiness, pellucidity, transillumination, limpidity, lucidity, thinness, sheerness, sleaziness, flimsiness, transpicuousness.

2. Silk, chiffon, nylon, gossamer, tissue, cobweb, gauze, rayon, tulle, crystal, glass, hyaline.

3. Intelligibility, comprehensibleness, palpability, plainness, clearness, perspicuity, lucidness, perspicuousness, explicitness, clarity, plain speaking, openness, frankness, candor, candidness, sincerity, ingenuousness, simplicity, honesty.

TRANSPARENT, *adj.* 1. Transmitting light through its substance, diaphanous, transpicuous, translucent, that may be seen through, lucent, limpid, crystalline, silken, silky, clear, sheer, gauzy, sleazy, thin, porous, flimsy, hyaline, vitreous, cloudless, glassy.

2. Plain, unequivocal, explicit, unambiguous, evident, distinct, apparent, patent, obvious, manifest, clear-cut, perspicuous, intelligible, lucid, visible, palpable, unmistakable, self-evident, perceptible.

3. Frank, candid, plain-speaking, open, direct, sincere, honest, artless, ingenuous, unsophisticated, simple, innocent, aboveboard, straightforward.

TRANSPIRE, *v.* 1. Emit waste matter, exhale, evaporate, ooze, perspire, volatilize, vaporize, distill, fume, smoke, steam, reek.

2. Happen, occur, take place, arise, appear, be met with, present itself, befall, fall out, come to pass, supervene, eventuate, betide, chance, turn up, crop up.

3. Be disclosed, escape from secrecy, become known, come out, come to light, get abroad, be made public, leak out, show its face.

TRANSPLANT, *v.* 1. Replant, plant in a new place, repot, slip, graft.

2. Transfer, carry, tote, remove, transport, transpose, transmit, transplace, bear, shift, conduct, fetch.

TRANSPORT, *v.* 1. Carry from one place to another, remove, conduct, transfer, transpose, transplant, truck, cart, ship, dispatch, convey, fetch, take, bear, bring, tote, lug, send, waft, move, translate, smuggle, run, transmit, deliver, consign, freight, post, mail, express, convey.

2. Banish to a penal colony, deport, relegate, ostracize, expel, drive out, exile, drum out.

3. Carry away by strong emotion, ravish, enrapture, enravish, enchant, entrance, captivate, possess, rivet, electrify, galvanize, thrill, send *(sl.)*, put into ecstasy, beatify, delight, overpower, gladden, intrigue, stimulate, allure, take one's fancy, charm, fascinate, ensorcel, bewitch.

TRANSPORT, *n.* 1. Violent excitement, passion, raptus, seizure, frenzy, vehemence, warmth, paroxysm, outburst, outbreak, furor, rage, madness, delirium, raving, distraction, hysterics.

2. Ecstatic joy, rapture, bliss, felicity, ecstasy, thrill, delight, elation, enchantment, exultation, delectation, enravishment, rejoicing, enthusiasm, happiness, beatitude, beatification, ravishment, titillation, enjoyment, oblectation, seventh heaven, paradise, elysium.

3. Transport vessel, transport ship, tender, store-ship, merchantman, packet, freighter, cargo ship, freight steamer, lighter, troopship, cruiser, liner.

TRANSPORTATION, *n.* 1. Transport, shipment, conveyance, dispatch, carriage, transmission, portage, freightage, haulage, transshipment, transportal, traduction, convection, truckage, transvection, movement, cartage, telpherage.

2. Transit, transition, passage, shift, removal, displacement, change, translocation.

3. Forced exile, banishment, deportation, asportation, relegation, ostracism, expulsion, proscription, expatriation.

TRANSPORTING, *adj.* Intensely pleasurable, thrilling, heavenly, entrancing, enchanting, ravishing, voluptuous, charming, exquisite, delightful, sensuous, delectable, luxurious, felicitous, rapturous, ecstatic, fascinating, magnetic, electrifying, galvanizing, alluring, seductive, captivating, bewitching, enticing, exciting.

TRANSPOSE, *v.* Alter the relative position of, change the order of, put one in place of the other, substitute one for another, interchange, reverse, shift, transfer, cause to change places, transplant, exchange, invert, counterchange, commute, alternate.

TRANSPOSITION, *n.* Transposal, changing, interchange, inversion, substitution, reversal, transference, exchange, counterchange, commutation, alternation, transmutation, permutation, transposal, intermutation, *quid pro quo (Lat.),* shuffle, contraposition.

TRANSUBSTANTIATION, *n.* 1. Change of one substance into another, transformation, conversion, mutation, alteration, transfiguration, metamorphosis, transmogrification, transmutation, metagenesis, catalysis.

2. Eucharist, Lord's Supper, communion, the holy sacrament, celebration of the mass, real presence, consubstantiation, consecration of the elements.

TRANSUDE, *v.* Ooze through interstices, pass through pores, exude, percolate, filter, strain, leak, transcolate, distill, seep, perspire, sweat, extravasate, effuse, disembogue.

TRANSVERSE, *adj.* Lying across, being in a cross direction, oblique, cross, thwart, athwart, intersecting, antiparallel, diagonal.

TRAP, *v.* 1. Catch in a trap, snare, entrap, ensnare, enmesh, noose, springe, entangle, forelay, bait the hook, lime, spread the toils, entoil, benet, illaqueate, sniggle, trepan.

2. Take by stratagem, lead on by artifice, bait, decoy, waylay, lure, inveigle, ambush, close in on, outmaneuver, surround, trick, deceive, delude, beguile, hook in, trip up.

TRAP, *n.* 1. Mechanical device to take game, snare, trapfall, gin, deadfall, pitfall, toil, net, spring, trepan, pit, springle, decoy, hook, noose, cobweb, meshes, birdlime.

2. Ambuscade, ambush, artifice, stratagem, ruse, feint, wile, trick, maneuver, cul-de-sac, blind, plant, fetch, bubble, machination, booby trap, mine, battery.

3. Percussion instrument, bass drum with a cymbal attached, snare drum.

4. Light two-wheeled carriage, gig, buggy, sulky, shay, droshky, surrey.

TRAPPINGS, *n., pl.* 1. Articles of dress, clothes, investment, clothing, raiment, attire, drapery, costume, toilette, guise, habiliment, trim, vesture, palliament, garb, things, apparel, array, finery, garniture, togs.

2. Equipment, outfit, uniform, gear, livery, harness, turnout, caparison, accouterments, rigging, suit, traps, khakis, canonicals, academicals, full dress, fittings.

3. Ornaments, frippery, finery, embellishments, paraphernalia, decorations, adornments, trimmings, trim, ornamentation, ornature, frills and furbelows.

TRASH, *n.* 1. Rubbish, litter, refuse, waste matter, worthless stuff, dross, trumpery, sweepings, dregs, scum, residue, scoriae, slag, residuum, leavings, offal, junk, odds and ends, castoffs, lumber, orts, rags, rubble, debris, dottle.

2. Balderdash, nonsense, twaddle, rigmarole, bosh, flummery, hogwash, moonshine, jargon, jabber, gibberish, patter, palaver, fudge, drivel, rot, flapdoodle.

3. Person of low repute, riffraff, scum, rabble, hoi polloi, good-for-nothing, *vaurien (Fr.),* *Taugenichts (Ger.),* flotsam and jetsam, chaff, canaille, ragtag and bobtail.

TRASHY, *adj.* Useless, worthless, trifling, flimsy, trumpery, insignificant, paltry, poor, unimportant, rubbishy, petty, inane, twaddling, trivial, inutile, futile, bootless, unavailing, inept, unserviceable, meritless, valueless, good-for-nothing, not worth a straw, worn-out, not worth powder and shot.

TRAUMA, *n.* 1. Bodily injury, lesion, wound, cut, laceration, bruise, hurt, stab, concussion.

2. *(Psychiatry)* Startling experience which has a lasting effect on mental life, shock, blow, ordeal, strain, jolt, succussion, disturbance, surprise, thunderclap, bolt from the blue.

TRAVAIL, *n.* 1. Childbirth, parturition, accouchement, lying-in, confinement, delivery, labor, birth pains, birth-throe, obstetrics.

2. Physical toil, exertion, strain, effort, stress, work, drudgery, sweat of one's brow, fagging, slavery.

TRAVEL, *n.* Excursion, trek, expedition, trip, tour, journey, peregrination, periegesis, pilgrimage, hadj, circuit, jaunt, ride, cruise, voyage, passage, sail, perambulation, tramp, wayfaring, sightseeing, globetrotting, nomadism, vagabondage, *Wanderlust (Ger.)*, migration, hoboism, flitting, gadding, route, itinerary, course, road.

TRAVEL, *v.* Go from one place to another, journey, take a trip, rove, roam, itinerate, peregrinate, perambulate, pererrate, make a tour, take a journey, make an excursion, range, wander, nomadize, march, commute, knock around, trek, ride a magic carpet, voyage, cruise, tour, sail, pilgrim, flit, migrate, drive, motor, auto, jaunt, stray, meander, gad about, straggle, promenade, visit, sightsee, globetrot.

TRAVELER, *n.* 1. Wayfarer, peripatetic, periegete, excursionist, tripper, tourist, wanderer, rover, nomad, itinerant, voyager, journeyer, globetrotter, sightseer, peregrinator, passenger, trekker, explorer, pilgrim, hadji, migrant, rambler, cosmopolite, polytopian, adventurer, bird of passage, gadling, gadabout, landloper, vagabond, beachcomber, gypsy.

2. Traveling salesman, drummer, representative, commercial traveler, retail man.

TRAVELING, *adj.* Itinerant, nomadic, ambulatory, periegetic, perambulatory, rambling, vagrant, roving, gadding, circumforaneous, migratory, migrant, wayfaring, globetrotting, sightseeing.

TRAVEL-WORN, *adj.* Wearied by traveling, wayworn, travel-stained, weather-beaten, footsore, fatigued, weary, spent, exhausted, ready to drop, out of breath, dog-tired, played-out, on one's last legs.

TRAVERSE, *v.* 1. Pass from point to point, travel, cross in traveling, travel over, go across, wander over, pass through, overpass, range, ply, ford, cut across, itinerate, track, roam, ramble, peregrinate, pererrate, course, perambulate, promenade, tramp, trek, patrol, march, walk, cruise, sail, navigate.

2. Pass in review, survey carefully, pass over and view, examine thoroughly, measure, scour, scan, inspect, reconnoiter, probe, plumb, gauge, fathom, sound.

3. Cross in opposition, go counter to, obstruct, thwart, balk, foil, frustrate, contravene, counteract, defeat, circumvent, disconcert.

4. Contradict, deny, negate, gainsay, controvert, negative, shake the head, disavow, disclaim, impugn, dispute, join issue upon, rebut, repudiate, give the lie to.

TRAVERSE, *adj.* Lying across, crosswise, cross, athwart, transverse, across, crossing, oblique, intersecting, adverse.

TRAVESTY, *v.* Turn to ridicule by burlesque imitation, imitate grotesquely, turn into burlesque, parody, ape, take off, make fun of, ridicule, deride, twit, poke fun at, rag, satirize, burlesque, caricature, pervert, misrepresent, garble, distort, overdraw, misinterpret, exaggerate.

TRAVESTY, *n.* Ludicrous literary treatment of a serious subject, burlesque, parody, take-off, caricature, mockery, farce, low comedy, imitation, satire, exaggeration, distortion, misrepresentation, perversion, falsification.

TRAY, *n.* Flat shallow container, receptacle with slightly raised edges, trencher, salver, waiter, coaster, server, hod, dorser, scuttle, utensil, patera.

TREACHEROUS, *adj.* 1. Violating faith, betraying trust, untrustworthy, faithless, Punic, disloyal, recreant, perfidious, two-faced, double-tongued, false-hearted, traitorous, unfaithful, treasonable, deceitful, untrue, false, betraying, insidious, undependable, malicious, sly, wily, fraudulent, tricky, designing, Iscariotic, devious, ill-intentioned, spiteful, venomous, unscrupulous, unprincipled, timeserving, Machiavellian, crooked, slippery, perjured, sneaking, purchasable, venal, deceptive.

2. Dangerous, risky, precarious, unstable, insecure, unsafe, unreliable, rotten, critical, hanging by a thread, between Scylla and Charybdis, on slippery ground, on the brink of a precipice, topheavy, shaky, tottering, ramshackle, tumble-down, crumbling, nodding to its fall, trembling in the balance, ominous, threatening, explosive.

TREACHERY, *n.* Violation of faith, betrayal of trust, faithlessness, breach of faith, deceitfulness, deception, Punic faith, double-dealing, insidiousness, Machiavellism, perfidy, perfidiousness, fraudulence, conspiracy, collusion, intrigue, machination, complot, cabal, betrayal, infidelity, breach of allegiance, treason, recreancy, disloyalty, foul play, perjury, dishonesty, guilefulness, wiliness, falsehood, duplicity, dissimulation, subtlety, cunning, misrepresentation, trickery, knavery, hanky-panky, improbity, Judas kiss, Iscariotism, apostasy, venality.

TREAD, *v.* 1. Step, pace, walk, tramp, march, go, trudge, plod, traipse, stump, pad, stride, stalk, wend, hike, bowl, strut, paddle, toddle, mince, shuffle, jog, promenade, peg on, stroll, stray, jaunt, saunter, meander, perambulate, straggle, gad about, ramble, prowl, range, roam, rove, trek, amble.

2. Dance, prance, waltz, fox-trot, tango, glide, trip, frisk, caper, caracole, curvet, cavort.

3. Crush, trample upon, subdue, subjugate, reduce, overcome, floor, thrash, settle.

TREAD, *n.* Step, pace, stride, rate, gait, port, clip, carriage, locomotion, trek, footstep, footfall.

TREASON, *n.* Treachery, breach of allegiance, lese majesty, disloyalty, sedition, rebellion, revolt, prodition, subversion, conspiracy, complot, machination, cabal, faithlessness, breach of faith, betrayal of a trust, perfidy, perfidiousness, insurgence, outbreak, mutiny, insurrection, revolution, secession, insubordination, disobedience, apostasy.

TREASONABLE, *adj.* Treacherous, disloyal, perfidious, faithless, traitorous, proditorious, unfaithful, perjured, Iscariotic, fraudulent, false-hearted, two-faced, double-tongued, mutinous, insurgent, rebellious, seditious, revolutionary.

TREASURE, *v.* 1. Put away for future use, keep in store, stow away, conserve, amass, lay by, garner, accumulate, lay in, hoard, save, treasure up, store, husband, collect and reposit, put by, fund, bank, *cacher (Fr.)*.

2. Cherish, value, prize, hold dear, esteem, revere, regard, cling to, idolize, dote upon, count precious, care greatly for, coddle.

TREASURE, *n.* Riches, wealth, savings, money hoarded up, cash, funds, hoardings, hoard, store, stock, abundance, reserve, thesaurus, nest egg, wherewithal, capital, finance, bullion, gold bricks, Spanish doubloons, pieces of eight, nugget, ingot, gold, silver, precious gems, wampum, cache, mazuma, jack, dough, spondulics, simoleons, shekels, millions.

TREASURER, *n.* Receiver of moneys, bursar, purser, cash-keeper, banker, cashier, trustee, depositary, cofferer, quaestor, financier, accountant, steward, paymaster, almoner, teller.

TREASURE-TROVE, *n.* Bullion found hidden away, cache, prize, windfall, godsend, unexpected good fortune, velvet, bonanza, El Dorado, trouvaille.

TREASURY, *n.* 1. Place where funds are kept, exchequer, fisc, repository, thesaurus, depository, bursary, coffer, strongbox, chest, money-box, till, moneybag, purse, bank, safe, fiscus.
2. Funds, revenue, securities, shares, stocks, bonds, gilt-edged securities.

TREAT, *v.* 1. Behave toward, manage, handle, use, behave to, deal with, act toward, wield, manipulate, exercise, utilize.
2. Doctor, dose, attend, prescribe for, remedy, relieve, palliate, heal, cure, medicate, minister, dress, nurse.
3. Entertain, gratify, refresh, feast, regale, indulge, divert, satisfy, amuse, gladden, stimulate, tickle the palate, satiate, quench, pamper, coddle, humor, cheer, enliven, pleasure.
4. Negotiate, bargain, covenant, make terms, come to terms, parley, temporize, stipulate, dicker, haggle, higgle, contract, agree, engage, adjust, settle.

TREAT, *n.* 1. Sweetmeat, tidbit, *bonne bouche (Fr.)*, candy, sugarplum, confectionery, comfits, confections, caramel, lollipop, bonbon, taffy, butterscotch, pastry, dessert, puff, *pâtisserie (Fr.)*, tart, pie, pudding, cake, kickshaw, mouthful, morsel, ambrosia, nectar, manna.
2. Entertainment given by way of friendly regard, feast, banquet, junket, repast, spread, feed, snack, collation, refection, potluck, picnic, tea, dinner, supper, luncheon, party, fete, fiesta, refreshment, festival, festivity, revelry, carnival, jollification, frolic, holiday.

TREATISE, *n.* Book treating of some particular subject, dissertation, thesis, disquisition, discourse, tract, tractate, commentary, essay, brochure, theme, composition, writing, homily, study, descant, memoir, discussion, investigation, exposition, review, appreciation, criticism, critique, article, publication, volume, tome, work, lucubration, codex, booklet, pamphlet, enchiridion, manual, handbook.

TREATMENT, *n.* 1. Handling, manner of dealing, course, procedure, management, manipulation, conduct, line of action, execution, practice, way, process, transaction.
2. Medical care, therapy, doctoring, regimen, dietary, rehabilitation, recruital.

TREATY, *n.* International compact, agreement between nations, interstate covenant, formal contract, alliance, concordat, pact, league, convention, charter, entente, protocol, *entente cordiale (Fr.)*, deal, understanding, bargain, bond, negotiation, Axis *(World War II)*.

TREBLE, *v.* Make threefold, multiply by three, triple, make three times as much, triplicate, cube.

TREBLE, *n. (Mus.)* Highest part for a human voice, shrill sound, high voice, high note, falsetto, soprano, tenor, *voce di testa (It.)*.

TREBLE, *adj.* 1. Threefold, triple, triplicate, triform, trinomial, triune, tertiary, trigonal, triquetral, deltoid, three-ply, tern, ternate, trinal, triplex, triadic, tripartite, trifid, trifurcate, trisulcate, tridental, tripodal, trifoliolate, triarch.

2. Of the highest pitch *or* range, shrill, acute, sharp, high, high-pitched, piercing, trumpet-toned, stridulous, strident, metallic, reedy.

TREE, *n.* 1. Perennial woody plant of considerable height, pollard, sapling, stand, bush, shrub, espalier, cordon, arbuscle, arbor, seedling, Yggdrasil *(Scand. Myth.)*, Baum *(Ger.)*, arbre *(Fr.)*, arbrisseau *(Fr.)*, árbol *(Sp.)*, albero *(It.)*, timber tree, fruit tree — dendron *(suffix)*.
2. Family tree, genealogy, pedigree, diagram indicating main stem and branches of a family, stock, lineage, line, stirps, house, family, clan, sept, extraction, descent, ancestry, birth, forebears, forefathers.
3. Gallows, gibbet, Tyburn tree, noose, halter, rope, drop, scaffold, cross, crucifix, rood.

TREE-SHAPED, *adj.* Dendriform, dendritic, arborescent, treelike, branched, arboreous, arboreal, arboriform, ramous, ramose, ramiform, dendroidal, dendroid, arborized, symmetrical.

TREK, *v.* Travel *(by ox wagon)*, migrate, journey, emigrate, roam, rove, patrol, peregrinate, traverse, peragrate, nomadize, wander, straggle, tramp, trudge, plod.

TREK, *n.* Migration, transhumance, emigration, expedition, journey, excursion, wayfaring, peregrination, pilgrimage, vagrancy, nomadism, roving, vagabondage.

TRELLIS, *n.* Structure of lattice-work, framework for the support of growing vines, lattice frame, *treillage (Fr.)*, arbor, kiosk, summerhouse, grille, wattle.

TREMBLE, *v.* Shake involuntarily with quick short movements, pulsate, quake, shiver, shudder, quaver, quiver, palpitate, flutter, twitter, falter, totter, rock, dodder, vibrate, quail, oscillate.

TREMENDOUS, *adj.* 1. Dreadful, frightful, alarming, horrific, terrible, horrible, fearful, horrid, horrendous, terrific, appalling, awful, direful, formidable, dire, portentous, dread, perilous, fell, shocking, redoubtable, ghastly, awe-inspiring.
2. Immense, monstrous, huge, elephantine, colossal, vast, mountainous, gargantuan, towering, strapping, lumbering, gigantic, titanic, megatherian, mammoth, Cyclopean, Brobdingnagian, giant.
3. Extraordinary, unusual, egregious, uncommon, singular, rare, unwonted, unique, remarkable, wonderful, wondrous, noteworthy.
4. Inordinate, undue, excessive, immoderate, extravagant, exorbitant, unreasonable, unconscionable, preposterous, extreme, gross, crass.

TREMOR, *n.* Vibratory movement, fit of trembling, involuntary shaking, quivering, quaking, quake, trepidation, tremulousness, agitation, perturbation, nervousness, flutter, shudder, shiver, shock, stir, jolt, twitter, pulsation, throe, spasm, palpitation, convulsion, throb, paroxysm, vellication, subsultus, jactation, jactitation.

TREMULOUS, *adj.* 1. Trembling, shaking, shivering, quivering, quavering, shaky, vibrating, quivery, quavery, tremulant, vibratory, saltatorial, jerky, spasmodic, convulsive, saltant.
2. Irresolute, infirm, undecided, fidgety, wobbly, hesitant, changeable, unstable, inconstant, mutable, vacillating, faltering.
3. Fearful, timorous, nervous, apprehensive, agitated, afraid, diffident, faint-hearted, panic-stricken, alarmed, anxious, cowardly, skittish.

TRENCH, *n.* 1. Long narrow excavation in the ground, ditch, gutter, fosse, drain, moat, furrow, sewer, pit, watercourse, trough, channel, deep cut, hollow, groove, sulcation, canaliculus, dike, depression, cutting.

2. Shelter from hostile fire, intrenchment, dugout, fortification, mine, bulwark, screen, safeguard, rampart, parapet, levee, embankment, breastwork, bank, mound, earthwork, fieldwork, redoubt.

TRENCHANT, *adj.* 1. Cutting, sharp, biting, keen, incisive, acute, pointed, knife-edged, sharp-edged, razor-edged.

2. Sarcastic, caustic, acrid, tart, ironical, pungent, piquant, poignant, penetrative, piercing.

3. Sententious, pithy, terse, crisp, dogmatic, arbitrary, concise, succinct, laconic, commatic, curt, epigrammatic, pregnant.

4. Emphatic, cogent, impressive, vivid, intense, salient, forcible, powerful, significant, explicit, graphic, spirited, thoroughgoing, vigorous, effective, clearly defined.

TREND, *v.* Have a general tendency, tend to take a particular direction, extend in some direction indicated, drift, gravitate, incline, turn, verge, stretch, run, sweep, lean, set, aim, steer for, bend, dip, level at, be bound for.

TREND, *n.* General course, tendency in a certain direction, drift, bent, inclination, leaning, direction, set, bearing, aim, run, tack, tenor, route, beeline, proclivity, propensity, proneness, impulse, bias, predisposition.

TREPAN, *v.* 1. Pierce, perforate, bore, tap, drill, puncture, pink, lance, trephine, prick, stick, punch, riddle, stave in, cut a passage through, open, uncover.

2. Trap, snare, entrap, ensnare, bait, forelay, spread the toils, decoy, waylay, hook in, benet, springe, entangle, illaqueate.

TREPIDATION, *n.* 1. Vibratory movement, vibration, oscillation, agitation, tremor, quivering, shaking, quaking, trembling, stir, jolt, shock, jar, succussion, jactitation.

2. State of terror, tremulous excitement, perturbation, panic, dismay, fear, terror, alarm, consternation, demoralization, disquietude, nervousness, jitteriness, pins and needles, flutter, cold sweat, cold feet, funk, fright, pavor, affright, awe, dread, horror, scare, stampede, bugaboo, nightmare, hobgoblin.

TRESPASS, *v.* 1. Pass unlawfully within the boundaries of another's property, overstep proper boundaries, invade, intrude, obtrude, infringe, encroach, trench, enter unlawfully, poach, violate, assume possession of others' property, crowd onto the rights of others.

2. Commit an offense, offend against, sin, transgress, err, misbehave, misconduct oneself, lapse, fall, trip, go astray, deviate from rectitude, stray, slip, misconduct oneself, break the Commandments.

TRESPASS, *n.* 1. Wrongful entry upon another's lands, invasion, intrusion, infringement, infraction, violation, encroachment, forced entrance, injury, overstepping, transilience, inroad, breach.

2. Transgression, sin, wrongdoing, fault, crime, misdeed, delinquency, misdemeanor, felony, error, evildoing, iniquity, the old Adam, corruption, viciousness, immorality, wickedness, criminality, misconduct, misbehavior, peccadillo, misdoing,

malpractice, turpitude, depravity, enormity, outrage, atrocity, lapse, slip, trip, misstep, failing.

TRESPASSER, *n.* 1. Intruder, encroacher, trencher, invader, poacher, violator, infringer.

2. Wrongdoer, evildoer, offender, transgressor, sinner, delinquent, misdoer, worker of iniquity, profligate, libertine, wanton, debauchee, bad example, reprobate, blackguard, culprit, malefactor, criminal, malfeasant, recidivist, felon, outlaw.

TRESS, *n.* Plait of hair, ringlet, curl, lock, braid, thatch.

TRIAL, *n.* 1. Subjection to grievous experiences, suffering, affliction, trouble, infliction, distress, heartache, sorrow, tribulation, hardship, cross, burden, grief, woe, wretchedness, misery, dolor, unhappiness, chagrin, vexation, pain, mortification, rue, misfortune, adversity, blow, shock, bad luck, adverse fortune, evil day, gathering clouds, hard times, ill wind, rainy day, blight, curse, humiliation, pressure, load, mischance, mishap, misadventure, calamity, disaster, catastrophe, casualty, accident, scourge, visitation, reverse, setback, ruin, fall, undoing, losing game, concern, solicitude, ordeal.

2. Putting to the proof, examination, inspection, investigation, assay, test, scrutiny, inquiry, review, analysis, study.

3. Attempt, experiment, essay, tryout, probation, verification, venture, speculation, leap in the dark, random shot, straw in the wind, pilot balloon, *ballon d'essai (Fr.),* flyer *(coll.),* effort, endeavor, aim, struggle, exertion, criterion, touchstone, proof.

4. Determination of a person's guilt or innocence by process of law, lawsuit, case, hearing, action, arbitration, litigation, cause, judicial contest, arraignment, prosecution, indictment, accusation, true bill, presentment.

TRIANGLE, *n.* Geometrical plane figure formed by three straight lines forming three angles, three-sided figure, trigon, delta, oxygon, wedge, triskelion, cube, trigraph.

TRIANGULAR, *adj.* Three-sided, three-cornered, trigonal, deltoid, triquetral, triquetrous, tricorn, wedge-shaped, trilateral, trigonous.

TRIBAL, *adj.* Pertaining to a tribe, tribular, phyletic, phylogenic, racial, consanguineous, kindred, allied, affiliated, sib, agnate, cognate, akin, related, lineal, ancestral, clannish.

TRIBE, *n.* 1. Aggregate of people united by ties of descent from a common ancestor, clan, sept, phyle, family, lineage, race, gens, stock, stirps, breed, strain, line, brotherhood, fraternity, local division of a primitive people, caste.

2. Class, order, genus, species, phylum, kind, sort, distinct portion, group, clique, coterie, lodge, society, association, set, faction.

TRIBULATION, *n.* Grievous trouble, severe trial, vexation of spirit, distress, affliction, misery, infliction, hard road, cross, grief, suffering, wretchedness, adversity, woe, sorrow, calamity, catastrophe, misfortune, hardship, pain, dolor, rue, unhappiness, visitation, worry, plague, mortification, *mauvais quart d'heure (Fr.),* blow, shock, anxiety, care, solicitude, load, burden, concern, heartache, extremity, desolation, prostration, despair, agony, anguish, throe, torment, torture, martyrdom, crucifixion, the stake, the rack, adverse fortune, evil day, curse, blight, scourge, setback, reverse, undoing, ordeal.

TRIBUNAL, *n.* 1. Raised platform for the seats of magistrates, judgment-seat, bench, dais, rostrum, board, mercy seat.

2. Court, bar, assizes, judicature, sessions, judicatory, Inquisition, forum, Areopagus, Star Chamber, woolsack, Chancery, High Court, judiciary, circuit.

TRIBUTARY, *adj.* Paying tribute, contributing, furnishing subsidiary aid, contributory, ancillary, auxiliary, subordinate, subject, inferior, sportulary, adjuvant, accessory, subsidiary.

TRIBUTARY, *n.* Stream contributing its flow to a larger body of water, affluent, feeder, reach, anabranch, brook, rivulet, streamlet, gill, brooklet, runnel, runlet, creek, burn, run, rill, rillet.

TRIBUTE, *n.* 1. Tax, duty, impost, levy, excise, toll, assessment, custom, charge, rent, payment, discharge, settlement, acquittance, fee, subsidy, bribe, ransom, gift, donation, remuneration, pay, subvention, subscription, aid, sportula, offering, grant, honorarium, bonus, oblation, consideration, largess, gratuity, tip, douceur, offertory, *pourboire (Fr.), Trinkgeld (Ger.),* cumshaw, handout, blood money, protection money, shake-down, peace offering, sop, graft, palm grease *(sl.).*

2. Personal testimonial, compliment given in acknowledgment of esteem, praise, laud, laudation, panegyric, eulogy, encomium, eulogium, commendation.

TRICE, *n.* Very short time, twinkling, instant, moment, second, minute, flash, jiffy, crack, breath, *coup (Fr.).*

TRICK, *n.* 1. Sleight, legerdemain, prestidigitation, jugglery, deftness, knack, craft, juggle, skill, adroitness, technic, featness, dexterity.

2. Prank, caprice, gambol, antic, joke, escapade, *espièglerie (Fr.),* whimsy, quirk, freak, mischievous behavior, caper, roguery.

3. Peculiar habit, peculiarity, idiosyncratic practice, mannerism, specialty, idiosyncrasy, trait, characteristic, singularity, eccentricity, crotchet, vagary.

4. Artifice, ruse, wile, fraudulent expedient, underhanded act designed to cheat someone, feint, shift, blind, hocus-pocus, stratagem, fetch, maneuver, gammon, fraud, fake, deception, crafty device, imposture, dodge, shuffle, imposition, hoax, trap, finesse, humbug, swindle, deceit, chicane, doubling, cheat, double-dealing, game, chouse, cog, circumvention, cozenage, delusion, subterfuge, sham, bunco, chicanery, machination, conspiracy, complot, jape, sharp practice, sophistry, intrigue, pretense, cunning contrivance.

TRICK, *v.* 1. Deceive by trickery, bamboozle, hoax, humbug, gammon, gull, take in, cheat, dupe, diddle, swindle, beguile, chouse, cozen, befool, play false, defraud, trap, delude, impose upon, bilk, trim, outmaneuver, flimflam, evade, lure, circumvent, overreach, hoodwink, fob, victimize, mislead, jockey, betray, bait, snare, outwit, outreach, practice upon, palm off on, inveigle, entangle, bluff, stuff, mystify, sell *(sl.),* counterfeit, sham, dissimulate, dissemble.

2. Trick out, set off, bedizen, deck, decorate, embellish, enhance, ornament, attire, apparel, beautify, adorn, dress, array, enrich, furbish, garnish, prink, bedight, spruce up, preen.

TRICKERY, *n.* Use of tricks, deceitfulness, chicanery, hocus-pocus, flimflam, charlatanry, mountebankery, quackery, imposture, imposition, bunkum, pretense, claptrap, knavery, pettifogging, skulduggery, circumvention, rascality, villainy, sharp practice, Machiavellianism, duplicity, intrigue, cunning, device, stratagem, blind, feint, ruse, wile, artifice, fraud, deception, chicane, craftiness, wiliness, insidiousness, slipperiness, crookedness, shiftiness, evasiveness, artfulness, ingeniousness, dexterity.

TRICKLE, *v.* Fall by drops, drip, drop, dribble, distill, percolate, trill, flow gently, seep, exude, transude, leak, ooze, drain, sweat, well out, plash, spurt, spirtle.

TRICKSTER, *n.* Sharper, swindler, charlatan, mountebank, impostor, faker, quack, cheat, empiric, pretender, juggler, prestidigitator, hocus-pocus, tricker, double-dealer, con man, shark, scoundrel, rascal, knave, deceiver, shifter, rogue, villain, dissimulator, deluder, dissembler, cozener, fourflusher, humbug, conjurer, magician, wizard, sorcerer, shaman.

TRICKSY, *adj.* 1. Tricky, crafty, wily, deceitful, cunning, roguish, scampish, guileful, knavish, villainous, crooked, shifty, timeserving, subtle, arch, artful, unprincipled, designing, unscrupulous, intriguing, rascally, fraudulent, foxy, deceptive, *rusé (Fr.),* sly, insidious, underhand, double-faced, canny, strategic, scheming, bogus, misleading, elusive, delusive.

2. Mischievous, frolicsome, playful, sportive, *folâtre (Fr.),* playsome, frisky, gamesome, waggish.

3. Trim, spruce, dapper, dandy, fine, neat, trig, goodly, jaunty, natty, smart, tidy, immaculate.

TRIDENDATE, *adj.* Three-toothed, having three points, tridented, tricuspid, tricuspidate.

TRIFLE, *v.* 1. Deal lightly, act with levity, toy, amuse oneself, dally, play, fribble, dabble, fiddle-faddle, putter, frivol, palter, dawdle, handle, finger, paw, diddle, quiddle, dillydally, fondle, flirt, pet, spoon, neck, spark, philander, coquet.

2. Neglect, slur, skim, scamp, skimp, skip, take a cursory view of, dip into, run over, not trouble oneself with, pass by, slight, omit, pass over.

TRIFLE, *n.* 1. Fragment, modicum, trace, particle, iota, small quantity, jot, atom, minimum, molecule, speck, point, fleabite, mote, dot, spark, tittle, drop, mite, nip, bit, dash, dab, dole, tinge, sprinkling, grain, minim, crumb, pinch, chip, fraction, shred, scrap, sliver, splinter.

2. Small matter, triviality, article of small value, bagatelle, bauble, trinket, gewgaw, gimcrack, knickknack, thing of no moment, matter of slight importance, bean, fig, straw, bubble, nothing, brass farthing, pin, red cent, peppercorn, button, halfpenny, rap, tinker's dam, feather, continental, plaything, toy, kickshaw, whimwham.

TRIFLER, *n.* Time waster, procrastinator, dallier, fribbler, idler, potterer, dawdler, piddler, waiter on Providence, neglector, drifter, dillydallier, shilly-shallier, slacker.

TRIFLING, *adj.* Inconsequential, insignificant, picayune, unimportant, of slight importance, trivial, frippery, petty, nugatory, piddling, of little value, slight, of no moment, finicking, worthless, immaterial, inconsiderable, paltry, puny, little, inappreciable, nominal, beggarly, weak, frivolous, shallow, superficial, light, airy, foolish, silly, idle, minute, sorry, flimsy, niggling, fribbling, trashy, second-rate, two-by-four, gimcrack, cheap, trumpery, catchpenny, brummagem.

TRIG, *adj.* 1. Tidy, trim, spruce, natty, neat, smart, chic, dapper, jaunty, stylish, debonair, comely, elegant.

2. In good physical condition, sound, hale, healthy, well, fit, strong, hearty, hardy, picture of health, in fine fettle.

TRILL, *v.* 1. Sing with a vibratory effect, warble, carol, cantillate, troll, intone, yodel, chirrup, twitter, sol-fa, lilt.

2. Resound vibrantly, shake, quaver, vibrate, tremble, quiver.

TRILL, *n.* Rapid alternation of two consecutive tones, tremolo, vibrato, warbling, quaver, shake, grace note, *appoggiatura, acciaccatura (It.),* turn, *fioritura (It.),* bravura, roulade, *coloratura (It.),* cadenza, run, *arpeggio (It.).*

TRIM, *v.* 1. Clip, cut, shear, lop, prune, mow, poll, shave, crop, cut off, pare, barber, curtail, truncate, dock, shorten, abbreviate, diminish, take in, abridge, check the growth of.

2. Adjust, arrange, balance, equalize, fill, set right, put in order, equate, make equal, dress, level, coördinate.

3. Decorate, adorn, ornament, embellish, bedeck, deck, trick out, set off, array, set out, garnish, beautify, perk, prink, prank, spruce, enrich, ornamentalize, bedizen, smarten, polish, furbish, spangle, bespangle, embroider, bead.

4. Rebuke, chastise, castigate, scold, chide, reprimand, berate, rate, disparage, abuse, upbraid, rail at, revile, denounce, vilify, recriminate, censure, blame, reproach, criticize, impugn, impeach, take to task, overhaul, dress down.

5. Defeat, vanquish, beat hollow, trounce, lick, drub, pommel, belabor, subjugate, subdue, floor, buffet, thrash, lambaste, overcome, conquer, master, overpower, discomfit, outdo, checkmate, rout, worst.

6. Pursue a neutral course, be cautious, be timeserving, be on the fence, temporize, shuffle, hedge, stall, shift, vacillate, fluctuate, blow hot and cold, play fast and loose, change sides, veer round, balance, dodge, straddle, wait to see how the wind blows.

TRIM, *adj.* 1. Neat, compact, lean, thin, slender, slight, slim, shapely, lithe, lissome, svelte, limber, supple, streamlined, well-proportioned, shipshape, athletic, fit, compact, dainty, delicate, petite, comely, personable, handsome, pretty, beauteous, seemly.

2. Spruce, chic, dapper, smart, elegant, finical, perky, natty, trig, jaunty.

TRIM, *n.* 1. State, fettle, kilter, good condition, form, frame, constitution, morphology, figure, configuration, conformation, make, set, build.

2. Dress, array, trappings, equipment, gear, attire, apparel, costume, panoply, decoration, ornamentation, garnish, decorative trimming, adornment, ornature, embellishment, finery, tinsel, spangle, frippery, clinquant, sequin, frills and furbelows.

TRIMMER, *n.* One who pursues a cautious policy between parties, temporizer, cunctator, Fabianist, timeserver, timist, timepleaser, ambidexter, weathercock, Janus, self-seeker, opportunist, worldling, egotist, profiteer, knave, renegade, turncoat, Proteus, apostate, traitor, Judas, betrayer, recreant, truant, sycophant, yes-man, toady, stooge, mugwump, rat, tergiversator, backslider, recidivist, chameleon.

TRINITY, *n.* 1. Group of three, triad, trio, triplets, trilogy, ternion, trine, tierce.

2. (With *The*) The Godhead, Triune God, the Holy Trinity, Father, Son and Holy Ghost,

Triunity, Threefold Unity, the Trinity in Unity, Three in One and One in Three.

TRINKET, *n.* Small fancy article, bauble, cheap piece of ornament, bit of jewelry, bijou, gewgaw, knickknack, guad, whimwham, gimcrack, bagatelle, trifle, plaything, toy, rickshaw, trumpery, frippery, souvenir, memento, keepsake, token.

TRIP, *v.* 1. Stumble, misstep, tumble, miss one's footing, fall, slip, lose footing, make a false step, make a false movement, flounder, founder, pitch, lurch, topple, plunge, sprawl, come a cropper *(coll.),* precipitate oneself, fall on one's nose.

2. Blunder, fail, err, be at fault, bungle, come short, mistake, commit an offense, commit a faux pas, make a mistake, slip up, misreckon, miscalculate, misjudge, go astray, be deluded, underestimate, flub *(coll.),* muff *(coll.),* fluff *(Theatrical).*

3. Throw off balance, overthrow, cause to fall, upset, subvert, overturn, level, floor.

4. Go with a light quick tread, skip, caper, frisk, cavort, prance, foot it, hop, dance, scamper, run, spring, leap, bound, gambado, frolic, gambol, demivolt, caracole, flounce, bob, buckjump.

5. Scud, speed, hie, spurt, hasten, post, whiz, dart, run, fly, whisk, swoop, shoot, race, tear along, scorch, dash, bolt, scamper, scurry, skedaddle, scuttle.

TRIP, *n.* 1. Excursion, outing, jaunt, sightseeing, globetrotting, expedition, journey, tour, route, circuit, voyage, cruise, pilgrimage, hadj, peregrination, trek, ride, ramble, stroll, hike, saunter, tramp, perambulation, turn, wayfaring, automobiling, motoring, nomadism, roving, vagrancy, wanderlust, vagabondage, migration, emigration, flit, gadding, itinerary, course, errand, mission.

2. False step, misstep, stumble, lurch, loss of balance, slip, tumble, plunge, drop, fall.

3. Mistake, bungle, faux pas, lapse, oversight, failure, error, blunder, fault, lapsus linguae, slip of the tongue, slip of the pen, lapsus calami, solecism, bull, Malapropism, Spoonerism, break *(coll.),* boner *(coll.),* flub *(coll.),* fluff *(Theatrical),* muff *(coll.).*

TRIPLE, *v.* Make threefold, treble, triplicate, cube, increase, magnify, enlarge, multiply, augment, add to.

TRIPLE, *adj.* Consisting of three parts, triplicate, threefold, treble, three-ply, ternary, triplex, tern, ternal, ternate, trinal, triadic, trinary, trilogistic, tripartite, three-parted, trifid, trifurcate, trisulcate, tridental, three-forked, tridentate, tripodal, triarch.

TRIPOD, *n.* Three-legged stand, trivet, teapoy, trestle, stool, taboret, footstool, faldstool.

TRIPPER, *n.* Excursionist, sightseer, globetrotter, tourist, voyager, motorist, pilgrim, hadji, peregrinator, trekker, hiker, tramp, perambulator, wayfarer, nomad, vagrant, vagabond, beachcomber, migrator, emigrant, gadder, flitter, journeyer, traveler, wanderer, rambler.

TRIPPING, *adj.* Agile, quick, nimble-footed, spry, fleet, light-footed, brisk, frisky, spirited, expeditious, fast, swift, rapid, galloping, flying, winged, light of heel, light-legged, graceful, fluent, rhythmic, flowing.

TRITE, *adj.* Hackneyed, stereotyped, platitudinous, bromidic, banal, commonplace, routine, thrice-familiar, threadbare, stale, oft-repeated, well-known, common, run-of-the-mill, wearisome, ordinary, shopworn, out-of-date, old, antiquated, ancient, archaic, hoary, obsolete, fossil, senile, whiskered, antediluvian, musty, venerable, gray-bearded, worn-out, beaten, much used, habitual, customary, traditional, everyday, wonted, household, vernacular, conventional, prescriptive, stock, set, established, proverbial.

TRITURATE, *v.* Reduce to fine particles, grind to powder, pulverize, comminute, levigate, granulate, abrade, scrape, grate, pound, thrash, rub, bray, beat, bruise, crush, crunch, disintegrate, crumble.

TRITURATION, *n.* Pulverization, levigation, comminution, attenuation, granulation, contusion, subaction, disintegration, detrition, abrasion, filing, grating.

TRIUMPH, *v.* 1. Win, succeed, be victorious, prevail, get the mastery, meet with success, obtain a victory, overcome, overwhelm, subdue, conquer, vanquish, subjugate, surpass, gain one's end, accomplish, manage to, prosper, make one's way, bring off, gain the day, take by storm, score a success, carry all before one, weather the storm, stem the torrent, take the prize, outwit, outmaster, outmaneuver, win one's spurs, come off with flying colors, have the best of it, have the ball at one's feet, win hands down, surmount an obstacle, make head against, turn the corner.

2. Exult, rejoice, celebrate a victory, glory, be elated, crow, boast, brag, vaunt, swagger, gloat, fling up one's cap, leap with joy, jubilate, hurrah.

TRIUMPH, *n.* Victory, conquest, ascendancy, mastery, walkover, pushover, upper hand, advantage, palm, masterstroke, coup, hit, feat, ten strike, trump card, prize, checkmate, killing *(sl.)*, smash *(sl.)*, feather in one's cap, accomplishment, success, acclamation, trophy, glory, gain, flourish of trumpets, fanfare, joy, exultation, jubilation, jubilee, ovation, celebration, prosperous issue, luck, smiles of fortune, achievement, attainment, expugnation, edge, subdual, medal, blue ribbon, laurels, citation, civic crown, wreath, flying colors, parade, state, glorification, paean, bonfire, triumphal arch.

TRIUMPHANT, *adj.* Rejoicing for victory, crowned with success, laurel-wreathed, palm-bearing, prosperous, felicitous, auspicious, in the ascendant, unbeaten, trophy-winning, prize-holding, bay-wreathed, garlanded, majestic, in high feather, cock-a-hoop, flushed with victory.

TRIVIAL, *adj.* Petty, picayune, trifling, slight, unimportant, of little consequence, inconsequential, insignificant, nugatory, inconsiderable, small, little, light, slim, flimsy, meager, inappreciable, dribbling, piddling, beggarly, scurvy, scanty, diminutive, nugacious, minute, niggling, atomic, sixpenny, no-account, worthless, shallow, idle, frivolous, foolish, frothy, gimcrack, sleazy, immaterial, brummagem, pinchbeck, of little value, trumpery, paltry, ordinary, common, everyday, puerile, childish, vain, futile, unessential, useless, commonplace, mean, nominal, puny, slender, poor, empty, inept, vulgar, quotidian, incidental, indifferent, subordinate, mediocre, passable, uneventful, so-so, airy, weak, petty, inane, fribble, namby-pamby, good-for-nothing, nonsensical, trashy, twaddling.

TRIVIALITY, *n.* Unimportance, insignificance, inconsequentiality, trivialness, indifference, flimsiness, paltriness, foolishness, emptiness, futility, nugatoriness, inconsiderableness, nothingness, immateriality, levity, frivolity, matter of indifference, smallness, trifling matter, fiddlestick, falderal, flimflam, fudge, joke, snap of the fingers, jest, *peu de chose (Fr.), ridiculus mus (Lat.),* incident, mere nothing, flash in the pan, tempest in a teapot, much ado about nothing, storm in a teacup, bagatelle, trifle, bauble, bubble, froth, fig, iota, jot, tittle, straw, rap, brass farthing, red cent, tinker's dam, continental, trinket, gewgaw, kickshaw, knickknack, frippery, balderdash, trash, dross, chaff.

TROGLODYTE, *n.* 1. Cave dweller, cave man, pithecanthrope, paleolithic man, Piltdown man, Neanderthal man, Cro-Magnon man, Heidelberg man.

2. Person living in seclusion, anchorite, recluse, hermit, stylite, ascetic, cenobite, eremite, Timon of Athens, *solitaire (Fr.),* outcast, pariah, outsider, castaway, pilgarlic, wretch, miserable fellow.

TROLL, *v.* 1. Sing loudly, yodel, carol, chant, trill, jubilate, crow, cantillate, warble, intone, chirrup, lilt, trill, sol-fa, solmizate.

2. Angle with a trolling line, fish, entice, allure, draw on, lure, bait.

TROLL, *n.* 1. Part song, round, roundelay, catch, chant, carol, psalm, hymn, canticle, canzonet, strain, chanson, ditty, lay, ballad.

2. Dwarf, gnome, elf, goblin, demon, kobold, Rumpelstiltskin, brownie, pixy, leprechaun, oaf, sprite, nix, pigwidgeon, Earl King, changeling, cluricaune, urchin, Puck.

TROLLOP, *n.* 1. Prostitute, whore, broad, jade, wench, trull, tart, strumpet, hustler, harlot, chippy, *fille de joie (Fr.),* streetwalker, fallen woman, Cyprian, baggage, demirep, drab, hussy, bitch, skirt, quean, demimondaine, cocotte, lorette, grisette, concubine, white slave, fancy woman, doxy, kept woman, frail, wanton, pick-up, wren *(sl.).*

2. Slovenly female, untidy woman, slut, slattern, harridan, minx, drab, dowdy, sloven, draggletail, scrubwoman, charwoman.

TROOP, *v.* 1. Come in great numbers, flock together, collect, crowd, muster, gather in crowds, throng, assemble, consort, meet, cluster, swarm, surge, rush, stream, mass, herd, huddle, congregate, forgather, concentrate, associate, resort, concur, converge, pour in, rally, mobilize.

2. March in a company, file, defile, deploy, goose-step, foot it, step, countermarch, parade, quickstep, plod, trudge, tramp, stride, strut, bowl along.

TROOP, *n.* 1. Great number, multitude, concourse, throng, press, crowd, flock, swarm, herd, horde, assemblage, conflux, levy, rally, ingathering, mobilization, muster, convergence, concentration, meet, congregation, forgathering, rush, mob, host, crush, gang, covey, shoal, roundup, drove, bevy, bunch, array, legion, scores, army, aggregation, brood, hive, flight, school.

2. Company, band, detachment, squad, party, body, division, crew, battery, force, posse, team, column, wing, garrison, brigade, regiment, squadron, battalion, platoon, section, detail, phalanx, cohort, patrol, guard, picket.

3. Company of stage-players, troupe, dramatis personae, cast.

TROOPER, *n.* Cavalry soldier, cavalryman, horse-soldier, horseman, dragoon, hussar, mounted policeman, Cossack, spahi, Uhlan, light-horseman, mounted rifleman.

TROOPS, *n., pl.* Army, soldiery, armed forces, militia, military force, soldiers, infantry, cavalry, military, standing army, regulars, yeomanry, host, reserves, horse and foot, military train, conscripts, recruits, rookies (sl.), campaigners, combatants, fighting men, belligerents, rank and file, sharpshooters, skirmishers, guerrillas.

TROPE, n. Figure of speech, image, metaphor, simile, metonymy, tralatition, enallage, synecdoche, catachresis, figurativeness, personification, prosopopoeia.

TROPHY, n. Token of victory, evidence of valor, symbol of achievement, memorial of conquest, spoil, spolia opima (Lat.), prize, laurels, palm, medal, wreath, civic crown, blue ribbon, bays, loving cup, citation, cordon bleu (Fr.), chaplet, Croix de Guerre, Victoria Cross, Congressional Medal, Medal of Honor, Distinguished Service Cross, Purple Heart, Iron Cross, insignia, feather in one's cap, garland, decoration, monument, memento, souvenir, remembrancer, relic, tablet, testimonial, order, keepsake.

TROPICAL, adj. 1. Torrid, humid, sultry, sweltering, blazing, fiery, sun-drenched, hot, thermic, roasting, baking, burning, close, stifling, oppressive, sudorific, canicular, estival.

2. Passionate, ardent, amorous, erotic, fervent, fervid, vehement, excitable, carnal, sexual, voluptuous, salacious, lewd, lustful, lascivious, libidinous, lecherous, wanton.

3. Figurative, allusive, metaphorical, catachrestical, tralatitious, allegorical, parabolic.

TROT, n. 1. Jogging gait between a walk and a run, canter, gallop, spurt, run, scamper, pace.

2. Quick continuous movement, go, move, motion, bustle, hustle, flurry, action, activity, animation, stir, **ado.**

3. Translation, crib, pony, rendition, reddition, key, commentary, annotation, scholium, interpretation, meaning.

TROTH, n. 1. Truth, veracity, verity, honesty, sincerity, candor, frankness, truthfulness, plain dealing, probity, ingenuousness.

2. Faithfulness, fidelity, allegiance, faith, belief, bona fides (Lat.), loyalty, trust, confidence, dependence, assurance, credence, credit, conviction, uberrima fides (Lat.).

3. Promise, pledge, vow, word, engagement, plight, parole, word of honor, oath, profession, guarantee, warranty, insurance, obligation, contract, affiance, betrothal, betrothment, marriage compact.

TROT OUT, v. Make manifest, bring forth, bring out, express, give notice, exhibit, show, set forth, represent, expose, set before one, produce, put through one's paces, show off, unfold, unveil, show forth, display, indicate, demonstrate, blazon forth.

TROUBADOUR, n. Lyric poet of chivalric love and gallantry, bard, singer, lyrist, laureate, trouvère (Fr.), skald, minstrel, Meistersinger, minnesinger, versifier, improvisatore (It.).

TROUBLE, v. Disconcert, annoy, discommode, incommode, harass, plague, perturb, disturb, agitate, derange, disarrange, confuse, stir up, discompose, affect, inconvenience, put to exertion, vex, torment, fret, worry, afflict, pester, distress, badger, grieve, molest, bother, perplex, infest, harry, disquiet, concern, cumber, embroil, embarrass, ruffle, pique, unsettle, render uneasy, exercise, oppress, upset, confound, depress, deject, irritate, displease, anger, provoke, thwart, frustrate, cross, irk, nettle, rile, ruffle, chafe, gall.

TROUBLE, n. 1. Affliction, tribulation, ordeal, infliction, dolor, calamity, catastrophe, hardship, adversity, woe, grief, sorrow, distress, misfortune, suffering, pain, misery, cross, disaster, reverse, grievance, ailment, ill, agony, frowns of fortune, evil day, gathering clouds, rainy day, ill wind, accident, casualty, trial, blow, scourge, visitation, check, setback, contretemps.

2. Annoyance, vexation, plague, perplexity, molestation, harassment, difficulty, worry, care, irritation, embarrassment, anxiety, inconvenience, pains, exertion, ado, fuss, pother, bother, discomfort, agitation, effort, to-do, turmoil, duty, strain, stress, struggle, labor, work, toil, travail, elbow grease.

3. Dissatisfaction, discontentment, uproar, rumpus, embroilment, riot, anarchy, anarchism, rebellion, revolt, revolution, sedition, strike, agitation, row, disturbance, disorder, commotion, ferment, convulsion, fracas, mêlée, pandemonium, Donnybrook, bedlam, chaos, discord.

4. Cause of distress, matter, ailment, bane, burden, pest, curse, nuisance, bug (coll.), fix, scrape, strait, pinch, mess, pickle, deep water, hot water, quandary, dilemma, muddle, crisis, emergency, critical situation, predicament, entanglement, intricacy, Gordian knot, poser, maze, labyrinth, puzzle, paradox, hard nut to crack, pass, rub, exigency, crux, hornets' nest, imbroglio, stew, stumbling block, obstruction, barrier, impediment, obstacle, snag, hindrance, clog, block, slough, hitch, quagmire, Augean task, labor of Hercules, uphill work, tough job, dead weight.

TROUBLEMAKER, n. Mischief-maker, marplot, rogue, knave, villain, traitor, snake in the grass, sneak, squealer, tattletale, scandalmonger, gossip, dissension-sower, recreant, truant, evildoer, anarchist, firebrand, incendiary, saboteur, agent provocateur (Fr.), communist, iconoclast, terrorist, racketeer, bully, hooligan, roughneck, larrikin, ugly customer, hornet, scorpion, adder, non-cooperator, striker, slacker, gold-bricker (coll.), critic, detractor, caviler, cynic, carper, backbiter, knocker, slanderer, satirist, libeler, traducer, calumniator, relator, informer, spy, delator, miscreant, scoundrel, caitiff, wretch, reptile, urchin, vandal, scamp, scapegrace, ne'er-do-well, black sheep, defaulter, culprit, malefactor, misdemeanant, felon, criminal, delinquent, jailbird, convict, outlaw, blackguard.

TROUBLE-SHOOTER, n. Expert in eliminating the cause of trouble in the operation of something, efficiency-expert, bug-eliminator, Mr. Fixit (coll.).

TROUBLESOME, adj. Vexatious, harassing, distressing, worrisome, annoying, grievous, galling, provoking, disturbing, perplexing, tough, difficult, hard, arduous, trying, laborious, onerous, operose, tedious, inconvenient, unwieldy, herculean, heavy, incommodious, knotty, thorny, spiny, plaguy, nasty, untoward, calamitous, cursed, pesky, bothersome, pestiferous, fatiguing, cumbersome, burdensome, irksome, tiresome, wearisome, exasperating, aggravating, unpleasant, disagreeable, distasteful, unsatisfactory, undesirable, unacceptable, unwelcome.

TROUBLOUS, adj. Full of trouble, †tumultuous, turbulent, disturbed, agitated, disquieted, disquieting, trying, disturbing, confused, restless, violent, boisterous, vicious, disorderly, blustering, raging, riotous, seditious, rebellious, revolutionary, tumultuary, uproarious, obstreperous, desperate, frenzied, frantic, explosive, volcanic, stormy, tempestuous.

TROUGH, *n.* 1. Channel, furrow, hollow, depression, trench, gutter, conduit, duct, race, watercourse, aqueduct, canal, flume, pantile, sewer, culvert, drain, ditch, moat, gully, main, gorge, ravine, canyon, dike.

2. Long and narrow open boxlike receptacle, long tray, hutch, manger.

TROUNCE, *v.* Thrash severely, trim, pommel, flog, larrup, castigate, baste, lambaste, whip, flagellate, punish, beat, lick hollow, drub, paste, spank, cuff, smite, bethwack, wham, thump, thwack, buffet, lace, belabor, cowhide, lash, scourge, horsewhip, cane, birch, lay about one, switch, sandbag.

TROUSERS, *n.* Loose-fitting outer garment for men, covering for the lower part of the trunk and each leg separately, pantaloons, pants, slacks, breeches, trews, overalls, jeans, knickerbockers, knickers, plus-fours, bloomers, shorts, kicks *(sl.)*, tights, drawers, galligaskins, leggings, spatterdashes, culottes.

TROUSSEAU, *n.* Outfit of a bride which she brings with her at marriage, hope chest, equipment, trappings, gear, accouterment, toggery, array, finery, wardrobe, apparel, wearing apparel, things, clothes, vesture, raiment.

TRUANT, *adj.* Staying away from without leave, shirking, malingering, wandering from business, loitering, idling, loafing, gold-bricking, absent, away, not present, A.W.O.L., absent without leave, missing, gone, runaway, fugitive, at large, decamped.

TRUANT, *n.* 1. One who neglects his duty, shirker, slacker, gold-bricker, quitter, laggard, loiterer, idler, lounger, loafer, evader of responsibility, skulker, school-skipper, draft-dodger, backslider, do-little, *fainéant (Fr.)*, floater, recreant.

2. One who stays away from without leave, A.W.O.L.'er, deserter, absentee, runaway, runagate, fugitive, absconder, decamper, refugee, renegade.

TRUCE, *n.* 1. Suspension of hostilities, cessation of arms, cease-fire, armistice, flag of truce, white flag, temporary peace.

2. Short rest, interval of rest, lull, pause, recess, respite, cessation, reprieve, short quiet, intermission, delay, breathing-spell, stay, stop, interruption, discontinuance, hitch, break, stoppage, halt, remission, abeyance, suspension, standstill.

TRUCK, *v.* 1. Transport, convey, transfer, carry, dispatch, transmit, deliver, consign, freight.

2. Give in exchange, barter, peddle, traffic, exchange, trade, deal, bargain, negotiate, have dealings, transact, interchange, swap, buy and sell, nundinate, keep shop, haggle, dicker, higgle, huckster, chaffer.

TRUCK, *n.* 1. Barter, exchange, dealings, nundination, bargain, deal, trade, commerce, buying and selling, business, jobbing, transaction, negotiation.

2. Small commodities, wares, goods, merchandise, articles, stock, staple commodities, staples, stock in trade, produce, cargo, effects.

3. Delivery wagon, motor lorry, van, automotive vehicle for carrying loads, wheeled frame for moving heavy articles.

TRUCKLE, *v.* Submit tamely, yield obsequiously, humble oneself, succumb, accede, defer to, draw in one's horns, knuckle down to, bootlick, crouch before, stoop, cringe, bend the knee, bow to, be servile, grovel, knock under, prostrate oneself, crawl, cower, lick the feet of, kiss the hem of one's garment, toady, dance attendance on, hang on the sleeve of, keep time to, fetch and carry, fawn upon, curry favor with, flatter, wheedle, coax, pet, slaver, butter, pander to, creep into the good graces of.

TRUCULENT, *adj.* Brutally harsh, savagely threatening, ferocious, feral, barbarous, fierce and cruel, savage, bloodthirsty, sanguinary, brutish, malevolent, relentless, dire, ruthless, inhuman, deadly, lethal, malign, malicious, rancorous, maleficent, fell, ferine, inexorable, slaughterous, murderous, sanguinolent, red-handed, mortiferous.

TRUDGE, *v.* March heavily, travel with labor, plod, jog on, walk heavily, drag, lumber, shamble, move along laboriously, travel wearily, lag, trail, inch along, traipse, slouch, waddle, shuffle, hobble, hitch, limp, falter, flag, stagger, totter, tramp, stump, bundle, stir one's stumps, slug, bundle on, claudicate.

TRUE, *adj.* 1. Real, authentic, pure, genuine, veritable, actual, solid, absolute, simon-pure, unadulterated, unvarnished, sound, not false.

2. Correct, exact, right, accurate, precise, conformable to truth, reliable, sure, unfailing, concrete, definite, well-defined, strict, clear-cut, scrupulous, punctilious, literal, textual, scientific, mathematical, valid, uncontradictable, express, unimpeachable, well-founded.

3. Legitimate, rightful, canonical, orthodox, official, proper, lawful, legal, bona fide.

4. Truthful, veracious, conforming to fact, factual, trustworthy, realistic, unimagined, substantial, tangible, ponderable, palpable, evident, manifest.

5. Faithful, firm in allegiance, loyal, true-blue, stanch, constant, steadfast, steady, trusty, truehearted, dependable, incorruptible, devoted, unswerving, unwavering.

6. Free from deceit, honest, upright, conscientious, honorable, just, virtuous, equitable, sincere, righteous, earnest, artless, ingenuous, fair and square, aboveboard.

7. Even, straight, undeviating, direct, in a line, rectilinear, inflexible, invariable, plumb, symmetrical, regular, normal, orderly.

TRUE, *v.* Regulate, adjust, set, square, fix, readjust, make true, straighten, put in order, rectify, correct.

TRUE-BLUE, *adj.* Loyal, faithful, unchanging, unwavering, stanch, incorruptible, honest, true, trustworthy, honorable, pledged, good as one's word, observant, virtuous, constant, true to the core, dependable, conscientious, high-minded, devoted.

TRUE-HEARTED, *adj.* Sincere, frank, candid, ingenuous, artless, guileless, honest, trusty, straightforward, aboveboard, undissembling, veracious, truthful, scrupulous, unreserved, simplehearted, pure, unperjured, bona fide, unfeigned, unaffected, undisguised, innocent, stainless, untarnished, unsullied, uncorrupted, chivalrous, jealous of honor, *sans peur et sans reproche (Fr.)*, inviolable, inviolate.

TRUELOVE, *n.* Beloved, lover, darling, sweetheart, love, dear, amoret, beau, inamorata, inamorato, swain, flame, gallant, girl friend, boy friend, amoroso, ladylove, idol, angel, duck, affianced, betrothed, fiancé, fiancée.

TRUISM, *n.* Self-evident truth, necessary truth, evident proposition, axiom, proverb, platitude, maxim, adage, saw. apothegm, cliché, bromide, aphorism, saying, dictum, gnome, epigram, mot, byword, sentence, motto, precept, phylactery, moral.

TRULL, *n.* Whore, bawd, harlot, prostitute, trollop, strumpet, streetwalker, broad *(sl.),* jade, chippy, tart, hustler, drab, wench, punk, courtesan, Cyprian, *fille de joie (Fr.), Hure (Ger.), puta (Sp.), meretrice (It.),* demirep, hussy, baggage, doxy, bitch, quean, fornicatress, wanton, white slave, demimondaine.

TRULY, *adv.* 1. Yes, aye, yea, very true, well and good, *placet (Lat.),* granted, even so, just so, to be sure, precisely, exactly, certainly, certes, of course, no doubt, assuredly, unquestionably, so be it.

2. Correctly, rightly, duly, justly, accurately, strictly, unequivocally, word for word, literally, *totidem verbis (Lat.),* to the letter, *ipsissimis verbis (Lat.),* to a T, to a nicety, chapter and verse, verbatim, literatim, *mot à mot (Fr.), ad unguem (Lat.),* to a hair, to a turn.

3. Verily, really, indeed, in truth, forsooth, in fact, in reality, actually, certainly, especially, surely, veritably, positively, absolutely, intrinsically, as a matter of fact, in effect, beyond question, beyond doubt.

4. Sincerely, frankly, candidly, truthfully, veraciously, honestly, plainly, in good earnest, I must say, marry, you may be sure, upon my word, egad, by my troth, of a truth, pardi, upon oath, in all conscience, so help me God.

TRUMP, *v.* Win with a trump card, excel, surpass, be better than, beat, checkmate, nonplus, confound, circumvent, settle, sink, swamp, reduce, roll in the dust, vanquish, defeat, discomfit, overpower, overmatch, rout, drub, lick, worst, floor, put *hors de combat (Fr.),* gain the ascendancy, get the upper hand, get the better of, triumph over, make short work of, score a success, win a point, put over.

TRUMP, *n.* 1. Playing card of a suit that outranks other suits, winning card, trump card, court card.

2. Masterstroke, coup, clever hit, lucky hit, bold move, *coup de maître (Fr.),* checkmate, advantage over, edge, upper hand, mastery, ascendancy, victory, subdual, conquest, success, triumph.

3. Person of great excellence, good fellow, brick, model, paragon, worthy, good example, rough diamond, one in ten thousand, salt of the earth, demigod, hero, saint, benefactor, good genius, guardian angel, good Samaritan, prince, admirable Crichton, phoenix, *beau idéal (Fr.).*

TRUMPERY, *n.* 1. Something showy but of little intrinsic value, worthless finery, frippery, pinchbeck, brummagem, clinquant, spangle, tinsel, knickknack, gimcrack, gewgaw, frills and furbelows, sequin, paste, brilliant, gaud, trickery, trinket, bauble, bagatelle, kickshaw, whim-wham.

2. Nonsense, trash, rubbish, stuff, humbug, fudge, moonshine, bosh, twaddle, jargon, gibberish, jabber, rant, fustian, balderdash, bombast, flummery, palaver, rodomontade, rigmarole, drivel, rot, flapdoodle.

TRUMPERY, *adj.* Showy but insubstantial *or* useless, of little *or* no value, good-for-nothing, worthless, trashy, trifling, pinchbeck, rubbishy, trivial, petty, beggarly, light, flimsy, airy, fribble, piddling, paltry, scrubby, mean, scurvy, shabby,

wretched, sorry, vile, cheap, gimcrack, catchpenny, inferior, meritless, not worth a straw, vain, inane, insignificant, unimportant, brummagem, flashy, meretricious, inconsequential, twopenny, nugatory, picayune.

TRUMPET, *v.* 1. Blare, blow, resound, reverberate, sound, boom, bellow, din, rumble.

2. Proclaim, herald, make known, publish, announce, blazon, bruit, noise abroad, emit, report, voice, promulgate, disseminate, diffuse, rumor.

TRUMPET, *n.* Cornet, horn, bugle, clarion, lituus, French horn, post horn, saxhorn, tuba, trombone, English horn, bombardon, ophicleide, serpent, baritone, euphonium.

TRUMPET-CALL, *n.* Bugle-call, reveille, taps, rappel, alarm, alarum, summons to arms, rallying cry, trumpet blast, battle cry, flourish of trumpets, blare, fanfare, din, tintamarre, boom.

TRUMPET-TONGUED, *adj.* Vociferous, sonorous, stentorian, ear-piercing, ear-rending, deafening, enough to wake the dead, obstreperous, ear-splitting, stentorophonic, shrill, loud, powerful, blatant, loud-voiced, bellowing.

TRUMP UP, *v.* Fabricate, devise deceitfully, forge, counterfeit, invent, concoct, hatch, get up, fake, feign, simulate, sham, pass off for, contrive, scheme, coin, strain one's imagination, set one's wits to work, fancy, imagine, conceive, originate, create, improvise.

TRUNCATE, *v.* Shorten by cutting off a part, cut short, lop, lop off, dock, cut off, maim, mutilate, detruncate, cripple, mangle, obtruncate, hew, hack, pare down, snip, clip, prune, crop, stunt, pollard.

TRUNCHEON, *n.* 1. Policeman's club, billy, shillelagh, cudgel, bludgeon, knuckle-duster, stick, cane, bat.

2. Staff of authority *or* office, baton, wand, mace, fasces, rod, scepter.

TRUNDLE, *v.* Revolve, roll, spin, wheel, turn round, rotate, gyrate, circulate, whirl, twist, swirl, twirl.

TRUNDLE, *n.* 1. Rotation, gyration, turning, revolution, turn, circulation, circumgyration, roll, circumrotation, circumvolution, turbination, convolution, whirligig, pirouette, twirl, spin, reel, whirl, swirl.

2. Little wheel, roller, caster, gyrostat, screw, turnspit, flywheel, gearwheel, cogwheel, pulley, sheave, axle, pivot, axis, swivel, gudgeon, hinge, spool, mandrel, quill, bobbin, pirn, cop, whorl.

TRUNK, *n.* 1. Chest, box, coffer, bin, caddy, casket, receptacle, caisson, container, portmanteau, bunker, bandbox, hat box, hamper, pannier, basket, crate.

2. Main part, torso, stock, butt, body, bole, shaft, stem, stalk, caudex, *tige (Fr.),* axis.

3. Proboscis, snout, nose, nozzle, neb, beak, antlia, appendage.

TRUSS, *v.* 1. Support, hold, bear, sustain, carry, bolster up, hold up, shore up, uphold, underprop, underset, bandage, brace, pillow, cradle, underpin, lend support, hold fast, keep tight, make fast.

2. Bind up, pack close, pack up, put up, cram, compress, constrict, confine, enclose, circumscribe.

3. Tie, fasten, secure, unite, hold together, clinch, tighten, pinion, strap, hitch.

TRUSS, *n.* 1. Collection of things tied together, package, pack, packet, bundle, batch, parcel, bale, tuft, fagot, clump, shock, thicket, rick, sheaf, stack, swath.

2. *(Med.)* Apparatus for maintaining a hernia in a reduced state, support, bandage, fitting, shore, stay, splint, supporter.

TRUST, *v.* 1. Confide in, depend upon, rely on, trust to, put confidence in, place reliance in, put hope in, pin one's faith upon, have faith in, swear by, put one's trust in, build upon, count upon.

2. Believe, give credence to, credit, give faith to, give credit to, take for granted, accept, assume, swallow *(coll.),* follow implicitly, take on faith.

3. Expect, anticipate, hope, feel sure, be confident, look for, contemplate, look forward to, reckon upon, calculate upon, foresee, forecast, prognosticate.

TRUST, *n.* 1. Feeling of security, faith, confidence, assurance, reliance, credence, belief, mainstay, sheet anchor, dependence, conviction, persuasion, certainty, certitude, gospel, sureness, assuredness, reassurance, safety.

2. Confident expectation, assured anticipation, expectancy, hope, hopefulness, optimism, presumption, reckoning, calculation, foresight, prospect, prognostication, prediction, premonition, presentiment, prognostic, presage, forecast.

3. Good name, credit, tick, cuff *(coll.),* score, account, tally, charge, deposit, security.

4. Combination of companies, merger, association, corporation, monopolistic organization, syndicate, combine, cartel, house, firm, copartnership, ring, pool. interlocking directorate.

5. Responsibility, obligation, devoir, duty, charge, office, bond of duty, incumbency, bounden duty, function, business, errand, mission, commission.

6. Right, use, interest, benefit, usufruct, title, holding, vested interest, property, assets, resources, belongings, estate, effects, income, means.

TRUSTEE, *n.* Person appointed to administer the affairs of a company, fiduciary, depositary, treasurer, bursar, purser, bookkeeper, quaestor, steward, accountant, liquidator, almoner, teller, cashier, financier, custodian, keeper, custos, nominee, consignee, commissioner, commissary, curator, functionary, agent, clerk, factor, proctor, caretaker, holder of the legal estate, regent, officer.

TRUSTEESHIP, *n.* Administrative control, stewardship, custodianship, custody, guardianship, management, direction, government, régime, ménage, conduct, regulation, guidance, superintendence, supervision, surveillance, control, charge, administration, proctorship, agency, wardship, wardenship, tutelage, safekeeping.

TRUSTFUL, *adj.* 1. Believing, confident, convinced, certain, assured, satisfied, cocksure, positive, sure, unhesitating, secure, under the impression.

2. Credulous, gullible, unsuspicious, unsuspecting, unquestioning, green, simple, naïve.

TRUSTLESS, *adj.* 1. False-hearted, unfaithful, false, unreliable, untrustworthy, dishonest, unscrupulous, unconscientious, dishonorable, fraudulent, knavish, disingenuous, two-faced, double-tongued, Machiavellian, treacherous, perfidious, perjured, Punic.

2. Suspicious, doubting, dubious, skeptical, from Missouri *(sl.),* unbelieving, incredulous, distrustful, inconvincible.

TRUSTWORTHINESS, *n.* Integrity, uprightness, faithfulness, reliability, reliableness, dependability,

dependableness, loyalty, constancy, trueness, probity, rectitude, honesty, good faith, honor, honorableness, *bona fides (Lat.),* fidelity, veracity, candor, singleness of heart, punctiliousness, scrupulosity, point of honor.

TRUSTWORTHY, *adj.* Reliable, dependable, unfailing, stable, steadfast, steady, firm, solid, valid, strong, abiding, lasting, permanent, durable, constant, unwavering, resolute, stanch, faithful, loyal, true, upright, straightforward, trusty, responsible, honest, honorable, aboveboard, sincere, conscientious, truthful, veracious, foursquare, true-blue, high-principled, noble, faithworthy, decent, respectable, worthy, scrupulous, reputable, good as one's word, uncorrupt, credible, confidential, virtuous, tried, incorruptible, devoted.

TRUTH, *n.* 1. Trueness, verity, authenticity, reality, existence, actuality, factuality, realness, principle, fact, gospel, veracity, naked truth, truthfulness, sooth, 'troth, unvarnished truth, realism, naturalism, truth to nature, graphicalness.

2. Fidelity, trustiness, faithfulness, steadfastness, devotion, constancy, loyalty, honor, fealty, faith, *bona fides (Lat.),* trustworthiness.

3. Sincerity, single-mindedness, candor, frankness, candidness, honesty, purity, genuineness, guilelessness, integrity, single-heartedness, probity, virtue, ingenuousness.

4. Accuracy, authenticity, orthodoxy, exactitude, correctness, nicety, preciseness, literalism, textualism, the very words, *ipsissima verba (Lat.),* exactness, precision, orthology.

5. Self-evident truth, axiom, truism, law, canon, oracle, proverb, maxim, platitude, apothegm, adage, cliché, saw, bromide, aphorism, saying, gnome, dictum, epigram, byword, mot, sentence, precept, motto, phylactery, moral.

TRUTHFUL, *adj.* 1. Conforming to truth, corresponding to reality, genuine, actual, veritable, **real,** authentic, sterling, orthodox, legitimate, rightful, official, authoritative, canonical, sound, pure, simon-pure, unadulterated, unimpeachable, undisguised, unvarnished, realistic, natural, naturalistic, true to life, unimaginary, true to the facts, factual.

2. Accurate, exact, precise, meticulous, punctilious, concrete, definite, well-defined, definitive, correct, just, strict, clear-cut, clean-cut, rigorous, literal, scrupulous, textual, scientific, mathematical, nice, particular, valid, solid, tangible, substantial, well-founded.

3. Sincere, ingenuous, frank, candid, honest, open, guileless, artless, straightforward, true, single-hearted, trusty, trustworthy, plain-spoken, plain-dealing, telling the truth, aboveboard, unsophisticated, veracious.

4. Faithful, loyal, steadfast, constant, stanch, trustworthy, unwavering, devoted, true-blue, unswerving, undeviating, reliable, dependable, steady, trusty, tried, tried and true, incorruptible.

TRUTHLESS, *adj.* False, deceitful, deceptive, dishonest, hypocritical, canting, insincere, disingenuous, treacherous. pharisaical, hollow, unfair, faithless, forsworn, mendacious, unveracious, fraudulent, untruthful, trothless, Jesuitical, tartuffish, two-faced, double-tongued, double-dealing, Janus-faced, barefaced, perfidious, Punic, artful, collusive.

TRY, *v.* 1. Strive, attempt, essay, endeavor, put forth effort toward, aim, undertake, venture, tempt fortune, speculate, experiment, test, have a fling at, take a crack at, have a go at, make trial of, tackle, compete, risk, take a chance, strain every nerve, make essay, make an effort, seek.

2. Examine, adjudicate, arbitrate, hear a cause, sit in judgment, adjudge, decide, judge, consider, deliberate, umpire, referee.

3. Sample, taste, smell, sound, sift, partake of, savor, smack, relish, roll on the tongue.

4. Refine, purify, depurate, elutriate, clarify.

TRY, *n.* Attempt, experiment, venture, trial, endeavor, effort, go, turn, essay, crack *(sl.),* whack *(sl.),* adventure, aim, speculation, struggle, undertaking, probation, sample, leap in the dark, random shot, feeler, *ballon d'essai (Fr.).*

TRYING, *adj.* 1. Irksome, tedious, tiresome, operose, hard, difficult, troublesome, fatiguing, wearisome, tough, toilsome, arduous, onerous, formidable, Herculean, rugged, knotty, thorny, plaguy, complicated, intricate, ticklish, perplexing, critical, painstaking.

2. Painful, grievous, distressing, afflictive, severe, calamitous, disastrous, catastrophic, dire, deplorable, lamentable, hurtful, harsh, sore, agonizing, excruciating, provoking, irritating, aggravating, disquieting, exasperating, vexatious, galling, burdensome, cumbrous, worrisome, oppressive, tormenting, harassing, grim, tremendous, harrowing, heartbreaking, unendurable, unbearable, intolerable, insufferable, repellent, odious, obnoxious, offensive, revolting, disgusting, loathsome, objectionable, desolating, tragic, ruinous, hapless.

TRYST, *n.* Appointment to meet, rendezvous, appointed meeting, date *(coll.),* assignation, reunion, communion, colloquy, commerce, tête-à-tête, vis-à-vis.

TUB, *n.* 1. Bathtub, bath, ablution, washing, immersion, humectation, balneation, douche, lavation, *bain (Fr.).*

2. Bucketlike vessel, receptacle, vat, keg, bucket, cask, keeler, firkin, caldron, barrel, rundlet, puncheon, butt, tun, hogshead, carboy, kilderkin.

3. Very corpulent person, fatty *(sl.),* hulk, mammoth, whale, hippopotamus, elephant, leviathan, behemoth, colossus, lump, clod, whopper, thumper, strapper, spanker, mountain.

TUBE, *n.* Hollow cylinder, pipe, duct, main, bore, hose, pipette, worm, bronchus, conduit, spout, tunnel, gut, canal, fistula, tubule, catheter *(Med.),* bronchiole, flue, chimney, shaft, outlet, inlet, passage, channel.

TUBERCULOSIS, *n.* Pulmonary disease, consumption, T.B., phthisis, churchyard cough, delicate health, scrofula, marasmus, cachexia, tabes, emaciation.

TUBERCULOUS, *adj.* Tubercular, consumptive, phthisic, scrofulous, hectic, marasmic, cachectic, delicate, emaciated, tabetic.

TUBULAR, *adj.* Tube-shaped, tube-like, fistulous, tubate, fistular, tubulate, tubiform, cannular, tubulous, pipe-shaped, tubuliform.

TUCK, *v.* 1. Fold, double, pleat, lap, plicate, gather, crease, plait, crinkle, cocker, wrinkle, ruffle, pucker, hem, ruck, dog's-ear, infold.

2. Insert, intromit, put into, implant, dovetail, stick in, stuff in, cram in, thrust in, obtrude, impact, embed.

3. Wrap, pack, stow, press together, cover snugly in, incase, envelop, enwrap, involve, muffle up, sheathe, overlap, swaddle, swathe, circumvest, shroud, roll up in.

TUCK, *n.* 1. Fold, pleat, plait, lap, doubling, plicature, plication, plica, ply, flexure, crease, gather, crumple, crinkle, dog's-ear, cockle, flounce, ruffle, pucker.

2. Dagger, rapier, Ferrara, Toledo, steel, creese, claymore, dirk, poniard, stiletto, dudgeon, stylet, blade, glaive, bilbo, cutlass, broadsword, falchion, saber.

TUFT, *n.* 1. Crest, topknot, brush, pompon, plume, knot, feather, fetlock, aigrette, scalp lock, elf locks, pompadour, mane, shag, shock, mop, thatch, quill, plumule, panache, hackle.

2. Group, cluster, tussock, clump, wisp, rick, swath, sheaf, sorus, nest, tissue, series, batch, set, pack, lot, assortment, bunch, bundle, parcel, fagot, packet, bale, truss, thicket.

TUFTHUNTER, *n.* One who seeks the acquaintance of celebrated persons, lion-hunter, celebrity-seeker, fortune-hunter, gold-digger *(sl.),* worldling, self-seeker, opportunist, jobber, egotist, timeserver, flunkey, yes-man, sycophant, toady, parasite, snob, hanger-on, stooge, pickthank, flatterer, courtier, truckler, sponge.

TUG, *v.* 1. Pull at with great force, haul, drag, draw, tow, lug, move by pulling forcibly, draggle, rake, trawl, yank, trail, twitch, snake, jerk, wrench.

2. Strive hard, exert oneself, labor, wrestle, struggle, toil, strain, endeavor, bestir oneself, fag, drudge, sweat, grub, grind, slave, ply, plod, do one's utmost.

TUG, *n.* 1. Hard pull, haul, yank, towage, draught, wrench, jerk, twitch.

2. Great effort, struggle, strenuous contest, spell, spurt, dead lift, heft, stretch, stress, strain, exercitation, exercise, toil, labor, work, travail, sweat of one's brow, grind, moil, drudgery.

TUITION, *n.* 1. Instruction, training, teaching, schooling, education, discipline, edification, pedagogy, tutelage, tutorship, tutorage, guidance, direction, preparation, exercitation, qualification, practice, drill.

2. Fee for instruction, charge, cost, expense, disbursement, price, outlay.

TUMBLE, *v.* 1. Roll about, wallow, heave, toss, pitch, move tumultuously, flounder, reel.

2. Trip, fall, sprawl, plunge, topple, be precipitated, drop, descend, lose footing, stumble, slide, slip, dive, glissade, titubate, swag, lurch, come a cropper.

3. Derange, put in disorder, disturb, disorder, rumple, dishevel, disarrange, tousle, tangle, entangle, ruffle.

TUMBLE-DOWN, *adj.* Ready to fall, dilapidated, rickety, decrepit, ramshackle, tottering, ruinous, unstable, shaky, crumbling, top-heavy, threatening, untrustworthy, insecure, parlous, perilous, periculous, unsafe.

TUMBLER, *n.* 1. Acrobat, somersaulter, athletic, gymnast, trampolinist, contortionist, posture-master, funambulist, tightrope-dancer, aërialist, highwire-performer.

2. Drinking vessel without handle *or* stem, glass, dipper, goblet, chalice, beaker.

TUMEFACTION, *n.* Swelling, intumescence, bloating, dilatation, turgescence, tumor, dropsy, distention, enlargement, growth, puffiness, excrescence, appendage, protuberance.

TUMEFY, *v.* Swell, distend, enlarge, puff up, inflate, increase, become larger, incrassate, inspissate, fill out, dilate, bloat, protuberate.

TUMID, *adj.* 1. Swollen, bloated, dropsical, edematous, swelled, distended, enlarged, turgid, puffed up, protuberant, puffy.

2. Pompous, bombastic, grandiloquent, altiloquent, magniloquent, turgid, stilted, grandiose, high-flown, fustian, ranting, inflated, rhetorical, declamatory, sesquipedalian, pedantic, orotund, Ciceronian, sonorous, Johnsonian, euphuistic, high-sounding, lexiphanic, flamboyant, plethoric.

TUMOR, *n.* Swelling, protuberance, tumefaction, morbid outgrowth of tissue, growth, boil, carbuncle, gathering, intumescence, pimple, wheal, wen, postule, goiter, sarcoma, furuncle, polyp, excrescence, tubercle.

TUMULT, *n.* 1. Commotion, agitation, disturbance, turbulence, ferment, confusion, turmoil, stir, hurly-burly, pother, stew, bustle, fuss, ado, to-do, flurry, helter-skelter, disorder, disquiet.

2. Mental agitation, trepidation, panic, state of high excitement, perturbation, discomposure, shock, twitter, fidgets, restlessness, disquietude, ruffle, flutter, transport, passion, heat, flush, fever, fume, outburst, paroxysm, furor, rage, desperation, distraction, hysterics, frenzy, raving, brain storm.

3. Riot, fracas, strife, melee, revolt, rebellion, sedition, infraction, outbreak, mutiny, uprising, insurrection, strike, *émeute (Fr.), Putsch (Ger.),* mutinousness, secession, revolution, sabotage.

4. Altercation, brawl, uproar, hubbub, quarrel, squabble, row, fray, feud, affray, hullabaloo, din, outcry, rumpus, Donnybrook, bedlam, pandemonium, squall, blowup, controversy, dispute, wrangle, discord, disagreement, dissension, contention, clash, disunion, faction, quarrel, bicker, tiff, high words, friction, open rupture, broil, imbroglio, scrimmage, bear garden.

TUMULTUOUS, *adj.* 1. Disturbed, restless, agitated, uneasy, excitable, high-strung, febrile, feverish, hysterical, delirious, chafing, fidgety, nettlesome, startlish, skittish, violent, demonstrative, hot-headed, temperamental, rabid, impulsive, passionate, impetuous, uncontrollable, irrepressible, ungovernable, volcanic, simmering, restive.

2. Clamorous, rampant, uproarious, turbulent, tumultuary, tempestuous, boisterous, obstreperous, noisy, vociferous, blustering, rowdy.

3. Mutinous, rebellious, insurgent, insurrectionary, insubordinate, disobedient, unruly, refractory, contumacious, recalcitrant, lawless, seditious, revolutionary, riotous.

TUMULUS, *n.* Artificial mound, hillock, earth bank, barrow, dolmen, cromlech, menhir, cairn, tope.

TUN, *n.* 1. Large cask, barrel, hogshead, rundlet, puncheon, firkin, butt, carboy, kilderkin, caldron, vat.

2. Measure of capacity for wine, 252 gallons, 4 hogsheads, 2 pipes.

TUNE, *v.* 1. Put in tune, bring into harmony, harmonize, attune, modulate, accord, test the pitch.

2. Adjust in due agreement, adapt, render accordant, make to chime with, regulate, accommodate, coördinate, temper, make conformable.

3. Put into proper condition, put into order, make ready, sound the note of preparation, settle preliminaries, prime, set, ramp up, screw up, put in trim, put in working order.

TUNE, *n.* 1. Pleasing succession of sounds, strain, air, aria, melody, measure, musical phrase, burden, chanson, canzonetta, lay, ditty, arietta, carol, *Lied (Ger.),* song, descant, modulation.

2. Harmony, concord, accord, accordance, concert, agreement, unison, chime, conformity, concurrence, consonance, euphony, tunefulness, concentus.

TUNEFUL, *adj.* Harmonious, melodious, musical, dulcet, sweet-sounding, canorous, resonant, lyrical, melic, in concord, sweet, mellifluous, mellow, euphonious, symphonious, rhythmical, measured, tunable, silvery.

TUNNEL, *n.* Subterranean passage, underground, subway, tube, shaft, mine, burrow, adit, gallery, drift, pit, airway, crosscut.

TURBAN, *n.* Scarf wound around the head, Eastern headdress, headgear, pugree, topee, toque, caftan, tarboosh, taj, fez, mandil, bandanna.

TURBID, *adj.* 1. Muddy, thick, roiled, feculent, befouled, smudgy, grimy, filthy, dreggy, thick, opaque, not clear, not transparent, dense, cloudy, roily, murky, foul, unclean, impure, nontranslucent, filmy, vaporous, foggy, dark, dim, fuliginous, smeared.

2. Disordered, unsettled, muddled, messy, confused, disturbed, slovenly, hugger-mugger, chaotic, deranged, disjointed, topsy-turvy, helter-skelter, harum-scarum.

TURBINATED, *adj.* Inversely conical, whorled, spiral, turbinate, top-shaped, convoluted, twisted, winding, tortile, coiled, helical, rotatory, trochilic, gyratory.

TURBULENCE, *n.* 1. Violence, vehemence, impetuosity, ebullition, bluster, uproar, row, riot, rumpus, fracas, ferocity, berserk, paroxysm, fit, convulsion, spasm, throe, hysterics, outburst, turmoil, ferment, tempest, storm, squall, fury, hubbub, agitation, commotion, excitement, disturbance, tumult, disorder, tumultuousness, restlessness, unruliness, confusion, excitation, perturbation, trepidation, ruffle, flurry, hurry-scurry, pother, stew, whirl, delirium, raving, frenzy, furor, rage, distraction, brain storm.

2. Riot, mutiny, revolt, rebellion, sedition, revolution, insurrection, insubordination, *bouleversement (Fr.),* uprising, rising, subversion, upheaval.

TURBULENT, *adj.* 1. Agitated, disturbed, tumultuous, restless, blustering, uproarious, boisterous, obstreperous, brawling, blatant, vociferous, noisy, rampant, unruly, furious, fierce, tumultuary, clamorous, rough, tempestuous, violent, stormy, raging, frenzied, infuriate, rabid, frantic, convulsive, spasmodic, paroxysmal, spastic, volcanic, explosive, savage, vehement.

2. Riotous, mutinous, rebellious, insurgent, factious, revolutionary, subversive, refractory, insubordinate, ungovernable, disorderly, seditious, intransigent, radical, bolshevistic, insurrectionary, restive, lawless, anarchistic.

TURF, *n.* 1. Grass, sward, greensward, sod, lawn, grassland, peat, mead, meadow, pasturage, plot, grassplat, heather, lea, herbage, pasture.

2. Racecourse, hippodrome, circus, arena, amphitheater, coliseum, track, corso, stadium.

TURFY, *adj.* Covered with grass, turf-like, cespitose, grassy, cespititious, campestrian, herbaceous, verdant, verdurous.

TURGID, *adj.* 1. Swollen, swelled, puffed up, distended, puffy, bloated, tumid, pudgy, pursy, dropsical, edematous, inflated.

2. Bombastic, pompous, grandiloquent, altisonant, magniloquent, fustian, ranting, high-flown, declamatory, turgent, rhetorical, grandiose, ostentatious, boastful, swaggering, florid, ornate, flowery, sonorous, euphuistic, euphemistic, big-sounding, stilted, pedantic, sesquipedalian, diffuse, digressive, redundant, wordy, profuse, prolix, pleonastic, periphrastic, circumlocutory, discursive, rambling, frothy, exuberant, tautological, fulsome, ambagious.

TURGIDITY, *n.* 1. Distention, swelling, bloatedness, turgidness, turgescence, tumidity, enlargement, dilation, dropsy, tumefaction, intumescence, inflation, puffiness.

2. Bombast, grandiloquence, altisonance, magniloquence, pompousness, pomposity, verbosity, diffuseness, tautology, pleonasm, profuseness, verbiage, wordiness, periphrasis, circumlocution, ambages, prolixity, redundance, exuberance, floridness, floweriness, altiloquence, orotundity, declamation, euphuism, macrology, sesquipedalianism, fustian, rant.

TURMOIL, *n.* Agitation, commotion, tumult, disturbance, bustle, ferment, hurly-burly, uproar, turbulence, welter, racket, din, pandemonium, babel, to-do, huddle, disorder, conflict, ado, pother, trouble, disquiet, activity, excitement, distraction, storm, tempest, perturbation, confusion, convulsion, row, charivari, rumpus, riot, fracas, melee, bear garden, Donnybrook Fair, bedlam, discord, anarchy, chaos, imbroglio.

TURN, *v.* 1. Cause to move round on an axis, turn round, revolve, rotate, make go round, spin, whirl, gyrate, wheel round, give a circular motion to, roll, rev, gyre, trundle, twiddle, twirl, caracole.

2. Cause to deviate, turn, flex, bend, deflect, inflect, cast, swivel, twist, sway, round, tack, cant, put about, change course, circumflex, spiral, veer, warp, slue, jibe, swing, haul, maneuver, deviate, detour, shift, swerve, divert, reverse the course of, transfer, meander, zigzag, serpentine, sinuate.

3. Wind, coil, twine, curl, wreathe, roll, crank, swivel, grind, wrench, contort, circle, circumscribe.

4. Change, alter, metamorphose, transmute, transfigure, transmogrify, transform, vary, convert, resolve, revolutionize, alternate, ring the changes, shuffle the cards, turn over a new leaf, shift the scene.

5. Shape as in a lathe, mold, form, fashion, reconstruct, remold, recast, re-form, reorganize.

6. Reverse the position of, bring under parts to the surface, turn topsy-turvy, invert, subvert, upset, overturn, transpose.

7. Put to some use, apply to some purpose, fit, suit, adapt, adjust, regulate, maneuver, employ, direct.

8. Come about, ensue, eventuate, result, issue, terminate, follow, arise, flow, spring, emanate, proceed, be derived.

9. Depend, pivot, hinge, hang, be conditioned, be contingent on.

10. Grow sour, become acid, ferment, curdle, acidify, work, sour, acetify, acidulate.

11. Change opinion, persuade, convert, proselyte, proselytize, prejudice, alter belief, induce, influence, actuate, impel, move, prevail upon, bring round, win over.

TURN, *n.* 1. Rotatory movement, rotation, revolution, movement about a center, gyration, cycle, circumvolution, circumgyration, circuit, volte, course, wheel, gyre, turning, circulation, roll,

circumrotation, turbination, whirligig, convolution, reel, spin, pirouette, twirl.

2. Bend, twist, curve, winding, meandering, sinuosity, zigzag, curvature, incurvation, flexure, deviation, deflexion, detour, sweep, arc, labyrinth, maze.

3. Change, vicissitude, alteration, variation, mutation, fluctuation, alternation, transmutation, conversion, innovation.

4. Successive course, due change, spell, round, bout, inning, opportunity, shift, hand, appropriate time, crack *(coll.),* go *(coll.).*

5. Aptitude, proclivity, talent, genius, forte, flair, faculty, gift, tendency, bias, bent, inclination, proneness, propensity, penchant, capacity, ability, ingenuity, aptness, disposition, frame of mind, liking, mood, humor, vein, parts, felicity, endowment, readiness, resourcefulness, savoir-faire, finesse, mother wit, tact.

6. Opportune deed, favor, service, hand, action, office, act, occasional kindness, benefaction, benefit, boon, dispensation.

7. Cast, fashion, mold, manner, phase, guise, shape, form, style, mode, conformation, format, contour, cut, build, construction, frame, set, stamp, pattern.

8. Short excursion, brief walk, airing, constitutional, promenade, stroll, ramble, run, drive, saunter, hike, tramp, perambulation, peregrination, trip, tour, circuit, expedition, journey, jaunt, outing, ride, trek.

TURN AGAINST, *v.* Revolt, rebel, mutiny, secede, take the law into one's own hands, disobey, kick over the traces, defy, transgress, set at naught, run riot, rise against, spurn, challenge, repudiate, abandon, reject, cast off, retract, rescind, resist, make a stand, oppose, fly in the face of.

TURN ASIDE, *v.* Avert, deflect, ward off, parry, divert, shunt, switch, warp, stave off, keep off, fend off, obviate, prevent, draw off, forfend, check, nip in the bud, preclude, countercheck, obstruct, stay, block the way, intercept, interrupt, interclude, frustrate, thwart, balk, circumvent, foil.

TURN BACK, *v.* Retrace one's steps, retrogress, retrograde, revert, return, retreat, recoil, repair, recede, retire, retrocede, withdraw, drop astern, put about, wheel, veer round, turn upon one's heel, double, dance the back step, go home, beat a retreat.

TURNCOAT, *n.* One who changes his party *or* principles, backslider, apostate, deserter, renegade, traitor, quitter, trimmer, rebel, weathercock, changeling, recreant, recidivist, double-dealer, timeserver, opportunist, temporizer, Judas, Iscariot, rat, turntippet, welsher, mugwump, Janus.

TURN IN, *v.* Go to bed, retire, hit the sack *(coll.),* hit the hay *(coll.),* call it a day, turn back the counterpane, shed one's clothes, bid good-night, say one's prayers.

TURNING POINT, *n.* Point at which a decisive change takes place, decisive moment, crisis, climacteric, juncture, turn, conjuncture, emergency, critical period, extremity, crux, crossroads, exigency, strait, nick of time, turn of the tide, calm before the storm, hinge, pivot, straw that broke the camel's back, last straw, crowning point, apex, zenith, acme, culmination, ne plus ultra, meridian, maximum, apogee, climax, Rubicon, boundary line.

TURNKEY, *n.* One who has charge of the keys of a prison, jailer, warden, custodian, keeper, castellan, ranger, guard.

TURN OUT, *v.* 1. Put out, extinguish, douse *(sl.)*, suppress, darken, smother, quell.

2. Expel, send away, dismiss, discharge, eject, oust, drive out, fire, banish, expatriate, relegate, ostracize, send to Coventry, *chasser (Fr.)*, dispatch, throw out, bundle out, sack, send packing, pack off, show the door to, evict, dislodge, deport.

3. Produce as the result of labor, manufacture, make, fabricate, build, construct, fashion, put together, set up, frame.

4. Happen, come to be, become ultimately, wax, get, come round to, undergo a change, resolve into, issue, eventuate, ensue, result, accrue, be the effect, be derived, emanate.

TURNOUT, *n.* 1. Body of persons who come to an assemblage, gathering, audience, assembly, forgathering, conflux, levy, concourse, meet, congregation, muster, convocation, congress, convention, throng, crowd, host, mob, multitude, crush, press, body, horde, gang.

2. Quantity produced, output, batch, aggregate, amount, bulk, volume, quantum, lot, mass.

3. Manner in which anything is equipped, style, getup, pattern, kind, sort, make, mode, fashion, vogue, appearance, guise, shape, cut, trim.

4. Equipage, outfit, equipment.

TURNPIKE, *n.* Tollroad, pike, highway, throughway, state road, speedway, parkway, roadway, route.

TURN TAIL, *v.* Retreat ignominiously, run away, flee, cut and run, make off, decamp, abscond, show a light pair of heels, retire, back out, draw back, veer round, turn upon one's heel, beat a retreat, dance the back step, take to one's heels, be off like a shot, fly, take flight, scamper off, desert, defect, give leg bail, take French leave, bolt, flit, levant, skedaddle, make oneself scarce, absquatulate *(sl.)*.

TURN TO ACCOUNT, *v.* Take advantage of, utilize, make use of, profit from, put to use, avail oneself of, convert to use, make the most of, make a shift with, make the best of, make capital out of, reap the fruits of, obtain a return from, gain an advantage, bring grist to the mill, make the pot boil, clear, realize.

TURN UP, *v.* 1. Bend upward, fold over, fold up, pleat, plicate, double, plait, lap, crease, crinkle, corrugate, pucker, ruffle, gather, hem, ruck, tuck, dog's-ear, infold.

2. Happen, occur, come to pass, transpire, eventuate, befall, chance, betide, take place, fall out, supervene, crop up, issue, ensue.

3. Appear, arise, come into view, be met with, present itself, be found, greet the eye, meet the eye, come to light, manifest itself, stand forth, drop from the clouds, come unawares, pop up, be unexpected, creep upon one, burst upon one, take by surprise.

TURPITUDE, *n.* Depravity, baseness, degradation, shameful wickedness, vileness, degeneracy, corruption, vice, obloquy, immorality, lewdness, obscenity, infamy, ill repute, bad odor, odium, opprobrium, ignominy, disgrace, dishonor, scandal, shame, defilement, tarnish, stain, stigma, brand, badge of infamy, blot on one's ecutcheon, bar sinister, improbity, deviation from virtue, villainy, abjection, debasement, laxity, roguery, knavery,

foul play, perfidy, perfidiousness, badness, wrongdoing.

TURPITUDINOUS, *adj.* Shameful, degraded, debased, degenerate, base, vile, ignominious, corrupt, vicious, immoral, lewd, obscene, libidinous, lustful, infamous, opprobrious, disgraceful, dishonorable, scandalous, abject, lax, bestial, animal, gross, impure, filthy, foul, dirty, indecent, coarse, ribald, incontinent, dissolute, sensual, lecherous, salacious, concupiscent, arrant, blackguard.

TURRET, *n.* Small tower, tourelle, minaret, cupola, steeple, pinnacle, column, lookout, observatory, campanile, *flèche (Fr.)*, spire, belfry, obelisk, pillar, dome, watchtower, crow's-nest, belvedere, gazebo.

TUSK, *n.* Pointed tooth, fang, tush, incisor, nib, cusp, spur, barb, spit, horn, antler, bristle, snag.

TUSSLE, *n.* Rough struggle, fracas, fray, affray, fight, set-to, shindy, scuffle, broil, colluctation, mêlée, scrimmage, skirmish, conflict, brush, battle royal, boxing, pugilism, wrestling, jujitsu, sparring, fisticuffs, bout, scrap, brawl, embroilment, rixation, embranglement, rumpus.

TUTELAGE, *n.* 1. Teaching, instruction, education, edification, pedagogy, tutorage, tuition, guidance, direction, preparation, schooling, training, discipline.

2. Learning, pupilage, apprenticeship, pupilarity, matriculation, novitiate.

3. Office of a guardian, tutorship, guardianship, protection, custody, charge, keeping, wardship, care, safekeeping, preservation, auspices.

TUTELARY, *adj.* Protective, guarding, tutelar, protecting, guardian, patron, preservative, patronal, preceptive, counseling, advisory.

TUTOR, *v.* Teach, school, instruct, edify, indoctrinate, inculcate, coach, prime, exercise, discipline, educate, cram, inform, enlighten, guide, direct, show, give lessons in, instill, infuse, impregnate, imbue, disseminate, expound, preach, lecture, enlarge the mind, rear, train, ground, qualify, prepare, drill, familiarize with, practice, initiate.

TUTOR, *n.* 1. Teacher, preceptor, mentor, instructor, coach, schoolmaster, dominie, counselor, adviser, professor, master, trainer, pedagogue, director, paedotribe, guru, educator, crammer, catechist, principal, lecturer, governess, nurse.

2. *(Law)* Guardian, custodian, keeper, warder, custos, protector, duenna.

TUXEDO, *n.* Men's dark tailless coat for semiformal wear, dinner jacket, tux *(abbr.)*, smoking jacket, dress suit.

TWADDLE, *v.* Talk in a trivial *or* foolish manner, prattle, prate, twattle, maunder, chatter, blather, jabber, gibber, babble, gabble, palaver, clack, rattle on, jaw.

TWADDLE, *n.* Meaningless talk, gibberish, babble, drivel, balderdash, nonsense, jargon, tosh *(sl.)*, hogwash *(sl.)*, jabber, *bavardage (Fr.)*, flapdoodle, *baragouin (Fr.)*, bosh, poppycock *(coll.)*, moonshine, rubbish, trash, inanity, stuff and nonsense, chatter, prate, prattle, tittle-tattle, gabble, fiddle-faddle.

TWANG, *v.* Give out a sharp ringing sound, twangle, twank, resound, ring, reverberate, jingle, ding, clink, chink, tinkle, chime.

TWANG, *n.* Harsh quick sound, vibrating sound, sharp ringing, resonance, stridency, reverberation, tintinnabulation, chime, clangor, vibration, nasality, dissonance, cacophony, sharpness, shrillness,

TWEAK, *v.* Seize and pull with a sharp jerk and twist, twitch, pinch, jerk, twinge, pull rudely, squeeze, nip, grip.

TWEEZERS, *n.* Small pincers for plucking out hairs, nippers, tongs, forceps, pliers, grippers.

TWELVE, *n.* Ten plus two, dozen, XII, long dozen, baker's dozen.

TWENTY, *n.* Ten times two, score, XX.

TWICE, *adv.* Two times in succession, doubly, over again, once more, bis, encore, double, on two occasions, in two instances, in twofold quantity, *da capo (It.), de novo (Lat.),* anew, *de nouveau (Fr.), noch einmal (Ger.).*

TWIDDLE, *v.* Turn round and round with the fingers, twirl, fidget, wiggle, play with, tweedle, touch lightly, finger, manipulate, fiddle with, toy with, trifle, twist, grabble, grope, handle, feel, pass the fingers over, stroke, palpate, rub, knead, massage.

TWIG, *n.* Offshoot, branch, shoot, withe, sprig, slip, stem, spray, stick, switch, sprout, scion, sucker, tendril, runner, sarmentum, bough, ramification.

TWILIGHT, *n.* Light from the sky when the sun is below the horizon, gloaming, crepuscule, dusk, crepuscular light, thin gray half-light, edge of darkness, faint light, nightfall, decline of day, *entre chien et loup (Fr.),* blind man's holiday, rushlight, eventide, vespers, evensong, curfew, sundown, *demi-jour (Fr.),* shades of evening, cockshut time.

TWILIGHT, *adj.* Crepuscular, dim, obscure, faint, pale, darkish, darkling, shadowy, shaded, dusky, blurred, darksome, sombrous, tenebrous, darkened, umbrageous, looming.

TWIN, *adj.* 1. Being one of two born at the same time, Siamese, sibling, cognate, congeneric, connatural, congenerous, kindred.

2. Forming a pair, constituting a couple, occurring in pairs, didymous, geminate, twain, two, duplex, doubled, second, double, twofold, dual, duplicate, dualistic, binate, binary, binomial, both, paired, coupled, conjugate, matched, bijugate.

3. Fellow, like, similar, alike, corresponding, resembling, consimilar, analogous, parallel, homologous, of a piece, akin to.

TWINE, *v.* 1. Twist together, unite closely, interwind, intertwine, interlace, weave, intertwist, interdigitate, entwine, inweave, wreathe, link, splice, plait, mat, plat, braid, knot, net, form by twisting strands.

2. Embrace, surround, wind around, wind about, encircle, enfold, clasp, throw tendrils about, involve.

3. Dispose by winding, wind in a sinuous course, meander, zigzag, undulate, wave.

TWINE, *n.* 1. Twist, coil, convolution, involution, anfractuosity, tortuosity, undulation, winding, sinuosity, twirl, ambages, inosculation, curl, spiral, corkscrew, helix, volute, worm, whorl, tendril, kink, labyrinth, maze.

2. Strong thread composed of strands twisted together, cord, cordage, string, packthread, cable, rope, yarn, hemp.

TWINGE, *v.* Affect with sudden sharp pain, ache, shoot, tingle, twitch, lancinate, smart, chafe, hurt, pain, gripe, gnaw, bite, sting, grind, stab, pinch,

convulse, harrow, wring, torture, torment, agonize, rack, excruciate.

TWINCE, *n.* Sudden sharp pain, pang, gripe, ache, throe, torment, torture, stab, smart, anguish, cramp, spasm, stitch, crick, kink, convulsion, throb, twitch, dolor, shooting, soreness, malaise, discomfort, tic douloureux.

TWINKLE, *v.* Shine with quick gleams of light, emit light in little flashes, sparkle, scintillate, coruscate, fulgurate, flash, glimmer, flicker, beam, radiate, gleam, glisten, glow, glare, flare, shimmer, blaze.

TWINKLING, *n.* 1. Shining with little gleams of light, scintillation, coruscation, fulguration, sparkling, flashing, gleaming, glitter, glint, shimmer, glistening, effulgence, refulgency, radiance, luminosity, glowing.

2. Time required for a wink, instant, second, minute, moment, trice, jiffy, split second, *coup (Fr.), coup d'oeil (Fr.),* crack, breath.

TWIRL, *v.* Swing circularly, revolve, whirl, rotate rapidly, circulate, turn round, twist, wind, coil, spin, wheel, move round, spiral, whisk, twine, reel, wreathe, worm, curl, swivel, roll, sinuate, meander, serpentine, undulate, wave, zigzag.

TWIRL, *n.* Circular motion, quick rotation, revolution, convolution, turn, twist, whirl, spin, spiral, involution, tortuosity, sinuosity, undulation, wave, circuit, contortion, meandering, maze, ambages, coil, helix, curl, roll, volute, corkscrew, scallop, scroll, worm, kink, labyrinth, circumflexion.

TWIST, *v.* 1. Combine by winding together, intertwine, entwine, twine, twist together, purl, wreathe, interlace, intersect, cross, coil, twirl, roll, reel, entwist.

2. Wheel, slue, tack, veer, alter one's course, zigzag, meander, deviate, vary, curve, bend, swerve, bear off, heel, jibe, sheer, yaw, go about, shift, switch, deflect, shunt, sidetrack, divaricate, fork, jib, shy.

3. Contort, gnarl, wrinkle, distort, writhe, warp, knot, wrench, screw, buckle, wrest, wring, misshape, deform, alter in shape.

TWIST, *n.* 1. Convolution, tortion, flexure, twirl, turn, bend, coil, spiral, bight, winding, torque, circumbendibus, curve, corkscrew, helix, maze, labyrinth, meander, zigzag, involution, tortuosity, undulation, wave, sinuousness, circuit, ambages, volute, scallop, scroll, serpent, eel.

2. Contortion, distortion, wrench, writhing, kink, tangle, deformation, warp, knot, screw, buckle, crookedness, malformation, kyphosis, asymmetry, misproportion, monstrosity, anamorphosis, grimace, disfigurement.

3. Peculiar bias, idiosyncrasy, eccentricity, crotchet, quirk, vagary, freak, caprice, whim, fancy, peculiarity, aberration, singularity, oddity, mannerism.

TWISTER, *n.* Whirlwind, tornado, cyclone, dust storm, hurricane, squall, blast, gale, tempest, storm, samiel, simoom, typhoon, monsoon, harmattan, mistral, sirocco.

TWIT, *v.* Reproach, taunt, blame, find fault with, nag, peck at, harass, fling at, upbraid, mock, ridicule, sneer at, scoff at, jeer at, gibe at, disparage, belittle, underrate, impute, charge, accuse, slur, stigmatize, incriminate, rebuke, reprehend, berate, chide, overhaul, take to task, blow up, lecture, reprimand, castigate, trounce, dress down, abuse, scold, rail at, decry, backbite, dispraise, depreciate, malign, slander, traduce, asperse, knock, discredit, lampoon, burlesque, travesty, satirize.

TWITCH, *v.* 1. Pull suddenly, jerk, snatch, pluck, tweak, pinch, nip, tug at, wrench.

2. Shake, agitate, convulse, bandy, toss, brandish, whisk, hitch, joggle, jolt, jounce, churn, vellicate, whip.

2. Quiver, move in a jerky way, shiver, quaver, wiggle, wriggle, squirm, throb, pulsate, palpitate, go pitapat, beat.

TWITCH, *n.* 1. Quick pull, sudden tug, jerk, wrench, tweak, pinch, nip, snatch.

2. Tremor, tic, shake, quiver, quaver, jactitation, ripple, spasm, throb, throe, palpitation, paroxysm, convulsion, contraction, vellication.

3. Ache, pain, twinge, lancination, stab, shooting, gripe.

TWITTER, *v.* 1. Utter a succession of small tremulous sounds, chirp, chirrup, cheep, peep, sing, screech, cluck, cackle, quack, coo, caw, chatter.

2. Be agitated, be excited, flutter, be flurried, tremble with excitement, be in a flutter, be in a tizzy, be wrought up, be in a ferment, fuss, fidget, be in a stew.

TWITTER, *n.* 1. Chirping, chirruping, chirp, peep, twittering, cheep, screech, cackle, cluck, quack, caw, coo.

2. Agitation, tremor, state of tremulous excitement, perturbation, trepidation, flutter, ferment, stew, ado, to-do, bustle, fuss, tizzy, flurry, impatience, turbulence, restlessness, disquietude, fidgets, ruffle, fluster, pother, whirl.

TWO, *n.* 1. Sum of two units, 2, II, plus one.

2. Pair, brace, couple, couplet, yoke, twain, deuce, span, doublet, team, set, twins, both, binary, gemini.

TWO-BY-FOUR, *adj.* Unimportant, insignificant, immaterial, trivial, trifling, piddling, niggling, fribbling, petty, paltry, worthless, inconsequential, picayune, second-rate, inferior, one-horse, beneath consideration, not worth a rap, wretched, miserable, meager, sorry, pitiful, poor, scrubby, mean, trashy, rubbishy, nugatory, inappreciable.

TWO-FACED, *adj.* Deceitful, double-dealing, Janus-faced, double-faced, hypocritical, Jesuitical, pharisaical, tartuffish, insincere, canting, affected, sanctimonious, perfidious, perjured, treacherous, faithless, forsworn, wily, tricky, sly, cunning, artful, disingenuous, evasive, hollow, dishonest, fraudulent, untruthful, falsified, lying, mendacious, false-hearted, untrue, unveracious, feigned, counterfeit, spurious, sham, pseudo, untrustworthy, casuistic, sophistical, fallacious, misleading, timeserving, crooked, slippery, Machiavellian, double-tongued, unscrupulous, unprincipled, rascally, recreant, knavish, villainous, Iscariotic, traitorous, disloyal, insidious.

TWOFOLD, *adj.* Having two elements *or* parts, double, dual, duplex, biform, dualistic, duplicate, geminate, binary, binomial.

TWO-SIDED, *adj.* Bilateral, bifacial, dihedral.

TYCOON, *n.* 1. Commander-in-chief, generalissimo, shogun, sultan, caesar, caliph, shah, imaum, padishah, mogul, khan, mikado, lama, imperator, commandant, chieftain, sirdar, sachem, sheik, potentate.

2. Businessman having great wealth and power, baron of industry, executive, director, boss, big gun (*sl.*), big wheel (*sl.*), magnate, big wig (*sl.*).

TYKE, *n.* 1. Mischievous child, urchin, gamin, street Arab, mudlark, imp, brat, whippersnapper, pixy, leprechaun, guttersnipe.

2. Low contemptible fellow, boor, cad, churl, caitiff, villain, lout, rowdy, roughneck, ruffian, hooligan, slubberdegullion, curmudgeon, hoodlum, desperado, brute, savage, barbarian, Mohock, larrikin.

TYPE, *n.* 1. Group distinguished by a particular character, kind, class, variety, genus, species, phylum, strain, breed, sort, division, subdivision, clan, category, grouping, feather, brand, stamp, classification, order, family, race, sept.

2. Manner, nature, character, gender, genre, description, denomination, style, color, sex, specification, designation, form, temper, disposition, cast, mold, figure.

3. Model, example, standard, pattern, original, representative specimen, prototype, archetype, protoplast, exemplar, exponent, copy, instance, sample, design, norm, precedent, criterion, rule, paradigm, ideal.

4. Image, symbol, figure, sign, token, emblem, cipher, mark, signum, device, indicium, indicant, prognostic, augury, foreshowing, adumbration.

5. Simile, comparison, metaphor, bird of a feather, duplicate, counterpart, analogue, facsimile, parallel, homologue, double, mate, pair, twin.

6. Printing character, letter, typography, figure, stamp, impressed sign, Italic, Roman, Gothic, boldface, font, pica.

TYPESETTING, *n.* Composing, typography, printing, presswork, linotype, monotype, composition, letterpress.

TYPHOON, *n.* Tropical cyclone, hurricane, tornado, simoom, violent storm, whirlwind, tempest, gale, squall, samiel, monsoon, harmattan, rainstorm, waterspout, deluge, cloudburst, downpour, inundation, drencher, serein.

TYPICAL, *adj.* Serving as a type, exemplary, illustrative, representative, indicative, characteristic, suggestive, symbolic, model, true-to-type, normal, ideal, emblematical, figurative, metaphorical, symbolical, emblematic, in character, distinctive, regular, ordinary, usual, indicatory, significatory, connotative, denotative, indicant, diagnostic, in point, canonical, standard, orthodox, prefigurative.

TYPIFY, *v.* Serve as the typical specimen of, exemplify, represent, indicate, stand for, signify, betoken, symbolize, denote, figure, shadow forth, prefigure, embody, image, impersonate, mean, connote, manifest, imply, evidence, evince, mark.

TYPOGRAPHIC, *adj.* Printed, in print, set, typographical, in type, published, typeset.

TYRANNICAL, *adj.* Arbitrary, despotic, absolute, autocratic, tyrannous, domineering, imperious, high-handed, iron-fisted, dictatorial, overbearing, ruthless, severe, cruel, severely oppressive, harsh, inhuman, grinding, galling, Draconian, barbarous, inquisitorial, arrogant, insolent, coercive, stringent, extortionate, imperative, peremptory, austere, relentless, pitiless, rigorous, unyielding, exigent, inexorable, obdurate, inflexible, unlawful, illegal, illicit, illegitimate, extrajudicial, unauthorized, summary, irresponsible, discretionary, intolerant, overweening, swaggering, blustering, abusive.

TYRANNIZE, *v.* Exercise power oppressively, rule despotically, despotize, domineer, dictate, rule with an iron rod, lord it, carry matters with a high hand, be despotic, oppress, grind the heel, hold the whip hand, persecute, maltreat, intimidate, put on the screws, usurp, arrogate, bully, ill-treat, override, ride roughshod over, destroy civil liberties, coerce, dragoon, enforce, constrain, subjugate, subdue, commandeer, require, overpower, exact, lay down the law, swagger, bluster, bulldoze.

TYRANNY, *n.* 1. Arbitrary exercise of power, despotic abuse of authority, absolutism, despotism, autocracy, absolute rule, dictatorship, Nazism, Fascism.

2. Brute force, oppression, iron rule, iron heel, iron fist, reign of terror, harshness, heavy hand, imperiousness, severity, cruelty, coercion, terrorism, inhumanity, persecution, strict censorship, inclemency, extreme severity, violence, mob law, usurpation, domination, martial law.

TYRANT, *n.* 1. Absolute ruler, despot, dictator, autocrat, Draco, Caesar, overlord, Führer, Duce.

2. Cruel master, oppressor, inquisitor, martinet, disciplinarian, stickler, bully, persecutor, bashaw, hard master, Simon Legree, taskmaster, slave driver.

TYRO, *n.* 1. Novice, greenhorn, neophyte, beginner, apprentice, freshman, learner, pupil, plebe, schoolboy, abecedarian, alphabetarian, tenderfoot, rooky, recruit, debutant, probationer, initiate, catechumen.

2. Smatterer, sciolist, dabbler, dilettante, amateur, half-scholar, wiseacre.

3. Booby, numskull, bonehead, duffer, dunce, ignoramus, bungler, butterfingers, lout, clod, blockhead, galoot, dolt, fumbler, yokel, oaf.

U

UBIQUITOUS, *adj.* Existing *or* being everywhere at the same time, omnipresent, ubiquitary, everywhere, pervading, ever-present, universal, worldwide.

UBIQUITY, *n.* Presence in more than one place at the same time, omnipresence, ubiquitariness, universality, diffusion, dispersion, pervasion, ubiquitousness.

UGLIFY, *v.* Make ugly, deform, blemish, distort, disfigure, impair, mar, mutilate, deface, scar, spoil, grimace, blight, twist, turn awry, contort, misshape, screw, gnarl, wring, wrench, torture, writhe.

UGLY, *adj.* 1. Offensive to the sight, contrary to beauty, hideous, homely, beautiless, plain, forbidding, uncomely, unsightly, unshapely, distorted, misshapen, frightful, horrid, monstrous, grotesque, unlovely, unseemly, ill-favored, unprepossessing, horrible, horrifying, repulsive, repellent, evil-looking, evil-favored, hard-favored, hard-featured, hard-visaged.

2. Offensive from a moral aspect, repulsive, noisome, odious, execrable, repugnant, repellent, vile, foul, obnoxious, noxious, fulsome, nasty, loathful, beastly, disgraceful, unendurable, insupportable, unbearable, intolerable, insufferable, nauseating, nauseous, serious, grave, hateful, despicable, loathsome, disgusting, abhorrent, sickening, contemptible, mean, low, abominable.

UKASE, *n.* Official decree, dictate, edict, rule, fiat, act, imperative, mandate, caveat, writ, declaration, dispensation, rescript, proclamation, pronouncement, pronunciamento, manifesto, decreement, firman *(Oriental)*.

ULCER, *n.* 1. *(Med.)* Superficial sore discharging pus, inflammation, canker, fester.

2. *(Fig.)* Anything that festers and corrupts like an open sore, curse, woe, visitation, sore, plague, nettle, infestation, affliction, provocation, infliction, offense, disease, torment, scourge, venom, poison, moth and rust, annoyance, fret, gall, grievance, bane, blight, canker, vexation, pest, worry, thorn, sting, mortification, pestilence, worm in the apple *or* rose.

ULCERATE, *v.* Affect with *or* as with an ulcer, undergo ulceration, corrupt, defile, contaminate, debase, degrade, deprave, pollute, infect, vitiate, taint, poison, envenom, eat at, destroy, afflict, canker, sphacelate *(Med.).*

ULCEROUS, *adj.* Ulcerated, cankerous, gangrened, gangrenous, mortified, cankered, tainted, morbid, corroded, sphacelate *(Med.).*

ULTERIOR, *adj.* 1. Situated beyond *or* on the farther side, exterior, external, far, remote, distant, outside, oversea, overseas, faraway, far-off, yonder, foreign, tramontane, ultramontane.

2. Further, remoter, beyond what is manifest *or* avowed, obscure, side, concealed, hidden, secret, unseen, unrevealed, undivulged, undisclosed, unperceived, unexpressed, unmentioned.

ULTIMATE, *adj.* 1. Farthest, most remote *(in space or time),* last, rear, hindermost, final, foremost, earliest.

2. Last in a train of progression *or* consequences, final, terminal, conclusive, conclusory, crowning, ending, completing, eventual, definitive, determinative, inevitable, unavoidable, predetermined, terminative.

3. Incapable of further analysis (division, separation), elemental, original, basic, unmixed, unmingled, pure, uncompounded, radical, root, essential, elementary, fundamental, incomplex, unadulterated, unsophisticated, unalloyed, distilled, primary, refined, purified, rudimentary, rudimental, incomposite.

ULTIMATUM, *n.* Final proposition *or* condition, terms offered, order, command, proposal, decision, demand, request, stipulation, obligation, provision, exaction, requirement.

ULTRA, *adj.* Going beyond others *or* beyond due limit, extreme, radical, startling, outstanding, ultimate, advanced, forward-looking, revolutionary, flagrant, glaring, pronounced, thorough, out-and-out, utter, complete, downright.

ULTRA, *n.* Extremist, radical, heretic, nonconformist, die-hard, dissenter, reformer, progressive, irreconcilable, progressist, progressionist, bitter-ender *(coll.),* intransigent.

ULTRACRITICAL, *adj.* Hypercritical, carping, caviling, finicking, finicky, fussy, exigent, censorious, exacting, squeamish, querulous, punctilious, precise, strict, finical, difficult, denunciatory, captious, contumelious, condemnatory, damnatory, overscrupulous, hairsplitting, overcritical, hard *or* difficult to please.

ULTRAISM, *n.* Principles of those who advocate extreme measures, radicalism, progressivism, revolution, extremism, aggravation, reform, reformism.

ULTRAMODERN, *adj.* Beyond the norm of the modern, extreme in typically modern ideas *or* tendencies, up-to-the-minute, modernistic, futuristic, neoteric.

ULTRAMONTANE, *adj.* Beyond the mountains *(esp. the Alps),* alien, foreign, distant, exotic, ulterior, exterior, external, remote, removed, far-off, faraway, tramontane, transalpine, hyperborean, out-of-the-way, outland, antipodean, antipodal, oversea, overseas, barbaric, outlandish, barbarian.

ULTRAMUNDANE, *adj.* Being beyond the world, beyond the limits of our system, otherworldly, celestial, extramundane, empyrean, supramundane, unworldly, spiritual, heavenly, unearthly, sphery.

ULTRANATIONALISM, *n.* Great *or* excessive devotion to *or* advocacy of national interests, chauvinism, overpatriotism, jingoism, spread-eagleism *(coll.),* patriolatry.

ULULANT, *adj.* Howling, wailing, lamenting, reboant, resounding, plaintive, mournful, crying, clamorous, blatant, latrant, mugient, ululatory, ululative, moaning, full-mouthed, full-toned, lowing, bellowing.

ULULATE, *v.* Howl, wail, hoot, bell, bellow, moan, yell, squall, blare, bay, bawl, pule, whine, call, cry, yowl, caterwaul.

UMBRA, *n.* Shade, shadow, shadiness, dimness, darkness, semidark, semidarkness, gloom, penumbra, dusk, twilight, duskiness, crepuscule, half-light.

UMBRAGE, *n.* 1. That which casts shade *(esp. foliage),* overhang, verdure, bower, arbor, leafage.
2. Offense, resentment, heat, warmth, rancor, choler, spleen, pique, displeasure, vexation, gall, soreness, bile, animosity, dudgeon, anger, wrath, indignation, annoyance, irritation, disaffection, alienation, estrangement, bad blood, hatred, dislike, ill humor, pet, tiff, huff, bitterness, enmity, hostility, miff *(sl.).*

UMBRAGEOUS, *adj.* 1. Forming *or* affording a shade, being shaded, shady, overhanging, over-shadowed, overshaded, overcast, enveloping, umbriferous, covering, protective, dim, gloomy, dark, semi-dark.
2. Feeling umbrage, taking *or* disposed to take umbrage, suspicious, resentful, bitter, acrimonious, indignant, offensive, hurt, rancorous, virulent, hasty, moody, wounded, injured, thin-skinned, up in arms, displeased, like touchwood *or* tinder, splenetic, hot-tempered, hot-headed, iracund, crabby, crabbed, crusty, bearish, touchy, peevish, huffy, petty, currish, out of sorts, cross, churlish, testy, humorsome, petulant, querulous, waspish, bristling, captious, ill-humored, ill-disposed, ill-affected, ill-tempered, in high dudgeon, in bad *or* ill humor.

UMBRELLA, *n.* Shade (screen, guard) for protection from rain *or* sun, sunshade, gamp, sun-shield, canopy, parasol, bumbershoot *(hum.).*

UMPIRAGE, *n.* Office *or* power of an umpire, act of umpiring, arbitrament, mediation, intermediation, intervention, pacification, arbitration, intercession, interagency, negotiation, conciliation, mollification, settlement, mediatorship, mediatorialism, mediatization, adjustment, modulation.

UMPIRE, *n.* Person who decides controversies *or* questions between parties, referee, judge, mediator, intermediator, go-between, referendary, peacemaker, reconciler, propitiator, pacificator, make-peace, negotiator, arbitrator, arbiter, moder-ator, negotiant, intervener, intercessor, interagent, intermediary, intermedium, intermediate agent.

UNABLE, *adj.* Not able, incapable, impotent, incompetent, powerless, forceless, ineffective, inefficacious, helpless, inept, inapt, unfit, defenseless, inadequate, not equal *or* up to, inoperative, worthless, useless, insufficient, disabled, unendowed, unqualified.

UNABRIDGED, *adj.* Not abridged *or* shortened *(as a book),* complete, full, unreduced, unexpurgated, as originally written, whole, entire, intact, uncut.

UNACCOMMODATED, *adj.* 1. Not accommodated, not adapted, strange, ill-suited, uncongenial, mismatched, at odds, uncomfortable, uneasy, misplaced, misjoined, ill-at-ease, divergent, inharmonious, discordant, contrary, dissonant, different, discrepant, incongruous, incompatible, irreconcilable, inconformable, disaccordant, lost, overwhelmed, nonplused, confused, disoriented.
2. Without accommodations, unhoused, homeless, houseless, out in the cold, unprovided for, unplaced, unsettled, unestablished.

UNACCOMPANIED, *adj.* Alone, unattended, solitary, unescorted, deserted, companionless, separate, apart, lonely.

UNACCOMPLISHED, *adj.* 1. Not accomplished, incomplete, unfulfilled, unfinished, undone, unperformed, unexecuted, half-baked, half-cocked, frustrated, sketchy.
2. Without accomplishments, unskilled, devoid of talents, untrained, unprepared, unpracticed, incompetent, ungifted, untalented, unendowed, uneducated, inexperienced, ignorant, inexpert, unproficient, unapt, uncultured, uncultivated, untutored, inapt, inadept, undexterous, unfacile.

UNACCOUNTABLE, *adj.* 1. Not accountable *or* answerable, irresponsible, immune, lawless, exempt, clear, free, spared, innocent, excused, unanswerable, unsubject, unliable.
2. Not to be accounted for *or* explained, strange, unusual, mysterious, surprising, unintelligible, incomprehensible, inexplicable, extraordinary, peculiar, singular, anomalous, irrational, erratic, astonishing, abnormal, unnatural, aberrant, unwonted, freakish, arbitrary, unheard-of.

UNACCUSTOMED, *adj.* 1. Unfamiliar, unusual, foreign, strange, new, unwonted, extraordinary, curious, odd, queer, out of the ordinary, irregular, uncommon, outlandish, far-fetched, eccentric, singular, peculiar, anomalous, exceptional, rare, unaccountable, irrational, surprising, astonishing, erratic, startling, amazing, remarkable, wild, grotesque, quaint, droll, bizarre, abnormal, unnatural, unique, out-of-the-way, unheard-of, original, fantastic, whimsical, inusitate, aberrant, unconventional, fanciful, freakish.
2. Not habituated, strange, unused, uninitiated, unskilled, ignorant, unpracticed, inexperienced, unseasoned, unacquainted, untried, raw, green, unfamiliar, a stranger to, a novice at, amateurish, naïve, unversed, unconversant, unenlightened, uninformed, new to, unwonted, ungiven to, unhabituated.

UNADVISED, *adj.* 1. Not advised, without advice, uninformed, unaware, unsuspecting, unwarned, inexpectant, unadmonished, off one's guard, unready, napping, ignorant, unwary, unprepared.
2. Indiscreet, rash, madcap, heady, hasty, careless, reckless, headlong, headstrong, heedless,

thoughtless, imprudent, precipitate, injudicious, impulsive, incautious, devil-may-care, irresponsible, premature, harum-scarum, impetuous, sudden, adventurous, harebrained, hot-brained, hot-headed, foolhardy, unwary, precipitous, foolish, unthinking, brash, unbridled, unchecked, abrupt, frantic, hotspur, immature, hurried, subitaneous, ungoverned, feverish, unwise, ill-managed, inconsiderate.

UNAFFECTED, *adj.* 1. Free from affectation, simple, plain, sincere, genuine, open, ingenuous, artless, innocent, direct, guileless, childlike, wholesome, frank, candid, unreserved, honest, undissembling, undesigning, naïve, plain-spoken, downright, open-hearted, single-minded, simpleminded, aboveboard, truthful, blunt, clear-eyed, unfeigning, unsophisticated, lamblike, outspoken, straightforward.

2. Not affected (acted upon, influenced), hard, unfeeling, unkind, severe, untender, austere, unsympathetic, unyielding, callous, obdurate, hardhearted, mean, harsh, remote, soulless, obtuse, untouched, unimpressible, unstirred, unemotional, cold, implacable, unresponsive, frigid, passionless, indifferent, hostile, unkindled, impervious, pitiless, insentient, chill, icy, unmoved, forbidding, heartless, stoical, stolid, unconcerned, inflexible, stony, flinty, steely, insensitive, thick-skinned, deadened, numbed, inured, hardened, remorseless, bowelless, inclement, uncompassionate, unnatural, uncaring, hard-boiled *(coll.)*, disdainful, proof against, aweless, bloodless, cold-blooded, cold-hearted, unmerciful, inhumane, inhuman.

UNANIMITY, *n.* Complete accord *or* agreement, harmony, unity, unison, concert, union, uniformity, oneness, accordance, like-mindedness, compliance, compatibility, coöperation, one voice, assent, concurrence, alliance, acceptance, acquiescence, concinnity, consonance, sympathy, rapport *(Fr.)*, conformation, sanction, consonance, meeting of minds, consentience, accession, correspondence, consistency, congeniality.

UNANIMOUS, *adj.* In complete accord, agreed, concordant, of one mind, united, solid, likeminded, agreeing, harmonious, accordant, acquiescent, concerted, sympathetic, of the same mind, correspondent, compatible, consistent, consonant, of one accord, allied, consentient, assenting, assonant.

UNAPPEALABLE, *adj.* Final, irrefutable, conclusive, determinative, ultimate, incontestable, unavoidable, irrevocable, incontrovertible, indisputable, unimpeachable, unanswerable, irrefragable, inescapable, binding, inexorable, inevitable.

UNAPPROACHABLE, *adj.* 1. Not to be approached, inaccessible, aloof, distant, remote, infinite, out-of-the-way, Godforsaken *(coll.)*, beyond reach, unattainable, impervious, impregnable, stern, austere, forbidding.

2. Unrivaled, inimitable, superior, unequaled, superlative, peerless, matchless, highest, unique, incomparable, superexcellent, unexcelled, exalted, quintessential, paramount, unparalleled, rare, sublime, noble, supreme, transcendent, nonpareil, preëminent, second to none, foremost, first, uppermost, ne plus ultra, beyond compare *or* comparison, priceless, unsurpassed, culminating.

UNAPT, *adj.* 1. Unsuited, unfitted, unsuitable, inapposite, untimely, malapropos, awkward, inapplicable, irrelevant, inopportune, ill-adapted, ill-timed, unseasonable, improper, inappropriate,

infelicitous, out of keeping, out of proportion, unbecoming, out of character, out of place, out of joint, out of tune, imprudent, indecorous, inconvenient, untoward, incorrect, illogical, inexpedient, inadvisable, not to the purpose, unbefitting, impertinent.

2. Not disposed (likely, liable), indisposed, unlikely, not inclined, disinclined, averse, slow to, opposed, unwilling, reluctant, out of concert with, loath, refusing, unconsenting, dissenting, not in the mood *or* vein.

3. Not quick to learn, slow, inapt, ill-qualified, inept, incompetent, inefficient, unendowed, incapable, dull, unskillful, unproductive, undexterous, unpromising, unfacile, unproficient, inexpert, unclever, stupid, retarded, insulse, thick *(coll.)*, dull-pated, mutton-headed *(coll.)*, numskull *(coll.)*, stolid, bovine, dull-witted, dumb *(coll.)*, sluggish, simple-minded, clodpated, thick-headed, dronish, muddle-brained, slow-witted, uncomprehending, unintelligent, blockish, unteachable, addlepated, green.

UNARM, *v.* 1. Deprive of weapons, disarm, render powerless, disable, incapacitate, weaken, unsinew, cripple, hamstring.

2. Lay down one's arms, disarm, surrender, end hostilities, make peace, come to terms, make matters up, smoke the pipe of peace *or* calumet, cease opposition, hand over one's sword, settle one's differences, hoist (show, wave) the white flag.

UNARMED, *adj.* Without arms *or* armor, unshielded, defenseless, naked, vulnerable, undefended, unprotected, unguarded, weaponless, exposed, open, unprepared.

UNASSUMING, *adj.* Modest, unpretending, simple, without pretensions, homely, informal, ordinary, prosy, common, commonplace, insignificant, lesser, mediocre, humble, obscure, bourgeois, undistinguished, minor, subordinate, matter-of-fact, workaday, household, plebeian, prosaic, unambitious, unaspiring, meek, without arrogance, lowly, diffident, retiring, reserved, unobtrusive, unostentatious, undissimulating, undissembling, plain, content, lamblike, mild, submissive, unassertive, docile, gentle.

UNATTACHED, *adj.* 1. Not attached, loose, unbound, unconnected, disconnected, unlocked, unlatched, unfastened, untethered, untied, unbuttoned, unshackled, unpinned, unhasped, unclasped, unhooked, adrift, free.

2. Not connected *or* associated with any particular body (group, organization, *etc.*), free, freethinking, independent, ungoverned, autonomous, unsubject, self-determined, self-governing, self-directing, self-reliant.

3. Not married *or* engaged, single, bachelor, mateless, spinster, old-maid, wifeless, spouseless, celibate, virgin, virginal, husbandless, maidenly, unwedded, unmarried.

UNATTENDED, *adj.* 1. Unaccompanied, alone, solitary, unescorted, deserted, companionless, apart, lonely, separate.

2. *(Often fol. by* TO*)* Not attended to, uncared for, abandoned, left undone, neglected, unheeded, unregarded, disregarded, shelved, postponed, put off, deferred, overlooked, ignored, passed over, on the shelf, slighted, cast aside, tabled, put aside, pigeonholed.

UNAVAILING, *adj.* Ineffectual, useless, fruitless, inoperative, invalid, bootless, futile, nugatory, inutile, ineffective, worthless, weak, lame, wide of the mark, to no end, sterile, inane, impotent, inadequate, vain, to no purpose, abortive, inept, of no avail, unprofitable, inefficacious, deficient, thrown away, unproductive, unsuccessful, profitless, unserviceable, idle, valueless, empty.

UNAVOIDABLE, *adj.* 1. Inevitable, certain, inescapable, compulsory, obligatory, uncontrollable, imperative, necessary, inevasible, irresistible, ineluctable, that must be suffered, irrevocable, fated, fixed, sure, inavertible, coercive, inexorable, requisite, ineludible, unpreventable, undeniable.

2. Incapable of being made null *or* void, compulsory, irrevocable, binding, fixed, settled, requisite, irrefutable, determined, indefeasible, unchangeable.

UNAWARE, *adj.* Unconscious, unknowing, unwarned, inattentive, heedless, unsuspecting, incognizant, ignorant, unadvised, unmindful, unapprised, unacquainted, unenlightened, uninitiated, unversed, unwary, unaccustomed, blinded, insensible, unanticipative, blindfold, in the dark, unprepared, napping, off one's guard.

UNAWARES, *adv.* 1. While not aware *or* conscious of a thing, unknowingly, inadvertently, ignorantly, unwittingly, unaware, unconsciously, mistakenly, unintentionally, accidentally, involuntarily, fortuitously.

2. While another is not aware, unexpectedly, suddenly, abruptly, without warning *or* notice, like a bolt from the blue, like a thunderbolt, like a thief in the night, by surprise.

UNBACKED, *adj.* Without backing *or* support, not endorsed, not guaranteed, not certified, unauthenticated, unratified, unfounded, unattested, assumed, hypothetical, suppositional.

UNBAKED, *adj.* 1. Not baked, raw, underdone, uncooked, green.

2. Crude, raw, immature, untrained, unfinished, unseasoned, untried, inexperienced, new, green, young, tender, youthful, uninured, callow, unripe, unpracticed, unfledged, uncivilized, undisciplined, tenderfoot, unhabituated, rookie *(sl.)*, inept, unskilled, artless, unconversant, amateurish, ignorant, uninitiated, undeveloped, half-baked *(coll.)*, half-cocked *(coll.)*, not dry behind the ears *(joc.)*.

UNBALANCE, *n.* Want of balance, unbalanced condition, imbalance, precariousness, shakiness, unsteadiness, instability.

UNBALANCE, *v.* 1. Throw out of balance, upset, shift the weight of, distort, topple, turn the scale, warp, capsize, overturn, overthrow.

2. Disorder *(as the mind)*, derange, dementate, dement, insanify, madden, drive insane, unhinge, craze, turn one's brain *or* head, possess, obsess, addle the wits, loco *(coll.)*.

UNBALANCED, *adj.* 1. Not balanced *or* poised, top-heavy, irregular, unequal, unballasted, unsymmetrical, lopsided, overbalanced, unstable, uneven, unsteady.

2. Lacking steadiness and soundness of judgment, injudicious, unwise, unreliable, prepossessed, unstable, biased, warped, interested, jaundiced, influenced, unjust, unfair, one-sided, undependable, imprudent, uncritical, untactful, indiscreet, undiscriminating, indiscriminate.

3. Mentally disordered *or* deranged, unsound, not sane, lunatic, maniacal, moonstruck, mad, maddened, crazy, crazed, demented, dementate, unsettled, unhinged, daft, touched, psychotic, psychopathic, non compos mentis *(Lat.)*, loco *(sl.)*,

off, bereft of reason, cracked *(coll.)*, not all there *(coll.)*, batty *(sl.)*, nutty *(sl.)*.

4. *(Of an account)* Not adjusted, not brought to an equality of debits and credits, unsettled, unequal, disparate, open, outstanding.

UNBAR, *v.* Open, unlock, unfasten, unclose, unbolt, unhasp, unhinge, unhitch, throw open, gape, undo, part, lay open.

UNBEARABLE, *adj.* Intolerable, unendurable, insufferable, that cannot be borne *or* endured, inadmissible, unacceptable, insupportable, enough to provoke a saint, enough to drive one mad.

UNBEATEN, *adj.* 1. Not defeated, victorious, flourishing, thriving, triumphant, unbowed, ascendant, fortunate, prosperous, successful.

2. Untrodden, new, fresh, unused, untouched, wild, virgin, virginal, untraveled, untrampled.

UNBECOMING, *adj.* 1. Unsuitable, unapt, inappropriate, unsuited, unfitted, inapposite, untimely, malapropos, awkward, inapplicable, irrelevant, inopportune, ill-adapted, ill-timed, unseasonable, improper, infelicitous, out of keeping, out of proportion, out of character, out of place, out of joint, out of tune, imprudent, indecorous, inconvenient, untoward, incorrect, illogical, inexpedient, inadvisable, not to the purpose, unbefitting, impertinent.

2. Improper, unseemly, indecent, indecorous, unworthy, gross, uncomely, indelicate, unhandsome, wrong, untasteful, mean, low, shameful, churlish, loutish, boorish, discreditable, beneath one, unmanly, unpraiseworthy, reprehensible, barbarous, barbaric, disreputable, undignified, ignoble, beggarly, barbarian, monstrous, base, crude, rude, coarse, extravagant, unladylike, ungentlemanly, ungenteel, vulgar, offensive, in bad taste.

UNBELIEF, *n.* Lack of belief *(esp. in divine revelation, etc.)*, incredulity, distrust, disbelief, dissent, unorthodoxy, atheism, agnosticism, irreligion, free thought, minimifidianism, nonconformity, skepticism, infidelity, freethinking, heresy, suspicion, faithlessness, heterodoxy, paganism, ungodliness, iconoclasm.

UNBELIEVER, *n.* One who does not believe, one who does not accept any *(or some particular)* religious belief, skeptic, heretic, deist, agnostic, nihilist, earthling, worldling, secularist, freethinker, heathen, apostate, infidel, disbeliever, idolater, iconoclast, latitudinarian, irreligionist, nullifidian, minimifidian, doubter, doubting Thomas.

UNBELIEVING, *adj.* 1. Not believing, skeptical, incredulous, inconvincible, suspicious, dubitative, dubious, requiring proof, from Missouri *(sl.)*, distrustful, mistrustful.

2. Not accepting any *(or some particular)* belief, faithless, infidelic, nullifidian, minimifidian, heretic, heterodox, materialistic, latitudinarian, freethinking, Pyrrhonic, unconverted, atheistic, pagan, heretical, earthly, worldly, deistic.

UNBEND, *v.* 1. Straighten from a bent form *or* position, make straight, rectify, align, adjust, right, correct, untangle, uncurl, unfold, square, regulate.

2. Release from the strain of effort *or* close application, relax, remit, slacken, ease up, let up, rest, pause, cease, take time out, be amused, be diverted, take recreation, recreate, stay one's hand, take breath, lie *or* rest upon one's oars.

3. Relax by laying aside formality *or* cere-

mony, act in an easy genial manner, put *or* be at ease, simplify, become natural, lay off restraint.

UNBENDING, *adj.* Not bending, inflexible, unyielding, rigid, firm, straight, unpliant, stiff, obstinate, stubborn, stark, set, fixed, inelastic, unlimber, tense, impliable, immobile, hard, petrified, ossified, congealed, inductile, brittle, crisp, wooden.

UNBENT, *adj.* 1. Not bent, unbowed, straight, without a bend (crook, curve), even, true, direct, rectilinear, right, near, linear, undistorted, unturned, in a line, undeviating, unswerving, inflexible, plumb, vertical, straightaway, virgate.

2. Not forced to yield *or* submit, unbowed, victorious, unbeaten, undefeated, flourishing, thriving, ascendant, fortunate, prosperous, successful, overcoming, firm, standing, surviving.

UNBIASED, *adj.* Not biased, unprejudiced, impartial, unwarped, unswayed, uninfluenced, disinterested, independent, unbigoted, unprepossessed, unjaundiced, just, fair-minded, open, openminded, indifferent, neutral, liberal, dispassionate, reasonable, undogmatic, broad-minded, tolerant.

UNBIDDEN, *adj.* 1. Unordered, uncommanded, free, optional, unforced, willing, spontaneous, volitional, instinctive, voluntary, by choice, volitionary, volitient, elective, optionary, discretional, discretionary.

2. Uninvited, unasked, unsolicited, gratuitous, unbesought, unwelcome, unwished, unwanted, unrequested, unsought.

UNBIND, *v.* 1. Unchain, release from bonds *or* restraint, set free, set at liberty, free, let go, clear, liberate, absolve, exculpate, unshackle, unfetter, reprieve, exempt, forgive, acquit, demobilize, disband, deliver, dismiss, discharge, manumit, emancipate, extricate, set at large, affranchise, loose, disenthrall, vindicate.

2. Loose, unfasten, unloose, untie, undo, disjoin, loosen, unlace, release, unchain, unbandage, unharness, unshackle, unleash, unlash, unbridle, unpinion, separate, part, detach, disjoint, extricate, disengage, cut off *or* adrift.

UNBLESSED, *adj.* 1. Excluded from a blessing, unhallowed, unholy, damned, accursed, graceless, cursed, unsanctified, hardened, reprobate, unregenerate.

2. Unhappy, wretched, miserable, unlucky, hapless, unprosperous, unfortunate, infelicitous, luckless, ill-fated, fortuneless, unblest, out of luck, woebegone, bereft, hopeless, evil-starred, under a cloud, clouded, born with a wooden ladle in one's mouth, scotched, victimized, stultified, woeful, forlorn, hoodooed *(coll.)*, born under an evil star.

UNBLUSHING, *adj.* Shameless, impudent, bold, brazen, immodest, indecent, unabashed, boldfaced, forward, barefaced, bluff, audacious, daring, unreserved, cheeky, insolent, indecorous, malapert, pert, unseemly, brash.

UNBORN, *adj.* Not yet born, future, still to appear, unmade, unconceived, unbegotten, uncreated, unproduced.

UNBOSOM, *v.* Disclose *(one's thoughts, feelings, etc.)* in confidence, open, reveal, unburden, confide, admit, acknowledge, disburden, lay bare, uncover, confess, divulge, communicate, unfold, make a clean breast, lay one's cards on the table, come clean *(sl.)*, show one's hand *or* cards, get it out of one's system *(sl.)*, get it off one's chest *(sl.)*, uncloak, unscreen, unveil.

UNBOUND, *adj.* Not bound, untied, loose, flyaway, flowing, streaming, unfastened, unprotected, without a cover *(as a book)*, uncovered, disunited, in separate parts.

UNBOUNDED, *adj.* 1. Infinite, boundless, unlimited, immeasurable, undefined, unstinting, unsparing, full, plenary, unconditioned, unconditional, all-inclusive, termless, universal, worldwide, illimitable, immense, measureless, endless, vast, interminable, absolute, undetermined, arbitrary, all-embracing, perpetual, inexhaustible, exhaustless, indeterminate.

2. Unrestricted, uncontrolled, unrestrained, unchecked, unhampered, unconstrained, unhindered, excessive, rampant, unbridled, unobstructed, intemperate, unconfined, libertine, uncurbed, unreined, untrammeled.

UNBRIDLED, *adj.* Unrestrained, licensed, uncontrolled, incontinent, free, loose, intemperate, lax, licentious, reinless, violent, ungoverned, intractable, uncurbed, unchecked, unruly, libertine, wanton, immoderate, dissolute, unmitigated, abandoned, lawless, rampant, prodigal, unchaste, free-living.

UNBROKEN, *adj.* 1. Whole, intact, undivided, complete, full, round, entire, uncut, total, unimpaired, even, level, flat, solid, perfect, undiminished, unreduced, undefective, indeficient, sound, undefaced.

2. Uninterrupted, continuous, successive, constant, continual, perennial, consecutive, unintermitting, eternal, linear, progressive, unremitting, ceaseless, sequential, endless, incessant.

3. Not tamed, wild, savage, unsubdued, brutish, bestial, ferine, barbarous, ungentle, feral, tameless, vicious, unruly, fierce, ferocious, uncivilized.

4. Undisturbed, unimpaired, sound, fast, profound, inviolate, unbetrayed, preserved, honored, respected, placid, calm, untouched, unspoiled, perfect, peaceful, unruffled, untampered-with.

UNBURDEN, *v.* 1. Free from a burden, relieve, unload, uplift, upraise, buoy up, unencumber, disburden, free from impediment, unpack, lighten, empty, rid of a load, ease the load.

2. Relieve *(one's mind, conscience, etc.)* by disclosure *or* confession, disclose, unbosom, free, cast off, get rid of, reveal, confide, open, admit, acknowledge, disburden, lay bare, uncover, confess, divulge, unfold, make a clean breast, lay one's cards on the table, come clean *(sl.)*, get it out of one's system *(sl.)*, get it off one's chest *(sl.)*, uncloak, unscreen, unveil.

UNCALLED-FOR, *adj.* Unnecessary and improper, unwarranted, superfluous, unrequired, overgreat, overdone, overwrought, inordinate, excessive, out of bounds, inexcusable, unbounded, distasteful, undue, prodigal, profuse, lavish, overweening, supernumerary, expletive, immoderate, extravagant.

UNCANNY, *adj.* 1. Preternaturally good, unerring, unfailing, infallible, inspired, intuitional, unnatural, remarkable, uncommon, rare, unheard-of, unaccountable, unexampled, incredible, singular, supernatural, exceptional, unbelievable, prodigious, marvelous, preternatural, inconceivable, striking, astonishing, wonderful, noteworthy, supernormal.

2. Such as to arouse superstitious uneasiness, unnaturally strange, spectral, weird, unnatural, ghostly, eerie, unearthly, spooky *(coll.)*, phantomlike, ethereal, spiritual, phantom, incorporeal,

shadowy, pale, unreal, specterlike, unsubstantial, gossamery, airy, vaporous, wraithlike, disembodied, bodiless, discarnate, unbodied, illusory, chimerical, immaterial, visionary, asomatous, animistic, intangible, imaginary.

UNCEREMONIOUS, *adj.* Not ceremonious, abrupt, blunt, bluff, ungracious, uncourtly, unmannerly, brusque, coarse, rude, homely, rough, informal, casual, hasty, cursory, hurried, slight, undignified, quick, summary, uncivil, brief, inelegant, unrefined, vulgar, rustic, ungenteel, indelicate, unpolished, superficial, offhand, curt, gruff.

UNCERTAIN, *adj.* 1. Not definitely *or* surely known, doubtful, open to question, speculative, conjectural, problematic, undiscovered, academic, ideal, dubious, questionable, abstract, theoretical, enigmatic, hypothetical, puzzling, notional, presumptive, putative, postulational, assumptive, empirical, trial-and-error, projected, unreal, experimental, tentative, probative, debatable, contestable, provisional, controvertible, unproven, indefinite, undemonstrated, unconfirmed.

2. Not confident (assured, decided), irresolute, wavering, hesitant, infirm of purpose, dubious, inconstant, undecided, vacillating, quibbling, fickle, unsure, timid, doubtful, fluctuating, unresolved, dallying, unsettled, faltering, debating, pausing, shilly-shallying, sitting on *or* straddling the fence, hanging back, hovering, wobbling, considering, seesawing, variable, alternating, halting, oscillating, oscillatory, equivocating, constrained, reserved, demurring.

3. Not fixed *or* determined, unsettled, undecided, irregular, unsystematic, fluctuating, inconstant, in flux, in question, casual, debatable, disputable, unsteady, indeterminate, erratic, hanging in the balance, sporadic, capricious, oscillating, fitful, spasmodic, eccentric, desultory, changeable, variable, mutable, plastic, protean, alterable, ever-changing, permutable, vagrant, vacillating, vicissitudinous, unstable, unfixed, broken, rambling, transient, wanton, unmethodical, deviative, changeful.

4. Doubtful, vague, indistinct, obscure, hazy, equivocal, shadowy, indeterminate, fugitive, mistakable, indefinite, ambiguous, unclear, enigmatic, nebulous, impenetrable, abtruse, confusing, confused, recondite, cryptic, unfathomable, difficult, perplexing, puzzling, imperspicuous.

5. Not to be depended on, variable, subject to change, unreliable, undependable, unpredictable, unstable, changeable, slippery, fickle, inconstant, changeful, unsteadfast, vacillating, mutable, untrustworthy, erratic, fitful, skittish, undisciplined, arbitrary, uncontrolled, contrary, wanton, wavering, vagrant, mercurial, wayward, vicissitudinous, tergiversating, timeserving.

6. Dependent on chance, risky, unsafe, shaky, fallible, insecure, precarious, ticklish, hazardous, dangerous, vicissitudinous, perilous, chancy *(coll.)*, unsound, unsure, infirm, tottery, slippery, critical, built on sand.

7. Unsteady *(as light)*, fitful, irregular, wavering, flickering, variable, unequal, erratic, fluctuating, inconstant, sporadic, spasmodic, intermittent, poor, feeble, dim, inadequate, coming and going.

UNCERTAINTY, *n.* 1. Uncertain state, doubt, dubiousness, unsureness, hesitation, indefiniteness, vagueness, insecurity, precariousness, doubtfulness, perplexity, dubiety, indetermination, irresolution, hesitancy, quandary, suspense, indecision,

obscurity, ambiguity, irregularity, vacillation, capriciousness, fluctuation, unsettlement, demur, scruple, shilly-shally, equivocation, boggle, diffidence, confusion.

2. Something uncertain, irregularity, gamble, chance, contingency, jeopardy, liability, risk, odds, accident, speculation.

UNCHAIN, *v.* Free from chains, set free, liberate, unbind, unshackle, set at liberty, discharge, emancipate, release, extricate, manumit, let loose, unfetter, loose, disenthrall, untie, deliver.

UNCHARITABLE, *adj.* Unforgiving, harsh, censorious, severe, illiberal, unkind, unfriendly, unchristian, selfish, ungenerous, ruthless, pitiless, ungentle, exacting, cruel, unsparing, merciless, inexorable, unremitting, uncompromising, exigent, unreasonable, stringent, inhuman, strict, hard, rough, unpleasant, stern, stiff, austere, rigorous, despotic, inquisitorial, iron-handed, iron-fisted, obdurate, tyrannical, mean, extortionate, biting, relentless, abusive, overbearing, inflexible, uncompassionate, unrelenting, unfeeling, cold, cool, implacable, unconcerned, insensitive, inclement, remorseless, unbending, hard-boiled *(coll.)*, cold-blooded, Draconian.

UNCHASTE, *adj.* 1. Not chaste *or* virtuous, loose, lewd, dissolute, libidinous, salacious, wicked, lubricious, lecherous, incontinent, immoral, indecent, obscene, impure, immodest, light, abandoned, unbridled, bestial, wanton, licentious, lascivious, ruttish, ribald, lustful, shameless, lickerish, satyric, smutty, unclean, dirty, filthy, pornographic, adulterous, lurid, goatish, indelicate, swinish, Cyprian, sensual, Fescennine.

2. Not marked by purity of taste, gross, coarse, common, vulgar, low, crude, unrefined, indifferent, depraved, distasteful, ostentatious, offensive, inferior, prosaic, undiscriminating, mediocre, pedestrian, indelicate, stock, banal, affected, ordinary, plebeian, ignoble, unrestrained.

UNCHRISTIAN, *adj.* 1. Not Christian, unworthy of Christians, irreligious, heterodox, infidelic, unrighteous, evil, wicked, uncharitable, sinful, atheistic, heathen, uncanonical, unconverted, unsound, unscriptural, unorthodox, misbelieving, pagan, heretical, ungodly, unholy.

2. Unseemly, improper, uncivil, churlish, harsh, uncharitable, unforgiving, illiberal, severe, unkind, ungenerous, selfish, unfriendly, hard, merciless, cruel, exacting, ungentle, ruthless, pitiless, unsparing, exigent, unreasonable, inhuman, despotic, tyrannical, extortionate, mean, relentless, overbearing, uncompassionate, unrelenting, unfeeling, cold, implacable, insensitive, unconcerned, inclement, hard-boiled *(coll.)*, cold-blooded, Draconian, obdurate.

UNCHURCH, *v.* Expel from a church, excommunicate, proscribe, exile, banish, oust, relegate, ostracize, unfrock, drum out, strike off the rolls, break, outlaw with bell, book and candle.

UNCIVIL, *adj.* Without good manners, rude, impolite, discourteous, unmannerly, ungentle, ungracious, unmannered, rough, disrespectful, gruff, ill-bred, ill-mannered, uncouth, boorish, churlish, clownish, brusque, ungentlemanly, unladylike, unpolished, uncultivated, misbehaved, coarse, surly, indecorous, harsh, unseemly, bearish, insulting, abrupt, sharp, obnoxious, sullen, crabbed, insolent, bluff, brutish, waspish, snappish, crusty, unamiable, gross, ugly, ill-tempered, morose, base, fractious, testy, low-bred, crude, of shabby behavior, loutish, cloddish, brash, curt, mordant, currish, short, irritable, contemptible.

UNCIVILIZED, *adj.* Unenlightened, barbarous, savage, rude, uncouth, untamed, heathenish, barbaric, barbarian, low, ungenteel, benighted, brutish, uncultivated, uncultured, crude, crass, raw, unpolished, rough, outlandish, untutored, ill-bred, unlettered, vulgar, uncivil, churlish, boorish.

UNCLEAN, *adj.* 1. Not clean, dirty, soiled, foul, filthy, grimy, muddy, miry, uncleanly, slovenly, grubby, stained, smeared, smirched, polluted, smudged, spotted, defiled, contaminated, tainted, blurred, purulent, nasty, unwashed, muddied, begrimed, besmeared, sullied, dirt-encrusted, squalid, befouled, sluttish.

2. Morally impure, evil, vile, obscene, indecent, polluted, foul, lewd, indecorous, off-color, smutty, risqué, ribald, suggestive, pornographic, coarse, bawdy, nasty, carnal, evil-minded, perverted, concupiscent, prurient, lascivious, lecherous, libidinous, licentious, salacious, lustful, lickerish, loose, unchaste, wanton.

UNCLOAK, *v.* 1. Remove the cloak from, divest, uncover, undress, disrobe, undrape, peel, unclothe.

2. Expose, reveal, manifest, evince, disclose, exhibit, evidence, demonstrate, present, bare, show, put in plain sight, make known, uncover, unscreen, unveil, produce, hold up to view, make visible, bring to light, proclaim, lay open, divulge, bring out in bold (high, strong) relief, unfold, unmask.

UNCLOTHE, *v.* Make naked, unrobe, strip, undress, lay bare, expose, unveil, uncloak, denude, denudate, reveal, bare, undrape, divest of clothing, disrobe, peel off.

UNCOMFORTABLE, *adj.* 1. Uneasy, on edge, rattled, disturbed, nervous, discomposed, ill-at-ease, discomfited, troubled, disquieted, edgy, perturbed, put out.

2. Unpleasant, hard, rough, irritating, wearisome, bothersome, wearying, irksome.

3. Gloomy, comfortless, dingy, lightless, grim, cold, somber, cheerless, sunless, bleak, uninviting, depressing, joyless, dreary, austere, murky, dismal, barren.

UNCOMMITTED, *adj.* Not bound by pledge *or* assurance *(as to a course),* reserved, reticent, evasive, close-mouthed, close, taciturn, secretive, independent, holding back, free, unanswerable, unsubject, unliable, undecided, neutral, choiceless, unaccountable, on the fence *(coll.),* indifferent, irresolute, in the middle of the road, neither one thing nor the other, impartial.

UNCOMMON, *adj.* 1. Rare, scarce, unusual, odd, strange, queer, unfamiliar, infrequent, extraordinary, noteworthy, out-of-the-way, exceptional, seldom met with, singular, unique, few and far between, occasional, unprecedented, unexampled, remarkable, unwonted, unheard-of, abnormal, eccentric, peculiar, novel, unparalleled, unequaled, incomparable, curious, freakish, unconventional, bizarre, surprising, fanciful, anomalous, unnatural, unaccountable, inusitate, whimsical, aberrant.

2. Unusual in amount *or* degree, above the ordinary, exceptional, superior, upper, uppermost, over, high, great, top, peerless, maximum, inimitable, matchless, superlative, transcendent, second to none, incomparable, unparagoned, unparalleled, unexcelled, unsurpassed, unapproached, unequaled, supreme, preëminent, paramount.

UNCOMMONLY, *adv.* 1. In an uncommon *or* unusual degree, remarkably, singularly, unusually, peculiarly, curiously, oddly, strangely, extraordinarily, signally, strikingly, incredibly, prominently, famously, egregiously, queerly, pointedly, glaringly, emphatically, marvelously, notably, particularly.

2. Rarely, infrequently, seldom, scarcely, hardly, barely, scantly, ill, no more than, not easily, but just, merely, sparsely, little, not often, only arduously, faintly, slightly, imperceptibly, once in a blue moon, once in a coon's age *(coll.).*

UNCOMMUNICATIVE, *adj.* Not disposed to impart information, reserved, close, taciturn, reticent, unsociable, unconversable, close-mouthed, secretive, curt, sparing of words, silent as the grave, speechless, mute, word-bound, silent, tongue-tied, evasive, laconic, retiring, mum, not loquacious, dumb, brief, concise, sententious, cautious, pauciloquent, obmutescent, wary.

UNCOMPROMISING, *adj.* Not admitting of compromise, unyielding, inflexible, strict, narrow, hidebound, obstinate, rigid, stiff, fanatical, arbitrary, strait-laced, firm, immovable, implacable, steadfast, unrelenting, incorruptible, resolved, resolute, inexorable, puritanical, obdurate, relentless, determined, exacting, heavy, unremitting, exigent, unreasonable, Spartan, stringent, hard, austere, ruthless, pitiless, grim, pressing, Draconian, unbending, unsparing.

UNCONCERN, *n.* Freedom from solicitude *or* anxiety, indifference, hardness, coldness, apathy, unfeeling, incuriosity, insensitiveness, nonchalance, coolness, carelessness, insensibility, deaf ears, impassiveness, callosity, obtundity, stoicism, unimpressibility, callousness, uncontriteness, ruthlessness, hard-heartedness, hardness of heart, want of compassion, mercilessness, inhumanity, unkindness, heart of stone, uncharity, uncharitableness.

UNCONCERNED, *adj.* Not concerned, free from solicitude *or* anxiety, indifferent, cold, unsolicitous, unmoved, apathetic, listless, nonchalant, easy, casual, cool, uninterested, reckless, heartless, unemotional, unsympathetic, unresponsive, phlegmatic, distant, stoical, cruel, unfeeling, aloof, hard, hard-hearted, unsusceptible, unimpressible, frigid, passionless, torpid, sluggish, lukewarm, neutral, impartial, untroubled, serene, supercilious, composed, unperturbed, unkindled, contemptuous, chill, icy, unapproachable, inaccessible, stiff, unmindful, harsh, listless, flinty, steely, adamantine, numb, supine, obdurate, thick-skinned, stony, soulless, insensitive, hardened, obtuse, incurious, unstirred, untouched, impervious, uncaring, insouciant, stolid.

UNCONDITIONAL, *adj.* Not limited by conditions, unrestricted, unconditioned, complete, absolute, unqualified, positive, full, entire, unlimited, free, unreserved, categorical, utter, allowing no doubt, definite, explicit, peremptory, decisive, certain, past dispute, conclusive, plain, inescapable, unconfuted, inappealable, unanswerable, undisputed, unquestioned, irrefutable, irrefragable, incontestable, undeniable, infallible, incontrovertible, indisputable, unambiguous, authoritative.

UNCONFORMITY, *n.* Lack of conformity, incongruity, inconsistency, disagreement, irregularity, dissent, irrelation, unrelatedness, irrelevance, divergence, dissimilarity, misalliance, opposition, conflict, disharmony, deviation, aberrance, variety, discordance, discord, impertinence, disaccord, anomaly, noncompliance, aberration, dissonance, incommensurability, inconsequence, inapplicability, independence, inaccordance, dissidence, nonobservance, sectarianism, unorthodoxy, unconventionality, Bohemianism, recusancy.

UNCONNECTED, *adj.* Separate, disjoined, detached, unattached, isolated, disconnected, cut, sundered, parted, disunited, disjunct, distinct, unassociated, disparate.

UNCONSCIONABLE, *adj.* 1. Not reasonable, unreasonable, without thought, thoughtless, groundless, unfair, unfounded, false, rash, preposterous, hurried, extravagant, impulsive, exaggerated, ungrounded, hasty.

2. Unscrupulous, blackguard, knavish, unprincipled, tricky, designing, dishonest, rascally, Machiavellian, corrupt, scheming, intriguing, conniving.

UNCONSCIOUS, *adj.* 1. Asleep, without consciousness, out *(coll.),* comatose, sleeping, in a coma, numb, senseless, insensible, deadened.

2. *(Often with* OF) Unaware, unsuspecting, ignorant, heedless, unknowing, incognizant, unapprised, unacquainted, unaccustomed, blinded, insensible, blindfold, off one's guard, unadvised, unmindful, unenlightened, uninitiated, unversed, unwary, unanticipating, in the dark, unprepared, napping.

UNCONTROLLABLE, *adj.* Unmalleable, opinionated, bullheaded, refractory, mulish, willful, pigheaded, unmanageable, self-willed, ungovernable, pervicacious, obdurate, obstinate, headstrong, intractable, stubborn, dogged.

UNCONVENTIONAL, *adj.* Strange, outlandish, unusual, off the beaten path, uncommon, bizarre, freakish, extraordinary, irregular, *outré (Fr.),* exceptional, abnormal, unaccustomed, original, curious, odd, queer, erratic, eccentric, idiosyncratic, wacky *(sl.),* bohemian, nonconformist, left-bank, aberrant, informal, peculiar, unique, lawless, quaint, in a class by itself, *sui generis (Lat.),* unorthodox, newfangled, fantastic.

UNCOUTH, *adj.* 1. Unfamiliar, uncanny, strange, mysterious, outlandish, unnatural, shadowy, phantomlike, unearthly, unreal, eerie, weird, bizarre, spooky *(coll.).*

2. Crude, rough-and-ready, boorish, rude, unrefined, brusque, ill-mannered, uncivil, bluff, impolite, unmannerly, brutish, rough, callow, doltish, indelicate, unlettered, crass, uneducated, illiterate, uncultivated, uncivilized, coarse, unripe, churlish, ignorant, loutish, graceless, barbaric, gross, roughcast.

UNCOVER, *v.* 1. Lay bare, disclose, reveal, remove the cover *or* covering from, unclose, unsheathe, uncase, undo, unwrap, uncork, unstop, uncurtain, undrape, expose, open, unfold, bare, set forth, produce, unveil, unearth, disinter, unseal, denude, strip, divest, peel, pare, skin, disrobe, undress, unclothe, dig up *or* out, bring to light, unmask, uncloak, make visible.

2. Remove the hat *or* other head covering, uncap, unbonnet, tip the cap, doff the cap, salute, raise *or* lift the hat.

UNCRITICAL, *adj.* 1. Lacking in acuteness of judgment *or* critical analysis, undiscriminating, imprudent, unjust, dull, pedestrian, mediocre, undiscerning, indiscriminate, injudicious, imperceptive, uninformed, ignorant, stupid, indiscreet, indiscretionary.

2. Not in accordance with the rules of just criticism, indiscriminate, imprudent, unjust, tactless, untactful, irrational, unwise, loose, inconsistent, ill-advised, ill-judged.

UNCROWN, *v.* Deprive *or* divest of a crown, reduce from dignity *or* preëminence, dethrone, depose, unseat, oust, humiliate, disenthrone, undermine the authority of, remove from office, disestablish, displace, unfrock, strike off the rolls, abase, lower, degrade, humble, weaken, break, disbar, disbench, dismiss, disgrace.

UNCTION, *n.* 1. Anointing *(esp. for medical purposes or as a religious rite),* lubrication, oiling, rubbing, smearing, chrism *(Eccles.).*

2. Something soothing *or* comforting, lubricant, lenitive, unguent, ointment, balm, salve, lotion, liniment, embrocation, abirritant, assuasive, demulcent, emollient *(Med.).*

3. Professional earnestness in utterance, soothing (sympathetic, persuasive) quality in discourse, fervor, ardor, warmth, enthusiasm, power, force, passion, fervency, zest, emotion, inducement, persuasion, feeling, verve, spirit, gusto, zeal, fire, gush *(coll.),* exhortation, heartiness, eagerness, glow, fullness of heart, cordiality, vehemence, rapture, ravishment, transport, ecstasy, animation.

UNCTUOUS, *adj.* 1. Of the nature of *or* characteristic of an unguent *or* ointment, unguent, oily, greasy, lenitive, lubricous, lubricatory, lubricant, lubricative, unguentary, unguentous.

2. Characterized by religious unction *or* fervor, excessively smooth, bland, suave, glib, smoothspoken, oily, complaisant, fervid, gushing *(coll.),* sycophantic, plausible, obsequious, honeyed, ingratiating, blandiloquent, fair-spoken, complimentary, adulatory, oily-tongued, buttery *(coll.),* smooth-tongued, fine-spoken, oleaginous, insincere, false, pharisaical, sanctimonious, hypocritical, fawning, servile, pietistic, canting, dissembling, self-righteous, conciliatory, flattering, disarming, mealy-mouthed.

3. Having an oily *or* soapy feel *(as certain minerals),* slippery, smooth, saponaceous, oleaginous, sleek, greasy, slick, waxy, lubricous.

UNDAMAGED, *adj.* Uninjured, unhurt, intact, safe, unharmed, unimpaired, unspoiled, undefaced, undeformed, perfect, scatheless, unscathed, sound, entire, whole, faultless, preserved, safe and sound, in perfect condition, unscratched.

UNDAUNTED, *adj.* Intrepid, daring, mettlesome, Spartan, fearless, gritty, valiant, invincible, dreadless, unappalled, stalwart, unflinching, unblenched, unalarmed, unshrinking, valorous, dauntless, hardy, manful, high-spirited, lion-hearted, doughty, plucky, gallant, heroic, unapprehensive, firm, indomitable, aweless, audacious, stouthearted, game, resolute, courageous, brave, bold, spunky *(coll.).*

UNDECEIVE, *v.* Free from deception (fallacy, mistake), set right, put straight, unblindfold, clear the mind of, disenchant, burst the bubble, disillusion, disabuse, correct, open the eyes of, tell the truth, show, inform, paint in its true colors, puncture one's balloon *(coll.).*

UNDECIDED, *adj.* 1. Not decided *or* determined, debatable, unsettled, pending, undetermined, tentative, open, in suspense, uncertain, doubtful, questionable, problematical, vague, indefinite, unfixed, moot, speculative, disputable, experimental.

undemonstrated, untried, unascertained, unconfirmed, contestable, dubious.

2. Not having one's mind made up, irresolute, open, doubtful, undetermined, unresolved, variable, dubious, unconvinced, of two minds, doubleminded, hesitant, indecisive, infirm of purpose, capricious, choiceless, tergiversating, changeful, in a dilemma, on the horns of a dilemma, up in the air, neither hot nor cold, open-minded, wavering, vacillating, oscillatory, shilly-shally, going around in circles, unsure, inconstant, unstable, fickle, Laodicean.

UNDECIPHERABLE, *adj.* Illegible, indistinct, indistinguishable, unrecognizable, inapprehensible, incomprehensible, not understandable, puzzling, unintelligible, unfathomable, incognizable, mysterious, enigmatic, inscrutable, impenetrable, inexplicable.

UNDEFEATED, *adj.* Unbeaten, triumphant, unbowed, prosperous, victorious, flourishing, successful, fortunate, ascendant, thriving, invincible, unconquerable.

UNDEFENDED, *adj.* Unprotected, unguarded, exposed, defenseless, uncovered, unsheltered, unshielded, unarmed, expugnable, vulnerable, guardless, open, helpless, pregnable, unarmored, unfortified, naked, weaponless.

UNDEFILED, *adj.* 1. Pure, spotless, clean, unspotted, unstained, stainless, unsullied, unblemished, untarnished, immaculate, perfect, clear, undefaced, flawless, white, unsoiled, untainted, faultless, snowy, bright, speckless, shining, washed, uncorrupted, unmarred, unpolluted, fair, uncontaminated, sterling, uninfected, expurgate, fresh.

2. Untainted with evil, innocent, chaste, guiltless, guileless, sinless, blameless, snowy, unsullied, virtuous, true, virgin, modest, holy, incorrupt, candid, unspoiled, spotless, virginal, immaculate, vestal, untarnished, unstained, unblemished, unsoiled, clean-minded, wholesome, above suspicion, uncorrupted, angelic, divine, inviolable, moral, white, continent, upright, righteous, inculpable, with clean hands, inviolate, impeccable, unimpeachable, faultless, stainless, heavenly, godlike, incontaminate, honorable.

UNDEFINED, *adj.* 1. Not definitely limited, indefinite, unbounded, boundless, limitless, infinite, unlimited, full, immeasurable, unconditioned, unconditional, all-inclusive, termless, illimitable, measureless, endless, vast, interminable, undetermined, all-embracing, perpetual, inexhaustible, exhaustless, indeterminate.

2. Not described by definition *or* explanation, not explained, obscure, vague, confused, blurred, loose, general, unclear, indistinct, hazy, mysterious, uncertain, shadowy, indeterminate, veiled, cryptic, indecisive, enigmatic, nebulous, abstruse, confusing, ambiguous, imperspicuous, puzzling, perplexing.

UNDEMONSTRATIVE, *adj.* Sedate, reserved, cold, unsusceptible, impassive, phlegmatic, self-controlled, calm, composed, sober, staid, quiet, modest, demure, placid, unemotional, unresponsive, unsympathetic, apathetic, stoical, distant, aloof, lukewarm, neutral, serene, frigid, poised, supercilious, unperturbed, unfriendly, chill, cool, listless, formal, unimpressible, insensible, halfhearted, steely, uncommunicative, inarticulate, unexcitable, supine, unmoved, unstirred, languid, callous, inert, unsolicitous, obdurate, thick-

skinned, stony, unfeeling, unanimated, indifferent, unconcerned, spiritless, stolid, uninterested.

UNDENIABLE, *adj.* 1. Not to be refuted, indisputable, indubitable, incontrovertible, incontestable, irrefutable, obvious, conclusive, ultimate, final, decisive, convincing, unanswerable, inappealable, clear, certain, firm, solid, secure, infallible, unimpeachable, beyond dispute, evident, irrefragable, convincing, determinative, without *or* beyond a doubt *or* question, established, demonstrable, proven, sound.

2. That cannot be refused, inevitable, unavoidable, binding, persuasive, convincing, necessary, strong, compulsory, required, requisite, irresistible, inescapable, compelling, coactive, obligatory, imperative, forcible, coercive, peremptory, importunate, strong-arm *(coll.)*.

3. Unquestionably good, unexceptionable, excellent, supreme, paramount, superior, superb, first-rate, beyond reproach *or* criticism, topnotch *(coll.),* extraordinary, inestimable, perfect, exceptional, invaluable, capital, first-class, picked, prime, elect, best, choice, of the first water, select, priceless, exquisite, superfine, superexcellent, superlative, peerless, unparalleled, matchless, crack *(coll.),* A-1 *(coll.),* A number 1 *(coll.)*.

UNDEPENDABLE, *adj.* Not to be depended upon, unreliable, untrustworthy, fickle, irresponsible, light, frivolous, variable, mercurial, without ballast, unauthentic, unauthenticated, unsound, perfidious, treacherous, insubstantial, shifty, two-faced, double-dealing, capricious, trimming, slippery, timeserving, deceitful, inconstant, changeable, unstable, wavering, tergiversating.

UNDER, *adj.* 1. Beneath, lower in position, inferior, nether, underlying, subjacent, submerged.

2. Lower in rank *or* degree, lower in amount, inferior, subject, subordinate, subaltern, less important, insignificant, inconsequential, lesser, smaller, in the shade, dependent, deficient, submissive, common, ineffectual, mediocre, auxiliary, ancillary, junior, secondary, subsidiary, underling.

UNDER, *adv.* 1. Beneath something, beneath the surface, in a lower place, underneath, below, submerged, short of, down, at the foot *or* base of.

2. In a subordinate position *or* condition, in *or* into subjection *or* submission, at the bottom of the scale, at the bottom of the heap *(sl.),* beneath, at a disadvantage, down, in submission, under the heel of, at the feet of, with no mind (will, soul) of one's own.

UNDER, *prep.* 1. Beneath and covered by, below the surface of, underneath, sunk in, engulfed by, buried in, submerged in, plunged in *or* into, drowned in, inundated by, immersed in, soaking in, lowered into.

2. At a position lower than *or* further down than, below, subordinate to, subjacent to, beneath, inferior to.

3. In the position *or* state of bearing (supporting, sustaining, undergoing, *etc.*), exposed to, open to, suffering, burdened with, subjected to, tasting, laboring, being the subject of, saddled with, carrying, entertaining, harboring, encountering, passing *or* going through, feeling, experiencing, liable to.

4. Beneath (a head, heading, *etc.*) as in classification, belonging to *or* with, within, with, placed in.

5. As designated (indicated, represented) by, bearing, known by, named, called, carrying, recognizable by, marked with.

6. Below in degree (amount, price, etc.), less than, short of, reduced from, below the mark, under par.

7. Below in rank (dignity, etc.), subject to the rule (direction, guidance, etc.) of, beneath, subordinate to, subject to, inferior to, at the feet of, under the heel of, second to, in bondage to, at one's beck and call, at one's mercy, in one's power, with no mind (will, soul) of one's own, in one's hands or clutches.

8. Subject to the influence (conditioning force, etc.) of, bound by, in light of, in view of, subject to, determined by, limited by, qualified by, restricted by, circumscribed by, taking into account, considering, owing to, on account of.

9. With the favor or aid of, sustained by, guided by, preserved by, strengthened by, supported by, upheld by, guarded by, backed by, fostered by, sponsored by.

10. Authorized by, warranted by, attested by, confirmed by, authenticated by, decreed by, ordered by, sanctioned by, enacted by, legalized by, certified by.

11. In accordance with, by right of, in agreement with, by authority of, supported by, in harmony with, justified by, upheld by, according to, with respect to, with regard to, at the command of, by virtue of, in the name of.

UNDERAGE, adj. Lacking the required age (esp. that of legal maturity), unfledged, juvenile, youthful, too young, immature, minor, junior.

UNDERBID, v. Make a lower bid than another, bargain, negotiate, haggle, higgle, cheapen, beat down, stickle, outbid, dicker, chaffer.

UNDERBRED, adj. 1. Of inferior breeding or manners, vulgar, uncivil, unmannerly, mongrel, impertinent, rude, impolite, discourteous, ungentle, ungracious, unmannered, rough, disrespectful, gruff, ill-bred, ill-mannered, uncouth, boorish, churlish, clownish, brusque, ungentlemanly, unladylike, unpolished, uncultivated, misbehaved, coarse, surly, indecorous, harsh, unseemly, bearish, insulting, abrupt, sharp, obnoxious, sullen, insolent, bluff, brutish, gross, ugly, base, lowbred, crude, of shabby behavior, loutish, cloddish, brash, currish, contemptible.

2. Not of pure breed (as a horse), half-breed, half-caste, half-bred, half-blooded, crossed, crossbred, mongrel, hybrid.

UNDERBRUSH, n. Shrubs or small trees growing under large trees, undergrowth, underwood, brush, brushwood, scrub, brake, thicket, boscage.

UNDERCLOTHES, n., pl. Underclothing, underwear, undies (coll.), woolens, undergarments, linen, lingerie, unmentionables (Victorian), panties, briefs, shorts, vests, jerseys, underdrawers, drawers, knickers.

UNDERCOVER, adj. Private, stealthy, obscured, screened, masked, veiled, underhand, shrouded, reserved, underhanded, taciturn, collusive, disguised, undisclosed, confidential, cunning, covert, dissembled, feigned, sly, evasive, cloaked, unrevealed, ensconced, unseen, secret, underground, skulking, surreptitious, furtive, secluded, clandestine, crafty, obreptitious, sneaking, huggermugger, hidden, privy, arcane, secretive, close, conspiring.

UNDERCURRENT, n. 1. Cross current, undertow, underset, riptide.

2. Hidden or secret influence, wind, tenor, drift,

atmosphere, trend, hidden feeling, hidden tendency, hidden opposition.

UNDERCUT, v. 1. Cut away under part of, cut out, excavate, undermine, gouge out, scoop out, mine, hollow out.

2. Undersell, sell cheaply, sell at a loss, undercharge.

UNDERDOG, n. Weaker party, loser, underling, victim, little fellow (coll.).

UNDERDONE, adj. Rare, raw, saignant (Fr.), uncooked, undercooked, plain, not cooked, unbaked.

UNDERESTIMATE, v. Rate too low, misjudge, undervalue, miscalculate, detract from, underrate, discredit, misprize, depreciate, belittle, minimize.

UNDERFED, adj. Suffering from lack of nourishment, attenuated, skinny, scurvy, undernourished, hungry, emaciated, starving, meager, ill-conditioned, ill-fed, starveling.

UNDERFOOT, adv. Under the feet, on the ground, beneath one's feet, below, down, against the ground.

UNDERGO, v. Pass through an experience, experience, go through, support, withstand, stomach, sustain, bear, submit to, weather, encounter, meet with, suffer, abide, brook, stand, brave, forbear.

UNDERGROUND, adj. 1. Subterranean, subterraneous, hypogeal, buried.

2. Secret, stealthy, obscured, shrouded, undisclosed, sly, evasive, undercover, underhand, clandestine, hidden, privy, arcane, conspiring, close, secretive, hugger-mugger, sneaking, obreptitious, crafty, secluded, skulking, surreptitious, furtive, cloaked, unseen, unrevealed, confidential, feigned, dissembled, covert, cunning, disguised, collusive, taciturn, veiled, masked, screened, obscured.

UNDERGROUND, n. 1. Subterranean channel, cave, etc., tunnel, underpass.

2. Subway, tube.

3. Underground movement, resistance, secret and organized rebellion.

UNDERGROWTH, n. 1. Shrubs or small trees growing under large trees, underwood, brush, brushwood, scrub, brake, thicket, boscage.

2. Soft hair underlying outer hair of animal's pelt, coat, etc., pelage.

UNDERHANDED, adj. 1. Stealthy, shrouded, undisclosed, secret, secretive, undercover, underground, hugger-mugger, sneaking, secluded, furtive, surreptitious, skulking, crafty, hidden, privy, conspiring, arcane, close, unseen, unrevealed, cloaked, evasive, feigned, dissembled, covert, cunning, confidential, disguised, collusive, taciturn, reserved, veiled, masked, screened, obscured, underhand.

2. Fraudulent, crooked, unfair, criminal, wicked, nefarious, tricky, dishonest, bogus, fake, sham, conniving, designing, unconscionable, unscrupulous, intriguing, scheming, corrupt, rascally, Machiavellian, unprincipled, knavish, blackguard, scampish, villainous, sneaking, dark, felonious, questionable, open to suspicion, not above board.

UNDERLAY, v. 1. Provide with something laid underneath, raise or support with something laid underneath, brace, shore up, bolster up, underpin, underbrace, prop, stay, buttress, underset, underprop.

2. Extend beneath, jut out from under, project, underhang, undershoot, underrun.

UNDERLIE, *v.* 1. Lie under *or* beneath, be situated under, be subjacent to, be inferior to, rest beneath.

2. Be at the basis of, form the foundation of, support, carry, bear, hold, ground, bed, sustain, uphold, found, base, bottom, shoulder, underset, bear up, underpin, underbrace, underprop, upbear, prop, brace.

UNDERLING, *n.* Inferior, subordinate, assistant, attendant, secondary, nonentity, servant, menial, thrall, vassal, subject, hireling, help, worker, serf, domestic, valet, servitor, hand, flunky *(contempt.),* understrapper, subaltern, employee.

UNDERMINE, *v.* 1. Form a mine *or* passage under, make an excavation under, mine, tunnel, scoop, dig, gouge, sink, sap *(Fort.),* excavate, burrow, drive.

2. Render unstable by digging into *or* wearing away the foundations, disable, impair, riddle, honeycomb, weaken, shake, mine.

3. Affect injuriously *or* weaken by secret *or* underhand means, weaken insidiously, demoralize, sap the foundations of, ruin secretly, disable, thwart, foil, frustrate, disenable, disarm, enfeeble, shake, unstring, exhaust, devitalize, debilitate, unsinew, cramp, enervate, blunt, incapacitate, cut the ground from under one, hock, hamstring, lame, maim, cripple, prostrate, paralyze, render powerless.

UNDERMOST, *adj.* Lowest, bottom, lowermost, nethermost, basic, basal, nadiral, root, radical, fundamental, rock-bottom, bedrock, bottommost.

UNDERNEATH, *adv.* Beneath, under, below, in a lower place, submerged, short of, down, at the foot *or* base of, subjacent to.

UNDERNOURISH, *v.* Feed inadequately to maintain normal health, underfeed, starve, impair the health of, deprive nutritionally.

UNDERPASS, *n.* Passage running underneath, tunnel, culvert, cave, covered way, passageway.

UNDERPRIVILEGED, *adj.* Denied the enjoyment of normal privileges *or* rights *(because of low economic or social position),* poor, indigent, necessitous, straitened, penniless, needy, impecunious, poverty-stricken, destitute, moneyless, pauperized, bereft, in need, stinted, excluded, hard up *(coll.),* on the rocks *(coll.),* restricted, discriminated against, down-and-out, distressed, beggarly, impoverished, on the edge *or* ragged edge *(coll.),* unable to make both ends meet, unable to keep the wolf from the door.

UNDERSCORE, *v.* 1. Draw a line under *(for emphasis),* underline, accentuate, stress, italicize.

2. Lay stress upon, accentuate, bring out forcibly, make distinct, mark, stress, press home, reiterate, iterate, dwell on, affirm, heighten, accent, feature, intensify, enforce, bring into relief, harp on.

UNDERSEA, *adj.* Underwater, marine, submersible, subaquatic, subaqueous, sunk, sunken, on the bottom, below the surface, submerged.

UNDERSELL, *v.* Sell cheaply, sell at a loss, undercut, undercharge.

UNDERSIDE, *n.* Lower side, underlying side, the underneath, undermost part, base, bottom.

UNDERSIZED, *adj.* Below normal *or* accepted size, immature, emaciated, nanoid, miniature, scrubby, Lilliputian, scanty, little, pint-sized, minikin, pygmy, minute, stunted, underdeveloped, atrophied, small, bantam, half-pint, dwarfed, dwarfish, puny, diminutive.

UNDERSTAND, *v.* 1. Conceive, appreciate, absorb, get *(coll.),* catch the idea, digest, know, comprehend, apprehend, discern, master, fathom, see into, get the hang of *(coll.),* savvy *(sl.),* penetrate, cognize, perceive, make out, recognize, seize.

2. Gather, infer, take to mean, take for granted, take, guess, conclude, interpret, presume, deduce, assume, conjecture, fancy, reason, dare say, estimate, think likely, reckon, opine, glean.

UNDERSTANDING, *n.* Ability to grasp *or* seize ideas, mental capacity, sense, intellect, intuition, conception, cognizance, conversancy, perspicacity, imagination, awareness of, mastery of thought, comprehension, apperception, enlightenment, penetration, command of thought, awareness, knowledge, recognition, perception, apprehension, discernment, realization, assimilation, cognition, ability to know, mental grasp, reason, insight, mind, capability.

UNDERSTATE, *v.* State *or* represent less strongly than the truth will admit, state too low, underdraw, underestimate, undervalue, minimize, reduce, detract from, make nothing of, make little *or* light of, be modest about, not do justice to.

UNDERSTUDY, *n.* Person trained to act as substitute for an actor *or* actress, pinch hitter, stand-in, alternate, fill-in, alternative, secondary, double, second.

UNDERTAKE, *v.* 1. Take on oneself *(a task, performance, etc.),* essay, take in hand, embark on *or* upon, endeavor, devote oneself to, set about, engage in, enter upon, tackle, try, commence, fall to, buckle to, plunge in, launch into *or* upon, put in *or* into execution, take up, assume, begin, aspire to *or* after, pursue, aim at, start, strive, set before oneself, bid for, determine upon, go in *or* out for *(coll.).*

2. Take on oneself by formal promise *or* agreement, lay oneself under obligation to perform *or* execute, agree, engage, be answerable for, give one's word for, contract, bargain, vow, vouch, avouch, indent, stipulate, covenant, pledge oneself.

3. *(Fol. by a clause)* Warrant, guarantee, wager, vouch, assure, pledge, promise, declare, swear, give one's word *or* word of honor, be answerable for, certify, bet, see to it.

UNDERTAKER, *n.* One who prepares and buries the dead, funeral director, mortician, embalmer.

UNDERTAKING, *n.* 1. Task undertaken, enterprise, matter in hand, venture, pursuit, quest, search, purpose, prospect, project, engagement, design, plan, transaction, experiment, game, resolution, ambition, concern, employment, occupation.

2. Promise, pledge, guarantee, compact, contract, oath, troth, covenant, vow, word, avowal, stipulation, warrant, insurance, parole, indemnity, assurance.

UNDERTONE, *n.* 1. Low *or* subdued tone, whisper, murmur, breath, sigh, underbreath, susurration, susurrus, rustle, hum, stage whisper, veiled voice, bombination, bombilation.

2. Underlying quality *or* element, undercurrent, essence, savor, taste, odor, hint, suggestion, flavor, redolence, intimation, indication, trace, manifestation, inkling, evidence, sign, mark, scent, tinge, coloring, connotation, implication, force, effect, innuendo, drift, tenor, signification.

UNDERTOW, *n.* Strong reverse current of water below the surface, underset, undercurrent, backflow, rip, riptide.

UNDERVALUE, *v.* Rate below the true value, esteem lightly, esteem too low, hold in low estimation, underrate, despise, underestimate, minimize, make light of, detract from, misjudge, misprize, discredit, depreciate, belittle.

UNDERWEAR, *n.* Lingerie, underclothing, underclothes, undergarments, linen, woolens, undies *(coll.)*, panties, shorts, briefs, jerseys, vests, unmentionables, bloomers, knickers.

UNDERWEIGHT, *adj.* Lacking usual *or* required weight, light, poor, skimpy, lean, undernourished, undersized, puny, thin, scrawny, underfed, emaciate, emaciated, half-starved, starved, stunted, scanty.

UNDERWORLD, *n.* 1. Lower (degraded *or* criminal) part of human society, dregs of society, chaff, riffraff, raff, scum (offscum, offscourings) of society, scum of the earth, rabble, ragtag and bobtail.

2. Lower *or* nether world, hell, Hades *(Gk. Myth.)*, place of departed spirits, abode of the damned, infernal regions, shades below, purgatory, perdition, Inferno, realms of Pluto, everlasting fire, bottomless pit, place of torment, abyss, limbo, hellfire, lake of fire and brimstone, place of the lost, habitation of fallen angels, Gehenna *(Jew. Hist.)*, Tartarus *(Gr. Myth.)*, Sheol *(Heb.)*, Pandemonium, Tophet *(Lit.)*, Avernus *(Gr. Myth.)*, Satan's kingdom, Naraka *(Hind. and Buddh.)*, Styx *(Gr. Myth.)*, Abaddon, Erebus *(Gr. Myth.)*, Malebolge, Avichi *(Buddh.)*, Acheron *(Class. Myth.)*.

UNDERWRITE, *v.* 1. Write something under a thing, sign, subscribe, affix a signature to, endorse, ratify, countersign, put one's name to, initial, mark, stamp, character, letter, inscribe, seal, undersign, set one's hand and seal to.

2. Subscribe to, agree to (give *or* pay, *etc.*), attest, sign, undersign, express assent *or* adhesion *(by signing)*, approve, accede, consent, second, endorse, sanction, set one's name to, affix one's signature to, acknowledge, ratify, countersign, inscribe, confirm, accept, corroborate, verify, certify, validate, O.K. *(coll.)*, okay *(coll.)*.

3. Guarantee, agree to meet the expense of, undertake to finance, subsidize, back, sponsor, aid, promote, befriend, patronize, subserve, keep, maintain, sustain, support, uphold, foster, shoulder.

UNDESIRABLE, *adj.* Objectionable, unwelcomed, unacceptable, distasteful, disliked, unsuitable, unadvisable, inexpedient, wrong, foolish, unmeet, unsatisfactory, out of place, out of character *or* keeping, inappropriate, unfit, inadvisable, unattractive, uninviting, disagreeable, unwished, thankless, unpopular, improper, unseemly, unworthy, unbefitting, unbecoming, unfortunate, infelicitous, inadmissible, ineligible, disadvantageous, incommodious, inconvenient.

UNDIGNIFIED, *adj.* Unbecoming, unbefitting, unworthy, degrading, inelegant, informal, unhandsome, ungraceful, unseemly, indecorous, improper, indecent, uncomely, indelicate, vulgar, untasteful, low, shameful, boorish, beneath one, discreditable, unmanly, unpraiseworthy, barbarous, barbaric, reprehensible, disreputable, ignoble, beggarly, barbarian, crude, rude, coarse,

monstrous, unladylike, ungentlemanly, ungenteel, offensive, in bad taste.

UNDISCERNING, *adj.* 1. Inattentive, unobservant, unheeding, heedless, unmindful, careless, thoughtless, regardless, negligent, neglectful, unwatchful, forgetful, mindless, oblivious, unobserving, remiss, unconcerned, abstracted, unwary, unthinking, unreflecting, deaf, blind, unaware, indifferent, scatterbrained, disregardant, insensible, not on the job *(coll.)*, unthoughtful, absent, witless, irresponsible, preoccupied, distracted.

2. Dull in discernment *or* understanding, purblind, stupid, obtuse, doltish, gauche, stolid, thick-headed, witless, dumb *(coll.)*, insensate, cloddish, ignorant, lumpish, oafish, foggy, mopeeyed, dense, uncomprehending, bovine, blunt, sluggish, slow, slow-witted, dull-pated, insulse, dull-witted, imbecile, idiotic, moronic, thick *(coll.)*, weak-minded, shallow-witted, muddle-brained, mutton-headed *(coll.)*, simple-minded, simple, dronish, numskull *(coll.)*, clodpated, addlepated, addleheaded, unintelligent, unenlightened.

UNDISCIPLINED, *adj.* 1. Untrained, unskilled, inexperienced, undrilled, unpracticed, raw, unaccomplished, unprepared, untaught, untutored, uninstructed, uneducated, unfinished, uninitiated, unschooled, unconformable.

2. Capricious, whimsical, skittish, fitful, vagrant, wanton, random, fanciful, wayward, freakish, fast and loose, uncontrolled, unrestrained, erratic, idiocratic, undependable, unreliable, irregular, idiosyncratic, eccentric, changeful, unstable, uncertain, unsteady, unpredictable, unmethodical, inconstant, volatile, fickle, mercurial.

UNDISGUISED, *adj.* Unconcealed, discernible, apparent, obvious, plain, conspicuous, manifest, distinct, palpable, bald, notable, unquestionable, visible, lucid, patent, unequivocal, unmistakable, undeniable, overt, perspicuous, glaring, recognizable, prominent, disclosed, plain as a pikestaff, plain as the nose on one's face, unhidden, uncamouflaged, open, undoubted, pronounced, explicit, unscreened, unmasked, unreserved, real, honest, barefaced, naked, out-and-out, candid, clear, evident, ingenuous, unfeigned.

UNDISMAYED, *adj.* Unafraid, undaunted, fearless, unappalled, unawed, high-spirited, unintimidated, plucky, intrepid, brave, bold, courageous, spirited, mettlesome, manly, stanch, gritty, game, stout, hardy, stout-hearted, unflinching, strong, strong-willed, gallant, heroic, resolute, high-mettled, lion-hearted, spunky *(coll.)*, indomitable, valiant, doughty *(hum.)*.

UNDISPUTED, *adj.* Accepted, received, uncontested, undoubted, acknowledged, conclusive, incontestable, indisputable, undeniable, unquestioned, doubtless, past dispute, without *or* beyond a doubt *or* question, irrefragable, unanswerable, irrefutable, incontrovertible.

UNDISTURBED, *adj.* Composed, calm, placid, imperturbable, unruffled, peaceful, serene, tranquil, still, quiescent, cool, collected, dormant, unmolested, unagitated, motionless, unexcitable, equable, untroubled, smooth, halcyon, self-possessed, unmoved, level-headed, steady, inirritable, pacific, orderly, concordant, reposeful.

UNDIVIDED, *adj.* 1. Whole, complete, intact, integral, perfect, uncut, solid, unbroken, unsevered, combined, compact, unseparated, entire.

2. United, one, joined, joint, conjoint, conjunct, corporate, unanimous, hand-in-hand, co-

öperative, whole, wedded, bonded, unified, undivided, inseparable, concordant, indissoluble, likeminded, in accord, of one mind, allied, cemented, congenial, compatible, accordant, harmonious, bound, integrated.

UNDO, *v.* 1. Reverse the doing of, annul, nullify, bring to naught, offset, defeat, abrogate, retract, revert, betray, neutralize, invalidate, void, cancel, frustrate, confute, obviate, counterbalance, counteract, run counter, withstand, vitiate, thwart, impede, be *or* play at cross-purposes, overbalance.

2. Loose, unfasten, open, untie, unravel, disentangle, unfold, unlace, unbutton, unhook, unbolt, unbind, release, disengage, set free, free, unchain, unbridle, unshackle, liberate, extricate, unwrap, uncover, unlock, lay open, unbar, throw open, separate.

3. Ruin, overthrow, crush, overturn, destroy, impoverish, cast down, vanquish, defeat, overcome, overpower, overwhelm, confound, subjugate, suppress, put down, bear down, prostrate, rout, beat, discomfit, master, worst, conquer, demolish, subvert, disorganize, annihilate, exterminate, do away with, level, invalidate, confute, quash, shatter, smash, fell, wreck, reduce, fling *or* dash down, tear down, extirpate, abolish, obliterate, quell, subdue, get the upper hand of, break, overmaster, thrash, whip, surmount.

UNDOING, *n.* Ruin, destruction, ruination, adversity, catastrophe, overthrow, calamity, affliction, reversal, trial, visitation, woe, downfall, misfortune, grief, loss, defeat, trouble, wreck, sorrow, cataclysm, disaster, reverse, casualty, failure, humiliation, disgrace, debasement, abasement, rout, extremity, stumble, tumble, doom, deposition, demolition, discomfiture, prostration, debacle, collapse, perdition, beating, havoc, ravage, extinction, breakdown, upset, overset, derangement, deathblow, crackup, vanquishment, jinx, hoodoo, nemesis.

UNDONE, *adj.* 1. Not done, not accomplished *or* completed, omitted, neglected, unfinished, overlooked, incomplete, unfulfilled, unexecuted, unperformed, uncared for, unattended to, shelved, postponed, ignored, slighted.

2. Brought to destruction *or* ruin, prostrate, hopeless, dejected, overcome, helpless, defenseless, impotent, overthrown, paralyzed, abject, down, downtrodden, cast down, with one's hands tied, despairing, abased, on one's last legs, *hors de combat (Fr.),* crippled, disabled, out of the fight, shattered, incapacitated, crushed, exhausted, spent, powerless, oppressed, downcast, overpowered, upset, fallen, collapsed, on one's beam ends, finished, worn out, at the end of one's resources.

UNDOUBTED, *adj.* Not called in question, accepted as beyond doubt, true, believed, received, undisputed, indisputable, indubitable, unquestionable, unchallenged, unmistakable, unequivocal, unquestioned, authoritative, uncontested, acknowledged, conclusive, incontestable, doubtless, irrefragable, irrefutable, incontrovertible.

UNDOUBTEDLY, *adv.* Actually, truly, without *or* beyond question *or* doubt, decidedly, undeniably, unmistakably, really, verily, absolutely, positively, assuredly, surely, certainly, unquestionably, incontrovertibly, indubitably, to be sure, sure enough, doubtless, indeed, in fact, in truth, as a matter of course, no doubt, of course.

UNDOUBTING, *adj.* Confident, sure, unsuspecting, unquestioning, credulous, certain, implicit, believing, trustful, trusting, unhesitating, indubious, convinced, positive, doubtless, decided, satisfied, assured, cocksure.

UNDRESS, *n.* Informality *or* carelessness of attire, dishabille, unadornment, disarray, informality, negligee.

UNDRESS, *v.* Make naked, uncover, expose, put off, doff, lay bare, unwrap, undress, unclothe, strip, disrobe, peel, undrape, unarray, cast off.

UNDUE, *adj.* 1. Not due, not yet payable.

2. Improper, not fitting, unsuitable, unseemly, objectionable, unmeet, imprudent, ill-advised, inappropriate, wrong, in bad taste, indiscreet, impolite, unworthy, unbecoming, inadmissible.

3. Not right, illegal, unlawful, not allowed, illicit, unallowed, illegitimate.

4. Too great, excessive, overmuch, superabundant, profuse, superfluous, prodigal, inordinate, fulsome, immoderate, lavish, uncalled for, copious, supernumerary, overflowing, de trop *(Fr.),* unnecessary, needless.

UNDULANT, *adj.* Having a waving *or* rolling surface, undulatory, ribbed, rolling, waving, wavy, rising and falling, undulating, hilly, rippling, cockled, wrinkled, surging, billowing, crinkled.

UNDULATE, *v.* 1. Rise and fall *(as waves),* surge, billow, ripple, corrugate, wave, roll, cockle, wrinkle, pucker.

2. Swing to and fro, pendulate, nutate, pulsate, beat, oscillate, agitate, librate, fluctuate, rock, ebb and flow, wave, vibrate, sway, nod, alternate, pitch, lurch, seesaw, wigwag.

UNDUTIFUL, *adj.* Slack, remiss, recreant, unfaithful, perfidious, apostate, double-tongued, two-faced, untrue, disaffected, renegade, disloyal, untrustworthy, false-hearted, traitorous, disobedient.

UNDYING, *adj.* Never-ending, never-failing, eternal, perennial, unceasing, unwearied, invariable, incessant, perpetual, endless, everlasting, undiminished, unimpeded, unfaltering, constant, untiring, steady, permanent, uninterrupted, stable, fixed, unremitting, unintermitting, lasting, protracted, unwavering, indestructible, imperishable, immortal.

UNEARNED, *adj.* Not earned by work, labor, service, *etc.,* free, gratis, unmerited, undeserved.

UNEARTH, *v.* 1. Exhume, dig up, excavate, disinter, unbury, disentomb, disinhume.

2. Bring to light, discover, reveal, divulge, disclose, make manifest, ferret out, uncover, dig up, root out, display, exhibit, show.

UNEARTHLY, *adj.* 1. Not terrestrial, not of this earth, not of this world, phantom-like, extramundane, eerie, disembodied, spiritual, incorporeal, spectral, ghostly, occult, supernatural, preternatural, wraithlike, immaterial, weird, uncanny, bodiless, macabre.

2. Terrible, terrifying, repulsive, bloodcurdling, ugly, loathsome, beastly, heinous, gruesome, base, unutterable, devilish, portentous, distasteful, terror-breathing, startling, creepy, scaring, formidable, disconcerting, disagreeable, dismaying, unsavory, ghostlike, cadaverous, evil-looking, ill-looking, astounding, misproportioned, fulsome, foul, Satanic, rank, evil, sinister, nauseating, revolting, misshappen, noisome, despicable, obnoxious, evil-shaped, awe-inspiring, disquieting, bestial, fiendish, hellish, black, evil-fashioned, Tartarean, stygian, infernal, unmanning, terror-breeding, lurid, baleful, repellent, malevolent, maleficent, harmful, demoniac, diabolical, un-

speakable, hateful, damnable, dreadful, nocuous, unpleasant, teratoid, insufferable, unbearable, abominable, grisly, ghoulish, atrocious, execrable, forbidding, horrid, horrible, horrific, shocking, ghastly, grim, fearful, awful, grotesque.

UNEASY, *adj.* 1. On edge, unquiet, restless, fidgety, rattled, discomposed, troubled, ill-at-ease, perturbed, put out, disturbed, nervous, disquieted, edgy, uncomfortable.

2. Constraining, cramping, bothersome, unpleasant, hard, crabbed, stiff, confining, wearying, irksome, limiting, restraining, difficult, restricting, uncomfortable.

UNECONOMICAL, *adj.* Expensive, unprofitable, costly, running into money, dear, wasteful, prodigal.

UNEDUCATED, *adj.* Without learning, knowledge, *etc.*, uninstructed, illiterate, unschooled, raw, unerudite, ignorant, unlettered, untutored, unrefined, undisciplined, unaccomplished, untaught, inexperienced, unread, rude, crude, lowbrow, uncultured.

UNEMBELLISHED, *adj.* Unornamental, bare, untrimmed, ungarnished, severe, simple, restrained, frugal, pure, clear, flat, unfigured, modest, unvaried, unadorned, unfurbished, blank, inelegant, spare, chaste, undecked, unarrayed.

UNEMOTIONAL, *adj.* Distant, reserved, apathetic, frigid, torpid, poised, composed, unkindled, chill, icy, nonchalant, unimpassioned, unexcitable, stony, insensitive, undemonstrative, unconcerned, unanimated, phlegmatic, passionless, lukewarm, serene, unperturbed, stiff, disdainful, unimpressionable, formal, languid, neutral, impartial, supine, soulless, unfeeling, calm, indifferent, inanimate.

UNEMPLOYABLE, *adj.* Unable to work *or* be used, useless, unfit, disabled, worthless, unusable, inoperative, ineffective.

UNEMPLOYED, *adj.* Out of work, jobless, workless, idle, inactive, laid off.

UNENDING, *adj.* Never-ending, invariable, incessant, unimpeded, undiminished, constant, permanent, fixed, protracted, eternal, unceasing, perpetual, endless, unfaltering, untiring, steady, uninterrupted, stable, unremitting, lasting, unwavering, enduring.

UNENDURABLE, *adj.* That cannot be borne *or* endured, insupportable, intolerable, insufferable, unbearable, inadmissible, unacceptable.

UNENTERPRISING, *adj.* Torpid, lumpish, indolent, remiss, lax, lazy, asleep, dilatory, inert, phlegmatic, listless, sluggish, lethargic, lentitudinous.

UNENTHUSIASTIC, *adj.* Distant, reserved, disdainful, lukewarm, indifferent, unperturbed, listless, phlegmatic, inert, uninterested, cold, unimpressionable, apathetic, unimpressed, neutral, nonchalant, unconcerned.

UNEQUAL, *adj.* 1. Not of the same size, *etc.*, different, differing, dissimilar, unlike, unmatched.

2. Unmatched, lopsided, top-heavy, uneven, unbalanced, ill-balanced, unfair, disparate, ill-matched, disquiparant *(Logic).*

3. Not uniform, variable, differing, changeable, incongruous, incompatible, dissimilar, deviative, fitful, mutable, heteroclite.

4. Not enough, inadequate, not sufficient, deficient, wanting, not up to, insufficient, lacking.

UNEQUALED, *adj.* Matchless, unparalleled, peerless, incomparable, superexcellent, unexcelled,

paramount, faultless, unapproached, rare, supreme, superior, transcendent, inimitable, unrivaled, best, second to none, consummate, flawless, ne plus ultra, beyond compare *or* comparison, priceless, unsurpassed.

UNEQUIVOCAL, *adj.* Unambiguous, certain, not doubtful, received, believed, true, incontrovertible, unchallenged, irrefragable, absolute, explicit, definite, undisputed, incontestable, decided, unanswerable.

UNERRING, *adj.* Without mistake, irreprehensible, irreproachable, certain, faithful, constant, sound, unimpeachable, unfailing, precise, infallible, faultless, correct, trustworthy, dependable, reliable, accurate.

UNESSENTIAL, *adj.* Not important, not indispensable, dispensable, minor, slight, secondary, trivial, of no account, trifling, meager, unnecessary, insignificant, negligible, inconsiderable, small, petty, paltry.

UNESTIMATED, *adj.* Of unknown quantity, quality, number, *etc.*, uncalculated, uncounted, untold, unnumbered, unfixed, undetermined.

UNETHICAL, *adj.* Wrong, unprincipled, unconscionable, disreputable, unworthy, dishonest, uncommendable, mean, ungentlemanly, shoddy, unbecoming, underhanded, dirty *(coll.)*, unfair, dishonorable, questionable, shady.

UNEVEN, *adj.* 1. Rough, not uniform, craggy, unlevel, unsmooth, unpolished, rough-hewn, coarse, jagged, rough-grained, broken, gnarled, lumpy.

2. Not of the same size, *etc.*, dissimilar, different, differing, unmatched, unequal, odd.

3. Unmatched, lopsided, unbalanced, top-heavy, ill-balanced, unequal, ill-matched, disparate, unfair.

UNEVENTFUL, *adj.* Lacking in important *or* striking occurrences, inconsequential, insignificant, dull, quiet, commonplace, eventless, smooth, humdrum, monotonous, uninteresting, common, immaterial, flat, usual, everyday, customary, average, daily, conventional, wonted, normal, accustomed, unexceptional, expected, regular, routine, standard, cut and dried, matter-of-fact, mediocre, unimpressive, tame, ordinary, tedious.

UNEXACTING, *adj.* Requiring little, easy, loose, lax, slack, soft, lenient, forbearing, forbearant, easygoing, tolerant, indulgent, long-suffering, undespotic, adespotic.

UNEXAMPLED, *adj.* Having no example *or* similar case, unprecedented, unparalleled, unusual, unequaled, archetypal, prototypal, prototypical, unheard-of, uncommon, unmatched, unapproached, matchless, original, unique, novel, incomparable, singular, unfamiliar, unpatterned, peerless, inimitable, exceptional.

UNEXCELLED, *adj.* Supreme, unsurpassed, superior, unequaled, unrivaled, matchless, unparalleled, peerless, incomparable, superexcellent, paramount, faultless, unapproached, rare, transcendent, inimitable, best, second to none, consummate, flawless, ne plus ultra, beyond compare *or* comparison, priceless.

UNEXCEPTIONABLE, *adj.* Not open *or* liable to any exception *or* objection, beyond criticism, unobjectionable, excellent, faultless, irreproachable, inculpable, uncensurable, above suspicion, unblamable, superfine, perfect, flawless, good, unimpeachable, unchallengeable, irreprovable, unblameworthy, irreprehensible, quite satisfactory, perfectly acceptable, unexceptional.

UNEXCEPTIONAL, *adj.* 1. Not unusual *or* extraordinary, commonplace, average, common, mediocre, tolerable, bearable, decent, middling, acceptable, admissible, ordinary, fair, passable, indifferent, so-so, undistinguished, medium, run-of-the-mill, humdrum, second-rate, trivial, insignificant, insipid, wishy-washy, pedestrian, stale, trite, hackneyed, unimpressive, prosaic, tame, banal, homely, stereotyped, uninspiring, uninspired, unimaginative, cohventional, usual, customary, accustomed, pat *(coll.),* stock, cut and dried, dime-a-dozen, typical.

2. Admitting of no exception, flat, rigid, inflexible, dogmatic, final, closed, peremptory, mandatory, absolute, decided, positive, categorical, explicit, inalterable.

UNEXPECTED, *adj.* Sudden, unforeseen, unanticipated, premature, unthought-of, unlooked-for, startling, astonishing, unwonted, accidental, abrupt, precipitate, previous, prevenient, unfamiliar, unaccountable, subitaneous, surprising, unpurposed, undesigned, extemporaneous, extempore, unintentional, fortuitous, unintended, untimely, unseasonable, out of the blue, out of one's reckoning.

UNEXPRESSIVE, *adj.* Lacking in expression of meaning *or* feeling, *etc.,* blank, characterless, empty, expressionless, cold, vacant, vacuous, foolish, inane, absurd, senseless, meaningless, stupid, unthinking, nonunderstanding, unintelligent, apathetic, unemotional, unsympathetic, unresponsive, phlegmatic, stoical, grim, distant, remote, hard, aloof, passionless, dead, neutral, sluggish, impartial, unkindled, nonchalant, unimpressionable, unimpassioned, listless, insensible, comatose, supine, inert, stony, soulless, insensitive, obtuse, unmoved, unstirred, untouched, impervious, stolid, unconcerned, indifferent, unanimated, inanimate.

UNFADING, *adj.* Unchanging, enduring, fast, fresh, lasting, endless, perpetual, everlasting, never-ending, constant, unceasing, permanent, undecaying, perennial, fadeless, sempiternal, infinite, ever-blooming, amaranthine, never-fading, deathless, evergreen, immortal, undying, perdurable, imperishable, sempervirent.

UNFAILING, *adj.* 1. Incapable of being exhausted, inexhaustible, constant, certain, unchanging, endless, deathless, intact, dependable, reliable, exhaustless, never-failing, infallible, eternal, sure, perennial, perpetual.

2. Not *or* never failing, not giving way, faithful, infallible, dependable, unchanging, loyal, stanch, true, steadfast, steady, reliable, unerring, firm, constant, resolute, inevitable, indefatigable, stable, unshaken, determined, unwavering, unhesitating, unmoved, stern, zealous, persevering, pertinacious, unyielding, strong, not to be shaken, sedulous, untiring, unflagging, enduring, patient, indomitable, undaunted, inexorable, fixed, gritty, persistent, relentless, uncompromising, tenacious, dedicated, devoted.

UNFAIR, *adj.* 1. Biased, partial, not just *or* equitable, unjust, warped, jaundiced, prepossessed, prejudiced, influenced, interested, false, hypocritical, insincere, uncandid, dishonest, dishonorable, inequitable, unrightful, underhand, unreasonable, backhanded, oblique, faithless, one-sided, unequal, disingenuous.

2. Using unethical business practices, false, underhand, unconscientious, unscrupulous, deceitful, unprincipled, dishonorable, unconscienced, unconscionable, dirty, dishonest, corrupt, lawless, unhandsome, foul, mean, crooked, misleading, of bad faith, fraudulent, venal, immoral.

UNFAITHFUL, *adj.* 1. False to duty *or* promises, faithless, perfidious, disloyal, deceitful, unreliable, treacherous, dishonest, recreant, heedless, traitorous, remiss, disregardful, slack, unsteadfast, untrue, inconstant, changeable, fickle, apostate, renegade, negligent, untrustworthy, undutiful, disobedient, careless, false-hearted, backsliding.

2. Not upright, dishonest, insincere, insidious, mendacious, uncandid, uningenuous, disingenuous, underhand, false, deceitful, two-faced, hypocritical, double-dealing, casuistic, jesuitical, truthless, temporizing, timeserving, scheming, shifty, misleading, deceptive, artful, cunning, unveracious, untruthful, lying.

3. Not faithfully accurate *or* exact, careless, erring, spurious, mendacious, sham, erroneous, false, faulty, untrue, defective, fallacious, counterfeit, subreptitious, wide of the mark, perverted, imperfect, distorted.

4. Guilty of adultery, unchaste, licentious, abandoned, profligate, loose, wanton, adulterous, free, fast, light, rakish, wild, prostituted, of easy morals *or* virtue.

UNFALTERING, *adj.* Resolute, firm, unwavering, steadfast, unswerving, unhesitating, determined, intrepid, unflagging, steady, indefatigable, firm of purpose, stanch, fixed, stable, unshaken, resolved, faithful, unreserved, pertinacious, persevering, zealous, true, unyielding, undeviating, unmoved, stern, inflexible, constant, strong, serious, decided, not to be shaken, sedulous, untiring, industrious, enduring, patient, grim, plodding, indomitable, undaunted, inexorable, settled, intransigent, persistent, relentless, strong-willed, uncompromising, obstinate, tenacious, dedicated, devoted.

UNFAMILIAR, *adj.* 1. Not well known, unaccustomed, strange, unusual, extraordinary, curious, odd, out of the ordinary, irregular, uncommon, outlandish, singular, rare, exceptional, unaccountable, surprising, astonishing, erratic, remarkable, bizarre, abnormal, unnatural, unique, out-of-the-way, unheard-of, original, whimsical, aberrant, unwonted, inusitate, unconventional, fanciful, freakish, new, fresh, novel, foreign, different, dissimilar, unlike, diverse, varied.

2. Not acquainted *or* conversant, strange, unaccustomed, unacquainted, inexperienced, untried, raw, green, a stranger to, a novice at, ignorant, unskilled, unpracticed, unversed, unseasoned, unconversant, unused, unenlightened, uninformed, uninitiated, new, uninured, unwonted, ungiven, unhabituated.

UNFASHIONABLE, *adj.* 1. Unconventional, unmodish, unaccustomed, unique, original, whimsical, nonobservant, unaccepted, not being done.

2. Old-fashioned, disused, obsolete, outmoded, out of fashion *or* date, out of use, antiquated, fallen into desuetude, superannuated, archaic, stale, fusty, moldy, passé, extinct, timeworn, dead, gone out, outworn, back-number, behind the age *or* times, of the old school.

UNFASTEN, *v.* Loose, unbind, unloose, untie, undo, unchain, set free, release, let go, disjoin, loosen, unlace, unharness, unshackle, unlash, separate, part, detach, disjoint, extricate, disengage, cut off *or* adrift, unlink, unhasp, open, unlock, unfix, unclasp, unhitch, unbar, unbuckle, unbolt, unpin.

UNFATHOMABLE, *adj.* 1. Incapable of being fathomed, fathomless, infinite, measureless, bottomless, soundless, abysmal, illimitable, limitless, incalculable, immeasurable, interminable, very deep, profound, unplumbed, boundless, unbounded, plumbless, eternal, yawning, immense, exhaustless, inexhaustible, indeterminate.

2. Impenetrable by the mind, unsearchable, inscrutable, profound, paradoxical, indecipherable, inexplicable, mysterious, inapprehensible, incognizable, undiscoverable, unknowable, unintelligible, crabbed, perplexed, deep, unaccountable, esoteric, puzzling, unanswerable, enigmatic, insoluble, incomprehensible.

UNFAVORABLE, *adj.* Adverse, disadvantageous, unpropitious, unlucky, unfortunate, untimely, inopportune, contrary, preventive, deterrent, evil, ill, inimical, preclusive, evil-starred, doomed, planet-struck, poor, bad, infelicitous, hostile, disparaging, derogatory, unpromising, sinister, cross, malign, indisposed, inauspicious, hindering, unseasonable, opposed, ominous, ill-boding, ill-fated, ill-omened, ill-suited, unsuited, unhappy, inconvenient, impedimentary, inhibitive, repugnant, noxious, awkward, at issue, at odds, conflicting, contradictory, antagonistic, discouraging, at war with.

UNFEELING, *adj.* 1. Devoid of feeling, insensate, insensible, numb, unconscious, unimpressionable, torpid, apathetic, callous, dead, dull, phlegmatic.

2. Callous, unsympathetic, hard-hearted, cruel, unkind, hardened, pitiless, merciless, cold-blooded, cold-hearted, inhuman, adamantine, stony, flinty, insensate, unmerciful, obdurate, unpitying, harsh, tough, stiff, unconcerned, supercilious, uncompassionate, unsparing, unmerciful, unforgiving, unimpassioned, unimpressible, untouched, unmoved, insentient, insensitive, relentless, remorseless, ironhearted, unresponsive, hard-bitten, indifferent, Laodicean, unstirred, thick-skinned, cold, hard, disdainful, indurated, impervious, implacable, uncaring, brutal, unnatural, emotionless.

UNFEIGNED, *adj.* Real, sincere, true, genuine, honest, unaffected, unassumed, undisguised, open, unvarnished, natural, deceitless, undeceitful, pure, straightforward, inartificial, candid, ingenuous, frank, artless, whole-hearted, aboveboard, heartfelt, veracious, cordial, innocent, serious, fervent, earnest, blunt, single-hearted, direct, simple, straight, plain, guileless, truthful, outspoken, undissembling, unreserved, uncorrupted, unclouded, forthright, childlike, open-hearted.

UNFILIAL, *adj.* Unbecoming of a child to a parent, not observing the obligations of a child to a parent, undutiful, unruly, ungovernable, intractable, unduteous, ungrateful, disobedient, insubordinate, wayward, impudent, insolent, defiant, rebellious.

UNFINISHED, *adj.* Incomplete, unexecuted, unperformed, imperfect, crude, rough, raw, sketchy, deficient, defective, immature, wanting, inadequate, half-baked, scanty, meager, poor, undone, perfunctory, half-cocked, unfulfilled, uncompleted.

UNFIT, *adj.* 1. Not fit, not adapted *or* suited, unsuitable, unmeet, malapropos, inapplicable, unsuited, undue, inadvisable, incongruous, inapt, inapposite, unfitting, unwise, injudicious, improvident, imprudent, inappropriate, irrelevant, idle,

ill-advised, ill-contrived, vain, foolish, empty, unseemly, unbefitting, unbecoming, improper, out of proportion, objectionable, infelicitous, ill-timed, inexpedient, untimely, unseasonable, inconvenient, inopportune, impertinent, out of keeping, out of place, unworthy.

2. Unqualified, ineligible, inadequate, incompetent, unprepared, unripe, ineffective, useless, unequipped, incapable, unready, inefficient, unequal, inept, maladjusted, unadjusted, disqualified, not cut out for, not equal *or* up to, unfitted, unable, inexpert.

3. Not physically fit *or* in due condition, puny, disabled, spent, impotent, frail, delicate, prostrate, exhausted, unmanned, decrepit, weak, devitalized, unnerved, enervated, emasculate, weakly, feeble, debilitated, soft, strengthless.

UNFIT, *v.* Render unfit *or* unsuitable, disqualify, invalidate, incapacitate, disenable, unsinew, undermine, lame, maim, cripple, hamstring, disarm, indispose, disable, handcuff, hock, blunt the edge of, blemish, mar, bruise, impair, tie the hands, render useless, deface.

UNFLAGGING, *adj.* Untiring, unremitting, indefatigable, undrooping, unfaltering, steady, steadfast, sedulous, constant, never-tiring, persevering, unweakened, unwearied, fixed, firm, resolute, stanch, determined, unshaken, resolved, faithful, unhesitating, unyielding, pertinacious, zealous, true, undeviating, unmoved, stern, serious, strong, inflexible, unswerving, decided, not to be shaken, industrious, enduring, grim, patient, plodding, indomitable, undaunted, inexorable, settled, devoted, intransigent, persistent, relentless, tenacious, obstinate, uncompromising, dedicated.

UNFLATTERING, *adj.* Plain, forthright, true, candid, frank, blunt, outspoken, honest, direct, unvarnished, unsparing, cruel, bitter, unaffected, untrimmed, unromantic, brusque, plain-speaking, uncomplimentary, straightforward, truthful, crude, undisguised, unfeigning.

UNFLEDGED, *adj.* 1. Without feathers sufficiently developed for flight, youthful, unfeathered, young, new-fledged, fledgling.

2. Inexperienced, immature, undeveloped, callow, untried, unripe, budding, raw, green, coarse, unhatched, unrefined, half-cocked, half-baked, unschooled, unlearned, rude, crude, unnurtured, uneducated, unprepared, unskilled, uninitiated, childish, childlike, puerile, roughcast, rough-hewn, unseasoned, unmellowed, uncultivated, unlicked, tender, ignorant, precocious, untaught, unfinished, unpolished.

UNFLINCHING, *adj.* Resolute, unshrinking, firm, steady, steadfast, plucky, fearless, indomitable, unabashed, game, unappalled, stanch, determined, unshaken, stable, resolved, faithful, unhesitating, unwavering, pertinacious, persevering, zealous, true, unfaltering, unyielding, undeviating, stern, unmoved, inflexible, unswerving, constant, strong, sedulous, untiring, indefatigable, unflagging, enduring, patient, undaunted, inexorable, fixed, intransigent, gritty, persistent, relentless, devoted, uncompromising, obstinate, tenacious, dedicated.

UNFOLD, *v.* 1. Open out, spread, release, unroll, expand, unfurl, separate, unravel, display, undo, disentangle, straighten, unwrap, fan out, untie, undouble, stretch, uncoil, unwind, extend, deploy (*Mil.*), disinvolve.

2. Develop, flower, uncurl, open, grow, wax, expand, increase, burst forth, put forth, evolve,

mature, blossom, bloom, bud, burgeon, sprout up, shoot up.

3. Reveal, display, show, exhibit, expose, set to view, spread out, unveil, undrape, uncurtain, bare, disclose, materialize, demonstrate, manifest, present, make visible, hold up to view, bring to light, uncloak, evince, lay open, evidence, publish, proclaim, unscreen, uncover, unmask.

4. Reveal in words, disclose, set forth, explain, divulge, tell, declare, amplify, narrate, unriddle, unravel, interpret, make clear, make known, show, bare, broadcast, expose, evolve, inform, interpret, whisper, tell, breathe, evulgate, divulgate, expound, explicate, elucidate, solve, amplify, give away, spill, let fall *or* drop, give utterance to.

UNFORESEEN, *adj.* Unexpected, unlooked for, sudden, accidental, unanticipated, startling, abrupt, surprise, unthought-of, unlooked-for, unwonted, unfamiliar, unaccountable, subitaneous, unpurposed, undesigned, fortuitous, unintended, out of the blue, out of one's reckoning.

UNFORGETTABLE, *adj.* Never to be forgotten, notable, noteworthy, etched on the memory, memorable, indelible, impressive, rememberable, exceptional, extraordinary, outstanding, indelibly impressed on the mind *or* memory.

UNFORGIVABLE, *adj.* Inexcusable, unjustifiable, unallowable, unreasonable, inexpiable, unpardonable, indefensible, unwarrantable.

UNFORGIVING, *adj.* Implacable, revengeful, vengeful, avenging, hard, inexorable, relentless, punitive, retaliative, vindictive, callous, rancorous, unappeasable, unrelenting, stony-hearted, merciless, Achillean, recriminatory, uncompassionate, inclement, bowelless, heartless, hard-hearted, severe.

UNFORTUNATE, *adj.* 1. Inauspicious, unlucky, ominous, adverse, untimely, unpropitious, disadvantageous, inopportune, contrary, evil, ill, inimical, preclusive, evil-starred, doomed, planet-struck, poor, bad, infelicitous, hostile, unpromising, sinister, malign, indisposed, unseasonable, cross, opposed, ill-boding, ill-fated, ill-omened, unhappy, inconvenient, impedimentary, inhibitive, noxious, antagonistic, discouraging, contradictory.

2. Unhappy, unlucky, hapless, unsuccessful, unprosperous, fortuneless, disastrous, unblest, miserable, jinxed, Jonahed, ill-starred, ill-fated, wretched, luckless, out of luck, woebegone, bereft, hopeless, evil-starred, under a cloud, clouded, down on one's luck *(coll.),* thwarted, born with a wooden ladle in one's mouth, scotched, foiled, crossed, victimized, stultified, balked, woeful, forlorn, hoodooed *(coll.),* born under an evil star, cursed, dashed *(coll.),* infelicitous.

UNFOUNDED, *adj.* Without foundation, baseless, unestablished, unproven, unattested, idle, vain, groundless, untrue, ungrounded, unsubstantial, forged, invented, trumped up, fabricated, false, erroneous, supposititious, factitious, fraudulent, unsupported, spurious, improbable, unauthenticated.

UNFRIENDLY, *adj.* Unkindly, inimical, hostile, unkind, cool, ill-disposed, antagonistic, unsympathetic, estranged, cold, unsociable, inhospitable, antipathetic, bristling, ill-willed, quarrelsome, fractious, contrary, disputatious, snappish, disobliging, ill-natured, spiteful, malevolent, uncongenial, contentious, unamiable, unneighborly,

disagreeable, ungracious, unaccommodating, unamicable.

UNFRUITFUL, *adj.* Not fruitful, unproductive, barren, fruitless, infertile, unprolific, infecund, otiose, sterile, arid, acarpous, issueless, impotent, poor, fallow.

UNGAINLY, *adj.* 1. Awkward, unhandy, inapt, unskillful, maladroit, bungling, unpolished, graceless, uncourtly, inelegant, without dexterity, like a bull in a china shop, clumsy, uncouth, clownish, rough, slovenly, without skill, stiff, gauche, left-handed, dull, dense, bovine, doltish, thick *(coll.),* dumb *(coll.),* insensitive, untoward, all thumbs *(coll.),* slatternly, stolid, insulse, obtuse, heavy-handed, oafish, butter-fingered, inexpert.

2. Unwieldy, awkwardly done, wooden, ill-contrived, lumbering, heavy, clumsy, ponderous, ill-made, rough, lumpish, crude, hulking, stodgy, heavy-handed, stupid, knocked together, makeshift, ugly, ill-shaped, lubberly, cumbersome, boorish, ungainly, crass, thoughtless, bulky, hulky, tactless, coarse, gross, obtuse, amorphous, uncouth, inept, dull, inelegant.

UNGENTLEMANLY, *adj.* Not refined, crude, rough, coarse, loutish, cloddish, impolite, ill-mannered, vulgar, uncivil, rude, unpolished, bearish, bluff, ungraceful, ill-bred.

UNGODLY, *adj.* Sinful, impious, wicked, sinning, heinous, pernicious, malevolent, mischievous, bestial, unwholesome, demoralized, accursed, base, rotten, unscrupulous, reprobate, sinister, depraved, disreputable, opprobrious, treacherous, false, untrustworthy, uncommendable, blameworthy, infernal, diabolic, Mephistophelian, culpable, virtueless, fiendish, hellish, stygian, vicious, baneful, baleful, noisome, malignant, malicious, noxious, poisonous, hurtful, naughty, spiteful, crooked, mean, injurious, corrupt, unprincipled, iniquitous, hardened, incorrigible, felonious, dissolute, profligate, libertine, infamous, unrighteous, vile, miscreant, unlawful, knavish, arrant, shameful, immoral, villainous, degenerate, criminal, dishonorable, brutal, foul, scandalous, black-hearted, flagitious, peccant, obliquitous, virtueless, censurable, atrocious, peccable, illaudable, obdurate, irreclaimable, atrocious, scampish, devilish, evil-disposed, inexpiable, evil-minded, facinorous, blackguard, Machiavellian, insidious, soulless, turpitudinous.

UNGOVERNABLE, *adj.* Unruly, impliable, refractory, uncontrollable, wayward, unmanageable, unbridled, contumacious, recalcitrant, contrary, unsubmissive, perverse, lawless, irrepressible, intractable.

UNGRACIOUS, *adj.* Not refined, crude, ill-mannered, impolite, cloddish, loutish, coarse, vulgar, uncivil, rude, unpolished, bearish, bluff.

UNGRAMMATICAL, *adj.* Inaccurate, solecistic, faulty, incorrect, badly constructed.

UNGRATEFUL, *adj.* Without thanks, uncivil, impolite, inconsiderate, unthankful, heedless, rude.

UNGUARDED, *adj.* 1. Uncircumspect, absentminded, sleeping, inobservant, unwary, unwatchful, unobservant, nonobservant, unvigilant, asleep.

2. Foolhardy, heedless, unguided, rash, impetuous, impulsive, precipitate, headstrong, reckless, thoughtless, irresponsible, imprudent, unchecked, unwary.

3. Without protection *or* defense, unwatched, weaponless, unarmed, unarmored, uncovered, weak, guardless, undefended, pregnable, defense-

less, unprotected, exposed, unpatrolled, unscreened, unshielded, vulnerable.

UNGUENT, n. Salve, ointment, balm, demulcent, emollient, lotion, cerate, embrocation, liniment.

UNGUINOUS, adj. Oily, oleaginous, fatty, oil-like, unctuous, oleoresinous, pinguid, sebaceous, lardaceous, buttery, emulsive, butyraceous, unguentary, unguentiferous, lardy, lardiform.

UNHALLOWED, adj. 1. Not hallowed or consecrated, unsanctified, unholy, unregenerate, impure, ungodly, unpurified, infidel, irreligious, unconverted.

2. Profane, impious, wicked, irreverent, polluted, reprobate, nefarious, infamous, vile, accursed, godless, dark, shameful, devilish, diabolical, demoniac, foul, black, cursed, vicious, bad, evil, base, immoral, hardened, sinful, debauched, depraved, guilty, corrupt, iniquitous, unrighteous, ungodly, blasphemous, sacrilegious, demonic.

UNHANDY, adj. 1. Not easy to handle or manage (as things), unmanageable, incommodious, untoward, intractable, refractory, obstinate, awkward, annoying, unwieldy, perverse, contrary, cumbersome, unruly, ungovernable, annoying, uncomfortable, inconvenient, balky, unyielding, ponderous, impliable, stubborn, resistant, inflexible, unbending, difficult or hard to deal with.

2. Unskillful (in use of the hands), awkward, clumsy, incompetent, lubberly, oafish, maladroit, bungling, gauche, inapt, inexpert, lumpish, blockish, butterfingered, gawky, ungraceful, undeft, left-handed, heavy-handed, clumsy-fisted, undexterous, inefficient, inadept, all thumbs (joc.).

UNHAPPY, adj. 1. Wretched, miserable, sad, sorrowful, dispirited, woeful, disconsolate, afflicted, comfortless, heartsick, dejected, mournful, lugubrious, melancholy, downcast, heavy, depressed, cheerless, crestfallen, pathetic, brokenhearted, joyless, desolate, funereal, woebegone, plaintive, somber, despondent, heavy-hearted, long-faced, long-visaged, blue, subdued, sober, grave, saturnine, pensive, doleful, dismal, gloomy, rueful, tearful, grief-stricken, burdened, bowed down, full of care, stricken, crushed, heavy-laden, pessimistic, grieved, tristful, infelicitous, despairing, forlorn, unmanned, inconsolable, prostrated, chapfallen, down in the mouth (coll.).

2. Unfortunate, unlucky, infelicitous, luckless, ill-starred, hapless, cursed, unsuccessful, unprosperous, fortuneless, unblest, jinxed, Jonahed, ill-fated, out of luck, bereft, hopeless, evil-starred, under a cloud, clouded, down on one's luck (coll.), thwarted, born with a wooden ladle in one's mouth, scotched, foiled, crossed, victimized, stultified, balked, hoodooed (coll.), born under an evil star, dashed (coll.), poor.

3. Unfavorable, inauspicious, unpropitious, unblest, sinister, evil, malign, unlucky, ominous, adverse, untimely, disadvantageous, inopportune, contrary, ill, inimical, preclusive, evil-starred, doomed, planet-struck, bad, poor, infelicitous, hostile, unpromising, indisposed, unseasonable, cross, opposed, ill-boding, ill-fated, ill-omened, contradictory, discouraging, antagonistic, noxious, inhibitive, impedimentary.

4. Unfortunate, unwise, unbecoming, foolish, ill-advised, infelicitous, indiscreet, injudicious, unapt, unsuited, unbefitting, inappropriate, inapposite, untimely, malapropos, awkward, inapplicable, seasonable, out of keeping, out of place, out of tune, imprudent, indecorous, incorrect, inexpedient, inadvisable, not to the purpose, impertinent.

UNHARMED, adj. Uninjured, unhurt, intact, safe, unimpaired, unspoiled, undefaced, undeformed, perfect, scatheless, unscathed, sound, entire, whole, preserved, safe and sound, in perfect condition, unscratched, inviolate, immune, unaffected.

UNHARMONIOUS, adj. 1. Discordant, dissonant, unmusical, harsh, untuneful, unmelodious, cacophonous, out of tune, inharmonic, unharmonious, off-key, off-pitch, sour, raucous, jarring, strident.

2. Discordant, disagreeing, at variance, uncongenial, divergent, dissentient, quarrelsome, dissonant, antagonistic, inaccordant, jarring, clashing, at odds, at war, discrepant, variant, dissimilar, hostile, differing, factious, unconformable, disproportioned, dissident, incongruous, inconsistent, incompatible, repugnant.

UNHEALTHFUL, adj. 1. Injurious to health, insalubrious, unwholesome, noxious, noisome, innutritious, indigestible, poisonous, morbific, morbiferous, detrimental, unhygienic, prejudicial, pernicious, venomous, pestilential, pestiferous, malevolent, unsanitary, bad, deleterious, deadly, hurtful, harmful, baneful, toxic, septic, unhealthy.

2. Not healthful, not possessing health, etc., (See UNHEALTHY, adj.).

UNHEALTHY, adj. 1. Unsound, unwell, indisposed, out of health, sickly, ailing, invalid, diseased, poorly (chiefly coll.), seedy (coll.), weak, feeble, infirm, valetudinary, valetudinarian, impaired, decrepit, drooping, languid, injured, tainted, morbid.

2. Hurtful to health, unwholesome, insalubrious, etc. (See UNHEALTHFUL, adj.).

3. Morally harmful, noxious, undesirable, dangerous, perilous, in question, doubtful, dubious, degrading, demoralizing, corrupting, dishonorable, polluting, contaminating, vitiating, sinful, bad, foul, filthy, dirty, ominous, destructive of character, hazardous, evil, tainted, vicious, depraved.

UNHEARD-OF, adj. 1. Obscure, unknown, renownless, concealed, hidden, unsung, out-of-the-way, insignificant, unhonored, nameless, inglorious, unnoted, inconspicuous.

2. Unprecedented, uncommon, unexpected, new, unexampled, unwonted, unbelievable, unequaled, strange, singular, surprising, improbable, inconceivable, abnormal, exceptional, unparalleled, unfamiliar, incomparable, unmatched, original, unique, outlandish, extraordinary, odd, queer, irregular, peculiar, anomalous, rare, unaccountable, outré, erratic, unaccustomed, freakish, foreign, novel, never encountered.

UNHEEDED, adj. Ignored, unnoticed, disregarded, unobserved, unseen, slighted, left out, left undone, overlooked, unperceived, passed over, unnoted, uncared-for, unattended to, neglected, unregarded, missed, unremarked, unmarked, unthought-of.

UNHEEDFUL, adj. Careless, heedless, unheeding, negligent, uncaring, insouciant, indifferent, inattentive, disregardful, thoughtless, unmindful, reckless, headlong, unobservant, neglectful, inconsiderate, unwatchful, rash, forgetful, listless, slovenly, mindless, oblivious, unobserving, unsolicitous, remiss, slack, unconcerned, abstracted, harebrained, unthinking, deaf, blind, unaware, inadvertent, insensible, scatterbrained, absent, witless, irresponsible, hasty, preoccupied, distracted, incautious.

UNHERALDED, *adj.* Unsung, unexpected, obscure, unannounced, unknown, unheard-of, nameless, renownless, unanticipated, sudden, without warning, premature, unproclaimed, unrecognized, as a thief in the night, unlooked for, unhoped for, unforeseen, precipitate, dropped from the clouds, out of the blue.

UNHESITATING, *adj.* Unfaltering, prompt, ready, unwavering, steadfast, undoubting, resolute, believing, forthright, immediate, instantaneous, quick, without delay, on the alert, on one's toes, wide-awake, eager, direct, unflinching, unshaken, determined, unreserved, undeviating, unmoved, unswerving, untiring, unflagging, not to be shaken, undaunted, relentless, intransigent.

UNHINGE, *v.* 1. Detach, separate, displace, dislocate, dislodge, disjoint, luxate, disunite, part, disconnect, sever, disengage, remove.
   2. Deprive of fixity *or* stability, throw into confusion *or* disorder, unfix, convulse, rout, complicate, perplex, confuse, disorder, unsettle, shatter, derange, confound, mix up, muddle, trouble, perturb, agitate, toss, embroil, bedevil, tangle, entangle.
   3. Unbalance *(the mind, etc.)*, dement, obsess, possess, madden, drive mad *or* insane, derange, craze, turn one's brain *or* head, dementate.
   4. Upset *(a person)*, discompose, unsettle *(opinions, etc.)*, disable, agitate, fluster, disturb, disconcert, disarm, unman, unnerve, rattle *(coll.)*, perturb, trouble, bewilder, confound, nonplus, throw on one's beam-ends, muddle, devitalize, enervate, undermine, paralyze, incapacitate, daze, unbrace, shake up, convulse.

UNHOPED-FOR, *adj.* Incredible, unanticipated, unlooked-for, chance, unforeseen, fortuitous, fluky *(sl.)*, surprising, unexpected, unbelievable, too good to be true, undreamed-of, not in one's wildest imaginings.

UNHURT, *adj.* Uninjured, unharmed, intact, safe, unimpaired, unspoiled, undefaced, undeformed, perfect, unscathed, scatheless, sound, entire, whole, safe and sound, preserved, unaffected, immune, inviolate, unscratched, in perfect condition.

UNHYGIENIC, *adj.* Unclean, unwashed, unpurified, unsanitary, dirty, impure, soiled, uncleanly, grimy, unhealthful, unhealthy, disease-producing.

UNIDENTIFIED, *adj.* Unknown, anonymous, undesignated, unspecified, unnamed, innominate, disclaimed, disowned, nameless, unacknowledged, disavowed, repudiated.

UNIFICATION, *n.* Union, alliance, junction, combination, incorporation, unity, consolidation, oneness, synthesis, coalition, fusion, coalescence, amalgamation, conjunction, confederation, cohesion, association.

UNIFORM, *adj.* 1. Unvarying, undeviating, unvaried, regular, constant, even, steady, monotonous, usual, tedious, customary, accustomed, habitual, normal, homogeneous, humdrum, reiterative, unbroken, smooth, equable, undiversified, jog-trot, regimented, of a piece, singsong, droning, repetitious, unchanging.
   2. Regular, even, plodding, unchanging, steady, constant, deliberate, rhythmical, metrical, set, mechanical, unbroken, measured, stable, consistent, unvaried, unaltered, unswerving, uninterrupted, systematic, methodical, orderly.

   3. Consistent, universal, agreeing, flat, stable, same, regular, in accord, orderly, in step, in line, standard, established, accepted, parallel, orthodox, conventional, related, correspondent, resembling, comparable, commensurate, proportionate.
   4. Agreeing with one another, alike, of the same form *or* character, equal, homologous, harmonious, symmetrical, identical, similar, same, consentaneous, consentient, reconcilable, compatible, congenial, consonant, conformable, at one, of a piece, of one mind, synchronized.

UNIFORM, *n.* Distinctive dress worn by members of an organization, livery, costume, regalia, regimentals.

UNIFORMITY, *n.* 1. Absence of variation *or* diversity, regularity, sameness, order, evenness, constancy, unison, permanence, continuity, stability, equableness, homogeneity, consistency, homology, symmetry, regulation, standardization, line, keeping.
   2. Agreement *(in form, character, etc.)*, unanimity, consonance, harmony, unity, accord, conformity, accordance, similarity, consistency, equivalence, sympathy, concord, rapport, keeping, line, union, correspondence, comparability, concordance, concinnity, approximation, affinity, congruity, congeniality.
   3. Wearisome sameness, monotony, routine, dullness, invariability, tediousness, humdrum.

UNIFY, *v.* Form into one, reduce to unity, join, combine, render one, unite, make into a unit, consolidate, coalesce, amalgamate, embody, mix, blend, lump together, weave, commingle, alloy, infuse, hybridize, mingle, compound, converge, couple, merge, coördinate, federate, synergize, confederate, ally.

UNILATERAL, *adj.* Pertaining to (occurring on, affecting) one side only, one-sided, undertaken *or* performed by one side only, independent, single, lone, unaided.

UNILLUMINATED, *adj.* Dark, unlighted, lightless, dusky, rayless, black, starless, moonless, sunless, caliginous, tenebrous, dim, shadowy, murky, gloomy, shady, dismal, somber, pitch-dark, pitch-black, pitchy, shrouded *or* clothed in darkness.

UNIMAGINABLE, *adj.* Inconceivable, unthinkable, incredible, unheard-of, unreasonable, fantastic, unlikely, contrary to reason *or* fact, implausible, incomprehensible.

UNIMAGINATIVE, *adj.* Literal, prosaic, pedestrian, matter-of-fact, practical, unromantic, unpoetical, barren, prosaical, commonplace, dull, flat, tame, humdrum, uninteresting, tiresome, tedious, vapid, usual, trite, stale, hackneyed, mediocre, common, stock, everyday, platitudinous, ordinary, dreary.

UNIMPAIRED, *adj.* Uninjured, perfect, sound, undiminished, preserved, unhurt, unharmed, intact, safe, undefaced, undeformed, unscathed, unchanged, unaltered.

UNIMPASSIONED, *adj.* Composed, calm, moderate, cool, deliberate, dispassionate, steady, rational, temperate, reasonable, self-possessed, self-controlled, philosophical, unruffled, collected, serene, imperturbable, undisturbed, unemotional, cool-headed, even-tempered, inexcitable, level-headed, tranquil, poised, sane, impartial, prudent, analytical, enlightened, judicious, objective, circumspect, impartial, unprejudiced, unbiased, stoical.

UNIMPEACHABLE, *adj.* Blameless, irreproachable, inculpable, perfect, above *or* beyond reproach, unassailable, unquestionable, unchallengeable, irreprehensible, faultless, ideal, excellent, consummate, pure, unqualified, unblemished, spotless, sublime, supreme, infallible, matchless, unexceptionable, unsurpassed, paramount, sinless, stainless, undefiled, inviolate, impeccable, highest, best, unexcelled, priceless, inestimable, superfine, unmarred, untainted.

UNIMPEDED, *adj.* Unchecked, unstopped, unconstrained, unhampered, unrestrained, free, unrestricted, unprevented, unhindered, unobstructed, unconfined, uncurbed, unbound, untrammeled, unreined, uninhibited.

UNIMPORTANT, *adj.* Insignificant, inconsequential, inferior, nugatory, piddling, ignoble, vain, negligible, worthless, idle, meaningless, light, slight, little, of no moment, of no consequence, petty, paltry, trivial, trifling, inconsiderable, minor, indifferent, mediocre, nonessential, immaterial, humble, not vital, irrelevant, evanescent, fair, inappreciable, meager, picayunish *(coll.),* superficial, ineffectual, lesser, depthless, shallow, slender, scant, below *or* under par, no great shakes *(coll.),* second-rate, subordinate.

UNIMPOSING, *adj.* Unimpressive, uninspired, unimportant, commonplace, insignificant, nugatory, ineffective, humble, inferior, slight, slender, little, inconsiderable, indifferent, mediocre, minor, inappreciable, meager, worthless, ineffectual, no great shakes *(coll.),* inconsequential.

UNIMPRESSED, *adj.* Uninspired, unstruck, unstirred, unexcited, inured, unmoved, unruffled, untouched, proof against, steeled against, unresponsive, unshocked, apathetic, indifferent.

UNINFLUENCED, *adj.* Unprejudiced, unbiased, impartial, unwarped, unswayed, unbigoted, fair, open, open-minded, even-handed, impersonal, conscientious, unjaundiced, unprepossessed, neutral, disinterested, dispassionate, just, equitable, liberal, unhidebound, undogmatic, persuadable, amenable, unopinionated.

UNINFORMED, *adj.* Uninstructed, ignorant, unlearned, unaware, in the dark, unacquainted, uneducated, unintelligent, unlettered, unenlightened, unapprised, untaught, unversed, uninitiated, unconversant, unschooled, green, nescient, a stranger to.

UNINHABITED, *adj.* Abandoned, desolate, unsettled, unpeopled, waste, untenanted, unoccupied, vacant, forsaken, deserted, lifeless, lone, lonely, solitary, unfrequented, isolated, depopulated, unpopulated, unvisited, barren .

UNINHIBITED, *adj.* Open, free, unimpeded, lax, loose, unrestrained, intemperate, unchecked, unstopped, unconstrained, unhampered, unrestricted, unprevented, unhindered, unobstructed, unconfined, uncurbed, unreined, untrammeled, unbound, unbridled, immoderate, unself-disciplined, incontinent, fast, abandoned, profligate, prodigal, lawless, rampant, uncontrolled.

UNINITIATED, *adj.* Uninformed, unskilled, inexperienced, raw, green, unripe, innocent, untried, ignorant, unacquainted, naïve, a stranger to, unused, unprepared, unseasoned, unaccustomed, unfamiliar, unconversant.

UNINSPIRED, *adj.* Unstirred, unexcited, unimpressed, unanimated, untouched, unmoved, uninfluenced, unaffected, indolent, indifferent, cursory, inattentive, unfeeling, perfunctory, emotionless.

UNINSPIRING, *adj.* Uninteresting, trite, banal, lifeless, common, commonplace, tame, flat, dull, dead, empty, barren, inadequate, devoid, insipid, arid, hollow, effete, inefficacious, meager, prosaic, wanting, insulse, lean, vapid, deficient, vacant, poor, weak, puerile, unsatisfactory, unsatisfying, colorless, otiose, unfruitful, stale, lame, infertile, inept.

UNINTELLIGENT, *adj.* Deficient in intelligence, stupid, dull, obtuse, unlearned, untaught, foolish, unenlightened, uneducated, uninstructed, doltish, bovine, oafish, sluggish, slow, slow-witted, lubberly, cloddish, ignorant, lumpish, dumb *(coll.),* uncomprehending, moronic, idiotic, imbecilic, dull-witted, thick *(coll.),* dull-pated, insulse, stolid, blundering, witless, addleheaded, addlepated, clodpated, numskull *(coll.),* simple, dronish, dense, asinine, vulgar, clownish, muttonheaded *(coll.),* beetleheaded *(coll.),* muddlebrained, shallow-witted.

UNINTELLIGIBLE, *adj.* Not capable of being understood, incomprehensible, meaningless, imperspicuous, inarticulate, indistinct, riddling, cryptic, crabbed, perplexed, incognizable, inexplicable, inscrutable, obscure, impenetrable, unaccountable, unfathomable, incoherent, occult, hidden, ambiguous, baffling, intricate, enigmatic, insoluble, puzzling, mumbled, confused, undecipherable.

UNINTENTIONAL, *adj.* Not done purposely, not designed, unthinking, chance, adventitious, incidental, contingent, side, involuntary, inadvertent, accidental, casual, fortuitous, spontaneous, unmeant, haphazard, unforeseen, unexpected, unconscious, blind, unwitting, unpremeditated.

UNINTERESTED, *adj.* Having *or* showing no feeling *or* interest, indifferent, unconcerned, not personally concerned *or* involved, uninvolved, aloof, detached, careless, regardless, Laodicean, disregardful, nonchalant, apathetic, pococurante, lukewarm, half-hearted, insouciant, incurious, unperturbed, blasé, cool, bored, neutral.

UNINTERESTING, *adj.* Dull, tiresome, dreary, jejune, flat, tasteless, trite, monotonous, prosaic, prosy, arid, barren, drab, dry, stupid, wearisome, tedious, boring, unattractive, slow, uneventful, devoid, insipid, tame, insulse, lean, vapid, uninspiring, weak, poor, puerile, unsatisfying, colorless, stale, without distinction, wishy-washy, characterless, sinewless, undistinctive, ineffective, unmoving, sapless, bloodless, insignificant, ordinary, mediocre, lifeless, commonplace, average, inconsequential, pallid, unrewarding, pithless.

UNINTERRUPTED, *adj.* Incessant, unintermitting, unceasing, continual, constant, perpetual, unbroken, endless, interminable, eternal, everlasting, solid, successive, consecutive, perennial, linear, ceaseless, sequential, progressive.

UNINVITED, *adj.* Unbidden, unasked, uncalled-for, unevoked, unwelcome, unbesought, unwished, unwanted, unsought, unrequested, unsolicited, gratuitous.

UNINVITING, *adj.* Unpleasant, unattractive, unsavory, disagreeable, unpalatable, unappetizing, distasteful, displeasing, insipid, unalluring, undesirable, unwelcome, unacceptable, dislikable.

UNION, *n.* 1. Combination, junction, coalition, conjunction, unification, incorporation, fusion, confluence, integration, cohesion, coherence, oneness, link, bond, symphysis *(Zool.),* attachment, coöperation, absorption, annexation, meeting, commixture, coalescence, alliance, incorporation, consolidation, synthesis, amalgamation, confederation, association.

2. Confederacy, league, alliance, merger, company, corporation, federation, convention, association, partnership, guild, club, society, fellowship, circle, body, congregation, fraternity, sorority, affiliation, consociation, camaraderie, amity, colleagueship, tribe.

3. Harmony, concord, agreement, concert, unison, unity, unanimity, accord, communion, amity, concurrence, sympathy, fraternity, congeniality, assent, amicability, oneness, accordance, affinity, acclamation, consentaneity, rapport, rapprochement, compliance, cordiality, consensus, compatibility, coöperation, one voice, brotherhood.

4. Marriage, wedlock, wedding, nuptuals, liaison, matrimony, match.

UNIQUE, *adj.* 1. Sole, single, alone, one and only, singular, azygous *(Anat.).*

2. Surpassing all others, unapproached, inimitable, unrivaled, nonpareil, unmatched, matchless, unequaled, unexampled, unparalleled, peerless, incomparable.

UNISON, *n.* 1. Concord, agreement, accord, order, consent, compatibility, chime, chord, beauty, melody, music, tune, chorus, cadence, polyphony, concentus, organum *(Mediev. Mus.),* collation, conformity, minstrelsy, sound, sympathy, uniformity, symphony, symmetry, unity, agreeableness, harmony, sweetness, blending, tunefulness, accordance, consonance, euphony, attunement, symphoniousness.

2. Agreement between things, ideas, people, *etc.,* consistency, suitableness, fitness, congruence, smoothness, correspondence, mutual fitness, proportion, coherence, propriety, accord, compatibility, harmony, affinity, fusion, consonance, agreement, connaturalness, homoöusia, correlation, conformation, adaptability, synchronization, congeniality, keeping, coincidence, concinnity, assonance, synthesis, amalgamation, organic totality, coalescence, aptitude, relevancy, conjunction, parallelism, apposition, integrality, concomitancy.

UNIT, *n.* 1. Member *(of a group),* item, element, monad, component, constituent, radicle, part.

2. Weight, unit of weight, quantity, *etc.,* measure.

3. *(Chiefly Military)* Group, squad, organization, outfit, corps, detachment, section, subdivision, wing.

UNITE, *v.* Coalesce, associate, amalgamate, pool, blend, mix, lump together, commingle, alloy, scramble, converge, couple, connect, marry, tie together, chain, band, link, merge, coördinate, join, league, federate, consolidate, confederate, agglomerate, synergize, hold together.

UNITY, *n.* 1. Peace, amity, friendship, agreement, accord, harmonious relations, harmony, tranquillity, amicableness, understanding, unanimity, concurrence, love, sympathy, fraternity, congeniality, communion, assent, amicability, oneness, union, accordance, mutual regard, rapprochement, good will, rapport, like-mindedness, brotherhood, compliance, cordiality, neighborliness, compatibility, fellowship, coöperation.

2. Composition from like parts, congruity of constitution, homogeneity, homogeneousness, oneness, evenness, identity, affinity, congruity, continuity, parity.

3. Sameness, sameliness, regularity, monotony, likeness, correspondence, uniformity, equivalence, connaturalness, parallelism, constancy, parity, consimilarity, alikeness.

UNIVERSAL, *adj.* 1. Liberal, latitudinarian, broad-minded, unbiased, unbigoted, unsectarian, dispassionate, uninfluenced, impartial, catholic, open-minded, unopinionated, freethinking.

2. Unlimited, infinite, unmeasurable, measureless, unbounded, uncircumscribed, endless, limitless.

3. Of *or* pertaining to the whole, general, generic, rampant, all-inclusive, all-embracing, world-wide, common, widespread, preponderant, ecumenical, catholic, predominant, prevailing, comprehensive.

UNIVERSALITY, *n.* 1. Generality, world-wideness, all-inclusiveness, predominance, comprehension, catholicity, ecumenicity, generalization.

2. Completeness, entirety, wholeness, whole, totality.

UNIVERSALLY, *adv.* Without exception, always, everywhere, in every instance, in all cases, predominantly, invariably, uniformly, comprehensively.

UNIVERSE, *n.* 1. Totality of existing *or* created things, cosmos, whole creation, macrocosm, infinity, nature, ether, interminability, illimitability, boundlessness, space, heavens, plenum, firmament, sky, empyrean, vault *or* canopy of heaven, macrocosmos, megacosm.

2. Whole world, mankind generally, length and breadth of the land, wide world, whole creation, earth, sphere, terra, globe, four corners of the earth.

3. World in which something exists *or* prevails, sphere, orbit, milieu, round, walk, ambit, circle, circuit, compass, bounds, area, beat, scope, reach, extent, range, span, limits, demesne, premises, realm, quarter, territory, region, zone, field, vicinage, latitude.

UNJUST, *adj.* 1. Not acting justly *or* fairly, unfair, partial, dishonest, dishonorable, prejudiced, warped, unreasonable, biased, prepossessed, one-sided, jaundiced, influenced, interested, uncandid, unprincipled, dead to honor, disingenuous, uningenuous, false, unscrupulous, deceitful, dirty, unconscienced, unconscionable, unhandsome, mean, crooked, of bad faith, venal, immoral, fraudulent, misleading, faithless, hypocritical.

2. Not in accordance with justice *or* fairness, partial, unfair, inequitable, unequal, unjustifiable, unwarrantable, undeserved, unmerited, wrong, wrongful, dishonest, unreasonable, unrightful, underhand, backhanded, oblique, one-sided.

UNJUSTIFIABLE, *adj.* Unwarrantable, unallowable, objectionable, wrong, indefensible, unreasonable, unjust, groundless, inexpiable, irremissible, censurable, impeachable, chargeable, culpable, guilty, reprehensible, wicked, blameworthy.

UNKEMPT, *adj.* In an uncared-for *or* neglected state, untidy, rough, uncombed *(as the hair),* messy, disheveled, disarranged, frowzy, dowdy, slouchy, mussy *(coll.),* slovenly, shaggy, wind-blown, disordered, disorderly, uneven, irregular, unsmooth, ungroomed, tously, tousled, careless, draggletailed, drabbletailed.

UNKIND, *adj.* Harsh, cruel, unfeeling, pitiless, unamiable, unfriendly, ungracious, unbenign, unbenevolent, unbeneficent, unsympathetic, heartless, unkindly, uncordial, uncomplacent, inconsiderate, brutal, unchristian, unmerciful, uncompassionate, rigorous, austere, uncharitable, inhospitable, disobliging, hard-hearted, ungenerous, callous, relentless, inexorable, inhuman, ruthless, stony, unpitying, unsparing, unresponsive, cold, flinty, uncaring, insensible, sharp, hostile, uninterested, disdainful, indifferent, unconcerned, cold-blooded.

UNKNOWN, *adj.* 1. Not within the range of one's knowledge (cognizance, acquaintance), strange, unfamiliar, new, unusual, unaccustomed, curious, odd, irregular, out of the ordinary, uncommon, exceptional, surprising, unique, out-of-the-way, unheard-of, unwonted, inusitate, freakish, fresh, foreign, different, novel, diverse, divergent, singular, rare, unaccountable.

2. Not ascertained (discovered, identified), unperceived, unexplored, latent, undeveloped, unrevealed, far-off, faraway, uninvestigated, unseen, concealed, undisclosed, unsuspected, untraced, untracked, invisible, foreign.

3. Obscure, unheard-of, unheralded, nameless, unnoted, renownless, unhonored, inglorious, unrecognized, unrenowned, undistinguished, ignored, incognito, anonymous, low, mean, insignificant, unsung, inconspicuous.

4. Mysterious, hidden, concealed, dark, secret, occult.

UNKNOWN, *n.* One who *or* that which is unknown, closed book, enigma, sealed book, mystery, x-y-z, virgin soil, unknown quantity, Dark Continent, unexplored territory, matter of ignorance, poser, dilemma, knotty point, vexed question, problem, query.

UNLADYLIKE, *adj.* Ungentle, unrefined, unseemly, unmannerly, uncivil, rude, impolite, ungracious, indelicate, inelegant, improper, coarse, rough, boisterous, indecorous, undignified, hoydenish, forward, bold, immodest, ill-bred, unfeminine, unbecoming, ungenteel, discourteous.

UNLAMENTED, *adj.* Unwept, unloved, uncared-for, unmourned, unmissed, unbeloved, unregretted, undeplored, no great loss, good riddance.

UNLATCH, *v.* Open *or* unfasten, undo, unclose, unlock, unbar, lay *or* throw open, part, unseal.

UNLAWFUL, *adj.* 1. Illegal, illicit, illegitimate, wrongful, nonlicit, nonlegal, actionable, unallowed, forbidden, undue, unauthorized, prohibited, unconstitutional, unwarrantable, unjustified, unchartered, against the law, criminal, spurious, fraudulent, outlawed, contraband.

2. Born out of wedlock, illegitimate, misbegotten, misbegot, bastard, natural.

UNLIKE, *adj.* Having no resemblance, different, dissimilar, variant, diverse, heterogeneous, opposite, alien, unconformable, irregular, varied, disparate, odd, divergent, contrary, distinct, ill-matched, irreconcilable, disaccordant, deviative, incongruous, unallied, discrepant, unequal, unrelated, not comparable, incommensurable, discordant.

UNLIKELIHOOD, *n.* Improbability, small *or* little chance, poor chance, poor *or* unfavorable prospect, not half a chance, long odds, inconceivability, doubtfulness, bare possibility, Chinaman's chance *(sl.)*, ghost of a chance.

UNLIKELY, *adj.* 1. Not likely, improbable, not going *(to do, to be, etc.)*, contrary to expectation, contrary to experience *or* fact, highly questionable, unsound, inconceivable, unimagi-

nable, incredible, unbelievable, unreasonable, illogical, implausible, doubtful, fishy *(coll.)*, uncertain, untenable, unsubstantial.

2. Holding out little prospect of success, unpromising, hopeless, unpropitious, unfavorable, ominous, adverse, disadvantageous, unlucky, unfortunate, untimely, inopportune, contrary, evil, ill, inimical, doomed, planet-struck, infelicitous, sinister, inauspicious, unseasonable, ill-boding, ill-fated, ill-omened, unhappy, awkward, discouraging, antagonistic, contradictory, conflicting, at odds, at issue, indisposed, evil-starred.

UNLIMITED, *adj.* 1. Unrestricted, unconstrained, absolute, full, unchecked, unmeasured, unconfined, uncontrolled, immoderate, despotic, undefined, indefinite, plenary, unqualified, total, arbitrary, unconditional, comprehending, encompassing, unbounded, unquestioned, unstinted, unsparing.

2. Boundless, unbounded, limitless, infinite, illimitable, vast, immeasurable, interminable, endless, immense, perpetual, inexhaustible, inexhaustless, universal, termless.

UNLOAD, *v.* 1. Take the load from, remove the burden (cargo, freight) from, unpack, unship, lighten, unburden, disburden, unlade, discharge, transfer, dump, empty, break bulk *(Naut.)*.

2. Relieve of anything burdensome, unburden, disburden, buoy up, uplift, ease, revive, alleviate, lighten the load, free from, disencumber.

UNLOCK, *v.* 1. Unfasten, open, release, unlatch, unhasp, disjoin, lay open, unbolt, loose, undo, disengage.

2. Open anything firmly closed *or* joined, relax, release, undo, separate, loosen, disengage, free, permit entry *or* passage, disconnect, disjoin, part, divide, unbar, unbind, unloose.

UNLOOKED-FOR, *adj.* Unexpected, unforeseen, unhoped-for, chance, sudden, unanticipated, accidental, startling, abrupt, surprise, unthought-of, unwonted, unfamiliar, unaccountable, subitaneous, unpurposed, undesigned, fortuitous, unintended, out of the blue, out of one's reckoning.

UNLOVED, *adj.* Disliked, hated, out of favor, unbeloved, despised, unlamented, loveless, lovelorn, forsaken, rejected, undeplored, unendeared, uncared-for, unmourned, unvalued, unpopular, crossed in love, jilted.

UNLUCKY, *adj.* Unfortunate, ill-fated, not having good luck, luckless, unprosperous, unsuccessful, ill-starred, hapless, unhappy, miserable, disastrous, baleful, unblest, jinxed, Jonahed, wretched, out of luck, woebegone, bereft, hopeless, under a cloud, clouded, down on one's luck *(coll.)*, thwarted, born with a wooden ladle in one's mouth, scotched, foiled, crossed, victimized, stultified, balked, woeful, forlorn, hoodooed *(coll.)*, born under an evil star, cursed, dashed *(coll.)*, infelicitous.

UNMAKE, *v.* 1. Cause to be as if never made, reduce to the original state (matter, elements), dissolve, disintegrate, annihilate, decompose, crumble, analyze, quench, snuff out, invalidate, put an end to, blow up, swallow up, devour, wipe out, abolish, do away with, exterminate, eradicate, kill, abrogate, obliterate, nullify, extinguish, erase.

2. Emasculate, deprive of virility, eunuchize, crush, separate, segment, cut up, break up, overthrow, dismantle, unbuild, dislimb, dismember, dissect, anatomize, mangle, mutilate, splinter,

decimate, powder, triturate, levigate, grind, bray, atomize, pulverize, comminute, divellicate.

3. Depose from office *or* authority, put down, overthrow, unseat, divest of power, disenthrone, discrown, uncrown, disestablish, displace, unfrock, dethrone, disbar, disbench, reduce, oust, suppress, destroy, ruin.

UNMAN, *v.* 1. Deprive of the character *or* qualities of a man *or* human being, bestialize, brutalize, blunt, dull, hebetate, callous, harden, deaden, vitiate, corrupt, brutify, deprave, degrade, debase, demoralize.

2. Emasculate, deprive of virility, enuchize, castrate, geld, effeminate, make effeminate, demasculinize, sterilize, alter *(coll.),* sissify *(coll.),* evirate.

3. Deprive of manly courage *or* fortitude, break down the manly spirit of, deject, make despondent, discourage, dishearten, disable, devitalize, depress, weaken, enfeeble, unnerve, enervate, unbrace, frighten, dispirit, grieve, sink, sorrow, sadden, appall, daunt, dismay, disconcert, intimidate, abash, terrorize, browbeat, horrify, terrify, wring, prostrate, stun, petrify, stupefy, make one tremble, make one's teeth chatter, make one's blood run cold, make one's hair stand on end.

4. Deprive of men, depopulate, reduce the force of, dispeople, abandon, leave unguarded.

UNMANAGEABLE, *adj.* 1. Not easily governed, ungovernable, unruly, refractory, stubborn, intractable, perverse, difficult, obstinate, uncontrollable, rebellious, indocile, obstreperous, impliable, wayward, unbridled, contumacious, recalcitrant, contrary, unsubmissive, lawless, irrepressible, fractious.

2. Unwieldy, unhandy, awkward, inconvenient, incommodious, cumbersome, perverse, untoward, intractable, refractory, obstinate, contrary, unruly, uncomfortable, balky, unyielding, ponderous, impliable, bulky, stubborn, resistant, inflexible, unbending, difficult *or* hard to deal with.

UNMANLY, *adj.* Not like *or* befitting a man, womanish, weak, childish, effeminate, feminine, cowardly, soft, timid, timorous, invaliant, uncourageous, faint-hearted, unmanful, chicken-hearted, sissyish *(col!.),* unvalorous, unheroic, fearful, spiritless, lily-livered, white-livered, pusillanimous, weak-hearted, yellow *(sl.).*

UNMANNERLY, *adj.* Impolite, uncivil, ungracious, uncourteous, rough, ill-bred, ill-mannered, ungentlemanly, boorish, unladylike, discourteous, ungentle, gruff, uncouth, disrespectful, uncultivated, misbehaved, coarse, surly, unseemly, bearish, insulting, crabbed, bluff, insolent, lowbred, crude, cloddish, loutish, caddish, impertinent.

UNMARRIED, *adj.* Single, unmated, unwedded, spouseless, lone, unwed, maiden, bachelor, husbandless, wifeless, celibate, virgin, old-maid, spinster, maidenly, companionless.

UNMASK, *v.* Expose in its true character, lay open *(anything concealed),* strip of disguise *or* mask, unveil, bare, disclose, uncover, reveal, uncase, unsheathe, undo, unwrap, uncurtain, undrape, unfold, unearth, disinter, unseal, divest, denude, dig up *or* out, bring to light, uncloak, make visible.

UNMELODIOUS, *adj.* Harsh, unmusical, unharmonious, dissonant, tuneless, inharmonious, discordant, absonant *(fol. by* FROM *or* TO),

diaphonic, untuneful, cacophonous, out-of-tune, off-key, off-pitch, sour, raucous, jarring, strident.

UNMENTIONABLE, *adj.* Unworthy *or* unfit to be mentioned, inexpressible, ineffable, shameful, disreputable, infamous, scandalous, unspeakable, unwhisperable, disgraceful, discreditable, dishonorable, shocking, ignoble, unrespectable, opprobrious, indescribable, incommunicable, unhintable.

UNMERCIFUL, *adj.* 1. Merciless, pitiless, unsparing, relentless, inhuman, unkind, cruel, inexorable, remorseless, heartless, unrelenting, ruthless, inclement, bowelless, unfeeling, unpitying, severe, uncompassionate, savage, unsparing, hardened, stern, brutal, callous, hard-hearted, stony, flinty, unbending, unyielding.

2. Unsparingly great, unconscionable, exorbitant, excessive, extravagant, immoderate, inordinate, fearful, frightful, whacking, whopping, roaring, thundering, outrageous, preposterous, monstrous, prodigious, gigantic, howling, huge, rousing, titanic, colossal, overwrought, overdone.

UNMINDFUL, *adj.* Careless, regardless, heedless, neglectful, mindless, disregardful, indifferent, absent-minded, unheeding, negligent, forgetful, unobservant, oblivious, reckless, thoughtless, unaware, blind, perfunctory, ungrateful, insensible, inconsiderate, remiss, unconcerned, unthinking, unreflecting, harebrained, unwary, scatterbrained, disregardant, lax, nonchalant, irresponsible, preoccupied, incautious, distracted, hasty.

UNMISTAKABLE, *adj.* Admitting of no mistake, clear, plain, evident, palpable, sure, manifest, obvious, open, unequivocal, apparent, distinct, express, signal, understandable, certain, conspicuous, unconcealed, discernible, bald, notable, unquestionable, lucid, undeniable, overt, perspicuous, glaring, recognizable, prominent, disclosed, undoubted, unmasked, undisguised, explicit, pronounced.

UNMITIGATED, *adj.* 1. Not softened *or* lessened, unquelled, unabated, unbridled, untamed, tameless, unsuppressed, unrepressed, unmollified, unyielding, severe, austere, unmodified, unreduced, oppressive, rigid, unbending.

2. Absolute, unqualified, complete, thorough, unredeemed, perfect, utter, sheer, stark, rank, bald, unlimited, unbounded, unqualified, consummate, downright, full, whole, entire, positive, veritable, plenary, out-and-out.

UNMOTIVATED, *adj.* Unprovoked, unelicited, unreasonable, unsolicited, senseless, reasonless, capricious, illogical, wanton, unjustifiable, unjustified, without rhyme *or* reason, unwarranted, groundless, unjust, ungrounded, incongruous.

UNMOVED, *adj.* 1. Steadfast, unshaken, obstinate, firm, unwavering, constant, unfaltering, unswerving, resolute, stanch, determined, stable, resolved, faithful, unhesitating, unflinching, undeviating, stern, steady, inflexible, strong, decided, sedulous, untiring, serious, unflagging, enduring, patient, grim, inflexible, indomitable, undaunted, settled, fixed, plodding, gritty, persistent, relentless, dedicated, devoted, uncompromising, tenacious, strong-willed.

2. Calm, collected, poised, undisturbed, cool, self-possessed, imperturbable, patient, quiescent, stoical, restrained, nonchalant, serene, placid, tranquil, level-headed, inexcitable, inirritable, unruffled, balanced, sane, even-tempered, dis-

passionate, unemotional, at ease, peaceful, temperate, undemonstrative.

3. Indifferent, insensible, hard-hearted, stony-hearted, unaffected, untouched, impassive, sullen, cold, stoical, unstirred, with dry eyes, unfeeling, cruel, unpitying, pitiless, heartless, unsympathetic, ruthless, merciless, implacable, unrelenting, stony, stern, inexorable, unsparing, callous, unforgiving, adamantine, apathetic, unresponsive, passionless, distant, aloof, hard, unsusceptible, unconcerned, unkindled, uninterested, stiff, unimpassioned, unimpressible, flinty, unsolicitous, indurated, uncaring, impervious, soulless.

UNNATURAL, *adj.* 1. Not proper to the natural constitution *or* character, contrary to the nature of things, unbefitting, unseemly, unexpected, eccentric, uneasy, unusual, peculiar, odd, uncomfortable, unconformable, unbecoming, irregular, foreign, uncommon, anomalous, aberrant, abnormal, exceptional.

2. Having *or* showing a lack of proper *or* natural instincts, heartless, inhuman, cold, unfeeling, cruel, evil, brutal, callous, unforgiving, insensible, insensitive, soulless, hardened, impervious, untouched, uncaring, stony, indurated, Laodicean, flinty, adverse, hostile, disdainful, unimpressible, cold-blooded, passionless, indifferent, unconcerned, frigid, aloof, pitiless, ruthless, unpitying, marble-hearted, insentient, savage, inexorable, relentless, remorseless.

3. At variance with the ordinary course of nature, strange, uncanny, monstrous, preternatural, queer, grotesque, prodigious, unusual, extraordinary, irregular, uncommon, outlandish, erratic, anomalous, rare, unaccountable, irrational, astonishing, wild, unaccustomed, bizarre, unique, out-of-the-way, unheard-of, fantastic, whimsical, inusitate, unwonted, aberrant, freakish.

4. Forced, strained, artificial, affected, stiff, stilted, constrained, insincere, self-conscious, feigned, labored, assumed, factitious, simulated, theatrical, mannered.

UNNECESSARY, *adj.* Needless, superfluous, uncalled-for, overplus, overmuch, surplus, unrequired, redundant, excessive, useless, inessential, dispensable, extra, spare, gratuitous, supererogatory, supplemental, auxiliary, extraneous, remaining, left, unused, unconsumed, leftover, supplementary, exceeding, accessory.

UNNERVE, *v.* Deprive of nerve (strength *or* physical *or* mental firmness), break down the self-control *or* courage of, unman, weaken, upset, discourage, dispirit, enervate, paralyze, enfeeble, unsettle, dishearten, deject, disable, devitalize, unbrace, sink, sorrow, daunt, dismay, disconcert, intimidate, wring, prostrate, stun, stupefy.

UNNOTICED, *adj.* Unobserved, overlooked, disregarded, unnoted, unseen, ignored, unheeded, neglected, unperceived, unregarded, slighted, obscure, surreptitious, missed, passed over, unwatched, forgotten, omitted, left out.

UNOBTRUSIVE, *adj.* Modest, retiring, unpretentious, humble, meek, shy, unaspiring, unboastful, deprecatory, passive, unassertive, shrinking, diffident, bashful, lowly, submissive, reserved, unassuming, unpretending, quiet, unostentatious, inconspicuous.

UNOCCUPIED, *adj.* 1. Vacant, not held *or* possessed, empty, untenanted, uninhabited, unfilled, abandoned, deserted, unpossessed, tenant-less, desolate, unpeopled, forsaken, unpopulated, depopulated.

2. Not employed, idle, inactive, loafing, disengaged, at leisure, free, resting, leisured, *(of soil, etc.)* fallow, unsown, unworked, untilled, uncultivated.

UNOFFICIAL, *adj.* Private, personal, informal, off the record, unprofessional, unauthoritative, unauthentic, illegal, unorthodox, unaccepted, unendorsed, unwarranted, unconstitutional, unchartered, unlawful.

UNOPPOSED, *adj.* Unanimous, uncontradicted, unchallenged, clear, free, uncontroverted, unhampered, unhindered, with free rein, unquestioned, unobstructed, total, entire.

UNORGANIZED, *adj.* Without organic structure, not formed into an organized *or* systematized whole, chaotic, random, unprepared, unready, unarranged, helter-skelter, disjointed, straggling, undirected, casual, aimless, unsystematized, unclassified, unfitted, loose, out of order, promiscuous, disorganized, confused, disordered, orderless, irregular, haphazard, unsystematic, unmethodical.

UNORTHODOX, *adj.* Heterodox, unconformable, unauthoritative, heretical, unconventional, eccentric, irregular, heteroclite, deviative, divergent, unobservant, nonobservant, nonconformable, wanton, stray, lawless, aberrant, anomalous, arbitrary, capricious, out of step, out of line *(coll.),* unauthenticated, unofficial, infidelic, nonjurant, unscriptural, unsound, uncanonical.

UNPACK, *v.* Undo *or* take out *(something packed),* remove the contents of, unload, unlade, empty, turn out, undo, discharge, disburden, unship, break bulk *(Naut.).*

UNPAID, *adj.* 1. Unrewarded, unsalaried, volunteer, gratuitous, unrequited, free, given, gratis, unremunerated.

2. Unsettled, in arrears, owing, outstanding, due, unliquidated, unsatisfied, uncollected, payable, ungathered.

UNPALATABLE, *adj.* 1. Savorless, vapid, untoothsome, dull, tedious, humdrum, monotonous, unattractive, uninviting, unalluring, unsavory, flat, tasteless, flavorless, undesirable, stale, dreary, indifferent, jejune, tiresome, wishy-washy, weak, commonplace, trite, prosaic, pedestrian, dry, uninteresting, unvaried, unimaginative, undiscriminating, stereotyped, platitudinous, vulgar, banal, trivial, tame, unimpressive, hackneyed.

2. Disagreeable to the taste, disgusting, nauseous, offensive, nauseating, unsavory, savorless, strong, unpleasant, disagreeable, inedible, uneatable, undelicious, undelectable, unappetizing, distasteful, unwelcome, unacceptable, sour, bitter.

UNPARALLELED, *adj.* Unequaled, unusual, unexampled, unmatched, without parallel, isolated, unprecedented, unparagoned, matchless, peerless, unique, unrivaled, exceptional, unheard-of, incomparable, rare, inimitable, beyond compare *or* comparison.

UNPARDONABLE, *adj.* Unforgivable, unjustifiable, unatonable, inexpiable, inexcusable, indefensible, irremissible, unallowable, unreasonable, unwarrantable.

UNPERTURBED, *adj.* Calm, serene, tranquil, peaceful, cool, poised, composed, unexcited, untroubled, quiet, undisturbed, halcyon, smooth, placid, unruffled, still, sedate, reconciled, philosophic, nonchalant, level-headed, unimpassioned, platonic.

UNPLEASANT, *adj.* 1. Unpleasing, displeasing, unacceptable, distasteful, repulsive, offensive, obnoxious, unlovely, unpalatable, unwelcome, disagreeable, repugnant, uninviting, ugly, grating, hard, noisome, vexatious, sickening, nasty, nauseous, irksome, pesky, painful, harsh, unsavory, thankless, uncomfortable, undesirable, unenviable, forbidding, uncongenial.

2. Disagreeable, ill-humored, ill-natured, ill-tempered, ungracious, churlish, brusque, sullen, crabbed, sour, rude, obnoxious, ill-mannered, sharp, abrupt, tart, acetous, surly, choleric, ill-bred, unmannerly, acerbic, irascible, grouchy (*coll.*), growling, sarcastic, insolent, uncivil, impolite, harsh, waspish, snarling, peppery, snappish, quarrelsome, splenetic, unamiable, unhandsome, boorish, perverse, ungallant, morose, spiteful, mean, discourteous, testy, resentful, loutish, curt, mordant, short, captious, thin-skinned, cross-grained, irritable, jaundiced, mordacious, saturnine, umbrageous, rancorous, contemptible, touchy, peevish, bilious, shrewish.

UNPOLISHED, *adj.* 1. Rough, unfinished, in the rough, uncut, dull, rustic, unvarnished, uneven, ununiform, unsmooth, unlevel, irregular, roughcast, rough-hewn.

2. (*Of speech, etc.*) Inelegant, coarse, vulgar, crude, ignorant, unaccepted, substandard, unrefined, tasteless, blunt, illiterate, uncouth, ungraceful, graceless, low, incorrect, undignified, offensive, improper.

3. Rude, unrefined, crude, vulgar, uncourtly, barbaric, unseemly, ill-bred, unseasoned, uncouth, uncourteous, ignorant, clumsy, churlish, unmellowed, undeveloped, uncultured, callow, unfledged, uncultivated, undisciplined, untaught, untrained, uncivilized, awkward, blunt, illiterate, half-baked.

UNPOPULAR, *adj.* Disliked, out of favor, unapproved, offensive, odious, unwelcome, uncared-for, unaccepted, unloved, hated, thankless, undesired, unvalued, offensive, odious, unacceptable, obnoxious, uncared-for, unbeloved, rejected, loveless, unendeared.

UNPRECEDENTED, *adj.* Having no preceding instance, never known before, unexampled, exceptional, unheard-of, unusual, unequaled, unrivaled, unparalleled, peculiar, first, unique, extraordinary, novel, new, infrequent, unmatched, isolated, incomparable, rare.

UNPREDICTABLE, *adj.* Erratic, irregular, uncertain, mutable, capricious, inconstant, eccentric, unsystematic, changeful, fitful, unsteady, uneven, spasmodic, variable, mercurial, aberrant, fickle, fanciful, discursive, arbitrary, unreliable, unreasonable, whimsical, vicissitudinous, desultory, wavering, unstable, unsteadfast, unmethodical, deviative, changeable.

UNPREJUDICED, *adj.* Unbiased, uninfluenced, impartial, just, fair, disinterested, judicial, unpassioned, dispassionate, unjaundiced, unwarped, unprepossessed, unswayed, independent, unbigoted, fair-minded, open-minded, neutral, indifferent, liberal, reasonable, undogmatic, tolerant, broad-minded.

UNPREMEDITATED, *adj.* Unstudied, undesigned, spontaneous, improvised, instinctive, impulsive, unintentional, blind, extemporaneous, involuntary, unprepared, accidental, automatic, impromptu,

offhand, unthinking, rash, chance, casual, fortuitous, improvisate, snap, unexpected, unforeseen, not meant, unpurposed.

UNPREPARED, *adj.* 1. Unready, inexpectant, napping, taken off guard, unwary, unguarded, unwarned, taken aback, unnotified, unaware, unadvised, unsuspecting.

2. Incompleted, premature, meager, sketchy, raw, crude, vulnerable, immature, unready, unfitted, unqualified, insufficient, unprovided, unfurnished, imperfect, deficient, inadequate, wanting, slight, skimpy, unorganized, defective, partial, fractional, unfinished, uncompleted, unequipped, untrimmed.

3. Untrained, unskilled, uninitiated, unpracticed, inexperienced, unqualified, inexpert, undrilled, unaccustomed, undisciplined, untried, raw, green, incompetent, ignorant, unfit, incapable, unable, unfitted, unfamiliar, unconversant, half-baked, unseasoned, unused, new to, a stranger to.

UNPRETENTIOUS, *adj.* Simple, unassuming, modest, retiring, humble, meek, unobtrusive, unostentatious, unambitious, unpretending, workday, household, plebeian, prosaic, homely, informal, everyday, prosy, ordinary, garden, common, commonplace, insignificant, lesser, mediocre, obscure, bourgeois, matter-of-fact, subordinate, undistinguished.

UNPRINCIPLED, *adj.* Lacking sound moral principles, unconscienced, dishonest, without integrity, faithless, false, disingenuous, fraudulent, knavish, unscrupulous, thievish, roguish, corrupt, crooked, wrongful, unconscientious, dishonorable, underhand, deceitful, unjust, untrustworthy, deceptive, unlawful, inequitable, unfair, treacherous, false-hearted, immoral, perfidious, collusive, hypocritical, double-tongued, two-faced, Janus-faced, wicked, vicious, bad, iniquitous, lawless, rascally, profligate, villainous.

UNPRODUCTIVE, *adj.* 1. Unfruitful, sterile, fruitless, useless, impotent, unprolific, arid, unyielding, unfertile, dead, barren, infecund, issueless, childless, teemless (*Poetic*), poor, dry, empty, bare, desert, fallow, acarpous (*Bot.*).

2. Ineffectual, inefficient, futile, otiose, useless, unsuccessful, abortive, unprofitable, nugatory, inefficacious, without effect, fruitless, stillborn, doomed, hopeless, jejune, in vain, worthless, barren, bootless, profitless, unavailing, impotent, inoperative, unrewarding, unremunerative, lame, dead, inane, empty, fatuous, effete, inadequate, null and void.

UNPROFESSIONAL, *adj.* Contrary to professional ethics, unbecoming to members of a profession, improper, unethical, undignified, unfitting, unbefitting, indiscreet, injudicious, imprudent, unsuitable, unseemly, unworthy, inappropriate, inexpedient, unscholarly.

UNPROMISING, *adj.* Unfavorable, hopeless, unlikely, ill-omened, unlucky, unpropitious, inauspicious, not encouraging, ominous, adverse, disadvantageous, untimely, inopportune, contrary, ill, evil, inimical, doomed, planet-struck, infelicitous, sinister, unseasonable, ill-boding, ill-fated, unhappy, discouraging, antagonistic, contradictory, conflicting, at odds, at issue, evil-starred, indisposed, inimical, hostile, malignant, portentous.

UNPROMPTED, *adj.* Spontaneous, gratis, unsolicited, freely given, impulsive, unpremeditated, natural, uncompelled, unconstrained, voluntary, unwitting, unthinking, instinctive, extempora-

hamstring, lame, maim, cripple, prostrate, paralyze, render powerless.

UNSETTLED, *adj.* 1. Not fixed in a place *or* abode, homeless, adrift, afloat, unestablished, itinerant, migratory, wandering, exiled, outcast, vagabond, unhoused, houseless, disinherited, derelict, unplaced, unharbored, dispossessed.

2. Not populated, uninhabited, unpeopled, desolate, abandoned, untenanted, unoccupied, vacant, empty, forsaken, deserted, lonely, unfrequented, isolated, depopulated, unvisited.

3. Not fixed *or* stable, without established order, unstable, perilous, hazardous, unsafe, unsound, infirm, evil, risky, alarming, precarious, threatening, ominous, portentous, menacing, unsteady, inauspicious, disquieting, grave, dire, arduous, serious, dark, critical, insecure, unpredictable, uncertain.

4. Liable to change (*as weather*), changeable, capricious, fickle, unstable, shifting, mutable, alterable, moody, protean, reversible, many-sided, changeful, inconstant, inconsistent, fluctuating, unreliable, vacillating, irregular, vicissitudinary, undependable.

5. Wavering, uncertain, fickle, unstable, unsteady, inconstant, irregular, shifting, fluctuating, not confident, irresolute, hesitant, infirm of purpose, vacillating, quibbling, unsure, timid, doubtful, unresolved, faltering, dallying, demurring, debating, pausing, shilly-shallying, hovering, wobbling, considering, seesawing, variable, halting, alternating, oscillating, equivocating, reserved, constrained.

6. Undetermined, undecided, pending, open, tentative, debatable, in suspense, drawn, doubtful, questionable, problematical, indefinite, vague, unfixed, moot, speculative, disputable, experimental, undemonstrated, untried, unascertained, unconfirmed, contestable, dubious, chance, random, unresolved, conjectural.

7. Owing, outstanding, due, unliquidated, in arrears, unsatisfied, payable, ungathered, uncollected, not adjusted (closed, disposed of).

UNSHAKEN, *adj.* Unmoved, unsteady, steadfast, unaffected, firm, stable, constant, obstinate, unwavering, unfaltering, unswerving, stanch, determined, resolved, faithful, unhesitating, unflinching, undeviating, stern, inflexible, strong, sedulous, decided, untiring, unflagging, enduring, patient, grim, indomitable, undaunted, fixed, gritty, plodding, persistent, relentless, dedicated, devoted, uncompromising, tenacious, strong-willed, undisturbed, calm, serene, stoical, quiescent, unperturbed, self-possessed, cool, tranquil, unruffled, balanced, level-headed.

UNSHEATHE, *v.* 1. Draw from a sheath (*as a sword, knife, etc.*), pull out, bare, wield, throw away the scabbard.

2. Bring *or* put forth from a covering, open, uncover, undrape, lay bare, disclose, reveal, unclose, undo, uncase, unwrap, uncurtain, expose, unfold, bare, set forth, unveil, produce, unearth, unseal, strip, divest, denude, unmask, uncloak, make visible.

UNSHELTERED, *adj.* Unprotected, exposed, unshielded, unscreened, uncovered, open, harborless, vulnerable, helpless, wind-swept, bleak, bare, undefended, unguarded, defenseless, stormy, expugnable, pregnable, whipped *or* lashed by every gale.

UNSHRINKING, *adj.* Unflinching, unblenching, persisting, resolute, indomitable, fearless, unabashed, intrepid, firm, determined, stanch, steadfast, steady, game, unappalled, unshaken, stable, faithful, resolved, unhesitating, unwavering, pertinacious, persevering, zealous, true, unfaltering, unyielding, undeviating, unmoved, stern, inflexible, unswerving, constant, strong, sedulous, untiring, indefatigable, unflagging, enduring, patient, undaunted, inexorable, fixed, intransigent, gritty, persistent, relentless, uncompromising, obstinate, tenacious, devoted, dedicated.

UNSIGHTLY, *adj.* Disagreeable to the sight, ugly, hideous, homely, unseemly, uncomely, unlovely, offensive, deformed, repulsive, repellent, forbidding, horrid, ill-favored, unattractive, plain, ordinary, not fit to be seen, unprepossessing, ungraceful, graceless, hard-favored, hard-featured, evil-favored, revolting, sickening, evil-fashioned.

UNSKILLFUL, *adj.* Awkward, bungling, inexpert, without dexterity, clumsy, unhandy, unskilled, inapt, green, unworkmanlike, incompetent, maladroit, lubberly, oafish, gauche, inexpert, lumpish, blockish, butterfingered, gawky, ungraceful, undeft, undexterous, inefficient, inadept, clumsy-fisted, heavy-handed, left-handed, all thumbs (*joc.*), blundering, amateurish, untrained, untaught, inexperienced, undrilled, undisciplined.

UNSOCIABLE, *adj.* Disinclined to friendly social relations, unfriendly, uncompanionable, distant, taciturn, solitary, ungenial, uncommunicative, inaffable, inhospitable, misanthropic, shy, reserved, retiring, unsocial, cool, cold, unkindly, hostile, inimical, ill-disposed, ill-natured, uncongenial, unamiable, unneighborly, disagreeable, ungracious, unamicable, unaccommodating.

UNSOLICITED, *adj.* Gratuitous, unwanted, undesired, unwished, unasked, unrequested, unbesought, unwelcome, offered, proffered, volunteered, voluntary, free, spontaneous, unforced, unbidden, gratis, complimentary.

UNSOLICITOUS, *adj.* Unconcerned, undesirous, neglectful, indifferent, cold, unmoved, apathetic, nonchalant, casual, cool, uninterested, unsympathetic, heartless, unresponsive, phlegmatic, distant, unfeeling, aloof, cruel, hard, hard-hearted, unsusceptible, frigid, unimpressible, passionless, lukewarm, neutral, untroubled, impartial, supercilious, unperturbed, unkindled, contemptuous, chill, inaccessible, unmindful, obdurate, thick-skinned, soulless, insensitive, hardened, obtuse, incurious, unstirred, untouched, uncaring, insouciant.

UNSOPHISTICATED, *adj.* 1. Artless, simple, unaffected, naïve, sincere, ingenuous, straightforward, natural, unstudied, candid, open, innocent, guileless, unpolluted, undepraved, undefiled, simple-hearted, childlike, undisguised, aboveboard, wholesome, incapable of deceit, direct, plain, rustic, undissembling, undissimulating, trustful, plain-spoken, blunt, downright, unpretentious, unassuming.

2. Pure, unadulterated, genuine, without extraneous matter, unmodified, uncontaminated, unmixed, real, true, fair, single, simple, homogeneous, flawless, undefiled, uninfected, clarified, unpolluted, unalloyed, perfect, unmingled, straight, authentic, untainted, undistorted, undisguised, uncorrupted, unqualified, uncolored, sterling.

neous, unguarded, self-directing, independent, self-determined, rash, snap, unforced, unstudied, unintentional, unconscious, involuntary, free, willing, unbidden, gratuitous.

UNPROTECTED, *adj.* Helpless, exposed, defenseless, pregnable, vulnerable, unmanned, unarmed, vincible, conquerable, weaponless, unguarded, aidless, naked, unaided, unstrengthened, open to attack, expugnable, unfortified, unfenced, insecure, unshielded, open, bare, surmountable, undefended, uncovered, unsheltered, guardless, unscreened.

UNQUALIFIED, *adj.* 1. Not having the requisite qualifications, unfit, incompetent, incapable, inadequate, disqualified, unsuited, ineligible, unadapted, unprepared, unripe, uneffective, unequipped, unready, unequal, inept, not cut out for, not equal *or* up to, unable, inexpert.

2. Not modified (limited, restricted), extravagant, excessive, exaggerated, sweeping, overwhelming, unrestrained, unsparing, unstinted, unbounded, immoderate, overmuch, lavish, exuberant, profuse, copious, disproportionate, uncalled-for, fulsome, superfluous, egregious, effusive.

3. Absolute, out-and-out, unconditional, unmeasured, limitless, unlimited, unmodified, arbitrary, utter, unbounded, boundless, full, unmitigated, unrestricted, unrestrained, unconstrained, unchecked, thorough, outright, unconfined, uncontrolled, immoderate, despotic, undefined, indefinite, plenary, total, comprehensive, all-encompassing, unquestioned, complete, entire, unreserved, undisputed, authoritative.

UNQUESTIONABLE, *adj.* 1. Beyond doubt *or* dispute, indisputable, indubitable, certain, sure, unmistakable, irrefutable, undeniable, clear, conclusive, obvious, beyond all question, self-evident, unimpeachable, evident, incontestable, irrefragable, incontrovertible, unanswerable, positive, undoubted, authoritative, manifest, dogmatic, unimpugnable, conspicuous, bald, patent, unequivocal, lucid, perspicuous, glaring, recognizable, prominent, plain, decided.

2. Beyond criticism, unexceptionable, unobjectionable, faultless, excellent, irreproachable, uncensurable, above suspicion, unblamable, perfect, flawless, unimpeachable, unchallengeable, irreprovable, unblameworthy, irreprehensible, unexceptional, quite satisfactory, perfectly acceptable.

UNRAVEL, *v.* 1. Disentangle, untangle, unroll, extricate, straighten, disengage, separate by unweaving, unwind, undo, unweave, untwist, comb, card, untie, disembroil, divide, part, dispart, unbind, ravel.

2. Solve, free from complication *or* difficulty, make plain *or* clear, explain, clear up, disclose, resolve, unfold, develop, decipher, interpret, understand, make out, rectify, unriddle, disembroil, decode, crack, do, work, work out, figure out, puzzle out, fathom, get to the bottom of, penetrate, see through, elucidate, define, enunciate, unknot, render intelligible.

UNREAL, *adj.* Unsubstantial, imaginary, artificial, nonexistent, spurious, visionary, fictitious, illusory, impalpable, intangible, false, ghostly, spectral, chimerical, deceptive, hallucinatory, maggoty, figmental, immaterial, incorporeal, castle-built, air-built, phantom, phantasmagorial, fabulous, idealistic, dreamy, cloud-built, imponderable, vaporous, airy, vain, romantic, delusive, gossamer, gaseous, uncertain, ethereal,

tenuous, dreamlike, fancy-bred, phantasmic, theoretical, impractical, counterfeit, Utopian, unsound, ideal, make-believe, sham, fancied, nebulous.

UNREASONABLE, *adj.* 1. Not endowed with reason, not guided by reason *or* good sense, unreasoning, hard to deal with, foolish, silly, irrational, stubborn, bigoted, biased, arbitrary, obstinate, fatuous, prejudiced, senseless, injudicious, stupid, fanatical, perverse, capricious, self-opinionated, opinioned, dogmatic, irreconcilable, narrow-minded, immovable, unbending, inflexible, headstrong, obdurate, unaffected, pervicacious, unmanageable, bullheaded, mulish, wilful, pig-headed, ungovernable, recalcitrant.

2. Contrary to reason, unwise, senseless, foolish, illogical, irrational, injudicious, ill-judged, ill-advised, unjustifiable, unwarrantable, nonsensical, impracticable, implausible, inexpedient, silly, absurd, preposterous, impossible, ridiculous, brainless, sophistical, fatuous, pointless, groundless, aimless, irrelevant, purposeless, untenable, unwarranted, unsound, self-contradictory, absonant, fallacious, ill-devised, incongruous.

—3. Exorbitant, immoderate, inordinate, undeserving, excessive, unfair, extravagant, undue, extortionate, overmuch, profuse, prodigal, effusive, fulsome, lavish, copious, unnecessary, needless, de trop (*Fr.*), uncalled-for, superfluous.

UNRECOGNIZABLE, *adj.* Indistinct, unintelligible, indefinite, undefined, unclear, indistinguishable, uncertain, blurred, incognizable, confused, unknowable, ill-marked, ill-defined, unfamiliar, distorted, changed, altered.

UNREFINED, *adj.* 1. Not purified, crude, coarse, impure, raw, unpurified, unmanufactured, in a natural state, unprocessed, unpolished.

2. Lacking nice feeling, taste, *etc.*, unpolished, uncultivated, rude, vulgar, boorish, gross, ill-bred, crude, barbaric, uncourtly, unseemly, unseasoned, uncouth, uncourteous, ignorant, clumsy, churlish, undeveloped, uncultured, callow, unfledged, undisciplined, untaught, untrained, unschooled, uncivilized, awkward, illiterate, half-baked.

UNREGENERATE, *adj.* Remaining at enmity with God, unconverted, wicked, impious, irreligious, godless, unholy, unhallowed, atheistic, infidel, sinful, unchristian, hardened, unsanctified, blasphemous, reprobate, unbelieving, disbelieving, profligate, carnal, profane.

UNRELATED, *adj.* Different, irrelative, unallied, unconnected, foreign, strange, isolated, irrespective, independent, disrelated, extraneous, unmatched, incongruous, incompatible, unconformable, not comparable, incommensurate, incommensurable, separate, differing, distinguished, discrepant, distinguishable, heterogeneous, disaccordant.

UNRELENTING, *adj.* 1. Not yielding to feelings of kindness *or* compassion, pitiless, inexorable, merciless, ruthless, cruel, hard, unpitying, stern, rigorous, unsparing, remorseless, rigid, severe, inflexible, stony, unyielding, vindictive, unforgiving, hard-hearted, unsympathetic, uncompassionate, relentless, implacable, heartless, obdurate, adamantine, unresponsive, indifferent, unconcerned, stiff, flinty, untouched, uncaring, hardened, hostile.

2. Not slackening in severity *or* determination, steadfast, unremitting, relentless, persevering,

incessant, sedulous, unwearied, indefatigable, unflagging, unrelieved, continuous, unintermitting, unbroken, ceaseless, interminable, endless, diligent, assiduous, unabated, continual, firm, determined, unshaken, resolved, unreserved, unwavering, pertinacious, unfaltering, unyielding, undeviating, stern, steady, unswerving, constant, enduring, patient, grim, indomitable, undaunted, intransigent, uncompromising, tenacious.

UNRELIABLE, *adj.* Undependable, not to be depended upon, untrustworthy, fickle, irresponsible, light, frivolous, variable, mercurial, without ballast, unauthentic, unauthenticated, unsound, treacherous, perfidious, insubstantial, shifty, double-dealing, two-faced, capricious, trimming, timeserving, slippery, deceitful, inconstant, changeable, unstable, tergiversating, wavering, faithless, false, precarious, fly-by-night, fallible.

UNREPENTANT, *adj.* Impenitent, hardened, obdurate, lost, profligate, abandoned, incontrite, recreant, shameless, irreclaimable, incorrigible, callous, seared, impious, habituated, seasoned, reprobate, remorseless, irreligious, profane, irredeemable, depraved, blasphemous, sacrilegious, unhallowed, unregenerate, irreverent, hard-hearted, unashamed, uncaring, inaccessible, recusant, hard-boiled *(coll.).*

UNREQUITED, *adj.* Unreturned, unrepaid, unthanked, unanswered, unrewarded, unremunerated, forgotten, unrecompensed, unacknowledged.

UNRESERVED, *adj.* 1. Full, entire, unlimited, out-and-out, unrestrained, absolute, unqualified, unconstrained, unchecked, unmeasured, unconfined, uncontrolled, immoderate, despotic, undefined, plenary, total, arbitrary, unconditional, comprehensive, all-encompassing, unbounded, unquestioned, unstinted.

2. Open, candid, ingenuous, frank, sincere, aboveboard, single-minded, plain-spoken, guileless, artless, undesigning, undissembling, communicative, easy, point-blank, inartificial, unaffected, natural, straightforward, honest, unvarnished, true, real, genuine, veracious, innocent, earnest, blunt, forthright, clean-cut, open-hearted, childlike, pure, unfeigning, undisguised, unsophisticated, unclouded, uncorrupted, truthful, outspoken, direct, simple, straight, plain, trustworthy.

UNRESOLVED, *adj.* Unfinished, inconclusive, unconcluded, unsolved, open, unanswered, indeterminate, undetermined, uncertain, unstable, undecided, unsettled, debatable, pending, tentative, in suspense, doubtful, questionable, problematical, drawn, vague, indefinite, unfixed, moot, speculative, disputable, undemonstrated, unascertained, unconfirmed, contestable.

UNREST, *n.* 1. Agitation, uneasiness, restlessness, excitement, fidgetiness, inquietude, disquietude, hubbub, perturbation, commotion, trepidation, trepidity, tumult, turbulence, turmoil, storm, bustle, disturbance, fluster, flurry, fomentation, ebullition, effervescence, ferment, stir, ado, pother, bother, stew *(coll.),* to-do *(coll.).*

2. Strong dissatisfaction, rebellion, discontentment, agitation, displeasure, dissent, nonassent, complaint, uprising, resentment, resistance, dissension, bad blood, uneasiness, difference, disagreement, disaffection, irritation, rancor, umbrage, annoyance, discord, asperity, disapproval, animosity, rankling, soreness, acerbity, acrimony, bitterness.

UNRESTRAINED, *adj.* 1. Free, capricious, skittish, whimsical, flighty, unreserved, unpredictable, unrepressed, erratic, undisciplined, wayward, wanton, fitful, fanciful, unconformable, arbitrary, lively, irrepressible, spirited, mettlesome, buoyant, active, vigorous, riotous, wild, immoderate, boisterous, joyous, saturnalian, rampageous, rampant.

2. Unburdened, unbounded, unhampered, unlimited, free, uncurbed, unconstrained, unconfined, unbridled, unfettered, unobstructed, independent, unchecked, unhindered, boundless, ungoverned, uncontrolled, unsuppressed, limitless, untrammeled, open, clear, free.

3. Intemperate, incontinent, lawless, inabstinent, excessive, licentious, wanton, voluptuous, light, loose, rampant, rampageous, dissolute, abandoned, wild, fast, indulgent, inordinate, prodigal, extravagant, immoderate, self-indulgent, profligate, broad, lax, libertine, passionate, effusive, fulsome.

UNRESTRICTED, *adj.* Unqualified, unconditioned, unlimited, carte blanche *(Fr.),* free, absolute, out-and-out, unmeasured, limitless, unmodifed, arbitrary, utter, unbounded, boundless, full, unmitigated, unrestrained, unconstrained, unchecked, thorough, outright, unconfined, uncontrolled, immoderate, despotic, undefined, plenary, total, comprehensive, encompassing, indefinite, unquestioned, complete, entire, unreserved, authoritative, undisputed.

UNRIDDLE, *v.* Solve, expound, explain, unfold, unravel, resolve, decipher, interpret, crack, enucleate, elucidate, disentangle, clear up, fathom, work out, make plain, translate, untangle, decode, unlock, find the key, penetrate, find the answer *or* solution.

UNRIGHTEOUS, *adj.* 1. Not upright *or* virtuous, wicked, ungodly, evil, sinful, unholy, vicious, wrong, iniquitous, depraved, transgressive, peccant, immoral, bad, guilty, infamous, devious, despicable, blamable, vile, culpable, profligate, villainous, unclean, errant, corrupt, profane, criminal, mischievous, degenerate, erring, wayward, recreant, reprobate, accursed, abandoned, nefarious, impious, defiled, peccable, heinous, flagitious, shameless.

2. Not in accordance with right, wrong, unjust, unfair, dishonest, iniquitous, heinous, inequitable, nefarious, unchristian, partial, unjustifiable, unwarrantable, unrightful, underhand, backhanded, wrongful, evil, wicked, immoral, bad, villainous, corrupt.

UNRIPE, *adj.* Not fully developed, immature, premature, crude, youthful, hard, green, sour, unprepared, unfitted, uncompleted, unfinished, wanting, raw, imperfect, sketchy, deficient, inadequate, half-baked, scanty, meager, half-cocked, unfulfilled, undone.

UNRIVALED, *adj.* Having no rival *or* competitor, having no equal, unequaled, unparalleled, matchless, peerless, unapproached, supreme, superior, transcendent, inimitable, second to none, consummate, flawless, faultless, ne plus ultra, priceless, unsurpassed, incomparable, of the first water, unique, unprecedented, unexcelled, unmatched.

UNROLL, *v.* 1. Unfold, open, spread out, undo, unfurl, draw out, expand, dilate, untwine, untwist, uncoil, unwind, lengthen, stretch, deploy *(Mil.),* broaden, enlarge.

2. Display, lay open, reveal, disclose, present, produce, manifest, flaunt, exhibit, bare, uncover, unscreen, uncloak, bring to light, divulge, unmask, unveil, hold up to view.

UNRUFFLED. *adj.* Quiet, tranquil, calm, serene, peaceful, equable, unexcitable, collected, untroubled, self-possessed, gentle, philosophical, unexcited, cool, composed, unmoved, undisturbed, imperturbable, level-headed, steady, inirritable, pacific, restful, orderly, reposeful, harmonious, concordant, patient, sober.

UNRULY, *adj.* Ungovernable, impliable, refractory, uncontrollable, wayward, unmanageable, unbridled, contumacious, recalcitrant, contrary, unsubmissive, perverse, lawless, irrepressible, intractable, turbulent.

UNSAFE, *adj.* Perilous, hazardous, dangerous, uncertain, risky, treacherous, unprotected, untrustworthy, insecure, fraught with danger, unreliable, unsound, unhealthy *(coll.),* threatening, ominous, menacing, portentous, shaky, tottery, unsteady, slippery, ticklish, sinister, hanging by a thread, unstable, built upon sand.

UNSANITARY, *adj.* Unhealthful, unhealthy, unhygienic, unwashed, unclean, unpurified, impure, soiled, uncleanly, disease-producing.

UNSATISFACTORY, *adj.* Not satisfying the desires *or* requirements, insufficient, deficient, disappointing, inadequate, unsuitable, undesirable, inappropriate, unbefitting, unfit, unworthy, unseemly, useless, unacceptable, exceptionable, objectionable, imperfect, faulty, poor, inconvenient, incommodious, unprofitable, troublesome, disadvantageous, inadmissible, ineligible, discommodious, inept, inapt, unapt, incommensurate, fruitless, displeasing, vain, short of one's expectations, not up to (below, under) par.

UNSAVORY, *adj.* 1. Unpalatable, tasteless, insipid, savorless, vapid, dull, tedious, humdrum, monotonous, unattractive, uninviting, unalluring, flat, flavorless, stale, dreary, undesirable, indifferent, jejune, tiresome, wishy-washy, commonplace, trite, weak, prosaic, pedestrian, dry, uninteresting, unvaried, unimaginative, undiscriminating, stereotyped, platitudinous, vulgar, banal, trivial, tame, unimpressive, hackneyed.

2. Disagreeable *or* unpleasant to the taste *or* smell, nauseous, disgusting, offensive, unsavory, nauseating, strong, savorless, inedible, uneatable, undelicious, undelectable, unappetizing, distasteful, unwelcome, unacceptable, sour, bitter, strong, revolting, rank, unpalatable.

3. Morally unpleasant, offensive, obnoxious, objectionable, evil-flavored, unpalatable, intolerable, disgusting, evil, hellish, peccant, rank, abominable, beastly, sickening, scurvy, infernal, infamous, revolting, evil-fashioned, devilish, base, putrid, insufferable, despicable, contemptible, nasty, foul, bad, tainted, opprobrious, rotten, monstrous, invidious, corrupt, heinous, ignominious, cursed, execrable, repugnant, loathsome, odious, abhorrent, detestable.

UNSAY, *v.* Retract, recant, take back, repudiate, revoke, recall, deny, disclaim, withdraw, eat one's words, disown, repent, renounce, apologize, back down *(coll.).*

UNSCATHED, *adj.* Unhurt, uninjured, unharmed, safe, whole, perfect, preserved, intact, unimpaired, unspoiled, undefaced, undeformed, scatheless, sound, entire, in perfect condition, safe and sound, unscratched, inviolate, unaffected, immune.

UNSCIENTIFIC, *adj.* Unsound, irrational,
scholarly, illogical, unreasonable, unsubstant
invalid, inconclusive, untenable, unproved,
philosophical, inconsistent, unwarranted, fau
ungrounded, groundless, self-contradictory.

UNSCRUPULOUS, *adj.* Unprincipled, conscie
less, lacking sound moral principles, witl
integrity, false, faithless, disingenuous, fraudu
knavish, thievish, roguish, corrupt, croc
wrongful, unconscientious, dishonorable, ur
hand, deceitful, unjust, untrustworthy, decep
unlawful, inequitable, unfair, treacherous,
hearted, immoral, perfidious, collusive,
critical, double-tongued, two-faced, Janus-f
wicked, vicious, bad, iniquitous, lawless, ras
profligate, villainous,.

UNSEASONABLE, *adj.* Untimely, inoppo
ill-timed, inappropriate, inexpedient, inapt,
timed, unapt, malapropos, awkward, ill-ad
improper, irrelevant, inapplicable, inapposit
suitable, infelicitous, unsuited, out of keepin
of proportion, out of character, out of plac
of tune, out of joint, unbecoming, impr
indecorous, inconvenient, untoward, illogic
correct, inadvisable, unbefitting, impertiner
to the purpose.

UNSAID, *adj.* Unspoken, unuttered,
nounced, unexpressed, tacit, unbreathed,
unmentioned, meant, inferred, implied, ir
suggested, hinted, untalked-of.

UNSEAT, *v.* 1. Throw from a saddle, un
displace from a seat, eject, expel, disloca
move, dislodge.

2. Depose from official seat *or* office, ur
disestablish, unthrone, reduce from dignity
ëminence, oust, humiliate, disenthrone,
from office, disbar, disbench, dismiss, bre
grace, humble, degrade, abase, lower, u
displace, replace, strike off the rolls.

UNSEEMLY, *adj.* Unbecoming, unbefitti
proper, indecorous, unsuitable, indecer
worthy, gross, uncomely, indelicate, unhar
wrong, untasteful, mean, distasteful, sh
churlish, loutish, boorish, discreditable,
one, unmanly, unpraiseworthy, reprehensil
reputable, undignified, ignoble, monstrou
crude, rude, coarse, unladylike, ungentl
ungenteel, offensive, vulgar, in bad taste,
place, out of tune, out of character.

UNSELFISH, *adj.* Disinterested, altruisti
denying, selfless, liberal, generous, high-
magnanimous, munificent, benevolent, cons
charitable, self-sacrificing, great-hearted,
ungrudging, lavish, beneficent, open-hanc
sparing, big-hearted, bounteous, bc
princely, handsome, humanitarian, eleem

UNSETTLE, *v.* 1. Render unstable, distu
order, disconcert, derange, upset, confuse
into disorder, agitate, unbalance, confou
ruffle, bother, fluster, convulse, startle,
put out, bewilder, perturb, discompose,
displace, make uncertain, unstring, stag
hinge, give a turn *(coll.),* throw off one's
bowl over *(coll.),* trouble, rattle *(coll.).*

2. Shake *(beliefs, feelings, etc.),* weaken
mine, derange *(the mind),* demoralize, sap tl
dations of, ruin, disable, thwart, foil, frus
disenable, disarm, enfeeble, unstring, exh
devitalize, debilitate, unsinew, enervate,
incapacitate, cut the ground from under

UNSOUGHT, *adj.* 1. Unasked, unrequested, unbidden, gratuitous, voluntary, unsolicited, unbesought, unwanted, undesired, unwelcome, spontaneous, unforced, gratis, complimentary, volunteered, free, offered, proffered.

2. Unpopular, unlamented, unmourned, shunned, avoided, eschewed, disliked, out of favor, unapproved, unloved, unaccepted, offensive, unwelcome, uncared-for, undesired, unvalued, thankless, unbeloved, rejected, unendeared, loveless, obnoxious.

UNSOUND, *adj.* 1. Diseased, sickly, unhealthy, feeble, ailing, deranged, unbalanced, morbid, infirm, weakly, unwell, indisposed, invalid, poorly (*chiefly coll.*), seedy (*coll.*), valetudinary, valetudinarian, impaired, decrepit, drooping, languid, tainted, injured, unsettled, unhinged, disordered, off.

2. Defective, imperfect, decayed, rotten, wasted, impaired, worn, poor, deformed, warped, injured, hurt, corrupt, unhealthy, reduced, effete, spent, deteriorated, exhausted, faulty, incomplete, inadequate, blemished, tainted, deficient, wanting, below par, second-rate.

3. Not solid *or* firm, unsafe, unsubstantial, shaky, decrepit, infirm, unstable, insecure, unsteady, rickety, tottery, teetery, built on sand, precarious, treacherous, perilous, hazardous, dangerous, risky, uncertain, untrustworthy, unreliable, slippery, ticklish.

4. Not well-founded *or* valid, erroneous, fallacious, illogical, invalid, faulty, hollow, false, wrong, incorrect, deceitful, sophistical, untenable, defective, unsubstantial, questionable, inconclusive, unwarranted, incongruous, ungrounded, groundless, unreasonable, heretical, flimsy, weak, feeble, unorthodox, unauthentic, loose, deceptive, spurious, poor, lame, illegitimate, worthless, mistaken, disputable, paralogistic (*Logic*), absurd, improbable, foolish.

5. (*Of sleep, etc.*) Easily broken, light, unquiet, uneasy, restless, disturbed, troubled, unpeaceful, agitated.

6. Not financially strong, unreliable, untrustworthy, bankrupt, insolvent, unbacked, unstable, on the rocks, precarious, insecure, unhealthy (*coll.*), shaky, tottery.

UNSPARING, *adj.* 1. Liberal, profuse, unlimited, abundant, plenteous, munificent, plentiful, unstinted, bountiful, generous, lavish, ungrudging, unrestricted, unconstrained, full, unchecked, unmeasured, unconfined, uncontrolled, immoderate, undefined, indefinite, unqualified, total, unconditional, comprehensive, encompassing, unbounded, unquestioned.

2. Unmerciful, unforgiving, inexorable, ruthless, hard, relentless, uncompromising, rigorous, harsh, severe, pitiless, merciless, hard-hearted, peremptory, arbitrary, inhuman, unkind, cruel, remorseless, heartless, inclement, bowelless, unfeeling, unpitying, uncompassionate, savage, stern, callous, brutal, unbending, unyielding, flinty, stony.

UNSPEAKABLE, *adj.* Unutterable, beyond expression, unmentionable, awful, immense, unheard-of, overwhelming, unimaginable, inconceivable, unnamable, preposterous, monstrous, marvelous, ineffable, inexpressible, indescribable, incredible, astonishing, remarkable, extraordinary, prodigious.

UNSPECIFIED, *adj.* General, undefined, indefinite, indeterminate, vague, anonymous, unfixed,

unsettled, unnamed, unacknowledged, undesignated.

UNSPOILED, *adj.* Perfect, preserved, scatheless, unharmed, spotless, fresh, unmarred, unblemished, unspotted, faultless, unimpaired, uninjured, undefaced, intact, safe, sound, whole, entire, unscratched, inviolate, immune, unaffected.

UNSPOKEN, *adj.* Understood, implicit, implied, unvoiced, unsaid, assumed, intimated, hinted, suggested, construed, meant, intended, insinuated.

UNSPORTSMANLIKE, *adj.* Unfair, unsporting, dissatisfied, malcontent, moody, disgruntled, dissentient, unchivalric, malcontented, ungentlemanly, unbecoming, disloyal, uncivil, uncourteous, rude, ungracious, inaffable, ill-mannered, ill-behaved, ungallant, unmannerly, unmanly, a poor loser *or* winner.

UNSTABLE, *adj.* 1. Not firm *or* firmly fixed, unsafe, infirm, insecure, unbalanced, overbalanced, lopsided, precarious, unballasted, top-heavy, rickety, flimsy, decrepit, jerry-built, pasteboardy, papery, gimcrack, unsubstantial, frail, fragile, unsteady, weak, tottering, tipsy, wobbly, perilous, hazardous, uncertain, unsound, shaky, built upon sand, slippery.

2. Liable to fall (change, cease), tenuous, infirm, precarious, weak, risky, unsure, doubtful, perilous, hazardous, wavering, in danger, unreliable, dubious, critical, ticklish, unsound, slippery, undependable, speculative, insecure, fallible, untrustworthy, uncertain, shaky, shifting, fluctuating, teetering, tottering, ill-omened, trembling in the balance, hanging by a thread, ominous.

3. Inconstant, wavering, fickle, unsteady, changeable, unsteadfast, undependable, untrustworthy, light, frivolous, irresponsible, variable, mercurial, unsound, treacherous, perfidious, shifty, double-dealing, two-faced, capricious, trimming, timeserving, slippery, deceitful, tergiversating, faithless, false, precarious, fly-by-night, fallible, undecided, inconsistent, unsettled, fitful, fluctuating, erratic, irresolute, vacillating, mutable, desultory, faltering, intemperate.

UNSTINTED, *adj.* Unlimited, unsparing, unstinting, liberal, lavish, abundant, plentiful, full, profuse, bountiful, prodigal, unmodified, unqualified, unbounded, unmeasured, generous, unrestricted, unconstrained, unchecked, unconfined, immoderate, unquestioned, uncurbed, unreined, excessive, unbridled.

UNSTRUNG, *adj.* Shaken, weak, overcome, unnerved, unsteady, spent, drained, oppressed, expended, debilitated, used up, haggard, played out, enfeebled, weighed down, enervated, emasculated, depleted, worn-out, exhausted, emptied, done in (*coll.*), hamstrung, unmanned, unsinewed, disarmed, prostrated, appalled, disabled, terror-stricken, dismayed, disconcerted, unbraced, dispirited, wrung, petrified, dejected.

UNSTUDIED, *adj.* 1. Unpremeditated, unlabored, unaffected, natural, spontaneous, impromptu, extempore, extemporaneous, offhand, undesigned, improvised, instinctive, impulsive, unintentional, involuntary, accidental, blind, automatic, unthinking, casual, chance, rash, snap, unforeseen, unpurposed, unexpected, fortuitous.

2. Unskilled, unversed, inexpert, untrained, untaught, amateur, undrilled, undisciplined, inexperienced, inadept, inapt, inefficient, undeft, incompetent, gauche, maladroit, green, unhandy, clumsy.

UNSUBMISSIVE, *adj.* Uncomplying, obstinate, refractory, disobedient, unmanageable, ungovernable, mutinous, insubordinate, unyielding, indocile, resistant, unruly, perverse, contumacious, impliable, uncontrollable, wayward, unbridled, recalcitrant, contrary, lawless, irrepressible, intractable, rebellious, stubborn, obstreperous, fractious.

UNSUBSTANTIAL, *adj.* 1. Not solid (firm, sound), fine, fragile, delicate, light, flimsy, frail, frothy, filmy, airy, thin, gossamer, shadowy, vaporous, subtile, elusive, tenuous, gaseous, uncertain, intangible, sleazy, gimcrack, will-o'-the-wisp, ethereal, dainty, gentle, attenuated, perishable, frangible, breakable.

2. Insubstantial, unreal, abstract, vaporous, visionary, imaginary, chimerical, vague, spectral, apparitional, dreamlike, imponderable, cloud-built, fantastical, illusory, ideal, bodiless, fictitious, impalpable, spurious, nonexistent, intangible, false, ghostly, deceptive, maggoty, hallucinatory, figmental, immaterial, incorporeal, castle-built, air-built, phantom, phantasmagorial, fabulous, idealistic, fancy-bred, phantasmic, theoretical, impractical, Utopian, unsound, make-believe, sham, nebulous, fancied, vain, romantic, gossamer, delusive, airy.

3. Unsound, unsolid, unstable, groundless, ungrounded, without foundation, fallacious, illogical, erroneous, untenable, weak, insignificant, slight, petty, paltry, unimportant, trifling, worthless, frivolous, idle, meager, foolish, inane, inconsiderable, negligible, ridiculous, indifferent, puerile, enervated, nugatory, passable, childish, airy, superficial, cursory, shallow, deficient, depthless, lame, poor, ephemeral, jejune.

UNSUBSTANTIATED, *adj.* Unconfirmed, unattested, tentative, speculative, experimental, unsupported, unsustained, debatable, doubtful, controvertible, refutable, disputable, equivocal, ambiguous, open to question *or* doubt, questionable.

UNSUCCESSFUL, *adj.* 1. Without success, unavailing, profitless, vain, futile, unproductive, fruitless, ineffectual, bootless, abortive, worthless, unremunerative, unprofitable, ungainful, losing, inexpedient, inefficacious, nugatory, useless, still-born, doomed, hopeless, jejune, barren, impotent, inane, effete, inadequate, inoperative, dead.

2. Unfortunate, unlucky, luckless, unhappy, unprosperous, infelicitous, ill-starred, hapless, cursed, fortuneless, unblest, jinxed, Jonahed, ill-fated, out of luck, bereft, evil-starred, under a cloud, thwarted, scotched, foiled, crossed, dashed (*coll.*), balked, stultified, poor, victimized, down on one's luck (*coll.*).

UNSUITABLE, *adj.* Unfit, unfitting, inappropriate, ill-adapted, improper, unbecoming, inexpedient, inapplicable, incongruous, inopportune, untimely, unbefitting, unseemly, unseasonable, inconvenient, incommodious, infelicitous, inapt, in bad taste, out of place, out of character, out of keeping, ill-advised, inapposite, disproportionate, inadvisable, incompatible, malapropos, awkward, irrelevant, ill-timed, imprudent, indecorous, untoward, illogical, not to the purpose, impertinent.

UNSUNG, *adj.* Not celebrated in song *or* verse, unhonored, unrecognized, unacknowledged, obscure, unheard-of, unheralded, unnoted, renownless, inglorious, nameless, unrenowned, undistinguished, ignored, anonymous, mean, low, inconspicuous, insignificant, unknown.

UNSURE, *adj.* Uncertain, unconfident, irresolute, wavering, hesitant, infirm of purpose, dubious, inconstant, undecided, vacillating, timid, doubtful, fluctuating, unresolved, unsettled, faltering, demurring, debating, pausing, shilly-shallying, hanging back, hovering, wobbling, considering, seesawing, variable, halting, alternating, oscillating, oscillatory, equivocating, constrained, reserved.

UNSURPASSED, *adj.* Unexcelled, unequaled, unmatched, unparalleled, matchless, supreme, superior, inimitable, peerless, transcendent, unparagoned, unexampled, unrivaled, unique, exceptional, incomparable, paramount, unapproached, second to none, best, consummate, ne plus ultra, beyond compare *or* comparison, alone, nonpareil.

UNSUSPECTED, *adj.* 1. Clear of *or* not under suspicion, unsuspicious, trusted, undisputed, uncontested, accepted, accredited, unquestioned, undoubted.

2. Not imagined to exist, unknown, unheard-of, unimaginable, undreamed-of, unconceived, unthought-of, unapprehended, unbelievable, unprecedented, improbable, original, unique, irregular, anomalous, freakish, foreign, novel, unwonted, unaccustomed, unmatched, exceptional, unaccountable.

UNSUSPECTING, *adj.* Unsuspicious, credulous, simple, believing, unaware, overtrustful, overcredulous, naïve, easily deceived, undoubting, gullible, confiding, trusting, off one's guard, uninformed, caught napping.

UNSWAYED, *adj.* Uninfluenced, unbiased, steadfast, unmoved, resolute, unprejudiced, impartial, unwarped, unbigoted, fair, open, open-minded, even-handed, impersonal, conscientious, unjaundiced, unprepossessed, neutral, disinterested, dispassionate, just, equitable, liberal, unhidebound, undogmatic, amenable, unopinionated, persuadable.

UNSWERVING, *adj.* 1. Undeviating, direct, straight, unbending, uncurved, even, true, unbent, the shortest possible, right, near, linear, unturned, undistorted, in a line, plumb, straightaway, virgate, fixed, steady, unflinching, unwavering, intent, steadfast.

2. Firm in purpose (resolution, faith, attachment, *etc.*), resolute, stanch, determined, stable, unshaken, resolved, faithful, unreserved, unhesitating, unwavering, pertinacious, persevering, zealous, true, unfaltering, unyielding, undeviating, unmoved, stern, steady, inflexible, constant, strong, serious, decided, not to be shaken, sedulous, untiring, industrious, unflagging, enduring, grim, patient, plodding, indomitable, undaunted, inexorable, settled, fixed, intransigent, gritty, persistent, strong-willed, uncompromising, obstinate, tenacious, dedicated, devoted, unswayed, unvaried, uniform.

UNSYMMETRICAL, *adj.* Asymmetrical, unbalanced, unequal, irregular, out of proportion, disproportionate, off-balance.

UNSYMPATHETIC, *adj.* Uncongenial, unresponsive, unbenevolent, pitiless, cold, uncharitable, unkind, unkindly, uncompassionate, hard-hearted, cruel, heartless, unaccommodating, mismatched, mismated, misjoined, ill-assorted, ill-sorted, unfeeling, callous, unstirred, unmoved, soulless, impervious, marble-hearted, unpitying, stony, inhuman, unmerciful, implacable, insentient, obdurate, unsparing, brutal, adamantine, frigid, aloof, distant, apathetic, cold-blooded, passionless, indifferent, unconcerned, uninterested, disdainful, hostile, unimpressible, flinty, indurated, Laodicean, uncaring, untouched, hardened, insensible, thick-skinned, iron-hearted.

UNSYSTEMATIC, *adj.* Irregular, disorderly, orderless, disorganized, chaotic, helter-skelter, sporadic, fitful, casual, planless, haphazard, perplexed, confused, broken, disconnected, deranged, anarchic, undisciplined, unmethodical, indiscriminate, desultory, random, promiscuous, undirected, straggling, aimless, purposeless, topsy-turvy.

UNTARNISHED, *adj.* 1. Pure, clean, fresh, sweet, wholesome, unstained, unspotted, unsullied, uncontaminated, unadulterated, undefiled, undefaced, clear, immaculate, flawless, perfect, unblemished, spotless, unsoiled, white, speckless, shining, bright, polished, unmarred, uncorrupted, unpolluted, fair, expurgate.

2. Incorrupt, unblemished, unpolluted, unvitiated, guiltless, uncorrupted, innocent, chaste, pure, unspotted, guileless, sinless, blameless, undefiled, unsullied, virtuous, candid, true, holy, virgin, unsoiled, spotless, immaculate, vestal, unstained, wholesome, clean-minded, above suspicion, unimpeachable, faultless, impeccable, inviolate, stainless, godlike, heavenly, incontaminate, righteous, inculpable, moral, clean, white, with clean hands, upright, inviolable, divine.

UNTAUGHT, *adj.* 1. Not acquired by teaching, unlearned, natural, native, intuitive, instinctive, unstudied, automatic, involuntary, spontaneous, innate, inherent, inspirational, uncultivated.

2. Not instructed *or* educated, unlearned, ignorant, uneducated, not scholarly *or* erudite, illiterate, unlettered, uninstructed, unscholarly, uninformed, unenlightened, unskilled, unread, benighted, inerudite, unschooled, untutored, unbookish, unguided, bookless, grammarless, uncultured, uncultivated, Philistine, lowbrow *(sl.).*

UNTENABLE, *adj.* Unmaintainable, indefensible, ridiculous, invalid, irrational, unreasonable, unsound, weak, fallacious, hollow, illogical, unjustifiable, insupportable, unsubstantial, defenseless, false, unsustainable, intolerable, baseless, groundless, untrustworthy, questionable, equivocal, debatable, controvertible, erroneous, refutable, open to question *or* doubt, contestable, improbable, unreliable, loose, feeble, poor, undemonstrable, unscientific, unphilosophical, disputable, suspicious, unwarrantable, faulty, spurious, unbelievable, self-contradictory.

UNTHINKABLE, *adj.* 1. Inconceivable, unbelievable, impossible, improbable, unimaginable, too much to grasp, beyond reach, beyond comprehension, disputable, incredible, controvertible, staggering, problematical, doubtful, questionable, hard of belief, hard to believe.

2. Not to be considered, impossible, out of the question, untenable, unworthy of notice *or* consideration, unachievable, unattainable, insuperable, unworkable, unsupportable, infeasible, impracticable, implausible, absurd, defenseless, insurmountable.

UNTHINKING, *adj.* 1. Heedless, thoughtless, unreasoning, inconsiderate, unreflecting, senseless, incogitant, witless, mindless, careless, unintellectual, unintelligent, irrational, blind, undiscerning, remiss, unwise, brainless, purblind, unmindful, regardless, reckless, inattentive, unobservant, negligent, neglectful, unwatchful, forget-

ful, oblivious, unsolicitous, slack, happy-go-lucky, unconcerned, abstracted, unwary, harebrained, uncircumspect, improvident, insouciant, unaware, indifferent, scatterbrained, insensible, not on the job *(coll.),* nonchalant, absent, fickle, irresponsible, preoccupied, distracted, incautious.

2. Indicating lack of thought *or* reflection, unintentional, casual, short-sighted, automatic, mechanical, rash, foolish, unwise, unwitting, irrational, instinctive, unconscious, spontaneous, inadvertent, imprudent, unpremeditated, undesigned, unpurposed, impulsive, accidental, blank, empty, vacuous, vacant, stupid, inane, senseless, involuntary, precipitate, headlong, loose, lax, harebrained, hasty, indiscreet.

UNTHRIFTY, *adj.* Wasteful, prodigal, dissipative, lavish, profuse, happy-go-lucky, insouciant, extravagant, unfrugal, shiftless, improvident, pennywise and pound-foolish, overliberal, thriftless.

UNTIDY, *adj.* Disorderly, slovenly, careless, unmethodical, confused, deranged, disarranged, straggling, chaotic, littered, helter-skelter, mussed, unkempt, unneat, slatternly, slipshod, aimless, messy, disheveled.

UNTIE, *v.* 1. Loose, unfasten, let *or* set loose, undo, unknot, disengage, liberate, unbind, unloose, free, disentangle, release, unlace, unshackle, extricate, unchain, open.

2. Resolve *(as complexities),* clear, solve, unfold, explain, set forth, unriddle, unravel, interpret, show, expound, explicate, elucidate, amplify, decipher, crack, enucleate, disentangle, fathom, work out, translate, decode, unlock, find the key, penetrate, get at the truth of, understand, rectify, disembroil, figure out, puzzle out, define, enunciate, unknot, render intelligible.

UNTIMELY, *adj.* Unseasonable, ill-timed, inapt, premature, unpunctual, immature, inopportune, mistimed, unfortunate, inconvenient, out of season, anachronous, inexpedient, ill-considered, inappropriate, unapt, malapropos, awkward, improper, irrelevant, inapplicable, inapposite, unsuitable, infelicitous, out of keeping, out of place, out of tune, unbecoming, imprudent, indecorous, untoward, unbefitting, impertinent.

UNTIRING, *adj.* Unwearied, unflagging, unremitting, indefatigable, undrooping, unfaltering, steady, steadfast, sedulous, constant, never-tiring, persevering, unweakened, fixed, firm, resolute, stanch, determined, unshaken, resolved, faithful, unhesitating, unyielding, pertinacious, zealous, true, undeviating, unmoved, stern, serious, inflexible, unswerving, strong, decided, not to be shaken, grim, enduring, industrious, patient, plodding, indomitable, undaunted, inexorable, settled, intransigent, persistent, relentless, tenacious, obstinate, uncompromising, devoted, dedicated, assiduous, incessant, unceasing.

UNTOLD, *adj.* 1. Not related *or* revealed, secret, hidden, unspoken, unexpressed, unmentioned, unavowed, private, mysterious, clandestine, occult, unknown, concealed, cloaked, veiled, disguised, unseen, unsuspected, suppressed, covert, undisclosed, dark, inward, unexposed, sequestered, withheld, invisible, undetected, imperspicuous, imperceptible, shrouded, unapparent.

2. Not enumerated, unnumbered, uncounted, countless, incalculable, innumerable, infinite, numberless, sumless, illimitable, indeterminate, indefinite, interminable, exhaustless, inexhaustible,

unfixed, undetermined, limitless, myriad, immeasurable, unbounded, endless, legion.

UNTOUCHED, *adj.* 1. New, unused, natural, fresh, unspent, unapplied, virginal, raw, unexercised, unessayed, unemployed, untried, unhandled, untrodden, unsullied, unbeaten, in a state of nature.

2. Unmoved, unaffected, unstirred, indifferent, insensible, hard-hearted, stony-hearted, impassive, sullen, cold, stoical, with dry eyes, unfeeling, cruel, unpitying, pitiless, heartless, unsympathetic, ruthless, merciless, implacable, unrelenting, stony, stern, inexorable, unsparing, callous, unforgiving, adamantine, apathetic, unresponsive, passionless, distant, aloof, hard, unsusceptible, unconcerned, unkindled, uninterested, stiff, unimpassioned, unimpressible, flinty, unsolicitous, indurated, uncaring, impervious, soulless.

3. Intact, unhurt, unharmed, uninjured, safe, secure, unmolested, scatheless, unimpaired, unspoiled, undefaced, undeformed, perfect, unscathed, sound, entire, whole, safe and sound, preserved, unaffected, immune, inviolate, unscratched, in perfect condition.

UNTOWARD, *adj.* Unfavorable, unfortunate, adverse, disadvantageous, unpropitious, unlucky, untimely, inopportune, contrary, preventive, deterrent, evil, ill, inimical, preclusive, evil-starred, doomed, planet-struck, poor, bad, infelicitous, hostile, disparaging, derogatory, unpromising, sinister, malign, indisposed, inauspicious, hindering, unseasonable, opposed, cross, ominous, ill-boding, ill-fated, ill-omened, ill-suited, unhappy, inconvenient, impedimentary, inhibitive, repugnant, noxious, awkward, at odds, conflicting, contradictory, antagonistic, discouraging, disastrous.

UNTRAINED, *adj.* Untaught, uneducated, undrilled, unskilled, raw, uninitiated, unbroken, green, undisciplined, uninstructed, untutored, inexperienced, unpracticed, ignorant, unlearned, illiterate, unlettered, uninformed, unenlightened, unread, benighted, unschooled, unguided, inexpert, bungling, awkward, unhandy, inapt, incompetent, undeft, amateurish.

UNTRAMMELED, *adj.* Unhampered, unchecked, unbound, unrestricted, unrestrained, unburdened, unfettered, unconfined, free, unencumbered, disburdened, disencumbered, independent, at large *or* liberty, loose, unobstructed, clear, liberated, unconstrained, foot-loose and fancy-free, uncontrolled, unshackled, uncoerced.

UNTRIED, *adj.* Not tested *or* put to the proof, not attempted, new, fresh, unassayed, virgin, maiden, inexperienced, raw, untested, novel, unused, uninitiated, naïve, ignorant, unpracticed, unskilled, unacquainted, unaccustomed, half-baked, unseasoned, unripe, green, unfamiliar, untrodden, immature, new-fledged, not dry behind the ears *(joc.)*.

UNTROUBLED, *adj.* Composed, calm, placid, imperturbable, unruffled, peaceful, serene, tranquil, still, quiescent, cool, collected, dormant, unmolested, unagitated, unexcitable, equable, smooth, halcyon, self-possessed, unmoved, level-headed, steady, unexcited, inirritable, pacific, orderly, concordant, reposeful, unvexed, careless, nonchalant, comfortable, carefree.

UNTRUE, *adj.* 1. Not true *(as to a person, cause, fact or standard),* nonobservant, out of line *or* step, contradictory, at variance, not corre-

sponding, at odds, disagreeing, inobservant, unobservant, deaf, blind, neglectful, negligent, heedless, careless, indifferent, inaccurate, disregardful, unfaithful, unmindful, lax, loose, remiss, slack, forgetful, respectless, disregardant, insensible, regardless, inattentive, erring, spurious, mendacious, false, faulty, defective, fallacious, perverted, distorted, sham, inconstant, unsteadfast, fickle, changeable, traitorous, unreliable, untrustworthy, undutiful, false-hearted, backsliding, disobedient, renegade, apostate, disloyal.

2. Faithless, false, unfaithful, perfidious, recreant, treacherous, disloyal, insincere, untruthful, dishonest, insidious, mendacious, uncandid, uningenuous, disingenuous, underhand, deceitful, two-faced, hypocritical, double-dealing, casuistic, Jesuitical, truthless, temporizing, timeserving, scheming, shifty, misleading, deceptive, artful, cunning, unveracious, untruthful, lying.

3. Inaccurate, incorrect, at variance with the facts, false, wrong, contrary to fact, unfounded, forged, erroneous, fictitious, groundless, specious, fake, spurious, unveracious, unattested, make-believe, peccant, dishonest, counterfeit, wide of the mark, distorted, perverted, sham, deceitful, deceptive, misleading, fraudulent, pseudo, mock, casuistic, Jesuitical, errant, fabulous, mythological, meretricious, impossible, trumped-up, mendacious, lying, truthless, untruthful.

UNTRUSTWORTHY, *adj.* Unreliable, undependable, fickle, irresponsible, light, frivolous, variable, mercurial, unauthenticated, unsound, treacherous, perfidious, insubstantial, shifty, double-dealing, two-faced, capricious, trimming, time-serving, slippery, deceitful, inconstant, changeable, unstable, tergiversating, wavering, faithless, false, precarious, fly-by-night, fallible, unstable, unsafe, uncertain, inaccurate, illusive, weak, questionable.

UNTRUTH, *n.* 1. Want of veracity, divergence from truth, falsehood, incorrectness, error, aberration, misrepresentation, want of fidelity, treachery, inveracity, falsity, faithlessness, falsification, lying, mendacity, sophistry, subreption, distortion, forgery, prevarication, counterfeiting, perjury, casuistry, Jesuitism, dissimulation, fraudulence, deceitfulness, subtlety, deception, imposition, imposture, duplicity, improbity, pseudology, fibbery.

2. Something untrue, falsehood, lie, evasion, fiction, fabrication, deception, tale, fable, myth, incorrectness, equivocation, fallacy, imposture, fib, deceit, error, misstatement, misrepresentation, invention, fraud.

UNTRUTHFUL, *adj.* Wanting in veracity, diverging from *or* contrary to truth, not corresponding with fact *or* reality, dishonest, truthless, dissembling, insincere, hypocritical, uncandid, subreptitious, uningenuous, disingenuous, dishonorable, misleading, questionable, crooked, corrupt, inaccurate, incorrect, false, wrong, unfounded, forged, erroneous, fictitious, groundless, specious, fake, spurious, unveracious, unattested, peccant, counterfeit, wide of the mark, distorted, perverted, sham, deceitful, deceptive, fraudulent, Jesuitical, casuistic, pseudo, meretricious, lying, trumped-up.

UNTUTORED, *adj.* Uninstructed, untaught, ignorant, unlearned, uneducated, illiterate, unlettered, uninformed, unenlightened, unskilled, unread, benighted, inerudite, unschooled, unbooked, unguided, bookless, grammarless, uncultured, uncultivated, Philistine, lowbrow *(sl.)*, untrained, undisciplined, undrilled, unpracticed, raw, green, unprepared, unaccomplished, uninitiated, artless, simple, unsophisticated, natural.

UNUSED, *adj.* 1. Not put to use, unemployed, never having been used, remaining, idle, new, untried, unconsumed, remanent, leftover, left, surplus, superfluous, unrequired, uncalled-for, supernumerary, over and above, fresh, unseasoned.

2. Unaccustomed, unfamiliar, inexperienced, unpracticed, new, strange, not habituated, uninitiated, unskilled, ignorant, unseasoned, unacquainted, untried, raw, green, a stranger to, a novice at, naïve, unversed, amateurish, unconversant, unenlightened, uninformed, new to, unwonted, ungiven to, unhabituated.

UNUSUAL, *adj.* Rare, scarce, uncommon, odd, strange, unfamiliar, queer, infrequent, extraordinary, noteworthy, out of the way, exceptional, seldom met with, singular, unique, few and far between, occasional, unprecedented, unexampled, remarkable, unwonted, unheard-of, abnormal, eccentric, peculiar, novel, unparalleled, unequaled, incomparable, curious, freakish, *outré (Fr.),* unconventional, bizarre, surprising, fanciful, anomalous, unnatural, unaccountable, inusitate, whimsical, aberrant, special, offbeat, outlandish, irregular, unorthodox, choice.

UNUTTERABLE, *adj.* Inexpressible, unspeakable, beyond expression, unmentionable, awful, immense, unheard-of, overwhelming, unimaginable, inconceivable, unnameable, preposterous, monstrous, marvelous, ineffable, indescribable, incredible, astonishing, remarkable, extraordinary, prodigious, incommunicable.

UNVARNISHED, *adj.* Unembellished, unadorned, true, simple, bare, candid, plain, unornamented, severe, pure, frugal, restrained, clear, flat, modest, blank, spare, chaste, undecked, unfurbished, unarrayed, naked, frank, overt, open, direct, barefaced, unqualified, outspoken, sincere, honest, unflattering, ingenuous, straightforward, blunt, undisguised, unreserved, unsophisticated, undissembling, artless, unfeigning, upright, guileless, veracious.

UNVARYING, *adj.* Unchanging, continuing, uniform, monotonous, even, smooth, constant, invariable, undeviating, regular, steady, usual, tedious, accustomed, customary, homogeneous, humdrum, reiterative, unbroken, undiversified, regimented, of a piece, singsong, droning, repetitious, rhythmical, metrical, consistent, measured, uninterrupted, systematic.

UNVEIL, *v.* Open, manifest, reveal, divulge, lay open, bare, disclose, expose, strip, uncover, uncase, unwrap, undrape, uncurtain, unfold, divest, denude, uncloak, make visible, bring to light.

UNVERIFIED, *adj.* Unproven, unproved, ungrounded, groundless, unattested, unestablished, uncorroborated, unsubstantiated, unwarranted, inconclusive, unsustained, disputable, controvertible, contestable, insupportable.

UNVERSED, *adj.* Uneducated, uninstructed, unschooled, ignorant, raw, unlettered, untutored, undisciplined, green, unread, rude, uncultured, inexperienced, untaught, unaccomplished, inexpert, unhandy, uninformed, unskilled, inefficient, untrained, blundering, bungling, awkward, clumsy, inapt.

UNWANTED, *adj.* Unwelcome, undesired, unlamented, unmourned, rejected, outcast, unwished, uninvited, derelict, estranged, unintroduced, under a cloud, under an embargo, excluded, unpleasing, ungrateful, unpleasant, thankless, gratuitous, unpopular, uncared-for, undesirable.

UNWARLIKE, *adj.* Peaceful, pacific, peaceable, peace-loving, gentle, mild, equable, clement, sober, amicable, friendly, kindly, inoffensive, amiable, neutral, noncombative, civil, long-suffering, tranquil, forbearant, forgiving, bland, unbellicose, unpugnacious, uncontentious, temperate, patient, well-disposed, conciliatory, slow to take offense.

UNWARNED, *adj.* Unprepared, unadvised, uninformed, unready, napping, taken off guard, inexpectant, unwary, unguarded, taken aback, unnotified, unaware, unsuspecting, ignorant, in the dark, unenlightened, unapprised.

UNWARRANTED, *adj.* 1. Undue, excessive, overmuch, superabundant, profuse, superfluous, prodigal, inordinate, fulsome, immoderate, lavish, uncalled-for, copious, supernumerary, overflowing, *de trop (Fr.),* unnecessary, needless.

2. Unjustifiable, unjust, unallowable, objectionable, wrong, indefensible, unreasonable, groundless, inexpiable, irremissible, censurable, impeachable, chargeable, culpable, guilty, reprehensible, blameworthy, heinous, unauthorized, improper, outrageous, inexcusable, wrongful, illegal, arbitrary, despotic, lawless, prohibited, unlawful.

UNWARY, *adj.* Heedless, careless, thoughtless, unmindful, reckless, regardless, headlong, unobservant, precipitate, negligent, neglectful, unwatchful, rash, oblivious, remiss, slack, happy-go-lucky, unconcerned, abstracted, hasty, harebrained, uncircumspect, unthinking, unreflecting, improvident, insouciant, blind, deaf, unaware, impulsive, imprudent, indifferent, disregardant, inadvertent, unheeding, indiscreet, incautious, preoccupied, witless, irresponsible, inexpectant.

UNWAVERING, *adj.* Unfaltering, unhesitating, resolute, firm, steadfast, unswerving, determined, intrepid, unflagging, steady, indefatigable, stanch, fixed, stable, unshaken, resolved, faithful, unreserved, pertinacious, persevering, zealous, true, unyielding, undeviating, unmoved, stern, inflexible, constant, strong, serious, decided, not to be shaken, sedulous, untiring, industrious, enduring, patient, grim, plodding, indomitable, undaunted, inexorable, settled, intransigent, persistent, relentless, strong-willed, uncompromising, obstinate, tenacious, dedicated, devoted, incessant, unremitting, unceasing.

UNWELCOME, *adj.* Unwanted, unwished, unpleasing, displeasing, thankless, gratuitous, unacceptable, undesirable, unpleasant, disagreeable, uncared-for, unpopular, ungrateful, outcast, rejected, uninvited, unintroduced, excluded.

UNWELL, *adj.* Ill, ailing, indisposed, sick, sickly *(coll.),* diseased, unhealthy, delicate, laid up, infirm, afflicted, qualmish, valetudinary, suffering, invalid, queasy, nauseated, valetudinarian, under the weather *(coll.),* seedy *(coll.),* poorly *(coll.).*

UNWHOLESOME, *adj.* 1. Deleterious to health *or* well-being, unhealthy, unhealthful, injurious, insalubrious, noxious, noisome, innutritious, indigestible, poisonous, morbific, morbiferous, detrimental, unhygienic, prejudicial, pernicious, venomous, pestilential, pestiferous, malevolent, unsanitary, bad, deadly, hurtful, harmful, baneful, toxic, septic.

2. Deleterious to moral health *or* well-being, pernicious, corrupting, unsound, injurious, demoralizing, immoral, evil, vitiating, degrading,

depraving, sinful, vicious, mortal, deadly, ruinous, destructive, undesirable, dangerous, perilous, in question, questionable, doubtful, dubious, dishonorable, polluting, contaminating, foul, filthy, dirty, ominous, destructive of character, tainted, hazardous.

3. Not sound in health, unhealthy (*esp. in appearance*), suggestive of disease, pale, ghostly, morbid, tainted, moribund, anemic, impaired, unwell, sickly (*coll.*), ailing, languid, drooping, decrepit, weak, feeble, seedy (*coll.*), poorly (*coll.*), invalid, valetudinary, valetudinarian.

UNWIELDY, *adj.* Unmanageable, unhandy, awkward, inconvenient, incommodious, cumbersome, perverse, untoward, intractable, refractory, obstinate, contrary, unruly, uncomfortable, balky, unyielding, ponderous, impliable, stubborn, resistant, heavy, inflexible, unbending, difficult *or* hard to deal with, burdensome, cumbrous, weighty, big, large, substantial, massive, dense, portly, corpulent, hefty (*coll.*).

UNWILLING, *adj.* Loath, reluctant, disinclined, grudging, forced, dissenting, dissentient, negative, refractory, renitent, shrinking, demurring, contrary, restive, constrained, involuntary, resistant, refusing, recalcitrant, not content, not in the mood *or* vein, recusant, unconsenting, rejective, declinatory, uncomplaisant, unacquiescent, averse, opposed, backward, indisposed.

UNWIND, *v.* Wind off, undo, separate, loose, unroll, uncoil, untwist, unravel, untwine, unreel, disentangle, unwrap.

UNWISE, *adj.* Foolish, injudicious, imprudent, senseless, stupid, ill-considered, absurd, unintelligent, ill-managed, short-sighted, ill-advised, silly, brainless, impolitic, unreasonable, indiscreet, unwary, inexpedient, irrational, idiotic, fatuous, inappropriate, inapplicable, incongruous, illogical, foolhardy, harebrained, crazy (*coll.*), irresponsible, madcap, witless, inane, reckless, flighty, giddy.

UNWITTING, *adj.* Not knowing, unconscious, ignorant, unaware, unintentional, inadvertent, undesigned, unknowing, thoughtless, unthinking, unpurposed, chance, adventitious, incidental, contingent, involuntary, accidental, casual, fortuitous, unmeant, unexpected, blind, unpremeditated

UNWONTED, *adj.* 1. Unaccustomed, unused, unfamiliar, inexperienced, unpracticed, new, strange, not habituated, uninitiated, unskilled, ignorant, unseasoned, unacquainted, untried, raw, green, a stranger to, naïve, unversed, unconversant, unenlightened, uninformed, new to, ungiven to, unhabituated.

2. Not customary (habitual, usual), unusual, rare, uncommon, infrequent, odd, strange, unfamiliar, queer, extraordinary, noteworthy, out-of-the-way, exceptional, seldom met with, singular, unique, occasional, unprecedented, unexampled, remarkable, unheard-of, abnormal, eccentric, peculiar, novel, unparalleled, unequaled, incomparable, curious, freakish, unconventional, bizarre, surprising, fanciful, anomalous, unnatural, unaccountable, outré (*Fr.*), inusitate, aberrant, offbeat, outlandish, irregular, unorthodox.

UNWORLDLY, *adj.* 1. Not seeking material advantage *or* gain, pious, righteous, spiritual, moral, ethical, devout, holy, solemn, pure, reverent, religious, worshipful, heavenly-minded, virtuous, believing, godlike, godly.

2. Not terrestrial, unearthly, not of this world, phantom, extramundane, eerie, disembodied, in-

corporeal, spiritual, spectral, ghostly, occult, supernatural, preternatural, wraithlike, weird, immaterial, bodiless, uncanny, unsubstantial, supersensible, psychical, transcendental, superphysical, supramundane, ethereal, metaphysical.

UNWORTHY, *adj.* 1. Lacking worth *or* excellence, inferior, paltry, pitiful, poor, worthless, bad, base, sorry, contemptible, cheap, scurvy, niggardly, mean, shabby, despicable, wretched, meager, beggarly, dismal, pitiable.

2. Not commendable *or* creditable, dishonorable, unhandsome, despicable, mean, contemptible, shameful, reprehensible, derogatory, small, objectionable, exceptionable, ignoble, unpraiseworthy, blameworthy, discreditable, disreputable, illaudable, uncommendable, ungenerous, illiberal, churlish, sordid, stinting.

3. (*With OF*) Unbecoming, of a kind not worthy, beneath the dignity of, unsuitable, unapt, inappropriate, unsuited, unfitted, inapposite, untimely, malapropos, awkward, inapplicable, irrelevant, inopportune, ill-adapted, ill-timed, unseasonable, improper, infelicitous, out of keeping, out of character, out of place, out of tune, imprudent, indecorous, inconvenient, untoward, incorrect, illogical, inexpedient, inadvisable, ill-advised, unbefitting, impertinent, not to the purpose.

4. Undeserving, not of adequate merit *or* character, unfit, ineligible, unmeriting, unqualified, inadequate, unprepared, unready, unequal, disqualified.

UNWRAP, *v.* Unfold, open, spread, release, unroll, unfurl, expand, undo, display, untie, unwind, extend, untwist, untwine, uncoil, stretch, lengthen.

UNWRITTEN, *adj.* 1. Not reduced to writing, verbal, unrecorded, word-of-mouth, vocal, oral, unregistered, nuncupative (*of will, etc.*), parol (*Law*), acroamatic.

2. Not actually formulated *or* expressed, oral, traditional, unpublished, taken for granted, customary, verbal, traditive, prescriptive, immemorial, rooted, inveterate, unsaid, untold, vocal, unmentioned, unarticulated, traditionary.

UNYIELDING, *adj.* 1. Unbending, stiff, hard, firm, immovable, implastic, relentless, adamantine, stubborn, rigid, inflexible, implacable, unchangeable, straight, impliant, obstinate, set, fixed, inelastic, unlimber, tense, stark, immobile, petrified, ossified, congealed, inductile, wooden.

2. Unmanageable, headstrong, perverse, stubborn, resistant, obstinate, willful, self-willed, intractable, unmalleable, pervicacious, unimpressible, obdurate, mulish, unbending, inflexible, uninfluenced, unmovable, refractory, bullheaded, pigheaded, opinionated, uncontrollable, bulletheaded (*coll.*), ungovernable, recalcitrant, bigoted, uncompliant, adamant, unreasonable.

3. Steadfast, uncompromising, unwavering, determined, tenacious, stanch, pertinacious, resolute, inflexible, constant, steady, unchanging, firm, stable, unshaken, faithful, unreserved, unhesitating, persevering, zealous, true, unfaltering, undeviating, unswerving, stern, strong, serious, decided, sedulous, untiring, industrious, unflagging, enduring, patient, grim, plodding, indomitable, undaunted, settled, intransigent, fixed, gritty, persistent, relentless, strong-willed, obstinate, dedicated, devoted.

UPBRAID, *v.* Reproach (*for a fault or offense*), reprove sternly, chide, blame, find fault with, lash, trounce, reprimand, rebuke, censure, berate, rail at, revile, accuse, denounce, overhaul, set down, scold, remonstrate, castigate, take down, take up, reprehend, exprobrate, execrate, have words with, correct, bring *or* call to account *or* order, rate, objurgate, admonish, vilify, vituperate, bawl out *(coll.)*, pick *or* pluck a crow with, roast *(sl.)*, rake *or* haul over the coals *(coll.)*, tongue-lash.

UPBRINGING, *n.* Bringing up of a person from childhood, rearing, care and training of the young, cultivation, nurture, training, breeding.

UPCOUNTRY, *adj.* 1. Being *or* living remote from the coast *or* border, interior, inland.

2. *(Derog.)* Unsophisticated, rustic, countrified, country, provincial, bucolic, upland, uplandish, uncouth, rural, inurbane, backwoods, backcountry, uncultivated, cloddish, clodhopping, churlish, rough-hewn, roughcast, rough, doltish, uncivilized, coarse, loutish, rude, unrefined.

UPGRADE, *n.* Incline *(going up in the direction of movement)*, rise, rising, ascent, acclivity, slope, hill, climb, grade, rising ground *or* grade, uphill, uplift, upgo, upclimb, upway.

UPGROWTH, *n.* 1. Process of growing up, development, budding, sprouting, expansion, increase, extension, heightening, burgeoning, enlargement.

2. Something that grows up, shoot, twig, branch, sprout, switch, tendril, stem, sprig, scion, offshoot, sucker *(Bot.)*, burgeon, sarmentum *(Bot.)*.

UPHEAVAL, *n.* Outburst, outbreak, convulsion, eruption, disruption, confusion, upcast, upthrust, rout, debacle, catastrophe, blowup, breakup, breakdown, collapse, explosion, quake, earthquake, volcano.

UPHEAVE, *v.* 1. Raise up *or* aloft, lift up, heave up, uprear, uplift, boost, sublevate, erect, pitch, rear, hoist, uphoist, upcast, upthrow, upend.

2. Shake, discompose, agitate, disturb, convulse, quake, toss, rock, unsettle, disorder, stagger, undermine, perturb, disquiet, perturbate, rattle, jolt, jar, rouse, excite, ruffle, startle, move, frighten, foment.

3. Be lifted up, rise as if thrust up, burst, break out, explode, blow out *or* up, heave, upleap, upturn, spring up, shoot up, erupt, buckle, warp, swell, rear, tilt up, lever, bulge, bilge, bouge, vault, arch.

UPHILL, *adj.* 1. Going *or* tending upward on *or* as on a hill, upward, ascending, rising, uprising, acclivitous, acclivous, acclinate.

2. At a high place *or* point, high, eminent, exalted, elevated, superior, lofty, prominent, towering, soaring, cloud-topped, cloud-capped, cloud-kissing, sky-high, skyscraping.

3. Laboriously fatiguing, heavy, arduous, wearisome, tiresome, bearing hard, burdensome, onerous, grievous, afflictive, intolerable, unbearable, severe, cruel, hard, difficult, wearying, trying, oppressive, toilsome, wearing, operose, tough, strenuous, rugged, formidable, exhausting, taxing, exacting, spiny, thorny, untoward.

UPHOLD, *v.* 1. Hold up, upbear, raise, elevate, support, sustain, bear up, carry, shoulder, shore up, bolster up, prop, brace, stay, buttress, underprop, underbrace, underpin, underset.

2. Support, espouse, sustain, maintain, defend, speak for, stand up for, contend for, advocate, back, help, protect, aid, guard, justify, assist, battle for, vindicate, champion, countenance, acknowledge, second, endorse, confirm, stand by,

demonstrate, corroborate, approve, preserve, encourage.

UPKEEP, *n.* 1. Keeping in operation (due condition, repair), maintenance, support, sustainment, sustenance, conservation, preservation, safekeeping.

2. Cost of maintenance, running expenses.

UPLAND, *n.* High land, elevated region, promontory, crest, heights, peak, pinnacle, summit, watershed, table, tableland, down, plateau, divide, crag, point, ridge, range, spine.

UPLIFT, *n.* 1. Act of lifting up *or* raising, elevation, upheaval, support, sustainment, sustentation, sustention, sustenance.

2. Raising socially *or* morally, improvement, melioration, betterment, edification, amelioration, rehabilitation, reclamation, amendment, furtherance, refinement, cultivation, enrichment, enhancement.

3. Emotional *or* spiritual exaltation, inspiration, excitation, awakening, stirring, thrill, kindling, illumination, intoxication, encouragement, quickening, animation, stimulation, fervor, exhilaration, transport, heat, fever, fire, flame.

UPLIFT, *v.* 1. Lift up, upbear, upraise, raise, elevate, lift aloft, hoist, heave, uprear, heighten, boost, sublevate.

2. Raise socially *or* morally, edify, elevate, improve, refine, better, meliorate, ameliorate, advance, cultivate, forward, emend, emendate, benefit, help, civilize.

3. Exalt emotionally *or* spiritually, inspire, inspirit, animate, buoy up, cheer, gladden, elate, hearten, exhilarate, encourage, stimulate, disburden, rejoice, excite, move, fire, inflame, kindle, enkindle, arouse, awaken, impassion, quicken, thrill, delight, enrapture, intoxicate.

UPPER, *adj.* 1. Higher *(as in place, position, or in a scale)*, superior, greater, over.

2. Superior *(as in rank, dignity, station)*, better, major, surpassing, eminent, distinguished, exceeding, ascendant.

UPPER-CLASS, *adj.* Relating to *or* typical of a high-ranking class in society, noble, wellborn, well-bred, of rank, highborn, patrician, aristocratic, exalted, thoroughbred, genteel, princely, gentle, blue-blooded, of gentle blood.

UPPER HAND, *n.* The dominating *or* controlling position, advantage, dominion, superiority, ascendancy, mastery, supremacy, preëminence, whip hand, control, dominance, primacy, influence, commanding position, sway, command, pressure, hold, grasp, suzerainty, sovereignty, weight, grasp.

UPPERMOST, *adj.* Highest *(in place, order, rank, power, etc.)*, topmost, predominant, supreme, foremost, loftiest, greatest, chief, main, paramount, maximum, summital, head, apical, principal, sovereign, top, controlling, peerless, hegemonic, crowning, leading, dominant, overruling, capital, prime, primary, cardinal, preëminent.

UPRIGHT, *adj.* 1. Erect, vertical, on end, upended, upstanding, standing, sheer, plumb, uplifted, perpendicular, straight-up-and-down, rampant *(Her.)*.

2. Honest, righteous, adhering to rectitude, in accord with what is right, straightforward, true, pure, upstanding, truthful, veracious, trustworthy, forthright, uncorrupt, fair, just, square, straight, conscientious, even-handed, innocent, open, guileless, candid, impartial, aboveboard, scrupulous, estimable, worthy, licit, foursquare, on the up-and-

up *(coll.)*, faithful, moral, ethical, rightful, high-principled, sincere, good, virtuous, incorruptible.

UPRISE, *v.* 1. Rise up *(as from lying or sitting)*, get up, arise, leap up, start up.

2. Rise in revolt, rebel, strike, kick over the traces, upheave, mutiny, mutineer, defy, rise up in arms.

3. Move upward, mount up, become high, upsurge, grow, go uphill, ascend, climb, slope upward, swarm up, scale, clamber up, escalade, scramble up, shin up *(coll.)*, wind *or* curl upwards, upstream.

UPRISING, *n.* 1. Overturn, overthrow, revolt, insurrection, outbreak, insurgence, mutiny, revolution, rebellion, rising, riot, commotion, coup d'état, sedition, upset, upheaval, confusion.

2. Ascent, acclivity, incline, upgrade, pitch, rise, climb, upgo, upclimb, grade, slope, uplift, uphill.

UPROAR, *n.* Violent and noisy disturbance, tumultuous *or* confused noise *or* din, commotion, hubbub, pandemonium, confusion, outcry, agitation, turmoil, tumult, upheaval, pother, ado, to-do *(coll.)*, altercation, ruckus, affray, furor, fuss, racket, stir, outbreak, clatter, row, riot, flurry, quarrel, hullabaloo, turbulence, encounter, fight, skirmish, conflict, tussle, scuffle, concussion, clash, ruction, imbroglio, struggle, mêlée, embroilment.

UPROARIOUS, *adj.* Disorderly, confused, noisy, loud, tumultuous, turbulent, excited, quarrelsome, stormy, violent, vociferous, boisterous, hysterical, obstreperous, raging, frenzied, contentious, fierce, rampageous, passionate, riotous, wild, agitated, furious, blustering, intense, fiery, feverish, kindled, disturbed, boiling, tempestuous, explosive, volcanic.

UPROOT, *v.* Eradicate, pull up by the roots, root out *or* up, remove utterly, do away with, destroy, annihilate, exterminate, extirpate, weed out, eject, eliminate, extract, deracinate, excavate, shake off, withdraw, pluck out.

UPSET, *adj.* 1. Overturned, capsized, overthrown, recumbent, prostrate, upside down, wrong side up, upturned, inverted, reversed, bottom *or* keel upwards, on one's *or* its head.

2. In disorder, untidy, disorderly, disordered, routed, overthrown, confused, topsy-turvy, chaotic, disorganized, slovenly, careless, deranged, disarranged, littered, helter-skelter, mussed, messy, disheveled, straggling.

3. In an irritable state of mind, overwrought, worried, distracted, agitated, flustered, affected, ruffled, perturbed, disturbed, distressed, hysterical, emotional, nervous, excessively stirred, tempest-tossed.

UPSET, *v.* 1. Overturn, invert, overthrow, tip over, capsize, swamp, overset, subvert, spill, tumble, turn topsy-turvy, upend, reverse, disarrange, precipitate.

2. Overthrow, defeat, destroy, vanquish, undo, ruin, topple, overcome, cast down, overpower, overwhelm, crush, confound, suppress, subjugate, put down, prostrate, rout, beat, discomfit, worst, demolish, subvert, disorganize, refute, do away with, confute, invalidate, obviate, quash, reduce, shatter, smash, nullify, break up, extirpate, abolish, quell, subdue, get the upper hand of, overmaster, whip, surmount, be victorious over.

3. Put out of order, throw into disorder, derange, disarrange, scatter, litter, invert, dishevel, convulse, disorganize, muddle, tumble, jumble,

mix up, complicate, tangle, mess, discompose, shuffle, botch, displace, confuse, strew about, lumber, turn topsy-turvy, toss at random.

4. Disturb mentally, perturb, agitate, confuse, startle, unnerve, disconcert, unsettle, toss, rattle, convulse, embroil, bewilder, bother, confound, discompose, embarrass, fluster, stun, shock, overwhelm, overcome.

UPSHOT, *n.* 1. Final issue, conclusion, result, end, outcome, consequence, aftermath, event, termination, consummation, eventuation, outgrowth, resultant, fruit, offshoot, offspring, settlement, product, aftereffect, sequel, finale, close, development, pay-off *(coll.)*.

2. Gist, sum, substance, pith, core, salient point, kernel, center, heart, nucleus, keystone, keynote, essence, quintessence, fundamental, principle, essential quality, cornerstone.

UPSIDE DOWN, *adj.* 1. With the top part undermost, inverted, upturned, reversed, wrong side up, turned over, overturned, bottom *or* keel upwards, on one's head, upset.

2. In complete disorder, topsy-turvy, helter-skelter, disorganized, disarranged, haphazard, chaotic, perplexed, deranged, untidy, messy, upset, mussed, routed, overthrown, confused, littered, disheveled.

UPSTANDING, *adj.* 1. Standing erect, tall, vigorous, upright, erect, vertical, upended, on end, uplifted, perpendicular, straight-up-and-down, rampant *(Her.)*.

2. Upright, honorable, honest, righteous, adhering to rectitude, straightforward, true, pure, just, fair, truthful, veracious, uncorrupt, forthright, trustworthy, square, straight, even-handed, conscientious, open, innocent, candid, impartial, guileless, aboveboard, estimable, worthy, licit, scrupulous, foursquare, faithful, ethical, moral, on the up-and-up *(coll.)*, rightful, sincere, good, virtuous, incorruptible, high-principled.

UPSTART, *n.* One who has risen suddenly from humble position, mushroom, parvenu, nouveau riche, pretender, newly-rich, sprout, snob, codfish aristocrat *(coll.)*, pig in clover *(sl.)*.

UP-TO-DATE, *adj.* 1. Extending to the present time, including the latest facts, current, complete, present, instant, prevalent, prevailing.

2. In accordance with the latest *or* newest standards (ideas, style), new, modern, up-to-the-minute, new-fashioned, neoteric, fashionable, the latest, all the rage, stylish, modish, being done, the last word, abreast of the times.

UPTURN, *n.* Upward turn, marked advance, upswing, upsurge, revival, lift, recovery, progress, headway, rise, increase, improvement, betterment, spring tide, restoration, flood tide.

UPTURNED, *adj.* 1. Turned upward, directed upward, uplifted, erect, scandent, upcast, upright, ascending, rising, raised, retroussé *(esp. of the nose)*.

2. Turned over, overturned, reversed, inverted, upside down, wrong side up, on one's *or* its head, upset, bottom *or* keel upwards.

UPWARD, *adj.* Moving *or* tending upward, directed to a higher place, aspiring, ascending, scandent, uphill, acclivitous, ascendant, uprising, acclivous, heavenward, up, higher.

UPWARD, *adv.* 1. Toward a higher place *or* position, skyward, upstream, uphill, northward, upstairs, heavenward.

2. More, beyond, above, over, additionally, in advance of, in addition, overplus, over and above.

URBAN, *adj.* 1. Of, pertaining to *or* comprising a city *or* town, city, metropolitan, civic, oppidan, municipal, burghal.

2. Living in a city *or* cities, characteristic of *or* accustomed to cities, citified, worldly-wise, sophisticated, cosmopolitan.

URBANE, *adj.* Polite *(esp. in a refined or elegant way),* agreeable, courteous, civil, complaisant, polished, well-bred, well-mannered, gracious, suave, gallant, gentlemanly, affable, diplomatic, bland, civilized, mannerly, conciliatory, obliging, genteel, ingratiating, social, courtly, tactful, ceremonious, cultivated, chivalrous.

URBANITY, *n.* 1. Refined *or* elegant politeness, suavity, courtesy, civility, refinement, courteousness, good manners, good breeding, amenity, gentleness, polish, gallantry, chivalry, complaisance, comity, affability, gentility, graciousness, social grace, observance of the proprieties, cultivation, mildness, tact, savoir-faire, finesse, deference.

2. Civilities, amenities, custom, propriety, convention, decorum, good form, etiquette, punctilio, dictates of society, *bienséance (Fr.).*

URCHIN, *n.* Small boy, mischievous child, youngster, brat, imp, elf, gamin, shaver *(coll.),* kid *(sl.),* guttersnipe *(coll.),* tot, tad.

URGE, *n.* Involuntary (instinctive, natural) impulse, impelling influence (action, force), motivation, provocation, stimulation, dictate, press, spur, stimulus, incentive, impulsion, prick, fillip, inspiration, rationale, reason, motive, prompting, inducement.

URGE, *v.* 1. Push along, force, drive, propel, impel with force *or* vigor, hasten, press, move, constrain, speed, help, aid, shove, boost, forward, hustle, prompt, actuate, jog, animate, poke, prod, thrust, speed up, accelerate, expedite, precipitate.

2. Incite to speed *or* effort, constrain, animate, encourage, hasten, inflame, speed, impel, hurry, spur, stimulate, instigate, quicken, goad, whip on, hound on, prick, lash, induce, rouse, incite, move, motivate, egg on, awaken, provoke, exhort, press, push, precipitate, catapult, advance, jolt, jog, vivify, bestir, flog, assist, boost, inspire.

3. Endeavor to induce, solicit, entreat, exhort, importune, persuade, earnestly recommend, prevail upon, press, beseech, beg, ply, advise, coax, plead with, sway, implore, pray, supplicate, conjure, crave, request, invoke, appeal to, apply to, adjure, obtest, postulate, agitate, sue, demand, claim, bespeak, clamor, impetrate, obsecrate, agitate.

4. Press *(something)* upon the attention, move, prompt, exhort, counsel, advise, admonish, suggest strongly, prescribe, recommend, advocate, remonstrate, expostulate, press by persuasion.

5. Insist on, allege, assert with earnestness, claim, argue for, uphold, justify, defend, support, sustain, plead, maintain, profess, contend for, champion, vindicate.

URGENCY, *n.* Urgent character, imperativeness, insistence, importunateness, importance, necessity, gravity, obligation, seriousness, spur, goad, stimulus, incitement, compulsion, pinch, demand, matter of life and death, instance, importunity, entreaty, haste, emergency, pressure, press, stress, drive, exigency.

URGENT, *adj.* 1. Requiring immediate action *or* attention, pressing, imperative, compelling, critical,

crucial, instant, cogent, indispensable, compulsory, necessitous, importunate, exigent, clamant, solicitous, pertinacious, crying, solemn, imperious, earnest, vehement, important, serious, absorbing, primary, salient, grave, vital, obligatory, essential, strong.

2. Earnest in solicitation, insistent, importunate, pressing, demanding, clamoring, crying, vehement, solicitous.

URN, *n.* 1. Vase *(esp. with foot or pedestal),* pot, amphora, ewer, cruse, jardiniere, bottle, jar, crock, ossuary, cinerarium, funeral *or* mortuary vessel.

2. Vessel with faucet *or* cock *(for making tea, coffee, etc.),* pot, samovar.

USABLE, *adj.* Available for use, in condition to be used, ready, applicable, adaptable, commodious, useful, on hand, at hand, handy, in working condition.

USAGE, *n.* 1. Customary way of doing, habit, long-continued practice, convention, tradition, mode, consuetude, fashion, custom, etiquette, wont, vogue, method, prescription, settled tendency of behavior, normal occurrence *or* procedure, way, system, form, pattern, groove, rut, regime, institution, routine, beaten path, grind *(coll.),* fixed procedure.

2. Way of using *or* treating, treatment, conduct, procedure, handling, management, conditions of life, control, manipulation, command, disposition, care, government, operation, supervision, regulation.

3. Act of using *or* employing, use, *etc. (See* USE, *n.,* 1.)

USE, *n.* 1. Act of employing *or* putting into service, state of being employed *or* used, instance *or* way of employing, purpose, employment, application, disposition, service, enjoyment, exercitation, adhibition, disposal, appliance, utilization, exercise, practice, exertion, occupancy, conversion to a purpose, usage.

2. Advantage, help, resulting good, utility, profit, service, benefit, avail, convenience, usefulness, aid, office, ministration, support, furtherance, serviceability, good, interest, assistance, applicability, instrumentality, benefaction, advancement, accommodation, subservience.

3. Occasion, need, necessity, indispensability, exigency, cause, ground, motive, reason, basis, call, provocation, inducement.

4. Continued (habitual, customary) employment *or* practice, usage, form, *etc. (See* USAGE, *n.,* 1.).

5. Way of using *or* treating, treatment, usage, *etc. (See* USAGE, *n.,* 2.).

USE, *v.* 1. Put into service, employ for a purpose, utilize, make use of, apply, wield, resort to, have recourse to, put into action, turn to account, recur to, play, operate, ply, bring into play, put in requisition, drive, administer, occupy, manipulate, handle.

2. Avail oneself of, take advantage of, utilize, profit by, exert, exercise, apply to one's own purposes, exploit, make the most of, turn to account.

3. Consume in use, expend, spend, exhaust, waste, devour, deplete, swallow up, wear out, squander, throw away, fritter away, run through, absorb, drain, dissipate.

4. Treat, act *or* behave toward, have to do with, deal with, manage, handle, direct, control, manipulate, command, dispose, conduct, care for, superintend, rule, hold the reins, govern, run, lead, regulate, drive, guide.

USEFUL, *adj.* Profitable, serving some purpose, of good effect, of practical use, advantageous, serviceable, helpful, instrumental, conducive, utilitarian, convenient, operative, beneficial, handy, effective, valuable, contributory, accessory, coöperative, functional, salutary, subservient, attendant, availing, commodious, suitable.

USELESS, *adj.* Of no use, not serving any purpose, unavailing, futile, unprofitable, superfluous, fruitless, unserviceable, unbeneficial, unhelpful, vain, idle, frivolous, ineffectual, inefficient, otiose, abortive, nugatory, inefficacious, jejune, worthless, barren, bootless, impotent, inoperative, effete, inadequate, to no end, impracticable, unnecessary, needless, inutile.

USHER, *n.* One who escorts persons to seats, officer *or* servant in charge of an entrance door, doorkeeper, escort, gatekeeper, porter, ostiary, bodyguard, concierge, conductor.

USHER, *v.* 1. Conduct *(fol. by* IN. INTO, OUT, *etc.),* show, direct, convoy, squire, guide, escort.
2. Attend *or* bring at the coming *or* beginning, herald, introduce, induct, announce, set up, set on foot, ring in *(sl.),* forerun, precede, launch, be the precursor of, lay the foundation, prepare, broach, inaugurate, antecede, institute, install, proclaim.

USUAL, *adj.* 1. Customary, ordinary, habitual, common, familiar, of frequent occurrence, rife, prevailing, plentiful, current, abundant, popular, everyday, often met with, prevalent, daily, conventional, wonted, normal, accustomed, natural, unexceptional, known, expected, stock, vernacular, commonplace, indiscriminate, well-trodden, regular, routine, repeated, established, standard, orthodox, cut and dried, acknowledged, received, traditional, workday, settled, normal.
2. In common use, common, commonplace, trite, stale, worn-out, tedious, threadbare, hackneyed, prosaic, monotonous, humdrum, unvaried, everyday, moth-eaten, platitudinous, stereotyped, ordinary, homely, workday, plebeian, Philistine, undistinguished, unrefined, uncultured, popular, casual, oft-repeated, bromidic *(coll.),* mediocre.

USURER, *n.* One who lends money at an exorbitant rate, Shylock, shyster, extortionist.

USURP, *v.* Seize and hold by force and without right, steal, arrogate, encroach, assume, appropriate unlawfully, lay hold of, take, exact, infringe, wrest, make free with, help oneself to, commandeer, lay under contribution, dispossess, deprive of, get under false pretenses, violate.

USURPATION, *n.* Wrongful seizure and occupation of another's place *or* power, *etc.,* seizure, infringement, assumption, arrogation, despotism, encroachment, disenthronement, dethronement, deprivation, deposal, appropriation.

USURY, *n.* Exorbitant amount *or* rate of interest, lending of money at an exorbitant rate, robbery, exploitation.

UTENSIL, *n.* Implement, instrument, vessel, dish, receptacle, container, tool, apparatus.

UTILITARIAN, *adj.* 1. Having regard to utility *or* usefulness rather than beauty *or* ornamentality, *etc.,* practical, useful, serviceable, profitable, serving some purpose, instrumental, helpful, conducive, convenient, operative, beneficial, advantageous, handy, commodious, subservient, functional, valuable, contributory, accessory, effective.
2. Public-spirited, benevolent, patriotic, philanthropic, charitable, generous, liberal, Benthamite.

UTILITARIANISM, *n.* Ethical doctrine that virtue is based on utility, belief that conduct should promote the greatest happiness of the greatest number of persons, philanthropy, public welfare (good, service), common *or* general welfare, commonweal, patriotism, public spirit, Benthamism.

UTILITY, *n.* 1. State *or* character of being useful, usefulness, advantageousness, help, aid, avail, efficiency, use, service, profit, benefit, value, efficacy, convenience, productivity, fruitfulness, productiveness, serviceability, profitability, timeliness, adaptability, suitability, applicability, advantage.
2. Well-being, happiness, public good, welfare, comfort, prosperity, contentment, interest, advantage, benefit, commonweal.

UTILIZE, *v.* Put to use, turn to account, employ, use, make use of, take advantage of, put into service, apply, resort to, have recourse to, ply, operate, bring into play, put into action, handle, manipulate, avail oneself of, profit by, exert, exercise, exploit, make the most of.

UTMOST, *adj.* 1. Being at the furthest point *or* extremity, furthest, extreme, most distant, most remote, outermost, outlying, exterior, external, peripheral, outside, extraneous.
2. Of the greatest *or* highest degree *or* quantity, *etc.,* supreme, uttermost, uppermost, maximum, superlative, topmost, predominant, foremost, loftiest, chief, main, paramount, maximal, summital, head, apical, principal, sovereign, top, controlling, peerless, hegemonic, crowning, leading, dominant, capital, prime, primary, cardinal, preëminent.

UTMOST, *n.* 1. Greatest degree *or* amount, the most possible, best, highest, limit, all, ultimate.
2. Extreme limit *or* extent, boundary, bound, border, periphery, enclosing line, ring, zone, horizon, orbit, ambit, margin, circumference, perimeter, circumscription.

UTOPIAN, *adj.* Founded upon *or* involving imaginary *or* ideal perfection, visionary, fanciful, air-built, unpractical, unreal, phantom, imaginary, vaporous, speculative, contemplative, castle-built, inoperable, infeasible, idealistic, cloud-born, impractical, quixotic.

UTOPIAN, *n.* Ardent but impractical political *or* social performer, visionary, idealist, daydreamer, romantic, romanticist, Don Quixote, fantasist, castle-builder, seer, imaginer, dreamer, enthusiast, rhapsodist, phantasmagorist.

UTRICLE, *n.* Small baglike body *(as air-filled cavity in seaweed),* vesicle, vesica, sac, bladder, saccule, pocket, bleb, blister, cyst.

UTTER, *adj.* Absolute, complete, total, perfect, unconditional, unqualified, entire, pure, downright, sheer, rank, unmitigated, thorough, consummate, extreme, unmodified, unrelieved, out-and-out, limitless, unlimited, unbounded, boundless, full, unchecked, unrestricted, unrestrained, unconstrained, outright, immoderate, despotic, comprehensive, all-encompassing, undisputed, egregious, sweeping, overwhelming, excessive, unsparing, unstinted, overmuch, lavish, exuberant, profuse, copious, disproportionate, peremptory, stark, blank.

UTTER, *v.* 1. Enunciate, pronounce, speak, give audible expression to, articulate, give forth, emit, voice, tell, deliver, reveal, disclose, divulge, say, proclaim, express, frame, sound, enounce, vocalize, accent.

2. Make publicly known, issue, announce, publish, circulate, declare, proclaim, promulgate, post, placard, trumpet, divulgate, communicate, disclose, advertise, spread, give out, air, tell, impart, blaze abroad, reveal, propagate, noise abroad, give to the world, broadcast, herald, publicize, enounce, give publicity to.

UTTERANCE, *n.* Vocal expression, pronunciation, articulation, speech, decision, opinion, report, notice, notification, declaration, enunciation, announcement, saying, dictum, proclamation, indication, fiat, edict, manifesto, pronunciamento, statement, affirmation, annunciation, assertion, remark, observation, comment, sentence, expression, word, order, profession, allegation, asseveration, averment, disclosure, publication, delivery.

UTTERMOST, *adj.* Extreme, utmost, furthest, of the greatest degree, outmost, most remote, greatest, most distant, last.

UXORIAL, *adj.* Of *or* pertaining to a wife, typical of *or* befitting a wife, wifely, womanly, matronly.

UXORIOUS, *adj.* Excessively *or* foolishly fond of one's wife, doting, loving, fawning, philogynous.

V

VACANCY, *n.* 1. Empty space, void, vacuum, vacuity, emptiness, vacuousness.

2. Poverty of intellect, unintelligence, thoughtlessness, incognizance, fatuity, silliness, asininity, inanity, expressionlessness, dead pan (*sl.*), poker face (*coll.*), inscrutability.

3. Fissure, breach, chink, hollow, hiatus, aperture, cavity, cleft, hole, crevice, cranny, gap, chasm, space, opening, oscitance, dehiscence, foramen, interstice, pore, mouth, crater, window, port, fenestration.

4. Unfilled place, unoccupied office, opportunity, chance, space, favorable conjuncture, suitable occasion.

5. Room, quarters, apartment, flat, residence, domicile, abode, home, lodging, housing, suite.

6. Freedom from activity, idleness, inactivity, interval of leisure, unemployment, spare time, otiosity, inertness, inaction, loafing, *dolce-far-niente* (*It.*), want of occupation, indolence, faineancy, do-nothingness, supineness, sloth, ergophobia, inexertion, deedlessness.

VACANT, *adj.* 1. Having no contents, unfilled, empty, blank, void, hollow, depleted, devoid, destitute of, exhausted.

2. Unoccupied, untenanted, uninhabited, not in use, tenantless, deserted, inutilized, abandoned, unfurnished, open to any claimant, without an incumbent, forsaken.

3. Unemployed, unoccupied, at leisure, idle, otiose, free, disengaged, unencumbered, loafing, inert, out of work, stagnant, indolent, slack, *fainéant* (*Fr.*), shiftless, do-nothing.

4. Thoughtless, vacuous, inane, fatuous, unthinking, brainless, unreflecting, unreasoning, unintellectual, unintelligent, expressionless, dead-pan (*sl.*), poker-faced (*coll.*), inscrutable, inexpressive.

VACATE, *v.* 1. Make vacant, cause to be unoccupied, leave empty, quit the occupancy of, quit possession of, depart from, abandon, disoccupy, withdraw from, relinquish, surrender,

evacuate, resign, give up, desert, hand over, abdicate.

2. Deprive of validity, render inoperative, nullify, annul, deprive of force, disannul, quash, make void, cancel, rescind, revoke, abrogate, abolish, do away with, overrule, set aside, invalidate, repeal, reverse, recall, retract, override, dissolve, nol-pros, disestablish, countermand, repudiate, disclaim.

VACATION, *n.* Freedom from duty, release from business activity, suspension of work, leisure, spare time, otiosity, furlough, leave, holiday, day of rest, Sabbath, *dies non* (*Lat.*), Lord's day, red-letter day, recess, relaxation, respite, repose, intermission, estivation, excursion, jaunt, sightseeing, travel, cruise, voyage.

VACATIONIST, *n.* One who is taking a holiday, holidayer, vacationer, summer resident, estivator, tripper, tourist, sightseer, excursionist, traveler, voyager.

VACCINATE, *v.* Inoculate with vaccine matter, immunize, inject with preventive substance.

VACILLATE, *v.* 1. Sway unsteadily, move to and fro, oscillate, waver, rock, stagger, reel, have an unsteady motion, totter, wobble, undulate, nutate, librate, pendulate, swing, waggle, bob, nod, falter, flutter, toss, roll, pitch, flounder, teeter, vibrate, pulsate, wriggle, waddle.

2. Be irresolute, be inconstant, be unsteady, be a weathercock, be unsettled, fluctuate, blow hot and cold, hesitate, box the compass, play fast and loose, run with the hare and hunt with the hound, think twice about, hang in suspense, dawdle, pause, shilly-shally, boggle, dillydally, be neutral, hem and haw, hover, demur, not know one's own mind, balance, debate, will and will not, dally over, palter, shuffle, trim.

VACILLATING, *adj.* Irresolute, vacillatory, wavering, shilly-shally, fluctuating, inconstant, unsteady, changeable, irresponsible, weak-kneed, unstable, indecisive, pliant, fickle, capricious, infirm of purpose, off-again on-again, unsettled, undecided, erratic, oscillating, unsteadfast, unreliable, without ballast, mercurial, volatile, frothy, light-minded, giddy, fast and loose, hot and cold, half-hearted, double-minded, unresolved, at a loss, fitful, inconsistent, crotchety, whimsical, fanciful, skittish.

VACILLATION, *n.* 1. Mobility, instability, changeableness, fluctuation, oscillation, alternation, libration, nutation, vibration, pulsation, undulation, seesaw, vibratility, to-and-fro, teeter, ebb and flow, systole and diastole, flux and reflux, up and down.

2. Indecision, irresolution, unsteadiness, wavering, inconstancy, hesitation, faltering, hesitancy, dubiety, infirmity of purpose, indetermination, absence of will power, uncertainty, demur, ambivalence, suspense, lukewarmness, half measures, pliancy, timidity, incertitude, dilemma, quandary, diaporesis, vagueness, contingency, something or other.

VACUITY, *n.* 1. Absence of contents, emptiness, void, vacancy, vacuum, empty space, gap, interval, hiatus, vacuousness, hollowness, voidness, interruption, space, interim, recess, pause, *tabula rasa* (*Lat.*).

2. Absence of ideas, poverty of intellect, vacancy of mind, inanity, unintelligence, nihility, expressionlessness, thoughtlessness, incognizancy, fatuity, woolgathering, heedlessness, inattention,

disregard, inadvertence, absent-mindedness, oversight, neglect, abstraction, detachment, distraction, preoccupation, reverie, daydream, brown study, engrossment, absorption.

VACUOUS, *adj.* 1. Without contents, empty, void, blank, vacant, unoccupied, unfilled, exhausted, depleted, drained of, idle, wanting, missing, hollow.

2. Purposeless, pointless, fatuous, inane, groundless, insubstantial, tenuous, baseless, flimsy, ungrounded, without foundation, imaginary, illusory, immaterial, unreal, vaporous, imponderable.

3. Unintellectual, unintelligent, showing mental vacancy, devoid of intelligence, empty of ideas, thoughtless, expressionless, poker-faced, dead-pan *(sl.),* inexpressive, stupid, dull, incogitative, irrational, unthinking, unreasoning, inattentive, heedless, woolgathering, diverted, preoccupied, absent-minded, distrait, dazed, in a fog, faraway.

VACUUM, *n.* Space entirely void of matter, enclosed space from which air has been removed, empty space, void.

VAGABOND, *adj.* 1. Wandering from place to place without settled habitation, homeless, vagrant, nomadic, landloping, journeying, ambulatory, itinerant, peripatetic, migratory, roving, wayfaring, weather-beaten, travel-stained, restless, transient, foot-loose.

2. Leading a disreputable life, loose-living, irregular, bohemian, gypsy, profligate, licentious, dissolute, lax, wanton, promiscuous.

3. Good-for-nothing, no-account, worthless, truant, recreant, blackguard.

VAGABOND, *n.* 1. One who is without a fixed abode, one who wanders from place to place, vagrant, nomad, itinerant, tramp, hobo, knight-of-the-road, roamer, gadabout, gadling, beachcomber, landloper, rover, sundowner, strolling beggar, panhandler, hedgebird, floater, lounger, loafer, idle wanderer, peripatetic, outcast, pariah, castaway, bum, tatterdemalion, down-and-outer, peregrinator, straggler, rambler, Bedouin, gypsy, *zingaro (It.),* Arab, migrant, wayfarer.

2. Worthless fellow, good-for-nothing, *vaurien (Fr.), Taugenichts (Ger.),* scamp, rascal, renegade, scoundrel, rogue, knave, blackguard, black sheep, hooligan, hoodlum, ne'er-do-well, wastrel, rapscallion, scapegrace, wretch, scalawag, rotter, ragtag and bobtail, riffraff, miscreant, caitiff, reprobate, profligate, wanton, libertine, rake, debauchee.

VAGARY, *n.* 1. Extravagant idea, wild notion, whim, caprice, crotchet, whimsy, freak, whimsicality, humor, fancy, whim-wham, maggot, quirk, fad, flimflam, fit.

2. Prank, antic, escapade, tomfoolery, practical joke, romp, gambol, spree, lark, monkeyshine, skylarking, *gambade (Fr.), espièglerie (Fr.),* horseplay, buffoonery, *boutade (Fr.).*

VAGRANCY, *n.* Vagabondage, nomadism, vagabondism, peripateticism, itinerancy, restlessness, mobility, wayfaring, globetrotting, Bohemianism, pererration, roving, flitting, gadding, migratoriness.

VAGRANT, *adj.* 1. Wandering, itinerant, peripatetic, roaming, roving, strolling, nomadic, straggling, foot-loose, wayfaring, unsettled, journeying, traveling, ambulatory, perambulative, gadding, rambling, migratory, transient.

2. Erratic, unstable, fickle, capricious, whimsical, irresolute, wayward, inconstant, fitful, wavering, indecisive, volatile, mercurial, desultory, skittish, shiftless.

VAGRANT, *n.* Wanderer, vagabond, nomad, gypsy, Bedouin, Arab, hobo, tramp, knight-of-the-road, panhandler, beggar, itinerant, unlicensed peddler, camp follower, Okie, sundowner, bum, floater, ragamuffin, outcast, traveler, wayfarer, journeyer, trekker, peregrinator, rover, straggler, gadabout, gadling, landloper, rambler, roamer, loafer, beachcomber, migrant.

VAGUE, *adj.* Of an indistinct character, not definite, not explicit, not precise, not clear, ill-defined, indefinite, dim, obscure, ambiguous, equivocal, enigmatic, cryptic, confused, doubtful, uncertain, unfixed, undetermined, unsettled, dubious, hazy, nebulous, cloudy, intangible, indistinguishable, muddy, blurred, misty, abstruse, incomprehensible, mysterious, loose, perplexing, confusing, paradoxical, apocryphal, oracular, problematical, casual, general, aimless, random.

VAGUENESS, *n.* Indefiniteness, ambiguity, ambiguousness, equivocalness, obscurity, nebulousness, indistinctness, obscuration, obfuscation, unclearness, inexactness, unintelligibleness, confusion, abstruseness, mysteriousness, mystery, uncertainty, doubtfulness, dubiousness, haziness, fogginess, dilemma, quandary, inexplicitness, inexactitude, indeterminateness, looseness, generality.

VAIN, *adj.* 1. Worthless, empty, useless, inane, unavailing, fruitless, trivial, unessential, unimportant, vapid, hollow, idle, inept, weak, foolish, bootless, ineffectual, profitless, nugatory, futile, unprofitable, abortive, to no purpose, to no end, valueless, ineffective, inutile, inefficacious, inadequate, unserviceable, meritless, good-for-nothing, barren, effete, sterile, worn-out, impotent.

2. Unsubstantial, unreal, shadowy, dreamy, false, supposititious, deceitful, imaginary, chimerical, baseless, delusive, unfounded, visionary, vaporous, frothy, air-spun, fabulous, fantastic, fanciful, mythical, legendary, fictitious, notional, whimsical, figmental, fairy, high-flown, romantic, poetic, idealistic, quixotic.

3. Conceited, haughty, self-important, pretentious, affected, proud, vainglorious, egotistical, self-complacent, arrogant, inflated, ostentatious, showy, overweening, self-sufficient, opinionated, flushed, self-satisfied, self-admiring, self-confident, self-opinioned, puffed up, self-flattering, uppish, stuck-up *(coll.),* upstage, pompous, fatuous, wise in one's own conceit, high and mighty, forward, high-flown, elated, boastful, supercilious, lordly, bumptious, disdainful, imperious, magisterial, toplofty, consequential, presumptuous, exultant, bombastic, cocky, swaggering, foppish, finical, dandyish, coxcombical, dandified, macaronic.

VAINGLORIOUS, *adj.* Proud beyond desert, conceited, inordinately elated, cock-a-hoop, pompous, arrogant, haughty, boastful, braggart, vaunting, pretentious, puffed up, presumptuous, overbearing, overweening, self-important, ostentatious, proud-crested, high-plumed, high-handed, high-toned, insolent, lofty, high and mighty, swollen, inflated, blown, disdainful, supercilious, bumptious, imperious, magisterial, consequential, stuck-up, on one's high horse, *en grand seigneur (Fr.),* forward, perky, magniloquent, Thrasonic, gasconading, exultant, jubilant.

VAINGLORY, *n.* Inordinate elation over one's achievements, empty pride, vanity, show, showiness, ostentatiousness, pretentiousness, empty boasting, rodomontade, gasconading, haughtiness, arrogance, swashbuckling, swaggering, *hauteur (Fr.),* high notions, crest, cheekiness, insolence, lordliness, pomposity, swank, showing-off, strut, dash, flourish, *amour-propre (Fr.)*, self-glorification, self-laudation, self-approbation, self-gratulation, self-applause, airs, egotism, coxcombry, foppishness, dandyism, dudism, dudishness, exquisitism, vaporing, heroics, exultation, jactitation.

VAINLY, *adv.* To no purpose, in vain, without effect, in a vain manner, ineffectually, uselessly, fruitlessly, unavailingly, bootlessly, futilely, unsuccessfully, *re infecta (Lat.)*, *frustra (Lat.)*, of no effect, unprofitably, inefficaciously.

VALE, *n.* Valley, glen, dale, dingle, dell, glade, ravine, gully, gorge, combe, coulee, *couloir (Fr.)*, bottom, gill, strath, intervale.

VALEDICTION, *n.* A bidding farewell, leave-taking, good-by, *adieu (Fr.)*, *addio (It.)*, *adiós (Sp.)*, *Lebewohl (Ger.)*, *sayonara (Jap.)*, parting, God-speed, valedictory, *congé (Fr.)*, bye-bye, bon voyage, *glückliche Reise (Ger.)*, *vive valeque (Lat.)*, *ave atque vale (Lat.)*, hail and farewell, *au revoir (Fr.)*, *auf Wiedersehen (Ger.)*, *a rivederci (It.)*, *hasta luego (Sp.)*, *hasta la vista (Sp.)*, fare-you-well, so long *(sl.)*.

VALEDICTORY, *adj.* Farewell, final, parting, leavetaking, terminal, last, latest, ultimate, conclusive, outward-bound, outbound, departing.

VALET, *n.* Manservant, valet-de-chambre, groom, servingman, lackey, flunky, attendant, servant, waiting-servant, menial, man, page, squire, cup-bearer, caddie, buttons *(coll.)*, *khitmutgar (India)*, orderly, boots *(Brit.)*, steward, butler, footman, boy, man Friday.

VALETUDINARIAN, *n.* Invalid, valetudinary, person of a sickly constitution, patient, case, martyr to disease, cripple, chronic complainer, "the halt, the lame and the blind," dyspeptic, consumptive, paralytic.

VALETUDINARIAN, *adj.* In poor health, sickly, ailing, valetudinary, invalid, infirm, indisposed, diseased, sick, unwell, unhealthy, bedfast, sick-abed, laid-up, confined, helpless, asthenic, impotent, enfeebled, prostrate, debilitated, frail, fragile, weakly, feeble, weak, groggy, spent, exhausted, neurasthenic, faint, delicate, poorly, languishing, wasted, laid-low, stricken, decrepit, strengthless, insalubrious, unsound, unhealthful, paralytic, palsied, paretic, tubercular, consumptive, phthisical, bedridden, under the weather, on the sick list.

VALIANT, *adj.* Courageous, valorous, bold, stout-hearted, brave, intrepid, dauntless, lion-hearted, fearless, doughty, daring, unafraid, undaunted, redoubtable, heroic, gallant, manly, virile, manful, unflinching, indomitable, defiant, puissant, powerful, unshrinking, spirited, chivalric, chivalrous, stalwart, plucky, self-reliant, resolute, audacious, soldierly, hardy, mettlesome, venturous, vigorous, adventurous, strenuous, high-spirited, undismayed, confident, enterprising, dashing, warlike.

VALID, *adj.* 1. Having legal force, executed with proper formalities, lawful, legal, legitimate, binding, authoritative, sustainable in law, cogent, efficacious, official, authentic, obligatory, licit, legalized, sound, constitutional, statutory, judicial, warranted, sanctioned, forcible.

2. Well-grounded, conclusive, factual, forceful, weighty, substantial, powerful, logical, tested, true, honest, well-founded, actual, accurate, solid, strong, grave, just, important, good, sufficient, justifiable, genuine, stable, tangible, veritable, canonical, orthodox, pure, sterling, veracious, realistic, truthful, concrete, definite, well-defined, precise, exact, clear-cut, scrupulous, rigorous, punctilious, literal, scientific, meticulous, nice.

VALIDATE, *v.* Make valid, give legal force to, authorize, sanction, warrant, legalize, enforce, confirm, ratify, attest, legitimize, legitimatize, regulate, formulate, ordain, codify, enact, decree, empower, charter, license, enfranchise, privilege, grant, entitle, prescribe, capacitate, qualify, sign, countersign, stamp, seal.

VALIDITY, *n.* 1. Legal binding force, legality, quality of being good in law, lawfulness, legitimacy, legitimateness, legitimization, legalization, authorization, legitimation, authority, power, right, warrant, sanction, permission, prerogative, permit, imprimatur.

2. Cogency, power, force, forcefulness, weight, strength, gravity, efficacy, soundness, solidness, importance, moment, consequence, materialness, significance, emphasis, caliber, urgency, pressure, stress, potency, puissance, might, vigor, authenticity, verity, reality, truth, trueness, realness, actuality, veracity.

VALISE, *n.* Traveler's case, traveling bag, overnight bag, portmanteau, satchel, grip, duffel bag, Gladstone bag, gripsack, kitbag, suitcase, bandbox, hatbox, carpetbag.

VALLEY, *n.* Elongated depression between uplands, flat region drained by a river system, dale, vale, glen, bottom, dingle, gully, gorge, canyon, ravine, dell, basin, hollow, pocket, low place, gap, dip, concavity, quarry, trough, combe, coulee, couloir, strath, intervale, gill.

VALOR, *n.* Firmness in braving danger, heroic courage, bravery, hardihood, mettle, daring, boldness, valiancy, valiance, intrepidity, dauntlessness, prowess, resolution, backbone, determination, fearlessness, manliness, virility, dash, derring-do, fortitude, spirit, heroism, gallantry, chivalrousness, pluck, chivalry, resoluteness, *élan (Fr.)*, audacity, confidence, defiance, self-reliance, manhood, grit, nerve, spunk, sand *(sl.)*.

VALOROUS, *adj.* Courageous, intrepid, fearless, dauntless, undaunted, mettlesome, doughty, valiant, brave, lion-hearted, stout-hearted, bold, heroic, resolute, hardy, manly, virile, gallant, chivalrous, stalwart, high-spirited, plucky, manful, soldierly, audacious, daring, unflinching, unafraid, unshrinking, undismayed, self-reliant, confident, adventurous, venturesome, venturous, warlike, dashing, indomitable.

VALUABLE, *adj.* 1. Of great monetary worth, costly, having pecuniary value, expensive, precious, rich, high-priced, dear, beyond one's means, lavish, extravagant, sumptuous, *impayable (Fr.)*, golden, priceless.

2. Capable of having the value estimated, estimable, admirable, worthy, prizable, treasurable, esteemed, gilt-edged, choice, desirable, rare, fine, agreeable, pleasing, excellent, above par, superior, select, recherché, inimitable, matchless, capital.

3. Of considerable use *or* service, useful, advantageous, serviceable, profitable, beneficial, important, helpful, gainful, good, favorable, utilitarian, effective, operative, active, effectual, efficacious, suitable.

VALUABLE, *n.* Valuable article of comparatively small size, treasure, prize, jewel, gem, precious possession, *bijou (Fr.)*, precious stone, chef d'oeuvre, masterpiece, nonpareil, *rara avis (Lat.)*, acquisition, bauble.

VALUATION, *n.* 1. Fixing of the value of a thing, assessment, appraisement, estimate, estimation, appreciation, appraisal, gauging, reckoning, rating, award, consideration.

2. Value, price, worth, cost, amount, charge, expense, quotation, rate, demand, figure, face value, par, money's worth, price current, market price.

VALUE, *v.* 1. Rate at a certain price, estimate the value of, appraise, assess, estimate, apprize, price, account, set a value on, determine, compute, weigh, balance, judge, adjudge, rank, count, size up, fix the price of, reckon.

2. Prize, esteem, treasure, regard highly, appreciate, hold in high esteem, set store by, cherish, respect, admire, care for.

VALUE, *n.* 1. Monetary worth, price, value in exchange, equivalent, market price, price current, cost, rate, amount, expense, charge, quotation, face value, money's worth, par, figure, assessment, valuation, estimation, appraisal, appraisement.

2. Merit, excellence, finish, perfection, superiority, eminence, greatness, advantage, influence, authority, power, prestige, importance, consequence, mark, consideration, caliber, standing, repute, materialness.

3. Usefulness, benefit, avail, beneficiality, advantage, utility, serviceableness, profitableness, profit, efficacy, productiveness.

4. Precise signification, significance, meaning, force, import, purport, drift, intent, purpose, sense, tenor, bearing, essence, force, denotation, implication, spirit, pith, interpretation, allusion, connotation, substance, upshot, effect, gist, burden, sum and substance, subject matter, content.

5. Color, shade, tone, nuance, tinge, tint, hue, chromatism, tincture, complexion, flush, glow, luminosity, coloring, coloration.

VALUELESS, *adj.* Of no value, worthless, miserable, inconsequential, piddling, niggling, picayune, of no use, profitless, vain, futile, inefficacious, inutile, bootless, unavailing, inadequate, ineffectual, dispensable, unsaleable, not worth a straw, inane, unserviceable, unprofitable, fit for the discard pile, good-for-nothing, of no earthly use, not worth having.

VAMP, *v.* 1. Patch up, repair, piece, mend, patch, refit, tinker, retouch, revamp, doctor up, restore, renovate, recondition, put in repair, cobble.

2. Lure, inveigle, seduce, tempt, overpower, persuade, coax, cajole, wheedle, blandish, prevail upon, induce, stimulate, move, entice, captivate, bewitch, fascinate, ensorcel, charm, hypnotize, magnetize.

VAMPIRE, *n.* 1. Reanimated corpse who sucks the blood of sleeping persons at night, bloodsucker, Dracula, succubus, incubus, ghoul, parasite, preternatural being, zombi, lamia, cacodemon, fiend, banshee, *loup-garou (Fr.)*, werewolf.

2. Seductive woman, vamp, temptress, siren, Lorelei, Circe, enchantress, flirt, coquette, Sheba.

3. One who preys ruthlessly on others, extortioner, vulture, harpy, gold digger *(coll.)*, extortionist.

VAN, *n.* 1. Front of an army, foremost division, forefront, avant-garde, advance guard, vanguard, head, forerank, front rank, first line, line of battle, outpost, scout, picket, sentinel, vedette.

2. Covered vehicle for transporting goods, lorry, dray, truck, motor truck, wagon, car, gondola car, wain, trailer truck.

VANDAL, *n.* One who willfully attacks *or* mars anything beautiful, destroyer, Hun, barbarian, iconoclast, image-breaker, savage, ravager, devastator, plunderer, pillager, sacker, looter, despoiler, marauder, spoliator, raider, freebooter.

VANDALIC, *adj.* Barbarous, destructive, vandalish, vandalistic, barbarian, iconoclastic, ruinous, subversive, incendiary, deletory, brutish, savage, terroristic, maleficent, anarchistic, spoliative, malicious, feral, ferocious, truculent, bellicose, inhuman, fell, untamed, atrocious.

VANDALISM, *n.* Willful destruction of artistic treasures, barbarity, barbarism, savagery, iconoclasm, spoliation, plunderage, pillage, rapine, depredation, devastation, disruption, annihilation, extinction, prostration, desolation, demolition, subversion, overthrow, abolition, suppression, ravage, incendiarism, terrorism.

VANE, *n.* Wind-indicator, weathercock, weather vane, windgauge, anemometer, wind vane, wind cone.

VANGUARD, *n.* 1. Foremost division of an army, advance-guard, avant-garde, first line, front rank, van, forward troops, front, spearhead, forefront, forerank, line of battle, outpost, vedette, sentinel, picket, scout.

2. Leading people of any intellectual *or* political movement, pioneers, precursors, heralds, forerunners, harbingers, avant-couriers, leaders, forelopers, *Bahnbrecher (Ger.)*, apostles, missionaries, propagandists, preparers.

VANISH, *v.* Disappear from sight, evanesce, be lost to view, go out of sight, become invisible, fade away, sink, evaporate, melt away, dissolve, pass away, fly, die, be lost, come to an end, cease, terminate, expire, conclude, become zero, die out, die away, perish, become extinct, be no more, dematerialize, avaunt, leave no trace, retire from view, undergo eclipse.

VANITY, *n.* 1. Self-conceit, conceitedness, egotism, excessive self-pride, *amour-propre (Fr.)*, self-esteem, self-love, narcissism, self-admiration, self-approbation, vaingloriousness, vainglory, self-complacency, self-praise, self-sufficiency, self-applause, self-glorification, self-laudation, self-worship, self-interest.

2. Arrogance, superciliousness, presumption, presumptuousness, airs, high horse, pretension, pretentiousness, affected manners, affectation, mannerism, egoism, ostentatious display, ostentation, fanfare, foppishness, foppery, dandyism, coxcombry, dog *(sl.)*, side *(sl.)*, frills and furbelows, dudism, exquisitism, haughtiness, hauteur, toploftiness, swagger, front, show, display, parade, flourish, pomposity, pomp, pageantry, array, splurge, dash, splash, glitter, frippery, high notions, lordliness, self-exaltation, elation, exultation, dazzle.

3. Worthless character, want of real value, hollowness, emptiness, inanity, unreality, unsubstantialness, unrealness, *vanitas vanitatum (Lat.)*, worthlessness, foolishness, folly, futility, falsity, sham, mirage, delusion, hallucination.

4. Vanity case, compact, powder box, rouge box, vanity box, vanity bag.

5. Dressing table, vanity dresser, dresser, mirror-table.

VANQUISH, *v.* Conquer, subdue, defeat, subjugate, overcome, overthrow, reduce to subjection, overpower, put down, rout, worst, discomfit, crush, quell, master, foil, outwit, overbear, outmaneuver, get the better of, get the upper hand over, overwhelm, triumph over, beat, surmount, outgeneral, outdo, thrash, checkmate, floor, drub, trim, lick to a frazzle, do for, suppress, nonplus, confound, circumvent, baffle, drive to the wall, take by storm, score a success, gain the day, carry all before one, prevail over, win, be triumphant, outdistance, surpass.

VANQUISHER, *n.* Conqueror, victor, subduer, subjugator, champion, master, winner, humbler, successful contestant.

VANTAGE GROUND, *n.* 1. Favorable position, position giving one an advantage, height, eminence, elevation, hill, ridge, rising ground, upland, highland, hillock, hummock, knoll, hog's back, butte, foreland, promontory, mound, barrow, bluff, summit, crest.

2. Control, authority, dominance, influence, prevalence, pull, sway, predominance, ascendancy, sway, potency, power, prepollence, superiority, advantage, drag, prestige, supremacy, paramountcy.

3. Footing, fulcrum, point d'appui, purchase, leverage, play.

VAPID, *adj.* 1. Tasteless, insipid, flat, stale, savorless, flavorless, unpalatable, watery, weak, unflavored, unsavory, *fade (Fr.),* milk-and-water, wishy-washy, diluted, pale, waterish.

2. Without animation, spiritless, lifeless, unanimated, dead, inanimate, feeble, barren, sterile, arid, dull, wearisome, tedious, pointless, monotonous, heavy, jejune, prosaic, prosy, tame, meager, lean, languid, namby-pamby, dry, bald, colorless.

VAPOR, *v.* 1. Cause to pass off in vapor, vaporize, evaporate, steam, reek, fume, smoke, exhale, transpire, volatilize.

2. Talk grandiloquently, speak boastfully, bluster, boast, brag, vaunt, crow, swagger, talk big, exult, show off, puff, flourish, bluff, trumpet, draw a long bow, jubilate, gloat, glory, preen oneself, *se faire valoir (Fr.),* blow one's horn, *faire claquer son fouet (Fr.),* act the *grand seigneur,* ride a high horse, assume a lofty bearing, toss the head, give oneself airs, swell, roister, rant, gasconade.

VAPOR, *n.* 1. Gaseous state of a substance, aeriform state, visible exhalation, fume, smoke, mist, steam, fog, reek, rack, cloud, haze, effluvium, emanation, gas, ether, air, flatus, damp, choke, scud.

2. Boasting, vaunting, pretensions, puffery, fanfaronade, flourish, gasconade, rodomontade, bombast, rant, highfaluting, braggartism, bluff, swagger, swank, bravado, jactitation, bluster, venditation, heroics, magniloquence, grandiloquence, altiloquence, hot air *(sl.).*

3. Something unsubstantial, fantasy, phantom, figment, vagary, daydream, vision, hallucination, illusion, delusion, mirage, will-o'-the-wisp, *ignis fatuus (Lat.),* unreal fancy, whimsy, whim-wham, fertile imagination, castle-building, maggot, myth, chimera, rhapsody, romance.

VAPORER, *n.* Boaster, braggart, braggadocio, blatherskite, vaunter, swaggerer, blusterer, bully, fanfaron, roisterer, swashbuckler, hot-air merchant, gascon, fourflusher, pretender, *soi-disant (Fr.),* blowhard, windbag, bluffer, trumpeter, charlatan, mountebank, quack, fire-eater, Thraso.

VAPORING, *adj.* Foolishly boastful, bragging, blustering, windy, grandiloquent, magniloquent, altiloquent, ostentatious, Thrasonic, gasconading, braggart, *soi-disant (Fr.),* pretentious, vainglorious, exultant, jubilant, elated, cock-a-hoop, high and mighty, supercilious, high-flown.

VAPORISH, *adj.* Depressed, melancholic, hypochondriacal, splenetic, petulant, peevish, humorsome, cheerless, joyless, unhappy, pining, languishing, lackadaisical, dismal, gloomy, somber, lugubrious, funereal, mournful, downhearted, down in the mouth, in the doldrums, low-spirited, heavy-hearted, in doleful dumps, mopish, glum, moody, out of heart, disheartened, despondent, tristful, woebegone, lachrymose, hipped, atrabilious, jaundiced, saturnine, forlorn, desolate, disconsolate, rueful, long-faced.

VAPORIZATION, *n.* Vaporescence, volatilization, atomization, gasification, evaporation, distillation, cohobation, sublimation, steaming, fumigation.

VAPORIZE, *v.* Convert into vapor, evaporate, sublimate, atomize, volatilize, spray, fumigate, gasify, finestill, distill, exhale, reek, steam, smoke, fume.

VAPOROUS, *adj.* 1. Vaporiferous, vaporific, vaporescent, volatilized, volatile, vaporizable, vaporable, evaporable.

2. Vaporish, vapory, halituous, gaseous, fumy, steamy, reeking, fumous, exhalant, gasiform, aeriform, etheric, ethereal, aerial.

3. Unsubstantial, unreal, illusive, illusory, imaginary, illusionary, vain, flimsy, tenuous, airdrawn, rhapsodic, fanciful, romantic, extravagant, quixotic, preposterous, legendary, fabulous, mythical, chimerical, mythological, visionary, notional, fantastic.

VAPORS, *n., pl.* Low spirits, doldrums, dumps, blues, hypochondriasis, hypochondria, despondency, melancholia, blue devils, melancholy, dejection, depression of spirits, spleen, *taedium vitae (Lat.),* dejectedness, prosternation, heart sinking, heaviness of heart, gloom, glumness, infestivity, weariness, disgust of life, sadness, dismals, mopes, lachrymals, megrims, pessimism, Slough of Despond, disconsolateness, despair, desperation, broken heart, prostration of soul.

VARIABLE, *adj.* 1. Apt to vary, changeable, shifting, alterable, mutable, altering, mobile, variant, modifiable, aberrant, changeful, unsteady, changing, protean, mercurial, volatile, fluctuating, oscillating, wavering, unstable, unsettled, uneven, metamorphic, kaleidoscopic, versatile.

2. Fickle, inconstant, capricious, fanciful, fitful, unsteadfast, faithless, erratic, irregular, spasmodic, touch-and-go, wayward, vagrant, irresponsible, unreliable, frothy, light-minded, giddy, fast and loose.

VARIANCE, *n.* 1. Disagreement, dissension, discord, difference, incompatibility, strife, dispute, quarrel, altercation, contention, dissidence, breach, division, rupture, controversy, split, hostility, misunderstanding, alienation.

2. Divergence, discrepancy, heterogeneity, incongruity, deviation, diversity, inconformity, inconsistency, nonconformity, fluctuation, oscillation, contrast, disparity, variety.

VARIATION, *n.* Modification, alteration, mutation, change, deviation, difference, divergency, aberration, deflection, discrepancy, disagreement, contrariety, diversity, discordance, departure, alternation, interchange, innovation, inequality, up and down, vicissitude, diversification, transformation, metamorphosis, transmogrification.

VARIEGATE, *v.* Make varied in appearance, mark with different colors, diversify, streak, mottle, checker, counterchange, fret, spot, stripe, diaper, speckle, fleck, dapple, dot, figure, striate, polychromatize, opalesce, iridize, marbleize, marble, sprinkle, besprinkle, bespot, tattoo, maculate, inlay, tessellate.

VARIEGATED, *adj.* 1. Multicolor, polychromatic, many-colored, varicolored, many-hued, particolored, pleochroic, versicolor, kaleidoscopic, daedal.

2. Prismatic, iridescent, irisated, rainbowlike, opaline, pavonine, chatoyant, opalescent, *gorge-de-pigeon (Fr.)*, nacreous, pearly, *nacré (Fr.)*, tortoise-shell, nacred, cymophanous, shot.

3. Pepper-and-salt, mottled, pied, skewbald, piebald, motley, marmoraceous, marbled, marmoreal, watered, clouded, dappled, flecked, speckled, studded, spotty, powdered, freckled, flecky, flea-bitten, diversified, spotted.

4. Striped, veined, brindled, lined, barred, banded, tabby, belted, striate, streaked, strigose, fasciate, checked, checkered, tessellated, mosaic, tartan, plaid.

VARIEGATION, *n.* 1. Spottiness, streakiness, maculation, marbling, striation, iridescence, opalescence, irisation, iridization, polychromatism, play of colors, diversification, pleochroism.

2. Rainbow, iris, spectrum, peacock, butterfly, tulip, chameleon, leopard, cheetah, zebra, ocelot, kaleidoscope, nacre, mother-of-pearl, tortoise shell, Joseph's coat, mackerel sky, harlequin, crazy quilt, mosaic, checkers, checkerboard, parquetry, checkerwork, chessboard, patchwork, plaid, check, tartan, tweed, vein, fleck, stria, stripe, streak.

VARIETY, *n.* 1. Difference, dissimilarity, discrepancy, disagreement, variance, variation, deviation, deflection, divergence, aberration, discordance, diversity, contrast, contrariety, innovation, alternation, unlikeness, antithesis, disparity, dissonance, distinction, inequality, incongruity, incompatibility, opposition, adverseness.

2. Miscellany, mixture, medley, intermixture, jumble, hodgepodge, mélange, mingle-mangle, hash, olla-podrida, olio, mulligatawny, salmagundi, omnium-gatherum *(coll.),* farrago, patchwork, pastiche, gallimaufry, chowchow, motley, heterogeneity, heterogeneousness, multiformity, multifariousness, multiplicity, collection, versatility, diversification.

3. Kind, class, species, subspecies, genus, phylum, sort, brand, group, type, breed, strain, race, tribe, family, category, genre, character, description, color, denomination, classification, division, subdivision, stamp, kidney, feather, order, suborder, nature, manner, gender, sex.

VARIOUS, *adj.* 1. Different, diversified, diverse, manifold, varied, heterogeneous, assorted, multifarious, sundry, several, galore, multiplex, multiple, variform, multifold, omniform, omnifarious, polymorphic, diversiform, proteiform, protean, miscellaneous, multiphase, variegated, motley, indiscriminate, mixed.

2. Dissimilar, unlike, distinct, contrastive, another, other, separate, not the same, unidentical, unequal, unmatched, incongruous.

VARLET, *n.* Low fellow, rascal, knave, scoundrel, scapegrace, rogue, blackguard, scalawag, wretch, rapscallion, scamp, villain, miscreant, caitiff, runagate, renegade, rip, ne'er-do-well, *vaurien (Fr.)*, *Taugenichts (Ger.)*, rake, reprobate, roué, blacksheep, *âme damnée (Fr.)*, fallen angel, *mauvais sujet (Fr.)*, recreant, delinquent, derelict, misdemeanant, malefactor, felon, outlaw, sneak, mongrel, dog, outcast, pariah.

VARNISH, *v.* 1. Stain, enamel, shellac, lacquer, glaze, japan, paint, coat, incrust, daub, smear, besmear, bedaub, plate, veneer, gild, calcimine, embellish, polish, adorn, garnish, decorate, invest with a glossy appearance.

2. Gloss over, justify, extenuate, palliate, disguise, excuse, glaze over, gloze, vindicate, whitewash, pardon, absolve, forgive, apologize for, make allowance for, smooth over, soften, mitigate, give the devil his due.

VARNISH, *n.* 1. Lacquer, shellac, stain, enamel, transparent coating, lac, mastic, oleoresin, colophony, resin, rosin, facing, veneer, layer, paint, wash.

2. Extenuation, palliation, gloss, cover, mitigation, vindication, justification, exoneration, acquittal, exculpation, whitewashing, softening, explanation, apology, extenuating circumstances, allowance, plea, apologia.

VARY, *v.* 1. Alter, modify, change, diversify, variegate, transform, transmute, transmogrify, metamorphose, convert, moderate, temper, modulate, translate, transfigure, alternate, innovate, recast, remodel, reconstruct, remold, resolve into, reorganize, re-form.

2. Veer, shift, deviate, diverge, fluctuate, depart, swerve, bend, turn, curve, heel, jibe, bear off, yaw, sheer, go about, tack, twist, slue, shy, wheel, deflect, switch, shunt, fork, divaricate, ramify.

3. Differ, disagree with, contrast, diverge from, disaccord, dissent, be unlike.

4. Alternate, rotate, interchange, reciprocate, revolve, turn, whirl, wheel, spin, go round, twirl.

VASE, *n.* Hollow vessel used for decoration, flower-container, urn, amphora, jar, *tazza (It.)*, receptacle, epergne, canister, murrhine, utensil.

VASSAL, *n.* Person holding lands involving obligation to render military service to his superior, feudal tenant, feudatory, thrall, liegeman, bondman, subject, helot, bondslave, serf, villein, churl, peon, dependent, creature, puppet, retainer, yeoman, satellite, adherent, follower, henchman.

VASSALAGE, *n.* 1. Servitude, subjection, slavery, dependence, enslavement, thralldom, bondage, enthrallment, yoke, serfdom, feudalism, subjugation, reduction.

2. Service, obligation, duty, devoir, aid, obedience, submission, homage, allegiance, fealty, loyalty, obeisance, deference, honor.

VAST, *adj.* Of very great area, extensive, immense, very spacious, boundless, measureless, infinite, wide, enormous, huge, gigantic, colossal, stupendous, prodigious, mighty, monstrous, tremendous, unbounded, unlimited, uncircumscribed, illimitable, monumental, world-wide, widespread, far-reaching, far-flung, immeasurable, mammoth, titanic, Brobdingnagian, bulky, voluminous, capacious, interminable, interminate, endless, Cyclopean, Gargantuan, megatherian, elephantine, hippopotamic, expansive.

VAT, *n.* Large container for liquids, caldron, cask, barrel, puncheon, rundlet, butt, keg, tun, hogshead, firkin, carboy, kilderkin, tub.

VATIC, *adj.* Prophetic, predictive, vaticinal, fatidical, sibylline, oracular, haruspical, presageful, portentous, ominous, auspicial, monitory, prescious, extispicious, premonitory.

VATICINATE, *v.* Predict, foretell, prognosticate, divine, prophesy, soothsay, augur, presage, forecast, forebode, augurate, cast a horoscope, forewarn, advise, bode, foretoken, prefigure, portend, foreshadow, ominate.

VATICINATION, n. Prognostication, prophecy, divination, prediction, augury, forecast, prognosis, premonition, mantology, premonstration, auguration, hariolation, bodement, foreboding, omination, auspices, horoscope, soothsaying, fortune-telling, necromancy, crystal gazing, horoscopy, astrology, astromancy, prefigurement.

VAUDEVILLE, n. Light theatrical piece interspersed with songs and dances, variety show, revue, mixed theatrical entertainment, music hall show.

VAULT, v. 1. Cover with an arch, arch over, arch, embow, arcuate, concamerate.

2. Jump, leap, spring, bound, hop, caracole, curvet, ramp, skip, clear, surmount, pole-vault, buck, buck-jump.

VAULT, n. 1. Dome, arch, fornix, camera, curvet, cupola, swell, curve, curvature, span, ogive, arcuation, arc, arcade, crescent, bow, parabola.

2. Underground cell, dungeon, subterraneous prison, crypt, cavern, oubliette, keep, hold, subbasement, black hole.

3. Repository for the dead, catacomb, tomb, mastaba, serdab, burial place, ossuarium, mausoleum, sepulcher, pit, deadhouse.

VAULTED, adj. Arched, cupolar, domed, concave, curved, bowed, camerated, concamerated, fornicated, embowed, hemispheric, crescentic, semicircular.

VAULTER, n. Leaper, jumper, pole-vaulter, highjumper, acrobat, athlete, tumbler, bounder, saltator, kangaroo, chamois, mountain goat.

VAULTING, adj. Overambitious, overeager, aspiring, impatient, avid, ardent, intent upon, set upon, sky-aspiring, high-reaching, eager for superiority, emulous, strongly desirous, self-seeking, opportunistic, impetuous.

VAUNT, v. Speak vaingloriously of, exult, jubilate, crow, gloat, rejoice, bluster, draw the long bow, put on side, swagger, swashbuckle, show off, make display of, boast of, brag of, blow (coll.), flourish, puff, strut, gasconade, blow one's own horn, trumpet, advertise, vapor, talk big, exaggerate, put on the dog, give oneself airs.

VAUNTER, n. Braggart, boaster, vaporer, braggadocio, swaggerer, swashbuckler, egoist, blusterer, windbag (sl.), hot-air merchant (coll.), four-flusher, Drawcansir, pretender, soi-disant (Fr.), hornblower (sl.), bluffer, ranter, roisterer, jingoist, Thraso, gascon, blatherskite, fanfaron, blowhard, charlatan, mountebank.

VEER, v. Shift to another point of the compass, change course, change direction, turn to another direction, turn about, wheel, change about, gybe, tack, yaw, slue, swing round, come round, turn aside, deviate, swerve, diverge, deflect, dodge, warp, chop, chop and change, vacillate, fluctuate, vary, alter, waver, whirl.

VEERING, n. 1. Change of course, deflection, alteration, deviation, divergence, shift, tack, jibe, swerve, warp, chop, turn, obliquation, sheer, drift, aberration, zigzag, detour.

2. Fickleness, vacillation, instability, change of mind. tergiversation, retraction, reversal, backsliding, recidivism, timeserving, apostasy, recreancy, recidivation, trimming, opportunism, temporizing.

VEGETABLE, n. Herbaceous plant used as food, produce, truck, greens, bulb, tuber, legume, pulse, bean, pea, lentil, herb, chive, corm, sprout, cabbage, potato, turnip, corn, lettuce, endive, cauliflower, broccoli, chard, spinach, string bean, lima bean, Brussels sprouts, parsley, water cress, onion, garlic, kale, rape, kohlrabi, squash, pumpkin, radish, dandelion, eggplant, mushroom, scallion, leek, shallot, rice, maize, tomato, cucumber, celery, carrot, artichoke, asparagus.

VEGETABLE, adj. 1. Vegetal, vegetarian, vegetative, leguminous, herbal, herbaceous, botanic, verdurous, verdant.

2. Inert, passive, sluggish, inactive, dull, monotonous, stupid, unprogressive, torpid, quiescent, vacant, disengaged, leaden, logy, tame, supine, stagnant, indolent, idle, lazy, otiose, lethargic, languid, comatose, dormant, slack, do-nothing, fainéant (Fr.).

VEGETATE, v. 1. Germinate, shoot, sprout, bud, put forth, pullulate, burgeon, shoot up, grow, swell, spring up, develop, increase, blossom, flourish, flower, bloom.

2. Lead a passive existence, do nothing, hibernate, estivate, rusticate, stagnate, be inactive, idle, become rooted, live a monotonous life, bask, luxuriate, cool one's heels, waste time, lag, dawdle, loll, loaf, lounge, loiter, take it easy, fritter away time, potter, dillydally, putter. snooze, doze, drowse, nap, languish.

VEGETATION, n. 1. Vegetable growth, vegetable life, plant life, flora, flowerage, herbage, shrubbery, foliage, leafage, frondescence, leaves, foliation, verdure.

2. Bush, copse, stand, woodland, forest, greenwood, timber, grove, spinney, coppice, canebrake, thicket, bosk, covert, plantation, underbrush, brushwood, brake, scrub, boscage, furze, bracken, heather, heath, fern, gorse, broom, sedge.

3. Inert existence, stagnation, inertia, vegetativeness, unprogressiveness, passivity, idleness, inertness, loafing, dolce far niente (It.), inactivity, inaction, do-nothingness, faineancy, sloth, sluggishness, ergophobia, indolence, otiosity, quiescence, languor, somnolence, torpor, lethargy, hibernation, estivation, rustication, dormancy.

VEHEMENCE, n. Violent ardor, fervor, fervency, ardency, enthusiasm, fire, dash, élan, vim, passion, warmth, transport, raptus, heat, zeal, intensity, glow, keenness, eagerness, vigor, impetuous force, impetuosity, fury, violence, hot-headedness, wildness, fieriness, excitability, boisterousness, turbulence, agitation, ferment, whirl, flurry, flush, fever, fume, flame, effervescence, tumult, ebulliency, ebullition, gust, furor, madness, raving, distraction, delirium, frenzy, intoxication, fanaticism, monomania, infatuation, fascination, animation, potency, puissance, might, strength, lustihood, energy, vitality, spirit, pep, punch, virility, vigorousness.

VEHEMENT, adj. Impetuous, impulsive, excited, agitated, headstrong, hot-headed, heated, inflamed, impassioned, passionate, ardent, fervent, perfervid, fierce, intense, glowing, fiery, burning, sanguine, enthusiastic, earnest, keen, eager, zealous, wrought up, overwrought, rampant, furious, violent, strenuous, forcible, strong, powerful, potent, puissant, mighty, lusty, boisterous, obstreperous, explosive, stormy, tempestuous, temperamental, mettlesome, clamorous, tumultuous, wild, excitable, skittish, high-strung, nervous, mercurial, galvanic, feverish, delirious, hysterical, demonstrative, inflammable, furious, rabid, fanatical, uproarious, turbulent, hasty, rash, uncontrollable, reckless, heedless, madcap, mad-brained, ungovernable, irrepressible, volcanic, torrid, precipitate, frenzied, vigorous, overwhelming, overpowering, cogent, striking, acute, poignant, vivid, trenchant, incisive, mordant, pungent, piquant, graphic, emphatic.

VEHICLE, *n.* 1. Means of transport, conveyance, transportation, carriage, wagon, *voiture (Fr.),* trap, coach, hack, equipage, rig, landau, brougham, turnout, barouche, chariot, victoria, calash, phaeton, buggy, buckboard, cab, droshky, hackney, fiacre, runabout, surrey, fly, growler, shay, hansom, *vettura (It.),* cabriolet, curricle, gig, cariole, tilbury, sulky, jinricksha, ricksha, team, tandem, span, four-in-hand, vis-à-vis, char-à-banc, wagonette, sociable, coupé, stanhope, stagecoach, diligence, stage, post chaise, wain, lorry, truck, Conestoga wagon, prairie schooner, van, dray, cart, tumbrel, sled, sleigh, bobsled, toboggan, palanquin, litter, sedan chair, stretcher, sedan, bicycle, tricycle, velocipede, wheel, motorcycle, automobile, motor car, machine, auto, limousine, berlin, roadster, speedster, landaulet, flivver, jitney, omnibus, autobus, taxicab, taxi.

2. Railroad train, express, special, passenger train, rolling stock, Pullman car, sleeping car, sleeper, parlor car, compartment, trolley car.

3. Agency, medium, means, instrument, intermediary, instrumentality, interagency, tool.

VEIL, *v.* Hide, conceal, disguise, mask, cloak, gloze, curtain, shroud, invest, cover, envelop, screen, shelter, throw a veil over, camouflage, canopy, ensconce, protect, obscure, beshade, cloud, dim, eclipse, obfuscate, becloud, adumbrate, overshadow, bedarken.

VEIL, *n.* Transparent material to conceal the face, domino, yashmak, peekaboo, mantilla, muffler, burnoose, mask, guise, visor, cloak, blind, screen, disguise, cover, covering, masquerade, camouflage, shroud, curtain, shade, film, mantle.

VEIN, *v.* Mark with lines, streak, stripe, striate, furrow, variegate, checker, fleck, speckle, sprinkle, maculate, stipple, score, hatch, sulcate.

VEIN, *n.* 1. Blood vessel, vena, venule, nervure, nerve, artery, aorta, capillary.

2. Line, streak, marking, stripe, variegation, rib, stria, fleck, thread, striation, streakiness, seam, channel, furrow, wave, sulcation.

3. Lode, stratum, bed, ledge, quarry, fund, mine.

4. Tinge, tincture, dash, soupçon, suspicion, small quantity, sprinkling, strain, shade, touch, infusion, smack.

5. Humor, disposition, mood, temperament, temper, bent, turn of mind, quality, faculty, talent, genius, prevailing spirit, affection, nature, character, tendency, idiosyncrasy, grain, predilection, predisposition, inclination, diathesis, bias, proclivity, propensity, proneness, aptitude.

VELLICATE, *v.* Pluck, twitch, jounce, whip, shake up, stir, churn, wallop, buffet, disturb, jostle, discompose, disarrange, jerk, jolt, jog, hitch, joggle, whisk, convulse, agitate.

VELOCITY, *n.* 1. Speed, swiftness, rapidity, expedition, celerity, acceleration, quickness, haste, fleetness, alacrity, agility, dispatch, briskness, dash, nimbleness, expeditiousness, promptitude, rush, precipitation, precipitancy, hustle, hurry, rate of motion, time rate of change of position.

2. Spurt, clip, burst, race, sprint, tantivy, swoop, scuttle, scamper, scurry, flight, fast pace, run, gallop, trot, canter.

3. Race horse, grayhound, courser, gazelle, antelope, doe, eagle, hare, ostrich, Mercury, Hermes, Ariel, Camilla, Puck, Iris.

4. Lightning, flash, greased lightning, electricity, light, sound, wind, cyclone, hurricane, bullet, cannon ball, arrow, rocket, quicksilver, dart, split second, thought.

VELVET, *n.* 1. Fabric with a thick soft pile, velveteen, duvetine, plush, down, satin, silk.

2. *(Slang)* Money gained through speculation, clear gain, profit, surplus, moneymaking, lucre, earnings, innings, winnings, cleanup, pickings, prize, sweepstakes, pool.

VELVET, *adj.* Velvety, velutinous, downy, smooth, soft, delicate, thick, silken, silky, glossy, sleek, lanate, wooly, lanated, lanuginous.

VENAL, *adj.* Ready to sell one's services unscrupulously, accessible to bribery, purchasable, mercenary, hireling, sordid, corrupt, vendible, mean, dirty, avaricious, covetous, grasping, extortionate, rapacious, greedy, selfish, self-seeking, exacting, dishonest, dishonorable, questionable, shady *(sl.),* fishy *(sl.).*

VENALITY, *n.* Prostitution of principles for money *or* reward, mercenariness, corruptness, accessibility to bribery, sordidness, vendibility, avariciousness, covetousness, extortionism, rapacity, dishonesty, dishonorableness, graft, sharp practice, jobbery, jobbing, baseness, knavery, roguery, cupidity.

VEND, *v.* Dispose of by sale, hawk, huckster, sell, market, peddle, effect a sale, retail, dispense, turn into money, auction, put up for sale, trade, traffic in, barter, offer, deal in, unload, dump.

VENDEE, *n.* Person to whom a thing is sold, buyer, purchaser, emptor, customer, client, patron, clientele *(pl.).*

VENDER, *n.* One who sells in the streets, peddler, huckster, hawker, monger, vendor, merchant, dealer, chandler, retailer, smous, trader, salesman, tradesman, chapman, sutler, costermonger, cheap-Jack, auctioneer, jobber.

VENDETTA, *n.* State of private war, blood feud, dispute, quarrel, altercation, squabble, outbreak, warfare, open rupture, embranglement, embroilment, imbroglio, hostilities, bloodshed, appeal to arms, the sword, warpath, war to the knife, *guerre à mort (Fr.),* conflict.

VENDIBLE, *adj.* Salable, merchantable, merchandisable, marketable, having a ready sale, in demand, popular, staple.

VENDUE, *n.* Public auction, public sale, sheriff's sale, auction sale, sale by outcry, roup, disposal, vendition.

VENEER, *v.* 1. Cover thinly, overlay, coat, face, superimpose, overspread, invest, envelop, incase, incrust, plate, stratify, foil, foliate, laminate.

2. Give a superficially fair appearance to, gloze, varnish, disguise, conceal, dissemble, cloak, hide, screen, paint, stucco, stain, gild, japan, enamel, lacquer, calcimine, whitewash.

VENEER, *n.* 1. Thin outer layer of fine material, facing, covering, sheath, casing, leaf, lamina, coat, scale, jacket, wrapper, envelope, plate, sheet.

2. Paint, varnish, wash, gloss, stain, enamel, lacquer, japan, plaster, whitewash, stucco, luster.

3. Superficial show, fair external appearance, outward display, *étalage (Fr.)*, glitter, frippery, clinquant, front *(sl.)*, splash *(coll.)*, splurge, ostentation, pretension, parade, ostentatiousness, flourish, magnificence, pomposity, pomp, splendor, array, pageantry, exhibition, spectacle.

VENERABLE, *adj.* 1. Deserving respect because of advanced age, patriarchal, hoary, aged, ancient, Noachian, old as Methuselah, elderly, senile, mellow, ripe, senescent, superannuated, white-headed, snowy-haired.

2. Time-honored, revered, respected, grave, solemn, esteemed, august, hallowed, awful, dread, sage, wise, awe-inspiring, venerated, reverenced, sagacious.

VENERATE, *v.* Revere, reverence, adore, esteem, respect, regard highly, honor, worship, look up to, admire, glorify, extol, fear, dread, hold in awe, hallow, defer to, do honor to, pay homage to, treat with deference.

VENERATION, *n.* Outward expression of reverent feeling, reverence, respect mingled with awe, high respect, esteem, homage, worship, devotion, adoration, admiration, consideration, regard, deference, estimation, obeisance, fealty, prostration, genuflection, kneeling, kowtow, salaam, proskynesis, glorification, laudation, magnification, idolization.

VENESECTION, *n.* Practice of opening a vein for letting blood, bloodletting, phlebotomy, bleeding, seton, cupping, leeching, tapping, paracentesis.

VENGEANCE, *n.* Vindictiveness, revengefulness, retaliation, reprisal, infliction of suffering in requital for wrong done, retributive punishment, avenging of injury, revenge, avengement, retribution, nemesis, vengefulness, rancor, implacability, malevolence, ruthlessness, death feud, vendetta, tooth for a tooth, eye for an eye, blood for blood, pound of flesh, day of reckoning, *dies irae (Lat.)*, day of judgment, *lex talionis (Lat.)*, counterstroke, retortion, *revanche (Fr.)*, recrimination, a Roland for an Oliver, tit for tat, measure for measure, blow for blow, the biter bit, boomerang.

VENGEFUL, *adj.* Revengeful, vindictive, rancorous, ruthless, resentful, remorseless, retributive, harsh, spiteful, malicious, malevolent, retaliative, avenging, unforgiving, inexorable, unrelenting, implacable, recriminatory, requiting, reciprocal, Draconian, inflexible, envenomed, venomous, virulent, cold-blooded, stony-hearted, grim, bloodthirsty, nemesic.

VENIAL, *adj.* Pardonable, excusable, forgivable, exculpable, defensible, justifiable, warrantable, allowable, not seriously wrong, slight, trivial.

VENOM, *n.* 1. Poison naturally secreted by various animals, virus, toxin, poisonous fluid.

2. Malevolence, bitterness, acerbity, virulence, ill will, hatred, hate, spite, gall, malice, rancor, spitefulness, rancorousness, maliciousness, malignity, grudge, pique, rankling, acrimony, bile, bad blood, bane, bale, enmity, animosity, resentment, malice aforethought, malice prepense, savagery, brutality, barbarity, ferocity, ferity, inhumanity, truculence, evil eye, atrocity, ill usage, hostility, dislike, vials of wrath, umbrage, dudgeon, spleen, indignation, exasperation, irascibility, choler, ire, dander, *acharnement (Fr.)*.

VENOMOUS, *adj.* 1. Noxious, poisonous, toxic, deadly, lethal, virulent, septic, morbiferous, morbific, toxiferous, pestilential, pestiferous, azotic.

2. Malicious, malevolent, malignant, malign, mischievous, caustic, envenomed, spiteful, rancorous, hostile, pernicious, treacherous, vicious, baneful, ill-disposed, maleficent, acrimonious, cruel, feral, ferine, fell, barbarous, brutal, bloodthirsty, truculent.

VENT, *v.* 1. Let out, pour forth, discharge, emit, throw out, exhale, escape, break forth, debouch, come forth, disembogue, ooze, gush, spout, well out, effuse, exude, give free course to.

2. Utter, express, publish, say, air, spread abroad, bruit, blazon, divulgate, disclose, reveal, divulge, expose, bring to light, bare, tell, breathe, blab, blurt out, let slip, let fall, communicate, make known, broadcast.

VENT, *n.* 1. Aperture serving for outlet, opening, venthole, hole, mouth, orifice, air hole, outlet, passage, bunghole, blowhole, spiracle, plug, spout, faucet, spigot, tap, touch hole, air pipe, chimney, nozzle, flue, smokestack.

2. Egress, emission, disemboguement, effusion, escape, issue, emanation, discharge, outburst, emersion, drainage, leakage, effluence, outpour, efflux, outflow.

3. Utterance, expression, divulgation, disclosure, revelation, publication, exposure, exposé, declaration.

VENTER, *n.* 1. Stomach, belly, abdomen, ventricle, paunch, gizzard, bread basket *(coll.)*, crop, ingluvies, craw.

2. Womb, uterus, matrix.

VENTILATE, *v.* 1. Provide with fresh air, oxygenate, air, air-condition, air-cool, aerate, expose to air, blow on so as to freshen, purify, circulate through, aerify, fan.

2. Discuss, comment on, review, criticize, discourse about, interpret, explain, elucidate, analyze, treat of, go into a subject, dissect.

3. Publish, vent, utter, broach, divulge, promulgate, divulgate, spread abroad, bring before the public, disseminate, propagate, report.

VENTILATION, *n.* 1. Circulation of fresh air through, air conditioning, air cooling, airing, aerification, oxygenation.

2. Publicity, utterance, outlet, vent, exposure, currency, publication, promulgation, announcement, *réclame (Fr.)*, flagrancy, hue and cry, propagation.

3. Public exposure, scrutiny, examination, discussion, investigation, sifting, winnowing, exploration, inquisition, inspection, searching inquiry.

VENTILATOR, *n.* Air shaft, air-conditioner, air-cooler, louver, flue, funnel, transom, fan, aerator, air pipe, blower.

VENTRAL, *adj.* Situated on the abdominal side of the body, pertaining to the belly, stomachal, abdominal, situated on the anterior or lower side.

VENTRILOQUISM, *n.* Art of speaking apparently from the belly, practice of uttering sounds in such a way that they appear to come from some source other than the speaker, ventriloquy, gastriloquism, polyphonism.

VENTURE, *v.* 1. Hazard, risk, stake, jeopardize, endanger, imperil, gamble, speculate, dare, bet on, put to hazard, tempt fortune, fly in the face of fate, wager, game.

2. Undertake, try, experiment, test, essay, endeavor, aim, attempt, strive, chance, take a flyer, plunge, go it blind, brave, face.

3. Put forward, advance, offer, proffer, broach, presume, make bold, take the liberty.

VENTURE, *n.* 1. Gamble, hazard, risk, chance, jeopardy, danger, peril, contingency, luck, stake, wager, bet, potluck, speculation, daring undertaking, trial, flyer, lot, fortune, fortuity, fate, destiny, odds, presumption, possibility, uncertainty, tossup, throw of the dice, heads or tails, parimutuel, wheel of fortune, plunge, gambling, gaming, sweepstakes, pool, lottery, fluke, random shot, pig in a poke, leap in the dark, blind bargain.

2. Enterprise, business, project, work, job, essay, undertaking, endeavor, attempt, task, move, affair, adventure, step, experiment, mission, errand, trip, crusade, campaign, excursion.

VENTURESOME, *adj.* 1. Showing a disposition to take risks, adventurous, presumptuous, daring, rash, brash, venturous, foolhardy, fearless, reckless, headstrong, daredevil, madcap, brave, mettlesome, undaunted, courageous, intrepid, bold, doughty, enterprising, ambitious, energetic, pushing, imprudent, hardy, hot-headed, headlong, harebrained, precipitate, quixotic, overconfident, impulsive, impetuous, indiscreet, temerarious.

2. Risky, hazardous, dangerous, perilous, shaky, unsafe, uncertain, problematical, dubious, doubtful, slippery, ticklish, critical, precarious.

VERACIOUS, *adj.* Truthful, speaking truly, observant of truth, truth-telling, true, trustworthy, reliable, veridical, veridic, straightforward, aboveboard, candid, frank, truth-loving, credible, honest, unfeigned, genuine, literal, sincere, conscientious, scrupulous, punctilious, outspoken, open, guileless, unreserved, true-blue, good as one's word.

VERACITY, *n.* Habitual observance of truth, truthfulness, love of truth, candor, frankness, factualness, correctness, conformity to facts, honesty, trueness, fidelity, probity, ingenuousness, sincerity, exactness, accuracy, verity, openness, integrity, faithfulness, artlessness, guilelessness, fairness, rectitude, exactitude, veridicality.

VERANDA, *n.* Open portico, roofed gallery, piazza, porch, stoop, arcade, stoa, vestibule, loggia, sun porch, solarium.

VERBAL, *adj.* 1. Spoken, oral, unwritten, nuncupative, vocal, expressed in words, acroamatic, parol *(Law)*, voiced, lingual, phonetic.

2. Word for word, *mot à mot (Fr.)*, literal, textual, verbatim, lexical.

VERBALIST, *n.* One skilled in words, linguist, vocabulist, lexicographer, etymologian, philologist, philologue, philologer, philologian, semanticist, glossologist, glossarist, terminologist, orismologist, neologist, word-coiner, logomachist.

VERBATIM, *adv.* In exactly the same words, *ipsissimis verbis (Lat.)*, literally, word for word, *mot à mot (Fr.), totidem verbis (Lat.), ad amussim (Lat.)*, to the letter, *sic (Lat.)*, chapter and verse, *au pied de la lettre (Fr.)*, literatim.

VERBIAGE, *n.* Abundance of useless words, wordiness, verbosity, verboseness, diffuseness, prolixity, *copia verborum (Lat.)*, flow of words, circumlocution, loquacity, periphrasis, ambages, tautology, exuberance, battology, redundancy, padding, roundaboutness, verbalism, grandiloquence, flowers of rhetoric, euphuism, rodomontade, bombast, rant, fustian, inflation, sesquipedality, fine writing, macrology, pleonasm, polyloquence, multiloquence, effusion, volubility, perissology, *flux de paroles (Fr.)*.

VERBOSE, *adj.* Wordy, long-winded, prolix, loquacious, diffuse, talkative, lengthy, garrulous, redundant, tedious, pleonastic, rhetorical, declamatory, orotund, plethoric, glib, multiloquent, polyloquent, eloquent, fluent, effusive, voluble.

VERBOSITY, *n.* Loquacity, loquaciousness, garrulity, talkativeness, volubility, fluency, eloquence, flow of words, gift of gab, gush, effusion, multiloquence, polylogy, chatter, prattle, jabber, gabble, prate, twaddle, rattle, *caqueterie (Fr.)*, blather, gibblegabble, talkee-talkee, jaw *(sl.)*.

VERDANCY, *n.* 1. Greenness, verdantness, viridity.

2. Verdure, greenery, vegetation, green plants, lawn, sward, greensward, green, commons, grassplot, turf, heath, campus.

3. Inexperience, callowness, gullibility, liability to be imposed upon, credulousness, overtrustfulness.

VERDANT, *adj.* 1. Green with vegetation, covered with growing plants, verdurous, grassy, luxuriant, flourishing, fresh, rural, rustic.

2. Immature, young, raw, undeveloped, unripe, crude, unfledged, tender, inexperienced, callow, untrained, unskilled, unsophisticated, unacquainted, gullible, credulous, dupable, unversed, uninformed, ignorant, inexpert, undisciplined.

VERDICT, *n.* Decision, finding, opinion, judgment, sentence, answer, judication, adjudication, arbitrament, award, determination, decree, dictum, assessment, valuation, *res judicata (Lat.)*, vote, deduction, estimation.

VERDURE, *n.* Vegetation, greenness of fresh plants, foliage, herbage, grass, greenery, vert, turf, sward, greensward, lawn, garden, sod, grassland, meadow, pasture, mead, pasturage, nursery, *jardin (Fr.)*, arboretum, shrubbery, patch.

VERECUND, *adj.* Modest, diffident, bashful, shy, reserved, timorous, timid, nervous, coy, shamefaced, sheepish, skittish, unobtrusive, unpretentious, unassuming, demure, constrained, humble, meek, lowly.

VERGE, *v.* 1. Border, be near, skirt, approach, approximate, coast, fringe, margin, hem, edge, marginate.

2. Incline, tend, trend, slope, bear, lean, gravitate towards, move towards, predispose, conduce, be directed to, dispose, affect, serve, influence, promote, lead, contribute.

VERGE, *n.* 1. Emblem of authority, staff, rod, mace, ensign of office, wand, crosier, baton, caduceus, fasces, scepter, truncheon.

2. Border, edge, skirt, hem, brim, brink, rim, margin, lip, brow, curb, frame, ledge, labium, flange, mouth, confine, extreme, boundary, limit, end, ne plus ultra, bourn, pale, terminus, term.

3. Beginning, inception, limen, threshold, groundsill, sill, portal, gate, entrance, door, doorway, doorsill, porch, point, eve, outset, debut.

VERIFICATION, *n.* Formal assertion of the truth of something, attestation, affirmation, asseveration, establishment, substantiation, confirmation, authentication, corroboration, proof, satisfactory evidence, probation, affidavit, certification, certificate, warranty, warrant, voucher, guarantee, guaranty, security, gage, pledge, pignoration, earnest, stake.

VERIFY, *v.* Substantiate, attest, confirm, corroborate, prove to be correct, establish as true, authenticate, certify, guarantee, support, demonstrate, make good, evidence, identify, witness, document, depose, testify, vouch for, swear, acknowledge, ratify, endorse, bear out, validate, sustain, clinch *(coll.)*, accredit, vindicate.

VERILY, *adv.* Truly, of a truth, really, indeed, absolutely, positively, in very truth, actually, in fact, certainly, in truth, confidently, sooth to say, veritably, in reality, as a matter of fact, beyond question, beyond doubt.

VERISIMILITUDE, *n.* Semblance of truth, appearance of truth, probability, likelihood, likeliness, *vraisemblance (Fr.),* plausibility, credibility, well-grounded hope, favorable prospect, reasonable chance.

VERITABLE, *adj.* Being really such, conformable to fact, factual, true, actual, bona-fide, real, genuine, absolute, positive, authentic, sterling, orthodox, legitimate, valid, true-blue, sound, pure, veracious, unimpeachable, certain.

VERITY, *n.* Truthfulness, truth, reality, veracity, actuality, consonance to the reality of what is claimed, trueness, authenticity, troth, gospel, *nuda veritas (Lat.),* naked truth, literalism, accuracy, correctness, nicety, textualism, fidelity, realism.

VERMICULAR, *adj.* 1. Wormlike, worm-shaped, vermiform, vermiculated, anguilliform, serpentiform, snake-like.

2. Sinuous, serpentine, twisting, tortuous, flexuous, winding, roundabout, ambagious, devious, meandering, labyrinthine, wavy, waving, undulating, undulant, convoluted, tortive, tortile, undulatory, snaky, anfractuous, mazy, sigmoidal, circuitous, spiral, helical, coiled, turbinated.

VERMILION, *n.* Brilliant red, scarlet, cochineal, cardinal, cinnabar, crimson, carmine, carnation, maroon, damask, ruby, garnet, *sang-de-boeuf (Fr.),* rose, minium, rouge.

VERMIN, *n., pl.* 1. Noxious insects, creeping parasitic animals, mice, rats, rodents, bugs, fleas, roaches, bedbugs, lice, flies, cooties *(sl.),* centipedes, silverfish, millipedes, termites.

2. Obnoxious persons, riffraff, scum, rabble, offscourings, mudlarks, draggletails, muckworms, tatterdemalions, ragamuffins, pariahs, outcasts.

VERNACULAR, *adj.* 1. Originating in the place of its occurrence, native, indigenous, autochthonous, naturalized, domesticated, national.

2. Peculiar to popular taste, vulgar, common, plebeian, ordinary, public, general.

VERNACULAR, *n.* Natural speech of a people, phraseology peculiar to a class, mother tongue, idiom, dialect, jargon, cant, lingo, slang, patois, brogue, argot.

VERSATILE, *adj.* 1. Many-sided in abilities, capable of turning with ease from one subject to another, adaptable, varied, plastic, protean, ready, handy, clever, endowed with many talents, gifted, talented, many-skilled, adroit, dexterous, expert, resourceful, proficient, master of, *au fait (Fr.),* accomplished, ingenious.

2. Changeable, kaleidoscopic, mobile, variable, alterable, mutable, manifold.

3. Unsteady, inconstant, mercurial, fickle, shifting, spasmodic, vacillating, wavering, unstable, spasmodic, restless, fitful.

VERSE, *n.* 1. Succession of metrical feet, line of a poem, stave, stich, number, measure, meter, rhythm, succession of lines, stanza, strophe, poem, versicle, canto, verselet, doggerel, jingle, limerick, macaronics.

2. Versification, poesy, prosody, rhyming, orthometry, scansion.

3. Passage of Scripture, text, short division, chapter, sentence.

VERSED, *adj.* At home with, skilled in, proficient, competent, qualified, conversant, *au fait (Fr.),* experienced, expert, adept, acquainted, accomplished,

gifted, talented, skillful, able, practiced, clever, familiar with, learned, well-informed, *au courant (Fr.),* erudite, scholarly, studious, cognizant of, instructed, lettered, well-conned, well-read, bookish, enlightened.

VERSION, *n.* Interpretation, translation, reading, rendering, rendition, lection, reddition, construction, light, exegesis, particular account of some matter, story, description, tale, narration, recital, enumeration, delineation, depiction, rehearsal, relation.

VERTEX, *n.* Highest point of something, culmen, zenith, apogee, acme, apex, summit, top, crown, crest, pinnacle, meridian, culmination, climax.

VERTICAL, *adj.* In the same direction as the axis, perpendicular to the horizon, upright, lengthwise, erect, plumb, steep, sheer, bolt upright, longitudinal, rampant.

VERTIGINOUS, *adj.* 1. Whirling, rotatory, rotary, trochilic, gyratory, circumrotatory, head over heels, round and round.

2. Dizzy, giddy, reeling, light-headed, confused, distracted, bewildered, distraught, flighty, wild, frantic, crazed, crazy, disordered, unhinged, frenzied, daft, deranged, incoherent, off one's head.

VERTIGO, *n.* 1. Whirl, verticity, vortex, swirl, surge, eddy, whirlpool, maelstrom, tornado, cyclone, twister, dizzy round, whirligig, merry-go-round, carrousel.

2. Swimming of the head, light-headedness, dizziness, reeling, siriasis, fainting, syncope, loss of equilibrium, giddiness.

VERVE, *n.* Enthusiasm, stimulation of the imagination, spirit, élan, esprit, dash, snap, animation, vigor, ardor, fervor, rapture, liveliness, energy, force, gusto, relish, vivacity, life, go, zeal, eagerness, abandon, inspiration, feeling, warmth, fire, glow, vehemence, passion.

VERY, *adj.* 1. True, actual, genuine, authentic, real, exact, veritable, sound, correct, pure, truthful, precise, right, literal, scrupulous, textual, unimpeachable.

2. Same, identical, selfsame, similar, ditto, one, like, equal, duplicate, twin, homologous, parallel, cast in the same mold.

3. Even, mere, sheer, downright, unconditional, unqualified, utter, unmitigated, simple, bare, stark, plain, such, sole.

VERY, *adv.* Exceedingly, extremely, highly, to a high degree, supremely, hugely, excessively, vastly, enormously, greatly, surpassingly, superlatively, quite, terribly *(coll.),* absolutely, remarkably, wondrously, jolly *(Brit. coll.),* extravagantly, unduly, exorbitantly, consummately, thoroughly, intensely, profoundly, most, indeed, powerfully, mightily, incalculably, immeasurably, truly, positively, decidedly, fundamentally, unconditionally, downright, unequivocally, essentially, radically, wholly, altogether, utterly, completely, entirely, fully.

VESICLE, *n.* Bladderlike cavity filled with fluid, little sac, cyst, follicle, utricle, cell, blister, circumscribed elevation of the epidermis containing serous fluid, eruption, blotch, vacuole, bleb, sacculus, vesica, saccule.

VESPERS, *n., pl.* Evensong, sixth of the seven canonical hours, evening services, evening prayer, compline (last of the canonical hours immediately after vespers).

VESPERTINE, *adj.* Nocturnal, vesper, nightly, crepuscular, twilight.

VESSEL, *n.* 1. Hollow article for holding of contents, utensil, receptacle, vase, jar, bowl, crock, jug, glass, cup, pot, pitcher, ewer, flask, horn, canteen, bottle, epergne, dish, plate, canister, amphora, decanter, cruse, carafe, flagon, urn, tankard, mug, basin, beaker, goblet, chalice, tumbler, platter, porringer, toby, pipkin, bucket, tub, vat, caldron, cask, barrel, keg, butt, tun, hogshead, carboy, ampulla, demijohn, phial, vial, cruet, pail, stein.

2. Blood vessel, artery, vein, capillary, duct, tube, canal, channel, tubule.

3. Sailing craft, boat, ship, steamship, clipper, sailer, windjammer, barque, brigantine, schooner, brig, yacht, sloop, ketch, cutter, yawl, junk, smack, felucca, caravel, galley, sampan, caique, kayak, trireme, gondola, motorboat, canoe, rowboat, skiff, gig, shallop, cockboat, dory, dinghy, tender, dugout, barge, punt, scow, lighter, catamaran, raft, tugboat, pilot boat, flatboat, ferry, launch, cruiser, tramp, whaler, slaver, whaleback, merchantman, cargo boat, packet, transport, tanker, collier, liner, freighter, trawler, corvette, pinnace, outrigger.

VEST, *n.* Waistcoat for men, short sleeveless garment, jacket, jerkin, doublet.

VEST, *v.* 1. Clothe, dress, array, envelop, cover, deck out, drape, invest, enwrap, robe, attire, habilitate, garb, accouter, fit out, apparel, rig.

2. Place in the control of, clothe with possession, put in possession, furnish, endow, put into the hands of, make over, entrust, consign, settle upon, leave to, bequeath, devise.

VESTAL, *adj.* Virginal, chaste, virgin, pure, stainless, immaculate, unmarried, maidenly, undefiled, continent, virtuous.

VESTAL, *n.* Chaste unmarried woman, virgin, maiden, damsel, spinster, old maid, celibate, nun.

VESTED, *adj.* 1. Robed, clothed, outfitted, clad, costumed, habited, appareled, garmented, arrayed.

2. Authorized, sanctioned, fixed, legalized, lawful, valid, legitimate, legal, licit, constitutional, sound, statutory, chartered, according to law, established.

VESTIBULE, *n.* Anteroom, antechamber, lobby, hall, passage, entranceway, porch, hallway, propylaeum, narthex, loggia, court, corridor, foyer, lounge, waiting room.

VESTIGE, *n.* Visible evidence of something no longer present, surviving memorial, relic, evidence, remains, mark, token, record, memento, sign, footprint, footstep, track, trail, *piste (Fr.),* footmark, wake, spoor, scent, pug, cicatrix, scar, trace, very slight amount of something.

VESTMENTS, *n., pl.* 1. Priestly garments, canonicals, pontificalia, pontificals, surplice, gown, cassock, robe, dalmatic, alb, stole, scapular, maniple, cope, pallium, chasuble, tunic, mantelletta, tunicle, cotta.

2. Clothing, clothes, attire, raiment, apparel, array, dress, habiliment, vesture, garb, costume, outfit, livery, regalia, toilette, wardrobe, finery, regimentals, harness, gear, trappings, rigging, turnout, caparison, accouterment, uniform.

VESTRY, *n.* 1. Church room in which vestments and sacred vessels are kept, sacristy, vestry room.

2. Ecclesiastical council, conclave, synod, convocation, consistory, presbytery.

VETERAN, *adj.* 1. Experienced, expert, practiced, seasoned, long-exercised, long-practiced, skilled, proficient, skillful, adroit, deft, apt, adept, crack,

finished, polished, dexterous, facile, ready, qualified, up in, capable, trained, disciplined, initiated, primed, talented, *aguerri (Fr.).*

2. Aged, old, gray-headed, hoary, venerable.

VETERAN, *n.* 1. One who has seen long service, old campaigner, old soldier, old stager, expert, old hand, proficient, adept, practiced hand, master, prizeman, medalist.

2. Old timer, old man, graybeard, oldster, patriarch, grisard, dean, *doyen (Fr.),* Nestor, Methuselah, centenarian, nonagenarian, octogenarian, sexagenarian.

VETERINARIAN, *n.* One who practices medical and surgical treatment of domesticated animals, veterinary, horse doctor, veterinary surgeon, vet *(coll.),* farrier, hippiatrist.

VETO, *v.* Withhold assent to, refuse to consent to, negative, vote down, reject, turn down, turn thumbs down on, enjoin, prohibit, prevent, hinder, restrain, taboo, interdict, forbid, disallow.

VETO, *n.* Right to negative a governmental determination, prohibition directed against some proposed act, refusal to sanction, restriction, interdiction, rejection, taboo, thumbs down, power of preventing action, forbiddance, prevention, inhibition, disallowance, interdict, injunction, ban, proscription, embargo.

VEX, *v.* Irritate, annoy, anger, displease, provoke, irk, rile, nettle, pique, offend, try the patience, fret, discompose, put out, discommode, affront, chafe, gall, distress, worry, plague, perturb, ruffle, miff, madden, distract, grate, exasperate, inflame, chagrin, grieve, pain, persecute, molest, bother, torment, tantalize, taunt, mortify, pester, hector, tease, harass, harry, perplex, pother, cross, trouble, badger, tire, bore, weary, infest, tantalize, beset, incense.

VEXATION, *n.* Irritation, annoyance, pique, agitation, displeasure, chagrin, mortification, embarrassment, distress, disquiet, trouble, uneasiness, affliction, sorrow, grief, discomfort, bother, heartache, anguish, unhappiness, discontent, regret, rue, wretchedness, anxiety, botheration, worry, discomfiture, ordeal, misery, anger, dissatisfaction, exasperation, spleen, plague, torment, curse, nuisance, affliction, affront, trial, visitation, grievance, discomposure, resentment, animosity, choler, ire, indignation, wrath, irascibility, dudgeon, huff, umbrage, tiff, pet, indignity.

VEXATIOUS, *adj.* Irritating, galling, provoking, irksome, aggravating, vexing, annoying, exasperating, maddening, bothersome, grievous, disturbing, afflictive, harassing, distressing, painful, troublesome, bothering, pestering, tormenting, worrying, odious, objectionable, obnoxious, insufferable, hateful, mortifying, unaccommodating, invidious, wearisome, plaguy, thorny, pesky, pestiferous, oppressive, grating, stinging.

VEXED, *adj.* 1. Irritated, annoyed, provoked, harassed, troubled, worried, disquieted, plagued, disturbed, in high dudgeon, discontented, sulky, pettish, irascible, sore, out of temper, exasperated.

2. Disputed, controversial, much discussed, moot, in dispute, contested, causing contention, polemic.

VIA, *adv.* By a route that passes through, by way of, through, on the road to.

VIADUCT, *n.* Arched bridge for carrying a roadway over a ravine, causeway, gantry, catwalk, drawbridge, span, ramp, pontoon.

VIAL, *n.* Glass vessel for liquids, small bottle, phial, cruet, carafe, decanter, ampoule, jar, ewer, cruse, flagon, flask, test tube.

VIANDS, *n., pl.* Choice articles of food, delicate fare, gastronomic victuals, nutriment, aliment, nourishment, diet, provisions, repast, refreshment, sustentation, sustenance, subsistence, nurture, provender, rations, commons, board, dietary, cheer, regimen, comestibles, edibles, dainties, delicacies, ambrosia, good living, pabulum, *pièce de résistance (Fr.)*, cuisine, table, bill of fare, menu, spread, feed, collation, refection, banquet, feast.

VIBRANT, *adj.* 1. Moving to and fro rapidly, oscillating, fluctuating, undulous, oscillatory, pulsatory, libratory, undulatory, vibratory, vibratile, pendulous, shutterwise, seesaw, zigzag, swaying, wavering.

2. Resonant, sonorous, plangent, quivering, reverberant, resounding, ringing, deep-toned, bell-like, soniferous, sonoric, melodious, throbbing, tintinnabulous, clanging, pealing.

3. Pulsating with energy, full of vigor, powerful, energetic, forcible, puissant, potent, mettlesome, strenuous, vivacious, alert, brisk, active, lively, spirited, sparkling, glowing, vehement, ardent, fervent, eager.

VIBRATE, *v.* 1. Move to and fro, go backward and forward, fluctuate, oscillate, librate, pendulate, swing, undulate, nutate, wave, sway, pulsate, vary, waver, alternate, wobble, rock, dangle, beat, throb, waggle, bob, reel, seesaw, teeter, ebb and flow, flutter, flap.

2. Quiver, quaver, quake, palpitate, flutter, resound, reverberate, reëcho, tintinnabulate, peel, ring, chime.

3. Brandish, flourish, wag, wave, wield, agitate, convulse, shake, switch, whisk.

VIBRATION, *n.* 1. Oscillation, fluctuation, nutation, libration, pendulation, undulation, swinging, pulsation, variation, vibratility, throb, beat, teeter, seesaw, to-and-fro, alternation, ebb and flow, flux and reflux.

2. Resonance, reverberation, tintinnabulation, ringing, chime, boom, clangor, roar, charivari, tingle, tinkle, thunder, rumble, roll.

3. Tremor, earthquake, seismos, temblor, shock, explosion, convulsion, throe, upheaval.

VIBRATO, *n.* Pulsating sound, tremolo, quaver, reverberation, shake, appoggiatura, acciaccatura, grace note, quiver.

VICAR, *n.* 1. Priest of a parish, rector, clergyman, cleric, minister, curate, ecclesiastic, parson, curé, padre, father, churchman, divine, presbyter, pastor, abbé, reverend, sky pilot, chaplain, preacher.

2. Deputy, emissary, substitute, lieutenant, delegate, representative, vice-regent, proxy, locum tenens, surrogate, regent, commissioner, plenipotentiary.

VICARIOUS, *adj.* 1. Taking the place of another, acting as substitute for, delegated, deputed, commissioned, vice, acting, accredited, substitutional, subdititious, substituted, intermediary.

2. Suffered in place of another, sympathetic, empathic, understanding, mental, perceptive, sympathizing.

VICE, *n.* 1. Fault, defect, imperfection, blemish, flaw, frailty, shortcoming, infirmity, failing, weakness, deficiency, demerit, inadequacy, weak point, error, foible, want, lack, failure, besetting sin, lapse.

2. Indulgence in degrading practices, immoral habit, iniquity, wickedness, sinfulness, sin, depravity, immorality, turpitude, evil, corruption, wrongdoing, badness, evildoing, viciousness, obliquity, the old Adam, vileness, pollution, offense, crime, felony, perversion, depravation, profligacy, enormity, flagrancy, atrocity, excess, infamy, brutality, debauchery, impurity, unchastity, looseness, unnatural desire, licentiousness, lechery, lust, fornication, rape, bastardy, sensuality, carnality, lewdness, prostitution, incest, sadism, masochism, sodomy, pederasty, Lesbianism, obscenity, indecency, incontinence, concupiscence, libertinism, dissipation, venery, harlotry, animalism.

VICEROY, *n.* One appointed to rule a country as the deputy of a sovereign, vice-king, vice-regent, regent, consul, deputy ruler, satrap, khedive, nawab, pasha, bey, governor, imaum, caliph, padishah, shah, khan, mogul, emir, rajah, Nizam, Negus, palatine, exarch, hospodar, bashaw, dey, tetrarch, mandarin, subahdar, maharajah, burgrave, sherif, vizier, prefect, archon, proconsul, plenipotentiary, commissioner, legate.

VICE VERSA Conversely, the order being changed, turn about, contrariwise, reversely, in exchange, inversely, *mutatis mutandis (Lat.)*.

VICINITY, *n.* Region near *or* about a place, environs, neighborhood, vicinage, purlieus, suburbs, outskirts, banlieue, surroundings, milieu, circumjacencies, precincts, background, scene, setting, propinquity, proximity, *alentours (Fr.)*, faubourg, confines, periphery.

VICIOUS, *adj.* 1. Faulty, blemished, marred, unsound, imperfect, defective, flawed, irregular, deficient, impaired, injured, warped, disfigured, mutilated.

2. Reprehensible, blameworthy, wrong, culpable, guilty, offensive, flagrant, egregious, flagitious, condemnable, censurable, blamable, uncommendable, reprovable, refractory, recalcitrant, recidivistic, discreditable, disreputable, disgraceful, unworthy, recreant, disorderly, lawless, irreclaimable, incorrigible, irreformable, reprobate, unruly, unmanageable, obdurate.

3. Immoral, wicked, sinful, depraved, degenerate, perverse, perverted, turpitudinous, iniquitous, abandoned, unprincipled, corrupt, shameless, hellish, diabolical, demoniac, atrocious, evil-minded, foul-mouthed, obscene, smutty, pornographic, ribald, lewd, lustful, lecherous, salacious, libidinous, libertine, debauched, loose-living, dissolute, felonious, criminal, base, gross, foul, vile, scandalous, opprobrious, scurvy, villainous, heinous, monstrous, infamous, fiendish, satanic.

4. Malicious, spiteful, rancorous, venomous, virulent, malevolent, malign, malignant, maleficent, ill-tempered, ill-disposed, inimical, unfriendly, bitter, ill-natured, ill-intentioned, treacherous, envenomed, caustic, acrimonious, disobliging, harsh, churlish, sullen, surly, cruel, brutal, feral, ferine, inhuman, ferocious, savage, fell, truculent, barbarous.

VICISSITUDE, *n.* Variation occuring in the course of a thing, successive phase, alternating condition, ups and downs, shifting sands, alteration, fluctuation, change, mutation, revolution, mutual succession, interchange, alternation, kaleidoscope, moon, wheel of fortune.

VICTIM, *n.* 1. Living creature sacrificed in religious rites, martyr, sacrifice, sufferer, prey, wretch, shorn lamb.

2. Culprit, malefactor, *condamné (Fr.)*, criminal, convict, felon.

3. Dupe, puppet, cat's-paw, gull, cully, gudgeon, fall guy *(sl.)*, patsy *(sl.)*, scapegoat, tool, hireling, come-on, sucker *(sl.)*, easy mark, softy *(coll.)*, boob, booby, pigeon *(sl.)*, fool, greenhorn, butt, target, laughingstock, April fool.

VICTIMIZE, *v.* Dupe, play upon, take in, impose upon, practice upon, put upon, hoodwink, swindle, cheat, defraud, diddle, fool, gull, jockey, bamboozle, befool, chouse, trick, beguile, deceive, overreach, circumvent, hoax, cozen, outwit, throw sand in the eyes, mislead, thwart, abuse, ensnare, waylay, decoy, inveigle, lure, entangle, betray, bluff, humbug, stuff, sell *(sl.)*, palm off, foist upon, take advantage of.

VICTOR, *n.* One who has defeated an adversary, winner, conqueror, vanquisher, master, conquistador, subduer, champion, hero, prizeman, medalist, lion.

VICTORIOUS, *adj.* Conquering, triumphant, successful, winning, undefeated, exultant, triumphal, unbeaten, crowned with success, wearing the laurel, in the ascendant, set up, prize-winning.

VICTORY, *n.* Ultimate superiority, successful outcome of a struggle, decisive defeat of an opponent, achievement, triumph, conquest, palm, laurels, mastery, vanquishment, subdual, success, walkover, lucky stroke, master stroke, supremacy, *coup de grâce (Fr.)*, favorable issue, smiles of fortune, *coup de maître (Fr.)*, feat, trump card, prize, checkmate, feather in one's cap, ascendancy, whip hand, upper hand, expungation, subjugation.

VICTUAL, *v.* Provide with food, feed, supply with victuals, furnish sustenance, supply with provisions, nourish, board.

VICTUALS, *n., pl.* Food, provisions, eatables, edibles, comestibles, sustenance, viands, meat, repast, fare, refreshment, nourishment, sustentation, diet, meal, nutriment, pabulum, subsistence, provender, board, rations, commissariat, cheer, dietary, regimen, staff of life, foodstuffs, grub *(sl.)*, eats *(coll.)*, ambrosia, creature comforts, manna, spread, table, cuisine, collation, refection.

VIDELICET, *adv.* Namely, that is to say, in other words, viz. *(abbr.)*, to wit, to be more explicit, to particularize, that is, *i.e., id est (Lat.)*, in explanation, in plain terms, more simply.

VIE, *v.* Strive in competition with, contend for superiority, compete, emulate, rival, enter the lists, challenge comparison, endeavor to excel, contest, tilt with, measure swords, cope with, race with.

VIEW, *v.* Survey, behold, inspect, scan, contemplate, eye, look at, watch, see, attend, observe, turn the eyes to, explore, witness, have in sight, look upon, reconnoiter, glance at, study, regard, consider, examine, reflect upon, think about, scrutinize, ransack, review, search, probe, take stock of, notice, note, pore over, look askance.

VIEW, *n.* 1. Prospect, vista, panorama, outlook, scene, landscape, range, perspective, conspectus, spectacle, scenery, seascape, treescape, *paysage (Fr.)*, bird's-eye view, diorama, horizon.

2. Vision, sight, ocular range, eyesight, reach of the sight, ken, perception, seeing, discernment.

3. Glimpse, peep, look, *coup d'oeil (Fr.)*, blink, glint, glance, peek, gaze.

4. Regard, contemplation, survey, inspection, examination, observation, scrutiny, reconnaissance.

5. Lookout, watchtower, gazebo, post of observation, tower, beacon, crow's-nest, observatory, belvedere.

6. Appearance, phenomenon, show, tableau, picture, spectacle, representation, display, exhibition, exposition.

7. Opinion, judgment, belief, notion, idea, impression, conception, theory, sentiment, thought, creed, tenet, credo, apprehension, doctrine, supposition.

8. Object, purpose, objective, design, aim, intention, intent, drift, scope, expectation, anticipation.

VIEWPOINT, *n.* Point of view, standpoint, attitude of mind, aspect, angle, train of thought.

VIGIL, *n.* Watch kept by night, keeping awake during the natural hours of sleep, period of watchful attention, abstinence from sleep, sleeplessness, wake.

VIGILANCE, *n.* Watchfulness, circumspection, wakefulness, caution, alertness, weariness, lookout, *surveillance (Fr.), l'oeil du maître (Fr.)*, eyes of Argus, precaution, forethought, prudence, watch and ward, heedfulness, heed, cautiousness, scrupulous attention, incessant care, carefulness, watching, solicitude, sleeplessness, insomnia, concern, anxiety, pains, guardedness, providence, reconnoitering.

VIGILANT, *adj.* Watchful, keenly attentive to detect danger, ever-awake and alert, Argus-eyed, wary, on the *qui vive*, on the alert, unsleeping, wakeful, circumspect, unslumbering, on the lookout, cautious, careful, prudent, provident, wideawake, guarded, observant, heedful, sleepless, hawk-eyed, keen-eyed, lynx-eyed, chary, on one's guard, suspicious, scrupulous, canny, discreet, regardful, judicious, precautious, foresighted, foreseeing, anticipatory, prescient, far-seeing, searching.

VIGNETTE, *n.* 1. Decorative design used on the title page of a book, picture at the beginning or end of a chapter, headpiece, tailpiece, *cul de lampe (Fr.), fleuron (Fr.)*, engraving, illumination, print, illustration, drawing shading off at the edges, design without a border line, arabesque.

2. Pleasing view, delineation, sketch, graphic account, graceful sketch, historiette.

VIGOR, *n.* 1. Strength, vitality, physical force, healthy physical energy, potency, power, puissance, stamina, hardiness, hardihood, might, pith, sap, steel, nerve, mettle, soundness, robustness, sturdiness, health, efficacy, virility, vim, pep, vigorousness, punch, haleness, heartiness, bloom, flourishing condition, tone, elasticity, dash, snap, go *(coll.)*.

2. Keenness, forcibleness, intellectuality, cogency, penetration, forcefulness, trenchancy, animation, enthusiasm, verve, ardor, fervor, fire, glow, warmth, sprightliness, liveliness, vivacity, raciness, pungency, piquancy, vehemence, intensity, élan.

VIGOROUS, *adj.* 1. Strong, robust, virile, sinewy, muscular, lusty, sturdy, hale, masculine, sound, powerful, mighty, able-bodied, brawny, stout, robustious, stalwart, athletic, hardy, husky, strapping, wiry, well-knit, doughty, rugged.

2. Energetic, forceful, strenuous, active, dynamic, forcible, mighty, aggressive, spry, resolute, spirited, sparkling, lively, bold, sharp, trenchant, emphatic, impassioned, cogent, irresistible, telling, mettlesome, sparkling, glowing, slashing, racy, mordant, incisive, pungent, piquant, biting, pointed, meaty, marrowy, pithy, graphic,

striking, vivid, picturesque, terse, sententious, epigrammatic.

3. Vehement, violent, burning, fervent, ardent, zealous, eager, industrious, assiduous, enterprising, resolute, inexorable.

VILE, *adj.* 1. Ignoble, low, common, baseborn, plebeian, mean, contemptible, despicable, slavish, beggarly, scurvy, degraded, ignominious, abject, shabby, paltry, dirty, groveling, sordid, menial, servile, scrubby, sorry, vulgar, shabby, seedy, humble, obscure, inglorious.

2. Disreputable, disgraceful, notorious, foul, gross, flagitious, evil, sinful, vicious, iniquitous, immoral, wicked, criminal, degenerate, facinorous, depraved, perverted, corrupt, recreant, lawless, abandoned, infamous, felonious, black, nefarious, opprobrious, villainous, scandalous, heinous, flagrant, incorrigible, lewd, foul-mouthed, pornographic, smutty, ribald, coarse, obscene, impure, salacious, risqué, broad, lustful, blackguard, profligate, dissipated, shameful, filthy, nasty, scurrilous, turpitudinous.

3. Disgusting, revolting, odious, repulsive, repellent, objectionable, obnoxious, offensive, repugnant, hateful, abhorrent, execrable, detestable.

VILENESS, *n.* 1. Baseness, ignobleness, ignominiousness, ignominy, abjectness, abjection, menialness, servility, vulgarity, uncouthness, seediness, humbleness, ingloriousness, commonness, shabbiness, abasement, common herd, rank and file, rabble, canaille, mob, vulgus, riffraff, trash, ragtag and bobtail.

2. Sinfulness, wickedness, criminality, depravity, degeneracy, perversion, depravation, turpitude, reprobacy, profligacy, dissipation, villainy, knavery, roguery, disrepute, disreputableness, notoriety, grossness, foulness, flagitiousness, vice, viciousness, iniquity, immorality, recreancy, corruption, infamy, feloniousness, felony, nefariousness, flagrancy, lewdness, salacity, pornography, smuttiness, ribaldry, coarseness, obscenity, impurity, lustfulness, lechery, libidinousness, lasciviousness, filthiness.

3. Odiousness, repulsiveness, repellence, obnoxiousness, objectionableness, offensiveness, repugnancy, abhorrence, hatefulness, heinousness.

VILIFY, *v.* Speak evil of, calumniate, blacken, denigrate, defame, slander, traduce, stigmatize, disparage, abuse, revile, vilipend, asperse, slur, malign, run down, vituperate, scandalize, libel, blemish, brand, lampoon, decry, backbite, berate, depreciate, degrade, denounce, accuse falsely, contemn, detract from, ridicule, debase, sneer at, tongue-lash, upbraid, censure, belittle, derogate, criticize, bespatter, pull to pieces, anathematize.

VILLA, *n.* Suburban dwelling house, country residence, country house, rural mansion, country seat, estate, hacienda, cottage, hermitage, lodge.

VILLAGE, *n.* Small assemblage of houses in a country district, small rural community, hamlet, settlement, town, thorp, borough, kraal, clachan (*Gaelic*), bustee (*India*), kampong, compound, dorp (*Dutch*), wick, pueblo, burgh.

VILLAIN, *n.* Wicked person, bad man, evildoer, knave, rascal, scoundrel, blackguard, reprobate, rogue, ruffian, scapegrace, scamp, wretch, caitiff, miscreant, malefactor, scalawag, knave-of-spades, mischief-maker, wrongdoer, desperado, brute, hoodlum, hooligan, tough, transgressor, lawbreaker, worker of iniquity, felon, criminal, scapegallows, profligate, debauchee, libertine, cur,

hound, trickster, sneak, hellhound, forger, thief, sharper, swindler, embezzler, peculator, crook, hellion, terrorist, roughneck, black sheep, gangster, hijacker, jailbird, convict, outlaw, murderer, cutthroat, assassin, rotter, delinquent, ne'er-do-well, rapscallion, snake-in-the-grass, bravo, traitor, Judas, Iscariot.

VILLAINOUS, *adj.* Base, depraved, vicious, iniquitous, corrupt, unprincipled, ruffianly, knavish, roguish, rascally, scoundrelly, wicked, sinful, felonious, criminal, nefarious, heinous, atrocious, flagitious, abominable, infamous, profligate, foul, arrant, black-hearted, blackguardly, notorious, turpitudinous, reprehensible, opprobrious, monstrous, accursed, evil, bad, unregenerate, mischievous, malefic, baleful, maleficent, hateful, abominable, abhorrent, repugnant, repellent, detestable, execrable, odious, devilish, diabolic, demoniac, satanic, pernicious, malignant, malevolent, ill-intentioned, evil-minded, malicious, venomous, treacherous, perfidious, cold-blooded, grim, fell, pitiless, rancorous, merciless, unfeeling, brutal, cruel, barbarous, truculent.

VILLAINY, *n.* Knavery, roguery, miscreancy, rascality, trickery, iniquity, wrongdoing, dishonesty, sin, crime, felony, outrage, enormity, foul play, atrocity, injury, depravity, turpitude, corruption, unregeneracy, immorality, viciousness, vice, evildoing, wickedness, depravity, profligacy, excess, flagrancy, infamy, obliquity, debauchery, laxity, unchastity, criminality.

VIM, *n.* Vigor in action, dash, pep, élan, snap, energy, spirit, zeal, force, liveliness, briskness, efficacy, potency, intensity, might, fervor, verve, animation, go, punch, mettle.

VINCULUM, *n.* Bond, connection, tie, link, nexus, copula, ligature, cord, leader, stepping stone, bridge, hyphen, dash, string, funiculus, line, cable, catena, chain, lace, strap, thong, leash, brace, binder, cincture, surcingle, sash, cestus, zone, cummerbund, belt, hitch, noose, loop, slipknot, halter, clamp, clip, rivet, clinch, staple, catch, ring, clasp, hook, buckle, latch, shackle, coupling, tack, nail, dowel, thole, pin, spike, peg, toggle.

VINDICATE, *v.* 1. Clear from a charge, exonerate, exculpate, acquit, reprieve, respite.

2. Excuse, extenuate, forgive, pardon, absolve, palliate, gloss over, apologize for, smooth over, give the devil his due, whitewash, make allowance for, varnish, gloze, soften, remit.

3. Stand up for, champion, espouse, advocate, uphold, justify, support, stand by, maintain, make good, defend against opposition, claim, assert, plead, speak for, stick up for, bear out, contend for, bolster up.

4. Avenge, revenge, retaliate, requite, right.

VINDICATION, *n.* 1. Acquittal, exoneration, exculpation, reprieve, pardon, respite, clearance, absolution, release, discharge, quietus.

2. Justification, authorization, warrant, sanction, right.

3. Extenuation, whitewashing, mitigation, softening, palliation, explanation, apology, apologia, gloss, acknowledgment, extenuating circumstances, varnish, allowance.

4. Reply, rejoinder, defense, plea, answer, response, objection, denial, excuse, demurrer, recrimination, rebutter, countercharge, retort.

VINDICATIVE, *adj.* Vindicatory, justificatory, vindicating, exculpatory, exonerative, extenuating, palliative, mitigative, mitigatory, apologetic, excusatory, plausible, specious, venial.

VINDICTIVE, *adj.* Vengeful, revengeful, retaliative, punitive, unrelenting, avenging, implacable, rancorous, remorseless, unforgiving, relentless, spiteful, resentful, malicious, malevolent, maleficent, malignant, ruthless, pitiless, rigorous, inexorable, stony-hearted.

VIOLATE, *v.* 1. Infringe, trespass, transgress, encroach upon, trench upon, invade, break, set at naught, break through, disregard, disobey, enter without right, pass by force, contravene, repudiate, trample on, take the law into one's own hands.

2. Desecrate, profane, dishonor, pollute, defile, outrage, abuse, blaspheme, contaminate, revile, commit sacrilege.

3. Rape, ravish, constuprate, debauch, attack, ruin, seduce, deflower, devirginate, force.

4. Usurp, arrogate, exact, extort, take under false pretenses, dispossess.

VIOLATION, *n.* 1. Infraction, transgression, trespass, breach, infringement, nonobservance, evasion, misuse, illegality, dereliction, delinquency.

2. Profanation, desecration, sacrilege, dishonor, impiety, irreverence, blasphemy, profanity, apostasy, recreancy, recusancy, nonconformity.

3. Rape, ravishment, constupration, stupration, debauchment, devirgination, pollution, defilement, abuse, defloration, ruination, seduction.

4. Usurpation, seizure, assumption, dispossession, tort, encroachment, imposition, exaction.

VIOLENCE, *n.* 1. Rough force in action, brute force, might, ferocity, brunt, vehemence, shock, strain, fury, impetuosity, rage, severity, fierceness, intensity, acuteness, exasperation, irritation, furiousness, sharpness, impact, *acharnement (Fr.),* savagery, brutality, malignity, ferociousness, outrage, injurious treatment, injury, wrong, injustice, violation, poignancy, stress, assault, attack, onslaught, foul play, rape, desecration, profanation.

2. Turbulence, disorder, commotion, fracas, excitement, boisterousness, disturbance, ebullition, tumultuousness, riot, tumult, bluster, row, uproar, rumpus, outbreak.

3. Eruption, outburst, debacle, disruption, explosion, volley, discharge, detonation, blast, blow-up, roar, earthquake, crash, temblor, quake, storm, squall.

4. Convulsion, throe, paroxysm, fit, spasm, frenzy, ictus, raptus, access, hysterics, madness, raving.

VIOLENT, *adj.* 1. Turbulent, stormy, tumultuous, raging, disorderly, disturbed, restless, obstreperous, riotous, troublous, boisterous, refractory, uproarious, ungovernable, rabid, rampant, berserk, amuck, fuming, fiery, fierce, roaring, tearing, rough, towering, infuriate, passionate, explosive, raving, flaming, rampageous, frenzied, frantic, frothing, furious, desperate, ferocious, hysterical, uncontrollable, unbridled, tempestuous, impetuous, forcible, wild, insane, demented, headstrong, unruly, intractable, obdurate, unrestrainable, irrepressible, convulsive, spasmodic, spastic, paroxysmal, volcanic, explosive, murderous, homicidal, bloody, bloodthirsty, suicidal, maniacal, demoniac, inflamed, hot-headed, impassioned, ardent.

2. Intense, severe, acute, extreme, drastic, excessive, virulent, poignant, sharp, lancinating, cutting, excruciating, exquisite, cruel, abrupt, rude, brusque, unnatural, unexpected, abnormal, irregular, accidental.

VIOLIN, *n.* Fiddle, stringed instrument, Stradivarius, Strad, Guarnerius, Cremona, Amati, kit.

VIPER, *n.* 1. Poisonous snake, venomous serpent, horned viper, puff adder, reptile, asp, scorpion, cobra, rattler.

2. Malignant person, bad man, evildoer, snake-in-the-grass, fiend, monster, hellhound, cutthroat, miscreant, scoundrel, rascal, villain, caitiff, wretch, devil incarnate, recreant, malefactor, blackguard, criminal, delinquent, culprit, misdemeanant, felon, rogue, reprobate.

VIPEROUS, *adj.* Poisonous, venomous, lethal, deadly, malignant, spiteful, rancorous, baneful, baleful, maleficent, malicious, malign, vicious, treacherous.

VIRAGO, *n.* Turbulent ill-tempered woman, termagant, shrew, vixen, scold, brawler, tartar, Xanthippe, she-devil, fury, beldam, hag, dragon, spitfire, Tisiphone, Alecto, Megaera, Medusa, amazon.

VIRGIN, *n.* Young woman who has had no sexual intercourse, vestal, spinster, celibate, old maid, damsel, lass, girl, maiden, maid, Diana, Parthenos, Lucretia, nun, sister, *religieuse (Fr.),* St. Agnes, bachelor-girl.

VIRGINAL, *adj.* Chaste, continent, stainless, vestal, unpolluted, undefiled, unsullied, pure, parthenic, immaculate, maidenly, modest, untouched, untried, unused, celibate, unwedded, unmarried, husbandless, innocent, spotless, clean, unblemished, virtuous.

VIRGINITY, *n.* Virginal chastity, maidenhood, purity, celibacy, innocence, continence, virtue, modesty, pudicity, immaculacy, immaculateness.

VIRIDESCENT, *adj.* Slightly green, greenish, virescent, glaucous, olive, verdant, porraceous, leek-green, emerald, virent, verdurous, grass-green, chlorine, citrine, olivaceous, aquamarine, berylline.

VIRIDITY, *n.* Greenness, verdancy, viridness, verdure, viridescence, verdigris, emerald, malachite, aquamarine, beryl, chlorophyl, bice.

VIRILE, *adj.* Manly, masculine, manlike, adult, vigorous, forceful, strong, robust, powerful, hardy, mighty, masterful, potent, brave, courageous, stout-hearted, husky, sturdy, strapping, brawny, muscular, sinewy, lusty, stalwart, able-bodied, athletic, wiry, well-knit, manful, energetic, undaunted, resolute, heroic, bold, fearless, gallant, valiant, lion-hearted, audacious, self-reliant, soldierly, dashing, chivalrous, adventurous.

VIRILITY, *n.* Maturity, manhood, adulthood, majority, full age, flower of age, prime of life, masculinity, male energy, masculineness, masculine spirit, manly vigor, manliness, sexual power, potency, strength, puissance, force, vigor, physical force, stamina, lustihood, brawn, muscle, thews, sinews, vitality, grit, physique, bravery, courage, resoluteness, valor, resolution, spirit, dash, daring, heroism, gallantry, soldierliness, prowess, self-reliance, nerve, pluck, spunk, sand, fortitude, hardihood, backbone.

VIRTUAL, *adj.* Practical, potential, substantial, tantamount to, essential, equivalent, constructive, implicit, implied, indirect, moral, effective.

VIRTUALLY, *adv.* Substantially, in effect, in essence, practically, essentially, to all intents and purposes, potentially, in principle, in substance.

VIRTUE, *n.* 1. Self-disciplined goodness, rectitude, integrity, morality, probity, honesty, honor, uprightness, moral excellence, worth, worthiness, soundness, nobleness, nobility, moral practice, good actions, well-doing, self-control, well-spent life, good behavior, cardinal virtues, duty, prudence, fortitude, justice, merit, grace, value, desert, credit, quality, high-mindedness, righteousness.

2. Effective force, effectiveness, efficacy, efficacity, inherent power, potentiality, potency, power, puissance, energy, strength, efficiency, efficaciousness, effectuality.

3. Chastity, virginity, pudicity, purity, innocence, continence, decency, immaculacy, decorum, delicacy, modesty, sanctity, impeccability, sinlessness, guiltlessness, incorruption.

VIRTUOSO, *n.* 1. One who excels in artistic technique *or* execution, technician, bravura performer, *artiste (Fr.)*, master, expert, adept.

2. One who has a cultivated appreciation of fine arts, person skilled in the fine arts, connoisseur, student, collector, dilettante, amateur, man of taste, critic, judge, *conoscente (It.)*, *arbiter elegantiarum (Lat.)*, savant, ardent admirer.

VIRTUOUS, *adj.* 1. Conforming to moral laws, morally excellent, righteous, upright, worthy, honorable, noble, honest, morally right, exemplary, good, estimable, equitable, dutiful, bound to do what is right, just, correct, conscientious, whole-souled, sterling, right-minded, duteous, deserving, meritorious, commendable, creditable, praiseworthy, laudable, peerless, matchless, god-like, holy, angelic, saintly, religious, strict, high-principled, respectable, fair, veracious, truthful, reputable, aboveboard, punctilious.

2. Chaste, pure, virginal, continent, clean, unsullied, immaculate, uncontaminated, undefiled, unpolluted, spotless, unspotted, innocent, modest.

VIRULENCE, *n.* 1. Poisonousness, toxicity, venomousness, deadliness, lethality, perniciousness.

2. Maliciousness, malignity, malignancy, malevolence, hostility, animosity, rancor, malice, spitefulness, enmity, acrimony, acerbity, asperity, corrosiveness, acridity, sourness, bitterness.

VIRULENT, *adj.* 1. Poisonous, toxic, venomous, noxious, deadly, malignant, lethal, pernicious, cancerous, deleterious, hurtful, baneful, injurious.

2. Malicious, malevolent, malign, hostile, spiteful, rancorous, baleful, implacable, corrosive, violent, bitter, acrimonious, acerbous, caustic, indignant, resentful.

VIRUS, *n.* Infective agent requiring living cells for multiplication, morbid poison, venom, toxin, septicity, infection, pestilence, disease-producing microörganism, germ, bug *(sl.)*.

VISAGE, *n.* 1. Face, physiognomy, countenance, profile, features, lineaments, mug *(sl.)*, map *(sl.)*.

2. Appearance, aspect, guise, mien, semblance, likeness, look, image, complexion, expression, presence, demeanor, port, carriage, cast, air, shape, form.

VIS-A-VIS, *adj., adv.* Face-to-face, tête-à-tête, cheek by jowl, before one's face, eye-to-eye, side by side, situated opposite to another, confronting one another.

VISCERA, *n., pl.* Intestines, entrails, bowels, splanchna, inner parts, soft interior organs in the cavity of the body, inwards, insides, guts, internals, ventrals, haslets.

VISCID, *adj.* Sticky, mucilaginous, viscous, slimy, glutinous, adhesive, sizy, ropy, clammy, thick, tenacious, tough, gluey, stringy, dauby, tacky,

pasty, gummy, albuminous, gummous, mucid, pituitous, mucous, gelatinous.

VISCOSITY, *n.* Stickiness, viscidity, viscousness, viscidness, glutinousness, ropiness, sliminess, cohesiveness, mucilaginousness, adhesiveness, tenacity, clamminess, thickness, toughness, stringiness, pastiness, gumminess, mucosity, gummosity, glutinosity, spissitude, inspissation, coagulation, incrassation, jellification, gelatinousness.

VISIBILITY, *n.* 1. Capability of being seen, perceptibility, exposure to view, distinctness, discernibleness, clearness, clarity, apparentness, perceivability, atmospheric transparency, visuality, appearance, apparency, manifestation, conspicuousness, ocular demonstration, precision, definition, sharp outline.

2. Reach of the sight, field of observation, field of view, range, ceiling, horizon.

VISIBLE, *adj.* 1. Capable of being seen, perceivable, perceptible, visual, seeable, in view, to be seen, discernible, in sight, distinct, well-defined, unclouded, in focus, clear, conspicuous, recognizable, observable.

2. Evident, obvious, patent, noticeable, unhidden, plain, discoverable, unmistakable, open, manifest, apparent, *en évidence (Fr.)*, revealed, palpable, glaring, salient.

VISION, *n.* 1. Faculty of seeing, eyesight, sight, perception, discernment, optics, light.

2. Glance, glimpse, look, peep, blink, peek, glint, stare, ken, gaze, *coup d'oeil (Fr.)*, ogle, leer, regard, inspection, observation, survey, contemplation, view, lookout, watch.

3. Field of view, eyeshot, range of vision, panoramic view, arena, theater, amphitheater, vista, prospect, horizon, perspective.

4. Visual organ, eye, orb, oculus, optic, ocular, peeper, lamps *(sl.)*, peepers *(sl.)*, naked eye.

5. Observatory, lookout, tower, watchtower, beacon, belvedere, crow's-nest, gazebo.

6. Spectacle, apparition, sight, phenomenon, specter, phantom, ghost, shade, *revenant (Fr.)*, phantasm, hallucination, chimera, illusion, image, supernatural appearance, wraith, spirit, sprite, banshee, spook, materialization, will-o'-the-wisp, ignis fatuus, friar's lantern, lemures, jack-o'-lantern, St. Elmo's fire, mirage, Fata Morgana.

7. Imagination, imaginativeness, mental image, conception, notion, fancy, figment, fiction, creation, belief, thought, idea, daydream, air castle, castle in Spain, air-drawn dagger, man in the moon, dream.

VISIONARY, *adj.* 1. Given to flights of fancy, romantic, imaginative, impractical, quixotic, unpractical, idealistic, wild-eyed, starry-eyed.

2. Unreal, fancied, fanciful, imaginary, fantastic, ideal, illusory, wild, chimerical, dreamy, unsubstantial, shadowy, utopian, air-built, rhapsodic, Laputan, delusive, vain, unfounded, vague, airy, aerial, fabulous, mythical, legendary, mythological, fictional.

VISIONARY, *n.* One given to impractical ideas *or* schemes, castle-builder, dreamer, daydreamer, visionist, fantast, utopian, Don Quixote, optimist, idealist, Laputan, theorist, speculator, unpractical enthusiast, fanatic, bug *(sl.)*, zealot, seer, *exalté (Fr.)*, romancer, rhapsodist, romanticist.

VISIT, *v.* 1. Call upon, look in on, go to see, pay a visit to, drop in, arrive, call at, leave a card.

2. Sojourn with, stay with, tarry with, frequent, haunt.

3. Affect, afflict, smite, assail, attack, punish, act upon.

VISITATION, *n.* 1. Misfortune, affliction, blow, infliction, trial, adversity, sorrow, cross, calamity, punishment, disaster, catastrophe, stroke, hardship, trouble, ill-fortune, ill-luck, broken fortunes, evil day, rainy day, hard times, ill wind, gathering clouds, blight, curse, load, harm, evil, humiliation, mishap, misadventure, mischance, casualty, accident, reverse, scourge, setback, debacle, extremity, undoing.

2. Seizure, attack, paroxysm, stroke, ictus, raptus, fit, convulsion, apoplexy, epilepsy, falling sickness.

3. Official inspection, visiting in order to examine, official visit, *surveillance (Fr.),* supervision, superintendence.

VISITOR, *n.* Visitant, caller, frequenter, sojourner, habitué, company, guest, newcomer, stranger, incomer, transient.

VISTA, *n.* Field of view, perspective, prospect, outlook, horizon, picture, sight, scenery, landscape, seascape, panorama, bird's-eye view, arena, theater.

VISUAL, *adj.* Optical, ocular, optic, ophthalmic, pertaining to the sight *or* vision, of the eye.

VISUALIZE, *v.* Call up mental images, envisage, envision, conceive, imagine, invent, objectify, actualize, exteriorize, externalize, dream of, fancy, picture.

VITAL, *adj.* 1. Existing, living, vivifying, alive, having life, animate, mortal, live, viable, quick, breathing.

2. Essential, necessary, requisite, cardinal, radical, elementary, paramount, highly important, indispensable, urgent, pressing, critical, serious, significant, material, foremost, principle, primary, chief, basic.

VITALITY, *n.* Vital power, virility, life, animation, the vital spark, energy, vigor, strength, animal spirits, physical exuberance, essence, life force, lifeblood, vital flame.

VITALIZE, *v.* Give life to, quicken, vivify, animate, make alive, strengthen, furnish with vital principle, vigorize, invigorate, energize, fire, resuscitate, reanimate, revivify, restore.

VITALS, *n., pl.* Vital organs, parts essential to life, viscera, heart, entrails, intestines, splanchna, chitterlings, womb, internal organs, penetralia.

VITIATE, *v.* 1. Make void, cancel, abolish, make legally invalid, invalidate, destroy, abrogate, rescind, undo, nullify, annul, overthrow, quash, suppress, erase, efface, obliterate, expunge, delete.

2. Impair the quality of, make faulty, render defective, injure, spoil, mar, contaminate, pervert, wrest, despoil, defile, pollute, sully, taint, corrupt, debase, degrade, deprave, deteriorate, adulterate, infect, poison, demoralize, debauch, damage, alloy, tamper with, rot, blight, canker.

VITIATION, *n.* 1. Voidance, annulment, nullification, cancellation, invalidation, abolition, destruction, abrogation, undoing, suppression, erasure, obliteration, effacement, deletion.

2. Deterioration, impairment, depravation, debasement, contamination, pollution, defilement, degradation, adulteration, degeneration, degeneracy, decadence, corruption, perversion, prostitution, demoralization, detriment.

VITREOUS, *adj.* Glassy, crystalline, transparent,

diaphanous, translucent, transpicuous, hyaline, brittle, fragile, frangible.

VITRIOLIC, *adj.* Severely critical, caustic, corrosive, scathing, censorious, acrimonious, acerbous, abusive, trenchant, sarcastic, satirical, sardonic, sharp, cutting, withering, virulent, carping, captious, hypercritical.

VITUPERATE, *v.* Find fault with abusively, rail at, objurgate, scold, berate, dress down, overwhelm with abuse, censure, denounce, revile, vilify, abuse verbally, rate, reproach, upbraid, assail, condemn, declaim against, reprove, traduce, brand, stigmatize, malign, slander, exprobrate, beshrew, execrate, anathematize, fulminate, disparage, slate, impugn, castigate, reprimand, lash, chastise, impeach, backbite, decry, inveigh against, calumniate, lampoon.

VITUPERATION, *n.* Verbal abuse, criticism, reviling, billingsgate, railing, upbraiding, reproach, blame, denunciation, malediction, dispraise, slander, severe censure, scolding, invective, objurgation, increpation, castigation, jobation, obloquy, philippic, calumniation, lampoon, squib, exprobration.

VITUPERATIVE, *adj.* Abusive, censorious, critical, insulting, reproachful, scurrilous, scolding, condemnatory, opprobrious, objurgatory, damnatory, contemptuous, defamatory, slanderous, sarcastic, satirical, sardonic, cutting, sharp-tongued, virulent, withering, caustic, corrosive, disparaging, denunciatory, exprobratory.

VITUPERATOR, *n.* Critic, censurer, censor, detractor, reprover, caviler, backbiter, defamer, knocker, slanderer, lampooner, traducer, satirist, calumniator, reviler, castigator, disapprover.

VIVACIOUS, *adj.* Lively, light-hearted, sprightly, gay, bubbling, effervescent, full of life, chipper, frolicsome, mirthful, jocund, breezy, debonair, gladsome, airy, jovial, merry, jolly, playful, sportive, cheerful, bright, pleasant, animated, full of ginger, brisk, volatile, buxom, spirited, active, genial, sunny, optimistic, blithe, buoyant, jaunty, pert, saucy, dashing, social, convivial, waggish, frisky, alive, enthusiastic, mettlesome.

VIVACITY, *n.* Liveliness, sprightliness, lightheartedness, effervescence, gaiety, cheerfulness, jocundity, breeziness, gladsomeness, airiness, joviality, jollity, playfulness, sportiveness, animation, ebullience, ginger, volatility, geniality, blitheness, buoyancy, jauntiness, pertness, conviviality, friskiness, waggishness, enthusiasm, energy, élan, spirit, activity, good spirits, high spirits, alacrity, hilarity, levity, animal spirits, vigor, alertness, snap, go *(coll.),* dash, briskness, ardor, zeal, flurry, joyousness.

VIVA VOCE *(Lat.)* By word of mouth, orally, vocally, from the lips of, articulately, expressively.

VIVID, *adj.* 1. Radiant, effulgent, resplendent, shining, luminous, brilliant, lustrous, nitid, lucid, splendid, refulgent, fulgurant, scintillant, lucent, shiny, luminescent.

2. Gay, bright, intense, deep, gorgeous, rich, bright-colored, glowing, chromatic, chromatous, colorific, florid, showy, garish, flashy, fresh, strong, distinct, loud, colorful.

3. Expressive, graphic, picturesque, pictorial, telling, striking, dramatic, descriptive, emphatic, impressive, incisive, forceful, trenchant, stirring, delineatory, depictive, picaresque, narrative, realistic, true to life, energetic, forcible, vigorous, rousing, racy, illustrative.

VIVIDNESS, *n.* Sharpness, distinctness, prominence, distinction, definition, clarity, relief, picturesqueness, pictorialness, graphicalness, atmosphere, chiaroscuro, perspective, realism, realness, naturalism, truth to nature, fidelity.

VIVIFY, *v.* Animate, enliven, vitalize, quicken, give life to, stir up, invigorate, inspire, make alive, arouse, awake, revive, refresh, excite, stimulate, brighten, energize, inspirit, sharpen.

VIXEN, *n.* Ill-tempered quarrelsome woman, termagant, scold, shrew, spitfire, Xanthippe, tartar, brawler, fury, virago, beldam, catamaran *(coll.),* dragon, pepperpot *(coll.),* battle-ax *(sl.).*

VOCABULARY, *n.* 1. Stock of words used regularly by a person *or* class, range of language, speech, verbiage, language, dialect, patois, brogue, lingo, vernacular, slang, argot, diction, phraseology, idiom, style, verbal expression, cant.

2. List of words in alphabetical order and defined, lexicon, dictionary, wordbook, glossary, nomenclature, thesaurus, *Wörterbuch (Ger.),* gloss.

VOCAL, *adj.* 1. Voiced, articulate, sonant, oral, spoken, phonetic, vocalized, phthongal, tonic, intonated.

2. Lyric, choral, operatic, melic.

VOCALIST, *n.* Singer, chanter, songstress, warbler, caroler, cantatrice, *chanteuse (Fr.),* diva, thrush *(coll.),* nightingale *(coll.),* songbird, minstrel, melodist, songster, chorister, lark *(coll.),* wren *(coll.).*

VOCATION, *n.* Profession, trade, calling, occupation, pursuit, business, work, lifework, employment, job, career, task, stint, mission, chore, assignment, charge, incumbency, post, berth, billet, situation, métier, craft, handicraft, cloth, line, industry, commerce.

VOCIFERATE, *v.* Cry aloud, utter loudly, shout, bawl, roar, bellow, holler, yell, exclaim, clamor, rant, mouth, roar out, halloo, yoick, whoop, screech, scream, shriek, squall, give cry, proclaim, shout from the rooftops, rend the air, make the welkin ring, din, thunder, rap out, ejaculate, brawl, hoop, howl.

VOCIFERATION, *n.* Loud utterance, noisy outcry, clamor, din, hue and cry, racket, howl, bellow, hullabaloo, hubbub, roar, squall, screech, scream, yell, bark, shriek, ejaculation, clatter, uproar, charivari, pandemonium, fracas, bombilation.

VOCIFEROUS, *adj.* Crying out noisily, clamorous, obstreperous, uproarious, blatant, noisy, trumpet-tongued, tumultuous, stentorian, sonorous, powerful, thundering, ear-splitting, deafening, shrill, piercing, blustering, turbulent, clamant, vociferant, full-mouthed, loud-mouthed, loud-voiced.

VOGUE, *n.* 1. Fashion at a particular time, usage, style, mode, fad, rage, go *(coll.),* the thing, practice, custom, *dernier cri (Fr.),* ton *(Fr.),* the latest thing, craze, prevailing taste, *haut ton (Fr.),* bon ton *(Fr.),* high fashion, chic.

2. Popular favor, popularity, currency, acceptance, acceptation, repute, esteem.

VOICE, *n.* 1. Articulate sound, intonation, articulation, utterance, vocalization, enunciation, delivery, ecphonesis, modulation, tongue, speech, tone, *vox (Lat.),* accentuation, accent, stress, emphasis, ictus, orthoëpy, pronunciation, inflection, distinctive quality of tone, mode of speaking.

2. Choice, vote, preference, option, wish, suffrage, say *(coll.),* opinion, right to express an opinion.

3. Admonition, injunction, instruction, caution, warning, exhortation, reprehension, caveat, monition, summons.

VOICE, *v.* Give expression to, express, declare, proclaim, state, vent, utter, pronounce, announce, divulge, articulate, breathe, enunciate, murmur, whisper, vocalize, emit, hold forth, mouth, orate, deliver, publish, bruit.

VOICELESS, *adj.* 1. Speechless, mute, dumb, wordless, mum, reticent, taciturn, silent, inarticulate, tongue-tied.

2. Aphonic, surd, nonvocal, nonsonant, toneless, nonintoned.

VOID, *adj.* 1. Without legal force, not legally enforceable, not binding, invalid, inoperative, not in force, ineffectual, null, of no effect, vain, idle, nugatory, useless, inane, inept.

2. Empty, vacuous, without contents, blank, vacant, hollow, clear, free, destitute, wanting, without, lacking, devoid.

3. Without an incumbent, unoccupied, untenanted, unfilled, unsupplied, unfurnished, desolate, forsaken, waste, tenantless.

VOID, *n.* 1. Empty space, vacuum, blank, emptiness, vacuity, vacancy, hollow, cavity, hole, chasm, abyss, gap, opening, break.

2. Naught, zero, cipher, goose-egg *(coll.),* nothing, nil, nihil, nix *(sl.).*

VOID, *v.* 1. Make of no effect, invalidate, nullify, annul, make null, cancel, disannul, abrogate, repeal, recant, abolish, quash, repudiate, revoke, reverse, countermand, rescind, negate, offset, neutralize.

2. Eject, emit, discharge, throw out, empty, clear, evacuate, send out, pour out, egest, pass, defecate, purge.

VOLATILE, *adj.* 1. Passing off in the form of vapor, vaporizing, vaporous, vaporizable, vaporific, vaporable, gaseous, gasiform, aeriferous, aeriform, evaporable, etheric, aery, volatilized, superheated, vaporescent, vaporiferous, halituous.

2. Buoyant, light, airy, lively, levitative, gossamery, floaty, ethereal, floating, subtle, imponderous, incoercible, sprightly, vivacious, spirited, jocund, jolly, frivolous.

3. Fickle, inconstant, changeable, mercurial, giddy, light-headed, capricious, whimsical, flighty, flyaway, unsteady, wild, reckless, brash, humorsome, harebrained, skittish, harum-scarum, instable, mobile, protean, kaleidoscopic, erratic, irresolute, desultory, vagrant, fitful, spasmodic, wavering, vacillating.

4. Fleeting, transient, evanescent, ephemeral, fugacious, fugatory, fugitive, transitory, passing, elusive, caducous, diurnal, short-lived, monohemerous.

VOLATILITY, *n.* 1. Disposition to evaporate, evaporableness, gaseity, gaseousness, vaporousness, aerification, gasification, vaporization, volatilization, vaporescence, evaporation, cohobation, distillation, sublimation.

2. Buoyancy, lightness, airiness, levitativeness, gossameriness, etherealness, levity, imponderability, levitation.

3. Fickleness, inconstancy, mercurialness, changeableness, giddiness, light-headedness, capriciousness, whimsicality, flightiness, unsteadiness, wildness, recklessness, skittishness, brashness, in-

stability, mobility, irresolution, desultoriness, vagrancy, fitfulness, spasmodicalness.

4. Transiency, evanescence, impermanence, fugaciousness, fugacity, ephemerality, temporariness, caducity, mortality, transitoriness.

VOLITION, *n.* Free exercise of the will power of conscious choice, will, preference, determination, choice, option, free agency, free will, elective preference, power of willing, use of choice to determine action, purpose, volitiency, conation (*Psychol.*), velleity. voluntarism, spontaneity, power of choosing, discretion, unhampered choice, force of will, intent, resolution, will of one's own, decision.

VOLITIONAL, *adj.* Voluntary, freewill, spontaneous, volitionary, optional, volitient, volitive, unconstrained, free, discretionary, facultative, discretional, conative.

VOLLEY, *n.* 1. Simultaneous shooting, flight of shot, salvo, fusillade, round, enfilade, cross fire, firing, broadside, *rafale (Fr.),* sharpshooting, barrage, curtain of fire.

2. Explosion, report, discharge, detonation, burst, blast, outpouring, shot, pop, crash, clap, thunderclap, fulmination, fulguration, outbreak, emission, shower, storm.

VOLUBILITY, *n.* Facility of expression, copiousness of speech, *copia verborum (Lat.), flux de paroles (Fr.),* glibness, loquacity, loquaciousness, multiloquence, fluency, garrulity, garrulousness, talkativeness, command of language, wordiness, largiloquence, eloquence, polylogy, verbosity, gift of gab, effusiveness, gush, jabber, chatter, twaddle, prattle, gabble, prate, gossip, *bavardage (Fr.),* gibble-gabble, *caqueterie (Fr.),* cackle, clack, rattle, blather.

VOLUBLE, *adj.* Characterized by a continuous flow of words, loquacious, garrulous, wordy, verbose, windy *(sl.),* glib, talkative, fluent, nimble of speech, ready-tongued, multiloquent, polyloquent, chattering, long-winded, eloquent, declamatory, effusive, profuse, copious, exuberant, prolix, pleonastic, periphrastic, circumlocutory, discursive, rambling, turgid, elocutionary, rhetorical, mellifluent, mellifluous.

VOLUME, *n.* 1. Tome, large book, folio, quarto, work, opus, writing, publication, treatise, codex, monograph, dissertation, libretto, brochure, tract, essay, tractate.

2. Bulk, quantity, vastness, mass, size, measure, measurement, amplitude, contents, capacity, magnitude, bigness, compass, body, substance, dimensions.

VOLUMINOUS, *adj.* Of great volume, bulky, large, big, ample, great, full, copious, considerable, huge, titanic, abundant, goodly, immense, sizable, massive, substantial, capacious, comprehensive, hulky, unwieldy, cumbersome, cumbrous, ponderous, weighty, enormous, gigantic, mighty, stupendous, elephantine, mammoth, colossal, giant, monstrous.

VOLUNTARILY, *adv.* Spontaneously, willingly, freely, purposely, deliberately, of one's own accord, intentionally, of one's own free will, unconstrainedly, gratuitously, *proprio motu (Lat.),* by choice, *ex mero motu (Lat.),* on one's own responsibility, at will, *à discrétion (Fr.), al piacere (It.), ad libitum (Lat.), libenter (Lat.), à volonté (Fr.),* at pleasure, *a beneplacito (It.), ad arbitrium (Lat.),* as one thinks fit, by preference, optionally.

VOLUNTARY, *adj.* Spontaneous, intentional, purposeful, deliberate, free, unasked, gratuitous, unbidden, unconstrained, volitional, volitionary, volitient, optional, discretionary, facultative, discretional, willing, unforced, unimpelled, intended, purposed, designed, unaccidental, prepense, without compulsion, freewill, self-willed, uncompelled, *sua sponte (Lat.).*

VOLUNTEER, *v.* Enter into a service of one's own free will, attempt to do something, come forward with, proffer, present, offer, tender, propose, bid, propound, suggest, lay before, put forward, submit, extend, advance, hold out, urge upon, place at one's disposal, bestow, make an offer, express willingness, express readiness, be at one's service, undertake.

VOLUNTEER, *n.* 1. Freewill worker, unpaid worker, nonprofessional, amateur.

2. National guardsman, home guard, territorial.

VOLUPTUARY, *n.* One given up to luxurious pleasures, man of pleasure, sensualist, hedonist, libertine, debauchee, bon vivant, high-liver, gallant, silk-stocking, softling, effeminate, sybarite, epicure, gourmet, gastronome, gourmand, Heliogabalus, rake, roué, Lothario, Casanova, Don Juan.

VOLUPTUOUS, *adj.* 1. Ministering to pleasure, promoting full gratification of the senses, directed toward sensuous enjoyment, luxurious, sybaritic, sensuous, sensual, effeminate, silk-stocking, self-indulgent, pleasure-loving, hedonistic, epicurean, self-gratifying.

2. Carnal, fleshly, sexual, erotic, amorous, wanton, licentious, dissolute, animal, libidinous, dissipated, lewd, lecherous, lascivious, salacious, debauched, profligate, gross, intemperate, bestial, crapulous, gluttonous, hoggish, porcine, brutish, swinish, piggish, lustful, concupiscent, goatish.

VOLUPTUOUSNESS, *n.* Sensuousness, sensuality, animal gratification, self-indulgence, self-enjoyment, pleasure, luxuriousness, luxury, witchery, seduction, seductiveness, sex appeal, prodigalism, dissipation, self-gratification, free-living, high-living, dissoluteness, fastness, license, animalism, debauchery, fleshpots of Babylon, sybaritism, epicureanism, epicurism.

VOMIT, *v.* Cast up from the stomach, puke up, throw up, upchuck *(coll.),* puke, disgorge, belch forth, eructate, eject copiously, emit, spew forth, bring up.

VOMITORY, *adj.* Inducing vomiting, vomitive, emetic, emetocathartic.

VOODOO, *n.* Sorcery, witchcraft, conjuration, fetishism, superstition, magic, divination, black art, enchantment, necromancy, occult art, theurgy, thaumaturgy, *diablerie (Fr.),* witchery, demonology, hoodoo, shamanism, incantation, exorcism, obsession, hocus-pocus.

VOODOO, *n.* Sorcerer, magician, necromancer, conjuror, witch, warlock, wizard, seer, thaumaturgist, exorcist, powwow, *Hexe (Ger.),* witch doctor, shaman, dowser, medicine man, diviner, mage.

VORACIOUS, *adj.* Gluttonous, greedy in eating, devouring food in large quantities, ravenous, omnivorous, ravening, edacious, rapacious, insatiable, hungry, hoggish, porcine, piggish, swinish, gormandizing, overfed, gross, gorging, pantophagous, predacious, insatiate, unsated.

VORACITY, *n.* Gluttonous appetite, gluttony, ravenousness, omnivorousness, insatiable hunger, voraciousness, edacity, edaciousness, gulosity, greediness, gormandizing, piggishness, hoggishness, polyphagia, rapacity, rapaciousness, gastronomy.

VORTEX, *n.* 1. Rotation, circulation, circumrotation, gyration, circumgyration, circumvolution, rolling, volutation, turbination, circination, convolution, verticity.

2. Eddy, whirlpool, swirl, maelstrom, gurge, surge, whirl, *tourbillon (Fr.),* undercurrent, reflux, undertow, rapids, bore.

3. Whirlwind, tornado, twister, cyclone, tempest, storm, typhoon, samiel.

VORTICAL, *adj.* Turning, whirling, churning, twisting, rotating, rotary, rotatory, trochilic, circumrotatory, gyratory, vorticose, round and round, head over heels.

VOTARY, *n.* 1. One who is bound by a religious vow, votarist, monk, nun, sister, holy man, conventual, cenobite, friar, prior, abbot, lay brother, mendicant, *religieuse (Fr.),* devotionalist, saintly person.

2. Devotee, enthusiast, fan *(coll.),* devoted admirer, bug *(sl.),* zealot, adherent, partisan, disciple, follower, hanger-on, adjuvant, auxiliary, satellite, champion.

VOTE, *n.* Formal expression of choice, voice, franchise, suffrage, say, ballot, elective privilege, judgment, approval, election, poll, plebiscite, ticket, referendum, option, selection, determination, preference, discretion, adoption, volition, decision, coöptation, coöption, *vox populi (Lat.).*

VOTER, *n.* Elector, balloter, constituent, electorate *(collective),* suffragist.

VOTIVE, *adj.* Offered in accordance with a vow, given by vow, dedicated, devoted, promissory, pledged, committed.

VOUCH, *v.* Answer for, warrant, certify, attest, guarantee, maintain by affirmation, affirm, aver, evidence, declare, confirm, corroborate, authenticate, asseverate, protest, obtest, call to witness, testify, take affidavit, witness, swear to, endorse, subscribe to, give assurance, support, uphold, back, sustain, acknowledge, depose, vow, be surety for.

VOUCHER, *n.* Receipt, verification, certificate, authentication, security, guaranty, guarantee, warranty, warrant, attested copy.

VOUCHSAFE, *v.* Grant by favor, give by graciousness, concede, accord, condescend to grant, deign to confer. allow, permit, tolerate, suffer, let, yield, stoop, admit, bear with, recognize, gratify, humor, indulge, consent to, assent, acquiesce.

VOW, *v.* 1. Promise solemnly, pledge one's word, swear, make a solemn resolution of, dedicate, consecrate, devote, contract, subscribe.

2. Assert emphatically, asseverate, declare earnestly, vouch, certify, affirm, assure, warrant, attest, stress, emphasize.

VOW, *n.* Solemn promise, personal engagement, pledge, word, parole, solemn affirmation, oath, undertaking, troth, plight, word of honor, assurance, profession, deposition.

VOYAGE, *v.* Take a cruise, take a voyage, travel by water, travel by sea, sail, take ship, cruise, plough the deep, skim the waves, steam, navigate, circumnavigate, set sail, put to sea.

VOYAGE, *n.* Cruise, journey by water, crossing, passage by sea, sail, circumnavigation, course of travel, route, itinerary.

VULGAR, *adj.* 1. Constituting the common people of society, plebeian, proletarian, common, lowborn, lowly, baseborn, ignoble, untitled, underbred, inferior, mean, homespun, uncultivated, boorish, ill-bred, rustic, coarse, unrefined, cheap, discourteous, crude, rude, uncouth, brutish, illmannered, unmannerly, uncivil, impolite, carlish, ungentlemanly, disrespectful, unpolished, unkempt, countrified, rough, provincial, clownish, awkward, wild, barbarous, rowdyish, raffish, outlandish.

2. Obscene, foul, vile, gross, base, smutty, pornographic, ribald, offensive, indecent, abusive, scurrilous, blackguardly, lewd, risqué, off-color, suggestive, Fescennine, filthy, licentious, immoral, libidinous, lecherous, lascivious, sensual, salacious, concupiscent, shameless.

3. Gaudy, loud, tawdry, meretricious, showy, ostentatious, obtrusive, flashy, garish, brummagem, gimcrack, gingerbread, cheap, tinsel.

VULGARIAN, *n.* Vulgar rich person, upstart, *nouveau riche (Fr.),* parvenu, rough diamond, *novus homo (Lat.),* snob, barbarian, boor, churl, Boeotian, clod, clown, bumpkin, nobody, mushroom, *bourgeois gentilhomme (Fr.),* adventurer, opportunist.

VULGARISM, *n.* Vulgar idiom, vulgar expression, barbarism, slang, colloquialism, vulgar phrase, instance of substandard speech, solecism.

VULGARITY, *n.* 1. Ill-breeding, bad taste, *mauvais ton (Fr.), mauvais goût (Fr.),* gaucherie, ungentlemanliness, plebeianism, commonness, boorishness, awkwardness, inelegance, clownishness, indecorum, want of tact, misbehavior, want of refinement, rudeness.

2. Ostentation, tawdriness, loudness, gaudiness, frippery, flashiness, trickery, trumpery, gingerbread, clinquant, tinsel, brummagem.

3. Ribaldry, smuttiness, obscenity, pornography, indecency, coarseness, grossness, vileness, bawdiness.

VULGUS, *n.* Rabble, hoi polloi, the masses, canaille, the common people, the great unwashed, mob, horde, scum, riffraff, ragtag and bobtail, trash, dregs of society, the crowd, common herd, *profanum vulgus (Lat.),* rank and file, lower classes, *bourgeoisie (Fr.),* commonalty, populace, proletariat.

VULNERABLE, *adj.* Capable of being wounded, liable to injury, open to physical hurt, woundable, exposed, assailable, unprotected, unguarded, accessible, defenseless, not proof against attack, weak in defense, susceptible, unshielded, insecure, fallible, hazardous, dangerous, precarious, risky, unprepared.

VULPINE, *adj.* Foxy, foxlike, cunning, wily, sly, artful, crafty, subtle, designing, insidious, tricky, subdolous, deceitful, arch, acute, shrewd, astute, canny, knowing, clever.

VULTURE, *n.* 1. Large carrion-eating bird, buzzard, kite, hawk, falcon, eagle, bird of prey.

2. Person who preys ruthlessly, extortioner, harpy, depredator, spoliator, oppressor.

VULTURINE, *adj.* Rapacious, ravenous, ravening, avaricious, spoliative, voracious, devouring, greedy, omnivorous, insatiable, insatiate, ferocious, feral, raptorial, predacious.

W

WADDLE, *v.* Sway from side to side, rock, waggle, wobble, toddle, totter, stagger, swerve, walk with short steps, mince, paddle, swing, pendulate, wag, bob.

WADE, *v.* 1. Walk through water, ford, traverse afoot, cross, pass through, go across.

2. Wade through, read, peruse, pore over, thumb through, dip into, turn over the leaves, run the eye over, study, burn the midnight oil, lucubrate.

3. Make one's way with difficulty, toil, exert oneself, labor, moil, tax one's energies, work hard, fag, slave, drudge, strain, strive, tug, pull, ply, bestir oneself, trouble oneself, rough it, put forth a strong arm, bend the bow, buckle to, set one's shoulder to the wheel, redouble one's efforts, lay about one, take pains, hammer at, put all one's strength into, strain every nerve, go all lengths.

WAFER, *n.* Thin disk of unleavened bread, biscuit, tablet, thin cake, cachet, lozenge, obley, slice, shaving.

WAFT, *v.* Bear through a buoyant medium, convey lightly as if in flight, carry through the air, transport, transmit, flat, shunt, blow, puff, whiff.

WAG, *v.* 1. Move from side to side rapidly, move up and down repeatedly, vibrate, oscillate, pendulate, nutate, waggle, wigwag, shake, wave, undulate, dangle, swing, beat, pulsate, vacillate, throb, quiver, wriggle, flutter, flicker, switch, swish, sweep, convulse, agitate, tumble, toss, flap, flourish, whisk, hitch, joggle.

2. Get along, travel, fare, proceed, advance, progress, move.

WAG, *n.* 1. Shake, jerk, twitch, toss, quiver, wriggle, flick, switch, swish, flap, flourish, whisk, hitch, joggle, throb, pulsation, vacillation, nutation, oscillation, vibration, sway, swing, fluctuation, beat, undulation, wave.

2. Humorist, wit, joker, jokester, droll fellow, jester, farceur, buffoon, banterer, wisecracker *(sl.), bel esprit (Fr.),* comedian, merry-andrew, clown, montebank, pantaloon, harlequin, punchinello, life of the party, antic, Scaramouch, card *(coll.).*

WAGE, *v.* 1. Undertake, engage in, carry on, conduct, manage, practice, set about, take up, attempt, begin, assume, embark on, take in hand, enter upon.

2. Stake, bet, hazard, pledge, wager, lay, plight.

WAGE, *n.* That which is paid for work, hire, pay, payment, compensation, remuneration, recompense, salary, stipend, emolument, earnings, return, income, revenue, allowance, reward, fee, meed, quittance.

WAGER, *v.* Stake, bet, hazard, risk, venture, pledge, gamble, punt, speculate, take a flyer, plunge, lay, back, wage, tempt fortune, game, cast lots, toss up, try one's luck, play for.

WAGER, *n.* Gamble, bet, hazard, venture, stake, pot, jackpot, ante, pledge, tossup, heads *or* tails, throw of the dice, wheel of fortune, flyer, speculation, pari-mutuel, plunge, gambling, gaming, game of chance, sweepstakes, drawing lots, pool, lottery, random shot, pig in a poke, leap in the dark.

WAGGERY, *n.* Drollery, jocularity, waggishness, facetiousness, mischievous merriment, humor, jocosity, sport, sportiveness, jocoseness, pleasantry, roguery, practical joke, fun, wit, jesting, *esprit (Fr.),* buffoonery, clowning, wittiness, Attic salt, cleverness, harlequinade, tomfoolery, clownery, broad farce, *espièglerie (Fr.),* comicality, witticism, wisecrack, sally, smart saying, gag, flash of wit, *mot pour rire (Fr.), jeu d'esprit (Fr.),* epigram, bon mot, quip, *plaisanterie (Fr.),* conceit, wordplay, *jeu de mots (Fr.),* pun, *double-entendre (Fr.), calembour (Fr.),* conundrum, riddle, quibble, quillet, quiddity, raillery, banter, persiflage, badinage, chaffing, repartee, brightness, smartness, piquancy, horseplay, burlesque, parody, mimicry, travesty, caricature.

WAGGISH, *adj.* Good-humored, facetious, sparkling, jocular, humorous, prankish, witty, jocose, funny, mirthful, droll, comical, ridiculous, jolly, laughable, gay, jesting, sportive, frolicsome, merry, tricksy, roguish, gamesome, smart, clever, keen-witted, pungent, piquant, brilliant, quick-witted, sprightly, whimsical, epigrammatic, *ben trovato (It.),* paronomastic, amusing, burlesque, ludicrous, quizzical, risible, farcical, diverting, entertaining, sidesplitting, festive, high-spirited, festal, jovial, arch, delightful, pleasing, pleasurable, genial, gladsome.

WAGON, *n.* Four-wheeled vehicle for transport, lorry, truck, wain, dray, van, cart, prairie schooner, Conestoga wagon, gondola car, tipcart, tumbrel, barrow.

WAIF, *n.* Homeless child, foundling, stray, estray, wanderer, castaway, vagrant, beggar, tramp, hobo, knight of the road, vagabond, gypsy, beachcomber, floater, sundowner, panhandler, bum, ragamuffin, street Arab, gamin, outcast, pariah, mudlark, straggler, itinerant, peripatetic, nomad.

WAIL, *v.* Utter a prolonged, high-pitched mournful cry, lament, bewail, moan, deplore, keen, ululate, bemoan, mourn over, cry in lamentation, sound mournfully, grieve audibly for, weep, howl, whine, blubber, snivel, caterwaul, fret, sorrow, rend the air, sob, whimper, groan.

WAIL, *n.* Plaint, mournful sound, ululation, keening, loud weeping, lamentation, deploration, crying, complaint, moan, lament, wailing cry, howling, jeremiad, dirge, coronach, threnody, elegy, nenia, epicedium, requiem, murmur, whimper, whine, sob, suspiration, outcry, fit of crying, squall, mewl, boohoo.

WAIST, *n.* 1. Middle part of the human body, *taille (Fr.), talle (Sp.), cintura (It.).*

2. Waistline, bodice, *corsage (Fr.),* basque, blouse.

3. Midpoint constriction, neck, isthmus, stricture, hourglass, wasp, angustation, coarctation, tapering, contraction.

WAISTCOAT, *n.* Man's vest, doublet, jerkin, jacket, jumper, weskit *(coll.).*

WAIT, *v.* 1. Rest in expectation, continue stationary in expectation of, remain inactive until something expected happens, tarry, linger, bide one's time, cool one's heels, abide, delay, stay, loiter, hesitate, procrastinate, defer, pause, postpone, dally, take it easy, dawdle, hang fire, lie over, put off, suspend, retard, remand, prorogue, table, shelve.

2. Be in readiness for, be reserved for, keep a sharp lookout, sit tight, set a trap for, lay an ambuscade for, lie in ambush, watch for, look for.

WAIT, *n.* 1. Delay, halt, stop, pause, interval of waiting, respite, suspension, remand, moratorium, continuance *(Law),* stay, reprieve, deferment, postponement, prorogation, procrastination, adjournment, retardation, lagging, loitering, lingering, tardiness, dilatoriness, hindrance, obstacle, obstruction.

2. Ambuscade, ambushment, hiding, cover, lurking-place, retreat, concealment, latency, secretion, camouflage, shelter, secretness.

WAITER, *n.* Steward, *garçon (Fr.),* boy, flunky, lackey, footman, butler, cupbearer, manservant, menial, domestic, servitor, servant, attendant, *khidmutgar (India), khansamah (India), mozo (Sp.), cameriere (It.), Kellner (Ger.),* tapster, busboy.

WAIT ON, *v.* 1. Perform services for, supply the wants of a person, attend to, attend as a servant, serve, minister to, wait upon, tend, set on table, furnish, provide, accommodate.

2. Accompany, squire, escort, conduct, convoy, show the way, guard, usher, take care of, go along with, keep company with.

3. Follow as a consequence, ensue, result, issue, succeed, come after, proceed, spring, arise.

WAIVE, *v.* 1. Forbear to insist on, remit, relinquish, give up, surrender, forgo, renounce, give up claim to, yield, let go, abandon, abstain, reject, not vote, refrain from, not use, dispense with, spare, supersede, dismiss.

2. Put aside for the time, defer, shelve, table, put off, lay over, remand, retard, adjourn, postpone, procrastinate, protract, prolong, prorogue.

WAKE, *v.* 1. Awaken, awake, waken, rouse from sleep, wake up, get up.

2. Put in motion, arouse, put in action, rouse, stimulate, animate, enliven, vivify, stir up, kindle, revive, provoke, bring to life again, resuscitate, reanimate, summon up, excite, exsuscitate, inspirit, infuse life into, quicken, work upon, foment, foster.

WAKE, *n.* 1. Track of a vessel, wash, backwash, trail, path, train, rear, course of anything, trace, pug, scent, spoor, *piste (Fr.).*

2. All-night watch of a corpse before burial, vigil, pervigilium, watching, pernoctation.

WAKEFUL, *adj.* 1. Indisposed to sleep, insomnious, sleepless, unsleeping, waking, awake, restless, wide-awake, slumberless, insomnolent.

2. Vigilant, watchful, wary, cautious, alert, observant, circumspect, careful, heedful, regardful, prudent, discreet, judicious, guarded, on the *qui vive,* precautious, chary, on the lookout, lynx-eyed, Argus-eyed.

WAKEFULNESS, *n.* 1. Indisposition to sleep, sleeplessness, restlessness, want of sleep, insomnia, insomnolence, pernoctation, pervigilium.

2. Vigilance, watchfulness, alertness, circumspection, providence, wariness, chariness, cautiousness, caution, precaution, carefulness, discretion, judiciousness.

WALE, *n.* 1. Mark on the skin made by stroke of a whip *or* rod, stripe, raised line, weal, ridge, whelk, welt, streak.

2. Texture, weave, fabric, contexture, intertexture, warp and woof, weft, web, tissue, grain, surface, nap, hand, feel.

WALK, *v.* Proceed by steps at a moderate pace, travel on foot, advance by steps, pace, tread, step, saunter, tramp, march, stride, stroll, perambulate, promenade, ambulate, hike, strut, parade, waddle, traipse, trudge, trundle, plod, shamble, stomp, mince, foot it, shuffle, gad, stalk, tiptoe, ramble, toddle, trample, roam, traverse, move, trek, journey, take a turn, peregrinate, migrate, flit, wander, range, rove, jaunt, prowl, stray, straggle, meander, nomadize, pad, wend, bowl along, paddle, peg on, jog on, defile, gallivant.

WALK, *n.* 1. Promenade, constitutional, stroll, saunter, journey by foot, march, trek, tramp, hike, excursion, ramble, airing, turn, expedition, trip, tour, circuit, peregrination, pilgrimage, hadj, jaunt, outing, stalk, perambulation.

2. Manner of walking, carriage, gait, step, pace, tread, stride, amble, bearing, conduct, deportment, comportment, behavior, address.

3. Way for foot passengers, path, sidewalk, *trottoir (Fr.), Bürgersteig (Ger.), acera (Sp.), marciapiede (It.),* footway, pavement, footpath, pathway, avenue, aisle, passage, boulevard, ambulatory, promenade, esplanade.

4. Branch of activity, sphere, career, beat, frequented track, bailiwick, course, habitual field of action, province, department, business, employment, occupation, pursuit, vocation, realm, station, arena, office, position, incumbency, place, job, situation, berth, billet, engagement, enterprise, undertaking, calling, profession, métier, line, trade, industry, commerce.

WALKER, *n.* Foot passenger, pedestrian, peripatetic, hiker, tramper, traveler afoot, wayfarer, trekker, tripper, excursionist, commuter, rover, wanderer, peregrinator, itinerant, rambler, straggler, roamer, gadabout, landloper, tramp, vagrant, knight of the road, vagabond, hobo, nomad, pilgrim, hadji, stroller, promenader, saunterer.

WALKING STICK, *n.* Staff, cane, crutch, stick, rod, Malacca, alpenstock, crosier, shepherd's crook.

WALKOUT, *n.* Strike of laborers, concerted work-stoppage, sit-down, uprising, outbreak, defiance, riot, *émeute (Fr.),* noncompliance, tumult, sabotage, rebellion, *Putsch (Ger.).*

WALKOVER, *n.* Easy victory, walkaway, pushover, cinch, conquest, triumph, ascendancy, palm, upper hand, advantage, mastery, *coup (Fr.),* feat, hit, checkmate, ten strike *(coll.),* master stroke, killing *(sl.).*

WALL, *n.* 1. Upright structure serving for enclosure *or* division, enclosing side of a building *or* room, solid fence of masonry *or* wood, partition, bulkhead, party wall, septum, rail, paling, barricade, barrier, stockade, cordon, obstruction, parapet, rampart, bulwark, breastwork, battlement, fortification, protection, dike, levee, embankment, fieldwork, bastion, redoubt, buttress, abutment, abattis, barbed wire.

2. Bluff, cliff, precipice, crag, steep, scaur.

WALLET, *n.* 1. Purse, pocketbook, *portemonnaie (Fr.),* wad *(sl.),* roll.

2. Pouch, bag, knapsack, sack, pocket, poke, rucksack, satchel, haversack, portfolio.

WALLOP, *v.* Beat soundly, thrash, pommel, drub, lambaste, strike, buffet, deal a blow to, slap, smite, smack, cuff, thwack, spank, thump, swinge, lay on, leather, belabor, trounce, bang, strap, larrup, whip, fustigate, pitch into, sandbag, defeat thoroughly, overcome, rout, lick.

WALLOW, *v.* 1. Grovel, toss, flounder, welter, roll about in, tumble, squat, cower, crouch.

W
Z

2. Live self-indulgently, luxuriate, relish, enjoy, riot in, bask in, revel in, swim in, feast on, gloat over, live on the fat of the land, have money to burn.

WAMPUM, *n.* 1. Cylindrical beads made from shells and used by North American Indians as money, peag, wampumpeag, seawan, cowrie, roanoke.

2. Money, hard cash, jack, dough, spondulix, simoleons, rhino, kale, mazuma, long green, velvet, chips, clinkers, iron men, bucks, mopuses, shekels, specie, coins, ready money.

WAN, *adj.* Of a sickly color, of an unnatural hue, showing ill-health, pale, pallid, colorless, ashen, bloodless, anemic, haggard, cadaverous, ghastly, white, sallow, etiolated, pasty, dull, blanched, pale-faced, dun.

WAND, *n.* Rod, stick, scepter, mace, caduceus, kerykeion, staff, truncheon, divining rod, Aaron's rod, verge, lituus, fasces, thyrsus.

WANDER, *v.* 1. Deviate, digress, stray, swerve, take another direction, turn aside, divagate, veer, alter course, curve, heel, bear off, yaw, jibe, sheer, wear, tack, sidle, twist, slew, wheel, glance off, shift, deflect, switch, divert, shunt.

2. Roam, prowl, range, meander, straggle, gad about, go aimlessly, saunter, traipse, rove, ramble, peregrinate, tramp, promenade, travel, journey, trek, knock about, vagabondize, nomadize, jaunt, perambulate, trudge, plod, wend, bend one's steps, gallivant.

3. Speak incoherently, be delirious, rave, moon, ramble, be crazed, dote, rhapsodize, drivel, go off one's head.

WANDERER, *n.* Itinerant, vagrant, knight of the road, peripatetic, vagabond, nomad, gypsy, Okie, landloper, roamer, rover, gadabout, gadling, runagate, straggler, rambler, stroller, traveler, runabout, peregrinator, wayfarer, pilgrim, palmer, journeyer, voyager, trekker, sightseer, globetrotter, beachcomber, excursionist, tourist, tripper, adventurer, explorer, tramp, loafer, hobo, Arab, bedouin, hadji, tramper, hiker, walker, pedestrian.

WANDERING, *adj.* 1. Vagrant, peripatetic, itinerant, vagabond, nomadic, roving, roaming, rambling, straying, traveling, journeying, ambulatory, gadding, migratory, migrant, wayfaring.

2. Devious, circuitous, indirect, roundabout, circumlocutory, circumlocutionary, periphrastic, circumlocutional, ambagious, discursive, digressive.

WANE, *v.* Decline, decrease, diminish, grow smaller, fall off, dwindle, flag, wither, subside, abate, ebb, fade, fail, die, sink, draw to a close, approach an end, narrow, lessen, contract, shrink, shrivel, waste, retrograde, droop.

WANE, *n.* Decline, gradual decrease, falling off, declension, failure, decay, downgrade, diminution, subsidence, ebb, abatement, contraction, wasting, loss, recession, retrogradation, declination, attenuation, atrophy.

WANT, *n.* 1. Lack, absence, need, requirement, deficiency, dearth, defect, default, exigency, necessity, inexistence, scarcity, scantiness, meagerness, insufficiency, failure, shortness, paucity, defectiveness, shortage.

2. Poverty, pennilessness, penury, pauperism, neediness, necessitude, indigence, destitution, straits, distress, privation, starvation, hunger, famine, thirst, drought, wolf at the door, im-

pecuniosity, insolvency, mendicancy, beggary, mendicity.

WANT, *v.* 1. Desire, crave, wish, long for, desiderate, wish for, covet, fancy, pine for, hanker for, hope for, yearn for.

2. Need, lack, require, have need of, stand in need of, be without, be destitute of, be deficient in, miss, fall short in, be lacking in, not reach, come short of.

WANTING, *adj.* Deficient in, lacking, absent, defective, faulty, void, missing, inadequate, short, minus, scarce, destitute, needy, slack, insufficient, incomplete, imperfect, scanty, scant, out of, devoid of, bereft of, denuded of, vacant, empty, bare, at low ebb, drained, dry, thin, spare, meager, barren, arid, stinted, vacuous, blank.

WANTON, *adj.* 1. Reckless, inconsiderate, deliberate, malicious, careless, heedless, needless, willful, froward, perverse, wayward, gratuitous, groundless, headstrong, hot-headed, devil-may-care, unruly, irresponsible, disregardful, irrepressible, wild.

2. Sportive, playful, frolicsome, gay, coltish, capricious, skittish, frisky, airy, debonair, merry, arch, whimsical, frivolous, fickle, flighty, volatile, mercurial, notional.

3. Lewd, lustful, libidinous, lecherous, lascivious, promiscuous, unchaste, concupiscent, lickerish, immoral, salacious, carnal, incontinent, prurient, voluptuous, licentious, libertine, loose, sybaritic, erotic, amorous, obscene, immodest, fast, sensual, impure, gross, intemperate, bestial, animal.

WANTON, *n.* 1. Lewd *or* dissolute man, profligate, voluptuary, rake, roué, debauchee, rakehell, rip, lecher, fast man, wolf *(coll.)*, goat, satyr, whoremonger, adulterer, fornicator, seducer, Don Juan, Lothario, Casanova, sybarite, libertine, silk-stocking, sensualist, Sardanapalus, hedonist.

2. Lascivious woman, baggage, hussy, jade, trollop, bitch, courtesan, light-o'-love, flirt, coquette, tart, strumpet, hustler, streetwalker, prostitute, broad, chippy, whore, harlot, *fille de joie (Fr.)*, wench, trull, demirep, drab, slut, Jezebel, minx, cocotte, grisette, demimondaine, fancy woman, concubine, kept woman, doxy, quean.

WAR, *n.* Active military operations, declared hostilities, warfare, fighting, *la guerre (Fr.)*, *la guerra (Sp. and It.)*, *der Krieg (Ger.)*, arbitrament of the sword, armed conflict, contest of arms, force of arms, the sword, appeal to arms, bloodshed, Armageddon, Mars, Ares, Bellona *(Roman goddess of war)*, mobilization, declaration of war, battle array, warpath, campaign, tented field, battle, combat, struggle, fray, contest, strategy, castrametation, war to the death, *guerre à outrance (Fr.)*, *guerre à mort (Fr.)*, belligerence, strife, antagonism, state of opposition, enmity, inimicality, battlefield, battleground, Aceldama, theater of war, aggression, attack, invasion, outbreak, sortie, sally, raid, zero hour, bombardment, beleaguerment, blockade, investment, siege, clash of arms, pitched battle, death struggle, *Blitzkrieg (Ger.)*, carnage, slaughter, butchery, jihad *(Moham.)*, crusade, holy war, fiery cross.

WAR, *v.* Carry on war, make war, declare war, go to war, wage war, take up arms, take the field, battle with, join battle, let slip the dogs of war, combat, fight, wield the sword, arm to the teeth, campaign, see active service, be under fire, go over the top, be on the warpath, attack, invade, take the offensive, enter the lists, march against, raid, blitz, bombard, fire upon, open fire, bomb, invest, besiege, blockade, beleaguer, storm, join issue, exchange shots, come to blows, measure swords, take up the gantlet, shed blood, slaughter, butcher, decimate.

WARBLE, *v.* Sing like a bird, trill, carol, yodel, chant, modulate, utter musically, hum, hymn, chirp, lilt, chirrup, twitter, intone, sol-fa, troll, cantilate, vocalize, quaver.

WARBLER, *n.* Songster, songbird, singer, vocalist, *chanteuse (Fr.),* cantatrice, diva, thrush, nightingale, wren, caroler, chanter, melodist, songstress, chorister, lark, philomel.

WAR CRY, *n.* Battle cry, war whoop, whoop, alarm, defiance, slogan.

WARD, *v.* Turn aside, avert, repel, parry, act on the defensive, fend, stave off, forfend, keep off, obviate, antevert, check, countercheck, obstruct, preclude, defend, guard against, beat off, hinder, propugn, hold at arm's length, keep at bay, bear the brunt.

WARD, *n.* 1. Guardianship, care, custody, charge, protection, guard, defense, security, safeguard, preservation, vigilance, watchfulness, surveillance, watch and ward, lookout, vigil, eyes of Argus.
2. Dependent, protégé, minor, pupil.
3. Division of a city, precinct, zone, quarter, district, *arrondissement (Fr.),* department.

WARDEN, *n.* One charged with the custody of, keeper, warder, guardian, curator, superintendent, guard, sentry, protector, watchman, jailer, claviger, castellan, turnkey, ranger, watchdog, concierge, janitor, maintenance man, conservator, doorkeeper, doorman, picket, patrol, tutor, governor, chaperon, duenna, patrolman, Cerberus.

WARDROBE, *n.* 1. Piece of furniture for holding clothes, portable closet, clothespress, chest, bureau, chiffonier, chest of drawers, commode, corner cupboard.
2. Stock of clothes, clothing, raiment, apparel, garments, vestments, attire, habiliments, togs, toilette, trousseau, wearing apparel, toggery.

WARDSHIP, *n.* 1. Right of guardianship, custody, guardianship, tutelage, safekeeping, auspices, protection, safeguard, preservation, keeping, trust, security, defense, shelter, safety, bulwark, aegis, palladium.
2. Minority, pupilage, pupilarity, nonage.

WAREHOUSE, *n.* Storehouse, storeroom, store, repository, magazine, depot, *entrepôt (Fr.),* depository, pantechnicon, loft, *étape (Fr.),* cache, vault, arsenal, armory.

WARES, *n., pl.* Articles of manufacture, goods, chattels, merchandise, commodities, stock, effects, movables, staples, stock in trade, cargo, supplies, reserves.

WARFARE, *n.* 1. Military operations, state of war, operations against an enemy, hostilities, fighting, strategy, tactics, bloodshed, appeal to arms, the sword, declaration of war, campaign, mobilization, crusade, jihad, tented field, warpath, military expedition, Mars, Ares, Bellona, war to the death, *guerre à outrance (Fr.), guerre à mort (Fr.),* castrametation, attack, force of arms, Armageddon, battlefield, battleground, theater of war, Aceldama, bombardment, blockade, investment, beleaguerment, siege, clash of arms, carnage, slaughter, butchery, fiery cross.

2. Onslaught, battle, combat, conflict, fray, affray, contest, militancy, strife, struggle, discord, engagement, encounter, skirmish, dogfight, brush.

WARILY, *adv.* Cautiously, circumspectly, heedfully, carefully, vigilantly, watchfully, charily, discreetly, prudently, judiciously, guardedly, suspiciously, on one's guard, on the *qui vive,* cannily, gingerly, stealthily, furtively.

WARINESS, *n.* Cautiousness, caution, precaution, circumspection, vigilance, alertness, care, carefulness, foresight, prudence, forethought, scrupulousness, wakefulness, secretiveness, calculation, discretion, discreetness, heed, deliberation, safety first, self-possession, coolness, presence of mind, *sangfroid (Fr.),* solicitude, surveillance, eyes of Argus, lookout, watch and ward, Fabian policy, watchful waiting, watchfulness.

WARLIKE, *adj.* 1. Soldierly, martial, military, militant, bellicose, belligerent, combative, stratonic, pugnacious, truculent, hostile, inimical, unfriendly, militaristic, armigerous.
2. Under arms, armed to the teeth, embattled, in battle array, panoplied, sword in hand, threatening.

WARLOCK, *n.* Magician, sorcerer, wizard, thaumaturgist, necromancer, witch, seer, exorcist, charmer, mage, voodoo, dowser, diviner, witch doctor, medicine man, shaman, soothsayer, fortuneteller, prophet, sage, oracle, augur, clairvoyant, haruspice.

WARM, *v.* 1. Heat moderately, tepefy, make warm, make hot, mull, thaw, melt, liquefy, dissolve, torrefy, cook, stew, seethe, simmer, steam, grill, curry, pan, braise, bake, roast, griddle, fricassee, frizzle, fry, parboil, toast, broil.
2. Excite, animate, waken, rouse, stir up, foment, chafe, kindle, arouse, whet, incite, quicken.
3. Prepare for play, practice, exercise, rehearse, drill, train.

WARM, *adj.* 1. Of moderately high temperature, not cold, thermal, calid, tepid, lukewarm, heated, hot, torrid, calorific.
2. Close, sweltering, oppressive, canicular, muggy, steaming, sultry, tropical, uncomfortable, sudorific, stifling, stuffy, suffocating.
3. Sunny, bright, sunshiny, pleasant, mild, genial, clement.
4. Feverish, febrile, pyretic, feverous, fevered, burning, inflamed, fiery, excitable, irascible, highstrung, temperamental, nervous, irritable, inflammable, impatient, hasty, hot-headed, wrathful, irate, choleric, passionate, agitated, violent, vehement, ardent, fervid, furious, raging, impetuous, precipitate, frantic, frenzied, phrenetic, emotional, flushed.
5. Lively, vivacious, animated, vigorous, zealous, enthusiastic, earnest, cordial, hearty, gushing, effusive, glowing.
6. Warm-hearted, affectionate, tender, loving, sympathetic, sincere, kind-hearted, kindly, kind, fond, devoted, attached.

WARMTH, *n.* Glow, fervency, fervor, ardor, ardency, hotness, fire, fever, flush, zeal, enthusiasm, eagerness, earnestness, excitement, animation, vivacity, passion, cordiality, spirit, intensity, emotionalism, vigor, verve, liveliness, piquancy, feeling, sentiment, emotion, sympathy, pathos, tenderness, affection, concern, solicitude, gusto, unction, vehemence, cordiality, heartiness, *empressement (Fr.).*

WARN, *v.* 1. Forewarn of something unfavorable, give intimation of impending evil, give warning of possible harm, caution against danger, put on one's guard, premonish, urge to take heed, sound the alarm, ring the tocsin, forebode, threaten, predict, augur, presage, foretell, cry out against, dissuade, expostulate, remonstrate, discourage, deter, restrain, portend, augur.

2. Give notice to, serve notice, apprise, notify, inform, communicate to, disclose to, make aware, mention to, make acquainted, alert, signal, advertise, counsel, advise, exhort, admonish, bid, order, call, summon, make aware.

WARNING, *adj.* Cautionary, precautionary, admonitory, cautioning, monitory, monitorial, premonitory, ominous, portentous, threatening, minatory, significant, menacing, lowering, symptomatic, indicative, dissuasive, remonstrative, expostulatory, dehortatory, boding, presageful, unfavorable, inauspicious, ill-boding, ill-omened, augural, minacious, forbidding, comminatory, black, sinister, dire.

WARNING, *n.* Caution, admonition, monition, caveat, notice, notification, forewarning, intimation, premonishment, prediction, indication, premonition, sign, token, symptom, handwriting on the wall, *tekel upharsin (Biblical),* bird of ill omen, stormy petrel, Mother Carey's chickens, warning voice, gathering clouds, lowering sky, presage, omen, portent, augury, prognostic, auspice, foretoken, bodement, signs of the times, alarm, tocsin, alarum, sign of distress, SOS, foghorn, siren, danger signal, red flag, red light, fire alarm, fiery cross, threat, commination, thunder, fulmination.

WARP, *v.* 1. Twist out of shape, distort, pervert, bend, contort, gnarl, buckle, knot, wrench, screw, wrest, wring, misshape, deform, writhe, spring.

2. Misinterpret, misconstrue, garble, color, misrender, exaggerate, misrepresent, torture, misapply, misuse.

3. Deviate, swerve, turn, jibe, tack, veer, wear, diverge from, chop, deflect, slew.

4. Prejudice, bias, influence, prepossess, misguide, beguile, falsify.

5. Tend, lean to, incline, predispose, promote, dispose, verge, gravitate towards.

WARP, *n.* 1. Proclivity, trend, drift, gravitation, penchant, proneness, propensity, tendency, inclination, bent, disposition, leaning, set, bias, predisposition, susceptibility, liability, one-sidedness, partiality, favor, prepossession, predilection.

2. Variation, deflection, deviation, divergence, tack, sidling, yaw, zigzag, drift, sweep, declination, alteration, aberration, divagation, digression, swerve, switch, sheer.

WARRANT, *v.* 1. Guarantee, certify, attest, promise, assure, foretoken, vouch for, answer for, underwrite, secure, subscribe, swear, pledge, plight, stipulate, affirm, asseverate, aver, depose, avow, avouch, depone.

2. Uphold, sustain, ratify, confirm, corroborate, bear out, indorse, validate, vindicate, authenticate, establish, substantiate, prove, verify, circumstantiate.

3. Sanction, authorize, license, justify, empower, privilege, grant, charter.

WARRANT, *n.* 1. Verification, authentication, commission, authority, authorization, sanction, justification, security.

2. Certificate, voucher, paper, charter, receipt,

guarantee, surety, security, warranty, pledge, stipulation, agreement, covenant, compact.

3. Permit, pass, *laissez-passer (Fr.),* passport, credentials, imprimatur, safe-conduct, safeguard, *carte blanche (Fr.),* admission.

4. Summons, writ, order, subpoena, decree, prescript, mandate, rescript, decretal, edict.

WARRANTABLE, *adj.* Permissible, lawful, legitimate, proper, admissible, allowable, justifiable, vindicable, defensible, right.

WARRIOR, *n.* Soldier, man-at-arms, military man, fighting man, fighter, combatant, belligerent, brave, private, doughboy, poilu, rank and file, skirmisher, infantryman, guerrilla, sharpshooter, trooper, conscript, rookie, recruit, volunteer, enlisted man, veteran, campaigner, hussar, dragoon, cavalryman, chasseur, zouave, grenadier, guardsman, fusileer, *franc-tireur (Fr.),* mercenary, sepoy, musketeer, free lance, soldier of fortune, armigerent, janissary, myrmidon, Cossack, legionary, subaltern, shavetail, ensign, non-com, standard bearer, cannon-fodder, gunner, artilleryman, bombardier, cannoneer, sapper.

WARSHIP, *n.* Man-of-war, war vessel, battleship, cruiser, dreadnought, ironsides, gunboat, destroyer, torpedoboat, minesweeper, submarine, U-boat, submersible, flagship, corvet, capital ship, turretship, aircraft carrier, tender.

WART, *n.* Small hard abnormal elevation on the skin, morbid excrescence, fungous growth, small protuberance on the skin, bristly tubercle, hyperplasia, verruca, thymion, condyloma.

WARY, *adj.* Cautious, heedful, guarded, on one's guard, vigilant, watchful, careful, provident, prudent, discreet, circumspect, canny, chary, shy, secretive, sly, shrewd, wise, judicious, politic, leery, foxy, suspicious, close-mouthed, wide-awake, alert, mindful, attentive, wakeful, calculating, deliberate, scrupulous, noncommittal, strategic, Fabian.

WASH, *v.* 1. Lave, cleanse, scrub, launder, swab, purge, purify, clean, ablute, mop, scour, immerse, drench, sprinkle, rinse, bathe, wet, moisten, flush, irrigate, remove dirt by the action of water, free from dirt, apply a liquid to for the purpose of cleansing, sponge, rub, wipe.

2. Cover with a thin coat of color, paint, stain, color, tint, dye, tinge, coat, calcimine, whitewash, gild, imbue, hue, ingrain.

WASH, *n.* 1. Washing, ablution, bath, lavation, bathing, cleansing, immersion, tubbing, tub, sponge bath, shower, dip, dipping, balneation, humectation, douche, sprinkling, drenching, submersion.

2. Laundry, buck.

3. Lotion, embrocation, liquid for toilet purposes, detergent, purgative, disinfectant, deodorant, cologne, diluent.

4. Varnish, paint, stain, enamel, gloss, washing, plaster, whitewash, stucco.

5. Fen, marsh, bog, morass, quagmire, swamp, slough, sump.

WASPISH, *adj.* Irritable, snappish, irascible, splenetic, peevish, testy, petulant, resentful, pettish, captious, fretful, touchy, snarly, choleric, perverse, quick, moody, peppery, temperamental, thin-skinned, fiery, crusty, crabby, morose, sullen, sulky, churlish, quarrelsome, surly, fractious, frumpish, grumpy, cross-grained, humorsome, cantankerous, sinistrous, exceptious, froward, intractable, refractory, spleenish, cankered, ill-tempered, sharp-tongued, rude, brusque, abrupt.

WASSAIL, *n.* 1. Carousal, festivity, conviviality, revelry, revels, orgy, debauch, rout, saturnalia, convivial entertainment, drunken spree, potation, jollification, compotation, symposium, jollity, bacchanalia, whoopee, merrymaking, high jinks, brawl, party, shindig *(sl.),* feast, carnival, junket.

2. Salutation wishing health to a person, toast, prosit, *à votre santé (Fr.),* a su salud *(Sp.),* alla salute *(It.),* Gesundheit *(Ger.).*

WASTE, *v.* 1. Lay waste, devastate, ravage, spoil, despoil, desolate, pillage, loot, sack, plunder, destroy, strip, overrun, scour, raze, ruin, harry, demolish, dilapidate, prey upon, overthrow, fell, crush, shatter, smash, overturn, dismantle, gut, blast, extirpate, eradicate, deracinate, annihilate.

2. Use up, expend, consume, devour, exhaust, empty, drain, deplete, dissipate, squander, misspend, disperse, spill, lavish, prodigalize, burn up, fritter away, throw away, wear out, burn the candle at both ends, misuse, fool away, muddle away, lose, run through, misemploy, misapply, impoverish, scatter, make ducks and drakes of one's money, pour forth like water, overdraw.

3. Decrease, reduce, diminish, corrode, erode, wear away, gnaw, eat, wear out, impair gradually.

4. Disappear, evaporate, run to waste, leak, ebb, melt away, vanish, evanesce, dissolve, dry up, run dry, wither, decay, perish, crumble, decline, molder, run to seed.

WASTE, *n.* 1. Use without adequate return, useless consumption, diminution, loss, expenditure, decrement, dissipation, wasting, wear and tear, exhaustion, depletion, dispersion, detriment, injury, damage, havoc, ravage, misuse, devastation, decay, ruination, ruin, desolation, rapine, pillage, sack, spoliation, demolition, dilapidation, extirpation, eradication, annihilation.

2. Ineconomy, extravagance, wastefulness, prodigality, squandering, lavishness, unthriftiness, profusion, effusion, profuse liberality, excessive generosity.

3. Wilderness, desert, Sahara, barren expanse, dreary void, deserted region, solitude, lonely place, wild, uncultivated tract of land, howling wilderness, bush, tundra, steppe, alkali flat, mesa, veldt, savanna, prairie.

4. Trash, rubbish, refuse, wastage, offal, chaff, waste material, scraps, leavings, husks, dross, remnants, detritus, alluvium, culm, spilth, debris, junk, slops, scum, dregs, lees, sediment, offscourings, odds and ends, shoddy, orts, garbage, sweepings, litter.

WASTE, *adj.* 1. Uncultivated, wild, untilled, barren, arid, desert, desolate, uninhabited, unoccupied, unimproved, bare, void, empty, stripped, cheerless, gloomy, dreary, dismal, monotonous, forlorn, bleak, ruined, destroyed, ravaged, spoiled, despoiled, devastated, desolated, vacant, unproductive, effete, infertile, sterile, unprolific, infecund, infructuose, acarpous, unfruitful, fallow, lifeless, dead.

2. Worthless, useless, losel, valueless, refuse, trashy, unprofitable, unserviceable, superfluous, leftover, rejected as refuse, good-for-nothing, not worth a straw.

WASTEFUL, *adj.* Extravagant, prodigal, spendthrift, thriftless, squandering, profligate, over-liberal, too free, improvident, profuse, lavish, unthrifty, penny-wise and pound-foolish, free-handed,

inordinate, exorbitant, superfluous, excessive, exuberant, superabundant, overmuch, fulsome, replete, immoderate, *de trop (Fr.).*

WASTER, *n.* 1. Spendthrift, prodigal, wastrel, free spender, squanderer, Prodigal Son, profligate, lavisher.

2. Idler, loafer, bum, good-for-nothing, *vaurien (Fr.),* Taugenichts *(Ger.),* trifler, slacker, goldbricker, malingerer, beachcomber, hobo, vagrant, scatterling, tramp, knight of the road.

WATCH, *v.* 1. Fix the attention upon, keep the eye on, look attentively, notice, eye, espy, look on, observe, perceive, see, remark, attend, regard, mark, ogle, stare at, gaze at, behold, descry, sight, witness, contemplate, view, survey, inspect, scan, reconnoiter, peer, squint, pry, peep, goggle, rivet the eyes upon, pore over, cock the eye, be closely observant, be a spectator, make note of, examine, scrutinize, investigate, take stock of.

2. Be cautious, take care, heed, take heed, be on the alert, be on guard, be on the lookout, keep a sharp lookout, be careful, keep a close check on, not lose sight of, be Argus-eyed, pay attention to, guard, tend, scout, patrol, oversee, superintend, look after, chaperon, mind, picket, escort, conduct, convoy, ward, safeguard, preserve, take care of.

WATCH, *n.* 1. Close observation, inspection, superintendence, surveillance, oversight, attention, heed, advertency, note, regard, circumspection, alertness, observance, consideration, heedfulness, view, survey, contemplation, charge, custody, supervision, vigilance, watchfulness, wariness, vigil, lookout, watch and ward, reconnoitering, safekeeping, safeguard.

2. Guard, sentry, picket, outpost, watchman, sentinel, patrolman, scout.

3. Small timepiece, pocket watch, wrist watch, ticker *(coll.),* Ingersoll, chronometer, clock, horologe.

WATCHFUL, *adj.* Closely observant, vigilant, circumspect, on the alert, on the lookout, wide-awake, wakeful, on one's guard, guarded, cautious, wary, prudent, careful, alert, heedful, Argus-eyed, lynx-eyed, aware, cognizant, regardful, mindful, shrewd, discreet, politic, unsleeping, not caught napping, on the *qui vive,* open-eyed, hawk-eyed, attentive, chary, canny, scrupulous, discerning, searching.

WATCHMAN, *n.* One who keeps guard over at night, guard, picket, sentry, sentinel, scout, patrol, lookout, guardsman, watch, warden, keeper, Argus, Cerberus, watchdog, warder, bloodhound, policeman, copper, bobby *(Brit.),* dick *(sl.),* flatfoot *(sl.),* guardian, custodian, patrolman, roundsman, bull *(sl.),* spotter, night watchman, vedette *(Military),* outpost, doorkeeper, gatekeeper, concierge, janitor, porter.

WATCHTOWER, *n.* Observation post, belvedere, gazebo, turret, beacon, lookout, crow's-nest, observatory.

WATCHWORD, *n.* Short phrase to be communicated for recognition, countersign, password, shibboleth, catchword, word, parole, signal, cry, slogan, *mot de passe (Fr.),* mot d'ordre *(Fr.).*

WATER, *n.* 1. Transparent and tasteless liquid, H_2O *(Chem.),* aqua *(Lat.),* eau *(Fr.),* Wasser *(Ger.),* agua *(Sp.),* acqua *(It.),* hydor *(Greek),* Adam's ale *(humorous),* city gin *(humorous),* pani *(Hindu),* lymph, crystal, fluid, rheum, diluent.

2. Ablution, bath, immersion, baptism, lavation, lavabo, elution, dip, tub, shower, balneation, humectation.

WATER, v. 1. Wet, moisten, irrigate, drench, souse, steep, soak, damp, sprinkle, dampen, macerate, douse, slosh, immerse, dip, submerge, baptize, duck, lave, wash, bathe, spatter, asperge, sparge, besprinkle, splash, deluge, flood, inundate, saturate, bedew, sodden.

2. Dilute, adulterate, attenuate, add water to, thin, weaken, humidify, humectate, infiltrate.

3. Tabby, calender, moiré, dapple, variegate.

WATER CLOSET, n. Toilet, privy, necessary, backhouse, outhouse, outbuilding, lavatory, powder room, urinal, jakes, W.C.

WATERCOURSE, n. 1. Waterway, stream, river, brook, creek, run, rivulet, rill, streamlet, affluent, tributary, reach, branch, feeder, anabranch, gill, runnel, runlet, burn, beck, current, race, sluice, torrent.

2. Canal, channel, drain, ditch, trench, moat, fosse, sewer, gutter.

WATERFALL, n. Cascade, cataract, falls, Niagara, linn, chute, rapid, shoot, foss, whirlpool, maelstrom, vortex, eddy, gurge, Charybdis.

WATER NYMPH, n. Naiad, Nereid, Oceanid, Undine, Thetis, sea nymph, mermaid, Siren, kelpie, Lorelei.

WATERPROOF, n. Raincoat, impermeable, slicker, mackintosh, ulster, poncho, oilskin.

WATERY, adj. 1. Aqueous, liquid, wet, moist, humid, overmoist, lymphatic, serous, soggy, sodden, fluid, fluent, liquefied, soluble, uncongealed, sanious, ichorous, rheumy, hydrous, lush, juicy, succulent.

2. Diluted, waterish, watered, adulterated, transparent, thin, weak.

3. Tasteless, insipid, vapid, flat, wishy-washy, tame, poor, feeble, dull, uninteresting, jejune.

4. Tearful, lachrymose, weepy, sorrowful, crying, mournful, dissolved in tears.

WATTLE, n. 1. Mat, plait, trellis, lattice, grille, grating, gridiron, reticle, tracery, filigree, fretwork, netting, plexus, web.

2. Hurdle of twigs, switch, withe, twig, wand, stick, rod, stake, branch.

3. Fleshy appendage hanging down from the throat or chin, dewlap, jowl, double chin.

WAVE, v. 1. Undulate, oscillate, fluctuate, meander, flutter, vibrate, heave, wallow, float, move to and fro, flap, rock, swing, shake, sway, move alternately in opposite directions, librate, nutate, wobble, pendulate, dangle, pulsate, waggle, bob, waver, reel, quiver, wriggle, toss, teeter, seesaw, crossruff, ebb and flow, come and go.

2. Direct by a waving motion, signal, beckon, gesticulate, gesture, signalize, saw the air.

WAVE, n. 1. Disturbance of the surface of a body of water, comber, breaker, whitecap, swell, roller, billow, bore, ridge on the surface of water, surf, ripple, surge, undulation, wavelet, tide, flood, riffle, ground swell, heave, white horse.

2. Coil, curl, convolution, winding, roll, involution, tortuosity, sinuosity, circuit, meandering, ambages, circumbendibus, twirl, twist, contortion, spiral, volute, corkscrew, scallop, helix, tendril, worm, kink, scroll.

3. Gesture, sign, gesticulation, flourish, sway, motion, chironomy, pantomime, dactylology.

WAVER, v. 1. Sway, totter, falter, reel, become unsteady, begin to give way, stagger, be in danger of falling, stumble, flounder.

2. Vacillate, alternate, fluctuate, straddle, palter, undulate, wave, flutter, flicker, quiver, tremble, shake, wag, vibrate, shift, boggle, vary, hesitate between two choices, be unsettled, show indecision, feel doubt, shilly-shally, be undetermined.

WAVERER, n. Trimmer, shuffler, tergiversator, timeserver, shilly-shallier, shuttlecock, turncoat, apostate, Vicar of Bray, opportunist, weathercock, chameleon.

WAVERING, adj. Vacillating, fluctuating, oscillatory, changeable, unsettled, unsteady, varying, unstable, variable, mutable, lubricous, inconstant, mercurial, volatile, unsteadfast, irresponsible, indecisive, infirm, undetermined, shilly-shallying, uncertain, irresolute, undecided, faltering, hesitating, double-minded, fickle, unreliable, half-hearted, capricious.

WAVY, adj. Curving alternately in opposite directions, bending with successive curves, undulating, undulant, billowy, rough, choppy, waving, flickering, sinuous, meandering, curly, crinkly, playing to and fro, vibrating, tremulous, wavering, unsteady, undulatory, undulative, undose, sinuate, flexuose, ripply.

WAX, v. Become larger, increase, become fuller, develop, expand, enlarge, extend, widen, incrassate, gather, swell, fill out, dilate, spread, spread out, amplify, magnify, puff out, inflate, blow up, fatten.

WAXEN, adj. Waxlike, ceruminous, waxy, soft, tender, yielding, plastic, impressible, pliable, malleable, pliant, supple, flexible, ductile, tractile, extensile, mollient, flaccid, argillaceous, doughy.

WAY, n. 1. Road, path, street, pathway, avenue, boulevard, highway, artery, turnpike, highroad, pike, thoroughfare, throughway, roadway, alley, parkway, speedway, route, trail, lane, footpath, towpath, track, fairway, channel, pavement, sidewalk, trottoir (Fr.), flagging, causeway, viaduct, cobbles, overpass, underpass.

2. Orbit, trajectory, course, direction, bearing, progression, trend, transit, journey, march, passage, progress.

3. Method, mode, fashion, manner, procedure, system, modus operandi (Lat.), wise, style, form, practice, guise, habit, conduct, custom, behavior, tone, usage, habitude, wont, plan of conduct, second nature.

4. Space, stretch, interval, interspace, remoteness, extent.

5. Detail, point, respect, aspect, particular, feature, item.

WAYFARER, n. Passenger, traveler, itinerant, peripatetic, rambler, voyager, pilgrim, periegete, wanderer, tourist, journeyer, trekker, walker, excursionist, tripper, migrant, hiker, knight of the road, rover, nomad, gypsy, Bedouin, hadji, globetrotter, sightseer, explorer, adventurer, peregrinator, roamer, landloper, gadabout, gadling, hobo, tramp, vagabond, pedestrian.

WAYFARING, adj. Journeying, itinerant, ambulatory, peripatetic, perambulatory, rambling, roving, roaming, gadding, migratory, vagrant, nomadic, circumforaneous, traveling, wayworn.

WAYLAY, v. Fall upon from ambush, ambuscade, ambush, lie in wait for, lie in ambush for, assail, attack, accost unexpectedly, lay a trap for, decoy, lure, inveigle, illaqueate.

WAYWARD, *adj.* Turned away from what is right *or* proper, perverse, willful, froward, contrary, self-willed, headstrong, cross-grained, obstinate, intractable, stubborn, mulish, unruly, captious, refractory, recalcitrant, capricious, disobedient, balky, humorsome, restive, wanton, arbitrary, unyielding, moody, morose, sulky, untoward, erratic, whimsical, eccentric, irregular, pertinacious, fluctuating, changeable, mercurial, volatile, inconsistent, fitful, crotchety, unreasonable, irresolute, mutable, inconstant, notional, fickle, opinionated, opinionative, ungovernable, heady, contumacious, incorrigible.

WEAK, *adj.* 1. Deficient in bodily vigor, enfeebled, feeble, debilitated, spent, exhausted, weakly, not strong, languid, languishing, enervated, infirm, delicate, faint, invalid, fragile, frail, unsound, strengthless, impotent, impuissant, asthenic, atonic, prostrate, valetudinarian, wasted, valetudinary, inert, passive, sapless, poorly, haggard, emaciated, shaky, unnerved, unstrung, limp, slack, flaccid, groggy, unsteady, helpless, powerless, laid low, decrepit, sickly, unhealthy, ill, indisposed, unwell, ailing.

2. Effeminate, unmanly, soft, womanish, spineless, timorous, sissy, tender.

3. Breakable, brittle, frangible, sleazy, flimsy, gimcrack, jerry-built, unsubstantial, paper.

4. Worn, deteriorated, the worse for wear, used up, on its last legs, wasted, seedy, rotten, decayed, rickety, tumble-down, dilapidated.

5. Exposed, vulnerable, defenseless, assailable, unguarded, unprotected, unfortified, accessible, wide-open, woundable, unsafe, untrustworthy.

6. Inefficacious, ineffective, futile, useless, inefficient, ineffectual, lame, unavailing, vain.

7. Illogical, unconvincing, poor, inconclusive, unsupported, unsatisfactory, untenable.

8. Faint, feeble, low, indistinct, gentle, small, thin, watery, waterish, diluted, attenuated, vapid, adulterated, tasteless, insipid.

WEAKEN, *v.* 1. Enfeeble, deprive of strength, impair, sap, undermine, enervate, debilitate, unnerve, unman, invalidate, effeminize, soften, exhaust, reduce, devitalize, emasculate, incapacitate, cripple, impoverish, strain, dilute, adulterate, lower, debase, minimize, tone down, water, diminish, thin, make weak, deplete, lessen, lower.

2. Droop, languish, give way, fade, decline, faint, fail, flag, tremble, totter, shake, dodder, crumble, drop.

WEAK-KNEED, *adj.* Irresolute, undecided, wavering, changeable, fickle, vacillating, inconstant, unstable, mercurial, volatile, pliable, spineless, unmanly, womanish, timorous, craven, pusillanimous, cowardly, chicken *(sl.),* feeble, timid, dastardly, recreant, effeminate, lily-livered, spiritless, faint-hearted.

WEAK-MINDED, *adj.* Feeble-minded, weakheaded, half-witted, doting, witless, sappy, shallow, foolish, irrational, deranged, inane, imbecilic, moronic, idiotic, crackbrained, touched, asinine, daft, insensate, insulse, fatuous, silly, cretinous, driveling, weak in the upper story, vacant, nutty *(sl.),* mentally deficient, half-baked.

WEAKNESS, *n.* 1. Feebleness, infirmity, debility, debilitation, enervation, impotence, impuissance, languor, atony, asthenia, adynamia, decrepitude, neurasthenia, cachexia, loss of strength, anemia, malnutrition, invalidism, valetudinarianism, invalidity, prostration, attenuation.

2. Vulnerability, susceptibility, vulnerableness, susceptibleness, accessibility, openness to attack, assailableness.

3. Frailty, imperfection, defect, failing, deficiency, fault, foible, lapse.

4. Liking, propensity, penchant, proclivity, leaning, inclination, proneness, tendency, bias, prejudice, aptitude, bent, appetite, hunger, thirst, passion.

WEAL, *n.* 1. Welfare, well-being, advantage, benefit, good, happiness, profit, interest, utility, prosperity, improvement, service, behalf, summum bonum, gain, good turn, boon, blessing, benison, good fortune.

2. Welt, streak, ridge, wale, mark, stripe, lump.

WEALTH, *n.* Great store of riches, affluence, prosperity, easy street, resources, possessions, property, capital, assets, goods, chattels, estate, belongings, substance, lucre, revenue, money, riches, pelf, mammon, gold, treasure, funds, moneybags, cash, means, fortune, luxury, opulence, independence, competency, profusion, plenty, cornucopia, horn of plenty, golden calf, abundance, wealthiness, easy circumstances, mint of money, El Dorado, bonanza, Pactolian sands, Golconda, the golden touch, Midas' touch, purse of Fortunatus, *embarras de richesses (Fr.),* income, livelihood, capitalism, plutology, plutocracy.

WEALTHY, *adj.* 1. Rich, affluent, prosperous, moneyed, well-to-do, well-off, well-heeled *(coll.),* flush *(coll.),* opulent, independent, rolling in riches, capitalistic, plutocratic, propertied, landed, flourishing, aristocratic, luxurious, luxuried, silk-stocking, silver-spoon, patrician, lordly, princely, blue-blooded, regal, made of money, on easy street, well provided for, pecunious.

2. Abundant, copious, plentiful, full, ample, bountiful, profuse, luxuriant, exuberant, lavish, bounteous, superabundant.

WEAN, *v.* Withdraw from any object of habit, disengage from a form of enjoyment, reconcile to the loss of anything, detach, disaccustom, alienate, estrange, transfer, set against, abalienate, relinquish, surrender, give up, let slip, drop, yield, forgo, abjure, renounce, lay aside, part with, cast off, discard, quit.

WEAPON, *n.* Instrument for use in combat, deadly device, lethal instrument, club, truncheon, cudgel, bludgeon, mace, shillelagh, quarterstaff, blackjack, brass knuckles, billy, slingshot, bow, crossbow, catapult, sling, poleax, battle-ax, tomahawk, halberd, lance, spear, assegai, pike, harpoon, javelin, boomerang, dart, missile, arrow, shaft, machete, kukri, cutlass, bolo, saber, sword, scimitar, broadsword, rapier, brand, claymore, foil, glaive, poniard, dagger, dirk, creese, stiletto, knife, blade, bayonet, cold steel, firearm, small arm, pistol, revolver, rifle, Colt, gun, fowling piece, firelock, musket, carbine, matchlock, blunderbuss, harquebus, breechloader, repeater, shotgun, muzzle-loader, automatic, six-gun, shooting iron, six-shooter, rod, bomb, grenade, torpedo, ordnance, artillery, cannon, battery, fieldpiece, Big Bertha, howitzer, mortar, pompom, aerogun, antiaircraft gun, ack-ack, machine gun.

WEAR, *v.* 1. Have on the body as covering, don, put on, carry upon the person, bear, step into, deck, rig out, fit out, enrobe, drape, attire, gown, costume, apparel, invest, garb, endue, enclothe, dight, accouter, array, wrap, swathe, muffle, swaddle, shroud, slip on, dress in, assume, get on, sport.

2. Consume, waste, impair by use, destroy by gradual attrition, wear away, use up, wear out, fray, frazzle, eat away, corrode, erode, scrape, rub away, wash away, shred, gnaw into, diminish, reduce, deteriorate, dwindle, chafe, fret, abrade.

3. Weary, exhaust, tire, fatigue, drain, spend, jade, irk, annoy, bore, flag, harass, prostrate, tax, overtask, strain, overburden, overwork.

4. *(Naut.)* Veer, jibe, yaw, tack, sheer, slue, alter course, turn, swerve, deviate, curve, bend, heel, bear off, go about.

WEAR, *n.* 1. Wear and tear, disrepair, impairment, disintegration, deterioration, dilapidation, decrepitude, damage, detriment, injury, havoc, depreciation, decadence, decay, erosion, corrosion, dry rot, moth and rust, atrophy, ruination, dissolution, ravage.

2. Service, use, employment, utility, appliance, adhibition, application, exercise, consumption, utilization.

WEARINESS, *n.* 1. Fatigue, exhaustion, defatigation, lassitude, languor, prostration, tiredness, languidness, enervation, debility, drowsiness, faintness, heaviness, lentor, sluggishness, toilsome effort, dull work, long hours, drudgery.

2. Boredom, ennui, tedium, tediousness, monotony, monotonousness, sameness, wearisomeness, repletion, satiety, surfeit, glut, dullness, uninterestingness, dryness, torpor, stupor.

WEARISOME, *adj.* Fatiguing, exhausting, toilsome, arduous, onerous, operose, burdensome, laborious, tiresome, tiring, backbreaking, uphill, wearing, tedious, irksome, prolix, long-winded, diffuse, dull, flat, dry, boring, uninteresting, bald, stupid, monotonous, jejune, unrewarding, arid, dry-as-dust, humdrum, routine, prosy, prosaic, soporific, somniferous, dismal, heavy, leaden, torpid, slack, slow, vexatious, annoying, trying, insipid, vapid, dreary, troublesome, plaguy, sluggish.

WEARY, *adj.* 1. Fatigued, exhausted, spent, tired, footsore, fagged out, defatigated, done in, worn out, wearied, wayworn, toilworn, prostrate, faint, used up, haggard, all in, dog-tired, ready to drop, played out, shattered, enfeebled, careworn, sleepy, drowsy, languid, enervated.

2. Harassed, dissatisfied, discontented, dispirited, blasé, *ennuyé (Fr.),* disgusted, sick and tired, impatient.

3. Irksome, tedious, operose, tiresome, wearisome, weariful, wearing, prolix, tiring, laborious, arduous, onerous, boring, uninteresting, dull, heavy, insipid, vapid, prosaic, prosy, humdrum, routine, arid, dry, monotonous, bald, slow, stupid, jejune, somniferous, soporific.

WEARY, *v.* 1. Exhaust, fatigue, defatigate, tire out, fag out, wear out, tire, overburden, overtax, jade.

2. Irk, annoy, harass, buttonhole, bore, make impatient, fret, chafe, harp on the same string, bother, distress, vex, glut, surfeit, cloy, pall, sicken, disgust, revolt, nauseate, dishearten, discourage, depress, deject, displease, pain, dun, importune.

WEATHER, *n.* Climate, atmospheric conditions, clime, mercury, barometric reading, meteorology, aerology, climatography, climatology.

WEATHER, *v.* 1. Expose to the weather, dry, season, undergo change because of exposure to atmospheric conditions, discolor, bleach, tan, rust, oxidize, toughen.

2. Come safely through trouble, accomplish against opposition, bear up against, encounter and sustain, endure, get the better of, stand, resist, overcome, surmount, *se tirer d'affaire (Fr.),* keep one's head above water, ride out the storm, light upon one's feet, pull through, recover, rally, survive.

WEATHER PROPHET, *n.* Weather forecaster, meteorologist, weather man *(coll.),* goosebone man *(coll.),* climatologist.

WEATHER VANE, *n.* Weathercock, vane, cock, weather gauge, aerometer, anemoscope, wind vane, anemometer.

WEAVE, *v.* 1. Twine the threads of a fabric, interlace, plait, entwine, lace, braid, plat, mat, interweave, intertwine, decussate, cross, intertwist, crisscross, interlink, wattle, loom, knit, interknit.

2. Fabricate, make, construct, compose, form, design.

3. Move from side to side, proceed in a winding course, meander, zigzag, sinuate.

WEB, *n.* Thin spun fabric, tissue, woven structure, textile fabric, texture, mesh, net, lace, netting, plait, interlacement, network, reticulation, warp and woof, warp and weft, gossamer, cobweb.

WED, *v.* 1. Bind in marriage, give in wedlock, join, marry, couple, espouse, splice, make one.

2. Lead to the altar, take for better *or* worse, take for husband *or* wife, bind oneself to in marriage.

WEDDING, *n.* Marriage ceremony, nuptial rite, nuptials, bridal, marriage, espousals, hymeneals, spousals, hymeneal rites, hymen, confarreation, leading to the altar, epithalamium.

WEDGE, *n.* V-shaped piece of material, chock, keystone, cuneus, arrowhead, cleat, quoin, shim, block, voussoir, cotter, embolus, key, glut.

WEDLOCK, *n.* Nuptial state, matrimony, nuptial tie, marriage, holy matrimony, intermarriage, nuptial knot, match, *vinculum matrimonii (Lat.),* union.

WEE, *adj.* Very small, tiny, little, diminutive, minute, minikin, picayunish, pygmean, microscopic, atomic, molecular, Lilliputian, miniature, exiguous, elfin, puny, pocket-size, runty, undersized, dwarf, stunted, nanoid, infinitesimal, animalcular, microbic, microbial, homeopathic, embryonic, slight, petite.

WEED, *v.* Free from troublesome plants, rid of weeds, clear of weeds, root up, uproot, deracinate, root out, extirpate, eradicate, take away, eliminate, remove as undesirable, eject, reject, extrude, unearth, dig out, delve, hoe, dibble, harrow, thin out.

WEED, *n.* 1. Useless *or* troublesome plant that grows profusely, tare, thistle, thorn, rush, sedge, spur, prickle, underbrush, bush.

2. Tobacco, cigar, cigarette, gasper, fag, cheroot, smoke, coffin nail *(coll.).*

3. *(Pl.)* Symbol of sorrow, mourning, widow's weeds, sables, sackcloth, deep mourning, crepe.

WEEK, *n.* Period of seven successive days, sevennight, sennight, *semaine (Fr.),* *settimana (It.),* *semana (Sp.),* *Woche (Ger.).*

WEEKLY, *adj.* Happening once a week, occurring weekly, hebdomadal, hebdomadary, *hebdomadaire (Fr.),* *wöchentlich (Ger.),* *semanal (Sp.),* *settimanale (It.).*

WEEN, *v.* Think, opine, suppose, conjecture, fancy, presume, imagine, expect, judge, conclude, gather, deduce, infer, consider, regard, believe, trow, conceive, deem, surmise, know, ken, wot.

WEEP, *v.* Shed tears, manifest grief by tears, cry, sob, mourn with tears, boohoo, blubber, lament, keen, greet *(Scot.),* wail, ululate, bemoan, grieve, deplore, whimper, snivel.

WEEPING, *n.* Crying, shedding tears, sobbing, lachrymation, cry *(coll.),* flood of tears, lachrymals, tears, mourning, keening, ululation, elegy, nenia, dirge, threnody, outcry, lament, plaint, wail, moan, whimper, suspiration.

WEEPY, *adj.* Bathed in tears, lachrymose, mournful, sorrowful, blubbering, boohooing, sniveling, whimpering, tearful, lamenting, querulous, plaintive.

WEIGH, *v.* 1. Ascertain the weight of by means of a scale *or* balance, try in the balance, determine the heaviness of, measure according to weight, counterweigh, equiponderate, counterbalance, balance.

2. Carry weight, have influence, count, tell, be potent, be influential, bias, incline, work upon, impel, induce, persuade.

3. Consider carefully, estimate deliberately, meditate upon, ponder, balance in the mind, examine, realize, contemplate, investigate, brood over, mull over, reflect upon, cogitate, consult, reason, speculate, ruminate, con over, study, set one's wits to work.

WEIGHT, *n.* 1. Heaviness, heft, ponderosity, ponderousness, tonnage, gravity, pounds, relative density, load, pressure, burden, ballast, mass, counterpoise, lading, cargo.

2. Importance, magnitude, significance, seriousness, import, enormity, moment, concern, consideration, consequence, value, prominence, materialness, emphasis, interest, caliber, solemnity, urgency, pressure, stress.

3. Power, preponderance, ascendancy, impressiveness, favor, influentiality, potency, puissance, drag *(sl.),* pull *(coll.),* authority, domination, sway.

WEIGHTY, *adj.* 1. Heavy, ponderous, massive, onerous, unwieldy, burdensome, hefty, ponderable, cumbersome, cumbrous.

2. Important, consequential, telling, influential, forcible, considerable, significant, efficacious, momentous, determinative, serious, grave, pregnant, cogent, persuasive, valid, formidable, earnest, solemn, substantial, sound, solid, strong, urgent, pressing, critical, outstanding, salient, predominant, material, notable, prominent, marked, signal, crucial, imperative, exigent, vital, essential, emphatic, decided, forceful, potent, effective, powerful, puissant, authoritative.

WEIR, *n.* Obstruction placed across a stream, dam, fence, floodgate, sluice, conduit, penstock, watergate, lock.

WEIRD, *adj.* Outside natural law, supernatural, preternatural, uncanny, unearthly, eerie, eldritch, spooky, witching, ghostly, wraithlike, haunted, phantasmal, spiritistic, hyperphysical, awe-inspiring, portentous, mystic, cabalistic, magical, incantatory, strange, odd, queer, spectral, singular.

WEIRD SISTERS, *n.* The Fates, Parcae, Moerae, The Sisters Three, Norns; Clotho, Altropos, Lachesis.

WELCOME, *v.* Receive with kindly pleasure, greet with courtesy, offer hospitality to, treat hospitably, bid welcome, roll out the welcome mat, open the door to, embrace, hail, gratulate, accept eagerly, admit, do the honors, usher in, smile upon, entertain, have the latchstring out, keep open house, kill the fatted calf, hold out the hand to, drink to, pledge, toast, shake hands with, befriend, receive with open arms, fraternize, salute.

WELCOME, *adj.* Cordial, agreeable, acceptable, genial, pleasing, pleasant, gratifying, grateful, delightful, pleasurable, admitted with pleasure, gladly received, hospitably entertained, given full right to by the cordial consent of others, free to enjoy gratuitously, free to have, amiable, charming, heartfelt, felicitous, joyful, gladsome, jolly, glad, invigorating, refreshing, comfortable, restful, inviting, engaging, prepossessing, winning, entrancing, enticing, cheering.

WELCOME, *n.* 1. Salutation, greeting, *bienvenue (Fr.), benvenuto (It.), bienvenida (Sp.), Willkommen (Ger.),* hearty reception, the glad hand, open door, entrée.

2. Entertainment, at-home, party, soirée, social gathering, housewarming, social, tea party, dinner party, cocktail party, open-house, fete, dinner dance.

WELFARE, *n.* Well-being, weal, happiness, affluence, prosperity, success, good fortune, good, benefit, advantage, progress, profit, thrift, prosperousness, good luck, godsend, blessing, gain, boon, benison, interest, behalf, favorable issue, favor, advance, smiles of fortune, good health, vigor, soundness, haleness, euphoria.

WELKIN, *n.* Sky, the heavens, canopy of heaven, firmament, vault of heaven, empyrean, starry heavens, azure, starry host, celestial spaces, milky way, *via lactea (Lat.),* open air, stratosphere, troposphere, blue sky.

WELL, *n.* 1. Natural source of water, spring, fountain, fountainhead, wellspring, font, reservoir, pool, springhead.

2. Pit, hole, shaft, depression, hollow, crater, abyss, crevasse, chasm, deep, bowels of the earth.

WELL, *v.* Flow, pour, jet, issue, gush, spring, spout, stream, roll, run, spurt, ooze, trickle, geyser, drip, drop, dribble, gurgle, purl, surge, babble, overflow, swirl, inundate, plash, splash.

WELL, *adv.* 1. Worthily, meritoriously, excellently, commendably, satisfactorily, favorably, advantageously, fortunately, happily, auspiciously, propitiously, agreeably, famously, splendidly, finely, skillfully, rightly, properly, correctly, suitably, accurately, nobly, nicely, capitally, laudably.

2. Abundantly, sufficiently, fully, amply, thoroughly, adequately, completely, quite, highly, considerably, very much, not a little, soundly.

3. Rightly, in a proper manner, properly, first-rate, justly, not amiss.

WELL, *adj.* 1. Healthy, hearty, hale, sound, in good health, wholesome, salubrious, salutary, strong, robust, vigorous, euphoric, rosy-cheeked, blooming, in fine fettle, chipper, florid.

2. Fortunate, happy, auspicious, propitious, lucky, felicitous, successful, prosperous, advantageous, favorable, promising, halcyon.

3. Opportune, seasonable, timely, convenient, well-timed, suitable, fit.

WELL-BALANCED, *adj.* Rational, sane, sensible, in one's right mind, sober, reasonable, reasoning, intelligent, sagacious, judicious, prudent, discreet, wise, intellectual, cognizant, understanding, keen, quick-witted, knowing, hard-headed, smart, discerning, thoughtful, brainy.

WELL-BEHAVED, *adj.* Well-bred, mannerly, polite, urbane, polished, courteous, well-mannered, decorous, orderly, civil, suave, refined, cultivated, chivalrous, gallant, gracious, tactful, diplomatic, bland, fair-spoken, well-conducted, seemly, *bienséant (Fr.),* decent.

WELL-BEING, *n.* Welfare, weal, euphoria, happiness, prosperity, affluence, success, luck, godsend, smiles of fortune, wealth, riches, fortune, good, blessing, comfort, advantage, profit, benefit, boon, benison, behalf, interest, health, good luck, prosperousness, pleasure, felicity, beatitude, gratification, ease, joy, gladness.

WELLBORN, *adj.* Of gentle birth, highborn, of good stock, of good descent, thoroughbred, of good family, pedigreed, princely, patrician, silk-stocking, aristocratic, blue-blooded, noble, distinguished, courtly, titled, genteel, illustrious.

WELL-BRED, *adj.* Thoroughbred, showing good breeding, well brought up, genteel, urbane, aristocratic, patrician, gentlemanly, urbane, suave, cultivated, refined, courteous, mannerly, polite, polished, debonair, wellborn, gently bred, civil, chivalrous, gallant, courtly, poised, *dégagé (Fr.),* distinguished, *distingué (Fr.),* highborn, titled, princely, pedigreed, blue-blooded, silk-stocking.

WELL-DEFINED, *adj.* Clear-cut, distinct, clear, sharp-cut, clean-cut, definite, well-marked, patent, palpable, conspicuous, salient, cameo-like, sculptured.

WELL-FAVORED, *adj.* Good-looking, comely, fair, handsome, personable, bonny, elegant, dapper, beauteous, beautiful, lovely, pretty, pleasing, goodly, well-made, well-formed, well-proportioned, bright-eyed, ruddy, rosy-cheeked, easy to look at, easy on the eyes, *beau (Fr.), hübsch (Ger.), schön (Ger.), hermoso (Sp.), bello (It.).*

WELL-GROOMED, *adj.* Well-dressed, neat in appearance, *bien soigné (Fr.),* chic, dapper, spruce, trig, jaunty, stylish, natty, silk-stocking, dudish, dandified, dandyish, coxcombical, foppish, fashionable, modish, smart, presentable, trim, tony *(sl.),* snappy *(coll.),* dressy, elegant.

WELL-KNOWN, *adj.* 1. Renowned, reputable, famous, recognized, known, widely known, celebrated, eminent, prominent, illustrious, distinguished, notable, noted, notorious, egregious, flagrant, arrant, estimable, honorable, popular, honored, far-famed, conspicuous.

2. Familiar, commonplace, trite, stereotyped, bromidic, platitudinous, cliché, proverbial, hackneyed, banal, routine, habitual, wonted, customary, usual, household, everyday, conventional.

WELL-NIGH, *adv.* Very nearly, almost, for the most part, about, nigh unto, near to, fast by, hard by, close to, close upon, next door to, within range of, not far from, within an acre of, but a step from, on the brink, on the verge, at no great distance from, in the environs of, at one's elbow, under one's nose, in sight of, within a stone's throw of, cheek-by-jowl, at close quarters, verging on, bordering upon, thereabouts, approximately, in round numbers, as good as.

WELL-OFF, *adj.* Moderately rich, prosperous, flush, well-heeled, in easy circumstances, moneyed, wealthy, affluent, well-to-do, propertied, influential, thriving, possessed of a competence, flourishing, fortunate, born with a silver spoon in one's mouth, silk-stocking, opulent, well provided for, pecunious.

WELL-TIMED, *adj.* Timely, opportune, seasonable, timeous, timeful, in the nick of time, providential, fortunate, lucky, propitious, favorable, auspicious, critical.

WELL-TO-DO, *adj.* Wealthy, affluent, rich, moneyed, landed, propertied, well-off, prosperous, in easy circumstances, comfortable, opulent, fortunate, influential, flourishing, booming, thriving, at one's ease, lucky, palmy, halcyon, favorable, independent, rolling in riches, flush, capitalistic, luxurious, silk-stocking, aristocratic, patrician, blue-blooded, responsible, substantial, solvent, pecunious.

WELT, *n.* Ridge on the body from a blow, wale, streak, stripe, lump, swelling, mark, black-and-blue spot, contusion, bruise, scratch, blemish, injury, maculation, excrescence.

WELTER, *v.* Tumble about, flounder, wallow, rise and fall, toss, heave, roll, founder, surge, plunge, pitch.

WELTER, *n.* Commotion, hubbub, fracas, turmoil, to-do, bustle, flurry, tumult, turbulence, rout, racket, spasm, convulsion, throe, ferment, hurly-burly, storm, tempest, vortex, confusion, riot.

WENCH, *n.* 1. Peasant girl, young rustic woman, serving woman, maid, country lass.

2. Strumpet, jade, trull, whore, harlot, prostitute, slut, courtesan, baggage, *fille de joie (Fr.),* tart, hustler, broad, chippy, streetwalker, trollop, demirep, bitch, hussy, minx, drab, wanton, demimondaine, fancy woman.

WEND, *v.* Direct one's path, pursue one's way, betake oneself, steer toward, hie to, move along, trek, range, roam, pace around, traverse, perambulate, pace, promenade, stalk, foot it.

WEREWOLF, *n.* Human being turned preternaturally into a wolf, man-wolf, *loup-garou (Fr.),* lycanthrope, changeling, berserker.

WEST, *n.* Cardinal point of the compass 90 degrees to the left of North, sunset, occident, setting sun.

WET, *v.* Make wet, dampen, moisten, soak, damp, sprinkle, shower, humidify, humectate, water, drench, saturate, hose down, splash, wash, bathe, irrigate, imbrue, dip, immerse, submerge, souse, duck, steep, drown, sparge, lave, swash, slosh, inundate, slop, deluge, bedew.

WET, *adj.* Damp, dampened, soaked, drenched, moist, dank, humid, dripping, dewy, bedewed, clammy, sloppy, aqueous, soaking, sodden, spongy, wringing wet, swashy, saturated, rainy, sprinkly, showery, watery, vaporous, soggy, squishy.

WET, *n.* 1. Moistness, wetness, moisture, humidity, dampness, mugginess, wateriness, water, dew, drip, exudation, humidification, condensation, precipitation, rain, shower, downpour, cloudburst, rainstorm, drizzle, mizzle, scud, serein, drencher, flood, deluge, waterspout, inundation, monsoon.

2. Antiprohibitionist, boozer, John Barleycorn, tippler, dipsomaniac, alcoholic, lush *(sl.),* drinker, inebriate, toper, sot, tosspot, winebibber, soak *(sl.).*

WHACK, *n.* 1. Smart resounding blow, thwack, buffet, thump, bang, rap, whang, knock, stroke, fillip, dab, smack, slap, slam, hit, clout, cuff, punch, swipe, jab.

2. Trial, endeavor, attempt, go, turn, essay, try, crack *(sl.),* venture.

WHALE, *n.* Cetacean, sperm whale, finback, cete, finner, sulphur-bottom, rorqual, humpback, killer whale, grampus, narwhal, behemoth.

WHARF, *n.* Landing, dock, pier, jetty, quay, landing place, mole, bund, basin, port, harbor.

WHEEDLE, *v.* Endeavor to influence by smooth words, cajole, flatter, coax, humor, use artful persuasions, soft-soap, butter up *(coll.),* entice, lure, inveigle, court, beguile, pay court to, fawn upon, blandish, honey, truckle to, ingratiate oneself with, curry favor with, pander to, allure, charm, magnetize, hypnotize, mesmerize, prevail on, influence, rouse, predispose, bias, carry, bring round.

WHEEDLER, *n.* Flatterer, adulator, coaxer, sycophant, bootlicker, truckler, hanger-on, parasite, soft-soaper, toady, fawner, flunky, pickthank.

WHEEL, *v.* 1. Turn round, rotate, turn, revolve, gyrate, circumgyrate, circumrotate, spin, swirl, twirl, rev, gyre, trundle, twiddle, roll, whirl.

2. Turn aside, twist, wind, deviate, diverge, deflect, alter one's course, veer, double, countermarch, swerve, bend, bear off, heel, yaw, jibe, sheer, go about, tack, slue, sidle, shift, shunt, sidetrack.

WHEEL, *n.* 1. Disk, circle, circlet, annulus, ring, annulet, roller, hoop, caster, drum, orb, trolley, disc, orbit.

2. Revolution, turn, rotation, gyration, circumrotation, circumgyration, circulation, roll, turbination, circumvolution, convolution, whirlabout, whirligig, reel, whirl, twirl, pirouette, spin, gyre, vortex, twister.

3. Cycle, unicycle, bicycle, bike *(coll.),* tricycle, tandem, velocipede.

WHEEZE, *v.* Breathe hard and audibly, whistle, snuffle, puff, huff and puff, gasp, pant, whiffle, sniffle.

WHELP, *n.* 1. Young dog, puppy, pup, cub, mutt.

2. Stripling, lad, youth, whippersnapper, child, chick, pickaninny, brat, urchin, bratling, bantling, slip, elf, sprig, boy, whipster, youngster, hobbledehoy, kid.

WHEN, *adv., conj.* 1. At what time? how soon? how long ago? on what occasion?

2. At the time that, as soon as, whenever, while, whereas, upon which, after which, and then, at any time, whensoever, at whatever time, whereupon.

WHENCE, *adv., conj.* 1. From what place? wherefrom? from what source? from what origin? from what cause? how? howso? why? wherefore? how does it happen? how comes it? what is the reason?

2. Forasmuch as, *propter hoc (Lat.),* thanks to, on that account, owing to, on account of, because of, since, thence, hence, therefore, from this cause, accordingly, somehow or other, in some such way.

WHERE, *adv., conj.* 1. In what place? at which place? whither? to which place? where to? to what? wherever?

2. Here, there, on the spot, everywhere, in the presence of, in the face of, under the eyes of, before the nose of.

WHEREABOUTS, *n.* Location, place, locality, residence, habitat, milieu, position, situation, locale, latitude and longitude, post, site, station, base, environment, neighborhood, spot, vicinity, vicinage, adjacency, environs, purlieus, propinquity, proximity.

WHEREAS, *adv.* and *conj.* It being the case that, seeing that, considering that, since, inasmuch as, because, forasmuch as, *ex concesso (Lat.),* in con-

sideration of, ergo, consequently, accordingly, thus, *a fortiori (Lat.).*

WHEREWITHAL, *n.* That wherewith to do something, the means with which to accomplish a purpose, supplies for the purpose, means for an end, *de quoi (Fr.),* reserve, nest egg, savings, money, finance, treasure, funds, assets, capital, ways and means, wealth, needful cash, almighty dollar, amount, sum, boodle *(sl.),* coin, specie, greenbacks, wampum, ready money, lucre, bankroll, shekels, jack, dough, spondulix *(sl.),* wad, pile, rupees, bucks, simoleons.

WHET, *v.* 1. Sharpen by friction, grind, hone, strop, point, barb, acuminate, spiculate, cuspidate.

2. Stimulate, excite, awaken, rouse, arouse, make eager, make keen, make avid, stir up, kindle, warm, quicken, animate, inspire, fire, inspirit, goad, urge, fillip, spur, foster, fan, foment, provoke, instigate, egg on, incite, induce, prompt, entice, tempt, allure, coax, wheedle, compel, impel.

WHETHER, *conj.* If, in case, supposing that, provided, if so be, in the event of, on the supposition that, granting that, allowing that, for all one knows.

WHIFF, *n.* 1. Breath of air, slight blast of wind, puff, sudden gust, zephyr, flatus, draught, blow, breeze.

2. Single inhalation of odor, waft of smell, sniff, scent, aroma, bouquet, effluvium, emanation, odoriferousness, redolence, fume, reek, noseful.

WHIFF, *v.* 1. Inhale, exhale, respire, breathe, puff, whiffle, snuffle.

2. Smell, whiff, sniff, scent, nose.

WHILE, *n.* 1. Space of time, season, spell, time, tide, term, period, stage, snap, span.

2. Interval, meantime, interim, recess, interlude, pause, respite, intermission, interruption.

WHILE, *conj.* 1. During the time that, in the time that, throughout the time that, as long as, at the same time that, whilst.

2. Although, albeit, whereas, though, even if, even though, notwithstanding that.

WHIM, *n.* Fanciful notion, capricious desire, odd humor, passing fancy, vagary, caprice, fantasy, quirk, wrinkle, crotchet, whimsy, maggot, kink, conceit, chimera, vapor, fit, fad, eccentricity, bent, inclination, wish, leaning, mind, partiality, propensity, predilection, fondness, liking, relish, passion, mania, furor, rage, craze, monomania, hunger, appetite, thirst, twist.

WHIMPER, *v.* Whine plaintively, cry in low tones, sob brokenly, sniffle, snivel, blubber, weep, pule, pipe, yammer, maunder.

WHIMSICAL, *adj.* 1. Given to odd notions, notional, crotchety, humorsome, capricious, vagarious, fitful, volatile, chimerical, wayward, imaginative, romantic, rhapsodic, quixotic, changeable, fickle, freakish, queer, erratic, eccentric, inconsistent, bohemian, wanton, frivolous, moody, extravagant, preposterous, imaginational, dreamy.

2. Outlandish, grotesque, bizarre, fantastic, quaint, odd, curious, singular, quizzical, droll, rum *(sl.),* out-of-the-way, strange, baroque, rococo, preposterous, irrational, unreasonable, absurd, monstrous, *outré (Fr.).*

WHINE, *v.* Cry plaintively, snivel, blubber, whimper, pule, mewl, wail, bewail, moan, bemoan, cant, utter a low uneasy sound, keen, fret, groan, yelp, grumble, complain, murmur, grouse, growl, croak, clamor, grunt.

WHINE, *n.* Whimper, moan, sob, wail, cry, outcry, lachrymation, complaint, murmur, plaint, grumble, grunt, mutter, suspiration, fit of crying, tears, lamentation.

WHIP, *v.* 1. Strike with thongs, lash, scourge, flog, punish with a whip, beat, flagellate, rawhide, horsewhip, bastinado, slash, castigate, smite, thrash, birch, switch, trounce, maul, drub, lambaste, spank, strap, stripe, bethwack, cuff, wham, thwack, buffet, thump, pommel, lace, belabor, trim, cane, goad.
2. Hurry, impel, egg on, urge, hasten, press, spur, precipitate, speed up, dispatch, instigate, hound on, prick, propel, drive.
3. Outdo, defeat, vanquish, overcome, conquer, outwit, overpower, rout, discomfit, worst, floor, beat hollow, lick *(coll.),* overthrow.
4. Move quickly and suddenly, pull with a sudden movement, snatch, whisk, jerk, snap, flick, twitch, jolt.

WHIP, *n.* Lash, scourge, rawhide, horsewhip, flagellum, thong, strap, cowhide, knout, cat-o'-nine-tails, bullwhack, cat, blacksnake, quirt, kurbash, chabouk, switch, birch rod, rattan.

WHIP HAND, *n.* Upper hand, dominating position, advantage, better, mastery, ascendancy, triumph, victory, walkover, palm, conquest, trump card, edge, command, domination, supremacy, control, dictation.

WHIPPING, *n.* Thrashing, flogging, castigation, beating, flagellation, bastinado, dusting, licking, breeching, trouncing, lashing, punishment, chastisement, mauling, birching, caning, rawhiding, scourging, strapping, pommeling.

WHIRL, *v.* Turn round rapidly, wheel, spin, pirouette, twirl, revolve, rotate, gyrate, circumgyrate, reel, circulate, gyre, swirl.

WHIRL, *n.* 1. Rapid rotation, circumrotation, gyration, circumgyration, revolution, circumvolution, spin, swirl, twirl, pirouette, eddy, vortex, maelstrom, turning, turn, wheel, circulation, roll, turbination, reeling.
2. Rapid round of events, dizzying succession, dizzy round, whirligig, whirlabout, carrousel, merry-go-round.
3. Flurry, flutter, fluster, ferment, turbulence, excitability, vertigo.

WHIRLING, *adj.* Circumgyratory, circumrotatory, gyral, revolving, vortical, rotary, rotating, rotational, rotative, trochilic, gyratory, vertiginous, gyrational, vorticose, circumvolutory.

WHIRLPOOL, *n.* Whirling current, maelstrom, vortex, surge, eddy, swirl, gurge, Charybdis, gulf.

WHIRLWIND, *n.* Mass of rotating air, cyclone, twister, tornado, funnel cloud *(Meteor.),* windstorm, typhoon, baguio *(Philippines),* simoom, samiel, harmattan, gale, blow, tempest, sirocco, dust spout.

WHIRRING, *n.* 1. Flying, skimming, darting, revolving, rotating, wheeling, turning, gyrating, circumgyrating, circumrotating, turbinating, rushing.
2. Vibratory sound, buzzing noise, whizzing, humming, hissing, burring.

WHISK, *v.* 1. Move rapidly, go lightly and fast, sweep, hie, hasten, rush, speed, scud, move nimbly, trip, post, dash, haste, cut along, flit, fly, push on, spurt, sprint, scuttle, scurry, scamper, tear, shoot, race, skim, whiz, bowl along, bolt, gallop, trot, bound, spring, dart, accelerate, quicken one's pace.

2. Shake, agitate, toss, wield, convulse, tumble, brandish, bandy, flourish, flap, jerk, jolt, hitch.

WHISKER, *n.* 1. Bristle, seta, striga, setula, feeler, pappus, vibrissa, arista, awn, filament, hair, villus.
2. Beard, imperial, goatee, Vandyke, burnsides, mutton chops, sideburns, moustache.

WHISPER, *v.* 1. Utter under the breath, murmur, mutter, breathe, sigh, suspirate, speak softly, susurrate, rustle, hum, buzz, drone, sough.
2. Divulge, disclose, reveal, intimate, hint, insinuate, rumor, bruit, confide, blab, blurt, betray, vent, let fall, gossip, tell.

WHISPER, *n.* 1. Indistinct utterance, mutter, murmur, susurrus, susurration, suspiration, sigh, sough, rustle, drone, buzz, hum, sibilant sound, sibilation, sibilance, undertone.
2. Intimation, insinuation, innuendo, hint, inkling, disclosure, rumor, suggestion, revelation, grapevine *(coll.),* scuttlebutt *(sl.),* gossip.

WHIST, *interj.* Hush! silence! 'sh! silence! hold your tongue! soft! mum's the word! *pax!* be silent! be still! shut up! be quiet! keep quiet! make no noise! dry up! *tais-toi (Fr.)! schweige (Ger.)!*

WHISTLE, *n.* Shrill pipe, fipple flute, siren, Pan-pipe, syrinx, Pandean pipe, reed instrument, fife, penny-whistle, flute, piccolo, flageolet.

WHISTLE, *v.* 1. Pipe, flute, trill, chirp, quaver, twitter, warble, yodel, troll.
2. Sibilate, hiss, catcall, wolf-whistle, siss *(coll.),* wheeze.

WHIT, *n.* Little bit, particle, iota, jot, mite, tittle, scintilla, mote, atom, molecule, electron, corpuscle, speck, dot, point, scrap, minim, grain, modicum, drop, nip, dab, dash, pinch, slip, snick, morsel, fragment, fraction, trifle, crumb, sliver, snip, hair, shaving, chip, splinter, drop in the bucket, fig, peppercorn, straw, button, pin, rap, cent, farthing, tinker's dam, continental.

WHITE, *adj.* 1. Of the color of pure snow, snow-white, niveous, snowy, hoar, frosted, hoary, canescent, candent, milk-white, milky, lactescent, marmoreal, chalky, cretaceous, pearly, nacreous, opalescent, opaline, semiopaque, semitransparent, ivory, silver, silvery, argent, argentine, whitish, creamy, albescent, albinistic, albicant, etiolated, bleached, blanched, blond, fair, light, wan, pallid, pale, ashen, cinereous, ashy, gray, lackluster, colorless, hueless, achromatous, achromatic, pasty, bloodless, anemic, leucocytic, cadaverous, ghastly, dingy, dun, sallow, glassy, faint, leaden, grizzled, griseous, cloudy, nubilous, nebulous, misty, hazy, foggy, smoky, filmy, vaporous.
2. Pure, immaculate, clean, stainless, spotless, unstained, unspotted, undefiled, innocent, chaste, virtuous, unblemished, candid, clear, unsullied.
3. Honorable, honest, trustworthy, upright, rectitudinous, righteous, just, equitable, foursquare, true-blue, straightforward, aboveboard, trusty, fair, veracious, truthful, incorruptible, loyal, faithful, stanch, constant, true, frank, openhearted.

WHITEN, *v.* 1. Make white, etiolate, blanch, bleach, albify, blench, silver, frost, pale, dealbate, grizzle, decolorize, decolor, achromatize, wash out.
2. Lose color, fade, grow white, become colorless, turn pale.

WHITENESS, *n.* 1. Canescence, whitishness, milkiness, lactescence, frostiness, hoariness, colorlessness, achromatousness, achromatism, paleness, decoloration, etiolation, achromatization, pallor, pallidness, sallowness, pearliness, nacreousness, silveriness, albescence, albification, dealbation, albinism.

2. Driven snow, ivory, silver, alabaster, lily, milk.

WHITE SLAVE, *n.* Love slave, hustler, prostitute, whore, harlot, *fille de joie (Fr.),* strumpet, broad, punk, fallen woman, frail sister, piece, tart, trull, trollop, wench, baggage, drab, hussy, bitch, slut, jade, fornicatress, wanton, demirep, demimondaine, grisette, cocotte, lorette, fancy woman, kept woman, doxy, concubine, courtesan, streetwalker.

WHITEWASH, *v.* 1. Calcimine, white, paint white, whiten, coat, plaster, stucco, daub, smear.

2. Justify, palliate, extenuate, exonerate, clear, gloze over, vindicate, exculpate, absolve, excuse, apologize for, soften, gloss over, make allowance for, forgive, pardon, acquit.

3. Defeat, overthrow, conquer, vanquish, drub, lick *(coll.),* best, worst, rout, floor, beat, discomfit, overcome, overpower, master, thrash, trim *(coll.).*

WHIZ, *v.* 1. Move rapidly, rush, hie, speed, hasten, scud, scurry, post, spurt, scuttle, scamper, trip, fly, cut away, race, dart, whisk, tear, shoot, sweep, skim, bowl along, bolt ahead, flit, bound, spring, accelerate, hurry, quicken, outstrip the wind, plunge headlong.

2. Whir, buzz, hum, hiss, rustle, fizzle, swish, sizzle, whistle, wheeze, sibilate.

WHOA, *interj.* Stop! hold hard! stay! wait up! just a minute! avast! halt! enough! have done! leave off! cease! slow up! come to a stop! make an end of! decelerate! slow down! retard! check! moderate! slacken speed! relax! brake! take it easy! break off! desist! discontinue! pause!

WHOLE, *n.* 1. Allness, wholeness, totality, integrality, integrity, omnitude, integer, entirety, ensemble, *tout ensemble (Fr.),* completeness, complexus, collectiveness, intactness, undividedness, indivisibility, universality, indiscerptibility, assemblage, integration, compaction, organic unity, integral.

2. The whole, everything, all, aggregate, total, sum total, be-all, alpha and omega, length and breadth of, gross amount, bulk, body, mass, lump sum, lion's share, major part, Benjamin's mess, main part, torso, bole, trunk, caudex, stock, body, axis, shaft, stem, thing complete in itself, *das Ding an sich (Ger.),* entity, essence, quintessence.

WHOLE, *adj.* 1. Containing all the elements properly belonging, entire, undivided, integral, in one piece, not fractional, complete, inclusive, unabridged, all-embracing, round, plenary, full, total, all, intact, inviolate, uninjured, unscathed, unbroken, unimpaired, unsevered, undamaged, scatheless, gross, integrate, unshorn, uncut, indiscrete, undiminished, indivisible, indiscerptible, indissoluble, inseparable.

2. Comprehensive, wholesale, extensive, sweeping, indiscriminate, widespread, all-inclusive, general.

3. Sound, healthy, hale, robust, well, in good health.

WHOLE-HEARTED, *adj.* Hearty, cordial, earnest, sincere, frank, candid, straightforward, wholesouled, single-hearted, open, unreserved, veracious, simple-hearted, trustworthy, true-blue, honest, undissembling, pure, guileless, unfeigned, unaffected, ingenuous, bona-fide, undisguised.

WHOLESOME, *adj.* 1. Conducive to physical well-being, conducive to bodily health, healthful, salutiferous, salubrious, healthy, nutritious,

nourishing, invigorating, strengthening, roborant, tonic, stomachic, nutritive, health-giving, beneficial, helpful, salutary, good, improving, sanative, benign, benignant, healing, prophylactic, sanitary, bracing, hygienic, nutrient, eutrophic, alimental, eupeptic, digestible, substantial, sustentative.

2. Hale, sound, blooming, robust, whole, hardy, vigorous, florid, rosy-cheeked, chipper *(coll.),* in fine fettle, well, hearty, strong, euphoric, fresh.

3. Sane, rational, well-balanced, normal, underanged, right-minded, sound-minded, *compos mentis (Lat.),* sensible, intelligent, reasonable, moderate, sober, understanding, clear-minded.

WHOLLY, *adv.* Altogether, entirely, fully, totally, as a whole, completely, *in extenso (Lat.),* perfectly, in the main, in the aggregate, *en bloc (Fr.), en masse (Fr.),* in the mass, on the whole, all in all, all, collectively, in a body, substantially, bodily, utterly, quite, *in toto (Lat.),* out-and-out, from top to toe, throughout, outright, in all respects, in every respect, from head to foot, from first to last, cap-a-pie, every inch, every whit, root and branch, heart and soul, to perfection, with a finish, *ad unguem (Lat.),* to a nicety.

WHOOP, *v.* Utter a loud cry, yell, shout, cry out, halloo, holler, hollo, vociferate, roar, bawl, bellow, scream, howl, shriek, screech, squall, shrill, hoot, hurrah, cheer, rend the air, shout at the top of one's voice.

WHOOP, *n.* Outcry, shout, vociferation, halloo, yell, hoot, shriek, squall, scream, holler, hollo, roar, bellow, howl, screech, cheer, hurrah, hullabaloo, hue and cry, clamor, battle cry, war cry.

WHOPPER, *n. (coll.)* 1. Something uncommonly large of its kind, monstrosity, behemoth, juggernaut, thumper, stunner, whale, elephant, hippopotamus, mammoth, monster, Cyclops, colossus, leviathan, strapper, spanker.

2. Lie, falsehood, prevarication, fabrication, bouncer, untruth, story, trumped-up tale, canard, cock-and-bull story.

WHORE, *n.* Prostitute, harlot, bawd, demirep, woman of ill fame, streetwalker, strumpet, wench, trull, bitch, jade, baggage, drab, punk, *fille de joie (Fr.),* call girl, courtesan, Cyprian, white slave, hustler, tart, broad, chippy, frail sister, fallen woman, demimondaine, trollop, hussy, minx, slut, woman of easy virtue, wanton, fornicatress, fancy woman, concubine, doxy, kept woman, mistress.

WHOREMONGER, *n.* 1. Whoremaster, libertine, rake, debauchee, rakehell, rip, roué, fornicator, rapist, seducer, goat, lecher, adulterer, voluptuary.

2. Pimp, pander, go-between, procurer.

WHORL, *n.* Circumvolution, convolution, involution, undulation, wave, anfractuosity, tortuosity, sinuosity, sinuation, circumbendibus, twirl, twist, ambages, inosculation, coil, curl, roll, spire, buckle, spiral, corkscrew, helix, volute, rundle, worm, tendril, scallop, escallop, kink, labyrinth, maze.

WHY, *adv.* For what reason? wherefore? on what account? for what cause? to what end? to what purpose? *pourquoi (Fr.)? warum (Ger.)? por qué (Sp.)? perchè (It.)?* with what intent? how so? whence? *quare (Lat.)?* whither? what is the reason? what's the matter? what's up? what's in the wind?

WICKED, *adj.* Sinful, evil, iniquitous, bad, vile, depraved, infamous, vicious, flagitious, abominable, nefarious, heinous, criminal, monstrous, atrocious, flagrant, felonious, profligate, reprobate, immoral, dissolute, lewd, corrupt, outrageous, foul, wrong, naughty, mischievous, base, gross, facinorous, black, shameful, scandalous, villainous, incorrigible, vitiated, unholy, godless, profane, ungodly, irreverent, sacrilegious, irreligious, graceless, impious, devilish, abandoned, unprincipled, worthless, unrighteous, ignominious, black-hearted, satanic, pernicious, malicious, malignant, malign, malevolent, maleficent, dark, hellish, unjust, perverse, demoniacal, accursed, infernal, obdurate, unhallowed, evil-minded, obscene, smutty, pornographic, impure, indecent, indelicate, coarse, bawdy, ribald, prurient, concupiscent, lustful, lecherous, salacious, incestuous, adulterous, unchaste, debauched, bestial, reprehensible, dishonorable, dishonest, disgraceful, knavish, rascally, blackguard, lawless, degenerate, opprobrious, wrongdoing, guilty, blameworthy, peccable.

WICKEDNESS, *n.* Sinfulness, turpitude, criminality, depravity, corruption, flagitiousness, heinousness, nefariousness, immorality, wrongdoing, facinorousness, improbity, infamy, iniquitousness, badness, vileness, evilness, unrighteousness, ungodliness, godlessness, sacrilegiousness, irreverence, impiety, guilt, offense, abomination, atrocity, enormity, flagrancy, rascality, villainy, malignity, maleficence, malefaction, transgression, sin, vice, crime, iniquity, deviltry, evil, perversity, unregeneracy, gracelessness, monstrousness, pollution, diabolism, demoralization, debauchery, obscenity, fornication, adultery, lustfulness, carnality, rape, perversion, venery, sodomy, pederasty, buggery, bestiality, bawdry, impudicity, indecency, grossness, lechery, salacity, lewdness, libertinism, defilement, stupration, impenitence, seared conscience, felony, misdemeanor, trespass, outrage, peccability, deviation from rectitude, dishonor, foul play, knavery.

WICKER, *n.* Pliant twig, withe, slender osier, sprig, offshoot, branch, slip, scion, bough, ramification, spray, spur, switch, tendril, runner, sarmentum.

WIDE, *adj.* 1. Having great extent from side to side, not narrow, broad, of great horizontal extent, vast, ample, spacious, roomy, large, extensive, expanded, distended, open to the full extent, of great scope, capacious, splay, full, extended, outspread, outstretched, immense, beamy, commodious.

2. Embracing a great number of subjects, comprehensive, all-inclusive, encyclopedic, general, world-wide, ecumenical, universal, widespread, boundless, infinite, far-flung.

WIDE-AWAKE, *adj.* Vigilant, watchful, sleepless, alert, Argus-eyed, lynx-eyed, sharp-sighted, keen, astute, shrewd, knowing, observant, careful, attentive, heedful, wary, circumspect, cautious, prudent, thoughtful, sagacious, artful, cunning, canny, wily, sly, acute, crafty.

WIDEN, *v.* Spread, amplify, enlarge, expand, stretch, broaden, open, dilate, mushroom, outstretch, distend, unfurl, deploy, unfold, aggrandize, augment, develop, magnify, spread out.

WIDTH, *n.* Wideness, broadness, girth, circumference, span, beam, diameter, amplitude, breadth, latitude, size, extent, spaciousness, roominess, expanse, stretch, measure, scope, area, reach, bore, caliber, radius.

WIELD, *v.* 1. Flourish, shake, brandish, manipulate, agitate, handle, ply, work, tumble, toss, convulse, switch, whisk, sweep, swing, hitch, jerk, joggle, jolt, jostle, flap, wave.

2. Manage, control, handle, make use of, use, utilize, employ, exercise.

WIFE, *n.* Married woman, helpmate, consort, helpmeet, spouse, matron, better half, life's partner, mate, bride, wife of one's bosom, housewife, wedded wife, rib *(humorous),* squaw, gray mare, lady, soul mate, affinity.

WIG, *n.* Artificial covering of hair, periwig, toupee, hairpiece, peruke, scratch, transformation, Gregorian, Ramillie, Brutus, jasey, pigtail, front.

WIGGLE, *v.* Move irregularly from side to side, wriggle, quiver, shimmy, writhe, twitch, waggle, squirm, jerk, shake, sway, flitter, flutter, bustle, convulse.

WIGHT, *n.* Human being, person, creature, fellow, man, male, swain, yeoman, guy, gaffer, blade, chap, homo, hombre, beau, individual, personage, body, mortal, someone, living soul, party, countryman, peasant, clodhopper, hind, churl, yokel, bumpkin, rustic, commoner, plebeian, oaf, lout, boor.

WIGWAM, *n.* Hut of an American Indian, tepee, lodge, cabin, lair, dugout, tent, pavilion, booth, "A" tent, canoe tent, fly tent, bell tent, lean-to tent, dog tent, wall tent, shelter tent.

WILD, *adj.* 1. Living in a state of nature, undomesticated, untamed, ferine, feral, unbroken.

2. Uncultivated, produced without the care of man, native, dense, luxuriant, exuberant, rank, indigenous, autochthonous, sylvan, wooded, verdurous.

3. Uninhabited, desolate, desert, waste, bleak, rugged, abandoned.

4. Uncivilized, barbarous, savage, barbaric, fierce, ferocious, rude, rough, unrefined, cannibalistic, anthropophagous, outlandish.

5. Lawless, disorderly, unruly, ungovernable, turbulent, tumultuous, violent, unrestrained, uncontrolled, rampant, berserk, frantic, distracted, frenzied, raving, raging, furious, mad, crazed, excited, undisciplined, impetuous, impulsive, riotous, tempestuous, desperate, insane, maddened, unhinged, demented, maniacal, homicidal, murderous, rabid, fanatical.

6. Stormy, obstreperous, noisy, boisterous, uproarious, squally, blustering, windy, inclement, howling, foul, dirty, blusterous, wind-swept, storm-lashed, raw.

7. Flighty, giddy, bewildered, vertiginous, reckless, heedless, light-headed, harebrained, thoughtless, harum-scarum, pell-mell, inconsiderate, ill-advised, foolish, precipitate, unwise, injudicious, indiscreet, wanton, rash, brash, self-willed, froward, wayward, rattlebrained, volatile, mercurial, madcap, uncircumspect.

8. Dissolute, profligate, loose-living, fast, dissipated, debauched, self-indulgent, intemperate, incontinent, unbridled, inordinate, uncurbed, crapulous, voluptuous, sensual, fleshly, carnal, bestial, gross, lecherous, lustful, licentious, libidinous, concupiscent, salacious.

9. Romantic, fanciful, impractical, extravagant, bizarre, visionary, chimerical, quixotic, utopian, absurd, fantastic, queer, imaginative, preposterous, legendary, fabulous, mythical, mythological, notional, dreamy, fictitious.

WILDERNESS, *n.* Desolate tract, desert, wasteland, wild, Sahara, waste, steppe, tundra, bush, veldt, barren, howling wilderness.

WILD-GOOSE CHASE, *n.* Senseless undertaking, foolish enterprise, useless pursuit, sleeveless errand, lost labor, escapade, caprice.

WILE, *n.* Deceitful cunning, stratagem, trick, artifice, ruse, finesse, chicanery, trickery, deception, deceit, chicane, maneuver, plot, dodge, fetch, imposition, fraud, chouse, cheat, crafty device, imposture, cunning contrivance, machination, intrigue, guile, snare, trap, subtlety, artfulness, pretense, craftiness, craft, strategy, circumvention, sharp practice, jugglery, knavery, concealment, duplicity, address, diplomacy, savoirfaire, politics, jobbery, shift, hoax, subterfuge, flimflam, hocus-pocus, swindle, bunco, insidiousness, wiliness, sophistry, dissimulation, misrepresentation, hanky-panky, double-dealing.

WILL, *v.* 1. Exercise volition, elect, choose, desire, wish for, want, prefer, long for, hanker after, list, incline to, be inclined, be disposed, be pleased, have a mind, intend, purpose.

2. Decide by act of will, determine, ordain, enjoin, decree, direct, command, resolve, see fit, think fit, use one's discretion, dominate, impel, order, prescribe.

3. Leave by testament, bequeath, devise, convey, demise, give by will, bestow, proffer, donate, award, confer, allot, apportion, distribute, transfer, turn over, dower, invest, endow, settle upon.

WILL, *n.* 1. Faculty of conscious and deliberate action, power of choosing one's own actions, free will, power of determination, faculty of volition, conation, voluntarism, volitiency, spontaneity, velleity, voluntariness, originality, freedom of option, unhampered choice, discretion, preference, intent, desire, wish, inclination, pleasure, disposition, mind, craving, longing, yearning, hankering, purpose.

2. Determination, self-reliance, resolution, decision, resoluteness, force of will, will power, moral courage, grit, sand, backbone, strength of purpose, self-control, self-discipline, energy of intention.

3. Order, command, requirement, behest, direction, demand, request, decree.

4. Last will and testament, testament.

WILLFUL, *adj.* 1. Deliberate, intentional, prepense, intended, planned, premeditated, studied, designed, contemplated, purposed.

2. Self-willed, stubborn, obstinate, headstrong, perverse, unyielding, contumacious, unruly, refractory, recalcitrant, intractable, dogged, mulish, pigheaded, inflexible, intransigent, uncompromising, self-opinionated, heady, cantankerous, obdurate, high-handed, wayward, persistent, pertinacious, arbitrary, capricious.

3. Determined, resolute, decided, resolved, bent, set, purposeful, strong-willed, autocratic, domineering, bossy, dictatorial, despotic.

4. Volitive, volitional, volitient, volitionary, freewill, unconstrained, spontaneous, voluntary, discretionary, optional, facultative, discretional.

WILLING, *adj.* 1. Ready, enthusiastic, eager, fain, zealous, prompt, desirous, earnest, favorable, lief, minded, favorably inclined, bent upon, disposed, willing-hearted, content, forward, cordial, desiring, partial to, anxious, fervent, ardent, fervid, burning, impatient, agog, avid, wishful, solicitous, longing, hankering, assenting, acquiescent, compliant, easily persuaded, amenable, nothing loath, not averse, not unwilling, unreluctant, of a mind, adaptable, tractable, yielding, agreeable, ac-

cordant, persuadable, susceptible, manageable, facile, genial, docile, ductile, sequacious, gracious, easygoing.

2. Voluntary, intentional, unconstrained, free, uncompelled, spontaneous, unforced, deliberate, unbidden, unasked, gratuitous, unimpelled, purposed, intended.

WILLINGLY, *adv.* Cheerfully, gladly, readily, fain, lief, with pleasure, freely, voluntarily, *ex animo* (*Lat.*), of one's own accord, with all one's heart, *de bonne volonté* (*Fr.*), *con amore* (*It.*), graciously, with good will, without hesitancy, without demur, with good grace, *de bonne grâce* (*Fr.*), spontaneously, ungrudgingly, gratuitously, unconstrainedly, compliantly, acquiescently, agreeably, intentionally, deliberately, by choice, purposely, of one's own responsibility.

WILLINGNESS, *n.* 1. Eagerness, enthusiasm, readiness, zeal, promptness, good will, alacrity, desire, ardor, ardency, fervor, fervidness, voluntariness, earnestness, geniality, cordiality, heartiness, acquiescence, assent, consent, compliance, good nature, concurrence, approval, inclination, wish, leaning, fancy, partiality, mind, bent, whim, propensity, predilection, proclivity, relish, liking, hankering, yen, yearning, longing, anxiety, solicitude, mood, humor, disposition, proneness, tendency, penchant, turn, frame of mind, aptitude, vein.

2. Labor of love, gratuitous service, unrewarded effort, voluntary labor, self-appointed task, tender, overture, proposal, proffer, offer, bid, proposition, invitation, offering.

WILL-O'-THE-WISP, *n.* 1. Flitting phosphorescent light seen over marshy ground at night, swamp fire, marsh fire, jack-o'-lantern, friar's lantern, St. Elmo's fire, *ignis fatuus* (*Lat.*), corposant.

2. Elusive object, mirage, illusion, shadow, dream, vision, phantom, phantasm, specter, apparition, chimera.

WILLOWY, *adj.* Gracefully slender, lissome, svelte, wasp-waisted, limber, supple, graceful, flexible, pliant, lithe.

WILT, *v.* Lose freshness, wither, droop, limp, fade, languish, deteriorate, fall off, degenerate, have seen better days, decline, decay, shrivel, go off.

WILY, *adj.* Cunning, crafty, deceitful, insidious, sly, subtle, scheming, intriguing, machinating, treacherous, designing, artful, disingenuous, arch, tricky, foxy, vulpine, shifty, shrewd, guileful, Jesuitical, trickish, politic, diplomatic, crooked, Machiavellian, snaky, *rusé* (*Fr.*), timeserving, feline, underhand, stealthy, double-faced, deceptive, canny, sharp, strategic.

WIN, *v.* 1. Triumph, surpass, conquer, vanquish, subdue, overcome, overpower, overwhelm, subjugate, be triumphant, gain a victory, take by storm, carry all before one, gain the day, gain the prize, score a success, succeed, defeat, discomfit, master, overthrow, outmaneuver, outgeneral, rout, beat hollow, worst, floor, crush.

2. Get, gain, procure, make, obtain, secure, acquire, earn, achieve, attain, accomplish, reach, recover, catch, gather, reclaim, reap, score, effect, receive, execute, realize, pick up, collect, glean, scrape up, come at, bag, net, come by, take.

3. Win over, convince, wean, convert, proselytize, influence, sway, prevail on, persuade, induce, get the compliance of, bring round, conciliate,

indoctrinate, talk over, engage, enlist, incline, predispose.

WINCE, *v.* Start back, flinch, startle, shrink, quail, shy, blench, recoil, draw back, funk, falter, be afraid, dread, distrust, hesitate, crouch, cower, skulk, take alarm, tremble, shudder, quiver, quake, shiver, writhe, grimace, make faces, groan, scream, moan, whine, blubber, snivel, whimper, make a wry face, gnash one's teeth.

WIND, *v.* 1. Twine, entwine, curl, coil, roll, reel, infold, twist, entwist, wreathe, involve, crank, encircle, loop, twirl, lap, fold, indent, scallop, serpentine, sinuate.

2. Take a bending course, change direction, proceed circuitously, meander, zigzag, turn in and out, curve, bend, be devious, be tortuous, detour, deviate, ramble, swerve, tack, heel, jibe, slue, swing round, veer, put about, warp, haul.

WIND, *n.* 1. Air in natural motion, stream of air, breeze, zephyr, draught, flatus, whiff, puff, breath, current, wiffet, afflatus, indraught, inflow, sough.

2. Squall, flurry, gust, hurricane, blast, gale, storm, cyclone, tornado, twister, whirlwind, tempest, typhoon, monsoon, simoom, windstorm, blow, blizzard, northeaster, baguio, harmattan, samiel, mistral, sirocco.

3. Aeolus, Eurus, Favonius, Zephyrus, Boreas, Notus, Vulturnus, Afer, Corus.

4. Respiration, breath, inhalation, inspiration, exhalation, expiration, eupnoea.

5. Gas, flatulence, windiness, eructation, borborygmus, belch, burp *(coll.)*.

6. Empty talk, mere words, bombast, hot air *(sl.)*, twaddle, babble, claptrap, rodomontade, fustian, boasting, bull *(sl.)*, humbug, sesquipedalianism, bluff, altiloquence, grandiloquence, magniloquence, braggadocio, gasconade, fanfaronade, brag, swagger, *blague (Fr.)*, bunk *(sl.)*.

7. Hint, intimation, inkling, innuendo, insinuation, suggestion, ear to the ground, enlightenment, news, information, knowledge, intelligence, cue, whisper, pointer, word to the wise, report, tidings.

WINDBAG, *n.* *(Coll.)* Voluble talker, empty chatterer, blatherskite, chatterbox, gossip, boaster, braggart, braggadocio, vaporer, hot-air artist, bluffer, ranter, blower, stump orator.

WINDFALL, *n.* Unexpected piece of good fortune, unanticipated legacy, stroke of good luck, piece of good fortune, godsend, run of luck, boon, blessing, prize, weal, boot, treasure-trove.

WINDING, *adj.* Curving, bending, twisting, turning, twining, meandering, spiral, corkscrew, sinuous, serpentine, flexuous, tortuous, anfractuous, circuitous, ambagious, snaky, crooked, devious, labyrinthian, indirect, roundabout, vermicular, mazy, helical, labyrinthine, convoluted, circling, intricate, curly, kinky, wavy, undulant, turbinate, cochleate, ripply.

WINDING, *n.* Involution, convolution, tortuosity, meandering, circuit, sinuosity, flexure, curvature, contortion, coiling, turning, twisting, kink, crook, bend, wave, undulation, ambages, anfractuosity, circumbendibus, twirl, roll, spiral, curl, helix, labyrinth, maze, corkscrew, volute, worm, scallop, tendril, scroll.

WINDOW, *n.* Opening for admission of air *or* light, aperture, orifice, fenestra, fenestration, fenestella, dormer, casement, oriel, skylight, bow, bay, transom, ventilator, lattice, porthole, port, fanlight, bull's-eye, *oeil-de-boeuf (Fr.)*, embrasure.

WINDPIPE, *n.* Trachea, airpipe, throat, weasand, gullet, fauces, gorge.

WINDUP, *n.* Conclusion, end, close, finale, termination, denouement, crisis, finis, completion, finish, consummation, catastrophe *(Drama)*, final event, epilogue, postlude, fall of the curtain, peroration, ending.

WINDY, *adj.* 1. Breezy, blustery, blasty, blowy, blusterous, gusty, wind-swept, raw, bleak, foul, dirty, stormy, turbulent, tempestuous, typhonic, cyclonic, raging, violent, squally.

2. Wordy, diffuse, long-winded, prolix, talkative, garrulous, voluble, verbose, empty, loquacious, polyloquent, multiloquent, declamatory, eloquent, fluent, glib, effusive.

WINEBIBBER, *n.* Wine-addict, vinolent person, oenophilist, sot, toper, vino *(sl.)*, lush *(sl.)*, drunkard, tippler, intemperate man, hard drinker, guzzler, soak, tosspot, lovepot, dipsomaniac, alcoholic, thirsty soul, inebriate, boozer *(coll.)*, sponge *(sl.)*, reveler, carouser.

WING, *n.* 1. Pinion, ala, pennon, arm, plane, patagium, pteron, sail, alula, elytron, supporting surface, aileron.

2. Flying, flight, volitation, volation, aviation, airmanship, aerial navigation, aeronautics, avigation.

3. Ell, sidepiece, adjunct, extension, ramification, annex, branch, addition, affix, attachment, appendage, flank.

WINGED, *adj.* 1. Having wings, alar, alary, alate, pteroid, pterous *(suffix)*.

2. Fleet, swift, flying, speedy, rapid, quick, fast, agile, nimble, express, light-footed, mercurial, light-legged, expeditious, hasty, hurried, precipitate, headlong, instant, immediate, prompt.

3. Aspiring, inspired, elevated, lofty, exalted, soaring.

WINK, *v.* Close and open the eyes quickly, blink, twinkle, nictate, squint, nictitate, screw up the eyes.

WINK AT, *v.* Be purposely blind to, pretend not to see, overlook, shut one's eyes to, connive at, condone, ignore, excuse, pass over, skim over, humor, tolerate, allow by inaction, gloss over, favor, let pass, let slip, indulge, suffer, brook, stretch a point.

WINNING, *adj.* 1. Successful, victorious, triumphant, jubilant, crowned with success, unbeaten.

2. Alluring, inviting, prepossessing, attractive, charming, fetching, taking, engaging, bewitching, fascinating, captivating, enchanting, winsome, lovely, delightful, persuasive, sweet, lovable, agreeable, gratifying, entrancing, appealing, pleasant, amiable, cordial, affable, seductive, ravishing.

WINNOW, *v.* Clear of chaff, ventilate, blow upon, fan, separate, sift, glean, divide, part, select, cull, distinguish, differentiate, analyze, sieve, bolt, riddle, screen, weed.

WINSOME, *adj.* Charming, engaging, entrancing, captivating, bewitching, prepossessing, fascinating, attractive, alluring, seductive, enticing, enchanting, lovely, beautiful, beauteous, bonny, lovable, cheerful, amiable, affable, cordial, sweet, gay, blithe, sportive, lively, vivacious, sparkling, blithesome, jocund, buoyant, debonair, light-hearted.

WINTER, *n.* Cold season, *hiems (Lat.)*, depth of winter, hard winter, Arctic, Antarctic, North Pole, South Pole, zero weather, frozenness, gelidity, algidity, frigidity, iciness, coldness, bleakness, inclemency.

WINTRY, *adj.* Hiemal, hibernal, brumal, brumous, boreal, hyperborean, arctic, antarctic, polar, icy, snowy, frosty, hoary, cold, glacial, freezing, gelid, algid, frore, bitter, nipping, raw, inclement, harsh, frozen, bleak.

WIPE, *v.* Rub lightly with a cloth, clean, mop, dry, swab, cleanse, sponge, scour, scrub.

WIPE OUT, *v.* Take out by rubbing, erase, expunge, blot out, delete, rub out, eradicate, remove, cancel, scratch out, raze, obliterate, efface, annihilate, eliminate, exterminate, extinguish, destroy, extirpate, deracinate, strike out.

WIRE, *n.* 1. Strand of slender flexible metal, metallic thread, filament, harl.

2. Telegraph, telephone, cable, radiotelegraph, radio, radiophone.

WIRELESS, *n.* Telegraphic communication, telegram, cable, night letter, wire, cablegram, radiogram, radiotelegram, marconigram, dispatch, bulletin, broadcast, flash *(coll.).*

WIREPULLER, *n.* Controller of others' actions by secret means, tactician, adroit manager, diplomatist, maneuverer, intriguing politician, pipelayer, friend at court, power behind the throne, latent influence, strategist.

WIRY, *adj.* 1. Filiform, filamentous, filamentary, threadlike, filar, fibrillose, stringy, thready.

2. Lean and sinewy, strong, robust, athletic, gymnastic, tough, supple, limber, agile, husky, sturdy, muscular, brawny, well-knit, stalwart, strapping, lusty, doughty.

WISDOM, *n.* 1. Good judgment, clear thinking, rationality, horse sense *(coll.),* wiseness, sense, common sense, sapience, reason, discernment, insight, profundity, sagacity, understanding, judiciousness, depth, prescience, good sense, solidity, reach of thought, enlarged views, foresight, prudence, providence, judgment of ends, knowledge how to live, acumen, astuteness, shrewdness, comprehension, intelligence, penetration, brains, wit, savvy *(sl.),* capacity for reasoning, long-headedness, perspicuity, apperception, mother wit, *esprit (Fr.),* intellectuality, circumspection, gumption.

2. Learning, erudition, enlightenment, information, lore, scholarship, knowledge, attainment, education, culture.

3. Advisability, expediency, policy, discreetness, tact, vigilance, carefulness, aplomb, sobriety.

WISE, *adj.* 1. Sagacious, sage, sensible, sapient, reasonable, rational, intelligent, intellectual, perceptive, strong-minded, far-sighted, perspicacious, prudent, provident, discerning, profound, enlightened, philosophical, having good judgment, sound, penetrating, deep-thinking, judicious, worldly-wise, informed, knowing, erudite, lettered, educated, accomplished, scholarly, bookish, learned, sophisticated, skilled, circumspect, wary, politic, discreet, tactful, cautious, vigilant, prepared, watchful, careful, staid, well-balanced, sober, regardful, heedful, alert, observant, chary, guarded, wide-awake, long-headed.

2. Well-advised, expedient, diplomatic, politic, well-judged, punctilious, scrupulous, conscientious, strategic.

WISE, *n.* Way of proceeding, *modus operandi (Lat.),* manner, mode, fashion, method, procedure, respect, detail, degree.

WISE MAN, *n.* Savant, sage, pundit, philosopher, magus, scholar, intellectual, Brahmin, solon, oracle, authority, walking encyclopedia *(humorous),* luminary, mentor, thinker, mastermind, man of learning, specialist, expert, shining light, Solomon, Nestor, guru *(Hindu),* colossus of learning, *homo multarum literarum (Lat.),* prodigy, pantologist, pedant, seer, wizard, connoisseur, mine of information.

WISH, *v.* Desire, want, long for, set one's heart upon, hanker after, covet, crave, yearn for, hope for, entertain wishes for, list, have an inclination toward, sigh for, care for, fancy, have an eye to, be bent upon, court, pine after, woo, fish for, will, prefer.

WISH, *n.* Desire, longing, craving, hankering, liking, yearning, inclination, aspiration, aim, want, hunger, appetite, appetency, leaning, bent, partiality, predilection, penchant, fondness, love, relish, eagerness, ambition, itch, ardor, keenness, thirst, cupidity, avidity, passion, mania, furor, pleasure, behest, hest, mind, will, whim, propensity.

WISHBONE, *n.* Furcula, merrythought, united pair of clavicles, furculum.

WISHFUL, *adj.* Desirous, eager, bent upon, hankering, longing, craving, yearning, appetitive, hungry, thirsty, fain, inclined, partial to, solicitous, anxious, dreamy-eyed, wistful, ardent, keen, fervent, avid, ambitious, aspiring, impatient, insatiable, in hopes, hopeful, expectant, sanguine, anticipative, optimistic, anticipatory, enthusiastic.

WISHY-WASHY, *adj.* 1. Watery, diluted, thin, weak, watered, aqueous, attenuated, adulterated, tasteless, insipid, mawkish, savorless, milk-and-water, flat, vapid, mild.

2. Without strength, unforceful, feeble, poor, languid, irresolute, impotent, powerless, feckless, weakly, soft, effeminate, emasculate, namby-pamby.

WISTFUL, *adj.* 1. Pensive, musing, contemplative, thoughtful, reflective, cogitative, meditative, studious, speculative, introspective, absorbed in thought, rapt, deliberative, dreamy-eyed, serious, sedate, sober, solemn, demure.

2. Expressive of sadness, melancholy, triste, mournful, woeful, doleful, woebegone, hypochondriacal, lachrymose, sorrowful, disconsolate, grieving, dismal, desolate, forlorn, heartsick.

3. Longing, fervent, ardent, desirous, wishful, fain, eager, keen, avid.

WIT, *n.* 1. Quick perception, mental power, intelligence, intellect, brains, rationality, understanding, nous, sense, mind, reason, intellectual faculties, genius, *esprit (Fr.),* mother wit, parts, sagacity, astuteness, shrewdness, discernment, ingenuity, smartness, judgment, insight, intuition, perspicacity, penetration, acumen, wisdom, cognition, comprehension, intellectuality, percipience, mentality, apperception, capacity, gumption, hardheadedness, long-headedness, cunning, subtlety.

2. Facetiousness, sense of humor, drollery, waggishness, cleverness, Attic salt, Atticism, quickness at repartee, waggery, jocularity, readiness, sparkle, vivacity, whimsicality, piquancy, brightness, point.

3. Witticism, repartee, riposte, badinage, persiflage, raillery, banter, satire, playfulness, burlesque, irony, buffoonery, ridicule, sally, epigram, bon mot, joke, wordplay, jest, pun, *calembour (Fr.),* quip, conceit, pleasantry, joshing, chaff, airy nothings, retort, *quid pro quo (Lat.),*

wisecrack, smart saying, gag *(sl.)*, quibble, double-entendre.

4. Humorist, jokester, jester, wag, banterer, reparteeist, *persifleur (Fr.)*, *bel esprit (Fr.)*, wisecracker *(sl.)*, punster, epigrammatist, buffoon, joker, comedian, droll, merry-andrew, pantaloon, harlequin, clown.

WITCH, *v.* Affect by witchcraft, charm, fascinate, enchant, ensorcel, enamor, captivate, put under a spell, spellbind, bewitch, ravish, practice sorcery upon, hoodoo, hex, entrance, bedevil, hypnotize, mesmerize, allure, enrapture.

WITCH, *n.* 1. Female magican, sorceress, sibyl, pythoness, weird sister, witch of Endor, warlock, prophetess, seeress, soothsayer, fortuneteller, evocatrix, medium, palmist, clairvoyant, Pythia, Hecate.

2. Enchantress, charmer, fascinator, Circe, siren, Lorelei, Lilith, succubus, succuba, incubus, vampire, vamp.

3. Ugly old woman, hag, crone, beldam, harridan.

WITCHCRAFT, *n.* 1. Supernatural power, magical influence, black art, *Hexerei (Ger.)*, voodoo, hoodoo, voodooism, sorcery, black magic, wonderworking, thaumaturgy, demonology, necromancy, witchery, shamanism, incantation, conjuration, exorcism, enchantment, invocation, hocus-pocus, sortilege, divination, spell, spellbinding, possession, obsession, theurgy, charm, fascination, entrancement, enravishment, captivation, glamor, attraction, allurement, wizardry, fetishism, obiism, abracadabra, open sesame, jinx, evil eye, talisman, phylactery, amulet, philter, seduction.

2. Wand, divining rod, caduceus, magic ring, Aladdin's lamp, wishing cap, magic carpet.

WITH, *prep.* 1. In company with, between, among, amongst, amidst, beside, along with, accompanying, attending, in the midst of, plus, by the side of.

2. Through the agency of, by means of, by the instrumentality of, with the help of, by the aid of, by the use of.

3. Using, having, employing, utilizing, showing, owing to, due to.

4. Notwithstanding, despite, in spite of, without regard to, not the less for.

WITHDRAW, *v.* 1. Retreat, retire, depart, be off, go away, vamoose *(sl.)*, abscond, decamp, take French leave, go off, secede, regress, recede, vacate, leave, absent oneself, evacuate, fall back, retrograde, disappear, elope, give way, give ground, play truant, quit, make oneself scarce, back out, crawfish, backtrack.

2. Retract, recall, recant, revoke, abjure, disavow, annul, abrogate, cancel, repeal, rescind, overrule, reverse, set aside, override, disannul, invalidate, nullify, quash, disestablish, abolish.

3. Abdicate, resign, relinquish, desert, lay down, give up, hand over, surrender.

WITHDRAWAL, *n.* 1. Departure, retirement, recession, leave-taking, exit, leave, retreat, going away, *congé (Fr.)*, setting out, sailing, hegira, exodus, flight, parting, farewell, adieu, valediction, good-by, regression, secession, evacuation, disappearance, elopement, desertion.

2. Retraction, revocation, recall, abjuration, annulment, disavowal, abrogation, cancellation, reversal, repeal, disannulment, invalidation, nullification, abolition.

3. Abdication, resignation, relinquishment, surrender, retirement.

WITHE, *n.* Willow twig, slender stem, osier, wicker, wattle, switch, shoot, branch, bough, sprig, branchlet, ramulus, runner, ramule, offshoot, spray, tendril, sarmentum, scion.

WITHER, *v.* Shrivel, droop, waste, wilt, fade, wane, decay, decline, contract, sear, wizen, lose freshness, dry up, wrinkle, shrink, lose moisture, blight, die, languish, collapse, fall off, deteriorate, retrograde, degenerate, run to seed, molder.

WITHERING, *adj.* 1. Shriveling, shrinking, wilting, fading, decaying, marcescent, shrunken.

2. Disdainful, scornful, contumelious, arrogant, supercilious, contemptuous, haughty, derisive, bumptious, upstage, toplofty, cavalier, icy, aloof, cool, chilly, superior, with nose in air, high-hat.

3. Cutting, biting, trenchant, mordant, cynical, sarcastic, severe, harsh, acerbous, acidulous, sardonic, satirical, sharp-tongued, derogatory, disparaging, depreciatory, abusive, critical, faultfinding, censorious, hypercritical, captious.

WITHHOLD, *v.* 1. Reserve, keep from, hide, suppress, conceal, keep back, not disclose, keep secret, hush up, stifle, smother, gag, censor, muzzle.

2. Restrain, hold back, restrict, check, hinder, prohibit, detain, repress, rein in, curb, keep in, desist, cease, abstain, forbear, refrain, debar, constrain, harness, coerce, bridle, control, hold in leash, stop short, inhibit.

WITHIN, *adv.* 1. Indoors, at home, withindoors, in the house, in, inside.

2. Interiorly, inwardly, internally, in the inside of, *ab intra (Lat.)*, inly.

WITHIN, *prep.* 1. Inside of, enclosed by, in, inside, in the inside of.

2. Not exceeding, not beyond, not farther than, to some point not beyond, not transgressing, inside of the limits required by, in the compass of, not above, not more than.

3. In the field of, within the sphere of, in the scope of, in the reach of, in the course of, during, in the period of.

WITHOUT, *adv.* 1. Outdoors, outside, out, out-of-doors, *extra muros (Lat.)*, *al fresco (It.)*, in open air, *à la belle étoile (Fr.)*.

2. Externally, outwardly, exteriorly, in space without, outwards.

3. Lacking, short of, requiring, unaccompanied by.

WITHOUT, *prep.* 1. Destitute of, lacking, short of, requiring, not with, with no, unaccompanied by, less, free from, *sans (Fr.)*, *senza (It.)*, *sin (Sp.)*, *ohne (Ger.)*, in the absence of, independently of, in default of, in want of, deprived of, excluding, unburdened by, exclusively of.

2. On the outside of, beyond, outside of, out of, beyond the limits of.

WITHSTAND, *v.* Oppose, resist, defy, challenge, confront, stand against, face, make a stand against, hold out against, strive against, oppugn, stand off, thwart, impede, stem, breast, weather, endure, stay, obstruct, stop, stand fast, stand firm, check, frustrate, foil, hinder, counteract, countervail, grapple with, encounter, show a bold front, defend, repulse, buffet the waves, cope with, repel.

WITLESS, *adj.* Slow of apprehension, slow-witted, unintelligent, stupid, obtuse, dull-witted, fatuous, weak-minded, addleheaded, half-witted, feeble-minded, fat-witted, brainless, unwise, foolish, inane, empty-headed, short-witted, muddleheaded, muddy-brained, senseless, dull, silly, shallow, daft, deranged, duncical, idiotic, driveling, besotted, imbecilic, moronic, dense, nitwitted, weak in the upper story, *borné (Fr.),* vacant.

WITLING, *n.* 1. Would-be wit, smart aleck, wiseacre, gag-man, humorist, clown, jester, jokesmith, farceur, buffoon, merry-andrew, wearer of the cap and bells, zany.

2. Booby, nincompoop, fool, simpleton, goose, imbecile, moron, idiot, Simple Simon, tomfool, nitwit, ass, donkey, dizzard, dolt, ninny, hoddydoddy, looby, oaf, dullard, lout, loon, blockhead.

WITNESS, *n.* 1. Testifier, deponent, attestor, one who gives testimony, person affording evidence, corroborator.

2. Proof, evidence, testimony, attestation, surety, confirmation, corroboration, testification, averment, affirmation, deposition, declaration, facts, data.

3. Eyewitness, looker-on, beholder, observer, bystander, spectator, onlooker, *assistant (Fr.),* passer-by.

WITNESS, *v.* 1. Give evidence, give testimony, attest, certify, confirm, corroborate, testify, depose, swear, vouch for, endorse, validate, bear out, sustain, establish, uphold, authenticate, warrant, verify, substantiate, acknowledge, document, circumstantiate.

2. Observe, see, take cognizance of, note, mark, notice, look on, behold, view, know by personal perception, perceive, be present at, attend, *assister (Fr.).*

WITTICISM, *n.* Witty remark, sally of humor, quip, jest, joke, flash of wit, bon mot, pleasantry, conceit, pun, *calembour (Fr.), jeu d'esprit (Fr.),* play on words, quirk, crank, wisecrack *(sl.),* scintillation, gag *(sl.),* epigram, quiddity, *mot pour rire (Fr.), jeu de mots (Fr.),* quibble, doubleentendre, conundrum, riddle, chaff, banter, badinage, joshing, persiflage, raillery, repartee, riposte, retort, *quid pro quo (Lat.).*

WITTY, *adj.* Amusingly clever, jocular, facetious, droll, jocose, funny, waggish, bright, sparkling, scintillating, pleasant, original, mirthful, smart, jolly, gay, sprightly, penetrating, quick-witted, *spirituel (Fr.),* humorous, risible, laughable, comic, whimsical, *ben trovato (It.),* epigrammatic, wellturned, brilliant, ludicrous, farcical.

WIZARD, *n.* 1. Sorcerer, seer, magician, enchanter, charmer, wonderworker, thaumaturge, thaumaturgist, miracle man, necromancer, soothsayer, diviner, conjurer, juggler, prestidigitator, witch, warlock, exorcist, mage, voodoo, dowser, shaman, medicine man, witch doctor, clairvoyant, astrologer, Merlin, Cagliostro, Katerfelto, Comus, prophet, oracle, augur, geomancer, haruspex.

2. Wise man, sage, pundit, magus, mastermind, walking encyclopedia, luminary, *esprit fort (Fr.),* shining light, virtuoso, expert, adept, Solomon, Solon, connoisseur, top sawyer, past master, specialist, veteran, good hand, genius, pantologist, prodigy.

WIZENED, *adj.* Shriveled, shrunken, dried up, desiccated, lean, withered, wilted, faded, decayed, moldered, tabid, stunted, tabescent.

WOBBLE, *v.* Incline alternately to one side and the other, be improperly balanced, move unsteadily from side to side, teeter, totter, dodder, be unsteady, vacillate, waver, tremble, quaver, shake, quiver, quake, stagger, shuffle, waggle, flounder.

WOE, *n.* Trial, tribulation, sorrow, misery, suffering, grievous distress, adversity, misfortune, trouble, affliction, wretchedness, heartache, grief, unhappiness, disconsolateness, heavy heart, anguish, broken heart, pain of mind, agony, torture, torment, melancholy, depression, bitterness, disaster, calamity, catastrophe, gloom, dolor, dejection, worry, anxiety, care, ordeal, blow, shock, heavy load, burden, bleeding heart, infelicity, despair, prostration, extremity, depth of misery, throe, stab, pang, the rack.

WOEBEGONE, *adj.* Beset with woe, wretched, doleful, dolorous, downcast, sad, miserable, chapfallen, despondent, hypochondriacal, melancholy, forlorn, disconsolate, depressed, dejected, cast down, lugubrious, funereal, rueful, sorrowful, comfortless, pitiable, cheerless, joyless, crestfallen, mournful, dismal, gloomy, long-faced, down-inthe-mouth, worried, afflicted, stricken, heavyladen, crushed, doomed, undone, infelicitous, unhappy, careworn, cut up, mortified, chagrined, broken-hearted, somber, glum, low-spirited, discouraged, disheartened, lachrymose, heartsick.

WOEFUL, *adj.* Heart-rending, grievous, calamitous, disastrous, catastrophic, tragic, lamentable, deplorable, dreadful, distressing, pitiable, saddening, afflictive, piteous, depressing, sorrowful, wretched, dolorific, painful, bitter, disheartening, dreary, cruel, harsh, severe, excruciating, racking, ruinous, oppressive, onerous.

WOMAN, *n.* 1. Adult female, she, petticoat, skirt *(sl.),* weaker sex, dame, belle, mother, wife, spouse, helpmate, better half, dowager, matron, *Frau (Ger.), madame (Fr.), donna (It.), señora (Sp.),* Mrs., mistress, lady, mem-sahib *(Anglo-Indian),* squaw, *femme (Fr.), signora (It.),* spinster, old maid, damsel, maiden, lass, virgin, damosel, colleen, nymph, girl, miss, *mademoiselle (Fr.), Fräulein (Ger.), señorita (Sp.), signorina (It.),* fair sex.

2. Paramour, concubine, doxy, broad, courtesan, tart, strumpet, chippy, piece, demimondaine, demirep, fancy woman, kept woman.

3. Maidservant, female attendant, handmaiden, chambermaid, lady in waiting, maid, ancilla, abigail, *bonne (Fr.),* nurse, ayah, amah.

WOMAN-HATER, *n.* Misogynist, misogyne.

WOMANHOOD, *n.* 1. Adult feminine quality, womanliness, femininity, feminineness, matronhood, muliebrity, female maturity, feminality, femineity.

2. The distaff side, the fair sex, womenfolk, eternal feminine, world of women, the female sex.

WOMANISH, *adj.* Unnaturally feminine, effeminate, sissyish *(coll.),* milksopish, unmanly, emasculate, mollycoddle, weak, soft, emasculated, tender, delicate, unvirile.

WOMANLY, *adj.* Appropriately feminine, becoming a woman, womanlike, ladylike, matronly, feminine, muliebrous, tender, gentle, motherly, gynecic, feministic, sympathetic.

WOMB, *n.* 1. Uterus, venter, matrix, belly.

2. Innermost recesses, penetralia, interior recess, arcanum, hollow, depth, abyss, cavern, antrum.

WONDER, *n.* 1. Feeling of surprise, puzzled interest, wonderment, amazement, astonishment, bewilderment, consternation, stupefaction, awe, amazedness, wondering, fascination, stupor, bolt out of the blue, shock, curious awe, curiosity.

2. Phenomenon, prodigy, miracle, marvel, portent, rarity, *rara avis (Lat.)*, eye opener, oddity, sight, spectacle, wonderwork, *coup de théâtre (Fr.)*

WONDER, *v.* 1. Feel surprise, marvel, be amazed, be surprised, admire, stare, start, hold one's breath, gape, be taken aback, be dumbstruck, stand aghast, be overcome by awe, be stunned, be petrified, be stupefied, feel bewilderment, be flabbergasted, be wonderstruck, stand agog, look blank, open one's mouth, be dazed.

2. Speculate, meditate, cogitate, excogitate, ponder, conjecture, query, be in a state of uncertainty, be curious about, be inquisitive, be curiously doubtful, question.

WONDERFUL, *adj.* Astonishing, amazing, astounding, awesome, awe-inspiring, stupendous, surprising, startling, wondrous, marvelous, incredible, inconceivable, portentous, miraculous, prodigious, staggering, extraordinary, very strange, unique, odd, queer, fantastic, fabulous, mythical, phenomenal, stunning, striking, fascinating, remarkable, curious, admirable, exceptional, unexpected, monstrous, mysterious, singular, unprecedented, unwonted, signal, unusual, mirific, thaumaturgic.

WONDERWORKER, *n.* Worker of marvels, miracle man, thaumaturge, thaumaturgist, magician, wizard, conjurer, prestidigitator, necromancer, sorcerer, seer, fairy, exorcist, charmer, warlock, voodoo, diviner, magus, dowser, witch doctor, medicine man, shaman, soothsayer, Merlin, Cagliostro, Katerfelto.

WONT, *n.* Habit, custom, usage, practice, use, consuetude, routine, habitude, rule, way, run, fashion, mode, vogue, procedure, conventionalism, prescription, beaten path, matter of course, second nature, standing order, groove, rut, convention, precedent.

WONTED, *adj.* 1. Accustomed, habituated, used, in the habit of, wont to, given to, used to, addicted to, wedded to, devoted to, *ex more (Lat.)*.

2. Habitual, customary, usual, familiar, conventional, frequent, common, ordinary, regular, everyday, consuetudinary, routine, general, trite, well-trodden, hackneyed, commonplace, stock, set, established, stereotyped, prescriptive, prescribed, inveterate, confirmed, ingrained, prevailing.

WOO, *v.* 1. Seek the love of, spark, blandish, ogle, serenade, make love to, court, pay one's addresses to, dance attendance on, solicit, spoon *(sl.)*, bill and coo, wear one's heart upon one's sleeve, fold to the heart, smile upon, wheedle, make much of, philander, coquet, set one's cap at, address.

2. Seek to persuade, solicit, address, sue, importune, pursue, aim after.

WOOD, *n.* 1. Large collection of growing trees, woods, woodland, grove, forest, copse, coppice, timberland, greenwood, covert, thicket, spinney, bosk, brush, bush, brake, jungle, virgin forest, wildwood, canebrake, boscage.

2. Lumber, timber, kindling, fuel, firewood, xylem *(Bot.)*, lignum.

WOODED, *adj.* Abounding in trees, forest-covered, forested, timbered, covered with woods, forest-crowned, overgrown, sylvan, arboreal, arboreous, copsy, bosky, dense, luxuriant, rank, shady, umbrageous.

WOODEN, *adj.* 1. Made of wood, woody, ligneous, xyloid, lignose.

2. Awkward, clumsy, gauche, maladroit, ungainly, rigid, stiff, hard, unplastic, unpliable, unmalleable, unpliant, unhandy, unskillful, inept, without dexterity.

3. Without animation, spiritless, expressionless, poker-faced, dead-pan, inscrutable, passive, dull, stupid, inert, lethargic, comatose.

WOODLAND, *n.* Land covered with trees, grove, forest, woods, timberland, thicket, greenwood, virgin forest, wildwood, coppice, copse, spinney, bosk, covert, canebrake, bush, jungle, brush, plantation, shrubbery, bosquet, hurst, holt, chaparral.

WOOER, *n.* Suitor, lover, gallant, spark, paramour, swain, cicisbeo, carpet knight, sheik *(sl.)*, philanderer, spooner *(sl.)*, petter, aspirant, boy friend, adorer, admirer, fiancé, beau, inamorato, sweetheart, flame, truelove, amorist, Lothario, Casanova, cavalier, *amoroso (It.)*.

WOOF, *n.* 1. Loom yarns interlacing with the warp weft, filling, weft.

2. Fabric, texture, cloth, tooth, nap, fineness *or* coarseness of grain, contexture, intertexture, tissue, web, grain, surface.

WOOLGATHERING, *n.* Inattentiveness, abstraction, castle-building, absence of mind, absent-mindedness, distraction, preoccupation, brown study, reverie, fit of abstraction, deep musing, bemusedness, raptness, engrossment, dreaminess, napping, daydream, detachment.

WOOLLY, *adj.* Lanate, lanuginous, flocculent, fluffy, downy, fleecy, tomentose, flocky, villous.

WORD, *n.* 1. Written *or* spoken sign for a concept, element standing alone as an utterance, term, vocable, name, expression, phrase, etymon, monosyllable, ideophone, derivative, root, unit of discourse, part of speech, remark, metonym, synonym, antonym, homonym, heteronym, neologism, locution, idiom, noun, adjective, pronoun, preposition, verb, adverb, conjunction, interjection, particle, enclitic, coined word, neoterism.

2. Promise, assurance, pledge, parole, agreement, word of honor, plight, warrant, engagement, troth, plighted faith, undertaking, affiance, avowal, affirmation, declaration, statement, averment, assertion.

3. News, report, tidings, advice, account, intelligence, message, information, hearsay, rumor, bruit, *oui-dire (Fr.)*, scoop, beat, gossip, talk, canard, tittle-tattle, communication, bulletin, letter, dispatch, broadcast, wire, telegram, cable, flash, telephone call.

4. Command, order, behest, direction, bidding, precept, mandate, injunction, fiat, decree, ukase, firman, ordinance, regulation, act, beck, call, nod, hest, commandment, dictation, ruling, instructions, charge, dictate, caveat, prescript, writ, edict, enactment, dispensation, bull, ultimatum, summons, subpoena, citation, word of command, order of the day, *l'ordre du jour (Fr.)*, password, shibboleth, *mot de passe (Fr.)*, watchword, signal, countersign, *mot d'ordre (Fr.)*.

5. Word of God, Scriptures, Holy Writ, Bible, Logos, God's Word.

6. *(Pl.)* Conversation, parley, speech, chat, *causerie (Fr.)*, discourse, intercourse, language, converse, palaver, colloquy, communion, interlocution, commerce, chitchat, gossip, tattle, babble,

dialogue, conference, consultation, tête-à-tête, discussion, audience, interview, reception, pow-wow.

7. *(Pl.)* Argument, quarrel, dispute, wrangling, bickering, altercation, contention, jangle, logomachy, war of words.

WORD, *v.* Express, utter, call, term, name, phrase, put it, voice, clothe in words, give expression to, designate, style, describe, dub, denominate, couch in terms.

WORD-FOR-WORD, *adv.* Literally, exactly, verbally, in the exact words, verbatim, literatim, *ad amussim (Lat.), sic (Lat.), totidem verbis (Lat.),* chapter and verse, to the letter, *ipsissimis verbis (Lat.), au pied de la lettre (Fr.), sous tous les rapports (Fr.),* strictly speaking.

WORDINESS, *n.* Verbosity, prolixity, diffuseness, verbiage, verbalism, loquacity, multiloquence, *copia verborum (Lat.), flux de paroles (Fr.),* profuseness, flow of words, gift of gab, amplification, circumlocution, periphrasis, indirection, ambages, tautology, roundaboutness, windiness *(coll.),* padding, redundancy, polylogy, volubility, garrulity, talkativeness, fluency, eloquence, effusiveness, effusion, gush.

WORDPLAY, *n.* Pun, riddle, quibble, conundrum, *jeu de mots (Fr.),* paronomasia, *équivoque (Fr.), calembour (Fr.),* double-entendre, carriwitchet, quillet, subtlety.

WORDY, *adj.* Given to the use of too many words, verbose, prolix, circumlocutory, periphrastic, diffuse, redundant, tautological, ambagious, roundabout, pleonastic, long-winded, windy *(coll.),* bombastic, fustian, spun-out, multiloquent, polylogistic, polyloquent, grandiloquent, magniloquent, inflated, rambling, garrulous, voluble, talkative, loquacious, tedious, discursive, digressive, lengthy, profuse, gushing, exuberant, copious, protracted, maundering, episodic, rhapsodic, turgid, eloquent, declamatory, rhetorical.

WORK, *v.* 1. Labor, toil, drudge, be busily employed, moil, slave, sweat, fag, grind, grub, be industrious, be diligent, exert oneself, exercise, practice, plod, endeavor, strive, attempt, aim, try, contend, vie, buckle to, put forth one's strength, do double duty, set one's shoulder to the wheel, ply the oar, take pains, do one's utmost, strain one's nerve, do one's best, leave no stone unturned, spare no effort.

2. Carry on, do, perform, be in action, operate, act, run, have an effect, have influence, be effective *(coll.),* succeed, get on, function, execute, achieve, transact, enact.

3. Wield, manipulate, use, ply, utilize, employ, turn to account, occupy, apply, put to use, set in motion, adhibit, bring into play, handle.

4. Originate, cause, engender, produce, effect, accomplish, lead to, beget, bring about, make, fashion, form, forge, shape, mold, hammer out.

5. Ferment, leaven, raise, effervesce, pepsinate.

WORK, *n.* 1. Toil, grind, drudgery, exertion, elbow grease *(coll.),* sweat of one's brow, labor, pains, effort, industry, diligence, slavery, chore, endeavor, exercitation, exercise, travail, manual labor, energy, stress, strain, tug, dead lift, heft, discipline, training, drill.

2. Employment, task, occupation, vocation, avocation, office, function, business, trade, craft, handicraft, pursuit, job, profession, calling, métier, line.

3. Deed, feat, transaction, act, doing, maneuver, enterprise, coup, stunt, achievement, exploit.

4. Production, performance, output, turnout, handiwork, fabric, yield, harvest, manufacture, structure, product, composition, fruit.

5. Book, volume, tome, publication, writing, opus, novel, article, essay, paper, monograph, theme, thesis, biography, history, story, piece of fiction, annals, poem, treatise, codex, pamphlet, booklet, tract, brochure, tractate, dissertation, manual, handbook, textbook, libretto, reference book, dictionary, encyclopedia, glossary, lexicon, thesaurus, anthology, concordance, almanac, gazetteer, compilation.

WORKER, *n* 1. Performer, doer, operator, agent, actor, perpetrator, executor, practitioner.

2. Workman, workingman, laborer, artisan, handicraftsman, craftsman, operative, mechanic, laboring man, manual laborer, handworker, navvy, hand, hired man, journeyman, day laborer, drudge, hack, toiler, hustler, busy bee, artificer, grind, grubber, fag, moiler, coolie, peon, slave, serf, employee, wright, carpenter, joiner, machinist, electrician, engineer, plodder, proletarian, mason, hewers of wood and drawers of water.

WORKHOUSE, *n.* 1. Jail, penitentiary, reformatory, prison, house of correction, bridewell, dungeon, keep, prison house, clink *(sl.),* stir *(sl.),* pen, lockup, hoosegow *(sl.),* oubliette, Bastille, cell, coop, jug *(sl.).*

2. Poorhouse, eleemosynary institution, county home, almshouse, asylum.

WORKMANSHIP, *n.* Skill in working, quality of execution, handiwork, handicraft, craftsmanship, work, achievement, manufacture, fabric, texture, execution, manipulation, technique, fabrication, construction, performance.

WORKOUT, *n.* Drill, discipline, practice, preliminary trial in preparation for an exhibition, rehearsal, performance for practice *or* training, test run, trial, conditioning, shakedown.

WORKSHOP, *n.* Atelier, studio, workroom, works, plant, factory, mill, manufactory, foundry, establishment, laboratory, hive of industry, yard, forge, furnace, dock, wharf, pier, slip.

WORLD, *n.* 1. Entire system of created things, cosmos, macrocosm, creation, universe, nature, planetary system, heavenly bodies, Galaxy, Milky Way, *Via Lactea (Lat.),* celestial bodies, galactic circle, constellations, stars, luminaries, planetoids, asteroids, satellites, planets, solar system, heavens, welkin, empyrean, sky, firmament, starry host, celestial spaces, vault of heaven, megacosm, Midgard, cosmogony, cosmology, cosmography, cosmic evolution, cosmism.

2. Earth, terrestrial ball, terraqueous globe, terrestrial globe, terra, Ge, terrene, wide world.

3. Orb of day, sun, daystar, Sol, sun god, Helios, Hyperion, Phoebus, Apollo, Phaëthon, Shamash, Ra, moon, Queen of Night, Luna, Selene, Diana, Phoebe, Artemis, Cynthia, Hecate, Astarte, comet, meteor, meteorite, shooting star, aerolite, cosmic dust, meteoric trail, astronomy, astrology, astrography, uranography, uranology, astrophysics.

4. Human affairs, secular things, material matters, life, mundane interests, affairs of life, worldly aims, course of life, course of human affairs, current of events, stream of time, ways of men.

5. Social intercourse, social life, society, *haut monde (Fr.),* fashionable world, worldly people, *le beau monde (Fr.),* the great world.

6. Mankind, humankind, humanity, men, public, people, human race, inhabitants.

7. Sphere, department, domain, realm, division, kingdom, section, part, region, class, group, system.

WORLDLY, *adj.* 1. Earthly, terrestrial, terraqueous, sublunary, terrene, mundane, telluric, subastral, cosmic, cosmogonal, cosmographic, cosmogonical, celestial, empyrean, heavenly, empyreal, uranic, astronomical, sidereal, starry, stellary, astral, stellar, planetary, solar, heliacal, lunar, planetesimal, nebular, interstellar, interplanetary, intersidereal.

2. Temporal, secular, profane, fleshly, earthy, carnal, ungodly, unsanctified, unspiritual, irreligious, unregenerate.

3. Worldly-minded, sordid, pleasure-loving, moneygrubbing, selfish, proud, ambitious, hireling, mercenary, venal, covetous, grasping, timeserving, self-seeking.

WORLDLY WISDOM, *n.* Tact, savoir-faire, diplomacy, strategy, prudence, discretion, heed, forethought, cautiousness, caution, wariness, deliberation, foresight, self-assurance, aplomb, coolness, self-possession, presence of mind, sangfroid, knowledge of the world, *l'usage du monde (Fr.),* finesse, mother wit.

WORLD-WIDE, *adj.* Universal, ecumenical, global, international, general, extensive, prevailing, vast, planetary, catholic, widespread, far-reaching, cosmopolitan, pandemic, uncircumscribed.

WORM, *v.* Advance stealthily, work secretly and gradually, insinuate slowly, wriggle, creep, crawl, writhe, steal, get by insidious procedure, ingratiate, infiltrate, slip in, interpenetrate.

WORMLIKE, *adj.* Vermiform, vermicular, vermiculate, worm-shaped, sinuous, serpentine, winding, convoluted, tortile, undulatory, snaky, anguilliform, coiled, spiral, helical.

WORN, *adj.* 1. Dilapidated, decrepit, brokendown, used up, threadbare, shabby, impaired by wear *or* use, worn to a thread, worse for wear, consumed, abraded, wasted, decayed, wellused, seedy, faded, dingy, rusty, deteriorated, battered, weather-beaten, wilted, gone by, antiquated, timeworn, frayed, crumbling, moldering, mildewed, moth-eaten, useless, ruinous, trashy, rickety, tumble-down.

2. Worn-out, wearied, exhausted, spent, weary, footsore, fatigued, tired, haggard, *épuisé (Fr.),* *ausgespielt (Ger.),* played out, done up, toilworn, faint, drooping, prostrate, all in, ready to drop, dog-tired, enfeebled, blown, weak, debilitated.

WORRY, *v.* 1. Feel uneasy, be anxious, be solicitous, torment oneself with disturbing thoughts, be troubled, think anxiously upon, fret, fidget, chafe, fuss, fume, be vexed, be restive, be heavyhearted, brood over, take to heart, take on about, mope over, grieve over, sit on thorns, agonize, despair, despond, lose heart, dread, be afraid, distrust, be apprehensive, have prey on the mind.

2. Harass, harry, molest, persecute, vex, trouble, annoy, plague, harry, bother, torment, badger, pester, hector, beset, disturb, disquiet, gall, infest, bait, irritate, haze, discompose, pain, taunt, dog, tantalize, nag, distract, ruffle, distress, displease, confound, confuse, embarrass, mortify, chagrin, incommode, perturb, exercise, bedevil, hound,

dragoon, oppress, grind, abuse, maltreat, pique, rile, affront.

WORRY, *n.* Anxiety, solicitude, apprehension, trouble, misgiving, fear, premonition, uneasiness, perturbation, disquiet, restiveness, discomposure, concern, fretting, chafing, care, vexation, annoyance, perplexity, affliction, grief, difficulty, mental agitation, fearfulness, apprehensiveness, dread, consternation, dismay, trepidation, fear and trembling, bugaboo, bogy, *bête noire (Fr.),* trial, Slough of Despond, misery, despair, torment, thorn in the flesh, sore subject, hornets' nest, plague, sea of troubles.

WORSHIP, *n.* 1. Spiritual-mindedness, devotion, heavenly-mindedness, adoration, homage, cult, vow, latria, dulia, hyperdulia, cultus, service, idolization, reverence, idolizing, idolatry, veneration, deification, apotheosis, glorification, exaltation, invocation, supplication, prayer, laudation, praise, orison, petition, litany, miserere, rogation, benediction, doxology, alleluia, *Gloria (Lat.),* Te Deum *(Lat.),* hosanna, hymn, psalm, genuflection, kneeling, prostration, libation, offertory, oblation, incense, sacrifice.

2. Divine service, office, Eucharist, Mass, Holy Communion, Lord's Supper, matins, prayer meeting, revival, evensong, vespers, compline, novena.

3. Respect, deference, honor, repute, esteem, estimation, dignity, admiration, adoring regard, aspiration.

WORSHIP, *v.* 1. Render religious reverence to, venerate, revere, reverence, adore, give homage to, lift up the heart, bow down before, invoke, pray to, supplicate, entreat, beseech, commune with God, implore, glorify, exalt, magnify, hymn, extol, celebrate, laud, praise, chant, bless, hallow, return thanks, say grace, deify, apotheosize, canonize, beatify, consecrate, enshrine.

2. Admire extravagantly, dote upon, love, idolize, treasure, idolatrize, make an idol of, put on a pedestal, hold dear, make much of, set one's affections on, cherish.

WORSHIPER, *n.* 1. Celebrant, churchgoer, pillar of the church, communicant, congregation *(collective),* liturgist, ritualist, devotionalist, devotionist, pietist, theist, convert, believer, the faithful *(collective).*

2. Admirer, adorer, suitor, follower, swain, wooer, beau, inamorato, sweetheart, flame, truelove, amorist, cavalier, gallant, boy friend *(coll.),* Lothario, Don Juan, Casanova.

3. Idolater, idolist, idolizer, fetishist, iconodulist, iconolater.

WORSHIPFUL, *adj.* 1. Devout, pious, sanctified, saintly, prayerful, solemn, reverent, adoring, devotional, fervent, religious, holy, heavenly-minded, spiritual-minded, godly, reverential, pure in heart, believing, regenerate, consecrated, prostrate, kneeling, genuflecting, idolatrous.

2. Revered, venerated, estimable, honorable, esteemed, respected, worthy, venerable.

WORST, *v.* Defeat, vanquish, overthrow, conquer, beat, overcome, rout, subdue, overpower, subjugate, master, overwhelm, crush, get the better of, discomfit, quell, put down, foil, frustrate, balk, disappoint, outgeneral, outmaneuver, drub, floor, put to flight, put hors de combat, confound, upset, do for, settle, reduce, make bite the dust, trample under foot, roll in the dust.

WORTH, *n.* 1. Value, cost, price, valuation, estimation, appraisement, appraisal, expense, amount, charge, quotation, rate, face value, par, market price, price current.

2. Merit, worthiness, desert, excellence, importance, quality, credit, character, account, dignity, virtue, nobleness, integrity, probity, honor, goodness, respectability, trustworthiness.

3. Benefit, advantage, avail, good, usefulness, utility, serviceableness, profitableness, advantageousness, helpfulness, efficacy, help, use, service, aid, profit.

WORTHLESS, *adj.* 1. Useless, inutile, valueless, unserviceable, unavailing, of no account, of no use, good-for-nothing, nugatory, meritless, unsalable, unproductive, refuse, superfluous, bootless, inadequate, inefficacious, ineffectual, inefficient, incompetent, inept, fruitless, gainless, not worth a straw, trashy, vain, empty, idle, of no moment, piddling, inane, slight, paltry, trivial, trifling, frivolous, insignificant, petty, superficial, showy, trumpery, gaudy, glittering, tinsel, brummagem, pinchbeck, meretricious, vapid, pointless, claptrap, sleazy, jerry-built.

2. Vile, base, ne'er-do-well, abandoned, ignoble, depraved, abject, corrupt, blackguardly, rascally, wicked, vicious, scurvy, shabby, despicable, contemptible, dissolute, profligate.

WORTHY, *adj.* 1. Meritorious, deserving, of adequate merit, fit, suitable, appropriate, due, rightful, just, fitting, meet, decorous, befitting, creditable, right, becoming, proper, seemly, equitable, deserved.

2. Of commendable excellence, estimable, virtuous, good, exemplary, excellent, righteous, rectitudinous, honorable, honest, reputable, upright, noble, sterling, morally pure, commendable, matchless, laudable, praiseworthy, trustworthy, reliable, blameless, admirable, decent, incorruptible, respectable, irreproachable.

WOULD-BE, *adj.* Pretended, pseudo, bogus, counterfeit, spurious, supposititious, self-styled, *soi-disant (Fr.)*, *so-genannt (Ger.)*, false, illegitimate, bastard, pretentious, presumptuous, hopeful, assuming, precocious, bumptious, bold-faced, bluffing.

WOUND, *n.* 1. Bodily injury, blow, trauma, cut, stab, lesion, laceration, tear, bruise, gash, scratch, mutilation, slit, split, cleft, incision.

2. Mishap, injury, damage, hurt, harm, detriment, load, burden, stroke, curse, pang, pain, anguish, grief, torture, torment, agony, rack.

WOUND, *v.* 1. Cut, lacerate, stab, pierce, hurt, prick, injure, maul, scathe, maim, mutilate, disable, mangle, tear, truncate, amputate, damage, harm, gash, slit, carve, sever, rend, rive, cleave, chop, hew, hack, slice, slash, dissect, quarter, anatomize.

2. Offend, pique, annoy, provoke, irritate, mortify, pain, hurt the feelings of, affront, distress, trouble, grieve, afflict, gall, harrow, harry, harass, ruffle, incense, heckle, insult, nettle, peeve, inflame, chafe, fret, exasperate, sting, infuriate, embitter.

WRAITH, *n.* Visible spirit, apparition, specter, vision, ghost, revenant, unreal image, sprite, banshee, fetch, shade, spook, shadow, phantasm, phantom, materialization.

WRANGLE, *v.* Quarrel, dispute, squabble, contend, bicker, have an altercation, have a set-to, brawl, jangle, tiff, spat, have words, argue, cavil, spar, fall out, haggle, be at variance, contest,

disagree, differ, altercate, clash, controvert, litigate, row *(coll.)*, chop logic, split hairs.

WRANGLE, *n.* Altercation, squabble, brawl, controversy, bickering, jangle, clash, quarrel, contention, angry dispute, scrap *(sl.)*, contest, hot words, jar, strife, verbal affray, difference, conflict, disagreement, debate, Donnybrook, fracas, imbroglio, logomachy, discord, dissension, variance, faction, feud, tiff, high words, polemics, friction, litigation, open rupture, broil, row *(coll.)*, rumpus, scrimmage, squall, disturbance, riot, commotion, bear garden, apple of discord, bone of contention, vexed question, *casus belli (Lat.)*, disputation, polemics.

WRANGLER, *n.* Disputant, quarrelsome fellow, hothead *(coll.)*, jangler, controversialist, polemicist, logomachist, hairsplitter, caviler, eristic, arguer, casuist, dialectician, debater, oppositionist, obscurantist, brawler, extremist, brangler, irreconcilable, bitter-ender, die-hard, reactionist, malcontent, antagonist, opponent.

WRAP, *v.* 1. Enclose and make fast, bind about, roll together, wrap up, wind around, secure, enwrap, encase, enclose, swathe, enfold, envelop, surround.

2. Hide, conceal, cloak, muffle, shroud, mask, furl, involve, swaddle, cover, hood, screen, shelter, protect.

WRAP, *n.* 1. Shawl, cape, stole, mantle, scarf, wrapper, fur piece, collar, cloak, robe, cope, capote, burnoose, hood, cardinal, pelerine, redingote, overcoat, raglan.

2. Coverlet, quilt, blanket, cover, spread, comforter, bed quilt, puff.

WRAPPER, *n.* 1. Envelope, covering, wrapping, integument, container, sheath, case, involucrum, casing, jacket, capsule, pod, investment, shell.

2. Dressing gown, long loose outer garment, housecoat, kimono, negligee, peignoir.

WRATH, *n.* 1. Resentful indignation, fierce anger, rage, ire, choler, spleen, fury, passion, exasperation, dudgeon, pique, huff, umbrage, resentment, irritation, heat, madness, offense, animosity, displeasure, animus, hostility, irascibility, vexation, ferment, acrimony, bitterness, bile, virulence, gall, soreness, acerbity, tiff, pet, sulks, *acharnement (Fr.)*, paroxysm, explosion, vials of wrath, hot blood, rancor.

2. Ill will, malignity, malevolence, vengeance, revenge, retaliation, reprisal, punishment, revengefulness, vindictiveness, implacability, vengefulness, vendetta, day of reckoning.

WRATHFUL, *adj.* Fiercely angry, infuriate, wroth, ireful, irate, furious, incensed, raging, choleric, fuming, enraged, mad, sore *(coll.)*, irritated, resentful, rageful, indignant, provoked, exacerbated, exasperated, passionate, hot under the collar, out of temper, huffy, touchy, offended, up in arms, in high dudgeon, acrimonious, bitter, on one's high ropes, *acharné (Fr.)*, rabid, fiery, violent, bad-tempered, splenetic, nettlesome, waspish, peppery, cross, snappish.

WREAK, *v.* Carry out the promptings of ill humor on a victim, execute, inflict, work, give rein to, indulge, exercise, visit, hound, persecute, give no quarter, be hard upon, tyrannize, lay a heavy hand on, put the screws on, deal harshly with.

WREATH, *n.* Circular band for adorning the head, diadem, coronal, coronet, garland, crown, chaplet, laurel, bays, festoon.

WREATHE, *v.* Twist, festoon, garland, twine, interweave, interbraid, intertwine, surround in curling masses, envelop, enfold, encircle, curl, coil, wind around, adorn with a wreath.

WRECK, *v.* 1. Cause the wreck of in navigation, shipwreck, cast away, founder, strand, scuttle, swamp, sink, submerge.
2. Destroy, ruin, shatter, break up, demolish, blast, dynamite, sabotage, raze, smash, overthrow, undo, devastate, despoil, blight, ravage, desolate, level, annihilate, eradicate, overturn, pull down, dismantle, batter, crash.

WRECK, *n.* 1. Shipwrecked vessel, stranded ship, derelict, flotsam and jetsam, ruins, relic.
2. Destruction, wreckage, havoc, devastation, debris, smash-up, crackup, crash, desolation, prostration, undoing, ruination, ruin, perdition, demolition, blasting, razing, leveling, subversion, overthrow, dissolution, disruption, ravaging, downfall, breakup, debacle, cataclysm.

WRENCH, *v.* 1. Twist forcibly, strain, sprain, overturn, pull suddenly, jerk, force, tear, rip, contort, wring.
2. Turn out of its true meaning, put a violent construction on, misconstrue, falsify, pervert, distort, garble, wrest, misrender, misinterpret, torture the sense.
3. Extort, extract, wring from, draw forth, pluck out.

WRENCH, *n.* 1. Sudden violent twist, sprain, strain, wrick, wring, contortion, distortion, deformation, screw.
2. Extraction, ejection, eradication, extirpation, deracination, evulsion, removal, extrication, dislodgment.
3. Tool for gripping and turning, monkey wrench, spanner, screw-key, pliers, pincers.

WRESTLE, *v.* Contend in a struggle for mastery, grapple, struggle, strive, contest, tug, grasp, throw, pin down, embrace, hug, clasp, force back on the mat.

WRESTLER, *n.* Mat man, grunt and groan artist *(coll.)*, grappler, bruiser, bone-crusher, gladiator.

WRESTLING, *n.* Grappling, contention, throwing, pinning to the mat, struggle, luctation, jujitsu, *sumo (Jap.)*, catch-as-catch-can, Greco-Roman contest, the mat, the ring, bout, set-to, modified murder *(coll.)*.

WRETCH, *n.* 1. Deplorably unfortunate person, poor creature, outcast, victim, sufferer, miserable being, unfortunate, vagabond, pariah, pilgarlic, tatterdemalion, ragamuffin, tramp, underling, menial, martyr, shorn lamb, prey.
2. Bad man, miscreant, person of base character, bezonian, scullion, vile fellow, outlaw, knave, scoundrel, ruffian, thug, criminal, blackguard, reprobate, viper, varlet, renegade, scamp, caitiff, scapegrace, *âme damnée (Fr.)*, black sheep, skunk *(sl.)*, cur, hound, rascal, villain, rogue, Judas, traitor, rake, worker of iniquity, wrongdoer, scapegallows, debauchee, libertine, wanton, hellion, delinquent, culprit, malefactor, felon, jailbird, rotter, ne'er-do-well, rapscallion, scalawag.

WRETCHED, *adj.* 1. Sad, pitiable, unhappy, unfortunate, woeful, woebegone, piteous, miserable, dejected, infelicitous, broken-hearted, heartbroken, forlorn, distressed, inconsolable, comfortless, disconsolate, doleful, dolorous, lachrymose, hapless, crushed, afflicted, melancholic, depressed, downcast, cheerless, sorrowful, abject, lamentable, dismal, drear, grievous, desperate, careworn, worried, gloomy, spiritless, joyless, dispirited, disheartened, despondent, low-spirited, discouraged, crestfallen, sick at heart, downhearted, somber, mournful, funereal, pensive, pathetic, stricken, heavy-laden.
2. Beggarly, shabby, scurvy, worthless, mean, abominable, despicable, base, vile, poor, bad, sorry, contemptible, paltry, rubbishy, trashy, scrubby, niggardly, catchpenny, cheap, gimcrack, sleazy, inferior, trumpery, two-penny.

WRIGGLE, *v.* Twist to and fro, writhe, squirm, worm, wiggle, struggle, churn, flail, turn, contort, quiver, shake, quaver, flicker, toss, roll, flounder, hitch, convulse, jolt, jerk, twitch.

WRING, *v.* 1. Twist violently, squeeze, compress, wrench, contort, force, wrest, extract, extort, expel, eject.
2. Torment, torture, rack, pain, hurt, oppress, distress, agonize, harass, excruciate, rend, stab, pierce, lancinate, martyrize, lacerate, wound, harrow, crucify, abuse, maltreat.

WRINKLE, *v.* Crease, knit, raddle, ruck, purse up, ruffle, rumple, corrugate, cockle, crumple, pucker, plicate, fold, pleat, gather, plait, contract, cocker, crinkle.

WRINKLE, *n.* 1. Crease, furrow, contraction, corrugation, pucker, cockle, gather, rimple, crow's-foot, crinkle, crumple, plait, fold, rumple, ridge, seam, crimp, plica, flexure, pleat.
2. Notion, fancy, whim, whimsy, conceit, crotchet, freak, vagary, maggot, quirk, caprice, kink, humor, idea.
3. Artful procedure, ingenious method, knack, flair, novel device, clever trick, gadget.

WRINKLED, *adj.* Rugose, marked with crow's-feet, seamed, corrugated, rugous, crinkly, leathery, wrinkly, creased, crumpled, rumpled, puckered, gathered, ridged, cockled, shriveled, parched.

WRIT, *n.* 1. *(Law)* Formal order under seal, warrant, habeas corpus, mandamus, summons, subpoena, brevet, decretal, decree, caveat, injunction, prescript, ordination, edict, placet, command, bidding, dictum.
2. Holy Writ, Scripture, the Bible, the Logos, Word of God, the Book of Books, Gospel, divine revelation.

WRITE, *v.* 1. Inscribe, transcribe, pen, scribble, scrawl, pencil, scrabble, record, scratch, scriven, write down, set down, note down, copy, address, engross, superscribe, take up the pen, take pen in hand, shed ink, typewrite, type, put on paper, jot down, set down in black and white, commit to paper, autograph, sign.
2. Compose, author, draft, draw up, indite, execute, frame, produce, compile, give a written account of, narrate, tell, describe, relate, rehearse, invent literarily, practice authorship, dash off, turn out, formulate, dictate.

WRITER, *n.* 1. Penman, calligrapher, calligraphist, scribe, scrivener, clerk, notary, secretary, amanuensis, quill-driver, scribbler, scrawler, copyist, transcriber, penner, chirographer, scriptor, stenographer, typist.
2. One engaged in literary work, author, composer, inditer, word-painter, fictioneer, novelist, storyist, historian, annalist, biographer, essayist, epistolographer, correspondent, *littérateur (Fr.)*, dramatist, playwright, poet, versifier, paragraphist, columnist, gentleman of the press, reporter, journalist, hack, pamphleteer, penny-a-liner, editorialist, contributor, editor, commentator,

annotator, lexicographer, publicist, reviewer, critic, newspaper man, magazinist, potboiler (*coll.*), free lance, librettist, encyclopedist, anthologist.

WRITHE, *v.* Twist about, squirm, wriggle, flail, thrash, thresh, struggle, suffer, contort, jerk, hitch, wiggle, twinge, wince, knot, gnarl, buckle, misshape, deform.

WRITING, *n.* 1. Handwriting, chirography, penmanship, calligraphy, hand, scription, longhand, fist (*coll.*), quill-driving, pencraft, stylography, lexigraphy, cerography, hieroglyphics, cuneiform, macrography, micrography, dash of the pen, *coup de plume (Fr.)*, flowing hand, Spencerian hand, cacography, scrawl, *griffonage (Fr.)*, scribble, doodling, fly tracks, *pattes de mouche (Fr.)*, cramped hand, *barbouillage (Fr.)*, shorhand, stenography, brachygraphy, pasigraphy, tachygraphy, logography, cryptography, steganography, code, haplography, dittography, autography, engrossment, legend, title, inscription, indenture.

2. Manuscript, document, script, writ, author's copy, original, instrument, deed, script, holograph, *litterae scriptae (Lat.)*, codex, scroll, parchment, opisthograph, palimpsest, transcript, certificate, charter, diploma, these presents (*Law*).

3. Literary production, literary labor, literature, work, opus, book, volume, tome, publication, composition, lucubration, authorship, inditement, conflation, article, bulletin, record, screed, theme, paper, thesis, dissertation, tract, pamphlet, tractate, communication, correspondence, textbook, novel, fiction, story, biography, history, annals, drama, play, poem, verse.

WRITING DESK, *n.* Secretary, desk, *escritoire (Fr.)*, break front.

WRONG, *v.* 1. Do injury to, harm, hurt, injure, abuse, maltreat, ill-treat, treat unjustly, damage, misserve, serve ill, defraud, cheat, swindle, bilk, fleece, impose upon, encroach, oppress, be inequitable, favor, show partiality, aggrieve, persecute, victimize, trample upon.

2. Seduce, rape, deflower, constuprate, devirginate, molest, violate, ravish, force, defile, debauch, ruin, attack, assault, prostitute, dishonor, outrage.

WRONG, *adj.* 1. Deviating from truth, incorrect, erroneous, faulty, inaccurate, mistaken, inexact, untrue, false, wide of the mark, illogical, unsound, unjustified.

2. Improper, indecorous, unfit, inappropriate, inapt, unsuitable, inapposite, malapropos, incongruous, unbecoming, unseemly, unbefitting, *contra bonos mores (Lat.)*, indelicate, immoral, immodest, indecent, impure.

3. Wicked, evil, bad, sinful, iniquitous, criminal, felonious, vicious, guilty, culpable, inexcusable, blameworthy, reprehensible, indefensible, unwarrantable, base, evil-minded, illegal, illegitimate, unlawful, lawless.

4. Injurious, harmful, scatheful, deleterious, hurtful, noxious, baneful, pernicious.

5. Faulty, amiss, kaput, ruined, done for, out of gear, out of order, disordered, out of kilter, deranged, disturbed, disarranged, in bad condition, shaky, unreliable, untrustworthy, awry.

6. Unfair, unjust, partial, one-sided, unilateral, prejudicial, unequal.

WRONG, *adv.* Erroneously, inaccurately, wrongly, incorrectly, improperly, falsely, at fault, faultily, amiss, awry, astray, athwart, unjustly, unfairly, inequitably, injuriously, harmfully, feloniously, criminally, immorally, sinfully, iniquitously, basely.

WRONG, *n.* 1. Error, falsity, inaccuracy, untruthfulness, untruth, slip, mistake, faux pas, blunder, oversight, fault, flaw, bungle, boner, fallacy.

2. Crime, transgression, trespass, felony, tort, offense, grievance, injury, villainy, *malum in se (Lat.)*, malpractice, misdoing, misdeed, malfeasance, delinquency, obliquity, guilt, wrongdoing, sin, evil, shame, improbity, disobedience, infraction, violation, iniquity, unrighteousness, wickedness, vice, blame, misdemeanor, dereliction, mistreatment, disservice, outrage, abomination, atrocity, enormity, foul play, knavery.

3. Injustice, inequity, unfairness, imposition, hardship, oppression, violation of right, exaction, extortion, prejudice, partiality, bias, nepotism, prepossession, favoritism, partisanship, illegality, unlawfulness.

WRONGDOER, *n.* Criminal, felon, convict, jailbird, gallowsbird, malefactor, evildoer, worker of iniquity, transgressor, sinner, profligate, libertine, wanton, debauchee, reprobate, rascal, villain, scoundrel, blackguard, miscreant, caitiff, shyster, sneak, cheat, thief, robber, trickster, swindler, peculator, sharper, forger, counterfeiter, contrabandist, smuggler, crook, delinquent, culprit, malfeasant, outlaw, murderer, assassin, cutthroat, pickpocket, safecracker, footpad, housebreaker, thug, gangster, hijacker, ruffian, hooligan, roughneck, rowdy, terrorist, apache, gunman, hoodlum, arsonist, pyromaniac, incendiary, firebrand, vandal, anarchist knave, desperado, racketeer, bootlegger, traitor, conspirator, accomplice, fence (*sl.*), recreant, renegade, blackmailer, kidnapper, bandit, brigand, highwayman, freebooter, pirate, embezzler, fleecer, burglar.

WRONG-HEADED, *adj.* Obstinate, stubborn, pigheaded, mulish, dogged, intractable, recalcitrant, perverse, wayward, wanton, cross-grained, headstrong, crotchety, misguided, froward, refractory, prejudiced, biased, short-sighted, partial, purblind, one-sided, narrow-minded, insular, parochial, provincial, intolerant, illiberal, narrow, fanatical, warped, cracked, *entêté (Fr.)*, dogmatic, opinionated, dictatorial, tyrannical, despotic, bigoted, unreasonable.

WROUGHT-UP, *adj.* Excited, beside oneself, perturbed, worked up, fired, maddened, agog, hysterical, melodramatic, in a ferment, feverish, all of a flutter, atwitter, in a dither, raving, wild, carried away, distraught, frantic, amuck, out of one's wits, violent, angered, irate, wroth, wrathful, ireful, raging, fuming, hot under the collar, boiling mad, foaming at the mouth, wavy, *acharné (Fr.)*, peeved, sore, indignant, resentful, furious, rabid, huffy, in high dudgeon.

WRY, *adj.* Twisted, crooked, askew, awry, contorted, abnormally turned to one side, distorted, unsymmetric, out of shape, irregular, asymmetrical, gnarled, deformed, kyphotic, not straight, misshapen, grotesque, oblique, aslant.

X

XANTHIPPE, *n.* Shrewish woman, ill-tempered wife, scold, virago, vixen, termagant, spitfire, battle-ax (*sl.*), dragon, shrew, fury, Tartar, beldam, demon, tiger, amazon, harridan, tigress, ripsnorter, carper, porcupine, bacchante, vituperator, backbiter, calumniator, detractor, defamer.

XANTHOUS, *adj.* Tending to yellow, yellowish, yellow, xanthic, fulvous, fulvid, golden, citron-colored, tawny, saffron, aureate, citrine, gilded, luteous, sallow, sandy, lemon-colored, amber, flaxen, cream-colored, buff, straw-colored, blond, fair, auricomous, golden-haired, ochreous, ecru, festucine, stramineous, fulvescent, croconic, xanthocroid.

XIPHOID, *adj.* Sword-shaped, gladiate, ensiform, swordlike, ensate, scimitared, pointed, tapering, acicular, barbed, sharp, acuminate, cuspidate, mucronate, peaked, keen-edged, knife-edged.

X-RAY, *n.* Electromagnetic radiation of extremely short wave length *(approximately 1 angstrom),* Roentgen ray, radiograph, roentgenogram, roentgenograph, photograph made with Roentgen rays, refractometry, skiagram, radiogram, radiotherapy, radioscopy, ray-therapy, ultraviolet ray, infrared ray.

XYLOGRAPH, *n.* Engraving on wood, woodcut, cut, wood engraving, lignograph, block, woodblock, print, picture.

XYLOGRAPHY, *n.* Woodcutting, engraving on wood, wood-graver's art, lignography, wood-engraving, decorative printing on wood, printed wood decorating.

XYLOID, *adj.* Resembling wood, ligneous, woody, lignose, wooden, lignous.

XYLOPHAGOUS, *adj.* Wood-eating, feeding on wood, living on wood, wood-nourished, subsisting on timber.

XYLOPHONE, *n.* Musical instrument consisting of a graduated series of wooden bars sounded by striking with small wooden hammers, marimba, celeste, harmonicon, orchestrion.

Y

YACHT, *n.* Private cruising vessel, sloop, pleasure boat, racing vessel, craft, ship, schooner, brigantine, barkentine, yawl, cutter, smack, ketch, sailboat, lugger, pinnace, launch, cabin cruiser, motor launch, speedboat.

YAHOO, *n.* Brute with degrading passions, coarse fellow, rough uncouth person, barbarian, savage, Hottentot, vandal, ruffian, rowdy, roughneck, hoodlum, hooligan, terrorist, larrikin, Mohock, desperado, apache, gangster, gunman, racketeer, ugly customer.

YAMMER, *v.* 1. Whine, complain, mew, moan, groan, murmur, mutter, grumble, maunder, croak, lament, bewail, mourn, bemoan, keen, fret, blubber, whimper, snivel.

2. Make an outcry, raise a clamor, talk loudly and persistently, vociferate, bellow, roar, yell, rend the air, scream, shout, bawl, howl, whoop, shriek, squall, shout at the top of one's voice, thunder.

YANK, *v.* Pull with a sudden jerking motion, jerk, twitch, snatch, pull suddenly and roughly, wrench, tug, drag, jolt, whisk, hitch, buffet, jostle, wallop, jounce, churn, shake up, hustle, convulse, agitate.

YAP, *v.* 1. Bark snappishly, yelp, yawp, ululate, snarl, bellow, roar, blare, latrate, yarr, yawl, snort, neigh, bray, caterwaul, mewl, bleat, croak,

screech, crow, quack, gobble, caw, gaggle, cackle, cluck, clack, hoot, blatter.

2. Talk foolishly, gibblegabble, twaddle, rant, jabber, prate, pour forth, chatter, palaver, prattle, blather, talk nonsense.

YARD, *n.* 1. Enclosed ground, enclosure, compound, close, courtyard, court, garth, curtilage, garden, croft, quadrangle, confine, grounds, area, pasture, barnyard, farmyard, bailey, barton, stockyard, cattlefold, pound, fold, pen, paddock.

2. Three feet, thirty-six inches, 0.9144 meter, unit of linear measure.

3. *(Naut.)* Long cylindrical spar suspending a sail and slung crosswise to a mast.

YARDSTICK, *n.* Yard-long stick marked with subdivisions used to measure with, three-foot ruler, measure, measuring stick.

YARN, *n.* 1. Knitting and weaving thread made by twisting fibers, woolen thread, spun wool, worsted, packthread, twist, strand, sewing silk, linen, cotton, lisle.

2. Anecdote, story, tale, narrative, romance, short story, mystery story, thriller, whodunit *(coll.),* fairy tale, myth, legend, parable, fable, detective story, experiences, adventures, life, ana, autobiography, biography, memoirs, explanation, description, report, account, sketch, delineation.

3. Boasting, exaggeration, amplification, high coloring, stretch, embroidery, traveler's tale, tall story, fish story, rant, extravagance, fiction, cock-and-bull story, bedtime story, moonshine, canard, bosh, hoax, imagination, concoction, bouncer, false coloring, *suggestio falsi (Lat.),* falsification, perversion, fabrication, invention, forgery, misrepresentation, gloss.

YAW, *v.* Deviate from a straight course, curve, bend, swerve, trend, turn, heel, bear off, tack, veer, sheer, wheel, drift, dodge, glance off, wobble.

YAWL, *n.* Fore-and-aft rigged vessel, ship, boat, ketch, schooner, cutter, sloop, yacht, clipper, corvette, dandy, smack, lugger, catboat, windjammer, brig, barque, brigantine.

YAWL, *v.* Roar, howl, yowl, ululate, bellow, cry, rebellow, yelp, bark, blare, bay, growl, yap, yarr, snarl.

YAWN, *v.* 1. Open the mouth involuntarily with a deep inspiration, gape, oscitate, express fatigue, get sleepy.

2. Open wide, extend wide, stretch wide, lay open, dehisce, part, spread out, divaricate, split, crack, fly open.

YEA, *adv.* Yes, aye, ay, true, very true, good, well, well and good, *placet (Lat.),* granted, just so, even so, truly, to be sure, assuredly, precisely, exactly, certainly, indeed, certes, of course, unquestionably, no doubt, so be it, amen, in the affirmative, affirmatively.

YEAR, *n.* Twelve months, fifty-two weeks, 365 days, leap year (366 days), calendar year, civil year, legal year, astronomical year, solar year, tropical year, lunar year, sidereal year, true period of the earth's revolution around the sun, time interval between one vernal equinox and the next, full round of the seasons, cycle of seasons, *annus (Lat.).*

YEARLING, *n.* One-year old animal, animal in the second year of its age, suckling, nursling, weanling.

YEARLY, *adj.* Pertaining to a year, annual, happening once a year, anniversary, coming every year, cyclic, cyclical.

YEARLY, *adv.* 1. Once a year, annually, every year, at regular intervals, serially, recurrently.

2. Per annum, by the year.

YEARN, *v.* Have an earnest desire, long, feel strong desire, be eager, hanker, covet, crave, long fondly, pine after, burn, be moved tenderly, lust for, languish, aspire to, desire, thirst for, wish for, want, have at heart, have a fancy for, be bent upon, set one's heart upon, hope for, sigh for, miss, need, lack.

YEARNING, *n.* Consuming desire, deep longing, importunate craving, tender passion, fervor, inclination, appetite, appetency, thirst, hunger, eager hankering, craving, avidity, lusting, itching, ardor, concupiscence, libido, keenness, ambition, zeal, eagerness, aspiration.

YEARS, *n., pl.* Time of life, age, agedness, oldness, advanced age, old age, senility, grand climacteric, gray hairs, decrepitude, declining years, superannuation, anility, dotage, second childhood, decline of life, vale of years, senescence, ripe age, longevity, ravages of time.

YEAST, *n.* Ferment, leaven, barm, rising, zyme, top yeast, surface yeast, bottom yeast, sediment yeast, spume, foam, froth, enzyme, suds, lather, fume, head.

YEASTY, *adj.* Fermenting, barmy, fermentative, zymotic, frothy, foamy, spumous, lathery.

YEGG, *n.* Criminal, malefactor, ruffian, evildoer, bad man, misdemeanant, felon, outlaw, jailbird, convict, rowdy, rough, ugly customer, hoodlum, hooligan, thief, robber, footpad, safecracker, yeggman, housebreaker, depredator, marauder, pillager, pilferer, bandit, brigand, gangster, hijacker, thug, gunman, apache, plunderer, smuggler, racketeer, highwayman, pickpocket, cutthroat, blackleg, crook, burglar, cat man, fence, blackmailer.

YELL, *v.* Cry out with a strong loud clear sound, shriek, screech, scream, shout, bellow, roar, halloo, howl, squeal, bawl, squall, yammer, ululate, vociferate, yowl, yap, hoot, whoop, yoick, yelp, raise the voice, cheer, huzza, hurrah, call out, exclaim, proclaim, clamor, give cry, rend the air, make the welkin ring, ejaculate.

YELLOW, *adj.* 1. Of a bright color like that of butter *or* lemons, golden, gold-colored, aureate, fulvid, fulvous, xanthous, xanthic, xanthochroid, gilt, saffron, luteous, citron-colored, citrine, citreous, croconic, fulvescent, creamy, cream-colored, buff, stramineous, straw-colored, flaxen, festucine, yellowish, amber-colored, primrose, ecru, ocherous, tawny, ochreous, ochery, auricomous, icteritious, icteroid, sallow, fallow, icterine, gambogian, sulfurous, jonquil, sandy, lutescent, daffodil.

2. Lurid, sensational, melodramatic, thrilling, emotional, exciting, jingoistic, stirring, hysterical, vivid, sordid, cheap.

3. Cowardly, craven, afraid, pusillanimous, lily-livered, showing the white feather, unmanly, timorous, white-livered, despicable, contemptible, mean, cringing, sneaking, slinking, groveling, dishonorable.

4. Jealous, envious, jaundiced, covetous, distrustful, prejudiced, suspicious, melancholic, green-eyed.

YELP, *v.* Give a sharp shrill cry, yawp, yap, cry, bark, bay, ululate, snarl, growl, whine, wail, howl, bray, neigh, snort, grunt, squeak, caterwaul, mew, blat, bleat, bellow, roar, moo, low, trumpet, screech, crow, caw, croak, cackle quack, cluck, peep, chirp, hoot.

YEN, *n.* Desire, longing, craving, hankering, yearning, vaulting ambition, ardor, itch, appetency, lust, appetite, keenness, thirst, hunger, prurience, cacoëthes, concupiscence, cupidity, sheep's-eye, passion, mania, monomania, obsession, zeal, eagerness, *empressement (Fr.),* breathless impatience, fondness, relish, love, liking, penchant, propensity, predilection, leaning, partiality, inclination, mind, bent, fancy, wish, want, temptation, lure, attraction, fascination, maggot, whim, hobby, wishing cap.

YEOMAN, *n.* 1. One of a class of lesser freeholders *(below the gentry)* who cultivated their own land, independent farmer, freeholder, commoner, small landowner, agriculturist, laird *(Scot.),* duniewassal *(Scot.),* agronomist, husbandman, granger, landed gentry, countryman, country gentleman.

2. Yeoman of the guard, beefeater *(Eng.),* guardsman, grenadier, chasseur, fusileer, trooper, cavalryman, dragoon, hussar, cuirassier, lancer.

3. Subordinate official in a great household, attendant, servant, retainer, servitor, gillie *(Scot.),* follower, henchman, squire.

4. Petty Officer in the U. S. Navy, clerk, scrivener, scribe, scriptor, copyist.

YES, *adv.* It is so, yea, aye, ay, true, granted, acknowledged, recognized, just so, even so, to be sure, assuredly, as you say, surely, certes, certainly, no doubt, exactly, doubtless, precisely, of course, unquestionably, by common consent, admittedly.

YESTERDAY, *n.* 1. The day preceding today, yestermorn, yestereve, yestereven, *hier (Fr.),* ayer *(Sp.),* ieri *(It.),* Gestern *(Ger.).*

2. A short time ago, time in the immediate past, days of yore, time gone by, good old days, bygone days, former times, fore time, eld, auld lang syne.

YET, *conj.* And yet, but yet, at the same time, nevertheless, however, notwithstanding, still, though.

YET, *adv.* 1. At this *or* that time, as previously, to this time, even now, now, still.

2. In addition, besides, over and above, further, again, moreover, even, still.

3. Though the case be such, nevertheless, but, unless, if, provided, according as, conditionally, supposing, with the understanding, on the supposition, at all events, after all, for all that, though, although.

4. Up to a particular time, hitherto, thus far, up to the present time, as soon as the present time, in the time still remaining.

YIELD, *v.* 1. Produce in return for cultivation, bear, give forth by a natural process, bring forth, furnish, bear fruit, flower, blossom, fructify, give birth to, throw, farrow, drop, lamb, yean, calve, foal, whelp, fawn, kitten, hatch, progenerate, breed, spawn, conceive, form in the womb, generate, proliferate, engender, beget, reproduce, fecundate, propagate.

2. Give a return for, give as due *or* required, return, render, confer, bestow, communicate, impart, afford, supply.

3. Sell for, fetch, bring in, accrue.

4. Relent, bend, give, relax, flex, deflect, thaw, melt, dissolve.

5. Submit, obey, capitulate, surrender, give in, give oneself up, succumb, resign oneself, defer to, be submissive, acquiesce, comply, stoop, accede, yield obeisance, kneel to, bow down before, cringe to, pay homage to, truckle to, bow submission, kowtow, kiss the rod.

6. Relinquish, cede, forbear, let go, lay down, cease from, demit, vacate, resign, abdicate, quit, leave, part with, give up, desert, abandon, forsake, dispose of, give away, dismiss, jettison, throw away, renounce, waive, forgo, drop, have done with, revoke, nol-pros (*Law*), reject, lay aside, cast off, discard, disavow, disclaim, repudiate, disown, give up the point (*Debate*), table.

7. Concede, acknowledge, allow, concur, accept, assent, consent, admit, grant, agree to, give consent, vouchsafe, satisfy, come to terms, settle, close with.

YIELD, *n.* Crop, harvest, fruit, produce, reaping, return, product, result, effect, proceeds, gain, net, output, vintage, mow, gleanings, income, revenue, earnings, receipts, *rente (Fr.)*, bounty, reward, premium.

YIELDING, *adj.* 1. Soft, pliant, pliable, plastic, ductile, malleable, waxy, flabby, flaccid, fictile, limber, spongy, supple, flexible, mollient, resilient, impressible, softened, relaxed, limp, flexuous, extensible, tractile, doughy, pulpy, clayey, argillaceous, unresistant, facile, gentle.

2. Obedient, manageable, compliant, tractable, amenable, docile, submissive, morigerous, obsequious, sequacious, credulous, deferential, subservient, complaisant, meek, acquiescent, easily persuaded, obliging.

3. Productive, fertile, prolific, workable, cultivable, arable, fructiferous, fruit-bearing, uberous, fruitful, luxuriant, fructuous, teeming, plenteous, generative, life-giving.

YODEL, *v.* Sing with frequent changes to falsetto and back again, troll, carol, warble, chaunt, chirp, lilt, trill, purl, quaver, twitter, sol-fa, intone, vocalize, croon.

YOGI, *n.* One who practices the Yoga beliefs, Hindu ascetic, fakir, anchorite, mendicant priest, holy man, devotee, mortifier of the flesh, *solitaire (Fr.)*, hermit, recluse, eremite, mental-disciplinarian, one who withdraws the senses from all external objects, one who concentrates the mind on some central truth, one who practices controlled breathing.

YOKE, *n.* 1. Contrivance for joining together, oxbow and bar, crosspiece with two bow-shaped pieces beneath, *jugum (Lat.)*, bond, tie, ligature, coupler, link, chain, union, vinculum, nexus, connective, interconnection, copula, bond of union, halter, harness, collar.

2. Pair (*of oxen*), couple, brace, team, match, twain, span.

3. Servitude, bondage, enslavement, vassalage, thralldom, slavery, subjection, dependence, dependency, enthrallment, serfdom, feudalism, subjugation, reduction, conquest, service, constraint, employment.

YOKE, *v.* Couple by means of a yoke, attach to a plow *or* vehicle, harness, hitch, bracket, link, join, conjoin, connect, interlink, unite, fasten together, bind, mate, marry, associate, clinch, entwine, knot, splice, tether, truss, buckle, picket, gird, chain.

YOKEFELLOW, *n.* 1. Intimate associate, partner, colleague, coworker, confrere, collaborator, coadjutor, co-laborer, co-aid, ally, teammate, yokemate, companion, comrade, fellow, compeer, chum, crony, pal, bedfellow, messmate, sidekick, buddy, bunkie.

2. Spouse, consort, mate, husband, wife, better half, helpmate, helpmeet.

YOKEL, *n.* Countryman, rustic, bumpkin, rube, hayseed, clodhopper, boor, clod, hick, lubber, peasant, churl, swain, hind, hobnail, cider squeezer, plowboy, bogtrotter, chawbacon, lout, looby, booby.

YOLK, *n.* 1. Yellow substance of an egg, vitellus, formative yoke, archiblast, nutritive yolk, parablast, deutoplasm, oviplasm.

2. Essential part, inner core, essence, pith, quintessence, quiddity, hypostasis, elixir, substance.

YONDER, *adj.* Distant, far-off, faraway, remote, yon, incontiguous, ulterior, distal, antipodean, hyperborean, ultramontane, tramontane, ultramundane, transatlantic, transmarine, transpontine, transalpine, out of the way, inaccessible, unapproachable, unapproached.

YONDER, *adv.* At a distance (*within view*), yon, faraway, far-off, away, off, a good way off, aloof, out of the way, farther, beyond, further, clear of, abroad, over the horizon, *outre mer (Fr.)*, overseas, over the hills and faraway, out of range, *à perte de vue (Fr.)*, a far cry to, out of the sphere of, asunder, apart, wide asunder, at arm's length, *longo intervallo (Lat.)*.

YORE, *adv.* Of old, years ago, long ago, in times past, formerly, erstwhile, anciently, whilom, erst, aforetime, bygone, heretofore, time was, erewhile, over, in olden times, long since, ages ago, some time back, no longer, in time immemorial, time out of mind.

YOUNG, *adj.* 1. Being in the early stage of life, in process of growth, having the freshness of youth, not far advanced in years, youthful, childlike, juvenile, junior, in one's teens, not old, undeveloped, adolescent, infantile, infantine, pubescent, unripe, green, inexperienced, immature, callow, fresh, vigorous, puerile, youthsome, juvenescent, underage, tender, *in statu pupillari (Lat.)*, unfledged, newfledged, beardless, budding, boyish, blooming, fresh, buoyant, light-hearted.

2. More recent, newer, modern, early, novel, advocating progressive policies, forward-looking.

YOUNGSTER, *n.* Young person, youth, adolescent, lad, stripling, boy, schoolboy, young man, shaver, whippersnapper, child, bantling, slip, scion, sprig, cub, laddie, hobbledehoy, boykin, cadet, kid, hopeful, urchin, gamin, street Arab, brat, chit, chick, little tot, bairn, pickaninny, elf, whipster, callant, minor, nestling, whelp, fry, puppy, maverick, cherub, imp, mite, teen-ager.

YOUTH, *n.* 1. Early life, period of life from puberty to the attainment of full growth, time of being young, juvenility, juvenescence, juniority, adolescence, teens, minority, nonage, leading strings, pupilage, childhood, wardship, immaturity, youthfulness, youthhead, boyishness, girlishness, Juventas (*Roman Myth.*), Hebe (*Greek Myth.*), boyhood, girlhood, infancy, incunabula, babyhood, tender age, flower of life, bloom, virginity, pucilage, seedtime of life, springtime of life, golden season of life, heyday of youth, prime of life, school days, salad days.

2. Boy, schoolboy, teen-ager, stripling, strip, sprig, slip, scion, lad, laddie, youngster, adolescent, young man, youngling, younker, whelp, cub, callant, shaver, whippersnapper, bantling, child, hobbledehoy, boykin, kid, cadet, gamin, urchin, street Arab, hopeful, chit, brat, chick, bairn, whipster, minor, elf, nestling, fry, puppy, cherub, maverick, imp, mite.

3. Young persons collectively, the rising generation, young men, young women.

YOUTHFUL, adj. 1. Young, juvenile, teen-aged, adolescent, juvenescent, boyish, beardless, downy-cheeked, pubescent, puerile, immature, callow, childish, under age, in one's teens, budding, in statu pupillari (Lat.), unfledged, newfledged, boy-like, childlike, tender, green, unripe, blooming, kiddish, kittenish, bright-eyed, rosy-cheeked, fresh.

2. Vigorous, enthusiastic, keen, active, buoyant, light-hearted, hopeful, optimistic, cheerful, laughing, starry-eyed, sanguine, confident, high-hearted.

YOWL, n. Long distressful or dismal cry, howl, ululation, latration, reboation, bark, yelp, bay, yap, yawl, bray, snarl, growl, snort, neigh, caterwaul, mewl, meow, pule, purr, low, moo, bleat.

YULE, n. Christmas, Christmas season, yuletide, Advent, Noël (Fr.), Weihnachtszeit (Ger.), Navidad (Sp.), Natale (It.), Epiphany.

Z

ZANY, n. 1. Apish buffoon, merry-andrew, scaramouch, punch, droll, punchinello, harlequin, clown, jester, mimic, court jester, fool, pickle-herring, jack-pudding, antic, pierrot, pantaloon, farceur, grimacier (Fr.), pantomimist, buffo.

2. Simpleton, half-wit, nitwit, tomfool, witling, dunce, Simple Simon, booby, dolt, noodle, ass, donkey, imbecile, blockhead, nincompoop, bonehead, calf, mooncalf, numskull, goose, lunkhead.

ZANYISM, n. Buffoonery, drollery, foolery, tomfoolery, clownishness, harlequinism, cap and bells, harlequinade, jocularity, facetiousness, waggishness, comicality.

ZEAL, n. Ardor for a cause, eagerness, fervor, enthusiasm, alacrity, fervency, enthusiastic diligency, eager endeavor, devotedness, heartiness, devotion, zealotry, energy, fanaticism, passion, intensity, earnestness, vehemence, intentness, warmth, spirit, soul, feeling, glow, cordiality, willingness, readiness, promptness, labor of love, proneness, propensity, inclination, proclivity, bent, penchant, liking, empressement (Fr.), keenness, exertion, industry, sedulousness, assiduity, persistence, perseverance, application, vigilance, watchfulness, dispatch, enterprise, energy, activity, vim, vigor, vivacity, snap, go, animation, dash, expedition, promptitude, stir, bustle, ado, hustle, flurry, rustle, verve, warm fancy, ecstasy, frenzy, rhapsody.

ZEALOT, n. 1. One carried away by an excess of zeal, fanatic, enthusiast, devotee, aficionado (Sp.), partisan, champion, bigot, fan.

2. Visionary, dreamer, idealist, romanticist, romancer, rhapsodist, Don Quixote.

3. Pharisee, puritan, sabbatarian, pietist, religionist, ranter, whirling dervish.

ZEALOTRY, n. Fanaticism, infatuation, opinionativeness, monomania, obsession, fixed idea, idée fixe (Fr.), bigotry, dogmatism, ruling passion, dogged resolution, inflexibility, tenacity, obstinateness, perseverance, persistence, partiality, partisanship, prepossession, bias, twist, warp.

ZEALOUS, adj. Ardently active, fervent, perfervid, ardent, fervid, burning, impassioned, glowing, enthusiastic, fanatical, eager, passionate, devoted, warm, fiery, keen, prompt, earnest, diligent, assiduous, sedulous, persistent, attentive, solicitous, ready, swift, expeditious, forward, industrious, strenuous, devout, devoted, loving, affectionate, cordial, willing, bent upon, minded, desirous, inclined, gushing, hearty, impetuous, rabid, feverish, raging, raving, infatuated.

ZENITH, n. Highest point, summit, apex, top, pinnacle, utmost height, culmination, culminating point, acme, climax, vertex, extreme limit, meridian, ne plus ultra (Lat.), turning point, heyday, prime, flower, bloom, high tide, maximum, apogee, crown.

ZEPHYR, n. West wind, soft mild breeze, gentle wind, Favonius, puff, current, breath, draft, flatus, afflatus.

ZEPPELIN, n. Large cylindrical balloon filled with gas, dirigible, blimp, sausage-balloon, pilot-balloon, observation-balloon.

ZERO, n. 1. Cipher, symbol 0, lowest degree, absence of quantity, naught, nothing, none, nil, goose egg, duck's egg, nix (sl.).

2. Point from which all divisions of a scale are measured in a positive or a negative direction, origin of any kind of measurement, point of commencement, lowest point, nadir, nullity, nothingness.

ZEST, n. 1. Flavor, relish, piquancy, tang, smack, tinge, goût (Fr.), taste, savor, twang, edge, salt, spice.

2. Gusto, exhilaration, thrill, enjoyment, kick (sl.), liking, interest, charm, appetite, pleasure, stimulus, satisfaction, delectation, cheer, glee, jubilation, elation, delight, joy, gratification, gladness, bliss, felicity, happiness, exaltation, beatitude, enchantment, rapture, ecstasy, transport, treat, diversion, refreshment, entertainment, amusement, sport, indulgence, jollity, gaiety, hilarity, merriment.

ZESTFUL, adj. 1. Savory, toothsome, piquant, tasty, delectable, palatable, delicious, appetizing, luscious, nectareous, ambrosial, rich, spicy, salty, well-seasoned, delicate, exquisite.

2. Pleased, glad, blissful, happy, ecstatic, enthusiastic, blithe, joyous, gratified, overjoyed, enchanted, entranced, enraptured, transported, ravished, fascinated, captivated, beatific, ardent, vehement, fervent, fervid, perfervid, zealous, impassioned, passionate, burning, glowing, flaming.

ZIGZAG, adj. Turning sharply first to one side and then to the other, staggered, angled, serpentine, sinuous, circuitous, anfractuous, meandering, labyrinthine, daedalian, mazy, forked, like a worm fence, oblique, crooked, indirect, askew, round-about, devious.

ZIP, n. Energy, vim, go, push, drive, élan, vigor, liveliness, briskness, force, spirit, forcefulness, potency, power, efficacy, puissance, strength, intensity, fervor, might, verve, animation, dash, pep, punch, fire, mettle.

ZONE, n. 1. (Poetic) Girdle, cestus, cincture, belt, baldric, girth, band, zonule, sash, surcingle, cummerbund, zoster, circlet, cordon.

2. Region, area, theater, locality, district, site, arena, circuit, climate, clime, meridian, realm, latitude, hemisphere, tract, sphere, domain, territory, quarter, locale, location, spot, part, situation.

ZOO, *n.* Zoölogical garden, menagerie, *Tiergarten (Ger.), Jardin des Plantes (Fr.),* vivarium, *giardino zoölògico (It.).*

ZOOLOGIST, *n.* Student of the animal kingdom, naturalist, zoögrapher, zoötomist, mammalogist, mastologist, therologist, ornithologist, entomologist, herpetologist, helminthologist, ophiologist, ichthyologist, malacologist, cetologist, conchologist, crustaceologist, carcinologist, morphologist.

ZOOLOGY, *n.* Science of animals, natural history, therology, mastology, mammalogy, ornithology, herpetology, entomology, ophiology, helminthology, ichthyology, conchology, cetology, crustaceology, carcinology, malacology, zoötechnics, ecology, bionomy, zoönomy, zoögeography, zoögraphy, thremmatology, paleontology, taxonomy, morphology.

ZYMOTIC, *adj.* Infectious by the action of a ferment, fermentative, bacterial, diffused by germs, originating from decomposition, germinating, morbiferous, deleterious, injurious, pernicious, noxious, noisome, pestiferous, epizoötic, endemic, pestilential, pandemic, epidemic, taking, inoculable, communicable, catching, contagious, virulent, toxic, azotic, deadly, toxiferous, septic.